2019

Harris

Ohio

Services Directory

MERGENT

Exclusive Provider of
Dun & Bradstreet Library Solutions

dun & bradstreet

 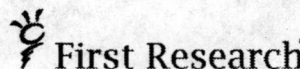 

HOOVERS™   First Research   HARRIS INFOSOURCE™

Published July 2019 next update July 2020

Publisher

Mergent Inc.
444 Madison Ave
New York, NY 10022

2019 Mergent Business Press
ISSN 1080-2614
ISBN 978-1-64141-222-3

MERGENT
BUSINESS PRESS
by FTSE Russell

TABLE OF CONTENTS

SUMMARY OF CONTENTS

Number of Companies.. 20,388
Number of Decision Makers....................................... 46,721
Minimum Number of Employees............................... 25

EXPLANATORY NOTES

How to Cross-Reference in This Directory

Sequential Entry Numbers. Each establishment in the Geographic Section is numbered sequentially (G-0000). The number assigned to each establishment is referred to as its "entry number." To make cross-referencing easier, each listing in the Geographic, SIC, Alphabetic and Product Sections includes the establishment's entry number. To facilitate locating an entry in the Geographic Section, the entry numbers for the first listing on the left page and the last listing on the right page are printed at the top of the page next to the city name.

Source Suggestions Welcome

Although all known sources were used to compile this directory, it is possible that companies were inadvertently omitted. Your assistance in calling attention to such omissions would be greatly appreciated. A special form on the facing page will help you in the reporting process.

Analysis

Every effort has been made to contact all firms to verify their information. The one exception to this rule is the annual sales figure, which is considered by many companies to be confidential information. Therefore, estimated sales have been calculated by multiplying the nationwide average sales per employee for the firm's major SIC/NAICS code by the firm's number of employees. Nationwide averages for sales per employee by SIC/NAICS codes are provided by the U.S. Department of Commerce and are updated annually. All sales—sales (est)—have been estimated by this method. The exceptions are parent companies (PA), division headquarters (DH) and headquarter locations (HQ) which may include an actual corporate sales figure—sales (corporate-wide) if available.

Types of Companies

Descriptive and statistical data are included for companies in the entire state. These comprise manufacturers, machine shops, fabricators, assemblers and printers. Also identified are corporate offices in the state.

Employment Data

This directory contains companies with 25 or more employees in the service industry. The actual employment shown in the Geographic Section includes male & female employees and embraces all levels of the company. This figure is for the facility listed and does not include other offices or branches. It should be recognized that these figures represent an approximate year-round average. These employment figures are broken into codes A-E and used in the SIC and Services Sections to further help you in qualifying a company. Be sure to check the footnotes on the bottom of the page for the code breakdowns.

Standard Industrial Classification (SIC)

The Standard Industrial Classification (SIC) system used in this directory was developed by the federal government for use in classifying establishments by the type of activity they are engaged in. The SIC classifications used in this directory are from the 1987 edition published by the U.S. Government's Office of Management and Budget. The SIC system separates all activities into broad industrial divisions (e.g., manufacturing, mining, retail trade). It further subdivides each division. The range of manufacturing industry classes extends from two-digit codes (major industry group) to four-digit codes (product).

For example:

Industry Breakdown	Code	Industry, Product, etc.
*Major industry group	20	Food and kindred products
Industry group	203	Canned and frozen foods
*Industry	2033	Fruits and vegetables, etc.

*Classifications used in this directory

Only two-digit and four-digit codes are used in this directory.

Arrangement

1. The **Geographic Section** contains complete in-depth corporate data. This section is sorted by cities listed in alphabetical order and companies listed alphabetically within each city. A County/City Index for referencing cities within counties precedes this section.

IMPORTANT NOTICE: It is a violation of both federal and state law to transmit an unsolicited advertisement to a facsimile machine. Any user of this product that violates such laws may be subject to civil and criminal penalties, which may exceed $500 for each transmission of an unsolicited facsimile. Mergent Inc. provides fax numbers for lawful purposes only and expressly forbids the use of these numbers in any unlawful manner.

2. The **Standard Industrial Classification (SIC) Section** lists companies under approximately 500 four-digit SIC codes. An alphabetical and a numerical index precedes this section. A company can be listed under several codes. The codes are in numerical order with companies listed alphabetically under each code.

3. The **Alphabetic Section** lists all companies with their full physical or mailing addresses and telephone number.

4. The **Services Section** lists companies under unique Harris categories. An index precedes this section. Companies can be listed under several categories.

USER'S GUIDE TO LISTINGS

GEOGRAPHIC SECTION

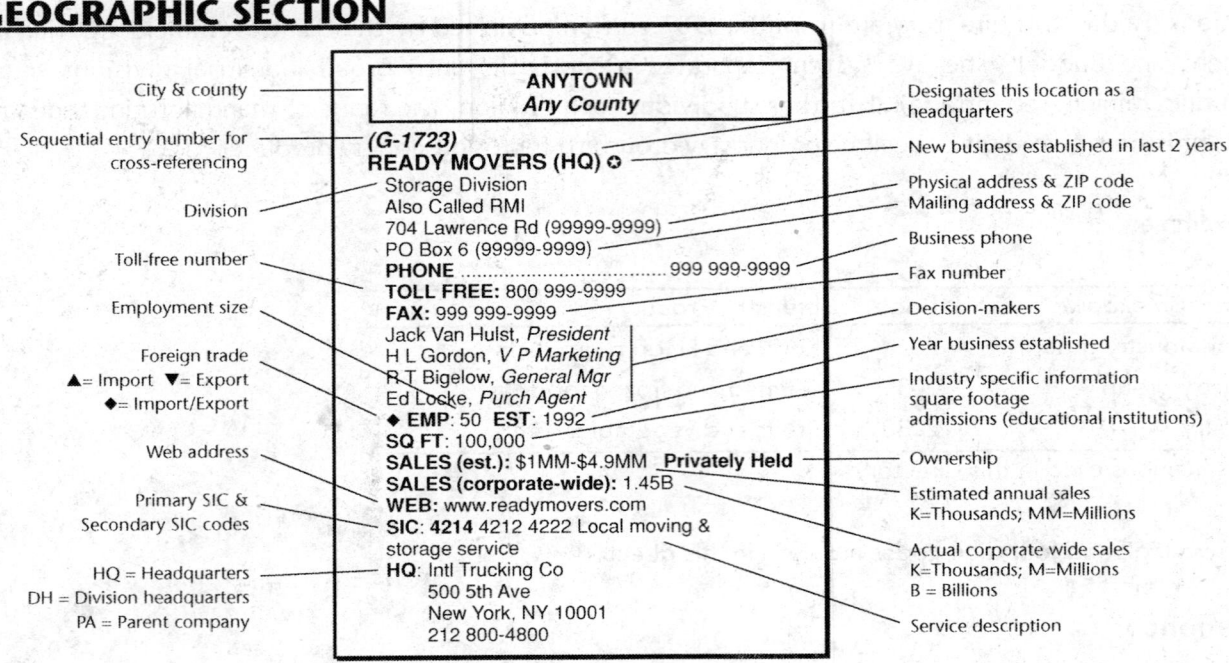

City & county

Sequential entry number for cross-referencing

Division

Toll-free number

Employment size

Foreign trade
▲= Import ▼= Export
◆= Import/Export

Web address

Primary SIC & Secondary SIC codes

HQ = Headquarters
DH = Division headquarters
PA = Parent company

ANYTOWN
Any County

(G-1723)
READY MOVERS (HQ) ✪
Storage Division
Also Called RMI
704 Lawrence Rd (99999-9999)
PO Box 6 (99999-9999)
PHONE 999 999-9999
TOLL FREE: 800 999-9999
FAX: 999 999-9999
Jack Van Hulst, *President*
H L Gordon, *V P Marketing*
R T Bigelow, *General Mgr*
Ed Locke, *Purch Agent*
◆ **EMP:** 50 **EST:** 1992
SQ FT: 100,000
SALES (est.): $1MM-$4.9MM **Privately Held**
SALES (corporate-wide): 1.45B
WEB: www.readymovers.com
SIC: 4214 4212 4222 Local moving & storage service
HQ: Intl Trucking Co
500 5th Ave
New York, NY 10001
212 800-4800

Designates this location as a headquarters

New business established in last 2 years

Physical address & ZIP code
Mailing address & ZIP code

Business phone

Fax number

Decision-makers

Year business established

Industry specific information square footage admissions (educational institutions)

Ownership

Estimated annual sales
K=Thousands; MM=Millions

Actual corporate wide sales
K=Thousands; M=Millions
B = Billions

Service description

SIC SECTION

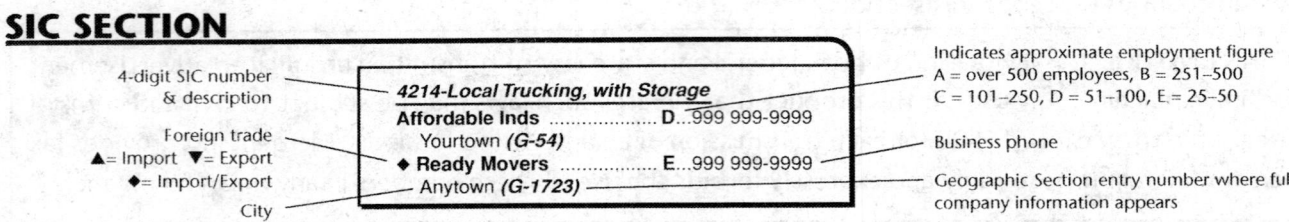

4-digit SIC number & description

Foreign trade
▲= Import ▼= Export
◆= Import/Export
City

4214-Local Trucking, with Storage
Affordable Inds .... D...999 999-9999
Yourtown *(G-54)*
◆ **Ready Movers** .... E...999 999-9999
Anytown *(G-1723)*

Indicates approximate employment figure
A = over 500 employees, B = 251–500
C = 101–250, D = 51–100, E = 25–50

Business phone

Geographic Section entry number where full company information appears

ALPHABETIC SECTION

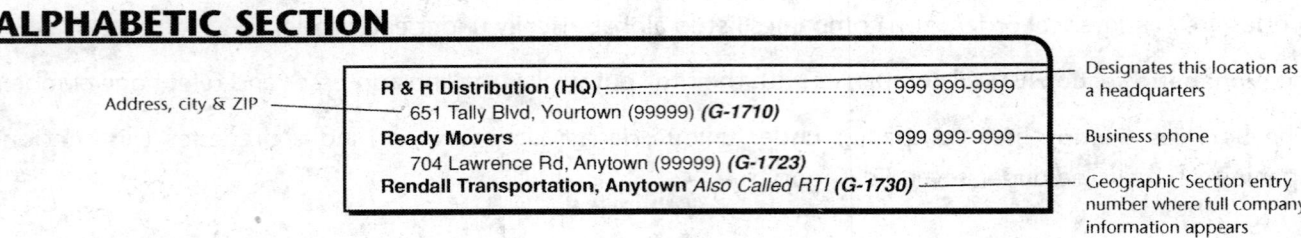

Address, city & ZIP

R & R Distribution (HQ) ----------------999 999-9999
651 Tally Blvd, Yourtown (99999) *(G-1710)*
Ready Movers 999 999-9999
704 Lawrence Rd, Anytown (99999) *(G-1723)*
Rendall Transportation, Anytown *Also Called RTI* *(G-1730)*

Designates this location as a headquarters

Business phone

Geographic Section entry number where full company information appears

SERVICES SECTION

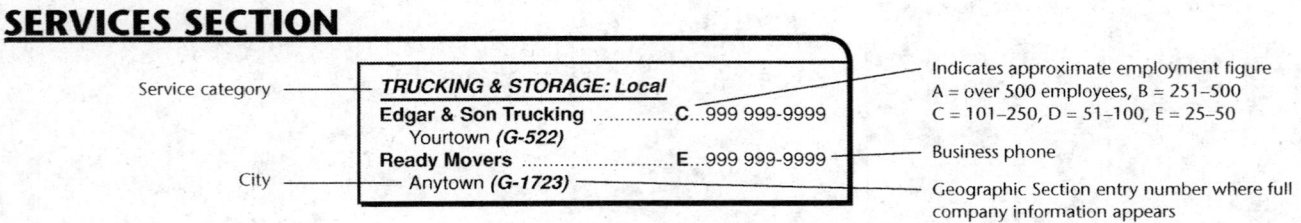

Service category

City

TRUCKING & STORAGE: Local
Edgar & Son Trucking ....C...999 999-9999
Yourtown *(G-522)*
Ready Movers ....E...999 999-9999
Anytown *(G-1723)*

Indicates approximate employment figure
A = over 500 employees, B = 251–500
C = 101–250, D = 51–100, E = 25–50

Business phone

Geographic Section entry number where full company information appears

GEOGRAPHIC SECTION
Companies sorted by city in alphabetical order
In-depth company data listed

STANDARD INDUSTRIAL CLASSIFICATIONS
Alphabetical index of classifcation descriptions
Numerical index of classifcation descriptions
Companies sorted by SIC product groupings

ALPHABETIC SECTION
Company listings in alphabetical order

SERVICES INDEX
Service categories are listed in alphabetical order

SERVICES SECTION
Companies sorted by service classifications

GEOGRAPHIC

SIC

ALPHABETIC

SVCS INDEX

SERVICES

Ohio
County Map

COUNTY/CITY CROSS-REFERENCE INDEX

	ENTRY #		ENTRY #		ENTRY #		ENTRY #		ENTRY #

Hardin
Ada .... (G-2)
Dunkirk .... (G-10384)
Forest .... (G-10982)
Kenton .... (G-12271)
Mc Guffey .... (G-13898)
Mount Victory .... (G-14796)

Harrison
Bowerston .... (G-1710)
Cadiz .... (G-2027)
Freeport .... (G-11055)
Hopedale .... (G-11936)
Scio .... (G-16662)

Henry
Deshler .... (G-10057)
Holgate .... (G-11866)
Liberty Center .... (G-12575)
Mc Clure .... (G-13893)
Napoleon .... (G-14800)
New Bavaria .... (G-14879)
Ridgeville Corners .... (G-16398)

Highland
Greenfield .... (G-11358)
Hillsboro .... (G-11833)
Lynchburg .... (G-13055)

Hocking
Logan .... (G-12830)
Rockbridge .... (G-16413)

Holmes
Berlin .... (G-1445)
Big Prairie .... (G-1472)
Holmesville .... (G-11928)
Killbuck .... (G-12310)
Millersburg .... (G-14452)
Mount Hope .... (G-14737)
Walnut Creek .... (G-18631)
Winesburg .... (G-19666)

Huron
Bellevue .... (G-1371)
Greenwich .... (G-11402)
Monroeville .... (G-14588)
New Haven .... (G-14916)
New London .... (G-14930)
North Fairfield .... (G-15245)
Norwalk .... (G-15424)
Plymouth .... (G-16076)
Wakeman .... (G-18619)
Willard .... (G-19479)

Jackson
Jackson .... (G-12168)
Oak Hill .... (G-15480)
Wellston .... (G-18847)

Jefferson
Adena .... (G-7)
Amsterdam .... (G-600)
Bergholz .... (G-1444)
Bloomingdale .... (G-1490)
Brilliant .... (G-1819)
Dillonvale .... (G-10062)
East Springfield ...... (G-10426)
Hammondsville .... (G-11657)
Mingo Junction .... (G-14527)
Rayland .... (G-16272)
Richmond .... (G-16386)
Steubenville .... (G-17139)
Stratton .... (G-17242)

Toronto .... (G-18181)
Wintersville .... (G-19667)

Knox
Centerburg .... (G-2614)
Danville .... (G-9149)
Fredericktown .... (G-11052)
Gambier .... (G-11224)
Howard .... (G-11939)
Mount Vernon .... (G-14748)

Lake
Concord Township .... (G-8943)
Concord Twp .... (G-8945)
Eastlake .... (G-10427)
Grand River .... (G-11331)
Kirtland .... (G-12322)
Madison .... (G-13092)
Mentor .... (G-14016)
Mentor On The Lake . (G-14128)
Painesville .... (G-15691)
Perry .... (G-15820)
Wickliffe .... (G-19453)
Willoughby .... (G-19501)
Willoughby Hills ...... (G-19586)
Willowick .... (G-19596)

Lawrence
Chesapeake .... (G-2727)
Coal Grove .... (G-6756)
Ironton .... (G-12144)
Pedro .... (G-15800)
Proctorville .... (G-16215)
South Point .... (G-16928)
Willow Wood .... (G-19595)

Licking
Buckeye Lake .... (G-1974)
Croton .... (G-9065)
Etna .... (G-10612)
Granville .... (G-11334)
Heath .... (G-11702)
Hebron .... (G-11710)
Homer .... (G-11933)
Johnstown .... (G-12195)
Kirkersville .... (G-12320)
Newark .... (G-15008)
Pataskala .... (G-15782)
Saint Louisville .... (G-16518)
Utica .... (G-18454)

Logan
Belle Center .... (G-1342)
Bellefontaine .... (G-1343)
De Graff .... (G-9900)
East Liberty .... (G-10390)
Lakeview .... (G-12332)
Lewistown .... (G-12572)
West Liberty .... (G-19117)
West Mansfield .... (G-19124)
Zanesfield .... (G-20272)

Lorain
Amherst .... (G-578)
Avon .... (G-862)
Avon Lake .... (G-907)
Columbia Station ..... (G-6769)
Elyria .... (G-10475)
Grafton .... (G-11316)
Lagrange .... (G-12325)
Lorain .... (G-12878)
North Ridgeville ...... (G-15318)
Oberlin .... (G-15497)

Sheffield Village .... (G-16731)
South Amherst .... (G-16921)
Wellington .... (G-18838)

Lucas
Holland .... (G-11868)
Maumee .... (G-13744)
Monclova .... (G-14559)
Oregon .... (G-15580)
Ottawa Hills .... (G-15668)
Sylvania .... (G-17411)
Toledo .... (G-17573)
Waterville .... (G-18788)
Whitehouse .... (G-19443)

Madison
London .... (G-12858)
Mount Sterling .... (G-14745)
Plain City .... (G-16040)
West Jefferson .... (G-19103)

Mahoning
Austintown .... (G-855)
Beloit .... (G-1398)
Berlin Center .... (G-1449)
Boardman .... (G-1695)
Campbell .... (G-2090)
Canfield .... (G-2130)
Lowellville .... (G-13039)
New Middletown ...... (G-14939)
New Springfield .... (G-14996)
North Jackson .... (G-15246)
North Lima .... (G-15261)
Petersburg .... (G-15943)
Poland .... (G-16079)
Sebring .... (G-16666)
Struthers .... (G-17360)
Youngstown .... (G-19943)

Marion
La Rue .... (G-12324)
Marion .... (G-13404)
Morral .... (G-14711)
Prospect .... (G-16221)
Waldo .... (G-18629)

Medina
Brunswick .... (G-1918)
Chippewa Lake .... (G-2838)
Hinckley .... (G-11857)
Lodi .... (G-12827)
Medina .... (G-13906)
Seville .... (G-16682)
Sharon Center .... (G-16722)
Spencer .... (G-16953)
Valley City .... (G-18459)
Wadsworth .... (G-18587)
Westfield Center ...... (G-19307)

Meigs
Long Bottom .... (G-12877)
Middleport .... (G-14280)
Pomeroy .... (G-16093)
Racine .... (G-16229)
Syracuse .... (G-17469)

Mercer
Burkettsville .... (G-2012)
Celina .... (G-2581)
Coldwater .... (G-6757)
Fort Recovery .... (G-10987)
Maria Stein .... (G-13306)
Rockford .... (G-16414)
Saint Henry .... (G-16515)

Miami
Bradford .... (G-1761)
Covington .... (G-9045)
Piqua .... (G-15994)
Tipp City .... (G-17548)
Troy .... (G-18194)
West Milton .... (G-19126)

Monroe
Beallsville .... (G-1119)
Lewisville .... (G-12573)
Sardis .... (G-16661)
Woodsfield .... (G-19671)

Montgomery
Beavercreek .... (G-1202)
Beavercreek Township (G-1264)
Brookville .... (G-1909)
Centerville .... (G-2618)
Clayton .... (G-4856)
Dayton .... (G-9193)
Englewood .... (G-10578)
Farmersville .... (G-10857)
Germantown .... (G-11276)
Huber Heights .... (G-11953)
Kettering .... (G-12290)
Miamisburg .... (G-14134)
Moraine .... (G-14619)
Oakwood .... (G-15482)
Trotwood .... (G-18191)
Union .... (G-18350)
Vandalia .... (G-18500)
Washington Township (G-18785)
West Carrollton .... (G-18856)

Morgan
Malta .... (G-13121)
Mc Connelsville .... (G-13895)
McConnelsville .... (G-13899)
Stockport .... (G-17183)

Morrow
Chesterville .... (G-2748)
Marengo .... (G-13302)
Mount Gilead .... (G-14724)

Muskingum
Dresden .... (G-10115)
Duncan Falls .... (G-10381)
East Fultonham .... (G-10388)
Frazeysburg .... (G-11048)
Nashport .... (G-14819)
New Concord .... (G-14900)
Roseville .... (G-16453)
South Zanesville ...... (G-16951)
Zanesville .... (G-20273)

Noble
Caldwell .... (G-2036)
Dexter City .... (G-10059)

Ottawa
Clay Center .... (G-4855)
Curtice .... (G-9066)
Elmore .... (G-10472)
Genoa .... (G-11251)
Lakeside .... (G-12329)
Lakeside Marblehead (G-12331)
Marblehead .... (G-13301)
Oak Harbor .... (G-15468)
Port Clinton .... (G-16099)

Put In Bay .... (G-16224)
Rocky Ridge .... (G-16419)
Williston .... (G-19500)

Paulding
Antwerp .... (G-613)
Oakwood .... (G-15483)
Paulding .... (G-15790)

Perry
Crooksville .... (G-9064)
Glenford .... (G-11308)
New Lexington .... (G-14918)
Somerset .... (G-16918)
Thornville .... (G-17504)

Pickaway
Ashville .... (G-761)
Circleville .... (G-4821)
Orient .... (G-15619)
Williamsport .... (G-19498)

Pike
Beaver .... (G-1120)
Piketon .... (G-15970)
Waverly .... (G-18813)

Portage
Aurora .... (G-815)
Deerfield .... (G-9901)
Diamond .... (G-10061)
Garrettsville .... (G-11229)
Hiram .... (G-11864)
Kent .... (G-12212)
Mantua .... (G-13264)
Mogadore .... (G-14541)
Randolph .... (G-16230)
Ravenna .... (G-16232)
Rootstown .... (G-16450)
Streetsboro .... (G-17243)
Windham .... (G-19663)

Preble
Camden .... (G-2088)
Eaton .... (G-10436)
Lewisburg .... (G-12568)
New Paris .... (G-14940)
West Alexandria .... (G-18855)
West Manchester ...... (G-19123)

Putnam
Columbus Grove .... (G-8940)
Continental .... (G-8961)
Fort Jennings .... (G-10983)
Glandorf .... (G-11307)
Kalida .... (G-12207)
Leipsic .... (G-12520)
Ottawa .... (G-15657)
Ottoville .... (G-15670)
Pandora .... (G-15750)

Richland
Bellville .... (G-1387)
Butler .... (G-2021)
Lexington .... (G-12574)
Mansfield .... (G-13130)
Ontario .... (G-15542)
Shelby .... (G-16743)

Ross
Bainbridge .... (G-930)
Chillicothe .... (G-2749)
Frankfort .... (G-11018)
Kingston .... (G-12315)

	ENTRY #		ENTRY #		ENTRY #		ENTRY #		ENTRY #

Sandusky

Burgoon .... (G-2011)
Clyde .... (G-6738)
Fremont .... (G-11056)
Gibsonburg .... (G-11278)
Millersville .... (G-14504)
Vickery .... (G-18575)
Woodville .... (G-19682)

Scioto

Franklin Furnace .... (G-11042)
Lucasville .... (G-13045)
Mc Dermott .... (G-13896)
Minford .... (G-14526)
New Boston .... (G-14880)
Portsmouth .... (G-16123)
South Webster .... (G-16950)
Wheelersburg .... (G-19427)

Seneca

Alvada .... (G-559)
Attica .... (G-813)
Bascom .... (G-981)
Bettsville .... (G-1458)
Bloomville .... (G-1492)
Flat Rock .... (G-10978)
Fostoria .... (G-10996)
Green Springs .... (G-11350)
Kansas .... (G-12208)
Tiffin .... (G-17509)

Shelby

Anna .... (G-610)
Botkins .... (G-1706)
Fort Loramie .... (G-10985)
Jackson Center .... (G-12183)
Russia .... (G-16466)
Sidney .... (G-16755)

Stark

Alliance .... (G-512)
Beach City .... (G-1024)
Brewster .... (G-1809)

Canal Fulton .... (G-2092)
Canton .... (G-2167)
East Canton .... (G-10385)
East Sparta .... (G-10423)
Hartville .... (G-11682)
Louisville .... (G-12959)
Magnolia .... (G-13111)
Massillon .... (G-13656)
Minerva .... (G-14515)
Navarre .... (G-14822)
North Canton .... (G-15184)
North Lawrence .... (G-15258)
Paris .... (G-15756)
Uniontown .... (G-18357)
Waynesburg .... (G-18827)
Wilmot .... (G-19657)

Summit

Akron .... (G-9)
Barberton .... (G-938)
Bath .... (G-1017)
Clinton .... (G-6737)
Copley .... (G-8963)
Coventry Township ... (G-9032)
Cuyahoga Falls .... (G-9067)
Fairlawn .... (G-10816)
Hudson .... (G-11960)
Macedonia .... (G-13057)
Munroe Falls .... (G-14797)
New Franklin .... (G-14907)
Northfield .... (G-15371)
Norton .... (G-15417)
Peninsula .... (G-15808)
Richfield .... (G-16342)
Silver Lake .... (G-16807)
Stow .... (G-17187)
Tallmadge .... (G-17470)
Twinsburg .... (G-18241)

Trumbull

Bristolville .... (G-1825)
Brookfield .... (G-1851)

Burghill .... (G-2010)
Cortland .... (G-8983)
Fowler .... (G-11016)
Girard .... (G-11281)
Hubbard .... (G-11941)
Kinsman .... (G-12317)
Masury .... (G-13740)
Mc Donald .... (G-13897)
Mesopotamia .... (G-14130)
Mineral Ridge .... (G-14508)
Newton Falls .... (G-15135)
Niles .... (G-15142)
Southington .... (G-16952)
Vienna .... (G-18577)
Warren .... (G-18660)
West Farmington ...... (G-19102)

Tuscarawas

Baltic .... (G-933)
Bolivar .... (G-1702)
Dennison .... (G-10049)
Dover .... (G-10064)
Dundee .... (G-10382)
Gnadenhutten .... (G-11312)
Midvale .... (G-14357)
Mineral City .... (G-14506)
New Philadelphia ...... (G-14945)
Newcomerstown .... (G-15129)
Port Washington .... (G-16121)
Strasburg .... (G-17240)
Sugarcreek .... (G-17376)
Uhrichsville .... (G-18339)

Union

Marysville .... (G-13482)
Milford Center .... (G-14444)
Raymond .... (G-16275)
Richwood .... (G-16397)

Van Wert

Convoy .... (G-8962)
Middle Point .... (G-14246)
Van Wert .... (G-18471)

Vinton

Creola .... (G-9050)
Hamden .... (G-11552)
Mc Arthur .... (G-13889)
New Plymouth .... (G-14991)

Warren

Carlisle .... (G-2551)
Franklin .... (G-11020)
Kings Mills .... (G-12313)
Lebanon .... (G-12446)
Maineville .... (G-13112)
Mason .... (G-13536)
Middletown .... (G-14341)
Morrow .... (G-14714)
Oregonia .... (G-15616)
Pleasant Plain .... (G-16073)
South Lebanon .... (G-16926)
Springboro .... (G-16960)
Waynesville .... (G-18831)

Washington

Belpre .... (G-1399)
Beverly .... (G-1459)
Little Hocking .... (G-12807)
Lowell .... (G-13036)
Marietta .... (G-13309)
Reno .... (G-16276)
Vincent .... (G-18585)
Waterford .... (G-18786)
Whipple .... (G-19442)

Wayne

Apple Creek .... (G-617)
Burbank .... (G-2008)
Creston .... (G-9061)
Dalton .... (G-9143)
Doylestown .... (G-10108)
Fredericksburg .... (G-11051)
Kidron .... (G-12305)
Marshallville .... (G-13474)
Mount Eaton .... (G-14723)
Orrville .... (G-15622)

Rittman .... (G-16403)
Shreve .... (G-16753)
Smithville .... (G-16811)
West Salem .... (G-19128)
Wooster .... (G-19684)

Williams

Alvordton .... (G-562)
Bryan .... (G-1950)
Edgerton .... (G-10466)
Edon .... (G-10470)
Montpelier .... (G-14605)
Stryker .... (G-17369)
West Unity .... (G-19140)

Wood

Bowling Green .... (G-1711)
Bradner .... (G-1763)
Cygnet .... (G-9142)
Grand Rapids .... (G-11323)
Luckey .... (G-13054)
Millbury .... (G-14446)
North Baltimore .... (G-15176)
Northwood .... (G-15388)
Pemberville .... (G-15804)
Perrysburg .... (G-15831)
Portage .... (G-16122)
Rossford .... (G-16459)
Stony Ridge .... (G-17184)
Walbridge .... (G-18622)
Wayne .... (G-18825)

Wyandot

Carey .... (G-2545)
Nevada .... (G-14838)
Sycamore .... (G-17410)
Upper Sandusky .... (G-18403)

GEOGRAPHIC SECTION

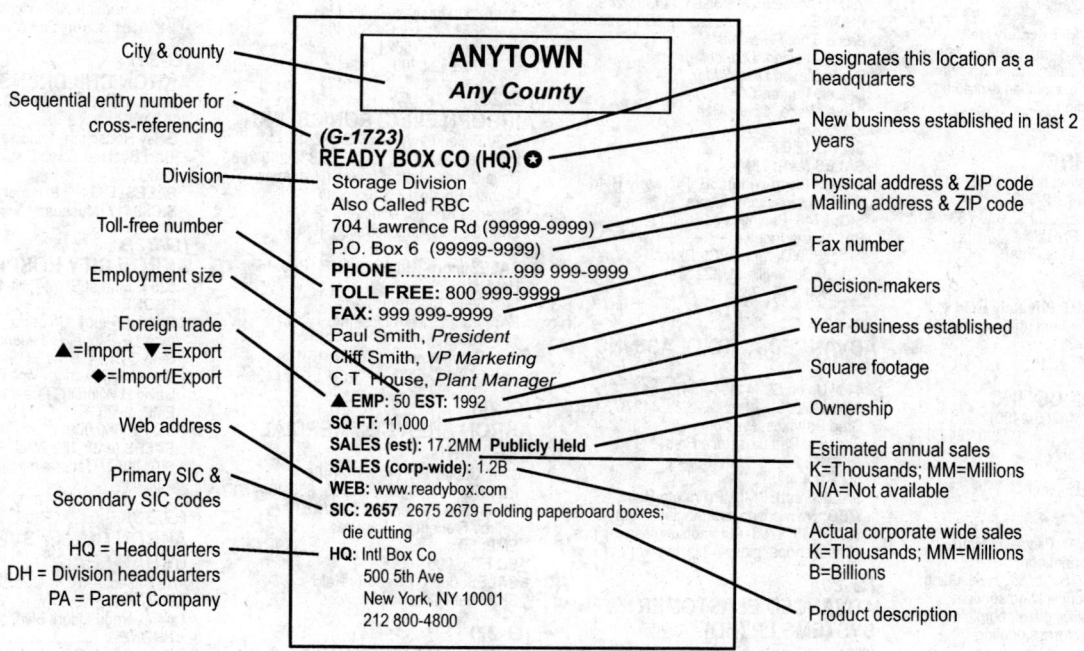

City & county → **ANYTOWN** *Any County*

Sequential entry number for cross-referencing → **(G-1723)**

Division → **READY BOX CO (HQ)** ✪
Storage Division
Also Called RBC

Toll-free number → 704 Lawrence Rd (99999-9999)
P.O. Box 6 (99999-9999)

Employment size → **PHONE** 999 999-9999
TOLL FREE: 800 999-9999
FAX: 999 999-9999

Foreign trade
▲=Import ▼=Export
◆=Import/Export → Paul Smith, *President*
Cliff Smith, *VP Marketing*
C T House, *Plant Manager*
▲ **EMP:** 50 **EST:** 1992
SQ FT: 11,000

Web address → **SALES (est):** 17.2MM **Publicly Held**
SALES (corp-wide): 1.2B
WEB: www.readybox.com

Primary SIC & Secondary SIC codes → **SIC: 2657** 2675 2679 Folding paperboard boxes; die cutting

HQ = Headquarters
DH = Division headquarters
PA = Parent Company → **HQ:** Intl Box Co
500 5th Ave
New York, NY 10001
212 800-4800

Designates this location as a headquarters

New business established in last 2 years

Physical address & ZIP code
Mailing address & ZIP code

Fax number

Decision-makers

Year business established

Square footage

Ownership

Estimated annual sales
K=Thousands; MM=Millions
N/A=Not available

Actual corporate wide sales
K=Thousands; MM=Millions
B=Billions

Product description

See footnotes for symbols and codes identification.
- This section is in alphabetical order by city.
- Companies are sorted alphabetically under their respective cities.
- To locate cities within a county refer to the County/City Cross Reference Index.

IMPORTANT NOTICE: It is a violation of both federal and state law to transmit an unsolicited advertisement to a facsimile machine. Any user of this product that violates such laws may be subject to civil and criminal penalties which may exceed $500 for each transmission of an unsolicited facsimile. Harris InfoSource provides fax numbers for lawful purposes only and expressly forbids the use of these numbers in any unlawful manner.

GEOGRAPHIC

Aberdeen
Brown County

(G-1)
BEVERLY HILLS INN LA LLC
1830 Us Highway 52 (45101-2503)
PHONE..........................859 494-9151
Anette Mineer, *Mng Member*
EMP: 30
SALES: 1MM **Privately Held**
SIC: 7011 5812 7231 Hotels; American restaurant; unisex hair salons

Ada
Hardin County

(G-2)
BRENT BURRIS TRUCKING LLC
2445 County Road 75 (45810-9786)
P.O. Box 227 (45810-0227)
PHONE..........................419 759-2020
Brent Burris,
EMP: 50
SALES (est): 4.6MM **Privately Held**
SIC: 4213 Trucking, except local

(G-3)
COMMUNITY HLTH PRFSSIONALS INC
Also Called: Ada Visiting Nurses
1200 S Main St (45810-2616)
PHONE..........................419 634-7443
Claudia Crawford, *Manager*
EMP: 25

SALES (corp-wide): 13.1MM **Privately Held**
SIC: 8082 8051 Visiting nurse service; skilled nursing care facilities
PA: Community Health Professionals, Inc.
1159 Westwood Dr
Van Wert OH 45891
419 238-9223

(G-4)
COUNTY OF HARDIN
Also Called: Ada Lberty Joint Ambulance Dst
530 N Gilbert St (45810-1012)
P.O. Box 204 (45810-0204)
PHONE..........................419 634-7729
Keith Shaw, *Chief*
EMP: 27 **Privately Held**
WEB: www.kenton.com
SIC: 4119 Ambulance service
PA: County Of Hardin
1 Court House Sq Rm 100
Kenton OH 43326
419 674-2205

(G-5)
MIDWEST REHAB INC
118 E Highland Ave (45810-1120)
PHONE..........................419 692-3405
Steve Zuber, *President*
EMP: 60
SALES (est): 3.1MM **Privately Held**
SIC: 8093 Rehabilitation center, outpatient treatment

(G-6)
WILSON SPORTING GOODS CO
217 Liberty St (45810-1135)
P.O. Box 116 (45810-0116)
PHONE..........................419 634-9901
Dan Riegle, *Manager*
Pam Clark, *Manager*

EMP: 150
SQ FT: 30,000 **Privately Held**
SIC: 5091 Sporting & recreation goods
HQ: Wilson Sporting Goods Co.
1 Prudential Pl
Chicago IL 60601
773 714-6400

Adena
Jefferson County

(G-7)
ADENA NH LLC
Also Called: Altercare Adena
213 U S Route 250 (43901-7925)
PHONE..........................740 546-3620
Ronald Swartz, *Vice Pres*
Mordecai Rosenberg, *Mng Member*
Lisa Schwartz, *Admin Sec*
Dawn Wozniak, *Exec Sec*
EMP: 40
SALES (est): 600K **Privately Held**
SIC: 8051 8322 Skilled nursing care facilities; rehabilitation services

(G-8)
SIENNA HILLS NURSING & REHAB
73841 Pleasant Grove Rd (43901-9514)
PHONE..........................740 546-3013
Oscar Jarnicke, *President*
EMP: 45
SALES (est): 1.2MM **Privately Held**
SIC: 8051 Skilled nursing care facilities

Akron
Summit County

(G-9)
21ST CENTURY FINANCIAL INC
130 Springside Dr Ste 100 (44333-4543)
PHONE..........................330 668-9065
Charlie Parks, *President*
Charles Parks, *Managing Prtnr*
Robert Slater, *Business Mgr*
Joseph Dazey, *Vice Pres*
James Greenwell, *Vice Pres*
EMP: 40 **EST:** 1996
SALES (est): 15.5MM **Privately Held**
SIC: 6311 Life insurance

(G-10)
50 X 20 HOLDING COMPANY INC
779 White Pond Dr (44320-1136)
PHONE..........................330 865-4663
Walt Myers, *General Mgr*
Guy Robinson, *Branch Mgr*
EMP: 40
SALES (corp-wide): 116MM **Privately Held**
SIC: 1521 Single-family housing construction
PA: 50 X 20 Holding Company, Inc.
2715 Wise Ave Nw
Canton OH 44708
330 478-4500

(G-11)
A CRANO EXCAVATING INC
1505 Industrial Pkwy (44310-2603)
PHONE..........................330 630-1061

James V Riter, *President*
Anthony Riter, *Vice Pres*
Raymond Riter, *Treasurer*
EMP: 40
SALES (est): 8.6MM **Privately Held**
SIC: 1623 1794 Oil & gas line & compressor station construction; water & sewer line construction; excavation & grading, building construction

(G-12)
A TO ZOFF CO INC
Also Called: Zoff Heating & Plumbing
1105 Canton Rd (44312-3320)
PHONE................................330 733-7902
Elizabeth Zofchak, *President*
Joseph Zofchak Jr, *Vice Pres*
EMP: 25
SQ FT: 4,800
SALES (est): 3.1MM **Privately Held**
SIC: 1711 Warm air heating & air conditioning contractor

(G-13)
A-A BLUEPRINT CO INC
2757 Gilchrist Rd (44305-4400)
PHONE................................330 794-8803
John Scalia, *President*
Daisy Scalia, *Principal*
Joseph Brown, *Production*
EMP: 32
SQ FT: 30,000
SALES (est): 5.7MM **Privately Held**
WEB: www.aablueprint.com
SIC: 2791 7334 2752 2789 Typesetting; photocopying & duplicating services; commercial printing, offset; bookbinding & related work; letterpress printing

(G-14)
ABACUS CHILD CARE CENTERS INC
839 S Arlington St (44306-2452)
P.O. Box 7333 (44306-0333)
PHONE................................330 773-4200
Kim Herburgh, *President*
Talisa Salaam, *Director*
Kimberly Herbulh, *Director*
EMP: 32
SALES (est): 785.9K **Privately Held**
SIC: 8351 Child day care services

(G-15)
ACC AUTOMATION CO INC
475 Wolf Ledges Pkwy (44311-1199)
PHONE................................330 928-3821
Frank Rzicznek, *Vice Pres*
EMP: 25
SQ FT: 7,500
SALES (est): 2.3MM **Privately Held**
SIC: 8711 3536 Consulting engineer; cranes, overhead traveling

(G-16)
ACCESS INC
Also Called: AKRON CITIZEN'S COALITION FOR
230 W Market St (44303-2197)
P.O. Box 1007 (44309-1007)
PHONE................................330 535-2999
Silvia Hines, *Exec Dir*
EMP: 30
SQ FT: 9,050
SALES: 1.6MM **Privately Held**
SIC: 8322 Individual & family services

(G-17)
ACRO TOOL & DIE COMPANY
Also Called: Landscape & Christmas Tree
325 Morgan Ave (44311-2494)
PHONE................................330 773-5173
T T Thompson, *President*
Steve Wilcox, *Purchasing*
Randy Farnsworth, *QC Mgr*
Terry Ellis, *Technology*
Pamela Perrin, *Admin Sec*
▲ **EMP:** 60
SQ FT: 27,000
SALES (est): 9.1MM **Privately Held**
WEB: www.acrotool.com
SIC: 3544 3469 0781 0811 Special dies & tools; stamping metal for the trade; landscape services; Christmas tree farm; machine tools, metal cutting type; sheet metalwork

(G-18)
ACTIONLINK LLC
286 N Cleveland Massillon (44333-2492)
PHONE................................888 737-8757
Bruce Finn, *President*
Bobby Lessing, *District Mgr*
Roger Meyer, *District Mgr*
Delbert Tanner, *COO*
Ashley Pace, *Opers Mgr*
EMP: 2000
SQ FT: 12,000
SALES (est): 78MM
SALES (corp-wide): 6B **Privately Held**
WEB: www.actionlink.com
SIC: 8748 Business consulting
PA: Acosta Inc.
　　6600 Corporate Ctr Pkwy
　　Jacksonville FL 32216
　　904 332-7986

(G-19)
ADVANCED AUTO GLASS INC (PA)
44 N Union St (44304-1347)
PHONE................................412 373-6675
Greg Pattakos, *President*
Christina Pattakos, *Vice Pres*
▲ **EMP:** 29
SQ FT: 4,400
SALES (est): 7MM **Privately Held**
WEB: www.advancedautoglass.com
SIC: 7536 1793 Automotive glass replacement shops; glass & glazing work

(G-20)
ADVANCED ELASTOMER SYSTEMS LP (HQ)
Also Called: AES
388 S Main St Ste 600 (44311-1065)
PHONE................................800 352-7866
Rogerf Sellew, *CEO*
Loic Vivier, *President*
Stacy Johnson, *Purchasing*
Lynell Maenza, *Executive*
▲ **EMP:** 150
SQ FT: 150,000
SALES (est): 130.6MM
SALES (corp-wide): 290.2B **Publicly Held**
WEB: www.santoprene.com
SIC: 5162 5085 Plastics materials & basic shapes; rubber goods, mechanical
PA: Exxon Mobil Corporation
　　5959 Las Colinas Blvd
　　Irving TX 75039
　　972 940-6000

(G-21)
AERODYNAMIC CONCRETE & CNSTR
1726 Massillon Rd (44312-4207)
PHONE................................330 906-7477
John Chafe, *Partner*
Geneie Chafe, *Partner*
EMP: 50
SALES (est): 3.8MM **Privately Held**
SIC: 1771 Concrete work

(G-22)
AEROTEK INC
540 White Pond Dr B (44320-1100)
PHONE................................330 517-7330
Pat Hoyle, *Director*
EMP: 27
SALES (corp-wide): 12.3B **Privately Held**
SIC: 7363 Temporary help service
HQ: Aerotek, Inc.
　　7301 Parkway Dr
　　Hanover MD 21076
　　410 694-5100

(G-23)
AFM EAST ARCHWOOD OIL INC
745 E Archwood Ave (44306-2657)
PHONE................................330 786-1000
EMP: 46 **EST:** 2010
SALES: 46.2MM **Privately Held**
SIC: 5172 Whol Petroleum Products

(G-24)
AIMBRIDGE HOSPITALITY LLC
100 Springside Dr (44333-2431)
PHONE................................330 668-9090
EMP: 584

SALES (corp-wide): 605.6MM **Privately Held**
SIC: 7011 Hotels & motels
PA: Aimbridge Hospitality, Llc
　　5851 Legacy Cir Ste 400
　　Plano TX 75024
　　972 952-0200

(G-25)
AIRBORN ELECTRONICS INC
2230 Picton Pkwy (44312-4269)
PHONE................................330 245-2630
Dave Soederstrom, *Human Resources*
Michael Brustoski, *Sales Staff*
Suzanne Runals, *Director*
Brian Selzer, *Administration*
EMP: 27
SALES (corp-wide): 39.8MM **Privately Held**
SIC: 5065 Electronic parts
PA: Airborn Electronics, Inc.
　　3500 Airborn Cir
　　Georgetown TX 78626
　　512 863-5585

(G-26)
AKRON AREA COMMERCIAL CLEANING
1264 Copley Rd (44320-2748)
PHONE................................330 434-0767
Annamarie Frederick, *President*
Jeffrey Frederick, *Vice Pres*
EMP: 50
SQ FT: 5,000
SALES: 500K **Privately Held**
SIC: 7699 Cleaning services

(G-27)
AKRON ART MUSEUM
1 S High St (44308-1801)
PHONE................................330 376-9185
Mitchell Kahan, *President*
Sherry Streb, *General Mgr*
Susan Schweitzer, *Vice Pres*
John Kane, *Opers Mgr*
Bridgette Beard, *Comms Mgr*
EMP: 75
SQ FT: 3,312
SALES: 4.5MM **Privately Held**
WEB: www.akronartmuseum.org
SIC: 8412 Museum

(G-28)
AKRON AUTOMOBILE ASSOCIATION (PA)
Also Called: AKRON AUTOMOBILE CLUB
100 Rosa Parks Dr (44311-2015)
PHONE................................330 762-0631
Brian Thomas, *President*
Gail Lee, *Treasurer*
EMP: 83
SQ FT: 20,000
SALES: 7MM **Privately Held**
SIC: 8699 Automobile owners' association; travel club

(G-29)
AKRON BLIND CENTER & WORKSHOP (PA)
Also Called: VISON SUPPORT SERVICES
325 E Market St (44304-1340)
P.O. Box 1864 (44309-1864)
PHONE................................330 253-2555
Kristen Baysinger, *Exec Dir*
EMP: 53
SQ FT: 15,000
SALES: 91.6K **Privately Held**
SIC: 8331 Job training services

(G-30)
AKRON CENTL ENGRV MOLD MCH INC
1625 Massillon Rd (44312-4204)
PHONE................................330 794-8704
John Kaeberlein, *President*
Bob Simone, *Plant Mgr*
Linda Gibson, *Manager*
Frank Muhl, *Manager*
James Muhl, *Technology*
EMP: 50 **EST:** 1969
SQ FT: 15,000

SALES (est): 10.8MM **Privately Held**
WEB: www.acemm.com
SIC: 3544 8742 4213 Industrial molds; new products & services consultants; automobiles, transport & delivery

(G-31)
AKRON CHILDRENS MUSEUM
216 S Main St (44308-1315)
PHONE................................330 396-6103
Betsy Hartschuh, *Principal*
Traci Buckner, *Exec Dir*
EMP: 25
SALES: 583.2K **Privately Held**
SIC: 8412 Museum

(G-32)
AKRON CITY HOSPITAL INC
525 E Market St (44304-1698)
PHONE................................330 253-5046
Barbara Hiney, *Ch of Bd*
Albert F Gilbert, *President*
Beth O'Brien, *Exec VP*
James B Pickering, *Vice Pres*
David H Wilhoite, *Treasurer*
EMP: 2900
SQ FT: 850,000
SALES (est): 152.2MM **Privately Held**
SIC: 8062 General medical & surgical hospitals

(G-33)
AKRON CMNTY SVC CTR URBAN LEAG
Also Called: AKRON COMMUNITY SERV CENTER
440 Vernon Odom Blvd (44307-2108)
PHONE................................234 542-4141
Fred Wright, *President*
EMP: 28
SALES: 1.7MM **Privately Held**
SIC: 8399 Community action agency

(G-34)
AKRON COCA-COLA BOTTLING CO
1560 Triplett Blvd (44306-3306)
PHONE................................330 784-2653
Matt Cartaglia, *General Mgr*
▲ **EMP:** 1300 **EST:** 1985
SALES: 164.4MM
SALES (corp-wide): 35.4B **Publicly Held**
WEB: www.colasic.net
SIC: 5149 Soft drinks
HQ: Coca-Cola Refreshments Usa, Inc.
　　2500 Windy Ridge Pkwy Se
　　Atlanta GA 30339
　　770 989-3000

(G-35)
AKRON CONCRETE CORP
910 White Pond Dr (44320-1502)
PHONE................................330 864-1188
David Ochsenhirt, *President*
Mary Cavalier, *Human Resources*
EMP: 40
SALES (est): 4.1MM **Privately Held**
WEB: www.akronconcrete.com
SIC: 1771 Concrete pumping

(G-36)
AKRON COUNCIL OF ENGINEERING
411 Wolf Ledges Pkwy (44311-1028)
P.O. Box 2993 (44309-2993)
PHONE................................330 535-8835
Michael B Dowell, *Principal*
EMP: 30
SALES (corp-wide): 2.5MM **Privately Held**
SIC: 8621 Professional membership organizations
PA: Akron Council Of Engineering & Scientific Societies
　　411 Wolf Ledges Pkwy # 105
　　Akron OH 44311
　　330 535-8835

(G-37)
AKRON ELECTRIC INC
1025 Eaton Ave (44303)
PHONE................................330 745-8891
George Ostich, *President*
EMP: 65
SQ FT: 13,000

SALES (est): 14.5MM
SALES (corp-wide): 22MM **Privately Held**
WEB: www.akronelectric.com
SIC: 5063 Boxes & fittings, electrical
PA: Akron Foundry Co.
2728 Wingate Ave
Akron OH 44314
330 745-3101

(G-38)
AKRON ENERGY SYSTEMS LLC
226 Opportunity Pkwy (44307-2232)
PHONE..................330 374-0600
Marc Divis, *President*
Donald J Hoffman, *Chairman*
Rick Hawkins, *Plant Engr*
Paul Conlon, *Controller*
Robert Douglas, *Controller*
EMP: 54
SALES (est): 11.1MM **Privately Held**
SIC: 4961 Steam heating systems (suppliers of heat)

(G-39)
AKRON ERECTORS INC
8098 W Waterloo Rd (44314)
P.O. Box 3710 (44314-0710)
PHONE..................330 745-7100
Dennis Stump, *CEO*
EMP: 25
SQ FT: 1,000
SALES (est): 1.3MM **Privately Held**
SIC: 1791 Structural steel erection

(G-40)
AKRON FOUNDRY CO (PA)
2728 Wingate Ave (44314-1300)
P.O. Box 27028 (44319-7028)
PHONE..................330 745-3101
George Ostich, *President*
Ronald C Allan, *Principal*
Geraldine Ostich, *Vice Pres*
Michael Ostich, *VP Opers*
John Varga, *Supervisor*
EMP: 175 EST: 1969
SQ FT: 100,000
SALES: 22MM **Privately Held**
WEB: www.akronfoundry.com
SIC: 3369 5063 3365 3363 Castings, except die-castings, precision; boxes & fittings, electrical; aluminum foundries; aluminum die-castings

(G-41)
AKRON GENERAL FOUNDATION
Also Called: AKRON GENERAL HEALTH SYSTEM
400 Wabash Ave (44307)
PHONE..................330 344-6888
Karen Bozzelli, *President*
EMP: 45
SALES: 3MM
SALES (corp-wide): 8.9B **Privately Held**
SIC: 8322 Individual & family services
HQ: Akron General Medical Center Inc
1 Akron General Ave
Akron OH 44307
330 344-6000

(G-42)
AKRON GENERAL HEALTH SYSTEM
4125 Medina Rd Ste 104 (44333-4514)
PHONE..................330 665-8200
Doris Volk, *Principal*
EMP: 30
SALES (corp-wide): 8.9B **Privately Held**
SIC: 8011 Surgeon
HQ: Akron General Health System
1 Akron General Ave
Akron OH 44307
330 344-6000

(G-43)
AKRON GENERAL MEDICAL CENTER (DH)
Also Called: Edwin Shaw Rehabilitation Hosp
1 Akron General Ave (44307-2432)
PHONE..................330 344-6000
F William Steere, *Ch of Bd*
Cathy Ceccio, *Exec VP*
Mary Beth Carroll, *Director*
Phillip G Moser, *Nursing Dir*
EMP: 56 EST: 1914
SQ FT: 1,027,000

SALES: 544.4MM
SALES (corp-wide): 8.9B **Privately Held**
SIC: 8322 Rehabilitation services
HQ: Akron General Health System
1 Akron General Ave
Akron OH 44307
330 344-6000

(G-44)
AKRON GENERAL MEDICAL CENTER
224 W Exchange St Ste 330 (44302-1715)
PHONE..................330 344-1980
David Baumgardner, *Principal*
EMP: 103
SQ FT: 79,879
SALES (corp-wide): 8.9B **Privately Held**
SIC: 8062 General medical & surgical hospitals
HQ: Akron General Medical Center Inc
1 Akron General Ave
Akron OH 44307
330 344-6000

(G-45)
AKRON GENERAL MEDICAL CENTER
Akron Gen Employee Hlth Dept
1 Akron General Ave (44307-2432)
PHONE..................330 344-1444
Ken Bulen MD, *Director*
EMP: 103
SALES (corp-wide): 8.9B **Privately Held**
SIC: 8062 General medical & surgical hospitals
HQ: Akron General Medical Center Inc
1 Akron General Ave
Akron OH 44307
330 344-6000

(G-46)
AKRON GENERAL MEDICAL CENTER
Also Called: Akron Gen Hlth & Wellness Ctr
4125 Medina Rd Ste 1 (44333-4505)
PHONE..................330 665-8000
Doug Ribley, *Manager*
EMP: 200
SALES (corp-wide): 8.9B **Privately Held**
SIC: 8062 8093 7991 General medical & surgical hospitals; specialty outpatient clinics; health club
HQ: Akron General Medical Center Inc
1 Akron General Ave
Akron OH 44307
330 344-6000

(G-47)
AKRON HARDWARE CONSULTANTS INC (PA)
1100 Killian Rd (44312-4730)
PHONE..................330 644-7167
Roy Crute, *President*
Thomas Orihel, *COO*
Tim Kane, *Warehouse Mgr*
Dwayne Spencer, *Sales Mgr*
Craig Hoffman, *Manager*
EMP: 37
SQ FT: 28,000
SALES (est): 21.6MM **Privately Held**
SIC: 5072 Builders' hardware

(G-48)
AKRON MANAGEMENT CORP
Also Called: Firestone Country Club
452 E Warner Rd (44319-1925)
PHONE..................330 644-8441
Mark Gore, *General Mgr*
EMP: 260 EST: 1950
SQ FT: 3,700
SALES (est): 15.4MM
SALES (corp-wide): 477MM **Privately Held**
WEB: www.firestonecountryclub.com
SIC: 7997 5941 5812 5813 Golf club, membership; golf goods & equipment; eating places; cocktail lounge
HQ: Clubcorp Usa, Inc.
3030 Lyndon B Johnson Fwy
Dallas TX 75234
972 243-6191

(G-49)
AKRON NEONATOLOGY INC
300 Locust St (44302-1821)
PHONE..................330 379-9473
Anand D Kantak MD, *President*
William H Considine, *Principal*
EMP: 30
SALES (est): 1.2MM **Publicly Held**
WEB: www.pediatrix.com
SIC: 8011 Specialized medical practitioners, except internal; physical medicine, physician/surgeon; pediatrician
PA: Mednax, Inc.
1301 Concord Ter
Sunrise FL 33323

(G-50)
AKRON PLASTIC SURGEONS INC
Also Called: Parker, Michael G MD
1 Park West Blvd Ste 350 (44320-4226)
P.O. Box 1706, Stow (44224-0706)
PHONE..................330 253-9161
James Lehman Jr, *President*
Michael G Parker MD, *Principal*
Douglas S Wagner MD, *Principal*
Frank Quirk, *Corp Secy*
M D Tantri MD, *Vice Pres*
EMP: 37
SQ FT: 6,800
SALES (est): 3.9MM **Privately Held**
WEB: www.akronplasticsurgeons.com
SIC: 8011 Plastic surgeon

(G-51)
AKRON PUBLIC SCHOOL MAINT SVCS
Also Called: Facility Services
515 Grant St (44311-1109)
PHONE..................330 761-2640
Mike Critchfield, *Principal*
Ken Phares, *Administration*
EMP: 62
SALES (est): 1.1MM **Privately Held**
SIC: 7349 Building maintenance services

(G-52)
AKRON PUBLIC SCHOOLS
70 N Broadway St (44308-1911)
PHONE..................330 761-1660
David James, *Exec Dir*
EMP: 300
SALES (corp-wide): 260.1MM **Privately Held**
WEB: www.akronschools.com
SIC: 1541 Industrial buildings & warehouses
PA: Akron Public Schools
70 N Broadway St
Akron OH 44308
330 761-1661

(G-53)
AKRON RADIOLOGY INC
525 E Market St (44304-1619)
PHONE..................330 375-3043
Malay Mody, *President*
Edward Bury, *President*
Angelique Rogers, *Controller*
Brian L Hayes, *Diag Radio*
EMP: 28
SALES (est): 3.1MM **Privately Held**
WEB: www.akronradiology.com
SIC: 8062 General medical & surgical hospitals

(G-54)
AKRON RUBBER DEV LAB INC (PA)
2887 Gilchrist Rd (44305-4415)
PHONE..................330 794-6600
Charles R Samples, *CEO*
Jerry Leyden, *President*
Tim Samples, *Principal*
Lisa Jursik, *Manager*
Debbie Coffee, *Executive*
EMP: 100
SALES (est): 15.2MM **Privately Held**
WEB: www.ardl-india.com
SIC: 8731 Commercial research laboratory

(G-55)
AKRON SCHOOL TRNSP SVCS
500 E North St (44304-1220)
PHONE..................330 761-1390

Kathy Kiel, *Principal*
EMP: 80
SALES (est): 1.6MM **Privately Held**
SIC: 4151 School buses

(G-56)
AKRON SUMMIT CMNTY ACTION AGCY
Also Called: Foster Grandparent Program
670 W Exchange St (44302-1300)
PHONE..................330 572-8532
Sonia Williams, *Manager*
Jessica Hurst, *Director*
Robert Dowdell, *Administration*
Rebecca Davison, *Personnel Assit*
EMP: 150
SALES (corp-wide): 18MM **Privately Held**
WEB: www.ascainc.org
SIC: 8399 8361 Antipoverty board; group foster home
PA: Akron Summit Community Action Agency
55 E Mill St
Akron OH 44308
330 376-7730

(G-57)
AKRON SUMMIT CMNTY ACTION AGCY
1335 Massillon Rd (44306-4137)
PHONE..................330 733-2290
Alice Owen, *Manager*
EMP: 56
SALES (corp-wide): 18MM **Privately Held**
SIC: 8399 8351 Antipoverty board; child day care services
PA: Akron Summit Community Action Agency
55 E Mill St
Akron OH 44308
330 376-7730

(G-58)
AKRON SUMMIT CMNTY ACTION AGCY (PA)
Also Called: COMMUNITY ACTION AKRON SUMMIT
55 E Mill St (44308-1405)
P.O. Box 2000 (44309-2000)
PHONE..................330 376-7730
Malcolm J Costa, *President*
David Gabelman, *Vice Pres*
Richard Nelson, *CFO*
Parivash Naini, *Supervisor*
Matt Hoyt, *Database Admin*
EMP: 331
SQ FT: 8,908
SALES: 18MM **Privately Held**
WEB: www.ascainc.org
SIC: 8399 Community action agency

(G-59)
AKRON WOMANS CITY CLUB INC
732 W Exchange St (44302-1308)
PHONE..................330 762-6261
Judith Wishnek, *General Mgr*
Tina Nary, *General Mgr*
EMP: 25
SQ FT: 32,897
SALES: 916.8K **Privately Held**
SIC: 7997 Membership sports & recreation clubs

(G-60)
AKRON ZOOLOGICAL PARK
500 Edgewood Ave (44307-2199)
PHONE..................330 375-2550
L Patricia Simmons, *CEO*
Linda Criss, *Vice Pres*
Pete Mohan, *Opers Staff*
Robert Littman, *Treasurer*
Wendy Buck, *Director*
EMP: 50 EST: 1950
SQ FT: 35,000
SALES: 12.1MM **Privately Held**
WEB: www.akronzoo.com
SIC: 8422 Zoological garden, noncommercial

G E O G R A P H I C

(G-61)
AKRON-CANTON REGIONAL FOODBANK (PA)
350 Opportunity Pkwy (44307-2234)
PHONE....................330 535-6900
Daniel R Flowers, *CEO*
Peggy Susniskas, *COO*
Laura Bennett, *Vice Pres*
Patricia Gibbs, *Treasurer*
Michelle Hinton, *Marketing Staff*
EMP: 50
SQ FT: 87,000
SALES: 38.4MM **Privately Held**
WEB: www.akroncantonfoodbank.com
SIC: 8699 Charitable organization

(G-62)
AKRON-SUMMIT CONVENTION
Also Called: John S Knight Center
77 E Mill St (44308-1459)
PHONE....................330 374-7560
Gregg Mervis, *President*
Raven Gayheart, *Sales Mgr*
Jill Raymond, *Sales Mgr*
Chuck Wolfe, *Client Mgr*
Leslie O'Neal, *Sales Staff*
▲ **EMP:** 35 **EST:** 1973
SALES: 7.5MM **Privately Held**
WEB: www.johnsknightcenter.com
SIC: 7389 Convention & show services; tourist information bureau

(G-63)
ALCO-CHEM INC (PA)
45 N Summit St (44308-1933)
PHONE....................330 253-3535
Anthony Mandala Jr, *President*
Bart Mandala, *Vice Pres*
Robert Mandala, *Vice Pres*
▲ **EMP:** 34
SQ FT: 22,000
SALES: 26.7MM **Privately Held**
WEB: www.alco-chem.com
SIC: 5087 2869 2842 Janitors' supplies; industrial organic chemicals; specialty cleaning, polishes & sanitation goods

(G-64)
ALL STAR TRAINING CLUB
3108 Sparrows Crst (44319-5401)
PHONE....................330 352-5602
Catherine Lancianese, *Principal*
EMP: 25
SALES (est): 395.3K **Privately Held**
SIC: 8322 Individual & family services

(G-65)
ALLAN HUNTER CONSTRUCTION LLC
931 Evans Ave (44305-1041)
P.O. Box 1552 (44309-1552)
PHONE....................330 634-9882
Chris Moore, *Owner*
EMP: 25 **EST:** 2007
SQ FT: 4,000
SALES (est): 2.6MM **Privately Held**
SIC: 1521 4212 New construction, single-family houses; local trucking, without storage

(G-66)
ALLIED INFOTECH CORPORATION
2170 Romig Rd (44320-3879)
PHONE....................330 745-8529
Michael Zulia, *President*
Pam Fretz, *Info Tech Mgr*
EMP: 51
SQ FT: 18,000
SALES (est): 5.1MM **Privately Held**
WEB: www.alliedinfotech.com
SIC: 7389 Document storage service

(G-67)
ALMOST FAMILY INC
1225 E Waterloo Rd (44306-3805)
PHONE....................330 724-7545
Renea Thompson, *Branch Mgr*
EMP: 30
SALES (corp-wide): 1.8B **Publicly Held**
SIC: 8082 Home health care services
HQ: Almost Family, Inc.
9510 Ormsby Station Rd # 300
Louisville KY 40223
502 891-1000

(G-68)
ALPHA PHI ALPHA HOMES INC
730 Callis Dr (44311-1313)
PHONE....................330 376-2115
Beverly Lomax, *General Mgr*
EMP: 57
SALES (corp-wide): 2.3MM **Privately Held**
SIC: 7299 6513 Apartment locating service; apartment building operators
PA: Alpha Phi Alpha Homes Incorporated
662 Wolf Ledges Pkwy
Akron OH
330 376-8787

(G-69)
AMERICAN MED
1265 Triplett Blvd (44306-3162)
PHONE....................330 762-8999
Jerry Key, *CEO*
EMP: 300
SALES (corp-wide): 643.1MM **Privately Held**
WEB: www.amr-inc.com
SIC: 4119 8741 Ambulance service; management services
HQ: American Medical Response, Inc.
6363 S Fiddlers Green Cir # 1400
Greenwood Village CO 80111

(G-70)
AMERICAN NATIONAL RED CROSS
Also Called: American Natl Red CRS-Bld Svcs
501 W Market St (44303-1842)
PHONE....................330 535-6131
EMP: 33
SALES (corp-wide): 2.5B **Privately Held**
WEB: www.redcross.org
SIC: 8322 Emergency social services; disaster service; first aid service
PA: The American National Red Cross
430 17th St Nw
Washington DC 20006
202 737-8300

(G-71)
AMERICAS BEST MEDICAL EQP CO
Also Called: Americas Best Medical Eqp
1566 Akron Peninsula Rd # 2 (44313-7980)
PHONE....................330 928-0884
Jeffrey E Gregory, *President*
Sharon Gregory, *Vice Pres*
EMP: 40
SQ FT: 12,000
SALES (est): 6.4MM **Privately Held**
SIC: 5169 7352 5047 Oxygen; invalid supplies rental; medical & hospital equipment

(G-72)
AMERIPRISE FINANCIAL SVCS INC
3333 Massillon Rd Ste 110 (44312-5993)
PHONE....................330 494-9300
Kile Lewis, *Chairman*
EMP: 50
SALES (corp-wide): 12.8B **Publicly Held**
WEB: www.amps.com
SIC: 6282 Investment advisory service
HQ: Ameriprise Financial Services Inc.
707 2nd Ave S
Minneapolis MN 55402
612 671-2733

(G-73)
AMPERSAND GROUP LLC
1946 S Arlington St (44306-4285)
PHONE....................330 379-0044
Robert Penn, *Officer*
Todd Mellon,
EMP: 46
SALES: 13.6MM **Privately Held**
SIC: 5961 7389 ; financial services

(G-74)
ANESTHESIOLOGY ASSOC OF AKRON
224 W Exchange St Ste 220 (44302-1726)
PHONE....................330 344-6401
Paul Korytkowski, *President*
Dr Michael Di Cioccio,
EMP: 50
SALES (est): 4.6MM **Privately Held**
SIC: 8011 Anesthesiologist

(G-75)
ANSTINE DRYWALL INC
2215 E Waterloo Rd # 403 (44312-3857)
PHONE....................330 784-3867
Danny Anstine, *President*
EMP: 30 **EST:** 1987
SALES (est): 2.9MM **Privately Held**
SIC: 1742 Drywall

(G-76)
APPLE GROWTH PARTNERS INC (PA)
1540 W Market St (44313-7114)
PHONE....................330 867-7350
Harold Gaar, *CEO*
Ivan Mahovlic, *President*
Rick Archer, *Principal*
James Gornik, *Principal*
Sean McKiernan, *Principal*
EMP: 70
SQ FT: 2,500
SALES (est): 20.1MM **Privately Held**
SIC: 8748 8721 Business consulting; certified public accountant

(G-77)
ARCADIA SERVICES INC
Also Called: Arcadia Health Care
1650 W Market St Ste 27 (44313-7007)
PHONE....................330 869-9520
Kathy Kozachenko, *Manager*
EMP: 51
SALES (corp-wide): 147.7MM **Privately Held**
SIC: 7363 8082 Medical help service; home health care services
PA: Arcadia Services, Inc.
20750 Civic Center Dr # 100
Southfield MI 48076
248 352-7530

(G-78)
ARCADIS US INC
222 S Main St Ste 200 (44308-1538)
PHONE....................330 434-1995
Gary Johnson, *Branch Mgr*
EMP: 61
SALES (corp-wide): 2.8B **Privately Held**
SIC: 8711 Sanitary engineers
HQ: Arcadis U.S., Inc.
630 Plaza Dr Ste 200
Highlands Ranch CO 80129
720 344-3500

(G-79)
ARDMORE INC
981 E Market St (44305-2443)
PHONE....................330 535-2601
Deborah Dutton, *Finance*
Joyce Fox, *Manager*
Yvette Diaz, *Exec Dir*
Michael Trace, *Exec Dir*
Sheryl Weber, *Director*
EMP: 180 **EST:** 1975
SQ FT: 12,000
SALES: 6.4MM **Privately Held**
SIC: 8361 8699 Home for the mentally retarded; home for the physically handicapped; charitable organization

(G-80)
AT&T CORP
3890 Medina Rd Ste B (44333-2470)
PHONE....................330 665-3100
Derek Swan, *Branch Mgr*
EMP: 69
SALES (corp-wide): 170.7B **Publicly Held**
WEB: www.sbc.com
SIC: 4812 Cellular telephone services
HQ: At&T Corp.
1 At&T Way
Bedminster NJ 07921
800 403-3302

(G-81)
AT&T CORP
45 E Market St (44308-2009)
PHONE....................330 752-7776
Chad Elwell, *Manager*
EMP: 109

SALES (corp-wide): 170.7B **Publicly Held**
SIC: 4813 Local & long distance telephone communications
HQ: At&T Corp.
1 At&T Way
Bedminster NJ 07921
800 403-3302

(G-82)
AUTOMOTIVE DISTRIBUTORS CO INC
1329 E Archwood Ave (44306-2832)
PHONE....................330 785-7290
Robert Yeoman, *Owner*
EMP: 40
SALES (corp-wide): 132.8MM **Privately Held**
WEB: www.adw1.com
SIC: 5013 Automotive supplies
PA: Automotive Distributors Co., Inc.
2981 Morse Rd
Columbus OH 43231
614 476-1315

(G-83)
AXESSPOINTE CMNTY HLTH CTR INC (PA)
Also Called: Axesspointe Community Hlth Ctr
1400 S Arlington St # 38 (44306-3750)
P.O. Box 7695 (44306-0695)
PHONE....................330 724-5471
Mark Batson, *CEO*
Kathy Frank, *Site Mgr*
Gary Collins, *CFO*
Kristie Engler, *Officer*
EMP: 25
SALES (est): 4.3MM **Privately Held**
SIC: 8011 Clinic, operated by physicians

(G-84)
B F G FEDERAL CREDIT UNION (PA)
445 S Main St Ste B (44311-1056)
PHONE....................330 374-2990
Owen Dibert, *Ch of Bd*
Betty Phillips, *President*
Cheryl Foster, *Exec VP*
Paul Bush, *Credit Mgr*
EMP: 64
SQ FT: 29,000
SALES: 4.5MM **Privately Held**
WEB: www.bfgcu.net
SIC: 6061 Federal credit unions

(G-85)
BABCOX MEDIA INC
3550 Embassy Pkwy (44333-8318)
PHONE....................330 670-1234
William E Babcox, *President*
Nichole Anderson, *Design Engr*
Greg Cira, *CFO*
Bryan Hess, *Accounting Mgr*
Dawn Andrews, *Manager*
EMP: 75
SQ FT: 40,000
SALES (est): 11.7MM **Privately Held**
WEB: www.bodyshopbusiness.com
SIC: 8742 Marketing consulting services

(G-86)
BARBICAS CONSTRUCTION CO
124 Darrow Rd Ste 1 (44305-3835)
PHONE....................330 733-9101
Carla Barbicas, *President*
Lee Barbicas, *General Mgr*
Valas Winters, *Superintendent*
Elia Barbicas, *Corp Secy*
Alan Potter, *Safety Dir*
EMP: 36 **EST:** 1947
SQ FT: 9,600
SALES: 9.1MM **Privately Held**
SIC: 1771 1611 Blacktop (asphalt) work; surfacing & paving; grading; highway & street paving contractor; general contractor, highway & street construction

(G-87)
BATH MANOR LIMITED PARTNERSHIP
Also Called: BATH MANOR SPECIAL CARE CENTRE
2330 Smith Rd (44333-2927)
PHONE....................330 836-1006
Morton J Weisburg, *President*

Vernie Venture, *Education*
EMP: 50
SALES: 10.9MM
SALES (corp-wide): 157.7MM **Privately Held**
SIC: 8051 Skilled nursing care facilities
PA: Saber Healthcare Group, L.L.C.
26691 Richmond Rd Frnt
Bedford OH 44146
216 292-5706

(G-88)
BATTERED WOMENS SHELTER (PA)
Also Called: B W S
974 E Market St (44305-2445)
PHONE..............................330 374-0740
Terri Heckman, *Director*
EMP: 75
SQ FT: 5,542
SALES: 5MM **Privately Held**
WEB: www.scmcbws.org
SIC: 8322 Emergency shelters

(G-89)
BBS & ASSOCIATES INC
130 Springside Dr Ste 200 (44333-4553)
PHONE..............................330 665-5227
Dale Berkey, *President*
Jim Alexander, *Vice Pres*
Phyllis Laskowski, *CFO*
Amy Nicely, *Sr Project Mgr*
EMP: 32
SALES (est): 2.6MM **Privately Held**
SIC: 7389 7311 8748 Fund raising organizations; advertising agencies; business consulting

(G-90)
BCG SYSTEMS THAT WORK INC
Also Called: B C G Systems
1735 Merriman Rd Ste 3000 (44313-9005)
PHONE..............................330 864-4816
Mark Goodson, *President*
Jim Coats, *Vice Pres*
EMP: 35
SQ FT: 12,000
SALES (est): 5.6MM **Privately Held**
WEB: www.systemsthatwork.com
SIC: 7379 Computer related consulting services
PA: Brockman, Coats, Gedelian & Co.
1735 Merriman Rd Ste 300
Akron OH

(G-91)
BDO USA LLP
301 Springside Dr (44333-2434)
PHONE..............................330 668-9696
James Dannemiller, *Partner*
EMP: 90
SALES (corp-wide): 940.4MM **Privately Held**
SIC: 8721 Certified public accountant
PA: Bdo Usa, Llp
330 N Wabash Ave Ste 3200
Chicago IL 60611
312 240-1236

(G-92)
BEACON COMPANY (PA)
Also Called: Northeast Furniture Rental
2350 Gilchrist Rd (44305-3810)
PHONE..............................330 733-8322
Jerry Karkowski, *President*
Jean Conrad, *Corp Secy*
Rick Macken, *Controller*
EMP: 26
SQ FT: 12,000
SALES (est): 4.3MM **Privately Held**
SIC: 7359 5712 Furniture rental; furniture stores

(G-93)
BELL MUSIC COMPANY
533 W Market St (44303-1892)
PHONE..............................330 376-6337
Fax: 330 376-3776
EMP: 25
SQ FT: 12,000
SALES (est): 1.3MM **Privately Held**
SIC: 7993 Amusement Device Operator

(G-94)
BENEFICIAL BUILDING SERVICES (PA)
1830 13th St Sw (44314-2907)
PHONE..............................330 848-2556
James Lawson, *President*
Paul Carnifac, *Vice Pres*
Tom Lesiczka, *Vice Pres*
EMP: 55
SQ FT: 500
SALES (est): 1.6MM **Privately Held**
SIC: 7349 Building cleaning service; building maintenance, except repairs; janitorial service, contract basis; window cleaning

(G-95)
BERNARD BUSSON BUILDER
Also Called: Timbertop Apartments
1551 Treetop Trl (44313-4986)
P.O. Box 5480 (44334-0480)
PHONE..............................330 929-4926
Bernard D Busson, *Owner*
EMP: 41
SQ FT: 4,000
SALES (est): 3.4MM **Privately Held**
SIC: 1522 1531 8741 1521 Apartment building construction; speculative builder, multi-family dwellings; management services; single-family housing construction

(G-96)
BERNS ONEILL SEC & SAFETY LLC
Also Called: Boss Investigations
1000 N Main St (44310-1452)
PHONE..............................330 374-9133
Dan O'Neill, *Mng Member*
Maurice Berns,
EMP: 30
SQ FT: 2,000
SALES (est): 55K
SALES (corp-wide): 6.4MM **Privately Held**
SIC: 7361 Placement agencies
PA: Professional Placement Services Llc
34200 Solon Rd
Solon OH 44139
440 914-0090

(G-97)
BEST WESTERN EXECUTIVE INN
2677 Gilchrist Rd Unit 1 (44305-4439)
PHONE..............................330 794-1050
Dilu Dinani, *Partner*
Haider Ladha, *Partner*
EMP: 25
SQ FT: 73,823
SALES (est): 1.3MM **Privately Held**
SIC: 7011 Hotels

(G-98)
BIO-MDCAL APPLCATIONS OHIO INC
Also Called: Greater Akron Dialysis Center
345 Bishop St (44307-2401)
PHONE..............................330 376-4905
Dottie Sample, *Exec Dir*
EMP: 28
SQ FT: 2,000
SALES (corp-wide): 18.9B **Privately Held**
WEB: www.fresenius.org
SIC: 8092 Kidney dialysis centers
HQ: Bio-Medical Applications Of Ohio, Inc.
920 Winter St
Waltham MA 02451

(G-99)
BLICK CLINIC INC (PA)
640 W Market St (44303-1465)
PHONE..............................330 762-5425
Karin Loper-Orr, *President*
Michelle Clark, *Purchasing*
Gayle Breedlove, *Bookkeeper*
Judy Colvin, *Human Res Dir*
Tonia Bogema, *Manager*
EMP: 215 EST: 1969
SQ FT: 15,600
SALES: 14.7MM **Privately Held**
WEB: www.blickclinic.org
SIC: 8093 8322 Mental health clinic, outpatient; individual & family services

(G-100)
BLICK CLINIC INC
682 W Market St (44303-1414)
PHONE..............................330 762-5425
Dr G Lafoarme, *Exec Dir*
EMP: 60
SQ FT: 11,400
SALES (corp-wide): 14.7MM **Privately Held**
WEB: www.blickclinic.org
SIC: 8093 Mental health clinic, outpatient
PA: Blick Clinic, Inc.
640 W Market St
Akron OH 44303
330 762-5425

(G-101)
BLUELINX CORPORATION
550 Munroe Falls Rd (44305)
P.O. Box 218, Mogadore (44260-0218)
PHONE..............................330 794-1141
Bob Jacobus, *Manager*
EMP: 30
SALES (corp-wide): 1.8B **Publicly Held**
WEB: www.bluelinx.com
SIC: 5031 Building materials, exterior; doors & windows; building materials, interior
HQ: Bluelinx Corporation
1950 Spectrum Cir Se # 300
Marietta GA 30067
770 953-7000

(G-102)
BOGIE INDUSTRIES INC LTD
Also Called: Weaver Fab & Finishing
1100 Home Ave (44310-3504)
PHONE..............................330 745-3105
Jim Lauer, *President*
Marian Lauer, *Owner*
Fuzzy Helton, *Vice Pres*
Anthony Tarulli, *Purch Agent*
EMP: 38 EST: 1998
SQ FT: 40,000
SALES (est): 10.7MM **Privately Held**
WEB: www.weaverfab.com
SIC: 3444 1799 3399 Sheet metalwork; coating of metal structures at construction site; powder, metal

(G-103)
BRAKEFIRE INCORPORATED
Also Called: Akron Welding & Spring Co
451 Kennedy Rd (44305-4423)
PHONE..............................330 535-4343
Kenneth G May, *Manager*
EMP: 34
SALES (corp-wide): 31MM **Privately Held**
WEB: www.silcofireprotection.com
SIC: 5087 Firefighting equipment
PA: Brakefire, Incorporated
10765 Medallion Dr
Cincinnati OH 45241
513 733-5655

(G-104)
BRAUN & STEIDL ARCHITECTS INC (HQ)
Also Called: Studio of Prime Ae Group
450 White Pond Dr Ste 200 (44320-4209)
PHONE..............................330 864-7755
Kumar Buvanendaran, *President*
Olivia Evans, *Opers Mgr*
Kathy Cyphert, *CFO*
Josh Drummond, *Internal Med*
Matt Tolodzieski, *Internal Med*
EMP: 25
SALES (est): 3.5MM **Privately Held**
WEB: www.bsa-net.com
SIC: 8712 Architectural engineering

(G-105)
BRENNAN MANNA & DIAMOND LLC (PA)
75 E Market St (44308-2010)
PHONE..............................330 253-5060
Nancy Grams, *President*
Joy Westfall, *Office Mgr*
Anthony S Manna,
Jack T Diamond,
Michael R Freed,
EMP: 50
SQ FT: 6,800

SALES (est): 7.9MM **Privately Held**
WEB: www.bmdllc.com
SIC: 8111 General practice law office

(G-106)
BRIDGESTONE RESEARCH LLC
Also Called: Bridgestone Americas Center
1655 S Main St (44301-2035)
PHONE..............................330 379-7570
H Mouri, *President*
EMP: 1468
SALES (est): 98.4MM
SALES (corp-wide): 32.4B **Privately Held**
WEB: www.bridgestone-firestone.com
SIC: 8731 Commercial physical research
HQ: Bridgestone Americas Tire Operations, Llc
200 4th Ave S Ste 100
Nashville TN 37201
615 937-1000

(G-107)
BRIGHT HORIZONS CHLD CTRS LLC
475 Ohio St (44304-1421)
PHONE..............................330 375-7633
Cindy Usner, *Exec Dir*
EMP: 27
SALES (corp-wide): 1.9B **Publicly Held**
WEB: www.atlantaga.ncr.com
SIC: 8351 Group day care center
HQ: Bright Horizons Children's Centers Llc
200 Talcott Ave
Watertown MA 02472
617 673-8000

(G-108)
BRINKS INCORPORATED
1601 Industrial Pkwy (44310-2695)
PHONE..............................330 633-5351
Steve Seredich, *General Mgr*
Mike Nace, *Manager*
EMP: 40
SALES (corp-wide): 3.4B **Publicly Held**
WEB: www.brinksinc.com
SIC: 7381 Armored car services
HQ: Brink's, Incorporated
1801 Bayberry Ct Ste 400
Richmond VA 23226
804 289-9600

(G-109)
BROOKDALE LVING CMMUNITIES INC
100 Brookmont Rd Ofc (44333-9268)
PHONE..............................330 666-4545
Debra Haueter, *Manager*
Carol Shemenski, *Hlthcr Dir*
EMP: 50
SALES (corp-wide): 4.5B **Publicly Held**
WEB: www.parkplace-spokane.com
SIC: 6513 Retirement hotel operation
HQ: Brookdale Living Communities, Inc.
515 N State St Ste 1750
Chicago IL 60654

(G-110)
BROOKDALE SENIOR LIVING INC
101 N Clvland Mssilon Rd (44333-2422)
PHONE..............................330 666-7011
John Rijos, *Branch Mgr*
EMP: 61
SALES (corp-wide): 4.5B **Publicly Held**
SIC: 8059 Nursing home, except skilled & intermediate care facility
PA: Brookdale Senior Living
111 Westwood Pl Ste 400
Brentwood TN 37027
615 221-2250

(G-111)
BROTT MARDIS & CO
1540 W Market St (44313-7114)
PHONE..............................330 762-5022
Denise M Griggs, *President*
Donald A Brott, *President*
William B Mardis, *Vice Pres*
Kevin L Snyder, *Asst Treas*
Robert A Kazar, *Admin Sec*
EMP: 30
SQ FT: 4,300

SALES (est): 1.5MM **Privately Held**
WEB: www.brottmardis.com
SIC: **8721** Accounting services, except auditing

(G-112)
**BUCKEYE CMNTY THIRTY FIVE
LP**
2228 11th St Sw (44314)
PHONE.............................614 942-2020
Steve Boone, *Partner*
Trenda Cooper, *Clerk*
EMP: 99 EST: 2013
SALES (est): 3.8MM **Privately Held**
SIC: **6513** Apartment building operators

(G-113)
**BUCKEYE STATE CREDIT UNION
(PA)**
197 E Thornton St (44311-1537)
P.O. Box 848 (44309-0848)
PHONE.............................330 253-9197
Norma Sue Preston, *CEO*
EMP: 65
SALES (est): 3.1MM **Privately Held**
WEB: www.buckeyecu.com
SIC: **6062** State credit unions, not federally chartered

(G-114)
**BUCKINGHAM DLTTLE
BRROUGHS LLC (PA)**
3800 Embassy Pkwy (44333-8387)
PHONE.............................330 376-5300
Nicholas T George, *President*
Chelsea Gehring, *President*
Terry Lehner, *President*
David Drechsler, *Managing Prtnr*
Aimee Muzic, *Managing Prtnr*
EMP: 165
SQ FT: 70,000
SALES (est): 40.6MM **Privately Held**
SIC: **8111** General practice law office

(G-115)
**BUREAU VERITAS NORTH AMER
INC**
520 S Main St Ste 2444 (44311-1087)
PHONE.............................330 252-5100
Barb Hana, *President*
EMP: 30
SALES (corp-wide): 280.5MM **Privately
Held**
SIC: **8748** Environmental consultant
HQ: Bureau Veritas North America, Inc.
1601 Sawgrs Corp Pkwy
Sunrise FL 33323
954 236-8100

(G-116)
CANAL PHYSICIAN GROUP
1 Akron General Ave (44307-2432)
PHONE.............................330 344-4000
Lakshman Negi, *Med Doctor*
Kim Roberts, *Practice Mgr*
EMP: 25
SALES (est): 2MM **Privately Held**
SIC: **8011** General & family practice, physician/surgeon

(G-117)
**CARDINAL ENVIRONMENTAL
SVC INC**
180 E Miller Ave (44301-1349)
PHONE.............................330 252-0220
Daniel Pohl, *President*
Ray Brophy, *Vice Pres*
Allen Linger, *Manager*
EMP: 25
SQ FT: 10,000
SALES (est): 3.1MM **Privately Held**
SIC: **1799** Asbestos removal & encapsulation

(G-118)
**CARDINAL MAINTENANCE &
SVC CO**
180 E Miller Ave (44301-1349)
PHONE.............................330 252-0282
Dan Pohl, *President*
EMP: 120
SQ FT: 7,000

SALES (est): 5.5MM **Privately Held**
SIC: **7349 8748 1761** Janitorial service, contract basis; business consulting; roofing, siding & sheet metal work

(G-119)
**CARTER-JONES LUMBER
COMPANY**
Also Called: Carter Lumber
172 N Case Ave (44305-2599)
PHONE.............................330 784-5441
Mike Smead, *Manager*
EMP: 70
SALES (corp-wide): 1.4B **Privately Held**
SIC: **5211 5031 5251** Lumber products; lumber, plywood & millwork; hardware
HQ: The Carter-Jones Lumber Company
601 Tallmadge Rd
Kent OH 44240
330 673-6100

(G-120)
CBIZ ACCOUNTING TAX
4040 Embassy Pkwy Ste 100
(44333-8354)
PHONE.............................330 668-6500
Bradford Hale, *Managing Dir*
Betty Isler, *Managing Dir*
Tracey McDonald, *Managing Dir*
Laura Plotner, *Managing Dir*
Kathleen Watson, *Managing Dir*
EMP: 60
SALES (est): 4MM **Publicly Held**
WEB: www.cbizinc.com
SIC: **8721** Accounting, auditing & bookkeeping
PA: Cbiz, Inc.
6050 Oak Tree Blvd # 500
Cleveland OH 44131

(G-121)
**CEDARWOOD CONSTRUCTION
COMPANY**
1765 Merriman Rd (44313-9003)
PHONE.............................330 836-9971
Anthony Petrarca, *President*
EMP: 100
SQ FT: 15,500
SALES (est): 6.3MM **Privately Held**
SIC: **8741 1542** Construction management; commercial & office building, new construction

(G-122)
CELLCO PARTNERSHIP
Also Called: Verizon Wireless
50 W Bowery St (44308-1102)
PHONE.............................330 376-8275
EMP: 71
SALES (corp-wide): 130.8B **Publicly
Held**
SIC: **4812** Cellular telephone services
HQ: Cellco Partnership
1 Verizon Way
Basking Ridge NJ 07920

(G-123)
CENTER 5
Also Called: Suma Health Sys St Thomas
Hosp
444 N Main St (44310-3110)
PHONE.............................330 379-5900
Fax: 330 379-5515
EMP: 85
SALES (est): 3MM **Privately Held**
SIC: **8093** Specialty Outpatient Clinic

(G-124)
**CENTER FOR UROLOGIC
HEALTH LLC (PA)**
Also Called: Physicians Urology Centre
95 Arch St Ste 165 (44304-1488)
PHONE.............................330 375-0924
Fabian Breaux MD, *President*
Joseph Dankoff, *Corp Secy*
John Chulik MD, *Vice Pres*
Ray Bologna, *Med Doctor*
Kevin Spear, *Med Doctor*
EMP: 49
SALES (est): 4.9MM **Privately Held**
WEB: www.physiciansurology.com
SIC: **8011** Medical centers; urologist

(G-125)
**CHAPEL HILL MANAGEMENT
INC**
2000 Brittain Rd Ste 830 (44310-4303)
PHONE.............................330 633-7100
Richard B Buchholzer, *President*
Robert P Dunn, *Vice Pres*
Mildred R Blount, *Admin Sec*
EMP: 65
SQ FT: 12,590
SALES (est): 4.3MM **Privately Held**
SIC: **6512** Shopping center, community (100,000 - 300,000 sq ft)

(G-126)
**CHEMSTRESS CONSULTANT
COMPANY (PA)**
39 S Main St Ste 315 (44308-1856)
PHONE.............................330 535-5591
James Kehres, *President*
Paul K Christoff, *Principal*
Rod Clark, *Principal*
Wiliam R Ferguson, *Principal*
Jean E Hagen, *Principal*
EMP: 150 EST: 1965
SQ FT: 70,000
SALES (est): 27.7MM **Privately Held**
WEB: www.chemstress.com
SIC: **8711 8712 8741** Consulting engineer; architectural services; construction management

(G-127)
CHESTER WEST DENTISTRY
1575 Vernon Odom Blvd (44320-4091)
PHONE.............................330 753-7734
Dr Jeffrey S Rosenthal, *President*
EMP: 30
SALES (est): 274.1K **Privately Held**
SIC: **8011 8021** Offices & clinics of medical doctors; dentists' office

(G-128)
CHICAGO TITLE INSURANCE CO
799 White Pond Dr Ste A (44320-1189)
PHONE.............................330 873-9393
Lorie Finney, *Banking Exec*
Shelly Maggard, *Manager*
EMP: 80
SALES (corp-wide): 7.5B **Publicly Held**
WEB: www.goldleaf-tech.com
SIC: **6361** Real estate title insurance
HQ: Chicago Title Insurance Company
601 Riverside Ave
Jacksonville FL 32204

(G-129)
**CHILDRENS HOME CARE
GROUP**
185 W Cedar St Ste 203 (44307-2447)
PHONE.............................330 543-5000
Polly Herchek, *Director*
Sally Hartline, *Director*
EMP: 280
SALES: 11.2MM **Privately Held**
SIC: **8082** Home health care services

(G-130)
**CHILDRENS HOSP MED CTR
AKRON (PA)**
Also Called: Akron Children's Hospital
1 Perkins Sq (44308-1063)
PHONE.............................330 543-1000
William Considine, *CEO*
Daniel McMahon, *Trustee*
Michael Rubin, *Ch Radiology*
Karen Richter, *Vice Pres*
Walt Schwoeble, *Vice Pres*
EMP: 3462
SQ FT: 356,000
SALES: 747.4MM **Privately Held**
SIC: **8069** Children's hospital

(G-131)
**CHILDRENS HOSP MED CTR
AKRON**
Also Called: Ask Childrens
1 Perkins Sq (44308-1063)
PHONE.............................330 543-8004
Cheryl Ballentine, *Principal*
Kay Kirtley, *Manager*
Kristene Nagy, *Manager*
Christine Perebzak, *Education*
EMP: 40

SALES (corp-wide): 747.4MM **Privately
Held**
SIC: **8069 8011** Children's hospital; offices & clinics of medical doctors
PA: Childrens Hospital Medical Center Of Akron
1 Perkins Sq
Akron OH 44308
330 543-1000

(G-132)
CIOFFI & SON CONSTRUCTION
1001 Eastwood Ave (44305-1127)
PHONE.............................330 794-9448
Frank Cioffi, *President*
Mark Rittenhour, *Superintendent*
Dominic Cioffi, *Vice Pres*
Maria Palcko, *Admin Sec*
Jamie Stone, *Admin Sec*
EMP: 30 EST: 1975
SQ FT: 5,000
SALES (est): 4.4MM **Privately Held**
SIC: **1771** Sidewalk contractor; curb construction; driveway contractor

(G-133)
CITY OF AKRON
Also Called: Alcohol, Drug Addiction
100 W Cedar St Ste 300 (44307-2572)
PHONE.............................330 564-4075
Gerald Craig, *Manager*
EMP: 51 **Privately Held**
SIC: **9431 6513** Administration of public health programs; apartment building operators
PA: City Of Akron
166 S High St Rm 502
Akron OH 44308
330 375-2720

(G-134)
CITY OF AKRON
Also Called: Good Park Golf Course
530 Nome Ave (44320-1234)
PHONE.............................330 864-0020
Dante Deandrea, *Branch Mgr*
EMP: 30 **Privately Held**
SIC: **7992** Public golf courses
PA: City Of Akron
166 S High St Rm 502
Akron OH 44308
330 375-2720

(G-135)
CITY OF AKRON
Also Called: Akron Water Distribution Div
1460 Triplett Blvd (44306-3304)
PHONE.............................330 375-2420
David Crundell, *Principal*
EMP: 120 **Privately Held**
SIC: **4941** Water supply
PA: City Of Akron
166 S High St Rm 502
Akron OH 44308
330 375-2720

(G-136)
CITY OF AKRON
Bureau of Engineering
166 S High St Rm 701 (44308-1627)
PHONE.............................330 375-2355
Jim Hewitt, *Office Mgr*
EMP: 80 **Privately Held**
SIC: **8711 9111** Engineering services; mayors' offices
PA: City Of Akron
166 S High St Rm 502
Akron OH 44308
330 375-2720

(G-137)
CITY OF AKRON
Sewer Department
2460 Akron Peninsula Rd (44313-4710)
PHONE.............................330 375-2666
Jim Six, *Branch Mgr*
EMP: 50
SQ FT: 240 **Privately Held**
SIC: **4952** Sewerage systems
PA: City Of Akron
166 S High St Rm 502
Akron OH 44308
330 375-2720

(G-138)
CITY OF AKRON
Also Called: Traffic Engineering
1420 Triplett Blvd (44306-3304)
PHONE..................................330 375-2851
David Gester, *Manager*
EMP: 33 **Privately Held**
SIC: 8748 9111 Traffic consultant; mayors'
offices
PA: City Of Akron
166 S High St Rm 502
Akron OH 44308
330 375-2720

(G-139)
CITY SCRAP & SALVAGE CO
760 Flora Ave (44314-1755)
PHONE..................................330 753-5051
Steven Katz, *CEO*
Randy Katz, *Vice Pres*
EMP: 31
SQ FT: 10,000
SALES (est): 7.7MM
SALES (corp-wide): 1.3B **Publicly Held**
SIC: 5093 3341 Ferrous metal scrap &
waste; nonferrous metals scrap; second-
ary nonferrous metals
HQ: Tsb Metal Recycling Llc
1835 Dueber Ave Sw
Canton OH 44706

(G-140)
CITY YELLOW CAB COMPANY
650 Home Ave (44310-4102)
PHONE..................................330 253-3141
Derek McClenathen, *President*
Derek Mc Clenathen, *President*
Cornelius P Chima, *Corp Secy*
EMP: 30 EST: 1933
SQ FT: 6,000
SALES (est): 2.7MM **Privately Held**
SIC: 7515 4121 Passenger car leasing;
taxicabs

(G-141)
**CLEARPATH HM HLTH HOSPICE
LLC**
475 Wolf Ledges Pkwy (44311-1199)
PHONE..................................330 784-2162
Ruth Self, *Mng Member*
EMP: 90
SALES (est): 3.5MM **Privately Held**
SIC: 8082 Visiting nurse service

(G-142)
CLEARWATER SERVICES INC
Also Called: Clearwater Systems
1411 Vernon Odom Blvd (44320-4086)
PHONE..................................330 836-4946
Jerome P Kovach Jr, *CEO*
EMP: 61 EST: 2014
SQ FT: 13,000
SALES (est): 7.4MM **Privately Held**
SIC: 4941 7389 Water supply; water sof-
tener service

(G-143)
**CLEVELAND ELC ILLUMINATING
CO (HQ)**
76 S Main St (44308-1812)
PHONE..................................800 589-3101
John E Skory, *President*
L L Vespoli, *Exec VP*
Harvey L Wagner, *Vice Pres*
Michael Deflorville, *Opers Staff*
Mark T Clark, *CFO*
EMP: 91 EST: 1892
SALES: 928.4MM **Publicly Held**
SIC: 4911 Generation, electric power;
transmission, electric power

(G-144)
CLIFTONLARSONALLEN LLP
388 S Main St Ste 403 (44311-4407)
PHONE..................................330 376-0100
Mike Markowski, *Manager*
EMP: 26
SALES (corp-wide): 755.1MM **Privately
Held**
WEB: www.brunercox.com
SIC: 8721 Accounting services, except au-
diting

PA: Cliftonlarsonallen Llp
220 S 6th St Ste 300
Minneapolis MN 55402
612 376-4500

(G-145)
CLUBCORP USA INC
600 Swartz Rd (44319-1332)
PHONE..................................330 724-4444
Mark Gore, *Manager*
EMP: 25
SALES (corp-wide): 477MM **Privately
Held**
WEB: www.remington-gc.com
SIC: 7997 Country club, membership
HQ: Clubcorp Usa, Inc.
3030 Lyndon B Johnson Fwy
Dallas TX 75234
972 243-6191

(G-146)
COHEN & COMPANY LTD
3500 Embassy Pkwy (44333-8373)
PHONE..................................330 374-1040
J Michael Kolk, *Partner*
Tracy Campbell, *Manager*
Sean Detwiler, *Manager*
Jenn Pederson, *Manager*
Adam Timblin, *Manager*
EMP: 100
SALES (corp-wide): 36MM **Privately
Held**
WEB: www.cohencpa.com
SIC: 8721 Certified public accountant
PA: Cohen & Company, Ltd.
1350 Euclid Ave Ste 800
Cleveland OH 44115
216 579-1040

(G-147)
**COLEMAN PROFESSIONAL
SVCS INC**
Sage Computer
3043 Sanitarium Rd Ste 2 (44312-4600)
PHONE..................................330 628-2275
Fred Brown, *Technology*
Debra Prioletti, *Director*
EMP: 220
SALES (corp-wide): 51.3MM **Privately
Held**
SIC: 7374 Data entry service
PA: Coleman Professional Services, Inc.
5982 Rhodes Rd
Kent OH 44240
330 673-1347

(G-148)
**COMMERCIAL TIME SHARING
INC**
Also Called: C T I
2740 Cory Ave (44314-1339)
PHONE..................................330 644-3059
David L Poling, *Ch of Bd*
Ronald Symens, *President*
Gerard Beisler, *VP Opers*
Furst Daniel, *Mfg Spvr*
Susan Mikulin, *Purchasing*
EMP: 29
SQ FT: 8,000
SALES (est): 6MM **Privately Held**
WEB: www.ipobox.net
SIC: 7373 7371 5045 Systems integration
services; computer software develop-
ment; computer software

(G-149)
**COMMUNITY DRUG BOARD INC
(PA)**
725 E Market St (44305-2421)
PHONE..................................330 315-5590
Theodore P Ziegler, *CEO*
Janet Wagner, *COO*
Pamela J Crislip, *CFO*
Pamela Crislip, *CFO*
EMP: 90
SQ FT: 17,000
SALES: 12.5MM **Privately Held**
SIC: 8093 8322 Substance abuse clinics
(outpatient); substance abuse counseling

(G-150)
COMMUNITY DRUG BOARD INC
Also Called: Ramar-Genesis
380 S Portage Path (44320-2326)
PHONE..................................330 996-5114

Rozanne Hindman, *Branch Mgr*
EMP: 90
SALES (corp-wide): 12.5MM **Privately
Held**
SIC: 8322 Rehabilitation services
PA: Community Drug Board, Inc.
725 E Market St
Akron OH 44305
330 315-5590

(G-151)
**COMMUNITY HBILITATION SVCS
INC (PA)**
Also Called: University of Individuality
493 Canton Rd (44312-1647)
P.O. Box 1028 (44309-1028)
PHONE..................................234 334-4288
Wanda Haines, *President*
EMP: 25
SQ FT: 100
SALES: 40.5MM **Privately Held**
SIC: 8361 Home for the mentally retarded

(G-152)
**COMMUNITY LEGAL AID
SERVICES (PA)**
Also Called: WESTERN RESERVE LEGAL
SERVICES
50 S Main St Ste 800 (44308-1823)
PHONE..................................330 535-4191
Nancy Grim, *President*
Ereka Langford, *Office Mgr*
Linda Duffy, *Manager*
Laureen Moore, *Manager*
John Petit, *Manager*
EMP: 70
SALES: 5.7MM **Privately Held**
SIC: 8111 Legal aid service; general prac-
tice attorney, lawyer

(G-153)
**COMMUNITY SUPPORT
SERVICES INC (PA)**
150 Cross St (44311-1026)
PHONE..................................330 253-9388
Terry Dalton, *CEO*
Terrence B Dalton, *President*
Frank Sepetauc, *COO*
James E Bournival, *Vice Pres*
Suzanne Gorman, *Opers Staff*
EMP: 201
SQ FT: 45,000
SALES: 18.3MM **Privately Held**
WEB: www.cssbh.org
SIC: 8093 8331 8361 Mental health clinic,
outpatient; vocational rehabilitation
agency; home for the emotionally dis-
turbed

(G-154)
**COMMUNITY SUPPORT
SERVICES INC**
Also Called: Work Tech
150 Cross St (44311-1026)
PHONE..................................330 253-9675
Frank Sepetauc, *Manager*
EMP: 75
SALES (corp-wide): 18.3MM **Privately
Held**
WEB: www.cssbh.org
SIC: 8093 Mental health clinic, outpatient
PA: Community Support Services, Inc.
150 Cross St
Akron OH 44311
330 253-9388

(G-155)
**COMMUNITY SUPPORT
SERVICES INC**
Also Called: Keebler Hall
403 Canton Rd (44312-1603)
PHONE..................................330 733-6203
Rebecca Sandlin, *Manager*
EMP: 74
SALES (corp-wide): 18.3MM **Privately
Held**
WEB: www.cssbh.org
SIC: 8093 Mental health clinic, outpatient
PA: Community Support Services, Inc.
150 Cross St
Akron OH 44311
330 253-9388

(G-156)
**CONCORD TESTA HOTEL
ASSOC LLC**
Also Called: Courtyard By Marriott
41 Furnace St (44308-1914)
PHONE..................................330 252-9228
Garry Kirkland, *General Mgr*
Dena St Clair,
EMP: 99
SALES (est): 587.2K **Privately Held**
SIC: 7011 Hotels & motels

(G-157)
**CONWED PLAS ACQUISITION V
LLC**
Also Called: Filtrexx International
61 N Clevlnd Mssln Rd (44333-4558)
PHONE..................................440 926-2607
Chris Hatzenbuhler, *CEO*
Ray Swartzwelder, *President*
EMP: 99
SQ FT: 1,000
SALES (est): 17.6MM **Publicly Held**
SIC: 8731 Environmental research
PA: Schweitzer-Mauduit International, Inc.
100 N Point Ctr E Ste 600
Alpharetta GA 30022

(G-158)
**COOPER BROTHERS TRUCKING
LLC (PA)**
1355 E Archwood Ave (44306-2832)
P.O. Box 7725 (44306-0725)
PHONE..................................330 784-1717
Annalee Cooper, *Mng Member*
Mark Cooper, *Manager*
Adam Khattab, *Manager*
EMP: 29
SQ FT: 60,000
SALES: 7MM **Privately Held**
WEB: www.cooperbrostrucking.com
SIC: 4213 Heavy hauling

(G-159)
**CORNERSTONE MEDICAL
ASSOCIATES**
453 S High St Ste 201 (44311-4417)
PHONE..................................330 374-0229
Jessica Deluke,
EMP: 35
SQ FT: 11,000
SALES (est): 5MM **Privately Held**
SIC: 7352 5047 Medical equipment rental;
medical equipment & supplies

(G-160)
COTTER MDSE STOR OF OHIO
1564 Firestone Pkwy (44301-1626)
P.O. Box 808 (44309-0808)
PHONE..................................330 773-9177
Chris Geib, *President*
Howard D Heater, *Vice Pres*
Tonya Bridgeland, *Executive*
EMP: 45
SQ FT: 500,000
SALES (est): 4.1MM
SALES (corp-wide): 12.8MM **Privately
Held**
SIC: 4225 General warehousing
PA: The Cotter Merchandise Storage Com-
pany
1564 Firestone Pkwy
Akron OH 44301
330 315-2755

(G-161)
**COTTER MOVING & STORAGE
CO (PA)**
Also Called: A-Advnced Mvg Stor Systms-Self
265 W Bowery St (44308-1034)
P.O. Box 529 (44309-0529)
PHONE..................................330 535-5115
Harry L Bord, *President*
Fred Bord, *Vice Pres*
William C Bord, *Treasurer*
EMP: 25
SQ FT: 250,000
SALES (est): 1.6MM **Privately Held**
SIC: 4213 4225 4212 Trucking, except
local; general warehousing & storage;
local trucking, without storage

(G-162)
COUNTY OF SUMMIT
Also Called: Summit County Probation Offs
25 N Main St (44308-1919)
PHONE..............................330 643-2300
Pete Hoost, *Director*
EMP: 62
SQ FT: 29,236 **Privately Held**
WEB: www.cpcourt.summitoh.net
SIC: 8322 9111 Probation office; county
supervisors' & executives' offices
PA: County Of Summit
650 Dan St
Akron OH 44310
330 643-2500

(G-163)
COUNTY OF SUMMIT
Also Called: Summit Cnty Juvenile CT
650 Dan St (44310-3909)
PHONE..............................330 643-2943
Dave Alexander, *Administration*
EMP: 150 **Privately Held**
WEB: www.cpcourt.summitoh.net
SIC: 8361 9211 Juvenile correctional facili-
ties; courts
PA: County Of Summit
650 Dan St
Akron OH 44310
330 643-2500

(G-164)
COUNTY OF SUMMIT
538 E South St (44311-1848)
PHONE..............................330 643-2850
Gene Esser, *General Mgr*
Dennis Tubbs, *Engineer*
Allan Brubaker, *Branch Mgr*
Geordie Kissos, *Manager*
Bob Warren, *Manager*
EMP: 120
SQ FT: 1,368 **Privately Held**
WEB: www.cpcourt.summitoh.net
SIC: 8711 9111 Engineering services;
county supervisors' & executives' offices
PA: County Of Summit
650 Dan St
Akron OH 44310
330 643-2500

(G-165)
COUNTY OF SUMMIT
Also Called: Highway Maintenance
601 E Crosier St (44311-1808)
PHONE..............................330 643-2860
Gary Ellison, *Director*
EMP: 200 **Privately Held**
WEB: www.cpcourt.summitoh.net
SIC: 1611 Highway & street maintenance
PA: County Of Summit
650 Dan St
Akron OH 44310
330 643-2500

(G-166)
COUNTY OF SUMMIT
Social Services
47 N Main St (44308-1971)
PHONE..............................330 643-7217
Dr Daisy Alfred Smith, *Director*
EMP: 500 **Privately Held**
WEB: www.cpcourt.summitoh.net
SIC: 8322 Probation office
PA: County Of Summit
650 Dan St
Akron OH 44310
330 643-2500

(G-167)
COUNTY OF SUMMIT BOARD OF MNTL
636 W Exchange St (44302-1306)
PHONE..............................330 634-8100
EMP: 700
SALES (est): 5MM **Privately Held**
SIC: 8699 Membership Organization

(G-168)
CRAFTSMEN RESTORATION LLC (PA)
Also Called: Village Handyman, The
2013 N Clvland Mssllon Rd (44333-1258)
PHONE..............................877 442-3424
Jeffrey Sartori, *Mng Member*
Michael Farist,

EMP: 26 EST: 2008
SALES: 12.6MM **Privately Held**
SIC: 1521 General remodeling, single-fam-
ily houses

(G-169)
CRAIN COMMUNICATIONS INC
Also Called: Rubber & Plastics News
1725 Merriman Rd Ste 300 (44313-5283)
PHONE..............................330 836-9180
Robert S Simmons, *Vice Pres*
Christine Zernick, *Sales Mgr*
Sarah Arnold, *Marketing Staff*
EMP: 90
SALES (corp-wide): 225MM **Privately Held**
WEB: www.crainsnewyork.com
SIC: 2711 2721 7389 Newspapers: pub-
lishing only, not printed on site; periodi-
cals; advertising, promotional & trade
show services
PA: Crain Communications, Inc.
1155 Gratiot Ave
Detroit MI 48207
313 446-6000

(G-170)
CRAWFORD GROUP INC
3960 Medina Rd (44333-2445)
PHONE..............................330 665-5432
EMP: 54
SALES (corp-wide): 4.9B **Privately Held**
SIC: 7514 Passenger car rental
PA: The Crawford Group Inc
600 Corporate Park Dr
Saint Louis MO 63105
314 512-5000

(G-171)
CRYSTAL ARTHRITIS CENTER INC
3975 Embassy Pkwy Ste 101
(44333-8325)
PHONE..............................330 668-4045
Raymond Federman MD, *President*
EMP: 36
SQ FT: 2,200
SALES (est): 3.8MM **Privately Held**
SIC: 8011 Rheumatology specialist, physi-
cian/surgeon

(G-172)
CRYSTAL CLINIC SURGERY CTR INC
3975 Embassy Pkwy Ste 202
(44333-8395)
PHONE..............................330 668-4040
Ronald R Suntken, *President*
Holli Cholley, *President*
Gregory P Zolton, *President*
Gordon L Bennett MD, *Vice Pres*
Daniel J Ferry, *CFO*
EMP: 700
SQ FT: 6,800
SALES (est): 45.1MM **Privately Held**
WEB: www.crystalclinic.com
SIC: 8011 Surgeon

(G-173)
CRYSTAL CLNIC ORTHPDIC CTR LLC (PA)
3925 Embassy Pkwy Ste 250
(44333-1799)
PHONE..............................330 668-4040
Ronald R Suntken, *President*
Holli Cholley, *Opers Staff*
Daniel Ferry, *CFO*
Gregg Zolton, *CIO*
EMP: 99 EST: 2007
SALES (est): 19.7MM **Privately Held**
SIC: 8069 Orthopedic hospital

(G-174)
CRYSTAL CLNIC ORTHPDIC CTR LLC
20 Olive St Ste 200 (44310-3169)
PHONE..............................330 535-3396
EMP: 62
SALES (corp-wide): 19.7MM **Privately Held**
SIC: 8069 Orthopedic hospital
PA: Crystal Clinic Orthopaedic Center, Llc
3925 Embassy Pkwy Ste 250
Akron OH 44333
330 668-4040

(G-175)
CSL PLASMA INC
727 Grant St Lowr (44311-2128)
PHONE..............................330 535-4338
Jane Mueller, *Branch Mgr*
EMP: 65 **Privately Held**
WEB: www.zlbplasma.com
SIC: 8099 Blood donor station; blood bank
HQ: Csl Plasma Inc.
900 Broken Sound Pkwy Nw # 4
Boca Raton FL 33487
561 981-3700

(G-176)
CTI ENGINEERS INC
1 Cascade Plz Ste 710 (44308-1136)
PHONE..............................330 294-5996
Richard W Reed, *Principal*
EMP: 54
SALES (est): 1.1MM **Privately Held**
SIC: 8711 Engineering services

(G-177)
CUTLER AND ASSOCIATES INC
Also Called: Cutler Realtor
971 E Turkeyfoot Lake Rd (44312-5240)
PHONE..............................330 896-1680
Bonnie Wagler, *Manager*
EMP: 55
SALES (corp-wide): 8.4MM **Privately Held**
WEB: www.cutlerhomes.com
SIC: 6531 Real estate agents & managers
PA: Cutler And Associates, Inc
4618 Dressler Rd Nw
Canton OH 44718
330 493-9323

(G-178)
CYO & COMMUNITY SERVICES INC (PA)
795 Russell Ave (44307-1115)
PHONE..............................330 762-2961
Celeste Thayer, *Office Mgr*
Donald P Finn, *Exec Dir*
EMP: 40
SALES (est): 1.2MM **Privately Held**
SIC: 8661 8322 Religious organizations;
individual & family services

(G-179)
CYPRESS COMPANIES INC (PA)
670 W Market St (44303-1448)
PHONE..............................330 849-6500
Rollie Bauer, *CEO*
Dennis Raney, *Exec VP*
Matt McGinnes, *Vice Pres*
EMP: 50
SALES (est): 7.2MM **Privately Held**
WEB: www.cypresscos.com
SIC: 8741 Management services

(G-180)
DAN MARCHETTA CNSTR CO INC
525 N Cleveland Massillon (44333-3332)
PHONE..............................330 668-4800
Daniel T Marchetta Jr, *President*
Joseph Marchetta, *Vice Pres*
Michael Marchetta, *Vice Pres*
EMP: 30
SQ FT: 3,000
SALES (est): 7.9MM **Privately Held**
SIC: 1542 1521 Commercial & office build-
ing, new construction; commercial & of-
fice buildings, renovation & repair; new
construction, single-family houses

(G-181)
DATZAP LLC
1520 S Arlington St (44306-3863)
PHONE..............................330 785-2100
Donald Jacob, *Mng Member*
EMP: 30 EST: 2002
SALES (est): 868.5K **Privately Held**
SIC: 4813

(G-182)
DAVITA INC
73 Massillon Rd (44312-1028)
PHONE..............................330 733-1861
Candi Willoughby, *Branch Mgr*
EMP: 35 **Publicly Held**
SIC: 8092 Kidney dialysis centers

PA: Davita Inc.
2000 16th St
Denver CO 80202

(G-183)
DENTAL HEALTH GROUP PA
Also Called: Great Expressions
2000 Brittain Rd Ste 91 (44310-4320)
PHONE..............................330 630-9222
Sam Jaffe, *Manager*
EMP: 30
SALES (corp-wide): 112.8MM **Privately Held**
SIC: 8021 Dentists' office
PA: Dental Health Group, P.A.
29777 Telg Rd St 3000
Southfield MI 48034
248 203-2330

(G-184)
DETROIT WESTFIELD LLC
Also Called: Holiday Inn
4073 Medina Rd (44333-2476)
PHONE..............................330 666-4131
Fred Lami, *Partner*
Louie Lemaster, *General Mgr*
Theodore Sahley,
EMP: 60
SQ FT: 106,335
SALES (est): 3.1MM **Privately Held**
SIC: 7011 5812 Motels; restaurant, family:
independent

(G-185)
DI FEO & SONS POULTRY INC
1075 Grant St (44301-1434)
P.O. Box 530 (44309-0530)
PHONE..............................330 564-8172
Robert Di Feo, *President*
John Di Feo, *Vice Pres*
Edward Di Feo, *Treasurer*
EMP: 30
SQ FT: 7,000
SALES (est): 11.5MM **Privately Held**
SIC: 5144 5499 Poultry: live, dressed or
frozen (unpackaged); eggs; eggs & poul-
try

(G-186)
DIET CENTER WORLDWIDE INC (PA)
395 Springside Dr (44333-2434)
PHONE..............................330 665-5861
Charles E Sekeres, *President*
EMP: 25
SQ FT: 53,684
SALES (est): 1.7MM **Privately Held**
SIC: 7299 6794 Diet center, without med-
ical staff; franchises, selling or licensing

(G-187)
DIGITAL COLOR INTL LLC
Also Called: D C I
1653 Merriman Rd Ste 211 (44313-5276)
PHONE..............................330 762-6959
Christopher Che, *CEO*
David Fusselman,
David Welner,
EMP: 43
SQ FT: 38,000
SALES (est): 8.5MM **Privately Held**
WEB: www.digitalcolorinternational.com
SIC: 7336 2653 7319 7331 Creative
services to advertisers, except writers;
display items, solid fiber: made from pur-
chased materials; display advertising
service; transit advertising services; direct
mail advertising services; commercial
printing, lithographic

(G-188)
DIVERSIFIED AIR SYSTEMS INC
1201 George Wash Blvd (44312-3007)
PHONE..............................330 784-3366
John Smelko, *Manager*
EMP: 35
SALES (corp-wide): 13.5MM **Privately Held**
WEB: www.diversifiedair.com
SIC: 5075 7699 Compressors, air condi-
tioning; compressor repair
PA: Diversified Air Systems, Inc.
4760 Van Epps Rd
Brooklyn Heights OH 44131
216 741-1700

▲ = Import ▼=Export
◆ =Import/Export

(G-189)
DLZ OHIO INC
1 Canal Square Plz # 1300 (44308-1037)
PHONE..............................330 923-0401
Thomas Sisley, *Senior VP*
EMP: 25
SQ FT: 11,667
SALES (corp-wide): 93MM **Privately Held**
SIC: 8711 Consulting engineer
HQ: Dlz Ohio, Inc.
6121 Huntley Rd
Columbus OH 43229
614 888-0040

(G-190)
DON DRUMM STUDIOS & GALLERY
437 Crouse St (44311-1220)
PHONE..............................330 253-6840
Don Drumm, *President*
Jill Parr, *General Mgr*
Elizabeth B Drumm, *Treasurer*
Judy Kelly, *Bookkeeper*
Mary Cistone, *Marketing Staff*
EMP: 32
SALES (est): 4.1MM **Privately Held**
WEB: www.dondrummstudios.com
SIC: 5999 5199 8999 7336 Artists' supplies & materials; art goods; sculptor's studio; commercial art & graphic design

(G-191)
DONZELLS FLOWER & GRDN CTR INC
Also Called: Donzell's
937 E Waterloo Rd (44306-3996)
PHONE..............................330 724-0550
Sam Donzelli, *President*
Wm Gale, *Principal*
Harold D Parker, *Principal*
Julie Difeo, *Admin Sec*
▲ **EMP:** 30
SQ FT: 52,000
SALES (est): 4.5MM **Privately Held**
WEB: www.donzells.com
SIC: 5999 5181 Christmas lights & decorations; beer & ale

(G-192)
DOUG BIGELOW CHEVROLET INC
Also Called: Doug Chevrolet
894 Robinwood Hills Dr (44333-1550)
PHONE..............................330 644-7500
Doug Bigelow, *CEO*
Christopher Bigelow, *Principal*
Mike Treml, *Parts Mgr*
Patricia Bigelow, *Treasurer*
Doreen Sisley, *Sales Staff*
EMP: 75
SQ FT: 10,000
SALES (est): 29.2MM **Privately Held**
WEB: www.dougchevrolet.com
SIC: 5511 5521 7538 7532 Automobiles, new & used; used car dealers; general automotive repair shops; top & body repair & paint shops; automobiles & other motor vehicles

(G-193)
DOWNTOWN AKRON PARTNERSHIP INC
Also Called: DAT
103 S High St Fl 4 (44308-1461)
PHONE..............................330 374-7676
Clair Dickinson, *Ch of Bd*
Holly Mattucci, *Business Mgr*
Suzie Graham, *Exec Dir*
EMP: 50
SALES: 1.7MM **Privately Held**
WEB: www.downtownakron.com
SIC: 8699 Charitable organization

(G-194)
DRB HOLDINGS LLC (PA)
3245 Pickle Rd (44312-5333)
PHONE..............................330 645-3299
Bill Morgenstern, *CEO*
EMP: 85
SALES (est): 11.6MM **Privately Held**
SIC: 6719 Investment holding companies, except banks

(G-195)
DRB SYSTEMS LLC (HQ)
3245 Pickle Rd (44312-5333)
P.O. Box 550, Uniontown (44685-0550)
PHONE..............................330 645-3299
Dale Brott, *President*
William Ritter, *Project Mgr*
Kenneth Brott, *Treasurer*
Amy Abraham, *Manager*
Andy Clugston, *Manager*
EMP: 104
SALES (est): 35.9MM
SALES (corp-wide): 11.6MM **Privately Held**
WEB: www.drbsystems.com
SIC: 7373 7371 7372 Systems software development services; custom computer programming services; prepackaged software
PA: Drb Holdings Llc
3245 Pickle Rd
Akron OH 44312
330 645-3299

(G-196)
DSI EAST
73 Massillon Rd (44312-1028)
PHONE..............................330 733-1861
EMP: 31
SALES (est): 309.1K **Publicly Held**
SIC: 8092 Kidney dialysis centers
PA: Davita Inc.
2000 16th St
Denver CO 80202

(G-197)
DUER CONSTRUCTION CO INC
70 E North St (44304-1203)
PHONE..............................330 848-9930
Lawrence Griebel, *President*
David Griebel, *Vice Pres*
Tom Griebel, *Vice Pres*
EMP: 75
SQ FT: 20,000
SALES (est): 4.5MM **Privately Held**
WEB: www.duerconstructioncompany.com
SIC: 1741 Bricklaying

(G-198)
E & V VENTURES INC (PA)
Also Called: Two Men and A Truck
1511 E Market St (44305-4208)
PHONE..............................330 794-6683
Victoria Slama, *President*
Kenneth Slama Jr, *Vice Pres*
Eric Voth, *Vice Pres*
EMP: 46
SALES (est): 6.5MM **Privately Held**
SIC: 4212 Moving services

(G-199)
EARTH N WOOD PRODUCTS INC
2436 S Arlington Rd (44319-2029)
PHONE..............................330 644-1858
EMP: 49
SALES (corp-wide): 15.4MM **Privately Held**
SIC: 5099 Whol Durable Goods
PA: Earth 'n Wood Products, Inc.
5335 Strausser St Nw
Canton OH 44720
330 499-8309

(G-200)
EAST AKRON NEIGHBORHOOD DEV
Also Called: Akron Lead Base Program
550 S Arlington St (44306-1740)
PHONE..............................330 773-6838
Grady Appleton, *Exec Dir*
Susan Schweitzer, *Director*
Charles Small, *Maintence Staff*
EMP: 45
SQ FT: 1,701
SALES (est): 4.9MM **Privately Held**
SIC: 8699 Charitable organization

(G-201)
ECHOGEN POWER SYSTEMS DEL INC
365 Water St (44308-1044)
PHONE..............................234 542-4379
Philip Brennan, *CEO*
Timothy Held, *Principal*

Mark Terzola, *COO*
Edward Zdankiewicz,
▲ **EMP:** 36 **EST:** 2011
SALES: 30.4MM **Privately Held**
SIC: 4911 Generation, electric power

(G-202)
EMERGE COUNSELING SERVICE
900 Mull Ave (44313-7502)
PHONE..............................330 865-8351
John Palmer, *President*
Lee Wetherbee, *Principal*
EMP: 30
SALES (est): 124.2K **Privately Held**
SIC: 8049 8093 8322 Clinical psychologist; mental health clinic, outpatient; family counseling services

(G-203)
EMERGE MINISTRIES INC
900 Mull Ave (44313-7597)
PHONE..............................330 865-8351
Clayton Glickert, *President*
Richard D Dobbins, *President*
Dr Donald A Lichi, *Vice Pres*
Julie Carpenter, *Treasurer*
Norma Rowe, *Treasurer*
EMP: 44
SQ FT: 25,000
SALES: 2.9MM **Privately Held**
WEB: www.emerge.org
SIC: 8322 7841 5942 General counseling services; video disk/tape rental to the general public; books, religious

(G-204)
EPIPHANY MANAGEMENT GROUP LLC
283 E Waterloo Rd (44319-1238)
PHONE..............................330 706-4056
Suranjan Shome, *Principal*
Frank Cikach, *Vice Pres*
Larry Hughes, *Manager*
Timothy Houston, *Info Tech Dir*
EMP: 30
SALES (est): 5.5MM **Privately Held**
WEB: www.epiphanymgmt.com
SIC: 8742 Business consultant

(G-205)
EXECUTIVE INSURANCE AGENCY (PA)
130 Springside Dr Ste 300 (44333-2489)
PHONE..............................330 576-1234
Lawrence S Rybka, *Ch of Bd*
Sarah Lee, *Manager*
James Pfeifer, *Advisor*
EMP: 28 **EST:** 1963
SQ FT: 7,000
SALES (est): 4.2MM **Privately Held**
SIC: 6411 Insurance agents

(G-206)
EXECUTIVE PROPERTIES INC (PA)
733 W Market St Ste 102 (44303-1088)
PHONE..............................330 376-4037
Thomas J Dillon, *President*
Francis Dillon Kline, *Vice Pres*
EMP: 30
SQ FT: 600
SALES (est): 5.1MM **Privately Held**
WEB: www.execprop.com
SIC: 6531 Real estate managers; rental agent, real estate

(G-207)
EXONIC SYSTEMS LLC
380 Water St (44308-1045)
P.O. Box 1030 (44309-1030)
PHONE..............................330 315-3100
Richard Rogers, *President*
EMP: 35
SQ FT: 17,000
SALES: 12MM **Privately Held**
SIC: 5065 Electronic parts & equipment

(G-208)
FAIRLAWN COUNTRY CLUB COMPANY
200 N Wheaton Rd (44313-3963)
P.O. Box 5423 (44334-0423)
PHONE..............................330 836-5541
Kelly Butler, *President*

William Shea, *General Mgr*
Mike Balso, *Vice Pres*
Elizabeth Wecker, *Marketing Mgr*
EMP: 70 **EST:** 1917
SQ FT: 40,000
SALES: 5.5MM **Privately Held**
WEB: www.fairlawncountryclub.com
SIC: 7997 5813 5812 Country club, membership; drinking places; eating places

(G-209)
FALLSWAY EQUIPMENT CO INC (PA)
Also Called: Fallsway Equipment Company
1277 Devalera St (44310-2454)
P.O. Box 4537 (44310-0537)
PHONE..............................330 633-6000
Harry Fairhurst, *CEO*
Gregory Fairhurst, *COO*
Jackie Maynard, *Controller*
▲ **EMP:** 133
SQ FT: 92,140
SALES (est): 81.8MM **Privately Held**
WEB: www.fallsway.com
SIC: 5084 5511 7699 7359 Trucks, industrial; trucks, tractors & trailers: new & used; industrial truck repair; industrial truck rental

(G-210)
FAMOUS DISTRIBUTION INC (HQ)
Also Called: Famous Supply Companies
2620 Ridgewood Rd Ste 200 (44313-3507)
P.O. Box 951344, Cleveland (44193-0011)
PHONE..............................330 762-9621
Jay Blaushild, *CEO*
Marc Blaushild, *President*
Nick Ezzone, *Vice Pres*
Callie St Clair, *Opers Mgr*
Dale Newman, *Treasurer*
EMP: 60
SQ FT: 200,000
SALES (est): 210.7MM **Privately Held**
WEB: www.famous-supply.com
SIC: 5074 5075 5085 5023 Plumbing & hydronic heating supplies; furnaces, warm air; warm air heating equipment & supplies; valves & fittings; kitchenware

(G-211)
FAMOUS DISTRIBUTION INC
Also Called: Johnson Contrls Authorized Dlr
166 N Union St (44304-1355)
PHONE..............................330 434-5194
Steve Greer, *Manager*
EMP: 50 **Privately Held**
WEB: www.famous-supply.com
SIC: 5075 5074 Furnaces, warm air; plumbing & hydronic heating supplies
HQ: Famous Distribution Inc
2620 Ridgewood Rd Ste 200
Akron OH 44313
330 762-9621

(G-212)
FAMOUS ENTERPRISES INC (PA)
Also Called: Famous Manufacturing
2620 Ridgewood Rd Ste 200 (44313-3507)
PHONE..............................330 762-9621
Marc Blaushild, *President*
Jay Blaushild, *Chairman*
Dale J Newman, *Treasurer*
EMP: 45
SQ FT: 20,000
SALES (est): 292.4MM **Privately Held**
WEB: www.jfgood.com
SIC: 5075 5031 5074 7699 Warm air heating equipment & supplies; lumber, plywood & millwork; plumbing & hydronic heating supplies; industrial equipment services

(G-213)
FAMOUS II INC (PA)
Also Called: Pittsburgh Plumbing & Htg Sup
2620 Ridgewood Rd Ste 200 (44313-3507)
PHONE..............................330 762-9621
Jay Blaushild, *President*
Pete Isaacs, *Sales Staff*
Chris Odom, *Sales Staff*
Cory Williams, *Sales Staff*
Richard Newman, *Shareholder*
EMP: 55

SALES (est): 61.9MM **Privately Held**
WEB: www.famoussupply.com
SIC: 5075 5074 Furnaces, heating: electric; furnaces, warm air; plumbing & hydronic heating supplies

(G-214)
FAMOUS INDUSTRIES INC (HQ)
Also Called: Johnson Contrls Authorized Dlr
2620 Ridgewood Rd Ste 200 (44313-3507)
PHONE....................................330 535-1811
Jay Blaushild, *President*
Marc Blaushild, *Vice Pres*
EMP: 50
SALES (est): 69.2MM **Privately Held**
WEB: www.jfgoodco.com
SIC: 3444 5065 5074 Metal ventilating equipment; telephone equipment; intercommunication equipment, electronic; plumbing & heating valves

(G-215)
FAMOUS INDUSTRIES INC
Also Called: J F Good Co
166 N Union St (44304-1355)
PHONE....................................330 535-1811
Jim Vinson, *Manager*
EMP: 40 **Privately Held**
WEB: www.jfgoodco.com
SIC: 5074 Plumbing & hydronic heating supplies
HQ: Famous Industries, Inc.
2620 Ridgewood Rd Ste 200
Akron OH 44313
330 535-1811

(G-216)
FC 1346 LLC
118 Hollywood Ave (44313-6724)
PHONE....................................330 864-8170
Duane Bishop, *Vice Pres*
James Prohaska, *Vice Pres*
Karen Travers Rake, *Vice Pres*
Edward Pelavin,
David Levy,
EMP: 47
SALES (est): 2.4MM
SALES (corp-wide): 4.5MM **Privately Held**
SIC: 1522 Multi-family dwellings, new construction
PA: Epdl, Llc
118 Hollywood Ave
Akron OH 44313
330 864-8170

(G-217)
FC SCHWENDLER LLC
724 Canton Rd (44312-2607)
P.O. Box 6341 (44312-0341)
PHONE....................................330 733-8715
Fred Schwendler, *Partner*
Anne Schwendler,
EMP: 27
SQ FT: 29,000
SALES: 526K **Privately Held**
SIC: 8741 Management services

(G-218)
FEDEX FREIGHT INC
678 Killian Rd (44319-2528)
PHONE....................................330 645-0879
EMP: 80
SALES (corp-wide): 47.4B **Publicly Held**
SIC: 4213 4212 Trucking Operator-Nonlocal Local Trucking Operator
HQ: Fedex Freight, Inc.
2200 Forward Dr
Harrison AR 72601
870 741-9000

(G-219)
FIRST AMRCN CASH ADVNCE SC LLC
3100 Manchester Rd (44319-1464)
PHONE....................................330 644-9144
Fax: 330 644-9144
EMP: 52 **Privately Held**
SIC: 6361 Title Insurance Carrier
HQ: First American Cash Advance Of South Carolina, Llc
1603 N Longstreet St
Kingstree SC

(G-220)
FIRST ENERGY LINDE
76 S Main St Bsmt (44308-1890)
PHONE....................................330 384-4959
Anthony J Alexander, *President*
Rob Corbett, *Engineer*
Larry Shade, *Engineer*
Rey Y Jimenez, *Manager*
John Wagner, *Technology*
EMP: 62
SALES (est): 30.6MM **Privately Held**
SIC: 4911 Electric services

(G-221)
FIRSTENERGY CORP (PA)
76 S Main St Bsmt (44308-1817)
PHONE....................................800 736-3402
George M Smart, *Ch of Bd*
Charles E Jones, *President*
Jeffrey Elser, *Vice Pres*
Jim Haney, *Vice Pres*
Bob Mattiuz, *Vice Pres*
EMP: 1618
SALES (est): 11.2B **Publicly Held**
WEB: www.firstenergycorp.com
SIC: 4911 Distribution, electric power

(G-222)
FIRSTENERGY NUCLEAR OPER CO (HQ)
76 S Main St Bsmt (44308-1817)
PHONE....................................800 646-0400
Anthony J Alexander, *CEO*
James H Lash, *President*
Garry Leidich, *President*
Lew Myers, *COO*
Charles E Jones, *Exec VP*
EMP: 13000
SQ FT: 250,000
SALES (est): 4.3B **Publicly Held**
SIC: 4911 Electric services

(G-223)
FIRSTENERGY SOLUTIONS CORP (HQ)
Also Called: Fes
341 White Pond Dr Bldg B3 (44320-1119)
PHONE....................................800 736-3402
Donald R Schneider, *Ch of Bd*
John W Judge, *President*
Stephen Burnazian, *Exec VP*
Brian Farley, *Exec VP*
Jay Bellingham, *Senior VP*
EMP: 28
SALES: 3.1B **Publicly Held**
WEB: www.firstenergysolutions.com
SIC: 4911 Distribution, electric power; generation, electric power; transmission, electric power

(G-224)
FLEX-TEAM INC (PA)
Also Called: Flex Team
753 W Waterloo Rd (44314-1525)
PHONE....................................330 745-3838
Rick Pollock, *President*
Jacob Pollock, *President*
Julie Horinger, *Manager*
EMP: 300
SALES: 6MM **Privately Held**
WEB: www.flex-team.com
SIC: 7363 Temporary help service

(G-225)
FLEXSYS AMERICA LP (DH)
260 Springside Dr (44333-4554)
PHONE....................................330 666-4111
Enrique Bolanos, *CEO*
James Voss, *President*
◆ EMP: 65
SQ FT: 85,000
SALES (est): 22.7MM **Publicly Held**
SIC: 3069 8731 2899 2823 Reclaimed rubber & specialty rubber compounds; commercial physical research; chemical preparations; cellulosic manmade fibers; synthetic rubber; plastics materials & resins
HQ: Solutia Inc.
575 Maryville Centre Dr
Saint Louis MO 63141
423 229-2000

(G-226)
FOR EVERS KIDS LLC
775 Copley Rd (44320-2957)
PHONE....................................330 258-9014
Yvette Harris, *Mng Member*
EMP: 25
SALES (est): 190K **Privately Held**
SIC: 8641 Youth organizations

(G-227)
FORMU3 INTERNATIONAL INC (PA)
395 Springside Dr (44333-2434)
PHONE....................................330 668-1461
Charles Sekeres, *President*
EMP: 35
SALES (est): 1.3MM **Privately Held**
SIC: 8093 7299 Weight loss clinic, with medical staff; diet center, without medical staff

(G-228)
FRED MARTIN NISSAN LLC
3388 S Arlington Rd (44312-5257)
PHONE....................................330 644-8888
Anthony Hernandez, *Parts Mgr*
Fred Kodroff, *Finance Mgr*
Duane Huff,
Adam Huff,
EMP: 45
SALES (est): 12.7MM **Privately Held**
SIC: 5511 7539 Automobiles, new & used; automotive repair shops

(G-229)
FRED W ALBRECHT GROCERY CO
Also Called: Acme
3979 Medina Rd (44333-2444)
PHONE....................................330 666-6781
Bill Haliko, *Manager*
EMP: 180
SALES (corp-wide): 419.7MM **Privately Held**
WEB: www.acmefreshmarket.com
SIC: 5411 5912 7384 Grocery stores, chain; drug stores & proprietary stores; photofinish laboratories
PA: The Fred W Albrecht Grocery Company
2700 Gilchrist Rd Ste A
Akron OH 44305
330 733-2861

(G-230)
FRITO-LAY NORTH AMERICA INC
1460 E Turkeyfoot Lake Rd (44312-5349)
PHONE....................................330 786-6000
Jessica Wolf, *Sales Mgr*
Doug Evans, *Branch Mgr*
EMP: 40
SQ FT: 14,832
SALES (corp-wide): 64.6B **Publicly Held**
WEB: www.fritolay.com
SIC: 5145 Snack foods
HQ: Frito-Lay North America, Inc.
7701 Legacy Dr
Plano TX 75024

(G-231)
G & O RESOURCES LTD
96 E Crosier St (44311-2342)
PHONE....................................330 253-2525
Robert Nelson, *CEO*
EMP: 60
SALES (est): 3.4MM **Privately Held**
WEB: www.goresources.com
SIC: 4932 Gas & other services combined

(G-232)
GBC DESIGN INC
565 White Pond Dr (44320-1123)
PHONE....................................330 283-6870
Sy Cymerman, *President*
EMP: 37
SQ FT: 10,000
SALES (est): 5.1MM **Privately Held**
WEB: www.gbcdesign.com
SIC: 8711 8712 Consulting engineer; architectural services

(G-233)
GENERAL TRANSPORT INCORPORATED
1100 Jenkins Blvd (44306-3754)
P.O. Box 7727 (44306-0727)
PHONE....................................330 786-3400
Harold Joseph Ostrowske, *President*
Michelle Troy, *Corp Secy*
John Troy, *Vice Pres*
EMP: 42
SQ FT: 5,000
SALES (est): 14.9MM **Privately Held**
WEB: www.generaltrans.com
SIC: 4213 Trucking, except local

(G-234)
GENESIS CORP
Also Called: Genesis 10
1 Cascade Plz Ste 1230 (44308-1144)
PHONE....................................330 597-4100
Nate Gram, *Branch Mgr*
EMP: 85
SALES (corp-wide): 179.7MM **Privately Held**
SIC: 7379
PA: Genesis Corp.
950 3rd Ave Ste 900
New York NY 10022
212 688-5522

(G-235)
GIRONDA VITO & BROS INC
1130 Brittain Rd (44305-1005)
PHONE....................................330 630-9399
Frank Gironda, *President*
Pamela Gironda, *Vice Pres*
EMP: 40
SQ FT: 7,200
SALES (est): 4.6MM **Privately Held**
WEB: www.vgconstruction.com
SIC: 1771 Concrete work

(G-236)
GLENCOE RESTORATION GROUP LLC
Also Called: Grgstormpro
575 Canton Rd (44312-2511)
PHONE....................................330 752-1244
Whitney Philips, *Mng Member*
EMP: 32
SQ FT: 1,600
SALES: 500K **Privately Held**
SIC: 1531 Operative builders

(G-237)
GLOBAL EXEC SLUTIONS GROUP LLC
Also Called: Mri Network
3505 Embassy Pkwy Ste 200 (44333-8404)
PHONE....................................330 666-3354
Jim Chadbourne, *Managing Prtnr*
Scott Chadbourne, *Managing Dir*
Carolyn Chadbourne, *Finance*
Pat Lucia, *Senior Mgr*
Linda Marmash, *Senior Mgr*
EMP: 27 EST: 2001
SQ FT: 14,000
SALES (est): 2.5MM **Privately Held**
WEB: www.mriexecutivesolutions.com
SIC: 7361 Executive placement

(G-238)
GMI HOLDINGS INC
Genie Company, The
2850 Gilchrist Rd (44305-4444)
PHONE....................................330 794-0846
EMP: 55
SALES (corp-wide): 2.8B **Privately Held**
SIC: 4225 5072 General Warehouse/Storage Whol Hardware
HQ: Gmi Holdings, Inc.
1 Door Dr
Mount Hope OH 44660
330 821-5360

(G-239)
GOLDEN LIVING LLC
Also Called: Beverly
721 Hickory St (44303-2213)
PHONE....................................330 762-6486
Michael Jordan, *Manager*
EMP: 200

SALES (corp-wide): 7.4MM **Privately Held**
SIC: 8059 8051 Convalescent home; skilled nursing care facilities
PA: Golden Living Llc
5220 Tennyson Pkwy # 400
Plano TX 75024
972 372-6300

(G-240)
GOODWILL INDUSTRIES INC
Also Called: Pic
570 E Waterloo Rd (44319-1223)
PHONE..................330 724-6995
Nan McClenagham, *President*
Barry Thoman, *Treasurer*
EMP: 50
SALES (est): 4.5MM **Privately Held**
SIC: 8322 8331 7361 Individual & family services; job training & vocational rehabilitation services; employment agencies

(G-241)
GOODWILL INDUSTRIES OF AKRON (PA)
570 E Waterloo Rd (44319-1223)
PHONE..................330 724-6995
Nancy Ellis McClenaghan, *CEO*
M M Montis, *Principal*
Janet Morrison, *Vice Pres*
Greg Morton, *Vice Pres*
Brent R Thompson, *Treasurer*
EMP: 150
SQ FT: 112,000
SALES: 18.5MM **Privately Held**
WEB: www.goodwillakron.org
SIC: 8331 Vocational rehabilitation agency

(G-242)
GOODYEAR TIRE & RUBBER COMPANY (PA)
200 E Innovation Way (44316-0001)
PHONE..................330 796-2121
Richard J Kramer, *Ch of Bd*
Christopher R Delaney, *President*
Stephen R McClellan, *President*
Ryan G Patterson, *President*
Jose Asencio, *District Mgr*
◆ EMP: 3000 EST: 1898
SALES: 15.4B **Publicly Held**
WEB: www.goodyear.com
SIC: 3052 7534 7538 7539 Rubber & plastics hose & beltings; automobile hose, rubber; rubber belting; tire retreading & repair shops; rebuilding & retreading tires; general automotive repair shops; truck engine repair, except industrial; automotive repair shops; brake services; shock absorber replacement; tune-up service, automotive; motor vehicle supplies & new parts; automotive servicing equipment; automotive supplies & parts; inner tubes, all types

(G-243)
GPD SERVICES COMPANY INC (PA)
Also Called: Gpd Associates
520 S Main St Ste 2531 (44311-1073)
PHONE..................330 572-2100
David B Granger, *President*
Darrin Kotecki, *President*
Tim Ledrich, *Project Mgr*
EMP: 62
SALES (est): 20MM **Privately Held**
SIC: 8712 Architectural services

(G-244)
GREAT LAKES HOME HLTH SVCS INC
1530 W Market St (44313-7141)
PHONE..................888 260-9835
EMP: 50 **Privately Held**
SIC: 8082 Home health care services
PA: Great Lakes Home Health Services, Inc.
900 Cooper St
Jackson MI 49202

(G-245)
GREENLEAF FAMILY CENTER (PA)
580 Grant St (44311-9910)
PHONE..................330 376-9494
Judy Joyce, *President*

EMP: 28
SQ FT: 8,000
SALES: 3MM **Privately Held**
WEB: www.greenleafctr.org
SIC: 8322 Family service agency; family counseling services

(G-246)
GREENSTAR MID-AMERICA LLC
1535 Exeter Rd (44306-3889)
PHONE..................330 784-1167
Tom Jackson, *Branch Mgr*
EMP: 25
SALES (corp-wide): 14.9B **Publicly Held**
SIC: 4953 Recycling, waste materials
HQ: Greenstar Mid-America, Llc
1001 Fannin St Ste 4000
Houston TX 77002

(G-247)
GUYS PARTY CENTER
Also Called: Guy's Party Ctr
500 E Waterloo Rd (44319-1272)
PHONE..................330 724-6373
Rocky Zimbardi, *President*
Michael Nyeste, *Sales Executive*
EMP: 50
SALES (est): 1.3MM **Privately Held**
WEB: www.guyspartycenter.com
SIC: 7299 5812 Banquet hall facilities; eating places

(G-248)
GYNECLGIC ONCLGISTS OF NE OHIO (PA)
224 W Exchange St Ste 140 (44302-1705)
PHONE..................330 384-6041
Eric Jenison, *President*
John R Karlin, *Vice Pres*
Michael P Hopkins, *Admin Sec*
EMP: 25
SALES (est): 1.3MM **Privately Held**
SIC: 8011 Gynecologist

(G-249)
HAND REHABILITATION ASSOCIATES
3925 Embassy Pkwy Ste 200 (44333-8400)
PHONE..................330 668-4055
Joyce E Baldwin, *President*
Adele L Wargo, *Corp Secy*
EMP: 25
SQ FT: 4,000
SALES (est): 662.8K **Privately Held**
SIC: 8011 Orthopedic physician

(G-250)
HANNA CAMBELL & POWELL
3737 Embassy Pkwy Ste 100 (44333-8380)
PHONE..................330 670-7300
Timothy Campbell, *Partner*
Timothy Cambell, *Partner*
David Hanna, *Partner*
Donald Powell, *Partner*
Juliana Gall, *Editor*
EMP: 50
SALES (est): 8.6MM **Privately Held**
WEB: www.hcplaw.net
SIC: 8111 Corporate, partnership & business law; general practice attorney, lawyer

(G-251)
HARRY C LOBALZO & SONS INC (PA)
Also Called: Hobart Sales & Service
61 N Cleveland (44333)
PHONE..................330 666-6758
Mike Lobalzo, *CEO*
Joe Saporito, *President*
Rick Lobalzo, *Exec VP*
Douglas Fox, *Financial Exec*
▲ EMP: 35
SQ FT: 20,000
SALES: 6.3MM **Privately Held**
WEB: www.lobalzo.com
SIC: 5046 7699 3556 Commercial cooking & food service equipment; bakery equipment & supplies; restaurant equipment repair; food products machinery

(G-252)
HARTVILLE GROUP INC (PA)
1210 Massillon Rd (44306-3327)
PHONE..................330 484-8166
Nicholas J Leighton, *Ch of Bd*
Dennis C Rushovich, *President*
Chris Chaney, *President*
Scott Taylor, *President*
Liz Watson, *President*
EMP: 39
SQ FT: 12,395
SALES (est): 35.5MM **Privately Held**
WEB: www.hartvillegroup.com
SIC: 6399 Health insurance for pets

(G-253)
HARWICK STANDARD DIST CORP (PA)
60 S Seiberling St (44305-4217)
P.O. Box 9360 (44305-0360)
PHONE..................330 798-9300
Ernie Pouttu, *CEO*
Jeffrey J Buda, *President*
Richard A Chenoweth, *Principal*
Brian Johnson, *Principal*
Bill Knezevich, *Principal*
◆ EMP: 60
SQ FT: 160,000
SALES (est): 65.6MM **Privately Held**
WEB: www.harwickstandard.com
SIC: 5169 Chemicals, industrial & heavy

(G-254)
HASENSTAB ARCHITECTS INC (PA)
190 N Union St Ste 400 (44304-1362)
PHONE..................330 434-4464
Dennis Check, *President*
Robert Medziuch, *Treasurer*
EMP: 37
SALES (est): 7.5MM **Privately Held**
WEB: www.hainc.cc
SIC: 8712 Architectural engineering

(G-255)
HAT WHITE MANAGEMENT LLC (PA)
Also Called: Life Skills Center
121 S Main St Ste 107 (44308-1436)
PHONE..................800 525-7967
Rodd Coker, *Vice Pres*
Robert L Fox, *Vice Pres*
Kerry Jupina, *Vice Pres*
John Morris,
EMP: 40
SALES (est): 21.7MM **Privately Held**
WEB: www.whitehatmgmt.com
SIC: 4142 8741 Bus charter service, except local; business management

(G-256)
HAVEN REST MINISTRIES INC (PA)
175 E Market St (44308-2011)
P.O. Box 547 (44309-0547)
PHONE..................330 535-1563
James Cummins, *President*
Dr Forest Crocker, *Vice Pres*
EMP: 90
SQ FT: 45,851
SALES (est): 3.9MM **Privately Held**
WEB: www.havenofrest.org
SIC: 8661 8322 Non-denominational church; individual & family services

(G-257)
HCR MANORCARE MED SVCS FLA LLC
Also Called: Arden Courts of Akron Bath
171 N Clvland Mssillon Rd (44333-2422)
PHONE..................330 668-6889
Richard Winslow, *Exec Dir*
EMP: 60
SQ FT: 25,448
SALES (corp-wide): 2.4B **Publicly Held**
WEB: www.manorcare.com
SIC: 8051 Convalescent home with continuous nursing care
HQ: Hcr Manorcare Medical Services Of Florida, Llc
333 N Summit St Ste 100
Toledo OH 43604
419 252-5500

(G-258)
HEALTHCARE FACILITY MGT LLC
Also Called: Wyant Woods Care Center
200 Wyant Rd (44313-4228)
PHONE..................330 836-7953
Jim Burke, *Administration*
EMP: 115
SALES (corp-wide): 125.8MM **Privately Held**
WEB: www.communicarehealth.com
SIC: 8051 8052 Skilled nursing care facilities; intermediate care facilities
PA: Communicare Health Services, Inc.
4700 Ashwood Dr Ste 200
Blue Ash OH 45241
513 530-1654

(G-259)
HERNANDEZ CNSTR SVCS INC
1160 Gorge Blvd Ste D (44310)
PHONE..................330 796-0500
Scott Hernandez, *President*
Alyssa Wieland, *Executive Asst*
EMP: 45 EST: 2005
SALES (est): 8.1MM **Privately Held**
SIC: 8741 Construction management

(G-260)
HICKORY HEALTH CARE INC
721 Hickory St (44303-2213)
PHONE..................330 762-6486
Brian Colleran, *President*
EMP: 99
SALES (est): 1.9MM **Privately Held**
SIC: 8051 Skilled nursing care facilities

(G-261)
HIGH LINE CORPORATION
Also Called: Casnet
2420 Wedgewood Dr Ste 20 (44312-2414)
PHONE..................330 848-8800
Bradley D Bowers, *President*
Brian Bowers, *Manager*
Jeff Comer, *CTO*
Elena Fiocca, *Software Engr*
Larry Jezior, *Director*
EMP: 50
SALES (est): 5.3MM **Privately Held**
WEB: www.gotocasnet.com
SIC: 7389 5999 7629 4226 Microfilm recording & developing service; telephone & communication equipment; electrical repair shops; document & office records storage

(G-262)
HILLANDALE FARMS CORPORATION (PA)
1330 Austin Ave (44306-3106)
PHONE..................330 724-3199
Orland Bethel, *President*
Gary Bethel, *Corp Secy*
EMP: 45
SQ FT: 10,000
SALES (est): 27.5MM **Privately Held**
WEB: www.hillandalefarms.com
SIC: 5144 5143 5147 5141 Eggs; butter; cheese; meats & meat products; groceries, general line

(G-263)
HITCHCOCK FLEMING & ASSOC INC
Also Called: H F A
500 Wolf Ledges Pkwy (44311-1080)
PHONE..................330 376-2111
Jack Deleo, *CEO*
Nick Betro, *President*
Charles Abraham, *Managing Prtnr*
Gina Page, *Accounts Mgr*
EMP: 90
SQ FT: 16,000
SALES: 19MM **Privately Held**
SIC: 7311 Advertising consultant

(G-264)
HOC TRANSPORT COMPANY
1569 Industrial Pkwy (44310-2603)
PHONE..................330 630-0100
Carl Hummel, *Principal*
EMP: 26
SALES (est): 4.1MM **Privately Held**
SIC: 4789 Cargo loading & unloading services

(G-265)
HOGLUND CHWLKOWSKI MROZIK PLLC
Also Called: Hoglund Law
520 S Main St (44311-1072)
PHONE.................................330 252-8009
Robert Hoglund, *Branch Mgr*
EMP: 110 **Privately Held**
SIC: 8111 General practice law office
PA: Hoglund, Chwialkowski & Mrozik Pllc
1781 County Road B W
Saint Paul MN 55113

(G-266)
HOLLAND OIL COMPANY (PA)
1485 Marion Ave (44313-7625)
PHONE.................................330 835-1815
Lisa M Holland-Toth, *President*
Lynn Gorman, *Exec VP*
Michael J Toth, *Senior VP*
Carl Hummel, *VP Opers*
John Ballard, *VP Merchandise*
EMP: 70
SQ FT: 20,000
SALES (est): 179.2MM **Privately Held**
WEB: www.hollandoil.com
SIC: 5541 5172 5411 Gasoline service
stations; gasoline; service station sup-
plies, petroleum; convenience stores

(G-267)
HOLUB IRON & STEEL COMPANY
470 N Arlington St (44305-1604)
PHONE.................................330 252-5655
Stephen Carroll, *President*
EMP: 25 EST: 1924
SQ FT: 7,500
SALES (est): 2.8MM **Privately Held**
SIC: 5093 5051 Ferrous metal scrap &
waste; nonferrous metals scrap; steel

(G-268)
HOME DEPOT USA INC
Also Called: Home Depot, The
2811 S Arlington Rd (44312-4715)
PHONE.................................330 245-0280
Eric Hilgert, *Branch Mgr*
EMP: 200
SQ FT: 119,856
SALES (corp-wide): 108.2B **Publicly Held**
WEB: www.homerentalsdepot.com
SIC: 5211 7359 Home centers; tool rental
HQ: Home Depot U.S.A., Inc.
2455 Paces Ferry Ave
Atlanta GA 30339

(G-269)
HOME HELPER DIRECT LINK
1720 Merriman Rd Unit B (44313-5280)
PHONE.................................330 865-5730
Ryan O'Callaghan, *Owner*
EMP: 84 EST: 2007
SALES (est): 358.8K **Privately Held**
SIC: 8082 Home health care services

(G-270)
HOWARD HANNA SMYTHE CRAMER
2603 W Market St Ste 100a (44313-4214)
PHONE.................................216 447-4477
Cris Burdick, *Manager*
EMP: 70
SALES (corp-wide): 73.7MM **Privately Held**
WEB: www.smythecramer.com
SIC: 6531 Real estate brokers & agents
HQ: Howard Hanna Smythe Cramer
6000 Parkland Blvd
Cleveland OH 44124
216 447-4477

(G-271)
HUNTINGTON NATIONAL BANK
Iii Cascade Plz Fl 7 Flr 7 (44308)
PHONE.................................330 996-6300
EMP: 4814
SALES (corp-wide): 5.2B **Publicly Held**
SIC: 6021 National commercial banks
HQ: The Huntington National Bank
17 S High St Fl 1
Columbus OH 43215
614 480-4293

(G-272)
HUNTINGTON NATIONAL BANK
Also Called: Firstmerit
106 S Main St Fl 5 (44308-1412)
PHONE.................................330 384-7201
Daniel Zoeller, *Senior VP*
Eric Bowers, *Vice Pres*
Randy Oswald, *Project Mgr*
Jeremy Jones, *Engineer*
Lori Dyer, *Loan Officer*
EMP: 2836
SALES (corp-wide): 5.2B **Publicly Held**
SIC: 6021 National commercial banks
HQ: The Huntington National Bank
17 S High St Fl 1
Columbus OH 43215
614 480-4293

(G-273)
HUNTINGTON NATIONAL BANK
121 S Main St Ste 200 (44308-1426)
PHONE.................................330 384-7092
EMP: 25
SALES (corp-wide): 5.2B **Publicly Held**
SIC: 6021 National commercial banks
HQ: The Huntington National Bank
17 S High St Fl 1
Columbus OH 43215
614 480-4293

(G-274)
IACOMINIS PAPA JOES INC
1561 Akron Peninsula Rd (44313-5159)
PHONE.................................330 923-7999
Judith Amato, *President*
Jeffrey Bruno, *Treasurer*
EMP: 89
SALES (est): 3.8MM **Privately Held**
WEB: www.lopico.com
SIC: 7299 5812 5921 Banquet hall facili-
ties; eating places; wine

(G-275)
INFO LINE INC
703 S Main St Ste 200 (44311-1098)
PHONE.................................330 252-8064
Richard Stahl, *President*
EMP: 47
SALES: 3.2MM **Privately Held**
SIC: 8322 Referral service for personal &
social problems

(G-276)
INFOCISION MANAGEMENT CORP (PA)
325 Springside Dr (44333-4504)
PHONE.................................330 668-1411
Craig Taylor, *CEO*
Gary Taylor, *Ch of Bd*
Steve Boyazis, *President*
Steve Brubaker, *Senior VP*
Ken Dawson, *Senior VP*
EMP: 356
SQ FT: 38,000
SALES (est): 242.3MM **Privately Held**
WEB: www.infocision.com
SIC: 7389 Telemarketing services

(G-277)
INFOCISION MANAGEMENT CORP
250 N Clvland Mssilon Rd (44333-2479)
PHONE.................................330 668-6615
Marshal Larsen, *Branch Mgr*
EMP: 227
SALES (corp-wide): 242.3MM **Privately Held**
WEB: www.infocision.com
SIC: 7389 Telemarketing services
PA: Infocision Management Corporation
325 Springside Dr
Akron OH 44333
330 668-1411

(G-278)
INSTALLED BUILDING PDTS LLC
Also Called: Nooney & Moses
2783 Gilchrist Rd Unit B (44305-4406)
PHONE.................................330 798-9640
James Pope, *Principal*
EMP: 30
SALES (corp-wide): 1.3B **Publicly Held**
WEB: www.dwdcpa.com
SIC: 1742 Insulation, buildings

HQ: Installed Building Products Llc
495 S High St Ste 50
Columbus OH 43215
614 221-3399

(G-279)
INTERNAL MEDICINE OF AKRON
150 Springside Dr 320c (44333-2486)
PHONE.................................330 376-2728
Erwin A Maseelall MD, *President*
Jeffrey Eckman, *Principal*
Michael Giddeon, *Principal*
EMP: 25
SALES (est): 2.7MM **Privately Held**
SIC: 8062 General medical & surgical hos-
pitals

(G-280)
INTERNATIONAL CHEM WKRS CR UN (PA)
1655 W Market St Fl 6 (44313-7004)
PHONE.................................330 926-1444
Frank Cyphers, *Principal*
Eric Bray, *Treasurer*
EMP: 40
SQ FT: 60,000
SALES (est): 4.2MM **Privately Held**
SIC: 8631 Labor union

(G-281)
IRACE INC
Also Called: Irace Automotive
2265 W Market St (44313-6907)
PHONE.................................330 836-7247
Jim Irace, *Principal*
EMP: 25 EST: 2001
SQ FT: 2,448
SALES (est): 4.8MM **Privately Held**
SIC: 5541 7538 7539 Filling stations,
gasoline; general automotive repair
shops; automotive repair shops

(G-282)
ISD RENAL INC
Also Called: Akron Renal Center
525 E Market St Bldg 50 (44304-1619)
P.O. Box 102407, Atlanta GA (30368-2407)
PHONE.................................330 375-6848
James K Hilger,
EMP: 85 **Publicly Held**
SIC: 8092 Kidney dialysis centers
HQ: Isd Renal, Inc.
2000 16th St
Denver CO 80202

(G-283)
J F BERNARD INC
359 Stanton Ave (44301-1468)
PHONE.................................330 785-3830
Joseph Bernard Jr, *President*
Eric Bernard, *Vice Pres*
Rob Hampton, *Project Mgr*
Johnathan Meade, *Project Mgr*
Steve Noffert, *Accounts Mgr*
EMP: 30
SALES (est): 3.8MM **Privately Held**
WEB: www.jfbinc.com
SIC: 1711 Warm air heating & air condi-
tioning contractor

(G-284)
J W DIDADO ELECTRIC INC
1033 Kelly Ave (44306-3143)
PHONE.................................330 374-0070
Gary Didado, *President*
Rhonda Didado, *Corp Secy*
Tony Didado, *Vice Pres*
EMP: 150
SQ FT: 6,500
SALES (est): 32.4MM
SALES (corp-wide): 11.1B **Publicly Held**
WEB: www.jwdidadoelectric.com
SIC: 1731 General electrical contractor
PA: Quanta Services, Inc.
2800 Post Oak Blvd # 2600
Houston TX 77056
713 629-7600

(G-285)
J W GEOPFERT CO INC
Also Called: Geopfert Company, The
1024 Home Ave (44310-3579)
PHONE.................................330 762-2293
Thomas Geopfert Jr, *President*
Thomas Geopfert Sr, *Chairman*
Joe Geopfert, *Vice Pres*

Joseph Geopfert, *Vice Pres*
Jean Geopfert, *Treasurer*
EMP: 32 EST: 1953
SQ FT: 6,100
SALES (est): 6.7MM **Privately Held**
WEB: www.geopfert.com
SIC: 1711 Plumbing/Heating/Air Cond
Contractor

(G-286)
J&B SPRAFKA ENTERPRISES INC (PA)
1430 Goodyear Blvd (44305-4168)
PHONE.................................330 733-4212
Brian Sprafka, *President*
Jennifer Sprafka, *Vice Pres*
EMP: 28
SQ FT: 4,000
SALES (est): 1.1MM **Privately Held**
WEB: www.colorourrainbow.com
SIC: 8351 8211 7999 Preschool center;
kindergarten; day camp

(G-287)
JACKSON KELLY PLLC
17 S Main St 1 (44308-1803)
PHONE.................................330 252-9060
Cheryl Green, *Branch Mgr*
EMP: 56
SALES (corp-wide): 80.4MM **Privately Held**
SIC: 8111 General practice attorney,
lawyer
PA: Jackson Kelly Pllc
500 Lee St E Ste 1600
Charleston WV 25301
304 340-1000

(G-288)
JC PENNEY CORPORATION INC
Also Called: JC Penney
2000 Brittain Rd Ste 600 (44310-1814)
PHONE.................................330 633-7700
Carton Sanders, *Manager*
Richard Gotch, *Manager*
EMP: 300
SALES (corp-wide): 12B **Publicly Held**
SIC: 5311 7231 Department stores, non-
discount; beauty shops
HQ: J. C. Penney Corporation, Inc.
6501 Legacy Dr
Plano TX 75024
972 431-1000

(G-289)
JEFF PLUMBER INC (PA)
1100 Tower Dr (44305-1090)
PHONE.................................330 940-2600
Jeffrey L Thompson, *CEO*
Kevin Thompson, *Treasurer*
EMP: 25
SQ FT: 6,000
SALES (est): 4.1MM **Privately Held**
WEB: www.jefftheplumber.com
SIC: 1711 Plumbing contractors

(G-290)
JENNINGS HEATING COMPANY INC
Also Called: Jennings Heating & Cooling
1671 E Market St (44305-4210)
P.O. Box 9442 (44305-0442)
PHONE.................................330 784-1286
Mike Foraker, *President*
Fred S Jennings, *Vice Pres*
Marshall Jennings, *Vice Pres*
EMP: 38
SQ FT: 10,000
SALES (est): 6.9MM **Privately Held**
WEB: www.jenningsheating.com
SIC: 1711 Warm air heating & air condi-
tioning contractor

(G-291)
JERSEY CENTRAL PWR & LIGHT CO (HQ)
76 S Main St (44308-1812)
PHONE.................................800 736-3402
Donald M Lynch, *President*
Chad Hampson, *General Mgr*
William D Byrd, *Vice Pres*
Mark A Jones, *Vice Pres*
Alex Patton, *VP Opers*
▲ EMP: 170 EST: 1925

SALES: 1.8B **Publicly Held**
WEB: www.jersey-central-power-light.mon-mouth.n
SIC: 4911 Generation, electric power; distribution, electric power; transmission, electric power

(G-292)
JOHN DELLAGNESE & ASSOC INC
4000 Embassy Pkwy Ste 400 (44333-8357)
PHONE..................................330 668-4000
Regina Shaw, *President*
Christina Kallio, *Accountant*
EMP: 25
SQ FT: 8,600
SALES: 1MM **Privately Held**
WEB: www.dellagnese.com
SIC: 6531 Real estate managers

(G-293)
JOHN P NOVATNY ELECTRIC CO
955 Evans Ave (44305-1041)
PHONE..................................330 630-8900
Mark Trudics, *President*
Mike Panaciulli, *Vice Pres*
Dennis Pennington, *Technology*
EMP: 50 EST: 1920
SQ FT: 10,000
SALES (est): 9.3MM **Privately Held**
SIC: 1731 General electrical contractor

(G-294)
JONES GROUP INTERIORS INC
701 S Broadway St Ste 200 (44311-1500)
PHONE..................................330 253-9180
Robert J Jones, *President*
Robert F Linton, *Principal*
Linda E Miller, *Principal*
Patricia Wendling, *Principal*
EMP: 25
SQ FT: 64,575
SALES (est): 3.4MM **Privately Held**
WEB: www.bie1.com
SIC: 7389 8748 5021 Interior designer; lighting consultant; office furniture

(G-295)
JPMORGAN CHASE BANK NAT ASSN
1805 Brittain Rd (44310-1803)
PHONE..................................330 972-1915
Eric Vanhorn, *Branch Mgr*
EMP: 26
SALES (corp-wide): 131.4B **Publicly Held**
WEB: www.chase.com
SIC: 6021 National commercial banks
HQ: Jpmorgan Chase Bank, National Association
1111 Polaris Pkwy
Columbus OH 43240
614 436-3055

(G-296)
KAISER FOUNDATION HOSPITALS
Also Called: Chapel Hill Medical Offices
1260 Independence Ave (44310-1812)
PHONE..................................330 633-8400
EMP: 593
SALES (corp-wide): 93B **Privately Held**
SIC: 8011 Medical Doctor's Office
HQ: Kaiser Foundation Hospitals Inc
1 Kaiser Plz
Oakland CA 94612
510 271-6611

(G-297)
KALLAS ENTERPRISES INC
Also Called: Custom Trim of America
916 E Buchtel Ave (44305-2337)
PHONE..................................330 253-6893
Alex Kallas, *President*
EMP: 26
SQ FT: 20,000
SALES (est): 2MM **Privately Held**
SIC: 7532 Upholstery & trim shop, automotive; tops (canvas or plastic), installation or repair: automotive

(G-298)
KANDY KANE CHILDRENS LRNG CTR (PA)
Also Called: Kandy Kane Chrstn Day Care Ctr
1010 S Hawkins Ave (44320-2615)
P.O. Box 3395 (44309-3395)
PHONE..................................330 864-6642
Mamie Gardner, *President*
Morris Gardner, *Vice Pres*
EMP: 30 EST: 1974
SQ FT: 9,796
SALES: 0 **Privately Held**
SIC: 8351 Christian Day Care

(G-299)
KENMORE CONSTRUCTION CO INC (PA)
700 Home Ave (44310-4190)
PHONE..................................330 762-8936
William A Scala, *President*
Bill Scala, *Superintendent*
Matt Moravec, *Vice Pres*
Paul Scala, *Vice Pres*
Jerry Stanoch, *Vice Pres*
▲ EMP: 151
SQ FT: 3,000
SALES (est): 93MM **Privately Held**
WEB: www.kenmorecompanies.com
SIC: 1611 5032 General contractor, highway & street construction; sand, construction

(G-300)
KENNY OBAYASHI JOINT VENTURE V
144 Cuyahoga St (44304-1067)
PHONE..................................703 969-0611
Michael Stoecker, *Vice Pres*
EMP: 150
SALES (est): 4.4MM **Privately Held**
SIC: 1542 Commercial & office building, new construction

(G-301)
KEVIN C MCDONNELL MD
224 W Exchange St Ste 220 (44302-1726)
PHONE..................................330 344-6401
Kevin McDonnell MD, *Co-Owner*
EMP: 77 EST: 2013
SALES (est): 94.4K **Privately Held**
SIC: 8011 Anesthesiologist

(G-302)
KEYSTONE TECHNOLOGY CONS
Also Called: Keystone Business Solutions
787 Wye Rd (44333-2268)
PHONE..................................330 666-6200
Greg Cordray, *President*
Brian Fontanella, *Managing Prtnr*
David Howard, *Managing Prtnr*
Stephanie Thoma, *Finance Asst*
Rochelle Schenk, *Accounts Mgr*
EMP: 25
SALES (est): 4.7MM **Privately Held**
SIC: 7371 Computer software development & applications

(G-303)
KINDRED HEALTHCARE OPERATING
Also Called: Ridgepark Center
145 Olive St (44310-3236)
PHONE..................................330 762-0901
Jim Kallevig, *Admin Director*
EMP: 172
SALES (corp-wide): 6B **Privately Held**
WEB: www.salemhaven.com
SIC: 8051 Skilled nursing care facilities
HQ: Kindred Healthcare Operating, Llc
680 S 4th St
Louisville KY 40202
502 596-7300

(G-304)
KNOTICE LLC
526 S Main St Ste 705 (44311-4402)
PHONE..................................800 801-4194
Will Margiloff,
EMP: 60

(G-305)
KRUMROY-COZAD CNSTR CORP
376 W Exchange St (44302-1703)
PHONE..................................330 376-4136
Daniel J Cozad, *President*
EMP: 50
SQ FT: 3,226
SALES (est): 12.3MM **Privately Held**
WEB: www.krumroy-cozad.com
SIC: 1542 Commercial & office building, new construction

(G-306)
KURTZ BROS COMPOST SERVICES
2677 Riverview Rd (44313-4719)
PHONE..................................330 864-2621
Thomas Kurtz, *President*
EMP: 30
SALES (est): 4.3MM **Privately Held**
WEB: www.kbcompost.com
SIC: 2875 8741 Compost; management services

(G-307)
LABORATORY CORPORATION AMERICA
1 Park West Blvd Ste 290 (44320-4231)
PHONE..................................330 865-3624
Barb Hoskinson, *Manager*
EMP: 25 **Publicly Held**
SIC: 8071 Testing laboratories
HQ: Laboratory Corporation Of America
358 S Main St Ste 458
Burlington NC 27215
336 229-1127

(G-308)
LAKE ERIE ELECTRIC INC
1888 Brown St (44301-3143)
PHONE..................................330 724-1241
Gregg Juchum, *Warehouse Mgr*
John Kellamis, *Branch Mgr*
EMP: 33
SALES (corp-wide): 137.9MM **Privately Held**
SIC: 1731 General electrical contractor
PA: Erie Lake Electric Inc
25730 1st St
Westlake OH 44145
440 835-5565

(G-309)
LAWRENCE A CERVINO MD
Also Called: Wells, Mark D MD
3975 Embassy Pkwy Ste 203 (44333-8396)
PHONE..................................330 668-4065
Lawrence A Cervino MD, *Owner*
EMP: 25
SALES (est): 632.7K **Privately Held**
SIC: 8011 Plastic surgeon

(G-310)
LEVEL 3 COMMUNICATIONS INC
520 S Main St Ste 2435 (44311-1071)
PHONE..................................330 256-8999
Scott Farley, *Manager*
EMP: 50
SALES (corp-wide): 23.4B **Publicly Held**
WEB: www.level3.com
SIC: 4813 Telephone communication, except radio
HQ: Level 3 Parent, Llc
1025 Eldorado Blvd # 4000
Broomfield CO 80021
720 888-1000

(G-311)
LEVEL 3 TELECOM LLC
Also Called: Time Warner Cable
1019 E Turkeyfoot Lake Rd (44312-5242)
PHONE..................................234 542-6279
EMP: 29
SALES (corp-wide): 23.4B **Publicly Held**
SIC: 4813
HQ: Level 3 Telecom, Llc
10475 Park Meadows Dr
Lone Tree CO 80124
303 566-1000

(G-312)
LHA DEVELOPMENTS
910 Eller Ave (44306-3705)
PHONE..................................330 785-3219
Kathy McCormick, *Manager*
EMP: 25 EST: 2009
SALES (est): 977.4K **Privately Held**
SIC: 6552 Subdividers & developers

(G-313)
LIFE INSURANCE MKTG CO INC
91 Mayfield Ave (44313-6827)
PHONE..................................330 867-1707
Lawrence S Rybka, *President*
Elaine Pressler, *Treasurer*
EMP: 50
SALES (est): 5MM **Privately Held**
SIC: 6411 Insurance agents & brokers

(G-314)
LIFELINE SYSTEMS COMPANY
703 S Main St Ste 211 (44311-1098)
PHONE..................................330 762-5627
Richard Stahal, *CEO*
EMP: 50
SALES (corp-wide): 20.9B **Privately Held**
SIC: 8399 Social service information exchange
HQ: Lifeline Systems Company
111 Lawrence St
Framingham MA 01702
508 988-1000

(G-315)
LINCARE INC
Also Called: America's Best Medical
1566 Akron Peninsula Rd # 2 (44313-7980)
PHONE..................................330 928-0884
Rob Dellaposta, *Manager*
EMP: 35
SALES (corp-wide): 20.1B **Privately Held**
WEB: www.lincare.com
SIC: 8399 Advocacy group
PA: Lincare Inc.
19387 Us Highway 19 N
Clearwater FL 33764
727 530-7700

(G-316)
LINDSEY CNSTR & DESIGN INC
2151 S Arlington Rd (44306-4207)
PHONE..................................330 785-9931
Eric Lindsey, *CEO*
EMP: 26
SQ FT: 2,400
SALES (est): 6.4MM **Privately Held**
SIC: 7389 5033 Design services; roofing, siding & insulation

(G-317)
LKQ TRIPLETTASAP INC (HQ)
Also Called: Triplett ASAP
1435 Triplett Blvd (44306-3303)
P.O. Box 7667 (44306-0667)
PHONE..................................330 733-6333
Stuart Willen, *President*
EMP: 120
SQ FT: 25,000
SALES (est): 31.8MM
SALES (corp-wide): 11.8B **Publicly Held**
WEB: www.triplettasap.com
SIC: 5015 5521 Automotive supplies, used; used car dealers
PA: Lkq Corporation
500 W Madison St Ste 2800
Chicago IL 60661
312 621-1950

(G-318)
LOCAL UNION 856 UAW BLDG CORP
501 Kelly Ave (44306-2573)
PHONE..................................330 733-6231
Gene Steele, *President*
Renee Kaplinger, *Admin Sec*
EMP: 25
SQ FT: 2,100

SALES (est): 1.1MM **Privately Held**
SIC: 8631 Labor union

(G-319)
LOCKHART CONCRETE CO (PA)
800 W Waterloo Rd (44314-1528)
PHONE.................................330 745-6520
Robert Lockart, *President*
Alexander R Lockhart, *Principal*
Jill Lockhart, *Vice Pres*
Rick Stanley, *Admin Sec*
EMP: 55
SALES (est): 7.1MM **Privately Held**
SIC: 1771 Concrete work

(G-320)
LOCUST DENTAL CENTER
300 Locust St Ste 430 (44302-1880)
PHONE.................................330 535-7876
Gail Kamlowski, *Office Mgr*
EMP: 25
SALES (est): 1.6MM **Privately Held**
SIC: 8021 Dentists' office

(G-321)
LOWES HOME CENTERS LLC
186 N Clvland Mssillon Rd (44333-2467)
PHONE.................................330 665-9356
Mike Hoffmeier, *Manager*
EMP: 150
SALES (corp-wide): 68.6B **Publicly Held**
SIC: 5211 5031 5722 5064 Home centers; building materials, exterior; building materials, interior; household appliance stores; electrical appliances, television & radio
HQ: Lowe's Home Centers, Llc
1605 Curtis Bridge Rd
Wilkesboro NC 28697
336 658-4000

(G-322)
LOWES HOME CENTERS LLC
940 Interstate Pkwy (44312-5286)
PHONE.................................330 245-4300
Scott Adkins, *Manager*
EMP: 150
SALES (corp-wide): 68.6B **Publicly Held**
SIC: 5211 5031 5722 5064 Lumber & other building materials; building materials, exterior; building materials, interior; household appliance stores; electrical appliances, television & radio
HQ: Lowe's Home Centers, Llc
1605 Curtis Bridge Rd
Wilkesboro NC 28697
336 658-4000

(G-323)
LUMBERJACKS INC (PA)
Also Called: Lumberjack's Creative Bldg Ctr
723 E Tallmadge Ave Ste 1 (44310-2419)
PHONE.................................330 762-2401
Todd Allen, *President*
Jack D Allen, *Treasurer*
EMP: 50 **EST:** 1978
SQ FT: 31,500
SALES (est): 10.5MM **Privately Held**
WEB: www.lumberjacks.com
SIC: 5211 5031 Cabinets, kitchen; counter tops; lumber: rough, dressed & finished; kitchen cabinets

(G-324)
M & R FREDERICKTOWN LTD INC
Also Called: Spectra Medical Distribution
895 Home Ave (44310-4115)
PHONE.................................440 801-1563
Mike Houska, *President*
Clarence Palgua, *Partner*
Shawn Dellafave, *Opers Mgr*
Debbie Maggiore, *Manager*
EMP: 25
SQ FT: 4,000
SALES (est): 3.7MM **Privately Held**
SIC: 5139 5047 Footwear; medical equipment & supplies

(G-325)
MANOR CARE OF AMERICA INC
1211 W Market St (44313-7180)
PHONE.................................330 867-8530
Kim Nelson, *Manager*
EMP: 110

SALES (corp-wide): 2.4B **Publicly Held**
WEB: www.trisunhealthcare.com
SIC: 8051 Convalescent home with continuous nursing care
HQ: Manor Care Of America, Inc.
333 N Summit St Ste 103
Toledo OH 43604
419 252-5500

(G-326)
MCDONALDS 3490
578 E Market St (44304-1660)
PHONE.................................330 762-7747
V Gorsmith, *General Mgr*
Victoria Gorsmith, *General Mgr*
EMP: 46
SALES (est): 970K **Privately Held**
SIC: 5812 7389 Fast-food restaurant, independent;

(G-327)
MCKINLEY EARLY CHILDHOOD CTR
440 Vernon Odom Blvd (44307-2108)
PHONE.................................330 252-2552
Dianna Sigmon, *Administration*
EMP: 25
SALES (est): 446K
SALES (corp-wide): 1MM **Privately Held**
SIC: 8351 Group day care center
PA: Mckinley Early Childhood Ctr
1350 Cherry Ave Ne
Canton OH 44714
330 454-4800

(G-328)
MED ASSIST PRGRAM OF INFO LINE
703 S Main St Ste 211 (44311-1098)
PHONE.................................330 762-0609
Elaine Woloshyn, *Director*
EMP: 40
SALES (est): 577.2K **Privately Held**
SIC: 8399 Social service information exchange

(G-329)
MEDIC MANAGEMENT GROUP LLC (PA)
275 Springside Dr (44333-4548)
PHONE.................................330 670-5316
Thomas Ferkovic, *President*
Jennifer Evans, *Manager*
Helen Simmons, *Information Mgr*
EMP: 87
SALES (est): 5.4MM **Privately Held**
SIC: 8721 Billing & bookkeeping service

(G-330)
MEDLINK OF OHIO INC
Also Called: Nursefinders
1225 E Waterloo Rd (44306-3805)
PHONE.................................330 773-9434
Tina Janok, *Marketing Staff*
Doti Johnson, *Manager*
EMP: 300
SALES (corp-wide): 1.8B **Publicly Held**
SIC: 8049 7363 Nurses, registered & practical; temporary help service
HQ: Medlink Of Ohio, Inc
20600 Chagrin Blvd # 290
Cleveland OH 44122
216 751-5900

(G-331)
MERRILL LYNCH PIERCE FENNER
4000 Embassy Pkwy Ste 300 (44333-8357)
PHONE.................................330 670-2400
Peter Calleri, *Director*
EMP: 40
SALES (corp-wide): 110.5B **Publicly Held**
WEB: www.merlyn.com
SIC: 6211 Security brokers & dealers
HQ: Merrill Lynch, Pierce, Fenner & Smith Incorporated
111 8th Ave
New York NY 10011
800 637-7455

(G-332)
MERRILL LYNCH PIERCE FENNER
4000 Embassy Pkwy Ste 300 (44333-8357)
PHONE.................................330 670-2400
Jerry Huffman, *Branch Mgr*
Robert Wright, *Director*
EMP: 100
SALES (corp-wide): 110.5B **Publicly Held**
WEB: www.merlyn.com
SIC: 6211 8742 6282 6221 Security brokers & dealers; management consulting services; investment advice; commodity contracts brokers, dealers
HQ: Merrill Lynch, Pierce, Fenner & Smith Incorporated
111 8th Ave
New York NY 10011
800 637-7455

(G-333)
METALICO AKRON INC (HQ)
Also Called: Metalico Annaco
943 Hazel St (44305-1609)
P.O. Box 1148 (44309-1148)
PHONE.................................330 376-1400
Jeffery Bauer, *General Mgr*
EMP: 35 **EST:** 1930
SQ FT: 30,000
SALES (est): 9.5MM
SALES (corp-wide): 110.5MM **Privately Held**
WEB: www.annaco.com
SIC: 5093 4953 3341 Ferrous metal scrap & waste; nonferrous metals scrap; refuse systems; secondary nonferrous metals
PA: Metalico, Inc.
135 Dermody St
Cranford NJ 07016
908 497-9610

(G-334)
METRO REGIONAL TRANSIT AUTH
631 S Broadway St (44311-1000)
PHONE.................................330 762-0341
Shawn Metcalf, *Supervisor*
Jarrod Hampshire, *Maintence Staff*
EMP: 272
SALES (corp-wide): 28.9MM **Privately Held**
SIC: 4111 Bus line operations
PA: Metro Regional Transit Authority
416 Kenmore Blvd
Akron OH 44301
330 762-0341

(G-335)
METRO REGIONAL TRANSIT AUTH (PA)
416 Kenmore Blvd (44301-1099)
PHONE.................................330 762-0341
Bernard Bear, *President*
Saundra Foster, *President*
Scott C Meyer, *Vice Pres*
Troy Webb, *Facilities Mgr*
Dean J Harris, *CFO*
EMP: 90
SQ FT: 300,000
SALES (est): 28.9MM **Privately Held**
SIC: 4111 Bus transportation

(G-336)
METROPOLITAN EDISON COMPANY (HQ)
Also Called: Met-Ed
76 S Main St (44308-1812)
PHONE.................................800 736-3402
Charles E Jones, *President*
Leila L Vespoli, *Exec VP*
Harvey L Wagner, *Vice Pres*
James Frey, *Opers Staff*
Alfred Nerino, *Engineer*
EMP: 144 **EST:** 1922
SALES: 837.1MM **Publicly Held**
SIC: 4911 Generation, electric power

(G-337)
METROPOLITAN SECURITY SVCS INC
Also Called: Walden Security
2 S Main St (44308-1813)
PHONE.................................330 253-6459
EMP: 439 **Privately Held**
SIC: 7381 Guard services
PA: Metropolitan Security Services, Inc.
100 E 10th St Ste 400
Chattanooga TN 37402

(G-338)
MID-OHIO FORKLIFTS INC
1336 Home Ave (44310-2551)
PHONE.................................330 633-1230
Art Sherwood, *President*
Matthew Welhouse, *Opers Mgr*
Jeremy Petros, *Manager*
Roger Wright, *Executive*
EMP: 25
SQ FT: 17,250
SALES (est): 14.8MM **Privately Held**
WEB: www.midohioforklift.com
SIC: 5084 Materials handling machinery

(G-339)
MILLERS RENTAL AND SLS CO INC (PA)
2023 Romig Rd (44320-3819)
PHONE.................................330 753-8600
John J Miller, *CEO*
John P Miller, *President*
Daniel E Craig, *Vice Pres*
Frank P Pamer, *Vice Pres*
Jackie Paulik, *Vice Pres*
EMP: 95
SQ FT: 14,000
SALES (est): 23.9MM **Privately Held**
WEB: www.millers.com
SIC: 7352 5999 Medical equipment rental; hospital equipment & supplies

(G-340)
MOBILE MEALS (PA)
1357 Home Ave Ste 1 (44310-2549)
PHONE.................................330 376-7717
Dana Downing, *President*
Kathleen Downing, *Director*
EMP: 88 **EST:** 1971
SQ FT: 6,500
SALES: 3.6MM **Privately Held**
SIC: 8322 Meal delivery program

(G-341)
MORGAN STANLEY
3700 Embassy Pkwy Ste 340 (44333-8339)
PHONE.................................330 670-4600
Teri Deal, *Manager*
EMP: 25
SALES (corp-wide): 40.1B **Publicly Held**
SIC: 6153 Short-term business credit
PA: Morgan Stanley
1585 Broadway
New York NY 10036
212 761-4000

(G-342)
MYERS INDUSTRIES INC (PA)
1293 S Main St (44301-1339)
PHONE.................................330 253-5592
F Jack Liebau Jr, *Ch of Bd*
R David Banyard, *President*
Kevin Brackman, *Vice Pres*
Matteo Anversa, *CFO*
Kevin L Brackman, *CFO*
EMP: 50
SQ FT: 129,000
SALES: 566.7MM **Publicly Held**
WEB: www.myersind.com
SIC: 3089 3086 3069 3052 Pallets, plastic; stock shapes, plastic; boxes, plastic; blow molded finished plastic products; plastics foam products; packaging & shipping materials, foamed plastic; insulation or cushioning material, foamed plastic; padding, foamed plastic; rubber automotive products; automobile hose, rubber; tools & equipment, automotive; tire & tube repair materials

(G-343)
NATIONWIDE CHILDRENS HOSPITAL
Also Called: Central Billing Office
1 Canal Square Plz # 110 (44308-1037)
PHONE.................................(330) 253-5200
Melanie Polack, *Manager*
EMP: 38
SALES (corp-wide): 2.3B **Privately Held**
SIC: 8069 8721 Children's hospital; billing & bookkeeping service
PA: Nationwide Children's Hospital
700 Childrens Dr
Columbus OH 43205
614 722-2000

(G-344)
NEUROLOGY NROSCIENCE ASSOC INC (PA)
701 White Pond Dr (44320-1155)
PHONE.................................(330) 572-1011
Lawrence M Saltis, *Principal*
EMP: 26
SALES (est): 5.5MM **Privately Held**
SIC: 8011 Neurologist

(G-345)
NEWTOWN NINE ` INC
568 E Crosier St (44311-1809)
PHONE.................................(330) 376-7741
Kevin Akers, *Branch Mgr*
EMP: 49
SALES (corp-wide): 40MM **Privately Held**
WEB: www.ohiomaterialshandling.com
SIC: 7538 5084 Truck engine repair, except industrial; materials handling machinery
PA: Newtown Nine, Inc.
8155 Roll And Hold Pkwy
Macedonia OH 44056
440 781-0623

(G-346)
NIGHTINGALE HOLDINGS LLC (PA)
Also Called: Pebble Creek
670 Jarvis Rd (44319-2538)
PHONE.................................(330) 645-0200
Lisa Richardson, *Executive*
Jim Egli,
EMP: 441
SALES (est): 10.3MM **Privately Held**
SIC: 8051 Convalescent home with continuous nursing care

(G-347)
NORTHAST OHIO EYE SURGEONS INC
4099 Embassy Pkwy (44333-1781)
PHONE.................................(330) 836-8545
Todd E Woodruff, *Principal*
EMP: 37
SALES (corp-wide): 1.1MM **Privately Held**
SIC: 8011 Ophthalmologist
PA: Northeast Ohio Eye Surgeons, Inc.
2013 State Route 59
Kent OH 44240
330 678-0201

(G-348)
NORTHAST OHIO ORTHPEDICS ASSOC
224 W Exchange St Ste 440 (44302-1718)
PHONE.................................(330) 344-1980
Michael J Smith, *Principal*
EMP: 50
SALES (est): 3.4MM **Privately Held**
SIC: 8011 Orthopedic physician

(G-349)
NORTHAST OHIO SSTNBLE CMMNTIES
146 S High St Ste 800 (44308-1432)
PHONE.................................(216) 410-7698
EMP: 55
SALES (est): 262.8K **Privately Held**
SIC: 8699 Charitable organization

(G-350)
NORTHEAST OHIO CARDIOLOGY SVCS
95 Arch St Ste 300350 (44304-1437)
PHONE.................................(330) 253-8195
Alexander Ormond, *President*
Dr Vincent Johnson Jr, *Corp Secy*
Dr William Bauman, *Vice Pres*
EMP: 34
SQ FT: 8,200
SALES (est): 3.1MM **Privately Held**
SIC: 8011 Cardiologist & cardio-vascular specialist

(G-351)
NORTHERN DATACOMM CORP
3700 Embassy Pkwy Ste 141 (44333-8384)
PHONE.................................(330) 665-0344
Michael D Sheers, *President*
EMP: 25
SALES (est): 2.3MM **Privately Held**
SIC: 7373 Systems integration services

(G-352)
NORTHERN STYLE CNSTR LLC
344 Lease St Ste 104 (44306-1021)
PHONE.................................(330) 412-9594
Burton Pierce, *Mng Member*
James Pierce,
EMP: 60
SQ FT: 3,000
SALES: 2.1MM **Privately Held**
SIC: 1521 Single-family housing construction

(G-353)
NSA TECHNOLOGIES LLC
3867 Medina Rd Ste 256 (44333-4525)
PHONE.................................(330) 576-4600
Vincent E Fischer,
Victor J Bierman III,
Mark W Jenney,
EMP: 150
SALES (est): 6.1MM **Privately Held**
SIC: 7372 8742 8731 Publishers' computer software; marketing consulting services; commercial physical research; biological research

(G-354)
OAK ASSOCIATES LTD
3875 Embassy Pkwy Ste 250 (44333-8355)
PHONE.................................(330) 666-5263
Carol Zollars, *Financial Exec*
James D Oelschlager, *Mng Member*
Vanita B Oelschlager,
Vanita Oelschlager,
Edward Yardeni,
EMP: 45
SQ FT: 35,000
SALES (est): 11.6MM **Privately Held**
SIC: 6282 Investment advisory service

(G-355)
OBSTETRICS GYNCLOGY OF RESERVE
799 Wye Rd (44333-2268)
PHONE.................................(330) 666-1166
Ross Marchetta, *President*
EMP: 35
SQ FT: 1,600
SALES (est): 2.8MM **Privately Held**
SIC: 8011 Gynecologist; obstetrician

(G-356)
OHIO CHAMBER BALLET
Also Called: Ohio Ballet
354 E Market St (44325-0036)
PHONE.................................(330) 972-7900
Stephen Newenhisen, *Principal*
EMP: 35
SALES (est): 497.3K **Privately Held**
SIC: 7922 7911 Ballet production; dance studios, schools & halls

(G-357)
OHIO DEPT OF JOB & FMLY SVCS
Also Called: Job Service of Ohio
161 S High St Ste 300 (44308-1615)
PHONE.................................(330) 484-5402
Barbara Frank, *Director*
EMP: 60 **Privately Held**

WEB: www.job.com
SIC: 7361 9441 Employment agencies;
HQ: The Ohio Department Of Job And Family Services
30 E Broad St Fl 32
Columbus OH 43215

(G-358)
OHIO EDISON COMPANY (HQ)
76 S Main St Bsmt (44308-1817)
PHONE.................................(800) 736-3402
Charles E Jones Jr, *President*
Harvey L Wagner, *Vice Pres*
Tracy Mayse, *Opers Staff*
Darren Puffinburger, *Opers Staff*
Gregory Macmaster, *Engineer*
EMP: 143 EST: 1930
SALES: 1.3B **Publicly Held**
SIC: 4911 Generation, electric power

(G-359)
OHIO GASKET AND SHIM CO INC (PA)
Also Called: Ogs Industries
976 Evans Ave (44305-1019)
PHONE.................................(330) 630-0626
John S Bader, *President*
Thomas Bader, *Principal*
▲ EMP: 45 EST: 1959
SQ FT: 84,000
SALES (est): 21.7MM **Privately Held**
WEB: www.ogsindustries.com
SIC: 3469 3053 3599 3499 Stamping metal for the trade; gaskets, all materials; machine shop, jobbing & repair; shims, metal; packaging & labeling services

(G-360)
OHIO MAINT & RENOVATION INC (PA)
Also Called: Commercial Maintenance & Repr
124 Darrow Rd (44305-3835)
PHONE.................................(330) 315-3101
Steven Harvey, *CEO*
Steven E Harvey, *CEO*
Mike Abel, *Vice Pres*
EMP: 40
SALES (est): 6.4MM **Privately Held**
SIC: 1542 Commercial & office building contractors

(G-361)
OHIO PRESBT RETIREMENT SVCS
Also Called: Rockynol Reritment Community
1150 W Market St (44313-7129)
PHONE.................................(330) 867-2150
Thomas R Miller, *Branch Mgr*
EMP: 150 **Privately Held**
WEB: www.nwo.oprs.org
SIC: 8051 Skilled nursing care facilities
PA: Ohio Living
1001 Kingsmill Pkwy
Columbus OH 43229

(G-362)
OHIO REHABILITATION SVCS COMM
Also Called: Bureau Vctional Rehabilitation
161 S High St Ste 103 (44308-1615)
PHONE.................................(330) 643-3080
Bonita Susko, *Branch Mgr*
EMP: 35 **Privately Held**
WEB: www.rsc.ohio.gov
SIC: 9441 8331 ; vocational rehabilitation agency
HQ: Opportunities For Ohioans With Disabilities Agency
150 E Campus View Blvd
Columbus OH 43235
614 438-1200

(G-363)
OID ASSOCIATES
Also Called: Springside Racquet Fitnes CLB
215 Springside Dr (44333-2432)
PHONE.................................(330) 666-3161
Ken Channels, *General Mgr*
Val Murphy, *Manager*
EMP: 25
SQ FT: 86,000
SALES (est): 1.1MM **Privately Held**
SIC: 7991 Health club

(G-364)
OMNOVA SOLUTIONS INC
2990 Gilchrist Rd (44305-4418)
PHONE.................................(330) 794-6300
Jennifer Muffley, *Opers Staff*
Bill Beers, *Manager*
Brian Grant, *Manager*
Andrew Tisler, *Technology*
Marshall Moore, *Officer*
EMP: 65
SQ FT: 117,299
SALES (corp-wide): 769.8MM **Publicly Held**
WEB: www.omnova.com
SIC: 8731 Commercial physical research
PA: Omnova Solutions Inc.
25435 Harvard Rd
Beachwood OH 44122
216 682-7000

(G-365)
ORIANA HOUSE INC
941 Sherman St (44311-2467)
P.O. Box 1501 (44309-1501)
PHONE.................................(330) 374-9610
James Lawrence, *President*
EMP: 700
SALES (corp-wide): 51.1MM **Privately Held**
SIC: 8322 Substance abuse counseling
PA: Oriana House, Inc.
885 E Buchtel Ave
Akron OH 44305
330 535-8116

(G-366)
ORIANA HOUSE INC (PA)
885 E Buchtel Ave (44305-2338)
P.O. Box 1501 (44309-1501)
PHONE.................................(330) 535-8116
James Lawrence, *President*
William Scheub, *Managing Dir*
Gina D'Aurelio, *Principal*
Anne Connell-Freund, *Exec VP*
Bernard Rochford, *Exec VP*
EMP: 65 EST: 1981
SALES: 51.1MM **Privately Held**
WEB: www.orianahouse.org
SIC: 8322 9111 Alcoholism counseling, nontreatment; rehabilitation services; county supervisors' & executives' offices

(G-367)
ORIANA HOUSE INC
Also Called: A D M Crisis Center
15 Frederick Ave (44310-2904)
PHONE.................................(330) 996-7730
Tammy Johnson, *Manager*
EMP: 60
SALES (corp-wide): 51.1MM **Privately Held**
WEB: www.orianahouse.org
SIC: 8322 8069 Emergency social services; drug addiction rehabilitation hospital
PA: Oriana House, Inc.
885 E Buchtel Ave
Akron OH 44305
330 535-8116

(G-368)
ORIANA HOUSE INC
Also Called: Summit County Jail
205 E Crosier St (44311-2351)
PHONE.................................(330) 643-2171
Steven Finical, *Branch Mgr*
EMP: 200
SALES (corp-wide): 51.1MM **Privately Held**
WEB: www.orianahouse.org
SIC: 8322 Substance abuse counseling
PA: Oriana House, Inc.
885 E Buchtel Ave
Akron OH 44305
330 535-8116

(G-369)
ORIN GROUP LLC
537 N Clvland Mssillon Rd (44333-2457)
PHONE.................................(330) 630-3937
John Krusinski,
EMP: 35
SQ FT: 7,888
SALES (est): 2MM **Privately Held**
WEB: www.oringroup.com
SIC: 8748 Environmental consultant

(G-370)
PARKLANE MANOR OF AKRON INC
Also Called: Rti
744 Colette Dr (44306-2208)
PHONE..................330 724-3315
Robert Abassi, *President*
EMP: 50
SALES: 1.8MM **Privately Held**
SIC: 6513 Apartment building operators

(G-371)
PASTORAL COUNSELING SVC SUMMIT
Also Called: P C S
611 W Market St (44303-1406)
PHONE..................330 996-4600
Byron Arledge, *CEO*
EMP: 140
SALES: 8.3MM **Privately Held**
SIC: 8322 8049 General counseling services; psychiatric social worker

(G-372)
PEBBLE CREEK CNVLSCNT CTR
Also Called: Communicare
670 Jarvis Rd (44319-2538)
PHONE..................330 645-0200
Jim Egli, *Administration*
EMP: 220
SQ FT: 60,000
SALES (est): 2.4MM
SALES (corp-wide): 10.3MM **Privately Held**
SIC: 8051 Extended care facility
PA: Nightingale Holdings, Llc
  670 Jarvis Rd
  Akron OH 44319
  330 645-0200

(G-373)
PEDIATRICS OF AKRON INC
300 Locust St Ste 200 (44302-1889)
PHONE..................330 253-7753
Rajneefh Jain, *President*
Dr Robert Sobieski, *Vice Pres*
Dr William Ginther, *Treasurer*
Jennifer Czarnecki, *Manager*
EMP: 25
SALES (est): 4.8MM **Privately Held**
SIC: 8011 Pediatrician

(G-374)
PENN MUTUAL LIFE INSURANCE CO
130 Springside Dr Ste 100 (44333-4543)
PHONE..................330 668-9065
Charles R Parks, *Manager*
Barbara Marvin, *Director*
EMP: 50
SALES (corp-wide): 2.8B **Privately Held**
WEB: www.thepfggroup.com
SIC: 6311 Life insurance
PA: The Penn Mutual Life Insurance Co
  600 Dresher Rd
  Horsham PA 19044
  215 956-8000

(G-375)
PENNSYLVANIA ELECTRIC COMPANY (HQ)
76 S Main St Bsmt (44308-1817)
PHONE..................800 545-7741
Charles E Jones, *President*
Leila L Vespoli, *Exec VP*
Harvey L Wagner, *Vice Pres*
Mark T Clark, *CFO*
James F Pearson, *Treasurer*
EMP: 80
SALES: 893.8MM **Publicly Held**
SIC: 4911 Electric services

(G-376)
PENNSYLVANIA POWER COMPANY (DH)
Also Called: PENN POWER
76 S Main St Bsmt (44308-1817)
PHONE..................800 720-3600
Anthony J Alexander, *President*
T M Welsh, *Senior VP*
Robert Wuschinske, *Vice Pres*
Harvey Wagner, *Finance Other*
Leila Vespoli, *General Counsel*

EMP: 140 **EST:** 1930
SQ FT: 40,000
SALES: 243.8MM **Publicly Held**
SIC: 4911 Distribution, electric power; generation, electric power; transmission, electric power
HQ: Ohio Edison Company
  76 S Main St Bsmt
  Akron OH 44308
  800 736-3402

(G-377)
PENSKE TRUCK LEASING CO LP
3000 Fortuna Dr (44312-5252)
PHONE..................330 645-3100
John Kushan, *Manager*
EMP: 25
SQ FT: 9,520
SALES (corp-wide): 2.6B **Privately Held**
WEB: www.pensketruckleasing.com
SIC: 7513 Truck leasing, without drivers; truck rental, without drivers
PA: Penske Truck Leasing Co., L.P.
  2675 Morgantown Rd
  Reading PA 19607
  610 775-6000

(G-378)
PERKINELMER HLTH SCIENCES INC
520 S Main St Ste 2423 (44311-1086)
PHONE..................330 825-4525
Susan Monaco, *Human Res Mgr*
Chritine Gradisher, *Manager*
Jim Bailey, *Manager*
Aniket Parekh, *Software Engr*
Mallory Petrolla, *Software Dev*
EMP: 32
SALES (corp-wide): 2.7B **Publicly Held**
SIC: 2835 2836 5049 In vitro & in vivo diagnostic substances; biological products, except diagnostic; laboratory equipment, except medical or dental
HQ: Perkinelmer Health Sciences, Inc.
  940 Winter St
  Waltham MA 02451
  781 663-6900

(G-379)
PERRIN ASPHALT CO INC
525 Dan St (44310-3987)
PHONE..................330 253-1020
Charles W Perrin, *President*
Pamela J Perrin, *Corp Secy*
Keith D Perrin, *Vice Pres*
Kimberly A Perrin, *Vice Pres*
Michael A Perrin, *Vice Pres*
EMP: 100
SALES: 25MM **Privately Held**
WEB: www.perrinasphalt.com
SIC: 1771 Blacktop (asphalt) work

(G-380)
PETER M KOSTOFF
222 S Main St Fl 4 (44308-1533)
PHONE..................330 849-6681
Peter M Kostoff, *Principal*
EMP: 65
SALES (est): 3.1MM **Privately Held**
SIC: 8111 General practice attorney, lawyer

(G-381)
PETERS TSCHANTZ & ASSOC INC
275 Springside Dr Ste 300 (44333-4550)
PHONE..................330 666-3702
James Peters, *President*
Dave Tzchantz, *Corp Secy*
Tom Bandwin, *Vice Pres*
EMP: 25 **EST:** 1954
SQ FT: 120,000
SALES (est): 3.4MM **Privately Held**
WEB: www.ptbengineering.com
SIC: 8711 Electrical or electronic engineering

(G-382)
PHYSICIANS WEIGHT LS CTR AMER (PA)
395 Springside Dr (44333-2434)
PHONE..................330 666-7952
Charles E Sekeres, *President*
EMP: 25 **EST:** 1979

SQ FT: 45,000
SALES (est): 124MM **Privately Held**
SIC: 5141 5122 6794 Groceries, general line; vitamins & minerals; franchises, selling or licensing

(G-383)
PINNACLE RECYCLING LLC
2330 Romig Rd (44320-3825)
P.O. Box 3857 (44314-0857)
PHONE..................330 745-3700
Kelly Brock, *Office Mgr*
Gary M Dalessandro, ...
EMP: 33 **EST:** 2010
SALES (est): 7.2MM **Privately Held**
SIC: 4953 Refuse System

(G-384)
PLANNED PRENTHOOD GREATER OHIO
Also Called: Akron Health Center
444 W Exchange St (44302-1711)
PHONE..................330 535-2671
Stephanie Kight, *CEO*
EMP: 48
SALES (corp-wide): 20.7MM **Privately Held**
SIC: 8093 Family planning clinic
PA: Planned Parenthood Of Greater Ohio
  206 E State St
  Columbus OH 43215
  614 224-2235

(G-385)
PLATINUM TECHNOLOGIES
121 S Main St Ste 200 (44308-1426)
PHONE..................216 926-1080
Jody Anderson, *Principal*
EMP: 38
SALES (est): 2.5MM **Privately Held**
SIC: 7379

(G-386)
PLUS ONE COMMUNICATIONS LLC
1115 S Main St (44301-1205)
PHONE..................330 255-4500
Robert Madden, *CEO*
Bobby Cart, *President*
Jill Madden, *Vice Pres*
EMP: 500 **EST:** 2008
SQ FT: 50,000
SALES (est): 20MM **Privately Held**
SIC: 7379 Computer related maintenance services

(G-387)
PNC BANK NATIONAL ASSOCIATION
Also Called: National City Bank
1 Cascade Plz Ste 200 (44308-1198)
PHONE..................330 375-8342
Elena K'Meyer, *Vice Pres*
Susan Brenner, *Branch Mgr*
EMP: 125
SALES (corp-wide): 19.9B **Publicly Held**
WEB: www.allegiantbank.com
SIC: 6021 National commercial banks
HQ: Pnc Bank, National Association
  222 Delaware Ave
  Wilmington DE 19801
  877 762-2000

(G-388)
POLISH AMERICAN CITIZENS CLUB
Also Called: Polish-American Club
472 E Glenwood Ave (44310-3421)
P.O. Box 414, Tallmadge (44278-0414)
PHONE..................330 253-0496
Tom Buehl, *President*
Stan Oziomek, *Admin Sec*
EMP: 50
SQ FT: 9,665
SALES (est): 1MM **Privately Held**
SIC: 8641 Fraternal associations

(G-389)
PORTAGE COUNTRY CLUB COMPANY
240 N Portage Path (44303-1299)
PHONE..................330 836-8565
Robert J Le Fever, *General Mgr*
Jim Albanese, *Facilities Mgr*
Gregory Relyea, *Controller*

Stephen Goczo, *Director*
EMP: 80
SQ FT: 52,275
SALES: 4MM **Privately Held**
WEB: www.portagecc.com
SIC: 7997 Country club, membership

(G-390)
PORTAGE PATH BEHAVORIAL HEALTH (PA)
340 S Broadway St (44308-1529)
PHONE..................330 253-3100
Jerome Kraker, *President*
Tim Morgan, *President*
Phil Heislman, *Vice Pres*
Jeffrey Moore, *Vice Pres*
Ravinder Brar, *Controller*
EMP: 68
SQ FT: 12,000
SALES: 11.7MM **Privately Held**
WEB: www.portagepath.org
SIC: 8093 Mental health clinic, outpatient

(G-391)
PORTAGE PATH BEHAVORIAL HEALTH
Also Called: Emergency Psychiatric Svc
10 Penfield Ave (44310-2912)
PHONE..................330 762-6110
Candy Pallante, *Financial Exec*
Antonio Montinola, *Manager*
Tracy M Dawyduk, *Manager*
EMP: 60
SALES (corp-wide): 11.7MM **Privately Held**
WEB: www.portagepath.org
SIC: 8093 4119 Mental health clinic, outpatient; ambulance service
PA: Portage Path Behavorial Health
  340 S Broadway St
  Akron OH 44308
  330 253-3100

(G-392)
POWER ENGINEERS INCORPORATED
Also Called: P E I
1 S Main St Ste 501 (44308-1867)
PHONE..................234 678-9875
EMP: 49
SALES (corp-wide): 460.2MM **Privately Held**
SIC: 8711 Consulting engineer
PA: Power Engineers, Incorporated
  3940 Glenbrook Dr
  Hailey ID 83333
  208 788-3456

(G-393)
PRAXAIR DISTRIBUTION INC
1760 E Market St (44305-4245)
PHONE..................330 376-2242
Brian McCormick, *Branch Mgr*
EMP: 30 **Privately Held**
SIC: 5084 Welding machinery & equipment
HQ: Praxair Distribution, Inc.
  10 Riverview Dr
  Danbury CT 06810
  203 837-2000

(G-394)
QT EQUIPMENT COMPANY (PA)
151 W Dartmore Ave (44301-2462)
PHONE..................330 724-3055
Daniel Root, *President*
Dave Root, *Treasurer*
Mitch Langford, *Manager*
▼ **EMP:** 35
SQ FT: 20,000
SALES (est): 6.3MM **Privately Held**
SIC: 7532 5531 3713 Body shop, trucks; automotive tires; utility truck bodies

(G-395)
R & R TRUCK SALES INC
1650 E Waterloo Rd (44306-4103)
P.O. Box 7309 (44306-0309)
PHONE..................330 784-5881
George Ralich, *President*
Steven Ralich, *Corp Secy*
Daniel Ralich, *Vice Pres*
Larry Chapman, *Parts Mgr*
Steve Ralich, *Treasurer*
EMP: 30
SQ FT: 30,000

▲ = Import ▼=Export
◆ =Import/Export

SALES (est): 14.5MM **Privately Held**
WEB: www.rrtrucksales.com
SIC: **5511** 5012 Ret New/Used Automobiles Whol Autos/Motor Vehicles

(G-396)
R B STOUT INC
1285 N Clvland Mssllon Rd (44333-1805)
PHONE..................................330 666-8811
Rodney B Stout, *CEO*
Jerry Kusar, *President*
Allen D Keefer, *Vice Pres*
Paul Revoldt, *Sales Staff*
EMP: 50
SQ FT: 3,500
SALES (est): 5.9MM **Privately Held**
SIC: **0782** 5261 Landscape contractors; lawn & garden supplies

(G-397)
RAY BERTOLINI TRUCKING CO
2070 Wright Rd (44320-2440)
P.O. Box 8155 (44320-0155)
PHONE..................................330 867-0666
Joseph F Bertolini, *President*
EMP: 26
SQ FT: 14,000
SALES (est): 3.8MM **Privately Held**
SIC: **4212** 4213 1611 1794 Dump truck haulage; trucking, except local; general contractor, highway & street construction; excavation work; wrecking & demolition work; demolition, buildings & other structures

(G-398)
REGAL CINEMAS INC
Also Called: Montrose Cinema 12
4020 Medina Rd Ste 100 (44333-4524)
PHONE..................................330 666-9373
Mandy Hught, *Manager*
EMP: 30 **Privately Held**
WEB: www.regalcinemas.com
SIC: **7832** Motion picture theaters, except drive-in
HQ: Regal Cinemas, Inc.
101 E Blount Ave Ste 100
Knoxville TN 37920
865 922-1123

(G-399)
REGAL CINEMAS INC
Also Called: Independence 10
1210 Independence Ave (44310-1812)
PHONE..................................330 633-7668
Mark Schneider, *Branch Mgr*
EMP: 35 **Privately Held**
WEB: www.regalcinemas.com
SIC: **7832** Motion picture theaters, except drive-in
HQ: Regal Cinemas, Inc.
101 E Blount Ave Ste 100
Knoxville TN 37920
865 922-1123

(G-400)
REGENCY SEATING INC
Also Called: Regency Office Furniture
2375 Romig Rd (44320-3824)
PHONE..................................330 848-3700
John Summerville, *CEO*
Aaron Summerville, *CFO*
▲ EMP: 35
SQ FT: 100,000
SALES (est): 10.1MM **Privately Held**
WEB: www.regencyseating.com
SIC: **5021** Office furniture

(G-401)
RELIABLE APPL INSTALLATION INC
2850 Gilchrist Rd Ste 1b (44305-4431)
PHONE..................................330 784-7474
EMP: 38
SALES (corp-wide): 10.7MM **Privately Held**
SIC: **4212** Local trucking, without storage
PA: Reliable Appliance Installation, Inc.
604 Office Pkwy
Westerville OH 43082
614 794-3307

(G-402)
RENNER KENNER GRIEVE BOBAK (PA)
106 S Main St (44308-1417)
PHONE..................................330 376-1242
Edward Grieve, *Partner*
Donald J Bobak, *Partner*
Tama Drenski, *Partner*
Phillip Kenner, *Partner*
Reese Taylor, *Partner*
EMP: 37
SQ FT: 4,500
SALES: 7.2MM **Privately Held**
SIC: **8111** General practice attorney, lawyer

(G-403)
REPRODUCTIVE GYNECOLOGY INC
95 Arch St Ste 250 (44304-1496)
PHONE..................................330 375-7722
Richard Moretuzzo, *President*
Brad Hambert, *Branch Mgr*
EMP: 25
SALES (est): 4.3MM **Privately Held**
WEB: www.reproductivegynecologyinc.com
SIC: **8011** Gynecologist

(G-404)
REPUBLIC SERVICES INC
964 Hazel St (44305-1610)
PHONE..................................330 434-9183
Patti Reder, *Facilities Mgr*
Al Marino, *Manager*
EMP: 34
SALES (corp-wide): 10B **Publicly Held**
WEB: www.republicservices.com
SIC: **4953** Garbage: collecting, destroying & processing; non-hazardous waste disposal sites; recycling, waste materials; sanitary landfill operation
PA: Republic Services, Inc.
18500 N Allied Way # 100
Phoenix AZ 85054
480 627-2700

(G-405)
RESERVE
3636 Yellow Creek Rd (44333-2269)
PHONE..................................330 666-1166
Ross Marchetta, *Owner*
EMP: 30
SALES (est): 889.5K **Privately Held**
WEB: www.reserveinc.org
SIC: **8011** Gynecologist

(G-406)
RGIS LLC
767 E Turkey Foot Lake Rd (44319)
PHONE..................................330 896-9802
Frank Altir, *Branch Mgr*
EMP: 90
SALES (corp-wide): 6.8B **Publicly Held**
WEB: www.rgisinv.com
SIC: **7389** Inventory computing service
HQ: Rgis, Llc
2000 Taylor Rd
Auburn Hills MI 48326
248 651-2511

(G-407)
RICHARDS WHL FENCE CO INC
Also Called: Richard's Fence Company
1600 Firestone Pkwy (44301-1659)
PHONE..................................330 773-0423
Richard Peterson, *President*
Bill Peterson, *Vice Pres*
▲ EMP: 30
SQ FT: 235,000
SALES: 11.1MM **Privately Held**
SIC: **3315** 5039 Chain link fencing; wire fence, gates & accessories

(G-408)
RICOH USA INC
Also Called: Nightrider Overnite Copy Svc
80 W Center St (44308-1037)
PHONE..................................330 384-9111
Mike Perkins, *Manager*
EMP: 25
SALES (corp-wide): 19.3B **Privately Held**
WEB: www.ikon.com
SIC: **5044** Office equipment

HQ: Ricoh Usa, Inc.
70 Valley Stream Pkwy
Malvern PA 19355
610 296-8000

(G-409)
RODERICK LINTON BELFANCE LLP
50 S Main St Fl 10 (44308-1849)
PHONE..................................330 434-3000
Katherine Belfance, *Partner*
EMP: 43
SALES (est): 1.7MM **Privately Held**
SIC: **8111** General practice law office

(G-410)
ROETZEL AND ANDRESS A LEGAL P (PA)
222 S Main St Ste 400 (44308-1500)
PHONE..................................330 376-2700
Robert E Blackham, *CEO*
Anita Gill, *Manager*
Paul L Jackson, *President*
John Coyne, *Vice Pres*
Chondra Dangerfield, *Vice Pres*
EMP: 130 EST: 1872
SQ FT: 115,000
SALES (est): 53.4MM **Privately Held**
WEB: www.ralaw.com
SIC: **8111** General practice law office

(G-411)
RUBBER CITY MACHINERY CORP
Also Called: R C M
1 Thousand Sweitzer Ave (44311)
P.O. Box 2043 (44309-2043)
PHONE..................................330 434-3500
George B Sobieraj, *President*
Daniel Abraham, *General Mgr*
Bernie Sobieraj, *Vice Pres*
Robert J Westfall, *Vice Pres*
Doug Fulwell, *Engineer*
▲ EMP: 32
SQ FT: 100,000
SALES (est): 7.7MM **Privately Held**
SIC: **3559** 5084 7629 Rubber working machinery, including tires; plastics working machinery; industrial machinery & equipment; electrical repair shops

(G-412)
RUBBER CITY RADIO GROUP (PA)
Also Called: Wqmx 94.9 FM
1795 W Market St (44313-7001)
PHONE..................................330 869-9800
Thomas Mandel, *President*
Henry Zelman, *Vice Pres*
Nancy Bittner, *Accounts Exec*
Daniel Dipasquale, *Accounts Exec*
Chloe Jefferson, *Accounts Exec*
EMP: 80
SALES (est): 5.8MM **Privately Held**
SIC: **4832** Rock

(G-413)
RUBBER CITY REALTY INC
942 Kenmore Blvd (44314-2148)
PHONE..................................330 745-9034
George W Turchin, *President*
Helen Turchin, *Vice Pres*
EMP: 70
SQ FT: 2,500
SALES (est): 3.3MM **Privately Held**
SIC: **6531** 1521 1522 Real estate brokers & agents; general remodeling, single-family houses; remodeling, multi-family dwellings

(G-414)
S & K ASPHALT & CONCRETE
2275 Manchester Rd (44314-3745)
PHONE..................................330 848-6284
Nick Skeriotis, *CEO*
EMP: 25 EST: 2008
SALES (est): 2.7MM **Privately Held**
SIC: **1771** 1611 Blacktop (asphalt) work; surfacing & paving

(G-415)
SACS CNSLTING TRAINING CTR INC
Also Called: Sacs Cnsltng Invstigative Svc
520 S Main St Ste 2516 (44311-1073)
PHONE..................................330 255-1101
Timothy Dimoff, *President*
Anthony Wellendorf, *COO*
Michelle Dimoff, *CFO*
Lori Ann Crowe, *Software Dev*
EMP: 25
SALES: 287.1K **Privately Held**
WEB: www.sacsconsulting.com
SIC: **8742** Management consulting services

(G-416)
SADGURU KRUPA LLC
897 Arlington Rdg E (44312-5276)
PHONE..................................330 644-2111
Naresh Patel,
EMP: 35 EST: 2008
SALES (est): 541.5K **Privately Held**
SIC: **7011** Hotels & motels

(G-417)
SALOMA INTL CO SINCE 1978
Also Called: Salomanetics
430 Grant St (44311-1190)
P.O. Box 24370, Fort Lauderdale FL (33307-4370)
PHONE..................................440 941-1527
Henry Drake Stull, *Owner*
EMP: 27
SALES (est): 747.7K **Privately Held**
SIC: **8748** Business consulting

(G-418)
SALVATION ARMY
1006 Grant St (44311-2442)
P.O. Box 1743 (44309-1743)
PHONE..................................330 773-3331
Gregory Cole, *Branch Mgr*
EMP: 102
SALES (corp-wide): 4.3B **Privately Held**
WEB: www.salvationarmy-usaeast.org
SIC: **8069** 5932 8741 Specialty hospitals, except psychiatric; used merchandise stores; administrative management
HQ: The Salvation Army
440 W Nyack Rd Ofc
West Nyack NY 10994
845 620-7200

(G-419)
SBM BUSINESS SERVICES INC (DH)
Also Called: GMAC Insurance
333 S Main St Ste 200 (44308-1205)
PHONE..................................330 396-7000
Steven B Shechter, *President*
Ron Buzek, *Vice Pres*
Scott Gill, *Vice Pres*
Edward Morrison, *Vice Pres*
Donna Syroid, *Vice Pres*
EMP: 26
SQ FT: 9,000
SALES (est): 5.2MM **Privately Held**
SIC: **6411** Insurance agents, brokers & service
HQ: Dawson Insurance, Inc.
3900 Kinross Lakes Pkwy
Richfield OH 44286
440 333-9000

(G-420)
SCHOMER GLAUS PYLE (PA)
Also Called: Gpd Group
520 S Main St Ste 2531 (44311-1073)
PHONE..................................330 572-2100
Darrin Kotecki, *President*
Jim Riche, *President*
Brent Hughes, *Chief*
Fred Trautman, *COO*
Jeff Evans, *Senior VP*
EMP: 270
SQ FT: 20,000
SALES (est): 93.9MM **Privately Held**
WEB: www.gpdgroup.com
SIC: **8711** 8712 Consulting engineer; architectural services

(G-421)
SEGMINT INC
365 Water St (44308-1044)
PHONE................................330 594-5379
Russel Heiser, *CEO*
EMP: 33
SQ FT: 5,800
SALES (est): 4.7MM **Privately Held**
SIC: 7313 Electronic media advertising
representatives

(G-422)
**SELECT MEDICAL
CORPORATION**
Select Specialty Hosp Akron
200 E Market St (44308-2015)
PHONE................................330 761-7500
Doug McGee, *COO*
Kathy Calhoun, *Vice Pres*
Donna Moore, *QA Dir*
Karl Schwartz, *Director*
EMP: 88
SALES (corp-wide): 3.7B **Publicly Held**
WEB: www.selectmedicalcorp.com
SIC: 8062 General medical & surgical hos-
pitals
HQ: Select Medical Corporation
4714 Gettysburg Rd
Mechanicsburg PA 17055
717 972-1100

(G-423)
**SELECT SPCLTY HSPTAL-
AKRON LLC**
200 E Market St (44308-2015)
P.O. Box 2090 (44309-2090)
PHONE................................330 761-7500
Jeffrey Houck, *Principal*
Kathy Beltz, *Med Doctor*
Brad Martin, *Med Doctor*
Debra Adams, *Director*
Merv Tierney, *Director*
EMP: 100 EST: 2000
SALES (est): 4.3MM
SALES (corp-wide): 3.7B **Publicly Held**
SIC: 8069 8361 8051 Alcoholism rehabili-
tation hospital; residential care; skilled
nursing care facilities
HQ: Sempercare, Inc
4716 Old Gettysburg Rd
Mechanicsburg PA 17055
717 972-1100

(G-424)
**SERVICE CORPS RETIRED
EXECS**
Also Called: S C O R E 81
1 Cascade Plz Fl 18 (44308-1166)
PHONE................................330 379-3163
Ron Stallings, *Chairman*
EMP: 42
SALES (corp-wide): 13.1MM **Privately
Held**
WEB: www.score199.mv.com
SIC: 8748 Business consulting
PA: Service Corps Of Retired Executives
Association
1175 Herndon Pkwy Ste 900
Herndon VA 20170
703 487-3612

(G-425)
SERVICE EXPERTS LLC
847 Home Ave (44310-4114)
PHONE................................330 577-3918
EMP: 27
SALES (corp-wide): 985.7MM **Privately
Held**
SIC: 1711 Warm air heating & air condi-
tioning contractor
HQ: Service Experts Llc
3820 American Dr Ste 200
Plano TX 75075

(G-426)
SH-91 LIMITED PARTNERSHIP
Also Called: Spring Hill Apartments
1221 Everton Dr (44307-1468)
PHONE................................330 535-1581
Gerald A Krueger, *Partner*
Janice Rubrich, *Principal*
EMP: 26
SALES (est): 1MM **Privately Held**
SIC: 6513 Apartment building operators

(G-427)
**SHAW JEWISH COMMUNITY
CENTER**
750 White Pond Dr (44320-1128)
PHONE................................330 867-7850
Michael Wise, *CEO*
Irving Sugerman, *President*
EMP: 105 EST: 1924
SQ FT: 100,000
SALES: 5MM **Privately Held**
SIC: 8322 Community center

(G-428)
SIGNET MANAGEMENT CO LTD
19 N High St (44308-1912)
PHONE................................330 762-9102
Anthony S Manna, *Chairman*
Martin Berry,
Patrick James,
EMP: 200
SALES (est): 21.2MM **Privately Held**
WEB: www.signet-enterprises.com
SIC: 8742 Management consulting serv-
ices

(G-429)
**SILCO FIRE PROTECTION
COMPANY**
451 Kennedy Rd (44305-4423)
PHONE................................330 535-4343
James Fraser, *President*
Marc Ollier, *Vice Pres*
EMP: 31
SQ FT: 7,500
SALES (est): 2.1MM **Privately Held**
SIC: 7389 Fire extinguisher servicing

(G-430)
**SIRPILLA RECRTL VHCL CTR
INC**
Also Called: Freedom Rv
1005 Interstate Pkwy (44312-5289)
PHONE................................330 494-2525
John A Sirpilla Jr, *President*
Todd Bleichrodt, *Site Mgr*
Karen Snyder, *Executive*
EMP: 74
SQ FT: 23,000
SALES (est): 17MM **Privately Held**
WEB: www.sirpillarv.com
SIC: 5561 7699 Travel trailers: automo-
bile, new & used; motor homes; campers
(pickup coaches) for mounting on trucks;
mobile home repair

(G-431)
SKYCASTERS LLC
1520 S Arlington St # 100 (44306-3863)
PHONE................................330 785-2100
Tina Carl, *Controller*
Danielle Rodriguez, *Supervisor*
Julie Long, *Web Dvlpr*
Sam Corbin, *Technical Staff*
Don Jacobs,
▼ EMP: 32
SQ FT: 1,608
SALES: 7.1MM **Privately Held**
WEB: www.satellite-asp.com
SIC: 4813

(G-432)
SMITHERS GROUP INC (PA)
121 S Main St Ste 300 (44308-1426)
PHONE................................330 762-7441
Volker Bornemann, *President*
Michael J Hochschwender, *President*
Prasad Raje, *President*
Gregory J Dziak, *Principal*
Steve Mihnovets, *Vice Pres*
EMP: 55
SALES (est): 63.6MM **Privately Held**
WEB: www.smithersgroup.com
SIC: 8742 Business consultant

(G-433)
**SMITHERS QUALITY
ASSESSMENTS**
Also Called: Sqa
121 S Main St Ste 300 (44308-1426)
PHONE................................330 762-4231
Jeanette Preston, *President*
Kimberle Rohrer, *Production*
Spencer Clark, *Manager*
Michelle Butcher, *Associate*
EMP: 25

SALES (est): 2.6MM
SALES (corp-wide): 63.6MM **Privately
Held**
WEB: www.smithersregistrar.com
SIC: 8742 8734 8748 Quality assurance
consultant; product testing laboratories;
testing services; test development & eval-
uation service
PA: The Smithers Group Inc
121 S Main St Ste 300
Akron OH 44308
330 762-7441

(G-434)
SMITHERS RAPRA INC (HQ)
425 W Market St (44303-2044)
PHONE................................330 762-7441
J Michael Hochschwender, *President*
Bruce D Lambillotte, *General Mgr*
Gregory J Dziak, *Principal*
Douglas Domeck, *Vice Pres*
Raymond Farmer, *Vice Pres*
EMP: 51
SQ FT: 20,000
SALES: 1MM
SALES (corp-wide): 63.6MM **Privately
Held**
WEB: www.smithersconsulting.com
SIC: 8734 8742 Product testing laborato-
ries; automobile proving & testing ground;
business consultant
PA: The Smithers Group Inc
121 S Main St Ste 300
Akron OH 44308
330 762-7441

(G-435)
**SMITHERS TIRE & AUTO
TESTNG TX**
Also Called: Smithers Trnsp Test Ctrs
425 W Market St (44303-2044)
PHONE................................330 762-7441
J Hoschschwender, *President*
EMP: 47
SALES (est): 133.5K
SALES (corp-wide): 63.6MM **Privately
Held**
WEB: www.smitherstiretest.com
SIC: 8734 Product testing laboratories; au-
tomobile proving & testing ground
HQ: Smithers Rapra Inc.
425 W Market St
Akron OH 44303
330 762-7441

(G-436)
SPANO BROTHERS CNSTR CO
2595 Pressler Rd (44312-5553)
PHONE................................330 645-1544
Vito Spano, *President*
EMP: 30
SQ FT: 20,000
SALES (est): 4.7MM **Privately Held**
SIC: 1794 1771 Excavation work; con-
crete work

(G-437)
**SPECTRUM MGT HOLDG CO
LLC**
530 Suth Main St Ste 1751 (44311)
PHONE................................330 208-9028
Steve Frey, *Branch Mgr*
EMP: 27
SALES (corp-wide): 43.6B **Publicly Held**
SIC: 4841 Cable television services
HQ: Spectrum Management Holding Com-
pany, Llc
400 Atlantic St
Stamford CT 06901
203 905-7801

(G-438)
ST GEORGE & CO INC
Also Called: St George Company
2586 Robindale Ave (44312-1653)
PHONE................................330 733-7528
EMP: 32
SALES (est): 1.8MM **Privately Held**
SIC: 8741 Management Services

(G-439)
**ST PAULS CATHOLIC CHURCH
(PA)**
433 Mission Dr (44301-2710)
PHONE................................330 724-1263

Ralph Thomas, *Pastor*
EMP: 50
SQ FT: 2,000
SALES: 450K **Privately Held**
SIC: 8661 8351 8211 Catholic Church;
preschool center; Catholic elementary
school

(G-440)
**STAN HYWET HALL AND GRDNS
INC**
714 N Portage Path (44303-1399)
PHONE................................330 836-5533
Harry Lynch, *CEO*
Dianne Ketler, *General Mgr*
William Binnie, *COO*
Joyce Johnson, *Accountant*
Melissa Agner, *Hum Res Coord*
EMP: 62 EST: 1955
SQ FT: 5,000
SALES: 3.9MM **Privately Held**
WEB: www.stanhywet.org
SIC: 8412 8422 Museum; arboreta &
botanical or zoological gardens

(G-441)
STARK KNOLL
3475 Richwood Rd (44333)
PHONE................................330 376-3300
Michael L Stark, *Principal*
EMP: 40
SALES (est): 3.4MM **Privately Held**
SIC: 8111 General practice law office

(G-442)
**STONEHEDGE ENTERPRISES
INC**
Also Called: Stonehedge Place
580 E Cuyahoga Falls Ave (44310-1540)
PHONE................................330 928-2161
Fred Borden, *President*
Frank Bevilacqua, *Sr Exec VP*
Ron Winer, *Vice Pres*
Shelly Siegenthaler, *Financial Exec*
EMP: 48
SQ FT: 50,000
SALES (est): 1.7MM **Privately Held**
SIC: 7933 5813 7948 7999 Ten pin cen-
ter; cocktail lounge; race track operation;
miniature golf course operation; snack
bar; coin-operated amusement devices

(G-443)
SUMMA HEALTH
1 Park West Blvd Ste 130 (44320-4230)
PHONE................................330 873-1518
Barb Pisaneli, *Branch Mgr*
Paula Russell, *Receptionist*
EMP: 747
SALES (corp-wide): 1B **Privately Held**
SIC: 8062 General medical & surgical hos-
pitals
PA: Summa Health
525 E Market St
Akron OH 44304
330 375-3000

(G-444)
SUMMA HEALTH
Also Called: Summa Rehabilitation Services
750 White Pond Dr Ste 500 (44320-1128)
PHONE................................330 836-9023
EMP: 830
SALES (corp-wide): 1B **Privately Held**
SIC: 8062 General medical & surgical hos-
pitals
PA: Summa Health
525 E Market St
Akron OH 44304
330 375-3000

(G-445)
SUMMA HEALTH
1077 Gorge Blvd (44310-2408)
PHONE................................330 252-0095
Elizabeth Bender, *Surgeon*
EMP: 332
SALES (corp-wide): 1B **Privately Held**
SIC: 8062 General medical & surgical hos-
pitals
PA: Summa Health
525 E Market St
Akron OH 44304
330 375-3000

(G-446)
SUMMA HEALTH
Also Called: Akron City Hospital
55 Arch St Ste 1b (44304-1436)
PHONE....................................330 375-3315
Steven Radwany, *Director*
EMP: 200
SALES (corp-wide): 1B **Privately Held**
WEB: www.summahealth.org
SIC: 8062 General medical & surgical hospitals
PA: Summa Health
525 E Market St
Akron OH 44304
330 375-3000

(G-447)
SUMMA HEALTH
Also Called: Summa Park West
1 Park West Blvd Ste 130 (44320-4230)
PHONE....................................330 864-8060
Deanna Frye, *Branch Mgr*
EMP: 415
SALES (corp-wide): 1B **Privately Held**
SIC: 8062 General medical & surgical hospitals
PA: Summa Health
525 E Market St
Akron OH 44304
330 375-3000

(G-448)
SUMMA HEALTH SYSTEM
Also Called: Summa Care
168 E Market St Ste 208 (44308-2014)
PHONE....................................330 535-7319
Charles Vignos, *Branch Mgr*
EMP: 52
SALES (corp-wide): 1B **Privately Held**
WEB: www.summahealth.org
SIC: 8062 General medical & surgical hospitals
PA: Summa Health
525 E Market St
Akron OH 44304
330 375-3000

(G-449)
SUMMA HEALTH SYSTEM
Also Called: Summa Akron City Hospital
525 E Market St (44304-1698)
PHONE....................................330 375-3000
Dale Murphy, *Vice Pres*
Nicholas Fulton, *Med Doctor*
Shayda Mirhaidari, *Med Doctor*
Dylan Childs, *Surgeon*
Stephanie Zaugg, *Internal Med*
EMP: 45
SALES (corp-wide): 1B **Privately Held**
SIC: 8062 General medical & surgical hospitals
PA: Summa Health
525 E Market St
Akron OH 44304
330 375-3000

(G-450)
SUMMA HEALTH SYSTEM
Also Called: Family Practice Center Akron
75 Arch St Ste 303 (44304-1432)
PHONE....................................330 375-3584
Dr Richard Hines, *Director*
John Feucht, *Director*
EMP: 70
SALES (corp-wide): 1B **Privately Held**
WEB: www.summahealth.org
SIC: 8062 8011 General medical & surgical hospitals; general & family practice, physician/surgeon
PA: Summa Health
525 E Market St
Akron OH 44304
330 375-3000

(G-451)
SUMMA HEALTH SYSTEM
Also Called: Internal Medical Center
75 Arch St Ste 302 (44304-1432)
PHONE....................................330 375-3315
Steven M Radwany, *Manager*
EMP: 130
SALES (corp-wide): 1B **Privately Held**
WEB: www.summahealth.org
SIC: 8062 8093 8011 General medical & surgical hospitals; specialty outpatient clinics; offices & clinics of medical doctors

PA: Summa Health
525 E Market St
Akron OH 44304
330 375-3000

(G-452)
SUMMA HEALTH SYSTEM
Also Called: Family Mdcine Ctr At St Thomas
444 N Main St (44310-3110)
PHONE....................................330 375-3000
Dr J Flanagan, *Director*
Diane Kramanak, *Director*
Victoria Sanelli, *Psychiatry*
William Pakan, *Surg-Orthopdc*
EMP: 25
SALES (corp-wide): 1B **Privately Held**
WEB: www.summahealth.org
SIC: 8062 8011 General medical & surgical hospitals; offices & clinics of medical doctors
PA: Summa Health
525 E Market St
Akron OH 44304
330 375-3000

(G-453)
SUMMA INSURANCE COMPANY INC (DH)
Also Called: Summacare
10 N Main St (44308-1958)
P.O. Box 3620 (44309-3620)
PHONE....................................800 996-8411
Claude Vincenti, *CEO*
Martin P Hauser, *President*
Annette M Ruby, *Vice Pres*
EMP: 290
SALES (est): 346.8MM
SALES (corp-wide): 1B **Privately Held**
SIC: 6321 6311 Health insurance carriers; life insurance

(G-454)
SUMMA REHAB HOSPITAL LLC
29 N Adams St (44304-1641)
PHONE....................................330 572-7300
Pam Mackintosh, *Director*
William A Powel III,
EMP: 25
SALES (est): 2.2MM **Privately Held**
SIC: 8049 Physiotherapist

(G-455)
SUMMACARE INC
10 N Main St Unit 1 (44308-1958)
PHONE....................................330 996-8410
Martin Hauser, *President*
Jim Mc Nutt, *Financial Exec*
EMP: 325
SALES (est): 6.5MM
SALES (corp-wide): 1B **Privately Held**
WEB: www.summacare.com
SIC: 8099 Medical services organization
HQ: Summa Insurance Company, Inc.
10 N Main St
Akron OH 44308
800 996-8411

(G-456)
SUMMIT CNTY DEPT JOB FMLY SVCS
1180 S Main St Ste 102 (44301-1253)
PHONE....................................330 643-8200
Michelle Moore, *Principal*
EMP: 99
SALES (est): 1.5MM **Privately Held**
SIC: 8322 Family counseling services

(G-457)
SUMMIT CNTY INTERNISTS & ASSOC (PA)
55 Arch St Ste 1a (44304-1424)
PHONE....................................330 375-3690
Dale P Murphy MD, *Owner*
EMP: 37
SALES (est): 3.3MM **Privately Held**
SIC: 8011 Internal medicine, physician/surgeon

(G-458)
SUMMIT HAND CENTER INC
3975 Embassy Pkwy Ste 201
(44333-8393)
PHONE....................................330 668-4055
William McCue, *President*
John X Biondi MD, *Principal*

John W Dietrich MD, *Principal*
William Mc Cue MD, *Principal*
Nina M Njus MD, *Principal*
EMP: 30
SALES (est): 1.7MM **Privately Held**
SIC: 8011 Orthopedic physician

(G-459)
SUMMIT OPTHOMOLOGY OPTICAL
Also Called: West Market Optical Service
1 Park West Blvd Ste 150 (44320-4230)
PHONE....................................330 864-8060
Dr J Cannatti, *Partner*
EMP: 50
SALES (est): 846.4K **Privately Held**
SIC: 8011 5995 Ophthalmologist; optical goods stores

(G-460)
SUMMIT PSYCHOLOGICAL ASSOC INC (PA)
37 N Broadway St (44308-1910)
PHONE....................................330 535-8181
James Orlando, *President*
Rachel Wade, *CFO*
EMP: 46
SALES (est): 4.2MM **Privately Held**
WEB: www.summit-psychological.com
SIC: 8049 Clinical psychologist

(G-461)
SUPERR-SPDIE PORTABLE SVCS INC
1050 Killian Rd (44312-4744)
PHONE....................................330 733-9000
Jeffrey M Grubbs, *President*
Patrick Flynn, *Vice Pres*
Shelley Grubbs, *Treasurer*
Scott Savage, *Marketing Staff*
Brian Rayl, *Manager*
EMP: 32
SQ FT: 24,000
SALES: 6.5MM **Privately Held**
SIC: 7359 5099 Portable toilet rental; toilets, portable

(G-462)
SWS EQUIPMENT SERVICES INC
Also Called: S W S
712 Palisades Dr (44303-1708)
PHONE....................................330 806-2767
Loyd McCoy, *President*
◆ EMP: 30
SALES (est): 1.4MM **Privately Held**
SIC: 1799 Rigging & scaffolding

(G-463)
TARRY HOUSE INC
564 Diagonal Rd (44320-3010)
PHONE....................................330 253-6689
Natalie Grier, *Program Mgr*
Ron Rett, *Program Mgr*
Michael Bullock, *Director*
EMP: 25
SALES: 1MM **Privately Held**
SIC: 8322 Social service center

(G-464)
TASTY PURE FOOD COMPANY (PA)
1557 Industrial Pkwy (44310-2603)
PHONE....................................330 434-8141
Jim K Heilmeier, *President*
Bill Heilmeier, *CFO*
William Heilmeier, *CFO*
Andrew Heilmeier, *Sales Staff*
EMP: 34
SQ FT: 20,000
SALES (est): 28.9MM **Privately Held**
WEB: www.tastypure.com
SIC: 5147 5142 5141 Meats, fresh; packaged frozen goods; groceries, general line

(G-465)
TECH CENTER INC
265 S Main St Ste 200 (44308-1223)
P.O. Box 22489 (44302-0489)
PHONE....................................330 762-6212
Doug Eilertson, *President*
EMP: 25
SALES (est): 1.3MM **Privately Held**
WEB: www.techcenterinc.com
SIC: 7361 Employment Agency

(G-466)
TECH PRO INC
3030 Gilchrist Rd (44305-4420)
PHONE....................................330 923-3546
John Putman, *President*
Kay Putman, *Vice Pres*
▲ EMP: 28
SQ FT: 30,000
SALES (est): 2.6MM **Privately Held**
WEB: www.techpro-usa.com
SIC: 7699 3821 3829 3825 Laboratory instrument repair; laboratory apparatus & furniture; measuring & controlling devices; instruments to measure electricity; computer peripheral equipment

(G-467)
TENNIS UNLIMITED INC
Also Called: TOWPATH RACQUET CLUB
2108 Akron Peninsula Rd (44313-4804)
PHONE....................................330 928-8763
Dallas Aleman, *President*
Nancy Aleman, *Vice Pres*
Kristianne Bontempo, *Manager*
EMP: 30
SQ FT: 50,000
SALES: 1MM **Privately Held**
WEB: www.towpathtennis.com
SIC: 7997 5941 Tennis club, membership; tennis goods & equipment

(G-468)
THE BOYS AND GIRLS CLUB OF (PA)
889 Jonathan Ave (44306-3606)
PHONE....................................330 773-3375
Lashawrida Fellows, *Manager*
Teresa Le Grair, *Director*
John Morgan, *Director*
James Warner, *Director*
Michelle Alley, *Executive Asst*
EMP: 27
SALES: 1MM **Privately Held**
SIC: 8641 Youth organizations

(G-469)
THE FAMOUS MANUFACTURING CO
2620 Ridgewood Rd Ste 200 (44313-3507)
PHONE....................................330 762-9621
Jay Blaushild, *President*
EMP: 35 EST: 2001
SALES (est): 4.3MM **Privately Held**
SIC: 5075 5074 Furnaces, heating: electric; furnaces, warm air; air conditioning & ventilation equipment & supplies; plumbing & hydronic heating supplies
PA: Famous Enterprises, Inc.
2620 Ridgewood Rd Ste 200
Akron OH 44313

(G-470)
TIME WARNER CABLE INC
1919 Brittain Rd (44310-1843)
PHONE....................................330 800-3874
John Duran, *Director*
Stephen Fry, *Director*
EMP: 25
SALES (corp-wide): 43.6B **Publicly Held**
SIC: 4841 4813 Cable television services;
HQ: Spectrum Management Holding Company, Llc
400 Atlantic St
Stamford CT 06901
203 905-7801

(G-471)
TOLEDO EDISON COMPANY (HQ)
Also Called: Toledo Railways and Light Co
76 S Main St Bsmt (44308-1817)
PHONE....................................800 447-3333
Anthony J Alexander, *CEO*
C E Jones, *President*
Jasmine Witherspoon, *Principal*
L L Vespoli, *Exec VP*
Harvey L Wagner, *Vice Pres*
EMP: 94
SALES: 484.3MM **Publicly Held**
SIC: 4911 Distribution, electric power; transmission, electric power

(G-472)
TPUSA INC
Also Called: Teleperformance USA
150 E Market St (44308-2014)
PHONE..................................330 374-1232
EMP: 500
SALES (corp-wide): 123.7MM **Privately Held**
SIC: 7389 Telemarketing services
HQ: Tpusa, Inc.
5295 S Commerce Dr # 600
Murray UT 84107
801 257-5800

(G-473)
TRI-COUNTY PALLET RECYCL INC
Also Called: Tri-County Mulch
900 Flora Ave (44314-1722)
PHONE..................................330 848-0313
William C Bowling, *President*
EMP: 40
SALES (est): 6.3MM **Privately Held**
SIC: 5031 Lumber, plywood & millwork

(G-474)
TW TELECOM INC
Also Called: Time Warner Cable
1019 E Turkeyfoot Lake Rd (44312-5242)
PHONE..................................234 542-6279
EMP: 29
SALES (corp-wide): 1.4B **Publicly Held**
SIC: 4813 Telephone Communications
PA: Tw Telecom Inc.
10475 Park Meadows Dr
Littleton CO 80124
303 566-1000

(G-475)
UNIFIED CNSTR SYSTEMS LTD (PA)
1920 S Main St (44301-2851)
PHONE..................................330 773-2511
Bob Lucius, *Sales Staff*
Terry Arny, *Webmaster*
Jason Haws,
Scott Wyler,
EMP: 30
SQ FT: 6,000
SALES (est): 4.3MM **Privately Held**
WEB: www.foundsystems.com
SIC: 1742 1799 Insulation, buildings; waterproofing

(G-476)
UNITED DISABILITY SERVICES INC (PA)
701 S Main St (44311-1019)
PHONE..................................330 374-1169
Marianne Riggenbach, *Manager*
Jim Acton, *Supervisor*
Shawn Murtagh, *Supervisor*
Gary Knuth, *Exec Dir*
Howard Taylor, *Exec Dir*
EMP: 160
SQ FT: 78,000
SALES: 12.2MM **Privately Held**
SIC: 8331 8322 8093 Job training & vocational rehabilitation services; social services for the handicapped; rehabilitation center, outpatient treatment

(G-477)
UNITED WAY OF SUMMIT COUNTY
37 N High St Ste A (44308-1973)
PHONE..................................330 762-7601
Robert A Kulinski, *President*
Brett Kimmell, *CFO*
EMP: 29
SQ FT: 13,000
SALES: 13.3MM **Privately Held**
SIC: 8399 Fund raising organization, non-fee basis

(G-478)
UNIVERSAL NURSING SERVICES (PA)
483 Augusta Dr (44333-9214)
PHONE..................................330 434-7318
Gloria Rookard, *President*
Derrick Rookard, *Vice Pres*
David Rookard, *Treasurer*
EMP: 50

SQ FT: 4,800
SALES (est): 7.6MM **Privately Held**
SIC: 8082 Home health care services

(G-479)
UNIVERSITY OF AKRON
Also Called: College Polymr Science & Engrg
170 University Ave (44325-0044)
PHONE..................................330 972-6008
Steven Cheng, *Dean*
EMP: 60
SALES (corp-wide): 449.6MM **Privately Held**
WEB: www.uakron.edu
SIC: 8221 8711 University; engineering services
PA: The University Of Akron
302 Buchtel Mall
Akron OH 44325
330 972-7111

(G-480)
UNIVERSITY OF AKRON
Also Called: Center For Child Development
108 Fir HI (44325-0004)
PHONE..................................330 972-8210
Sophia Kraun, *Director*
EMP: 30
SALES (corp-wide): 449.6MM **Privately Held**
WEB: www.uakron.edu
SIC: 8351 8221 Child day care services; university
PA: The University Of Akron
302 Buchtel Mall
Akron OH 44325
330 972-7111

(G-481)
URS GROUP INC
564 White Pond Dr (44320-1100)
PHONE..................................330 836-9111
Mark Buchenic, *Vice Pres*
Michael Stepic, *Project Mgr*
Scott Buchanan, *Engineer*
Ryan Schuster, *Engineer*
Michael Burgess, *Director*
EMP: 90
SALES (corp-wide): 20.1B **Publicly Held**
SIC: 8712 8711 Architectural engineering; professional engineer
HQ: Urs Group, Inc.
300 S Grand Ave Ste 1100
Los Angeles CA 90071
213 593-8000

(G-482)
USIC LOCATING SERVICES LLC
441 Munroe Falls Rd (44312)
PHONE..................................330 733-9393
Shaun Corrin, *Manager*
EMP: 125 **Privately Held**
WEB: www.sm-p.com
SIC: 8713 Surveying services
HQ: Usic Locating Services, Llc
9045 River Rd Ste 300
Indianapolis IN 46240
317 575-7800

(G-483)
VALMARK FINANCIAL GROUP LLC
130 Springside Dr Ste 300 (44333-2489)
PHONE..................................330 576-1234
Lawrence J Rybka, *President*
Caleb Callahan, *COO*
Mark White, *Executive*
EMP: 60
SQ FT: 15,000
SALES (est): 8.5MM **Privately Held**
WEB: www.abellassociates.com
SIC: 6411 6211 Insurance agents, brokers & service; security brokers & dealers

(G-484)
VALMARK SECURITIES INC (HQ)
130 Springside Dr Ste 300 (44333-2489)
PHONE..................................330 576-1234
Lawrence J Rybka, *President*
David K Critzer, *CFO*
EMP: 28
SALES (est): 6.6MM
SALES (corp-wide): 4.2MM **Privately Held**
SIC: 6211 Security brokers & dealers

PA: Executive Insurance Agency, Inc
130 Springside Dr Ste 300
Akron OH 44333
330 576-1234

(G-485)
VAN DEVERE INC (PA)
Also Called: Van Devere Buick
300 W Market St (44303-2185)
PHONE..................................330 253-6137
Michael Van Devere, *President*
Shirley A Van Devere, *Corp Secy*
Brian Vandevere, *Finance Mgr*
Randy Browne, *Sales Mgr*
Mack Gilchrist, *Sales Mgr*
EMP: 77
SALES (est): 98.9MM **Privately Held**
WEB: www.vandevere.com
SIC: 5511 7515 Automobiles, new & used; passenger car leasing

(G-486)
VANTAGE AGING (PA)
2279 Romig Rd (44320-3823)
PHONE..................................330 253-4597
Karen Hrdlicka, *President*
Melinda Smith Yeargin, *Chairman*
Paul Magnus, *Vice Pres*
Amy Marsteller, *Admin Sec*
EMP: 67 EST: 1975
SQ FT: 17,000
SALES: 13.1MM **Privately Held**
SIC: 8322 Senior citizens' center or association

(G-487)
VANTAGE AGING
1155 E Tallmadge Ave (44310-3529)
PHONE..................................330 785-9770
Catherine Lewis, *President*
EMP: 620
SALES (corp-wide): 13.1MM **Privately Held**
SIC: 8999 Artists & artists' studios
PA: Vantage Aging
2279 Romig Rd
Akron OH 44320
330 253-4597

(G-488)
VIP HOMECARE INC
Also Called: VIP Home Care
545 E Cuyahoga Falls Ave (44310-1550)
PHONE..................................330 929-2838
Diane Johnson, *President*
EMP: 85 EST: 1995
SALES (est): 1.2MM **Privately Held**
SIC: 8082 Home health care services

(G-489)
VIRTUAL HOLD TECHNOLOGY LLC (PA)
3875 Embassy Pkwy Ste 350 (44333-8343)
PHONE..................................330 670-2200
Wes Hayden, *CEO*
Thomas Jameson, *Exec VP*
Ted Bray, *Vice Pres*
Kevin Shinseki, *Vice Pres*
Mark Williams, *Mng Member*
EMP: 80
SQ FT: 18,000
SALES (est): 19.1MM **Privately Held**
WEB: www.virtualhold.com
SIC: 7371 7372 Computer software development; prepackaged software

(G-490)
VISITING NURSE SERVICE INC (PA)
1 Home Care Pl (44320-3999)
PHONE..................................330 745-1601
Karen Talbott, *President*
Jerry Bauman, *Vice Pres*
Tom Lyzen, *Vice Pres*
Kelly Ward, *Corp Comm Staff*
Mike Hornfeck, *Info Tech Dir*
EMP: 325
SQ FT: 20,000
SALES: 21.8MM **Privately Held**
WEB: www.vnsa.com
SIC: 8082 Visiting nurse service

(G-491)
VULCAN MACHINERY CORPORATION
20 N Case Ave (44305-2598)
PHONE..................................330 376-6025
David Jacobs, *President*
Bradley J Jacobs, *Vice Pres*
Steph Wensel, *Purchasing*
EMP: 25
SALES (est): 3.9MM **Privately Held**
WEB: www.vulcanmachinery.com
SIC: 3559 7299 Plastics working machinery; banquet hall facilities

(G-492)
W G LOCKHART CONSTRUCTION CO
800 W Waterloo Rd (44314-1528)
PHONE..................................330 745-6520
Alexander R Lockhart, *President*
Richard Stanley, *Admin Sec*
EMP: 100 EST: 1918
SQ FT: 5,000
SALES (est): 8.1MM **Privately Held**
SIC: 1611 3273 Highway & street construction; ready-mixed concrete

(G-493)
WAIDS RAINBOW RENTAL INC
1050 Killian Rd (44312-4744)
PHONE..................................216 524-3736
Patricia Waid, *President*
Ron Waid, *Treasurer*
Bernadette Waid, *Shareholder*
Claire Waid, *Admin Sec*
EMP: 25
SQ FT: 3,400
SALES (est): 2.2MM **Privately Held**
SIC: 7359 Portable toilet rental

(G-494)
WALGREEN CO
Also Called: Walgreens
302 Canton Rd (44312-1544)
PHONE..................................330 733-4237
Jess Roeger, *Branch Mgr*
EMP: 30
SALES (corp-wide): 131.5B **Publicly Held**
WEB: www.walgreens.com
SIC: 5912 7384 Drug stores; photofinishing laboratory
HQ: Walgreen Co.
200 Wilmot Rd
Deerfield IL 60015
847 315-2500

(G-495)
WALNUT RIDGE MANAGEMENT
520 S Main St Ste 2457 (44311-1095)
PHONE..................................234 678-3900
Jeanette M Thomas, *Principal*
EMP: 70 EST: 2010
SALES (est): 6.7MM **Privately Held**
SIC: 8741 Business management

(G-496)
WEAVER INDUSTRIES INC
636 W Exchange St (44302-1306)
PHONE..................................330 379-3606
Jean Fish, *Manager*
EMP: 120
SALES (corp-wide): 6.9MM **Privately Held**
SIC: 7389 Packaging & labeling services
PA: Weaver Industries Inc.
520 S Main St Ste 2441
Akron OH 44311
330 379-3660

(G-497)
WEAVER INDUSTRIES INC (PA)
520 S Main St Ste 2441 (44311-1071)
PHONE..................................330 379-3660
Jeff Johnson, *Exec Dir*
EMP: 30
SQ FT: 20,000
SALES: 6.9MM **Privately Held**
WEB: www.weaverindustries.org
SIC: 7389 8331 Packaging & labeling services; job training & vocational rehabilitation services

(G-498)
WEAVER INDUSTRIES INC
340 N Clvland Mssillon Rd (44333-9302)
PHONE.....................330 666-5114
Claire Poirer-Keys, *Manager*
EMP: 175
SALES (corp-wide): 6.9MM **Privately Held**
SIC: 7389 8331 Packaging & labeling services; job training & vocational rehabilitation services
PA: Weaver Industries Inc.
520 S Main St Ste 2441
Akron OH 44311
330 379-3660

(G-499)
WEAVER INDUSTRIES INC
Also Called: Weaver Secure Shred
2337 Romig Rd Ste 2 (44320-3824)
PHONE.....................330 745-2400
Jack Skinner, *Branch Mgr*
EMP: 127
SALES (corp-wide): 6.9MM **Privately Held**
SIC: 7389 Document & office record destruction
PA: Weaver Industries Inc.
520 S Main St Ste 2441
Akron OH 44311
330 379-3660

(G-500)
WHITE POND GARDENS INC
Also Called: Graf Growers
1015 White Pond Dr (44320-1503)
PHONE.....................330 836-2727
Lisa Graf, *President*
Scott Graf, *Vice Pres*
Craig Graf, *Treasurer*
Scott Burdeshaw, *Manager*
EMP: 32
SQ FT: 5,000
SALES (est): 4.2MM **Privately Held**
WEB: www.grafgrowers.com
SIC: 0182 0181 5261 0161 Food crops grown under cover; flowers: grown under cover (e.g. greenhouse production); nurseries & garden centers; vegetables & melons

(G-501)
WHITESPACE DESIGN GROUP INC
Also Called: Whitespace Creative
243 Furnace St (44304-1284)
PHONE.....................330 762-9320
Keeven White, *President*
Gregory Kiskadden, *Vice Pres*
Samantha Warnock, *Admin Asst*
EMP: 30
SQ FT: 17,000
SALES (est): 8.7MM **Privately Held**
WEB: www.whitespace-creative.com
SIC: 8743 7336 7311 Public relations services; public relations & publicity; sales promotion; commercial art & graphic design; graphic arts & related design; advertising agencies; advertising consultant

(G-502)
WINDSONG HEALTHCARE GROUP LLC
Also Called: Windsong Care Center
120 Brookmont Rd (44333-3089)
PHONE.....................216 292-5706
Teresa Lane, *Administration*
EMP: 40
SALES (corp-wide): 1MM **Privately Held**
WEB: www.parkplace-spokane.com
SIC: 8051 Skilled nursing care facilities
PA: Windsong Healthcare Group, Llc
120 Brookmont Rd
Akron OH 44333
330 666-7373

(G-503)
WOLFF BROS SUPPLY INC
1200 Kelly Ave (44306-3735)
PHONE.....................330 786-4140
Bob Doherty, *Sales & Mktg St*
Denise Alt, *Consultant*
Diane Gilles, *Consultant*
EMP: 30

SALES (corp-wide): 114.4MM **Privately Held**
WEB: www.wolffbros.com
SIC: 5063 5074 5075 Electrical apparatus & equipment; plumbing & hydronic heating supplies; warm air heating & air conditioning
PA: Wolff Bros. Supply, Inc
6078 Wolff Rd
Medina OH 44256
330 725-3451

(G-504)
WQMX LOVE FUND
1795 W Market St (44313-7001)
PHONE.....................330 869-9800
Thomas Mandel, *President*
EMP: 75
SALES (est): 824.5K **Privately Held**
SIC: 4832 Radio broadcasting stations

(G-505)
WYANT LEASING CO LLC
Also Called: Wyant Woods Care Center
200 Wyant Rd (44313-4228)
PHONE.....................330 836-7953
Gail McFadden, *Social Dir*
Stephen Rosedale,
EMP: 270
SALES (est): 9MM **Privately Held**
SIC: 8051 Skilled nursing care facilities

(G-506)
WZ MANAGEMENT INC
3417 E Waterloo Rd (44312-4036)
P.O. Box 6258 (44312-0258)
PHONE.....................330 628-4881
Sidney Zetzer, *President*
John Miskar, *Parts Mgr*
Robert Zetzer, *Executive*
Shirley Zetzer, *Admin Sec*
◆ EMP: 32 EST: 1946
SALES (est): 9.8MM **Privately Held**
WEB: www.samwinermotors.com
SIC: 5013 5531 Truck parts & accessories; truck equipment & parts

(G-507)
YOUNG MENS CHRISTIAN ASSOC
Also Called: Phoenix School Program
888 Jonathan Ave (44306-3607)
PHONE.....................330 784-0408
Wendy Neloms, *Principal*
EMP: 25
SQ FT: 17,127
SALES (corp-wide): 16.8MM **Privately Held**
WEB: www.campynoah.com
SIC: 8641 7991 8351 7032 Youth organizations; physical fitness facilities; child day care services; youth camps; individual & family services
PA: The Young Men's Christian Association Of Akron Ohio
50 S Mn St Ste LI100
Akron OH 44308
330 376-1335

(G-508)
YOUNG MENS CHRISTIAN ASSOC
Also Called: YMCA
350 E Wilbeth Rd (44301-2624)
PHONE.....................330 724-1255
Melissa Roddy, *Executive*
EMP: 35
SALES (corp-wide): 16.8MM **Privately Held**
WEB: www.campynoah.com
SIC: 8641 8351 Youth organizations; child day care services
PA: The Young Men's Christian Association Of Akron Ohio
50 S Mn St Ste LI100
Akron OH 44308
330 376-1335

(G-509)
YOUNG MENS CHRISTIAN ASSOC
Also Called: Canal Square Branch
80 W Center St (44308-1037)
PHONE.....................330 376-1335
Douglas R Kohl, *President*

EMP: 550
SALES (corp-wide): 16.8MM **Privately Held**
WEB: www.campynoah.com
SIC: 8641 8351 Recreation association; child day care services
PA: The Young Men's Christian Association Of Akron Ohio
50 S Mn St Ste LI100
Akron OH 44308
330 376-1335

Albany
Athens County

(G-510)
FARM CREDIT MID-AMERICA
2368 Blizzard Ln (45710-9287)
PHONE.....................740 441-9312
Donna Crabtree, *Manager*
EMP: 39
SALES (corp-wide): 568.6MM **Privately Held**
SIC: 6029 6141 6162 Commercial banks; personal credit institutions; mortgage bankers & correspondents
PA: Farm Credit Mid-America
1601 Ups Dr
Louisville KY 40223
502 420-3700

(G-511)
OASIS THRPTIC FSTER CARE NTWRK
34265 State Route 681 S (45710-9083)
PHONE.....................740 698-0340
Kay Wheeler, *President*
Charles Wheeler, *President*
EMP: 25
SALES: 1.9MM **Privately Held**
SIC: 8361 Group foster home

Alliance
Stark County

(G-512)
A J OSTER FOILS LLC
2081 Mccrea St (44601-2793)
PHONE.....................330 823-1700
Kevin Bense, *President*
Brian Vonder Haar, *General Mgr*
Alexander B Jourdan, *General Mgr*
Robert M James, *Vice Pres*
Scott Riordan, *Plant Mgr*
▲ EMP: 53
SQ FT: 80,000
SALES (est): 14.9MM **Publicly Held**
SIC: 3341 3353 3471 3497 Secondary nonferrous metals; aluminum sheet, plate & foil; plating & polishing; metal foil & leaf; metals service centers & offices
HQ: A.J. Oster, Llc
301 Metro Center Blvd # 204
Warwick RI 02886
401 736-2600

(G-513)
AARONS INC
2102 W State St (44601-3527)
PHONE.....................330 823-1879
Anthony Hunter, *Manager*
EMP: 25
SALES (corp-wide): 3.8B **Publicly Held**
WEB: www.aaronrents.com
SIC: 7359 Home appliance, furniture & entertainment rental services
PA: Aaron's, Inc.
400 Galleria Pkwy Se # 300
Atlanta GA 30339
678 402-3000

(G-514)
ALLIANALCE HOSPITALIST GROUP
200 E State St (44601-4936)
PHONE.....................330 823-5626
Stan Jonas, *Principal*
EMP: 25
SALES: 63.6K **Privately Held**
SIC: 8062 General medical & surgical hospitals

(G-515)
ALLIANCE CITIZENS HEALTH ASSN
200 E State St (44601-4936)
PHONE.....................330 596-6000
Stan Jonas, *CEO*
Louise Roth, *Director*
EMP: 1200
SQ FT: 30,000
SALES: 109.9MM **Privately Held**
SIC: 8062 General medical & surgical hospitals

(G-516)
ALLIANCE HOT STOVE BASEBALL L
1127 Forest Ave (44601-3261)
P.O. Box 2681 (44601-0681)
PHONE.....................330 823-7034
Bill Fast, *President*
Jim Newman, *Vice Pres*
William Clark, *Treasurer*
Barry Benedict, *Admin Sec*
EMP: 25
SALES: 78.5K **Privately Held**
SIC: 7941 Baseball club, professional & semi-professional

(G-517)
ALLIANCE TOWERS LLC
350 S Arch Ave Apt 106 (44601-2677)
PHONE.....................330 823-1063
Leeann Morein, *Partner*
David Robertson, *Principal*
EMP: 3924
SALES (est): 33.1MM **Publicly Held**
WEB: www.aimco.com
SIC: 6513 Apartment building operators
HQ: Aimco Properties, L.P.
4582 S Ulster St Ste 1100
Denver CO 80237

(G-518)
BEL AIR CARE CENTER
2350 Cherry Ave (44601-5022)
PHONE.....................330 821-3939
David Childs, *Owner*
Arnold Yost, *Administration*
EMP: 90
SALES (est): 2.6MM **Privately Held**
SIC: 8052 8059 8051 Intermediate care facilities; convalescent home; skilled nursing care facilities

(G-519)
BROOKDALE SENIOR LIVING COMMUN
Also Called: Sterling House of Alliance
1277 S Sawburg Ave (44601-5755)
PHONE.....................330 829-0180
Andrea Williams, *Director*
EMP: 34
SALES (corp-wide): 4.5B **Publicly Held**
WEB: www.assisted.com
SIC: 8059 Rest home, with health care
HQ: Brookdale Senior Living Communities, Inc.
6737 W Wa St Ste 2300
Milwaukee WI 53214
414 918-5000

(G-520)
CANTERBURY VLLA OPRATIONS CORP
Also Called: Canterbury Villa Alliance Ctr
1785 N Freshley Ave (44601-8772)
PHONE.....................330 821-4000
Brian Colleran, *President*
EMP: 100
SALES: 7.1MM
SALES (corp-wide): 8MM **Privately Held**
SIC: 8051 Skilled nursing care facilities
PA: Ballantrae Healthcare, Llc
1128 Pennsylvania St Ne
Albuquerque NM 87110
505 366-5200

(G-521)
CARING HANDS INC
885 S Sawburg Ave Ste 107 (44601-5905)
PHONE.....................330 821-6310
Malenda Sever, *Director*
EMP: 150
SALES: 1.3MM **Privately Held**
SIC: 8082 Home health care services

(G-522)
**CARPENTER METAL
SOLUTIONS INC (PA)**
803 S Mahoning Ave (44601-3233)
PHONE.................................330 829-2771
Gregg Carpenter Sr, *President*
Gregg Carpenter Jr, *Exec VP*
Daniel Hammer, *CFO*
EMP: 30
SQ FT: 70,000
SALES: 16MM **Privately Held**
WEB: www.carpentermetal.com
SIC: 5093 Metal scrap & waste materials

(G-523)
CELLCO PARTNERSHIP
Also Called: Verizon
2700 W State St (44601-5611)
PHONE.................................330 823-7758
William Sanford, *Branch Mgr*
EMP: 71
SALES (corp-wide): 130.8B **Publicly
Held**
SIC: 4812 Cellular telephone services
HQ: Cellco Partnership
1 Verizon Way
Basking Ridge NJ 07920

(G-524)
CINTAS CORPORATION
12445 Rockhill Ave Ne (44601-1065)
PHONE.................................330 821-2220
Joe Caruthers, *General Mgr*
EMP: 100
SQ FT: 38,000
SALES (corp-wide): 6.4B **Publicly Held**
WEB: www.cintas-corp.com
SIC: 7218 Industrial launderers
PA: Cintas Corporation
6800 Cintas Blvd
Cincinnati OH 45262
513 459-1200

(G-525)
**CITY ALLIANCE WATER SEWER
DST**
1015 Walnut Ave (44601-1367)
PHONE.................................330 823-5216
Doug Hastings, *Superintendent*
EMP: 31
SQ FT: 4,048
SALES (est): 2MM **Privately Held**
SIC: 4941 Water supply

(G-526)
CLEM LUMBER AND DISTRG CO
16055 Waverly St Ne (44601-1441)
P.O. Box 2238 (44601-0238)
PHONE.................................330 821-2130
Don McAlister, *President*
James McAlister, *President*
Peter Fahey, *Division Mgr*
David McAlister, *Corp Secy*
Rich Wollaim, *Purch Agent*
▲ EMP: 65 EST: 1946
SQ FT: 60,000
SALES (est): 43.3MM **Privately Held**
SIC: 5031 Millwork; building materials, interior; building materials, exterior

(G-527)
**CONCORDE THERAPY GROUP
INC**
Also Called: Concord Therapy Group
2484 W State St (44601-5608)
PHONE.................................330 493-4210
Marcy Woost, *Manager*
EMP: 30 **Privately Held**
WEB: www.concordehealth.com
SIC: 8049 8011 Physical therapist; offices
& clinics of medical doctors
PA: Concorde Therapy Group Inc
4645 Belpar St Nw
Canton OH 44718

(G-528)
**COPE FARM EQUIPMENT INC
(PA)**
Also Called: John Deere Authorized Dealer
24915 State Route 62 (44601-9000)
PHONE.................................330 821-5867
Alan W Cope, *President*
Evan W Morris Jr, *Principal*
Carol A Ricci, *Admin Sec*
EMP: 26

SQ FT: 20,000
SALES (est): 4.2MM **Privately Held**
WEB: www.copefarm.com
SIC: 7699 5999 5082 Farm machinery repair; farm equipment & supplies; construction & mining machinery

(G-529)
D A PETERSON INC
Also Called: Wdpn
393 Smyth Ave (44601-1562)
P.O. Box 2356 (44601-0356)
PHONE.................................330 821-1111
Donald A Peterson Jr, *President*
Jill P Mc Carty, *Treasurer*
Josephine H Peterson, *Admin Sec*
EMP: 35
SQ FT: 3,500
SALES (est): 2.5MM **Privately Held**
WEB: www.dapeterson.com
SIC: 4832 Radio broadcasting stations,
music format

(G-530)
DINO PERSICHETTI
Also Called: Perkins Family Restaurant
20040 Hrrsburg Wstvlle Rd (44601)
PHONE.................................330 821-9600
Dino Persichetti, *President*
Richard Fielgar, *General Mgr*
Phillip Constantine, *Corp Secy*
Richard Felgar, *Manager*
EMP: 40
SQ FT: 2,788
SALES (est): 1.5MM **Privately Held**
SIC: 5812 7011 Restaurant, family: chain;
motor inn

(G-531)
FIDELITY PROPERTIES INC
220 E Main St (44601-2423)
P.O. Box 2055 (44601-0055)
PHONE.................................330 821-9700
Paul D Boggs, *President*
Gregory A Robb, *Treasurer*
James E Thorpe Jr, *Admin Sec*
EMP: 37
SQ FT: 10,000
SALES (est): 3.3MM **Privately Held**
SIC: 7322 Collection agency, except real
estate

(G-532)
FILNOR INC (PA)
227 N Freedom Ave (44601-1897)
P.O. Box 2328 (44601-0328)
PHONE.................................330 821-8731
Ronald L Neely, *CEO*
James C Neely, *President*
Craig Clarke, *Vice Pres*
Daren Szekely, *Vice Pres*
Mike Higgins, *Production*
◆ EMP: 50 EST: 1970
SQ FT: 72,000
SALES (est): 14.3MM **Privately Held**
WEB: www.filnor.com
SIC: 3625 5063 Electric controls & control
accessories, industrial; switches, electric
power; resistors & resistor units; electrical
apparatus & equipment

(G-533)
GNW ALUMINUM INC
1356 Beeson St Ne (44601-6201)
P.O. Box 2418 (44601-0418)
PHONE.................................330 821-7955
Nathan Hoopes, *President*
Adam Hoopes, *Vice Pres*
Beatrice K Hoopes, *Treasurer*
EMP: 40
SALES (est): 19.2MM **Privately Held**
SIC: 5051 Aluminum bars, rods, ingots,
sheets, pipes, plates, etc.

(G-534)
**IMMEDIATE MEDICAL SERVICE
INC**
2461 W State St Ste E (44601-5609)
PHONE.................................330 823-0400
EMP: 25
SQ FT: 12,000
SALES: 200K
SALES (corp-wide): 103.2MM **Privately
Held**
SIC: 8011 Freestanding Emergency Medical Center

PA: Alliance Community Hospital
200 E State St
Alliance OH 44601
330 596-6000

(G-535)
**INTERNTIONAL ASSN
FIREFIGHTERS**
Also Called: Alliance Fire Dept
63 E Broadway St (44601-2646)
PHONE.................................330 823-5222
Jim Reese, *Chief*
EMP: 30
SALES (corp-wide): 56.3MM **Privately
Held**
WEB: www.sjff.org
SIC: 8631 Labor union
PA: International Association Of Firefighters
1750 New York Ave Nw # 300
Washington DC 20006
202 737-8484

(G-536)
KUNTZMAN TRUCKING INC (PA)
13515 Oyster Rd (44601-2064)
PHONE.................................330 821-9160
Virgil Waters, *Ch of Bd*
Kenneth Boatright, *President*
EMP: 47 EST: 1997
SQ FT: 32,000
SALES (est): 6.9MM **Privately Held**
SIC: 4213 4212 Contract haulers; local
trucking, without storage

(G-537)
**LAVERY CHEVROLET-BUICK
INC (PA)**
Also Called: Lavery Buick
1096 W State St (44601-4694)
P.O. Box 3545 (44601-7545)
PHONE.................................330 823-1100
Thomas C Lavery, *Ch of Bd*
William Lavery, *President*
Tom Nezbeth, *Parts Mgr*
Pat Bland, *Treasurer*
Nikki Pettit, *Office Mgr*
EMP: 50
SQ FT: 31,000
SALES (est): 17.3MM **Privately Held**
WEB: www.laverychevy.com
SIC: 5511 7538 7532 7515 Automobiles,
new & used; pickups, new & used; general automotive repair shops; top & body
repair & paint shops; passenger car leasing; used car dealers

(G-538)
LOWES HOME CENTERS LLC
2595 W State St (44601-5604)
PHONE.................................330 829-2700
Keith Fosse, *Manager*
EMP: 150
SALES (corp-wide): 68.6B **Publicly Held**
SIC: 5211 5031 5722 5064 Home centers; building materials, exterior; building
materials, interior; household appliance
stores; electrical appliances, television &
radio
HQ: Lowe's Home Centers, Llc
1605 Curtis Bridge Rd
Wilkesboro NC 28697
336 658-4000

(G-539)
**MAC MANUFACTURING INC
(PA)**
14599 Commerce St Ne (44601-1003)
PHONE.................................330 823-9900
Michael Conny, *Principal*
Jenny Conny, *Corp Secy*
Dan Tubbs, *Vice Pres*
▲ EMP: 700
SALES (est): 270.9MM **Privately Held**
SIC: 3715 5012 Truck trailers; trailers for
trucks, new & used; truck bodies

(G-540)
**MAC TRAILER
MANUFACTURING INC (PA)**
14599 Commerce St Ne (44601-1003)
PHONE.................................330 823-9900
Mike Conny, *President*
Ben Childers, *Vice Pres*
David Sandor, *Vice Pres*
Bill Ogden, *CFO*

Jenny Conny, *Treasurer*
▲ EMP: 193
SQ FT: 220,000
SALES (est): 140.2MM **Privately Held**
SIC: 3715 5012 5013 5015 Truck trailers;
trailers for trucks, new & used; truck bodies; motor vehicle supplies & new parts;
motor vehicle parts, used; trailer repair

(G-541)
MILLER PRODUCTS INC
Also Called: Mpi Label Systems Eqp Rfid Div
1421 W Main St (44601-2153)
PHONE.................................330 238-4200
Carey Weingart, *Branch Mgr*
EMP: 35
SALES (corp-wide): 36.3MM **Privately
Held**
SIC: 7389 Packaging & labeling services
PA: Miller Products, Inc.
450 Courtney Rd
Sebring OH 44672
330 938-2134

(G-542)
OHIO EYE ALLIANCE (PA)
985 S Sawburg Ave (44601-3515)
PHONE.................................330 823-1680
Sanjeev Dewan MD, *President*
Richard Lehrer MD, *President*
Tammy Ulbricht, *Financial Exec*
EMP: 32 EST: 1892
SQ FT: 8,000
SALES (est): 5MM **Privately Held**
WEB: www.ohioeye.com
SIC: 8011 Ophthalmologist

(G-543)
**PEREGRINE HEALTH SERVICES
INC**
Also Called: McCrea Manor Nursing
2040 Mccrea St (44601-2703)
PHONE.................................330 823-9005
Nicole Dandee, *Branch Mgr*
EMP: 92
SALES (corp-wide): 6.8MM **Privately
Held**
SIC: 8051 8093 Skilled nursing care facilities; rehabilitation center, outpatient treatment
PA: Peregrine Health Services, Inc.
1661 Old Henderson Rd
Columbus OH 43220
614 459-2656

(G-544)
QBS INC
Also Called: Fedvendor
1548 S Linden Ave (44601-4211)
PHONE.................................330 821-8801
Jim Franks, *President*
EMP: 31
SQ FT: 6,000
SALES (est): 9.5MM **Privately Held**
WEB: www.qbsinc.com
SIC: 1542 1541 Commercial & office building, new construction; commercial & office building contractors; industrial
buildings, new construction

(G-545)
**ROBERTSON HEATING SUP CO
OHIO (PA)**
2155 W Main St (44601-2190)
P.O. Box 2448 (44601-0448)
PHONE.................................800 433-9532
Scott Robertson, *President*
Ed Robertson, *Vice Pres*
Susan Neil, *Admin Sec*
EMP: 41 EST: 1946
SQ FT: 137,000
SALES (est): 36.4MM **Privately Held**
SIC: 5075 5074 Warm air heating & air
conditioning; plumbing & hydronic heating
supplies

(G-546)
**ROBERTSON HTG SUP ALIANCE
OHIO (PA)**
2155 W Main St (44601-2190)
P.O. Box 2448 (44601-0448)
PHONE.................................330 821-9180
Scott Robertson, *President*
Edward Robertson, *Vice Pres*
Larry Smith, *Manager*

Susan Neil, *Admin Sec*
▲ EMP: 110 EST: 1946
SALES (est): 19.5MM **Privately Held**
SIC: 5074 5999 5722 Plumbing fittings & supplies; plumbing & heating supplies; air conditioning room units, self-contained

(G-547)
ROBERTSON HTG SUP CANTON OHIO (PA)
2155 W Main St (44601-2190)
P.O. Box 2448 (44601-0448)
PHONE...................................330 821-9180
John J Robertson, *Principal*
Ed Robertson, *Exec VP*
Kevin Duro, *Vice Pres*
EMP: 35
SQ FT: 137,000
SALES (est): 11.8MM **Privately Held**
WEB: www.rhs1.com
SIC: 5074 Plumbing fittings & supplies

(G-548)
ROBERTSON HTG SUP CLUMBUS OHIO (PA)
2155 W Main St (44601-2190)
P.O. Box 2448 (44601-0448)
PHONE...................................330 821-9180
Scott Robertson, *President*
Geoff Alpert, *Vice Pres*
Kevin Duro, *Vice Pres*
Scott Middleton, *Vice Pres*
Ed Robertson, *Vice Pres*
EMP: 105
SQ FT: 60,000
SALES (est): 85.5MM **Privately Held**
SIC: 5075 Warm air heating & air conditioning

(G-549)
ROGER S PALUTSIS MD
Also Called: Carnation Clinic
1401 S Arch Ave (44601-4288)
PHONE...................................330 821-0201
Roger S Palutsis MD, *Owner*
EMP: 25
SALES (est): 2MM **Privately Held**
WEB: www.carnationclinic.com
SIC: 8011 Internal medicine, physician/surgeon

(G-550)
ROSELAWN HEALTH SERVICES CORP
Also Called: Roselawn Terrace
11999 Klinger Ave Ne (44601-1116)
PHONE...................................330 823-0618
Jeffrey Donner, *President*
Brian Colleran, *President*
EMP: 50
SQ FT: 3,824
SALES (est): 2MM **Privately Held**
WEB: www.roselawn-terrace.net
SIC: 8059 Nursing home, except skilled & intermediate care facility

(G-551)
RUHL ELECTRIC CO
6428 Union Ave Ne (44601-8140)
PHONE...................................330 823-7230
Kenneth W Ruhl Jr, *President*
Traci Ruhl, *Vice Pres*
Tracy Ruhl, *Vice Pres*
Patricia Ruhl, *Treasurer*
Paula Baum, *Manager*
EMP: 25
SQ FT: 30,000
SALES (est): 3.2MM **Privately Held**
WEB: www.ruhlelectric.com
SIC: 1731 General electrical contractor

(G-552)
SSOE INC
885 S Sawburg Ave Ste 106 (44601-5905)
PHONE...................................330 821-7198
Michael Hickman, *Principal*
EMP: 27
SALES (corp-wide): 186MM **Privately Held**
SIC: 8711 8712 8741 Structural engineering; architectural engineering; management services

PA: Ssoe, Inc.
1001 Madison Ave Ste A
Toledo OH 43604
419 255-3830

(G-553)
STARK COUNTY CMNTY ACTION AGCY
Also Called: Alliance Franklin Head Start
321 Franklin Ave (44601-1908)
PHONE...................................330 821-5977
Betty Thompson, *Office Mgr*
EMP: 35
SALES (est): 464.1K
SALES (corp-wide): 11.3MM **Privately Held**
SIC: 8399 Community action agency
PA: Stark County Community Action Agency
1366 Market Ave N
Canton OH 44714
330 454-1676

(G-554)
STARK METAL SALES INC
Also Called: SMS
432 Keystone St (44601-1722)
PHONE...................................330 823-7383
Charle B Reiber, *Incorporator*
EMP: 35
SQ FT: 70,000
SALES (est): 33.8MM **Privately Held**
WEB: www.starkmetal.com
SIC: 5051 Steel

(G-555)
STEEL EQP SPECIALISTS INC (PA)
Also Called: S.E.S.
1507 Beeson St Ne (44601-2142)
PHONE...................................330 823-8260
James R Boughton, *CEO*
T Virgil Huggett, *Ch of Bd*
Doris Gulyas, *Principal*
Said S Kabalan, *Principal*
Richard G Pinkett, *Principal*
▲ EMP: 72 EST: 1976
SQ FT: 32,000
SALES (est): 23.5MM **Privately Held**
WEB: www.seseng.com
SIC: 7699 3599 7629 3593 Industrial machinery & equipment repair; custom machinery; electrical repair shops; fluid power cylinders & actuators; rolling mill machinery; fabricated structural metal

(G-556)
TRAFFIC CTRL SAFETY SVCS LLC
8970 Allen Dr Ne (44601-9702)
PHONE...................................330 904-2732
Donald Peterson, *President*
EMP: 30
SQ FT: 2,500
SALES (est): 1.1MM **Privately Held**
SIC: 7389 Flagging service (traffic control)

(G-557)
WINKLE INDUSTRIES INC
2080 W Main St (44601-2187)
PHONE...................................330 823-9730
Joe Schatz, *CEO*
Shawn Babington, *General Mgr*
Jeff McCartney, *Engineer*
Beth A Felger, *Treasurer*
Paul Bean, *Regl Sales Mgr*
▲ EMP: 55
SQ FT: 85,000
SALES (est): 12.8MM **Privately Held**
WEB: www.winkleindustries.com
SIC: 7699 3499 5063 Industrial machinery & equipment repair; magnets, permanent: metallic; control & signal wire & cable, including coaxial

(G-558)
YMCA
205 S Union Ave (44601-2593)
PHONE...................................330 823-1930
Dale Nissley, *Director*
EMP: 50
SQ FT: 12,000

SALES: 1.2MM **Privately Held**
SIC: 8641 7991 8351 7032 Youth organizations; physical fitness facilities; child day care services; youth camps; individual & family services

---

Alvada
Seneca County

(G-559)
ACI CONST CO INC
Also Called: Alvada Trucking
2959 S Us Highway 23 (44802-9713)
PHONE...................................419 595-4284
Richard C Kirk, *Principal*
EMP: 25 EST: 2003
SALES (est): 4MM **Privately Held**
SIC: 4212 Dump truck haulage

(G-560)
ALVADA CONST INC
Also Called: Alvada Construction
2959 S Us Highway 23 (44802-9713)
PHONE...................................419 595-4224
Richard Kirk, *President*
Kevin Kurtz, *Project Mgr*
Matt Leonard, *Project Mgr*
Vicky Coppus, *Accountant*
Kim Phlipot, *Info Tech Mgr*
EMP: 150
SQ FT: 1,500
SALES (est): 32.7MM **Privately Held**
SIC: 1542 Commercial & office building, new construction

(G-561)
KIRK BROS CO INC
11942 Us Highway 224 (44802-9609)
P.O. Box 49 (44802-0049)
PHONE...................................419 595-4020
Richard C Kirk, *President*
Robert Kirk, *Treasurer*
EMP: 65 EST: 1969
SQ FT: 4,000
SALES (est): 22.8MM **Privately Held**
SIC: 1629 1623 Waste water & sewage treatment plant construction; water & sewer line construction

---

Alvordton
Williams County

(G-562)
KUNKLE FARM LIMITED
20674 Us Highway 20 (43501-9753)
PHONE...................................419 237-2748
Richard Kuncle, *President*
Don Kunkle, *Principal*
EMP: 80
SALES: 2.4MM **Privately Held**
SIC: 0191 General farms, primarily crop

Amelia
Clermont County

(G-563)
A & A SAFETY INC (PA)
1126 Ferris Rd Bldg B (45102-2376)
PHONE...................................513 943-6100
William N Luttmer, *President*
Billy Luttmer, *Vice Pres*
Steve Clough, *Project Mgr*
Francis Luttmer, *Treasurer*
Tom McLaughlin, *Manager*
EMP: 50
SQ FT: 12,300
SALES (est): 20.2MM **Privately Held**
WEB: www.aasafetyinc.com
SIC: 7359 3993 5084 1721 Work zone traffic equipment (flags, cones, barrels, etc.); signs & advertising specialties; safety equipment; painting & paper hanging; highway & street sign installation

(G-564)
AMELIA DAVITA DIALYSIS CENTER
1761 E Ohio Pike (45102-2007)
PHONE...................................513 797-0713
Donald Wolfer, *Manager*
EMP: 30 EST: 2010
SALES (est): 336.2K **Publicly Held**
SIC: 8092 Kidney dialysis centers
PA: Davita Inc.
2000 16th St
Denver CO 80202

(G-565)
AMERICAN FAMILY HOME INSUR CO
7000 Midland Blvd (45102-2608)
P.O. Box 5323, Cincinnati (45201-5323)
PHONE...................................513 943-7100
Thomas J Rohs, *President*
John W Hayden, *Senior VP*
Brad Fisher, *Vice Pres*
Tina Edmondson, *Mktg Dir*
Lee Pinkerton, *Sr Project Mgr*
EMP: 51
SALES (est): 6.8MM
SALES (corp-wide): 15.6B **Privately Held**
SIC: 6411 Insurance agents
HQ: American Modern Insurance Group, Inc.
7000 Midland Blvd
Amelia OH 45102

(G-566)
AMERICAN MODERN HOME INSUR CO (DH)
Also Called: American Mdrn Srpls Lnes Insur
7000 Midland Blvd (45102-2608)
P.O. Box 5323, Cincinnati (45201-5323)
PHONE...................................513 943-7100
John Hayden, *President*
Tomothy S Hogan, *Principal*
W Gary King, *Principal*
William McD Kite, *Principal*
Ken Boberg, *Exec VP*
EMP: 60 EST: 1965
SALES (est): 156.6MM
SALES (corp-wide): 15.6B **Privately Held**
WEB: www.americanmodernhomeinsurancecompany.com
SIC: 6331 Fire, marine & casualty insurance

(G-567)
AMERICAN MODERN HOME SVC CO
7000 Midland Blvd (45102-2608)
PHONE...................................513 943-7100
W Todd Gray, *President*
EMP: 28
SALES (est): 9MM
SALES (corp-wide): 15.6B **Privately Held**
SIC: 6321 Reinsurance carriers, accident & health
HQ: American Modern Insurance Group, Inc.
7000 Midland Blvd
Amelia OH 45102

(G-568)
AMERICAN MODRN INSUR GROUP INC (DH)
Also Called: American Modern Home Insur Co
7000 Midland Blvd (45102-2608)
P.O. Box 5323, Cincinnati (45201-5323)
PHONE...................................800 543-2644
John W Hayden, *President*
Kevin Barber, *President*
Tony Dirksing, *President*
Sharon Epling, *President*
Eric Hunziker, *President*
EMP: 108
SALES (est): 599.6MM
SALES (corp-wide): 15.6B **Privately Held**
WEB: www.amig.com
SIC: 6321 6411 Accident & health insurance carriers; insurance agents & brokers
HQ: Midland-Guardian Co.
7000 Midland Blvd
Amelia OH 45102
513 943-7100

(G-569)
AMERICAN WESTERN HOME INSUR CO
7000 Midland Blvd (45102-2608)
PHONE.................................513 943-7100
Joseph P Hayden Jr, *Ch of Bd*
Thomas Rohs, *President*
Charlie Hill, *President*
Michael Conaton, *Exec VP*
Ken Boberg, *Senior VP*
EMP: 428
SALES (est): 105.4MM
SALES (corp-wide): 15.6B **Privately Held**
WEB: www.amig.com
SIC: 6331 Fire, marine & casualty insurance
HQ: American Modern Home Insurance Company
   7000 Midland Blvd
   Amelia OH 45102
   513 943-7100

(G-570)
BANTAM LEASING INC
2291 State Route 125 (45102-9700)
P.O. Box 249, Bethel (45106-0249)
PHONE.................................513 734-6696
Shanda Douglas, *President*
EMP: 25
SQ FT: 1,050
SALES (est): 2.4MM **Privately Held**
SIC: 4213 Trucking Operator-Nonlocal

(G-571)
CLERMONT COUNSELING CENTER (PA)
Also Called: Lifepoint Solutions
43 E Main St (45102-1993)
PHONE.................................513 947-7000
Arlene Herman, *CEO*
Annette Cook, *Manager*
EMP: 30
SALES: 2.7MM **Privately Held**
WEB: www.clermontcounseling.org
SIC: 8322 General counseling services

(G-572)
EGER PRODUCTS INC (PA)
1132 Ferris Rd (45102-1020)
PHONE.................................513 753-4200
Dick Koebbe, *President*
EMP: 60 EST: 1969
SQ FT: 38,400
SALES: 28MM **Privately Held**
WEB: www.egerproducts.com
SIC: 3644 3544 5039 Insulators & insulation materials, electrical; forms (molds), for foundry & plastics working machinery; ceiling systems & products

(G-573)
INTERPHACE PHTGRPHY CMMNCTIONS
Also Called: Awis Designs
1365 Meadowlark Ln (45102-2612)
PHONE.................................254 289-6270
Todd A Fair, *President*
Todd Fair, *President*
EMP: 25
SALES (est): 1.1MM **Privately Held**
WEB: www.awisdesigns.com
SIC: 7335 Commercial photography

(G-574)
MIDLAND COMPANY
Also Called: American Western Home Insur
7000 Midland Blvd (45102-2608)
PHONE.................................513 947-5503
Joseph P Hayden III, *Ch of Bd*
John W Hayden, *President*
Paul T Brizzolara, *Exec VP*
John I Von Lehman, *Exec VP*
John Lehman, *Exec VP*
EMP: 1200
SQ FT: 275,000
SALES (est): 2.1MM
SALES (corp-wide): 15.6B **Privately Held**
WEB: www.motorcycle-insurance.com
SIC: 6331 4449 Property damage insurance; fire, marine & casualty insurance: stock; intracoastal (freight) transportation
HQ: Munich-American Holding Corporation
   555 College Rd E
   Princeton NJ 08540
   609 243-4876

(G-575)
MIDLAND-GUARDIAN CO (HQ)
7000 Midland Blvd (45102-2608)
P.O. Box 5323, Cincinnati (45201-5323)
PHONE.................................513 943-7100
Andreas Kleiner, *President*
John Von Lehman, *Exec VP*
Todd Gray, *CFO*
Matt McConnell, *Treasurer*
Rob Young, *Manager*
EMP: 650 EST: 1952
SALES: 733.4MM
SALES (corp-wide): 15.6B **Privately Held**
SIC: 6311 6331 Life insurance carriers; fire, marine & casualty insurance: stock
PA: Muncherner Ruckversicherungs-Gesellschaft Ag In Munchen
   Koniginstr. 107
   Munchen 80802
   893 891-0

(G-576)
SUNRISE MANOR CONVALESCENT CTR
3434 State Route 125 (45102-2012)
P.O. Box 54923, Cincinnati (45254-0923)
PHONE.................................513 797-5144
Howard L Meeker, *President*
Steve Meeker, *Principal*
Florel Meeker, *Vice Pres*
Patricia Meeker, *Administration*
EMP: 80
SALES (est): 2.5MM **Privately Held**
SIC: 8051 Skilled nursing care facilities

(G-577)
WHITT INC
Also Called: Whitt Plumbing
1152 Ferris Rd (45102-1020)
PHONE.................................513 753-7707
Richard Whitt, *President*
Lila Whitt, *Corp Secy*
EMP: 25
SQ FT: 8,500
SALES (est): 3.1MM **Privately Held**
WEB: www.whitt.com
SIC: 1711 Plumbing contractors

Amherst
Lorain County

(G-578)
AMHERST ANIMAL HOSPITAL INC
1425 Cooper Foster Pk Rd (44001-1297)
PHONE.................................440 282-5220
Thomas Gigliotti, *President*
Jerome Gigliotti, *Vice Pres*
EMP: 30
SQ FT: 6,000
SALES (est): 1.3MM **Privately Held**
SIC: 0742 Veterinarian, animal specialties

(G-579)
AMHERST EXEMPTED VLG SCHOOLS
Also Called: Bus Garage
225 Washington St (44001)
PHONE.................................440 988-2633
Kathy Moyer, *Supervisor*
Rebecca Bunnell, *Teacher*
Angie Deleon, *Teacher*
Al McConihe, *Teacher*
EMP: 48 **Privately Held**
SIC: 7521 Parking garage
PA: Amherst Exempted Village Schools
   185 Forest St
   Amherst OH 44001

(G-580)
AMHERST HOSPITAL ASSOCIATION
Also Called: E M H Regional Medical Center
254 Cleveland Ave (44001-1699)
PHONE.................................440 988-6000
Kristi Sink, *President*
David Cook, *CFO*
Chad Cohen, *Radiology*
James Frank, *Radiology*
EMP: 152 EST: 1917
SQ FT: 90,000

SALES (est): 7.4MM **Privately Held**
WEB: www.emh-healthcare.org
SIC: 8011 Freestanding emergency medical center

(G-581)
AMHERST MANOR NURSING HOME
175 N Lake St (44001-1332)
P.O. Box 260 (44001-0260)
PHONE.................................440 988-4415
Donel Sprenger, *President*
Anthony Sprenger, *Vice Pres*
EMP: 70
SQ FT: 30,000
SALES (est): 2.3MM **Privately Held**
WEB: www.sprengerretirement.com
SIC: 8052 Intermediate care facilities
PA: Sprenger Enterprises, Inc.
   2198 Gladstone Ct
   Glendale Heights IL 60139

(G-582)
BUTCHKO ELECTRIC INC
7333 S Dewey Rd (44001-2507)
PHONE.................................440 985-3180
Gary A Butchko, *President*
Bill Butchko, *Vice Pres*
EMP: 25
SQ FT: 2,000
SALES (est): 1.8MM **Privately Held**
WEB: www.butchkoelectric.com
SIC: 7349 1731 Building maintenance, except repairs; general electrical contractor

(G-583)
CELLCO PARTNERSHIP
Also Called: Verizon Wireless
7566 Oak Point Rd (44001-9658)
PHONE.................................440 984-5200
Andrew Schimd, *Branch Mgr*
EMP: 25
SALES (corp-wide): 130.8B **Publicly Held**
SIC: 4813 4812 Telephone communication, except radio; cellular telephone services
HQ: Cellco Partnership
   1 Verizon Way
   Basking Ridge NJ 07920

(G-584)
ED MULLINAX FORD LLC
Also Called: Autonation Ford Amherst
8000 Leavitt Rd (44001-2712)
P.O. Box 280 (44001-0280)
PHONE.................................440 984-2431
Michael J Jackson, *Ch of Bd*
Dennis Pritt, *General Mgr*
EMP: 250
SALES (est): 41.4MM
SALES (corp-wide): 21.4B **Publicly Held**
SIC: 5511 7538 7532 5521 Automobiles, new & used; general automotive repair shops; top & body repair & paint shops; used car dealers
HQ: An Dealership Holding Corp.
   200 Sw 1st Ave
   Fort Lauderdale FL 33301
   954 769-7000

(G-585)
EDWARDS LAND CLEARING INC
Also Called: Edwards Tree Service
49090 Cooper Foster Pk Rd (44001-9649)
PHONE.................................440 988-4477
Carl Kopocs,
EMP: 40
SALES: 1.2MM **Privately Held**
SIC: 0783 1629 Ornamental shrub & tree services; land clearing contractor

(G-586)
ENVIROTEST SYSTEMS CORP
205 Sandstone Blvd (44001-1273)
PHONE.................................330 963-4464
EMP: 34 **Privately Held**
WEB: www.il.etest.com
SIC: 7549 Emissions testing without repairs, automotive
HQ: Envirotest Systems Corp.
   7 Kripes Rd
   East Granby CT 06026

(G-587)
FIFTH THIRD BANK
309 N Leavitt Rd (44001-1126)
PHONE.................................440 984-2402
Tina Graham, *Branch Mgr*
EMP: 109
SALES (corp-wide): 7.9B **Publicly Held**
SIC: 6022 State commercial banks
HQ: The Fifth Third Bank
   38 Fountain Square Plz
   Cincinnati OH 45202
   513 579-5203

(G-588)
GRACE HOSPITAL
254 Cleveland Ave (44001-1620)
PHONE.................................216 687-4013
Vickie Kayatin, *Principal*
EMP: 90
SALES (corp-wide): 17.4MM **Privately Held**
SIC: 8062 General medical & surgical hospitals
PA: Grace Hospital
   2307 W 14th St
   Cleveland OH 44113
   216 687-1500

(G-589)
H&R BLOCK INC
1980 G Coper Foster Pk Rd (44001)
PHONE.................................440 282-4288
Sharon Griffith, *Director*
EMP: 27
SALES (corp-wide): 3.1B **Publicly Held**
SIC: 7291 Tax return preparation services
PA: H&R Block, Inc.
   1 H&R Block Way
   Kansas City MO 64105
   816 854-3000

(G-590)
HOWARD HANNA SMYTHE CRAMER
1711 Cooper Foster Pk Rd (44001-1205)
PHONE.................................440 282-8002
Rick Edler, *Branch Mgr*
EMP: 30
SALES (corp-wide): 72.1MM **Privately Held**
WEB: www.smythecramer.com
SIC: 6531 Real estate agent, residential
HQ: Howard Hanna Smythe Cramer
   6000 Parkland Blvd
   Cleveland OH 44124
   216 447-4477

(G-591)
KTM NORTH AMERICA INC (PA)
1119 Milan Ave (44001-1319)
PHONE.................................855 215-6360
Di Stefan Pierer, *CEO*
Rod Bush, *President*
John S Harden, *Vice Pres*
Selvaraj Narayana, *Vice Pres*
Jon-Erik Burleson, *Treasurer*
▲ EMP: 87
SQ FT: 5,000
SALES (est): 36.8MM **Privately Held**
SIC: 5012 3751 Motorcycles; motorcycles, bicycles & parts

(G-592)
LORAIN CNTY STY OFF EQP CO INC
1953 Cooper Foster Pk Rd (44001-1207)
PHONE.................................440 960-7070
Pamelynn C Carver, *President*
James A Adkins, *Vice Pres*
Alan T Shaffstall, *Vice Pres*
EMP: 40 EST: 1947
SQ FT: 33,000
SALES (est): 11.2MM **Privately Held**
WEB: www.bobels.com
SIC: 5044 5943 Office equipment; office forms & supplies

(G-593)
MERCY HEALTH
578 N Leavitt Rd (44001-1131)
PHONE.................................440 988-1009
Marsha Heuring, *Branch Mgr*
Ilona E Jurek, *Family Practiti*
EMP: 33

▲ = Import ▼=Export
◆ =Import/Export

SALES (corp-wide): 4.7B **Privately Held**
SIC: 8062 General medical & surgical hospitals
PA: Mercy Health
 1701 Mercy Health Pl
 Cincinnati OH 45237
 513 639-2800

(G-594)
NORDSON CORPORATION
300 Nordson Dr (44001-2422)
PHONE...................................440 985-4496
Janice Bailey, *Opers Staff*
Wendy Jordan, *Branch Mgr*
Mary White, *Manager*
Jeff Wasko, *Info Tech Mgr*
Chris Park, *Director*
EMP: 432
SALES (corp-wide): 2.2B **Publicly Held**
SIC: 5084 Industrial machinery & equipment
PA: Nordson Corporation
 28601 Clemens Rd
 Westlake OH 44145
 440 892-1580

(G-595)
PET CENTRAL LODGE & GROOMING
1425 C Foster Pk Rd C (44001)
PHONE...................................440 282-1811
Dawn Roberts, *Manager*
EMP: 25
SALES (est): 670K **Privately Held**
SIC: 0752 Grooming services, pet & animal specialties

(G-596)
RAK CORROSION CONTROL INC
7455 S Dewey Rd (44001-2509)
PHONE...................................440 985-2171
Clinton Reph, *Ch of Bd*
Guy A Reph, *President*
Tari Reph, *Vice Pres*
EMP: 25
SQ FT: 20,000
SALES (est): 4.1MM **Privately Held**
SIC: 1799 1742 Sandblasting of building exteriors; corrosion control installation; insulation, buildings

(G-597)
SLIMANS SALES & SERVICE INC
Also Called: Slimans Chrysler Plymuth Dodge
7498 Leavitt Rd (44001-2457)
PHONE...................................440 988-4484
Paul Sliman, *President*
Barbara Sliman, *Treasurer*
Ben Gray, *Director*
Wendy Sliman, *Admin Sec*
EMP: 42
SQ FT: 20,000
SALES (est): 17.7MM **Privately Held**
SIC: 5511 5012 Automobiles, new & used; pickups, new & used; automobiles & other motor vehicles

(G-598)
SPITZER AUTO WORLD AMHERST
200 N Leavitt Rd (44001-1125)
PHONE...................................440 988-4444
Alan Spitzer, *President*
EMP: 55 EST: 1995
SALES (est): 18.4MM
SALES (corp-wide): 52.2MM **Privately Held**
WEB: www.spitzerauto.com
SIC: 5511 7515 5521 Automobiles, new & used; passenger car leasing; used car dealers
PA: Spitzer Management, Inc.
 150 E Bridge St
 Elyria OH 44035
 440 323-4671

(G-599)
STAR BUILDERS INC
46405 Telegraph Rd (44001-2855)
P.O. Box 109 (44001-0109)
PHONE...................................440 986-5951
Richard Molder, *CEO*
Kalyn Wise, *President*

Todd Mealwitz, *Vice Pres*
EMP: 45
SQ FT: 30,000
SALES (est): 11.4MM **Privately Held**
SIC: 1542 1541 Commercial & office building contractors; farm building construction; industrial buildings & warehouses; warehouse construction

Amsterdam
Jefferson County

(G-600)
APEX ENVIRONMENTAL LLC
11 County Road 78 (43903)
P.O. Box 157 (43903-0157)
PHONE...................................740 543-4389
Antony Rosso, *CEO*
EMP: 90
SQ FT: 2,500
SALES (est): 15.8MM **Privately Held**
SIC: 1629 Waste disposal plant construction

(G-601)
EDISON LOCAL SCHOOL DISTRICT
Also Called: Edison Bus Garage
8235 Amsterdam Rd Se (43903-9794)
PHONE...................................740 543-4011
Florence Mader, *Manager*
EMP: 33
SALES (corp-wide): 21.2MM **Privately Held**
SIC: 8211 7514 Public senior high school; passenger car rental
PA: Edison Local School District
 14890 State Route 213
 Hammondsville OH 43930
 740 282-0065

(G-602)
WEBA OUTREACH FOOD PANTRY
346 N Main St (43903-7956)
PHONE...................................740 543-3227
Pauline Wagner, *Principal*
EMP: 25
SALES (est): 165.7K **Privately Held**
SIC: 8322 Outreach program

Andover
Ashtabula County

(G-603)
ANDOVER BANCORP INC (PA)
19 Public Sq (44003-9316)
P.O. Box 1300 (44003-1300)
PHONE...................................440 293-7605
Larry W Park, *President*
James Greenfield, *Vice Pres*
EMP: 50
SALES: 16.8MM **Privately Held**
WEB: www.andoverbancorp.com
SIC: 6022 State commercial banks

(G-604)
ANDOVER VLG RETIREMENT CMNTY
486 S Main St (44003-9602)
PHONE...................................440 293-5416
Gina A Richardson,
EMP: 235
SALES (est): 10.8MM **Privately Held**
WEB: www.andoverretirement.com
SIC: 8051 Convalescent home with continuous nursing care

(G-605)
DAVITA INC
Also Called: Davita Kidney Dialysis
486 S Main St (44003-9602)
PHONE...................................440 293-6028
Tracy Meure, *Branch Mgr*
EMP: 26 **Publicly Held**
SIC: 8092 Kidney dialysis centers
PA: Davita Inc.
 2000 16th St
 Denver CO 80202

(G-606)
FRATERNAL ORDER EAGLES INC
Also Called: Foe 4035
6210 State Route 85 (44003-9702)
P.O. Box 1175 (44003-1175)
PHONE...................................440 293-5997
Marlene Waters, *Branch Mgr*
EMP: 26
SQ FT: 1,248
SALES (corp-wide): 5.7MM **Privately Held**
WEB: www.fraternalorderofeagles.tribe.net
SIC: 8641 Fraternal associations
PA: Fraternal Order Of Eagles, Bryan Aerie
 2233 Of Bryan, Ohio
 221 S Walnut St
 Bryan OH 43506
 419 636-7812

(G-607)
PYMATUNING AMBULANCE SERVICE
153 Station St (44003)
P.O. Box 1509 (44003-1509)
PHONE...................................440 293-7991
EMP: 25 EST: 1997
SALES: 101.2K **Privately Held**
SIC: 4119 Ambulance Service

(G-608)
SEELEY ENTERPRISES COMPANY (PA)
Also Called: Seeley Medical
104 Parker Dr (44003-9481)
PHONE...................................440 293-6600
Mario Lacute, *CEO*
Joe Petrolla, *President*
Glenna Gallagher, *Principal*
Ron Adamov, *Vice Pres*
Donald Bellante, *Vice Pres*
EMP: 35
SQ FT: 12,000
SALES (est): 18.5MM **Privately Held**
WEB: www.seeleymedical.com
SIC: 5999 7352 Medical apparatus & supplies; medical equipment rental

(G-609)
SEELEY MEDICAL OXYGEN CO (HQ)
104 Parker Dr (44003-9481)
PHONE...................................440 255-7163
Mario Lacute, *President*
Donald Bellante, *Vice Pres*
Ann Lacute, *Vice Pres*
EMP: 45 EST: 1955
SQ FT: 15,000
SALES (est): 11.6MM
SALES (corp-wide): 18.5MM **Privately Held**
SIC: 5047 7352 Medical equipment & supplies; medical equipment rental
PA: Seeley Enterprises Company
 104 Parker Dr
 Andover OH 44003
 440 293-6600

Anna
Shelby County

(G-610)
ANNA RESCUE SQUAD
203 S Linden St (45302-8712)
P.O. Box 201 (45302-0201)
PHONE...................................937 394-7377
Melinda Gerlich, *President*
Jessica Rickart, *Administration*
EMP: 25
SALES: 276.8K **Privately Held**
SIC: 4119 Ambulance service

(G-611)
WELLS BROTHERS INC
Also Called: Honeywell Authorized Dealer
105 Shue Dr (45302-8402)
PHONE...................................937 394-7559
Curt Wells, *President*
Scott Robinson, *Business Mgr*
Ken Steinke, *Vice Pres*
Scott Vanfossen, *Vice Pres*
Jerry Wells, *Vice Pres*

EMP: 82
SALES (est): 27MM **Privately Held**
SIC: 1731 1711 General electrical contractor; plumbing contractors; heating & air conditioning contractors

Ansonia
Darke County

(G-612)
ANSONIA AREA EMERGENCY SERVICE
225 W Elroy Ansonia Rd (45303)
P.O. Box 171 (45303-0171)
PHONE...................................937 337-2651
Ron Thompson, *President*
Kris Eb, *Chief*
EMP: 30
SALES: 287.1K **Privately Held**
SIC: 8322 Emergency social services

Antwerp
Paulding County

(G-613)
ANTWERP MNOR ASSSTED LVING LLC
204 Archer Dr (45813-8499)
P.O. Box 759 (45813-0759)
PHONE...................................419 258-1500
Kenneth Wilson, *President*
EMP: 40
SALES (est): 324.8K **Privately Held**
SIC: 8361 Geriatric residential care

(G-614)
SCHROEDER ASSOCIATES INC (PA)
5554 County Road 424 (45813)
PHONE...................................419 258-5075
Easther H Schroeder, *Principal*
Charles Schroeder, *Principal*
EMP: 30
SQ FT: 10,000
SALES (est): 4.3MM **Privately Held**
SIC: 4212 4789 4213 Local trucking, without storage; pipeline terminal facilities, independently operated; trucking, except local

(G-615)
VILLAGE OF ANTWERP (PA)
118 N Main St (45813)
P.O. Box 1046 (45813-1046)
PHONE...................................419 258-7422
Ray Delong, *Mayor*
Sarah Keerman, *Administration*
EMP: 42 EST: 1846 **Privately Held**
SIC: 9111 8611 City & town managers' offices; business associations

(G-616)
VILLAGE OF ANTWERP
Also Called: Fire Department
203 S Cleveland St (45813)
P.O. Box 1046 (45813-1046)
PHONE...................................419 258-6631
Ray Friend, *Chief*
EMP: 25 **Privately Held**
SIC: 4119 9224 Ambulance service; fire department, not including volunteer;
PA: Village Of Antwerp
 118 N Main St
 Antwerp OH 45813
 419 258-7422

Apple Creek
Wayne County

(G-617)
APPLE CREEK BANKING CO (INC) (PA)
3 W Main St (44606)
PHONE...................................330 698-2631
Carol Meek, *CEO*
Leo Miller, *Senior VP*
Margo Broehl, *Admin Sec*

EMP: 43
SQ FT: 12,000
SALES: 5.4MM **Privately Held**
WEB: www.applecreekbank.com
SIC: 6022 State commercial banks

(G-618)
ESPT LIQUIDATION INC
339 Mill St (44606-9541)
P.O. Box 458 (44606-0458)
PHONE.................................330 698-4711
Leonard Buckner, *President*
EMP: 75 **EST:** 1960
SQ FT: 88,000
SALES (est): 21.1MM **Privately Held**
WEB: www.euclidspiral.com
SIC: 5047 5113 Medical & hospital equipment; paper tubes & cores

(G-619)
GROSS LUMBER INC
8848 Ely Rd (44606-9799)
PHONE.................................330 683-2055
Rick Grossniklaus, *President*
Don Grossniklaus, *President*
EMP: 35 **EST:** 1957
SQ FT: 30,000
SALES (est): 5MM **Privately Held**
SIC: 2448 5031 5099 2426 Pallets, wood; lumber: rough, dressed & finished; wood & wood by-products; hardwood dimension & flooring mills; sawmills & planing mills, general

(G-620)
PRECISION PRODUCTS GROUP INC
Also Called: Euclid Medical Products
339 Mill St (44606-9541)
PHONE.................................330 698-4711
Ray Schroeder, *Manager*
EMP: 75 **Privately Held**
SIC: 5047 5113 Medical & hospital equipment; paper tubes & cores
PA: Precision Products Group, Inc.
10201 N Illinois St # 390
Indianapolis IN 46290

(G-621)
TROYERS HOME PANTRY (PA)
668 W Main St (44606-9092)
PHONE.................................330 698-4182
Abe Troyer, *Owner*
EMP: 25
SQ FT: 5,000
SALES (est): 1.5MM **Privately Held**
SIC: 5149 5461 Bakery products; bakeries

(G-622)
WESTHAFER TRUCKING INC
6333 E Messner Rd (44606-9642)
PHONE.................................330 698-3030
Glen Westhafer, *President*
Terri Sinder, *Admin Sec*
EMP: 30
SALES (est): 2.7MM **Privately Held**
SIC: 4212 Local trucking, without storage

Arcanum
Darke County

(G-623)
BRUMBAUGH CONSTRUCTION INC
3520 State Route 49 (45304-9731)
P.O. Box 309 (45304-0309)
PHONE.................................937 692-5107
Scott Myers, *President*
Fred A Garber, *Principal*
Jason Willis, *Executive*
Ralph Brumbaugh, *Shareholder*
Diane Wills, *Admin Sec*
▲ **EMP:** 43 **EST:** 1961
SQ FT: 3,000
SALES (est): 14.7MM **Privately Held**
WEB: www.brumbaughconstruction.com
SIC: 1542 1622 Commercial & office building, new construction; bridge construction

(G-624)
CALVIN ELECTRIC LLC
4957 Hursch Rd (45304-9273)
PHONE.................................937 670-2558

Brandon Wombold, *Mng Member*
EMP: 25
SALES: 3.5MM **Privately Held**
SIC: 1731 General electrical contractor

(G-625)
MIKESELL TRANSPORTATION BROKER
Also Called: Beach Golf Course
1476 State Route 503 (45304-9237)
PHONE.................................937 996-5731
Bruce Mikesell, *President*
Terri Mikesell, *Corp Secy*
EMP: 35
SALES (est): 912.6K **Privately Held**
SIC: 4789 Transportation services

Archbold
Fulton County

(G-626)
ARCHBOLD ELEVATOR INC
3265 County Road 24 (43502-9415)
PHONE.................................419 445-2451
William Fricke, *President*
Carolyn Fricke, *Corp Secy*
EMP: 30
SQ FT: 4,000
SALES (est): 4.8MM **Privately Held**
WEB: www.archboldelevator.com
SIC: 5153 5191 Grain elevators; farm supplies

(G-627)
BLACK SWAMP EQUIPMENT LLC (PA)
700 E Lugbill Rd (43502-1566)
P.O. Box 427 (43502-0427)
PHONE.................................419 445-0030
Jeff Fryman, *Principal*
Kearen S Burkholder,
EMP: 32
SQ FT: 3,500
SALES (est): 5.4MM **Privately Held**
WEB: www.blackswampequipment.com
SIC: 7359 Tool rental

(G-628)
COMMUNITY HLTH PRFSSIONALS INC
230 Westfield Dr (43502-1047)
PHONE.................................419 445-5128
Brent Tow, *Branch Mgr*
EMP: 46
SALES (corp-wide): 13.1MM **Privately Held**
SIC: 8082 Visiting nurse service
PA: Community Health Professionals, Inc.
1159 Westwood Dr
Van Wert OH 45891
419 238-9223

(G-629)
COMMUNITY HSPTALS WLLNESS CTRS
Also Called: Archbold Hospital
121 Westfield Dr Ste 1 (43502-1005)
PHONE.................................419 445-2015
Greg Flattery, *President*
Rusty O Brunicardi, *COO*
EMP: 76
SALES (corp-wide): 77.2MM **Privately Held**
SIC: 8062 General medical & surgical hospitals
PA: Community Hospitals And Wellness Centers
433 W High St
Bryan OH 43506
419 636-1131

(G-630)
FARMERS & MERCHANTS STATE BANK (HQ)
307-11 N Defiance St (43502)
P.O. Box 216 (43502-0216)
PHONE.................................419 446-2501
Brenda Mossing, *President*
Rex D Rice, *Exec VP*
Edward A Leininger, *Vice Pres*
John Kantner, *Vice Pres*
Chris Kurt, *Vice Pres*

EMP: 115 **EST:** 1897
SALES: 51.2MM
SALES (corp-wide): 57.2MM **Publicly Held**
WEB: www.fm-bank.com
SIC: 6022 State trust companies accepting deposits, commercial
PA: Farmers & Merchants Bancorp, Inc.
307 N Defiance St
Archbold OH 43502
419 446-2501

(G-631)
LIECHTY INC (HQ)
1701 S Defiance St (43502-9798)
P.O. Box 67 (43502-0067)
PHONE.................................419 445-1565
Orval Jay Beck, *President*
EMP: 30
SALES (est): 26.1MM **Privately Held**
WEB: www.liechtyfarmequipment.com
SIC: 5083 Agricultural machinery & equipment

(G-632)
MBC HOLDINGS INC (PA)
1613 S Defiance St (43502-9488)
P.O. Box 30 (43502-0030)
PHONE.................................419 445-1015
Dean E Miller, *President*
Steven A Everhart, *Corp Secy*
Robert Miller, *Vice Pres*
EMP: 39
SALES (est): 110.2MM **Privately Held**
WEB: www.mbcholdings.com
SIC: 1622 1611 Bridge construction; highway & street paving contractor

(G-633)
MILLER BROS CONST INC
1613 S Defiance St (43502-9488)
P.O. Box 30 (43502-0030)
PHONE.................................419 445-1015
Bradley D Miller, *President*
Terry Moore, *Corp Secy*
Mark F Murray, *Exec VP*
Scott Jaskela, *Vice Pres*
David Lersch, *Vice Pres*
EMP: 30 **EST:** 1945
SQ FT: 48,000
SALES (est): 15.2MM **Privately Held**
WEB: www.millerbrosconst.com
SIC: 1611 Highway & street paving contractor
PA: Mbc Holdings, Inc.
1613 S Defiance St
Archbold OH 43502

(G-634)
NORTHWEST OHIO COMPUTER ASSN (PA)
Also Called: Northern Bckeye Edcatn Council
209 Nolan Pkwy (43502-8404)
PHONE.................................419 267-5565
Jason Klinger, *Programmer Anys*
Kim Olson, *Programmer Anys*
John Mohler, *Exec Dir*
Christine Ziegler, *Director*
Robin Pfund, *Executive*
EMP: 69
SQ FT: 6,000
SALES (est): 7.9MM **Privately Held**
SIC: 7374 8211 Data processing service; elementary & secondary schools

(G-635)
PROGRESSIVE FURNITURE INC (HQ)
Also Called: Progressive International
502 Middle St (43502-1559)
P.O. Box 308 (43502-0308)
PHONE.................................419 446-4500
Kevin Sauder, *President*
Dan Kendrick, *Exec VP*
John Boring, *VP Finance*
Janys Etts, *Credit Mgr*
▲ **EMP:** 25
SQ FT: 8,000

SALES (est): 23.1MM
SALES (corp-wide): 500MM **Privately Held**
WEB: www.progressivefurniture.com
SIC: 2511 2517 5021 Bed frames, except water bed frames: wood; dressers, household: wood; home entertainment unit cabinets, wood; tables, occasional; beds; dining room furniture
PA: Sauder Woodworking Co.
502 Middle St
Archbold OH 43502
419 446-2711

(G-636)
QUADCO REHABILITATION CENTER
Also Called: Northwest Products Div
600 Oak St (43502-1579)
PHONE.................................419 445-1950
Phillip Zuver, *Branch Mgr*
Shannon Zellers, *Program Mgr*
EMP: 90
SALES (corp-wide): 247.7K **Privately Held**
SIC: 8331 2448 Vocational rehabilitation agency; wood pallets & skids
PA: Quadco Rehabilitation Center, Inc.
427 N Defiance St
Stryker OH 43557
419 682-1011

(G-637)
SAUDER HARITAGE INN
22611 State Route 2 (43502-9452)
PHONE.................................419 445-6408
Debbie David, *CEO*
EMP: 40
SALES (est): 687.9K **Privately Held**
SIC: 7011 Tourist camps, cabins, cottages & courts

(G-638)
SAUDER VILLAGE
22611 State Route 2 (43502-9452)
PHONE.................................419 446-2541
Maynard Sauder, *President*
Harold Plassman, *Vice Pres*
Greg Bontrager, *Treasurer*
Debbie Sauder David, *Exec Dir*
Kris Jemmott, *Director*
EMP: 300
SQ FT: 20,000
SALES: 8MM **Privately Held**
SIC: 5812 7299 8412 5947 Restaurant, family: independent; banquet hall facilities; museum; gift shop

(G-639)
SAUDER WOODWORKING CO (PA)
502 Middle St (43502-1500)
P.O. Box 156 (43502-0156)
PHONE.................................419 446-2711
Kevin J Sauder, *President*
Patrick Sauder, *CFO*
Paige Miller, *Admin Sec*
◆ **EMP:** 2100
SQ FT: 5,000,000
SALES (est): 500MM **Privately Held**
WEB: www.sauder.com
SIC: 2512 5021 Upholstered household furniture; wood upholstered chairs & couches; couches, sofas & davenports: upholstered on wood frames; living room furniture: upholstered on wood frames; furniture

(G-640)
SONIT SYSTEMS LLC
130 Westfield Dr (43502-1060)
PHONE.................................419 446-2151
Lana Rising, *Purchasing*
Brenda Farnsworth, *CFO*
Douglas Nofziger, *Accounts Exec*
Marvin R Meck, *Mng Member*
EMP: 41
SALES (est): 6.6MM **Privately Held**
SIC: 7379

(G-641)
T J AUTOMATION INC
U075 State Route 66 (43502-9505)
PHONE.................................419 267-5687
Tracy Hammersmith, *President*
EMP: 30

SQ FT: 12,000
SALES (est): 12.9MM **Privately Held**
SIC: 5084 Industrial machinery & equipment

Arlington
Hancock County

(G-642)
EVANGELICAL LUTHERAN
Also Called: Good Samaritan Soc - Arlington
100 Powell Dr (45814-9688)
P.O. Box 5038, Sioux Falls SD (57117-5038)
PHONE..............................419 365-5115
Rayenae Nylander, *Treasurer*
Sally Balentage, *Human Res Dir*
Teresa Buck, *Director*
Johnna Shaferly, *Director*
Susan Lawrence, *Nursing Dir*
EMP: 95 **Privately Held**
WEB: www.good-sam.com
SIC: 8059 8051 Nursing home, except skilled & intermediate care facility; skilled nursing care facilities
HQ: The Evangelical Lutheran Good Samaritan Society
4800 W 57th St
Sioux Falls SD 57108
866 928-1635

Arlington Heights
Hamilton County

(G-643)
MITER MASONRY CONTRACTORS
421 Maple Ave (45215-5425)
PHONE..............................513 821-3334
Thomas Krallman, *President*
Anne M Krallman, *Corp Secy*
EMP: 40
SQ FT: 8,000
SALES (est): 3.9MM **Privately Held**
SIC: 1741 Masonry & other stonework

Ashland
Ashland County

(G-644)
ABERS GARAGE INC (PA)
Also Called: Aber's Truck Center
1729 Claremont Ave (44805-3594)
PHONE..............................419 281-5500
Danny Aber, *President*
Frances Aber, *Corp Secy*
Allen Aber, *Vice Pres*
Jerry Aber, *Vice Pres*
EMP: 45 **EST:** 1950
SQ FT: 26,000
SALES (est): 24.9MM **Privately Held**
WEB: www.aberstrucks.com
SIC: 5511 7538 7549 5012 Trucks, tractors & trailers: new & used; general truck repair; towing service, automotive; automobiles & other motor vehicles

(G-645)
APPLESEED CMNTY MNTAL HLTH CTR
Also Called: APPLESEED COUNSELING
2233 Rocky Ln (44805-4701)
PHONE..............................419 281-3716
Karen Carroll, *General Mgr*
Jerry Strausaugh, *Director*
EMP: 25
SALES (est): 4.6MM **Privately Held**
WEB: www.appleseedcmhc.org
SIC: 8049 8093 Clinical psychologist; specialty outpatient clinics

(G-646)
ASHLAND CITY SCHOOL DISTRICT
Also Called: Reagan Elementary School
850 Jackson Dr (44805-4254)
PHONE..............................419 289-7967
Stephen McDonnell, *Principal*

EMP: 50
SALES (corp-wide): 4.8MM **Privately Held**
SIC: 8211 8351 Public junior high school; public elementary school; preschool center
PA: Ashland City School District
1407 Claremont Ave
Ashland OH 44805
419 289-1117

(G-647)
ASHLAND CLEANING LLC
48 W Main St (44805-2237)
PHONE..............................419 281-1747
Melinda Turk, *President*
EMP: 40
SQ FT: 1,800
SALES (est): 230.8K **Privately Held**
SIC: 7349 Building & office cleaning services; floor waxing; janitorial service, contract basis; maid services, contract or fee basis

(G-648)
ASHLAND CLEANING LLC
Also Called: Ahsland Cleaning
48 W Main St (44805-2237)
PHONE..............................419 281-1747
Melinda Turk, *Principal*
EMP: 50
SALES: 600K **Privately Held**
SIC: 7349 Janitorial service, contract basis

(G-649)
ASHLAND CNTY COUNCIL ON AGING
240 E 3rd St (44805-2405)
PHONE..............................419 281-1477
James A Dalenberg, *Exec Dir*
EMP: 50
SALES: 943.7K **Privately Held**
SIC: 8322 Old age assistance

(G-650)
ASHLAND COMFORT CONTROL INC (PA)
Also Called: Honeywell Authorized Dealer
805 E Main St (44805-2620)
PHONE..............................419 281-0144
Jeffrey Reep, *President*
Joy Reep, *Corp Secy*
Jeff Reep, *Sales Executive*
EMP: 29
SQ FT: 17,000
SALES (est): 5MM **Privately Held**
WEB: www.ashlandcomfortcontrol.com
SIC: 1711 Warm air heating & air conditioning contractor; refrigeration contractor

(G-651)
ASHLAND GOLF CLUB
1333 Center St (44805-4142)
PHONE..............................419 289-2917
Cindy Mitchell, *General Mgr*
EMP: 35
SQ FT: 3,500
SALES (est): 27.7K **Privately Held**
WEB: www.ccashland.com
SIC: 7992 Public Golf Course

(G-652)
ASHLAND LLC
Also Called: Ashland Distribution
1745 Cottage St (44805-1237)
PHONE..............................419 289-9588
Norma Malcolm, *Controller*
David A Tobolski, *Branch Mgr*
EMP: 100
SALES (corp-wide): 3.7B **Publicly Held**
WEB: www.ashland.com
SIC: 5169 Alkalines & chlorine
HQ: Ashland Llc
50 E Rivercenter Blvd # 1600
Covington KY 41011
859 815-3333

(G-653)
ATLAS BOLT & SCREW COMPANY LLC (DH)
Also Called: Atlas Fasteners For Cnstr
1628 Troy Rd (44805-1398)
PHONE..............................419 289-6171
Robert W Moore, *President*
Robert C Gluth, *Treasurer*

Robert Webb, *Admin Sec*
▲ **EMP:** 175
SQ FT: 75,000
SALES (est): 30.1MM
SALES (corp-wide): 225.3B **Publicly Held**
WEB: www.atlasfasteners.com
SIC: 3452 5085 5051 5072 Washers, metal; screws, metal; fasteners, industrial: nuts, bolts, screws, etc.; metals service centers & offices; hardware
HQ: Marmon Group Llc
181 W Madison St Ste 2600
Chicago IL 60602
312 372-9500

(G-654)
BALL BOUNCE AND SPORT INC (PA)
Also Called: Hedstrom Fitness
1 Hedstrom Dr (44805-3586)
PHONE..............................419 289-9310
David Faulkner, *President*
Scott Fickes, *CFO*
Michael Kelly, *CFO*
Jeremy Rohr, *Associate*
◆ **EMP:** 270
SQ FT: 187,000
SALES (est): 195.8MM **Privately Held**
SIC: 5092 5091 3089 Toys; fitness equipment & supplies; plastic processing

(G-655)
BALL BOUNCE AND SPORT INC
Also Called: Hedstrom Plastics
100 Hedstrom Dr (44805-3586)
PHONE..............................419 289-9310
Dave Braeunig, *General Mgr*
EMP: 50
SALES (corp-wide): 195.8MM **Privately Held**
SIC: 5092 Toys
PA: Ball, Bounce And Sport, Inc.
1 Hedstrom Dr
Ashland OH 44805
419 289-9310

(G-656)
BCU ELECTRIC INC
1019 Us Highway 250 N (44805-9474)
PHONE..............................419 281-8944
Bennie Uselton, *President*
Brenda Uselton, *Treasurer*
EMP: 40
SQ FT: 6,000
SALES (est): 10.5MM **Privately Held**
WEB: www.bcuelectric.com
SIC: 1731 General electrical contractor

(G-657)
BENDON INC (PA)
1840 S Baney Rd (44805-3524)
PHONE..............................419 207-3600
Benjamin Ferguson, *President*
Brent Bowers, *Editor*
Terry Gerwig, *Exec VP*
Jenny Hastings, *Exec VP*
Don Myers II, *Senior VP*
▲ **EMP:** 54
SQ FT: 220,000
SALES (est): 31.4MM **Privately Held**
WEB: www.bendonpub.com
SIC: 2731 5999 5961 5092 Books: publishing only; educational aids & electronic training materials; educational supplies & equipment, mail order; educational toys

(G-658)
BOOKMASTERS INC (PA)
Also Called: Atlasbooks
30 Amberwood Pkwy (44805-9765)
PHONE..............................419 281-1802
Tony Proe, *President*
Raymond Sevin, *President*
Karen Broach, *Publisher*
Jessica Phillips, *Publisher*
Ken Fultz, *General Mgr*
◆ **EMP:** 122
SQ FT: 180,000

SALES (est): 58.4MM **Privately Held**
WEB: www.atlasbooks.com
SIC: 7389 2752 2731 2791 Printers' services: folding, collating; commercial printing, lithographic; book publishing; typesetting; books, periodicals & newspapers

(G-659)
BRETHREN CARE INC
Also Called: BLOOMFIELD COTTAGES
2140 Center St Ofc (44805-4380)
PHONE..............................419 289-0803
Jay Brooks, *CEO*
Lori Spring, *Food Svc Dir*
Tim Pond, *Associate*
EMP: 200
SQ FT: 38,000
SALES (est): 15.1MM **Privately Held**
WEB: www.brethrencarevillage.org
SIC: 8052 6513 8051 Intermediate care facilities; apartment building operators; skilled nursing care facilities

(G-660)
BRETHREN CARE VILLAGE LLC
2140 Center St (44805-4376)
PHONE..............................419 289-1585
Troy Snyder, *CEO*
Matthew McFarland, *CFO*
Mindy Wilson, *Social Dir*
Kim Messer, *Food Svc Dir*
EMP: 99
SQ FT: 49,810
SALES (est): 299.2K **Privately Held**
SIC: 8059 Personal care home, with health care

(G-661)
BUREN INSURANCE GROUP INC (PA)
Also Called: Padgett-Young & Associates
1101 Sugarbush Dr (44805-9400)
PHONE..............................419 281-8060
Tim Buren, *President*
Jeffrey Buren, *Vice Pres*
Dale Roberts, *CFO*
EMP: 38
SQ FT: 1,200
SALES (est): 12.8MM **Privately Held**
WEB: www.barnardagency.com
SIC: 6411 Insurance agents

(G-662)
CASTLE CONSTRUCTION CO INC
588 Us Highway 250 E (44805-8919)
PHONE..............................419 289-1122
John Makuch, *President*
EMP: 38
SALES (est): 3.7MM **Privately Held**
SIC: 1751 Framing contractor

(G-663)
CATHOLIC CHARITIES CORPORATION
Also Called: Catholic Charities Services
34 W 2nd St Ste 18 (44805-2201)
PHONE..............................419 289-1903
Cathy Themens, *Director*
EMP: 25 **Privately Held**
WEB: www.catholic-action.org
SIC: 8399 8322 Fund raising organization, non-fee basis; child related social services
PA: Catholic Charities Corporation
7911 Detroit Ave
Cleveland OH 44102

(G-664)
CATHOLIC DIOCESE OF CLEVELAND
Also Called: Saint Edward's Church
501 Cottage St (44805-2125)
PHONE..............................419 289-7224
James J Cassidy, *Pastor*
EMP: 30
SALES (corp-wide): 79.9MM **Privately Held**
WEB: www.oce-ocs.org
SIC: 8661 6512 Catholic Church; auditorium & hall operation

PA: Catholic Diocese Of Cleveland
1404 E 9th St Ste 201
Cleveland OH 44114
216 696-6525

(G-665)
CENTERRA CO-OP (PA)
813 Clark Ave (44805-1967)
PHONE..................................419 281-2153
Jean Bratton, *CEO*
William Bullock, *CFO*
EMP: 30
SALES: 174.6MM **Privately Held**
WEB: www.tc-feed.com
SIC: 5983 5261 5999 2048 Fuel oil dealers; fertilizer; feed & farm supply; bird food, prepared; gases, liquefied petroleum (propane)

(G-666)
CHANDLER SYSTEMS INCORPORATED
Also Called: Best Controls Company
710 Orange St (44805-1725)
PHONE..................................888 363-9434
William Chandler III, *President*
Bill Chandler, *Principal*
Polly Chandler, *Admin Sec*
▲ **EMP:** 65
SQ FT: 52,000
SALES (est): 25.3MM **Privately Held**
WEB: www.chandlersystemsinc.com
SIC: 5074 3625 3823 Water purification equipment; relays & industrial controls

(G-667)
CHARLES RIVER LABS ASHLAND LLC (DH)
1407 George Rd (44805-8946)
PHONE..................................419 282-8700
David Spaight, *CEO*
Lynn Myers, *COO*
Evelyn Tanchevski, *Project Mgr*
Robert Wally, *Opers Mgr*
Heather Reynolds, *Purchasing*
EMP: 111
SALES (est): 111.8MM
SALES (corp-wide): 2.2B **Publicly Held**
SIC: 8733 Research institute
HQ: Charles River Laboratories Sa Usa, Inc.
30 Two Bridges Rd Ste 200
Fairfield NJ 07004
919 245-3114

(G-668)
COMPAK INC
605 Westlake Dr (44805-4710)
PHONE..................................419 207-8888
Jerry Baker, *President*
▲ **EMP:** 50
SQ FT: 240,000
SALES (est): 3.6MM **Privately Held**
SIC: 1541 7699 Industrial buildings & warehouses; pumps & pumping equipment repair

(G-669)
COMPANIONS OF ASHLAND LLC (PA)
1241 E Main St (44805-2810)
PHONE..................................419 281-2273
Tiffany Behrendsen,
EMP: 42
SALES (est): 3.1MM **Privately Held**
SIC: 8082 Home health care services

(G-670)
CRYSTAL CARE CENTERS INC
1251 E Main St (44805-2810)
PHONE..................................419 281-9595
Jerry Smith, *Owner*
EMP: 40 **Privately Held**
SIC: 8051 Convalescent home with continuous nursing care
PA: Crystal Care Centers Inc
1159 Wyandotte Ave
Mansfield OH 44906

(G-671)
D-R TRAINING CENTER & WORKSHOP
Also Called: Dale-Roy School & Training Ctr
1256 Center St (44805-4139)
PHONE..................................419 289-0470

Jerry Simon, *Ch of Bd*
Ron Pagano, *Superintendent*
Kathy Wallace, *Principal*
EMP: 185
SQ FT: 5,000
SALES: 253.8K **Privately Held**
WEB: www.daleroy.org
SIC: 8211 8331 8361 School for the retarded; school for physically handicapped; public special education school; sheltered workshop; residential care

(G-672)
DONLEY FORD-LINCOLN INC (PA)
1641 Claremont Ave (44805-3536)
P.O. Box 405 (44805-0405)
PHONE..................................419 281-3673
Scott Donley, *President*
Ryan Sponsler, *Vice Pres*
Chuck Griffith, *Manager*
Jane Vines, *Executive Asst*
EMP: 45
SQ FT: 25,000
SALES (est): 19.8MM **Privately Held**
WEB: www.donleyford.com
SIC: 5511 5012 Automobiles, new & used; automobiles & other motor vehicles

(G-673)
GOOD SHEPHERD HOME FOR AGED
Also Called: The Good Shepherd
622 Center St (44805-3343)
PHONE..................................614 228-5200
Marshall G Moore, *CEO*
Larry Crowell, *President*
Phil Helser, *CFO*
Henry Kassab, *Accounting Mgr*
Mary Schalmo, *Human Res Dir*
EMP: 170
SQ FT: 82,651
SALES: 10.8MM **Privately Held**
SIC: 8051 Convalescent home with continuous nursing care

(G-674)
GUENTHER MECHANICAL INC
1248 Middle Rowsburg Rd (44805-2813)
P.O. Box 97 (44805-0097)
PHONE..................................419 289-6900
Herbert E Guenther, *President*
James B Andrews, *Vice Pres*
Jim Cutright, *Vice Pres*
EMP: 120
SQ FT: 35,000
SALES (est): 32.2MM **Privately Held**
SIC: 1711 Mechanical contractor

(G-675)
HOSPICE OF NORTH CENTRAL OHIO (PA)
1050 Dauch Dr (44805-8845)
PHONE..................................419 281-7107
Larry McConnell, *COO*
Betty Hennessey, *Marketing Staff*
Ruth Lindsey, *Exec Dir*
EMP: 32
SQ FT: 6,500
SALES: 8.4MM **Privately Held**
WEB: www.hospiceofnorthcentralohio.org
SIC: 8082 8051 8059 Home health care services; skilled nursing care facilities; rest home, with health care

(G-676)
IHEARTCOMMUNICATIONS INC
1197 Us Highway 42 (44805-4575)
PHONE..................................419 289-2605
EMP: 26 **Publicly Held**
SIC: 4832 Radio Broadcast Station
HQ: Iheartcommunications, Inc.
20880 Stone Oak Pkwy
San Antonio TX 78258
210 822-2828

(G-677)
KINGSTON HEALTHCARE COMPANY
Also Called: Kingston of Ashland
20 Amberwood Pkwy (44805-9765)
PHONE..................................419 289-3859
Timothy Callahan, *Branch Mgr*
EMP: 114

SALES (corp-wide): 95.5MM **Privately Held**
WEB: www.kingstonhealthcare.com
SIC: 8051 Convalescent home with continuous nursing care
PA: Kingston Healthcare Company
1 Seagate Ste 1960
Toledo OH 43604
419 247-2880

(G-678)
LUTHERAN SCIAL SVCS CENTL OHIO
Also Called: Good Shepard, The
622 Center St (44805-3343)
PHONE..................................419 289-3523
Michele Cenci, *Vice Pres*
Joe Abraham, *Manager*
Jay Crane, *Records Dir*
EMP: 165
SALES (corp-wide): 49.2MM **Privately Held**
SIC: 8051 Skilled nursing care facilities
PA: Lutheran Social Services Of Central Ohio
500 W Wilson Bridge Rd
Worthington OH 43085
419 289-3523

(G-679)
MCGRAW-HILL SCHOOL EDUCATION H
Also Called: Mc Graw-Hill Educational Pubg
1250 George Rd (44805-8916)
PHONE..................................419 207-7400
Maryellen Valaitis, *Principal*
EMP: 401
SALES (corp-wide): 158MM **Privately Held**
WEB: www.mcgraw-hill.com
SIC: 2731 5192 Books: publishing & printing; books, periodicals & newspapers
HQ: Mcgraw-Hill School Education Holdings, Llc
2 Penn Plz Fl 20
New York NY 10121
646 766-2000

(G-680)
MEDICAL ASSOCIATES OF MID-OHIO
2109 Claremont Ave (44805-3547)
PHONE..................................419 289-1331
Michael Stencel MD, *President*
Christopher D Boyd, *Family Practiti*
EMP: 25
SALES (est): 2MM **Privately Held**
SIC: 8062 General medical & surgical hospitals

(G-681)
MITCHELL & SONS MOVING & STOR
1217 Township Road 1153 (44805-3474)
PHONE..................................419 289-3311
Mitchell Goshinski Jr, *President*
Jennifer McQuellan, *Vice Pres*
Sue Goshinki, *CFO*
EMP: 25
SQ FT: 12,000
SALES: 1.4MM **Privately Held**
WEB: www.mitchellandsons.com
SIC: 4214 4213 Household goods moving & storage, local; household goods transport

(G-682)
MOWRY CONSTRUCTION & ENGRG INC
2105 Claremont Ave (44805-3590)
P.O. Box 188 (44805-0188)
PHONE..................................419 289-2262
Michael Dana Mowry, *President*
Ronald Lee Mowry, *Vice Pres*
EMP: 25
SQ FT: 6,660
SALES: 5MM **Privately Held**
SIC: 1542 1541 Commercial & office building, new construction; commercial & office buildings, renovation & repair; industrial buildings, new construction; renovation, remodeling & repairs: industrial buildings

(G-683)
NATIONAL ASSN LTR CARRIERS
530 Claremont Ave (44805-3177)
PHONE..................................419 289-8359
Kim Dellinger, *Manager*
EMP: 50
SALES (corp-wide): 1.4B **Privately Held**
WEB: www.nalc.org
SIC: 8631 Labor union
PA: National Association Of Letter Carriers
100 Indana Ave Nw Ste 709
Washington DC 20001
202 393-4695

(G-684)
PUMP HOUSE MINISTRIES
1661 Cleveland Rd (44805-1929)
PHONE..................................419 207-3900
Gerald Bruce Wilkinson, *President*
Rich Pate, *Manager*
Rebecca Zickefoose, *Manager*
EMP: 35
SALES (est): 1.2MM **Privately Held**
WEB: www.pumphouseministries.com
SIC: 8322 Social service center

(G-685)
RANDALL R LEAB
Also Called: Accessibility
1895 Township Road 1215 (44805-9414)
PHONE..................................330 689-6263
Randall R Leab, *CFO*
EMP: 45
SALES (est): 434.8K **Privately Held**
SIC: 8399 Community development groups

(G-686)
RETURN POLYMERS INC
400 Westlake Dr (44805-1397)
PHONE..................................419 289-1998
David Foell, *President*
EMP: 65
SQ FT: 26,000
SALES (est): 1.4MM **Privately Held**
WEB: www.returnpolymers.com
SIC: 7389 Custom compound purchased resins

(G-687)
RPG INC
400 Westlake Dr (44805-1397)
PHONE..................................419 289-2757
William Hutira, *President*
Michael Hutira, *Vice Pres*
EMP: 60
SQ FT: 50,000
SALES (est): 5.3MM **Privately Held**
SIC: 4953 Recycling, waste materials

(G-688)
SAMARITAN PROFESSIONAL CORP
1025 Center St (44805-4011)
PHONE..................................419 289-0491
Danny Boggs, *President*
EMP: 50
SALES: 8.3MM **Privately Held**
SIC: 8062 General medical & surgical hospitals

(G-689)
SAMARITAN REGIONAL HEALTH SYS
Also Called: Samaritan Health & Rehab Ctr
2163 Claremont Ave (44805-3547)
PHONE..................................419 281-1330
Don Harris, *Director*
EMP: 30
SALES (corp-wide): 74.6MM **Privately Held**
WEB: www.samaritanhospital.org
SIC: 8062 8049 General medical & surgical hospitals; occupational therapist
PA: Samaritan Regional Health System
1025 Center St
Ashland OH 44805
419 289-0491

(G-690)
SAMARITAN REGIONAL HEALTH SYS (PA)
Also Called: Peoples Hospital
1025 Center St (44805-4097)
PHONE..................................419 289-0491
Danny L Boggs, *CEO*

Matthew Bernhard, *Vice Pres*
Chris Hunt, *Vice Pres*
Alyce Legg, *Vice Pres*
Ron Manchester, *Vice Pres*
EMP: 349
SQ FT: 128,700
SALES: 74.6MM **Privately Held**
WEB: www.samaritanhospital.org
SIC: 8062 General medical & surgical hospitals

(G-691)
SIMONSON CONSTRUCTION SVCS INC
2112 Troy Rd (44805-1396)
PHONE..............................419 281-8299
Robert M Simonson, *President*
Doug Beattie, *Superintendent*
Daniel Moore, *Vice Pres*
Robert Msimonson, *Vice Pres*
Jay Myers, *Vice Pres*
EMP: 72
SQ FT: 11,532
SALES (est): 22.3MM **Privately Held**
SIC: 1542 1521 8741 8712 Commercial & office building, new construction; new construction, single-family houses; construction management; architectural services

(G-692)
SNYDERS-LANCE INC
2041 Claremont Ave (44805-3545)
PHONE..............................419 289-0787
Brenda Marker, *Purch Mgr*
Bob Remington, *Manager*
EMP: 205
SALES (corp-wide): 8.6B **Publicly Held**
SIC: 5145 Snack foods
HQ: Snyder's-Lance, Inc.
13515 Balntyn Corp Pl
Charlotte NC 28277
704 554-1421

(G-693)
SUNSHINE HOMECARE
320 Pleasant St (44805-2029)
P.O. Box 450 (44805-0450)
PHONE..............................419 207-9900
Wendy Maust, *Partner*
Tim Maust, *Partner*
EMP: 25
SALES (est): 936K **Privately Held**
SIC: 8082 Home health care services

(G-694)
THIELS REPLACEMENT SYSTEMS INC
Also Called: Cabinet Restylers
419 E 8th St (44805-1953)
PHONE..............................419 289-6139
Eric Thiel, *President*
Denise Appleby, *Vice Pres*
Anthony Thiel, *Wholesale*
Bobbie Browne, *Manager*
EMP: 56
SQ FT: 50,000
SALES (est): 7.7MM **Privately Held**
SIC: 1751 2541 5211 1799 Window & door (prefabricated) installation; cabinet & finish carpentry; cabinets, lockers & shelving; cabinets, kitchen; bathtub refinishing; gutter & downspout contractor

(G-695)
TRANSFORMATION NETWORK (PA)
1310 Claremont Ave Unit A (44805-3529)
PHONE..............................419 207-1188
Dan Phillip, *President*
Bob Bufford, *Administration*
EMP: 28
SALES: 4.3MM **Privately Held**
WEB: www.transformationnetwork.org
SIC: 8322 Individual & family services

(G-696)
VALLEY TRANSPORTATION INC
Also Called: Valley Fleet
1 Valley Dr (44805)
P.O. Box 305 (44805-0305)
PHONE..............................419 289-6200
Steven Aber, *President*
Karen Aber, *Corp Secy*
Shawn Aber, *Vice Pres*

Michelle Aber, *Manager*
Robert Peck, *Manager*
EMP: 150
SQ FT: 20,000
SALES (est): 22.6MM **Privately Held**
WEB: www.valleytransportation.com
SIC: 4213 Contract haulers

(G-697)
VISITING NRSE ASSN OF CLVELAND
Also Called: Visiting Nurse Assn Ashland
1165 E Main St (44805-2831)
PHONE..............................419 281-2480
Daniel Fedeli, *Exec VP*
Jennifer Hale, *Manager*
Robert Solich, *Manager*
Barbara Walker, *Admin Sec*
EMP: 257
SALES (corp-wide): 11.8MM **Privately Held**
SIC: 8082 Visiting nurse service
PA: The Visiting Nurse Association Of Cleveland
925 Keynote Cir Ste 300
Brooklyn Heights OH 44131
216 931-1400

(G-698)
WARD REALESTATE INC
Also Called: Coldwell Banker
600 E Main St (44805-2699)
PHONE..............................419 281-2000
Robert Ward II, *President*
Polly Ward Chandler, *Vice Pres*
EMP: 25
SQ FT: 1,800
SALES (est): 1.9MM **Privately Held**
WEB: www.wardrealestate.com
SIC: 6531 Real estate agent, residential

(G-699)
WHITCOMB & HESS INC
1020 Cleveland Ave (44805-2710)
PHONE..............................419 289-7007
Jim Hess, *President*
Eric Key, *Partner*
Allison Smith, *Accounting Dir*
Beau Carpenter, *Accountant*
Bruce Ronk, *CPA*
EMP: 25
SALES (est): 2MM **Privately Held**
SIC: 8721 Certified public accountant

(G-700)
Y M C A OF ASHLAND OHIO INC
Also Called: YMCA
207 Miller St (44805-2484)
PHONE..............................419 289-0626
Jerry Seiter, *Exec Dir*
Tiffany Roberts, *Director*
EMP: 55
SQ FT: 443,000
SALES: 1MM **Privately Held**
WEB: www.ashlandymcaoh.org
SIC: 8641 7991 8351 7032 Youth organizations; physical fitness facilities; child day care services; youth camps; individual & family services

---

Ashley
Delaware County

(G-701)
BUCKEYE VLY E ELEMENTARY PTO
522 E High St (43003-9748)
PHONE..............................740 747-2266
Katie Karacson, *Principal*
Katie Karcson, *Principal*
EMP: 70
SALES: 23.7K **Privately Held**
SIC: 8641 Parent-teachers' association

Ashtabula
Ashtabula County

(G-702)
ABC CHILD CARE & LEARNING CTR
Also Called: ABC Day Care
2012 W 11th St (44004-2625)
PHONE..............................440 964-8799
Lireena Spring, *Director*
EMP: 38
SALES: 1MM **Privately Held**
WEB: www.abc-childcare.com
SIC: 8351 Preschool center

(G-703)
ABC PHONES NORTH CAROLINA INC
Also Called: A Wireless
2411 W Prospect Rd (44004-6357)
PHONE..............................440 319-3654
EMP: 26
SALES (corp-wide): 149.9MM **Privately Held**
SIC: 4812 Cellular telephone services
PA: Abc Phones Of North Carolina, Inc.
8510 Colonnade Center Dr
Raleigh NC 27615
252 317-0388

(G-704)
ASH CRAFT INDUSTRIES INC
5959 Green Rd (44004-4746)
PHONE..............................440 224-2177
Linda Perry, *Director*
EMP: 220
SQ FT: 45,000
SALES: 70K **Privately Held**
SIC: 8331 Vocational rehabilitation agency; sheltered workshop

(G-705)
ASHTABULA AREA CITY SCHOOL DST
Also Called: Transportation Department
5921 Gerald Rd (44004-9450)
PHONE..............................440 992-1221
Al Peck, *Principal*
EMP: 35
SALES (corp-wide): 51.3MM **Privately Held**
SIC: 8211 7538 Public senior high school; general automotive repair shops
PA: Ashtabula Area City School District
6610 Sanborn Rd
Ashtabula OH 44004
440 992-1200

(G-706)
ASHTABULA BROADCASTING STATION
Also Called: Wzoo-FM
3226 Jefferson Rd (44004-9112)
P.O. Box 980 (44005-0980)
PHONE..............................440 993-2126
Dana Schulte, *Principal*
EMP: 50
SALES (est): 1.5MM **Privately Held**
SIC: 4832 Radio broadcasting stations, music format

(G-707)
ASHTABULA CHEMICAL CORP
Also Called: Green Leaf Motor Express
4606 State Rd (44004-6210)
P.O. Box 667 (44005-0667)
PHONE..............................440 998-0100
Mark Jarvis, *President*
Jack Jarvis, *Vice Pres*
David Jarvis, *Treasurer*
EMP: 25
SQ FT: 150,000
SALES (est): 1.3MM **Privately Held**
SIC: 4789 6512 Cargo loading & unloading services; commercial & industrial building operation

(G-708)
ASHTABULA CLINIC INC (PA)
2422 Lake Ave (44004-4982)
PHONE..............................440 997-6980
Morris Wasylenki MD, *President*

Glenn E Eippert MD, *Vice Pres*
Suk K Choi, *Treasurer*
John Lee MD, *Med Doctor*
Sang Kim, *Surgeon*
EMP: 81
SQ FT: 13,000
SALES (est): 7.9MM **Privately Held**
WEB: www.ashtabulaclinic.com
SIC: 8011 Clinic, operated by physicians

(G-709)
ASHTABULA CNTY EDUCTL SVC CTR
2630 W 13th St Ste A (44004-2405)
PHONE..............................440 576-4085
John Rubesich, *Superintendent*
Christina Ray, *Human Resources*
EMP: 56
SALES: 40.3K **Privately Held**
SIC: 8211 8748 Specialty education; business consulting

(G-710)
ASHTABULA COMMUNITY COUNSELING
Also Called: Friendship Home
2801 C Ct Unit 2 (44004-4578)
PHONE..............................440 998-6032
Dale Brinker, *Exec Dir*
Stephen Cervas, *Director*
EMP: 55
SALES: 3.8MM **Privately Held**
SIC: 8322 Individual & family services

(G-711)
ASHTABULA COUNTY COMMNTY ACTN (PA)
Also Called: ACCAA
6920 Austinburg Rd (44004-9393)
P.O. Box 2610 (44005-2610)
PHONE..............................440 997-1721
Steve Cervas, *CFO*
Richard J Pepperney, *Exec Dir*
Judith Barris, *Admin Sec*
EMP: 168
SQ FT: 17,380
SALES: 92.1K **Privately Held**
SIC: 8399 Antipoverty board

(G-712)
ASHTABULA COUNTY COMMNTY ACTN
4510 Main Ave (44004-6925)
PHONE..............................440 993-7716
Stephanie Patriarco, *Branch Mgr*
EMP: 78
SALES (corp-wide): 92.1K **Privately Held**
SIC: 8399 Antipoverty board
PA: Ashtabula County Community Action Agency Properties Corporation
6920 Austinburg Rd
Ashtabula OH 44004
440 997-1721

(G-713)
ASHTABULA COUNTY COMMNTY ACTN
3215 Lake Ave (44004-5758)
PHONE..............................440 997-5957
David Jordan, *Branch Mgr*
EMP: 73
SALES (corp-wide): 92.1K **Privately Held**
SIC: 8399 Community action agency
PA: Ashtabula County Community Action Agency Properties Corporation
6920 Austinburg Rd
Ashtabula OH 44004
440 997-1721

(G-714)
ASHTABULA COUNTY COMMUNITY
6920 Austinburg Rd (44004-9393)
PHONE..............................440 997-1721
Richard Pepperney, *CEO*
Steve Cervas, *Director*
EMP: 180
SALES: 9.3MM **Privately Held**
SIC: 8322 Social service center

(G-715)
ASHTABULA COUNTY MEDICAL CTR (PA)
2420 Lake Ave (44004-4970)
PHONE.....................................440 997-2262
Michael Habowski, *CEO*
Mohammad Varghai, *Managing Dir*
Joe Giangola, *Chairman*
Rajwinder Kaur, *Vice Chairman*
Bill Dingledine, *Corp Secy*
EMP: 750
SQ FT: 270,000
SALES: 123.4MM **Privately Held**
WEB: www.ashtabulacountymedicalcen-ter.com
SIC: **8062** General medical & surgical hospitals

(G-716)
ASHTABULA COUNTY MEDICAL CTR
2422 Lake Ave (44004-4985)
PHONE.....................................440 997-6960
David Alpeter, *Manager*
Mark Verdun, *Surgeon*
Crystal Severino, *Asst Director*
EMP: 200
SALES (corp-wide): 119.6MM **Privately Held**
WEB: www.ashtabulacountymedicalcen-ter.com
SIC: **8062 8011** General medical & surgical hospitals; offices & clinics of medical doctors
PA: Ashtabula County Medical Center
  2420 Lake Ave
  Ashtabula OH 44004
  440 997-2262

(G-717)
ASHTABULA DENTAL ASSOCIATES
Also Called: Laukhuf, Gary DDS
5005 State Rd (44004-6265)
PHONE.....................................440 992-3146
William Sockman, *President*
Gregory Seymour DDS, *Vice Pres*
▲ EMP: 45
SQ FT: 7,700
SALES (est): 4.2MM **Privately Held**
SIC: **8021** Dentists' office

(G-718)
ASHTABULA JOB AND FAMILY SVCS
2924 Donahoe Dr (44004-4540)
PHONE.....................................440 994-2020
Ronald Smith, *CFO*
Patrick Arcaro, *Director*
EMP: 170
SALES (est): 2.1MM **Privately Held**
SIC: **8322** Senior citizens' center or association

(G-719)
ASHTABULA RGIONAL HM HLTH SVCS
2131 Lake Ave Ste 2 (44004-3466)
P.O. Box 1428 (44005-1428)
PHONE.....................................440 992-4663
Kerry Gerken, *President*
Sue Shadle, *Info Tech Dir*
Connie Forinash, *Executive*
EMP: 80 EST: 1974
SQ FT: 1,200
SALES (est): 5.3MM **Privately Held**
SIC: **8082** Home health care services

(G-720)
ASHTABULA STEVEDORE COMPANY
Also Called: Pinney Doc Co
1149 E 5th St (44004-3513)
PHONE.....................................440 964-7186
Maynard B Walker, *President*
Joe Del Priore, *Vice Pres*
EMP: 40
SQ FT: 120
SALES (est): 1.1MM **Privately Held**
SIC: **7363** Help supply services

(G-721)
AYRSHIRE INC
1432 E 21st St (44004-4062)
PHONE.....................................440 992-0743
Ed Furman, *Manager*
EMP: 70
SALES (est): 4MM **Privately Held**
SIC: **1711 7359** Mechanical contractor; equipment rental & leasing

(G-722)
BEATITUDE HOUSE
3404 Lake Ave (44004-5700)
PHONE.....................................440 992-0265
Sarah Masek, *Branch Mgr*
EMP: 26 **Privately Held**
SIC: **8322** Emergency shelters
PA: Beatitude House
  238 Tod Ln
  Youngstown OH

(G-723)
C TED FORSBERG
5005 State Rd (44004-6265)
PHONE.....................................440 992-3145
C Ted Forsberg, *Owner*
EMP: 40
SALES (est): 1.3MM **Privately Held**
SIC: **8021** Offices & clinics of dentists

(G-724)
CELLCO PARTNERSHIP
Also Called: Verizon Wireless
3315 N Ridge Rd E (44004-4300)
PHONE.....................................440 998-3111
EMP: 76
SALES (corp-wide): 130.8B **Publicly Held**
SIC: **4812** Cellular telephone services
HQ: Cellco Partnership
  1 Verizon Way
  Basking Ridge NJ 07920

(G-725)
CHALK BOX GET FIT LLC
5521 Main Ave (44004-7037)
PHONE.....................................440 992-9619
Kathy Speelman, *Mng Member*
David Speelman,
EMP: 25
SALES: 250K **Privately Held**
SIC: **5941 5699 7991** Gymnasium equipment; sports apparel; physical fitness facilities

(G-726)
CHS-LAKE ERIE INC
Also Called: CARINGTON PARK
2217 West Ave (44004-3107)
PHONE.....................................440 964-8446
Brian Colleran, *President*
Kelly Johnson,
EMP: 200
SALES: 11.8MM **Privately Held**
SIC: **8051** Mental retardation hospital

(G-727)
CITY TAXICAB & TRANSFER CO
Also Called: Black Eagle Transfer Company
1753 W Prospect Rd (44004-6621)
P.O. Box 3076 (44005-3076)
PHONE.....................................440 992-2156
Bill Peek, *President*
EMP: 30
SQ FT: 600
SALES (est): 2.1MM **Privately Held**
SIC: **4111 4121 4215** Local & suburban transit; taxicabs; package delivery, vehicular

(G-728)
COMMUNITY CARE AMBLANCE NETWRK (PA)
115 E 24th St (44004-3417)
P.O. Box 1340 (44005-1340)
PHONE.....................................440 992-1401
Julie Rose, *Exec Dir*
Ashtabula County Medical Cente, *Shareholder*
Memorial Hospital of Geneva, *Shareholder*
EMP: 75
SQ FT: 36,000
SALES: 15.6MM **Privately Held**
WEB: www.ccan.org
SIC: **4119** Ambulance service

(G-729)
COMMUNITY COUNSLNG CTR ASHTABU (PA)
2801 C Ct Unit 2 (44004-4578)
PHONE.....................................440 998-4210
Kathy L Regal, *CEO*
Lynton Becker, *Med Doctor*
Christine Schulz, *Med Doctor*
EMP: 85 EST: 1961
SALES: 5.7MM **Privately Held**
SIC: **8093** Mental health clinic, outpatient

(G-730)
CONTINUUM HOME CARE INC
Also Called: Home Health Care
1100 Lake Ave (44004-2930)
PHONE.....................................440 964-3332
Robert L Huff, *President*
Lynne Huff, *President*
EMP: 37
SALES (est): 1.6MM **Privately Held**
SIC: **8082** Home health care services

(G-731)
COUNTRY CLUB RETIREMENT CENTER
Also Called: Country Club Center III
925 E 26th St (44004-5061)
PHONE.....................................440 992-0022
Gabriella Vendetti, *Manager*
Paul Mikulin, *Info Tech Mgr*
EMP: 70
SALES (corp-wide): 5.4MM **Privately Held**
SIC: **8059** Nursing home, except skilled & intermediate care facility
PA: Country Club Retirement Center, Inc
  55801 Conno Mara Dr
  Bellaire OH 43906
  740 671-9330

(G-732)
COUNTY OF ASHTABULA
Also Called: Ashtabula Board of Mental
2505 S Ridge Rd E (44004-4464)
PHONE.....................................440 224-2157
Patrick Guliano, *Principal*
EMP: 125 **Privately Held**
WEB: www.help-a-child.com
SIC: **8322** Rehabilitation services
PA: County Of Ashtabula
  25 W Jefferson St
  Jefferson OH 44047

(G-733)
COUNTY OF ASHTABULA
Also Called: Ashtabula Cnty Chldren Svcs Bd
3914 C Ct (44004-4572)
P.O. Box 1175 (44005-1175)
PHONE.....................................440 998-1811
Diane Solembrino, *Director*
EMP: 80 **Privately Held**
WEB: www.help-a-child.com
SIC: **8322** Child related social services
PA: County Of Ashtabula
  2505 S Ridge Rd E
  Ashtabula OH 44004
  440 224-2155

(G-734)
COUNTY OF ASHTABULA
Also Called: Ashtabula Welfare Department
2924 Donahoe Dr (44004-4540)
P.O. Box 1650 (44005-1650)
PHONE.....................................440 994-1206
Paul Fuller, *Director*
EMP: 100 **Privately Held**
SIC: **6371** Pension, health & welfare funds
PA: County Of Ashtabula
  25 W Jefferson St
  Jefferson OH 44047

(G-735)
CSX TRANSPORTATION INC
1709 E Prospect Rd (44004-5815)
PHONE.....................................440 992-0871
EMP: 39
SALES (corp-wide): 12.2B **Publicly Held**
SIC: **4011** Railroads, line-haul operating
HQ: Csx Transportation, Inc.
  500 Water St
  Jacksonville FL 32202
  904 359-3100

(G-736)
DELTA RAILROAD CNSTR INC (PA)
2648 W Prospect Rd Frnt (44004-6372)
P.O. Box 1398 (44005-1398)
PHONE.....................................440 992-2997
Larry F Laurello, *President*
Michael A Laurello, *Vice Pres*
Paul J Laurello, *Vice Pres*
Rick R Ryel, *Vice Pres*
Linda Laurello, *CFO*
▲ EMP: 100
SQ FT: 82,000
SALES: 29.5MM **Privately Held**
WEB: www.deltarr.com
SIC: **1629** Railroad & railway roadbed construction

(G-737)
EAST OHIO GAS COMPANY
Also Called: Dominion Energy Ohio
7001 Center Rd (44004-8948)
PHONE.....................................216 736-6120
Dave Findley, *Branch Mgr*
EMP: 59
SALES (corp-wide): 13.3B **Publicly Held**
SIC: **4924** Natural gas distribution
HQ: The East Ohio Gas Company
  1201 E 55th St
  Cleveland OH 44103
  800 362-7557

(G-738)
GOODWILL INDS OF ASHTABULA (PA)
Also Called: Goodwill Industry
621 Goodwill Dr (44004-3232)
P.O. Box 2926 (44005-2926)
PHONE.....................................440 964-3565
Doreen Costello, *Finance Dir*
Dorthey Altonen, *Exec Dir*
EMP: 100
SQ FT: 35,000
SALES: 3.4MM **Privately Held**
SIC: **8331 5932** Vocational rehabilitation agency; used merchandise stores

(G-739)
HEALTH SMILE CENTER
Also Called: Healthy Smile Center The
2010 W 19th St (44004-9709)
PHONE.....................................440 992-2700
Martin Crombie, *Owner*
EMP: 25
SALES (est): 1.3MM **Privately Held**
SIC: **8072 8021** Artificial teeth production; offices & clinics of dentists

(G-740)
HOSPICE OF THE WESTERN RESERVE
1166 Lake Ave (44004-2930)
PHONE.....................................440 997-6619
Cathy Westcott, *Manager*
Mary Temperney, *Director*
EMP: 57
SALES (corp-wide): 89.8MM **Privately Held**
SIC: **8082 8322** Home health care services; individual & family services
PA: Hospice Of The Western Reserve, Inc
  17876 Saint Clair Ave
  Cleveland OH 44110
  216 383-2222

(G-741)
ID NETWORKS INC
7720 Jefferson Rd (44004-9025)
P.O. Box 2986 (44005-2986)
PHONE.....................................440 992-0062
Douglas G Blenman, *President*
Bonnie Blenman, *Corp Secy*
Patrick Foster, *Project Mgr*
Corey Yovich, *Project Mgr*
Doug Bleman, *Manager*
EMP: 31
SALES (est): 5.9MM **Privately Held**
WEB: www.idnetworks.com
SIC: **7373** Systems software development services

(G-742)
IHEARTCOMMUNICATIONS INC
Port Erie Communications
3226 Jefferson Rd (44004-9112)
P.O. Box 980 (44005-0980)
PHONE.....................440 992-9700
Bill Kelly, *Manager*
EMP: 50 Publicly Held
SIC: 4832 Radio broadcasting stations
HQ: Iheartcommunications, Inc.
20880 Stone Oak Pkwy
San Antonio TX 78258
210 822-2828

(G-743)
JBJ ENTERPRISES INC
Also Called: Top Performance
2450 W Prospect Rd (44004-6358)
PHONE.....................440 992-6051
James Monday Jr, *President*
Elizabeth Monday, *Vice Pres*
John Monday, *Treasurer*
EMP: 45
SQ FT: 2,000
SALES (est): 1.3MM Privately Held
WEB: www.jbjenterprises.com
SIC: 7231 Hairdressers

(G-744)
JERSEY CENTRAL PWR & LIGHT CO
Also Called: Firstenergy
2210 S Ridge W (44004-9047)
PHONE.....................440 994-8271
Bill Larson, *Manager*
EMP: 67 Publicly Held
WEB: www.jersey-central-power-
light.monmouth.n
SIC: 4911 Electric services
HQ: Jersey Central Power & Light Com-
pany
76 S Main St
Akron OH 44308
800 736-3402

(G-745)
LOWES HOME CENTERS LLC
2416 Dillon Dr (44004-4102)
PHONE.....................440 998-6555
John Matras, *Manager*
Deanna Schultz,
EMP: 150
SALES (corp-wide): 68.6B Publicly Held
SIC: 5211 5031 5722 5064 Home cen-
ters; building materials, exterior; building
materials, interior; household appliance
stores; electrical appliances, television &
radio
HQ: Lowe's Home Centers, Llc
1605 Curtis Bridge Rd
Wilkesboro NC 28697
336 658-4000

(G-746)
LT HARNETT TRUCKING INC
2440 State Rd (44004-4163)
PHONE.....................440 997-5528
Chuck Hughes, *Branch Mgr*
EMP: 50
**SALES (corp-wide): 11.9MM Privately
Held**
SIC: 4212 4213 Local trucking, without
storage; trucking; trucking, except local
PA: L.T. Harnett Trucking, Inc.
7431 State Route 7
Kinsman OH 44428
330 876-2701

(G-747)
LT TRUCKING INC
Also Called: Harnett Vision Transportation
2440 State Rd (44004-4163)
PHONE.....................440 997-5528
David Harnett, *President*
Chuck Hughes, *Manager*
Kevin Rybaik, *Manager*
EMP: 50
SALES: 15MM Privately Held
SIC: 4213 Contract haulers

(G-748)
**NEW AVENUES TO
INDEPENDENCE**
4230 Lake Ave (44004-6845)
PHONE.....................888 853-8905

Carol Blaasco, *President*
EMP: 25
**SALES (corp-wide): 14.6MM Privately
Held**
SIC: 8361 Home for the mentally handi-
capped
PA: New Avenues To Independence Inc
17608 Euclid Ave
Cleveland OH 44112
216 481-1907

(G-749)
**NORFOLK SOUTHERN
CORPORATION**
645 E 6th St (44004-3517)
PHONE.....................440 992-2274
Ben Johnson, *Manager*
EMP: 40
SALES (corp-wide): 11.4B Publicly Held
WEB: www.nscorp.com
SIC: 4011 Railroads, line-haul operating
PA: Norfolk Southern Corporation
3 Commercial Pl Ste 1a
Norfolk VA 23510
757 629-2680

(G-750)
**NORFOLK SOUTHERN
CORPORATION**
Also Called: Norfolk Sthern Ashtbula Cltock
2886 Harbor Sta (44004)
PHONE.....................440 992-2215
Brian Johnson, *Manager*
EMP: 55
SALES (corp-wide): 11.4B Publicly Held
WEB: www.nscorp.com
SIC: 4011 Railroads, line-haul operating
PA: Norfolk Southern Corporation
3 Commercial Pl Ste 1a
Norfolk VA 23510
757 629-2680

(G-751)
PARK HAVEN INC
Also Called: Park Haven Home
6434 Lee Road Ext (44004-4814)
PHONE.....................440 992-9441
Fax: 440 992-7592
EMP: 50
SALES (est): 1.5MM Privately Held
SIC: 8059 Nursing Home

(G-752)
**PINNEY DOCK & TRANSPORT
LLC**
1149 E 5th St (44004-3513)
P.O. Box 41 (44005-0041)
PHONE.....................440 964-7186
Lee Demers,
Bradley Frank,
◆ **EMP: 33 EST: 1953**
SQ FT: 20,000
SALES (est): 36.1MM Publicly Held
SIC: 3731 4491 5032 Drydocks, floating;
docks, piers & terminals; limestone
PA: Kinder Morgan Inc
1001 La St Ste 1000
Houston TX 77002

(G-753)
SALUTARY PROVIDERS INC
Also Called: Carington Park
2217 West Ave (44004-3107)
PHONE.....................440 964-8446
Cindy Woodburn, *Manager*
EMP: 203
**SALES (corp-wide): 2.1MM Privately
Held**
SIC: 8059 8052 8051 Convalescent
home; intermediate care facilities; skilled
nursing care facilities
PA: Salutary Providers Inc
8230 Beckett Park Dr
West Chester OH

(G-754)
SHAWNEE OPTICAL INC
3705 State Rd (44004-5957)
PHONE.....................440 997-2020
Bob Leonardi, *Branch Mgr*
EMP: 51

**SALES (corp-wide): 2.4MM Privately
Held**
SIC: 8042 5995 5049 Contact lense specialist optometrist; optical goods stores;
optical goods
PA: Shawnee Optical Inc
2240 E 38th St Ste 2
Erie PA 16510
814 824-3937

(G-755)
SHELLEY ELIZABETH BLUM
Also Called: Hobby Smile Center
2614 W 13th St (44004-2405)
PHONE.....................440 964-0542
Shelley E Blum, *Owner*
Martin Crombie DDS, *Principal*
Shelley Blum, *Manager*
EMP: 26
SALES (est): 576.6K Privately Held
SIC: 8021 Dentists' office

(G-756)
**SPECTRUM MGT HOLDG CO
LLC**
2904 State Rd (44004-5328)
PHONE.....................440 319-3271
Valentin Vargas, *Branch Mgr*
EMP: 83
SALES (corp-wide): 43.6B Publicly Held
SIC: 4841 Cable television services
HQ: Spectrum Management Holding Com-
pany, Llc
400 Atlantic St
Stamford CT 06901
203 905-7801

(G-757)
**UNION INDUSTRIAL
CONTRACTORS**
Also Called: UIC General Contractors
1800 E 21st St (44004-4012)
P.O. Box 1718 (44005-1718)
PHONE.....................440 998-7871
Kim Kidner, *President*
Ryan Cochran, *Admin Sec*
EMP: 40 EST: 1978
SQ FT: 22,000
SALES: 10.9MM Privately Held
WEB: www.uicconstruction.com
SIC: 1542 1541 Commercial & office build-
ing, new construction; industrial buildings,
new construction

(G-758)
**VETERANS HEALTH
ADMINISTRATION**
Also Called: Ashtabula County V A Clinic
4314 Main Ave Frnt (44004-6894)
PHONE.....................866 463-0912
EMP: 264 Publicly Held
WEB: www.veterans-ru.org
SIC: 8011 9451 Clinic, operated by physi-
cians; psychiatric clinic;
HQ: Veterans Health Administration
810 Vermont Ave Nw
Washington DC 20420

(G-759)
VOLPONE ENTERPRISES INC
Also Called: Ziggler Heating
5223 N Ridge Rd W Ste 2 (44004-8851)
PHONE.....................440 969-1141
Tim Volpone, *President*
EMP: 27
SALES (est): 1.3MM Privately Held
SIC: 1711 Warm air heating & air condi-
tioning contractor

(G-760)
**YMCA OF ASHTABULA COUNTY
INC**
Also Called: ASHTABULA COUNTY FAMILY
Y
263 W Prospect Rd (44004-5841)
PHONE.....................440 997-5321
Stacy Herr, *Vice Pres*
Henri De Villiers, *Finance*
Carol Molnar, *Director*
Bonnie Bordeau, *Admin Sec*
EMP: 75
SALES: 1.3MM Privately Held
SIC: 8641 7997 Social associations;
recreation association; membership
sports & recreation clubs

Ashville
Pickaway County

(G-761)
**CITIZENS BANK OF ASHVILLE
OHIO**
26 Main St E (43103-1512)
P.O. Box 227 (43103-0227)
PHONE.....................740 983-2511
Calvin Gebhart, *President*
Lafern Bailey, *Vice Pres*
David Moody, *Vice Pres*
Chris Yingling, *Vice Pres*
Robert Black, *Director*
EMP: 27
SALES: 4.4MM Privately Held
SIC: 6022 State trust companies accepting
deposits, commercial

(G-762)
**NOXIOUS VEGETATION
CONTROL INC**
Also Called: Novco
14923 State Route 104 (43103-9411)
P.O. Box 21757, Columbus (43221-0757)
PHONE.....................614 486-8994
Charles W Thomas, *President*
Clarence Wissinger, *General Mgr*
Todd Thomas, *Vice Pres*
Clarence Wissiner, *Vice Pres*
Sandy Harris, *Accountant*
EMP: 100
SQ FT: 8,000
SALES (est): 29.1MM Privately Held
WEB: www.helicopterminitmen.com
SIC: 5191 Herbicides

Athens
Athens County

(G-763)
**AMERICAN ELECTRIC POWER
CO INC**
9135 State Route 682 (45701-9102)
PHONE.....................740 594-1988
Dave Corrigan, *Principal*
Charles Spires, *Opers Mgr*
EMP: 45
SALES (corp-wide): 16.2B Publicly Held
SIC: 4911 Distribution, electric power
PA: American Electric Power Company, Inc.
1 Riverside Plz Fl 1 # 1
Columbus OH 43215
614 716-1000

(G-764)
APPALACHIAN COMMUNITY VISI
444 W Union St Ste C (45701-2494)
PHONE.....................740 594-8226
Deborah Sechkar, *Vice Pres*
Margaret Frey, *Director*
EMP: 75
SQ FT: 8,000
SALES: 3.5MM Privately Held
WEB: www.acvna.org
SIC: 8082 Visiting nurse service

(G-765)
ATCO INC
1002 E State St Ste 5 (45701-2149)
PHONE.....................740 592-6659
Jodi Harris, *Superintendent*
▲ **EMP: 150**
SALES: 356.6K Privately Held
WEB: www.atcoinc.org
SIC: 8331 7331 Sheltered workshop; di-
rect mail advertising services

(G-766)
**ATHENS COUNTY BOARD OF
DEV (PA)**
801 W Union St (45701-9411)
PHONE.....................740 594-3539
Kevin Davis, *Superintendent*
EMP: 93
SQ FT: 1,200
SALES: 10.7MM Privately Held
SIC: 8322 Social services for the handi-
capped

GEOGRAPHIC

(G-767)
ATHENS GOLF & COUNTRY CLUB (PA)
Also Called: ATHENS COUNTRY CLUB
7606 Country Club Rd (45701-8844)
PHONE..................740 592-1655
Rick Oremus, *President*
Rick Frame, *General Mgr*
Mark Felcman, *Vice Pres*
EMP: 50
SQ FT: 5,000
SALES: 922.2K **Privately Held**
SIC: 7997 Country club, membership; golf club, membership; swimming club, membership; tennis club, membership

(G-768)
ATHENS MOLD AND MACHINE INC
180 Mill St (45701-2627)
PHONE..................740 593-6613
Jack D Thornton, *President*
Mark Thornton, *Vice Pres*
EMP: 81
SQ FT: 70,000
SALES (est): 11.5MM **Privately Held**
SIC: 3544 3599 7692 Special dies & tools; machine shop, jobbing & repair; welding repair

(G-769)
ATHENS OH 1013 LLC
Also Called: Fairfield Inn
924 E State St (45701-2116)
PHONE..................740 589-5839
Jack Bortle, *Mng Member*
EMP: 25
SQ FT: 47,613
SALES (est): 785.6K **Privately Held**
SIC: 7011 Hotels & motels

(G-770)
ATHENS-HCKING CNTY RECYCL CTRS
Also Called: Refuse / Recycling
5991 Industrial Park Rd (45701-8736)
P.O. Box 2607 (45701-5407)
PHONE..................740 594-5312
Joe Kalser, *Principal*
Joe Kasler, *Manager*
EMP: 26
SQ FT: 150,000
SALES: 3MM **Privately Held**
SIC: 4953 Recycling, waste materials

(G-771)
ATTRACTIONS
19 N Court St (45701-2420)
PHONE..................740 592-5600
Leslie Cornwell, *Owner*
EMP: 29
SALES (est): 690K **Privately Held**
SIC: 7231 7299 7241 Hairdressers; tanning salon; barber shops

(G-772)
CORPORATION FOR OH APPALACHIAN (PA)
Also Called: Coad
1 Pinchot Pl (45701-2135)
P.O. Box 787 (45701-0787)
PHONE..................740 594-8499
Owen Yoder, *CFO*
Ronald Rees, *Director*
EMP: 32 **EST:** 1972
SQ FT: 168
SALES: 25.3MM **Privately Held**
WEB: www.coadinc.org
SIC: 8322 Individual & family services

(G-773)
COUNTY OF ATHENS
Also Called: County Engineers Office
16000 Canineville Rd (45701)
PHONE..................740 593-5514
Archie Stanley, *Principal*
EMP: 27
SQ FT: 20,000 **Privately Held**
SIC: 8711 9111 Consulting engineer; county supervisors' & executives' offices
PA: County Of Athens
15 S Court St Rm 234
Athens OH 45701
740 592-3219

(G-774)
COUNTY OF ATHENS
Also Called: Athens County Childrens Svcs
18 Stonybrook Dr (45701-1451)
P.O. Box 1046 (45701-1046)
PHONE..................740 592-3061
Catherine Hill, *Director*
EMP: 80 **Privately Held**
WEB: www.opd.state.oh.us
SIC: 8351 9111 Child day care services; county supervisors' & executives' offices
PA: County Of Athens
15 S Court St Rm 234
Athens OH 45701
740 592-3219

(G-775)
DAVID R WHITE SERVICES INC (PA)
Also Called: David White Services
5315 Hebbardsville Rd (45701-8973)
P.O. Box 250 (45701-0250)
PHONE..................740 594-8381
Gayman Chambers, *President*
EMP: 38
SQ FT: 16,000
SALES (est): 6.9MM **Privately Held**
SIC: 1711 Warm air heating & air conditioning contractor

(G-776)
DON WOOD INC
Also Called: Don Wood Buick, Oldsmobile
900 E State St (45701-2116)
PHONE..................740 593-6641
Don Wood, *CEO*
EMP: 100
SQ FT: 10,000
SALES (est): 17.7MM **Privately Held**
SIC: 5511 7538 Automobiles, new & used; general automotive repair shops

(G-777)
DON WOOD INC
Also Called: Don Wood GMC & Toyota
900 E State St (45701-2116)
PHONE..................740 593-6641
Donald Wood, *President*
Jeff Wood, *President*
Ryan Leadbetter, *General Mgr*
Brenda K Wood, *Treasurer*
Scott Carpenter, *Sales Mgr*
EMP: 70
SALES (est): 29.9MM **Privately Held**
WEB: www.donwood.com
SIC: 5511 7538 5521 Automobiles, new & used; general automotive repair shops; used car dealers

(G-778)
ECHOING HILLS VILLAGE INC
Also Called: Echoing Meadows
528 1/2 Richland Ave (45701-3748)
PHONE..................740 594-3541
Heather Buckley, *Social Dir*
Mark Hutchinson, *Administration*
EMP: 65
SALES (corp-wide): 27MM **Privately Held**
WEB: www.echoinghillsvillage.org
SIC: 7032 8361 Sporting & recreational camps; residential care
PA: Echoing Hills Village, Inc.
36272 County Road 79
Warsaw OH 43844
740 327-2311

(G-779)
EDISON BIOTECHNOLOGY INSTITUTE
101 Konneker The Rdgs (45701)
PHONE..................740 593-4713
Shiyong Wu, *Director*
EMP: 45
SALES (est): 1.9MM **Privately Held**
SIC: 8731 Biological research

(G-780)
ERIC HASEMEIER DO
Also Called: On Call Medical
510 W Union St Ste A (45701-2331)
PHONE..................740 594-7979
Eric Hasemeier Do, *Owner*
EMP: 25

SALES (est): 780K **Privately Held**
SIC: 8031 8011 Offices & clinics of osteopathic physicians; offices & clinics of medical doctors

(G-781)
G & J PEPSI-COLA BOTTLERS INC
2001 E State St (45701-2125)
PHONE..................740 593-3366
Curt Allison, *Branch Mgr*
EMP: 51
SALES (corp-wide): 418.3MM **Privately Held**
WEB: www.gjpepsi.com
SIC: 4225 5149 2086 General warehousing; beverages, except coffee & tea; carbonated beverages, nonalcoholic: bottled & canned
PA: G & J Pepsi-Cola Bottlers Inc
9435 Waterstone Blvd # 390
Cincinnati OH 45249
513 785-6060

(G-782)
HAVAR INC (PA)
396 Richland Ave (45701-3204)
P.O. Box 460 (45701-0460)
PHONE..................740 594-3533
Jerrad Willis, *Business Mgr*
Mitch Daugherty, *Program Mgr*
Barb Mugrage, *Program Mgr*
Lisa Simpson, *Program Mgr*
Carla Perry, *Manager*
EMP: 75
SQ FT: 3,300
SALES: 3.6MM **Privately Held**
WEB: www.havar.org
SIC: 8361 8322 Residential care; individual & family services

(G-783)
HEALTH RECOVERY SERVICES INC (PA)
224 Columbus Rd Ste 102 (45701-1350)
P.O. Box 724 (45701-0724)
PHONE..................740 592-6720
Virgina Smith, *Finance Dir*
Jacob Jones, *Manager*
Joe Gay, *Exec Dir*
EMP: 185 **EST:** 1975
SALES: 13.2MM **Privately Held**
WEB: www.hrs.org
SIC: 8069 8361 Alcoholism rehabilitation hospital; rehabilitation center, residential: health care incidental

(G-784)
HOCKING VLY BNK OF ATHENS CO (PA)
7 W Stimson Ave (45701-2649)
PHONE..................740 592-4441
Benedict Weissenrieder, *CEO*
Tammy Bobo, *Vice Pres*
Candy Kemmerer, *Vice Pres*
EMP: 45 **EST:** 1963
SALES: 10.3MM **Privately Held**
SIC: 6022 State trust companies accepting deposits, commercial

(G-785)
HOLZER CLINIC LLC
2131 E State St (45701-2138)
PHONE..................740 589-3100
Sue Campbell, *Manager*
EMP: 112
SALES (corp-wide): 323.8MM **Privately Held**
SIC: 8011 Clinic, operated by physicians
HQ: Holzer Clinic Llc
90 Jackson Pike
Gallipolis OH 45631
740 446-5411

(G-786)
INTEGRATED SERVICES OF APPALA
11 Graham Dr (45701-1430)
P.O. Box 132 (45701-0132)
PHONE..................740 594-6807
Susan Isaac, *President*
Kelly Arbaugh, *Area Mgr*
Karen Kaufman, *Area Mgr*
Samantha Shafer, *Area Mgr*
Beth Flum, *COO*

EMP: 80
SQ FT: 1,000
SALES: 12.9MM **Privately Held**
WEB: www.integratedservice.org
SIC: 8322 8399 8331 Individual & family services; health systems agency; job training & vocational rehabilitation services

(G-787)
JOEY BOYLE
Also Called: Athens Bicycle Club
11 Garfield Ave (45701-1650)
P.O. Box 624 (45701-0624)
PHONE..................216 273-8317
Joey Boyle, *Owner*
EMP: 30
SALES (est): 114K **Privately Held**
SIC: 8641 Civic social & fraternal associations

(G-788)
KAL ELECTRIC INC
5265 Hebbardsville Rd (45701-8973)
PHONE..................740 593-8720
Dirk Walton, *CEO*
Kay Proffitt, *Vice Pres*
Katlyn Walton, *Treasurer*
Laurie Walton, *Treasurer*
EMP: 46
SALES (est): 6.1MM **Privately Held**
WEB: www.kalelectric.com
SIC: 1731 General electrical contractor

(G-789)
KIMES CONVALESCENT CENTER
75 Kimes Ln (45701-3899)
PHONE..................740 593-3391
Richard Buckley, *Owner*
EMP: 45
SALES: 5MM **Privately Held**
SIC: 8051 Convalescent home with continuous nursing care

(G-790)
LAUGHLIN MUSIC & VENDING SVC (PA)
Also Called: Laughlin Music and Vending Svc
148 W Union St (45701-2728)
P.O. Box 547 (45701-0547)
PHONE..................740 593-7778
Harold D Laughlin, *President*
Dewey Laughlin, *Corp Secy*
Naomi Laughlin, *Vice Pres*
EMP: 29
SQ FT: 100,000
SALES (est): 4.3MM **Privately Held**
SIC: 5962 5063 5087 Sandwich & hot food vending machines; electrical apparatus & equipment; laundry equipment & supplies

(G-791)
LOWES HOME CENTERS LLC
983 E State St (45701-2117)
PHONE..................740 589-3750
Dave Matter, *Principal*
Mike Grueser, *Manager*
EMP: 150
SALES (corp-wide): 68.6B **Publicly Held**
SIC: 5211 5031 5722 5064 Home centers; building materials, exterior; building materials, interior; household appliance stores; electrical appliances, television & radio
HQ: Lowe's Home Centers, Llc
1605 Curtis Bridge Rd
Wilkesboro NC 28697
336 658-4000

(G-792)
MENTAL HEALTH AND ADDI SERV
Also Called: Appalchian Bhvioral Healthcare
100 Hospital Dr (45701-2301)
PHONE..................740 594-5000
EMP: 35 **Privately Held**
SIC: 8093 9431 Mental health clinic, outpatient;
HQ: Ohio Department Of Mental Health And Addiction Services
30 E Broad St Fl 8
Columbus OH 43215

(G-793)
OHIO HEALTH PHYSICIAN GROUP
Also Called: River Rose Obstetrics & Gyneco
75 Hospital Dr Ste 216 (45701-2859)
PHONE..............................740 594-8819
Richard F Castrop, *Mng Member*
EMP: 56
SALES (est): 5.1MM **Privately Held**
SIC: 8099 Medical services organization

(G-794)
OHIO STATE UNIVERSITY
Also Called: Southeast Asia Collection
1 Park Pl (45701-5005)
PHONE..............................740 593-2657
Jeff Ferrier, *Manager*
EMP: 100
SALES (corp-wide): 5.8B **Privately Held**
WEB: www.ohio-state.edu
SIC: 8732 8221 Educational research; university
PA: The Ohio State University
Student Acade Servi Bldg
Columbus OH 43210
614 292-6446

(G-795)
OHIO UNIVERSITY
Also Called: Computer Services
3 Station St Apt D (45701-2760)
PHONE..............................740 593-1000
Dewayne Starkey, *Principal*
EMP: 60
SALES (corp-wide): 531.5MM **Privately Held**
WEB: www.zanesville.ohiou.edu
SIC: 7371 8221 Custom computer programming services; university
PA: Ohio University
1 Ohio University
Athens OH 45701
740 593-1000

(G-796)
OHIO UNIVERSITY
Also Called: Woub Public Media
Woub 35 S Cllg St 395 (45701)
PHONE..............................740 593-1771
Tom Hodson, *Director*
EMP: 38
SQ FT: 120,982
SALES (corp-wide): 531.5MM **Privately Held**
SIC: 4833 4832 Television broadcasting stations; radio broadcasting stations, except music format
PA: Ohio University
1 Ohio University
Athens OH 45701
740 593-1000

(G-797)
OHIO UNIVERSITY
Also Called: Woub Channel 20 & 44
35 S College St (45701-2933)
PHONE..............................740 593-1771
Mark Brower, *General Mgr*
Cheri Russo, *Manager*
Steve N Skidmore, *CTO*
Jeannie Jeffers, *Director*
EMP: 35
SALES (corp-wide): 531.5MM **Privately Held**
WEB: www.zanesville.ohiou.edu
SIC: 4832 4833 Radio broadcasting stations; television broadcasting stations
PA: Ohio University
1 Ohio University
Athens OH 45701
740 593-1000

(G-798)
OHIO UNIVERSITY
Also Called: Medical Office
227 W Washington St Apt 1 (45701-2442)
PHONE..............................740 593-2195
Peter Dane, *Principal*
EMP: 52
SALES (corp-wide): 531.5MM **Privately Held**
WEB: www.zanesville.ohiou.edu
SIC: 8011 8211 Medical centers; elementary & secondary schools

PA: Ohio University
1 Ohio University
Athens OH 45701
740 593-1000

(G-799)
OHIO UNIVERSITY
Ohio Univ Student Health Svcs
2 Health Center Dr Rm 110 (45701-2907)
PHONE..............................740 593-1660
Jacqueline Legg, *Manager*
Dave Steortz, *Manager*
EMP: 35
SALES (corp-wide): 531.5MM **Privately Held**
WEB: www.zanesville.ohiou.edu
SIC: 8011 8221 Offices & clinics of medical doctors; university
PA: Ohio University
1 Ohio University
Athens OH 45701
740 593-1000

(G-800)
OHIO VALLEY HOME HEALTH INC
2097 E State St Ste B1 (45701-2156)
PHONE..............................740 249-4219
Donna Williams, *Marketing Staff*
Summer Atkinson, *Branch Mgr*
EMP: 31
SALES (corp-wide): 3.5MM **Privately Held**
SIC: 8082 Home health care services
PA: Ohio Valley Home Health Inc
1480 Jackson Pike
Gallipolis OH 45631
740 441-1393

(G-801)
PARKS RECREATION ATHENS
Also Called: Community Center
701 E State St (45701-2110)
PHONE..............................740 592-0046
Richard Campitelli, *Director*
EMP: 50 EST: 2000
SALES (est): 1.7MM **Privately Held**
SIC: 7033 Recreational vehicle parks

(G-802)
SHELTERING ARMS HOSPITAL FOUND
Also Called: Ohiohealth O'Bleness Hospital
55 Hospital Dr (45701-2302)
PHONE..............................740 592-9300
Larry Thornhill, *CEO*
Mark Seckinger, *President*
Greg Long, *President*
Clifford Young, *Principal*
Lynn Anastas, *Vice Pres*
EMP: 368
SQ FT: 127,500
SALES: 96.3MM
SALES (corp-wide): 4B **Privately Held**
SIC: 8062 General medical & surgical hospitals
PA: Ohiohealth Corporation
180 E Broad St
Columbus OH 43215
614 788-8860

(G-803)
SPECTRUM MGT HOLDG CO LLC
28 Station St (45701-2757)
PHONE..............................740 200-3385
Steve Hewitt, *Branch Mgr*
EMP: 83
SALES (corp-wide): 43.6B **Publicly Held**
SIC: 4841 Cable television services
HQ: Spectrum Management Holding Company, Llc
400 Atlantic St
Stamford CT 06901
203 905-7801

(G-804)
SUNPOWER INC
2005 E State St Ste 104 (45701-2125)
PHONE..............................740 594-2221
Jeffrey Hatfield, *Vice Pres*
Douglas Richards, *Vice Pres*
Mike Blair, *Info Tech Mgr*
EMP: 95
SQ FT: 16,000

SALES (est): 15.6MM
SALES (corp-wide): 4.8B **Publicly Held**
WEB: www.sunpower.com
SIC: 8731 8711 8733 3769 Commercial physical research; engineering services; physical research, noncommercial; scientific research agency; guided missile & space vehicle parts & auxiliary equipment
HQ: Advanced Measurement Technology, Inc.
801 S Illinois Ave
Oak Ridge TN 37830
865 482-4411

(G-805)
TASC OF SOUTHEAST OHIO
86 Columbus Rd (45701-1300)
PHONE..............................740 594-2276
Stephen Thomas, *CEO*
Cherilyn Warner, *President*
EMP: 28 EST: 2003
SALES (est): 175.9K **Privately Held**
SIC: 8322 Individual & family services

(G-806)
TRI COUNTY MENTAL HEALTH SVCS (PA)
Also Called: TRAC
90 Hospital Dr (45701-2301)
PHONE..............................740 592-3091
Toll Free:.............................888 -
George P Weigly, *CEO*
George Weigly, *Exec Dir*
EMP: 204
SALES: 168.1K **Privately Held**
WEB: www.epilepsyservices.org
SIC: 8093 8361 8011 Mental health clinic, outpatient; home for the mentally handicapped; offices & clinics of medical doctors

(G-807)
TRI COUNTY MENTAL HEALTH SVCS
90 Hospital Dr (45701-2301)
PHONE..............................740 594-5045
George Weigly, *Branch Mgr*
EMP: 99
SALES (corp-wide): 168.1K **Privately Held**
SIC: 8093 Mental health clinic, outpatient
PA: Tri County Mental Health Services Inc
90 Hospital Dr
Athens OH 45701
740 592-3091

(G-808)
TS TECH AMERICAS INC
TS Tech North America
10 Kenny Dr (45701-9406)
PHONE..............................740 593-5958
Bill Hass, *Manager*
EMP: 43
SALES (corp-wide): 4.5B **Privately Held**
SIC: 5099 Child restraint seats, automotive
HQ: Ts Tech Americas, Inc.
8458 E Broad St
Reynoldsburg OH 43068
614 575-4100

(G-809)
UNITED PARCEL SERVICE INC OH
Also Called: UPS
1 Kenny Dr (45701-9406)
PHONE..............................740 592-4570
Matthew Kazmirski, *Manager*
EMP: 50
SALES (corp-wide): 71.8B **Publicly Held**
WEB: www.upsscs.com
SIC: 4215 Parcel delivery, vehicular
HQ: United Parcel Service, Inc. (Oh)
55 Glenlake Pkwy
Atlanta GA 30328
404 828-6000

(G-810)
UNIVERSITY MEDICAL ASSOC INC
350 Parks Hall (45701-1359)
PHONE..............................740 593-0753
Scott Jenkinson, *Principal*
Nuzhat Nisa, *Family Practiti*
EMP: 150

SALES: 11MM **Privately Held**
SIC: 8011 Offices & clinics of medical doctors

(G-811)
WHITE & CHAMBERS PARTNERSHIP
Also Called: Manufactured Comfort
5315 Hebbardsville Rd (45701-8973)
P.O. Box 250 (45701-0250)
PHONE..............................740 594-8381
David R White, *Partner*
Gayman Chambers, *Partner*
Sandra White, *Partner*
EMP: 40
SALES (est): 1.9MM **Privately Held**
WEB: www.davidwhiteservices.com
SIC: 6512 Commercial & industrial building operation

(G-812)
XEROX CORPORATION
35 Elliott St (45701-2608)
PHONE..............................740 592-5609
Jeffrey Wenger, *Owner*
Scott Smith, *Sales Staff*
EMP: 84
SALES (corp-wide): 9.8B **Publicly Held**
SIC: 5044 Office equipment
PA: Xerox Corporation
201 Merritt 7
Norwalk CT 06851
203 968-3000

Attica
Seneca County

(G-813)
CLAY DISTRIBUTING CO
15025 E Us 224 (44807)
P.O. Box 581 (44807-0581)
PHONE..............................419 426-3051
Doug Beck, *President*
Dean Beck, *Corp Secy*
Brian Beck, *Vice Pres*
EMP: 30
SALES (est): 8.7MM
SALES (corp-wide): 188.3MM **Privately Held**
WEB: www.beckoil.com
SIC: 5172 Petroleum products
PA: Beck Suppliers, Inc.
1000 N Front St
Fremont OH 43420
800 232-5645

(G-814)
NORTH CENTRAL ELC COOP INC
350 Stump Pike Rd (44807-9571)
P.O. Box 475 (44807-0475)
PHONE..............................800 426-3072
Richard Reichert, *President*
Markus I Bryant, *General Mgr*
Denny Schendler, *Vice Pres*
Duane E Frankard, *Treasurer*
Terry Mazzone, *Comms Dir*
EMP: 44 EST: 1936
SQ FT: 27,000
SALES: 25.4MM **Privately Held**
WEB: www.ncelec.org
SIC: 4911 Distribution, electric power

Aurora
Portage County

(G-815)
ANNA MARIA OF AURORA INC (PA)
Also Called: Kensington Care Center
889 N Aurora Rd (44202-9537)
PHONE..............................330 562-6171
Robert J Norton Jr, *President*
George Norton, *VP Admin*
Carol Conteen, *Controller*
Mindy Hershey, *Human Res Mgr*
Jason Reed, *Director*
EMP: 200
SQ FT: 100,000

SALES (est): 20.4MM **Privately Held**
WEB: www.annamariaofaurora.com
SIC: 8051 Skilled nursing care facilities

(G-816)
ANNA MARIA OF AURORA INC
849 Rural Rd (44202)
PHONE....................................330 562-3120
Robert J Norton Jr, *President*
EMP: 100
SALES (corp-wide): 20.4MM **Privately Held**
WEB: www.annamariaofaurora.com
SIC: 8051 Skilled nursing care facilities
PA: Anna Maria Of Aurora, Inc.
    889 N Aurora Rd
    Aurora OH 44202
    330 562-6171

(G-817)
AURORA HOTEL PARTNERS LLC
Also Called: Aurora Inn Hotel & Event Ctr
30 Shawnee Trl (44202-9385)
PHONE....................................330 562-0767
Stephen Mansfield,
EMP: 50
SQ FT: 42,682
SALES (est): 184.9K **Privately Held**
SIC: 7011 6513 5812 Resort hotel, franchised; residential hotel operation; American restaurant

(G-818)
AURORA MANOR LTD PARTNERSHIP
Also Called: Aurora Mnor Spcial Care Centre
101 S Bissell Rd (44202-9170)
PHONE....................................330 562-5000
Christa Mayes, *Administration*
EMP: 40
SALES: 7.4MM
SALES (corp-wide): 157.7MM **Privately Held**
WEB: www.nursehome.com
SIC: 8051 8093 Convalescent home with continuous nursing care; rehabilitation center, outpatient treatment
PA: Saber Healthcare Group, L.L.C.
    26691 Richmond Rd Frnt
    Bedford OH 44146
    216 292-5706

(G-819)
B & I HOTEL MANAGEMENT LLC
Also Called: Bertram Inn
600 N Aurora Rd (44202-7107)
PHONE....................................330 995-0200
Dale A Bradford, *Mng Member*
EMP: 150
SALES (est): 10.1MM **Privately Held**
WEB: www.thebertraminn.com
SIC: 7011 7991 5813 5812 Inns; physical fitness facilities; drinking places; eating places

(G-820)
BARRINGTON GOLF CLUB INC (PA)
350 N Aurora Rd (44202-7104)
PHONE....................................330 995-0600
Dave Roberts, *General Mgr*
Jack Nicklaus, *Principal*
Richard A Rosner, *Principal*
EMP: 61
SALES (est): 9.6MM **Privately Held**
SIC: 7997 Golf club, membership

(G-821)
BARRINGTON GOLF CLUB INC
680 N Aurora Rd (44202-7107)
PHONE....................................330 995-0821
EMP: 59
SALES (corp-wide): 9.6MM **Privately Held**
SIC: 7997 Golf club, membership
PA: Barrington Golf Club, Inc.
    350 N Aurora Rd
    Aurora OH 44202
    330 995-0600

(G-822)
BREEZY POINT LTD PARTNERSHIP
Also Called: Barrington Golf Club
350 N Aurora Rd (44202-7104)
PHONE....................................330 995-0600
James A Schoff, *Branch Mgr*
EMP: 40
SALES (est): 763.1K **Privately Held**
SIC: 7997 7991 5813 5812 Golf club, membership; physical fitness facilities; drinking places; eating places
PA: Breezy Point Limited Partnership
    30575 Bnbridge Rd Ste 100
    Solon OH 44139

(G-823)
CABIN RESTAURANT
34 N Chillicothe Rd (44202-7780)
PHONE....................................330 562-9171
Mario Liuzzo, *President*
EMP: 40
SALES (est): 215.2K **Privately Held**
SIC: 5812 7299 7011 Italian restaurant; miscellaneous personal service; hotels & motels

(G-824)
CERTANTEED GYPS CILING MFG INC
1192 S Chillicothe Rd (44202)
PHONE....................................800 233-8990
EMP: 44
SALES (est): 5.6MM
SALES (corp-wide): 215.9MM **Privately Held**
SIC: 1742 Acoustical & ceiling work
HQ: Certainteed Corporation
    20 Moores Rd
    Malvern PA 19355
    610 893-5000

(G-825)
CITY OF AURORA
158 W Pioneer Trl (44202-9103)
PHONE....................................330 562-8662
Ann Womer Benjamin, *Mayor*
EMP: 99 **Privately Held**
SIC: 1611 9111 Highway & street maintenance;
PA: City Of Aurora
    130 S Chillicothe Rd
    Aurora OH 44202
    330 562-6131

(G-826)
ELECTROVATIONS INC
350 Harris Dr (44202-7536)
PHONE....................................330 274-3558
R Charles Vermerris, *President*
EMP: 25
SQ FT: 4,500
SALES (est): 1.9MM **Privately Held**
SIC: 8711 7389 3357 Electrical or electronic engineering; design, commercial & industrial; nonferrous wiredrawing & insulating

(G-827)
FUNTIME PARKS INC
Also Called: Six Flags Ohio
1060 N Aurora Rd (44202-8749)
PHONE....................................330 562-7131
EMP: 175
SQ FT: 20,000
SALES (est): 2.2MM
SALES (corp-wide): 64.8MM **Privately Held**
SIC: 7996 Theme Amusement Park
PA: Six Flags Theme Parks Inc.
    924 E Avenue J
    Grand Prairie TX 75050
    972 595-5000

(G-828)
GODFREY & WING INC (PA)
220 Campus Dr (44202-6663)
PHONE....................................330 562-1440
Christopher Gilmore, *President*
Brad Welch, *Corp Secy*
Karen Gilmore, *Vice Pres*
▲ EMP: 50 EST: 1947
SQ FT: 68,000

(G-829)
HOWARD HANNA SMYTHE CRAMER
195 Barrington Town Sq Dr (44202-7790)
PHONE....................................330 562-6188
Dottie Dupree, *Manager*
EMP: 55
SALES (corp-wide): 72.1MM **Privately Held**
WEB: www.smythecramer.com
SIC: 6531 Real estate brokers & agents
HQ: Howard Hanna Smythe Cramer
    6000 Parkland Blvd
    Cleveland OH 44124
    216 447-4477

(G-830)
ILPEA INDUSTRIES INC
OEM/Miller
1300 Danner Dr (44202-9284)
PHONE....................................330 562-2916
Ken Chenoweth, *Manager*
EMP: 135 **Privately Held**
WEB: www.holmindustries.com
SIC: 3089 5162 3083 Plastic containers, except foam; plastics sheets & rods; laminated plastics plate & sheet
HQ: Ilpea Industries, Inc.
    745 S Gardner St
    Scottsburg IN 47170
    812 752-2526

(G-831)
JIT PACKAGING INC (PA)
Also Called: Jit Milrob
250 Page Rd (44202)
PHONE....................................330 562-8080
Dan Harrison, *General Mgr*
David R Jones, *Chairman*
Elaine Jones, *Vice Pres*
Marian Maulis, *Purchasing*
EMP: 34
SQ FT: 60,000
SALES (est): 11.7MM **Privately Held**
SIC: 2448 5113 5085 2653 Pallets, wood; corrugated & solid fiber boxes; industrial supplies; corrugated & solid fiber boxes

(G-832)
KAPSTONE CONTAINER CORPORATION
Also Called: Filmco
1450 S Chillicothe Rd (44202-9282)
P.O. Box 239 (44202-0239)
PHONE....................................330 562-6111
Richard Pohland, *Branch Mgr*
EMP: 106
SQ FT: 20,000
SALES (corp-wide): 16.2B **Publicly Held**
SIC: 3081 5199 2671 Packing materials, plastic sheet; packaging materials; packaging paper & plastics film, coated & laminated
HQ: Kapstone Container Corporation
    1601 Blairs Ferry Rd Ne
    Cedar Rapids IA 52402
    319 393-3610

(G-833)
LYNK PACKAGING INC
1250 Page Rd (44202-6666)
PHONE....................................330 562-8080
Rick Macdonald, *President*
Albert N Salvatore, *Principal*
Marian Maulis, *Purchasing*
Kenneth Ddagg, *CFO*
Gwenn Bamer-Flynn, *Sales Mgr*
EMP: 27
SALES (est): 12.2MM **Privately Held**
SIC: 5113 Corrugated & solid fiber boxes

(G-834)
MARC GLASSMAN INC
Also Called: Marc's 45
300 Aurora Commons Cir (44202-8828)
PHONE....................................330 995-9246
Michael Lamay, *Manager*
EMP: 160
SALES (corp-wide): 1.1B **Privately Held**
WEB: www.marcs.com
SIC: 5331 7384 5912 Variety stores; photofinish laboratories; drug stores & proprietary stores
PA: Marc Glassman, Inc.
    5841 W 130th St
    Cleveland OH 44130
    216 265-7700

(G-835)
MARIOS INTERNATIONAL SPA & HT (PA)
Also Called: Mario's Beauty Salon
34 N Chillicothe Rd (44202-7780)
PHONE....................................330 562-5141
Mario Liuzzo, *President*
Sheryl Greve, *Corp Secy*
Joanne Liuzzo, *Vice Pres*
Bryon Miller, *Controller*
EMP: 140
SALES: 2.2MM **Privately Held**
SIC: 7231 7991 7011 5812 Beauty Shop Physical Fitness Faclty Hotel/Motel Operation Eating Place

(G-836)
MARK DURA INC
11384 Chamberlain Rd (44202-9360)
P.O. Box 868 (44202-0868)
PHONE....................................330 995-0883
Curtis Britton, *CEO*
Frank Gibson, *CFO*
EMP: 30
SQ FT: 13,000
SALES: 8MM **Privately Held**
SIC: 1721 Pavement marking contractor

(G-837)
MILL DISTRIBUTORS INC
45 Aurora Industrial Pkwy (44202-8088)
PHONE....................................330 995-9200
Thomas H Wieder, *President*
Douglas M Wieder, *Corp Secy*
Chris Sorna, *Purch Mgr*
Sharon Dolan, *Controller*
Angela Steed, *Accounting Mgr*
▲ EMP: 53 EST: 1926
SQ FT: 40,000
SALES (est): 44.3MM **Privately Held**
WEB: www.milldist.com
SIC: 5023 5021 Blankets; bedspreads; sheets, textile; pillowcases; furniture; mattresses; chairs

(G-838)
PARTSSOURCE INC
777 Lena Dr (44202-8025)
PHONE....................................330 562-9900
Philip Settimi, *President*
Mike Maguire, *Senior VP*
David Brennan, *Vice Pres*
Mark Critchfield, *Vice Pres*
Patrick Blake, *CFO*
EMP: 210
SQ FT: 75,000
SALES (est): 147.9MM **Privately Held**
WEB: www.partssource.com
SIC: 5047 Medical equipment & supplies

(G-839)
PNC BANK NATIONAL ASSOCIATION
7044 N Aurora Rd (44202-9626)
PHONE....................................330 562-9700
Jeff Dyrlund, *Branch Mgr*
EMP: 162
SALES (corp-wide): 19.9B **Publicly Held**
SIC: 6029 6021 Commercial banks; national commercial banks
HQ: Pnc Bank, National Association
    222 Delaware Ave
    Wilmington DE 19801
    877 762-2000

(G-840)
ROBECK FLUID POWER CO
350 Lena Dr (44202-8098)
PHONE....................................330 562-1140
Peter Becker, *President*
Ken Traeger, *Corp Secy*
Don Louis, *Opers Mgr*
Sherri Meloy, *Purchasing*
Bob Long, *Engineer*
▲ EMP: 65
SQ FT: 6,000

GEOGRAPHIC

SALES (est): 71.1MM Privately Held
WEB: www.robeckfluidpower.com
SIC: **5084** 3593 3594 3494 Hydraulic systems equipment & supplies; fluid power cylinders & actuators; fluid power pumps & motors; valves & pipe fittings

(G-841)
ROVISYS BUILDING TECH LLC (PA)
Also Called: Rovisys Building Tech Rbt
260 Campus Dr (44202-6663)
PHONE.................................330 954-7600
Derek Drayer, *Managing Prtnr*
EMP: 32
SQ FT: 1,000
SALES (est): 1.3MM Privately Held
SIC: **7373** Computer integrated systems design

(G-842)
ROVISYS COMPANY (PA)
1455 Danner Dr (44202-9273)
PHONE.................................330 562-8600
John W Robertson, *President*
Chris Otto, *Vice Pres*
Jonathan Hynes, *Engineer*
Joel Spafford, *Director*
EMP: 148
SQ FT: 35,000
SALES (est): 69.6MM Privately Held
WEB: www.rovisys.com
SIC: **8711** Consulting engineer

(G-843)
SEAWORLD ENTERTAINMENT INC
1100 Squires Rd (44202-8706)
PHONE.................................330 562-8101
Fax: 330 995-2091
EMP: 32
SALES (corp-wide): 1.3B Publicly Held
SIC: **7996** Marine Theme Park
PA: Seaworld Entertainment, Inc.
9205 Southpark Center Loo
Orlando FL 32819
407 226-5011

(G-844)
TECHNICAL CONSUMER PDTS INC
Also Called: T C P
325 Campus Dr (44202-6662)
PHONE.................................800 324-1496
Kaj Den Daas, *CEO*
Solomon Yan, *President*
Chris Lindner, *General Mgr*
Hope Brown, *Business Mgr*
Jim Connolly, *Senior VP*
▲ EMP: 292
SQ FT: 159,000
SALES (est): 221.8MM Privately Held
WEB:
www.technicalconsumerproducts.com
SIC: **5063** Lighting fittings & accessories
HQ: Quality Light Source Gmbh
C/O Sibla Services Ag
Zug ZG

(G-845)
TWO-X ENGNERS CONSTRUCTERS LLC
570 Club Dr (44202-6305)
P.O. Box 906 (44202-0906)
PHONE.................................330 995-0592
Kenneth Finnerty, *Mng Member*
Sam Waren, *Mng Member*
EMP: 45
SALES: 7.8MM Privately Held
SIC: **1521** Single-family housing construction

(G-846)
UNITED TECHNICAL SUPPORT SVCS
206 E Garfield Rd (44202-9301)
PHONE.................................330 562-3330
EMP: 50
SQ FT: 5,000
SALES: 3MM
SALES (corp-wide): 13.4MM Privately Held
SIC: **7699** Repair Services

PA: United Technical Support Services, Inc
206 E Garfield Rd
Aurora OH 44241
330 562-3330

(G-847)
VWR CHEMICALS LLC
Also Called: VWR International
220 Lena Dr (44202-9244)
PHONE.................................330 425-2522
EMP: 36 Privately Held
SIC: **5169** Chemicals & allied products
HQ: Vwr Chemicals, Llc
28600 Fountain Pkwy
Solon OH 44139
800 448-4442

(G-848)
WALDEN CLUB
1119 Aurora Hudson Rd (44202-7512)
PHONE.................................330 995-7162
Manuel Barenholtz, *President*
EMP: 80 EST: 1969
SQ FT: 10,000
SALES (est): 2.4MM Privately Held
SIC: **7997** 5941 5812 Golf club, membership; tennis club, membership; golf goods & equipment; tennis goods & equipment; eating places

(G-849)
WALDEN COMPANY LTD
Also Called: Walden Country Club
1119 Aurora Hudson Rd (44202-7512)
PHONE.................................330 562-7145
Robert J Rosencrans, *Managing Prtnr*
Manuel Barenholtz, *Partner*
EMP: 135
SALES (est): 5MM Privately Held
SIC: **5812** 7997 Eating places; country club, membership

(G-850)
WALDEN TURF CENTER
375 Deer Island Dr (44202-8202)
PHONE.................................330 995-0023
Rob Rosencrans, *Owner*
EMP: 50
SALES (est): 657.9K Privately Held
SIC: **0782** Turf installation services, except artificial

(G-851)
WATERWAY GAS & WASH COMPANY
Also Called: BP
7010 N Aurora Rd (44202-9626)
PHONE.................................330 995-2900
Shayne Roche, *General Mgr*
Cathy Hemp, *Manager*
EMP: 47
SALES (corp-wide): 350.2MM Privately Held
SIC: **7542** Washing & polishing, automotive
PA: Waterway Gas & Wash Company
727 Goddard Ave
Chesterfield MO 63005
636 537-1111

(G-852)
WS ONE INVESTMENT USA LLC (PA)
Also Called: Ws1
1263 S Chillicothe Rd (44202-8002)
PHONE.................................855 895-3728
Shiraz Khan, *President*
EMP: 100
SALES (est): 27.8MM Privately Held
SIC: **6799** Investors

Austinburg
Ashtabula County

(G-853)
NASSIEF AUTOMOTIVE INC
Also Called: Nassief Honda
2920 Gh Dr (44010-9793)
PHONE.................................440 997-5151
George Nassief, *CEO*
Todd Nassief, *President*
Ann Nassief, *Corp Secy*
Helen Nassief, *Vice Pres*

EMP: 32
SQ FT: 10,000
SALES (est): 10.4MM Privately Held
WEB: www.nassief.com
SIC: **5511** 7538 Automobiles, new & used; trucks, tractors & trailers: new & used; general automotive repair shops

(G-854)
UNITED PARCEL SERVICE INC OH
Also Called: UPS
1553 State Route 45 (44010-9749)
PHONE.................................440 275-3301
Carol Bianchi, *Manager*
EMP: 65
SALES (corp-wide): 71.8B Publicly Held
WEB: www.upsscs.com
SIC: **4215** Parcel delivery, vehicular
HQ: United Parcel Service, Inc. (Oh)
55 Glenlake Pkwy
Atlanta GA 30328
404 828-6000

Austintown
Mahoning County

(G-855)
44444 LLC
Also Called: Target Trans-Logic
5783 Norquest Blvd (44515-2201)
P.O. Box 4043 (44515-0043)
PHONE.................................330 502-2023
George Rood Jr, *Mng Member*
EMP: 38
SALES: 200K Privately Held
SIC: **4212** Mail carriers, contract

(G-856)
BROOKDALE SNIOR LVING CMMNTIES
Also Called: Brookdale Austintown
1420 S Canfield Niles Rd (44515-4040)
PHONE.................................330 249-1071
Anna Jannecti, *Manager*
EMP: 36
SALES (corp-wide): 4.5B Publicly Held
WEB: www.assisted.com
SIC: **8059** 8051 Rest home, with health care; extended care facility
HQ: Brookdale Senior Living Communities, Inc.
6737 W Wa St Ste 2300
Milwaukee WI 53214
414 918-5000

(G-857)
CHCC HOME HEALTH CARE
Also Called: Community Home Health
60 N Canfield Niles Rd # 50 (44515-2340)
PHONE.................................330 759-4069
Brad Contel, *Administration*
EMP: 40
SALES (est): 94.9K Privately Held
SIC: **8082** 8049 8059 Home health care services; occupational therapist; convalescent home

(G-858)
OHIO DEPARTMENT OF HEALTH
Also Called: Wic Program
50 Westchester Dr Ste 202 (44515-3991)
PHONE.................................330 792-2397
EMP: 269 Privately Held
SIC: **8322** Individual & family services
HQ: Department Of Health Ohio
246 N High St
Columbus OH 43215

(G-859)
PRIMO PROPERTIES LLC
5555 Cerni Pl (44515-1159)
PHONE.................................330 606-6746
Frank Pasqualetti, *Owner*
EMP: 36 EST: 2009
SQ FT: 50,400
SALES: 20MM Privately Held
SIC: **6512** Nonresidential building operators

(G-860)
R L LIPTON DISTRIBUTING LLC
425 Victoria Rd Ste B (44515-2029)
PHONE.................................800 321-6553
Martin Lipton, *President*
Jim Gill, *Info Tech Dir*
EMP: 70
SALES (est): 13.1MM Privately Held
WEB: www.rllipton.com
SIC: **5181** Beer & other fermented malt liquors

(G-861)
RHIEL SUPPLY CO INC (PA)
Also Called: Rhiel Supply Co, The
3735 Oakwood Ave (44515-3050)
PHONE.................................330 799-7777
Toby Mirto, *CEO*
Daniel F Mirto, *President*
J D Mirto, *Vice Pres*
James Wade, *Sales Mgr*
Karen Blasko, *Cust Mgr*
EMP: 33
SQ FT: 30,000
SALES (est): 11.7MM Privately Held
WEB: www.rhiel.com
SIC: **5087** 5169 Janitors' supplies; swimming pool & spa chemicals

---

Avon
Lorain County

(G-862)
APEX INTERIORS INC
3233 Waterford Way (44011-2910)
PHONE.................................330 327-2226
Tom Hershey, *President*
EMP: 26
SALES: 1.5MM Privately Held
SIC: **1742** Drywall

(G-863)
AVON OAKS COUNTRY CLUB
32300 Detroit Rd Ste A (44011-2097)
PHONE.................................440 892-0660
Barb Russell, *Controller*
Ann Patterson, *Mktg Coord*
Judd Stevenson, *Director*
EMP: 65
SQ FT: 30,000
SALES (est): 4.3MM Privately Held
WEB: www.avonoakscc.com
SIC: **7997** Country club, membership

(G-864)
AVON PROPERTIES INC
Also Called: Bob O Link Golf Course
4141 Center Rd (44011-2347)
PHONE.................................440 934-6217
William Fitch, *President*
Donna Fitch, *Treasurer*
EMP: 35
SQ FT: 1,500
SALES (est): 2.5MM Privately Held
SIC: **7992** 5941 Public golf courses; golf goods & equipment

(G-865)
AVONDALE GOLF CLUB
3111 Moon Rd (44011-1743)
PHONE.................................440 934-4398
Jane K Egger, *President*
Carol Noll, *Partner*
George Noll, *Partner*
EMP: 32 EST: 1972
SALES (est): 1.2MM Privately Held
WEB: www.avondalegolfclub.com
SIC: **7992** 7997 Public golf courses; membership sports & recreation clubs

(G-866)
BEARING TECHNOLOGIES LTD (PA)
1141 Jaycox Rd (44011-1366)
PHONE.................................440 937-4770
Laz Tromler, *CEO*
▲ EMP: 60 EST: 1997
SQ FT: 230,000
SALES (est): 29.5MM Privately Held
SIC: **5085** Bearings

(G-867)
BRADY HOMES INC
36741 Chester Rd (44011)
PHONE..............................440 937-6255
Shaun P Brady, *President*
Trevor Miller, *Pub Rel Dir*
EMP: 40
SQ FT: 900
SALES (est): 2.7MM **Privately Held**
WEB: www.bradyhomesinc.com
SIC: 1521 New construction, single-family
  houses; general remodeling, single-family
  houses

(G-868)
**BRAMHALL ENGRG &
SURVEYING CO (PA)**
801 Moore Rd (44011-4051)
PHONE..............................440 934-7878
Michael Bramhall, *President*
Chris Howard, *Vice Pres*
Valerie Kilmer, *Project Mgr*
Nicholas Sheffield, *Engineer*
James Scott, *Project Engr*
EMP: 33
SQ FT: 11,000
SALES: 3MM **Privately Held**
WEB: www.bramhall-engineering.com
SIC: 8711 8713 Civil engineering; survey-
  ing services

(G-869)
**BRIGHTVIEW LANDSCAPES
LLC**
1051 Lear Industrial Pkwy A (44011-1386)
PHONE..............................440 937-5126
Matt Krems, *Manager*
John Chagin, *Manager*
EMP: 47
SALES (corp-wide): 2.8B **Publicly Held**
SIC: 0781 Landscape services
HQ: Brightview Landscapes, Llc
  401 Plymouth Rd Ste 500
  Plymouth Meeting PA 19462
  484 567-7204

(G-870)
CARAVAN GOLF COMPANY LTD
Also Called: Red Tail Golf Club
4400 Nagel Rd (44011-2736)
PHONE..............................440 937-6018
Bob Buck, *General Mgr*
EMP: 60
SALES (est): 3.2MM
SALES (corp-wide): 4.6MM **Privately
Held**
WEB: www.redtailgolfclub.com
SIC: 7992 Public golf courses
PA: Caravan Golf Company, Ltd.
  27500 Detroit Rd Ste 300
  Cleveland OH 44145
  440 892-6800

(G-871)
**CARROLL MANUFACTURING &
SALES**
Also Called: CMS
35179 Avon Commerce Pkwy
(44011-1374)
PHONE..............................440 937-3900
Chris Carroll, *President*
Jessica Neal, *Sales Staff*
Jill Teufel, *Sales Staff*
Stacey Brown, *Marketing Mgr*
Pat Poorman, *Manager*
▲ EMP: 50
SALES (est): 11MM **Privately Held**
WEB: www.carrollmfg.com
SIC: 5046 Commercial cooking & food
  service equipment

(G-872)
CELLCO PARTNERSHIP
Also Called: Verizon Wireless
36050 Detroit Rd (44011-1683)
PHONE..............................440 934-0576
EMP: 71
SALES (corp-wide): 130.8B **Publicly
Held**
SIC: 4812 Cellular telephone services
HQ: Cellco Partnership
  1 Verizon Way
  Basking Ridge NJ 07920

(G-873)
CHAMBERLAIN HR
36368 Detroit Rd Ste A (44011-2843)
PHONE..............................216 589-9280
Henry Chamberlain, *Branch Mgr*
EMP: 102
SALES (corp-wide): 55.6MM **Privately
Held**
SIC: 8111 General practice attorney,
  lawyer
PA: Chamberlain, Hrdlicka, White, Williams
  & Aughtry, P.C.
  1200 Smith St
  Houston TX 77002
  713 658-1818

(G-874)
CHAPMAN & CHAPMAN INC
36711 American Way Ste 2f (44011-4061)
PHONE..............................440 934-4102
Walter K Chapman, *CEO*
EMP: 35 EST: 1963
SALES (est): 3.6MM **Privately Held**
SIC: 6411 8742 Insurance information &
  consulting services; financial consultant

(G-875)
CHEMTRON CORPORATION
35850 Schneider Ct (44011-1298)
PHONE..............................440 937-6348
Andrew Kuhar, *President*
Michael Guenther, *Vice Pres*
EMP: 50
SQ FT: 16,500
SALES (est): 26.4MM **Privately Held**
WEB: www.chemtron-corp.com
SIC: 4953 4959 Recycling, waste materi-
  als; refuse collection & disposal services;
  environmental cleanup services

(G-876)
CITY OF AVON
36080 Chester Rd (44011-1070)
PHONE..............................440 937-5740
Jerry Plas, *Director*
EMP: 30 **Privately Held**
WEB: www.cityofavon.com
SIC: 1611 Highway & street maintenance
PA: City Of Avon
  36080 Chester Rd
  Avon OH 44011
  440 937-7800

(G-877)
CLEVELAND WHEELS
Also Called: Aircraft Wheels and Breaks
1160 Center Rd (44011-1208)
PHONE..............................440 937-6211
Manny Nnay Bajakfoujian, *CEO*
EMP: 99
SALES (est): 6.5MM **Privately Held**
SIC: 5088 3799 Aircraft equipment & sup-
  plies; transportation equipment

(G-878)
COCHIN TECHNOLOGIES LLC
Also Called: Delight Connection
37854 Briar Lakes Dr (44011-3105)
PHONE..............................440 941-4856
Robin Roy, *Principal*
EMP: 50
SALES: 2MM **Privately Held**
SIC: 7371 Computer software develop-
  ment

(G-879)
DIVERSICARE OF AVON LLC
Also Called: Avon Skilled Nursing
32900 Detroit Rd (44011-2018)
PHONE..............................440 937-6201
Edgar Rios, *Human Res Dir*
EMP: 116
SALES (est): 5.8MM
SALES (corp-wide): 563.4MM **Publicly
Held**
SIC: 8051 Skilled nursing care facilities
PA: Diversicare Healthcare Services, Inc.
  1621 Galleria Blvd
  Brentwood TN 37027
  615 771-7575

(G-880)
**EMH REGIONAL MEDICAL
CENTER**
Also Called: Fitness Center
1997 Healthway Dr (44011-2834)
PHONE..............................440 988-6800
Connie Hurst, *Buyer*
Sabarras George, *Manager*
EMP: 100
SALES (corp-wide): 580MM **Privately
Held**
SIC: 8062 7991 Hospital, affiliated with
  AMA residency; physical fitness facilities
HQ: Emh Regional Medical Center
  630 E River St
  Elyria OH 44035
  440 329-7500

(G-881)
**FREEMAN MANUFACTURING &
SUP CO (PA)**
1101 Moore Rd (44011-4043)
PHONE..............................440 934-1902
Gerald W Rusk, *Ch of Bd*
Lou Turco, *President*
Mike Porter, *Business Mgr*
Jon Hofener, *Export Mgr*
Ben Inman, *Export Mgr*
EMP: 50
SQ FT: 110,000
SALES (est): 70.2MM **Privately Held**
WEB: www.freemansupply.com
SIC: 5084 3087 3543 2821 Industrial ma-
  chinery & equipment; custom compound
  purchased resins; industrial patterns;
  plastics materials & resins

(G-882)
GODDARD SCHOOL OF AVON
2555 Hale St (44011-1856)
PHONE..............................440 934-3300
John Keshock, *Owner*
Mark Reinhart, *Director*
EMP: 25
SALES (est): 517.4K **Privately Held**
SIC: 8351 Preschool center

(G-883)
**GREAT LAKES COMPUTER
CORP**
33675 Lear Indus Pkwy (44011-1370)
PHONE..............................440 937-1100
Jim Manco, *CEO*
Robert Martin, *Vice Pres*
EMP: 60
SQ FT: 20,000
SALES (est): 5MM **Privately Held**
WEB: www.grlakes.com
SIC: 7378 5734 Computer peripheral
  equipment repair & maintenance; com-
  puter & software stores

(G-884)
HANNA HOLDINGS INC
Also Called: Howard Hanna Real Estate
2100 Center Rd Ste L (44011-1892)
PHONE..............................440 933-6195
Meghan Kopp, *Branch Mgr*
EMP: 25
SALES (corp-wide): 73.7MM **Privately
Held**
SIC: 6531 Real estate agent, residential
PA: Hanna Holdings, Inc.
  1090 Freeport Rd Ste 1a
  Pittsburgh PA 15238
  412 967-9000

(G-885)
**HEALTHSPAN INTEGRATED
CARE**
Also Called: Kaiser Foundation Health Plan
36711 American Way Fl 1 (44011-4061)
PHONE..............................440 937-2350
John Alfes, *Principal*
Melanie B Rolsen, *Branch Mgr*
EMP: 25
SALES (corp-wide): 4.7B **Privately Held**
SIC: 6324 Health maintenance organiza-
  tion (HMO), insurance only
HQ: Healthspan Integrated Care
  1001 Lakeside Ave E # 1200
  Cleveland OH 44114
  216 621-5600

(G-886)
HOME DEPOT USA INC
Also Called: Home Depot, The
35930 Detroit Rd (44011-1653)
PHONE..............................440 937-2240
Ronald W Salazar, *Manager*
EMP: 100
SALES (corp-wide): 108.2B **Publicly
Held**
WEB: www.homerentalsdepot.com
SIC: 5211 7359 Home centers; tool rental
HQ: Home Depot U.S.A., Inc.
  2455 Paces Ferry Ave
  Atlanta GA 30339

(G-887)
J WAY LEASING LTD
1284 Miller Rd (44011-1004)
PHONE..............................440 934-1020
Alan N Johnson,
Susan Lutz,
EMP: 30 EST: 1997
SQ FT: 26,000
SALES (est): 2.9MM **Privately Held**
SIC: 1629 7359 Marine construction;
  equipment rental & leasing

(G-888)
JENNE INC
33665 Chester Rd (44011-1307)
PHONE..............................440 835-0040
Dave Johnson, *CEO*
Rose M Jenne, *Ch of Bd*
Dean M Jenne, *President*
Ray Jenne Jr, *President*
Chip Fincher, *Business Mgr*
▲ EMP: 200
SQ FT: 126,000
SALES (est): 243.4MM **Privately Held**
WEB: www.jenne.com
SIC: 7371 7382 Software programming
  applications; security systems services

(G-889)
**KAISER FOUNDATION
HOSPITALS**
Also Called: Avon Medical Offices
36711 American Way (44011-4062)
PHONE..............................216 524-7377
EMP: 593
SALES (corp-wide): 93B **Privately Held**
SIC: 8011 Medical centers
HQ: Kaiser Foundation Hospitals Inc
  1 Kaiser Plz
  Oakland CA 94612
  510 271-6611

(G-890)
KMU TRUCKING & EXCVTG INC
4436 Center Rd (44011-2369)
PHONE..............................440 934-1008
Kevin Urig, *President*
Lorie Urig, *Vice Pres*
Keith Urig, *Admin Sec*
EMP: 30
SALES: 20MM **Privately Held**
SIC: 1794 4212 Excavation & grading,
  building construction; local trucking, with-
  out storage

(G-891)
KUNO CREATIVE GROUP LLC
36901 American Way Ste 2a (44011-4058)
PHONE..............................440 225-4144
Cali Thomson, *Marketing Staff*
Christopher Knipper,
EMP: 27
SALES (est): 1.9MM **Privately Held**
WEB: www.kunocreative.com
SIC: 7374 7311 Computer graphics serv-
  ice; advertising agencies

(G-892)
LE CHAPERON ROUGE (PA)
1504 Travelers Pt (44011-4046)
PHONE..............................440 934-0296
Stella Moga, *Principal*
Marie Bentley, *Director*
EMP: 41
SALES (est): 4.3MM **Privately Held**
SIC: 8351 Child day care services

(G-893)
LOWES HOME CENTERS LLC
1445 Center Rd (44011-1238)
PHONE..............................440 937-3500
Greg Fillar, *Manager*
EMP: 130
SALES (corp-wide): 68.6B **Publicly Held**
SIC: 5211 5031 5722 5064 Home centers; building materials, exterior; building materials, interior; household appliance stores; electrical appliances, television & radio
HQ: Lowe's Home Centers, Llc
1605 Curtis Bridge Rd
Wilkesboro NC 28697
336 658-4000

(G-894)
MEDICAL DIAGNOSTIC LAB INC (PA)
Also Called: Premier Physican Centers
36711 American Way Ste 2a (44011-4061)
P.O. Box 74692, Cleveland (44194-0775)
PHONE..............................440 333-1375
Robert Harrison, *Corp Comm Staff*
M Sowden, *Manager*
EMP: 30
SALES (est): 5.7MM **Privately Held**
SIC: 8011 8071 General & family practice, physician/surgeon; testing laboratories

(G-895)
MERCY HEALTH
1480 Center Rd Ste A (44011-1239)
PHONE..............................440 937-4600
John W Escolas Do, *Principal*
EMP: 37
SALES (corp-wide): 4.7B **Privately Held**
SIC: 8062 General medical & surgical hospitals
PA: Mercy Health
1701 Mercy Health Pl
Cincinnati OH 45237
513 639-2800

(G-896)
NORTH COAST BEARINGS LLC
Also Called: After Market Products
1050 Jaycox Rd (44011-1312)
PHONE..............................440 930-7600
William Hagy, *President*
▲ EMP: 50
SQ FT: 30,000
SALES (est): 32.3MM **Privately Held**
SIC: 5085 Bearings

(G-897)
NORTH OHIO HEART CENTER INC
Also Called: Ohio Medical Group
1220 Moore Rd Ste B (44011-4044)
P.O. Box 714363, Columbus (43271-4363)
PHONE..............................440 204-4000
Ali N Assaad MD, *Med Doctor*
Gary Thome, *Manager*
EMP: 40
SALES (corp-wide): 13.5MM **Privately Held**
WEB: www.nohc.com
SIC: 8011 Cardiologist & cardio-vascular specialist
PA: North Ohio Heart Center, Inc
3600 Kolbe Rd Ste 127
Lorain OH 44053
440 204-4000

(G-898)
NVR INC
2553 Palmer Ln (44011-2048)
PHONE..............................440 933-7734
EMP: 33 **Publicly Held**
SIC: 1521 New construction, single-family houses
PA: Nvr, Inc.
11700 Plaza America Dr # 500
Reston VA 20190

(G-899)
PAT YOUNG SERVICE CO INC
1260 Moore Rd Ste K (44011-4021)
PHONE..............................440 891-1550
Kirk Young, *Branch Mgr*
EMP: 40

SALES (corp-wide): 54MM **Privately Held**
WEB: www.pysfederated.com
SIC: 5013 Motor vehicle supplies & new parts
PA: Pat Young Service Co Inc
6100 Hillcrest Dr
Cleveland OH 44125
216 447-8550

(G-900)
PERSONAL LAWN CARE INC
3910 Long Rd (44011-2244)
PHONE..............................440 934-5296
Thomas Brunner, *President*
EMP: 30
SQ FT: 4,500
SALES (est): 2.7MM **Privately Held**
SIC: 0781 0782 Landscape architects; lawn care services

(G-901)
PHOENIX COSMOPOLITAN GROUP LLC
36550 Chester Rd Apt 1505 (44011-4003)
PHONE..............................814 746-4863
Tamarah Black, *CEO*
Michele Zieziula, *COO*
Leon Wilson, *CFO*
EMP: 26
SALES (est): 1.8MM **Privately Held**
SIC: 8742 Management consulting services

(G-902)
R & J INVESTMENT CO INC
Also Called: Avon Oaks Nursing Home
37800 French Creek Rd (44011-1763)
PHONE..............................440 934-5204
Joan E Reidy, *President*
Juliette Reidy, *Corp Secy*
Karen Ortiz, *Vice Pres*
Richard J Reidy, *Vice Pres*
Chris Brown, *Office Mgr*
EMP: 130 EST: 1965
SQ FT: 75,000
SALES (est): 8.1MM **Privately Held**
WEB: www.avonoaks.net
SIC: 8051 8351 Convalescent home with continuous nursing care; child day care services

(G-903)
RIVER PLUMBING INC
Also Called: River Plumbing & Supply
1756 Moore Rd (44011-1024)
P.O. Box 270 (44011-0270)
PHONE..............................440 934-3720
David Dobos, *President*
John Janner, *General Mgr*
Douglas Vaught, *Vice Pres*
EMP: 38
SQ FT: 8,000
SALES: 3.5MM **Privately Held**
SIC: 5074 Plumbing fittings & supplies

(G-904)
WHITTGUARD SECURITY SERVICES
37435 Colorado Ave (44011-1531)
PHONE..............................440 288-7233
James Whitt, *Owner*
Art Keller, *Opers Mgr*
EMP: 130
SQ FT: 3,000
SALES: 1MM **Privately Held**
SIC: 7381 Security guard service

(G-905)
WICKENS HRZER PNZA COOK BTISTA
35765 Chester Rd (44011-1262)
PHONE..............................440 695-8000
David L Herzer, *President*
Corri Burns, *President*
Matthew Nakon, *Principal*
Joseph Cirigliano, *Vice Pres*
Rochelle Kuznicki, *Vice Pres*
EMP: 75
SQ FT: 30,000
SALES (est): 9.9MM **Privately Held**
SIC: 8111 General practice law office; general practice attorney, lawyer

(G-906)
WILLOWAY NURSERIES INC (PA)
4534 Center Rd (44011-2368)
P.O. Box 299 (44011-0299)
PHONE..............................440 934-4435
Tom Demaline, *President*
Cathy Kowalczyk, *Vice Pres*
Paul Doherty, *Buyer*
Tim Cullinan, *Purchasing*
Ken Didion, *CFO*
▲ EMP: 105
SQ FT: 5,000
SALES (est): 28.5MM **Privately Held**
WEB: www.willowaynurseries.com
SIC: 0181 Shrubberies grown in field nurseries; nursery stock, growing of; foliage, growing of

---

Avon Lake
Lorain County

(G-907)
ALUMALLOY METALCASTING COMPANY
33665 Walker Rd (44012-1044)
PHONE..............................440 930-2222
Dennis Daniels, *President*
Chris Daniels, *Vice Pres*
Tom Schroeder, *Manager*
Mary Rumsey, *Administration*
Judy Spencer, *Administration*
EMP: 65
SQ FT: 11,000
SALES (est): 29.5MM **Privately Held**
WEB: www.alumalloy.com
SIC: 5051 Metals service centers & offices

(G-908)
APL LOGISTICS LTD
32608 Surrey Ln (44012-1643)
PHONE..............................440 930-2822
EMP: 245
SALES (corp-wide): 5.1B **Privately Held**
SIC: 4412 Deep sea foreign transportation of freight
HQ: Apl Logistics, Ltd.
17600 N Perimeter Dr # 150
Scottsdale AZ 85255
602 357-9100

(G-909)
AVON LAKE ANIMAL CLINIC INC
Also Called: Avon Lake Animal Care Center
124 Miller Rd (44012-1015)
PHONE..............................440 933-5297
James Haddad, *President*
John H Simpson Dvm, *Principal*
Frank J Krupka Jr, *Vice Pres*
EMP: 45 EST: 1956
SQ FT: 2,000
SALES (est): 5MM **Privately Held**
SIC: 0742 0752 Animal hospital services, pets & other animal specialties; veterinarian, animal specialties; grooming services, pet & animal specialties

(G-910)
AVON LAKE SHEET METAL CO
33574 Pin Oak Pkwy (44012-2320)
P.O. Box 64 (44012-0064)
PHONE..............................440 933-3505
Carl Wetzig Jr, *President*
Gary Wightman, *Corp Secy*
Dennis Lightfoot, *Draft/Design*
EMP: 38
SQ FT: 32,000
SALES (est): 8.8MM **Privately Held**
WEB: www.avonlakesheetmetal.com
SIC: 3444 1761 Sheet metalwork; sheet metalwork

(G-911)
CATAMARAN HOME DLVRY OHIO INC
Also Called: Ips
33381 Walker Rd (44012-1456)
PHONE..............................440 930-5520
Douglas Boodjeh, *Chairman*
Thomas Mc Connell, *VP Finance*
Stacy Kendeigh Cain, *Cust Mgr*
EMP: 65

SALES (est): 6.8MM
SALES (corp-wide): 226.2B **Publicly Held**
WEB: www.ipsrx.com
SIC: 5961 5122 Pharmaceuticals, mail order; drugs, proprietaries & sundries
HQ: Catamaran Health Solutions Llc
800 King Farm Blvd # 400
Rockville MD 20850

(G-912)
CITY OF AVON LAKE
Also Called: Water & Sewer Department
201 Miller Rd (44012-1004)
PHONE..............................440 933-6226
Todd A Danielson, *Branch Mgr*
EMP: 36 **Privately Held**
WEB: www.sunsetshoresbb.com
SIC: 4941 4952 Water supply; sewerage systems
PA: City Of Avon Lake
150 Avon Belden Rd
Avon Lake OH 44012
440 933-6141

(G-913)
CLEVELAND CLINIC FOUNDATION
450 Avon Belden Rd (44012-2282)
PHONE..............................440 930-6800
Toby Cosgrove, *Manager*
EMP: 85
SALES (corp-wide): 8.9B **Privately Held**
SIC: 6733 Trusts
PA: The Cleveland Clinic Foundation
9500 Euclid Ave
Cleveland OH 44195
216 636-8335

(G-914)
COMPREHENSIVE LOGISTICS CO INC
1200 Chester Indus Pkwy (44012)
PHONE..............................330 233-2627
Daryl Legg, *Branch Mgr*
EMP: 33 **Privately Held**
SIC: 8742 Management consulting services
PA: Comprehensive Logistics, Co., Inc.
4944 Belmont Ave Ste 202
Youngstown OH 44505

(G-915)
DMR MANAGEMENT INC
Also Called: Fast Track Auction Sales
109 Brookfield Rd (44012-1504)
PHONE..............................513 771-1700
Ray Donsante, *President*
Carmen Donsante, *Vice Pres*
Michael Vescio, *Vice Pres*
EMP: 50
SALES: 12MM **Privately Held**
SIC: 7389 Auction, appraisal & exchange services

(G-916)
ED TOMKO CHRYSLR JEP DGE INC
33725 Walker Rd (44012-1010)
PHONE..............................440 835-5900
Edward P Tomko, *President*
Dolores Tomko, *Vice Pres*
Paul E Tomko, *Admin Sec*
EMP: 30
SQ FT: 8,000
SALES (est): 10.9MM **Privately Held**
SIC: 5511 7538 7515 5012 Automobiles, new & used; general automotive repair shops; passenger car leasing; automobiles & other motor vehicles

(G-917)
FLUID MECHANICS LLC (PA)
760 Moore Rd (44012-2317)
PHONE..............................216 362-7800
Thomas Koenig, *Treasurer*
Herwig Flug, *Mng Member*
James Stevenot, *Admin Sec*
Joanna Vardas, *Asst Sec*
EMP: 25 EST: 2015
SQ FT: 10,000
SALES (est): 9.7MM **Privately Held**
SIC: 5084 Engines & parts, diesel

(G-918)
H & B WINDOW CLEANING INC
753 Avon Belden Rd Ste D (44012-2253)
P.O. Box 42, Avon (44011-0042)
PHONE....................................440 934-6158
John Aunspaw, *President*
Donna Aunspaw, *Vice Pres*
EMP: 25
SQ FT: 1,777
SALES (est): 743.2K **Privately Held**
SIC: 7349 Window cleaning

(G-919)
HALL CONTRACTING SERVICES INC
33540 Pin Oak Pkwy (44012-2665)
P.O. Box 144, Florissant CO (80816-0144)
PHONE....................................440 930-0050
Richard Palmer, *President*
Graham Hall, *Chairman*
▲ **EMP:** 55
SQ FT: 24,000
SALES (est): 5.4MM **Privately Held**
WEB: www.grhall.com
SIC: 7699 Printing trades machinery & equipment repair

(G-920)
HINKLEY LIGHTING INC (PA)
Also Called: Fredrick Ramond
33000 Pin Oak Pkwy (44012-2641)
PHONE....................................440 653-5500
Richard A Wiedemer Jr, *President*
Eric Wiedemer, *Vice Pres*
Jess Wiedemer, *Vice Pres*
Richard Wiedemer, *VP Opers*
Matt McKnight, *Opers Mgr*
◆ **EMP:** 60 **EST:** 1920
SQ FT: 100,000
SALES (est): 42.2MM **Privately Held**
WEB: www.hinkleylighting.com
SIC: 5063 Lighting fixtures

(G-921)
KOPF CONSTRUCTION CORPORATION (PA)
420 Avon Belden Rd Ste A (44012-2294)
PHONE....................................440 933-6908
Herman R Kopf Jr, *President*
EMP: 125
SQ FT: 1,609
SALES (est): 14.2MM **Privately Held**
SIC: 1521 1522 New construction, single-family houses; multi-family dwelling construction

(G-922)
KOPF CONSTRUCTION CORPORATION
Also Called: Aqua Marine Luxury Apartments
750 Aqua Marine Blvd (44012-2585)
PHONE....................................440 933-0250
David Klima, *Branch Mgr*
EMP: 73
SALES (corp-wide): 14.2MM **Privately Held**
SIC: 6513 Apartment building operators
PA: Kopf Construction Corporation
420 Avon Belden Rd Ste A
Avon Lake OH 44012
440 933-6908

(G-923)
LUBRIZOL ADVANCED MTLS INC
Also Called: LUBRIZOL ADVANCED MATERIALS, INC.
550 Moore Rd (44012-2313)
P.O. Box 134 (44012-0134)
PHONE....................................440 933-0400
Joeri Plusnin, *Engineer*
Dmitry Shuster, *Engineer*
Stan Biel, *Project Engr*
Meredith Bruder, *Marketing Staff*
Joseph Lazeunick, *Branch Mgr*
EMP: 50
SALES (corp-wide): 225.3B **Publicly Held**
WEB: www.pharma.noveoninc.com
SIC: 8731 2821 2899 Commercial physical research; plastics materials & resins; chemical preparations

HQ: Lubrizol Global Management, Inc
9911 Brecksville Rd
Brecksville OH 44141
216 447-5000

(G-924)
M T BUSINESS TECHNOLOGIES
Also Called: Mt Business Technologies
33588 Pin Oak Pkwy (44012-2320)
PHONE....................................440 933-7682
Donald Cole, *Manager*
EMP: 45
SALES (corp-wide): 9.8B **Publicly Held**
WEB: www.mtbustech.com
SIC: 5044 Office equipment
HQ: Mt Business Technologies, Inc.
1150 National Pkwy
Mansfield OH 44906
419 529-6100

(G-925)
NRG POWER MIDWEST LP
Also Called: Avon Lake Generating Station
33570 Lake Rd (44012-1108)
PHONE....................................440 930-6401
Dan Rogatto, *Branch Mgr*
EMP: 54 **Publicly Held**
SIC: 4911 Generation, electric power
HQ: Nrg Power Midwest Lp
1000 Main St
Houston TX 77002

(G-926)
POLYONE CORPORATION (PA)
33587 Walker Rd (44012-1145)
PHONE....................................440 930-1000
Robert M Patterson, *Ch of Bd*
Richard N Altice, *President*
Robert Bindner, *President*
Mark D Crist, *President*
Michael A Garratt, *President*
◆ **EMP:** 73
SALES: 3.5B **Publicly Held**
WEB: www.polyone.com
SIC: 2821 3087 5162 3081 Thermoplastic materials; polyvinyl chloride resins (PVC); vinyl resins; custom compound purchased resins; resins; plastics basic shapes; unsupported plastics film & sheet

(G-927)
SEMINOLE THEATER CO LLC
Also Called: Seminole 8 Theaters
32818 Walker Rd (44012-1473)
PHONE....................................440 934-6998
EMP: 25
SALES: 1.9MM **Privately Held**
SIC: 7832 Motion Picture Theater

(G-928)
TRUENORTH CULTURAL ARTS
739 Moore Rd Ste 1 (44012-2661)
PHONE....................................440 949-5200
Rick Fortney, *President*
Richard Fortney, *President*
EMP: 25
SALES: 179.7K **Privately Held**
SIC: 8733 7911 Noncommercial social research organization; dance studio & school

(G-929)
WATTEREDGE LLC (DH)
567 Miller Rd (44012-2304)
PHONE....................................440 933-6110
Joseph P Langhenry, *President*
Craig Smith, *Engineer*
George Sass, *Project Engr*
Janet Collins, *Human Res Mgr*
Brenda Westfall, *Sales Staff*
◆ **EMP:** 64
SQ FT: 65,000
SALES (est): 41.1MM
SALES (corp-wide): 2.3B **Privately Held**
WEB: www.watteredge.com
SIC: 5085 3643 5051 3052 Industrial supplies; current-carrying wiring devices; metals service centers & offices; rubber & plastics hose & beltings; miscellaneous metalwork
HQ: Coleman Cable, Llc
1 Overlook Pt
Lincolnshire IL 60069
847 672-2300

Bainbridge
Ross County

(G-930)
COUNTRYSIDE RENTALS INC (PA)
Also Called: Rent To Own
210 S Quarry St (45612-9482)
P.O. Box 547 (45612-0547)
PHONE....................................740 634-2666
Michael D Tissot, *President*
James D Hapner, *Principal*
Ronald L Magee, *Principal*
Jane Tissot, *Corp Secy*
Jason Salyers, *Cust Mgr*
▲ **EMP:** 26
SQ FT: 8,000
SALES (est): 34MM **Privately Held**
WEB: www.r2o.com
SIC: 7359 Television rental; electronic equipment rental, except computers; furniture rental

(G-931)
LIGHTHOUSE YOUTH SERVICES INC
Also Called: Paint Creek Youth Center
1071 Tong Hollow Rd (45612-1500)
P.O. Box 586 (45612-0586)
PHONE....................................740 634-3094
Renee Hagan, *Director*
EMP: 60
SALES (corp-wide): 25.2MM **Privately Held**
SIC: 8322 8361 Youth center; juvenile correctional facilities
PA: Lighthouse Youth Services, Inc.
401 E Mcmillan St
Cincinnati OH 45206
513 221-3350

(G-932)
W K H R RADIO
Also Called: FM 91 Point 5
17425 Snyder Rd (45612)
PHONE....................................440 708-0915
Rowland Shepard, *Vice Pres*
EMP: 30 **EST:** 1999
SALES (est): 122.8K **Privately Held**
SIC: 4832 Radio broadcasting stations

Baltic
Tuscarawas County

(G-933)
BALTIC HEALTH CARE CORP
Also Called: Oakponte Nrsing Rehabilitation
130 Buena Vista St (43804-9091)
PHONE....................................330 897-4311
Brian Colleran, *President*
EMP: 99
SALES (est): 2.6MM **Privately Held**
SIC: 8051 Skilled nursing care facilities

(G-934)
FLEX TECHNOLOGIES INC
Also Called: Poly Flex
3430 State Route 93 (43804-9705)
P.O. Box 300 (43804-0300)
PHONE....................................330 897-6311
Gglenn Burket, *Division Mgr*
Brian Harrison, *Manager*
Ken Ziegembusch, *Info Tech Mgr*
EMP: 35
SQ FT: 20,000
SALES (corp-wide): 6MM **Privately Held**
WEB: www.flextechnologies.com
SIC: 2821 5169 3087 Molding compounds, plastics; synthetic resins, rubber & plastic materials; custom compound purchased resins
PA: Flex Technologies, Inc.
5479 Gundy Dr
Midvale OH 44653
740 922-5992

(G-935)
KEIM LUMBER COMPANY
State Rte 557 (43804)
PHONE....................................330 893-2251

Bill Keim, *Branch Mgr*
EMP: 41
SALES (corp-wide): 41MM **Privately Held**
WEB: www.keimlumber.com
SIC: 5211 5031 Planing mill products & lumber; lumber: rough, dressed & finished
PA: Keim Lumber Company
4465 St Rte 557
Charm OH 44617
330 893-2251

(G-936)
SCHLABACH WOOD DESIGN INC
52567 State Route 651 (43804-9520)
PHONE....................................330 897-2600
Willis Schlabach, *President*
EMP: 32
SQ FT: 9,000
SALES (est): 3.3MM **Privately Held**
WEB: www.schlabachwooddesign.com
SIC: 1751 5211 Cabinet & finish carpentry; cabinets, kitchen

Baltimore
Fairfield County

(G-937)
MICRO CONSTRUCTION LLC
Also Called: Micro Roll Off Containers
8675 Lncster Newark Rd Ne (43105-9659)
P.O. Box 202 (43105-0202)
PHONE....................................740 862-0751
Rusty Mock, *Mng Member*
Tony P Mock,
EMP: 25
SALES (est): 1.7MM **Privately Held**
SIC: 4953 5032 Garbage: collecting, destroying & processing; granite building stone

---

Barberton
Summit County

(G-938)
AKROCHEM CORPORATION
2845 Newpark Dr (44203-1047)
PHONE....................................330 535-2108
Jack Hale, *Branch Mgr*
EMP: 25
SALES (corp-wide): 118.8MM **Privately Held**
SIC: 5169 Chemicals & allied products
PA: Akrochem Corporation
3770 Embassy Pkwy
Akron OH 44333
330 535-2100

(G-939)
AKRON FOUNDRY CO
Also Called: Akron Electric
1025 Eagon St (44203-1603)
PHONE....................................330 745-3101
Mike Pancoe, *General Mgr*
Sukhwant Puri, *Mfg Mgr*
EMP: 40
SALES (corp-wide): 22MM **Privately Held**
WEB: www.akronfoundry.com
SIC: 1731 3699 3643 3444 Electrical work; electrical equipment & supplies; noncurrent-carrying wiring services; sheet metalwork; aluminum foundries
PA: Akron Foundry Co.
2728 Wingate Ave
Akron OH 44314
330 745-3101

(G-940)
AKRON PORCELAIN & PLASTICS CO
83 E State St (44203-2755)
P.O. Box 15157, Akron (44314-5157)
PHONE....................................330 745-2159
George H Lewis III, *President*
EMP: 26
SQ FT: 47,900

SALES (est): 1.6MM
SALES (corp-wide): 21.1MM **Privately Held**
WEB: www.akronporcelain.com
SIC: **4225** General warehousing & storage
PA: The Akron Porcelain & Plastics Co
2739 Cory Ave
Akron OH 44314
330 745-2159

(G-941)
APPLE HEATING INC (PA)
Also Called: Apple Electric
344 4th St Nw (44203-2212)
PHONE...............................440 997-1212
Scott Robinson, *President*
David Pinelli, *Vice Pres*
EMP: 26
SQ FT: 8,000
SALES (est): 3.1MM **Privately Held**
WEB: www.appleheating.com
SIC: **1711** Warm air heating & air conditioning contractor; hydronics heating contractor

(G-942)
ARIS HORTICULTURE INC (PA)
Also Called: Yoder Trading Company
115 3rd St Se (44203-4208)
PHONE...............................330 745-2143
William Rasbach, *President*
Thomas D Doak, *Principal*
G Ramsey Yoder, *Chairman*
William Riffey, *Vice Pres*
Scott Schaefer, *CFO*
▲ EMP: 85 EST: 1919
SQ FT: 28,000
SALES (est): 216.3MM **Privately Held**
WEB: www.yoder.com
SIC: **0181** Nursery stock, growing of; florists' greens & flowers

(G-943)
BABCOCK & WILCOX CNSTR CO INC (DH)
74 Robinson Ave (44203-2630)
PHONE...............................330 860-6301
E James Ferland, *CEO*
Brian Kelly, *Superintendent*
Mark S Low, *Senior VP*
D Paul Scavuzzo, *Senior VP*
Rod Carlson, *Vice Pres*
EMP: 94
SALES (est): 467.8MM
SALES (corp-wide): 1B **Publicly Held**
SIC: **1629** Power plant construction
HQ: The Babcock & Wilcox Company
20 S Van Buren Ave
Barberton OH 44203
330 753-4511

(G-944)
BABCOCK & WILCOX COMPANY (HQ)
20 S Van Buren Ave (44203-3585)
P.O. Box 351 (44203-0351)
PHONE...............................330 753-4511
Gregory Calvin, *President*
Pete Campanizzi, *General Mgr*
Kevin Brolly, *Regional Mgr*
Mark S Low, *Senior VP*
Jenny L Apker, *Senior VP*
◆ EMP: 1000 EST: 1867
SQ FT: 16,000
SALES (est): 1.3B
SALES (corp-wide): 1B **Publicly Held**
SIC: **1629 1711 3443 7699** Industrial plant construction; power plant construction; plumbing, heating, air-conditioning contractors; fabricated plate work (boiler shop); boilers: industrial, power, or marine; boiler & heating repair services; management services; auto controls regulating residntl & coml environmt & applncs
PA: Babcock & Wilcox Enterprises, Inc.
20 S Van Buren Ave
Barberton OH 44203
330 753-4511

(G-945)
BARBERTON AREA FAMILY PRACTICE
155 5th St Ne (44203-3332)
PHONE...............................330 615-3205
James Randall Richard, *Director*

EMP: 40
SALES (est): 1.3MM **Privately Held**
SIC: **8011** General & family practice, physician/surgeon

(G-946)
BARBERTON JAYCEES
541 W Tuscarawas Ave # 104 (44203-2592)
P.O. Box 148 (44203-0148)
PHONE...............................330 745-3733
Teri Dwyer, *President*
EMP: 45
SALES: 39.1K **Privately Held**
SIC: **8399** Community development groups

(G-947)
BARBERTON LAUNDRY & CLEANING
Also Called: Liniform Service
1050 Northview Ave (44203-7197)
PHONE...............................330 825-6911
Bertha Jenkins, *President*
A Edward Good, *Chairman*
Patricia Shultz, *Vice Pres*
EMP: 58
SQ FT: 35,000
SALES (est): 5MM **Privately Held**
WEB: www.liniform.com
SIC: **7299 7213 4215** Clothing rental services; uniform supply; package delivery, vehicular

(G-948)
BLIND & SON LLC
Also Called: Tri-County Heating & Cooling
344 4th St Nw (44203-2212)
PHONE...............................330 753-7711
William Blind, *Mng Member*
Joe Bilota,
John Hartman,
David Zahn,
EMP: 80
SQ FT: 15,000
SALES (est): 16.4MM **Privately Held**
SIC: **1711** Warm air heating & air conditioning contractor; heating & air conditioning contractors

(G-949)
CASEGOODS INC
130 31st St Nw (44203-7238)
PHONE...............................330 825-2461
Mitchell Volk, *President*
Denise Volk, *Corp Secy*
EMP: 30
SALES (est): 2.8MM **Privately Held**
WEB: www.casegoods.com
SIC: **1751** Cabinet & finish carpentry

(G-950)
CHRISTIAN HEALTHCARE
127 Hazelwood Ave (44203-1316)
PHONE...............................330 848-1511
Roger Kittelson, *CFO*
Charity Beall, *Finance*
Lauren Selleck, *Comms Dir*
Norma Mull, *Supervisor*
Howard Russell, *Exec Dir*
EMP: 40
SALES (est): 220.3MM **Privately Held**
WEB: www.christianbrotherhood.org
SIC: **8011** Offices & clinics of medical doctors

(G-951)
CORPORATE ELECTRIC COMPANY LLC
Also Called: Electrical Construction
378 S Van Buren Ave (44203-4014)
P.O. Box 390, Akron (44309-0390)
PHONE...............................330 331-7517
Crystal Bowers, *Office Mgr*
Marcus Sabo,
Rachel Collins,
EMP: 33
SALES (est): 2.7MM **Privately Held**
SIC: **1731** General electrical contractor

(G-952)
FOUR CORNERS CLEANING INC
3479 E Tuscarawas Ext (44203-3843)
PHONE...............................330 644-0834
Timothy Horvath, *President*

Rebecca Horvath, *Vice Pres*
EMP: 50
SALES (est): 1.1MM **Privately Held**
SIC: **7349** Cleaning service, industrial or commercial

(G-953)
GENERAL PLASTEX INC
35 Stuver Pl (44203-2417)
PHONE...............................330 745-7775
Renee Hershberger, *President*
EMP: 31
SQ FT: 52,500
SALES (est): 5.1MM **Privately Held**
SIC: **7699 3452** Industrial machinery & equipment repair; screws, metal

(G-954)
HCR MANORCARE MED SVCS FLA LLC
Also Called: Manor Care
85 3rd St Se (44203-4208)
PHONE...............................330 753-5005
Sara Fielding-Russell, *Director*
EMP: 150
SQ FT: 31,749
SALES (corp-wide): 2.4B **Publicly Held**
WEB: www.manorcare.com
SIC: **8051** Convalescent home with continuous nursing care
HQ: Hcr Manorcare Medical Services Of Florida, Llc
333 N Summit St Ste 100
Toledo OH 43604
419 252-5500

(G-955)
INTEGRITY PROCESSING LLC
1055 Wooster Rd N (44203-1352)
P.O. Box 342, Chagrin Falls (44022-0342)
PHONE...............................330 285-6937
Gerald F Robinson,
EMP: 30
SALES (est): 1.1MM **Privately Held**
SIC: **7699** Plastics products repair

(G-956)
JOSEPH R HARRISON COMPANY LPA
36 37th St Sw (44203-7321)
PHONE...............................330 666-6900
Joseph R Harrison, *President*
Lazar John,
EMP: 42
SQ FT: 5,500
SALES (est): 3.3MM **Privately Held**
WEB: www.jrhlpa.com
SIC: **8111** General practice law office

(G-957)
JR ENGINEERING INC
123 9th St Nw (44203-2455)
P.O. Box 189 (44203-0189)
PHONE...............................330 848-0960
Louis Bilinovich Jr, *President*
EMP: 115
SQ FT: 725,000
SALES (corp-wide): 70.6MM **Privately Held**
SIC: **5084 5013** Industrial machinery & equipment; motor vehicle supplies & new parts
PA: Jr Engineering, Inc.
123 9th St Nw
Barberton OH 44203
330 848-0960

(G-958)
LABCARE
165 5th St Se Ste A (44203-9001)
PHONE...............................330 753-3649
Bobbi Butterfield, *Principal*
EMP: 30
SALES (est): 419.4K **Privately Held**
SIC: **8071 8011** Medical laboratories; medical centers

(G-959)
LENNYS AUTO SALES INC
Also Called: Lenny's Collision Center
893 Wooster Rd N (44203-1637)
PHONE...............................330 848-2993
Leonard K Eicher, *President*
Brenda L Eicher, *Vice Pres*
EMP: 25
SQ FT: 7,000

SALES: 1MM **Privately Held**
WEB: www.lennyscollision.com
SIC: **7532** Collision shops, automotive; lettering & painting services

(G-960)
LOYAL OAK GOLF COURSE INC
2909 Clvland Massillon Rd (44203-5228)
PHONE...............................330 825-2904
Arthur Gruber, *President*
Katheryn Gruber, *Vice Pres*
Harold Corzin, *Admin Sec*
EMP: 30 EST: 1938
SALES (est): 1.3MM **Privately Held**
SIC: **7992 5813 5812 5941** Public golf courses; bar (drinking places); snack bar; golf goods & equipment

(G-961)
PLEASANT VIEW NURSING HOME (PA)
Also Called: Pleasant View Health Care Ctr
401 Snyder Ave (44203-4131)
PHONE...............................330 745-6028
Richard Morris, *President*
Lucy Majorkiewicz, *Admin Sec*
Eileen Morris,
EMP: 99
SALES (est): 9.3MM **Privately Held**
SIC: **8051** Convalescent home with continuous nursing care

(G-962)
PLEASANT VIEW NURSING HOME
220 3rd St Se (44203-4235)
PHONE...............................330 848-5028
Richard Morris, *Branch Mgr*
EMP: 50
SALES (corp-wide): 9.3MM **Privately Held**
SIC: **8052** Personal care facility
PA: Pleasant View Nursing Home
401 Snyder Ave
Barberton OH 44203
330 745-6028

(G-963)
PSC METALS INC
284 7th St Nw (44203-2125)
PHONE...............................234 208-2331
EMP: 51
SALES (corp-wide): 11.7B **Publicly Held**
SIC: **5093** Metal scrap & waste materials
HQ: Psc Metals, Llc
5875 Landerbrook Dr # 200
Mayfield Heights OH 44124
440 753-5400

(G-964)
PSC METALS INC
701 W Hopocan Ave (44203-2159)
PHONE...............................330 745-4437
Dave Casalinova, *Manager*
EMP: 42
SQ FT: 16,000
SALES (corp-wide): 11.7B **Publicly Held**
WEB: www.pscmetals.com
SIC: **5093** Metal scrap & waste materials
HQ: Psc Metals, Llc
5875 Landerbrook Dr # 200
Mayfield Heights OH 44124
440 753-5400

(G-965)
RONDY FLEET SERVICES INC
255 Wooster Rd N (44203-8206)
PHONE...............................330 745-9016
Donald Rondy, *President*
Ronna Rondy, *Corp Secy*
Frank Moore, *Vice Pres*
EMP: 150
SALES (est): 13.5MM
SALES (corp-wide): 33.1MM **Privately Held**
WEB: www.rondy.net
SIC: **4731 7538** Freight transportation arrangement; general automotive repair shops
HQ: Tahoma Rubber & Plastics, Inc.
255 Wooster Rd N
Barberton OH 44203
330 745-9016

GEOGRAPHIC

(G-966)
RT80 EXPRESS INC
4409 Clvland Massillon Rd (44203-5703)
P.O. Box 269 (44203-0269)
PHONE....................330 706-0900
David Bilinovich, *President*
Pam Bilinovich, *Vice Pres*
EMP: 30
SQ FT: 140,000
SALES (est): 4.7MM **Privately Held**
SIC: 4212 4213 Local trucking, without storage; trucking, except local

(G-967)
SUMMA HEALTH
Also Called: Lab Care
165 5th St Se Ste A (44203-9001)
PHONE....................330 753-3649
Fran Royer, *Manager*
EMP: 70
SALES (corp-wide): 1B **Privately Held**
WEB: www.barbhosp.com
SIC: 8062 8071 General medical & surgical hospitals; medical laboratories
PA: Summa Health
     525 E Market St
     Akron OH 44304
     330 375-3000

(G-968)
SUMMA HEALTH SYSTEM
Also Called: Summa Barberton Hospital
155 5th St Ne (44203-3332)
PHONE....................330 615-3000
Ronald J Elder, *Principal*
Mark Matthews, *Vice Pres*
Dawn Barabasch, *Facilities Mgr*
Stephen A Dabreau Do, *Osteopathy*
Eddie Sveda,
EMP: 2490
SALES (corp-wide): 1B **Privately Held**
SIC: 8062 General medical & surgical hospitals
PA: Summa Health
     525 E Market St
     Akron OH 44304
     330 375-3000

(G-969)
TAHOMA ENTERPRISES INC (PA)
255 Wooster Rd N (44203-2560)
PHONE....................330 745-9016
William P Herrington, *CEO*
EMP: 100
SALES (est): 33.1MM **Privately Held**
SIC: 3069 3089 5199 5162 Reclaimed rubber (reworked by manufacturing processes); plastic processing; foams & rubber; plastics products

(G-970)
TAHOMA RUBBER & PLASTICS INC (HQ)
Also Called: Rondy & Co.
255 Wooster Rd N (44203-2560)
PHONE....................330 745-9016
William P Herrington, *CEO*
Mary Wilcox, *Manager*
▼ **EMP:** 100
SQ FT: 750,000
SALES (est): 23.8MM
SALES (corp-wide): 33.1MM **Privately Held**
WEB: www.rondy.net
SIC: 3069 3089 5199 5162 Reclaimed rubber (reworked by manufacturing processes); plastic processing; foams & rubber; plastics products
PA: Tahoma Enterprises, Inc.
     255 Wooster Rd N
     Barberton OH 44203
     330 745-9016

(G-971)
WALGREEN CO
Also Called: Walgreens
900 Wooster Rd N (44203-1659)
PHONE....................330 745-2674
Steve Krausa, *Manager*
EMP: 30

SALES (corp-wide): 131.5B **Publicly Held**
WEB: www.walgreens.com
SIC: 5912 7384 Drug stores; photofinishing laboratory
HQ: Walgreen Co.
     200 Wilmot Rd
     Deerfield IL 60015
     847 315-2500

(G-972)
WESTERN & SOUTHERN LF INSUR CO
4172 Clvland Massillon Rd (44203-5704)
PHONE....................330 825-9935
Joseph Parker, *Marketing Mgr*
Roger Sanford, *Branch Mgr*
EMP: 34 **Privately Held**
SIC: 6411 Life insurance agents
HQ: The Western & Southern Life Insurance Company
     400 Broadway St
     Cincinnati OH 45202
     513 629-1800

(G-973)
YERMAN & YOUNG PAINTING INC
811 Brady Ave (44203-6661)
PHONE....................330 861-0022
Michael Yerman, *President*
Beth Yerman, *Corp Secy*
EMP: 30
SALES (est): 2.6MM **Privately Held**
SIC: 1721 Commercial painting

Barnesville
Belmont County

(G-974)
BARNESVILLE HEALTHCARE REHAB
Also Called: Astoria Place of Barnesville
400 Carrie Ave (43713-1317)
PHONE....................740 425-3648
Joseph Brandman,
Jeremy Goldberg,
Matt Gotter,
Michael Nudell,
EMP: 78 **EST:** 2012
SALES (est): 1.9MM **Privately Held**
SIC: 8051 Skilled nursing care facilities

(G-975)
BARNESVILLE HOSPITAL ASSN INC (PA)
639 W Main St (43713-1039)
P.O. Box 309 (43713-0309)
PHONE....................740 425-3941
Richard Doan, *CEO*
David Phillips, *COO*
Michael Carpenter, *Facilities Dir*
Willie Cooper-Lohr, *CFO*
Dorothy Minnich, *Finance Mgr*
EMP: 68
SQ FT: 60,000
SALES: 19.5MM **Privately Held**
WEB: www.barnesvillehospital.com
SIC: 8062 Hospital, affiliated with AMA residency

(G-976)
BARNESVILLE LIVESTOCK SALES CO
Also Called: Barnesville Live Stock Ofc
315 S Gardner St (43713-1379)
P.O. Box 166, New Concord (43762-0166)
PHONE....................740 425-3611
Mike N Morris, *Owner*
Gary Fogle, *Owner*
EMP: 25
SQ FT: 3,600
SALES (est): 1.5MM **Privately Held**
SIC: 5154 Auctioning livestock

(G-977)
BELMONT PROFESSIONAL ASSOC INC
100 Hospital Dr Ste 109 (43713-1099)
P.O. Box 309 (43713-0309)
PHONE....................740 425-5140
EMP: 247

SALES: 2.5MM
SALES (corp-wide): 19.5MM **Privately Held**
SIC: 8011 Primary care medical clinic
PA: Barnesville Hospital Association, Inc.
     639 W Main St
     Barnesville OH 43713
     740 425-3941

(G-978)
OHIO HILLS HEALTH SERVICES (PA)
101 E Main St (43713-1005)
PHONE....................740 425-5165
William E Chaney, *President*
Charles Bardell, *Vice Pres*
Candy Lendon, *Treasurer*
Linda Tacosik, *Admin Sec*
EMP: 80
SALES: 5.1MM **Privately Held**
SIC: 8011 Clinic, operated by physicians

(G-979)
SOUTH CENTRAL POWER COMPANY
Also Called: Belmont Division
37801 Brnsvlle Bthesda Rd (43713)
PHONE....................740 425-4018
Jim Meyers, *Branch Mgr*
EMP: 30
SALES (corp-wide): 282.1MM **Privately Held**
WEB: www.southcentralpower.com
SIC: 4911 Distribution, electric power
PA: South Central Power Company Inc
     2780 Coonpath Rd Ne
     Lancaster OH 43130
     740 653-4422

(G-980)
WESBANCO BANK INC
230 E Main St (43713-1006)
PHONE....................740 425-1927
EMP: 53
SALES (corp-wide): 284.5MM **Publicly Held**
SIC: 6022 State Commercial Bank
HQ: Wesbanco Bank, Inc.
     1 Bank Plz
     Wheeling WV 26003
     304 234-9000

Bascom
Seneca County

(G-981)
COUNTY OF SENECA
P.O. Box 119 (44809-0119)
PHONE....................419 937-2340
EMP: 25 **Privately Held**
SIC: 4119 Ambulance service
PA: County Of Seneca
     111 Madison St
     Tiffin OH 44883
     419 447-4550

Batavia
Clermont County

(G-982)
AECOM TECHNICAL SERVICES INC
4386 Haskell Ln (45103-2958)
P.O. Box 24099, Dayton (45424-0099)
PHONE....................937 233-1898
Todd Webster, *Branch Mgr*
EMP: 35
SALES (corp-wide): 20.1B **Publicly Held**
WEB: www.earthtech.com
SIC: 8711 Sanitary engineers
HQ: Aecom Technical Services, Inc.
     300 S Grand Ave Ste 1100
     Los Angeles CA 90071
     213 593-8000

(G-983)
BACHMANS INC
Also Called: Honeywell Authorized Dealer
4058 Clough Woods Dr (45103-2586)
PHONE....................513 943-5300

Marc E Bachman, *President*
Rod E Bachman, *Exec VP*
Dan Hughes, *Sales Mgr*
Hubert Acton, *Sales Staff*
Keith Finitzer, *Manager*
EMP: 30 **EST:** 1955
SQ FT: 16,500
SALES (est): 6.1MM **Privately Held**
WEB: www.bachmansinc.com
SIC: 1711 Warm air heating & air conditioning contractor; refrigeration contractor

(G-984)
BURD BROTHERS INC (PA)
4005 Borman Dr (45103-1684)
P.O. Box 324 (45103-0324)
PHONE....................800 538-2873
Dick Burdick, *CEO*
Tyler Burdick, *President*
Gayle Burdick, *Chairman*
Ryan Meiers, *Warehouse Mgr*
Erin Burdick, *Admin Sec*
EMP: 45
SQ FT: 30,000
SALES: 7.2MM **Privately Held**
WEB: www.burdbrothers.com
SIC: 4213 4225 Contract haulers; general warehousing

(G-985)
CARINGTON HEALTH SYSTEMS
Also Called: Batavia Nrsing Cnvalescent Inn
4000 Golden Age Dr (45103-1913)
PHONE....................513 732-6500
Steve Chaney, *Administration*
EMP: 300
SALES (corp-wide): 85.7MM **Privately Held**
SIC: 8051 Convalescent home with continuous nursing care
PA: Carington Health Systems
     8200 Beckett Park Dr
     Hamilton OH 45011
     513 682-2700

(G-986)
CHILD FOCUS INC
2337 Clermont Center Dr (45103-1959)
PHONE....................513 732-8800
Jim Carter, *Branch Mgr*
EMP: 32
SALES (corp-wide): 17MM **Privately Held**
WEB: www.childfocus.com
SIC: 8322 Child related social services
PA: Child Focus, Inc.
     4629 Aicholtz Rd Ste 2
     Cincinnati OH 45244
     513 752-1555

(G-987)
CLERMONT CNTY WTR RSOURCES DEPT
Also Called: Clermont County Wtr Resources
4400 Haskell Ln (45103-2990)
PHONE....................513 732-7970
Robert Sander, *Vice Pres*
Tom Yeager, *Director*
EMP: 97
SQ FT: 11,000
SALES: 27.9MM **Privately Held**
SIC: 4952 Sewerage systems

(G-988)
CLERMONT COUNTY COMMUNITY SVCS (PA)
3003 Hospital Dr (45103-2689)
PHONE....................513 732-2277
Joyce A Richardson, *President*
Billie Kuntz, *Director*
Joe Spaulding, *Director*
EMP: 35
SQ FT: 10,000
SALES: 2.4MM **Privately Held**
WEB: www.clermontsupportskids.org
SIC: 8322 9111 Individual & family services; county supervisors' & executives' offices

(G-989)
CLERMONT COUNTY GEN HLTH DST
2275 Bauer Rd Ste 300 (45103-1914)
PHONE....................513 732-7499
Timothy Kelly, *Principal*

Julianne Nesbit, *Commissioner*
EMP: 49 **Privately Held**
WEB: www.clermontauditor.org
SIC: 9431 8748 ; business consulting

(G-990)
CLERMONT NORTH EAST SCHOOL DST (PA)
2792 Us Highway 50 (45103-8532)
PHONE..................................513 625-8283
EMP: 39
SALES (est): 8.2MM **Privately Held**
SIC: 8211 8741 Elementary/Secondary School Management Services

(G-991)
CLERMONT RECOVERY CENTER INC
1088 Wasserman Way Ste C (45103-1974)
PHONE..................................513 735-8100
Steve Goldsberry, *President*
Cathy McClain, *Opers Spvr*
Doris Sigel, *Psychologist*
Tina Gullett, *Supervisor*
Joyce Long, *Administration*
EMP: 50
SALES: 7.4MM **Privately Held**
SIC: 8093 Drug clinic, outpatient

(G-992)
CLERMONT SENIOR SERVICES INC (PA)
Also Called: CLERMONT SENIOR SERVICES
2085 James E Sauls Sr Dr (45103-3255)
PHONE..................................513 724-1255
Cynthia Jenkins-Gramke, *CEO*
Gregory Carson, *CFO*
EMP: 119
SQ FT: 33,000
SALES: 8.3MM **Privately Held**
WEB: www.clermontseniors.com
SIC: 8322 Senior citizens' center or association

(G-993)
COUNTY OF CLERMONT
Also Called: Information Systems Dept
2279 Clermont Center Dr (45103-1956)
PHONE..................................513 732-7661
Steve Rybolt, *Manager*
EMP: 35
SQ FT: 1,320 **Privately Held**
WEB: www.clermontauditor.org
SIC: 8999 9121 Information bureau; county commissioner;
PA: County Of Clermont
177 E Main St
Batavia OH 45103
513 732-7980

(G-994)
COUNTY OF CLERMONT
Also Called: Division of Water Resources
4400 Haskell Ln (45103-2990)
PHONE..................................513 732-7970
Lyle Bloom, *Director*
EMP: 45 **Privately Held**
SIC: 1623 Water, sewer & utility lines
PA: County Of Clermont
177 E Main St
Batavia OH 45103
513 732-7980

(G-995)
CURTISS-WRIGHT FLOW CONTROL
Also Called: Qualtech NP
750 Kent Rd (45103-1704)
PHONE..................................513 735-2538
EMP: 85
SALES (corp-wide): 2.1B **Publicly Held**
SIC: 3491 3443 3599 1799 Mfg Industrial Valves Mfg Fabricated Plate Wrk Mfg Industrial Machinery Special Trade Contractor
HQ: Curtiss-Wright Flow Control Service Corporation
2950 E Birch St
Brea CA 92821
714 982-1898

(G-996)
DEVELPMNTAL DSBLTIES OHIO DEPT
Also Called: Southwest Ohio Dvlopmental Ctr
4399 E Bauman Ln (45103-1685)
PHONE..................................513 732-9200
Nancy McAvoy, *Principal*
EMP: 225 **Privately Held**
SIC: 8322 9431 Family counseling services;
HQ: Ohio Department Of Developmental Disabilities
30 E Broad St Fl 13
Columbus OH 43215

(G-997)
EDUCATIONAL AND COMMUNITY RDO
Rr 276 (45103)
P.O. Box 338, Owensville (45160-0338)
PHONE..................................513 724-3939
Mel Riffen, *President*
Paul Bodde, *Treasurer*
Don Littman, *Admin Sec*
EMP: 45
SALES: 180.5K **Privately Held**
SIC: 4832 Radio broadcasting stations

(G-998)
EDWARD ROSE ASSOCIATES INC
Also Called: Eastgate Woods Apts
4412 Eastwood Dr (45103-2440)
PHONE..................................513 752-2727
Gary Mounts, *Manager*
EMP: 25
SALES (corp-wide): 7.1MM **Privately Held**
SIC: 6513 Apartment building operators
PA: Edward Rose Associates, Inc.
38525 Woodward Ave
Bloomfield Hills MI 48304
248 539-2255

(G-999)
FIRST TRANSIT INC
2040 Us Highway 50 (45103-8694)
PHONE..................................513 732-1206
Carolyn Kelley, *Principal*
EMP: 86
SALES (corp-wide): 8.9B **Privately Held**
SIC: 4111 Local & suburban transit
HQ: First Transit, Inc.
600 Vine St Ste 1400
Cincinnati OH 45202
513 241-2200

(G-1000)
GC AT STONELICK HILLS
3155 Sherilyn Ln (45103-8674)
PHONE..................................513 735-4653
Jeff Osterfeld, *Owner*
Mike Sowards, *General Mgr*
EMP: 40
SALES (est): 1.5MM **Privately Held**
SIC: 7992 Public golf courses

(G-1001)
HEALTHSOURCE OF OHIO INC
2055 Hospital Dr Ste 320 (45103-1978)
PHONE..................................513 707-1997
EMP: 48
SALES (corp-wide): 47.8MM **Privately Held**
SIC: 8093 Specialty outpatient clinics
PA: Healthsource Of Ohio, Inc.
5400 Dupont Cir Ste A
Milford OH 45150
513 576-7700

(G-1002)
J & B SYSTEMS COMPANY INC
5055 State Route 276 (45103-1211)
P.O. Box 56, Owensville (45160-0056)
PHONE..................................513 732-2000
Jerrilyn Kearney, *President*
William Kearney, *Owner*
EMP: 120
SQ FT: 45,000
SALES (est): 4MM **Privately Held**
SIC: 7389 Packaging & labeling services

(G-1003)
LEHN PAINTING INC (PA)
4175 Taylor Rd (45103-9792)
PHONE..................................513 732-1515
William R Lehn, *President*
Kimberly E Lehn, *Corp Secy*
EMP: 46
SQ FT: 8,000
SALES (est): 5.1MM **Privately Held**
SIC: 1721 Residential painting

(G-1004)
MERCY HLTH - CLERMONT HOSP LLC (DH)
3000 Hospital Dr (45103-1921)
PHONE..................................513 732-8200
Mark Shuagerman, *President*
Arlene Cooper, *Vice Pres*
Julie Porter, *Director*
EMP: 79 **EST:** 1973
SQ FT: 230,000
SALES: 121.1MM
SALES (corp-wide): 4.7B **Privately Held**
SIC: 8062 8011 General medical & surgical hospitals; clinic, operated by physicians
HQ: Mercy Health Cincinnati Llc
1701 Mercy Health Pl
Cincinnati OH 45237
513 952-5000

(G-1005)
PAK LAB
5069 State Route 276 (45103-1211)
P.O. Box 550, Owensville (45160-0550)
PHONE..................................513 735-4777
William Kearney, *Mng Member*
George McIlroy,
▲ **EMP:** 45
SQ FT: 17,000
SALES (est): 5.2MM **Privately Held**
SIC: 7389 Packaging & labeling services

(G-1006)
PERRY INTERIORS INC
4054 Clough Woods Dr (45103-2586)
PHONE..................................513 761-9333
Karen Perry, *President*
Rick Perry, *Vice Pres*
EMP: 30 **EST:** 1999
SQ FT: 3,500
SALES (est): 2.6MM **Privately Held**
SIC: 1721 Residential painting

(G-1007)
R & R WIRING CONTRACTORS INC
1269 Clough Pike (45103-2501)
PHONE..................................513 752-6304
Mark Rettinger, *President*
Rick Rettinger, *Vice Pres*
Deborah Rettinger, *Admin Sec*
EMP: 34
SQ FT: 5,000
SALES (est): 4.2MM **Privately Held**
SIC: 1731 General electrical contractor

(G-1008)
RECORD EXPRESS LLC
4295 Armstrong Blvd (45103-1697)
PHONE..................................513 685-7329
Nadine Albenze-Smith, *CEO*
Beverly Tackett, *Director*
EMP: 25
SALES (est): 2.4MM **Privately Held**
SIC: 7374 Optical scanning data service

(G-1009)
SPORTSMANS MARKET INC
Also Called: Sportys Pilot Shop
2001 Sportys Dr (45103-9719)
PHONE..................................513 735-9100
Harold Shevers Jr, *Ch of Bd*
Michael J Wolf, *President*
Marc A Liggett, *Exec VP*
Jack Lynch, *Exec VP*
John P Lynch, *Exec VP*
▲ **EMP:** 172 **EST:** 1961
SQ FT: 120,000
SALES (est): 71.8MM **Privately Held**
WEB: www.sportys.com
SIC: 5599 5088 Aircraft instruments, equipment or parts; aircraft equipment & supplies

(G-1010)
STRICKER BROS INC
Also Called: Stricker Auto Sales
4955 Benton Rd (45103-1203)
PHONE..................................513 732-1152
John M Stricker, *President*
Arthur J Stricker, *Vice Pres*
▼ **EMP:** 50 **EST:** 1956
SQ FT: 2,500
SALES (est): 11.8MM **Privately Held**
WEB: www.gmusedpartsonline.com
SIC: 5521 5015 5531 Automobiles, used cars only; automotive supplies, used; automobile & truck equipment & parts

(G-1011)
THREE D GOLF LLC
Also Called: Elks Run Golf Club
2000 Elklick Rd (45103-9401)
PHONE..................................513 732-0295
Daryll Landrum, *Mng Member*
Kim Day,
William Landrum,
David Shearer,
EMP: 40
SALES (est): 1.1MM **Privately Held**
SIC: 7999 Miniature golf course operation

(G-1012)
TOWNE CONSTRUCTION SVCS LLC
Also Called: Towne Properties Machine Group
500 Kent Rd Ste A (45103-1703)
PHONE..................................513 561-3700
Christopher Bortz, *President*
Neil Bortz,
EMP: 150 **EST:** 2005
SALES: 14.5MM
SALES (corp-wide): 16.7MM **Privately Held**
SIC: 1771 Concrete work
PA: Original Partners Limited Partnership
1055 Saint Paul Pl
Cincinnati OH 45202
513 381-8696

(G-1013)
UNIVERSAL PACKG SYSTEMS INC
Also Called: Paklab
5055 State Route 276 (45103-1211)
PHONE..................................513 732-2000
Richard Burton, *Branch Mgr*
EMP: 388
SALES (corp-wide): 399.6MM **Privately Held**
SIC: 2844 7389 3565 2671 Cosmetic preparations; packaging & labeling services; bottling machinery: filling, capping, labeling; plastic film, coated or laminated for packaging
PA: Universal Packaging Systems, Inc.
380 Townline Rd Ste 130
Hauppauge NY 11788
631 543-2277

(G-1014)
UNIVERSAL PACKG SYSTEMS INC
5069 State Route 276 (45103-1211)
PHONE..................................513 735-4777
Rick Zellen, *Site Mgr*
EMP: 40
SALES (corp-wide): 423.8MM **Privately Held**
SIC: 2844 7389 3565 2671 Cosmetic preparations; packaging & labeling services; bottling machinery: filling, capping, labeling; plastic film, coated or laminated for packaging
PA: Universal Packaging Systems, Inc.
380 Townline Rd Ste 130
Hauppauge NY 11788
631 543-2277

(G-1015)
UTILITY TRAILER MFG CO
4225 Curliss Ln (45103-3217)
PHONE..................................513 436-2600
Del Eastman, *General Mgr*
Jason Pautvein, *Cust Mgr*
Joe Musnicky, *Manager*
EMP: 30

GEOGRAPHIC

SALES (corp-wide): 1.2B **Privately Held**
WEB: www.utm.com
SIC: 4225 General warehousing & storage
PA: Utility Trailer Manufacturing Company
  17295 Railroad St Ste A
  City Of Industry CA 91748
  626 964-7319

(G-1016)
YMCA OF CLERMONT COUNTY INC
2075 James E Sauls Sr Dr (45103-3256)
PHONE.................................513 724-9622
Whit Hitckmin, *Principal*
EMP: 40
SQ FT: 33,000
SALES: 750K **Privately Held**
SIC: 8641 7991 8351 7032 Youth organizations; physical fitness facilities; child day care services; youth camps; individual & family services

Bath
Summit County

(G-1017)
MERRILL LYNCH PIERCE FENNER
4000 Embassy Pkwy Ste 210 (44210)
PHONE.................................330 670-2400
Peter J Calleri, *Manager*
EMP: 26
SALES (corp-wide): 110.5B **Publicly Held**
WEB: www.merlyn.com
SIC: 6211 Security brokers & dealers
HQ: Merrill Lynch, Pierce, Fenner & Smith Incorporated
  111 8th Ave
  New York NY 10011
  800 637-7455

(G-1018)
OLD TRAIL SCHOOL
2315 Ira Rd (44210)
PHONE.................................330 666-1118
John Farber, *Headmaster*
Laurie Arnold, *Headmaster*
Robert Morgan, *Facilities Dir*
Meeta Nosrati, *CFO*
Kathy Pockett, *Supervisor*
EMP: 95
SQ FT: 100,000
SALES: 12MM **Privately Held**
WEB: www.oldtrail.org
SIC: 8211 8351 Private elementary school; preschool center

(G-1019)
WESTERN RESERVE HISTORICAL SOC
Also Called: Hale Farm & Village
2686 Oak Hill Dr (44210)
P.O. Box 296 (44210-0296)
PHONE.................................330 666-3711
Margaret Tramontine, *Director*
Gregory Bean, *Admin Sec*
EMP: 75
SALES (corp-wide): 7.4MM **Privately Held**
SIC: 8412 Museum
PA: Western Reserve Historical Society
  10825 East Blvd
  Cleveland OH 44106
  216 721-5722

(G-1020)
WILLORY LLC
1970 N Cleveland Mssilln (44210-5367)
P.O. Box 50 (44210-0050)
PHONE.................................330 576-5486
John Bernatovicz,
EMP: 37
SALES: 3MM **Privately Held**
SIC: 7361 Executive placement

Bay Village
Cuyahoga County

(G-1021)
BRADLEY BAY ASSISTED LIVING
605 Bradley Rd (44140-1670)
PHONE.................................440 871-4509
John O'Neal, *Owner*
John O' Neal, *Owner*
EMP: 25
SALES (est): 442.8K **Privately Held**
SIC: 8361 8082 Rest home, with health care incidental; home health care services

(G-1022)
LAKE ERIE NATURE & SCIENCE CTR
28728 Wolf Rd (44140-1350)
PHONE.................................440 871-2900
Patrick J Mazur, *Ch of Bd*
Larry D Richardson, *Principal*
Morgan Paskert, *Marketing Staff*
Catherine Timko, *Exec Dir*
EMP: 36
SQ FT: 22,240
SALES: 1.4MM **Privately Held**
WEB: www.lensc.org
SIC: 8299 0752 8412 Educational service, nondegree granting: continuing educ.; animal specialty services; planetarium

(G-1023)
US SWIMMING LAKE ERIE SWIMMING
301 Rockledge Dr (44140-2712)
PHONE.................................330 423-0485
Edward L Bettendorf, *Principal*
EMP: 25
SALES: 228.7K **Privately Held**
SIC: 7997 Swimming club, membership

Beach City
Stark County

(G-1024)
GRABILL PLUMBING & HEATING
Also Called: Graybill Gallery Kitchens Bath
10235 Manchester Ave Sw (44608-9756)
PHONE.................................330 756-2075
Luke Grabill, *President*
Karla Ferguson, *Principal*
Grant Grabill, *Vice Pres*
EMP: 28 EST: 1965
SALES (est): 6MM **Privately Held**
WEB: www.grabill.com
SIC: 1711 Plumbing contractors

Beachwood
Cuyahoga County

(G-1025)
A+ SOLUTIONS LLC
Also Called: Ohiosolutions.org
3659 Green Rd Ste 112 (44122-5715)
PHONE.................................216 896-0111
Hadassa Meyers, *Mng Member*
Callie McCleery, *Admin Asst*
Oren Meyers,
EMP: 49
SQ FT: 1,877
SALES (est): 911.9K **Privately Held**
SIC: 8049 8093 8299 Speech therapist; clinical psychologist; occupational therapist; mental health clinic, outpatient; educational services

(G-1026)
ADVANCE PAYROLL FUNDING LTD
Also Called: Advance Partners
3401 Entp Pkwy Fl 5 Flr 5 (44122)
PHONE.................................216 831-8900
Joel Adelman, *CEO*
Adam C Stern, *President*

Michael Turk, *CFO*
EMP: 114
SQ FT: 4,000
SALES (est): 16.2MM
SALES (corp-wide): 3.3B **Publicly Held**
WEB: www.advancepayroll.com
SIC: 8721 Payroll accounting service
PA: Paychex, Inc.
  911 Panorama Trl S
  Rochester NY 14625
  585 385-6666

(G-1027)
ADVANTAGE IMAGING LLC (PA)
Also Called: Advantage Diagnostic
3733 Park East Dr Ste 100 (44122-4334)
PHONE.................................216 292-9998
Jonathan Metzler MD, *Principal*
Donna Iacobacci, *Marketing Staff*
Kristina Van Deusen, *Mng Member*
EMP: 25
SALES (est): 1.9MM **Privately Held**
SIC: 8099 Health screening service

(G-1028)
ALTRUISM SOCIETY INC
3695 Green Rd Unit 22896 (44122-7945)
PHONE.................................877 283-4001
James Abrams, *CEO*
Jaicynthia Farmer, *Vice Pres*
EMP: 99
SALES (est): 2.3MM **Privately Held**
SIC: 6732 8611 8322 1611 Trusts: educational, religious, etc.; community affairs & services; emergency social services; general contractor, highway & street construction

(G-1029)
AMIN TUROCY & WATSON LLP (PA)
200 Park Ave Ste 300 (44122-4296)
PHONE.................................216 696-8730
Gregory Turocy, *Partner*
Himanshu S Amin, *General Ptnr*
Erin C Keller, *Patent Law*
Jeff Neterval,
Nicole Lockett, *Legal Staff*
EMP: 49
SALES (est): 5.8MM **Privately Held**
WEB: www.thepatentattorneys.com
SIC: 8111 Corporate, partnership & business law

(G-1030)
APOLLO PROPERTY MANAGEMENT LLC (PA)
200 Park Ave Ste 410 (44122-4297)
PHONE.................................216 468-0050
Gary Murphy, *CFO*
Steve Pogozelski, *Accounting Dir*
Joyce Nelson, *Accountant*
Mihaela Nita, *Accountant*
Paul Kiebler, *Mng Member*
EMP: 35
SALES (est): 6.2MM **Privately Held**
SIC: 8741 Management services

(G-1031)
ATLANTIC HOSPITALITY & MGT LLC
26300 Chagrin Blvd (44122-4229)
PHONE.................................216 454-5450
Theodore A Sahley,
EMP: 44
SALES (est): 3.6MM **Privately Held**
WEB: www.atlantichospitalityinc.com
SIC: 8741 Hotel or motel management

(G-1032)
ATTEVO INC
24500 Chagrin Blvd # 300 (44122-5646)
PHONE.................................216 928-2800
EMP: 70
SALES (est): 4.9MM **Privately Held**
SIC: 8742 7373 7379 Management Consulting Services Computer Systems Design Computer Related Services

(G-1033)
AVNET INC
Also Called: Avnet Computers
2000 Auburn Dr Ste 200 (44122-4328)
PHONE.................................440 349-7600
Kimberly Marriott, *Accounts Mgr*

Melinda Hicks, *Manager*
EMP: 27
SALES (corp-wide): 19B **Publicly Held**
WEB: www.avnet.com
SIC: 5065 Electronic parts
PA: Avnet, Inc.
  2211 S 47th St
  Phoenix AZ 85034
  480 643-2000

(G-1034)
BEACHWOOD CITY SCHOOLS
Also Called: Beachwood Board of Education
24601 Fairmount Blvd (44122-2239)
PHONE.................................216 464-2600
Karen Leeds, *Principal*
Gregory Perry, *Marketing Staff*
Nate Smith, *Athletic Dir*
Lisa Brockwell, *Asst Director*
Alison Lemieux, *Teacher*
EMP: 74
SALES (corp-wide): 43.3MM **Privately Held**
SIC: 8351 Preschool center
PA: Beachwood City Schools
  24601 Fairmount Blvd
  Cleveland OH 44122
  216 464-2600

(G-1035)
BEACHWOOD PROF FIRE FIGHTERS C
P.O. Box 221250 (44122-0996)
PHONE.................................216 292-1968
Mark Russo, *President*
EMP: 42
SALES: 32.4K **Privately Held**
SIC: 8699 Membership organizations

(G-1036)
BRE DDR PARKER PAVILIONS LLC
3300 Enterprise Pkwy (44122-7200)
PHONE.................................216 755-6451
Daniel Hurwitz, *CEO*
EMP: 50 EST: 2012
SALES (est): 2.9MM
SALES (corp-wide): 707.2MM **Privately Held**
SIC: 6798 Real estate investment trusts
PA: Site Centers Corp.
  3300 Enterprise Pkwy
  Beachwood OH 44122
  216 755-5500

(G-1037)
BROADWAY CARE CTR MPLE HTS LLC
25201 Chagrin Blvd # 190 (44122-5600)
PHONE.................................216 662-0551
Louis Kraus,
EMP: 25
SALES (est): 2.1MM **Privately Held**
SIC: 8361 Residential care

(G-1038)
BRYDEN PLACE INC
25201 Chagrin Blvd # 190 (44122-5633)
PHONE.................................614 258-6623
Roger King, *President*
Glyndon Powell, *President*
Edward L Byington, *Vice Pres*
EMP: 150
SALES (est): 5.8MM **Privately Held**
SIC: 8051 Convalescent home with continuous nursing care

(G-1039)
BUCKEYE RUBBER & PACKING CO
23940 Mercantile Rd (44122-5989)
PHONE.................................216 464-8900
Donaldcatlin, *Principal*
Donald Catlin, *Exec VP*
Irene Papp, *Exec VP*
James Sampson, *Vice Pres*
Bob Hurst, *QC Mgr*
▲ EMP: 45 EST: 1937
SQ FT: 30,000
SALES: 20.2MM **Privately Held**
WEB: www.buckeyerubber.com
SIC: 5085 Gaskets & seals; gaskets

(G-1040)
BUFFALO-GTB ASSOCIATES LLC
Also Called: Hampton Inn and Suites
3840 Orange Pl (44122-4488)
PHONE..............................216 831-3735
Ryan Mattlack, *Manager*
EMP: 28
SALES (corp-wide): 3MM **Privately Held**
WEB: www.buffalolodging.com
SIC: 7011 Hotels
PA: Buffalo-Gtb Associates, Llc
570 Delaware Ave
Buffalo NY 14202
781 344-4435

(G-1041)
CARLISLE MCNELLIE RINI KRAM
24755 Chagrin Blvd (44122-5682)
PHONE..............................216 360-7200
Richard McNellie, *President*
Herbert Kramer, *Vice Pres*
William Rini, *Vice Pres*
James Sassano, *Vice Pres*
Phyllis Ulrich, *Vice Pres*
EMP: 40 **EST:** 1979
SQ FT: 5,000
SALES (est): 6.1MM **Privately Held**
SIC: 8111 Real estate law; debt collection law; bankruptcy law; will, estate & trust law

(G-1042)
CELLCO PARTNERSHIP
Also Called: Verizon Wireless
400 Park Ave Apt 210 (44122-4283)
PHONE..............................216 765-1444
Brian Liao, *Engineer*
EMP: 124
SALES (corp-wide): 130.8B **Publicly Held**
SIC: 4812 Cellular telephone services
HQ: Cellco Partnership
1 Verizon Way
Basking Ridge NJ 07920

(G-1043)
CHAMPION OPTICAL NETWORK
Also Called: Champion One
23645 Mercantile Rd Ste A (44122-5936)
PHONE..............................216 831-1800
John Jutila, *CEO*
EMP: 33
SQ FT: 5,000
SALES (est): 8.6MM **Privately Held**
WEB: www.cctupgrades.com
SIC: 5049 Optical goods

(G-1044)
CLEVELAND BCHWOOD HSPTLITY LLC
Also Called: Hilton Cleveland/Beachwood
3663 Park East Dr (44122-4315)
PHONE..............................216 464-5950
Scott Schmelzer, *Manager*
EMP: 99
SALES (est): 5.1MM **Privately Held**
SIC: 7011 Hotels

(G-1045)
CLEVELAND CENTER FOR ETNG DSOR
25550 Chagrin Blvd # 200 (44122-5638)
PHONE..............................216 765-2535
Mark Warren, *Principal*
Lucene Wisniewski, *Director*
EMP: 28
SALES: 950K **Privately Held**
SIC: 8322 General counseling services

(G-1046)
CLEVELAND CLINIC FOUNDATION
25875 Science Park Dr (44122-7304)
PHONE..............................216 448-0116
Brian Rockwell, *Counsel*
Jaime Winer, *Project Mgr*
Lisa Cummins, *Manager*
Amy Cossette, *Consultant*
Pamela Holmes, *Director*
EMP: 2931

SALES (corp-wide): 8.9B **Privately Held**
SIC: 8062 General medical & surgical hospitals
PA: The Cleveland Clinic Foundation
9500 Euclid Ave
Cleveland OH 44195
216 636-8335

(G-1047)
COMMUNITY HEALTH CENTERS OHIO
3355 Richmond Rd Ste 225a (44122-4180)
PHONE..............................216 831-1494
Arun Chattree, *Exec Dir*
EMP: 54
SALES: 800K **Privately Held**
SIC: 8093 Specialty outpatient clinics

(G-1048)
CORNELIA C HODGSON - ARCHITEC (PA)
23240 Chagrin Blvd # 300 (44122-5405)
PHONE..............................216 593-0057
Cornelia Hodgson, *President*
EMP: 47
SQ FT: 5,000
SALES (est): 5.7MM **Privately Held**
SIC: 8712 Architectural engineering

(G-1049)
CTPARTNERS EXEC SEARCH INC
28601 Chagrin Blvd # 600 (44122-4557)
PHONE..............................216 464-8710
Fax: 216 464-6172
EMP: 65
SALES (corp-wide): 176.8MM **Publicly Held**
SIC: 7361 Employment Agency
PA: Ctpartners Executive Search Inc.
1166 Avenue Of The Amrcs
New York NY 10036
212 588-3500

(G-1050)
CW FINANCIAL LLC
Also Called: Press Wood Management
23550 Commerce Park # 5000 (44122-5862)
PHONE..............................941 907-9490
Johanna Brooks, *Principal*
EMP: 325 **EST:** 1991
SALES (est): 38.1MM **Privately Held**
SIC: 6282 Investment advice

(G-1051)
DDR TUCSON SPECTRUM I LLC
3300 Enterprise Pkwy (44122-7200)
PHONE..............................216 755-5500
Daniel Hurwitz, *President*
EMP: 25
SALES (est): 1.5MM
SALES (corp-wide): 707.2MM **Privately Held**
SIC: 6798 Real estate investment trusts
PA: Site Centers Corp.
3300 Enterprise Pkwy
Beachwood OH 44122
216 755-5500

(G-1052)
DEALERS GROUP LIMITED
Also Called: Scher Group
23240 Chagrin Blvd # 802 (44122-5404)
PHONE..............................440 352-4970
Robert Scher, *CFO*
Jan Benroth, *Treasurer*
Pete Hallahan ME, *Director*
EMP: 25
SQ FT: 12,500
SALES: 4MM **Privately Held**
WEB: www.dlrgrp.com
SIC: 8742 7514 Industry specialist consultants; rent-a-car service

(G-1053)
EATON CORPORATION
1000 Eaton Blvd (44122-6058)
PHONE..............................440 523-5000
Brian Braley, *Project Mgr*
John Schindler, *Branch Mgr*
Ron Mueller, *Manager*
David Soldat, *Manager*
Jeff Oko, *Senior Mgr*
EMP: 400 **Privately Held**

WEB: www.eaton.com
SIC: 7549 Automotive maintenance services
HQ: Eaton Corporation
1000 Eaton Blvd
Cleveland OH 44122
440 523-5000

(G-1054)
EATON CORPORATION
Eastlake Office
1000 Eaton Blvd (44122-6058)
PHONE..............................216 523-5000
Manuel Prieto, *Project Mgr*
Keith Cozart, *Purch Mgr*
Bernie Beier, *Engineer*
Sell Craig, *Engineer*
Doug Koch, *Manager*
EMP: 260 **Privately Held**
WEB: www.eaton.com
SIC: 3714 5084 Hydraulic fluid power pumps for auto steering mechanism; hydraulic systems equipment & supplies
HQ: Eaton Corporation
1000 Eaton Blvd
Cleveland OH 44122
440 523-5000

(G-1055)
ENVIRNMENTAL RESOURCES MGT INC
Also Called: Erm Midatlantic
3333 Richmond Rd Ste 160 (44122-4196)
PHONE..............................216 593-5200
Cheryl Garson, *Branch Mgr*
EMP: 31
SALES (corp-wide): 358.4MM **Privately Held**
SIC: 8748 Environmental consultant
HQ: Environmental Resources Management, Inc.
75 Valley Stream Pkwy
Malvern PA 19355
484 913-0300

(G-1056)
EZRA HEALTH CARE INC
Also Called: Beachwood Nrsing Hlthcare Ctr
23258 Fernwood Dr (44122-1569)
PHONE..............................440 498-3000
Will Grunspan, *President*
Sharona Grunspan, *Vice Pres*
EMP: 130
SQ FT: 160,000
SALES: 963.6MM **Privately Held**
WEB: www.ezrahealthcareinc.com
SIC: 8051 Extended care facility

(G-1057)
FEDEX OFFICE & PRINT SVCS INC
27450 Chagrin Blvd (44122-4423)
PHONE..............................216 292-2679
EMP: 25
SALES (corp-wide): 65.4B **Publicly Held**
WEB: www.kinkos.com
SIC: 7334 Photocopying & duplicating services
HQ: Fedex Office And Print Services, Inc.
7900 Legacy Dr
Plano TX 75024
800 463-3339

(G-1058)
FOX INTERNATIONAL LIMITED INC (PA)
23645 Merc Rd Ste B (44122)
PHONE..............................216 454-1001
Ronald D Ordway, *CEO*
David Heiden, *President*
Murray Fox, *Principal*
Richard H Siegel, *Principal*
Greg Osborn, *CFO*
▼ **EMP:** 47
SQ FT: 50,000
SALES (est): 22.2MM **Privately Held**
WEB: www.fox-intl.com
SIC: 5065 7389 5087 Electronic parts & equipment; telemarketing services; fire-fighting equipment

(G-1059)
FRANKLIN & SEIDELMANN INC (PA)
3700 Park East Dr Ste 300 (44122-4399)
PHONE..............................216 255-5700
Peter Franklin, *President*
Clayton T Larsen, *Senior VP*
Frank Seidelmann, *Vice Pres*
EMP: 26 **EST:** 2001
SALES (est): 4.9MM **Privately Held**
WEB: www.franklin-seidelmann.com
SIC: 8011 Radiologist

(G-1060)
FRANKLIN & SEIDELMANN LLC
3700 Park East Dr Ste 300 (44122-4399)
PHONE..............................216 255-5700
Bill O' Neal, *Controller*
Frank E Seidelmann MD,
Peter D Franklin MD,
EMP: 80 **EST:** 2001
SQ FT: 11,508
SALES (est): 4.9MM **Privately Held**
SIC: 8741 Management services

(G-1061)
GCI CONSTRUCTION LLC (PA)
25101 Chagrin Blvd (44122-5643)
PHONE..............................216 831-6100
Larry Goldberg, *President*
EMP: 33
SALES (est): 28.1MM **Privately Held**
SIC: 1522 1521 Multi-family dwelling construction; single-family housing construction

(G-1062)
HEALTH DATA MGT SOLUTIONS INC
3201 Enterprise Pkwy (44122-7330)
PHONE..............................216 595-1232
Denise Zeman, *Branch Mgr*
Steve Young, *Technology*
Marilyn Morrow, *Director*
EMP: 86 **Privately Held**
SIC: 8099 Blood related health services
PA: Health Data & Management Solutions, Inc.
123 N Wacker Dr Ste 650
Chicago IL 60606

(G-1063)
HEMODIALYSIS SERVICES INC
Also Called: Hsi Hemodialysis Services
25550 Chagrin Blvd # 404 (44122-4640)
P.O. Box 22330 (44122-0330)
PHONE..............................216 378-2691
Charles Wilson, *President*
Steven Lovelace, *CFO*
EMP: 43 **EST:** 1991
SALES (est): 4.3MM **Privately Held**
WEB: www.hsihd.com
SIC: 8092 Kidney dialysis centers

(G-1064)
HOWARD HANNA SMYTHE CRAMER
28879 Chagrin Blvd (44122-4603)
PHONE..............................216 831-0210
Howard Hanna, *Branch Mgr*
EMP: 30
SALES (corp-wide): 72.1MM **Privately Held**
SIC: 6531 Real estate brokers & agents
HQ: Howard Hanna Smythe Cramer
6000 Parkland Blvd
Cleveland OH 44124
216 447-4477

(G-1065)
HOWARD HANNA SMYTHE CRAMER
24465 Greenwich Ln (44122-1646)
PHONE..............................216 751-8550
Len Okuly, *Branch Mgr*
EMP: 30
SALES (corp-wide): 73.7MM **Privately Held**
SIC: 6531 Real estate agent, residential
HQ: Howard Hanna Smythe Cramer
6000 Parkland Blvd
Cleveland OH 44124
216 447-4477

G E O G R A P H I C

(G-1066)
IA URBAN HTELS BCHWOOD TRS LLC
Also Called: Embassy Suites
3775 Park East Dr (44122-4307)
PHONE...............................216 765-8066
Kelly Norcini, *Manager*
Mark Herron,
EMP: 99
SQ FT: 66,940
SALES (est): 5.8MM **Privately Held**
SIC: 7011 Hotels & motels

(G-1067)
INTELLICORP RECORDS INC
3000 Auburn Dr Ste 410 (44122-4340)
PHONE...............................216 450-5200
Todd Carpenter, *President*
Bob Berichon, *Vice Pres*
Chad Ascar, *Opers Staff*
Kelly Georgiou, *Finance*
Rhoda Reid, *Natl Sales Mgr*
EMP: 65
SQ FT: 16,000
SALES (est): 11.6MM **Publicly Held**
WEB: www.intellicorp.net
SIC: 7375 Information retrieval services
HQ: Insurance Services Office, Inc.
   545 Washington Blvd Fl 12
   Jersey City NJ 07310
   201 469-2000

(G-1068)
JACOBS REAL ESTATE SERVICES
1000 Eaton Blvd (44122-6058)
PHONE...............................216 514-9830
James Eppele, *CEO*
EMP: 39
SALES (est): 674.8K **Privately Held**
SIC: 6531 6512 Real Estate Agent/Manager Nonresidential Building Operator

(G-1069)
JEWISH COMMUNITY CTR CLEVELAND
Also Called: MANDEL JEWISH COMMUNITY OF CLE
26001 S Woodland Rd (44122-3367)
PHONE...............................216 831-0700
Michael Hyman, *CEO*
Gilon Rubanenko, *COO*
Traci Felder, *Vice Pres*
Lauri Baker, *Accountant*
Julia Yang, *Finance*
EMP: 225 EST: 1948
SQ FT: 93,000
SALES: 13.1MM **Privately Held**
SIC: 8322 Social service center

(G-1070)
JOSEPH AND FLORENCE MANDEL
26500 Shaker Blvd (44122-7116)
PHONE...............................216 464-4055
Jerry D Isaac-Shapiro, *Principal*
Bennet Kleinman, *Principal*
L C Sherman, *Principal*
Bennett Yanowitz, *Principal*
Janet Keane, *CFO*
EMP: 90
SQ FT: 28,600
SALES: 22MM **Privately Held**
WEB: www.agnon.org
SIC: 8211 8351 Catholic elementary & secondary schools; Catholic combined elementary & secondary school; private elementary school; preschool center

(G-1071)
KALYPSO LP (PA)
3659 Green Rd Ste 100 (44122-5715)
PHONE...............................216 378-4290
Bill Poston, *Managing Prtnr*
Greg Adkins, *Partner*
Mick Broekhof, *Partner*
Niels Ebbing, *Partner*
Michael Friedman, *Partner*
EMP: 70
SALES (est): 7.1MM **Privately Held**
SIC: 8742 Business consultant

(G-1072)
KAREN FUNKE INC
Also Called: Funke & Co Hair Design
27730 Chagrin Blvd (44122-4473)
PHONE...............................216 464-4311
Karen Funke, *President*
Robert Fisher, *Principal*
Patrick Funke, *Vice Pres*
Kris Fisher, *Admin Sec*
EMP: 34
SALES (est): 697.8K **Privately Held**
SIC: 7991 7231 Spas; facial salons

(G-1073)
KING GROUP INC
25550 Chagrin Blvd # 300 (44122-4640)
PHONE...............................216 831-9330
Donald M King, *President*
EMP: 25
SQ FT: 3,500
SALES (est): 1MM **Privately Held**
SIC: 6512 Nonresidential building operators

(G-1074)
LINCOLN FINCL ADVISORS CORP
28601 Chagrin Blvd # 300 (44122-4500)
PHONE...............................216 765-7400
Karen Lasher, *Manager*
EMP: 50
SALES (corp-wide): 16.4B **Publicly Held**
WEB: www.lfaonline.com
SIC: 6282 Investment advisory service
HQ: Lincoln Financial Advisors Corporation
   1300 S Clinton St
   Fort Wayne IN 46802
   800 237-3813

(G-1075)
MARSH BERRY & COMPANY INC (PA)
28601 Chagrin Blvd # 400 (44122-4556)
PHONE...............................440 354-3230
John Wepler, *President*
Douglas A Yoh, *President*
Dale Myer, *Managing Dir*
Lawrence J Marsh, *Chairman*
Rob Lieblein, *Exec VP*
EMP: 27
SALES (est): 11.2MM **Privately Held**
SIC: 8742 8741 Business consultant; management services

(G-1076)
MASTER BUILDERS LLC (DH)
Also Called: Degussa Construction
23700 Chagrin Blvd (44122-5506)
PHONE...............................216 831-5500
John Salvatore, *President*
Michael Pelsozy, *Research*
Donald Kehr, *Treasurer*
◆ EMP: 50
SALES (est): 336.8MM
SALES (corp-wide): 71.7B **Privately Held**
WEB: www.basf-admixtures.com
SIC: 2899 2851 1799 Concrete curing & hardening compounds; epoxy coatings; caulking (construction)
HQ: Basf Corporation
   100 Park Ave
   Florham Park NJ 07932
   973 245-6000

(G-1077)
MCM CAPITAL PARTNERS
25201 Chagrin Blvd # 360 (44122-5600)
PHONE...............................216 514-1840
Mark Mansour, *Managing Prtnr*
James Poffenberger, *Exec Dir*
Steve Ross, *Exec Dir*
Gerry Weimann, *Exec Dir*
EMP: 343
SQ FT: 5,000
SALES (est): 37.1MM **Privately Held**
WEB: www.mcmcapital.com
SIC: 6799 Investors

(G-1078)
MEDICAL MUTUAL OF OHIO
Also Called: Antares Management Solutions
23700 Commerce Park (44122-5827)
PHONE...............................216 292-0400
Monica Klag, *Purch Agent*
Eric Lazar, *Engineer*

Jay Hader, *Auditor*
Robert Trombly, *Branch Mgr*
Keith Garner, *Manager*
EMP: 300
SALES (corp-wide): 1.2B **Privately Held**
SIC: 6411 6321 Insurance agents; accident & health insurance carriers
PA: Medical Mutual Of Ohio
   2060 E 9th St Frnt Ste
   Cleveland OH 44115
   216 687-7000

(G-1079)
MENORAH PARK CENTER FOR SENIO
Also Called: Rh Meyers Apartments
27200 Cedar Rd (44122-8104)
PHONE...............................216 831-6515
Stewart Collins, *Branch Mgr*
EMP: 50
SQ FT: 195,000
SALES (corp-wide): 71.1MM **Privately Held**
WEB: www.menorahpark.org
SIC: 6513 Retirement hotel operation
PA: Menorah Park Center For Senior Living
   Bet Moshav Zekenim Hadati
   27100 Cedar Rd
   Cleveland OH 44122
   216 831-6500

(G-1080)
METROHEALTH SYSTEM
Also Called: Metrohealth Beachwood Hlth Ctr
3609 Park East Dr Ste 300 (44122-4309)
PHONE...............................216 765-0733
Michael Phillips, *Officer*
Kathleen Hale,
Carolyn Pounds-Lewis,
EMP: 26
SALES (corp-wide): 1B **Privately Held**
SIC: 8062 General medical & surgical hospitals
PA: The Metrohealth System
   2500 Metrohealth Dr
   Cleveland OH 44109
   216 398-6000

(G-1081)
METROHEALTH SYSTEM
Also Called: Metrohlth Pepper Pike Hlth Ctr
3609 Park East Dr Ste 206 (44122-4309)
PHONE...............................216 591-0523
Frances Ballo, *Branch Mgr*
Lisa Gelles, *Dermatology*
EMP: 26
SALES (corp-wide): 1B **Privately Held**
SIC: 8062 General medical & surgical hospitals
PA: The Metrohealth System
   2500 Metrohealth Dr
   Cleveland OH 44109
   216 398-6000

(G-1082)
MIM SOFTWARE INC (PA)
25800 Science Park Dr # 180 (44122-7339)
PHONE...............................216 896-9798
Dennis Nelson, *President*
Peter Simmelink, *General Mgr*
Pete Zimmelink, *COO*
Kelly Mastromonaco, *Vice Pres*
Aaron Greene, *Opers Staff*
EMP: 49
SALES (est): 16.3MM **Privately Held**
WEB: www.mimvista.com
SIC: 7372 Application computer software

(G-1083)
MONTEFIORE HOME
1 David N Myers Pkwy (44122)
PHONE...............................216 360-9080
Lauren B Rock, *CEO*
Mark Weiss, *CFO*
Althea Johnson, *Human Res Dir*
Kristen Morelli, *Program Mgr*
Jacqulyn Gutowski, *Manager*
EMP: 450
SQ FT: 180,000
SALES (est): 29.7MM **Privately Held**
SIC: 8051 Skilled nursing care facilities

(G-1084)
MR MAGIC CARNEGIE INC
Also Called: Mr Magic Car Wash & Detail Ctr
23511 Chagrin Blvd # 306 (44122-5528)
PHONE...............................440 461-7572
Sterling Kassoff, *President*
EMP: 25
SQ FT: 7,800
SALES (est): 967.5K **Privately Held**
SIC: 7542 Washing & polishing, automotive; carwash, automatic

(G-1085)
MURWOOD REAL ESTATE GROUP LLC
Also Called: Keller Williams Realtors
29225 Chagrin Blvd (44122-4645)
PHONE...............................216 839-5500
Laird Wynn, *Manager*
John Ludwick,
EMP: 50
SALES (est): 4.2MM **Privately Held**
SIC: 6531 Real estate agent, residential

(G-1086)
NORTH EAST OHIO HEALTH SVCS (PA)
Also Called: CONNECTIONS
24200 Chagrin Blvd # 126 (44122-5529)
P.O. Box 22955 (44122-0955)
PHONE...............................216 831-6466
Esther Pla, *CEO*
James Nagle, *CFO*
Pamela Holmes, *Manager*
Randy Bradford, *Info Tech Dir*
EMP: 57
SQ FT: 12,000
SALES: 18.6MM **Privately Held**
WEB: www.neohs.org
SIC: 8322 8093 General counseling services; specialty outpatient clinics

(G-1087)
NORTHCOAST HEALTHCARE MGT
23611 Chagrin Blvd # 380 (44122-5540)
PHONE...............................216 591-2000
Fran Voll, *President*
Dr Kenneth Weiner, *President*
Jack Koenig, *Vice Pres*
R W Brockman, *Treasurer*
Clyde Rhein, *Admin Sec*
EMP: 120
SQ FT: 22,000
SALES (est): 5.8MM
SALES (corp-wide): 208.3B **Publicly Held**
SIC: 8741 8721 Management services; billing & bookkeeping service
HQ: Ndchealth Corporation
   1564 Northeast Expy Ne
   Brookhaven GA 30329
   404 728-2000

(G-1088)
NPA ASSOCIATES
Also Called: Nelson Park Apartments
23875 Commerce Park # 120 (44122-5835)
PHONE...............................614 258-4053
Angelica Stoves, *Principal*
Mira Debevc, *Principal*
Larry Looney, *Principal*
EMP: 99
SALES: 950K **Privately Held**
SIC: 6513 Apartment building operators

(G-1089)
OHIO CLLBRTIVE LRNG SLTONS INC (PA)
Also Called: Smart Solutions
24700 Chagrin Blvd # 104 (44122-5647)
PHONE...............................216 595-5289
Anand Julka, *President*
Frank Hanis, *Purchasing*
Stephanie Green, *Accountant*
Ray Baumiller, *Comp Tech*
EMP: 50
SQ FT: 6,000
SALES (est): 15MM **Privately Held**
WEB: www.smartsolutionsonline.com
SIC: 7372 8741 Business oriented computer software; business management

(G-1090)
OHIO DESIGN CENTRE
23533 Mercantile Rd (44122-5959)
PHONE.................................216 831-1245
Jeffery Davis, *Owner*
Davis Development, *Mng Member*
EMP: 100
SQ FT: 100,000
SALES (est): 4.8MM **Privately Held**
SIC: 7389 Interior designer

(G-1091)
**OMNI CONSTRUCTION
COMPANY INC**
25825 Science Park Dr # 100
(44122-7315)
PHONE.................................216 514-6664
Richard Stone, *President*
Bryan Stone, *Vice Pres*
EMP: 25
SQ FT: 8,500
SALES: 20MM **Privately Held**
WEB: www.omni-construction.com
SIC: 1799 Home/office interiors finishing,
furnishing & remodeling

(G-1092)
**ORACLE SYSTEMS
CORPORATION**
3333 Richmond Rd Ste 420 (44122-4198)
PHONE.................................513 826-6000
Carol Beebe, *Manager*
EMP: 50
SALES (corp-wide): 39.8B **Publicly Held**
WEB: www.forcecapital.com
SIC: 7372 Prepackaged software
HQ: Oracle Systems Corporation
500 Oracle Pkwy
Redwood City CA 94065
650 506-7000

(G-1093)
**ORACLE SYSTEMS
CORPORATION**
3333 Richmond Rd Ste 420 (44122-4198)
PHONE.................................216 328-9100
Tom Bregar, *Opers Staff*
John Bitzan, *Sales Staff*
Stewart Flemming, *Manager*
Matthew Zorich, *Supervisor*
EMP: 94
SALES (corp-wide): 39.8B **Publicly Held**
WEB: www.forcecapital.com
SIC: 8748 5045 Systems analysis & engi-
neering consulting services; computers,
peripherals & software
HQ: Oracle Systems Corporation
500 Oracle Pkwy
Redwood City CA 94065
650 506-7000

(G-1094)
**ORPHAN FOUNDATION OF
AMERICA**
Also Called: FOSTER CARE TO SUCCESS
23811 Chagrin Blvd # 210 (44122-5525)
PHONE.................................571 203-0270
Gina Stracuzzi, *President*
Eileen McCaffrey, *Director*
EMP: 26
SALES: 13.1MM **Privately Held**
WEB: www.orphan.org
SIC: 8399 Fund raising organization, non-
fee basis

(G-1095)
PENSKE LOGISTICS LLC
3000 Auburn Dr Ste 100 (44122-4333)
PHONE.................................216 765-5475
Peter Smith, *Ch of Bd*
Caleb Soetanto, *Project Mgr*
David McClish, *Manager*
Carlos Zalla, *Manager*
EMP: 75
SALES (corp-wide): 2.6B **Privately Held**
WEB: www.penskelogistics.com
SIC: 4213 Contract haulers
HQ: Penske Logistics Llc
2675 Morgantown Rd
Reading PA 19607
610 775-6000

(G-1096)
**PREFERRED MEDICAL GROUP
INC**
23600 Commerce Park (44122-5817)
PHONE.................................404 403-8310
EMP: 189
SALES (corp-wide): 11.3MM **Privately
Held**
SIC: 8082 Home health care services
PA: Preferred Medical Group, Inc.
9140 Crsea Del Fntana Way
Naples FL 34109
239 597-2010

(G-1097)
**PSYCHLGCAL BEHAVIORAL
CONS LLC (PA)**
25101 Chagrin Blvd # 100 (44122-5643)
PHONE.................................216 456-8123
Donald Sykes, *Managing Dir*
EMP: 25
SQ FT: 12,719
SALES: 13MM **Privately Held**
SIC: 8093 Mental health clinic, outpatient

(G-1098)
QUALCHOICE INC
Also Called: University Hospitals Hlth Sys
3605 Warrensville Ctr Rd (44122-5203)
PHONE.................................330 656-1231
Thomas A Sullivan, *President*
Rebecca N Ho, *Vice Pres*
Bryan A James, *Vice Pres*
Karen Fifer Ferry, *CFO*
EMP: 300
SQ FT: 17,000
SALES: 2.5MM
SALES (corp-wide): 580MM **Privately
Held**
WEB: www.qchp.com
SIC: 6411 Medical insurance claim pro-
cessing, contract or fee basis
PA: University Hospitals Health System,
Inc.
3605 Warrensville Ctr Rd
Shaker Heights OH 44122
216 767-8900

(G-1099)
RCT ENGINEERING INC (PA)
24880 Shaker Blvd (44122-2356)
PHONE.................................561 684-7534
James V Burphy, *President*
Ralph S Tyler Jr, *Chairman*
EMP: 28
SQ FT: 3,800
SALES: 2.8MM **Privately Held**
WEB: www.rctengineering.com
SIC: 8711 Structural engineering

(G-1100)
**RETINA ASSOCIATE OF
CLEVELAND (PA)**
3401 Entp Pkwy Ste 300 (44122)
PHONE.................................216 831-5700
Dr Lawrence J Singerman, *President*
David Miller, *President*
Dr Michael Novak, *Vice Pres*
EMP: 35
SQ FT: 5,000
SALES (est): 10.8MM **Privately Held**
SIC: 8011 Ophthalmologist

(G-1101)
ROBOTS AND PENCILS LP
24245 Mercantile Rd (44122)
PHONE.................................587 350-4095
Dave Aikenhead, *CFO*
EMP: 63 EST: 2017
SALES (est): 1.6MM **Privately Held**
SIC: 7373 Systems software development
services

(G-1102)
RODDY GROUP INC
24500 Chagrin Blvd # 200 (44122-5646)
PHONE.................................216 763-0088
Matthew Roddy, *President*
EMP: 30
SALES (est): 158.4K **Privately Held**
SIC: 7322 Adjustment bureau, except in-
surance

(G-1103)
RURALOGIC INC
24500 Chagrin Blvd # 300 (44122-5646)
PHONE.................................419 630-0500
David Snyder, *Principal*
Jim Armstead, *Principal*
EMP: 55 EST: 2010
SALES (est): 2.7MM **Privately Held**
SIC: 8742 Management consulting serv-
ices

(G-1104)
**SHIELDS CAPITAL
CORPORATION**
20600 Chagrin Blvd # 800 (44122-5327)
PHONE.................................216 767-1340
Robert Snapper, *Principal*
Max Georgatos, *Sales Staff*
Sunny Jain, *Associate*
EMP: 55
SALES (corp-wide): 26.3MM **Privately
Held**
SIC: 6799 Investors
PA: Shields Capital Corporation
140 Broadway Ste 4400
New York NY 10005
212 320-3000

(G-1105)
**SIEGEL SIEGEL J & JENNINGS
CO (PA)**
23425 Commerce Park # 103
(44122-5848)
PHONE.................................216 763-1004
Fred Siegel, *President*
J K Jennings,
EMP: 29
SALES (est): 3.5MM **Privately Held**
SIC: 8111 General practice attorney,
lawyer

(G-1106)
**SIGNATURE BOUTIQUE HOTEL
LP**
1010 Eaton Blvd (44122-6058)
PHONE.................................216 595-0900
J T Norville, *Managing Prtnr*
EMP: 36
SQ FT: 70,176
SALES (est): 686.5K **Privately Held**
SIC: 7011 Hotels

(G-1107)
SITE CENTERS CORP (PA)
3300 Enterprise Pkwy (44122-7200)
PHONE.................................216 755-5500
Terrance R Ahern, *Ch of Bd*
David R Lukes, *President*
Michael A Makinen, *COO*
Maria Manley-Dutton, *Counsel*
Christa A Vesy, *Exec VP*
EMP: 150
SALES: 707.2MM **Privately Held**
WEB: www.ddrc.com
SIC: 6798 Real estate investment trusts

(G-1108)
**STRATOS WEALTH PARTNERS
LTD**
3750 Park East Dr Ste 200 (44122-4350)
PHONE.................................440 519-2500
Jeffrey Concepcion, *CEO*
Richard Gibson, *Partner*
Rick Maloyan, *Partner*
Jeremy Thompson, *Partner*
Chad Tom, *Partner*
EMP: 56
SALES (est): 789.8K
SALES (corp-wide): 401K **Privately Held**
SIC: 6282 Investment advisory service
PA: Man On The Moon, Llc
6241 Riverside Dr Ste 1n
Dublin OH 43017
614 886-9395

(G-1109)
SUNSTORM GAMES LLC
23245 Mercantile Rd Ste A (44122-5922)
PHONE.................................216 403-4820
Ron Laneve, *COO*
Anthony Campiti,
Len Tagon,
EMP: 38

SALES: 10MM **Privately Held**
SIC: 7371 Computer software development

(G-1110)
**SURESITE CONSULTING GROUP
LLC (PA)**
3659 Green Rd Ste 214 (44122-5715)
PHONE.................................216 593-0400
Kelly Warsaw, *CEO*
Jerry Warsaw, *President*
Courtney Schmidt, *Exec VP*
Jerald Warsaw,
EMP: 30
SALES (est): 11.5MM **Privately Held**
WEB: www.sure-site.com
SIC: 1541 Industrial buildings, new con-
struction

(G-1111)
**TELARC INTERNATIONAL CORP
(PA)**
23412 Commerce Park (44122-5813)
PHONE.................................216 464-2313
Jack Renner, *Ch of Bd*
Robert Woods, *President*
Scott Peplin, *Vice Pres*
Lawrence Blake, *Admin Sec*
EMP: 42
SQ FT: 14,000
SALES (est): 6.5MM **Privately Held**
WEB: www.telarc.com
SIC: 5099 7389 Compact discs; music
recording producer

(G-1112)
TOA TECHNOLOGIES INC (PA)
3333 Richmond Rd Ste 420 (44122-4198)
PHONE.................................216 360-8106
Yuval Brisker, *President*
Irad Carmi, *President*
Bruce Grainger, *Senior VP*
Francis S Barassi, *Vice Pres*
Daniel Little, *Vice Pres*
EMP: 73
SALES: 204.2K **Privately Held**
WEB: www.toatechnologies.com
SIC: 7371 Custom Computer Programing

(G-1113)
TODD ASSOCIATES INC (PA)
23825 Commerce Park Ste A (44122-5837)
PHONE.................................440 461-1101
Edward J Hyland Jr, *President*
Wayne A Leach, *Vice Pres*
Bryan Swicicki, *Broker*
Carol Maier, *Accounts Mgr*
Mick Stryffeler, *Sales Staff*
EMP: 55
SQ FT: 5,000
SALES (est): 15.8MM **Privately Held**
WEB: www.toddassociates.com
SIC: 6411 Insurance agents

(G-1114)
TREMCO INCORPORATED (HQ)
3735 Green Rd (44122-5730)
PHONE.................................216 292-5000
Jeffrey L Korach, *CEO*
Randall J Korach, *President*
Donna Teffer, *President*
Deryl Kratzer, *Division Pres*
Moorman Scott, *Division Pres*
◆ EMP: 300
SQ FT: 93,000
SALES (est): 581.4MM
SALES (corp-wide): 5.3B **Publicly Held**
WEB: www.tremcoinc.com
SIC: 2891 2952 1761 1752 Sealants;
caulking compounds; adhesives; epoxy
adhesives; roofing materials; coating
compounds, tar; asphalt saturated board;
roofing contractor; floor laying & floor
work; paints & allied products; specialty
cleaning, polishes & sanitation goods
PA: Rpm International Inc.
2628 Pearl Rd
Medina OH 44256
330 273-5090

GEOGRAPHIC

(G-1115)
UNITED INSURANCE COMPANY AMER
23215 Commerce Park # 310
(44122-5843)
PHONE..........................216 514-1904
Chris Powell, *General Mgr*
EMP: 30
SALES (corp-wide): 3.7B **Publicly Held**
WEB: www.unitedinsure.com
SIC: 6411 Insurance agents, brokers & service
HQ: United Insurance Company Of America
12115 Lackland Rd
Saint Louis MO 63146
314 819-4300

(G-1116)
UNIVERSITY HOSPITALS CLEVELAND
Also Called: Alzheimer Center
23215 Commerce Park # 300
(44122-5803)
PHONE..........................216 342-5556
Karl Herrup, *Principal*
EMP: 60
SALES (corp-wide): 580MM **Privately Held**
SIC: 8062 8011 General medical & surgical hospitals; offices & clinics of medical doctors
HQ: University Hospitals Of Cleveland
11100 Euclid Ave
Cleveland OH 44106
216 844-1000

(G-1117)
WEATHERPROOFING TECH INC (DH)
3735 Green Rd (44122-5705)
PHONE..........................216 292-5000
Robert Beckner, *President*
Deryl Kratzer, *President*
Jeffrey L Korach, *Principal*
Amie Grant, *Engineer*
Mike Drumm, *CFO*
EMP: 66
SALES (est): 70.7MM
SALES (corp-wide): 5.3B **Publicly Held**
WEB: www.wtiservices.com
SIC: 1761 Roofing contractor
HQ: Tremco Incorporated
3735 Green Rd
Beachwood OH 44122
216 292-5000

(G-1118)
ZINNER & CO
3201 Entp Pkwy Ste 410 (44122)
PHONE..........................216 831-0733
Robin Baum, *Managing Prtnr*
Donald J Zinner, *Partner*
David Antine, *Partner*
Sidney Brode, *Partner*
Jill Giesy, *Partner*
EMP: 41 EST: 1939
SQ FT: 5,000
SALES (est): 3.3MM **Privately Held**
WEB: www.zinnerco.com
SIC: 8721 Certified public accountant

Beallsville
Monroe County

(G-1119)
EMORY ROTHENBUHLER & SONS
47126 Sunfish Creek Rd (43716-9592)
PHONE..........................740 458-1432
Joyce Bonar, *President*
Gene Rothenbuhler, *Vice Pres*
EMP: 35
SQ FT: 8,000
SALES (est): 708.6K **Privately Held**
SIC: 4212 Local trucking, without storage

Beaver
Pike County

(G-1120)
D G M INC
1881 Adams Rd (45613-3500)
P.O. Box 207 (45613-0207)
PHONE..........................740 226-1950
Gerry Salsbury, *President*
Denny Salsbury, *Vice Pres*
Janet Salsbury, *Vice Pres*
Mark Salsbury, *Vice Pres*
Thomas Salsbury, *Vice Pres*
EMP: 61
SALES (est): 11.6MM **Privately Held**
SIC: 1611 General contractor, highway & street construction

Beavercreek
Greene County

(G-1121)
22ND CENTURY TECHNOLOGIES INC
2601 Commons Blvd Ste 130
(45431-3830)
PHONE..........................866 537-9191
Satvinder Singh, *President*
EMP: 129
SALES (corp-wide): 89.9MM **Privately Held**
SIC: 7371 Computer software systems analysis & design, custom
PA: 22nd Century Technologies Inc.
220 Davidson Ave Ste 100b
Somerset NJ 08873
732 537-9191

(G-1122)
A M MANAGEMENT INC
2000 Zink Rd (45324-2018)
PHONE..........................937 426-6500
Diana Spiegel, *Branch Mgr*
EMP: 44
SALES (corp-wide): 3.1MM **Privately Held**
SIC: 7021 Dormitory, commercially operated
PA: A M Management Inc
2871 Heinz Rd Ste B
Iowa City IA 52240
319 354-1961

(G-1123)
AAA CLUB ALLIANCE INC
3321 Dayton Xenia Rd (45432-2728)
PHONE..........................937 427-5884
EMP: 121
SALES (corp-wide): 408.5MM **Privately Held**
SIC: 6411 Insurance agents
PA: Aaa Club Alliance Inc.
1 River Pl
Wilmington DE 19801
302 299-4700

(G-1124)
ALTAMIRA TECHNOLOGIES CORP
2850 Presidential Dr # 200 (45324-6298)
PHONE..........................937 490-4804
Amber Scott, *Vice Pres*
Steve Betts, *Sr Software Eng*
EMP: 170
SALES (corp-wide): 50.2MM **Privately Held**
SIC: 7373 Systems integration services
HQ: Altamira Technologies Corporation
8201 Greensboro Dr # 800
Mc Lean VA 22102
703 813-2100

(G-1125)
APPLIED OPTIMIZATION INC
3040 Presidential Dr # 100 (45324-6272)
PHONE..........................937 431-5100
Anil Chaudhary, *President*
Katy Keenan, *Marketing Staff*
Jessica Piekenbrock, *Comp Scientist*
EMP: 101

SQ FT: 1,450
SALES (est): 8MM **Privately Held**
WEB: www.appliedo.com
SIC: 8733 Physical research, noncommercial

(G-1126)
ARCADIA SERVICES INC
Arcadia Health Care
2440 Dayton Xenia Rd C (45434-7124)
PHONE..........................937 912-5800
Cathy Sparling, *COO*
EMP: 51
SALES (corp-wide): 147.7MM **Privately Held**
SIC: 7363 8082 Medical help service; home health care services
PA: Arcadia Services, Inc.
20750 Civic Center Dr # 100
Southfield MI 48076
248 352-7530

(G-1127)
ASSURED INFORMATION SEC INC
3500 Pentagon Blvd # 310 (45431-2374)
PHONE..........................937 427-9720
Charles Green, *CEO*
Shannon M Secor, *Branch Mgr*
EMP: 54
SALES (corp-wide): 40.2MM **Privately Held**
SIC: 7371 7373 8733 Computer software development & applications; computer integrated systems design; physical research, noncommercial
PA: Assured Information Security, Inc.
153 Brooks Rd
Rome NY 13441
315 336-3306

(G-1128)
AT&T GOVERNMENT SOLUTIONS INC
2940 Presidential Dr # 390 (45324-6762)
PHONE..........................937 306-3030
Kirk Dunker, *General Mgr*
EMP: 75
SQ FT: 1,500
SALES (corp-wide): 170.7B **Publicly Held**
SIC: 3829 8742 Measuring & controlling devices; management consulting services
HQ: At&T Government Solutions, Inc.
1900 Gallows Rd Ste 105
Vienna VA 22182
703 506-5000

(G-1129)
BATTELLE MEMORIAL INSTITUTE
5100 Springfield St (45431-1261)
PHONE..........................937 258-6717
Aimee Kennedy, *Vice Pres*
Elizabeth Combs, *Branch Mgr*
EMP: 99
SALES (corp-wide): 2.5B **Privately Held**
SIC: 8731 Biotechnical research, commercial
PA: Battelle Memorial Institute Inc
505 King Ave
Columbus OH 43201
614 424-6424

(G-1130)
BEAVER-VU BOWL
1238 N Fairfield Rd (45432-2634)
PHONE..........................937 426-6771
Doug Wilson, *President*
Ron Rentz, *Principal*
Tom Wilson, *Principal*
Bob Rentz, *Corp Secy*
Bob Wilson, *Vice Pres*
EMP: 40
SQ FT: 5,500
SALES: 1.2MM **Privately Held**
WEB: www.daytonbowling.com
SIC: 7933 7999 5091 Ten pin center; bowling instruction; bowling equipment

(G-1131)
BEAVERCREEK CHURCH OF NAZARENE
1850 N Fairfield Rd (45432-2714)
PHONE..........................937 426-0079

Debbie Black, *Director*
EMP: 50
SALES (est): 2.4MM **Privately Held**
SIC: 8351 Preschool center

(G-1132)
BEAVERCREEK MEDICAL CENTER
2510 Commons Blvd Ste 120
(45431-3821)
PHONE..........................937 558-3000
Ann Hopkins, *Manager*
EMP: 68
SALES (est): 2MM
SALES (corp-wide): 1.7B **Privately Held**
SIC: 8062 General medical & surgical hospitals
HQ: Dayton Osteopathic Hospital
405 W Grand Ave
Dayton OH 45405
937 762-1629

(G-1133)
BEAVERCREEK MEDICAL CENTER
2510 Commons Blvd Ste 120
(45431-3821)
PHONE..........................937 558-3000
EMP: 52
SALES (est): 269K
SALES (corp-wide): 1.7B **Privately Held**
SIC: 8062 General Hospital
HQ: Dayton Osteopathic Hospital
405 W Grand Ave
Dayton OH 45405
937 762-1629

(G-1134)
BOOZ ALLEN HAMILTON INC
3800 Pentagon Blvd # 110 (45431-2199)
PHONE..........................937 429-5580
Charles Flowers, *Branch Mgr*
EMP: 50 **Publicly Held**
WEB: www.arinc.com
SIC: 8711 Engineering services
HQ: Booz Allen Hamilton Inc.
8283 Greensboro Dr # 700
Mc Lean VA 22102
703 902-5000

(G-1135)
BTAS INC (PA)
Also Called: Business Tech & Solutions
4391 Dayton Xenia Rd (45432-1803)
PHONE..........................937 431-9431
Angela Fronista, *President*
Charles Dyer, *Vice Pres*
John Sotman, *Vice Pres*
George Vlahos, *Vice Pres*
Chad Rayburn, *CFO*
EMP: 185
SQ FT: 7,500
SALES (est): 23.4MM **Privately Held**
WEB: www.btas.com
SIC: 8742 7374 7371 Business consultant; data processing & preparation; custom computer programming services

(G-1136)
C H DEAN INC (PA)
Also Called: Dean Financial Management
3500 Pentagon Blvd # 200 (45431-2376)
PHONE..........................937 222-9531
Dennis D Dean, *CEO*
Stephen M Miller, *President*
Mark E Schutter, *Exec VP*
Ronald A Best Phr, *Vice Pres*
Debra E Rindler, *CFO*
EMP: 60
SQ FT: 26,000
SALES (est): 11.8MM **Privately Held**
WEB: www.chdean.com
SIC: 6282 8721 8742 Investment counselors; accounting services, except auditing; management consulting services

(G-1137)
CADX SYSTEMS INC
2689 Commons Blvd Ste 100
(45431-3832)
PHONE..........................937 431-1464
EMP: 71

SALES (est): 789.9K
SALES (corp-wide): 26.3MM **Publicly Held**
SIC: 8071 Research And Development Of Computer Aided Detection Systems
PA: Icad, Inc.
  98 Spit Brook Rd Ste 100
  Nashua NH 03062
  603 882-5200

(G-1138)
CELLCO PARTNERSHIP
Also Called: Verizon
2755 Fairfield Cmns (45431-3777)
PHONE................937 429-4000
Steve Hamlin, *Branch Mgr*
EMP: 30
SALES (corp-wide): 130.8B **Publicly Held**
SIC: 4812 5999 Cellular telephone services; mobile telephones & equipment
HQ: Cellco Partnership
  1 Verizon Way
  Basking Ridge NJ 07920

(G-1139)
CHOICE HEALTHCARE LIMITED
1257 N Fairfield Rd (45432-2633)
PHONE................937 254-6220
Cammy Burns, *Principal*
Megan Upchurch, *Administration*
EMP: 80 **EST:** 2000
SALES: 5.9MM **Privately Held**
SIC: 8082 Visiting nurse service

(G-1140)
CISCO SYSTEMS INC
2661 Commons Blvd Ste 133
(45431-3704)
PHONE................937 427-4264
Helen Yep, *Principal*
EMP: 691
SALES (corp-wide): 48B **Publicly Held**
SIC: 3577 7379 Data conversion equipment, media-to-media: computer;
PA: Cisco Systems, Inc.
  170 W Tasman Dr
  San Jose CA 95134
  408 526-4000

(G-1141)
CITY OF BEAVERCREEK
2800 New Germany Trebein (45431-8531)
PHONE................937 320-0742
Mike Gafkjen, *Superintendent*
Steve Klick, *Opers Staff*
Steve Click, *Manager*
Leslie Heller, *Manager*
EMP: 60 **Privately Held**
SIC: 7992 7299 Public golf courses; banquet hall facilities
PA: City Of Beavercreek
  1368 Research Park Dr
  Beavercreek OH 45432
  937 427-5510

(G-1142)
CREEK TECHNOLOGIES COMPANY
2372 Lakeview Dr Ste H (45431-2566)
PHONE................937 272-4581
Lee Allen Culver, *President*
Steve Kaine, *CTO*
EMP: 120
SQ FT: 16,000
SALES: 14.8MM **Privately Held**
SIC: 7379 Computer related maintenance services

(G-1143)
CSRA LLC
3560 Pentagon Blvd (45431-1706)
PHONE................937 429-9774
David Edmondson, *Branch Mgr*
EMP: 320
SALES (corp-wide): 36.1B **Publicly Held**
WEB: www.csc.com
SIC: 7379 Computer related consulting services
HQ: Csra Llc
  3170 Fairview Park Dr
  Falls Church VA 22042
  703 641-2000

(G-1144)
DAUGWOOD INC
Also Called: Right At Home
3183 Beaver Vu Dr Ste B (45434-6385)
PHONE................937 429-9465
Lynn Daugherty, *President*
EMP: 35
SALES (est): 498.4K **Privately Held**
SIC: 8082 4729 Home health care services; carpool/vanpool arrangement

(G-1145)
DAVITA INC
3070 Presidential Dr A (45324-6273)
PHONE................937 426-6475
Tony Herd, *Principal*
EMP: 27 **Publicly Held**
SIC: 8092 Kidney dialysis centers
PA: Davita Inc.
  2000 16th St
  Denver CO 80202

(G-1146)
DAYTON ROOF & REMODELING CO
418 Merrick Dr (45434-5812)
PHONE................937 224-7667
William A Landefeld, *President*
Terryl Oyer, *Vice Pres*
EMP: 25 **EST:** 1948
SQ FT: 2,500
SALES (est): 1.9MM **Privately Held**
SIC: 1521 1761 New construction, single-family houses; roofing, siding & sheet metal work

(G-1147)
DESIGN KNOWLEDGE COMPANY
3100 Presidential Dr # 103 (45324-7145)
PHONE................937 320-9244
James R McCracken, *CEO*
Daniel Schiavone, *President*
Eric Loomis, *Vice Pres*
Daniel P Schaivone, *Engineer*
John Hutton, *Sr Project Mgr*
EMP: 63
SQ FT: 13,000
SALES (est): 8.8MM **Privately Held**
WEB: www.tdkc.com
SIC: 8711 Engineering services

(G-1148)
DRS SIGNAL TECHNOLOGIES INC
4393 Dayton Xenia Rd (45432)
PHONE................937 429-7470
Leo Torresani, *President*
EMP: 30
SALES (est): 10.3MM
SALES (corp-wide): 9.2B **Privately Held**
WEB: www.drs-st.com
SIC: 3825 7371 Electrical energy measuring equipment; custom computer programming services
HQ: Leonardo Drs, Inc.
  2345 Crystal Dr Ste 1000
  Arlington VA 22202
  703 416-8000

(G-1149)
DYN MARINE SERVICES INC
3040 Presidential Dr (45324-6294)
PHONE................937 427-2663
Ernie Carrillo, *Manager*
EMP: 40
SALES (corp-wide): 30.7B **Privately Held**
SIC: 7376 Computer facilities management
HQ: Dyn Marine Services, Inc.
  3190 Frview Pk Dr Ste 350
  Falls Church VA 22042

(G-1150)
E&I SOLUTIONS LLC
3610 Pentagon Blvd # 220 (45431-6700)
PHONE................937 912-0288
David Judson, *President*
EMP: 30
SALES (est): 612.1K **Privately Held**
SIC: 7373 7376 7379 Computer integrated systems design; computer facilities management; computer related maintenance services

(G-1151)
EDICT SYSTEMS INC
2434 Esquire Dr (45431-2573)
PHONE................937 429-4288
Ason K Wadzinski, *Ch of Bd*
David J Rike, *VP Sales*
Michael Byers, *Accounts Exec*
Derrik Moerner, *Accounts Exec*
Chuck Stuckert, *Accounts Exec*
EMP: 45
SQ FT: 12,000
SALES: 11.8MM
SALES (corp-wide): 12.6MM **Publicly Held**
WEB: www.retailec.com
SIC: 7372 Prepackaged software
PA: Advant-E Corporation
  2434 Esquire Dr
  Beavercreek OH 45431
  937 429-4288

(G-1152)
FITNESS INTERNATIONAL LLC
2500 N Fairfield Rd Ste F (45431-1781)
PHONE................937 427-0700
Christina Watson, *Branch Mgr*
EMP: 29
SALES (corp-wide): 173.1MM **Privately Held**
SIC: 7991 Physical fitness clubs with training equipment
PA: Fitness International, Llc
  3161 Michelson Dr Ste 600
  Irvine CA 92612
  949 255-7200

(G-1153)
G M A SURGERY INC
3359 Kemp Rd Ste 120 (45431-2565)
PHONE................937 429-7350
Larry Gault, *Administration*
EMP: 26
SALES (est): 1.2MM **Privately Held**
SIC: 8062 General medical & surgical hospitals

(G-1154)
GREENE MEMORIAL HOSPITAL INC
Also Called: Beavercreek Health Park
3359 Kemp Rd (45431-2565)
PHONE................937 458-4500
Larry Gault, *Branch Mgr*
EMP: 45
SQ FT: 1,782
SALES (corp-wide): 1.7B **Privately Held**
WEB: www.greenememorialhospital.com
SIC: 8062 Hospital, affiliated with AMA residency
HQ: Greene Memorial Hospital Inc.
  1141 N Monroe Dr
  Xenia OH 45385
  937 352-2000

(G-1155)
HJ FORD ASSOCIATES INC
2940 Presidential Dr # 150 (45324-6762)
PHONE................937 429-9711
Frank Grosso, *Vice Pres*
EMP: 125
SALES (corp-wide): 4.6B **Publicly Held**
WEB: www.hjford.com
SIC: 8711 8742 7361 Industrial engineers; management consulting services; employment agencies
HQ: H.J. Ford Associates, Inc.
  2900 Presidential Dr # 150
  Beavercreek OH 45324
  937 490-1482

(G-1156)
HOME DEPOT USA INC
Also Called: Home Depot, The
3775 Presidential Dr (45324-9095)
PHONE................937 431-7346
Tiffany A Collinsworth, *Manager*
EMP: 95
SALES (corp-wide): 108.2B **Publicly Held**
WEB: www.homerentalsdepot.com
SIC: 5211 7359 Home centers; tool rental
HQ: Home Depot U.S.A., Inc.
  2455 Paces Ferry Ave
  Atlanta GA 30339

(G-1157)
ILLUMINATION WORKS LLC
2689 Commons Blvd Ste 120
(45431-3832)
PHONE................937 938-1321
Jonathon J Mitchell, *Mng Member*
Kim Buchhalter, *Consultant*
Glen Pennington, *Software Dev*
EMP: 85
SQ FT: 6,200
SALES: 12.9MM **Privately Held**
WEB: www.illuminationworksllc.com
SIC: 7379 7374 8711 8748 Data processing consultant; data processing & preparation; consulting engineer; business consulting

(G-1158)
INTERNATIONAL BUS MCHS CORP
Also Called: IBM
3000 Presidential Dr # 300 (45324-6208)
PHONE................917 406-7400
EMP: 381
SALES (corp-wide): 79.5B **Publicly Held**
WEB: www.ibm.com
SIC: 7379 Computer related consulting services
PA: International Business Machines Corporation
  1 New Orchard Rd Ste 1 # 1
  Armonk NY 10504
  914 499-1900

(G-1159)
JJR SOLUTIONS LLC
3610 Pentagon Blvd # 220 (45431-6700)
PHONE................937 912-0288
Joseph Skinner, *General Mgr*
Linda Skinner, *COO*
David L Judson Jr, *Mng Member*
Jean Kuns, *Database Admin*
Alan Hensley, *Analyst*
EMP: 35
SALES: 4MM **Privately Held**
WEB: www.jjrsolutions.com
SIC: 8742 7371 7376 8711 Management information systems consultant; computer software development & applications; computer facilities management; engineering services; computer related maintenance services; physical research, noncommercial

(G-1160)
KETTERING ADVENTIST HEALTHCARE
2510 Commons Blvd Ste 100
(45431-3821)
PHONE................937 426-0049
Ronald Klein, *Branch Mgr*
Victoria Buckner, *Med Doctor*
Dale Hamilton, *Manager*
EMP: 49
SALES (corp-wide): 1.7B **Privately Held**
SIC: 8062 General medical & surgical hospitals
PA: Kettering Adventist Healthcare
  3535 Southern Blvd
  Dayton OH 45429
  937 298-4331

(G-1161)
KETTERING MEDICAL CENTER
Also Called: Soin Medical Center
3535 Pentagon Park Blvd (45431)
PHONE................937 702-4000
EMP: 54
SALES (corp-wide): 1.7B **Privately Held**
SIC: 8062 General medical & surgical hospitals
HQ: Kettering Medical Center
  3535 Southern Blvd
  Kettering OH 45429
  937 298-4331

(G-1162)
KEYW CORPORATION
1415 Research Park Dr (45432-2842)
PHONE................937 702-9512
EMP: 30 **Publicly Held**
SIC: 8711 8748 Engineering services; testing services

HQ: The Keyw Corporation
7740 Milestone Pkwy # 400
Hanover MD 21076

(G-1163)
KNOLLWOOD FLORISTS INC
Also Called: Knollwood Garden Center
3766 Dayton Xenia Rd (45432-2887)
P.O. Box 517, Dayton (45434-0517)
PHONE....................937 426-0861
Robert Scott, *President*
John Scott, *Vice Pres*
EMP: 35 **EST:** 1930
SQ FT: 35,000
SALES (est): 4.3MM **Privately Held**
WEB: www.knollwoodgardens.com
SIC: 5261 0181 Garden supplies & tools; flowers: grown under cover (e.g. greenhouse production)

(G-1164)
LEIDOS INC
Also Called: Mission Support
3745 Pentagon Blvd (45431-2369)
PHONE....................937 431-2270
Dennis Anders, *Branch Mgr*
EMP: 77
SALES (corp-wide): 10.1B **Publicly Held**
WEB: www.saic.com
SIC: 8731 7371 7373 8742 Commercial physical research; energy research; environmental research; medical research, commercial; computer software development; systems engineering, computer related; training & development consultant; recording & playback apparatus, including phonograph; integrated circuits, semiconductor networks, etc.
HQ: Leidos, Inc.
11951 Freedom Dr Ste 500
Reston VA 20190
571 526-6000

(G-1165)
LEIDOS INC
3745 Pentagon Blvd (45431-2369)
PHONE....................937 431-2220
John Jumper, *CEO*
Daniel Shrum, *Principal*
Sarita Ambris, *Administration*
Susan Little, *Analyst*
EMP: 304
SALES (corp-wide): 10.1B **Publicly Held**
WEB: www.saic.com
SIC: 8732 8731 Market analysis or research; commercial physical research
HQ: Leidos, Inc.
11951 Freedom Dr Ste 500
Reston VA 20190
571 526-6000

(G-1166)
LIBERTY INSULATION CO INC (PA)
2903 Kant Pl (45431-8573)
PHONE....................513 621-0108
Denver Smith, *President*
Nancy Smith, *Corp Secy*
Laura Meo, *Vice Pres*
Sarah Smith, *Office Mgr*
EMP: 60
SALES (est): 4.7MM **Privately Held**
SIC: 1742 Insulation, buildings

(G-1167)
LIFECYCLE SOLUTIONS JV LLC
2689 Cmmons Blvd Ste 120 (45431)
PHONE....................937 938-1321
Jonathon Mitchell, *Partner*
EMP: 99 **EST:** 2017
SALES (est): 1.4MM **Privately Held**
SIC: 7371 Custom computer programming services

(G-1168)
LOWES HOME CENTERS LLC
2850 Centre Dr Ste I (45324-2675)
PHONE....................937 427-1110
Brian Oletti, *Branch Mgr*
EMP: 150
SALES (corp-wide): 68.6B **Publicly Held**
SIC: 5211 5031 5722 5064 Home centers; building materials, exterior; building materials, interior; household appliance stores; electrical appliances, television & radio

HQ: Lowe's Home Centers, Llc
1605 Curtis Bridge Rd
Wilkesboro NC 28697
336 658-4000

(G-1169)
MCKEEVER & NIEKAMP ELC INC
1834 Woods Dr (45432-2261)
PHONE....................937 431-9363
Larry A McKeever, *President*
Doug Niekamp, *Vice Pres*
EMP: 25
SQ FT: 3,000
SALES (est): 4.4MM **Privately Held**
WEB: www.mckeeverniekamp.com
SIC: 1731 General electrical contractor

(G-1170)
MCR LLC
2601 Missi Point Blvd Ste (45431)
PHONE....................937 879-5055
Kurt Gwaltney, *Manager*
EMP: 100
SALES (corp-wide): 46.8MM **Privately Held**
WEB: www.innolog.com
SIC: 8741 Administrative management
PA: Mcr, Llc
2010 Corp Rdg Ste 350
Mclean VA 22102
703 506-4600

(G-1171)
MINTEK RESOURCES INC
3725 Pentagon Blvd # 100 (45431-2775)
P.O. Box 340187 (45434-0187)
PHONE....................937 431-0218
Christopher Myer, *CEO*
EMP: 25
SQ FT: 1,200
SALES (est): 7.2MM **Privately Held**
WEB: www.calciment.com
SIC: 5032 Lime building products; lime, except agricultural
HQ: Carmeuse Lime & Stone, Inc.
11 Stanwix St Fl 21
Pittsburgh PA 15222
412 995-5500

(G-1172)
N & C ACTIVE LEARNING LLC
1380 N Fairfield Rd (45432-2644)
PHONE....................937 545-1342
Colleen Clemens,
Nathan Clemens,
EMP: 30
SALES (est): 315.7K **Privately Held**
SIC: 8351 Child day care services

(G-1173)
NOVA TECHNOLOGY SOLUTIONS LLC
3100 Presidential Dr # 310 (45324-9039)
PHONE....................937 426-2596
Rick Denezza,
Brad Hart,
EMP: 48
SQ FT: 4,000
SALES: 3.9MM **Privately Held**
WEB: www.novatechsol.com
SIC: 7379

(G-1174)
ORACLE CORPORATION
3610 Pentagon Blvd # 205 (45431-6700)
PHONE....................513 826-5632
Peter Burton, *Principal*
EMP: 191
SALES (corp-wide): 39.8B **Publicly Held**
SIC: 7372 Business oriented computer software
PA: Oracle Corporation
500 Oracle Pkwy
Redwood City CA 94065
650 506-7000

(G-1175)
PERDUCO GROUP INC
2647 Commons Blvd (45431)
PHONE....................937 401-0271
Toyzanne Mason, *President*
Stephen Chambal, *Exec VP*
Christopher Mason, *Vice Pres*
Neil Ranly, *Software Engr*
Kevin Gaudette, *Director*
EMP: 44

SQ FT: 4,580
SALES: 500K **Privately Held**
SIC: 8741 8742 Management services; management consulting services

(G-1176)
PH FAIRBORN HT OWNER 2800 LLC
Also Called: Holiday Inn
2800 Presidential Dr (45324-6296)
PHONE....................937 426-7800
Nathaniel Hamilton, *General Mgr*
EMP: 85
SALES (est): 1.1MM **Privately Held**
SIC: 7011 Hotels & motels

(G-1177)
PREMIER RADIOLOGY GROUP INC
2145 N Fairfield Rd Ste A (45431-2783)
P.O. Box 1365, Springfield (45501-1365)
PHONE....................937 431-9729
EMP: 27
SQ FT: 16,000
SALES (est): 5MM **Privately Held**
SIC: 8011 Medical Doctor's Office

(G-1178)
PRIMARY CR NTWRK PRMR HLTH PRT
722 N Fairfield Rd (45434-5918)
PHONE....................937 208-7000
EMP: 63
SALES (corp-wide): 33.7MM **Privately Held**
SIC: 8011 General & family practice, physician/surgeon
PA: Primary Care Network Of Premier Health Partners
110 N Main St Ste 350
Dayton OH 45402
937 226-7085

(G-1179)
QBASE LLC (PA)
3725 Pentagon Blvd # 100 (45431-2775)
PHONE....................888 458-0345
Steve Baldwin, *President*
Brian Nightingale, *Exec VP*
Scott Reynolds, *Exec VP*
Steve Schlosser, *Exec VP*
Jose Gomes, *Senior VP*
EMP: 32
SQ FT: 9,000
SALES (est): 28.9MM **Privately Held**
WEB: www.qbase.us
SIC: 7379 Data processing consultant

(G-1180)
RAINBOW DATA SYSTEMS INC
2358 Lakeview Dr Ste A (45431-2569)
PHONE....................937 431-8000
John H Kim, *President*
David Reynolds, *Business Mgr*
Tom Steuer, *Business Mgr*
Doug Mummert, *COO*
Sam Morgan, *Vice Pres*
EMP: 34
SQ FT: 7,100
SALES: 5.9MM **Privately Held**
WEB: www.rainbowdata.com
SIC: 7379 7371 7373 Computer related consulting services; custom computer programming services; computer software development; computer integrated systems design

(G-1181)
REGAL CINEMAS INC
Also Called: Hollywood 20
2651 Fairfield Cmns (45431-3775)
PHONE....................937 431-9418
Gwen Watts, *Manager*
EMP: 35 **Privately Held**
WEB: www.regalcinemas.com
SIC: 7832 Motion picture theaters, except drive-in
HQ: Regal Cinemas, Inc.
101 E Blount Ave Ste 100
Knoxville TN 37920
865 922-1123

(G-1182)
RESIDENCE INN BY MARRIOTT BEAV
2779 Frfield Commons Blvd (45431)
PHONE....................937 427-3914
Carroll Hamann, *Manager*
Ryann McCoy, *Manager*
EMP: 50
SALES (est): 1.3MM **Privately Held**
SIC: 7011 Hotels

(G-1183)
RIVERSIDE RESEARCH INSTITUTE
2640 Hibiscus Way (45431-1798)
PHONE....................937 431-3810
Steve Omick, *President*
Brian O'Connor, *Manager*
EMP: 99
SALES (corp-wide): 88.1MM **Privately Held**
SIC: 8733 Research institute
PA: Riverside Research Institute
156 William St Fl 9
New York NY 10038
212 563-4545

(G-1184)
ROUND ROOM LLC
Also Called: Unknown
3301 Dayton Xenia Rd (45432-2758)
PHONE....................937 429-2230
EMP: 44 **Privately Held**
SIC: 4813 Local & long distance telephone communications
PA: Round Room, Llc
525 Congressional Blvd
Carmel IN 46032

(G-1185)
SEARS ROEBUCK AND CO
Also Called: Sears Auto Center
2727 Fairfield Cmns (45431-3778)
PHONE....................937 427-8528
EMP: 25
SALES (corp-wide): 16.7B **Publicly Held**
SIC: 7549 Automotive Services
HQ: Sears, Roebuck And Co.
3333 Beverly Rd
Hoffman Estates IL 60179
847 286-2500

(G-1186)
SIBCY CLINE INC
2476 Commons Blvd Ste E (45431-3808)
PHONE....................937 429-2101
Rob Sibcy, *Owner*
EMP: 42
SALES (corp-wide): 2.1B **Privately Held**
SIC: 6531 Real estate agent, residential
PA: Sibcy Cline, Inc.
8044 Montgomery Rd # 300
Cincinnati OH 45236
513 984-4100

(G-1187)
SOLUTIONS THROUGH INNOVATIVE T
Also Called: STI Technologies
3152 Presidential Dr (45324-2039)
PHONE....................937 320-9994
Dr Alvin E Hall Sr, *President*
Charles A Colon III, *Vice Pres*
EMP: 65 **EST:** 2000
SQ FT: 2,000
SALES (est): 5.6MM **Privately Held**
WEB: www.sti-tec.com
SIC: 7371 Computer software development & applications

(G-1188)
SUMARIA SYSTEMS INC
3164 Presidential Dr (45324-2039)
PHONE....................937 429-6070
Don Kurtz, *President*
Ron Goerges, *Branch Mgr*
EMP: 80
SALES (corp-wide): 31.8MM **Privately Held**
WEB: www.sumaria.com
SIC: 7373 8711 7374 7371 Computer integrated systems design; consulting engineer; data processing & preparation; custom computer programming services

▲ = Import ▼=Export
◆ =Import/Export

PA: Sumaria Systems, Inc.
99 Rosewood Dr Ste 140
Danvers MA 01923
978 739-4200

(G-1189)
SYTRONICS INC
4433 Dayton Xenia Rd # 1 (45432-1805)
PHONE..........................937 431-6100
Barrett Myers, *President*
Sonja Johannes, *Corp Secy*
Steve Myers, *Vice Pres*
Gregory Hubbard, *Engineer*
Cherrie Zindorf, *Accounting Mgr*
EMP: 35
SQ FT: 22,000
SALES: 5MM **Privately Held**
WEB: www.sytronics.com
SIC: 8732 8731 7373 Commercial non-physical research; commercial physical research; computer systems analysis & design

(G-1190)
UES INC (PA)
4401 Dayton Xenia Rd (45432-1805)
PHONE..........................937 426-6900
Nina Joshi, *CEO*
Johnson Tang, *Managing Dir*
John Gruenwald, *Vice Pres*
Brian Byg, *Opers Staff*
Ronda Boles, *Purch Agent*
EMP: 180
SQ FT: 80,000
SALES (est): 39.4MM **Privately Held**
WEB: www.ues.com
SIC: 8731 Biotechnical research, commercial

(G-1191)
UES METALS GROUP
4401 Dayton Xenia Rd (45432-1805)
PHONE..........................937 255-9340
T Parthaswrthy, *Office Mgr*
Triplicane Parthaswrthy, *Office Mgr*
EMP: 30 **EST:** 2008
SALES (est): 1.6MM **Privately Held**
SIC: 6411 Research services, insurance

(G-1192)
UNISON INDUSTRIES LLC
Also Called: Elano Div
2070 Heller Dr (45434-7210)
PHONE..........................937 427-0550
Robert Hessel, *Branch Mgr*
EMP: 400
SALES (corp-wide): 121.6B **Publicly Held**
WEB: www.unisonindustries.com
SIC: 3728 4581 Aircraft parts & equipment; aircraft servicing & repairing
HQ: Unison Industries, Llc
7575 Baymeadows Way
Jacksonville FL 32256
904 739-4000

(G-1193)
UNIVERSAL TECHNOLOGY CORP (PA)
Also Called: U T C
1270 N Fairfield Rd (45432-2600)
PHONE..........................937 426-2808
Bob Gran, *CEO*
Donna Walker, *General Mgr*
Norman C Carey, *Principal*
Charles J Giemza, *Principal*
Robert D Guyton, *Principal*
EMP: 72 **EST:** 1961
SQ FT: 24,000
SALES (est): 48.4MM **Privately Held**
WEB: www.utcdayton.com
SIC: 8711 7812 7221 Engineering services; audio-visual program production; photographic studios; portrait

(G-1194)
VANA SOLUTIONS LLC
4027 Col Glenn Hwy 110 (45431)
PHONE..........................937 242-6399
Srujal Sheth,
EMP: 50
SALES (est): 2.7MM **Privately Held**
SIC: 7379 Computer related maintenance services

(G-1195)
VOSS TOYOTA INC
2110 Heller Dr (45434-7211)
P.O. Box 340100, Dayton (45434-0100)
PHONE..........................937 431-2100
John E Voss, *President*
Rob George, *General Mgr*
EMP: 40
SQ FT: 23,000
SALES (est): 12.9MM **Privately Held**
WEB: www.vosstoyota.com
SIC: 5511 7538 5531 5521 Automobiles, new & used; general automotive repair shops; automotive parts; used car dealers; automotive supplies & parts

(G-1196)
WRIGHT EXECUTIVE HT LTD PARTNR (PA)
Also Called: Holiday Inn
2800 Presidential Dr (45324-6296)
PHONE..........................937 426-7800
Western and Southern Life Insu, *Partner*
Steve Groppe, *General Mgr*
Karl Williard, *Director*
EMP: 180
SALES (est): 6.1MM **Privately Held**
WEB: www.hwdaytonfairborn.com
SIC: 7011 Hotels & motels

(G-1197)
WRIGHT EXECUTIVE HT LTD PARTNR
Also Called: Homewood Suites
2750 Presidential Dr (45324-6262)
PHONE..........................937 429-0600
Janelle Richards, *Branch Mgr*
EMP: 128 **Privately Held**
WEB: www.hwdaytonfairborn.com
SIC: 7011 Hotels & motels
PA: Wright Executive Hotel Limited Partnership
2800 Presidential Dr
Beavercreek OH 45324

(G-1198)
WRIGHT STATE PHYSCANS DRMTLOGY (PA)
725 University Blvd (45324-2640)
PHONE..........................937 224-7546
Jeffrey Travers, *Dermatology*
Marc Raslich, *Pediatrics*
Iva Staats,
EMP: 45
SALES (est): 8.1MM **Privately Held**
SIC: 8011 Dermatologist

(G-1199)
WRIGHT STATE UNIVERSITY
Also Called: Quest Diagnostics
3640 Colonel Glenn Hwy (45324-2096)
PHONE..........................937 775-3333
Simone Polk, *Manager*
EMP: 851
SALES (corp-wide): 230.3MM **Privately Held**
SIC: 5063 8221 Electrical apparatus & equipment; university
PA: Wright State University
3640 Colonel Glenn Hwy
Dayton OH 45435
937 775-3333

(G-1200)
WRIGHT-PATT CREDIT UNION INC (PA)
3560 Pentagon Blvd (45431-1706)
P.O. Box 286, Fairborn (45324-0286)
PHONE..........................937 912-7000
Doug Fecher, *President*
Kim Test, *Principal*
EMP: 254
SQ FT: 46,000
SALES: 137MM **Privately Held**
WEB: www.wrightpattcu.com
SIC: 6062 State credit unions, not federally chartered

(G-1201)
WYLE LABORATORIES INC
2601 Mission Point Blvd # 300
(45431-6600)
PHONE..........................937 912-3470
Douglas Van Kirk, *Admin Sec*
EMP: 40 **Publicly Held**

WEB: www.wylelabs.com
SIC: 8734 Testing laboratories
HQ: Wyle Laboratories, Inc.
970 W 190th St Ste 890
Torrance CA 90502

Beavercreek
Montgomery County

(G-1202)
APPLIED RESEARCH SOLUTIONS INC (HQ)
51 Plum St Ste 240 (45440-1397)
PHONE..........................937 912-6100
Gary Wittinger, *CEO*
Kevin Sullivan, *President*
Juan Lopez, *Engineer*
Chris Colvin, *Sr Software Eng*
EMP: 67
SALES (est): 8MM
SALES (corp-wide): 88.1MM **Privately Held**
WEB: www.arsiresearch.com
SIC: 8733 Research institute
PA: Riverside Research Institute
156 William St Fl 9
New York NY 10038
212 563-4545

(G-1203)
AT&T CORP
4467 Walnut St (45440-1379)
PHONE..........................937 320-9648
Jonathon Gohmann, *Branch Mgr*
EMP: 69
SALES (corp-wide): 170.7B **Publicly Held**
WEB: www.att.com
SIC: 4812 Cellular telephone services
HQ: At&T Corp.
1 At&T Way
Bedminster NJ 07921
800 403-3302

(G-1204)
AT&T INC
4467 Walnut St Ste A120 (45440-1379)
PHONE..........................937 320-9648
EMP: 30
SALES (corp-wide): 170.7B **Publicly Held**
SIC: 4812 Cellular telephone services
PA: At&T Inc.
208 S Akard St
Dallas TX 75202
210 821-4105

(G-1205)
ATK SPACE SYSTEMS INC
1365 Technology Ct (45430-2212)
PHONE..........................937 490-4121
James Dillon, *General Mgr*
Mark Cottle, *Principal*
Joseph Scheckel, *Principal*
Blake Larson, *COO*
Todd Henrich, *Vice Pres*
EMP: 50 **Publicly Held**
WEB: www.psi-pci.com
SIC: 8731 Commercial physical research
HQ: Atk Space Systems Inc.
6033 Bandini Blvd
Commerce CA 90040
323 722-0222

(G-1206)
BIG HILL REALTY CORP
Also Called: Suzie Roselius Real Estate
4011 Danern Dr (45430-2040)
PHONE..........................937 426-4420
Suzie Roselius, *Branch Mgr*
EMP: 75
SALES (est): 1.2MM
SALES (corp-wide): 9.3MM **Privately Held**
WEB: www.bighillgmac.com
SIC: 6531 Real estate brokers & agents
PA: Big Hill Realty Corp
5580 Far Hills Ave
Dayton OH 45429
937 435-1177

(G-1207)
BIG HILL REALTY CORP
Also Called: Better Homes and Gardens
3944 Indian Ripple Rd (45440-3450)
PHONE..........................937 429-2200
Jeff Owens, *Manager*
EMP: 29
SALES (est): 1.2MM
SALES (corp-wide): 9.3MM **Privately Held**
WEB: www.bighillgmac.com
SIC: 6531 Real estate agent, residential
PA: Big Hill Realty Corp
5580 Far Hills Ave
Dayton OH 45429
937 435-1177

(G-1208)
BROOKDALE SENIOR LIVING COMMUN
Also Called: Brookdale Beavercreek
3839 Indian Ripple Rd (45440-3468)
PHONE..........................937 203-8443
Chris Mattox, *Manager*
EMP: 25
SALES (corp-wide): 4.5B **Publicly Held**
WEB: www.assisted.com
SIC: 8059 Rest home, with health care
HQ: Brookdale Senior Living Communities, Inc.
6737 W Wa St Ste 2300
Milwaukee WI 53214
414 918-5000

(G-1209)
CENTRE COMMUNICATIONS CORP
70 Birch Aly Ste 240 (45440-1477)
PHONE..........................440 454-3262
Eman Shawkey Kailini, *President*
Rick Stadelman, *Principal*
Eric Denis Weiss, *Director*
EMP: 25
SQ FT: 15,000
SALES (est): 249K **Privately Held**
SIC: 8999 Communication services

(G-1210)
CITIGROUP GLOBAL MARKETS INC
Also Called: Smith Barney
4380 Buckeye Ln Ste 200 (45440-7310)
PHONE..........................860 291-4181
Rusty Clark, *Branch Mgr*
EMP: 70
SALES (corp-wide): 72.8B **Publicly Held**
WEB: www.salomonsmithbarney.com
SIC: 6211 Security brokers & dealers; stock brokers & dealers
HQ: Citigroup Global Markets Inc.
388 Greenwich St Fl 18
New York NY 10013
212 816-6000

(G-1211)
COMPUNET CLINICAL LABS LLC
75 Sylvania Dr (45440-3237)
PHONE..........................937 427-2655
Linda Blumme, *Manager*
EMP: 57
SALES (corp-wide): 17.2K **Privately Held**
SIC: 8071 Medical laboratories
HQ: Compunet Clinical Laboratories, Llc
2308 Sandridge Dr
Moraine OH 45439
937 296-0844

(G-1212)
CONTECH-GDCG
4197 Research Blvd (45430-2203)
PHONE..........................937 426-3577
Greg Thompson, *Partner*
EMP: 40
SQ FT: 14,000
SALES (est): 1.5MM **Privately Held**
SIC: 8741 Construction management

(G-1213)
DAYTON EYE SURGERY CENTER
81 Sylvania Dr (45440-3271)
PHONE..........................937 431-9531
Charles Kidwell Jr, *Principal*

Melody Audia, *Executive*
Judith L Doell, *Administration*
EMP: 40
SALES (est): 4.8MM **Privately Held**
SIC: 8011 Medical centers; ophthalmologist

(G-1214)
DEDICATED NURSING ASSOC INC
70 Birch Aly Ste 240 (45440-1477)
PHONE....................888 465-6929
EMP: 177 **Privately Held**
SIC: 8051 7361 7363 Skilled nursing care facilities; nurses' registry; medical help service
PA: Dedicated Nursing Associates, Inc.
6536 State Route 22
Delmont PA 15626

(G-1215)
DIGESTIVE CARE INC
75 Sylvania Dr (45440-3237)
PHONE....................937 320-5050
Jonhathan Saxe MD, *President*
William Wilson, *Principal*
Richard C Cammerer MD, *Vice Pres*
Craig W Penno, *Office Mgr*
Giti Rostami MD, *Med Doctor*
EMP: 100
SALES (est): 9.3MM **Privately Held**
WEB: www.digestivecare.net
SIC: 8011 Gastronomist

(G-1216)
ENDOSCOPY CENTER OF DAYTON (PA)
4200 Indian Ripple Rd (45440-3248)
PHONE....................937 320-5050
Dr Larry Weprin, *President*
EMP: 32
SQ FT: 10,000
SALES (est): 2.1MM **Privately Held**
SIC: 8011 Gastronomist

(G-1217)
FARMERS FINANCIAL SERVICES
3888 Indian Ripple Rd (45440-3448)
PHONE....................937 424-0643
Pete Dutton, *Owner*
EMP: 40
SALES (est): 1.7MM **Privately Held**
SIC: 6411 Insurance agents, brokers & service

(G-1218)
FIRST COMMAND FINCL PLG INC
51 Plum St Ste 260 (45440-1397)
PHONE....................937 429-4490
John Deraper, *Manager*
EMP: 30
SALES (corp-wide): 440.8MM **Privately Held**
SIC: 8742 Financial consultant
HQ: First Command Financial Planning, Inc.
1 Firstcomm Plz
Fort Worth TX 76109
817 731-8621

(G-1219)
GLOBAL MILITARY EXPERT CO
Also Called: Spotlight Labs
2670e Indian Ripple Rd (45440-3605)
PHONE....................800 738-9795
Nathaniel C Dickman,
Bradford Everman,
EMP: 50
SALES (est): 3.1MM **Privately Held**
SIC: 8742 8711 Training & development consultant; electrical or electronic engineering

(G-1220)
GREATER DAYTON CNSTR LTD
Also Called: OBERER THOMPSON CO
4197 Research Blvd (45430-2203)
PHONE....................937 426-3577
Greg Thompson, *Partner*
Robin Collier, *Partner*
Jerry Woodruff, *Project Mgr*
Bryan Sowder, *Director*
EMP: 74
SQ FT: 13,500

SALES: 43.1MM **Privately Held**
SIC: 1542 1521 1522 Commercial & office building, new construction; specialized public building contractors; new construction, single-family houses; residential construction; apartment building construction; multi-family dwellings, new construction; remodeling, multi-family dwellings

(G-1221)
GREENE TOWN CENTER LLC
Also Called: Greene, The
4452 Buckeye Ln (45440-3100)
PHONE....................937 490-4990
David Lukes, *CEO*
Andrea Olshan, *President*
Brad Warvel, *Opers Dir*
Kelli Kooken, *Marketing Staff*
EMP: 90
SALES (est): 4.3MM **Privately Held**
SIC: 6531 Real estate agents & managers

(G-1222)
HAROLD J BECKER COMPANY INC
3946 Indian Ripple Rd (45440-3499)
P.O. Box 340970, Dayton (45434-0970)
PHONE....................614 279-1414
Kevin L Bechtel, *President*
Nicholas Bechtel, *Vice Pres*
Dave Fromma, *Project Mgr*
Naomi Terry, *Controller*
EMP: 30 EST: 1949
SQ FT: 12,000
SALES (est): 5.1MM **Privately Held**
WEB: www.hjbecker.com
SIC: 1761 1799 Roofing contractor; waterproofing

(G-1223)
HCF OF CRESTVIEW INC
Also Called: Village At The Greene
4381 Tonawanda Trl (45430-1961)
PHONE....................937 426-5033
Patrice Gerber, *Principal*
Nema Samples, *Nursing Dir*
EMP: 99
SQ FT: 26,580
SALES (est): 3.7MM **Privately Held**
SIC: 8051 Convalescent home with continuous nursing care

(G-1224)
ITS FINANCIAL LLC
Also Called: Instant Tax Service
51 Plum St Ste 260 (45440-1397)
PHONE....................937 425-6889
Peter Samborsky, *CFO*
Fesum Ogbazion,
EMP: 77
SQ FT: 4,000
SALES (est): 8.8MM **Privately Held**
SIC: 8742 Franchising consultant

(G-1225)
LARUE ENTERPRISES INC
Also Called: Merry Maids
3331 Seajay Dr (45430-1365)
PHONE....................937 438-5711
Judith Larue, *Owner*
EMP: 35
SALES: 1MM **Privately Held**
SIC: 7349 7363 Maid services, contract or fee basis; domestic help service

(G-1226)
LEWIS P C JACKSON
70 Birch Aly (45440-1479)
PHONE....................937 306-6304
EMP: 38
SALES (corp-wide): 249.8MM **Privately Held**
SIC: 8111 General practice law office
PA: Lewis P C Jackson
1133 Weschester Ave
White Plains NY 10604
914 872-8060

(G-1227)
MACAULAY-BROWN INC (PA)
Also Called: Macb
4021 Executive Dr (45430-1062)
PHONE....................937 426-3421
Sid Fuchs, *CEO*
Sidney E Fuchs, *President*

Mike Beauchamp, *Senior VP*
Duane Shugars, *Senior VP*
Dave Bramlage, *Vice Pres*
EMP: 400 EST: 1979
SQ FT: 64,000
SALES (est): 230MM **Privately Held**
WEB: www.macaulaybrown.com
SIC: 8711 8733 Consulting engineer; research institute

(G-1228)
MANATRON INC (DH)
4105 Executive Dr (45430-1071)
PHONE....................937 431-4000
Allen Peat, *President*
Nan W Warner, *Regional Mgr*
EMP: 34
SQ FT: 12,000
SALES (est): 3.5MM
SALES (corp-wide): 10.6B **Publicly Held**
SIC: 7373 5045 Turnkey vendors, computer systems; local area network (LAN) systems integrator; computer peripheral equipment; computers & accessories, personal & home entertainment
HQ: Manatron, Inc.
510 E Milham Ave
Portage MI 49002
269 567-2900

(G-1229)
MANATRON SABRE SYSTEMS AND SVC (DH)
4105 Executive Dr (45430-1071)
PHONE....................937 431-4000
Dan Muthard, *President*
EMP: 68
SALES (est): 7.7MM
SALES (corp-wide): 10.6B **Publicly Held**
WEB: www.manatron.com
SIC: 5045 6531 Computer software; appraiser, real estate
HQ: Manatron, Inc.
510 E Milham Ave
Portage MI 49002
269 567-2900

(G-1230)
MATRIX RESEARCH INC
3844 Research Blvd (45430-2104)
PHONE....................937 427-8433
James Lutz, *Ch of Bd*
Robert Hawley, *President*
Robert W Hawley, *President*
William Pierson, *Vice Pres*
EMP: 80
SQ FT: 4,000
SALES (est): 23.3MM **Privately Held**
SIC: 3829 8711 Measuring & controlling devices; engineering services

(G-1231)
MINI UNIVERSITY INC (PA)
115 Harbert Dr Ste A (45440-5117)
PHONE....................937 426-1414
Julie Thorner, *President*
Donna Mowles, *Human Res Dir*
Sarah Cannon, *Mktg Coord*
Bess John, *Director*
Karen Mackay, *Director*
EMP: 125
SALES (est): 1MM **Privately Held**
WEB: www.miniuniversity.net
SIC: 8351 Preschool center

(G-1232)
NORTHROP GRUMMAN SYSTEMS CORP
4020 Executive Dr (45430-1061)
PHONE....................937 429-6450
Mel Meadows, *Branch Mgr*
Thomas Seibert, *Director*
EMP: 45 **Publicly Held**
SIC: 7373 Computer systems analysis & design
HQ: Northrop Grumman Systems Corporation
2980 Fairview Park Dr
Falls Church VA 22042
703 280-2900

(G-1233)
POND-WOOLPERT LLC
4454 Idea Center Blvd (45430-1500)
PHONE....................937 461-5660
David Ziegman,

EMP: 60
SALES (est): 1MM **Privately Held**
SIC: 8712 Architectural engineering

(G-1234)
RE/MAX
51 Plum St Ste 220 (45440-1397)
PHONE....................937 477-4997
Stan Haper, *Owner*
Marsha Conner, *Broker*
Kathryn Dixon, *Broker*
Cheri Knedler, *Broker*
Jill Aldineh, *Consultant*
EMP: 45 EST: 2011
SALES: 150K **Privately Held**
SIC: 6531 Real estate agent, residential

(G-1235)
RICHARD L LISTON MD
Also Called: Danton Eye Associates
89 Sylvania Dr (45440-3281)
PHONE....................937 320-2020
Dr R Liston, *Partner*
EMP: 52
SALES (est): 925K **Privately Held**
SIC: 8011 General & family practice, physician/surgeon

(G-1236)
SAWDEY SOLUTION SERVICES INC (PA)
1430 Oak Ct Ste 304 (45430-1065)
PHONE....................937 490-4060
Constance Sawdey, *President*
Jeffrey Sawdey, *Vice Pres*
Sterling Fenwick, *Opers Staff*
Brittney Ream, *Opers Staff*
Michael Duckworth, *QC Mgr*
EMP: 27 EST: 2001
SALES: 65MM **Privately Held**
WEB: www.sawdeysolutionservices.com
SIC: 7371 8748 8711 Custom computer programming services; systems engineering consultant, ex. computer or professional; consulting engineer

(G-1237)
TACG LLC (PA)
1430 Oak Ct Ste 100 (45430-1064)
PHONE....................937 203-8201
Brian Chaney, *President*
Todd Vikan, *COO*
John Graves, *Project Mgr*
Derron Hunt, *Production*
Keith Harvey, *Engineer*
EMP: 175
SALES (est): 8MM **Privately Held**
SIC: 7382 8742 Security systems services; business consultant

(G-1238)
TM CAPTURE SERVICES LLC
Also Called: Macalogic
4380 Buckeye Ln Ste 222 (45440-3199)
PHONE....................937 728-1781
Teresa Macalolooy,
EMP: 70
SALES: 8MM **Privately Held**
SIC: 8741 7389 8742 Administrative management; ; sales (including sales management) consultant

(G-1239)
UNITED CHURCH HOMES INC
Also Called: Trinity Community
3218 Indian Ripple Rd (45440-3637)
PHONE....................937 426-8481
Laura Farrell, *Director*
EMP: 200
SALES (corp-wide): 78.1MM **Privately Held**
WEB: www.altenheimcommunity.org
SIC: 8051 8052 8361 Convalescent home with continuous nursing care; intermediate care facilities; geriatric residential care
PA: United Church Homes Inc
170 E Center St
Marion OH 43302
740 382-4885

(G-1240)
WERNLI REALTY INC
1300 Grange Hall Rd (45430-1013)
PHONE....................937 258-7878
Richard L Schaefer, *President*
John Miltenberger, *Asst Sec*

EMP: 75
SQ FT: 20,000
SALES (est): 8.6MM **Privately Held**
SIC: 3441 6512 Building components, structural steel; nonresidential building operators

(G-1241)
WOOLPRT-MRRICK JOINT VENTR LLP
4454 Idea Center Blvd (45430-1500)
PHONE....................................937 461-5660
David Ziegman, *Principal*
EMP: 50 EST: 2014
SQ FT: 4,800
SALES (est): 1.7MM **Privately Held**
SIC: 8712 Architectural engineering

(G-1242)
WYLE LABORATORIES INC
2700 Indian Ripple Rd (45440-3638)
PHONE....................................937 320-2712
Mike Gilkey, *Branch Mgr*
EMP: 150 **Publicly Held**
WEB: www.wylelabs.com
SIC: 8731 Commercial physical research
HQ: Wyle Laboratories, Inc.
970 W 190th St Ste 890
Torrance CA 90502

Beavercreek Township
Greene County

(G-1243)
AZIMUTH CORPORATION
4027 Colonel Glenn Hwy # 230 (45431-1695)
PHONE....................................937 256-8571
James Michael Livingston, *CEO*
Valerie Rossi, *President*
Charles Rossi, *Vice Pres*
EMP: 49
SQ FT: 3,286
SALES: 8.5MM **Privately Held**
WEB: www.azimuth-corp.com
SIC: 8711 8731 8742 Consulting engineer; commercial physical research; management consulting services

(G-1244)
COLDWELL BNKR HRITG RLTORS LLC
4139 Colonel Glenn Hwy (45431-1652)
PHONE....................................937 426-6060
Bruce Doldeer, *Manager*
EMP: 32
SALES (corp-wide): 6.5MM **Privately Held**
WEB: www.coldwellbankerdayton.com
SIC: 6531 Real estate agent, residential
PA: Coldwell Banker Heritage Realtors Llc
2000 Hewitt Ave
Dayton OH 45440
937 434-7600

(G-1245)
DAVE DNNIS CHRYSLER JEEP DODGE
Also Called: Dave Dennis Auto Group
4232 Colonel Glenn Hwy (45431-1604)
PHONE....................................937 429-5566
Jason Dennis, *President*
Ulysses Ponder, *Treasurer*
JB Davis, *Sales Mgr*
Joe Eldridge, *Sales Mgr*
Ryan McGee, *Sales Mgr*
EMP: 60 EST: 1969
SQ FT: 31,000
SALES (est): 25.7MM **Privately Held**
WEB: www.davedennis.com
SIC: 5511 7532 7538 5531 Automobiles, new & used; body shop, automotive; general automotive repair shops; automotive parts; automotive accessories

(G-1246)
DAYTON AEROSPACE INC
4141 Colonel Glenn Hwy # 252 (45431-5102)
PHONE....................................937 426-4300
Robert Matthews, *President*
Charles Craw Jr, *Vice Pres*
Gary Poleskey, *Vice Pres*

Robert Raggio, *Vice Pres*
David Waite, *Vice Pres*
EMP: 30
SQ FT: 6,337
SALES (est): 5.5MM **Privately Held**
WEB: www.daytonaero.com
SIC: 8742 Business consultant

(G-1247)
DCS CORPORATION
4027 Colonel Glenn Hwy (45431-1673)
PHONE....................................937 306-7180
EMP: 28
SALES (corp-wide): 229.8MM **Privately Held**
SIC: 8711 Consulting engineer
PA: Dcs Corporation
6909 Metro Park Dr # 500
Alexandria VA 22310
571 227-6000

(G-1248)
FRONTIER TECHNOLOGY INC (PA)
Also Called: Fti
4141 Colonel Glenn Hwy # 140 (45431-1662)
PHONE....................................937 429-3302
Ron Shroder, *CEO*
Connie R Edwards, *Vice Pres*
Jose L Hidalgo, *CFO*
Tim Hinds, *Human Resources*
Thomas P Karmondy, *Manager*
EMP: 30
SQ FT: 3,834
SALES: 101.6MM **Privately Held**
WEB: www.fti-net.com
SIC: 7371 8711 Computer software development & applications; consulting engineer

(G-1249)
INFOSCITEX CORPORATION
4027 Colonel Glenn Hwy # 210 (45431-1661)
PHONE....................................937 429-9008
Lori Walton, *Branch Mgr*
EMP: 27
SALES (corp-wide): 229.8MM **Privately Held**
SIC: 8711 Engineering services
HQ: Infoscitex Corporation
295 Foster St Ste 210
Littleton MA 01460
781 419-6370

(G-1250)
JACOBS TECHNOLOGY INC
Also Called: Advanced Systems Group
4027 Colonel Glenn Hwy (45431-1673)
PHONE....................................937 429-5056
EMP: 40
SALES (corp-wide): 12.1B **Publicly Held**
SIC: 8711 Engineering Services
HQ: Jacobs Technology Inc.
600 William Northern Blvd
Tullahoma TN 37388
931 455-6400

(G-1251)
JOES LDSCPG BEAVERCREEK INC
2500 National Rd (45324-2011)
PHONE....................................937 427-1133
Joe Leopard, *President*
EMP: 30
SQ FT: 5,000
SALES: 3MM **Privately Held**
WEB: www.joeslandscaping.com
SIC: 0781 Landscape services

(G-1252)
LANE CHEVROLET
635 S Orchard Ln (45434-6163)
P.O. Box 340910, Dayton (45434-0910)
PHONE....................................937 426-2313
Jason Laughlin, *Principal*
Keith Bockbrader, *Purch Mgr*
Jaime Holbrook, *Sales Mgr*
EMP: 92
SALES (est): 11.3MM **Privately Held**
SIC: 5511 7538 Automobiles, new & used; general automotive repair shops

(G-1253)
LANG CHEVROLET CO
Also Called: Lang Chevrolet Geo
635 Orchard Ln (45434-6163)
P.O. Box 340910, Dayton (45434-0910)
PHONE....................................937 426-2313
Richard F Lang, *Owner*
Gerry Laughlin, *General Mgr*
Keith Bockbrader, *Co-Owner*
Judy Lang, *Co-Owner*
Steve Sexton, *Opers Mgr*
EMP: 100
SQ FT: 35,000
SALES (est): 32.8MM **Privately Held**
WEB: www.langs.com
SIC: 5511 7538 7532 7515 Automobiles, new & used; trucks, tractors & trailers: new & used; general automotive repair shops; top & body repair & paint shops; passenger car leasing; used car dealers

(G-1254)
MODERN TECH SOLUTIONS INC
Also Called: Mtsi
4141 Colonel Glenn Hwy # 115 (45431-5100)
PHONE....................................937 426-9025
Scott Coale, *Principal*
Benjamin Downing, *Senior Engr*
EMP: 65
SALES (est): 5.7MM **Privately Held**
WEB: www.mtsi-va.com
SIC: 8711 8731 Consulting engineer; commercial physical research
PA: Modern Technology Solutions, Inc.
5285 Shawnee Rd Ste 400
Alexandria VA 22312

(G-1255)
NORTHROP GRUMMAN TECHNICAL
Also Called: Ngts
4065 Colonel Glenn Hwy (45431-1601)
PHONE....................................937 320-3100
Dale A Brookhart, *Principal*
Saju Kuruvilla, *Branch Mgr*
Garin Clint, *Program Mgr*
Donald Howell, *Consultant*
Eve Beavers, *Admin Asst*
EMP: 150 **Publicly Held**
WEB: www.afqrc.com
SIC: 8732 8711 7373 Market analysis or research; engineering services; computer integrated systems design
HQ: Northrop Grumman Technical Services, Inc.
2340 Dulles Corner Blvd
Herndon VA 20171
703 713-4096

(G-1256)
OASIS SYSTEMS INC
4141 Colonel Glenn Hwy (45431-1600)
PHONE....................................937 426-1295
Tome Challea, *President*
EMP: 48
SALES (est): 2.2MM **Privately Held**
SIC: 7379 Computer related consulting services

(G-1257)
PEERLESS TECHNOLOGIES CORP
2300 National Rd (45324-2009)
PHONE....................................937 490-5000
Michael C Bridges, *President*
Doug Burkett, *Senior VP*
Don Greiman, *Senior VP*
Julie Jones, *Senior VP*
Brian Carron, *Vice Pres*
EMP: 60
SQ FT: 17,000
SALES (est): 13.5MM **Privately Held**
WEB: www.epeerless.com
SIC: 7373 Computer systems analysis & design

(G-1258)
PHILLIPS COMPANIES
Also Called: Phillips Sand & Gravel Co
620 Phillips Dr (45434-7230)
PHONE....................................937 426-5461
Richard L Phillips II, *President*
EMP: 29

SALES (corp-wide): 13.3MM **Privately Held**
WEB: www.phillipscompanies.com
SIC: 3273 1771 Ready-mixed concrete; concrete pumping
PA: Phillips Companies
620 Phillips Dr
Beavercreek Township OH 45434
937 426-5461

(G-1259)
PHILLIPS READY MIX CO
620 Phillips Dr (45434-7230)
P.O. Box 187, Alpha (45301-0187)
PHONE....................................937 426-5151
Rick Phillips, *President*
Dennis Phillips, *Treasurer*
EMP: 100
SALES (est): 4.2MM **Privately Held**
SIC: 1771 3273 7353 5191 Concrete pumping; ready-mixed concrete; heavy construction equipment rental; farm supplies; excavation work; construction sand & gravel

(G-1260)
PRIORITY BUILDING SERVICES INC
2370 National Rd (45324-2009)
P.O. Box 1881, Fairborn (45324-7881)
PHONE....................................937 233-7030
EMP: 65
SQ FT: 7,500
SALES (est): 2.6MM **Privately Held**
SIC: 7349 Building Maintenance Services

(G-1261)
QUANTECH SERVICES INC
4141 Colonel Glenn Hwy # 273 (45431-1676)
PHONE....................................937 490-8461
Maryanne E Cromwell, *Principal*
EMP: 133
SALES (corp-wide): 81MM **Privately Held**
SIC: 8999 Artists & artists' studios
PA: Quantech Services Inc.
91 Hartwell Ave Ste 3
Lexington MA 02421
781 271-9757

(G-1262)
SMITH CONSTRUCTION GROUP INC
731 Orchard Ln (45434-7214)
PHONE....................................937 426-0500
Sean Smith, *President*
EMP: 25
SALES (est): 10.7MM **Privately Held**
SIC: 1542 Commercial & office building, new construction

(G-1263)
SONOCO PRODUCTS COMPANY
Sonoco Consumer Products
761 Space Dr (45434-7171)
PHONE....................................937 429-0040
Norwood Bizzell, *Manager*
EMP: 60
SALES (corp-wide): 5.3B **Publicly Held**
WEB: www.sonoco.com
SIC: 2655 5113 2891 Cans, fiber: made from purchased material; paper tubes & cores; adhesives & sealants
PA: Sonoco Products Company
1 N 2nd St
Hartsville SC 29550
843 383-7000

Beavercreek Township
Montgomery County

(G-1264)
BROOKDALE SENIOR LIVING INC
Also Called: Brookdale Kettering
280 Walden Way Ofc (45440-4402)
PHONE....................................937 203-8596
Sharon Bristow, *Manager*
EMP: 65
SALES (corp-wide): 4.5B **Publicly Held**
WEB: www.grandcourtlifestyles.com
SIC: 8051 Skilled nursing care facilities

PA: Brookdale Senior Living
111 Westwood Pl Ste 400
Brentwood TN 37027
615 221-2250

Beavercrk Twp
Greene County

(G-1265)
HORTICULTURAL MANAGEMENT INC
1350 Shaw Ln (45385-7134)
PHONE..................................937 427-8835
James Campbell, *Ch of Bd*
James Mason, *President*
Danny K Mason, *Treasurer*
Mark Stone, *Admin Sec*
EMP: 28
SALES (est): 589.7K **Privately Held**
SIC: 0781 0782 Landscape counseling services; landscape contractors; lawn care services

Beaverdam
Allen County

(G-1266)
BEAVERDAM FLEET SERVICES INC
424 E Main St (45808-9724)
PHONE..................................419 643-8880
Joe Seeling, *President*
EMP: 31
SQ FT: 11,000
SALES (est): 2.3MM **Privately Held**
WEB: www.beaverdamfleetservice.com
SIC: 7538 7549 General truck repair; towing service, automotive

(G-1267)
BLUE BEACON USA LP II
Also Called: Blue Beacon of Beaverdam
413 E Main St (45808-9728)
PHONE..................................419 643-8146
Mike Kreager, *Branch Mgr*
EMP: 30
SALES (corp-wide): 99MM **Privately Held**
SIC: 7542 Truck wash
PA: Blue Beacon U.S.A., L.P. Ii
500 Graves Blvd
Salina KS 67401
785 825-2221

Bedford
Cuyahoga County

(G-1268)
AKE MARKETING
503 Broadway Ave (44146-2723)
PHONE..................................440 232-1661
Jennifer Marriott, *Manager*
EMP: 30 EST: 2001
SALES (est): 1.9MM **Privately Held**
SIC: 8742 Management Consulting Services

(G-1269)
AM CASTLE & CO
Also Called: Oliver Steel Plate
26800 Miles Rd (44146-1405)
PHONE..................................330 425-7000
Tony Prybuto, *Transportation*
Scott J Dolan, *Branch Mgr*
EMP: 65
SALES (corp-wide): 581.9MM **Publicly Held**
SIC: 5051 3444 3443 3398 Steel; sheet metalwork; fabricated plate work (boiler shop); metal heat treating
PA: A.M. Castle & Co.
1420 Kensington Rd # 220
Oak Brook IL 60523
847 455-7111

(G-1270)
BEDFORD HEIGHTS CITY WASTE
Also Called: Bedford Heights City Waste Wtr
25301 Solon Rd (44146-4727)
PHONE..................................440 439-5343
Dave Pocaro, *Director*
EMP: 25
SALES (est): 1MM **Privately Held**
SIC: 7699 Waste cleaning services

(G-1271)
CBF INDUSTRIES INC
Also Called: Cleveland Business Furniture
23600 Aurora Rd (44146-1712)
PHONE..................................216 229-9300
Gary Bunge, *President*
Joe Fixler, *Vice Pres*
Terry Kopania, *Treasurer*
Gary Grecar, *Admin Sec*
EMP: 30
SQ FT: 92,000
SALES (est): 5.7MM
SALES (corp-wide): 6MM **Privately Held**
WEB: www.ebo.com
SIC: 5046 5021 5712 Shelving, commercial & industrial; office furniture; office furniture
PA: Ebo Inc
23600 Aurora Rd
Bedford OH 44146
216 229-9300

(G-1272)
CHAGRIN VALLEY DISPATCH
88 Center Rd Ste B100 (44146-2700)
PHONE..................................440 247-7321
Nick Dicicco, *Director*
EMP: 39
SQ FT: 5,000
SALES: 4.2MM **Privately Held**
SIC: 8322 Hotline

(G-1273)
COMFORT SYSTEMS USA OHIO INC (HQ)
7401 First Pl Ste A (44146-6723)
PHONE..................................440 703-1600
Daniel Lemons, *President*
EMP: 50
SQ FT: 21,000
SALES (est): 903K
SALES (corp-wide): 2.1B **Publicly Held**
SIC: 1711 Warm air heating & air conditioning contractor
PA: Comfort Systems Usa, Inc.
675 Bering Dr Ste 400
Houston TX 77057
713 830-9600

(G-1274)
COMMUNITY HOSPITAL OF BEDFORD
Also Called: University Hospitals Hlth Sys
44 Blaine Ave (44146-2709)
PHONE..................................440 735-3900
Arlene Rak, *President*
Nancy De Santis, *Sls & Mktg Exec*
Don Paulson, *CFO*
Velibor Drobnjak, *Pharmacist*
EMP: 425
SQ FT: 155,000
SALES (est): 3.6MM
SALES (corp-wide): 580MM **Privately Held**
WEB: www.uhhsbmc.com
SIC: 8062 General medical & surgical hospitals
PA: University Hospitals Health System, Inc.
3605 Warrensville Ctr Rd
Shaker Heights OH 44122
216 767-8900

(G-1275)
CUNNINGHAM PAVING COMPANY
20814 Aurora Rd (44146-1006)
PHONE..................................216 581-8600
Timothy Cunningham, *President*
EMP: 30
SALES: 9MM **Privately Held**
SIC: 1611 Highway & street paving contractor; surfacing & paving

(G-1276)
DEUFOL WORLDWIDE PACKAGING LLC
19800 Alexander Rd (44146-5346)
PHONE..................................440 232-1100
EMP: 54
SALES (est): 1MM **Privately Held**
SIC: 4783 5113 Packing And Crating, Nsk

(G-1277)
DINO PALMIERI BEAUTY SALON (PA)
Also Called: Palmieri Enterprises
5201 Richmond Rd Ste 1 (44146-1357)
PHONE..................................440 498-9411
Dino Palmieri, *President*
EMP: 52
SQ FT: 1,275
SALES (est): 2.9MM **Privately Held**
WEB: www.dinolots.com
SIC: 7231 Unisex hair salons

(G-1278)
DONE-RITE BOWLING SERVICE CO (PA)
Also Called: Paragon Machine Company
20434 Krick Rd (44146-4422)
PHONE..................................440 232-3280
Robert W Gable, *CEO*
Glenn Gable, *President*
Gale Burns, *Vice Pres*
Dave Patz, *Vice Pres*
Ann Gable, *Shareholder*
▲ EMP: 25 EST: 1950
SQ FT: 20,000
SALES (est): 2.6MM **Privately Held**
WEB: www.donerite.com
SIC: 3949 1752 5091 Bowling equipment & supplies; floor laying & floor work; bowling equipment

(G-1279)
EBO INC (PA)
Also Called: Cbf Industries
23600 Aurora Rd (44146-1712)
PHONE..................................216 229-9300
Terrance Kopania, *President*
Gary Bunge, *President*
Joe Fixler, *Vice Pres*
Terry Kopania, *Treasurer*
Gary Grecar, *Admin Sec*
EMP: 50
SQ FT: 100,000
SALES (est): 6MM **Privately Held**
WEB: www.ebo.com
SIC: 5046 5021 5712 Shelving, commercial & industrial; office furniture; office furniture

(G-1280)
FEDERAL EXPRESS CORPORATION
Also Called: Fedex
5313 Majestic Pkwy (44146-1743)
PHONE..................................800 463-3339
EMP: 150
SALES (corp-wide): 65.4B **Publicly Held**
WEB: www.federalexpress.com
SIC: 4212 Local trucking, without storage
HQ: Federal Express Corporation
3610 Hacks Cross Rd
Memphis TN 38125
901 369-3600

(G-1281)
FOWLER ELECTRIC CO
26185 Broadway Ave (44146-6512)
PHONE..................................440 735-2385
Tim Phillips, *Project Mgr*
Richard Trela, *Mng Member*
Scott Jordan, *Mng Member*
Tim Fowler, *Sr Project Mgr*
EMP: 53
SALES: 24MM **Privately Held**
SIC: 1711 1731 Mechanical contractor; general electrical contractor

(G-1282)
GRACE HOSPITAL
44 Blaine Ave (44146-2709)
PHONE..................................216 687-1500
EMP: 55

SALES (corp-wide): 17.4MM **Privately Held**
SIC: 8062 General medical & surgical hospitals
PA: Grace Hospital
2307 W 14th St
Cleveland OH 44113
216 687-1500

(G-1283)
HANDL-IT INC
7120 Krick Rd Ste 1a (44146-4444)
PHONE..................................440 439-9400
Jerry Peters, *Branch Mgr*
EMP: 100 **Privately Held**
WEB: www.handlit.net
SIC: 5063 Light bulbs & related supplies
PA: Handl-It, Inc
360 Highland Rd E 2
Macedonia OH 44056

(G-1284)
HAVSCO INC
5018 Richmond Rd (44146)
PHONE..................................440 439-8900
Rick Coates, *General Mgr*
Bob Haines, *Service Mgr*
EMP: 40
SQ FT: 10,000
SALES (est): 2.4MM **Privately Held**
SIC: 1711 Warm air heating & air conditioning contractor; ventilation & duct work contractor

(G-1285)
HAWTHORNE VALLEY COUNTRY CLUB
25250 Rockside Rd Ste 1 (44146-1839)
PHONE..................................440 232-1400
Bob Zeman, *General Mgr*
EMP: 100
SQ FT: 46,500
SALES (est): 2.8MM **Privately Held**
SIC: 7997 5941 Country club, membership; sporting goods & bicycle shops

(G-1286)
INDUSTRIAL FIRST INC (PA)
25840 Miles Rd Ste 2 (44146-1426)
PHONE..................................216 991-8605
Steven F Lau, *President*
Robin Harvey, *Superintendent*
Frank Burkosky, *Exec VP*
Carmen Santamaria, *Vice Pres*
Dale Leboda, *Project Mgr*
EMP: 125
SQ FT: 6,400
SALES (est): 32.3MM **Privately Held**
WEB: www.industrialfirst.com
SIC: 1741 1761 1791 Masonry & other stonework; siding contractor; roofing contractor; sheet metalwork; structural steel erection

(G-1287)
KOLTCZ CONCRETE BLOCK CO
7660 Oak Leaf Rd (44146-5554)
PHONE..................................440 232-3630
Stanley M Koltcz, *President*
EMP: 26 EST: 1938
SQ FT: 55,000
SALES (est): 4.8MM **Privately Held**
WEB: www.koltcz.com
SIC: 3271 5032 5211 Blocks, concrete or cinder: standard; masons' materials; masonry materials & supplies

(G-1288)
LEGACY CONSULTANT PHARMACY
Also Called: Autumn
26691 Richmond Rd (44146-1421)
PHONE..................................336 760-1670
EMP: 40
SALES (est): 3.3MM **Privately Held**
SIC: 8748 Business Consulting Services

(G-1289)
LOVEMAN STEEL CORPORATION
5455 Perkins Rd (44146-1856)
PHONE..................................440 232-6200
Anthony Murru, *CEO*
James Loveman, *COO*
David Loveman, *Exec VP*

Rob Loveman, *Vice Pres*
◆ **EMP:** 75
SQ FT: 80,000
SALES: 17MM **Privately Held**
WEB: www.lovemansteel.com
SIC: 5051 3443 Plates, metal; weldments

(G-1290)
LOWES HOME CENTERS LLC
24500 Miles Rd (44146-1314)
PHONE..................................216 831-2860
William Sandy, *Store Mgr*
John Lerch, *Manager*
EMP: 300
SALES (corp-wide): 68.6B **Publicly Held**
SIC: 5211 5031 5722 5064 Home centers; building materials, exterior; building materials, interior; household appliance stores; electrical appliances, television & radio
HQ: Lowe's Home Centers, Llc
1605 Curtis Bridge Rd
Wilkesboro NC 28697
336 658-4000

(G-1291)
MAINES PAPER & FOOD SVC INC
199 Oak Leaf Oval (44146-6156)
PHONE..................................216 643-7500
Dennis Kee, *Manager*
Vance Ferrari, *Supervisor*
EMP: 50
SALES (corp-wide): 1.9B **Privately Held**
WEB: www.maines.net
SIC: 5142 5169 5113 Packaged frozen goods; chemicals & allied products; groceries & related products; industrial & personal service paper
PA: Maines Paper & Food Service, Inc.
101 Broome Corporate Pkwy
Conklin NY 13748
607 779-1200

(G-1292)
MCCARTHY BURGESS & WOLFF INC (PA)
26000 Cannon Rd (44146-1807)
PHONE..................................440 735-5100
Freida M Wolff, *President*
Brian Nagle, *General Mgr*
Stephen Wolff, *Principal*
Michael Sands, *Opers Staff*
Monica Ziman, *CFO*
EMP: 140
SQ FT: 21,000
SALES (est): 19.1MM **Privately Held**
WEB: www.mbandw.com
SIC: 7322 Collection agency, except real estate

(G-1293)
MEDICAL SERVICE COMPANY (PA)
24000 Broadway Ave (44146-6329)
PHONE..................................440 232-3000
Joel D Marx, *President*
Darrel Lowery, *President*
John Geller, *Vice Pres*
Michelle Leighton, *Vice Pres*
Dana McLaughlin, *Vice Pres*
EMP: 62
SQ FT: 4,000
SALES (est): 25.7MM **Privately Held**
WEB: www.medicalserviceco.com
SIC: 5912 7352 Drug stores; medical equipment rental

(G-1294)
NORFOLK SOUTHERN RAILWAY CO
7847 Northfield Rd (44146)
PHONE..................................440 439-1827
Allan Carter, *Superintendent*
EMP: 57
SALES (corp-wide): 11.4B **Publicly Held**
SIC: 4011 Railroads, line-haul operating
HQ: Norfolk Southern Railway Company
3 Commercial Pl Ste 1a
Norfolk VA 23510
757 629-2680

(G-1295)
NPK CONSTRUCTION EQUIPMENT INC (HQ)
7550 Independence Dr (44146-5541)
PHONE..................................440 232-7900
Dan Tyrell, *President*
Bob Gerhardstein, *Opers Mgr*
Robert Truelsch, *Executive*
◆ **EMP:** 60
SQ FT: 150,000
SALES (est): 45.5MM
SALES (corp-wide): 85.8MM **Privately Held**
WEB: www.npkce.com
SIC: 5082 3599 3546 3532 General construction machinery & equipment; machine shop, jobbing & repair; power-driven handtools; mining machinery; construction machinery; cutlery
PA: Nippon Pneumatic Manufacturing Co.,Ltd.
4-11-5, Kamiji, Higashinari-Ku
Osaka OSK 537-0
669 739-100

(G-1296)
OAKWOOD HOSPITALITY CORP
Also Called: Holiday Inn
23303 Oakwood Commons Dr (44146-5700)
PHONE..................................440 786-1998
Vinu Patel, *President*
Chris Ellis, *Manager*
EMP: 25
SALES (est): 1.1MM **Privately Held**
SIC: 7011 Hotels

(G-1297)
OHIO CONCRETE RESURFACING INC (PA)
Also Called: Nature Stone
15 N Park St (44146-3634)
PHONE..................................440 786-9100
Antonia Masetta, *President*
Cherry Lockett, *Technology*
Sean Burton, *Lab Dir*
Russell Masetta, *Admin Sec*
Nicholas A Papa, *Legal Staff*
EMP: 30
SQ FT: 8,000
SALES (est): 12.9MM **Privately Held**
WEB: www.naturestonefloors.com
SIC: 1799 Epoxy application

(G-1298)
OLYMPIC STEEL INC
5080 Richmond Rd (44146-1329)
PHONE..................................216 292-3800
Timothy Hippely, *Engineer*
Beverly Christie, *Sales Staff*
Rich Manson, *Branch Mgr*
EMP: 156
SALES (corp-wide): 1.3B **Publicly Held**
WEB: www.olysteel.com
SIC: 5051 Steel; sheets, metal; plates, metal; aluminum bars, rods, ingots, sheets, pipes, plates, etc.
PA: Olympic Steel, Inc.
22901 Millcreek Blvd # 650
Cleveland OH 44122
216 292-3800

(G-1299)
PARTNERS AUTO GROUP BDFORD INC
Also Called: Mazda Saab of Bedford
11 Broadway Ave (44146-2001)
PHONE..................................440 439-2323
Chris Hudak, *President*
Jerald Loretitsch, *Corp Secy*
Scott Newman, *Sales Mgr*
Shannon Clark, *Manager*
Patrick Sheehan, *Manager*
EMP: 52
SQ FT: 30,000
SALES (est): 20.9MM **Privately Held**
WEB: www.saabofbedford.com
SIC: 5511 7515 Automobiles, new & used; passenger car leasing

(G-1300)
PENSKE TRUCK LEASING CO LP
7600 First Pl (44146-6700)
PHONE..................................440 232-5811

Daniel O Florig, *Manager*
EMP: 30
SQ FT: 15,068
SALES (corp-wide): 2.6B **Privately Held**
WEB: www.pensketruckleasing.com
SIC: 7513 Truck leasing, without drivers
PA: Penske Truck Leasing Co., L.P.
2675 Morgantown Rd
Reading PA 19607
610 775-6000

(G-1301)
RENAISSANCE HOME HEALTH CARE
5311 Northfield Rd (44146-1188)
PHONE..................................216 662-8702
Patricia Eady, *President*
EMP: 95
SALES (est): 1.5MM **Privately Held**
SIC: 8099 Health screening service

(G-1302)
ROSELAND LANES INC
26383 Broadway Ave (44146-6516)
PHONE..................................440 439-0097
Peter Scimone, *President*
Anna Marie Slaby, *Vice Pres*
Rosalie Scimone, *Treasurer*
EMP: 60 EST: 1961
SQ FT: 20,000
SALES (est): 2.5MM **Privately Held**
WEB: www.roselandlanes.com
SIC: 7933 5812 Ten pin center; snack bar; caterers

(G-1303)
SABER HEALTHCARE GROUP LLC (PA)
26691 Richmond Rd Frnt (44146-1422)
PHONE..................................216 292-5706
William Weisberg, *Mng Member*
Dahlia Black, *Exec Dir*
Dawn Norton, *Director*
Corey Bennici, *Administration*
Michael E Defrank,
EMP: 50
SQ FT: 3,600
SALES (est): 157.7MM **Privately Held**
SIC: 8051 8741 Convalescent home with continuous nursing care; nursing & personal care facility management

(G-1304)
SAFELY HOME INC
121 Center Rd Ofc (44146-2758)
PHONE..................................440 232-9310
George Purgert, *Exec Dir*
Tisha Chambers, *Program Dir*
Wanda Lugo, *Teacher*
EMP: 25
SALES: 2.3MM **Privately Held**
SIC: 8322 Child related social services

(G-1305)
SIGNATURE HEALTHCARE LLC
5386 Majestic Pkwy (44146-1784)
PHONE..................................440 232-1800
EMP: 140 **Privately Held**
SIC: 8011 6321 Offices & clinics of medical doctors; accident & health insurance
PA: Signature Healthcare, Llc
12201 Bluegrass Pkwy
Louisville KY 40299

(G-1306)
SMITH & OBY SERVICE CO
7676 Northfield Rd (44146-5519)
PHONE..................................440 735-5322
Gary Y Klie, *President*
EMP: 30
SALES (est): 3.3MM **Privately Held**
WEB: www.smithandoby.com
SIC: 1711 7699 7623 Warm air heating & air conditioning contractor; ventilation & duct work contractor; boiler & heating repair services; air conditioning repair

(G-1307)
SMYLIE ONE HEATING & COOLING
Also Called: Honeywell Authorized Dealer
5108 Richmond Rd (44146-1331)
PHONE..................................440 449-4328
Shari Rosen, *President*
Steven Smiley, *Vice Pres*

Scott Fisher, *Warehouse Mgr*
Dennis Blankenburg, *Manager*
Joseph Rosen, *Consultant*
EMP: 25
SALES (est): 5.1MM **Privately Held**
SIC: 1711 Warm air heating & air conditioning contractor

(G-1308)
SOUTHEAST AREA LAW ENFORCEMENT
165 Center Rd (44146-2738)
PHONE..................................216 475-1234
Thomas P Murphy, *Director*
EMP: 30
SALES (est): 489.7K **Privately Held**
SIC: 8611 Business associations

(G-1309)
STATE CREST CARPET & FLOORING (PA)
5400 Perkins Rd (44146-1857)
PHONE..................................440 232-3980
Dennis Chiancone, *President*
Janice Redina, *Corp Secy*
◆ **EMP:** 30
SQ FT: 36,000
SALES (est): 10.7MM **Privately Held**
SIC: 5023 Carpets; resilient floor coverings: tile or sheet

(G-1310)
TOYOTA OF BEDFORD
18151 Rockside Rd (44146-2039)
PHONE..................................440 439-8600
Mike Damato, *Partner*
Greg Figueroa, *General Mgr*
Nick Snyder, *Finance Mgr*
Kari Morgan, *Cust Mgr*
EMP: 56
SALES (est): 16.5MM **Privately Held**
WEB: www.toyotaofbedford.com
SIC: 5511 7515 5521 Automobiles, new & used; passenger car leasing; used car dealers

(G-1311)
TRUGREEN LIMITED PARTNERSHIP
Also Called: Tru Green-Chemlawn
20375 Hannan Pkwy (44146-5354)
P.O. Box 46429, Cleveland (44146-0429)
PHONE..................................440 786-7200
Steve Chaney, *Manager*
EMP: 100
SALES (corp-wide): 3.4B **Privately Held**
SIC: 0782 Lawn care services
HQ: Trugreen Limited Partnership
1790 Kirby Pkwy
Memphis TN 38138
901 251-4128

(G-1312)
TUCKER LANDSCAPING INC
Also Called: Tucker Landscaping Company
1000 Broadway Ave (44146-4521)
PHONE..................................440 786-9840
Austin W Tucker, *Partner*
EMP: 90 EST: 2004
SQ FT: 4,160
SALES (est): 1.3MM **Privately Held**
WEB: www.tuckerlandscaping.net
SIC: 0781 Landscape services

(G-1313)
UNIVERSITY MEDNET
22750 Rockside Rd Ste 210 (44146-1576)
PHONE..................................440 285-9079
Yvonne Maret, *Manager*
EMP: 50
SALES (corp-wide): 10.4MM **Privately Held**
SIC: 8011 Clinic, operated by physicians
PA: University Mednet
18599 Lake Shore Blvd
Euclid OH 44119
216 383-0100

(G-1314)
WINDOW FACTORY OF AMERICA (PA)
21600 Alexander Rd (44146-5509)
PHONE..................................440 439-3050
Sheldon Fromson, *Ch of Bd*
Scott Berman, *President*

Cindy Obringer, *CFO*
EMP: 100
SQ FT: 20,000
SALES (est): 8.3MM **Privately Held**
WEB: www.wadf.com
SIC: 5211 5031 1751 Door & window products; windows; window & door (pre-fabricated) installation

---

Bedford Heights
Cuyahoga County

(G-1315)
ALLOY METAL EXCHANGE LLC
Also Called: Dynamic Metal Services
26000 Corbin Dr (44128)
PHONE..................................216 478-0200
Brian Ducovna, *President*
Ben Henson, *Vice Pres*
Bill Mills, *Vice Pres*
Frank Lochiatto, *Director*
EMP: 25
SQ FT: 40,000
SALES (est): 12MM **Privately Held**
SIC: 1081 Metal mining services

(G-1316)
AMERICAS FLOOR SOURCE LLC
26000 Richmond Rd Ste 1 (44146-1420)
PHONE..................................216 342-4929
Glenn Gould, *Branch Mgr*
EMP: 41 **Privately Held**
SIC: 7217 5713 Carpet & upholstery cleaning; floor covering stores
PA: America's Floor Source, Llc
3442 Millennium Ct
Columbus OH 43219

(G-1317)
BASS SECURITY SERVICES INC
26701 Richmond Rd (44146-1449)
PHONE..................................216 755-1200
Dale Bass, *CEO*
Ron Brown, *COO*
Paul Fisher, *Vice Pres*
Kenneth Kossin Jr, *Vice Pres*
Ken Koffin, *CFO*
EMP: 159
SQ FT: 31,000
SALES (est): 39.1MM **Privately Held**
WEB: www.bass-security.com
SIC: 5251 7382 Door locks & lock sets; security systems services

(G-1318)
BUCKEYE HEATING AND AC SUP INC (PA)
5075 Richmond Rd (44146-1384)
PHONE..................................216 831-0066
John Wortendyke, *President*
Louis Tisch, *Vice Pres*
Chris Wortendyke, *Sales Mgr*
EMP: 35
SQ FT: 30,000
SALES (est): 9.3MM **Privately Held**
SIC: 5078 5075 Refrigeration equipment & supplies; warm air heating & air conditioning

(G-1319)
CHAPEL STEEL CORP
26400 Richmond Rd (44146-1444)
PHONE..................................800 570-7674
EMP: 25
SALES (corp-wide): 11.5B **Publicly Held**
SIC: 5051 Steel
HQ: Chapel Steel Corp.
590 N Bethlehem Pike
Ambler PA 19002
215 793-0899

(G-1320)
CHORES UNLIMITED INC
Also Called: Cui
26150 Richmond Rd Unit C (44146-1438)
P.O. Box 46760, Bedford (44146-0760)
PHONE..................................440 439-5455
Robin Gray, *Vice Pres*
Bryan Gray, *Vice Pres*
Gary Gray, *Vice Pres*
EMP: 85
SQ FT: 10,000

SALES: 3.8MM **Privately Held**
SIC: 0782 Mowing services, lawn

(G-1321)
CRAFTED SURFACE AND STONE LLC
26050 Richmond Rd Ste D (44146-1436)
PHONE..................................440 658-3799
Allen Gleine, *Mng Member*
EMP: 25
SQ FT: 38,000
SALES: 7MM **Privately Held**
SIC: 1799 2541 Counter top installation; counter & sink tops

(G-1322)
EDELMAN PLUMBING SUPPLY INC (PA)
26201 Richmond Rd Ste 4 (44146-1454)
PHONE..................................216 591-0150
Alan Edelman, *Ch of Bd*
Sheldon Edelman, *President*
Paula Williams, *Purchasing*
Steve Caldwell, *Sales Staff*
Andrew Gerber, *Sales Staff*
EMP: 30
SQ FT: 40,000
SALES (est): 10.1MM **Privately Held**
WEB: www.edelmanplumbing.com
SIC: 5074 Plumbing fittings & supplies

(G-1323)
INTERGRATED CONSULTING
Also Called: ICM
5311 Northfield Rd (44146-1188)
PHONE..................................216 214-7547
Cynthia Weston,
Joe Fouche,
EMP: 40
SALES (est): 1.7MM **Privately Held**
WEB: www.integrated-consulting.net
SIC: 8741 Management services

(G-1324)
PLANNED PRENTHOOD GREATER OHIO
Also Called: Bedford Heights Health Center
25350 Rockside Rd (44146-7110)
PHONE..................................216 961-8804
Tara Broderick, *Manager*
EMP: 50
SALES (corp-wide): 20.7MM **Privately Held**
SIC: 8093 Family planning clinic; family planning & birth control clinics
PA: Planned Parenthood Of Greater Ohio
206 E State St
Columbus OH 43215
614 224-2235

(G-1325)
PUBLIC STORAGE
22800 Miles Rd (44128-5447)
PHONE..................................216 220-7978
Barbara Lawrence, *Manager*
EMP: 50
SQ FT: 80,050
SALES (corp-wide): 2.7B **Publicly Held**
WEB: www.publicstorage.com
SIC: 4225 Miniwarehouse, warehousing; warehousing, self-storage
PA: Public Storage
701 Western Ave
Glendale CA 91201
818 244-8080

(G-1326)
R J MARTIN ELEC SVCS INC
22841 Aurora Rd (44146-1244)
PHONE..................................216 662-7100
Robert J Martin Jr, *President*
Marie Schenkel, *CFO*
EMP: 51
SQ FT: 50,000
SALES (est): 3.1MM **Privately Held**
SIC: 1731 General electrical contractor

(G-1327)
RISER FOODS COMPANY (HQ)
Also Called: American Seaway
5300 Richmond Rd (44146-1389)
PHONE..................................216 292-7000
Laura Shapira Karet, *CEO*
John Lucot, *President*
David S Shapiro, *Chairman*

Mark Minnaugh, *CFO*
EMP: 100
SQ FT: 1,000,000
SALES: 63.1MM
SALES (corp-wide): 6.9B **Privately Held**
SIC: 5411 5141 5146 5199 Supermarkets, chain; supermarkets, 55,000-65,000 square feet (superstore); supermarkets, 66,000-99,000 square feet; groceries, general line; seafoods; general merchandise, non-durable; druggists' sundries
PA: Giant Eagle, Inc.
101 Kappa Dr
Pittsburgh PA 15238
800 362-8899

(G-1328)
THE MAIDS
23480 Aurora Rd Ste 1 (44146-1757)
PHONE..................................440 735-6243
Michael Manhoff, *Owner*
EMP: 60
SALES (est): 97.1K **Privately Held**
SIC: 7349 Maid services, contract or fee basis

Bellaire
Belmont County

(G-1329)
BELLAIRE HARBOR SERVICE LLC
Also Called: Harbor Services
4102 Jefferson St (43906-1282)
P.O. Box 29 (43906-0029)
PHONE..................................740 676-4305
Charles Appleby, *Manager*
Bob Harrison,
EMP: 43
SALES (est): 5.5MM **Privately Held**
SIC: 4491 Marine loading & unloading services

(G-1330)
BELMONT COMMUNITY HOSPITAL (HQ)
4697 Harrison St (43906-1338)
P.O. Box 653 (43906-0653)
PHONE..................................740 671-1200
Terry L L Stake, *Ch Radiology*
Darla Kuri, *Director*
Daniel Palmer, *Director*
Beth Bednar, *Food Svc Dir*
John De Blasis, *Administration*
EMP: 259
SQ FT: 98,000
SALES: 18MM
SALES (corp-wide): 395.3MM **Privately Held**
SIC: 8062 General medical & surgical hospitals
PA: Wheeling Hospital, Inc.
1 Medical Park
Wheeling WV 26003
304 243-3000

(G-1331)
BELMONT FEDERAL SAV & LN ASSN (PA)
3301 Guernsey St (43906-1527)
P.O. Box 654 (43906-0654)
PHONE..................................740 676-1165
Thomas Poe, *President*
Nancy Veres, *Vice Pres*
Ray Wise, *Vice Pres*
James Trouten, *Admin Sec*
EMP: 48 **EST:** 1885
SQ FT: 5,000
SALES: 13.4MM **Privately Held**
SIC: 6035 Federal savings & loan associations

(G-1332)
COMMUNITY ACTION COMSN BELMONT
Also Called: Indian Learning Head Start
4129 Noble St (43906-1246)
PHONE..................................740 676-0800
Miche le Davidson, *Principal*
EMP: 93

SALES (corp-wide): 4.1MM **Privately Held**
SIC: 8351 Head start center, except in conjunction with school
PA: Community Action Commission Of Belmont County
153 1/2 W Main St
Saint Clairsville OH 43950
740 695-0293

(G-1333)
COUNTRY CLUB RETIREMENT CENTER (PA)
55801 Conno Mara Dr (43906-9698)
PHONE..................................740 671-9330
David Taylor, *Principal*
Mark Bradley, *Principal*
John E Holland, *Principal*
EMP: 169
SALES (est): 5.4MM **Privately Held**
SIC: 8059 8052 8051 Nursing home, except skilled & intermediate care facility; intermediate care facilities; skilled nursing care facilities

(G-1334)
JPMORGAN CHASE BANK NAT ASSN
3201 Belmont St Ste 100 (43906-1547)
P.O. Box 10 (43906-0010)
PHONE..................................740 676-2671
Beth Kaufman, *Principal*
EMP: 26
SALES (corp-wide): 131.4B **Publicly Held**
SIC: 6021 National commercial banks
HQ: Jpmorgan Chase Bank, National Association
1111 Polaris Pkwy
Columbus OH 43240
614 436-3055

(G-1335)
S-L DISTRIBUTION COMPANY LLC
Also Called: Snyder's Potato Chips
3157 Guernsey St (43906-1541)
PHONE..................................740 676-6932
Dennis Delbert, *Partner*
EMP: 100
SALES (corp-wide): 8.6B **Publicly Held**
SIC: 5145 Snack foods
HQ: S-L Distribution Company, Llc
1250 York St
Hanover PA 17331
717 632-4477

(G-1336)
WHEELING HOSPITAL INC
Also Called: Belmont Community Hlth Ctr
3000 Guernsey St (43906-1540)
PHONE..................................740 676-4623
Sherri Harvey, *Vice Pres*
Gurbachan Chawla, *Branch Mgr*
Carla Seals, *Admin Sec*
EMP: 62
SALES (corp-wide): 395.3MM **Privately Held**
SIC: 8099 Blood related health services
PA: Wheeling Hospital, Inc.
1 Medical Park
Wheeling WV 26003
304 243-3000

(G-1337)
XTO ENERGY INC
2358 W 23rd St (43906-9614)
PHONE..................................740 671-9901
EMP: 73
SALES (corp-wide): 290.2B **Publicly Held**
SIC: 1311 Crude petroleum production
HQ: Xto Energy Inc.
22777 Sprngwoods Vlg Pkwy
Spring TX 77389

Bellbrook
Greene County

(G-1338)
BELLBROOK RHBLTTION HEALTHCARE
Also Called: Bellbrook Rhblttion Healthcare
1957 N Lakeman Dr (45305-1245)
PHONE..................937 848-8421
Dawn Di Lorenzo,
EMP: 99
SQ FT: 21,950
SALES: 10MM **Privately Held**
SIC: 8051 Skilled Nursing Care Facility

(G-1339)
LBK HEALTH CARE INC (PA)
4336 W Franklin St Ste A (45305-1551)
PHONE..................937 296-1550
Linda Miles, *Accountant*
Linda Black, *CPA*
EMP: 42
SALES (est): 8.1MM **Privately Held**
SIC: 8721 Accounting, auditing & book-keeping

(G-1340)
LIBERTY HEALTH CARE CENTER INC
4336 W Franklin St 100 (45305-1551)
PHONE..................937 296-1550
Linda Black, *Principal*
EMP: 25
SALES (est): 1.6MM **Privately Held**
SIC: 8051 Skilled nursing care facilities

(G-1341)
LITTLE MIAMI RIVER CATERING CO
80 E Franklin St (45305-2005)
PHONE..................937 848-2464
Glen Penquite, *President*
Molly McCowell, *Manager*
Joan Emtite, *Admin Sec*
EMP: 50
SALES (est): 1.6MM **Privately Held**
WEB: www.lmrcatering.com
SIC: 5812 7299 Caterers; banquet hall facilities

Belle Center
Logan County

(G-1342)
WALMART INC
11040 Pear Ln (43310-9771)
PHONE..................937 843-3681
EMP: 283
SALES (corp-wide): 514.4B **Publicly Held**
SIC: 4225 General warehousing & storage
PA: Walmart Inc.
702 Sw 8th St
Bentonville AR 72716
479 273-4000

Bellefontaine
Logan County

(G-1343)
AGC AUTOMOTIVE AMERICAS
1465 W Sandusky Ave (43311-1082)
PHONE..................937 599-3131
Arkady Doorman, *Vice Pres*
Dean Wright, *Plant Mgr*
Scott Keller, *Buyer*
▲ EMP: 81
SALES (est): 11.4MM **Privately Held**
SIC: 7549 1541 1799 3231 Automotive customizing services, non-factory basis; glass & glazing work; glass tinting, architectural or automotive; products of purchased glass

(G-1344)
ALLIED WASTE SYSTEMS INC
Also Called: Site 046
2946 Us Highway 68 N (43311-9218)
PHONE..................937 593-3566
Randy Traub, *General Mgr*
EMP: 60
SALES (corp-wide): 10B **Publicly Held**
WEB: www.fennellgrp.com
SIC: 4953 Garbage: collecting, destroying & processing
HQ: Allied Waste Systems, Inc.
18500 N Allied Way # 100
Phoenix AZ 85054
480 627-2700

(G-1345)
ASPC CORP (PA)
Also Called: Acusport Corporation
1 Hunter Pl (43311-3002)
PHONE..................937 593-7010
William L Fraim, *Ch of Bd*
Chris Murfield, *Engineer*
Nalin Prabhu, *Engineer*
Ben Seibert, *Sales Mgr*
Mark Buckley, *Regl Sales Mgr*
EMP: 120
SQ FT: 120,000
SALES (est): 227.4MM **Privately Held**
WEB: www.acusport.com
SIC: 5091 Firearms, sporting; archery equipment; ammunition, sporting; hunting equipment & supplies

(G-1346)
BELLEFONTAINE PHYSICAL THERAPY
711 Rush Ave (43311-2250)
PHONE..................937 592-1625
Rodney Kerns, *President*
EMP: 25
SALES (est): 1MM **Privately Held**
WEB: www.bellefontainept.com
SIC: 8049 Physiotherapist; physical therapist

(G-1347)
BELLETECH CORP (HQ)
700 W Lake Ave (43311-9647)
P.O. Box 790 (43311-0790)
PHONE..................937 599-3774
Masaaki Mori, *President*
Mark Mc Intyre, *COO*
Mark McIntyre, *Vice Pres*
Brad Pearson, *Production*
Rick Nelson, *Finance Mgr*
▲ EMP: 75
SQ FT: 100,000
SALES (est): 17.2MM
SALES (corp-wide): 13.5B **Privately Held**
WEB: www.belletechcorp.com
SIC: 7536 Automotive glass replacement shops
PA: Agc Inc.
1-5-1, Marunouchi
Chiyoda-Ku TKY 100-0
332 185-741

(G-1348)
CITIZENS FEDERAL SAV & LN ASSN
110 N Main St (43311-2084)
PHONE..................937 593-0015
Charles Earick, *President*
Christi Skidmore, *Assistant VP*
Kim Norton, *Bd of Directors*
Niki Ropp, *Bd of Directors*
EMP: 30
SALES: 4.7MM **Privately Held**
WEB: www.citizensfederalsl.com
SIC: 6035 Federal savings & loan associations

(G-1349)
COUNTY OF LOGAN
Also Called: Logan Cnty Prbate Juvenile Crt
101 S Main St Rm 1 (43311-2055)
PHONE..................937 599-7252
Annette Deao, *General Mgr*
Linda Brunke, *Principal*
Brandie Stonerock, *Manager*
EMP: 35 **Privately Held**
WEB: www.co.logan.oh.us
SIC: 8743 9211 Public relations services; courts

PA: County Of Logan
100 S Madriver St
Bellefontaine OH 43311
937 599-7209

(G-1350)
COUNTY OF LOGAN
121 S Opera St Rm 12 (43311-2057)
PHONE..................937 599-4221
Sara J Tracey, *Branch Mgr*
EMP: 37 **Privately Held**
SIC: 8999 Artists & artists' studios
PA: County Of Logan
100 S Madriver St
Bellefontaine OH 43311
937 599-7209

(G-1351)
COUNTY OF LOGAN
Also Called: Logan Acres
2739 County Road 91 (43311-9007)
PHONE..................937 592-2901
Andrew Hershderger, *Manager*
Liz Salyer, *Nursing Dir*
Lorraine Fischio, *Administration*
EMP: 115 **Privately Held**
WEB: www.co.logan.oh.us
SIC: 8361 8051 Home for the aged; skilled nursing care facilities
PA: County Of Logan
100 S Madriver St
Bellefontaine OH 43311
937 599-7209

(G-1352)
COUNTY OF LOGAN
Also Called: Logan County Childrens Svcs
1100 S Detroit St (43311-9702)
PHONE..................937 599-7290
John Holtkamp, *Director*
EMP: 26 **Privately Held**
WEB: www.co.logan.oh.us
SIC: 8322 Child related social services
PA: County Of Logan
100 S Madriver St
Bellefontaine OH 43311
937 599-7209

(G-1353)
HEALTH CARE RTREMENT CORP AMER
Also Called: Heartland of Bellefontaine
221 School St (43311-1078)
PHONE..................937 599-5123
Iva Dewitt-Hoblit, *Manager*
EMP: 100
SALES (corp-wide): 2.4B **Publicly Held**
WEB: www.hrc-manorcare.com
SIC: 8051 Convalescent home with continuous nursing care
HQ: Health Care And Retirement Corporation Of America
333 N Summit St Ste 103
Toledo OH 43604
419 252-5500

(G-1354)
LINK CONSTRUCTION GROUP INC
895 County Road 32 N (43311-9210)
PHONE..................937 292-7774
David Link, *President*
Richard Dyer, *Treasurer*
Reno Stapleton, *Admin Sec*
EMP: 40
SQ FT: 1,500
SALES: 14.2MM **Privately Held**
SIC: 1542 1541 Commercial & office building contractors; industrial buildings & warehouses

(G-1355)
LOGAN COUNTY ENGINEERING OFF
1991 County Road 13 (43311-9322)
PHONE..................937 592-2791
Scott Coleman, *President*
EMP: 39 EST: 1819
SALES (est): 4.7MM **Privately Held**
SIC: 8711 Engineering services

(G-1356)
LOGAN HOUSING CORP INC
Also Called: Logan County Board of Mrdd
1973 State Route 47 W (43311-9328)
P.O. Box 710 (43311-0710)
PHONE..................937 592-2009
Joy Badenhop, *Principal*
Susan Jones, *Director*
Susan Holycross, *Director*
EMP: 80
SALES (est): 83.8K **Privately Held**
WEB: www.mrdd.co.logan.oh.us
SIC: 8351 Preschool center

(G-1357)
LOWES HOME CENTERS LLC
2168 Us Highway 68 S (43311-8904)
PHONE..................937 599-4000
Jeremy Givens, *Manager*
EMP: 150
SALES (corp-wide): 68.6B **Publicly Held**
SIC: 5211 5031 5722 5064 Home centers; building materials, exterior; building materials, interior; household appliance stores; electrical appliances, television & radio
HQ: Lowe's Home Centers, Llc
1605 Curtis Bridge Rd
Wilkesboro NC 28697
336 658-4000

(G-1358)
MARY RTAN HLTH ASSN LOGAN CNTY (PA)
Also Called: Mary Rutan Hospital
205 E Palmer Rd (43311-2281)
PHONE..................937 592-4015
Mandy Goble, *President*
Mary Ann Kelly, *Vice Pres*
Ron Carmin, *CFO*
Vickie Thomas, *Supervisor*
Robert Reynolds, *Info Tech Dir*
EMP: 44
SQ FT: 145,000
SALES: 4.1MM **Privately Held**
WEB: www.maryrutanhospital.com
SIC: 8741 Hospital management

(G-1359)
MARY RUTAN HOSPITAL (HQ)
205 E Palmer Rd (43311-2298)
PHONE..................937 592-4015
Thomas Simon, *Ch of Bd*
Mary Rutan, *COO*
Ron Carmen, *Vice Pres*
Marcia Davis, *Vice Pres*
Rebecca Nicholl, *Vice Pres*
EMP: 650
SQ FT: 90,000
SALES: 96MM
SALES (corp-wide): 4.1MM **Privately Held**
WEB: www.maryrutan.org
SIC: 8062 General medical & surgical hospitals
PA: Mary Rutan Health Association Of Logan County
205 E Palmer Rd
Bellefontaine OH 43311
937 592-4015

(G-1360)
MOBILE INSTR SVC & REPR INC (PA)
333 Water Ave (43311-1733)
PHONE..................937 592-5025
Dwight E Reed, *President*
Charles Reed, *Corp Secy*
Ann Reed, *Vice Pres*
Charlie Reed, *Vice Pres*
Pam Wasson, *CFO*
EMP: 142 EST: 1980
SQ FT: 85,000
SALES (est): 19.8MM **Privately Held**
WEB: www.mobileinstrument.com
SIC: 7699 Surgical instrument repair

(G-1361)
REPUBLIC SERVICES INC
2946 Us Rt 68 N (43311)
PHONE..................937 593-3566
Jim Speirs, *Controller*
EMP: 34
SALES (corp-wide): 10B **Publicly Held**
SIC: 4953 Sanitary landfill operation

GEOGRAPHIC

PA: Republic Services, Inc.
18500 N Allied Way # 100
Phoenix AZ 85054
480 627-2700

(G-1362)
ROBINSON INVESTMENTS LTD
811 N Main St (43311-2376)
P.O. Box 508 (43311-0508)
PHONE................................937 593-1849
Mark Robinson, *President*
Matt Robinson, *President*
Ashley Shepherd, *Human Res Mgr*
John Baker, *Officer*
Lisa Keller, *Executive Asst*
EMP: 37 **EST:** 1998
SQ FT: 70,000
SALES (est): 6.2MM **Privately Held**
SIC: 6512 Commercial & industrial building operation

(G-1363)
ROSS TRAINING CENTER INC
334 E Columbus Ave (43311-2002)
PHONE................................937 592-0025
Brian Reimes, *President*
Joe Mancufl, *Superintendent*
EMP: 90
SALES (est): 1.2MM **Privately Held**
SIC: 8331 Sheltered workshop

(G-1364)
RTC INDUSTRIES INC
Also Called: RTC Employment Services
36 County Road 32 S (43311-1152)
P.O. Box 710 (43311-0710)
PHONE................................937 592-0534
Tina Burrey, *Finance Dir*
Nancy Evans Donley, *Manager*
Abby Alexander, *Manager*
EMP: 50
SALES: 3.7MM **Privately Held**
SIC: 8331 Sheltered workshop

(G-1365)
SHAW GROUP INC
2946 Us Highway 68 N (43311-9218)
PHONE................................937 593-2022
EMP: 502
SALES (corp-wide): 10.6B **Privately Held**
SIC: 8734 Provides Services To Environmental Andinfrastructure
HQ: The Shaw Group Inc
4171 Essen Ln
Baton Rouge LA 70809

(G-1366)
SPARTANNASH COMPANY
Fame
4067 County Road 130 (43311-9359)
P.O. Box 219 (43311-0219)
PHONE................................937 599-1110
Gary Bickmore, *Managing Dir*
Max Earick, *Principal*
Tom Keller, *Vice Pres*
David Tuttle, *Opers Staff*
EMP: 675
SALES (corp-wide): 8B **Publicly Held**
SIC: 5141 Food brokers
PA: Spartannash Company
850 76th St Sw
Byron Center MI 49315
616 878-2000

(G-1367)
SPARTANNASH COMPANY
Also Called: Bellefontaine Distribution Ctr
4067 County Road 130 (43311-9359)
PHONE................................937 599-1110
Glenn Curtis, *Manager*
EMP: 93
SALES (corp-wide): 8B **Publicly Held**
WEB: www.nashfinch.com
SIC: 5141 Groceries, general line
PA: Spartannash Company
850 76th St Sw
Byron Center MI 49315
616 878-2000

(G-1368)
STEVE AUSTIN AUTO GROUP
Also Called: Steve Austins of Hardin County
2500 S Main St (43311)
P.O. Box 247 (43311-0247)
PHONE................................937 592-3015
Steve Austin, *President*

EMP: 40
SALES (est): 2MM **Privately Held**
WEB: www.steveaustins.com
SIC: 7549 High performance auto repair & service

(G-1369)
VIEIRA INC
Also Called: Cherokee Hills Golf Course
4622 County Road 49 (43311-9038)
PHONE................................937 599-3221
James Vieira, *President*
Michael A Vieira, *Vice Pres*
EMP: 27
SQ FT: 3,000
SALES (est): 1.1MM **Privately Held**
WEB: www.cherokeehillsgolfclub.com
SIC: 7992 Public golf courses

(G-1370)
YOUNG MENS CHRISTIAN ASSOC
Also Called: Camp Willson
2732 County Road 11 (43311-9306)
PHONE................................937 593-9001
Brian Kridler, *Senior VP*
Anne Brienza, *Branch Mgr*
Jean Fry, *Director*
EMP: 50
SALES (corp-wide): 44.9MM **Privately Held**
WEB: www.ymca-columbus.com
SIC: 8641 7991 8351 7032 Youth organizations; physical fitness facilities; child day care services; youth camps; individual & family services
PA: Young Men's Christian Association Of Central Ohio
40 W Long St
Columbus OH 43215
614 389-4409

Bellevue
Huron County

(G-1371)
AMRSTRONG DISTRIBUTORS INC
Also Called: Hart-Greer
421 Monroe St (44811-1730)
PHONE................................419 483-4840
John W Norris Jr, *Ch of Bd*
EMP: 35 **EST:** 1999
SALES (corp-wide): 3.8B **Publicly Held**
WEB: www.magicpak.com
SIC: 6719 Personal holding companies, except banks
HQ: Armstrong Air Conditioning Inc.
215 Metropolitan Dr
West Columbia SC 29170
803 738-4000

(G-1372)
BELLEVUE HEALTHCARE GROUP LLC
Also Called: Bellevue Care Center
1 Audrich Sq (44811-9700)
PHONE................................419 483-6225
Cindy Starkey, *Administration*
Sarah Depompei, *Assistant*
EMP: 36
SALES (corp-wide): 4.8MM **Privately Held**
SIC: 8051 Skilled nursing care facilities
PA: Bellevue Healthcare Group, Llc
26691 Richmond Rd
Bedford OH 44146
216 292-5706

(G-1373)
BELLEVUE HOSPITAL (PA)
1400 W Main St Unit Front (44811-9088)
PHONE................................419 483-4040
Mike Winthrop, *President*
Dr Valerie Hepburn, *President*
David West, *Ch Radiology*
Alan Ganci, *Exec VP*
Lisa Sartain, *Human Res Dir*
EMP: 400 **EST:** 1915
SQ FT: 70,000
SALES: 51.3MM **Privately Held**
SIC: 8062 General medical & surgical hospitals

(G-1374)
BELLEVUE HOSPITAL
811 Northwest St (44811)
PHONE................................419 547-0074
Michael Winthrop, *Principal*
Maryanne Shane, *Invest Mgr*
Tony Lombardi, *Human Res Dir*
Joann Ventura, *Asst Director*
EMP: 307
SALES (corp-wide): 51.3MM **Privately Held**
SIC: 8062 General medical & surgical hospitals
PA: The Bellevue Hospital
1400 W Main St Unit Front
Bellevue OH 44811
419 483-4040

(G-1375)
CROGAN COLONIAL BANK
1 Union Sq (44811-1400)
P.O. Box 150 (44811-0150)
PHONE................................419 483-2541
EMP: 45 **EST:** 1930
SALES (est): 4.8MM **Privately Held**
SIC: 6022 State Commercial Bank

(G-1376)
DONALD E DIDION II
Also Called: Didion's Mechanical
1027b County Road 308 (44811-9497)
PHONE................................419 483-2226
Donald E Didion II, *Principal*
EMP: 25
SQ FT: 20,000
SALES: 1.4MM **Privately Held**
WEB: www.didionsmech.com
SIC: 3499 8711 Fire- or burglary-resistive products; engineering services

(G-1377)
FIRELANDS FEDERAL CREDIT UNION (PA)
221 E Main St (44811-1410)
P.O. Box 8005 (44811-8005)
PHONE................................419 483-4180
Kevin L Wadsworth, *President*
Deborah Houle, *Vice Pres*
Jacquelyn Wells, *Vice Pres*
EMP: 47
SQ FT: 10,000
SALES: 10.8MM **Privately Held**
SIC: 6061 6163 Federal credit unions; loan brokers

(G-1378)
FIRST NATIONAL BANK BELLEVUE (HQ)
120 North St (44811-1452)
P.O. Box 210 (44811-0210)
PHONE................................419 483-7340
Dean Miller, *President*
Brandon Barr, *Assistant VP*
Valerie Bumb, *Vice Pres*
Deborah Hawkins, *Vice Pres*
Karalee Siesel, *Officer*
EMP: 30
SQ FT: 10,000
SALES: 10.4MM **Privately Held**
WEB: www.fnblifetime.com
SIC: 6021 National commercial banks

(G-1379)
GREAT LAKES PACKERS INC
400 Great Lakes Pkwy (44811-1165)
P.O. Box 366 (44811-0366)
PHONE................................419 483-2956
Jerome Fritz, *President*
EMP: 50
SQ FT: 31,500
SALES: 16MM **Privately Held**
SIC: 0723 Vegetable packing services; fruit (fresh) packing services

(G-1380)
LIFETOUCH NAT SCHL STUDIOS INC
102 Commerce Park Dr (44811-9095)
PHONE................................419 483-8200
Douglas Barr, *Branch Mgr*
EMP: 41
SALES (corp-wide): 1.9B **Publicly Held**
SIC: 7221 School photographer

HQ: Lifetouch National School Studios Inc.
11000 Viking Dr Ste 300
Eden Prairie MN 55344
952 826-4000

(G-1381)
NEW BEGINNINGS PEDIATRICS INC
Also Called: Trippe, Glen MD
1400 W Main St Ste G (44811-9088)
PHONE................................419 483-4122
Glen Trippe MD, *Director*
EMP: 25 **Privately Held**
SIC: 8011 Pediatrician
PA: New Beginnings Pediatrics Inc
282 Benedict Ave Ste B
Norwalk OH 44857

(G-1382)
NORFOLK SOUTHERN CORPORATION
24424 N Prairie Rd (44811)
PHONE................................419 483-1423
Paula Stiffler, *Manager*
EMP: 133
SALES (corp-wide): 11.4B **Publicly Held**
WEB: www.nscorp.com
SIC: 4011 Railroads, line-haul operating
PA: Norfolk Southern Corporation
3 Commercial Pl Ste 1a
Norfolk VA 23510
757 629-2680

(G-1383)
PLOGER TRANSPORTATION LLC (PA)
15581 County Road 46 (44811-9507)
PHONE................................419 465-2100
Tanya Morrow, *Principal*
Jerry Morrow, *Office Mgr*
EMP: 40
SQ FT: 2,000
SALES (est): 9.2MM **Privately Held**
SIC: 4213 Trucking, except local

(G-1384)
QUALITY WELDING INC
104 Ronald Ln (44811)
P.O. Box 273 (44811-0273)
PHONE................................419 483-6067
Charles Tinnel, *President*
EMP: 25
SQ FT: 2,800
SALES: 1.5MM **Privately Held**
SIC: 7692 Welding repair

(G-1385)
ROYAL COLOR INC
Also Called: Ohio School Pictures
550 Goodrich Rd (44811-1139)
P.O. Box 769, Berea (44017-0769)
PHONE................................440 234-1337
Adam Barr, *CEO*
Douglas H Barr, *President*
Elaine Barr, *Vice Pres*
EMP: 490
SQ FT: 7,500
SALES: 8MM **Privately Held**
WEB: www.ohioschoolpictures.com
SIC: 7221 Photographer, still or video

(G-1386)
WOODARD PHOTOGRAPHIC INC (DH)
550 Goodrich Rd (44811-1163)
P.O. Box 8001 (44811-8001)
PHONE................................419 483-3364
George Woodard, *President*
Marc Woodard, *President*
Roger Wilburn, *Vice Pres*
EMP: 40 **EST:** 1965
SQ FT: 18,763
SALES (est): 5.4MM
SALES (corp-wide): 1.9B **Publicly Held**
WEB: www.woodardphoto.com
SIC: 7335 7221 Commercial photography; school photographer
HQ: Lifetouch Inc.
11000 Viking Dr
Eden Prairie MN 55344
952 826-4000

Bellville
Richland County

(G-1387)
BELLVILLE HOTEL COMPANY
Also Called: Quality Inn
1000 Comfort Plaza Dr (44813-8820)
PHONE..............................419 886-7000
Dan Galat, *Owner*
Steve Hering, *Partner*
Jim Hering, *Partner*
Annette Lemaster, *Manager*
Greg Loesch, *Manager*
EMP: 30 EST: 1996
SQ FT: 40,000
SALES: 1.2MM **Privately Held**
SIC: 7011 Hotels & motels

(G-1388)
COMPETITIVE TRANSPORTATION
7086 State Route 546 (44813-9316)
P.O. Box 1177, Mansfield (44901-1177)
PHONE..............................419 529-5300
Merle D Shaffner, *President*
Jeffery Shaffner, *Corp Secy*
Robin Shaffner, *Vice Pres*
EMP: 42
SQ FT: 27,500
SALES: 3.2MM **Privately Held**
SIC: 4212 4213 Local trucking, without storage; trucking, except local

(G-1389)
CONSULATE MANAGEMENT CO LLC
Also Called: Country Meadow Care Center
4910 Algire Rd (44813-9263)
PHONE..............................419 886-3922
Phil Critcher, *Director*
EMP: 55
SALES (corp-wide): 580.2MM **Privately Held**
WEB: www.tandemhealthcare.com
SIC: 8051 Skilled nursing care facilities
PA: Consulate Management Company, Llc
800 Concourse Pkwy S
Maitland FL 32751
407 571-1550

(G-1390)
COUNTRY MDOW FCLTY OPRTONS LLC
Also Called: Country Meadow Care Center
4910 Algire Rd (44813-9263)
PHONE..............................419 886-3922
Phil Critcher, *Administration*
Carla Naegele,
EMP: 53
SALES (est): 2.1MM **Privately Held**
SIC: 8051 Skilled nursing care facilities

(G-1391)
COUNTRY MEADOW CARE CENTER LLC
Also Called: Country Meadow Rehabilitation
4910 Algire Rd (44813-9263)
PHONE..............................419 886-3922
Phil Kritcher, *Exec Dir*
EMP: 47 EST: 2017
SALES (est): 631.6K **Privately Held**
SIC: 8093 8059 Rehabilitation center, outpatient treatment; nursing home, except skilled & intermediate care facility

(G-1392)
VALLEYVIEW MANAGEMENT CO INC
Also Called: Comfort Inn
855 Comfort Plaza Dr (44813-1267)
PHONE..............................419 886-4000
James W Haring, *President*
Daniel Galat, *Vice Pres*
EMP: 29
SALES (est): 1.5MM **Privately Held**
SIC: 7011 Hotels & motels

(G-1393)
WADE & GATTON NURSERIES
1288 Gatton Rock Rd (44813-9106)
PHONE..............................419 883-3191
Van R Wade, *Owner*

EMP: 65
SQ FT: 1,000
SALES (est): 3.4MM **Privately Held**
SIC: 0181 5261 Nursery stock, growing of; nurseries & garden centers

Belmont
Belmont County

(G-1394)
50 X 20 HOLDING COMPANY INC
Also Called: Schumacher Homes
41201 Bond Dr (43718-7502)
PHONE..............................740 238-4262
Greg McQuaid, *Branch Mgr*
EMP: 31
SALES (corp-wide): 117MM **Privately Held**
SIC: 1521 Single-family housing construction
PA: 50 X 20 Holding Company, Inc.
2715 Wise Ave Nw
Canton OH 44708
330 478-4500

(G-1395)
RECO EQUIPMENT INC (PA)
Also Called: Bobcat of Pittsburgh
41245 Reco Rd (43718-9542)
P.O. Box 160, Morristown (43759-0160)
PHONE..............................740 619-8071
Reed B Mahany, *President*
Paul Di Tullio, *Vice Pres*
Josh Gasber, *Vice Pres*
Tom Kerr, *Sales Staff*
Tony Zappia, *Sales Staff*
▲ EMP: 25
SQ FT: 26,000
SALES (est): 59.3MM **Privately Held**
WEB: www.recoequip.com
SIC: 5082 Cranes, construction; excavating machinery & equipment; power shovels

(G-1396)
STINGRAY PRESSURE PUMPING LLC (PA)
42739 National Rd (43718-9669)
PHONE..............................405 648-4177
Bob Maughmer, *Mng Member*
▲ EMP: 42
SALES (est): 130.1MM **Privately Held**
SIC: 1389 Gas field services

(G-1397)
VALLEY HARLEY DAVIDSON CO (PA)
Also Called: Valley Harley Davidson-Buell
41255 Reco Rd (43718-9542)
PHONE..............................740 695-9591
William Paul Jr, *President*
Jon Toohey, *Manager*
EMP: 42
SQ FT: 16,000
SALES (est): 8.1MM **Privately Held**
SIC: 5571 7699 Motorcycles; motorcycle repair service

Beloit
Mahoning County

(G-1398)
STRATTON CHEVROLET CO
16050 State Route 14a (44609-9734)
PHONE..............................330 537-3151
Don L Stratton Jr, *President*
Theresa Stratton, *Corp Secy*
Don L Stratton Sr, *Shareholder*
EMP: 25 EST: 1928
SQ FT: 7,800
SALES (est): 146.4K **Privately Held**
SIC: 5511 7538 5012 Automobiles, new & used; pickups, new & used; vans, new & used; general automotive repair shops; automobiles & other motor vehicles

Belpre
Washington County

(G-1399)
BELPRE HISTORICAL SOCIETY
Also Called: FARMERS CASTLE MUSEUM EDUCATIO
509 Ridge St (45714-2454)
P.O. Box 731 (45714-0731)
PHONE..............................740 423-7588
Nancy Sams, *President*
John King, *Vice Pres*
EMP: 40
SALES: 171K **Privately Held**
WEB: www.belprehistory.org
SIC: 8412 Museum

(G-1400)
BLENNERHASSETT YACHT CLUB INC
800 Oneal St (45714-1754)
PHONE..............................740 423-9062
David Ruble, *CEO*
EMP: 45
SALES: 68.6K **Privately Held**
SIC: 7997 Yacht club, membership

(G-1401)
DAVITA INC
Also Called: Da Vita
2906 Washington Blvd (45714-1848)
PHONE..............................740 401-0607
Traci Lancaster, *Branch Mgr*
EMP: 39 **Publicly Held**
SIC: 8092 Kidney dialysis centers
PA: Davita Inc.
2000 16th St
Denver CO 80202

(G-1402)
ENTERPRISE SERVICES LLC
2505 Washington Blvd Frnt (45714-1982)
P.O. Box 219 (45714-0219)
PHONE..............................740 423-9501
EMP: 78
SALES (corp-wide): 13.5B **Publicly Held**
SIC: 7374 Data Processing Service Center
HQ: Enterprise Services Llc
5400 Legacy Dr
Plano TX 20171
703 245-9675

(G-1403)
ESTES EXPRESS LINES INC
12140 State Road 7 (45714)
PHONE..............................740 401-0410
Sam Kirbe, *Manager*
EMP: 26
SALES (corp-wide): 2.7B **Privately Held**
WEB: www.estes-express.com
SIC: 4213 Contract haulers
PA: Estes Express Lines, Inc.
3901 W Broad St
Richmond VA 23230
804 353-1900

(G-1404)
FRONTIER BASSMASTERS INC
904 Boulevard Dr (45714-1210)
PHONE..............................740 423-9293
Jerry Burkhart, *President*
Tim William, *Corp Secy*
John Trunk, *Vice Pres*
EMP: 25
SALES (est): 443K **Privately Held**
SIC: 7997 Outdoor field clubs

(G-1405)
JPMORGAN CHASE BANK NAT ASSN
321 Main St (45714-1613)
P.O. Box 710 (45714-0710)
PHONE..............................740 423-4111
Drew Smith, *Branch Mgr*
EMP: 32
SALES (corp-wide): 131.4B **Publicly Held**
SIC: 6022 State commercial banks
HQ: Jpmorgan Chase Bank, National Association
1111 Polaris Pkwy
Columbus OH 43240
614 436-3055

(G-1406)
JUSTICE & BUSINESS SVCS LLC
210 Florence St (45714-1757)
PHONE..............................740 423-5005
Gary L Justice,
EMP: 40
SALES: 2MM **Privately Held**
SIC: 1541 1542 Industrial buildings, new construction; commercial & office building, new construction

(G-1407)
KRATON POLYMERS US LLC
2419 State Rd 618 (45714)
P.O. Box 235 (45714-0235)
PHONE..............................740 423-7571
Robert Roesh, *Plant Mgr*
Kathleen Ervine, *Engineer*
Gabriel Guevara, *Engineer*
Ben Hayes, *Engineer*
Bob Rose, *Branch Mgr*
EMP: 400 **Publicly Held**
WEB: www.kraton.com
SIC: 2822 5169 2821 Synthetic rubber; synthetic resins, rubber & plastic materials; plastics materials & resins
HQ: Kraton Polymers U.S. Llc
15710 John F Kennedy Blvd # 300
Houston TX 77032
281 504-4700

(G-1408)
MARIETTA MEMORIAL HOSPITAL
809 Farson St (45714-1066)
PHONE..............................740 401-0362
EMP: 470
SALES (corp-wide): 400.4MM **Privately Held**
SIC: 8062 General medical & surgical hospitals
PA: Marietta Memorial Hospital Inc
401 Matthew St
Marietta OH 45750
740 374-1400

(G-1409)
OHIO VALLEY AMBULATORY SURGERY
608 Washington Blvd (45714-2465)
P.O. Box 369 (45714-0369)
PHONE..............................740 423-4684
David Catalino Mendoza, *Principal*
Tracey Hood, *Financial Exec*
EMP: 26
SALES (est): 3.8MM **Privately Held**
SIC: 8011 Ambulatory surgical center

(G-1410)
STONEGATE CONSTRUCTION INC
1378 Way Rd (45714-9633)
PHONE..............................740 423-9170
Karen Hiehle, *President*
Michael Hiehle, *Corp Secy*
James Robertson, *Vice Pres*
EMP: 70
SQ FT: 1,800
SALES (est): 12.8MM **Privately Held**
SIC: 1611 1794 General contractor, highway & street construction; excavation work

Berea
Cuyahoga County

(G-1411)
AMERICAN INTERNATIONAL CNSTR
1180 Berea Indus Pkwy (44017-2947)
PHONE..............................440 243-5535
Michael Petrasek, *President*
William Perry, *Vice Pres*
Joel Garn, *Project Mgr*
Adam Petrasek, *Project Mgr*
Lee Petrasek, *Project Mgr*
EMP: 25 EST: 1978
SQ FT: 9,000

G E O G R A P H I C

SALES (est): 3.3MM **Privately Held**
SIC: **1799 1741** Caulking (construction); waterproofing; coating of concrete structures with plastic; exterior cleaning, including sandblasting; tuckpointing or restoration

(G-1412)
ASANA HOSPICE CLEVELAND LLC
Also Called: Asana Hospice Palliative Care
885 W Bagley Rd (44017-2903)
PHONE..................................419 903-0300
Tina Krajnikovich, *Principal*
EMP: 35
SALES (est): 227.8K **Privately Held**
SIC: **8052** Personal care facility

(G-1413)
BALDWIN WALLACE UNIVERSITY
Also Called: Recreational Sports & Svc
136 E Bagley Rd (44017-2011)
PHONE..................................440 826-2285
Tim Miller, *Director*
Susan C Warner, *Director*
Jay Bush, *Training Spec*
EMP: 30
SALES (corp-wide): 103.2MM **Privately Held**
WEB: www.baldwinw.edu
SIC: **7999 8221** Recreation center; college, except junior
PA: Baldwin Wallace University
275 Eastland Rd
Berea OH 44017
440 826-2900

(G-1414)
BEREA B O E TRNSP DEPT
235 Riveredge Pkwy (44017-1123)
PHONE..................................216 898-8300
Al Fiekle, *Manager*
EMP: 80
SALES (est): 2.5MM **Privately Held**
SIC: **4151** School buses

(G-1415)
BEREA LAKE TOWERS INC
4 Berea Cmns Ste 1 (44017-2524)
PHONE..................................440 243-9050
Michael Coury, *President*
John Coury, *Corp Secy*
Phillip Coury, *Vice Pres*
EMP: 50
SQ FT: 60,000
SALES (est): 3.2MM **Privately Held**
SIC: **8361** Home for the aged

(G-1416)
BEREA LK TWERS RTIREMENT CMNTY
3 Berea Cmns (44017-2524)
PHONE..................................440 243-9050
Tammy Cummins, *CEO*
Fran Reynolds, *Manager*
EMP: 45
SALES (est): 846.5K **Privately Held**
SIC: **8059** Rest home, with health care

(G-1417)
CHARLIE TOWING SERVICE INC
Also Called: Charlie's Towing Svc
55 Lou Groza Blvd (44017-1237)
PHONE..................................440 234-5300
Charles Valentine, *President*
EMP: 30
SQ FT: 8,000
SALES (est): 2.8MM **Privately Held**
SIC: **7549** Towing service, automotive

(G-1418)
CITY OF BEREA
Also Called: Berea Service Garage
400 Barrett Rd (44017-1021)
PHONE..................................440 826-5853
Cyril Kleem, *Mayor*
EMP: 40
SQ FT: 23,124
SALES (est): 1.5MM **Privately Held**
SIC: **7538 9532** General automotive repair shops; county planning & development agency, government

PA: City Of Berea
11 Berea Cmns
Berea OH 44017
440 826-5800

(G-1419)
CLEVELAND BROWNS FOOTBALL LLC
76 Lou Groza Blvd (44017-1269)
PHONE..................................440 891-5000
Joe Banner, *CEO*
Andrew Berry, *President*
Alec Scheiner, *President*
Sashi Brown, *Exec VP*
Brent Stehlik, *Exec VP*
EMP: 150
SQ FT: 10,000
SALES (est): 18.4MM **Privately Held**
WEB: www.clevelandbrowns.com
SIC: **7941** Football club

(G-1420)
COMMUNICARE HEALTH SVCS INC
Also Called: Berea Alzheimer's Care Center
49 Sheldon Rd (44017-1136)
PHONE..................................440 234-0454
Haleigh Niece, *Exec Dir*
EMP: 100
SALES (corp-wide): 125.8MM **Privately Held**
SIC: **8051** Skilled nursing care facilities
PA: Communicare Health Services, Inc.
4700 Ashwood Dr Ste 200
Blue Ash OH 45241
513 530-1654

(G-1421)
CUYAHOGA COUNTY AG SOC
Also Called: Cuyahoga County Fair
164 Eastland Rd (44017-2066)
P.O. Box 135 (44017-0135)
PHONE..................................440 243-0090
Timothy Fowler, *President*
EMP: 30
SALES: 1.2MM **Privately Held**
WEB: www.cuyfair.com
SIC: **8641 7999** Civic associations; agricultural fair

(G-1422)
CYPRESS HOSPICE LLC
2 Berea Cmns Ste 1 (44017-2535)
PHONE..................................440 973-0250
Jay Coury, *President*
EMP: 25
SALES (est): 286.2K **Privately Held**
SIC: **8052** Personal care facility

(G-1423)
ENVIROTEST SYSTEMS CORP
1291 W Bagley Rd (44017-2911)
PHONE..................................330 963-4464
EMP: 34
SQ FT: 7,545 **Privately Held**
WEB: www.il.etest.com
SIC: **7549** Emissions testing without repairs, automotive
HQ: Envirotest Systems Corp.
7 Kripes Rd
East Granby CT 06026

(G-1424)
ESTABROOK CORPORATION (PA)
700 W Bagley Rd (44017-2900)
P.O. Box 804 (44017-0804)
PHONE..................................440 234-8566
Kelly Sutula, *Ch of Bd*
Jeffrey W Tarr, *President*
Bob Abramczyk, *Sales Mgr*
Brad Tarr, *Accounts Mgr*
Kevin McKenzie, *Sales Engr*
EMP: 30
SQ FT: 25,000
SALES (est): 40.4MM **Privately Held**
WEB: www.estabrookcorp.com
SIC: **5084 7699** Pumps & pumping equipment; industrial machinery & equipment repair

(G-1425)
ETB UNIVERSITY PROPERTIES LLC
343 W Bagley Rd (44017-1370)
PHONE..................................440 826-2212
Robert C Helmer, *President*
EMP: 142
SQ FT: 40,000
SALES: 110K
SALES (corp-wide): 103.2MM **Privately Held**
SIC: **6519** Real property lessors
PA: Baldwin Wallace University
275 Eastland Rd
Berea OH 44017
440 826-2900

(G-1426)
FASTENER INDUSTRIES INC
Also Called: Ohio Nut & Bolt Company Div
33 Lou Groza Blvd (44017-1237)
PHONE..................................440 891-2031
Susan Croft, *Purch Mgr*
Jim Thomas, *Engineer*
Tim Morgan, *Manager*
Patrick Finnegan, *Manager*
EMP: 50
SALES (corp-wide): 42.3MM **Privately Held**
WEB: www.on-b.com
SIC: **3452 5084** Bolts, nuts, rivets & washers; lift trucks & parts
PA: Fastener Industries, Inc.
1 Berea Cmns Ste 209
Berea OH 44017
440 243-0034

(G-1427)
FRONT LEASING CO LLC
Also Called: Aristocrat Berea Skilled
255 Front St (44017-1943)
PHONE..................................440 243-4000
Stephen L Rosedale,
Charles Stoltz,
EMP: 245
SALES (est): 6.6MM **Privately Held**
SIC: **8051** Convalescent home with continuous nursing care

(G-1428)
INTERCNNECT CBLING NETWRK SVCS
125 Pelret Indus Pkwy (44017-2940)
PHONE..................................440 891-0465
Diana O Fretwell, *President*
Sarah Mitchell, *Business Mgr*
Jim Fretwell, *Corp Secy*
Sung Pyo, *Consultant*
Todd Penna, *Info Tech Mgr*
EMP: 32
SALES (est): 4.2MM **Privately Held**
WEB: www.icns-interconnect.com
SIC: **1731** Computer installation; telephone & telephone equipment installation

(G-1429)
L O G TRANSPORTATION INC
Also Called: Eagle Freight
120 Blaze Industrial Pkwy (44017-2930)
PHONE..................................440 891-0850
Kelly Hoban, *President*
EMP: 25
SQ FT: 46,000
SALES (est): 2.7MM **Privately Held**
SIC: **4213** Heavy hauling

(G-1430)
MERRICK BODY SHOP
520 Front St (44017-1758)
PHONE..................................440 243-6700
Robert Serpentini, *Owner*
EMP: 25
SALES (est): 1.5MM **Privately Held**
SIC: **5511 5521 7532** Automobiles, new & used; automobiles, used cars only; paint shop, automotive

(G-1431)
NORTHSTAR ALLOYS & MACHINE CO
631 Wyleswood Dr (44017-2264)
P.O. Box 684 (44017-0684)
PHONE..................................440 234-3069
Jane Wagner, *President*
EMP: 40

SQ FT: 3,000
SALES (est): 805.2K **Privately Held**
SIC: **5051** Steel

(G-1432)
OHIO TPK & INFRASTRUCTURE COMM (DH)
682 Prospect St (44017-2711)
P.O. Box 460 (44017-0460)
PHONE..................................440 234-2081
Randy Cole, *CEO*
Jerry N Hruby, *Chairman*
Sandy Barber, *Corp Secy*
Martin S Seekely, *CFO*
George Dixon, *Manager*
EMP: 125
SQ FT: 55,000
SALES: 321.9MM **Privately Held**
WEB: www.ohioturnpike.net
SIC: **4785** Toll road operation

(G-1433)
OHIO TPK & INFRASTRUCTURE COMM
Also Called: Amherst Maintenance Bldg
682 Prospect St (44017-2711)
PHONE..................................440 234-2081
Dan Castrigano, *Chief*
EMP: 160 **Privately Held**
WEB: www.ohioturnpike.net
SIC: **1611 0782 9621** Highway & street maintenance; highway lawn & garden maintenance services; regulation, administration of transportation;
HQ: Ohio Turnpike And Infrastructure Commission
682 Prospect St
Berea OH 44017
440 234-2081

(G-1434)
OHIOGUIDESTONE (PA)
434 Eastland Rd (44017-1217)
PHONE..................................440 234-2006
Richard Frank, *CEO*
Donna Keegan, *Vice Pres*
EMP: 50
SQ FT: 53,000
SALES: 62.8MM **Privately Held**
WEB: www.bchfs.org
SIC: **8322 8361 8351 8051** Child related social services; home for the emotionally disturbed; child day care services; skilled nursing care facilities

(G-1435)
PUCHER PAINT CO INC (PA)
Also Called: Pucher's Decorating Center
50 Park St (44017-1506)
PHONE..................................440 234-0991
Randy Pucher, *President*
Alisa Pucher, *Vice Pres*
EMP: 25
SQ FT: 11,700
SALES (est): 3.4MM **Privately Held**
WEB: www.puchers.com
SIC: **1799 7389 5211 5231** Window treatment installation; interior decorating; tile, ceramic; wallpaper

(G-1436)
ROCKY RIVER LEASING CO LLC
Also Called: Northwestern Healthcare Center
570 N Rocky River Dr (44017-1613)
PHONE..................................440 243-5688
Stephen L Rosedale, *Chairman*
EMP: 150
SALES (est): 5.3MM **Privately Held**
SIC: **8051** Skilled nursing care facilities

(G-1437)
SOUND COM CORPORATION
Also Called: Sound Com System
227 Depot St (44017-1860)
PHONE..................................440 234-2604
Paul Winkler, *President*
Paul Fussner, *President*
Carl McLaughlin, *COO*
Stephon Hall, *Project Mgr*
Mike Richley, *Project Mgr*
EMP: 70 EST: 1974
SQ FT: 10,500

SALES (est): 60.7MM
SALES (corp-wide): 4.8B **Publicly Held**
SIC: 5065 Communication equipment; sound equipment, electronic
PA: Ametek, Inc.
1100 Cassatt Rd
Berwyn PA 19312
610 647-2121

(G-1438)
SUBURBAN COLLISION CENTERS
Also Called: Surburan Collision Ctr
1151 W Bagley Rd (44017-2909)
PHONE...................................440 243-5533
Angelo Papotto, *Owner*
EMP: 36
SQ FT: 8,617
SALES (est): 2.2MM **Privately Held**
WEB: www.suburbancollision.com
SIC: 7532 Body shop, automotive

(G-1439)
T & L ENTERPRISES INC
Also Called: ServiceMaster
1060 W Bagley Rd Ste 101 (44017-2938)
PHONE...................................440 234-5900
Terry D Litt, *President*
Elizabeth Litt, *Corp Secy*
Burnie Wright, *Technical Staff*
EMP: 30
SQ FT: 3,000
SALES (est): 900K **Privately Held**
SIC: 7349 Building maintenance services

(G-1440)
T ALLEN INC
200 Depot St (44017-1810)
PHONE...................................440 234-2366
Thomas Krivos, *President*
Randy Hamilton, *Vice Pres*
EMP: 30
SQ FT: 4,500
SALES (est): 7MM **Privately Held**
WEB: www.rogue-cavern.net
SIC: 1542 Commercial & office building contractors

(G-1441)
TJM EXPRESS INC
212 Sandstone Ridge Way (44017-1085)
PHONE...................................216 385-4164
James R McCarthy, *President*
EMP: 27
SALES: 2.2MM **Privately Held**
SIC: 4731 Freight forwarding

(G-1442)
TRICOR EMPLYMENT SCREENING LTD
110 Blaze Industrial Pkwy (44017-2950)
PHONE...................................800 818-5116
Mary Morrison,
EMP: 39
SQ FT: 7,200
SALES (est): 2.5MM **Privately Held**
SIC: 7389 Personal investigation service

(G-1443)
WEEKLEYS MAILING SERVICE INC
1420 W Bagley Rd (44017-2935)
PHONE...................................440 234-4325
Thomas Weekley, *President*
Gerald Milton, *Vice Pres*
Vera Rutz, *Treasurer*
EMP: 100
SQ FT: 63,000
SALES (est): 15.1MM **Privately Held**
WEB: www.weekleysmailing.com
SIC: 7331 Mailing service

Bergholz
Jefferson County

(G-1444)
ROSEBUD MINING COMPANY
Also Called: Bergholz 7
9076 County Road 53 (43908-7948)
PHONE...................................740 768-2097
William Denoon, *Branch Mgr*
EMP: 33

SALES (corp-wide): 605.3MM **Privately Held**
SIC: 1222 1221 Bituminous coal-underground mining; bituminous coal & lignite-surface mining
PA: Rosebud Mining Company
301 Market St
Kittanning PA 16201
724 545-6222

Berlin
Holmes County

(G-1445)
BERLIN CONTRACTORS
Also Called: Holmes Crane
5233 Township Rd 359 (44610)
P.O. Box 257 (44610-0257)
PHONE...................................330 893-2904
Perry Chupp, *Owner*
EMP: 25
SALES (est): 2.3MM **Privately Held**
SIC: 1771 Concrete work

(G-1446)
DUTCH HERITAGE FARMS INC
Also Called: Amish Farm, The
Hc 39 (44610)
P.O. Box 270 (44610-0270)
PHONE...................................330 893-3232
John Schrock, *President*
James Schrock, *Corp Secy*
EMP: 40
SALES (est): 1.4MM **Privately Held**
SIC: 7999 5947 Tourist attraction, commercial; gift shop

(G-1447)
ZINCKS IN BERLIN INC (PA)
4799 E Main St (44610)
P.O. Box 153 (44610-0153)
PHONE...................................330 893-2071
Alan R Zinck, *President*
Monika Zinck, *Treasurer*
EMP: 30
SQ FT: 2,000
SALES (est): 2MM **Privately Held**
SIC: 5949 5131 Fabric stores piece goods; yard goods, woven

(G-1448)
ZINCKS INN (PA)
4703 State Rt 39 (44610)
P.O. Box 441 (44610-0441)
PHONE...................................330 893-6600
Alan Zincks, *Owner*
EMP: 25
SALES (est): 793K **Privately Held**
SIC: 7011 Inns

Berlin Center
Mahoning County

(G-1449)
BECDIR CONSTRUCTION COMPANY
15764 W Akron Canfield Rd (44401-9786)
PHONE...................................330 547-2134
David Dirusso, *President*
Rebecca Dirusso, *Vice Pres*
EMP: 50
SQ FT: 6,000
SALES (est): 10.5MM **Privately Held**
SIC: 1622 1611 Bridge construction; highway & street construction

Berlin Heights
Erie County

(G-1450)
DANIELS BASEMENT WATERPROOFING
Also Called: Daniel's Construction
10407 Main Rd (44814-9585)
PHONE...................................440 965-4332
Daniel Polling, *Owner*
EMP: 30

SALES (est): 1.1MM **Privately Held**
WEB: www.danielswaterproofing.com
SIC: 1799 Waterproofing

(G-1451)
SHAN-ROD INC
7308 Driver Rd (44814-9661)
P.O. Box 380 (44814-0380)
PHONE...................................419 588-2066
Dave Hatala, *President*
Edward F Norton, *Principal*
Robert Rodwancy, *Principal*
H V Pat Shannon, *Principal*
Greg Seeley, *Admin Sec*
EMP: 25 EST: 1970
SALES (est): 9.6MM **Privately Held**
WEB: www.shanrod.com
SIC: 5085 Valves & fittings

Bethel
Clermont County

(G-1452)
BASTIN HOME INC
656 W Plane St (45106-9721)
PHONE...................................513 734-2662
Debbie Bastin, *CEO*
EMP: 35
SALES (est): 1.6MM **Privately Held**
SIC: 8361 Home for the mentally handicapped

(G-1453)
M M CONSTRUCTION
1924 St Routee 222 (45106)
PHONE...................................513 553-0106
Mark Sturgill, *President*
EMP: 50
SALES (est): 100K **Privately Held**
SIC: 1521 Single-family housing construction

(G-1454)
SMYTH AUTOMOTIVE INC
Also Called: Parts Plus
685 W Plane St (45106-9573)
PHONE...................................513 734-7800
John Eowman, *Manager*
EMP: 29
SQ FT: 2,080
SALES (corp-wide): 122.3MM **Privately Held**
WEB: www.smythautomotive.com
SIC: 5013 Automotive supplies & parts
PA: Smyth Automotive, Inc.
4275 Mt Carmel Tobasco Rd
Cincinnati OH 45244
513 528-2800

(G-1455)
UTTER CONSTRUCTION INC
1302 State Route 133 (45106-8449)
PHONE...................................513 876-2246
Doug Utter, *President*
Jim Messmer, *President*
Dwayne K Utter, *Vice Pres*
Shiela G Defau, *CFO*
EMP: 150
SALES (est): 41.7MM **Privately Held**
WEB: www.utterconstruction.net
SIC: 1794 Excavation work

Bethesda
Belmont County

(G-1456)
NEW HORIZON YOUTH CENTER CO
40060 National Rd (43719-9763)
PHONE...................................740 782-0092
Tom Perrone, *President*
EMP: 50
SQ FT: 1,296
SALES (est): 1.8MM **Privately Held**
SIC: 8322 Youth center

(G-1457)
RES-CARE INC
39555 National Rd (43719-9762)
PHONE...................................740 782-1476

Gloria Llewellyn, *Exec Dir*
EMP: 37
SALES (corp-wide): 23.7B **Privately Held**
SIC: 8082 Home health care services
HQ: Res-Care, Inc.
805 N Whittington Pkwy
Louisville KY 40222
502 394-2100

Bettsville
Seneca County

(G-1458)
CARMEUSE LIME INC
Also Called: Carmeuse Natural Chemicals
1967 W County Rd 42 (44815)
P.O. Box 708 (44815-0708)
PHONE...................................419 986-5200
Thomas A Buck, *CEO*
Matt Rogish, *Safety Mgr*
Bobby Hay, *Production*
Nathaniel Freeborn, *Project Engr*
Dwayne Knee, *CFO*
EMP: 49 **Privately Held**
SIC: 1422 Crushed & broken limestone
HQ: Carmeuse Lime, Inc.
11 Stanwix St Fl 21
Pittsburgh PA 15222
412 995-5500

Beverly
Washington County

(G-1459)
ADKINS TIMBER PRODUCTS INC
Also Called: Nmoble Hardwoods
22180 State Rte 60 (45715)
P.O. Box 387 (45715-0387)
PHONE...................................740 984-2768
Allen Adkins, *President*
Kevin Adkins, *Treasurer*
Randy Adkins, *Admin Sec*
EMP: 25
SALES (est): 3.9MM **Privately Held**
SIC: 5031 Lumber: rough, dressed & finished

(G-1460)
APPALACHIAN RESPITE CARE LTD
Also Called: Dayspring Healthcare Center
501 Pinecrest Dr (45715-8909)
PHONE...................................740 984-4262
Meg Suermondt, *Partner*
Brian Casey, *Administration*
EMP: 75
SQ FT: 17,000
SALES (est): 441.2MM **Privately Held**
SIC: 8051 Skilled nursing care facilities

(G-1461)
CITIZENS BANK COMPANY (PA)
501 5th St (45715-8916)
PHONE...................................740 984-2381
Todd A Hilverding, *CEO*
Loretta Linn, *Vice Pres*
Josh Arnold, *Marketing Mgr*
Lisa Keeney, *Officer*
Linda Flowers, *Administration*
EMP: 28
SALES: 9.2MM **Privately Held**
WEB: www.thecitizens.com
SIC: 6022 State trust companies accepting deposits, commercial

(G-1462)
DAY SPRING HEALTH CARE CORP
501 Pinecrest Dr (45715-8909)
PHONE...................................740 984-4262
Brian Colleran, *President*
EMP: 62
SALES (est): 669.1K **Privately Held**
SIC: 8051 Skilled nursing care facilities

(G-1463)
LARRY LANG EXCAVATING INC
19371 State Route 60 (45715-5055)
PHONE...................................740 984-4750
Larry D Lang, *President*

EMP: 30
SALES (est): 3MM **Privately Held**
SIC: 1794 Excavation & grading, building construction

(G-1464)
MUSKINGUM VLY BANCSHARES INC
Ullman & Fifth Sts # 5 (45715)
P.O. Box 128 (45715-0128)
PHONE..................................740 984-2381
Todd Hilverding, *President*
S Richard Arnold, *Incorporator*
EMP: 32 **Privately Held**
SIC: 6712 Bank holding companies

(G-1465)
MUSKINGUM VLY NRSING RHBLTTION
501 Pinecrest Dr (45715-8909)
PHONE..................................740 984-4262
Clay Enslen, *Administration*
EMP: 65 **EST:** 2007
SALES (est): 1.5MM **Privately Held**
SIC: 8051 Skilled nursing care facilities

(G-1466)
STEPHENS-MATTHEWS MKTG INC
605 Center St (45715-2504)
P.O. Box 1208 (45715-1208)
PHONE..................................740 984-8011
David Stephens, *President*
Dave Russell, *Vice Pres*
Kerri Stephens, *Vice Pres*
Tessa Wolfe, *Vice Pres*
Larry L Mathews, *Treasurer*
EMP: 32
SQ FT: 3,500
SALES: 7.3MM **Privately Held**
SIC: 6411 Insurance brokers

Bidwell
Gallia County

(G-1467)
CARMICHAEL EQUIPMENT INC (PA)
668 Pinecrest Dr (45614-9275)
PHONE..................................740 446-2412
John Carmichael, *President*
Loralee Carmichael, *Vice Pres*
EMP: 35
SQ FT: 39,000
SALES (est): 11.1MM **Privately Held**
WEB: www.careq.com
SIC: 5999 5261 5082 Farm equipment & supplies; lawn & garden equipment; contractors' materials

(G-1468)
FOSTER SALES & DELIVERY INC
35 Corporate Dr (45614)
P.O. Box 5 (45614-0005)
PHONE..................................740 245-0200
Robert D Foster, *President*
Dave Casto, *Manager*
Howard Joseph Foster, *Admin Sec*
EMP: 55
SQ FT: 5,000
SALES (est): 10.1MM **Privately Held**
SIC: 4213 Trucking, except local

(G-1469)
HOLZER SENIOR CARE CENTER
380 Colonial Dr (45614-9215)
PHONE..................................740 446-5001
Charles I Adkins Jr, *Principal*
EMP: 25
SALES (est): 9.2MM **Privately Held**
WEB: www.holzer.org
SIC: 8051 8741 Skilled nursing care facilities; nursing & personal care facility management

(G-1470)
TRIMAT CONSTRUCTION INC
13621 State Route 554 (45614-9425)
P.O. Box 10 (45614-0010)
PHONE..................................740 388-9515
Matthew Toler, *President*

Patrica Toler, *Treasurer*
EMP: 50
SQ FT: 3,000
SALES (est): 6.4MM **Privately Held**
WEB: www.trimatconstruction.com
SIC: 1521 1794 New construction, single-family houses; excavation work; excavation & grading, building construction

(G-1471)
VRABLE III INC
Also Called: Abbyshire Place Skilled Nurse
311 Buck Ridge Rd (45614-9016)
PHONE..................................740 446-7150
Al Vrable, *President*
James Merrill, *CFO*
Amber Frum, *Nursing Dir*
EMP: 81
SALES (est): 5.6MM **Privately Held**
SIC: 8082 Home health care services
PA: Vrable Healthcare, Inc.
3248 Henderson Rd
Columbus OH 43220

Big Prairie
Holmes County

(G-1472)
MANSFIELD PLUMBING PDTS LLC
13211 State Route 226 (44611-9584)
P.O. Box 68 (44611-0068)
PHONE..................................330 496-2301
Paul Conrad, *Manager*
EMP: 40 **Privately Held**
SIC: 1711 3088 Plumbing contractors; plastics plumbing fixtures
HQ: Mansfield Plumbing Products Llc
150 E 1st St
Perrysville OH 44864
419 938-5211

Blacklick
Franklin County

(G-1473)
AMERISCAPE INC
6751 Taylor Rd Unit D1 (43004-8313)
P.O. Box 663, New Albany (43054-0663)
PHONE..................................614 863-5400
Bill Duraney, *President*
EMP: 45
SALES (est): 2.1MM **Privately Held**
SIC: 0782 Landscape contractors; lawn care services

(G-1474)
ATRIUM BUYING CORPORATION
Also Called: David Hirsh
1010 Jackson Hole Dr # 100 (43004-6050)
PHONE..................................740 966-8200
David Hirsh, *President*
Douglas Tu, *CFO*
Jason Tu, *CFO*
Brittany Baker, *Sales Staff*
Mike Carroll, *Prgrmr*
▲ **EMP:** 100
SQ FT: 25,000
SALES (est): 100MM **Privately Held**
SIC: 5137 Handbags

(G-1475)
BUCKEYE LANDSCAPE SERVICE INC
6608 Taylor Rd (43004-8661)
PHONE..................................614 866-0088
Kevin McIntyre, *President*
Garry Schwartzkopf, *Chairman*
Paul Barlow, *Sales Staff*
Joyce Kasper, *Admin Sec*
▲ **EMP:** 100
SQ FT: 4,000
SALES (est): 5.8MM **Privately Held**
WEB: www.buckeyelandscape.com
SIC: 0781 1629 0782 1711 Landscape services; golf course construction; lawn care services; seeding services, lawn; sodding contractor; irrigation sprinkler system installation

(G-1476)
CBRE INC
860 Taylor Station Rd (43004-9540)
PHONE..................................614 419-7429
EMP: 29
SALES (corp-wide): 21.3B **Publicly Held**
SIC: 6531 Real estate agent, commercial
HQ: Cbre, Inc.
400 S Hope St Ste 25
Los Angeles CA 90071
213 613-3333

(G-1477)
CINTAS CORPORATION NO 2
1275 Research Rd (43004-9534)
P.O. Box 400 (43004-0400)
PHONE..................................614 860-9152
Matt Schwinghammer, *Manager*
EMP: 120
SQ FT: 27,948
SALES (corp-wide): 6.4B **Publicly Held**
WEB: www.cintas-corp.com
SIC: 7213 7218 Uniform supply; industrial launderers
HQ: Cintas Corporation No. 2
6800 Cintas Blvd
Mason OH 45040

(G-1478)
COAST TO COAST STUDIOS LLC
7522 Blacklick Ridge Blvd (43004-9144)
PHONE..................................614 861-9800
Charles H Morgan,
EMP: 45
SQ FT: 3,000
SALES (est): 1.3MM **Privately Held**
SIC: 7389 Personal service agents, brokers & bureaus

(G-1479)
HENLEY & ASSOC SEC GROUP LLC
967 Jefferson Chase Way (43004-9154)
PHONE..................................614 378-3727
EMP: 25
SQ FT: 10,000
SALES (est): 719.2K **Privately Held**
SIC: 7382 Security Services

(G-1480)
JEFFERSON GOLF & COUNTRY CLUB
7271 Jefferson Meadows Dr (43004-9811)
PHONE..................................614 759-7500
Earl Berry, *President*
Brianne Stone, *Director*
EMP: 35
SQ FT: 7,980
SALES (est): 3.6MM **Privately Held**
WEB: www.jeffersoncountryclub.com
SIC: 7997 Golf club, membership; country club, membership

(G-1481)
JESS HOWARD ELECTRIC COMPANY
6630 Taylor Rd (43004-8661)
P.O. Box 400 (43004-0400)
PHONE..................................614 864-2167
Jess E Howard, *CEO*
John Howard, *President*
Bill Walt, *Exec VP*
Mel Haywood, *Vice Pres*
Tim Howard Sr, *Vice Pres*
EMP: 140
SQ FT: 70,000
SALES (est): 45.6MM **Privately Held**
WEB: www.jesshoward.com
SIC: 1731 General electrical contractor

(G-1482)
MANHATTAN MORTGAGE GROUP LTD
6833 Clark State Rd (43004-7500)
PHONE..................................614 933-8955
Michael Matalka, *President*
EMP: 60
SQ FT: 7,500
SALES (est): 5.1MM **Privately Held**
WEB: www.manhattanmortgagegroup.com
SIC: 6163 Mortgage brokers arranging for loans, using money of others

(G-1483)
UNIFIRST CORPORATION
211 Reynoldsburg New Albn (43004-8700)
PHONE..................................614 575-9999
Brandon Craft, *District Mgr*
Douglas Parfker, *Branch Mgr*
EMP: 50
SALES (corp-wide): 1.7B **Publicly Held**
WEB: www.unifirst.com
SIC: 7218 7213 Work clothing supply; uniform supply
PA: Unifirst Corporation
68 Jonspin Rd
Wilmington MA 01887
978 658-8888

(G-1484)
VESCO OIL CORPORATION
254 Business Center Dr (43004-9240)
PHONE..................................614 367-1412
EMP: 27
SALES (corp-wide): 223.7MM **Privately Held**
SIC: 5172 Crude oil
PA: Vesco Oil Corporation
16055 W 12 Mile Rd
Southfield MI 48076
800 527-5358

(G-1485)
YARDMASTER OF COLUMBUS INC
570 Rynldsburg New Albany (43004-9688)
P.O. Box 650 (43004-0650)
PHONE..................................614 863-4510
Robert Slingluff, *President*
Rick Colwell, *Corp Secy*
Kurt Kluznik, *Vice Pres*
EMP: 30
SALES (est): 2.2MM **Privately Held**
SIC: 0781 4959 Landscape architects; landscape planning services; snowplowing

Blanchester
Clinton County

(G-1486)
FIRST RICHMOND CORP
Also Called: Continental Manor
820 E Center St (45107-1310)
PHONE..................................937 783-4949
Howard W Reifsteck, *Branch Mgr*
EMP: 57
SALES (corp-wide): 7.5MM **Privately Held**
SIC: 8051 Skilled nursing care facilities
PA: First Richmond Corp
900 N E St
Richmond IN 47374
765 962-2947

(G-1487)
HEALTHQUEST BLANCHESTER INC
Also Called: Quantum Health
661 W Main St (45107-9401)
PHONE..................................937 783-4535
Robert Prewitt, *President*
Marc Littrell, *Chiropractor*
EMP: 48
SALES (est): 2.5MM **Privately Held**
SIC: 7299 8041 8049 8748 Massage parlor & steam bath services; offices & clinics of chiropractors; physical therapist; business consulting

(G-1488)
J-C-R TECH INC
936 Cherry St (45107-1318)
P.O. Box 65 (45107-0065)
PHONE..................................937 783-2296
Rick Carmean, *President*
Larry Hinz, *Electrical Engi*
Caleb Maxwell, *Electrical Engi*
▲ **EMP:** 27
SQ FT: 18,000
SALES (est): 4.5MM **Privately Held**
WEB: www.jcrtech.com
SIC: 3541 7629 3544 Machine tool replacement & repair parts, metal cutting types; electrical repair shops; special dies, tools, jigs & fixtures

(G-1489)
RUTHMAN PUMP AND ENGINEERING
Fulflo Specialties Co
459 E Fancy St (45107-1462)
PHONE...................................937 783-2411
David Locaputo, *Manager*
EMP: 25
SALES (corp-wide): 45.4MM **Privately Held**
WEB: www.ruthmannpumpen.de
SIC: 3494 5085 3491 Valves & pipe fittings; valves & fittings; industrial valves
PA: Ruthman Pump And Engineering, Inc
1212 Streng St
Cincinnati OH 45223
513 559-1901

Bloomingdale
Jefferson County

(G-1490)
KUESTER IMPLEMENT COMPANY INC
Also Called: John Deere Authorized Dealer
1436 State Route 152 (43910-7997)
PHONE...................................740 944-1502
Dave Boring, *President*
Dean Boring, *Manager*
EMP: 25
SQ FT: 13,360
SALES (est): 3.8MM **Privately Held**
WEB: www.kuesterimplement.com
SIC: 5999 5261 5082 Farm machinery; nurseries & garden centers; construction & mining machinery

(G-1491)
WILLIAM WOOD
8392 County Road 39 (43910-7808)
PHONE...................................740 543-4052
William Wood, *CEO*
EMP: 37
SALES (est): 4MM **Privately Held**
SIC: 5051 Steel

Bloomville
Seneca County

(G-1492)
ELMCO TRUCKING INC
30 Railroad St (44818-9108)
P.O. Box 218 (44818-0218)
PHONE...................................419 983-2010
Elmer Cole, *President*
Wendy Seyer, *Principal*
EMP: 25
SALES (est): 1.1MM **Privately Held**
SIC: 4213 Trucking, except local

Blue Ash
Hamilton County

(G-1493)
1 FINANCIAL CORPORATION
10123 Alliance Rd Ste 110 (45242-4714)
PHONE...................................513 936-1400
William V Carroll, *President*
EMP: 25
SALES: 2MM **Privately Held**
SIC: 7389 Financial services

(G-1494)
4MYBENEFITS INC
4665 Cornell Rd Ste 331 (45241-2455)
PHONE...................................513 891-6648
Gerald A Peter, *President*
Jason Peter, *Vice Pres*
Justin Peter, *Vice Pres*
Penny Garner, *Human Resources*
Tina Stringer, *Accounts Mgr*
▲ EMP: 25
SALES (est): 1.5MM **Privately Held**
WEB: www.4mybenefits.com
SIC: 4813

(G-1495)
5901 PFFFER RD HTELS SITES LLC
Also Called: Clarion Hotel Suites
5901 Pfeiffer Rd (45242-4821)
PHONE...................................513 793-4500
Jose Machuca, *General Mgr*
EMP: 80
SALES (est): 2.6MM **Privately Held**
SIC: 7011 5812 Hotels; eating places

(G-1496)
ADVANCED COMPUTER GRAPHICS
10895 Indeco Dr (45241-2926)
PHONE...................................513 936-5060
Tony Butrum, *CEO*
Mary Sue Harpenau, *Vice Pres*
EMP: 25
SQ FT: 11,564
SALES (est): 2.4MM **Privately Held**
WEB: www.acgmultimedia.com
SIC: 8742 Marketing consulting services

(G-1497)
ADVANCED INTGRTED SLUTIONS LLC
11140 Deerfield Rd (45242-2022)
PHONE...................................313 724-8600
Vanessa Willett, *President*
EMP: 30
SALES (corp-wide): 10.8MM **Privately Held**
SIC: 1542 Commercial & office buildings, renovation & repair
PA: Advanced Integrated Solutions, Llc
27016 Princeton St
Inkster MI 48141
313 724-8600

(G-1498)
ADVANCED TESTING LAB INC
Also Called: Advanced Testing Laboratories
6954 Cornell Rd Ste 200 (45242-3001)
PHONE...................................513 489-8447
Greg Neal, *President*
Paula Brooks, *Manager*
EMP: 250
SALES (est): 41.3MM **Privately Held**
SIC: 8734 Testing laboratories

(G-1499)
ADVANCED TESTING MGT GROUP INC
6954 Cornell Rd Ste 200 (45242-3001)
PHONE...................................513 489-8447
Greg Neal, *President*
Dorothy S Stammer, *Corp Secy*
Elizabeth Horton, *Vice Pres*
Dieter Stammer, *Vice Pres*
EMP: 250
SQ FT: 6,000
SALES (est): 15.5MM **Privately Held**
WEB: www.advancedtesting.net
SIC: 8734 Testing laboratories

(G-1500)
ADVANTAGE SALES & MKTG LLC
Also Called: Advantage Sales & Mktg
10300 Alliance Rd Ste 400 (45242-4761)
PHONE...................................513 841-0500
John Mazza, *President*
Dave Weeks, *Manager*
EMP: 80
SALES (corp-wide): 9.2B **Privately Held**
SIC: 5141 Food brokers
HQ: Advantage Sales & Marketing Llc
18100 Von Karman Ave # 900
Irvine CA 92612
949 797-2900

(G-1501)
ADVANTECH CORPORATION
Also Called: Advantech Indus Automtn Group
11380 Reed Hartman Hwy (45241-2430)
PHONE...................................513 742-8895
Troy Matus, *Engineer*
Roy Schroeder, *Sales Engr*
Darren Leu, *Sales Staff*
Kayla Nakai, *Sales Staff*
Roy Wang, *Branch Mgr*
EMP: 70

SALES (corp-wide): 1.4B **Privately Held**
SIC: 5045 Computer peripheral equipment
HQ: Advantech Corporation
380 Fairview Way
Milpitas CA 95035
408 519-3800

(G-1502)
ALPHA & OMEGA BLDG SVCS INC
11319 Grooms Rd (45242-1405)
PHONE...................................513 429-5082
Jim Baker, *CEO*
EMP: 38
SALES (corp-wide): 11.3MM **Privately Held**
SIC: 7349 Janitorial service, contract basis
PA: Alpha & Omega Building Services, Inc.
2843 Culver Ave Ste B
Dayton OH 45429
937 298-2125

(G-1503)
ALS GROUP USA CORP
4388 Glendale Milford Rd (45242-3706)
PHONE...................................513 733-5336
James Baxter, *Branch Mgr*
EMP: 26
SQ FT: 5,645 **Privately Held**
WEB: www.paragonlabs.com
SIC: 8734 8748 Testing laboratories; environmental consultant
HQ: Als Group Usa, Corp.
10450 Stncliff Rd Ste 210
Houston TX 77099
281 530-5656

(G-1504)
AMERIGROUP OHIO INC
10123 Alliance Rd Ste 140 (45242-4714)
P.O. Box 62509, Virginia Beach VA (23466-2509)
PHONE...................................513 733-2300
Gary Radke, *Principal*
EMP: 35
SALES (est): 11.4MM
SALES (corp-wide): 92.1B **Publicly Held**
WEB: www.amerigroupcorp.com
SIC: 6324 Health maintenance organization (HMO), insurance only
HQ: Amerigroup Corporation
4425 Corp Ln Ste 160
Virginia Beach VA 23462

(G-1505)
AMERIPATH CINCINNATI INC
Also Called: Richfield Labs
9670 Kenwood Rd (45242-6141)
PHONE...................................513 745-8330
David R Barron MD, *President*
David Barron, *Lab Dir*
EMP: 35
SALES (est): 2.8MM
SALES (corp-wide): 7.5B **Publicly Held**
WEB: www.ameripath.com
SIC: 8071 Medical laboratories
HQ: Ameripath, Inc.
7111 Fairway Dr Ste 101
Palm Beach Gardens FL 33418
561 712-6200

(G-1506)
APRECIA PHARMACEUTICALS CO
10901 Kenwood Rd (45242-2813)
PHONE...................................513 864-4107
EMP: 112
SQ FT: 14,000 **Privately Held**
SIC: 6719 Holding Company

(G-1507)
ARDUS MEDICAL INC
9407 Kenwood Rd (45242-6811)
P.O. Box 42122, Cincinnati (45242-0122)
PHONE...................................855 592-7387
Kevin Williams, *President*
George Pettesch, *Purch Mgr*
EMP: 78
SQ FT: 23,000
SALES (est): 8.2MM **Privately Held**
WEB: www.ardusmedical.com
SIC: 5047 Medical equipment & supplies

(G-1508)
ARSZMAN & LYONS LLC
Also Called: A&L Imaging
9933 Alliance Rd Ste 2 (45242-5662)
PHONE...................................513 527-4900
William Lyons,
Jason Arszman,
EMP: 25
SQ FT: 8,000
SALES (est): 1.8MM **Privately Held**
WEB: www.alimaging.com
SIC: 7379

(G-1509)
BELCAN LLC
Multimedia Services Division
10200 Anderson Way (45242-4718)
PHONE...................................513 985-7777
Patrick Wagonfield, *Principal*
EMP: 749
SALES (corp-wide): 813.3MM **Privately Held**
SIC: 7363 Engineering help service
PA: Belcan, Llc
10200 Anderson Way
Blue Ash OH 45242
513 891-0972

(G-1510)
BELCAN LLC (PA)
10200 Anderson Way (45242-4718)
PHONE...................................513 891-0972
Lance H Kwasneiwski, *CEO*
Lee Shabe, *President*
Joe Triompo, *President*
Kerry Byrne, *Vice Pres*
Steve Houghtaling, *Vice Pres*
EMP: 3000 EST: 1958
SQ FT: 104,000
SALES (est): 813.3MM **Privately Held**
SIC: 7363 8711 Engineering help service; engineering services

(G-1511)
BELCAN ENGINEERING GROUP LLC (HQ)
10200 Anderson Way (45242-4718)
PHONE...................................513 891-0972
Lance Kwasniewski, *CEO*
Neal Montour, *Senior VP*
Beth Ferris, *CFO*
Terry Williams, *CIO*
EMP: 1100 EST: 1991
SQ FT: 104,000
SALES (est): 294.3MM
SALES (corp-wide): 813.3MM **Privately Held**
SIC: 8711 Engineering services
PA: Belcan, Llc
10200 Anderson Way
Blue Ash OH 45242
513 891-0972

(G-1512)
BELCAN SVCS GROUP LTD PARTNR (HQ)
10200 Anderson Way (45242-4718)
PHONE...................................513 891-0972
Arnold Johnson, *Partner*
John Kuprionis, *Partner*
Michael McCaw, *Partner*
Candace McCaw, *General Ptnr*
Mike Wirth, *CFO*
EMP: 200
SALES: 260.6MM
SALES (corp-wide): 813.3MM **Privately Held**
SIC: 7363 Engineering help service
PA: Belcan, Llc
10200 Anderson Way
Blue Ash OH 45242
513 891-0972

(G-1513)
BEST & DONOVAN N A INC
5570 Creek Rd (45242-4004)
P.O. Box 42235, Cincinnati (45242-0235)
PHONE...................................513 791-9180
Scott Andre, *President*
L George Andre, *Chairman*
Keith Jameson, *Purch Dir*
Karen Proctor, *Purchasing*
Ken Park, *CFO*
▲ EMP: 25
SQ FT: 50,000

SALES: 5MM **Privately Held**
SIC: **5084** Industrial machinery & equipment

(G-1514)
BLUE CHIP MAILING SERVICES INC
9933 Alliance Rd Ste 1 (45242-5662)
PHONE.................................513 541-4800
EMP: 35
SQ FT: 35,000
SALES (est): 4.3MM **Privately Held**
SIC: **7331 7299** Direct Mail Advertising Services Misc Personal Services

(G-1515)
BLUE-KENWOOD LLC
Also Called: Hilton Garden Blue Ash
5300 Cornell Rd (45242-2002)
PHONE.................................513 469-6900
Greg Culey Od, *Principal*
Peter Winchester, *Director*
EMP: 40
SALES (est): 470.8K **Privately Held**
SIC: **7011** Hotels & motels

(G-1516)
BRIGHTSTAR HEALTHCARE
10999 Reed Hartman Hwy # 209
(45242-8331)
PHONE.................................513 321-4688
John Apler,
EMP: 25
SALES (est): 443.8K **Privately Held**
SIC: **8082** Home health care services

(G-1517)
BUCKEYE HOME HEALTH CARE
10921 Reed Hartman Hwy # 310
(45242-2880)
PHONE.................................513 791-6446
EMP: 125 **Privately Held**
SIC: **8082** Home health care services
PA: Buckeye Home Health Care
　　7700 Paragon Rd Ste A
　　Dayton OH 45459

(G-1518)
BUNZL USA INC
Also Called: Bunzl Cincinnati
4699 Malsbary Rd (45242-5632)
PHONE.................................513 891-9010
Donna Rey, *Branch Mgr*
EMP: 25
SQ FT: 60,000
SALES (corp-wide): 11.3B **Privately Held**
SIC: **5113** Industrial & personal service paper
HQ: Bunzl Usa, Inc.
　　1 Cityplace Dr Ste 200
　　Saint Louis MO 63141
　　314 997-5959

(G-1519)
CASSADY SCHILLER & ASSOCIATES
4555 Lake Forest Dr # 400 (45242-3732)
PHONE.................................513 483-6699
David Cassady, *President*
Michael Clark, *Managing Prtnr*
James McGrath, *Director*
Helen McElvogue, *Executive*
EMP: 40
SALES (est): 3.9MM **Privately Held**
WEB: www.csa-cpa.com
SIC: **8721** Certified public accountant

(G-1520)
CAVALIER DISTRIBUTING COMPANY
4650 Lake Forest Dr # 580 (45242-3756)
PHONE.................................513 247-9222
George T Fisher, *President*
Kiel Weber, *Warehouse Mgr*
Ian Sroufe, *Purch Mgr*
Kyle Allen, *Human Res Mgr*
Tara Jones, *Human Resources*
▲ EMP: 70
SQ FT: 12,000
SALES (est): 39MM **Privately Held**
SIC: **5181** Beer & other fermented malt liquors

(G-1521)
CEI PHYSICIANS INC
Also Called: Cincinnati Eye Institute
1945 Cei Dr (45242-5664)
PHONE.................................513 984-5133
Richard Kerstine MD, *President*
John Cohen MD, *Principal*
James D Faulkner MD, *Principal*
William Faulkner MD, *Principal*
Robert H Osher MD, *Principal*
EMP: 400
SALES (est): 19.7MM **Privately Held**
SIC: **8011** Ophthalmologist

(G-1522)
CEI PHYSICIANS PSC LLC (PA)
Also Called: Cincinnati Eye Institute
1945 Cei Dr (45242-5664)
PHONE.................................513 984-5133
Clyde Bell, *President*
Kavitha Sivaraman, *Managing Dir*
Robert E Brant, *Principal*
Carry McGehee, *Vice Pres*
Ron Sprinkle, *Vice Pres*
EMP: 160
SQ FT: 44,000
SALES (est): 40.9MM **Privately Held**
SIC: **8011** Ophthalmologist

(G-1523)
CENTENE CORPORATION
4665 Cornell Rd Ste 300 (45241-2455)
PHONE.................................513 469-4500
Ron Supernant, *Manager*
EMP: 153 **Publicly Held**
SIC: **6324** Hospital & medical service plans
PA: Centene Corporation
　　7700 Forsyth Blvd Ste 800
　　Saint Louis MO 63105

(G-1524)
CINCINNATI COLLISION CENTER
Also Called: Carstar
9323 Blue Ash Rd (45242-6818)
PHONE.................................513 984-4445
Greg Theobald, *President*
EMP: 30
SQ FT: 29,239
SALES (est): 2.8MM **Privately Held**
SIC: **7532** Body shop, automotive

(G-1525)
CINCINNATI COPIERS INC (PA)
Also Called: Prosource
4720 Glendale Milford Rd (45242-3847)
PHONE.................................513 769-0606
Benjamin J Russert, *Chairman*
Chris Shersky, *CFO*
Geoff Griffiths, *Controller*
Ryan Burlas, *Accounts Mgr*
Scott Crouch, *Manager*
EMP: 110
SQ FT: 26,000
SALES (est): 52.1MM **Privately Held**
WEB: www.totalprosource.com
SIC: **7378 5999** Computer maintenance & repair; business machines & equipment

(G-1526)
CINCINNATI OCCUPATIONAL THERAP (PA)
Also Called: Coti
4440 Carver Woods Dr # 200
(45242-5524)
PHONE.................................513 791-5688
Kathryn Reese, *COO*
Tara Brock, *Practice Mgr*
Deborah Whitcomb, *Exec Dir*
Joan Dostal, *Executive*
Deb Whitcomb, *Administration*
EMP: 26
SALES (est): 2.5MM **Privately Held**
WEB: www.cintiotinstitute.com
SIC: **8049** Occupational therapist

(G-1527)
CITY OF BLUE ASH
Also Called: Fire Department
10647 Kenwood Rd (45242-3846)
PHONE.................................513 745-8534
EMP: 41 **Privately Held**
SIC: **9224 8049** Fire department, not including volunteer; ; paramedic

PA: City Of Blue Ash
　　4343 Cooper Rd
　　Cincinnati OH 45242
　　513 745-8500

(G-1528)
CITY OF BLUE ASH
Also Called: Blue Ash Golf Course
4040 Cooper Rd (45241-3331)
PHONE.................................513 745-8577
David Waltz, *Manager*
EMP: 32
SQ FT: 3,756
SALES (est): 671.6K **Privately Held**
SIC: **7992** Public golf courses
PA: City Of Blue Ash
　　4343 Cooper Rd
　　Cincinnati OH 45242
　　513 745-8500

(G-1529)
CLIPPER MAGAZINE LLC
4601 Malsbary Rd 1 (45242-5632)
PHONE.................................513 794-4100
EMP: 60 **Privately Held**
SIC: **7331** Direct mail advertising services
HQ: Clipper Magazine, Llc
　　3708 Hempland Rd
　　Mountville PA 17554
　　717 569-5100

(G-1530)
CLUBESSENTIAL LLC (PA)
Also Called: Clubessential Holdings
4600 Mcauley Pl Ste 350 (45242-4765)
PHONE.................................800 448-1475
Randy Eckels, *CEO*
Frederick Prescott, *Project Mgr*
Carrie Seddon, *Opers Staff*
Brenda Nunnally, *Accountant*
Jackie Xu, *Accountant*
EMP: 41
SQ FT: 6,341
SALES (est): 8.2MM **Privately Held**
SIC: **7371 7374** Computer software development; computer graphics service

(G-1531)
CMP I BLUE ASH OWNER LLC
Also Called: Courtyard Cincinnati Blue Ash
4625 Lake Forest Dr (45242-3729)
PHONE.................................513 733-4334
Rick Kimmel, *Executive*
EMP: 26
SALES (est): 1.6MM
SALES (corp-wide): 50.6MM **Privately Held**
SIC: **7011** Hotels
PA: Cmp I Owner-T, Llc
　　399 Park Ave Fl 18
　　New York NY 10022
　　212 547-2609

(G-1532)
CMP I OWNER-T LLC
4625 Lake Forest Dr (45242-3729)
PHONE.................................513 733-4334
Rick Kimmel, *Manager*
EMP: 26
SALES (corp-wide): 50.6MM **Privately Held**
SIC: **8741** Hotel or motel management
PA: Cmp I Owner-T, Llc
　　399 Park Ave Fl 18
　　New York NY 10022
　　212 547-2609

(G-1533)
COHESION CONSULTING LLC
5151 Pfeiffer Rd Ste 105 (45242-4871)
PHONE.................................513 587-7700
EMP: 68
SALES (corp-wide): 11MM **Privately Held**
SIC: **8748** Systems engineering consultant, ex. computer or professional
PA: Cohesion Consulting Llc
　　511 W Bay St Ste 480
　　Tampa FL 33606
　　813 999-3100

(G-1534)
COLUMBUS HOTEL PARTNERS
4243 Hunt Rd (45242-6645)
PHONE.................................513 891-1066
Mike Conway, *President*
EMP: 40

SALES (est): 5.8MM **Privately Held**
SIC: **7011** Hotels

(G-1535)
COMMUNICARE HEALTH SVCS INC (PA)
4700 Ashwood Dr Ste 200 (45241-2424)
PHONE.................................513 530-1654
Stephen L Rosedale, *President*
Beatrice Rosedale, *Vice Pres*
Jerry Williams, *IT/INT Sup*
Michele Hoft, *Exec Dir*
Randy Penwell, *Director*
EMP: 40
SALES (est): 125.8MM **Privately Held**
WEB: www.communicarehealth.com
SIC: **8741** Hospital management; nursing & personal care facility management

(G-1536)
COMPLETE MECHANICAL SVCS LLC
11399 Grooms Rd (45242-1405)
PHONE.................................513 489-3080
Tom Blaha,
Bruce Ducker,
Daniel G Dulle,
Wyane Miller,
Robert Sambrookes,
EMP: 86
SQ FT: 20,000
SALES: 17.4MM **Privately Held**
WEB: www.completemech.com
SIC: **1711** Mechanical contractor

(G-1537)
CORNERSTONE MED SVCS MIDWEST
4570 Cornell Rd (45241-2425)
PHONE.................................513 554-0222
EMP: 40
SALES (est): 2MM **Privately Held**
SIC: **7352** Medical equipment rental

(G-1538)
CORNERSTONE MEDICAL SERVICES
4570 Cornell Rd (45241-2425)
PHONE.................................513 554-0222
Tom Sayre, *President*
EMP: 40
SALES (est): 5MM **Privately Held**
WEB: www.cornerstoneonecall.com
SIC: **7352** Medical equipment rental

(G-1539)
COUNSELING SOURCE INC
Also Called: Rehab Continuum, The
10921 Reed Hartman Hwy # 134
(45242-2881)
PHONE.................................513 984-9838
David Turner, *President*
OH Akron, *President*
Catherine Staskavich, *Manager*
Merilee Wale, *Social Worker*
EMP: 40
SALES (est): 2.9MM **Privately Held**
WEB: www.thecounselingsource.com
SIC: **8093** Mental health clinic, outpatient

(G-1540)
CREATIVE CRAFTS GROUP LLC
10151 Carver Rd Ste 200 (45242-4760)
PHONE.................................303 215-5600
Tina Battock,
EMP: 85
SALES (est): 4.8MM **Privately Held**
SIC: **7313** Radio, television, publisher representatives

(G-1541)
CRESTLINE HOTELS & RESORTS LLC
11435 Reed Hartman Hwy (45241-2418)
PHONE.................................513 489-3666
April Collins, *Manager*
EMP: 26
SALES (corp-wide): 49.8MM **Privately Held**
SIC: **8741** Hotel or motel management
PA: Crestline Hotels & Resorts, Llc
　　3950 University Dr # 301
　　Fairfax VA 22030
　　571 529-6100

(G-1542)
CROSSGATE LANES INC
Also Called: Crossgate Bowling Lanes
4230 Hunt Rd (45242-6612)
PHONE.....................513 891-0310
Ronald C Bedinghaus, *President*
Cathy Ely, *General Mgr*
Rosemary Bedinghaus, *Vice Pres*
Janet Terry, *Admin Sec*
EMP: 30
SQ FT: 27,000
SALES (est): 1.4MM **Privately Held**
WEB: www.crossgatelanes.com
SIC: 7933 5812 Ten pin center; eating
places

(G-1543)
CT CONSULTANTS INC
11120 Kenwood Rd (45242-1818)
PHONE.....................513 791-1700
Mark Brueggemann, *Vice Pres*
EMP: 44
SALES (corp-wide): 40MM **Privately
Held**
SIC: 8711 8712 8713 Consulting engi-
neer; architectural engineering; surveying
services
PA: C.T. Consultants, Inc.
8150 Sterling Ct
Mentor OH 44060
440 951-9000

(G-1544)
DESIGN CENTER
Also Called: Architechs Plus
10816 Millington Ct # 100 (45242-4025)
PHONE.....................513 618-3133
Rick Koehler, *Partner*
EMP: 30
SALES (est): 3.8MM **Privately Held**
SIC: 8712 Architectural services

(G-1545)
DHL SUPPLY CHAIN (USA)
4550 Creek Rd (45242-2804)
PHONE.....................513 745-7445
Dave Pendeton, *Branch Mgr*
EMP: 25
SALES (corp-wide): 70.4B **Privately Held**
WEB: www.exel-logistics.com
SIC: 4225 General warehousing
HQ: Exel Inc.
570 Polaris Pkwy
Westerville OH 43082
614 865-8500

(G-1546)
**DUGAN & MEYERS
CONSTRUCTION CO (HQ)**
11110 Kenwood Rd (45242-1818)
PHONE.....................513 891-4300
Francis Dugan, *CEO*
Jerome E Meyers Jr, *President*
Keith Hall, *Superintendent*
Tim Dugan, *Vice Pres*
Jeffrey Kelly, *Treasurer*
EMP: 150
SQ FT: 20,000
SALES (est): 59.1MM
SALES (corp-wide): 103.1MM **Privately
Held**
WEB: www.dugan-meyers.com
SIC: 1541 1542 1522 Industrial buildings,
new construction; commercial & office
building, new construction; institutional
building construction; condominium con-
struction
PA: Dugan & Meyers Interests, Inc.
11110 Kenwood Rd
Blue Ash OH 45242
513 891-4300

(G-1547)
**DUGAN & MEYERS INTERESTS
INC (PA)**
11110 Kenwood Rd (45242-1818)
PHONE.....................513 891-4300
Jerome E Meyers Jr, *CEO*
Jeffrey Kelly, *CFO*
EMP: 25
SQ FT: 15,100

SALES (est): 103.1MM **Privately Held**
SIC: 1541 1542 1522 Industrial buildings,
new construction; renovation, remodeling
& repairs; industrial buildings; commercial
& office building, new construction; commercial & office buildings, renovation &
repair; institutional building construction;
condominium construction

(G-1548)
DUGAN & MEYERS LLC
11110 Kenwood Rd (45242-1818)
PHONE.....................513 891-4300
Jeff Kelly, *CFO*
EMP: 250
SALES: 100MM **Privately Held**
SIC: 1542 Commercial & office building
contractors

(G-1549)
EASTER SEALS TRISTATE (HQ)
4300 Rossplain Dr (45236-1208)
PHONE.....................513 985-0515
Pamela Green, *President*
Peter Bloch, *President*
Rich Davis, *Vice Pres*
Amy Balson, *CFO*
Dan Feigelson, *Admin Sec*
EMP: 115
SQ FT: 30,000
SALES: 9.5MM
SALES (corp-wide): 17.4MM **Privately
Held**
SIC: 8331 8322 Vocational rehabilitation
agency; individual & family services
PA: Easter Seals Tristate Llc
2901 Gilbert Ave
Cincinnati OH 45206
513 281-2316

(G-1550)
ELIASSEN GROUP LLC
10101 Alliance Rd Ste 195 (45242-4715)
PHONE.....................781 205-8100
EMP: 49
SALES (corp-wide): 107.6MM **Privately
Held**
SIC: 7371 7374 Custom computer pro-
gramming services; data processing &
preparation
PA: Eliassen Group, Llc
55 Walkers Brook Dr Fl 6
Reading MA 01867
781 246-1600

(G-1551)
**EMPLOYERS MUTUAL
CASUALTY CO**
Also Called: EMC Insurance Companies
11311 Cornell Park Dr # 500 (45242-1889)
PHONE.....................513 221-6010
Phil Goedde, *Manager*
EMP: 77
SALES (corp-wide): 1.1B **Publicly Held**
SIC: 6411 6321 6311 6519 Insurance
agents; reinsurance carriers; accident &
health; life insurance carriers; real prop-
erty lessors
PA: Employers Mutual Casualty Company
717 Mulberry St
Des Moines IA 50309
515 280-2511

(G-1552)
ENERVISE INCORPORATED (PA)
Also Called: Engineering Excellence
4360 Glendale Milford Rd (45242-3706)
PHONE.....................513 761-6000
Daniel J Temming, *CEO*
Andrew Beto, *General Mgr*
Ann Moran, *Vice Pres*
Steve Ferguson, *Project Mgr*
Tara Boze, *Opers Staff*
EMP: 104
SQ FT: 22,000
SALES (est): 40.9MM **Privately Held**
WEB: www.engineeringexcellence.com
SIC: 1711 Mechanical contractor

(G-1553)
ENGINEERING EXCELLENCE
Blue Ash Business Park (45242)
PHONE.....................972 535-3756
Andy Beto, *General Mgr*
Holly Baas, *Manager*
Scott Boxer,

EMP: 85 EST: 2008
SALES: 2.5MM **Privately Held**
SIC: 1711 Heating & air conditioning con-
tractors

(G-1554)
**ENTERPRISE DATA
MANAGEMENT INC (HQ)**
Also Called: Datalliance
4380 Malsbary Rd Ste 250 (45242-5648)
PHONE.....................513 791-7272
Carl Hall, *President*
Doug Bethea, *Vice Pres*
Jennifer Warner, *Vice Pres*
Ellen Campbell-Kaminski, *VP Mktg*
EMP: 80
SALES (est): 8.9MM
SALES (corp-wide): 14.3MM **Privately
Held**
WEB: www.edm1.com
SIC: 7379 8742 7378 7374 Computer re-
lated consulting services; management
consulting services; computer mainte-
nance & repair; data processing & prepa-
ration
PA: True Commerce, Inc.
210 W Kensinger Dr # 100
Cranberry Township PA 16066
724 940-5520

(G-1555)
ENTERPRISE HOLDINGS INC
Also Called: Enterprise Rent-A-Car
4600 Mcauley Pl Ste 150 (45242-4765)
PHONE.....................937 879-0023
Mike Cullen, *Controller*
Leandra Carlfeldt, *Manager*
Madeline Stoddard, *Supervisor*
EMP: 40
SALES (corp-wide): 4.9B **Privately Held**
SIC: 7514 7515 Rent-a-car service; pas-
senger car leasing
HQ: Enterprise Holdings, Inc.
600 Corporate Park Dr
Saint Louis MO 63105
314 512-5000

(G-1556)
**ENVIRNMENTAL RESOURCES
MGT INC**
9825 Kenwood Rd Ste 100 (45242-6252)
PHONE.....................513 830-9030
Jodi Keller, *Branch Mgr*
EMP: 31
SALES (corp-wide): 358.4MM **Privately
Held**
SIC: 8748 Environmental consultant
HQ: Environmental Resources Manage-
ment, Inc.
75 Valley Stream Pkwy
Malvern PA 19355
484 913-0300

(G-1557)
**EQUIPMENT DEPOT OHIO INC
(DH)**
4331 Rossplain Dr (45236-1207)
PHONE.....................513 891-0600
Edward Neyer, *President*
John Herrmann, *General Mgr*
John Ventre, *Vice Pres*
Joe Spriggs, *Materials Mgr*
Judi Fischer, *Parts Mgr*
▲ EMP: 25 EST: 1960
SQ FT: 106,000
SALES (est): 90.2MM
SALES (corp-wide): 1.8B **Privately Held**
WEB: www.portmanpeople.com
SIC: 5084 Materials handling machinery
HQ: Pon North America, Inc.
840 Gessner Rd Ste 950
Houston TX 77024
713 365-2547

(G-1558)
**ETHICON ENDO-SURGERY INC
(HQ)**
4545 Creek Rd (45242-2839)
PHONE.....................513 337-7000
Andrew K Ekdahl, *President*
RC Caldwell, *Partner*
Dawn Rauen, *Division Mgr*
Amy Maxson, *Project Mgr*
Michael Boehm, *Research*
▲ EMP: 1440

SQ FT: 31,330
SALES: 430.4MM
SALES (corp-wide): 81.5B **Publicly Held**
WEB: www.ethiconendo.com
SIC: 3841 5047 Surgical instruments &
apparatus; medical equipment & supplies;
surgical equipment & supplies
PA: Johnson & Johnson
1 Johnson And Johnson Plz
New Brunswick NJ 08933
732 524-0400

(G-1559)
F+W MEDIA INC (HQ)
Also Called: Novel Writing Workshop
10151 Carver Rd Ste 200 (45242-4760)
P.O. Box 78000, Detroit MI (48278-0001)
PHONE.....................513 531-2690
Gregory J Osberg, *CEO*
David Nussbaum, *Ch of Bd*
Sara Domville, *President*
Gwenael Nicolas, *Principal*
Chris Berens, *Editor*
▲ EMP: 265 EST: 2005
SQ FT: 250,000
SALES (est): 256.7MM
SALES (corp-wide): 259.2MM **Privately
Held**
WEB: www.decorativeartist.com
SIC: 2721 2731 4813 Magazines: pub-
lishing only, not printed on site; trade jour-
nals: publishing only, not printed on site;
books: publishing only;

(G-1560)
FEG CONSULTING LLC
3587 Tiffany Ridge Ln (45241-3810)
PHONE.....................412 224-2263
Adam Stalczynski, *Principal*
Christa Lachenmayr, *Business Mgr*
Tanya Boudreau,
EMP: 25
SALES: 2MM **Privately Held**
WEB: www.feg-consulting.com
SIC: 8748 Agricultural consultant

(G-1561)
**FEINTOOL EQUIPMENT
CORPORATION**
6833 Creek Rd (45242-4121)
PHONE.....................513 791-1118
Lars Reich, *General Mgr*
Mark Rowlett, *Facilities Mgr*
Lyle Hargis, *Production*
Beat Andres, *Executive*
▲ EMP: 35
SQ FT: 29,000
SALES (est): 8.1MM
SALES (corp-wide): 2.9B **Privately Held**
SIC: 5084 Industrial machinery & equip-
ment
HQ: Feintool U.S. Operations, Inc.
11280 Cornell Park Dr
Blue Ash OH 45242
513 247-4061

(G-1562)
**FIRST DATA GVRNMENT
SLTIONS LP**
11311 Cornell Park Dr (45242-1889)
PHONE.....................513 489-9599
Jeffrey D Myers, *Partner*
EMP: 93
SALES (est): 15.6MM **Privately Held**
SIC: 6099 8742 Electronic funds transfer
network, including switching; business
planning & organizing services

(G-1563)
**FIRST DATA GVRNMNT
SOLUTNS INC (HQ)**
11311 Cornell Park Dr (45242-1889)
PHONE.....................513 489-9599
Michael D Capellas, *CEO*
EMP: 125
SALES (est): 8.7MM
SALES (corp-wide): 9.5B **Publicly Held**
WEB: www.fdgs.com
SIC: 7371 Custom computer programming
services
PA: First Data Corporation
225 Liberty St Fl 29
New York NY 10281
800 735-3362

G
E
O
G
R
A
P
H
I
C

(G-1564)
FISHBECK THMPSON CARR HBER INC
11353 Reed Hartman Hwy # 500 (45241-2443)
PHONE.................................513 469-2370
Peter Soltys, *Manager*
Richard Miller, *Associate*
EMP: 29
SALES (corp-wide): 78.1MM **Privately Held**
SIC: 8711 Consulting engineer
PA: Fishbeck, Thompson, Carr & Huber, Inc.
    1515 Arboretum Dr Se
    Grand Rapids MI 49546
    616 575-3824

(G-1565)
FUSION ALLIANCE LLC
4555 Lake Forest Dr # 325 (45242-3785)
PHONE.................................513 563-8444
Julie Kimmel, *Principal*
Jason Lee, *Consultant*
Rob Pfister, *Consultant*
EMP: 27
SALES (corp-wide): 58.5MM **Privately Held**
SIC: 8742 Management information systems consultant
HQ: Fusion Alliance, Llc
    301 Pennsylvania Pkwy 2
    Carmel IN 46032
    317 955-1300

(G-1566)
G & G INVESTMENT LLC
4901 Hunt Rd Ste 300 (45242-6990)
PHONE.................................513 984-0300
Stephen Guttman, *President*
EMP: 65
SALES (est): 5.3MM **Privately Held**
SIC: 6162 Mortgage companies, urban

(G-1567)
GENERAL ELECTRIC COMPANY
11240 Cornell Park Dr # 114 (45242-1800)
PHONE.................................513 530-7107
Gary Ernst, *Branch Mgr*
EMP: 30
SALES (corp-wide): 121.6B **Publicly Held**
SIC: 5084 Industrial machinery & equipment
PA: General Electric Company
    41 Farnsworth St
    Boston MA 02210
    617 443-3000

(G-1568)
GFK CUSTOM RESEARCH LLC
11240 Cornell Park Dr (45242-1800)
PHONE.................................513 562-1507
EMP: 112
SALES (corp-wide): 1.5B **Privately Held**
SIC: 8732 Commercial Nonphysical Research
HQ: Gfk Custom Research, Llc
    200 Liberty St Fl 4
    New York NY 10281
    212 240-5300

(G-1569)
GINGERBREAD INC
Also Called: Gingerbread Academy
4215 Malsbary Rd (45242-5509)
PHONE.................................513 793-4122
Louise Yakubisin, *President*
EMP: 35
SALES (est): 910.3K **Privately Held**
WEB: www.gingerbread.net
SIC: 8351 Group day care center

(G-1570)
GIRL SCOUTS OF WESTERN OHIO (PA)
4930 Cornell Rd (45242-1804)
PHONE.................................513 489-1025
Barbara J Bonifas, *CEO*
EMP: 45 EST: 1963
SQ FT: 6,000
SALES: 13.7MM **Privately Held**
WEB: www.grgsc.org
SIC: 8641 Girl Scout organization

(G-1571)
GLOBALTRANZ ENTERPRISES INC
10945 Reed Hartman Hwy (45242-2828)
PHONE.................................513 745-0138
EMP: 103
SALES (corp-wide): 484MM **Privately Held**
SIC: 4731 Freight Transportation Arrangement
PA: Globaltranz Enterprises, Inc.
    7350 N Dobson Rd Ste 135
    Scottsdale AZ 85256
    480 339-5600

(G-1572)
GOETTSCH INTERNATIONAL INC
9852 Redhill Dr (45242-5627)
PHONE.................................513 563-6500
Edith Goettsch, *Ch of Bd*
Eric Goettsch, *President*
Mike Goettsch, *Vice Pres*
Nate Patterson, *Warehouse Mgr*
Ingrid Riester, *Export Mgr*
◆ EMP: 25
SQ FT: 11,500
SALES (est): 22.6MM **Privately Held**
WEB: www.goettsch.com
SIC: 5084 Paper manufacturing machinery

(G-1573)
GROUNDSYSTEMS INC (PA)
11315 Williamson Rd (45241-2232)
PHONE.................................800 570-0213
Rachel Rorie, *President*
Michael Rorie, *Vice Pres*
Kris Marsh, *VP Accounting*
Jay Witte, *Accounts Mgr*
EMP: 35 EST: 2013
SALES (est): 22.3MM **Privately Held**
SIC: 0782 Landscape contractors

(G-1574)
HAL HOMES INC (PA)
9545 Kenwood Rd Ste 401 (45242-6100)
PHONE.................................513 984-5360
Harold Silverman, *President*
EMP: 25
SQ FT: 30,000
SALES (est): 5.7MM **Privately Held**
WEB: www.halhomes.com
SIC: 1542 Commercial & office building, new construction

(G-1575)
HARRIS & BURGIN
9545 Kenwood Rd Ste 301 (45242-6100)
PHONE.................................513 891-3270
Jerald D Harris, *Partner*
Lester J Burgin, *Partner*
EMP: 30
SALES (est): 1.8MM **Privately Held**
WEB: www.harris-burgin.com
SIC: 8111 General practice attorney, lawyer

(G-1576)
HEALTH CARE FACILITY MGT LLC (HQ)
Also Called: Communicare Family of Company
4700 Ashwood Dr Ste 200 (45241-2424)
PHONE.................................513 489-7100
Stephen L Rosedale, *CEO*
EMP: 65
SALES (est): 13.3MM
SALES (corp-wide): 114.3MM **Privately Held**
SIC: 8082 Home health care services
PA: Communicare Health Services, Inc.
    4700 Ashwood Dr Ste 200
    Blue Ash OH 45241
    513 530-1654

(G-1577)
HEALTHCARE HOLDINGS INC
4700 Ashwood Dr Ste 200 (45241-2424)
PHONE.................................513 530-1600
Steve Rosedale, *President*
EMP: 60
SALES (est): 1.5MM **Privately Held**
SIC: 8082 Home health care services

(G-1578)
HENNINGSON DRHAM RICHARDSON PC
9987 Carver Rd Ste 200 (45242-5552)
PHONE.................................513 984-7500
Brad Hyre, *Vice Pres*
EMP: 66
SALES (est): 2.3MM **Privately Held**
SIC: 8711 Designing: ship, boat, machine & product

(G-1579)
HILLS COMMUNITIES INC
4901 Hunt Rd Ste 300 (45242-6990)
PHONE.................................513 984-0300
Stephen Guttman, *President*
Harold Guttman, *Vice Pres*
Seth Guttman, *Vice Pres*
Louis Guttman, *Treasurer*
Lynn Iori, *Human Res Dir*
EMP: 120
SQ FT: 5,000
SALES (est): 15.8MM **Privately Held**
WEB: www.hillscommunities.com
SIC: 1522 Condominium construction

(G-1580)
HILLS DEVELOPERS INC
4901 Hunt Rd Ste 300 (45242-6990)
PHONE.................................513 984-0300
Murray Guttman, *Ch of Bd*
Stephen Guttman, *President*
Louis Guttman, *Corp Secy*
Harold Guttman, *Vice Pres*
Diane Ficker, *Manager*
EMP: 175
SQ FT: 16,000
SALES: 50MM **Privately Held**
WEB: www.hillsinc.com
SIC: 8741 Construction management

(G-1581)
HILLS PROPERTY MANAGEMENT INC (PA)
Also Called: Hills Real Estate Group
4901 Hunt Rd Ste 300 (45242-6990)
PHONE.................................513 984-0300
Steve Guttman, *President*
Louis Guttman, *Vice Pres*
Reginna Bray, *Property Mgr*
Patty Andrew, *Manager*
EMP: 70
SQ FT: 2,000
SALES (est): 11.4MM **Privately Held**
SIC: 6513 6512 Apartment building operators; nonresidential building operators

(G-1582)
HOMECARE SERVICE INC
10979 Reed Hartman Hwy # 320 (45242-2800)
PHONE.................................513 655-5022
EMP: 50
SALES (est): 1.4MM **Privately Held**
SIC: 8082 4119 Home health care services; ambulance service

(G-1583)
ILLINOIS TOOL WORKS INC
Paxton Products
10125 Carver Rd (45242-4719)
PHONE.................................513 891-7485
Tony King, *Principal*
Margaret W Comey, *Principal*
EMP: 28
SALES (corp-wide): 14.7B **Publicly Held**
SIC: 8741 Management services
PA: Illinois Tool Works Inc.
    155 Harlem Ave
    Glenview IL 60025
    847 724-7500

(G-1584)
INNOVTIVE CLLECTN CONCEPTS INC
Also Called: National Child Support Center
11353 Reed Hartman Hwy # 100 (45241-2443)
P.O. Box 42437, Cincinnati (45242-0437)
PHONE.................................513 489-5500
Michael T Higgins, *CEO*
James Durham, *President*
EMP: 25
SQ FT: 5,500
SALES (est): 2.7MM **Privately Held**
WEB: www.nationalchildsupport.com
SIC: 7322 Adjustment & collection services

(G-1585)
INTERACT ONE INC
4665 Cornell Rd Ste 255 (45241-2455)
PHONE.................................513 469-7042
Maryellen Dwyer, *Ch of Bd*
Brian Dwyer, *President*
Zach Stutzman, *Vice Pres*
Joe Williams, *Vice Pres*
Amanda Watkins, *Corp Comm Staff*
EMP: 32
SALES (est): 2.5MM **Privately Held**
WEB: www.interactone.com
SIC: 7374 Computer graphics service

(G-1586)
IRON MOUNTAIN INFO MGT LLC
11350 Deerfield Rd (45242-2105)
PHONE.................................513 247-2183
Jay Geisler, *General Mgr*
EMP: 30
SALES (corp-wide): 4.2B **Publicly Held**
SIC: 4226 Document & office records storage
HQ: Iron Mountain Information Management, Llc
    1 Federal St
    Boston MA 02110
    800 899-4766

(G-1587)
ITCUBE LLC
10999 Reed Hartman Hwy (45242-8331)
PHONE.................................513 891-7300
Hiten Patel,
EMP: 99
SALES (est): 4.2MM **Privately Held**
WEB: www.itcube.net
SIC: 7371 Computer software systems analysis & design, custom; computer software development & applications

(G-1588)
J PETERMAN COMPANY LLC
Also Called: J. Peterman
5345 Creek Rd (45242-3935)
PHONE.................................888 647-2555
John Peterman,
Tim Peterman,
▲ EMP: 35
SQ FT: 15,000
SALES (est): 7.3MM **Privately Held**
SIC: 5136 5611 5621 5137 Apparel belts, men's & boys'; men's & boys' clothing stores; women's clothing stores; women's & children's clothing

(G-1589)
JANELL INC (PA)
Also Called: Janell Concrete & Masonry Eqp
6130 Cornell Rd (45242-2082)
PHONE.................................513 489-9111
Andrew Roth, *President*
Peggy Sullivan, *Vice Pres*
EMP: 40 EST: 1964
SQ FT: 20,000
SALES (est): 29MM **Privately Held**
WEB: www.janell.com
SIC: 5082 7359 5961 5032 General construction machinery & equipment; tool rental; catalog & mail-order houses; concrete building products

(G-1590)
JOHNSON MIRMIRAN THOMPSON INC
4600 Mcauley Pl Ste 150 (45242-4765)
PHONE.................................614 714-0270
Andrew Barr, *Manager*
EMP: 86
SALES (corp-wide): 259.1MM **Privately Held**
SIC: 8711 Civil engineering
PA: Johnson, Mirmiran & Thompson, Inc.
    40 Wight Ave
    Hunt Valley MD 21030
    410 329-3100

(G-1591)
JPMORGAN CHASE BANK NAT ASSN
9019 Plainfield Rd (45236-1201)
PHONE.................................513 826-2317

▲ = Import ▼=Export
◆ =Import/Export

EMP: 26
SALES (corp-wide): 131.4B **Publicly Held**
SIC: 6022 State commercial banks
HQ: Jpmorgan Chase Bank, National Association
    1111 Polaris Pkwy
    Columbus OH 43240
    614 436-3055

(G-1592)
KINDER GARDEN SCHOOL
10969 Reed Hartman Hwy (45242-2821)
PHONE..................................513 791-4300
Tami Lanham, *Owner*
EMP: 45
SALES: 800K **Privately Held**
WEB: www.kindergardenschool.com
SIC: 8351 Preschool center

(G-1593)
L J F MANAGEMENT INC
Also Called: Oxford Square
4719 Alma Ave Ofc 200 (45242-6172)
P.O. Box 54844, Cincinnati (45254-0844)
PHONE..................................513 688-0104
Aristide Belfiore, *President*
Linda Fox, *Corp Secy*
EMP: 25
SALES (est): 1.3MM **Privately Held**
SIC: 6531 Real estate managers

(G-1594)
LAN SOLUTIONS INC
Also Called: Intrust It
9850 Redhill Dr (45242-5627)
PHONE..................................513 469-6500
Timothy J Rettig, *President*
Jeff Andrews, *President*
EMP: 30
SQ FT: 4,300
SALES (est): 4.9MM **Privately Held**
SIC: 7379

(G-1595)
LANDRUM & BROWN INCORPORATED (PA)
4445 Lake Forest Dr # 400 (45242-3784)
PHONE..................................513 530-5333
Mark Perryman, *CEO*
James Adams, *Exec VP*
Daniel Benzon, *Exec VP*
Berta Fernandez, *Exec VP*
Robert Gibb, *Exec VP*
EMP: 50 EST: 1949
SALES: 44.9MM **Privately Held**
SIC: 8748 8742 Business consulting; transportation consultant

(G-1596)
LANG FINANCIAL GROUP INC
4225 Malsbary Rd Ste 100 (45242-5561)
PHONE..................................513 699-2966
Stanford L Lang, *Ch of Bd*
EMP: 26
SQ FT: 8,700
SALES (est): 5.6MM **Privately Held**
WEB: www.langgroup.com
SIC: 6411 8742 6282 Insurance agents; financial consultant; investment advice

(G-1597)
LEADEC CORP (DH)
9395 Kenwood Rd Ste 200 (45242-6819)
PHONE..................................513 731-3590
William Bell, *CEO*
Donald G Morsch, *Treasurer*
▲ EMP: 34
SQ FT: 18,000
SALES (est): 341.3MM **Privately Held**
WEB: www.premiermss.com
SIC: 7349 8741 3714 Building cleaning service; management services; motor vehicle parts & accessories
HQ: Leadec Holding Bv & Co. Kg
    Meitnerstr. 11
    Stuttgart 70563
    711 784-10

(G-1598)
LITERATURE FULFILLMENT SVCS
11400 Grooms Rd Ste 112 (45242-1435)
PHONE..................................513 774-8600
Rank Grande, *President*
Francesco Grande, *President*

Perry Frey, *Vice Pres*
EMP: 25
SALES (est): 3.1MM **Privately Held**
WEB: www.lfsmail.com
SIC: 7331 Mailing service

(G-1599)
LODGE STONE WOOD
11350 Swing Rd (45241-2227)
PHONE..................................513 769-4325
Sandy Johnson, *Director*
EMP: 39
SALES (est): 215.2K **Privately Held**
SIC: 7996 Theme park, amusement

(G-1600)
LSI INDUSTRIES INC
LSI Midwest Lighting
10000 Alliance Rd (45242-4706)
PHONE..................................913 281-1100
Dennis Oberling, *Manager*
EMP: 200
SALES (corp-wide): 331.3MM **Publicly Held**
WEB: www.lsi-industries.com
SIC: 3646 5063 Commercial indusl & institutional electric lighting fixtures; lighting fixtures
PA: Lsi Industries Inc.
    10000 Alliance Rd
    Blue Ash OH 45242
    513 793-3200

(G-1601)
LUMINEX HOME DECOR (PA)
Also Called: Luminex HD&f Company
10521 Millington Ct (45242-4022)
PHONE..................................513 563-1113
Calvin Johnston, *CEO*
EMP: 709
SALES (est): 259.4MM **Privately Held**
SIC: 5023 2844 Decorative home furnishings & supplies; toilet preparations

(G-1602)
MAPP BUILDING SERVICE LLC
11367 Deerfield Rd 200 (45242-2121)
PHONE..................................513 253-3990
Curtis Mapp,
Joette Mapp,
EMP: 30
SQ FT: 4,400
SALES (est): 740K **Privately Held**
SIC: 7349 5087 Janitorial service, contract basis; cleaning & maintenance equipment & supplies

(G-1603)
MARKET INQUIRY LLC
5825 Creek Rd (45242-4009)
PHONE..................................513 794-1088
Cathy Noyes, *Owner*
John Ganster, *Controller*
Lee Anne Adams, *Vice Pres*
Kathi Stewart, *Admin Asst*
EMP: 30
SALES (est): 2.5MM **Privately Held**
WEB: www.marketinquiry.com
SIC: 8732 Market analysis or research

(G-1604)
MARKETVISION RESEARCH INC (PA)
5151 Pfeiffer Rd Ste 300 (45242-4854)
PHONE..................................513 791-3100
Tyler McMullen, *CEO*
Chad Davis, *Vice Pres*
Lisa Fridley, *Vice Pres*
Michelle Jefferys, *Vice Pres*
Melinda Kizer, *Vice Pres*
EMP: 70
SQ FT: 20,500
SALES (est): 13.7MM **Privately Held**
WEB: www.copyvision.com
SIC: 8732 Market analysis or research

(G-1605)
MARRIOTT INTERNATIONAL INC
Also Called: Residence Inn By Marriott
11401 Reed Hartman Hwy (45241-2418)
PHONE..................................513 530-5060
John Secola, *Branch Mgr*
EMP: 167
SALES (corp-wide): 20.7B **Publicly Held**
SIC: 7011 Hotels & motels

PA: Marriott International, Inc.
    10400 Fernwood Rd
    Bethesda MD 20817
    301 380-3000

(G-1606)
MD BUSINESS SOLUTIONS INC
9825 Kenwood Rd Ste 108 (45242-6252)
P.O. Box 630110, Cincinnati (45263-0110)
PHONE..................................513 872-4500
Mark S Grossman, *President*
Tom Merchant, *Controller*
Eric Anderson, *Info Tech Dir*
Joseph E Bernstein MD, *Director*
Robert V Bulas MD, *Director*
EMP: 40
SQ FT: 10,000
SALES (est): 3.3MM **Privately Held**
WEB: www.mdbiz.com
SIC: 8721 8741 Billing & bookkeeping service; management services

(G-1607)
MEDICAL SOLUTIONS LLC
9987 Carver Rd Ste 510 (45242-5563)
PHONE..................................513 936-3468
Kelly Anderson, *Branch Mgr*
EMP: 60 **Privately Held**
SIC: 7361 Nurses' registry
PA: Medical Solutions L.L.C.
    1010 N 102nd St Ste 300
    Omaha NE 68114

(G-1608)
MERCHANDISING SERVICES CO
10999 Reed Hartman Hwy (45242-8331)
PHONE..................................866 479-8246
Mike Buschelmann, *President*
EMP: 62
SALES (corp-wide): 5.2MM **Privately Held**
SIC: 8742 Merchandising consultant
PA: Merchandising Services, Co.
    9891 Montgomery Rd # 320
    Cincinnati OH 45242
    866 479-8246

(G-1609)
MERCY HEALTH
9403 Kenwood Rd Ste D203 (45242-6878)
PHONE..................................513 686-8100
EMP: 32
SALES (corp-wide): 4.7B **Privately Held**
SIC: 8011 Offices & clinics of medical doctors
PA: Mercy Health
    1701 Mercy Health Pl
    Cincinnati OH 45237
    513 639-2800

(G-1610)
MERCY HEALTH PARTNERS
4600 Mcauley Pl Ste A (45242-4765)
PHONE..................................513 981-5056
EMP: 58
SALES (corp-wide): 4.5B **Privately Held**
SIC: 8062 General Hospital
HQ: Mercy Health Partners
    4600 Mcauley Pl Ste A
    Blue Ash OH 45237
    513 981-6000

(G-1611)
MERRILL LYNCH BUSINESS
5151 Pfeiffer Rd Ste 100 (45242-8400)
PHONE..................................513 791-5700
Fax: 513 791-5685
EMP: 44
SQ FT: 9,000
SALES (corp-wide): 95.1B **Publicly Held**
SIC: 6021 Business Credit Institution
HQ: Merrill Lynch Business Financial Services Inc.
    540 W Madison St Fl 1
    Chicago IL 60661
    312 325-2625

(G-1612)
META MANUFACTURING CORPORATION
8901 Blue Ash Rd Ste 1 (45242-7809)
PHONE..................................513 793-6382
David Mc Swain, *President*
Bruce Fille, *QC Mgr*
Jeff Theis, *Manager*

EMP: 50
SQ FT: 54,000
SALES (est): 9.2MM **Privately Held**
WEB: www.metamfg.com
SIC: 3599 7692 Machine shop, jobbing & repair; welding repair

(G-1613)
MODERN OFFICE METHODS INC (PA)
Also Called: M.O.M.
4747 Lake Forest Dr # 200 (45242-3853)
PHONE..................................513 791-0909
Robert J McCarthy, *Ch of Bd*
Kevin P McCarthy, *President*
Eric Hall, *District Mgr*
Steven Bandy, *Vice Pres*
Silas P Rose, *Vice Pres*
EMP: 85 EST: 1957
SQ FT: 10,000
SALES (est): 27.8MM **Privately Held**
WEB: www.momnet.com
SIC: 7359 7629 5044 Office machine rental, except computers; business machine repair, electric; office equipment

(G-1614)
MOLLOY ROOFING COMPANY
Also Called: Blue Ash Roofing Co
11099 Deerfield Rd (45242-4111)
PHONE..................................513 791-7400
Donald A Molloy, *President*
Joyce Molloy, *Corp Secy*
EMP: 45
SQ FT: 10,000
SALES (est): 6.6MM **Privately Held**
SIC: 1761 Roofing contractor

(G-1615)
MORPHICK INC
4555 Lake Forest Dr # 150 (45242-3781)
PHONE..................................844 506-6774
Brian Minick, *Principal*
David Lavinder, *Vice Pres*
Paul Schaefer, *Vice Pres*
Janet Rubleske, *Controller*
Tushar Shah, *Sr Software Eng*
EMP: 32
SALES (est): 2.2MM **Privately Held**
SIC: 7371 Computer software development

(G-1616)
MPF SALES AND MKTG GROUP LLC
11243 Cornell Park Dr (45242-1811)
PHONE..................................513 793-6241
Mike Marek, *Mng Member*
EMP: 200 EST: 2010
SALES (est): 140.2K **Privately Held**
SIC: 5141 Food brokers

(G-1617)
MURRAY GUTTMAN
Also Called: M G Management
4901 Hunt Rd Ste 300 (45242-6990)
PHONE..................................513 984-0300
Murray Guttman, *Chairman*
EMP: 70
SQ FT: 2,000
SALES (est): 3MM **Privately Held**
SIC: 6513 Apartment building operators

(G-1618)
MYCA MLTMDIA TRNING SLTONS LLC
4555 Lake Forest Dr # 650 (45242-3785)
PHONE..................................513 544-2379
Sandra Vogel, *Vice Pres*
Patricia Massey, *Mng Member*
Dave Schwiegeraht, *Info Tech Mgr*
EMP: 35
SALES: 700K **Privately Held**
SIC: 7379

(G-1619)
N SERVICES INC
Also Called: A Miracle Home Care
10901 Reed Hartman Hwy (45242-2831)
PHONE..................................513 793-2000
Natalya Chernova, *President*
EMP: 55
SALES: 140K **Privately Held**
SIC: 7349 Building maintenance services

(G-1620)
NIELSEN CONSUMER INSIGHTS INC
Also Called: Answer Group, The
4665 Cornell Rd Ste 160 (45241-2455)
PHONE.................................513 489-9000
Jack Korte, *Vice Pres*
EMP: 100
SALES (corp-wide): 6.5B **Privately Held**
WEB: www.harrisi.com
SIC: 8732 Market analysis or research
HQ: Nielsen Consumer Insights, Inc.
155 Corporate Woods
Rochester NY 14623
585 272-8400

(G-1621)
NIGHTNGL-ALAN MED EQP SVCS LLC
11418 Deerfield Rd Bldg 1 (45242-2116)
PHONE.................................513 247-8200
Paul Meyer, *Mng Member*
Tiffany Galloway, *Info Tech Mgr*
Richard Almasy,
Steve Steigelman,
EMP: 33
SQ FT: 4,000
SALES (est): 7.6MM **Privately Held**
WEB: www.namedinc.com
SIC: 5047 Medical equipment & supplies

(G-1622)
NORMANDY GROUP LLC
5151 Pfeiffer Rd Ste 210 (45242-4854)
PHONE.................................513 745-0990
Peter Von Nessi, *Managing Dir*
Charles C Burke, *Mng Member*
EMP: 25
SALES (est): 4.2MM **Privately Held**
WEB: www.thenormandygroup.com
SIC: 8742 Business consultant

(G-1623)
OHIO VALLEY ELEC SVCS LLC
4585 Cornell Rd (45241-2439)
PHONE.................................513 771-2410
Steve Ortner, *President*
Brent Foster, *Project Mgr*
Troy Phelps, *Warehouse Mgr*
Darren Jones, *Foreman/Supr*
Roger Brockman, *Cust Mgr*
EMP: 85
SQ FT: 8,000
SALES: 17.3MM **Privately Held**
SIC: 1731 General electrical contractor

(G-1624)
OHS LLC
Also Called: Ohs Media Group
11427 Reed Hartman Hwy (45242-2418)
PHONE.................................513 252-2249
Chris Schlueter,
EMP: 43
SALES: 950K **Privately Held**
SIC: 7319 Advertising

(G-1625)
OMYA INDUSTRIES INC (HQ)
9987 Carver Rd Ste 300 (45242-5563)
PHONE.................................513 387-4600
Anthony Colak, *President*
John Suddarth, *Vice Pres*
Don Stewart, *Safety Mgr*
Roland Meier, *Facilities Mgr*
Lester Cantrell, *Buyer*
◆ EMP: 85 EST: 1977
SQ FT: 21,700
SALES (est): 279.8MM
SALES (corp-wide): 4B **Privately Held**
SIC: 1422 Crushed & broken limestone
PA: Omya Ag
Baslerstrasse 42
Oftringen AG 4665
627 892-929

(G-1626)
ORTHOPAEDIC OFFICES INC
Also Called: Freiberg Spine Institute
9825 Kenwood Rd Ste 200 (45242-6252)
PHONE.................................513 221-5500
Michael Swank, *Branch Mgr*
EMP: 29

SALES (corp-wide): 2.9MM **Privately Held**
WEB: www.freibergortho.com
SIC: 8011 Orthopedic physician
PA: Orthopaedic Offices, Inc
8250 Kenwood Crossing Way # 100
Cincinnati OH 45236
513 221-5500

(G-1627)
ORTHOPEDIC CONS CINCINNATI (PA)
Also Called: Wellington Orthpd Spt Medicine
4701 Creek Rd Ste 110 (45242-8330)
PHONE.................................513 733-8894
Robert S Heidt MD Sr, *President*
Edward Miller, *Chairman*
Michael Welch, *Treasurer*
Mark Snyder, *Med Doctor*
Warren G Harding, *Admin Sec*
▲ EMP: 224 EST: 1968
SQ FT: 14,000
SALES (est): 16.7MM **Privately Held**
SIC: 8011 Orthopedic physician

(G-1628)
PCM SALES INC
Also Called: Educational Services
4600 Mcauley Pl Ste 200 (45242-4775)
PHONE.................................513 842-3500
Brian Koehl, *General Mgr*
John McGoff, *Accounts Exec*
Mike Krieger, *Manager*
David Schawe, *Manager*
Tim Jung, *Software Engr*
EMP: 150
SALES (corp-wide): 2.1B **Publicly Held**
WEB: www.sarcom.com
SIC: 5045 Computers
HQ: Pcm Sales, Inc.
1940 E Mariposa Ave
El Segundo CA 90245
310 354-5600

(G-1629)
PCMS DATAFIT INC
4270 Glendale Milford Rd (45242-3704)
PHONE.................................513 587-3100
Richard Smith, *President*
Jason Wingert, *General Mgr*
Thomas Schuetz, *Senior VP*
Melissa Donnelly, *Vice Pres*
Matthew Reardon, *Project Mgr*
EMP: 68
SALES (est): 14.6MM
SALES (corp-wide): 571K **Privately Held**
WEB: www.pcmsdatafit.com
SIC: 7371 7373 Computer software writing services; computer integrated systems design
HQ: The Pcms Group Limited
P C M S House, Torwood Close
Coventry W MIDLANDS CV4 8
247 669-4455

(G-1630)
PREMIER HEALTH CARE MGT INC
4750 Ashwood Dr Ste 300 (45241-2453)
PHONE.................................248 644-5522
Harold Sosna, *President*
EMP: 30
SALES: 3.1MM **Privately Held**
SIC: 8051 Skilled nursing care facilities

(G-1631)
PRIORITY DISPATCH INC (PA)
4665 Malsbary Rd (45242-5645)
PHONE.................................513 791-3900
R Jeffrey Thomas, *President*
David Castator, *General Mgr*
Beth Dusha, *Treasurer*
Kathleen Grady, *Human Res Dir*
Julie Thomas, *Manager*
EMP: 40 EST: 1973
SQ FT: 20,000
SALES (est): 14.7MM **Privately Held**
SIC: 4212 Delivery service, vehicular

(G-1632)
PROCAMPS INC
4600 Mcauley Pl Fl 4 (45242-4776)
PHONE.................................513 745-5855
Gregg Darbyshire, *President*
EMP: 30
SQ FT: 2,000

SALES: 4.8MM **Privately Held**
SIC: 7032 Sporting & recreational camps

(G-1633)
PROFESSIONAL DATA RESOURCES INC (PA)
4555 Lake Forest Dr # 220 (45242-3785)
PHONE.................................513 792-5100
Phyllis Adams, *President*
EMP: 101
SQ FT: 5,000
SALES (est): 3.9MM **Privately Held**
WEB: www.pdrinc.com
SIC: 7379 7361 Data processing consultant; employment agencies

(G-1634)
QVIDIAN CORPORATION
10260 Alliance Rd Ste 210 (45242-4743)
PHONE.................................513 631-1155
Lewis Miller, *President*
EMP: 50
SQ FT: 5,500 **Publicly Held**
SIC: 7371 Computer software development
HQ: Qvidian Corporation
1 Executive Dr Ste 302
Chelmsford MA 01824

(G-1635)
RA CONSULTANTS LLC
10856 Kenwood Rd (45242-2812)
PHONE.................................513 469-6600
John P Allen,
Marijo Flamm, *Admin Asst*
EMP: 30
SALES (est): 4.5MM **Privately Held**
WEB: www.raconsultantsllc.com
SIC: 8711 3679 Civil engineering; commutators, electronic

(G-1636)
RACO INDUSTRIES LLC (HQ)
5481 Creek Rd (45242-4001)
PHONE.................................513 984-2101
Don Mech, *President*
Tracey Veith, *General Mgr*
Tina Shuemake, *Purch Mgr*
Brittany Moore, *Purch Agent*
Amy Reddy, *Human Res Dir*
EMP: 85
SQ FT: 82,000
SALES (est): 25.8MM
SALES (corp-wide): 38.4MM **Privately Held**
SIC: 5045 5199 7389 Printers, computer; badges; packaging & labeling services; printers' services: folding, collating
PA: Digitalinc, Company, Inc.
5481 Creek Rd
Blue Ash OH 45242
513 984-2101

(G-1637)
RACO WIRELESS LLC (HQ)
4460 Carver Woods Dr # 100 (45242-5520)
PHONE.................................513 870-6480
Ariel Gonzalez, *VP Opers*
Jeff Lehn, *Senior Engr*
Herman Rivas, *VP Sales*
Melissa Bryant, *Accounts Mgr*
Judith Maria, *Sales Staff*
EMP: 46
SALES (est): 24.1MM
SALES (corp-wide): 31.1MM **Privately Held**
WEB: www.racoindustries.com
SIC: 4813 7371 ; computer software development & applications
PA: Kore Wireless Group, Inc.
3700 Mansell Rd Ste 300
Alpharetta GA 30022
416 621-1232

(G-1638)
RANDSTAD PROFESSIONAL US LP
Also Called: Randstad Engineering
4555 Lake Forest Dr # 300 (45242-3785)
PHONE.................................513 792-6658
Ed Anderson, *General Mgr*
EMP: 39
SALES (corp-wide): 27.2B **Privately Held**
SIC: 7361 Employment agencies

HQ: Randstad Professionals Us, Llc
150 Presidential Way Fl 4
Woburn MA 01801

(G-1639)
RANDSTAD PROFESSIONALS US LP
Also Called: Mergis Group, The
5151 Pfeiffer Rd Ste 120 (45242-4854)
PHONE.................................513 791-8600
EMP: 39
SALES (corp-wide): 21.7B **Privately Held**
SIC: 7363 Help Supply Services
HQ: Randstad Professionals Us, Lp
150 Presidential Way # 300
Woburn MA 01801
781 213-1500

(G-1640)
RAY HAMILTON COMPANIES
Also Called: Ray Hamilton Company
11083 Kenwood Rd (45242-1815)
PHONE.................................513 641-5400
Jay Wallis, *President*
EMP: 43
SQ FT: 67,000
SALES (est): 412.2K **Privately Held**
WEB: www.rayhamilton.com
SIC: 4226 4212 4731 4214 Document & office records storage; safe moving, local; freight transportation arrangement; domestic freight forwarding; furniture moving & storage, local

(G-1641)
RAYMOND STORAGE CONCEPTS INC (PA)
5480 Creek Rd Unit 1 (45242-4029)
PHONE.................................513 891-7290
Scott Wolcott, *President*
Tim Crowe, *Vice Pres*
Matt Gordon, *Research*
Tim Fahey, *CFO*
Nancy Delong, *Accounting Mgr*
▲ EMP: 90
SQ FT: 15,000
SALES: 50MM **Privately Held**
SIC: 5084 7699 Materials handling machinery; industrial equipment services

(G-1642)
REED HARTMAN CORPORATE CENTER
10925 Reed Hartman Hwy # 200 (45242-2836)
PHONE.................................513 984-3030
Robert Blatt, *President*
David Wolfe, *Vice Pres*
EMP: 50
SALES (est): 1.7MM **Privately Held**
SIC: 6512 Commercial & industrial building operation

(G-1643)
REHAB CONTINUUM INC
Also Called: Rehab Continuum, The
10921 Reed Hartman Hwy # 133 (45242-2830)
P.O. Box 428666, Cincinnati (45242-8666)
PHONE.................................513 984-8070
David Turner, *President*
EMP: 30
SQ FT: 500
SALES (est): 927.3K **Privately Held**
SIC: 8049 8011 8063 Physical therapist; offices & clinics of medical doctors; hospital for the mentally ill

(G-1644)
REPUBLIC BANK
9683 Kenwood Rd (45242-6128)
PHONE.................................513 793-7666
EMP: 460
SALES (corp-wide): 202.1MM **Privately Held**
SIC: 6029 Commercial Bank
PA: Republic Bank
328 S Saginaw St Lbby
Flint MI 48502
810 257-2506

(G-1645)
REQ/JQH HOLDINGS INC (PA)
Also Called: International Merchants
4243 Hunt Rd Ste 2 (45242-6645)
PHONE..................................513 891-1066
J Erik Kamfjord, *Ch of Bd*
John Q Hammons, *Vice Ch Bd*
Roy E Winegardner, *Vice Ch Bd*
Keith W Daub, *President*
John J Slaboch, *Senior VP*
EMP: 90 **EST:** 1966
SQ FT: 24,000
SALES (est): 84.3MM **Privately Held**
WEB: www.whihotels.com
SIC: 8741 6552 Hotel or motel manage-
ment; land subdividers & developers,
commercial

(G-1646)
RESOURCE INTERNATIONAL
4480 Lake Forest Dr # 308 (45242-3753)
PHONE..................................513 769-6998
Farah Majadzadeh, *President*
Steve Johnson, *Vice Pres*
Cameron Majadzadeh, *Vice Pres*
George Yousef, *Research*
Darin Crain, *Technician*
EMP: 100
SALES (est): 4.9MM **Privately Held**
SIC: 8711 Consulting engineer

(G-1647)
**ROBERT HALF INTERNATIONAL
INC**
10300 Alliance Rd Ste 220 (45242-4764)
PHONE..................................513 563-0770
Donna Connor, *Branch Mgr*
EMP: 92
SALES (corp-wide): 5.8B **Publicly Held**
SIC: 7361 Placement agencies
PA: Robert Half International Inc.
2884 Sand Hill Rd Ste 200
Menlo Park CA 94025
650 234-6000

(G-1648)
RUN JUMP-N-PLAY
5897 Pfeiffer Rd (45242-4819)
PHONE..................................513 701-7529
David E Powell, *Owner*
EMP: 30
SALES (est): 499.8K **Privately Held**
SIC: 7929 Entertainment service

(G-1649)
SAMUELS PRODUCTS INC
9851 Redhill Dr (45242-5694)
PHONE..................................513 891-4456
Millard Samuels, *President*
Thomas J Samuels, *Vice Pres*
William Fitzpatric, *Admin Sec*
EMP: 30 **EST:** 1903
SQ FT: 61,000
SALES (est): 4.3MM **Privately Held**
WEB: www.samuelsproducts.com
SIC: 2759 5122 Flexographic printing;
bags, plastic: printing; druggists' sundries

(G-1650)
**SERVICE EXPERTS HTG & AC
LLC**
Also Called: Stevenson Service Experts
4610 Carlynn Dr (45241-2202)
PHONE..................................513 489-3361
Chris Knochelmann, *Branch Mgr*
EMP: 30
SALES (corp-wide): 985.7MM **Privately
Held**
SIC: 1711 Heating & air conditioning con-
tractors
HQ: Service Experts Heating & Air Condi-
tioning Llc
3820 American Dr Ste 200
Plano TX 75075
972 535-3800

(G-1651)
SOGETI USA LLC
4445 Lake Forest Dr # 550 (45242-3734)
PHONE..................................513 824-3000
Mike Buob, *Vice Pres*
Patrick Keyser, *Opers Staff*
Emily McClimon, *Accounts Exec*
John Rogan, *Manager*
Srini Datla, *Sr Consultant*

EMP: 50
SALES (corp-wide): 355MM **Privately
Held**
WEB: www.sogeti-usa.com
SIC: 7379
HQ: Sogeti Usa Llc
10100 Innovation Dr # 200
Miamisburg OH 45342
937 291-8100

(G-1652)
ST JOSEPH LEASING CO LLC
Also Called: Rolling Hills Health Care Ctr
4700 Ashwood Dr (45241-2465)
PHONE..................................513 530-1654
Thomas Phillppe Jr,
Rod Benson,
Joesph Phillppe,
William Phillppe,
EMP: 100
SQ FT: 32,000
SALES (est): 2.4MM
SALES (corp-wide): 125.8MM **Privately
Held**
SIC: 8051 Skilled nursing care facilities
PA: Communicare Health Services, Inc.
4700 Ashwood Dr Ste 200
Blue Ash OH 45241
513 530-1654

(G-1653)
SUGAR CREEK PACKING CO
4360 Creek Rd (45241-2924)
PHONE..................................513 551-5255
EMP: 25
SALES (corp-wide): 700MM **Privately
Held**
SIC: 4783 Packing & crating
PA: Sugar Creek Packing Co.
2101 Kenskill Ave
Wshngtn Ct Hs OH 43160
740 335-3586

(G-1654)
**SYCAMORE SENIOR CENTER
(PA)**
Also Called: Mt View Terrace
4455 Carver Woods Dr (45242-5560)
PHONE..................................513 984-1234
Jim Formal, *President*
Ray Kingsbury, *Vice Pres*
Cynthia Holloway, *Volunteer Dir*
EMP: 90
SALES (est): 4MM **Privately Held**
SIC: 8322 Senior citizens' center or associ-
ation

(G-1655)
TDG FACILITIES LLC
6819 Ashfield Dr (45242-4108)
PHONE..................................513 834-6105
Paul Jostworth, *Mng Member*
EMP: 110
SQ FT: 10,000
SALES: 10MM **Privately Held**
SIC: 7349 Building maintenance services

(G-1656)
**TECHNCAL SLTONS
SPCIALISTS INC**
4250 Creek Rd (45241-2956)
PHONE..................................513 792-8930
George D Mihal, *President*
George Mihal, *President*
John Baher, *Engineer*
Robin Mihal, *Admin Sec*
EMP: 25 **EST:** 1990
SALES (est): 1.5MM **Privately Held**
SIC: 8742 Business planning & organizing
services

(G-1657)
THERAPY SUPPORT INC
4351 Creek Rd (45241-2923)
PHONE..................................513 469-6999
Brain Pavlin, *Owner*
EMP: 100
SALES (corp-wide): 265.2MM **Privately
Held**
WEB: www.therapysupport.com
SIC: 5047 Medical equipment & supplies
HQ: Therapy Support, Inc.
2803 N Oak Grove Ave
Springfield MO 65803

(G-1658)
**TIME WARNER CABLE ENTPS
LLC**
11325 Reed Hartman Hwy # 110
(45241-2493)
PHONE..................................513 489-5000
Mary Egloff, *Manager*
EMP: 900
SALES (corp-wide): 43.6B **Publicly Held**
SIC: 4841 Cable television services
HQ: Time Warner Cable Enterprises Llc
400 Atlantic St Ste 6
Stamford CT 06901

(G-1659)
TIME WARNER CABLE INC
9825 Kenwood Rd Ste 102 (45242-6252)
PHONE..................................513 354-1100
Mike Barbetta, *Manager*
Susie V Boom, *Manager*
EMP: 25
SALES (corp-wide): 43.6B **Publicly Held**
SIC: 4899 Data communication services
HQ: Spectrum Management Holding Com-
pany, Llc
400 Atlantic St
Stamford CT 06901
203 905-7801

(G-1660)
TIME WARNER CABLE INC
11252 Cornell Park Dr (45242-1886)
PHONE..................................513 489-5000
Wilfredo Juan R Baez, *Pastor*
Virgil Reed, *Director*
EMP: 83
SQ FT: 7,038
SALES (corp-wide): 43.6B **Publicly Held**
SIC: 4841 Cable/Pay Television Service
HQ: Spectrum Management Holding Com-
pany, Llc
400 Atlantic St
Stamford CT 06901
203 905-7801

(G-1661)
**TRADESMEN INTERNATIONAL
LLC**
4398 Glendale Milford Rd (45242-3706)
PHONE..................................513 771-1115
Dave Henderson, *Manager*
EMP: 80 **Privately Held**
WEB: www.tradesmen-intl.com
SIC: 7361 Labor contractors (employment
agency)
PA: Tradesmen International, Llc
9760 Shepard Rd
Macedonia OH 44056

(G-1662)
TREMOR LLC
9545 Kenwood Rd Ste 303 (45242-6270)
PHONE..................................513 983-1100
Paulette Yarosz, *Vice Pres*
Geoffry Schroeder, *Manager*
Heather Johnson, *Director*
Laura S Raines,
EMP: 30
SALES (est): 1.2MM **Privately Held**
WEB: www.tremor.com
SIC: 4813

(G-1663)
TRI-CON INCORPORATED
11160 Kenwood Rd Ste 200 (45242-1818)
P.O. Box 498457, Cincinnati (45249-7457)
PHONE..................................513 530-9844
Raymond A Conn, *President*
Camilla Warren, *Vice Pres*
Andrew Conn, *Project Mgr*
Joan Conn, *Admin Sec*
EMP: 25
SALES (est): 6.7MM **Privately Held**
SIC: 1542 Commercial & office building,
new construction

(G-1664)
TRIHEALTH INC
4665 Cornell Rd Ste 350 (45241-2460)
PHONE..................................513 891-1627
Stacey Bodenstein, *Manager*
Rick Hassler, *Director*
Kelly Lang, *Director*
Ranga Brahmamdam, *Hematology*
James Maher, *Hematology*

EMP: 35 **Privately Held**
WEB: www.trihealth.com
SIC: 8741 8011 Hospital management; of-
fices & clinics of medical doctors
HQ: Trihealth, Inc.
619 Oak St
Cincinnati OH 45206
513 569-6111

(G-1665)
TRIPLEFIN LLC (PA)
11333 Cornell Park Dr (45242-1813)
PHONE..................................855 877-5346
Gregory T Lalonde, *CEO*
Joseph Conda, *President*
Rick Randall, *President*
Michael Eckstein, *COO*
Sandy Piscitello, *Vice Pres*
▲ **EMP:** 100 **EST:** 1983
SALES (est): 84.8MM **Privately Held**
WEB: www.triplefin.com
SIC: 5122 Pharmaceuticals

(G-1666)
TRIPLEFIN LLC
11333 Cornell Park Dr (45242-1813)
PHONE..................................513 794-9870
Wendy Ficke, *Branch Mgr*
Geri Mittelhauser, *Executive*
EMP: 40
SALES (corp-wide): 84.8MM **Privately
Held**
WEB: www.triplefin.com
SIC: 7389 Telemarketing services
PA: Triplefin Llc
11333 Cornell Park Dr
Blue Ash OH 45242
855 877-5346

(G-1667)
TRUEPOINT INC
4901 Hunt Rd Ste 200 (45242-6990)
PHONE..................................513 792-6648
Michael J Chasnoff, *President*
Janel Carroll, *General Mgr*
Christopher L Sheldon Jr, *Accountant*
John Azens, *Director*
EMP: 27
SALES (est): 3.9MM **Privately Held**
WEB: www.acsadvisors.com
SIC: 8742 Financial consultant

(G-1668)
TRUSTAFF MANAGEMENT INC
Also Called: Trustaff Travel Nurses
4675 Cornell Rd Ste 100 (45241-2498)
PHONE..................................513 272-3999
Brent Loring, *CEO*
Doug Dean, *President*
Sean Loring, *President*
Pam Oliver, *COO*
Michelle Filipkowski, *Vice Pres*
EMP: 2000
SQ FT: 40,000
SALES (est): 305.7MM **Privately Held**
WEB: www.trustaff.com
SIC: 7361 Executive placement

(G-1669)
TSG-CINCINNATI LLC
11243 Cornell Park Dr (45242-1811)
PHONE..................................513 793-6241
Paul E Towle,
EMP: 54
SALES (est): 10.1MM **Privately Held**
SIC: 5147 Meat brokers

(G-1670)
ULTIMATE REHAB LTD
11305 Reed Hartman Hwy # 226
(45241-2435)
PHONE..................................513 563-8777
Lorie Macdonald, *CEO*
Tom Macdonald, *COO*
Sheryl Marler, *Vice Pres*
Kelley Robinson, *Vice Pres*
Thomas Macdonald, *CFO*
EMP: 85
SALES (est): 2.8MM **Privately Held**
SIC: 8093 Rehabilitation center, outpatient
treatment

(G-1671)
UNIFUND CCR LLC
10625 Techwoods Cir (45242-2846)
PHONE..................................513 489-8877

David G Rosenberg, *CEO*
EMP: 100
SALES (est): 11.7MM **Privately Held**
SIC: 6153 Buying of installment notes

(G-1672)
UNIFUND CORPORATION
Also Called: Rushcard
10625 Techwoods Cir (45242-2846)
PHONE.................................513 489-8877
David G Rosenberg, *CEO*
Jeffrey Shaffer, *Vice Pres*
David Stringer, *Auditor*
Autumn Hopkins, *Agent*
Autumn Bloom, *Director*
EMP: 50
SQ FT: 12,000
SALES (est): 36.9MM **Privately Held**
SIC: 6153 Buying of installment notes

(G-1673)
UNIQUE CONSTRUCTION SVCS INC
10999 Reed Hartman Hwy # 313
(45242-8331)
PHONE.................................513 608-1363
EMP: 33
SALES: 850K **Privately Held**
SIC: 1721 Contractor Of Commercial And Residentail Painting

(G-1674)
UNIRUSH LLC (HQ)
Also Called: Babyphat
4701 Creek Rd Ste 200 (45242-8330)
P.O. Box 42482, Cincinnati (45242-0482)
PHONE.................................866 766-2229
Ron Hynes, *CEO*
Douglas McGann, *President*
Paul Flanigan, *VP Opers*
Ward Saunier, *Project Mgr*
Kim Kenney, *Opers Mgr*
EMP: 68
SALES (est): 25.1MM
SALES (corp-wide): 1B **Publicly Held**
SIC: 7389 Financial services
PA: Green Dot Corporation
3465 E Foothill Blvd # 100
Pasadena CA 91107
626 765-2000

(G-1675)
VARIOUS VIEWS RESEARCH INC
11353 Reed Hartman Hwy # 200
(45241-2443)
PHONE.................................513 489-9000
Mirjana Popovich, *CEO*
Sharon Lally, *President*
Kevin Vaselakes, *President*
Brendan Burns, *Marketing Staff*
Elizabeth Parish, *Marketing Staff*
EMP: 55
SQ FT: 13,788
SALES (est): 6.4MM **Privately Held**
SIC: 8732 Market analysis or research

(G-1676)
VORA VENTURES LLC
10290 Alliance Rd (45242-4710)
PHONE.................................513 792-5100
Kevin Dooley, *Exec VP*
Mahendra B Vora, *Mng Member*
EMP: 200
SALES (est): 13.1MM **Privately Held**
SIC: 8741 Business management; financial management for business

(G-1677)
W & H REALTY INC (PA)
Also Called: Holiday Inn
4243 Hunt Rd (45242-6645)
PHONE.................................513 891-1066
J Erik Kamfjord, *Ch of Bd*
John J Slaboch, *Treasurer*
EMP: 50
SALES (est): 15MM **Privately Held**
SIC: 7011 Hotels & motels

(G-1678)
WINEGRDNER HMMONS HT GROUP LLC (PA)
4243 Hunt Rd (45242-6645)
PHONE.................................513 891-1066
Terry Dammeyer, *President*

Mike Conway, *Chairman*
Brian Perkins, *COO*
Kent Bruggeman, *CFO*
EMP: 38
SALES (est): 3.3MM **Privately Held**
SIC: 7011 Hotels & motels

(G-1679)
WOLF MACHINE COMPANY (PA)
5570 Creek Rd (45242-4004)
PHONE.................................513 791-5194
Scott E Andre, *President*
Greg Russell, *Vice Pres*
Dave Smith, *Plant Mgr*
EMP: 160
SQ FT: 50,000
SALES (est): 41.3MM **Privately Held**
WEB: www.wolfmachine.com
SIC: 5084 3552 3556 3546 Machine tools & accessories; textile machinery; food products machinery; power-driven handtools

(G-1680)
WOLF SENSORY INC
Also Called: Wolf Group, The
10860 Kenwood Rd (45242-2812)
PHONE.................................513 891-9100
Mona Wolf, *President*
EMP: 50
SQ FT: 17,000
SALES (est): 4.9MM **Privately Held**
WEB: www.wolfsensory.com
SIC: 8732 Market analysis or research

(G-1681)
WOOD ENVIRONMENT &
4460 Lake Forest Dr # 200 (45242-3741)
PHONE.................................513 489-6611
Rick Campbell, *Manager*
EMP: 30
SALES (corp-wide): 5.3B **Privately Held**
SIC: 8711 Consulting engineer
HQ: Wood Environment & Infrastructure Solutions, Inc.
1105 Lakewood Pkwy # 300
Alpharetta GA 30009
770 360-0600

(G-1682)
WOODWARD CONSTRUCTION INC
11425 Deerfield Rd (45242-2106)
PHONE.................................513 247-9241
Jeff Woodward, *President*
Brent Sebesy, *Vice Pres*
Wally Szymanski, *Project Mgr*
EMP: 26
SQ FT: 5,000
SALES (est): 3MM **Privately Held**
SIC: 1542 Commercial & office building, new construction

(G-1683)
WW GRAINGER INC
Also Called: Grainger 152
4420 Glendale Milford Rd (45242-3708)
PHONE.................................513 563-7100
Gary Brown, *General Mgr*
EMP: 25
SQ FT: 2,450
SALES (corp-wide): 11.2B **Publicly Held**
WEB: www.grainger.com
SIC: 5084 5063 Industrial machinery & equipment; motors, electric
PA: W.W. Grainger, Inc.
100 Grainger Pkwy
Lake Forest IL 60045
847 535-1000

(G-1684)
XEROX CORPORATION
10560 Ashview Pl (45242-3735)
PHONE.................................513 554-3200
Lonnie Stiff, *Plant Mgr*
EMP: 500
SALES (corp-wide): 9.8B **Publicly Held**
WEB: www.xerox.com
SIC: 3861 5044 Photocopy machines; office equipment
PA: Xerox Corporation
201 Merritt 7
Norwalk CT 06851
203 968-3000

(G-1685)
YOUNG MENS CHRISTIAN ASSOCIAT
Also Called: Blue Ash YMCA
5000 Ymca Dr (45242-7444)
PHONE.................................513 791-5000
Morgan Perry, *Business Mgr*
Paul Waldsmith, *Exec Dir*
Emily Momberger, *Program Dir*
EMP: 150
SQ FT: 16,506
SALES (corp-wide): 33.6MM **Privately Held**
WEB: www.cincinnatiymca.org
SIC: 8641 7336 8351 7997 Youth organizations; commercial art & graphic design; child day care services; membership sports & recreation clubs
PA: Young Mens Christian Association Of Greater Cincinnati
1105 Elm St
Cincinnati OH 45202
513 651-2100

Bluffton
Allen County

(G-1686)
A TO Z PORTION CTRL MEATS INC
201 N Main St (45817-1283)
PHONE.................................419 358-2926
Lee Ann Kagy, *President*
Leslie Barnes, *Corp Secy*
Sean Kagy, *COO*
Ed Bucher, *Engineer*
EMP: 34 **EST:** 1945
SQ FT: 20,000
SALES (est): 10.2MM **Privately Held**
SIC: 5142 2013 Meat, frozen: packaged; sausages & other prepared meats

(G-1687)
BLANCHARD VLY RGIONAL HLTH CTR
Also Called: Bluffton Campus
139 Garau St (45817-1027)
P.O. Box 48 (45817-0048)
PHONE.................................419 358-9010
Gary Blosser, *Supervisor*
William Watkins, *Director*
Bonnie Van Schoik, *Lab Dir*
EMP: 150
SALES (corp-wide): 32.5MM **Privately Held**
SIC: 8011 Health maintenance organization
HQ: Blanchard Valley Regional Health Center
1900 S Main St
Findlay OH 45840
419 423-4500

(G-1688)
BLUFFTON FAMILY RECREATION
Also Called: BFR
215 Snider Rd (45817-9572)
PHONE.................................419 358-6978
Mandy Kinn, *President*
Carole Enneking, *Director*
EMP: 30
SALES: 289.2K **Privately Held**
WEB: www.bfronline.com
SIC: 8641 Recreation association

(G-1689)
CARPE DIEM INDUSTRIES LLC
Also Called: Diamond Machine and Mfg
505 E Jefferson St (45817-1349)
PHONE.................................419 358-0129
Ryan Smith, *Manager*
EMP: 30
SQ FT: 271,000

SALES (corp-wide): 18.1MM **Privately Held**
WEB: www.colonialsurfacesolutions.com
SIC: 3471 3398 3479 1799 Cleaning & descaling metal products; sand blasting of metal parts; tumbling (cleaning & polishing) of machine parts; metal heat treating; tempering of metal; painting of metal products; coating of metal structures at construction site
PA: Carpe Diem Industries, Llc
4599 Campbell Rd
Columbus Grove OH 45830
419 659-5639

(G-1690)
CITIZENS NAT BNK OF BLUFFTON (HQ)
102 S Main St (45817-1250)
P.O. Box 88 (45817-0088)
PHONE.................................419 358-8040
J Michael Romey, *President*
Robert D Everett, *Exec VP*
Bob Inniger, *Vice Pres*
Brent Kohn, *Vice Pres*
Becky Reichenbach, *Vice Pres*
EMP: 43
SALES: 40.3MM **Privately Held**
WEB: www.cnbohio.com
SIC: 6021 National commercial banks

(G-1691)
GROB SYSTEMS INC
Also Called: Machine Tool Division
1070 Navajo Dr (45817-9666)
PHONE.................................419 358-9015
Michael Hutecker, *CEO*
Jason Cartright, *President*
Michael Salger, *COO*
David Stephan, *Maint Spvr*
Brian Wolke, *Purch Agent*
◆ **EMP:** 198 **EST:** 1981
SQ FT: 262,000
SALES (est): 137.8MM
SALES (corp-wide): 276.6MM **Privately Held**
WEB: www.grobsystems.com
SIC: 3535 7699 Robotic conveyors; industrial equipment services
PA: Grob-Werke Burkhart Grob E.K.
Industriestr. 4
Mindelheim 87719
826 199-60

(G-1692)
JPMORGAN CHASE BANK NAT ASSN
135 S Main St (45817-1249)
PHONE.................................419 358-4055
Chad Grieser, *Branch Mgr*
EMP: 26
SALES (corp-wide): 131.4B **Publicly Held**
SIC: 6021 National commercial banks
HQ: Jpmorgan Chase Bank, National Association
1111 Polaris Pkwy
Columbus OH 43240
614 436-3055

(G-1693)
MENNONITE MEMORIAL HOME (PA)
Also Called: Maple Crest Senior Living Vlg
410 W Elm St (45817-1122)
PHONE.................................419 358-1015
Laura Voth, *CEO*
David Lynn Thompson, *CEO*
Chris Moser, *Marketing Staff*
Neil Morrison, *Director*
Sue Richard, *Director*
EMP: 275
SQ FT: 65,000
SALES: 5.5MM **Privately Held**
SIC: 8052 8059 8051 Intermediate care facilities; personal care home, with health care; skilled nursing care facilities

(G-1694)
MENNONITE MEMORIAL HOME
Also Called: Maple Crest
700 Maple Crest Ct (45817-8552)
PHONE.................................419 358-7654
Daren Lee, *Manager*
EMP: 40

SALES (est): 1MM
SALES (corp-wide): 5.3MM **Privately Held**
SIC: 8051 Skilled nursing care facilities
PA: Mennonite Memorial Home
410 W Elm St
Bluffton OH 45817
419 358-1015

Boardman
Mahoning County

(G-1695)
ASHLEY ENTERPRISES LLC (PA)
Also Called: Briarfield At Ashley Circle
1419 Boardman Canfield Rd (44512-8062)
PHONE..................................330 726-5790
Rob Rupeka, *CFO*
Edward Reese, *Mng Member*
Diane Reese,
EMP: 93
SQ FT: 33,991
SALES (est): 2.5MM **Privately Held**
SIC: 8051 Skilled nursing care facilities

(G-1696)
BEEGHLY OAKS OPERATING LLC
Also Called: Beeghly Oaks Center For Rehabi
6505 Market St Bldg D (44512-3459)
PHONE..................................330 884-2300
Mark Friedman, *Mng Member*
EMP: 130 EST: 2014
SALES (est): 85.8K **Privately Held**
SIC: 8322 8052 Rehabilitation services; home for the mentally retarded, with health care

(G-1697)
FINANCIAL ENGINES INC
1449 Boardman Canfield Rd (44512-8061)
PHONE..................................330 726-3100
Ronald Tabus, *Branch Mgr*
EMP: 43
SALES (corp-wide): 480.5MM **Privately Held**
SIC: 6282 Investment advice
HQ: Financial Engines, Llc
1050 Enterprise Way Fl 3
Sunnyvale CA 94089
408 498-6000

(G-1698)
GORANT CHOCOLATIER LLC (PA)
Also Called: Gorant's Yum Yum Tree
8301 Market St (44512-6257)
PHONE..................................330 726-8821
Gary Weiss, *President*
Joseph M Miller, *Mng Member*
EMP: 120 EST: 1946
SQ FT: 60,000
SALES (est): 63.7MM **Privately Held**
SIC: 5441 5947 5145 3999 Candy; greeting cards; gift shop; candy; candles; chocolate & cocoa products

(G-1699)
HOME DEPOT USA INC
Also Called: Home Depot, The
7001 Southern Blvd (44512-4637)
PHONE..................................330 965-4790
Audrey Elias, *Manager*
EMP: 160
SALES (corp-wide): 108.2B **Publicly Held**
WEB: www.homerentalsdepot.com
SIC: 5211 7359 Home centers; tool rental
HQ: Home Depot U.S.A., Inc.
2455 Paces Ferry Ave
Atlanta GA 30339

(G-1700)
OREILLY AUTOMOTIVE INC
8308 Market St (44512-6256)
PHONE..................................330 318-3136
EMP: 49 **Publicly Held**
SIC: 5531 5013 Batteries, automotive & truck; automotive supplies & parts
PA: O'reilly Automotive, Inc.
233 S Patterson Ave
Springfield MO 65802

(G-1701)
RL BEST COMPANY
723 Bev Rd (44512-6423)
PHONE..................................330 758-8601
Ted A Best, *President*
Ted Best, *President*
Mark Best, *Vice Pres*
William Kavanaugh, *Vice Pres*
◆ EMP: 26
SQ FT: 35,000
SALES: 9MM **Privately Held**
WEB: www.rlbest.com
SIC: 3599 7539 Machine shop, jobbing & repair; machine shop, automotive

Bolivar
Tuscarawas County

(G-1702)
ELEET CRYOGENICS INC (PA)
11132 Industrial Pkwy Nw (44612-8993)
PHONE..................................330 874-4009
Garry Sears, *President*
Tenia Sears, *Vice Pres*
▲ EMP: 33
SQ FT: 47,000
SALES (est): 10.1MM **Privately Held**
WEB: www.eleetcryogenics.com
SIC: 3443 7353 2761 5088 Cryogenic tanks, for liquids & gases; oil field equipment, rental or leasing; manifold business forms; tanks & tank components; trailer rental; management services

(G-1703)
FSRC TANKS INC
11029 Industrial Pkwy Nw (44612-8992)
PHONE..................................234 221-2015
Andrew Feucht, *President*
EMP: 35
SALES (est): 1.5MM **Privately Held**
SIC: 1791 3443 Storage tanks, metal: erection; reactor containment vessels, metal plate

(G-1704)
MEGCO MANAGEMENT INC
Also Called: HENNIS CARE CENTER OF BOLIVAR
300 Yant St (44612-9712)
PHONE..................................330 874-9999
Stephanie Erb, *Director*
Matthew Ridgway, *Food Svc Dir*
David Hennis, *Administration*
Kim Zontini, *Administration*
EMP: 120 EST: 1999
SALES: 10MM **Privately Held**
SIC: 8051 Convalescent home with continuous nursing care

(G-1705)
OHIO MACHINERY CO
Also Called: Caterpillar Authorized Dealer
10955 Industrial Pkwy Nw (44612-8991)
PHONE..................................330 874-1003
Glen Smith, *General Mgr*
Janie Rogers, *Branch Mgr*
Matt Mole, *Manager*
EMP: 38
SALES (corp-wide): 222.7MM **Privately Held**
WEB: www.enginesnow.com
SIC: 7699 5082 Hydraulic equipment repair; construction & mining machinery
PA: Ohio Machinery Co.
3993 E Royalton Rd
Broadview Heights OH 44147
440 526-6200

Botkins
Shelby County

(G-1706)
AGRANA FRUIT US INC
16197 County Road 25a (45306-9646)
PHONE..................................937 693-3821
Sean Augustus, *Opers Mgr*
Jeff Elliott, *Opers Mgr*
Salvador Vazquez, *Opers Mgr*
Salvador Alvarez, *Engineer*
Tony Kerns, *Engineer*

EMP: 150
SALES (corp-wide): 51.7MM **Privately Held**
SIC: 8734 2099 2087 Food testing service; food preparations; flavoring extracts & syrups
HQ: Agrana Fruit Us, Inc.
6850 Southpointe Pkwy
Brecksville OH 44141
440 546-1199

(G-1707)
BEEM CONSTRUCTION INC
225 S Mill St (45306-8023)
P.O. Box 208 (45306-0208)
PHONE..................................937 693-3176
Roger Barlage, *President*
Steven Eilerman, *Vice Pres*
Donald Eilerman, *Treasurer*
EMP: 45
SQ FT: 8,000
SALES (est): 8.6MM **Privately Held**
WEB: www.beemconstruction.com
SIC: 1541 Industrial buildings, new construction; warehouse construction

(G-1708)
BROWN INDUSTRIAL INC
311 W South St (45306-8019)
P.O. Box 74 (45306-0074)
PHONE..................................937 693-3838
Christopher D Brown, *President*
Ruth C Brown, *Corp Secy*
Craig D Brown, *Vice Pres*
Boyce Branscrum, *Manager*
EMP: 45
SQ FT: 32,000
SALES (est): 12.5MM **Privately Held**
WEB: www.brownindustrial.com
SIC: 3713 5012 5084 7692 Truck bodies (motor vehicles); truck bodies; industrial machinery & equipment; packaging machinery & equipment; automotive welding

(G-1709)
SCHNIPPEL CONSTRUCTION INC
302 N Main St (45306-8039)
P.O. Box 477 (45306-0477)
PHONE..................................937 693-3831
Thomas J Schnippel, *President*
Tracy Cooper, *Corp Secy*
Rob Jenkins, *Purch Mgr*
EMP: 30
SQ FT: 10,000
SALES: 3.5MM **Privately Held**
WEB: www.schnippelconstruction.com
SIC: 1522 1541 1542 Multi-family dwelling construction; industrial buildings, new construction; commercial & office building, new construction

Bowerston
Harrison County

(G-1710)
CARRIAGE INN OF BOWERSTON INC
Also Called: Sunny Slope Nursing Home
102 Boyce Dr (44695-9701)
PHONE..................................740 269-8001
Bob Huff, *President*
EMP: 65
SQ FT: 9,700
SALES (est): 3.5MM **Privately Held**
SIC: 8051 Skilled nursing care facilities

Bowling Green
Wood County

(G-1711)
AA GREEN REALTY INC
1045 N Main St Ste 2 (43402-1360)
PHONE..................................419 352-5331
Allen A Green, *President*
EMP: 32
SALES: 1.1MM **Privately Held**
WEB: www.aagreen.com
SIC: 6531 Real estate agent, residential; real estate brokers & agents

(G-1712)
ADVANCED SPECIALTY PRODUCTS
428 Clough St (43402-2914)
P.O. Box 210 (43402-0210)
PHONE..................................419 882-6528
Kenneth T Kujawa, *President*
Eugene Kujawa, *Vice Pres*
▼ EMP: 60
SQ FT: 24,000
SALES (est): 7.8MM **Privately Held**
SIC: 5082 7389 2759 Construction & mining machinery; packaging & labeling services; commercial printing

(G-1713)
AL-MAR LANES
Also Called: Cj's Sports Bar
1010 N Main St (43402-1301)
PHONE..................................419 352-4637
Bill Wammes, *Owner*
EMP: 36
SQ FT: 16,500
SALES: 980K **Privately Held**
SIC: 7933 5941 7389 6531 Ten pin center; sporting goods & bicycle shops; auction, appraisal & exchange services; appraiser, real estate; cocktail lounge; warehousing, self-storage

(G-1714)
ARGO-HYTOS INC
1835 N Research Dr (43402-8548)
P.O. Box 28 (43402-0028)
PHONE..................................419 353-6070
Christian H Kienzle, *President*
Larry Gerken, *Vice Pres*
Patrick Green, *Vice Pres*
George Hartwell, *Engineer*
Walter Bader, *CFO*
▲ EMP: 1200
SQ FT: 6,200
SALES (est): 192.2MM **Privately Held**
WEB: www.argo-hytos.com
SIC: 5084 Hydraulic systems equipment & supplies
PA: Fsp Fluid Systems Partners Holding Ag
Rebmattli 20
Baar ZG
417 632-905

(G-1715)
B G NEWS
Also Called: Bg News
214 W Hall Bgsu (43403-0001)
PHONE..................................419 372-2601
Fax: 419 372-6967
EMP: 50
SALES (est): 2MM **Privately Held**
SIC: 2711 7313 2741 Newspapers-Publishing/Printing Advertising Representative Misc Publishing

(G-1716)
BEHAVRAL CNNCTIONS WD CNTY INC (PA)
280 S Main St (43402-3053)
P.O. Box 29 (43402-0029)
PHONE..................................419 352-5387
Richard Goldberg, *CEO*
Sajid Khan, *President*
Deborah Smith, *CFO*
Michelle Klement, *Treasurer*
Janel Haas, *Admin Sec*
EMP: 171 EST: 1979
SQ FT: 5,500
SALES: 4.8MM **Privately Held**
SIC: 8093 Alcohol clinic, outpatient; drug clinic, outpatient

(G-1717)
BEHAVRAL CNNCTIONS WD CNTY INC
320 W Gypsy Lane Rd Ste A (43402-4571)
PHONE..................................419 352-5387
Richard Goldberg, *Director*
EMP: 26
SALES (corp-wide): 4.8MM **Privately Held**
SIC: 8093 8069 Alcohol clinic, outpatient; drug addiction rehabilitation hospital

PA: Behavioral Connections Of Wood
County, Inc.
280 S Main St
Bowling Green OH 43402
419 352-5387

(G-1718)
BEHAVRAL CNNCTIONS WD CNTY INC
1010 N Prospect St (43402-1335)
P.O. Box 8970, Toledo (43623-0970)
PHONE..............................419 352-5387
John Betts, *Manager*
EMP: 150
SALES (corp-wide): 4.8MM **Privately Held**
SIC: 8093 Mental health clinic, outpatient
PA: Behavioral Connections Of Wood
County, Inc.
280 S Main St
Bowling Green OH 43402
419 352-5387

(G-1719)
BETCO CORPORATION (PA)
400 Van Camp Rd (43402-9062)
PHONE..............................419 241-2156
Paul C Betz, *CEO*
Greg Gangelhoff, *Regional Mgr*
Terry Huber, *COO*
Tom Green, *Vice Pres*
Jeff Iverson, *Vice Pres*
EMP: 200 **EST:** 1950
SQ FT: 90,000
SALES (est): 138.8MM **Privately Held**
WEB: www.betco.com
SIC: 6719 Investment holding companies,
except banks

(G-1720)
BIOTEST PHARMACEUTICALS CORP
Also Called: Biotest Plasma Center
1616 E Wooster St Unit 39 (43402-3478)
PHONE..............................419 819-3068
Ileana Carlisle, *Principal*
EMP: 50
SALES (est): 641.1K **Privately Held**
SIC: 7389 Inspection & testing services

(G-1721)
BOWLING GREEN COOP NURS SCHL
Also Called: Bright Beginnings Preschool
315 S College Dr (43402-4001)
PHONE..............................419 352-8675
Kelly McHugh, *President*
EMP: 32
SALES (est): 44.5K **Privately Held**
SIC: 8351 Preschool center

(G-1722)
BOWLING GREEN LNCLN-MRCURY INC
Also Called: Bowling Green Lincoln Auto SL
1079 N Main St (43402-1302)
PHONE..............................419 352-2553
John Heffernan, *President*
Carl Heffernan Jr, *President*
Kay C Heffernan, *Vice Pres*
Jesse Lane, *Store Mgr*
Lisa Kline, *Finance Mgr*
EMP: 35
SQ FT: 37,000
SALES (est): 13.1MM **Privately Held**
WEB: www.bglmj.com
SIC: 5511 7538 Automobiles, new & used;
general automotive repair shops

(G-1723)
BOWLING GREEN STATE UNIVERSITY
Also Called: Wbgu FM 88 1
120 W Hall (43403-0001)
PHONE..............................419 372-8657
Jon Meinhold, *Manager*
James Barnes, *Manager*
EMP: 60
SALES (corp-wide): 260.3MM **Privately Held**
WEB: www.bgsu.edu
SIC: 4832 8221 Radio broadcasting stations; university

PA: Bowling Green State University
110 Mcfall Ctr
Bowling Green OH 43403
419 372-2311

(G-1724)
BOWLING GREEN STATE UNIVERSITY
Also Called: College of Musical Arts
516 Admin Bldg (43403-0001)
PHONE..............................419 372-2186
Richard Tennell, *Principal*
EMP: 80
SALES (corp-wide): 260.3MM **Privately Held**
WEB: www.bgsu.edu
SIC: 8221 8641 University; civic social & fraternal associations
PA: Bowling Green State University
110 Mcfall Ctr
Bowling Green OH 43403
419 372-2311

(G-1725)
BOWLING GREEN STATE UNIVERSITY
W B G U TV
245 Troup Ave (43402-3158)
PHONE..............................419 372-2700
Patrick Fitzgerald, *Opers-Prdtn-Mfg*
EMP: 45
SALES (corp-wide): 260.3MM **Privately Held**
WEB: www.bgsu.edu
SIC: 4833 8221 Television broadcasting stations; university
PA: Bowling Green State University
110 Mcfall Ctr
Bowling Green OH 43403
419 372-2311

(G-1726)
BROOKDALE SNIOR LVING CMMNTIES
Also Called: Sterling House Bowling Green
121 N Wintergarden Rd Ofc (43402-2199)
PHONE..............................419 354-5300
Cynthia Walsh, *Manager*
EMP: 40
SALES (corp-wide): 4.5B **Publicly Held**
WEB: www.assisted.com
SIC: 8059 Rest home, with health care
HQ: Brookdale Senior Living Communities,
Inc.
6737 W Wa St Ste 2300
Milwaukee WI 53214
414 918-5000

(G-1727)
CENTURY MARKETING CORPORATION (HQ)
Also Called: Centurylabel
12836 S Dixie Hwy (43402-9230)
PHONE..............................419 354-2591
Albert J Caperna, *President*
Craig E Dixon, *President*
William Horner, *Corp Secy*
▼ **EMP:** 150
SQ FT: 58,000
SALES (est): 21.2MM
SALES (corp-wide): 41.9MM **Privately Held**
WEB: www.centurylabel.com
SIC: 2759 2679 5046 5199 Labels & seals: printing; flexographic printing; tags & labels, paper; price marking equipment & supplies; packaging materials; commercial printing, lithographic
PA: Cmc Group, Inc.
12836 S Dixie Hwy
Bowling Green OH 43402
419 354-2591

(G-1728)
CMC DAYMARK CORPORATION
Also Called: Daymark Security Systems
12830 S Dixie Hwy (43402-9697)
PHONE..............................419 354-2591
Jeffery Palmer, *General Mgr*
▲ **EMP:** 140

SALES (est): 24.9MM
SALES (corp-wide): 41.9MM **Privately Held**
WEB: www.centurylabel.com
SIC: 2679 5046 Labels, paper: made from purchased material; commercial equipment
PA: Cmc Group, Inc.
12836 S Dixie Hwy
Bowling Green OH 43402
419 354-2591

(G-1729)
DAYMARK FOOD SAFETY SYSTEMS
12830 S Dixie Hwy Bldg B (43402-9697)
PHONE..............................419 353-2458
Jeff Palmer, *President*
EMP: 140
SALES (est): 12.8MM **Privately Held**
WEB: www.daymarklabel.com
SIC: 8734 Food testing service

(G-1730)
FALCON PLAZA LLC
Also Called: Best Western Falcon Plaza Mtl
1450 E Wooster St Ste 401 (43402-3260)
PHONE..............................419 352-4671
Jacob C Bishop, *President*
EMP: 27 **EST:** 1963
SALES (est): 992.6K **Privately Held**
SIC: 7011 Hotels & motels

(G-1731)
FIRST DEFIANCE FINANCIAL CORP
209 W Poe Rd (43402-1767)
PHONE..............................419 353-8611
EMP: 42 **Publicly Held**
SIC: 6035 6411 Savings institutions, federally chartered; insurance agents, brokers & service
PA: First Defiance Financial Corp.
601 Clinton St
Defiance OH 43512

(G-1732)
GREENLINE FOODS INC (DH)
12700 S Dixie Hwy (43402-9697)
PHONE..............................419 354-1149
George Benson, *CEO*
Thomas Harteis, *Opers Staff*
Michael Salsbury, *Production*
Doug Bargiel, *Engineer*
Mervyn McCulloch, *CFO*
EMP: 59
SQ FT: 10,000
SALES (est): 61.1MM
SALES (corp-wide): 524.2MM **Publicly Held**
SIC: 5148 Vegetables, fresh
HQ: Curation Foods, Inc.
4575 W Main St
Guadalupe CA 93434
800 454-1355

(G-1733)
H & R BLOCK
241 S Main St (43402-3026)
PHONE..............................419 352-9467
Judy McGraw, *Owner*
EMP: 25
SALES (est): 456.4K **Privately Held**
SIC: 7291 Tax return preparation services

(G-1734)
HARTUNG BROTHERS INC
815 S Dunbridge Rd (43402-8720)
PHONE..............................419 352-3000
Neil Schilling, *Branch Mgr*
EMP: 50
SALES (corp-wide): 120MM **Privately Held**
WEB: www.hartungbrothers.com
SIC: 0115 Corn
PA: Hartung Brothers, Inc.
708 Heartland Trl # 2000
Madison WI 53717
608 829-6000

(G-1735)
HCF OF BOWL GREEN CARE CTR INC
850 W Poe Rd (43402-1219)
PHONE..............................419 352-7558

Tom Blakely, *CEO*
EMP: 82
SALES (est): 1.9MM
SALES (corp-wide): 154.8MM **Privately Held**
SIC: 8051 Convalescent home with continuous nursing care
PA: Hcf Management, Inc.
1100 Shawnee Rd
Lima OH 45805
419 999-2010

(G-1736)
HCF OF BOWLING GREEN INC
1021 W Poe Rd (43402-9362)
PHONE..............................419 352-4694
Maranda Hafner, *Director*
Kerri Trabbic, *Food Svc Dir*
Rita Kohler, *Executive*
EMP: 280
SALES (est): 9.4MM
SALES (corp-wide): 154.8MM **Privately Held**
SIC: 8051 Skilled nursing care facilities
PA: Hcf Management, Inc.
1100 Shawnee Rd
Lima OH 45805
419 999-2010

(G-1737)
IOOF HOME OF OHIO INC
139 Eberly Ave (43402-2702)
PHONE..............................419 352-3014
David Taylor, *Branch Mgr*
Charles Miner, *Admin Sec*
EMP: 115
SALES (corp-wide): 2.6MM **Privately Held**
SIC: 8641 Fraternal associations
PA: Ioof Home Of Ohio Inc
404 E Mccreight Ave
Springfield OH 45503
937 399-8631

(G-1738)
ISHIKAWA GASKET AMERICA INC
828 Van Camp Rd (43402-9379)
PHONE..............................419 353-7300
Gary Stasiak, *Manager*
EMP: 190
SALES (corp-wide): 54MM **Privately Held**
WEB: www.ishikawaamerica.com
SIC: 3053 5085 3714 Gaskets & sealing devices; gaskets; motor vehicle parts & accessories
HQ: Ishikawa Gasket America, Inc.
828 Van Camp Rd
Bowling Green OH 43402

(G-1739)
LANE WOOD INDUSTRIES
Also Called: Work Leads To Independence
991 S Main St (43402-4708)
PHONE..............................419 352-5059
Vic Gable, *CEO*
Richard Harris, *Principal*
Virginia Melchert, *Principal*
Patricia K Keul, *Vice Pres*
Melinda Kale, *CFO*
EMP: 350
SALES: 6MM **Privately Held**
SIC: 7361 Employment agencies

(G-1740)
MACK INDUSTRIES
507 Derby Ave (43402-3973)
PHONE..............................419 353-7081
Betsie Mack, *President*
EMP: 173
SALES: 19.3MM
SALES (corp-wide): 170.9MM **Privately Held**
WEB: www.mackconcrete.com
SIC: 3272 5211 1711 Burial vaults, concrete or precast terrazzo; masonry materials & supplies; septic system construction
PA: Mack Industries, Inc.
1321 Industrial Pkwy N # 500
Brunswick OH 44212
330 460-7005

▲ = Import ▼=Export
◆ =Import/Export

(G-1741)
NEWELL BRANDS INC
Also Called: Calphalon
20750 Midstar Dr (43402-9215)
PHONE..........................419 662-2225
Zachary Graffice, *Branch Mgr*
EMP: 200
SALES (corp-wide): 8.6B **Publicly Held**
SIC: 5023 Kitchen tools & utensils
PA: Newell Brands Inc.
        221 River St Ste 13
        Hoboken NJ 07030
        201 610-6600

(G-1742)
NORTHWESTERN WATER &
SEWER DST
12560 Middleton Pike (43402-8289)
P.O. Box 348 (43402-0348)
PHONE..........................419 354-9090
Dick Heyman, *Project Mgr*
Tom Stalter, *Engineer*
Jerry Greiner, *Exec Dir*
Theresa Pollick, *Officer*
Rob Armstrong,
EMP: 49
SQ FT: 30,000
SALES (est): 25MM **Privately Held**
WEB: www.nwwsd.org
SIC: 4952 4941 Sewerage systems; water
supply

(G-1743)
OHIO BILIFFS CRT OFFICERS
ASSN
Also Called: Obaco
1 Court House Sq (43402-2427)
PHONE..........................419 354-9302
Tom Chidester,
EMP: 99
SALES (est): 4.1MM **Privately Held**
SIC: 8611 Business associations

(G-1744)
PHOENIX TECHNOLOGIES INTL
LLC (PA)
Also Called: Pti
1098 Fairview Ave (43402-1233)
PHONE..........................419 353-7738
Shari McCague, *Finance*
Adam Bechstein, *Sales Staff*
Lori Carson, *Sales Staff*
Thomas E Brady, *Mng Member*
Henrey Schworm, *Maintence Staff*
▲ **EMP:** 50
SQ FT: 100,000
SALES (est): 12.3MM **Privately Held**
WEB: www.phoenixtechnologies.net
SIC: 3085 5169 Plastics bottles; synthetic
resins, rubber & plastic materials

(G-1745)
PIONEER PACKING CO
510 Napoleon Rd (43402-4821)
P.O. Box 171 (43402-0171)
PHONE..........................419 352-5283
Brian Contris, *President*
EMP: 70 **EST:** 1945
SQ FT: 30,000
SALES (est): 7.3MM **Privately Held**
WEB: www.pioneeroakland.com
SIC: 5147 Meats & meat products

(G-1746)
POGGEMEYER DESIGN GROUP
INC (PA)
Also Called: PDG
1168 N Main St (43402-1352)
PHONE..........................419 244-8074
Michael Atherine, *Principal*
Jack A Jones, *Chairman*
Larry Carroll, *Treasurer*
Charlene Kerr, *Admin Sec*
EMP: 110
SQ FT: 50,000
SALES (est): 36.2MM **Privately Held**
WEB: www.poggemeyer.com
SIC: 8711 8712 8713 8748 Professional
engineer; architectural services; survey-
ing services; city planning

(G-1747)
R & Y HOLDING
Also Called: Hampton Inn
142 Campbell Hill Rd (43402-3458)
PHONE..........................419 353-3464
Jabbar Youssif, *Owner*
EMP: 25
SALES (est): 1MM **Privately Held**
SIC: 7011 Hotels & motels

(G-1748)
SAM BS RESTAURANT
163 S Main St (43402-2910)
PHONE..........................419 353-2277
Jim Ferell, *Owner*
EMP: 45
SQ FT: 4,000
SALES (est): 1MM **Privately Held**
WEB: www.sambs.com
SIC: 5812 7299 American restaurant; ban-
quet hall facilities

(G-1749)
SPECK SALES INCORPORATED
17746 N Dixie Hwy (43402-9324)
PHONE..........................419 353-8312
Esther Speck, *President*
Bruce Speck, *Vice Pres*
Terry Speck, *Treasurer*
▲ **EMP:** 27
SQ FT: 6,000
SALES (est): 6.7MM **Privately Held**
WEB: www.specksales.com
SIC: 5014 5531 5083 7539 Automobile
tires & tubes; automotive tires; agricultural
machinery; wheel alignment, automotive

(G-1750)
USF HOLLAND LLC
20820 Midstar Dr (43402-8611)
PHONE..........................419 354-6633
Tod Weadock, *Manager*
EMP: 100
SALES (corp-wide): 5B **Publicly Held**
WEB: www.usfc.com
SIC: 4213 Less-than-truckload (LTL) trans-
port
HQ: Usf Holland Llc
        700 S Waverly Rd
        Holland MI 49423
        616 395-5000

(G-1751)
WIRELESS SOURCE ENTPS LLC
16545 Euler Rd (43402-9709)
PHONE..........................419 266-5556
Don Stichler, *Mng Member*
Donald Stichler, *Mng Member*
EMP: 35
SALES: 2MM **Privately Held**
SIC: 8999 Communication services

(G-1752)
WOOD COUNTY CHLD SVCS
ASSN
Also Called: CHILDREN'S RESOURCE CEN-
TER
1045 Klotz Rd (43402-4820)
P.O. Box 738 (43402-0738)
PHONE..........................419 352-7588
Toll Free:........................888 -
J Lafond, *Exec Dir*
Janelle Lafond, *Exec Dir*
Timothy Scherer, *Exec Dir*
EMP: 90
SQ FT: 29,900
SALES (est): 5.2MM **Privately Held**
WEB: www.crc.wcnet.org
SIC: 8322 8361 8093 Child related social
services; residential care; specialty outpa-
tient clinics

(G-1753)
WOOD COUNTY COMMITTEE ON
AGING (PA)
305 N Main St (43402-2424)
PHONE..........................419 353-5661
Sandy Abke, *Site Mgr*
James Stainbrook, *VP Finance*
Denise Niese, *Exec Dir*
Angie Bradford, *Director*
Sandra Gerety, *Director*
EMP: 32

SALES: 3MM **Privately Held**
WEB: www.bowlinggreenhomeinfo.com
SIC: 8322 Senior citizens' center or associa-
tion

(G-1754)
WOOD COUNTY HOSPITAL
ASSOC (PA)
Also Called: WCH
960 W Wooster St (43402-2644)
PHONE..........................419 354-8900
Stanley Korducki, *President*
George Massar, *COO*
Charles Genson, *Ch Radiology*
John EBY, *Vice Pres*
Joe Williford, *Vice Pres*
EMP: 530
SQ FT: 130,000
SALES: 110.4MM **Privately Held**
WEB: www.wch.net
SIC: 8062 General medical & surgical hos-
pitals

(G-1755)
WOOD COUNTY OHIO
1 Court House Sq (43402-2427)
PHONE..........................419 354-9201
James Carter, *Branch Mgr*
EMP: 200 **Privately Held**
WEB: www.woodmrdd.org
SIC: 8322 Probation office
PA: County Of Wood
        1 Courthouse Sq
        Bowling Green OH 43402
        419 354-9100

(G-1756)
WOOD COUNTY OHIO
Also Called: Wood Haven Health Care
1965 E Gypsy Lane Rd (43402-9396)
PHONE..........................419 353-8411
David Cecil, *Administration*
EMP: 125
SQ FT: 400,000
SALES (est): 7.7MM **Privately Held**
WEB: www.woodmrdd.org
SIC: 8051 9111 Convalescent home with
continuous nursing care; county supervi-
sors' & executives' offices
PA: County Of Wood
        1 Courthouse Sq
        Bowling Green OH 43402
        419 354-9100

(G-1757)
WOOD COUNTY OHIO
Also Called: Wood County Health Department
1840 E Gypsy Lane Rd (43402-9173)
PHONE..........................419 353-6914
Lori Heideman, *Comms Mgr*
Pam Butler, *Director*
Nancy Levy, *Admin Asst*
Kathy Teeple, *Nurse*
EMP: 61 **Privately Held**
WEB: www.woodmrdd.org
SIC: 9431 8399 ; health systems agency
PA: County Of Wood
        1 Courthouse Sq
        Bowling Green OH 43402
        419 354-9100

(G-1758)
WOOD COUNTY OHIO
Also Called: Community Emplyment Svcs WD
Ln
705 W Newton Rd (43402-9026)
PHONE..........................419 352-5059
Vic Gable, *Director*
EMP: 30 **Privately Held**
WEB: www.woodmrdd.org
SIC: 7361 8331 Placement agencies; job
training & vocational rehabilitation serv-
ices
PA: County Of Wood
        1 Courthouse Sq
        Bowling Green OH 43402
        419 354-9100

(G-1759)
WOOD HEALTH COMPANY LLC
745 Haskins Rd Ste B (43402-1600)
PHONE..........................419 353-7069
Standley Korducki, *President*
EMP: 100
SALES (est): 765.5K **Privately Held**
SIC: 8011 Medical centers

(G-1760)
WRYNECK DEVELOPMENT LLC
Also Called: Stone Ridge Golf Club
1553 Muirfield Dr (43402-5230)
PHONE..........................419 354-2535
Joe Ghesquiere, *General Mgr*
Joann Whittaker, *Accountant*
Kara Higdon, *Sales Staff*
Paul E Thayer, *Mng Member*
Jonathon Lenox, *Director*
EMP: 25
SQ FT: 20,000
SALES (est): 5MM **Privately Held**
SIC: 6552 Land subdividers & developers,
residential

Bradford
Miami County

(G-1761)
DICK LAVY TRUCKING INC
8848 State Route 121 (45308-9631)
PHONE..........................937 448-2104
Richard Lavy, *President*
Ray Lavy, *Vice Pres*
Steve Burke, *Maintenance Dir*
Heather Applegate, *Opers Mgr*
Krista Wulber, *Human Res Dir*
EMP: 243
SQ FT: 18,000
SALES (est): 48.1MM **Privately Held**
WEB: www.dicklavytrucking.com
SIC: 4213 4731 Contract haulers; freight
transportation arrangement

(G-1762)
METCON LTD (PA)
6730 Greentree Rd (45308-9756)
PHONE..........................937 447-9200
Glen Garber, *President*
Kirby Crist, *Vice Pres*
Simon King, *Vice Pres*
Anthony Miller, *Vice Pres*
Kidron Crist, *Supervisor*
EMP: 33
SALES (est): 9.7MM **Privately Held**
SIC: 1771 Foundation & footing contractor

Bradner
Wood County

(G-1763)
AMERICAN WARMING AND
VENT
120 Plin St (43406-7735)
P.O. Box 677 (43406-0677)
PHONE..........................419 288-2703
Stewart E Reed, *President*
John Reed, *President*
EMP: 75
SALES (est): 21.2MM **Privately Held**
SIC: 5031 5039 Doors & windows; air
ducts, sheet metal

(G-1764)
DAVIDSON TRUCKING INC
1227 Bowling Green Rd E (43406-9789)
P.O. Box 162 (43406-0162)
PHONE..........................419 288-2318
Dan Davidson, *President*
Jessica Davidson, *Corp Secy*
EMP: 25
SALES (est): 3.1MM **Privately Held**
SIC: 4212 4213 Local Trucking Operator
Trucking Operator-Nonlocal

Brecksville
Cuyahoga County

(G-1765)
A SAINATO ENTERPRISES INC
Also Called: Jmax Enterprises
11160 Snowville Rd (44141-3402)
PHONE..........................216 795-5167
Alex Sainato, *CEO*
EMP: 25

GEOGRAPHIC

SALES (est): 3MM **Privately Held**
SIC: 7389 Personal service agents, brokers & bureaus

(G-1766)
AB RESOURCES LLC
6802 W Snowville Rd Ste E (44141-3296)
PHONE..........................440 922-1098
Gordon O Yonel,
EMP: 25
SQ FT: 7,500
SALES (est): 3.5MM **Privately Held**
SIC: 1311 Crude petroleum & natural gas production

(G-1767)
AHOLA CORPORATION
6820 W Snowville Rd (44141-3214)
PHONE..........................440 717-7620
Mark Ahola, *President*
Cheryl Laskowski, *General Mgr*
Paula Tresger, *Sales Associate*
Jeffrey B Ahola, *Chief Mktg Ofcr*
Eve Serrano, *Executive Asst*
EMP: 60
SQ FT: 21,000
SALES (est): 6.9MM **Privately Held**
WEB: www.ahola.com
SIC: 8721 Payroll accounting service

(G-1768)
ANGEL CARE INC
7033 Oakes Rd (44141-2737)
PHONE..........................440 736-7267
Peggy Haladyna, *President*
EMP: 25
SALES (est): 800K **Privately Held**
SIC: 8351 Child day care services

(G-1769)
APPLIED MEDICAL TECHNOLOGY INC
Also Called: Amt
8006 Katherine Blvd (44141-4202)
PHONE..........................440 717-4000
George J Picha, *President*
Robert J Crump, *Director*
EMP: 30
SQ FT: 14,000
SALES (est): 9.5MM **Privately Held**
SIC: 3841 3083 8731 Surgical & medical instruments; laminated plastics plate & sheet; medical research, commercial

(G-1770)
ARISE INCORPORATED
7000 S Edgerton Rd # 100 (44141-3199)
PHONE..........................440 746-8860
William Ramonas, *President*
EMP: 30
SALES (est): 2.9MM
SALES (corp-wide): 257.2K **Privately Held**
WEB: www.globalriskconsultants.com
SIC: 1711 Boiler maintenance contractor
HQ: Tuv Sud America Inc.
10 Centennial Dr Ste 207
Peabody MA 01960
978 573-2500

(G-1771)
BPI INFRMTION SYSTEMS OHIO INC
6055 W Snowville Rd (44141-3245)
PHONE..........................440 717-4112
Gary Ellis, *President*
George Stoll, *Vice Pres*
Cheri Wilmoth, *Accounts Mgr*
Joyce Ellis, *Admin Sec*
EMP: 50
SQ FT: 12,000
SALES (est): 6.7MM **Privately Held**
WEB: www.bpiohio.com
SIC: 7378 7373 Computer maintenance & repair; computer integrated systems design; systems engineering, computer related; value-added resellers, computer systems

(G-1772)
BRECKSVLLE HALTHCARE GROUP INC
Also Called: Oaks of Brecksville, The
8757 Brecksville Rd (44141-1919)
PHONE..........................440 546-0643

Repchick S George, *President*
EMP: 98
SALES (est): 2.6MM **Privately Held**
SIC: 8093 8099 Rehabilitation center, outpatient treatment; physical examination & testing services

(G-1773)
CINTAS CORPORATION NO 2
55 Andrews Cir Ste 1a (44141-3270)
PHONE..........................440 746-7777
EMP: 88
SALES (corp-wide): 6.4B **Publicly Held**
SIC: 7218 Industrial uniform supply
HQ: Cintas Corporation No. 2
6800 Cintas Blvd
Mason OH 45040

(G-1774)
CITY OF BRECKSVILLE
Also Called: Brecksville City Service Dept
9069 Brecksville Rd (44141-2367)
PHONE..........................440 526-1384
Virginia Price, *General Mgr*
Robert Pech, *Director*
EMP: 40 **Privately Held**
SIC: 1611 Highway & street maintenance
PA: City Of Brecksville
9069 Brecksville Rd
Cleveland OH 44141
440 526-4351

(G-1775)
CITY OF BRECKSVILLE
Also Called: Brecksville Community Center
1 Community Dr (44141-2326)
PHONE..........................440 526-4109
Padmini Patnaik, *Finance Mgr*
Tom Tupa, *Director*
Bob Pliske, *Director*
EMP: 80 **Privately Held**
SIC: 8322 7991 Community center; physical fitness facilities
PA: City Of Brecksville
9069 Brecksville Rd
Cleveland OH 44141
440 526-4351

(G-1776)
CLEVELAND METROPARKS
Also Called: Sleepy Hollow Golf Course
9445 Brecksville Rd (44141-2711)
PHONE..........................440 526-4285
John Fiander, *Manager*
EMP: 60
SALES (corp-wide): 57.3MM **Privately Held**
WEB: www.clemetparks.com
SIC: 7992 Public golf courses
PA: Cleveland Metroparks
4101 Fulton Pkwy
Cleveland OH 44144
216 635-3200

(G-1777)
CLINICAL TECHNOLOGY INC
7005 S Edgerton Rd (44141-4203)
PHONE..........................440 526-0160
Dennis Forchione, *President*
Dennis A Forchione, *President*
Dominic Verrilli, *Vice Pres*
Michael Forchione, *Treasurer*
EMP: 40
SQ FT: 11,000
SALES (est): 15.1MM **Privately Held**
SIC: 5047 Patient monitoring equipment

(G-1778)
CSI MANAGED CARE INC
Also Called: Csi Network Services
6955 Treeline Dr Ste A (44141-3373)
PHONE..........................440 717-1700
Ed Rivalsky, *CEO*
EMP: 99
SALES (est): 2.4MM **Privately Held**
SIC: 8059 Nursing & personal care

(G-1779)
DEERFIELD ESTATES INC (PA)
7000 S Edgerton Rd # 108 (44141-3172)
PHONE..........................440 838-1400
Earl Linden, *President*
Marc Rosenthal, *Human Res Dir*
EMP: 48

SALES (est): 2MM **Privately Held**
SIC: 6531 Real estate brokers & agents; real estate managers

(G-1780)
ELLISON TECHNOLOGIES INC
6955 Treeline Dr Ste J (44141-3373)
PHONE..........................440 546-1920
Matt Bujoll, *Branch Mgr*
Kurt Schaldach, *Manager*
EMP: 30
SALES (corp-wide): 45.9B **Privately Held**
WEB: www.ellisonmw.com
SIC: 5084 Machine tools & metalworking machinery
HQ: Ellison Technologies, Inc.
9912 Pioneer Blvd
Santa Fe Springs CA 90670
562 949-8311

(G-1781)
GLOBAL RISK CONSULTANTS CORP
7000 S Edgerton Rd # 100 (44141-3172)
PHONE..........................440 746-8861
Doris Barnhouse, *Administration*
EMP: 31
SALES (corp-wide): 257.2K **Privately Held**
WEB: www.globalriskconsultants.com
SIC: 8711 Consulting engineer
HQ: Global Risk Consultants Corp.
100 Walnut Ave Ste 501
Clark NJ 07066
732 680-1370

(G-1782)
HASTINGS WATER WORKS INC (PA)
10331 Brecksville Rd (44141-3335)
PHONE..........................440 832-7700
David J Hastings, *President*
Mike Johnson, *Manager*
Brent Stanley, *Manager*
Scott Waite, *Director*
EMP: 35
SQ FT: 17,000
SALES (est): 5.8MM **Privately Held**
WEB: www.hastingswaterworks.com
SIC: 7389 Swimming pool & hot tub service & maintenance

(G-1783)
HOUSE OF LA ROSE CLEVELAND
6745 Southpointe Pkwy (44141-3267)
PHONE..........................440 746-7500
Thomas A La Rose, *Ch of Bd*
Joseph F La Rose, *Vice Ch Bd*
James P La Rose, *President*
Peter C La Rose, *Vice Pres*
Mark Yakubowski, *CFO*
EMP: 210 EST: 1979
SQ FT: 153,000
SALES (est): 105MM **Privately Held**
WEB: www.la-rose.com
SIC: 5181 Beer & other fermented malt liquors

(G-1784)
HUDEC DENTAL ASSOCIATES INC (PA)
6700 W Snowville Rd (44141-3285)
PHONE..........................216 485-5788
John Hudec, *Principal*
John A Hudec, *Principal*
EMP: 70
SALES (est): 12.1MM **Privately Held**
SIC: 8021 Dentists' office

(G-1785)
JERSEY CENTRAL PWR & LIGHT CO
Also Called: Firstenergy
6896 Miller Rd (44141-3222)
PHONE..........................440 546-8609
Dennis Chack, *President*
Thedore Rader III, *Supervisor*
Lori Sombati, *Supervisor*
Gregory Gawlik, *Director*
EMP: 980
SQ FT: 48,531 **Publicly Held**
WEB: www.jersey-central-power-light.monmouth.n
SIC: 4911 Distribution, electric power

HQ: Jersey Central Power & Light Company
76 S Main St
Akron OH 44308
800 736-3402

(G-1786)
JOHNSON CNTRLS SEC SLTIONS LLC
6650 W Snowville Rd Ste K (44141-4301)
PHONE..........................440 262-1084
Mark Altsman, *General Mgr*
EMP: 65
SQ FT: 4,000 **Privately Held**
WEB: www.adt.com
SIC: 7382 5063 Burglar alarm maintenance & monitoring; fire alarm maintenance & monitoring; electrical apparatus & equipment
HQ: Johnson Controls Security Solutions Llc
6600 Congress Ave
Boca Raton FL 33487
561 264-2071

(G-1787)
JONES LANG LSALLE AMERICAS INC
Also Called: J.L.L.
9921 Brecksville Rd (44141-3201)
PHONE..........................216 447-5276
Ed Prabucki, *General Mgr*
EMP: 37
SALES (corp-wide): 16.3B **Publicly Held**
WEB: www.am.joneslanglasalle.com
SIC: 6531 Real estate agents & managers
HQ: Jones Lang Lasalle Americas, Inc.
200 E Randolph St # 4300
Chicago IL 60601
312 782-5800

(G-1788)
LUCE SMITH & SCOTT INC
Also Called: Allstate
6860 W Snwlle Rd Ste 110 (44141)
PHONE..........................440 746-1700
William Killea, *CEO*
Daniel Skaljac, *President*
Janice M Dwyer, *Vice Pres*
Greg Skaljac, *Vice Pres*
EMP: 28 EST: 1923
SALES: 2.8MM **Privately Held**
WEB: www.lucesmithscott.com
SIC: 6411 Insurance agents, brokers & service

(G-1789)
MEDIQUANT INC (PA)
6900 S Edgerton Rd # 100 (44141-3193)
PHONE..........................440 746-2300
Tony Papalera, *President*
EMP: 30
SALES (est): 20.1MM **Privately Held**
WEB: www.mediquant.com
SIC: 5045 Computer software

(G-1790)
MICHAEL BENZA AND ASSOC INC
6860 W Snowville Rd # 100 (44141-3279)
P.O. Box 469, Richfield (44286-0469)
PHONE..........................440 526-4206
EMP: 26
SALES (est): 3.5MM **Privately Held**
SIC: 8711 Engineering Services

(G-1791)
NATIONAL STAFFING GROUP LTD
8221 Brecksville Rd # 202 (44141-1390)
P.O. Box 41444 (44141-0444)
PHONE..........................440 546-0800
Kim Barnett, *President*
EMP: 42
SALES (est): 1.8MM **Privately Held**
WEB: www.nsgl.com
SIC: 7361 Executive placement

(G-1792)
NEOPOST USA INC
6670 W Snowville Rd Ste 2 (44141-4300)
PHONE..........................440 526-3196
John Moss, *Manager*
EMP: 25

SALES (corp-wide): 53.4MM **Privately Held**
WEB: www.neopostinc.com
SIC: 5044 Office equipment
HQ: Neopost Usa Inc.
478 Wheelers Farms Rd
Milford CT 06461
203 301-3400

(G-1793)
NGN ELECTRIC CORP
10310 Brecksville Rd (44141-3338)
P.O. Box 1119, Hudson (44236-6319)
PHONE..................................330 923-2777
Gene Piscitello, *President*
▼ EMP: 40
SALES (est): 4.7MM **Privately Held**
WEB: www.ngnelectric.com
SIC: 1731 General electrical contractor

(G-1794)
NVR INC
6770 W Snowville Rd 100 (44141-3212)
PHONE..................................440 584-4250
Michael Gould, *President*
EMP: 36 **Publicly Held**
SIC: 1521 New construction, single-family houses
PA: Nvr, Inc.
11700 Plaza America Dr # 500
Reston VA 20190

(G-1795)
PAUL DENNIS
Also Called: Chippewa Place
7005 Stadium Dr Ofc (44141-1843)
PHONE..................................440 746-8600
Paul Dennis, *Owner*
EMP: 30
SQ FT: 28,910
SALES (est): 1.5MM **Privately Held**
SIC: 8361 6513 Home for the aged; apartment building operators

(G-1796)
PITNEY BOWES INC
6910 Treeline Dr Ste C (44141-3366)
P.O. Box 75007, Fort Thomas KY (41075-0007)
PHONE..................................203 426-7025
Brian Philbin, *Director*
EMP: 75
SALES (corp-wide): 3.5B **Publicly Held**
SIC: 3579 7359 Postage meters; business machine & electronic equipment rental services
PA: Pitney Bowes Inc.
3001 Summer St Ste 3
Stamford CT 06905
203 356-5000

(G-1797)
PNC BANK NATIONAL ASSOCIATION
National City Bank
6750 Miller Rd (44141-3239)
PHONE..................................440 546-6760
Lynne Sheley Baker, *Branch Mgr*
EMP: 77
SALES (corp-wide): 19.9B **Publicly Held**
WEB: www.allegiantbank.com
SIC: 6141 Personal credit institutions
HQ: Pnc Bank, National Association
222 Delaware Ave
Wilmington DE 19801
877 762-2000

(G-1798)
POMEROY IT SOLUTIONS SLS INC
6670 W Snowville Rd Ste 3 (44141-4300)
PHONE..................................440 717-1364
Hal Loughry, *General Mgr*
EMP: 25 **Privately Held**
WEB: www.pomeroy.com
SIC: 1731 7373 8243 7378 Computer installation; voice, data & video wiring contractor; computer integrated systems design; systems software development services; computer systems analysis & design; data processing schools; computer maintenance & repair; computer rental & leasing; computer peripheral equipment

HQ: Pomeroy It Solutions Sales Company, Inc.
1020 Petersburg Rd
Hebron KY 41048

(G-1799)
PROMERUS LLC
9921 Brecksville Rd (44141-3201)
PHONE..................................440 922-0300
Nobuaki Sugimoto, *CEO*
Robert Shick, *President*
Geert Casteleyn, *CFO*
EMP: 42
SQ FT: 40,000
SALES (est): 7.1MM
SALES (corp-wide): 1.9B **Privately Held**
WEB: www.promerus.com
SIC: 8731 Electronic research
HQ: Sumitomo Bakelite North America Holding, Inc.
46820 Magellan Dr Ste C
Novi MI 48377
248 313-7000

(G-1800)
PROVATO LLC
8748 Brecksville Rd # 125 (44141-1988)
PHONE..................................440 546-0768
Kevin Marquirt, *President*
EMP: 50
SQ FT: 1,400
SALES (est): 1.6MM **Privately Held**
SIC: 8999 Information bureau

(G-1801)
REGIONAL INCOME TAX AGENCY (PA)
10107 Brecksville Rd (44141-3205)
PHONE..................................800 860-7482
Amy L Arrighi, *Counsel*
Liam Malue, *Supervisor*
Thomas Wojnarowski, *CIO*
Rick Carbone, *Exec Dir*
EMP: 150 EST: 1971
SQ FT: 33,000
SALES (est): 14.2MM **Privately Held**
WEB: www.ritaohio.com
SIC: 7291 Tax return preparation services

(G-1802)
RICHFIELD FINANCIAL GROUP INC
8223 Brecksville Rd # 201 (44141-1367)
PHONE..................................440 546-4288
Maura Prentiss, *Administration*
EMP: 30
SALES (est): 3MM **Privately Held**
SIC: 6411 Insurance brokers

(G-1803)
SABER HEALTHCARE GROUP LLC
Also Called: Oaks of Brecksville, The
8757 Brecksville Rd (44141-1919)
PHONE..................................440 546-0643
Sue Doherty, *Administration*
EMP: 36
SALES (corp-wide): 157.7MM **Privately Held**
PA: Saber Healthcare Group, L.L.C.
26691 Richmond Rd Frnt
Bedford OH 44146
216 292-5706

(G-1804)
SCG FIELDS LLC
10303 Brecksville Rd (44141-3335)
PHONE..................................440 546-1200
Michael Sherman, *CEO*
Joseph Smith, *COO*
Christopher Franks, *Director*
EMP: 50
SALES (est): 242.1K **Privately Held**
SIC: 1629 Athletic field construction

(G-1805)
SIEMENS INDUSTRY INC
Also Called: Rapistan Systems
6930 Treeline Dr Ste A (44141-3367)
PHONE..................................440 526-2770
Charles McBride, *Manager*
EMP: 30

SALES (corp-wide): 95B **Privately Held**
WEB: www.sea.siemens.com
SIC: 5084 3535 Industrial machinery & equipment; conveyors & conveying equipment
HQ: Siemens Industry, Inc.
1000 Deerfield Pkwy
Buffalo Grove IL 60089
800 743-6367

(G-1806)
SOFTWARE ANSWERS INC
6770 W Snowville Rd 200 (44141-3212)
PHONE..................................440 526-0095
Paul Chaffee, *President*
Scott Miller, *Vice Pres*
Lia Hardy, *QA Dir*
Cindy Chaffee, *Human Resources*
Christopher Aiello, *Info Tech Mgr*
EMP: 30
SQ FT: 7,700
SALES (est): 3.3MM **Privately Held**
SIC: 7371 Computer software development

(G-1807)
SPORTS SURFACES CNSTR LLC
Also Called: Sports Construction Group
10303 Brecksville Rd (44141-3335)
PHONE..................................440 546-1200
Ed Berichon, *Controller*
Steve Hines, *Asst Controller*
Jim Henry, *Sales Mgr*
Joel Desguin, *Sales Staff*
Keith Froelich, *Sales Staff*
EMP: 25
SALES (est): 6.3MM **Privately Held**
SIC: 1629 Athletic field construction

(G-1808)
TRUE NORTH ENERGY LLC (PA)
10346 Brecksville Rd (44141-3338)
PHONE..................................877 245-9336
Mark E Lyden, *President*
Ben Sunderlin, *General Mgr*
Jaime Martinez, *District Mgr*
Ryan Howard, *COO*
Keith A McIntyre, *Vice Pres*
EMP: 35
SQ FT: 18,000
SALES (est): 265.4MM **Privately Held**
WEB: www.case.edu
SIC: 5541 5172 Filling stations, gasoline; gasoline; engine fuels & oils; service station supplies, petroleum

---

Brewster
Stark County

(G-1809)
BREWSTER PARKE INC
Also Called: Brewster Convalescent Center
264 Mohican St Ne (44613-1126)
PHONE..................................330 767-4179
David E Childs, *President*
Cheryl Childs, *Vice Pres*
EMP: 84
SQ FT: 9,000
SALES (est): 6.2MM **Privately Held**
SIC: 8059 8052 8051 Convalescent home; intermediate care facilities; skilled nursing care facilities

(G-1810)
HEALTHSPAN INTEGRATED CARE
Also Called: Kaiser Foundation Health Plan
360 Wabash Ave N (44613-1042)
PHONE..................................330 767-3436
Charles Cather, *Principal*
EMP: 29
SALES (corp-wide): 4.7B **Privately Held**
SIC: 6324 Hospital & medical service plans
HQ: Healthspan Integrated Care
1001 Lakeside Ave E # 1200
Cleveland OH 44114
216 621-5600

(G-1811)
MIKE MORRIS
Also Called: Five Star Power Clg & Pntg
505 Wabash Ave N (44613-1045)
PHONE..................................330 767-4122

Mike Morris, *Owner*
EMP: 28
SQ FT: 5,000
SALES (est): 1.4MM **Privately Held**
SIC: 1799 1721 Exterior cleaning, including sandblasting; exterior commercial painting contractor; interior commercial painting contractor; industrial painting

(G-1812)
WHEELING & LAKE ERIE RLWY CO (HQ)
100 1st St Se (44613-1202)
P.O. Box 96 (44613-0096)
PHONE..................................330 767-3401
Larry R Parsons, *CEO*
William Callison, *President*
Jonathan Chastek, *Exec VP*
James I Northcraft, *Vice Pres*
Mike Mokodean, *Vice Pres*
EMP: 303
SQ FT: 33,000
SALES: 100.6MM
SALES (corp-wide): 103MM **Privately Held**
WEB: www.wlerwy.com
SIC: 4011 Railroads, line-haul operating
PA: Wheeling Corporation
100 1st St Se
Brewster OH 44613
330 767-3401

Bridgeport
Belmont County

(G-1813)
BELMONT CNTY FIRE & SQUAD OFFI
69604 Sunset Hts (43912-1688)
PHONE..................................740 312-5058
Allan Ketzell III, *President*
Jim Delman, *Treasurer*
EMP: 30
SALES (est): 400.3K **Privately Held**
SIC: 0851 Fire fighting services, forest

(G-1814)
BRIDGEPORT AUTO PARTS INC (PA)
890 National Rd (43912-1444)
P.O. Box 390 (43912-0390)
PHONE..................................740 635-0441
Tim Conway, *President*
Timothy A Conway, *President*
EMP: 35
SQ FT: 19,000
SALES (est): 3.3MM **Privately Held**
SIC: 5013 5531 Automotive supplies & parts; automotive parts

(G-1815)
COMCAST CORPORATION
908 National Rd (43912-1532)
PHONE..................................740 633-3437
Paul Luicart, *Principal*
Michael King, *Opers Staff*
EMP: 57
SALES (corp-wide): 94.5B **Publicly Held**
WEB: www.comcast.com
SIC: 4841 Cable television services
PA: Comcast Corporation
1701 Jfk Blvd
Philadelphia PA 19103
215 286-1700

(G-1816)
ERB ELECTRIC CO
500 Hall St Ste 1 (43912-1324)
PHONE..................................740 633-5055
Tom Knight, *President*
Wayne McCracken, *COO*
Marianne Knight, *Vice Pres*
John Satkowski, *Foreman/Supr*
Paul Simmons, *Engineer*
EMP: 200 EST: 1958
SALES (est): 30.9MM **Privately Held**
WEB: www.erbelectric.com
SIC: 1731 General electrical contractor

(G-1817)
HEALTH CARE RTREMENT CORP AMER
Also Called: Heartland - Lansing
300 Commercial Dr (43912)
PHONE..............................740 635-4600
Jamie Dangelo, *Manager*
EMP: 100
SALES (corp-wide): 2.4B **Publicly Held**
WEB: www.hrc-manorcare.com
SIC: 8051 Skilled nursing care facilities
HQ: Health Care And Retirement Corporation Of America
333 N Summit St Ste 103
Toledo OH 43604
419 252-5500

(G-1818)
LASH PAVING INC
70700 Swingle Rd (43912-8800)
P.O. Box 296, Colerain (43916-0296)
PHONE..............................740 635-4335
David Lash, *President*
Brian Barrato, *Vice Pres*
Daniel Lash, *Vice Pres*
EMP: 70
SALES (est): 8.4MM **Privately Held**
SIC: 1611 Contractor - Highway & Street Construction

Brilliant
Jefferson County

(G-1819)
AMERICAN ELECTRIC POWER CO INC
306 County Road 7e (43913-1079)
PHONE..............................740 598-4164
Dwight Pittenger, *Branch Mgr*
EMP: 46
SALES (corp-wide): 16.2B **Publicly Held**
SIC: 4911 Distribution, electric power
PA: American Electric Power Company, Inc.
1 Riverside Plz Fl 1 # 1
Columbus OH 43215
614 716-1000

(G-1820)
BUCKEYE POWER INC
Also Called: Cardinal Plant
306 County Road 7e (43913-1079)
PHONE..............................740 598-6534
Doug Shearn, *Manager*
EMP: 300
SALES (corp-wide): 708.2MM **Privately Held**
WEB: www.buckeyepower.com
SIC: 4911 Generation, electric power
PA: Buckeye Power, Inc.
6677 Busch Blvd
Columbus OH 43229
614 781-0573

(G-1821)
CARDINAL OPERATING COMPANY
Also Called: American Electric Power
306 County Road 7e (43913-1079)
PHONE..............................740 598-4164
Douglas Shem, *Manager*
Gale Nation, *Manager*
Eli Mamula, *Supervisor*
EMP: 250 **Privately Held**
SIC: 4911 Electric services

(G-1822)
FRALEY & SCHILLING INC
708 Dandy Ln (43913)
PHONE..............................740 598-4118
Jon Patton, *Manager*
EMP: 115
SALES (corp-wide): 77.5MM **Privately Held**
SIC: 4213 4212 Contract haulers; local trucking, without storage
PA: Fraley & Schilling Inc
1920 S State Road 3
Rushville IN 46173
765 932-5977

(G-1823)
TRUGREEN LIMITED PARTNERSHIP
Also Called: Tru Green-Chemlawn
198 Penn St (43913-1232)
P.O. Box 157 (43913)
PHONE..............................740 598-4724
EMP: 30
SALES (corp-wide): 3.3B **Privately Held**
SIC: 0782 Lawn/Garden Services
PA: Trugreen Limited Partnership
860 Ridge Lake Blvd G02
Memphis TN 38138
901 681-1800

(G-1824)
UNITED PARCEL SERVICE INC OH
Also Called: UPS
500 Labelle St (43913-1165)
PHONE..............................740 598-4293
EMP: 158
SALES (corp-wide): 71.8B **Publicly Held**
WEB: www.upsscs.com
SIC: 4215 Parcel delivery, vehicular
HQ: United Parcel Service, Inc. (Oh)
55 Glenlake Pkwy
Atlanta GA 30328
404 828-6000

Bristolville
Trumbull County

(G-1825)
FINLAW CONSTRUCTION INC
5213 State Route 45 (44402-9608)
PHONE..............................330 889-2074
EMP: 25
SALES (est): 2.9MM **Privately Held**
SIC: 1623 Water/Sewer/Utility Construction

(G-1826)
K M B INC
Also Called: King Bros Feed & Supply
1306 State Route 88 (44402-8743)
P.O. Box 240 (44402-0240)
PHONE..............................330 889-3451
Marlene King, *President*
Rex King, *Vice Pres*
EMP: 35 EST: 1956
SQ FT: 4,200
SALES (est): 6.2MM **Privately Held**
WEB: www.kingbrosracing.com
SIC: 3273 5211 5261 5191 Ready-mixed concrete; lumber & other building materials; fertilizer; feed; concrete products

Broadview Heights
Cuyahoga County

(G-1827)
CLEVELAND CLINIC FOUNDATION
Also Called: Broadview Heights
2001 E Royalton Rd (44147-2811)
PHONE..............................440 986-4000
Mark Lang, *Manager*
EMP: 2656
SALES (corp-wide): 8.9B **Privately Held**
SIC: 8062 General medical & surgical hospitals
PA: The Cleveland Clinic Foundation
9500 Euclid Ave
Cleveland OH 44195
216 636-8335

(G-1828)
CLINICL OTCMS MNGMNT SYST LLC
Also Called: Coms Interactive
9200 S Hills Blvd Ste 200 (44147-3520)
PHONE..............................330 650-9900
Edward J Tromczynski, *CEO*
Libby Manthei, *Opers Staff*
Bill Stuart, *CFO*
Terry Sullivan, *Chief Mktg Ofcr*
Nichole Fetterman, *Manager*
EMP: 59
SQ FT: 1,400

SALES (est): 8.7MM
SALES (corp-wide): 77.3MM **Privately Held**
WEB: www.comsllc.com
SIC: 7372 Business oriented computer software
HQ: Pointclickcare Technologies Inc
5570 Explorer Dr
Mississauga ON L4W 0
905 858-8885

(G-1829)
CT MEDICAL ELECTRONICS CO
1 Corporation Ctr (44147-3265)
PHONE..............................440 526-3551
Dennis Forchione, *President*
EMP: 40
SALES (est): 3.3MM **Privately Held**
SIC: 5047 Medical & hospital equipment

(G-1830)
DANA LAUREN SALON & SPA
8076 Broadview Rd (44147-1204)
PHONE..............................440 262-1092
Dana Lauren,
EMP: 30 EST: 2009
SALES (est): 445.2K **Privately Held**
SIC: 7231 Hairdressers

(G-1831)
DEUTSCHE BANK SECURITIES INC
3152 Oakwood Trl (44147-3918)
PHONE..............................440 237-0188
Charles Dunham, *Branch Mgr*
EMP: 43
SALES (corp-wide): 13.6B **Privately Held**
SIC: 6211 Brokers, security
HQ: Deutsche Bank Securities Inc.
60 Wall St Bsmt 1
New York NY 10005
212 250-2500

(G-1832)
FAMILY HERITG LF INSUR CO AMER (HQ)
6001 E Royalton Rd # 200 (44147-3527)
P.O. Box 470608 (44147-0608)
PHONE..............................440 922-5200
Howard Lewis, *CEO*
Tracey Bell, *President*
Dave Deliz, *President*
Brandy Khamesi, *President*
Ken Matson, *President*
EMP: 40
SQ FT: 16,000
SALES (est): 48.3MM
SALES (corp-wide): 4.3B **Publicly Held**
SIC: 6311 Life insurance
PA: Torchmark Corporation
3700 S Stonebridge Dr
Mckinney TX 75070
972 569-4000

(G-1833)
FLEXNOVA INC
8452 Windsor Way (44147-1788)
PHONE..............................216 288-6961
Steve Rossi, *President*
EMP: 26
SALES (corp-wide): 2.9MM **Privately Held**
SIC: 7371 Computer software development & applications
PA: Flexnova, Inc.
6100 Oak Tree Blvd
Cleveland OH 44131
216 288-6961

(G-1834)
GREAT LAKES ENERGY
332 Clearview Ct (44147-3091)
PHONE..............................440 582-4662
EMP: 50
SALES (est): 3.9MM **Privately Held**
SIC: 4911 Electric Services

(G-1835)
HARBORSIDE CLVELAND LTD PARTNR
Also Called: Harborside Healthcarebroadview
2801 E Royalton Rd (44147-2827)
PHONE..............................440 526-4770
Joe Garrett, *Administration*
EMP: 150 **Publicly Held**

SIC: 8051 Convalescent home with continuous nursing care
HQ: Harborside Of Cleveland Limited Partnership
101 Sun Ave Ne
Albuquerque NM 87109
505 821-3355

(G-1836)
HMT ASSOCIATES INC
335 Treeworth Blvd (44147-2985)
PHONE..............................216 369-0109
Patti Conti, *Principal*
Jenny Williams, *Controller*
Rick Einhaus, *IT/INT Sup*
EMP: 43
SALES (est): 7.4MM **Privately Held**
SIC: 8742 Marketing consulting services

(G-1837)
KONICA MINOLTA BUSINESS SOLUTI
9150 S Hills Blvd Ste 100 (44147-3511)
PHONE..............................440 546-5795
Chris Kaskey, *Manager*
EMP: 75
SALES (corp-wide): 9.6B **Privately Held**
WEB: www.konicabt.com
SIC: 5044 Photocopy machines
HQ: Konica Minolta Business Solutions U.S.A., Inc.
100 Williams Dr
Ramsey NJ 07446
201 825-4000

(G-1838)
MUTUAL SHAREHOLDER SVCS LLC
8000 Town Centre Dr # 400 (44147-4030)
PHONE..............................440 922-0067
Dave Kocurkovic, *Opers Staff*
Tanya Vegera, *Accountant*
Greg Getts,
Ceola Eastwood, *Administration*
EMP: 27
SQ FT: 7,000
SALES (est): 6.1MM **Privately Held**
WEB: www.mutualss.com
SIC: 6282 8721 Manager of mutual funds, contract or fee basis; accounting services, except auditing

(G-1839)
NORTHAST OHIO MED RSERVE CORPS
3612 Ridge Park Dr (44147-2042)
P.O. Box 33524, Cleveland (44133-0524)
PHONE..............................216 789-6653
Thomas J Powell, *President*
Bob Fehlner, *Vice Pres*
EMP: 50
SALES (est): 931.6K **Privately Held**
WEB: www.neomrc.org
SIC: 8099 Medical services organization

(G-1840)
OHIO MACHINERY CO (PA)
Also Called: Caterpillar Authorized Dealer
3993 E Royalton Rd (44147-2898)
PHONE..............................440 526-6200
Ken Taylor, *President*
Janie Hovan, *Division Mgr*
Cathy Bican, *COO*
Eric W Emch, *Vice Pres*
Eric Emch, *Vice Pres*
◆ EMP: 160
SQ FT: 92,000
SALES (est): 222.7MM **Privately Held**
WEB: www.enginesnow.com
SIC: 7513 6159 7699 5082 Truck rental, without drivers; machinery & equipment finance leasing; aircraft & heavy equipment repair services; construction equipment repair; general construction machinery & equipment; mining machinery & equipment, except petroleum; heavy construction equipment rental

(G-1841)
OHIO MACHINERY CO
Also Called: Caterpillar
900 Ken Mar Indus Pkwy (44147-2992)
PHONE..............................440 526-0520
Jeff Dress, *Accounts Mgr*
Mike Graham, *Sales Staff*

▲ = Import ▼=Export
◆ =Import/Export

Erik Laps, *Sales Staff*
Chuck Vorhees, *Sales Staff*
Greg Deanna, *Manager*
EMP: 80
SALES (corp-wide): 222.7MM **Privately Held**
WEB: www.enginesnow.com
SIC: 5082 General construction machinery & equipment
PA: Ohio Machinery Co.
3993 E Royalton Rd
Broadview Heights OH 44147
440 526-6200

(G-1842)
OMNI FASTENERS INC
909 Towpath Trl (44147-3676)
PHONE....................440 838-1800
Ron Kuczmarski, *President*
Lynn Kuczmarski, *Vice Pres*
Jon Goodman, *Purchasing*
Brian Cicco, *Sales Staff*
▲ **EMP:** 25
SQ FT: 23,000
SALES (est): 8.2MM **Privately Held**
WEB: www.omnifasteners.com
SIC: 5072 Nuts (hardware); bolts; screws

(G-1843)
PEAK PERFORMANCE CENTER INC
1 Eagle Valley Ct (44147-2982)
PHONE....................440 838-5600
John Collis PHD, *President*
EMP: 50
SQ FT: 45,000
SALES (est): 1.6MM **Privately Held**
WEB: www.peakperformancecenter.com
SIC: 8093 Rehabilitation center, outpatient treatment

(G-1844)
RAM CONSTRUCTION SERVICES
100 Corporation Ctr # 4 (44147-3265)
PHONE....................440 740-0100
Robert Mazur, *President*
EMP: 50
SALES (est): 2MM
SALES (corp-wide): 106.8MM **Privately Held**
SIC: 1799 Waterproofing
PA: Ram Construction Services Of Michigan, Inc.
13800 Eckles Rd
Livonia MI 48150
734 464-3800

(G-1845)
SEASON CONTRACTORS INC
55 Eagle Valley Ct (44147-2982)
PHONE....................440 717-0188
Don Cacciacarne, *President*
Sharon Vasickanin, *IT/INT Sup*
▲ **EMP:** 30
SQ FT: 8,000
SALES (est): 3.7MM **Privately Held**
WEB: www.bxohio.net
SIC: 1521 1542 1751 New construction, single-family houses; commercial & office building, new construction; framing contractor

(G-1846)
SOTERA HEALTH LLC (PA)
9100 S Hills Blvd Ste 300 (44147-3525)
PHONE....................440 262-1410
Michael B Petras Jr, *CEO*
EMP: 100
SALES (est): 678.3MM **Privately Held**
SIC: 7389 Product sterilization service

(G-1847)
T M C SYSTEMS LLC
7655 Town Centre Dr (44147-4032)
PHONE....................440 740-1234
Martin Camloh,
Theresa Camloh,
EMP: 28
SALES (est): 869.5K **Privately Held**
SIC: 8351 Preschool center

(G-1848)
THYSSENKRUPP ELEVATOR CORP
9200 Market Pl (44147-2863)
PHONE....................440 717-0080
Lou Cozza, *Sales Staff*
Phil Resparc, *Office Mgr*
EMP: 40
SALES (corp-wide): 39.8B **Privately Held**
WEB: www.tyssenkrupp.com
SIC: 5084 7699 Elevators; elevators: inspection, service & repair
HQ: Thyssenkrupp Elevator Corporation
11605 Haynes Bridge Rd # 650
Alpharetta GA 30009
678 319-3240

(G-1849)
UNITED FD & COML WKRS INTL UN
9199 Market Pl (44147-2869)
PHONE....................216 241-2828
Tom Robertson, *Principal*
EMP: 50
SALES (corp-wide): 250.4MM **Privately Held**
SIC: 8631 Labor union
PA: United Food And Commercial Workers International Union
1775 K St Nw
Washington DC 20006
202 223-3111

(G-1850)
WARWICK COMMUNICATIONS INC (PA)
Also Called: C C I
405 Ken Mar Indus Pkwy (44147-4614)
PHONE....................216 787-0300
Steve Leopold, *CEO*
Laura Green, *Vice Pres*
Heidi Murphy, *Vice Pres*
Tonia Earley, *Project Mgr*
Jay Londahl, *Opers Mgr*
EMP: 30
SQ FT: 25,000
SALES (est): 8.1MM **Privately Held**
WEB: www.warwickinc.com
SIC: 7359 5065 Electronic equipment rental, except computers; telephone equipment

---

Brookfield
Trumbull County

(G-1851)
A TARA TIFFANYS PROPERTY
Also Called: Tiffany's Banquet Center
601 Bedford Rd Se (44403-9756)
PHONE....................330 448-0778
James Winner, *Owner*
EMP: 50
SQ FT: 20,000
SALES (est): 1.3MM **Privately Held**
WEB: www.tiffanysbanquet.com
SIC: 7299 5812 Banquet hall facilities; caterers

(G-1852)
K-Y RESIDENTIAL COML INDUS DEV
Also Called: Kirila Realty
505 Bedford Rd Se (44403-9750)
P.O. Box 179 (44403-0179)
PHONE....................330 448-4055
Ronald Kirila, *President*
David Pringle, *Executive*
EMP: 75
SQ FT: 40,000
SALES (est): 5.8MM **Privately Held**
SIC: 1542 1522 Shopping center construction; apartment building construction

(G-1853)
KIRILA CONTRACTORS INC
505 Bedford Rd Se (44403-9750)
P.O. Box 179 (44403-0179)
PHONE....................330 448-4055
Ronald Kirila Jr, *President*
Paul Kirila, *Vice Pres*
Robert Kirila, *Vice Pres*
William Kirila Jr, *Vice Pres*

Michael Kirila, *Supervisor*
EMP: 70
SQ FT: 50,000
SALES: 18.3MM **Privately Held**
WEB: www.kirila.com
SIC: 1611 Highway & street paving contractor

(G-1854)
KIRILA FIRE TRNING FCLTIES INC
509 Bedford Rd Se (44403-9750)
P.O. Box 2 (44403-0002)
PHONE....................724 854-5207
Jerry Kirila, *President*
EMP: 25
SQ FT: 30,000
SALES (est): 6.4MM **Privately Held**
SIC: 8748 Safety training service

(G-1855)
NICK STRIMBU INC (PA)
3500 Parkway Dr (44403-9755)
P.O. Box 268 (44403-0268)
PHONE....................330 448-4046
William Strimbu, *President*
Nicholas Strimbu III, *Exec VP*
Elizabeth Murray, *Senior VP*
Tom Nesbit, *Vice Pres*
Cory Knowlton, *Opers Staff*
EMP: 72
SQ FT: 200,000
SALES (est): 23.9MM **Privately Held**
WEB: www.nickstrimbu.com
SIC: 4213 Trucking, except local

(G-1856)
T R L INC
3500 Parkway Dr (44403-9755)
P.O. Box 268 (44403-0268)
PHONE....................330 448-4071
William Strimbu, *President*
EMP: 150
SQ FT: 200,000
SALES (est): 11.1MM **Privately Held**
WEB: www.trl.com
SIC: 4212 Truck rental with drivers

(G-1857)
UNITED STEEL SERVICE LLC (PA)
Also Called: Uniserv
4500 Parkway Dr (44403-8720)
P.O. Box 149 (44403-0149)
PHONE....................330 448-4057
Steven A Friedman, *CEO*
Mark Jones, *Safety Mgr*
Joel Miller, *Treasurer*
Gary Komsa, *Controller*
Bob States, *Manager*
▲ **EMP:** 120
SQ FT: 50,000
SALES (est): 26.8MM **Privately Held**
WEB: www.uniserv.com
SIC: 5051 Steel

(G-1858)
YANKEE RUN GOLF COURSE
7610 Warren Sharon Rd (44403-9626)
PHONE....................330 448-8096
Paul McMullen, *President*
William Gary McMullen, *Treasurer*
Patti Luchette, *Manager*
EMP: 53 **EST:** 1931
SALES (est): 1.8MM **Privately Held**
WEB: www.yankeerun.com
SIC: 7992 5941 Public golf courses; sporting goods & bicycle shops

---

Brooklyn
Cuyahoga County

(G-1859)
AMC ENTERTAINMENT INC
4788 Ridge Rd (44144-3327)
PHONE....................216 749-0260
Paul Gellott, *Branch Mgr*
EMP: 27
SALES (corp-wide): 7.3MM **Publicly Held**
WEB: www.amctheatres.com
SIC: 7832 Motion picture theaters, except drive-in

HQ: Amc Entertainment Inc.
11500 Ash St
Leawood KS 66211
913 213-2000

(G-1860)
CRESTVIEW PARTNERS II GP LP
4900 Tiedeman Rd Fl 4 (44144-2338)
PHONE....................216 898-2400
David C Brown, *Ch of Bd*
EMP: 276
SALES (est): 6.3MM **Privately Held**
SIC: 6282 Investment advisory service

(G-1861)
FERROUS METAL TRANSFER
11103 Memphis Ave (44144-2055)
PHONE....................216 671-8500
Eduardo Gonzalez, *President*
Reed McGivney, *Exec VP*
Anthony Potelicki, *Vice Pres*
Jim Stratton, *Vice Pres*
David Hill, *Treasurer*
EMP: 36
SQ FT: 1,000
SALES (est): 3.1MM **Privately Held**
SIC: 4212 4213 1541 1611 Lumber & timber trucking; steel hauling, local; heavy hauling; steel building construction; general contractor, highway & street construction

(G-1862)
VICTORY CAPITAL MANAGEMENT INC (HQ)
Also Called: Cemp
4900 Tiedeman Rd Fl 4 (44144-2338)
PHONE....................216 898-2400
David Brown, *CEO*
Kelly S Cliff, *President*
Kelly Cliff, *President*
Mannik S Dhillon, *President*
Chris Dyer, *Managing Dir*
EMP: 219
SALES (est): 294.8MM
SALES (corp-wide): 413.4MM **Publicly Held**
SIC: 6722 Money market mutual funds
PA: Victory Capital Holdings, Inc.
4900 Tiedeman Rd Fl 4
Brooklyn OH 44144
216 898-2400

Brooklyn Heights
Cuyahoga County

(G-1863)
ABC PIPING CO
1277 E Schaaf Rd Ste 5 (44131-1336)
PHONE....................216 398-4000
Aldo Campellone, *President*
Robert Campellone, *Vice Pres*
Adam Campellone, *Project Mgr*
John Ranucci, *Project Mgr*
Tom Whitby, *Project Mgr*
EMP: 34
SQ FT: 15,000
SALES (est): 13.2MM **Privately Held**
WEB: www.abcpipingco.com
SIC: 1623 1711 Pipeline construction; plumbing contractors

(G-1864)
ADELMOS ELECTRIC SEWER CLG CO
4917 Van Epps Rd (44131-1017)
PHONE....................216 641-2301
Joseph Di Franco, *President*
EMP: 35
SALES (est): 2.5MM **Privately Held**
SIC: 7699 1711 1799 Sewer cleaning & rodding; plumbing contractors; waterproofing

(G-1865)
AIR SYSTEMS OF OHIO INC (PA)
4760 Van Epps Rd (44131-1014)
PHONE....................216 741-1700
Vince Lisi, *President*
Bob Lisi, *Treasurer*
EMP: 26
SQ FT: 10,000

SALES (est): 4.3MM **Privately Held**
SIC: 5084 5075 Compressors, except air conditioning; compressors, air conditioning

(G-1866)
BRILLIANT ELECTRIC SIGN CO LTD
4811 Van Epps Rd (44131-1082)
PHONE...................................216 741-3800
Rob Kraus, *Plant Mgr*
Patty Molnar, *Project Mgr*
Jo Janos, *Accounting Mgr*
Lee Rodenfels, *Accounts Exec*
John Walsh, *Sales Staff*
EMP: 55
SQ FT: 55,000
SALES (est): 7.6MM **Privately Held**
WEB: www.brilliantsign.com
SIC: 3993 1799 Electric signs; sign installation & maintenance

(G-1867)
CI DISPOSITION CO
1000 Valley Belt Rd (44131-1433)
PHONE...................................216 587-5200
Gary Tarnowski, *Vice Pres*
EMP: 38
SQ FT: 56,000
SALES (est): 8MM **Privately Held**
WEB: www.comptrolinc.com
SIC: 3699 5085 Linear accelerators; industrial supplies

(G-1868)
CLEVELAND CONCRETE CNSTR INC (PA)
Also Called: Cleveland Cement Contractors
4823 Van Epps Rd (44131-1015)
PHONE...................................216 741-3954
Ronald Simonetti, *CEO*
Michael H Simonetti, *President*
Steven Murphy, *Vice Pres*
Jim Simonetti, *Vice Pres*
EMP: 98 EST: 1944
SQ FT: 10,000
SALES (est): 21.2MM **Privately Held**
WEB: www.clevelandcement.com
SIC: 1771 Foundation & footing contractor

(G-1869)
DEDICATED TRANSPORT LLC (HQ)
700 W Resource Dr (44131-1836)
PHONE...................................216 641-2500
Tom McDermott, *President*
Tim Jarus, *Opers Mgr*
F Fred Price, *CFO*
Franklin Price, *CFO*
Barb Stapleton, *Marketing Mgr*
EMP: 120
SQ FT: 6,000
SALES (est): 22.3MM **Privately Held**
WEB: www.dedicatedtransport.com
SIC: 4212 4213 Local trucking, without storage; contract haulers

(G-1870)
ELECTRICAL APPL REPR SVC INC
5805 Valley Belt Rd (44131-1423)
PHONE...................................216 459-8700
Tom Roberts, *President*
Kenneth Roberts, *Treasurer*
Raymond Busher, *Director*
Gloria Crist, *Admin Sec*
Dave Stettin,
EMP: 26
SQ FT: 12,500
SALES (est): 3.1MM **Privately Held**
WEB: www.electapplrep.com
SIC: 7629 7623 Electrical equipment repair services; refrigeration service & repair

(G-1871)
FLAVORFRESH DISPENSERS INC
4705 Van Epps Rd (44131-1013)
PHONE...................................216 641-0200
Stanley Klein, *President*
David Fischer, *General Mgr*
Michael O'Malley, *Corp Secy*
EMP: 50

SALES (est): 3.2MM **Privately Held**
SIC: 5149 Beverage concentrates; juices; soft drinks; water, distilled

(G-1872)
JANTECH BUILDING SERVICES INC
4963 Schaaf Ln (44131-1034)
PHONE...................................216 661-6102
William Rosby, *President*
Jeff Thayer, *Vice Pres*
EMP: 200
SQ FT: 3,000
SALES (est): 6.5MM **Privately Held**
WEB: www.jantechinc.com
SIC: 7349 Janitorial service, contract basis

(G-1873)
KAISER FOUNDATION HOSPITALS
Also Called: Bedford Medical Offices
5400 Lancaster Dr (44131-1832)
PHONE...................................216 524-7377
EMP: 593
SALES (corp-wide): 93B **Privately Held**
SIC: 8011 Offices & clinics of medical doctors
HQ: Kaiser Foundation Hospitals Inc
1 Kaiser Plz
Oakland CA 94612
510 271-6611

(G-1874)
KAISER FOUNDATION HOSPITALS
Also Called: Parma Medical Center
5400 Lancaster Dr (44131-1832)
PHONE...................................800 524-7377
EMP: 593
SALES (corp-wide): 93B **Privately Held**
SIC: 8011 Medical centers
HQ: Kaiser Foundation Hospitals Inc
1 Kaiser Plz
Oakland CA 94612
510 271-6611

(G-1875)
MULTI FLOW TRANSPORT INC
4705 Van Epps Rd (44131-1013)
PHONE...................................216 641-0200
Stanley Klein, *President*
EMP: 50
SALES (est): 2.1MM **Privately Held**
WEB: www.mftransport.net
SIC: 4789 Cargo loading & unloading services

(G-1876)
MULTI-FLOW DISPENSERS OHIO INC (PA)
4705 Van Epps Rd (44131-1013)
PHONE...................................216 641-0200
Stanley Klein, *President*
Bill Fazzone, *Vice Pres*
Tim Baird, *Finance Mgr*
Michelle Frankiewicz, *Technology*
EMP: 100
SQ FT: 17,000
SALES (est): 46.8MM **Privately Held**
SIC: 5145 7359 Syrups, fountain; vending machine rental

(G-1877)
OHIO DESK CO
4851 Van Epps Rd Ste B (44131-1052)
PHONE...................................216 623-0600
Ralph Gervasi, *Manager*
Randy Spence, *Consultant*
EMP: 45
SALES (corp-wide): 39.6MM **Privately Held**
WEB: www.ohiodesk.com
SIC: 4225 General warehousing & storage
PA: The Ohio Desk Company
1122 Prospect Ave E
Cleveland OH 44115
216 623-0600

(G-1878)
PEN BRANDS LLC (HQ)
220 Eastview Dr Ste 102 (44131-1040)
PHONE...................................216 447-1199
Scott Rickert, *CEO*
Anne Marie Thomas, *President*
Bruce Vereecken, *President*

Krish RAO, *Vice Pres*
Harvey Brush,
EMP: 42
SQ FT: 19,200
SALES (est): 2MM
SALES (corp-wide): 7.8MM **Publicly Held**
WEB: www.nanofilm.cc
SIC: 8731 5995 Optical goods stores; biological research
PA: Pen Inc.
701 Brickell Ave Ste 1550
Miami FL 33131
844 273-6462

(G-1879)
RENTOKIL NORTH AMERICA INC
1240 Valley Belt Rd (44131-1437)
PHONE...................................216 328-0700
J Ehrlich, *Principal*
EMP: 26
SALES (corp-wide): 3.1B **Privately Held**
SIC: 7342 Pest control services
HQ: Rentokil North America, Inc.
1125 Berkshire Blvd # 150
Wyomissing PA 19610
610 372-9700

(G-1880)
RENTOKIL NORTH AMERICA INC
Also Called: Ambius
1240 Valley Belt Rd (44131-1437)
PHONE...................................216 328-0700
Connie Brock, *Branch Mgr*
EMP: 33
SALES (corp-wide): 3.1B **Privately Held**
SIC: 7342 Pest control in structures
HQ: Rentokil North America, Inc.
1125 Berkshire Blvd # 150
Wyomissing PA 19610
610 372-9700

(G-1881)
SOLAR TESTING LABORATORIES INC (PA)
1125 Valley Belt Rd (44131-1434)
PHONE...................................216 741-7007
George J Ata, *President*
Michele Palmateer, *Business Mgr*
Anthony Kichurchak, *Exec VP*
Edward A Zielinski, *Exec VP*
Michael Kichurchak, *Vice Pres*
EMP: 135
SQ FT: 20,000
SALES (est): 11.6MM **Privately Held**
WEB: www.solartestinglabs.com
SIC: 8748 Testing services

(G-1882)
SPECIALTY EQUIPMENT SALES CO
Also Called: Sesco
5705 Valley Belt Rd (44131-1421)
PHONE...................................216 351-2559
Edward Ahern, *President*
Scott Reitano, *President*
Steve Wright, *President*
Kevin Leonard, *Regional Mgr*
Jim Ania, *Purch Mgr*
▲ EMP: 26
SQ FT: 15,000
SALES (est): 10.2MM **Privately Held**
SIC: 5046 Restaurant equipment & supplies

(G-1883)
TOP DAWG GROUP LLC
220 Eastview Dr Ste 103 (44131-1040)
PHONE...................................216 398-1066
George A Sagaris, *President*
Antoinette Koleno, *Vice Pres*
Tony Koleno, *Vice Pres*
Anthony Sagaris, *Vice Pres*
Patrick McCabe, *Opers Mgr*
EMP: 25
SQ FT: 12,000
SALES (est): 4.9MM **Privately Held**
WEB: www.topdawgdelivery.com
SIC: 4212 4225 Local Trucking Operator General Warehouse/Storage

(G-1884)
TOWLIFT INC (PA)
1395 Valley Belt Rd (44131-1474)
PHONE...................................216 749-6800
David H Cannon, *President*
David Bongorno, *Vice Pres*
▲ EMP: 121
SQ FT: 28,000
SALES (est): 106.6MM **Privately Held**
WEB: www.towlift.com/about_towlift.html
SIC: 5084 7699 7359 Materials handling machinery; industrial machine parts; industrial machinery & equipment repair; industrial truck repair; equipment rental & leasing

(G-1885)
UPTIME CORPORATION
4820 Van Epps Rd (44131-1016)
PHONE...................................216 661-1655
Jay Ross, *President*
EMP: 30
SQ FT: 25,000
SALES (est): 1.7MM
SALES (corp-wide): 12MM **Privately Held**
SIC: 7378 Computer maintenance & repair
PA: Ultimate Technology Corporation
100 Rawson Rd Ste 210
Victor NY 14564
585 924-9500

(G-1886)
VIRGINIA TILE COMPANY
4749 Spring Rd (44131-1025)
PHONE...................................216 741-8400
Jeff Dudzik, *Branch Mgr*
EMP: 29
SALES (corp-wide): 117.8MM **Privately Held**
SIC: 5032 Ceramic wall & floor tile
PA: Virginia Tile Company
28320 Plymouth Rd
Livonia MI 48150
248 476-7850

(G-1887)
VISTA COLOR IMAGING INC
4770 Van Epps Rd Ste 1 (44131-1058)
PHONE...................................216 651-2830
Paul E Gallo, *CEO*
Kevin Vesely, *President*
Herb Byers, *Vice Pres*
Joanne Mociolek, *Vice Pres*
Scott Ney, *Vice Pres*
EMP: 25 EST: 1970
SALES (est): 3.7MM **Privately Held**
WEB: www.vistacolorlab.com
SIC: 7384 Photograph developing & retouching; photograph enlarging; photographic services

(G-1888)
WELTMAN WEINBERG & REIS CO LPA
965 Keynote Cir (44131-1829)
PHONE...................................216 739-5100
Ruben Moreno, *Opers Mgr*
Dawn Stawicki, *Purch Agent*
Kt Heil, *Mktg Coord*
Lorri Skubon, *Business Anlyst*
Emily Berger, *Marketing Staff*
EMP: 240
SALES (corp-wide): 151.3MM **Privately Held**
SIC: 8111 General practice law office
PA: Weltman, Weinberg & Reis Co., L.P.A.
323 W Lkeside Ave Ste 200
Cleveland OH 44113
216 685-1000

Brookpark
Cuyahoga County

(G-1889)
16644 SNOW RD LLC
Also Called: Howard Johnson
16644 Snow Rd (44142-2767)
PHONE...................................216 676-5200
Praveeen Auror,
EMP: 28
SALES (est): 2.5MM **Privately Held**
SIC: 7011 Hotels & motels

(G-1890)
AM INDUSTRIAL GROUP LLC (PA)
16000 Commerce Park Dr (44142-2023)
PHONE...................................216 433-7171
Reginald Wyman, *Owner*
Luke Wootten, *Opers Mgr*
Ryan Wyman, *Engineer*
Jason Cottle, *Sales Staff*
Robert Wootten, *Sales Staff*
▲ EMP: 40
SQ FT: 5,000
SALES (est): 23.6MM **Privately Held**
WEB: www.amindustrial.com
SIC: 5084 3541 1799 Machine tools & accessories; sawing & cutoff machines (metalworking machinery); rigging & scaffolding

(G-1891)
AVALON PRECISION CAST CO LLC
Also Called: Avalon Precision Metalsmiths
15583 Brookpark Rd (44142-1618)
PHONE...................................216 362-4100
David Palivec, *President*
▲ EMP: 238 EST: 2012
SALES (est): 91.8MM
SALES (corp-wide): 51.3MM **Privately Held**
SIC: 5051 Steel
PA: Xapc, Co.
   15583 Brookpark Rd
   Cleveland OH 44142
   216 362-4100

(G-1892)
CAR PARTS WAREHOUSE INC (PA)
Also Called: C P W
5200 W 130th St (44142-1804)
PHONE...................................216 281-4500
Tony Difiore, *President*
Carmelina Di Fiore, *Corp Secy*
Carl Lambert, *Manager*
▲ EMP: 30
SQ FT: 70,000
SALES (est): 96.9MM **Privately Held**
WEB: www.carpartswarehouse.com
SIC: 5013 5531 Automotive supplies; automotive parts

(G-1893)
CEC COMBUSTION SAFETY LLC (DH)
2100 Apollo Dr (44142-4103)
PHONE...................................216 749-2992
EMP: 43
SQ FT: 25,000
SALES: 12MM
SALES (corp-wide): 41.8B **Publicly Held**
WEB: www.cec-consultants.com
SIC: 8711 7389 Consulting engineer; mechanical engineering; industrial & commercial equipment inspection service
HQ: Eclipse, Inc.
   1665 Elmwood Rd
   Rockford IL 61103
   815 877-3031

(G-1894)
CREDIT FIRST NA
Also Called: AMTS
6275 Eastland Rd (44142-1399)
PHONE...................................216 362-5000
Alfred Policy, *CEO*
Alan Meier, *CFO*
EMP: 199
SQ FT: 25,000
SALES: 44.2MM
SALES (corp-wide): 32.4B **Privately Held**
WEB: www.bfis.com
SIC: 6021 National commercial banks
HQ: Bridgestone Retail Operations, Llc
   333 E Lake St Ste 300
   Bloomingdale IL 60108
   630 259-9000

(G-1895)
CUSA LL INC
Also Called: A Coach USA Company
13315 Brookpark Rd (44142-1822)
P.O. Box 81172, Cleveland (44181-0172)
PHONE...................................216 267-8810
Tom Goebel, *President*

Mike Goebel, *Corp Secy*
Jack Goebel, *Vice Pres*
EMP: 200
SQ FT: 48,000
SALES (est): 372.7K **Privately Held**
WEB: www.lakefrontlines.com
SIC: 4119 4142 4141 Local passenger transportation; bus charter service, except local; local bus charter service

(G-1896)
DISTRIBUTION DATA INCORPORATED (PA)
Also Called: Ddi
16101 Snow Rd Ste 200 (44142-2817)
P.O. Box 818019, Cleveland (44181-8019)
PHONE...................................216 362-3009
Robert W Hartig, *President*
Charles C Deems, *Exec VP*
Lynn M Hartig, *Vice Pres*
Debbie Zillich, *Vice Pres*
EMP: 38
SQ FT: 34,000
SALES (est): 66.2MM **Privately Held**
WEB: www.ddiservices.com
SIC: 5199 7371 8742 4731 Art goods & supplies; custom computer programming services; transportation consultant; freight forwarding; management services

(G-1897)
EDUCATION ALTERNATIVES (PA)
5445 Smith Rd (44142-2026)
PHONE...................................216 332-9360
Gerald Swartz, *CEO*
Jerry Swartz, *Exec Dir*
EMP: 93
SALES (est): 11.2MM **Privately Held**
SIC: 8211 8093 Private special education school; rehabilitation center, outpatient treatment

(G-1898)
J & R ASSOCIATES
Also Called: Windsor Construction
14803 Holland Rd (44142-3065)
PHONE...................................440 250-4080
John Coury Sr, *President*
EMP: 1000
SALES (est): 53.3MM **Privately Held**
SIC: 1542 8361 6514 Institutional building construction; home for the aged; dwelling operators, except apartments

(G-1899)
K-M-S INDUSTRIES INC
Also Called: K.M.S.
6519 Eastland Rd Ste 1 (44142-1347)
PHONE...................................440 243-6680
Gerald Korman, *President*
Richard Malone Jr, *Vice Pres*
Diane Malone, *Treasurer*
EMP: 30
SQ FT: 25,000
SALES (est): 5.6MM **Privately Held**
SIC: 3599 5531 7692 Machine shop, jobbing & repair; automotive parts; automotive accessories; welding repair

(G-1900)
LAKEFRONT LINES INC (DH)
13315 Brookpark Rd (44142-1822)
P.O. Box 81172, Cleveland (44181-0172)
PHONE...................................216 267-8810
Chris Goebel, *CEO*
Christopher Goebel, *General Mgr*
Tom Goebel, *General Mgr*
Sue Koetter, *Accountant*
EMP: 175
SQ FT: 48,000
SALES (est): 31.7MM
SALES (corp-wide): 4.5B **Privately Held**
SIC: 4119 4142 4141 Local passenger transportation; bus charter service, except local; local bus charter service

(G-1901)
LAKEWOOD CHRYSLER-PLYMOUTH
Also Called: Spitzer Lakewood
13001 Brookpark Rd (44142-1819)
PHONE...................................216 521-1000
Allan Spitzer, *President*
William Burke, *Vice Pres*

EMP: 30
SQ FT: 30,000
SALES (est): 7.2MM **Privately Held**
SIC: 5511 7538 7515 Automobiles, new & used; general automotive repair shops; passenger car leasing

(G-1902)
MCPC INC (PA)
Also Called: McPc Tech Pdts & Solutions
21500 Aerospace Pkwy (44142-1071)
PHONE...................................440 238-0102
Michael Trebilcock, *CEO*
Lance Frew, *President*
Andy Jones, *President*
Jason Taylor, *Exec VP*
Seth Gray, *Engineer*
EMP: 120
SQ FT: 80,000
SALES (est): 445.3MM **Privately Held**
WEB: www.mcpc.com
SIC: 5045 Computers, peripherals & software

(G-1903)
NORTH COAST LOGISTICS INC (PA)
18901 Snow Rd Frnt (44142-1471)
PHONE...................................216 362-7159
Patricia A Gazey, *President*
Dante Granados, *General Mgr*
Bob Hamill, *General Mgr*
William Harrison, *Vice Pres*
Gary Watts, *Transptn Dir*
EMP: 40
SQ FT: 575,000
SALES: 18.5MM **Privately Held**
WEB: www.northcoastlogistics.com
SIC: 4225 General warehousing

(G-1904)
NORTH PARK CARE CENTER LLC
14803 Holland Rd (44142-3065)
PHONE...................................440 250-4080
EMP: 65
SQ FT: 66,000
SALES (est): 2.5MM **Privately Held**
SIC: 6514 Dwelling Operator

(G-1905)
ROBERT ERNEY
Also Called: Elite Proofing
14830 Larkfield Dr (44142-3005)
P.O. Box 5087, Chicago IL (60680-5004)
PHONE...................................312 788-9005
Robert Erney, *President*
EMP: 25
SQ FT: 1,500
SALES: 250K **Privately Held**
SIC: 7338 Proofreading service

(G-1906)
STANDARD CONTG & ENGRG INC
Also Called: S C E
6356 Eastland Rd (44142-1302)
PHONE...................................440 243-1001
Russell Metzger, *President*
Brad Metzger, *General Mgr*
Gary Barnhill, *Vice Pres*
George Wonkovich, *Vice Pres*
Jerry Snodgrass, *Project Mgr*
EMP: 75
SQ FT: 6,000
SALES (est): 17.4MM **Privately Held**
WEB: www.standardcontracting.com
SIC: 1541 1771 1794 1796 Industrial buildings, new construction; renovation, remodeling & repairs: industrial buildings; concrete work; excavation work; machine moving & rigging

(G-1907)
SWX ENTERPRISES INC
5231 Engle Rd (44142-1531)
PHONE...................................216 676-4600
Dean Armanini, *President*
EMP: 50
SQ FT: 25,000
SALES (est): 8.3MM **Privately Held**
SIC: 4213 Trucking, except local

(G-1908)
VANTAGE PARTNERS LLC
3000 Aerospace Pkwy (44142-1001)
PHONE...................................216 925-1302
Joseph Polk, *President*
EMP: 25
SALES (est): 5.5MM **Privately Held**
SIC: 8711 Aviation &/or aeronautical engineering

Brookville
Montgomery County

(G-1909)
A BROWN & SONS NURSERY (PA)
11506 Dyton Grnville Pike (45309-8652)
P.O. Box 427, Phillipsburg (45354-0427)
PHONE...................................937 836-5826
Kenneth Brown, *President*
Harry Brown, *Vice Pres*
John Brown, *Vice Pres*
Michael Brown, *Vice Pres*
Kenda Henson, *Finance*
EMP: 33
SALES (est): 6.1MM **Privately Held**
SIC: 0181 5431 Nursery stock, growing of; vegetable stands or markets

(G-1910)
BROOK HAVEN HOME HEALTH CARE
Also Called: Brookhaven Home Care
850 Albert Rd (45309-9275)
PHONE...................................937 833-6945
Dale Baughman, *President*
EMP: 40
SALES (est): 1.2MM **Privately Held**
SIC: 8071 8082 Medical laboratories; home health care services

(G-1911)
BROOKVILLE ENTERPRISES INC
Also Called: BROOKHAVEN NURSING & CARE CENT
1 Country Ln (45309-9268)
PHONE...................................937 833-2133
Dale Baughman, *President*
Terry Miller, *Treasurer*
Mike McKinniss, *Exec Dir*
EMP: 255 EST: 1972
SQ FT: 32,500
SALES: 11MM **Privately Held**
SIC: 8052 8051 Intermediate care facilities; skilled nursing care facilities

(G-1912)
BROOKVILLE ROADSTER INC
718 Albert Rd (45309-9202)
PHONE...................................937 833-4605
Ray Gollahon, *President*
EMP: 40
SALES (est): 5.8MM **Privately Held**
WEB: www.brookvilleroadster.com
SIC: 3711 5013 Automobile assembly, including specialty automobiles; automotive supplies & parts

(G-1913)
DAYTON TALL TIMBERS RESORT
Also Called: KOA Dayton Tall Timbers Resort
7796 Wellbaum Rd (45309-9421)
PHONE...................................937 833-3888
Rhonda Landis, *President*
Joseph Landis, *Vice Pres*
EMP: 25
SALES: 630K **Privately Held**
SIC: 7033 Campgrounds; campsite

(G-1914)
IMAGE PAVEMENT MAINTENANCE
425 Carr Dr (45309-1935)
P.O. Box 157 (45309-0157)
PHONE...................................937 833-9200
Michael Gartrell, *President*
EMP: 42

SALES (est): 3.9MM **Privately Held**
SIC: **1611** 2951 1799 1771 Surfacing & paving; asphalt paving mixtures & blocks; parking lot maintenance; driveway contractor; sweeping service: road, airport, parking lot, etc.; tennis court construction

(G-1915)
MACKIL INC
Also Called: Rob's Restaurant & Catering
705 Arlington Rd (45309-9728)
PHONE.............................937 833-3310
Joe Schwartzberger, *President*
Gerard Schwartz, *President*
EMP: 45
SALES (est): 1.7MM **Privately Held**
SIC: **7299** 5812 Banquet hall facilities; American restaurant

(G-1916)
PROVIMI NORTH AMERICA INC (HQ)
Also Called: Cargill Premix and Nutrition
10 Collective Way (45309-8878)
P.O. Box 69 (45309-0069)
PHONE.............................937 770-2400
Thomas Taylor, *President*
Terrence Quinlan, *President*
Scott Swenson, *Plant Mgr*
Mark Hemrick, *Safety Mgr*
Chad Nate, *Purch Dir*
◆ EMP: 253
SALES (est): 516.9MM
SALES (corp-wide): 114.7B **Privately Held**
WEB: www.vigortone.com
SIC: **5191** 2048 Animal feeds; prepared feeds
PA: Cargill, Incorporated
15407 Mcginty Rd W
Wayzata MN 55391
952 742-7575

(G-1917)
SHILOH GROUP
Also Called: Shiloh Springs Care Center
14336 Amity Rd (45309-8764)
PHONE.............................937 833-2219
Joe Hardy, *Partner*
Joe Barnett, *Partner*
Margaret Barnett, *Partner*
Katherine Gibson, *Partner*
Debra Hardy, *Partner*
EMP: 120
SQ FT: 30,000
SALES (est): 3.4MM **Privately Held**
SIC: **8059** Nursing home, except skilled & intermediate care facility

---

Brunswick
Medina County

(G-1918)
ALL CONSTRUCTION SERVICES INC
Also Called: All Construction/Mooney Moses
945 Industrial Pkwy N (44212-4321)
PHONE.............................330 225-1653
David J Le Hotan, *President*
Michael J Fox, *Vice Pres*
David Lehotan, *Manager*
EMP: 40
SQ FT: 12,000
SALES (est): 4MM
SALES (corp-wide): 1.3B **Publicly Held**
WEB: www.dwdcpa.com
SIC: **1742** Insulation, buildings
HQ: Installed Building Products Llc
495 S High St Ste 50
Columbus OH 43215
614 221-3399

(G-1919)
ALLSTATE PAINTING & CONTG CO
1256 Industrial Pkwy N # 2 (44212-2369)
P.O. Box 369 (44212-0369)
PHONE.............................330 220-5533
Elias Kafantaris, *President*
George Rodits, *Vice Pres*
EMP: 90 EST: 1962
SQ FT: 5,000

SALES (est): 3.4MM **Privately Held**
SIC: **1721** 1799 Exterior commercial painting contractor; sandblasting of building exteriors

(G-1920)
BLACKHAWK INDUSTRIES
2845 Interstate Pkwy (44212-4326)
PHONE.............................918 610-4719
Bill Scheller, *Principal*
Ormond J Hamilton, *Principal*
EMP: 32 EST: 2013
SALES (est): 13.8MM **Privately Held**
SIC: **5085** Industrial supplies

(G-1921)
BRUNSWICK CITY SCHOOLS (PA)
3643 Center Rd (44212-3619)
PHONE.............................330 225-7731
Michael Mayell, *Superintendent*
Tracy Wheeler, *Asst Supt*
Richard Nowak, *School Board Pr*
Mary Korud, *Treasurer*
Jeanine Scally, *Psychologist*
EMP: 811 EST: 1968
SQ FT: 10,000
SALES: 92.1MM **Privately Held**
SIC: **8211** 8351 Public elementary & secondary schools; secondary school; child day care services

(G-1922)
BRUNSWICK FOOD PANTRY INC
2876 Center Rd (44212)
PHONE.............................330 225-0395
Kathryn Pick, *Director*
EMP: 30 EST: 1976
SALES (est): 44.1K **Privately Held**
SIC: **8699** Charitable organization

(G-1923)
CARLSON AMBLNCE TRNSPT SVC INC
1642 Pearl Rd (44212-3406)
PHONE.............................330 225-2400
Neil Carlson, *President*
EMP: 32
SQ FT: 7,000
SALES (est): 967.5K
SALES (corp-wide): 1.2MM **Privately Held**
SIC: **4119** Ambulance service
PA: Carlson-Brunswick Funeral Home Inc
1642 Pearl Rd
Brunswick OH 44212
330 225-2400

(G-1924)
CITY OF BRUNSWICK
Animal Control
4095 Center Rd (44212-2944)
PHONE.............................330 225-9144
Sam Scaffide, *Director*
EMP: 200 **Privately Held**
SIC: **8699** Animal humane society
PA: City Of Brunswick
4095 Center Rd
Brunswick OH 44212
330 225-9144

(G-1925)
CONTROL CLEANING SOLUTIONS
780 Pearl Rd (44212-2177)
PHONE.............................330 220-3333
Nicholas Cummings, *CEO*
EMP: 45
SQ FT: 3,000
SALES (est): 1.2MM **Privately Held**
SIC: **7349** Cleaning service, industrial or commercial

(G-1926)
DEED REALTY CO
4600 Center Rd (44212-3345)
PHONE.............................330 225-5220
Bonnie Scahel, *President*
Thomas Scahel, *Corp Secy*
EMP: 29 EST: 1975
SALES (est): 1.4MM **Privately Held**
WEB: www.deedrealty.com
SIC: **6531** Real estate brokers & agents

(G-1927)
DIGESTIVE DISEASE CONSULTANTS
1299 Industrial Pkwy N # 110 (44212-6366)
PHONE.............................330 225-6468
David Myers, *Owner*
Helen Sharma, *Office Mgr*
Fadi Bashour, *Med Doctor*
EMP: 25
SALES (est): 2.6MM **Privately Held**
SIC: **8011** Gastronomist

(G-1928)
DW TOGETHER LLC
Also Called: H & R Block Brunswick
3698 Center Rd (44212-3620)
PHONE.............................330 225-8200
Joseph Destro, *President*
Debra Destro, *Treasurer*
EMP: 32
SALES (est): 850K **Privately Held**
SIC: **7291** Tax return preparation services

(G-1929)
ESBI INTERNATIONAL SALON
4193 Center Rd (44212-2935)
PHONE.............................330 220-3724
Nuccio Basilisco, *Partner*
Cheryl Basilisco, *Partner*
EMP: 35
SALES (est): 656.2K **Privately Held**
SIC: **7231** Manicurist, pedicurist

(G-1930)
FOOD SAMPLE EXPRESS LLC
2945 Carquest Dr (44212-4447)
PHONE.............................330 225-3550
Jeffrey M Wood, *Mng Member*
Judi Flynn,
EMP: 90
SALES (est): 12MM **Privately Held**
WEB: www.imtco.com
SIC: **5141** Groceries, general line

(G-1931)
GENERAL PARTS INC
Also Called: Advance Auto Parts
2830 Carquest Dr (44212-4352)
PHONE.............................330 220-6500
Tom Kenney, *Manager*
EMP: 80
SALES (corp-wide): 9.3B **Publicly Held**
WEB: www.carquest.com
SIC: **5013** Automotive supplies & parts
HQ: General Parts, Inc.
2635 E Millbrook Rd Ste C
Raleigh NC 27604
919 573-3000

(G-1932)
HOME DEPOT USA INC
Also Called: Home Depot, The
3330 Center Rd (44212-6510)
PHONE.............................330 220-2654
Jason Werny, *Branch Mgr*
EMP: 150
SALES (corp-wide): 108.2B **Publicly Held**
WEB: www.homerentalsdepot.com
SIC: **5211** 7359 Home centers; tool rental
HQ: Home Depot U.S.A., Inc.
2455 Paces Ferry Ave
Atlanta GA 30339

(G-1933)
INTEGRATED MARKETING TECH INC
Also Called: IMT
2945 Carquest Dr (44212-4447)
PHONE.............................330 225-3550
Jeff Wood, *President*
▲ EMP: 100
SQ FT: 120,000
SALES (est): 8.9MM **Privately Held**
SIC: **7363** 7374 Labor resource services; data processing service

(G-1934)
JOSEPH SCHMIDT REALTY INC
47 Pearl Rd (44212-1114)
PHONE.............................330 225-6688
Joseph Schmidt, *President*
EMP: 29
SQ FT: 1,904

SALES (est): 1.4MM **Privately Held**
WEB: www.josephschmidrealty.com
SIC: **6531** Real estate brokers & agents

(G-1935)
KHM CONSULTING INC
Also Called: Khm Travel Group
1152 Pearl Rd (44212-2888)
PHONE.............................330 460-5635
Richard Zimmerman, *President*
Holly Peck, *Agent*
Karen Tyler, *Agent*
Tyler Parvu, *Training Spec*
EMP: 45 EST: 2007
SALES (est): 13.8MM **Privately Held**
SIC: **4724** Tourist agency arranging transport, lodging & car rental

(G-1936)
LOU-RAY ASSOCIATES INC
1378 Pearl Rd Ste 201 (44212-3469)
PHONE.............................330 220-1999
John Herman, *CEO*
Murray Herman, *President*
Doug Fabian, *Vice Pres*
Scott Katzenmeyer, *Agent*
Joseph M Herman, *Shareholder*
EMP: 25
SQ FT: 7,500
SALES (est): 2.3MM **Privately Held**
WEB: www.louray.com
SIC: **7374** Data processing & preparation

(G-1937)
MAPLESIDE VALLEY LLC (PA)
Also Called: Mapleside Bakery
294 Pearl Rd (44212-1118)
PHONE.............................330 225-5576
William Eyssen Jr, *Principal*
David Eyssen, *Principal*
Robert Romph, *Manager*
EMP: 75
SQ FT: 9,900
SALES (est): 8.4MM **Privately Held**
WEB: www.mapleside.com
SIC: **0175** 0172 5947 5812 Apple orchard; peach orchard; plum orchard; grapes; gift shop; novelties; eating places; bakeries; fruit stands or markets

(G-1938)
PRECISION SUPPLY COMPANY INC
2845 Interstate Pkwy (44212-4326)
PHONE.............................330 225-5530
Alfred J Koch, *CEO*
Bob Koch, *President*
Tracy Lehnecker, *CFO*
EMP: 75 EST: 1973
SQ FT: 18,630
SALES (est): 38.6MM **Privately Held**
WEB: www.precisionsupply.com
SIC: **5084** 5085 Machine tools & accessories; industrial supplies
PA: Blackhawk Industrial Distribution, Inc.
1501 Sw Expressway Dr
Broken Arrow OK 74012

(G-1939)
ROLLING HLLS RHAB WELLNESS CTR
4426 Homestead Dr (44212-2506)
P.O. Box 70 (44212-0070)
PHONE.............................330 225-9121
Dan Shiller, *President*
Basil Gaitanaros, *Vice Pres*
Mary Traczyk, *Vice Pres*
Michael Traczyk, *Vice Pres*
EMP: 125 EST: 1967
SQ FT: 15,000
SALES (est): 5MM **Privately Held**
SIC: **8051** Extended care facility

(G-1940)
SUBURBAN TRANSPORTATION CO INC
Also Called: Suburban School
1289 Pearl Rd (44212-2868)
PHONE.............................440 846-9291
James Ondrejcak, *Principal*
EMP: 26
SALES (corp-wide): 4.8MM **Privately Held**
SIC: **4151** School buses

PA: Suburban Transportation Company, Inc.
26 River Rd
Hinckley OH 44233
440 582-5553

(G-1941)
SYMATIC INC
Also Called: Ancom Business Products
2831 Center Rd (44212-2331)
PHONE...................................330 225-1510
Walter H Tanner, *President*
Cindy Holton, *Vice Pres*
Nancy Hanshue, *Sales Staff*
Michelle McDonald, *Manager*
EMP: 35
SALES (est): 5.4MM **Privately Held**
WEB: www.ancom-filing.com
SIC: 3579 5044 2541 2521 Paper handling machines; office equipment; wood partitions & fixtures; wood office furniture

(G-1942)
TMR INC
2945 Carquest Dr (44212-4447)
PHONE...................................330 220-8564
Peter Howe, *Ch of Bd*
Jason Atkins, *President*
Marjorie Zychowski, *Founder*
EMP: 120
SQ FT: 210,000
SALES (est): 10.2MM **Privately Held**
WEB: www.themailroom.com
SIC: 7334 7331 Photocopying & duplicating services; direct mail advertising services

(G-1943)
TOTAL MARKETING RESOURCES LLC
Also Called: T M R
2811 Carquest Dr (44212-4332)
PHONE...................................330 220-1275
Jeff Wood,
Linda Wood,
EMP: 27
SQ FT: 125,000
SALES (est): 2.2MM **Privately Held**
SIC: 8742 Business planning & organizing services

(G-1944)
VOESTLPINE PRECISION STRIP LLC (HQ)
3052 Interstate Pkwy (44212-4324)
PHONE...................................330 220-7800
Udo Koehler, *Mng Member*
◆ EMP: 45
SALES (est): 24.7MM
SALES (corp-wide): 16B **Privately Held**
SIC: 5051 Iron or steel semifinished products
PA: Voestalpine Ag
Voest-Alpine-StraBe 1
Linz 4020
503 041-50

(G-1945)
W W WILLIAMS COMPANY LLC
Also Called: Midwest Division - Brunswick
1176 Industrial Pkwy N (44212-2342)
PHONE...................................330 225-7751
Alan Gatlin, *CEO*
EMP: 50
SALES (corp-wide): 4.8B **Privately Held**
SIC: 7538 7537 5084 Diesel engine repair; automotive; automotive transmission repair shops; engines & parts, diesel
HQ: The W W Williams Company Llc
5025 Bradenton Ave # 130
Dublin OH 43017
614 228-5000

(G-1946)
WHITAKER MASONRY INC
4910 Grafton Rd (44212-1002)
PHONE...................................330 225-7970
Frank Whitaker, *President*
EMP: 48 EST: 2000
SALES: 2.6MM **Privately Held**
SIC: 1741 Masonry & other stonework

(G-1947)
WILLOWOOD CARE CENTER
Also Called: SAND T NURSING HOME
1186 Hadcock Rd (44212-3061)
PHONE...................................330 225-3156
Edward Telle, *President*
Deborah Lougheed, *Director*
EMP: 121
SQ FT: 27,150
SALES: 8.7MM **Privately Held**
WEB: www.willowoodcare.com
SIC: 8051 8742 Convalescent home with continuous nursing care; management consulting services

(G-1948)
WINKING LIZARD INC
3634 Center Rd (44212-4446)
PHONE...................................330 220-9944
Jim Callam, *Branch Mgr*
EMP: 90
SALES (corp-wide): 103.7MM **Privately Held**
SIC: 5812 7299 Fast food restaurants & stands; banquet hall facilities
PA: Winking Lizard, Inc.
25380 Miles Rd
Bedford OH 44146
216 831-0022

(G-1949)
WOLVERTON INC
3048 Nationwide Pkwy (44212-2360)
PHONE...................................330 220-3320
Fax: 330 273-4361
EMP: 25
SALES (corp-wide): 663.9MM **Privately Held**
SIC: 5199 Whol Pet Supplies
HQ: Wolverton, Inc.
5542 W Grand River Ave
Lansing MI 48906
517 327-0738

Bryan
Williams County

(G-1950)
AIRMATE COMPANY
16280 County Road D (43506-9552)
PHONE...................................419 636-3184
Carol Schreder Czech, *President*
Carol Schreder, *President*
Neil Oberlin, *Vice Pres*
Ed Dewitt, *Production*
Todd Moyer, *Purch Agent*
▲ EMP: 57
SQ FT: 24,000
SALES (est): 6.8MM **Privately Held**
WEB: www.airmatecompany.com
SIC: 3823 7311 Industrial instrmnts msrmnt display/control process variable; advertising consultant

(G-1951)
ALLIED WASTE SYSTEMS INC
Also Called: Site 091b
12604 County Road G (43506-9596)
PHONE...................................419 636-2242
Chris Carpenter, *Manager*
EMP: 49
SALES (corp-wide): 10B **Publicly Held**
WEB: www.fennellgrp.com
SIC: 4953 Garbage: collecting, destroying & processing
HQ: Allied Waste Systems, Inc.
18500 N Allied Way # 100
Phoenix AZ 85054
480 627-2700

(G-1952)
ANDERSON & VREELAND INC
Also Called: Anderson Vreeland Midwest
15348 State Rte 127 E (43506)
P.O. Box 527 (43506-0527)
PHONE...................................419 636-5002
Scott Gordon, *Vice Pres*
Graig Sanderson, *Buyer*
Gary Goll, *Purchasing*
Keith Vreeland, *Engineer*
Lauren Wenz, *Finance Mgr*
EMP: 80
SQ FT: 3,000

SALES (corp-wide): 73.7MM **Privately Held**
WEB: www.andersonvreeland.com
SIC: 5084 3555 3542 2796 Printing trades machinery, equipment & supplies; printing trades machinery; machine tools, metal forming type; platemaking services
PA: Anderson & Vreeland, Inc.
8 Evans St
Fairfield NJ 07004
973 227-2270

(G-1953)
BUCKEYE GOLF CLUB CO INC
Also Called: Orchard Hills Country Club
10277 County Road D (43506-9548)
PHONE...................................419 636-6984
Rob Vogelsong, *President*
EMP: 35
SQ FT: 7,000
SALES (est): 977.7K **Privately Held**
WEB: www.orchardhillscountryclub.com
SIC: 7997 Country club, membership

(G-1954)
COMMUNITY HOSPITALS
433 W High St (43506-1690)
PHONE...................................419 636-1131
Phillip Ennen, *CEO*
EMP: 399
SALES (est): 1MM
SALES (corp-wide): 77.2MM **Privately Held**
SIC: 8062 General medical & surgical hospitals
PA: Community Hospitals And Wellness Centers
433 W High St
Bryan OH 43506
419 636-1131

(G-1955)
COMMUNITY HSPTALS WLLNESS CTRS (PA)
Also Called: Chwc
433 W High St (43506-1690)
PHONE...................................419 636-1131
Phil Ennen, *CEO*
Mike Culler, *COO*
Janice David, *Vice Pres*
Greg Slattery, *Vice Pres*
Chad Tinkel, *Vice Pres*
EMP: 101
SQ FT: 50,000
SALES: 77.2MM **Privately Held**
SIC: 8062 General medical & surgical hospitals

(G-1956)
COUNTY OF WILLIAMS
Also Called: Williams Conty Hllsd Cntry Lvg
9876 County Road 16 (43506-9781)
PHONE...................................419 636-4508
Marcia Hauer, *Manager*
EMP: 120 **Privately Held**
SIC: 8051 9111 Skilled nursing care facilities; county supervisors' & executives' offices
PA: County Of Williams
1 Courthouse Sq Ste L
Bryan OH 43506
419 636-2059

(G-1957)
FRATERNAL ORDER OF EAGLES BR (PA)
Also Called: Foe 2233
221 S Walnut St (43506-1720)
PHONE...................................419 636-7812
Denny Baer, *President*
Chuck Cunnigham, *Vice Pres*
Tim Lewis, *Treasurer*
EMP: 33
SQ FT: 21,000
SALES: 5.7MM **Privately Held**
WEB: www.fraternalorderofeagles.tribe.net
SIC: 8641 7371 Fraternal associations; computer software development & applications

(G-1958)
GEORGE GARDNER
Also Called: Custom Cleaners
1420 W High St (43506-1595)
PHONE...................................419 636-4277
George Gardner, *Owner*

EMP: 65
SQ FT: 10,500
SALES (est): 913.7K **Privately Held**
SIC: 7216 7211 7349 Drycleaning plants, except rugs; power laundries, family & commercial; janitorial service, contract basis

(G-1959)
HARBORSIDE HEALTHCARE NW OHIO
1104 Wesley Ave (43506-2579)
PHONE...................................419 636-5071
Katy Hithcock, *Administration*
EMP: 180 EST: 1976
SALES (est): 2.5MM **Privately Held**
SIC: 8059 8051 Nursing home, except skilled & intermediate care facility; skilled nursing care facilities

(G-1960)
INGERSOLL-RAND COMPANY
209 N Main St (43506-1319)
P.O. Box 151 (43506-0151)
PHONE...................................419 633-6800
Larry White, *Manager*
EMP: 50 **Privately Held**
WEB: www.ingersoll-rand.com
SIC: 3546 4225 3823 3594 Power-driven handtools; general warehousing & storage; industrial instrmnts msrmnt display/control process variable; fluid power pumps & motors; pumps & pumping equipment; hoists, cranes & monorails
HQ: Ingersoll-Rand Company
800 Beaty St Ste B
Davidson NC 28036
704 655-4000

(G-1961)
LE SMITH COMPANY (PA)
1030 E Wilson St (43506-9358)
P.O. Box 766 (43506-0766)
PHONE...................................419 636-4555
Laura Juarez, *President*
Steve Smith, *Principal*
Craig Francisco, *COO*
Mari Ivan, *COO*
Mindy Hess, *CFO*
▲ EMP: 100 EST: 1950
SQ FT: 90,000
SALES (est): 18.8MM **Privately Held**
WEB: www.lesmith.com
SIC: 2431 5072 2541 Interior & ornamental woodwork & trim; builders' hardware; wood partitions & fixtures

(G-1962)
MAJAAC INC
Also Called: Brust Pipeline
820 E Edgerton St (43506-1412)
P.O. Box 624 (43506-0624)
PHONE...................................419 636-5678
Nicholas Arnold II, *President*
EMP: 25 EST: 1940
SQ FT: 7,000
SALES (est): 1.8MM **Privately Held**
WEB: www.majaac.com
SIC: 1623 Gas main construction

(G-1963)
MANUFACTURED HOUSING ENTPS INC
Also Called: MANSION HOMES
9302 Us Highway 6 (43506-9516)
PHONE...................................419 636-4511
Mary Jane Fitzcharles, *CEO*
Janet Rice, *Corp Secy*
Nathan Kimpel, *Vice Pres*
Robert Confer, *Purch Agent*
John Bailey, *Engineer*
EMP: 150
SQ FT: 250,000
SALES: 28.1MM **Privately Held**
WEB: www.mheinc.com
SIC: 2451 1521 Mobile homes, except recreational; single-family housing construction

(G-1964)
MIDWEST CMNTY HLTH ASSOC INC (HQ)
Also Called: Parkview Physicians Group
442 W High St Ste 3 (43506-1685)
PHONE...................................419 633-4034

Randall Bauman, *President*
James Hamilton, *COO*
Stacey Beck, *CFO*
Luvenia Tantoco, *Med Doctor*
EMP: 175
SALES (est): 18.7MM **Privately Held**
SIC: 8011 Medical centers

(G-1965)
NWO RESOURCES INC (PA)
200 W High St (43506-1612)
P.O. Box 528 (43506-0528)
PHONE.............................419 636-1117
James N Blue, *President*
Richard Hallett, *President*
Gerlad Richards, *Treasurer*
EMP: 105
SALES (est): 2.3MM **Publicly Held**
SIC: 4924 6719 Natural gas distribution;
public utility holding companies

(G-1966)
OHIO GAS COMPANY (HQ)
200 W High St (43506-1677)
P.O. Box 528 (43506-0528)
PHONE.............................419 636-1117
Richard Hallett, *President*
Bob Eyre, *Vice Pres*
Douglas Saul, *Vice Pres*
Dee Swanson, *Vice Pres*
Kim Watkins, *Vice Pres*
EMP: 30 **EST:** 1914
SQ FT: 15,000
SALES (est): 38.3MM
SALES (corp-wide): 2.3MM **Publicly Held**
WEB: www.ohiogas.com
SIC: 4924 Natural gas distribution
PA: Nwo Resources Inc
200 W High St
Bryan OH 43506
419 636-1117

(G-1967)
OHIO GAS COMPANY
715 E Wilson St (43506-1848)
P.O. Box 528 (43506-0528)
PHONE.............................419 636-3642
Doug Saul, *Director*
EMP: 30
SALES (corp-wide): 2.3MM **Publicly Held**
WEB: www.ohiogas.com
SIC: 4922 Natural gas transmission
HQ: Ohio Gas Company
200 W High St
Bryan OH 43506
419 636-1117

(G-1968)
OREILLY AUTOMOTIVE INC
1116 S Main St (43506-2439)
PHONE.............................419 630-0811
EMP: 40 **Publicly Held**
SIC: 5531 5013 Batteries, automotive &
truck; automotive supplies & parts
PA: O'reilly Automotive, Inc.
233 S Patterson Ave
Springfield MO 65802

(G-1969)
PEOPLEWORKS DEV OF HR LLC
3440 County Road 9 (43506-9708)
PHONE.............................419 636-4637
John Murray,
Sam Stuck,
EMP: 27
SALES (est): 1.7MM **Privately Held**
SIC: 8742 Human resource consulting
services

(G-1970)
POTTER INC (PA)
630 Commerce Dr (43506-8864)
P.O. Box 685 (43506-0685)
PHONE.............................419 636-5624
Dave Gorzelanczyk, *President*
Marie Campbell Watkins, *Vice Pres*
Pam Klein, *Analyst*
▲ **EMP:** 30
SQ FT: 37,000
SALES (est): 26MM **Privately Held**
WEB: www.potter-inc.com
SIC: 5199 Baskets; gifts & novelties

(G-1971)
POWER TRAIN COMPONENTS INC
509 E Edgerton St (43506-1315)
P.O. Box 805 (43506-0805)
PHONE.............................419 636-4430
Delton R Nihart, *Ch of Bd*
Jack Nihart, *President*
▲ **EMP:** 55 **EST:** 1978
SQ FT: 60,000
SALES (est): 17.5MM **Privately Held**
WEB: www.ptcauto.com
SIC: 5013 Truck parts & accessories; auto-
motive supplies & parts

(G-1972)
PULASKI HEAD START
Also Called: Northwest Cmmuntiy Action
Comm
6678 Us Highway 127 (43506-8607)
PHONE.............................419 636-8862
Deb Gerken, *President*
Carmen Coy, *Manager*
EMP: 25
SALES (est): 444.9K **Privately Held**
SIC: 8351 Head start center, except in con-
junction with school

(G-1973)
REPUBLIC SERVICES INC
Also Called: Williams County Landfill
12359 County Road G (43506-9596)
PHONE.............................419 636-5109
John Bolyard, *Branch Mgr*
EMP: 34
SALES (corp-wide): 10B **Publicly Held**
SIC: 4953 Sanitary landfill operation
PA: Republic Services, Inc.
18500 N Allied Way # 100
Phoenix AZ 85054
480 627-2700

Buckeye Lake
Licking County

(G-1974)
BUCKEYE LAKE YACHT CLUB INC
5019 Northbank Rd (43008-7862)
P.O. Box 867 (43008-0867)
PHONE.............................740 929-4466
Fritz Riderman, *General Mgr*
EMP: 30
SALES (est): 983.8K **Privately Held**
WEB: www.buckeyelakeyc.com
SIC: 7997 Yacht club, membership

(G-1975)
NORTONE SERVICE INC
164 Slocum Ave (43008-7826)
P.O. Box 82, Canal Winchester (43110-
0082)
PHONE.............................740 527-2057
William Hubbard, *President*
Aaron Sott, *Vice Pres*
EMP: 42 **EST:** 1989
SALES (est): 968K **Privately Held**
SIC: 7349 Janitorial service, contract basis

Bucyrus
Crawford County

(G-1976)
ALTERCARE OF BUCYRUS INC
1929 Whetstone St (44820-3564)
PHONE.............................419 562-7644
Brenda Wachtel, *Executive*
Cathy Rox, *Administration*
Josh Snyder, *Administration*
EMP: 130
SALES (est): 5.4MM **Privately Held**
SIC: 8051 Convalescent home with contin-
uous nursing care

(G-1977)
BROKEN ARROW INC
1649 Marion Rd (44820-3116)
PHONE.............................419 562-3480
Jayne Hanning, *Exec Dir*
EMP: 32

SALES: 1.2MM **Privately Held**
SIC: 8322 8699 8059 Social services for
the handicapped; charitable organization;
personal care home, with health care

(G-1978)
BUCKEYE DRAG RACING ASSN LLC
201 Penn Ave (44820-2032)
PHONE.............................419 562-0869
Fred Nolen, *President*
EMP: 30
SALES (est): 440.5K **Privately Held**
SIC: 8699 Automobile owners' association

(G-1979)
BUCYRUS COMMUNITY HOSPITAL INC
629 N Sandusky Ave (44820-1821)
PHONE.............................419 562-4677
Jerry Morasko, *Principal*
Andrew Daniels, *COO*
EMP: 165 **EST:** 1956
SQ FT: 75,000
SALES (est): 27MM
SALES (corp-wide): 444.6K **Privately Held**
WEB: www.bchonline.org
SIC: 8062 Hospital, affiliated with AMA res-
idency
PA: Avita Health System
269 Portland Way S
Galion OH 44833
419 468-4841

(G-1980)
BUCYRUS COMMUNITY HOSPITAL LLC
629 N Sandusky Ave (44820-1821)
PHONE.............................419 562-4677
Jerome Morasko, *Mng Member*
Andy Daniels,
Eric Draime,
Shirley Fitz,
Traci Oswald,
EMP: 95
SALES: 53.5MM
SALES (corp-wide): 444.6K **Privately Held**
SIC: 8062 General medical & surgical hospi-
tals
PA: Avita Health System
269 Portland Way S
Galion OH 44833
419 468-4841

(G-1981)
CARLES BRATWURST INC
1210 E Mansfield St (44820-1943)
PHONE.............................419 562-7741
Chris Berry, *President*
EMP: 25
SQ FT: 4,000
SALES (est): 1.8MM **Privately Held**
WEB: www.carlesbrats.com
SIC: 5421 5147 Meat markets, including
freezer provisioners; meats, fresh

(G-1982)
CITY OF BUCYRUS
Also Called: Crawford Cnty Council On Aging
200 S Spring St (44820-2227)
P.O. Box 166 (44820-0166)
PHONE.............................419 562-3050
Margaret Wells, *Director*
EMP: 45 **Privately Held**
WEB: www.crawfordcountyaging.com
SIC: 8322 Senior citizens' center or associ-
ation
PA: City Of Bucyrus
500 S Sandusky Ave
Bucyrus OH 44820
419 562-6767

(G-1983)
CNB BANK
105 Washington Sq (44820-2252)
PHONE.............................419 562-7040
Joseph B Bower, *Branch Mgr*
EMP: 60
SALES (corp-wide): 152.5MM **Publicly Held**
SIC: 6022 State commercial banks

HQ: Cnb Bank
1 S 2nd St
Clearfield PA 16830
814 765-4577

(G-1984)
COMMUNITY COUNSELING SERVICES
2458 Stetzer Rd (44820-2066)
P.O. Box 765 (44820-0765)
PHONE.............................419 468-8211
Paul Sipes, *VP Finance*
Tom Saccenti, *Director*
EMP: 35
SQ FT: 4,600
SALES (est): 2.9MM **Privately Held**
SIC: 8093 8322 8069 Mental health clinic,
outpatient; crisis intervention center; alco-
holism rehabilitation hospital

(G-1985)
COMMUNITY INVSTORS BANCORP INC
119 S Sandusky Ave (44820-2220)
PHONE.............................419 562-7055
Phillip Gerber, *President*
David M Auck, *Principal*
Brent D Fissel, *Principal*
Phillip E Harris, *Principal*
Dale C Hoyles, *Principal*
EMP: 42
SALES: 7.4MM **Privately Held**
WEB: www.ffcb.com
SIC: 6712 Bank holding companies

(G-1986)
COUNTY OF CRAWFORD
Also Called: Crawford Cnty Job & Fmly Svcs
224 Norton Way (44820-1831)
PHONE.............................419 562-0015
Thomas M O'Leary, *Director*
EMP: 75 **Privately Held**
SIC: 8331 Job training services
PA: County Of Crawford
112 E Mansfield St # 304
Bucyrus OH 44820
419 562-5871

(G-1987)
COUNTY OF CRAWFORD
815 Whetstone St (44820-3359)
PHONE.............................419 562-7731
Tim Marcom, *Principal*
EMP: 44 **Privately Held**
SIC: 8711 Engineering services
PA: County Of Crawford
112 E Mansfield St # 304
Bucyrus OH 44820
419 562-5871

(G-1988)
CRAWFORD COUNTY CHILDREN SVCS (PA)
Also Called: Children's Service Board
224 Norton Way (44820-1831)
PHONE.............................419 562-1200
Brian Star, *Principal*
Kathy Scott, *Director*
EMP: 28
SALES (est): 843.6K **Privately Held**
SIC: 8322 Child related social services

(G-1989)
CRAWFORD COUNTY COUNCIL ON AGI
200 S Spring St (44820-2227)
PHONE.............................419 562-3050
Bruce Grafmiller, *Manager*
Margaret Wells, *Director*
EMP: 45
SALES: 1.8MM **Privately Held**
SIC: 8322 Senior citizens' center or associ-
ation

(G-1990)
FARMERS CITIZENS BANK (DH)
105 Washington Sq (44820-2252)
P.O. Box 567 (44820-0567)
PHONE.............................419 562-7040
Coleman Clougherty, *CEO*
Robert D Hord, *Chairman*
EMP: 43 **EST:** 1907
SQ FT: 24,000

SALES (est): 14.3MM
SALES (corp-wide): 152.5MM **Publicly Held**
WEB: www.farmerscitizensbank.com
SIC: 6022 State commercial banks
HQ: Cnb Bank
1 S 2nd St
Clearfield PA 16830
814 765-4577

(G-1991)
HEALTH CARE RTREMENT CORP AMER
Also Called: Heartland of Bucyrus
1170 W Mansfield St (44820-8509)
PHONE.............................419 562-9907
Tiffany Remmert, *Principal*
EMP: 99
SALES (est): 2.4B **Publicly Held**
WEB: www.hrc-manorcare.com
SIC: 8051 Skilled nursing care facilities
HQ: Health Care And Retirement Corporation Of America
333 N Summit St Ste 103
Toledo OH 43604
419 252-5500

(G-1992)
HEBCO PRODUCTS INC
1232 Whetstone St (44820-3539)
PHONE.............................419 562-7987
Andrew Ason, *President*
Ralph Reins, *Vice Pres*
EMP: 862
SALES (est): 73.7MM **Privately Held**
WEB: www.hebcoproducts.com
SIC: 3714 3451 3429 5013 Motor vehicle brake systems & parts; screw machine products; manufactured hardware (general); automotive supplies & parts
HQ: Qualitor, Inc.
1840 Mccullough St
Lima OH 45801
248 204-8600

(G-1993)
HOMECARE MTTERS HM HLTH HSPICE
133 S Sandusky Ave (44820-2220)
P.O. Box 327, Galion (44833-0327)
PHONE.............................419 562-2001
B Maglott, *Exec Dir*
Bertha Maglott, *Exec Dir*
EMP: 73 EST: 2007
SALES (est): 1MM **Privately Held**
SIC: 8082 Visiting nurse service

(G-1994)
HORD LIVESTOCK COMPANY INC
887 State Route 98 (44820-8646)
PHONE.............................419 562-0277
Robert Hord, *Principal*
EMP: 46
SALES (corp-wide): 9.7MM **Privately Held**
SIC: 5154 Livestock
PA: Hord Livestock Company Inc.
911 State Route 98
Bucyrus OH 44820
419 562-9885

(G-1995)
J & F CONSTRUCTION AND DEV INC
2141 State Route 19 (44820-9569)
PHONE.............................419 562-6662
James Mayes, *President*
Steve Bridgford, *Vice Pres*
Brock Mayes, *Vice Pres*
Ronda Scott, *Manager*
EMP: 28
SQ FT: 5,000
SALES (est): 9.3MM **Privately Held**
WEB: www.jfconstruction.com
SIC: 1542 1541 Commercial & office building, new construction; industrial buildings & warehouses

(G-1996)
MAPLECRST ASISTD LVG INTL ORDR
Also Called: Maple Crest Assisted Living
717 Rogers St (44820-2735)
PHONE.............................419 562-4988

Judy Wilkins, *Director*
EMP: 25
SALES: 584.3K **Privately Held**
SIC: 8082 5812 Home health care services; eating places

(G-1997)
NATIONAL LIME AND STONE CO
4580 Bethel Rd (44820-9754)
P.O. Box 69 (44820-0069)
PHONE.............................419 562-0771
Eric Johnson, *Principal*
Rick Dehays, *Purchasing*
Roger Nye, *Maintence Staff*
EMP: 62
SALES (corp-wide): 3.2B **Privately Held**
WEB: www.natlime.com
SIC: 1411 3281 1422 Limestone, dimension-quarrying; cut stone & stone products; crushed & broken limestone
PA: The National Lime And Stone Company
551 Lake Cascade Pkwy
Findlay OH 45840
419 422-4341

(G-1998)
OBERLANDERS TREE & LDSCP LTD
1874 E Mansfield St (44820-2018)
PHONE.............................419 562-8733
Roger Oberlander, *Principal*
EMP: 25
SALES (est): 1.4MM **Privately Held**
SIC: 0781 0783 Landscape services; ornamental shrub & tree services

(G-1999)
OHIO MUTUAL INSURANCE COMPANY (PA)
1725 Hopley Ave (44820-3596)
P.O. Box 111 (44820-0111)
PHONE.............................419 562-3011
Jim Kennedy, *President*
Todd Albert, *Vice Pres*
Michael Brogan, *Vice Pres*
Kathy Guinther, *Vice Pres*
Thomas Holtshouse, *Vice Pres*
EMP: 120 EST: 1901
SQ FT: 26,000
SALES (est): 190.3MM **Privately Held**
SIC: 6411 6331 Insurance brokers & service; fire, marine & casualty insurance: mutual; fire, marine & casualty insurance: stock

(G-2000)
PEOPLES SAVINGS AND LOAN CO (PA)
300 S Walnut St (44820-2330)
PHONE.............................419 562-6896
Steven Shields, *CEO*
Renae Cox, *Treasurer*
EMP: 30
SALES (est): 3.8MM **Privately Held**
SIC: 6035 Federal savings & loan associations

(G-2001)
SUBURBAN GALA LANES INC (PA)
975 Hopley Ave (44820-3506)
PHONE.............................419 468-7488
David Skaggs, *President*
Sherry Ransom, *Treasurer*
EMP: 40 EST: 1962
SALES (est): 600K **Privately Held**
SIC: 7933 Ten pin center

(G-2002)
TOTAL WAREHOUSING SERVICES
115 Crossroads Blvd (44820-1362)
P.O. Box 149 (44820-0149)
PHONE.............................419 562-2878
Jason McMullen, *President*
Justin McMullen, *Vice Pres*
EMP: 60
SQ FT: 71,000
SALES (est): 4.7MM **Privately Held**
SIC: 4225 General warehousing

(G-2003)
UNITED BANK NATIONAL ASSN (HQ)
Also Called: United Bank N A
401 S Sandusky Ave (44820-2624)
P.O. Box 568 (44820-0568)
PHONE.............................419 562-3040
Don Stone, *President*
EMP: 25
SQ FT: 5,000
SALES (est): 2.6MM
SALES (corp-wide): 411.9MM **Publicly Held**
WEB: www.unitedbankna.com
SIC: 6021 National commercial banks
PA: Park National Corporation
50 N 3rd St
Newark OH 43055
740 349-8451

(G-2004)
UNITED OHIO INSURANCE COMPANY
1725 Hopley Ave (44820-3569)
P.O. Box 111 (44820-0111)
PHONE.............................419 562-3011
James Kennedy, *President*
Randu O'Conner, *Vice Pres*
David Hendrix, *CFO*
EMP: 150
SQ FT: 15,000
SALES (est): 6.1MM
SALES (corp-wide): 190.3MM **Privately Held**
SIC: 6411 Insurance agents, brokers & service
PA: Ohio Mutual Insurance Company
1725 Hopley Ave
Bucyrus OH 44820
419 562-3011

(G-2005)
WAYCRAFT INC (PA)
118 River St (44820-1536)
PHONE.............................419 563-0550
Mark Barron, *President*
W Michael Miller, *Exec Dir*
EMP: 125
SQ FT: 44,000
SALES (est): 3.3MM **Privately Held**
SIC: 8331 Vocational rehabilitation agency

(G-2006)
WAYCRAFT INC
118 River St (44820-1536)
PHONE.............................419 562-3321
Nancy Whiteamire, *Branch Mgr*
EMP: 70
SALES (est): 1MM
SALES (corp-wide): 3.3MM **Privately Held**
SIC: 8331 Job training & vocational rehabilitation services
PA: Waycraft, Inc.
118 River St
Bucyrus OH 44820
419 563-0550

Buffalo
Guernsey County

(G-2007)
UNITED HSPTALITY SOLUTIONS LLC
11998 Clay Pike Rd (43722)
P.O. Box 98 (43722-0098)
PHONE.............................800 238-0487
Jennifer Yontz-Orlando, *Mng Member*
Marc Orlando,
Hugo Vargas,
Marieclaire Yontz,
EMP: 600
SQ FT: 1,200
SALES (est): 7.1MM **Privately Held**
SIC: 7011 Hotels & motels

Burbank
Wayne County

(G-2008)
4TH AND GOAL DISTRIBUTION LLC
9911 Avon Lake Rd (44214-9631)
PHONE.............................440 212-0769
Chris Mares,
EMP: 25
SALES (est): 374.2K **Privately Held**
SIC: 5091 Sporting & recreation goods

(G-2009)
RON BURGE TRUCKING INC
Also Called: Burge, Ron
1876 W Britton Rd (44214-9729)
PHONE.............................330 624-5373
Mike Burge, *President*
Annette Burge, *Corp Secy*
Scott Burge, *Vice Pres*
Sandra Burge, *Shareholder*
EMP: 30 EST: 1957
SQ FT: 2,000
SALES: 6.5MM **Privately Held**
WEB: www.ronburgetrucking.com
SIC: 4213 Contract haulers

Burghill
Trumbull County

(G-2010)
WILLIAM KERFOOT MASONRY INC
4948 State Route 7 (44404-9778)
PHONE.............................330 772-6460
William Kerfoot, *President*
EMP: 26
SALES (est): 983.6K **Privately Held**
SIC: 1741 Masonry & other stonework

Burgoon
Sandusky County

(G-2011)
C I E INC
2704 County Road 13 (43407-9750)
PHONE.............................419 986-5566
Marylin Broski, *Branch Mgr*
EMP: 273
SALES (corp-wide): 4.2MM **Privately Held**
SIC: 6513 8361 Retirement hotel operation; geriatric residential care
PA: C I E Inc
2036 E Township Road 122
Tiffin OH 44883
419 443-0767

Burkettsville
Mercer County

(G-2012)
KLINGSHIRN & SONS TRUCKING
Also Called: Klingshirn, Tom & Sons Trckng
14884 St Rt 118 S (45310)
P.O. Box 98 (45310-0098)
PHONE.............................937 338-5000
Thomas P Klingshirn, *President*
Paul Klingshirn, *Vice Pres*
Robert Klingshirn, *Vice Pres*
Joe Klingshirn, *Treasurer*
Mary Ann Klingshirn, *Admin Sec*
EMP: 40
SALES (est): 5.8MM **Privately Held**
SIC: 4213 4212 Contract haulers; local trucking, without storage

Burton
Geauga County

(G-2013)
AMERICAN LEGION
Also Called: Atwood Mock Post 459
14052 Goodwin St (44021-9522)
P.O. Box 261 (44021-0261)
PHONE..................................440 834-8621
Bob Hams, *Vice Pres*
EMP: 25
SALES (est): 302.5K **Privately Held**
SIC: 8641 Veterans' organization

(G-2014)
BAMA MASONRY INC
14379 Aquilla Rd (44021-9558)
PHONE..................................440 834-4175
Susan Saurman, *President*
EMP: 25
SALES (est): 2MM **Privately Held**
SIC: 1741 Masonry & other stonework

(G-2015)
BFG SUPPLY CO LLC (DH)
Also Called: Tricor Pacific Capital Partner
14500 Kinsman Rd (44021-9423)
P.O. Box 479 (44021-0479)
PHONE..................................440 834-1883
Rob Glockner, *President*
Doug Scott, *President*
Charles Fulks, *Partner*
Daniel Dignan, *General Mgr*
Nicole Krizner, *Vice Pres*
▲ EMP: 30
SQ FT: 32,000
SALES (est): 162.9MM
SALES (corp-wide): 3.6MM **Privately Held**
WEB: www.bfgsupply.com
SIC: 5191 5261 Garden supplies; garden supplies & tools

(G-2016)
HEXPOL COMPOUNDING LLC
Also Called: Burton Rubber Processing
14330 Kinsman Rd (44021-9648)
PHONE..................................440 834-4644
John Gorrell, *Manager*
EMP: 200
SALES (corp-wide): 1.4B **Privately Held**
SIC: 3087 2865 5162 2899 Custom compound purchased resins; dyes & pigments; resins; plastics basic shapes; chemical preparations; adhesives & sealants; paints & allied products
HQ: Hexpol Compounding Llc
　14330 Kinsman Rd
　Burton OH 44021
　440 834-4644

(G-2017)
IMPULLITTI LANDSCAPING INC
14659 Ravenna Rd (44021-9713)
PHONE..................................440 834-1866
Wayne Impullitti, *President*
EMP: 75
SALES: 9.5MM **Privately Held**
SIC: 0781 Landscape services

(G-2018)
MIDEAST BAPTIST CONFERENCE
14282 Butternut Rd (44021-9572)
PHONE..................................440 834-8984
Dave Scull, *Director*
John Lundwall, *Director*
EMP: 50 EST: 1956
SQ FT: 1,296
SALES (est): 438.6K **Privately Held**
WEB: www.campburton.org
SIC: 7032 8661 Sporting & recreational camps; religious organizations

(G-2019)
STEPHEN M TRUDICK
Also Called: Hardwood Lumber Co
13813 Station Rd (44021)
P.O. Box 15 (44021-0015)
PHONE..................................440 834-1891
Stephen M Trudick, *Owner*
Jayne Shaffer, *Director*
▲ EMP: 41

SQ FT: 80,000
SALES (est): 5.5MM **Privately Held**
WEB: www.hardwood-lumber.com
SIC: 3991 2426 5031 3442 Brooms & brushes; dimension, hardwood; lumber: rough, dressed & finished; metal doors, sash & trim; millwork; sawmills & planing mills, general

(G-2020)
WINDSOR HOUSE INC
Also Called: Burton Health Care Center
14095 E Center St (44021-9651)
PHONE..................................440 834-0544
Clara Brown, *Food Svc Dir*
Erin Kostas, *Administration*
EMP: 40
SALES (corp-wide): 14.1MM **Privately Held**
SIC: 8741 8051 Nursing & personal care facility management; skilled nursing care facilities
PA: Windsor House, Inc.
　101 W Liberty St
　Girard OH
　330 545-1550

Butler
Richland County

(G-2021)
OTS-NJ LLC
21 Traxler St (44822-8827)
PHONE..................................732 833-0600
James T O Connor, *Owner*
James White,
EMP: 55
SQ FT: 1,700
SALES (est): 7.8MM **Privately Held**
WEB: www.vikingelectronics.com
SIC: 1623 Water, sewer & utility lines

(G-2022)
SUSAN A SMITH CRYSTAL CARE
5375 Teeter Rd (44822-9623)
PHONE..................................419 747-2666
Jerry Smith, *President*
Kyann Miner, *Vice Pres*
Jennifer Coile, *Treasurer*
Mindy Caudill, *Controller*
Susan Smith, *Admin Sec*
EMP: 45 EST: 1993
SALES (est): 670.6K **Privately Held**
SIC: 8059 7542 Nursing home, except skilled & intermediate care facility; carwashes

Byesville
Guernsey County

(G-2023)
CAMBRIDGE COUNTRY CLUB COMPANY
60755 Southgate Rd (43723-9643)
PHONE..................................740 439-2744
Gary Farmer, *President*
Tom Fischer, *Vice Pres*
EMP: 25 EST: 1907
SQ FT: 25,000
SALES (est): 890K **Privately Held**
SIC: 7997 7992 5941 5813 Country club, membership; golf club, membership; swimming club, membership; tennis club, membership; public golf courses; sporting goods & bicycle shops; drinking places; eating places

(G-2024)
CAMBRIDGE COUNTRY CLUB CORP
60755 Southgate Rd (43723-9643)
PHONE..................................740 432-2107
Shawn Thompson, *General Mgr*
EMP: 40
SALES (est): 543.3K **Privately Held**
SIC: 7997 Country club, membership

(G-2025)
KEN HARPER
Also Called: GUERNSEY INDUSTRIES
60772 Southgate Rd (43723-9731)
PHONE..................................740 439-4452
Ken Harper, *Exec Dir*
EMP: 110
SALES: 997.3K **Privately Held**
SIC: 8331 2511 2448 Sheltered workshop; wood household furniture; wood pallets & skids

(G-2026)
VILLAGE OF BYESVILLE
221 Main St (43723-1338)
P.O. Box 8 (43723-0008)
PHONE..................................740 685-5901
Jay Jackson, *Mayor*
Annette Whealdon, *Treasurer*
EMP: 25
SALES: 852.1K **Privately Held**
SIC: 8721 Billing & bookkeeping service

Cadiz
Harrison County

(G-2027)
CARRIAGE INN OF CADIZ INC
308 W Warren St (43907-1077)
PHONE..................................740 942-8084
Ken Bernsen, *President*
Lynne Huff, *Vice Pres*
Sarah Manning, *Relations*
EMP: 32 EST: 1982
SALES: 4.5MM **Privately Held**
SIC: 8051 8322 Convalescent home with continuous nursing care; rehabilitation services

(G-2028)
HARRISON CO COUNTY HOME
41500 Cadiz Dennison Rd (43907-9575)
PHONE..................................740 942-3573
William G Rogers, *Superintendent*
EMP: 30
SALES (est): 686K **Privately Held**
SIC: 8361 Home for the aged

(G-2029)
HARRISON INDUSTRIES INC
82460 Cadiz Jewett Rd (43907-9427)
PHONE..................................740 942-2988
C L Strahl, *Dir Ops-Prd-Mfg*
F Scott Brace, *Director*
EMP: 55
SQ FT: 8,000
SALES (est): 230.3K **Privately Held**
WEB: www.harrisonindustries.com
SIC: 8331 5712 7349 Sheltered workshop; outdoor & garden furniture; building maintenance services

(G-2030)
ISI SYSTEMS INC (PA)
43029 Industrial Park Rd (43907-9621)
P.O. Box 156, Bellaire (43906-0156)
PHONE..................................740 942-0050
Christine Wallace, *President*
William Wallace, *Exec VP*
EMP: 30
SQ FT: 10,000
SALES: 1.5MM **Privately Held**
WEB: www.isisystems.net
SIC: 1629 Industrial plant construction

(G-2031)
MANNIK & SMITH GROUP INC
Also Called: Mannik Smith Group, The
104 S Main St (43907-1171)
PHONE..................................740 942-4222
EMP: 38
SALES (est): 1.8MM
SALES (corp-wide): 34.3MM **Privately Held**
SIC: 8711 Consulting engineer
PA: The Mannik & Smith Group Inc
　1800 Indian Wood Cir
　Maumee OH 43537
　419 891-2222

(G-2032)
OHIO MACHINERY CO
Also Called: Ohio Cat
1016 E Market St (43907-9728)
PHONE..................................740 942-4626
Rick Wagstaff, *General Mgr*
Frank Keller, *Manager*
Ken Skapik, *Manager*
EMP: 50
SALES (corp-wide): 222.7MM **Privately Held**
WEB: www.enginesnow.com
SIC: 5082 General construction machinery & equipment
PA: Ohio Machinery Co.
　3993 E Royalton Rd
　Broadview Heights OH 44147
　440 526-6200

(G-2033)
VERIZON NORTH INC
994 E Market St (43907-9799)
PHONE..................................740 942-2566
Jim Woods, *President*
EMP: 25
SALES (corp-wide): 130.8B **Publicly Held**
SIC: 4813 Local telephone communications; long distance telephone communications
HQ: Verizon North Inc
　140 West St
　New York NY 10007
　212 395-1000

(G-2034)
WHEELING HOSPITAL INC
Also Called: Harrison Community Hospital
951 E Market St (43907-9799)
PHONE..................................740 942-4631
Anthony Martinelli, *Branch Mgr*
EMP: 150
SALES (corp-wide): 395.3MM **Privately Held**
SIC: 8062 Hospital, affiliated with AMA residency
PA: Wheeling Hospital, Inc.
　1 Medical Park
　Wheeling WV 26003
　304 243-3000

(G-2035)
WHEELING HOSPITAL INC
Also Called: Harrison Community Hospital
943 E Market St (43907-9783)
PHONE..................................740 942-4116
Janis Olinski, *Vice Pres*
Peter Giordano, *Director*
EMP: 79
SALES (corp-wide): 395.3MM **Privately Held**
WEB: www.srprasad.com
SIC: 8062 General medical & surgical hospitals
PA: Wheeling Hospital, Inc.
　1 Medical Park
　Wheeling WV 26003
　304 243-3000

Caldwell
Noble County

(G-2036)
BRADEN MED SERVICES INC
Also Called: Gillespie Drug
44519 Marietta Rd (43724-9209)
PHONE..................................740 732-2356
James Scott Braden, *President*
Diane Braden, *General Mgr*
Kyle Huck, *General Mgr*
Diane R Braden, *Treasurer*
John Turner, *Sales Executive*
EMP: 35
SQ FT: 5,000
SALES (est): 2MM **Privately Held**
WEB: www.bradenmed.com
SIC: 8082 7352 5122 5169 Home health care services; medical equipment rental; pharmaceuticals; oxygen; hospital equipment & furniture

(G-2037)
COMMUNITY IMPRV CORP NBLE CNTY
44523 Marietta Rd (43724-9209)
P.O. Box 41 (43724-0041)
PHONE...................................740 509-0248
Scott Braden, *President*
EMP: 99
SALES: 0 **Privately Held**
SIC: 8399 Community development groups

(G-2038)
CROCK CONSTRUCTION CO
17990 Woodsfield Rd (43724-9435)
PHONE...................................740 732-2306
Edward Crock, *CEO*
Brandon Crock, *Vice Pres*
Leander Crock, *Vice Pres*
EMP: 25 **EST:** 1948
SQ FT: 15,000
SALES (est): 4.3MM **Privately Held**
SIC: 1542 1521 Commercial & office building, new construction; new construction, single-family houses

(G-2039)
G M N TRI CNTY COMMUNITY ACTION (PA)
615 North St (43724-1123)
PHONE...................................740 732-2388
Gary Ricer, *Exec Dir*
EMP: 150
SQ FT: 4,000
SALES: 7.2MM **Privately Held**
WEB: www.gmncac.org
SIC: 8322 Social service center

(G-2040)
IEH AUTO PARTS LLC
218 West St (43724-1337)
PHONE...................................740 732-2395
Wally Olson, *Branch Mgr*
EMP: 27
SALES (corp-wide): 11.7B **Publicly Held**
SIC: 5013 Automotive supplies & parts
HQ: Ieh Auto Parts Llc
    1155 Roberts Blvd Nw # 175
    Kennesaw GA 30144
    770 701-5000

(G-2041)
NOBEL COUNTY ENGINEERS OFFICE
Courthouse Rm 220 St Rm 2 (43724)
PHONE...................................740 732-4400
Kris Stritz, *Principal*
Greg Tilton, *Principal*
EMP: 30
SALES (est): 931.7K **Privately Held**
SIC: 4789 Transportation services

(G-2042)
NOBEL LEARNING CENTER
44135 Marietta Rd (43724-9124)
PHONE...................................740 732-4722
Lashona D Volld, *Director*
EMP: 30
SALES: 860.5K **Privately Held**
SIC: 8351 Preschool center

(G-2043)
NOBLE CNTY NBLE CNTY CMMSONERS
Also Called: Noble County Health Department
44069 Marietta Rd (43724-9124)
PHONE...................................740 732-4958
Shawn Ray, *Branch Mgr*
EMP: 32 **Privately Held**
SIC: 8093 9111 Family planning & birth control clinics; county supervisors' & executives' offices
PA: Noble, County Of Noble County Commisioners
    200 Court House Fl 2
    Caldwell OH 43724
    740 732-4044

(G-2044)
SUMMIT ACRES INC (PA)
Also Called: SUMMIT ACRES NURSING HOME
44565 Sunset Rd (43724-9731)
PHONE...................................740 732-2364
Leander Crock, *President*
Malcolm Parks, *Treasurer*

Edward Hupp, *Admin Sec*
Donald Crock, *Administration*
EMP: 200 **EST:** 1965
SQ FT: 54,000
SALES: 6.5MM **Privately Held**
SIC: 8093 8052 8082 Rehabilitation center, outpatient treatment; intermediate care facilities; home health care services

(G-2045)
TLC HOME HEALTH CARE INC
43 Kennedy Dr (43724-9004)
PHONE...................................740 732-5211
Betty Postelwait, *President*
EMP: 40
SALES (est): 1.3MM **Privately Held**
SIC: 8082 Home health care services

(G-2046)
UNITED AMBULANCE SERVICE
523 Main St (43724-1324)
PHONE...................................740 732-5653
Jim Starr, *Director*
EMP: 40
SALES (est): 604.4K **Privately Held**
SIC: 4119 Ambulance service

Cambridge
Guernsey County

(G-2047)
AFC CABLE SYSTEMS INC
829 Georgetown Rd (43725)
PHONE...................................740 435-3340
Bob Koscoe, *Branch Mgr*
EMP: 52 **Publicly Held**
WEB: www.afcweb.com
SIC: 5063 Wire & cable
HQ: Afc Cable Systems, Inc.
    16100 Lathrop Ave
    Harvey IL 60426
    508 998-1131

(G-2048)
ALL FOR KIDS INC
1405 E Wheeling Ave (43725-2563)
P.O. Box 1266 (43725-6266)
PHONE...................................740 435-8050
Lisa Brown, *Director*
EMP: 25
SALES (est): 625.9K **Privately Held**
SIC: 8351 Preschool center

(G-2049)
ALLWELL BEHAVIORAL HEALTH SVCS
Also Called: Guernsy Counseling Center
2500 Glenn Hwy (43725-9028)
PHONE...................................740 439-4428
Barbara Stclair, *Manager*
EMP: 25
SALES (corp-wide): 14.2MM **Privately Held**
SIC: 8093 8322 Mental health clinic, outpatient; family counseling services
PA: Allwell Behavioral Health Services
    2845 Bell St
    Zanesville OH 43701
    740 454-9766

(G-2050)
AREA AGENCY ON AGING REG 9 INC
1730 Southgate Pkwy (43725-3024)
PHONE...................................740 439-4478
James Endly, *CEO*
EMP: 98
SQ FT: 15,000
SALES: 46.6MM **Privately Held**
WEB: www.aaa9.org
SIC: 8322 Outreach program; senior citizens' center or association

(G-2051)
CAMBRIDGE ASSOCIATES LTD
Also Called: Holiday Inn
2248 Southgate Pkwy (43725-3038)
P.O. Box 15395, Columbus (43215-0395)
PHONE...................................740 432-7313
Ralph Ray, *General Mgr*
EMP: 50

SALES (corp-wide): 1.4MM **Privately Held**
SIC: 7011 Hotels & motels
PA: Cambridge Associates Ltd
    2002 Richard Jones Rd 105c
    Nashville TN 37215
    615 385-4946

(G-2052)
CAMBRIDGE BEHAVIORAL HOSPITAL
66755 State St (43725-8757)
PHONE...................................740 432-4906
EMP: 130
SALES: 14.6MM **Privately Held**
SIC: 8063 8069 Hospital for the mentally ill; substance abuse hospitals

(G-2053)
CAMBRIDGE HOME HEALTHCARE
1300 Clark St Unit 7 (43725-8875)
PHONE...................................740 432-6191
Connie Stone, *Manager*
EMP: 50
SALES (est): 1.5MM **Privately Held**
SIC: 8051 Skilled Nursing Care Facility

(G-2054)
CAMBRIDGE NH LLC
Also Called: Greystone Health and
66731 Old Twenty One Rd (43725-8987)
PHONE...................................740 432-7717
Mordecai Rosenberg, *President*
Ronald Swartz, *CFO*
Lisa Schwartz, *Admin Sec*
Dawn Wozniak, *Exec Sec*
EMP: 80
SALES (est): 264.1K **Privately Held**
SIC: 8051 Skilled nursing care facilities

(G-2055)
CAMBRIDGE PACKAGING INC
Also Called: Cambridge Box & Gift Shop
60794 Southgate Rd (43725-9414)
PHONE...................................740 432-3351
Larry Knellinger, *President*
Bill Knellinger, *Vice Pres*
Rick Knellinger, *Vice Pres*
John Common, *Purch Mgr*
John Luskevich, *Purch Mgr*
EMP: 31
SQ FT: 26,000
SALES (est): 7.6MM **Privately Held**
WEB: www.cambridgepackaging.com
SIC: 2653 5199 Boxes, corrugated: made from purchased materials; packaging materials

(G-2056)
CAMBRIDGE PROPERTY INVESTORS
Also Called: Holiday Inn
2248 Southgate Pkwy (43725-3038)
P.O. Box 96, Byesville (43723-0096)
PHONE...................................740 432-7313
Richard Lenhart, *Partner*
Kelly Lenhart,
EMP: 47
SALES (est): 1.9MM **Privately Held**
SIC: 7011 Hotels & motels

(G-2057)
CELLCO PARTNERSHIP
Also Called: Verizon Wireless
2103 Southgate Pkwy (43725-3080)
PHONE...................................740 432-7785
Jeff Fluharty, *Principal*
EMP: 71
SALES (corp-wide): 130.8B **Publicly Held**
SIC: 4812 Cellular telephone services
HQ: Cellco Partnership
    1 Verizon Way
    Basking Ridge NJ 07920

(G-2058)
CHILDRENS ADVOCACY CENTER
274 Highland Ave (43725-2571)
P.O. Box 1725 (43725-6725)
PHONE...................................740 432-6581
Melissa Kaylor, *Director*
EMP: 32

SALES (est): 705.1K **Privately Held**
SIC: 8322 Child related social services

(G-2059)
COLUMBIA GAS TRANSMISSION LLC
Also Called: Columbia Energy
11296 E Pike Rd (43725-9669)
PHONE...................................740 432-1612
Rod Graham, *Manager*
EMP: 45
SALES (corp-wide): 10.5B **Privately Held**
SIC: 4923 Gas transmission & distribution
HQ: Columbia Gas Transmission, Llc
    200 Cizzic Ctr Dr
    Columbus OH 43216
    614 460-6000

(G-2060)
COUNTY OF GUERNSEY
Also Called: Guernsey Cnty Children Svcs Bd
274 Highland Ave (43725-2571)
PHONE...................................740 439-5555
Kelly Lynch, *Exec Dir*
EMP: 35 **Privately Held**
WEB: www.visitguernseycounty.com
SIC: 8351 9111 Child day care services; county supervisors' & executives' offices
PA: County Of Guernsey
    627 Wheeling Ave Rm 301
    Cambridge OH 43725
    740 432-9243

(G-2061)
COUNTY OF GUERNSEY
Also Called: Guernsey Co Public Info Agency
324 Highland Ave (43725-2530)
PHONE...................................800 307-8422
Kathy Jamiel, *Director*
EMP: 80 **Privately Held**
WEB: www.visitguernseycounty.com
SIC: 8743 Public relations services
PA: County Of Guernsey
    627 Wheeling Ave Rm 301
    Cambridge OH 43725
    740 432-9243

(G-2062)
COUNTY OF GUERNSEY
Also Called: Department of Jobs & Family
324 Highland Ave (43725-2530)
PHONE...................................740 432-2381
Kathy Jamiel, *Director*
EMP: 82 **Privately Held**
WEB: www.visitguernseycounty.com
SIC: 7361 8322 Employment agencies; community center
PA: County Of Guernsey
    627 Wheeling Ave Rm 301
    Cambridge OH 43725
    740 432-9243

(G-2063)
COUNTY OF GUERNSEY
Also Called: Guernsey County Senior Center
1022 Carlisle Ave (43725-2420)
PHONE...................................740 439-6681
Shon Gress, *Director*
EMP: 50 **Privately Held**
WEB: www.visitguernseycounty.com
SIC: 8322 Individual & family services
PA: County Of Guernsey
    627 Wheeling Ave Rm 301
    Cambridge OH 43725
    740 432-9243

(G-2064)
DUNNING MOTOR SALES INC
9108 Southgate Rd (43725-8005)
PHONE...................................740 439-4465
John Dunning Jr, *General Mgr*
Nancy S Dunning, *Vice Pres*
Sal Gard, *Parts Mgr*
Craig Abner, *Sales Mgr*
Connie Daugherty, *Office Mgr*
EMP: 45
SALES (est): 18.8MM **Privately Held**
WEB: www.dunningmotorsales.com
SIC: 5511 7538 7515 Automobiles, new & used; general automotive repair shops; passenger car leasing

---

(G-2065)
DYNO NOBEL TRANSPORTATION
Also Called: Dyno Transportation
850 Woodlawn Ave (43725-2959)
PHONE......................................740 439-5050
Bobby Bickford, *Manager*
EMP: 30 **Privately Held**
SIC: 4212 Delivery service, vehicular
HQ: Dyno Nobel Transportation, Inc
  2795 E Cottonwood Pkwy # 500
  Salt Lake City UT 84121
  801 364-4800

(G-2066)
FAMILY PLANNING CENTER
326 Highland Ave (43725-2530)
PHONE......................................740 439-3340
Maryland Moorehead, *Partner*
EMP: 25
SALES (est): 596.8K **Privately Held**
SIC: 8093 Family planning clinic

(G-2067)
FEDERAL-MOGUL POWERTRAIN LLC
6420 Glenn Hwy (43725-9755)
PHONE......................................740 432-2393
Robb Junker, *Branch Mgr*
EMP: 170
SALES (corp-wide): 11.7B **Publicly Held**
SIC: 3053 3592 3562 5085 Gaskets & sealing devices; oil seals, rubber; gaskets, all materials; pistons & piston rings; ball bearings & parts; bearings; motor vehicle parts & accessories; bearings, motor vehicle; transmission housings or parts, motor vehicle; steering mechanisms, motor vehicle; motor vehicle lighting equipment
HQ: Federal-Mogul Powertrain Llc
  27300 W 11 Mile Rd # 101
  Southfield MI 48034

(G-2068)
FOOD DISTRIBUTORS INC
449 N 1st St (43725-1256)
P.O. Box 607 (43725-0607)
PHONE......................................740 439-2764
Charles E Smith, *President*
Darla Perkins, *Manager*
EMP: 25 EST: 1973
SQ FT: 25,000
SALES (est): 5.3MM **Privately Held**
SIC: 5149 5142 5113 Canned goods: fruit, vegetables, seafood, meats, etc.; packaged frozen goods; industrial & personal service paper

(G-2069)
GEORGETOWN VINEYARDS INC
62920 Georgetown Rd (43725-9749)
PHONE......................................740 435-3222
John Nicolozakes, *President*
Kay Nicolozakes, *Vice Pres*
Sam Nicolozakes, *Treasurer*
Emma McVicker, *Admin Sec*
EMP: 25
SQ FT: 600
SALES (est): 113.3K **Privately Held**
SIC: 0721 2084 5812 2082 Vines, cultivation of; wine cellars, bonded: engaged in blending wines; pizza restaurants; near beer

(G-2070)
GOODWILL INDS CENTL OHIO INC
1712 Southgate Pkwy (43725-3024)
PHONE......................................740 439-7000
Vickie Frick, *Manager*
EMP: 50
SALES (corp-wide): 48.1MM **Privately Held**
SIC: 8699 8331 5932 Charitable organization; vocational rehabilitation agency; used merchandise stores
PA: Goodwill Industries Of Central Ohio, Inc.
  1331 Edgehill Rd
  Columbus OH 43212
  614 294-5181

(G-2071)
GUERNSEY COUNTY CMNTY DEV CORP
Also Called: GUERNSEY COUNTY CDC
905 Wheeling Ave (43725-2318)
P.O. Box 1175 (43725-6175)
PHONE......................................740 439-0020
Ron Gombida, *Exec Dir*
EMP: 36
SALES: 424.8K **Privately Held**
SIC: 8399 Community development groups

(G-2072)
GUERNSEY HEALTH ENTERPRISES
1341 Clark St (43725-9614)
P.O. Box 610 (43725-0610)
PHONE......................................740 439-3561
Raymond Shorey, *President*
EMP: 700
SQ FT: 211,000
SALES (est): 2.3MM
SALES (corp-wide): 105.5MM **Privately Held**
SIC: 4119 8059 5912 Ambulance service; rest home, with health care; drug stores
HQ: Guernsey Health Systems
  1341 Clark St
  Cambridge OH 43725
  740 439-3561

(G-2073)
GUERNSEY HEALTH SYSTEMS (HQ)
1341 Clark St (43725-9614)
P.O. Box 610 (43725-0610)
PHONE......................................740 439-3561
Philip Hearing, *CEO*
Donald P Huelskamp, *CFO*
EMP: 550
SQ FT: 211,000
SALES: 2MM
SALES (corp-wide): 105.5MM **Privately Held**
SIC: 4119 8062 8052 Local passenger transportation; general medical & surgical hospitals; intermediate care facilities
PA: Southeastern Ohio Regional Medical Center
  1341 Clark St
  Cambridge OH 43725
  740 439-3561

(G-2074)
HIGGINS BUILDING COMPANY INC
11342 E Pike Rd (43725-9669)
PHONE......................................740 439-5553
James R Higgins, *President*
Darlene Higgins, *Corp Secy*
Martin Higgins, *Vice Pres*
EMP: 40
SQ FT: 11,000
SALES (est): 5.2MM **Privately Held**
WEB: www.higginsbuildingcoinc.org
SIC: 1541 1542 Industrial Building Construction Nonresidential Construction

(G-2075)
KINDRED HEALTHCARE OPER INC
Also Called: Kindred Nursing
1471 Wills Creek Vly Dr (43725-8620)
PHONE......................................740 439-4437
Debbie Morse, *Manager*
Mary Jo Yonker, *Receptionist*
EMP: 140
SALES (corp-wide): 6B **Privately Held**
WEB: www.salemhaven.com
SIC: 8051 Skilled nursing care facilities
HQ: Kindred Healthcare Operating, Llc
  680 S 4th St
  Louisville KY 40202
  502 596-7300

(G-2076)
MEDICAL ASSOC CAMBRIDGE INC
1515 Maple Dr Ste 1 (43725-1162)
PHONE......................................740 439-3515
Mark T Goggin, *Principal*
Patrick D Goggin, *Principal*
Kayode Ojedele, *Principal*
Douglas A Rush, *Principal*
EMP: 34
SALES (est): 2.8MM **Privately Held**
SIC: 8011 Clinic, operated by physicians; psychiatrists & psychoanalysts; surgeon

(G-2077)
MOSSER GLASS INCORPORATED
9279 Cadiz Rd (43725-9564)
PHONE......................................740 439-1827
Timmy J Mosser, *President*
Thomas R Mosser, *President*
Mindy Hartly, *Manager*
▲ EMP: 30
SALES (est): 3.9MM **Privately Held**
WEB: www.mosserglass.com
SIC: 3229 5199 5719 Novelty glassware; glassware, industrial; glassware, novelty; glassware

(G-2078)
NICOLOZAKES TRCKG & CNSTR INC
8555 Georgetown Rd (43725-8866)
P.O. Box 670 (43725-0670)
PHONE......................................740 432-5648
William A Nicolozakes, *President*
Basil J Nicolozakes, *Vice Pres*
Dean S Nicolozakes, *Vice Pres*
James A Nicolozakes, *Vice Pres*
EMP: 30 EST: 1953
SQ FT: 32,600
SALES: 5.1MM **Privately Held**
WEB: www.nicolozakes.com
SIC: 1541 4212 4213 1794 Industrial buildings, new construction; light haulage & cartage, local; heavy machinery transport; excavation & grading, building construction

(G-2079)
OHIO BRIDGE CORPORATION
Also Called: U.S. Bridge
201 Wheeling Ave (43725-2256)
P.O. Box 757 (43725-0757)
PHONE......................................740 432-6334
Daniel Rogovin, *CEO*
Jeff Lawson, *Division Mgr*
Richard Rogovin, *Chairman*
Scott Flaten, *Project Engr*
David Morgan, *Design Engr*
▼ EMP: 140 EST: 1952
SQ FT: 250,000
SALES (est): 56.6MM **Privately Held**
SIC: 1622 3449 Bridge construction; bars, concrete reinforcing: fabricated steel

(G-2080)
PEOPLES BANK
845 Wheeling Ave (43725-2316)
PHONE......................................740 439-2767
Larry Miller, *Manager*
EMP: 27
SALES (corp-wide): 208MM **Publicly Held**
SIC: 6021 National commercial banks
HQ: Peoples Bank
  138 Putnam St
  Marietta OH 45750
  740 373-3155

(G-2081)
RED CARPET HEALTH CARE CENTER
8420 Georgetown Rd (43725-9770)
PHONE......................................740 439-4401
Arnold Tuber, *Corp Secy*
Dale Shonk, *Vice Pres*
Mary Jirles, *Chf Purch Ofc*
Michael Shade, *Director*
Vern Beynon, *Administration*
EMP: 130
SQ FT: 35,000
SALES (est): 4.9MM
SALES (corp-wide): 10.3MM **Privately Held**
WEB: www.redcarpetcc.com
SIC: 8059 8051 Rest home, with health care; skilled nursing care facilities
PA: S.F.T. Health Care Inc
  5890 Mayfair Rd
  Canton OH 44720
  330 499-6358

(G-2082)
SOUTHEAST DIVERSIFIED INDS
1401 Burgess Ave (43725-3003)
PHONE......................................740 432-4241
Ed Rolan Dee, *Chairman*
Daniel Duniver, *Manager*
EMP: 70
SQ FT: 20,000
SALES: 69.7K **Privately Held**
SIC: 8322 4783 8331 Association for the handicapped; packing & crating; job training & vocational rehabilitation services

(G-2083)
SOUTHSTERN OHIO RGONAL MED CTR (PA)
Also Called: Southeastern Med
1341 Clark St (43725-9614)
P.O. Box 610 (43725-0610)
PHONE......................................740 439-3561
Raymond Chorey, *President*
Troy Mills, *Maint Spvr*
Donald Huelskamp, *CFO*
Nabiel Alkhouri, *Med Doctor*
Clark Carpenter, *Supervisor*
EMP: 40 EST: 1954
SQ FT: 211,000
SALES: 105.5MM **Privately Held**
SIC: 8062 General medical & surgical hospitals

(G-2084)
SUPERIOR MED LLC (PA)
1251 Clark St (43725-9612)
P.O. Box 501 (43725-0501)
PHONE......................................740 439-8839
EMP: 37
SALES (est): 5.8MM **Privately Held**
WEB: www.superiormed.com
SIC: 8011 Medical centers

(G-2085)
THE C-Z COMPANY (PA)
Also Called: C-Z Realtors
201 Wheeling Ave (43725-2256)
P.O. Box 757 (43725-0757)
PHONE......................................740 432-6334
Arthur Rogovin, *Vice Pres*
Casey Frame, *Accountant*
Casey Rich, *Accountant*
Nate Wutrick, *Regl Sales Mgr*
Julie Meldrum, *Business Anlyst*
EMP: 40 EST: 1947
SQ FT: 4,000
SALES (est): 3.9MM **Privately Held**
SIC: 6512 4225 Commercial & industrial building operation; general warehousing & storage

(G-2086)
UNITED AMBLNCE SVC OF CMBRIDGE (DH)
1331 Campbell Ave (43725-2928)
P.O. Box 1118 (43725-6118)
PHONE......................................740 439-7787
Raymond Chorey, *President*
Andrew D Eddy, *Vice Pres*
James Michael Starr, *Director*
EMP: 25
SQ FT: 1,500
SALES (est): 109.8K
SALES (corp-wide): 105.5MM **Privately Held**
SIC: 4119 Ambulance service
HQ: Guernsey Health Systems
  1341 Clark St
  Cambridge OH 43725
  740 439-3561

(G-2087)
ZEKELMAN INDUSTRIES INC
Also Called: Wheatland Tube Company
9208 Jeffrey Dr (43725-9417)
PHONE......................................740 432-2146
Ned Feeney, *President*
EMP: 104
SQ FT: 58,000 **Privately Held**
SIC: 3317 3498 5074 3644 Pipes, seamless steel; fabricated pipe & fittings; plumbing fittings & supplies; noncurrent-carrying wiring services; plumbing fixture fittings & trim; blast furnaces & steel mills
PA: Zekelman Industries, Inc.
  227 W Monroe St Ste 2600
  Chicago IL 60606

Camden
Preble County

(G-2088)
BARNETS INC
Also Called: G & J Kartway
1619 Barnetts Mill Rd (45311-9728)
PHONE.................................937 452-3275
Gary Gregg, *President*
Jane Simpson, *Vice Pres*
Travis Gregg, *Treasurer*
Elaine Gregg, *Admin Sec*
EMP: 48
SQ FT: 25,000
SALES: 9MM **Privately Held**
SIC: 5153 4213 Grain elevators; trucking, except local

(G-2089)
COUNCIL ON RUR SVC PRGRAMS INC
8263 Us Route 127 (45311-8798)
PHONE.................................937 452-1090
EMP: 97
SALES (corp-wide): 15.7MM **Privately Held**
SIC: 8351 Head start center, except in conjunction with school
PA: Council On Rural Service Programs, Inc.
201 Robert M Davis Pkwy B
Piqua OH 45356
937 778-5220

Campbell
Mahoning County

(G-2090)
APBN INC
670 Robinson Rd (44405-2031)
P.O. Box 637 (44405-0637)
PHONE.................................724 964-8252
Diane Katsourakis, *President*
Vasilis Katsourakis, *Partner*
Nikita Katsourakis, *Vice Pres*
Vasalis Katsourakis, *Vice Pres*
Sean Tress, *Officer*
EMP: 37
SALES (est): 3.1MM **Privately Held**
SIC: 1721 Bridge painting

(G-2091)
LIBERTY-ALPHA III JV
24 Madison St (44405-1800)
PHONE.................................330 755-7711
Emanouel Frangos, *Principal*
EMP: 40
SALES: 950K **Privately Held**
SIC: 1721 Bridge painting

Canal Fulton
Stark County

(G-2092)
AVALON FOODSERVICE INC
1 Avalon Dr (44614-8893)
P.O. Box 536 (44614-0536)
PHONE.................................330 854-4551
Andrew Schroer, *President*
Jeff Fix, *President*
John Holdren, *President*
Alan Dade, *Vice Pres*
Alan Durell, *Vice Pres*
EMP: 120 EST: 1957
SQ FT: 100,000
SALES (est): 188.3MM **Privately Held**
WEB: www.avalonfoods.com
SIC: 5142 5149 5169 5113 Packaged frozen goods; canned goods: fruit, vegetables, seafood, meats, etc.; chemicals & allied products; industrial & personal service paper; individual & family services; eating places

(G-2093)
BJAAM ENVIRONMENTAL INC
472 Elm Ridge Ave (44614-9369)
P.O. Box 523 (44614-0523)
PHONE.................................330 854-5300
Brett Urian, *President*
Williams Pidcock, *Principal*
Troy Schultz, *Vice Pres*
Sean Hetrick, *Treasurer*
EMP: 50
SQ FT: 26,000
SALES (est): 6.9MM **Privately Held**
WEB: www.bjaam.com
SIC: 8748 Environmental consultant

(G-2094)
CLARK SON ACTN LIQUIDATION INC
4500 Erie Ave Nw (44614-8598)
PHONE.................................330 837-9710
Clark Barkheimer, *President*
EMP: 25
SALES (est): 5.7MM **Privately Held**
SIC: 5031 Kitchen cabinets

(G-2095)
GASLITE VILLA CONVALESCENT CTR
7055 High Mill Ave Nw (44614-9344)
PHONE.................................330 494-4500
Corita C Childs, *President*
EMP: 95 EST: 1964
SQ FT: 22,000
SALES (est): 4.1MM **Privately Held**
WEB: www.gaslitevilla.com
SIC: 8059 8052 Convalescent home; intermediate care facilities

(G-2096)
PNC BANK NATIONAL ASSOCIATION
420 Beverly Ave (44614-9338)
P.O. Box 289 (44614-0289)
PHONE.................................330 854-0974
Doug Choven, *Manager*
EMP: 162
SALES (corp-wide): 19.9B **Publicly Held**
WEB: www.allegiantbank.com
SIC: 6021 National commercial banks
HQ: Pnc Bank, National Association
222 Delaware Ave
Wilmington DE 19801
877 762-2000

(G-2097)
SKIPCO FINANCIAL ADJUSTERS (PA)
2306 Locust St S (44614-9388)
P.O. Box 606 (44614-0606)
PHONE.................................330 854-4800
Robert Blowers, *President*
Cynthia Blowers, *Vice Pres*
EMP: 60
SQ FT: 17,000
SALES (est): 8MM **Privately Held**
WEB: www.skipcoautoauction.com
SIC: 7389 5521 Auctioneers, fee basis; used car dealers

(G-2098)
TOWN OF CANAL FULTON (PA)
155 Market St E Ste A (44614-1305)
PHONE.................................330 854-9448
John Grogan, *Mayor*
Scott M Svab, *Finance Dir*
Patricia Schauwecker, *Council Mbr*
EMP: 42
SQ FT: 2,145 **Privately Held**
SIC: 9121 8611 Town council; ; business associations

(G-2099)
UNITED CHURCH HOMES INC
12200 Strausser St Nw (44614-9479)
PHONE.................................330 854-4177
Susan Strutner, *Administration*
EMP: 150
SALES (corp-wide): 78.1MM **Privately Held**
WEB: www.altenheimcommunity.org
SIC: 8051 Convalescent home with continuous nursing care

PA: United Church Homes Inc
170 E Center St
Marion OH 43302
740 382-4885

(G-2100)
ZVN PROPERTIES INC
957 Cherry St E (44614-9609)
P.O. Box 583 (44614-0583)
PHONE.................................330 854-5890
Bryan Lysikowski, *CEO*
Rick Hoback, *President*
Richard Hoback, *President*
David Dolan, *COO*
EMP: 65 EST: 2007
SQ FT: 5,000
SALES (est): 7MM **Privately Held**
SIC: 6512 Nonresidential building operators

Canal Winchester
Franklin County

(G-2101)
A FOX CONSTRUCTION
6478 Winchester Blvd # 156 (43110-2004)
PHONE.................................614 506-1685
Lisa M Fox, *Owner*
EMP: 40
SALES: 300K **Privately Held**
SIC: 8611 Business associations

(G-2102)
A K ATHLETIC EQUIPMENT INC
8015 Howe Industrial Pkwy (43110-7890)
PHONE.................................614 920-3069
Angela Katz, *President*
Paige Ludwin, *Sales Staff*
EMP: 25
SQ FT: 32,000
SALES (est): 4.2MM **Privately Held**
WEB: www.akathletics.com
SIC: 3086 5091 Plastics foam products; gymnasium equipment

(G-2103)
AERO ELECTRICAL CONTRACTORS
8020 Dove Pkwy Ste A (43110-9559)
PHONE.................................614 834-8181
George R Wolfenbarker, *President*
Caren Wolfenbarker, *Corp Secy*
Paul Hollingshead, *Vice Pres*
EMP: 36
SALES (est): 4.7MM **Privately Held**
SIC: 1731 General electrical contractor

(G-2104)
BERWICK ELECTRIC COMPANY
6863 Eliza Dr (43110-1338)
P.O. Box 241 (43110-0241)
PHONE.................................614 834-2301
Theodore Philput, *President*
EMP: 37
SALES (est): 2.7MM **Privately Held**
SIC: 1731 General electrical contractor

(G-2105)
CAMGEN LTD
6693 Axtel Dr (43110-8417)
PHONE.................................330 204-8636
William Genkins,
EMP: 35
SALES: 5MM **Privately Held**
SIC: 7371 8711 Custom computer programming services; electrical or electronic engineering

(G-2106)
CENTRAL OHIO PRIMARY CARE
6201 Gender Rd (43110-2007)
PHONE.................................614 834-8042
EMP: 42 **Privately Held**
SIC: 8011 General & family practice, physician/surgeon
PA: Central Ohio Primary Care Physicians, Inc.
570 Polaris Pkwy Ste 250
Westerville OH 43082

(G-2107)
CITY OF CANAL WINCHESTER
22 S Trine St (43110-1230)
PHONE.................................614 837-8276
Will Bennett, *Vice Pres*
Jennifer Paswell, *Director*
EMP: 26 **Privately Held**
WEB: www.cwcvb.com
SIC: 8322 9111 Senior citizens' center or association; mayors' offices
PA: City Of Canal Winchester
36 S High St
Canal Winchester OH 43110
614 837-6937

(G-2108)
FEECORP CORPORATION (PA)
Also Called: F E E
7995 Allen Rd Nw (43110-9206)
P.O. Box 447, Pickerington (43147-0447)
PHONE.................................614 837-3010
Karen Fee, *President*
Dawn Fee, *Vice Pres*
Casandra Fee, *Admin Sec*
EMP: 50
SQ FT: 2,400
SALES (est): 16.1MM **Privately Held**
SIC: 1799 Exterior cleaning, including sandblasting; petroleum storage tanks, pumping & draining; petroleum storage tank installation, underground

(G-2109)
GENERAL TEMPERATURE CTRL INC
970 W Walnut St (43110-9757)
PHONE.................................614 837-3888
Bob Billings, *CEO*
Brenda Billings, *President*
L R Billings Jr, *Principal*
Brian Ray Woodard, *Principal*
Patricia Ann Woodard, *Principal*
EMP: 30
SQ FT: 10,000
SALES (est): 7.9MM **Privately Held**
WEB: www.gtc.cc
SIC: 1711 Warm air heating & air conditioning contractor

(G-2110)
GODDARD SCHOOL
6405 Canal St (43110-2044)
PHONE.................................614 920-9810
Eric Park, *Principal*
EMP: 26 EST: 2015
SALES (est): 215K **Privately Held**
SIC: 8351 Group day care center

(G-2111)
JPMORGAN CHASE BANK NAT ASSN
6314 Gender Rd (43110-2052)
PHONE.................................614 920-4182
Steve Rouch, *Branch Mgr*
EMP: 26
SALES (corp-wide): 131.4B **Publicly Held**
WEB: www.chasebank.com
SIC: 6029 Commercial banks
HQ: Jpmorgan Chase Bank, National Association
1111 Polaris Pkwy
Columbus OH 43240
614 436-3055

(G-2112)
KEN HEIBERGER PAVING INC
458 W Waterloo St (43110-1019)
PHONE.................................614 837-0290
EMP: 70
SALES (est): 175.6K **Privately Held**
SIC: 1611 Highway/Street Construction

(G-2113)
KESSLER HEATING & COOLING
Also Called: Honeywell Authorized Dealer
9793 Basil Western Rd Nw (43110-9278)
P.O. Box 245 (43110-0245)
PHONE.................................614 837-9961
Ervin Kessler, *Owner*
EMP: 30
SALES (est): 3MM **Privately Held**
WEB: www.kesslerheating.com
SIC: 1711 Warm air heating & air conditioning contractor

(G-2114)
KINDRED NURSING CENTERS E LLC
Also Called: MGM Health Care Winchstr
36 Lehman Dr (43110-1006)
PHONE..................................614 837-9666
Seth White, *Administration*
EMP: 150
SALES (corp-wide): 6B **Privately Held**
WEB: www.salemhaven.com
SIC: 8051 Convalescent home with continuous nursing care
HQ: Kindred Nursing Centers East, L.L.C.
680 S 4th St
Louisville KY 40202
502 596-7300

(G-2115)
ONEIL AWNING AND TENT INC
895 W Walnut St (43110-9436)
PHONE..................................614 837-6352
Dennis Ritchey, *President*
Tim Ritchey, *Vice Pres*
Fred Waller, *Vice Pres*
Suzanne Wagner, *Sales Staff*
Brian Ritchey, *Admin Sec*
EMP: 65
SQ FT: 40,000
SALES (est): 8.3MM **Privately Held**
WEB: www.oneiltents.com
SIC: 7359 Tent & tarpaulin rental

(G-2116)
REI TELECOM INC (PA)
7890 Robinett Way (43110-8165)
PHONE..................................614 255-3100
Tim Roehrenbeck, *President*
EMP: 25 EST: 1999
SQ FT: 4,000
SALES: 1.5MM **Privately Held**
WEB: www.reitelecom.com
SIC: 1731 Telephone & telephone equipment installation; general electrical contractor

(G-2117)
RENTOKIL NORTH AMERICA INC
Also Called: I P S Interior Landscaping
6300 Cmmerce Ctr Dr Ste G (43110)
PHONE..................................614 837-0099
Monica Desch, *Manager*
EMP: 30
SALES (corp-wide): 3.1B **Privately Held**
WEB: www.primescapeproducts.com
SIC: 7342 Pest control services
HQ: Rentokil North America, Inc.
1125 Berkshire Blvd # 150
Wyomissing PA 19610
610 372-9700

(G-2118)
RUDOLPH BROTHERS & CO
6550 Oley Speaks Way (43110-8274)
PHONE..................................614 833-0707
Kevin Rudolph, *CEO*
Rick Rudolph, *President*
William Coontz Jr, *Vice Pres*
Eric Watson, *Purch Mgr*
Jonathon Elliott, *Engineer*
EMP: 31 EST: 1966
SQ FT: 25,000
SALES (est): 6.3MM **Privately Held**
WEB: www.rudolphbros.com
SIC: 7389 5169 Packaging & labeling services; adhesives, chemical

(G-2119)
SEALS CONSTRUCTION INC
10283 Busey Rd Nw (43110-9629)
PHONE..................................614 836-7200
Andy Seals, *President*
EMP: 47 EST: 1999
SQ FT: 12,000
SALES (est): 7.4MM **Privately Held**
WEB: www.sealscoinc.com
SIC: 1794 Excavation & grading, building construction

(G-2120)
SOUTH CENTRAL POWER COMPANY
10229 Busey Rd Nw (43110-9629)
PHONE..................................614 837-4351
Tom Musick, *President*

Cyndi Arledge, *Principal*
EMP: 35
SALES (corp-wide): 282.1MM **Privately Held**
WEB: www.southcentralpower.com
SIC: 4911 Distribution, electric power
PA: South Central Power Company Inc
2780 Coonpath Rd Ne
Lancaster OH 43130
740 653-4422

(G-2121)
TNT MOBILE POWERWASH INC
260 Pfeifer Dr (43110-2031)
PHONE..................................614 402-7474
Seth Bromberg, *President*
EMP: 25
SALES (est): 922.7K **Privately Held**
SIC: 1799 Steam cleaning of building exteriors

(G-2122)
TRI COUNTY FAMILY PHYSICIANS
11925 Lithopolis Rd Nw (43110-9535)
PHONE..................................614 837-6363
Fred Hennis, *Principal*
EMP: 40
SALES (est): 2.4MM **Privately Held**
SIC: 8011 General & family practice, physician/surgeon

(G-2123)
UNITED CHURCH RESIDENCES OF
Also Called: CANAL VILLAGE
85 Covenant Way (43110-1080)
P.O. Box 1806, Marion (43301-1806)
PHONE..................................614 837-2008
Brian Allen, *President*
EMP: 60
SQ FT: 20,000
SALES: 520.6K **Privately Held**
SIC: 6513 Apartment building operators

(G-2124)
VOGEL DIALYSIS LLC
Also Called: Canal Winchester Dialysis
3568 Gender Rd (43110-8007)
PHONE..................................614 834-3564
James K Hilger,
EMP: 39
SALES (est): 548.5K **Publicly Held**
SIC: 8092 Kidney dialysis centers
PA: Davita Inc.
2000 16th St
Denver CO 80202

(G-2125)
WASTE MANAGEMENT OHIO INC
1006 W Walnut St (43110-9757)
PHONE..................................614 382-6342
John Copas, *Sales Staff*
Gene Meredith, *Branch Mgr*
Kendall Stephens, *Manager*
EMP: 36
SALES (corp-wide): 14.9B **Publicly Held**
WEB: www.wm.com
SIC: 4953 Refuse systems
HQ: Waste Management Of Ohio, Inc.
1700 N Broad St
Fairborn OH 45324

(G-2126)
WASTE MANAGEMENT OHIO INC
1046 W Walnut St (43110-9757)
PHONE..................................614 833-5290
Karen Factor, *Principal*
Steven Mignone, *Safety Mgr*
EMP: 99
SALES (corp-wide): 14.9B **Publicly Held**
WEB: www.wm.com
SIC: 4953 Refuse systems
HQ: Waste Management Of Ohio, Inc.
1700 N Broad St
Fairborn OH 45324

(G-2127)
WINCHESTER PLACE LEASING LLC
Also Called: WINCHESTER CARE & REHABILITATION
36 Lehman Dr (43110-1099)
PHONE..................................614 834-2273
Eli Gunzburg, *Manager*
EMP: 99
SQ FT: 52,214
SALES (est): 901.4K
SALES (corp-wide): 1.5MM **Privately Held**
SIC: 8051 Mental retardation hospital
PA: Aspenwood Holdings, Llc
29225 Chagrin Blvd # 230
Cleveland OH 44122
216 367-1214

(G-2128)
WORLD HARVEST CHURCH INC (PA)
Also Called: Breakthrough Media Ministries
4595 Gender Rd (43110-9149)
P.O. Box 428 (43110-0428)
PHONE..................................614 837-1990
Rodney Parsley, *Pastor*
Rod Parsley, *Pastor*
Darrin Endicott, *Maintenance Dir*
Jeff Barnhart, *Director*
EMP: 300
SQ FT: 200,000
SALES (est): 14.4MM **Privately Held**
WEB: www.breakthrough.net
SIC: 7812 2731 Video tape production; books; publishing & printing

(G-2129)
YOUNG MENS CHRISTIAN ASSOC
Also Called: Jerry L Garver Branch
6767 Refugee Rd (43110-8682)
PHONE..................................614 834-9622
Joanna Heck, *Superintendent*
Mike Sabin, *Branch Mgr*
Marcus Parham, *Director*
EMP: 200
SALES (corp-wide): 44.9MM **Privately Held**
WEB: www.ymca-columbus.com
SIC: 8641 8661 8322 7997 Youth organizations; religious organizations; individual & family services; membership sports & recreation clubs; physical fitness facilities
PA: Young Men's Christian Association Of Central Ohio
40 W Long St
Columbus OH 43215
614 389-4409

Canfield
Mahoning County

(G-2130)
ALLY FINANCIAL INC
Also Called: GMAC
3731 Boardman Canfield Rd (44406-9013)
PHONE..................................330 533-7300
Steve Hidell, *Branch Mgr*
EMP: 45
SALES (corp-wide): 10.4B **Publicly Held**
WEB: www.gmacfs.com
SIC: 6153 Short-term business credit
PA: Ally Financial Inc.
500 Woodward Ave Fl 10
Detroit MI 48226
866 710-4623

(G-2131)
BODINE PERRY LLC (PA)
3711 Strrs Cntre Dr Ste 2 (44406)
PHONE..................................330 702-8100
Larry Parker, *Partner*
Justin Yost, *Accountant*
Amy Troiano, *CPA*
Mathew Bodine,
Jim Hunter,
EMP: 50
SALES (est): 8.9MM **Privately Held**
WEB: www.bodineperry.com
SIC: 8721 8742 Certified public accountant; financial consultant

(G-2132)
CASALS HAIR SALON INC (PA)
Also Called: Casal Day Spa and Salon
4030 Boardman Canfield Rd (44406-9505)
PHONE..................................330 533-6766
Thomas Ciarniello, *President*
EMP: 35
SALES (est): 2.3MM **Privately Held**
SIC: 7231 Manicurist, pedicurist

(G-2133)
CENTER FOR DLYSIS CRE OF CNFLD
3695 Stutz Dr Ste 1 (44406-9144)
PHONE..................................330 702-3040
Kim Blankenship, *Manager*
Erdal Sarac, *Director*
EMP: 30
SALES (est): 1.6MM **Privately Held**
SIC: 8092 Kidney dialysis centers

(G-2134)
COY BROTHERS INC
433 Fairground Blvd (44406-1551)
PHONE..................................330 533-6864
Arlan Coy, *President*
Patricia Coy, *Admin Sec*
EMP: 32 EST: 1920
SALES: 3MM **Privately Held**
SIC: 4213 Trucking, except local

(G-2135)
DANIELS LUMBER CO INC
Also Called: Bernard Daniels Lumber Co
250 Railroad St (44406-1443)
PHONE..................................330 533-2211
Paul B Daniels, *President*
Tom Paranzino, *President*
EMP: 60
SQ FT: 100,000
SALES (est): 8.9MM **Privately Held**
SIC: 5031 5211 5251 Lumber, plywood & millwork; lumber & other building materials; hardware

(G-2136)
FACILITY PRODUCTS & SVCS LLC
330 Newton St (44406-1435)
PHONE..................................330 533-8943
Frank Bostardi, *General Mgr*
John Christopher, *Principal*
Mike Carlozzi, *Manager*
Edward Petruzzi, *Supervisor*
EMP: 44
SALES (est): 6.5MM **Privately Held**
SIC: 1761 Roofing, siding & sheet metal work

(G-2137)
FARMERS NATIONAL BANK (HQ)
20 S Broad St (44406-1401)
P.O. Box 555 (44406-0555)
PHONE..................................330 533-3341
Kevin Helmick, *President*
Gregg Strollo, *Principal*
Carl Culp, *Sr Exec VP*
Carl D Culp, *Exec VP*
James R Vansickle, *Senior VP*
EMP: 120
SQ FT: 25,000
SALES: 96.2MM
SALES (corp-wide): 117.2MM **Publicly Held**
SIC: 6021 National commercial banks
PA: Farmers National Banc Corp.
20 S Broad St
Canfield OH 44406
330 533-3341

(G-2138)
GATEWAYS TO BETTER LIVING INC
3220 S Raccoon Rd (44406-9359)
PHONE..................................330 797-1764
EMP: 25
SALES (corp-wide): 18.3MM **Privately Held**
SIC: 8361 Home for the mentally retarded
PA: Gateways To Better Living Inc
6000 Mahoning Ave Ste 234
Youngstown OH 44515
330 792-2854

(G-2139)
GREEN HAVEN MEMORIAL GARDENS
3495 S Canfield Niles Rd (44406-9698)
PHONE...................................330 533-6811
Merrill O Fisher, *Principal*
EMP: 30
SALES (est): 1.6MM **Privately Held**
SIC: 6553 Cemeteries, real estate operation

(G-2140)
HILL BARTH & KING LLC (PA)
6603 Summit Dr (44406-9509)
P.O. Box 3406, Youngstown (44513-3406)
PHONE...................................330 758-8613
Christopher M Allegretti, *CEO*
Doug Stahl, *CFO*
Nicholas Belcastro, *Accountant*
Michael Byrwa, *Accountant*
Stephen Horne, *Accountant*
EMP: 50
SQ FT: 15,000
SALES (est): 49.7MM **Privately Held**
WEB: www.hbkcpa.com
SIC: 8721 8741 Certified public accountant; financial management for business

(G-2141)
HILL BARTH & KING LLC
Also Called: Hbk
6603 Summit Dr (44406-9509)
PHONE...................................330 747-1903
Richard A Keyse, *Principal*
Steven Steer, *Principal*
Rose Depinet-Foss, *CPA*
Phil Kocon, *Manager*
EMP: 27
SALES (corp-wide): 49.7MM **Privately Held**
WEB: www.hbkcpa.com
SIC: 8721 Certified public accountant
PA: Hill, Barth & King Llc
6603 Summit Dr
Canfield OH 44406
330 758-8613

(G-2142)
HOWARD HANNA SMYTHE CRAMER
4374 Boardman Canfield Rd (44406-8092)
PHONE...................................800 656-7356
Gina Shutrump, *Principal*
EMP: 30
SALES (corp-wide): 72.1MM **Privately Held**
SIC: 6531 Real estate brokers & agents
HQ: Howard Hanna Smythe Cramer
6000 Parkland Blvd
Cleveland OH 44124
216 447-4477

(G-2143)
IES SYSTEMS INC
464 Lisbon St (44406-1423)
P.O. Box 89 (44406-0089)
PHONE...................................330 533-6683
Mark Brucoli, *President*
Kelly Weiss, *Corp Secy*
Rob McAndrew, *Exec VP*
David Wigal, *Exec VP*
Bill Yobi, *Exec VP*
EMP: 45
SQ FT: 27,000
SALES (est): 7.5MM **Privately Held**
WEB: www.ies-us.com
SIC: 7389 3821 Design, commercial & industrial; laboratory apparatus & furniture

(G-2144)
J A DONADEE CORPORATION (PA)
535 N Broad St Ste 5 (44406-8221)
PHONE...................................330 533-3305
John A Donadee, *President*
Bill Burnside, *Plant Supt*
Jane Donadee, *Treasurer*
EMP: 39
SQ FT: 4,200
SALES (est): 3.6MM **Privately Held**
SIC: 1611 General contractor, highway & street construction

(G-2145)
L CALVIN JONES & COMPANY
3744 Starrs Centre Dr (44406-8001)
P.O. Box 159 (44406-0159)
PHONE...................................330 533-1195
Alvin Miller Jr, *President*
EMP: 25
SALES (est): 7.7MM **Privately Held**
WEB: www.lcalvinjones.com
SIC: 6331 Fire, marine & casualty insurance & carriers

(G-2146)
MEANDER HOSPITALITY GROUP INC
Also Called: Staybridge Suites
6599 Seville Dr Ste 100 (44406-7010)
PHONE...................................330 702-0226
Bill Kovas, *President*
EMP: 35
SALES (est): 2.3MM **Privately Held**
SIC: 7011 Hotels & motels

(G-2147)
MERRILL LYNCH PIERCE FENNER
4137 Boardman Canfield Rd (44406-8087)
PHONE...................................330 702-7300
Gordon Raynor, *Manager*
EMP: 40
SALES (corp-wide): 110.5B **Publicly Held**
SIC: 6211 Stock brokers & dealers
HQ: Merrill Lynch, Pierce, Fenner & Smith
Incorporated
111 8th Ave
New York NY 10011
800 637-7455

(G-2148)
MERRILL LYNCH PIERCE FENNER
4137 Boardman Canfield Rd # 201
(44406-7004)
PHONE...................................330 702-0535
Fax: 330 702-7301
EMP: 27
SALES (corp-wide): 95.1B **Publicly Held**
SIC: 6211 Security Broker/Dealer
HQ: Merrill Lynch, Pierce, Fenner & Smith
Incorporated
111 8th Ave
New York NY 10011
800 637-7455

(G-2149)
MILL CREEK METROPOLITAN PARK (PA)
Also Called: Mill Creek Metro Parks
7574 Clmbiana Canfield Rd (44406-9441)
P.O. Box 596 (44406-0596)
PHONE...................................330 702-3000
M V Dailey, *Commissioner*
Susan Dicken, *Exec Dir*
Stacie Butler, *Administration*
EMP: 70 EST: 1891
SALES (est): 6.7MM **Privately Held**
WEB: www.millcreekmetroparks.com
SIC: 7999 Tourist attractions, amusement park concessions & rides; recreation services

(G-2150)
MYERS BUS PARTS AND SUPS CO
Also Called: Myers Equipment
8860 Akron Canfield Rd (44406-8770)
PHONE...................................330 533-2275
David Myers, *President*
Richard Myers, *Vice Pres*
EMP: 40
SALES (est): 2.9MM **Privately Held**
SIC: 5015 Automotive parts & supplies, used

(G-2151)
MYERS EQUIPMENT CORPORATION
8860 Akron Canfield Rd (44406-8770)
PHONE...................................330 533-5556
David Myers, *President*
Doug Spencer, *Parts Mgr*
Rick Scarazzo, *Controller*
Paul Myers, *Sales Staff*

Rob Spencer, *Sales Staff*
▼ EMP: 40
SQ FT: 40,000
SALES (est): 15.1MM **Privately Held**
WEB: www.myersequip.com
SIC: 5083 Farm equipment parts & supplies

(G-2152)
NADLER NADLER & BURDMAN CO LPA
6550 Seville Dr Ste B (44406-9138)
PHONE...................................330 533-6195
Jay Skolnick, *President*
Michael A Gallo, *Treasurer*
Robert S Hartford Jr,
William A Myers,
Donn D Rosenblum,
EMP: 35
SQ FT: 12,000
SALES (est): 3.5MM **Privately Held**
WEB: www.nnblaw.com
SIC: 8111 General practice law office

(G-2153)
OHIO DEPARTMENT TRANSPORTATION
Also Called: Odot District 4
501 W Main St (44406)
PHONE...................................330 533-4351
Charles Miner, *Manager*
EMP: 34 **Privately Held**
SIC: 1611 9621 Highway & street maintenance;
HQ: Ohio Department Of Transportation
1980 W Broad St
Columbus OH 43223

(G-2154)
OHIO STRUCTURES INC (HQ)
535 N Broad St Ste 5 (44406-8221)
PHONE...................................330 533-0084
John Donadee, *President*
Julie Hlebovy, *Corp Secy*
Sean Giblin, *Vice Pres*
David Spurio, *Treasurer*
Thomas Kostelic, *Admin Sec*
EMP: 50
SALES (est): 13.2MM
SALES (corp-wide): 3.6MM **Privately Held**
SIC: 3441 8711 Fabricated structural metal; engineering services
PA: J A Donadee Corporation
535 N Broad St Ste 5
Canfield OH 44406
330 533-3305

(G-2155)
PAUL HRNCHAR FORD-MERCURY INC
Also Called: Hrnchar's Fairway Ford
366 W Main St (44406-1477)
PHONE...................................330 533-3673
Paul J Hrnchar, *President*
Bob Davis, *General Mgr*
Ed Jarzen, *General Mgr*
Jeff Stockman, *Information Mgr*
EMP: 40
SQ FT: 30,000
SALES (est): 16.5MM **Privately Held**
SIC: 5511 7539 7532 Automobiles, new & used; trucks, tractors & trailers: new & used; automotive repair shops; body shop, automotive

(G-2156)
ROHOLT VISION INSTITUTE INC
25 Manor Hill Dr (44406-1596)
PHONE...................................330 702-8755
Philip Roholt, *President*
EMP: 30
SALES (corp-wide): 2MM **Privately Held**
SIC: 8011 Ophthalmologist
PA: Roholt Vision Institute Inc
5890 Mayfair Rd
Canton OH 44720
330 305-2200

(G-2157)
SCHROEDEL SCULLIN & BESTIC LLC
196 N Broad St Ste A (44406-1291)
PHONE...................................330 533-1131
Karl Schroedel, *Principal*

Mark R Heagerty, *Principal*
Gregory Bestic, *Admin Sec*
Richard Scullin,
EMP: 40
SALES (est): 2.5MM **Privately Held**
WEB: www.ssb-cpa.com
SIC: 8721 Certified public accountant

(G-2158)
SEBASTIANI TRUCKING INC
61 Railroad St (44406-1440)
PHONE...................................330 286-0059
Daniel Sebastiani, *CEO*
Emilio Sebastiani, *President*
Angelica Sebastiani, *Corp Secy*
EMP: 56
SQ FT: 2,500
SALES (est): 6.6MM **Privately Held**
SIC: 4212 Dump truck haulage

(G-2159)
TALMER BANK AND TRUST
2 S Broad St (44406-1401)
PHONE...................................330 726-3396
EMP: 38
SALES (corp-wide): 321.3MM **Publicly Held**
SIC: 6035 Savings Bank
HQ: Talmer Bank And Trust
2301 W Big Beaver Rd # 525
Troy MI 48084
248 649-2301

(G-2160)
THOMAS PACKER & CO (PA)
6601 Westford Pl Ste 101 (44406-7005)
PHONE...................................330 533-9777
Phillip Dennison, *President*
Patricia Czechowski, *Opers Staff*
Bridgette Bukofchan, *Accountant*
Stefanie Flyak, *Accountant*
Joe Gabriel, *Accountant*
EMP: 40
SALES (est): 7.8MM **Privately Held**
SIC: 8721 Certified public accountant

(G-2161)
TIPPECANOE COUNTRY CLUB INC
Also Called: TIPPECANOE PRO SHOP
5870 Tippecanoe Rd (44406-9538)
P.O. Box 86 (44406-0086)
PHONE...................................330 758-7518
Adnan Folloum, *Manager*
EMP: 35
SQ FT: 34,000
SALES: 3MM **Privately Held**
SIC: 7997 5941 7991 5812 Country club, membership; golf club, membership; swimming club, membership; tennis club, membership; golf goods & equipment; physical fitness facilities; eating places

(G-2162)
UNITED METHODIST COMMUNITY CTR
4580 Canfield Rd (44406-9349)
PHONE...................................330 743-5149
Robert L Faulkner, *President*
Rev Jerry Krueger, *Vice Pres*
Jerry Savo, *Treasurer*
Amanda Crosby, *Director*
Judy Yungbluth, *Admin Sec*
EMP: 40
SALES: 476.8K **Privately Held**
SIC: 8661 8399 Religious Organization Social Services

(G-2163)
UNITED SRGCAL PRTNERS INTL INC
4147 Westford Dr (44406-8086)
PHONE...................................330 702-1489
Cheryl Lambros, *Branch Mgr*
EMP: 30
SALES (corp-wide): 18.3B **Publicly Held**
WEB: www.surgisinc.com
SIC: 8011 Ambulatory surgical center
HQ: United Surgical Partners International, Inc.
15305 Dallas Pkwy # 1600
Addison TX 75001
972 713-3500

(G-2164)
VECTOR SECURITY INC
4259 Boardman Canfield Rd # 5
(44406-8064)
PHONE....................330 726-9841
Chris Toombs, *Sales Mgr*
Jennifer Petrock, *Branch Mgr*
EMP: 26
SALES (corp-wide): 422.7MM **Privately Held**
WEB: www.vectorsecurity.com
SIC: 7382 1731 Burglar alarm mainte-
nance & monitoring; fire detection & bur-
glar alarm systems specialization
HQ: Vector Security Inc.
2000 Ericsson Dr Ste 250
Warrendale PA 15086
724 741-2200

(G-2165)
**WSB REHABILITATION SVCS
INC (PA)**
Also Called: Blue Sky Therapy
510 W Main St Ste B (44406-1454)
PHONE....................330 533-1338
Renee Bucci Halfhill, *President*
Mellisa Urioste, *Finance*
EMP: 60
SALES (est): 26.6MM **Privately Held**
WEB: www.blueskytherapy.net
SIC: 8049 Physical Therapy

(G-2166)
**YOUNGSTOWN ORTHOPAEDIC
ASSOC**
6470 Tippecanoe Rd Ste A (44406-9568)
PHONE....................330 726-1466
James Solmen, *Surgeon*
Robert Cutticakuo, *Director*
James Jamison, *Director*
James Kerrigan, *Director*
Leslie Schwendeman, *Director*
EMP: 30
SQ FT: 2,000
SALES (est): 5.8MM **Privately Held**
SIC: 8011 Orthopedic physician; surgeon

Canton
Stark County

(G-2167)
415 GROUP INC (PA)
4100 Holiday St Nw # 100 (44718-2589)
P.O. Box 35334 (44735-5334)
PHONE....................330 492-0094
Frank Monaco, *President*
Rich Craig, *General Ptnr*
Scott Whetstone, *Vice Pres*
Kelby Kraft, *Accountant*
Patricia Metz, *Accountant*
EMP: 38
SQ FT: 13,000
SALES: 3.5MM **Privately Held**
WEB: www.415group.com
SIC: 8721 Certified public accountant

(G-2168)
**50 X 20 HOLDING COMPANY
INC (PA)**
Also Called: Schumacher Homes
2715 Wise Ave Nw (44708-1641)
PHONE....................330 478-4500
Paul T Schumacher, *President*
Larry Scheetz, *President*
Dave Boldman, *General Mgr*
Keith Fluharty, *General Mgr*
Scott Lantz, *General Mgr*
EMP: 57
SQ FT: 250,000
SALES (est): 116MM **Privately Held**
SIC: 1521 New construction, single-family
houses

(G-2169)
**A CHILDS PLACE NURSERY
SCHOOL**
4770 Higbee Ave Nw (44718-2550)
PHONE....................330 493-1333
EMP: 55
SQ FT: 6,100
SALES (est): 978K **Privately Held**
SIC: 8351 Nursery School

(G-2170)
ABBOTT ELECTRIC (PA)
1935 Allen Ave Se (44707-3605)
PHONE....................330 452-6601
James D Abbott, *President*
Michael C Abbott, *Vice Pres*
Nancy Abbott, *Vice Pres*
Mike Thomas, *Project Mgr*
Brent R Fatzinger, *Treasurer*
EMP: 63
SQ FT: 5,000
SALES: 25.2MM **Privately Held**
SIC: 1731 General electrical contractor

(G-2171)
ABCD INC (PA)
Also Called: A B C D
1225 Gross Ave Ne (44705-1605)
PHONE....................330 455-6385
William Dent, *CEO*
EMP: 30
SQ FT: 114,000
SALES: 1MM **Privately Held**
SIC: 8399 Community action agency

(G-2172)
**ACUTE CARE SPECIALTY
HOSPITAL**
2600 6th St Sw (44710-1702)
PHONE....................330 363-4860
Ileen Good, *Principal*
EMP: 638 EST: 2009
SALES (est): 7.3MM **Privately Held**
SIC: 8062 General medical & surgical hos-
pitals

(G-2173)
**ADELMANS TRUCK PARTS
CORP (PA)**
Also Called: Adelman's Truck Sales
2000 Waynesburg Dr Se (44707-2194)
PHONE....................330 456-0206
Carl Adelman, *President*
Larry Adelman, *Vice Pres*
◆ EMP: 30
SQ FT: 120,000
SALES (est): 8.8MM **Privately Held**
WEB: www.adelmans.com
SIC: 5013 3714 Truck parts & acces-
sories; power transmission equipment,
motor vehicle; differentials & parts, motor
vehicle

(G-2174)
**ADVANTAGE APPLIANCE
SERVICES**
Also Called: Absolute Health Services
7235 Whipple Ave Nw (44720-7461)
P.O. Box 2279, North Canton (44720-0279)
PHONE....................330 498-8101
Gereld Schroer Sr, *President*
Jerry Schroer Jr, *Vice Pres*
EMP: 175
SQ FT: 27,000
SALES (est): 10.9MM **Privately Held**
WEB: www.abshealth.com
SIC: 5047 Medical equipment & supplies

(G-2175)
**ADVENTURE CMBAT
OPERATIONS LLC**
4501 Hlls Dls Rd Nw A (44708-1572)
P.O. Box 35063 (44735-5063)
PHONE....................330 818-1029
Travis Krauss, *Owner*
Melissa Laskovski, *Manager*
EMP: 30
SQ FT: 2,300
SALES (est): 450K **Privately Held**
SIC: 7929 7389 Entertainers & entertain-
ment groups;

(G-2176)
AEEA LLC
Also Called: Meriprise Financial
4383 Executive Cir Nw (44718-2999)
PHONE....................330 497-5304
Mike Dougherty, *Partner*
EMP: 30
SALES (est): 1.7MM **Privately Held**
SIC: 8742 Planning consultant

(G-2177)
ALCO-CHEM INC
1303 Park Ave Sw (44706-5403)
PHONE....................330 833-8551
Alco Chem, *President*
EMP: 34
SALES (corp-wide): 26.7MM **Privately
Held**
SIC: 7629 5113 5087 Electrical household
appliance repair; paper & products, wrap-
ping or coarse; janitors' supplies
PA: Alco-Chem, Inc.
45 N Summit St
Akron OH 44308
330 253-3535

(G-2178)
**ALLEN-KEITH CONSTRUCTION
CO (PA)**
Also Called: Service Master By Allen Keith
2735 Greensburg Rd (44720-1423)
PHONE....................330 266-2220
Daniel Hanlon, *CEO*
Thomas Hocking, *Vice Pres*
EMP: 57
SQ FT: 38,000
SALES (est): 8MM **Privately Held**
WEB: www.allenkeith.com
SIC: 7349 1541 7217 Building mainte-
nance services; industrial buildings &
warehouses; carpet & upholstery cleaning

(G-2179)
ALLIANCE IMAGING INC
4825 Higbee Ave Nw # 201 (44718-2567)
PHONE....................330 493-5100
Shawn Smith, *Vice Pres*
Steven J Ossakow, *Vice Pres*
Randy Skiles, *Treasurer*
EMP: 115
SQ FT: 5,000
SALES (est): 3.6MM **Privately Held**
WEB: www.mvhs.org
SIC: 8071 8731 X-ray laboratory, including
dental; commercial physical research
HQ: Alliance Healthcare Services, Inc.
18201 Von Karman Ave
Irvine CA 92612
949 242-5300

(G-2180)
**ALLIANCE PETROLEUM
CORPORATION (HQ)**
4150 Belden Village Mall (44718-2502)
PHONE....................330 493-0440
Dora L Silvis, *COO*
Martin L Miller, *VP Opers*
EMP: 61
SQ FT: 2,900
SALES (est): 75.2MM **Privately Held**
WEB: www.alliancepetroleumcorp.com
SIC: 1311 1382 Crude petroleum produc-
tion; natural gas production; oil & gas ex-
ploration services
PA: Diversified Gas & Oil Corporation
1800 Corporate Dr
Birmingham AL 35242
205 408-0909

(G-2181)
ALLIED TRUCK PARTS CO
4216 Southway St Sw (44706-1876)
PHONE....................330 477-8127
Lorel L Molder, *President*
Lee Hochstetler, *Vice Pres*
William Rudner, *Treasurer*
EMP: 35
SQ FT: 35,000
SALES: 4.7MM **Privately Held**
SIC: 5013 5511 7538 Truck parts & ac-
cessories; trucks, tractors & trailers: new
& used; truck engine repair, except indus-
trial

(G-2182)
**ALTERCARE NOBLES POND
INC**
Also Called: Altercare of Ohio
7006 Fulton Dr Nw (44718-1521)
PHONE....................330 834-4800
Brenda Pedro, *Administration*
EMP: 70
SQ FT: 38,892

SALES: 7.7MM **Privately Held**
SIC: 8052 Intermediate care facilities; skilled nursing care facilities

(G-2183)
**ALTERNATIVE RESIDENCES
TWO**
Also Called: Canton Group Home
2832 34th St Ne (44705-3886)
PHONE....................330 453-0200
Fax: 330 453-3895
EMP: 45
SALES (corp-wide): 5K **Privately Held**
SIC: 8361 8052 Residential Care Services
Intermediate Care Facility
PA: Alternative Residences Two, Inc
67051 Executive Dr
Saint Clairsville OH 43950
740 526-0514

(G-2184)
**AMERICAN ELECTRIC POWER
CO INC**
Also Called: AEP Texas North Company
301 Cleveland Ave Sw (44702-1623)
P.O. Box 24400 (44701-4400)
PHONE....................330 438-7024
John Fabian, *Engineer*
Michael Ickes, *Engineer*
Ello Bafello, *Branch Mgr*
Gregory Sohovich, *Manager*
Morgan Howe, *Admin Asst*
EMP: 208
SALES (corp-wide): 16.2B **Publicly Held**
WEB: www.myenviroassistant.com
SIC: 4911 Distribution, electric power
PA: American Electric Power Company, Inc.
1 Riverside Plz Fl 1 # 1
Columbus OH 43215
614 716-1000

(G-2185)
**AMERICAN ELECTRIC POWER
CO INC**
Also Called: AEP
5300 Navarre Rd Sw (44706-3315)
PHONE....................330 580-5085
EMP: 46
SALES (corp-wide): 16.2B **Publicly Held**
SIC: 4911 Distribution, electric power
PA: American Electric Power Company, Inc.
1 Riverside Plz Fl 1 # 1
Columbus OH 43215
614 716-1000

(G-2186)
**AMERICAN MEDICAL
RESPONSE INC**
817 3rd St Sw (44707-4511)
PHONE....................330 455-3579
Bart Liberator, *Manager*
EMP: 45
SALES (corp-wide): 643.1MM **Privately
Held**
WEB: www.amr-inc.com
SIC: 4119 Ambulance service
HQ: American Medical Response, Inc.
6363 S Fiddlers Green Cir # 1400
Greenwood Village CO 80111

(G-2187)
**AMERICAN PRPRTY-
MNAGEMENT CORP**
Also Called: Marriott McKinley Grande Hotel
320 Market Ave S (44702-2108)
PHONE....................330 454-5000
Kevin Goebel, *Manager*
EMP: 100
SALES (corp-wide): 183MM **Privately
Held**
WEB: www.americanpropertymanagement-
corp.com
SIC: 7011 Hotels & motels
PA: American Property-Management Cor-
poration
8910 University Center Ln # 100
San Diego CA 92122
858 964-5500

(G-2188)
AMERIDIAL INC
4877 Higbee Ave Nw (44718-2566)
PHONE....................800 445-7128
Michael McCarthy, *Branch Mgr*
EMP: 350

SALES (corp-wide): 40MM **Privately Held**
SIC: **7389** Telemarketing services
HQ: Ameridial, Inc.
4535 Strausser St Nw
North Canton OH 44720
330 497-4888

(G-2189)
ANHEUSER-BUSCH LLC
1611 Marietta Ave Se (44707-2573)
PHONE..................................330 438-2036
Dan Kessler, *Manager*
EMP: 64
SQ FT: 34,360
SALES (corp-wide): 1.9B **Privately Held**
WEB: www.hispanicbud.com
SIC: **5181** Beer & other fermented malt liquors
HQ: Anheuser-Busch, Llc
1 Busch Pl
Saint Louis MO 63118
314 632-6777

(G-2190)
ANSWERCARE LLC
4150 Belden Village St Nw # 307 (44718-2595)
PHONE..................................855 213-1511
Jordan P Bucar, *Mng Member*
EMP: 55
SQ FT: 1,500
SALES (est): 502K **Privately Held**
SIC: **8082** Home health care services

(G-2191)
ANTHEM INSURANCE COMPANIES INC
Also Called: Blue Cross
4150 Belden Village St Nw # 506 (44718-2595)
PHONE..................................330 492-2151
Eloise Walls, *Branch Mgr*
EMP: 30
SALES (corp-wide): 92.1B **Publicly Held**
WEB: www.anthem-inc.com
SIC: **6324** Group hospitalization plans
HQ: Anthem Insurance Companies, Inc.
220 Virginia Ave
Indianapolis IN 46204
317 488-6000

(G-2192)
APPALACHIAN POWER COMPANY
301 Cleveland Ave Sw (44702-1623)
P.O. Box 24400 (44701-4400)
PHONE..................................330 438-7102
EMP: 98
SALES (corp-wide): 16.2B **Publicly Held**
SIC: **4911** Electric services
HQ: Appalachian Power Company
1 Riverside Plz
Columbus OH 43215
614 716-1000

(G-2193)
ARCHER CORPORATION
Also Called: Archer Sign
1917 Henry Ave Sw (44706-2941)
PHONE..................................330 455-9995
Jerry Archer, *CEO*
Michael Minor, *Vice Pres*
EMP: 40
SQ FT: 70,000
SALES (est): 6.4MM **Privately Held**
WEB: www.archersign.com
SIC: **1799 3993** Sign installation & maintenance; signs & advertising specialties

(G-2194)
ARTHUR MIDDLETON CAPITAL HOLDN
8000 Freedom Ave Nw (44720-6912)
PHONE..................................330 966-3033
Monica Wallace, *Branch Mgr*
EMP: 208 **Privately Held**
SIC: **6799** Investors
PA: Arthur Middleton Capital Holdings, Inc.
8000 Freedom Ave Nw
North Canton OH 44720

(G-2195)
ASAP HOMECARE INC
4150 Belden Village St Nw (44718-2595)
PHONE..................................330 491-0700
Roy Batista, *Manager*
EMP: 52
SALES (corp-wide): 6.9MM **Privately Held**
SIC: **8082** Home health care services
PA: Asap Homecare Inc
1 Park Centre Dr Ste 107
Wadsworth OH 44281
330 334-7027

(G-2196)
ASW GLOBAL LLC
Also Called: Asw Akron Logistic
2150 International Pkwy (44720-1373)
PHONE..................................330 899-1003
Bruce Paisley, *Branch Mgr*
EMP: 60
SALES (corp-wide): 84.5MM **Privately Held**
WEB: www.aswservices.com
SIC: **4225** General warehousing
PA: Asw Global, Llc
3375 Gilchrist Rd
Mogadore OH 44260
330 733-6291

(G-2197)
ATLANTIC FISH & DISTRG CO
Also Called: Atlantic Food Distributors
430 6th St Se (44702-1158)
PHONE..................................330 454-1307
Debbi Vinton, *Vice Pres*
Tiffany Manolakis, *Admin Sec*
EMP: 41
SQ FT: 3,000
SALES (est): 37.2MM **Privately Held**
SIC: **5141** Food brokers

(G-2198)
AULTCARE CORP
2600 6th St Sw (44710-1702)
PHONE..................................330 363-6360
Rick Haines, *President*
Allen Rovner MD, *President*
Frank Getz, *Vice Pres*
Frank Hayden, *Vice Pres*
Kevin Pete, *Vice Pres*
EMP: 300
SALES (est): 185.1MM **Privately Held**
SIC: **6324** Group hospitalization plans

(G-2199)
AULTCARE INSURANCE COMPANY
2600 6th St Sw (44710-1702)
P.O. Box 6910 (44706-0910)
PHONE..................................330 363-6360
Rick Haines, *President*
Melissa Shelton, *Vice Pres*
Kathryn Hayden, *Administration*
EMP: 400
SALES (est): 117.4MM **Privately Held**
WEB: www.aultcare.com
SIC: **6321** Health insurance carriers

(G-2200)
AULTMAN HEALTH FOUNDATION
6100 Whipple Ave Nw (44720-7618)
PHONE..................................330 305-6999
Cindy Spondsellar, *Manager*
Casey Allison, *Surgeon*
EMP: 150
SALES (corp-wide): 1.1MM **Privately Held**
SIC: **8062** General medical & surgical hospitals
PA: Aultman Health Foundation
2600 6th St Sw
Canton OH 44710
330 452-9911

(G-2201)
AULTMAN HEALTH FOUNDATION (PA)
2600 6th St Sw (44710-1702)
PHONE..................................330 452-9911
Christopher Remark, *CEO*
Joseph R Halter Jr, *Vice Chairman*
Kimberly Hager, *Buyer*
Melissa Warrington, *Controller*

Judy Simonson, *Marketing Staff*
EMP: 37
SQ FT: 1,000,000
SALES: 1.1MM **Privately Held**
SIC: **8011** Health maintenance organization

(G-2202)
AULTMAN HOSPITAL (PA)
2600 6th St Sw (44710-1799)
PHONE..................................330 452-9911
Christopher E Remark, *CEO*
Edward J Roth III, *President*
Chris Parrish, *Assistant VP*
Liz Edmunds, *Vice Pres*
Jean Paddock, *Vice Pres*
EMP: 2900
SQ FT: 700,000
SALES: 315.1MM **Privately Held**
WEB: www.aultmanresidencies.com
SIC: **8062 8069 8221** General medical & surgical hospitals; specialty hospitals, except psychiatric; colleges universities & professional schools

(G-2203)
AULTMAN HOSPITAL
2600 6th St Sw (44710-1799)
PHONE..................................330 452-9911
Doug Kirby, *Supervisor*
EMP: 272
SALES (corp-wide): 315.1MM **Privately Held**
WEB: www.aultmanresidencies.com
SIC: **8062 8069** General medical & surgical hospitals; specialty hospitals, except psychiatric
PA: The Aultman Hospital
2600 6th St Sw
Canton OH 44710
330 452-9911

(G-2204)
AULTMAN HOSPITAL
Also Called: Primetime
2600 6th St Sw (44710-1799)
PHONE..................................330 363-6262
Edward Ross, *President*
EMP: 2100
SALES (corp-wide): 315.1MM **Privately Held**
WEB: www.aultmanresidencies.com
SIC: **8062 6324 8322** General medical & surgical hospitals; hospital & medical service plans; geriatric social service
PA: The Aultman Hospital
2600 6th St Sw
Canton OH 44710
330 452-9911

(G-2205)
AULTMAN HOSPITAL
Also Called: Child Care Center
125 Dartmouth Ave Sw (44710-1716)
PHONE..................................330 452-2273
Kerri Gollbach, *Director*
EMP: 30
SALES (corp-wide): 315.1MM **Privately Held**
WEB: www.aultmanresidencies.com
SIC: **8062 8351** General medical & surgical hospitals; group day care center
PA: The Aultman Hospital
2600 6th St Sw
Canton OH 44710
330 452-9911

(G-2206)
AULTMAN NORTH CANTON MED GROUP (PA)
Also Called: NCMF
6046 Whipple Ave Nw (44720-7616)
PHONE..................................330 433-1200
Nicholas Cleary, *CEO*
Carol Pontius, *COO*
Tmothy Murphy, *CFO*
John Humphrey M D, *Exec Dir*
EMP: 300
SQ FT: 93,398
SALES: 365.6K **Privately Held**
WEB: www.ncmf.com
SIC: **8011** Clinic, operated by physicians

(G-2207)
AULTMAN NORTH INC
6100 Whipple Ave Nw (44720-7618)
PHONE..................................330 305-6999
Edward Roth, *President*
David Thiel, *Vice Pres*
Mark Wright, *CFO*
Tieryn Trissel, *Manager*
Lori Hatton,
EMP: 40
SALES (est): 2.4MM
SALES (corp-wide): 315.1MM **Privately Held**
WEB: www.aultmanresidencies.com
SIC: **8062 8011** General medical & surgical hospitals; ophthalmologist
PA: The Aultman Hospital
2600 6th St Sw
Canton OH 44710
330 452-9911

(G-2208)
B-TEK SCALES LLC
1510 Metric Ave Sw (44706-3088)
PHONE..................................330 471-8900
Kraig F Brechbuhler, *President*
Rei Tritt, *Corp Secy*
Andrew Brechbuhler, *Vice Pres*
Matthew Mulinix, *Draft/Design*
Brian Wheatley, *Engineer*
◆ EMP: 50
SQ FT: 65,000
SALES (est): 18.6MM
SALES (corp-wide): 48.1MM **Privately Held**
WEB: www.b-tek.com
SIC: **3325 7371** Steel foundries; software programming applications
PA: Brechbuhler Scales, Inc.
1424 Scales St Sw
Canton OH 44706
330 458-3060

(G-2209)
BAKER DBLKAR BECK WLEY MATHEWS
Also Called: Baker Dublikar
400 S Main St (44720-3028)
PHONE..................................330 499-6000
Jack Baker, *Partner*
Gregory Beck, *Partner*
Ralph Dublikar, *Partner*
Daniel Funk, *Partner*
James Hanratti, *Partner*
EMP: 30
SALES (est): 3.9MM **Privately Held**
WEB: www.bakerfirm.com
SIC: **8111** General practice attorney, lawyer

(G-2210)
BEAVER CONSTRUCTORS INC
2000 Beaver Place Ave Sw (44706-1963)
P.O. Box 6059 (44706-0059)
PHONE..................................330 478-2151
W Mark Sterling, *President*
Jeffrey W Sterling, *Vice Pres*
Richard Williams, *CFO*
EMP: 80
SALES: 48.6MM **Privately Held**
SIC: **1741 1611** Masonry & other stonework; general contractor, highway & street construction

(G-2211)
BETHANY NURSING HOME INC
626 34th St Nw (44709-2977)
PHONE..................................330 492-7171
John Baum, *President*
Susan Kelly, *Business Mgr*
Elizabeth Baum, *Treasurer*
Mary Meyer, *Manager*
Trisha Ross, *Director*
EMP: 50 EST: 1968
SQ FT: 16,000
SALES (est): 4.7MM **Privately Held**
WEB: www.bethanynh.com
SIC: **8051** Convalescent home with continuous nursing care

(G-2212)
BILFINGER WESTCON INC
4525 Vliet St Sw (44710-1311)
PHONE..................................330 818-9734
EMP: 26

SALES (corp-wide): 4.7B **Privately Held**
SIC: 1541 Industrial buildings & warehouses
HQ: Bilfinger Westcon Inc.
7401 Yukon Dr
Bismarck ND 58503
701 222-0076

(G-2213)
BIOTECH MEDICAL INC
7800 Whipple Ave Nw (44767-0001)
PHONE................................330 494-5504
Suarez Corporation Industries, *Mng Member*
Benjamin Suarez,
◆ EMP: 800
SQ FT: 50,000
SALES (est): 108.7MM **Privately Held**
SIC: 5047 Medical equipment & supplies

(G-2214)
BITZEL EXCAVATING INC
4141 Southway St Sw (44706-1809)
PHONE................................330 477-9653
EMP: 30 EST: 1982
SQ FT: 5,000
SALES (est): 3.3MM **Privately Held**
SIC: 1623 Water/Sewer/Utility Construction

(G-2215)
BLUE TECHNOLOGIES INC
5701 Mayfair Rd (44720-1546)
PHONE................................330 499-9300
Keith Stump, *Manager*
EMP: 25 **Privately Held**
SIC: 7629 5044 5045 Business machine repair, electric; copying equipment; word processing equipment
PA: Blue Technologies, Inc.
5885 Grant Ave
Cleveland OH 44105

(G-2216)
BRAWNSTONE SECURITY LLC
6986 Fenwick Ave Ne (44721-2560)
PHONE................................330 800-9006
Daniel Unsworth, *President*
EMP: 71
SALES (est): 2.1MM
SALES (corp-wide): 822.1K **Publicly Held**
SIC: 7382 Security systems services
PA: Fastfunds Financial Corp
7315 E Peakview Ave
Centennial CO 80111
561 514-9042

(G-2217)
BRECHBUHLER SCALES INC (PA)
1424 Scales St Sw (44706-3096)
PHONE................................330 458-3060
Kraig Brechbuhler, *President*
Jason Ammerman, *Regional Mgr*
Bob Musgrove, *Regional Mgr*
Raymond Tritt, *Vice Pres*
Eric Wolfe, *Project Mgr*
EMP: 50
SQ FT: 90,000
SALES (est): 48.1MM **Privately Held**
WEB: www.brechbuhler.com
SIC: 5046 7699 Scales, except laboratory; scale repair service

(G-2218)
BROOKSIDE COUNTRY CLUB INC
1800 Canton Ave Nw (44708-1803)
PHONE................................330 477-6505
Andrew Grove, *General Mgr*
EMP: 60
SQ FT: 70,000
SALES: 3.7MM **Privately Held**
SIC: 7997 Country club, membership

(G-2219)
BROOKWOOD MANAGEMENT COMPANY (PA)
Also Called: Versailles Gardens Apts
1201 S Main St Ste 220 (44720-4283)
PHONE................................330 497-6565
William Lemmon, *President*
EMP: 32
SQ FT: 4,800

SALES (est): 7.3MM **Privately Held**
WEB: www.brookwoodmgnt.com
SIC: 6531 Condominium manager

(G-2220)
BUCKEYE PAPER CO INC
5233 Southway St Sw # 523 (44706-1943)
P.O. Box 711, Massillon (44648-0711)
PHONE................................330 477-5925
Edward N Bast Sr, *President*
Edward Bast Jr, *Vice Pres*
Debby Olson, *Plant Mgr*
▼ EMP: 32
SQ FT: 54,000
SALES (est): 8.9MM **Privately Held**
WEB: www.buckeyepaper.com
SIC: 2679 5113 Paper products, converted; industrial & personal service paper

(G-2221)
BUCKEYE PROF IMAGING INC
5143 Stoneham Rd (44720-1585)
PHONE................................800 433-1292
EMP: 25
SQ FT: 27,000
SALES (est): 2.7MM **Privately Held**
SIC: 7384 Photofinishing Laboratory

(G-2222)
BUCKINGHAM DLTTLE BRROUGHS LLC
4277 Munson St Nw (44718-2982)
PHONE................................330 492-8717
Joseph J Feltes, *Partner*
Joseph L Ackerman, *Partner*
Ronald C Allan, *Partner*
Samuel A Peppers, *Partner*
EMP: 73
SALES (corp-wide): 40.6MM **Privately Held**
SIC: 8111 General practice attorney, lawyer
PA: Buckingham, Doolittle & Burroughs, Llc
3800 Embassy Pkwy
Akron OH 44333
330 376-5300

(G-2223)
CA-MJ HOTEL ASSOCIATES LTD
Also Called: Courtyard By Marriott Canton
4375 Metro Cir Nw (44720-7715)
PHONE................................330 494-6494
Richard Jabara, *General Ptnr*
William Meyer, *General Ptnr*
Jeff Hach, *Director*
EMP: 61
SALES (est): 2.4MM **Privately Held**
SIC: 7011 Hotels
PA: Meyer Jabara Hotels
7 Kenosia Ave Ste 2a
Danbury CT 06810

(G-2224)
CAEP-DUNLAP LLC
2600 6th St Sw (44710-1702)
PHONE................................330 456-2695
Timothy M O'Toole, *Principal*
EMP: 35
SALES (est): 247K **Privately Held**
SIC: 8062 General medical & surgical hospitals

(G-2225)
CAIN MOTORS INC
Also Called: Cain B M W
6527 Whipple Ave Nw (44720-7339)
PHONE................................330 494-5588
David Cain, *President*
Brian Cain, *Vice Pres*
Brian Conner, *Parts Mgr*
Tim Barnes, *Sales Mgr*
Mike Bann, *Sales Staff*
EMP: 49
SQ FT: 17,000
SALES (est): 23.3MM **Privately Held**
SIC: 5511 7538 5521 Automobiles, new & used; pickups, new & used; vans, new & used; general automotive repair shops; used car dealers

(G-2226)
CANTON ALTMAN EMRGNCY PHYSCANS
2600 6th St Sw (44710-1702)
PHONE................................330 456-2695
Paul Ricks, *President*
EMP: 36
SALES (est): 3.6MM **Privately Held**
SIC: 8062 General medical & surgical hospitals

(G-2227)
CANTON ASSISTED LIVING
836 34th St Nw (44709-2947)
PHONE................................330 492-7131
Max Hagee, *CEO*
EMP: 200
SALES (est): 1.9MM **Privately Held**
SIC: 8051 8052 Convalescent home with continuous nursing care; intermediate care facilities

(G-2228)
CANTON CHRISTIAN HOME INC
Also Called: C C H
2550 Cleveland Ave Nw (44709-3306)
PHONE................................330 456-0004
Tom K Strobl, *Exec Dir*
Bonnie Lepley, *Nursing Dir*
EMP: 180
SQ FT: 154,000
SALES: 12.1MM **Privately Held**
WEB: www.cantonchristianhome.org
SIC: 8322 Senior citizens' center or association

(G-2229)
CANTON CITY SCHOOL DISTRICT
Also Called: Fairmount Elementary School
2701 Coventry Blvd Ne (44705-4165)
PHONE................................330 456-3167
Marilyn Vanalmen, *Principal*
EMP: 30
SALES (corp-wide): 55.4MM **Privately Held**
SIC: 8351 Preschool center
PA: Canton City School District
305 Mckinley Ave Nw
Canton OH 44702
330 438-2500

(G-2230)
CANTON CITY SCHOOL DISTRICT
Also Called: Canton School Trnsp Dept
2030 Cleveland Ave Sw (44707-3657)
PHONE................................330 456-6710
Sheena Miller, *Director*
EMP: 100
SALES (corp-wide): 55.4MM **Privately Held**
SIC: 4151 School buses
PA: Canton City School District
305 Mckinley Ave Nw
Canton OH 44702
330 438-2500

(G-2231)
CANTON COUNTRY DAY SCHOOL
3000 Demington Ave Nw (44718-3399)
PHONE................................330 453-8279
Doug Donavan, *Business Mgr*
David Costello, *Headmaster*
Pam Shaw, *Headmaster*
Lucian Barbur, *Info Tech Dir*
Claudia Sommers, *Teacher*
EMP: 48
SQ FT: 30,000
SALES (est): 2.9MM **Privately Held**
WEB: www.cantoncountryday.org
SIC: 8211 8351 Private elementary school; child day care services

(G-2232)
CANTON ERECTORS INC
Also Called: C E I
2009 Quimby Ave Sw (44706-2491)
PHONE................................330 453-7363
Brian Selinsky, *President*
Susan Smith, *Corp Secy*
Bryan Grove, *Vice Pres*
▲ EMP: 30
SQ FT: 18,500

SALES (est): 6.7MM **Privately Held**
WEB: www.cantonerectors.com
SIC: 1796 7353 Machine moving & rigging; cranes & aerial lift equipment, rental or leasing

(G-2233)
CANTON FLOORS INC
Also Called: CFI Interiors
3944 Fulton Dr Nw (44718-3094)
PHONE................................330 492-1121
Rollie L Layfield, *President*
I K Sapienza, *Principal*
Wayne Kroll, *Exec VP*
Gary W Frank, *Vice Pres*
Dan Schwab, *Vice Pres*
EMP: 40
SQ FT: 15,200
SALES (est): 10MM **Privately Held**
WEB: www.cfiinteriors.com
SIC: 1542 Commercial & office buildings, renovation & repair

(G-2234)
CANTON HOTEL HOLDINGS INC
Also Called: Comfort Inn
5345 Broadmoor Cir Nw (44709-4026)
PHONE................................330 492-1331
Mike Koker, *Manager*
EMP: 30
SALES (est): 1MM
SALES (corp-wide): 198.1MM **Privately Held**
WEB: www.sunbursthospitality.com
SIC: 7011 Hotels
PA: Sunburst Hospitality Corporation
10750 Columbia Pike # 300
Silver Spring MD 20901
301 592-3800

(G-2235)
CANTON INVENTORY SERVICE
2204 38th St Ne (44705-2822)
P.O. Box 9068 (44711-9068)
PHONE................................330 453-1633
Michael Pierce, *Owner*
EMP: 30
SALES (est): 1.2MM **Privately Held**
SIC: 7389 Inventory computing service

(G-2236)
CANTON JEWISH COMMUNITY CENTER
Also Called: CANTON JEWISH COMMUNITY FEDERA
432 30th St Nw (44709-3108)
PHONE................................330 452-6444
Paul Spiegal, *Director*
Bonnie Manello, *Asst Director*
EMP: 55
SQ FT: 70,000
SALES: 1.5MM **Privately Held**
WEB: www.jewishcanton.org
SIC: 8322 Community center

(G-2237)
CANTON MED EDUCATN FOUNDATION
Also Called: C M E F
2600 6th St Sw (44710-1702)
PHONE................................330 363-6783
Carol Young, *Director*
Kathleen Senger, *Director*
EMP: 50 EST: 1977
SQ FT: 100
SALES: 4.3MM **Privately Held**
SIC: 8732 Educational research

(G-2238)
CANTON MONTESSORI ASSOCIATION
Also Called: Canton Montessori School
125 15th St Nw (44703-3207)
PHONE................................330 452-0148
Maryann McLellan, *Manager*
EMP: 39
SALES (corp-wide): 953.4K **Privately Held**
WEB: www.cantonmontessori.com
SIC: 8351 Montessori child development center
PA: Canton Montessori Association, Inc
125 15th St Nw
Canton OH 44703
330 452-0148

(G-2239)
CANTON OPHTHALMOLOGY ASSOC
2600 Tuscarawas St W # 200
(44708-4693)
PHONE..................................330 994-1286
Frank J Weinstock MD, *President*
Dr Jamie Zucker, *Corp Secy*
EMP: 25
SALES (est): 1.9MM Privately Held
WEB: www.coaeye.com
SIC: 8011 Ophthalmologist

(G-2240)
CANTON PUBLIC WORKS
Also Called: Canton Street Department
2436 30th St Ne (44705-2568)
PHONE..................................330 489-3030
Michael Roar, *Superintendent*
EMP: 37
SALES (est): 2MM Privately Held
SIC: 1611 Highway & street construction

(G-2241)
CANTON REG CHAM OF COMM FDN
222 Market Ave N (44702-1418)
PHONE..................................330 456-7253
Dennis Saunier, *President*
EMP: 40
SALES: 555.8K Privately Held
SIC: 8611 Chamber of Commerce

(G-2242)
CANTON RGNAL CHMBER OF CMMERCE
222 Market Ave N Ste 122 (44702-1418)
PHONE..................................330 456-7253
Dennis Saunier, *President*
Linnea Gallagher-Olbon, *Principal*
John A Murphy Jr, *Vice Chairman*
Steve Katz, *Vice Pres*
EMP: 40 EST: 2009
SALES: 4.5MM Privately Held
SIC: 8611 Community affairs & services;
Chamber of Commerce

(G-2243)
CANTON SCHOOL EMPLOYEES FED CR (PA)
1380 Market Ave N (44714-2606)
PHONE..................................330 452-9801
Robert Hallier, *President*
Jeannie Fye, *COO*
Kara Chambers, *Loan Officer*
Steve Pflugh, *Loan Officer*
Angie Burgess, *Human Res Mgr*
EMP: 40
SALES: 12.4MM Privately Held
WEB: www.csefcu.com
SIC: 6061 Federal credit unions

(G-2244)
CARDIOLOGY CONSULTANTS INC
2600 Tuscarawas St W # 600
(44708-4644)
PHONE..................................330 454-8076
Alan Kamen MD, *President*
Ira Friedlander MD, *Principal*
Srinivasu Paranandi MD, *Principal*
Dennis Ruff MD, *Principal*
Henry Seto MD, *Principal*
EMP: 60
SALES (est): 1.6MM Privately Held
SIC: 8011 Cardiologist & cardio-vascular
specialist

(G-2245)
CARDIOVASCULAR CONSULTANTS INC
2600 6th St Sw Ste A2710 (44710-1702)
PHONE..................................330 454-8076
Milan Dopirak, *President*
Alan Kamen, *Med Doctor*
EMP: 70
SALES (est): 6.5MM Privately Held
SIC: 8011 Cardiologist & cardio-vascular
specialist

(G-2246)
CARPET SERVICES PLUS INC
Also Called: Carpet Restoration Plus
1807 Allen Ave Se Ste 8 (44707-3696)
PHONE..................................330 458-2409
Andrew C Miller, *President*
EMP: 47
SQ FT: 2,500
SALES (est): 1.4MM Privately Held
SIC: 7217 Carpet & furniture cleaning on
location

(G-2247)
CELLCO PARTNERSHIP
Also Called: Verizon
4926 Dressler Rd Nw (44718-2557)
PHONE..................................330 493-7979
Rick Pawlack, *Branch Mgr*
Diane Bach, *Manager*
Matt Reed, *Manager*
EMP: 30
SALES (corp-wide): 130.8B Publicly
Held
SIC: 4812 5999 Cellular telephone serv-
ices; telephone equipment & systems
HQ: Cellco Partnership
1 Verizon Way
Basking Ridge NJ 07920

(G-2248)
CHASE PHIPPS
2993 Perry Dr Sw (44706-2269)
PHONE..................................330 754-0467
Mike Madal, *General Mgr*
EMP: 40 EST: 2010
SALES (est): 2.4MM Privately Held
SIC: 7359 Tool rental

(G-2249)
CHILD ADLSCENT BEHAVIORAL HLTH (PA)
919 2nd St Ne (44704-1132)
PHONE..................................330 454-7917
Sandra Vaughn, *COO*
Lillian Blosfield, *CFO*
Susan Finsel, *Supervisor*
Michael Johnson, *Exec Dir*
Georgene Voros, *Officer*
EMP: 50
SALES: 7.3MM Privately Held
WEB: www.casrv.org
SIC: 8093 Mental health clinic, outpatient

(G-2250)
CHILD ADLSCENT BEHAVIORAL HLTH
4641 Fulton Dr Nw (44718-2384)
PHONE..................................330 433-6075
Sandy Vaughn, *Manager*
Ryan Beale, *Technology*
Mary Frazier, *Exec Dir*
Amelia Kocher, *Director*
EMP: 65
SALES (corp-wide): 7.3MM Privately
Held
WEB: www.casrv.org
SIC: 8322 Child guidance agency
PA: Child And Adolescent Behavioral
Health
919 2nd St Ne
Canton OH 44704
330 454-7917

(G-2251)
CHILDRENS PHYSICIAN INC
4575 Everhard Rd Nw (44718-2406)
PHONE..................................330 494-5600
Michael Motz, *President*
Douglas Blocker, *Vice Pres*
EMP: 31
SALES (est): 3.7MM Privately Held
SIC: 8011 Pediatrician

(G-2252)
CHRISTIAN PERRY PRE SCHOOL
139 Perry Dr Nw (44708-5048)
PHONE..................................330 477-7262
Sarah Modlin, *Director*
Sharon Skogen, *Director*
Anna Deiters, *Asst Director*
EMP: 30
SALES (est): 675.2K Privately Held
SIC: 8211 8351 Private elementary & sec-
ondary schools; group day care center

(G-2253)
CINEMARK USA INC
Also Called: Cinemark Movies 10
6284 Dressler Rd Nw (44720-7608)
PHONE..................................330 497-9118
Jeremy Thomas, *Manager*
EMP: 40 Publicly Held
SIC: 7832 Motion picture theaters, except
drive-in
HQ: Cinemark Usa, Inc.
3900 Dallas Pkwy Ste 500
Plano TX 75093
972 665-1000

(G-2254)
CINTAS CORPORATION NO 2
3865 Highland Park Nw (44720-4537)
P.O. Box 3010 (44720-8010)
PHONE..................................330 966-7800
Allen Kocsis, *Manager*
EMP: 100
SQ FT: 17,084
SALES (corp-wide): 6.4B Publicly Held
WEB: www.cintas-corp.com
SIC: 7218 2326 2337 Industrial uniform
supply; treated equipment supply: mats,
rugs, mops, cloths, etc.; wiping towel sup-
ply; work uniforms; uniforms, except ath-
letic: women's, misses' & juniors'
HQ: Cintas Corporation No. 2
6800 Cintas Blvd
Mason OH 45040

(G-2255)
CITIZENS BANK NATIONAL ASSN
400 Tuscarawas St W Ste 1 (44702-2044)
PHONE..................................330 580-1913
Kevin Kamper, *Branch Mgr*
EMP: 100
SALES (corp-wide): 7.3B Publicly Held
SIC: 6022 State commercial banks
HQ: Citizens Bank, National Association
1 Citizens Plz Ste 1 # 1
Providence RI 02903
401 282-7000

(G-2256)
CITY OF CANTON
Also Called: Water Pollution Control Ctrl
3530 Central Ave Se (44707-1404)
PHONE..................................330 489-3080
Tracy Mills, *Superintendent*
EMP: 42 Privately Held
WEB: www.cantonincometax.com
SIC: 4953
PA: City Of Canton
218 Cleveland Ave Sw
Canton OH 44702
330 438-4300

(G-2257)
CLAYS HERITAGE CARPET INC (PA)
Also Called: Heritage Carpet & HM Dctg Ctrs
1440 N Main St (44720-1640)
PHONE..................................330 497-1280
Dennis Clay, *President*
Paula Clay, *Admin Sec*
EMP: 38 EST: 1979
SQ FT: 3,850
SALES (est): 6.5MM Privately Held
WEB: www.heritage-carpet.com
SIC: 5713 5211 1752 Carpets; rugs; lum-
ber & other building materials; floor laying
& floor work

(G-2258)
CLEARMOUNT ELEMENTARY SCHOOL
150 Clearmount Ave Se (44720-3214)
PHONE..................................330 497-5640
Beth Humbert, *President*
Mary Lynn Grande, *Vice Pres*
Rickie Irwin, *Treasurer*
Sue Roush, *Admin Sec*
EMP: 48
SALES: 15.8K Privately Held
SIC: 8641 Parent-teachers' association

(G-2259)
CLIFTONLARSONALLEN LLP
4505 Stephens Cir Nw # 200 (44718-3683)
PHONE..................................330 497-2000
Steven Pittman, *Partner*

EMP: 100
SALES (corp-wide): 755.1MM Privately
Held
SIC: 8721 Certified public accountant
PA: Cliftonlarsonallen Llp
220 S 6th St Ste 300
Minneapolis MN 55402
612 376-4500

(G-2260)
COLUMBIA-CSA/HS GREATER CANTON
Also Called: Columbia Mercy Medical Center
1320 Mercy Dr Nw 30 (44708-2614)
PHONE..................................330 489-1000
Jack Topoleski, *CEO*
Csa Health Network, *General Ptnr*
Columbia HCA Healthcare Corp, *Ltd Ptnr*
Michael Rieger, *CFO*
Allyson Kelly, *Director*
EMP: 2185 EST: 1908
SQ FT: 652,760
SALES (est): 15.3MM Privately Held
SIC: 8062 General medical & surgical hos-
pitals

(G-2261)
COMMQUEST SERVICES INC
Also Called: COMMUNITY SERVICES OF
STARK CO
625 Cleveland Ave Nw (44702-1805)
PHONE..................................330 455-0374
Keith Hochadel, *CEO*
John Kaminiski, *President*
Richard Craig, *President*
Shannon English-Hexamer, *Vice Pres*
Jennifer Peveich, *CFO*
EMP: 103
SQ FT: 8,500
SALES: 7.5MM Privately Held
SIC: 8322 8742 Family service agency;
management consulting services

(G-2262)
COMMUNICARE HEALTH SVCS INC
Also Called: Pines Healthcare Center, The
3015 17th St Nw (44708-6004)
PHONE..................................330 454-6508
Elisa Taylor, *President*
Jason Jones, *Division Mgr*
Adam Berry, *Vice Pres*
Deborah Jones, *Vice Pres*
Bob Linder, *Vice Pres*
EMP: 25
SALES (corp-wide): 125.8MM Privately
Held
WEB: www.atriumlivingcenters.com
SIC: 8051 Skilled nursing care facilities
PA: Communicare Health Services, Inc.
4700 Ashwood Dr Ste 200
Blue Ash OH 45241
513 530-1654

(G-2263)
COMMUNICARE HEALTH SVCS INC
Also Called: Canton Healthcare Center
3015 17th St Nw (44708-6004)
PHONE..................................330 454-2152
Kim Frankieberger, *Administration*
EMP: 200
SQ FT: 38,794
SALES (corp-wide): 125.8MM Privately
Held
WEB: www.atriumlivingcenters.com
SIC: 6531 8051 Real estate agents &
managers; skilled nursing care facilities
PA: Communicare Health Services, Inc.
4700 Ashwood Dr Ste 200
Blue Ash OH 45241
513 530-1654

(G-2264)
CONCORDE THERAPY GROUP INC (PA)
4645 Belpar St Nw (44718-3602)
PHONE..................................330 493-4210
Timothy C Murphy, *President*
Mark Mottice, *Shareholder*
EMP: 180
SQ FT: 21,000

SALES (est): 6.7MM **Privately Held**
WEB: www.concordehealth.com
SIC: 8049 8021 Physiotherapist; speech specialist; occupational therapist; offices & clinics of dentists

(G-2265)
CONCORDE THERAPY GROUP INC
5156 Whipple Ave Nw (44718-2663)
PHONE.................................330 478-1752
Janet Murphy, *Branch Mgr*
EMP: 30 **Privately Held**
SIC: 8049 Physical therapist
PA: Concorde Therapy Group Inc
    4645 Belpar St Nw
    Canton OH 44718

(G-2266)
CONSOLIDATED COMMUNICATIONS
Also Called: C.C.i
7015 Sunset Strip Ave Nw (44720-7078)
PHONE.................................330 896-3905
Richard Lutz, *Principal*
Melissa Leasure, *VP Finance*
Nick Shaheen, *Sales Mgr*
Christine McDonnell, *Sales Associate*
EMP: 28
SALES (est): 1.7MM **Privately Held**
WEB: www.cci-solutions.com
SIC: 7622 5065 Communication equipment repair; communication equipment

(G-2267)
COUNTY OF STARK
Also Called: Higgins Sheltered Workshop
3041 Cleveland Ave S (44707-3625)
PHONE.................................330 484-4814
Margalie Belivaire, *Manager*
EMP: 100 **Privately Held**
WEB: www.starkadas.org
SIC: 9431 8331 Mental health agency administration, government; job training & vocational rehabilitation services
PA: County of Stark
    110 Central Plz S Ste 240
    Canton OH 44702
    330 451-7371

(G-2268)
COUNTY OF STARK
Also Called: Stark County Sewer Dept
1701 Mahoning Rd Ne (44705-1471)
PHONE.................................330 451-2303
Kayla Herron, *Engineer*
Mike Armogida, *Manager*
EMP: 790
SQ FT: 17,924 **Privately Held**
WEB: www.starkadas.org
SIC: 4952 Sewerage systems
PA: County of Stark
    110 Central Plz S Ste 240
    Canton OH 44702
    330 451-7371

(G-2269)
COUNTY OF STARK
Also Called: Stark County Engineer
5165 Southway St Sw (44706-1962)
PHONE.................................330 477-6781
Keith Bennett, *Principal*
Stephen Gronow, *Safety Mgr*
EMP: 105
SQ FT: 20,626 **Privately Held**
WEB: www.starkadas.org
SIC: 8711 Engineering services
PA: County Of Stark
    110 Central Plz S Ste 240
    Canton OH 44702
    330 451-7371

(G-2270)
COUNTY OF STARK
Also Called: Mhrs Board of Stark County
121 Cleveland Ave Sw (44702-1903)
PHONE.................................330 455-6644
EMP: 36 **Privately Held**
WEB: www.starkadas.org
SIC: 8069 Drug addiction rehabilitation hospital
PA: County Of Stark
    110 Central Plz S Ste 240
    Canton OH 44702
    330 451-7371

(G-2271)
COURTVIEW JUSTICE SOLUTIONS (DH)
4825 Higbee Ave Nw # 101 (44718-2567)
PHONE.................................330 497-0033
John H Hines III, *President*
Monica Middleton, *General Mgr*
Barbara Petroc, *General Mgr*
Tor Gudmundsen, *Managing Dir*
Jeffrey Harmon, *Managing Dir*
EMP: 32
SALES (est): 15.1MM
SALES (corp-wide): 2.1B **Privately Held**
SIC: 7373 Systems software development services

(G-2272)
CRISIS INTERVENTION & RCVY CTR
832 Mckinley Ave Nw (44703-2463)
PHONE.................................330 455-9407
Bernard Jesiolowski, *Director*
Jeff Allen, *Director*
Sharon Saunier, *Executive Asst*
EMP: 59
SALES (est): 6.8MM **Privately Held**
SIC: 8322 8049 Crisis center; psychologist, psychotherapist & hypnotist

(G-2273)
CRISIS INTVNTN CTR STARK CNTY
2421 13th St Nw (44708-3116)
PHONE.................................330 452-9812
Ryan McNair, *Info Tech Dir*
Bernard Jesiolowski, *Director*
EMP: 90
SQ FT: 7,570
SALES (est): 6.6MM **Privately Held**
WEB: www.cicstark.org
SIC: 8322 Crisis intervention center

(G-2274)
CROSS TRUCK EQUIPMENT CO INC
1801 Perry Dr Sw (44706-1923)
P.O. Box 80509 (44708-0509)
PHONE.................................330 477-8151
M Lucille Cross, *President*
Glenn G Cross, *Principal*
Ivan Bruce Hart, *Principal*
John Cross, *Vice Pres*
William Cross, *Purch Agent*
EMP: 30 EST: 1950
SQ FT: 45,000
SALES (est): 18.2MM **Privately Held**
WEB: www.crosstruck.com
SIC: 5084 5013 Trucks, industrial; truck parts & accessories

(G-2275)
CROXTON REALTY COMPANY
410 47th St Nw (44709-1417)
PHONE.................................330 492-1697
Elaine Croxton, *CEO*
EMP: 25
SQ FT: 3,500
SALES (est): 1.3MM **Privately Held**
WEB: www.croxtonrealty.com
SIC: 6531 Real estate agents & managers

(G-2276)
CUTLER AND ASSOCIATES INC (PA)
Also Called: Cutler/Gmac Real Estate
4618 Dressler Rd Nw (44718-2500)
PHONE.................................330 493-9323
James L Bray, *President*
James H Camp, *Vice Pres*
Jay L Cutler, *Vice Pres*
EMP: 25
SQ FT: 9,500
SALES (est): 8.4MM **Privately Held**
WEB: www.cutlerhomes.com
SIC: 6531 Buying agent, real estate; selling agent, real estate

(G-2277)
CUTLER REAL ESTATE (PA)
Also Called: Cutler G M A C Real Estate
4618 Dressler Rd Nw (44718-2500)
PHONE.................................330 492-7230
James Bray, *President*
James Camp, *Principal*

Jay Cutler, *Vice Pres*
EMP: 90
SALES (est): 4.2MM **Privately Held**
SIC: 6531 Real estate brokers & agents

(G-2278)
DAMARC INC
Also Called: Harding Park Cycle
4330 Kirby Ave Ne (44705-4348)
PHONE.................................330 454-6171
Daniel Harding, *President*
EMP: 43
SQ FT: 40,000
SALES (est): 11.9MM **Privately Held**
WEB: www.hardingsparkcycle.com
SIC: 5571 7699 Motorcycles; motorcycle repair service

(G-2279)
DAVID W STEINBACH INC
Also Called: Steinbach Painiting
6824 Wise Ave Nw (44720-7359)
PHONE.................................330 497-5959
David Steinbach, *President*
EMP: 31
SALES (est): 900K **Privately Held**
SIC: 1721 Painting & paper hanging

(G-2280)
DAVITA INC
Also Called: Da Vita
4685 Fulton Dr Nw (44718-2379)
PHONE.................................330 494-2091
James Jenni, *Branch Mgr*
EMP: 26 **Publicly Held**
SIC: 8092 Kidney dialysis centers
PA: Davita Inc.
    2000 16th St
    Denver CO 80202

(G-2281)
DAY KETTERER LTD (PA)
200 Market Ave N Ste 300 (44702-1436)
P.O. Box 24213 (44701-4213)
PHONE.................................330 455-0173
Blake Gerney, *Managing Prtnr*
James R Blake, *Partner*
Gail Tabron, *Opers Staff*
Rick Arnold,
Matthew Hochstetler, *Associate*
EMP: 73
SQ FT: 35,000
SALES (est): 10.2MM **Privately Held**
WEB: www.dayketterer.com
SIC: 8111 General practice law office

(G-2282)
DDR CORP
5539 Dressler Rd Nw (44720)
PHONE.................................216 755-5547
Scott Woolstine, *President*
EMP: 50
SALES (corp-wide): 707.2MM **Privately Held**
WEB: www.ddrc.com
SIC: 6531 Real estate brokers & agents
PA: Site Centers Corp.
    3300 Enterprise Pkwy
    Beachwood OH 44122
    216 755-5500

(G-2283)
DELTA MEDIA GROUP INC
4726 Hills And Dales Rd N (44708-1571)
PHONE.................................330 493-0350
Mike Minard, *President*
EMP: 40
SALES (est): 4.3MM **Privately Held**
WEB: www.deltagroup.com
SIC: 7372 Application computer software

(G-2284)
DETROIT DIESEL CORPORATION
515 11th St Se (44707-3811)
PHONE.................................330 430-4300
Cathy Bradshaw, *Human Res Mgr*
Greg France, *Manager*
Troy Bannister, *Relg Ldr*
Kevin Ray, *Technology*
Jerry Reaves, *Exec Dir*
EMP: 264
SALES (corp-wide): 191.6B **Privately Held**
WEB: www.detroitdeisel.com
SIC: 5084 Engines & parts, diesel

HQ: Detroit Diesel Corporation
    13400 W Outer Dr
    Detroit MI 48239
    313 592-5000

(G-2285)
DIEBOLD INCORPORATED
217 2nd St Nw Fl 6 (44702-1567)
PHONE.................................330 588-3619
Sharon Pinckard, *Branch Mgr*
EMP: 125
SALES (corp-wide): 4.5B **Publicly Held**
SIC: 5049 1731 Bank equipment & supplies; banking machine installation & service
PA: Diebold Nixdorf, Incorporated
    5995 Mayfair Rd
    North Canton OH 44720
    330 490-4000

(G-2286)
DIEBOLD SELF SERVICE SYSTEMS (PA)
5995 Mayfair Rd (44720-1550)
P.O. Box 3077 (44720-8077)
PHONE.................................330 490-5099
Thomas Swidarski, *CEO*
Patrick Green, *General Mgr*
Leslie Pierce, *Controller*
Louis V Bockius, *Director*
▲ EMP: 600
SQ FT: 1,000
SALES (est): 300MM **Privately Held**
SIC: 5049 Bank equipment & supplies

(G-2287)
DIGNITY HEALTH
Also Called: Emergency Physicians Med Group
4535 Dressler Rd Nw (44718-2545)
PHONE.................................330 493-4443
Josh Rubin, *Principal*
EMP: 150 **Privately Held**
WEB: www.chw.edu
SIC: 8011 8621 Medical centers; professional membership organizations
HQ: Dignity Health
    185 Berry St Ste 300
    San Francisco CA 94107
    415 438-5500

(G-2288)
DLHBOWLES INC (PA)
2422 Leo Ave Sw (44706-2344)
PHONE.................................330 478-2503
John W Saxon, *CEO*
SRI Sridhara, *President*
Dennis Whittington, *Buyer*
Mike Ramsay, *CFO*
Matt Nyeste, *Controller*
◆ EMP: 450
SQ FT: 107,000
SALES (est): 271.5MM **Privately Held**
WEB: www.dlh-inc.com
SIC: 8711 3089 3082 Engineering services; injection molding of plastics; tubes, unsupported plastic

(G-2289)
DOMESTIC VIOLENCE PROJECT INC
720 19th St Ne (44714-2213)
P.O. Box 9459 (44711-9459)
PHONE.................................330 445-2000
Connie Kincaid, *CFO*
Cheli Curran, *Exec Dir*
EMP: 33
SQ FT: 24,575
SALES: 1.5MM **Privately Held**
SIC: 8322 8361 Emergency shelters; hotline; residential care

(G-2290)
DOWNTOWN FORD LINCOLN INC
1423 Tuscarawas St W (44702-2037)
PHONE.................................330 456-2781
Donald Schneider, *President*
Jayne A Montgomery, *Corp Secy*
Brad A Black, *Vice Pres*
Christina Barbato, *Sales Staff*
Randy Upperman, *Sales Staff*
EMP: 98
SQ FT: 35,000

SALES (est): 35.2MM **Privately Held**
SIC: 5511 5012 7538 7532 Automobiles, new & used; trucks, tractors & trailers: new & used; vans, new & used; automobiles & other motor vehicles; general automotive repair shops; collision shops, automotive

(G-2291)
EAST OHIO GAS COMPANY
Dominion Energy Ohio
4725 Southway St Sw (44706-1936)
PHONE.................................330 477-9411
Nancy McClenaghan, *Branch Mgr*
EMP: 120
SALES (corp-wide): 13.3B **Publicly Held**
SIC: 4924 Natural gas distribution
HQ: The East Ohio Gas Company
1201 E 55th St
Cleveland OH 44103
800 362-7557

(G-2292)
EAST OHIO GAS COMPANY
Dominion Energy Ohio
7015 Freedom Ave Nw (44720-7381)
PHONE.................................330 499-2501
Greg Theirl, *Branch Mgr*
EMP: 90
SALES (corp-wide): 13.3B **Publicly Held**
SIC: 4924 Natural gas distribution
HQ: The East Ohio Gas Company
1201 E 55th St
Cleveland OH 44103
800 362-7557

(G-2293)
EAST OHIO GAS COMPANY
Also Called: Dominion Energy Ohio
332 2nd St Nw (44702-1704)
P.O. Box 26666, Richmond VA (23261-6666)
PHONE.................................330 478-1700
Nancy Mc Lanihan, *Branch Mgr*
EMP: 200
SALES (corp-wide): 13.3B **Publicly Held**
SIC: 4924 4923 Natural gas distribution; gas transmission & distribution
HQ: The East Ohio Gas Company
1201 E 55th St
Cleveland OH 44103
800 362-7557

(G-2294)
EASTBURY BOWLING CENTER
3000 Atl Blvd Ne Unit A (44705-3908)
PHONE.................................330 452-3700
Rocco Ferruccio, *President*
Rocco Feruccio, *President*
EMP: 30 EST: 1979
SQ FT: 86,000
SALES (est): 945.7K **Privately Held**
SIC: 7933 5813 Ten pin center; cocktail lounge

(G-2295)
EBSCO INDUSTRIES INC
Also Called: Ebsco Teleservice
4150 Belden Village Mall (44718-2502)
PHONE.................................330 478-0281
EMP: 337
SALES (corp-wide): 2.3B **Privately Held**
SIC: 7389 Business Services
PA: Ebsco Industries, Inc.
5724 Highway 280 E
Birmingham AL 35242
205 991-6600

(G-2296)
ECKINGER CONSTRUCTION COMPANY
2340 Shepler Ch Ave Sw (44706-3093)
PHONE.................................330 453-2566
Tom Eckinger, *CEO*
Philip Eckinger, *President*
Jeremy Eckinger, *Vice Pres*
Rick Eckinger, *Vice Pres*
Fred Eckhardt, *Project Mgr*
EMP: 47 EST: 1923
SQ FT: 18,740
SALES (est): 24.7MM **Privately Held**
WEB: www.eckinger.com
SIC: 1542 Shopping center construction

(G-2297)
EDCO CLEANERS INC
Also Called: Dutch Girl Cleaners
2455 Whipple Ave Nw (44708-1513)
PHONE.................................330 477-3357
Mark Edwards, *President*
Linda Edwards, *Corp Secy*
EMP: 35
SQ FT: 3,400
SALES (est): 1.4MM **Privately Held**
SIC: 7216 Drycleaning plants, except rugs

(G-2298)
EDGE HAIR DESIGN & SPA
4655 Dressler Rd Nw (44718-3657)
PHONE.................................330 477-2300
· Patti Bower Chaney, *Owner*
EMP: 25
SALES (est): 126.1K **Privately Held**
SIC: 7231 Hairdressers

(G-2299)
EMERITUS CORPORATION
Also Called: Emeritus Assisted Living
4507 22nd St Nw Apt 33 (44708-6211)
PHONE.................................330 477-5727
Sue Rohr, *Branch Mgr*
EMP: 35
SALES (corp-wide): 4.5B **Publicly Held**
WEB: www.emeraldestatesslc.com
SIC: 8361 Residential care
HQ: Emeritus Corporation
3131 Elliott Ave Ste 500
Milwaukee WI 53214

(G-2300)
EMP HOLDINGS LTD
4535 Dressler Rd Nw (44718-2545)
PHONE.................................330 493-4443
Dominic Bagnoli, *COO*
Ashley Holder, *Accountant*
Marty Richmond, *Director*
David Peppard,
Dustin Parsons, *Analyst*
EMP: 900
SALES (est): 57.7MM **Privately Held**
SIC: 7363 Medical help service

(G-2301)
EMP MANAGEMENT GROUP LTD
Also Called: Emergency Medicine Physicians
4535 Dressler Rd Nw (44718-2545)
PHONE.................................330 493-4443
Dominic J Bagnoli Jr, *CEO*
David C Packo MD, *President*
William B White MD, *Partner*
Broida Robert I, *COO*
Denise Works, *Exec VP*
EMP: 60
SQ FT: 24,000
SALES (est): 9.8MM **Privately Held**
SIC: 8741 8011 Hospital management; nursing & personal care facility management; offices & clinics of medical doctors

(G-2302)
ENVIRITE OF OHIO INC
Also Called: Eq Ohio
2050 Central Ave Se (44707-3540)
PHONE.................................330 456-6238
Jeffrey R Feeler, *President*
Simon Bell, *Vice Pres*
Eric Gerratt, *Treasurer*
Wayne Ipsen, *Admin Sec*
EMP: 50
SALES (est): 12MM
SALES (corp-wide): 565.9MM **Publicly Held**
WEB: www.envirite.com
SIC: 4953 8734 Recycling, waste materials; hazardous waste testing
PA: Us Ecology, Inc.
101 S Capitol Blvd # 1000
Boise ID 83702
208 331-8400

(G-2303)
ERIE INDEMNITY COMPANY
4690 Munson St Nw (44718-3636)
PHONE.................................330 433-6300
EMP: 75
SALES (corp-wide): 2.3B **Publicly Held**
WEB: www.erieinsurance.com
SIC: 6411 8741 Insurance agents; management services

PA: Erie Indemnity Company
100 Erie Insurance Pl
Erie PA 16530
814 870-2000

(G-2304)
ERIE INSURANCE EXCHANGE
1120 Valleyview Ave Sw (44710-1426)
PHONE.................................330 479-1010
EMP: 67
SALES (corp-wide): 373.8MM **Privately Held**
WEB: www.erie-insurance.com
SIC: 6331 Reciprocal interinsurance exchanges: fire, marine, casualty
PA: Erie Insurance Exchange
100 Erie Insurance Pl
Erie PA 16530
800 458-0811

(G-2305)
ERIE INSURANCE EXCHANGE
4690 Munson St Nw Ste A (44718-3636)
P.O. Box 9031 (44711-9031)
PHONE.................................330 433-1925
Mark Hammerstein, *Manager*
EMP: 100
SALES (corp-wide): 373.8MM **Privately Held**
WEB: www.erie-insurance.com
SIC: 6331 Reciprocal interinsurance exchanges: fire, marine, casualty
PA: Erie Insurance Exchange
100 Erie Insurance Pl
Erie PA 16530
800 458-0811

(G-2306)
ESBER BEVERAGE COMPANY
2217 Bolivar Rd Sw (44706-3099)
PHONE.................................330 456-4361
Gary Esber, *President*
Lou Mahshie, *Controller*
Patricia McCrimmon, *Manager*
Fred Nida, *Manager*
Cindy Esber, *Info Tech Mgr*
▲ EMP: 50
SQ FT: 40,000
SALES (est): 26.7MM **Privately Held**
WEB: www.esberbeverage.com
SIC: 5181 5182 5149 Ale; beer & other fermented malt liquors; wine & distilled beverages; beverages, except coffee & tea

(G-2307)
EXTENDED FAMILY CONCEPTS INC
Also Called: Heather Ridge Commons
913 Pittsburg Ave Nw (44720-1814)
PHONE.................................330 966-2555
Gloria Prose, *President*
Coleen Neifeldt, *Director*
EMP: 50
SALES (est): 1.9MM **Privately Held**
SIC: 8361 Residential care

(G-2308)
EYE CENTERS OF OHIO INC
800 Mckinley Ave Nw (44703-2463)
PHONE.................................330 966-1111
John Malik, *Branch Mgr*
EMP: 30
SALES (est): 996K
SALES (corp-wide): 4.7MM **Privately Held**
WEB: www.eyecentersofohio.com
SIC: 8011 Ophthalmologist
PA: Eye Centers Of Ohio Inc
1330 Mercy Dr Nw Ste 310
Canton OH 44708
330 489-1441

(G-2309)
FAMILY MEDICINE STARK COUNTY
6512 Whipple Ave Nw (44720-7340)
PHONE.................................330 499-5600
Gust Pantelas MD, *President*
Matthew L Cause MD, *Vice Pres*
Bryan Lewis, *Nurse Practr*
EMP: 25
SALES (est): 3.5MM **Privately Held**
SIC: 8011 General & family practice, physician/surgeon

(G-2310)
FAMILY PHYSICIANS INC
4860 Frank Ave Nw (44720-7498)
PHONE.................................330 494-7099
Thomas Shemory, *President*
Melanie Mirande, *Principal*
Dr Gregory A Haban, *Vice Pres*
Dr Howard Marshall, *Treasurer*
Dr Paul Bortos, *Admin Sec*
EMP: 38
SQ FT: 20,000
SALES (est): 5.6MM **Privately Held**
SIC: 8011 Physicians' office, including specialists; general & family practice, physician/surgeon

(G-2311)
FEDERAL EXPRESS CORPORATION
Also Called: Fedex
3301 Bruening Ave Sw (44706-4100)
PHONE.................................800 463-3339
EMP: 34
SALES (corp-wide): 65.4B **Publicly Held**
WEB: www.fedex.com
SIC: 4513 Package delivery, private air
HQ: Federal Express Corporation
3610 Hacks Cross Rd
Memphis TN 38125
901 369-3600

(G-2312)
FEDEX GROUND PACKAGE SYS INC
8033 Pittsburg Ave Nw (44720-5673)
PHONE.................................330 244-1534
EMP: 40
SALES (corp-wide): 47.4B **Publicly Held**
SIC: 4215 Courier Service
HQ: Fedex Ground Package System, Inc.
1000 Fed Ex Dr
Coraopolis PA 15108
412 269-1000

(G-2313)
FIRST CHRISTIAN CHURCH
6900 Market Ave N (44721-2437)
PHONE.................................330 445-2700
John Hampton, *Pastor*
Bill Webster, *Facilities Dir*
Scott McPeek, *Transportation*
Joe Beltz, *Opers Staff*
Kathy Wahl, *Manager*
EMP: 50
SQ FT: 107,000
SALES: 2.5MM **Privately Held**
WEB: www.trychurchagain.com
SIC: 8661 8351 Miscellaneous denomination church; preschool center

(G-2314)
FIRSTMERIT MORTGAGE CORP
4455 Hills & Dales Rd Nw (44708-1505)
PHONE.................................330 478-3400
Stephen D Steinour, *President*
EMP: 85
SALES (est): 16.9MM
SALES (corp-wide): 5.2B **Publicly Held**
WEB: www.firstmerit.com
SIC: 6162 Mortgage bankers
HQ: The Huntington National Bank
17 S High St Fl 1
Columbus OH 43215
614 480-4293

(G-2315)
FLAMOS ENTERPRISES INC
Also Called: Stark Sandblasting & Pntg Co
1501 Raff Rd Sw Ste 1 (44710-2356)
PHONE.................................330 478-0009
Stelio Flamos, *President*
EMP: 50
SQ FT: 30,000
SALES (est): 7MM **Privately Held**
WEB: www.sandblastandpaint.com
SIC: 1799 7389 1721 Sandblasting of building exteriors; waterproofing; interior decorating; industrial painting

(G-2316)
FRATERNAL ORDER EAGLES INC
Also Called: Foe 2370
5024 Monticello Ave Nw (44708-3445)
P.O. Box 80032 (44708-0032)
PHONE.................................330 477-8059
Tom Preda, *Manager*
EMP: 32
SALES (corp-wide): 5.7MM Privately Held
WEB: www.fraternalorderofeagles.tribe.net
SIC: 8641 Fraternal associations
PA: Fraternal Order Of Eagles, Bryan Aerie
2233 Of Bryan, Ohio
221 S Walnut St
Bryan OH 43506
419 636-7812

(G-2317)
FREEDOM HARLEY-DAVIDSON INC
7233 Sunset Strip Ave Nw (44720-7038)
PHONE.................................330 494-2453
David M Smith Sr, *President*
Kathy Hartmann, *General Mgr*
Josephine Smith, *Corp Secy*
Kathy Hartman, *Vice Pres*
Sam Huff, *Sales Mgr*
EMP: 33
SQ FT: 22,000
SALES (est): 3.1MM Privately Held
WEB: www.freedomharley.com
SIC: 7699 5571 Motorcycle repair service;
motorcycle parts & accessories

(G-2318)
FRIEND-SHIP CHILD CARE CTR LLC
425 45th St Sw (44706-4429)
PHONE.................................330 484-2051
Susan Neading, *Director*
Joan Gray,
EMP: 28
SALES (est): 552.3K Privately Held
SIC: 8351 Group day care center

(G-2319)
FURBAY ELECTRIC SUPPLY CO (PA)
208 Schroyer Ave Sw (44702-2039)
P.O. Box 6268 (44706-0268)
PHONE.................................330 454-3033
Timothy Furbay, *President*
Peggy Miller, *COO*
Jean Furbay, *Vice Pres*
Homer Miller, *Warehouse Mgr*
Jeff Kutz, *Purch Mgr*
EMP: 37
SQ FT: 35,000
SALES (est): 51.2MM Privately Held
SIC: 5063 Electrical supplies; lighting fixtures

(G-2320)
G E G ENTERPRISES INC
Also Called: Gary's Place Salon & Spa
4080 Fulton Dr Nw (44718-2866)
PHONE.................................330 494-9160
Jeff Scott, *Manager*
EMP: 34
SQ FT: 960
SALES (corp-wide): 887.9K Privately Held
WEB: www.garysplacesalons.com
SIC: 7231 Beauty shops
PA: G E G Enterprises Inc
4345 Tuscarawas St W
Canton OH 44708
330 477-3133

(G-2321)
G E G ENTERPRISES INC (PA)
Also Called: Gary's Place
4345 Tuscarawas St W (44708-5461)
PHONE.................................330 477-3133
Jeff Scott, *President*
Shelly Talbot, *Vice Pres*
EMP: 25
SQ FT: 2,500
SALES: 887.9K Privately Held
WEB: www.garysplacesalons.com
SIC: 7231 5999 5122 7299 Beauty Shop
Salon & Spa Ret Misc Merchandise Whol
Hair Preparations

(G-2322)
GASPAR INC
1545 Whipple Ave Sw (44710-1373)
PHONE.................................330 477-2222
Gary W Gaspar, *President*
Wesley M Morgan, *Managing Dir*
Chuck Clark, *Editor*
Rodney Shaffer, *Materials Mgr*
Bob Frederick, *Purch Mgr*
EMP: 55
SQ FT: 36,000
SALES (est): 15.6MM Privately Held
WEB: www.gasparinc.com
SIC: 3443 7692 3444 Tanks, standard or
custom fabricated: metal plate; heat ex-
changers, condensers & components;
welding repair; sheet metalwork

(G-2323)
GASTROENTEROLOGY ASSOCIATES
4665 Belpar St Nw (44718-3602)
P.O. Box 36329 (44735-6329)
PHONE.................................330 493-1480
Sanjiv Khetarpal, *President*
Kathy Farley-White, *Manager*
EMP: 38 EST: 1971
SQ FT: 4,500
SALES (est): 3.9MM Privately Held
SIC: 8011 Gastronomist

(G-2324)
GENERAL ELECTRIC COMPANY
4500 Munson St Nw (44718-3607)
P.O. Box 36960 (44735-6960)
PHONE.................................330 433-5163
Ken Scheller, *Vice Pres*
EMP: 1200
SQ FT: 73,234
SALES (corp-wide): 121.6B Publicly Held
WEB: www.gecapital.com
SIC: 6141 Installment sales finance, other
than banks
PA: General Electric Company
41 Farnsworth St
Boston MA 02210
617 443-3000

(G-2325)
GERDAU MACSTEEL ATMOSPHERE ANN
Also Called: Advanced Bar Technology
1501 Raff Rd Sw (44710-2356)
PHONE.................................330 478-0314
Saminathan Ramaswamy, *Principal*
Scott C Pence, *Principal*
EMP: 80
SQ FT: 31,316 Privately Held
WEB: www.aaimac.com
SIC: 7389 3398 Metal cutting services;
metal heat treating
HQ: Gerdau Macsteel Atmosphere Anneal-
ing
209 W Mount Hope Ave # 1
Lansing MI 48910
517 782-0415

(G-2326)
GLENMOOR COUNTRY CLUB INC
4191 Glenmoor Rd Nw Lowr (44718-4077)
PHONE.................................330 966-3600
Iris Wolstein, *Ch of Bd*
Myron Vernis, *General Mgr*
Bob Hon, *Opers Staff*
Jocelyn Piper, *Mktg Dir*
Shannon Evans, *Director*
EMP: 120
SQ FT: 167,000
SALES (est): 11.8MM Privately Held
WEB: www.glenmoorcc.com
SIC: 7997 Country club, membership

(G-2327)
GLOBAL INSULATION INC (PA)
Also Called: Chempower Sheetmetal
4450 Belden Village St Nw # 306
(44718-2588)
PHONE.................................330 479-3100
Patrick F Byrne, *President*
Dale Crumley, *Vice Pres*
EMP: 38
SQ FT: 1,200

SALES (est): 10.8MM Privately Held
SIC: 1742 1761 Insulation, buildings;
sheet metalwork

(G-2328)
GOLDEN KEY CTR FOR EXCPTNL CHL
1431 30th St Nw (44709-2926)
PHONE.................................330 493-4400
Terry Frank, *Exec Dir*
EMP: 40
SALES (est): 1.5MM Privately Held
SIC: 8351 Preschool center

(G-2329)
GOODWILL IDSTRS GRTR CLVLND L (PA)
408 9th St Sw (44707-4714)
PHONE.................................330 454-9461
Anne Richards, *President*
Craig Chaffinch, *CFO*
Ann McBrian, *Accountant*
Trish Dawson, *Human Res Dir*
Cheryl Musgrove, *Human Res Dir*
EMP: 100
SQ FT: 96,000
SALES: 27.6MM Privately Held
SIC: 8331 Vocational rehabilitation agency

(G-2330)
GOODWILL INDS RHBILITATION CTR (PA)
408 9th St Sw (44707-4799)
PHONE.................................330 454-9461
Ken Weber, *CEO*
Gene Dechellis, *CFO*
Anne Richards, *VP Human Res*
Lisa Strong, *Manager*
David Schollaert, *Info Tech Mgr*
EMP: 225
SQ FT: 76,000
SALES (est): 10.9MM Privately Held
WEB: www.goodwillcanton.org
SIC: 8322 8331 Rehabilitation services;
community service employment training
program

(G-2331)
GRACO OHIO INC
Also Called: Profiol
8400 Port Jackson Ave Nw (44720-5464)
PHONE.................................330 494-1313
Mike Sowd, *Controller*
V V Thiel, *Manager*
EMP: 100
SQ FT: 832
SALES (corp-wide): 1.6B Publicly Held
WEB: www.dispensit.com
SIC: 5084 Pumps & pumping equipment
HQ: Graco Ohio Inc.
8400 Port Jackson Ave Nw
North Canton OH 44720
330 494-1313

(G-2332)
H & H AUTO PARTS INC (PA)
300 15th St Sw (44707-4095)
P.O. Box 6440 (44706-0440)
PHONE.................................330 456-4778
James Green, *President*
Richard Green, *Vice Pres*
EMP: 55
SQ FT: 10,000
SALES (est): 10.1MM Privately Held
SIC: 5013 5531 Automotive supplies &
parts; automotive parts

(G-2333)
H & H AUTO PARTS INC
6434 Wise Ave Nw (44720-7385)
PHONE.................................330 494-2975
Curt Price, *Manager*
EMP: 25
SALES (corp-wide): 10.1MM Privately Held
SIC: 5013 5531 Automotive supplies &
parts; automotive accessories
PA: H & H Auto Parts Inc
300 15th St Sw
Canton OH 44707
330 456-4778

(G-2334)
HAIR SHOPPE INC
6460 Wise Ave Nw (44720-7351)
PHONE.................................330 497-1651
Karen Volzer, *President*
EMP: 60
SALES (est): 1.2MM Privately Held
WEB: www.thehairshoppe.com
SIC: 7231 Hairdressers

(G-2335)
HAMMOND CONSTRUCTION INC
1278 Park Ave Sw (44706-1599)
PHONE.................................330 455-7039
William A Schurman, *President*
Victor Gramoy Jr, *Corp Secy*
John Kirkpatrick, *Exec VP*
Bill Schurman, *Vice Pres*
Kirk George, *Project Mgr*
EMP: 80 EST: 1973
SQ FT: 20,000
SALES (est): 32.7MM Privately Held
WEB: www.hammondconstruction.com
SIC: 1542 1541 8741 Commercial & of-
fice building contractors; industrial build-
ings & warehouses; construction
management

(G-2336)
HAMMONTREE & ASSOCIATES LTD (PA)
5233 Stoneham Rd (44720-1594)
PHONE.................................330 499-8817
Bruce Bair, *Partner*
Barbara H Bennett, *Partner*
Keith A Bennett, *Partner*
Charles F Hammontree, *Partner*
EMP: 46
SQ FT: 10,800
SALES (est): 8.6MM Privately Held
WEB: www.hammontree-engineers.com
SIC: 8711 8713 Consulting engineer; sur-
veying services

(G-2337)
HAMPTON INNS LLC
5335 Broadmoor Cir Nw (44709-4097)
PHONE.................................330 492-0151
Jeremiah Louden, *Manager*
EMP: 29
SALES (corp-wide): 2.7B Publicly Held
WEB: www.premierhotels.us
SIC: 7011 Hotels & motels
HQ: Hampton Inns, Llc
755 Crossover Ln
Memphis TN 38117
901 374-5000

(G-2338)
HANCO INTERNATIONAL
Also Called: Hannon Co, The
1605 Waynesburg Dr Se (44707-2196)
PHONE.................................330 456-9407
Tom Hannan, *Chairman*
EMP: 75
SALES (est): 1.5MM Privately Held
SIC: 7389 Design, commercial & industrial

(G-2339)
HANNON COMPANY (PA)
Also Called: Charles Rewinding Div
1605 Waynesburg Dr Se (44707-2137)
PHONE.................................330 456-4728
Christopher Meister, *President*
Mike McAllister, *Superintendent*
Steven Harper, *COO*
Gary Gonzalez, *Plant Mgr*
Gary Griswold, *CFO*
EMP: 75 EST: 1926
SQ FT: 65,000
SALES (est): 25.8MM Privately Held
WEB: www.hanco.com
SIC: 3621 3825 5084 3699 Motors, elec-
tric; test equipment for electronic & elec-
trical circuits; transformers, portable;
instrument; industrial machinery & equip-
ment; electrical equipment & supplies;
transformers, except electric; industrial
furnaces & ovens

(G-2340)
HARMON MEDIA GROUP
4650 Hills And Dales Rd N (44708-6222)
PHONE.................................330 478-5325

Ernest Blood, *Owner*
Marlene Poole, *Sales Associate*
EMP: 49
SALES (est): 3MM **Privately Held**
SIC: 7319 Media buying service

(G-2341)
HART ROOFING INC
Also Called: (PARENT COMPANY IS HART, EDWARD R COMPANY)
437 Mcgregor Ave Nw (44703-2831)
P.O. Box 6207 (44706-0207)
PHONE...................................330 452-4055
Harry Rennecker, *Ch of Bd*
Michael McAndrew, *President*
Michael Mc Andrew, *President*
EMP: 25
SALES (est): 1.2MM **Privately Held**
SIC: 1761 Roofing contractor

(G-2342)
HEARTBEATS TO CITY INC
1352 Market Ave S (44707-4811)
PHONE...................................330 452-4524
EMP: 36
SQ FT: 5,000
SALES (est): 774.3K **Privately Held**
SIC: 8699 8299 Membership Organization School/Educational Services

(G-2343)
HIGHPOINT HOME HEALTHCARE AGCY
4767 Higbee Ave Nw (44718-2551)
PHONE...................................330 491-1805
Joseph Kuntz,
EMP: 37
SALES (est): 742.2K **Privately Held**
WEB: www.hphomecare.net
SIC: 8082 Home health care services

(G-2344)
HILAND GROUP INCORPORATED (PA)
Also Called: Delano Foods
7600 Supreme St Nw (44720-6920)
P.O. Box 36737 (44735-6737)
PHONE...................................330 499-8404
EMP: 65 EST: 1955
SQ FT: 10,000
SALES (est): 8.3MM **Privately Held**
SIC: 5149 2099 Whol Groceries Mfg Food Preparations

(G-2345)
HILSCHER-CLARKE ELECTRIC CO (PA)
519 4th St Nw (44703-2699)
PHONE...................................330 452-9806
Ronald Becker, *CEO*
Ronald D Becker, *CEO*
Scott A Goodspeed, *President*
Scott Goodspeed, *President*
Tony Fay, *Division Mgr*
EMP: 30
SQ FT: 26,000
SALES (est): 48.2MM **Privately Held**
WEB: www.hilscher-clarke.com
SIC: 1731 General electrical contractor

(G-2346)
HILTON GARDEN INN AKRON
5251 Landmark Blvd (44720-1575)
PHONE...................................330 966-4907
Lindsey Misconish, *General Mgr*
EMP: 35
SALES (est): 1.3MM **Privately Held**
SIC: 7011 Hotels & motels

(G-2347)
HOME DEPOT USA INC
Also Called: Home Depot, The
4873 Portage St Nw (44720-7246)
PHONE...................................330 497-1810
Jay Hissom, *Branch Mgr*
EMP: 150
SQ FT: 111,806
SALES (corp-wide): 108.2B **Publicly Held**
WEB: www.homerentalsdepot.com
SIC: 5211 7359 Home centers; tool rental
HQ: Home Depot U.S.A., Inc.
  2455 Paces Ferry Ave
  Atlanta GA 30339

(G-2348)
HOSPITALISTS MGT GROUP LLC (DH)
Also Called: Cogent-Hmg
4535 Dressler Rd Nw (44718-2545)
PHONE...................................866 464-7497
David Hess, *Vice Pres*
Susan Brownie, *CFO*
M F Maida MD, *Chief Mktg Ofcr*
Linda J Ellis, *Mng Member*
Ronald Greeno, *Officer*
EMP: 560
SQ FT: 8,000
SALES (est): 42.5MM
SALES (corp-wide): 18.9B **Privately Held**
SIC: 8741 Management Services
HQ: Hmg Holding Corporation
  920 Winter St
  Waltham MA 02451
  781 699-9000

(G-2349)
HOUSE OF LORETO
2812 Harvard Ave Nw (44709-3195)
PHONE...................................330 453-8137
Sister Claire Batterson, *Vice Pres*
Sister Gladis, *Exec Dir*
EMP: 75
SQ FT: 350,000
SALES: 2.3MM **Privately Held**
WEB: www.houseofloreto.com
SIC: 8051 Extended care facility

(G-2350)
HOWARD HANNA SMYTHE CRAMER
4758 Dressler Rd Nw (44718-2555)
PHONE...................................330 493-6555
Ron Tomblin, *Branch Mgr*
EMP: 45
SALES (corp-wide): 72.1MM **Privately Held**
WEB: www.smythecramer.com
SIC: 6531 Real estate brokers & agents
HQ: Howard Hanna Smythe Cramer
  6000 Parkland Blvd
  Cleveland OH 44124
  216 447-4477

(G-2351)
HUGHES KITCHENS AND BATH LLC
1258 Cleveland Ave Nw (44703-3147)
PHONE...................................330 455-5269
Michael Pierce,
EMP: 30
SQ FT: 80,000
SALES (est): 2.6MM **Privately Held**
SIC: 1799 Kitchen & bathroom remodeling

(G-2352)
HUMANA INC
4690 Munson St Nw Ste C (44718-3636)
PHONE...................................330 498-0537
EMP: 701
SALES (corp-wide): 56.9B **Publicly Held**
SIC: 8062 General medical & surgical hospitals
PA: Humana Inc.
  500 W Main St Ste 300
  Louisville KY 40202
  502 580-1000

(G-2353)
HUNTINGTON INSURANCE INC
Also Called: Canton Insurance
220 Market Ave S Ste 40 (44702-2182)
PHONE...................................330 430-1300
Scott Dodds, *Branch Mgr*
EMP: 37
SALES (corp-wide): 5.2B **Publicly Held**
SIC: 6411 Insurance agents
HQ: Huntington Insurance, Inc.
  519 Madison Ave
  Toledo OH 43604
  419 720-7900

(G-2354)
INCEPT CORPORATION
4150 Belden Village St Nw # 205 (44718-3643)
PHONE...................................330 649-8000
Jeffrey White, *President*
Sam Falletta, *President*
Brad White, *Vice Pres*

EMP: 200
SQ FT: 10,000
SALES (est): 22.2MM **Privately Held**
WEB: www.inceptcorp.com
SIC: 7389 Telemarketing services

(G-2355)
INDUSTRIAL PARTS & SERVICE CO
Also Called: Industrial Parts and Service
6440 Promler St Nw (44720-7625)
PHONE...................................330 966-5025
Edwin Mauser, *President*
Auston Papay, *Warehouse Mgr*
Mark Mauser, *Treasurer*
Jason Schoeppner, *Sales Staff*
Amie Baringer, *Office Mgr*
◆ EMP: 26
SQ FT: 19,000
SALES (est): 14.9MM **Privately Held**
SIC: 5084 7699 Materials handling machinery; industrial equipment services

(G-2356)
INTEGRITY GLOBAL MARKETING LLC
4735 Belpar St Nw (44718-3648)
PHONE...................................330 492-9989
Paul Monea,
▲ EMP: 40
SALES (est): 1.1MM **Privately Held**
SIC: 7999 Gymnastic instruction, nonmembership

(G-2357)
INTERNATIONAL ASSOCIATION OF (PA)
Also Called: Iaitam
4848 Munson St Nw (44718-3631)
PHONE...................................330 628-3012
Barbara Rembiesa, *President*
Glenn Wilson, *Exec VP*
Regina Rupnik, *Opers Dir*
Larry Shoup, *Training Spec*
Steve Reid,
EMP: 25
SQ FT: 3,000
SALES (est): 6.2MM **Privately Held**
SIC: 7379 8249 ; business training services

(G-2358)
INTRIGUE SALON & DAY SPA
4762 Dressler Rd Nw (44718-2555)
PHONE...................................330 493-7003
Yevonne Reese, *Owner*
EMP: 26 EST: 1998
SALES (est): 440.1K **Privately Held**
SIC: 7231 Manicurist, pedicurist

(G-2359)
J M T CARTAGE INC
4925 Southway St Sw (44706-1939)
PHONE...................................330 478-2430
Jeffrey M Tomich, *President*
EMP: 35
SQ FT: 11,000
SALES: 3.1MM **Privately Held**
WEB: www.jmtcartage.com
SIC: 4212 4213 Light haulage & cartage, local; contract haulers

(G-2360)
JANSON INDUSTRIES
1200 Garfield Ave Sw (44706-1639)
P.O. Box 6090 (44706-0090)
PHONE...................................330 455-7029
Richard Janson, *Partner*
Eric H Janson, *Partner*
Tim Brindack, *Design Engr*
Will Harper, *Manager*
Lisa Whitt, *Manager*
EMP: 100
SQ FT: 120,000
SALES (est): 13.6MM **Privately Held**
WEB: www.jansonindustries.com
SIC: 1799 2391 3999 Rigging & scaffolding; curtains & draperies; stage hardware & equipment, except lighting

(G-2361)
JMW WELDING AND MFG
512 45th St Sw (44706-4432)
PHONE...................................330 484-2428
John Slutz, *President*

Michael Slutz, *Vice Pres*
Neal Slutz, *Treasurer*
EMP: 30
SQ FT: 12,000
SALES (est): 6MM **Privately Held**
SIC: 3443 7692 Industrial vessels, tanks & containers; dumpsters, garbage; welding repair

(G-2362)
JOHNSON CNTRLS SEC SLTIONS LLC
5590 Lauby Rd Ste 6 (44720-1500)
PHONE...................................330 497-0850
Brad Wilamson, *General Mgr*
EMP: 110 **Privately Held**
WEB: www.adt.com
SIC: 7382 Burglar alarm maintenance & monitoring; fire alarm maintenance & monitoring
HQ: Johnson Controls Security Solutions Llc
  6600 Congress Ave
  Boca Raton FL 33487
  561 264-2071

(G-2363)
K & L FLOORMASTERS LLC
1518 Cadney St Ne (44714-1189)
PHONE...................................330 493-0869
Kenneth D Wallace Sr, *Mng Member*
EMP: 29
SALES (est): 703.7K **Privately Held**
SIC: 7349 Janitorial service, contract basis

(G-2364)
K HOVNANIAN SUMMIT HOMES LLC (HQ)
2000 10th St Ne (44705-1414)
PHONE...................................330 454-4048
Burce Grosse,
Ricky Haney,
EMP: 50
SALES (corp-wide): 1.9B **Publicly Held**
SIC: 1521 New construction, single-family houses
PA: Hovnanian Enterprises, Inc.
  90 Matawan Rd Fl 5
  Matawan NJ 07747
  732 747-7800

(G-2365)
KEMPTHORN MOTORS INC (PA)
Also Called: Jaguar Volvo
1449 Cleveland Ave Nw (44703-3181)
PHONE...................................800 451-3877
Richard Kempthorn, *President*
Marilyn Kempthorn, *Vice Pres*
Grant Huston, *Sales Staff*
Bob Helm, *Manager*
Jim Kempthorn, *Manager*
EMP: 105
SQ FT: 25,000
SALES (est): 29.4MM **Privately Held**
SIC: 5511 5521 7538 7515 Automobiles, new & used; vans, new & used; pickups, new & used; used car dealers; general automotive repair shops; passenger car leasing; truck rental & leasing, no drivers

(G-2366)
KEMPTHORN MOTORS INC
1449 Cleveland Ave Nw (44703-3181)
PHONE...................................330 452-6511
Richard Kempthorn, *President*
Dwayne Holbrook, *Sales Mgr*
John Titus, *Tech/Comp Coord*
EMP: 100 EST: 1938
SALES (est): 23.2MM **Privately Held**
SIC: 6159 Automobile finance leasing

(G-2367)
KIDNEY & HYPERTENSION CONS
4689 Fulton Dr Nw (44718-2379)
PHONE...................................330 649-9400
Jehad Yusef Asfoura, *Principal*
Jehad Asfoura, *Med Doctor*
Dave Ruckey, *Executive*
James Rajan,
EMP: 28 EST: 2001
SALES (est): 6.1MM **Privately Held**
SIC: 6211 Security brokers & dealers

(G-2368)
KIDS-PLAY INC
1651 Boettler Rd (44721)
PHONE.................................330 896-2400
David Schipper, *President*
EMP: 31
SALES (est): 125.8K
SALES (corp-wide): 4.8MM **Privately Held**
SIC: 8351 Preschool center
PA: Kids-Play Inc
388 S Main St Ste 100
Akron OH 44311
330 253-2373

(G-2369)
KLASE ENTERPRISES INC (PA)
Also Called: United Sales Co
713 12th St Ne (44704-1315)
PHONE.................................330 452-6300
Marlin Klase, *President*
David D Klase, *Vice Pres*
EMP: 42 EST: 1970
SQ FT: 3,000
SALES (est): 7.5MM **Privately Held**
SIC: 5013 Body repair or paint shop supplies, automotive

(G-2370)
KNOCH CORPORATION
1015 Schneider St Se 1a (44720-3800)
PHONE.................................330 244-1440
James B Fenske, *President*
David J Walker, *Vice Pres*
Mike Jirele, *Sr Project Mgr*
Annette Destefano, *Admin Sec*
EMP: 53 EST: 1983
SQ FT: 3,000
SALES (est): 13.8MM **Privately Held**
SIC: 1542 1541 Commercial & office building, new construction; industrial buildings, new construction

(G-2371)
KOZMIC KORNER
8282 Port Jackson Ave Nw (44720-5471)
PHONE.................................330 494-4148
Barb Hanna, *Owner*
EMP: 25
SALES (est): 626.9K **Privately Held**
SIC: 8351 Group day care center

(G-2372)
KRUGLIAK WILKINS GRIFIYHD & (PA)
4775 Munson St Nw (44718-3612)
P.O. Box 36963 (44735-6963)
PHONE.................................330 497-0700
F Stuart Wilkins, *Partner*
John Bogniard, *Managing Dir*
Gregory Watts, *COO*
Paul Malesick, *Vice Pres*
Sue Wilson, *Accountant*
EMP: 68 EST: 1965
SQ FT: 23,000
SALES (est): 11.2MM **Privately Held**
WEB: www.kwgd.com
SIC: 8111 General practice law office

(G-2373)
LED TRANSPORTATION
4645 Monica Ave Sw (44706-4525)
PHONE.................................330 484-2772
Gregg Elliott, *Principal*
EMP: 25
SALES: 1MM **Privately Held**
SIC: 4111 Airport transportation

(G-2374)
LEO A DICK & SONS CO (PA)
935 Mckinley Ave Nw (44703-2072)
PHONE.................................330 452-5010
Leo A Dick, *President*
Lawrence J Dick, *Corp Secy*
Donna Widford, *Accountant*
Victoria Harper, *Executive Asst*
▲ EMP: 65 EST: 1922
SQ FT: 50,000
SALES (est): 9.7MM **Privately Held**
SIC: 5149 Specialty food items

(G-2375)
LEONARD INSUR SVCS AGCY INC (DH)
4244 Mount Pleasant St Nw (44720-5469)
P.O. Box 9160 (44711-9160)
PHONE.................................330 266-1904
W Fred Kloots Jr, *President*
Richard Martindale, *Vice Pres*
W Todd Witham, *Vice Pres*
Heather Cheetham, *Manager*
Jason Vermillion, *Agent*
EMP: 30
SQ FT: 8,500
SALES (est): 16.4MM **Privately Held**
WEB: www.leonardinsurance.com
SIC: 6411 Insurance agents, brokers & service
HQ: Dawson Insurance, Inc.
3900 Kinross Lakes Pkwy
Richfield OH 44286
440 333-9000

(G-2376)
LEPPO INC
Also Called: Leppo Equipment
1534 Shepler Ch Ave Sw (44706-3017)
PHONE.................................330 456-2930
Jeff Ulman, *Branch Mgr*
EMP: 26
SQ FT: 1,890
SALES (corp-wide): 70.6MM **Privately Held**
WEB: www.leppos.com
SIC: 7353 7699 Heavy construction equipment rental; construction equipment repair
PA: Leppo, Inc.
176 West Ave
Tallmadge OH 44278
330 633-3999

(G-2377)
LIBERTY HEALTHSHARE INC
4845 Fulton Dr Nw Ste 1 (44718-2300)
PHONE.................................855 585-4237
Tammy McAvinew, *Agent*
Dale Bellis, *Exec Dir*
EMP: 26
SALES: 1.9MM **Privately Held**
SIC: 7389 Financial services

(G-2378)
LIFECARE FMLY HLTH & DNTL CTR
2725 Lincoln St E (44707-2769)
PHONE.................................330 454-2000
Kay Seeberger, *CEO*
Janet McPeek, *CFO*
Eric D Riley, *Director*
EMP: 35
SQ FT: 16,552
SALES: 5.5MM **Privately Held**
SIC: 8011 Clinic, operated by physicians

(G-2379)
LIFETOUCH NAT SCHL STUDIOS INC
1300 S Main St Ste 300 (44720-4252)
PHONE.................................330 497-1291
Todd Weber, *Site Mgr*
Barry Weber, *Manager*
EMP: 40
SALES (corp-wide): 1.9B **Publicly Held**
SIC: 7221 School photographer
HQ: Lifetouch National School Studios Inc.
11000 Viking Dr Ste 300
Eden Prairie MN 55344
952 826-4000

(G-2380)
LOCKER MOVING & STORAGE INC (PA)
131 Perry Dr Nw (44708)
PHONE.................................330 784-0477
Gregory Stephens, *President*
Wendy Menegay, *Principal*
Kenneth Keller, *Vice Pres*
Sherry L Stephens, *Treasurer*
Jackie Pinter, *Admin Sec*
EMP: 25
SQ FT: 22,000

SALES: 2.1MM **Privately Held**
SIC: 4214 4213 4226 4212 Local trucking with storage; household goods transport; special warehousing & storage; local trucking, without storage; general warehousing & storage

(G-2381)
LOWES HOME CENTERS LLC
6375 Strip Ave Nw (44720-7097)
PHONE.................................330 497-2720
Jim Weirick, *General Mgr*
EMP: 150
SALES (corp-wide): 68.6B **Publicly Held**
SIC: 5211 5031 5722 5064 Home centers; building materials, exterior; building materials, interior; household appliance stores; electrical appliances, television & radio
HQ: Lowe's Home Centers, Llc
1605 Curtis Bridge Rd
Wilkesboro NC 28697
336 658-4000

(G-2382)
LUIS F SOTO MD
Also Called: Asfoura, Jehad MD
4689 Fulton Dr Nw (44718-2379)
PHONE.................................330 649-9400
Luis F Soto MD, *Principal*
Asfoura Jehad MD, *Principal*
EMP: 25
SALES (est): 484K **Privately Held**
SIC: 8011 Offices & clinics of medical doctors

(G-2383)
M CONLEY COMPANY (PA)
Also Called: Network
1312 4th St Se (44707-3243)
P.O. Box 21270 (44701-1270)
PHONE.................................330 456-8243
Robert Stuart III, *CEO*
Eric Conley, *President*
Michael Conley, *Principal*
Ernest A Gerber, *Principal*
Robert H Stewart III, *COO*
EMP: 110
SQ FT: 75,000
SALES (est): 57.9MM **Privately Held**
WEB: www.conleypackaging.com
SIC: 5087 5084 5113 Janitors' supplies; safety equipment; paper & products; wrapping or coarse

(G-2384)
MALONEY & ASSOCIATES INC
Also Called: Canton Chair Rental
4850 Southway St Sw (44706-1947)
PHONE.................................330 479-7084
Tim Moloney Sr, *President*
R C Maloney, *Vice Pres*
Helen L Maloney, *Admin Sec*
EMP: 40
SQ FT: 20,000
SALES (est): 6.4MM **Privately Held**
WEB: www.cantonchairrental.com
SIC: 7359 Party supplies rental services

(G-2385)
MANO LOGISTICS LLC
1934 Navarre Rd Sw (44706-1570)
PHONE.................................330 454-1307
Tiffany Manolakis, *Manager*
Stan Manolakis,
EMP: 34
SALES (est): 1.2MM **Privately Held**
SIC: 4214 Local trucking with storage

(G-2386)
MANOR CARE OF AMERICA INC
5005 Higbee Ave Nw (44718-2521)
PHONE.................................330 492-7835
Megan Lublin, *Manager*
EMP: 110
SALES (corp-wide): 2.4B **Publicly Held**
WEB: www.trisunhealthcare.com
SIC: 8051 Convalescent home with continuous nursing care
HQ: Manor Care Of America, Inc.
333 N Summit St Ste 103
Toledo OH 43604
419 252-5500

(G-2387)
MARATHON PETROLEUM COMPANY LP
3500 21st St Sw (44706-2457)
PHONE.................................330 479-5688
Brad McKain, *General Mgr*
EMP: 350 **Publicly Held**
SIC: 5172 Gasoline
HQ: Marathon Petroleum Company Lp
539 S Main St
Findlay OH 45840

(G-2388)
MARGARET B SHIPLEY CHILD HLTH (PA)
919 2nd St Ne (44704-1132)
PHONE.................................330 478-6333
Steve Muckley, *President*
Karen Coughlin, *Trustee*
Dr Allison Oprandi, *Vice Pres*
James Rossi, *Treasurer*
Laurie Inskeep, *Exec Dir*
EMP: 30
SALES (est): 809K **Privately Held**
SIC: 8011 Clinic, operated by physicians

(G-2389)
MARQUIS MOBILITY INC
4051 Whipple Ave Nw Ste E (44718-3059)
PHONE.................................330 497-5373
Rick Worstell, *President*
EMP: 100
SALES (est): 10.1MM **Privately Held**
SIC: 5047 Medical equipment & supplies

(G-2390)
MARRIOTT INTERNATIONAL INC
Also Called: Fairfield Inn
4025 Greentree Ave Sw (44706-4016)
PHONE.................................330 484-0300
Jennifer Ruiz, *Manager*
EMP: 25
SALES (corp-wide): 20.7B **Publicly Held**
SIC: 7011 Hotels
PA: Marriott International, Inc.
10400 Fernwood Rd
Bethesda MD 20817
301 380-3000

(G-2391)
MARTIN LOGISTICS INC
4526 Louisville St Ne (44705-4850)
PHONE.................................330 456-8000
Alice F Martin, *President*
EMP: 51 EST: 1997
SQ FT: 30,000
SALES (est): 7MM **Privately Held**
SIC: 4731 Freight forwarding

(G-2392)
MATRIX MANAGEMENT SOLUTIONS
5200 Stoneham Rd (44720-1584)
PHONE.................................330 470-3700
Mark Terpylak, *President*
EMP: 140
SALES (est): 7.9MM
SALES (corp-wide): 531MM **Publicly Held**
SIC: 7372 7373 Prepackaged software; computer integrated systems design
PA: Nextgen Healthcare, Inc.
18111 Von Karman Ave
Irvine CA 92612
949 255-2600

(G-2393)
MAYFLOWER NURSING HOME INC
Also Called: Sumser Health Care Center
836 34th St Nw (44709-2947)
PHONE.................................330 492-7131
Shirley Armstrong, *President*
EMP: 150
SQ FT: 55,000
SALES (est): 1.4MM **Privately Held**
SIC: 8051 8059 Convalescent home with continuous nursing care; personal care home, with health care

(G-2394)
MCKINLEY AIR TRANSPORT INC
5430 Lauby Rd Bldg 4 (44720-1576)
P.O. Box 2406 (44720-0406)
PHONE..................................330 497-6956
Don J Armen, *President*
Sara Armen, *Admin Mgr*
EMP: 40 EST: 1934
SQ FT: 38,000
SALES (est): 7.1MM **Privately Held**
SIC: 5599 4581 5172 4522 Aircraft, self-propelled; aircraft cleaning & janitorial service; aircraft fueling services; flying charter service

(G-2395)
MCKINLEY EARLY CHILDHOOD CTR (PA)
1350 Cherry Ave Ne (44714-2529)
PHONE..................................330 454-4800
Lucas Tindell, *Manager*
Michelle Wiggin, *Administration*
EMP: 42
SQ FT: 5,000
SALES (est): 1MM **Privately Held**
SIC: 8351 Group day care center; pre-school center

(G-2396)
MCKINLEY LIFE CARE CENTER LLC
800 Market Ave N Ste 1560 (44702-2303)
PHONE..................................330 456-1014
Bob Knapp,
EMP: 100 EST: 1999
SALES (est): 4.9MM
SALES (corp-wide): 28MM **Privately Held**
SIC: 8051 Extended care facility
PA: Extended Care Consulting, Llc
   2201 Main St Ste A
   Evanston IL 60202
   847 905-3000

(G-2397)
MEADOWLAKE CORPORATION
Also Called: Golf and Swim Club
1211 39th St Ne Ste A (44714-1237)
PHONE..................................330 492-2010
Roy Barr, *President*
EMP: 25
SQ FT: 1,500
SALES (est): 1.1MM **Privately Held**
SIC: 7992 5941 Public golf courses; sporting goods & bicycle shops

(G-2398)
MEDLINE DIAMED LLC (HQ)
3800 Commerce St Sw (44706-3367)
PHONE..................................330 484-1450
Scott Wakser, *Mng Member*
Howard Fried,
Jerry Fried,
Michael Fried,
Douglas Sharpe,
▲ EMP: 46
SQ FT: 15,000
SALES (est): 7.4MM
SALES (corp-wide): 5.9B **Privately Held**
WEB: www.diamedinc.com
SIC: 5047 Medical equipment & supplies
PA: Medline Industries, Inc.
   3 Lakes Dr
   Northfield IL 60093
   847 949-5500

(G-2399)
MERCY MEDICAL CENTER INC
Also Called: Mercy Medical Center Hospice
4369 Whipple Ave Nw (44718-2643)
PHONE..................................330 649-4380
Maria Thompson, *Administration*
EMP: 60
SALES (corp-wide): 321.4MM **Privately Held**
SIC: 8062 General medical & surgical hospitals
HQ: Mercy Medical Center, Inc.
   1320 Mercy Dr Nw
   Canton OH 44708
   330 489-1000

(G-2400)
MERCY MEDICAL CENTER INC (HQ)
1320 Mercy Dr Nw (44708-2641)
PHONE..................................330 489-1000
Thomas E Cecconi, *President*
Christopher J Swift, *Principal*
David D Cemate, *COO*
Joseph Mendiola, *Ch Radiology*
Sister Carolyn Capuano, *Vice Pres*
EMP: 40
SQ FT: 1,000,000
SALES: 299.8MM
SALES (corp-wide): 321.4MM **Privately Held**
WEB: www.cantonmercy.com
SIC: 8062 General medical & surgical hospitals
PA: The Sisters Of Charity Of St Augustine Health System Inc
   2475 E 22nd St Ste 404
   Cleveland OH 44115
   216 696-5560

(G-2401)
MERRILL LYNCH PIERCE FENNER
4300 Munson St Nw Ste 300 (44718-3647)
PHONE..................................330 497-6600
Anastasia Cozer, *Manager*
Gregory Dinarda, *Manager*
Antha Poleondakis, *Advisor*
EMP: 50
SALES (corp-wide): 110.5B **Publicly Held**
WEB: www.merlyn.com
SIC: 6211 Security brokers & dealers
HQ: Merrill Lynch, Pierce, Fenner & Smith Incorporated
   111 8th Ave
   New York NY 10011
   800 637-7455

(G-2402)
MICHAEL BAKER INTL INC
101 Cleveland Ave Nw # 106 (44702-1707)
PHONE..................................330 453-3110
Kurt Bergman, *CEO*
Michael Baker, *Branch Mgr*
EMP: 140
SALES (corp-wide): 592.9MM **Privately Held**
SIC: 8711 8741 Civil engineering; management services
HQ: Baker Michael International Inc
   500 Grant St Ste 5400
   Pittsburgh PA 15219
   412 269-6300

(G-2403)
MIDLANDS MILLROOM SUPPLY INC
1911 36th St Ne (44705-5023)
P.O. Box 7007 (44705-0007)
PHONE..................................330 453-9100
Fred Clark, *President*
David Salvino, *Accounting Mgr*
John Husser, *Manager*
Dee Sohal, *Manager*
▲ EMP: 28
SQ FT: 17,000
SALES: 15MM **Privately Held**
WEB: www.batch-off.com
SIC: 5084 3061 Materials handling machinery; mechanical rubber goods

(G-2404)
MIDWEST INDUSTRIAL SUPPLY INC (PA)
1101 3rd St Se (44707-3230)
P.O. Box 8431 (44711-8431)
PHONE..................................330 456-3121
Robert Vitale, *President*
Steven Vitale, *Vice Pres*
Michael Darke, *Prdtn Mgr*
▲ EMP: 70
SQ FT: 40,000
SALES (est): 67MM **Privately Held**
WEB: www.midwestind.com
SIC: 5084 Industrial machinery & equipment

(G-2405)
MILLER & CO PORTABLE TOIL SVCS
2400 Shepler Ch Ave Sw (44706-4112)
PHONE..................................330 453-9472
Ronald Miller Jr, *President*
EMP: 30 EST: 1999
SQ FT: 40,000
SALES (est): 4MM **Privately Held**
WEB: www.millerandcompany.com
SIC: 7359 Portable toilet rental

(G-2406)
MIRACLE PLUMBING & HEATING CO
Also Called: Honeywell Authorized Dealer
2121 Whipple Ave Nw (44708-2361)
PHONE..................................330 477-2402
Steven J Brown, *President*
EMP: 35
SALES (est): 5.4MM **Privately Held**
WEB: www.miracleplumbing.com
SIC: 1711 1623 Warm air heating & air conditioning contractor; plumbing contractors; irrigation sprinkler system installation; water main construction

(G-2407)
MISTRAS GROUP INC
1415 Raff Rd Sw (44710-2319)
PHONE..................................330 244-1541
EMP: 54 **Publicly Held**
SIC: 8711 Engineering services
PA: Mistras Group, Inc.
   195 Clarksville Rd Ste 2
   Princeton Junction NJ 08550

(G-2408)
MORROW CONTROL AND SUPPLY INC (PA)
Also Called: Johnson Contrls Authorized Dlr
810 Marion Motley Ave Ne (44705-1430)
PHONE..................................330 452-9791
Richard Schwane, *President*
EMP: 35
SQ FT: 100,000
SALES: 13MM **Privately Held**
SIC: 5074 Heating equipment (hydronic)

(G-2409)
MPLX TERMINALS LLC
Also Called: Marathon Canton Refinery
2408 Gambrinus Ave Sw (44706-2365)
PHONE..................................330 479-5539
Mike Armbrester, *Branch Mgr*
EMP: 350
SALES (corp-wide): 6.4B **Publicly Held**
WEB: www.mapllc.com
SIC: 5172 2951 Gasoline; asphalt paving mixtures & blocks
HQ: Mplx Terminals Llc
   200 E Hardin St
   Findlay OH

(G-2410)
MPW INDUSTRIAL SERVICES INC
Also Called: Industrial Cleaning
907 Belden Ave Se (44707-2613)
PHONE..................................330 454-1898
Kevin Smith, *Branch Mgr*
EMP: 70
SALES (corp-wide): 208.7MM **Privately Held**
SIC: 7349 Building component cleaning service; cleaning service, industrial or commercial
HQ: Mpw Industrial Services, Inc.
   9711 Lancaster Rd
   Hebron OH 43025
   800 827-8790

(G-2411)
MULLINAX FORD NORTH CANTON INC
Also Called: Autonation Ford North Canton
5900 Whipple Ave Nw (44720-7614)
PHONE..................................330 238-3206
Charles E Mullinax, *President*
Larry Mullinax, *Treasurer*
Brian Gilmore, *Manager*
Janet Mullinax, *Admin Sec*
EMP: 125
SQ FT: 40,000

SALES (est): 40.1MM
SALES (corp-wide): 21.4B **Publicly Held**
WEB: www.mullinaxfordcanton.com
SIC: 5511 5521 7515 Automobiles, new & used; pickups, new & used; vans, new & used; used car dealers; passenger car leasing
HQ: An Dealership Holding Corp.
   200 Sw 1st Ave
   Fort Lauderdale FL 33301
   954 769-7000

(G-2412)
MULTI-CNTY JVNILE ATTNTION SYS (PA)
815 Faircrest St Sw (44706-4844)
PHONE..................................330 484-6471
Mellissa Clark, *General Mgr*
Donald Thernes, *Superintendent*
David Riker, *Superintendent*
Walter Thornsley, *Supervisor*
Ruth Martin, *Admin Sec*
EMP: 100
SALES: 12.7MM **Privately Held**
SIC: 8361 Juvenile correctional home

(G-2413)
MY COMMUNITY HEALTH CENTER
2600 7th St Sw (44710-1709)
PHONE..................................330 363-6242
Terry L Regula, *CEO*
Terry Regula, *CEO*
EMP: 40 EST: 2016
SALES: 2.4MM **Privately Held**
SIC: 8011 Physicians' office, including specialists

(G-2414)
NATIONAL FOOTBALL MUSEUM INC
Also Called: Professional Football Hall Fame
2121 George Halas Dr Nw (44708-2630)
PHONE..................................330 456-8207
David Baker, *President*
Tim Mara, *General Mgr*
George Veras, *COO*
Pat Lindesmith, *Senior VP*
Pete Fierle, *Vice Pres*
EMP: 31
SQ FT: 83,000
SALES (est): 30.4MM **Privately Held**
WEB: www.profootballhof.com
SIC: 7941 Football club

(G-2415)
NATIONWIDE CORPORATION
1000 Market Ave N (44702-1025)
P.O. Box 8379 (44711-8379)
PHONE..................................330 452-8705
Lisa Hodkinson, *Vice Pres*
Larry Ray, *Manager*
EMP: 600
SALES (corp-wide): 13.2B **Privately Held**
WEB: www.nationwide.com
SIC: 6411 Insurance agents
HQ: Nationwide Corporation
   1 Nationwide Plz
   Columbus OH 43215
   614 249-7111

(G-2416)
NATIONWIDE MUTUAL INSURANCE CO
1000 Market Ave N (44702-1025)
P.O. Box 8379 (44711-8379)
PHONE..................................330 489-5000
Barbara Moses, *Manager*
Jeff Elliot, *Senior Mgr*
EMP: 520
SALES (corp-wide): 13.2B **Privately Held**
WEB: www.nirassn.com
SIC: 6411 Insurance agents
PA: Nationwide Mutual Insurance Company
   1 Nationwide Plz
   Columbus OH 43215
   614 249-7111

(G-2417)
NCR CORPORATION
5590 Lauby Rd Ste J (44720-1500)
PHONE..................................330 497-7300
Karen Bowling, *Branch Mgr*
EMP: 70

SALES (corp-wide): 6.4B **Publicly Held**
WEB: www.ncr.com
SIC: 7629 Business machine repair, electric
PA: Ncr Corporation
    864 Spring St Nw
    Atlanta GA 30308
    937 445-5000

(G-2418)
NIMISHILLEN & TUSCARAWAS LLC
2633 8th St Ne (44704-2311)
PHONE..................................330 438-5821
Steve Sinnott, *General Mgr*
EMP: 32
SALES (est): 2.4MM **Privately Held**
SIC: 4011 Railroads, line-haul operating
HQ: Republic Steel
    2633 8th St Ne
    Canton OH 44704
    330 438-5435

(G-2419)
NORCIA BAKERY
624 Belden Ave Ne (44704-2229)
PHONE..................................330 454-1077
Donald C Horne, *President*
Jim Butler, *Vice Pres*
EMP: 25 EST: 1920
SQ FT: 3,200
SALES (est): 3MM **Privately Held**
SIC: 2051 5461 5149 2052 Bakery:
wholesale or wholesale/retail combined;
bread; groceries & related products; cookies & crackers

(G-2420)
NORTH CANTON CITY SCHOOL DST
Also Called: North Canton Schl Transprtatn
387 Pershing Ave Ne (44720)
PHONE..................................330 497-5615
Thomas Shoup, *Superintendent*
EMP: 66
SALES (corp-wide): 52.7MM **Privately Held**
WEB: www.northcantoncityschools.com
SIC: 4151 School buses
PA: North Canton City School District
    525 7th St Ne
    Canton OH 44720
    330 497-5600

(G-2421)
NORTHEAST PROFESSIONAL HM CARE (PA)
1177 S Main St Ste 11 (44720-4200)
PHONE..................................330 966-2311
Anthony John Vallone, *President*
Eusnook Vallone, *Corp Secy*
EMP: 46 EST: 1995
SALES (est): 4.5MM **Privately Held**
SIC: 8082 Visiting nurse service

(G-2422)
NORTHERN INDUS ENRGY DEV INC
4100 Holiday St Nw # 201 (44718-2589)
PHONE..................................330 498-9130
Andy Duckworth, *President*
EMP: 100
SALES (est): 2.2MM **Privately Held**
SIC: 8748 Energy conservation consultant

(G-2423)
NUEROCARE CENTER INC
4105 Holiday St Nw (44718-2531)
P.O. Box 35006 (44735-5006)
PHONE..................................330 494-2917
EMP: 70 EST: 2002
SALES (est): 3MM **Privately Held**
SIC: 8011 Medical Doctor's Office

(G-2424)
OHIO AUTO SUPPLY COMPANY
Also Called: Professional Detailing Pdts
1128 Tuscarawas St W (44702-2086)
PHONE..................................330 454-5105
Michael Dickson, *President*
Stanley R Rubin, *Admin Sec*
EMP: 29 EST: 1933
SQ FT: 15,000

SALES (est): 6.7MM **Privately Held**
WEB: www.ohioautosupply.com
SIC: 5013 2842 5531 3714 Automotive
supplies & parts; cleaning or polishing
preparations; automotive parts; motor vehicle parts & accessories

(G-2425)
OHIO FARMERS INSURANCE COMPANY
1801 Faircrest St Se (44707-1243)
PHONE..................................330 484-5660
Willian Edwards, *Owner*
EMP: 242
SALES (corp-wide): 1.7B **Privately Held**
SIC: 6411 6399 Property & casualty insurance agent; health insurance for pets
PA: Ohio Farmers Insurance Company
    1 Park Cir
    Westfield Center OH 44251
    800 243-0210

(G-2426)
OHIO HEAD & NECK SURGEONS INC (PA)
Also Called: Canton Allergy Lab
4912 Higbee Ave Nw # 200 (44718-2599)
PHONE..................................330 492-2844
Steven J Ossakow, *President*
Lecia Stark, *Manager*
Chuck Bogdan, *Surgeon*
EMP: 36
SALES (est): 4.7MM **Privately Held**
SIC: 8011 Ears, nose & throat specialist:
physician/surgeon; physicians' office, including specialists; surgeon; allergist

(G-2427)
OHIO MACHINERY CO
Also Called: Caterpillar Authorized Dealer
4731 Corporate St Sw (44706-1906)
PHONE..................................330 478-6525
Gabe Hoffa, *Manager*
EMP: 40
SALES (corp-wide): 222.7MM **Privately Held**
WEB: www.enginesnow.com
SIC: 5082 General construction machinery
& equipment
PA: Ohio Machinery Co.
    3993 E Royalton Rd
    Broadview Heights OH 44147
    440 526-6200

(G-2428)
OHIO POOLS & SPAS INC (PA)
6815 Whipple Ave Nw (44720-7335)
PHONE..................................330 494-7755
Richard A Annis, *President*
▲ EMP: 40
SQ FT: 8,000
SALES (est): 5.3MM **Privately Held**
WEB: www.ohiopools.com
SIC: 1799 Swimming pool construction

(G-2429)
OHIO POWER COMPANY
1 Riverside Plz (44701)
P.O. Box 24421 (44701-4421)
PHONE..................................888 216-3523
Thomas Nohl, *Branch Mgr*
EMP: 30
SALES (corp-wide): 16.2B **Publicly Held**
SIC: 1731 Electrical work
HQ: Ohio Power Company
    1 Riverside Plz
    Columbus OH 43215
    614 716-1000

(G-2430)
OHIO RETINA ASSOCIATES INC (PA)
4690 Munson St Nw Ste D (44718-3636)
PHONE..................................330 966-9800
Thomas Tsai, *President*
Jeffery C Lamkin, *Principal*
Arnold F Nothnagel, *Corp Secy*
EMP: 25
SQ FT: 3,300
SALES (est): 3.8MM **Privately Held**
SIC: 8011 Eyes, ears, nose & throat specialist: physician/surgeon

(G-2431)
OHIO STATE UNIVERSITY
Also Called: Stark and Summit Regional EXT
5119 Lauby Rd (44720)
PHONE..................................330 263-3725
Ernest Oelker, *Branch Mgr*
EMP: 25
SALES (corp-wide): 5.8B **Privately Held**
WEB: www.ohio-state.edu
SIC: 8221 8731 University; agricultural research
PA: The Ohio State University
    Student Acade Servi Bldg
    Columbus OH 43210
    614 292-6446

(G-2432)
OHIO STEEL SLITTERS INC
1401 Raff Rd Sw (44710-2319)
P.O. Box 80168 (44708-0168)
PHONE..................................330 477-6741
Warren Selinsky, *President*
Craig Selinsky, *President*
Florence Selinsky, *Admin Sec*
EMP: 25
SQ FT: 165,000
SALES: 400K **Privately Held**
SIC: 7389 Metal slitting & shearing

(G-2433)
ORTHORPDICS MLTSPCIALTY NETWRK (PA)
4760 Belpar St Nw (44718-3603)
PHONE..................................330 493-1630
Stephen A Lohr, *CEO*
Michael D London, *Admin Sec*
EMP: 50
SALES (est): 3.5MM **Privately Held**
SIC: 8011 Orthopedic physician; surgeon

(G-2434)
PARK CENTRE LANES INC
7313 Whipple Ave Nw (44720-7194)
PHONE..................................330 499-0555
Timmy Brendle, *President*
EMP: 40 EST: 1976
SQ FT: 12,000
SALES: 800.7K **Privately Held**
WEB: www.parkcentrelanes.com
SIC: 7933 Ten pin center

(G-2435)
PATHWAY CARING FOR CHILDREN (PA)
4895 Dressler Rd Nw Ste A (44718-2571)
PHONE..................................330 493-0083
Eric Belden, *CEO*
Gregg Umberger, *CFO*
EMP: 60
SQ FT: 21,000
SALES: 4.2MM **Privately Held**
SIC: 8361 Children's home

(G-2436)
PATRIOT SOFTWARE LLC
4883 Dressler Rd Nw # 301 (44718-3665)
PHONE..................................877 968-7147
Michael J Kappel, *President*
Todd Schmitt, *Treasurer*
Michele Bossart, *Marketing Staff*
Zach Masters, *Marketing Staff*
Wendy Smith, *Payroll Mgr*
EMP: 100
SQ FT: 1,120
SALES: 2.4MM **Privately Held**
WEB: www.patriothr.com
SIC: 7372 Business oriented computer software

(G-2437)
PEOPLES SERVICES INC (PA)
2207 Kimball Rd Se (44707-3631)
P.O. Box 20109 (44701-0109)
PHONE..................................330 453-3709
Ronald R Sibila, *Ch of Bd*
Douglas J Sibila, *President*
Chuck Bridwell, *General Mgr*
James Morgan, *General Mgr*
Shawn Stilphen, *General Mgr*
▲ EMP: 25
SQ FT: 110,000
SALES: 72.9MM **Privately Held**
SIC: 4225 4213 4212 General warehousing; trucking, except local; local trucking, without storage

(G-2438)
POWELL ELECTRICAL SYSTEMS INC
Also Called: Pemco North Canton Division
8967 Pleasantwood Ave Nw (44720-4761)
PHONE..................................330 966-1750
Randy Mulheim, *Project Mgr*
Donald Vrudney, *Mfg Staff*
Allen Marshall, *Engineer*
Kristin Heller, *Human Res Mgr*
Jarc Tana, *Department Mgr*
EMP: 92
SQ FT: 41,600
SALES (corp-wide): 395.9MM **Publicly Held**
WEB: www.powl.com
SIC: 3678 5063 3699 Electronic connectors; electrical apparatus & equipment;
electrical equipment & supplies
HQ: Powell Electrical Systems, Inc.
    8550 Mosley Rd
    Houston TX 77075
    713 944-6900

(G-2439)
PREFERRED TEMPORARY SERVICES
4791 Munson St Nw (44718-3612)
PHONE..................................330 494-5502
Charles Hill, *CEO*
EMP: 30
SALES (est): 1.4MM **Privately Held**
SIC: 7363 Temporary help service

(G-2440)
PRIMARY CARE PHYSICIANS ASSN
4575 Stephens Cir Nw (44718-3629)
PHONE..................................330 499-9944
Karin Triggs, *Partner*
Karin T Riggs, *Partner*
Lynn Ferry, *Manager*
EMP: 25
SALES (est): 3.3MM **Privately Held**
SIC: 8011 Pediatrician

(G-2441)
PROJECT REBUILD INC
406 Shorb Ave Nw (44703-2617)
PHONE..................................330 639-1559
Jake Martin, *Manager*
Joanna James, *Exec Dir*
Carolyn Hess, *Director*
Don Brighenti, *Director*
EMP: 25
SQ FT: 3,600
SALES: 856.9K **Privately Held**
WEB: www.projectrebuild.com
SIC: 8331 Community service employment
training program

(G-2442)
PROTECH SECURITY INC
Also Called: Protech Alarm Systems
7026 Sunset Strip Ave Nw (44720-7077)
P.O. Box 35034 (44735-5034)
PHONE..................................330 499-3555
Daniel Mc Kimm, *President*
Laura Mc Kimm, *Corp Secy*
EMP: 27 EST: 1980
SQ FT: 7,500
SALES (est): 5MM **Privately Held**
WEB: www.protech-security.com
SIC: 1731 7382 Fire detection & burglar
alarm systems specialization; closed circuit television installation; security systems services

(G-2443)
PSC METALS INC
237 Tuscarawas St E (44702-1214)
P.O. Box 21070 (44701-1070)
PHONE..................................330 455-0212
EMP: 42
SALES (corp-wide): 19.1B **Publicly Held**
SIC: 5093 Wholesales Scrap Metals
HQ: Psc Metals, Inc.
    5875 Landerbrook Dr # 200
    Mayfield Heights OH 44124
    216 752-4000

(G-2444)
PSC METALS INC
3101 Varley Ave Sw (44706-3544)
PHONE..................................330 484-7610

▲ = Import ▼=Export
◆ =Import/Export

Andrew Luntz, *Branch Mgr*
EMP: 42
SALES (corp-wide): 11.7B **Publicly Held**
WEB: www.pscmetals.com
SIC: 5093 Metal scrap & waste materials
HQ: Psc Metals, Llc
5875 Landerbrook Dr # 200
Mayfield Heights OH 44124
440 753-5400

(G-2445)
PTA OHIO CNGRSS - MSN ELEM PTA
316 30th St Nw (44709-3106)
PHONE................................330 588-2156
Janelle Schuler, *Principal*
EMP: 31
SALES (est): 308.8K **Privately Held**
SIC: 8641 Parent-teachers' association

(G-2446)
QUEST RECOVERY PREVENTION SVCS (PA)
1341 Market Ave N (44714-2624)
PHONE................................330 453-8252
Keith Hochadel, *CEO*
Ivan Rosa, *COO*
Beth Devitt, *CFO*
Kelly Sober, *Recruiter*
EMP: 111
SQ FT: 12,000
SALES: 13MM **Privately Held**
WEB: www.questrecoveryservices.com
SIC: 8322 Substance abuse counseling; outreach program

(G-2447)
QUICK DELIVERY SERVICE INC (HQ)
2207 Kimball Rd Se (44707-3631)
P.O. Box 20109 (44701-0109)
PHONE................................330 453-3709
Douglas J Sibila, *President*
Larry Kelley, *CFO*
EMP: 30
SALES (est): 2.7MM **Privately Held**
SIC: 4212 Delivery service, vehicular

(G-2448)
R E RICHARDS INC
Also Called: Eecutive Directions
9701 Cleveland Ave Nw # 100 (44720-9833)
P.O. Box 3006 (44720-8006)
PHONE................................330 499-1001
Paul Richards, *President*
Cecilly Lisik, *Research*
Amanda Robinson, *Research*
EMP: 25
SALES (est): 1.6MM **Privately Held**
SIC: 7361 Executive placement

(G-2449)
R S SEWING INC
1387 Clarendon Ave Sw # 10 (44710-2190)
PHONE................................330 478-3360
Richard Spencer, *President*
EMP: 25
SALES (est): 5.8MM **Privately Held**
SIC: 5131 Sewing supplies & notions

(G-2450)
RADIOLOGY ASSOC CANTON INC
2600 6th St Sw (44710-1702)
PHONE................................330 363-2842
John Vizzuso, *CEO*
EMP: 50
SALES (est): 1.9MM **Privately Held**
SIC: 8721 Billing & bookkeeping service

(G-2451)
RED CARPET CAR WASH INC
4546 Tuscarawas St W (44708-5337)
PHONE................................330 477-5772
Jonathan Shaw, *President*
EMP: 41
SQ FT: 10,000
SALES (est): 1.4MM **Privately Held**
SIC: 7542 Washing & polishing, automotive

(G-2452)
RED ROBIN GOURMET BURGERS INC
6522 Strip Ave Nw (44720-9203)
PHONE................................330 305-1080
Jason Myers, *Manager*
EMP: 65
SALES (corp-wide): 1.3B **Publicly Held**
SIC: 5812 6794 Restaurant, family: chain; franchises, selling or licensing
PA: Red Robin Gourmet Burgers Inc
6312 S Fiddlers Green Cir 200n
Greenwood Village CO 80111
303 846-6000

(G-2453)
RENTWEAR INC
7944 Whipple Ave Nw (44720-6992)
PHONE................................330 535-2301
Roger Clay, *President*
Patricia Clay, *Corp Secy*
Christopher Clay, *Vice Pres*
Dan Clay, *Vice Pres*
Daniel Clay, *Vice Pres*
EMP: 72 **EST:** 1972
SQ FT: 31,000
SALES (est): 5.6MM **Privately Held**
SIC: 7218 Industrial uniform supply; wiping towel supply; laundered mat & rug supply

(G-2454)
REPRODUCTIVE GYNECOLOGY INC
2600 Tuscarawas St W # 560 (44708-4699)
PHONE................................330 452-6010
Richard Moretuzzo, *President*
EMP: 35
SALES (est): 780.8K **Privately Held**
SIC: 8011 Endocrinologist; fertility specialist, physician

(G-2455)
REPUBLIC N&T RAILROAD INC
2633 8th St Ne (44704-2311)
PHONE................................330 438-5826
Jim Murphy, *Manager*
EMP: 110
SALES (est): 8.8MM **Privately Held**
SIC: 4011 Railroads, line-haul operating
HQ: Republic Steel
2633 8th St Ne
Canton OH 44704
330 438-5435

(G-2456)
REPUBLIC TELCOM WORLDWIDE LLC (HQ)
3939 Everhard Rd Nw (44709-4004)
PHONE................................330 966-4586
Aaron Stryker, *General Mgr*
Valerie Moreland, *Manager*
EMP: 150
SALES (est): 7.4MM **Privately Held**
SIC: 7389 Telephone services

(G-2457)
RES-CARE INC
2915 33rd St Ne (44705-3827)
PHONE................................330 453-4144
Molly Maher, *Branch Mgr*
EMP: 48
SALES (corp-wide): 23.7B **Privately Held**
WEB: www.rescare.com
SIC: 8052 Home for the mentally retarded, with health care
HQ: Res-Care, Inc.
805 N Whittington Pkwy
Louisville KY 40222
502 394-2100

(G-2458)
RESCARE OHIO INC
2821 Whipple Ave Nw # 100 (44708-6215)
PHONE................................330 479-9841
Lisa Javersak, *Branch Mgr*
EMP: 39
SALES (corp-wide): 23.7B **Privately Held**
SIC: 8361 Self-help group home
HQ: Rescare Ohio Inc
348 W Main St
Williamsburg OH 45176

(G-2459)
RESERVE FTL LLC
Also Called: Reserve Iron Ohio
1451 Trump Ave Ne (44730-1651)
PHONE................................773 721-8740
Guy Peake, *Branch Mgr*
EMP: 30 **Privately Held**
SIC: 5093 Ferrous metal scrap & waste
PA: Reserve Ftl, Llc
11600 S Burley Ave
Chicago IL 60617

(G-2460)
REXS AIR CONDITIONING COMPANY
Also Called: Rex Reliable
7801 Freedom Ave Nw (44720-6907)
P.O. Box 1030, Uniontown (44685-1030)
PHONE................................330 499-8733
Scott Seifert, *President*
Eugene Seifert, *Shareholder*
EMP: 25
SALES (est): 1.8MM **Privately Held**
SIC: 1711 Plumbing, heating, air-conditioning contractors

(G-2461)
RICK ALLMAN
Also Called: Primerica
4450 Belden Village St Nw Nw800 (44718-2552)
PHONE................................330 699-1660
Rick Allman, *Owner*
EMP: 40
SALES (est): 4.1MM **Privately Held**
SIC: 6411 Insurance agents & brokers

(G-2462)
ROMAN PLUMBING COMPANY
2411 Shepler Ch Ave Sw (44706-4199)
PHONE................................330 455-5155
Scott Kocher, *President*
Doug Kocher, *Vice Pres*
EMP: 55
SQ FT: 2,500
SALES (est): 7.5MM **Privately Held**
SIC: 1711 Plumbing contractors; warm air heating & air conditioning contractor

(G-2463)
RORICKS INC
Also Called: Roricks Ceiling Center
4701 Eagle St Nw (44720-7083)
PHONE................................330 497-6888
Richard L Rorick, *President*
Mike Arters, *Opers Mgr*
Krissy Greene, *Controller*
Lewis W Devore, *Manager*
Floyd E Oryszak, *Manager*
EMP: 50
SQ FT: 23,000
SALES (est): 5.7MM **Privately Held**
WEB: www.roricks.com
SIC: 1742 Drywall; plastering, plain or ornamental

(G-2464)
ROYAL SHEEN SERVICE CENTER
Also Called: Royal Car Wash
6720 Bridgestone Cir Ne (44721-2466)
PHONE................................330 966-7200
Scott Walker, *General Mgr*
Lonn Swinehart, *Vice Pres*
Pam Walker, *Admin Sec*
EMP: 25
SQ FT: 5,720
SALES (est): 1.1MM **Privately Held**
SIC: 7542 Carwash, automatic

(G-2465)
RUKH-JAGI HOLDINGS LLC
Also Called: Holiday Inn Canton
4520 Everhard Rd Nw (44718-2407)
PHONE................................330 494-2770
Rupen Patel,
EMP: 100
SALES (est): 6.1MM **Privately Held**
WEB: www.hicanton.com
SIC: 7011 Hotels & motels

(G-2466)
RUNT WARE & SANITARY SERVICE
7944 Whipple Ave Nw (44720-6930)
PHONE................................330 494-5776
Roger Clay, *General Mgr*
Chris Clay, *Principal*
Tadd Clay, *Principal*
Dan Clay, *Manager*
EMP: 50
SALES (est): 598.7K **Privately Held**
WEB: www.saniserv.biz
SIC: 7218 Industrial uniform supply

(G-2467)
RUSSELL D ENS DO
Also Called: Ohio Anestisia
4665 Douglas Cir Nw # 101 (44718-3673)
PHONE................................330 499-5700
Mark Fellow, *Owner*
EMP: 50
SALES (est): 142.6K **Privately Held**
SIC: 8011 Anesthesiologist

(G-2468)
S&S CAR CARE INC
5340 Mayfair Rd (44720-1533)
PHONE................................330 494-9535
Lonn Swinehart, *President*
EMP: 25
SQ FT: 20,000
SALES (est): 1.3MM **Privately Held**
SIC: 7539 Automotive repair shops

(G-2469)
SAFETY RESOURCES COMPANY OHIO
4650 Southway St Sw (44706-1935)
P.O. Box 80425 (44708-0425)
PHONE................................330 477-1100
Curt Speck, *President*
Curtis Speck, *General Mgr*
Chuck Householder, *Finance Mgr*
Gordon Snyder, *Consultant*
EMP: 33
SALES (est): 4.5MM **Privately Held**
SIC: 8742 Quality assurance consultant

(G-2470)
SBS OF CANTON JV LLC
Also Called: Staybridge Suites Canton
3879 Everhard Rd Nw (44709-4003)
PHONE................................330 966-6620
Mona Rigdon, *Principal*
Richard Larson, *Principal*
EMP: 25
SALES (est): 166.1K **Privately Held**
SIC: 7011 Hotels & motels

(G-2471)
SCHAUER GROUP INCORPORATED
200 Market Ave N Ste 100 (44702-1435)
PHONE................................330 453-7721
David T Schauer, *President*
Tim Pentivegna, *Vice Pres*
Ronald Repp, *Vice Pres*
Aimee B Belden, *Assoc VP*
Peter Butler, *Assoc VP*
EMP: 40
SQ FT: 11,000
SALES (est): 7.4MM **Privately Held**
WEB: www.schauergroup.com
SIC: 6411 Insurance agents; advisory services, insurance

(G-2472)
SECURITY SAVINGS MORTGAGE CORP
Also Called: Mortgage Service Center
300 Tuscarawas St W Fl 8 (44702-1914)
P.O. Box 8469 (44711-8469)
PHONE................................330 455-2833
Clara E Preston, *President*
Libe Preston, *President*
EMP: 60
SQ FT: 22,100
SALES (est): 8MM
SALES (corp-wide): 312MM **Privately Held**
WEB: www.dollarbank.com
SIC: 6162 Mortgage bankers

PA: Dollar Bank, Federal Savings Bank
340 4th Ave
Pittsburgh PA 15222
412 261-4900

(G-2473)
SELINSKY FORCE LLC
4015 23rd St Sw (44706-2313)
PHONE..................................330 477-4527
Steve Miller, *Branch Mgr*
EMP: 200 **Privately Held**
SIC: 5085 Industrial supplies
PA: The Selinsky Force Llc
5365 E Center Dr Ne
Canton OH 44721

(G-2474)
SERVICEMASTER BY STEINBACH
6824 Wise Ave Nw (44720-7359)
PHONE..................................330 497-5959
Dave Steinbach, *President*
Thomas Baer, *President*
EMP: 25
SQ FT: 3,000
SALES: 750K **Privately Held**
SIC: 7349 Janitorial service, contract basis

(G-2475)
SHARED PET IMAGING LLC
4825 Higbee Ave Nw # 201 (44718-2567)
PHONE..................................330 491-0480
Randy Skiles,
Steven J Ossakow,
Raymond Rosedale,
EMP: 175 EST: 1999
SQ FT: 10,000
SALES (est): 3.6MM **Privately Held**
WEB: www.sharedpet.com
SIC: 8071 Medical laboratories
HQ: Alliance Healthcare Services, Inc.
18201 Von Karman Ave
Irvine CA 92612
949 242-5300

(G-2476)
SIMPLY YOUTH LLC
123 Cleveland Ave Nw (44702-1707)
PHONE..................................330 284-2537
Terrance Jones, *Exec Dir*
EMP: 89
SALES (est): 300.6K **Privately Held**
SIC: 8322 Child related social services

(G-2477)
SIRAK FINANCIAL SERVICES INC (PA)
Also Called: Sirak Financial Companies
4700 Dressler Rd Nw (44718-2511)
PHONE..................................330 493-0642
Gary D Sirak, *President*
Wayne E S Arnold, *CFO*
EMP: 60 EST: 1956
SQ FT: 22,000
SALES (est): 10.4MM **Privately Held**
WEB: www.sirakfinancial.com
SIC: 6211 6411 Stock brokers & dealers;
pension & retirement plan consultants; in-
surance agents

(G-2478)
SIRAK-MOORE INSURANCE AGCY INC
Also Called: Kemper Insurance
4700 Dressler Rd Nw (44718-2511)
PHONE..................................330 493-3211
Corbin Moore, *President*
Mark L Sirak, *Vice Pres*
Wayne Arnold, *CFO*
Stanford Sirak, *Treasurer*
Gary Sirak, *Admin Sec*
EMP: 30
SQ FT: 20,000
SALES (est): 4.2MM **Privately Held**
SIC: 6411 Insurance agents, brokers &
service

(G-2479)
SLESNICK IRON & METAL CO
Also Called: Auto Crushers
927 Warner Rd Se (44707-3337)
PHONE..................................330 453-8475
W Stanley Slesnick, *President*
Edward Slesnick, *Vice Pres*
Jeffrey Slesnick, *Admin Sec*

EMP: 50 EST: 1920
SQ FT: 3,000
SALES (est): 12MM **Privately Held**
WEB: www.autocrushers.com
SIC: 5093 Junk & scrap

(G-2480)
SOUTHWAY FENCE COMPANY
5156 Southway St Sw (44706-1944)
PHONE..................................330 477-5251
Peter Williams Sr, *President*
EMP: 30
SQ FT: 8,800
SALES (est): 4.2MM **Privately Held**
WEB: www.southwayfence.com
SIC: 1799 Fence construction

(G-2481)
SPAULDING CONSTRUCTION CO INC
7640 Whipple Ave Nw (44720-6924)
PHONE..................................330 494-1776
EMP: 52 EST: 1987
SALES (est): 5.1MM **Privately Held**
SIC: 1771 Cement Contractor

(G-2482)
SPITZER CHEVROLET COMPANY
7111 Sunset Strip Ave Nw (44720-7080)
PHONE..................................330 966-9524
Alan Spitzer, *President*
Kevin Spitzer, *Vice Pres*
EMP: 40 EST: 1959
SQ FT: 7,140
SALES (est): 12.8MM **Privately Held**
SIC: 5511 7514 Automobiles, new & used;
vans, new & used; pickups, new & used;
passenger car rental

(G-2483)
SPRAYWORKS EQUIPMENT GROUP LLC
945 Mckinley Ave Sw (44707-4163)
P.O. Box 20388 (44701-0388)
PHONE..................................330 587-4141
Debra Davidson,
James Davidson,
EMP: 30
SALES (est): 8.9MM **Privately Held**
SIC: 5046 Commercial equipment

(G-2484)
SPRINT SPECTRUM LP
4470 Belden Village St Nw (44718-2516)
PHONE..................................330 470-4614
Kevin Finn, *Branch Mgr*
EMP: 30
SALES (corp-wide): 85.9B **Publicly Held**
WEB: www.sprintpcs.com
SIC: 4813 Local & long distance telephone
communications
HQ: Sprint Spectrum L.P.
6800 Sprint Pkwy
Overland Park KS 66251

(G-2485)
STANDARD PLUMBING & HEATING CO (PA)
435 Walnut Ave Se (44702-1348)
P.O. Box 20650 (44701-0650)
PHONE..................................330 453-5150
David Grabowsky, *President*
Herman C Grabowsky, *Principal*
May C Grabowsky, *Principal*
Robert W Grabowsky, *Principal*
Bruce Humbert, *Project Mgr*
EMP: 75
SQ FT: 20,000
SALES (est): 25.1MM **Privately Held**
WEB: www.standardpandh.net
SIC: 1711 Plumbing contractors; warm air
heating & air conditioning contractor; ven-
tilation & duct work contractor; process
piping contractor

(G-2486)
STAR COUNTY HOME CONSORTIUM
201 3rd St Ne Fl 2201 (44702-1212)
PHONE..................................330 451-7395
Beth Pearson, *Principal*
Bill James, *Technology*
EMP: 25

SALES (est): 940.9K **Privately Held**
SIC: 8748 Urban planning & consulting
services

(G-2487)
STARK AREA REGIONAL TRNST AUTH (PA)
Also Called: Sarta
1600 Gateway Blvd Se (44707-3544)
PHONE..................................330 477-2782
Debbie Swickard, *Manager*
Kirt Conrad, *Exec Dir*
EMP: 207
SQ FT: 100,000
SALES: 18.7MM **Privately Held**
WEB: www.sartaonline.com
SIC: 4131 4111 Intercity & rural bus trans-
portation; local & suburban transit

(G-2488)
STARK CNTY DEPT JOB FMLY SVCS
221 3rd St Se (44702-1302)
PHONE..................................330 451-8400
Jane Bethel, *Finance*
Susan Lenigar, *Director*
Nedra Petro, *Director*
Rob Pierson, *Director*
Julie Barnes, *Administration*
EMP: 485
SQ FT: 121,700
SALES (est): 9.4MM **Privately Held**
SIC: 8322 Public welfare center
PA: County Of Stark
110 Central Plz S Ste 240
Canton OH 44702
330 451-7371

(G-2489)
STARK CNTY HISTORICAL SOC INC
Also Called: MCKINLEY NATIONAL MEMO-
RIAL
800 Mckinley Monu Dr Nw (44708-4832)
PHONE..................................330 455-7043
Joyce Yut, *Director*
EMP: 25
SALES: 935.7K **Privately Held**
WEB: www.mckinleymuseum.org
SIC: 8412 Museum; historical society

(G-2490)
STARK COUNTY BOARD OF DEVELOPM
Also Called: Workshops, The
4065 Bradley Cir Nw (44718-2565)
PHONE..................................330 477-5200
H Michael Miller, *CEO*
Gary Braun, *President*
EMP: 600
SALES (est): 19.5MM **Privately Held**
WEB: www.theworkshopsinc.com
SIC: 8331 8093 Sheltered workshop;
mental health clinic, outpatient

(G-2491)
STARK COUNTY CMNTY ACTION AGCY (PA)
Also Called: SCCAA
1366 Market Ave N (44714-2606)
PHONE..................................330 454-1676
Rodney Reasonover, *CEO*
Rudolph Herter, *Human Res Dir*
EMP: 170
SQ FT: 11,500
SALES: 11.3MM **Privately Held**
SIC: 8399 Community action agency

(G-2492)
STARK COUNTY FEDERATION OF CON
6323 Richville Dr Sw (44706-3131)
PHONE..................................330 268-1652
Michael W Rutledge, *Principal*
Jim Adkins, *Principal*
Debbie Bonk, *Principal*
Kathy Griffin, *Principal*
Bob Hess, *Principal*
EMP: 25
SALES (est): 371.6K **Privately Held**
SIC: 7389 Business services

(G-2493)
STARK COUNTY NEUROLOGISTS INC
4105 Holiday St Nw (44718-2531)
P.O. Box 35006 (44735-5006)
PHONE..................................330 494-2097
Alok Bhagap, *President*
Dr Morris Kinast, *Vice Pres*
Dr Leon Rosenberg, *Treasurer*
Dr Jay P Berke, *Admin Sec*
EMP: 56
SQ FT: 3,100
SALES (est): 2.9MM **Privately Held**
WEB: www.neurocarecenter.com
SIC: 8011 Neurologist; physical medicine,
physician/surgeon

(G-2494)
STARK COUNTY PARK DISTRICT
5300 Tyner Ave Nw (44708-5041)
PHONE..................................330 477-3552
Bob Fonte, *Director*
EMP: 60
SQ FT: 2,912
SALES: 5.3MM **Privately Held**
SIC: 7999 Recreation services

(G-2495)
STARK COUNTY WOMENS CLINIC INC
5000 Higbee Ave Nw (44718-2582)
PHONE..................................330 493-0313
William Alford Do, *President*
Carl Schlech MD, *Principal*
EMP: 70
SQ FT: 11,000
SALES (est): 9.9MM **Privately Held**
SIC: 8011 Gynecologist; obstetrician

(G-2496)
STB ENTERPRISES
4417 17th St Nw (44708-2709)
PHONE..................................330 478-0044
Bernice Guist, *Owner*
EMP: 25
SQ FT: 1,700
SALES (est): 763K **Privately Held**
SIC: 7349 Office cleaning or charring

(G-2497)
STEELE W W JR AGENCY INC
Also Called: Schauer Indpendence Insur Agcy
200 Market Ave N Ste 100 (44702-1435)
PHONE..................................330 453-7721
David Shauer, *President*
Aimee B Belden, *Assoc VP*
Heather Nau, *Personnel*
Carolyn Nupp, *Executive*
EMP: 40
SQ FT: 2,500
SALES (est): 5.8MM **Privately Held**
SIC: 6411 Insurance agents

(G-2498)
STOLLE MACHINERY COMPANY LLC
4150 Belden Village St Nw (44718-2595)
PHONE..................................330 493-0444
Jim McClung, *Branch Mgr*
EMP: 50
SALES (corp-wide): 262.3MM **Privately Held**
WEB: www.stollemachinery.com
SIC: 5084 Industrial machinery & equip-
ment
PA: Stolle Machinery Company, Llc
6949 S Potomac St
Centennial CO 80112
303 708-9044

(G-2499)
STONE CROSSING ASSISTED LIVING
Also Called: Glenwood Assisted Living
820 34th St Nw (44709-2966)
PHONE..................................330 492-7131
Tracy Imhoff, *Administration*
EMP: 250
SALES (est): 561.8K **Privately Held**
SIC: 8051 Skilled nursing care facilities

(G-2500)
STONE PRODUCTS INC (HQ)
Also Called: GREY STONE
3105 Varley Ave Sw (44706-3544)
P.O. Box 6059 (44706-0059)
PHONE..............................800 235-6088
W Mark Sterling, *President*
Jeffrey Sterling, *Vice Pres*
Richard Williams, *CFO*
Bruce Manwaring, *Sales Mgr*
Dan Fugate, *Sales Staff*
▼ EMP: 25
SQ FT: 5,000
SALES: 10.5MM
SALES (corp-wide): 249.5MM **Privately Held**
WEB: www.stonepro.com
SIC: 5082 Construction & mining machinery
PA: The Beaver Excavating Co
    2000 Beaver Place Ave Sw
    Canton OH 44706
    330 478-2151

(G-2501)
STONEMOR PARTNERS LP
4450 Belden Village St Nw # 802
(44718-2552)
PHONE..............................330 491-8001
Cathy Konen, *Manager*
EMP: 50
SALES (corp-wide): 316.1MM **Publicly Held**
WEB: www.stonemor.com
SIC: 6553 Cemetery subdividers & developers
PA: Stonemor Partners L.P.
    3600 Horizon Blvd Ste 100
    Trevose PA 19053
    215 826-2800

(G-2502)
SUAREZ CORPORATION INDUSTRIES
Biotech Research Division
7800 Whipple Ave Nw (44767-0002)
PHONE..............................330 494-4282
Benjamin Suarez, *Manager*
EMP: 73
SALES (corp-wide): 71.8MM **Privately Held**
WEB: www.suarez.com
SIC: 3841 5091 2834 5122 Veterinarians' instruments & apparatus; fitness equipment & supplies; vitamin, nutrient & hematinic preparations for human use; vitamins & minerals
PA: Suarez Corporation Industries
    7800 Whipple Ave Nw
    North Canton OH 44720
    330 494-5504

(G-2503)
SUNSET HILLS CEMETERY CORP
5001 Everhard Rd Nw (44718-2473)
PHONE..............................330 494-2051
Victor M Evans, *President*
Floyd E Bennett, *Treasurer*
E Keith Payne, *Admin Sec*
EMP: 35
SQ FT: 12,600
SALES (est): 1.4MM
SALES (corp-wide): 3.1B **Publicly Held**
WEB: www.sci-corp.com
SIC: 6553 Cemetery association
PA: Service Corporation International
    1929 Allen Pkwy
    Houston TX 77019
    713 522-5141

(G-2504)
SUPERIOR PAVING & MATERIALS
5947 Whipple Ave Nw (44720-7613)
PHONE..............................330 499-5849
Marlene Oster, *President*
EMP: 35
SQ FT: 3,000
SALES (est): 4.6MM **Privately Held**
SIC: 1611 Highway & street paving contractor

(G-2505)
T & B TRANSPORTATION INC
4938 Southway St Sw (44706-1940)
PHONE..............................330 495-0316
Edward Braun, *President*
EMP: 25
SALES (est): 2.5MM **Privately Held**
SIC: 4214 Local trucking with storage

(G-2506)
TAB CONSTRUCTION COMPANY INC
530 Walnut Ave Ne (44702-1273)
PHONE..............................330 454-5228
William E Richardson III, *President*
EMP: 50
SQ FT: 3,900
SALES (est): 9.8MM **Privately Held**
WEB: www.tab-construction.com
SIC: 1611 1542 Highway & street construction; nonresidential construction

(G-2507)
TEBO FINANCIAL SERVICES INC
4740 Belpar St Nw Ste A (44718-3685)
PHONE..............................234 207-2500
Robert L Bowman, *President*
Roy A Baker Jr, *CFO*
Robert M James, *Admin Sec*
EMP: 48
SALES: 12.3MM **Privately Held**
WEB: www.tebofinancialservices.com
SIC: 6141 Personal credit institutions

(G-2508)
TERMINAL WAREHOUSE INC (HQ)
2207 Kimball Rd Se (44707-3631)
P.O. Box 20109 (44701-0109)
PHONE..............................330 773-2056
Ronald R Goson, *CEO*
Douglas J Sibila, *CEO*
William Hanlon, *President*
Bill Hanlon, *COO*
Dan Stemple, *Vice Pres*
▲ EMP: 64
SQ FT: 1,700,000
SALES (est): 18.3MM **Privately Held**
WEB: www.terminalwhse.com
SIC: 4225 General warehousing

(G-2509)
TERMINIX INTL CO LTD PARTNR
2680 Roberts Ave Nw Ste A (44709-3484)
PHONE..............................978 744-2402
Sam Bodila, *Manager*
EMP: 30
SALES (corp-wide): 1.9B **Publicly Held**
SIC: 7342 Pest control services
HQ: The Terminix International Company
    Limited Partnership
    150 Peabody Pl
    Memphis TN 38103
    901 766-1400

(G-2510)
THOMAS AND ASSOCIATES
1421 Portage St Nw Ste C (44702-2289)
PHONE..............................330 494-2111
Dr Michael L Thomas, *President*
EMP: 30
SQ FT: 3,920
SALES (est): 3.1MM **Privately Held**
SIC: 8021 Dentists' office

(G-2511)
TIME WARNER CABLE INC
5520 Whipple Ave Nw (44720-7700)
P.O. Box 8559 (44711-8559)
PHONE..............................330 494-9200
Ken Fuchs, *Vice Pres*
EMP: 83
SQ FT: 30,000
SALES (corp-wide): 43.6B **Publicly Held**
SIC: 4841 Cable television services
HQ: Spectrum Management Holding Company, Llc
    400 Atlantic St
    Stamford CT 06901
    203 905-7801

(G-2512)
TIMKEN COMPANY
Research Division
4500 Mount Pleasant St Nw (44720-5450)
P.O. Box 6930 (44706-0930)
PHONE..............................330 471-2121
Sal Miraglia, *Manager*
EMP: 250
SALES (corp-wide): 3.5B **Publicly Held**
SIC: 5085 Bearings
PA: The Timken Company
    4500 Mount Pleasant St Nw
    North Canton OH 44720
    234 262-3000

(G-2513)
TOM BAIER & ASSOC INC
Also Called: Coldwell Banker
4686 Douglas Cir Nw (44718-3619)
PHONE..............................330 497-3115
Thomas Baier, *President*
Ben Emerick, *Agent*
EMP: 25
SALES (est): 1.2MM **Privately Held**
WEB: www.ohiohomesbypat.com
SIC: 6531 Real estate agent, residential

(G-2514)
TOP ECHELON CONTRACTING INC
4883 Dressler Rd Nw # 200 (44718-3665)
PHONE..............................330 454-3508
Debra M Fledderjohann, *President*
Diane Marzec, *Hum Res Coord*
Lisa Kovac, *Manager*
Michael J Kappel, *Shareholder*
Tammi Shields, *Admin Asst*
EMP: 364
SQ FT: 1,095
SALES: 26.7MM **Privately Held**
WEB: www.topecheloncontracting.com
SIC: 8742 8721 7363 Materials mgmt. (purchasing, handling, inventory) consultant; payroll accounting service; engineering help service

(G-2515)
TRUGREEN LIMITED PARTNERSHIP
Also Called: Tru Green-Chemlawn
6302 Promway Ave Nw (44720-7620)
P.O. Box 36120 (44735-6120)
PHONE..............................330 409-2861
Bill Brown, *Manager*
EMP: 40
SALES (corp-wide): 3.4B **Privately Held**
SIC: 0782 Lawn care services
HQ: Trugreen Limited Partnership
    1790 Kirby Pkwy
    Memphis TN 38138
    901 251-4128

(G-2516)
TYCOR ROOFING INC
1704 Warner Rd Se (44707-2276)
PHONE..............................330 452-8150
Bruce Martin, *President*
Cynthia Soos, *Treasurer*
Lisa Lint, *Bookkeeper*
Cinde L Martin, *Admin Sec*
EMP: 25
SQ FT: 5,664
SALES (est): 4.3MM **Privately Held**
WEB: www.haljones.com
SIC: 1761 Roofing contractor

(G-2517)
UNITED FOOD & COMMERCIAL WKR
Also Called: LOCAL 17A
1800 Cleveland Ave Nw (44709-3602)
PHONE..............................330 452-4850
Sonja Campbell, *President*
Gary Feiock, *Principal*
EMP: 40
SALES: 671.5K **Privately Held**
SIC: 8631 Labor union

(G-2518)
UNITED GL & PANL SYSTEMS INC
4250 Strausser St Nw (44720-7114)
PHONE..............................330 244-9745
Thomas M Nesbitt, *President*
Shelly M Nesbitt, *Corp Secy*

EMP: 42
SQ FT: 36,000
SALES (est): 9MM **Privately Held**
WEB: www.ugps.com
SIC: 1793 1761 Glass & glazing work; roofing, siding & sheet metal work

(G-2519)
UNITED HEALTH NETWORK LTD
4455 Dressler Rd Nw (44718-2785)
PHONE..............................330 492-2102
Jeff Russell, *President*
EMP: 48
SALES: 2.1MM **Privately Held**
WEB: www.unitedhealthnetwork.com
SIC: 8011 Offices & clinics of medical doctors

(G-2520)
UNITED PARCEL SERVICE INC OH
Also Called: UPS
4850 Navarre Rd Sw (44706-2238)
PHONE..............................330 478-1007
Roger Mattock, *Branch Mgr*
EMP: 152
SALES (corp-wide): 71.8B **Publicly Held**
WEB: www.upsscs.com
SIC: 4215 Parcel delivery, vehicular
HQ: United Parcel Service, Inc. (Oh)
    55 Glenlake Pkwy
    Atlanta GA 30328
    404 828-6000

(G-2521)
UNITED STATES COMMEMRTV ART GA
7800 Whipple Ave Nw (44767-0001)
PHONE..............................330 494-5504
Fax: 330 497-6807
EMP: 25
SALES (est): 3.4MM **Privately Held**
SIC: 5094 Whol Jewelry/Precious Stones

(G-2522)
UNITED STEELWORKERS OF AMERICA
Also Called: Uswa
4069 Bradley Cir Nw (44718-2565)
PHONE..............................330 493-7721
Dave McCall, *Director*
EMP: 111
SALES (corp-wide): 4.9MM **Privately Held**
WEB: www.uswa.org
SIC: 8631 Labor union
PA: United Steelworkers
    60 Blvd Of The Allies # 902
    Pittsburgh PA 15222
    412 562-2400

(G-2523)
UNITED WAY GREATER STARK CNTY
401 Market Ave N Ste 300 (44702-1502)
PHONE..............................330 491-0445
Maria Heege, *President*
EMP: 25
SALES: 6.5MM **Privately Held**
SIC: 8399 Fund raising organization, non-fee basis

(G-2524)
US TECH AROSPC ENGRG CORP (PA)
Also Called: US Technology Aerospace
4200 Munson St Nw (44718-2981)
PHONE..............................330 455-1181
Raymond F Williams, *President*
Robert Putnam, *Vice Pres*
Nimmie E Wasson, *Vice Pres*
EMP: 70
SALES (est): 8.1MM **Privately Held**
WEB: www.ustae.com
SIC: 8711 Engineering services

(G-2525)
USAM INC
Also Called: United Studios of America
4450 Belden Village St Nw # 305
(44718-2552)
PHONE..............................330 244-8782
Dean Nelson, *President*
Robert Humphries, *Admin Sec*
EMP: 75 EST: 1996

GEOGRAPHIC

SQ FT: 35,000
SALES (est): 1.6MM **Privately Held**
WEB: www.unitedstudiosofamerica.com
SIC: 7221 Photographer, still or video

(G-2526)
**VETERANS HEALTH
ADMINISTRATION**
Also Called: Veterans Clinic
733 Market Ave S (44702-2165)
PHONE.................................330 489-4600
Nancye Jackson, *Branch Mgr*
EMP: 70 **Publicly Held**
WEB: www.veterans-ru.org
SIC: 8011 9451 Clinic, operated by physicians;
HQ: Veterans Health Administration
810 Vermont Ave Nw
Washington DC 20420

(G-2527)
**VICTORY SQ APRTMNTS LTD
PARTNR**
1206 Lppert Rd Ne Apt 211 (44705)
PHONE.................................330 455-8035
George Buchanan, *Principal*
Leeann Morein, *Manager*
EMP: 99
SALES: 950K **Privately Held**
SIC: 6513 Apartment building operators

(G-2528)
**VISUAL EDGE TECHNOLOGY
INC (PA)**
3874 Highland Park Nw (44720-4538)
PHONE.................................330 494-9694
Austin Vanchieri, *Ch of Bd*
Yvonne Brown, *Vice Pres*
Gennie Snider, *Purch Dir*
Charles Bergdorf, *Engineer*
Terry Kikkert, *Info Tech Mgr*
EMP: 130
SQ FT: 52,000
SALES: 270MM **Privately Held**
WEB: www.visualedgetechnology.com
SIC: 5044 5065 Copying equipment; facsimile equipment

(G-2529)
**W L LOGAN TRUCKING
COMPANY**
Also Called: Logan Logistics
3224 Navarre Rd Sw (44706-1897)
PHONE.................................330 478-1404
William L Logan Sr, *Ch of Bd*
Betty Jane Logan, *President*
Robert Logan, *Corp Secy*
William L Logan Jr, *Vice Pres*
Dave Pritchard, *Human Res Mgr*
EMP: 125
SQ FT: 30,000
SALES (est): 37.5MM **Privately Held**
WEB: www.logantrucking.com
SIC: 4212 4213 Local trucking, without storage; contract haulers

(G-2530)
W W SCHAUB ELECTRIC CO
501 Applegrove St Nw (44720-1619)
PHONE.................................330 494-3560
Wesley W Schaub III, *President*
Robert Schaub, *Vice Pres*
Pam Hess, *Purchasing*
EMP: 40
SQ FT: 16,000
SALES (est): 4MM **Privately Held**
WEB: www.wwschaub.com
SIC: 1731 General electrical contractor

(G-2531)
**WARSTLER BROTHERS
LANDSCAPING**
4125 Salway Ave Nw (44718-2953)
PHONE.................................330 492-9500
Shawn Warstlet, *President*
Shawn Warstler, *President*
EMP: 33
SQ FT: 3,360
SALES: 2MM **Privately Held**
SIC: 0782 4959 8748 4971 Landscape contractors; snowplowing; lighting consultant; irrigation systems

(G-2532)
**WASTE MANAGEMENT OHIO
INC**
1800 9th St Ne (44705-1404)
PHONE.................................330 452-9000
Dave Bower, *Opers Staff*
Don Leisure, *Manager*
EMP: 30
SALES (corp-wide): 14.9B **Publicly Held**
WEB: www.metrodisposal.com
SIC: 4953 Garbage: collecting, destroying & processing; waste materials, disposal at sea
HQ: Waste Management Of Ohio, Inc.
1700 N Broad St
Fairborn OH 45324

(G-2533)
**WERN-RAUSCH LOCKE
ADVERTISING**
Also Called: Wrl Advertising
4470 Dressler Rd Nw (44718-2716)
PHONE.................................330 493-8866
Todd Locke, *President*
Robert Isenberg, *Principal*
Charles T Locke, *Vice Pres*
Thomas Locke, *Vice Pres*
Tom Locke, *Vice Pres*
EMP: 28 **EST** 1956
SQ FT: 5,500
SALES (est): 6.4MM **Privately Held**
WEB: www.wrladv.com
SIC: 7311 Advertising agencies

(G-2534)
WESTERN BRANCH DIESEL INC
Also Called: John Deere Authorized Dealer
1616 Metric Ave Sw (44706-3087)
PHONE.................................330 454-8800
Mike McElwain, *Branch Mgr*
EMP: 28
SQ FT: 22,400
SALES (corp-wide): 84MM **Privately
Held**
WEB: www.westernbranchdiesel.com
SIC: 5084 5531 5063 3714 Engines & parts, diesel; truck equipment & parts; generators; motor vehicle parts & accessories; power transmission equipment; internal combustion engines
PA: Western Branch Diesel, Incorporated
3504 Shipwright St
Portsmouth VA 23703
757 673-7000

(G-2535)
WESTFIELD BELDEN VILLAGE
4230 Belden Village Mall (44718-2504)
PHONE.................................330 494-5490
Katrina Barton, *General Mgr*
EMP: 40
SALES (est): 2.5MM **Privately Held**
SIC: 8611 Merchants' association

(G-2536)
**WINDSOR MEDICAL CENTER
INC**
1454 E Maple St (44720-2634)
PHONE.................................330 499-8300
Thomas Sawllen, *President*
EMP: 100
SQ FT: 10,000
SALES (est): 7.1MM **Privately Held**
SIC: 8059 8661 8052 8051 Personal care home, with health care; religious organizations; intermediate care facilities; skilled nursing care facilities

(G-2537)
**WORKFORCE INITIATIVE ASSN
(PA)**
822 30th St Nw (44709-2902)
PHONE.................................330 433-9675
Alice Stephens, *Director*
EMP: 25
SQ FT: 15,000
SALES: 10.6MM **Privately Held**
WEB: www.eswork.org
SIC: 8331 Job training services

(G-2538)
**WORKFORCE SERVICES INC
(PA)**
Also Called: Wf Services
6245 Sherman Ch Ave Sw (44706-3770)
PHONE.................................330 484-2566
John Kissell, *President*
EMP: 40
SQ FT: 2,400
SALES (est): 4.2MM **Privately Held**
SIC: 7538 General truck repair

(G-2539)
**Y M C A CENTRAL STARK
COUNTY**
Also Called: YMCA Child Care
200 Charlotte St Nw (44720-2404)
PHONE.................................330 305-5437
Sherry Sampson, *Branch Mgr*
EMP: 45
SALES (corp-wide): 16.5MM **Privately
Held**
WEB: www.ymcastark.org
SIC: 8641 7991 8351 7032 Youth organizations; physical fitness facilities; child day care services; youth camps; individual & family services
PA: Y M C A Of Central Stark County
1201 30th St Nw Ste 200a
Canton OH 44709
330 491-9622

(G-2540)
**Y M C A CENTRAL STARK
COUNTY**
Also Called: Gymnastics Center
7241 Whipple Ave Nw (44720-7137)
PHONE.................................330 498-4082
Colleen Ekle, *Branch Mgr*
EMP: 33
SALES (corp-wide): 16.5MM **Privately
Held**
WEB: www.ymcastark.org
SIC: 8641 7991 8351 7032 Youth organizations; physical fitness facilities; child day care services; youth camps; individual & family services
PA: Y M C A Of Central Stark County
1201 30th St Nw Ste 200a
Canton OH 44709
330 491-9622

(G-2541)
YOUNG TRUCK SALES INC (PA)
Also Called: Jay-Mac
4970 Southway St Sw (44706-1940)
P.O. Box 6118 (44706-0118)
PHONE.................................330 477-6271
Richard A Young, *Ch of Bd*
Craig Young, *President*
Nellie M Young, *Principal*
Robert P Young, *Vice Pres*
EMP: 50
SQ FT: 31,000
SALES (est): 39.5MM **Privately Held**
SIC: 5511 5013 7538 Automobiles, new & used; truck parts & accessories; general automotive repair shops

(G-2542)
**YOUNG WNS CHRISTN ASSN
CANTON (PA)**
Also Called: YWCA of Canton
231 6th St Ne (44702-1035)
PHONE.................................330 453-7644
Kelly Bah, *CEO*
Darcy Anderson, *Mktg Dir*
Samantha Dunn, *Admin Sec*
EMP: 55
SQ FT: 71,749
SALES (est): 5.1MM **Privately Held**
SIC: 8641 Youth organizations

(G-2543)
**YOUNG WOMNS CHRSTN ASSC
CANTON**
1700 Gateway Blvd Se (44707-3518)
PHONE.................................330 453-0789
Sandy Markert, *Branch Mgr*
EMP: 51

SALES (corp-wide): 5.1MM **Privately
Held**
SIC: 8641 7991 8351 7032 Youth organizations; physical fitness facilities; child day care services; youth camps; individual & family services
PA: Young Womens Christian Association
Canton
231 6th St Ne
Canton OH 44702
330 453-7644

(G-2544)
**ZIEGLER BOLT & PARTS CO
(PA)**
Also Called: Ziegler Bolt & Nut House
4848 Corporate St Sw (44706-1907)
P.O. Box 80369 (44708-0369)
PHONE.................................330 478-2542
William A Ziegler Jr, *President*
Jim Spadone, *Purch Agent*
Janet Hanacek, *Treasurer*
William Tgaut, *Human Res Mgr*
Timothy McNichol, *Sales Mgr*
EMP: 86
SQ FT: 80,000
SALES (est): 33MM **Privately Held**
WEB: www.zieglerbolt.com
SIC: 5085 5072 Fasteners, industrial: nuts, bolts, screws, etc.; hardware

---

Carey
Wyandot County

(G-2545)
NATIONAL LIME AND STONE CO
370 N Patterson St (43316-1057)
P.O. Box 8 (43316-0008)
PHONE.................................419 396-7671
Chris Beeman, *Exec VP*
Ron Wike, *Mktg Dir*
Ryan Phillips, *Branch Mgr*
David Beltz, *Info Tech Dir*
EMP: 130
SALES (corp-wide): 3.2B **Privately Held**
WEB: www.natlime.com
SIC: 1422 3291 3281 3274 Lime rock, ground; abrasive products; cut stone & stone products; lime; alkalies & chlorine; construction sand & gravel
PA: The National Lime And Stone Company
551 Lake Cascade Pkwy
Findlay OH 45840
419 422-4341

(G-2546)
REPUBLIC SERVICES INC
11164 Co Rd 4 (43316)
PHONE.................................419 396-3581
Thomas Weelden V, *Branch Mgr*
EMP: 34
SALES (corp-wide): 10B **Publicly Held**
SIC: 4953 Refuse collection & disposal services
PA: Republic Services, Inc.
18500 N Allied Way # 100
Phoenix AZ 85054
480 627-2700

(G-2547)
SHELLY COMPANY
1794 County Highway 99 (43316-9722)
PHONE.................................419 396-7641
Marc Bader, *Branch Mgr*
EMP: 42
SALES (corp-wide): 29.7B **Privately Held**
SIC: 1611 Highway & street paving contractor
HQ: Shelly Company
80 Park Dr
Thornville OH 43076
740 246-6315

(G-2548)
VAUGHN INDUSTRIES LLC (PA)
1201 E Findlay St (43316-9686)
P.O. Box 96 (43316-0096)
PHONE.................................419 396-3900
Brian Tschanen, *Division Mgr*
Shawn Lucas, *Superintendent*
Monte Seifert, *Superintendent*
Gregg Vaughn, *Exec VP*
Robert Livingston, *Safety Dir*

▲ EMP: 500
SQ FT: 12,800
SALES (est): 158.5MM **Privately Held**
SIC: **1731** 1711 General electrical contractor; mechanical contractor

(G-2549)
VULCAN ENTERPRISES INC
Also Called: Vulcan Fire Protection
2600 State Highway 568 A (43316-1142)
PHONE..................................419 396-3535
Joyce Hunter, *CEO*
Larry Walters, *President*
Armando A Madrigal, *Principal*
Michael Kenn, *Vice Pres*
EMP: 37
SQ FT: 10,000
SALES (est): 5.9MM **Privately Held**
SIC: **1711** Fire sprinkler system installation

(G-2550)
WAGNER LINCOLN-MERCURY INC
1200 S Vance St (43316-7502)
PHONE..................................419 435-8131
Rick Wagner, *President*
EMP: 28
SALES (est): 9.6MM **Privately Held**
SIC: **5511** 7538 5521 Automobiles, new & used; general automotive repair shops; used car dealers

Carlisle
Warren County

(G-2551)
CARLISLE HEALTH CARE INC
730 Hillcrest Ave (45005-3305)
PHONE..................................937 746-2662
Aaron Handler, *President*
Abe Wagshal, *President*
EMP: 45 EST: 1981
SQ FT: 36,338
SALES: 4.3MM **Privately Held**
WEB: www.carlislemanor.com
SIC: **8051** Convalescent home with continuous nursing care

(G-2552)
MPS GROUP INC
512 Linden Ave (45005-3345)
PHONE..................................937 746-2117
Charlie Williams, *Ch of Bd*
EMP: 100 **Privately Held**
SIC: **1799** Cleaning new buildings after construction
PA: Mps Group, Inc.
   38755 Hills Tech Dr
   Farmington Hills MI 48331

(G-2553)
NARROW WAY CUSTOM TECHNOLOGY
100 Industry Dr (45005-6304)
PHONE..................................937 743-1611
Timothy Williams, *President*
EMP: 29 EST: 1998
SQ FT: 5,600
SALES (est): 5.3MM **Privately Held**
SIC: **3599** 7629 Custom machinery; electrical repair shops

(G-2554)
SOCIETY FOR HANDICAPPED CITZNS
Also Called: FAIRVIEW HOMES
624 Fairview Dr (45005-3145)
PHONE..................................937 746-4201
Bobby Seebach, *Exec Dir*
EMP: 33
SALES: 1.2MM **Privately Held**
SIC: **8322** 8361 Social services for the handicapped; residential care

Carroll
Fairfield County

(G-2555)
AMERICAN BORING INC
6895 Pickerington Rd (43112-9614)
PHONE..................................740 969-8000
Rocky E Roark, *President*
EMP: 35
SQ FT: 4,800
SALES: 2.6MM **Privately Held**
SIC: **1623** Underground utilities contractor

(G-2556)
BOBBY LAYMAN CADILLAC GMC INC
3733 Claypool Dr (43112-9795)
PHONE..................................740 654-9590
Mick Layman, *President*
Robert A Layman, *President*
Linda Layman, *Corp Secy*
EMP: 32
SALES (est): 3.9MM **Privately Held**
SIC: **5511** 7539 Automobiles, new & used; automotive repair shops

(G-2557)
FAIRFIELD INDUSTRIES INC
P.O. Box 160 (43112-0160)
PHONE..................................740 409-1539
Terry Morris, *Principal*
Cindy Hillberry, *Human Res Dir*
EMP: 37
SALES: 1.1MM **Privately Held**
SIC: **5812** 8699 8412 Coffee shop; charitable organization; art gallery

(G-2558)
THOMPSON CONCRETE LTD
6182 Winchester Rd (43112-9764)
P.O. Box 440 (43112-0440)
PHONE..................................740 756-7256
Erik Avesil, *Foreman/Supr*
Nate Wilson, *Manager*
Owen Wyss, *Manager*
Scott Thompson,
EMP: 260
SQ FT: 4,000
SALES (est): 27.6MM **Privately Held**
WEB: www.thompsonconcrete.com
SIC: **1771** 1794 Concrete work; excavation work

(G-2559)
WRENCH LTD COMPANY (PA)
4805 Scooby Ln (43112-9446)
PHONE..................................740 654-5304
Cameron Gabbard, *President*
Mike Santore, *President*
Brad Hutchinson, *Chairman*
Jason Templeton, *Vice Pres*
John Hales, *Parts Mgr*
▲ EMP: 65 EST: 1999
SQ FT: 40,000
SALES: 90MM **Privately Held**
WEB: www.companywrench.com
SIC: **5082** General construction machinery & equipment

Carrollton
Carroll County

(G-2560)
CARROLL ELECTRIC COOP INC
250 Canton Rd Nw (44615)
P.O. Box 67 (44615-0067)
PHONE..................................330 627-2116
Lary Sanders, *President*
Tim Dingess, *Engineer*
Yvonne Ackerman, *Marketing Staff*
Bill Meese, *Supervisor*
EMP: 33 EST: 1937
SQ FT: 11,000
SALES: 21.8MM **Privately Held**
WEB: www.carrollelectriccoop.com
SIC: **4911** Distribution, electric power

(G-2561)
CARROLL GOLDEN AGE RETREAT
2202 Kensington Rd Ne (44615-8678)
PHONE..................................330 627-4665
Ollie Hawkins, *Superintendent*
EMP: 40
SALES (est): 951K **Privately Held**
SIC: **8059** 8052 Rest home, with health care; intermediate care facilities

(G-2562)
CARROLL HEALTH CARE CENTER
Also Called: Carroll Healthcare Center
648 Longhorn St Nw (44615-9469)
PHONE..................................330 627-5501
Erma Mc Cullough, *Corp Secy*
Alan Miller, *Administration*
EMP: 110 EST: 1980
SQ FT: 27,000
SALES (est): 6.5MM **Privately Held**
SIC: **8051** 8052 Convalescent home with continuous nursing care; intermediate care facilities

(G-2563)
CARROLL HILLS INDUSTRIES INC
540 High St Nw (44615-1116)
P.O. Box 567 (44615-0567)
PHONE..................................330 627-5524
Matt Champbell, *Superintendent*
Shannan Boone, *Administration*
Diana Strader, *Administration*
EMP: 60
SQ FT: 4,640
SALES: 499.3K **Privately Held**
SIC: **8331** 3999 Sheltered workshop; barber & beauty shop equipment

(G-2564)
COUNTY OF CARROLL
P.O. Box 98 (44615-0098)
PHONE..................................330 627-4866
Robert Wirkner, *Vice Pres*
Nick Cascarelli, *Branch Mgr*
Patricia Oyer, *Recorder*
EMP: 30 **Privately Held**
SIC: **8099** Blood related health services
PA: County Of Carroll
   119 S Lisbon St Ste 203
   Carrollton OH 44615
   330 627-2250

(G-2565)
COUNTY OF CARROLL
Also Called: Board of Mental Retardation
2167 Kensington Rd Ne (44615-8626)
P.O. Box 429 (44615-0429)
PHONE..................................330 627-7651
Alicia Hall, *Principal*
EMP: 34 **Privately Held**
SIC: **9431** 8093 Mental health agency administration, government; rehabilitation center, outpatient treatment
PA: County Of Carroll
   119 S Lisbon St Ste 203
   Carrollton OH 44615
   330 627-2250

(G-2566)
CPX CARROLLTON ES LLC
Also Called: Candlewood Carrollton
1296 Canton Rd Nw (44615-9453)
PHONE..................................330 627-1200
Paul Stanton, *Vice Pres*
Jennifer Schneider, *Marketing Staff*
EMP: 25 EST: 2014
SQ FT: 80,000
SALES (est): 680.2K **Privately Held**
SIC: **7011** Hotels & motels

(G-2567)
EAST CARROLL NURSING HOME
Also Called: Countryview Manor
2193 Commerce Dr (44615-8677)
PHONE..................................330 627-6900
Thelma Miller, *Owner*
Sheryl Wallace, *Co-Owner*
EMP: 55

SALES (est): 1.5MM **Privately Held**
SIC: **8051** 8059 Convalescent home with continuous nursing care; home for the mentally retarded, exc. skilled or intermediate

(G-2568)
EFFICIENT SERVICES OHIO INC
Also Called: Eso
277 Steubenville Rd Se (44615-9601)
PHONE..................................330 627-4440
Bryan T Shaw, *CEO*
EMP: 30
SALES (est): 7.2MM **Privately Held**
SIC: **5039** Soil erosion control fabrics

(G-2569)
FUSION CERAMICS INC
237 High St Sw (44615-1523)
P.O. Box 127 (44615-0127)
PHONE..................................330 627-5821
Dick Hannon Jr, *Manager*
EMP: 30
SALES (corp-wide): 7.1MM **Privately Held**
WEB: www.fusionceramics.com
SIC: **4225** General warehousing & storage
PA: Fusion Ceramics, Inc.
   160 Scio Rd Se
   Carrollton OH 44615
   330 627-5821

(G-2570)
GRADY RENTALS LLC
4094 Canton Rd Nw (44615-9340)
PHONE..................................330 627-2022
Michael Pence,
EMP: 36
SALES: 5.6MM **Privately Held**
SIC: **7353** Oil equipment rental services

(G-2571)
GUESS MOTORS INC (PA)
457 Steubenville Rd Se (44615-9608)
PHONE..................................866 890-0522
Toll Free:.............................888 -
Paul Guess, *President*
Michael Guess, *Vice Pres*
EMP: 30
SQ FT: 12,000
SALES (est): 12.5MM **Privately Held**
WEB: www.guessmotors.com
SIC: **5511** 7538 Automobiles, new & used; general automotive repair shops

(G-2572)
MERCY MEDICAL CENTER INC
Also Called: Timken Mercy Health Center
125 Canton Rd Nw (44615-1009)
PHONE..................................330 627-7641
Jack Topeleski, *Owner*
EMP: 25
SALES (corp-wide): 321.4MM **Privately Held**
WEB: www.cantonmercy.com
SIC: **8011** 8093 Clinic, operated by physicians; specialty outpatient clinics
HQ: Mercy Medical Center, Inc.
   1320 Mercy Dr Nw
   Canton OH 44708
   330 489-1000

(G-2573)
NORTH AMERICAN PLAS CHEM INC
Also Called: Noramco
750 Garfield Ave Nw (44615-1114)
PHONE..................................330 627-2210
John Boggs, *Manager*
EMP: 35
SALES (est): 5.3MM
SALES (corp-wide): 37.5MM **Privately Held**
WEB: www.nap-bag.com
SIC: **5113** Bags, paper & disposable plastic
PA: North American Plastics Chemicals Incorporated
   1400 E 222nd St
   Euclid OH 44117
   216 531-3400

(G-2574)
OHIO F F A CAMPS INC
Also Called: F F A Camp Muskingum
3266 Dyewood Rd Sw (44615-9246)
PHONE.................................330 627-2208
Todd Davis, *Director*
EMP: 35
SQ FT: 1,000
SALES: 1.6MM **Privately Held**
SIC: 7032 Recreational camps

(G-2575)
RES-CARE INC
Also Called: RES Care OH
520 S Lisbon St (44615-9582)
PHONE.................................330 627-7552
Jenny Brendel, *Manager*
EMP: 47
SALES (corp-wide): 23.7B **Privately Held**
SIC: 8052 Home for the mentally retarded,
with health care
HQ: Res-Care, Inc.
805 N Whittington Pkwy
Louisville KY 40222
502 394-2100

(G-2576)
SAINT JOHNS VILLA
Also Called: Villa Restaurant
701 Crest St Nw (44615-8425)
P.O. Box 457 (44615-0457)
PHONE.................................330 627-4662
Sister Elaine Weber, *President*
Sandy Kucera, *Human Resources*
Susan Dechiara, *Director*
EMP: 145
SQ FT: 60,000
SALES: 4.7MM **Privately Held**
WEB: www.stjohnsvilla.net
SIC: 5812 8351 8052 8361 Eating
places; child day care services; intermedi-
ate care facilities; home for the mentally
handicapped

(G-2577)
SALVATION ARMY
5037 Edgewood Rd Sw (44615-9278)
PHONE.................................330 735-2671
Josh Lyle, *Director*
EMP: 80
SALES (corp-wide): 4.3B **Privately Held**
WEB: www.salvationarmy-usaeast.org
SIC: 7032 Sporting & recreational camps
HQ: The Salvation Army
440 W Nyack Rd Ofc
West Nyack NY 10994
845 620-7200

Castalia
Erie County

(G-2578)
**HANSON AGGREGATES EAST
LLC**
9220 Portland Rd (44824-9260)
PHONE.................................419 483-4390
Gregory Russell, *Plant Mgr*
Tera Thornhill, *Manager*
EMP: 67
SQ FT: 3,200
SALES (corp-wide): 20.6B **Privately Held**
SIC: 1422 3274 Limestones, ground; lime
HQ: Hanson Aggregates East Llc
3131 Rdu Center Dr
Morrisville NC 27560
919 380-2500

Cedarville
Greene County

(G-2579)
APPLIED SCIENCES INC (PA)
141 W Xenia Ave (45314-9529)
P.O. Box 579 (45314-0579)
PHONE.................................937 766-2020
Max Lake, *President*
Inga Lake, *Vice Pres*
Loren Goins, *Technician*
EMP: 29
SQ FT: 6,600

SALES (est): 4.7MM **Privately Held**
SIC: 8731 3624 Commercial research laboratory; carbon & graphite products

(G-2580)
DALES TRUCK PARTS INC
2891 Us Route 42 E (45314-9443)
P.O. Box 2 (45314-0002)
PHONE.................................937 766-2551
Edward Dale Hughes, *President*
Ron Staker, *Finance*
Criss Snider, *Manager*
▼ EMP: 28
SQ FT: 6,000
SALES (est): 6.3MM **Privately Held**
WEB: www.dalestruckparts.com
SIC: 5015 5531 Motor vehicle parts, used;
truck equipment & parts

Celina
Mercer County

(G-2581)
ALLIED WASTE SYSTEMS INC
6141 Depweg Rd (45822-9573)
PHONE.................................419 925-4592
Randy Traub, *Sales/Mktg Mgr*
EMP: 30
SQ FT: 1,000
SALES (corp-wide): 10B **Publicly Held**
SIC: 4953 Garbage: collecting, destroying
& processing
HQ: Allied Waste Systems, Inc.
18500 N Allied Way # 100
Phoenix AZ 85054
480 627-2700

(G-2582)
**AMERI INTERNTL TRADE GRP
INC**
Also Called: Aitg
1 Visions Pkwy (45822-7500)
PHONE.................................419 586-6433
Murray L Dorfman, *President*
Joan C Dorfman, *Exec VP*
Leslie C Dorfman, *Exec VP*
William Dorfman, *Exec VP*
▲ EMP: 25
SQ FT: 25,000
SALES (est): 2.6MM **Privately Held**
WEB: www.aitginc.com
SIC: 5199 Gifts & novelties

(G-2583)
ARMCORP CONSTRUCTION INC
8511 State Route 703 C (45822-2979)
PHONE.................................419 778-7024
Timothy J Rosengarten, *President*
Mary Rosengarten, *Corp Secy*
EMP: 43
SQ FT: 2,200
SALES: 7MM **Privately Held**
SIC: 1542 Commercial & office building,
new construction

(G-2584)
**ASSISTED LIVING CONCEPTS
LLC**
Also Called: Miller House
1506 Meadowview Dr Ofc (45822-4101)
PHONE.................................419 586-2484
Celena Wolff, *Branch Mgr*
Bryan R Davenport, *Manager*
EMP: 25
SALES (corp-wide): 380.7MM **Privately
Held**
WEB: www.assistedlivingconcepts.com
SIC: 8051 Skilled nursing care facilities
HQ: Assisted Living Concepts, Llc
330 N Wabash Ave Ste 3700
Chicago IL 60611

(G-2585)
**BRIDGESTONE RET
OPERATIONS LLC**
Also Called: Michel Tires Plus 227571
1109 N Main St (45822-1076)
PHONE.................................419 586-1600
Stephan Brancaleone, *Manager*
EMP: 30
SALES (corp-wide): 32.4B **Privately Held**
WEB: www.tiresplus.com
SIC: 7534 Tire retreading & repair shops

HQ: Bridgestone Retail Operations, Llc
333 E Lake St Ste 300
Bloomingdale IL 60108
630 259-9000

(G-2586)
CA GROUP
Also Called: CA INDUSTRIES
4980 Mud Pike Rd (45822-9274)
PHONE.................................419 586-2137
Beth Butler, *CEO*
EMP: 40
SQ FT: 8,000
SALES: 2.6MM **Privately Held**
WEB: www.c;aindustries.com
SIC: 8322 Adult day care center

(G-2587)
**CELINA MUTUAL INSURANCE
CO (PA)**
Also Called: Celina Insurance Group
1 Insurance Sq (45822-1659)
PHONE.................................419 586-5181
Donald W Montgomery, *Ch of Bd*
William W Montgomery, *President*
Phil Fullenkamp, *CFO*
Phillip Fullenkamp, *Treasurer*
Angie Didier, *Manager*
EMP: 130 EST: 1919
SQ FT: 75,000
SALES (est): 97.3MM **Privately Held**
WEB: www.celinagroup.com
SIC: 6331 Fire, marine & casualty insur-
ance: mutual

(G-2588)
CITY OF CELINA
Also Called: Celina Waste Water Plant
1125 S Elm St (45822-2375)
PHONE.................................419 586-2451
Kerry Duncan, *Manager*
EMP: 45 **Privately Held**
WEB: www.celinaohio.org
SIC: 4941 Water supply
PA: City Of Celina
225 N Main St
Celina OH 45822
419 586-5823

(G-2589)
**COMMUNITY HLTH
PRFSSIONALS INC**
Also Called: Celina Visting Nurses
816 Pro Dr (45822-1360)
PHONE.................................419 586-1999
Deb Garwood, *Manager*
EMP: 40
SALES (corp-wide): 13.1MM **Privately
Held**
SIC: 8082 Visiting nurse service
PA: Community Health Professionals, Inc.
1159 Westwood Dr
Van Wert OH 45891
419 238-9223

(G-2590)
**COMMUNITY HLTH
PRFSSIONALS INC**
Also Called: Private Duty & Visiting Nurses
816 Pro Dr (45822-1360)
PHONE.................................419 586-6266
Caprice Smith, *Manager*
EMP: 60
SALES (corp-wide): 13.1MM **Privately
Held**
SIC: 8082 7361 Visiting nurse service;
nurses' registry
PA: Community Health Professionals, Inc.
1159 Westwood Dr
Van Wert OH 45891
419 238-9223

(G-2591)
COUNTY OF MERCER
Also Called: Cheryl Ann Special Olympics
4980 Mud Pike Rd (45822-9274)
PHONE.................................419 586-2369
Mike Overman, *Superintendent*
EMP: 60 **Privately Held**
WEB: www.mercercountyohio.org
SIC: 8322 8351 8331 Association for the
handicapped; child day care services; job
training & vocational rehabilitation serv-
ices

PA: County Of Mercer
220 W Livingston St A201
Celina OH 45822
419 586-3178

(G-2592)
COUNTY OF MERCER
220 W Livingston St # 10 (45822-1670)
PHONE.................................419 586-5106
Dale Borger, *Director*
EMP: 30 **Privately Held**
WEB: www.mercercountyohio.org
SIC: 8322 9111 Individual & family serv-
ices; county supervisors' & executives' of-
fices
PA: County Of Mercer
220 W Livingston St A201
Celina OH 45822
419 586-3178

(G-2593)
DELTA KAPPA GAMMA SOCIETY
Also Called: Beta PHI
1030 Canterbury Dr (45822-1169)
PHONE.................................419 586-6016
Dolores Irish, *President*
Eline Marbaugh, *Treasurer*
Jenny Jamison, *Admin Sec*
EMP: 50 EST: 2001
SALES (est): 254.8K **Privately Held**
WEB: www.betaphi.com
SIC: 8641 University club

(G-2594)
DOCTORS URGENT CARE
950 S Main St Ste 10 (45822-2475)
PHONE.................................419 586-1611
James Wermert, *President*
Lisa Klenke, *Vice Pres*
Cindy Berning, *CFO*
EMP: 30 EST: 2007
SALES (est): 809.3K **Privately Held**
SIC: 8011 Clinic, operated by physicians

(G-2595)
**FOUNDTION BEHAVIORAL HLTH
SVCS**
4761 State Route 29 (45822-8216)
PHONE.................................419 584-1000
Brian Angle, *Director*
EMP: 30
SALES: 2.7MM **Privately Held**
SIC: 8093 Mental health clinic, outpatient

(G-2596)
**JPMORGAN CHASE BANK NAT
ASSN**
205 W Market St (45822-2122)
PHONE.................................419 586-6668
Curt Cramer, *Site Mgr*
Ken Watts, *Manager*
EMP: 26
SALES (corp-wide): 131.4B **Publicly
Held**
WEB: www.chase.com
SIC: 6021 National commercial banks
HQ: Jpmorgan Chase Bank, National Asso-
ciation
1111 Polaris Pkwy
Columbus OH 43240
614 436-3055

(G-2597)
**KERNS CHEVROLET-BUICK-
GMC INC**
Also Called: Kerns Chevrolet Buick GMC
218 S Walnut St (45822-2145)
P.O. Box 27 (45822-0027)
PHONE.................................419 586-5131
Michael Kerns, *President*
George Heiser, *Principal*
J J Kerns, *Principal*
Mary Ellen Kerns, *Principal*
Chris Kerns, *Vice Pres*
EMP: 27
SQ FT: 10,000
SALES (est): 8MM **Privately Held**
WEB: www.kernschevyolds.com
SIC: 5511 7515 5521 7538 Automobiles,
new & used; passenger car leasing; used
car dealers; general automotive repair
shops

(G-2598)
KIDS KASTLE DAY CARE
6783 Staeger Rd (45822-2800)
PHONE...................................419 586-0903
Jodi Will,
EMP: 35
SALES (est): 266.5K Privately Held
SIC: 8351 Preschool center

(G-2599)
MERCELINA MOBILE HOME PARK
424 Elmgrove Dr (45822-1804)
PHONE...................................419 586-5407
Jerry Brandts, President
Verdice Brandts, Manager
EMP: 64
SALES (est): 1.6MM Privately Held
SIC: 6515 Mobile home site operators

(G-2600)
MERCER CNTY JOINT TOWNSHP HOSP
Mercer Health Home Care
909 E Wayne St Ste 126 (45822-3304)
PHONE...................................419 584-0143
Lisa Muhlenkamp, Branch Mgr
EMP: 42
SALES (corp-wide): 54.5MM Privately Held
SIC: 8082 Home health care services
PA: Mercer County Joint Township Community Hospital
800 W Main St
Coldwater OH 45828
419 678-2341

(G-2601)
MERCER CNTY JOINT TOWNSHP HOSP
Also Called: Community Medical Center
950 S Main St (45822-2413)
PHONE...................................419 586-1611
Vivian Hillwaret, Manager
EMP: 30
SALES (corp-wide): 54.5MM Privately Held
WEB: www.mercerhospital.com
SIC: 8062 8011 General medical & surgical hospitals; offices & clinics of medical doctors
PA: Mercer County Joint Township Community Hospital
800 W Main St
Coldwater OH 45828
419 678-2341

(G-2602)
MERCER LANDMARK INC
417 W Market St (45822-2126)
PHONE...................................419 586-7443
Scott Boulis, Manager
EMP: 29
SALES (corp-wide): 242.2MM Privately Held
SIC: 5153 Grains
PA: Mercer Landmark, Inc.
426 W Market St
Celina OH 45822
419 628-3093

(G-2603)
MERCER RESIDENTIAL SERVICES
Also Called: Mud Pike Group Home The
334 Godfrey Ave (45822-2120)
P.O. Box 603 (45822-0603)
PHONE...................................419 586-4709
Garry Mosier, Director
EMP: 50
SALES (est): 1.6MM Privately Held
WEB: www.mrsinc.org
SIC: 8059 Nursing home, except skilled & intermediate care facility; personal care home, with health care

(G-2604)
MERCER RESIDENTIAL SVCS INC
420 S Sugar St (45822-2431)
P.O. Box 603 (45822-0603)
PHONE...................................419 586-4709
Garry Mosier, CEO
EMP: 65

SQ FT: 1,500
SALES: 2.9MM Privately Held
SIC: 8052 Personal care facility

(G-2605)
MIDWEST LOGISTICS SYSTEMS
8779 State Route 703 (45822-2936)
PHONE...................................419 584-1414
F Edward Voelker, President
James Duvall, Principal
Ellen Welker, Vice Pres
David L Demoss, Admin Sec
EMP: 389
SALES (est): 78.6MM Privately Held
SIC: 4213 4212 Trucking, except local; local trucking, without storage

(G-2606)
PEREGRINE HEALTH SERVICES INC
Also Called: Gardens At Celina The
1301 Myers Rd (45822-4114)
PHONE...................................419 586-4135
Ed Fodrea, Branch Mgr
EMP: 54
SALES (corp-wide): 6.8MM Privately Held
SIC: 8099 Blood related health services
PA: Peregrine Health Services, Inc.
1661 Old Henderson Rd
Columbus OH 43220
614 459-2656

(G-2607)
RAF CELINA LLC
1915-1955 Haveman Rd (45822)
PHONE...................................216 464-6626
Andrew Kline, Vice Pres
EMP: 25
SALES (est): 396.5K Privately Held
SIC: 6512 Shopping center, community (100,000 - 300,000 sq ft)

(G-2608)
RAYMOND JAMES FINCL SVCS INC
225 N Main St (45822-1601)
PHONE...................................419 586-5121
Deny Knapschaefer, Branch Mgr
EMP: 30
SALES (corp-wide): 7.4B Publicly Held
SIC: 6211 6733 6029 Brokers, security; trusts; commercial banks
HQ: Raymond James Financial Services, Inc.
880 Carillon Pkwy
Saint Petersburg FL 33716
727 567-1000

(G-2609)
REPUBLIC SERVICES INC
6141 Depweg Rd (45822-9573)
PHONE...................................419 925-4592
Dan Jackson, Branch Mgr
EMP: 34
SALES (corp-wide): 10B Publicly Held
SIC: 4953 Sanitary landfill operation
PA: Republic Services, Inc.
18500 N Allied Way # 100
Phoenix AZ 85054
480 627-2700

(G-2610)
SAMPLES CHUCK-GENERAL CONTR
1460 E Wayne St (45822-9394)
PHONE...................................419 586-1434
EMP: 28
SQ FT: 6,000
SALES (est): 2.9MM Privately Held
SIC: 1611 Highway/Street Construction

(G-2611)
STAMMEN INSURANCE AGENCY LLC
115-117 S Main St (45822)
P.O. Box 268 (45822-0268)
PHONE...................................419 586-7500
Charles Stammen, President
Rob Howell, Mng Member
Dodie Bruggeman, Agent
EMP: 31
SQ FT: 2,400
SALES (est): 3.2MM Privately Held
SIC: 6411 Insurance agents

(G-2612)
TOMS INSTALLATION CO INC
5349 State Route 29 (45822-9210)
P.O. Box 30 (45822-0030)
PHONE...................................419 584-1218
Tom Slusser, President
Samuel Slusser, Vice Pres
Toni Slusser, CFO
EMP: 30
SALES (est): 1.2MM Privately Held
WEB: www.tomsinstallationco.com
SIC: 7389 Telephone services

(G-2613)
UNITED PARCEL SERVICE INC OH
Also Called: UPS
1851 Industrial Dr (45822-1377)
PHONE...................................419 586-8556
Steve Hoyne, Branch Mgr
EMP: 200
SALES (corp-wide): 71.8B Publicly Held
WEB: www.upsscs.com
SIC: 4215 Parcel delivery, vehicular
HQ: United Parcel Service, Inc. (Oh)
55 Glenlake Pkwy
Atlanta GA 30328
404 828-6000

Centerburg
Knox County

(G-2614)
CENTERBURG TWO LLC
Also Called: Centerburg Resp & Spclty Rehab
212 Fairview St (43011-8314)
PHONE...................................740 625-5774
George Repchick, President
William Weisberg, Vice Pres
EMP: 73
SALES: 5.9MM
SALES (corp-wide): 157.7MM Privately Held
SIC: 8051 Convalescent home with continuous nursing care
PA: Saber Healthcare Group, L.L.C.
26691 Richmond Rd Frnt
Bedford OH 44146
216 292-5706

(G-2615)
RESCARE OHIO INC
Also Called: Canterbury Villa
80 Miller St (43011-7023)
P.O. Box 10, Marengo (43334-0010)
PHONE...................................740 625-6873
Lisa Wood, Branch Mgr
EMP: 50
SALES (corp-wide): 23.7B Privately Held
WEB: www.schoenbrunnhealthcare.com
SIC: 8051 Skilled nursing care facilities
HQ: Rescare Ohio Inc
348 W Main St
Williamsburg OH 45176

(G-2616)
SHREDDED BEDDING CORPORATION (PA)
Also Called: SBC Recycling
6589 Bennington Chapel Rd (43011-9312)
PHONE...................................740 893-3567
D Lynn Hatfield, President
Betty L Hatfield, Corp Secy
Michael Hatfield, Vice Pres
Ryan Hatfield, Vice Pres
EMP: 50
SQ FT: 25,000
SALES (est): 15.4MM Privately Held
WEB: www.sbcrecycling.com
SIC: 7389 4953 5093 Brokers' services; document & office record destruction; recycling, waste materials; scrap & waste materials

(G-2617)
TABLE ROCK GOLF CLUB INC
3005 Wilson Rd (43011-9467)
PHONE...................................740 625-6859
Kathy Butler, President
Jim Butler, Vice Pres
EMP: 35
SQ FT: 4,500

SALES (est): 1.1MM Privately Held
WEB: www.tablerock.com
SIC: 7992 Public golf courses

Centerville
Montgomery County

(G-2618)
AGJ KIDZ LLC
Also Called: Kidz Watch
101 E Alexville 1 Rd 110 (45459)
PHONE...................................937 350-1001
Emily W Weaner, Mng Member
Bradley W Weaner,
EMP: 25 EST: 2013
SALES (est): 185.1K Privately Held
SIC: 8351 Group day care center

(G-2619)
AISLING ENTERPRISES LLC
9747 Crooked Creek Dr (45458-3029)
PHONE...................................937 203-1757
Jason Terry, President
EMP: 30 EST: 2014
SALES (est): 1.9MM Privately Held
SIC: 7373 Systems software development services

(G-2620)
ALL ABOUT KIDS
1300 E Social Row Rd (45458-4718)
PHONE...................................937 885-7480
Lisa Rizzo, Director
EMP: 30
SALES (est): 365K Privately Held
SIC: 8351 Preschool center

(G-2621)
ALLERGY & ASTHMA CENTRE DAYTON (PA)
Also Called: Allergy & Asthma Centre Dayton
8039 Wash Vlg Dr Ste 100 (45458-1877)
PHONE...................................937 435-8999
Arturo J Bonnin, Principal
Arturo Bonnin, Med Doctor
EMP: 26
SALES (est): 3.7MM Privately Held
SIC: 8011 8031 Allergist; offices & clinics of osteopathic physicians

(G-2622)
AT&T MOBILITY LLC
199 E Alex Bell Rd # 418 (45459-2797)
PHONE...................................937 439-4900
Brad Wimsatt, Manager
EMP: 26
SALES (corp-wide): 170.7B Publicly Held
WEB: www.cingular.com
SIC: 4812 Cellular telephone services
HQ: At&t Mobility Llc
1025 Lenox Park Blvd Ne
Brookhaven GA 30319
800 331-0500

(G-2623)
CENTERVILLE FITNESS INC
Also Called: Club 51 Fitness
51 E Spring Valley Pike (45458-3801)
PHONE...................................937 291-7990
Michael Brunett, President
Lisa Ostrom, Training Dir
EMP: 35
SQ FT: 40,000
SALES (est): 200.8K Privately Held
SIC: 7991 Health club

(G-2624)
CLYO INTERNAL MEDICINE INC
7073 Clyo Rd (45459-4816)
PHONE...................................937 435-5857
R Jeffrey Taylor, President
EMP: 78
SALES: 2.4MM
SALES (corp-wide): 287.4MM Privately Held
SIC: 8011 Physicians' office, including specialists
HQ: Ipc Healthcare, Inc.
4605 Lankershim Blvd
North Hollywood CA 91602
888 447-2362

(G-2625)
DAYTON OB GYN
330 N Main St Ste 200 (45459-4459)
PHONE..................................937 439-7550
Ahmed Moezzi, *President*
Brent Imbody, *Vice Pres*
Michael Thesing, *Vice Pres*
EMP: 25
SQ FT: 46,000
SALES (est): 2.9MM **Privately Held**
SIC: 8011 Fertility specialist, physician;
specialized medical practitioners, except
internal; gynecologist

(G-2626)
GRISMER TIRE COMPANY (PA)
1099 S Main St (45458-3840)
P.O. Box 337, Dayton (45401-0337)
PHONE..................................937 643-2526
Charles L Marshall II, *President*
Robert Hupp, *Treasurer*
John L Marshall, *Admin Sec*
John Marshall, *Admin Sec*
▲ EMP: 28 EST: 1932
SQ FT: 40,000
SALES (est): 25.5MM **Privately Held**
WEB: www.grismertire.com
SIC: 5531 7538 5014 7534 Automotive
tires; general automotive repair shops;
automobile tires & tubes; truck tires &
tubes; rebuilding & retreading tires

(G-2627)
**HCR MANORCARE MED SVCS
FLA LLC**
Also Called: Manor Care Hlth Svcs Cntrville
1001 A Alex Bell Rd (45459-2637)
PHONE..................................937 436-9700
Lee Elliot, *Administration*
EMP: 200
SALES (corp-wide): 2.4B **Publicly Held**
WEB: www.manorcare.com
SIC: 8051 Convalescent home with contin-
uous nursing care
HQ: Hcr Manorcare Medical Services Of
Florida, Llc
333 N Summit St Ste 100
Toledo OH 43604
419 252-5500

(G-2628)
IRONGATE INC (PA)
Also Called: Irongate Realtors
122 N Main St (45459-4621)
PHONE..................................937 433-3300
Steven Brown, *President*
Greg Gillen, *Vice Pres*
Scot Sutherland, *Broker*
Ed Griffith, *Sales Mgr*
Mark Stokoe, *Mktg Dir*
EMP: 225
SALES (est): 12.9MM **Privately Held**
WEB: www.irongate-realtors.com
SIC: 6531 6311 Real estate agent, resi-
dential; selling agent, real estate; mutual
association life insurance

(G-2629)
**KETTERING ADVENTIST
HEALTHCARE**
1989 Miamisbg Cntrvll Rd (45459-3859)
PHONE..................................937 401-6306
EMP: 31
SALES (corp-wide): 1.7B **Privately Held**
SIC: 8062 General medical & surgical hos-
pitals
PA: Kettering Adventist Healthcare
3535 Southern Blvd
Dayton OH 45429
937 298-4331

(G-2630)
MCM ELECTRONICS INC (DH)
650 Congress Park Dr (45459-4072)
PHONE..................................888 235-4692
Chris Haworth, *President*
Ed Bunch, *Business Mgr*
Eric Lockwood, *Business Mgr*
Stephen Campbell, *Vice Pres*
Joseph R Daprile, *Vice Pres*
▲ EMP: 80
SQ FT: 22,000

SALES: 62.4MM
SALES (corp-wide): 19B **Publicly Held**
WEB: www.mcmelectronics.com
SIC: 5065 Electronic parts & equipment
HQ: Newark Electronics Corporation
300 S Riverside Plz
Chicago IL 60606
773 784-5100

(G-2631)
ORTHOPEDIC ASSOCIATES (PA)
7677 Yankee St Ste 110 (45459-3475)
PHONE..................................937 415-9100
Jan E Faunders, *President*
H Brent Bamberger, *Treasurer*
Jessica Weihrauch, *Mktg Dir*
Jeffrey Rogers, *Manager*
Donna Beaudion, *Supervisor*
EMP: 30
SALES (est): 9.8MM **Privately Held**
WEB: www.oaswo.com
SIC: 8011 Orthopedic physician

(G-2632)
**PREMIER INTEGRATED MED
ASSOC (PA)**
Also Called: Primed Physicians
6520 Acro Ct (45459-2679)
PHONE..................................937 291-6813
Mark Couch, *President*
EMP: 67
SQ FT: 16,345
SALES (est): 4.8MM **Privately Held**
SIC: 8011 Internal medicine, physician/sur-
geon; oncologist; hematologist; cardiolo-
gist & cardio-vascular specialist

(G-2633)
SELECTTECH SERVICES CORP
8045 Washington Vlg Dr (45458-1847)
PHONE..................................937 438-9905
Robert B Finch, *CEO*
Scott A Sullivan, *President*
Robert Finch, *General Mgr*
Maxine Orum, *Chairman*
Linda Vikmanis, *Vice Pres*
EMP: 140
SQ FT: 4,300
SALES (est): 19.8MM **Privately Held**
WEB: www.selecttechservices.com
SIC: 8744 7376 Facilities support serv-
ices; computer facilities management

(G-2634)
**SUPPORT FINCL RESOURCES
INC**
830 E Franklin St Ste A (45459-5621)
P.O. Box 291767, Dayton (45429-0767)
PHONE..................................800 444-5465
EMP: 40
SQ FT: 5,000
SALES: 1MM
SALES (corp-wide): 4.9MM **Privately
Held**
SIC: 8742 Management Consulting Serv-
ices
PA: Support Insurance Systems Agency,
Inc.
830 E Franklin St Ste A
Centerville OH 45459
937 434-5700

(G-2635)
**TOTAL QUALITY LOGISTICS
LLC**
6525 Centervl Bus Pkwy (45459-2686)
PHONE..................................800 580-3101
Matt Howard, *Principal*
EMP: 39
SALES (corp-wide): 2.9B **Privately Held**
SIC: 4789 Cargo loading & unloading serv-
ices
HQ: Total Quality Logistics, Llc
4289 Ivy Pointe Blvd
Cincinnati OH 45245

(G-2636)
**WASHINGTON TOWNSHIP PARK
DST (PA)**
Also Called: Centerville Washington Pk Dst
221 N Main St (45459-4617)
PHONE..................................937 433-5155
Arnie Biono, *Director*
Carol Kennard, *Director*
EMP: 30

SQ FT: 3,500
SALES (est): 1.8MM **Privately Held**
WEB: www.cwpd.org
SIC: 7999 Recreation services

Chagrin Falls
Cuyahoga County

(G-2637)
ACTIVE CHIROPRACTIC
1 S Main St Ste 1 # 1 (44022-3225)
PHONE..................................440 893-8800
George Heathcote, *Owner*
EMP: 46
SQ FT: 34,354
SALES (est): 2.1MM **Privately Held**
SIC: 8041 Offices & clinics of chiropractors

(G-2638)
**ALTHANS INSURANCE AGENCY
INC**
543 Washington St (44022-4446)
P.O. Box 570 (44022-0570)
PHONE..................................440 247-6422
James C Althans, *President*
Michael A Althans, *COO*
John S Althans, *CFO*
EMP: 40
SQ FT: 15,000
SALES (est): 13.2MM **Privately Held**
WEB: www.althans.com
SIC: 6411 Insurance agents

(G-2639)
BARKLEY OF CLEVELAND LLC
Also Called: Barkley Pet Hotel & Day Spa
27349 Miles Rd (44022-2133)
PHONE..................................440 248-2275
Howard Perlmuter,
Howard J Babrow,
EMP: 30
SALES (est): 1.1MM **Privately Held**
SIC: 0752 Boarding services, kennels

(G-2640)
**CHAGRIN FALLS HISTORICAL
SOC**
87 E Washington St (44022-3001)
PHONE..................................440 247-4695
Jane Babinksy, *Director*
EMP: 35
SALES: 466.3K **Privately Held**
SIC: 8412 Museum

(G-2641)
**CHAGRIN VALLEY COUNTRY
CLUB CO**
4700 Som Center Rd (44022-2399)
PHONE..................................440 248-4310
Alan Matta, *CFO*
Jack Goldberg, *Exec Dir*
EMP: 100
SQ FT: 30,000
SALES: 5MM **Privately Held**
WEB: www.cvcclub.com
SIC: 7997 Country club, membership

(G-2642)
**CLEVELND CLNC CHAGRN
FLLS FMLY**
551 Washington St (44022-4403)
PHONE..................................440 893-9393
Kim Reidel, *Principal*
Lisa Ramage, *Manager*
Christopher M Young, *Family Practiti*
EMP: 35
SALES (est): 1.9MM
SALES (corp-wide): 8.9B **Privately Held**
SIC: 8011 Clinic, operated by physicians
PA: The Cleveland Clinic Foundation
9500 Euclid Ave
Cleveland OH 44195
216 636-8335

(G-2643)
CLUB AT HILLBROOK INC
14800 Hillbrook Dr (44022-2634)
P.O. Box 603 (44022-0603)
PHONE..................................440 247-4940
Jim Kaufman, *President*
EMP: 25

SALES (est): 1.1MM **Privately Held**
WEB: www.clubhillbrook.com
SIC: 7997 Country club, membership

(G-2644)
D E WILLIAMS ELECTRIC INC
168 Solon Rd Ste B (44022-3100)
P.O. Box 180 (44022-0180)
PHONE..................................440 543-1222
Dan E Williams, *Ch of Bd*
Briana Harper, *President*
Douglas Williams, *Vice Pres*
Ted Williams, *Vice Pres*
EMP: 50 EST: 1952
SQ FT: 12,000
SALES (est): 8.7MM **Privately Held**
WEB: www.dewilliamselectric.com
SIC: 1731 General electrical contractor

(G-2645)
FOR WOMEN LIKE ME INC (PA)
Also Called: Fwlm
46 Shopping Plz Ste 155 (44022-3022)
PHONE..................................407 848-7339
Arline Burks, *CEO*
Dakkota Gant, *President*
Marsha Robles, *Vice Pres*
Kathy Chislom, *Treasurer*
Julie Turner, *Admin Sec*
◆ EMP: 42
SQ FT: 5,000
SALES: 53MM **Privately Held**
WEB: www.forwomenlikeme.com
SIC: 7812 5137 5621 5136 Television
film production; women's & children's
clothing; women's clothing stores; men's
& boys' clothing; men's & boys' clothing
stores

(G-2646)
**GARFIELD HTS COACH LINE
INC**
Also Called: Cleveland Southeastern Trails
119 Manor Brook Dr (44022-4163)
P.O. Box 46670, Bedford (44146-0670)
PHONE..................................440 232-4550
Anthony J Walters, *President*
Diane Hyland, *Corp Secy*
Patrick J Hyland, *Vice Pres*
Frank D Walters, *Vice Pres*
EMP: 75
SQ FT: 85,000
SALES (est): 3.4MM **Privately Held**
SIC: 4142 Bus charter service, except local

(G-2647)
GOLDEN LIVING LLC
Also Called: Hamlet Manor
150 Cleveland St (44022-2985)
PHONE..................................440 247-4200
Bartlett T Bell, *Branch Mgr*
EMP: 185
SQ FT: 41,000
SALES (corp-wide): 7.4MM **Privately
Held**
SIC: 8059 Convalescent home
PA: Golden Living Llc
5220 Tennyson Pkwy # 400
Plano TX 75024
972 372-6300

(G-2648)
**HAMLET VILLAGE IN CHAGRIN
FLS**
Also Called: Hamlet Nursing Home
150 Cleveland St (44022-2985)
PHONE..................................440 247-4200
John Eigen, *Branch Mgr*
EMP: 72
SALES (corp-wide): 10.8MM **Privately
Held**
SIC: 8059 Rest home, with health care
PA: Hamlet Village In Chagrin Falls
200 Hamlet Hills Dr Ofc
Chagrin Falls OH 44022
216 263-6033

(G-2649)
**HAMLET VILLAGE IN CHAGRIN
FLS (PA)**
200 Hamlet Hills Dr Ofc (44022-2838)
PHONE..................................216 263-6033
John Eigen, *Exec Dir*
EMP: 78

▲ = Import ▼=Export
◆ =Import/Export

SALES (est): 10.8MM Privately Held
WEB: www.hamletretirement.com
SIC: 8051 Convalescent home with continuous nursing care

(G-2650)
INVESTMERICA LIMITED
547 Washington St Ste 10 (44022-4436)
PHONE.............................216 618-3296
Monty Warren,
EMP: 67
SQ FT: 1,500
SALES (est): 5.2MM Privately Held
SIC: 6798 1521 Real estate investment trusts; single-family housing construction

(G-2651)
LAKE HORRY ELECTRIC (PA)
Also Called: Hirsch Division
255 Bramley Ct (44022-3613)
PHONE.............................440 808-8791
Ronald Hirsch, President
Michael Simon, Vice Pres
Birdie Hirsch, Admin Sec
EMP: 100
SQ FT: 12,000
SALES (est): 6.5MM Privately Held
SIC: 1731 Electrical work

(G-2652)
OPINIONS LTD (PA)
33 River St (44022-3020)
PHONE.............................440 893-0300
Chris Sluder, Vice Pres
Rick Hammar, Opers Mgr
Sean Kehoe, Facilities Mgr
Brian Hargrove, Research
Erika Harris, Research
EMP: 50 EST: 1998
SALES (est): 11.5MM Privately Held
WEB: www.opinionsltd.com
SIC: 8732 Market analysis or research

(G-2653)
REAL ESTATE MORTGAGE CORP
200 Jackson Dr (44022-1556)
PHONE.............................440 356-5373
Mark Johnston, President
EMP: 100
SQ FT: 4,000
SALES (est): 7.1MM
SALES (corp-wide): 24.2MM Privately Held
WEB: www.remcorp.com
SIC: 6163 Mortgage brokers arranging for loans, using money of others
PA: The American Eagle Mortgage Co Llc
6145 Park Square Dr Ste 4
Lorain OH 44053
440 988-2900

(G-2654)
SNAVELY BUILDING COMPANY (PA)
7139 Pine St Ste 110 (44022-3401)
PHONE.............................440 585-9091
John P Snavely, President
Peter Snavely, Principal
Paul Snavely, Vice Pres
John E Withrow, CFO
Victor Epelbaum, Asst Controller
EMP: 30
SQ FT: 6,000
SALES (est): 19MM Privately Held
WEB: www.benefit-svcs.com
SIC: 1542 1521 1522 Commercial & office building contractors; new construction, single-family houses; general remodeling, single-family houses; apartment building construction; multi-family dwellings, new construction; remodeling, multi-family dwellings

(G-2655)
SNAVELY DEVELOPMENT COMPANY (PA)
7139 Pine St (44022-3401)
PHONE.............................440 585-9091
Peter Snavely, President
John P Snavely, Chairman
Paul Snavely, Vice Pres
Dennis Zanath, Project Mgr
Stacy Andrulis, Administration
EMP: 40

SQ FT: 6,000
SALES: 75MM Privately Held
SIC: 1521 1522 New construction, single-family houses; multi-family dwellings, new construction

(G-2656)
SNL DESIGNS LTD
13 N Franklin St (44022-3009)
PHONE.............................440 247-2344
Nancy Lyons, Owner
EMP: 30
SALES (est): 1.4MM Privately Held
SIC: 7389 Design services

(G-2657)
SUNPOINT SENIOR LIVING HAMLET
150 Cleveland St (44022-2985)
PHONE.............................440 247-4200
Alan Rosenfield, Principal
EMP: 50
SALES (est): 981.6K Privately Held
SIC: 6513 Retirement hotel operation

(G-2658)
VERTICAL KNOWLEDGE LLC (PA)
8 E Washington St Ste 200 (44022-3057)
PHONE.............................216 920-7790
Matt Carpenter, CEO
EMP: 45
SALES (est): 7.1MM Privately Held
SIC: 7379

(G-2659)
WESTERN RESERVE REALTY LLC
Also Called: Remax Traditions
26 S Main St Ste 100 (44022-3268)
PHONE.............................440 247-3707
Janeann Bell,
Dwight Milko,
EMP: 38
SQ FT: 3,000
SALES (est): 2.1MM Privately Held
SIC: 6531 Real estate agent, residential

(G-2660)
WESTERN RSRVE LAND CONSERVANCY (PA)
3850 Chagrin River Rd (44022-1131)
PHONE.............................440 729-9621
Richard Cochran, CEO
James Spira, President
Joanie O'Brien, General Mgr
Julia Musson, Principal
Andy McDowell, Vice Pres
EMP: 32
SALES: 18.5MM Privately Held
SIC: 8641 Environmental protection organization

(G-2661)
WIREFREE HOME AUTOMATION
Also Called: Martguild
576 Industrial Pkwy (44022-4492)
P.O. Box 382 (44022-0382)
PHONE.............................440 247-8978
EMP: 25
SQ FT: 8,400
SALES (est): 1.3MM Privately Held
SIC: 8742 Management Consulting Services

Chagrin Falls
Geauga County

(G-2662)
CHAGRIN VALLEY ATHLETIC CLUB
17260 Snyder Rd (44023-2724)
PHONE.............................440 543-5141
James M Rosenberger, President
Hollis H Rosenberger, Treasurer
Annie Bartlett, Controller
Maria Eidam, Manager
Kate Lukwinski, Manager
EMP: 100

SALES (est): 3.8MM Privately Held
WEB: www.cvaclub.com
SIC: 7997 Membership sports & recreation clubs

(G-2663)
CUSTOM MATERIALS INC
Also Called: C M I Group
16865 Park Circle Dr (44023-4591)
PHONE.............................440 543-8284
Anthony D Borrelli, Principal
Taylor D Robinson, Treasurer
Debbie Lurch, Human Resources
Debby Zarzour, Sales Mgr
Nick Iacano, Supervisor
▲ EMP: 70 EST: 1964
SQ FT: 50,000
SALES (est): 12.9MM Privately Held
WEB: www.custommaterials.com
SIC: 8711 Engineering services

(G-2664)
ENDO-SURGICAL CENTER FLA LLC
8185 Washington St (44023-4574)
PHONE.............................440 708-0582
EMP: 370
SALES (corp-wide): 14.3MM Privately Held
SIC: 8011 Endocrinologist
PA: Endo-Surgical Center Of Florida, Llc
2500 York Rd Ste 300
Jamison PA 18929
877 442-3687

(G-2665)
ENVIROTEST SYSTEMS CORP
17202 Munn Rd (44023-5417)
PHONE.............................330 963-4464
Steve Peterson, Branch Mgr
EMP: 34 Privately Held
WEB: www.il.etest.com
SIC: 7549 Emissions testing without repairs, automotive
HQ: Envirotest Systems Corp.
7 Kripes Rd
East Granby CT 06026

(G-2666)
FIELDSTONE FARM THERAPEUTIC RI
16497 Snyder Rd (44023-4313)
PHONE.............................440 708-0013
Linette Stuart, Exec Dir
James B Rucker Jr,
John H Wilharm Jr,
EMP: 29
SQ FT: 1,901
SALES: 1MM Privately Held
WEB: www.fieldstonefarmtrc.com
SIC: 7999 8093 Riding stable; rehabilitation center, outpatient treatment

(G-2667)
HEMLOCK LANDSCAPES INC
7209 Chagrin Rd Ste A (44023-1129)
PHONE.............................440 247-3631
Dennis Barriball, President
Mark Lefelhoc, Opers Mgr
Lauren Barriball, Treasurer
Brian Barriball, Finance
Emily Barriball, Executive Asst
EMP: 25
SQ FT: 4,500
SALES (est): 1.3MM Privately Held
WEB: www.hemlocklandscapes.com
SIC: 0781 0782 Landscape services; landscape contractors

(G-2668)
IMS COMPANY
Also Called: Injection Molders Supply
10373 Stafford Rd (44023-5296)
PHONE.............................440 543-1615
Brad G Morse, CEO
Mary Ann Morris, Co-CEO
Jeffrey Sawicki, COO
Andrew J Evans, Controller
Tracy Leva, Accounting Dir
◆ EMP: 60 EST: 1960
SQ FT: 62,000
SALES (est): 40.4MM Privately Held
SIC: 5084 Plastic products machinery

(G-2669)
INDUSTRIAL MAINT SVCS INC
9824 Washington St Ste A (44023-5455)
P.O. Box 265, Chesterland (44026-0265)
PHONE.............................440 729-2068
Bryce Vasko, President
Shane Dangy, Vice Pres
Dan Okay, Admin Sec
EMP: 47
SQ FT: 2,000
SALES (est): 3.3MM Privately Held
SIC: 7699 5084 Printing trades machinery & equipment repair; paper manufacturing machinery

(G-2670)
LOWES GRNHSE & GIFT SP INC
Also Called: Lowe's Greenhouses & Gift Shop
16540 Chillicothe Rd (44023-4328)
PHONE.............................440 543-5123
Jeffrey B Griff, President
Mary Lynn Griff, Vice Pres
EMP: 35
SQ FT: 40,000
SALES: 1MM Privately Held
WEB: www.lowesgreenhouse.com
SIC: 5992 0181 5947 Flowers, fresh; foliage, growing of; nursery stock, growing of; plants, potted: growing of; flowers: grown under cover (e.g. greenhouse production); gift shop

(G-2671)
M&C HOTEL INTERESTS INC
Also Called: Pine Lake Trout Club
17021 Chillicothe Rd (44023-4617)
P.O. Box 23282 (44023-0282)
PHONE.............................440 543-1331
Sandra Hughes, Branch Mgr
EMP: 30 Privately Held
WEB: www.richfield.com
SIC: 8741 7997 Hotel or motel management; membership sports & recreation clubs
HQ: M&C Hotel Interests, Inc.
6560 Greenwood Plaza Blvd # 300
Greenwood Village CO 80111

(G-2672)
MANAGEMENT RECRUITERS INTL INC
Also Called: Management Recruiters Intl
17632 Walnut Trl (44023-6414)
PHONE.............................440 543-1284
Lou Radakovich, Branch Mgr
EMP: 90
SALES (corp-wide): 864.3MM Privately Held
WEB: www.mrwg.com
SIC: 7361 Executive placement
HQ: Management Recruiters International, Inc.
1735 Market St Ste 200
Philadelphia PA 19103
800 875-4000

(G-2673)
MANOR CARE OF AMERICA INC
Also Called: Arden Courts of Bainbridge
8100 Washington St (44023-4506)
PHONE.............................440 543-6766
Erin Tfenning, Manager
EMP: 60
SALES (corp-wide): 2.4B Publicly Held
WEB: www.trisunhealthcare.com
SIC: 8051 Extended care facility
HQ: Manor Care Of America, Inc.
333 N Summit St Ste 103
Toledo OH 43604
419 252-5500

(G-2674)
MEDHURST MASON CONTRACTORS INC
17111 Munn Rd Ste 1 (44023-5427)
PHONE.............................440 543-8885
Robert Medhurst, President
Carol Medhurst, Treasurer
EMP: 115 EST: 1976
SQ FT: 7,900
SALES (est): 10MM Privately Held
WEB: www.medhurstmason.com
SIC: 1741 Masonry/Stone Contractor

G E O G R A P H I C

(G-2675)
NEW WEMBLEY LLC
Also Called: Wembley Club, The
8345 Woodberry Blvd (44023-4520)
PHONE.....................440 543-8171
Marc Duvin, *President*
Sandy Cadman, *Manager*
Kelly Barr, *Director*
Ali Hively, *Director*
Maggie Nash, *Director*
EMP: 50
SALES (est): 1.8MM **Privately Held**
SIC: 7997 Country club, membership

(G-2676)
OHIO VALLEY GROUP INC
16965 Park Circle Dr (44023-6502)
PHONE.....................440 543-0500
Andrew F Dangelo, *President*
Kathleen Dangelo, *Vice Pres*
EMP: 25
SALES (est): 3.9MM **Privately Held**
SIC: 0781 Landscape services

(G-2677)
PARK PLACE INTERNATIONAL LLC
8401 Chagrin Rd Ste 15a (44023-4702)
PHONE.....................877 991-1991
Erik Littlejohn, *President*
Steve Larabee, *Engineer*
Ken Brasch, *Regl Sales Mgr*
Carol Digaetano, *Branch Mgr*
Jesse Nehoda, *Manager*
EMP: 55
SALES (corp-wide): 43.1MM **Privately Held**
WEB: www.parkplaceintl.com
SIC: 5045 Computer peripheral equipment
PA: Park Place International, Llc
100 Crowley Dr
Marlborough MA 01752
877 991-1991

(G-2678)
PRINTING SERVICES
16750 Park Circle Dr (44023-4563)
PHONE.....................440 708-1999
Robert Roulan, *President*
EMP: 25
SQ FT: 16,000
SALES (est): 1.2MM **Privately Held**
SIC: 7389 2752 Printers' services: folding, collating; commercial printing, lithographic

(G-2679)
PROS FREIGHT CORPORATION
16687 Hilltop Park Pl (44023-4500)
PHONE.....................440 543-7555
Elaine R Moore, *President*
EMP: 30 EST: 1975
SQ FT: 2,000
SALES (est): 3.6MM **Privately Held**
SIC: 4213 Contract haulers

(G-2680)
ROUNDTABLE ONLINE LEARNING LLC
8401 Chagrin Rd Ste 6 (44023-4702)
PHONE.....................440 220-5252
Dan Grajzl, *President*
James Lorentz, *Partner*
Jim Wenger, *Exec VP*
Tanya Loncar, *Vice Pres*
Robert Baskette, *CTO*
EMP: 25
SQ FT: 3,500
SALES: 1.5MM **Privately Held**
WEB: www.knowbasenetworks.com
SIC: 8299 4813 Educational services;

(G-2681)
RURAL/METRO CORPORATION
8401 Chagrin Rd Ste 15a (44023-4702)
PHONE.....................440 543-3313
Fax: 440 543-3361
EMP: 110
SALES (corp-wide): 431.3MM **Privately Held**
SIC: 4119 Local Passenger Transportation
HQ: Rural/Metro Corporation
9221 E Via De Ventura
Scottsdale AZ 85258
480 606-3886

(G-2682)
SCHNEIDER SADDLERY LLC
Also Called: Billy Royal
8255 Washington St (44023-4507)
PHONE.....................440 543-2700
Donald Schneider, *President*
Stanley Schneider, *Vice Pres*
Jerry Nairn, *Manager*
▲ EMP: 35
SQ FT: 40,000
SALES (est): 16.2MM **Privately Held**
WEB: www.sstack.com
SIC: 5941 5699 5091 5961 Saddlery & equestrian equipment; riding apparel; western apparel; sporting & recreation goods; mail order house; women's accessory & specialty stores

(G-2683)
SOUTH FRANKLIN CIRCLE
16575 S Franklin St (44023-1002)
PHONE.....................440 247-1300
Bill Fehrenbach, *Vice Pres*
Rob Lucarelli, *Director*
EMP: 140
SALES (est): 2.7MM
SALES (corp-wide): 14.8MM **Privately Held**
SIC: 6513 Retirement hotel operation
PA: South Franklin Circle
16600 Warren Ct
Chagrin Falls OH 44023
440 247-1300

(G-2684)
STOCK FAIRFIELD CORPORATION
Also Called: Stock Equipment Company
16490 Chillicothe Rd (44023-4326)
PHONE.....................440 543-6000
Robert Ciavarella, *President*
Xitao Wang, *General Mgr*
Ihor Yakovenko, *Project Mgr*
Michal Cerych, *Prdtn Mgr*
Felipe Fonseca, *Production*
EMP: 170 EST: 2007
SALES (est): 34.3MM **Privately Held**
WEB: www.stockequipment.com
SIC: 5063 8711 3535 3823 Power transmission equipment, electric; electrical or electronic engineering; conveyors & conveying equipment; industrial instrmnts msrmnt display/control process variable; relays & industrial controls; industrial trucks & tractors
HQ: Schenck Process Llc
7901 Nw 107th Ter
Kansas City MO 64153
816 891-9300

(G-2685)
ULL INC (PA)
9812 Washington St (44023-5486)
P.O. Box 23399 (44023-0399)
PHONE.....................440 543-5195
Marilyn Ullman, *President*
Joshua R Cilley, *President*
Kim Ullman, *Vice Pres*
Bernd O Bryant, *Admin Sec*
EMP: 35
SQ FT: 20,000
SALES (est): 17.5MM **Privately Held**
WEB: www.ullmanoil.com
SIC: 5172 5983 Petroleum products; fuel oil dealers

Chardon
Geauga County

(G-2686)
ALLTEL COMMUNICATIONS CORP
205 S Hambden St (44024-1228)
P.O. Box 428 (44024-0428)
PHONE.....................330 656-8000
Dennis McGiles, *Branch Mgr*
EMP: 42
SALES (corp-wide): 170.7B **Publicly Held**
SIC: 4813 Local & long distance telephone communications

HQ: Alltel Communications Corp
66 N 4th St
Newark OH 43055
740 349-8551

(G-2687)
AYRSHIRE INC
191 Fifth Ave (44024-1005)
P.O. Box 172 (44024-0172)
PHONE.....................440 286-9507
Randall Darling, *President*
H W Bernstein, *Principal*
D M Dworken, *Principal*
M E Resnick, *Principal*
Ken Jamison, *Vice Pres*
EMP: 50 EST: 1975
SQ FT: 5,000
SALES (est): 12.9MM **Privately Held**
WEB: www.ayrshireinc.com
SIC: 1541 Industrial buildings, new construction

(G-2688)
BASS LAKE TAVERN INC
Also Called: Bass Lake Inn
426 South St (44024-1448)
PHONE.....................440 285-3100
Thomas Lutz, *President*
Erik Heatwole, *Vice Pres*
EMP: 60
SQ FT: 8,000
SALES (est): 1.5MM **Privately Held**
WEB: www.basslakeinn.com
SIC: 5812 5813 7011 American restaurant; bar (drinking places); bed & breakfast inn

(G-2689)
CHARDON LAKES GOLF COURSE INC (PA)
470 South St (44024-2804)
PHONE.....................440 285-4653
Jerry Peterson, *President*
Tom Bond, *General Mgr*
Rick Heterstrom, *General Mgr*
Bob Acquaviva, *Asst Mgr*
EMP: 40
SQ FT: 300
SALES (est): 1.2MM **Privately Held**
SIC: 7992 Public golf courses

(G-2690)
CHARDON TOOL & SUPPLY CO INC
115 Parker Ct (44024-1112)
P.O. Box 291 (44024-0291)
PHONE.....................440 286-6440
Weldon Bennett, *President*
Donna Blewett, *Principal*
Marshall Meadows, *Principal*
Andrew O'Dell, *Principal*
EMP: 35
SQ FT: 4,800
SALES: 3MM **Privately Held**
SIC: 3545 5085 Diamond cutting tools for turning, boring, burnishing, etc.; diamonds, industrial: natural, crude

(G-2691)
COUNTY OF GEAUGA
Also Called: Job and Family Service
12480 Ravenwood Dr (44024-9009)
P.O. Box 309 (44024-0309)
PHONE.....................440 564-2246
EMP: 85 **Privately Held**
SIC: 8331 8322 Job Training/Related Services Individual/Family Services
PA: County Of Geauga
470 Center St Bldg 4
Chardon OH 44024

(G-2692)
COUNTY OF GEAUGA
Also Called: Geauga County Jobs & Fmly Svcs
12480 Ravenwood Dr (44024-9009)
P.O. Box 309 (44024-0309)
PHONE.....................440 285-9141
Tim Taylor, *Director*
EMP: 80 **Privately Held**
SIC: 8322 Public welfare center
PA: County Of Geauga
470 Center St Bldg 4
Chardon OH 44024
440 285-2222

(G-2693)
E2B TEKNOLOGIES INC (PA)
Also Called: Anytime Collect
521 5th Ave (44024-1088)
PHONE.....................440 352-4700
William Henslee, *President*
Frank Nisenboum, *Vice Pres*
Mary A Griffith, *Controller*
James Mallory, *Credit Mgr*
Jeanne Lee, *Corp Comm Staff*
EMP: 45
SQ FT: 10,000
SALES (est): 6MM **Privately Held**
WEB: www.e2btek.com
SIC: 7379 Computer related consulting services

(G-2694)
ENVIROTEST SYSTEMS CORP
10632 Auburn Rd (44024-9646)
PHONE.....................330 963-4464
Mike Hensley, *Branch Mgr*
EMP: 34 **Privately Held**
WEB: www.il.etest.com
SIC: 7549 Emissions testing without repairs, automotive
HQ: Envirotest Systems Corp.
7 Kripes Rd
East Granby CT 06026

(G-2695)
GEAUGA COUNTY HEALTH DISTRICT
Also Called: Geauga County General Hlth Dst
470 Center St Bldg 8 (44024-1071)
PHONE.....................440 279-1940
Robert Weisdack, *Chief Engr*
Frank Varga, *Manager*
EMP: 29 EST: 2016
SALES (est): 2MM **Privately Held**
SIC: 8621 Health association

(G-2696)
GEAUGA MECHANICAL COMPANY
12585 Chardon Windsor Rd (44024-8968)
PHONE.....................440 285-2000
Bruce Berman, *President*
Ted R Berman, *Vice Pres*
Bryan Wadsworth, *Project Mgr*
Jeff Fishman, *Foreman/Supr*
Tim Berman, *Treasurer*
EMP: 72
SQ FT: 15,000
SALES (est): 15.1MM **Privately Held**
WEB: www.geaugamechanical.com
SIC: 1711 1761 Warm air heating & air conditioning contractor; sheet metalwork

(G-2697)
GEM ELECTRIC
12577 Gar Hwy (44024-9201)
PHONE.....................440 286-6200
Patrick Nusrala, *Owner*
EMP: 25
SQ FT: 3,000
SALES: 4MM **Privately Held**
SIC: 1731 General electrical contractor

(G-2698)
HEATHERHILL CARE COMMUNITIES
12340 Bass Lake Rd (44024-8327)
PHONE.....................440 285-4040
Jim Homa, *President*
Andy Bragalone, *Principal*
Beejadi Makunda, *COO*
Lynette Gesicki, *HR Admin*
Margaret Milyo, *Human Resources*
EMP: 42
SALES (est): 3.2MM **Privately Held**
SIC: 8051 Skilled nursing care facilities

(G-2699)
JPMORGAN CHASE BANK NAT ASSN
100 Center St Ste 100 # 100 (44024-1181)
PHONE.....................440 286-6111
Lisa Timms, *Manager*
EMP: 26
SALES (corp-wide): 131.4B **Publicly Held**
WEB: www.chase.com
SIC: 6021 National commercial banks

▲ = Import ▼=Export
◆ =Import/Export

HQ: Jpmorgan Chase Bank, National Association
1111 Polaris Pkwy
Columbus OH 43240
614 436-3055

(G-2700)
JUST 4 KIDZ CHILDCARE
13896 Gar Hwy (44024-9251)
PHONE..................................440 285-2221
Tina Prince, *Director*
EMP: 25
SALES (est): 636.3K **Privately Held**
SIC: 8351 Child day care services

(G-2701)
LANXESS CORPORATION
145 Parker Ct (44024-1112)
PHONE..................................440 279-2367
Margie Durkos, *Safety Mgr*
Lou Mueller, *Manager*
EMP: 250
SALES (corp-wide): 8.2B **Privately Held**
SIC: 3069 5169 Reclaimed rubber & specialty rubber compounds; industrial chemicals
HQ: Lanxess Corporation
111 Ridc Park West Dr
Pittsburgh PA 15275
800 526-9377

(G-2702)
LEGEND LAKE GOLF CLUB INC
11135 Auburn Rd (44024-9306)
PHONE..................................440 285-3110
Lou Alexander, *President*
Orion McCarty, *General Mgr*
Doug Garrett, *Executive*
Martha Happ, *Admin Sec*
EMP: 40
SQ FT: 5,400
SALES (est): 1.7MM **Privately Held**
SIC: 7997 Golf club, membership

(G-2703)
LIQUID WSTE SOLIDIFICATION LLC (PA)
Also Called: Lws
12488 Gar Hwy (44024-9299)
P.O. Box 245 (44024-0245)
PHONE..................................440 285-4648
EMP: 25
SQ FT: 25,000
SALES (est): 17.5MM **Privately Held**
SIC: 4953 Refuse systems

(G-2704)
MCI COMMUNICATIONS SVCS INC
Also Called: Verizon Business
12956 Taylor Wells Rd (44024-7910)
PHONE..................................440 635-0418
Dane Oneill, *Branch Mgr*
EMP: 450
SALES (corp-wide): 130.8B **Publicly Held**
SIC: 4813 Long distance telephone communications
HQ: Mci Communications Services, Inc.
22001 Loudoun County Pkwy
Ashburn VA 20147
703 886-5600

(G-2705)
MOUNTAIN FOODS INC
9761 Ravenna Rd (44024-9114)
PHONE..................................440 286-7177
John Youdath, *President*
Sandra Youdath, *Vice Pres*
◆ EMP: 30
SQ FT: 20,000
SALES (est): 11.4MM **Privately Held**
SIC: 5141 Groceries, general line

(G-2706)
NMS INC CERTIF PUB ACCOUNTANTS (PA)
121 South St (44024-1306)
PHONE..................................440 286-5222
Shawn Neece, *President*
George Malec, *Vice Pres*
Brian Seifert, *Treasurer*
Jessica Marker, *Controller*
Michael Duffy, *CPA*
EMP: 31

SQ FT: 9,000
SALES (est): 3.5MM **Privately Held**
WEB: www.neececpa.com
SIC: 8721 Certified public accountant

(G-2707)
PARKSIDE CARE CORPORATION
Also Called: Hospice of Care
831 South St (44024-1438)
PHONE..................................440 286-2273
Jason Baker, *CEO*
Cindy Brostek, *Office Mgr*
EMP: 80
SALES (est): 3.1MM **Privately Held**
SIC: 8082 Home health care services

(G-2708)
PENTAIR RSDNTIAL FLTRATION LLC
220 Park Dr (44024-1091)
PHONE..................................440 286-4116
Kevin Williams, *Principal*
Tom Zbiegien, *Controller*
◆ EMP: 32 EST: 2008
SALES (est): 4.5MM **Privately Held**
SIC: 4971 Irrigation systems

(G-2709)
RAVENWOOD MENTAL HLTH CTR INC (PA)
Also Called: RAVENWOOD HEALTH
12557 Ravenwood Dr (44024-9009)
PHONE..................................440 285-3568
Vicki Clark, *CEO*
Paula Atwood, *Vice Pres*
EMP: 110
SALES (est): 7.5MM **Privately Held**
SIC: 8093 Mental health clinic, outpatient

(G-2710)
RESIDENCE ARTISTS INC
220 5th Ave (44024-1075)
PHONE..................................440 286-8822
Keith Landies, *President*
Tina Vankan, *Admin Sec*
EMP: 40
SALES (est): 3.7MM **Privately Held**
WEB: www.residenceartists.com
SIC: 1721 1521 1542 Residential painting; exterior commercial painting contractor; new construction, single-family houses; commercial & office buildings, renovation & repair

(G-2711)
RESIDENCE OF CHARDON
Also Called: Residents of Chardon
501 Chardon Windsor Rd (44024-8944)
PHONE..................................440 286-2277
Debbie Bowman, *Executive*
Christin Johnson, *Administration*
EMP: 60 EST: 2000
SALES (est): 1.9MM **Privately Held**
SIC: 8052 Intermediate care facilities

(G-2712)
SAINT MARY PARISH
Also Called: Church of St Mary Catholic
401 North St (44024-1035)
PHONE..................................440 285-7051
Tom Behrend, *Principal*
Sandy Nativio, *Principal*
Daniel P Redmond, *Pastor*
Thomas C Gilles, *Pastor*
Jeanette Stone, *Senior Mgr*
EMP: 55
SALES (est): 2.3MM **Privately Held**
SIC: 8661 8611 Catholic Church; community affairs & services

(G-2713)
SAND RIDGE GOLF CLUB
12150 Mayfield Rd (44024-8448)
PHONE..................................440 285-8088
Peter Conway, *President*
Bill Conway, *Chairman*
EMP: 100
SALES (est): 5.2MM **Privately Held**
SIC: 7997 5941 5812 Golf club, membership; sporting goods & bicycle shops; box lunch stand

(G-2714)
SISTERS OF NOTRE DAME OF CHARD
Also Called: Notre Dame Pre-School
13000 Auburn Rd (44024-9337)
PHONE..................................440 279-0575
Daniel Schilling, *Human Res Dir*
David Bellini, *Psychologist*
Jennifer Hanna, *Director*
Christine Nemecek, *Teacher*
Jane Vajda, *Teacher*
EMP: 32
SALES (corp-wide): 27.1MM **Privately Held**
SIC: 8351 Preschool center
PA: The Sisters Of Notre Dame Of Chardon Ohio
13000 Auburn Rd
Chardon OH 44024
440 286-7101

(G-2715)
SOMMERSET DEVELOPMENT LTD
10585 Somerset Dr (44024-8946)
P.O. Box 1102 (44024-5102)
PHONE..................................440 286-6194
Sharon Sommers, *President*
EMP: 155
SQ FT: 1,000
SALES (est): 10.5MM **Privately Held**
SIC: 6552 7353 Land subdividers & developers, commercial; heavy construction equipment rental

(G-2716)
STAT INTEGRATED TECH INC (PA)
Also Called: Aqua Doc Lake & Pond MGT
10779 Mayfield Rd (44024-9323)
P.O. Box 625, Chesterland (44026-0625)
PHONE..................................440 286-7663
Jeanine Wilson, *President*
EMP: 34
SALES (est): 8.6MM **Privately Held**
SIC: 8741 Management services

(G-2717)
STEMBANC INC
100 7th Ave Ste 200 (44024-7805)
PHONE..................................440 332-4279
Archibald Grabinski, *CEO*
Edward Cup, *CFO*
EMP: 40
SALES (est): 2.3MM **Privately Held**
WEB: www.stembanc.com
SIC: 8071 8731 Biological laboratory; biological research

(G-2718)
THRASHER DINSMORE & DOLAN (PA)
Also Called: Thrasher Dinsmore & Doland
100 7th Ave Ste 150 (44024)
PHONE..................................440 285-2242
Lawrence J Dolan, *President*
Matthew J Dolan, *Principal*
Brandon Dynes, *Counsel*
David E Lowe, *Vice Pres*
Dale H Markowitz, *Treasurer*
EMP: 25
SALES (est): 4.1MM **Privately Held**
WEB: www.dolan.law.pro
SIC: 8111 General practice law office

(G-2719)
UAHS HEATHER HILL HOME HEALTH
12340 Bass Lake Rd (44024-8327)
PHONE..................................440 285-5098
Fax: 440 285-0946
EMP: 50
SQ FT: 7,915
SALES: 3.3MM
SALES (corp-wide): 19.4MM **Privately Held**
SIC: 8082 Home Health Care
PA: University Hospitals Health System-Heather Hill, Inc.
12340 Bass Lake Rd
Chardon OH 44024
440 285-4040

(G-2720)
UNIVERSAL DISPOSAL INC
9954 Old State Rd (44024-9521)
P.O. Box 1065 (44024-5065)
PHONE..................................440 286-3153
Murl Clemson, *President*
Shirley Clemson, *Corp Secy*
Bill Clemson, *Vice Pres*
EMP: 50 EST: 1962
SQ FT: 1,500
SALES (est): 6.3MM **Privately Held**
SIC: 4212 Garbage collection & transport, no disposal

(G-2721)
UNIVERSITY HOSPITALS
Also Called: Uhhs-Geauga Regional Hospital
13207 Ravenna Rd (44024-7032)
PHONE..................................440 285-6000
Steven Jones, *President*
Judy Ernest, *Editor*
Robert Forino, *Vice Chairman*
Theresa Weaver, *Vice Pres*
Wendy Brock, *Research*
EMP: 613 EST: 1952
SQ FT: 280,000
SALES: 140.4MM
SALES (corp-wide): 580MM **Privately Held**
SIC: 8062 General medical & surgical hospitals
PA: University Hospitals Health System, Inc.
3605 Warrensville Ctr Rd
Shaker Heights OH 44122
216 767-8900

(G-2722)
UNIVERSITY HOSPITALS HEALTH (PA)
Also Called: Heather HI Rehabilitation Hosp
12340 Bass Lake Rd (44024-8327)
PHONE..................................440 285-4040
Louise Alexander, *Ch of Bd*
Susan Juris, *President*
David Pasco, *Vice Pres*
Mark Ceja, *Buyer*
Rita Johnson, *Manager*
EMP: 41 EST: 1935
SQ FT: 39,000
SALES: 19.4MM **Privately Held**
SIC: 8069 8059 8052 8051 Specialty hospitals, except psychiatric; convalescent home; rest home, with health care; intermediate care facilities; skilled nursing care facilities

(G-2723)
VISITING NURSE SERVICE INC
Also Called: Geauga Cnty Visiting Nurse Svc
13221 Ravenna Rd Ste 1 (44024-9016)
PHONE..................................440 286-9461
Pat Stagner, *Principal*
EMP: 30
SALES (corp-wide): 21.8MM **Privately Held**
WEB: www.vnsa.com
SIC: 8082 Visiting nurse service
PA: Visiting Nurse Service, Inc.
1 Home Care Pl
Akron OH 44320
330 745-1601

(G-2724)
WASTE MANAGEMENT OHIO INC
9954 Old State Rd (44024-9521)
PHONE..................................440 286-7116
Bill Skidmore, *Manager*
Marlyn Gallus, *Director*
EMP: 49
SALES (corp-wide): 14.9B **Publicly Held**
WEB: www.wm.com
SIC: 4953 4212 Refuse collection & disposal services; local trucking, without storage
HQ: Waste Management Of Ohio, Inc.
1700 N Broad St
Fairborn OH 45324

(G-2725)
WATER LEASING CO LLC
Also Called: Chardon Healthcare Center
620 Water St (44024-1149)
PHONE..................................440 285-9400

Stephen L Rosedale, *Mng Member*
Ronald S Wilheim, *Mng Member*
EMP: 150
SALES (est): 5.9MM **Privately Held**
SIC: 8051 Convalescent home with continuous nursing care

(G-2726)
YOUNG MNS CHRSTN ASSN CLVELAND
Also Called: YMCA
12460 Bass Lake Rd (44024-8315)
PHONE....................................440 285-7543
Alexandria Nichols, *Branch Mgr*
EMP: 90
SALES (corp-wide): 29.2MM **Privately Held**
SIC: 8641 7991 8351 7032 Youth organizations; physical fitness facilities; child day care services; youth camps; individual & family services
PA: Young Men's Christian Association Of Cleveland
1801 Superior Ave E # 130
Cleveland OH 44114
216 781-1337

Chesapeake
Lawrence County

(G-2727)
BIG SANDY FURNITURE INC
Also Called: Big Sandy Superstore
45 County Rd 407 (45619)
PHONE....................................740 894-4242
Buck Ellis, *Manager*
EMP: 50 **Privately Held**
WEB: www.bigsandyfurniture.com
SIC: 4225 5712 General warehousing & storage; furniture stores
HQ: Big Sandy Furniture, Inc.
8375 Gallia Pike
Franklin Furnace OH 45629
740 574-2113

(G-2728)
COLLINS CAREER CENTER
11627 State Route 243 (45619-7962)
PHONE....................................740 867-6641
Gerald Love, *President*
Steve Dodgion, *Superintendent*
Jim Howard, *Principal*
Jerry Frye, *Vice Pres*
Richard Sketel, *Treasurer*
EMP: 90
SALES (est): 5.7MM **Privately Held**
WEB: www.collinscareercenter.com
SIC: 8331 Job training & vocational rehabilitation services

(G-2729)
G BIG INC (PA)
Also Called: Pickett Concrete
441 Rockwood Ave (45619-1120)
PHONE....................................740 867-5758
John W Galloway, *President*
James W Galloway, *Vice Pres*
Todd A Galloway, *Vice Pres*
Todd Galloway, *Vice Pres*
EMP: 25
SQ FT: 2,000
SALES (est): 3.8MM **Privately Held**
WEB: www.gbig.com
SIC: 3273 1771 Ready-mixed concrete; concrete work

(G-2730)
KLLEE TRUCKING INC
1714 Township Road 278 (45619-7606)
PHONE....................................740 867-6454
Sandra Adkins, *President*
David Stump, *Manager*
Kelly Stump, *Admin Sec*
EMP: 55
SALES (est): 2.5MM **Privately Held**
SIC: 4213 Trucking, except local

(G-2731)
PREMIER MANAGEMENT CO INC
805 3rd Ave (45619-1045)
P.O. Box 274 (45619-0274)
PHONE....................................740 867-2144

Jon Barker, *President*
Teffaney Barker, *Admin Sec*
EMP: 25
SQ FT: 3,500
SALES (est): 1.3MM **Privately Held**
SIC: 8741 Management services

(G-2732)
RESCARE OHIO INC
1107 Us Hwy 52 (45619)
PHONE....................................740 867-4568
Sherrie Carter, *Manager*
EMP: 25
SALES (corp-wide): 23.7B **Privately Held**
SIC: 8082 Home health care services
HQ: Rescare Ohio Inc
348 W Main St
Williamsburg OH 45176

Cheshire
Gallia County

(G-2733)
DISABLED AMERICAN VETERANS
Also Called: Dav Chapter 53
28051 State Route 7 (45620-9603)
PHONE....................................740 367-7973
Danver Curtis, *Principal*
EMP: 374
SALES (corp-wide): 137MM **Privately Held**
SIC: 8641 Veterans' organization
PA: Disabled American Veterans
3725 Alexandria Pike
Cold Spring KY 41076
859 441-7300

(G-2734)
GALLIA-MEIGS COMMUNITY ACTION (PA)
8010 State Route 7 N (45620)
P.O. Box 272 (45620-0272)
PHONE....................................740 367-7341
Michael Davenport, *Ch of Bd*
Tony Gallagher, *Vice Pres*
Tom Reed, *Exec Dir*
Linda Lester, *Admin Sec*
EMP: 35
SQ FT: 3,600
SALES: 2.5MM **Privately Held**
SIC: 8322 Individual & family services

(G-2735)
GAVIN AEP PLANT
7397 State Route 7 N (45620-7500)
P.O. Box 271 (45620-0271)
PHONE....................................740 925-3166
EMP: 27 **EST:** 2010
SALES (est): 13.3MM **Privately Held**
SIC: 4911 Electric services

Chesterland
Geauga County

(G-2736)
AMERICAN GOLF CORPORATION
Also Called: Fowlers Mill Golf Course
13095 Rockhaven Rd (44026-3311)
PHONE....................................440 286-9544
Mike Mucciarone, *General Mgr*
David Scull, *Manager*
EMP: 55 **Publicly Held**
WEB: www.americangolf.com
SIC: 7997 Golf club, membership
HQ: American Golf Corporation
909 N Pacific Coast Hwy
El Segundo CA 90245
310 664-4000

(G-2737)
BRIGHTVIEW LANDSCAPES LLC
7901 Old Ranger Rd (44026)
PHONE....................................440 729-2302
Tim Korte, *Manager*
EMP: 50

SALES (corp-wide): 2.8B **Publicly Held**
SIC: 0781 0782 Landscape services; lawn services
HQ: Brightview Landscapes, Llc
401 Plymouth Rd Ste 500
Plymouth Meeting PA 19462
484 567-7204

(G-2738)
COUNTY OF GEAUGA
8389 Mayfield Rd Ste A-2 (44026-2553)
PHONE....................................440 286-6264
Linda Reed, *Director*
EMP: 123
SALES (est): 118.6K **Privately Held**
SIC: 8093 Mental health clinic, outpatient
PA: County Of Geauga
470 Center St Bldg 4
Chardon OH 44024
440 285-2222

(G-2739)
G H A INC
Also Called: Turney's
12670 W Geauga Plz (44026-2505)
PHONE....................................440 729-2130
Howard Adelman, *President*
Ann Adelman, *Vice Pres*
EMP: 30
SQ FT: 34,000
SALES (est): 873.3K **Privately Held**
SIC: 6531 Real estate managers

(G-2740)
MATO INC
Also Called: Avanti Salon
8027 Mayfield Rd (44026-2438)
PHONE....................................440 729-9008
Marisa Paterniti, *President*
Tony Paterniti, *Vice Pres*
EMP: 30
SQ FT: 1,450
SALES (est): 1MM **Privately Held**
SIC: 7231 Cosmetology & personal hygiene salons

(G-2741)
METZENBAUM SHELTERED INDS INC
Also Called: MSI
8090 Cedar Rd (44026-3400)
PHONE....................................440 729-1919
Robert Preston, *Chairman*
Robert Voss, *Manager*
Diane Buehner, *Admin Sec*
EMP: 160
SQ FT: 12,000
SALES: 2.3MM **Privately Held**
SIC: 8331 7389 3672 Sheltered workshop; packaging & labeling services; presorted mail service; printed circuit boards

(G-2742)
MISS PATS DAY CARE CENTER (PA)
Also Called: Foot Steps Toward Discovery
8553 Herrick Dr (44026-2619)
PHONE....................................440 729-8255
Michael T Jasko, *President*
Patricia R Jasko, *Corp Secy*
Michelle Cole, *Vice Pres*
EMP: 32
SQ FT: 5,500
SALES: 1.3MM **Privately Held**
SIC: 8351 Group day care center

(G-2743)
PROFESSIONAL HSE CLG SVCS INC
8228 Mayfield Rd Ste 1b (44026-2542)
PHONE....................................440 729-7866
Shawn Day, *President*
EMP: 30
SQ FT: 1,200
SALES (est): 797.5K **Privately Held**
SIC: 7349 Cleaning service, industrial or commercial

(G-2744)
RES-CARE INC
Also Called: Raise
8228 Mayfield Rd Ste 5b (44026-2542)
PHONE....................................440 729-2432
Kevin Cook, *Director*
EMP: 34

SALES (corp-wide): 23.7B **Privately Held**
WEB: www.rescare.com
SIC: 8082 Home health care services
HQ: Res-Care, Inc.
805 N Whittington Pkwy
Louisville KY 40222
502 394-2100

(G-2745)
SPORTY EVENTS
8430 Mayfield Rd (44026-2580)
PHONE....................................440 342-5046
David Gordon, *COO*
EMP: 25
SALES: 1.1MM **Privately Held**
WEB: www.sportyevents.com
SIC: 8699 5999 Amateur sports promotion; trophies & plaques

(G-2746)
SYCAMORE LAKE INC
Also Called: Alpine Valley Ski Area
10620 Mayfield Rd (44026-2738)
PHONE....................................440 729-9775
Thomas Apthorp, *President*
S Sandy Sutlo, *Treasurer*
EMP: 200 **EST:** 1963
SQ FT: 22,000
SALES (est): 5.4MM **Privately Held**
WEB: www.alpinevalleyohio.com
SIC: 7011 5812 Ski lodge; caterers

(G-2747)
TOWNSHIP OF CHESTER
Also Called: Chester Township Fire Rescue
8552 Parkside Dr (44026-2643)
PHONE....................................440 729-9951
John Wargelin, *Chief*
EMP: 40 **Privately Held**
SIC: 9224 7363 Fire Protection Help Supply Services
PA: Township Of Chester
12701 Chillicothe Rd
Chesterland OH 44026
440 729-7058

Chesterville
Morrow County

(G-2748)
LEVERING MANAGEMENT INC
Also Called: Morrow Manor Nursing Home
115 N Portland St (43317-5006)
PHONE....................................419 768-2401
Darlene Yake, *Administration*
EMP: 50
SALES (corp-wide): 27.7MM **Privately Held**
SIC: 8741 8059 Management services; nursing home, except skilled & intermediate care facility
PA: Levering Management, Inc.
201 N Main St
Mount Vernon OH 43050
740 397-3897

Chillicothe
Ross County

(G-2749)
ACCURATE HEATING & COOLING
3001 River Rd (45601-8178)
PHONE....................................740 775-5005
Tom White, *Owner*
EMP: 40
SALES (est): 2.5MM **Privately Held**
WEB: www.accuratehvac.com
SIC: 1711 Warm air heating & air conditioning contractor; heating & air conditioning contractors

(G-2750)
ADENA HEALTH SYSTEM
Also Called: Parks Ob Gyn Assoc
4439 State Route 159 # 120 (45601-8207)
PHONE....................................740 779-7201
Heidi Streitenberger, *Manager*
EMP: 29

SALES (corp-wide): 470.6MM **Privately Held**
WEB: www.adena.org
SIC: **8062** 8031 Hospital, medical school affiliated with nursing & residency; offices & clinics of osteopathic physicians
PA: Adena Health System
272 Hospital Rd
Chillicothe OH 45601
740 779-7360

(G-2751)
ADENA HEALTH SYSTEM (PA)
Also Called: GREENFIELD AREA MEDICAL CENTER
272 Hospital Rd (45601-9031)
PHONE.................................740 779-7360
Jeffrey J Graham, *President*
Carolyn Hice, *President*
Dale Hume, *Ch Radiology*
David Magee, *Ch Radiology*
George Hatfield, *Plant Mgr*
EMP: 1130
SQ FT: 690,000
SALES: 470.6MM **Privately Held**
WEB: www.adena.org
SIC: **8062** Hospital, medical school affiliated with nursing & residency

(G-2752)
ADENA HEALTH SYSTEM
85 River Trce (45601-2686)
PHONE.................................740 779-8995
EMP: 213
SALES (corp-wide): 470.6MM **Privately Held**
SIC: **8062** Hospital, medical school affiliated with nursing & residency
PA: Adena Health System
272 Hospital Rd
Chillicothe OH 45601
740 779-7360

(G-2753)
ADENA HEALTH SYSTEM
Also Called: Adena Rhblitation Wellness Ctr
445 Shawnee Ln (45601-4145)
PHONE.................................740 779-4801
R Sorrell, *Manager*
Jason Folk, *Manager*
EMP: 25
SALES (corp-wide): 470.6MM **Privately Held**
WEB: www.adena.org
SIC: **8062** Hospital, medical school affiliated with nursing & residency
PA: Adena Health System
272 Hospital Rd
Chillicothe OH 45601
740 779-7360

(G-2754)
ADENA HEALTH SYSTEM
Also Called: Adena Counseling Center
455 Shawnee Dr Ln (45601)
PHONE.................................740 779-4888
R Sorrell, *Branch Mgr*
EMP: 25
SALES (corp-wide): 470.6MM **Privately Held**
WEB: www.adena.org
SIC: **8322** General counseling services
PA: Adena Health System
272 Hospital Rd
Chillicothe OH 45601
740 779-7360

(G-2755)
ADENA PCKWY-ROSS FMLY PHYSCANS
100 N Walnut St (45601-2420)
PHONE.................................740 779-4500
April Dollison, *General Mgr*
Alan D Noel, *Principal*
EMP: 30 EST: 2010
SALES (est): 110.4K **Privately Held**
SIC: **8011** General & family practice, physician/surgeon

(G-2756)
AMERICAN ELECTRIC POWER CO INC
701 Hardin Dr (45601-2780)
PHONE.................................740 779-5261
EMP: 44

SALES (corp-wide): 16.2B **Publicly Held**
SIC: **4911** Generation, electric power
PA: American Electric Power Company, Inc.
1 Riverside Plz Fl 1 # 1
Columbus OH 43215
614 716-1000

(G-2757)
B & B ROOFING INC
150 Cooks Hill Rd (45601-8220)
P.O. Box 6351 (45601-6351)
PHONE.................................740 772-4759
James Butt, *President*
Joe Zupi, *Vice Pres*
Melissa Butt, *Treasurer*
Jennifer Grooms, *Admin Sec*
EMP: 25
SQ FT: 9,000
SALES: 5.6K **Privately Held**
WEB: www.bandbroofing.com
SIC: **1761** Roofing contractor

(G-2758)
BIG SANDY FURNITURE INC
1404 N Bridge St (45601-4101)
PHONE.................................740 775-4244
Annette Dickess, *Financial Exec*
Mike Farmer, *Branch Mgr*
EMP: 30 **Privately Held**
WEB: www.bigsandyfurniture.com
SIC: **4225** 5722 5712 General warehousing & storage; electric household appliances, major; furniture stores
HQ: Big Sandy Furniture, Inc.
8375 Gallia Pike
Franklin Furnace OH 45629
740 574-2113

(G-2759)
CHILLICOTHE BOWLING LANES INC
Also Called: Shawnee Trophies & Sptg Gds
1680 N Bridge St (45601-4105)
PHONE.................................740 773-3300
John Corcoran, *President*
Walter Highland, *Treasurer*
Kenneth De Long, *Admin Sec*
EMP: 26
SQ FT: 39,600
SALES (est): 1.2MM **Privately Held**
SIC: **7933** 5812 5813 5941 Ten pin center; snack bar; cocktail lounge; bowling equipment & supplies

(G-2760)
CHILLICOTHE CITY SCHOOL DST
Also Called: Chillicothe Cty Sch Trans Off
89 Riverside St (45601-2547)
PHONE.................................740 775-2936
Bobbi Lowry, *Director*
EMP: 26
SALES (est): 601.7K
SALES (corp-wide): 53.1MM **Privately Held**
SIC: **4151** 7521 7538 School Bus Service Automobile Parking General Auto Repair
PA: Chillicothe City School District
425 Yoctangee Pkwy
Chillicothe OH 45601
740 775-4250

(G-2761)
CHILLICOTHE COUNTRY CLUB CO
Woodbridge Ave & Arch St (45601)
PHONE.................................740 775-0150
Bill Jones, *President*
Chris Frey, *General Mgr*
Carvel Simmons, *Vice Pres*
Noble Yoshida, *Treasurer*
Beth Gilmore, *Manager*
EMP: 30 EST: 1915
SALES: 995.3K **Privately Held**
SIC: **7997** Country club, membership

(G-2762)
CHILLICOTHE FAMILY PHYSICIANS
60 Capital Dr (45601-1186)
PHONE.................................740 779-4100
Paul Mc Carter, *President*
Andrew Varney, *Manager*
Wayne W Beam Jr, *Family Practiti*
EMP: 25

SALES (est): 1.5MM **Privately Held**
SIC: **8011** General & family practice, physician/surgeon

(G-2763)
CHILLICOTHE LONG TERM CARE
Also Called: Westmoreland Place
230 Cherry St (45601-2301)
PHONE.................................740 773-6161
David Dixon, *Administration*
EMP: 140
SALES (est): 5.2MM
SALES (corp-wide): 970.6MM **Privately Held**
WEB: www.westmorelandplace.com
SIC: **8051** Extended care facility
PA: Chillicothe Long Term Care Inc
7265 Kenwood Rd Ste 300
Cincinnati OH 45236
513 793-8804

(G-2764)
CHILLICOTHE MOTEL LLC
Also Called: Comfort Inn
20 N Plaza Blvd (45601-1757)
PHONE.................................740 773-3903
John Woods, *General Mgr*
Patrick K McCalister,
Wen F Chen MD,
Ron Fewster,
Tom White,
EMP: 34
SQ FT: 40,000
SALES (est): 1.3MM **Privately Held**
SIC: **7011** 7991 Hotel, franchised; physical fitness facilities

(G-2765)
CHILLICOTHE OPCO LLC
60 Marietta Rd (45601-9433)
PHONE.................................740 772-5900
William D Orand, *CEO*
Scott Burleyson,
EMP: 99
SALES (est): 2MM **Privately Held**
SIC: **8051** Skilled nursing care facilities
PA: Signature Healthcare, Llc
12201 Bluegrass Pkwy
Louisville KY 40299

(G-2766)
CHILLICOTHE RACQUET CLUB
Also Called: Csrc
1245 Western Ave (45601-1169)
PHONE.................................740 773-4928
Aaron Koch, *Partner*
Charles Halm, *Partner*
EMP: 30 EST: 1977
SQ FT: 32,000
SALES (est): 672.6K **Privately Held**
SIC: **7997** 7991 Tennis club, membership; racquetball club, membership; physical fitness facilities

(G-2767)
CHILLICOTHE TELEPHONE COMPANY (HQ)
68 E Main St (45601-2503)
P.O. Box 480 (45601-0480)
PHONE.................................740 772-8200
William Mc Kell, *CEO*
Joe Corbin, *VP Opers*
Ed McKell, *VP Opers*
Tom Krouse, *Mktg Dir*
Pamela Cox, *Manager*
EMP: 200 EST: 1927
SQ FT: 80,000
SALES (est): 31.7MM **Privately Held**
SIC: **4813** 4841 Local telephone communications; cable television services

(G-2768)
CHILLICOTHE TELEPHONE COMPANY
861 Orange St (45601-1341)
P.O. Box 480 (45601-0480)
PHONE.................................740 772-8361
Greg Haas, *Manager*
Rick Mitten, *Network Tech*
EMP: 75
SALES (est): 2.7MM **Privately Held**
SIC: **4813** 5999 Local telephone communications; telephone equipment & systems

HQ: The Chillicothe Telephone Company
68 E Main St
Chillicothe OH 45601
740 772-8200

(G-2769)
CLARY TRUCKING INC
1177 Eastern Ave (45601-9102)
PHONE.................................740 702-4242
Jesse Clary, *President*
EMP: 49
SALES (est): 763K **Privately Held**
SIC: **4212** Local trucking, without storage

(G-2770)
CORPORATE HEALTH DIMENSIONS
Also Called: Mead Family Medical Ctr
311 Caldwell St (45601-3332)
PHONE.................................740 775-6119
Dawn Limle, *Manager*
EMP: 25
SALES (corp-wide): 685MM **Privately Held**
SIC: **8741** 8011 Hospital management; general & family practice, physician/surgeon
HQ: Corporate Health Dimensions, Inc
40 British American Blvd # 2
Latham NY 12110
518 843-2300

(G-2771)
COUNTY ENGINEERS OFFICE
Also Called: Garage, The
755 Fairgrounds Rd (45601-9702)
PHONE.................................740 702-3130
Charles Ortman, *Director*
EMP: 25
SALES (est): 3.2MM **Privately Held**
SIC: **8711** 7538 Engineering services; general automotive repair shops

(G-2772)
COUNTY OF ROSS
Also Called: South Cntrl OH Rgnl Juv Dtn CT
182 Cattail Rd (45601-9404)
PHONE.................................740 773-4169
Cathy Fenner, *Superintendent*
EMP: 36 **Privately Held**
WEB: www.rosscountycommissioners.com
SIC: **8361** 9223 Juvenile correctional facilities; detention center, government
PA: County Of Ross
2 N Paint St Ste H
Chillicothe OH 45601
740 702-3085

(G-2773)
COURT DIALYSIS LLC
Also Called: Adena Dialysis
1180 N Bridge St (45601-1793)
PHONE.................................740 773-3733
Jim Hilger, *Principal*
EMP: 39
SALES (est): 707.1K **Publicly Held**
SIC: **8092** Kidney dialysis centers
PA: Davita Inc.
2000 16th St
Denver CO 80202

(G-2774)
DANBARRY LINEMAS INC
119 Pawnee Rd (45601-1770)
PHONE.................................740 779-6115
Danny Heilbrun, *Principal*
EMP: 30
SALES (est): 374.7K **Privately Held**
SIC: **7832** Exhibitors, itinerant: motion picture

(G-2775)
DAVE PINKERTON
Also Called: Advance Services
221 Renick Ave (45601-2852)
PHONE.................................740 477-8888
Dave Pinkerton, *Owner*
EMP: 25
SALES (est): 2.6MM **Privately Held**
SIC: **1711** Heating & air conditioning contractors

(G-2776)
DE HUDDLESTON INC
283 S Paint St (45601-3829)
P.O. Box 207 (45601-0207)
PHONE......................................740 773-2130
Jeffrey Huddleston, *President*
Don Huddleston, *President*
Don Anderson, *Vice Pres*
Jeff Huddleston, *Admin Sec*
EMP: 25
SQ FT: 2,000
SALES: 4MM Privately Held
WEB: www.dehuddleston.com
SIC: 1541 1542 Industrial buildings, new
construction; commercial & office build-
ing, new construction

(G-2777)
**DETILLION LANDSCAPING CO
INC**
20337 State Route 104 (45601-8489)
PHONE......................................740 775-5305
Randy Detillion, *President*
Cynthia Detillion, *Corp Secy*
EMP: 40
SQ FT: 800
SALES (est): 2.7MM Privately Held
SIC: 0781 0782 Landscape planning serv-
ices; lawn care services

(G-2778)
**FEDEX GROUND PACKAGE SYS
INC**
1415 Industrial Dr (45601-3977)
PHONE......................................800 463-3339
EMP: 34
SALES (corp-wide): 65.4B Publicly Held
WEB: www.fedex.com
SIC: 4513 Package delivery, private air
HQ: Fedex Ground Package System, Inc.
1000 Fed Ex Dr
Coraopolis PA 15108
800 463-3339

(G-2779)
**FIRST CAPITAL BANCSHARES
INC**
33 W Main St (45601-3131)
P.O. Box 463 (45601-0463)
PHONE......................................740 775-6777
Thomas Beard, *President*
John H Kochensparger III, *Chairman*
EMP: 55 EST: 1998 Privately Held
SIC: 6712 6021 Bank holding companies;
national commercial banks

(G-2780)
**FIRST CAPITAL ENTERPRISES
INC**
505 E 7th St (45601-3632)
PHONE......................................740 773-2166
Ron Sarrar, *Director*
EMP: 60
SQ FT: 18,000
SALES: 3MM Privately Held
WEB: www.fce-mrdd.net
SIC: 8331 8699 Sheltered workshop;
charitable organization

(G-2781)
FNS INC
Also Called: Family Nursing Services
24 Star Dr (45601-9845)
PHONE......................................740 775-5463
Ken Kevorkian, *Finance*
EMP: 50
SALES (est): 154.8K
SALES (corp-wide): 1.8MM Privately
Held
SIC: 8082 Home health care services
PA: Hcf Home Care, Inc.
1100 Shawnee Rd
Lima OH 45805
419 999-2010

(G-2782)
**G & J PEPSI-COLA BOTTLERS
INC**
Also Called: Pepsico
400 E 7th St (45601-3455)
PHONE......................................740 774-2148
Henry Thrapp, *Sales & Mktg St*
John Miller, *Finance Mgr*
EMP: 45

SALES (corp-wide): 418.3MM Privately
Held
WEB: www.gjpepsi.com
SIC: 5149 2086 Starch; bottled & canned
soft drinks
PA: G & J Pepsi-Cola Bottlers Inc
9435 Waterstone Blvd # 390
Cincinnati OH 45249
513 785-6060

(G-2783)
**GOOD SMARITAN NETWRK
ROSS CNTY**
133 E 7th St (45601-3352)
P.O. Box 1781 (45601-5781)
PHONE......................................740 774-6303
Steve Delmoe, *Chairman*
EMP: 25
SALES (est): 164.8K Privately Held
SIC: 8322 Individual & family services

(G-2784)
**HANSON AGGREGATES EAST
LLC**
Hanson Aggregates Davon
33 Renick Ave (45601-2895)
PHONE......................................740 773-2172
Leonard McFerren, *Manager*
EMP: 25
SALES (corp-wide): 20.6B Privately Held
SIC: 3273 3271 3272 1442 Ready-mixed
concrete; blocks, concrete or cinder: stan-
dard; concrete products; construction
sand & gravel
HQ: Hanson Aggregates East Llc
3131 Rdu Center Dr
Morrisville NC 27560
919 380-2500

(G-2785)
**HEALTH CARE RTREMENT
CORP AMER**
Also Called: Heartland of Chillicothe
1058 Columbus St (45601-2810)
PHONE......................................740 773-5000
Mike Armstrong, *Branch Mgr*
EMP: 100
SALES (corp-wide): 2.4B Publicly Held
WEB: www.hrc-manorcare.com
SIC: 8051 Skilled nursing care facilities
HQ: Health Care And Retirement Corpora-
tion Of America
333 N Summit St Ste 103
Toledo OH 43604
419 252-5500

(G-2786)
**HERRNSTEIN CHRYSLER INC
(PA)**
Also Called: Herrnstein Auto Group
133 Marietta Rd (45601-9433)
P.O. Box 266 (45601-0266)
PHONE......................................740 773-2203
Bart Herrnstein, *President*
Linda Herrnstein, *Corp Secy*
William B Herrnstein, *Vice Pres*
EMP: 72
SQ FT: 11,500
SALES (est): 48.2MM Privately Held
SIC: 5511 7549 Automobiles, new & used;
automotive maintenance services

(G-2787)
**HOMELAND CREDIT UNION INC
(PA)**
310 Caldwell St (45601-3331)
P.O. Box 1974 (45601-5974)
PHONE......................................740 775-3024
Michael Spindler, *CEO*
EMP: 65
SQ FT: 3,500
SALES: 10.8MM Privately Held
WEB: www.homelandcreditunion.com
SIC: 6062 State credit unions, not federally
chartered

(G-2788)
HOMELAND CREDIT UNION INC
25 Consumer Center Dr (45601-2676)
P.O. Box 1974 (45601-5974)
PHONE......................................740 775-3331
Shayne Poe, *CEO*
EMP: 31

SALES (corp-wide): 10.8MM Privately
Held
WEB: www.homelandcreditunion.com
SIC: 6062 6141 State credit unions, not
federally chartered; personal finance li-
censed loan companies, small
PA: Homeland Credit Union, Inc.
310 Caldwell St
Chillicothe OH 45601
740 775-3024

(G-2789)
**HOPEWELL HEALTH CENTERS
INC (PA)**
1049 Western Ave (45601-1104)
P.O. Box 188 (45601-0188)
PHONE......................................740 773-1006
Mark Bridenbaugh, *CEO*
Kathy Cecil, *President*
Brad Nelson, *CFO*
Amanda Putnam, *Human Res Dir*
Lori McCullough, *Hum Res Coord*
EMP: 50
SALES (est): 33.1MM Privately Held
SIC: 8093 Mental health clinic, outpatient

(G-2790)
HORIZON PCS INC (HQ)
68 E Main St (45601-2503)
PHONE......................................740 772-8200
William A McKell, *Ch of Bd*
Steven Burkhardt, *Corp Secy*
Alan G Morse, *COO*
Shawn Moorman, *Asst Controller*
Peter M Holland, *Director*
EMP: 200
SALES (est): 39MM Privately Held
SIC: 4812 Radio telephone communication

(G-2791)
HORIZON TELCOM INC (PA)
68 E Main St (45601-2503)
PHONE......................................740 772-8200
Bill McKell, *President*
Joey Holibaugh, *Vice Pres*
Nina Guysinger, *Data Admn*
Rob Painter, *Network Tech*
Peter Holland, *Executive*
EMP: 285
SQ FT: 80,000
SALES (est): 31.8MM Privately Held
WEB: www.horizontel.com
SIC: 4813 Local telephone communica-
tions

(G-2792)
HUNTINGTON NATIONAL BANK
Also Called: Home Mortgage
445 Western Ave (45601-2243)
PHONE......................................740 773-2681
Delbert Bochard, *President*
EMP: 50
SALES (corp-wide): 5.2B Publicly Held
WEB: www.huntingtonnationalbank.com
SIC: 6029 6162 6021 Commercial banks;
mortgage bankers; national commercial
banks
HQ: The Huntington National Bank
17 S High St Fl 1
Columbus OH 43215
614 480-4293

(G-2793)
INGLE-BARR INC (PA)
Also Called: Ibi
20 Plyleys Ln (45601-2005)
PHONE......................................740 702-6117
Jeffrey Poole, *President*
Rod Poole, *Vice Pres*
Mike Moss, *Sr Project Mgr*
Steve Bettendorf, *Technology*
EMP: 130
SQ FT: 6,500
SALES (est): 19.4MM Privately Held
WEB: www.4ibi.com
SIC: 1521 1541 1542 1389 General re-
modeling, single-family houses; renova-
tion, remodeling & repair: industrial
buildings; steel building construction;
commercial & office building, new con-
struction; commercial & office buildings,
renovation & repair; construction, repair &
dismantling services; construction management

(G-2794)
J B EXPRESS INC
27311 Old Route 35 (45601-8110)
P.O. Box 91 (45601-0091)
PHONE......................................740 702-9830
Jon Bell, *President*
Josh Bell, *Vice Pres*
Deana Bell, *Treasurer*
EMP: 60
SQ FT: 24,440
SALES (est): 12.1MM Privately Held
WEB: www.jbexpress.com
SIC: 4731 1623 4225 Transportation
agents & brokers; oil & gas pipeline con-
struction; general warehousing & storage

(G-2795)
J L SWANEY INC
975 Vigo Rd (45601-8993)
PHONE......................................740 884-4450
Jared Swaney, *President*
EMP: 27
SALES (est): 3.2MM Privately Held
SIC: 5094 Beads

(G-2796)
J W ENTERPRISES INC (PA)
Also Called: ERA
159 E Main St (45601-2507)
P.O. Box 2066 (45601-8066)
PHONE......................................740 774-4500
Wayne Martin Jr, *CEO*
Mark Cenci, *President*
EMP: 30
SQ FT: 6,000
SALES (est): 3MM Privately Held
WEB: www.benchmarkrealtyllc.com
SIC: 6531 1521 Real estate agent, resi-
dential; appraiser, real estate; auction,
real estate; new construction, single-fam-
ily houses

(G-2797)
KHC INC
Also Called: Kendal Home Care
24 Star Dr (45601-9845)
PHONE......................................740 775-5463
Marilyn Haines, *Administration*
EMP: 100
SALES (est): 230.7K
SALES (corp-wide): 1.8MM Privately
Held
SIC: 8082 Home health care services
PA: Hcf Home Care, Inc.
1100 Shawnee Rd
Lima OH 45805
419 999-2010

(G-2798)
**KINDRED NURSING CENTERS E
LLC**
Also Called: Kindred Transitional
60 Marietta Rd (45601-9433)
PHONE......................................740 772-5900
Christina Schramm, *Director*
EMP: 113
SALES (corp-wide): 6B Privately Held
WEB: www.salemhaven.com
SIC: 8051 Skilled nursing care facilities
HQ: Kindred Nursing Centers East, L.L.C.
680 S 4th St
Louisville KY 40202
502 596-7300

(G-2799)
KITCHEN COLLECTION LLC
133 Redd St (45601-3400)
PHONE......................................740 773-9150
Mike White, *Branch Mgr*
EMP: 40
SALES (corp-wide): 740.7MM Publicly
Held
WEB: www.kitchencollection.com
SIC: 4226 Special warehousing & storage
HQ: The Kitchen Collection Llc
71 E Water St
Chillicothe OH 45601
740 773-9150

(G-2800)
LCNB NATIONAL BANK
33 W Main St Frnt (45601-3132)
PHONE......................................740 775-6777
Jeff Meeker, *COO*
Ryan Adams, *Assoc VP*
EMP: 49

SALES (corp-wide): 65.6MM **Publicly Held**
SIC: 6021 National trust companies with deposits, commercial
HQ: Lcnb National Bank
2 N Broadway St Lowr
Lebanon OH 45036
513 932-1414

(G-2801)
LITTER BOB FUEL & HEATING CO (HQ)
Also Called: Litter Quality Propane
524 Eastern Ave (45601-3471)
P.O. Box 297 (45601-0297)
PHONE................................740 773-2196
Robert W Litter, President
Anna Roseberry, Corp Secy
EMP: 32
SQ FT: 1,500
SALES (est): 9.3MM **Privately Held**
SIC: 5984 1711 Propane gas, bottled; liquefied petroleum gas, delivered to customers' premises; plumbing, heating, air-conditioning contractors

(G-2802)
LITTER DISTRIBUTING CO INC
Also Called: Classic Brands
656 Hospital Rd (45601-9030)
PHONE................................740 774-2831
Ken Bartley, Warehouse Mgr
John Lodge, Manager
EMP: 53 **Privately Held**
SIC: 5181 Beer & other fermented malt liquors
HQ: Litter Distributing Company, Inc.
656 Hospital Rd
Chillicothe OH 45601
740 775-2063

(G-2803)
LOWES HOME CENTERS LLC
867 N Bridge St (45601-1775)
PHONE................................740 773-7777
Denny Gray, Office Mgr
EMP: 150
SALES (corp-wide): 68.6B **Publicly Held**
SIC: 5211 5031 5722 5064 Home centers; building materials, exterior; building materials, interior; household appliance stores; electrical appliances, television & radio
HQ: Lowe's Home Centers, Llc
1605 Curtis Bridge Rd
Wilkesboro NC 28697
336 658-4000

(G-2804)
MAXIM HEALTHCARE SERVICES INC
83 E Water St (45601-2535)
PHONE................................740 772-4100
Rachel Fuller, Branch Mgr
EMP: 93
SALES (corp-wide): 1.5B **Privately Held**
SIC: 8099 8049 Blood related health services; nurses & other medical assistants
PA: Maxim Healthcare Services, Inc.
7227 Lee Deforest Dr
Columbia MD 21046
410 910-1500

(G-2805)
MPW INDUSTRIAL SERVICES INC
65 Kenworth Dr (45601-8829)
PHONE................................740 774-5251
EMP: 89
SALES (corp-wide): 208.7MM **Privately Held**
SIC: 7349 Cleaning service, industrial or commercial
HQ: Mpw Industrial Services, Inc.
9711 Lancaster Rd
Hebron OH 43025
800 827-8790

(G-2806)
OAKWOOD MANAGEMENT COMPANY
402 W Main St (45601-3049)
PHONE................................740 774-3570
Fred Carlisle, Branch Mgr
EMP: 46

SALES (corp-wide): 4.3MM **Privately Held**
SIC: 6513 Apartment hotel operation
PA: Oakwood Management Company Inc
6950 Americana Pkwy Ste A
Reynoldsburg OH 43068
614 866-8702

(G-2807)
OHIO EYE SPECIALISTS INC
Also Called: Vision America of Ohio
50 N Plaza Blvd (45601-1757)
PHONE................................800 948-3937
Harmet Chawla, President
EMP: 30 **Privately Held**
SIC: 8011 Ophthalmologist
PA: Ohio Eye Specialists, Inc.
155 E Circle Ln
Circleville OH 43113

(G-2808)
OVERBROOK PARK LTD
Also Called: Overbrook Park
2179 Anderson Station Rd (45601-8856)
PHONE................................740 773-1159
Leeann Morein, Principal
Jennifer Hardee, Principal
EMP: 99
SALES (est): 3.2MM **Privately Held**
SIC: 6513 Apartment building operators

(G-2809)
OYER ELECTRIC INC
Also Called: S.O.S. Electric
14650 Pleasant Valley Rd (45601-4049)
P.O. Box 1800 (45601-5800)
PHONE................................740 773-2828
Larry Oyer, President
Sandra Scherer, Manager
EMP: 60
SQ FT: 11,000
SALES: 3MM **Privately Held**
WEB: www.soselectric.net
SIC: 1731 General electrical contractor

(G-2810)
PACE INTERNATIONAL UNION
Also Called: Paper Alied Indus Chem & Enrgy
170 S Hickory St (45601-3336)
PHONE................................740 772-2038
Keith Staggs, President
EMP: 35
SALES (corp-wide): 26.9MM **Privately Held**
SIC: 8631 Labor unions & similar labor organizations
PA: Pace International Union
5 Gateway Ctr
Pittsburgh PA 15222
412 562-2400

(G-2811)
PETLAND INC (PA)
250 Riverside St (45601-2611)
P.O. Box 1606 (45601-5606)
PHONE................................740 775-2464
Edward R Kunzelman, President
Greg Hudson, COO
Rondon Bettin, Exec VP
Steve Huggins, Vice Pres
Kari Mercer, Project Mgr
EMP: 50
SQ FT: 40,000
SALES (est): 61.5MM **Privately Held**
WEB: www.petland.com
SIC: 5199 6794 Pet supplies; franchises, selling or licensing

(G-2812)
R L S CORPORATION
Also Called: R L S Recycling
990 Eastern Ave (45601-3658)
P.O. Box 327 (45601-0327)
PHONE................................740 773-1440
Charles Stevens, President
EMP: 25 EST: 1923
SQ FT: 14,000
SALES (est): 3.3MM **Privately Held**
SIC: 5093 3341 Metal scrap & waste materials; waste paper; secondary nonferrous metals

(G-2813)
RECORDING WORKSHOP
Also Called: Recording Workshop, The
455 Massieville Rd (45601-9395)
PHONE................................740 663-1000
William Joseph Waters, Owner
EMP: 30
SQ FT: 10,500
SALES (est): 1.6MM **Privately Held**
WEB: www.recordingworkshop.com
SIC: 8249 7389 Trade school; recording studio, noncommercial records

(G-2814)
REHABCARE GROUP MGT SVCS INC
230 Cherry St (45601-2301)
PHONE................................740 779-6732
EMP: 26
SALES (corp-wide): 6B **Privately Held**
SIC: 8093 Rehabilitation center, outpatient treatment
HQ: Rehabcare Group Mgt Svcs Inc
680 S 4th St
Louisville KY 40202
502 596-7300

(G-2815)
RLS DISPOSAL COMPANY INC
990 Eastern Ave (45601-3658)
PHONE................................740 773-1440
Charlies N Stevens, President
Vincent Stevens, Manager
EMP: 50
SALES: 950K **Privately Held**
SIC: 4953 Refuse systems

(G-2816)
RON NEFF REAL ESTATE (PA)
Also Called: Ron Neff Her Realtors
153 S Paint St (45601-3215)
PHONE................................740 773-4670
Ron Neff, Owner
EMP: 27
SQ FT: 2,500
SALES: 650K **Privately Held**
SIC: 6531 Real estate brokers & agents

(G-2817)
ROSS CNTY CMMITTEE FOR ELDERLY
Also Called: Senior Center
1824 Western Ave (45601-1036)
PHONE................................740 773-3544
Jodi Riley, Director
Janet Elliott, Director
EMP: 45 EST: 1975
SALES: 1.4MM **Privately Held**
SIC: 8322 Outreach program; referral service for personal & social problems

(G-2818)
ROSS COUNTY CHILDREN SVCS CTR (PA)
Also Called: Ross Cnty Job & Family Svcs
150 E 2nd St (45601-2525)
P.O. Box 469 (45601-0469)
PHONE................................740 773-2651
Robert Gallagher, CEO
Thomas E Williamson, Director
EMP: 100
SALES (est): 2.3MM **Privately Held**
SIC: 8322 Individual & family services

(G-2819)
ROSS COUNTY COMMUNITY (PA)
250 N Woodbridge Ave (45601-2245)
PHONE................................740 702-7222
Ed Alexinas, Principal
EMP: 75
SALES: 4.8MM **Privately Held**
WEB: www.rossccac.com
SIC: 8399 Community action agency

(G-2820)
ROSS COUNTY HEALTH DISTRICT
150 E 2nd St (45601-2295)
PHONE................................740 775-1114
Tyler Gillenwater, Manager
Wanda Medcalf, Director
Michelle Long, Asst Director
EMP: 133

SALES (est): 3.5MM **Privately Held**
SIC: 8082 Home health care services

(G-2821)
ROSS COUNTY SPORTSMEN AND WILD
550 Musselman Mill Rd (45601)
P.O. Box 102, Bourneville (45617-0102)
PHONE................................740 649-9614
George Lockard, President
Oscar Rhoades, Vice Pres
Gene Frasure, Treasurer
EMP: 25
SALES (est): 42.4K **Privately Held**
SIC: 8699 Membership organizations

(G-2822)
ROSS COUNTY WATER COMPANY INC
Also Called: RURAL WATER UTILITY
663 Fairgrounds Rd (45601-9715)
P.O. Box 1690 (45601-5690)
PHONE................................740 774-4117
Michael Riffle, President
William Neal, Corp Secy
Clyde Hawkins, Vice Pres
Clint Martz, Sls & Mktg Exec
EMP: 33
SQ FT: 3,000
SALES: 8MM **Privately Held**
WEB: www.rosscowater.org
SIC: 4941 Water supply

(G-2823)
ROSS COUNTY YMCA
100 Mill St (45601-1662)
PHONE................................740 772-4340
Terry Conrad, Facilities Dir
Debby White, Exec Dir
Samantha Daniels,
EMP: 65
SALES: 947K **Privately Held**
SIC: 8641 8611 8351 8661 Youth organizations; business associations; child day care services; religious organizations; individual & family services; physical fitness facilities

(G-2824)
RUMPKE/KENWORTH CONTRACT
Also Called: Kenworth Truck Co
65 Kenworth Dr (45601-8829)
PHONE................................740 774-5111
Judy Nctigue, Branch Mgr
▲ EMP: 69 EST: 2010
SALES (est): 46.7MM **Privately Held**
SIC: 5084 5511 Trucks, industrial; trucks, tractors & trailers: new & used

(G-2825)
SCIOTO PNT VLY MENTAL HLTH CTR (PA)
4449 State Route 159 (45601-8620)
P.O. Box 6179 (45601-6179)
PHONE................................740 775-1260
Gary Kreuchauf, Exec Dir
EMP: 220
SQ FT: 25,000
SALES: 14.2MM **Privately Held**
SIC: 8322 8093 General counseling services; mental health clinic, outpatient

(G-2826)
SIOTO PAINTSVILLE MENTAL HLTH
Also Called: Crisis Center
4449 State Route 159 (45601-8620)
P.O. Box 6179 (45601-6179)
PHONE................................740 775-1260
Ed Sythe, Director
Robyn Lett, Director
EMP: 26
SALES (est): 315.5K **Privately Held**
SIC: 8322 Crisis center

(G-2827)
SOUTHERN OHIO EYE ASSOC LLC (PA)
159 E 2nd St (45601-2526)
PHONE................................740 773-6347
Toll Free:................................888 -
Stephen Demick,
EMP: 42

SALES (est): 5.7MM **Privately Held**
SIC: 8011 Ophthalmologist

(G-2828)
SOUTHERN OHIO WNS CANCER PRJ
Also Called: Bccp
150 E 2nd St (45601-2525)
PHONE....................................740 775-7332
Timothy Angel, *Commissioner*
Jamie Eselgroth, *Commissioner*
Frank Hirsch, *Commissioner*
EMP: 100
SALES (est): 1.5MM **Privately Held**
SIC: 8011 Offices & clinics of medical doctors

(G-2829)
SPECTRUM MGT HOLDG CO LLC
Also Called: Time Warner
32 Enterprise Pl (45601-8600)
PHONE....................................740 762-0291
Jim Cavender, *Manager*
EMP: 83
SALES (corp-wide): 43.6B **Publicly Held**
SIC: 4841 Cable television services
HQ: Spectrum Management Holding Company, Llc
400 Atlantic St
Stamford CT 06901
203 905-7801

(G-2830)
SUNRUSH CONSTRUCTION CO INC (PA)
1988 Western Ave (45601-1048)
PHONE....................................740 775-1300
Greg Wells, *President*
Michael Long, *Vice Pres*
EMP: 30
SQ FT: 10,000
SALES (est): 7.2MM **Privately Held**
WEB: www.sunrushconstruction.com
SIC: 1541 1542 Industrial buildings, new construction; commercial & office building, new construction

(G-2831)
TRADITIONS OF CHILLICOTHE
Also Called: Assisted Living Facilities
142 University Dr Ofc (45601-2119)
PHONE....................................740 773-8107
Pat Nichols, *Director*
EMP: 30
SALES (est): 1.3MM **Privately Held**
WEB: www.traditionshealth.org
SIC: 8059 Nursing home, except skilled & intermediate care facility

(G-2832)
TRANSPORTATION OHIO DEPARTMENT
Also Called: State Highway Garage
255 Larrick Ln (45601-4067)
PHONE....................................740 773-3191
Aaron Mitten, *Director*
EMP: 30 **Privately Held**
SIC: 1611 9621 Highway & street maintenance; bureau of public roads
HQ: Ohio Department Of Transportation
1980 W Broad St
Columbus OH 43223

(G-2833)
UNITED PARCEL SERVICE INC
Also Called: UPS
1536 N Bridge St (45601-4104)
PHONE....................................800 742-5877
EMP: 38
SALES (corp-wide): 71.8B **Publicly Held**
SIC: 4215 Package delivery, vehicular; parcel delivery, vehicular
PA: United Parcel Service, Inc.
55 Glenlake Pkwy
Atlanta GA 30328
404 828-6000

(G-2834)
UNITED STEELWORKERS
Also Called: Uswa
196 Burbridge Ave (45601-3358)
PHONE....................................740 772-5988
James Bowers, *President*
EMP: 45

SALES (corp-wide): 4.9MM **Privately Held**
SIC: 8631 Labor union
PA: United Steelworkers
60 Bolevard Of The Allies
Pittsburgh PA 15222
412 562-2400

(G-2835)
VA MEDICAL CENTER AUTOMATED RE
17273 State Route 104 (45601-9718)
PHONE....................................740 772-7118
Sheila E Jordan, *Principal*
EMP: 31
SALES (est): 3.8MM **Privately Held**
SIC: 8062 General medical & surgical hospitals

(G-2836)
VETERANS HEALTH ADMINISTRATION
Also Called: Chillicothe VA Medical Center
17273 State Route 104 (45601-9718)
PHONE....................................740 773-1141
Kitty Hess, *Principal*
Gary Mack, *Principal*
Michael Murphy, *Principal*
John Tribuiano, *Principal*
Jack Wilkins, *Principal*
EMP: 1100 **Publicly Held**
WEB: www.veterans-ru.org
SIC: 8011 9451 Medical centers; psychiatric clinic;
HQ: Veterans Health Administration
810 Vermont Ave Nw
Washington DC 20420

(G-2837)
WHITED SEIGNEUR SAMS & RAHE
Also Called: Wssr Cpas
213 S Paint St (45601-3828)
PHONE....................................740 702-2600
Kathleen M Alderman, *Partner*
Nathan Baldwin, *Partner*
Barry Rhea, *Partner*
John Sams, *Partner*
Donald Seigneur, *Partner*
EMP: 25
SALES (est): 2MM **Privately Held**
WEB: www.wssrcpa.com
SIC: 8721 Certified public accountant

Chippewa Lake
Medina County

(G-2838)
THE OAKS LODGE
5878 Longacre Ln (44215-9778)
P.O. Box 32 (44215-0032)
PHONE....................................330 769-2601
Bonnie Druschel, *President*
Donald R Casper, *President*
EMP: 50 **EST:** 1949
SQ FT: 10,393
SALES: 1MM **Privately Held**
WEB: www.theoakslodge.com
SIC: 5812 5813 7299 Restaurant, family; independent; cocktail lounge; banquet hall facilities

---

Cincinnati
Clermont County

(G-2839)
5ME LLC
4270 Ivy Pointe Blvd # 100 (45245-0004)
PHONE....................................513 719-1600
William A Horwarth, *President*
Jeffery Price, *Vice Pres*
Chris Chapman, *CFO*
EMP: 45
SALES (est): 9.1MM
SALES (corp-wide): 9.9MM **Privately Held**
SIC: 3544 8742 Special dies, tools, jigs & fixtures; business consultant

PA: 5me Holdings Llc
4270 Ivy Pointe Blvd # 100
Cincinnati OH 45245
859 534-4872

(G-2840)
ABILITY NETWORK INC
4357 Ferguson Dr Ste 100 (45245-1684)
PHONE....................................513 943-8888
James Donaldson, *Principal*
EMP: 30
SALES (corp-wide): 449.3MM **Publicly Held**
SIC: 7376 6411 Computer facilities management; insurance agents, brokers & service
HQ: Ability Network Inc.
100 N 6th St Ste 900a
Minneapolis MN 55403
612 460-4301

(G-2841)
AMERATHON LLC (HQ)
671 Ohio Pike Ste K (45245-2136)
PHONE....................................513 752-7300
Debbie Martin, *President*
Christopher Martin, *Vice Pres*
Tom Kaylor, *CFO*
Jim Jackson, *Admin Sec*
EMP: 450 **EST:** 2014
SQ FT: 25,000
SALES: 82MM **Privately Held**
SIC: 8071 Ultrasound laboratory
PA: American Health Associates, Inc.
15712 Sw 41st St Ste 16
Davie FL 33331
954 919-5005

(G-2842)
BEECHMONT FORD INC (PA)
600 Ohio Pike (45245-2118)
PHONE....................................513 752-6611
Mark Williams, *President*
Dan Rapier, *Corp Secy*
Lorine Williams, *Vice Pres*
EMP: 120
SQ FT: 25,000
SALES (est): 54.8MM **Privately Held**
SIC: 5511 7538 7515 5531 Automobiles, new & used; pickups, new & used; vans, new & used; general automotive repair shops; passenger car leasing; automotive & home supply stores; motor vehicle supplies & new parts

(G-2843)
CGH-GLOBAL EMERG MNGMT STRATEG
Also Called: Cgh Global
851 Ohio Pike Ste 203 (45245-2203)
PHONE....................................800 376-0655
Andrew Glassmeyer, *CEO*
Eric Mitchell, *President*
EMP: 48 **EST:** 2011
SALES (est): 180.2K
SALES (corp-wide): 8MM **Privately Held**
SIC: 8711 8322 1389 0851 Fire protection engineering; emergency social services; fire fighting, oil & gas field; fire fighting services, forest; fire prevention services, forest
PA: Cgh-Global, Llc
851 Ohio Pike Ste 203
Cincinnati OH 45245
800 376-0655

(G-2844)
CHILDRENS HOSPITAL MEDICAL CTR
796 Cncnnati Batavia Pike (45245-1262)
PHONE....................................513 636-6036
Jean Kinman, *Branch Mgr*
EMP: 848
SALES (corp-wide): 1.6B **Privately Held**
SIC: 8069 Children's hospital
PA: Children's Hospital Medical Center
3333 Burnet Ave
Cincinnati OH 45229
513 636-4200

(G-2845)
CINCINNATI DENTAL SERVICES
4360 Ferguson Dr Ste 140 (45245-1683)
PHONE....................................513 753-6446
Sherry Gifford, *Branch Mgr*
EMP: 45

SALES (corp-wide): 5.5MM **Privately Held**
SIC: 8021 Dentists' office
PA: Cincinnati Dental Services Inc
121 E Mcmillan St
Cincinnati OH 45219
513 721-8888

(G-2846)
CLERMONT HILLS CO LLC
Also Called: Holiday Inn
4501 Eastgate Blvd (45245-1201)
PHONE....................................513 752-4400
Jacquie A Dowdy, *Mng Member*
Dennis Flannigan, *Director*
EMP: 80
SALES (est): 2.5MM **Privately Held**
SIC: 7011 Hotels & motels

(G-2847)
CURTISS-WRIGHT FLOW CONTROL
Also Called: Qualtech NP
4600 E Tech Dr (45245-1000)
PHONE....................................513 528-7900
Kurt Mitchell, *Branch Mgr*
EMP: 88
SALES (corp-wide): 2.4B **Publicly Held**
SIC: 3491 8734 3441 Industrial valves; testing laboratories; fabricated structural metal
HQ: Curtiss-Wright Flow Control Service Corporation
2950 E Birch St
Brea CA 92821
714 982-1898

(G-2848)
CURTISS-WRIGHT FLOW CTRL CORP
Also Called: Qualtech NP
4600 E Tech Dr (45245-1000)
PHONE....................................513 528-7900
Wayne Laib, *Chief Engr*
David Holmes, *Controller*
Marion Mitchell, *Branch Mgr*
Michael Bell, *Supervisor*
Brett Runyon, *Administration*
EMP: 82
SALES (corp-wide): 2.4B **Publicly Held**
SIC: 3443 8734 Fabricated plate work (boiler shop); testing laboratories
HQ: Curtiss-Wright Flow Control Service, Llc
1966 Broadhollow Rd Ste E
Farmingdale NY 11735
631 293-3800

(G-2849)
DAVID M SCHNEIDER MD INC (PA)
Also Called: Midwest Eye Center
4452 Estgate Blvd Ste 305 (45245)
PHONE....................................513 752-5700
David M Schneider MD, *President*
Holly Schwab, *Nursing Dir*
Annie Taylor, *Nursing Dir*
Susan O'Neill, *Executive*
EMP: 33
SALES (est): 6.4MM **Privately Held**
SIC: 8011 Medical Doctor's Office

(G-2850)
EASTGATE HEALTH CARE CENTER
Also Called: CARESPRING
4400 Glen Este Withamsvil (45245)
PHONE....................................513 752-3710
Henry Schneider, *President*
Barry Bortz, *Vice Pres*
EMP: 211
SQ FT: 87,000
SALES: 18.4MM
SALES (corp-wide): 97.1MM **Privately Held**
WEB: www.carespring.com
SIC: 8051 Skilled nursing care facilities
PA: Carespring Health Care Management, Llc
390 Wards Corner Rd
Loveland OH 45140
513 943-4000

(G-2851)
EASTGATE PROFESSIONAL OFF PK V
4357 Ferguson Dr Ste 220 (45245-1689)
PHONE....................513 943-0050
EMP: 25
SALES (est): 793.3K **Privately Held**
SIC: 6531 Real Estate Agent/Manager

(G-2852)
EASTGATE VILLAGE
776 Cincinnati Batavia Pi (45245-1260)
PHONE....................513 753-4400
Oscar Jarnicki, *President*
EMP: 40
SQ FT: 500,000
SALES (est): 2.2MM **Privately Held**
WEB: www.eastgatevillage.com
SIC: 8361 Home for the aged

(G-2853)
GENERAL DATA COMPANY INC (PA)
4354 Ferguson Dr (45245-1667)
P.O. Box 541165 (45254-1165)
PHONE....................513 752-7978
Peter Wenzel, *President*
Jim Burns, *Vice Pres*
Tom Maue, *Safety Mgr*
Amy Clark, *Purchasing*
Rhonda Utley, *Purchasing*
▲ EMP: 230 EST: 1980
SQ FT: 45,000
SALES (est): 62.5MM **Privately Held**
WEB: www.general-data.com
SIC: 2679 5046 5084 2759 Labels, paper: made from purchased material; commercial equipment; printing trades machinery, equipment & supplies; commercial printing; surgical & medical instruments; unsupported plastics film & sheet

(G-2854)
GENERAL FNCL TAX CNSULTING LLC
1004 Seabrook Way (45245-1963)
P.O. Box 541032 (45254-1032)
PHONE....................888 496-2679
Sarah Gelter, *COO*
Mike Cunningham, *Exec VP*
Jessica Brown, *Senior VP*
Jason Walter, *Senior VP*
Richard Cunnigham, *Senior VP*
EMP: 32 EST: 2009
SALES (est): 2MM **Privately Held**
SIC: 8742 Financial consultant

(G-2855)
JEFF WYLER AUTOMOTIVE FMLY INC (PA)
Also Called: Wyler, Jeff, Dealer Group
829 Eastgate South Dr (45245)
PHONE....................513 752-7450
Jeff Wyler, *CEO*
Jeff Scheper, *General Mgr*
Robbie Graybeal, *Parts Mgr*
Jon Bowman, *CFO*
Kathy Roberts, *Human Res Dir*
EMP: 26
SQ FT: 4,400
SALES (est): 7.8MM **Privately Held**
SIC: 8741 5511 Business management; new & used car dealers

(G-2856)
JEFF WYLER FT THOMAS INC
829 Eastgate South Dr (45245-1547)
PHONE....................513 752-7450
Jeffrey L Wyler, *Principal*
EMP: 80
SALES (est): 1.3MM **Privately Held**
SIC: 7532 Body shop, automotive

(G-2857)
JENKINS ENTERPRISES LLC
Also Called: Janiking
849 Locust Corner Rd (45245-3111)
PHONE....................513 752-7896
Pat Jenkins, *President*
EMP: 50
SALES (est): 1.3MM **Privately Held**
SIC: 7349 Janitorial service, contract basis

(G-2858)
JOE DODGE KIDD INC
1065 Ohio Pike (45245-2329)
PHONE....................513 752-1804
Ron Kidd, *CEO*
Trudi Schwarz, *Corp Secy*
EMP: 39 EST: 1978
SQ FT: 20,000
SALES (est): 13.8MM **Privately Held**
WEB: www.joekidddodge.com
SIC: 5511 7538 7532 7515 Automobiles, new & used; general automotive repair shops; top & body repair & paint shops; passenger car leasing; automotive & home supply stores

(G-2859)
KGBO HOLDINGS INC (PA)
4289 Ivy Pointe Blvd (45245-0002)
P.O. Box 799, Milford (45150-0799)
PHONE....................513 831-2600
Kenneth Oaks, *President*
Kate Lucas Stump, *Controller*
EMP: 27
SQ FT: 100,000
SALES: 2.9B **Privately Held**
WEB: www.totalqualitylogistics.com
SIC: 4731 Truck transportation brokers

(G-2860)
LNS AMERICA INC (DH)
4621 E Tech Dr (45245-1044)
PHONE....................513 528-5674
Jeff McMullen, *CEO*
Andrew Valerius, *Controller*
▲ EMP: 63
SQ FT: 52,000
SALES (est): 29.1MM **Privately Held**
SIC: 5084 Industrial machinery & equipment
HQ: Lns Sa
Route De Frinvillier
Orvin BE
323 580-200

(G-2861)
LOWES HOME CENTERS LLC
618 Mount Moriah Dr (45245-2113)
PHONE....................513 753-5094
Mark Houndshed, *Manager*
EMP: 300
SQ FT: 1,753
SALES (corp-wide): 68.6B **Publicly Held**
SIC: 5211 5031 5722 5064 Home centers; building materials, exterior; building materials, interior; household appliance stores; electrical appliances, television & radio
HQ: Lowe's Home Centers, Llc
1605 Curtis Bridge Rd
Wilkesboro NC 28697
336 658-4000

(G-2862)
NATIONWIDE CHILDRENS HOSPITAL
796 Old State Route 74 # 200 (45245-1262)
PHONE....................513 636-6000
Donna Kinnemeyer, *Manager*
EMP: 473
SALES (corp-wide): 2.3B **Privately Held**
SIC: 8062 General medical & surgical hospitals
PA: Nationwide Children's Hospital
700 Childrens Dr
Columbus OH 43205
614 722-2000

(G-2863)
ORTHOPEDIC CONS CINCINNATI
4440 Glnste Wthmsville Rd (45245-1318)
PHONE....................513 753-7488
Robert S Hiedt Sr, *President*
EMP: 30
SALES (corp-wide): 16.7MM **Privately Held**
SIC: 8011 Orthopedic physician
PA: Orthopedic Consultants Of Cincinnati
4701 Creek Rd Ste 110
Blue Ash OH 45242
513 733-8894

(G-2864)
PEDIATRICS ASSOC OF MT CARMEL
4371 Ferguson Dr (45245-1668)
PHONE....................513 752-3650
Robert Carson MD, *Principal*
Helene Blitzer, *Principal*
Emanuel O Doyne, *Principal*
Cathryn Yost, *Principal*
Christopher Peltier, *Pediatrics*
EMP: 30 EST: 1973
SQ FT: 1,040
SALES (est): 4MM **Privately Held**
SIC: 8011 Pediatrician

(G-2865)
PETSMART INC
650 Eastgate South Dr B (45245-1772)
PHONE....................513 752-8463
Scott King, *Manager*
EMP: 28
SALES (corp-wide): 12.1B **Privately Held**
WEB: www.petsmart.com
SIC: 5999 0752 Pet food; animal specialty services
HQ: Petsmart, Inc.
19601 N 27th Ave
Phoenix AZ 85027
623 580-6100

(G-2866)
PRESSLEY RIDGE FOUNDATION
4355 Ferguson Dr Ste 125 (45245-5149)
PHONE....................513 752-4548
Matthew Mitchell, *Branch Mgr*
EMP: 584 **Privately Held**
SIC: 8322 Individual & family services
PA: Pressley Ridge Foundation
5500 Corporate Dr Ste 400
Pittsburgh PA 15237

(G-2867)
SCHNELLER HEATING AND AC CO
1079 Ohio Pike (45245-2339)
PHONE....................859 341-1200
Kris Knochelmann, *President*
Jacob C Grisham, *President*
Chris Knochelmann, *President*
Clay Hager, *Train & Dev Mgr*
Jeremy Lee, *Sales Staff*
EMP: 25
SQ FT: 4,500
SALES (est): 3.9MM **Privately Held**
WEB: www.schnellerheating.com
SIC: 1711 Warm air heating & air conditioning contractor

(G-2868)
SIBCY CLINE INC
792 Eastgate South Dr # 800 (45245-1563)
PHONE....................513 752-4000
Lori Schlagheck, *Financial Exec*
Mary Stone, *Manager*
EMP: 45
SALES (corp-wide): 2.1B **Privately Held**
WEB: www.sibcycline.com
SIC: 6531 Real estate agent, residential; real estate brokers & agents
PA: Sibcy Cline, Inc.
8044 Montgomery Rd # 300
Cincinnati OH 45236
513 984-4100

(G-2869)
SPIRIT WOMEN HEALTH NETWRK LLC
Also Called: Spirit Health
4270 Ivy Pointe Blvd # 220 (45245-0003)
PHONE....................561 544-2004
Tanya Abreau,
Sharon Bittner,
Joshua Max Davis,
EMP: 30 EST: 2006
SALES (est): 3.3MM **Privately Held**
SIC: 8742 Hospital & health services consultant

(G-2870)
STEWART ADVNCED LAND TITLE LTD (PA)
792 Eastgate South Dr (45245-1592)
PHONE....................513 753-2800
Gregory Traynor,
EMP: 37

SALES (est): 6.5MM **Privately Held**
SIC: 6361 Title insurance

(G-2871)
SURGERY CENTER CINCINNATI LLC
4415 Aicholtz Rd (45245-1506)
PHONE....................513 947-1130
Nestor Aquino,
Sabino Baluyout Et Al,
Rolando Go,
Hari Kothegal,
Michael Maggio,
EMP: 100
SALES (est): 4.5MM **Privately Held**
WEB: www.phcps.com
SIC: 8011 Surgeon

(G-2872)
THARALDSON HOSPITALITY MGT
Also Called: Fairfield Inn
4521 Eastgate Blvd (45245-1201)
PHONE....................513 947-9402
Joyce Jabornick, *Manager*
EMP: 25 **Privately Held**
SIC: 7011 Inns
PA: Tharaldson Hospitality Management
1201 Page Dr S Ste 200
Fargo ND 58103

(G-2873)
TOTAL QUALITY LOGISTICS LLC (HQ)
Also Called: Tql
4289 Ivy Pointe Blvd (45245-0002)
P.O. Box 799, Milford (45150-0799)
PHONE....................513 831-2600
Kenneth G Oaks, *CEO*
Kerry Bryne, *President*
Kate Lucas Stump, *Controller*
Zachary Stephenson, *Marketing Staff*
EMP: 264
SQ FT: 100,000
SALES (est): 2.6B
SALES (corp-wide): 2.9B **Privately Held**
WEB: www.totalqualitylogistics.com
SIC: 4731 Truck transportation brokers
PA: Kgbo Holdings, Inc
4289 Ivy Pointe Blvd
Cincinnati OH 45245
513 831-2600

(G-2874)
VERITAS ENTERPRISES INC
918 Tall Trees Dr (45245-1158)
PHONE....................513 578-2748
Richard Cox, *President*
EMP: 26
SALES: 1.1MM **Privately Held**
SIC: 5021 4212 5149 Furniture; delivery service, vehicular; sandwiches

(G-2875)
WILLIS ONE HOUR HEATING & AC
756 Cncnnati Batavia Pike (45245-1276)
PHONE....................513 752-2512
Joseph Gertz, *General Mgr*
EMP: 75
SALES (est): 5MM **Privately Held**
SIC: 1711 Warm air heating & air conditioning contractor

Cincinnati
Hamilton County

(G-2876)
16 BIT BAR
1331 Walnut St (45202-7120)
PHONE....................513 381-1616
Mike Bowling, *General Mgr*
EMP: 45
SALES (est): 65.6K **Privately Held**
SIC: 7993 5813 Arcades; tavern (drinking places)

(G-2877)
1ST CHOICE SECURITY INC
2245 Gilbert Ave Ste 400 (45206-3000)
PHONE....................513 381-6789
Alan Grissinger, *President*

EMP: 175
SQ FT: 1,200
SALES: 4MM **Privately Held**
SIC: 7381 Security guard service

(G-2878)
2060 DIGITAL LLC
2060 Reading Rd (45202-1454)
PHONE....................................513 699-5012
James Bryant, *President*
Andy Shepherd, *Director*
EMP: 41
SALES (est): 1.4MM **Privately Held**
SIC: 8742 Marketing consulting services

(G-2879)
21C CINCINNATI LLC
Also Called: 21c Museum Hotel Cincinnati
609 Walnut St Ste 2 (45202-1191)
PHONE....................................513 578-6600
Gerry Link Cha, *General Mgr*
Laura Lee Brown,
Steve Wilson,
EMP: 54
SALES (est): 5.2MM **Privately Held**
SIC: 7011 Hotel, franchised; hotels

(G-2880)
2444 MDSON RD CNDO OWNERS ASSN
Also Called: Regency, The
2444 Madison Rd Ste 101 (45208-1278)
PHONE....................................513 871-0100
Mary Lawson, *President*
James R Schafer, *General Mgr*
Anita Saylor, *Accountant*
EMP: 30
SALES: 300K **Privately Held**
WEB: www.homebuildingpitfalls.com
SIC: 8641 Condominium association

(G-2881)
2780 AIRPORT DRIVE LLC
2135 Dana Ave Ste 200 (45207-1327)
PHONE....................................513 563-7555
Jeff Tell, *CFO*
William Sayer, *Clerk*
EMP: 30 **EST:** 2015
SQ FT: 104,069
SALES (est): 437.2K **Privately Held**
SIC: 6531 Real estate agents & managers

(G-2882)
36 E SEVENTH LLC
2135 Dana Ave Ste 200 (45207-1327)
PHONE....................................513 699-2279
Will Sayer, *Clerk*
EMP: 30 **EST:** 2016
SALES (est): 480.9K **Privately Held**
SIC: 6531 Real estate agents & managers

(G-2883)
506 PHELPS HOLDINGS LLC
Also Called: Residnce Inn Cincinnati Dwntwn
506 E 4th St (45202-3303)
PHONE....................................513 651-1234
John Slaboch, *Vice Pres*
EMP: 42
SALES (est): 3.3MM **Privately Held**
SIC: 7011 Hotels

(G-2884)
6300 SHARONVILLE ASSOC LLC
Also Called: Doubletree Hotel
6300 E Kemper Rd (45241-2360)
PHONE....................................513 489-3636
David Sundermann, *Principal*
EMP: 182
SALES (est): 5.1MM **Privately Held**
WEB: www.dtwarrenplace.com
SIC: 7011 Hotels & motels

(G-2885)
722 REDEMPTION FUNDING INC
Also Called: Newstart Loan , The
169 Northland Blvd Ste 2 (45246-3154)
PHONE....................................513 679-8302
Stan Zappin, *President*
Greg Sweeny, *Chairman*
Steven Elmer, *Counsel*
Bob Freppon, *CFO*
Jake Sweeney, *Shareholder*
EMP: 35
SQ FT: 3,000

SALES: 22MM **Privately Held**
WEB: www.722redemption.com
SIC: 6141 Financing: automobiles, furniture, etc., not a deposit bank

(G-2886)
8451 LLC (HQ)
100 W 5th St (45202-2704)
PHONE....................................513 632-1020
Simon Hay, *CEO*
Bob Bo Mihalovich, *Director*
EMP: 124
SQ FT: 40,000
SALES (est): 61.3MM
SALES (corp-wide): 121.1B **Publicly Held**
WEB: www.dunnhumby.com
SIC: 8732 Market analysis or research
PA: The Kroger Co
1014 Vine St Ste 1000
Cincinnati OH 45202
513 762-4000

(G-2887)
A & A WALL SYSTEMS INC
11589 Deerfield Rd (45242-1419)
PHONE....................................513 489-0086
Michele McIntyre, *President*
Dale Adkins, *Vice Pres*
EMP: 45
SQ FT: 6,000
SALES (est): 7.4MM **Privately Held**
SIC: 1542 Commercial & office building, new construction; commercial & office buildings, renovation & repair

(G-2888)
A AND A MLLWRIGHT RIGGING SVCS
2205 Langdon Farm Rd (45237-4712)
PHONE....................................513 396-6212
Clifford Applegate, *President*
EMP: 50
SQ FT: 28,959
SALES (est): 2MM **Privately Held**
SIC: 1796 7353 7699 Machinery installation; millwright; machine moving & rigging; cranes & aerial lift equipment, rental or leasing; industrial machinery & equipment repair

(G-2889)
A BETTER CHILD CARE CORP
6945 Harrison Ave (45247-3205)
PHONE....................................513 353-5437
Alice Osborne, *Manager*
EMP: 25 **EST:** 2009
SALES (est): 357.9K **Privately Held**
SIC: 8351 Preschool center

(G-2890)
A C LEASING COMPANY
Also Called: A C Trucking
3023 E Kemper Rd Bldg 9 (45241-1509)
PHONE....................................513 771-3676
Joseph Zembrodt, *President*
John Zembrodt, *Treasurer*
Rob Schutzman, *Controller*
EMP: 42
SQ FT: 525,000
SALES (est): 6MM **Privately Held**
WEB: www.acleasing.net
SIC: 4214 4213 Local trucking with storage; trucking, except local

(G-2891)
A CCS DAY CARE CENTERS INC
1705 Section Rd (45237-3313)
PHONE....................................513 841-2227
Jamica Thomas, *President*
Derek Edwards, *General Mgr*
EMP: 28 **EST:** 2013
SALES (est): 156.9K **Privately Held**
SIC: 8351 Group day care center

(G-2892)
A ONE FINE DRY CLEANERS INC (PA)
6223 Montgomery Rd (45213-1403)
PHONE....................................513 351-2663
Mark Folzenlogen, *President*
EMP: 65
SALES (est): 1.8MM **Privately Held**
WEB: www.a-onecleaners.com
SIC: 7216 Cleaning & dyeing, except rugs

(G-2893)
A-1 QUALITY LABOR SERVICES LLC
3055 Blue Rock Rd (45239-6302)
PHONE....................................513 353-0173
William J Foster III,
EMP: 25
SALES (est): 450K **Privately Held**
SIC: 4491 Marine cargo handling

(G-2894)
AAA ALLIED GROUP INC (PA)
Also Called: World Wide Travel Service
15 W Central Pkwy (45202-1005)
PHONE....................................513 762-3301
James L Pease III, *President*
Johnathan Morley, *Exec VP*
Mike Hughes, *Project Mgr*
Michele Deutsch, *Sales Staff*
Karen Collins, *Property Mgr*
EMP: 300 **EST:** 1901
SQ FT: 50,000
SALES (est): 142.4MM **Privately Held**
WEB: www.aaacincinnati.com
SIC: 4724 8699 Travel agencies; automobile owners' association

(G-2895)
AAA CINCINNATI INSURANCE SVC
15 W Central Pkwy (45202-1005)
PHONE....................................513 345-5600
David Mc Millon, *President*
EMP: 30
SALES: 184.7K **Privately Held**
SIC: 6411 Insurance agents

(G-2896)
ABCO FIRE LLC
Also Called: Abco Fire Protection
510 W Benson St (45215-3106)
PHONE....................................800 875-7200
Meghan Cunningham, *Manager*
EMP: 46
SALES (corp-wide): 14.2MM **Privately Held**
SIC: 5099 7389 Safety equipment & supplies; fire extinguisher servicing
HQ: Abco Fire, Llc
4545 W 160th St
Cleveland OH 44135
216 433-7200

(G-2897)
ABM AVIATION INC
790 Grenoble Ct (45255-4540)
PHONE....................................859 767-7507
Bill Ray, *General Mgr*
EMP: 400
SALES (corp-wide): 6.4B **Publicly Held**
SIC: 4581 Airport
HQ: Abm Aviation, Inc.
3399 Peachtree Rd Ne
Atlanta GA 30326
404 926-4200

(G-2898)
ABM FACILITY SERVICES INC
Also Called: ABM Engineering
3087 B Terminal Dr (45275)
P.O. Box 75338 (45275-0338)
PHONE....................................859 767-4393
EMP: 36
SALES (corp-wide): 6.4B **Publicly Held**
SIC: 7349 Building maintenance services
HQ: Abm Facility Services, Inc.
1266 14th St Ste 103
Oakland CA 94607

(G-2899)
ABM JANITORIAL SERVICES INC
354 Gest St (45203-1822)
PHONE....................................513 731-1418
Brian Planicka, *Manager*
EMP: 105
SALES (corp-wide): 6.4B **Publicly Held**
SIC: 7349 Janitorial service, contract basis
HQ: Abm Janitorial Services, Inc.
1111 Fannin St Ste 1500
Houston TX 77002
713 654-8924

(G-2900)
ACCENTURE LLP
201 E 4th St Ste 1600 (45202-4249)
PHONE....................................513 455-1000
David Zalla, *Partner*
Nathan Beadle, *Manager*
Sameer Thakur, *Analyst*
EMP: 62 **Privately Held**
WEB: www.wavesecurities.com
SIC: 8742 Business consultant; business planning & organizing services
HQ: Accenture Llp
161 N Clark St Ste 1100
Chicago IL 60601
312 693-0161

(G-2901)
ACCENTURE LLP
425 Walnut St Ste 1200 (45202-3928)
PHONE....................................513 651-2444
Edward Harbach, *Branch Mgr*
EMP: 85 **Privately Held**
SIC: 8742 Business consultant
HQ: Accenture Llp
161 N Clark St Ste 1100
Chicago IL 60601
312 693-0161

(G-2902)
ACCOUNTANTS TO YOU LLC
Also Called: Consultants To You
430 Reading Rd Ste 100 (45202-1477)
PHONE....................................513 651-2855
EMP: 35
SALES (est): 2MM **Privately Held**
SIC: 7361 Employment Agency

(G-2903)
ACE DORAN HAULING & RIGGING CO
1601 Blue Rock St (45223-2579)
PHONE....................................513 681-7900
Daniel J Doran, *President*
EMP: 60
SQ FT: 3,000
SALES (est): 13.1MM **Privately Held**
SIC: 4213 Trucking, except local
HQ: Bennett Motor Express, Llc
1001 Industrial Pkwy
Mcdonough GA 30253
770 957-1866

(G-2904)
ACE-MERIT LLC
30 Garfield Pl Ste 540 (45202-4366)
PHONE....................................513 241-3200
Alicia Hardin,
Angelia Portune,
EMP: 30
SQ FT: 3,000
SALES: 2.2MM **Privately Held**
WEB: www.acemerit.com
SIC: 7338 Court reporting service

(G-2905)
ACS ACQCO CORP
201 E 4th St Ste 900 (45202-4160)
PHONE....................................513 719-2600
Elizabeth A Haley, *President*
EMP: 126 **EST:** 2014
SALES (est): 342.8K
SALES (corp-wide): 194.5B **Publicly Held**
SIC: 5122 Drugs, proprietaries & sundries
HQ: Omnicare, Inc.
900 Omnicare Ctr 201e4t
Cincinnati OH 45202
513 719-2600

(G-2906)
ACUREN INSPECTION INC
502 W Crescentville Rd (45246-1222)
PHONE....................................513 671-7073
Mike Ross, *District Mgr*
EMP: 27
SALES (corp-wide): 1.6B **Privately Held**
SIC: 8734 Testing laboratories
HQ: Acuren Inspection, Inc.
30 Main St Ste 402
Danbury CT 06810
203 702-8740

▲ = Import ▼=Export
◆ =Import/Export

(G-2907)
ADDICTION SERVICES COUNCIL
Also Called: CASA
2828 Vernon Pl (45219-2414)
PHONE..................................513 281-7880
Nan Franks, *CEO*
Daina Dennis, *COO*
EMP: 32
SQ FT: 4,000
SALES: 2.2MM **Privately Held**
WEB: www.alcoholismcouncil.org
SIC: 8322 Alcoholism counseling, nontreatment; drug abuse counselor, nontreatment

(G-2908)
ADLETA INC
Also Called: Adleta Construction
389 S Wayne Ave (45215-4522)
PHONE..................................513 554-1469
Robert Adleta Sr, *President*
Robert Adleta II, *Vice Pres*
Tim Adleta, *Vice Pres*
Bob Dunn, *Vice Pres*
Mary Lee Holthous, *Admin Sec*
EMP: 35
SQ FT: 2,000
SALES (est): 6.9MM **Privately Held**
SIC: 1771 1623 Concrete work; sewer line construction

(G-2909)
ADVANCE IMPLANT DENTISTRY INC
5823 Wooster Pike (45227-4505)
PHONE..................................513 271-0821
Scott E Sayre, *President*
Janet Sayre, *Vice Pres*
Clay Griffith, *Mktg Dir*
Robert Buechner, *Admin Sec*
EMP: 40
SQ FT: 1,600
SALES (est): 3.3MM **Privately Held**
WEB: www.advanced-dentistry.net
SIC: 8021 Dentists' office

(G-2910)
ADVANCE TRNSP SYSTEMS INC
Also Called: Ats Transportation Services
10558 Taconic Ter (45215-1125)
PHONE..................................513 818-4311
Robert L Wyenandt, *President*
EMP: 25
SQ FT: 10,000
SALES: 50MM **Privately Held**
WEB: www.atslogistics.com
SIC: 4731 Truck transportation brokers

(G-2911)
ADVANTAGE HUMAN RESOURCING INC (DH)
Also Called: Advantage Staffing
201 E 4th St Ste 800 (45202-4248)
PHONE..................................318 324-8060
Toshio Oka, *CEO*
Hitoshi Motohara, *Ch of Bd*
Mark Marheineke, *President*
Reiki Muratake, *CFO*
EMP: 60
SALES (est): 226.3MM
SALES (corp-wide): 20.4B **Privately Held**
SIC: 7363 Temporary help service

(G-2912)
ADVANTAGE RESOURCING AMER INC (HQ)
Also Called: Advantage Staffing
201 E 4th St Ste 800 (45202-4248)
PHONE..................................781 472-8900
Stacey Lane, *Exec VP*
Erin Kamenoff, *Senior VP*
Tom Schmidt, *Senior VP*
Matt Anderson, *Vice Pres*
Judy Culpepper, *Vice Pres*
EMP: 30
SALES (est): 631.1MM
SALES (corp-wide): 20.4B **Privately Held**
SIC: 7361 Labor contractors (employment agency)
PA: Recruit Holdings Co.,Ltd.
    1-9-2, Marunouchi
    Chiyoda-Ku TKY 100-0
    368 351-111

(G-2913)
ADVANTAGE TCHNCAL RSURCING INC
201 E 4th St Ste 800 (45202-4248)
PHONE..................................513 651-1111
Geno Cutolo, *CEO*
Hitoshi Motohara, *Chairman*
Jennifer Prospero, *CFO*
Michael Whitmer, *CIO*
Paula McMahon, *Technology*
EMP: 500
SALES (est): 47MM
SALES (corp-wide): 20.4B **Privately Held**
SIC: 7363 Help supply services
HQ: Advantage Resourcing America, Inc.
    201 E 4th St Ste 800
    Cincinnati OH 45202

(G-2914)
AECOM
525 Vine St Ste 1800 (45202-3142)
PHONE..................................513 651-3440
Perry Sole, *Branch Mgr*
Casey Oakes, *Admin Asst*
EMP: 60
SALES (corp-wide): 20.1B **Publicly Held**
SIC: 8748 Environmental consultant
PA: Aecom
    1999 Avenue Of The Stars # 2600
    Los Angeles CA 90067
    213 593-8000

(G-2915)
AFFINITY DISP EXPOSITIONS INC
Also Called: Adex International
1301 Glendale Milford Rd (45215-1210)
PHONE..................................513 771-2339
Tim Murphy, *President*
EMP: 110
SALES (corp-wide): 24.3MM **Privately Held**
WEB: www.adex-intl.com
SIC: 7389 Trade show arrangement
PA: Affinity Displays & Expositions, Inc.
    1301 Glendale Milford Rd
    Cincinnati OH 45215
    513 771-2339

(G-2916)
AIRGAS USA LLC
Also Called: Linde Gas
10031 Cncnnati Dyton Pike (45241-1003)
PHONE..................................513 563-8070
Hal Magers, *Branch Mgr*
EMP: 35
SALES (corp-wide): 125.9MM **Privately Held**
WEB: www.us.linde-gas.com
SIC: 5084 5169 Welding machinery & equipment; chemicals & allied products
HQ: Airgas Usa, Llc
    259 N Radnor Chester Rd # 100
    Radnor PA 19087
    610 687-5253

(G-2917)
AL NEYER LLC (PA)
302 W 3rd St Ste 800 (45202-3426)
PHONE..................................513 271-6400
Molly North, *President*
Rob Marks, *Sr Project Mgr*
Kathy Feller, *Payroll Mgr*
Collin Dekker, *Manager*
David Neyer,
EMP: 56
SQ FT: 22,570
SALES (est): 9.1MM **Privately Held**
SIC: 6531 Real estate managers

(G-2918)
AL NEYER LLC
302 W 3rd St Ste 800 (45202-3426)
PHONE..................................513 271-6400
Molly North, *President*
David F Neyer, *President*
William L Neyer, *Exec VP*
Cassie J Belmonte, *Vice Pres*
James T Neyer, *Vice Pres*
EMP: 80
SQ FT: 17,837

SALES (est): 15MM **Privately Held**
WEB: www.neyer.com
SIC: 6552 1522 1541 1542 Land subdividers & developers, commercial; land subdividers & developers, residential; multi-family dwelling construction; industrial buildings & warehouses; commercial & office building contractors

(G-2919)
ALBERT MIKE LEASING INC (PA)
10340 Evendale Dr (45241-2512)
PHONE..................................513 563-1400
Robert Betagole, *CEO*
Marty Betagole, *President*
Jason Henning, *Business Mgr*
Nate Shadoin, *Business Mgr*
W Patrick Stull, *COO*
▼ EMP: 169
SQ FT: 56,000
SALES (est): 36.1MM **Privately Held**
WEB: www.cvgrentacar.com
SIC: 7515 7513 5521 5012 Passenger car leasing; truck leasing, without drivers; automobiles, used cars only; trucks, tractors & trailers: used; automobiles; trucks, noncommercial; automotive & home supply stores; new & used car dealers

(G-2920)
ALEXANDER & ASSOCIATES CO (PA)
360 Mclean Dr (45237-1643)
PHONE..................................513 731-7800
Thomas Luebbe, *President*
Thomas Rowe, *Vice Pres*
Russ Miller, *Manager*
Bob Stock, *Manager*
Tom Rowe, *Technology*
EMP: 130
SQ FT: 15,000
SALES (est): 28.1MM **Privately Held**
WEB: www.alexanderandassoc.com
SIC: 8711 Consulting engineer

(G-2921)
ALL ABOUT HEATING COOLING
7861 Palace Dr (45249-1635)
PHONE..................................513 621-4620
DOT Braun, *Owner*
EMP: 30 EST: 2012
SALES (est): 901.6K **Privately Held**
SIC: 1711 Warm air heating & air conditioning contractor

(G-2922)
ALL OCCASIONS EVENT RENTAL
10629 Reading Rd (45241-2526)
PHONE..................................513 563-0600
Elizabeth Wilson, *President*
Eric Easterling, *Manager*
Brittany Koulias, *Consultant*
Kristen Mueller, *Consultant*
Matthew Brown, *Asst Mgr*
EMP: 25 EST: 1996
SALES (est): 4.7MM **Privately Held**
SIC: 7359 Party supplies rental services

(G-2923)
ALLAN PEACE & ASSOCIATES INC
Also Called: C A I Insurance Agency
2035 Reading Rd (45202-1415)
PHONE..................................513 579-1700
Carl Schloteman, *President*
EMP: 40
SALES (est): 3MM **Privately Held**
WEB: www.allanpeace.com
SIC: 6411 Insurance agents

(G-2924)
ALLCAN GLOBAL SERVICES INC (PA)
11235 Sebring Dr (45240-2714)
PHONE..................................513 825-1655
Anthony Lacey, *CEO*
EMP: 48
SQ FT: 50,000
SALES (est): 3MM **Privately Held**
SIC: 1731 8741 7361 Electrical work; management services; placement agencies

(G-2925)
ALLGEIER & SON INC (PA)
6386 Bridgetown Rd (45248-2933)
PHONE..................................513 574-3735
Michael Allgeier, *Owner*
Margaret A Steigerwald, *Treasurer*
EMP: 40
SQ FT: 800
SALES (est): 5MM **Privately Held**
SIC: 1794 1422 1795 Excavation & grading, building construction; crushed & broken limestone; wrecking & demolition work

(G-2926)
ALLIED BUILDING PRODUCTS CORP
1735 Eastern Ave (45202-1710)
PHONE..................................513 784-9090
Jim Francis, *Manager*
Tom Morrison, *Manager*
EMP: 25
SQ FT: 20,000
SALES (corp-wide): 4.3B **Publicly Held**
WEB: www.alliedbuilding.com
SIC: 5033 5031 Roofing & siding materials; windows
HQ: Allied Building Products Corp.
    15 E Union Ave
    East Rutherford NJ 07073
    201 507-8400

(G-2927)
ALLIED CAR WASH INC
Also Called: AAA Auto Wash
3330 Central Pkwy (45225-2307)
PHONE..................................513 559-1733
Emina Short, *Finance Dir*
EMP: 45
SALES (est): 177.2K **Privately Held**
SIC: 7542 Carwash, automatic

(G-2928)
ALLIED CASH HOLDINGS LLC (PA)
Also Called: Allied Cash Advance
7755 Montgomery Rd # 400 (45236-4197)
PHONE..................................305 371-3141
David Davis, *President*
Douglas Clark, *Vice Pres*
Roger Dean, *CFO*
Stephen Schaller, *Admin Sec*
Tracy Parks,
EMP: 58
SQ FT: 5,400
SALES (est): 138.4MM **Privately Held**
SIC: 6099 Check cashing agencies

(G-2929)
ALLIED SECURITY LLC
110 Boggs Ln Ste 140 (45246-3143)
PHONE..................................513 771-3776
Derrick Newman, *Client Mgr*
Tim Cember, *Manager*
EMP: 430
SALES (corp-wide): 13.5MM **Privately Held**
WEB: www.alliedsecurity.com
SIC: 7381 Security guard service
HQ: Allied Security, Llc
    161 Washington St
    Conshohocken PA 19428
    610 239-1100

(G-2930)
ALMOST FAMILY INC
2135 Dana Ave Ste 220 (45207-1342)
PHONE..................................513 662-3400
EMP: 30
SALES (corp-wide): 1.8B **Publicly Held**
SIC: 7389 Automobile recovery service
HQ: Almost Family, Inc.
    9510 Ormsby Station Rd # 300
    Louisville KY 40223
    502 891-1000

(G-2931)
ALPHA INVESTMENT PARTNERSHIP (PA)
Also Called: Cincinnati Equitable Insurance
525 Vine St Ste 1925 (45202-3125)
P.O. Box 3428 (45201-3428)
PHONE..................................513 621-1826
Peter Alpaugh, *President*
Greg Baker, *President*

George T Holmes, *Sales Staff*
Jay Keener, *Sales Staff*
Heather West, *Consultant*
EMP: 60
SALES (est): 13MM **Privately Held**
SIC: 6311 Life insurance

(G-2932)
ALRO STEEL CORPORATION
10310 S Medallion Dr (45241-4836)
PHONE..............................513 769-9999
Rick Tennenholtz, *Branch Mgr*
EMP: 85
SALES (corp-wide): 1.9B **Privately Held**
SIC: 5051 Steel
PA: Alro Steel Corporation
        3100 E High St
        Jackson MI 49203
        517 787-5500

(G-2933)
ALSTOM SIGNALING OPERATION LLC
25 Merchant St (45246-3700)
PHONE..............................513 552-6485
Bill Dwyer, *Branch Mgr*
EMP: 259
SALES (corp-wide): 1.5B **Privately Held**
WEB: www.proyard.com
SIC: 4789 Cargo loading & unloading services
PA: Alstom Signaling Operation, Llc
        2901 E Lake Rd Bldg 122
        Erie PA 16531
        800 825-3178

(G-2934)
ALTERNATIVE HOME CARE & STFFNG
7759 Montgomery Rd (45236-4201)
PHONE..............................513 794-0571
Kelly Wickline, *Principal*
EMP: 40 **EST:** 2012
SALES (est): 225.7K **Privately Held**
SIC: 8082 Home health care services

(G-2935)
ALTERNATIVE HOME HEALTH CARE
5150 E Galbraith Rd # 200 (45236-2872)
PHONE..............................513 794-0555
Kelly Wickline, *President*
EMP: 40
SALES (est): 2.8MM **Privately Held**
WEB: www.alternativehomehealthcare.com
SIC: 8741 8082 Nursing & personal care facility management; home health care services

(G-2936)
ALVEO HEALTH LLC
700 W Pete Rose Way # 426 (45203-1892)
PHONE..............................513 557-3502
Jeff Loney, *CEO*
EMP: 25 **EST:** 1988
SQ FT: 3,600
SALES (est): 113.6K **Privately Held**
SIC: 8099 Physical examination service, insurance

(G-2937)
AMENITY HOME HEALTH CARE LLC
3025 W Galbraith Rd (45239-4222)
P.O. Box 18307, Fairfield (45018-0307)
PHONE..............................513 931-3689
Patricia Carter, *Partner*
EMP: 40
SALES (est): 614.9K **Privately Held**
SIC: 8082 Home Health Care Services

(G-2938)
AMERICAN CONTRS INDEMNITY CO
7794 5 Mile Rd (45230-2368)
PHONE..............................513 688-0800
Paul Abrams, *Branch Mgr*
EMP: 34
SALES (corp-wide): 2.1B **Privately Held**
SIC: 6399 Bank deposit insurance
HQ: American Contractors Indemnity Company
        801 S Figueroa St Ste 700
        Los Angeles CA 90017

(G-2939)
AMERICAN EMPIRE SURPLUS LINES
Also Called: American Empire Insurance
515 Main St (45202)
PHONE..............................513 369-3000
Bob Nelson, *President*
Thomas Matthew Held, *Assistant VP*
Chet Nalepa, *Vice Pres*
Matt Held, *Admin Sec*
EMP: 43
SQ FT: 20,000
SALES (est): 4.7MM **Publicly Held**
SIC: 6331 Fire, marine & casualty insurance
HQ: American Empire Surplus Lines Insurance Company
        580 Walnut St
        Cincinnati OH 45202
        513 369-3000

(G-2940)
AMERICAN EMPRIE SRPLS LINES IN (DH)
580 Walnut St (45202-3127)
PHONE..............................513 369-3000
Robert A Nelson, *Ch of Bd*
Mark R Lonneman, *President*
EMP: 57
SQ FT: 33,000
SALES (est): 23.9MM **Publicly Held**
SIC: 6331 Fire, marine & casualty insurance: stock; property damage insurance
HQ: Great American Insurance Company
        301 E 4th St Fl 8
        Cincinnati OH 45202
        513 369-5000

(G-2941)
AMERICAN FEDERATION OF GOV
3200 Vine St (45220-2213)
P.O. Box 29093 (45229-0093)
PHONE..............................513 861-6047
EMP: 25
SALES (corp-wide): 42.4MM **Privately Held**
SIC: 8631 Labor union
PA: American Federation Of Government Employees, Afl-Cio
        80 F St Nw Fl 7
        Washington DC 20001
        202 737-8700

(G-2942)
AMERICAN FINANCIAL CORPORATION
580 Walnut St Fl 9 (45202-3193)
PHONE..............................513 579-2121
James Evans, *Principal*
Steve Brewer, *Manager*
Joseph Wermes, *Manager*
EMP: 92
SALES (est): 1MM **Publicly Held**
SIC: 8111 General practice attorney, lawyer
HQ: Afc Holding Company Inc
        1 E 4th St
        Cincinnati OH 45202

(G-2943)
AMERICAN FINANCIAL GROUP INC (PA)
301 E 4th St Fl 8 (45202-4257)
PHONE..............................513 579-2121
Carl H Lindner III, *CEO*
S Craig Lindner, *President*
Alicia Yoo, *Exec VP*
Mary Ford, *Senior VP*
Vito C Peraino, *Senior VP*
EMP: 146
SQ FT: 675,000
SALES (est): 7.1B **Publicly Held**
WEB: www.amfnl.com
SIC: 6331 6311 6321 Fire, marine & casualty insurance; life insurance; life insurance carriers; accident & health insurance; accident associations, mutual

(G-2944)
AMERICAN GEN LF INSUR CO DEL
Also Called: AIG
250 E 5th St Ste 1500 (45202-4252)
PHONE..............................513 762-7807
Fax: 513 762-7811
EMP: 49
SALES (corp-wide): 49.5B **Publicly Held**
SIC: 6411 Insurance Agent/Broker
HQ: American General Life Insurance Company Of Delaware
        2727 Allen Pkwy Ste A
        Houston TX 77019
        713 522-1111

(G-2945)
AMERICAN HERITAGE GIRLS INC
175 Tri County Pkwy # 100 (45246-3250)
PHONE..............................513 771-2025
Patty Garibay, *Exec Dir*
EMP: 70
SALES (est): 3.4MM **Privately Held**
WEB: www.ahgonline.org
SIC: 8641 Civic social & fraternal associations

(G-2946)
AMERICAN MONEY MANAGEMENT CORP
301 E 4th St Fl 27 (45202-4245)
PHONE..............................513 579-2592
S Craig Lindner, *Ch of Bd*
John B Berding, *President*
Sandra W Heimann, *Vice Pres*
EMP: 38 **EST:** 1973
SQ FT: 2,000
SALES (est): 6MM **Publicly Held**
WEB: www.amfnl.com
SIC: 6282 Investment advisory service
PA: American Financial Group, Inc.
        301 E 4th St Fl 8
        Cincinnati OH 45202

(G-2947)
AMERICAN NURSING CARE INC
4750 Wesley Ave Ste Q (45212-2273)
PHONE..............................513 731-4600
Amy Owens, *Manager*
EMP: 40 **Privately Held**
WEB: www.americannursingcare.com
SIC: 8051 8082 Skilled nursing care facilities; home health care services
HQ: American Nursing Care, Inc.
        1700 Edison Dr Ste 300
        Milford OH 45150
        513 576-0262

(G-2948)
AMERICAN NURSING CARE INC
4460 Red Bank Rd Ste 100 (45227-2173)
PHONE..............................513 245-1500
Victoria Dixon, *Principal*
EMP: 68 **Privately Held**
SIC: 8051 Skilled nursing care facilities
HQ: American Nursing Care, Inc.
        1700 Edison Dr Ste 300
        Milford OH 45150
        513 576-0262

(G-2949)
AMERICAN PARA PROF SYSTEMS INC
Also Called: A P P S
6056 Montgomery Rd (45213-1612)
P.O. Box 36166 (45236-0166)
PHONE..............................513 531-2900
Sarah Swisher, *Manager*
EMP: 30
SQ FT: 350
SALES (corp-wide): 9.3MM **Privately Held**
WEB: www.appsms.com
SIC: 8011 Medical insurance plan
PA: American Para Professional Systems, Inc.
        1 Jericho Plz Ste 101
        Jericho NY 11753
        516 822-6230

(G-2950)
AMERICAN RED CROSS
Also Called: Cincinnati Area Chapter
2111 Dana Ave (45207-1303)
PHONE..............................513 579-3000
Trish Smitson, *CEO*
Becky Willis, *Accountant*
EMP: 75
SQ FT: 26,147
SALES (est): 7.2MM
SALES (corp-wide): 2.5B **Privately Held**
SIC: 8322 Disaster service; first aid service; youth center
PA: The American National Red Cross
        430 17th St Nw
        Washington DC 20006
        202 737-8300

(G-2951)
AMERICAN RISK SERVICES LLC
1130 Congress Ave Ste A (45246-4485)
PHONE..............................513 772-3712
Robert Simpson III, *Principal*
EMP: 27
SALES (est): 3.5MM **Privately Held**
WEB: www.americanriskservices.com
SIC: 6411 Insurance brokers

(G-2952)
AMERIDIAN SPECIALTY SERVICES
11520 Rockfield Ct (45241-1919)
P.O. Box 62808 (45262-0808)
PHONE..............................513 769-0150
Betty Owens, *President*
EMP: 50
SQ FT: 32,000
SALES (est): 6.6MM **Privately Held**
WEB: www.ameridiansvcs.com
SIC: 8741 1761 3441 Construction management; architectural sheet metal work; gutter & downspout contractor; fabricated structural metal

(G-2953)
AMERITAS LIFE INSURANCE CORP
1876 Waycross Rd (45240-2825)
P.O. Box 40888 (45240-0888)
PHONE..............................513 595-2334
Joann M Martin, *CEO*
Steven J Valerius, *President*
Tim L Stonehocker, *Exec VP*
J Thomas Burkhard, *Senior VP*
Cheryl L Heilman, *Senior VP*
EMP: 40
SALES (est): 27.7MM **Privately Held**
SIC: 6311 Life insurance

(G-2954)
AMP ADVERTISING INC
700 Walnut St Ste 500 (45202-2011)
PHONE..............................513 333-4100
George Sabert, *President*
Jim Browning, *Vice Pres*
EMP: 38
SALES (est): 3.1MM **Privately Held**
WEB: www.sunriseadvertising.com
SIC: 7311 Advertising agencies

(G-2955)
AMPAC HOLDINGS LLC (HQ)
Also Called: Proampac
12025 Tricon Rd (45246-1719)
PHONE..............................513 671-1777
Greg Tucker, *Mng Member*
Eric Bradford,
Jon Dill,
Tom Geyer,
◆ **EMP:** 700 **EST:** 2001
SQ FT: 220,000
SALES (est): 354.9MM
SALES (corp-wide): 1.1B **Privately Held**
WEB: www.ampaconline.com
SIC: 2673 2677 3081 2674 Plastic bags: made from purchased materials; pliofilm bags: made from purchased materials; envelopes; unsupported plastics film & sheet; shopping bags: made from purchased materials; investment holding companies, except banks

PA: Proampac Holdings Inc.
12025 Tricon Rd
Cincinnati OH 45246
513 671-1777

(G-2956)
AMPACET CORPORATION
4705 Duke Dr 400 (45249)
PHONE..................................513 247-5400
Vicky Willsey, *Manager*
EMP: 25
SALES (corp-wide): 584.5MM **Privately Held**
WEB: www.ampacet.com
SIC: 3089 5162 Coloring & finishing of plastic products; plastics materials & basic shapes
PA: Ampacet Corporation
660 White Plains Rd # 360
Tarrytown NY 10591
914 631-6600

(G-2957)
AMPLE TRAILER LEASING & SALES
610 Wayne Park Dr (45215-2847)
PHONE..................................513 563-2550
Edward Focke, *President*
EMP: 27
SQ FT: 6,000
SALES (est): 1.8MM **Privately Held**
SIC: 7519 Trailer rental

(G-2958)
ANARK INC
Also Called: Animal Ark Pet Resort
2150 Struble Rd (45231-1736)
PHONE..................................513 825-7387
Vicki Gumpbush, *President*
Dave Gump, *Vice Pres*
George Gump, *Treasurer*
Jan Gump, *Admin Sec*
EMP: 30
SQ FT: 12,768
SALES (est): 697K **Privately Held**
WEB: www.anark.com
SIC: 0752 5999 Animal boarding services; animal training services; grooming services, pet & animal specialties; pets & pet supplies

(G-2959)
ANDERSON HEALTHCARE LTD
Also Called: Anderson, The
8139 Beechmont Ave (45255-3152)
P.O. Box 541084 (45254-1084)
PHONE..................................513 474-6200
Nikki Gerber, *Director*
Darrell Ross, *Telecom Exec*
Akiva Wagschal, *Administration*
Linda Wagschal,
EMP: 96
SQ FT: 44,000
SALES (est): 6.6MM **Privately Held**
SIC: 8051 8069 Convalescent home with continuous nursing care; specialty hospitals, except psychiatric

(G-2960)
ANDERSON HILLS PEDIATRICS INC
7400 Jager Ct (45230-4344)
PHONE..................................513 232-8100
Roger Herman, *President*
Brian Vanderhorst, *Manager*
EMP: 70 EST: 1975
SQ FT: 4,750
SALES (est): 10.6MM **Privately Held**
WEB: www.ahpediatrics.com
SIC: 8011 Pediatrician

(G-2961)
ANDERSON JEFFERY R RE INC
3805 Edwards Rd Ste 700 (45209-1955)
PHONE..................................513 241-5800
Jeffrey R Anderson, *President*
Mark Fallon, *Vice Pres*
Tom Hoffman, *Vice Pres*
Ryan Garlitz, *Controller*
Tracy Schwegmann, *Marketing Staff*
EMP: 50
SQ FT: 30,000
SALES (est): 3.1MM **Privately Held**
WEB: www.anderson-realestate.com
SIC: 6512 Commercial & industrial building operation

(G-2962)
ANDERSON LITTLE
8516 Beechmont Ave (45255-4708)
PHONE..................................513 474-7800
Robin Beier, *Director*
Robin L Beier, *Director*
EMP: 38
SALES (est): 823.3K **Privately Held**
SIC: 8351 Group day care center

(G-2963)
ANDERSON TOWNSHIP PARK DST
Also Called: Beech Acres Park
6910 Salem Rd (45230-2959)
PHONE..................................513 474-0003
Brian Jordan, *Finance*
EMP: 40
SALES (corp-wide): 1.2MM **Privately Held**
SIC: 7999 Recreation services
PA: Anderson Township Park District
8249 Clough Pike
Cincinnati OH 45244
513 474-0003

(G-2964)
ANDERSON TWNSHIP HSTORICAL SOC
6550 Clough Pike (45244-4029)
P.O. Box 30174 (45230-0174)
PHONE..................................513 231-2114
Sue A Wettstein, *President*
Carol Voorhees, *Corp Secy*
Albert Wettstein, *COO*
Robert Radcliffe, *Exec VP*
Bruce Bromen,
EMP: 45 EST: 1975
SALES: 92.3K **Privately Held**
SIC: 8412 Historical society

(G-2965)
ANDREW BELMONT SARGENT (PA)
Also Called: ABS Business Products
10855 Medallion Dr (45241-4829)
PHONE..................................513 769-7800
James Donnellon, *President*
Terry Dunigan, *Office Mgr*
Grant Hilty, *Consultant*
EMP: 31
SQ FT: 17,000
SALES (est): 19.8MM **Privately Held**
WEB: www.absproducts.com
SIC: 5044 7699 Copying equipment; office equipment & accessory customizing

(G-2966)
ANESTHSIA ASSOC CINCINNATI INC
2139 Auburn Ave (45219-2906)
P.O. Box 40574 (45240-0574)
PHONE..................................513 585-0577
Mark Manley, *President*
EMP: 60
SALES (est): 3.8MM
SALES (corp-wide): 287.4MM **Privately Held**
SIC: 8011 Anesthesiologist
HQ: Team Health Holdings, Inc.
265 Brookview Centre Way
Knoxville TN 37919
865 693-1000

(G-2967)
ANGEL ABOVE BYOND HM HLTH SVCS
8320 Beechmont Ave (45255-3146)
PHONE..................................513 553-9955
Scott Wolf, *President*
Nicholas Wolf, *Corp Secy*
EMP: 40
SALES (est): 1.6MM **Privately Held**
SIC: 8082 Home health care services

(G-2968)
ANGELS 4 LIFE LLC
431 Ohio Pike Ste 182s (45255-3717)
PHONE..................................513 474-5683
Shellie Fischer,
EMP: 30

SALES: 1MM **Privately Held**
SIC: 8082 8052 Home health care services; home for the mentally retarded, with health care

(G-2969)
ANGELS TOUCH NURSING CARE
3619 Harrison Ave (45211-5540)
P.O. Box 58244 (45258-0244)
PHONE..................................513 661-4111
Bonnie Perrino, *President*
Beverly Rosemeyer, *Assistant*
EMP: 30
SALES (est): 762K **Privately Held**
SIC: 8082 Visiting nurse service

(G-2970)
ANHEUSER-BUSCH LLC
600 Vine St Ste 1002 (45202-2400)
PHONE..................................513 381-3927
Dirk Disper, *Branch Mgr*
EMP: 113
SALES (corp-wide): 1.9B **Privately Held**
SIC: 5181 Beer & other fermented malt liquors
HQ: Anheuser-Busch, Llc
1 Busch Pl
Saint Louis MO 63118
314 632-6777

(G-2971)
AP CCHMC
3333 Burnet Ave (45229-3026)
PHONE..................................513 636-4200
Julia Bahar, *Opers Staff*
Diane Wall, *Human Res Mgr*
Patricia Holshouser, *Admin Asst*
Steve Koehne, *Analyst*
Cris Lewin,
EMP: 45
SALES (est): 8.4MM **Privately Held**
SIC: 8011 Pediatrician

(G-2972)
APC2 INC (PA)
Also Called: Appearance Plus
6812 Clough Pike (45244-4037)
PHONE..................................513 231-5540
Jonathon Lindy, *President*
EMP: 63
SALES (est): 4.4MM **Privately Held**
WEB: www.appearanceplus.com
SIC: 7216 7212 Cleaning & dyeing, except rugs; laundry & drycleaner agents

(G-2973)
APEX ENVIRONMENTAL SVCS LLC
295 Northland Blvd (45246-3603)
PHONE..................................513 772-2739
Bill Evans,
EMP: 85 EST: 1998
SALES (est): 2.3MM **Privately Held**
WEB: www.apexservicesllc.com
SIC: 7349 Janitorial service, contract basis

(G-2974)
APEX RESTORATION CONTRS LTD (PA)
6315 Warrick St (45227-2540)
P.O. Box 80850, Rochester MI (48308-0850)
PHONE..................................513 489-1795
Laeron Evans, *Vice Pres*
Daniel P Mc Neil, *Mng Member*
EMP: 30
SQ FT: 10,200
SALES (est): 4.6MM **Privately Held**
WEB: www.apexrest.com
SIC: 1521 1542 General remodeling, single-family houses; commercial & office buildings, renovation & repair

(G-2975)
APOLLO HEATING AND AC INC
Also Called: Three Rivers Heating & Air
1730 Tennessee Ave (45229-1202)
PHONE..................................513 271-3600
James Gerdsen, *President*
EMP: 35
SQ FT: 6,700

SALES (est): 6.6MM **Privately Held**
WEB: www.apollo-hvac.com
SIC: 1711 1731 Warm air heating & air conditioning contractor; electrical work

(G-2976)
APPLIED MECHANICAL SYSTEMS INC
12082 Champion Way (45241-6406)
PHONE..................................513 825-1800
Drew Mitakides, *Branch Mgr*
EMP: 75
SQ FT: 3,500
SALES (corp-wide): 33.5MM **Privately Held**
WEB: www.appliedmechanicalsys.com
SIC: 1711 Plumbing contractors; warm air heating & air conditioning contractor
PA: Applied Mechanical Systems, Inc.
5598 Wolf Creek Pike
Dayton OH 45426
937 854-3073

(G-2977)
APTIM CORP
5050 Section Ave (45212-2055)
PHONE..................................513 782-4700
William Pier, *Manager*
EMP: 40
SALES (corp-wide): 2B **Privately Held**
WEB: www.shawgrp.com
SIC: 8711 Engineering services
HQ: Aptim Corp.
1780 Hughes Landing Blvd # 1000
The Woodlands TX 77380
832 823-2700

(G-2978)
ARAMARK UNF & CAREER AP LLC
P.O. Box 12131 (45212-0131)
PHONE..................................513 533-1000
Rick Lachrop, *General Mgr*
John Green, *Plant Mgr*
EMP: 121 **Publicly Held**
SIC: 7218 Industrial uniform supply; treated equipment supply: mats, rugs, mops, cloths, etc.; wiping towel supply
HQ: Aramark Uniform & Career Apparel, Llc
115 N First St Ste 203
Burbank CA 91502
818 973-3700

(G-2979)
ARC DOCUMENT SOLUTIONS INC
7157 E Kemper Rd (45249-1028)
PHONE..................................513 326-2300
Joe Hipps, *Manager*
EMP: 27
SALES (corp-wide): 400.7MM **Publicly Held**
SIC: 7334 Photocopying & duplicating services
PA: Arc Document Solutions, Inc.
12657 Alcosta Blvd # 200
San Ramon CA 94583
925 949-5100

(G-2980)
ARCHDIOCESE OF CINCINNATI
Also Called: St Bartholomew Cons School
9375 Winton Rd (45231-3967)
PHONE..................................513 729-1725
Leanora Roach, *Principal*
EMP: 55
SALES (corp-wide): 229.4MM **Privately Held**
WEB: www.catholiccincinnati.org
SIC: 7032 Girls' camp
PA: Archdiocese Of Cincinnati
100 E 8th St Fl 8
Cincinnati OH 45202
513 421-3131

(G-2981)
ARCHDIOCESE OF CINCINNATI
Also Called: Altercrest
274 Sutton Rd (45230-3521)
PHONE..................................513 231-5010
Robert Wehr, *Exec Dir*
EMP: 50

SALES (corp-wide): 229.4MM **Privately Held**
WEB: www.catholiccincinnati.org
SIC: 8361 Residential care
PA: Archdiocese Of Cincinnati
   100 E 8th St Fl 8
   Cincinnati OH 45202
   513 421-3131

(G-2982)
ARCHIABLE ELECTRIC COMPANY
3803 Ford Cir (45227-3403)
PHONE....................513 621-1307
James D Schroth, *President*
David Bogenschutz, *Opers Mgr*
Ryan Ford, *Foreman/Supr*
Jan Praechter, *Foreman/Supr*
Howie Vollmer, *Purch Mgr*
EMP: 65 **EST:** 1919
SQ FT: 10,000
SALES (est): 9.5MM **Privately Held**
SIC: 1731 General electrical contractor

(G-2983)
ARCHITECTURAL METAL ERECTORS
869 W North Bend Rd (45224-1340)
P.O. Box 24 (45224)
PHONE....................513 242-5106
Chris Geiger, *President*
EMP: 25
SQ FT: 10,000
SALES (est): 1.5MM
SALES (corp-wide): 11.1MM **Privately Held**
SIC: 1799 Ornamental metal work
PA: Geiger Construction Products Inc.
   869 W North Bend Rd
   Cincinnati OH 45224
   513 242-5106

(G-2984)
ARENA MANAGEMENT HOLDINGS LLC
Also Called: U S Bank Arena
100 Broadway St (45202-3514)
PHONE....................513 421-4111
Jim Moehring, *Vice Pres*
Kristin Ropp, *Vice Pres*
Sarah Blevins, *Sales Mgr*
Kimberly Barry, *Manager*
EMP: 600
SQ FT: 123,208
SALES (est): 20.3MM **Privately Held**
WEB: www.usbankarena.com
SIC: 7941 6531 Sports field or stadium operator, promoting sports events; real estate agents & managers

(G-2985)
ARGUS INTERNATIONAL INC
4240 Airport Rd Ste 300 (45226-1623)
P.O. Box 10, South Lebanon (45065-0010)
PHONE....................513 852-1010
Kathy Tyler, *Principal*
Scott Liston, *Exec VP*
Aaron Greenwald, *Senior VP*
Josh Olds, *VP Opers*
Dave Parran, *Controller*
EMP: 30 **EST:** 1999
SALES (est): 4.7MM **Privately Held**
SIC: 4785 7389 Transportation inspection services; industrial & commercial equipment inspection service

(G-2986)
ARGUS INTERNATIONAL INC (PA)
4240 Airport Rd Ste 300 (45226-1623)
P.O. Box 10, South Lebanon (45065-0010)
PHONE....................513 852-5110
Joseph J Moeggenberg, *President*
Scott Shroyer, *QC Mgr*
David Parran, *Controller*
Michael Volpe, *Regl Sales Mgr*
Jenn Stone, *Sales Staff*
EMP: 38
SQ FT: 4,000
SALES (est): 4.8MM **Privately Held**
WEB: www.aviationresearch.com
SIC: 8711 Aviation &/or aeronautical engineering

(G-2987)
ARLINGTON MEMORIAL GRDNS ASSN
2145 Compton Rd (45231-3009)
PHONE....................513 521-7003
Leroy Meier, *Ch of Bd*
Edwin Friedhoff, *Ch of Bd*
Daniel Applegate, *President*
Julie Hoffman, *Vice Pres*
EMP: 35
SQ FT: 10,000
SALES: 3.7MM **Privately Held**
WEB: www.amgardens.org
SIC: 6553 Cemeteries, real estate operation

(G-2988)
ARLITT CHILD DEVELOPMENT CTR
44 W Corry St (45219)
PHONE....................513 556-3802
Larry Johnson, *Exec Dir*
EMP: 60
SALES (est): 540.5K **Privately Held**
SIC: 8351 Child day care services

(G-2989)
ARS OHIO LLC
947 Sundance Dr (45233-4567)
PHONE....................513 327-7645
Karen Finn, *Accountant*
EMP: 25
SALES (est): 1.9MM **Privately Held**
SIC: 7389 ;

(G-2990)
ART HAUSER INSURANCE INC
Also Called: Hauser Group, The
8260 Northcreek Dr # 200 (45236-2296)
PHONE....................513 745-9200
Mark J Hauser, *President*
Gary L Morgan, *COO*
Paul M Swanson, *Exec VP*
Jim Hyer, *Senior VP*
Jeri S Harrison, *Vice Pres*
EMP: 54
SALES (est): 18.1MM **Privately Held**
SIC: 6411 Insurance agents

(G-2991)
ARTHUR J GALLAGHER & CO
Also Called: Gallagher Sks
201 E 4th St Ste 625 (45202-4267)
PHONE....................513 977-3100
Bob Murphy, *Vice Pres*
Thomas Dietz, *Branch Mgr*
Brad Cooley, *Info Tech Dir*
EMP: 50
SALES (corp-wide): 6.9B **Publicly Held**
SIC: 6411 Insurance brokers
PA: Arthur J. Gallagher & Co.
   2850 Golf Rd Ste 1000
   Rolling Meadows IL 60008
   630 773-3800

(G-2992)
AT HOSPITALITY LLC
5375 Medpace Way (45227-1543)
PHONE....................513 527-9962
August J Troendle, *Owner*
EMP: 100
SALES: 13MM **Privately Held**
SIC: 7011 Hotels

(G-2993)
AT&T CORP
3612 Stonecreek Blvd (45251-1450)
PHONE....................513 741-1700
Gary Goldstein, *Branch Mgr*
EMP: 85
SALES (corp-wide): 170.7B **Publicly Held**
SIC: 4812 Cellular telephone services
HQ: At&T Corp.
   1 At&T Way
   Bedminster NJ 07921
   800 403-3302

(G-2994)
AT&T CORP
221 E 4th St (45202-4124)
PHONE....................513 629-5000
Jan Ojdana, *Technical Mgr*
Dennis Beck, *Branch Mgr*
EMP: 800

SALES (corp-wide): 170.7B **Publicly Held**
WEB: www.att.com
SIC: 4813 4822 4812 Long distance telephone communications; telegram services; radio telephone communication
HQ: At&T Corp.
   1 At&T Way
   Bedminster NJ 07921
   800 403-3302

(G-2995)
AT&T MOBILITY LLC
1605 Western Ave (45214-2001)
PHONE....................513 381-6800
EMP: 26
SALES (corp-wide): 160.5B **Publicly Held**
SIC: 4812 Radiotelephone Communication
HQ: At&T Mobility Llc
   1025 Lenox Park Blvd Ne
   Brookhaven GA 30319
   800 331-0500

(G-2996)
ATC GROUP SERVICES LLC
Also Called: Atc Associates
11121 Canal Rd (45241-1861)
PHONE....................513 771-2112
Daniel Distler, *Project Mgr*
Keith Arend, *Branch Mgr*
EMP: 56 **Privately Held**
WEB: www.atc-enviro.com
SIC: 8711 8734 Sanitary engineers; testing laboratories
HQ: Atc Group Services Llc
   221 Rue De Jean Ste 300
   Lafayette LA 70503
   337 234-8777

(G-2997)
ATKINS & STANG INC
1031 Meta Dr (45237-5007)
PHONE....................513 242-8300
Fred Stang, *President*
Randall Stortz, *Vice Pres*
Susan Ochs, *Treasurer*
EMP: 69
SQ FT: 28,000
SALES (est): 9.6MM **Privately Held**
WEB: www.atkinsandstang.com
SIC: 1731 General electrical contractor

(G-2998)
ATLANTIC FOODS CORP
1999 Section Rd (45237-3343)
PHONE....................513 772-3535
Gary Grefer, *President*
Jeff Busch, *COO*
Mike Kluener, *COO*
Stuart Berning, *Vice Pres*
Stuart Goret, *Vice Pres*
▲ **EMP:** 65
SALES (est): 36.4MM **Privately Held**
SIC: 5149 Specialty food items

(G-2999)
ATLAS TOWING SERVICE
5675 Glenway Ave (45238-2130)
PHONE....................513 451-1854
Mike Kaeser, *Owner*
EMP: 26
SALES (est): 490K **Privately Held**
SIC: 7549 Towing service, automotive

(G-3000)
ATM SOLUTIONS INC (PA)
551 Northland Blvd (45240-3212)
PHONE....................513 742-4900
Paul Scott, *President*
Mike Hines, *President*
Christy McMurry, *President*
Shaun Lyston, *Regional Mgr*
Scott Nelson, *Sales Executive*
EMP: 100 **EST:** 1996
SALES (est): 17.4MM **Privately Held**
WEB: www.atm-solutions.com
SIC: 7699 Automated teller machine (ATM) repair

(G-3001)
ATRIA SENIOR LIVING INC
Also Called: Northgate Pk Retirement Cmnty
9191 Round Top Rd Ofc (45251-2465)
PHONE....................513 923-3711
Natalie May, *Principal*

EMP: 50
SALES (corp-wide): 3.7B **Publicly Held**
WEB: www.atriacom.com
SIC: 8361 Residential care
HQ: Atria Senior Living Inc.
   300 E Market St Ste 100
   Louisville KY 40202

(G-3002)
ATTERRO INC (DH)
Also Called: Atterro Human Capital Group
201 E 4th St Ste 800 (45202-4248)
PHONE....................800 938-9675
Toshio Oka, *CEO*
Clay E Morel, *CEO*
Michael E Morris, *Exec VP*
Greg D Jensen, *Senior VP*
Susan Y Rylance, *Senior VP*
EMP: 50
SQ FT: 26,000
SALES (est): 179.8MM
SALES (corp-wide): 20.4B **Privately Held**
WEB: www.prostaff.com
SIC: 7363 7361 Temporary help service; employment agencies; placement agencies

(G-3003)
AUGUST FOOD & WINE LLC
Also Called: Nate
1214 Vine St (45202-7298)
PHONE....................513 421-2020
Lana Wright,
EMP: 40 **EST:** 2010
SALES (est): 3.7MM **Privately Held**
SIC: 5182 Wine

(G-3004)
AUGUST GROH & SONS INC
8832 Reading Rd (45215-4815)
PHONE....................513 821-0090
Jo Groh, *President*
Tom Mooran, *General Mgr*
Richard T Groh, *Vice Pres*
Rick Groh, *Vice Pres*
EMP: 50 **EST:** 1926
SQ FT: 10,000
SALES (est): 2.9MM **Privately Held**
WEB: www.groh.com
SIC: 1721 7349 Commercial painting; building & office cleaning services; janitorial service, contract basis

(G-3005)
AUTO AFTERMARKET CONCEPTS
Also Called: Calafonia Dream By AAC
1031 Redna Ter (45215-1114)
PHONE....................513 942-2535
John Miller, *Partner*
Mike Eckel, *Partner*
▲ **EMP:** 25
SQ FT: 24,720
SALES: 4MM **Privately Held**
SIC: 5013 Automotive engines & engine parts

(G-3006)
AUTO CENTER USA INC
Also Called: Kings Mazda Kia
4544 Kings Water Dr (45249-8201)
PHONE....................513 683-4900
Robert C Reichert, *President*
Louis K Galbraith, *Corp Secy*
Gerald Carmichael, *Vice Pres*
Mark Pittman, *Vice Pres*
Chris Parsley, *Finance Mgr*
EMP: 49
SALES: 25MM **Privately Held**
SIC: 5511 7538 7515 5521 Automobiles, new & used; pickups, new & used; general automotive repair shops; passenger car leasing; used car dealers

(G-3007)
AUTO CONCEPTS CINCINNATTI LLC
3428 Hauck Rd Ste I (45241-4603)
PHONE....................513 769-4540
Thomas Reader, *Principal*
Charles Deringer, *Mng Member*
Joseph Hart, *Mng Member*
Thomas Richards, *Mng Member*
Wayne Maupin, *Manager*
EMP: 30 **EST:** 2000
SQ FT: 20,000

SALES (est): 1MM **Privately Held**
SIC: 7549 Automotive customizing services, non-factory basis

(G-3008)
AWH HOLDINGS INC
Also Called: Woods Hardware
125 E 9th St (45202-2127)
PHONE....................................513 241-2614
Laura Woods, *President*
Steven Woods, *Principal*
Matthew Woods, *COO*
EMP: 80 **Privately Held**
SIC: 6719 Holding companies

(G-3009)
AWRS LLC
Also Called: Ekomovers USA
10866 Newmarket Dr (45251-1027)
PHONE....................................888 611-2292
Aaron Williams,
EMP: 40
SALES (est): 2.5MM **Privately Held**
SIC: 4213 Household goods transport

(G-3010)
AXA ADVISORS LLC
4000 Smith Rd Ste 300 (45209-1967)
PHONE....................................513 762-7700
Chris Dolly, *Branch Mgr*
Carol Rodgers, *Advisor*
EMP: 40
SALES (corp-wide): 1MM **Publicly Held**
WEB: www.axacs.com
SIC: 6411 Insurance agents
HQ: Axa Advisors, Llc
1290 Ave Of Amrcs Fl Cnc1
New York NY 10104
212 554-1234

(G-3011)
**AXCESS RCVERY CR
SOLUTIONS INC**
4540 Cooper Rd Ste 305 (45242-5649)
PHONE....................................513 229-6700
Jerry R Williams, *President*
Robert W Neu, *Treasurer*
Stephen J Schaller, *Admin Sec*
EMP: 50
SALES (est): 3MM **Privately Held**
SIC: 7322 Adjustment & collection services

(G-3012)
AZTEC SERVICES GROUP INC
3814 William P Dooley Byp (45223-2664)
PHONE....................................513 541-2002
Albert C Meininger, *President*
Tom Coon, *COO*
Melinda Boyd, *Office Mgr*
EMP: 100 **EST:** 2013
SQ FT: 2,000
SALES: 12MM **Privately Held**
SIC: 1795 8744 Wrecking & demolition work;

(G-3013)
**B & B EMPLOYMENT
RESOURCE LLC**
260 Northland Blvd # 216 (45246-3651)
PHONE....................................513 370-5542
Shonna Bryant, *Mng Member*
EMP: 25
SALES (est): 709.7K **Privately Held**
SIC: 7361 Employment agencies

(G-3014)
**B & J ELECTRICAL COMPANY
INC**
6316 Wiehe Rd (45237-4214)
PHONE....................................513 351-7100
Debbie Janzen, *President*
Gary Lee Janzen, *Chairman*
Shannon Ernst, *Chairman*
Peggy Deorger, *Vice Pres*
Kirsten Janzen, *Vice Pres*
EMP: 45
SQ FT: 1,000
SALES: 8MM **Privately Held**
WEB: www.bjelectrical.com
SIC: 1731 General electrical contractor

(G-3015)
BAKER & HOSTETLER LLP
312 Walnut St Ste 3200 (45202-4074)
PHONE....................................513 929-3400

David G Holcombe, *Managing Prtnr*
Kathy Dean, *Marketing Mgr*
Sharon Jesse, *Manager*
Sharon Kellum, *Supervisor*
David Gray, *Network Enginr*
EMP: 41
SALES (corp-wide): 313.3MM **Privately Held**
SIC: 8111 General practice attorney, lawyer; bankruptcy law; labor & employment law; real estate law
PA: Baker & Hostetler Llp
127 Public Sq Ste 2000
Cleveland OH 44114
216 621-0200

(G-3016)
**BANNOCKBURN GLOBAL
FOREX LLC**
312 Walnut St Ste 3580 (45202-4088)
PHONE....................................513 386-7400
Joe Areddy, *Managing Prtnr*
Michael Bourke, *Managing Prtnr*
Neil Brenner, *Managing Prtnr*
Sean Cahill, *Managing Prtnr*
Andrew Collins, *Managing Prtnr*
EMP: 27
SALES (est): 19MM **Privately Held**
SIC: 8742 6099 Foreign trade consultant; foreign currency exchange

(G-3017)
BANQUETS UNLIMITED
Also Called: Briarwood Banquet Center
1320 Ethan Ave (45225-1810)
P.O. Box 461, Hebron KY (41048-0461)
PHONE....................................859 689-4000
EMP: 25
SQ FT: 19,000
SALES (est): 353.3K **Privately Held**
SIC: 7299 Miscellaneous Personal Services, Nec, Nsk

(G-3018)
BAPTIST HOME AND CENTER
Also Called: JUDSON VILLAGE
2373 Harrison Ave (45211-7927)
PHONE....................................513 662-5880
Roland S Sedziol, *President*
Rev Michael Brandy, *Vice Pres*
Al Meyer, *Treasurer*
Mary Loesch, *Admin Sec*
EMP: 150
SQ FT: 8,500
SALES: 4.7K **Privately Held**
WEB: www.judsonvillage.com
SIC: 6513 8052 8051 Retirement hotel operation; intermediate care facilities; skilled nursing care facilities

(G-3019)
BARBARA S DESALVO INC
800 Compton Rd Unit 18 (45231-3846)
PHONE....................................513 729-2111
Barbara S Desalvo, *President*
EMP: 30
SALES (est): 2.9MM **Privately Held**
SIC: 8748 Educational consultant

(G-3020)
BAREFOOT LLC
700 W Pete Rose Way (45203-1892)
PHONE....................................513 861-3668
Douglas Worple, *President*
Sean Brown, *Partner*
Fran Dicari, *Partner*
Jodi Greene, *Partner*
Steve Kissing, *Partner*
EMP: 47
SALES (est): 82.8K **Privately Held**
SIC: 7311 Advertising agencies

(G-3021)
**BARNES DENNIG & CO LTD
(PA)**
150 E 4th St Ste 300 (45202-4186)
PHONE....................................513 241-8313
Thomas Groskopf, *Owner*
Richard L Batterbery, *Partner*
Alan E Bieber, *Partner*
Bradley S Chaffin, *Partner*
Alvin B Denning Jr, *Partner*
EMP: 70
SQ FT: 19,549
SALES: 8MM **Privately Held**
SIC: 8721 Certified public accountant

(G-3022)
**BARRETT CENTER FOR
CANCER PREV**
234 Goodman St (45219-2364)
PHONE....................................513 558-3200
EMP: 100
SALES (est): 3.8MM **Privately Held**
SIC: 8733 Research Institute

(G-3023)
BARTLETT & CO LLC
600 Vine St Ste 2100 (45202-3896)
PHONE....................................513 621-4612
Kelley J Downing, *President*
David P Francis, *Portfolio Mgr*
Woodrow Uible, *Portfolio Mgr*
Terry Kelly, *CPA*
Kelly Muthert, *Human Res Dir*
EMP: 56
SQ FT: 28,000
SALES (est): 9.4MM **Privately Held**
WEB: www.bartlett1898.com
SIC: 6282 Investment advisory service

(G-3024)
**BAXTER BURIAL VAULT
SERVICE**
Also Called: Baxter-Wilbert Burial Vault
909 E Ross Ave (45217-1159)
PHONE....................................513 641-1010
R Douglas Baxter, *President*
EMP: 25
SALES: 2.4MM **Privately Held**
SIC: 5087 3272 Concrete burial vaults & boxes; funeral directors' equipment & supplies; concrete products

(G-3025)
**BAXTER HODELL DONNELLY
PRESTON (PA)**
Also Called: BHDP ARCHITECTURE
302 W 3rd St Ste 500 (45202-3434)
PHONE....................................513 271-1634
Michael J Habel, *CEO*
Thomas Arends, *Vice Pres*
Barry J Bayer, *Vice Pres*
Anthony E Berger, *Vice Pres*
Larry Digennaro, *Vice Pres*
EMP: 104 **EST:** 1937
SQ FT: 24,000
SALES: 30.1MM **Privately Held**
WEB: www.bhdp.com
SIC: 8741 8712 8742 7373 Construction management; architectural engineering; management consulting services; computer integrated systems design

(G-3026)
BBDO WORLDWIDE INC
700 W Pete Rose Way (45203-1892)
PHONE....................................513 861-3668
Sean Brown, *Vice Pres*
Tim Lemke, *Vice Pres*
Susan Davidson, *Production*
Scott Schierberg, *Accounts Exec*
Matthew Raybuck, *Sr Project Mgr*
EMP: 47
SALES (corp-wide): 15.2B **Publicly Held**
WEB: www.bbdo.com
SIC: 7311 Advertising agencies
HQ: Bbdo Worldwide Inc.
1285 Ave Of The Amer
New York NY 10019
212 459-5000

(G-3027)
BDO USA LLP
221 E 4th St Ste 2600 (45202-4100)
PHONE....................................513 592-2400
Brian Berning, *Branch Mgr*
EMP: 35
SALES (corp-wide): 940.4MM **Privately Held**
SIC: 8721 7389 Certified public accountant; financial services
PA: Bdo Usa, Llp
330 N Wabash Ave Ste 3200
Chicago IL 60611
312 240-1236

(G-3028)
BDS INC (PA)
3500 Southside Ave (45204-1138)
PHONE....................................513 921-8441
William Lindsey, *President*

EMP: 35
SALES (est): 3.3MM **Privately Held**
WEB: www.bds.net
SIC: 4226 4225 Liquid storage; general warehousing & storage

(G-3029)
BEACON ELECTRIC COMPANY
Also Called: Beacon Electrical Contractors
7815 Redsky Dr (45249-1636)
PHONE....................................513 851-0711
William K Schubert, *CEO*
Joe Mellencamp, *President*
Kenneth K Butler, *Vice Pres*
David Earlywine, *Vice Pres*
Bonnie Klein, *Vice Pres*
EMP: 100 **EST:** 1983
SQ FT: 10,000
SALES (est): 30.6MM **Privately Held**
WEB: www.beacon-electric.com
SIC: 1731 General electrical contractor

(G-3030)
**BEECH ACRES PARENTING
CENTER (PA)**
Also Called: Beech Acres Thrptic Fster Care
6881 Beechmont Ave (45230-2907)
PHONE....................................513 231-6630
James Mason, *President*
Karen Sandker, *President*
Dianne Jordan Grizzard, *COO*
Betty Young, *COO*
Richard Sorg, *Vice Pres*
EMP: 85
SQ FT: 25,000
SALES: 9MM **Privately Held**
WEB: www.beechacres.net
SIC: 8322 Adoption services; child related social services

(G-3031)
BEECHMONT MOTORS INC (PA)
Also Called: Beechmont Porsche
8639 Beechmont Ave (45255-4709)
PHONE....................................513 388-3883
William Woeste Jr, *President*
Margo Woeste, *Treasurer*
Dennis Homan, *Info Tech Mgr*
Cynthia S Mac Connell, *Admin Sec*
EMP: 30 **EST:** 1971
SQ FT: 60,000
SALES (est): 27.1MM **Privately Held**
WEB: www.beechmontvolvo.com
SIC: 5511 7539 5012 5013 Automobiles, new & used; pickups, new & used; automotive repair shops; automobiles; motor vehicle supplies & new parts

(G-3032)
**BEECHMONT PET HOSPITAL
INC**
6400 Salem Rd (45230-2811)
PHONE....................................513 232-0300
Stewart Smith Dvm, *President*
EMP: 30
SALES (est): 1MM **Privately Held**
SIC: 0742 Veterinarian, animal specialties

(G-3033)
**BEECHMONT RACQUET CLUB
INC**
Also Called: Beechmont Racquet and Fitness
435 Ohio Pike (45255-3712)
PHONE....................................513 528-5700
William Atkins, *President*
Bradon Atkins, *Manager*
Helen Atkins, *Admin Sec*
EMP: 40
SQ FT: 160,000
SALES (est): 1.9MM **Privately Held**
WEB: www.beechmontracquetclub.com
SIC: 7991 7997 Health club; racquetball club, membership

(G-3034)
BEECHMONT TOYOTA INC
8667 Beechmont Ave (45255-4709)
PHONE....................................513 388-3800
William F Woeste Jr, *President*
Cathy Brock, *General Mgr*
Cynthia Mac Connell, *Corp Secy*
Margot Woeste, *Vice Pres*
James Woodall, *VP Opers*
EMP: 70
SQ FT: 20,000

SALES (est): 24.7MM **Privately Held**
WEB: www.beechmonttoyota.com
SIC: 5511 7539 5012 5013 Automobiles,
new & used; pickups, new & used; automotive repair shops; automobiles; motor
vehicle supplies & new parts

(G-3035)
BEECHWOOD HOME
2140 Pogue Ave (45208-3299)
PHONE.............................513 321-9294
Patricia Clark, CEO
Tim Owens, CFO
Beth Hils, Human Res Dir
Mauer Rosen, Manager
Belinda Rose, Nursing Dir
EMP: 150
SQ FT: 53,000
SALES: 9.6MM **Privately Held**
WEB: www.beechwoodhome.com
SIC: 8051 Skilled nursing care facilities

(G-3036)
**BEECHWOOD TERRACE CARE
CTR INC**
Also Called: Forest Hills Care Center
8700 Moran Rd (45244-1986)
PHONE.............................513 578-6200
Harold Sosna, President
EMP: 160 EST: 2007
SALES: 11.5MM **Privately Held**
SIC: 8051 Convalescent home with contin-
uous nursing care

(G-3037)
BELCAN CORPORATION
Also Called: Belcan Engineering Services
7785 E Kemper Rd (45249-1611)
PHONE.............................513 277-3100
RG Lee, Principal
EMP: 250
SALES (corp-wide): 813.3MM **Privately
Held**
SIC: 8711 Engineering services
PA: Belcan, Llc
10200 Anderson Way
Blue Ash OH 45242
513 891-0972

(G-3038)
**BELFLEX STAFFING NETWORK
LLC (PA)**
11591 Goldcoast Dr (45249-1633)
PHONE.............................513 488-8588
Mike McCaw, CEO
Todd Cross, President
Candace McCaw, Chairman
Bob Baer, Vice Pres
Tim Mueller, CFO
EMP: 125
SALES (est): 110.1MM **Privately Held**
SIC: 7361 7363 Labor contractors (em-
ployment agency); help supply services

(G-3039)
**BELTING COMPANY OF
CINCINNATI (PA)**
Also Called: Cbt Company
5500 Ridge Ave (45213-2516)
P.O. Box 14639 (45250-0639)
PHONE.............................513 621-9050
James E Stahl Jr, President
Jerry Perkins, General Mgr
Keith Harsh, Vice Pres
Mike Kiniyalocts, Vice Pres
Gary Osterbrock, Vice Pres
▲ EMP: 110
SQ FT: 95,000
SALES: 207.7MM **Privately Held**
WEB: www.cinbelt.com
SIC: 5085 5063 Bearings; power transmis-
sion equipment, electric

(G-3040)
BENCO DENTAL SUPPLY CO
10014 Intl Blvd Bldg 9 (45246)
PHONE.............................513 874-2990
Charles Chen, Owner
EMP: 98
SALES (corp-wide): 621.9MM **Privately
Held**
SIC: 5047 Whol Medical/Hospital Equip-
ment

PA: Benco Dental Supply Co.
295 Centerpoint Blvd
Pittston PA 18640
570 602-7781

(G-3041)
**BERNSTEIN ALLERGY GROUP
INC**
8444 Winton Rd (45231-4927)
PHONE.............................513 931-0775
Jonathan A Bernstein, President
David I Bernstein, Vice Pres
Justin C Greiwe, Admin Sec
EMP: 26
SALES (est): 3.3MM **Privately Held**
SIC: 8011 Allergist

(G-3042)
BESL TRANSFER CO
5700 Este Ave (45232-1435)
PHONE.............................513 242-3456
David Rusch, CEO
John M Smith, Ch of Bd
Kelly M Dehan, General Mgr
Michael Beckett, Opers Mgr
Michael J Meyer, Controller
EMP: 25
SQ FT: 8,500
SALES (est): 9.8MM
SALES (corp-wide): 2B **Privately Held**
WEB: www.besl.com
SIC: 4213 4212 Contract haulers; local
trucking, without storage
PA: Crst International, Inc.
201 1st St Se
Cedar Rapids IA 52401
319 396-4400

(G-3043)
BEST EXPRESS FOODS INC
2368 Victory Pkwy Ste 410 (45206-2810)
P.O. Box 8039 (45208-0039)
PHONE.............................513 531-2378
Allan Berliant, President
EMP: 60
SQ FT: 2,600
SALES (est): 27.5MM **Privately Held**
WEB: www.bestexpressfoods.com
SIC: 5142 Packaged frozen goods

(G-3044)
**BEST UPON REQUEST CORP
INC**
8170 Corp Pk Dr Ste 300 (45242)
PHONE.............................513 605-7800
Tillie Hidalgo Lima, President
EMP: 93
SALES (est): 6.9MM **Privately Held**
WEB: www.bestuponrequest.com
SIC: 7299 Consumer buying service

(G-3045)
**BETA RHO HOUSE ASSOC
KAPPA**
2801 Clifton Ave (45220-2401)
PHONE.............................513 221-1280
Betsy Kampman, Principal
EMP: 60
SALES (est): 298.5K **Privately Held**
SIC: 8641 Fraternal associations

(G-3046)
BETHESDA FOUNDATION INC
619 Oak St (45206-1613)
PHONE.............................513 569-6575
John Prout, Principal
EMP: 33
SALES: 621K **Privately Held**
SIC: 8051 Skilled nursing care facilities

(G-3047)
BETHESDA HOSPITAL INC (DH)
Also Called: Bethesda North Hospital
4750 Wesley Ave (45212-2244)
PHONE.............................513 569-6100
John Prout, President
Craig Rucker, CFO
Brian Krause, Controller
Nicholas S Mirkopoulos, Surgeon
Thomas Barnes, Information Mgr
EMP: 1390
SALES: 639.8MM **Privately Held**
SIC: 8062 General medical & surgical hos-
pitals

HQ: Bethesda, Inc.
619 Oak St 7n
Cincinnati OH 45206
513 569-6400

(G-3048)
BETHESDA HOSPITAL INC
Also Called: Bethesda North Hospital
10500 Montgomery Rd (45242-4402)
P.O. Box 422410 (45242-2410)
PHONE.............................513 745-1111
John Prout, President
Dana Hopper, Purch Dir
Michael Smith, Director
Anthony Suchoski, Director
Lorraine Stephens, Program Dir
EMP: 1500 **Privately Held**
SIC: 8062 General medical & surgical hos-
pitals
HQ: Bethesda Hospital, Inc.
4750 Wesley Ave
Cincinnati OH 45212
513 569-6100

(G-3049)
BETHESDA HOSPITAL INC
Bethesda Care-Sharonville
3801 Hauck Rd Frnt (45241-4607)
PHONE.............................513 563-1505
Jay Fultz, Principal
EMP: 35 **Privately Held**
SIC: 8011 8062 Primary care medical
clinic; general medical & surgical hospi-
tals
HQ: Bethesda Hospital, Inc.
4750 Wesley Ave
Cincinnati OH 45212
513 569-6100

(G-3050)
BILLS BATTERY COMPANY INC
5221 Crookshank Rd (45238-3392)
P.O. Box 58305 (45258-0305)
PHONE.............................513 922-0100
Michael F Hartoin, President
Michael Hartoin, President
Ronald Hartoin, Vice Pres
Helen Hartoin, Admin Sec
EMP: 28 EST: 1946
SQ FT: 40,000
SALES: 12.1MM **Privately Held**
SIC: 5013 Automotive batteries

(G-3051)
BIORX LLC (HQ)
Also Called: Thriverx
7167 E Kemper Rd (45249-1028)
PHONE.............................866 442-4679
Al Ranz, Partner
Megan Champagne, Business Mgr
Paul Costello, Business Mgr
Alex Zlatanoff, Business Mgr
Eric Hill, COO
EMP: 105
SALES (est): 81.7MM
SALES (corp-wide): 5.4B **Publicly Held**
WEB: www.biorx.net
SIC: 5122 8748 2834 5047 Pharmaceuti-
cals; business consulting; pharmaceutical
preparations; intravenous solutions; med-
ical & hospital equipment; medical equip-
ment & supplies; skilled nursing care
facilities; extended care facility; convales-
cent home with continuous nursing care
PA: Diplomat Pharmacy, Inc.
4100 S Saginaw St
Flint MI 48507
810 768-9000

(G-3052)
BIZ COM ELECTRIC INC
2867 Stanton Ave (45206-1122)
PHONE.............................513 961-7200
Bruce M Cummins, President
Larry Ayer, Vice Pres
EMP: 35
SQ FT: 7,000
SALES (est): 5.5MM **Privately Held**
WEB: www.bizcomelec.com
SIC: 1731 General electrical contractor

(G-3053)
BKD LLP
312 Walnut St Ste 3000 (45202-4025)
P.O. Box 5367 (45202)
PHONE.............................513 621-8300

Judy Haefling, Office Mgr
J Scott Golan, Administration
EMP: 54
SALES (corp-wide): 421.5MM **Privately
Held**
SIC: 8721 8748 Certified public account-
ant; business consulting
PA: Bkd, Llp
910 E Saint Louis St # 400
Springfield MO 65806
417 831-7283

(G-3054)
**BLACK STONE CINCINNATI LLC
(PA)**
Also Called: Assisted Care By Black Stone
4700 E Galbraith Rd Fl 3 (45236-2754)
PHONE.............................513 924-1370
David Tramontana, CEO
Christine Doggett, Vice Pres
Ronnell Spears, CIO
Kimberly Neikirk, Director
EMP: 45
SALES (est): 13.8MM **Privately Held**
SIC: 8082 Home health care services

(G-3055)
**BLACKBIRD CAPITAL GROUP
LLC**
312 Walnut St Ste 1600 (45202-4038)
PHONE.............................513 762-7890
John P Vota,
EMP: 170 EST: 2006
SALES (est): 7.2MM **Privately Held**
SIC: 6799 Real estate investors, except
property operators

(G-3056)
BLEUX HOLDINGS LLC
7257 Wooster Pike (45227-3830)
PHONE.............................859 414-5060
Jon Henson, Principal
EMP: 35 **Privately Held**
SIC: 6719 Holding companies

(G-3057)
BLUE & CO LLC
720 E Pete Rose Way # 100 (45202-3583)
PHONE.............................513 241-4507
Stephen Mann, Branch Mgr
EMP: 149
SALES (corp-wide): 37.6MM **Privately
Held**
SIC: 8721 Certified public accountant
PA: Blue & Co., Llc
12800 N Meridian St # 400
Carmel IN 46032
317 848-8920

(G-3058)
**BLUE ASH BUSINESS
ASSOCIATION**
P.O. Box 429277 (45242-9277)
PHONE.............................513 253-1006
Larry Bresko, Vice Pres
EMP: 100
SALES (est): 1MM **Privately Held**
SIC: 8611 Business associations

(G-3059)
**BLUE ASH DISTRIBUTION CTR
LLC**
2135 Dana Ave Ste 200 (45207-1327)
PHONE.............................513 699-2279
Will Sayer, Finance
EMP: 30
SALES (est): 397.4K **Privately Held**
SIC: 6531 Real estate agents & managers

(G-3060)
**BLUE ASH HEALTHCARE
GROUP INC**
Also Called: Blue Ash Care Center
4900 Cooper Rd (45242-6915)
PHONE.............................513 793-3362
George Repchick, President
EMP: 40
SALES (est): 2.8MM **Privately Held**
WEB: www.saberhealth.com
SIC: 8051 8059 Skilled nursing care facili-
ties; nursing home, except skilled & inter-
mediate care facility

(G-3061)

BLUE CHIP 2000 COML CLG INC
Also Called: Blue Chip Pros
7250 Edington Dr (45249-1063)
PHONE.................................513 561-2999
Daniel F Hopkins, *President*
Gary J Hopkins, *Vice Pres*
Debbie Gadberry, *CFO*
EMP: 450
SALES (est): 18.2MM **Privately Held**
SIC: 7349 Cleaning service, industrial or commercial

(G-3062)

BLUE CHIP PLUMBING INC
1950 Waycross Rd (45240-2827)
PHONE.................................513 941-4010
Bryan Gilbert, *President*
EMP: 60
SALES (est): 614.9K **Privately Held**
SIC: 1711 Plumbing contractors

(G-3063)

BLUE CHP SRGCL CTR PTNS LLC
4760 Red Bank Rd Ste 222 (45227-1549)
P.O. Box 42666 (45242-0666)
PHONE.................................513 561-8900
Jay Rom, *President*
EMP: 51
SALES (est): 7.8MM **Privately Held**
WEB: www.bluechipsurgical.com
SIC: 8062 General medical & surgical hospitals

(G-3064)

BLUE STAR LUBRICATION TECH LLC
3630 E Kemper Rd (45241-2011)
PHONE.................................847 285-1888
Jeff Worth, *Mng Member*
Tim Davis,
EMP: 28
SQ FT: 3,200
SALES (est): 13.2MM **Privately Held**
WEB: www.bluestarlt.com
SIC: 5172 Lubricating oils & greases

(G-3065)

BOB SUMEREL TIRE CO INC
2540 Annuity Dr (45241-1502)
PHONE.................................513 792-6600
Bill Mountford, *Manager*
EMP: 35
SALES (corp-wide): 89.7MM **Privately Held**
WEB: www.bobsumereltire.com
SIC: 5012 5014 Trucks, commercial; automobile tires & tubes; truck tires & tubes
PA: Bob Sumerel Tire Co., Inc.
    1257 Cox Ave
    Erlanger KY 41018
    859 283-2700

(G-3066)

BOISE CASCADE COMPANY
771 Neeb Rd (45233-4698)
PHONE.................................513 451-5700
P J Arling, *Branch Mgr*
EMP: 30
SALES (corp-wide): 5B **Publicly Held**
SIC: 5031 Lumber, plywood & millwork; lumber: rough, dressed & finished
PA: Boise Cascade Company
    1111 W Jefferson St # 300
    Boise ID 83702
    208 384-6161

(G-3067)

BONNEVILLE INTERNATIONAL CORP
2060 Reading Rd Ste 400 (45202-1456)
PHONE.................................513 699-5102
Duke Hamilton, *Branch Mgr*
EMP: 83
SALES (corp-wide): 3.9B **Privately Held**
WEB: www.boncom.com
SIC: 4832 Radio broadcasting stations
HQ: Bonneville International Corporation
    55 N 300 W Ste 315
    Salt Lake City UT 84101
    303 321-0950

(G-3068)

BORDEN DAIRY CO CINCINNATI LLC
Also Called: H. Meyer Dairy
415 John St (45215-5481)
PHONE.................................513 948-8811
David R Meyer, *President*
Mike Campe, *Info Tech Mgr*
James Houchin, *Maintence Staff*
EMP: 154 EST: 1976
SALES (est): 54MM **Privately Held**
WEB: www.meyerdairy.com
SIC: 2026 2086 5143 5144 Milk processing (pasteurizing, homogenizing, bottling); bottled & canned soft drinks; dairy products, except dried or canned; poultry & poultry products
PA: Borden Dairy Company
    8750 N Central Expy # 400
    Dallas TX 75231

(G-3069)

BOY SCOUTS OF AMERICA (PA)
Also Called: Dan Beard Council
10078 Reading Rd (45241-4833)
PHONE.................................513 961-2336
Laura Brunner, *President*
EMP: 50
SQ FT: 13,400
SALES (est): 6.5MM **Privately Held**
WEB: www.danbeard.org
SIC: 8641 Boy Scout organization

(G-3070)

BOYS & GIRLS CLUBS GRTR CINC (PA)
600 Dalton Ave (45203-1214)
PHONE.................................513 421-8909
Laura Baumann, *President*
EMP: 70
SQ FT: 4,500
SALES (est): 3.8MM **Privately Held**
WEB: www.bgcgc.org
SIC: 8641 Youth organizations

(G-3071)

BRENDAMOUR MOVING & STOR INC
2630 Glendale Milford Rd D (45241-4835)
PHONE.................................800 354-9715
Jack Brendamour, *CEO*
Michael Brendamour, *President*
Joan Brendamour, *Vice Pres*
Jeff Brendamour, *Opers Mgr*
Chuck Wolfe, *Treasurer*
EMP: 65
SALES (est): 7.7MM **Privately Held**
WEB: www.brendamourmoving.com
SIC: 4214 4213 Household goods moving & storage, local; trucking, except local

(G-3072)

BRG REALTY GROUP LLC (PA)
Also Called: Berkshire Realty Group
7265 Kenwood Rd Ste 111 (45236-4411)
PHONE.................................513 936-5960
Sheilah Johnson, *Vice Pres*
Dennis L Laake, *CFO*
Andrew R Giannelli,
Kellie Davis, *Executive Asst*
Pam Abner, *Administration*
EMP: 156
SALES (est): 17.5MM **Privately Held**
SIC: 6531 Rental agent, real estate

(G-3073)

BRICKER & ECKLER LLP
201 E 5th St Ste 1110 (45202-4135)
PHONE.................................513 870-6700
Kurt Tunnell, *Managing Prtnr*
Robert Woods, *Administration*
EMP: 163
SALES (corp-wide): 51.9MM **Privately Held**
SIC: 8111 9222 General practice attorney, lawyer; Attorney General's office
PA: Bricker & Eckler Llp
    100 S 3rd St Ste B
    Columbus OH 43215
    614 227-2300

(G-3074)

BRIDGETOWN MIDDLE SCHOOL PTA
3900 Race Rd (45211-4300)
PHONE.................................513 574-3511
Kim Cybulski, *Principal*
EMP: 65
SALES (est): 821.9K **Privately Held**
SIC: 8641 Parent-teachers' association

(G-3075)

BRINKS INCORPORATED
1105 Hopkins St (45203-1119)
PHONE.................................513 621-9310
Mike Moorman, *Manager*
EMP: 65
SALES (corp-wide): 3.4B **Publicly Held**
WEB: www.brinksinc.com
SIC: 7381 Armored car services
HQ: Brink's, Incorporated
    1801 Bayberry Ct Ste 400
    Richmond VA 23226
    804 289-9600

(G-3076)

BROADBAND EXPRESS LLC
11359 Mosteller Rd (45241-1827)
PHONE.................................513 834-8085
Dusty Banks, *Branch Mgr*
EMP: 48
SALES (corp-wide): 3.1B **Publicly Held**
SIC: 1731 Cable television installation
HQ: Broadband Express, Llc
    374 Westdale Ave Ste B
    Westerville OH 43082
    614 823-6464

(G-3077)

BROOKDALE DEER PARK
3801 E Galbraith Rd Ofc (45236-1585)
PHONE.................................513 745-7600
Noreen Bouley, *Manager*
EMP: 57
SQ FT: 20,075
SALES (est): 1MM **Privately Held**
SIC: 8059 Domiciliary care

(G-3078)

BROOKDALE SENIOR LIVING INC
9101 Winton Rd (45231-3829)
PHONE.................................855 308-2438
Christine Butler, *Director*
EMP: 74
SALES (corp-wide): 4.5B **Publicly Held**
SIC: 8059 Nursing home, except skilled & intermediate care facility
PA: Brookdale Senior Living
    111 Westwood Pl Ste 400
    Brentwood TN 37027
    615 221-2250

(G-3079)

BROOKDALE SENIOR LIVING INC
9090 Montgomery Rd (45242-7712)
PHONE.................................513 745-9292
Kelli Marshall-Pope, *Marketing Staff*
Mark Ohlendorf, *Branch Mgr*
EMP: 37
SALES (corp-wide): 4.5B **Publicly Held**
SIC: 8059 Nursing home, except skilled & intermediate care facility
PA: Brookdale Senior Living
    111 Westwood Pl Ste 400
    Brentwood TN 37027
    615 221-2250

(G-3080)

BROOKDALE SENIOR LIVING INC
3801 E Galbraith Rd Ofc (45236-1585)
PHONE.................................513 745-7600
EMP: 63
SALES (corp-wide): 4.5B **Publicly Held**
SIC: 8059 Nursing home, except skilled & intermediate care facility
PA: Brookdale Senior Living
    111 Westwood Pl Ste 400
    Brentwood TN 37027
    615 221-2250

(G-3081)

BROTHERS PROPERTIES CORP
Also Called: Cinncinnatian Hotel, The
601 Vine St Ste 1 (45202-2408)
PHONE.................................513 381-3000
Victor Fuller, *President*
Stephen Fuller, *Vice Pres*
EMP: 125
SALES (est): 9.5MM **Privately Held**
WEB: www.cincinnatianhotel.com
SIC: 7011 5812 5813 Hotels; eating places; bar (drinking places)

(G-3082)

BROWER PRODUCTS INC (DH)
Also Called: Cabinet Solutions By Design
401 Northland Blvd (45240-3210)
PHONE.................................937 563-1111
Daniel C Brower, *Ch of Bd*
William Brower, *President*
Mark Frericks, *Vice Pres*
EMP: 65
SQ FT: 125,000
SALES (est): 11.2MM **Privately Held**
SIC: 5031 2434 5211 3281 Whol Lumber/Plywd/Millwk Mfg Wood Kitchen Cabinet
HQ: Nisbet, Inc.
    11575 Reading Rd
    Cincinnati OH 45241
    513 563-1111

(G-3083)

BRUCE M ALLMAN
312 Walnut St Ste 1400 (45202-4029)
PHONE.................................513 352-6712
Bruce M Allman, *Partner*
EMP: 80
SALES (est): 2.1MM **Privately Held**
SIC: 8111 General practice attorney, lawyer

(G-3084)

BRUCE R BRACKEN
Also Called: Uc Physician
222 Piedmont Ave (45219-4231)
PHONE.................................513 558-3700
Bruce R Bracken, *Owner*
EMP: 30
SALES (est): 649.1K **Privately Held**
SIC: 8011 Urologist

(G-3085)

BSI ENGINEERING LLC (PA)
300 E Bus Way Ste 300 (45241)
PHONE.................................513 201-3100
Phil Beirne, *President*
Blake Leclair, *Project Mgr*
Dan Prickel, *CFO*
John Garmany, *Admin Sec*
EMP: 130
SQ FT: 17,000
SALES (est): 36.2MM **Privately Held**
SIC: 8711 Consulting engineer

(G-3086)

BUDCO GROUP INC (PA)
Also Called: O/B Leasing Company
1100 Gest St (45203-1114)
PHONE.................................513 621-6111
Otto Budig Jr, *President*
George J Budig, *Vice Pres*
Brian Schwartz, *Controller*
EMP: 25
SQ FT: 55,000
SALES (est): 195.1MM **Privately Held**
SIC: 7359 Equipment rental & leasing

(G-3087)

BUILDERS FIRSTSOURCE INC
10059 Princeton Glendale (45246-1223)
PHONE.................................513 874-9950
Mike Stimpfl, *Sales & Mktg St*
Josh Gross, *Manager*
EMP: 28
SALES (corp-wide): 7.7B **Publicly Held**
WEB: www.hopelumber.com
SIC: 5211 5031 Home centers; lumber, plywood & millwork
PA: Builders Firstsource, Inc.
    2001 Bryan St Ste 1600
    Dallas TX 75201
    214 880-3500

(G-3088)
BUILDING 8 INC
Also Called: J & N
10995 Canal Rd (45241-1886)
PHONE....................................513 771-8000
Thomas J Kuechly, *President*
David W Blocker, *Vice Pres*
Nick Kuechly, *Vice Pres*
Edoardo D Poffo, *Vice Pres*
Rich Mitchell, *Warehouse Mgr*
▲ **EMP:** 27 **EST:** 1954
SQ FT: 68,000
SALES (est): 38.8MM
SALES (corp-wide): 301.1MM **Privately Held**
WEB: www.jnae.com
SIC: 5013 Automotive supplies & parts; alternators
HQ: Arrowhead Electrical Products, Inc.
3705 95th Ave Ne
Circle Pines MN 55014
763 255-2555

(G-3089)
BURGESS & NIPLE INC
312 Plum St Ste 1210 (45202-2678)
PHONE....................................513 579-0042
Barry Y Dixon, *Director*
EMP: 105
SALES (corp-wide): 122.1MM **Privately Held**
WEB: www.burgessniple.com
SIC: 8712 8711 Architectural engineering; consulting engineer
PA: Burgess & Niple, Inc.
5085 Reed Rd
Columbus OH 43220
502 254-2344

(G-3090)
BURKE INC (PA)
Also Called: Burke Institute
500 W 7th St (45203-1543)
PHONE....................................513 241-5663
Jeff Miller, *CEO*
Micheal H Baumgardner, *President*
Stacy McWhorter, *Senior VP*
Andrew MA, *Senior VP*
Mike Webster, *Senior VP*
EMP: 202
SQ FT: 51,000
SALES (est): 55MM **Privately Held**
SIC: 8732 8742 Market analysis or research; management consulting services

(G-3091)
BURKE & SCHINDLER PLLC
901 Evans St (45204)
PHONE....................................859 344-8887
Linda Sloan, *Manager*
Lynnda Kasanicky, *Consultant*
Gene Schindler,
Patrick Burke,
Harold Jarner,
EMP: 30
SALES (est): 1.1MM **Privately Held**
SIC: 8721 Certified public accountant

(G-3092)
BURKE MANLEY LPA
225 W Court St (45202-1012)
PHONE....................................513 721-5525
Robert Manley, *President*
Kathie Thomas, *President*
Bonnie Bockelman, *Manager*
EMP: 27
SALES (est): 3MM **Privately Held**
WEB: www.mbl-law.com
SIC: 8111 General practice attorney, lawyer

(G-3093)
BURLINGTON HOUSE INC
2222 Springdale Rd (45231-1805)
PHONE....................................513 851-7888
Stephen L Rosedale, *President*
Beatrice W Rosedale, *Vice Pres*
Thomas Van Hook, *Director*
EMP: 100
SQ FT: 2,682
SALES (est): 2.9MM **Privately Held**
SIC: 8051 Convalescent home with continuous nursing care

(G-3094)
BURTONS COLLISION
Also Called: Burtons Collision & Auto Repr
4384 E Galbraith Rd (45236-2618)
PHONE....................................513 984-3396
Duane Burton, *Owner*
Kathy Penter, *Asst Mgr*
EMP: 35
SALES (est): 2.2MM **Privately Held**
WEB: www.burtonscollision.com
SIC: 7532 7538 7539 Body shop, automotive; general automotive repair shops; engine repair; engine rebuilding: automotive; frame & front end repair services; powertrain components repair services; electrical services; brake services

(G-3095)
BUSINESS BACKER LLC
10856 Reed Hartman Hwy # 100
(45242-2820)
PHONE....................................513 792-6866
Jim Salters, *President*
David Polaniecki, *Partner*
Steve Tosh, *COO*
Candace Levine, *VP Finance*
Chelsea Franklin, *Human Resources*
EMP: 25
SALES (est): 7.7MM
SALES (corp-wide): 1.1B **Publicly Held**
SIC: 6153 7389 Working capital financing; financial services
PA: Enova International, Inc.
175 W Jackson Blvd Fl 10
Chicago IL 60604
312 568-4200

(G-3096)
BUSINESS EQUIPMENT CO INC
Also Called: Beco Legal Systems
175 Tri County Pkwy # 120 (45246-3237)
PHONE....................................513 948-1500
Michael Brookbank, *President*
John Brookbank, *Vice Pres*
Therese Shumate, *Manager*
Jim Brun, *IT/INT Sup*
EMP: 25
SQ FT: 10,000
SALES (est): 4.5MM **Privately Held**
SIC: 7371 Computer software development

(G-3097)
BUSKEN BAKERY INC (PA)
2675 Madison Rd (45208-1389)
PHONE....................................513 871-2114
D Page Busken, *President*
Marilyn Buskirk, *General Mgr*
Brian Busken, *Senior VP*
Tina Toole, *Vice Pres*
Jaime Solis, *Prdtn Mgr*
EMP: 90 **EST:** 1928
SQ FT: 21,000
SALES (est): 33.4MM **Privately Held**
WEB: www.busken.com
SIC: 5461 5149 Bread; bakery products

(G-3098)
BYER STEEL RECYCLING INC (PA)
Also Called: Byer Steel Division
200 W North Bend Rd (45216-1728)
P.O. Box 1817 (45201-1817)
PHONE....................................513 948-0300
Burke Byer, *President*
Jay Binder, *COO*
Jonas Allen, *Vice Pres*
Larry Byer, *Vice Pres*
Shawn Eddy, *Vice Pres*
EMP: 38
SQ FT: 100,000
SALES (est): 22MM **Privately Held**
WEB: www.acomsteel.com
SIC: 5093 Ferrous metal scrap & waste

(G-3099)
C J & L CONSTRUCTION INC
11980 Runyan Dr (45241-1623)
PHONE....................................513 769-3600
James J Kossen Jr, *President*
Matt Brannigan, *Marketing Staff*
Marc Rees, *Manager*
EMP: 25
SQ FT: 2,100

SALES (est): 4.5MM **Privately Held**
WEB: www.cjlconstruction.com
SIC: 1611 Highway & street maintenance

(G-3100)
C K OF CINCINNATI INC
Also Called: Comfort Keepers
7525 State Rd Ste B (45255-6406)
PHONE....................................513 752-5533
Veronica Disimile, *President*
Chris Disimile, *Vice Pres*
EMP: 105 **EST:** 2001
SALES (est): 2.7MM **Privately Held**
SIC: 8082 Home health care services

(G-3101)
C MICAH RAND INC
Also Called: Brookwood Retirement Community
12100 Reed Hartman Hwy (45241-6071)
PHONE....................................513 605-2000
Steve Boymel, *President*
Stan Silverman, *Purchasing*
Wilkins Teresa, *Sls & Mktg Exec*
Beth Liesch, *Office Mgr*
Shari Turner, *Director*
EMP: 150
SQ FT: 180,000
SALES: 15.5MM **Privately Held**
SIC: 8051 Skilled nursing care facilities

(G-3102)
C&C CLEAN TEAM ENTERPRISES LLC
Also Called: Widmer's
2016 Madison Rd (45208-3238)
PHONE....................................513 321-5100
Lisa Younger, *Marketing Staff*
Steve Carico, *Mng Member*
Jack Cunningham,
EMP: 250
SALES (est): 13.5MM **Privately Held**
SIC: 7212 7217 Garment pressing & cleaners' agents; carpet & upholstery cleaning

(G-3103)
CADRE COMPUTER RESOURCES CO (PA)
Also Called: Cadre Information Security
201 E 5th St Ste 1800 (45202-4162)
PHONE....................................513 762-7350
Sandra E Laney, *CEO*
Steven W Snider, *President*
Stephen M Krumpelman, *Vice Pres*
Melissa Majewski, *Sales Mgr*
Greg Stewart, *Accounts Exec*
EMP: 48
SQ FT: 8,000
SALES (est): 37.2MM **Privately Held**
WEB: www.cadre.net
SIC: 7379 ; computer related consulting services

(G-3104)
CAI/INSURANCE AGENCY INC (PA)
Also Called: ACTUARIAL & EMPLOYEE BENEFIT S
2035 Reading Rd (45202-1415)
PHONE....................................513 221-1140
Carl R Schlotman III, *CEO*
Michael Schlotman, *COO*
Jimmie Foster, *Senior VP*
Kevin Schlotman, *Senior VP*
James T Schlotman, *Admin Sec*
EMP: 42
SQ FT: 17,000
SALES: 7MM **Privately Held**
SIC: 6411 Insurance agents

(G-3105)
CALFEE HALTER & GRISWOLD LLP
255 E 5th St (45202-4700)
PHONE....................................513 693-4880
Shelli Spine, *Office Mgr*
EMP: 192
SALES (corp-wide): 49.3MM **Privately Held**
SIC: 8111 General practice attorney, lawyer

PA: Calfee, Halter & Griswold Llp
1405 E 6th St Ste 1
Cleveland OH 44114
216 831-2732

(G-3106)
CAMARGO CLUB
8605 Shawnee Run Rd (45243-2811)
PHONE....................................513 561-9292
Joseph Beech III, *Vice Pres*
Doug Postler, *Treasurer*
EMP: 105 **EST:** 1925
SQ FT: 7,000
SALES: 3.9MM **Privately Held**
SIC: 7997 Country club, membership

(G-3107)
CAMARGO CONSTRUCTION COMPANY
6801 Shawnee Run Rd (45243-2417)
PHONE....................................513 248-1500
Harry W Adler Jr, *President*
Rita Adler, *Manager*
EMP: 35
SQ FT: 1,200
SALES (est): 3.7MM **Privately Held**
WEB: www.camargoconstruction.com
SIC: 1611 1794 1542 Surfacing & paving; excavation work; commercial & office building, new construction

(G-3108)
CAMARGO MANOR INC
Also Called: Pavillion At Camargo, The
12100 Reed Hartman Hwy (45241-6071)
PHONE....................................513 605-3000
Henry Schneider, *President*
Steven Boymel, *Vice Pres*
Jerry Stanislaw, *Treasurer*
James E Lark, *Director*
EMP: 80
SQ FT: 10,000
SALES (est): 1.2MM **Privately Held**
SIC: 8051 8052 Skilled nursing care facilities; intermediate care facilities

(G-3109)
CAMARGO RENTAL CENTER INC
8149 Camargo Rd (45243-2203)
PHONE....................................513 271-6510
David Murphy, *CEO*
Natalie S Currin, *President*
EMP: 28
SQ FT: 30,000
SALES (est): 3MM **Privately Held**
WEB: www.camargorental.com
SIC: 7299 7359 7389 Facility rental & party planning services; party planning service; party supplies rental services; decoration service for special events

(G-3110)
CAMDEN MANAGEMENT INC
Also Called: Real Estate
463 Ohio Pike Ste 304 (45255-3722)
P.O. Box 960, Milford (45150-0960)
PHONE....................................513 383-1635
Robert Camden, *President*
EMP: 26
SALES (est): 966.4K **Privately Held**
SIC: 8741 Business management

(G-3111)
CAMPBELL SALES COMPANY
8805 Governors Hill Dr # 300
(45249-3318)
PHONE....................................513 697-2900
Keith Olscamp, *Manager*
EMP: 30
SALES (corp-wide): 8.6B **Publicly Held**
WEB: www.campbellsoup.com
SIC: 8743 Sales promotion
HQ: Campbell Sales Company
1 Campbell Pl
Camden NJ 08103
856 342-4800

(G-3112)
CAMPEON ROOFG & WATERPROOFING
3535 Round Bottom Rd (45244-3025)
PHONE....................................513 271-8972
Mary B Barnes, *President*
Peter A Barnes, *Treasurer*

EMP: 50
SQ FT: 10,000
SALES (est): 5.2MM **Privately Held**
WEB: www.campeon.com
SIC: **1761** Roofing contractor; sheet metal-work

(G-3113)
CAPITAL INVESTMENT GROUP INC
226 E 8th St (45202-2104)
PHONE....................513 241-5090
David Bastos, *President*
Teresa Haas, *Accountant*
EMP: 40
SALES (est): 2.1MM **Privately Held**
SIC: **6799** Investors

(G-3114)
CAR WASH PLUS LTD
12105 Montgomery Rd (45249-1730)
PHONE....................513 683-4228
Bill Austin, *Owner*
EMP: 30
SQ FT: 5,000
SALES (est): 594.5K **Privately Held**
SIC: **7542** Washing & polishing, automotive

(G-3115)
CARACOLE INC
4138 Hamilton Ave (45223-2293)
PHONE....................513 761-1480
Mark McComas, *CFO*
Dean Clevenger, *Office Mgr*
Linda Seiter, *Exec Dir*
EMP: 41
SQ FT: 4,800
SALES: 4.5MM **Privately Held**
WEB: www.caracole.org
SIC: **8361 8322** Home for destitute men & women; referral service for personal & social problems

(G-3116)
CARDIAC VSCLAR THRCIC SURGEONS
4030 Smith Rd Ste 300 (45209-1974)
PHONE....................513 421-3494
Steven Park, *President*
Creighton Wright, *Vice Pres*
EMP: 38
SALES (est): 5MM
SALES (corp-wide): 4.7B **Privately Held**
WEB: www.cvts.com
SIC: **8011** Cardiologist & cardio-vascular specialist
PA: Mercy Health
 1701 Mercy Health Pl
 Cincinnati OH 45237
 513 639-2800

(G-3117)
CARDINAL PACELLI SCHOOL
927 Ellison Ave (45226-1287)
PHONE....................513 321-1048
Fax: 513 533-6114
EMP: 360 EST: 2012
SALES (est): 3.1MM **Privately Held**
SIC: **8211 8351** Elementary/Secondary School Child Day Care Services

(G-3118)
CARDINAL SOLUTIONS GROUP INC (HQ)
7755 Montgomery Rd # 510 (45236-7923)
PHONE....................513 984-6700
Kelly P Conway, *President*
Kristi Lell, *Human Res Mgr*
Nan Hatch, *Sr Consultant*
EMP: 98 EST: 1996
SALES (est): 18MM **Publicly Held**
WEB: www.cardinalsolutions.com
SIC: **7379** ; computer related consulting services

(G-3119)
CARDIOLOGY CTR OF CINCINNATI (PA)
Also Called: Cardiology Center Cincinnati
10525 Montgomery Rd A (45242-4401)
P.O. Box 631834 (45263-0001)
PHONE....................513 745-9800
Edward J Loughery, *President*
EMP: 30

SALES (est): 6.7MM **Privately Held**
WEB: www.thecardiologycenter.com
SIC: **8011** Cardiologist & cardio-vascular specialist

(G-3120)
CARE CONNECTION OF CINCINNATI
4420 Cooper Rd Ste 100 (45242-5660)
PHONE....................513 842-1101
Bob James,
Tony Izquierdo,
EMP: 70
SALES (est): 22.9MM **Privately Held**
WEB: www.ccohomecare.com
SIC: **8082** Visiting nurse service

(G-3121)
CAREGIVERS HEALTH NETWORK INC
2135 Dana Ave Ste 200 (45207-1327)
PHONE....................513 662-3400
Mary S Allen, *Principal*
Rebecca Miars, *Vice Pres*
EMP: 70
SALES (est): 1.3MM
SALES (corp-wide): 1.8B **Publicly Held**
WEB: www.caregivershealthnetwork.com
SIC: **8082** Home health care services
HQ: Almost Family, Inc.
 9510 Ormsby Station Rd # 300
 Louisville KY 40223
 502 891-1000

(G-3122)
CARESTAR INC (PA)
5566 Cheviot Rd (45247-7094)
PHONE....................513 618-8300
Thomas J Gruber, *President*
EMP: 112
SQ FT: 15,000
SALES (est): 25.9MM **Privately Held**
SIC: **7361 8082** Nurses' registry; home health care services

(G-3123)
CAREW REALTY INC
441 Vine St Ste 3900 (45202-3011)
PHONE....................513 241-3888
Stewart Warm, *Ch of Bd*
Alex Warm, *Vice Ch Bd*
Steven N Stein, *President*
James F Bastin, *CFO*
EMP: 45
SALES (est): 3.8MM **Privately Held**
SIC: **6512** Commercial & industrial building operation

(G-3124)
CARINGTON HEALTH SYSTEMS
Also Called: Glencare Center
3627 Harvey Ave (45229-2005)
PHONE....................513 961-8881
Bob Bishop, *Administration*
EMP: 110
SALES (corp-wide): 85.7MM **Privately Held**
SIC: **8051 8049** Convalescent home with continuous nursing care; physical therapist
PA: Carington Health Systems
 8200 Beckett Park Dr
 Hamilton OH 45011
 513 682-2700

(G-3125)
CAROL A & RALP V H US B FDN TR
425 Walnut St Fl 11f (45202-3944)
PHONE....................513 632-4426
EMP: 35
SALES: 24.1MM **Privately Held**
SIC: **8699** Charitable organization

(G-3126)
CAROL REESE
Also Called: Center Service
421 Anderson Ferry Rd (45238-5228)
PHONE....................513 347-0252
Carol Reese, *Owner*
Carol Mefford, *Owner*
EMP: 25
SALES (est): 642.3K **Privately Held**
SIC: **7389** Telephone answering service

(G-3127)
CARUSO INC (PA)
3465 Hauck Rd (45241-1601)
PHONE....................513 860-9200
Jim Caruso, *CEO*
James S Caruso, *Principal*
Steve Caruso, *Exec VP*
Mike Caruso, *Vice Pres*
Wayne Kramer, *Vice Pres*
▲ EMP: 105 EST: 1926
SQ FT: 155,000
SALES (est): 83.2MM **Privately Held**
WEB: www.carusofoods.com
SIC: **5148** General warehousing & storage

(G-3128)
CAS-KER COMPANY INC
2550 Civic Center Dr (45231-1310)
PHONE....................513 674-7700
Patrick J Cassedy, *President*
Daniel B Cassedy, *Corp Secy*
Thomas J Cassedy, *Vice Pres*
Richard Foster, *Vice Pres*
▲ EMP: 38
SQ FT: 21,750
SALES (est): 8.6MM **Privately Held**
WEB: www.casker.com
SIC: **5094** Clocks, watches & parts

(G-3129)
CASCO MFG SOLUTIONS INC
3107 Spring Grove Ave (45225-1821)
PHONE....................513 681-0003
Melissa Mangold, *President*
Thomas Mangold, *Chairman*
Terri Mangold, *Vice Pres*
Scott Clifford, *CFO*
David Stewart, *Human Res Mgr*
▲ EMP: 60 EST: 1959
SQ FT: 72,000
SALES (est): 10.6MM **Privately Held**
WEB: www.cascosolutions.com
SIC: **2515 7641 3841 2522** Mattresses, containing felt, foam rubber, urethane, etc.; upholstery work; surgical & medical instruments; office furniture, except wood; household furnishings

(G-3130)
CASSIDY TRLEY COML RE SVCS INC
Also Called: Colliers Turley Martin Tucker
300 E Bus Way Ste 190 (45241)
PHONE....................513 771-2580
Marnie Castleberry, *Branch Mgr*
EMP: 25
SALES (corp-wide): 1.2MM **Privately Held**
SIC: **6531** Real estate agent, commercial
HQ: Cassidy Turley Commercial Real Estate Services Inc.
 7700 Forsyth Blvd Ste 900
 Saint Louis MO 63105
 314 862-7100

(G-3131)
CATALINA MARKETING CORPORATION
525 Vine St Ste 2200 (45202-3123)
PHONE....................513 564-8200
Kriss Jones, *Manager*
EMP: 36
SALES (corp-wide): 53.3MM **Privately Held**
WEB: www.catalinamktg.com
SIC: **8742** Marketing consulting services
HQ: Catalina Marketing Corporation
 200 Carillon Pkwy
 Saint Petersburg FL 33716
 727 579-5000

(G-3132)
CATHOLIC CHARITIES OF SW OHIO (PA)
7162 Reading Rd Ste 604 (45237-3819)
PHONE....................513 241-7745
M Kathleen Donnellan, *Exec Dir*
Gene Johnson, *Asst Director*
EMP: 90
SALES: 16.7MM **Privately Held**
SIC: **8322 4119** Social service center; local passenger transportation

(G-3133)
CATHOLIC RESIDENTIAL SERVICE
100 E 8th St Ste 5 (45202-2195)
PHONE....................513 784-0400
Christy Hoekzema, *Director*
EMP: 30
SALES: 3.1MM **Privately Held**
SIC: **8322** Social services for the handicapped

(G-3134)
CBRE INC
201 E 5th St Ste 2200 (45202-4113)
PHONE....................513 369-1300
Ken Murawski, *Managing Dir*
David Lockard, *Vice Pres*
Tim Schenke, *Vice Pres*
Robert Calhoun, *Engineer*
Kevin Schutte, *Vice Pres*
EMP: 71
SALES (corp-wide): 21.3B **Publicly Held**
SIC: **6531** Real estate agent, commercial
HQ: Cbre, Inc.
 400 S Hope St Ste 25
 Los Angeles CA 90071
 213 613-3333

(G-3135)
CBS CORPORATION
2060 Reading Rd Fl 34 (45202-1454)
PHONE....................513 749-1035
Jim Bryant, *Manager*
EMP: 130
SALES (corp-wide): 14.5B **Publicly Held**
SIC: **4832** Radio broadcasting stations
HQ: Cbs Corporation
 51 W 52nd St Bsmt 1
 New York NY 10019
 212 975-4321

(G-3136)
CBS RADIO INC
2060 Reading Rd (45202-1454)
PHONE....................513 699-5105
Jim Bryant, *Manager*
EMP: 60
SALES (corp-wide): 1.4B **Publicly Held**
WEB: www.infinityradio.com
SIC: **4832** Radio broadcasting stations, music format
HQ: Cbs Radio Inc.
 345 Hudson St Fl 10
 New York NY 10014
 212 314-9200

(G-3137)
CBTS TECHNOLOGY SOLUTIONS LLC (HQ)
221 E 4th St (45202-4124)
P.O. Box 2301 (45201-2301)
PHONE....................513 841-2287
Theodore H Torbeck, *CEO*
John Burns, *President*
Leigh Fox, *President*
Scott Seger, *Vice Pres*
Don Verdon, *Vice Pres*
▼ EMP: 300
SQ FT: 10,000
SALES (est): 144.8MM
SALES (corp-wide): 1.3B **Publicly Held**
SIC: **7379 5734** Computer related consulting services; computer peripheral equipment
PA: Cincinnati Bell Inc.
 221 E 4th St Ste 700
 Cincinnati OH 45202
 513 397-9900

(G-3138)
CDW TECHNOLOGIES LLC
9349 Waterstone Blvd (45249-8320)
PHONE....................513 677-4100
Sean Eveslage, *Accounts Exec*
Marvin Gentry, *Sales Staff*
Chris Ashcraft, *Branch Mgr*
Adam Childers, *Manager*
Jeff Singleton, *Consultant*
EMP: 52 **Publicly Held**
WEB: www.berbee.com
SIC: **5045** Computers, peripherals & software
HQ: Cdw Technologies Llc
 5520 Research Park Dr
 Fitchburg WI 53711

(G-3139)
CE POWER ENGINEERED SVCS LLC (HQ)
4040 Rev Dr (45232-1914)
PHONE....................513 563-6150
Paul Cody, *CEO*
Mark Levine, *COO*
EMP: 69 EST: 2015
SALES: 80MM
SALES (corp-wide): 13.7MM **Privately Held**
SIC: 7629 Electrical repair shops
PA: Ce Power Holdings, Inc.
4040 Rev Dr
Cincinnati OH 45232
513 563-6150

(G-3140)
CE POWER HOLDINGS INC (PA)
4040 Rev Dr (45232-1914)
PHONE....................513 563-6150
William McCloy, *CEO*
EMP: 80
SALES (est): 13.7MM **Privately Held**
SIC: 6719 7629 Investment holding companies, except banks; electrical repair shops

(G-3141)
CEI PHYSICIANS PSC INC
7794 5 Mile Rd Ste 270 (45230-2369)
PHONE....................513 233-2700
Wendy Lippert, *Admin Mgr*
EMP: 31
SALES (corp-wide): 40.9MM **Privately Held**
SIC: 8011 Ophthalmologist
PA: Cei Physicians, P.S.C., Llc
1945 Cei Dr
Blue Ash OH 45242
513 984-5133

(G-3142)
CEI PHYSICIANS PSC INC
4760 Red Bank Rd Ste 108 (45227-1549)
PHONE....................513 531-2020
Heather Statton, *Branch Mgr*
EMP: 31
SALES (corp-wide): 40.9MM **Privately Held**
SIC: 8011 Ophthalmologist
PA: Cei Physicians, P.S.C., Llc
1945 Cei Dr
Blue Ash OH 45242
513 984-5133

(G-3143)
CELLCO PARTNERSHIP
Also Called: Verizon
9674 Colerain Ave (45251-2006)
PHONE....................513 923-2700
Ralph Wright, *Manager*
EMP: 71
SALES (corp-wide): 130.8B **Publicly Held**
SIC: 4812 Cellular telephone services
HQ: Cellco Partnership
1 Verizon Way
Basking Ridge NJ 07920

(G-3144)
CELLCO PARTNERSHIP
8650 Governors Hill Dr (45249-1372)
PHONE....................513 697-1190
Sharon Goldston, *Associate*
EMP: 71
SALES (corp-wide): 130.8B **Publicly Held**
SIC: 4812 Cellular telephone services
HQ: Cellco Partnership
1 Verizon Way
Basking Ridge NJ 07920

(G-3145)
CELLCO PARTNERSHIP
Also Called: Verizon
482 Ohio Pike Ste 1 (45255-7300)
PHONE....................513 688-1300
Pam Baird, *Branch Mgr*
EMP: 25
SALES (corp-wide): 130.8B **Publicly Held**
SIC: 4812 5731 Cellular telephone services; radio, television & electronic stores

HQ: Cellco Partnership
1 Verizon Way
Basking Ridge NJ 07920

(G-3146)
CELLCO PARTNERSHIP
Also Called: Verizon
55 E Kemper Rd (45246-3224)
PHONE....................513 671-2200
Lyn Boigt, *Branch Mgr*
EMP: 25
SALES (corp-wide): 130.8B **Publicly Held**
SIC: 4812 5999 Cellular telephone services; mobile telephones & equipment
HQ: Cellco Partnership
1 Verizon Way
Basking Ridge NJ 07920

(G-3147)
CELLCO PARTNERSHIP
Also Called: Verizon
9040 Union Cemetery Rd (45249-2016)
PHONE....................513 697-0222
Sue Milam, *Branch Mgr*
EMP: 30
SALES (corp-wide): 130.8B **Publicly Held**
SIC: 4812 5999 Cellular telephone services; mobile telephones & equipment
HQ: Cellco Partnership
1 Verizon Way
Basking Ridge NJ 07920

(G-3148)
CENTER FOR ADDICTION TREATMENT
830 Ezzard Charles Dr (45214-2525)
PHONE....................513 381-6672
Ronald T Derstadt, *VP Admin*
Nancy Blamer, *Manager*
Gladys Evans, *Supervisor*
Sandra L Keuhn, *Exec Dir*
EMP: 70
SQ FT: 31,000
SALES: 4.1MM **Privately Held**
SIC: 8069 8093 8063 Alcoholism rehabilitation hospital; drug addiction rehabilitation hospital; specialty outpatient clinics; psychiatric hospitals

(G-3149)
CENTRAL ACCOUNTING SYSTEMS (PA)
Also Called: Health Care Management Group
12500 Reed Hartman Hwy (45241-1892)
PHONE....................513 605-2700
Steven Boymel, *President*
Evan Boymel, *Vice Pres*
Stan Silverman, *Purchasing*
Allan Acheson, *CFO*
Renee Sharp, *Director*
EMP: 26
SALES (est): 20MM **Privately Held**
WEB: www.hcmg.com
SIC: 8721 Accounting, auditing & bookkeeping

(G-3150)
CENTRAL BUSINESS EQUIPMENT CO (HQ)
Also Called: Patterson Pope
10321 S Medallion Dr (45241-4825)
PHONE....................513 891-4430
Dennis Hammack, *President*
EMP: 27
SALES (est): 7.5MM
SALES (corp-wide): 108MM **Privately Held**
WEB: www.centralbusinessgroup.com
SIC: 5021 Filing units
PA: Patterson Pope, Inc.
3001 N Graham St
Charlotte NC 28206
704 523-4400

(G-3151)
CENTRAL CLINIC OUTPATIENT SVCS
311 Albert Sabin Way (45229-2838)
PHONE....................513 558-9005
Walter Smitson, *CEO*
Kathleen Fields, *CFO*
EMP: 99

SALES (est): 576.8K **Privately Held**
SIC: 8099 Health & allied services

(G-3152)
CENTRAL COMMNTY HLTH BRD OF HA (PA)
532 Maxwell Ave (45219-2408)
PHONE....................513 559-2000
Andy McCleese, *Engineer*
Larry Sykes, *Manager*
Deborah Smith, *Supervisor*
Charlie Bogenschutz, *MIS Dir*
Bennett Cooper Jr, *Exec Dir*
EMP: 100
SQ FT: 2,500
SALES: 10.1MM **Privately Held**
SIC: 8063 8093 Hospital for the mentally ill; specialty outpatient clinics

(G-3153)
CENTRAL COMMNTY HLTH BRD OF HA
Also Called: Crisis Stablization Center
536 Elliott Ave (45215-5416)
PHONE....................513 559-2000
Venessa Jetters, *Manager*
EMP: 100
SALES (corp-wide): 10.1MM **Privately Held**
SIC: 8063 Hospital for the mentally ill
PA: Central Community Health Board Of Hamilton County, The Inc.
532 Maxwell Ave
Cincinnati OH 45219
513 559-2000

(G-3154)
CENTRAL COMMNTY HLTH BRD OF HA
3020 Vernon Pl (45219-2418)
PHONE....................513 559-2981
Bennett Cooper, *Director*
EMP: 50
SALES (corp-wide): 10.1MM **Privately Held**
SIC: 8093 Drug clinic, outpatient
PA: Central Community Health Board Of Hamilton County, The Inc.
532 Maxwell Ave
Cincinnati OH 45219
513 559-2000

(G-3155)
CENTRAL INSULATION SYSTEMS INC
300 Murray Rd (45217-1011)
PHONE....................513 242-0600
Steve Kirby, *President*
Kathy Kirby, *Vice Pres*
Larry Kissel, *Vice Pres*
Dan Cross, *Project Mgr*
Jerry Lichtenfeld, *Project Mgr*
EMP: 50
SQ FT: 30,000
SALES (est): 8.9MM **Privately Held**
WEB: www.centralinsulation.com
SIC: 1799 1742 Asbestos removal & encapsulation; insulation, buildings

(G-3156)
CENTRAL PARKING SYSTEM INC
303 Broadway St Lot A (45202-4203)
PHONE....................513 381-2621
EMP: 35
SALES (corp-wide): 1.4B **Publicly Held**
SIC: 7521 Parking lots
HQ: Central Parking System, Inc.
1225 I St Nw Ste C100
Washington DC 20005
202 496-9650

(G-3157)
CENTRAL READY MIX LLC (PA)
6310 E Kemper Rd Ste 125 (45241-2370)
P.O. Box 70, Monroe (45050-0070)
PHONE....................513 402-5001
Toll Free:....................888 -
Robert Cherry,
EMP: 30 EST: 1934
SQ FT: 8,000
SALES (est): 11.1MM **Privately Held**
WEB: www.morainematerials.com
SIC: 3273 1442 Ready-mixed concrete; sand mining

(G-3158)
CENTRAL STEEL AND WIRE COMPANY
525 Township Ave (45216-2399)
PHONE....................513 242-2233
Mike Staggs, *Warehouse Mgr*
Tom Rogina, *Branch Mgr*
EMP: 150 **Publicly Held**
WEB: www.centralsteel.com
SIC: 5051 Steel
HQ: Central Steel And Wire Company
3000 W 51st St
Chicago IL 60632
773 471-3800

(G-3159)
CENTRAL USA WIRELESS LLC
11210 Montgomery Rd (45249-2311)
PHONE....................513 469-1500
Angie Flottemesch, *Opers Staff*
Mike Dalton, *CFO*
Chris Hildebrant, *Sales Staff*
EMP: 28
SALES (est): 2.9MM **Privately Held**
SIC: 7622 3663 Antenna repair & installation; antennas, transmitting & communications

(G-3160)
CENTRIC CONSULTING LLC
9380 Montgomery Rd # 207 (45242-7756)
PHONE....................513 791-3061
EMP: 33
SALES (corp-wide): 37.5MM **Privately Held**
SIC: 8999 Scientific consulting
PA: Centric Consulting, Llc
1215 Lyons Rd F
Dayton OH 45458
888 781-7567

(G-3161)
CENTURY MECH SOLUTIONS INC
Also Called: Honeywell Authorized Dealer
1554 Chase Ave (45223-2146)
P.O. Box 15948 (45215-0948)
PHONE....................513 681-5700
Thomas Lienhart Pe, *President*
Margaret Lienhart, *Corp Secy*
Doug S Nerhaus, *Vice Pres*
Kenneth J Weller, *Vice Pres*
EMP: 31 EST: 1938
SQ FT: 4,500
SALES (est): 1.8MM
SALES (corp-wide): 2.1B **Publicly Held**
SIC: 1711 Warm air heating & air conditioning contractor; mechanical contractor
PA: Comfort Systems Usa, Inc.
675 Bering Dr Ste 400
Houston TX 77057
713 830-9600

(G-3162)
CFM RELIGION PUBG GROUP LLC (PA)
8805 Governors Hill Dr # 400 (45249-3319)
PHONE....................513 931-4050
Matthew Thibeau, *President*
EMP: 31
SALES (est): 34.4MM **Privately Held**
SIC: 2721 8741 Magazines: publishing only, not printed on site; management services

(G-3163)
CFS CONSTRUCTION INC
2170 Gilbert Ave Ste 100 (45206-3019)
PHONE....................513 559-4500
Dan Scullin, *President*
EMP: 46
SQ FT: 5,000
SALES (est): 2.9MM **Privately Held**
WEB: www.cfsoh.com
SIC: 1522 1542 Hotel/motel & multi-family home renovation & remodeling; multi-family dwellings, new construction; commercial & office buildings, renovation & repair; commercial & office building, new construction

(G-3164)
CGH-GLOBAL SECURITY LLC
4957 Cinnamon Cir (45244-1210)
PHONE.....................................800 376-0655
Andrew Glassmeyer, *CEO*
EMP: 32 EST: 2016
SALES (est): 496.4K
SALES (corp-wide): 8MM **Privately Held**
SIC: 7389
PA: Cgh-Global, Llc
851 Ohio Pike Ste 203
Cincinnati OH 45245
800 376-0655

(G-3165)
CGH-GLOBAL TECHNOLOGIES LLC
4957 Cinnamon Cir (45244-1210)
PHONE.....................................800 376-0655
Andrew Glassmeyer, *CEO*
EMP: 32 EST: 2016
SALES (est): 524.3K
SALES (corp-wide): 8MM **Privately Held**
SIC: 8748 Business consulting
PA: Cgh-Global, Llc
851 Ohio Pike Ste 203
Cincinnati OH 45245
800 376-0655

(G-3166)
CH2M HILL INC
400 E Bus Way Ste 400 (45241)
PHONE.....................................513 243-5070
Mike Bartlett, *Principal*
EMP: 77
SALES (est): 22.3MM **Privately Held**
SIC: 8711 Consulting engineer

(G-3167)
CHAMPION CLG SPECIALISTS INC
8391 Blue Ash Rd (45236-1986)
PHONE.....................................513 871-2333
Toll Free:....................................888 -
Chris Kurtz, *President*
Pat Kurtz, *Vice Pres*
John Parnell, *Project Mgr*
EMP: 30 EST: 1982
SQ FT: 12,000
SALES (est): 1.5MM **Privately Held**
WEB: www.championcleaning.net
SIC: 7349 Cleaning service, industrial or commercial; air duct cleaning

(G-3168)
CHAMPION OPCO LLC (PA)
Also Called: Champion Windows Manufacturing
12121 Champion Way (45241-6419)
PHONE.....................................513 327-7338
Jim Mishler, *CEO*
Donald R Jones, *President*
Joe Faisant, *CFO*
▲ **EMP:** 300 EST: 1953
SQ FT: 500,000
SALES (est): 516.4MM **Privately Held**
WEB: www.championfactorydirct.com
SIC: 3089 1761 3442 Window frames & sash, plastic; siding contractor; storm doors or windows, metal

(G-3169)
CHAMPLIN HAUPT ARCHITECTS INC (PA)
Also Called: Champlin Architecture
720 E Pete Rose Way # 140 (45202-3375)
PHONE.....................................513 241-4474
Robert A Schilling Jr, *President*
Jay D Derenthal, *Principal*
Melissa M Lutz, *Principal*
Joan Tepe Wurtenberger, *Vice Pres*
Priya Dhuru, *Project Mgr*
EMP: 52
SQ FT: 6,900
SALES (est): 9.3MM **Privately Held**
WEB: www.charchitects.com
SIC: 8712 Architectural engineering

(G-3170)
CHARLES V FRANCIS TRUST
Also Called: Metro Recycling
19 W Vine St (45215-3233)
PHONE.....................................513 528-5600
Charles V Francis, *Owner*
EMP: 40

SALES (est): 2.8MM **Privately Held**
SIC: 6733 Personal investment trust management

(G-3171)
CHARLES W POWERS & ASSOC INC
Also Called: Powers Agency
1 W 4th St Ste 500 (45202-3610)
PHONE.....................................513 721-5353
Lori Powers, *CEO*
Charles W Powers, *President*
Jennifer King, *Vice Pres*
Mark Wesling, *Vice Pres*
Melissa McCann, *CFO*
EMP: 30
SALES (est): 5.6MM **Privately Held**
WEB: www.powersagency.com
SIC: 7311 Advertising consultant

(G-3172)
CHAS G BUCHY PACKING COMPANY
Also Called: Buchy Food Service
10510 Evendale Dr (45241-2516)
PHONE.....................................800 762-1060
G James Buchy, *President*
Sharon Buchy, *Vice Pres*
Kate Kerg, *Vice Pres*
EMP: 38 EST: 1878
SQ FT: 30,000
SALES (est): 11.7MM **Privately Held**
WEB: www.buchyfoods.com
SIC: 5141 Whol General Groceries

(G-3173)
CHECK IT OUT 4 ME LLC
7709 Greenland Pl Ste 1 (45237-2711)
PHONE.....................................513 568-4269
Carlton Eddins,
EMP: 25
SALES (est): 392.5K **Privately Held**
SIC: 8748 Business consulting

(G-3174)
CHEEK-O INC
639 Northland Blvd (45240-5202)
PHONE.....................................513 942-4880
EMP: 25
SALES (est): 3.7MM **Privately Held**
SIC: 5137 Whol Women's & Children's Clothing

(G-3175)
CHEMED CORPORATION (PA)
255 E 5th St Ste 2600 (45202-4138)
PHONE.....................................513 762-6690
George J Walsh III, *Ch of Bd*
Kevin J McNamara, *President*
Spencer S Lee, *Exec VP*
Nicholas M Westfall, *Exec VP*
Michael D Witzeman, *Vice Pres*
EMP: 86 EST: 1970
SALES: 1.7B **Publicly Held**
WEB: www.chemed.com
SIC: 1711 7699 8082 Plumbing, heating, air-conditioning contractors; plumbing contractors; sewer cleaning & rodding; visiting nurse service

(G-3176)
CHEMICAL BANK
7373 Beechmont Ave # 100 (45230-4100)
PHONE.....................................513 232-0800
Jim Sollars, *Manager*
EMP: 39
SALES (corp-wide): 924.5MM **Publicly Held**
SIC: 6035 Federal savings & loan associations
HQ: Chemical Bank
333 E Main St
Midland MI 48640
989 631-9200

(G-3177)
CHERRY GROVE SPORTS CENTER
Also Called: Cherry Grove Lanes
4005 Hopper Hill Rd (45255-4945)
PHONE.....................................513 232-7199
Jack Betts, *President*
Larry Roberts, *Principal*
EMP: 30
SQ FT: 852

SALES (est): 1.1MM **Privately Held**
WEB: www.cglanes.com
SIC: 7933 Ten pin center

(G-3178)
CHESAPEAKE RESEARCH REVIEW LLC
9380 Main St (45242-7657)
PHONE.....................................410 884-2900
Jeffrey Wendel,
EMP: 30
SALES (corp-wide): 7.8MM **Privately Held**
SIC: 8621 Professional standards review board
PA: Chesapeake Research Review, Llc
6940 Columbia Gateway Dr
Columbia MD 21046
410 884-2900

(G-3179)
CHEVIOT MUTUAL HOLDING COMPANY
3723 Glenmore Ave (45211-4720)
PHONE.....................................513 661-0457
Thomas J Linneman, *President*
EMP: 52
SALES (est): 3.5MM **Privately Held**
SIC: 6035 Federal savings & loan associations

(G-3180)
CHILD FOCUS INC (PA)
4629 Aicholtz Rd Ste 2 (45244-1560)
PHONE.....................................513 752-1555
James Carter, *CEO*
Sandy Lock, *COO*
Kevin Depew, *Manager*
EMP: 75
SQ FT: 27,000
SALES: 17MM **Privately Held**
WEB: www.child-focus.org
SIC: 8322 8093 8351 Child related social services; child guidance agency; family (marriage) counseling; mental health clinic, outpatient; head start center, except in conjunction with school

(G-3181)
CHILD FOCUS LEARNING CENTER
Also Called: Head Start
4629 Aicholtz Rd Ste 2 (45244-1560)
PHONE.....................................513 528-7224
Berta Zelilla, *Director*
EMP: 50
SALES (est): 1.1MM **Privately Held**
SIC: 8351 Preschool center

(G-3182)
CHILDRENS HM OF CNCINNATI OHIO
Also Called: CHILDREN'S HOME SCHOOL
5050 Madison Rd (45227-1491)
PHONE.....................................513 272-2800
Ellen Johnson, *CEO*
Roderick Hinton, *Vice Pres*
EMP: 200
SQ FT: 84,000
SALES: 25MM **Privately Held**
WEB: www.thechildrenshomecinti.org
SIC: 8322 Child related social services

(G-3183)
CHILDRENS HOSPITAL
3373 Burnet Ave (45229)
PHONE.....................................513 636-4051
Diane Holbrook, *Principal*
Melissa Stamper, *Pharmacist*
Todd Arthur, *Med Doctor*
Elizabeth Dupont, *Med Doctor*
Kathleen Ball, *Manager*
EMP: 28
SALES (est): 1.8MM **Privately Held**
SIC: 8062 General medical & surgical hospitals

(G-3184)
CHILDRENS HOSPITAL MEDICAL CTR
2750 Beekman St (45225-2049)
PHONE.....................................513 541-4500
Denia Redford,
EMP: 848

SALES (corp-wide): 1.6B **Privately Held**
SIC: 8062 General medical & surgical hospitals
PA: Children's Hospital Medical Center
3333 Burnet Ave
Cincinnati OH 45229
513 636-4200

(G-3185)
CHILDRENS HOSPITAL MEDICAL CTR
Also Called: Cincinnati Chld Hosp Med Ctr
3333 Burnet Ave (45229-3039)
PHONE.....................................513 636-4200
Jill Guilfoile, *Principal*
Dianna Mitchell, *Manager*
Melissa McCray, *Nurse Practr*
EMP: 727
SALES (corp-wide): 1.6B **Privately Held**
SIC: 8062 General medical & surgical hospitals
PA: Children's Hospital Medical Center
3333 Burnet Ave
Cincinnati OH 45229
513 636-4200

(G-3186)
CHILDRENS HOSPITAL MEDICAL CTR
Heart Institute Diagnostic Lab
240 Albert Sabin Way (45229-2842)
PHONE.....................................513 803-1751
Wenying Zhang, *Director*
EMP: 1332
SALES (corp-wide): 1.6B **Privately Held**
SIC: 8062 General medical & surgical hospitals
PA: Children's Hospital Medical Center
3333 Burnet Ave
Cincinnati OH 45229
513 636-4200

(G-3187)
CHILDRENS HOSPITAL MEDICAL CTR
2900 Vernon Pl (45219-2436)
PHONE.....................................513 636-4200
David Burns, *Sr Ntwrk Engine*
EMP: 848
SALES (corp-wide): 1.6B **Privately Held**
SIC: 8062 General medical & surgical hospitals
PA: Children's Hospital Medical Center
3333 Burnet Ave
Cincinnati OH 45229
513 636-4200

(G-3188)
CHILDRENS HOSPITAL MEDICAL CTR
Cincinnati Chld Hosp Med Ctr
2800 Winslow Ave Fl 3 (45206-1144)
PHONE.....................................513 636-4366
Yi-Ting Tsai, *Research*
Cynthia Wetzel, *Manager*
Todd Lehkamp, *Podiatrist*
Cynthia Kuelbs, *Director*
Kristen Wright, *Director*
EMP: 848
SALES (corp-wide): 1.6B **Privately Held**
SIC: 8062 General medical & surgical hospitals
PA: Children's Hospital Medical Center
3333 Burnet Ave
Cincinnati OH 45229
513 636-4200

(G-3189)
CHILDRENS HOSPITAL MEDICAL CTR
Also Called: Outpatient Anderson
7495 State Rd Ste 355 (45255-6402)
PHONE.....................................513 636-6100
Vince Paradisco, *Manager*
EMP: 40
SALES (corp-wide): 1.6B **Privately Held**
WEB: www.cincinnatichildrens.org
SIC: 8733 8093 Medical research; specialty outpatient clinics
PA: Children's Hospital Medical Center
3333 Burnet Ave
Cincinnati OH 45229
513 636-4200

(G-3190)
CHILDRENS HOSPITAL MEDICAL CTR (PA)
Also Called: Children's Home Healthcare
3333 Burnet Ave (45229-3039)
PHONE..................................513 636-4200
Michael Fisher, *President*
Dorine Seaquist, *Senior VP*
Maria Britto, *Assistant VP*
Thomas Kinman, *Vice Pres*
Jim Burger, *Opers Staff*
EMP: 3189
SQ FT: 1,803,000
SALES: 1.6B **Privately Held**
WEB: www.cincinnatichildrens.org
SIC: 8733 8011 8069 8731 Medical research; clinic, operated by physicians; children's hospital; biotechnical research, commercial

(G-3191)
CHILDRENS HOSPITAL MEDICAL CTR
Also Called: Cincinnati Children's Hospital
3350 Elland Ave (45229-3039)
PHONE..................................513 636-4200
Jing Xiang, *Research*
Walter Flynn, *Branch Mgr*
James McCarthy, *Med Doctor*
Lee Denson, *Director*
John Harley, *Director*
EMP: 3149
SALES (corp-wide): 1.6B **Privately Held**
SIC: 4225 General warehousing
PA: Children's Hospital Medical Center
3333 Burnet Ave
Cincinnati OH 45229
513 636-4200

(G-3192)
CHILDRENS HOSPITAL MEDICAL CTR
3333 Burnet Ave (45229-3039)
PHONE..................................513 636-8778
Michelle Stultz, *Branch Mgr*
EMP: 511
SALES (corp-wide): 1.6B **Privately Held**
SIC: 8011 Pediatrician
PA: Children's Hospital Medical Center
3333 Burnet Ave
Cincinnati OH 45229
513 636-4200

(G-3193)
CHILDRENS HOSPITAL MEDICAL CTR
3333 Burnet Ave (45229-3039)
PHONE..................................513 636-8778
Robby Thompson, *Branch Mgr*
EMP: 848
SALES (corp-wide): 1.6B **Privately Held**
SIC: 8062 General medical & surgical hospitals
PA: Children's Hospital Medical Center
3333 Burnet Ave
Cincinnati OH 45229
513 636-4200

(G-3194)
CHILLICOTHE LONG TERM CARE (PA)
Also Called: Westmoreland Place
7265 Kenwood Rd Ste 300 (45236-4414)
PHONE..................................513 793-8804
James Farley, *President*
Michael Scharfenberger, *Exec VP*
EMP: 220
SQ FT: 50,000
SALES (est): 970.6MM **Privately Held**
WEB: www.westmorelandplace.com
SIC: 8051 Skilled nursing care facilities

(G-3195)
CHIRST HOSPITAL SURGERY CENTER
4850 Red Bank Rd Fl 1 (45227-1546)
PHONE..................................513 272-3448
Tammy Wood,
Mary Ann,
Cindy Law,
EMP: 35

SALES (est): 2.6MM **Privately Held**
WEB: www.redbanksurgery.com
SIC: 8062 General medical & surgical hospitals

(G-3196)
CHMC CMNTY HLTH SVCS NETWRK
Also Called: CHILDREN'S HOME HEALTHCARE
3333 Burnet Ave (45229-3026)
PHONE..................................513 636-8778
Frank C Woodside III, *President*
EMP: 1454
SALES: 4.3MM
SALES (corp-wide): 1.6B **Privately Held**
SIC: 8322 Community center
PA: Children's Hospital Medical Center
3333 Burnet Ave
Cincinnati OH 45229
513 636-4200

(G-3197)
CHP AP SHARED SERVICES
P.O. Box 5203 (45201-5203)
PHONE..................................513 981-6704
EMP: 26
SALES (est): 1.9MM **Privately Held**
SIC: 8999 Services

(G-3198)
CHRIST HOSPITAL
Also Called: Glenway Family Medicine
5885 Harrison Ave # 2900 (45248-1728)
PHONE..................................513 347-2300
EMP: 186
SALES (corp-wide): 2.4MM **Privately Held**
SIC: 8062 General medical & surgical hospitals
PA: The Christ Hospital
2139 Auburn Ave
Cincinnati OH 45219
513 585-2000

(G-3199)
CHRIST HOSPITAL
2139 Auburn Ave (45219-2989)
PHONE..................................513 721-8272
EMP: 49
SALES (corp-wide): 929.7MM **Privately Held**
SIC: 8062 General medical & surgical hospitals
PA: The Christ Hospital
2139 Auburn Ave
Cincinnati OH 45219
513 585-2000

(G-3200)
CHRIST HOSPITAL
7545 Beechmont Ave Ste F (45255-4238)
PHONE..................................513 564-4000
Richard F Kammerer, *Branch Mgr*
EMP: 32
SALES (corp-wide): 2.4MM **Privately Held**
SIC: 8062 8011 General medical & surgical hospitals; gynecologist
PA: The Christ Hospital
2139 Auburn Ave
Cincinnati OH 45219
513 585-2000

(G-3201)
CHRIST HOSPITAL
11140 Montgomery Rd (45249-2309)
PHONE..................................513 561-7809
EMP: 113
SALES (corp-wide): 2.4MM **Privately Held**
SIC: 8062 8031 8011 General medical & surgical hospitals; offices & clinics of osteopathic physicians; offices & clinics of medical doctors
PA: The Christ Hospital
2139 Auburn Ave
Cincinnati OH 45219
513 585-2000

(G-3202)
CHRIST HOSPITAL
Also Called: Spectrum Rehabilitation
7545 Beechmont Ave Ste E (45255-4238)
PHONE..................................513 688-1111
Raymond C Rost, *Principal*

EMP: 311
SALES (corp-wide): 929.7MM **Privately Held**
SIC: 8062 8049 Hospital, medical school affiliated with nursing & residency; physical therapist
PA: The Christ Hospital
2139 Auburn Ave
Cincinnati OH 45219
513 585-2000

(G-3203)
CHRIST HOSPITAL
4440 Red Bank Rd Ste 100 (45227-2177)
PHONE..................................513 564-1340
Lisa Jarman, *Office Mgr*
EMP: 146
SALES (corp-wide): 929.7MM **Privately Held**
SIC: 8062 General medical & surgical hospitals
PA: The Christ Hospital
2139 Auburn Ave
Cincinnati OH 45219
513 585-2000

(G-3204)
CHRIST HOSPITAL
2123 Auburn Ave Ste 722 (45219-2906)
PHONE..................................513 651-0094
EMP: 243
SALES (corp-wide): 2.4MM **Privately Held**
SIC: 8062 General medical & surgical hospitals
PA: The Christ Hospital
2139 Auburn Ave
Cincinnati OH 45219
513 585-2000

(G-3205)
CHRIST HOSPITAL
Also Called: Surgery Center
4850 Red Bank Rd Fl 1 (45227-1546)
PHONE..................................513 272-3448
EMP: 311
SALES (corp-wide): 929.7MM **Privately Held**
SIC: 8062 General medical & surgical hospitals
PA: The Christ Hospital
2139 Auburn Ave
Cincinnati OH 45219
513 585-2000

(G-3206)
CHRIST HOSPITAL
2123 Auburn Ave Ste 341 (45219-2906)
PHONE..................................513 585-0050
Karthikeyan Kanagarajan, *Med Doctor*
EMP: 49
SALES (corp-wide): 2.4MM **Privately Held**
SIC: 8062 General medical & surgical hospitals
PA: The Christ Hospital
2139 Auburn Ave
Cincinnati OH 45219
513 585-2000

(G-3207)
CHRIST HOSPITAL (PA)
Also Called: CHRIST HOSPITAL HEALTH NETWORK
2139 Auburn Ave (45219-2989)
PHONE..................................513 585-2000
Jack Cook, *CEO*
Allan Jones, *President*
Mike Keating, *President*
Heather Adkins, *Vice Pres*
Berc Gawne, *Vice Pres*
EMP: 1500
SALES: 929.7MM **Privately Held**
SIC: 8062 Hospital, medical school affiliated with nursing & residency

(G-3208)
CHRIST HOSPITAL
4803 Montgomery Rd # 114 (45212-1152)
PHONE..................................513 631-3300
Mona Fry, *Branch Mgr*
EMP: 97
SALES (corp-wide): 2.4MM **Privately Held**
SIC: 8062 General medical & surgical hospitals

PA: The Christ Hospital
2139 Auburn Ave
Cincinnati OH 45219
513 585-2000

(G-3209)
CHRIST HOSPITAL
Also Called: Christ Hospital, The
2355 Norwood Ave Ste 1 (45212-2750)
PHONE..................................513 351-0800
EMP: 97
SALES (corp-wide): 2.4MM **Privately Held**
SIC: 8062 General medical & surgical hospitals
PA: The Christ Hospital
2139 Auburn Ave
Cincinnati OH 45219
513 585-2000

(G-3210)
CHRIST HOSPITAL
7545 Beechmont Ave Ste J (45255-4231)
PHONE..................................513 791-5200
EMP: 235
SALES (corp-wide): 2.4MM **Privately Held**
SIC: 8062 General medical & surgical hospitals
PA: The Christ Hospital
2139 Auburn Ave
Cincinnati OH 45219
513 585-2000

(G-3211)
CHRIST HOSPITAL SPINE SURGERY
4020 Smith Rd (45209-1936)
PHONE..................................513 619-5899
Mike Judge, *General Mgr*
EMP: 28
SALES (est): 4.4MM **Privately Held**
SIC: 8062 8093 General medical & surgical hospitals; specialty outpatient clinics

(G-3212)
CHRISTIAN BENEVOLENT ASSN (PA)
8097 Hamilton Ave (45231-2321)
PHONE..................................513 931-5000
J Donald Sams, *CEO*
Lizz Stephens, *VP Bus Dvlpt*
Vickie Brashear, *CFO*
John Hutcherson, *Exec Dir*
Bob Slade, *Exec Dir*
EMP: 350
SALES: 2.3MM **Privately Held**
SIC: 8741 Nursing & personal care facility management

(G-3213)
CHRISTIAN COMMUNITY HLTH SVCS
Also Called: CROSSROAD HEALTH CENTER
5 E Liberty St Ste 4 (45202-8202)
PHONE..................................513 381-2247
Anne Scheid, *Manager*
Sally Stewart, *Exec Dir*
▲ EMP: 37
SALES: 7MM **Privately Held**
WEB: www.crossrd.org
SIC: 8011 Clinic, operated by physicians

(G-3214)
CHS NORWOOD INC
Also Called: Woods Edge Point
1171 Towne St (45216-2227)
PHONE..................................513 242-1360
Carol Bottonari, *Director*
EMP: 70
SALES: 7MM **Privately Held**
SIC: 8051 Skilled nursing care facilities

(G-3215)
CHS-NORWOOD INC
Also Called: Harmony Court
6969 Glenmeadow Ln (45237-3001)
PHONE..................................513 351-7007
Glyndon Powell, *Principal*
Laurie Westermeyer, *Administration*
EMP: 160

SALES: 8.7MM
SALES (corp-wide): 85.7MM **Privately Held**
SIC: 8051 Convalescent home with continuous nursing care
PA: Carington Health Systems
8200 Beckett Park Dr
Hamilton OH 45011
513 682-2700

(G-3216)
CIMCOOL INDUSTRIAL PDTS LLC (DH)
3000 Disney St (45209-5028)
PHONE...................................888 246-2665
Tom Goeke, *CEO*
Robert McKee, *President*
Michael Crawford, *District Mgr*
Richard Marrone, *District Mgr*
Dale Morehouse, *Business Mgr*
▲ EMP: 56
SALES (est): 161.1MM
SALES (corp-wide): 1.2B **Publicly Held**
SIC: 5169 Chemicals & allied products

(G-3217)
CIMX LLC
Also Called: Cimx Software
4625 Red Bank Rd Ste 200 (45227-1552)
PHONE...................................513 248-7700
Anthony Cuilwik, *Principal*
Kristin Cuilwik, *Manager*
Comfort Wendel, *Director*
EMP: 30
SQ FT: 12,000
SALES (est): 3.3MM **Privately Held**
WEB: www.cimx.com
SIC: 7372 7371 Prepackaged software; custom computer programming services

(G-3218)
CINCILINGUA INC
322 E 4th St (45202-4202)
PHONE...................................513 721-8782
Hubert Collet, *President*
Edda Collet, *Corp Secy*
Sylvie Sum, *Program Mgr*
EMP: 45
SQ FT: 4,257
SALES (est): 1.6MM **Privately Held**
WEB: www.cincilingua.com
SIC: 8299 7389 Language school; translation services

(G-3219)
CINCINNATI - VULCAN COMPANY
5353 Spring Grove Ave (45217-1026)
PHONE...................................513 242-5300
Garry C Ferraris, *President*
Kathy Hughes, *Office Mgr*
EMP: 60
SQ FT: 6,000
SALES (est): 11.6MM
SALES (corp-wide): 13.4MM **Privately Held**
WEB: www.vulcanoil.com
SIC: 5983 2992 5171 2899 Fuel oil dealers; oils & greases, blending & compounding; petroleum bulk stations; petroleum terminals; chemical preparations; specialty cleaning, polishes & sanitation goods; soap & other detergents
PA: Coolant Control, Inc.
5353 Spring Grove Ave
Cincinnati OH 45217
513 471-8770

(G-3220)
CINCINNATI AIR CONDITIONING CO
Also Called: Honeywell Authorized Dealer
2080 Northwest Dr (45231-1700)
PHONE...................................513 721-5622
Mark Radtke, *President*
Michael Geiger, *Corp Secy*
Bill Wolf, *Project Mgr*
Patrick Doan, *Engineer*
Chris Fahrenholz, *Engineer*
EMP: 55 EST: 1939
SQ FT: 30,000

SALES (est): 17.2MM **Privately Held**
WEB: www.cincinnatiair.com
SIC: 1711 3822 Warm air heating & air conditioning contractor; refrigeration contractor; auto controls regulating residntl & coml environmt & applncs

(G-3221)
CINCINNATI ANML RFRRL
Also Called: Care Center
6995 E Kemper Rd (45249-1024)
PHONE...................................513 530-0911
Doug Hoffman, *CFO*
Angie Gleason, *Finance*
Douglas Hoffman,
Beth McElravy, *Internal Med*
Daniel Carey,
EMP: 85 EST: 2000
SALES (est): 6.5MM **Privately Held**
SIC: 0742 Animal hospital services, pets & other animal specialties

(G-3222)
CINCINNATI AREA SENIOR SVCS (PA)
2368 Victory Pkwy Ste 300 (45206-2810)
PHONE...................................513 721-4330
Jim Boesch, *CFO*
Elizabeth Patterson, *Exec Dir*
Tracy Collins, *Deputy Dir*
EMP: 130 EST: 1966
SQ FT: 9,000
SALES (est): 4MM **Privately Held**
WEB: www.senserv.org
SIC: 8322 Senior citizens' center or association

(G-3223)
CINCINNATI ASSN FOR THE BLIND
2045 Gilbert Ave (45202-1403)
PHONE...................................513 221-8558
Toll Free:...................................888 -
John Mitchell, *CEO*
Amy Scrivner, *Development*
Jennifer Dubois, *Finance*
Hanna Firestone, *Marketing Staff*
Judy Hale, *Info Tech Mgr*
▲ EMP: 120 EST: 1910
SQ FT: 88,000
SALES (est): 9.4MM **Privately Held**
SIC: 8331 8322 2891 Sheltered workshop; association for the handicapped; adhesives & sealants

(G-3224)
CINCINNATI BALLET COMPANY INC
1555 Central Pkwy (45214-2863)
PHONE...................................513 621-5219
Victoria Morgan, *CEO*
Melissa Santomo, *COO*
Tanya Cornejo, *Vice Pres*
Julie Sunderland, *Transptn Dir*
Kyle Lemoi, *Production*
EMP: 30 EST: 1958
SQ FT: 27,595
SALES (est): 8.4MM **Privately Held**
WEB: www.cincinnatiballet.com
SIC: 7911 Dance studios, schools & halls

(G-3225)
CINCINNATI BAR ASSOCIATION
225 E 6th St Fl 2 (45202-3213)
PHONE...................................513 381-8213
Catherine Glover, *Exec Dir*
Terrie Minniti, *Director*
EMP: 28
SQ FT: 37,000
SALES (est): 2.6MM **Privately Held**
WEB: www.cincybar.org
SIC: 8621 Bar association

(G-3226)
CINCINNATI BELL INC (PA)
221 E 4th St Ste 700 (45202-4118)
P.O. Box 2301 (45201-2301)
PHONE...................................513 397-9900
Phillip R Cox, *Ch of Bd*
Leigh R Fox, *President*
Ronald Bonner, *Managing Prtnr*
Rose Curnutte, *Regional Mgr*
Danielle Purdon, *Business Mgr*
▲ EMP: 100

SALES: 1.3B **Publicly Held**
WEB: www.broadwing.com
SIC: 7373 7374 7379 4813 Systems software development services; data processing service; computer related consulting services; ; local & long distance telephone communications

(G-3227)
CINCINNATI BELL TECHNO
4600 Montgomery Rd # 400 (45212-2600)
PHONE...................................513 841-6700
Tera Boster, *Business Anlyst*
John Burns, *Manager*
EMP: 100
SALES (corp-wide): 1.3B **Publicly Held**
SIC: 7379 5045 Computer related consulting services; computer peripheral equipment
HQ: Cbts Technology Solutions Llc
221 E 4th St
Cincinnati OH 45202

(G-3228)
CINCINNATI BELL TELE CO LLC (HQ)
209 W 7th St Fl 1 (45202-2394)
P.O. Box 2301 (45201-2301)
PHONE...................................513 565-9402
Rodney D Dir, *COO*
Judy Newberry, *Project Mgr*
Robert Monaghan, *Engineer*
Brian A Ross, *CFO*
Mark Peterson, *Treasurer*
EMP: 119 EST: 1873
SQ FT: 100,000
SALES (est): 565.1MM
SALES (corp-wide): 1.3B **Publicly Held**
SIC: 4813 Local telephone communications
PA: Cincinnati Bell Inc.
221 E 4th St Ste 700
Cincinnati OH 45202
513 397-9900

(G-3229)
CINCINNATI BELT AND TRANSM
5500 Ridge Ave (45213-2516)
PHONE...................................513 621-9050
Gerald Perkins, *Vice Pres*
Jerry Reichert, *Vice Pres*
Jay Stahl, *Vice Pres*
Rob Zielsdorf, *Vice Pres*
Mark Dorsey, *Credit Staff*
EMP: 62
SALES (est): 6.4MM **Privately Held**
SIC: 5063 Electrical apparatus & equipment

(G-3230)
CINCINNATI BENGALS INC (PA)
Also Called: Ohio Valley Sports, Inc.
1 Paul Brown Stadium (45202-3492)
PHONE...................................513 621-3550
Michael Brown, *CEO*
Andrew R Berger, *Ch of Bd*
Bill Connelly, *Business Mgr*
William Scanlom, *CFO*
Matt Sikich, *Sales Staff*
EMP: 164
SALES (est): 8.4MM **Privately Held**
SIC: 7941 Football club

(G-3231)
CINCINNATI BULK TERMINALS LLC
895 Mehring Way (45203-1906)
PHONE...................................513 621-4800
Jack Weiss, *Mng Member*
EMP: 50
SALES (est): 9.6MM **Privately Held**
WEB: www.progressfuels.com
SIC: 4491 Marine terminals

(G-3232)
CINCINNATI CENTRAL CR UN INC (PA)
1717 Western Ave (45214-2007)
P.O. Box 14699 (45250-0699)
PHONE...................................513 241-2050
William A Herring, *President*
John Nunns, *President*
Karen Rokich,
EMP: 55
SQ FT: 15,000

SALES: 4.7MM **Privately Held**
WEB:
www.cincinnaticentralcreditunion.com
SIC: 6061 Federal credit unions

(G-3233)
CINCINNATI CIRCUS COMPANY LLC
6433 Wiehe Rd (45237-4215)
PHONE...................................513 921-5454
Dave Willacker, *Mng Member*
Max Cormendy, *Manager*
EMP: 85
SALES (est): 192K **Privately Held**
SIC: 7299 Party planning service

(G-3234)
CINCINNATI CNSLTING CONSORTIUM
220 Wyoming Ave (45215-4308)
PHONE...................................513 233-0011
Richard Bruder, *President*
EMP: 35
SALES (est): 2.5MM **Privately Held**
WEB: www.cincconsult.com
SIC: 8748 Business consulting

(G-3235)
CINCINNATI COML CONTG LLC
4760 Red Bank Rd Ste 226 (45227-1549)
PHONE...................................513 561-6633
John Westheimer, *President*
Lawrence Knasel, *Vice Pres*
Heather Moore, *Vice Pres*
Justin Platt, *Vice Pres*
Joseph Lawwill, *Project Mgr*
EMP: 25
SQ FT: 6,000
SALES (est): 7.8MM **Privately Held**
SIC: 1542 6531 Commercial & office building, new construction; real estate agents & managers

(G-3236)
CINCINNATI COUNTRY CLUB
2348 Grandin Rd (45208-3399)
PHONE...................................513 533-5200
Pat O'Callaghan, *General Mgr*
EMP: 125
SQ FT: 75,000
SALES: 9.2MM **Privately Held**
SIC: 7997 Country club, membership

(G-3237)
CINCINNATI CTR/PSYCHOANALYSIS
3001 Highland Ave (45219-2315)
PHONE...................................513 961-8484
Phyllis Donovan, *Manager*
EMP: 25
SALES (est): 2.1MM **Privately Held**
WEB: www.cps-i.org
SIC: 8322 Family counseling services

(G-3238)
CINCINNATI DENTAL SERVICES
8111 Cheviot Rd Ste 102 (45247-4013)
PHONE...................................513 741-7779
Judy Farrell, *Office Mgr*
EMP: 45
SALES (corp-wide): 5.5MM **Privately Held**
SIC: 8021 Dentists' office
PA: Cincinnati Dental Services Inc
121 E Mcmillan St
Cincinnati OH 45219
513 721-8888

(G-3239)
CINCINNATI DENTAL SERVICES (PA)
121 E Mcmillan St (45219-2606)
PHONE...................................513 721-8888
Larry Faust, *President*
Missy Garvin, *Vice Pres*
Steve Jones, *Vice Pres*
Fred White Jr, *Manager*
EMP: 75
SQ FT: 18,500
SALES (est): 5.5MM **Privately Held**
SIC: 8021 Dentists' office; dental clinic

G
E
O
G
R
A
P
H
I
C

(G-3240)
CINCINNATI DRYWALL INC
659 Wilmer Ave (45226-1859)
PHONE.................................513 321-7322
Michael W Mott, *President*
David Mott, *Treasurer*
Christy Alfieri, *Admin Sec*
EMP: 50 EST: 1973
SQ FT: 7,800
SALES (est): 3.7MM **Privately Held**
WEB: www.cincinnatidrywall.net
SIC: 1742 Drywall

(G-3241)
**CINCINNATI EARLY LEARNING
CTR (PA)**
1301 E Mcmillan St (45206-2222)
PHONE.................................513 961-2690
Valerie Taylor, *Finance Mgr*
Patricia Gleason, *Exec Dir*
Deanna Lane, *Director*
Lissa Shackelford, *Admin Dir*
EMP: 30
SALES: 5.3MM **Privately Held**
SIC: 8351 Preschool center

(G-3242)
**CINCINNATI EQUITABLE INSUR
CO (DH)**
525 Vine St Ste 1925 (45202-3125)
P.O. Box 3428 (45201-3428)
PHONE.................................513 621-1826
Greg Baker, *CEO*
Gregory Baker, *President*
Peter Alpaugh, *Chairman*
Linda Bales, *Admin Sec*
EMP: 40
SQ FT: 5,000
SALES (est): 14.3MM **Privately Held**
WEB: www.1826.com
SIC: 6331 6321 Fire, marine & casualty in-
surance: stock; property damage insur-
ance; health insurance carriers
HQ: Cincinnati Equitable Companies, Inc
525 Vine St Ste 1925
Cincinnati OH 45202
513 621-1826

(G-3243)
**CINCINNATI FIFTH STREET HT
LLC**
Also Called: Cincinnati Hyatt Regency
151 W 5th St (45202-2703)
PHONE.................................513 579-1234
Hank Artime, *Agent*
Lakeisha Walker, *Agent*
EMP: 99
SQ FT: 100,000
SALES (est): 420.4K **Privately Held**
SIC: 7041 Membership-basis organization
hotels

(G-3244)
CINCINNATI FILL INC
900 Kieley Pl (45217-1153)
PHONE.................................513 242-7526
Steve Roth, *Manager*
EMP: 30
SALES (est): 2.2MM **Privately Held**
WEB: www.cincinnatireadymix.com
SIC: 1611 General contractor, highway &
street construction

(G-3245)
**CINCINNATI FLOOR COMPANY
INC (PA)**
5162 Broerman Ave (45217-1140)
PHONE.................................513 641-4500
Douglas J Drenik, *CEO*
Charle Maricle, *President*
Jill Drenik, *Treasurer*
EMP: 50 EST: 1894
SQ FT: 12,000
SALES (est): 9.2MM **Privately Held**
WEB: www.cincifloor.com
SIC: 1752 Wood floor installation & refin-
ishing

(G-3246)
**CINCINNATI HAND SURGERY
CONS (PA)**
10700 Montgomery Rd # 150
(45242-3255)
PHONE.................................513 961-4263

Peter Stern, *President*
Andrew Markiewitz, *COO*
Dr John Mc Donough, *Vice Pres*
Sarah Auxier, *Supervisor*
Dr Thomas Kiefhaber, *Admin Sec*
EMP: 32
SQ FT: 9,000
SALES (est): 2.5MM **Privately Held**
SIC: 8011 Surgeon

(G-3247)
**CINCINNATI HEAD AND NECK
INC (PA)**
Also Called: Cincinnati Better Hearing Ctr
2123 Auburn Ave (45219-2906)
PHONE.................................513 232-3277
Michael Wood MD, *President*
Joseph Hellmann, *Corp Secy*
Thomas Kereiakes, *Vice Pres*
Roxanne Reed, *Administration*
EMP: 25
SQ FT: 1,300
SALES: 500K **Privately Held**
SIC: 8011 Ears, nose & throat specialist:
physician/surgeon

(G-3248)
**CINCINNATI HEALTH NETWORK
INC**
2825 Burnet Ave Ste 232 (45219-2426)
PHONE.................................513 961-0600
Kate Bennett, *CEO*
Austin Maddox, *CFO*
EMP: 25
SQ FT: 2,200
SALES: 3.6MM **Privately Held**
WEB: www.cincihomeless.org
SIC: 8741 8699 Hospital management;
nursing & personal care facility manage-
ment; charitable organization

(G-3249)
**CINCINNATI HUMN RELATIONS
COMM**
Also Called: CHRC
801 Plum St Rm 158 (45202-5704)
PHONE.................................513 352-3237
Ericka King-Betts, *Director*
EMP: 33
SALES: 900.6K **Privately Held**
SIC: 8699 Charitable organization

(G-3250)
**CINCINNATI INDUS ACTONEERS
INC**
2020 Dunlap St (45214-2310)
PHONE.................................513 241-9701
Jerome A Luggen, *President*
Jeffrey L Luggen, *Vice Pres*
Jeffrey M Luggen, *Vice Pres*
Gary Rogg, *Marketing Staff*
Jim Stern, *Manager*
▼ EMP: 25
SQ FT: 20,000
SALES: 16MM **Privately Held**
WEB: www.cia-auction.com
SIC: 7389 Auction, appraisal & exchange
services

(G-3251)
**CINCINNATI INSTITUTE FINE
ARTS (PA)**
Also Called: ARTSWAVE
20 East Central Pkwy # 2 (45202-7239)
PHONE.................................513 871-2787
Mary McCullough-Hudson, *CEO*
Sue Reichelderfer, *Principal*
Teri Haught, *Vice Pres*
Theresa Haught, *Vice Pres*
Ryan Strand, *Opers Staff*
EMP: 27
SQ FT: 4,000
SALES: 14.7MM **Privately Held**
WEB: www.taftmuseum.org
SIC: 8399 Fund raising organization, non-
fee basis

(G-3252)
**CINCINNATI INSTITUTE FINE
ARTS**
Also Called: Taft Museum
316 Pike St (45202-4214)
PHONE.................................513 241-0343
Phillip C Long, *Director*
EMP: 25

SQ FT: 7,880
SALES (est): 654K
SALES (corp-wide): 14.7MM **Privately
Held**
WEB: www.taftmuseum.org
SIC: 8412 Museum
PA: Cincinnati Institute Of Fine Arts
20 East Central Pkwy # 2
Cincinnati OH 45202
513 871-2787

(G-3253)
**CINCINNATI MEDICAL BILLING
SVC**
8160 Corp Pk Dr Ste 330 (45242)
P.O. Box 42417 (45242-0417)
PHONE.................................513 965-8041
Beverly Shelton, *President*
Charles K D, *Vice Pres*
EMP: 50
SQ FT: 7,500
SALES (est): 2.7MM **Privately Held**
SIC: 8721 Billing & bookkeeping service

(G-3254)
**CINCINNATI METRO HSING
AUTH**
Also Called: Cmha
1635 Western Ave (45214-2001)
PHONE.................................513 421-2642
Gene Reed, *Manager*
EMP: 31
SALES (corp-wide): 116MM **Privately
Held**
WEB: www.cmha.com
SIC: 6513 Housing agency, government
PA: Cincinnati Metropolitan Housing Au-
thority
1635 Western Ave
Cincinnati OH 45214
513 421-8190

(G-3255)
**CINCINNATI METRO HSING
AUTH (PA)**
1635 Western Ave (45214-2001)
PHONE.................................513 421-8190
Reema Ruberg, *Finance*
Donald J Troendle, *Exec Dir*
EMP: 42
SQ FT: 10,000
SALES: 116MM **Privately Held**
WEB: www.cintimha.com
SIC: 6514 Housing agency, government

(G-3256)
**CINCINNATI METRO HSING
AUTH**
Also Called: Section 8
1627 Western Ave (45214-2001)
PHONE.................................513 333-0670
Joan Roark, *Director*
EMP: 36
SQ FT: 10,347
SALES (corp-wide): 116MM **Privately
Held**
WEB: www.cintimha.com
SIC: 6513 6514 Operator Of Apartment
Complexes And Single Family Houses
For Low Income And Elderly Families
PA: Cincinnati Metropolitan Housing Au-
thority
1635 Western Ave
Cincinnati OH 45214
513 421-8190

(G-3257)
**CINCINNATI MUSEUM
ASSOCIATION (PA)**
Also Called: CINCINNATI ART MUSEUM
953 Eden Park Dr (45202-1557)
PHONE.................................513 721-5204
Andrew Dewitt, *President*
Valerie Newell, *Vice Pres*
Ted Forrest, *Human Res Dir*
Laura Biaglow, *Human Res Mgr*
Jill Dunne, *Marketing Staff*
▲ EMP: 170
SQ FT: 300,000
SALES: 18MM **Privately Held**
WEB: www.artacademy.edu
SIC: 8412 8299 Museum; art gallery, non-
commercial; art school, except commer-
cial

(G-3258)
**CINCINNATI MUSEUM CENTER
(PA)**
1301 Western Ave (45203-1138)
PHONE.................................513 287-7000
Douglass McDonald, *President*
Sarah Stoutamire, *Marketing Staff*
Vanessa Vanzant, *Director*
Brian Sekerak, *Administration*
EMP: 286
SALES: 60.1MM **Privately Held**
WEB: www.cincymuseum.com
SIC: 7832 8412 8231 Motion picture the-
aters, except drive-in; museums & art gal-
leries; libraries

(G-3259)
**CINCINNATI NETHERLAND HT
LLC**
Also Called: Hilton Cncnnati Netherland Plz
35 W 5th St (45202-2801)
PHONE.................................513 421-9100
Greg Power,
EMP: 350
SALES (est): 12.5MM **Privately Held**
SIC: 7011 Hotels

(G-3260)
**CINCINNATI OPERA
ASSOCIATION**
1243 Elm St (45202-7531)
PHONE.................................513 768-5500
Patricia K Beggs, *CEO*
Robert W Olson, *President*
Cathy Crain, *Chairman*
Glenn Plott, *Production*
Darlene Zoz, *Controller*
EMP: 27
SALES: 7.7MM **Privately Held**
WEB: www.cincinnatiopera.org
SIC: 7922 Theatrical companies; perform-
ing arts center production

(G-3261)
**CINCINNATI POOL
MANAGEMENT INC**
3461 Mustafa Dr (45241-1668)
P.O. Box 603, West Chester (45071-0603)
PHONE.................................513 777-1444
Gary Toner, *President*
EMP: 507
SQ FT: 15,000
SALES (est): 7.6MM **Privately Held**
WEB: www.cincinnatipoolmgmt.com
SIC: 7999 Lifeguard service

(G-3262)
CINCINNATI PUBLIC RADIO INC
Also Called: W G U C-FM RADIO
1223 Central Pkwy (45214-2834)
PHONE.................................513 241-8282
Richard Eiswerth, *President*
Don Danko, *Vice Pres*
Sherri Mancini, *Vice Pres*
Barry S Weinstein, *CFO*
Juri Tults, *Sales Staff*
EMP: 36
SQ FT: 20,000
SALES: 7.2MM **Privately Held**
WEB: www.cinradio.org
SIC: 4832 Radio broadcasting stations,
music format

(G-3263)
CINCINNATI REDS LLC (PA)
100 Joe Nuxhall Way (45202-4109)
PHONE.................................513 765-7000
Robert Castellini, *CEO*
Carl Lindnert,
▼ EMP: 125 EST: 1869
SQ FT: 5,000
SALES (est): 2.3MM **Privately Held**
WEB: www.cincinnatireds.com
SIC: 7941 Baseball club, professional &
semi-professional

(G-3264)
CINCINNATI REDS LLC
100 Main St (45202)
PHONE.................................513 765-7923
Anthony V Ward, *Principal*
EMP: 92

▲ = Import ▼=Export
◆ =Import/Export

SALES (corp-wide): 2.3MM **Privately Held**
SIC: 7941 Baseball club, professional & semi-professional
PA: The Cincinnati Reds Llc
100 Joe Nuxhall Way
Cincinnati OH 45202
513 765-7000

(G-3265)
CINCINNATI SCHOLAR HOUSE LP
1826 Race St (45202-7720)
PHONE..................................513 559-0048
EMP: 28 EST: 2017
SALES (est): 93.6K
SALES (corp-wide): 5.7MM **Privately Held**
SIC: 8641 Dwelling-related associations
HQ: Cincinnati Scholar House Cub, Llc
2401 Reading Rd
Cincinnati OH 45202
513 768-6903

(G-3266)
CINCINNATI SENIOR CARE LLC
4001 Rosslyn Dr (45209-1111)
PHONE..................................513 272-0600
John E Marshall,
Karen Marshall,
EMP: 28
SALES (est): 1.4MM **Privately Held**
SIC: 8051 Convalescent home with continuous nursing care

(G-3267)
CINCINNATI SHAKESPEARE COMPANY
217 W 12th St (45202-7501)
PHONE..................................513 381-2273
Maddie Regan, Prdtn Mgr
Jeanna Vella, Marketing Staff
Brian Phillips, Exec Dir
Jay Woffington, Exec Dir
Joeliene Magoto, Director
EMP: 35
SALES: 3.4MM **Privately Held**
WEB: www.cincyshakes.com
SIC: 7922 Theatrical companies

(G-3268)
CINCINNATI SPEECH HEARING CTR (PA)
2825 Burnet Ave Ste 401 (45219-2426)
PHONE..................................513 221-0527
Carol P Leslie, Exec Dir
EMP: 34 EST: 1925
SQ FT: 9,000
SALES (est): 1.1MM **Privately Held**
WEB: www.hearingspeechdeaf.com
SIC: 8099 8093 Hearing testing service; speech defect clinic

(G-3269)
CINCINNATI SPORTS MALL INC
Also Called: Cincinnati Sports Club
3950 Red Bank Rd Ste A (45227-3430)
PHONE..................................513 527-4000
Christopher L Fister, President
Daniel A Funk MD, Owner
Charles Reynolds, Admin Sec
EMP: 60
SQ FT: 100,000
SALES (est): 6.2MM **Privately Held**
WEB: www.cincinnatisportsclub.com
SIC: 6512 7991 7997 Nonresidential building operators; athletic club & gymnasiums, membership; membership sports & recreation clubs

(G-3270)
CINCINNATI STEEL PRODUCTS CO
4540 Steel Pl (45209-1161)
PHONE..................................513 871-4444
James S Todd, CEO
Tom Brown, President
Thomas Rutter, Corp Secy
EMP: 50 EST: 1933
SQ FT: 75,000
SALES: 14.5MM **Privately Held**
WEB: www.cincinnatisteel.com
SIC: 5051 Steel; sheets, metal; bars, metal; strip, metal

(G-3271)
CINCINNATI SYMPHONY ORCHESTRA (PA)
Also Called: Riverbend Music Center
1241 Elm St (45202-7531)
PHONE..................................513 621-1919
Melody Sawyer Richardson, Chairman
L Timothy Giglio, Treasurer
Kenneth Goode, Director
Leonard M Randolph Jr, Admin Sec
EMP: 150
SQ FT: 10,000
SALES: 75.6MM **Privately Held**
WEB: www.cincinnatisymphony.org
SIC: 7929 Symphony orchestras; orchestras or bands

(G-3272)
CINCINNATI TAE KWON DO INC
Also Called: Cincinnati Tae Kwon Do Cntr
4325 Red Bank Rd Ste A (45227-2175)
PHONE..................................513 271-6900
Paul Korchak, President
EMP: 30
SQ FT: 4,200
SALES (est): 768.8K **Privately Held**
WEB: www.cincytaekwondo.com
SIC: 7999 Martial arts school

(G-3273)
CINCINNATI TRAINING TRML SVCS (PA)
Also Called: Ctts
4000 Executive Park Dr # 402 (45241-4008)
PHONE..................................513 563-4474
Patricia E Fraley, President
Kathleen A Mc Connell, Vice Pres
Jeannette Cruey, Office Mgr
EMP: 75
SQ FT: 2,600
SALES: 4.7MM **Privately Held**
SIC: 7379 7373 Data processing consultant; computer integrated systems design

(G-3274)
CINCINNATI USA RGIONAL CHAMBER
3 E 4th St Ste 200 (45202-3746)
PHONE..................................513 579-3100
Jill P Meyer, President
Brendon J Cull, COO
Cynthia Oxley, COO
John Bosse, Vice Pres
Thomas Farrell, Vice Pres
EMP: 75 EST: 1839
SQ FT: 24,900
SALES: 20.4MM **Privately Held**
WEB: www.cincinnatichamber.com
SIC: 8611 Chamber of Commerce

(G-3275)
CINCINNATI YOUTH COLLABORATIVE
301 Oak St (45219-2508)
PHONE..................................513 475-4165
Jenny Keller, Vice Pres
Bill Russel, Vice Pres
Myrtis Powell, Exec Dir
EMP: 25
SQ FT: 800
SALES: 2.9MM **Privately Held**
WEB: www.cycyouth.org
SIC: 8322 Youth center

(G-3276)
CINCINNATI-HMLTN CNTY COMM ACT (PA)
1740 Langdon Farm Rd (45237-1157)
PHONE..................................513 569-1840
Gwen L Robinson, President
Mark B Lawson, Principal
Chandra Mathews-Smith, Principal
Diana Paternoster, Treasurer
Earlene Newton, Case Mgr
EMP: 145
SQ FT: 28,000
SALES: 28.6MM **Privately Held**
SIC: 8322 Individual & family services

(G-3277)
CINCINNATI-HMLTN CNTY COMM ACT
1740 Langdon Farm Rd (45237-1157)
PHONE..................................513 569-4510
Gwen Robinson, President
EMP: 52
SALES (corp-wide): 28.6MM **Privately Held**
SIC: 8322 Individual & family services
PA: Cincinnati-Hamilton County Community Action Agency
1740 Langdon Farm Rd
Cincinnati OH 45237
513 569-1840

(G-3278)
CINCINNATI-HMLTN CNTY COMM ACT
880 W Court St (45203-1309)
PHONE..................................513 354-3900
Gwen Robinson, Manager
EMP: 28
SALES (corp-wide): 28.6MM **Privately Held**
SIC: 8322 Individual & family services
PA: Cincinnati-Hamilton County Community Action Agency
1740 Langdon Farm Rd
Cincinnati OH 45237
513 569-1840

(G-3279)
CINCINNATIAN HOTEL
Also Called: Cincinnatian Hotel, The
601 Vine St (45202-2408)
PHONE..................................513 381-3000
Rick Foreman, Controller
EMP: 140
SQ FT: 105,160
SALES (est): 8.8MM **Privately Held**
SIC: 7011 Hotels

(G-3280)
CINCINNATIS OPTIMUM RES ENVIR
Also Called: Core
75 Tri County Pkwy (45246-3218)
PHONE..................................513 771-2673
Martha A Adams, Exec Dir
Beth Pagano, Director
Cathy Graf, Asst Director
EMP: 150
SALES: 6.9MM **Privately Held**
WEB: www.coreinc.org
SIC: 8361 Home for the mentally handicapped; residential care for the handicapped

(G-3281)
CINCINNATUS SAVINGS & LOAN (PA)
3300 Harrison Ave (45211-5697)
PHONE..................................513 661-6903
Steven E Shultz, President
Michael St John, Vice Pres
Terry Todd, Vice Pres
Jeffery Beerman, CFO
EMP: 25
SALES: 4.1MM **Privately Held**
WEB: www.cincinnatussl.com
SIC: 6035 Federal savings & loan associations

(G-3282)
CINCINNTI EDUC & RES FOR VETRN
Also Called: Biomedical Research & Educatn
3200 Vine St (45220-2213)
PHONE..................................513 861-3100
Ronn Hayks, CEO
EMP: 25
SQ FT: 3,502
SALES (est): 1.5MM **Privately Held**
SIC: 8733 Educational research agency

(G-3283)
CINCITI BL ETD TRTS LLC
221 E 4th St Fl 1290 (45202-4124)
PHONE..................................513 397-0963
Rochelle Brown, Principal
EMP: 99

(G-3284)
CINCO CREDIT UNION (PA)
Also Called: CINCO FAMILY FINANCIAL CENTER
49 William Howard Taft Rd (45219-1760)
PHONE..................................513 281-9988
William C Page, President
Terry Tracey, VP Admin
Mark Schweinfurth, CFO
Bob Niehaus,
EMP: 50
SQ FT: 17,400
SALES: 3.5MM **Privately Held**
SIC: 6061 Federal credit unions

(G-3285)
CINCOM INTRNATIONAL OPERATIONS (HQ)
55 Merchant St Ste 100 (45246-3761)
PHONE..................................513 612-2300
Thomas M Nies, Ch of Bd
Gerald Shawhan, Treasurer
Kenneth L Byrne, Admin Sec
EMP: 350
SALES (est): 26.2MM
SALES (corp-wide): 109.6MM **Privately Held**
SIC: 7371 7373 Computer software development; computer integrated systems design
PA: Cincom Systems, Inc.
55 Merchant St Ste 100
Cincinnati OH 45246
513 612-2300

(G-3286)
CINCOM SYSTEMS INC (PA)
55 Merchant St Ste 100 (45246-3761)
PHONE..................................513 612-2300
Thomas M Nies, Ch of Bd
Greg Mills, President
Paul Schumacher, Principal
Sandy Truitt, Business Mgr
Jill Hicks, Project Mgr
EMP: 300
SQ FT: 180,000
SALES (est): 109.6MM **Privately Held**
SIC: 7373 Systems software development services

(G-3287)
CINCOM SYSTEMS INC
Also Called: Cincom Helpdesk
2300 Montana Ave Ste 235 (45211-3890)
PHONE..................................513 389-2344
Mike Aichele, Branch Mgr
EMP: 30
SALES (corp-wide): 109.6MM **Privately Held**
SIC: 7379 Computer related consulting services
PA: Cincom Systems, Inc.
55 Merchant St Ste 100
Cincinnati OH 45246
513 612-2300

(G-3288)
CINCYSMILES FOUNDATION INC
Also Called: GREATER CINCINNATI ORAL HEALTH
635 W 7th St Ste 405 (45203-1549)
PHONE..................................513 621-0248
Sonya Dreves, Exec Dir
Lawrence F Hill, Director
EMP: 35
SQ FT: 800
SALES: 1.6MM **Privately Held**
SIC: 8322 Individual & family services

(G-3289)
CINERGY CORP (DH)
139 E 4th St (45202-4003)
P.O. Box 960 (45201-0960)
PHONE..................................513 421-9500
David L Hauser, President
Steven K Young, CFO

Jaime Wells, *Director*
▲ **EMP:** 1700
SQ FT: 300,000
SALES (est): 2B
SALES (corp-wide): 24.5B **Publicly Held**
WEB: www.cinergy.com
SIC: 4911 4924 Distribution, electric
power; generation, electric power; transmission, electric power; natural gas distribution
HQ: Duke Energy Carolinas, Llc
526 S Church St
Charlotte NC 28202
704 382-3853

(G-3290)
CINFED FEDERAL CREDIT UNION (PA)
Also Called: Cinfed Credit Union
4801 Kennedy Ave (45209-7543)
PHONE.................................513 333-3800
Jay Sigler, *CEO*
Christine Kunnen, *President*
Eric Ketcham, *COO*
Frank Broermann, *Vice Pres*
Wanda Handley, *Vice Pres*
EMP: 93
SQ FT: 1,500
SALES: 15.9MM **Privately Held**
SIC: 6061 Federal credit unions

(G-3291)
CINTAS CORPORATION (PA)
6800 Cintas Blvd (45262)
PHONE.................................513 459-1200
Scott D Farmer, *Ch of Bd*
Pablo Almeida, *General Mgr*
Todd Schneider, *COO*
Michael Hansen, *Exec VP*
Thomas E Frooman, *Senior VP*
◆ **EMP:** 1500
SALES: 6.4B **Publicly Held**
WEB: www.cintas-corp.com
SIC: 7218 2337 2326 5084 Industrial uniform supply; uniforms, except athletic: women's, misses' & juniors'; work uniforms; safety equipment

(G-3292)
CINTAS CORPORATION
Also Called: Cintas Uniforms AP Fcilty Svcs
5570 Ridge Ave (45213-2516)
PHONE.................................513 631-5750
Marie Seng, *Branch Mgr*
EMP: 100
SALES (corp-wide): 6.4B **Publicly Held**
SIC: 2326 2337 7218 5084 Work uniforms; uniforms, except athletic: women's, misses' & juniors'; industrial uniform supply; wiping towel supply; treated equipment supply: mats, rugs, mops, cloths, etc.; safety equipment
PA: Cintas Corporation
6800 Cintas Blvd
Cincinnati OH 45262
513 459-1200

(G-3293)
CINTAS CORPORATION
690 E Crscntvlle Rd Ste A (45246)
PHONE.................................513 671-7717
Phil Adamson, *General Mgr*
Kevin Femal, *General Mgr*
John Hains, *General Mgr*
David Marta, *General Mgr*
Mark McKinney, *General Mgr*
EMP: 60
SALES (corp-wide): 6.4B **Publicly Held**
SIC: 7218 Industrial uniform supply
PA: Cintas Corporation
6800 Cintas Blvd
Cincinnati OH 45262
513 459-1200

(G-3294)
CINTAS R US INC
6800 Cintas Blvd (45262)
PHONE.................................513 459-1200
Scott Farmer, *CEO*
Richard T Farmer, *President*
EMP: 1500
SALES (est): 8.3MM
SALES (corp-wide): 6.4B **Publicly Held**
SIC: 7218 Industrial uniform supply

PA: Cintas Corporation
6800 Cintas Blvd
Cincinnati OH 45262
513 459-1200

(G-3295)
CINTAS SALES CORPORATION (HQ)
6800 Cintas Blvd (45262)
PHONE.................................513 459-1200
Richard T Farmer, *Ch of Bd*
Robert J Kohlhepp, *Vice Ch Bd*
Scott Farmer, *President*
Arrika Garcia, *Plant Mgr*
Nick Watkins, *Plant Mgr*
EMP: 450
SALES (est): 32.2MM
SALES (corp-wide): 6.4B **Publicly Held**
SIC: 7218 2326 5136 5137 Industrial uniform supply; work clothing supply; work uniforms; uniforms, men's & boys'; uniforms, women's & children's
PA: Cintas Corporation
6800 Cintas Blvd
Cincinnati OH 45262
513 459-1200

(G-3296)
CITIGROUP GLOBAL MARKETS INC
Also Called: Smithbarney
4030 Smith Rd Ste 200 (45209-1937)
PHONE.................................513 579-8300
John A Whalen, *Manager*
EMP: 100
SALES (corp-wide): 72.8B **Publicly Held**
WEB: www.salomonsmithbarney.com
SIC: 6211 Security brokers & dealers; stock brokers & dealers
HQ: Citigroup Global Markets Inc.
388 Greenwich St Fl 18
New York NY 10013
212 816-6000

(G-3297)
CITIZENS FINANCIAL SVCS INC
9620 Colerain Ave # 60 (45251-2018)
PHONE.................................513 385-3200
EMP: 93
SALES (corp-wide): 64.4MM **Publicly Held**
SIC: 7389 Financial services
PA: Citizens Financial Services, Inc.
15 S Main St
Mansfield PA 16933
570 662-2121

(G-3298)
CITY DASH LLC
949 Laidlaw Ave (45237-5003)
PHONE.................................513 562-2000
Troy Burt, *President*
Jeff Fine, *Vice Pres*
Chad Switzer, *Controller*
Nancy Flickinger, *Accountant*
EMP: 170
SQ FT: 10,000
SALES: 19.3MM **Privately Held**
SIC: 4213 4215 4212 Less-than-truckload (LTL) transport; courier services, except by air; local trucking, without storage

(G-3299)
CITY GOSPEL MISSION
1805 Dalton Ave (45214-2055)
PHONE.................................513 241-5525
Sterling Hawks, *Director*
Melissa Triantafillou, *Director*
Robin Wagner, *Volunteer Dir*
EMP: 45
SALES: 6.8MM **Privately Held**
WEB: www.citygospelmission.com
SIC: 8322 Individual & family services

(G-3300)
CLARITAS LLC (HQ)
8044 Montgomery Rd # 455 (45236-0714)
PHONE.................................513 739-6869
Mike Nazzaro, *CEO*
Tracy Roller, *Human Resources*
Jodi Kahn,
EMP: 34
SQ FT: 7,800
SALES (est): 272.9MM
SALES (corp-wide): 2.4B **Publicly Held**
SIC: 8742 Marketing consulting services

PA: The Carlyle Group L P
1001 Pennsylvania Ave Nw 220s
Washington DC 20004
202 729-5626

(G-3301)
CLARK SCHAEFER HACKETT & CO (PA)
1 E 4th St Ste 1200 (45202-4294)
PHONE.................................513 241-3111
Thomas D Hazelbaker, *Ch of Bd*
Carl R Coburn, *President*
Jennifer Steward, *Partner*
David Eichert, *Managing Dir*
Neil O'Connor, *Chairman*
EMP: 45
SQ FT: 8,700
SALES (est): 37.2MM **Privately Held**
WEB: www.cshco.com
SIC: 8721 Certified public accountant

(G-3302)
CLARKE POWER SERVICES INC (PA)
3133 E Kemper Rd (45241-1516)
PHONE.................................513 771-2200
Mark Andreae, *CEO*
Kirk Andreae, *President*
Riley Asher, *Vice Pres*
Don Bixler, *Vice Pres*
Randy Keach, *Vice Pres*
◆ **EMP:** 100
SQ FT: 62,000
SALES: 252.9MM **Privately Held**
WEB: www.clarkedda.com
SIC: 5083 Farm & garden machinery

(G-3303)
CLEAN HARBORS ENVMTL SVCS INC
Also Called: Ohio Valley Technical Services
4880 Spring Grove Ave (45232)
PHONE.................................513 681-6242
Mike Jana, *Manager*
Brian Ludwig, *Manager*
Becky Plant, *Executive*
Scott Fryman, *Maintence Staff*
EMP: 33
SALES (corp-wide): 3.3B **Publicly Held**
SIC: 4953 Refuse systems
HQ: Clean Harbors Environmental Services, Inc.
42 Longwater Dr
Norwell MA 02061
781 792-5000

(G-3304)
CLEAN LIVING LAUNDRY LLC
Also Called: Super Laundry
2437 Gilbert Ave (45206-2518)
PHONE.................................513 569-0439
Benjamin Krupp,
Paul Meise,
Daniel Wente,
EMP: 25
SALES (est): 871.4K **Privately Held**
SIC: 7219 Laundry, except power & coin-operated

(G-3305)
CLERMONT COUNSELING CENTER
3730 Glenway Ave (45205-1354)
PHONE.................................513 345-8555
Arlene Herman, *Branch Mgr*
EMP: 25
SALES (est): 397.2K
SALES (corp-wide): 2.9MM **Privately Held**
SIC: 8322 General counseling services
PA: Clermont Counseling Center
43 E Main St
Amelia OH 45102
513 947-7000

(G-3306)
CLIFF NORTH CONSULTANTS INC
3747 Warsaw Ave (45205-1773)
PHONE.................................513 251-4930
Paul Mc Osker, *President*
Teresa Kluener, *Supervisor*
Lizabeth Mc Osker, *Admin Sec*
EMP: 25
SQ FT: 12,123

SALES (est): 2.5MM **Privately Held**
SIC: 8748 8734 Testing services; product testing laboratories

(G-3307)
CLIFTON CARE CENTER INC
Also Called: Communicare of Clifton
625 Probasco St (45220-2710)
PHONE.................................513 530-1600
Stephen L Rosedale, *President*
Charles R Stoltz, *Exec VP*
Ronald S Wilhelm, *Exec VP*
Joe Hancock, *Facilities Dir*
Katherine Allen, *Project Mgr*
EMP: 200
SQ FT: 26,000
SALES: 950K
SALES (corp-wide): 125.8MM **Privately Held**
WEB: www.communicarehealth.com
SIC: 8051 Skilled nursing care facilities
PA: Communicare Health Services, Inc.
4700 Ashwood Dr Ste 200
Blue Ash OH 45241
513 530-1654

(G-3308)
CLINICAL RESEARCH CENTER
3333 Burnet Ave Rm 3641 (45229-3026)
PHONE.................................513 636-4412
Jim Heubi, *Principal*
EMP: 60
SALES (est): 18.4MM **Privately Held**
SIC: 6324 8062 Hospital & medical service plans; general medical & surgical hospitals

(G-3309)
CLIPPARD INSTRUMENT LAB INC (PA)
Also Called: Clippard Minimatic
7390 Colerain Ave (45239-5396)
PHONE.................................513 521-4261
Harriet H Clippard, *Principal*
Steve Schutte, *Prdtn Mgr*
◆ **EMP:** 200 **EST:** 1941
SQ FT: 84,000
SALES: 1.7MM **Privately Held**
WEB: www.clippard.com
SIC: 5085 Pistons & valves; diamonds, industrial: natural, crude

(G-3310)
CLOVERNOOK INC (PA)
Also Called: Clovernook Hlth Care Pavilion
7025 Clovernook Ave (45231-5557)
P.O. Box 246, Mason (45040-0246)
PHONE.................................513 605-4000
Steve Boymel, *President*
Patricia Jett, *Nursing Dir*
Catherine Curran, *Officer*
Deborah Bisel, *Administration*
EMP: 120
SQ FT: 15,000
SALES: 11MM **Privately Held**
SIC: 8051 Skilled nursing care facilities

(G-3311)
CLOVERNOOK CENTER FOR THE BLI (PA)
7000 Hamilton Ave (45231-5240)
PHONE.................................513 522-3860
Robin Usalis, *President*
Christopher Faust, *President*
Betsy Baugh, *Vice Pres*
Jacqueline L Conner, *Vice Pres*
Douglas Jacques, *Vice Pres*
EMP: 125
SQ FT: 40,000
SALES: 8.5MM **Privately Held**
WEB: www.clovernook.org
SIC: 2656 8322 7389 Paper cups, plates, dishes & utensils; rehabilitation services; fund raising organizations

(G-3312)
CLOVERNOOK COUNTRY CLUB
2035 W Galbraith Rd (45239-4364)
PHONE.................................513 521-0333
Leslie Huesman, *President*
EMP: 70
SQ FT: 12,000
SALES: 2.3MM **Privately Held**
SIC: 7997 Country club, membership

▲ = Import ▼=Export
◆ =Import/Export

(G-3313)
CM-GC LLC
1810 Section Rd (45237-3306)
PHONE..................................513 527-4141
Schuyler Murdock,
EMP: 39
SQ FT: 5,000
SALES (est): 2.8MM **Privately Held**
WEB: www.cm-gc.com
SIC: 1542 1541 Commercial & office building, new construction; commercial & office buildings, renovation & repair; renovation, remodeling & repairs: industrial buildings

(G-3314)
CMTA INC
222 E 14th St (45202-7385)
PHONE..................................502 326-3085
Jeff Millard, Opers-Prdtn-Mfg
EMP: 150
SALES (corp-wide): 32.5MM **Privately Held**
SIC: 8711 Consulting engineer
PA: Cmta, Inc.
10411 Meeting St
Prospect KY
502 326-3085

(G-3315)
CNG FINANCIAL CORP
7755 Montgomery Rd # 400 (45236-4197)
PHONE..................................513 336-7735
David Davis, President
Debbie Kessen, Executive Asst
EMP: 3000
SALES (est): 442.8K **Privately Held**
SIC: 6282 Investment advice

(G-3316)
CNG FINANCIAL CORPORATION (PA)
Also Called: Check N Go
7755 Montgomery Rd # 400 (45236-4197)
PHONE..................................513 336-7735
Jared A Davis, President
Robert M Beck Jr, Principal
David Davis, Exec VP
Caronis Christie, Vice Pres
David Mitchell, Vice Pres
EMP: 300 EST: 1994
SQ FT: 66,000
SALES (est): 541.8MM **Privately Held**
WEB: www.checkngo.com
SIC: 6099 Check cashing agencies

(G-3317)
CNSLD HUMACARE- EMPLOYEE MGT (PA)
9435 Waterstone Blvd # 250 (45249-8226)
PHONE..................................513 605-3522
William B Southerland, CEO
Troy Lammers, Human Res Dir
Ashley Meuser, Director
Brandy Meader, Personnel Assit
EMP: 45 EST: 1995
SALES (est): 5.1MM **Privately Held**
SIC: 7361 Employment agencies

(G-3318)
COFFEE BREAK CORPORATION
Also Called: Restaurant Refreshment Service
1940 Losantiville Ave (45237-4106)
PHONE..................................513 841-1100
Robert Walter, Principal
Robert C Porter Jr, Principal
Edward Walter, Vice Pres
Mary A Walter, Vice Pres
EMP: 35 EST: 1973
SQ FT: 7,500
SALES (est): 10.7MM **Privately Held**
WEB: www.coffeebreakroasting.com
SIC: 5149 5962 Coffee, green or roasted; beverage vending machines

(G-3319)
COHEN TODD KITE STANFORD LLC
250 E 5th St Ste 2350 (45202-5136)
PHONE..................................513 205-7286
Maria Masterson, Marketing Staff
Robin Fischer, Executive
Terrence E Mire,
John G Cobey,
Alfred M Cohen,

EMP: 40 EST: 1894
SALES (est): 5.9MM **Privately Held**
WEB: www.ctks.com
SIC: 8111 General practice attorney, lawyer

(G-3320)
COHO CREATIVE LLC
2331 Victory Pkwy (45206-2888)
PHONE..................................513 751-7500
Daniel Brod, Principal
Mallory Beane, Project Mgr
Maxine Springer, Project Mgr
Julie Knight, VP Finance
Lisa Adams, Manager
EMP: 26
SALES (est): 2.9MM **Privately Held**
WEB: www.cohocreative.com
SIC: 8742 Marketing consulting services

(G-3321)
COLAS SOLUTIONS INC
7374 Main St (45244-3015)
PHONE..................................513 272-5348
Roger Hayner, President
EMP: 25
SALES (est): 4.2MM **Privately Held**
SALES (corp-wide): 83.5MM **Privately Held**
SIC: 1611 1622 Highway & street construction; bridge construction
HQ: Colas Inc.
73 Headquarters Plz 10t
Morristown NJ 07960
973 290-9082

(G-3322)
COLDSTREAM COUNTRY CLUB
400 Asbury Rd (45255-4657)
PHONE..................................513 231-3900
Mike Haehnle, General Mgr
Irene Gonzalez, Asst Mgr
EMP: 50 EST: 1959
SQ FT: 5,000
SALES: 3.5MM **Privately Held**
SIC: 7997 Country club, membership

(G-3323)
COLDWELL BANKER
2721 Erie Ave (45208-2103)
PHONE..................................513 321-9944
Fax: 513 321-9944
EMP: 50
SALES (est): 146.2K **Privately Held**
SIC: 6531 Real Estate Agent/Manager

(G-3324)
COLDWELL BANKER WEST SHELL
3260 Westbourne Dr (45248-5107)
PHONE..................................513 922-9400
Judith Jones, Branch Mgr
Kevin Kelly, Manager
Susan Booth, Real Est Agnt
Chris Fay, Real Est Agnt
Carole M Jones, Real Est Agnt
EMP: 53
SALES (corp-wide): 15.3MM **Privately Held**
SIC: 6531 Real estate agent, residential
PA: Coldwell Banker West Shell
9321 Montgomery Rd Ste C
Cincinnati OH 45242
513 794-9494

(G-3325)
COLDWELL BANKER WEST SHELL
6700 Ruwes Oak Dr (45248-1032)
PHONE..................................513 385-9300
Dan Stefanou, Broker
Ann Williams, Broker
Anna Bisher, Sales Associate
Guy Cagney, Sales Associate
Steve Oyler, Manager
EMP: 90
SALES (corp-wide): 15.3MM **Privately Held**
WEB: www.coldwellbankerwestshell.com
SIC: 6531 Real estate agent, residential
PA: Coldwell Banker West Shell
9321 Montgomery Rd Ste C
Cincinnati OH 45242
513 794-9494

(G-3326)
COLDWELL BANKER WEST SHELL
7203 Wooster Pike (45227-3830)
PHONE..................................513 271-7200
Beth Rouse, Branch Mgr
Timothy W Annett, Real Est Agnt
EMP: 30
SALES (corp-wide): 15.3MM **Privately Held**
WEB: www.coldwellbankerwestshell.com
SIC: 6531 Real estate agent, residential
PA: Coldwell Banker West Shell
9321 Montgomery Rd Ste C
Cincinnati OH 45242
513 794-9494

(G-3327)
COLE + RUSSELL ARCHITECTS INC (PA)
Also Called: Cr Architecture and Design
600 Vine St Ste 2210 (45202-2491)
PHONE..................................513 721-8080
John Russell, President
Bill Dandy, COO
Kelly Gaddes, Vice Pres
Bruce Quisno, Vice Pres
Declan McCormack, Exec Dir
EMP: 30
SALES (est): 5.2MM **Privately Held**
WEB: www.colerussell.com
SIC: 8712 Architectural engineering

(G-3328)
COLERAIN DRY RDGE CHLDCARE LTD
Also Called: ABC Early Childhood Lrng Ctr
3998 Dry Ridge Rd (45252-1910)
PHONE..................................513 923-4300
David Maumey,
Lawrence Day,
David Mauney,
Kimmy Mauney,
EMP: 29
SQ FT: 8,700
SALES (est): 1.1MM **Privately Held**
SIC: 8351 Preschool center

(G-3329)
COLLINS KAO INC
8911 Rossash Rd (45236-1209)
PHONE..................................513 948-9000
EMP: 25 **Privately Held**
SIC: 5043 5946 Photographic equipment & supplies; camera & photographic supply stores
PA: Kao Collins Inc
1201 Edison Dr
Cincinnati OH 45216

(G-3330)
COLUMBUS EQUIPMENT COMPANY
712 Shepherd Ave (45215-3118)
PHONE..................................513 771-3922
Jeff McVey, Regional Mgr
Al Shepherd, Manager
Ben Sutkamp, Manager
EMP: 28
SQ FT: 3,000
SALES (corp-wide): 84.2MM **Privately Held**
WEB: www.colsequipment.com
SIC: 5082 5084 General construction machinery & equipment; industrial machinery & equipment
PA: The Columbus Equipment Company
2323 Performance Way
Columbus OH 43207
614 437-0352

(G-3331)
COLUMBUS LIFE INSURANCE CO
400 E 4th St (45202-3302)
P.O. Box 5737 (45201-5737)
PHONE..................................513 361-6700
Jj Miller, CEO
Cynthia Funcheon, President
James Acton, Exec VP
Janet Stehlin, Assistant VP
Brian Ballou, Vice Pres
EMP: 52

SALES (est): 21.4MM **Privately Held**
WEB: www.columbuslife.com
SIC: 6311 6411 Life insurance carriers; insurance agents, brokers & service
HQ: The Western & Southern Life Insurance Company
400 Broadway St
Cincinnati OH 45202
513 629-1800

(G-3332)
COMEY & SHEPHERD LLC
7870 E Kemper Rd Ste 100 (45249-1675)
PHONE..................................513 489-2100
Mike Wolfer, Sales Staff
Jonathan Amster, Branch Mgr
Ken Parchman, Executive
EMP: 28
SALES (corp-wide): 11.1MM **Privately Held**
SIC: 6531 Real estate brokers & agents
PA: Comey & Shepherd, Llc
6901 Wooster Pike
Cincinnati OH 45227
513 561-5800

(G-3333)
COMEY & SHEPHERD LLC
2716 Observatory Ave (45208-2108)
PHONE..................................513 321-4343
Carol Harris, Vice Pres
Erik Zimmerman, Branch Mgr
Meg Collier, Real Est Agnt
Melanie Jackson, Real Est Agnt
June Newman, Real Est Agnt
EMP: 50
SALES (corp-wide): 11.1MM **Privately Held**
WEB: www.comey.com
SIC: 6531 Real estate brokers & agents
PA: Comey & Shepherd, Llc
6901 Wooster Pike
Cincinnati OH 45227
513 561-5800

(G-3334)
COMEY & SHEPHERD LLC
7333 Beechmont Ave (45230-4118)
PHONE..................................513 231-2800
Amy Minor, Vice Pres
Jack Wolking, VP Sales
Cindy Aiken, Manager
Bobbi Hart, CIO
Karen Shaffer, Real Est Agnt
EMP: 35
SALES (corp-wide): 11.1MM **Privately Held**
WEB: www.comey.com
SIC: 6531 Real estate agent, residential; real estate brokers & agents
PA: Comey & Shepherd, Llc
6901 Wooster Pike
Cincinnati OH 45227
513 561-5800

(G-3335)
COMEY & SHEPHERD LLC
9857 Montgomery Rd (45242-6424)
PHONE..................................513 891-4444
Carol Buckley, Vice Pres
Larry J Heidler, Vice Pres
Sandra Peters, Vice Pres
Paddy Ward, Vice Pres
Brady Wolfer, Vice Pres
EMP: 38
SALES (corp-wide): 11.1MM **Privately Held**
WEB: www.comey.com
SIC: 6531 Real estate agent, residential
PA: Comey & Shepherd, Llc
6901 Wooster Pike
Cincinnati OH 45227
513 561-5800

(G-3336)
COMFORT INN NORTHEAST
9011 Fields Ertel Rd (45249-8261)
P.O. Box 498278 (45249-7278)
PHONE..................................513 683-9700
Gregory Roetting, General Mgr
Subhash Patel, Principal
EMP: 30
SALES (est): 704.8K **Privately Held**
SIC: 7011 Hotels & motels

(G-3337)
COMMERCE HOLDINGS INC
312 Elm St Ste 1150 (45202-2763)
PHONE.................................513 579-1950
V Daniel Magarian, *President*
EMP: 40
SQ FT: 12,000
SALES (est): 5.5MM **Privately Held**
WEB: www.eminetwork.com
SIC: 7311 Advertising Agency

(G-3338)
COMMERCIAL HVAC INC
Also Called: Honeywell Authorized Dealer
5240 Lester Rd Ste 200 (45213-2522)
PHONE.................................513 396-6100
Roger Clark, *President*
EMP: 30
SALES (est): 4MM
SALES (corp-wide): 11.4MM **Privately Held**
WEB: www.commhvac.com
SIC: 1711 Mechanical contractor
PA: Grote Enterprises Llc
5240 Lester Rd
Cincinnati OH 45213
513 731-5700

(G-3339)
COMMITTED TO CARE INC
155 Tri County Pkwy # 220 (45246-3238)
PHONE.................................513 245-1190
Naomi L Sims, *CEO*
Naomi Sim, *CEO*
Brenda Sims-Caldwell, *CFO*
EMP: 28
SQ FT: 1,000
SALES (est): 916.9K **Privately Held**
SIC: 8082 Visiting nurse service

(G-3340)
COMMUNITY INSURANCE COMPANY
Also Called: Anthem
1351 Wm Howard Taft (45206-1721)
PHONE.................................859 282-7888
Craig Gentry, *Human Res Mgr*
Kellie Gomia, *Mktg Dir*
Karen Bass, *Corp Comm Staff*
Dawn Caudill, *Manager*
Vicki King, *Manager*
EMP: 25
SALES (corp-wide): 92.1B **Publicly Held**
SIC: 6324 Hospital & medical service plans
HQ: Community Insurance Company
4361 Irwin Simpson Rd
Mason OH 45040

(G-3341)
COMMUNITY MANAGEMENT CORP
375 W Galbraith Rd (45215-5037)
PHONE.................................513 761-6339
Mary Cieger, *Branch Mgr*
EMP: 84
SALES (corp-wide): 1.7MM **Privately Held**
SIC: 1522 Apartment building construction
PA: Community Management Corp
10925 Reed Hartman Hwy # 200
Blue Ash OH 45242
513 984-3030

(G-3342)
COMPEL FITNESS LLC
10711 Princeton Pike (45246)
PHONE.................................216 965-5694
William Dane, *Mng Member*
EMP: 150
SALES (est): 448.2K **Privately Held**
SIC: 7991 Physical fitness clubs with training equipment

(G-3343)
COMPLETE BUILDING MAINT LLC
3629 Wabash Ave (45207-1223)
PHONE.................................513 235-7511
Anthony Boulding, *President*
EMP: 35
SALES: 250K **Privately Held**
SIC: 7349 Building maintenance services

(G-3344)
COMPLETE QLTY TRNSP SLTONS LLC
3055 Blue Rock Rd Ste T (45239-6302)
PHONE.................................513 914-4882
Richard Mursinna,
William Foster,
EMP: 25
SALES: 2.3MM **Privately Held**
SIC: 4731 Brokers, shipping

(G-3345)
COMPREHENSIVE CMNTY CHILD CARE (PA)
Also Called: 4C FOR CHILDREN
2100 Sherman Ave Ste 300 (45212-2775)
PHONE.................................513 221-0033
Vanessa Freytag, *President*
Ann Thomas, *Human Resources*
Terri Alekzander, *Manager*
Holly Grass, *Technical Staff*
Sallie Westheimer, *Exec Dir*
EMP: 37
SQ FT: 12,000
SALES: 9.6MM **Privately Held**
WEB: www.4c-cinci.org
SIC: 8322 Child guidance agency

(G-3346)
COMPREHENSIVE HR SOLUTIONS LLC
Also Called: Sheakley
1 Sheakley Way (45246-3778)
PHONE.................................513 771-2277
Shari Herper, *Vice Pres*
James Terris, *Opers Staff*
Steve Wilson, *Controller*
Denise Brownstone, *Accounts Mgr*
Dan Dattilo, *Sales Staff*
EMP: 32
SALES (est): 3.6MM **Privately Held**
SIC: 8742 Management consulting services

(G-3347)
COMPREHENSIVE MANAGED CARE SYS
Also Called: C M C S
3380 Erie Ave (45208-1626)
PHONE.................................513 533-0021
Fax: 513 533-2841
EMP: 40
SQ FT: 2,500
SALES (est): 2.7MM **Privately Held**
SIC: 8741 Managed Care

(G-3348)
CONCENTRIX CVG CORPORATION (HQ)
201 E 4th St (45202-4248)
P.O. Box 1895 (45201-1895)
PHONE.................................513 723-7000
Dennis J Polk, *CEO*
Christopher A Caldwell, *President*
Steven L Richie, *Senior VP*
Thomas Lightfoot, *Engineer*
Marshall W Witt, *CFO*
EMP: 800 EST: 1996
SALES: 3B
SALES (corp-wide): 20B **Publicly Held**
WEB: www.convergys.com
SIC: 7374 7373 Data processing service; computer integrated systems design
PA: Synnex Corporation
44201 Nobel Dr
Fremont CA 94538
510 656-3333

(G-3349)
CONCORDIA PROPERTIES LLC
Also Called: Tri County Mall Promotion Fund
11700 Princeton Pike B213 (45246-2535)
PHONE.................................513 671-0120
Sandra Holzwarth, *Director*
EMP: 25 EST: 1960
SQ FT: 50
SALES (est): 2.7MM **Privately Held**
WEB: www.concordiaproperties.com
SIC: 8742 Marketing consulting services

(G-3350)
CONEY ISLAND INC
6201 Kellogg Ave (45230-7199)
PHONE.................................513 232-8230

Victor W Nolting, *CEO*
Linda Layton, *Senior VP*
Linda L Layton, *Vice Pres*
Jennifer Reder, *Treasurer*
Susan Whitaker, *Accounts Exec*
▲ EMP: 36
SQ FT: 2,560
SALES (est): 4.7MM **Privately Held**
WEB: www.coneyislandpark.com
SIC: 7999 Tourist attractions, amusement park concessions & rides

(G-3351)
CONSOLIDATED GRAIN & BARGE CO
Also Called: Anderson Ferry
4837 River Rd (45233-1634)
PHONE.................................513 941-4805
EMP: 30 **Privately Held**
SIC: 4221 5153 4449 4491 Grain elevator, storage only; grain & field beans; canal barge operations; marine cargo handling
HQ: Consolidated Grain & Barge Company
1127 Hwy 190 E Service Rd
Covington LA 70433
985 867-3500

(G-3352)
CONTEMPORARY ARTS CENTER
44 E 6th St (45202-3998)
PHONE.................................513 721-0390
Glen Gruber, *CFO*
Margaux Higgins, *Controller*
Erin Sansalone, *Sales Staff*
Raphaela Platow, *Director*
EMP: 40
SQ FT: 80,000
SALES: 5MM **Privately Held**
WEB: www.cacmail.org
SIC: 8412 Arts or science center; museum

(G-3353)
CONTRACTORS MATERIALS COMPANY
Also Called: Mmi of Kentucky
10320 S Medallion Dr (45241-4836)
P.O. Box 621227 (45262-1227)
PHONE.................................513 733-3000
Martha C Luken, *President*
David L Friedman, *Vice Pres*
Daniel P King, *Vice Pres*
William H Luken, *Admin Sec*
▲ EMP: 50
SQ FT: 95,000
SALES (est): 29.6MM **Privately Held**
WEB: www.cmcmmi.com
SIC: 5211 5051 Lumber & other building materials; concrete reinforcing bars

(G-3354)
CONTROLLED CREDIT CORPORATION
644 Linn St Ste 1101 (45203-1742)
P.O. Box 5154 (45205-0154)
PHONE.................................513 921-2600
Daniel J Heisel, *President*
Dan Heisel Jr, *Vice Pres*
Robert W Leuenberger, *Vice Pres*
Becky Kelly, *Accounting Mgr*
Michelle Schneider, *Client Mgr*
EMP: 42 EST: 1967
SQ FT: 7,000
SALES (est): 5.7MM **Privately Held**
WEB: www.controlledcredit.com
SIC: 7322 Collection agency, except real estate

(G-3355)
CONTROLS AND SHEET METAL INC (PA)
1051 Sargent St (45203-1858)
PHONE.................................513 721-3610
Rick Schaible, *President*
EMP: 35 EST: 1983
SQ FT: 40,000
SALES (est): 10.8MM **Privately Held**
WEB: www.csm-inc.com
SIC: 5075 3444 Warm air heating & air conditioning; ducts, sheet metal

(G-3356)
CONTROLS CENTER INC (PA)
Also Called: Johnson Contrls Authorized Dlr
1640 E Kemper Rd Ste 2 (45246-2806)
PHONE.................................513 772-2665
Gregory E Grimme, *President*
Mark J Grimme, *Vice Pres*
EMP: 65
SQ FT: 45,000
SALES (est): 29.1MM **Privately Held**
WEB: www.johnstonecincinnati.com
SIC: 5075 5078 Air conditioning equipment, except room units; warm air heating equipment & supplies; refrigeration equipment & supplies

(G-3357)
CONVERGINT TECHNOLOGIES LLC
Also Called: Post Browning
7812 Redsky Dr (45249-1632)
PHONE.................................513 771-1717
EMP: 130
SALES (corp-wide): 624.4MM **Privately Held**
SIC: 5065 7699 Security control equipment & systems; industrial machinery & equipment repair
PA: Convergint Technologies Llc
1 Commerce Dr
Schaumburg IL 60173
847 620-5000

(G-3358)
CONVERGYS CSTMER MGT GROUP INC (DH)
201 E 4th St Bsmt (45202-4248)
P.O. Box 1638 (45201-1638)
PHONE.................................513 723-6104
David F Dougherty, *President*
Ronald E Schultz, *COO*
Andre S Valentine, *CFO*
▼ EMP: 300
SQ FT: 100,000
SALES (est): 373.7MM
SALES (corp-wide): 20B **Publicly Held**
SIC: 7389 8732 Telemarketing services; market analysis or research
HQ: Concentrix Cvg Corporation
201 E 4th St
Cincinnati OH 45202
513 723-7000

(G-3359)
CONVERGYS GVRNMENT SLTIONS LLC
201 E 4th St Bsmt (45202-4248)
PHONE.................................513 723-7006
David Dougherty, *Mng Member*
Roger V Goddu, *Bd of Directors*
Doug Thompson,
EMP: 99
SQ FT: 60,000
SALES (est): 8.9MM
SALES (corp-wide): 20B **Publicly Held**
WEB: www.convergys.com
SIC: 7374 Data processing service
HQ: Concentrix Cvg Corporation
201 E 4th St
Cincinnati OH 45202
513 723-7000

(G-3360)
CONVERSA LANGUAGE CENTER INC
817 Main St Ste 600 (45202-2183)
PHONE.................................513 651-5679
Jerry Thiemann, *President*
Gerry Thiemann, *Director*
EMP: 25
SQ FT: 5,000
SALES (est): 1.5MM **Privately Held**
WEB: www.conversa1.com
SIC: 7389 Translation services

(G-3361)
CORCORAN AND HARNIST HTG & AC
Also Called: Honeywell Authorized Dealer
1457 Harrison Ave (45214-1605)
PHONE.................................513 921-2227
Tim Corcoran, *President*
Greg Harnist, *Vice Pres*
EMP: 35
SQ FT: 300,000

▲ = Import ▼=Export
◆ =Import/Export

SALES: 3.5MM **Privately Held**
WEB: www.corcoranharnist.com
SIC: 1711 Warm air heating & air condi-
tioning contractor

(G-3362)
CORE RESOURCES INC
7795 5 Mile Rd (45230-2355)
PHONE..................................513 731-1771
Paul Kitzmiller, *CEO*
David Kitzmiller, *COO*
EMP: 52
SQ FT: 7,000
SALES (est): 9.6MM **Privately Held**
WEB: www.core-1.com
SIC: 8741 Construction management

(G-3363)
CORNERSTONE BROKER INS SVCS AG (PA)
Also Called: Cornerstone Brkrg Ins Svc Agn
2101 Florence Ave (45206-2426)
PHONE..................................513 241-7675
John Carroll, *CEO*
John Clark, *Vice Pres*
Steve Geis, *Vice Pres*
Mark Welcer, *Vice Pres*
Colleen Glaser, *Broker*
EMP: 40
SALES (est): 10.8MM **Privately Held**
SIC: 6411 Insurance agents

(G-3364)
CORPOREX REALTY & INV LLC
P.O. Box 75020 (45275-0020)
PHONE..................................859 292-5500
EMP: 419 **Privately Held**
SIC: 7997 Country club, membership
PA: Corporex Realty & Investment, Llc
100 E Riverctr Ste 1100
Covington KY 41011

(G-3365)
CORS & BASSETT LLC (PA)
537 E Pete Rose Way # 400 (45202-3578)
PHONE..................................513 852-8200
Janet Houston, *Partner*
Hans Zimmer, *Partner*
David L Barth, *Business Mgr*
Thomas Kilcoyne, *Counsel*
Stephen Holmes, *VP Mktg*
EMP: 75
SALES (est): 12.1MM **Privately Held**
SIC: 8111 General practice attorney,
lawyer

(G-3366)
COSTELLO PNTG BLDG RESTORATION
1113 Halpin Ave (45208-2907)
PHONE..................................513 321-3326
EMP: 25
SQ FT: 800
SALES (est): 1.3MM **Privately Held**
SIC: 1721 Painting Contractor

(G-3367)
COTTINGHAM RETIREMENT CMNTY
3995 Cottingham Dr # 102 (45241-1680)
PHONE..................................513 563-3600
Melanie Walden, *Human Res Dir*
Lesa Dean-Day, *Office Mgr*
Margie Berryman, *Store Dir*
EMP: 160
SALES: 5.1MM **Privately Held**
SIC: 8051 Skilled nursing care facilities

(G-3368)
COUNCIL ON AGING OF SOUTHWESTE
175 Tri County Pkwy # 200 (45246-3237)
PHONE..................................513 721-1025
Lindsay Alexander, *Opers Staff*
Ken Wilson, *Opers Staff*
Jacqueline Golston, *Human Res Dir*
Eduardo Garcia, *Manager*
Jacque Martens, *Manager*
EMP: 200 EST: 1971
SQ FT: 31,000
SALES: 81.1MM **Privately Held**
WEB: www.help4seniors.org
SIC: 8399 8322 Council for social agency;
individual & family services

(G-3369)
COUNTY OF HAMILTON
Also Called: Mental Retardation & Dev
2600 Civic Center Dr (45231-1312)
PHONE..................................513 742-1576
Charles Alteneau, *Director*
EMP: 359
SQ FT: 3,000 **Privately Held**
WEB: www.mhrecovery.com
SIC: 8331 9431 8322 Sheltered work-
shop; mental health agency administra-
tion, government; ; individual & family
services
PA: County Of Hamilton
138 E Court St Rm 607
Cincinnati OH 45202
513 946-4400

(G-3370)
COUNTY OF HAMILTON
Also Called: Hillcrest Training School
246 Bonham Rd (45215-2054)
PHONE..................................513 552-1200
Dennis Johnson, *Principal*
EMP: 150
SQ FT: 3,192 **Privately Held**
WEB: www.mhrecovery.com
SIC: 8361 9411 9211 Training school for
delinquents; administration of educational
programs; ; courts;
PA: County Of Hamilton
138 E Court St Rm 607
Cincinnati OH 45202
513 946-4400

(G-3371)
COUNTY OF HAMILTON
138 E Court St Rm 700 (45202-1224)
PHONE..................................513 946-4250
Teodore Hubbard, *Chief*
EMP: 100 **Privately Held**
WEB: www.mhrecovery.com
SIC: 8711 9511 Civil engineering; air,
water & solid waste management;
PA: County Of Hamilton
138 E Court St Rm 607
Cincinnati OH 45202
513 946-4400

(G-3372)
COUNTY OF HAMILTON
Also Called: Mental Retardation & Dev
5884 Bridgetown Rd (45248-3106)
PHONE..................................513 598-2965
Elizabeth Bellew, *Branch Mgr*
Bill Hoffman, *Director*
EMP: 260 **Privately Held**
WEB: www.mhrecovery.com
SIC: 8093 9431 Mental health clinic, out-
patient; mental health agency administra-
tion, government;
PA: County Of Hamilton
138 E Court St Rm 607
Cincinnati OH 45202
513 946-4400

(G-3373)
COUNTY OF HAMILTON
Also Called: Health Dept
7162 Reading Rd Ste 800 (45237-3845)
PHONE..................................513 821-6946
Patsy Matillar, *Program Dir*
EMP: 45 **Privately Held**
WEB: www.mhrecovery.com
SIC: 8322 9431 Child related social serv-
ices; administration of public health pro-
grams;
PA: County Of Hamilton
138 E Court St Rm 607
Cincinnati OH 45202
513 946-4400

(G-3374)
COUPLE TO COUPLE LEAG INTL INC (PA)
Also Called: FOUNDATION FOR THE FAM-
ILY
4290 Delhi Rd (45238-5829)
P.O. Box 111184 (45211-1184)
PHONE..................................513 471-2000
Sheila K Kippley, *Principal*
Mike Manhart, *Exec Dir*
EMP: 25
SQ FT: 13,500

SALES: 1.6MM **Privately Held**
SIC: 8322 Family service agency; family
counseling services

(G-3375)
COURT STRET CENTER ASSOCIATES
Also Called: Parking Company of America
250 W Court St Ste 200e (45202-1064)
PHONE..................................513 241-0415
Martin Chavez, *President*
EMP: 42
SQ FT: 105,000
SALES (est): 1.9MM **Privately Held**
WEB: www.pca-star.com
SIC: 6512 Commercial & industrial building
operation

(G-3376)
COWAN SYSTEMS LLC
10801 Evendale Dr (45241-7508)
PHONE..................................513 769-4774
EMP: 129 **Privately Held**
SIC: 4213 Trucking, except local
PA: Cowan Systems, Llc
4555 Hollins Ferry Rd
Baltimore MD 21227

(G-3377)
CRAFTSMAN ELECTRIC INC
3855 Alta Ave Ste 1 (45236-3932)
PHONE..................................513 891-4426
Kathleen Fischer, *President*
Charles Fischer, *Vice Pres*
▲ EMP: 55
SQ FT: 16,000
SALES: 9.5MM **Privately Held**
SIC: 1731 General electrical contractor

(G-3378)
CRANE HEATING & AC CO
Also Called: Honeywell Authorized Dealer
24 Clay St (45217-1193)
PHONE..................................513 641-4700
Frank J Crane III, *President*
Edward Crane, *Vice Pres*
Jim Lohbeck, *Sales Mgr*
Karen Crane, *Admin Sec*
EMP: 40 EST: 1953
SQ FT: 6,000
SALES (est): 5.8MM **Privately Held**
WEB: www.crane-htg-air.com
SIC: 1711 Warm air heating & air condi-
tioning contractor

(G-3379)
CRANLEY SURGICAL ASSOCIATES
3747 W Fork Rd (45247-7548)
PHONE..................................513 961-4335
L R Roedersheimer, *President*
James J Arbough, *Principal*
John J Cranley, *Principal*
Robert Cranley, *Principal*
EMP: 33
SALES (est): 2.6MM **Privately Held**
WEB: www.cranleysurgical.com
SIC: 8011 Cardiologist & cardio-vascular
specialist

(G-3380)
CRONINS INC
Also Called: Joseph Northland Porsche Audi
9847 Kings Auto Mall Rd (45249-8245)
PHONE..................................513 851-5900
Ronald Joseph, *President*
Greg Joseph, *General Mgr*
EMP: 37
SQ FT: 13,000
SALES (est): 9.3MM **Privately Held**
SIC: 5511 5531 7389 Automobiles, new &
used; automotive & home supply stores;
drive-a-way automobile service

(G-3381)
CROOKED TREE GOLF COURSE
1250 Springfield Pike # 100 (45215-2148)
PHONE..................................513 398-3933
Joe Bischoff, *Manager*
EMP: 40
SQ FT: 8,500
SALES (est): 1.1MM **Privately Held**
SIC: 7992 Public golf courses

(G-3382)
CROSSROADS CENTER
311 Mrtin Lther King Dr E (45219-2581)
PHONE..................................513 475-5300
Janice Bishop, *Senior VP*
Carl Tucker, *QA Dir*
Jacqueline P Butler, *Officer*
EMP: 150
SALES: 7MM **Privately Held**
SIC: 8069 8361 8093 Alcoholism rehabili-
tation hospital; drug addiction rehabilita-
tion hospital; residential care; specialty
outpatient clinics

(G-3383)
CRYSTALWOOD INC
Also Called: Alois Alzheimer Center, The
70 Damon Rd (45218-1041)
PHONE..................................513 605-1000
Stephen Boymel, *President*
Tamra Bell, *Accountant*
Jon Rarick, *Exec Dir*
EMP: 85
SQ FT: 30,000
SALES (est): 123.9K **Privately Held**
WEB: www.alois.com
SIC: 8059 8361 8052 Rest home, with
health care; residential care; intermediate
care facilities

(G-3384)
CSX TRANSPORTATION INC
3601 Geringer St (45223-2405)
PHONE..................................513 369-5514
Bob Babcock, *Branch Mgr*
Jimmy Spencer, *Manager*
EMP: 38
SALES (corp-wide): 12.2B **Publicly Held**
WEB: www.csxt.com
SIC: 4011 Railroads, line-haul operating
HQ: Csx Transportation, Inc.
500 Water St
Jacksonville FL 32202
904 359-3100

(G-3385)
CTS CONSTRUCTION INC
Also Called: CTS Telecommunications
7275 Edington Dr (45249-1064)
PHONE..................................513 489-8290
Rick Stezer, *President*
John Diss, *Superintendent*
William Coate, *Vice Pres*
Andrew Rotunno, *Vice Pres*
Joe Skinner, *Vice Pres*
EMP: 100
SQ FT: 15,000
SALES (est): 17.1MM **Privately Held**
WEB: www.ctstelecomm.com
SIC: 7378 8748 1796 1731 Computer
maintenance & repair; telecommunica-
tions consultant; installing building equip-
ment; electrical work

(G-3386)
CUMBERLAND GAP LLC
Also Called: Ramada Inn Cumberland Hotel
2285 Banning Rd (45239-6611)
PHONE..................................513 681-9300
Toni Winston, *President*
Jackie Iovine, *General Mgr*
EMP: 30
SALES (est): 1.1MM **Privately Held**
SIC: 7011 Hotels & motels

(G-3387)
CUMULUS BROADCASTING LLC
4805 Montgomery Rd (45212-2198)
PHONE..................................850 243-7676
Chris Huneke, *Branch Mgr*
EMP: 38
SALES (corp-wide): 1.1B **Publicly Held**
SIC: 4832 Radio broadcasting stations
HQ: Cumulus Broadcasting, Llc
3280 Peachtree Rd Nw Ste
Atlanta GA 30305
404 949-0700

(G-3388)
CUMULUS MEDIA INC
Also Called: Warm 98
4805 Montgomery Rd # 300 (45212-2198)
PHONE..................................513 241-9898
Karrie Subbrick, *Manager*
EMP: 65

G
E
O
G
R
A
P
H
I
C

SALES (corp-wide): 1.1B **Publicly Held**
WEB: www.cumulusmedia.com
SIC: **4832** Radio broadcasting stations
PA: Cm Wind Down Topco Inc.
　3280 Peachtree Rd Ne Ne2300
　Atlanta GA 30305
　404 949-0700

(G-3389)
CURIOSITY LLC
Also Called: Curiosity Advertising
35 E 7th St Ste 800 (45202-2411)
PHONE...............................513 744-6000
Gregory Livingston, *COO*
Stephanie Anglavar, *Vice Pres*
Kevin Clark, *Project Mgr*
April Martini, *Accounting Mgr*
Kathy Puckett, *Accounting Mgr*
EMP: 62
SQ FT: 14,000
SALES: 4MM **Privately Held**
WEB: www.Curiosity360.com
SIC: **7311** Advertising consultant

(G-3390)
CUSO CORPORATION
10485 Reading Rd (45241-2523)
PHONE...............................513 984-2876
Patrick Taylor, *CEO*
Tim Ballinger, *President*
Tina Wander, *COO*
Todd Blessing, *Advisor*
EMP: 100
SALES (est): 6.1MM **Privately Held**
SIC: **6062** State credit unions

(G-3391)
CUSTOM DESIGN BENEFITS INC
5589 Cheviot Rd (45247-7020)
PHONE...............................513 598-2929
M Steven Chapel, *CEO*
Julie Muller, *President*
EMP: 38
SQ FT: 10,000
SALES (est): 22.3MM **Privately Held**
WEB: www.customdesignbenefits.com
SIC: **6324** Hospital & medical service plans

(G-3392)
CUSTOM MAID CLEANING SERVICES
3840 Burwood Ave (45212-3944)
P.O. Box 12688 (45212-0688)
PHONE...............................513 351-6571
Walter H Ford, *President*
EMP: 50 EST: 1972
SALES (est): 1.1MM **Privately Held**
SIC: **7349** Janitorial service, contract basis

(G-3393)
D & D ADVERTISING ENTERPRISES
801 Evans St Ste 203 (45204-2075)
PHONE...............................513 921-6827
Diane Carpenter, *President*
Edwin D Hottinger, *President*
EMP: 25
SALES: 2MM **Privately Held**
WEB: www.coverads.com
SIC: **5199** Advertising specialties

(G-3394)
D B A INC
Also Called: Active Detective Bureau
4239 Hamilton Ave (45223-2088)
PHONE...............................513 541-6600
Celine M Estill, *President*
Bari Mairose, *Network Mgr*
Bari Venn Mairose, *Web Proj Mgr*
EMP: 50
SALES: 2MM **Privately Held**
SIC: **7381** 1731 7382 Private investigator; security guard service; fire detection & burglar alarm systems specialization; security systems services

(G-3395)
D JAMES INCORPORATED
Also Called: Hillebrand Nursing & Rehab
4320 Bridgetown Rd (45211-4428)
PHONE...............................513 574-4550
James Glass, *President*
Lynn Schroeder, *Purch Mgr*
Donna Masminster, *Mktg Dir*

EMP: 200
SQ FT: 2,953
SALES: 12.4MM **Privately Held**
WEB: www.hillebrandhealth.com
SIC: **8051** Convalescent home with continuous nursing care

(G-3396)
D-G CUSTOM CHROME LLC
5200 Lester Rd (45213-2522)
PHONE...............................513 531-1881
Alex Wyatt, *President*
Don Gorman, *President*
Victoria Gorman, *Vice Pres*
EMP: 58
SQ FT: 10,162
SALES (est): 7.2MM **Privately Held**
WEB: www.dgcustomchrome.com
SIC: **5013** 3471 Automotive supplies & parts; plating & polishing

(G-3397)
DAG CONSTRUCTION CO INC
4924 Winton Rd (45232-1505)
PHONE...............................513 542-8597
Dale S White Sr, *CEO*
Stephanie A Hall, *President*
Lindsay A Wilhelm, *President*
Gregory J Webb, *COO*
Dale White Jr, *Vice Pres*
EMP: 40
SALES (est): 11.1MM **Privately Held**
WEB: www.dag-cons.com
SIC: **1542** 1541 Commercial & office building, new construction; commercial & office buildings, renovation & repair; renovation, remodeling & repairs: industrial buildings

(G-3398)
DALTON ROOFING CO
4477 Eastern Ave (45226-1803)
PHONE...............................513 871-2800
M Thomas Dalton, *President*
Frank Dalton, *Vice Pres*
Martha Dalton, *Admin Sec*
EMP: 60
SQ FT: 8,000
SALES (est): 6.4MM **Privately Held**
WEB: www.daltonroofing.net
SIC: **1761** Roofing contractor

(G-3399)
DAMON TAX SERVICE
6572 Glenway Ave (45211-4410)
PHONE...............................513 574-9087
Damon Robins, *President*
EMP: 40
SQ FT: 1,400
SALES: 200K **Privately Held**
WEB: www.damontaxservice.com
SIC: **7291** Tax return preparation services

(G-3400)
DANSON INC
Also Called: Aegis Protective Services
3033 Robertson Ave (45209-1233)
PHONE...............................513 948-0066
Justin Dutro, *President*
Daniel G Dutro, *Vice Pres*
Dee Dutro, *Manager*
EMP: 210
SQ FT: 2,400
SALES (est): 7.3MM **Privately Held**
WEB: www.danson.com
SIC: **7381** Security guard service

(G-3401)
DAVEY RESOURCE GROUP INC
Also Called: New Age Communications Cnstr
1230 W 8th St (45203-1005)
PHONE...............................859 630-9879
Jay Martin, *Manager*
EMP: 40
SALES (corp-wide): 1B **Privately Held**
SIC: **1623** Water, sewer & utility lines
HQ: Davey Resource Group, Inc.
　1500 N Mantua St
　Kent OH 44240
　330 673-9511

(G-3402)
DAVID L BARTH LWYR
537 E Pete Rose Way (45202-3567)
PHONE...............................513 852-8228
David Barth, *Principal*

EMP: 60
SALES (est): 1.5MM **Privately Held**
SIC: **8111** General practice attorney, lawyer

(G-3403)
DAVITA INC
2109 Reading Rd (45202-1417)
PHONE...............................513 784-1800
Barbara Frommeyer, *Branch Mgr*
EMP: 27 **Publicly Held**
SIC: **8092** Kidney dialysis centers
PA: Davita Inc.
　2000 16th St
　Denver CO 80202

(G-3404)
DAVITA INC
7502 State Rd (45255-2596)
PHONE...............................513 624-0400
Laurie Johnson, *Branch Mgr*
EMP: 27 **Publicly Held**
SIC: **8092** Kidney dialysis centers
PA: Davita Inc.
　2000 16th St
　Denver CO 80202

(G-3405)
DAY SHARE LTD
5915 Glenway Ave (45238-2008)
PHONE...............................513 451-1100
Jeff Gault, *COO*
Thoams Gault, *Mng Member*
Thomas Gault, *Mng Member*
Patricia Gault,
EMP: 48
SALES (est): 1.1MM **Privately Held**
WEB: www.dayshare.com
SIC: **8322** Senior citizens' center or association

(G-3406)
DAYTON HEIDELBERG DISTRG CO
1518 Dalton Ave (45214-2018)
PHONE...............................513 421-5000
Lee Oberlag, *President*
Kevin McNamara, *Sales Mgr*
Albert Vontz, *Branch Mgr*
Mary Horn, *Manager*
Sebastian Palicki, *Manager*
EMP: 98
SALES (corp-wide): 369.4MM **Privately Held**
SIC: **5181** Beer & other fermented malt liquors
PA: Dayton Heidelberg Distributing Co.
　3601 Dryden Rd
　Moraine OH 45439
　937 222-8692

(G-3407)
DCS SANITATION MANAGEMENT INC (PA)
7864 Camargo Rd (45243-4300)
P.O. Box 43215 (45243-0215)
PHONE...............................513 891-4980
Lance White, *CEO*
Thomas Murray, *President*
James Gillespie, *CFO*
EMP: 85
SQ FT: 3,000
SALES (est): 42.4MM **Privately Held**
SIC: **7349** 7342 Building cleaning service; disinfecting services

(G-3408)
DE FOXX & ASSOCIATES INC (PA)
Also Called: Validex
324 W 9th St Fl 5 (45202-2043)
PHONE...............................513 621-5522
David E Foxx, *President*
Patricia Foxx, *Admin Sec*
EMP: 350
SQ FT: 25,000
SALES (est): 137.4MM **Privately Held**
WEB: www.xlcservices.com
SIC: **8742** 8741 Business consultant; general management consultant; construction management

(G-3409)
DEACONESS ASSOCIATIONS INC (PA)
615 Elsinore Pl Bldg B (45202-1459)
PHONE...............................513 559-2100
E Anthony Woods, *President*
Dave Mc Adams, *CFO*
EMP: 300
SALES: 23.6MM **Privately Held**
SIC: **6324** Hospital & medical service plans

(G-3410)
DEACONESS HOSPITAL OF CINCINNA (PA)
615 Elsinore Pl Bldg B (45202-1459)
PHONE...............................513 559-2100
James L Pahls, *Ch of Bd*
E Anthony Woods, *Chairman*
Scott Woods MD, *Med Doctor*
EMP: 81 EST: 1888
SQ FT: 649,000
SALES: 4.4MM **Privately Held**
SIC: **8062** General medical & surgical hospitals

(G-3411)
DEACONESS LONG TERM CARE INC (HQ)
330 Straight St Ste 310 (45219-1068)
P.O. Box 198027 (45219-8027)
PHONE...............................513 861-0400
Bryan Burklow, *President*
Kenneth Raupach, *CFO*
EMP: 89
SQ FT: 1,891
SALES: 5.6K
SALES (corp-wide): 23.6MM **Privately Held**
SIC: **8741** Nursing & personal care facility management
PA: The Deaconess Associations Inc
　615 Elsinore Pl Bldg B
　Cincinnati OH 45202
　513 559-2100

(G-3412)
DEACONESS LONG TERM CARE OF MI (PA)
Also Called: Camden Health Center
330 Straight St Ste 310 (45219-1068)
PHONE...............................513 487-3600
Ken Raupach, *COO*
EMP: 1500
SALES: 22K **Privately Held**
WEB: www.deaconessltc.org
SIC: **8059** 8361 8052 8051 Nursing home, except skilled & intermediate care facility; residential care; intermediate care facilities; skilled nursing care facilities

(G-3413)
DEANHOUSTON CREATIVE GROUP INC (PA)
310 Culvert St Ste 300 (45202-2229)
PHONE...............................513 421-6622
Dale Dean, *President*
Andy Dean, *Vice Pres*
Greg Houston, *Vice Pres*
Jim Molloy, *Vice Pres*
Pam Houston, *Treasurer*
EMP: 33
SQ FT: 4,100
SALES (est): 7.8MM **Privately Held**
SIC: **7311** Advertising consultant

(G-3414)
DEBRA-KUEMPEL INC (HQ)
Also Called: De Bra - Kuempel
3976 Southern Ave (45227-3562)
P.O. Box 701620 (45270-1620)
PHONE...............................513 271-6500
Joe D Clark, *CEO*
Fred B De Bra, *Ch of Bd*
Morris H Reed, *Corp Secy*
Robert E Cupp, *Vice Pres*
John Kuempel Jr, *Vice Pres*
EMP: 80 EST: 1944
SQ FT: 20,079
SALES (est): 29.3MM
SALES (corp-wide): 8.1B **Publicly Held**
SIC: **3446** 1711 3443 3441 Architectural metalwork; mechanical contractor; fabricated plate work (boiler shop); fabricated structural metal

PA: Emcor Group, Inc.
301 Merritt 7 Fl 6
Norwalk CT 06851
203 849-7800

(G-3415)
DEDICATED NURSING ASSOC INC
11542 Springfield Pike (45246-3516)
PHONE...................................866 450-5550
EMP: 44 **Privately Held**
SIC: 7361 7363 8051 Nurses' registry; medical help service; skilled nursing care facilities
PA: Dedicated Nursing Associates, Inc.
6536 State Route 22
Delmont PA 15626

(G-3416)
DEER PARK ROOFING INC (PA)
7201 Blue Ash Rd (45236-3665)
PHONE...................................513 891-9151
Nicholas A Sabino, *President*
EMP: 45
SQ FT: 23,000
SALES (est): 13.5MM **Privately Held**
WEB: www.deerparkroofing.com
SIC: 1761 Roofing contractor

(G-3417)
DEFINITIVE SOLUTIONS CO INC
Also Called: DSC Consulting
8180 Corp Pk Dr Ste 305 (45242)
PHONE...................................513 719-9100
Tim Osborn, *President*
Tony Manzo, *Vice Pres*
Ken Reece, *Vice Pres*
EMP: 82
SQ FT: 6,000
SALES (est): 6.1MM **Privately Held**
SIC: 7389 7379 7374 7373 Trade show arrangement; data processing consultant; data processing & preparation; computer integrated systems design

(G-3418)
DEI INCORPORATED
1550 Kemper Meadow Dr (45240-1638)
PHONE...................................513 825-5800
Richard D Grow, *Ch of Bd*
Nedd Compton, *President*
Don Neill, *President*
Jay Browning, *Site Mgr*
Richard Thatcher, *Site Mgr*
EMP: 74
SQ FT: 15,000
SALES (est): 14.5MM **Privately Held**
WEB: www.dei-corp.com
SIC: 8712 Architectural engineering

(G-3419)
DELHI TOWNSHIP (PA)
934 Neeb Rd (45233-4101)
PHONE...................................513 922-0060
Ken Ryan, *Principal*
Michael Davis, *Trustee*
Al Duebber, *Trustee*
Jerome Luebbers, *Trustee*
Melanie Hermes, *Human Res Mgr*
EMP: 70 **Privately Held**
SIC: 9111 8322 City & town managers' offices; ; senior citizens' center or association

(G-3420)
DELOITTE & TOUCHE LLP
Also Called: Deloitte Consulting
250 E 5th St Fl 1600 (45202-4263)
P.O. Box 5340 (45201-5340)
PHONE...................................513 784-7100
Clifford L Oppenheim, *Principal*
Cathy Melching, *Administration*
EMP: 440
SALES (corp-wide): 6.2B **Privately Held**
WEB: www.deloitte.com
SIC: 8721 8748 8742 7291 Certified public accountant; business consulting; management consulting services; tax return preparation services
HQ: Deloitte & Touche Llp
30 Rockefeller Plz # 4350
New York NY 10112
212 492-4000

(G-3421)
DELTA ELECTRICAL CONTRS LTD
4890 Gray Rd (45232-1512)
PHONE...................................513 421-7744
Dale Scheidt, *Owner*
Brad Scheidt, *Project Mgr*
Eric Scheidt, *Project Mgr*
EMP: 31
SQ FT: 18,000
SALES: 1MM **Privately Held**
SIC: 1731 General electrical contractor

(G-3422)
DENMARK CONSULTANTS INC
11464 Lippelman Rd # 200 (45246-6001)
PHONE...................................513 530-9984
Mark Hoskins, *President*
Dennis Runyan, *Vice Pres*
Phil Hoskins, *Electrical Engi*
John Wilcox, *Consultant*
Tim Ramil, *Software Engr*
EMP: 28
SALES (est): 2.9MM **Privately Held**
WEB: www.dennmark.com
SIC: 8711 Electrical or electronic engineering; mechanical engineering

(G-3423)
DESKEY ASSOCIATES INC
120 E 8th St (45202-2118)
PHONE...................................513 721-6800
Michael Busher, *President*
Douglas Studer, *Vice Pres*
EMP: 90 EST: 1925
SALES (est): 9.5MM **Privately Held**
WEB: www.deskey.com
SIC: 8711 8732 Designing: ship, boat, machine & product; market analysis or research

(G-3424)
DETOX HEALTH CARE CORP OHIO
Also Called: Vitas Healthcare Corp of Ohio
11500 Northlake Dr # 400 (45249-1650)
PHONE...................................513 742-6310
Kim Toole, *President*
EMP: 350
SALES (est): 5.2MM **Privately Held**
SIC: 8082 Home health care services

(G-3425)
DHL SUPPLY CHAIN (USA)
401 Murray Rd (45217-1012)
PHONE...................................513 482-6015
EMP: 55
SALES (corp-wide): 70.4B **Privately Held**
SIC: 4225 General warehousing
HQ: Exel Inc.
570 Polaris Pkwy
Westerville OH 43082
614 865-8500

(G-3426)
DHL SUPPLY CHAIN (USA)
10121 Princtn Glndle Rd B (45246-1211)
PHONE...................................513 942-1575
Ed Magoon, *Publisher*
Skip Riley, *Branch Mgr*
Meagan Schipper, *Maintence Staff*
EMP: 30
SALES (corp-wide): 70.4B **Privately Held**
WEB: www.exel-logistics.com
SIC: 4225 4213 General warehousing; trucking, except local
HQ: Exel Inc.
570 Polaris Pkwy
Westerville OH 43082
614 865-8500

(G-3427)
DIA ELECTRIC INC
3326 Reading Rd (45229-3114)
PHONE...................................513 281-0783
Thomas Gangloff, *President*
Joe Gangloff, *Sales Staff*
Joyce Gangloff, *Admin Sec*
EMP: 25 EST: 1951
SQ FT: 3,000
SALES (est): 2.3MM **Privately Held**
SIC: 1731 General electrical contractor

(G-3428)
DIALYSIS CLINIC INC
499 E Mcmillan St (45206-1924)
PHONE...................................513 281-0091
Roy Danfro, *Manager*
EMP: 60
SQ FT: 3,840
SALES (corp-wide): 760.1MM **Privately Held**
WEB: www.dciinc.org
SIC: 8092 Kidney dialysis centers
PA: Dialysis Clinic, Inc.
1633 Church St Ste 500
Nashville TN 37203
615 327-3061

(G-3429)
DICKINSON FLEET SERVICES LLC
11536 Gondola St Ste B (45241-5802)
PHONE...................................513 772-3629
John Demers, *Manager*
EMP: 25 **Privately Held**
WEB: www.dickinsonfleetservices.com
SIC: 7538 General truck repair
PA: Dickinson Fleet Services, Llc
4709 W 96th St
Indianapolis IN 46268

(G-3430)
DINSMORE & SHOHL LLP (PA)
255 E 5th St Ste 1900 (45202-1971)
PHONE...................................513 977-8200
Kirk Wall, *Partner*
Natalie Rauf, *Counsel*
Thomas J Westerfield, *Counsel*
Nicole Donohue, *Benefits Mgr*
Hannah Means, *Mktg Coord*
EMP: 406
SQ FT: 158,000
SALES: 2.4MM **Privately Held**
SIC: 8111 General practice attorney, lawyer

(G-3431)
DIRECT EXPRESS DELIVERY SVC
Also Called: Direct-X
2841 Colerain Ave (45225-2205)
P.O. Box 14028 (45250-0028)
PHONE...................................513 541-0600
Joseph Griffin, *President*
John C Griffin, *Vice Pres*
EMP: 30
SQ FT: 10,000
SALES (est): 5.1MM **Privately Held**
SIC: 4212 Delivery service, vehicular

(G-3432)
DIRECTIONS RESEARCH INC (PA)
401 E Court St Ste 200 (45202-1379)
PHONE...................................513 651-2990
Randolph Brooks, *President*
Beth Daush, *Vice Pres*
Howard Lax, *Vice Pres*
Brian Major, *Vice Pres*
Greg Widmeyer, *Vice Pres*
EMP: 150
SQ FT: 46,374
SALES (est): 19.5MM **Privately Held**
WEB: www.i-dri.com
SIC: 8732 Market analysis or research

(G-3433)
DITSCH USA LLC
311 Northland Blvd (45246-3690)
PHONE...................................513 782-8888
Gary Gottenbusch, *CEO*
Brian Tooley, *CFO*
EMP: 50
SQ FT: 100,000
SALES: 4MM
SALES (corp-wide): 2.1B **Privately Held**
SIC: 2052 5149 Pretzels; bakery products
PA: Valora Holding Ag
Hofackerstrasse 40
Muttenz BL
614 672-020

(G-3434)
DIVERSCARE HEALTHCARE SVCS INC
Also Called: Diversicare of St. Theresa
7010 Rowan Hill Dr (45227-3380)
PHONE...................................513 271-7010
Stephanie Hess, *Vice Pres*
Brenda Wimsatt, *Director*
EMP: 36
SALES (corp-wide): 563.4MM **Publicly Held**
SIC: 8051 Skilled nursing care facilities
PA: Diversicare Healthcare Services, Inc.
1621 Galleria Blvd
Brentwood TN 37027
615 771-7575

(G-3435)
DIVERSIFIED EMPLOYMENT GRP II
8530 Pringle Dr (45231-4904)
PHONE...................................513 428-6525
Tina Kunze, *Mng Member*
EMP: 26
SALES: 100K **Privately Held**
SIC: 7363 Manpower pools

(G-3436)
DIVERSIPAK INC (PA)
Also Called: Questmark
838 Reedy St (45202-2216)
PHONE...................................513 321-7884
Dan Kunkemoeller, *CEO*
Jennifer Kunkemoeller, *Principal*
Douglas Hearn, *Project Mgr*
Ted Trammel, *CFO*
EMP: 125
SQ FT: 15,000
SALES (est): 22.4MM **Privately Held**
WEB: www.diversipak.com
SIC: 2631 7336 Container, packaging & boxboard; package design

(G-3437)
DJJ HOLDING CORPORATION (HQ)
Also Called: David J Joseph Company, The
300 Pike St (45202-4222)
PHONE...................................513 621-8770
Craig A Feldman, *President*
Mark D Schaefer, *Exec VP*
David J Steigerwald, *Exec VP*
Karen A Arnold, *Senior VP*
Christopher J Bedel, *Senior VP*
▼ **EMP:** 175
SQ FT: 160,000
SALES: 1.6B
SALES (corp-wide): 25B **Publicly Held**
SIC: 5093 5088 4741 Ferrous metal scrap & waste; nonferrous metals scrap; railroad equipment & supplies; rental of railroad cars
PA: Nucor Corporation
1915 Rexford Rd Ste 400
Charlotte NC 28211
704 366-7000

(G-3438)
DOMAJAPARO INC (PA)
Also Called: Thompson Hall & Jordan Fnrl HM
11400 Winton Rd (45240-2354)
PHONE...................................513 742-3600
Fax: 513 674-2467
EMP: 44 EST: 1935
SQ FT: 3,536
SALES (est): 7.8MM **Privately Held**
SIC: 7261 Funeral Home

(G-3439)
DONNELLON MC CARTHY INC
4141 Turrill St (45223-2200)
PHONE...................................513 681-3200
EMP: 35
SALES (corp-wide): 34.3MM **Privately Held**
SIC: 5044 Photocopy machines
PA: Donnellon Mc Carthy, Inc.
10855 Medallion Dr
Cincinnati OH 45241
513 769-7800

(G-3440)
**DONTY HORTON HM CARE
DHHC LLC**
2692 Madison Rd Ste N1192 (45208-1321)
PHONE.................................513 463-3442
Donty Horton,
EMP: 35
SALES (est): 986.1K **Privately Held**
SIC: 8361 7381 4119 Residential care for
the handicapped; fingerprint service; local
passenger transportation

(G-3441)
DOTLOOP LLC
700 W Pete Rose Way # 436 (45203-1919)
PHONE.................................513 257-0550
Austin Allison, CEO
Daivak Shah, President
Michael Graham, COO
Allan Wallander, CFO
Matt Vorst, CTO
EMP: 168
SALES (est): 3MM
SALES (corp-wide): 1.3B **Publicly Held**
SIC: 7371 Computer software develop-
ment
HQ: Zillow, Inc.
1301 2nd Ave Fl 31
Seattle WA 98101
206 470-7000

(G-3442)
DRAKE CENTER LLC
151 W Galbraith Rd (45216-1015)
PHONE.................................513 418-2500
Karri Dickenson, Director
Jill Stegman, Director
Pamela Clinkenbeard, Phys Thrpy Dir
Lisa Clark, Telecom Exec
James A Jim Kingsbury,
EMP: 800
SQ FT: 400,000
SALES: 57MM **Privately Held**
WEB: www.drakecenter.com
SIC: 8051 Skilled nursing care facilities
PA: Uc Health, Llc.
3200 Burnet Ave
Cincinnati OH 45229

(G-3443)
DRAKE DEVELOPMENT INC
Also Called: Bridgeway Pointe
165 W Galbraith Rd Ofc (45216-1034)
PHONE.................................513 418-4370
W Wexler, Exec Dir
Daphne U Glenn, Exec Dir
William Wexler, Exec Dir
EMP: 65
SQ FT: 94,256
SALES: 2.9MM **Privately Held**
SIC: 8361 Residential care

(G-3444)
DRURY HOTELS COMPANY LLC
Also Called: Drury Inn Suites Cincinnati N
2265 E Sharon Rd (45241-1870)
PHONE.................................513 771-5601
Kam Siu, Branch Mgr
EMP: 29
SALES (corp-wide): 397.7MM **Privately
Held**
WEB: www.druryhotels.com
SIC: 7011 Hotels
PA: Drury Hotels Company, Llc
721 Emerson Rd Ste 400
Saint Louis MO 63141
314 429-2255

(G-3445)
**DRY RUN LIMITED
PARTNERSHIP**
Also Called: Ivy Hills Country Club
7711 Ivy Hills Dr (45244-2575)
PHONE.................................513 561-9119
William Hines, General Ptnr
E Michael Zicka, Ltd Ptnr
EMP: 30
SALES (est): 2.2MM **Privately Held**
SIC: 7997 Country club, membership

(G-3446)
DSS INSTALLATIONS LTD
Also Called: Dss/Direct TV
6717 Montgomery Rd (45236-3816)
P.O. Box 36520 (45236-0520)
PHONE.................................513 761-7000
Allen Sheff, Partner
EMP: 30 EST: 1990
SQ FT: 12,000
SALES: 2.8MM **Privately Held**
SIC: 5731 1731 7622 Antennas, satellite
dish; cable television installation; antenna
repair & installation

(G-3447)
DUBOIS CHEMICALS INC (PA)
3630 E Kemper Rd (45241-2011)
PHONE.................................513 731-6350
Jeff Welsh, CEO
Scott McManis, General Mgr
Roger Anderson, District Mgr
Jake Harris, Vice Pres
Martin Forsythe, Warehouse Mgr
▼ EMP: 153
SALES (est): 533.3MM **Privately Held**
WEB: www.riversidecompany.com
SIC: 5169 Chemicals & allied products

(G-3448)
DUKE ENERGY BECKJORD LLC
139 E 4th St (45202-4034)
PHONE.................................513 287-2561
Charles Whitlock, Principal
Tracy Hemsink,
EMP: 1963
SALES (est): 79MM
SALES (corp-wide): 24.5B **Publicly Held**
SIC: 4911 Electric services
HQ: Duke Energy Ohio, Inc.
139 E 4th St
Cincinnati OH 45202
704 382-3853

(G-3449)
DUKE ENERGY KENTUCKY INC
139 E 4th St (45202-4034)
PHONE.................................704 594-6200
James Rogers, CEO
Jim Henning, President
Jackson H Randolph, Chairman
Jim Lance, Vice Pres
William Grealis, Plant Mgr
EMP: 200
SQ FT: 300,000
SALES: 440.7MM
SALES (corp-wide): 24.5B **Publicly Held**
SIC: 4932 4931 Gas & other services
combined; electric & other services com-
bined
HQ: Duke Energy Ohio, Inc.
139 E 4th St
Cincinnati OH 45202
704 382-3853

(G-3450)
DUKE ENERGY OHIO INC (HQ)
139 E 4th St (45202-4034)
PHONE.................................704 382-3853
Lynn J Good, CEO
Kimberly Timmons, General Mgr
Brian D Savoy, Senior VP
Patti Resor, Buyer
Steven K Young, CFO
▲ EMP: 100
SALES: 1.9B
SALES (corp-wide): 24.5B **Publicly Held**
SIC: 4922 4924 4931 4911 Natural gas
transmission; natural gas distribution;
electric & other services combined; distri-
bution, electric power
PA: Duke Energy Corporation
550 S Tryon St
Charlotte NC 28202
704 382-3853

(G-3451)
DUKE ENERGY OHIO INC
Also Called: Montford Heights
5445 Audro Dr (45247-7001)
PHONE.................................800 544-6900
Eric Stolzenberger, Branch Mgr
EMP: 129
SALES (corp-wide): 24.5B **Publicly Held**
SIC: 4911 Electric services

HQ: Duke Energy Ohio, Inc.
139 E 4th St
Cincinnati OH 45202
704 382-3853

(G-3452)
DUKE ENERGY OHIO INC
Also Called: Brecon Distribution Center
7600 E Kemper Rd (45249-1610)
P.O. Box 5385 (45201-5385)
PHONE.................................513 287-1120
Darrell Ingel, Branch Mgr
Glenn Storer, Supervisor
EMP: 25
SALES (corp-wide): 24.5B **Publicly Held**
SIC: 4911 Electric services
HQ: Duke Energy Ohio, Inc.
139 E 4th St
Cincinnati OH 45202
704 382-3853

(G-3453)
DUKE ENERGY OHIO INC
Also Called: Duke Enrgy Ohio Cstmer Svc Ctr
3300 Central Pkwy (45225-2307)
PHONE.................................513 421-9500
Barb Stang, Manager
EMP: 200
SALES (corp-wide): 24.5B **Publicly Held**
SIC: 8742 Management consulting serv-
ices
HQ: Duke Energy Ohio, Inc.
139 E 4th St
Cincinnati OH 45202
704 382-3853

(G-3454)
DUNBAR ARMORED INC
1257 W 7th St (45203-1001)
PHONE.................................513 381-8000
Brian Baker, Manager
EMP: 40
SALES (corp-wide): 3.4B **Publicly Held**
WEB: www.dunbararmored.com
SIC: 7381 Armored car services
HQ: Dunbar Armored, Inc.
50 Schilling Rd
Hunt Valley MD 21031
410 584-9800

(G-3455)
DUNCAN AVIATION INC
358 Wilmer Ave 121 (45226-1832)
PHONE.................................513 873-7523
Jeremy Rutherford, Branch Mgr
EMP: 66
SALES (corp-wide): 242.5MM **Privately
Held**
SIC: 4581 Aircraft maintenance & repair
services
PA: Duncan Aviation, Inc.
3701 Aviation Rd
Lincoln NE 68524
402 475-2611

(G-3456)
DUNNHUMBY INC
3825 Edwards Rd Ste 600 (45209-1293)
PHONE.................................513 579-3400
Simon Hay, CEO
EMP: 59
SALES (est): 15.7MM
SALES (corp-wide): 80.1B **Privately Held**
SIC: 8742 Marketing consulting services
PA: Tesco Plc
Cirrus A
Welwyn Garden City HERTS AL7 1
170 791-8800

(G-3457)
DURGA LLC
11320 Chester Rd (45246-4003)
PHONE.................................513 771-2080
Vijaya K Vemulapalli, Mng Member
Sasikala Vemulapalli,
EMP: 99
SALES (est): 4MM **Privately Held**
SIC: 7011 5812 5091 Hotels; American
restaurant; water slides (recreation park)

(G-3458)
DVA HEALTHCARE - SOUTH
Also Called: Western Hills Dialysis
3267 Westbourne Dr (45248-5110)
PHONE.................................513 347-0444
Theresa Underwood, Principal

EMP: 25 **Publicly Held**
WEB: www.us.gambro.com
SIC: 8092 Kidney dialysis centers
HQ: Dva Healthcare - Southwest Ohio, Llc
1210 Hicks Blvd
Fairfield OH 45014

(G-3459)
DXP ENTERPRISES INC
5177 Spring Grove Ave (45217-1050)
PHONE.................................513 242-2227
Scott McCarthy, Site Mgr
EMP: 28 **Publicly Held**
SIC: 5084 5063 Industrial machinery &
equipment; electrical apparatus & equip-
ment
PA: Dxp Enterprises, Inc.
7272 Pinemont Dr
Houston TX 77040

(G-3460)
DYNCORP
26 W Mrtin Lther King Dr (45220-2242)
PHONE.................................513 569-7415
Dennis M McMullen, Prgrmr
Michael Johnson,
EMP: 70
SALES (corp-wide): 16.3B **Privately Held**
WEB: www.dyncorp.com
SIC: 7373 Systems integration services
PA: Dyncorp Llc
1700 Old Meadow Rd
Mc Lean VA 22102
571 722-0210

(G-3461)
E & A PEDCO SERVICES INC
11499 Chester Rd Ste 501 (45246-4012)
PHONE.................................513 782-4920
Kenneth Hover, CEO
William Giesler, President
Steve Weidner, Vice Pres
Jerome Doerger, Project Mgr
David Gilland, Project Mgr
EMP: 75
SQ FT: 12,250
SALES (est): 10.9MM **Privately Held**
WEB: www.pedcoea.com
SIC: 8711 8712 7389 Consulting engi-
neer; architectural engineering; interior
designer

(G-3462)
E & J TRAILER LEASING INC
610 Wayne Park Dr Ste 5 (45215-2847)
PHONE.................................513 563-7366
Edward John Focke, President
Edward John Focke Jr, Vice Pres
EMP: 30
SALES (est): 2MM **Privately Held**
SIC: 7519 Trailer rental

(G-3463)
**E & J TRAILER SALES &
SERVICE**
610 Wayne Park Dr Ste 5 (45215-2847)
PHONE.................................513 563-2550
Edward Focke, President
EMP: 35
SQ FT: 40,000
SALES (est): 1.4MM **Privately Held**
WEB: www.ejtrailer.com
SIC: 7519 Trailer rental

(G-3464)
E A ZICKA CO
2714 East Tower Dr Ofc (45238-2699)
PHONE.................................513 451-1440
Fax: 513 451-1499
EMP: 50 EST: 1938
SQ FT: 1,500
SALES (est): 1.8MM **Privately Held**
SIC: 6513 1521 6531 Apartment Building
Operator Single-Family House Construc-
tion Real Estate Agent/Manager

(G-3465)
E J ROBINSON GLASS CO
Also Called: Andy's Mirror and Glass
5618 Center Hill Ave (45216-2306)
PHONE.................................513 242-9250
Robert Diers, CEO
Rick Schiller, President
EMP: 30
SQ FT: 22,000

SALES: 4MM **Privately Held**
WEB: www.andysmirror.com
SIC: 1793 Glass & glazing work

(G-3466)
E&I CONSTRUCTION LLC
1210 Sycamore St Ste 200 (45202-7321)
PHONE.............................513 421-2045
EMP: 35 EST: 2001
SQ FT: 6,000
SALES (est): 2.6MM **Privately Held**
SIC: 1771 Concrete Contractors

(G-3467)
EA VICA CO
Also Called: Four Towers Apts
2714 E Twr Dr Ofc Ste 007 (45238)
PHONE.............................513 481-3500
Edwin Vica, *Owner*
Jamie Stockum, *Manager*
EMP: 30
SALES (est): 906.3K **Privately Held**
SIC: 6513 Apartment building operators

(G-3468)
EAGLE FINANCIAL BANCORP INC (PA)
6415 Bridgetown Rd (45248-2934)
PHONE.............................513 574-0700
James W Braun, *Ch of Bd*
Gary J Koester, *President*
Patricia L Walter, *Exec VP*
Kevin R Schramm, *CFO*
Guy Cagney, *Bd of Directors*
EMP: 28
SALES: 6.7MM **Publicly Held**
SIC: 6035 Savings institutions, federally chartered

(G-3469)
EAGLE REALTY GROUP LLC (DH)
421 E 4th St (45202-3317)
P.O. Box 1091 (45201-1091)
PHONE.............................513 361-7700
Mario San Marco, *President*
Shirley Scherzinger, *District Mgr*
Thomas M Stapleton, *Senior VP*
Cynthia Bucco, *Assistant VP*
Mike Dehart, *Vice Pres*
EMP: 37
SQ FT: 49,200
SALES (est): 8.1MM **Privately Held**
SIC: 6531 6552 Real estate managers; land subdividers & developers, commercial
HQ: The Western & Southern Life Insurance Company
400 Broadway St
Cincinnati OH 45202
513 629-1800

(G-3470)
EARLE M JORGENSEN COMPANY
Also Called: EMJ Cincinnati
601 Redna Ter (45215-1108)
PHONE.............................513 771-3223
Matt Hinkel, *Sales Staff*
Jeff Stethens, *Manager*
Lisa Wieman, *Director*
EMP: 30
SQ FT: 10,000
SALES (corp-wide): 11.5B **Publicly Held**
WEB: www.emjmetals.com
SIC: 5051 Steel
HQ: Earle M. Jorgensen Company
10650 Alameda St
Lynwood CA 90262
323 567-1122

(G-3471)
EAST GALBRAITH HEALTH CARE CTR (PA)
3889 E Galbraith Rd (45236-1514)
PHONE.............................513 984-5220
Henry Schneider, *President*
Raymond Schneider, *Treasurer*
EMP: 252
SQ FT: 7,245
SALES (est): 6.3MM **Privately Held**
SIC: 8059 Nursing home, except skilled & intermediate care facility

(G-3472)
EAST GALBRAITH NURSING HOME
3889 E Galbraith Rd (45236-1597)
PHONE.............................513 984-5220
Henry Schneider, *President*
EMP: 250
SQ FT: 48,000
SALES (est): 4.8MM **Privately Held**
SIC: 8052 8051 Intermediate care facilities; skilled nursing care facilities

(G-3473)
EASTER SEALS TRISTATE LLC (PA)
2901 Gilbert Ave (45206-1211)
PHONE.............................513 281-2316
David Wolfzorn, *CFO*
Christina Wolnitzek, *Accountant*
Pam Green, *Mng Member*
John Clancy, *Director*
EMP: 180
SQ FT: 22,000
SALES: 17.4MM **Privately Held**
SIC: 8331 Individual & family services

(G-3474)
EASTER SEALS TRISTATE LLC
Also Called: Walnut Hills Center Location
447 Morgan St (45206-2347)
PHONE.............................513 475-6791
David Dreith, *Manager*
EMP: 120
SQ FT: 4,000
SALES (corp-wide): 17.4MM **Privately Held**
SIC: 8322 Individual & family services
PA: Easter Seals Tristate Llc
2901 Gilbert Ave
Cincinnati OH 45206
513 281-2316

(G-3475)
EASTERN HILL INTERNAL MEDICINE
8000 5 Mile Rd Ste 305 (45230-2188)
PHONE.............................513 232-3500
David G Wilson MD, *Owner*
Jerry Bishop, *Executive*
EMP: 25
SALES (est): 1.5MM **Privately Held**
SIC: 8011 Internal medicine, physician/surgeon

(G-3476)
EASTERN HILLS PEDIATRIC ASSOC
Also Called: Eastern Hills Pediatrics
7502 State Rd Ste 3350 (45255-2801)
PHONE.............................513 231-3345
John E Furby, *Principal*
Nancy Chabot, *Administration*
EMP: 35
SALES (est): 4.2MM **Privately Held**
WEB: www.ehpeds.com
SIC: 8011 Pediatrician

(G-3477)
EASTGATE ANIMAL HOSPITAL INC
459 Old State Route 74 (45244-4210)
PHONE.............................513 528-0700
Todd A Phillips, *President*
EMP: 25
SALES (est): 1.4MM **Privately Held**
WEB: www.eastgateanimal.com
SIC: 0742 Veterinarian, animal specialties; animal hospital services, pets & other animal specialties

(G-3478)
EASTSIDE BODY SHOP
7636 Beechmont Ave (45255-4202)
PHONE.............................513 624-1145
Bill Woeste, *President*
Dennis Homan, *General Mgr*
EMP: 25
SALES (est): 1.2MM **Privately Held**
SIC: 7532 Body shop, automotive

(G-3479)
EASTSIDE ROOFG RESTORATION CO
417 Purcell Ave (45205-2245)
PHONE.............................513 471-0434
James Connaire, *Owner*
EMP: 30
SALES (est): 855.1K **Privately Held**
SIC: 1761 Roof repair

(G-3480)
EBENEZER ROAD CORP
Also Called: Western Hills Retirement Vlg
6210 Cleves Warsaw Pike (45233-4510)
PHONE.............................513 941-0099
Barry A Kohn, *President*
Sam Boymel, *Chairman*
Harold Sosna, *Vice Pres*
Lisa Varney, *Supervisor*
Michael Peterson, *Food Svc Dir*
EMP: 250
SQ FT: 150,000
SALES (est): 17.8MM **Privately Held**
SIC: 6513 8052 8051 Retirement hotel operation; intermediate care facilities; skilled nursing care facilities

(G-3481)
ECKERT FIRE PROTECTION SYSTEMS
510 W Benson St (45215-3106)
PHONE.............................513 948-1030
Don Eckert, *President*
Mary Ann Eckert, *Admin Sec*
EMP: 50
SQ FT: 6,000
SALES (est): 6.8MM **Privately Held**
WEB: www.eckertfireprotection.com
SIC: 1711 Fire sprinkler system installation

(G-3482)
ECKSTEIN ROOFING COMPANY
264 Stille Dr (45233-1647)
PHONE.............................513 941-1511
James Eckstein Jr, *President*
EMP: 30
SQ FT: 12,000
SALES (est): 5.6MM **Privately Held**
SIC: 1761 Sheet metalwork; roofing contractor

(G-3483)
ECO ENGINEERING INC
Also Called: Consolidated Lighting Svcs Co
11815 Highway Dr Ste 600 (45241-2065)
PHONE.............................513 985-8300
Thomas Kirkpatrick, *President*
Garry G Buttermann I, *Manager*
Susan Kirkpatrick, *Admin Sec*
EMP: 58
SQ FT: 11,000
SALES (est): 12.8MM **Privately Held**
WEB: www.ecoengineering.com
SIC: 8748 Energy conservation consultant

(G-3484)
ECOTAGE
11700 Princeton Pike # 4 (45246-2535)
PHONE.............................513 782-2229
Teggy Sova, *Manager*
EMP: 40
SALES (est): 293.7K **Privately Held**
SIC: 7231 Beauty shops

(G-3485)
ELBE PROPERTIES (PA)
Also Called: Janus Hotel and Resort
8534 E Kemper Rd (45249-3701)
PHONE.............................513 489-1955
Louis S Beck, *Partner*
Harry Yeaggy, *Partner*
EMP: 700
SQ FT: 6,000
SALES (est): 19.4MM **Privately Held**
SIC: 7011 7033 Motels; campgrounds

(G-3486)
ELECTRIC MOTOR TECH LLC (PA)
Also Called: Emt
5217 Beech St (45217-1021)
PHONE.............................513 821-9999
F Daniel Freshley, *Mng Member*
Andy Butz,
Dwaine York,

EMP: 46 EST: 1999
SQ FT: 30,000
SALES (est): 13.6MM **Privately Held**
WEB: www.electricmotortech.com
SIC: 7629 5063 Electrical repair shops; motors, electric

(G-3487)
ELECTRIC SERVICE CO INC
5331 Hetzell St (45227-1513)
PHONE.............................513 271-6387
Helen Snyder, *President*
EMP: 34
SQ FT: 35,000
SALES (est): 6.1MM **Privately Held**
WEB: www.electricservice.com
SIC: 7629 3677 3621 Electronic equipment repair; transformers power supply, electronic type; phase or rotary converters (electrical equipment)

(G-3488)
ELECTROL SYSTEMS INC
1380 Kemper Meadow Dr (45240-1634)
PHONE.............................513 942-7777
David C Staiger, *President*
EMP: 25
SQ FT: 13,750
SALES (est): 4MM **Privately Held**
WEB: www.electrolsystems.cc
SIC: 8711 Electrical or electronic engineering

(G-3489)
ELECTRONIC REGISTRY SYSTEMS
155 Tri County Pkwy # 110 (45246-3238)
PHONE.............................513 771-7330
Ashok Ramaswamy, *President*
Todd Carter, *Manager*
Elijah Bialik, *Software Dev*
EMP: 25
SQ FT: 1,000
SALES (est): 2.6MM **Privately Held**
WEB: www.ers-can.com
SIC: 7371 Computer software development

(G-3490)
ELEVAR DESIGN GROUP INC
Also Called: Sfa Architects
555 Carr St (45203-1815)
PHONE.............................513 721-0600
Emilio Thomas Fernandez, *CEO*
John Rademacher, *Sales Executive*
EMP: 49
SQ FT: 35,656
SALES: 4.8MM **Privately Held**
WEB: www.sfa-architects.com
SIC: 7389 8712 8711 Design services; architectural engineering; engineering services; mechanical engineering; heating & ventilation engineering; electrical or electronic engineering

(G-3491)
ELLIOTT DAVIS LLC
201 E 5th St Ste 2100 (45202-4230)
PHONE.............................513 579-1717
Kathy Mitts,
EMP: 25
SALES (corp-wide): 60.8MM **Privately Held**
SIC: 8721 Accounting services, except auditing; certified public accountant
PA: Elliott Davis, Llc
200 E Broad St Ste 500
Greenville SC 29601
864 242-3370

(G-3492)
EMCOR FACILITIES SERVICES INC (HQ)
Also Called: Viox Services
9655 Reading Rd (45215-3513)
PHONE.............................888 846-9462
Mike Viox, *President*
Mike Orebaugh, *Business Mgr*
Frank Riley, *Vice Pres*
Dan Viox, *Vice Pres*
Tim Viox, *Vice Pres*
EMP: 100 EST: 1946
SQ FT: 38,000

SALES (est): 241.7MM
SALES (corp-wide): 8.1B **Publicly Held**
WEB: www.viox-services.com
SIC: 7349 Building maintenance services
PA: Emcor Group, Inc.
　301 Merritt 7 Fl 6
　Norwalk CT 06851
　203 849-7800

(G-3493)
EMERALD HILTON DAVIS LLC
Also Called: Emerald Specialties Group
2235 Langdon Farm Rd (45237-4712)
PHONE..................................513 841-0057
James Donnelly, *Mng Member*
▲ **EMP:** 70
SALES (est): 20.6MM
SALES (corp-wide): 2.7B **Privately Held**
SIC: 5169 Chemicals & allied products
HQ: Dystar L.P.
　9844 Southern Pine Blvd A
　Charlotte NC 28273

(G-3494)
EMERSION DESIGN LLC
310 Culvert St Ste 100 (45202-2229)
PHONE..................................513 841-9100
Alan Hautman,
James Cheng,
Roger Curran,
Chad Edwards,
Steve Kimball,
EMP: 28
SQ FT: 5,000
SALES (est): 4MM **Privately Held**
WEB: www.emersiondesign.com
SIC: 8711 7389 8748 8712 Structural engineering; design services; urban planning & consulting services; architectural services; architectural engineering

(G-3495)
EMPOWER MEDIAMARKETING INC (PA)
15 E 14th St (45202-7001)
PHONE..................................513 871-7779
Jim Price, *President*
Joseph Lowry, *CFO*
EMP: 150
SQ FT: 40,000
SALES (est): 18.3MM **Privately Held**
WEB: www.empowermm.com
SIC: 7319 Media buying service

(G-3496)
ENCLOSURE SUPPLIERS LLC
Also Called: Champion
12119 Champion Way (45241-6419)
PHONE..................................513 782-3900
Dennis Manes,
▲ **EMP:** 30
SQ FT: 160,000
SALES (est): 12.1MM
SALES (corp-wide): 516.4MM **Privately Held**
SIC: 3448 5031 3231 Prefabricated metal buildings; lumber, plywood & millwork; products of purchased glass
PA: Champion Opco, Llc
　12121 Champion Way
　Cincinnati OH 45241
　513 327-7338

(G-3497)
ENCOMPASS HEALTH CORPORATION
Also Called: HealthSouth
151 W Galbraith Rd (45216-1015)
PHONE..................................513 418-5600
Joseph Steger, *Branch Mgr*
Joe Walsh, *Business Dir*
EMP: 113
SALES (corp-wide): 4.2B **Publicly Held**
SIC: 8069 Specialty hospitals, except psychiatric
PA: Encompass Health Corporation
　9001 Liberty Pkwy
　Birmingham AL 35242
　205 967-7116

(G-3498)
ENERFAB INC (PA)
4955 Spring Grove Ave (45232-1925)
PHONE..................................513 641-0500
Wendell R Bell, *CEO*
Jeffrey P Hock, *President*

Dave Herche, *Chairman*
Mark Schoettmer, *Vice Pres*
Daniel J Sillies, *CFO*
▲ **EMP:** 330
SQ FT: 180,000
SALES (est): 621.1MM **Privately Held**
WEB: www.enerfab.com
SIC: 3443 1629 1541 1711 Tanks, standard or custom fabricated: metal plate; power plant construction; land reclamation; industrial buildings & warehouses; mechanical contractor; process piping contractor; painting, coating & hot dipping

(G-3499)
ENGLE MANAGEMENT GROUP
867 Yarger Dr (45230-3540)
PHONE..................................513 232-9729
EMP: 51
SALES (est): 1.7MM **Privately Held**
SIC: 7299 Misc Personal Services

(G-3500)
ENTERPRISE VENDING INC
895 Glendale Milford Rd (45215-1136)
PHONE..................................513 772-1373
Ron Patiya, *Manager*
EMP: 30
SALES (corp-wide): 14MM **Privately Held**
SIC: 4225 7699 General warehousing & storage; vending machine repair
PA: Enterprise Vending, Inc.
　895 Glendale Milford Rd
　Cincinnati OH
　513 791-7070

(G-3501)
ENVIRONMENTAL ENTERPRISES INC
Also Called: Eei-Plant
4650 Spring Grove Ave (45232-1920)
PHONE..................................513 541-1823
Gary Brunner, *Info Tech Mgr*
Dan McCabe, *Systems Staff*
EMP: 82
SALES (corp-wide): 24.7MM **Privately Held**
WEB: www.eeienv.com
SIC: 4953 Recycling, waste materials
PA: Environmental Enterprises Inc
　10163 Cncinnati Dayton Rd
　Cincinnati OH 45241
　513 772-2818

(G-3502)
ENVIRONMENTAL QUALITY MGT (HQ)
Also Called: E Q M
1800 Carillion Blvd 100 (45240-2788)
PHONE..................................513 825-7500
Fred Nichols, *President*
Brenda Reid, *General Mgr*
Ronald L Hawks, *Vice Pres*
John R Kominsky, *Vice Pres*
Robert G McCullough, *Vice Pres*
EMP: 88
SQ FT: 30,000
SALES (est): 47.1MM **Publicly Held**
WEB: www.eqm.com
SIC: 8748 Environmental consultant

(G-3503)
ENVIRONMENTAL SOLUTIONS (PA)
4525 Este Ave (45232-1762)
PHONE..................................513 451-1777
Virgil Brack Jr, *President*
Taina Pankiewicz, *COO*
Casey Swecker, *Vice Pres*
Scott Berliner, *Controller*
Michael Wellman, *Client Mgr*
EMP: 34
SQ FT: 8,000
SALES (est): 5.4MM **Privately Held**
WEB: www.environmentalsi.com
SIC: 8748 Environmental consultant

(G-3504)
ENVISION CORPORATION
Also Called: Envision Children
8 Enfield St Ste 4 (45218-1433)
PHONE..................................513 772-5437
Matthew Hughes, *Exec Dir*
EMP: 53

SQ FT: 2,000
SALES: 248K **Privately Held**
SIC: 8748 Testing service, educational or personnel

(G-3505)
EPILEPSY CNCL/GRTER CINCINNATI (PA)
Also Called: Epilepsy Council Foundation
895 Central Ave Ste 550 (45202-5757)
PHONE..................................513 721-2905
Debbie Bedinghaus, *Bookkeeper*
Kathy Schrag, *Exec Dir*
Shelley Parrish, *Program Dir*
Mark Findley, *Asst Director*
EMP: 40
SALES (est): 1.6MM **Privately Held**
SIC: 8399 Fund raising organization, non-fee basis

(G-3506)
EPIPHEO INCORPORATED
Also Called: Epipheo Studios
700 W Pete Rose Way 450 (45203-1892)
PHONE..................................888 687-7620
John Herman, *CEO*
Lucas Cole, *Principal*
Dan Chaney, *Controller*
Jonathan Lapps, *Marketing Staff*
Nick Derington, *Producer*
EMP: 40 **EST:** 2009
SALES: 20MM **Privately Held**
SIC: 7311 8742 Advertising agencies; marketing consulting services

(G-3507)
EPISCOPAL RETIREMENT HOMES
3870 Virginia Ave Ste 2 (45227-3427)
PHONE..................................513 271-9610
Kathleen Ison-Lind,
EMP: 68
SALES (est): 897.2K **Privately Held**
SIC: 6513 Retirement hotel operation

(G-3508)
EPISCOPAL RETIREMENT HOMES INC (PA)
3870 Virginia Ave Ste 2 (45227-3427)
PHONE..................................513 271-9610
R Douglas Spitler, *CEO*
Jim Hanisian, *Vice Pres*
Nel Paul Scheper, *Vice Pres*
Paul Scheper, *CFO*
Paul J Scheper, *CFO*
EMP: 25
SQ FT: 6,900
SALES: 32.8MM **Privately Held**
WEB: www.erhinc.com
SIC: 8361 8322 8051 Home for the aged; senior citizens' center or association; old age assistance; skilled nursing care facilities

(G-3509)
EPISCOPAL RETIREMENT HOMES INC
Also Called: Dupree House
3939 Erie Ave (45208-1954)
PHONE..................................513 561-6363
Laura Lamb, *Branch Mgr*
EMP: 36
SALES (corp-wide): 32.8MM **Privately Held**
WEB: www.erhinc.com
SIC: 8361 Home for the aged
PA: Episcopal Retirement Homes, Inc.
　3870 Virginia Ave Ste 2
　Cincinnati OH 45227
　513 271-9610

(G-3510)
EPISCOPAL RETIREMENT HOMES INC
Also Called: Marjorie P Lee Rtirement Cmnty
3550 Shaw Ave Ofc (45208-1416)
PHONE..................................513 871-2090
Ginny Uehlin, *Administration*
EMP: 180
SQ FT: 2,850
SALES (corp-wide): 32.8MM **Privately Held**
WEB: www.erhinc.com
SIC: 8361 Home for the aged

PA: Episcopal Retirement Homes, Inc.
　3870 Virginia Ave Ste 2
　Cincinnati OH 45227
　513 271-9610

(G-3511)
EQUITY DIAMOND BROKERS INC (PA)
Also Called: Eddie Lane's Diamond Showroom
9301 Montgomery Rd Ste 2a (45242-7752)
PHONE..................................513 793-4760
Edmund Lane, *President*
Ted Bevis, *Corp Secy*
Patrick Higgins, *Vice Pres*
Cindy Lange, *Vice Pres*
EMP: 45
SQ FT: 7,000
SALES (est): 11.1MM **Privately Held**
WEB: www.edbsonline.com
SIC: 5094 5944 Jewelry; jewelry stores

(G-3512)
EQUITY RESOURCES INC
130 Tri County Pkwy # 108 (45246-3212)
PHONE..................................513 518-6318
Ed Rivor, *President*
EMP: 100
SALES (est): 78.9K **Privately Held**
SIC: 8742 6211 Business planning & organizing services; mortgages, buying & selling

(G-3513)
ERHAL INC
3870 Virginia Ave (45227-3431)
PHONE..................................513 272-5555
Paul Scheper, *CFO*
Elizabeth Ison, *Accountant*
EMP: 30
SALES (est): 1.1MM **Privately Held**
SIC: 6531 Cooperative apartment manager

(G-3514)
ERNEST V THOMAS JR (PA)
Also Called: Thomas & Thomas
2323 Park Ave (45206-2711)
PHONE..................................513 961-5311
Ernest V Thomas III, *Owner*
EMP: 50
SQ FT: 4,500
SALES (est): 4.7MM **Privately Held**
WEB: www.thomaslawfirm.com
SIC: 8111 General practice law office

(G-3515)
ERNST & YOUNG LLP
Also Called: Ey
312 Walnut St Ste 1900 (45202-4028)
PHONE..................................513 612-1400
Stanley Brown, *Partner*
Mark Doll, *Partner*
Steven Krekeler, *Partner*
Thomas O Neil, *Partner*
Jerry Hensley, *Principal*
EMP: 200
SALES (corp-wide): 4.3B **Privately Held**
WEB: www.ey.com
SIC: 8721 8742 Certified public accountant; auditing services; business consultant; management information systems consultant
PA: Ernst & Young Llp
　5 Times Sq Fl Conlv1
　New York NY 10036
　212 773-3000

(G-3516)
ESTREAMZ INC
1118 Groesbeck Rd (45224-3276)
PHONE..................................513 278-7836
Travis Bea, *President*
EMP: 30
SALES (est): 730.8K **Privately Held**
SIC: 7379 7372 7812 ; home entertainment computer software; motion picture production & distribution, television

(G-3517)
EUCLID HEALTH CARE INC (PA)
Also Called: Madeira Health Care Center
6940 Stiegler Ln (45243-2635)
PHONE..................................513 561-4105
Harold Sosna, *President*
EMP: 128

▲ = Import ▼=Export
◆ =Import/Export

SALES: 8MM **Privately Held**
SIC: 8051 Skilled nursing care facilities

(G-3518)
EVANSTON BULLDOGS YOUTH FOOTBA
3060 Durrell Ave (45207-1716)
PHONE..................................513 254-9500
EMP: 30
SALES (est): 428.9K **Privately Held**
SIC: 7389 Business Serv Non-Commercial Site

(G-3519)
EVERGREEN PHARMACEUTICAL LLC (DH)
201 E 4th St Ste 900 (45202-4160)
PHONE..................................513 719-2600
Carl Wood, *President*
EMP: 300
SQ FT: 40,000
SALES (est): 66.4MM
SALES (corp-wide): 194.5B **Publicly Held**
SIC: 5122 Pharmaceuticals
HQ: Omnicare Holding Company
1105 Market St Ste 1300
Cincinnati OH 45215
513 719-2600

(G-3520)
EVERGREEN PHRM CAL INC (DH)
201 E 4th St Ste 900 (45202-4160)
PHONE..................................513 719-2600
Elizabeth A Haley, *President*
EMP: 38 EST: 2004
SALES (est): 20.6MM
SALES (corp-wide): 194.5B **Publicly Held**
WEB: www.omnicare.com
SIC: 5122 Pharmaceuticals
HQ: Omnicare Holding Company
1105 Market St Ste 1300
Cincinnati OH 45215
513 719-2600

(G-3521)
EVERS WELDING CO INC
4849 Blue Rock Rd (45247-5504)
P.O. Box 53426 (45253-0426)
PHONE..................................513 385-7352
Edward G Evers, *President*
Jacqueline Evers, *Corp Secy*
EMP: 40 EST: 1957
SQ FT: 3,000
SALES (est): 4.5MM **Privately Held**
WEB: www.everssteel.com
SIC: 1791 3441 Structural steel erection; fabricated structural metal

(G-3522)
EVERY CHILD SUCCEEDS
3333 Burnet Ave (45229-3026)
PHONE..................................513 636-2830
Judith Van Ginkle, *President*
Jodie Short, *Research*
Julie Massie, *Consultant*
EMP: 150
SALES: 8.5MM **Privately Held**
WEB: www.everychildsucceeds.org
SIC: 8082 Home health care services

(G-3523)
EVOLUTION CRTIVE SOLUTIONS LLC
7107 Shona Dr Ste 110 (45237-3808)
PHONE..................................513 681-4450
Cathy Lindemann, *President*
Cathy Welz, *Accounting Mgr*
EMP: 25
SQ FT: 14,000
SALES: 3MM **Privately Held**
SIC: 7336 2759 5199 7389 Graphic arts & related design; commercial printing; advertising specialties; embroidering of advertising on shirts, etc.; screen printing; manmade fiber & silk broadwoven fabrics

(G-3524)
EXCELLENCE ALLIANCE GROUP INC
700 Walnut St Ste 210 (45202-2015)
PHONE..................................513 619-4800
Michael Baker, *President*

Justin Baker, *Marketing Staff*
EMP: 25
SQ FT: 20,000
SALES (est): 1.5MM **Privately Held**
WEB: www.eainet.net
SIC: 8742 1711 Business consultant; mechanical contractor

(G-3525)
EXECUTIVE JET MANAGEMENT INC (DH)
4556 Airport Rd (45226-1601)
PHONE..................................513 979-6600
Robert Molsbergen, *President*
Colleen Nissl, *Vice Pres*
Christine Leber, *CFO*
EMP: 280
SQ FT: 78,000
SALES (est): 59.3MM
SALES (corp-wide): 225.3B **Publicly Held**
WEB: www.executivejetmanagement.com
SIC: 4522 8741 4581 4512 Flying charter service; management services; airports, flying fields & services; air transportation, scheduled
HQ: Netjets Inc.
4111 Bridgeway Ave
Columbus OH 43219
614 239-5500

(G-3526)
FACILITIES MGT SOLUTIONS LLC
250 W Court St (45202-1088)
PHONE..................................513 639-2230
EMP: 25
SALES (est): 1.6MM
SALES (corp-wide): 579.6MM **Privately Held**
SIC: 8742 Management Consulting Services
HQ: Hochtief Ag
Opernplatz 2
Essen 45128
201 824-0

(G-3527)
FACTORY MUTUAL INSURANCE CO
Also Called: FM Global
9 Woodcrest Dr (45246-2363)
PHONE..................................513 742-9516
Mary Breighner, *Branch Mgr*
EMP: 90
SALES (corp-wide): 4.4B **Privately Held**
SIC: 6331 Fire, marine & casualty insurance
PA: Factory Mutual Insurance Co
270 Central Ave
Johnston RI 02919
401 275-3000

(G-3528)
FALU CORPORATION
Also Called: Falu Security
9435 Waterstone Blvd # 140 (45249-8229)
PHONE..................................502 641-8106
Hector Falu, *CEO*
EMP: 33
SALES (est): 75.9K **Privately Held**
SIC: 7381 Guard services

(G-3529)
FAMILY MEDICAL GROUP
6331 Glenway Ave (45211-6301)
PHONE..................................513 389-1400
Linda Behlmer, *Principal*
EMP: 26
SALES (est): 2.2MM **Privately Held**
SIC: 8011 General & family practice, physician/surgeon

(G-3530)
FAMILY MOTOR COACH ASSN INC (PA)
8291 Clough Pike (45244-2756)
PHONE..................................513 474-3622
Lana Makin, *CEO*
Bill Mallory, *Vice Pres*
Tina Henry, *Sales Staff*
Pamela Kay, *Comms Dir*
Barbara Greenwood, *Manager*
EMP: 111
SQ FT: 22,000

SALES: 3.1MM **Privately Held**
WEB: www.fmca.com
SIC: 8641 2721 Social associations; magazines: publishing & printing

(G-3531)
FAMILY SERVICE (PA)
Also Called: UNITED WAY
3730 Glenway Ave (45205-1354)
PHONE..................................513 381-6300
Arlene Herman, *President*
John Sarra, *Vice Pres*
Mark Schneider, *Vice Pres*
Jeannine Anderson, *Personnel Assit*
EMP: 50 EST: 1879
SQ FT: 10,500
SALES: 2.8MM **Privately Held**
WEB: www.mricinci.com
SIC: 8322 Social service center

(G-3532)
FARM INC
239 Anderson Ferry Rd (45238-5638)
PHONE..................................513 922-7020
Dan Elsaesser, *President*
Daniel Elsaesser, *Chairman*
Michael Siebert, *Admin Sec*
▲ EMP: 40 EST: 1940
SQ FT: 21,600
SALES: 100K **Privately Held**
WEB: www.theplacetohaveaparty.com
SIC: 7299 5812 Banquet hall facilities; eating places

(G-3533)
FASCOR INC
11260 Chester Rd Ste 100 (45246-4079)
PHONE..................................513 421-1777
John Klare Jr, *President*
John Klare Sr, *Chairman*
Andrew Klare, *Vice Pres*
EMP: 40 EST: 1978
SQ FT: 4,625
SALES (est): 4.7MM **Privately Held**
WEB: www.fascor.com
SIC: 7371 Computer software systems analysis & design, custom; computer software development

(G-3534)
FAY LIMITED PARTNERSHIP
Also Called: Fay Apartments
3710 President Dr (45225-1016)
PHONE..................................513 542-8333
Jerry Bowen, *Manager*
EMP: 35
SQ FT: 2,501
SALES (corp-wide): 2.3MM **Privately Held**
SIC: 6513 Apartment building operators
PA: Fay Limited Partnership
36 E 4th St 1320
Cincinnati OH 45202
513 241-1911

(G-3535)
FAY LIMITED PARTNERSHIP (PA)
36 E 4th St 1320 (45202-3725)
PHONE..................................513 241-1911
David Hendy, *Partner*
Ken Kerr, *Partner*
EMP: 35
SQ FT: 1,000,000
SALES (est): 2.3MM **Privately Held**
SIC: 6513 6531 Apartment building operators; real estate agents & managers

(G-3536)
FEDERAL HOME LN BNK CINCINNATI (PA)
600 Atrium Two # 2 (45201)
P.O. Box 598 (45201-0598)
PHONE..................................513 852-7500
Donald J Mullineaux, *Ch of Bd*
James A England, *Vice Ch Bd*
Andrew S Howell, *President*
Donald R Able, *COO*
James G Dooley Sr, *Exec VP*
EMP: 660
SQ FT: 79,000
SALES: 2.3B **Privately Held**
WEB: www.fhlbcin.com
SIC: 6111 Federal & federally sponsored credit agencies

(G-3537)
FEDERAL HOME LN BNK CINCINNATI
1000 Atrium 2 (45202)
P.O. Box 598 (45201-0598)
PHONE..................................513 852-5719
Charles Thiemann, *Manager*
EMP: 80
SALES (corp-wide): 2.3B **Privately Held**
WEB: www.fhlbcin.com
SIC: 6022 State commercial banks
PA: Federal Home Loan Bank Of Cincinnati
600 Atrium Two # 2
Cincinnati OH 45201
513 852-7500

(G-3538)
FEDERAL INSURANCE COMPANY
Also Called: Chubb
312 Walnut St Ste 2100 (45202-4083)
PHONE..................................513 721-0601
John Lafrance, *Opers Mgr*
Gary Delong, *Manager*
EMP: 80
SALES (corp-wide): 29B **Privately Held**
WEB: www.federalinsurancecompany.com
SIC: 6411 Insurance agents, brokers & service
HQ: Federal Insurance Company
202 N Illinois St # 2600
Indianapolis IN 46204
908 903-2000

(G-3539)
FEDERAL RSRVE BNK OF CLEVELAND
150 E 4th St Fl 3 (45202-4181)
P.O. Box 999 (45201-0999)
PHONE..................................513 721-4787
James M Anderson, *Ch of Bd*
Barbara Henshaw, *General Mgr*
Glenn D Leveridge, *Director*
Janet B Reid, *Director*
EMP: 225 **Privately Held**
WEB: www.clevelandfed.com
SIC: 6011 Federal reserve branches
HQ: The Federal Reserve Bank Of Cleveland
1455 E 6th St
Cleveland OH 44114
216 579-2000

(G-3540)
FELDKAMP ENTERPRISES INC
Also Called: Honeywell Authorized Dealer
3642 Muddy Creek Rd (45238-2044)
PHONE..................................513 347-4500
James E Feldkamp Jr, *President*
Bob Keseday, *Superintendent*
Chadd Feldkamp, *Vice Pres*
Connie Matchett, *Human Res Dir*
Pat Heeney, *Sales Staff*
EMP: 200
SQ FT: 40,000
SALES (est): 70.5MM **Privately Held**
SIC: 1711 Ventilation & duct work contractor

(G-3541)
FELDYS
8060 Beechmont Ave (45255-3145)
PHONE..................................513 474-2212
Brian Feldkamp, *Owner*
EMP: 70
SALES (est): 501.5K **Privately Held**
SIC: 8641 Bars & restaurants, members only

(G-3542)
FENTON RIGGING & CONTG INC
2150 Langdon Farm Rd (45237-4791)
PHONE..................................513 631-5500
Michael Besl, *President*
William C Besl, *Vice Pres*
Rafe Fowee, *Project Mgr*
Garry Miller, *Project Mgr*
David Williams, *Project Mgr*
▲ EMP: 150 EST: 1893
SQ FT: 6,800
SALES (est): 78.5MM **Privately Held**
WEB: www.fentonrigging.com
SIC: 1622 1796 Bridge, tunnel & elevated highway; machine moving & rigging

---

(G-3543)
FERN EXPOSITION SERVICES LLC (PA)
Also Called: George Fern Company
645 Linn St (45203-1722)
PHONE...................................513 621-6111
Aaron Bludworth, *President*
Michael Cox, *Exec VP*
Mark Epstein, *Vice Pres*
Sheila Pannell, *Vice Pres*
John Barclay, *CFO*
EMP: 30
SQ FT: 500,000
SALES (est): 44.5MM **Privately Held**
WEB: www.geofern.com
SIC: 7359 Electronic equipment rental, except computers

(G-3544)
FIDELITY CHARITABLE GIFT FUND
P.O. Box 770001 (45277-0001)
PHONE...................................800 952-4438
Sarah Libbey, *President*
Julia McCarthy, *Exec VP*
Paul Johnson, *Vice Pres*
Michael Manning, *Vice Pres*
Monna Steinhard, *Vice Pres*
EMP: 122
SALES (est): 5MM **Privately Held**
SIC: 8399 Fund raising organization, non-fee basis

(G-3545)
FIELDS MARKETING RESEARCH INC
Also Called: Fields Research
3814 West St Ste 110 (45227-3743)
PHONE...................................513 821-6266
Ken Fields, *President*
Jeff Streets, *Supervisor*
Patrick Colletta, *Technical Staff*
EMP: 55
SQ FT: 4,000
SALES (est): 4.1MM **Privately Held**
WEB: www.fieldsresearch.com
SIC: 8732 Market analysis or research

(G-3546)
FIFTH THIRD BANCORP (PA)
38 Fountain Square Plz (45202-3102)
PHONE...................................800 972-3030
Greg D Carmichael, *Ch of Bd*
Scott Silvas, *President*
Lars C Anderson, *COO*
Aravind Immaneni, *Exec VP*
Philip R McHugh, *Exec VP*
▲ EMP: 86 EST: 1975
SALES: 7.9B **Publicly Held**
WEB: www.53.com
SIC: 6022 State trust companies accepting deposits, commercial

(G-3547)
FIFTH THIRD BANK
5830 Harrison Ave (45248-1623)
PHONE...................................513 574-4457
Jason Beccaccio, *Manager*
EMP: 117
SALES (corp-wide): 7.9B **Publicly Held**
SIC: 6022 State commercial banks
HQ: The Fifth Third Bank
38 Fountain Square Plz
Cincinnati OH 45202
513 579-5203

(G-3548)
FIFTH THIRD BANK (DH)
38 Fountain Square Plz (45202-3191)
PHONE...................................513 579-5203
George A Schaefer, *CEO*
Greg Carmichael, *President*
Thomas R Quinn Jr, *President*
Eric Smith, *President*
Don Coleman, *Senior VP*
▲ EMP: 1800
SALES: 7.6B
SALES (corp-wide): 7.9B **Publicly Held**
WEB: www.53rd.com
SIC: 6022 State trust companies accepting deposits, commercial

(G-3549)
FIFTH THIRD BANK
Fifth 3rd Ctr 38 Fountain (45263-0001)
PHONE...................................513 579-5203
Richard Arendale, *Managing Dir*
Nick Jevic, *Managing Dir*
George Schaefer, *Principal*
Howard Kathey, *Assistant VP*
Demitrius Pettaway, *Assistant VP*
EMP: 100
SALES (corp-wide): 7.9B **Publicly Held**
SIC: 6022 State commercial banks
HQ: The Fifth Third Bank
38 Fountain Square Plz
Cincinnati OH 45202
513 579-5203

(G-3550)
FIFTH THIRD EQUIPMENT FIN CO (DH)
38 Fountain Square Plz (45202-3102)
PHONE...................................800 972-3030
George Schaefer Jr, *President*
David Jackson, *Senior VP*
Kelly McClain, *Investment Ofcr*
Carolyn David, *Manager*
August Foundation, *Manager*
EMP: 44
SQ FT: 1,000
SALES (est): 20.3MM
SALES (corp-wide): 7.9B **Publicly Held**
SIC: 7359 Equipment rental & leasing
HQ: The Fifth Third Bank
38 Fountain Square Plz
Cincinnati OH 45202
513 579-5203

(G-3551)
FINIT GROUP LLC
Also Called: Finit Solutions
8050 Hosbrook Rd Ste 326 (45236-2907)
PHONE...................................513 793-4648
Angie Apple,
EMP: 60
SALES (est): 243.9K **Privately Held**
SIC: 8742 Business consultant

(G-3552)
FINNEYTOWN CONTRACTING CORP
Also Called: Universal Contracting
5151 Fishwick Dr (45216-2215)
PHONE...................................513 482-2700
Philip Neumann, *President*
Greg Neumann, *Vice Pres*
EMP: 40
SQ FT: 7,500
SALES (est): 4.8MM **Privately Held**
SIC: 1542 Commercial & office building, new construction

(G-3553)
FIRST ACCEPTANCE CORPORATION
6150 Colerain Ave (45239-6418)
PHONE...................................513 741-0811
Deana Hayes, *Principal*
EMP: 27
SALES (corp-wide): 347.5MM **Publicly Held**
SIC: 6411 Insurance agents, brokers & service
PA: First Acceptance Corporation
3813 Green Hills Vlg Dr
Nashville TN 37215
615 844-2800

(G-3554)
FIRST CHOICE MEDICAL STAFFING
Also Called: First Choice Cincinnati Branch
1008 Marshall Ave Frnt (45225-2347)
PHONE...................................513 631-5656
Sheena Bell, *Branch Mgr*
EMP: 76
SALES (corp-wide): 4.6MM **Privately Held**
SIC: 8099 Blood related health services
PA: First Choice Medical Staffing Of Ohio, Inc.
1457 W 117th St
Cleveland OH 44107
216 521-2222

(G-3555)
FIRST FINANCIAL BANCORP
225 Pictoria Dr Ste 700 (45246-1620)
PHONE...................................513 551-5640
Jerry Begley, *Manager*
EMP: 200
SALES (corp-wide): 643.7MM **Publicly Held**
WEB: www.ffbc-oh.com
SIC: 6035 6021 Savings institutions, federally chartered; national commercial banks
PA: First Financial Bancorp.
255 E 5th St Ste 700
Cincinnati OH 45202
877 322-9530

(G-3556)
FIRST FINANCIAL BANK
255 E 5th St Ste 2900 (45202-4704)
PHONE...................................513 979-5800
Benjamin Cornist, *Assistant VP*
Dan Polly, *Vice Pres*
Andrew Chapman, *Engineer*
Dustin Strickler, *Engineer*
Damon Divari, *Manager*
EMP: 30
SALES (corp-wide): 643.7MM **Publicly Held**
SIC: 6021 National commercial banks
HQ: First Financial Bank
255 E 5th St Ste 2900
Cincinnati OH 45202
877 322-9530

(G-3557)
FIRST FINANCIAL BANK (HQ)
255 E 5th St Ste 2900 (45202-4704)
PHONE...................................877 322-9530
Claude E Davis, *President*
Matthew Burgess, *Exec VP*
Cathy Belding, *Assistant VP*
Mark Gregg, *Assistant VP*
Ruthann Warman, *Assistant VP*
EMP: 228
SALES: 406.3MM
SALES (corp-wide): 643.7MM **Publicly Held**
WEB: www.firstfb.com
SIC: 6022 State commercial banks
PA: First Financial Bancorp.
255 E 5th St Ste 700
Cincinnati OH 45202
877 322-9530

(G-3558)
FIRST GROUP INVESTMENT PARTNR (DH)
600 Vine St Ste 1200 (45202-2474)
PHONE...................................513 241-2200
Alton Sloan, *Partner*
Phil Crookes, *Partner*
EMP: 100
SALES (est): 210.5MM
SALES (corp-wide): 8.9B **Privately Held**
SIC: 7513 4212 4213 4225 Truck leasing, without drivers; truck rental, without drivers; local trucking, without storage; trucking, except local; general warehousing; school buses; local & suburban transit
HQ: Firstbus Investments Limited
Oldmixon Crescent
Weston-Super-Mare BS24
122 465-0100

(G-3559)
FIRST SERVICES INC
600 Vine St Ste 1200 (45202-2474)
PHONE...................................513 241-2200
Brad Thomas, *President*
Wayne Johnson, *CFO*
EMP: 5006
SALES (est): 135.8K
SALES (corp-wide): 8.9B **Privately Held**
SIC: 8741 7539 Management services; automotive repair shops
HQ: Firstgroup Usa, Inc.
600 Vine St Ste 1400
Cincinnati OH 45202
513 241-2200

(G-3560)
FIRST STUDENT INC
1801 Transpark Dr (45229-1239)
PHONE...................................513 531-6888

John Nardini, *Branch Mgr*
EMP: 100
SALES (corp-wide): 8.9B **Privately Held**
WEB: www.firststudentinc.com
SIC: 4151 School buses
HQ: First Student, Inc.
600 Vine St Ste 1400
Cincinnati OH 45202

(G-3561)
FIRST STUDENT INC
Also Called: Laidlaw Education Services
100 Hamilton Blvd (45215-5471)
PHONE...................................513 761-6100
Lisa Jajowka, *Manager*
EMP: 66
SALES (corp-wide): 8.9B **Privately Held**
WEB: www.leag.com
SIC: 4151 School buses
HQ: First Student, Inc.
600 Vine St Ste 1400
Cincinnati OH 45202

(G-3562)
FIRST STUDENT INC
Also Called: First Group America
100 Hamilton Blvd (45215-5471)
PHONE...................................513 761-5136
B Echelbarger, *Branch Mgr*
EMP: 400
SALES (corp-wide): 8.9B **Privately Held**
WEB: www.firststudentinc.com
SIC: 4151 School buses
HQ: First Student, Inc.
600 Vine St Ste 1400
Cincinnati OH 45202

(G-3563)
FIRST STUDENT INC (DH)
600 Vine St Ste 1400 (45202-2426)
PHONE...................................513 241-2200
Dennis Maple, *President*
Christian Gartner, *Senior VP*
Bruce Rasch, *Senior VP*
Kathy Vask, *Marketing Mgr*
Jeremy Rogers, *Director*
EMP: 50
SQ FT: 12,500
SALES (est): 7.6B
SALES (corp-wide): 8.9B **Privately Held**
WEB: www.firststudentinc.com
SIC: 4151 School buses
HQ: Firstgroup America, Inc.
600 Vine St Ste 1400
Cincinnati OH 45202
513 241-2200

(G-3564)
FIRST TRANSIT INC (DH)
600 Vine St Ste 1400 (45202-2426)
PHONE...................................513 241-2200
Brad Thomas, *President*
Mark Elias, *Vice Pres*
Jim Tippen, *CFO*
Christian Gartner, *Treasurer*
EMP: 300
SQ FT: 15,000
SALES (est): 1B
SALES (corp-wide): 8.9B **Privately Held**
WEB: www.firsttransit.com
SIC: 8741 7539 8742 Management services; automotive repair shops; transportation consultant
HQ: Firstgroup America, Inc.
600 Vine St Ste 1400
Cincinnati OH 45202
513 241-2200

(G-3565)
FIRST VEHICLE SERVICES INC (DH)
600 Vine St Ste 1400 (45202-2426)
PHONE...................................513 241-2200
Brad Thomas, *President*
Dale Domish, *Senior VP*
EMP: 200
SALES (est): 81.2MM
SALES (corp-wide): 8.9B **Privately Held**
SIC: 7549 Automotive maintenance services
HQ: First Transit, Inc.
600 Vine St Ste 1400
Cincinnati OH 45202
513 241-2200

(G-3566)
FIRSTGROUP AMERICA INC (DH)
Also Called: First Group of America
600 Vine St Ste 1400 (45202-2426)
PHONE.................................513 241-2200
Dennis Maple, *President*
Brad Thomas, *President*
John Joseph, *General Mgr*
William Rischow, *General Mgr*
Christian Gartner, *Senior VP*
EMP: 58
SQ FT: 350,000
SALES (est): 9B
SALES (corp-wide): 8.9B **Privately Held**
WEB: www.firstgroupamerica.com
SIC: 4151 4111 4119 4131 School buses;
local & suburban transit; local passenger
transportation; intercity & rural bus trans-
portation; local bus charter service; facili-
ties support services; base maintenance
(providing personnel on continuing basis);
HQ: Firstgroup Usa, Inc.
600 Vine St Ste 1400
Cincinnati OH 45202
513 241-2200

(G-3567)
FIRSTGROUP AMERICA INC
Also Called: Laidlaw Educational Services
600 Vine St Ste 1400 (45202-2426)
PHONE.................................513 419-8611
Martin Gilbert, *Chairman*
Scott Spivey, *Exec VP*
William Nichols, *Financial Analy*
Regina Snow, *Manager*
Denise Lang, *Representative*
EMP: 400
SALES (corp-wide): 8.9B **Privately Held**
WEB: www.firstgroup.com
SIC: 4151 School buses
HQ: Firstgroup America, Inc.
600 Vine St Ste 1400
Cincinnati OH 45202
513 241-2200

(G-3568)
FIRSTGROUP AMERICA INC
705 Central Ave (45202-1967)
PHONE.................................513 241-2200
Bruce Ballard, *Manager*
EMP: 75
SALES (corp-wide): 8.9B **Privately Held**
SIC: 4151 4111 4119 School buses; local
& suburban transit; local passenger trans-
portation
HQ: Firstgroup America, Inc.
600 Vine St Ste 1400
Cincinnati OH 45202
513 241-2200

(G-3569)
FIRSTGROUP USA INC (HQ)
Also Called: First Transit
600 Vine St Ste 1400 (45202-2426)
PHONE.................................513 241-2200
Bruce Ballard, *CEO*
Tim O'Toole, *Chairman*
Dave Hickie, *Vice Pres*
Paul Sears, *Director*
EMP: 425
SALES: 2.3MM
SALES (corp-wide): 8.9B **Privately Held**
SIC: 7513 4212 4213 4225 Truck leas-
ing, without drivers; truck rental, without
drivers; local trucking, without storage;
trucking, except local; general warehous-
ing; school buses; local & suburban tran-
sit
PA: Firstgroup Plc
Exchequer House
Aberdeen AB24
122 465-0100

(G-3570)
FISHER DESIGN INC (PA)
4101 Spring Grove Ave B (45223-1180)
PHONE.................................513 417-8235
Bryan Librandi, *CEO*
William Fisher, *Chairman*
Mary Frazier, *Business Mgr*
Randy Braun, *CFO*
Mary Kay, *Manager*
EMP: 40
SQ FT: 20,000
SALES (est): 5MM **Privately Held**
WEB: www.fisherdesign.com
SIC: 7336 Commercial art & illustration;
graphic arts & related design; package
design

(G-3571)
FITWORKS HOLDING LLC
5840 Cheviot Rd (45247-6225)
PHONE.................................513 923-9931
Mike Korn, *Branch Mgr*
EMP: 362 **Privately Held**
WEB: www.fitworks.com
SIC: 7991 Health club
PA: Fitworks Holding, Llc
849 Brainard Rd
Cleveland OH 44143

(G-3572)
FITWORKS HOLDING LLC
Also Called: Fitworks Fitness & Spt Therapy
4600 Smith Rd Ste G (45212-2784)
PHONE.................................513 531-1500
Andrew Bradley, *General Mgr*
EMP: 36 **Privately Held**
SIC: 7991 Health club
PA: Fitworks Holding, Llc
849 Brainard Rd
Cleveland OH 44143

(G-3573)
FIVE SEASONS SPT CNTRY CLB INC
11790 Snider Rd (45249-1223)
PHONE.................................513 842-1188
Ben Goodyear, *Manager*
EMP: 100 **Privately Held**
WEB: www.fiveseasonsday.com
SIC: 7997 Country club, membership
HQ: Five Seasons Sports Country Club,
Inc.
100 E Rivercenter Blvd # 1100
Covington KY 41011

(G-3574)
FLYPAPER STUDIO INC
311 Elm St Ste 200 (45202-2743)
PHONE.................................602 801-2208
Patrick Sullivan, *CEO*
Greg Head, *President*
Pat Stoner, *Treasurer*
Sunil Padiyar, *CTO*
Don Perison, *Admin Sec*
EMP: 30
SQ FT: 16,778
SALES: 1.9MM **Privately Held**
WEB: www.interactivealchemy.com
SIC: 7372 Educational computer software

(G-3575)
FOCUS SOLUTIONS INC
Also Called: Focus Staffing
1821 Summit Rd Ste 103 (45237-2818)
PHONE.................................513 376-8349
Zola Stewart, *President*
Barbara Johnson, *COO*
EMP: 101
SALES (est): 3.1MM **Privately Held**
SIC: 7363 8742 8741 Employee leasing
service; management consulting services;
management services

(G-3576)
FOLKERS MANAGEMENT CORPORATION (PA)
7741 Thompson Rd (45247-2252)
P.O. Box 54947 (45254-0947)
PHONE.................................513 421-0230
David Folkers, *President*
Winston Folkers, *Vice Pres*
Marilyn Compton, *Treasurer*
EMP: 25
SQ FT: 150,000
SALES (est): 2.7MM **Privately Held**
SIC: 8741 Management services

(G-3577)
FORD DEVELOPMENT CORP
Also Called: Trend Construction
11148 Woodward Ln (45241-1876)
PHONE.................................513 772-1521
Robert J Henderson, *CEO*
Robert F Henderson, *President*
Andrew Kloenne, *Vice Pres*
Mike Frey, *Project Mgr*
Christy Duhme, *Office Mgr*
EMP: 100
SQ FT: 22,000
SALES (est): 34.9MM **Privately Held**
WEB: www.forddevelopment.com
SIC: 1542 1623 1794 Commercial & of-
fice building, new construction; water,
sewer & utility lines; excavation work

(G-3578)
FORSYTHE TECHNOLOGY LLC
8845 Governors Hill Dr # 201
(45249-3316)
PHONE.................................513 697-5100
Andrew Anderson, *Branch Mgr*
EMP: 58
SALES (corp-wide): 3.1B **Privately Held**
SIC: 7379 Computer related consulting
services
HQ: Forsythe Technology, Llc
7770 Frontage Rd
Skokie IL 60077
847 213-7000

(G-3579)
FORT WASH INV ADVISORS INC (DH)
303 Broadway St Ste 1100 (45202-4203)
P.O. Box 2388 (45201-2388)
PHONE.................................513 361-7600
Maribeth S Rahe, *President*
Larry Carone, *President*
Bunn William, *President*
Stephen A Baker, *Managing Dir*
Margaret C Bell, *Managing Dir*
EMP: 76
SALES (est): 126.8MM **Privately Held**
WEB: www.fortwashington.com
SIC: 6282 Investment advisory service
HQ: The Western & Southern Life Insur-
ance Company
400 Broadway St
Cincinnati OH 45202
513 629-1800

(G-3580)
FORTEC MEDICAL INC
2050 Northwest Dr (45231-1700)
PHONE.................................513 742-9100
Paul Dierks, *Manager*
EMP: 25
SALES (corp-wide): 14.7MM **Privately Held**
SIC: 7352 Medical equipment rental
PA: Fortec Medical, Inc.
6245 Hudson Crossing Pkwy
Hudson OH 44236
330 463-1265

(G-3581)
FOSDICK & HILMER INC
525 Vine St Ste 1100 (45202-3141)
PHONE.................................513 241-5640
Jim Pretz, *Ch of Bd*
Joel Grubbs, *Senior VP*
Dennis Burns, *Vice Pres*
David Garrison, *Vice Pres*
Richard M Saunders, *Vice Pres*
EMP: 56
SQ FT: 16,000
SALES: 9.1MM **Privately Held**
WEB: www.fosdickandhilmer.com
SIC: 8711 Consulting engineer

(G-3582)
FOUNTAIN SQUARE MGT GROUP LLC
Also Called: Fsmg
1203 Walnut St Fl 4 (45202-7153)
PHONE.................................513 621-4400
Timothy Szilasi, *CFO*
Bill Donabedian, *Manager*
EMP: 50
SQ FT: 12,000
SALES (est): 142.1K **Privately Held**
SIC: 7929 Entertainment service

(G-3583)
FOXX & COMPANY
324 W 9th St Fl 5 (45202-2043)
PHONE.................................513 241-1616
Patricia Foxx, *President*
Martin O'Neill, *Vice Pres*
EMP: 30 EST: 1977
SQ FT: 5,000
SALES (est): 2.3MM **Privately Held**
SIC: 8721 Certified public accountant

(G-3584)
FRCH DESIGN WORLDWIDE - CINCIN
311 Elm St Ste 600 (45202-2774)
PHONE.................................513 241-3000
James R Tippmann, *CEO*
James R Lazzari, *President*
Thomas E Horwitz, *Senior VP*
Monica Gerhardt, *Vice Pres*
Shane Kavanagh, *Vice Pres*
EMP: 275
SQ FT: 22,000
SALES (est): 47.4MM
SALES (corp-wide): 87.3MM **Privately Held**
SIC: 8712 House designer
PA: Nelson Worldwide, Llc
100 S Independence Mall W
Philadelphia PA 19106
215 925-6562

(G-3585)
FRED A NEMANN CO
6480 Bender Rd (45233-1552)
PHONE.................................513 467-9400
Fred Nemann III, *President*
Sandra Timler, *Vice Pres*
Tim Nemann, *Treasurer*
EMP: 40
SQ FT: 3,000
SALES: 9.7MM **Privately Held**
SIC: 1611 1623 Highway & street con-
struction; water, sewer & utility lines

(G-3586)
FREDERICK STEEL COMPANY LLC
Also Called: Bfs Supply
630 Glendale Milford Rd (45215-1105)
PHONE.................................513 821-6400
Burke Byer, *Principal*
Mark Kurtz, *Vice Pres*
Timothy Nagy, *Asst Sec*
EMP: 60 EST: 2013
SALES (est): 8.1MM
SALES (corp-wide): 86.5MM **Privately Held**
SIC: 1791 3441 Structural steel erection;
building components, structural steel
PA: Benjamin Steel Company, Inc.
777 Benjamin Dr
Springfield OH 45502
937 322-8600

(G-3587)
FREDERICKS LANDSCAPING INC
301 S Cooper Ave (45215-4519)
PHONE.................................513 821-9407
Frederick Hollmann, *President*
Katie Clark, *Office Mgr*
Tina Pfeifer, *Manager*
EMP: 50 EST: 1977
SQ FT: 9,000
SALES: 2MM **Privately Held**
WEB: www.frederickslandscaping.com
SIC: 0782 Lawn care services; landscape
contractors

(G-3588)
FREE STORE/FOOD BANK INC (PA)
1250 Tennessee Ave (45229-1012)
PHONE.................................513 482-4526
John Young, *President*
Bernice Cooper, *Vice Pres*
Bill Kolb, *Manager*
Sarah Humphries, *Supervisor*
Mindy Hammer, *Director*
EMP: 45 EST: 1971
SQ FT: 100,000
SALES (est): 5.8MM **Privately Held**
SIC: 8322 Social service center; emer-
gency social services

(G-3589)
FREE STORE/FOOD BANK INC
Meyerson Food Distribution
1250 Tennessee Ave (45229-1012)
PHONE.................................513 241-1064
Steve Gibbs, *Manager*
EMP: 30

SALES (corp-wide): 5.8MM **Privately Held**
SIC: 8322 Social services for the handicapped; public welfare center
PA: Free Store/Food Bank, Inc
　1250 Tennessee Ave
　Cincinnati OH 45229
　513 482-4526

(G-3590)
FREESTORE FOODBANK INC
1141 Central Pkwy (45202-2050)
PHONE......................513 482-4500
Kurt Reiber, *President*
Tim Weidner, *CFO*
Kevin Lynam, *Supervisor*
Anthony Lavatori, *Technology*
Stephanie Togneri, *Volunteer Dir*
EMP: 50
SALES: 54.3MM **Privately Held**
SIC: 8322 Social service center

(G-3591)
FREIGHTLNER TRCKS OF CNCINNATI
1 Freightliner Dr (45241-6418)
PHONE......................513 772-7171
Gary Gibson, *President*
EMP: 40
SALES (est): 9.7MM **Privately Held**
SIC: 5511 5012 Trucks, tractors & trailers: new & used; trucks, commercial

(G-3592)
FREKING BETZ
525 Vine St Fl 6 (45202-3151)
PHONE......................513 721-1975
Randolph H Freking, *Partner*
Carrie Myers, *Partner*
Sheila Smith, *Partner*
Heather Waldron, *Manager*
Debbie Graham, *Admin Sec*
EMP: 30
SQ FT: 5,360
SALES (est): 4.2MM **Privately Held**
WEB: www.frekingandbetz.com
SIC: 8111 Labor & employment law

(G-3593)
FREY ELECTRIC INC
5700 Cheviot Rd Ste A (45247-7101)
P.O. Box 53785 (45253-0785)
PHONE......................513 385-0700
David Frey, *President*
EMP: 60
SQ FT: 16,000
SALES (est): 9.2MM **Privately Held**
WEB: www.freyelectric.com
SIC: 1731 General electrical contractor

(G-3594)
FRIARS CLUB INC
Also Called: FRANCISCAN FRIARS
4300 Vine St (45217-1542)
PHONE......................513 488-8777
Mike Besl, *Ch of Bd*
Beth Bowsky, *Director*
EMP: 71
SQ FT: 20,000
SALES: 826.6K
SALES (corp-wide): 12MM **Privately Held**
WEB: www.rogerbacon.org
SIC: 8361 7032 7991 Boys' Towns; summer camp, except day & sports instructional; athletic club & gymnasiums, membership
PA: The Province Of St John Baptist Order Friars Minor
　1615 Vine St
　Cincinnati OH 45202
　513 721-4700

(G-3595)
FRIEDMAN-SWIFT ASSOCIATES INC
110 Boggs Ln Ste 200 (45246-3147)
P.O. Box 9185 (45209-0185)
PHONE......................513 772-9200
Jeffrey Friedman, *President*
Judith George, *Senior VP*
EMP: 100
SQ FT: 5,500
SALES (est): 6.8MM **Privately Held**
WEB: www.friedmanswift.com
SIC: 8732 Market analysis or research

(G-3596)
FROST BROWN TODD LLC (PA)
3300 Grt Amrcn Towe 301e (45202)
PHONE......................513 651-6800
Bernard L McKay, *Partner*
Richard Moore, *Trustee*
James D Anderson, *Counsel*
Scott Hankins, *Counsel*
Angie Birkenhauer, *Vice Pres*
EMP: 294
SALES (est): 138MM **Privately Held**
WEB: www.fbtextra.com
SIC: 8111 General practice attorney, lawyer; labor & employment law; environmental law; patent, trademark & copyright law

(G-3597)
FUND EVALUATION GROUP LLC (PA)
201 E 5th St Ste 1600 (45202-4156)
PHONE......................513 977-4400
Rebecca Wood, *Sr Corp Ofcr*
Tim O'Donnell, *Senior VP*
Christina Drake, *Vice Pres*
Anthony Festa, *Vice Pres*
Douglas Harrell, *Vice Pres*
EMP: 50
SQ FT: 12,000
SALES (est): 11MM **Privately Held**
WEB: www.feg.com
SIC: 6282 7371 Investment advisory service; computer software development & applications

(G-3598)
FX FACILITY GROUP LLC (HQ)
Also Called: Foxx Construction LLC
324 W 9th St (45202-2043)
PHONE......................513 639-2509
Levon Thompson Jr, *COO*
Richard E Cleveland, *Vice Pres*
EMP: 30
SALES (est): 1.4MM
SALES (corp-wide): 137.4MM **Privately Held**
WEB: www.xlcservices.com
SIC: 8741 7389 Construction management;
PA: D.E. Foxx & Associates, Inc.
　324 W 9th St Fl 5
　Cincinnati OH 45202
　513 621-5522

(G-3599)
G4S SECURE SOLUTIONS (USA)
625 Eden Park Dr Ste 700 (45202-6016)
PHONE......................513 874-0941
Ryan Krause, *Manager*
EMP: 250 **Privately Held**
SIC: 7381 Security guard service
HQ: G4s Secure Solutions (Usa) Inc.
　1395 University Blvd
　Jupiter FL 33458
　561 622-5656

(G-3600)
GALAXY ASSOCIATES INC (HQ)
3630 E Kemper Rd (45241-2011)
PHONE......................513 731-6350
William D Oeters, *President*
Philip P Dober, *CFO*
Shawn Garver, *CFO*
Marty Burke, *Accounts Mgr*
EMP: 34
SQ FT: 12,300
SALES (est): 17MM **Privately Held**
SIC: 5169 Industrial chemicals

(G-3601)
GAMBLE ELZBETH DCNESS HM ASSN (PA)
2139 Auburn Ave (45219-2906)
PHONE......................513 751-4224
Thomas Petry, *Ch of Bd*
Theodore H Emmerich, *President*
Thomas R Gerdes, *Bd of Directors*
Michael Keating, *Bd of Directors*
Scott Farmer,
EMP: 2900 EST: 1888
SALES: 66.6MM **Privately Held**
WEB: www.elizabethgamble.com
SIC: 8062 8082 General Hospital Home Health Care Services

(G-3602)
GANNETT MEDIA TECH INTL (HQ)
Also Called: Gmti
312 Elm St Ste 2g (45202-2763)
PHONE......................513 665-3777
Daniel D Zito, *CEO*
Chris Ruffieux, *Vice Pres*
Ed Osiecki, *Manager*
John Larsen, *Technology*
EMP: 44
SALES (est): 10.2MM
SALES (corp-wide): 2.9B **Publicly Held**
WEB: www.gmti.com
SIC: 7371 Computer software development
PA: Gannett Co., Inc.
　7950 Jones Branch Dr
　Mc Lean VA 22102
　703 854-6000

(G-3603)
GARDEN STREET IRON & METAL (PA)
2885 Spring Grove Ave (45225-2222)
PHONE......................513 853-3700
Earl J Weber Jr, *President*
Dave Hollbroke, *General Mgr*
Margaret Weber, *Vice Pres*
Sarah Weber, *Office Mgr*
▲ EMP: 40
SQ FT: 43,000
SALES (est): 7.2MM **Privately Held**
SIC: 4953 3341 3312 Refuse System Secondary Nonferrous Metal Producer Blast Furnace-Steel Works

(G-3604)
GATEWAY DISTRIBUTION INC (PA)
11755 Lebanon Rd (45241-2038)
PHONE......................513 891-4477
Wayne Carucci, *CEO*
Dave Neely, *President*
Benjamin P Kenner, *Vice Pres*
Benny Kenner, *VP Opers*
Jeremy Kramer, *Opers Staff*
EMP: 40
SQ FT: 100,000
SALES: 17MM **Privately Held**
WEB: www.gatewaydistribution.com
SIC: 4225 7389 General warehousing & storage; brokers' services

(G-3605)
GE ENGINE SERVICES LLC
201 W Crescentville Rd (45246-1713)
PHONE......................513 977-1500
Brad Mottier, *Vice Pres*
Russell Sparks, *Vice Pres*
David L Clendenen, *Marketing Staff*
John Ousley, *Branch Mgr*
EMP: 300
SALES (corp-wide): 121.6B **Publicly Held**
SIC: 5088 Aircraft equipment & supplies
HQ: Ge Engine Services, Llc
　1 Neumann Way
　Cincinnati OH 45215
　513 243-2000

(G-3606)
GEARS GARDEN CENTER INC (PA)
Also Called: Gear's Florists & Garden Ctrs
1579 Goodman Ave (45224-1004)
PHONE......................513 931-3800
William H Gear IV, *President*
William H Gear III, *Vice Pres*
David W Gear, *Admin Sec*
EMP: 30
SQ FT: 25,000
SALES (est): 3.5MM **Privately Held**
WEB: www.busseborgmann.com
SIC: 5992 5261 0782 Ret Florist & Lawn & Garden Supplies & Landscape Contractors

(G-3607)
GEICO GENERAL INSURANCE CO
5050 Section Ave Ste 420 (45212-2057)
PHONE......................513 794-3426
Sidney Taghiof, *Manager*
EMP: 384

SALES (corp-wide): 225.3B **Publicly Held**
SIC: 6411 Insurance agents, brokers & service
HQ: Geico General Insurance Company
　1 Geico Plz
　Washington DC 20076

(G-3608)
GENERAL ELECTRIC COMPANY
201 W Crescentville Rd (45246-1733)
PHONE......................513 977-1500
Josh Mason, *Engineer*
Dave Kircher, *Sales Staff*
Bill Fitzgerald, *Manager*
EMP: 500
SALES (corp-wide): 121.6B **Publicly Held**
SIC: 7629 3769 3728 3537 Aircraft electrical equipment repair; electrical equipment repair, high voltage; guided missile & space vehicle parts & auxiliary equipment; aircraft parts & equipment; industrial trucks & tractors
PA: General Electric Company
　41 Farnsworth St
　Boston MA 02210
　617 443-3000

(G-3609)
GENERAL ELECTRIC COMPANY
1 Neumann Way (45215-1988)
PHONE......................513 552-2000
Partha Sreenivasan, *Program Mgr*
Randy Bates, *Manager*
Diane Orr, *Senior Mgr*
EMP: 1000
SQ FT: 84,308
SALES (corp-wide): 121.6B **Publicly Held**
SIC: 4581 3724 Hangar operation; aircraft engines & engine parts
PA: General Electric Company
　41 Farnsworth St
　Boston MA 02210
　617 443-3000

(G-3610)
GENERAL ELECTRIC COMPANY
8700 Governors Hill Dr (45249-1363)
PHONE......................513 583-3500
Robert Gatch Jr, *Business Mgr*
Debbie Beke, *Buyer*
Michael Andersen, *Engineer*
Justin Hill, *Engineer*
Dennis Jonassen, *Engineer*
EMP: 150
SQ FT: 7,273
SALES (corp-wide): 121.6B **Publicly Held**
SIC: 1731 7376 Electrical work; computer facilities management
PA: General Electric Company
　41 Farnsworth St
　Boston MA 02210
　617 443-3000

(G-3611)
GENERAL ELECTRIC COMPANY
2411 Glendale Milford Rd (45241-3120)
PHONE......................513 243-9404
William Roe, *Vice Pres*
Robert Pawlowski, *Manager*
Duwayne Scott, *Supervisor*
EMP: 30
SALES (corp-wide): 121.6B **Publicly Held**
SIC: 7991 Physical fitness facilities
PA: General Electric Company
　41 Farnsworth St
　Boston MA 02210
　617 443-3000

(G-3612)
GENERAL ELECTRIC CREDIT UNION (PA)
Also Called: Gecu
10485 Reading Rd (45241-2580)
PHONE......................513 243-4328
Timothy D Ballinger, *CEO*
Joan Moore, *CFO*
EMP: 90 EST: 1954
SQ FT: 23,000
SALES: 88MM **Privately Held**
WEB: www.gecreditunion.org
SIC: 6061 Federal credit unions

▲ = Import ▼=Export
◆ =Import/Export

(G-3613)
GENERAL ELECTRIC EMPLOYEES
Also Called: Geeaa Park Golf Course
12110 Princeton Pike (45246-1726)
PHONE..................513 243-2129
Gene Neff, *Manager*
EMP: 45
SQ FT: 10,000
SALES: 399.1K **Privately Held**
WEB: www.geeaa.org
SIC: 7997 Membership sports & recreation clubs

(G-3614)
GENERAL ELECTRIC INTL INC (HQ)
191 Rosa Parks St (45202-2573)
PHONE..................617 443-3000
Giuseppe Recchi, *President*
Candace F Carson, *Vice Pres*
Daniel Janki, *Vice Pres*
Michael J Geary, *Treasurer*
Pierrot Christophe, *Admin Sec*
◆ EMP: 125
SQ FT: 11,390
SALES: 14.1B
SALES (corp-wide): 121.6B **Publicly Held**
SIC: 8711 Engineering services
PA: General Electric Company
41 Farnsworth St
Boston MA 02210
617 443-3000

(G-3615)
GENERAL FACTORY SUPS CO INC
Also Called: Gfwd Supply
4811 Winton Rd (45232-1502)
PHONE..................513 681-6300
Tim Stautberg, *President*
Jeff Stautberg, *CFO*
EMP: 37 EST: 1946
SQ FT: 33,000
SALES (est): 50MM **Privately Held**
SIC: 5085 Industrial supplies
PA: Waltz-Dettmer Supply Co.
4811 Winton Rd
Cincinnati OH 45232

(G-3616)
GENERAL TOOL COMPANY (PA)
101 Landy Ln (45215-3495)
PHONE..................513 733-5500
William J Kramer Jr, *CEO*
John Cozad, *COO*
Elliot Adams, *Exec VP*
William J Kramer III, *CFO*
Paul Kramer, *Treasurer*
▲ EMP: 235 EST: 1947
SQ FT: 150,000
SALES: 47.5MM **Privately Held**
WEB: www.gentool.com
SIC: 3599 3443 3444 3544 Machine shop, jobbing & repair; fabricated plate work (boiler shop); sheet metalwork; special dies & tools; welding repair

(G-3617)
GENESIS TECHNOLOGY PARTNERS
Also Called: Masterplan
3200 Burnet Ave (45229-3019)
PHONE..................513 585-5800
Joe Happ, *Manager*
EMP: 50
SALES (est): 1.8MM **Privately Held**
WEB: www.genesispartners.net
SIC: 8741 Management services

(G-3618)
GENTHERM MEDICAL LLC
Also Called: Cincinnati Sub-Zero Products
12011 Mosteller Rd (45241-1528)
PHONE..................513 326-5252
Lesley Durik, *QC Mgr*
Steve Berke, *Manager*
EMP: 100
SALES (corp-wide): 1B **Publicly Held**
WEB: www.cszinc.com
SIC: 8734 Testing laboratories
HQ: Gentherm Medical, Llc
12011 Mosteller Rd
Cincinnati OH 45241

(G-3619)
GLENDALE PLACE CARE CENTER LLC
779 Glendale Milford Rd (45215-1161)
PHONE..................513 771-1779
Barry Kohn, *Mng Member*
EMP: 39
SALES (est): 3.6MM **Privately Held**
SIC: 8051 Convalescent home with continuous nursing care

(G-3620)
GLENWAY AUTOMOTIVE SERVICE
Also Called: Sanfillipos Automotive Service
4033 Glenway Ave (45205-1444)
PHONE..................513 921-2117
Joseph Sanfillipo Jr, *President*
Marty Sanfillipo, *Vice Pres*
Maria Sanfillipo, *Treasurer*
Joseph Sanfillipo III, *Admin Sec*
EMP: 28
SQ FT: 25,000
SALES (est): 2.8MM **Privately Held**
SIC: 7538 General automotive repair shops

(G-3621)
GODDARD SCHOOL
Also Called: Goddard School, The
4430 Red Bank Rd (45227-2116)
PHONE..................513 271-6311
Kate Joseph, *Owner*
EMP: 25
SALES (est): 335.2K **Privately Held**
SIC: 8351 Nursery school

(G-3622)
GOETTLE CO
12071 Hamilton Ave (45231-1032)
PHONE..................513 825-8100
Regina Hartfiel, *General Mgr*
Tyler Grow, *Project Mgr*
Kris King, *Project Mgr*
Chad Linz, *Project Mgr*
Tony Eckert, *Opers Mgr*
EMP: 75
SALES (est): 10.2MM **Privately Held**
SIC: 1521 Single-family housing construction

(G-3623)
GOETTLE HOLDING COMPANY INC (PA)
Also Called: Goettle Construction
12071 Hamilton Ave (45231-1032)
PHONE..................513 825-8100
Larry P Rayburn, *Ch of Bd*
Doug Keller, *President*
Terrence Tucker, *President*
Roger W Healey, *Principal*
Janet E Goettle, *Principal*
▲ EMP: 129
SQ FT: 15,000
SALES (est): 75.2MM **Privately Held**
WEB: www.goettle.com
SIC: 1799 1629 1771 1794 Shoring & underpinning work; pile driving contractor; foundation & footing contractor; excavation work

(G-3624)
GOLD STAR CHILI INC (PA)
650 Lunken Park Dr (45226-1800)
PHONE..................513 231-4541
Roger David, *President*
Jeremy Hildebrand, *Project Mgr*
James Conover, *CFO*
Jodi Kelly, *Asst Controller*
Jenny Endres, *Credit Mgr*
EMP: 33 EST: 1965
SQ FT: 5,000
SALES (est): 61.4MM **Privately Held**
SIC: 2032 2099 6794 5499 Chili with or without meat: packaged in cans, jars, etc.; food preparations; franchises, selling or licensing; spices & herbs

(G-3625)
GOOD SAMARITAN HOSP CINCINNATI (HQ)
375 Dixmyth Ave (45220-2489)
PHONE..................513 569-6251
John S Prout, *President*
Robert L Walker, *Chairman*

Gerald Oliphant, *COO*
John R Robinson, *Senior VP*
Craig Rucker, *CFO*
EMP: 50
SALES: 579.5MM **Privately Held**
SIC: 8062 8082 8011 General medical & surgical hospitals; home health care services; offices & clinics of medical doctors

(G-3626)
GOODALL PROPERTIES LTD
Also Called: Goodall Complex
324 W 9th St Ste 500 (45202-2043)
PHONE..................513 621-5522
David E Foxx, *President*
EMP: 40
SALES (est): 1.6MM **Privately Held**
SIC: 6512 Commercial & industrial building operation

(G-3627)
GORILLA GLUE COMPANY (PA)
2101 E Kemper Rd (45241-1805)
PHONE..................513 271-3300
Howard N Ragland III, *President*
Joe Ragland, *COO*
Michael F Ragland, *Vice Pres*
Scott Vilagi, *Vice Pres*
Sally Davidson, *Senior Buyer*
◆ EMP: 49 EST: 1904
SQ FT: 44,000
SALES (est): 62.8MM **Privately Held**
WEB: www.gorillaglue.com
SIC: 5169 5085 Glue; adhesives, tape & plasters

(G-3628)
GOVERNMENT ACQUISITIONS INC
720 E Pete Rose Way # 330 (45202-3583)
PHONE..................513 721-8700
Roger Brown, *Owner*
Kathy Meece, *Project Mgr*
Bobby Brown, *CFO*
Stan Jones, *CFO*
Corliss Baker, *Accountant*
EMP: 35
SQ FT: 20,000
SALES (est): 11.8MM **Privately Held**
WEB: www.gov-acq.com
SIC: 7378 3577 5045 Computer maintenance & repair; computer peripheral equipment; computer software

(G-3629)
GP STRATEGIES CORPORATION
3794 E Galbraith Rd (45236-1506)
PHONE..................513 583-8810
Terry Donahue, *Principal*
EMP: 35
SALES (corp-wide): 515.1MM **Publicly Held**
WEB: www.rwd.com
SIC: 7379 8742 8331 Computer related consulting services; management consulting services; job training services
PA: Gp Strategies Corporation
11000 Broken Land Pkwy # 200
Columbia MD 21044
443 367-9600

(G-3630)
GRACE HOSPICE LLC
4850 Smith Rd Ste 100 (45212-2797)
PHONE..................513 458-5545
Mark Mitchell, *Branch Mgr*
EMP: 102 **Privately Held**
SIC: 8052 Personal care facility
PA: Grace Hospice, Llc
500 Kirts Blvd Ste 250
Troy MI 48084

(G-3631)
GRADIENT CORPORATION
9900 Princtn Glndl Rd 1 (45246)
PHONE..................513 779-0000
Gregory Manhardt, *President*
George Taylor, *Vice Pres*
Thomas Ewers, *Treasurer*
Jamie Ertel, *Admin Sec*
EMP: 36
SQ FT: 2,400
SALES: 5.9MM **Privately Held**
SIC: 1623 1799 1721 Underground utilities contractor; building site preparation; pavement marking contractor

(G-3632)
GRADY VETERINARY HOSPITAL INC
9255 Winton Rd (45231-3935)
PHONE..................513 931-8675
Jeff Grady, *President*
Marsha Weiss, *Office Mgr*
James Auvil,
Jessica Brownfield,
Cameron Stanley,
EMP: 50 EST: 1957
SQ FT: 5,000
SALES (est): 3MM **Privately Held**
WEB: www.gradyvet.com
SIC: 0742 Animal hospital services, pets & other animal specialties

(G-3633)
GRANGE MUTUAL CASUALTY COMPANY
Also Called: Grange Mutual Casualty Co 721
12021 Sheraton Ln (45246-1611)
P.O. Box 46645 (45246-0645)
PHONE..................513 671-3722
George Carol, *Manager*
EMP: 30
SALES (corp-wide): 992.5MM **Privately Held**
SIC: 6331 Fire, marine & casualty insurance
PA: Grange Mutual Casualty Company
671 S High St
Columbus OH 43206
614 445-2900

(G-3634)
GRANT THORNTON LLP
4000 Smith Rd Ste 500 (45209-1967)
PHONE..................513 762-5000
Steve Albert, *Partner*
Sean V McGrory, *Partner*
Bob Taylor, *Branch Mgr*
EMP: 95
SALES (corp-wide): 65MM **Privately Held**
WEB: www.gt.com
SIC: 8721 Accounting services, except auditing
HQ: Grant Thornton Llp
171 N Clark St Ste 200
Chicago IL 60601
312 856-0200

(G-3635)
GRAY & PAPE INC (PA)
1318 Main St Fl 1 (45202-6619)
PHONE..................513 287-7700
W Kevin Pape, *President*
Mirna Colon, *General Mgr*
Christina Inman, *Financial Exec*
Beth McCord, *Branch Mgr*
Patrick O'Bannon, *Manager*
EMP: 47
SQ FT: 16,000
SALES (est): 7.7MM **Privately Held**
WEB: www.graypape.com
SIC: 8999 Earth science services

(G-3636)
GRAY MEDIA GROUP INC
Also Called: W X I X
635 W 7th St Ste 200 (45203-1549)
PHONE..................513 421-1919
Bill Lansey, *General Mgr*
EMP: 144
SALES (corp-wide): 1B **Publicly Held**
WEB: www.kwwl.com
SIC: 4833 Television broadcasting stations
HQ: Gray Media Group, Inc.
201 Monroe St Fl 20
Montgomery AL 36104

(G-3637)
GRAYBAR ELECTRIC COMPANY INC
1022 W 8th St (45203-1269)
PHONE..................513 719-7400
Phil Grimes, *Branch Mgr*
Justin Bass, *Manager*
Edward Kremer, *Supervisor*
EMP: 56
SQ FT: 60,000
SALES (corp-wide): 7.2B **Privately Held**
WEB: www.graybar.com
SIC: 5063 Electrical supplies

PA: Graybar Electric Company, Inc.
34 N Meramec Ave
Saint Louis MO 63105
314 573-9200

(G-3638)
GREAT AMERICAN ADVISORS INC (DH)
301 E 4th St Fl 8 (45202-4257)
P.O. Box 357 (45201-0357)
PHONE....................................513 357-3300
Jim Henderson, *President*
Bill Bair, *Vice Pres*
James Mc Vey, *Vice Pres*
Mark F Muething, *Admin Sec*
Tara Wright, *Administration*
EMP: 30
SQ FT: 9,000
SALES (est): 4.3MM **Publicly Held**
SIC: 6411 Insurance agents, brokers & service
HQ: Great American Financial Resources, Inc.
250 E 5th St Ste 1000
Cincinnati OH 45202
513 333-5300

(G-3639)
GREAT AMERICAN INSURANCE CO (HQ)
301 E 4th St Fl 8 (45202-4257)
P.O. Box 5420 (45201-5420)
PHONE....................................513 369-5000
Carl H Lindner III, *CEO*
Michael E Chevrette, *President*
Freeman Durham, *President*
William T Gaynor Jr, *President*
Julie F Kadnar, *President*
◆ **EMP:** 3000
SQ FT: 250,000
SALES (est): 1.5B **Publicly Held**
SIC: 6331 Automobile insurance

(G-3640)
GREAT AMERICAN LIFE INSUR CO (HQ)
250 E 5th St Ste 1000 (45202-4127)
P.O. Box 5420 (45201-5420)
PHONE....................................513 357-3300
Charles Scheper, *President*
Brad Garland, *Project Mgr*
Chris Miliano, *Asst Treas*
Robert Hodder, *Sales Staff*
Tonia Page, *Business Anlyst*
EMP: 27
SALES (est): 16.3MM **Publicly Held**
WEB: www.galic.com
SIC: 6311 Life insurance carriers

(G-3641)
GREAT AMRCN FNCL RESOURCES INC (HQ)
250 E 5th St Ste 1000 (45202-4127)
PHONE....................................513 333-5300
Carl H Lindner, *Ch of Bd*
S Craig Lindner, *President*
Charles R Scheper, *COO*
Mark F Muething, *Exec VP*
Richard E Beavers, *Vice Pres*
EMP: 150
SQ FT: 140,000
SALES (est): 548MM **Publicly Held**
WEB: www.aagcorp.com
SIC: 6371 Union welfare, benefit & health funds

(G-3642)
GREAT AMRCN PLAN ADMIN INC
525 Vine St Fl 7 (45202-3169)
PHONE....................................513 412-2316
Mark Muething, *President*
Kevin Kelley, *Vice Pres*
Minh Huynh, *Accounting Mgr*
Brian Beiting, *Underwriter*
Meriwether Moore, *Supervisor*
EMP: 55
SALES (est): 15MM **Privately Held**
SIC: 6371 Pension, health & welfare funds

(G-3643)
GREAT LAKES COMPANIES INC
925 Laidlaw Ave (45237-5003)
PHONE....................................513 554-0720
Eric Reed, *Superintendent*

Mark Grdina, *Vice Pres*
Albert Leonard, *Vice Pres*
Deb Wagner, *Manager*
EMP: 125
SALES (corp-wide): 68.1MM **Privately Held**
SIC: 1521 Single-family housing construction
PA: Great Lakes Companies Inc
2608 Great Lakes Way
Hinckley OH
330 220-3900

(G-3644)
GREAT OAKS INST TECH CREER DEV (PA)
110 Great Oaks Dr (45241-1573)
P.O. Box 62627 (45262-0627)
PHONE....................................513 613-3657
Harry Snyder, *President*
Jon Quatman, *Vice Pres*
Michelle Means Walker, *Vice Pres*
Robert Giuffre, *CFO*
EMP: 98 **EST:** 1971
SQ FT: 10,000
SALES: 67.1MM **Privately Held**
SIC: 8211 8299 8331 8249 Public vocational/technical school; educational service, nondegree granting: continuing educ.; job training & vocational rehabilitation services; vocational schools

(G-3645)
GREAT OAKS INST TECH CREER DEV
Also Called: Center For Employment Resource
3254 E Kemper Rd (45241-6421)
PHONE....................................513 771-8840
Gary Gebhert, *Director*
EMP: 50
SALES (corp-wide): 67.1MM **Privately Held**
SIC: 8211 8299 8331 8249 Public adult education school; educational service, nondegree granting: continuing educ.; job training & vocational rehabilitation services; vocational schools
PA: Great Oaks Institute Of Technology & Career Development
110 Great Oaks Dr
Cincinnati OH 45241
513 613-3657

(G-3646)
GREAT TRADITIONS DEV GROUP INC (PA)
4000 Executive Park Dr # 250 (45241-4008)
PHONE....................................513 563-4070
Thomas H Humes, *President*
Kathy Schroeder, *President*
Edward H Rogerson, *Vice Pres*
James P Sullivan, *Treasurer*
EMP: 25
SQ FT: 4,100
SALES (est): 3.8MM **Privately Held**
WEB: www.gtldc.com
SIC: 6552 Subdividers & developers

(G-3647)
GREATER ANDRSON PREMOTES PEACE
7642 Athenia Dr (45244-2900)
PHONE....................................513 588-8391
Luise Lawarre, *CEO*
EMP: 35
SALES (est): 299.1K **Privately Held**
WEB: www.gappeace.org
SIC: 8412 Museums & art galleries

(G-3648)
GREATER ARMS HOLISTIC HEALTH
260 Northland Blvd 131b (45246-4908)
PHONE....................................513 970-2767
Yarnell Crawford,
EMP: 25 **EST:** 2016
SALES: 156K **Privately Held**
SIC: 8052 Personal care facility

(G-3649)
GREATER CIN CARDI CONSULTS IN
Also Called: Greater Cnti Crdovascular Cons
2123 Auburn Ave (45219-2906)
PHONE....................................513 751-4222
F Thomas Jenike, *President*
David G Babbitt, *Vice Pres*
John S Held, *Vice Pres*
Lester E Suna, *Vice Pres*
Byron W Gustin, *Treasurer*
EMP: 50
SQ FT: 7,000
SALES (est): 3.4MM **Privately Held**
SIC: 8011 Cardiologist & cardio-vascular specialist

(G-3650)
GREATER CINCINNATI CNVNTN/VSTR
525 Vine St Ste 1500 (45202-3147)
PHONE....................................513 621-2142
Ben Lincoln, *President*
Cindi Flick, *Vice Pres*
Barrie Perks, *Vice Pres*
EMP: 32
SQ FT: 10,000
SALES: 9.5MM **Privately Held**
WEB: www.cincyusa.com
SIC: 7389 Convention & show services

(G-3651)
GREATER CINCINNATI DENTAL LABS
3719 Struble Rd (45251-4951)
P.O. Box 53070 (45253-0070)
PHONE....................................513 385-4222
Ken Blaylock, *President*
Robert Blaylock, *Treasurer*
Darlene Rogg, *Admin Sec*
EMP: 49
SALES (est): 4MM **Privately Held**
WEB: www.gcapmd.com
SIC: 8072 Denture production

(G-3652)
GREATER CINCINNATI GASTRO ASSC (PA)
2925 Vernon Pl Ste 100 (45219-2425)
PHONE....................................513 336-8636
Ronald Schneider, *President*
George Waissbluth, *Vice Pres*
Alan Safdi, *Treasurer*
Michael Safdi, *Admin Sec*
EMP: 60
SQ FT: 6,000
SALES (est): 9.9MM **Privately Held**
WEB: www.cincygastro.com
SIC: 8011 Gastronomist

(G-3653)
GREATER CINCINNATI OB/GYN INC (PA)
2830 Victory Pkwy Ste 140 (45206-1786)
PHONE....................................513 245-3103
Baha Sivai, *President*
Thomas Frerick, *Treasurer*
Clarence R McLaine, *Admin Sec*
EMP: 60
SALES (est): 12.9MM **Privately Held**
SIC: 8011 Obstetrician

(G-3654)
GREATER CINCINNATI TV EDUC FND
Also Called: CHANNEL 48
1223 Central Pkwy (45214-2834)
PHONE....................................513 381-4033
Susan Howarth, *CEO*
Kellie May, *Corp Comm Staff*
Jason Dennison, *Manager*
Lauren Hess, *Manager*
EMP: 70
SQ FT: 84,210
SALES: 5.1MM **Privately Held**
WEB: www.ohiomathworks.net
SIC: 4833 7812 Television broadcasting stations; television film production

(G-3655)
GREATER CNNCNATI CRIME STOPPER
P.O. Box 14330 (45250-0330)
PHONE....................................859 468-1310

Gene Farrari, *President*
Michele Peers,
EMP: 25
SALES (est): 314.8K **Privately Held**
SIC: 8641 Civic associations

(G-3656)
GREEN TOWNSHIP HOSPITALITY LLC (PA)
Also Called: Holiday Inn
5505 Rybolt Rd (45248-1029)
PHONE....................................513 574-6000
Katen Patel, *Mng Member*
Sanjiv Mehrotra,
Sejal Patel,
EMP: 294
SQ FT: 100,000
SALES (est): 9.3MM **Privately Held**
SIC: 7011 5812 Hotels; eating places

(G-3657)
GREYHOUND LINES INC
1005 Gilbert Ave (45202-1425)
PHONE....................................513 421-7442
Virginia Purdy, *Manager*
EMP: 50
SALES (corp-wide): 8.9B **Privately Held**
WEB: www.greyhound.com
SIC: 4131 Interstate bus line
HQ: Greyhound Lines, Inc.
350 N Saint Paul St # 300
Dallas TX 75201
214 849-8000

(G-3658)
GRIPPO FOODS INC
6750 Colerain Ave (45239-5542)
PHONE....................................513 923-1900
Ralph W Pagel II, *President*
Teri Baker, *Vice Pres*
Linda Foster, *Vice Pres*
James Pagel, *Vice Pres*
Nancy Schreiber, *Vice Pres*
EMP: 50 **EST:** 1919
SQ FT: 27,000
SALES (est): 8.9MM **Privately Held**
SIC: 5145 Snack foods; potato chips

(G-3659)
GROTE ENTERPRISES LLC (PA)
5240 Lester Rd (45213-2522)
PHONE....................................513 731-5700
Tom Grote Jr, *Principal*
Kim Valmore, *Human Res Dir*
Shannon Kemme, *Human Resources*
Resa Young, *Office Mgr*
EMP: 85
SALES (est): 11.4MM **Privately Held**
SIC: 8741 Management services

(G-3660)
GUARDIAN LIFE INSUR CO OF AMER
419 Plum St (45202-2632)
PHONE....................................513 579-1114
Patrick Wilson, *Branch Mgr*
Richard Shurmer, *Agent*
William Hoover, *Advisor*
Erin Knodel, *Advisor*
EMP: 30
SALES (corp-wide): 9.7B **Privately Held**
WEB: www.glic.com
SIC: 6311 Life insurance
PA: The Guardian Life Insurance Company Of America
7 Hanover Sq Fl 14
New York NY 10004
212 598-8000

(G-3661)
GUARDIAN SAVINGS BANK
560 Ohio Pike (45255-3315)
PHONE....................................513 528-8787
Tracy Royse, *Manager*
Andrew Shaffer, *Technology*
EMP: 30
SALES (corp-wide): 42.4MM **Privately Held**
SIC: 6163 6035 Loan brokers; savings institutions, federally chartered
PA: Guardian Savings Bank
6100 W Chester Rd
West Chester OH 45069
513 942-3535

(G-3662)
GUARDSMARK LLC
4050 Executive Park Dr # 350
(45241-2077)
PHONE................................513 851-5523
Mark Morrissey, *Manager*
EMP: 250
SALES (corp-wide): 741.7MM **Privately Held**
WEB: www.guardsmark.com
SIC: 7381 Security guard service
HQ: Guardsmark, Llc
    1551 N Tustin Ave Ste 650
    Santa Ana CA 92705
    714 619-9700

(G-3663)
GUNNING & ASSOCAITES MARKETING
Also Called: G&A Marketing
6355 E Kemper Rd Ste 250 (45241-3092)
PHONE................................513 688-1370
Patrick Gunning, *President*
EMP: 40
SQ FT: 3,700
SALES (est): 2.7MM **Privately Held**
SIC: 8748 Business consulting

(G-3664)
GUS HOLTHAUS SIGNS INC
Also Called: Holthaus Lackner Signs
817 Ridgeway Ave (45229-3222)
P.O. Box 29373 (45229-0373)
PHONE................................513 861-0060
Kevin Holthaus, *President*
Scott Holthaus, *Vice Pres*
Rick Souder, *Prdtn Mgr*
Charlie Holthaus, *Purch Mgr*
Jon Holthaus, *Sales Staff*
EMP: 40 EST: 1929
SQ FT: 38,600
SALES (est): 6.5MM **Privately Held**
WEB: www.holthaussigns.com
SIC: 3993 1799 Electric signs; sign installation & maintenance

(G-3665)
GUS PERDIKAKIS ASSOCIATES
Also Called: GPA
9155 Governors Way Unit A (45249-4005)
P.O. Box 498612 (45249-8612)
PHONE................................513 583-0900
Gus G Perdikakis, *President*
Joann L Perdikakis, *Treasurer*
George Perdikakis, *Marketing Staff*
Steve Saunders, *Marketing Staff*
Lynn Perdikakis, *Admin Sec*
EMP: 70
SQ FT: 1,600
SALES (est): 9.7MM **Privately Held**
WEB: www.gpainc.net
SIC: 8711 7361 Engineering services; employment agencies

(G-3666)
H DENNERT DISTRIBUTING CORP
351 Wilmer Ave (45226-1831)
P.O. Box 721768, Newport KY (41072-1768)
PHONE................................513 871-7272
Ronald J Plattner, *President*
▲ EMP: 110
SALES (est): 10.1MM **Privately Held**
SIC: 5182 Wine

(G-3667)
H P PRODUCTS CORPORATION
7135 E Kemper Rd (45249-1028)
PHONE................................513 683-8553
Mike Brown, *Branch Mgr*
EMP: 75
SALES (corp-wide): 20.7B **Privately Held**
SIC: 5087 Janitors' supplies
HQ: H P Products Corporation
    4220 Saguaro Trl
    Indianapolis IN 46268
    317 298-9957

(G-3668)
HABEGGER CORPORATION (PA)
Also Called: Johnson Contrls Authorized Dlr
4995 Winton Rd (45232-1504)
PHONE................................513 853-6644
Fred Habegger III, *Ch of Bd*

John Dor, *President*
Susan Brickweg, *Business Mgr*
Shawn Calton, *Opers Mgr*
Angie Gardner, *Opers Mgr*
▲ EMP: 49
SQ FT: 20,000
SALES (est): 91.9MM **Privately Held**
WEB: www.habeggercorp.com
SIC: 5075 Warm air heating equipment & supplies; air conditioning & ventilation equipment & supplies

(G-3669)
HABEGGER CORPORATION
Also Called: C A C Distributing
11413 Enterprise Park Dr (45241-1561)
PHONE................................513 612-4700
Ken Kellogg, *Opers Mgr*
Adam Cole, *Technical Mgr*
John R Kinnamon, *Sales/Mktg Mgr*
Trish Glazier, *Credit Mgr*
Jeff Achilles, *Sales Mgr*
EMP: 60
SQ FT: 29,320
SALES (corp-wide): 91.9MM **Privately Held**
WEB: www.habeggercorp.com
SIC: 5074 5075 Heating equipment (hydronic); air conditioning equipment, except room units
PA: The Habegger Corporation
    4995 Winton Rd
    Cincinnati OH 45232
    513 853-6644

(G-3670)
HACKENSACK MERIDIAN HEALTH INC
Also Called: Carriage Court of Kenwood
4650 E Galbraith Rd (45236-2792)
PHONE................................513 792-9697
K Pfeifer, *Finance*
EMP: 80
SALES (corp-wide): 4.4B **Privately Held**
SIC: 8051 Skilled nursing care facilities
PA: Hackensack Meridian Health, Inc.
    343 Thornall St
    Edison NJ 08837
    732 751-7500

(G-3671)
HAGGERTY LOGISTICS INC
95 W Crescentville Rd (45246)
PHONE................................734 713-9800
EMP: 44
SALES (corp-wide): 11.5MM **Privately Held**
SIC: 4789 Pipeline terminal facilities, independently operated
PA: Haggerty Logistics, Inc.
    17900 Woodland Dr
    New Boston MI 48164
    734 397-6300

(G-3672)
HAID ACQUISITIONS LLC
1053 Ebenezer Rd (45233-4820)
PHONE................................513 941-8700
Aaron Haid, *Mng Member*
EMP: 75 EST: 2015
SALES (est): 3.2MM **Privately Held**
SIC: 4731 Transportation agents & brokers

(G-3673)
HAIR FORUM
5801 Cheviot Rd Unit 1 (45247-6206)
PHONE................................513 245-0800
Don Feldmann, *Owner*
EMP: 25
SALES (est): 417.7K **Privately Held**
WEB: www.hairforum.com
SIC: 7231 Hairdressers

(G-3674)
HAMILTON CNTY AUDITOR OFFICE
138 E Court St Rm 501 (45202-1226)
PHONE................................513 946-4000
Dusty Rhodes, *Auditor*
David Nurre, *Supervisor*
Bradley A Bookheimer, *Real Est Agnt*
EMP: 142
SALES (est): 6.4MM **Privately Held**
WEB: www.auditor.hamilton.org
SIC: 7389 Personal service agents, brokers & bureaus

(G-3675)
HAMILTON COUNTY EDUCTL SVC CTR
924 Waycross Rd (45240-3022)
PHONE................................513 674-4200
Kathy Tirey, *Exec Dir*
EMP: 100
SALES (corp-wide): 75MM **Privately Held**
SIC: 8351 Head start center, except in conjunction with school
PA: Hamilton County Educational Service Center
    11083 Hamilton Ave
    Cincinnati OH 45231
    513 674-4200

(G-3676)
HAMILTON COUNTY PARKS DISTRICT
10999 Mill Rd (45240-3515)
PHONE................................513 825-3701
Andi Lanz, *Office Mgr*
Matt Starr, *Director*
Andrew Horner, *Director*
Doug Stulz, *Director*
EMP: 50
SALES (est): 804K **Privately Held**
SIC: 7999 Golf driving range

(G-3677)
HAMILTON COUNTY SOCIETY (PA)
Also Called: S P C A Cincinnati
3949 Colerain Ave (45223-2518)
PHONE................................513 541-6100
Harold Dates, *Director*
EMP: 36
SQ FT: 15,255
SALES (est): 4.2MM **Privately Held**
SIC: 8699 Animal humane society

(G-3678)
HAMMOND LAW GROUP LLC
441 Vine St Ste 3200 (45202-2800)
PHONE................................513 381-2011
Krystle Bryant, *COO*
Michael F Hammond,
Kimi Rolfsen, *Legal Exec*
Jonathan A Hammond, *Legal Staff*
Colleen Sullivan, *Legal Staff*
EMP: 30
SALES (est): 3.7MM **Privately Held**
WEB: www.hammondlawfirm.com
SIC: 8111 General practice law office

(G-3679)
HANEY INC
Also Called: Haney PRC
5657 Wooster Pike (45227-4120)
PHONE................................513 561-1441
Matthew J Haney, *CEO*
Daniel E Haney, *President*
EMP: 52
SQ FT: 4,000
SALES (est): 10.1MM **Privately Held**
SIC: 7336 Graphic arts & related design

(G-3680)
HANSON MCCLAIN INC
Also Called: Hanson McClain Advisors
7890 E Kemper Rd Ste 200 (45249-1657)
PHONE................................513 469-7500
Patrick C McClain, *Branch Mgr*
EMP: 30
SALES (est): 511.1K **Privately Held**
SIC: 8742 6282 Financial consultant; investment advisory service
PA: Hanson Mcclain, Lp
    8775 Folsom Blvd Ste 100
    Sacramento CA 95826

(G-3681)
HARRIS DISTRIBUTING CO
4261 Crawford Ave (45223-1857)
PHONE................................513 541-4222
Irma Harris, *President*
Carl Harris Jr, *Vice Pres*
Dennis A Harris, *Vice Pres*
Patricia Junker, *Treasurer*
EMP: 30
SALES (est): 3.6MM **Privately Held**
SIC: 4213 Contract haulers

(G-3682)
HARRISON PAVILION
2171 Harrison Ave (45211-8159)
PHONE................................513 662-5800
Skip Roos, *Principal*
EMP: 32
SALES: 6MM **Privately Held**
SIC: 8322 8059 Rehabilitation services; nursing home, except skilled & intermediate care facility

(G-3683)
HARTWIG TRANSIT INC
11971 Reading Rd (45241-1543)
PHONE................................513 563-1765
Caleb France, *Manager*
EMP: 40
SQ FT: 3,648
SALES (corp-wide): 29.6MM **Privately Held**
WEB: www.hartwigtransit.com
SIC: 7538 Truck engine repair, except industrial
PA: Hartwig Transit, Inc.
    204 Christina Dr
    Dundee IL 60118
    847 749-1101

(G-3684)
HAUCK HOSPITALITY LLC
Also Called: Holiday Inn
3855 Hauck Rd (45241-1609)
PHONE................................513 563-8330
Robin Rankin, *Sales Dir*
John Gieseke, *Director*
Reddy Kummetha,
Jennifer Davis, *Executive Asst*
EMP: 80
SQ FT: 24,311
SALES (est): 4.3MM **Privately Held**
WEB: www.hicincy.com
SIC: 7011 5812 Hotels; eating places

(G-3685)
HAYES CONCRETE CONSTRUCTION
2120 Waycross Rd (45240-2719)
PHONE................................513 648-9400
Ed Hayes, *President*
Steve Hawkins, *Project Mgr*
EMP: 35
SALES (est): 4.3MM **Privately Held**
SIC: 1771 Foundation & footing contractor

(G-3686)
HAYS & SONS CONSTRUCTION INC
190 Container Pl (45246-1709)
PHONE................................513 671-9110
Grant Saunders, *President*
EMP: 27
SALES (corp-wide): 49.6MM **Privately Held**
SIC: 1521 Single-family home remodeling, additions & repairs
PA: Hays & Sons Construction, Inc.
    800 E Thompson Rd
    Indianapolis IN 46227
    317 788-0911

(G-3687)
HC TRANSPORT INC
Also Called: For Hire Carrier
6045 Bridgetown Rd (45248-3049)
P.O. Box 111116 (45211-1116)
PHONE................................513 574-1800
Edward Sedler, *President*
Cliff Riegler, *Manager*
Clifford Riegler, *Director*
EMP: 30
SQ FT: 16,000
SALES (est): 7MM **Privately Held**
SIC: 4212 Delivery service, vehicular

(G-3688)
HCR MANORCARE MED SVCS FLA LLC
Also Called: Manor Care
4580 E Galbraith Rd (45236-2799)
PHONE................................513 745-9600
Jana Longbons-Saab, *Manager*
EMP: 50
SALES (corp-wide): 2.4B **Publicly Held**
WEB: www.manorcare.com
SIC: 8051 Extended care facility

HQ: Hcr Manorcare Medical Services Of
    Florida, Llc
    333 N Summit St Ste 100
    Toledo OH 43604
    419 252-5500

(G-3689)
**HCR MANORCARE MED SVCS
FLA LLC**
Also Called: Arden Courts of Anderson Twp.
6870 Clough Pike (45244-4161)
PHONE.................................513 233-0831
Jay Boyce, *Exec Dir*
EMP: 60
SQ FT: 1,220
SALES (corp-wide): 2.4B **Publicly Held**
WEB: www.manorcare.com
SIC: 8051 8082 Convalescent home with
continuous nursing care; home health
care services
HQ: Hcr Manorcare Medical Services Of
    Florida, Llc
    333 N Summit St Ste 100
    Toledo OH 43604
    419 252-5500

(G-3690)
**HCR MANORCARE MED SVCS
FLA LLC**
Also Called: Manor Care
4900 Cooper Rd (45242-6915)
PHONE.................................513 561-4111
Cindy Tipton, *Manager*
EMP: 170
SALES (corp-wide): 2.4B **Publicly Held**
WEB: www.manorcare.com
SIC: 8051 Convalescent home with contin-
uous nursing care
HQ: Hcr Manorcare Medical Services Of
    Florida, Llc
    333 N Summit St Ste 100
    Toledo OH 43604
    419 252-5500

(G-3691)
**HCR MANORCARE MED SVCS
FLA LLC**
2250 Banning Rd (45239-6608)
PHONE.................................513 591-0400
Brett Kirkpatrick, *Administration*
EMP: 105
SALES (corp-wide): 2.4B **Publicly Held**
WEB: www.manorcare.com
SIC: 8051 Convalescent home with contin-
uous nursing care
HQ: Hcr Manorcare Medical Services Of
    Florida, Llc
    333 N Summit St Ste 100
    Toledo OH 43604
    419 252-5500

(G-3692)
**HEALTH CARE RTREMENT
CORP AMER**
Also Called: Oak Pavilion Nursing & Rehabil
510 Oak St (45219-2507)
PHONE.................................513 751-0880
Dorothy Dew, *Chf Purch Ofc*
Shelley Owens, *Branch Mgr*
EMP: 113
SALES (corp-wide): 2.4B **Publicly Held**
WEB: www.hrc-manorcare.com
SIC: 8051 Skilled nursing care facilities
HQ: Health Care And Retirement Corpora-
    tion Of America
    333 N Summit St Ste 103
    Toledo OH 43604
    419 252-5500

(G-3693)
HEALTH CAROUSEL LLC (PA)
Also Called: Tailored Healthcare Staffing
3805 Edwards Rd Ste 700 (45209-1955)
PHONE.................................866 665-4544
William Deville, *CEO*
Jonathan Kukulski, *Vice Pres*
Lair Kennedy, *CFO*
Lawrence Kennedy, *CFO*
Tom Herbert, *Controller*
EMP: 96
SALES (est): 24.1MM **Privately Held**
WEB: www.globalscholarship.net
SIC: 7363 Temporary help service

(G-3694)
HEALTH COLLABORATIVE
615 Elsinore Pl Ste 500 (45202-1475)
PHONE.................................513 618-3600
Craig Brammer, *CEO*
Judy Bradford, *Pastor*
Jason Buckner, *Vice Pres*
Sharon Trainer, *Facilities Mgr*
Keith Hepp, *CFO*
EMP: 97
SQ FT: 18,300
SALES: 11.5MM **Privately Held**
SIC: 8621 8011 Professional membership
organizations; health maintenance organi-
zation

(G-3695)
HEALTHLINX INC
Also Called: ARA Staffing Services
602 Main St Ste 300 (45202-2554)
PHONE.................................513 402-2018
Brian Hubbard, *President*
EMP: 50
SALES (est): 493.1K **Privately Held**
SIC: 8082 Home health care services

(G-3696)
**HEARING SPCH DEAF CTR
GRTR CNC**
2825 Burnet Ave Ste 330 (45219-2426)
PHONE.................................513 221-0527
Janet Boothe, *CEO*
EMP: 35
SALES: 2MM **Privately Held**
SIC: 8322 8699 Rehabilitation services;
charitable organization

(G-3697)
**HEITS BUILDING SVCS CNKD
LLC**
Also Called: Heits Building Services Cincin
52 E Crescentville Rd (45246-1344)
PHONE.................................£55 464-3487
Joseph Okum, *CEO*
Robert Okum, *CFO*
David Okum,
Elizabeth Okum,
EMP: 75
SQ FT: 2,900
SALES: 750K **Privately Held**
SIC: 7349 Janitorial service, contract basis

(G-3698)
HENSLEY INDUSTRIES INC (PA)
2150 Langdon Farm Rd (45237-4711)
PHONE.................................513 769-6666
Trina Ewald, *President*
Linda Hensley, *President*
Bill Besl, *COO*
David Metzcar, *COO*
Dalaina Fancher, *Vice Pres*
EMP: 50
SQ FT: 182,000
SALES (est): 6.4MM **Privately Held**
WEB: www.hensleyindustries.com
SIC: 1796 Machine moving & rigging

(G-3699)
HERTZ CORPORATION
Cincinnati N Kentucky A P (45275)
P.O. Box 75016 (45275-0016)
PHONE.................................513 533-3161
Art Gunpher, *Branch Mgr*
EMP: 30
SALES (corp-wide): 8.8B **Publicly Held**
WEB: www.hertz.com
SIC: 7514 Rent-a-car service
HQ: The Hertz Corporation
    8501 Williams Rd
    Estero FL 33928
    239 301-7000

(G-3700)
HGC CONSTRUCTION CO (PA)
Also Called: H G C
2814 Stanton Ave (45206-1123)
PHONE.................................513 861-8866
Mike Huseman, *President*
EMP: 84
SQ FT: 22,000
SALES (est): 27.4MM **Privately Held**
WEB: www.hgc1040.com
SIC: 1751 1796 Carpentry work; millwright

(G-3701)
HICON INC
93 Caldwell Dr A (45216-1541)
PHONE.................................513 242-3612
Wayne Moratschek, *President*
Daniel Verst, *Exec VP*
Steve Sprengard, *Vice Pres*
Dave Wetzel, *Project Mgr*
Frank Brown, *Financial Exec*
EMP: 60
SQ FT: 6,000
SALES (est): 6.6MM **Privately Held**
WEB: www.hiconinc.com
SIC: 1741 1611 Masonry & other
stonework; highway & street paving con-
tractor

(G-3702)
**HILLEBRAND HOME HEALTH
INC**
4343 Bridgetown Rd (45211-4427)
PHONE.................................513 598-6648
Michelle Schneider, *President*
DOT Kemper, *Vice Pres*
Janet Cella, *Nursing Dir*
Vicki Dirr, *Administration*
Bobbie Knue, *Administration*
EMP: 50
SALES (est): 1.6MM **Privately Held**
WEB: www.hillebrandhomehealth.com
SIC: 8082 Visiting nurse service

(G-3703)
HILLMAN COMPANIES INC
Also Called: Hillman Group Anchor Wire
10590 Hamilton Ave (45231-1764)
PHONE.................................513 851-4900
Steve Seaford, *Branch Mgr*
EMP: 57
SALES (corp-wide): 838.3MM **Privately
Held**
WEB: www.quicktag.com
SIC: 5072 Hardware
HQ: The Hillman Companies Inc
    10590 Hamilton Ave
    Cincinnati OH 45231
    513 851-4900

(G-3704)
HILLMAN COMPANIES INC
1700 Carillion Blvd (45240-2795)
PHONE.................................513 851-4900
Rick Bore, *Branch Mgr*
EMP: 300
SALES (corp-wide): 838.3MM **Privately
Held**
WEB: www.quicktag.com
SIC: 5072 Hardware
HQ: The Hillman Companies Inc
    10590 Hamilton Ave
    Cincinnati OH 45231
    513 851-4900

(G-3705)
HILLMAN COMPANIES INC (DH)
10590 Hamilton Ave (45231-1764)
PHONE.................................513 851-4900
Douglas J Cahill, *Ch of Bd*
Gregory J Gluchowski Jr, *President*
Timothy Harkins, *District Mgr*
Leigh Piersol, *Business Mgr*
John Marshall, *Vice Pres*
◆ EMP: 400
SQ FT: 270,000
SALES: 974.1MM
SALES (corp-wide): 484.2MM **Privately
Held**
SIC: 5072 7699 Hardware; miscellaneous
fasteners; bolts, nuts & screws; key dupli-
cating shop
HQ: Hman Intermediate Ii Holdings Corp.
    10590 Hamilton Ave
    Cincinnati OH 45231
    513 851-4900

(G-3706)
HILLMAN GROUP INC (DH)
10590 Hamilton Ave (45231-1764)
PHONE.................................513 851-4900
Gregory J Gluchowski Jr, *CEO*
Douglas J Cahill, *Chairman*
Kim Corbitt, *Chairman*
Todd Spangler, *Vice Pres*
Cabot Mary, *Human Resources*
◆ EMP: 153

SALES (est): 733.1MM
SALES (corp-wide): 484.2MM **Privately
Held**
WEB: www.quicktag.com
SIC: 5072 Hardware
HQ: The Hillman Companies Inc
    10590 Hamilton Ave
    Cincinnati OH 45231
    513 851-4900

(G-3707)
**HILLSBORO TRANSPORTATION
CO**
2889 E Crescentville Rd (45246)
P.O. Box 62595 (45262-0595)
PHONE.................................513 772-9223
Jeff Duckwall, *Vice Pres*
EMP: 35
SQ FT: 4,800
SALES (corp-wide): 4.9MM **Privately
Held**
WEB: www.hillsborotransportation.com
SIC: 4213 Contract haulers
PA: Hillsboro Transportation Co.
    6256 Us Route 50
    Hillsboro OH 45133

(G-3708)
HILLSIDE MAINT SUP CO INC
3300 Spring Grove Ave (45225-1327)
PHONE.................................513 751-4100
Thomas R Glueck, *President*
James Glueck, *Vice Pres*
EMP: 25
SQ FT: 100,000
SALES (est): 8.6MM **Privately Held**
WEB: www.hillsideonline.com
SIC: 5087 5169 Janitors' supplies; chemi-
cals & allied products

(G-3709)
**HILLTOP BASIC RESOURCES
INC**
Also Called: Hilltop Concrete
511 W Water St (45202-3400)
PHONE.................................513 621-1500
Mike Marchioni, *Manager*
EMP: 45
SQ FT: 1,758
SALES (corp-wide): 116.7MM **Privately
Held**
WEB: www.hilltopbasicresources.com
SIC: 3273 3272 1442 Ready-mixed con-
crete; concrete products; construction
sand & gravel
PA: Hilltop Basic Resources, Inc.
    1 W 4th St Ste 1100
    Cincinnati OH 45202
    513 651-5000

(G-3710)
**HIRSCH INTERNATIONAL
HOLDINGS**
4 Kovach Dr Ste 470a (45215-1061)
PHONE.................................513 733-4111
Leo Stenger, *Branch Mgr*
EMP: 133 **Privately Held**
SIC: 5084 Printing trades machinery,
equipment & supplies
PA: Hirsch Holdings, Inc.
    490 Wheeler Rd Ste 285
    Hauppauge NY 11788

(G-3711)
HIT PORTFOLIO I MISC TRS LLC
Also Called: Hyatt Hotel
151 W 5th St (45202-2703)
PHONE.................................513 241-3575
Herb Rackliff, *General Mgr*
Chris Sejman, *Engineer*
Michelle Logel, *Sales Mgr*
Melissa Buday, *Manager*
Susan Flyer, *Manager*
EMP: 225
SALES (corp-wide): 4.4B **Publicly Held**
WEB: www.hyatt.com
SIC: 7011 Hotels And Motels
HQ: Hyatt Corporation
    150 N Riverside Plz
    Chicago IL 60606
    312 750-1234

(G-3712)
HIXSON INCORPORATED
Also Called: Hixson Archtcts/Ngnrs/Nteriors
659 Van Meter St Ste 300 (45202-1568)
PHONE.....................................513 241-1230
J Wickliffe Ach, *President*
Scott Schroeder, *Business Mgr*
Mitch Vanover, *Business Mgr*
Bruce Mirrielees, *Senior VP*
Bill Sander, *Senior VP*
EMP: 125 EST: 1948
SQ FT: 125,000
SALES (est): 26.1MM **Privately Held**
WEB: www.hixson-inc.com
SIC: 8712 Architectural engineering

(G-3713)
HJ BENKEN FLOR &
GREENHOUSES
6000 Plainfield Rd (45213-2335)
PHONE.....................................513 891-1040
Michael Benken, *President*
Timothy Clark, *General Mgr*
Kathleen A Benken, *Vice Pres*
John Clark, *Manager*
Doug Young, *Manager*
EMP: 75 EST: 1938
SQ FT: 6,500
SALES (est): 5.4MM **Privately Held**
WEB: www.benkens.com
SIC: 5992 0181 5261 Flowers, fresh;
plants, potted; nursery stock, growing of;
nurseries & garden centers

(G-3714)
HOBSONS INC (DH)
50 E-Business Way Ste 300 (45241-2398)
PHONE.....................................513 891-5444
Craig Heldman, *President*
Todd Jibby, *President*
Howard Bell, *Vice Pres*
Lee Wall, *CFO*
Bobby Tahir, *CTO*
EMP: 200
SALES (est): 68.3MM **Privately Held**
WEB: www.hobsons.com
SIC: 8748 Educational consultant
HQ: Daily Mail And General Trust P L C
Northcliffe House
London W8 5T
207 938-6000

(G-3715)
HOETING INC (PA)
Also Called: Hoeting Realtors
6048 Bridgetown Rd (45248-3021)
PHONE.....................................513 451-4800
Robert Bartholomew, *President*
Steve Florian, *Partner*
Steven Florian, *Vice Pres*
Dan Grote, *Vice Pres*
Jack Hoeting, *Vice Pres*
EMP: 52
SALES (est): 3.8MM **Privately Held**
WEB: www.hoeting.com
SIC: 6531 Real estate agent, residential

(G-3716)
HOLT RENTAL SERVICES (PA)
Also Called: Cat The Rental Store
11330 Mosteller Rd (45241-1828)
PHONE.....................................513 771-0515
Toll Free:...............................888 -
Peter Holt, *Owner*
Chris Kirk, *Sales Staff*
Mike Manny, *Sales Staff*
Craig Peters, *Sales Staff*
Paul Lorenze, *Sales Executive*
EMP: 45
SQ FT: 20,000
SALES (est): 7.9MM **Privately Held**
WEB: www.cattherentalstore.com
SIC: 7353 Heavy construction equipment
rental

(G-3717)
HOME BLDRS ASSN GRTER
CNCNNATI
11260 Chester Rd Ste 800 (45246-4007)
PHONE.....................................513 851-6300
Dan Dressman, *Exec Dir*
EMP: 60
SQ FT: 3,000

SALES: 19.7K **Privately Held**
WEB: www.cincybuilders.com
SIC: 8611 Contractors' association

(G-3718)
HOME CITY ICE COMPANY (PA)
6045 Bridgetown Rd Ste 1 (45248-3047)
P.O. Box 111116 (45211-1116)
PHONE.....................................513 574-1800
Thomas E Sedler, *President*
Joel Heck, *Division Mgr*
Joseph H Head, *Principal*
Edward T Sedler, *COO*
Kathy Winters, *Safety Dir*
EMP: 130
SQ FT: 10,000
SALES (est): 232.5MM **Privately Held**
WEB: www.homecityice.com
SIC: 4225 General warehousing & storage

(G-3719)
HOME DEPOT USA INC
Also Called: Home Depot, The
520 Ohio Pike (45255-3728)
PHONE.....................................513 688-1654
Matt Hingle, *Manager*
EMP: 150
SALES (corp-wide): 108.2B **Publicly
Held**
WEB: www.homerentalsdepot.com
SIC: 5211 7359 Home centers; tool rental
HQ: Home Depot U.S.A., Inc.
2455 Paces Ferry Ave
Atlanta GA 30339

(G-3720)
HOME DEPOT USA INC
Also Called: Home Depot, The
6300 Glenway Ave (45211-6303)
PHONE.....................................513 661-2413
Ken Hedges, *Principal*
EMP: 200
SALES (corp-wide): 108.2B **Publicly
Held**
WEB: www.homerentalsdepot.com
SIC: 5211 7359 Home centers; tool rental
HQ: Home Depot U.S.A., Inc.
2455 Paces Ferry Ave
Atlanta GA 30339

(G-3721)
HOME DEPOT USA INC
Also Called: Home Depot, The
3400 Highland Ave (45213-2612)
PHONE.....................................513 631-1705
Brenda Brown, *Manager*
EMP: 150
SALES (corp-wide): 108.2B **Publicly
Held**
WEB: www.homerentalsdepot.com
SIC: 5211 7359 Home centers; tool rental
HQ: Home Depot U.S.A., Inc.
2455 Paces Ferry Ave
Atlanta GA 30339

(G-3722)
HOME STATE PROTECTIVE
SVCS LLC
Also Called: Hsps Special Operations
1821 Summit Rd Ste 0-11 (45237-2822)
P.O. Box 11593 (45211-0593)
PHONE.....................................513 253-3095
Bobby Long, *Mng Member*
EMP: 50
SALES (est): 99.4K **Privately Held**
SIC: 7381 Detective & armored car serv-
ices

(G-3723)
HOMELAND DEFENSE
SOLUTIONS
128 E 6th St (45202-3211)
PHONE.....................................513 333-7800
James Noe, *Principal*
EMP: 40
SALES (est): 1.2MM **Privately Held**
SIC: 8748 Business consulting

(G-3724)
HONEYWELL INTERNATIONAL
INC
1280 Kemper Meadow Dr (45240-1632)
PHONE.....................................513 745-7200
Tracy Glendy, *Branch Mgr*
Bill Mc Afoos, *Manager*

EMP: 100
SALES (corp-wide): 41.8B **Publicly Held**
SIC: 7373 7372 Computer systems analy-
sis & design; prepackaged software
PA: Honeywell International Inc.
115 Tabor Rd
Morris Plains NJ 07950
973 455-2000

(G-3725)
HORIZON HEALTH
MANAGEMENT LLC
3889 E Galbraith Rd (45236-1514)
PHONE.....................................513 793-5220
Raymond Schneider, *Principal*
EMP: 100
SALES (est): 3.7MM **Privately Held**
SIC: 8051 Skilled nursing care facilities

(G-3726)
HORMEL FOODS CORP SVCS
LLC
4055 Executive Park Dr # 300
(45241-4020)
PHONE.....................................513 563-0211
Jim Tupy, *Manager*
EMP: 40
SALES (corp-wide): 9.5B **Publicly Held**
SIC: 5147 Meats & meat products
HQ: Hormel Foods Corporate Services, Llc
1 Hormel Pl
Austin MN 55912
507 437-5611

(G-3727)
HORTER INVESTMENT MGT LLC
11726 7 Gables Rd (45249-1735)
PHONE.....................................513 984-9933
Jack Peters, *Senior VP*
Tim Becker, *Vice Pres*
Casey Croysdale, *Vice Pres*
Kirk Horter, *Opers Staff*
Drew Horter, *Mng Member*
EMP: 40
SALES (est): 746.6K **Privately Held**
SIC: 7389 Financial services

(G-3728)
HOSPICE CINCINNATI INC
Also Called: Trihealth Work Capacity Center
2800 Winslow Ave (45206-1144)
PHONE.....................................513 862-1100
Dave Bertke, *Vice Pres*
Donna Giancola, *Vice Pres*
Barbara Pasztor, *Vice Pres*
Doug Roush, *Project Mgr*
Lee Storm, *Engineer*
EMP: 29 **Privately Held**
SIC: 8082 8051 Home health care serv-
ices; skilled nursing care facilities
HQ: Hospice Of Cincinnati, Incorporated
4360 Cooper Rd Ste 300
Cincinnati OH 45242
513 891-7700

(G-3729)
HOSPICE CINCINNATI INC (DH)
Also Called: TRIHEALTH
4360 Cooper Rd Ste 300 (45242-5636)
PHONE.....................................513 891-7700
Sandra Lobert, *President*
Adhrain Griffith, *Finance*
Stephen Fritsch, *Psychologist*
James Kahl, *Med Doctor*
Leigh Gerdsen, *Director*
EMP: 100
SALES: 54.5MM **Privately Held**
SIC: 8082 8051 Home health care serv-
ices; skilled nursing care facilities
HQ: Trihealth, Inc.
619 Oak St
Cincinnati OH 45206
513 569-6111

(G-3730)
HOSPICE SOUTHWEST OHIO
INC
7625 Camargo Rd (45243-3107)
PHONE.....................................513 770-0820
Joseph Killian, *CEO*
Steven Boymel, *Ch of Bd*
Michael Doddy, *Principal*
Brent Dixon, *Treasurer*
James Farley, *Director*
EMP: 100

SALES (est): 52.6K **Privately Held**
WEB: www.hswo.org
SIC: 8082 Home health care services

(G-3731)
HOST CINCINNATI HOTEL LLC
Also Called: Starwood Hotels & Resorts
21 E 5th St Ste A (45202-3120)
PHONE.....................................513 621-7700
Wayne Bodington, *General Mgr*
Jon Coleman, *General Mgr*
Gary Tarpinian, *Sales Dir*
Melanie Gandy, *Sales Mgr*
Tara Mullins, *Sales Mgr*
EMP: 200
SALES (est): 9.6MM **Privately Held**
WEB: www.hostmarriott.com
SIC: 7011 Hotels & motels
PA: Host Hotels & Resorts, Inc.
6903 Rockledge Dr # 1500
Bethesda MD 20817
240 744-1000

(G-3732)
HOUSE CALLS LLC
1936 Elm Ave (45212-2536)
PHONE.....................................513 841-9800
Stephanie Harden,
Darrell Harden,
EMP: 25
SQ FT: 1,200
SALES (est): 2.3MM **Privately Held**
WEB: www.housecallsllc.com
SIC: 7699 Cleaning services

(G-3733)
HOWARD JOHNSON
400 Glensprin Dr.L 275 Sr (45246)
PHONE.....................................513 825-3129
Howard Johnson, *Principal*
EMP: 177
SALES (est): 1.2MM **Publicly Held**
SIC: 7011 Hotels & motels
HQ: Howard Johnson International Inc
22 Sylvan Way
Parsippany NJ 07054

(G-3734)
HOWLAND LOGISTICS LLC
930 Tennessee Ave (45229-1006)
PHONE.....................................513 469-5263
Jennifer Howland, *Mng Member*
Matthew Howland,
EMP: 31
SALES (est): 919.5K **Privately Held**
SIC: 4212 Petroleum haulage, local

(G-3735)
HSR MARKETING
COMMUNICATIONS
Also Called: Hsr Business To Business
300 E Bus Way Ste 500 (45241)
PHONE.....................................513 671-3811
EMP: 75
SQ FT: 30,000
SALES (est): 6.6MM
SALES (corp-wide): 8.2B **Privately Held**
SIC: 7311 Marketing Communications
HQ: Gyro, Llc
7755 Montgomery Rd # 300
Cincinnati OH 45236

(G-3736)
HST LESSEE CINCINNATI LLC
Also Called: Westin Cincinnati, The
21 E 5th St (45202-3114)
PHONE.....................................513 852-2702
Monique Taylor, *Manager*
EMP: 160
SALES (est): 500K
SALES (corp-wide): 5.5B **Publicly Held**
SIC: 7011 Hotels & motels
HQ: Host Hotels & Resorts, L.P.
6903 Rockledge Dr # 1500
Bethesda MD 20817
240 744-1000

(G-3737)
HUBBARD RADIO CINCINNATI
LLC
Also Called: Queen City Jobs
2060 Reading Rd Ste 400 (45202-1456)
PHONE.....................................513 699-5102
James Bryant, *Partner*
Terry Moore, *Natl Sales Mgr*

Mikl Gabbard, *Info Tech Mgr*
Angela Mitchell, *Info Tech Mgr*
Kim Grant, *Director*
EMP: 99
SALES (est): 5.4MM **Privately Held**
SIC: 4832 Radio broadcasting stations

(G-3738)
HUMAN RESOURCE PROFILE INC
Also Called: Hr Profile
8506 Beechmont Ave (45255-4708)
PHONE................................513 388-4300
Mark Owens, *President*
Tanya Catron, *COO*
Robin Paraska, *Natl Sales Mgr*
John Robinson, *Manager*
Todd Shafer, *Manager*
EMP: 34
SQ FT: 4,500
SALES: 3.1MM **Privately Held**
WEB: www.hrprofile.com
SIC: 7389 Personal investigation service

(G-3739)
HUMANA HEALTH PLAN OHIO INC
111 Merchant St (45246-3730)
PHONE................................513 784-5200
Wayne Thomas Smith, *President*
Amanda Scheller, *Sales Staff*
Bill Cooney, *Info Tech Mgr*
Pamela Beltz, *Director*
Walter Emerson Neely, *Admin Sec*
EMP: 100
SALES (est): 48.8MM
SALES (corp-wide): 56.9B **Publicly Held**
WEB: www.humanahealth.com
SIC: 6324 Health maintenance organization (HMO), insurance only
PA: Humana Inc.
    500 W Main St Ste 300
    Louisville KY 40202
    502 580-1000

(G-3740)
HUMASERVE HR LLC
9435 Waterstone Blvd (45249-8226)
PHONE................................513 605-3522
Billy Southerland, *President*
Debbie Church, *Office Mgr*
EMP: 30
SALES (est): 347.8K **Privately Held**
SIC: 8631 8721 Employees' association; payroll accounting service

(G-3741)
HUMMEL INDUSTRIES INCORPORATED
Also Called: David Hummel Building
93 Caldwell Dr B (45216-1541)
PHONE................................513 242-1321
Greg Moratschek, *President*
Carl Kappes III, *Exec VP*
Frank Brown, *Controller*
Matt Privett, *Manager*
EMP: 30
SQ FT: 6,000
SALES (est): 3.5MM **Privately Held**
WEB: www.hummelindustries.com
SIC: 1799 1741 Caulking (construction); waterproofing; masonry & other stonework

(G-3742)
HUNTINGTON NATIONAL BANK
525 Vine St Ste 14 (45202-3133)
PHONE................................513 762-1860
Eric Winkler, *Loan Officer*
Francie Martin, *Business Anlyst*
Chad Todd, *Branch Mgr*
EMP: 120
SALES (corp-wide): 5.2B **Publicly Held**
WEB: www.huntingtonnationalbank.com
SIC: 6029 6162 6021 Commercial banks; mortgage bankers; national commercial banks
HQ: The Huntington National Bank
    17 S High St Fl 1
    Columbus OH 43215
    614 480-4293

(G-3743)
HYDE PARK GOLF & COUNTRY CLUB
3740 Erie Ave (45208-1923)
PHONE................................513 321-3721
Jeff McGrath, *President*
Eric O'Bryan, *General Mgr*
EMP: 75
SALES: 2.1MM **Privately Held**
WEB: www.hydeparkcc.com
SIC: 7997 Country club, membership

(G-3744)
HYDE PARK HEALTH CENTER
3763 Hopper Hill Rd (45255-5051)
PHONE................................513 272-0600
Aileen Jones, *Principal*
Booker Betts, *Director*
Kathy Johnson, *Director*
EMP: 34 **EST:** 2008
SALES (est): 2.7MM **Privately Held**
SIC: 8051 Skilled nursing care facilities

(G-3745)
HYDE PARK LDSCP & TREE SVC INC
Also Called: Hyde Park Landscaping
5055 Wooster Rd (45226-2326)
P.O. Box 8100 (45208-0100)
PHONE................................513 731-1334
Michael Shumrick, *President*
Vicki Seiter, *Admin Sec*
EMP: 49
SQ FT: 9,622
SALES (est): 5MM **Privately Held**
WEB: www.hydeparklandscaping.com
SIC: 0782 0783 Lawn & garden services; planting, pruning & trimming services

(G-3746)
HYDE PARK PLAY SCHOOL
3846 Drake Ave (45209-2124)
PHONE................................513 631-2095
Nancy Philpott, *Owner*
EMP: 35
SQ FT: 2,768
SALES (est): 788K **Privately Held**
WEB: www.thehydeparkplayschool.com
SIC: 8351 Preschool center

(G-3747)
HYLANT GROUP INC
Also Called: Hylant Group of Cincinnati
50 E-Business Way Ste 420 (45241-2398)
PHONE................................513 985-2400
Crystal Goodwin, *Client Mgr*
Craig Markos, *Branch Mgr*
EMP: 29
SALES (corp-wide): 129.8MM **Privately Held**
WEB: www.hylant.com
SIC: 6411 Insurance agents
PA: Hylant Group, Inc.
    811 Madison Ave Fl 11
    Toledo OH 43604
    419 255-1020

(G-3748)
HYPERQUAKE LLC
205 W 4th St Ste 1010 (45202-2628)
PHONE................................513 563-6555
Steve Bruce, *CEO*
Colin Crotty, *President*
Jeanne Bruce, *CFO*
Lauren McKenna, *Project Leader*
Sherwood Macveigh, *Director*
EMP: 40
SALES (est): 4.8MM **Privately Held**
SIC: 7374 Computer graphics service

(G-3749)
IBI GROUP ENGRG SVCS USA INC
23 Triangle Park Dr # 2300 (45246-3411)
PHONE................................513 942-3141
Dick Longenecker, *Principal*
EMP: 30
SALES (corp-wide): 283.1MM **Privately Held**
SIC: 8711 Consulting engineer
HQ: Ibi Group Engineering Services (Usa) Inc.
    635 Brooksedge Blvd
    Westerville OH 43081
    614 818-4900

(G-3750)
IHEARTCOMMUNICATIONS INC
8044 Montgomery Rd # 650 (45236-2919)
PHONE................................513 241-1550
Toni Smith, *Manager*
EMP: 250 **Publicly Held**
SIC: 4832 Radio broadcasting stations
HQ: Iheartcommunications, Inc.
    20880 Stone Oak Pkwy
    San Antonio TX 78258
    210 822-2828

(G-3751)
IHEARTCOMMUNICATIONS INC
Also Called: Wkrc-Tv/Cbs
1906 Highland Ave (45219-3104)
PHONE................................513 763-5500
John Lawhead, *General Mgr*
Tim Fair, *Editor*
EMP: 290 **Publicly Held**
SIC: 4832 Radio broadcasting stations
HQ: Iheartcommunications, Inc.
    20880 Stone Oak Pkwy
    San Antonio TX 78258
    210 822-2828

(G-3752)
IMAGE ENGINEERING INC
Also Called: Great Clips
7038 Golfway Dr (45239-5632)
PHONE................................513 541-8544
Alfred Scheide, *President*
Sally Sheide, *Vice Pres*
EMP: 25
SALES (est): 488K **Privately Held**
WEB: www.imageengineering.com
SIC: 7231 Unisex hair salons

(G-3753)
IMAGEPACE LLC
5375 Medpace Way (45227-1543)
PHONE................................513 579-9911
EMP: 497
SALES (est): 68.2K
SALES (corp-wide): 704.5MM **Publicly Held**
SIC: 5122 Biotherapeutics
PA: Medpace Holdings, Inc.
    5375 Medpace Way
    Cincinnati OH 45227
    513 579-9911

(G-3754)
IN HOME HEALTH LLC
Also Called: Heartland Hospice Services
3960 Red Bank Rd Ste 140 (45227-3421)
PHONE................................513 831-5800
EMP: 38
SALES (corp-wide): 2.4B **Publicly Held**
SIC: 8082 Home health care services
HQ: In Home Health, Llc
    333 N Summit St
    Toledo OH 43604

(G-3755)
IN-PLAS RECYCLING INC
4211 Crawford Ave (45223-1838)
PHONE................................513 541-9800
Dennis Boyer, *President*
Richard Smith, *Vice Pres*
Paul Markland, *Opers Mgr*
EMP: 30
SALES (est): 6.5MM **Privately Held**
SIC: 4953 Recycling, waste materials

(G-3756)
INDIANA & OHIO RAIL CORP (DH)
Also Called: Central Railroad of Indiana
2856 Cypress Way (45212-2446)
PHONE................................513 860-1000
Bill Hudran, *CEO*
Gary Mareno, *Ch of Bd*
EMP: 30
SQ FT: 5,700
SALES (est): 16.8MM
SALES (corp-wide): 2.3B **Publicly Held**
SIC: 4011 Railroads, line-haul operating
HQ: Railtex, Inc.
    1355 Central Pkwy S # 700
    San Antonio TX 78232
    210 301-7600

(G-3757)
INDIANA & OHIO RAILWAY COMPANY
2856 Cypress Way (45212-2446)
PHONE................................513 860-1000
Ryan Ratledge, *President*
EMP: 90
SALES: 950K **Privately Held**
SIC: 4011 Railroads, line-haul operating

(G-3758)
INDROLECT CO
630 W Wyoming Ave (45215-4527)
P.O. Box 15492 (45215-0492)
PHONE................................513 821-4788
Dave Schlager, *President*
Joseph Schlager, *President*
EMP: 30
SQ FT: 11,000
SALES (est): 3.9MM **Privately Held**
WEB: www.indrolect.com
SIC: 1731 General electrical contractor

(G-3759)
INDUSTRIAL COMM & SOUND INC
Also Called: I C S
2105 Schappelle Ln (45240-2724)
PHONE................................614 276-8123
C K Satyapriya, *President*
Thomas A Volz, *President*
Allen Volz, *Vice Pres*
EMP: 28 **EST:** 1948
SQ FT: 11,000
SALES (est): 5.2MM
SALES (corp-wide): 36.1MM **Privately Held**
WEB: www.icands.com
SIC: 1731 Electronic controls installation; sound equipment specialization
PA: Ctl Engineering, Inc.
    2860 Fisher Rd
    Columbus OH 43204
    614 276-8123

(G-3760)
INDUSTRIAL SORTING SERVICES
2599 Commerce Blvd (45241-1536)
PHONE................................513 772-6501
Joe Walden, *President*
Dan Grammer, *Opers Staff*
Mary Tabor, *Accounting Mgr*
EMP: 35
SQ FT: 10,000
SALES (est): 5.1MM **Privately Held**
SIC: 7549 Automotive maintenance services; inspection & diagnostic service, automotive

(G-3761)
INFUSION PARTNERS INC (HQ)
Also Called: Texas Infusion Partners
4623 Wesley Ave Ste H (45212-2272)
PHONE................................513 396-6060
Dana Soper, *Vice Pres*
Ray Di Saldo, *Vice Pres*
Tonya Osborne, *Accounts Exec*
▲ **EMP:** 27
SQ FT: 12,000
SALES (est): 12.6MM
SALES (corp-wide): 23.6MM **Privately Held**
SIC: 8082 Home health care services
PA: The Deaconess Associations Inc
    615 Elsinore Pl Bldg B
    Cincinnati OH 45202
    513 559-2100

(G-3762)
INNERWORKINGS INC
7141 E Kemper Rd (45249-1028)
PHONE................................513 984-9500
Danny Roundtree, *Opers Staff*
EMP: 32
SALES (corp-wide): 1.1B **Publicly Held**
SIC: 8742 Marketing consulting services
PA: Innerworkings, Inc.
    600 W Chicago Ave Ste 850
    Chicago IL 60654
    312 642-3700

(G-3763)
INREALITY LLC
403 Vine St Ste 200 (45202-2830)
PHONE...................................513 218-9603
John Decaprio, *CEO*
Michelle Murcia, *CFO*
EMP: 27
SALES: 5MM **Privately Held**
SIC: 7371 Computer software development & applications

(G-3764)
INSTITUTE/REPRODUCTIVE HEALTH
2123 Auburn Ave Ste A44 (45219-2906)
PHONE...................................513 585-2355
Michael D Scheiber MD, *Partner*
Sheris Awadalla MD, *Partner*
EMP: 25
SALES (est): 1.1MM **Privately Held**
SIC: 8011 General & family practice, physician/surgeon; fertility specialist, physician

(G-3765)
INSTRMNTATION CTRL SYSTEMS INC
Also Called: Ics Electrical Services
11355 Sebring Dr (45240-2796)
PHONE...................................513 662-2600
John Guenther, *President*
Darrenn Pegg, *Project Mgr*
▲ EMP: 43
SQ FT: 15,500
SALES (est): 7.6MM **Privately Held**
WEB: www.icselectricalservices.com
SIC: 1731 7629 3613 General electrical contractor; electric power systems contractors; electronic controls installation; fiber optic cable installation; electrical measuring instrument repair & calibration; control panels, electric

(G-3766)
INSULATING SALES CO INC
11430 Sebring Dr (45240-2791)
PHONE...................................513 742-2600
Steve Adam, *President*
Josh Adam, *Vice Pres*
Rebbeca Adam, *Vice Pres*
Thomas E Meckstroth, *Treasurer*
Becky Adam, *Info Tech Mgr*
EMP: 30
SQ FT: 8,000
SALES (est): 3MM **Privately Held**
SIC: 1742 Insulation, buildings

(G-3767)
INTEGRA GROUP INC
Also Called: Health Service Preferred
16 Triangle Park Dr # 1600 (45246-3411)
PHONE...................................513 326-5600
Kathleen Lutz, *President*
Mark Warner, *CIO*
Rose Longworth, *Executive*
Karen Cassidy, *Admin Asst*
EMP: 28
SALES (est): 2.5MM **Privately Held**
WEB: www.integragrp.com
SIC: 8742 Hospital & health services consultant

(G-3768)
INTEGRA OHIO INC
4900 Charlemar Dr Bldg A (45227-1595)
PHONE...................................513 378-5214
Chuck Gomien, *Principal*
EMP: 288
SALES (est): 1.8MM **Publicly Held**
WEB: www.integra-ls.com
SIC: 8741 Business management
PA: Integra Lifesciences Holdings Corporation
311 Enterprise Dr
Plainsboro NJ 08536

(G-3769)
INTEGRA REALTY RESOURCES - CIN
8241 Cornell Rd Ste 210 (45249-2285)
PHONE...................................513 561-2305
Gary Wright, *Principal*
EMP: 277

SALES (est): 7.2MM
SALES (corp-wide): 164.9MM **Privately Held**
SIC: 8742 Management consulting services
PA: Integra Realty Resources, Inc.
7800 E Union Ave Ste 400
Denver CO 80237
212 255-7858

(G-3770)
INTEGRATED PROTECTION SVCS INC (PA)
Also Called: I P S
5303 Lester Rd (45213-2523)
PHONE...................................513 631-5505
Garfield Hartman, *President*
Richard Keller, *COO*
Tim Kersting, *COO*
Andy Boyd, *Vice Pres*
Marla Ruffin, *Research*
EMP: 55
SQ FT: 15,000
SALES (est): 12.8MM **Privately Held**
WEB: www.integratedprotection.com
SIC: 7382 Burglar alarm maintenance & monitoring

(G-3771)
INTEGRITY EX LOGISTICS LLC (PA)
4420 Cooper Rd Ste 400 (45242-5660)
P.O. Box 42275 (45242-0275)
PHONE...................................888 374-5138
James Steger, *President*
Greg Hamilton, *Controller*
Eric Arling, *Director*
Matt Ventura,
Pete Ventura,
EMP: 287
SQ FT: 60,000
SALES (est): 139.9MM **Privately Held**
SIC: 4212 4731 Local trucking, without storage; truck transportation brokers

(G-3772)
INTELLIQ HEALTH
5050 Section Ave Ste 320 (45212-2052)
PHONE...................................513 489-8838
Robert V Miller, *President*
Ronald L Garner, *Vice Pres*
Lyn Kummer, *Vice Pres*
EMP: 60
SQ FT: 8,500
SALES (est): 3.7MM **Privately Held**
WEB: www.cooper-research.com
SIC: 8732 Marketing Analysis & Research

(G-3773)
INTER HEALT CARE OF CAMBR ZANE
Also Called: Interim Services
8050 Hosbrook Rd Ste 406 (45236-2907)
PHONE...................................513 984-1110
Tom Kirker, *Branch Mgr*
EMP: 27 **Privately Held**
SIC: 8049 8082 Nurses & other medical assistants; home health care services
PA: Interim Health Care Of Cambridge-Zanesville, Inc
960 Checkrein Ave Ste A
Columbus OH 43229

(G-3774)
INTERACT FOR HEALTH
Also Called: HEALTH FOUNDATION OF GREATER C
3805 Edwards Rd Ste 500 (45209-1948)
PHONE...................................513 458-6600
Donald E Hoffman, *CEO*
Jennifer Chubinski, *Vice Pres*
Patricia O'Connor, *Vice Pres*
Aaron Fleming, *Buyer*
Daniel Geeding, *CFO*
EMP: 30 **EST: 1978**
SQ FT: 27,490
SALES: 5.7MM **Privately Held**
SIC: 8399 Fund raising organization, non-fee basis

(G-3775)
INTERACTIVE BUS SYSTEMS INC
130 Tri County Pkwy # 208 (45246-3289)
PHONE...................................513 984-2205

Jeff Jorgensen, *General Mgr*
EMP: 40
SALES (corp-wide): 22MM **Privately Held**
WEB: www.ibs.com
SIC: 7379 Data processing consultant
PA: Interactive Business Systems, Inc.
2625 Bttrfeld Rd Ste 114w
Oak Brook IL 60523
630 571-9100

(G-3776)
INTERACTIVE SOLUTIONS INTL LLC
155 Tri County Pkwy 111 (45246-3238)
PHONE...................................513 619-5100
Rodney Sizemore, *Mng Member*
EMP: 26
SALES (est): 978.6K
SALES (corp-wide): 51.5MM **Privately Held**
WEB: www.citywatch.com
SIC: 8748 Communications consulting
PA: Avtex Solutions, Llc
3500 Amrcn Blvd W Ste 300
Minneapolis MN 55431
952 831-0888

(G-3777)
INTERBRAND DESIGN FORUM LLC
700 W Pete Rose Way # 460 (45203-1870)
PHONE...................................513 421-2210
D Lee Carpenter, *CEO*
Joseph Poulous, *Manager*
Scott Jeffrey, *Officer*
EMP: 225
SQ FT: 35,000
SALES (est): 26.3MM
SALES (corp-wide): 15.2B **Publicly Held**
WEB: www.designforum.com
SIC: 8742 7389 8711 Planning consultant; merchandising consultant; interior design services; engineering services
HQ: Interbrand Corporation
195 Broadway Fl 18
New York NY 10007
212 798-7500

(G-3778)
INTERBRAND HULEFELD INC
700 W Pete Rose Way (45203-1892)
PHONE...................................513 421-2210
Bruce Dyvbad, *President*
EMP: 80
SQ FT: 23,000
SALES: 16MM
SALES (corp-wide): 15.2B **Publicly Held**
WEB: www.interbrandcinti.com
SIC: 7336 Graphic arts & related design
HQ: Interbrand Corporation
195 Broadway Fl 18
New York NY 10007
212 798-7500

(G-3779)
INTERNATIONAL HEALTHCARE CORP
2837 Burnet Ave (45219-2401)
PHONE...................................513 731-3338
EMP: 85
SQ FT: 2,288
SIC: 8082 6411 Home health care services; insurance agents, brokers & service
PA: International Healthcare Corporation
6937 N Main St
Dayton OH 45415

(G-3780)
INTERNATIONAL UNION UNITED AU
Also Called: Uaw Local 863
10708 Reading Rd (45241-2529)
PHONE...................................513 563-1252
Tom Klein, *Branch Mgr*
EMP: 82
SALES (corp-wide): 237.6MM **Privately Held**
SIC: 8631 Labor union

PA: International Union, United Automobile, Aerospace And Agricultural Implement Workers Of Am
8000 E Jefferson Ave
Detroit MI 48214
313 926-5000

(G-3781)
INTERSTATE TRUCKWAY INC (PA)
Also Called: Truckway Leasing
1755 Dreman Ave (45223-2445)
PHONE...................................513 542-5500
Ron Horstman, *President*
Jeff Barber, *Vice Pres*
Robert Jones, *Vice Pres*
Shawn Watson, *Vice Pres*
Howard Elmore, *Opers Staff*
EMP: 70
SALES: 68.6MM **Privately Held**
WEB: www.itdsdedicated.com
SIC: 7513 5012 Truck rental & leasing, no drivers; commercial vehicles

(G-3782)
INTGRTED BRIDGE COMMUNICATIONS
302 W 3rd St Ste 900 (45202-3424)
PHONE...................................513 381-1380
Jay Woffington, *President*
Steve Fader, *Principal*
EMP: 35
SALES (est): 2MM **Privately Held**
WEB: www.bridgeagency.com
SIC: 4813 7812 ; audio-visual program production

(G-3783)
INTITLE AGENCY INC
120 E 4th St Ste 400 (45202-4010)
PHONE...................................513 241-8780
Richard Rothfuss, *CFO*
Janis Dorgan, *CFO*
Jan Dorgan, *Treasurer*
EMP: 100
SALES (est): 3.3MM **Privately Held**
SIC: 6541 Title & trust companies

(G-3784)
INTREN INC
Also Called: Midwest East Division
1267 Tennessee Ave (45229-1011)
PHONE...................................815 482-0651
Brian Carlin, *Manager*
EMP: 44
SALES (corp-wide): 159.6MM **Privately Held**
SIC: 8711 Construction & civil engineering; consulting engineer
PA: Intren, Llc
18202 W Union Rd
Union IL 60180
815 923-2300

(G-3785)
IPSOS-ASI LLC
Also Called: Ipsos-Asi, Inc.
3505 Columbia Pkwy # 300 (45226-2181)
PHONE...................................513 872-4300
Denice Patton, *Principal*
Marilyn O'Brien, *Co-Owner*
EMP: 60
SQ FT: 1,000
SALES (est): 4.8MM
SALES (corp-wide): 475.9K **Privately Held**
WEB: www.understandingunlimited.com
SIC: 8742 8732 Marketing consulting services; commercial nonphysical research
HQ: Ipsos America, Inc
360 Park Ave S Fl 17
New York NY 10010
212 265-3200

(G-3786)
IPSOS-INSIGHT LLC
11499 Chester Rd Ste 401 (45246-4012)
PHONE...................................513 552-1100
Lisa Lanier, *Principal*
EMP: 120
SALES (corp-wide): 475.9K **Privately Held**
WEB: www.ipsos-asi.com
SIC: 8732 Market analysis or research

HQ: Ipsos-Insight, Llc
   1600 Stewart Ave Ste 500
   Westbury NY 11590
   248 332-5000

(G-3787)
IRON MOUNTAIN INFO MGT LLC
5845 Highland Ridge Dr (45232-1441)
PHONE...................................513 297-3268
Brian Burnhard, *Manager*
EMP: 38
SALES (corp-wide): 4.2B **Publicly Held**
SIC: 4226 Document & office records storage
HQ: Iron Mountain Information Management, Llc
   1 Federal St
   Boston MA 02110
   800 899-4766

(G-3788)
ISQFT INC (HQ)
Also Called: Constructconnect
3825 Edwards Rd Ste 800 (45209-1289)
PHONE...................................513 645-8004
Dave Conway, *President*
Maria Sagrati, *Regional Mgr*
Fred Pugh, *COO*
Scott Waterbury, *COO*
Jon Kost, *Exec VP*
EMP: 132
SQ FT: 30,000
SALES (est): 75.7MM
SALES (corp-wide): 5.1B **Publicly Held**
WEB: www.isqft.com
SIC: 7371 5045 Computer software development; computer software
PA: Roper Technologies, Inc.
   6901 Prof Pkwy E Ste 200
   Sarasota FL 34240
   941 556-2601

(G-3789)
ISRAEL ADATH (PA)
3201 E Galbraith Rd (45236-1307)
PHONE...................................513 793-1800
Irvin Wise, *President*
Debbie Lempert, *Vice Pres*
Mollie Newman, *Marketing Staff*
Barbara Bresler, *Librarian*
Mitch Cohen, *Director*
EMP: 25
SALES (est): 1.3MM **Privately Held**
SIC: 8351 8661 Child day care services; synagogue

(G-3790)
ITELLIGENCE INC (DH)
10856 Reed Hartman Hwy (45242-2820)
PHONE...................................513 956-2000
Herbert Vogel, *CEO*
Steven Niesman, *President*
Shauna Keating-Schroot, *Business Mgr*
Uwe Bohnhorst, *Exec VP*
Andreas Pauls, *Exec VP*
EMP: 110
SALES (est): 95.9MM
SALES (corp-wide): 110.7B **Privately Held**
SIC: 7379 Computer related consulting services
HQ: Itelligence Ag
   Konigsbreede 1
   Bielefeld 33605
   521 914-480

(G-3791)
ITELLIGENCE OUTSOURCING INC (DH)
Also Called: Schmidt-Vogel Consulting
10856 Reed Hartman Hwy (45242-2820)
PHONE...................................513 956-2000
Steven Niesman, *President*
Brad Wolfe, *Vice Pres*
Ken Golisch, *CFO*
Ryan Schisler, *Sr Software Eng*
EMP: 80
SQ FT: 4,000
SALES (est): 10.7MM
SALES (corp-wide): 110.7B **Privately Held**
WEB: www.itelligencegroup.com
SIC: 7379

(G-3792)
IVY HEALTH CARE INC (PA)
Also Called: Ivy Woods Care Center
2025 Wyoming Ave (45205-1112)
PHONE...................................513 251-2557
Harold Sosna, *President*
EMP: 105
SALES: 7.5MM **Privately Held**
WEB: www.ivywoodscare.com
SIC: 8051 Convalescent home with continuous nursing care

(G-3793)
J & E LLC
Also Called: Chavez Properties
250 W Court St Ste 200e (45202-1064)
PHONE...................................513 241-0429
Robert Chavez, *Partner*
Manuel Chavez Sr, *Partner*
Carl Fisher, *Finance*
Pete Guggenheim, *Marketing Staff*
Beth Freemal, *General Counsel*
EMP: 30
SQ FT: 8,100
SALES (est): 3MM **Privately Held**
SIC: 6519 Real property lessors

(G-3794)
J E F INC
Also Called: Westside Health Care
1857 Grand Ave (45214-1503)
PHONE...................................513 921-4130
Jacob Fischer, *President*
Eta Fischer, *Vice Pres*
Abe Fischer, *Treasurer*
EMP: 55
SQ FT: 20,000
SALES (est): 1.6MM **Privately Held**
WEB: www.jef.com
SIC: 8059 Convalescent home; rest home, with health care

(G-3795)
J FELDKAMP DESIGN BUILD LTD
10036 Springfield Pike (45215-1452)
PHONE...................................513 870-0601
Jody Feldkamp, *President*
Robert Boggs, *Principal*
Jonathan Feldkamp, *Vice Pres*
Jonathan W Feldkamp, *Vice Pres*
Elisa Feldkamp, *CFO*
EMP: 42
SQ FT: 18,000
SALES: 3.7MM **Privately Held**
SIC: 1711 3499 Heating & air conditioning contractors; plumbing contractors; aerosol valves, metal

(G-3796)
J RUTLEDGE ENTERPRISES INC
Also Called: Rutledge Environmental Svcs
3512 Spring Grove Ave (45223-2448)
PHONE...................................502 241-4100
H Jack Rutledge, *President*
EMP: 35
SQ FT: 15,000
SALES (est): 1.3MM **Privately Held**
WEB: www.rutledgeenvironmental.com
SIC: 7349 Building maintenance services

(G-3797)
JACK & JILL BABYSITTING SVC
Also Called: Jack & Jill Babysitter Serv
6252 Beechmont Ave Apt 11 (45230-1930)
PHONE...................................513 731-5261
Nancy Yeatts, *Owner*
N Yates, *Owner*
EMP: 28
SALES (est): 290.3K **Privately Held**
SIC: 7299 Babysitting bureau

(G-3798)
JACK CINCINNATI CASINO LLC
1000 Broadway St (45202-1364)
PHONE...................................513 252-0777
Dougy Phillips, *Owner*
Deborah Davis, *Vice Pres*
EMP: 32
SALES (est): 3.2MM **Privately Held**
SIC: 7011 Casino hotel

(G-3799)
JACK GRAY
Also Called: Jack, The
8044 Montgomery Rd (45236-2919)
PHONE...................................216 688-0466
Jack Gray, *Owner*
EMP: 51
SALES: 6MM **Privately Held**
SIC: 1521 6552 General remodeling, single-family houses; subdividers & developers

(G-3800)
JACOBS CONSTRUCTORS INC
1880 Waycross Rd (45240-2825)
PHONE...................................513 595-7900
John Kadkah, *Manager*
EMP: 35
SALES (corp-wide): 14.9B **Publicly Held**
SIC: 1629 Land preparation construction
HQ: Jacobs Constructors, Inc.
   4949 Essen Ln
   Baton Rouge LA 70809
   225 769-7700

(G-3801)
JACOBS ENGINEERING GROUP INC
1880 Waycross Rd (45240-2825)
PHONE...................................513 595-7500
Craig Martin, *President*
Greg Rumsord, *General Mgr*
Pat Sanders, *Project Mgr*
Vijay Doshi, *Engineer*
Chet Kovaleski, *Engineer*
EMP: 40
SALES (corp-wide): 10B **Publicly Held**
WEB: www.jacobs.com
SIC: 8711 Consulting engineer
PA: Jacobs Engineering Group Inc.
   1999 Bryan St Ste 1200
   Dallas TX 75201
   214 583-8500

(G-3802)
JACOBS ENGINEERING GROUP INC
1880 Waycross Rd (45240-2825)
PHONE...................................513 595-7500
Ken Alkema, *Manager*
EMP: 88
SALES (corp-wide): 10B **Publicly Held**
WEB: www.jacobs.com
SIC: 8711 Consulting engineer
PA: Jacobs Engineering Group Inc.
   1999 Bryan St Ste 1200
   Dallas TX 75201
   214 583-8500

(G-3803)
JACOBS MECHANICAL CO
4500 W Mitchell Ave (45232-1912)
PHONE...................................513 681-6800
John E Mc Donald, *President*
EMP: 125
SQ FT: 20,000
SALES (est): 24.4MM **Privately Held**
WEB: www.jacobsmech.com
SIC: 1711 3444 Ventilation & duct work contractor; sheet metalwork

(G-3804)
JAGI JUNO LLC (PA)
Also Called: Holiday Inn
8534 E Kemper Rd (45249-3701)
PHONE...................................513 489-1955
Barb Soete,
EMP: 40
SALES (est): 1.5MM **Privately Held**
SIC: 7011 Hotels & motels

(G-3805)
JAKE SWEENEY AUTOMOTIVE INC
33 W Kemper Rd (45246-2509)
PHONE...................................513 782-2800
Jake Sweeney Jr, *President*
Gregory D Sweeney, *Vice Pres*
Rob Hall, *Sales Staff*
EMP: 200
SQ FT: 60,000
SALES (est): 19.8MM **Privately Held**
WEB: www.jakesweeney.com
SIC: 8741 7538 7532 7515 Management services; general automotive repair shops; top & body repair & paint shops; passenger car leasing; used car dealers; new & used car dealers

(G-3806)
JAKE SWEENEY BODY SHOP
Also Called: Jake Sweeney Chevrolet Imports
169 Northland Blvd Ste 1 (45246-3154)
PHONE...................................513 782-1100
Jake Sweeney, *Owner*
Fred Mangold, *General Mgr*
Scotty Rienschield, *Sales Mgr*
Morgan Thomas, *Sales Staff*
EMP: 30
SQ FT: 21,892
SALES (est): 1.9MM **Privately Held**
SIC: 7532 Body shop, automotive

(G-3807)
JAMES HUNT CONSTRUCTION CO INC
1865 Summit Rd (45237-2803)
PHONE...................................513 721-0559
Veronica Davis, *President*
David Thierry, *Superintendent*
Chris Davis, *Vice Pres*
Rich Hinton, *Project Mgr*
Danny Rusconi, *Project Mgr*
EMP: 30
SQ FT: 5,000
SALES (est): 18.2MM **Privately Held**
SIC: 1542 Commercial & office buildings, renovation & repair; commercial & office building, new construction

(G-3808)
JANCOA JANITORIAL SERVICES INC
5235 Montgomery Rd (45212-1655)
PHONE...................................513 351-7200
Mary Miller, *CEO*
Anthony Miller, *President*
Clint Bard, *COO*
Soraya Bass, *Human Res Mgr*
Amy Miller, *Accounts Mgr*
EMP: 275
SALES (est): 10.2MM **Privately Held**
WEB: www.jancoa.com
SIC: 7349 Janitorial service, contract basis

(G-3809)
JAVITCH BLOCK LLC
Also Called: Mapother & Mapother Attorneys
700 Walnut St Ste 300 (45202-2011)
PHONE...................................513 381-3051
Robert Hogan, *Managing Prtnr*
Robert K Hogan, *Manager*
EMP: 31
SALES (corp-wide): 58.1MM **Privately Held**
WEB: www.jber.com
SIC: 8111 General practice law office
PA: Javitch Block Llc
   1100 Superior Ave E Fl 19
   Cleveland OH 44114
   216 623-0000

(G-3810)
JBJS ACQUISITIONS LLC
Also Called: Alleen Company, The
11939 Tramway Dr (45241-1666)
PHONE...................................513 769-0393
Rachael Barnes, *COO*
Kenny Kaeser, *Warehouse Mgr*
Barbara Schull, *Mng Member*
Roger Hail, *Social Dir*
EMP: 35 EST: 1951
SQ FT: 36,000
SALES (est): 5.2MM **Privately Held**
SIC: 7359 7389 Party supplies rental services; convention & show services

(G-3811)
JEDSON ENGINEERING INC (PA)
705 Central Ave (45202-1967)
PHONE...................................513 965-5999
Rachid Abdallah, *CEO*
John Vignale, *President*
Tom Cress, *Project Mgr*
Angela Carroll, *CFO*

Jeff Holloman, *Manager*
EMP: 90
SQ FT: 20,000
SALES (est): 44.2MM Privately Held
WEB: www.jedson.com
SIC: 8711 Industrial engineers; electrical or electronic engineering; consulting engineer

(G-3812)
JESS HAUER MASONRY INC
2400 W Kemper Rd (45231-1137)
PHONE...................................513 521-2178
Michael Hauer, *President*
Jason Hauer, *Vice Pres*
Jess Hauer, *Vice Pres*
Denise Dunn, *Treasurer*
EMP: 40
SQ FT: 2,450
SALES: 4MM Privately Held
SIC: 1741 Bricklaying; concrete block masonry laying

(G-3813)
JETSON ENGINEERING
705 Central Ave (45202-1967)
PHONE...................................513 965-5999
Judson Tammy, *Principal*
EMP: 69
SALES (est): 13.4MM Privately Held
SIC: 8711 Consulting engineer

(G-3814)
JEWISH COMMUNITY CENTER INC
8485 Ridge Rd (45236-1300)
PHONE...................................513 761-7500
Roz Kaplan, *Exec Dir*
Tsipora Gopplieb, *Director*
Erika Aanestad, *Asst Director*
EMP: 90
SQ FT: 150,000
SALES (est): 7.9MM Privately Held
WEB: www.jcc-cinci.com
SIC: 8641 Community membership club

(G-3815)
JEWISH FAMILY SERVICE OF
8487 Ridge Rd (45236-1300)
PHONE...................................513 469-1188
John Youkilif, *President*
Doug Sandor, *CFO*
Hannah Gessendorf, *Marketing Staff*
Paula Tompkins, *Office Mgr*
Lilly Narusevich, *Case Mgr*
EMP: 40
SALES: 4.8MM Privately Held
WEB: www.jfscinti.org
SIC: 8322 Family service agency

(G-3816)
JEWISH FDERATION OF CINCINNATI
8499 Ridge Rd (45236-1300)
PHONE...................................513 985-1500
Shepard Englander, *CEO*
Bret Caller, *President*
AVI Ram, *COO*
Reagan Kuhn, *Project Mgr*
Ellen Daniel, *Pub Rel Mgr*
EMP: 35
SALES: 20.5MM Privately Held
SIC: 8322 Social service center

(G-3817)
JEWISH HOSPITAL LLC
4777 E Galbraith Rd (45236-2814)
P.O. Box 636641 (45263-6641)
PHONE...................................513 686-3000
Pam Vansant, *Vice Pres*
Sam Cordary, *Safety Mgr*
John Herold III, *Anesthesiology*
Shaka James, *Anesthesiology*
Anuradha Kulkarni, *Anesthesiology*
▲ EMP: 1700
SALES (est): 185.5MM Privately Held
SIC: 8062 General medical & surgical hospitals

(G-3818)
JEWISH HOSPITAL CINCINNATI INC
4777 E Galbraith Rd (45236-2814)
PHONE...................................513 686-3303
Patricia Davis-Hagens, *President*

Craig Schmidt, *COO*
▲ EMP: 2500
SQ FT: 1,000,000
SALES: 21.9K
SALES (corp-wide): 4.7B Privately Held
SIC: 8062 General medical & surgical hospitals
HQ: Mercy Health Cincinnati Llc
1701 Mercy Health Pl
Cincinnati OH 45237
513 952-5000

(G-3819)
JIM HAYDEN INC
3154 Exon Ave (45241-2548)
PHONE...................................513 563-8828
Jim Hayden, *President*
Ruth Hayden, *Treasurer*
Lisa Hayden, *Admin Sec*
EMP: 86
SQ FT: 24,000
SALES: 9.1MM Privately Held
SIC: 5013 5531 5731 Seat covers; automotive supplies & parts; automotive accessories; sound equipment, automotive

(G-3820)
JLW MARKETING LLC
4240 Airport Rd Ste 106 (45226-1629)
PHONE...................................513 260-8418
Jerry Jenkins, *Principal*
Daniel Listo, *Principal*
EMP: 80
SQ FT: 2,500
SALES (est): 3MM Privately Held
SIC: 7389

(G-3821)
JOE LASITA & SONS INC
940 W 5th St (45203-1848)
PHONE...................................513 241-5288
Dan Lasita, *President*
Joe Lasita, *Principal*
John M Lasita, *Principal*
Vincent C Lasita, *Principal*
Jerry Lasita, *CFO*
EMP: 35
SQ FT: 30,000
SALES (est): 19.8MM Privately Held
WEB: www.lasitaproduce.com
SIC: 5148 Fruits, fresh; vegetables, fresh

(G-3822)
JOHN A BECKER CO
Also Called: Becker Electric Supply
11310 Mosteller Rd (45241-1828)
PHONE...................................513 771-2550
Jim Dichito, *Sales/Mktg Mgr*
EMP: 65
SQ FT: 18,880
SALES (corp-wide): 219.3MM Privately Held
WEB: www.beckerelectric.com
SIC: 5063 Electrical supplies
PA: The John A Becker Co
1341 E 4th St
Dayton OH 45402
937 226-1341

(G-3823)
JOHN H COOPER ELEC CONTG CO
1769 Elmore St (45223-2482)
PHONE...................................513 471-9900
Gregory T Hyland, *President*
Martha A Hyland, *Admin Sec*
EMP: 26
SQ FT: 3,200
SALES (est): 4.8MM Privately Held
WEB: www.cooper-electric.net
SIC: 1731 General electrical contractor

(G-3824)
JOHN STEWART COMPANY
6819 Montgomery Rd (45236-3818)
PHONE...................................513 703-5412
John Stewart, *Branch Mgr*
EMP: 57
SALES (corp-wide): 106.4MM Privately Held
SIC: 6531 Real estate managers
PA: John Stewart Company
1388 Sutter St Ste 1100
San Francisco CA 94109
213 833-1860

(G-3825)
JOHNNYS CARWASH
7901 Beechmont Ave (45255-4212)
PHONE...................................513 474-6603
Kevin Mc Clurley, *Owner*
EMP: 55
SALES (est): 830.4K Privately Held
SIC: 7542 Washing & polishing, automotive

(G-3826)
JOHNSON CNTRLS SEC SLTIONS LLC
4750 Wesley Ave Ste Q (45212-2273)
PHONE...................................513 277-4966
Tereasa Schott, *Manager*
EMP: 25 Privately Held
WEB: www.adt.com
SIC: 7382 Protective devices, security
HQ: Johnson Controls Security Solutions Llc
6600 Congress Ave
Boca Raton FL 33487
561 264-2071

(G-3827)
JOHNSON CONTROLS INC
7863 Palace Dr (45249-1635)
PHONE...................................513 489-0950
Brian Ballitch, *Branch Mgr*
EMP: 52 Privately Held
SIC: 1711 Plumbing, heating, air-conditioning contractors
HQ: Johnson Controls, Inc.
5757 N Green Bay Ave
Milwaukee WI 53209
414 524-1200

(G-3828)
JOHNSON ELECTRIC SUPPLY CO (PA)
1841 Riverside Dr (45202-1738)
PHONE...................................513 421-3700
Douglas Johnson, *President*
W M Beinhart, *Principal*
A B Horton, *Principal*
Wm J McCauley, *Principal*
Robert White, *Corp Secy*
EMP: 34 EST: 1907
SQ FT: 48,000
SALES: 15MM Privately Held
WEB: www.johnson-electric.com
SIC: 5063 Electrical construction materials; lighting fixtures

(G-3829)
JOHNSON HOWARD INTERNATIONAL
Also Called: Howard Johnson
400 Glensprings Dr (45246-2306)
PHONE...................................513 401-8683
Robert Eckley, *Branch Mgr*
EMP: 30 Privately Held
SIC: 7011 Hotels & motels
HQ: Howard Johnson International Inc
22 Sylvan Way
Parsippany NJ 07054

(G-3830)
JOHNSON TRUST CO
Also Called: Johnson Institutional MGT
3777 W Fork Rd Fl 2 (45247-7575)
PHONE...................................513 598-8859
Timothy E Johnson, *CEO*
Ryan W Easter, *Project Mgr*
Dale Coates, *Portfolio Mgr*
Maria Seda, *Financial Exec*
Joyce Waters, *Business Dir*
EMP: 120
SALES (est): 10.3MM Privately Held
SIC: 6282 Investment counselors

(G-3831)
JONLE CO INC
Also Called: Jonle Heating & Cooling
4117 Bridgetown Rd (45211-4503)
PHONE...................................513 662-2282
Gregory Leisgang, *President*
Julie Gerhardt, *Treasurer*
Mike Breiner, *Sales Staff*
Ray Huber, *Manager*
Trishia Doyle, *Office Admin*
EMP: 38
SQ FT: 9,000

SALES (est): 5.2MM Privately Held
SIC: 1711 Warm air heating & air conditioning contractor; heating & air conditioning contractors

(G-3832)
JORDAN REALTORS INC
7658 Montgomery Rd (45236-4204)
PHONE...................................513 791-0281
Kenneth G Jordan, *President*
Jeffrey L Jordan, *Exec VP*
Michael W Jordan, *Exec VP*
Jeanne Jordan, *Broker*
Shannon Goodman, *Assistant*
EMP: 44
SQ FT: 4,000
SALES (est): 2.2MM Privately Held
WEB: www.jordan-realtors.com
SIC: 6531 Real estate agent, residential

(G-3833)
JOSEPH CHEVROLET OLDSMOBILE CO
8733 Colerain Ave (45251-2992)
PHONE...................................513 741-6700
Ronald Joseph, *Ch of Bd*
Louis Rouse, *Corp Secy*
EMP: 110 EST: 1965
SQ FT: 50,000
SALES (est): 38MM Privately Held
WEB: www.josephchevrolet.com
SIC: 5511 5521 7538 7532 Automobiles, new & used; trucks, tractors & trailers: new & used; used car dealers; general automotive repair shops; top & body repair & paint shops

(G-3834)
JOSEPH S MISCHELL
5109 Winton Rd (45232-1508)
PHONE...................................513 542-9800
Joseph S Mischell, *Principal*
EMP: 30 EST: 2012
SALES (est): 267.4K Privately Held
SIC: 7215 Laundry machine routes, coin-operated

(G-3835)
JOSTIN CONSTRUCTION INC
2335 Florence Ave (45206-2430)
PHONE...................................513 559-9390
Albert C Smitherman, *President*
Mike Mattis, *Vice Pres*
Mike Vieth, *VP Opers*
Andrew Brueggen, *Project Mgr*
Vince Enderle, *Project Mgr*
EMP: 50
SQ FT: 16,000
SALES (est): 7.9MM Privately Held
WEB: www.jostinconcrete.com
SIC: 1771 Concrete work

(G-3836)
JPMORGAN CHASE BANK NAT ASSN
4805 Montgomery Rd (45212-2198)
PHONE...................................513 221-1040
EMP: 26
SALES (corp-wide): 131.4B Publicly Held
SIC: 6021 National commercial banks
HQ: Jpmorgan Chase Bank, National Association
1111 Polaris Pkwy
Columbus OH 43240
614 436-3055

(G-3837)
JPMORGAN CHASE BANK NAT ASSN
822 Delta Ave (45226-1256)
PHONE...................................513 985-5120
Sheree Rosfeld, *Principal*
EMP: 26
SALES (corp-wide): 131.4B Publicly Held
SIC: 6021 National commercial banks
HQ: Jpmorgan Chase Bank, National Association
1111 Polaris Pkwy
Columbus OH 43240
614 436-3055

(G-3838)
JPMORGAN CHASE BANK NAT ASSN
45 E 4th St (45202-3731)
PHONE..................513 784-0770
Erik P Hoffman, *Principal*
EMP: 26
SALES (corp-wide): 131.4B **Publicly Held**
SIC: 6029 Commercial banks
HQ: Jpmorgan Chase Bank, National Association
1111 Polaris Pkwy
Columbus OH 43240
614 436-3055

(G-3839)
JPMORGAN CHASE BANK NAT ASSN
11745 Princeton Pike (45246-2521)
PHONE..................513 595-6450
Diane Draman, *Principal*
Kevin Jordan, *Site Mgr*
EMP: 26
SALES (corp-wide): 131.4B **Publicly Held**
SIC: 6021 National commercial banks
HQ: Jpmorgan Chase Bank, National Association
1111 Polaris Pkwy
Columbus OH 43240
614 436-3055

(G-3840)
JUDSON CARE CENTER INC
2373 Harrison Ave (45211-7927)
PHONE..................513 662-5880
George Repchick, *President*
William Weisberg, *Vice Pres*
Sarah Depompei, *Assistant*
EMP: 40
SQ FT: 59,607
SALES: 8MM
SALES (corp-wide): 157.7MM **Privately Held**
SIC: 8051 8052 Skilled nursing care facilities; personal care facility
PA: Saber Healthcare Group, L.L.C.
26691 Richmond Rd Frnt
Bedford OH 44146
216 292-5706

(G-3841)
JUDY MILLS COMPANY INC (PA)
3360 Red Bank Rd (45227-4107)
PHONE..................513 271-4241
Mike Judy, *President*
EMP: 36 EST: 1922
SALES (est): 6.9MM **Privately Held**
SIC: 6512 5211 2431 Commercial & industrial building operation; lumber & other building materials; millwork

(G-3842)
K - O - I WAREHOUSE INC (DH)
Also Called: K O I Auto Parts
2701 Spring Grove Ave (45225-2221)
P.O. Box 14240 (45250-0240)
PHONE..................513 357-2400
David Wesselman, *President*
Mary Riesenbeck, *Corp Secy*
Tom Frank, *CFO*
▲ EMP: 50 EST: 1966
SQ FT: 9,000
SALES (est): 50.8MM
SALES (corp-wide): 834.8MM **Privately Held**
WEB: www.koiwarehouse.com
SIC: 5013 Automotive supplies & parts
HQ: K.O.I. Enterprises, Inc.
2701 Spring Grove Ave
Cincinnati OH 45225
513 357-2400

(G-3843)
K F T INC
726 Mehring Way (45203-1809)
PHONE..................513 241-5910
Ronald Eubanks, *President*
EMP: 60
SQ FT: 45,000
SALES (est): 6.1MM **Privately Held**
WEB: www.tkf.com
SIC: 1796 3535 Millwright; machinery installation; overhead conveyor systems

(G-3844)
K R DRENTH TRUCKING INC
119 E Court St (45202-1203)
PHONE..................708 983-6340
Kristine Roy, *Principal*
EMP: 67 **Privately Held**
SIC: 4212 Dump truck haulage
PA: K. R. Drenth Trucking, Inc.
20340 Stoney Island Ave
Chicago Heights IL 60411

(G-3845)
K4 ARCHITECTURE LLC
555 Gest St (45203-1716)
PHONE..................513 455-5005
David Noell, *Vice Pres*
John A Schaefer, *Vice Pres*
Sandy Tenhundfeld, *Project Mgr*
John Schaefer, *Sales Executive*
Dale Schultz, *Director*
EMP: 60 EST: 1998
SQ FT: 25,000
SALES (est): 10MM **Privately Held**
WEB: www.k4arch.com
SIC: 8712 Architectural engineering

(G-3846)
KAFFENBARGER TRUCK EQP CO
3260 E Kemper Rd (45241-1519)
PHONE..................513 772-6800
Rodney Swigert, *Manager*
EMP: 35
SQ FT: 18,280
SALES (corp-wide): 38MM **Privately Held**
WEB: www.kaffenbarger.com
SIC: 7538 5531 3713 3532 Truck engine repair, except industrial; truck equipment & parts; truck bodies & parts; mining machinery; construction machinery
PA: Kaffenbarger Truck Equipment Co Inc
10100 Ballentine Pike
New Carlisle OH 45344
937 845-3804

(G-3847)
KAO COLLINS INC (PA)
1201 Edison Dr (45216-2277)
PHONE..................513 948-9000
Lawrence Gamblin, *President*
Chris Rogers, *Vice Pres*
Bob Hendricks, *CFO*
Lisa Gamblin, *Treasurer*
▲ EMP: 57
SQ FT: 8,700
SALES (est): 70.8MM **Privately Held**
WEB: www.collinsink.com
SIC: 5043 5946 Photographic equipment & supplies; camera & photographic supply stores

(G-3848)
KATZ TELLER BRANT HILD CO LPA
Also Called: Katz Teller
255 E 5th St Fl 24 (45202-4724)
PHONE..................513 721-4532
Katz Teller, *President*
Mark Jahnke, *President*
Joseph A Brant, *Counsel*
Jerome S Teller, *Vice Pres*
Guy Hild, *Treasurer*
EMP: 65 EST: 1967
SALES (est): 8.9MM **Privately Held**
WEB: www.katzteller.com
SIC: 8111 General practice attorney, lawyer; general practice law office

(G-3849)
KCBS LLC
7800 E Kemper Rd Ste 160 (45249-1665)
PHONE..................513 421-9422
Robert Lynn Sarsgard,
EMP: 35
SQ FT: 1,500
SALES (est): 3.8MM **Privately Held**
SIC: 5141 Food brokers

(G-3850)
KEATING MUETHING & KLEKAMP PLL (PA)
Also Called: Kmk
1 E 4th St Ste 1400 (45202-3752)
PHONE..................513 579-6400

Donald P Klekamp, *Senior Partner*
Stephen Goodson, *Senior Partner*
Gary Kreider, *Senior Partner*
Joseph Mellen, *Senior Partner*
David Rosenberg, *Senior Partner*
EMP: 400
SQ FT: 60,000
SALES (est): 49MM **Privately Held**
WEB: www.kmklaw.com
SIC: 8111 General practice attorney, lawyer

(G-3851)
KEEN & CROSS ENVMTL SVCS INC
504 Northland Blvd (45240-3213)
PHONE..................513 674-1700
Edwin Keen, *President*
Don Cross, *Vice Pres*
EMP: 30
SQ FT: 6,500
SALES: 3.4MM **Privately Held**
SIC: 1799 Asbestos removal & encapsulation

(G-3852)
KEIDEL SUPPLY COMPANY INC (PA)
1150 Tennessee Ave (45229-1010)
PHONE..................513 351-1600
Michael Barton, *Ch of Bd*
Barry Keidel, *President*
Gordon Hemsink, *Store Mgr*
Andy Hemsath, *Purch Mgr*
Chris Siemer, *Buyer*
EMP: 49 EST: 1954
SQ FT: 20,000
SALES (est): 50.8MM **Privately Held**
WEB: www.keidel.com
SIC: 5074 5031 5099 Plumbing fittings & supplies; kitchen cabinets; firearms & ammunition, except sporting

(G-3853)
KELLER WILLIAMS ADVISORS LLC
3505 Columbia Pkwy # 125 (45226-2188)
PHONE..................513 766-9200
Sarah Benza, *Mng Member*
EMP: 40
SALES (est): 1.9MM **Privately Held**
SIC: 6531 Real estate agent, residential

(G-3854)
KELLER WILLIAMS ADVISORY RLTY
8276 Beechmont Ave (45255-3153)
PHONE..................513 372-6500
Monica Weakley, *Principal*
Julie E Evans, *COO*
EMP: 25 EST: 2012
SALES (est): 744.8K **Privately Held**
SIC: 6531 Real estate agent, residential; real estate brokers & agents

(G-3855)
KELLY FARRISH LPA
Also Called: Farrish & Farrish Lpa
810 Sycamore St Fl 6 (45202-2182)
PHONE..................513 621-8700
Kelly Farrish, *Owner*
Linda Kenkel, *Office Mgr*
Stephan D Madden, *Vice Pres*
Walter C Wurster,
EMP: 30
SALES (est): 2.6MM **Privately Held**
SIC: 8111 General practice attorney, lawyer

(G-3856)
KELLY YOUTH SERVICES INC
800 Compton Rd Unit 11 (45231-3846)
PHONE..................513 761-0700
Joe Kelly, *President*
Bob Kelly, *Administration*
EMP: 25 EST: 1997
SALES: 1.4MM **Privately Held**
SIC: 8322 Youth center

(G-3857)
KENCOR PROPERTIES INC
7565 Kenwood Rd Ste 100 (45236-2835)
PHONE..................513 984-3870
Greg Pancero, *President*
EMP: 50

SALES (est): 1.1MM **Privately Held**
SIC: 6531 Real estate managers

(G-3858)
KENDLE INTERNATIONAL INC
441 Vine St Ste 500 (45202-2858)
PHONE..................513 763-1414
Thomas Stilgenbauer, *Vice Pres*
EMP: 31 EST: 2014
SALES (est): 2.8MM **Privately Held**
SIC: 8733 Medical research

(G-3859)
KENMARC INC
Also Called: Kenmarc Electrical Contractors
1055 Heywood St (45225-2209)
PHONE..................513 541-2791
Ken Stenger, *President*
Mark Baverman, *Treasurer*
William Seitz III, *Admin Sec*
EMP: 25
SQ FT: 5,000
SALES: 3MM **Privately Held**
WEB: www.kenmarcelectric.com
SIC: 1731 General electrical contractor

(G-3860)
KENWOOD COUNTRY CLUB INC
6501 Kenwood Rd (45243-2315)
PHONE..................513 527-3590
Fred Habegger, *President*
Christy Pearman, *Office Mgr*
Alan Adolphson, *Manager*
Jason Kidd, *Manager*
Dan Plunkett, *Manager*
EMP: 200
SQ FT: 40,000
SALES: 9.1MM **Privately Held**
SIC: 7997 Country club, membership

(G-3861)
KENWOOD TER HLTH CARE CTR INC
Also Called: Kenwood Terrace Care Center
7450 Keller Rd (45243-1028)
PHONE..................513 793-2255
Harold Sosna, *President*
EMP: 145
SALES: 9.2MM **Privately Held**
SIC: 8051 Convalescent home with continuous nursing care

(G-3862)
KENWORTH OF CINCINNATI INC
Also Called: PacLease
65 Partnership Way (45241-1570)
P.O. Box 62477 (45262-0477)
PHONE..................513 771-5831
John Nichols, *President*
Ken Townley, *General Mgr*
Eldon Palmer, *Chairman*
Jeffrey Curry, *Vice Pres*
Steve Hedger, *Store Mgr*
EMP: 90
SQ FT: 32,000
SALES (est): 33.1MM **Privately Held**
SIC: 5012 5013 7538 7513 Trucks, commercial; truck parts & accessories; general automotive repair shops; truck leasing, without drivers

(G-3863)
KERKAN ROOFING INC
721 W Wyoming Ave (45215-4528)
PHONE..................513 821-0556
Dave Kern, *President*
Ken Hunt, *General Mgr*
Paul Snarski, *Opers Mgr*
Dave Reinhart, *Treasurer*
Mary Sparks, *Human Res Dir*
EMP: 72
SQ FT: 20,000
SALES (est): 12.7MM **Privately Held**
WEB: www.kerkan.com
SIC: 1761 Roofing contractor

(G-3864)
KERRY FORD INC (PA)
Also Called: Kerry Mitsubishi
155 W Kemper Rd (45246-2590)
PHONE..................513 671-6400
Patrick De Castro, *President*
Paul W Krone, *Principal*
Daniel J Brady, *Corp Secy*
Mark Chaney, *Parts Mgr*
Justin Hiatt, *Finance Mgr*

▲ = Import ▼=Export
◆ =Import/Export

EMP: 100
SQ FT: 50,000
SALES (est): 46MM **Privately Held**
SIC: 5511 7538 7532 7515 Automobiles, new & used; pickups, new & used; vans, new & used; general automotive repair shops; top & body repair & paint shops; passenger car leasing; automotive & home supply stores

(G-3865)
KEYSOURCE ACQUISITION LLC
Also Called: Keysource Medical
7820 Palace Dr (45249-1631)
PHONE.................................513 469-7881
Albert Paonessa, CEO
Stephanie Ring, Exec VP
Dyann Harris, Human Resources
Molly Borgquist, Sales Staff
Ryne Clark, Sales Staff
EMP: 45
SQ FT: 22,000
SALES (est): 21MM **Privately Held**
WEB: www.keysourcemedical.com
SIC: 5122 5047 Pharmaceuticals; medical equipment & supplies

(G-3866)
KEYSTONE AUTOMOTIVE INDS INC
2831 Stanton Ave (45206-1122)
PHONE.................................513 961-5500
Paul Howell, Manager
Crystal Garrett, Manager
EMP: 58
SALES (corp-wide): 11.8B **Publicly Held**
WEB: www.kool-vue.com
SIC: 5013 Automotive supplies & parts
HQ: Keystone Automotive Industries, Inc.
5846 Crossings Blvd
Antioch TN 37013
615 781-5200

(G-3867)
KIDNEY & HYPERTENSION CENTER (PA)
Also Called: Good Samaritan Hospital Med
2123 Auburn Ave 404 (45219-2906)
PHONE.................................513 861-0800
Kenneth Newmark, President
Mary K McMurry, Nurse Practr
EMP: 25
SALES (est): 6.4MM **Privately Held**
WEB: www.khc.cc
SIC: 8011 Nephrologist

(G-3868)
KILGORE GROUP INC
Also Called: Columbia Staffing
201 E 4th St Ste 800 (45202-4248)
PHONE.................................513 684-3721
Sasha Garcia, Accounts Mgr
Suzanne Perry, Director
Juli Strawn, Receptionist
EMP: 35
SALES (corp-wide): 20.4B **Privately Held**
SIC: 7363 7361 Temporary help service; employment agencies
HQ: Kilgore Group, Inc.
4700 Forest Dr Ste 200
Columbia SC 29206
803 782-2000

(G-3869)
KILLER SPOTSCOM INC
Also Called: Killer Creative Media
463 Ohio Pike Ste 301 (45255-3722)
PHONE.................................513 201-1380
Storm Bennett, CEO
James H Bennet III, Vice Pres
EMP: 75
SQ FT: 4,000
SALES (est): 6.5MM **Privately Held**
WEB: www.killerspots.com
SIC: 7313 7812 5065 Radio advertising representative; video production; tapes, audio & video recording

(G-3870)
KINDER MRGAN LQDS TRMINALS LLC
5297 River Rd (45233-1642)
P.O. Box 33041 (45233-0041)
PHONE.................................513 841-0500
Connie Santa Vicca,

EMP: 48 **Publicly Held**
SIC: 4922 Natural gas transmission
HQ: Kinder Morgan Liquids Terminals Llc
1001 La St Ste 1000
Houston TX 77002
713 369-9000

(G-3871)
KINDERCARE LEARNING CTRS LLC
Also Called: Kindercare Child Care Network
1459 E Kemper Rd (45246-3905)
PHONE.................................513 771-8787
Jamie Schumacher, Manager
Lynnette Dowers, Director
EMP: 30
SALES (corp-wide): 1.2B **Privately Held**
WEB: www.kindercare.com
SIC: 8351 Group day care center
HQ: Kindercare Learning Centers, Llc
650 Ne Holladay St # 1400
Portland OR 97232
503 872-1300

(G-3872)
KINDERCARE LEARNING CTRS LLC
Also Called: Kindercare Child Care Network
2850 Winslow Ave (45206-1169)
PHONE.................................513 961-3164
Pam Daudistel, Director
EMP: 26
SALES (corp-wide): 1.2B **Privately Held**
WEB: www.kindercare.com
SIC: 8351 Child day care services
HQ: Kindercare Learning Centers, Llc
650 Ne Holladay St # 1400
Portland OR 97232
503 872-1300

(G-3873)
KINDERCARE LEARNING CTRS LLC
Also Called: Kindercare Child Care Network
10580 Montgomery Rd (45242-4469)
P.O. Box 6760 (45206-0760)
PHONE.................................513 791-4712
Ruby Kalyani, Director
EMP: 25
SALES (corp-wide): 1.2B **Privately Held**
WEB: www.kindercare.com
SIC: 8351 Group day care center
HQ: Kindercare Learning Centers, Llc
650 Ne Holladay St # 1400
Portland OR 97232
503 872-1300

(G-3874)
KINGS TOYOTA INC
Also Called: Kings Toyota Scion
4700 Fields Ertel Rd (45249-8200)
PHONE.................................513 583-4333
Gerald Carmichael, President
Darren Fay, Business Mgr
Dan Precht, Business Mgr
Dennis Collins, Sales Mgr
Mike Rutherford, Sales Mgr
EMP: 95
SALES (est): 34.1MM **Privately Held**
SIC: 5511 7515 7538 Automobiles, new & used; passenger car leasing; general automotive repair shops

(G-3875)
KIRK & BLUM MANUFACTURING CO (DH)
4625 Red Bank Rd Ste 200 (45227-1552)
PHONE.................................513 458-2600
◆ EMP: 200 EST: 1907
SQ FT: 250,000
SALES (corp-wide): 337.3MM **Publicly Held**
SIC: 1761 3444 3443 Sheet metalwork; sheet metal specialties, not stamped; fabricated plate work (boiler shop)
HQ: Ceco Group, Inc.
4625 Red Bank Rd Ste 200
Cincinnati OH 45227
513 458-2600

(G-3876)
KISSEL BROS SHOWS INC
6104 Rose Petal Dr (45247-5864)
PHONE.................................513 741-1080

Barbara Kissel, President
Dwayne Masek, Admin Sec
EMP: 50
SALES (est): 1.5MM **Privately Held**
WEB: www.kisselbros.com
SIC: 7999 Amusement ride; amusement concession

(G-3877)
KIWI HOSPITALITY - CINCINNATI
800 W 8th St (45203-1602)
PHONE.................................513 241-8660
Rakesh Sharma,
EMP: 25
SALES (est): 186.1K **Privately Held**
SIC: 7011 Hotels & motels

(G-3878)
KIWIPLAN INC
7870 E Kemper Rd Ste 200 (45249-1675)
PHONE.................................513 554-1500
Rodney McGee, President
EMP: 45
SQ FT: 17,000
SALES (est): 6.5MM
SALES (corp-wide): 1MM **Privately Held**
SIC: 7371 5045 Computer software development; computer software
HQ: Signode Packaging Group Nz
Level 7
Wellington 6011
800 744-663

(G-3879)
KLOECKNER METALS CORPORATION
11501 Reading Rd (45241-2240)
PHONE.................................513 769-4000
Darryl Grinstead, Branch Mgr
EMP: 76
SALES (corp-wide): 7.7B **Privately Held**
WEB: www.macsteelusa.com
SIC: 5051 Steel
HQ: Kloeckner Metals Corporation
500 Colonial Center Pkwy # 500
Roswell GA 30076

(G-3880)
KLOSTERMAN BAKING CO
1000 E Ross Ave (45217-1191)
PHONE.................................513 242-1004
Larry Moore, Manager
EMP: 85
SALES (corp-wide): 207.2MM **Privately Held**
SIC: 5149 2051 Bakery products; bread, cake & related products
PA: Klosterman Baking Co.
4760 Paddock Rd
Cincinnati OH 45229
513 242-5667

(G-3881)
KMH SYSTEMS INC
675 Redna Ter (45215-1108)
PHONE.................................513 469-9400
Phil Thomas, Branch Mgr
EMP: 30
SALES (corp-wide): 56.3MM **Privately Held**
SIC: 5084 Materials handling machinery
PA: Kmh Systems, Inc.
6900 Poe Ave
Dayton OH 45414
800 962-3178

(G-3882)
KNEISEL CONTRACTING CORP
3461 Mustafa Dr (45241-1668)
P.O. Box 158, West Chester (45071-0158)
PHONE.................................513 615-8816
Francis P Kneisel, President
Dennis Bustle, General Mgr
Richard Kneisel, Vice Pres
EMP: 30
SQ FT: 8,000
SALES (est): 1.5MM **Privately Held**
SIC: 1721 Pavement marking contractor

(G-3883)
KNOW THEATRE OF CINCINNATI
1120 Jackson St (45202-7215)
PHONE.................................513 300-5669
Alice Flanders, Managing Dir
Alexandra Kesman, Marketing Staff
Jay Kalagayan, Exec Dir

Maggie Rader, Director
Tamara Winters, Director
EMP: 25
SALES: 615K **Privately Held**
SIC: 7929 Entertainers & entertainment groups

(G-3884)
KNOWLEDGEWORKS FOUNDATION (PA)
1 W 4th St Ste 200 (45202-3624)
PHONE.................................513 241-1422
Tim Tuff, CEO
Brian Ross, President
William E McNeese, Senior VP
Andrew Benson, Vice Pres
Holly A Brinkman, Vice Pres
EMP: 43
SQ FT: 8,000
SALES: 8.8MM **Privately Held**
WEB: www.kwfdn.org
SIC: 8299 8742 Educational services; management consulting services

(G-3885)
KOHNEN & PATTON
201 E 5th St Ste 800 (45202-4190)
PHONE.................................513 381-0656
Malinda L Langston, Partner
EMP: 50
SALES (est): 1.2MM **Privately Held**
SIC: 8111 General practice attorney, lawyer

(G-3886)
KOI ENTERPRISES INC (HQ)
Also Called: K O I
2701 Spring Grove Ave (45225-2221)
P.O. Box 14240 (45250-0240)
PHONE.................................513 357-2400
David Wesselman, President
Bill Beckman, General Mgr
Joe Eagan, Regional Mgr
Michael Wesselman, VP Opers
Al Krautsack, Maint Spvr
▲ EMP: 100
SALES (est): 325.3MM
SALES (corp-wide): 834.8MM **Privately Held**
SIC: 5013 5531 Automotive supplies & parts; automotive & home supply stores
PA: Fisher Auto Parts, Inc.
512 Greenville Ave
Staunton VA 24401
540 885-8901

(G-3887)
KPMG LLP
312 Walnut Strste 3400 (45202)
PHONE.................................513 421-6430
Rick Siebert, Branch Mgr
Patty Basti, Director
EMP: 120
SALES (corp-wide): 3.8B **Privately Held**
SIC: 8721 Certified public accountant
PA: Kpmg Llp
1676 Intl Dr Ste 1200
Mclean VA 22102
703 286-8000

(G-3888)
KRAFT ELECTRICAL CONTG INC (PA)
Also Called: Kraft Electrical & Telecom Svs
5710 Hillside Ave (45233-1508)
PHONE.................................513 467-0500
Kelly Degregorio, President
Mike Jungkunz, Vice Pres
John Kraft, Vice Pres
Brian Knox, Engineer
Craig Adams, Manager
EMP: 39
SALES (est): 13.4MM **Privately Held**
WEB: www.kecc.com
SIC: 1731 General electrical contractor

(G-3889)
KRAMER & FELDMAN INC
7636 Production Dr (45237-3209)
PHONE.................................513 821-7444
Daniel Kramer, President
Lori Feldman, Corp Secy
Michael Feldman, Vice Pres
Renee Kraus, Office Mgr
EMP: 27
SQ FT: 8,000

SALES: 10.8MM **Privately Held**
WEB: www.kfigeneralcontractor.com
SIC: **1542** 1541 Commercial & office building contractors; industrial buildings & warehouses

(G-3890)
KREBS STEVE BP OIL CO
930 Tennessee Ave (45229-1006)
P.O. Box 17108 (45217-0108)
PHONE...............................513 641-0150
Steven Krebs, *Owner*
Kristen Krebbs, *Co-Owner*
EMP: 40 EST: 1967
SALES (est): 5.2MM **Privately Held**
SIC: **5172** Gasoline

(G-3891)
KRELLER BUS INFO GROUP INC
Also Called: Kreller Group
817 Main St Ste 300 (45202-2153)
PHONE...............................513 723-8900
Joe Davidoski, *President*
Harvey Rosen, *COO*
Scott Shaffer, *Vice Pres*
EMP: 30
SQ FT: 5,000
SALES (est): 8.1MM **Privately Held**
WEB: www.kreller.com
SIC: **7323** 7381 Credit reporting services; private investigator

(G-3892)
KROGER CO
150 Tri County Pkwy (45246-3246)
P.O. Box 46234 0234 (45246)
PHONE...............................513 782-3300
Jeff Covert, *President*
EMP: 200
SALES (corp-wide): 121.1B **Publicly Held**
SIC: **5411** 8741 Supermarkets, chain; management services
PA: The Kroger Co
1014 Vine St Ste 1000
Cincinnati OH 45202
513 762-4000

(G-3893)
KROGER CO FOUNDATION
1014 Vine St Ste 1000 (45202-1119)
P.O. Box 305261, Nashville TN (37230-5261)
PHONE...............................513 762-4000
Donald Becker, *Exec VP*
Christopher Hjelm, *Senior VP*
J M Schlotman, *Senior VP*
W Rodney McMullen, *Exec Dir*
John Lamacchia, *Director*
EMP: 44
SALES (est): 3.3MM **Privately Held**
SIC: **8699** Charitable organization

(G-3894)
KUEMPEL SERVICE INC
3976 Southern Ave (45227-3562)
PHONE...............................513 271-6500
Joseph Clark, *CEO*
John L Kuempel Jr, *Vice Pres*
Dave Gleason, *Project Mgr*
Tom Sucher, *Project Mgr*
Nancy Adkins, *Accounting Mgr*
EMP: 30 EST: 1981
SQ FT: 35,000
SALES (est): 5.2MM
SALES (corp-wide): 8.1B **Publicly Held**
WEB: www.emcorgroup.com
SIC: **1711** Mechanical contractor
PA: Emcor Group, Inc.
301 Merritt 7 Fl 6
Norwalk CT 06851
203 849-7800

(G-3895)
KUNKEL PHARMACEUTICALS INC
Also Called: Kunkel Apothecary
7717 Beechmont Ave (45255-4203)
PHONE...............................513 231-1943
John Dinkelaker, *President*
Donna Dinkelaker, *Vice Pres*
Tom Wynn, *Pharmacist*
Lynn Lewis, *Admin Sec*
EMP: 35
SQ FT: 10,600

SALES (est): 5.4MM **Privately Held**
WEB: www.kunkelrx.com
SIC: **5912** 5047 Drug stores; surgical equipment & supplies

(G-3896)
KURZHALS INC
6847 Menz Ln (45233-4312)
PHONE...............................513 941-4624
John Kurzhals, *President*
Ed Kurzhals, *Vice Pres*
Rick Kurzhals, *Vice Pres*
Margaret Kurzhals, *Admin Sec*
EMP: 35
SALES (est): 3MM **Privately Held**
SIC: **1741** Bricklaying

(G-3897)
KZF BWSC JOINT VENTURE
700 Broadway St (45202-2237)
PHONE...............................513 621-6211
Bill Wilson, *President*
EMP: 50
SALES (est): 1.6MM **Privately Held**
SIC: **8712** 8711 Architectural services; engineering services

(G-3898)
KZF DESIGN INC
700 Broadway St (45202-6010)
PHONE...............................513 621-6211
Robert B Steele, *CEO*
William H Wilson III, *President*
Doug Marsh, *Senior VP*
Alexis Ludtke, *CPA*
Susan Williams, *Admin Sec*
EMP: 74 EST: 1956
SQ FT: 36,000
SALES (est): 12.1MM **Privately Held**
SIC: **8712** 8711 Architectural engineering; engineering services

(G-3899)
L & W SUPPLY CORPORATION
Also Called: Nexgen Building Supply
3274 Spring Grove Ave (45225-1338)
PHONE...............................513 723-1150
Jeff Worthington, *Manager*
EMP: 35
SALES (corp-wide): 438.1MM **Privately Held**
WEB: www.nexgenbuildingsupply.com
SIC: **5211** 5032 Lumber products; drywall materials
HQ: L & W Supply Corporation
300 S Riverside Plz # 200
Chicago IL 60606
312 606-4000

(G-3900)
L M BERRY AND COMPANY
312 Plum St Ste 600 (45202-4809)
PHONE...............................513 768-7700
Michele Emmert, *Manager*
EMP: 100
SALES (corp-wide): 69.2MM **Privately Held**
SIC: **5199** Advertising specialties
PA: L. M. Berry And Company
3170 Kettering Blvd
Moraine OH 45439
937 296-2121

(G-3901)
L W LIMITED (PA)
Also Called: Old Montgomery
212 E 3rd St Ste 300 (45202-5500)
PHONE...............................513 721-2744
W J Williams Jr, *Partner*
L W Limited, *Partner*
EMP: 30
SQ FT: 500
SALES (est): 2.1MM **Privately Held**
WEB: www.oldemontgomery.com
SIC: **6513** Apartment building operators

(G-3902)
LA FORCE INC
2851 E Kemper Rd (45241-1819)
P.O. Box 10068, Green Bay WI (54307-0068)
PHONE...............................513 772-0783
Tom Gaible, *Branch Mgr*
EMP: 30

SALES (corp-wide): 156.3MM **Privately Held**
WEB: www.laforceinc.com
SIC: **5031** Doors; metal doors, sash & trim; building materials, interior
PA: La Force, Inc.
1060 W Mason St
Green Bay WI 54303
920 497-7100

(G-3903)
LABONE INC
3200 Burnet Ave (45229-3019)
PHONE...............................513 585-9000
Dr Wendell O'Neal, *VP Opers*
EMP: 600
SALES (corp-wide): 7.5B **Publicly Held**
SIC: **8071** Medical laboratories
HQ: Labone, Inc.
10101 Renner Blvd
Lenexa KS 66219
913 888-1770

(G-3904)
LABORATORY CORPORATION AMERICA
Also Called: Genetica Dna Laboratories
1737 Tennessee Ave (45229-1201)
PHONE...............................513 242-6800
Joshua Wismann, *Project Mgr*
Teri Baira, *Pathologist*
EMP: 25 **Publicly Held**
SIC: **8071** Testing laboratories
HQ: Laboratory Corporation Of America
358 S Main St Ste 458
Burlington NC 27215
336 229-1127

(G-3905)
LACAISSE INC
700 Broadway St (45202-2237)
PHONE...............................513 621-6211
Bill Wilson, *President*
Robert Steele, *CFO*
EMP: 80
SALES (est): 3.8MM **Privately Held**
SIC: **8712** Architectural engineering

(G-3906)
LADD INC
3603 Victory Pkwy (45229-2297)
PHONE...............................513 861-4089
David Robinson, *Principal*
Wylie Jones, *QA Dir*
David Wolfzorn, *Director*
EMP: 26
SALES: 7.5MM **Privately Held**
SIC: **8361** Home for the mentally handicapped

(G-3907)
LAFAYETTE LIFE INSURANCE CO (DH)
400 Broadway St (45202-3312)
P.O. Box 5740 (45201-5740)
PHONE...............................800 443-8793
Larry Griypp, *President*
Vincent Serpe, *President*
William Olds, *COO*
Jeffrey A Poxon, *Senior VP*
G Allhands, *Assistant VP*
EMP: 185
SQ FT: 102,000
SALES: 35.3MM **Privately Held**
WEB: www.llic.com
SIC: **6311** Life insurance
HQ: Western & Southern Financial Group, Inc.
400 Broadway St
Cincinnati OH 45202
866 832-7719

(G-3908)
LAIDLAW TRANSIT SERVICES INC (DH)
600 Vine St Ste 1400 (45202-2426)
PHONE...............................513 241-2200
Mike Rushin, *President*
Jeff C Baker, *Vice Pres*
EMP: 45
SQ FT: 23,000
SALES (est): 103MM
SALES (corp-wide): 8.9B **Privately Held**
SIC: **4111** Local & suburban transit

HQ: Firstgroup America, Inc.
600 Vine St 1400
Cincinnati OH 45202
513 241-2200

(G-3909)
LANGDON INC
9865 Wayne Ave (45215-1403)
P.O. Box 15308 (45215-0308)
PHONE...............................513 733-5955
David Sandman, *President*
Michael Sandman, *Vice Pres*
Bill Seibert, *Project Mgr*
▲ EMP: 40
SQ FT: 42,000
SALES (est): 11.6MM **Privately Held**
WEB: www.langdonsheetmetal.com
SIC: **3444** 1711 3564 3446 Ducts, sheet metal; warm air heating & air conditioning contractor; ventilation & duct work contractor; blowers & fans; architectural metalwork; fabricated plate work (boiler shop); fabricated structural metal

(G-3910)
LANGUAGE LOGIC
600 Vine St Ste 2020 (45202-2430)
PHONE...............................513 241-9112
Richard Thoman, *Partner*
Charles Baylis, *Partner*
EMP: 30
SQ FT: 1,500
SALES: 428K **Privately Held**
WEB: www.languagelogic.net
SIC: **8742** Marketing consulting services

(G-3911)
LAROSAS INC (PA)
2334 Boudinot Ave (45238-3492)
PHONE...............................513 347-5660
Marlenia Bennett, *General Mgr*
David Burns, *General Mgr*
Denise Gemmer, *General Mgr*
Donald S Larosa, *Principal*
Rob Kaiser, *District Mgr*
EMP: 515
SQ FT: 10,000
SALES (est): 73.9MM **Privately Held**
WEB: www.larosas.com
SIC: **5812** 6794 5141 5921 Pizzeria, chain; franchises, selling or licensing; groceries, general line; wine

(G-3912)
LASIK PLUS VISION CENTER
7840 Montgomery Rd (45236-4301)
PHONE...............................513 794-9964
Steven Jeoffe, *Principal*
EMP: 65
SALES (est): 4.4MM **Privately Held**
SIC: **8011** Physical medicine, physician/surgeon; ophthalmologist

(G-3913)
LAWN MANAGEMENT SPRINKLER CO
3828 Round Bottom Rd F (45244-2456)
PHONE...............................513 272-3808
Steven J Blauwkamp, *President*
Jill Blauwkamp, *Vice Pres*
EMP: 30
SALES (est): 2.6MM **Privately Held**
SIC: **1711** 1731 1799 Irrigation sprinkler system installation; lighting contractor; fountain installation

(G-3914)
LAWYERS TITLE CINCINNATI INC (HQ)
3500 Red Bank Rd (45227-4111)
PHONE...............................513 421-1313
Timothy Griffin, *President*
Michael Fletcher, *Exec VP*
Ernie Overstreet, *Manager*
EMP: 60
SQ FT: 10,000
SALES (est): 10.7MM
SALES (corp-wide): 7.5B **Publicly Held**
SIC: **6361** Real estate title insurance
PA: Fidelity National Financial, Inc.
601 Riverside Ave Fl 4
Jacksonville FL 32204
904 854-8100

(G-3915)
LCA-VISION INC (HQ)
7840 Montgomery Rd (45236-4348)
PHONE................................513 792-9292
Craig Joffe, *CEO*
Marcello J Celentano, *Senior VP*
Janet V Vest, *Executive Asst*
EMP: 107
SQ FT: 30,000
SALES (est): 33.8MM **Privately Held**
WEB: www.lca-vision.com
SIC: 8011 Eyes, ears, nose & throat specialist: physician/surgeon
PA: Vision Acquisition, Llc
7840 Montgomery Rd
Cincinnati OH 45236
513 792-9292

(G-3916)
LEE PERSONNEL INC
621 E Mehring Way # 807 (45202-3528)
P.O. Box 1175 (45201-1175)
PHONE................................513 744-6780
Gloria Sustor, *President*
EMP: 30 **EST:** 2008
SALES (est): 709.6K **Privately Held**
SIC: 7363 Temporary help service

(G-3917)
LEGAL AID SOCIETY CINCINNATI (PA)
Also Called: LEGAL AID SOCIETY OF GREATER C
215 E 9th St Ste 200 (45202-1084)
PHONE................................513 241-9400
Mary Asbury, *Exec Dir*
Gayle Bogardus, *Director*
EMP: 75
SQ FT: 21,000
SALES: 8MM **Privately Held**
WEB: www.lascinti.org
SIC: 8111 Legal aid service

(G-3918)
LERNER SAMPSON & ROTHFUSS (PA)
Also Called: L S R
120 E 4th St (45202-4070)
PHONE................................513 241-3100
Richard M Rothfuss, *President*
Donald M Lerner, *Principal*
Lisa Wayne, *Opers Mgr*
Maria Divita, *Human Res Dir*
Rachel Faris, *Human Res Dir*
EMP: 351 **EST:** 1975
SALES (est): 39.8MM **Privately Held**
SIC: 8111 General practice law office

(G-3919)
LEVEL 3 TELECOM LLC
Also Called: Time Warner Cable
3268 Highland Ave (45213-2508)
PHONE................................513 841-0000
Jeffrey Bewkes, *Branch Mgr*
EMP: 29
SALES (corp-wide): 23.4B **Publicly Held**
SIC: 4813
HQ: Level 3 Telecom, Llc
10475 Park Meadows Dr
Lone Tree CO 80124
303 566-1000

(G-3920)
LEVEL 3 TELECOM LLC
Also Called: Time Warner Cable
3268 Highland Ave (45213-2508)
PHONE................................513 841-0000
EMP: 29
SALES (corp-wide): 23.4B **Publicly Held**
SIC: 4813 Telephone communication, except radio
HQ: Level 3 Telecom, Llc
10475 Park Meadows Dr
Lone Tree CO 80124
303 566-1000

(G-3921)
LEVEL 3 TELECOM LLC
Also Called: Time Warner Cable
3268 Highland Ave (45213-2508)
PHONE................................513 841-0000
EMP: 29
SALES (corp-wide): 23.4B **Publicly Held**
SIC: 4813 Telephone communication, except radio

HQ: Level 3 Telecom, Llc
10475 Park Meadows Dr
Lone Tree CO 80124
303 566-1000

(G-3922)
LEVINE ARNOLD S LAW OFFICES
324 Reading Rd (45202-1316)
PHONE................................513 241-6748
Arnold Levine, *President*
Michael A Lanzillotta,
Andrew Macfarland,
EMP: 25
SQ FT: 2,000
SALES (est): 2.5MM **Privately Held**
WEB: www.cincinnatiinjurylaw.com
SIC: 8111 General practice attorney, lawyer; general practice law office

(G-3923)
LIBBY PRSZYK KTHMAN HLDNGS INC (PA)
Also Called: L P K
19 Garfield Pl (45202-4310)
PHONE................................513 241-6401
Jerome Kathman, *President*
John Recker, *President*
Phil Best, *COO*
Dennis Geiger, *CFO*
Tonya Van Tine-Burns, *Director*
EMP: 400
SQ FT: 125,000
SALES (est): 48.4MM **Privately Held**
WEB: www.lpklive.com
SIC: 7336 Graphic arts & related design

(G-3924)
LIBERTY NRSING CTR RVRSIDE LLC
315 Lilienthal St (45204-1170)
P.O. Box 11499 (45211-0499)
PHONE................................513 557-3621
Brenda Spalding, *Systems Dir*
Linda B Kurek,
EMP: 100
SALES (est): 5MM **Privately Held**
SIC: 8051 8069 Convalescent home with continuous nursing care; specialty hospitals, except psychiatric

(G-3925)
LIBERTY NURSING CENTER OF THRE
7800 Jandaracres Dr (45248-2032)
PHONE................................513 941-0787
Linda Black-Kurek, *President*
Jessica Allen, *Nursing Dir*
EMP: 150
SQ FT: 20,000
SALES (est): 6.8MM **Privately Held**
SIC: 8052 8322 Intermediate care facilities; rehabilitation services

(G-3926)
LIEBEL-FLARSHEIM COMPANY LLC
Also Called: Guerbet
2111 E Galbraith Rd (45237-1624)
P.O. Box 152760567 (45237)
PHONE................................513 761-2700
Robert McGraw, *Plant Mgr*
Cliff Brown, *Purch Mgr*
Gary Barnhart, *Engineer*
Jeremy Riggle, *Engineer*
EMP: 186
SALES (corp-wide): 550.5MM **Privately Held**
SIC: 1541 Pharmaceutical manufacturing plant construction
HQ: Liebel-Flarsheim Company Llc
1034 S Brentwood Blvd
Saint Louis MO

(G-3927)
LIFECENTER ORGAN DONOR NETWORK (PA)
615 Elsinore Pl Ste 400 (45202-1475)
PHONE................................513 558-5555
Jeff Matthews MD, *Chairman*
David D Lewis, *Director*
EMP: 47
SQ FT: 4,500

SALES: 14.5MM **Privately Held**
WEB: www.lifecnt.org
SIC: 8099 Medical services organization

(G-3928)
LIFETOUCH NAT SCHL STUDIOS INC
11815 Highway Dr Ste 100 (45241-2064)
PHONE................................513 772-2110
Jody Mello, *Manager*
Jodi Sampson, *Manager*
EMP: 50
SALES (corp-wide): 1.9B **Publicly Held**
SIC: 7221 School photographer
HQ: Lifetouch National School Studios Inc.
11000 Viking Dr Ste 300
Eden Prairie MN 55344
952 826-4000

(G-3929)
LIGHTHOUSE YOUTH SERVICES INC
Also Called: Youth Development Center
3603 Washington Ave (45229-2009)
PHONE................................513 221-1017
Karen Doggett, *Exec Dir*
EMP: 72
SALES (corp-wide): 25.2MM **Privately Held**
SIC: 8322 Youth center
PA: Lighthouse Youth Services, Inc.
401 E Mcmillan St
Cincinnati OH 45206
513 221-3350

(G-3930)
LIGHTHOUSE YOUTH SERVICES INC
2522 Highland Ave (45219-2649)
PHONE................................513 861-1111
Debbie Latter, *Branch Mgr*
EMP: 57
SALES (corp-wide): 25.2MM **Privately Held**
SIC: 8999 7389 Artists & artists' studios; fund raising organizations
PA: Lighthouse Youth Services, Inc.
401 E Mcmillan St
Cincinnati OH 45206
513 221-3350

(G-3931)
LIGHTHOUSE YOUTH SERVICES INC (PA)
401 E Mcmillan St (45206-1922)
PHONE................................513 221-3350
Robert C Mecum, *President*
Jean Sepate, *Vice Pres*
Judy Oakman, *CFO*
EMP: 65
SQ FT: 13,710
SALES: 25.2MM **Privately Held**
SIC: 8322 Child related social services

(G-3932)
LINCOLN CRAWFORD NRSG/REHAB CT
1346 Lincoln Ave (45206-1341)
PHONE................................513 861-2044
Richard Binenfeld, *Principal*
EMP: 41
SALES (est): 2.9MM **Privately Held**
SIC: 8051 Convalescent home with continuous nursing care

(G-3933)
LINCOLN MRCURY KINGS AUTO MALL (PA)
Also Called: Montgomery Jeep Eagle
9600 Kings Auto Mall Rd (45249-8240)
PHONE................................513 683-3800
Robert C Reichert, *President*
Lou Galbraith, *Corp Secy*
Gerald M Car Michael, *Vice Pres*
Mark Pittman, *Vice Pres*
EMP: 163 **EST:** 1954
SQ FT: 23,000
SALES (est): 42.4MM **Privately Held**
WEB: www.kingslincolnmercury.com
SIC: 5511 7514 7518 7515 Automobiles, new & used; passenger car rental; general automotive repair shops; passenger car leasing; used car dealers

(G-3934)
LINDHORST & DREIDAME CO LPA
312 Walnut St Ste 3100 (45202-4091)
PHONE................................513 421-6630
William Kirkham, *President*
Michelle Korb, *Human Resources*
Paula Graszus, *Legal Staff*
Bradley McPeek, *Associate*
EMP: 51
SQ FT: 20,000
SALES (est): 5MM **Privately Held**
SIC: 8111 General practice attorney, lawyer

(G-3935)
LINDNER CLINICAL TRIAL CENTER
Also Called: Research and Education The
2123 Auburn Ave Ste 424 (45219-2906)
PHONE................................513 585-1777
Linda Martin, *Exec Dir*
EMP: 25
SALES: 2.4MM **Privately Held**
SIC: 8732 8731 Business research service; commercial physical research

(G-3936)
LINN STREET HOLDINGS LLC
2135 Dana Ave Ste 200 (45207-1327)
PHONE................................513 699-8825
Colleen Kroell, *Controller*
EMP: 25 **EST:** 2013
SALES (est): 1.3MM **Privately Held**
SIC: 6531 Real estate agents & managers

(G-3937)
LIQUID TRANSPORT CORP
10711 Evendale Dr (45241-2535)
PHONE................................513 769-4777
Greg Blair, *Manager*
EMP: 28
SALES (corp-wide): 231.3MM **Privately Held**
WEB: www.liquidtransport.com
SIC: 4213 Contract haulers
HQ: Liquid Transport Corp.
8470 Allison Pointe Blvd # 400
Indianapolis IN 46250
317 841-4200

(G-3938)
LISNR INC
920 Race St Ste 4 (45202-1040)
PHONE................................513 322-8400
Rodney Williams, *CEO*
Eric Allen, *President*
Vicky Sagehorn, *Vice Pres*
EMP: 31
SALES (est): 641.3K **Privately Held**
SIC: 7371 Computer software development

(G-3939)
LITHUANIAN WORLD COMMUNITY
5927 Monticello Ave (45224-2319)
PHONE................................513 542-0076
Horace Zibas, *Director*
EMP: 30
SALES (est): 1MM **Privately Held**
SIC: 8641 Civic social & fraternal associations

(G-3940)
LITIGATION SUPPORT SVCS INC
817 Main St Ste 400 (45202-2153)
PHONE................................513 241-5605
Kirk McCracken, *President*
Jo Sabrowsky, *Manager*
EMP: 25 **EST:** 1981
SALES (est): 1.5MM **Privately Held**
WEB: www.litsup.com
SIC: 7819 8111 Video tape or disk reproduction; legal services

(G-3941)
LOGIKOR LLC
463 Ohio Pike Ste 105 (45255-3722)
PHONE................................513 762-7678
Chris Painter, *President*
Greg Shelton, *Opers Staff*
Paul Silk, *CFO*
Cody Stanelle, *Manager*
Darryl King, *Exec Dir*

G
E
O
G
R
A
P
H
I
C

EMP: 45
SQ FT: 46,000
SALES: 5.5MM Privately Held
SIC: 4731 Freight transportation arrangement

(G-3942)
LONDON COMPUTER SYSTEMS INC
Also Called: Lcs
9140 Waterstone Blvd (45249-7501)
PHONE...................................513 583-0840
David Hegemann, *President*
Patrick O'Hearn, *Partner*
Abbie Huffman, *Business Mgr*
Matthew Purintun, *Purch Mgr*
Cheryl Huntenbrinker, *Human Res Mgr*
EMP: 100 EST: 1987
SQ FT: 20,000
SALES (est): 14.3MM Privately Held
WEB: www.rentmanager.com
SIC: 7379 7371 ; computer software development

(G-3943)
LOSANTIVILLE COUNTRY CLUB
3097 Losantiville Ave (45213-1398)
PHONE...................................513 631-4133
Steve Vanburen, *General Mgr*
Marilyn Sferra, *Asst Mgr*
EMP: 70
SQ FT: 36,000
SALES: 2.1MM Privately Held
SIC: 7997 Country club, membership

(G-3944)
LOTH INC (PA)
Also Called: Asset Solutions
3574 E Kemper Rd (45241-2009)
PHONE...................................513 554-4900
JB Buse Jr, *CEO*
Rick Naber, *President*
Eric Roach, *CFO*
Walter Homan, *Shareholder*
EMP: 143 EST: 1994
SQ FT: 212,000
SALES (est): 58.2MM Privately Held
WEB: www.lothmbi.com
SIC: 7389 8712 Design services; architectural services

(G-3945)
LOWES HOME CENTERS LLC
10235 Colerain Ave (45251-4903)
PHONE...................................513 741-0585
Bob Czerniak, *Manager*
EMP: 150
SQ FT: 1,476
SALES (corp-wide): 68.6B Publicly Held
SIC: 5211 5031 5722 5064 Home centers; building materials, exterior; building materials, interior; household appliance stores; electrical appliances, television & radio
HQ: Lowe's Home Centers, Llc
1605 Curtis Bridge Rd
Wilkesboro NC 28697
336 658-4000

(G-3946)
LOWES HOME CENTERS LLC
6150 Harrison Ave (45247-7848)
PHONE...................................513 598-7050
Fausto Fuentes, *Branch Mgr*
EMP: 150
SALES (corp-wide): 68.6B Publicly Held
SIC: 5211 5031 5722 5064 Home centers; building materials, exterior; building materials, interior; household appliance stores; electrical appliances, television & radio
HQ: Lowe's Home Centers, Llc
1605 Curtis Bridge Rd
Wilkesboro NC 28697
336 658-4000

(G-3947)
LOWES HOME CENTERS LLC
5385 Ridge Ave (45213-2543)
PHONE...................................513 731-6127
Rob Harbaum, *Manager*
EMP: 150

SALES (corp-wide): 68.6B Publicly Held
SIC: 5211 5031 5722 5064 Home centers; building materials, exterior; building materials, interior; household appliance stores; electrical appliances, television & radio
HQ: Lowe's Home Centers, Llc
1605 Curtis Bridge Rd
Wilkesboro NC 28697
336 658-4000

(G-3948)
LOWES HOME CENTERS LLC
505 E Kemper Rd (45246-3233)
PHONE...................................513 671-2093
Joe Madrigal, *Manager*
EMP: 150
SALES (corp-wide): 68.6B Publicly Held
SIC: 5211 5031 5722 5064 Home centers; building materials, exterior; building materials, interior; household appliance stores; electrical appliances, television & radio
HQ: Lowe's Home Centers, Llc
1605 Curtis Bridge Rd
Wilkesboro NC 28697
336 658-4000

(G-3949)
LOYAL AMERICAN LIFE INSUR CO (DH)
250 E 5th St Fl 8 (45202-4119)
PHONE...................................800 633-6752
Robert A Adams, *Ch of Bd*
Charles Scheper, *President*
Jane Rollinson, *COO*
Mark Muething, *Exec VP*
Edward C Dahmer Jr, *Senior VP*
EMP: 180
SALES: 125.4MM
SALES (corp-wide): 141.6B Publicly Held
SIC: 6311 Life insurance

(G-3950)
LPL FINANCIAL HOLDINGS INC
11260 Chester Rd Ste 250 (45246-0002)
PHONE...................................513 772-2592
Gary Mathews, *Branch Mgr*
Edwin G Garvin, *Agent*
EMP: 285 Publicly Held
SIC: 8742 Financial consultant
PA: Lpl Financial Holdings Inc.
75 State St Ste 2401
Boston MA 02109

(G-3951)
LQ MANAGEMENT LLC
Also Called: La Quinta Inn
11029 Dowlin Dr (45241-1833)
PHONE...................................513 771-0300
William Goetz, *Branch Mgr*
EMP: 80
SALES (corp-wide): 1.8B Publicly Held
WEB: www.neubayern.net
SIC: 7011 Hotels
HQ: Lq Management L.L.C.
909 Hidden Rdg Ste 600
Irving TX 75038
214 492-6600

(G-3952)
LUXFER MAGTECH INC (HQ)
Also Called: Heatermeals
2940 Highland Ave Ste 210 (45212-2402)
PHONE...................................513 772-3066
Brian Purves, *CEO*
Marc Lamensdorf, *President*
Tim Zimmerman, *Exec VP*
Deborah Simsen, *Treasurer*
Cindy Reinhardt, *Accountant*
EMP: 38
SALES (est): 8.5MM
SALES (corp-wide): 441.3MM Privately Held
SIC: 2899 5149 Desalter kits, sea water; groceries & related products; beverages, except coffee & tea
PA: Luxfer Holdings Plc
Ancorage Gateway
Salford LANCS M50 3
161 300-0611

(G-3953)
LYONDELL CHEMICAL COMPANY
11530 Northlake Dr (45249-1642)
PHONE...................................513 530-4000
James Simiskey, *Principal*
Michael Bridges, *Research*
Norma Maraschin, *Manager*
Anne Balthazar, *Manager*
Natalie Nichols, *Manager*
EMP: 79
SALES (corp-wide): 34.5B Privately Held
WEB: www.lyondell.com
SIC: 2869 2822 8731 Olefins; ethylene; polyethylene, chlorosulfonated (hypalon); commercial physical research
HQ: Lyondell Chemical Company
1221 Mckinney St Ste 300
Houston TX 77010
713 309-7200

(G-3954)
M & M METALS INTERNATIONAL INC
840 Dellway St (45229-3396)
PHONE...................................513 221-4411
Beatrice Brunner, *President*
Steve Schuler, *Principal*
Jim Davis, *Vice Pres*
Beryl Merritt, *Vice Pres*
EMP: 25
SQ FT: 50,000
SALES (est): 10MM Privately Held
SIC: 5093 Nonferrous metals scrap; metal scrap & waste materials

(G-3955)
M T GOLF COURSE MANAGMENT INC (PA)
Also Called: Pebble Creek Golf Course
9799 Prechtel Rd (45252-2117)
PHONE...................................513 923-1188
Michael R Macke, *CEO*
Carl F Tuke Jr, *Principal*
Mary J Padro, *Vice Pres*
Mike Faillece, *Manager*
EMP: 50
SQ FT: 15,000
SALES (est): 8MM Privately Held
WEB: www.pebblecreekgc.com
SIC: 1799 1629 Coating, caulking & weather, water & fireproofing; golf course construction

(G-3956)
MACKE BROTHERS INC
10355 Spartan Dr (45215-1220)
PHONE...................................513 771-7500
Joseph D Macke Sr, *President*
Joseph D Macke Jr, *Vice Pres*
Bill Macke, *Treasurer*
Nick Macke, *Admin Sec*
EMP: 85 EST: 1908
SQ FT: 43,000
SALES (est): 8.4MM Privately Held
SIC: 2789 7331 Pamphlets, binding; bookbinding & repairing: trade, edition, library, etc.; mailing service

(G-3957)
MADEIRA HEALTH CARE CENTER
6940 Stiegler Ln (45243-2635)
PHONE...................................513 561-4105
Fax: 513 561-2450
EMP: 110
SALES (est): 4.7MM Privately Held
SIC: 8051 Skilled Nursing Facility

(G-3958)
MADISON BOWL INC
4761 Madison Rd (45227-1425)
PHONE...................................513 271-2700
Harry S Osgood, *President*
Linda Osgood, *Admin Sec*
EMP: 35 EST: 1956
SQ FT: 15,000
SALES (est): 1.3MM Privately Held
WEB: www.madisonbowl.com
SIC: 7933 Ten pin center

(G-3959)
MAE HOLDING COMPANY (PA)
7290 Deaconsbench Ct (45244-3708)
PHONE...................................513 751-2424

George Thurner III, *President*
EMP: 32
SQ FT: 80,000
SALES (est): 18.4MM Privately Held
SIC: 5031 5072 Door frames, all materials; hardware

(G-3960)
MAGNUM MEDICAL OVERSEAS JV LLC
2936 Vernon Pl 3 (45219-2433)
PHONE...................................979 848-8169
Richard Blatt, *CEO*
Kevin Korb, *CFO*
EMP: 99
SALES (est): 1.2MM Privately Held
SIC: 8011 Offices & clinics of medical doctors

(G-3961)
MAIDS HOME SERVICE OF CINCY
1830 Sherman Ave (45212-2516)
PHONE...................................513 396-6900
Margie Hall, *President*
EMP: 25
SQ FT: 2,174
SALES (est): 709.1K Privately Held
SIC: 7349 Maid services, contract or fee basis

(G-3962)
MAIL CONTRACTORS AMERICA INC
3065 Cresecentville Rd (45262)
PHONE...................................513 769-5967
Sue Deserisy, *Manager*
EMP: 225
SALES (corp-wide): 368.4MM Privately Held
WEB: www.mailcontractors.com
SIC: 4212 Local trucking, without storage
HQ: Mail Contractors Of America, Inc.
3809 Roundtop Dr
North Little Rock AR 72117
501 280-0500

(G-3963)
MAKETEWAH COUNTRY CLUB COMPANY
5401 Reading Rd (45237-5398)
PHONE...................................513 242-9333
Charles Carpenter, *President*
EMP: 75
SQ FT: 59,007
SALES: 4.3MM Privately Held
WEB: www.maketewah.com
SIC: 7997 Country club, membership

(G-3964)
MAKING EVRLASTING MEMORIES LLC
11475 Northlake Dr (45249-1641)
PHONE...................................513 864-0100
Scott Mindrum, *President*
Steven Sefton, *COO*
Olga Piehler, *Director*
EMP: 30
SQ FT: 2,000
SALES (est): 3.2MM Privately Held
WEB: www.familyheritageregistry.com
SIC: 4813

(G-3965)
MALIK PUNAM
3333 Burnet Ave (45229-3026)
PHONE...................................513 636-1333
Dr Punam Malik, *Owner*
EMP: 99
SALES: 12K Privately Held
SIC: 8742 Hospital & health services consultant

(G-3966)
MALLARD COVE SENIOR DEV LLC
Also Called: Mallard Cove Senior Living
1410 Mallard Cove Dr Ofc (45246-3930)
PHONE...................................513 772-6655
Shamela Limbaugh, *Owner*
Jonathan Levey, *Mng Member*
David A Smith, *Mng Member*
EMP: 105 EST: 2008

SALES (est): 10.5MM Privately Held
SIC: 8051 Skilled nursing care facilities

(G-3967)
MAPLE KNOLL COMMUNITIES INC (PA)
Also Called: MAPLE KNOLL VILLAGE
11100 Springfield Pike (45246-4165)
PHONE....................................513 782-2400
Rose Denman, Vice Pres
Kenneth Huff, CFO
Nancy Hendricks, Controller
Beth Bolin, VP Human Res
Jessie Puls, Mktg Dir
EMP: 600
SQ FT: 323,000
SALES: 43.4MM Privately Held
SIC: 8051 8052 8082 Convalescent home with continuous nursing care; intermediate care facilities; home health care services

(G-3968)
MARCUMS DON POOL CARE INC
6841 Main St Ste 1 (45244-3475)
PHONE....................................513 561-7050
Donald Marcum, President
Darlene Marcum, Corp Secy
Dave Bachman, Vice Pres
Gene Pollack, Technician
EMP: 25 EST: 1981
SQ FT: 5,000
SALES (est): 4.2MM Privately Held
SIC: 5999 7389 Swimming pool chemicals, equipment & supplies; swimming pool & hot tub service & maintenance

(G-3969)
MARFRE INC
Also Called: Riggs School Buses
4785 Morse St (45226-2316)
PHONE....................................513 321-3377
Dennis Riggs, CEO
Rebecca Campbell, President
Terry Howard, Vice Pres
EMP: 103
SQ FT: 4,000
SALES (est): 3.2MM Privately Held
WEB: www.marfre.com
SIC: 4151 4141 School buses; local bus charter service

(G-3970)
MARKETING RESEARCH SVCS INC
110 Boggs Ln Ste 380 (45246-3150)
PHONE....................................513 772-7580
Valerie Enderle, Manager
EMP: 100 Privately Held
SIC: 8732 Market analysis or research
HQ: Marketing Research Services, Inc.
310 Culvert St Fl 2
Cincinnati OH 45202
513 579-1555

(G-3971)
MARKETING RESEARCH SVCS INC (DH)
Also Called: M R S I
310 Culvert St Fl 2 (45202-2229)
PHONE....................................513 579-1555
Todd Earhart, President
John Barth, Exec VP
Richard Brumfield, Exec VP
Elise Delahanty, Exec VP
Lori Kelley, Exec VP
EMP: 95
SQ FT: 30,000
SALES (est): 13.7MM Privately Held
SIC: 8732 Market analysis or research
HQ: Orc International, Inc
902 Carnegie Ctr Ste 220
Princeton NJ 08540
609 452-5400

(G-3972)
MARKETING SUPPORT SERVICES INC (PA)
4921 Para Dr (45237-5011)
PHONE....................................513 752-1200
Greg Fischer, President
Pam Fischer, Corp Secy
EMP: 51
SQ FT: 100,000

SALES (est): 9.3MM Privately Held
WEB: www.m-s-s.com
SIC: 7311 Advertising agencies

(G-3973)
MARRIOTT INTERNATIONAL INC
151 Goodman St (45219-2105)
PHONE....................................513 487-3800
Susan Graves, General Mgr
Jayne Wilder, Finance
EMP: 130
SALES (corp-wide): 20.7B Publicly Held
SIC: 7011 Hotels & motels
PA: Marriott International, Inc.
10400 Fernwood Rd
Bethesda MD 20817
301 380-3000

(G-3974)
MARRIOTT INTERNATIONAL INC
151 Goodman St (45219-2105)
PHONE....................................513 487-3800
Fax: 513 487-3810
EMP: 167
SALES (corp-wide): 14.4B Publicly Held
SIC: 7011 Hotels And Motels
PA: Marriott International, Inc.
10400 Fernwood Rd
Bethesda MD 20817
301 380-3000

(G-3975)
MARSH INC (PA)
333 E 8th St (45202-2205)
PHONE....................................513 421-1234
Edward E Betz, Ch of Bd
Ken Neiheisel, President
Peter Costanzo, Vice Pres
EMP: 27 EST: 1937
SQ FT: 12,000
SALES (est): 11MM Privately Held
WEB: www.marshinc.com
SIC: 7336 8743 7335 Package design; promotion service; commercial photography

(G-3976)
MARSH USA INC
525 Vine St Ste 1600 (45202-3132)
PHONE....................................513 287-1600
Wren Schnelle, Assistant VP
Bernie Calonge, Manager
EMP: 70
SALES (corp-wide): 14.9B Publicly Held
WEB: www.marsh.com
SIC: 6411 Insurance brokers
HQ: Marsh Usa Inc.
1166 Ave Of The Americas
New York NY 10036
212 345-6000

(G-3977)
MASSACHUSETTS MUTL LF INSUR CO
1 W 4th St Ste 1000 (45202-3632)
PHONE....................................513 579-8555
Clair Greenwell, Manager
EMP: 48
SALES (corp-wide): 16.7B Privately Held
WEB: www.massmutual.com
SIC: 6311 Life insurance
PA: Massachusetts Mutual Life Insurance Company
1295 State St
Springfield MA 01111
413 788-8411

(G-3978)
MASUR TRUCKING INC
11825 Reading Rd Ste 1 (45241-5515)
PHONE....................................513 860-9600
Joseph N Masur, President
Paul J Masur, Treasurer
Charles Masur, Admin Sec
EMP: 30 EST: 1932
SQ FT: 520
SALES (est): 5.1MM Privately Held
WEB: www.masurtrucking.com
SIC: 4212 Delivery service, vehicular

(G-3979)
MATLOCK ELECTRIC CO INC (PA)
2780 Highland Ave (45212-2494)
PHONE....................................513 731-9600
Joseph P Geoppinger, President
Thomas J Geoppinger, Chairman
Rick Mullaney, Controller
Casey McKenna, Manager
Phil Mohr, Manager
EMP: 38
SQ FT: 25,000
SALES (est): 9.2MM Privately Held
WEB: www.matlockelectric.com
SIC: 7694 5063 3699 3612 Electric motor repair; rebuilding motors, except automotive; motors, electric; electrical equipment & supplies; transformers, except electric; speed changers, drives & gears

(G-3980)
MATRIX CLAIMS MANAGEMENT INC
Also Called: Matrix Invstgations Consulting
644 Linn St Ste 900 (45203-1738)
PHONE....................................513 351-1222
Brent Messmer, President
Katie Jones, Business Mgr
Darla Iles, Manager
EMP: 80
SQ FT: 6,400
SALES (est): 2.6MM Privately Held
SIC: 8742 Management consulting services

(G-3981)
MAXIMUM COMMUNICATIONS INC
Also Called: Maximum Call Center
117 Williams St (45215-4601)
PHONE....................................513 489-3414
Clark Sarver, President
Carol Sarver,
EMP: 30
SQ FT: 3,500
SALES (est): 2.3MM Privately Held
WEB: www.maximumcallcenter.com
SIC: 4812 4822 7389 5999 Paging services; electronic mail; telephone answering service; telephone & communication equipment

(G-3982)
MAYERS ELECTRIC CO INC
4004 Erie Ct Ste B (45227-2167)
PHONE....................................513 272-2900
Howard Mayers, President
Jim Hopper, Vice Pres
Patrick Bates, Project Mgr
Bill Puthoff, Project Mgr
Josh Sebolt, Project Mgr
▲ EMP: 150 EST: 1948
SQ FT: 22,250
SALES: 22.1MM Privately Held
WEB: www.mayerselectric.com
SIC: 1731 General electrical contractor

(G-3983)
MAYFIELD CLINIC INC (PA)
3825 Edwards Rd Ste 300 (45209-1288)
PHONE....................................513 221-1100
Michael J Gilligan, President
Bradley Mullin, Principal
Hwa Shain Yeh, Principal
Mary Kemper, Editor
A L Greiner MD, Chairman
EMP: 82
SQ FT: 25,000
SALES (est): 14.4MM Privately Held
WEB: www.mayfieldspine.com
SIC: 8011 Neurologist; neurosurgeon

(G-3984)
MC GREGOR FAMILY ENTERPRISES (PA)
Also Called: Play It Again Sports
9990 Kings Auto Mall Rd (45249-8234)
PHONE....................................513 583-0040
John Mc Gregor, President
Mary Mc Gregor, Vice Pres
EMP: 30
SQ FT: 4,200

SALES (est): 3.3MM Privately Held
SIC: 5941 5091 5932 Sporting goods & bicycle shops; sporting & recreation goods; used merchandise stores

(G-3985)
MCCASLIN IMBUS & MCCASLIN LPA (PA)
600 Vine St Ste 400 (45202-2426)
PHONE....................................513 421-4646
Gary Lewis, President
▲ EMP: 30
SALES (est): 1.8MM Privately Held
WEB: www.mimlaw.com
SIC: 8111 General practice law office

(G-3986)
MCCLUSKEY CHEVROLET INC (PA)
Also Called: McCluskey Automotive
8525 Reading Rd (45215-5598)
P.O. Box 15309 (45215-0309)
PHONE....................................513 761-1111
Daniel McCluskey, CEO
Keith P McCluskey, President
Brent Martin, Buyer
Gina Owens, Treasurer
James Gamble, Finance Mgr
EMP: 140 EST: 1927
SQ FT: 100,000
SALES (est): 56.5MM Privately Held
WEB: www.7611111.com
SIC: 5511 7515 7513 5521 Automobiles, new & used; pickups, new & used; vans, new & used; passenger car leasing; truck rental & leasing, no drivers; used car dealers; automobiles & other motor vehicles

(G-3987)
MCGILL SMITH PUNSHON INC
3700 Park 42 Dr Ste 190b (45241-2081)
PHONE....................................513 759-0004
Stephen C Roat, President
J Craig Rambo, Chairman
Stephanie Kirschner, Corp Secy
Jim Watson, Vice Pres
EMP: 28
SQ FT: 17,000
SALES (est): 4.3MM Privately Held
WEB: www.mcgillsmithpunshon.com
SIC: 8711 8712 8713 0781 Consulting engineer; architectural engineering; surveying services; landscape architects

(G-3988)
MCGINNIS INC
5525 River Rd (45233-1511)
P.O. Box 33177 (45233-0177)
PHONE....................................513 941-8070
Chris Mc Ginnis, Manager
EMP: 35
SALES (corp-wide): 152.4MM Privately Held
WEB: www.mcginnisinc.com
SIC: 4491 Marine cargo handling
HQ: Mcginnis, Inc.
502 2nd St E
South Point OH 45680
740 377-4391

(G-3989)
MCKESSON MEDICAL-SURGICAL TOP
Also Called: Physician Sales & Service
12074 Champion Way (45241-6406)
PHONE....................................513 985-0525
Fax: 513 985-0236
EMP: 40
SALES (corp-wide): 208.3B Publicly Held
SIC: 5047 Whol Medical/Hospital Equipment
HQ: Mckesson Medical-Surgical Top Holdings Inc.
4345 Southpoint Blvd
Jacksonville FL 32216
904 332-3000

(G-3990)
MCNERNEY & ASSOCIATES LLC (PA)
Also Called: P J McNerney & Associates
440 Northland Blvd (45240-3211)
PHONE....................................513 241-9951

Patrick J McNerney, *President*
Jan McNerney, *Vice Pres*
Tim McNerney, *Mktg Dir*
◆ **EMP:** 25
SQ FT: 70,000
SALES (est): 4.7MM **Privately Held**
WEB: www.pjmcnerney.com
SIC: 2752 4783 Commercial printing, litho-
graphic; packing goods for shipping

(G-3991)
MECHANCAL/INDUSTRIAL CONTG INC
Also Called: Honeywell Authorized Dealer
11863 Solzman Rd (45249-1236)
PHONE................................513 489-8282
Clay Craig, *President*
Bill Sempsrott, *Vice Pres*
Kelly Smith, *Manager*
EMP: 29
SQ FT: 20,000
SALES: 6.5MM **Privately Held**
SIC: 1711 Mechanical contractor

(G-3992)
MEDA-CARE TRANSPORTATION INC
270 Northland Blvd # 227 (45246-3660)
PHONE................................513 521-4799
RAD Galitsky, *President*
Boris Galitsky, *Principal*
EMP: 30
SALES (est): 227.2K **Privately Held**
SIC: 4119 Ambulance service

(G-3993)
MEDICAL CARE PSC INC
Also Called: Medical Reimbursment
2950 Robertson Ave Fl 2 (45209-1267)
PHONE................................513 281-4400
Richard C Levy MD, *President*
EMP: 27
SALES (est): 1.1MM **Privately Held**
SIC: 8721 7322 Billing & bookkeeping
service; collection agency, except real es-
tate

(G-3994)
MEDICAL CARE REIMBURSEMENT
Also Called: Medical Reimbursement
2950 Robertson Ave Fl 2 (45209-1267)
PHONE................................513 281-4400
Michael Jeffery, *CEO*
Jay Ripa, *Exec VP*
Bonnie Collins, *Accounts Mgr*
Monica Fussinger, *Director*
EMP: 50
SALES (est): 2MM **Privately Held**
SIC: 8721 Billing & bookkeeping service

(G-3995)
MEDICAL RECOVERY SYSTEMS INC
Also Called: Mrsi
3372 Central Pkwy (45225-2307)
PHONE................................513 872-7000
Stephen I Caroll, *President*
EMP: 100
SALES (est): 9MM **Privately Held**
SIC: 8742 Hospital & health services con-
sultant

(G-3996)
MEDICINE MIDWEST LLC (PA)
4700 Smith Rd Ste A (45212-2777)
PHONE................................513 533-1199
Robert Roettker,
EMP: 80 EST: 1998
SALES (est): 1.5MM **Privately Held**
SIC: 8043 Offices & clinics of podiatrists

(G-3997)
MEDICOUNT MANAGEMENT INC
10361 Spartan Dr (45215-1220)
P.O. Box 621005 (45262-1005)
PHONE................................513 772-4465
Joseph D Newcomb, *Ch of Bd*
Joseph A Newcomb, *President*
Tim Newcomb, *Vice Pres*
Anne Riddiough, *Accounts Mgr*
Ted Jennings, *Accounts Exec*
EMP: 40
SQ FT: 7,500

SALES (est): 4.4MM **Privately Held**
WEB: www.medicount.com
SIC: 8721 Billing & bookkeeping service

(G-3998)
MEDISYNC MIDWEST LTD LBLTY CO
25 Merchant St Ste 220 (45246-3740)
PHONE................................513 533-1199
Robert E Matthews, *CEO*
Robert E Roettker, *CFO*
Dena Perella, *Accountant*
Karen Duke, *Manager*
Charlie Hardtke, *CIO*
EMP: 85
SQ FT: 12,000
SALES (est): 13.7MM **Privately Held**
WEB: www.medisync.com
SIC: 8742 Hospital & health services con-
sultant

(G-3999)
MEDPACE INC
5355 Medpace Way (45227-1543)
PHONE................................513 366-3220
August J Troendle, *Branch Mgr*
EMP: 1200
SALES (corp-wide): 704.5MM **Publicly Held**
SIC: 8071 Biological laboratory
HQ: Medpace, Inc.
    5375 Medpace Way
    Cincinnati OH 45227

(G-4000)
MEDPACE INC (DH)
5375 Medpace Way (45227-1543)
PHONE................................513 579-9911
August Troendle, *President*
Kurt Brykman, *COO*
Susan Burwig, *Vice Pres*
Bernard Ilson, *Vice Pres*
Yun Le, *Vice Pres*
EMP: 700
SQ FT: 30,000
SALES (est): 331.8MM
SALES (corp-wide): 704.5MM **Publicly Held**
WEB: www.medpace.com
SIC: 8731 5122 5047 Biotechnical re-
search, commercial; pharmaceuticals;
medical equipment & supplies
HQ: Medpace Intermediateco, Inc.
    5375 Medpace Way
    Cincinnati OH 45227
    513 579-9911

(G-4001)
MEDPACE BIOANALYTICAL LABS LLC
5365 Medpace Way (45227-1543)
PHONE................................513 366-3260
August Troendle, *President*
Jesse Geiger, *CFO*
Stephen Ewald, *Admin Sec*
EMP: 27
SQ FT: 140,000
SALES (est): 433.2K
SALES (corp-wide): 704.5MM **Publicly Held**
SIC: 8071 Testing laboratories
HQ: Medpace, Inc.
    5375 Medpace Way
    Cincinnati OH 45227

(G-4002)
MEES DISTRIBUTORS INC (PA)
1541 W Fork Rd (45223-1203)
PHONE................................513 541-2311
Howard L Mees, *President*
Mark Waites, *COO*
Dan Sander, *Controller*
▲ **EMP:** 50 EST: 1954
SQ FT: 58,000
SALES (est): 19.7MM **Privately Held**
WEB: www.meesdistributors.com
SIC: 5032 Ceramic construction materials,
excluding refractory; ceramic wall & floor
tile

(G-4003)
MEGEN CONSTRUCTION COMPANY INC (PA)
11130 Ashburn Rd (45240-3813)
PHONE................................513 742-9191

Evans N Nwankwo, *President*
Megan Chorey, *Principal*
Fleet P Fangman, *Vice Pres*
Fleet Fangman, *Vice Pres*
Frank A Regueyra, *Vice Pres*
EMP: 40
SQ FT: 4,000
SALES (est): 36.8MM **Privately Held**
SIC: 8741 Construction management

(G-4004)
MELLOTT & MELLOTT PLL
12 Walnut St Ste 2500 (45216-2453)
PHONE................................513 241-2940
Donald Mellott Jr, *Partner*
Donald Mellot Sr, *Partner*
John Mellot, *Partner*
Rick Rumper, *Partner*
EMP: 40
SALES (est): 3.3MM **Privately Held**
WEB: www.mellottcpa.com
SIC: 8721 Certified public accountant

(G-4005)
MELS AUTO GLASS INC
11775 Reading Rd (45241-1548)
PHONE................................513 563-7771
Lisa M Gabrielle, *President*
Melvin W Wolf, *Principal*
EMP: 30
SQ FT: 8,000
SALES (est): 5.3MM **Privately Held**
WEB: www.melsautoglass.com
SIC: 7536 Automotive glass replacement
shops

(G-4006)
MENTAL HEALTH AND ADDI SERV
Also Called: Summit Bhvioral Healthcare Ctr
1101 Summit Rd (45237-2621)
PHONE................................513 948-3600
Dan Moles, *COO*
EMP: 400 **Privately Held**
SIC: 8063 9431 Psychiatric hospitals;
mental health agency administration, gov-
ernment;
HQ: Ohio Department Of Mental Health
    And Addiction Services
    30 E Broad St Fl 8
    Columbus OH 43215

(G-4007)
MERCER (US) INC
525 Vine St Ste 1600 (45202-3132)
PHONE................................513 632-2600
James Jackson, *Principal*
Miriam R Leonard, *Principal*
William Burnette, *Branch Mgr*
Shirley Ferber, *Administration*
EMP: 40
SALES (corp-wide): 14.9B **Publicly Held**
SIC: 8742 Compensation & benefits plan-
ning consultant
HQ: Mercer (Us) Inc.
    1166 Ave Of The Americ
    New York NY 10036
    212 345-7000

(G-4008)
MERCY FRANCISCAN HOSP MT AIRY (PA)
2446 Kipling Ave (45239-6650)
PHONE................................513 853-5101
Rodney Reider, *President*
Ruby Hemphil Crowford, *Vice Pres*
Judy Daleiden, *Vice Pres*
EMP: 1000
SQ FT: 10,500
SALES (est): 95MM **Privately Held**
SIC: 8741 8062 Hospital management;
nursing & personal care facility manage-
ment; general medical & surgical hospi-
tals

(G-4009)
MERCY FRNCSCAN HOSP WSTN HILLS
3131 Queen City Ave (45238-2316)
PHONE................................513 389-5000
EMP: 886
SQ FT: 100,000
SALES: 81MM **Privately Held**
SIC: 8062 General Hospital

(G-4010)
MERCY HEALTH
4750 E Galbraith Rd # 207 (45236-6706)
PHONE................................513 686-5392
EMP: 32
SALES (corp-wide): 4.7B **Privately Held**
SIC: 8062 General medical & surgical hos-
pitals
PA: Mercy Health
    1701 Mercy Health Pl
    Cincinnati OH 45237
    513 639-2800

(G-4011)
MERCY HEALTH
P.O. Box 5203 (45201-5203)
PHONE................................513 639-0250
EMP: 76
SALES (corp-wide): 4.7B **Privately Held**
SIC: 8062 General medical & surgical hos-
pitals
PA: Mercy Health
    1701 Mercy Health Pl
    Cincinnati OH 45237
    513 639-2800

(G-4012)
MERCY HEALTH
3301 Mercy Health Blvd (45211-1105)
PHONE................................513 981-5750
EMP: 125
SALES (corp-wide): 4.7B **Privately Held**
SIC: 8062 General medical & surgical hos-
pitals
PA: Mercy Health
    1701 Mercy Health Pl
    Cincinnati OH 45237
    513 639-2800

(G-4013)
MERCY HEALTH (PA)
1701 Mercy Health Pl (45237-6147)
PHONE................................513 639-2800
Michael D Connelly, *President*
Randy Curnow, *President*
Cathy Follmer, *Vice Pres*
Carlos Ballinas, *Purch Agent*
Christine Swyres, *Director*
EMP: 125
SALES: 4.7B **Privately Held**
SIC: 8062 General medical & surgical
pitals

(G-4014)
MERCY HEALTH
8094 Beechmont Ave (45255-3145)
PHONE................................513 232-7100
EMP: 54
SALES (corp-wide): 4.7B **Privately Held**
SIC: 8062 General medical & surgical hos-
pitals
PA: Mercy Health
    1701 Mercy Health Pl
    Cincinnati OH 45237
    513 639-2800

(G-4015)
MERCY HEALTH
Also Called: National Conference of Veteran
3200 Vine St (45220-2213)
PHONE................................561 358-1619
Martin Smith, *Branch Mgr*
Jonathan L Steinberg, *Psychologist*
Crystal Williams, *Psychologist*
Muhammad Aslam, *Geriatrics*
EMP: 57
SALES (corp-wide): 4.7B **Privately Held**
SIC: 8062 General medical & surgical hos-
pitals
PA: Mercy Health
    1701 Mercy Health Pl
    Cincinnati OH 45237
    513 639-2800

(G-4016)
MERCY HEALTH
Also Called: Mercy Health - Westside
5525 Marie Ave (45248-3200)
PHONE................................513 981-5463
EMP: 74
SALES (corp-wide): 4.7B **Privately Held**
SIC: 8062 General medical & surgical hos-
pitals

▲ = Import ▼=Export
◆ =Import/Export

PA: Mercy Health
1701 Mercy Health Pl
Cincinnati OH 45237
513 639-2800

(G-4017)
MERCY HEALTH
Also Called: Mercy Health - Heart Institute
4750 E Galbraith Rd # 207 (45236-6706)
PHONE..................................513 985-0741
Becky Benerer, *Branch Mgr*
EMP: 38
SALES (corp-wide): 4.7B Privately Held
SIC: 8011 General & family practice, physician/surgeon
PA: Mercy Health
1701 Mercy Health Pl
Cincinnati OH 45237
513 639-2800

(G-4018)
MERCY HEALTH
Also Called: Accounts Payable Sso
1701 Mercy Health Pl (45237-6147)
P.O. Box 5203 (45201-5203)
PHONE..................................513 639-2800
EMP: 43
SALES (corp-wide): 4.7B Privately Held
SIC: 8062 General medical & surgical hospitals
PA: Mercy Health
1701 Mercy Health Pl
Cincinnati OH 45237
513 639-2800

(G-4019)
MERCY HEALTH
Also Called: Emergency
4101 Edwards Rd Fl 2 (45209-1678)
PHONE..................................513 979-2999
EMP: 75
SALES (corp-wide): 4.7B Privately Held
SIC: 8062 General medical & surgical hospitals
PA: Mercy Health
1701 Mercy Health Pl
Cincinnati OH 45237
513 639-2800

(G-4020)
MERCY HEALTH
Also Called: Catholic Healthcare Par
7500 State Rd (45255-2439)
PHONE..................................513 233-6736
EMP: 65
SALES (corp-wide): 4.7B Privately Held
SIC: 8011 Offices & clinics of medical doctors
PA: Mercy Health
1701 Mercy Health Pl
Cincinnati OH 45237
513 639-2800

(G-4021)
MERCY HEALTH
11550 Winton Rd (45240-2355)
PHONE..................................513 924-8200
Kathy Garland, *Branch Mgr*
EMP: 27
SALES (corp-wide): 4.7B Privately Held
SIC: 8011 Offices & clinics of medical doctors
PA: Mercy Health
1701 Mercy Health Pl
Cincinnati OH 45237
513 639-2800

(G-4022)
MERCY HEALTH
10475 Reading Rd Ste 209 (45241-2500)
PHONE..................................513 585-9600
EMP: 43
SALES (corp-wide): 4.7B Privately Held
SIC: 8011 Offices & clinics of medical doctors
PA: Mercy Health
1701 Mercy Health Pl
Cincinnati OH 45237
513 639-2800

(G-4023)
MERCY HEALTH
Also Called: Mercy Hlth - White Oak Imaging
5819 Cheviot Rd (45247-6224)
PHONE..................................513 741-8200
Weaver Elizabeth, *Branch Mgr*

EMP: 27
SALES (corp-wide): 4.7B Privately Held
SIC: 8062 General medical & surgical hospitals
PA: Mercy Health
1701 Mercy Health Pl
Cincinnati OH 45237
513 639-2800

(G-4024)
MERCY HEALTH ANDERSON HOSPITAL (DH)
Also Called: MERCY HOSPITAL ANDERSON
7500 State Rd (45255-2439)
PHONE..................................513 624-4500
Patricia Shroer, *President*
EMP: 728
SQ FT: 115,000
SALES: 244.4MM
SALES (corp-wide): 4.7B Privately Held
WEB: www.mercy.health-partners.org
SIC: 8062 General medical & surgical hospitals
HQ: Mercy Health Cincinnati Llc
1701 Mercy Health Pl
Cincinnati OH 45237
513 952-5000

(G-4025)
MERCY HEALTH ANDERSON HOSPITAL
Also Called: Mercy Anderson Ambulatory Ctr
7520 State Rd (45255-2439)
PHONE..................................513 624-1950
Julie Hanser, *Principal*
EMP: 35
SALES (corp-wide): 4.7B Privately Held
WEB: www.mercy.health-partners.org
SIC: 8062 General medical & surgical hospitals
HQ: Mercy Health Anderson Hospital
7500 State Rd
Cincinnati OH 45255
513 624-4500

(G-4026)
MERCY HEALTH ANDERSON HOSPITAL
Also Called: Mercy Anderson Cancer Center
8000 5 Mile Rd Ste 105 (45230-2187)
PHONE..................................513 624-4025
Terry Beckman, *Director*
EMP: 25
SALES (corp-wide): 4.7B Privately Held
WEB: www.mercy.health-partners.org
SIC: 8062 8069 General medical & surgical hospitals; cancer hospital
HQ: Mercy Health Anderson Hospital
7500 State Rd
Cincinnati OH 45255
513 624-4500

(G-4027)
MERCY HEALTH CINCINNATI LLC (HQ)
Also Called: Mercy Health - Cincinnati
1701 Mercy Health Pl (45237-6147)
PHONE..................................513 952-5000
Tom Urban, *CEO*
Michael W Garfield, *Principal*
Kenneth C Page, *Senior VP*
Don Harmeyer, *Finance*
Tonya Carter, *Director*
EMP: 100
SALES (est): 396.2MM
SALES (corp-wide): 4.7B Privately Held
WEB: www.mercyweb.org
SIC: 8062 General medical & surgical hospitals
PA: Mercy Health
1701 Mercy Health Pl
Cincinnati OH 45237
513 639-2800

(G-4028)
MERCY HEALTH PARTNERS
Also Called: MERCY HEALTH PARTNERS OF SOUTHWEST OHIO
8000 5 Mile Rd Ste 350 (45230-2192)
PHONE..................................513 233-2444
Kelly Franer, *Principal*
EMP: 58
SALES (corp-wide): 4.7B Privately Held
SIC: 8062 General medical & surgical hospitals

HQ: Mercy Health Cincinnati Llc
1701 Mercy Health Pl
Cincinnati OH 45237
513 952-5000

(G-4029)
MERCY HEALTH PARTNERS
Also Called: Mercy Franciscan Hospital
3301 Mercy Health Blvd # 100 (45211-1105)
P.O. Box 587101 (45258-7101)
PHONE..................................513 389-5000
Rodney Ryder, *CEO*
EMP: 58
SALES (corp-wide): 4.7B Privately Held
WEB: www.mercyweb.org
SIC: 8062 General medical & surgical hospitals
HQ: Mercy Health Cincinnati Llc
1701 Mercy Health Pl
Cincinnati OH 45237
513 952-5000

(G-4030)
MERCY HEALTH PARTNERS
Also Called: Mercy Franciscan Hosp Mt Airy
2446 Kipling Ave (45239-6650)
PHONE..................................513 853-5101
EMP: 130
SQ FT: 2,298
SALES (corp-wide): 4.7B Privately Held
SIC: 8062 Hospital
HQ: Mercy Health Cincinnati Llc
1701 Mercy Health Pl
Cincinnati OH 45237
513 952-5000

(G-4031)
MERCY HEALTH PARTNERS
Also Called: Mercy Franciscan Senior Netwrk
2950 West Park Dr Ofc (45238-3542)
PHONE..................................513 451-8900
Kendra Couch, *Administration*
EMP: 300
SALES (corp-wide): 4.7B Privately Held
WEB: www.mercyweb.org
SIC: 8322 Senior citizens' center or association
HQ: Mercy Health Cincinnati Llc
1701 Mercy Health Pl
Cincinnati OH 45237
513 952-5000

(G-4032)
MERCY HEALTH PARTNERS
4750 E Galbraith Rd # 207 (45236-6706)
PHONE..................................513 686-4800
Dr Cari Ogg, *Principal*
EMP: 58
SALES (corp-wide): 4.7B Privately Held
SIC: 8062 General medical & surgical hospitals
HQ: Mercy Health Cincinnati Llc
1701 Mercy Health Pl
Cincinnati OH 45237
513 952-5000

(G-4033)
MERCY HEALTH WEST PARK
Also Called: West Park Retirement Community
2950 West Park Dr (45238-3599)
PHONE..................................513 451-8900
Rachel Wirth, *President*
EMP: 250
SQ FT: 88,000
SALES (est): 4.7MM Privately Held
SIC: 6513 8059 8051 Apartment building operators; nursing home, except skilled & intermediate care facility; skilled nursing care facilities

(G-4034)
MERCY MEDICAL ASSOCIATES
4750 E Galbraith Rd # 207 (45236-6705)
PHONE..................................513 686-4840
Jim May, *CEO*
EMP: 30
SALES (est): 1.5MM Privately Held
SIC: 8011 Internal medicine, physician/surgeon

(G-4035)
MERCY ST THERESA CENTER INC
7010 Rowan Hill Dr # 200 (45227-3380)
PHONE..................................513 271-7010
Brian Forschner, *President*
EMP: 180
SALES (est): 5.3MM Privately Held
SIC: 8051 Skilled nursing care facilities

(G-4036)
MERRILL LYNCH PIERCE FENNER
425 Walnut St Ste 2500 (45202-3930)
PHONE..................................513 579-3600
Paul Hansen, *Assistant VP*
Harvey Knowles, *Vice Pres*
John Nicholson, *Branch Mgr*
Samuel Dy, *Advisor*
EMP: 130
SALES (corp-wide): 110.5B Publicly Held
WEB: www.merlyn.com
SIC: 6211 Security brokers & dealers
HQ: Merrill Lynch, Pierce, Fenner & Smith Incorporated
111 8th Ave
New York NY 10011
800 637-7455

(G-4037)
MERRILL LYNCH PIERCE FENNER
312 Walnut St Ste 2400 (45202-4060)
PHONE..................................513 562-2100
Timothy Sutherland, *Finance*
Chris Sprenkle, *Manager*
Anthony Duggan, *Agent*
Gregory A Hopkins, *Agent*
Ross Hambleton, *Advisor*
EMP: 30
SALES (corp-wide): 110.5B Publicly Held
WEB: www.merlyn.com
SIC: 6211 Brokers, security
HQ: Merrill Lynch, Pierce, Fenner & Smith Incorporated
111 8th Ave
New York NY 10011
800 637-7455

(G-4038)
MESA INDUSTRIES INC (PA)
Also Called: Airplaco Equipment Company
4027 Eastern Ave (45226-1747)
PHONE..................................513 321-2950
Terry S Segerberg, *CEO*
Kent Sexton, *President*
James R Sexton, *Vice Pres*
Melanie Roaden, *Buyer*
Kent Segerberg, *Director*
◆ EMP: 82
SQ FT: 100,000
SALES (est): 30.1MM Privately Held
WEB: www.mesa-ind.net
SIC: 3531 5085 5082 Bituminous, cement & concrete related products & equipment; hose, belting & packing; construction & mining machinery

(G-4039)
MESSER CONSTRUCTION CO
2495 Langdon Farm Rd (45237-4950)
PHONE..................................513 672-5000
Mark Leugering, *Principal*
Justin Angrick, *Project Mgr*
Laura Boerger, *Project Engr*
Lori Sullivan, *Accountant*
Allan Dinsmore, *Executive*
EMP: 25
SALES (corp-wide): 1B Privately Held
SIC: 1542 Commercial & office building, new construction
PA: Messer Construction Co.
643 W Court St
Cincinnati OH 45203
513 242-1541

(G-4040)
MESSER CONSTRUCTION CO (PA)
Also Called: Frank Messer & Sons Cnstr Co
643 W Court St (45203-1511)
PHONE..................................513 242-1541
Thomas M Keckeis, *CEO*

Matt Monnin, *President*
Timothy J Steigerwald, *President*
Tom Wall, *President*
Ryan Wise, *Superintendent*
EMP: 100 **EST:** 1968
SQ FT: 26,000
SALES: 1B **Privately Held**
WEB: www.messer.com
SIC: 1542 1541 1522 Hospital construction; commercial & office building, new construction; commercial & office buildings, renovation & repair; school building construction; industrial buildings & warehouses; renovation, remodeling & repairs: industrial buildings; warehouse construction; hotel/motel, new construction; multifamily dwellings, new construction

(G-4041)
METCUT RESEARCH ASSOCIATES INC (PA)
3980 Rosslyn Dr (45209-1110)
PHONE.................................513 271-5100
William P Koster, *Ch of Bd*
John P Kahles, *President*
John H Clippinger, *Principal*
Robert T Keeler, *Principal*
John H More, *Principal*
EMP: 85
SQ FT: 25,000
SALES: 12.6MM **Privately Held**
WEB: www.metcut.com
SIC: 8734 3599 Metallurgical testing laboratory; machine & other job shop work

(G-4042)
METROPOLITAN SEWER DISTRICT
Also Called: Msdgc
1600 Gest St (45204-2022)
PHONE.................................513 244-1300
John Shinn, *Supervisor*
Gerald Checco, *Director*
James Parrott, *Director*
EMP: 600
SALES: 291.4MM **Privately Held**
SIC: 4952 Sewerage systems

(G-4043)
MH EQUIPMENT COMPANY
2650 Spring Grove Ave (45214-1732)
PHONE.................................513 681-2200
Bob Risheill, *Vice Pres*
Pat McCucheon, *Sales Mgr*
EMP: 55
SALES (corp-wide): 247.9MM **Privately Held**
SIC: 5084 Materials handling machinery
HQ: Mh Equipment Company
8901 N Industrial Rd
Peoria IL 61615
309 579-8020

(G-4044)
MIAMI CORPORATION (PA)
720 Anderson Ferry Rd (45238-4742)
PHONE.................................800 543-0448
Timothy J Niehaus, *President*
Mike Maisonet, *General Mgr*
Edward Cappel, *Principal*
Brian Oeder, *Principal*
Robert Tomlinson, *Principal*
▲ **EMP:** 45 **EST:** 1923
SQ FT: 40,000
SALES: 22.7MM **Privately Held**
WEB: www.miamicorp.com
SIC: 5131 5091 Upholstery fabrics, woven; boat accessories & parts

(G-4045)
MIAMI VALLEY INTL TRCKS INC
Also Called: Idealease Miami Valley Intl
11775 Highway Dr Ste D (45241-2005)
PHONE.................................513 733-8500
Chuck Siebert, *Manager*
EMP: 100
SALES (corp-wide): 41.6MM **Privately Held**
WEB: www.mvi.com
SIC: 7513 Truck rental & leasing, no drivers
PA: Miami Valley International Trucks, Inc.
7655 Poe Ave
Dayton OH 45414
937 898-3660

(G-4046)
MICHAEL G LAWLEY
8099 Cornell Rd (45249-2231)
PHONE.................................513 793-3933
Michael G Lawley, *Principal*
EMP: 30
SALES (est): 863.5K **Privately Held**
SIC: 8031 Offices & clinics of osteopathic physicians

(G-4047)
MICHAEL SCHUSTER ASSOCIATES
Also Called: MSA Architects
316 W 4th St Ste 600 (45202-2677)
PHONE.................................513 241-5666
Michael Schuster, *Principal*
Richard Tripp, *Principal*
Andrew Rowekamp, *Architect*
EMP: 39
SQ FT: 10,000
SALES (est): 7.5MM **Privately Held**
WEB: www.msaarch.com
SIC: 8712 7389 Architectural engineering; interior designer

(G-4048)
MICRO ELECTRONICS INC
Also Called: Micro Center
11755 Mosteller Rd Rear (45241-5505)
PHONE.................................513 782-8500
Chuck Gammello, *Manager*
EMP: 125
SALES (corp-wide): 3.6B **Privately Held**
WEB: www.microcenter.com
SIC: 5734 5045 Personal computers; computer peripheral equipment
PA: Micro Electronics, Inc.
4119 Leap Rd
Hilliard OH 43026
614 850-3000

(G-4049)
MIDLAND ATLANTIC PRPTS LLC (PA)
8044 Montgomery Rd # 710 (45236-2919)
PHONE.................................513 792-5000
Scott Catz, *Principal*
John Silverman, *Principal*
Daniel Shick, *Vice Pres*
Sarah Gossett, *Accountant*
Julie Krause, *Property Mgr*
EMP: 25
SQ FT: 3,600
SALES (est): 2.8MM **Privately Held**
SIC: 6531 Real estate agent, commercial

(G-4050)
MIDWEST LAUNDRY INC
10110 Cncnnati Dyton Pike (45241-1006)
PHONE.................................513 563-5560
Tom Jaynes, *General Mgr*
EMP: 70
SQ FT: 32,000
SALES: 1.9MM **Privately Held**
WEB: www.midwestlaundryinc.com
SIC: 7211 7218 7216 7213 Power laundries, family & commercial; industrial launderers; drycleaning plants, except rugs; linen supply

(G-4051)
MIDWESTERN PLUMBING SERVICE
3984 Bach Buxton Rd (45202)
PHONE.................................513 753-0050
Gene Hehemann, *President*
Eugene Heheman, *President*
Archie Wilson, *Vice Pres*
Rockie Cox, *Project Mgr*
John Harmellng, *Manager*
EMP: 40 **EST:** 1978
SQ FT: 4,700
SALES (est): 8.6MM **Privately Held**
WEB: www.midwestern-plumbing.com
SIC: 1711 6552 Plumbing contractors; subdividers & developers

(G-4052)
MILLER BROS WALLPAPER COMPANY
Also Called: Miller Bros Paint & Decorating
8460 Beechmont Ave Ste A (45255-4782)
PHONE.................................513 231-4470
Eddy Mills, *Manager*

EMP: 35
SALES (corp-wide): 6.8MM **Privately Held**
SIC: 5198 5231 Paints; paint
PA: Miller Bros. Wallpaper Company
4343 Montgomery Rd
Cincinnati OH 45212
513 531-1517

(G-4053)
MILLER CNFELD PDDOCK STONE PLC
511 Walnut St (45202-3115)
PHONE.................................513 394-5252
Linda K Wells, *Branch Mgr*
EMP: 55
SALES (corp-wide): 103.6MM **Privately Held**
SIC: 8111 General practice attorney, lawyer
PA: Miller, Canfield, Paddock And Stone, P.L.C.
150 W Jefferson Ave # 2500
Detroit MI 48226
313 963-6420

(G-4054)
MILLER-VALENTINE PARTNERS LTD
Also Called: M-V Rlty Mller Valentine Group
9349 Waterstone Blvd # 200 (45249-8320)
PHONE.................................513 588-1000
Tom Adams, *Partner*
Jack Goodwin,
EMP: 30
SALES (corp-wide): 14.2MM **Privately Held**
SIC: 6531 Real estate agents & managers
PA: Miller-Valentine Partners Ltd.
137 N Main St Ste 900
Dayton OH 45402
937 293-0900

(G-4055)
MILLER-VLNTINE PARTNERS LTD LC
Also Called: Mv Communities
9349 Waterstone Blvd # 200 (45249-8320)
PHONE.................................513 588-1000
Jeff Ramsey, *Asst Controller*
EMP: 28
SALES (corp-wide): 14.2MM **Privately Held**
SIC: 6531 Real estate agent, residential
PA: Miller-Valentine Partners Ltd.
137 N Main St Ste 900
Dayton OH 45402
937 293-0900

(G-4056)
MILLS CORPORATION
Also Called: Forest Fair Mall
600 Cincinnati Mills Dr (45240-1260)
PHONE.................................513 671-2882
Jim Childress, *Manager*
EMP: 31 **Privately Held**
WEB: www.millscorp.com
SIC: 6512 Shopping center, property operation only
HQ: The Mills Corporation
5425 Wisconsin Ave # 300
Chevy Chase MD 20815
301 968-6000

(G-4057)
MILLS FENCE CO INC (PA)
6315 Wiehe Rd (45237-4213)
PHONE.................................513 631-0333
Kenneth Mills, *President*
John Lyttle, *Vice Pres*
▲ **EMP:** 50
SQ FT: 100,000
SALES: 18.3MM **Privately Held**
WEB: www.millsfence.com
SIC: 5039 1799 5211 Wire fence, gates & accessories; fence construction; fencing

(G-4058)
MILLS SECURITY ALARM SYSTEMS
490 Mount Hope Ave (45204-1394)
PHONE.................................513 921-4600
Michael J Mills, *President*
EMP: 25
SQ FT: 7,500

SALES (est): 1.5MM **Privately Held**
WEB: www.mills-security.com
SIC: 7382 1731 Burglar alarm maintenance & monitoring; safety & security specialization

(G-4059)
MINATURE SOCIETY CINCINNATI
6718 Siebern Ave (45236-3832)
PHONE.................................513 931-9708
Gail Palmer, *President*
EMP: 58 **EST:** 1975
SALES (est): 331.7K **Privately Held**
SIC: 8641 Social club, membership

(G-4060)
MIRACLE RENOVATIONS
2786 Shaffer Ave (45211-7113)
PHONE.................................513 371-0750
Merrick Collins, *Owner*
EMP: 25
SALES: 950K **Privately Held**
SIC: 1521 Single-family housing construction

(G-4061)
MITCHELLS SALON & DAY SPA (PA)
5901 E Galbraith Rd # 230 (45236-2230)
PHONE.................................513 793-0900
Deborah M Schmidt, *President*
Christine Gilbert, *Managing Dir*
Jeanine Kreimer, *Managing Dir*
Mindy Wilson, *Managing Dir*
Teresa Bussell, *Vice Pres*
EMP: 90 **EST:** 1983
SQ FT: 11,000
SALES (est): 7.7MM **Privately Held**
WEB: www.mitchellssalon.com
SIC: 7231 7991 Hairdressers; spas

(G-4062)
MITCHELLS SALON & DAY SPA
11330 Princeton Pike (45246-3202)
PHONE.................................513 772-3200
Susie Thorpe, *Manager*
EMP: 50
SALES (corp-wide): 7.7MM **Privately Held**
WEB: www.mitchellssalon.com
SIC: 7231 Beauty shops
PA: Mitchell's Salon & Day Spa Inc
5901 E Galbraith Rd # 230
Cincinnati OH 45236
513 793-0900

(G-4063)
MITCHELLS SALON & DAY SPA
2692 Madison Rd (45208-1321)
PHONE.................................513 731-0600
Kim Socha, *Branch Mgr*
EMP: 60
SALES (corp-wide): 7.7MM **Privately Held**
WEB: www.mitchellssalon.com
SIC: 7231 7991 Unisex hair salons; spas
PA: Mitchell's Salon & Day Spa Inc
5901 E Galbraith Rd # 230
Cincinnati OH 45236
513 793-0900

(G-4064)
MK CHILDCARE WARSAW AVE LLC
3711 Warsaw Ave (45205-1773)
PHONE.................................513 922-6279
Mary B Walker,
EMP: 40
SALES (est): 143K **Privately Held**
SIC: 8351 Child day care services

(G-4065)
MLM CHILDCARE LLC
16 Beaufort Hunt Ln (45242-4672)
PHONE.................................513 623-8243
Courtney Berling,
EMP: 35
SALES (est): 120.4K **Privately Held**
SIC: 8351 Child day care services

(G-4066)
MOBILCOMM INC
1211 W Sharon Rd (45240-2916)
PHONE.................................513 742-5555
Greg Conrad, *President*

▲ = Import ▼=Export
◆ =Import/Export

EMP: 97
SALES (est): 14.2MM
SALES (corp-wide): 14.9MM **Privately Held**
WEB: www.mobilcomm.com
SIC: 7622 7359 5999 5065 Communication equipment repair; mobile communication equipment rental; communication equipment; electronic parts & equipment; electrical appliances, television & radio
PA: Combined Tecnologies, Inc.
1211 W Sharon Rd
Cincinnati OH 45240
513 595-5900

(G-4067)
MODAL SHOP INC
Also Called: T M S
3149 E Kemper Rd (45241-1516)
PHONE.....................513 351-9919
Michael J Lally, *President*
Emily T O'Dell, *President*
Tom Clary, *Engineer*
Aaron Goosman, *Engineer*
Chad Kallmeyer, *Engineer*
EMP: 70
SQ FT: 17,000
SALES (est): 40.2MM
SALES (corp-wide): 778MM **Publicly Held**
WEB: www.modalshop.com
SIC: 5084 7359 8711 Controlling instruments & accessories; electronic equipment rental, except computers; engineering services
HQ: Pcb Piezotronics, Inc.
3425 Walden Ave
Depew NY 14043
716 684-0001

(G-4068)
MODEL GROUP INC
2170 Gilbert Ave Ste 100 (45206-2577)
PHONE.....................513 559-0048
Arthur Reckman, *President*
Sam Barnhorst, *Superintendent*
Bob Keppler, *Vice Pres*
Stephen Smith, *Vice Pres*
Jason Wehby, *Vice Pres*
EMP: 50
SQ FT: 3,540
SALES (est): 7.1MM **Privately Held**
WEB: www.modelmgt.com
SIC: 6531 Real estate managers

(G-4069)
MODERN BUILDERS SUPPLY INC
6225 Wiehe Rd (45237-4211)
PHONE.....................513 531-1000
Dave Thiem, *General Mgr*
David Phiem, *Manager*
EMP: 25
SQ FT: 26,000
SALES (corp-wide): 347.7MM **Privately Held**
WEB: www.polaristechnologies.com
SIC: 5033 5031 Roofing, siding & insulation; doors & windows
PA: Modern Builders Supply, Inc.
3500 Phillips Ave
Toledo OH 43608
419 241-3961

(G-4070)
MONARCH CONSTRUCTION COMPANY
1654 Sherman Ave (45212-2598)
P.O. Box 12249 (45212-0249)
PHONE.....................513 351-6900
Ronald A Koetters, *CEO*
Thomas P Butler, *President*
Jerome J Corbett Jr, *CFO*
EMP: 200
SQ FT: 21,500
SALES (est): 79MM **Privately Held**
SIC: 1542 1541 Commercial & office building, new construction; commercial & office buildings, renovation & repair; institutional building construction; school building construction; industrial buildings & warehouses

(G-4071)
MONSTER WORLDWIDE INC
10296 Springfield Pike # 500 (45215-1194)
PHONE.....................513 719-3331
Pat Obrien, *Branch Mgr*
EMP: 68
SALES (corp-wide): 27.2B **Privately Held**
SIC: 7311 Advertising agencies
HQ: Monster Worldwide, Inc.
133 Boston Post Rd
Weston MA 02493
978 461-8000

(G-4072)
MORELIA CONSULTANTS LLC
11210 Montgomery Rd (45249-2311)
PHONE.....................513 469-1500
Christopher Hildebrant,
EMP: 75
SQ FT: 10,200
SALES (est): 6.8MM **Privately Held**
SIC: 6798 6531 Real estate investment trusts; real estate managers

(G-4073)
MORELIA GROUP LLC
8600 Governors Hill Dr # 160 (45249-1360)
PHONE.....................513 469-1500
Christopher Hildebrant, *CEO*
EMP: 35
SALES (est): 482.8K **Privately Held**
SIC: 4813 Telephone communication, except radio

(G-4074)
MORGAN STANLEY
221 E 4th St Ste 2200 (45202-4147)
PHONE.....................513 721-2000
Matt Maloney, *Branch Mgr*
EMP: 50
SALES (corp-wide): 40.1B **Publicly Held**
SIC: 6211 6282 Brokers, security; investment advice
PA: Morgan Stanley
1585 Broadway
New York NY 10036
212 761-4000

(G-4075)
MORRIS TECHNOLOGIES INC
11988 Tramway Dr (45241-1664)
PHONE.....................513 733-1611
Gregory M Morris, *CEO*
William G Noack, *President*
Wendell H Morris, *Treasurer*
Sharon Wray, *Human Resources*
Tom Sinnett, *Director*
EMP: 105
SQ FT: 25,000
SALES (est): 11.5MM **Privately Held**
WEB: www.morristech.com
SIC: 8711 3999 3313 8731 Mechanical engineering; models, except toy; alloys, additive, except copper: not made in blast furnaces; engineering laboratory, except testing; electrical discharge machining (EDM); surgical & medical instruments

(G-4076)
MOSKOWITZ FAMILY LTD
Also Called: Moskowitz Family Trust
7220 Pippin Rd (45239-4607)
PHONE.....................513 729-2300
EMP: 115
SQ FT: 40,000
SALES (est): 8.4MM **Privately Held**
SIC: 6798 Real Estate Investment Trust

(G-4077)
MOTZ GROUP INC (PA)
3607 Church St Ste 300 (45244-3097)
PHONE.....................513 533-6452
Joseph Motz, *President*
Mark Heinlein, *Senior VP*
Allen Verdin, *Project Mgr*
Lou Schindler, *Safety Mgr*
Heather Loux, *Accountant*
▲ EMP: 50 EST: 1994
SQ FT: 1,600
SALES (est): 11.3MM **Privately Held**
WEB: www.themotzgroup.com
SIC: 1799 0782 Artificial turf installation; turf installation services, except artificial

(G-4078)
MOUNT AUBURN OBSTETRICS & GYNE (PA)
Also Called: Mt Auburn Women's Center
2123 Auburn Ave Ste 724 (45219-2906)
PHONE.....................513 241-4774
John D Adler MD, *President*
James S Wendel MD, *Treasurer*
EMP: 40 EST: 1976
SQ FT: 1,900
SALES (est): 4.9MM **Privately Held**
SIC: 8011 Obstetrician; gynecologist

(G-4079)
MPLX TERMINALS LLC
4015 River Rd (45204-1035)
PHONE.....................513 451-0485
Sam O'Koon, *Manager*
EMP: 30
SALES (corp-wide): 6.4B **Publicly Held**
WEB: www.mapllc.com
SIC: 5172 Petroleum products
HQ: Mplx Terminals Llc
200 E Hardin St
Findlay OH

(G-4080)
MSK HOSPITALITY INC
Also Called: Econo Lodge
11620 Chester Rd (45246-2804)
PHONE.....................513 771-0370
Sanmukh Patel, *President*
EMP: 25
SALES (est): 1.3MM **Privately Held**
SIC: 7011 Hotel, franchised

(G-4081)
MT HEALTHY CHRISTIAN HOME INC
Also Called: CHRISTIAN BENEVOLENT ASSOCIATI
8097 Hamilton Ave (45231-2395)
PHONE.....................513 931-5000
Rod Huron, *Ch of Bd*
Kitty Garner, *Treasurer*
David Philips, *Admin Sec*
EMP: 175 EST: 1964
SQ FT: 300,000
SALES: 7.1MM
SALES (corp-wide): 2.3MM **Privately Held**
SIC: 8059 Rest home, with health care
PA: Christian Benevolent Association
8097 Hamilton Ave
Cincinnati OH 45231
513 931-5000

(G-4082)
MT TEXAS LLC
3055 Colerain Ave (45225-1827)
PHONE.....................513 853-4400
Doug Lang, *Mng Member*
EMP: 35
SALES (est): 1.7MM **Privately Held**
SIC: 7699 Aircraft & heavy equipment repair services

(G-4083)
MT WASHINGTON CARE CENTER INC
6900 Beechmont Ave (45230-2910)
PHONE.....................513 231-4561
James Farley, *President*
Michael Scharfenberger, *Exec VP*
Estate of Robert Wynne, *Treasurer*
Dawn Duncan, *Nursing Dir*
EMP: 215
SALES (est): 11.6MM **Privately Held**
WEB: www.mtwcc.com
SIC: 8051 8322 6282 7389 Convalescent home with continuous nursing care; individual & family services; investment advice;

(G-4084)
MTM TECHNOLOGIES (TEXAS) INC
8044 Montgomery Rd # 700 (45236-2926)
PHONE.....................513 786-6600
Jeff Grahm, *General Mgr*
EMP: 27 **Privately Held**
SIC: 5045 Computers, peripherals & software

HQ: Mtm Technologies (Texas) Inc
12600 Northborough Dr # 200
Houston TX 77067
203 975-3700

(G-4085)
MUNICPAL CNTRS SALING PDTS INC
Also Called: Sewer Savors
7740 Reinhold Dr (45237-2806)
PHONE.....................513 482-3300
Robert O'Connor, *President*
EMP: 25 EST: 2000
SQ FT: 10,000
SALES (est): 3MM **Privately Held**
SIC: 1623 Sewer line construction

(G-4086)
MURPHY TRACTOR & EQP CO INC
Also Called: John Deere Authorized Dealer
11441 Mosteller Rd (45241-1829)
PHONE.....................513 772-3232
Thomas Udland, *President*
Mike Skiles, *Branch Mgr*
EMP: 40 **Privately Held**
SIC: 5082 General construction machinery & equipment
HQ: Murphy Tractor & Equipment Co., Inc.
5375 N Deere Rd
Park City KS 67219
855 246-9124

(G-4087)
MV RESIDENTIAL CNSTR INC
9349 Waterstone Blvd # 200 (45249-8325)
PHONE.....................513 588-1000
Mike Green, *CEO*
Randy Humbert, *President*
EMP: 750
SQ FT: 23,000
SALES (est): 106.8MM **Privately Held**
SIC: 1522 Residential construction

(G-4088)
MV TRANSPORTATION INC
Also Called: Lancaster Transportation
1801 Transpark Dr (45229-1239)
P.O. Box 2583, Lancaster (43130-5583)
PHONE.....................740 681-5086
Chad Hockmay, *Manager*
EMP: 78
SALES (corp-wide): 1.4B **Privately Held**
WEB: www.mvtransit.com
SIC: 4111 Bus transportation
PA: Mv Transportation, Inc.
2711 N Haskell Ave
Dallas TX 75204
214 265-3400

(G-4089)
N COOK INC
5762 Argus Rd (45224-3204)
PHONE.....................513 275-9872
Nathan Cook, *Principal*
EMP: 33
SALES (est): 1.2MM **Privately Held**
SIC: 1542 Commercial & office building contractors

(G-4090)
NATIONAL AMUSEMENTS INC
760 Cincinnati Mills Dr (45240-1261)
PHONE.....................513 699-1500
John Beinke, *Branch Mgr*
EMP: 41
SALES (corp-wide): 14.5B **Publicly Held**
WEB: www.nationalamusements.com
SIC: 7832 Motion picture theaters, except drive-in
PA: National Amusements, Inc.
846 University Ave
Norwood MA 02062
781 461-1600

(G-4091)
NATIONAL EXPRESS TRANSIT CORP
8041 Hosbrook Rd Ste 330 (45236-2909)
PHONE.....................513 322-6214
Gary Waits, *CEO*
Mark Foster, *Vice Pres*
Thomas M Greufe, *Vice Pres*
Greg Harrington, *Vice Pres*
Mike Rushin, *CFO*

EMP: 99
SALES (est): 2.4MM **Privately Held**
SIC: 4119 Local passenger transportation

(G-4092)
NATIONAL HERITG ACADEMIES INC
Also Called: Orion Academy
1798 Queen City Ave (45214-1427)
PHONE..............................513 251-6000
Terrez Thomas, *Branch Mgr*
EMP: 54 **Privately Held**
SIC: 8741 Management services
PA: National Heritage Academies, Inc.
　3850 Broadmoor Ave Se # 201
　Grand Rapids MI 49512

(G-4093)
NATIONAL HERITG ACADEMIES INC
Also Called: Alliance Academy of Cincinnati
1712 Duck Creek Rd (45207-1644)
PHONE..............................513 751-5555
Juanita Preston, *Principal*
EMP: 54 **Privately Held**
SIC: 8741 Management services
PA: National Heritage Academies, Inc.
　3850 Broadmoor Ave Se # 201
　Grand Rapids MI 49512

(G-4094)
NATIONAL MARKETSHARE GROUP (PA)
2155 W 8th St (45204-2051)
PHONE..............................513 921-0800
William Burwinkel, *President*
Beth A Burwinkel, *Treasurer*
Scott Boothe, *Sales Mgr*
Danny Havel, *Sales Mgr*
Bobbi Bahr, *Sales Associate*
EMP: 37
SQ FT: 18,000
SALES (est): 6.2MM **Privately Held**
SIC: 5023 5092 5013 5087 Home furnishings; toys; automotive supplies & parts; janitors' supplies; specialty food items

(G-4095)
NATIONAL UNDERGROUND RAILROAD
1301 Western Ave (45203-1138)
PHONE..............................513 333-7500
Kim Robinson, *CEO*
Edwin Rigaud, *Ch of Bd*
Spencer Crew, *President*
Daniel Hoffheimer, *Chairman*
Christopher Miller, *Manager*
EMP: 85 **EST:** 1995
SALES: 4.4MM **Privately Held**
WEB: www.nurfc.org
SIC: 8412 Historical society; museum

(G-4096)
NATIONAL VALUATION CONSULTANTS
441 Vine St (45202-2821)
PHONE..............................513 929-4100
Jim Moher, *Branch Mgr*
EMP: 34 **Privately Held**
SIC: 8999 Scientific consulting
PA: National Valuation Consultants
　7807 E Pkview Ave Ste 200
　Centennial CO 80111

(G-4097)
NATIONWIDE TRANSPORT LLC
4445 Lk Frest Dr Ste 475 (45242)
PHONE..............................513 554-0203
Alan Hiatt,
EMP: 33
SQ FT: 15,000
SALES (est): 7MM **Privately Held**
WEB: www.nationwidetransport.net
SIC: 4731 Truck transportation brokers

(G-4098)
NATL CITY COML CAPITOL LLC
995 Dalton Ave (45203-1100)
PHONE..............................513 455-9746
Vince Rinaldi, *Principal*
EMP: 31
SALES (est): 6.2MM **Privately Held**
SIC: 6799 Investors

(G-4099)
NATROP INC
4400 Reading Rd (45229-1254)
PHONE..............................513 242-1375
William Kenneth Natorp, *CEO*
John Schmidt, *President*
Marian Brush, *Admin Sec*
EMP: 80
SQ FT: 15,000
SALES (est): 1.5MM **Privately Held**
SIC: 0782 Landscape contractors

(G-4100)
NCS HEALTHCARE OF OHIO LLC (DH)
201 E 4th St Ste 900 (45202-4160)
PHONE..............................513 719-2600
James Cialdini, *President*
EMP: 56
SALES (est): 46.7MM
SALES (corp-wide): 194.5B **Publicly Held**
SIC: 5122 Drugs, proprietaries & sundries

(G-4101)
NEALS CONSTRUCTION COMPANY
Also Called: Neals Design Remodel
7770 E Kemper Rd (45249-1612)
PHONE..............................513 489-7700
Neal P Hendy, *CEO*
Allan Hendy, *Vice Pres*
Neal Hendy Jr, *Vice Pres*
Steve Hendy, *Vice Pres*
Kevin Dunn, *Prdtn Mgr*
EMP: 29 **EST:** 1972
SQ FT: 3,000
SALES (est): 4.8MM **Privately Held**
WEB: www.neals.com
SIC: 1521 General remodeling, single-family houses

(G-4102)
NEHEMIAH MANUFACTURING CO LLC
1907 South St (45204-2033)
PHONE..............................513 351-5700
Daniel Meyer, *CEO*
Richard T Palmer, *President*
Mike Pachko, *COO*
Rich Halsey, *Vice Pres*
Eric Wellinghoff, *Vice Pres*
▲ **EMP:** 50
SQ FT: 33,706
SALES (est): 29.2MM **Privately Held**
SIC: 5122 2844 Toilet preparations; toiletries

(G-4103)
NEIGHBORCARE INC (DH)
201 E 4th St Ste 900 (45202-4160)
PHONE..............................513 719-2600
Elizabeth A Haley, *President*
Robert A Smith, *COO*
John L Kordash, *Exec VP*
John F Gaither Jr, *Senior VP*
Richard W Hunt, *CFO*
EMP: 600
SQ FT: 90,000
SALES (est): 500.8MM
SALES (corp-wide): 194.5B **Publicly Held**
WEB: www.ghv.com
SIC: 5122 5912 5047 7389 Pharmaceuticals; drug stores & proprietary stores; medical equipment & supplies; purchasing service
HQ: Omnicare Holding Company
　1105 Market St Ste 1300
　Cincinnati OH 45215
　513 719-2600

(G-4104)
NEIGHBORHOOD HEALTH CARE INC (PA)
2415 Auburn Ave (45219-2701)
PHONE..............................513 221-4949
Johnny B Daniels, *President*
Tracy Tiller, *Pediatrics*
EMP: 37
SALES: 6.5MM **Privately Held**
SIC: 8399 Social services

(G-4105)
NEIL KRAVITZ GROUP SALES INC
412 S Cooper Ave (45215-4555)
PHONE..............................513 961-8697
Neil Kravitz, *President*
Chris Schlichter, *General Mgr*
Daniel Conwell, *Vice Pres*
Jason Ernst, *Vice Pres*
Mike Paniccia, *Vice Pres*
◆ **EMP:** 34
SQ FT: 370,000
SALES: 22.4MM **Privately Held**
WEB: www.groupsalesinc.com
SIC: 5092 Toys & hobby goods & supplies

(G-4106)
NELSON STARK COMPANY
7685 Fields Ertel Rd D2 (45241-6084)
PHONE..............................513 489-0866
Jeff Read, *President*
Mark Stark, *President*
Todd Elliott, *General Mgr*
Charles Nelson, *Senior VP*
H Joseph Iori, *Vice Pres*
EMP: 170
SQ FT: 45,000
SALES: 52.9MM **Privately Held**
WEB: www.nelsonstark.com
SIC: 1711 1623 1794 Plumbing contractors; water, sewer & utility lines; underground utilities contractor; excavation work

(G-4107)
NEW HOPE & HORIZONS
4055 Executive Park Dr # 100 (45241-4029)
PHONE..............................513 761-7999
Marvin W Sims, *Owner*
EMP: 40
SQ FT: 428
SALES (est): 4MM **Privately Held**
SIC: 8052 Intermediate care facilities

(G-4108)
NEW SCHOOL INC
Also Called: NEW SCHOOL MONTESSORI, THE
3 Burton Woods Ln (45229-1399)
PHONE..............................513 281-7999
Jeff Groh, *Director*
Eric Dustman, *Director*
Ceara Comstock, *Hlthcr Dir*
EMP: 38
SQ FT: 10,000
SALES: 1.7MM **Privately Held**
WEB: www.thenewschool.cc
SIC: 8211 8351 Private elementary school; preschool center

(G-4109)
NEW VULCO MFG & SALES CO LLC
Also Called: Vulcan Oil Company
5353 Spring Grove Ave (45217-1026)
PHONE..............................513 242-2672
Garry Ferraris,
Larry Schirmann,
EMP: 60
SALES (est): 14.6MM **Privately Held**
SIC: 5983 2992 5171 2899 Fuel oil dealers; oils & greases, blending & compounding; petroleum bulk stations; petroleum terminals; chemical preparations; specialty cleaning, polishes & sanitation goods; soap & other detergents

(G-4110)
NEW YORK LIFE INSURANCE CO
5905 E Galbraith Rd # 4000 (45236-2972)
PHONE..............................513 621-9999
Jeffrey Slattery, *Manager*
Jerome Geller, *Manager*
EMP: 58
SALES (corp-wide): 18.3B **Privately Held**
WEB: www.newyorklife.com
SIC: 6411 Insurance agents & brokers
PA: New York Life Insurance Company
　51 Madison Ave Bsmt 1b
　New York NY 10010
　212 576-7000

(G-4111)
NEWCOMER FUNERAL SVC GROUP INC
7830 Hamilton Ave (45231-3106)
PHONE..............................513 521-1971
John Fish, *Director*
EMP: 379
SALES (corp-wide): 22.8MM **Privately Held**
SIC: 7261 Funeral home
PA: Newcomer Funeral Service Group, Inc.
　520 Sw 27th St
　Topeka KS 66611
　785 233-6655

(G-4112)
NEWPORT WALKING TOURS LLC
Also Called: American Legacy Tours
6292 Eagles Lake Dr (45248-6857)
PHONE..............................859 951-8560
Brad Hill, *Mng Member*
EMP: 36
SALES (est): 805.2K **Privately Held**
SIC: 4725 Tours, conducted

(G-4113)
NEXTEL COMMUNICATIONS INC
7878 Montgomery Rd (45236-4301)
PHONE..............................513 891-9200
Kat Williams, *Principal*
EMP: 60
SALES (corp-wide): 85.9B **Publicly Held**
SIC: 4812 Cellular telephone services
HQ: Nextel Communications, Inc.
　12502 Sunrise Valley Dr
　Reston VA 20191
　703 433-4000

(G-4114)
NEXTMED SYSTEMS INC (PA)
16 Triangle Park Dr (45246-3411)
PHONE..............................216 674-0511
David Shute, *CEO*
James Bennett, *Ch of Bd*
EMP: 44
SQ FT: 3,000
SALES (est): 3.6MM **Privately Held**
SIC: 7372 Business oriented computer software

(G-4115)
NEXTT CORP
106 Koehler Ave Apt 4 (45215-4844)
PHONE..............................513 813-6398
Travis Bea, *Principal*
EMP: 25
SALES (est): 807K **Privately Held**
SIC: 1521 General remodeling, single-family houses; repairing fire damage, single-family houses

(G-4116)
NEXXTSHOW EXPOSITION SVCS LLC
645 Linn St (45203-1722)
PHONE..............................877 836-3131
Aaron Bludworth, *CEO*
Jt Barclay, *CFO*
EMP: 50
SALES (est): 2.5MM
SALES (corp-wide): 44.5MM **Privately Held**
SIC: 7389 Convention & show services
PA: Fern Exposition Services Llc
　645 Linn St
　Cincinnati OH 45203
　513 621-6111

(G-4117)
NEYER REAL ESTATE MGT LLC
Also Called: Neyer Management
3927 Brotherton Rd # 200 (45209-1100)
PHONE..............................513 618-6000
Kathy Macke, *Property Mgr*
John E Neyer,
EMP: 30
SALES (est): 5.6MM **Privately Held**
WEB: www.neyermanagement.com
SIC: 6531 Rental agent, real estate

(G-4118)
NGM INC
Also Called: Custom Mail Services
7676 Reinhold Dr (45237-3312)
P.O. Box 37387 (45222-0387)
PHONE................................513 821-7363
Gene Magers, *President*
Deborah Magers, *Vice Pres*
Tonya Trippel, *Accounts Exec*
Kammy Alessandrini, *Info Tech Mgr*
EMP: 25
SQ FT: 30,000
SALES (est): 2.6MM **Privately Held**
WEB: www.custommailservices.com
SIC: 7389 Mailbox rental & related service

(G-4119)
NIEMAN PLUMBING INC
2030 Stapleton Ct (45240-2778)
PHONE................................513 851-5588
Drew Nieman, *President*
Jo Ellen Nieman, *Corp Secy*
EMP: 95
SQ FT: 20,000
SALES (est): 14.3MM **Privately Held**
WEB: www.niemanplumbing.com
SIC: 1711 Septic system construction;
plumbing contractors

(G-4120)
NISBET CORPORATION
Also Called: West Shell Coml Encore Intl
11575 Reading Rd (45241-2240)
PHONE................................513 563-1111
Mark Rippe, *President*
EMP: 150
SALES (est): 3.9MM **Privately Held**
SIC: 6531 Real estate agents & managers

(G-4121)
NOGGINS HAIR DESIGN INC
8556 Beechmont Ave # 450 (45255-4787)
PHONE................................513 474-4405
Jeff Anderson, *President*
Lisa Cornetet, *Executive*
EMP: 26
SALES (est): 439 1K **Privately Held**
SIC: 7231 7299 Hairdressers; tanning
salon

(G-4122)
NORAMCO TRANSPORT CORP (PA)
9252 Colerain Ave Ste 4 (45251-2447)
PHONE................................513 245-9050
Michael A Wetterich, *President*
Mark Wetterich, *Vice Pres*
EMP: 25
SQ FT: 50,000
SALES (est): 8MM **Privately Held**
SIC: 4731 4213 Freight forwarding; truck-
ing, except local

(G-4123)
NORFOLK SOUTHERN CORPORATION
1410 Gest St Fl 2 (45203-1019)
PHONE................................513 977-3246
BJ Mackey, *Manager*
EMP: 70
SALES (corp-wide): 11.4B **Publicly Held**
WEB: www.nscorp.com
SIC: 4011 Railroads, line-haul operating
PA: Norfolk Southern Corporation
3 Commercial Pl Ste 1a
Norfolk VA 23510
757 629-2680

(G-4124)
NORMANDY OFFICE ASSOCIATES
Also Called: Normanity Town
1055 Saint Paul Pl (45202-6042)
PHONE................................513 381-8696
Neil K Bortz, *General Ptnr*
Marvin Rosenberg, *General Ptnr*
EMP: 75
SQ FT: 10,000
SALES (est): 1.7MM **Privately Held**
SIC: 6531 Real estate agents & managers

(G-4125)
NORTH AMERICAN PROPERTIES INC
212 E 3rd St Ste 300 (45202-5500)
PHONE................................513 721-2744
Thomas L Williams, *President*
Donel Autin, *Partner*
Dale Hafele, *Principal*
Anthony Hobson, *Principal*
William J Williams Jr, *Chairman*
EMP: 40
SQ FT: 5,500
SALES (est): 9.5MM **Privately Held**
SIC: 6531 6552 Real estate managers;
subdividers & developers

(G-4126)
NORTH SIDE BANK AND TRUST CO (PA)
4125 Hamilton Ave (45223-2246)
P.O. Box 23128 (45223-0128)
PHONE................................513 542-7800
Clifford Coors, *Ch of Bd*
John A Coors, *President*
Donald Beimesche, *Vice Pres*
Michael Wisniewski, *Vice Pres*
EMP: 100 **EST:** 1891
SQ FT: 19,348
SALES: 23.3MM **Privately Held**
WEB: www.nsbt.net
SIC: 6022 State trust companies accepting
deposits, commercial

(G-4127)
NORTH SIDE BANK AND TRUST CO
2739 Madison Rd (45209-2208)
PHONE................................513 533-8000
Clifford Coors, *CEO*
EMP: 99
SALES (corp-wide): 23.3MM **Privately Held**
SIC: 6022 State trust companies accepting
deposits, commercial
PA: The North Side Bank And Trust Com-
pany
4125 Hamilton Ave
Cincinnati OH 45223
513 542-7800

(G-4128)
NORTHBEND ARCHTCTURAL PDTS INC
2080 Waycross Rd (45240-2717)
PHONE................................513 577-7988
Mark Smith, *President*
Richard Perkins, *CFO*
▲ **EMP:** 38
SQ FT: 3,000
SALES (est): 5.4MM **Privately Held**
WEB: www.waltekltd.com
SIC: 1791 Structural steel erection

(G-4129)
NORTHGATE CHRYSLER JEEP INC
8536 Colerain Ave (45251-2914)
PHONE................................513 385-3900
Peter Pannier, *President*
Kathy Hettesheimer, *Treasurer*
EMP: 60 **EST:** 1967
SQ FT: 40,000
SALES (est): 26.2MM **Privately Held**
WEB: www.northgatechrysler.com
SIC: 5511 7538 7515 7532 Automobiles,
new & used; general automotive repair
shops; passenger car leasing; body shop,
automotive

(G-4130)
NORTHGATE PK RETIREMENT CMNTY
9191 Round Top Rd Ofc (45251-2465)
PHONE................................513 923-3711
Patricia Jett, *Director*
EMP: 60
SQ FT: 50,000
SALES (est): 2.2MM **Privately Held**
SIC: 8361 Residential care

(G-4131)
NORTHWEST LOCAL SCHOOL DST
3308 Compton Rd (45251-2508)
PHONE................................513 923-1000
EMP: 73
SALES (corp-wide): 111.8MM **Privately Held**
SIC: 8211 8351 Public elementary & sec-
ondary schools; preschool center
PA: Northwest Local School District
3240 Banning Rd
Cincinnati OH 45239
513 923-1000

(G-4132)
NORTHWESTERN MUTL LF INSUR CO
3805 Edwards Rd Ste 200 (45209-1939)
PHONE................................513 366-3600
Shawn Kelley, *Manager*
EMP: 100
SALES (corp-wide): 28.1B **Privately Held**
WEB: www.nmfn.com
SIC: 6411 Insurance agents, brokers &
service
PA: The Northwestern Mutual Life Insur-
ance Company
720 E Wisconsin Ave
Milwaukee WI 53202
414 271-1444

(G-4133)
NORWOOD ENDOSCOPY CENTER
4746 Montgomery Rd # 100 (45212-2626)
PHONE................................513 731-5600
Daniel G Walker, *Principal*
EMP: 25
SALES (est): 1.1MM **Privately Held**
SIC: 8011 Gastronomist; endocrinologist

(G-4134)
NORWOOD HARDWARE & SUPPLY CO (PA)
2906 Glendale Milford Rd (45241-3131)
PHONE................................513 733-1175
Matt Chabot, *CEO*
Matthew Chabot, *Vice Pres*
Paul Sylvester, *Treasurer*
Craig Chabot, *Admin Sec*
▲ **EMP:** 50
SQ FT: 58,000
SALES (est): 22.2MM **Privately Held**
WEB: www.norwoodhardware.com
SIC: 5072 5031 5023 Hardware; metal
doors, sash & trim; doors; home furnish-
ings

(G-4135)
NORWOOD HEALTH CARE CENTER LLC
1578 Sherman Ave (45212-2510)
PHONE................................513 351-0153
Herbert Seidner, *Mng Member*
EMP: 85
SQ FT: 23,000
SALES (est): 1.5MM **Privately Held**
SIC: 8051 8052 8059 Skilled nursing care
facilities; intermediate care facilities; nurs-
ing home, except skilled & intermediate
care facility

(G-4136)
NOVELART MANUFACTURING COMPANY (PA)
Also Called: Topicz
2121 Section Rd (45237-3509)
P.O. Box 37289 (45222-0289)
PHONE................................513 351-7700
Marvin H Schwartz, *President*
Darlene Miller, *Buyer*
Angela Steinke, *Buyer*
Mark Zimmer, *Buyer*
Mike Fields, *Controller*
EMP: 100 **EST:** 1903
SQ FT: 90,000
SALES: 379.5MM **Privately Held**
SIC: 5141 5145 5194 Food brokers; con-
fectionery; tobacco & tobacco products

(G-4137)
NTT DATA INC
3284 North Bend Rd # 107 (45239-7688)
PHONE................................513 794-1400
Fax: 513 794-1040
EMP: 58
SALES (corp-wide): 93.3B **Privately Held**
SIC: 7371 Custom Computer Programing
HQ: Ntt Data, Inc.
5601 Gran Pkwy Ste 1000
Plano TX 75024
800 745-3263

(G-4138)
NUEROLOGICAL & SLEEP DISORDERS
Also Called: Fleet Management Institute
8250 Kenwood Crossing Way
(45236-3668)
PHONE................................513 721-7533
James Armitage, *CEO*
Bruce Corser, *CEO*
EMP: 35
SALES (est): 3.1MM **Privately Held**
SIC: 8011 Specialized medical practition-
ers, except internal

(G-4139)
NURAY RADIOLOGISTS INC
8160 Corp Pk Dr Ste 330 (45242)
P.O. Box 42417 (45242-0417)
PHONE................................513 965-8059
Beverly Shilton, *Manager*
EMP: 50
SALES (est): 2.6MM **Privately Held**
SIC: 8011 Radiologist

(G-4140)
NUROTOCO MASSACHUSETTS INC
Also Called: Roto-Rooter
255 E 5th St (45202-4700)
PHONE................................513 762-6690
Spencer Lee, *CEO*
EMP: 110
SALES (est): 2.6MM
SALES (corp-wide): 1.7B **Publicly Held**
SIC: 7699 Sewer cleaning & rodding
HQ: Roto-Rooter Services Company
255 E 5th St Ste 2500
Cincinnati OH 45202
513 762-6690

(G-4141)
NURSES CARE INC
9200 Montgomery Rd 13b (45242-7792)
PHONE................................513 791-0233
Tammy Stover, *Branch Mgr*
EMP: 45
SALES (corp-wide): 3.9MM **Privately Held**
WEB: www.nursescareinc.com
SIC: 7361 Nurses' registry
PA: Nurses Care, Inc
9009 Springboro Pike
Miamisburg OH 45342
513 424-1141

(G-4142)
NURSING CARE MGT AMER INC
Also Called: Montgomery Care Center
7777 Cooper Rd (45242-7703)
PHONE................................513 793-5092
Mark Osendorf, *Manager*
EMP: 95
SALES (corp-wide): 26.1MM **Privately Held**
WEB: www.nursinghomeinfo.org
SIC: 8741 8051 8059 Nursing & personal
care facility management; skilled nursing
care facilities; nursing home, except
skilled & intermediate care facility
PA: Nursing Care Management Of America,
Inc.
7265 Kenwood Rd Ste 300
Cincinnati OH 45236
513 793-8804

(G-4143)
OAK HILLS SWIM & RACQUET
5850 Muddy Creek Rd (45233-1808)
P.O. Box 58202 (45258-0202)
PHONE................................513 922-1827
Brian Galliger, *Principal*
EMP: 40

SALES: 186.2K **Privately Held**
SIC: 7997　Swimming club, membership

(G-4144)
OAKDALE ELEMENTARY PTA
3850 Virginia Ct (45248-3212)
PHONE.................................513 574-1100
Sam Gibbs, *Principal*
EMP: 75
SALES: 39.3K **Privately Held**
SIC: 8641　Parent-teachers' association

(G-4145)
OAKTREE LLC
Also Called: Oak Hlls Nrsing Rehabilitation
4307 Bridgetown Rd (45211-4427)
PHONE.................................513 598-8000
Aharon Kibel,
EMP: 70 EST: 2010
SQ FT: 72,000
SALES: 6.7MM **Privately Held**
SIC: 8051　Skilled nursing care facilities

(G-4146)
OCEAN WIDE SEAFOOD COMPANY
2601 W 8th St Apt 10 (45204-1425)
PHONE.................................937 610-5740
Dale Hartlage, *President*
EMP: 35
SALES (est): 8.8MM **Privately Held**
WEB: www.owseafood.com
SIC: 5146　Seafoods

(G-4147)
OCONNOR ACCIANI & LEVY LLC (PA)
600 Vine St Ste 1600 (45202-1133)
PHONE.................................513 241-7111
Eric Rowe, *Technology*
Henry D Acciani,
Carrie L Budinger,
Barry D Levy,
Dennis C Mahoney,
EMP: 33
SALES (est): 7.9MM **Privately Held**
WEB: www.oal-law.com
SIC: 8111　General practice law office; general practice attorney, lawyer

(G-4148)
OCR SERVICES CORPORATION
201 E 4th St Ste 900 (45202-4160)
PHONE.................................513 719-2600
Joel F Dumunder, *President*
Kenneth Chesterman, *Vice Pres*
Patrick E Keefe, *Vice Pres*
Cheryl Hodge, *Admin Sec*
EMP: 180
SALES (corp-wide): 194.5B **Publicly Held**
WEB: www.omnicare.com
SIC: 6719　Investment holding companies, except banks
HQ: Omnicare Holding Company
　　1105 Market St Ste 1300
　　Cincinnati OH 45215
　　513 719-2600

(G-4149)
OFFICIAL INVESTIGATIONS INC
Also Called: Tri-State Mobile Notaries
3284 North Bend Rd # 302 (45239-7688)
PHONE.................................844 263-3424
Michael P Rolfes, *President*
EMP: 63
SQ FT: 900
SALES (est): 1.3MM **Privately Held**
WEB: www.officialinvestigations.com
SIC: 7381　7389　Guard services; private investigator; notary publics

(G-4150)
OGARA GROUP INC (PA)
9113 Le Street Dr (45249)
PHONE.................................513 338-0660
Bill T O'Gara, *CEO*
Thomas M O'Gara, *Ch of Bd*
Jeff Bozworth, *President*
Tony Russell, *President*
Ritchie Allen, *Business Mgr*
EMP: 62
SALES (est): 32.8MM **Privately Held**
SIC: 7382　Security systems services

(G-4151)
OHIO BUILDING SERVICE INC
2212 Losantiville Ave (45237-4206)
PHONE.................................513 761-0268
Lina Orr, *President*
Steven Statman, *Vice Pres*
EMP: 30
SQ FT: 2,500
SALES: 600K **Privately Held**
WEB: www.ohiobuildingservices.com
SIC: 7349　7217　Janitorial service, contract basis; building cleaning service; carpet & upholstery cleaning

(G-4152)
OHIO HEART
7545 Beechmont Ave Ste E (45255-4238)
PHONE.................................513 206-1320
John F Schneider, *President*
EMP: 25
SALES (est): 477.5K **Privately Held**
SIC: 8011　Cardiologist & cardio-vascular specialist

(G-4153)
OHIO HEART AND VASCULAR
5885 Harrison Ave # 1900 (45248-1721)
PHONE.................................513 206-1800
A Daniel Glassman, *Principal*
Andrew Daniel Glassman, *Principal*
Sarah Wilder, *Nurse Practr*
EMP: 25
SALES (est): 798.6K **Privately Held**
SIC: 8011　Cardiologist & cardio-vascular specialist

(G-4154)
OHIO HEART HEALTH CENTER INC (PA)
237 Wlliam Howard Taft Rd (45219-2610)
PHONE.................................513 351-9900
Dean Kereiakes, *President*
Pete L Caples MD, *Principal*
Andrew J Hear, *Internal Med*
EMP: 200
SALES (est): 9.8MM **Privately Held**
WEB: www.ohioheart.org
SIC: 8011　Cardiologist & cardio-vascular specialist

(G-4155)
OHIO HYDRAULICS INC
2510 E Sharon Rd Ste 1 (45241-1891)
PHONE.................................513 771-2590
John Davis, *Ch of Bd*
Kathleen Hilliard, *President*
Tamera Fair, *Corp Secy*
Dave Davis, *Vice Pres*
Robert Farwick, *Vice Pres*
EMP: 25 EST: 1971
SQ FT: 13,500
SALES (est): 6.5MM **Privately Held**
WEB: www.ohiohydraulics.com
SIC: 3492　3599　5084　7699　Hose & tube fittings & assemblies, hydraulic/pneumatic; flexible metal hose, tubing & bellows; hydraulic systems equipment & supplies; tank repair & cleaning services; welding repair; manufactured hardware (general)

(G-4156)
OHIO LIVING
Also Called: Llanfair Retirement Community
1701 Llanfair Ave (45224-2972)
PHONE.................................513 681-4230
Sheena Parton, *Branch Mgr*
EMP: 220 **Privately Held**
WEB: www.nwo.oprs.org
SIC: 8361　8052　8051　Home for the aged; intermediate care facilities; skilled nursing care facilities
PA: Ohio Living
　　1001 Kingsmill Pkwy
　　Columbus OH 43229

(G-4157)
OHIO MACHINERY CO
Also Called: Caterpillar Authorized Dealer
11330 Mosteller Rd (45241-1828)
PHONE.................................513 771-0515
Jeffrey Whaley, *Manager*
Greg Sanker,
EMP: 125

SALES (corp-wide): 222.7MM **Privately Held**
WEB: www.enginesnow.com
SIC: 5082　General construction machinery & equipment
PA: Ohio Machinery Co.
　　3993 E Royalton Rd
　　Broadview Heights OH 44147
　　440 526-6200

(G-4158)
OHIO RVER VLY WTR SNTTION COMM
Also Called: Orsanco
5735 Kellogg Ave (45230-7112)
PHONE.................................513 231-7719
Douglas Conrow, *Ch of Bd*
Alan Vicory Jr, *Exec Dir*
David Bailey, *Administration*
EMP: 26
SQ FT: 15,000
SALES: 202.8K **Privately Held**
WEB: www.orsanco.org
SIC: 8734　8641　Pollution testing; civic social & fraternal associations

(G-4159)
OHIO VALLEY ACQUISITION INC
Also Called: Ameristop Food Marts
250 E 5th St Ste 1200 (45202-4139)
PHONE.................................513 553-0768
Don Bloom, *President*
Tony Parnigoni, *COO*
William Zembrodt, *CFO*
EMP: 415
SQ FT: 13,500
SALES (est): 63MM **Privately Held**
SIC: 6794　Franchises, selling or licensing

(G-4160)
OHIO VALLEY FLOORING INC (PA)
5555 Murray Ave (45227-2707)
PHONE.................................513 271-3434
Al Hurt, *President*
Pat Seibert, *President*
Bev Burck, *Purch Agent*
Mike Spivey, *VP Bus Dvlpt*
Mark Roflow, *CFO*
▲ EMP: 70
SQ FT: 300,000
SALES: 119.6MM **Privately Held**
WEB: www.ovf.com
SIC: 5023　Carpets

(G-4161)
OHIO VALLEY WINE COMPANY (PA)
Also Called: Ohio Valley Wine & Beer
10975 Medallion Dr (45241-4830)
PHONE.................................513 771-9370
Steve Lowrey, *President*
Greg Maurer, *Exec VP*
Joe Noll, *Vice Pres*
Albert W Vontz III, *Vice Pres*
Sherrie Wiley, *Human Res Mgr*
▲ EMP: 100 EST: 1974
SQ FT: 86,000
SALES (est): 41.4MM **Privately Held**
SIC: 5182　5181　Wine; beer & other fermented malt liquors

(G-4162)
OHIO-KENTUCKY-INDIANA REGIONAL
720 E Pete Rose Way # 420 (45202-3576)
PHONE.................................513 621-6300
Mark Polinski, *Director*
Mark Poticentski, *Director*
EMP: 40
SQ FT: 15,400
SALES (est): 3.8MM **Privately Held**
SIC: 8742　Planning consultant

(G-4163)
OHIO/OKLAHOMA HEARST TV INC
1700 Young St (45202-6821)
PHONE.................................513 412-5000
Brent Hensely, *President*
EMP: 110
SQ FT: 37,285

SALES (est): 8.5MM
SALES (corp-wide): 6.4B **Privately Held**
WEB: www.kocotv.com
SIC: 4833　Television broadcasting stations
HQ: Hearst Television, Inc.
　　300 W 57th St
　　New York NY 10019

(G-4164)
OK INTERIORS CORP
11100 Ashburn Rd (45240-3813)
PHONE.................................513 742-3278
Todd Prewitt, *President*
Loren Schramm, *President*
Mark Konradi, *Superintendent*
Gregory J Meurer, *Principal*
Ernie Reed, *Vice Pres*
EMP: 150
SQ FT: 18,500
SALES: 27MM **Privately Held**
WEB: www.okinteriors.com
SIC: 1742　5031　1751　1752　Acoustical & ceiling work; doors; window & door (prefabricated) installation; access flooring system installation; partitions

(G-4165)
OKI AUCTION LLC
Also Called: Oki Auto Auction
120 Citycentre Dr (45216-1622)
PHONE.................................513 679-7910
Tony Schoenling, *Partner*
Anthony Schoenling, *General Mgr*
Lee Schoenling,
EMP: 75
SALES (est): 220.2K **Privately Held**
SIC: 7389　Auctioneers, fee basis; auction, appraisal & exchange services

(G-4166)
OKL CAN LINE INC
11235 Sebring Dr (45240-2714)
PHONE.................................513 825-1655
Anthony Lacey, *CEO*
Scott Feldmann, *Prdtn Mgr*
Richard Green, *Manager*
◆ EMP: 47
SQ FT: 50,000
SALES (est): 12.8MM
SALES (corp-wide): 3MM **Privately Held**
WEB: www.oklcan.com
SIC: 3565　7699　Bottling & canning machinery; industrial machinery & equipment repair
PA: Allcan Global Services, Inc
　　11235 Sebring Dr
　　Cincinnati OH 45240
　　513 825-1655

(G-4167)
OLD TIME POTTERY INC
1191 Smiley Ave (45240-1832)
PHONE.................................513 825-5211
Ron Gribbins, *Branch Mgr*
EMP: 70
SALES (corp-wide): 691.2MM **Privately Held**
WEB: www.oldtimepottery.com
SIC: 5999　5023　Art, picture frames & decorations; home furnishings
PA: Old Time Pottery, Llc
　　480 River Rock Blvd
　　Murfreesboro TN 37128
　　615 890-6060

(G-4168)
OMNICARE INC (DH)
900 Omnicare Ctr 201e4t (45202)
PHONE.................................513 719-2600
Nitin Sahney, *President*
Alexander M Kayne, *Senior VP*
Kirsten Marriner, *Senior VP*
Ashok Singh, *Senior VP*
Robert O Kraft, *CFO*
EMP: 250
SALES (est): 3.8B
SALES (corp-wide): 194.5B **Publicly Held**
WEB: www.omnicare.com
SIC: 5122　5047　8082　8741　Pharmaceuticals; medical & hospital equipment; home health care services; nursing & personal care facility management

HQ: Cvs Pharmacy, Inc.
1 Cvs Dr
Woonsocket RI 02895
401 765-1500

(G-4169)
OMNICARE DISTRIBUTION CTR LLC
201 E 4th St Ste 1 (45202-4248)
PHONE.............................419 720-8200
Dennis Holmes,
EMP: 100
SALES (est): 18.7MM
SALES (corp-wide): 194.5B **Publicly Held**
WEB: www.omnicare.com
SIC: 5122 Pharmaceuticals
HQ: Omnicare, Inc.
900 Omnicare Ctr 201e4t
Cincinnati OH 45202
513 719-2600

(G-4170)
OMNICARE MANAGEMENT COMPANY
201 E 4th St Ste 900 (45202-1513)
PHONE.............................513 719-1535
David Hileman, President
Cheryl Hodges, Vice Pres
Amkur Bhandari, Treasurer
Robert Kraft, Admin Sec
EMP: 3000
SALES (est): 65.6MM
SALES (corp-wide): 194.5B **Publicly Held**
SIC: 8741 Management services
HQ: Omnicare Holding Company
1105 Market St Ste 1300
Cincinnati OH 45215
513 719-2600

(G-4171)
OMNICARE PHRM OF MIDWEST LLC (DH)
201 E 4th St Ste 900 (45202-1513)
PHONE.............................513 719-2600
Joel Gemunder, Principal
EMP: 100
SALES (est): 33.5MM
SALES (corp-wide): 194.5B **Publicly Held**
SIC: 5122 5912 2834 Drugs & drug proprietaries; drug stores; pharmaceutical preparations

(G-4172)
OMNICARE PURCH LTD PARTNER INC
201 E 4th St Ste 900 (45202-1513)
PHONE.............................800 990-6664
Janice Rice, Principal
EMP: 121
SALES (est): 161.6K
SALES (corp-wide): 194.5B **Publicly Held**
SIC: 8741 Business management
HQ: Omnicare, Inc.
900 Omnicare Ctr 201e4t
Cincinnati OH 45202
513 719-2600

(G-4173)
ONCALL LLC
8044 Montgomery Rd # 700 (45236-2926)
PHONE.............................513 381-4320
Rolando Collado, Managing Dir
James Erion, Technology
Guy Bradley,
Walter R Dewees,
Bob Hauser,
EMP: 92 EST: 1996
SALES (est): 8.4MM
SALES (corp-wide): 20.1B **Privately Held**
WEB: www.oncall-llc.com
SIC: 8742 General management consultant
HQ: Grey Healthcare Group Inc.
200 5th Ave Ste 500
New York NY 10010
212 886-3000

(G-4174)
ONCOLGY/HMATOLOGY CARE INC PSC (PA)
Also Called: O C I
5053 Wooster Rd (45226-2326)
PHONE.............................513 751-2145
E Randolph Broun, CEO
Eric Lee, Controller
Kelly Donohue, Manager
Charlie Walls, Manager
Peter Ruehlman, Hematology
EMP: 70
SALES (est): 21.8MM **Privately Held**
SIC: 8011 Oncologist

(G-4175)
ONESTAFF INC
2358 Harrison Ave Apt 20 (45211-7929)
PHONE.............................859 815-1345
EMP: 40
SALES: 500K **Privately Held**
SIC: 7361 Employment Agency

(G-4176)
OPPENHEIMER & CO INC
5905 E Galbraith Rd # 6200 (45236-2376)
PHONE.............................513 723-9200
EMP: 27 **Publicly Held**
SIC: 8742 Financial consultant
HQ: Oppenheimer & Co. Inc.
85 Broad St Fl 3
New York NY 10004
212 668-8000

(G-4177)
OPPORTUNITIES FOR OHIOANS
Also Called: Vocational Rehabilitation
895 Central Ave Fl 7 (45202-1989)
PHONE.............................513 852-3260
Mark Fay, Manager
EMP: 40 **Privately Held**
WEB: www.rsc.ohio.gov
SIC: 8093 9431 Rehabilitation center, outpatient treatment;
HQ: Opportunities For Ohioans With Disabilities Agency
150 E Campus View Blvd
Columbus OH 43235
614 438-1200

(G-4178)
OPTIS SOLUTIONS
6705 Steger Dr (45237-3097)
PHONE.............................513 948-2070
Jon Iverson, CEO
Sven Thiesen, COO
EMP: 45
SALES: 605.6K **Privately Held**
SIC: 8711 Aviation &/or aeronautical engineering

(G-4179)
ORCHARD HILL SWIM CLUB
8601 Cheviot Rd (45251-5903)
P.O. Box 53114 (45253-0114)
PHONE.............................513 385-0211
Paul Jeanmougin, Administration
Linda Templin, Administration
EMP: 75
SQ FT: 1,568
SALES: 140.6K **Privately Held**
WEB: www.orchardhillswimclub.com
SIC: 7997 Swimming club, membership

(G-4180)
OREILLY AUTOMOTIVE INC
1198 W Galbraith Rd (45231-5610)
PHONE.............................513 800-1169
EMP: 29 **Publicly Held**
SIC: 7538 General automotive repair shops
PA: O'reilly Automotive, Inc.
233 S Patterson Ave
Springfield MO 65802

(G-4181)
OREILLY AUTOMOTIVE INC
3480 Spring Grove Ave (45223-2417)
PHONE.............................513 818-4166
EMP: 29 **Publicly Held**
SIC: 7538 General automotive repair shops
PA: O'reilly Automotive, Inc.
233 S Patterson Ave
Springfield MO 65802

(G-4182)
ORGANIZED LIVING LTD
3100 E Kemper Rd Ste A (45241-1517)
PHONE.............................513 674-5484
John D Kokenge, President
▲ EMP: 210
SQ FT: 16,000
SALES (est): 9.8MM
SALES (corp-wide): 31.8MM **Privately Held**
WEB: www.schultestorage.com
SIC: 1799 Closet organizers, installation & design
PA: Organized Living Inc.
3100 E Kemper Rd
Cincinnati OH 45241
513 489-9300

(G-4183)
ORIGINAL PARTNERS LTD PARTNR (PA)
Also Called: Towne Properties
1055 Saint Paul Pl (45202-6042)
PHONE.............................513 381-8696
Marvin Rosenberg, Partner
Brian J Bortz, Division Mgr
Neil K Bortz, General Ptnr
George Hope, District Mgr
Steve Lawson, Project Mgr
EMP: 150 EST: 1961
SQ FT: 5,000
SALES: 16.7MM **Privately Held**
SIC: 6514 6513 Dwelling operators, except apartments; apartment building operators

(G-4184)
OROURKE WRECKING COMPANY
660 Lunken Park Dr (45226-1800)
PHONE.............................513 871-1400
Michael Orourke, President
EMP: 75
SQ FT: 20,000
SALES: 24.7MM **Privately Held**
WEB: www.orourkewrecking.com
SIC: 1795 Demolition, buildings & other structures

(G-4185)
ORTHOPEDIC CONS CINCINNATI
Also Called: Wellington Orthopedics
7575 5 Mile Rd (45230-4346)
PHONE.............................513 232-6677
Julie Moore, Manager
EMP: 31
SALES (corp-wide): 16.7MM **Privately Held**
SIC: 8011 Orthopedic physician; sports medicine specialist, physician
PA: Orthopedic Consultants Of Cincinnati
4701 Creek Rd Ste 110
Blue Ash OH 45242
513 733-8894

(G-4186)
ORTHOPEDIC CONS CINCINNATI
Also Called: Wellington Orthpd Spt Medicine
7663 5 Mile Rd (45230-4340)
PHONE.............................513 245-2500
Sonya Hughes, General Mgr
S M Lawhon, Principal
Yvonne Gantenberg, Admin Asst
EMP: 32
SALES (corp-wide): 16.7MM **Privately Held**
SIC: 8011 Orthopedic physician
PA: Orthopedic Consultants Of Cincinnati
4701 Creek Rd Ste 110
Blue Ash OH 45242
513 733-8894

(G-4187)
ORTHOPEDIC CONS CINCINNATI
Also Called: Wellington Orthpd Spt Medicine
6909 Good Samaritan Dr (45247-5208)
PHONE.............................513 347-9999
Sonya Hughes, Manager
EMP: 30
SALES (corp-wide): 16.7MM **Privately Held**
SIC: 8011 Orthopedic physician

PA: Orthopedic Consultants Of Cincinnati
4701 Creek Rd Ste 110
Blue Ash OH 45242
513 733-8894

(G-4188)
ORTHOPEDIC DIAGNSTC TRTMNT CTR
4600 Smith Rd Ste B (45212-2784)
PHONE.............................513 221-4848
Thomas Shockley, Med Doctor
Errol Stern, Med Doctor
Valerie Berry, Administration
EMP: 30
SALES (corp-wide): 3MM **Privately Held**
SIC: 8011 Orthopedic physician
PA: Orthopedic Diagnostic & Treatment Center Inc
4600 Smith Rd Ste B
Cincinnati OH 45212
513 221-4848

(G-4189)
OSTERWISCH COMPANY INC
6755 Highland Ave (45236-3968)
PHONE.............................513 791-3282
James W Osterwisch, President
Donald Osterwisch, Vice Pres
EMP: 80
SQ FT: 30,000
SALES (est): 19.6MM **Privately Held**
WEB: www.osterwisch.com
SIC: 1731 1711 General electrical contractor; warm air heating & air conditioning contractor; refrigeration contractor; plumbing contractors

(G-4190)
OTIS ELEVATOR COMPANY
2463 Crowne Point Dr (45241-5407)
PHONE.............................513 531-7888
Dave Rettenmaier, Manager
EMP: 65
SALES (corp-wide): 66.5B **Publicly Held**
WEB: www.otis.com
SIC: 1796 7699 Elevator installation & conversion; elevators: inspection, service & repair
HQ: Otis Elevator Company
1 Carrier Pl
Farmington CT 06032
860 674-3000

(G-4191)
OUR LADY PRPTUL HLP CNMTY BNGO
9908 Shellbark Ln (45231-2328)
P.O. Box 31271 (45231-0271)
PHONE.............................513 742-3200
Celsus Griese, Pastor
EMP: 50
SALES (est): 392.9K **Privately Held**
SIC: 7999 Bingo hall

(G-4192)
OVATIONS FOOD SERVICES LP
525 Elm St (45202-2316)
PHONE.............................513 419-7254
Ian Saroyan, General Mgr
EMP: 85
SALES (corp-wide): 94.5B **Publicly Held**
SIC: 5141 Groceries, general line
HQ: Ovations Food Services, L.P.
18228 N Us Highway 41
Lutz FL 33549
813 948-6900

(G-4193)
OVERLAND XPRESS LLC (PA)
431 Ohio Pike Ste 311 (45255-3629)
PHONE.............................513 528-1158
Jason Brown, Mng Member
Bledar Andoni,
EMP: 40
SQ FT: 1,600
SALES (est): 15.9MM **Privately Held**
SIC: 4731 Freight forwarding

(G-4194)
P & D REMOVAL SERVICE
400 N Wayne Ave (45215-2845)
PHONE.............................513 226-7687
Dwayne Jordan, Owner
EMP: 25
SALES: 200K **Privately Held**
SIC: 8999 Services

(G-4195)
P & M EXHAUST SYSTEMS WHSE
Also Called: Car-X Muffler & Brake
11843 Kemper Springs Dr (45240-1641)
PHONE................................513 825-2660
Ranga Gorrepati, *President*
Sumeeta Chalasani, *Vice Pres*
Ajay Gorrepati, *Vice Pres*
Madhavi Gorrepati, *Vice Pres*
Pallavi Gorrepati, *Vice Pres*
EMP: 25
SQ FT: 15,000
SALES (est): 6MM **Privately Held**
SIC: 5013 Exhaust systems (mufflers, tail pipes, etc.)

(G-4196)
PAC WORLDWIDE CORPORATION
Also Called: Copac
12110 Champion Way (45241-6420)
PHONE................................800 535-0039
Lance Fletcher, *Branch Mgr*
EMP: 89 **Privately Held**
SIC: 5199 Packaging materials
HQ: Pac Worldwide Corporation
15435 Ne 92nd St
Redmond WA 98052
425 202-4000

(G-4197)
PAKTEEM TECHNICAL SERVICES
1201 Glendale Milford Rd (45215-1247)
PHONE................................513 772-1515
Denise Demoss, *President*
Kevin Haspings, *Manager*
Laura Bryant, *Admin Asst*
Paul Hartman, *Sr Consultant*
EMP: 51
SALES (est): 3.7MM **Privately Held**
WEB: www.pakteem.com
SIC: 8711 Consulting engineer

(G-4198)
PARAGON SALONS INC (PA)
6775 Harrison Ave (45247-3239)
PHONE................................513 574-7610
Deborah Celek, *President*
Steven Celek, *Corp Secy*
EMP: 40
SQ FT: 2,600
SALES (est): 2.3MM **Privately Held**
WEB: www.paragonsalon.com
SIC: 7991 Spas

(G-4199)
PARAGON SALONS INC
441 Race St (45202)
PHONE................................513 651-4600
Toni Maurer, *General Mgr*
EMP: 35
SALES (corp-wide): 2.3MM **Privately Held**
WEB: www.paragonsalon.com
SIC: 7231 Manicurist, pedicurist
PA: Paragon Salons, Inc
6775 Harrison Ave
Cincinnati OH 45247
513 574-7610

(G-4200)
PARAGON SALONS INC
12064 Montgomery Rd (45249-1729)
PHONE................................513 683-6700
Tanya Garnica, *Manager*
EMP: 40
SALES (corp-wide): 2.3MM **Privately Held**
WEB: www.paragonsalon.com
SIC: 7231 Hairdressers
PA: Paragon Salons, Inc
6775 Harrison Ave
Cincinnati OH 45247
513 574-7610

(G-4201)
PARK CINCINNATI BOARD
Also Called: Krohn Conservatory Gift Shop
1501 Eden Park Dr (45202-6030)
PHONE................................513 421-4086
Betty Moscofe, *Vice Pres*
Sue Kellogg, *Treasurer*
Andrea L Schepmann, *Manager*

Willy Carden, *Director*
Ellen Geohegan, *Admin Sec*
EMP: 100 EST: 1975
SQ FT: 150
SALES (est): 4.1MM **Privately Held**
SIC: 5992 5947 8422 6512 Plants, potted; flowers, fresh; gift shop; arboreta & botanical or zoological gardens; nonresidential building operators

(G-4202)
PARK HOTELS & RESORTS INC
Also Called: Hilton Cncnnati Netherland Plz
35 W 5th St (45202-2801)
PHONE................................513 421-9100
EMP: 27
SALES (corp-wide): 2.7B **Publicly Held**
SIC: 7011 Hotels
PA: Park Hotels & Resorts Inc.
1775 Tysons Blvd Fl 7
Tysons VA 22102
571 302-5757

(G-4203)
PARK INTERNATIONAL THEME SVCS
2195 Victory Pkwy (45206-2812)
PHONE................................513 381-6131
Dennis Speigel, *President*
Shawn Haas, *Vice Pres*
Pam Westerman, *Vice Pres*
Lisa Cooke, *Opers Mgr*
EMP: 25
SALES (est): 1.8MM **Privately Held**
WEB: www.interthemepark.com
SIC: 8742 Management consulting services

(G-4204)
PARKING COMPANY AMERICA INC
Also Called: Hartsfield Atlanta Intl Arprt
250 W Court St Ste 200e (45202-1078)
PHONE................................513 241-0415
William Miller, *Branch Mgr*
EMP: 350
SALES (corp-wide): 94.4MM **Privately Held**
WEB: www.airportfastparkandshuttle.com
SIC: 7521 Parking lots
PA: Parking Company Of America, Inc.
250 W Court St Ste 200e
Cincinnati OH 45202
513 241-0415

(G-4205)
PARKING COMPANY AMERICA INC
Also Called: Downtown Fast Park
250 W Court St Ste 100e (45202-1046)
P.O. Box 6187 (45206-0187)
PHONE................................513 381-2179
Ayo Owoeye, *Manager*
EMP: 40
SALES (corp-wide): 94.4MM **Privately Held**
WEB: www.airportfastparkandshuttle.com
SIC: 7521 Parking garage
PA: Parking Company Of America, Inc.
250 W Court St Ste 200e
Cincinnati OH 45202
513 241-0415

(G-4206)
PARSEC INC (PA)
Also Called: Parsec Intermodal Cannada
1100 Gest St (45203-1114)
PHONE................................513 621-6111
Otto Budig Jr, *President*
David H Budig, *COO*
George J Budig, *Vice Pres*
Chuck Letko, *Safety Mgr*
Lloyd Shadley, *Safety Mgr*
EMP: 26
SQ FT: 55,000
SALES (est): 171.3MM **Privately Held**
WEB: www.parsecinc.com
SIC: 4789 Cargo loading & unloading services

(G-4207)
PASTORAL CARE MANAGEMENT SVCS
1240 Rosemont Ave (45205-1424)
PHONE................................513 205-1398

Ruben D Brazzile, *Exec Dir*
Alex Brandon, *Bd of Directors*
Christina Adams, *Administration*
James Stanford, *Administration*
Robin Webb, *Administration*
EMP: 26
SALES (est): 397.1K **Privately Held**
SIC: 8661 8322 Religious organizations; individual & family services; substance abuse counseling

(G-4208)
PATHWAY 2 HOPE INC
3036 Gilbert Ave (45206-1021)
PHONE................................866 491-3040
Tyler P Powell, *Exec Dir*
EMP: 25
SALES (est): 183.3K **Privately Held**
SIC: 8322 Individual & family services

(G-4209)
PATIENTPINT HOSP SOLUTIONS LLC
8230 Montgomery Rd # 300 (45236-2200)
PHONE................................513 936-6800
EMP: 184 EST: 2009
SALES (est): 4.3MM
SALES (corp-wide): 35.1MM **Privately Held**
SIC: 8742 Marketing consulting services
HQ: Patientpoint Holdings, Inc.
8230 Montgomery Rd # 300
Cincinnati OH 45236
513 936-6800

(G-4210)
PATIENTPINT NTWRK SLUTIONS LLC (DH)
Also Called: Healthy Advice Networks
5901 E Galbraith Rd (45236-2230)
PHONE................................513 936-6800
Arthur Kemper, *Business Mgr*
Mike Collette, *Mng Member*
EMP: 63
SQ FT: 15,000
SALES (est): 18.8MM
SALES (corp-wide): 35.1MM **Privately Held**
WEB: www.ontargetmedia.com
SIC: 8742 Marketing consulting services
HQ: Patientpoint Holdings, Inc.
8230 Montgomery Rd # 300
Cincinnati OH 45236
513 936-6800

(G-4211)
PATIENTPOINT LLC (PA)
5901 E Galbraith Rd (45236-2230)
PHONE................................513 936-6800
Mike Colette, *CEO*
Wes Staggs, *Exec VP*
Cathy Goold, *Vice Pres*
Terry Wall, *Vice Pres*
Evan Beck, *Accounts Exec*
EMP: 48
SALES (est): 35.1MM **Privately Held**
SIC: 8742 Marketing consulting services

(G-4212)
PATRICK J BURKE & CO
Also Called: Burke & Company
901 Adams Crossing Fl 1 (45202-1693)
PHONE................................513 455-8200
Patrick Burke, *Owner*
Eugene Schindler, *Co-Owner*
Betty Hancock, *Controller*
Monica Cradler, *Accountant*
Julie Gady, *Accountant*
EMP: 25
SALES (est): 2.9MM **Privately Held**
SIC: 8721 7372 Certified public accountant; prepackaged software

(G-4213)
PATTERSON POPE INC
10321 S Medallion Dr (45241-4825)
PHONE................................513 891-4430
Jeff Pfohl, *Manager*
EMP: 80
SALES (corp-wide): 108MM **Privately Held**
SIC: 5021 7371 5712 Filing units; computer software development; furniture stores

PA: Patterson Pope, Inc.
3001 N Graham St
Charlotte NC 28206
704 523-4400

(G-4214)
PAUL R YOUNG FUNERAL HOMES (PA)
7345 Hamilton Ave (45231-4321)
PHONE................................513 521-9303
Paul R Young, *President*
Paul R Young Jr, *Office Mgr*
Paul Young III, *Manager*
Walter Mc Kay, *Admin Sec*
EMP: 30
SQ FT: 8,000
SALES (est): 3.6MM **Privately Held**
WEB: www.paulyoungfuneralhome.com
SIC: 7261 Funeral home

(G-4215)
PAULS BUS SERVICE INC
3561 W Kemper Rd (45251-4236)
PHONE................................513 851-5089
Dennis P Wurzelbacher, *President*
Cynthia Wurzelbacher, *Vice Pres*
EMP: 40 EST: 1952
SQ FT: 4,650
SALES: 1.5MM **Privately Held**
SIC: 4151 School buses

(G-4216)
PAXTON HARDWOODS LLC
Also Called: Frank Paxton Lumber Company
7455 Dawson Rd (45243-2537)
P.O. Box 16343, Denver CO (80216-0343)
PHONE................................513 984-8200
John Griffin, *Manager*
EMP: 30
SALES (corp-wide): 812.5MM **Privately Held**
SIC: 5031 Lumber: rough, dressed & finished
HQ: Paxton Hardwoods Llc
4837 Jackson St
Denver CO 80216
303 399-6810

(G-4217)
PAYCOM SOFTWARE INC
255 E 5th St Ste 1420 (45202-4709)
PHONE................................888 678-0796
EMP: 575
SALES (corp-wide): 566.3MM **Publicly Held**
SIC: 8721 Payroll accounting service
PA: Paycom Software, Inc.
7501 W Memorial Rd
Oklahoma City OK 73142
405 722-6900

(G-4218)
PAYCOR INC (PA)
4811 Montgomery Rd (45212-2163)
PHONE................................513 381-0505
Stacey Browning, *President*
Robert J Coughlin, *Chairman*
Rick Chouteau, *Senior VP*
Chris Power, *CFO*
Steven G Haussler, *Treasurer*
EMP: 200
SQ FT: 33,000
SALES (est): 105.2MM **Privately Held**
SIC: 8721 Payroll accounting service

(G-4219)
PCY ENTERPRISES INC
Also Called: Young & Bertke Air Systems
3111 Spring Grove Ave (45225-1821)
PHONE................................513 241-5566
Roger Young, *President*
Michael Munafo, *Vice Pres*
Tim Rohrer, *Vice Pres*
Phillip C Young, *Shareholder*
EMP: 28
SQ FT: 51,000
SALES: 4MM **Privately Held**
WEB: www.youngbertke.com
SIC: 1761 3441 3564 3444 Sheet metalwork; fabricated structural metal; blowers & fans; sheet metalwork; fabricated plate work (boiler shop)

(G-4220)
PECK-HANNAFORD BRIGGS SVC CORP
Also Called: Peck Hannaford Briggs Service
4673 Spring Grove Ave (45232-1952)
PHONE..................................513 681-1200
James G Briggs Jr, *President*
Jerry Govert, *Vice Pres*
Mark Shad, *Project Mgr*
Tony Caminiti, *Marketing Staff*
EMP: 57
SQ FT: 4,000
SALES (est): 12.9MM
SALES (corp-wide): 52.9MM **Privately Held**
SIC: **1711** Warm air heating & air conditioning contractor; refrigeration contractor
PA: Peck-Hannaford & Briggs Co, The (Inc)
4670 Chester Ave
Cincinnati OH 45232
513 681-4600

(G-4221)
PEDIATRIC ASSOC CINCINNATI
4360 Cooper Rd Ste 201 (45242-5646)
PHONE..................................513 791-1222
Robert C Schiff Jr, *Corp Secy*
Ann Lichtenberg, *Director*
EMP: 28
SQ FT: 2,000
SALES (est): 2.8MM **Privately Held**
SIC: **8011** Pediatrician

(G-4222)
PEDIATRIC CARE INC (PA)
800 Compton Rd Unit 25 (45231-5959)
PHONE..................................513 931-6357
Mark S Dine, *President*
Daniel L Friedberg, *Vice Pres*
EMP: 32 EST: 1955
SALES (est): 3.7MM **Privately Held**
SIC: **8011** Pediatrician

(G-4223)
PEGASUS TECHNICAL SERVICES INC
46 E Hollister St (45219-1704)
PHONE..................................513 793-0094
Asit B Saha, *President*
Bijoli Saha, *Vice Pres*
EMP: 50
SQ FT: 200
SALES: 6.3MM **Privately Held**
WEB: www.ptsied.com
SIC: **8711** 7371 7373 Consulting engineer; custom computer programming services; computer-aided design (CAD) systems service

(G-4224)
PELLA CORPORATION
145 B Colwell Dr (45216)
PHONE..................................513 948-8480
James M Frey, *President*
EMP: 60
SALES (corp-wide): 1.8B **Privately Held**
SIC: **5031** Windows
PA: Pella Corporation
102 Main St
Pella IA 50219
641 621-1000

(G-4225)
PENNINGTON INTERNATIONAL INC
1977 Section Rd Ste 1 (45237-3333)
PHONE..................................513 631-2130
Gladys Pennington, *President*
L Paulette Kihm, *Exec VP*
Sheila Pennington, *Asst Treas*
EMP: 36
SQ FT: 3,200
SALES (est): 583.6K **Privately Held**
WEB: www.penningtoninternational.com
SIC: **7381** Security guard service; detective agency

(G-4226)
PENSION CORPORATION AMERICA
Also Called: ABG Advisors
2133 Luray Ave (45206-2604)
PHONE..................................513 281-3366
Tom Seitz, *President*
Jim Eckeroe, *Vice Pres*

Gina Stebbins, *Opers Staff*
Tracy Ackerson, *Marketing Staff*
Lori Palmisano, *Marketing Staff*
EMP: 35
SQ FT: 3,500
SALES (est): 4.1MM **Privately Held**
WEB: www.pencorp.com
SIC: **8742** Financial consultant

(G-4227)
PENSKE TRUCK LEASING CO LP
2528 Commodity Cir (45241-1550)
PHONE..................................513 771-7701
Brad Brockhoff, *Accounts Mgr*
Chad Powell, *Manager*
EMP: 30
SQ FT: 2,000
SALES (corp-wide): 2.6B **Privately Held**
WEB: www.pensketruckleasing.com
SIC: **7513** Truck rental & leasing, no drivers
PA: Penske Truck Leasing Co., L.P.
2675 Morgantown Rd
Reading PA 19607
610 775-6000

(G-4228)
PEOPLES BANCORP INC
9813 Montgomery Rd (45242-6401)
PHONE..................................513 793-2422
Jessica Benge, *Manager*
EMP: 100
SALES (corp-wide): 208MM **Publicly Held**
SIC: **6035** Federal savings & loan associations
PA: Peoples Bancorp Inc.
138 Putnam St
Marietta OH 45750
740 373-3155

(G-4229)
PEOPLES BANCORP INC
7114 Miami Ave (45243-2617)
PHONE..................................513 271-9100
EMP: 40
SALES (corp-wide): 208MM **Publicly Held**
SIC: **6035** Savings institutions, federally chartered
PA: Peoples Bancorp Inc.
138 Putnam St
Marietta OH 45750
740 373-3155

(G-4230)
PERFECTION GROUP INC (PA)
Also Called: Honeywell Authorized Dealer
2649 Commerce Blvd (45241-1553)
PHONE..................................513 772-7545
William J Albrecht, *CEO*
Anthony Apro, *President*
Ryan Dillard, *Business Mgr*
Mike Smith, *Project Mgr*
James Taylor, *Opers Mgr*
EMP: 151
SQ FT: 10,000
SALES: 34.5MM **Privately Held**
WEB: www.perfectionservices.com
SIC: **1711** Warm air heating & air conditioning contractor

(G-4231)
PERFECTION SERVICES INC
2649 Commerce Blvd (45241-1553)
PHONE..................................513 772-7545
William Albrecht, *President*
John E Shaw, *Vice Pres*
EMP: 50 EST: 1972
SQ FT: 10,000
SALES: 4MM
SALES (corp-wide): 34.5MM **Privately Held**
SIC: **1711** Warm air heating & air conditioning contractor
PA: Perfection Group, Inc.
2649 Commerce Blvd
Cincinnati OH 45241
513 772-7545

(G-4232)
PERRY KELLY PLUMBING INC
4498 Mt Carmel Tobasco Rd (45244-2222)
PHONE..................................513 528-6554
Perry Kelly, *President*

Mary Jo Kelly, *Corp Secy*
EMP: 27
SQ FT: 1,000
SALES: 3.5MM **Privately Held**
WEB: www.perrykelly.com
SIC: **1711** Plumbing contractors

(G-4233)
PERSONAL TOUCH HM CARE IPA INC
8260 Northcreek Dr # 140 (45236-2293)
PHONE..................................513 984-9600
Ann Koller, *Human Resources*
Barbie Wenman, *Manager*
EMP: 60
SALES (corp-wide): 363MM **Privately Held**
WEB: www.pthomecare.com
SIC: **8082** Home health care services
PA: Personal Touch Home Care Ipa, Inc.
1985 Marcus Ave Ste 202
New Hyde Park NY 11042
718 468-4747

(G-4234)
PETER A WIMBERG COMPANY INC
Also Called: Wimberg Landscaping
5401 Hetzell St (45227-1515)
PHONE..................................513 271-2332
Peter A Wimberg, *President*
John Wimberg, *Vice Pres*
Connie Brasington, *Office Mgr*
EMP: 40
SALES (est): 3.1MM **Privately Held**
WEB: www.wimberglandscaping.com
SIC: **0782** Landscape contractors

(G-4235)
PETERBILT OF CINCINNATI
2550 Annuity Dr (45241-1502)
PHONE..................................513 772-1740
Taylor Edwards, *President*
EMP: 30
SQ FT: 50,000
SALES (est): 10MM
SALES (corp-wide): 132.6MM **Privately Held**
WEB: www.peterbiltofcincinnati.com
SIC: **5012** 5013 7538 Truck tractors; trailers for trucks, new & used; truck parts & accessories; trailer parts & accessories; general truck repair
PA: W. D. Larson Companies Ltd., Inc.
500 Ford Rd
St Louis Park MN 55426
952 888-4934

(G-4236)
PETERMANN NORTHEAST LLC
8041 Hosbrook Rd Ste 330 (45236-2909)
PHONE..................................513 351-7383
Michael J Settle, *COO*
EMP: 1212
SALES (est): 6.9MM **Privately Held**
SIC: **4151** School buses
HQ: National Express Llc
2601 Navistar Dr
Lisle IL 60532

(G-4237)
PETRO ENVIRONMENTAL TECH (PA)
Also Called: Petro Cells
8160 Corp Pk Dr Ste 300 (45242)
PHONE..................................513 489-6789
Pete Mather, *President*
Peter Mather, *President*
Mark Mather, *Corp Secy*
EMP: 40
SQ FT: 7,500
SALES (est): 8MM **Privately Held**
SIC: **1629** 4959 Land preparation construction; toxic or hazardous waste cleanup

(G-4238)
PETSUITES OF AMERICA INC
3701 Hauck Rd (45241-1607)
PHONE..................................513 554-4408
Joseph G Mason III, *Manager*
EMP: 25
SALES (corp-wide): 1.2MM **Privately Held**
SIC: **0752** Boarding services, kennels

PA: Petsuites Of America, Inc.
620 Holly Ln
Erlanger KY 41018
859 727-7880

(G-4239)
PFH PARTNERS LLC
Also Called: Jefferey Anderson Real Estate
3805 Edwards Rd Ste 700 (45209-1955)
PHONE..................................513 241-5800
Jefferey Anderson, *President*
EMP: 25
SALES (est): 823.2K **Privately Held**
SIC: **6531** Real estate leasing & rentals

(G-4240)
PFPC ENTERPRISES INC
5750 Hillside Ave (45233-1508)
PHONE..................................513 941-6200
Peter F Coffaro, *Ch of Bd*
James Coffaro, *President*
Stephen Stout, *CFO*
Chuck Williams, *Manager*
EMP: 300 EST: 1963
SQ FT: 52,000
SALES (est): 18.1MM **Privately Held**
WEB: www.pabcofluidpower.com
SIC: **5023** 5084 3594 3535 Floor coverings; industrial machinery & equipment; pumps & pumping equipment; water pumps (industrial); hydraulic systems equipment & supplies; fluid power pumps & motors; conveyors & conveying equipment; turbines & turbine generator sets

(G-4241)
PHILLIPS EDISON & COMPANY LLC (HQ)
11501 Northlake Dr Fl 1 (45249-1667)
PHONE..................................513 554-1110
Jeffrey S Edison, *CEO*
Bob Myers, *President*
Robert F Myers, *President*
Eric Richer, *Owner*
Dj Belock, *Senior VP*
EMP: 27
SQ FT: 5,000
SALES (est): 20MM **Privately Held**
WEB: www.phillipsedison.com
SIC: **6531** 6552 Real estate brokers & agents; real estate managers; land subdividers & developers, commercial

(G-4242)
PHILLIPS SUPPLY COMPANY (PA)
1230 Findlay St (45214-2096)
PHONE..................................513 579-1762
Pamela Rossmann, *President*
Eleanor Roth, *Principal*
Claire B Phillips, *Treasurer*
Donna Ashley, *Sales Staff*
Kevin Foy, *Sales Associate*
▲ EMP: 55 EST: 1965
SQ FT: 40,000
SALES (est): 29.9MM **Privately Held**
WEB: www.phillipssupply.com
SIC: **5087** Janitors' supplies

(G-4243)
PHOENIX
812 Race St (45202-2006)
PHONE..................................513 721-8901
Jeremy Luers, *General Mgr*
Justin Kittle, *General Mgr*
Watch M Corp, *General Ptnr*
EMP: 60
SQ FT: 40,000
SALES (est): 2.9MM **Privately Held**
WEB: www.thephx.com
SIC: **7941** Stadium event operator services

(G-4244)
PHOENIX RESOURCE NETWORK LLC
602 Main St Ste 202 (45202-2521)
PHONE..................................800 990-4948
Thomas L Jordan,
Roger C Noble,
EMP: 26
SQ FT: 1,400
SALES: 250K **Privately Held**
SIC: **8742** 5047 Business consultant; financial consultant; hospital equipment & supplies

(G-4245)
PHYLLIS AT MADISON
2324 Madison Rd Ste 1 (45208-2693)
PHONE....................................513 321-1300
Phyllis Rinaldi, *President*
EMP: 30
SQ FT: 2,200
SALES (est): 772.8K **Privately Held**
WEB: www.phyllisatthemadison.com
SIC: 7231 Facial salons

(G-4246)
PIATT PARK LTD PARTNERSHIP
1055 Saint Paul Pl # 300 (45202-6042)
PHONE....................................513 381-8696
Arn Bortz, *Partner*
Dan Bayer, *Partner*
Fred Casper, *Partner*
William Curran, *Partner*
Ralph Heyman, *Partner*
EMP: 70
SALES (est): 4.4MM **Privately Held**
SIC: 6552 Subdividers & developers

(G-4247)
PIER N PORT TRAVEL INC
Also Called: Virtuoso
2692 Madison Rd Ste H1 (45208-1350)
PHONE....................................513 841-9900
Richard Cronenberg, *Ch of Bd*
Kristin Tatman, *President*
Patricia J Cronenberg, *Principal*
Beverly Hardiman, *Exec VP*
Michele Uckotter, *Exec VP*
EMP: 34
SQ FT: 2,400
SALES (est): 3.6MM **Privately Held**
WEB: www.virtuoso.com
SIC: 4724 Travel agencies

(G-4248)
PILGRIM UNITED CHURCH CHRIST
4418 Bridgetown Rd (45211-4493)
PHONE....................................513 574-4208
Dave Bucey, *Pastor*
EMP: 25
SALES (est): 860K **Privately Held**
SIC: 8661 8351 Church of Christ; pre-school center

(G-4249)
PILLAR OF FIRE
Also Called: Star 93.3 FM
6275 Collegevue Pl (45224-1959)
PHONE....................................513 542-1212
Joseph W Gross, *President*
Hunter T Barnes, *Trustee*
Robert B Dallenbach, *Trustee*
Christopher M Stanko, *Vice Pres*
Nate Baldwin, *Accounts Exec*
EMP: 28 EST: 1921
SQ FT: 8,694
SALES (est): 5.7MM **Privately Held**
WEB: www.mystar933.com
SIC: 4832 8661 Radio broadcasting stations; religious organizations

(G-4250)
PINNACLE ENVIRONMENTAL CONS (PA)
486 Old State Route 74 (45244-4215)
PHONE....................................513 533-1823
Christopher A Belcher, *President*
Mike Strine, *Vice Pres*
Nikki Braun, *Manager*
Gregory Pauley, *Manager*
Miranda Bs, *Director*
EMP: 30
SQ FT: 3,000
SALES (est): 3.1MM **Privately Held**
WEB: www.pinnacleinc.biz
SIC: 8748 Environmental consultant

(G-4251)
PIQUA MATERIALS INC (PA)
11641 Mosteller Rd Ste 1 (45241-1520)
PHONE....................................513 771-0820
James Jurgensen, *President*
Tim Saintclair, *Corp Secy*
James Jurgenson II, *Vice Pres*
James P Jurgensen, *Plant Mgr*
Beth Baker, *Controller*
EMP: 100

SALES (est): 10.1MM **Privately Held**
SIC: 1422 Limestones, ground

(G-4252)
PLANNED PARENTHOOD OF SW OH (PA)
2314 Auburn Ave (45219-2802)
PHONE....................................513 721-7635
Jerry Lawson, *CEO*
Lee Bower, *COO*
Kelli Halter, *Vice Pres*
Leslie Mitchell, *Vice Pres*
Rick Pender, *Vice Pres*
EMP: 35
SQ FT: 35,000
SALES: 9.4MM **Privately Held**
SIC: 8093 Family planning clinic; birth control clinic; abortion clinic

(G-4253)
PLASTIC SURGERY GROUP INC (PA)
4050 Red Bank Rd Ste 42 (45227)
PHONE....................................513 791-4440
Richard Williams, *President*
Gene Ireland, *Vice Pres*
Michael Leadbetter, *Treasurer*
Debbie Thacker, *Office Mgr*
Michael J Columbus, *Plastic Surgeon*
EMP: 25
SALES (est): 2.5MM **Privately Held**
WEB: www.tpsg.net
SIC: 8093 8011 Specialty outpatient clinics; plastic surgeon

(G-4254)
PLAY TIME DAY NURSERY INC
9550 Colerain Ave (45251-2004)
PHONE....................................513 385-8281
Larry W Napier, *President*
Nancy Jo Napier, *Vice Pres*
EMP: 25
SQ FT: 8,000
SALES (est): 667.9K **Privately Held**
SIC: 8351 Nursery school; group day care center

(G-4255)
PLEASANT RIDGE CARE CENTER INC (PA)
5501 Verulam Ave (45213-2417)
PHONE....................................513 631-1310
Harold Sosna, *President*
EMP: 103
SALES: 6.5MM **Privately Held**
SIC: 8051 Skilled nursing care facilities

(G-4256)
PLS PROTECTIVE SERVICES
8263 Clara Ave (45239-4214)
PHONE....................................513 521-3581
Paul Smith, *President*
EMP: 30
SALES (est): 649K **Privately Held**
SIC: 7381 Security guard service

(G-4257)
PNC BANK NATIONAL ASSOCIATION
5 Main Dr (45231-2300)
PHONE....................................513 721-2500
Edward Korfhagen, *Branch Mgr*
EMP: 400
SALES (corp-wide): 19.9B **Publicly Held**
WEB: www.pncfunds.com
SIC: 6021 National trust companies with deposits, commercial
HQ: Pnc Bank, National Association
222 Delaware Ave
Wilmington DE 19801
877 762-2000

(G-4258)
PNC BANK NATIONAL ASSOCIATION
995 Dalton Ave (45203-1100)
PHONE....................................513 455-9522
Chris Kelley, *Vice Pres*
Terry Karageorges, *Vice Pres*
Dana Pace, *Vice Pres*
Angela Shields, *Program Mgr*
EMP: 26
SALES (corp-wide): 19.9B **Publicly Held**
SIC: 6021 National trust companies with deposits, commercial

HQ: Pnc Bank, National Association
222 Delaware Ave
Wilmington DE 19801
877 762-2000

(G-4259)
PNC EQUIPMENT FINANCE LLC
995 Dalton Ave (45203-1100)
PHONE....................................513 421-9191
Douglas Shaffer, *Branch Mgr*
EMP: 85
SALES (corp-wide): 19.9B **Publicly Held**
SIC: 6159 Equipment & vehicle finance leasing companies; machinery & equipment finance leasing
HQ: Pnc Equipment Finance, Llc
620 Liberty Ave
Pittsburgh PA 15222

(G-4260)
PNG TELECOMMUNICATIONS INC (PA)
Also Called: Powernet Global Communications
8805 Governors Hill Dr # 250 (45249-3314)
PHONE....................................513 942-7900
Allison Stevens, *CEO*
Bernie Stevens, *President*
Michael Macke, *Opers Staff*
Stephanie Sams, *Opers Staff*
Keith Bode, *Engineer*
EMP: 99
SQ FT: 55,000
SALES (est): 36.7MM **Privately Held**
WEB: www.pngnet.com
SIC: 4813 7375 Long distance telephone communications; ; information retrieval services

(G-4261)
PNK (OHIO) LLC
Also Called: River Downs
6301 Kellogg Rd (45230-5237)
PHONE....................................513 232-8000
Anthony San Filippo, *CEO*
John Engelhardt, *Marketing Staff*
Stephen Heis, *Med Doctor*
Phyllis Vogel, *Security Mgr*
Karen Mollaun, *Manager*
EMP: 700
SALES (est): 2.3MM
SALES (corp-wide): 2.6B **Publicly Held**
SIC: 7948 7993 Horse race track operation; coin-operated amusement devices
HQ: Boyd Tciv, Llc
3883 Howard Hughes Pkwy
Las Vegas NV 89169
702 792-7200

(G-4262)
POISON INFORMATION CENTER
Also Called: Drug & Poison Information Ctr
3333 Burnet Ave Fl 3 (45229-3026)
PHONE....................................513 636-5111
Earl Siegel, *Director*
EMP: 35
SALES (est): 3.3MM **Privately Held**
SIC: 8062 General medical & surgical hospitals

(G-4263)
PORT GRTER CINCINNATI DEV AUTH
Also Called: Greater Cincinnati Redevelopme
3 E 4th St Ste 300 (45202-3745)
PHONE....................................513 621-3000
Laura Brunner, *President*
Charlie Luken, *Chairman*
Liz Eddy, *Vice Pres*
Todd Castellini, *Finance*
Darin Hall, *Software Dev*
EMP: 25
SALES: 6.3MM **Privately Held**
SIC: 8748 Economic consultant

(G-4264)
PORTER WRGHT MORRIS ARTHUR LLP
250 E 5th St Ste 2200 (45202-5118)
PHONE....................................513 381-4700
Donna Wirt, *President*
David Croall, *Branch Mgr*
Christina Elam, *Director*
Kim Culp, *Legal Staff*

Chris Dutton, *Sr Associate*
EMP: 40
SALES (corp-wide): 83MM **Privately Held**
SIC: 8111 General practice attorney, lawyer
PA: Porter, Wright, Morris & Arthur Llp
41 S High St Ste 2900
Columbus OH 43215
614 227-2000

(G-4265)
POSITIVE BUS SOLUTIONS INC
Also Called: Pbsi
200 Northland Blvd 100 (45246-3604)
PHONE....................................513 772-2255
Ray Cool, *President*
Tim Latham, *Vice Pres*
Lloyd Mason, *Vice Pres*
EMP: 56
SQ FT: 15,000
SALES (est): 7.3MM **Privately Held**
WEB: www.pbsinet.com
SIC: 7378 5045 7371 Computer & data processing equipment repair/maintenance; computer software; computer software development

(G-4266)
POWER ENGINEERS INCORPORATED
Also Called: Environmental Division
11733 Chesterdale Rd (45246-3405)
PHONE....................................513 326-1500
Carrie Loyd, *Office Mgr*
Tim Gessner, *Branch Mgr*
EMP: 35
SALES (corp-wide): 460.2MM **Privately Held**
WEB: www.bheenv.com
SIC: 8711 Consulting engineer
PA: Power Engineers, Incorporated
3940 Glenbrook Dr
Hailey ID 83333
208 788-3456

(G-4267)
PPS HOLDING LLC
4605 E Galbraith Rd # 200 (45236-2887)
PHONE....................................513 985-6400
Greg Hopkins,
Terry Correll,
Bill Laverty,
EMP: 67
SALES: 34.7MM **Privately Held**
WEB: www.partnerps.com
SIC: 7361 Executive placement

(G-4268)
PRECISION VHCL SOLUTIONS LLC
559 Liberty Hl (45202-6869)
PHONE....................................513 651-9444
Bret Griffin, *Principal*
Darrin McElroy, *Principal*
EMP: 35
SQ FT: 2,000
SALES (est): 354.9K **Privately Held**
SIC: 4789 Freight car loading & unloading

(G-4269)
PREFERRED REAL ESTATE GROUP (PA)
Also Called: Re/Max
3522 Erie Ave (45208-1717)
PHONE....................................513 533-4111
Christine Beresford, *President*
Myles Beresford, *Vice Pres*
Chris Teeter, *Broker*
Dana Thomas, *Broker*
Kelly Bunker, *Real Est Agnt*
EMP: 30
SALES (est): 3MM **Privately Held**
WEB: www.preferredgrouprealtors.com
SIC: 6531 Real estate agent, residential

(G-4270)
PREGNANCY CARE OF CINCINNATI
2415 Auburn Ave (45219-2701)
PHONE....................................513 487-7777
Mary Beth Lacy, *Principal*
EMP: 25

SALES: 696.3K **Privately Held**
WEB: www.pregnancycareofcincinnati.com
SIC: 8322 8093 Referral service for personal & social problems; specialty outpatient clinics

(G-4271)
PREMIER ESTATES 521 LLC
Also Called: Premier Estate of Three Rivers
7800 Jandacres Dr (45248)
PHONE...................................765 288-2488
Shari Bench,
EMP: 99
SQ FT: 46,878
SALES (est): 431.6K **Privately Held**
SIC: 8051 Skilled nursing care facilities

(G-4272)
PREMIER ESTATES 525 LLC
Also Called: Pristine Senior Living
1578 Sherman Ave (45212-2510)
PHONE...................................513 631-6800
Shari Bench, *Manager*
EMP: 63 EST: 2017
SALES (est): 671.9K
SALES (corp-wide): 6.3MM **Privately Held**
SIC: 8361 Home for the aged
PA: Trillium Healthcare Group, Llc
5115 E State Road 64
Bradenton FL 34208
941 758-4745

(G-4273)
PREMIER ESTATES 526 LLC
Also Called: Premier Esttes Cncnnt-Rverview
5999 Bender Rd (45233-1601)
PHONE...................................513 922-1440
Brian McCoy, *COO*
EMP: 80
SALES (est): 1MM
SALES (corp-wide): 6.3MM **Privately Held**
SIC: 8361 Home for the aged
PA: Trillium Healthcare Group, Llc
5115 E State Road 64
Bradenton FL 34208
941 758-4745

(G-4274)
PREMIER TRANSCRIPTION SERVICE
Also Called: Premier Transcription Services
7 Hetherington Ct (45246-3743)
PHONE...................................513 741-1800
Gen Jim Brian, *President*
EMP: 25
SALES (est): 810.3K **Privately Held**
SIC: 7338 Secretarial & typing service

(G-4275)
PRESSLEY RIDGE PRYDE
7162 Reading Rd Ste 300 (45237-3899)
PHONE...................................513 559-1402
Jane Wingz, *Director*
Terry Clark, *Admin Asst*
EMP: 28
SALES (est): 1MM **Privately Held**
SIC: 8322 General counseling services

(G-4276)
PRESTIGE AUDIO VISUAL INC
Also Called: Prestige AV & Creative Svcs
4835 Para Dr (45237-5009)
PHONE...................................513 641-1600
Tony Ramstetter, *President*
Kathryne Gardette, *General Mgr*
Terry Ramstetter, *Vice Pres*
Tom Bell, *Project Mgr*
Cameron Wilson, *Project Mgr*
EMP: 58
SQ FT: 57,000
SALES (est): 9.2MM **Privately Held**
WEB: www.prestigeaudiovisual.com
SIC: 7359 Audio-visual equipment & supply rental

(G-4277)
PRESTIGE VALET INC
4220 Appleton St (45209-1204)
PHONE...................................513 871-4220
Jeff Blevins, *President*
Mark Nartker, *Manager*
EMP: 60
SALES (est): 881.8K **Privately Held**
SIC: 7521 Parking lots

(G-4278)
PRICEWATERHOUSECOOPERS LLP
201 E 5th St Ste 2300 (45202-4174)
PHONE...................................513 723-4700
Dennis Bartolucci, *Partner*
Douglas McHoney, *Partner*
Don Bush, *Manager*
Sherri Creighton, *Sr Associate*
Lauren Richey, *Sr Associate*
EMP: 100
SALES (corp-wide): 7.8B **Privately Held**
WEB: www.pwcglobal.com
SIC: 8721 Certified public accountant
PA: Pricewaterhousecoopers Llp
300 Madison Ave Fl 24
New York NY 10017
646 471-4000

(G-4279)
PRIMAX MARKETING GROUP
2300 Montana Ave Ste 102 (45211-3888)
PHONE...................................513 443-2797
Steve P Miklavic, *President*
Brian Gelhaus, *Web Dvlpr*
EMP: 40
SQ FT: 2,400
SALES: 3.5MM **Privately Held**
WEB: www.primax.com
SIC: 4813 7371 ; computer software development

(G-4280)
PRIMROSE SCHOOL OF SYMMES
Also Called: Geier School Company
9175 Governors Way (45249-2037)
PHONE...................................513 697-6970
Richard Geier, *President*
Karen Rice, *Director*
Stephanie Adams,
EMP: 35
SQ FT: 4,651
SALES (est): 1MM **Privately Held**
SIC: 8351 Preschool center

(G-4281)
PRINTPACK INC
8044 Montgomery Rd # 600 (45236-2976)
PHONE...................................513 891-7886
J Erskine Love, *Owner*
EMP: 200
SALES (corp-wide): 1.3B **Privately Held**
SIC: 5199 Packaging materials
HQ: Printpack, Inc.
2800 Overlook Pkwy Ne
Atlanta GA 30339
404 460-7000

(G-4282)
PRIORITY 1 CONSTRUCTION SVCS
5178 Crookshank Rd (45238-3304)
PHONE...................................513 922-0203
Barry Kirby, *President*
EMP: 34
SALES (est): 3.3MM **Privately Held**
SIC: 1742 1799 Insulation, buildings; asbestos removal & encapsulation

(G-4283)
PRIORITY III CONTRACTING INC
5178 Crookshank Rd (45238-3304)
PHONE...................................513 922-0203
Brian Kirby, *President*
EMP: 35
SQ FT: 33,000
SALES (est): 3.6MM **Privately Held**
WEB: www.priorityinsulation.com
SIC: 1799 Insulation of pipes & boilers; asbestos removal & encapsulation

(G-4284)
PRISTINE SENIOR LIVING
Also Called: Premier Esttes Cncnnt-Rverside
315 Lilienthal St (45204-1170)
PHONE...................................513 471-8667
Jensen Glaze,
EMP: 60 EST: 2017
SALES (est): 653.5K
SALES (corp-wide): 6.3MM **Privately Held**
SIC: 8361 Home for the aged

PA: Trillium Healthcare Group, Llc
5115 E State Road 64
Bradenton FL 34208
941 758-4745

(G-4285)
PRIVATE HM CARE FOUNDATION INC
Also Called: PHC Foundation
3808 Applegate Ave (45211-6503)
PHONE...................................513 662-8999
Linda Puthoff, *President*
Tracy Beiting, *Director*
EMP: 60
SALES (est): 2.5MM **Privately Held**
WEB: www.privatehcfoundation.org
SIC: 8082 Home health care services

(G-4286)
PRN HEALTH SERVICES INC
8044 Montgomery Rd # 700 (45236-2919)
PHONE...................................513 792-2217
Anne Dejewski, *Branch Mgr*
EMP: 68
SALES (est): 1.1MM **Privately Held**
SIC: 7361 Nurses' registry
PA: Prn Health Services, Inc.
1101 E South River St
Appleton WI 54915

(G-4287)
PRO ONCALL TECHNOLOGIES LLC (PA)
6902 E Kemper Rd (45249-1025)
P.O. Box 498337 (45249-7337)
PHONE...................................513 489-7660
John O Brian, *President*
Don Walter, *Vice Pres*
▲ EMP: 80
SQ FT: 10,000
SALES (est): 34.8MM **Privately Held**
SIC: 5065 Telephone equipment; communication equipment

(G-4288)
PRO SENIORS INC
7162 Reading Rd Ste 1150 (45237-3849)
PHONE...................................513 345-4160
Rhonda Moore, *Exec Dir*
EMP: 30
SALES: 2.2MM **Privately Held**
SIC: 8322 Senior citizens' center or association

(G-4289)
PROCESS CONSTRUCTION INC
2128 State Ave (45214-1614)
PHONE...................................513 251-2211
Klem Fennell, *President*
EMP: 55
SALES (corp-wide): 18.9MM **Privately Held**
SIC: 1711 Mechanical contractor
PA: Process Construction, Inc.
1421 Queen City Ave
Cincinnati OH 45214
513 251-2211

(G-4290)
PROCESS PLUS LLC (PA)
135 Merchant St Ste 300 (45246-3759)
PHONE...................................513 742-7590
Grant Mitchell P E, *President*
Jeff Rankin, *President*
Ken Popham R A, *Principal*
Larry Greis, *Principal*
Dennis McCullough, *Vice Pres*
EMP: 107
SQ FT: 32,000
SALES (est): 24.2MM **Privately Held**
WEB: www.processplus.com
SIC: 8711 Consulting engineer

(G-4291)
PROCTER & GAMBLE DISTRG LLC
2 P&G Plz Tn8 235 (45202)
PHONE...................................513 945-7960
EMP: 272
SALES (corp-wide): 66.8B **Publicly Held**
SIC: 5169 Detergents
HQ: Procter & Gamble Distributing Llc
1 Procter And Gamble Plz
Cincinnati OH 45202
513 983-1100

(G-4292)
PROFESSIONAL CONTRACT SYSTEMS
11804 Conrey Rd Ste 100 (45249-1076)
PHONE...................................513 469-8800
Larry Bayer, *President*
Mike Cariappa, *Vice Pres*
Stuart Meyers, *Manager*
Cindy Schatzel, *Admin Asst*
EMP: 120
SQ FT: 4,800
SALES (est): 6.5MM **Privately Held**
WEB: www.pcsts.com
SIC: 7361 Placement agencies

(G-4293)
PROFESSIONAL MAINT OF COLUMBUS
Also Called: Professnal Mint Lttle Ohio Div
1 Crosley Field Ln (45214-2004)
PHONE...................................513 579-1762
Eldon Hall, *Ch of Bd*
Dale Barnett, *President*
EMP: 290 EST: 1960
SALES (est): 1.7MM **Privately Held**
SIC: 8351 7349 Child day care services; janitorial service, contract basis

(G-4294)
PROFESSIONAL TELECOM SVCS
2119 Beechmont Ave (45230-5414)
PHONE...................................513 232-7700
Joey Hazenfield, *President*
Jamie Hazenfield, *Vice Pres*
Leah Hazenfield, *Finance*
Rick Reynolds, *Director*
EMP: 27
SQ FT: 3,665
SALES (est): 4MM **Privately Held**
WEB: www.ptscinti.com
SIC: 5999 1731 7622 7629 Communication equipment; communications specialization; communication equipment repair; telephone set repair; long distance telephone communications

(G-4295)
PROFESSNAL MINT CINCINNATI INC
1230 Findlay St (45214-2050)
PHONE...................................513 579-1161
James L Miller, *President*
EMP: 700
SALES (est): 9.9MM **Privately Held**
WEB: www.pmcincinnati.com
SIC: 7349 8742 Janitorial service, contract basis; management consulting services

(G-4296)
PROJETECH INC
3815 Harrison Ave (45211-4725)
PHONE...................................513 481-4900
Steven K Richmond, *President*
Christopher Winston, *Project Mgr*
Bryce Plitt, *Sales Staff*
Kyle Davis, *Technical Staff*
Mark Eaton, *Director*
EMP: 28
SALES (est): 3.7MM **Privately Held**
WEB: www.emaintenance.com
SIC: 8742 Business consultant

(G-4297)
PROKIDS INC
2605 Burnet Ave (45219-2502)
PHONE...................................513 281-2000
Candy Stemple, *Manager*
Tracy Cook, *Exec Dir*
Paul Hunt, *Director*
Carol Igoe, *Director*
EMP: 27
SALES: 4.2MM **Privately Held**
WEB: www.prokidscasa.com
SIC: 8322 Children's aid society

(G-4298)
PROPERTY ESTATE MANAGEMENT LLC
1526 Elm St Ste 1 (45202-6907)
PHONE...................................513 684-0418
EMP: 25

GEOGRAPHIC

SALES (est): 1.7MM **Privately Held**
SIC: 1522 1542 Residential Construction Nonresidential Construction

(G-4299)
PROSCAN IMAGING LLC (PA)
5400 Kennedy Ave Ste 1 (45213-2668)
PHONE...................................513 281-3400
Judith Turner, *General Mgr*
Tia Hutcherson, *Exec VP*
Dawn Baumgardner, *Vice Pres*
Jane Burk, *Vice Pres*
Tammy Lunsford, *QA Dir*
EMP: 100 **EST:** 1996
SALES (est): 37.6MM **Privately Held**
SIC: 8071 Ultrasound laboratory

(G-4300)
PROVIDENT TRAVEL CORPORATION
11309 Montgomery Rd Ste B (45249-2379)
PHONE...................................513 247-1100
Jane Jones, *Vice Pres*
Anne Linnemann, *Accounts Exec*
Janet McLaughlin, *Consultant*
EMP: 95
SALES (est): 12.3MM
SALES (corp-wide): 142.4MM **Privately Held**
WEB: www.providenttravel.com
SIC: 4724 Tourist agency arranging transport, lodging & car rental
PA: Aaa Allied Group, Inc.
15 W Central Pkwy
Cincinnati OH 45202
513 762-3301

(G-4301)
PROVINCE OF ST JOHN THE BAPTIS
Also Called: St Anthony Messenger Press
28 W Liberty St (45202-6442)
PHONE...................................513 241-5615
Jeremy Harrington, *Principal*
John Feister, *CIO*
EMP: 100
SQ FT: 30,514
SALES (corp-wide): 12MM **Privately Held**
WEB: www.rogerbacon.org
SIC: 2721 5942 7812 2752 Magazines: publishing only, not printed on site; book stores; motion picture & video production; commercial printing, lithographic; miscellaneous publishing; book publishing
PA: The Province Of St John Baptist Order Friars Minor
1615 Vine St
Cincinnati OH 45202
513 721-4700

(G-4302)
PRUDENTIAL INSUR CO OF AMER
3 Crowne Point Ct Ste 100 (45241-5430)
PHONE...................................513 612-6400
Jackie Charles, *Branch Mgr*
Anthony Fehring, *Officer*
EMP: 30
SALES (corp-wide): 62.9B **Publicly Held**
SIC: 6411 Insurance agents, brokers & service
HQ: The Prudential Insurance Company Of America
751 Broad St
Newark NJ 07102
973 802-6000

(G-4303)
PRUS CONSTRUCTION COMPANY
5325 Wooster Pike (45226-2224)
PHONE...................................513 321-7774
Joseph M Prus, *President*
William J Prus, *Vice Pres*
EMP: 130
SALES (est): 20.6MM **Privately Held**
WEB: www.prusconstruction.com
SIC: 1771 1622 Blacktop (asphalt) work; bridge construction

(G-4304)
PSYCHPROS INC
2404 Auburn Ave (45219-2735)
PHONE...................................513 651-9500

Holly Dorna, *CEO*
EMP: 30
SQ FT: 3,240
SALES: 3.3MM **Privately Held**
WEB: www.psychpros.com
SIC: 7361 Executive placement

(G-4305)
PURE CONCEPT SALON INC (PA)
8740 Montgomery Rd Ste 7 (45236-2100)
PHONE...................................513 794-0202
Renee Heidrich, *President*
Bill Spiegel, *Vice Pres*
EMP: 70
SQ FT: 4,700
SALES (est): 3.2MM **Privately Held**
WEB: www.pureconceptsalon.com
SIC: 7231 Cosmetology & personal hygiene salons

(G-4306)
PURE ROMANCE LLC (PA)
655 Plum St Ste 3 (45202-2367)
PHONE...................................513 248-8656
Chris Cicchinelli, *CEO*
Brian Parsley, *Senior VP*
Cheryl Force, *Vice Pres*
Heather Snell, *Vice Pres*
Matty Brisben, *Purchasing*
EMP: 61
SALES (est): 8.2MM **Privately Held**
WEB: www.pureromance.com
SIC: 7299 5961 5632 Party planning service; books, mail order (except book clubs); toys & games (including dolls & models), mail order; lingerie & corsets (underwear)

(G-4307)
PYRAMID CONTROL SYSTEMS INC
Also Called: Pyramid Controls
5546 Fair Ln (45227-3402)
PHONE...................................513 679-7400
Mukesh Ram, *President*
Thomas E Martin, *Principal*
Stephen Kley, *Admin Sec*
EMP: 31
SALES (est): 6.6MM **Privately Held**
WEB: www.pyramidcontrols.com
SIC: 8711 Electrical or electronic engineering

(G-4308)
Q FACT MARKETING RESEARCH INC (PA)
11767 Thayer Ln (45249-1573)
PHONE...................................513 891-2271
Joann Monroe, *President*
EMP: 104
SQ FT: 20,400
SALES (est): 5.4MM **Privately Held**
WEB: www.qfact.com
SIC: 8732 Market analysis or research

(G-4309)
Q LABS LLC (PA)
Also Called: Q Laboratories
1911 Radcliff Dr (45204-1824)
PHONE...................................513 471-1300
Jeffrey Rowe, *President*
Adam Morris, *CFO*
EMP: 143
SALES (est): 7.2MM **Privately Held**
WEB: www.qlaboratories.com
SIC: 8734 8731 Testing laboratories; commercial physical research

(G-4310)
QUALITY SUPPLY CO (PA)
Also Called: Quality Restaurant Supply
4020 Rev Dr (45232-1914)
PHONE...................................937 890-6114
Bruce Feldman, *Ch of Bd*
Leland D Manders, *President*
Alan Moscowitz, *Vice Pres*
Mark Foster, *Treasurer*
Irvin Moscowitz, *Admin Sec*
EMP: 35
SALES (est): 6MM **Privately Held**
SIC: 5046 Commercial cooking & food service equipment

(G-4311)
QUANTUM CONSTRUCTION COMPANY
1654 Sherman Ave (45212-2544)
P.O. Box 12249 (45212-0249)
PHONE...................................513 351-6903
Ronald A Koetters, *Ch of Bd*
H Timothy Kemme, *President*
EMP: 25
SQ FT: 1,400
SALES (est): 3.2MM **Privately Held**
SIC: 1542 1541 Commercial & office building, new construction; institutional building construction; industrial buildings & warehouses

(G-4312)
QUEEN CITY BLACKTOP COMPANY
2130 Osterfeld St (45214-1590)
PHONE...................................513 251-8400
Martin Steinbach, *President*
Nancy S Kuley, *Vice Pres*
Nathan Steinbach, *VP Opers*
Andrew Steinbach, *Info Tech Mgr*
EMP: 26
SQ FT: 3,000
SALES (est): 3.4MM **Privately Held**
WEB: www.qcbpave.com
SIC: 1771 1611 Blacktop (asphalt) work; highway & street construction

(G-4313)
QUEEN CITY ELECTRIC INC
4015 Cherry St Ste 2 (45223-2587)
PHONE...................................513 591-2600
Mike J Cavanaugh, *President*
EMP: 25
SALES: 1,000K **Privately Held**
WEB: www.queencityelectric.net
SIC: 1731 General electrical contractor

(G-4314)
QUEEN CITY GENERAL & VASCULAR (PA)
Also Called: Queen City Generl Consultants
10506 Montgomery Rd # 101 (45242-4487)
PHONE...................................513 232-8181
Bradley Osborne, *Principal*
EMP: 25
SALES (est): 3.4MM **Privately Held**
SIC: 8011 Surgeon

(G-4315)
QUEEN CITY HOSPICE LLC
Also Called: QUEEN CITY HOSPICE AND PALLIAT
8250 Kenwood Crossing Way # 200 (45236-3669)
PHONE...................................513 510-4406
Tony Izquierdo, *Principal*
James Vannelle, *Vice Pres*
EMP: 26
SALES: 17.4MM **Privately Held**
SIC: 8052 Personal care facility

(G-4316)
QUEEN CITY MECHANICALS INC
1950 Waycross Rd (45240-2827)
PHONE...................................513 353-1430
Gary W Gilbert, *President*
Bradley Gilbert, *Vice Pres*
Bryan Gilbert, *Vice Pres*
Beverly Gilbert, *Treasurer*
Kathy Ward, *Administration*
EMP: 29
SALES (est): 5.8MM **Privately Held**
WEB: www.queencitymech.com
SIC: 1711 Plumbing contractors

(G-4317)
QUEEN CITY MEDICAL GROUP
7991 Beechmont Ave (45255-3189)
PHONE...................................513 528-5600
Diane Dolensky, *Managing Prtnr*
Dr Georges M Feghali, *Partner*
EMP: 30
SALES (est): 2.8MM **Privately Held**
SIC: 8011 Internal medicine, physician/surgeon; pediatrician

(G-4318)
QUEEN CITY PHYSICIANS
Also Called: Queen City of Physicians
2475 W Galbraith Rd Ste 3 (45239-4369)
PHONE...................................513 872-2061
Neil Deithsel, *President*
Dr Charles Dietschel, *Partner*
Dr Susan N Finney, *Partner*
Dr Kathleen Lamping-Arar, *Partner*
Dr Ellen H Norby, *Partner*
EMP: 54
SQ FT: 1,800
SALES (est): 4.6MM **Privately Held**
SIC: 8011 Pediatrician

(G-4319)
QUEEN CITY PHYSICIANS LTD
7825 Laurel Ave (45243-2608)
P.O. Box 43192 (45243-0192)
PHONE...................................513 791-6992
Nan Matteson, *Branch Mgr*
Leo Wayne, *Med Doctor*
EMP: 40
SALES (corp-wide): 4.7MM **Privately Held**
SIC: 8011 Offices & clinics of medical doctors
PA: Queen City Physicians, Ltd.
619 Oak St
Cincinnati OH 45206
513 246-8000

(G-4320)
QUEEN CITY RACQUET CLUB LLC
11275 Chester Rd (45246-4014)
PHONE...................................513 771-2835
Keven Shell, *President*
Carl Myers, *Treasurer*
Nick Lockman, *Office Mgr*
Dorianna James, *Manager*
William P Martin, *Admin Sec*
EMP: 60
SQ FT: 100,000
SALES (est): 1.7MM **Privately Held**
WEB: www.queencityfitness.com
SIC: 7991 Physical fitness facilities
PA: Central Investment Llc
7265 Kenwood Rd Ste 240
Cincinnati OH 45236

(G-4321)
QUEEN CITY REPROGRAPHICS
2863 E Sharon Rd (45241-1923)
PHONE...................................513 326-2300
Joe Herbst, *CEO*
Chris Chalifoux, *President*
EMP: 105
SQ FT: 30,000
SALES (est): 16.8MM
SALES (corp-wide): 400.7MM **Publicly Held**
WEB: www.ohioblue.com
SIC: 5049 7334 7335 2752 Drafting supplies; blueprinting service; commercial photography; lithographing on metal
PA: Arc Document Solutions, Inc.
12657 Alcosta Blvd # 200
San Ramon CA 94583
925 949-5100

(G-4322)
QUEEN CITY TRANSPORTATION LLC
Also Called: Charter Bus Service
211 Township Ave Ste 2 (45216-2501)
PHONE...................................513 941-8700
Jeff Klug, *Manager*
Arron Haid,
EMP: 300
SALES (est): 9MM **Privately Held**
WEB: www.charterbusservice.com
SIC: 4141 4142 4151 Local bus charter service; bus charter service, except local; school buses

(G-4323)
QUEEN CY SPT MDCINE RHBLTATION
3950 Red Bank Rd (45227-3429)
PHONE...................................513 561-1111
John E Turba MD, *President*
EMP: 26
SQ FT: 12,000

SALES (est): 605.7K **Privately Held**
SIC: 8011 Orthopedic physician; sports medicine specialist, physician

(G-4324)
QUEENS TOWER RESTAURANT INC
Also Called: Primavista
810 Matson Pl Ph 3 (45204-1482)
PHONE...................................513 251-6467
Joan Lenkerd, *President*
Frank Lenkerd, *Admin Sec*
EMP: 45
SQ FT: 4,000
SALES (est): 1.5MM **Privately Held**
WEB: www.primavista.com
SIC: 5812 7299 Italian restaurant; facility rental & party planning services

(G-4325)
QUEENSGATE FOOD GROUP LLC
Also Called: Queensgate Food Service
619 Linn St (45203-1794)
P.O. Box 14120 (45250-0120)
PHONE...................................513 721-5503
Matt Mazza, *Manager*
Brian Williams, *Consultant*
Dave Baysore, *Director*
Patrick L O'Callaghan Jr,
EMP: 75
SQ FT: 55,000
SALES (est): 36.5MM **Publicly Held**
WEB: www.queensgatefoods.com
SIC: 5141 Food brokers
PA: The Chefs' Warehouse Inc
100 E Ridge Rd
Ridgefield CT 06877

(G-4326)
QUEST DEF SYSTEMS SLUTIONS INC
11499 Chester Rd Ste 600 (45246-4000)
PHONE...................................860 573-5950
Robert Harvey, *President*
EMP: 100
SALES (est): 1.3MM
SALES (corp-wide): 476.3MM **Privately Held**
SIC: 7379 Computer related consulting services
HQ: Quest Global Services-Na, Inc.
11499 Chester Rd Fl 7
Cincinnati OH 45246

(G-4327)
QUEST GLOBAL SERVICES-NA INC
11499 Chester Rd Ste 600 (45246-4000)
PHONE...................................513 563-8855
EMP: 59
SALES (corp-wide): 476.3MM **Privately Held**
SIC: 8731 Engineering laboratory, except testing
HQ: Quest Global Services-Na, Inc.
11499 Chester Rd Fl 7
Cincinnati OH 45246

(G-4328)
QUEST GLOBAL SERVICES-NA INC (DH)
Also Called: Quest Ase
11499 Chester Rd Fl 7 (45246-4012)
PHONE...................................860 787-1600
Ajit Prabhu, *CEO*
Bob Harvey, *President*
Ajay Prabhu, *COO*
Mani Subramanian, *Vice Pres*
Keith Gonshorek, *Project Engr*
EMP: 60
SALES (est): 209.6MM
SALES (corp-wide): 476.3MM **Privately Held**
WEB: www.asetech.com
SIC: 8731 8711 Engineering laboratory, except testing; aviation &/or aeronautical engineering; electrical or electronic engineering; mechanical engineering
HQ: Quality Engineering & Software Technologies Llc
111 Founders Plz Ste 601
East Hartford CT 06108
860 290-1145

(G-4329)
R A HERMES INC
4015 Cherry St Ste 27 (45223-2587)
PHONE...................................513 251-5200
Rudolph Hermes, *President*
Carole Hermes, *Treasurer*
EMP: 28
SQ FT: 1,500
SALES (est): 4.5MM **Privately Held**
SIC: 1542 1521 6531 Commercial & office building, new construction; commercial & office buildings, renovation & repair; new construction, single-family houses; general remodeling, single-family houses; real estate agents & managers

(G-4330)
R E KRAMIG & CO INC
323 S Wayne Ave (45215-4522)
P.O. Box 9909 (45209-0909)
PHONE...................................513 761-4010
George Kulesza, *President*
Dan Diersing, *Superintendent*
Howard H Horne, *Exec VP*
EMP: 200
SQ FT: 65,000
SALES (est): 20.2MM **Privately Held**
SIC: 1799 5033 1742 Insulation of pipes & boilers; insulation materials; acoustical & insulation work

(G-4331)
R KELLY INC
7645 Production Dr (45237-3208)
PHONE...................................513 631-8488
Raymond Kelly, *President*
EMP: 35
SQ FT: 7,800
SALES (est): 6MM **Privately Held**
WEB: www.rkelly.com
SIC: 1711 Mechanical contractor

(G-4332)
R W GODBEY RAILROAD SERVICES
Also Called: B & R Railroad Services
2815 Spring Grove Ave (45225-2222)
PHONE...................................513 651-3800
Richard W Godbey, *CEO*
Ric Godbey, *President*
EMP: 25
SALES (est): 1.7MM **Privately Held**
SIC: 4789 Railroad maintenance & repair services

(G-4333)
R&F ERECTORS INC
Also Called: South Eastern Erectors
5763 Snyder Rd (45247-5723)
PHONE...................................513 574-8273
Steve Rigney, *President*
Jerry Freidman, *Admin Sec*
EMP: 25
SALES (est): 2.3MM **Privately Held**
SIC: 1791 Structural steel erection

(G-4334)
RACK SEVEN PAVING CO INC
7208 Main St (45244-3014)
PHONE...................................513 271-4863
Tim Rack, *President*
Kim Rack, *President*
EMP: 28
SQ FT: 700
SALES (est): 3.6MM **Privately Held**
SIC: 1611 Surfacing & paving; highway & street paving contractor

(G-4335)
RADIO PROMOTIONS
2518 Spring Grove Ave (45214-1730)
P.O. Box 14928 (45250-0928)
PHONE...................................513 381-5000
Thomas O'Toole, *President*
Thomas Ludlow, *Vice Pres*
EMP: 150
SALES (est): 3.1MM **Privately Held**
SIC: 4832 Radio broadcasting stations

(G-4336)
RAITZ INC
Also Called: Alliance Calibration
11402 Reading Rd (45241-2247)
PHONE...................................513 769-1200
Charles Goodall, *CEO*

Bradley Combs, *President*
Richard Barrett, *Principal*
Phil Wiseman, *COO*
Carissa Goodall, *Vice Pres*
EMP: 25
SQ FT: 5,400
SALES (est): 4.6MM **Privately Held**
SIC: 8734 Calibration & certification

(G-4337)
RAPID DELIVERY SERVICE CO INC
529 N Wayne Ave (45215-2800)
P.O. Box 15819 (45215-0819)
PHONE...................................513 733-0500
Jerry Delp, *President*
Tina Delp, *President*
EMP: 40
SQ FT: 13,600
SALES (est): 3MM **Privately Held**
SIC: 4212 Delivery service, vehicular

(G-4338)
RAPID MORTGAGE COMPANY
Also Called: Rapid Aerial Imaging
7870 E Kemper Rd Ste 280 (45249-1675)
PHONE...................................937 748-8888
Dennis M Fisher, *President*
Chris Howard, *Vice Pres*
David Rawson, *Vice Pres*
EMP: 50
SALES (est): 7.2MM **Privately Held**
WEB: www.rapidmortgagecompany.com
SIC: 6162 7335 7389 7221 Bond & mortgage companies; commercial photography; mapmaking or drafting, including aerial; photographer, still or video

(G-4339)
RASSAK LLC
Also Called: Benchmark Outfitters
7680 Demar Rd (45243-3504)
PHONE...................................513 791-9453
Makr A Denney,
Richard Casser,
EMP: 25
SALES (est): 8.9MM **Privately Held**
SIC: 5136 5137 Men's & boys' clothing; women's & children's clothing

(G-4340)
RAYMOND JAMES FINCL SVCS INC
255 E 5th St Ste 2210 (45202-4701)
PHONE...................................513 287-6777
Robert W Niehaus, *Senior VP*
John Ryan, *Manager*
EMP: 30
SALES (corp-wide): 7.4B **Publicly Held**
WEB: www.raymondjames.com
SIC: 8742 Financial consultant
HQ: Raymond James Financial Services, Inc.
880 Carillon Pkwy
Saint Petersburg FL 33716
727 567-1000

(G-4341)
RCR EAST INC (PA)
Also Called: Residence At Garden Gate
6922 Ohio Ave (45236-3506)
PHONE...................................513 793-2090
Rodger King, *President*
Beth Ann Dailey, *Director*
EMP: 150
SALES (est): 6.6MM **Privately Held**
SIC: 8051 Convalescent home with continuous nursing care

(G-4342)
RCR EAST INC
Also Called: Residence At Salem Woods
6164 Salem Rd (45230-2743)
PHONE...................................513 231-8292
Rodger King, *Principal*
EMP: 150
SALES (est): 2.6MM
SALES (corp-wide): 6.6MM **Privately Held**
SIC: 8051 Convalescent home with continuous nursing care
PA: Rcr East Inc
6922 Ohio Ave
Cincinnati OH 45236
513 793-2090

(G-4343)
READING FAMILY PRACTICE
Also Called: Rivera, Mary
9400 Reading Rd Ste 2 (45215-3401)
PHONE...................................513 563-6934
John Nolan MD, *Owner*
EMP: 25
SQ FT: 7,960
SALES (est): 1.8MM **Privately Held**
SIC: 8011 General & family practice, physician/surgeon

(G-4344)
RECARO CHILD SAFETY LLC
4921 Para Dr (45237-5011)
PHONE...................................248 904-1570
Kai Weisskopf,
Bill Pierchala,
▲ **EMP:** 38
SQ FT: 40,000
SALES (est): 9.3MM **Privately Held**
SIC: 3944 5099 Child restraint seats, automotive; child restraint seats, automotive

(G-4345)
RECKER CONSULTING LLC
Also Called: Path Forward It
6871 Steger Dr (45237-3055)
PHONE...................................513 924-5500
Clint Holliday, *President*
David Schulz, *Director*
Nicholas Recker,
EMP: 60
SALES (est): 12.1MM **Privately Held**
SIC: 7379

(G-4346)
RECONSTRUCTIVE ORTHOPEDICS (PA)
Also Called: Reconstructive Ortho Sports
10615 Montgomery Rd # 200 (45242-4461)
PHONE...................................513 793-3933
Jonathan W Bell, *President*
EMP: 25
SQ FT: 8,500
SALES (est): 4.1MM **Privately Held**
WEB: www.reconstructiveorthopedics.com
SIC: 8011 Orthopedic physician

(G-4347)
RED CARPET JANITORIAL SERVICE (PA)
3478 Hauck Rd Ste D (45241-4604)
PHONE...................................513 242-7575
Dale E Euller, *President*
EMP: 300
SQ FT: 2,000
SALES (est): 10.2MM **Privately Held**
WEB: www.redcarpetjanitorial.com
SIC: 7349 Janitorial Service

(G-4348)
RED DOG PET RESORT & SPA
4975 Babson Pl (45227-2683)
PHONE...................................513 733-3647
Grant Johnson, *Managing Dir*
Raymond Schneider, *Mng Member*
Sherry Agar, *Director*
EMP: 30
SQ FT: 28,000
SALES (est): 760.6K **Privately Held**
SIC: 0752 5999 Shelters, animal; grooming services, pet & animal specialties; pets & pet supplies

(G-4349)
REECE-CAMPBELL INC
10839 Chester Rd (45246-4707)
PHONE...................................513 542-4600
Peter W Chronis, *CEO*
Rob Hekler, *Vice Pres*
James Kohne, *Vice Pres*
Elio Zerbini, *Vice Pres*
EMP: 60
SQ FT: 10,000
SALES (est): 17.4MM **Privately Held**
SIC: 1542 Commercial & office building contractors

(G-4350)
REGENCY HOSPITAL CINCINNATI
10500 Montgomery Rd (45242-4402)
PHONE...................................513 862-4700

Kathleen Cahill, *CEO*
Carolyn Gray, *Principal*
EMP: 33
SALES (est): 3.1MM **Privately Held**
SIC: 8062 General medical & surgical hospitals

(G-4351)
REHAB MEDICAL INC
1150 W 8th St Ste 110 (45203-1245)
PHONE..................................513 381-3740
Patrick McGinley, *Principal*
EMP: 89
SALES (corp-wide): 10.6MM **Privately Held**
SIC: 8093 Rehabilitation center, outpatient treatment
PA: Rehab Medical, Inc.
6365 Castleplace Dr
Indianapolis IN 46250
877 813-0205

(G-4352)
REHAB RESOURCES
8595 Beechmont Ave # 204 (45255-4740)
P.O. Box 541127 (45254-1127)
PHONE..................................513 474-4123
Teresa Hollenkany, *CEO*
EMP: 25
SALES (est): 927.7K **Privately Held**
SIC: 8322 Rehabilitation services

(G-4353)
REINHART FOODSERVICE LLC
535 Shepherd Ave (45215-3115)
PHONE..................................513 421-9184
Michelle Hogue, *Buyer*
Bill Devine, *Branch Mgr*
Shawna Ewell, *Manager*
EMP: 175 **Privately Held**
WEB: www.reinhartfoodservice.com
SIC: 5141 Groceries, general line
HQ: Reinhart Foodservice, L.L.C.
6250 N River Rd Ste 9000
Rosemont IL 60018
608 782-2660

(G-4354)
REISENFELD & ASSOC LPA LLC (PA)
Also Called: Fojournerf Title Agency
3962 Red Bank Rd (45227-3408)
PHONE..................................513 322-7000
Gregory Stout, *Counsel*
Bradley A Reisenfeld, *Mng Member*
Michael Hoehn, *Info Tech Dir*
Sallie A Conyers,
Steven M Giordullo,
EMP: 170
SQ FT: 38,000
SALES (est): 24.4MM **Privately Held**
WEB: www.rslegal.com
SIC: 8111 General practice law office

(G-4355)
RELADYNE LLC (DH)
8280 Montgomery Rd # 101 (45236-6101)
PHONE..................................513 489-6000
Larry J Stoddard, *CEO*
Jeff Hart, *Exec VP*
Jay Hurt, *Exec VP*
Doug Oehler, *Exec VP*
Glenn Pumpelly, *Exec VP*
EMP: 41
SALES (est): 21.8MM **Privately Held**
SIC: 7699 7549 Industrial equipment services; lubrication service, automotive
HQ: Rel Ii Llc
9395 Kenwood Rd Ste 104
Blue Ash OH 45242
513 489-6000

(G-4356)
REMINGER CO LPA
525 Vine St Ste 1700 (45202-3123)
PHONE..................................513 721-1311
Stephanie Cook, *Manager*
EMP: 28
SALES (corp-wide): 52.2MM **Privately Held**
WEB: www.reminger.com
SIC: 8111 General practice law office
PA: Reminger Co., L.P.A.
101 W Prospect Ave # 1400
Cleveland OH 44115
216 687-1311

(G-4357)
RENDIGS FRY KIELY & DENNIS LLP (PA)
600 Vine St Ste 2602 (45202-2491)
PHONE..................................513 381-9200
Donald C Adams, *Partner*
Lawrence E Barbiere, *Partner*
W Roger Fry, *Partner*
J W Gelwicks, *Partner*
Edward R Goldman, *Partner*
EMP: 76 **EST:** 1940
SQ FT: 33,000
SALES (est): 13.3MM **Privately Held**
WEB: www.rendigs.com
SIC: 8111 General practice law office

(G-4358)
RENNIE & JONSON MONTGOMERY
36 E 7th St Ste 2100 (45202-4452)
PHONE..................................513 241-4722
James Montgomery, *President*
George Jonson, *Principal*
Douglas Rennie, *Principal*
Lance Dickinson, *Financial Exec*
G Hoffpauir, *Executive*
EMP: 30
SQ FT: 1,400
SALES (est): 3.9MM **Privately Held**
WEB: www.mrj.cc
SIC: 8111 General practice attorney, lawyer

(G-4359)
RENT-N-ROLL
7841 Laurel Ave (45243-2608)
PHONE..................................513 528-6929
Gre Lewalle, *President*
EMP: 60 **EST:** 2013
SALES (est): 2.2MM **Privately Held**
SIC: 7359 Equipment rental & leasing

(G-4360)
REPUBLIC SERVICES INC
10751 Evendale Dr (45241-2535)
PHONE..................................513 554-0237
EMP: 34
SALES (corp-wide): 10B **Publicly Held**
SIC: 4953 Refuse collection & disposal services
PA: Republic Services, Inc.
18500 N Allied Way # 100
Phoenix AZ 85054
480 627-2700

(G-4361)
RESOLVIT RESOURCES LLC (PA)
895 Central Ave Ste 1050 (45202-5758)
PHONE..................................703 734-3330
Lowell Lehmann, *Partner*
Brian Murrow, *General Mgr*
Craig Scates, *Managing Dir*
Jack Garabedian, *Vice Pres*
Julie Sizelove, *Vice Pres*
EMP: 45
SALES (est): 72MM **Privately Held**
WEB: www.resolvit.com
SIC: 7379

(G-4362)
RESOLVIT RESOURCES LLC
895 Central Ave Ste 350 (45202-1975)
PHONE..................................513 619-5900
Lowell Lehmann, *Branch Mgr*
EMP: 42
SALES (corp-wide): 72MM **Privately Held**
SIC: 8748 Business consulting
PA: Resolvit Resources, Llc
895 Central Ave Ste 1050
Cincinnati OH 45202
703 734-3330

(G-4363)
RESOLVIT RESOURCES LLC
895 Central Ave Ste 1050 (45202-5758)
PHONE..................................703 564-2100
Brian Hepp, *Branch Mgr*
EMP: 60
SALES (corp-wide): 72MM **Privately Held**
SIC: 8748 Business consulting

PA: Resolvit Resources, Llc
895 Central Ave Ste 1050
Cincinnati OH 45202
703 734-3330

(G-4364)
RESTAURANT DEPOT LLC
4501 W Mitchell Ave (45232-1911)
PHONE..................................513 542-3000
Quentin Hershberger, *Manager*
EMP: 42 **Privately Held**
SIC: 5046 Restaurant equipment & supplies
HQ: Restaurant Depot, Llc
1524 132nd St
College Point NY 11356

(G-4365)
REUPERT HEATING AND AC CO INC
5137 Crookshank Rd (45238-3386)
PHONE..................................513 922-5050
Kenneth Reupert, *President*
Donald Reupert, *Corp Secy*
Richard Reupert, *Vice Pres*
EMP: 27
SQ FT: 3,200
SALES (est): 4.7MM **Privately Held**
SIC: 1711 Warm air heating & air conditioning contractor; heating & air conditioning contractors

(G-4366)
RGIS LLC
4000 Executive Park Dr # 105 (45241-2023)
PHONE..................................513 772-5990
Debbie Cappel, *General Mgr*
Steve Lighner, *Manager*
EMP: 110
SALES (corp-wide): 6.8B **Publicly Held**
WEB: www.rgisinv.com
SIC: 7389 Inventory computing service
HQ: Rgis, Llc
2000 Taylor Rd
Auburn Hills MI 48326
248 651-2511

(G-4367)
RHC INC (PA)
Also Called: RESIDENT HOME, THE
3030 W Fork Rd (45211-1944)
PHONE..................................513 389-7501
Peter Keiser, *President*
Robert South, *Chairman*
Russell Ferneding, *Treasurer*
EMP: 150
SQ FT: 11,077
SALES (est): 8.8MM **Privately Held**
WEB: www.rhcorp.org
SIC: 8361 Home for the mentally handicapped

(G-4368)
RHINEGEIST LLC
Also Called: Rhinegeist Brewery
1910 Elm St (45202-7751)
PHONE..................................513 381-1367
Jon Colasurd, *General Mgr*
Aaron Stryker, *Site Mgr*
Ryan Kelly, *Accountant*
Amie Ruggles, *Accountant*
Omar Elayan, *Sales Mgr*
▲ **EMP:** 71
SQ FT: 120,000
SALES: 10MM **Privately Held**
SIC: 5181 5813 Beer & other fermented malt liquors; bars & lounges

(G-4369)
RICHARD GOETTLE INC
12071 Hamilton Ave (45231-1032)
PHONE..................................513 825-8100
Douglas Keller, *CEO*
John Conety, *Superintendent*
Cordale Francis, *Superintendent*
Kelly Hedger, *Superintendent*
Chris Herth, *Superintendent*
◆ **EMP:** 99
SALES (est): 75.2MM **Privately Held**
SIC: 5082 Contractors' materials
PA: Goettle Holding Company, Inc.
12071 Hamilton Ave
Cincinnati OH 45231
513 825-8100

(G-4370)
RICHARDS ELECTRIC SUP CO INC (PA)
4620 Reading Rd (45229-1297)
P.O. Box 29860 (45229-0860)
PHONE..................................513 242-8800
Ivan S Misrach, *President*
Richard Misrach, *Principal*
Joseph Schwartz, *Principal*
Norma Strelow, *Principal*
Mark Schmidlin, *Vice Pres*
▲ **EMP:** 141
SQ FT: 62,500
SALES (est): 172.1MM **Privately Held**
WEB: www.richardselectric.com
SIC: 5063 Electrical supplies; electrical construction materials; lighting fixtures

(G-4371)
RICK BLAZING INSURANCE AGENCY
Also Called: Nationwide
300 E Bus Way Ste 200 (45241)
PHONE..................................513 677-8300
EMP: 30
SALES (est): 2.6MM **Privately Held**
SIC: 6411 Insurance Agent/Broker

(G-4372)
RICKING PAPER AND SPECIALTY CO
525 Northland Blvd (45240-3233)
PHONE..................................513 825-3551
Carl Ricking Jr, *President*
Preston M Simpson, *Principal*
Carla Droll, *Vice Pres*
Julie Ricking, *Vice Pres*
Joyce Ricking, *Treasurer*
EMP: 50
SQ FT: 84,000
SALES (est): 13.4MM **Privately Held**
WEB: www.ricking.com
SIC: 5141 2656 5113 Groceries, general line; cups, paper; made from purchased material; bags, paper & disposable plastic

(G-4373)
RIDE SHARE INFORMATION
Also Called: Oki Rgonal Council Governments
720 E Pete Rose Way # 420 (45202-3579)
PHONE..................................513 621-6300
Katie Hannum, *Accountant*
Summer Jones, *Corp Comm Staff*
Mark Policinski, *Exec Dir*
Hui Xie, *Sr Associate*
EMP: 32
SALES (est): 3.8MM **Privately Held**
WEB: www.oki.org
SIC: 8742 Administrative services consultant

(G-4374)
RILCO INDUSTRIAL CONTROLS INC (HQ)
649 Dorgene Ln (45244-1010)
PHONE..................................513 530-0055
Chris Cowell, *President*
EMP: 27
SALES (est): 6.7MM
SALES (corp-wide): 43.6MM **Privately Held**
WEB: www.cincinnaticontrols.com
SIC: 5084 Controlling instruments & accessories
PA: Triad Technologies, Llc
985 Falls Creek Dr
Vandalia OH 45377
937 832-2861

(G-4375)
RIPPE & KINGSTON SYSTEMS INC (PA)
Also Called: Broughton International
1077 Celestial St Ste 124 (45202-1628)
PHONE..................................513 977-4578
Tom Obermaier, *CEO*
Ron Sharp, *President*
Joyce Tabar, *General Mgr*
John Fink, *District Mgr*
Thomas Davidson, *Vice Pres*
EMP: 60
SQ FT: 15,000

▲ = Import ▼=Export
◆ =Import/Export

SALES (est): 9.3MM **Privately Held**
WEB: www.rippe.com
SIC: 7379 7371 Computer related consulting services; computer related maintenance services; computer software development

(G-4376)
RITTER & RANDOLPH LLC
1 E 4th St Ste 700 (45202-3705)
PHONE..................................513 381-5700
Daniel P Randolph, *Partner*
Maryann Jacobs, *Partner*
Marcia Beasley, *Legal Staff*
Lynette Cummins, *Legal Staff*
EMP: 32
SALES (est): 3.7MM **Privately Held**
WEB: www.ritterandrandolph.com
SIC: 8111 General practice attorney, lawyer

(G-4377)
RIVER DOWNS TURF CLUB INC
Also Called: River Downs Race Course
6301 Kellogg Rd (45230-5237)
P.O. Box 30286 (45230-0286)
PHONE..................................513 232-8000
EMP: 50
SQ FT: 2,000
SALES (est): 2MM **Privately Held**
SIC: 7948 Horse Race Track

(G-4378)
RIVERHILLS HEALTHCARE INC (PA)
111 Wellington Pl Lowr (45219)
PHONE..................................513 241-2370
P Robert Schwetschenau, *President*
Linda Burnhardt, *Principal*
Peter Vicente, *Vice Pres*
Colin Zadikoff MD, *Treasurer*
Philip Becker, *Med Doctor*
EMP: 38
SQ FT: 22,224
SALES (est): 11.7MM **Privately Held**
SIC: 8011 Neurologist

(G-4379)
RIVERHILLS HEALTHCARE INC
4805 Montgomery Rd # 150 (45212-2280)
PHONE..................................513 791-6400
Barbara Mitchell, *Office Mgr*
Maureen LI MD, *Director*
EMP: 44
SALES (corp-wide): 11.7MM **Privately Held**
SIC: 8011 Surgeon; neurologist
PA: Riverhills Healthcare Inc
111 Wellington Pl Lowr
Cincinnati OH 45219
513 241-2370

(G-4380)
RIVERSIDE CNSTR SVCS INC
218 W Mcmicken Ave (45214-2314)
PHONE..................................513 723-0900
Robert S Krejci, *President*
Timothy L Pierce, *Vice Pres*
EMP: 32
SQ FT: 21,000
SALES (est): 5.2MM **Privately Held**
WEB: www.riversidearchitectural.com
SIC: 2431 1751 2434 Millwork; carpentry work; wood kitchen cabinets

(G-4381)
RIVERSIDE ELECTRIC INC (PA)
680 Redna Ter (45215-1108)
PHONE..................................513 936-0100
Paul Gangloff, *President*
Janet Gangloff, *Vice Pres*
Gary Luce, *Project Mgr*
Krista Mahon, *Manager*
Jacqueline Hummel, *Admin Asst*
EMP: 28
SQ FT: 6,000
SALES (est): 7.1MM **Privately Held**
WEB: www.riverside-elec.com
SIC: 1731 Fire detection & burglar alarm systems specialization

(G-4382)
RJB ACQUISITIONS LLC
2915 Highland Ave (45219-2494)
PHONE..................................513 314-2711
Debron Betts, *Principal*

EMP: 25
SALES (est): 1.1MM **Privately Held**
SIC: 6799 Investors

(G-4383)
RK EXPRESS INTERNATIONAL LLC
5474 Sanrio Ct (45247-7408)
P.O. Box 531106 (45253-1106)
PHONE..................................513 574-2400
Randy Lee, *Principal*
EMP: 55
SQ FT: 30,000
SALES (est): 4.7MM **Privately Held**
SIC: 4731 Freight transportation arrangement

(G-4384)
RLA INVESTMENTS INC
389 Wade St (45214-2825)
PHONE..................................513 554-1470
Robert L Adleta II, *President*
Ron Hill, *Foreman/Supr*
EMP: 45
SALES (est): 9.9MM **Privately Held**
SIC: 1623 Sewer line construction

(G-4385)
RM ADVISORY GROUP INC
5300 Vine St (45217-1030)
PHONE..................................513 242-2100
Robert Moskowitz, *President*
Ira Moskowitz, *Principal*
Mark Moskowitz, *Vice Pres*
Linda Curtis, *VP Human Res*
EMP: 35 EST: 1901
SQ FT: 70,000
SALES (est): 13.1MM **Privately Held**
WEB: www.moskowitzbros.com
SIC: 5093 3341 Ferrous metal scrap & waste; nonferrous metals scrap; secondary nonferrous metals

(G-4386)
RMS OF OHIO INC
2824 E Kemper Rd (45241-1820)
PHONE..................................513 841-0990
Gwen Lee, *Director*
EMP: 30
SALES (corp-wide): 11.8MM **Privately Held**
SIC: 8059 Convalescent home
PA: Rms Of Ohio, Inc
733 E Dublin Granville Rd # 100
Columbus OH 43229
614 844-6767

(G-4387)
ROADTRIPPERS INC
131 E Mcmicken Ave (45202-6520)
PHONE..................................917 688-9887
James Fischer, *CEO*
Jonathan Richman, *General Mgr*
Joshua Smibert, *COO*
Eric Lutley, *Software Engr*
Cheryl Gilligan, *Technical Staff*
EMP: 25
SALES (est): 2MM **Privately Held**
SIC: 7371 Custom computer programming services

(G-4388)
ROBBINS KELLY PATTERSON TUCKER
7 W 7th St Ste 1400 (45202-2451)
PHONE..................................513 721-3330
Fredric J Robbins, *President*
Richard Lauer, *Partner*
Stephen Sager, *Chief*
James M Kelly, *Vice Pres*
Debra Staggs, *Bookkeeper*
EMP: 45 EST: 1965
SALES (est): 5.8MM **Privately Held**
SIC: 8111 General practice attorney, lawyer

(G-4389)
ROBERT E LUBOW MD
3001 Highland Ave (45219-2315)
PHONE..................................513 961-8861
Robedrt Lubow, *Owner*
EMP: 37
SALES (est): 460.4K **Privately Held**
SIC: 8011 Psychiatrist

(G-4390)
ROBERT ELLIS
175 W Galbraith Rd (45216-1015)
PHONE..................................513 821-0275
Robert Ellis, *Principal*
Jennifer Schneider, *Office Mgr*
EMP: 25 EST: 2011
SALES (est): 143.5K **Privately Held**
SIC: 8011 General & family practice, physician/surgeon

(G-4391)
ROBERT HALF INTERNATIONAL INC
201 E 5th St Ste 2000a (45202-4162)
PHONE..................................513 621-8367
Danielle Skelton, *Branch Mgr*
EMP: 92
SALES (corp-wide): 5.8B **Publicly Held**
SIC: 7361 Placement agencies
PA: Robert Half International Inc.
2884 Sand Hill Rd Ste 200
Menlo Park CA 94025
650 234-6000

(G-4392)
ROBERT LUCKE HOMES INC
8825 Chapelsquare Ln B (45249-4702)
PHONE..................................513 683-3300
Robert Lucke, *President*
Randy Lamar, *Sales Mgr*
Tyler Lamar, *Marketing Staff*
EMP: 30
SALES (est): 5MM **Privately Held**
SIC: 1521 New construction, single-family houses

(G-4393)
ROCKFISH INTERACTIVE CORP
659 Van Meter St Ste 520 (45202-1585)
PHONE..................................513 381-1583
Kenny Tomlin, *CEO*
EMP: 63
SALES (corp-wide): 20.1B **Privately Held**
SIC: 7311 Advertising agencies
HQ: Rockfish Interactive Llc
3100 S Market St Ste 100
Rogers AR 72758

(G-4394)
RODEM INC (PA)
Also Called: Rodem Process Equipment
5095 Crookshank Rd (45238-3366)
PHONE..................................513 922-6140
Christopher Diener, *President*
Christopher A Diener, *President*
Jeffrey L Diener, *Vice Pres*
Susan D Kerr, *Treasurer*
Nancy D Finke, *Admin Sec*
▲ EMP: 40
SQ FT: 15,000
SALES (est): 61.5MM **Privately Held**
WEB: www.rodem.com
SIC: 5084 Dairy products manufacturing machinery; food product manufacturing machinery

(G-4395)
RONALD MCDONALD HSE GRTR CINCI
341 Erkenbrecher Ave (45229-2806)
PHONE..................................513 636-7642
David Anderson, *President*
Michael Weinberg, *Director*
EMP: 27
SQ FT: 56,000
SALES (est): 5.9MM **Privately Held**
SIC: 8322 Individual & family services

(G-4396)
ROSS SINCLAIRE & ASSOC LLC (PA)
700 Walnut St Ste 600 (45202-2027)
PHONE..................................513 381-3939
Daniel Blank, *Managing Dir*
Omar Ganoom, *Managing Dir*
Melanie Smith, *COO*
Gregory Haidet, *Exec VP*
Mike Gallagher, *Vice Pres*
EMP: 40 EST: 1981
SQ FT: 6,000
SALES (est): 14.9MM **Privately Held**
WEB: www.rsanet.com
SIC: 6211 Stock brokers & dealers; investment bankers

(G-4397)
ROTO RT INC (DH)
Also Called: Roto-Rooter
255 E 5th St Ste 2500 (45202-4725)
PHONE..................................513 762-6690
Spencer Lee, *CEO*
Rick Arquilla, *President*
EMP: 29
SALES: 350K
SALES (corp-wide): 1.7B **Publicly Held**
SIC: 7699 Sewer cleaning & rodding
HQ: Roto-Rooter Services Company
255 E 5th St Ste 2500
Cincinnati OH 45202
513 762-6690

(G-4398)
ROTO-ROOTER DEVELOPMENT CO (HQ)
255 E 5th St Ste 2500 (45202-4793)
PHONE..................................513 762-6690
Spencer S Lee, *CEO*
Edward L Hutton, *Ch of Bd*
Kevin J McNamara, *Vice Ch Bd*
Rick Arquilla, *President*
David Williams, *CFO*
EMP: 95
SQ FT: 20,000
SALES (est): 256.8MM
SALES (corp-wide): 1.7B **Publicly Held**
SIC: 7699 Sewer cleaning & rodding; gas appliance repair service; plumbing contractors; septic system construction
PA: Chemed Corporation
255 E 5th St Ste 2600
Cincinnati OH 45202
513 762-6690

(G-4399)
ROTO-ROOTER GROUP INC (HQ)
2500 Chemed Ctr (45202-4725)
PHONE..................................513 762-6690
Spencer Lee, *CEO*
Rick Arquilla, *President*
Frank Castillo, *President*
Robert Goldschmidt, *Exec VP*
Gary H Sander, *Exec VP*
EMP: 135
SALES (est): 4.3MM
SALES (corp-wide): 1.7B **Publicly Held**
WEB: www.chemed.com
SIC: 7699 Sewer cleaning & rodding
PA: Chemed Corporation
255 E 5th St Ste 2600
Cincinnati OH 45202
513 762-6690

(G-4400)
ROTO-ROOTER SERVICES COMPANY (DH)
255 E 5th St Ste 2500 (45202-4793)
PHONE..................................513 762-6690
Spencer S Lee, *CEO*
Rick L Arquilla, *President*
David Williams, *CFO*
EMP: 100
SALES (est): 247.3MM
SALES (corp-wide): 1.7B **Publicly Held**
SIC: 7699 1711 Sewer cleaning & rodding; plumbing contractors
HQ: Roto-Rooter Development Company
255 E 5th St Ste 2500
Cincinnati OH 45202
513 762-6690

(G-4401)
ROTO-ROOTER SERVICES COMPANY
2125 Montana Ave (45211-2741)
PHONE..................................513 541-3840
Mike Walker, *Manager*
EMP: 70
SQ FT: 13,761
SALES (corp-wide): 1.7B **Publicly Held**
SIC: 7699 1711 7623 Sewer cleaning & rodding; plumbing, heating, air-conditioning contractors; heating systems repair & maintenance; refrigeration repair service
HQ: Roto-Rooter Services Company
255 E 5th St Ste 2500
Cincinnati OH 45202
513 762-6690

(G-4402)
ROUGH BROTHERS MFG INC
5513 Vine St Ste 1 (45217-1022)
PHONE....................................513 242-0310
Richard Reilly, *President*
James Parris, *General Mgr*
Nick Workman, *Superintendent*
Kevin Caron, *Vice Pres*
James Gross, *Safety Mgr*
◆ EMP: 90
SQ FT: 100,000
SALES (est): 96.7MM
SALES (corp-wide): 1B **Publicly Held**
SIC: 1542 3448 Greenhouse construction;
　greenhouses: prefabricated metal
HQ: Rough Brothers Holding Co., Inc
　　3556 Lake Shore Rd # 100
　　Buffalo NY 14219
　　716 826-6500

(G-4403)
**ROUNDTOWER TECHNOLOGIES
LLC (PA)**
5905 E Galbraith Rd # 3000 (45236-0702)
PHONE....................................513 247-7900
Stephen West, *President*
Gary Halloran, *Managing Prtnr*
Stephen Power, *Managing Prtnr*
Jason Pennington, *Partner*
Sean Daly, *Chief*
EMP: 62
SQ FT: 5,000
SALES (est): 61.7MM **Privately Held**
SIC: 7379 Computer related consulting
　services

(G-4404)
ROYAL CAR WASH INC
6925 Colerain Ave (45239-5545)
PHONE....................................513 385-2777
Rick Ennis, *President*
EMP: 34
SQ FT: 1,000
SALES (est): 873.9K **Privately Held**
SIC: 7542 Carwash, automatic

(G-4405)
**RPC MECHANICAL SERVICES
(HQ)**
5301 Lester Rd (45213-2523)
PHONE....................................513 733-1641
John Lowe, *President*
EMP: 164 EST: 1937
SQ FT: 40,000
SALES (est): 16MM
SALES (corp-wide): 68.9MM **Privately
Held**
SIC: 1711 Mechanical contractor
PA: The Thomas J Dyer Company
　　5240 Lester Rd
　　Cincinnati OH 45213
　　513 321-8100

(G-4406)
RPF CONSULTING LLC
7870 E Kemper Rd Ste 300 (45249-1675)
PHONE....................................678 494-8030
Robert Fiorillo,
Mary Katherine Fiorillo,
EMP: 28
SQ FT: 500
SALES (est): 979.9K
SALES (corp-wide): 110.7B **Privately
Held**
SIC: 8742 Management consulting serv-
　ices
HQ: Itelligence Ag
　　Konigsbreede 1
　　Bielefeld 33605
　　521 914-480

(G-4407)
RPM MIDWEST LLC
352 Gest St (45203-1822)
PHONE....................................513 762-9000
Sam Thompson,
EMP: 26
SALES: 3.4MM **Privately Held**
SIC: 6531 Real estate managers

(G-4408)
RUMPKE AMUSEMENTS INC
Also Called: Rumpke Softball Park
10795 Hughes Rd (45251-4598)
PHONE....................................513 738-2646

William Rumpke, *Branch Mgr*
EMP: 26
SALES (corp-wide): 783.2K **Privately
Held**
SIC: 7996 Amusement parks
PA: Rumpke Amusements Inc
　　10795 Hughes Rd
　　Cincinnati OH 45251
　　513 742-2900

(G-4409)
**RUMPKE SANITARY LANDFILL
INC**
10795 Hughes Rd (45251-4598)
PHONE....................................513 851-0122
William J Rumpke, *President*
EMP: 150
SQ FT: 25,000
SALES (est): 14.7MM **Privately Held**
SIC: 4953 Sanitary landfill operation
PA: Rumpke Consolidated Companies, Inc.
　　3963 Kraus Ln
　　Hamilton OH 45014

(G-4410)
**RUMPKE TRANSPORTATION CO
LLC**
Also Called: Rumpke Container Service
553 Vine St (45202-3105)
PHONE....................................513 242-4600
Jeff Rumpke, *Manager*
EMP: 150 **Privately Held**
SIC: 4953 3341 3231 2611 Recycling,
　waste materials; secondary nonferrous
　metals; products of purchased glass; pulp
　mills
HQ: Rumpke Transportation Company, Llc
　　10795 Hughes Rd
　　Cincinnati OH 45251
　　513 851-0122

(G-4411)
RUMPKE WASTE INC (HQ)
10795 Hughes Rd (45251-4598)
PHONE....................................513 851-0122
Bill Rumpke Jr, *President*
William J Rumpke, *President*
EMP: 60
SQ FT: 25,000
SALES (est): 949.5MM **Privately Held**
SIC: 4953 Garbage: collecting, destroying
　& processing

(G-4412)
RUMPKE WASTE INC
Also Called: Rumpke Recycling
5535 Vine St (45217-1003)
PHONE....................................513 242-4401
Larry Ochs, *Manager*
EMP: 100
SQ FT: 51,870 **Privately Held**
SIC: 4953 4212 Recycling, waste materi-
　als; local trucking, without storage
HQ: Rumpke Waste, Inc.
　　10795 Hughes Rd
　　Cincinnati OH 45251
　　513 851-0122

(G-4413)
RUSH PACKAGE DELIVERY INC
Also Called: Rush Trans
10091 Moteller Ln (45201)
PHONE....................................513 771-7874
Brian Kressin, *Branch Mgr*
EMP: 40
SALES (corp-wide): 15.7MM **Privately
Held**
WEB: www.rush-delivery.com
SIC: 4212 Delivery service, vehicular
PA: Rush Package Delivery, Inc.
　　2619 Needmore Rd
　　Dayton OH 45414
　　937 224-7874

(G-4414)
**RUSH TRUCK CENTERS OHIO
INC (HQ)**
Also Called: Rush Truck Center, Cincinnati
11775 Highway Dr (45241-2005)
PHONE....................................513 733-8500
EMP: 73

SALES (est): 56.7MM
SALES (est): 5.5B **Publicly Held**
SIC: 5012 7538 5531 5014 Automobiles
　& other motor vehicles; general automo-
　tive repair shops; automotive & home
　supply stores; tires & tubes; truck rental &
　leasing, no drivers
PA: Rush Enterprises, Inc.
　　555 S Ih 35 Ste 500
　　New Braunfels TX 78130
　　830 302-5200

(G-4415)
**RWB PROPERTIES AND CNSTR
LLC**
611 Shepherd Dr Unit 6 (45215-2172)
PHONE....................................513 541-0900
Rodrigo M Williams, *CEO*
Larry Bryant, *VP Opers*
Jimmy Hill,
EMP: 60
SQ FT: 40,000
SALES (est): 6.2MM **Privately Held**
SIC: 1622 Bridge, tunnel & elevated high-
　way

(G-4416)
RWS ENTERPRISES LLC
Also Called: Visiting Angels
9019 Colerain Ave (45251-2401)
PHONE....................................513 598-6770
Michael Schroth, *Owner*
Jody Reeder, *Client Mgr*
EMP: 60
SALES (est): 1.2MM **Privately Held**
SIC: 8082 Home health care services

(G-4417)
**RYANS ALL-GLASS
INCORPORATED (PA)**
9884 Springfield Pike (45215-1441)
PHONE....................................513 771-4440
Bruce Ryan, *President*
Dan Ryan, *Vice Pres*
Ken Ryan, *Vice Pres*
Kathi McKenzie, *Manager*
Anita Salyers, *Manager*
EMP: 30
SQ FT: 22,000
SALES (est): 8MM **Privately Held**
WEB: www.ryansallglass.com
SIC: 1793 7536 1751 Glass & glazing
　work; automotive glass replacement
　shops; window & door (prefabricated) in-
　stallation

(G-4418)
RYDER TRUCK RENTAL INC
1190 Gest St (45203-1114)
PHONE....................................513 241-7736
Pat Murphy, *Branch Mgr*
Shawn Watson, *Manager*
EMP: 40
SALES (corp-wide): 8.4B **Publicly Held**
SIC: 7513 Truck rental, without drivers
HQ: Ryder Truck Rental, Inc.
　　11690 Nw 105th St
　　Medley FL 33178
　　305 500-3726

(G-4419)
RYDER TRUCK RENTAL INC
2575 Commodity Cir (45241-1563)
PHONE....................................513 772-0223
Dan Niles, *Site Mgr*
Steve Lennon, *CPA*
Bob Anks, *Manager*
EMP: 30
SQ FT: 9,870
SALES (corp-wide): 8.4B **Publicly Held**
SIC: 7513 7519 Truck rental, without driv-
　ers; trailer rental
HQ: Ryder Truck Rental, Inc.
　　11690 Nw 105th St
　　Medley FL 33178
　　305 500-3726

(G-4420)
**S & S HALTHCARE STRATEGIES
LTD**
1385 Kemper Meadow Dr (45240-1635)
PHONE....................................513 772-8866
Gail Scheitzer, *President*
Gail Schweitzer, *President*
Richard Rostowsky, *Vice Pres*

Cindy Volz, *Accounts Mgr*
ARI Rostowsky, *Marketing Staff*
EMP: 120
SQ FT: 60,000
SALES (est): 36.3MM **Privately Held**
SIC: 6411 Insurance adjusters

(G-4421)
**SADLER-NECAMP FINANCIAL
SVCS**
Also Called: Proware
7621 E Kemper Rd (45249-1609)
PHONE....................................513 489-5477
Randal R Sadler, *CEO*
Don Flischel, *Vice Pres*
Bret Sadler, *Vice Pres*
Melissa Sadler, *Admin Sec*
EMP: 40
SQ FT: 7,400
SALES (est): 6.2MM **Privately Held**
WEB: www.proware.com
SIC: 7371 8748 5045 Computer software
　development; systems engineering con-
　sultant, ex. computer or professional;
　computers, peripherals & software; com-
　puter software

(G-4422)
SAEC/KINETIC VISION INC
10255 Evendale Commons Dr
(45241-3250)
PHONE....................................513 793-4959
Richard Schweet, *President*
Jeremy Jarrett, *Vice Pres*
Catherine Bennett, *Opers Staff*
Brian C Carovillano, *Purch Mgr*
Zachary Leavitt, *Engineer*
EMP: 130
SQ FT: 28,000
SALES (est): 3.7MM **Privately Held**
WEB: www.saec-kv.com
SIC: 8711 7371 Mechanical engineering;
　computer software development & appli-
　cations

(G-4423)
**SAFRAN HUMN RSRCES
SUPPORT INC (HQ)**
111 Merchant St (45246-3730)
P.O. Box 15514 (45215-0514)
PHONE....................................513 552-3230
Jacques Riboni, *Exec VP*
Luc Bramy, *Vice Pres*
EMP: 72
SQ FT: 5,000
SALES (est): 4.3MM
SALES (corp-wide): 833.4MM **Privately
Held**
SIC: 8711 Consulting engineer
PA: Safran
　　2 Bd Du General Martial Valin
　　Paris 15e Arrondissement 75015
　　140 608-080

(G-4424)
**SAGE HOSPITALITY
RESOURCES LLC**
Also Called: Crowne Plaza Ci
11320 Chester Rd (45246-4003)
PHONE....................................513 771-2080
Matthew Bryant, *Branch Mgr*
EMP: 67
SALES (corp-wide): 388MM **Privately
Held**
WEB: www.21chotel.com
SIC: 7011 Hotel, franchised
PA: Sage Hospitality Resources L.L.C.
　　1575 Welton St Ste 300
　　Denver CO 80202
　　303 595-7200

(G-4425)
**SAINT JAMES DAY CARE
CENTER**
3929 Boudinot Ave (45211-3603)
PHONE....................................513 662-2287
Joan Chouteau, *Director*
EMP: 25
SALES: 837.5K **Privately Held**
SIC: 8351 Child day care services

(G-4426)
SAINT JOSEPH ORPHANAGE
274 Sutton Rd (45230-3521)
PHONE....................................513 231-5010

Tom Uhl, *Branch Mgr*
EMP: 95
SALES (corp-wide): 16.2MM **Privately Held**
SIC: 8361 Orphanage
PA: Saint Joseph Orphanage
5400 Edalbert Dr
Cincinnati OH 45239
513 741-3100

(G-4427)
SAINT JOSEPH ORPHANAGE (PA)
5400 Edalbert Dr (45239-7695)
PHONE.................................513 741-3100
Eric Cummins, *CEO*
Janet Nobel, *Director*
EMP: 66
SALES: 16.2MM **Privately Held**
WEB: www.stjosephorphanage.org
SIC: 8361 Children's home

(G-4428)
SALON LA
2711 Edmondson Rd (45209-1912)
P.O. Box 912, Georgetown KY (40324-0912)
PHONE.................................513 784-1700
Linda August, *Owner*
EMP: 30
SQ FT: 2,700
SALES (est): 443.8K **Privately Held**
WEB: www.salonla.com
SIC: 7231 Beauty Shop

(G-4429)
SALVATION ARMY
2250 Park Ave (45212-3200)
P.O. Box 12546 (45212-0546)
PHONE.................................859 255-5791
Fax: 513 351-8084
EMP: 82
SALES (corp-wide): 4.3B **Privately Held**
SIC: 8322 Individual/Family Services
HQ: The Salvation Army
440 W Nyack Rd Ofc
West Nyack NY 10994
845 620-7200

(G-4430)
SALVATION ARMY
114 East Central Pkwy (45202-7234)
P.O. Box 596 (45201-0596)
PHONE.................................513 762-5600
Maj Kenneth Maynor, *Manager*
EMP: 100
SALES (corp-wide): 4.3B **Privately Held**
WEB: www.salvationarmyusa.org
SIC: 8399 8322 Advocacy group; individual & family services
HQ: The Salvation Army
440 W Nyack Rd Ofc
West Nyack NY 10994
845 620-7200

(G-4431)
SANDER WOODY FORD (PA)
235 W Mitchell Ave (45232-1907)
PHONE.................................513 541-5586
William G Sander, *President*
James Mullen, *Vice Pres*
Thomas Paul Sander, *Treasurer*
EMP: 60 **EST:** 1962
SQ FT: 30,000
SALES (est): 7.4MM **Privately Held**
SIC: 7389 Personal service agents, brokers & bureaus; balloons, novelty & toy; building scale models

(G-4432)
SANTA MARIA COMMUNITY SVCS INC (PA)
617 Steiner St (45204-1327)
PHONE.................................513 557-2720
H A Musser Jr, *President*
Blair Schoen, *Vice Pres*
EMP: 40
SQ FT: 4,608
SALES: 4.3MM **Privately Held**
WEB: www.santamaria-cincy.org
SIC: 8322 Social service center

(G-4433)
SAP AMERICA INC
312 Walnut St Ste 1600 (45202-4038)
PHONE.................................513 762-7630

Tim Mc Larkey, *Principal*
Chad Schmidt, *Sales Staff*
Greg Bishop, *Sr Software Eng*
EMP: 38
SALES (corp-wide): 28.2B **Privately Held**
SIC: 7371 Computer software development
HQ: Sap America, Inc.
3999 West Chester Pike
Newtown Square PA 19073
610 661-1000

(G-4434)
SCARLET & GRAY CLEANING SVC
3247 Glenmore Ave Apt 1 (45211-6628)
PHONE.................................513 661-4483
Mark Cappel, *President*
Tim Cappel, *Opers Mgr*
EMP: 135
SQ FT: 1,800
SALES (est): 2.7MM **Privately Held**
SIC: 7349 Office cleaning or charring

(G-4435)
SCHERZINGER CORP
Also Called: Scherzinger Trmt & Pest Ctrl
10557 Medallion Dr (45241-3193)
PHONE.................................513 531-7848
Steven Scherzinger, *President*
EMP: 75
SQ FT: 13,500
SALES (est): 7.3MM **Privately Held**
WEB: www.stopzbugs.com
SIC: 7342 0782 Termite control; pest control in structures; lawn care services

(G-4436)
SCHIBI HEATING & COOLING CORP
Also Called: Comfort Distributors
5025 Hubble Rd (45247-3660)
PHONE.................................513 385-3344
Kenneth A Schibi, *CEO*
Norb Kinross, *President*
Dale M Schibi, *Vice Pres*
Craig Hines, *Treasurer*
EMP: 25
SQ FT: 561
SALES (est): 4.8MM **Privately Held**
SIC: 1711 Heating & air conditioning contractors

(G-4437)
SCHIMPF GINOCCHIO MULLINS LPA
36 E 7th St Ste 2600 (45202-4452)
PHONE.................................513 977-5570
Richard Schimpf, *President*
EMP: 25 **EST:** 1971
SALES (est): 1.9MM **Privately Held**
SIC: 8111 General practice attorney, lawyer

(G-4438)
SCHNEIDER HOME EQUIPMENT CO (PA)
7948 Pippin Rd (45239-4696)
PHONE.................................513 522-1200
Michael Schneider, *President*
Stanley C Schneider, *Vice Pres*
Steven Scheider, *Treasurer*
Annette Littrell, *Controller*
EMP: 38 **EST:** 1936
SQ FT: 10,000
SALES (est): 6.5MM **Privately Held**
WEB: www.schneiderhomeequipment.com
SIC: 5031 5039 5211 Building materials, exterior; building materials, interior; doors & windows; awnings; door & window products

(G-4439)
SCHOCH TILE & CARPET INC
5282 Crookshank Rd (45238-3376)
PHONE.................................513 922-3466
Dennis Bley, *President*
Ruth Bley, *Corp Secy*
EMP: 40 **EST:** 1927
SQ FT: 5,000
SALES: 4.5MM **Privately Held**
WEB: www.schochtile.com
SIC: 1752 5713 Carpet laying; floor covering stores

(G-4440)
SCROGGINSGREAR INC
Also Called: William X Greene Bus Advisor
200 Northland Blvd (45246-3604)
PHONE.................................513 672-4281
Terry Grear, *President*
Mark D Scroggins, *Principal*
Robert C Scroggins, *Principal*
Luke R Trenz, *Principal*
Paul R Trenz, *Principal*
EMP: 105
SQ FT: 36,000
SALES (est): 15.8MM **Privately Held**
WEB: www.scroggins.com
SIC: 8742 Business consultant

(G-4441)
SCS CONSTRUCTION SERVICES INC
2130 Western Ave (45214-1744)
PHONE.................................513 929-0260
Jerry Back, *President*
Larry Back, *Vice Pres*
John Freibert, *Foreman/Supr*
Charlie Hull, *CFO*
Dave Roark, *Technology*
EMP: 45 **EST:** 2000
SQ FT: 8,000
SALES (est): 8.7MM **Privately Held**
SIC: 1542 3231 1761 3449 Commercial & office building, new construction; doors, glass; made from purchased glass; skylight installation; curtain walls for buildings, steel; metalware

(G-4442)
SEARS ROEBUCK AND CO
Also Called: Northgate Sears
9405 Colerain Ave (45251-2001)
PHONE.................................513 741-6422
EMP: 50
SALES (corp-wide): 16.7B **Publicly Held**
SIC: 8741 Management Services
HQ: Sears, Roebuck And Co.
3333 Beverly Rd
Hoffman Estates IL 60179
847 286-2500

(G-4443)
SECURITAS SEC SVCS USA INC
Automotive Services Division
655 Plum St 150 (45202-2339)
PHONE.................................513 639-7615
Jason Bricking, *Business Mgr*
Joe Donaldson, *Manager*
Angel M Poynter, *Manager*
EMP: 100
SALES (corp-wide): 10.9B **Privately Held**
WEB: www.securitasinc.com
SIC: 7381 Detective services
HQ: Securitas Security Services Usa, Inc.
9 Campus Dr
Parsippany NJ 07054
973 267-5300

(G-4444)
SECURITY FENCE GROUP INC (PA)
4260 Dane Ave (45223-1855)
PHONE.................................513 681-3700
Christine Frankenstein, *President*
Angela Case, *Corp Secy*
George Frankenstein, *Vice Pres*
EMP: 49
SQ FT: 140,000
SALES (est): 12.1MM **Privately Held**
SIC: 1611 1799 5039 1731 Guardrail construction, highways; highway & street sign installation; fence construction; wire fence, gates & accessories; general electrical contractor; traffic signals, electric

(G-4445)
SECURITY STORAGE CO INC
Also Called: Lewis and Michael SEC Stor
706 Oak St (45206-1616)
P.O. Box 6417 (45206-0417)
PHONE.................................513 961-2700
Dave Lewis, *President*
David M Lewis, *President*
EMP: 60
SALES (est): 4.3MM
SALES (corp-wide): 8MM **Privately Held**
SIC: 4214 4213 Household goods moving & storage, local; trucking, except local

PA: Lewis & Michael, Inc.
1827 Woodman Dr
Dayton OH 45420
937 252-6683

(G-4446)
SECURITY TITLE GUARANTEE AGCY
150 E 4th St Fl 4 (45202-4186)
PHONE.................................513 651-3393
William Strausse, *CEO*
William V Strauss, *President*
EMP: 110
SALES (est): 2.3MM **Privately Held**
SIC: 6541 Title & trust companies

(G-4447)
SEI - CINCINNATI LLC
7870 E Kemper Rd Ste 400 (45249-1675)
PHONE.................................513 459-1992
Maria Korengel, *Vice Pres*
EMP: 60
SALES (est): 881.9K **Privately Held**
SIC: 8742 Management consulting services

(G-4448)
SEILKOP INDUSTRIES INC (PA)
Also Called: Epcor Foundries
425 W North Bend Rd (45216-1731)
PHONE.................................513 761-1035
Ken Seilkop, *President*
Dave Seilkop, *Vice Pres*
Julie Hammons, *Purch Mgr*
Robin Vogel, *CFO*
EMP: 50
SQ FT: 35,000
SALES (est): 24.1MM **Privately Held**
WEB: www.epcorfoundry.com
SIC: 3363 3544 3553 3469 Aluminum die-castings; special dies & tools; pattern makers' machinery, woodworking; patterns on metal; industrial tool grinding

(G-4449)
SELECT SPECIALTY HOSPITAL
375 Dixmyth Ave Fl 15 (45220-2475)
PHONE.................................513 862-4700
John Baird, *Branch Mgr*
EMP: 90
SALES (corp-wide): 3.7B **Publicly Held**
SIC: 8062 General medical & surgical hospitals
HQ: Select Specialty Hospital-North Knoxville, Inc.
7557b Dannaher Dr Ste 145
Powell TN 37849
865 512-2450

(G-4450)
SELECTION MGT SYSTEMS INC
Also Called: Selection.com
155 Tri County Pkwy # 150 (45246-3240)
PHONE.................................513 522-8764
John Hart II, *CEO*
James Boeddeker, *President*
Thomas A Coz, *Vice Pres*
Charlie Bailey, *Manager*
Melissa Fleming, *Graphic Designe*
EMP: 65
SQ FT: 3,500
SALES (est): 7.2MM **Privately Held**
WEB: www.selection.com
SIC: 8742 Personnel management consultant

(G-4451)
SENA WELLER ROHS WILLIAMS
Also Called: Reynolds, De Witt Securities
300 Main St Fl 4 (45202-4185)
PHONE.................................513 241-6443
William T Sena, *Ch of Bd*
Edward Donohoe, *President*
Mercer Reynolds, *President*
J Grant Troja, *Exec VP*
William M Higgins, *Senior VP*
EMP: 35
SQ FT: 4,500
SALES (est): 6.5MM **Privately Held**
SIC: 6282 Investment Advisory Service

GEOGRAPHIC

(G-4452)
SENIOR LIFESTYLE
EVERGREEN LTD
230 W Galbraith Rd (45215-5223)
PHONE...................513 948-2308
Sharon Cranston, *Marketing Staff*
Martha Ingram, *Administration*
EMP: 150
SALES (est): 1.9MM **Privately Held**
SIC: 8361 Home for the aged

(G-4453)
SENIOR STAR MANAGEMENT
COMPANY
5435 Kenwood Rd (45227-1328)
PHONE...................513 271-1747
Terry Bigger, *Branch Mgr*
EMP: 323
SALES (corp-wide): 51.2MM **Privately
Held**
SIC: 8322 Senior citizens' center or associ-
ation
PA: Senior Star Management Company
1516 S Boston Ave Ste 301
Tulsa OK 74119
918 592-4400

(G-4454)
SERV-A-LITE PRODUCTS INC
(DH)
Also Called: A-1 Best Locksmith
10590 Hamilton Ave (45231-1764)
PHONE...................309 762-7741
Thomas L Rowe, *President*
Mary J Rowe, *Treasurer*
▲ EMP: 216
SQ FT: 115,000
SALES (est): 100.7MM
SALES (corp-wide): 484.2MM **Privately
Held**
WEB: www.servalite.com
SIC: 5072 Whol Hardware
HQ: The Hillman Companies Inc
10590 Hamilton Ave
Cincinnati OH 45231
513 851-4900

(G-4455)
SERVALL ELECTRIC COMPANY
INC
11697 Lebanon Rd (45241-2012)
P.O. Box 621078 (45262-1078)
PHONE...................513 771-5584
Ryan Pogozalski, *CEO*
EMP: 45 EST: 1954
SQ FT: 4,000
SALES (est): 5.9MM **Privately Held**
SIC: 1731 General electrical contractor

(G-4456)
SERVATII INC (PA)
Also Called: Servatii Pastry and Dealey
3888 Virginia Ave (45227-3410)
PHONE...................513 271-5040
Gregory Gottenbusch, *President*
Gary Gottenbusch, *Vice Pres*
EMP: 75 EST: 1963
SQ FT: 15,000
SALES (est): 35.5MM **Privately Held**
WEB: www.servati.com
SIC: 5461 5149 Bakeries; groceries & re-
lated products

(G-4457)
SETCO SALES COMPANY (HQ)
5880 Hillside Ave (45233-1599)
PHONE...................513 941-5110
Jeffrey J Clark, *President*
Joseph S Haas, *Vice Pres*
Jerry Abbott, *Purch Mgr*
Philip Sauerbeck, *Engineer*
William Schroer, *Engineer*
▲ EMP: 80 EST: 1986
SQ FT: 55,000
SALES: 30MM
SALES (corp-wide): 322.3MM **Privately
Held**
SIC: 3545 7694 Machine tool accessories;
armature rewinding shops
PA: Holden Industries, Inc.
500 Lake Cook Rd Ste 400
Deerfield IL 60015
847 940-1500

(G-4458)
SEVEN HILLS OBGYN
ASSOCIATES
6350 Glenway Ave Ste 205 (45211-6375)
PHONE...................513 922-6666
Robert Stephens, *President*
Eric Stamler, *Vice Pres*
Mabkaran Singh, *Treasurer*
EMP: 30
SALES (est): 1.1MM **Privately Held**
SIC: 8011 Obstetrician

(G-4459)
SEVEN HILLS WOMENS HEALTH
CTRS (PA)
2060 Reading Rd Ste 150 (45202-1488)
PHONE...................513 721-3200
Joseph Sclafani, *President*
Jennifer Dunaway, *Principal*
Ambrose Puttmann, *Vice Pres*
Michael Karram, *Treasurer*
Robert Stephens, *Admin Sec*
EMP: 120
SQ FT: 2,900
SALES (est): 13.6MM **Privately Held**
WEB: www.womenshealthcenters.com
SIC: 8011 Obstetrician; gynecologist

(G-4460)
SEVEN HLLS NEIGHBORHOOD
HOUSES (PA)
Also Called: FINDLAY STREET NEIGHBOR-
HOOD
901 Findlay St (45214-2135)
PHONE...................513 407-5362
Melinda Butsch Kovacic, *Ch of Bd*
Leonard Small, *President*
Alexis Kidd Zafer, *Exec Dir*
EMP: 60
SQ FT: 7,500
SALES: 584.5K **Privately Held**
SIC: 8322 Neighborhood center

(G-4461)
SGK LLC
Also Called: Schawk
537 E Pete Rose Way # 100 (45202-3578)
PHONE...................513 569-9900
Rhett Warner, *Opers Mgr*
EMP: 65
SALES (corp-wide): 1.6B **Publicly Held**
WEB: www.schawk.com
SIC: 7311 Advertising agencies
HQ: Sgk, Llc
1695 S River Rd
Des Plaines IL 60018
847 827-9494

(G-4462)
SGS NORTH AMERICA INC
Also Called: Automotive Div Of,
650 Northland Blvd # 600 (45240-3242)
PHONE...................513 674-7048
Mark Van Horck Vp, *Principal*
EMP: 50
SALES (est): 1.7MM
SALES (corp-wide): 6.4B **Privately Held**
SIC: 7549 Inspection & diagnostic service,
automotive
HQ: Sgs North America Inc.
201 Route 17
Rutherford NJ 07070
201 508-3000

(G-4463)
SHARED SERVICES LLC
5905 E Galbraith Rd # 8000 (45236-2375)
PHONE...................513 821-4278
Matthew Gockerman, *CFO*
EMP: 80 EST: 2014
SQ FT: 20,000
SALES: 3MM **Privately Held**
SIC: 8111 Legal services

(G-4464)
SHARONVILLE CAR WASH
11727 Lebanon Rd (45241-2038)
PHONE...................513 769-4219
O Doyle Barnett, *Owner*
Judith Barnett, *Co-Owner*
Karen Applegate, *Admin Asst*
EMP: 37
SALES (est): 861.2K **Privately Held**
SIC: 7542 7532 Washing & polishing, au-
tomotive; lettering & painting services

(G-4465)
SHARONVILLE MTHDIST
WKDAYS NRS
3751 Creek Rd (45241-2707)
PHONE...................513 563-8278
Barbara Pendelton, *Director*
EMP: 32
SALES (est): 372.7K **Privately Held**
WEB: www.pendleton.net
SIC: 8351 8661 Child day care services;
Methodist Church

(G-4466)
SHEAKLEY CENTE
401 E Mcmillan St (45206-1922)
PHONE...................513 487-7106
Robert Mecum, *CEO*
Judith Oakman, *CFO*
EMP: 30 EST: 2015
SALES (est): 137.5K **Privately Held**
SIC: 8322 Youth center

(G-4467)
SHEAKLEY UNICOMP INC
1 Sheakley Way Ste 100 (45246-3774)
PHONE...................513 771-2277
Larry Sheakley, *CEO*
Kimberly Broughton, *Financial Analy*
EMP: 175
SQ FT: 23,000
SALES (est): 7.3MM **Privately Held**
SIC: 8742 Human resource consulting
services

(G-4468)
SHEAKLEY-UNISERVICE INC
1 Sheakley Way Ste 100 (45246-3774)
PHONE...................513 771-2277
Larry A Sheakley, *CEO*
EMP: 120
SALES (est): 11.6MM **Privately Held**
SIC: 8742 8721 Human resource consult-
ing services; payroll accounting service

(G-4469)
SHELTER HOUSE VOLUNTEER
GROUP (PA)
Also Called: ALCOHOLIC DROP-IN CENTER
411 Gest St (45203-1730)
PHONE...................513 721-0643
Arlene Nolan, *CEO*
Don Gardner, *President*
John Wagers, *COO*
Nancy Campbell, *CFO*
Melissa Merritt, *Treasurer*
EMP: 39
SQ FT: 2,000
SALES: 6.7MM **Privately Held**
WEB: www.dropinn.org
SIC: 8322 Aid to families with dependent
children (AFDC); emergency shelters

(G-4470)
SHERMAN FINANCIAL GROUP
LLC
8600 Governors Hill Dr # 201
(45249-2515)
PHONE...................513 707-3000
Mark Rufail, *Controller*
Brian Gardner, *Branch Mgr*
Robert Muncy, *CIO*
EMP: 30
SALES (est): 6.5MM
SALES (corp-wide): 152.4MM **Privately
Held**
WEB: www.sfg.com
SIC: 6153 Buying of installment notes
PA: Sherman Financial Group Llc
200 Meeting St Ste 206
Charleston SC 29401
212 922-1616

(G-4471)
SHOPTECH INDUSTRIAL SFTWR
400 E Bus Way Ste 300 (45241)
PHONE...................513 985-9900
Paul Ventura, *VP Mktg*
EMP: 55
SALES (corp-wide): 30MM **Privately
Held**
WEB: www.shoptech.com
SIC: 7371 Computer software develop-
ment

PA: Shoptech Industrial Software Corp.
180 Glastonbury Blvd # 303
Glastonbury CT 06033
860 633-0740

(G-4472)
SHP LEADING DESIGN (PA)
312 Plum St Ste 700 (45202-2618)
PHONE...................513 381-2112
Gerald S Hammond, *President*
Lauren Dellabella, *Vice Pres*
Cindy Dingeldein, *Vice Pres*
Michael Dingeldein, *Vice Pres*
Tom Fernandez, *Vice Pres*
EMP: 80
SQ FT: 6,160
SALES (est): 11.5MM **Privately Held**
WEB: www.shp.com
SIC: 8742 8712 Planning consultant; ar-
chitectural services

(G-4473)
SHRINERS HSPITALS FOR
CHILDREN
3229 Burnet Ave (45229-3018)
PHONE...................513 872-6000
Paula Durkee, *Research*
Stephanie Spagnola, *Pub Rel Dir*
John Kitzmiller, *Plastic Surgeon*
Rick Johngrass, *Director*
Charles Torline, *Security Dir*
EMP: 320 **Privately Held**
SIC: 8062 General medical & surgical hos-
pitals
HQ: Shriners Hospitals For Children
12504 Usf Pine Dr
Tampa FL 33612
813 972-2250

(G-4474)
SIBCY CLINE INC
Also Called: Kenwood Office
8040 Montgomery Rd (45236-2903)
PHONE...................513 793-2121
Stephanie Busam, *Manager*
EMP: 100
SALES (corp-wide): 2.1B **Privately Held**
WEB: www.sibcycline.com
SIC: 6531 Real estate agent, residential;
real estate brokers & agents
PA: Sibcy Cline, Inc.
8044 Montgomery Rd # 300
Cincinnati OH 45236
513 984-4100

(G-4475)
SIBCY CLINE INC (PA)
Also Called: Sibcy Cline Realtors
8044 Montgomery Rd # 300 (45236-2922)
PHONE...................513 984-4100
Robert N Sibcy, *President*
William D Borek, *Corp Secy*
James A Stofko, *Exec VP*
Jim Haven, *Vice Pres*
David Moyer, *Vice Pres*
EMP: 82 EST: 1952
SQ FT: 30,000
SALES: 2.1B **Privately Held**
WEB: www.sibcycline.com
SIC: 6531 Real estate agent, residential;
real estate brokers & agents

(G-4476)
SIBCY CLINE INC
9979 Montgomery Rd (45242-5311)
PHONE...................513 793-2700
Tim Mahoney, *Manager*
EMP: 90
SALES (corp-wide): 2.1B **Privately Held**
WEB: www.sibcycline.com
SIC: 6531 Real estate brokers & agents
PA: Sibcy Cline, Inc.
8044 Montgomery Rd # 300
Cincinnati OH 45236
513 984-4100

(G-4477)
SIBCY CLINE INC
Also Called: Sibcy Cline Realtors
9250 Winton Rd (45231-3936)
PHONE...................513 931-7700
Beth Sehling, *Manager*
EMP: 50
SALES (corp-wide): 2.1B **Privately Held**
WEB: www.sibcycline.com
SIC: 6531 Real estate brokers & agents

▲ = Import ▼=Export
◆ =Import/Export

PA: Sibcy Cline, Inc.
8044 Montgomery Rd # 300
Cincinnati OH 45236
513 984-4100

(G-4478)
SIBCY CLINE MORTGAGE SERVICES
8044 Montgomery Rd # 301 (45236-2922)
PHONE....................513 984-6776
Patricia Kuether, *President*
William Borek, *Corp Secy*
EMP: 30
SQ FT: 4,182
SALES (est): 1.9MM **Privately Held**
WEB: www.foxchapelneighborhoods.com
SIC: 6163 Mortgage brokers arranging for loans, using money of others

(G-4479)
SICKLE CELL AWAREMESS GRP
3458 Reading Rd (45229-3128)
PHONE....................513 281-4450
Donna Jones Stanley, *CEO*
EMP: 43
SQ FT: 2,736
SALES: 60K **Privately Held**
WEB: www.gcul.org
SIC: 8322 Individual & family services

(G-4480)
SIEMENS INDUSTRY INC
1310 Kemper Meadow Dr # 500
(45240-4127)
PHONE....................513 742-5590
A Riccella, *General Mgr*
EMP: 70
SALES (corp-wide): 95B **Privately Held**
WEB: www.sibt.com
SIC: 5063 Electrical apparatus & equipment
HQ: Siemens Industry, Inc.
1000 Deerfield Pkwy
Buffalo Grove IL 60089
800 743-6367

(G-4481)
SIGMATEK SYSTEMS LLC (PA)
Also Called: Sigma T E K
1445 Kemper Meadow Dr (45240-1637)
PHONE....................513 674-0005
Ben Terreblanche, *CEO*
Chris Eldridge, *Controller*
Chris Cooper,
Joseph Keblesh,
John Leuzinger,
EMP: 65
SQ FT: 23,000
SALES (est): 17MM **Privately Held**
WEB: www.sigmanest.com
SIC: 7372 Prepackaged software

(G-4482)
SIGNAL OFFICE SUPPLY INC
Also Called: Sos2000
415 W Benson St (45215-3193)
PHONE....................513 821-2280
C G Thiergartner, *President*
Chris Thiergartner, *President*
Matt Thiergartner, *Vice Pres*
EMP: 40
SQ FT: 17,000
SALES (est): 18.7MM **Privately Held**
WEB: www.everybodysb2b.com
SIC: 5112 5021 Stationery & office supplies; office & public building furniture

(G-4483)
SIMS-LOHMAN INC (PA)
Also Called: Sims-Lohman Fine Kitchens Gran
6325 Este Ave (45232-1458)
PHONE....................513 651-3510
Steve Steinman, *CEO*
John Beiersdorfer, *President*
Dan Sullivan, *Opers Mgr*
James Mitchell, *Opers Staff*
▲ EMP: 50 EST: 1974
SQ FT: 153,000
SALES (est): 127.4MM **Privately Held**
WEB: www.moelleringindustries.com
SIC: 5031 2435 Kitchen cabinets; hardwood veneer & plywood

(G-4484)
SINCLAIR BROADCAST GROUP INC
Also Called: W S T R
1906 Highland Ave (45219-3104)
PHONE....................513 641-4400
Dale Thomas, *Accounts Exec*
Jon Lawhead, *Manager*
Mike Horsley, *Manager*
EMP: 40
SQ FT: 8,658
SALES (corp-wide): 3B **Publicly Held**
SIC: 4833 Television broadcasting stations
PA: Sinclair Broadcast Group, Inc.
10706 Beaver Dam Rd
Hunt Valley MD 21030
410 568-1500

(G-4485)
SINCLAIR BROADCAST GROUP INC
Also Called: Star 64
1906 Highland Ave (45219-3104)
PHONE....................513 641-4400
Mark Dillon, *Manager*
EMP: 55
SALES (corp-wide): 3B **Publicly Held**
SIC: 4833 Television broadcasting stations
PA: Sinclair Broadcast Group, Inc.
10706 Beaver Dam Rd
Hunt Valley MD 21030
410 568-1500

(G-4486)
SISTERS OF LITTLE
Also Called: Archbishop Leibold Home
476 Riddle Rd (45220-2411)
PHONE....................513 281-8001
Motherjoseph Grenon, *Manager*
EMP: 125
SQ FT: 13,932
SALES (corp-wide): 8.6MM **Privately Held**
SIC: 8361 8052 Home for the aged; intermediate care facilities
PA: Little Sisters Of The Poor, Baltimore, Inc.
601 Maiden Choice Ln
Baltimore MD 21228
410 744-9367

(G-4487)
SIX CONTINENTS HOTELS INC
Also Called: Holiday Inn
3855 Hauck Rd (45241-1609)
PHONE....................513 563-8330
Ted Von Den Benken, *Branch Mgr*
EMP: 110 **Privately Held**
WEB: www.sixcontinenthotels.com
SIC: 7011 5812 Hotels; eating places
HQ: Six Continents Hotels, Inc.
3 Ravinia Dr Ste 100
Atlanta GA 30346
770 604-2000

(G-4488)
SJN DATA CENTER LLC (PA)
Also Called: Encore Technologies
4620 Wesley Ave (45212-2234)
PHONE....................513 386-7871
John Burns, *President*
Clay Stevens, *Vice Pres*
EMP: 50
SQ FT: 90,000
SALES: 2.5MM **Privately Held**
WEB: www.elantech.net
SIC: 8748 7378 7379 Systems engineering consultant, ex. computer or professional; computer maintenance & repair;

(G-4489)
SJS PACKAGING GROUP INC
Also Called: EZ Pack
6545 Wiehe Rd (45237-4217)
PHONE....................513 841-1351
Barry Schwartz, *President*
Terry Junker, *Vice Pres*
EMP: 26
SALES: 4MM **Privately Held**
SIC: 5199 Packaging materials

(G-4490)
SK RIGGING CO INC
11515 Rockfield Ct (45241-1918)
P.O. Box 62092 (45262-0092)
PHONE....................513 771-7766
Alan Schneider, *President*
Mike Schneider, *Vice Pres*
▲ EMP: 25
SQ FT: 50,000
SALES (est): 3.8MM **Privately Held**
WEB: www.skrigging.com
SIC: 1796 Machine moving & rigging

(G-4491)
SKALLYS OLD WORLD BAKERY INC
Also Called: Skally's Restaurant
1933 W Galbraith Rd (45239-4767)
PHONE....................513 931-1411
Odette Skally, *President*
Drew Skally, *Vice Pres*
EMP: 45
SQ FT: 40,000
SALES (est): 13.9MM **Privately Held**
SIC: 5149 5812 Bakery products; eating places

(G-4492)
SKANSKA USA BUILDING INC
201 E 5th St Ste 2020 (45202-4164)
PHONE....................513 421-0082
Craig Eckert, *Branch Mgr*
EMP: 29
SALES (corp-wide): 18.7B **Privately Held**
SIC: 1541 1542 8741 Industrial buildings & warehouses; nonresidential construction; management services
HQ: Skanska Usa Building Inc.
389 Interpace Pkwy Ste 5
Parsippany NJ 07054
973 753-3500

(G-4493)
SKY ZONE INDOOR TRAMPOLINE PK
Also Called: Sky Zone Indoor Trampoline Pk
11745 Commons Dr (45246-2551)
PHONE....................614 302-6093
EMP: 75
SALES (est): 1MM **Privately Held**
SIC: 7999 Trampoline operation

(G-4494)
SL WELLSPRING LLC
Also Called: Wellspring Health Care
8000 Evergreen Ridge Dr (45215-5750)
PHONE....................513 948-2339
Lory J Ward,
EMP: 80
SQ FT: 70,000
SALES (est): 11.5MM
SALES (corp-wide): 320.8MM **Privately Held**
SIC: 5051 Metals service centers & offices
PA: Senior Lifestyle Corporation
303 E Wacker Dr Ste 2400
Chicago IL 60601
312 673-4333

(G-4495)
SMITH ROLFES & SKAZDAHL LPA (PA)
Also Called: Smith, Matthew J Co Lpa
600 Vine St Ste 2600 (45202-1170)
PHONE....................513 579-0080
Matthew J Smith, *President*
Diana Reynard, *President*
Rebecca Johnson, *Counsel*
Tyler Hull,
Tracy Cavender, *Legal Staff*
EMP: 29
SQ FT: 2,000
SALES (est): 8.5MM **Privately Held**
SIC: 8111 General practice attorney, lawyer

(G-4496)
SMYTH AUTOMOTIVE INC (PA)
4275 Mt Carmel Tobasco Rd (45244-2319)
PHONE....................513 528-2800
Joseph M Smyth, *President*
Lynette Smithson, *Corp Secy*
Jim Smyth, *Vice Pres*
EMP: 87 EST: 1963
SQ FT: 23,000

SALES (est): 122.3MM **Privately Held**
WEB: www.smythautomotive.com
SIC: 5013 5531 Automotive supplies & parts; automotive parts

(G-4497)
SMYTH AUTOMOTIVE INC
4271 Mt Carmel Tobasco Rd (45244-2319)
PHONE....................513 528-0061
Rita Summers, *Manager*
EMP: 77
SALES (corp-wide): 122.3MM **Privately Held**
WEB: www.smythautomotive.com
SIC: 5013 5531 Automotive supplies & parts; automotive parts
PA: Smyth Automotive, Inc.
4275 Mt Carmel Tobasco Rd
Cincinnati OH 45244
513 528-2800

(G-4498)
SNAPBLOX HOSTED SOLUTIONS LLC
131 Eight Mile Rd (45255-4612)
PHONE....................866 524-7707
Michael Earls, *Mng Member*
EMP: 30 EST: 2010
SALES: 300K **Privately Held**
SIC: 7379 7389 Computer related consulting services;

(G-4499)
SNOWS LAKESIDE TAVERN
4344 Dry Ridge Rd (45252-1918)
PHONE....................513 954-5626
Mark Fehring, *Owner*
EMP: 35
SQ FT: 1,000
SALES (est): 200.8K **Privately Held**
SIC: 5813 7999 Tavern (drinking places); fishing lakes & piers, operation

(G-4500)
SOCIETY OF ST VINCENT DE PAUL
1125 Bank St (45214-2130)
PHONE....................513 421-2273
Tim Hiele, *Director*
EMP: 50
SALES (corp-wide): 13.9MM **Privately Held**
SIC: 8322 Individual & family services
PA: Society Of St. Vincent De Paul Archdiocesan Council Of St. Louis
1310 Papin St Ste 104
Saint Louis MO 63103
314 881-6000

(G-4501)
SOCIETY OF THE TRANSFIGURATION (PA)
Also Called: Sisters of The Transfiguration
555 Albion Ave (45246-4649)
PHONE....................513 771-7462
Sister Ann, *Principal*
Barbara Collier, *Teacher*
Emily Huff, *Teacher*
Stephen Imwalle, *Teacher*
Jonathan Reardon, *Teacher*
EMP: 48
SALES (est): 4.6MM **Privately Held**
SIC: 8661 8211 8059 7999 Religious organizations; boarding school; nursing home, except skilled & intermediate care facility; recreation center

(G-4502)
SOFCO ERECTORS INC (PA)
10360 Wayne Ave (45215-1129)
PHONE....................513 771-1600
John Hesford, *President*
John C Hesford, *President*
Daniel Powell, *Vice Pres*
Jim Frondorf, *Manager*
Caroline Perkins, *Info Tech Mgr*
EMP: 218
SQ FT: 5,000
SALES (est): 22.4MM **Privately Held**
SIC: 1791 Iron work, structural

(G-4503)
SOFTWARE INFO SYSTEMS LLC
8805 Governors Hill Dr (45249-3314)
PHONE....................513 791-7777

GEOGRAPHIC

Steve Sigg, *Branch Mgr*
EMP: 26 **Privately Held**
SIC: 5045 Computers, peripherals & software
HQ: Software Information Systems, Llc
165 Barr St
Lexington KY 40507
859 977-4747

(G-4504)
SOFTWARE MANAGEMENT GROUP
1128 Main St Fl 6 (45202-7276)
PHONE..................................513 618-2165
Dave Nolnan, *President*
EMP: 25
SALES (est): 878.2K **Privately Held**
SIC: 7372 Prepackaged software

(G-4505)
SOUTHWEST FINANCIAL SVCS LTD
537 E Pete Rose Way Ste 3 (45202-3567)
PHONE..................................513 621-6699
Gregory Schroeder, *President*
Barbara Schroeder, *Vice Pres*
Kelley Harvey, *Controller*
Diane Sweeney, *Human Res Dir*
Regina Baker, *Data Proc Staff*
EMP: 160
SQ FT: 35,000
SALES (est): 46.1MM **Privately Held**
WEB: www.sfsltd.com
SIC: 6211 Mortgages, buying & selling

(G-4506)
SOUTHWEST OH TRANS AUTH (PA)
Also Called: S O R T A
602 Main St Ste 1100 (45202-2549)
PHONE..................................513 621-4455
Terry Garcia Cruz, *CEO*
Lee Bennett, *Vice Pres*
Mike Davenport, *Foreman/Supr*
Philip Lind, *Opers Staff*
Mary Huller, *Purch Agent*
EMP: 865 **EST:** 1880
SQ FT: 18,000
SALES (est): 66.4MM **Privately Held**
WEB: www.go-metro.com
SIC: 4111 Bus line operations

(G-4507)
SOUTHWEST OH TRANS AUTH
Also Called: Mreto
1401 Bank St (45214-1737)
PHONE..................................513 632-7511
Bill Speraul, *Manager*
EMP: 700
SALES (est): 17.2MM
SALES (corp-wide): 66.4MM **Privately Held**
SIC: 4111 Bus line operations
PA: Southwest Ohio Regional Transit Authority
602 Main St Ste 1100
Cincinnati OH 45202
513 621-4455

(G-4508)
SOUTHWSTERN PCF SPCLTY FIN INC (HQ)
7755 Montgomery Rd # 400 (45236-4291)
P.O. Box 36382 (45236-0382)
PHONE..................................513 336-7735
A David Davis, *President*
EMP: 25
SALES (est): 25.1MM
SALES (corp-wide): 573.1MM **Privately Held**
SIC: 6099 Check cashing agencies
PA: Cng Financial Corporation
7755 Montgomery Rd # 400
Cincinnati OH 45236
513 336-7735

(G-4509)
SPARTAN ASSET RCVERY GROUP INC
8483 Fields Ertel Rd (45249-8266)
PHONE..................................786 930-0188
Steve Gino Stevenson II, *Principal*
EMP: 56 **EST:** 2010
SQ FT: 15,000

SALES (est): 145.6K **Privately Held**
SIC: 7322 Adjustment & collection services

(G-4510)
SPARTANNASH COMPANY
1 Sheakley Way Ste 160 (45246-3779)
PHONE..................................513 793-6300
John Dietrich, *Branch Mgr*
Greg Neff, *Manager*
Shawn Farrell, *Retailers*
EMP: 94
SALES (corp-wide): 8B **Publicly Held**
SIC: 5141 5148 5142 5147 Food brokers; fruits, fresh; vegetables, fresh; packaged frozen goods; meats, fresh; meats, cured or smoked; supermarkets, chain
PA: Spartannash Company
850 76th St Sw
Byron Center MI 49315
616 878-2000

(G-4511)
SPECIALIZED PHARMACY SVCS LLC (DH)
Also Called: Specialized Pharmacy Svcs - N
201 E 4th St Ste 900 (45202-4160)
PHONE..................................513 719-2600
John Workman, *CEO*
Gary W Kadlec, *Vice Pres*
Cecilia Temple, *Project Mgr*
Cheryl D Hodges, *Admin Sec*
EMP: 29 **EST:** 1977
SQ FT: 28,000
SALES (est): 29.7MM
SALES (corp-wide): 194.5B **Publicly Held**
WEB: www.spsomnicare.com
SIC: 5122 Pharmaceuticals; druggists' sundries

(G-4512)
SPECIALTY LOGISTICS INC (PA)
Also Called: Vogt Warehouse
1440 W 8th St (45203-1009)
PHONE..................................513 421-2041
Stephen P Hayward, *President*
Thomas Hayward, *Warehouse Mgr*
Bryon Heflin, *Supervisor*
▲ **EMP:** 33
SALES (est): 6.9MM **Privately Held**
SIC: 4225 General warehousing & storage

(G-4513)
SPECTRUM MGT HOLDG CO LLC
3290 Westbourne Dr (45248-5107)
PHONE..................................513 469-1112
EMP: 87
SALES (corp-wide): 43.6B **Publicly Held**
SIC: 4841 Cable television services
HQ: Spectrum Management Holding Company, Llc
400 Atlantic St
Stamford CT 06901
203 905-7801

(G-4514)
SPECTRUM NETWORKS INC
9145 Governors Way (45249-2037)
PHONE..................................513 697-2000
Troy McCracken, *CEO*
EMP: 29
SALES (est): 4.3MM **Privately Held**
SIC: 4813 5999 7389 Telephone communication, except radio; telephone equipment & systems; telephone services

(G-4515)
SPORTS THERAPY INC
11729 Springfield Pike (45246-2311)
P.O. Box 658, Mason (45040-0658)
PHONE..................................513 671-5841
Kathleen Novicki, *President*
Eric Novicki, *Director*
EMP: 40
SALES (est): 1.9MM **Privately Held**
SIC: 8049 Physical therapist

(G-4516)
SPORTS THERAPY INC
4600 Smith Rd Ste B (45212-2784)
PHONE..................................513 531-1698
Eric Novici, *President*
EMP: 45

SALES (est): 485.3K **Privately Held**
WEB: www.sportstherapyinc.com
SIC: 8049 Physical therapist

(G-4517)
SPRING GROVE CMTRY & ARBORETUM (PA)
4521 Spring Grove Ave (45232-1954)
PHONE..................................513 681-7526
Gary M Freytag, *President*
Michael Burke, *Vice Pres*
Jeannette Humphries, *Purch Agent*
David Kelly, *CFO*
David P Kelley, *Financial Exec*
EMP: 75
SALES (est): 10.5MM **Privately Held**
WEB: www.springgrove.com
SIC: 6553 Cemetery association; mausoleum operation

(G-4518)
SPRING GROVE FUNERAL HOMES INC
4389 Spring Grove Ave (45223-1862)
PHONE..................................513 681-7526
Gary Freytag, *CEO*
Jerry Wantz, *VP Opers*
Samantha Brown, *Director*
EMP: 120 **EST:** 1999
SQ FT: 40,000
SALES (est): 4.8MM **Privately Held**
SIC: 7261 Funeral home

(G-4519)
SPRING GROVE RSRCE RCOVERY INC
4879 Spring Grove Ave (45232-1938)
PHONE..................................513 681-6242
Alan McKin, *CEO*
John P Lawton, *Senior VP*
Eugene Cookson, *Vice Pres*
Stephen E Dovell, *Vice Pres*
William J Geary, *Vice Pres*
EMP: 70
SQ FT: 50,000
SALES (est): 18.5MM
SALES (corp-wide): 3.3B **Publicly Held**
SIC: 4953 4212 Sanitary landfill operation; local trucking, without storage
PA: Clean Harbors, Inc.
42 Longwater Dr
Norwell MA 02061
781 792-5000

(G-4520)
SPRING HILL SUITES
Also Called: Springhill Suites
610 Eden Park Dr (45202-6031)
PHONE..................................513 381-8300
Volker Wellmann, *General Mgr*
EMP: 40 **EST:** 2009
SALES (est): 944.3K
SALES (corp-wide): 20.7B **Publicly Held**
SIC: 7011 Hotels & motels
PA: Marriott International, Inc.
10400 Fernwood Rd
Bethesda MD 20817
301 380-3000

(G-4521)
SPRINGDALE FAMILY MEDICINE PC
Also Called: Webb, Barry W
212 W Sharon Rd (45246-4137)
PHONE..................................513 771-7213
Thomas Todd, *President*
Dr Douglas L Hancher, *Corp Secy*
Dr Barry Webb, *Vice Pres*
Michael Todd, *Med Doctor*
EMP: 30
SALES (est): 1.7MM **Privately Held**
SIC: 8011 General & family practice, physician/surgeon

(G-4522)
SPRINGDALE ICE CREAM BEVERAGE
11801 Chesterdale Rd (45246-3407)
PHONE..................................513 699-4984
Fax: 513 671-2864
EMP: 35
SALES (est): 5.8MM **Privately Held**
SIC: 2024 0241 Mfg Ice Cream/Frozen Desert Dairy Farm

(G-4523)
SPRINGDOT INC
2611 Colerain Ave (45214-1711)
PHONE..................................513 542-4000
Jeff Deutsch, *Ch of Bd*
Josh Deutsch, *President*
John Brenner, *Vice Pres*
Craig Miller, *Vice Pres*
Bill Fultz, *Traffic Mgr*
EMP: 65 **EST:** 1904
SQ FT: 70,000
SALES (est): 13.5MM **Privately Held**
WEB: www.springdot.com
SIC: 2752 4899 2759 2675 Commercial printing, offset; color lithography; data communication services; commercial printing; die-cut paper & board; packaging paper & plastics film, coated & laminated

(G-4524)
SQUIRE PATTON BOGGS (US) LLP
201 E 4th St Ste 324 (45202-4248)
PHONE..................................513 361-1200
Scott Kane, *Managing Prtnr*
Colter Paulson, *Sr Associate*
Elliot M Smith, *Sr Associate*
Christina A Heithaus, *Associate*
Evan A Toebbe, *Associate*
EMP: 30
SALES (corp-wide): 294.4MM **Privately Held**
WEB: www.squiresandersdempsey.com
SIC: 8111 Specialized law offices, attorneys
PA: Squire Patton Boggs (Us) Llp
4900 Key Tower 127 Pub Sq
Cleveland OH 44114
216 479-8500

(G-4525)
SREE HOTELS LLC
Also Called: Hampton Inn
617 Vine St Ste A (45202-2418)
PHONE..................................513 354-2430
Ted Vondenbenken, *General Mgr*
EMP: 50
SALES (corp-wide): 61.8MM **Privately Held**
SIC: 7011 Hotels
PA: Sree Hotels, L.L.C.
5113 Piper Station Dr # 300
Charlotte NC 28277
704 364-6008

(G-4526)
ST ALOYSIUS SERVICES INC
4721 Reading Rd (45237-6107)
PHONE..................................513 482-1745
Joan Pumbelison, *COO*
Arlene Nolan, *CFO*
Carrie Hampton, *Director*
EMP: 35
SALES: 41.5K **Privately Held**
SIC: 8093 Mental health clinic, outpatient

(G-4527)
ST JOSEPH INFANT MATERNITY HM
Also Called: ST JOSEPH'S HOME
10722 Wyscarver Rd (45241-3061)
PHONE..................................513 563-2520
Lynn Heper, *Vice Pres*
Andrew Frakes, *Human Res Mgr*
Drew Curtis, *Manager*
Sister Marianne Van Vurst, *Director*
Sister Lynn Heper, *Asst Admin*
EMP: 136
SALES: 10.7MM **Privately Held**
WEB: www.stjosephshome.org
SIC: 8052 8322 Home for the mentally retarded, with health care; individual & family services

(G-4528)
STAFFMARK HOLDINGS INC (HQ)
201 E 4th St Ste 800 (45202-4248)
PHONE..................................513 651-1111
Geno A Cutolo, *CEO*
Hitoshi Motohara, *Chairman*
Yuichiro Miura, *COO*
Kathryn S Bernard, *Exec VP*
William E Aglinsky, *CFO*
EMP: 75

SALES (est): 178.5MM
SALES (corp-wide): 20.4B **Privately Held**
WEB: www.cbscompanies.com
SIC: **7361** **7363** Placement agencies; executive placement; labor resource services; temporary help service
PA: Recruit Holdings Co.,Ltd.
1-9-2, Marunouchi
Chiyoda-Ku TKY 100-0
368 351-111

(G-4529)
STAFFMARK INVESTMENT LLC (DH)
201 E 4th St Ste 800 (45202-4248)
PHONE.................................513 651-3600
W David Bartholomew, *CEO*
Clay Bullock, *President*
Hitoshi Motohara, *Principal*
Kenny Berkemeyer, *Vice Pres*
Sally Berrier, *Vice Pres*
EMP: 120
SALES (est): 178.4MM
SALES (corp-wide): 20.4B **Privately Held**
WEB: www.staffmark.com
SIC: **7361** Labor contractors (employment agency)
HQ: Staffmark Holdings, Inc.
201 E 4th St Ste 800
Cincinnati OH 45202
513 651-1111

(G-4530)
STAGE WORKS
7800 Perry St (45231-3426)
P.O. Box 31227 (45231-0227)
PHONE.................................513 522-3118
Tony Peters, *Partner*
Kevin Prows, *Partner*
EMP: 25 EST: 1994
SALES (est): 1.2MM **Privately Held**
SIC: **7363** Labor resource services

(G-4531)
STAGNARO SABA PATTERSON CO LPA
7373 Beechmont Ave (45230-4100)
PHONE.................................513 533-2700
William Patterson, *Branch Mgr*
EMP: 30 **Privately Held**
SIC: **8111** General practice law office
PA: Stagnaro, Saba & Patterson Co., L.P.A
2623 Erie Ave
Cincinnati OH 45208

(G-4532)
STAND ENERGY CORPORATION
1077 Celestial St Ste 110 (45202-1629)
PHONE.................................513 621-1113
Judith Phillips, *President*
Matth Toebben, *Chairman*
Lawrence Freeman, *Exec VP*
Jeff Clines, *Vice Pres*
Nan Hamilton, *Vice Pres*
EMP: 34
SQ FT: 4,580
SALES (est): 110.3MM **Privately Held**
SIC: **4924** Natural gas distribution

(G-4533)
STANDARD TEXTILE CO INC (PA)
Also Called: Pridecraft Enterprises
1 Knollcrest Dr (45237-1608)
P.O. Box 371805 (45222-1805)
PHONE.................................513 761-9256
Gary Heiman, *President*
Chris Bopp, *Senior VP*
Norman Frankel, *Senior VP*
Kim Heiman, *Senior VP*
Steve Tracey, *Senior VP*
◆ EMP: 300
SQ FT: 150,000
SALES (est): 906.9MM **Privately Held**
WEB: www.standardtextile.com
SIC: **2389** **2326** **2337** **2211** Hospital gowns; medical & hospital uniforms, men's; uniforms, except athletic: women's, misses' & juniors'; bandages, gauzes & surgical fabrics, cotton; surgical fabrics, cotton; draperies, plastic & textile: from purchased materials; uniforms, men's & boys'

(G-4534)
STANDEX ELECTRONICS INC (HQ)
4538 Camberwell Rd (45209-1186)
PHONE.................................513 871-3777
John Meeks, *CEO*
Robert Lintz, *Vice Pres*
Michelle Martin, *Production*
Rob Whitman, *Engineer*
Ken Hay, *VP Finance*
▲ EMP: 64
SQ FT: 22,022
SALES (est): 48.8MM
SALES (corp-wide): 868.3MM **Publicly Held**
SIC: **5065** Electronic parts & equipment
PA: Standex International Corporation
11 Keewaydin Dr Ste 300
Salem NH 03079
603 893-9701

(G-4535)
STANDRDAERO COMPONENT SVCS INC (DH)
11550 Mosteller Rd (45241-1832)
PHONE.................................513 618-9588
Russell Ford, *CEO*
Kim Olson, *Senior VP*
Brent Fawkes, *Vice Pres*
Clinton Kent, *Vice Pres*
Greg Massa, *Vice Pres*
EMP: 700
SQ FT: 236,000
SALES (est): 51.5MM **Privately Held**
WEB: www.tssaviation.com
SIC: **7699** Aviation propeller & blade repair
HQ: Standard Aero, Inc.
3523 General Hudnell Dr
San Antonio TX 78226
210 334-6000

(G-4536)
STANLEY STEEMER INTL INC
Also Called: Stanley Steemer Carpet Clr 07
637 Redna Ter (45215-1108)
PHONE.................................513 771-0213
Aaron Huffman, *Opers-Prdtn-Mfg*
EMP: 30
SALES (corp-wide): 240MM **Privately Held**
WEB: www.stanley-steemer.com
SIC: **7217** Carpet & furniture cleaning on location
PA: Stanley Steemer International, Inc.
5800 Innovation Dr
Dublin OH 43016
614 764-2007

(G-4537)
STANTEC CONSULTING SVCS INC
11687 Lebanon Rd (45241-2012)
PHONE.................................513 842-8200
David Hayson, *Project Engr*
Daniel Hoffman, *Project Engr*
Lori Van Dermark, *Marketing Staff*
John Montgomery, *Branch Mgr*
John Menninger, *Sr Associate*
EMP: 73
SALES (corp-wide): 4B **Privately Held**
WEB: www.fmsm.com
SIC: **8712** **8711** Architectural services; engineering services
HQ: Stantec Consulting Services Inc.
475 5th Ave Fl 12
New York NY 10017
212 352-5160

(G-4538)
STAR ONE HOLDINGS INC
8118 Beechmont Ave (45255-5112)
PHONE.................................513 474-9100
Karen Weber, *Vice Pres*
Larry Trame, *Sales Associate*
Karen Meyer, *Manager*
Deborah Henderson, *Agent*
EMP: 40
SALES (corp-wide): 8.8MM **Privately Held**
WEB: www.nkybuilders.com
SIC: **6531** Real estate agent, residential
PA: Star One Holdings, Inc.
3895 Woodridge Blvd
Fairfield OH 45014
513 870-9100

(G-4539)
STAR ONE HOLDINGS INC
9722 Montgomery Rd (45242-7208)
PHONE.................................513 300-6663
Karen Weber, *Manager*
EMP: 30
SQ FT: 9,402
SALES (corp-wide): 8.8MM **Privately Held**
WEB: www.nkybuilders.com
SIC: **6531** Real estate brokers & agents
PA: Star One Holdings, Inc.
3895 Woodridge Blvd
Fairfield OH 45014
513 870-9100

(G-4540)
STARFORCE NATIONAL CORPORATION
455 Delta Ave Ste 410 (45226-1178)
P.O. Box 21600, Georgetown (45121-0600)
PHONE.................................513 979-3600
Frank Mayfield Jr, *Ch of Bd*
Judith Mc Cullough, *Corp Secy*
Lauren Gibson, *Vice Pres*
EMP: 110 EST: 2001
SQ FT: 2,000
SALES (est): 6MM **Privately Held**
SIC: **4142** Bus charter service, except local

(G-4541)
STAUTBERG FAMILY LLC
3871 Deerpath Ln (45248-1343)
PHONE.................................513 941-5070
Timothy Stautberg,
EMP: 40
SALES (est): 1.3MM **Privately Held**
SIC: **6513** Apartment building operators

(G-4542)
STEELSUMMIT HOLDINGS INC
Steelsummit Ohio
11150 Southland Rd (45240-3202)
PHONE.................................513 825-8550
Arnie Killberw, *Principal*
EMP: 38
SALES (corp-wide): 45.3B **Privately Held**
SIC: **5051** Steel
HQ: Steelsummit Holdings, Inc.
1718 Jp Hennessy Dr
La Vergne TN 37086
615 641-3300

(G-4543)
STERLING BUYING GROUP LLC
3802 Ford Cir (45227-3403)
PHONE.................................513 564-9000
Paul L Hunter, *President*
Jill Barnett, *Vice Pres*
George Mahowald, *Vice Pres*
Howard Cooper, *Mng Member*
Kevin Schifrin,
EMP: 36
SALES (est): 2.8MM
SALES (corp-wide): 93.9MM **Privately Held**
SIC: **7389** **7373** Financial services; systems integration services
HQ: Sterling Payment Technologies, Llc
12750 Citrus Park Ln # 300
Tampa FL 33625
813 637-9696

(G-4544)
STERLING MEDICAL ASSOCIATES
411 Oak St (45219-2504)
PHONE.................................513 984-1800
Richard Blatt, *CEO*
Edwin Blatt, *President*
Brandon Blatt, *Treasurer*
Tammy Hinkle, *Manager*
Dr Ethel Blatt, *Admin Sec*
EMP: 70 EST: 1963
SQ FT: 15,000
SALES (est): 220.3K
SALES (corp-wide): 3.7MM **Privately Held**
SIC: **8099** Medical services organization
PA: Sterling Medical Corporation
411 Oak St
Cincinnati OH 45219
513 984-1800

(G-4545)
STERLING MEDICAL CORPORATION
411 Oak St (45219-2504)
PHONE.................................513 984-1800
Kevin Korb, *Branch Mgr*
EMP: 99
SALES (corp-wide): 3.7MM **Privately Held**
SIC: **8741** Hospital management; nursing & personal care facility management
PA: Sterling Medical Corporation
411 Oak St
Cincinnati OH 45219
513 984-1800

(G-4546)
STERLING MEDICAL CORPORATION (PA)
Also Called: Sterling Med Staffing Group
411 Oak St (45219-2504)
PHONE.................................513 984-1800
Richard Blatt, *CEO*
Edwin Blatt, *President*
Brandon Blatt, *Vice Pres*
Deborah Aldridge, *Site Mgr*
Carrie Daulton, *Opers Staff*
EMP: 127
SQ FT: 15,000
SALES: 3.7MM **Privately Held**
SIC: **8741** Administrative management

(G-4547)
STEVEN SCHAEFER ASSOCIATES INC (PA)
537 E Pete Rose Way # 400 (45202-3567)
PHONE.................................513 542-3300
Steven E Schaefer, *Ch of Bd*
James Miller, *President*
Ed Schwieter, *Vice Pres*
Jim Graham, *Safety Mgr*
Julian Antoine, *Info Tech Dir*
EMP: 56
SQ FT: 13,000
SALES (est): 9.6MM **Privately Held**
WEB: www.ssastructural.com
SIC: **8711** Structural engineering

(G-4548)
STRAND ASSOCIATES INC
615 Elsinore Pl Ste 320 (45202-1475)
PHONE.................................513 861-5600
Ted Richards, *CEO*
EMP: 36
SALES (est): 1.7MM
SALES (corp-wide): 55.2MM **Privately Held**
SIC: **8711** Consulting engineer
PA: Strand Associates, Inc.
910 W Wingra Dr
Madison WI 53715
608 251-4843

(G-4549)
STRATEGIC DATA SYSTEMS INC
11260 Chester Rd Ste 425 (45246-4040)
PHONE.................................513 772-7374
David Pledger, *President*
Keith Stafford, *Managing Prtnr*
Toni Chitwood, *Office Mgr*
Toni Urbanic, *Office Mgr*
Keith Callis, *Consultant*
EMP: 25
SQ FT: 1,500
SALES (est): 2.4MM **Privately Held**
WEB: www.sds-consulting.com
SIC: **7371** Custom computer programming services

(G-4550)
STUDENT LOAN STRATEGIES LLC
Also Called: Innovative Studnt Ln Solutions
151 W 4th St Frnt (45202-0026)
PHONE.................................513 645-5400
Stuart Smylie, *CEO*
Ross Weintraub, *Business Mgr*
Meghan Davis, *Manager*
Melissa Bedwell, *Advisor*
Lee Cahill, *Advisor*
EMP: 30
SALES (est): 1.5MM **Privately Held**
SIC: **6141** Personal credit institutions

(G-4551)
SUBURBAN PEDIATRICS INC (PA)
12061 Sheraton Ln (45246-1611)
PHONE...................................513 336-6700
Allan Robinson, *President*
EMP: 25
SALES (est): 2.2MM Privately Held
WEB: www.suburbanpediatrics.org
SIC: 8011 Pediatrician

(G-4552)
SUMMIT HOTEL ○
5345 Medpace Way (45227-1543)
PHONE...................................513 527-9900
Bruce Flyer, *General Mgr*
EMP: 100 EST: 2018
SALES (est): 693.9K Privately Held
SIC: 7011 Hotels

(G-4553)
SUMNER SOLUTIONS INC
3610 Sherbrooke Dr (45241-3286)
PHONE...................................513 531-6382
Mark Lacker, *President*
EMP: 26
SALES (est): 1.1MM Privately Held
WEB: www.sumnersolutions.com
SIC: 8742 Marketing consulting services

(G-4554)
SUNRISE SENIOR LIVING LLC
Also Called: Sunrise At Finneytown
9101 Winton Rd (45231-3829)
PHONE...................................513 729-5233
Valerie Heine, *Exec Dir*
EMP: 40
SALES (corp-wide): 4.7B Publicly Held
WEB: www.sunrise.com
SIC: 8051 Skilled nursing care facilities
HQ: Sunrise Senior Living, Llc
　　7902 Westpark Dr
　　Mc Lean VA 22102

(G-4555)
SUPER SYSTEMS INC (PA)
7205 Edington Dr (45249-1064)
PHONE...................................513 772-0060
Stephen Thompson, *President*
Jim Oakes, *President*
Scott Johnstone, *Vice Pres*
Bill Heckman, *Project Mgr*
Haoxiang Wang, *Engineer*
EMP: 45
SQ FT: 5,000
SALES (est): 6.9MM Privately Held
SIC: 3829 5084 Measuring & controlling
　devices; industrial machinery & equip-
　ment

(G-4556)
SUPERIOR CARE PHARMACY INC
Also Called: Omnicare of St. George
201 E 4th St Ste 900 (45202-4160)
PHONE...................................513 719-2600
Owen E Wood, *President*
Janet Wood, *Vice Pres*
Bradley S Abbott, *Treasurer*
Catherine I Geary, *Admin Sec*
EMP: 150
SALES (est): 17MM
SALES (corp-wide): 194.5B Publicly
　Held
WEB: www.omnicare.com
SIC: 5122 Pharmaceuticals
HQ: Omnicare Holding Company
　　1105 Market St Ste 1300
　　Cincinnati OH 45215
　　513 719-2600

(G-4557)
SUPERIOR LINEN & AP SVCS INC
Also Called: Superior Linen & Apparel Svcs
481 Wayne St (45206-2325)
PHONE...................................513 751-1345
G Jerry Ruwe, *President*
EMP: 60
SALES (est): 4.8MM Privately Held
WEB: www.superior-linen.com
SIC: 7213 Towel supply; coat supply; uni-
　form supply

(G-4558)
SUPREME COURT UNITED STATES
Also Called: US Probation & Parole Svc.
100 E 5th St Rm 110 (45202-3911)
PHONE...................................513 564-7575
John Dierna, *Chief*
EMP: 27 Publicly Held
SIC: 8322 9211 Probation office; courts;
HQ: Supreme Court, United States
　　1 1st St Ne
　　Washington DC 20543
　　202 479-3000

(G-4559)
SWEENEY TEAM INC (PA)
Also Called: Comey Shepherd Realtors Cy
Off
1440 Main St (45202-7642)
PHONE...................................513 241-3400
Michael Sweeney, *President*
Shaun Daley, *Real Est Agnt*
Thomas Porter, *Real Est Agnt*
EMP: 46
SQ FT: 10,000
SALES (est): 2.7MM Privately Held
SIC: 6531 Multiple listing service, real es-
　tate

(G-4560)
SYCAMORE BOARD OF EDUCATION
YMCA Child Care-Montgomery
9609 Montgomery Rd (45242-7205)
PHONE...................................513 489-3937
Charles Day, *Director*
EMP: 60
SALES (corp-wide): 100.8MM Privately
　Held
SIC: 8211 7991 8351 7032 Public ele-
　mentary & secondary schools; physical
　fitness facilities; child day care services;
　youth camps; individual & family services;
　youth organizations
PA: Sycamore Board Of Education
　　5959 Hagewa Dr
　　Blue Ash OH 45242
　　513 686-1700

(G-4561)
SYNEOS HEALTH LLC
441 Vine St Ste 1200 (45202-2902)
PHONE...................................513 381-5550
Naomi Croll, *Project Mgr*
Antony Lovrich, *Project Mgr*
Veronique Pichon, *Sr Project Mgr*
Letitia Wynn, *Manager*
Mike Whitener, *Info Tech Dir*
EMP: 215
SALES (corp-wide): 4.3B Publicly Held
SIC: 8731 Medical research, commercial
HQ: Syneos Health, Llc
　　1030 Sync St
　　Morrisville NC 27560

(G-4562)
SYSCO CINCINNATI LLC
10510 Evendale Dr (45241-2516)
PHONE...................................513 563-6300
Michael Haunert, *President*
Dwuan Hamond, *President*
Daniel Pinsel, *Vice Pres*
Tom Moyer, *Purch Dir*
Mike Seamon, *Marketing Staff*
EMP: 483
SALES (est): 176.1MM
SALES (corp-wide): 58.7B Publicly Held
SIC: 5144 5149 5143 5113 Poultry &
　poultry products; groceries & related
　products; dairy products, except dried or
　canned; industrial & personal service
　paper
PA: Sysco Corporation
　　1390 Enclave Pkwy
　　Houston TX 77077
　　281 584-1390

(G-4563)
SYSTEMS EVOLUTION INC
Also Called: SEI Cincinnati
7870 E Kemper Rd Ste 400 (45249-1675)
PHONE...................................513 459-1992
Paul Ratkovich, *Branch Mgr*
Jeff Bensman, *Consultant*
EMP: 70 Privately Held

SIC: 8748 Business consulting
PA: Systems Evolution, Inc.
　　7870 E Kemper Rd Ste 400
　　Cincinnati OH 45249

(G-4564)
SYSTEMS EVOLUTION INC (PA)
7870 E Kemper Rd Ste 400 (45249-1675)
PHONE...................................513 459-1992
Daniel J Pierce, *President*
Erin Sullivan, *Managing Dir*
Phil Murgatroyd, *Principal*
Maria Korengel, *Corp Secy*
Gina Bohannon, *Controller*
EMP: 64
SQ FT: 6,000
SALES (est): 12.5MM Privately Held
SIC: 7371 Computer software develop-
　ment

(G-4565)
T C RUMPKE WASTE COLLECTION
Also Called: Theodore C Rumpke
5665 Dunlap Rd (45252-1013)
PHONE...................................513 385-7627
Theodore C Rumpke, *President*
Alan Rumpke, *Vice Pres*
EMP: 29
SALES (est): 1.3MM Privately Held
SIC: 4953 Refuse systems

(G-4566)
T H WINSTON COMPANY
4817 Glenshade Ave (45227-2419)
PHONE...................................513 271-2123
William Underwood, *President*
Steve Hartig, *Vice Pres*
Terry Rusche, *Vice Pres*
Lois Maas, *Office Mgr*
▲ EMP: 25
SQ FT: 1,500
SALES: 1.9MM Privately Held
WEB: www.thwinston.com
SIC: 1743 Marble installation, interior; tile
　installation, ceramic; terrazzo work

(G-4567)
TAFARO JOHN
1 W 4th St Ste 800 (45202-3609)
PHONE...................................513 381-0656
N Cougherty, *General Mgr*
Natalie Cougherty, *General Mgr*
EMP: 60
SALES (est): 1.4MM Privately Held
SIC: 8111 General practice attorney,
　lawyer

(G-4568)
TAFT MUSEUM OF ART
316 Pike St (45202-4293)
P.O. Box 631419 (45263-1419)
PHONE...................................513 241-0343
Beth Siler, *Finance Dir*
EMP: 41
SALES: 4MM Privately Held
SIC: 8412 Museum

(G-4569)
TAFT STETTINIUS HOLLISTER LLP (PA)
425 Walnut St Ste 1800 (45202-3920)
PHONE...................................513 381-2838
Nicholas Davis, *Counsel*
Paul Kortepeter, *Counsel*
Fred Livingstone, *Counsel*
Greg Lockhart, *Counsel*
Laura Ringenbach, *Counsel*
EMP: 278
SQ FT: 114,000
SALES (est): 104.2MM Privately Held
SIC: 8111 General practice law office

(G-4570)
TALBERT HOUSE
Also Called: Spring Grove Center
3129 Spring Grove Ave (45225-1821)
PHONE...................................513 541-0127
William Marshall, *Branch Mgr*
EMP: 25
SALES (corp-wide): 59.6MM Privately
　Held
WEB: www.talberthouse.org
SIC: 8322 Rehabilitation services

PA: Talbert House
　　2600 Victory Pkwy
　　Cincinnati OH 45206
　　513 872-5863

(G-4571)
TALBERT HOUSE
5837 Hamilton Ave (45224-2923)
PHONE...................................513 751-7747
Suzanne Lukacs, *Branch Mgr*
Debbie Lutkenhoff, *Education*
EMP: 195
SALES (corp-wide): 59.6MM Privately
　Held
SIC: 8069 Drug addiction rehabilitation
　hospital
PA: Talbert House
　　2600 Victory Pkwy
　　Cincinnati OH 45206
　　513 872-5863

(G-4572)
TALBERT HOUSE
1611 Emerson Ave (45239-4932)
PHONE...................................513 541-1184
Neil F Tilow, *Branch Mgr*
EMP: 32
SALES (corp-wide): 59.6MM Privately
　Held
SIC: 8322 Substance abuse counseling
PA: Talbert House
　　2600 Victory Pkwy
　　Cincinnati OH 45206
　　513 872-5863

(G-4573)
TALBERT HOUSE (PA)
2600 Victory Pkwy (45206-1395)
PHONE...................................513 872-5863
Neil F Tilow, *President*
Josh Arnold, *Vice Pres*
Brad McMonigle, *Vice Pres*
James Wilson, *Vice Pres*
Kevin Corey, *Opers Spvr*
EMP: 70
SQ FT: 40,000
SALES: 59.6MM Privately Held
WEB: www.talberthouse.org
SIC: 8322 Rehabilitation services; sub-
　stance abuse counseling; family counsel-
　ing services

(G-4574)
TALBERT HOUSE
328 Mcgregor Ave Ste 106 (45219-3135)
PHONE...................................513 684-7968
Victor Gray, *Manager*
EMP: 89
SALES (corp-wide): 59.6MM Privately
　Held
WEB: www.talberthouse.org
SIC: 8069 Alcoholism rehabilitation hospi-
　tal
PA: Talbert House
　　2600 Victory Pkwy
　　Cincinnati OH 45206
　　513 872-5863

(G-4575)
TALBERT HOUSE HEALTH (HQ)
4868 Glenway Ave (45238)
PHONE...................................513 541-7577
Cordilia Schaber, *Opers Staff*
Paul Guggenheim, *Director*
John Francis, *Director*
Laura Schiele, *Administration*
EMP: 35 EST: 1972
SQ FT: 13,000
SALES (est): 2.5MM
SALES (corp-wide): 59.6MM Privately
　Held
SIC: 8322 General counseling services
PA: Talbert House
　　2600 Victory Pkwy
　　Cincinnati OH 45206
　　513 872-5863

(G-4576)
TAN PRODUCTS
406 Dexter Ave (45215-4741)
PHONE...................................513 288-9264
EMP: 25
SALES (est): 371.6K Privately Held
SIC: 7389 Telephone answering service

▲ = Import ▼=Export
◆ =Import/Export

(G-4577)
TAPE PRODUCTS COMPANY (PA)
11630 Deerfield Rd (45242-1499)
P.O. Box 42413 (45242-0413)
PHONE..................................513 489-8840
John Fette, *CEO*
Janet F Fette, *Chairman*
Gail B Frazier, *Vice Pres*
Carlos Jimenez, *Vice Pres*
Cindy Kagrise, *Vice Pres*
▲ **EMP:** 80 **EST:** 1967
SQ FT: 62,500
SALES (est): 60.4MM **Privately Held**
WEB: www.tapeproducts.com
SIC: 5113 5084 Pressure sensitive tape; packaging machinery & equipment

(G-4578)
TEASDALE FENTON CARPET CLEANIN
12145 Centron Pl (45246-1704)
PHONE..................................513 797-0900
James Olmstead, *President*
EMP: 110
SQ FT: 20,000
SALES: 15.3MM **Privately Held**
SIC: 1623 7217 7299 Pipeline construction; carpet & upholstery cleaning; home improvement & renovation contractor agency

(G-4579)
TECHNICAL CONSULTANTS INC
Also Called: TCI
8228 Winton Rd Ste 200a (45231)
PHONE..................................513 521-2696
Horst Steigerwald, *President*
EMP: 43
SQ FT: 5,000
SALES: 5MM **Privately Held**
SIC: 8711 8741 Consulting engineer; construction management

(G-4580)
TECHSOFT SYSTEMS INC
10296 Springfield Pike (45215-1193)
PHONE..................................513 772-5010
Clifford A Bailey, *President*
Ben Schneider, *Sr Project Mgr*
Danielle Prewitt, *Info Tech Mgr*
EMP: 25
SQ FT: 5,000
SALES: 3MM **Privately Held**
WEB: www.techsoftsystems.com
SIC: 7379 Computer related consulting services

(G-4581)
TECHSOLVE INC
6705 Steger Dr (45237-3097)
PHONE..................................513 948-2000
David R Linger, *President*
Rick Henkel, *Exec VP*
Dave Levine, *Exec VP*
Kara Valz, *Exec VP*
Jon Iverson, *Vice Pres*
EMP: 51
SQ FT: 22,000
SALES: 8.6MM **Privately Held**
WEB: www.techsolve.org
SIC: 8742 8748 8711 Manufacturing management consultant; business consulting; mechanical engineering

(G-4582)
TECTA AMERICA ZERO COMPANY LLC (DH)
6225 Wiehe Rd (45237-4211)
PHONE..................................513 541-1848
Jonathan Wolf, *President*
Jim Stark, *Senior VP*
Thomas M Miller, *Vice Pres*
Edward Phillip, *Vice Pres*
Judy Benzing, *Accountant*
EMP: 100
SQ FT: 30,000
SALES (est): 21.7MM
SALES (corp-wide): 12.9MM **Privately Held**
SIC: 1761 Roofing contractor; sheet metal-work

HQ: Tecta America Corp.
9450 Bryn Mawr Ave
Rosemont IL 60018
847 581-3888

(G-4583)
TEKSYSTEMS INC
Also Called: Teksystems 611
3825 Edwards Rd Ste 500 (45209-1288)
PHONE..................................513 719-3950
Sarah Downs, *Manager*
EMP: 40
SALES (corp-wide): 12.3B **Privately Held**
WEB: www.teksystems.com
SIC: 7379 Computer related consulting services
HQ: Teksystems, Inc.
7437 Race Rd
Hanover MD 21076

(G-4584)
TENABLE PROTECTIVE SVCS INC
5643 Cheviot Rd Ste 5 (45247-7080)
PHONE..................................513 741-3560
Karl Angelo, *Branch Mgr*
EMP: 950
SALES (est): 6.2MM
SALES (corp-wide): 85.3MM **Privately Held**
WEB: www.ac-products.com
SIC: 7381 Security guard service
PA: Tenable Protective Services, Inc.
2423 Payne Ave
Cleveland OH 44114
216 361-0002

(G-4585)
TENDER MERCIES INC (PA)
27 W 12th St (45202-7205)
P.O. Box 14465 (45250-0465)
PHONE..................................513 721-8666
Marsha Spaeth, *CEO*
Kirsch Mary, *COO*
EMP: 60
SQ FT: 40,000
SALES: 3MM **Privately Held**
SIC: 8322 Emergency shelters

(G-4586)
TERRACON CONSULTANTS INC
Also Called: Terracon Consultants N1
611 Lunken Park Dr (45226-1813)
PHONE..................................513 321-5816
Jason Sander, *Branch Mgr*
EMP: 130
SALES (corp-wide): 654.9MM **Privately Held**
SIC: 8711 Consulting engineer
HQ: Terracon Consultants, Inc.
10841 S Ridgeview Rd
Olathe KS 66061
913 599-6886

(G-4587)
TESTAMERICA LABORATORIES INC
11416 Reading Rd (45241-2247)
PHONE..................................513 733-5700
Steve West, *Manager*
EMP: 48
SALES (corp-wide): 983.9MM **Privately Held**
SIC: 8734 Soil analysis
HQ: Testamerica Laboratories, Inc.
4101 Shuffel St Nw # 100
North Canton OH 44720
800 456-9396

(G-4588)
TETRA TECH INC
250 W Court St Ste 200w (45202-1072)
PHONE..................................513 251-2730
Rust Murphy, *Principal*
Michael Gibbons, *Manager*
EMP: 30
SALES (corp-wide): 2.9B **Publicly Held**
WEB: www.ttnus.com
SIC: 8748 Environmental consultant
PA: Tetra Tech, Inc.
3475 E Foothill Blvd
Pasadena CA 91107
626 351-4664

(G-4589)
TEVA WOMENS HEALTH INC (DH)
5040 Duramed Rd (45213-2520)
PHONE..................................513 731-9900
Bruce L Downey, *Principal*
Timothy J Holt, *Principal*
Lawrence A Glassman, *Senior VP*
EMP: 250 **EST:** 1982
SQ FT: 28,200
SALES (est): 125.7MM
SALES (corp-wide): 18.8B **Privately Held**
WEB: www.barrlabs.com
SIC: 5122 2834 7389 Patent medicines; pharmaceutical preparations; tablets, pharmaceutical; medicines, capsuled or ampuled; solutions, pharmaceutical; packaging & labeling services
HQ: Teva Pharmaceuticals Usa, Inc.
1090 Horsham Rd
North Wales PA 19454
215 591-3000

(G-4590)
THE CINCINNATI CORDAGE PPR CO
Also Called: Cincinnati Division
800 E Ross Ave (45217-1177)
PHONE..................................513 242-3600
John F Church Jr, *Ch of Bd*
Lawrence Bresko, *President*
EMP: 45
SQ FT: 60,000
SALES (est): 7.1MM **Privately Held**
SIC: 5111 5113 Printing paper; industrial & personal service paper

(G-4591)
THE FOR CINCINNATI ASSOCIATION (PA)
650 Walnut St (45202-2517)
PHONE..................................513 744-3344
Steve Loftin, *President*
Dudly S Taft, *Chairman*
Van Ackerman, *Director*
EMP: 75 **EST:** 1878
SQ FT: 200,000
SALES: 14.2MM **Privately Held**
WEB: www.cincinnatiarts.org
SIC: 8641 Dwelling-related associations

(G-4592)
THE HEALTHCARE CONNECTION INC (PA)
Also Called: Lincoln Hts Hlth Connection
1401 Steffen Ave (45215-2338)
PHONE..................................513 588-3623
Dolores Lindsay, *President*
Joseph Stickle, *Facilities Dir*
Diane Becker, *Opers Mgr*
Joanne Dwyer, *CFO*
Shirley Madison, *Manager*
EMP: 33
SQ FT: 42,000
SALES: 8MM **Privately Held**
SIC: 8011 Ambulatory surgical center; clinic, operated by physicians

(G-4593)
THE HUNTINGTON INVESTMENT CO
Also Called: Huntington Wealth Advisors
525 Vine St Ste 2100 (45202-3121)
PHONE..................................513 351-2555
Mark Reitzes, *Manager*
EMP: 45
SALES (corp-wide): 5.2B **Publicly Held**
SIC: 6211 6799 Brokers, security; investors
HQ: The Huntington Investment Company
41 S High St Fl 7
Columbus OH 43215
614 480-3600

(G-4594)
THE IN CINCINNATI PLAYHOUSE
962 Mount Adams Cir (45202-6023)
PHONE..................................513 421-3888
Edward Stern, *Director*
EMP: 100
SALES (corp-wide): 13.7MM **Privately Held**
WEB: www.cincyplay.com
SIC: 7922 Community theater production

PA: The Cincinnati Playhouse In The Park Inc
962 Mount Adams Cir
Cincinnati OH 45202
513 345-2242

(G-4595)
THE PECK-HANNAFORD BRIGGS CO (PA)
Also Called: PH B
4670 Chester Ave (45232-1851)
PHONE..................................513 681-4600
James G Briggs Jr, *President*
Jerry A Govert, *Vice Pres*
Nicholas Paff, *Project Mgr*
Garrett Perkins, *Project Mgr*
Ken Shad, *Project Mgr*
EMP: 90 **EST:** 1899
SQ FT: 40,000
SALES (est): 52.9MM **Privately Held**
SIC: 1711 Mechanical contractor; warm air heating & air conditioning contractor; refrigeration contractor

(G-4596)
THE SHEAKLEY GROUP INC (PA)
Also Called: S G I
1 Sheakley Way Ste 100 (45246-3774)
PHONE..................................513 771-2277
Larry Sheakley, *CEO*
Jayne Gaffney, *Vice Pres*
Shari Herper, *Vice Pres*
Scott Herrmann, *Vice Pres*
David Massey, *Vice Pres*
EMP: 30
SQ FT: 5,500
SALES (est): 33.7MM **Privately Held**
WEB: www.sheakley.com
SIC: 8742 8721 8741 6411 Compensation & benefits planning consultant; accounting, auditing & bookkeeping; management services; administrative management; insurance agents, brokers & service; pension & retirement plan consultants

(G-4597)
THEATRE MANAGEMENT CORPORATION
125 E Court St Ste 1000 (45202-1227)
PHONE..................................513 723-1180
Gary Goldman, *President*
EMP: 50
SALES (est): 2MM **Privately Held**
SIC: 7832 Motion picture theaters, except drive-in

(G-4598)
THELEN ASSOCIATES INC
1780 Carillion Blvd (45240-2795)
PHONE..................................513 825-4350
Dale Proffitt, *Manager*
EMP: 30
SALES (est): 1.9MM
SALES (corp-wide): 15.9MM **Privately Held**
WEB: www.thelenassoc.com
SIC: 8711 Consulting engineer
PA: Thelen Associates, Inc.
1398 Cox Ave
Erlanger KY 41018
859 746-9400

(G-4599)
THERMALTECH ENGINEERING INC (PA)
3960 Red Bank Rd Ste 250 (45227-3437)
PHONE..................................513 561-2271
Jeff Celuch, *President*
Bill W Widman, *Managing Dir*
Jeremy Davis, *Engineer*
Brad Edgell, *Engineer*
Jeff Hiatt, *Engineer*
EMP: 33
SQ FT: 8,000
SALES: 25MM **Privately Held**
WEB: www.thermaltech.com
SIC: 8711 Electrical or electronic engineering

(G-4600)
THINKWARE INCORPORATED
7611 Cheviot Rd Ste 2 (45247-4015)
PHONE..................................513 598-3300

Kevin Eickmann, *President*
Jack Dossou, *Software Engr*
EMP: 28
SQ FT: 7,500
SALES: 5.4MM **Privately Held**
WEB: www.thinkwareinc.com
SIC: 7371 7374 7372 Computer software
development; data processing & prepara-
tion; prepackaged software

(G-4601)
THOMAN WEIL MOVING & STOR CO
Also Called: Bekins Van Lines
5151 Fischer Ave (45217-1157)
P.O. Box 17105 (45217-0105)
PHONE...................................513 251-5000
Joseph C Thoman, *President*
James B Thoman, *VP Sales*
EMP: 50 **EST:** 1900
SQ FT: 9,000
SALES (est): 4.9MM **Privately Held**
SIC: 4213 4214 Trucking, except local;
local trucking with storage

(G-4602)
THOMAS J DYER COMPANY (PA)
5240 Lester Rd (45213-2522)
PHONE...................................513 321-8100
Thomas D Grote Sr, *CEO*
EMP: 164 **EST:** 1908
SQ FT: 29,600
SALES (est): 68.9MM **Privately Held**
WEB: www.tjdyer.com
SIC: 1711 Plumbing contractors; ventilation
& duct work contractor; warm air heating
& air conditioning contractor

(G-4603)
THOMAS TRUCKING INC
2558 Apple Ridge Ln (45236-1331)
PHONE...................................513 731-8411
Callis A Thomas, *President*
Mark Thomas, *Vice Pres*
Christine Thomas, *Treasurer*
Kathy Thomas-Dawson, *Admin Sec*
EMP: 40
SQ FT: 2,000
SALES (est): 6MM **Privately Held**
SIC: 4213 Contract haulers

(G-4604)
THOMPSON HALL & JORDAN FNRL HM
400 N Wayne Ave (45215-2845)
PHONE...................................513 761-8881
Katherine Jordan, *President*
Donald Jordan, *Vice Pres*
EMP: 50
SALES (est): 1.6MM **Privately Held**
SIC: 6512 Commercial & industrial building
operation

(G-4605)
THOMPSON HEATING & COOLING
800 E Ross Ave (45217-1177)
PHONE...................................513 242-4450
Wesley Holm, *President*
EMP: 40
SALES (est): 2.6MM **Privately Held**
SIC: 1711 Heating systems repair & main-
tenance

(G-4606)
THOMPSON HEATING CORPORATION
Also Called: Thompson Plumbing Htg Coolg
6 N Commerce Park Dr (45215-3174)
PHONE...................................513 769-7696
Wesley R Holm, *CEO*
Cheryl Holm, *Admin Sec*
EMP: 75
SQ FT: 9,000
SALES (est): 12.1MM **Privately Held**
WEB: www.thompsonheatingcooling.com
SIC: 1711 5075 5722 Heating systems re-
pair & maintenance; air conditioning &
ventilation equipment & supplies; electric
household appliances

(G-4607)
THP LIMITED INC
100 E 8th St Ste 3 (45202-2133)
PHONE...................................513 241-3222

James Millar, *President*
E James Millar, *President*
Frank J Ellert, *Principal*
Mark H Hoffman, *Principal*
L Michael Hurley, *Principal*
EMP: 55
SQ FT: 20,000
SALES: 385K **Privately Held**
WEB: www.thpltd.com
SIC: 8711 Structural engineering; civil en-
gineering

(G-4608)
THYSSENKRUPP ELEVATOR CORP
934 Dalton Ave (45203-1102)
PHONE...................................513 241-0222
Jeff Jaudes, *President*
EMP: 54
SALES (corp-wide): 39.8B **Privately Held**
SIC: 5084 Elevators
HQ: Thyssenkrupp Elevator Corporation
11605 Haynes Bridge Rd # 650
Alpharetta GA 30009
678 319-3240

(G-4609)
THYSSENKRUPP ELEVATOR CORP
934 Dalton Ave (45203-1102)
PHONE...................................513 241-6000
Toll Free:.................................888 -
Tom Zwick, *Branch Mgr*
EMP: 50
SALES (corp-wide): 39.8B **Privately Held**
WEB: www.tyssenkrupp.com
SIC: 1796 7699 Elevator installation &
conversion; elevators: inspection, service
& repair
HQ: Thyssenkrupp Elevator Corporation
11605 Haynes Bridge Rd # 650
Alpharetta GA 30009
678 319-3240

(G-4610)
TNS NORTH AMERICA INC
Also Called: Tns Global
600 Vine St Ste 300 (45202-2413)
PHONE...................................513 621-7887
Michelle Johnson, *Manager*
EMP: 67
SALES (corp-wide): 20.1B **Privately Held**
SIC: 8732 Market analysis or research
HQ: Tns North America, Inc.
175 Greenwich St Fl 16
New York NY 10007
212 991-6100

(G-4611)
TOTAL PACKAGE EXPRESS INC (PA)
5871 Cheviot Rd Ste 1 (45247-6200)
P.O. Box 53435 (45253-0435)
PHONE...................................513 741-5500
Joseph Amareno, *President*
Dave Wilkins, *General Mgr*
Joseph S Amareno, *Shareholder*
EMP: 25
SQ FT: 900
SALES (est): 6.9MM **Privately Held**
SIC: 4212 4213 4731 Delivery service,
vehicular; trucking, except local; truck
transportation brokers

(G-4612)
TOTAL QUALITY LOGISTICS LLC
5130 Glncrssing Way Ste 3 (45238)
PHONE...................................513 831-2600
Joe Myers, *Branch Mgr*
EMP: 74
SALES (corp-wide): 2.9B **Privately Held**
SIC: 4731 Freight transportation arrange-
ment
HQ: Total Quality Logistics, Llc
4289 Ivy Pointe Blvd
Cincinnati OH 45245

(G-4613)
TOUCHSTONE GROUP ASSOC LLC
9675 Montgomery Rd # 201 (45242-7263)
PHONE...................................513 791-1717
Scott Estes,
EMP: 35

SALES (est): 20.2MM **Privately Held**
WEB: www.findthevine.com
SIC: 8742 Hospital & health services con-
sultant

(G-4614)
TOWNE BUILDING GROUP INC (PA)
1055 Saint Paul Pl (45202-6042)
PHONE...................................513 381-8696
Neil K Bortz, *President*
Philip T Montanus, *Principal*
Marvin Rosenberg, *Principal*
Max L Wiseman, *Vice Pres*
AM J Sekula, *Manager*
EMP: 90
SQ FT: 2,000
SALES (est): 4.5MM **Privately Held**
SIC: 1522 Apartment building construction;
multi-family dwellings, new construction

(G-4615)
TOWNE DEVELOPMENT GROUP LTD
1055 Saint Paul Pl # 300 (45202-6042)
PHONE...................................513 381-8696
Neil K Bortz,
Marvin Rosenberg,
EMP: 32
SQ FT: 1,200
SALES (est): 5.6MM **Privately Held**
WEB: www.townedevelopmentgroup.com
SIC: 6552 1521 Land subdividers & devel-
opers, residential; new construction, sin-
gle-family houses

(G-4616)
TOWNE INVESTMENT COMPANY LP
1055 Saint Paul Pl (45202-6042)
PHONE...................................513 381-8696
Marvin Rosenberg, *Partner*
Neil Bortz, *General Ptnr*
Beverly Casey, *Human Res Dir*
EMP: 70 **Privately Held**
SIC: 6719 Investment holding companies,
except banks

(G-4617)
TOWNE PROPERTIES ASSET MGT (PA)
Also Called: Towne Properties Asset MGT
1055 Saint Paul Pl # 100 (45202-1687)
PHONE...................................513 381-8696
Bob Wahlke, *President*
Robert Wahlke, *President*
Neil Bortz, *Partner*
Phil Montanus, *Partner*
Judd Oscherwitz, *Property Mgr*
EMP: 600
SQ FT: 5,000
SALES (est): 27.4MM **Privately Held**
SIC: 6513 Apartment building operators

(G-4618)
TOWNE PROPERTIES ASSOC INC
Also Called: Racquet Club At Harper's Point
8675 E Kemper Rd (45249-2503)
PHONE...................................513 489-9700
Laura Wagner, *Principal*
EMP: 25
SALES (corp-wide): 33.3MM **Privately Held**
WEB: www.towneprop.com
SIC: 7941 Sports field or stadium operator,
promoting sports events
PA: Towne Properties Associates, Inc.
1055 Saint Paul Pl # 100
Cincinnati OH 45202
513 381-8696

(G-4619)
TOWNE PROPERTIES ASSOC INC
Also Called: Towne Management Realty
11340 Montgomery Rd # 202 (45249-2377)
P.O. Box 691650 (45269-0001)
PHONE...................................513 489-4059
Nora Rust, *Office Mgr*
Char Ostholthoff, *Manager*
EMP: 27

SALES (corp-wide): 33.3MM **Privately Held**
WEB: www.towneprop.com
SIC: 6531 Real estate managers
PA: Towne Properties Associates, Inc.
1055 Saint Paul Pl # 100
Cincinnati OH 45202
513 381-8696

(G-4620)
TOWNE PROPERTIES ASSOC INC
11840 Kemper Springs Dr C (45240-4130)
PHONE...................................513 874-3737
Wil Browning, *Manager*
EMP: 50
SALES (corp-wide): 33.3MM **Privately Held**
WEB: www.towneprop.com
SIC: 6513 6514 6531 Apartment building
operators; dwelling operators, except
apartments; real estate agents & man-
agers
PA: Towne Properties Associates, Inc.
1055 Saint Paul Pl # 100
Cincinnati OH 45202
513 381-8696

(G-4621)
TOWNEPLACE SUITES BY MARRIOTT
9369 Waterstone Blvd (45249-8218)
PHONE...................................513 774-0610
Pete Pordash, *Principal*
EMP: 25
SALES (est): 1.2MM **Privately Held**
SIC: 7011 Hotel, franchised

(G-4622)
TOWNSHIP OF COLERAIN
Also Called: Fire Dept
3360 W Galbraith Rd (45239-3969)
PHONE...................................513 741-7551
Frank W Cook, *Director*
EMP: 173 **Privately Held**
WEB: www.coleraintwp.org
SIC: 9224 8011 Fire department, not in-
cluding volunteer; freestanding emer-
gency medical center
PA: Township Of Colerain
4200 Springdale Rd
Cincinnati OH 45251
513 923-5000

(G-4623)
TP MECHANICAL CONTRACTORS INC (PA)
Also Called: Honeywell Authorized Dealer
1500 Kemper Meadow Dr (45240-1638)
PHONE...................................513 851-8881
Scott Teepe Sr, *President*
Bill Riddle, *President*
Jeff Keller, *Partner*
Mark Hunter, *General Mgr*
Greg Robinson, *General Mgr*
EMP: 525
SQ FT: 3,200
SALES (est): 54.5MM **Privately Held**
SIC: 6552 Subdividers & developers

(G-4624)
TPG NORAMCO LLC
9252 Colerain Ave Ste 4 (45251-2447)
PHONE...................................513 245-9050
Mark Wetterich,
EMP: 30
SQ FT: 104,000
SALES (est): 3.8MM **Privately Held**
SIC: 4213 4731 Trucking, except local;
freight forwarding

(G-4625)
TRAK STAFFING SERVICES INC (PA)
625 Eden Park Dr Ste 300 (45202-6006)
PHONE...................................513 333-4199
Joseph McCullough, *President*
John Murley, *Vice Pres*
Marty Sizemore, *Vice Pres*
Jennifer Spaulding-Marsh, *Vice Pres*
Beth Taylor, *Accounts Mgr*
EMP: 25
SQ FT: 11,000

SALES (est): 2MM **Privately Held**
WEB: www.trakcincy.com
SIC: 7361 Executive placement

(G-4626)
TRANS-CONTINENTAL SYSTEMS INC (PA)
Also Called: TCS
10801 Evendale Dr Ste 105 (45241-7509)
PHONE..................................513 769-4774
Gary W Stone, *Principal*
Robin Wright, *Safety Dir*
William Danford, *Controller*
EMP: 40
SQ FT: 6,000
SALES (est): 17.9MM **Privately Held**
WEB: www.tcsohio.com
SIC: 4731 Freight transportation arrangement

(G-4627)
TRANS-STATES EXPRESS INC
7750 Reinhold Dr (45237-2806)
PHONE..................................513 679-7100
William Edmund, *President*
Herb Glischinski, *Opers Staff*
Mary Edmund, *Admin Sec*
EMP: 70
SQ FT: 23,000
SALES (est): 5.8MM **Privately Held**
WEB: www.onecalldoesall.com
SIC: 4213 4212 Contract haulers; local trucking, without storage

(G-4628)
TRANSPORT SPECIALISTS INC (PA)
Also Called: Thermo King
12130 Best Pl (45241-1569)
PHONE..................................513 771-2220
Jake Jennings, *President*
Jeff Jennings, *Purch Mgr*
Dan Jennings, *Parts Mgr*
Ryan Sines, *Parts Mgr*
Jerry Vogele, *Sales Staff*
▲ EMP: 25
SQ FT: 24,000
SALES (est): 31.1MM **Privately Held**
SIC: 5531 7623 Truck equipment & parts; refrigeration repair service

(G-4629)
TRAVEL AUTHORITY (PA)
6800 Wooster Pike (45227-4324)
PHONE..................................513 272-2887
Denise Daum, *President*
Joyce Dill, *President*
Thomas Fucito, *Corp Secy*
Thomas Herbert, *Vice Pres*
John Stump, *Vice Pres*
EMP: 27
SQ FT: 2,500
SALES (est): 3.6MM **Privately Held**
SIC: 4724 Travel agencies

(G-4630)
TRAVELERS PROPERTY CSLTY CORP
Also Called: Travelers Insurance
615 Elsinore Pl Bldg B (45202-1459)
PHONE..................................513 639-5300
Bruce Brizzi, *Manager*
EMP: 35
SALES (corp-wide): 30.2B **Publicly Held**
WEB: www.travelerspc.com
SIC: 6411 Insurance agents
HQ: Travelers Property Casualty Corp.
1 Tower Sq 8ms
Hartford CT 06183

(G-4631)
TRI STATE CORPORATION
923 Glenwood Ave (45229-2713)
PHONE..................................513 763-0215
Joseph Lentine, *Branch Mgr*
EMP: 46
SALES (est): 2.8MM
SALES (corp-wide): 6.3MM **Privately Held**
SIC: 1611 1622 1541 1542 Highway & street construction; bridge, tunnel & elevated highway; industrial buildings & warehouses; nonresidential construction

PA: Tri State Corporation
1633 Main St
Bridgeport CT 06604
513 763-0215

(G-4632)
TRI STATE URLOGIC SVCS PSC INC (PA)
Also Called: Urology Group
2000 Joseph E Sanker Blvd (45212-1979)
PHONE..................................513 841-7400
Earl L Walz, *CEO*
William Corbett, *Research*
Nicolle Taylor, *Controller*
Rebecca Rowland, *Human Resources*
Vicky Turner, *Office Mgr*
EMP: 225
SALES (est): 39.8MM **Privately Held**
SIC: 8011 Medical centers; urologist

(G-4633)
TRI-STATE BEEF CO INC
2124 Baymiller St (45214-2208)
PHONE..................................513 579-1722
Yong Woo Koo, *President*
EMP: 30
SALES (est): 6MM **Privately Held**
SIC: 2011 2013 5147 Meat packing plants; sausages & other prepared meats; meats & meat products

(G-4634)
TRIANGLE OFFICE PARK LLC
2135 Dana Ave Ste 200 (45207-1327)
PHONE..................................513 563-7555
Dan Neyer, *Principal*
Colleen Kroell, *Controller*
EMP: 25
SALES (est): 860K **Privately Held**
SIC: 6531 Real estate leasing & rentals

(G-4635)
TRIHEALTH INC
415 W Court St Ste 100 (45203-1552)
PHONE..................................513 929-0020
EMP: 50 **Privately Held**
SIC: 8741 Management Services
HQ: Trihealth, Inc.
619 Oak St
Cincinnati OH 45206
513 569-6111

(G-4636)
TRIHEALTH INC
Also Called: Bethesda North Hospital
10506 Montgomery Rd (45242-4487)
PHONE..................................513 865-1111
Jason Niehaus, *Senior VP*
Jennifer Messer, *Med Doctor*
Douglas Moody, *Med Doctor*
Smita Saraf, *Med Doctor*
Shannon Cult, *Manager*
EMP: 50 **Privately Held**
SIC: 8741 Hospital management
HQ: Trihealth, Inc.
619 Oak St
Cincinnati OH 45206
513 569-6111

(G-4637)
TRIHEALTH INC
Also Called: Senior Behaviroal Health
375 Dixmyth Ave (45220-2475)
PHONE..................................513 569-6777
Katie McGee, *Vice Pres*
Susan Dietrich, *Opers Staff*
Dennis Hein, *Purchasing*
Chris Meredith, *Controller*
Greg Green, *Human Resources*
EMP: 50 **Privately Held**
WEB: www.trihealth.com
SIC: 8741 8093 Hospital management; mental health clinic, outpatient
HQ: Trihealth, Inc.
619 Oak St
Cincinnati OH 45206
513 569-6111

(G-4638)
TRIHEALTH INC (HQ)
619 Oak St (45206-1613)
PHONE..................................513 569-6111
John Prout, *President*
Myra James Bradley, *Principal*
L Thomas Wilburn Jr, *Principal*
Pat McMahon, *Dean*

Will Groneman, *Exec VP*
EMP: 50
SALES: 184MM **Privately Held**
WEB: www.trihealth.com
SIC: 8741 8062 Hospital management; general medical & surgical hospitals

(G-4639)
TRIHEALTH INC
2753 Erie Ave (45208-2204)
PHONE..................................513 871-2340
Raejean Hardig, *Branch Mgr*
EMP: 50 **Privately Held**
WEB: www.trihealth.com
SIC: 8741 Hospital management
HQ: Trihealth, Inc.
619 Oak St
Cincinnati OH 45206
513 569-6111

(G-4640)
TRIHEALTH EVENDALE HOSPITAL (DH)
3155 Glendale Milford Rd (45241-3134)
PHONE..................................513 454-2222
Ajay Mangal, *President*
Rhonda Bunch, *Director*
Rita Becker, *Receptionist*
EMP: 166
SALES: 0 **Privately Held**
SIC: 8062 General medical & surgical hospitals
HQ: Trihealth, Inc.
619 Oak St
Cincinnati OH 45206
513 569-6111

(G-4641)
TRIHEALTH G LLC (DH)
Also Called: Cincinnati Group Health
4600 Wesley Ave Ste N (45212-2274)
PHONE..................................513 732-0700
Donna Nienaber, *Senior VP*
Joseph Hellmann, *Med Doctor*
Raymond Sterling, *Info Tech Mgr*
EMP: 75 EST: 1974
SQ FT: 50,000
SALES (est): 60.1MM **Privately Held**
WEB: www.cgha.com
SIC: 8011 Physicians' office, including specialists
HQ: Trihealth, Inc.
619 Oak St
Cincinnati OH 45206
513 569-6111

(G-4642)
TRIHEALTH G LLC
Also Called: Blumenthal, Barry
55 Progress Pl (45246-1715)
PHONE..................................513 346-5000
Diana Hendry, *Manager*
EMP: 45 **Privately Held**
WEB: www.cgha.com
SIC: 8093 8011 Rehabilitation center, outpatient treatment; offices & clinics of medical doctors
HQ: Trihealth G, Llc
4600 Wesley Ave Ste N
Cincinnati OH 45212
513 732-0700

(G-4643)
TRIHEALTH G LLC
7691 5 Mile Rd Ste 214 (45230-4348)
PHONE..................................513 624-5535
Sharon Nicholas, *Med Doctor*
Jo Ann Vill, *Manager*
EMP: 100 **Privately Held**
WEB: www.cgha.com
SIC: 8011 Pediatrician
HQ: Trihealth G, Llc
4600 Wesley Ave Ste N
Cincinnati OH 45212
513 732-0700

(G-4644)
TRIHEALTH G LLC
Also Called: Group Health Associates
2001 Anderson Ferry Rd (45238-3325)
PHONE..................................513 922-1200
Lee Moeller, *Manager*
Patrick Huhn, *Manager*
Scott L Firestein, *Obstetrician*
Yogesh Sharma, *Internal Med*
Thomas Maloney, *Pediatrics*

EMP: 100 **Privately Held**
WEB: www.cgha.com
SIC: 8049 8011 Physical therapist; offices & clinics of medical doctors
HQ: Trihealth G, Llc
4600 Wesley Ave Ste N
Cincinnati OH 45212
513 732-0700

(G-4645)
TRIHEALTH ONCOLOGY INST LLC
Also Called: Oncology Partners Network
5520 Cheviot Rd (45247-7069)
PHONE..................................513 451-4033
Daniel White, *Med Doctor*
Richard Louis Meyer, *Mng Member*
Faisal Adhami, *Hematology*
J Bhaskaran,
EMP: 35 EST: 1963
SQ FT: 1,900
SALES (est): 5.7MM **Privately Held**
SIC: 8011 Oncologist; hematologist

(G-4646)
TRIHEALTH REHABILITATION HOSP
2155 Dana Ave (45207-1340)
PHONE..................................513 601-0600
Mark Asmen, *CEO*
EMP: 160
SALES (est): 48.6K
SALES (corp-wide): 3.7B **Publicly Held**
SIC: 8322 Rehabilitation services
HQ: Select Medical Corporation
4714 Gettysburg Rd
Mechanicsburg PA 17055
717 972-1100

(G-4647)
TRINITY CREDIT COUNSELING INC
Also Called: TRINITY DEBT MANAGEMENT
11229 Reading Rd Ste 1 (45241-2238)
PHONE..................................513 769-0621
Gary Vosick, *President*
EMP: 28
SQ FT: 10,000
SALES: 4.9MM **Privately Held**
WEB: www.trinitycredit.org
SIC: 8742 Banking & finance consultant

(G-4648)
TRINITY HEALTHCARE CORPORATION
Also Called: Meadbrook Care Center
8211 Weller Rd (45242-3208)
PHONE..................................513 489-2444
Kathy Brown, *Administration*
EMP: 125
SALES (corp-wide): 10.6MM **Privately Held**
WEB: www.trinityusa.org
SIC: 8051 Convalescent home with continuous nursing care
PA: Trinity Healthcare Corporation
2640 Peerless Rd Nw
Cleveland TN 37312
423 476-3035

(G-4649)
TRIO TRUCKING INC
7750 Reinhold Dr (45237-2806)
PHONE..................................513 679-7100
Bill Edmond, *Branch Mgr*
EMP: 45
SALES (corp-wide): 6.5MM **Privately Held**
SIC: 4213 4212 Trucking, except local; local trucking, without storage
PA: Trio Trucking, Inc.
7750 Reinhold Dr
Cincinnati OH 45237
513 679-7100

(G-4650)
TRIVERSITY CONSTRUCTION CO LLC
5050 Section Ave Ste 330 (45212-2052)
PHONE..................................513 733-0046
Melvin J Gravely II, *Mng Member*
EMP: 32 EST: 2005
SQ FT: 2,585
SALES (est): 7.1MM **Privately Held**
SIC: 8741 Construction management

G
E
O
G
R
A
P
H
I
C

(G-4651)
TSC APPAREL LLC (PA)
Also Called: T-Shirt City
Centennial Plaza Iii 895 (45202)
PHONE.....................513 771-1138
Rick Mouty, *CEO*
Bob Winget, *President*
Denny Blazer, *CFO*
James Van Hook, *Marketing Staff*
▲ EMP: 55
SQ FT: 170,000
SALES (est): 18.8MM **Privately Held**
WEB: www.tscapparel.com
SIC: 5699 5137 T-shirts, custom printed;
shirts, custom made; sportswear,
women's & children's

(G-4652)
TURNER CONSTRUCTION COMPANY
250 W Court St Ste 300w (45202-1071)
PHONE.....................513 721-4224
Doug Rack, *Superintendent*
Steve Spaulding, *Safety Mgr*
Kenneth Butler, *Branch Mgr*
EMP: 200
SQ FT: 7,000
SALES (corp-wide): 579.6MM **Privately Held**
WEB: www.tcco.com
SIC: 1541 1542 1522 Industrial buildings,
new construction; commercial & office
building, new construction; multi-family
dwellings, new construction
HQ: Turner Construction Company Inc
375 Hudson St Fl 6
New York NY 10014
212 229-6000

(G-4653)
TURNER CONSTRUCTION COMPANY
2315 Iowa Ave (45206-2312)
PHONE.....................513 363-0883
EMP: 60
SALES (corp-wide): 579.6MM **Privately Held**
SIC: 1542 Commercial & office building,
new construction
HQ: Turner Construction Company Inc
375 Hudson St Fl 6
New York NY 10014
212 229-6000

(G-4654)
TURPIN HILLS SWIM RACQUET CLB
3814 West St Ste 311 (45227-3743)
PHONE.....................513 231-3242
Jane Tillinghast, *President*
EMP: 25
SQ FT: 2,870
SALES: 368K **Privately Held**
WEB: www.turpinswimclub.org
SIC: 7997 Swimming club, membership

(G-4655)
TUSCANY SPA SALON
11355 Montgomery Rd (45249-2312)
PHONE.....................513 489-8872
Amy Kobs, *Owner*
EMP: 30
SQ FT: 5,600
SALES (est): 668.1K **Privately Held**
WEB: www.tuscanyspaandsalon.com
SIC: 7991 Spas

(G-4656)
TWC CONCRETE SERVICES LLC
10737 Medallion Dr (45241-4837)
PHONE.....................513 771-8192
Anthony R Decarlo, *CEO*
Donald J Wagner, *President*
Anthony Decarlo Jr, *Exec VP*
James J Skillman, *Vice Pres*
Barry Galbraith, *Mng Member*
EMP: 70
SALES (est): 19.9MM **Privately Held**
SIC: 1541 Industrial buildings, new construction

(G-4657)
TWISM ENTERPRISES LLC
Also Called: Valucadd Solutions
12110 Regency Run Ct # 9 (45240-1090)
PHONE.....................513 800-1098
Shawn Alexander,
EMP: 50
SALES (est): 876.1K **Privately Held**
SIC: 8712 8711 7373 8748 Architectural
engineering; mechanical engineering;
electrical or electronic engineering; computer-aided engineering (CAE) systems
service; telecommunications consultant

(G-4658)
TYCO INTERNATIONAL MGT CO LLC
Also Called: Real Time Systems
2884 E Kemper Rd (45241-1820)
PHONE.....................888 787-8324
Ron Hartmann, *Branch Mgr*
EMP: 50 **Privately Held**
SIC: 7373 7371 Systems integration services; custom computer programming
services
HQ: Tyco International Management Company, Llc
9 Roszel Rd Ste 2
Princeton NJ 08540
609 720-4200

(G-4659)
U C CHILD CARE CENTER INC
3310 Ruther Ave (45220-2111)
PHONE.....................513 961-2825
Sally Wehby, *Director*
EMP: 30
SALES: 1.6MM **Privately Held**
SIC: 8351 Child day care services

(G-4660)
U S ARMY CORPS OF ENGINEERS
Regional Acquisition
550 Main St Ste 10022 (45202-3222)
PHONE.....................513 684-3048
Bruce Berwick, *Commissioner*
EMP: 100 **Publicly Held**
WEB: www.sac.usace.army.mil
SIC: 8711 9711 Engineering services;
Army
HQ: U S Army Corps Of Engineers
441 G St Nw
Washington DC 20314
202 761-0001

(G-4661)
UBS FINANCIAL SERVICES INC
312 Walnut St Ste 3300 (45202-4045)
PHONE.....................513 576-5000
Kevin Shepherd, *Vice Pres*
Daniel Driscoll, *Manager*
EMP: 100
SQ FT: 3,500
SALES (corp-wide): 29.4B **Privately Held**
SIC: 6211 Stock brokers & dealers; bond
dealers & brokers
HQ: Ubs Financial Services Inc.
1285 Ave Of The Americas
New York NY 10019
212 713-2000

(G-4662)
UBS FINANCIAL SERVICES INC
8044 Montgomery Rd # 200 (45236-2926)
PHONE.....................513 792-2146
Thomas Frank, *Manager*
EMP: 48
SALES (corp-wide): 29.4B **Privately Held**
SIC: 6211 Security brokers & dealers
HQ: Ubs Financial Services Inc.
1285 Ave Of The Americas
New York NY 10019
212 713-2000

(G-4663)
UBS FINANCIAL SERVICES INC
8044 Montgomery Rd # 200 (45236-2926)
PHONE.....................513 792-2100
James Burchenal, *Vice Pres*
Troy Debord, *Branch Mgr*
William Baylor Jr, *IT/INT Sup*
Sheila Vance, *Executive*
EMP: 50

SALES (corp-wide): 29.4B **Privately Held**
SIC: 6211 Security brokers & dealers
HQ: Ubs Financial Services Inc.
1285 Ave Of The Americas
New York NY 10019
212 713-2000

(G-4664)
UC HEALTH LLC
222 Piedmont Ave Ste 6000 (45219-4223)
PHONE.....................513 475-7880
Ruth Cooper, *Med Doctor*
EMP: 85 **Privately Held**
SIC: 8011 Internal medicine, physician/surgeon
PA: Uc Health, Llc.
3200 Burnet Ave
Cincinnati OH 45229

(G-4665)
UC HEALTH LLC
3200 Burnet Ave (45229-3019)
PHONE.....................513 585-7600
Donald Kegg, *CEO*
Timothy D Freeman, *Med Doctor*
Beth Heath, *Manager*
Tim Hafley, *Exec Dir*
Laura Allerding, *Director*
EMP: 38 **Privately Held**
SIC: 6324 Health maintenance organization (HMO), insurance only
PA: Uc Health, Llc.
3200 Burnet Ave
Cincinnati OH 45229

(G-4666)
UC HEALTH LLC
11590 Century Blvd # 102 (45246-3317)
PHONE.....................513 648-9077
Amy Mechley, *Director*
EMP: 85 **Privately Held**
SIC: 8011 Internal medicine, physician/surgeon
PA: Uc Health, Llc.
3200 Burnet Ave
Cincinnati OH 45229

(G-4667)
UC HEALTH LLC
Also Called: Alliance Health
3120 Burnet Ave Ste 203 (45229-3091)
PHONE.....................513 584-8600
Marlene Push, *Chiropractor*
James Peters, *Exec Dir*
Joseph N Bateman, *Family Practiti*
Christopher T Lewis, *Family Practiti*
EMP: 30 **Privately Held**
SIC: 8741 8062 Management services;
general medical & surgical hospitals
PA: Uc Health, Llc.
3200 Burnet Ave
Cincinnati OH 45229

(G-4668)
UC HEALTH LLC (PA)
3200 Burnet Ave (45229-3019)
PHONE.....................513 585-6000
James Kingsbury, *CEO*
William Barrett, *Ch of Bd*
Jay Brown, *Vice Pres*
Anthony Condia, *Vice Pres*
Andrew Cusher, *Vice Pres*
EMP: 800
SALES: 1.6B **Privately Held**
SIC: 8741 Hospital management

(G-4669)
ULMER & BERNE LLP
600 Vine St Ste 2800 (45202-2448)
PHONE.....................513 698-5000
Janine Gumbert, *President*
Sheryl Ritter, *President*
Scott Katish, *Managing Prtnr*
Dacia R Crum, *Principal*
B Scott Boster, *Administration*
EMP: 68 EST: 2010
SALES (est): 3.9MM **Privately Held**
SIC: 8111 General practice attorney,
lawyer

(G-4670)
ULMER & BERNE LLP
600 Vine St Ste 2800 (45202-2448)
PHONE.....................513 698-5000
Scott Kadish, *Manager*
EMP: 100

SALES (corp-wide): 85.9MM **Privately Held**
SIC: 8111 General practice law office
PA: Ulmer & Berne Llp
1660 W 2nd St Ste 1100
Cleveland OH 44113
216 583-7000

(G-4671)
ULMER & BERNE LLP
600 Vine St Ste 2800 (45202-2448)
PHONE.....................513 698-5058
Jennifer Snyder, *Branch Mgr*
EMP: 104
SALES (corp-wide): 85.9MM **Privately Held**
SIC: 8111 General practice attorney,
lawyer
PA: Ulmer & Berne Llp
1660 W 2nd St Ste 1100
Cleveland OH 44113
216 583-7000

(G-4672)
ULTIMUS FUND SOLUTIONS LLC (PA)
225 Pictoria Dr Ste 450 (45246-1617)
PHONE.....................513 587-3400
Gary Tenkman, *CEO*
Gary Harris, *Exec VP*
Todd Heim, *Assistant VP*
Matt Miller, *Assistant VP*
Frank Newbauer, *Assistant VP*
EMP: 35
SQ FT: 21,900
SALES (est): 10.8MM **Privately Held**
WEB: www.ultimusfundsolutions.com
SIC: 6211 Mutual funds, selling by independent salesperson

(G-4673)
UNION CENTRAL LIFE INSUR CO (DH)
1876 Waycross Rd (45240-2899)
P.O. Box 40888 (45240-0888)
PHONE.....................866 696-7478
Joann Martin, *CEO*
David F Westerbeck, *Exec VP*
Dale Donald Johnson, *Senior VP*
John Gephart, *Vice Pres*
Bob Herum, *Vice Pres*
EMP: 600
SQ FT: 165,000
SALES (est): 240.2MM
SALES (corp-wide): 2.2B **Privately Held**
WEB: www.uclfinancial.com
SIC: 6311 6321 Mutual association life insurance; mutual accident & health associations; accident associations, mutual
HQ: Ameritas Holding Company
5900 O St
Lincoln NE 68510
402 467-1122

(G-4674)
UNION SECURITY INSURANCE CO
Also Called: Assurant Employee Benefits
312 Elm St Ste 1500 (45202-2769)
PHONE.....................513 621-1924
EMP: 25
SALES (corp-wide): 7.5B **Publicly Held**
SIC: 6411 Insurance Agent/Broker
HQ: Union Security Insurance Company
6941 Vista Dr
West Des Moines IA 50266
651 361-4000

(G-4675)
UNITED AUDIT SYSTEMS INC
Also Called: Uasi
1924 Dana Ave (45207-1212)
PHONE.....................513 723-1122
Ty C Hare, *President*
Frank Kerley, *Exec VP*
Beverly J Bredenfoerder, *Vice Pres*
John De Fraites, *Vice Pres*
John A Defraites, *Vice Pres*
EMP: 206
SQ FT: 16,000
SALES (est): 27.1MM **Privately Held**
WEB: www.uasi-qc.com
SIC: 8742 Hospital & health services consultant

▲ = Import ▼=Export
◆ =Import/Export

(G-4676)
UNITED CEREBRAL PALSY GR CINC
Also Called: CEREBRAL PALSY SERVICES CENTER
2300 Drex Ave (45212-1216)
PHONE....................................513 221-4606
Susan Schiller, *Director*
Michelle Stewart,
EMP: 42
SALES: 3.5K **Privately Held**
WEB: www.ucp-cincinnati.org
SIC: 8361 Rehabilitation center, residential: health care incidental

(G-4677)
UNITED CHURCH HOMES INC
Also Called: Riverview Community
5999 Bender Rd (45233-1601)
PHONE....................................513 922-1440
Leigh Deaton, *Principal*
EMP: 200
SQ FT: 2,125
SALES (corp-wide): 78.1MM **Privately Held**
WEB: www.altenheimcommunity.org
SIC: 8051 8052 8361 Convalescent home with continuous nursing care; intermediate care facilities; home for the aged; rest home, with health care incidental
PA: United Church Homes Inc
170 E Center St
Marion OH 43302
740 382-4885

(G-4678)
UNITED DAIRY FARMERS INC (PA)
Also Called: U D F
3955 Montgomery Rd (45212-3798)
PHONE....................................513 396-8700
Brad Lindner, *President*
Frank Cogliano, *Vice Pres*
Ronald Anderson, *Opers Mgr*
Angelos Christon, *Opers Staff*
Daniel May, *Production*
EMP: 200
SALES (est): 614.2MM **Privately Held**
SIC: 5411 5143 2026 2024 Convenience stores, chain; ice cream & ices; frozen dairy desserts; milk processing (pasteurizing, homogenizing, bottling); ice cream & ice milk; filling stations, gasoline; dairy products stores

(G-4679)
UNITED ELECTRIC COMPANY INC
1309 Ethan Ave (45225-1809)
PHONE....................................502 459-5242
Larry Farrell, *General Mgr*
Tom Murray, *Office Mgr*
Randy Knopf, *Manager*
EMP: 50
SQ FT: 10,000
SALES (est): 5.3MM
SALES (corp-wide): 28.5MM **Privately Held**
WEB: www.unitedelec.com
SIC: 1731 General electrical contractor
PA: United Electric Company, Inc.
4333 Robards Ln
Louisville KY 40218
502 459-5242

(G-4680)
UNITED HEALTHCARE OHIO INC
400 E Bus Way Ste 100 (45241)
PHONE....................................513 603-6200
Dorothy Coleman, *CEO*
EMP: 250
SALES (corp-wide): 226.2B **Publicly Held**
WEB: www.uhc.com
SIC: 6324 Health maintenance organization (HMO), insurance only
HQ: United Healthcare Of Ohio, Inc.
9200 Worthington Rd
Columbus OH 43085
614 410-7000

(G-4681)
UNITED INSURANCE COMPANY AMER
135 Merchant St Ste 120 (45246-3773)
PHONE....................................513 771-6771
Randy Chasteen, *District Mgr*
EMP: 25
SALES (corp-wide): 3.7B **Publicly Held**
SIC: 6411 Insurance agents & brokers
HQ: United Insurance Company Of America
12115 Lackland Rd
Saint Louis MO 63146
314 819-4300

(G-4682)
UNITED MANAGEMENT INC
8280 Montgomery Rd # 303 (45236-6101)
PHONE....................................513 936-8568
Greg Malone, *Officer*
EMP: 30
SALES (corp-wide): 74.2MM **Privately Held**
SIC: 6531 Real estate managers
PA: United Management, Inc.
250 Civic Center Dr
Columbus OH 43215
614 228-5331

(G-4683)
UNITED PARCEL SERVICE INC OH
Also Called: UPS
500 Gest St (45203-1717)
PHONE....................................513 852-6135
EMP: 158
SALES (corp-wide): 71.8B **Publicly Held**
WEB: www.upsscs.com
SIC: 4215 Parcel delivery, vehicular
HQ: United Parcel Service, Inc. (Oh)
55 Glenlake Pkwy
Atlanta GA 30328
404 828-6000

(G-4684)
UNITED PARCEL SERVICE INC OH
Also Called: UPS
640 W 3rd St (45202-3483)
PHONE....................................513 241-5289
EMP: 158
SALES (corp-wide): 71.8B **Publicly Held**
WEB: www.upsscs.com
SIC: 4215 Parcel delivery, vehicular
HQ: United Parcel Service, Inc. (Oh)
55 Glenlake Pkwy
Atlanta GA 30328
404 828-6000

(G-4685)
UNITED PARCEL SERVICE INC OH
Also Called: UPS
11141 Canal Rd (45241-1861)
PHONE....................................513 782-4000
Jason Reynolds, *Opers Mgr*
Francis Ngumbi, *Plant Engr Mgr*
Bryan Schweinefus, *Human Res Mgr*
Todd Wachter, *Manager*
EMP: 158
SALES (corp-wide): 71.8B **Publicly Held**
WEB: www.upsscs.com
SIC: 4215 Parcel delivery, vehicular
HQ: United Parcel Service, Inc. (Oh)
55 Glenlake Pkwy
Atlanta GA 30328
404 828-6000

(G-4686)
UNITED PARCEL SERVICE INC OH
Also Called: UPS
644 Linn St Ste 325 (45203-1734)
PHONE....................................513 241-5316
Karma Hopper, *Branch Mgr*
EMP: 55
SALES (corp-wide): 71.8B **Publicly Held**
WEB: www.upsscs.com
SIC: 4215 Parcel delivery, vehicular
HQ: United Parcel Service, Inc. (Oh)
55 Glenlake Pkwy
Atlanta GA 30328
404 828-6000

(G-4687)
UNITED STEELWORKERS
Also Called: Uswa
8968 Blue Ash Rd (45242-7810)
PHONE....................................513 793-0272
Don Brammer, *Branch Mgr*
EMP: 44
SALES (corp-wide): 4.9MM **Privately Held**
WEB: www.uswa.org
SIC: 8631 Trade union
PA: United Steelworkers
60 Blvd Of The Allies # 902
Pittsburgh PA 15222
412 562-2400

(G-4688)
UNITED STTES BOWL CONGRESS INC
520 W Wyoming Ave (45215-4525)
PHONE....................................513 761-3338
Willie Dean, *Vice Pres*
EMP: 51
SALES (corp-wide): 32.9MM **Privately Held**
SIC: 8699 Athletic organizations
PA: United States Bowling Congress, Inc.
621 Six Flags Dr
Arlington TX 76011
817 385-8200

(G-4689)
UNITED WAY GREATER CINCINNATI (PA)
2400 Reading Rd (45202-1458)
PHONE....................................513 762-7100
Robert C Reifsnyder, *President*
Yvonne L Gray, *COO*
Jill Johnson, *Vice Pres*
Ross Meyer, *Vice Pres*
Lisa Kirk, *Accounting Mgr*
EMP: 100
SQ FT: 70,000
SALES: 61.2MM **Privately Held**
WEB: www.uwgc.org
SIC: 8322 Individual & family services

(G-4690)
UNITED-MAIER SIGNS INC
1030 Straight St (45214-1734)
PHONE....................................513 681-6600
Antony E Maier, *President*
Elvera Maier, *Vice Pres*
Chris Maier, *Opers Mgr*
Michele Wocher, *Human Resources*
EMP: 54 **EST:** 1964
SQ FT: 18,000
SALES (est): 7.9MM **Privately Held**
WEB: www.united-maier.com
SIC: 3993 1799 Electric signs; sign installation & maintenance

(G-4691)
UNITEDHEALTH GROUP INC
Also Called: United Healthcare
400 E Bus Way Ste 100 (45241)
PHONE....................................513 603-6200
Dorothy Coleman, *CEO*
Renee Cassella, *Facilities Mgr*
Laura Lynn, *Opers Staff*
Lucy Carr, *Accounts Exec*
Jennifer Michels, *Manager*
EMP: 270
SALES (corp-wide): 226.2B **Publicly Held**
WEB: www.unitedhealthgroup.com
SIC: 6324 Health maintenance organization (HMO), insurance only
PA: Unitedhealth Group Incorporated
9900 Bren Rd E Ste 300w
Minnetonka MN 55343
952 936-1300

(G-4692)
UNIV DERMATOLOGY
Also Called: Uc Health Dermatology
5575 Cheviot Rd Ste 1 (45247-7097)
PHONE....................................513 475-7630
Dr Raymond Ringenbach, *President*
BR Brian Adams, *President*
EMP: 100
SALES (est): 4.4MM **Privately Held**
SIC: 8011 8093 Dermatologist; specialty outpatient clinics

(G-4693)
UNIVERSAL ADVERTISING ASSOC
Also Called: Business Community Section
2530 Civic Center Dr (45231-1310)
P.O. Box 31132 (45231-0132)
PHONE....................................513 522-5000
Larry Vonderhaar, *President*
Ernie Yee Sr, *Sales Mgr*
Mary Fuhrman, *Sr Project Mgr*
Jane McCann, *Regional*
EMP: 49
SQ FT: 7,500
SALES (est): 7.2MM **Privately Held**
WEB: www.uaai.com
SIC: 7311 8611 Advertising consultant; business associations

(G-4694)
UNIVERSAL CONTRACTING CORP
5151 Fishwick Dr (45216-2215)
PHONE....................................513 482-2700
Phillip J Neumann, *President*
EMP: 30 **EST:** 1957
SQ FT: 7,500
SALES (est): 7.5MM **Privately Held**
SIC: 1541 1542 Industrial buildings, new construction; commercial & office building, new construction

(G-4695)
UNIVERSAL PACKG SYSTEMS INC
Also Called: Paklab
470 Northland Blvd (45240-3211)
PHONE....................................513 674-9400
Jeff Topits, *Branch Mgr*
EMP: 388
SALES (corp-wide): 399.6MM **Privately Held**
SIC: 2844 3565 7389 2671 Cosmetic preparations; bottling machinery: filling, capping, labeling; packaging & labeling services; plastic film, coated or laminated for packaging
PA: Universal Packaging Systems, Inc.
380 Townline Rd Ste 130
Hauppauge NY 11788
631 543-2277

(G-4696)
UNIVERSAL WORK AND POWER LLC
Also Called: Kemper Shuttle Services
6320 E Kemper Rd Ste 150 (45241-2394)
PHONE....................................513 981-1111
Miko Eminyan, *Mng Member*
Mkrtich Eminyan, *Mng Member*
EMP: 30
SALES (est): 316.7K **Privately Held**
SIC: 4111 4119 Local & suburban transit; local rental transportation

(G-4697)
UNIVERSITY CLUB INC
401 E 4th St (45202-3373)
PHONE....................................513 721-2600
Ron Koetters, *President*
Paul Satoril, *Treasurer*
EMP: 35
SQ FT: 35,000
SALES: 1.1MM **Privately Held**
SIC: 8641 Social club, membership

(G-4698)
UNIVERSITY DERMATOLOGY CONS
234 Goodman St A3 (45219-2364)
PHONE....................................513 584-4775
Diya Mutsin, *President*
David Astles, *Treasurer*
EMP: 40
SQ FT: 5,000
SALES (est): 1.6MM **Privately Held**
SIC: 8011 Dermatologist

(G-4699)
UNIVERSITY DERMATOLOGY CONS
222 Piedmont Ave Ste 5300 (45219-4215)
PHONE....................................513 475-7630
Diya F Mutasim, *President*
Brian Adams, *Med Doctor*

EMP: 50
SALES: 10.3MM **Privately Held**
SIC: 8011 Dermatologist

(G-4700)
UNIVERSITY FAMILY PHYSICIANS
2123 Auburn Ave (45219-2906)
PHONE....................513 929-0104
Laura J Ranz, *Branch Mgr*
EMP: 43
SALES (corp-wide): 3.6MM **Privately Held**
SIC: 8011 General & family practice, physician/surgeon
PA: University Family Physicians Inc
　3235 Eden Ave
　Cincinnati OH 45267
　513 558-4022

(G-4701)
UNIVERSITY FAMILY PHYSICIANS
Also Called: Wyoming Family Practice Center
175 W Galbraith Rd (45216-1015)
PHONE....................513 475-7505
Elouise Clark, *Manager*
Jean McAdams, *Manager*
EMP: 80
SALES (corp-wide): 3.6MM **Privately Held**
SIC: 8011 General & family practice, physician/surgeon
PA: University Family Physicians Inc
　3235 Eden Ave
　Cincinnati OH 45267
　513 558-4022

(G-4702)
UNIVERSITY NEUROLOGY INC
222 Piedmont Ave Ste 3200 (45219-4217)
PHONE....................513 475-8730
Joseph Broderick, *President*
Bratt Kissela, *Vice Pres*
Brett Kissela, *Vice Pres*
Neil Holsing, *Treasurer*
Alberto Espay, *Med Doctor*
EMP: 66
SALES: 7.7MM **Privately Held**
SIC: 8011 Neurologist

(G-4703)
UNIVERSITY OF CINCINNATI
Also Called: Department of Anesthetia
231 Albert Sabin Way (45267-2827)
PHONE....................513 558-4194
Mary Schaefer, *Business Mgr*
Steve Slezak, *Dept Chairman*
Arnold Miller, *Vice Pres*
Nancy C McNeal, *Electrical Engi*
John P Lawrence, *Med Doctor*
EMP: 35
SALES (corp-wide): 1.2B **Privately Held**
SIC: 8011 8221 Offices & clinics of medical doctors; university
PA: University Of Cincinnati
　2600 Clifton Ave
　Cincinnati OH 45220
　513 556-6000

(G-4704)
UNIVERSITY OF CINCINNATI
Also Called: University Hosp A & MBL Care
3200 Burnet Ave (45229-3019)
PHONE....................513 584-7522
Dudley Smith, *Principal*
EMP: 30
SALES (corp-wide): 1.2B **Privately Held**
SIC: 8062 8221 Hospital, medical school affiliation; university
PA: University Of Cincinnati
　2600 Clifton Ave
　Cincinnati OH 45220
　513 556-6000

(G-4705)
UNIVERSITY OF CINCINNATI
Also Called: University Hsptl-Uc Physicians
222 Piedmont Ave Ste 7000 (45219-4224)
PHONE....................513 475-8771
Michael Nussbaum, *CEO*
Tammy Millerwohl, *Opers Staff*
Cathy Maltbie, *Research*
George Meier, *Surgeon*
Rino Munda, *Surgeon*
EMP: 40

SALES (corp-wide): 1.2B **Privately Held**
SIC: 8011 8221 General & family practice, physician/surgeon; university
PA: University Of Cincinnati
　2600 Clifton Ave
　Cincinnati OH 45220
　513 556-6000

(G-4706)
UNIVERSITY OF CINCINNATI
Also Called: Blood Center
3130 Highland Ave Fl 3 (45219-2399)
P.O. Box 670055 (45267-0001)
PHONE....................513 558-1200
Howard Jackson, *Vice Pres*
Caroline Miller, *Assoc VP*
Ronald Sachner, *Director*
Jim Tinker, *Director*
Tina Sandfoss, *Program Dir*
EMP: 300
SALES (corp-wide): 1.2B **Privately Held**
SIC: 8011 8221 Offices & clinics of medical doctors; university
PA: University Of Cincinnati
　2600 Clifton Ave
　Cincinnati OH 45220
　513 556-6000

(G-4707)
UNIVERSITY OF CINCINNATI
Also Called: Administration Services Dept
51 Goodman St (45219-2477)
P.O. Box 210080 (45221-0080)
PHONE....................513 556-6381
James Tucker, *Director*
EMP: 1600
SALES (corp-wide): 1.2B **Privately Held**
SIC: 8221 7349 5812 0782 University; building maintenance services; eating places; lawn & garden services
PA: University Of Cincinnati
　2600 Clifton Ave
　Cincinnati OH 45220
　513 556-6000

(G-4708)
UNIVERSITY OF CINCINNATI
Also Called: Endocrine Lab
3125 Eden Ave (45219-2293)
P.O. Box 670547 (45267-0001)
PHONE....................513 558-4444
David A'Lessio, *Manager*
EMP: 30
SQ FT: 1,203
SALES (corp-wide): 1.2B **Privately Held**
SIC: 8071 8221 Medical laboratories; university
PA: University Of Cincinnati
　2600 Clifton Ave
　Cincinnati OH 45220
　513 556-6000

(G-4709)
UNIVERSITY OF CINCINNATI
260 Stetson St Ste 5300 (45219-2450)
P.O. Box 19614 (45219-0614)
PHONE....................513 556-5511
Michelle Altenau, *Director*
Joseph Broderick, *Program Dir*
Joanna Bordenave, *Administration*
Aristide Merola, *Neurology*
Katie Perkins, *Assistant*
EMP: 32
SALES (corp-wide): 1.2B **Privately Held**
SIC: 8731 Commercial physical research
PA: University Of Cincinnati
　2600 Clifton Ave
　Cincinnati OH 45220
　513 556-6000

(G-4710)
UNIVERSITY OF CINCINNATI
Also Called: University Hosp Rdilology Dept
234 Goodman St 761 (45219-2364)
PHONE....................513 584-4396
Robert Lukin MD, *Chairman*
Shelly Kirby, *Anesthesiology*
Andrea Merkel, *Anesthesiology*
Bethany Schmidt, *Anesthesiology*
Amanda Workman, *Anesthesiology*
EMP: 30
SALES (corp-wide): 1.2B **Privately Held**
SIC: 8062 8221 General medical & surgical hospitals; university

PA: University Of Cincinnati
　2600 Clifton Ave
　Cincinnati OH 45220
　513 556-6000

(G-4711)
UNIVERSITY OF CINCINNATI
Also Called: McMicken College of Asa
146 Mcmicken Hall (45221-0001)
PHONE....................513 556-5087
Peg Ellensworth, *Principal*
EMP: 2000
SALES (corp-wide): 1.2B **Privately Held**
SIC: 8999 8221 Communication services; university
PA: University Of Cincinnati
　2600 Clifton Ave
　Cincinnati OH 45220
　513 556-6000

(G-4712)
UNIVERSITY OF CINCINNATI
Also Called: Ucvp For Research
2614 Mecken Cir (45221-0001)
PHONE....................513 556-4054
Nedille Pinto, *Principal*
EMP: 28
SALES (corp-wide): 1.2B **Privately Held**
SIC: 8221 8732 University; educational research
PA: University Of Cincinnati
　2600 Clifton Ave
　Cincinnati OH 45220
　513 556-6000

(G-4713)
UNIVERSITY OF CINCINNATI
Also Called: Institute Environmental Health
3223 Eden Avenue (45267-0001)
P.O. Box 6756 (45206-0756)
PHONE....................513 558-5439
Neville Tam, *Research*
Marshall W Anderson, *Director*
Kenneth Skau, *Professor*
EMP: 200
SALES (corp-wide): 1.2B **Privately Held**
SIC: 8071 8221 Medical laboratories; university
PA: University Of Cincinnati
　2600 Clifton Ave
　Cincinnati OH 45220
　513 556-6000

(G-4714)
UNIVERSITY OF CINCINNATI
Also Called: University Cincinnati Book Str
51 W Goodman Dr (45221-0001)
PHONE....................513 556-4200
Mike Zimmerman, *Branch Mgr*
EMP: 50
SALES (corp-wide): 1.2B **Privately Held**
SIC: 8741 5942 Administrative management; book stores
PA: University Of Cincinnati
　2600 Clifton Ave
　Cincinnati OH 45220
　513 556-6000

(G-4715)
UNIVERSITY OF CINCINNATI
Also Called: Uima
231 Albert Sabin Way (45267-2827)
PHONE....................513 558-4231
B E Martin, *Treasurer*
Bradley Britigan, *Branch Mgr*
Robert Baughman, *Professor*
EMP: 150
SALES (corp-wide): 1.2B **Privately Held**
SIC: 8741 Administrative management; university
PA: University Of Cincinnati
　2600 Clifton Ave
　Cincinnati OH 45220
　513 556-6000

(G-4716)
UNIVERSITY OF CINCINNATI
Also Called: Breast Consultation Center
234 Goodman St (45219-2364)
PHONE....................513 584-5331
Mary Mahoney, *Exec Dir*
Carolyn Thomas, *Director*
Teresa Williams, *Lab Dir*
EMP: 55

PA: University Of Cincinnati
　2600 Clifton Ave
　Cincinnati OH 45220
　513 556-6000

(G-4717)
UNIVERSITY OF CINCINNATI
Also Called: Geological Department
500 Geo Physics Bldg 5f (45221-0001)
P.O. Box 2210030
PHONE....................513 556-3732
Arnold Miller, *Principal*
Jeff Havig, *Professor*
EMP: 40
SALES (corp-wide): 1.2B **Privately Held**
SIC: 8221 8711 University; engineering services
PA: University Of Cincinnati
　2600 Clifton Ave
　Cincinnati OH 45220
　513 556-6000

(G-4718)
UNIVERSITY OF CINCINNATI
Also Called: Athletics Dept
2751 O'vrsity Way Ste 880 (45221-0001)
P.O. Box 210021 (45221-0021)
PHONE....................513 556-4603
Greg Bruner, *Opers Staff*
Andrew Kolb, *Manager*
Mike Bohn, *Director*
Niki Cianciola, *Director*
Jennifer Sturm, *Director*
EMP: 140
SALES (corp-wide): 1.2B **Privately Held**
SIC: 8699 8221 Athletic organizations; university
PA: University Of Cincinnati
　2600 Clifton Ave
　Cincinnati OH 45220
　513 556-6000

(G-4719)
UNIVERSITY OF CINCINNATI
Also Called: Consolidated Utilities
3001 Short Vine St (45219-2024)
PHONE....................513 558-1799
Sallie Troutman, *Director*
EMP: 60
SALES (corp-wide): 1.2B **Privately Held**
SIC: 4939 8221 Combination utilities; university
PA: University Of Cincinnati
　2600 Clifton Ave
　Cincinnati OH 45220
　513 556-6000

(G-4720)
UNIVERSITY OF CINCINNATI
Also Called: Cancer Center
234 Goodman St (45219-2364)
PHONE....................513 584-3200
Barbara Stumps, *Manager*
EMP: 150
SALES (corp-wide): 1.2B **Privately Held**
SIC: 8093 8221 Specialty outpatient clinics; university
PA: University Of Cincinnati
　2600 Clifton Ave
　Cincinnati OH 45220
　513 556-6000

(G-4721)
UNIVERSITY OF CINCINNATI
Also Called: Nephrology Department
231 Albert Sabin Way G258 (45267-2827)
P.O. Box 670585 (45267-0001)
PHONE....................513 558-5471
Manoocher Soleimani, *Director*
Junhang Dong, *Professor*
Charuhas Thakar, *Assoc Prof*
EMP: 50
SALES (corp-wide): 1.2B **Privately Held**
SIC: 8011 8221 Nephrologist; university
PA: University Of Cincinnati
　2600 Clifton Ave
　Cincinnati OH 45220
　513 556-6000

(G-4722)
UNIVERSITY OF CINCINNATI
222 Piedmont Ave Ste 6000 (45219-4223)
PHONE....................513 475-8524

Faisal Syed, *Med Doctor*
Faisal M Syed, *Director*
EMP: 67
SALES (corp-wide): 1.2B **Privately Held**
SIC: 8011 Internal medicine, physician/surgeon
PA: University Of Cincinnati
2600 Clifton Ave
Cincinnati OH 45220
513 556-6000

(G-4723)
UNIVERSITY OF CINCINNATI
Also Called: Univ Hospital, The
331 Albert Sabin Way (45229-2838)
PHONE..............................513 584-1000
Mark Slye, *Branch Mgr*
Lisa Ann, *Director*
Stanley Corkin, *Professor*
EMP: 30
SALES (corp-wide): 1.2B **Privately Held**
SIC: 8062 8221 Hospital, medical school affiliation; university
PA: University Of Cincinnati
2600 Clifton Ave
Cincinnati OH 45220
513 556-6000

(G-4724)
UNIVERSITY OF CINCINNATI
Also Called: Pulmonary Division
231 Albert Sabin Way (45267-2827)
PHONE..............................513 558-4831
Melanie Maughlin, *Med Doctor*
Michael Newton, *Med Doctor*
Dee Douglas, *Manager*
EMP: 25
SALES (corp-wide): 1.2B **Privately Held**
SIC: 8011 8221 Pulmonary specialist, physician/surgeon; university
PA: University Of Cincinnati
2600 Clifton Ave
Cincinnati OH 45220
513 556-6000

(G-4725)
UNIVERSITY OF CINCINNATI
Also Called: University Hospital
234 Goodman St (45219-2364)
PHONE..............................513 584-1000
Yong Kim, *Ch of Bd*
Doug Jarrold, *VP Finance*
Kenneth Hanover, *Branch Mgr*
Breck D Finzer, *Med Doctor*
Arthur Pancioli, *Med Doctor*
EMP: 30
SALES (corp-wide): 1.2B **Privately Held**
SIC: 8062 8221 General medical & surgical hospitals; university
PA: University Of Cincinnati
2600 Clifton Ave
Cincinnati OH 45220
513 556-6000

(G-4726)
UNIVERSITY OF CINCINNATI
Also Called: Arlette Child Family Rese
Edwards 1 Bldg (45221-0001)
P.O. Box 210105 (45221-0105)
PHONE..............................513 556-3803
Vicky Carr, *Director*
EMP: 60
SALES (corp-wide): 1.2B **Privately Held**
SIC: 8322 8221 Child related social services; university
PA: University Of Cincinnati
2600 Clifton Ave
Cincinnati OH 45220
513 556-6000

(G-4727)
UNIVERSITY OF CNCNNATI
SRGEONS (PA)
2830 Victory Pkwy Ste 320 (45206-3700)
P.O. Box 630251 (45263-0251)
PHONE..........................,.513 245-3300
Tal Richards, *President*
EMP: 50
SALES (est): 11.9MM **Privately Held**
SIC: 8011 Surgeon

(G-4728)
UNIVERSITY ORTHOPAEDIC
CNSLTNT
Also Called: Angelo J Colosimo MD
222 Piedmont Ave Ste 2200 (45219-4238)
P.O. Box 670212 (45267-0001)
PHONE..............................513 475-8690
Peter Stern, *President*
Angelo Colosimo, *Med Doctor*
EMP: 50
SALES (est): 2.3MM **Privately Held**
SIC: 8011 Orthopedic physician

(G-4729)
UNIVERSITY RADIOLOGY
ASSOC
Also Called: Uc Health
222 Piedmont Ave Ste 2100 (45219-4238)
PHONE..............................513 475-8760
Karen Krebs, *Principal*
Lisa Renner, *Business Mgr*
Steven Knost, *Technology*
EMP: 100
SALES (est): 2MM **Privately Held**
SIC: 8011 8093 Radiologist; specialty outpatient clinics

(G-4730)
UNIVERSTY OF CINCINNTI
MEDCL C (HQ)
234 Goodman St (45219-2364)
PHONE..............................513 584-1000
Bryan Gibler, *CEO*
Arthur T Evans II, *Ch OB/GYN*
Christopher Johns, *Med Doctor*
Caitlyn Kenny, *Med Doctor*
Erin Requarth, *Med Doctor*
▲ **EMP:** 39
SALES (est): 913.1MM **Privately Held**
SIC: 8062 General medical & surgical hospitals

(G-4731)
UPSCALE LAWNCRE & PRPRTY
MAINT
Also Called: Upscale Lawn Care
4200 N Bend Rd (45211-2604)
PHONE..............................513 266-1165
Chris Gum, *President*
EMP: 35
SALES (est): 192.8K **Privately Held**
SIC: 0782 Lawn care services

(G-4732)
UPTOWN RENTAL PROPERTIES
LLC
2718 Short Vine St (45219-2019)
PHONE..............................513 861-9394
Shane Studer, *Opers Staff*
Jessica Stringfield, *Marketing Staff*
Angie Reynolds, *Property Mgr*
Patrice Burke, *Director*
Ann Johnston, *Director*
EMP: 45
SQ FT: 2,289
SALES (est): 6.9MM **Privately Held**
WEB: www.uptownrents.com
SIC: 6513 Apartment building operators

(G-4733)
URBAN LEAGUE OF GREATER
SOUTHW
3458 Reading Rd (45229-3128)
PHONE..............................513 281-9955
Donna Jones Baker, *President*
Jeanette Shoecraft, *General Mgr*
Cato Mayberry, *Vice Pres*
Angela Williams, *Vice Pres*
Angelina Hollis, *Info Tech Mgr*
EMP: 54
SQ FT: 27,000
SALES: 6.1MM **Privately Held**
SIC: 8399 Community development groups

(G-4734)
URBAN ONE INC
Also Called: Wizf-FM
1821 Summit Rd Ste 400 (45237-2822)
PHONE..............................513 749-1009
Alfred Leggins, *Owner*
EMP: 50

SALES (corp-wide): 439.1MM **Publicly Held**
WEB: www.radio-one.com
SIC: 4832 Radio broadcasting stations
PA: Urban One, Inc.
1010 Wayne Ave Fl 14
Silver Spring MD 20910
301 429-3200

(G-4735)
URBAN ONE INC
Also Called: Blue Chip Broadcasting
705 Central Ave Ste 200 (45202-1900)
PHONE..............................513 679-6000
Jeri Tolliver, *Branch Mgr*
EMP: 40
SALES (corp-wide): 439.1MM **Publicly Held**
WEB: www.radio-one.com
SIC: 4832 Radio broadcasting stations
PA: Urban One, Inc.
1010 Wayne Ave Fl 14
Silver Spring MD 20910
301 429-3200

(G-4736)
URBAN RETAIL PROPERTIES
LLC
Also Called: Kenwood Management
7875 Montgomery Rd (45236-4344)
PHONE..............................513 346-4482
Wanda Wagner, *General Mgr*
EMP: 25
SALES (corp-wide): 49.2MM **Privately Held**
WEB: www.kaanapali-golf.com
SIC: 6552 Subdividers & developers
HQ: Urban Retail Properties, Llc
111 E Wacker Dr Ste 2400
Chicago IL 60601

(G-4737)
URS GROUP INC
525 Vine St Ste 1900 (45202-3124)
PHONE..............................513 651-3440
Margaret Yocom, *Sales Executive*
Glenn Armstrong, *Branch Mgr*
EMP: 69
SALES (corp-wide): 20.1B **Publicly Held**
SIC: 8711 Engineering services
HQ: Urs Group, Inc.
300 S Grand Ave Ste 1100
Los Angeles CA 90071
213 593-8000

(G-4738)
US BANK NATIONAL
ASSOCIATION (HQ)
Also Called: US Bank
425 Walnut St Fl 14 (45202-3989)
PHONE..............................513 632-4234
Richard K Davis, *Ch of Bd*
Steven Bennett, *President*
Marsha Cruzan, *President*
Mahesh Kharkar, *President*
Donna McMillin, *President*
◆ **EMP:** 1150
SQ FT: 244,000
SALES: 23.4B
SALES (corp-wide): 25.7B **Publicly Held**
WEB: www.firstar.com
SIC: 6021 National commercial banks
PA: U.S. Bancorp
800 Nicollet Mall # 1500
Minneapolis MN 55402
651 466-3000

(G-4739)
US BANK NATIONAL
ASSOCIATION
Also Called: US Bank
5065 Wooster Rd (45226-2326)
PHONE..............................513 979-1000
Diane Johnson, *Branch Mgr*
EMP: 800
SALES (corp-wide): 25.7B **Publicly Held**
SIC: 6021 National commercial banks
HQ: U.S. Bank National Association
425 Walnut St Fl 14
Cincinnati OH 45202
513 632-4234

(G-4740)
US BANK NATIONAL
ASSOCIATION
Also Called: US Bank
2300 Wall St Ste A (45212-2742)
PHONE..............................513 458-2844
Sandy Metcalf, *Branch Mgr*
EMP: 50
SALES (corp-wide): 25.7B **Publicly Held**
SIC: 6021 National commercial banks
HQ: U.S. Bank National Association
425 Walnut St Fl 14
Cincinnati OH 45202
513 632-4234

(G-4741)
US INSPECTION SERVICES INC
502 W Crescentville Rd (45246-1222)
PHONE..............................513 671-7073
Ed Graham, *Branch Mgr*
EMP: 35
SALES (corp-wide): 1.6B **Privately Held**
SIC: 8734 Testing laboratories
HQ: U.S. Inspection Services, Inc.
7333 Paragon Rd Ste 240
Dayton OH 45459

(G-4742)
US PROTECTION SERVICE LLC
Also Called: Now Security Group
1850 W Galbraith Rd (45239-4851)
PHONE..............................513 422-7910
Michael Pendleton, *Branch Mgr*
EMP: 54
SALES (corp-wide): 4.9MM **Privately Held**
SIC: 7381 7389 Security guard service; private investigator; commodities sampling
PA: U.S. Protection Service Llc
5785 Emporium Sq
Columbus OH 43231
614 794-4950

(G-4743)
US SECURITY ASSOCIATES INC
230 Northland Blvd # 307 (45246-0016)
PHONE..............................513 381-7033
Lisa K Crawford, *Owner*
EMP: 108
SALES (corp-wide): 13.5MM **Privately Held**
SIC: 7381 Security guard service
HQ: U.S. Security Associates, Inc.
200 Mansell Ct E Fl 5
Roswell GA 30076

(G-4744)
USI MIDWEST LLC (DH)
312 Elm St Ste 24 (45202-2992)
PHONE..............................513 852-6300
Thomas Cassady, *CEO*
Tom Cassady, *President*
Ron Eslick, *Vice Pres*
Katone Roberts, *Executive Asst*
▲ **EMP:** 111
SQ FT: 24,000
SALES: 200MM **Privately Held**
SIC: 6411 Insurance agents

(G-4745)
USIC LOCATING SERVICES LLC
3478 Hauck Rd Ste D (45241-4604)
PHONE..............................513 554-0456
Tom Mox, *Director*
EMP: 100 **Privately Held**
SIC: 1623 Underground utilities contractor
HQ: Usic Locating Services, Llc
9045 River Rd Ste 300
Indianapolis IN 46240
317 575-7800

(G-4746)
UTS INC
P.O. Box 36342 (45236-0342)
PHONE..............................513 332-9000
John Broke, *Principal*
EMP: 25
SALES (est): 474.9K **Privately Held**
SIC: 8748 Telecommunications consultant

(G-4747)
VALLEY INTERIOR SYSTEMS INC (PA)
2203 Fowler St (45206-2307)
P.O. Box 68109 (45206-8109)
PHONE.................................513 961-0400
Mike Strawser, *CEO*
Jeff Hudepohl, *President*
Todd Brandenburg, *Superintendent*
Eric Johnson, *Superintendent*
Darrell Woodruff, *Superintendent*
EMP: 350
SQ FT: 9,000
SALES (est): 70.4MM **Privately Held**
SIC: 1742 Drywall; acoustical & ceiling work; plastering, plain or ornamental

(G-4748)
VALVOLINE INC
4050 River Rd (45204-1036)
PHONE.................................513 451-1753
Jerry Erow, *Branch Mgr*
EMP: 54
SALES (corp-wide): 2.2B **Publicly Held**
SIC: 5984 7549 Liquefied petroleum gas dealers; lubrication service, automotive
PA: Valvoline Inc.
  100 Valvoline Way
  Lexington KY 40509
  859 357-7777

(G-4749)
VALVOLINE LLC
3901 River Rd (45204-1033)
PHONE.................................513 557-3100
Patrick Nelson, *General Mgr*
Missy Voges, *Cust Svc Dir*
James Jones, *Branch Mgr*
EMP: 100
SALES (corp-wide): 2B **Publicly Held**
SIC: 7549 Automotive maintenance services
HQ: Valvoline Llc
  100 Valvoline Way
  Lexington KY 40509
  859 357-7777

(G-4750)
VAN PELT CORPORATION
Also Called: Service Steel Div
5170 Broerman Ave (45217-1140)
PHONE.................................513 242-6000
Ron Wood, *Branch Mgr*
Todd McEntyre, *Manager*
EMP: 25
SQ FT: 55,000
SALES (corp-wide): 30.5MM **Privately Held**
WEB: www.servicesteel.com
SIC: 5051 Steel
PA: Van Pelt Corporation
  36155 Mound Rd
  Sterling Heights MI 48310
  313 365-3600

(G-4751)
VARNEY DISPATCH INC
4 Triangle Park Dr # 404 (45246-3401)
PHONE.................................513 682-4200
EMP: 40
SQ FT: 22,000
SALES (est): 3.7MM **Privately Held**
SIC: 4212 Local Trucking Operator

(G-4752)
VELCO INC
Also Called: Coit
10280 Chester Rd (45215-1200)
PHONE.................................513 772-4226
Dennis Desserich, *President*
Douglas Desserich, *Treasurer*
EMP: 38
SQ FT: 27,000
SALES: 2.9MM **Privately Held**
WEB: www.restoraid.net
SIC: 7217 7216 Carpet & furniture cleaning on location; upholstery cleaning on customer premises; curtain cleaning & repair

(G-4753)
VENCO VENTURO INDUSTRIES LLC (PA)
Also Called: Venco/Venturo Div
12110 Best Pl (45241-1569)
PHONE.................................513 772-8448
Brett Collins, *President*
Dave Foster, *Vice Pres*
Mike Strittholt, *CFO*
▲ EMP: 41
SQ FT: 100,000
SALES (est): 18.3MM **Privately Held**
WEB: www.venturo.com
SIC: 3713 5012 3714 5084 Truck bodies (motor vehicles); truck bodies; motor vehicle parts & accessories; cranes, industrial

(G-4754)
VENTURO MANUFACTURING INC
12110 Best Pl (45241-1569)
PHONE.................................513 772-8448
Larry Collins, *President*
Ronald A Collins, *Vice Pres*
Jeremy Sapp, *Purchasing*
Joe Dirr, *QC Mgr*
Stuart Phipps, *Design Engr*
EMP: 32 EST: 1952
SQ FT: 5,000
SALES (est): 9MM
SALES (corp-wide): 18.3MM **Privately Held**
WEB: www.venturo.com
SIC: 3537 5084 Cranes, industrial truck; industrial machinery & equipment
PA: Venco Venturo Industries Llc
  12110 Best Pl
  Cincinnati OH 45241
  513 772-8448

(G-4755)
VERSATEX LLC
324 W 9th St (45202-2043)
PHONE.................................513 639-3119
Gerald Sparkman, *President*
Constance A Hill, *Legal Staff*
EMP: 40
SQ FT: 4,000
SALES (est): 6.5MM
SALES (corp-wide): 137.4MM **Privately Held**
SIC: 8742 Business consultant
PA: D.E. Foxx & Associates, Inc.
  324 W 9th St Fl 5
  Cincinnati OH 45202
  513 621-5522

(G-4756)
VERST GROUP LOGISTICS INC
Zenith Logistics
98 Glendale Milford Rd (45215-1101)
PHONE.................................513 782-1725
Rich Grau, *Vice Pres*
EMP: 240
SALES (corp-wide): 59.2MM **Privately Held**
SIC: 4225 General warehousing & storage
PA: Verst Group Logistics, Inc.
  300 Shorland Dr
  Walton KY 41094
  859 485-1212

(G-4757)
VERST GROUP LOGISTICS INC
11880 Enterprise Dr (45241-1512)
PHONE.................................513 772-2494
Jeff Antrobus, *Branch Mgr*
Pam Dumaine, *Technology*
EMP: 30
SALES (corp-wide): 59.2MM **Privately Held**
WEB: www.verstgroup.com
SIC: 4225 4731 8741 General warehousing & storage; freight transportation arrangement; management services
PA: Verst Group Logistics, Inc.
  300 Shorland Dr
  Walton KY 41094
  859 485-1212

(G-4758)
VETERAN SECURITY PATROL CO
36 E 7th St Ste 2201 (45202-4453)
PHONE.................................513 381-4482

Pat Navin, *Branch Mgr*
EMP: 225 **Privately Held**
WEB: www.veteransecurity.com
SIC: 7381 Security guard service
PA: Veteran Security Patrol Co.
  215 Taylor Ave
  Bellevue KY 41073

(G-4759)
VETERANS HEALTH ADMINISTRATION
Also Called: Cincinnati V A Medical Center
3200 Vine St (45220-2213)
PHONE.................................513 861-3100
Timothy Roth, *Manager*
Craig Ryan, *Director*
EMP: 1200 **Publicly Held**
WEB: www.veterans-ru.org
SIC: 8011 9451 Medical centers; administration of veterans' affairs;
HQ: Veterans Health Administration
  810 Vermont Ave Nw
  Washington DC 20420

(G-4760)
VETERANS HEALTH ADMINISTRATION
Also Called: Clermont County Community
4600 Beechwood Rd (45244-1809)
PHONE.................................513 943-3680
Donna Witt, *Branch Mgr*
EMP: 263 **Publicly Held**
WEB: www.veterans-ru.org
SIC: 8011 9451 Clinic, operated by physicians; psychiatric clinic;
HQ: Veterans Health Administration
  810 Vermont Ave Nw
  Washington DC 20420

(G-4761)
VISITING NURSE ASSOCIAT (PA)
2400 Reading Rd Ste 207 (45202-1468)
PHONE.................................513 345-8000
Valerie Landell, *CEO*
Trudy Schwab, *Exec VP*
EMP: 180
SQ FT: 11,492
SALES: 5.7MM **Privately Held**
SIC: 8082 Home health care services

(G-4762)
VITAS HEALTHCARE CORPORATION
11500 Northlake Dr # 400 (45249-1658)
PHONE.................................513 742-6310
Joe Killian, *General Mgr*
Daniel Lubrecht, *General Mgr*
EMP: 95
SALES (corp-wide): 1.7B **Publicly Held**
WEB: www.vitasinnovativehospicecare.com
SIC: 8052 Personal care facility
HQ: Vitas Healthcare Corporation
  201 S Biscayne Blvd # 400
  Miami FL 33131
  305 374-4143

(G-4763)
VIVIAL MEDIA LLC
720 E Pete Rose Way # 350 (45202-3576)
PHONE.................................513 768-7800
EMP: 37
SALES (corp-wide): 31.3MM **Privately Held**
SIC: 8721 Accounting, auditing & bookkeeping
PA: Vivial Media Llc
  160 Inverness Dr W # 250
  Englewood CO 80112
  303 867-1600

(G-4764)
VOLT MANAGEMENT CORP
Also Called: Volt Workforce Solutions
8044 Montgomery Rd # 630 (45236-2919)
PHONE.................................513 791-2600
Ed Coleman, *Branch Mgr*
EMP: 56
SALES (corp-wide): 1B **Publicly Held**
SIC: 7363 Help supply services
HQ: Volt Management Corp.
  50 Charles Lindbergh Blvd # 206
  Uniondale NY 11553

(G-4765)
VORYS SATER SEYMOUR PEASE LLP
301 E 4th St Ste 3410 (45202-4257)
P.O. Box 236 (45201-0236)
PHONE.................................513 723-4000
Thomas Gabelman, *Partner*
Roger Lautenhiser, *Principal*
Weigel W Breck,
Sheilah Duncan,
Eugene P Ruehlman,
EMP: 125
SALES (corp-wide): 133.4MM **Privately Held**
SIC: 8111 Corporate, partnership & business law
PA: Vorys, Sater, Seymour And Pease Llp
  52 E Gay St
  Columbus OH 43215
  614 464-6400

(G-4766)
W L W T T V 5
1700 Young St (45202-6821)
PHONE.................................513 412-5000
Fax: 513 412-6121
EMP: 150
SALES (est): 415.4K **Privately Held**
SIC: 4833 Television Station

(G-4767)
W P DOLLE LLC
201 E 5th St Ste 1000 (45202-4188)
PHONE.................................513 421-6515
Stephen Campbell, *CPA*
Marcie Carey, *Accounts Exec*
Gerry Stricker, *Accounts Exec*
David Poignard, *Sales Staff*
Mark Rummler,
EMP: 25
SQ FT: 18,000
SALES (est): 4.4MM **Privately Held**
SIC: 6411 Insurance agents

(G-4768)
WALNUT HILLS PRESERVATION LP
Also Called: Walnut Hills Apartments
861 Beecher St Ofc Ofc (45206-1571)
PHONE.................................513 281-1288
George Buchanan, *Partner*
Leeann Morein, *Principal*
EMP: 99
SALES: 950K **Privately Held**
SIC: 6513 Apartment building operators

(G-4769)
WALTER ALEXANDER ENTPS INC
Also Called: Cincinnati Vending Company
1940 Losantiville Ave (45237-4106)
PHONE.................................513 841-1100
Richard Walter, *President*
Norman Alexander, *COO*
EMP: 27
SQ FT: 8,000
SALES (est): 2.7MM **Privately Held**
WEB: www.cincinnativending.com
SIC: 5962 7389 Food vending machines; coffee service

(G-4770)
WATERFRONT & ASSOCIATES INC
Also Called: South Beach Grille
700 Walnut St Ste 200 (45202-2015)
PHONE.................................859 581-1414
Jeff Ruby, *President*
EMP: 400
SQ FT: 30,000
SALES (est): 6.3MM **Privately Held**
SIC: 5812 5813 6512 Grills (eating places); bar (drinking places); auditorium & hall operation

(G-4771)
WAYPOINT AVIATION LLC
4765 Airport Rd (45226-1613)
PHONE.................................800 769-4765
Mark Davis, *President*
EMP: 25
SQ FT: 50,000
SALES: 10K **Privately Held**
SIC: 7363 Pilot service, aviation

▲ = Import ▼=Export
◆ =Import/Export

(G-4772)
WEED MAN LAWNCARE LLC
12100 Phanpion Way (45241)
PHONE..................................513 683-6310
Mike Ward, *Mng Member*
EMP: 40
SALES (est): 703.5K **Privately Held**
SIC: 0782 Lawn care services

(G-4773)
WEGMAN CONSTRUCTION COMPANY
Also Called: Wegman Company
1101 York St Ste 500 (45214-2131)
PHONE..................................513 381-1111
Joseph Wegman, *Ch of Bd*
Scott Wegman, *President*
Melissa Wegman, *Vice Pres*
EMP: 50
SQ FT: 175,000
SALES (est): 9.2MM **Privately Held**
WEB: www.wegmancompany.com
SIC: 1799 7389 Office furniture installation; relocation service

(G-4774)
WELCH HOLDINGS INC
8953 E Miami River Rd (45247-2232)
PHONE..................................513 353-3220
James R Welch, *President*
Ronnie L Welch, *Treasurer*
EMP: 45
SQ FT: 3,400
SALES (est): 4.4MM **Privately Held**
WEB: www.welchsand.com
SIC: 1442 Common sand mining; gravel mining

(G-4775)
WELD PLUS INC
4790 River Rd (45233-1633)
PHONE..................................513 941-4411
Laurie Rensing, *Ch of Bd*
Paul Rensing, *President*
Elizabeth Byrum, *General Mgr*
Daniel Hughes, *Opers Mgr*
Matt Schumm, *Warehouse Mgr*
EMP: 30
SQ FT: 42,000
SALES: 8.4MM **Privately Held**
WEB: www.weldplus.com
SIC: 5084 Welding machinery & equipment

(G-4776)
WELLS FARGO CLEARING SVCS LLC
Also Called: Wells Fargo Advisors
255 E 5th St Ste 1400 (45202-4184)
PHONE..................................513 241-9900
Art Fischer, *Manager*
Adam Boerger, *Agent*
Eric Greenwell, *Advisor*
EMP: 40
SALES (corp-wide): 101B **Publicly Held**
SIC: 6211 Brokers, security
HQ: Wells Fargo Clearing Services, Llc
1 N Jefferson Ave Fl 7
Saint Louis MO 63103
314 955-3000

(G-4777)
WELTMAN WEINBERG & REIS CO LPA
525 Vine St Ste 800 (45202-3171)
PHONE..................................513 723-2200
Nicole Smith, *Chief Mktg Ofcr*
Frank Veneziano, *Manager*
EMP: 151
SALES (corp-wide): 151.3MM **Privately Held**
SIC: 8111 General practice law office
PA: Weltman, Weinberg & Reis Co., L.P.A.
323 W Lkeside Ave Ste 200
Cleveland OH 44113
216 685-1000

(G-4778)
WESBANCO BANK INC
5511 Cheviot Rd (45247-7003)
PHONE..................................513 741-5766
Susan Osterhage, *Manager*
EMP: 45
SQ FT: 4,670

SALES (corp-wide): 515.2MM **Publicly Held**
WEB: www.realtydoneright.net
SIC: 6022 State commercial banks
HQ: Wesbanco Bank, Inc.
1 Bank Plz
Wheeling WV 26003
304 234-9000

(G-4779)
WESLEY COMMUNITY SERVICES LLC
2091 Radcliff Dr (45204-1853)
PHONE..................................513 661-2777
Ericka Dansby, *Superintendent*
Robin Rodgers, *Principal*
Brenda Stier, *CFO*
Michael Durr, *Finance*
Barb Macke, *Human Res Mgr*
EMP: 90
SALES: 2.9MM **Privately Held**
SIC: 8322 Geriatric social service

(G-4780)
WESLEY EDUC CNTR FOR CHLDRN
525 Hale Ave (45229-3105)
PHONE..................................513 569-1840
Rita Bryant, *CEO*
Carla Butler, *Principal*
Rick Wagner, *Chairman*
Rose Palmieri, *Admin Sec*
EMP: 45 EST: 1920
SALES (est): 791.7K **Privately Held**
SIC: 8351 Group day care center

(G-4781)
WEST CHESTER HOLDINGS LLC
Also Called: West Chester Protective Gear
11500 Canal Rd (45241-1862)
PHONE..................................800 647-1900
Tim Fogarty, *CEO*
Mark J Jahnke, *President*
Ken Meyer, *President*
Robert W Fisher, *Corp Secy*
Mike Derge, *Vice Pres*
▲ EMP: 110
SQ FT: 200,000
SALES (corp-wide): 1.9B **Privately Held**
SIC: 3842 2381 5136 5137 Clothing, fire resistant & protective; gloves, work: woven or knit, made from purchased materials; men's & boys' clothing; women's & children's clothing; safety equipment & supplies
HQ: Protective Industrial Products, Inc.
968 Albany Shaker Rd
Latham NY 12110
518 861-0133

(G-4782)
WEST END HEALTH CENTER INC
1413 Linn St (45214-2605)
PHONE..................................513 621-2726
Wendell Walker, *Exec Dir*
EMP: 28
SQ FT: 4,500
SALES: 212.2K **Privately Held**
SIC: 8093 Specialty outpatient clinics

(G-4783)
WEST PARK RETIREMENT COMMUNITY
Also Called: Mercy House Partners
2950 West Park Dr Ofc (45238-3542)
PHONE..................................513 451-8900
Kendra Couch, *President*
Donald Stinnett, *Treasurer*
EMP: 200
SQ FT: 206,000
SALES (est): 1.5MM **Privately Held**
SIC: 8052 8051 Personal care facility; extended care facility

(G-4784)
WEST SHELL COMMERCIAL INC
Also Called: Colliers International
425 Walnut St Ste 1200 (45202-3993)
PHONE..................................513 721-4200
Shenan Murphy, *President*
Michael Daly, *Vice Pres*
Michael Finke, *Vice Pres*

William Keefer, *Vice Pres*
Meredith Gurren, *Sr Consultant*
EMP: 55 EST: 2000
SQ FT: 11,000
SALES (est): 6.7MM **Privately Held**
WEB: www.westshell.com
SIC: 6531 Real estate agent, commercial

(G-4785)
WEST SIDE PEDIATRICS INC (PA)
663 Anderson Ferry Rd # 1 (45238-4798)
PHONE..................................513 922-8200
Lee Burroughs MD, *President*
R Scott Hunter, *Vice Pres*
EMP: 44
SALES (est): 7.8MM **Privately Held**
SIC: 8011 Pediatrician

(G-4786)
WESTERN & SOUTHERN LF INSUR CO (DH)
Also Called: Western-Southern Life
400 Broadway St (45202-3341)
P.O. Box 1119 (45201-1119)
PHONE..................................513 629-1800
John F Barrett, *President*
Marilyn Cobb, *President*
Dennis Dietz, *President*
David Dimartino, *President*
Donna Parobek, *President*
EMP: 982 EST: 1888
SQ FT: 600,000
SALES (est): 1.6B **Privately Held**
SIC: 6211 6311 2511 Investment firm, general brokerage; life insurance; play pens, children's: wood
HQ: Western & Southern Financial Group, Inc.
400 Broadway St
Cincinnati OH 45202
866 832-7719

(G-4787)
WESTERN FAMILY PHYSICIANS
3425 North Bend Rd Ste A (45239-7660)
PHONE..................................513 853-4900
R Stephen EBY, *President*
Lisbeth Lazaron, *Vice Pres*
Lisa Cantor, *Officer*
Richard Goldfarb, *Officer*
Jean Siebenaler, *Officer*
EMP: 31
SQ FT: 2,000
SALES (est): 3.6MM **Privately Held**
WEB: www.westernfamilyphysicians.com
SIC: 8011 General & family practice, physician/surgeon

(G-4788)
WESTERN HILLS CARE CENTER
6210 Cleves Warsaw Pike (45233-4510)
PHONE..................................513 941-0099
Barry A Kohn, *President*
Sam Boymel, *Chairman*
Rick Friedman, *Vice Pres*
EMP: 200
SQ FT: 150,000
SALES (est): 4.3MM **Privately Held**
WEB: www.whrv.com
SIC: 8051 Skilled nursing care facilities

(G-4789)
WESTERN HILLS COUNTRY CLUB
5780 Cleves Warsaw Pike (45233-4900)
P.O. Box 58644 (45258-0644)
PHONE..................................513 922-0011
Paul Garrett, *General Mgr*
Dana Cinorell, *COO*
EMP: 75
SQ FT: 20,000
SALES: 2.8MM **Privately Held**
SIC: 7997 Country club, membership

(G-4790)
WESTERN HILLS SPORTSPLEX INC (PA)
Also Called: Western Sports Mall
2323 Ferguson Rd Ste 1 (45238-3500)
PHONE..................................513 451-4900
John P Torbeck, *President*
Bobby Farley, *Owner*
Robert Czerwinski, *Vice Pres*
John L Torbeck, *Treasurer*

EMP: 75 EST: 1972
SQ FT: 40,000
SALES (est): 2.4MM **Privately Held**
WEB: www.westernsportsmall.net
SIC: 7997 7999 Tennis club, membership; racquetball club, membership; swimming club, membership; indoor court clubs; baseball batting cage

(G-4791)
WESTERN SOUTHERN MUTL HOLDG CO (PA)
400 Broadway St (45202-3341)
PHONE..................................866 832-7719
John F Barrett, *President*
Jonathan Niemeyer, *Senior VP*
Todd Henderson, *Vice Pres*
Kim Demaria, *Marketing Staff*
Nadia Norris, *Manager*
EMP: 1450
SALES (est): 3.3B **Privately Held**
SIC: 6211 Investment firm, general brokerage

(G-4792)
WESTERN STHERN FINCL GROUP INC (HQ)
400 Broadway St (45202-3312)
P.O. Box 1119 (45201-1119)
PHONE..................................866 832-7719
John F Barrett, *President*
Gary Enzweiler, *President*
Lisa Fangman, *President*
Donna Parobek, *President*
Eric Walzer, *President*
EMP: 1800
SALES: 3.3B **Privately Held**
WEB: www.westernsouthern.com
SIC: 6211 Investment firm, general brokerage

(G-4793)
WESTWAY TRML CINCINNATI LLC
3500 Southside Ave (45204-1138)
PHONE..................................513 921-8441
William Lindsey, *Mng Member*
EMP: 30
SQ FT: 12,000
SALES (est): 3.2MM
SALES (corp-wide): 102.5MM **Privately Held**
WEB: www.ssrrt.com
SIC: 4225 General warehousing & storage
PA: Contanda Llc
1111 Bagby St Ste 1800
Houston TX 77002
832 699-4001

(G-4794)
WFTS
Also Called: W C P O - T V
1720 Gilbert Ave (45202-1401)
PHONE..................................513 721-9900
Bill Fee, *General Mgr*
Mike Canan, *Editor*
James Leggate, *Editor*
Ashley Harriman, *Marketing Staff*
Cindy Fay, *Executive*
EMP: 172
SALES (corp-wide): 2.9B **Publicly Held**
WEB: www.diytv.com
SIC: 4833 Television broadcasting stations
HQ: Wfts
4045 N Himes Ave
Tampa FL 33607
813 354-2800

(G-4795)
WIDMERS LLC (HQ)
Also Called: Widmer's Drycleaners
2016 Madison Rd (45208-3238)
PHONE..................................513 321-5100
Tod Krasnow,
Steve Carico,
EMP: 200
SQ FT: 33,000
SALES (est): 9.5MM
SALES (corp-wide): 67.7MM **Privately Held**
WEB: www.widmerscleaners.com
SIC: 7216 7217 Cleaning & dyeing, except rugs; carpet & upholstery cleaning

PA: Zoots Holding Corporation
153 Needham St Bldg 1
Newton MA
617 558-9666

(G-4796)
WILLIAM HAFER DRAYAGE INC
11320 Mosteller Rd Ste 1 (45241-5808)
PHONE.................................513 771-5000
Michael Fitzgibbons, *President*
Amy Marie Fitzgibbons, *Vice Pres*
EMP: 30
SQ FT: 4,800
SALES: 6.2MM **Privately Held**
SIC: 4212 Light haulage & cartage, local

(G-4797)
WILLIAM THOMAS GROUP INC
10795 Hughes Rd (45251-4523)
P.O. Box 538703 (45253-8703)
PHONE.................................800 582-3107
William Rumpke Jr, *President*
EMP: 85
SALES (est): 10.2MM **Privately Held**
SIC: 8742 Management consulting services
PA: Rumpke Consolidated Companies, Inc.
3963 Kraus Ln
Hamilton OH 45014

(G-4798)
WILLIAMSBURG OF CINCINNATI MGT
Also Called: Evergreen Kindervelt Gift Shop
230 W Galbraith Rd (45215-5223)
PHONE.................................513 948-2308
Lynn Saul, *Exec Dir*
EMP: 250
SALES (est): 8.1MM
SALES (corp-wide): 320.8MM **Privately Held**
SIC: 8059 5947 Rest home, with health care; gift, novelty & souvenir shop
PA: Senior Lifestyle Corporation
303 E Wacker Dr Ste 2400
Chicago IL 60601
312 673-4333

(G-4799)
WINGS INVESTORS COMPANY LTD
3805 Edwards Rd Ste 200 (45209-1939)
PHONE.................................513 241-5800
Jeffrey R Anderson, *President*
EMP: 25
SALES (est): 1.4MM **Privately Held**
SIC: 6799 8741 Investors; management services

(G-4800)
WITT GLVNZING - CINCINNATI INC
Also Called: Aaz Galvanizing Cincinnati
4454 Steel Pl (45209-1135)
PHONE.................................513 871-5700
Tom Ferguson, *President*
EMP: 45
SALES (est): 7.6MM
SALES (corp-wide): 810.4MM **Publicly Held**
SIC: 5051 Sheets, galvanized or other coated
PA: Azz Inc.
3100 W 7th St Ste 500
Fort Worth TX 76107
817 810-0095

(G-4801)
WNB GROUP LLC
Also Called: Ray Hamilton Company
4817 Section Ave (45212-2118)
P.O. Box 12370 (45212-0370)
PHONE.................................513 641-5400
James Wallis, *President*
EMP: 49 **EST:** 1892
SALES: 12.1MM **Privately Held**
SIC: 4212 4214 4731 Moving services; local trucking with storage; freight transportation arrangement

(G-4802)
WOOD HERRON & EVANS LLP (PA)
441 Vine St Ste 2700 (45202-2814)
PHONE.................................513 241-2324

Bruce Tittel, *President*
J Robert Chambers, *Principal*
Donald F Frei, *Principal*
Kurt Grossman, *Principal*
David J Josephic, *Principal*
EMP: 49
SQ FT: 15,000
SALES (est): 14.9MM **Privately Held**
WEB: www.whepatent.com
SIC: 8111 General practice attorney, lawyer

(G-4803)
WOOD & LAMPING LLP
600 Vine St Ste 2500 (45202-2491)
PHONE.................................513 852-6000
Diane Werner, *President*
Mark R Fitch, *Partner*
William Price, *Partner*
Mark Reckman, *Partner*
Thomas M Woebkenberg, *Partner*
EMP: 60
SALES (est): 9.4MM **Privately Held**
SIC: 8111 General practice attorney, lawyer

(G-4804)
WOOD GRAPHICS INC (HQ)
Also Called: United Engraving
8075 Reading Rd Ste 301 (45237-1416)
PHONE.................................513 771-6300
Mark Richler, *President*
Gaylord H Fill, *Corp Secy*
◆ **EMP:** 30 **EST:** 1972
SQ FT: 21,500
SALES (est): 2.7MM
SALES (corp-wide): 164.4MM **Privately Held**
SIC: 3555 7699 2796 Printing trades machinery; industrial machinery & equipment repair; platemaking services
PA: Rotation Dynamics Corporation
1101 Windham Pkwy
Romeoville IL 60446
630 769-9255

(G-4805)
WOODCRAFT SUPPLY LLC
11711 Princeton Pike # 251 (45246-2534)
PHONE.................................513 407-8371
Mark Miller, *Owner*
EMP: 76
SALES (corp-wide): 226.9MM **Privately Held**
SIC: 5084 Woodworking machinery
PA: Woodcraft Supply, Llc
1177 Rosemar Rd
Parkersburg WV 26105
304 422-5412

(G-4806)
WPH CINCINNATI LLC
Also Called: Crown Plaza
11320 Chester Rd (45246-4003)
PHONE.................................513 771-2080
Wilbert Schwartz,
EMP: 110
SQ FT: 150,000
SALES: 7MM **Privately Held**
SIC: 7011 Hotels

(G-4807)
WRIGHT BROTHERS INC (PA)
1930 Losantiville Ave (45237-4106)
PHONE.................................513 731-2222
Charles Wright, *President*
Josh Gerdes, *General Mgr*
Dee Wright, *Purchasing*
Tim Mooney, *Treasurer*
Ashley Werthaiser, *Marketing Mgr*
EMP: 35
SQ FT: 15,000
SALES (est): 8.7MM **Privately Held**
WEB: www.expectthebest.com
SIC: 2813 3446 5084 Industrial gases; architectural metalwork; welding machinery & equipment

(G-4808)
WULCO INC (PA)
Also Called: Jet Machine & Manufacturing
6899 Steger Dr Ste A (45237-3059)
PHONE.................................513 679-2600
Richard G Wulfeck, *President*
Adam Wulfeck, *Vice Pres*
Chris Wulfeck, *Safety Dir*

Jeff Wulfeck, *Opers Mgr*
Zach Stoeppel, *Mfg Mgr*
▲ **EMP:** 100
SQ FT: 100,000
SALES (est): 145.3MM **Privately Held**
WEB: www.wulco.com
SIC: 5085 3599 Industrial supplies; machine shop, jobbing & repair

(G-4809)
WULFF & ASSOCIATES CPA LLC (PA)
5554 Cheviot Rd G (45247-7039)
PHONE.................................513 245-1010
Scott Wulff,
EMP: 25
SALES (est): 1.8MM **Privately Held**
SIC: 8721 Certified public accountant

(G-4810)
XAVIER UNIVERSITY
Also Called: Wvxu Radio
3800 Victory Pkwy Unit 1 (45207-1092)
PHONE.................................513 745-3335
James King, *Manager*
EMP: 25
SALES (corp-wide): 166.6MM **Privately Held**
WEB: www.xu.edu
SIC: 4832 8221 Radio broadcasting stations; university
PA: Xavier University
3800 Victory Pkwy Unit 1
Cincinnati OH 45207
513 961-0133

(G-4811)
YOUNG & RUBICAM INC
Landor Associates
110 Shillito Pl (45202-2361)
PHONE.................................513 419-2300
Karen Floyd, *Human Res Dir*
Marie Zalla, *Manager*
Jaci St, *Manager*
Noelle Flood, *Director*
Sharon Hoppenjans, *Associate*
EMP: 150
SALES (corp-wide): 20.1B **Privately Held**
SIC: 7311 Advertising agencies
HQ: Young & Rubicam Llc
3 Columbus Cir
New York NY 10019
212 210-3000

(G-4812)
YOUNG MENS CHRISTIAN ASSOCIAT
Also Called: Powel Crosley Jr Branch
9601 Winton Rd (45231-2637)
PHONE.................................513 521-7112
Cindy Tomaszewski, *Manager*
EMP: 60
SALES (corp-wide): 33.6MM **Privately Held**
WEB: www.cincinnatiymca.org
SIC: 8641 7997 Youth organizations; membership sports & recreation clubs
PA: Young Mens Christian Association Of Greater Cincinnati
1105 Elm St
Cincinnati OH 45202
513 651-2100

(G-4813)
YOUNG MENS CHRISTIAN ASSOCIAT
Also Called: Y M C A
2039 Sherman Ave (45212-2634)
PHONE.................................513 731-0115
Alan Geans, *Director*
Jenna Igel, *Program Dir*
EMP: 40
SQ FT: 14,869
SALES (corp-wide): 33.6MM **Privately Held**
WEB: www.cincinnatiymca.org
SIC: 8641 8351 7997 7991 Youth organizations; child day care services; membership sports & recreation clubs; athletic club & gymnasiums, membership
PA: Young Mens Christian Association Of Greater Cincinnati
1105 Elm St
Cincinnati OH 45202
513 651-2100

(G-4814)
YOUNG MENS CHRISTIAN ASSOCIAT
Also Called: Ymca/M.e.lions
8108 Clough Pike Fl 1 (45244-2745)
PHONE.................................513 474-1400
Jennifer Snyder, *Director*
Jackie McNary, *Director*
EMP: 180
SQ FT: 5,320
SALES (corp-wide): 33.6MM **Privately Held**
WEB: www.cincinnatiymca.org
SIC: 8641 8351 7997 7991 Youth organizations; child day care services; membership sports & recreation clubs; physical fitness facilities
PA: Young Mens Christian Association Of Greater Cincinnati
1105 Elm St
Cincinnati OH 45202
513 651-2100

(G-4815)
YOUNG MENS CHRISTIAN ASSOCIAT
Also Called: West End YMCA
1425b Linn St (45214-2605)
PHONE.................................513 241-9622
Joseph C Calloway, *Branch Mgr*
Kerri Conner, *Program Dir*
Jean Roberts, *Receptionist*
EMP: 60
SALES (corp-wide): 33.6MM **Privately Held**
WEB: www.cincinnatiymca.org
SIC: 8641 7991 8351 7032 Youth organizations; physical fitness facilities; child day care services; youth camps; individual & family services
PA: Young Mens Christian Association Of Greater Cincinnati
1105 Elm St
Cincinnati OH 45202
513 651-2100

(G-4816)
YOUNG MENS CHRISTIAN ASSOCIAT
Also Called: William & Clippard YMCA
8920 Cheviot Rd (45251-5910)
PHONE.................................513 923-4466
Dirk Langfoss, *Director*
EMP: 75
SQ FT: 29,230
SALES (corp-wide): 33.6MM **Privately Held**
WEB: www.cincinnatiymca.org
SIC: 8641 7991 8351 7032 Youth organizations; physical fitness facilities; child day care services; youth camps; individual & family services
PA: Young Mens Christian Association Of Greater Cincinnati
1105 Elm St
Cincinnati OH 45202
513 651-2100

(G-4817)
YWCA OF GREATER CINCINNATI (PA)
898 Walnut St Fl 1 (45202-2088)
PHONE.................................513 241-7090
Charlene Ventura, *President*
Debbie Brook, *Vice Pres*
Sandra Genco, *VP Finance*
EMP: 65
SALES: 7.3MM **Privately Held**
SIC: 8641 7991 8351 7032 Youth organizations; physical fitness facilities; child day care services; youth camps; individual & family services

(G-4818)
ZICKA WALKER BUILDERS LTD
Also Called: Zicka Development
7861 E Kemper Rd (45249-1622)
PHONE.................................513 247-3500
E Michael Zicka, *President*
William L Martin Jr, *Principal*
Dennis Walker, *Vice Pres*
EMP: 40 **EST:** 1968
SQ FT: 6,500

SALES (est): 4.1MM **Privately Held**
WEB: www.zickahomes.com
SIC: **1531** Speculative builder, single-family houses

(G-4819)
ZIPSCENE LLC
615 Main St Fl 5 (45202-2538)
PHONE..................................513 201-5174
Sameer Mungur, *CEO*
Mohamed Berete, *Director*
Rick Lamy, *Officer*
EMP: 62
SQ FT: 2,000
SALES (est): 10.8MM **Privately Held**
SIC: **7372** Business oriented computer software

(G-4820)
ZOOLOGICAL SOCIETY CINCINNATI
Also Called: CINCINNATI ZOO & BOTANICAL GAR
3400 Vine St (45220-1333)
PHONE..................................513 281-4700
Lori Voss, *Vice Pres*
Michelle Curley, *Comms Dir*
Kim Denzler, *Manager*
Thane Maynard, *Director*
Bill Swanson, *Director*
▲ EMP: 320 EST: 1875
SALES: 49.3MM **Privately Held**
WEB: www.cincinnatizoo.org
SIC: **8422** Zoological garden, noncommercial

Circleville
Pickaway County

(G-4821)
1ST CARRIER CORP
177 Neville St (43113-9129)
PHONE..................................740 477-2587
Jeffrey Lanman, *President*
Jeffrey Beaver, *Vice Pres*
EMP: 80
SALES (est): 9.7MM **Privately Held**
WEB: www.1stcarrier.com
SIC: **4213** 4212 Trucking, except local; local trucking, without storage

(G-4822)
ACCENTCARE HOME HEALTH CAL INC
Also Called: Sunplus Home Health - Marion
119 S Court St Ste A (43113-1658)
PHONE..................................740 387-4568
Linda Davis, *Manager*
EMP: 108
SALES (corp-wide): 466.3MM **Privately Held**
WEB: www.dhsi.com
SIC: **8082** 7361 Home health care services; nurses' registry
HQ: Accentcare Home Health Of California, Inc.
17855 Dallas Pkwy
Dallas TX 75287

(G-4823)
ACCENTCARE HOME HEALTH CAL INC
Also Called: Sunplus HM Care - Circleville
119 S Court St Ste A (43113-1658)
PHONE..................................740 474-7826
Jenny Clark, *President*
EMP: 150
SALES (corp-wide): 466.3MM **Privately Held**
WEB: www.dhsi.com
SIC: **8082** Visiting nurse service
HQ: Accentcare Home Health Of California, Inc.
17855 Dallas Pkwy
Dallas TX 75287

(G-4824)
ADENA HEALTH SYSTEM
798 N Court St (43113-1262)
PHONE..................................740 420-3000
Christa Lagard, *Auditor*
Brandi Bogard, *Manager*
DOT Pettit, *Admin Asst*

EMP: 213
SALES (corp-wide): 470.6MM **Privately Held**
SIC: **8062** Hospital, medical school affiliated with nursing & residency
PA: Adena Health System
272 Hospital Rd
Chillicothe OH 45601
740 779-7360

(G-4825)
BLB TRANSPORT INC
20615 Us Highway 23 N (43113-8971)
PHONE..................................740 474-1341
William Fletcher, *President*
EMP: 40
SALES (est): 3.1MM **Privately Held**
SIC: **4212** 4213 Local trucking, without storage; trucking, except local

(G-4826)
BROWN MEMORIAL HOME INC
158 E Mound St (43113-1702)
PHONE..................................740 474-6238
Charles Gerhart, *Treasurer*
Luke Conley, *Administration*
EMP: 72
SALES: 3.2MM **Privately Held**
SIC: **8052** Personal care facility

(G-4827)
CAMCO INC
Also Called: Clean Image
24685 Us Highway 23 S (43113-9191)
P.O. Box 363 (43113-0363)
PHONE..................................740 477-3682
Clark Moats, *President*
Mary Moats, *Vice Pres*
EMP: 30
SALES: 3.4MM **Privately Held**
WEB: www.cleanimage.net
SIC: **1799** 7349 0782 Parking lot maintenance; building maintenance services; lawn & garden services

(G-4828)
CIRCLEVILLE OIL CO
315 Town St (43113-2220)
P.O. Box 189 (43113-0189)
PHONE..................................740 474-7568
Gary Scherer, *Branch Mgr*
EMP: 60
SALES (corp-wide): 43.7MM **Privately Held**
WEB: www.circlevilleoil.com
SIC: **5983** 5172 Fuel oil dealers; petroleum products
PA: Circleville Oil Co (Inc)
315 Town St
Circleville OH 43113
740 474-7544

(G-4829)
CITY OF CIRCLEVILLE
Also Called: Department of Public Utilities
108 E Franklin St (43113-1718)
PHONE..................................740 477-8255
Nathan Anderson, *Director*
EMP: 30 **Privately Held**
WEB: www.circlevillecourt.com
SIC: **8611** Public utility association
PA: City Of Circleville
133 S Court St
Circleville OH 43113
740 477-2551

(G-4830)
COUNTY OF PICKAWAY
Also Called: Dept of Human Service
110 Island Rd Ste E (43113-9197)
P.O. Box 610 (43113-0610)
PHONE..................................740 474-7588
Rojanne Woodward, *Branch Mgr*
EMP: 80 **Privately Held**
SIC: **8322** 9111 Individual & family services; county supervisors' & executives' offices
PA: County Of Pickaway
139 W Franklin St
Circleville OH 43113
740 474-6093

(G-4831)
DARBY CREEK EXCAVATING INC
19524 London Rd (43113-9614)
PHONE..................................740 477-8600
Kevin Steward, *President*
Mary Steward, *Corp Secy*
Cary Purcell, *Vice Pres*
EMP: 90
SQ FT: 7,000
SALES (est): 15.8MM **Privately Held**
SIC: **1794** 1623 Excavation & grading; building construction; sewer line construction

(G-4832)
EATON CONSTRUCTION CO INC
653 Island Rd (43113-9594)
P.O. Box 684 (43113-0684)
PHONE..................................740 474-3414
Debbie Manson, *CEO*
EMP: 60
SALES: 2MM **Privately Held**
SIC: **1611** Highway & street maintenance

(G-4833)
ELECT GENERAL CONTRACTORS INC
27634 Jackson Rd (43113-9039)
P.O. Box 1135 (43113-5135)
PHONE..................................740 420-3437
Timothy R Covell, *President*
Gary Smith, *Project Mgr*
Jeri Wallace, *Office Mgr*
EMP: 30 EST: 1989
SALES (est): 4.9MM **Privately Held**
WEB: www.electgeneralcontractors.com
SIC: **1731** Fiber optic cable installation

(G-4834)
HATZEL & BUEHLER INC
3381 Congo Dr (43113-9087)
P.O. Box 848 (43113-0848)
PHONE..................................740 420-3088
James Ivey, *Manager*
EMP: 50
SALES (corp-wide): 277MM **Privately Held**
WEB: www.hatzelandbuehler.com
SIC: **1731** General electrical contractor
HQ: Hatzel & Buehler, Inc.
3600 Silverside Rd Ste A
Wilmington DE 19810
302 478-4200

(G-4835)
HILLS SUPPLY INC
8476 Us Highway 22 E (43113)
PHONE..................................740 477-8994
David Hill, *CEO*
Dolores Hill, *President*
EMP: 40
SALES (est): 2.1MM **Privately Held**
SIC: **5159** Farm animals

(G-4836)
JAMES LAFONTAINE
Also Called: Captain D's
25050 Us Highway 23 S (43113-9131)
PHONE..................................740 474-5052
James Lafontaine, *Partner*
Steve Kay, *Partner*
George Sanson, *Partner*
EMP: 30
SQ FT: 2,800
SALES (est): 763K **Privately Held**
SIC: **5812** 6519 Seafood restaurants; landholding office

(G-4837)
JD MUSIC TILE CO
105 E Ohio St (43113-1917)
PHONE..................................740 420-9611
Joe Music, *President*
Deana Music, *Vice Pres*
EMP: 30
SALES (est): 4.2MM **Privately Held**
SIC: **1752** Ceramic floor tile installation

(G-4838)
NEW HOPE CHRISTIAN ACADEMY
2264 Walnut Creek Pike (43113-8938)
PHONE..................................740 477-6427
Julie Baumgardner, *Principal*

Tami McCallister, *CFO*
Dr Frank Martin III, *Director*
EMP: 35
SALES: 700K **Privately Held**
WEB: www.newhopechristianschool.org
SIC: **8351** 8211 Preschool center; private elementary & secondary schools

(G-4839)
PICKAWAY COUNTY COMMUNITY ACTI (PA)
Also Called: P I C C A
469 E Ohio St (43113-2034)
PHONE..................................740 477-1655
Dave Kline, *CFO*
Dave Hannahs, *Exec Dir*
EMP: 65
SQ FT: 6,000
SALES: 5.8MM **Privately Held**
SIC: **8322** 6513 4121 4119 Social service center; apartment building operators; taxicabs; local passenger transportation; local & suburban transit

(G-4840)
PICKAWAY COUNTY COMMUNITY ACTI
Also Called: Headstart Program
145 E Corwin St (43113-1904)
PHONE..................................740 474-7411
Donna Solovey, *Director*
EMP: 40
SALES (est): 1.4MM
SALES (corp-wide): 5.8MM **Privately Held**
SIC: **8322** 8351 Social service center; head start center, except in conjunction with school
PA: Pickaway County Community Action Organization
469 E Ohio St
Circleville OH 43113
740 477-1655

(G-4841)
PICKAWAY COUNTY COMMUNITY ACTI
Also Called: Pickaway Senior Citizen Center
590 E Ohio St (43113-2000)
PHONE..................................740 477-1655
Sue Frey, *Manager*
EMP: 25
SALES (est): 323.9K
SALES (corp-wide): 5.8MM **Privately Held**
SIC: **8322** Senior citizens' center or association
PA: Pickaway County Community Action Organization
469 E Ohio St
Circleville OH 43113
740 477-1655

(G-4842)
PICKAWAY DIVERSIFIED INDUSTRIES
548 Lancaster Pike (43113-9026)
PHONE..................................740 474-1522
Kim McPeek, *Director*
EMP: 93
SALES (est): 3.4MM **Privately Held**
SIC: **8331** 7331 Job training & vocational rehabilitation services; direct mail advertising services

(G-4843)
PICKAWAY DIVERSIFIED
548 Lancaster Pike (43113-9026)
PHONE..................................740 474-1522
Robert Hhuffer, *Principal*
Tammy Alvoid, *Director*
EMP: 25
SALES: 702K **Privately Held**
SIC: **8322** Social services for the handicapped

(G-4844)
PICKAWAY MANOR INC
391 Clark Dr (43113-1598)
PHONE..................................740 474-5400
Robert Kenworthy, *President*
Ned Hardin, *Treasurer*
EMP: 150 EST: 1969
SQ FT: 10,000

SALES: 8.5MM **Privately Held**
SIC: 8051 8052 Convalescent home with continuous nursing care; intermediate care facilities

(G-4845)
PICKAWAY PLAINS AMBULANCE SVC (PA)
Also Called: Pro Care Medical Trnsp Svc
1950 Stoneridge Dr (43113-8955)
PHONE...........................740 474-4180
Clyde Cook, *CEO*
Gary Cook, *President*
Jarrod Strouth, *General Mgr*
Elaine Cook, *Corp Secy*
EMP: 190
SALES (est): 7.5MM **Privately Held**
SIC: 4119 Ambulance service

(G-4846)
PRECISION ELECTRICAL SERVICES
201 W Main St (43113-1621)
PHONE...........................740 474-4490
John Seyfang II, *President*
Kelly Seyfang, *Treasurer*
EMP: 35
SQ FT: 12,000
SALES (est): 3.1MM **Privately Held**
WEB: www.precisionelectricalservices.com
SIC: 1731 General electrical contractor

(G-4847)
RUMPKE WASTE INC
Also Called: Rumpke Recycling
819 Island Rd (43113-9594)
PHONE...........................740 474-9790
Bill Rumpke, *President*
EMP: 55 **Privately Held**
SIC: 4953 Garbage: collecting, destroying & processing
HQ: Rumpke Waste, Inc.
10795 Hughes Rd
Cincinnati OH 45251
513 851-0122

(G-4848)
SAVINGS BANK (PA)
118 N Court St 120 (43113-1606)
P.O. Box 310 (43113-0310)
PHONE...........................740 474-3191
Steven Gary, *President*
Connie Campbell, *Exec VP*
EMP: 35 EST: 1912
SQ FT: 8,000
SALES: 14MM **Privately Held**
WEB: www.thesavingsbank.com
SIC: 6022 State commercial banks

(G-4849)
SHELLY COMPANY
24537 Canal Rd (43113-9691)
P.O. Box 600, Thornville (43076-0600)
PHONE...........................740 441-1714
EMP: 30
SALES (corp-wide): 29.7B **Privately Held**
SIC: 1611 Surfacing & paving
HQ: Shelly Company
80 Park Dr
Thornville OH 43076
740 246-6315

(G-4850)
SOUTH CENTRAL POWER COMPANY
2100 Chickasaw Dr (43113-9199)
PHONE...........................740 474-6045
Jan Bussert, *Branch Mgr*
EMP: 26
SALES (est): 2.8MM
SALES (corp-wide): 282.1MM **Privately Held**
WEB: www.southcentralpower.com
SIC: 4911 Distribution, electric power
PA: South Central Power Company Inc
2780 Coonpath Rd Ne
Lancaster OH 43130
740 653-4422

(G-4851)
SUNBRIDGE CIRCLEVILLE
Also Called: Circlville Care Rhblitation Ctr
1155 Atwater Ave (43113-1301)
PHONE...........................740 477-1695
Robert Banwart, *Administration*

EMP: 50 **Publicly Held**
SIC: 8051 Convalescent home with continuous nursing care
HQ: Sunbridge Circleville Health Care Llc
101 Sun Ave Ne
Albuquerque NM 87109
505 821-3355

(G-4852)
WESTFALL AGGREGATE & MTLS INC
19522 London Rd (43113-9614)
PHONE...........................740 420-9090
Kenneth Stewart, *President*
EMP: 80
SALES (est): 9.2MM **Privately Held**
SIC: 5032 Gravel

(G-4853)
WHETSTONE CARE CENTER LLC
Also Called: Pickaway Manor Care Center
391 Clark Dr (43113-1561)
PHONE...........................740 474-6036
Noah Moore, *Branch Mgr*
EMP: 130
SALES (corp-wide): 20.1MM **Privately Held**
WEB: www.macintoshcompany.com
SIC: 8051 8059 Convalescent home with continuous nursing care; convalescent home
PA: Whetstone Care Center Llc
3863 Trueman Ct
Hilliard OH 43026
614 345-9500

(G-4854)
YOUNG MENS CHRISTIAN ASSOC
Also Called: Y M C A
440 Nicholas Dr (43113-1535)
PHONE...........................740 477-1661
Hollie Queen, *Director*
Lauren Bunting, *Director*
EMP: 100
SALES (corp-wide): 44.9MM **Privately Held**
WEB: www.ymca-columbus.com
SIC: 8641 7997 7991 7999 Youth organizations; membership sports & recreation clubs; physical fitness facilities; recreation center
PA: Young Men's Christian Association Of Central Ohio
40 W Long St
Columbus OH 43215
614 389-4409

Clay Center
Ottawa County

(G-4855)
WHITE ROCK QUARRY L P
3800 Bolander Rd (43408-7713)
PHONE...........................419 855-8388
Ray Advnia, *Principal*
U S Aggregates, *General Ptnr*
Robert Simpson, *General Ptnr*
Jim Fehsenseld, *Ltd Ptnr*
Heritage Group, *Ltd Ptnr*
EMP: 590
SALES (est): 13.6MM
SALES (corp-wide): 248.2MM **Privately Held**
SIC: 1422 Crushed & broken limestone
PA: Asphalt Materials, Inc.
5400 W 86th St
Indianapolis IN 46268
317 872-6010

Clayton
Montgomery County

(G-4856)
DAYTON MDOWBROOK CNTRY CLB LLC
6001 Salem Ave (45315-9736)
PHONE...........................937 836-5186
Brian Early, *General Mgr*

EMP: 100
SQ FT: 35,000
SALES (est): 1.5MM **Privately Held**
SIC: 7997 Country club, membership

(G-4857)
ENGLEWOOD TRUCK INC
Also Called: Englewood Trck Towing Recovery
7510 Jacks Ln (45315-8779)
PHONE...........................937 836-5109
Frank Cecrle, *President*
Brookie Cercle, *Vice Pres*
EMP: 45 EST: 1947
SQ FT: 12,000
SALES (est): 2MM **Privately Held**
SIC: 7549 Towing service, automotive

(G-4858)
IDEAL COMPANY INC (PA)
Also Called: F & M Contractors
8313 Kimmel Rd Ste A (45315-8905)
P.O. Box 149 (45315-0149)
PHONE...........................937 836-8683
Fred A Sink, *President*
Kent Filbrun, *Principal*
Kevin G Filbrun, *Vice Pres*
Bruce Neador, *Vice Pres*
Gary Boothe, *Project Mgr*
EMP: 40 EST: 1960
SQ FT: 2,400
SALES (est): 19.2MM **Privately Held**
SIC: 1542 Commercial & office building, new construction

(G-4859)
LANDES FRESH MEATS INC
Also Called: Ol' Smokehaus
9476 Haber Rd (45315-9711)
PHONE...........................937 836-3613
Keith Landes, *President*
Mark Landes, *Vice Pres*
Joe Dunn, *Plant Mgr*
Ann Landes, *Admin Sec*
EMP: 50
SQ FT: 16,000
SALES (est): 3.9MM **Privately Held**
WEB: www.landesfreshmeats.com
SIC: 5421 0751 5147 Meat markets, including freezer provisioners; slaughtering: custom livestock services; meats, fresh

(G-4860)
MOYER INDUSTRIES INC
7555 Jacks Ln (45315-8778)
PHONE...........................937 832-7283
John Moyer, *President*
Jane Moyer, *Exec VP*
EMP: 50
SQ FT: 13,000
SALES (est): 9.7MM **Privately Held**
SIC: 1521 1611 Single-family housing construction; surfacing & paving

(G-4861)
SALEM CHURCH OF GOD INC
6500 Southway Rd Unit 2 (45315-7938)
P.O. Box 39 (45315-0039)
PHONE...........................937 836-6500
Rolland Daniels, *Pastor*
Paula Spear, *Teacher*
Craig Denise, *Assistant*
EMP: 27
SQ FT: 1,470
SALES (est): 1.8MM **Privately Held**
WEB: www.salemchurch.org
SIC: 8661 8351 Church of God; preschool center

(G-4862)
TOM TISE GOLF PROFESSIONAL
6001 Salem Ave (45315-9736)
PHONE...........................937 836-5186
Bill Williams, *Manager*
Steve Taylor, *Manager*
EMP: 75
SALES: 1.9MM **Privately Held**
SIC: 7999 5941 7997 7991 Golf professionals; golf, tennis & ski shops; membership sports & recreation clubs; physical fitness facilities; eating places

---

Cleveland
Cuyahoga County

(G-4863)
1 COMMUNITY
1375 Euclid Ave (44115-1826)
PHONE...........................216 923-2272
Charles Berry, *COO*
EMP: 37
SALES (est): 1.8MM **Privately Held**
SIC: 4813

(G-4864)
1-888 OHIO COMP LLC
2900 Carnegie Ave (44115-2649)
PHONE...........................216 426-0646
Lynn Munn, *Case Mgmt Dir*
Jay Lucarelli,
EMP: 80
SALES (est): 21.3MM **Privately Held**
WEB: www.1-888-ohiocomp.com
SIC: 6321 6324 Accident & health insurance; health maintenance organization (HMO), insurance only

(G-4865)
127 PS FEE OWNER LLC
1300 Key Tower 127 Pub Sq (44114)
PHONE...........................216 520-1250
Frank Sinito,
EMP: 99
SALES (est): 1.1MM **Privately Held**
SIC: 6512 Commercial & industrial building operation

(G-4866)
1460 NINTH ST ASSOC LTD PARTNR
Also Called: Brampton Inn
1460 E 9th St (44114-1700)
PHONE...........................216 241-6600
Ray Valle, *General Mgr*
EMP: 40
SQ FT: 18,836
SALES (est): 855.2K **Privately Held**
SIC: 7011 Hotels & motels

(G-4867)
1ST CHOICE LLC
600 Superior Ave E # 1300 (44114-2614)
PHONE...........................877 564-6658
Sartara Williams, *Manager*
EMP: 60 **Privately Held**
SIC: 7353 Heavy construction equipment rental
PA: 1st Choice, Llc
400 E Pratt St
Baltimore MD 21202

(G-4868)
1ST CHOICE ROOFING COMPANY
10311 Berea Rd (44102-2503)
PHONE...........................216 227-7755
Ian Fess, *President*
EMP: 37
SQ FT: 33,000
SALES (est): 1.2MM **Privately Held**
WEB: www.1stchoiceroofing.com
SIC: 1761 Roofing Contractor

(G-4869)
2100 LAKESIDE SHELTER FOR MEN
2100 Lakeside Ave E (44114-1126)
PHONE...........................216 566-0047
Dewayne Drotar, *Director*
EMP: 30
SALES (est): 300.7K **Privately Held**
SIC: 8322 Adult day care center

(G-4870)
21ST CENTURY CON CNSTR INC
13925 Enterprise Ave (44135-5117)
PHONE...........................216 362-0900
Patrick Butler, *President*
EMP: 50
SQ FT: 28,000
SALES (est): 9.3MM **Privately Held**
WEB: www.21stcenturyconcrete.com
SIC: 1771 Concrete work

▲ = Import ▼=Export
◆ =Import/Export

(G-4871)
3B HOLDINGS INC (PA)
Also Called: 3b Supply
11470 Euclid Ave Ste 407 (44106-3934)
PHONE.....................................800 791-7124
Leonard Dashkin, *President*
David L Porter, *President*
Watson Boxley, *Vice Pres*
Robert Dashkin, *VP Opers*
Nathan Keen, *Program Mgr*
EMP: 61
SQ FT: 250,000
SALES: 25MM **Privately Held**
SIC: 5085 Industrial supplies

(G-4872)
6200 ROCKSIDE LLC
Also Called: Vantage Financial Group
6200 Rockside Rd Ste 100 (44131)
PHONE.....................................216 642-8004
Manish Bhatt, *Partner*
EMP: 80
SALES (est): 3.7MM **Privately Held**
SIC: 7389 Financial services

(G-4873)
A A ASTRO SERVICE INC
5283 Pearl Rd (44129-1550)
PHONE.....................................216 459-0363
Philip Tromba, *President*
EMP: 56
SALES (est): 4.3MM **Privately Held**
SIC: 1711 Warm air heating & air conditioning contractor

(G-4874)
A B C RENTAL CENTER EAST INC
5204 Warrensville Ctr Rd (44137-1902)
PHONE.....................................216 475-8240
Howard R Kelley, *President*
Molly Kelley, *Corp Secy*
EMP: 25
SQ FT: 9,400
SALES (est): 2.4MM **Privately Held**
SIC: 7359 Party supplies rental services; tool rental

(G-4875)
A BEE C SERVICE INC (PA)
Also Called: Service-Tech
7589 First Pl Ste 1 (44146-6727)
PHONE.....................................440 735-1505
Alan Sutton, *President*
Barbara Sutton, *Treasurer*
Susan Sutton, *Admin Sec*
EMP: 42
SQ FT: 22,000
SALES (est): 7MM **Privately Held**
WEB: www.service-techcorp.com
SIC: 7349 Air duct cleaning

(G-4876)
A C MANAGEMENT INC
Also Called: Holiday Inn
780 Beta Dr (44143-2328)
PHONE.....................................440 461-9200
Alfred Quagliata, *President*
Kathy Quagliata, *Vice Pres*
EMP: 40
SALES (est): 2.6MM **Privately Held**
SIC: 7011 5813 5812 Hotels & motels; drinking places; eating places

(G-4877)
A D A ARCHITECTS INC
17710 Detroit Ave (44107-3451)
PHONE.....................................216 521-5134
Robert Acciarri, *President*
EMP: 35
SQ FT: 1,000
SALES (est): 5.1MM **Privately Held**
WEB: www.adaarchitects.cc
SIC: 8712 Architectural engineering

(G-4878)
A M MC GREGOR HOME
14900 Private Dr Ofc (44112-3495)
PHONE.....................................216 851-8200
Rob Hilton, *CEO*
Robertson Hilton, *CEO*
Kyle Callahan, *Opers Staff*
Ann Conn, *CFO*
Sue W Neff, *Exec Dir*
EMP: 275

SALES: 21.1MM **Privately Held**
SIC: 8051 Skilled nursing care facilities

(G-4879)
A NEW BEGINNING PRESCHOOL
18403 Euclid Ave (44112-1016)
PHONE.....................................216 531-7465
Monee Kidd, *Director*
EMP: 62
SALES (est): 49.7K **Privately Held**
SIC: 8351 Preschool center

(G-4880)
A RESSLER INC
Also Called: Down To Earth Landscaping
12750 Broadway Ave (44125-1855)
PHONE.....................................216 518-1804
Adam Ressler, *President*
Colleen Cunningham, *Prgrmr*
EMP: 25
SQ FT: 6,000
SALES (est): 1.4MM **Privately Held**
SIC: 0782 Landscape contractors

(G-4881)
A W S INC
Also Called: S A W Adult Training Center
4720 Hinckley Indus Pkwy (44109-6003)
PHONE.....................................216 749-0356
William Oliverio, *Manager*
EMP: 350
SALES (corp-wide): 7.8MM **Privately Held**
SIC: 8331 7331 Vocational training agency; direct mail advertising services
PA: A W S Inc
1275 Lakeside Ave E
Cleveland OH 44114
216 861-0250

(G-4882)
A W S INC
Also Called: Brooklyn Adult Activity Center
10991 Memphis Ave (44144-2055)
PHONE.....................................216 941-8800
David Nodge, *Manager*
EMP: 77
SALES (corp-wide): 7.8MM **Privately Held**
SIC: 8093 8331 Mental health clinic, outpatient; job training & vocational rehabilitation services
PA: A W S Inc
1275 Lakeside Ave E
Cleveland OH 44114
216 861-0250

(G-4883)
A-1 GENERAL INSURANCE AGENCY (DH)
9700 Rockside Rd Ste 250 (44125-6264)
PHONE.....................................216 986-3000
Steven Mason, *Ch of Bd*
Randy Parker, *President*
Randy P Parker, *President*
Dick Muma, *Principal*
EMP: 80
SQ FT: 24,000
SALES (est): 2.9MM
SALES (corp-wide): 10.3B **Privately Held**
WEB: www.thegeneral.com
SIC: 6411 Insurance agents
HQ: Pga Service Corporation
2636 Elm Hill Pike # 510
Nashville TN 37214
615 242-1961

(G-4884)
A-1 HEALTHCARE STAFFING LLC (PA)
Also Called: Synergy Healthcare Systems
2991 E 73rd St (44104-4163)
PHONE.....................................216 862-0906
Amie Sherman, *Manager*
Jennifer Fox,
EMP: 109
SALES: 6.5MM **Privately Held**
SIC: 8011 7361 Offices & clinics of medical doctors; employment agencies

(G-4885)
A-TEAM LLC
Also Called: Masters of Disasters
5280 W 161st St Frnt (44142-1607)
PHONE.....................................216 271-7223
Enzo Maddalena,

EMP: 30
SALES (est): 2MM **Privately Held**
WEB: www.a-team.com
SIC: 8322 1711 Disaster service; plumbing contractors

(G-4886)
AAA AMRICAN ABATEMENT ASB CORP
15401 Chatfield Ave (44111-4309)
PHONE.....................................216 281-9400
John P Donalon, *President*
Robert E Donalon, *Vice Pres*
Terry Donelon, *Vice Pres*
EMP: 75
SQ FT: 4,000
SALES: 2.5MM **Privately Held**
WEB: www.americanabatement.com
SIC: 1799 Asbestos removal & encapsulation

(G-4887)
AAA FLEXIBLE PIPE CLEANING
7277 Bessemer Ave (44127-1815)
P.O. Box 16692, Rocky River (44116-0692)
PHONE.....................................216 341-2900
Margaret Ziegenruecker, *President*
Carol Ann Fisco, *Treasurer*
Susan Kubach, *Director*
EMP: 45
SALES (est): 5.7MM **Privately Held**
SIC: 1623 Pipeline construction

(G-4888)
AAA PIPE CLEANING CORPORATION (PA)
Also Called: AAA Flexible Pipe
7277 Bessemer Ave (44127-1815)
PHONE.....................................216 341-2900
Ernest Fisco, *President*
Benjamin Fisco III, *Vice Pres*
Brian Nix, *Controller*
Susan Kubach, *Director*
EMP: 103 EST: 1935
SQ FT: 90,000
SALES (est): 9.5MM **Privately Held**
WEB: www.aaapipecleaning.com
SIC: 7699 1711 Sewer cleaning & rodding; plumbing, heating, air-conditioning contractors

(G-4889)
AARONS INC
11629 Lorain Ave (44111-5404)
PHONE.....................................216 251-4500
Pat Cassidy, *Manager*
EMP: 25
SALES (corp-wide): 3.8B **Publicly Held**
WEB: www.aaronrents.com
SIC: 7359 Furniture rental; home appliance, furniture & entertainment rental services
PA: Aaron's, Inc.
400 Galleria Pkwy Se # 300
Atlanta GA 30339
678 402-3000

(G-4890)
ABCO FIRE LLC (HQ)
4545 W 160th St (44135-2647)
PHONE.....................................216 433-7200
Steve Dejohn, *President*
EMP: 68
SALES (est): 3.2MM
SALES (corp-wide): 14.2MM **Privately Held**
SIC: 7389 Fire protection service other than forestry or public
PA: Abco Holdings, Llc
4545 W 160th St
Cleveland OH 44135
216 433-7200

(G-4891)
ABCO FIRE PROTECTION INC (PA)
4545 W 160th St (44135-2647)
PHONE.....................................800 875-7200
Matthew Aloisio, *President*
Scott Rose, *Division Mgr*
Bill Jellison, *Assistant VP*
Mike Frantz, *Facilities Mgr*
Linda Petrigan, *Controller*
EMP: 32

SALES (est): 8.8MM **Privately Held**
SIC: 5099 Fire extinguishers

(G-4892)
ABCO HOLDINGS LLC (PA)
Also Called: Abco Fire Protection
4545 W 160th St (44135-2647)
PHONE.....................................216 433-7200
Robert J Titmas Jr, *President*
Merrick E Murphy, *Vice Pres*
Stephen Dejohn, *CFO*
▼ EMP: 90
SQ FT: 12,000
SALES: 14.2MM **Privately Held**
WEB: www.abcofire.net
SIC: 5099 7389 Safety equipment & supplies; fire extinguisher servicing

(G-4893)
ABF FREIGHT SYSTEM INC
5630 Chevrolet Blvd (44130-1404)
PHONE.....................................440 843-4600
Richard De Santos, *Manager*
EMP: 70
SQ FT: 15,000
SALES (corp-wide): 3B **Publicly Held**
WEB: www.abfs.com
SIC: 4213 Contract haulers
HQ: Abf Freight System, Inc.
3801 Old Greenwood Rd
Fort Smith AR 72903
479 785-8700

(G-4894)
ABM JANITORIAL SERVICES INC
1501 Euclid Ave Ste 320 (44115-2108)
PHONE.....................................216 861-1199
Scott Sedio, *District Mgr*
Robert J Pfahl, *Manager*
Robert Castle, *Manager*
EMP: 105
SALES (corp-wide): 6.4B **Publicly Held**
SIC: 7349 Janitorial service, contract basis
HQ: Abm Janitorial Services, Inc.
1111 Fannin St Ste 1500
Houston TX 77002
713 654-8924

(G-4895)
ABM PARKING SERVICES INC
Also Called: Ampco System Parking
1459 Hamilton Ave (44114-1105)
PHONE.....................................216 621-6600
Steve Brown, *Manager*
EMP: 50
SALES (corp-wide): 6.4B **Publicly Held**
WEB: www.meyers.net
SIC: 7521 Parking lots
HQ: Abm Parking Services, Inc.
1150 S Olive St Fl 19
Los Angeles CA 90015
213 284-7600

(G-4896)
ACADEMY ANSWERING SERVICE INC
Also Called: Academy Communications
30 Alpha Park (44143-2208)
PHONE.....................................440 442-8500
Daniel J Day, *President*
EMP: 50
SALES (est): 2.7MM **Privately Held**
WEB: www.academycom.com
SIC: 7389 Telephone answering service

(G-4897)
ACADEMY GRAPHIC COMM INC
1000 Brookpark Rd (44109-5824)
PHONE.....................................216 661-2550
James M Champion, *President*
Erik Eichenberger, *General Mgr*
Elaine Champion, *Vice Pres*
Courtney Dolinar, *VP Sales*
Courtney Champion, *Mktg Dir*
EMP: 27
SQ FT: 1,400
SALES (est): 4.7MM **Privately Held**
WEB: www.visitagc.com
SIC: 2752 7336 Commercial printing, offset; graphic arts & related design

(G-4898)
ACCENTURE LLP
1400 W 10th St Ste 401 (44113-1361)
PHONE.....................................216 685-1435

James Dickey, *Branch Mgr*
Roberto Rando, *Manager*
EMP: 180 Privately Held
WEB: www.wavesecurities.com
SIC: 8742 8748 Business consultant; business consulting
HQ: Accenture Llp
161 N Clark St Ste 1100
Chicago IL 60601
312 693-0161

(G-4899)
ACHIEVEMENT CTRS FOR CHILDREN (PA)
4255 Northfield Rd (44128-2811)
PHONE..........................216 292-9700
Patricia Nobili, *President*
Sally Farwell, *Vice Pres*
Scott Peplin, *CFO*
Betsey Saffar, *Controller*
Scott Matson, *Info Tech Dir*
EMP: 70 EST: 1940
SQ FT: 38,000
SALES: 10MM Privately Held
WEB: www.achievementcenters.org
SIC: 8322 Social services for the handicapped

(G-4900)
ACTION TRAVEL CENTER INC (PA)
5900 Harper Rd Ste 101 (44139-1866)
PHONE..........................440 248-8388
Arlene Goldberg, *President*
EMP: 26
SQ FT: 9,500
SALES (est): 5.6MM Privately Held
WEB: www.actiontvl.com
SIC: 4724 Tourist agency arranging transport, lodging & car rental

(G-4901)
ADCOM GROUP INC
1370 W 6th St Fl 3 (44113-1315)
PHONE..........................216 574-9100
Joe Kubic, *CEO*
Loren Chylla, *Partner*
Tim Sieple, *COO*
Mike Derrick, *Exec VP*
Steve Dressig, *Vice Pres*
EMP: 110
SQ FT: 15,000
SALES (est): 10.6MM Privately Held
SIC: 7336 Graphic arts & related design

(G-4902)
ADRIAN M SCHNALL MD
1611 S Green Rd Lbby A (44121-4121)
PHONE..........................216 291-4300
Philip Junglas MD, *President*
Adrian M Schnall MD, *Owner*
Dr Debra Dejoseph, *Vice Pres*
Dr James Cobiello, *Treasurer*
Dr Steven Turocvi, *Admin Sec*
EMP: 62
SALES (est): 1MM Privately Held
SIC: 8011 Ears, nose & throat specialist: physician/surgeon

(G-4903)
ADVANCE DOOR COMPANY
4555 Willow Pkwy (44125-1081)
PHONE..........................216 883-2424
Bill Giordano, *President*
EMP: 30
SQ FT: 15,000
SALES (est): 6.5MM Privately Held
SIC: 7699 5031 1751 Door & window repair; doors; window & door (prefabricated) installation

(G-4904)
ADVANCED GROUP CORP (PA)
Also Called: Advanced Benefit Cons Agcy
3800 Lkside Ave E Ste 400 (44114)
PHONE..........................216 431-8800
Philip Galaska, *Ch of Bd*
James Kretzschmar, *President*
EMP: 40
SQ FT: 7,700
SALES (est): 5.1MM Privately Held
WEB: www.advanced-on-line.com
SIC: 6411 Insurance agents, brokers & service

(G-4905)
ADVOCARE INC
25001 Emery Rd (44128-5626)
PHONE..........................216 514-1451
Joseph M Cannelongo, *CEO*
Karen Agnich, *President*
George W Cyphers, *Director*
EMP: 75
SALES (est): 4.8MM Privately Held
WEB: www.advocare-inc.com
SIC: 8741 Administrative management

(G-4906)
AECOM ENERGY & CNSTR INC
Also Called: Washington Group
1300 E 9th St Ste 500 (44114-1503)
PHONE..........................216 622-2300
James Bickford, *Manager*
EMP: 400
SALES (corp-wide): 20.1B Publicly Held
WEB: www.wgint.com
SIC: 1622 1611 1629 1623 Bridge construction; tunnel construction; highway construction, elevated; general contractor, highway & street construction; dams, waterways, docks & other marine construction; industrial plant construction; power plant construction; pipeline construction; industrial buildings, new construction; institutional building construction; commercial & office building, new construction
HQ: Aecom Energy & Construction, Inc.
1999 Avenue Of The Stars
Los Angeles CA 90067
213 593-8100

(G-4907)
AECOM ENERGY & CNSTR INC
Also Called: URS
1500 W 3rd St Ste 200 (44113-1453)
P.O. Box 73, Boise ID (83729-0073)
PHONE..........................216 523-5600
EMP: 700
SALES (corp-wide): 20.1B Publicly Held
WEB: www.wgint.com
SIC: 7389 Personal service agents, brokers & bureaus
HQ: Aecom Energy & Construction, Inc.
1999 Avenue Of The Stars
Los Angeles CA 90067
213 593-8100

(G-4908)
AECOM ENERGY & CNSTR INC
Also Called: URS
1500 W 3rd St Ste 200 (44113-1453)
PHONE..........................216 523-5600
Mark Foster, *Engineer*
Larry Beers, *Manager*
EMP: 600
SALES (corp-wide): 20.1B Publicly Held
WEB: www.wgint.com
SIC: 7389 Personal service agents, brokers & bureaus
HQ: Aecom Energy & Construction, Inc.
1999 Avenue Of The Stars
Los Angeles CA 90067
213 593-8100

(G-4909)
AECOM ENERGY & CNSTR INC
Also Called: URS
1500 W 3rd St Ste 470 (44113-1440)
PHONE..........................216 523-5600
Steve Hanks, *Branch Mgr*
EMP: 99
SALES (corp-wide): 20.1B Publicly Held
WEB: www.wgint.com
SIC: 8711 Engineering services
HQ: Aecom Energy & Construction, Inc.
1999 Avenue Of The Stars
Los Angeles CA 90067
213 593-8100

(G-4910)
AECOM GLOBAL II LLC
1500 W 3rd St Fl 2 (44113-1467)
PHONE..........................216 523-5600
Diane Roth, *Manager*
EMP: 84
SALES (corp-wide): 20.1B Publicly Held
SIC: 8712 8741 8711 Architectural engineering; construction management; consulting engineer

HQ: Aecom Global Ii, Llc
1999 Avenue Of The Stars
Los Angeles CA 90067
213 593-8100

(G-4911)
AG INTERACTIVE INC (DH)
Also Called: American Greetings
1 American Rd (44144-2354)
PHONE..........................216 889-5000
David Ricanati, *President*
Josef Mandelbaum, *Chairman*
Sally Babcock, *Senior VP*
Kathy Hecht, *Senior VP*
Rajiv Jain, *Senior VP*
EMP: 120
SQ FT: 34,000
SALES (est): 34.5MM
SALES (corp-wide): 7.2B Privately Held
WEB: www.aginteractive.com
SIC: 5947 7335 Greeting cards; commercial photography
HQ: American Greetings Corporation
1 American Way
Cleveland OH 44145
216 252-7300

(G-4912)
AGE LINE INC
4350 Rocky River Dr (44135-2504)
PHONE..........................216 941-9990
June Pearce Novatney, *President*
Norma Robinette, *COO*
EMP: 30
SALES (est): 984.9K Privately Held
WEB: www.age-line.com
SIC: 8059 4789 Personal care home, with health care; cabs, horse drawn: for hire

(G-4913)
AGMET LLC (PA)
7800 Medusa Rd (44146-5549)
PHONE..........................440 439-7400
Dana Cassidy, *President*
Timothy Andel, *CFO*
Rajesh Shah, *CTO*
▲ **EMP: 35**
SQ FT: 78,000
SALES (est): 21.8MM Privately Held
SIC: 5093 Ferrous metal scrap & waste

(G-4914)
AIDS TSKFRCE GRTER CLVLAND INC
2829 Euclid Ave (44115-2413)
PHONE..........................216 357-3131
David Postero, *President*
Leon Hall, *Opers Staff*
EMP: 80
SALES: 1.6MM Privately Held
SIC: 8322 Social service center; self-help organization

(G-4915)
AIR COMFORT SYSTEMS INC
Also Called: Comfort Air
5108 Richmond Rd (44146-1331)
PHONE..........................216 587-4125
Frank Demarco, *President*
Steven Smylie, *Shareholder*
William Smylie, *Shareholder*
Elaine Weinberg, *Shareholder*
EMP: 50
SQ FT: 3,000
SALES (est): 3MM Privately Held
SIC: 1711 Warm air heating & air conditioning contractor; heating & air conditioning contractors

(G-4916)
AIR COMPLIANCE TESTING INC (PA)
5525 Canal Rd Ste 1 (44125-4866)
P.O. Box 41156 (44141-0156)
PHONE..........................216 525-0900
Philip J Billick, *President*
Alan Schreiner, *Exec VP*
EMP: 26
SQ FT: 15,000
SALES (est): 2.6MM Privately Held
WEB: www.aircomp.com
SIC: 8748 Environmental consultant

(G-4917)
AIR CONDITIONING ENTPS INC
1370 Ontario St Ste 450 (44113-1812)
PHONE..........................440 729-0900
EMP: 25 EST: 1970
SQ FT: 2,000
SALES (est): 2.1MM Privately Held
SIC: 1711 Heating & Air Conditioning Contractor

(G-4918)
AIR-TEMP CLIMATE CONTROL INC
Also Called: Air-Temp Mechanical
3013 Payne Ave (44114-4594)
PHONE..........................216 579-1552
Allen J Krupar, *President*
Timothy Holmes, *Vice Pres*
EMP: 40 EST: 1978
SQ FT: 11,000
SALES (est): 7MM Privately Held
WEB: www.air-tempmech.com
SIC: 1711 Warm air heating & air conditioning contractor; refrigeration contractor

(G-4919)
AIRGAS INC
2020 Train Ave (44113-4205)
PHONE..........................866 935-3370
Tom Kall, *Manager*
EMP: 269
SALES (corp-wide): 125.9MM Privately Held
SIC: 5084 Welding machinery & equipment
HQ: Airgas, Inc.
259 N Radnor Chester Rd # 100
Radnor PA 19087
610 687-5253

(G-4920)
AIRGAS MERCHANT GASES LLC (DH)
6055 Rckside Woods Blvd N (44131-2301)
PHONE..........................800 242-0105
Tom Thoman,
Chris Plitnick,
▲ **EMP: 335**
SALES (est): 218MM
SALES (corp-wide): 125.9MM Privately Held
WEB: www.airgas.com
SIC: 5169 Industrial gases
HQ: Airgas, Inc.
259 N Radnor Chester Rd # 100
Radnor PA 19087
610 687-5253

(G-4921)
AIRGAS USA LLC
6055 Rocksd Woods Blv 400 (44131)
PHONE..........................440 232-1590
Kevin McBride, *Branch Mgr*
EMP: 148
SALES (corp-wide): 125.9MM Privately Held
SIC: 8711 Engineering services
HQ: Airgas Usa, Llc
259 N Radnor Chester Rd # 100
Radnor PA 19087
610 687-5253

(G-4922)
AIRKO INC
20160 Center Ridge Rd # 101 (44116-3507)
PHONE..........................440 333-0133
James Gilbert, *President*
Raymond Gilbert, *Senior VP*
Barb Gilbert, *Assistant*
EMP: 35
SQ FT: 1,500
SALES: 2MM Privately Held
WEB: www.airkoinc.com
SIC: 1761 1751 1542 1521 Siding contractor; carpentry work; window & door installation & erection; commercial & office buildings, renovation & repair; general remodeling, single-family houses

(G-4923)
AITHERAS AVIATION GROUP LLC (PA)
2301 N Marginal Rd (44114-3708)
PHONE..........................216 298-9060
George Katsikas, *CEO*

Kevin Weir, *COO*
Marc Goldfarb, *Marketing Staff*
EMP: 29
SALES (est): 9.5MM **Privately Held**
WEB: www.aitherasaviationgroup.com
SIC: 4581 Aircraft maintenance & repair services

(G-4924)
AJAX CLEANING CONTRACTORS CO
1561 E 40th St (44103-2301)
P.O. Box 603126 (44103-0126)
PHONE..................................216 881-8484
Martin Presser, *President*
EMP: 100
SQ FT: 3,375
SALES (est): 1MM **Privately Held**
SIC: 7349 Window cleaning; janitorial service, contract basis

(G-4925)
ALADDINS BAKING COMPANY INC
1301 Carnegie Ave (44115-2809)
PHONE..................................216 861-0317
Carl E Nahra, *President*
Carl Nahra, *President*
Maurice Abood, *Vice Pres*
Rick Nahra, *Vice Pres*
Jean Yaacoub, *Site Mgr*
EMP: 48
SQ FT: 10,000
SALES (est): 7.8MM **Privately Held**
WEB: www.aladdinbaking.com
SIC: 5149 5461 Bakery products; bakeries

(G-4926)
ALBERT M HIGLEY CO LLC (PA)
3636 Euclid Ave Fl 3 (44115-2539)
PHONE..................................216 861-2050
Albert M Higley Jr, *Ch of Bd*
Charles Stephenson, *President*
Kurt Heinicke, *Vice Pres*
Rex Lewers, *Vice Pres*
Tom Lippert, *Vice Pres*
EMP: 180
SALES: 159MM **Privately Held**
WEB: www.amhigley.com
SIC: 1542 1541 Commercial & office building, new construction; institutional building construction; industrial buildings, new construction

(G-4927)
ALEPH HOME & SENIOR CARE INC
Also Called: Infinity
2448 Beachwood Blvd (44122-1547)
PHONE..................................216 382-7689
William Bein, *President*
EMP: 60 **EST:** 2001
SALES (est): 820.1K **Privately Held**
SIC: 8361 Home for the aged

(G-4928)
ALEXANDER MANN SOLUTIONS CORP
1301 E 9th St Ste 1200 (44114-1823)
PHONE..................................216 336-6756
Rosaleen M Blair, *President*
Mark Jones, *COO*
Richard Timmins, *CFO*
Lisa REA, *Asst Treas*
Tanya-Marie Nichols, *Human Res Dir*
EMP: 425
SQ FT: 13,000
SALES: 70.8MM **Privately Held**
SIC: 7361 Executive placement
HQ: Alexander Mann Solutions Limited
7-11 Bishopsgate
London EC2N
207 832-2700

(G-4929)
ALGART HEALTH CARE INC
8902 Detroit Ave (44102-1840)
PHONE..................................216 631-1550
Gary Klein, *President*
Tom Jacobs, *Treasurer*
Garth Ireland, *Admin Sec*
EMP: 85
SQ FT: 29,000

SALES (est): 5.2MM **Privately Held**
WEB: www.algart.com
SIC: 8052 Intermediate care facilities

(G-4930)
ALL ERECTION & CRANE RENTAL (PA)
4700 Acorn Dr Ste 100 (44131-6942)
P.O. Box 318047 (44131-8047)
PHONE..................................216 524-6550
Michael C Liptak Jr, *President*
John Mummert, *Transportation*
Lawrence Liptak, *Treasurer*
Wayne C Linson, *Credit Mgr*
Larry Jeppe, *Manager*
EMP: 225
SQ FT: 50,000
SALES (est): 93.3MM **Privately Held**
WEB: www.allcrane.com
SIC: 7353 7359 Heavy construction equipment rental; equipment rental & leasing

(G-4931)
ALL ERECTION & CRANE RENTAL
7809 Old Rockside Rd (44131-2384)
PHONE..................................216 524-6550
Sharon Voyten, *Accounting Mgr*
Shaune Rados, *Sales Staff*
Steve Stefancic, *Branch Mgr*
John Lohn, *Manager*
Patrick Rehmer, *Info Tech Mgr*
EMP: 69
SALES (corp-wide): 93.3MM **Privately Held**
SIC: 7353 7359 Heavy construction equipment rental; equipment rental & leasing
PA: All Erection & Crane Rental Corp
4700 Acorn Dr Ste 100
Cleveland OH 44131
216 524-6550

(G-4932)
ALL ERECTION CRANE RENTL CORP
4700 Acorn Dr Ste 100 (44131-6942)
PHONE..................................216 524-6550
John Martello, *General Mgr*
Rich Nomanson, *General Mgr*
Edward Kocsis, *Managing Dir*
John Mummert, *Transportation*
Michael Hernandez, *Controller*
EMP: 32
SALES (est): 5.2MM **Privately Held**
SIC: 7353 Cranes & aerial lift equipment, rental or leasing

(G-4933)
ALL HEARTS HOME HEALTH CARE
6009 Landerhaven Dr Ste D (44124-4192)
PHONE..................................440 342-2026
Kelli Goodrick, *President*
EMP: 50
SALES (est): 659.4K **Privately Held**
SIC: 8082 Home health care services

(G-4934)
ALL MY SONS BUSINESS DEV CORP
15224 Neo Pkwy (44128-3153)
PHONE..................................469 461-5000
EMP: 121 **Privately Held**
SIC: 4214 Local trucking with storage
PA: All My Sons Business Development Corporation
2400 Old Mill Rd
Carrollton TX 75007

(G-4935)
ALL OHIO THREADED ROD CO INC
5349 Saint Clair Ave (44103-1311)
PHONE..................................216 426-1800
James Wolford, *CEO*
Rick Fien, *President*
Brian Wolford, *Vice Pres*
Raechel Sanichar, *Office Mgr*
▲ **EMP:** 28
SQ FT: 40,000
SALES (est): 7.6MM **Privately Held**
SIC: 3312 5085 3316 Bar, rod & wire products; industrial supplies; cold finishing of steel shapes

(G-4936)
ALL-TYPE WELDING & FABRICATION
7690 Bond St (44139-5351)
PHONE..................................440 439-3990
Mike Distaulo, *President*
William Jones, *Vice Pres*
Dennis Whitaker, *Vice Pres*
Anton Wingren, *Plant Supt*
EMP: 40
SQ FT: 34,000
SALES (est): 8.1MM **Privately Held**
WEB: www.atwf-inc.com
SIC: 3599 7692 1761 Machine & other job shop work; welding repair; sheet metalwork

(G-4937)
ALLEGA RECYCLED MTLS & SUP CO
5585 Canal Rd (44125-4874)
PHONE..................................216 447-0814
Joe Allega, *President*
Jeffrey F Wallis, *Treasurer*
EMP: 25
SQ FT: 30,000
SALES (est): 4MM **Privately Held**
SIC: 5211 5032 Concrete & cinder block; concrete & cinder block

(G-4938)
ALLIED BUILDING PRODUCTS CORP
12800 Brookpark Rd (44130-1116)
PHONE..................................216 362-1764
George Botoulis, *Manager*
EMP: 30
SALES (corp-wide): 6.4B **Publicly Held**
WEB: www.alliedbuilding.com
SIC: 5031 Building materials, exterior
HQ: Allied Building Products Corp.
15 E Union Ave
East Rutherford NJ 07073
201 507-8400

(G-4939)
ALMOST FAMILY INC
23611 Chagrin Blvd # 130 (44122-5540)
PHONE..................................216 464-0443
EMP: 30
SALES (corp-wide): 1.8B **Publicly Held**
SIC: 8082 Home health care services
HQ: Almost Family, Inc.
9510 Ormsby Station Rd # 300
Louisville KY 40223
502 891-1000

(G-4940)
ALORICA CUSTOMER CARE INC
9525 Sweet Valley Dr (44125-4237)
PHONE..................................216 525-3311
EMP: 563
SALES (corp-wide): 7.6B **Privately Held**
SIC: 7389 Telemarketing services
HQ: Alorica Customer Care, Inc.
5085 W Park Blvd Ste 300
Plano TX

(G-4941)
ALPHAPORT INC
18013 Cleveland (44135)
PHONE..................................216 619-2400
Rosella Miranda, *CEO*
Jennifer Jones, *Vice Pres*
Grant Illenberger, *CFO*
Phyliss Mossbruger, *Human Res Mgr*
Michelle Wimmer, *Contract Mgr*
EMP: 50
SQ FT: 5,500
SALES (est): 6MM **Privately Held**
WEB: www.alpha-port.com
SIC: 8711 Consulting engineer

(G-4942)
ALPINE NURSING CARE
5555 Brecksville Rd (44131-1524)
PHONE..................................216 650-6295
Divyech Patel, *CEO*
Dermesh Patel, *President*
Mili Patel, *Vice Pres*
John Herman, *CFO*
EMP: 32

SALES (est): 1.4MM **Privately Held**
WEB: www.alpinehhc.com
SIC: 8082 Home health care services

(G-4943)
ALS SERVICES USA CORP
Also Called: Als Laboratory Group
6180 Halle Dr Ste D (44125-4636)
PHONE..................................604 998-5311
Mike Scruggs, *General Mgr*
EMP: 40 **Privately Held**
SIC: 8734 Testing laboratories
HQ: Als Services Usa, Corp.
10450 Stncliff Rd Ste 210
Houston TX 77099
281 530-5656

(G-4944)
AM INDUSTRIAL GROUP LLC
4680 Grayton Rd (44135-2357)
PHONE..................................216 267-6783
Reginald Wyman, *Owner*
EMP: 35 **Privately Held**
WEB: www.amindustrial.com
SIC: 4225 General warehousing & storage
PA: Am Industrial Group, Llc
16000 Commerce Park Dr
Brookpark OH 44142

(G-4945)
AMALGAMATED TRANSIT UNION
Also Called: Local 268
2428 Saint Clair Ave Ne (44114-4011)
PHONE..................................216 861-3350
Gary Johnson, *President*
EMP: 27
SQ FT: 4,620
SALES (corp-wide): 28.8MM **Privately Held**
WEB: www.atu1005.com
SIC: 8631 Trade union
PA: Amalgamated Transit Union
10000 New Hampshire Ave
Silver Spring MD 20903
202 537-1645

(G-4946)
AMERICAB INC
3380 W 137th St (44111-2412)
PHONE..................................216 429-1134
Jonathan Schwartz, *President*
Robert Zarin, *President*
Robert Roesch, *General Mgr*
Patrick Keenan, *General Mgr*
Robin Sue Lansburg, *Corp Secy*
EMP: 40
SQ FT: 3,500
SALES (est): 1.8MM **Privately Held**
SIC: 4121 Taxicabs

(G-4947)
AMERICAN AIRLINES INC
Also Called: US Airways
5300 Riverside Dr Ste 8a (44135-3147)
PHONE..................................216 706-0702
Robert Mitchell, *Manager*
EMP: 48
SALES (corp-wide): 44.5B **Publicly Held**
WEB: www.usair.com
SIC: 4512 Air passenger carrier, scheduled
HQ: American Airlines, Inc.
4333 Amon Carter Blvd
Fort Worth TX 76155
817 963-1234

(G-4948)
AMERICAN AIRLINES INC
5300 Riverside Dr Ste 1a (44135-3145)
PHONE..................................216 898-1347
Bob Mitchell, *Manager*
EMP: 50
SALES (corp-wide): 44.5B **Publicly Held**
WEB: www.aa.com
SIC: 4581 4512 Airport terminal services; air transportation, scheduled
HQ: American Airlines, Inc.
4333 Amon Carter Blvd
Fort Worth TX 76155
817 963-1234

(G-4949)
AMERICAN CANCER SOCIETY EAST
10501 Euclid Ave (44106-2204)
PHONE..................................800 227-2345

Rimas Jasin, *Exec Dir*
EMP: 25
SALES (corp-wide): 91.7MM **Privately Held**
SIC: 8322 Social service center
PA: American Cancer Society, East Central
Division, Inc.
Sipe Ave Rr 422
Hershey PA 17033
717 533-6144

(G-4950)
AMERICAN COMMODORE TU
(PA)
4130 Mayfield Rd (44121-3033)
PHONE..............................216 291-4601
Frank Simoni Jr, *President*
Joe N Simoni, *Principal*
Mary Simoni, *Principal*
Toni Wick, *Corp Secy*
Ray Caporale, *Vice Pres*
EMP: 60 EST: 1947
SQ FT: 35,000
SALES (est): 6.7MM **Privately Held**
WEB: www.actux.com
SIC: 7299 5699 Dress suit rental; tuxedo
rental; formal wear

(G-4951)
AMERICAN CONSOLIDATED
INDS INC (PA)
4650 Johnston Pkwy (44128-3219)
PHONE..............................216 587-8000
Joyce Kaufman, *Ch of Bd*
Josh Kaufman, *President*
Steve Lefkowitz, *CFO*
◆ EMP: 100
SQ FT: 118,000
SALES (est): 24.9MM **Privately Held**
SIC: 5051 Metals service centers & offices

(G-4952)
AMERICAN COPY EQUIPMENT
INC
Also Called: Online Imaging Solutions
6599 Granger Rd (44131-1415)
PHONE..............................330 722-9555
John Baron, *President*
Katherine L Huff, *Principal*
EMP: 195
SQ FT: 30,000
SALES (est): 73.1MM **Privately Held**
WEB: www.acecleveland.com
SIC: 5044 Office equipment

(G-4953)
AMERICAN HEART ASSN OHIO
VLY
Also Called: Great Rivers
1375 E 9th St Ste 600 (44114-1785)
PHONE..............................216 791-7500
Dawn Clark, *Director*
EMP: 25
SQ FT: 36,000
SALES (est): 1.8MM **Privately Held**
SIC: 8733 Research institute

(G-4954)
AMERICAN INCOME LIFE INSUR
CO
12301 Ridge Rd (44133-3744)
P.O. Box 33160, North Royalton (44133-
0160)
PHONE..............................440 582-0040
James M Surace, *Principal*
EMP: 60
SQ FT: 750
SALES (corp-wide): 4.3B **Publicly Held**
WEB: www.ailfl.com
SIC: 6311 6411 Life insurance carriers; in-
surance agents
HQ: American Income Life Insurance Com-
pany Inc
1200 Wooded Acres Dr
Waco TX 76710
254 741-5701

(G-4955)
AMERICAN INTL GROUP INC
1300 E 9th St Ste 1400 (44114-1573)
PHONE..............................216 479-8800
Richard Kudla, *Branch Mgr*
Kim Gallo, *Manager*
EMP: 150

SALES (corp-wide): 47.3B **Publicly Held**
SIC: 6411 Insurance agents
PA: American International Group, Inc.
80 Pine St Fl 4
New York NY 10005
212 770-7000

(G-4956)
AMERICAN LIVERY SERVICE
INC
Also Called: American Limousine Service
11723 Detroit Ave (44107-3001)
PHONE..............................216 221-9330
Robert Mazzarella, *President*
Joanne Mazzarella, *Corp Secy*
EMP: 45
SQ FT: 2,500
SALES (est): 2.4MM **Privately Held**
WEB: www.americanlimousineservice.com
SIC: 4119 Limousine rental, with driver;
hearse rental, with driver

(G-4957)
AMERICAN MARINE EXPRESS
INC
Also Called: Amx
765 E 140th St Ste A (44110-2181)
P.O. Box 32487 (44132-0487)
PHONE..............................216 268-3005
Harjit S Dhillon, *President*
Dan Cain, *General Mgr*
Julie Boothe-Rhodes, *Business Mgr*
Billy Kyle, *Opers Mgr*
EMP: 30
SALES: 10.4MM **Privately Held**
SIC: 4731 Truck transportation brokers

(G-4958)
AMERICAN MIDWEST
MORTGAGE CORP (PA)
6363 York Rd Ste 300 (44130-3031)
PHONE..............................440 882-5210
John Paulozzi, *President*
Dan Lease, *Broker*
Dianne Potok, *Office Mgr*
Shannon Gluck, *Technology*
Jocephine Paulozzi, *Admin Sec*
EMP: 50
SALES (est): 10.9MM **Privately Held**
SIC: 6162 Mortgage bankers

(G-4959)
AMERICAN MULTI-CINEMA INC
Also Called: AMC
4788 Ridge Rd (44144-3327)
PHONE..............................216 749-0260
Paul Gellott, *Branch Mgr*
EMP: 50
SALES (corp-wide): 7.3MM **Publicly Held**
WEB: www.arrowheadtownecenter.com
SIC: 7832 Motion picture theaters, except
drive-in
HQ: American Multi-Cinema, Inc.
1 Amc Way
Leawood KS 66211
913 213-2000

(G-4960)
AMERICAN MUTUAL LIFE ASSN
(PA)
Also Called: AMLA
19424 S Waterloo Rd (44119-3250)
PHONE..............................216 531-1900
Stanley Ziherl, *President*
Joseph Petric Jr, *Corp Secy*
Tereasa Aveni, *Exec VP*
Albert Amigoni, *Vice Pres*
Anna Mae Mannian, *Vice Pres*
EMP: 25
SQ FT: 1,500
SALES: 3.3MM **Privately Held**
WEB: www.americanmutual.org
SIC: 6311 Fraternal life insurance organi-
zations

(G-4961)
AMERICAN NAT FLEET SVC INC
Also Called: American Fleet Services
7714 Commerce Park Oval (44131-2306)
PHONE..............................216 447-6060
Joe Schuerger, *CEO*
EMP: 65
SQ FT: 40,000

SALES (est): 13.1MM **Privately Held**
WEB: www.fleetme.com
SIC: 7538 7532 General truck repair; body
shop, automotive; body shop, trucks

(G-4962)
AMERICAN NATIONAL RED
CROSS
3747 Euclid Ave (44115-2501)
PHONE..............................216 431-3152
David Plate, *CEO*
EMP: 29
SALES (corp-wide): 2.5B **Privately Held**
SIC: 8999 Artists & artists' studios
PA: The American National Red Cross
430 17th St Nw
Washington DC 20006
202 737-8300

(G-4963)
AMERICAN PRSERVATION
BLDRS LLC
127 Public Sq Ste 1300 (44114-1310)
PHONE..............................216 236-2007
Michael Kucera, *President*
Dennis Arian, *Vice Pres*
Harry Lee, *Vice Pres*
Todd Wallace, *Vice Pres*
Frank Sara, *Project Mgr*
EMP: 68
SALES (est): 45.6MM **Privately Held**
SIC: 1531 Operative builders

(G-4964)
AMERICAN RESIDENTIAL SVCS
LLC
4547 Hinckley Industrial (44109-6018)
PHONE..............................216 561-8880
Divyesh Patel, *Branch Mgr*
EMP: 59
SALES (corp-wide): 2.4B **Privately Held**
SIC: 1711 Plumbing contractors
PA: American Residential Services Llc
965 Ridge Lake Blvd # 201
Memphis TN 38120
901 271-9700

(G-4965)
AMERICAN RETIREMENT CORP
Also Called: Homewood Rsdnce At Rchmond
Hts
3 Homewood Way (44143-2955)
PHONE..............................216 291-6140
Kim Hutter, *Branch Mgr*
EMP: 55
SALES (corp-wide): 4.5B **Publicly Held**
WEB: www.arclp.com
SIC: 8051 8052 Skilled nursing care facili-
ties; intermediate care facilities
HQ: American Retirement Corporation
111 Westwood Pl Ste 200
Brentwood TN 37027
615 221-2250

(G-4966)
AMERICAN RETIREMENT CORP
Also Called: Homewood Residence At Rocke-
fel
3151 Mayfield Rd Apt 1105 (44118-1756)
PHONE..............................216 321-6331
Toni Colon, *Manager*
EMP: 60
SQ FT: 2,726
SALES (corp-wide): 4.5B **Publicly Held**
WEB: www.arclp.com
SIC: 8051 Skilled nursing care facilities
HQ: American Retirement Corporation
111 Westwood Pl Ste 200
Brentwood TN 37027
615 221-2250

(G-4967)
AMERICAN TANK &
FABRICATING CO (PA)
Also Called: A T & F Co
12314 Elmwood Ave (44111-5991)
PHONE..............................216 252-1500
Terry Ripich, *Ch of Bd*
Bob Ripich, *President*
Michael Ripich, *President*
Kevin Cantrell, *Vice Pres*
Michael Puleo, *Vice Pres*
▲ EMP: 190 EST: 1940
SQ FT: 300,000

SALES (est): 183.4MM **Privately Held**
WEB: www.amtank.com
SIC: 5051 3443 Metals service centers &
offices; iron & steel (ferrous) products;
weldments

(G-4968)
AMERICAN TITLE OF OHIO LLC
600 Superior Ave E # 1300 (44114-2654)
PHONE..............................303 868-2250
Richard Talley, *
EMP: 25
SALES: 950K **Privately Held**
SIC: 6411 Insurance agents, brokers &
service

(G-4969)
AMERIMARK HOLDINGS LLC
(PA)
Also Called: Complements
6864 Engle Rd (44130-7910)
PHONE..............................440 325-2000
Mark Ethier, *CEO*
Linda Dulcie, *Vice Pres*
Dawn Kelly, *Opers Staff*
Vicki Baker, *Buyer*
Joie Hill, *Buyer*
EMP: 425
SALES (est): 643.7MM **Privately Held**
SIC: 7331 5961 Direct mail advertising
services; catalog sales; mail order house

(G-4970)
AMITEL BEACHWOOD LTD
PARTNR (PA)
Also Called: Residence Inn By Marriott
6000 Rckside Woods Blvd N (44131-2330)
PHONE..............................216 707-9839
Resair Corp, *Partner*
Stonewood Investments III, *Partner*
Frank Crisafi, *General Ptnr*
John Phillips, *Controller*
EMP: 50 EST: 1997
SALES (est): 863.8K **Privately Held**
SIC: 7011 Hotels And Motels

(G-4971)
AMITEL BEACHWOOD LTD
PARTNR
Also Called: Residence Inn By Marriott
3628 Park Dr (44134)
PHONE..............................216 831-3030
Terry Knowlan, *General Mgr*
EMP: 25
SALES (est): 1MM
SALES (corp-wide): 863.8K **Privately
Held**
SIC: 7011 Hotels
PA: Amitel Beachwood Limited Partnership
6000 Rckside Woods Blvd N
Cleveland OH 44131
216 707-9839

(G-4972)
AMITEL ROCKSIDE LTD PARTNR
Also Called: Residence Inn By Marriott
5101 Independence (44131)
PHONE..............................216 520-1450
Darrell Glenn, *General Mgr*
EMP: 49
SQ FT: 41,267
SALES (est): 1.1MM
SALES (corp-wide): 2.8MM **Privately
Held**
SIC: 7011 Hotel, franchised
PA: Amitel Rockside Limited Partnership
6000 Rockside Woods Blvd
Cleveland OH

(G-4973)
AMOTEC INC (PA)
1701 E 12th St Apt 10b (44114-3271)
PHONE..............................440 250-4600
Carmine Izzo, *President*
Dennis George, *Business Mgr*
Lisa Peters, *Vice Pres*
David Brooks, *Accounts Mgr*
Mike Donahue, *Business Dir*
EMP: 31
SQ FT: 5,000
SALES: 3.5MM **Privately Held**
WEB: www.amotecinc.com
SIC: 7361 Employment agencies

(G-4974)

AMSDELL CONSTRUCTION INC (PA)

20445 Emerald Pkwy # 220 (44135-6009)
PHONE...................................216 458-0670
Berry Amsdell, *President*
Robert J Amsdell, *Vice Pres*
Robert Amsdell, *Vice Pres*
John Black, *CFO*
EMP: 180
SQ FT: 8,000
SALES (est): 17.4MM **Privately Held**
SIC: 1522 1541 1542 6531 Hotel/motel, new construction; warehouse construction; industrial buildings, new construction; commercial & office building, new construction; shopping center construction; real estate agents & managers

(G-4975)

AMTRUST NORTH AMERICA INC (DH)

Also Called: Amtrust Financial Services
800 Superior Ave E # 2100 (44114-2613)
PHONE...................................216 328-6100
Barry D Zyskind, *CEO*
Joey Andrews, *President*
Walter Lasley, *President*
Matt Gillespie, *Assistant VP*
Karen Owsiany, *Assistant VP*
EMP: 230
SQ FT: 60,000
SALES (est): 1.1B
SALES (corp-wide): 187.6MM **Privately Held**
SIC: 6331 6411 Workers' compensation insurance; insurance claim processing, except medical

(G-4976)

ANCHOR BRONZE AND METALS INC

11470 Euclid Ave Ste 509 (44106-3934)
PHONE...................................440 549-5653
Roger Moore, *President*
EMP: 32
SQ FT: 42,000
SALES (est): 5.4MM **Privately Held**
SIC: 5051 3366 Copper; copper products; miscellaneous nonferrous products; castings, rough: iron or steel; brass foundry

(G-4977)

ANCHOR CLEANING CONTRACTORS

1966 W 52nd St (44102-3367)
P.O. Box 602160 (44102-0160)
PHONE...................................216 961-7343
Paul Gwinn, *President*
EMP: 25
SQ FT: 750
SALES (est): 812.2K **Privately Held**
SIC: 7349 Janitorial service, contract basis; window cleaning

(G-4978)

ANCHOR METAL PROCESSING INC (PA)

11830 Brookpark Rd (44130-1103)
PHONE...................................216 362-1850
Edward Pfaff, *Ch of Bd*
Frederick Pfaff, *President*
Jeff Pfaff, *Vice Pres*
Dave Pippert, *Purchasing*
Robert Pfaff, *Admin Sec*
EMP: 30
SQ FT: 46,000
SALES (est): 9MM **Privately Held**
SIC: 3599 1761 3444 Machine shop, jobbing & repair; sheet metalwork; sheet metalwork

(G-4979)

ANGELS ON EARTH CHILD CARE CO

13439 Lorain Ave (44111-3433)
PHONE...................................216 476-8100
Robert Gonzalez, *President*
Marilyn Gonzalez, *Vice Pres*
EMP: 40
SQ FT: 7,500
SALES (est): 1.2MM **Privately Held**
SIC: 8351 Child day care services

(G-4980)

ANGSTROM GRAPHICS INC MIDWEST (HQ)

4437 E 49th St (44125-1005)
PHONE...................................216 271-5300
Wayne R Angstrom, *Ch of Bd*
Bruce Macdonald, *Vice Pres*
Rachel Malakoff, *CFO*
Tim Gailey, *Accounting Mgr*
Kathy Lazar, *Credit Mgr*
EMP: 295
SQ FT: 230,000
SALES (est): 56.9MM
SALES (corp-wide): 288.8MM **Privately Held**
SIC: 2752 7331 Commercial printing, offset; direct mail advertising services
PA: Angstrom Graphics Inc
4437 E 49th St
Cleveland OH 44125
216 271-5300

(G-4981)

ANGSTROM GRAPHICS INC MIDWEST

Also Called: New Channel Direct
4437 E 49th St (44125-1005)
PHONE...................................330 225-8950
Carol Swearingen, *Manager*
EMP: 45
SALES (corp-wide): 288.8MM **Privately Held**
SIC: 7331 Mailing service
HQ: Angstrom Graphics Inc Midwest
4437 E 49th St
Cleveland OH 44125
216 271-5300

(G-4982)

ANIMAL PROTECTIVE LEAGUE

1729 Willey Ave (44113-4391)
PHONE...................................216 771-4616
Jeffrey L Kocian, *President*
EMP: 35
SQ FT: 22,400
SALES: 4MM **Privately Held**
SIC: 8699 0742 Animal humane society; veterinary services, specialties

(G-4983)

ANSELMO RSSIS PREMIER PROD LTD

Also Called: Premiere Produce
4500 Willow Pkwy (44125-1042)
PHONE...................................800 229-5517
Anthony Anselmo, *President*
Anthony Rossi, *Partner*
Joe Harvey, *General Mgr*
Chad Witham, *Purchasing*
EMP: 43
SALES (est): 22.2MM **Privately Held**
SIC: 5148 Fruits, fresh

(G-4984)

ANSWERING SERVICE INC

Also Called: Radio Page Leasing
5767 Mayfield Rd Rear 1 (44124-2991)
PHONE...................................440 473-1200
William Smylie, *Ch of Bd*
Shari Rosen, *President*
EMP: 30
SQ FT: 800
SALES (est): 2.1MM **Privately Held**
SIC: 7389 4812 Telephone answering service; paging services

(G-4985)

ANTHONY ALLEGA CEMENT CONTR

5585 Canal Rd (44125-4874)
PHONE...................................216 447-0814
John Allega, *President*
James Allega, *Vice Pres*
Joseph Allega, *Vice Pres*
Jeffrey Wallis, *Controller*
Jeff Repenning, *Manager*
EMP: 50 **EST:** 1946
SQ FT: 5,000
SALES (est): 18.5MM **Privately Held**
WEB: www.allega.com
SIC: 1611 Concrete construction: roads, highways, sidewalks, etc.

(G-4986)

ANY DOMEST WORK INC

Also Called: Adw
5735 Pearl Rd (44129-2849)
PHONE...................................440 845-9911
Joseph Sokolowski, *President*
EMP: 80
SALES (est): 2.3MM **Privately Held**
SIC: 7349 Cleaning service, industrial or commercial

(G-4987)

AON CONSULTING INC

1660 W 2nd St Ste 650 (44113-1419)
PHONE...................................216 621-8100
Jerry Kysela, *Manager*
EMP: 40
SALES (corp-wide): 10B **Privately Held**
SIC: 6411 Insurance brokers
HQ: Aon Consulting, Inc.
200 E Randolph St Ll3
Chicago IL 60601
312 381-1000

(G-4988)

AON RISK SVCS NORTHEAST INC (HQ)

Also Called: A O N
1660 W 2nd St (44113-1454)
P.O. Box 7247, Philadelphia PA (19170-0001)
PHONE...................................216 621-8100
Richard Longyhore, *Principal*
Jerry G Kysela, *Director*
EMP: 1100
SALES (est): 358.5MM
SALES (corp-wide): 10B **Privately Held**
SIC: 6411 Insurance brokers
PA: Aon Plc
The Leadenhall Building
London EC3V
207 623-5500

(G-4989)

APG OFFICE FURNISHINGS INC

3615 Superior Ave E 4407a (44114-4139)
PHONE...................................216 621-4590
Sean Regan, *Branch Mgr*
EMP: 45
SALES (corp-wide): 28.9MM **Privately Held**
WEB: www.apgof.com
SIC: 5021 5044 Office furniture; office equipment
PA: Apg Office Furnishings, Inc.
12075 Northwest Blvd # 100
Cincinnati OH 45246
513 621-9111

(G-4990)

APPALACHIAN HARDWOOD LUMBER CO

5433 Perkins Rd (44146-1856)
PHONE...................................440 232-6767
Gary S Kaufman, *President*
Stephen Kaufman, *Vice Pres*
▲ **EMP:** 30
SQ FT: 100,000
SALES (est): 16.3MM **Privately Held**
WEB: www.appalachianlumber.com
SIC: 5031 Lumber: rough, dressed & finished; millwork; hardboard

(G-4991)

APPLEWOOD CENTERS INC (PA)

10427 Detroit Ave (44102-1645)
PHONE...................................216 696-6815
Adam Jacobs, *Exec Dir*
EMP: 60
SQ FT: 17,000
SALES: 17.4MM **Privately Held**
SIC: 8322 8699 Child related social services; charitable organization

(G-4992)

APPLEWOOD CENTERS INC

Also Called: Children's Aide Society Campus
10427 Detroit Ave (44102-1645)
PHONE...................................216 521-6511
Roberta King, *Manager*
EMP: 90
SALES (corp-wide): 17.4MM **Privately Held**
SIC: 8322 Child related social services

PA: Applewood Centers, Inc.
10427 Detroit Ave
Cleveland OH 44102
216 696-6815

(G-4993)

APPLEWOOD CENTERS INC

3518 W 25th St (44109-1951)
PHONE...................................216 741-2241
J Blumhagen, *Branch Mgr*
Elizabeth Frantz, *Psychologist*
Ellen Rosenblatt, *Psychiatry*
EMP: 143
SALES (corp-wide): 17.4MM **Privately Held**
SIC: 8322 Child related social services
PA: Applewood Centers, Inc.
10427 Detroit Ave
Cleveland OH 44102
216 696-6815

(G-4994)

APPLIED INDUS TECH - CA LLC (HQ)

1 Applied Plz (44115-2511)
PHONE...................................216 426-4000
Kevin Ramsland, *Manager*
David L Pugh,
▲ **EMP:** 307
SALES (est): 202.7MM
SALES (corp-wide): 3B **Publicly Held**
WEB: www.ait-applied.com
SIC: 5063 Power transmission equipment, electric
PA: Applied Industrial Technologies, Inc.
1 Applied Plz
Cleveland OH 44115
216 426-4000

(G-4995)

APPLIED INDUS TECH - DIXIE INC (HQ)

1 Applied Plz (44115-2511)
P.O. Box 6925 (44101-2193)
PHONE...................................216 426-4000
David L Pugh, *Ch of Bd*
Robert Christensen, *President*
Michael Coticchia, *President*
Krysta Dodd, *General Mgr*
Joseph M Bruening, *Principal*
▲ **EMP:** 153 **EST:** 1923
SQ FT: 146,000
SALES (est): 368.5MM
SALES (corp-wide): 3B **Publicly Held**
SIC: 5172 5169 Lubricating oils & greases; sealants
PA: Applied Industrial Technologies, Inc.
1 Applied Plz
Cleveland OH 44115
216 426-4000

(G-4996)

APPLIED INDUSTRIAL TECH INC (PA)

1 Applied Plz (44115-2511)
PHONE...................................216 426-4000
Peter C Wallace, *Ch of Bd*
Neil A Schrimsher, *President*
Eldon Hancock, *Partner*
Joe Alfonso, *General Mgr*
Randy Barnard, *General Mgr*
▲ **EMP:** 296 **EST:** 1923
SALES: 3B **Publicly Held**
WEB: www.appliedindustrial.com
SIC: 5169 7699 5085 Sealants; industrial machinery & equipment repair; bearings

(G-4997)

APRIA HEALTHCARE LLC

5480 Cloverleaf Pkwy # 4 (44125-4867)
PHONE...................................216 485-1180
Lynn Rampley, *Manager*
EMP: 37 **Privately Held**
WEB: www.apria.com
SIC: 7352 5999 Medical equipment rental; medical apparatus & supplies
HQ: Apria Healthcare Llc
26220 Enterprise Ct
Lake Forest CA 92630
949 639-2000

(G-4998)
ARAMARK FACILITY SERVICES LLC
2121 Euclid Ave (44115-2214)
PHONE.................................216 687-5000
Pat Underwood, *Manager*
EMP: 50 **Publicly Held**
SIC: 7349 8744 Janitorial service, contract basis; facilities support services
HQ: Aramark Facility Services, Llc
2400 Market St 209
Philadelphia PA 19103
215 238-3000

(G-4999)
ARAMARK UNF & CAREER AP LLC
3600 E 93rd St (44105-1686)
PHONE.................................216 341-7400
Douglas Johnson, *General Mgr*
Jason Cash, *District Mgr*
Chad Martuscelli, *District Mgr*
Scott Robbins, *District Mgr*
David Silveira, *District Mgr*
EMP: 140
SQ FT: 85,000 **Publicly Held**
WEB: www.aramark-uniform.com
SIC: 7218 7213 Industrial launderers; linen supply
HQ: Aramark Uniform & Career Apparel, Llc
115 N First St Ste 203
Burbank CA 91502
818 973-3700

(G-5000)
ARBOR CONSTRUCTION CO
1350 W 3rd St (44113-1806)
PHONE.................................216 360-8989
Robert Stark, *President*
Howard Beder, *Vice Pres*
Dominic Del Balso, *Info Tech Dir*
EMP: 30 EST: 1980
SQ FT: 3,400
SALES (est): 5.5MM **Privately Held**
SIC: 1542 Shopping center construction

(G-5001)
ARBOR PARK PHASE TWO ASSOC
Also Called: Arbor Park Village
3750 Fleming Ave (44115-3741)
PHONE.................................561 998-0700
Denniis Blackinton, *Partner*
EMP: 30
SALES: 950K **Privately Held**
SIC: 6513 Apartment building operators

(G-5002)
ARBOR PK PHASE THREE ASSOC LP
Also Called: ARBOR PARK VILLAGE
3750 Fleming Ave (44115-3741)
PHONE.................................561 998-0700
Dennis Blackinton, *Treasurer*
EMP: 30
SALES: 1.7MM **Privately Held**
SIC: 6513 Apartment building operators

(G-5003)
ARC DOCUMENT SOLUTIONS INC
Also Called: A R C
3666 Carnegie Ave (44115-2714)
PHONE.................................216 281-1234
Tina Lemanomcz, *Branch Mgr*
EMP: 92
SALES (corp-wide): 400.7MM **Publicly Held**
SIC: 7334 Blueprinting service
PA: Arc Document Solutions, Inc.
12657 Alcosta Blvd # 200
San Ramon CA 94583
925 949-5100

(G-5004)
ARC GAS & SUPPLY LLC
4560 Nicky Blvd Ste D (44125-1058)
PHONE.................................216 341-5882
Sam Strazzanti, *President*
Jim Kinser, *Vice Pres*
Danny Strazzanti, *Opers Mgr*
Dan Trappe, *Store Mgr*
Gary Mroczka, *Controller*
EMP: 38

SALES (est): 7.4MM **Privately Held**
SIC: 7692 Welding repair

(G-5005)
ARCADIS US INC
1111 Superior Ave E # 1300 (44114-2577)
PHONE.................................216 781-6177
Ben Webster, *Branch Mgr*
EMP: 35
SALES (corp-wide): 2.8B **Privately Held**
SIC: 8712 Architectural services
HQ: Arcadis U.S., Inc.
630 Plaza Dr Ste 200
Highlands Ranch CO 80129
720 344-3500

(G-5006)
ARCHITECTURAL INTR RESTORATION
2401 Train Ave Ste 100 (44113-4254)
PHONE.................................216 241-2255
John L Textoris Jr, *President*
EMP: 45
SQ FT: 11,000
SALES (est): 3.3MM **Privately Held**
SIC: 1742 Drywall; acoustical & ceiling work

(G-5007)
ARISTOCRAT W NURSING HM CORP (PA)
Also Called: Tuscan Villa
24340 Sperry Dr (44145-1565)
PHONE.................................440 835-0660
Elias J Coury, *President*
Norman Fox, *Corp Secy*
EMP: 125
SQ FT: 36,000
SALES: 3.2MM **Privately Held**
SIC: 8051 Skilled Nursing Care Facility

(G-5008)
ARISTOCRAT W NURSING HM CORP
Also Called: Call Traditions
4401 W 150th St (44135-1311)
PHONE.................................216 252-7730
Anthony M Coury, *President*
EMP: 105
SALES (corp-wide): 3.2MM **Privately Held**
SIC: 8051 Skilled nursing care facilities
PA: Aristocrat West Nursing Home Corporation
24340 Sperry Dr
Cleveland OH 44145
440 835-0660

(G-5009)
ARS RESCUE ROOTER INC
4547 Hinckley Industrial (44109-6018)
PHONE.................................440 842-8494
Bill Linn, *Manager*
EMP: 30 EST: 2008
SALES (est): 1MM **Privately Held**
SIC: 1711 Plumbing contractors

(G-5010)
ART-AMERICAN PRINTING PLATES
1138 W 9th St Fl 4 (44113-1007)
PHONE.................................216 241-4420
John T Mc Sweeney, *President*
Lawrence Mc Sweeney, *Vice Pres*
EMP: 25
SQ FT: 11,000
SALES (est): 3.5MM **Privately Held**
WEB: www.art-american.com
SIC: 2796 7336 Platemaking services; graphic arts & related design

(G-5011)
ARTISAN AND TRUCKERS CSLTY CO
6300 Wilson Mills Rd (44143-2109)
PHONE.................................440 461-5000
Tricia Griffith, *President*
EMP: 1612 EST: 1994
SALES: 42.4MM
SALES (corp-wide): 31.9B **Publicly Held**
SIC: 6331 Automobile insurance
HQ: Progressive Commercial Holdings, Inc.
6300 Wilson Mills Rd
Cleveland OH 44143

(G-5012)
ASHLAND LLC
Also Called: Ashland Distribution
2191 W 110th St (44102-3509)
PHONE.................................216 961-4690
Don Matson, *Branch Mgr*
EMP: 60
SALES (corp-wide): 3.7B **Publicly Held**
WEB: www.ashland.com
SIC: 5169 Alkalines & chlorine
HQ: Ashland Llc
50 E Rivercenter Blvd # 1600
Covington KY 41011
859 815-3333

(G-5013)
ASHLAND LLC
Ashland Distribution
4600 E 71st St (44125-1051)
PHONE.................................216 883-8200
Dana Cooper, *Manager*
EMP: 32
SQ FT: 95,730
SALES (corp-wide): 3.7B **Publicly Held**
WEB: www.ashland.com
SIC: 5169 Alkalines & chlorine
HQ: Ashland Llc
50 E Rivercenter Blvd # 1600
Covington KY 41011
859 815-3333

(G-5014)
ASPEN WOODSIDE VILLAGE
19455 Rockside Rd Ofc (44146-2056)
PHONE.................................440 439-8666
Renee Owens, *Exec VP*
Bill Way, *Exec Dir*
EMP: 80
SALES (est): 3.3MM **Privately Held**
SIC: 8361 Home for the aged

(G-5015)
ASSOCIATED STEEL COMPANY INC
Also Called: N-T Steel
18200 Miles Rd (44128-3484)
PHONE.................................216 475-8000
Ron Dekamp, *Manager*
EMP: 25
SALES (corp-wide): 9.4MM **Privately Held**
SIC: 5051 Steel
PA: Associated Steel Company, Inc.
18200 Miles Rd
Cleveland OH 44128
216 475-8200

(G-5016)
AT HOLDINGS CORPORATION
23555 Euclid Ave (44117-1703)
PHONE.................................216 692-6000
Michael S Lipscomb, *Ch of Bd*
David Scaife, *Vice Pres*
Frances S St Clair, *CFO*
Shawn Berry, *Accounts Exec*
Jeffrey Tomson, *Info Tech Mgr*
EMP: 736
SQ FT: 1,800,000
SALES (est): 42MM **Privately Held**
SIC: 3724 3728 6512 Pumps, aircraft engine; aircraft parts & equipment; commercial & industrial building operation
HQ: Eaton Corporation
1000 Eaton Blvd
Cleveland OH 44122
440 523-5000

(G-5017)
AT&T CORP
Also Called: ATT
3530 Ridge Rd (44102-5462)
PHONE.................................216 672-0809
EMP: 118
SALES (corp-wide): 170.7B **Publicly Held**
SIC: 4813 Local & long distance telephone communications
HQ: At&t Corp.
1 At&t Way
Bedminster NJ 07921
800 403-3302

(G-5018)
AT&T MOBILITY LLC
25309 Cedar Rd (44124-3785)
PHONE.................................216 382-0825

EMP: 26
SALES (corp-wide): 170.7B **Publicly Held**
SIC: 4812 Cellular telephone services
HQ: At&t Mobility Llc
1025 Lenox Park Blvd Ne
Brookhaven GA 30319
800 331-0500

(G-5019)
ATI AVIATION SERVICES LLC
12401 Taft Ave (44108-1627)
PHONE.................................216 268-4888
Lee Paschyn, *Controller*
Timothy Gurewicz, *Director*
Jeff Robbins, *Officer*
Pablo Prieto,
Chris Di Lillo,
EMP: 25 EST: 2001
SQ FT: 55,000
SALES: 2.5MM **Privately Held**
SIC: 4581 Aircraft maintenance & repair services; aircraft servicing & repairing

(G-5020)
ATLANTIS CO INC (PA)
Also Called: Atlantis Company, The
105 Ken Mar Indus Pkwy (44147)
PHONE.................................888 807-3272
Brian Whitaker, *President*
EMP: 70
SALES (est): 13.3MM **Privately Held**
WEB: www.atlantissecurity.com
SIC: 7349 7381 Building maintenance services; detective services

(G-5021)
ATLAS ROOFING COMPANY
4190 E 71st St (44105-5831)
PHONE.................................330 467-7683
Anthony J Hadala, *President*
EMP: 25
SALES (est): 2.3MM **Privately Held**
SIC: 1761 Roofing contractor

(G-5022)
ATOTECH USA INC
1000 Harvard Ave (44109-3048)
PHONE.................................216 398-0550
Steve Bellavita, *Branch Mgr*
Robin Taylor, *Manager*
EMP: 80
SALES (corp-wide): 8.4B **Publicly Held**
SIC: 2899 4225 Chemical supplies for foundries; general warehousing & storage
HQ: Atotech Usa, Llc
1750 Overview Dr
Rock Hill SC 29730

(G-5023)
AUSTIN BUILDING AND DESIGN INC (DH)
Also Called: Austin Company, The
6095 Parkland Blvd # 100 (44124-6139)
PHONE.................................440 544-2600
Michael G Pierce, *President*
Brandon Davis, *General Mgr*
Frank Spano, *Managing Dir*
Noriaki Ohashi, *Chairman*
Mark Phillips, *Senior VP*
EMP: 121
SQ FT: 21,869
SALES (est): 98.2MM
SALES (corp-wide): 17.1B **Privately Held**
WEB: www.kajimausa.com
SIC: 1541 1542 8742 8711 Industrial buildings, new construction; commercial & office building, new construction; institutional building construction; management consulting services; engineering services; architectural engineering
HQ: Kajima U.S.A. Inc.
3550 Lenox Rd Ne Ste 1850
Atlanta GA 30326
404 564-3900

(G-5024)
AUTOGRAPH INC
Also Called: Autograph Foliages
4419 Perkins Ave (44103-3543)
PHONE.................................216 881-1911
Thomas M Acklin, *Manager*
EMP: 32

SALES (corp-wide): 4.8MM **Privately Held**
WEB: www.autographfoliages.com
SIC: 5193 Flowers & florists' supplies
PA: Autograph, Inc.
3631 Perkins Ave
Cleveland OH
216 426-6151

(G-5025)
AUTOMOTIVE DISTRIBUTORS CO INC
990 Valley Belt Dr (44109)
PHONE..............................216 398-2014
Randy Primer, *Branch Mgr*
EMP: 30
SALES (corp-wide): 132.8MM **Privately Held**
WEB: www.adw1.com
SIC: 5013 Automotive supplies & parts
PA: Automotive Distributors Co., Inc.
2981 Morse Rd
Columbus OH 43231
614 476-1315

(G-5026)
AUXILIARY BD FAIRVIEW GEN HOSP
Also Called: FAIRVIEW WEST PHYSICIAN CENTER
18101 Lorain Ave (44111-5612)
PHONE..............................216 476-7000
EMP: 1115
SALES: 50.3K
SALES (corp-wide): 8.9B **Privately Held**
SIC: 8062 General medical & surgical hospitals
HQ: Fairview Hospital
18101 Lorain Ave
Cleveland OH 44111
216 476-7000

(G-5027)
AVANTIA INC
9655 Sweet Valley Dr # 1 (44125-4271)
PHONE..............................216 901-9366
Jennie Zamberlan, *President*
Jereme Willig, *Engineer*
Jack Gabriel, *VP Bus Dvlpt*
Michael Knoll, *Business Anlyst*
Bob Drake, *Manager*
EMP: 35
SQ FT: 4,500
SALES (est): 2.8MM **Privately Held**
WEB: www.avantia-inc.com
SIC: 8748 Business consulting

(G-5028)
AW FABER-CASTELL USA INC
Also Called: Creativity For Kids
9450 Allen Dr Ste B (44125-4602)
PHONE..............................216 643-4660
Jamie Gallagher, *CEO*
Phyllis Brody, *Vice Pres*
Don Fischer, *CFO*
Michael Smith, *Info Tech Dir*
▲ EMP: 100
SQ FT: 85,000
SALES (est): 37MM
SALES (corp-wide): 712.9MM **Privately Held**
WEB: www.faber-castell.com
SIC: 5092 5112 3944 Arts & crafts equipment & supplies; stationery & office supplies; writing instruments & supplies; games, toys & children's vehicles; craft & hobby kits & sets
HQ: Faber-Castell Ag
Nurnberger Str. 2
Stein 90547
911 996-50

(G-5029)
AXA ADVISORS LLC
1001 Lakeside Ave E # 1650 (44114-1158)
PHONE..............................216 621-7715
Greg Lastisa,
EMP: 60
SALES (corp-wide): 1MM **Publicly Held**
WEB: www.axacs.com
SIC: 8742 Financial consultant
HQ: Axa Advisors, Llc
1290 Ave Of Amrcs Fl Cnc1
New York NY 10104
212 554-1234

(G-5030)
AZALEA ALABAMA INVESTMENT LLC
8111 Rockside Rd Ste 200 (44125-6135)
PHONE..............................216 520-1250
EMP: 99
SALES (est): 789.1K **Privately Held**
SIC: 6513 Apartment building operators

(G-5031)
B & B WRECKING & EXCVTG INC
4510 E 71st St Ste 6 (44105-5638)
PHONE..............................216 429-1700
Pete Boyas, *Principal*
William A Baumann, *Vice Pres*
Nik Filippi, *Project Mgr*
EMP: 40 EST: 1957
SQ FT: 50,000
SALES (est): 10.8MM **Privately Held**
SIC: 1795 1794 Demolition, buildings & other structures; excavation & grading, building construction

(G-5032)
B&F CAPITAL MARKETS INC
635 W Lkeside Ave Apt 201 (44113)
PHONE..............................216 472-2700
Derek Beitzel, *Director*
EMP: 25
SQ FT: 4,000
SALES (est): 1.8MM **Privately Held**
WEB: www.bfcmi.com
SIC: 8742 Financial consultant

(G-5033)
BAKER & HOSTETLER LLP
127 Public Sq Ste 2000 (44114-1214)
PHONE..............................216 861-7587
Hewitt Shaw, *Managing Prtnr*
Edward L Friedman, *Partner*
Stacey Hutton, *Project Mgr*
Dave Fair, *Engineer*
Nick Thompson, *Business Anlyst*
EMP: 274
SALES (corp-wide): 313.3MM **Privately Held**
SIC: 8111 General practice attorney, lawyer; bankruptcy law; labor & employment law; taxation law
PA: Baker & Hostetler Llp
127 Public Sq Ste 2000
Cleveland OH 44114
216 621-0200

(G-5034)
BAKER & HOSTETLER LLP (PA)
127 Public Sq Ste 2000 (44114-1214)
PHONE..............................216 621-0200
W Ray Whitman, *Ch of Bd*
Ronald G Linville, *Managing Prtnr*
G Thomas Ball, *Managing Prtnr*
John F Cermak, *Managing Prtnr*
James V Etscorn, *Managing Prtnr*
EMP: 274 EST: 1916
SQ FT: 160,000
SALES (est): 313.3MM **Privately Held**
WEB: www.bakerlaw.com
SIC: 8111 General practice attorney, lawyer; bankruptcy law; labor & employment law; real estate law

(G-5035)
BARBS GRAFFITI INC
3111 Carnegie Ave (44115-2632)
PHONE..............................216 881-5550
Abe Miller, *Manager*
EMP: 65
SALES (corp-wide): 6.3MM **Privately Held**
WEB: www.graffiticaps.com
SIC: 5136 5137 Sportswear, men's & boys'; sportswear, women's & children's
PA: Barb's Graffiti, Inc.
3111 Carnegie Ave
Cleveland OH 44115
216 881-5550

(G-5036)
BARBS GRAFFITI INC (PA)
Also Called: Graffiti Co
3111 Carnegie Ave (44115-2632)
PHONE..............................216 881-5550
Abe Miller, *President*
Barbara Miller, *Corp Secy*

Monica McKinley, *Controller*
Mike Struk, *Sales Associate*
▲ EMP: 40
SQ FT: 18,000
SALES (est): 6.3MM **Privately Held**
WEB: www.graffiticaps.com
SIC: 2353 2395 5136 5137 Baseball caps; pleating & stitching; sportswear, men's & boys'; sportswear, women's & children's

(G-5037)
BARNES WENDLING CPAS INC (PA)
1350 Euclid Ave Ste 1400 (44115-1830)
PHONE..............................216 566-9000
Jeffrey Neuman, *President*
Janine Iacobelli, *Treasurer*
John Flannery, *Accountant*
Mandi Raneri, *Accountant*
Sondra Sofranko, *Accountant*
EMP: 45
SQ FT: 18,500
SALES (est): 11.2MM **Privately Held**
SIC: 8721 7291 Certified public accountant; tax return preparation services

(G-5038)
BASELINE CONSULTING LLC
21298 Endsley Ave (44116-2231)
PHONE..............................440 336-5382
David A Hein,
Douglas Drier,
EMP: 54
SALES (est): 2.2MM **Privately Held**
SIC: 7379 Computer related consulting services

(G-5039)
BASF CATALYSTS LLC
23800 Mercantile Rd (44122-5908)
P.O. Box 22126 (44122-0126)
PHONE..............................216 360-5005
John Ferek, *Branch Mgr*
EMP: 83
SALES (corp-wide): 71.7B **Privately Held**
SIC: 2819 8731 Catalysts, chemical; commercial physical research
HQ: Basf Catalysts Llc
33 Wood Ave S
Iselin NJ 08830
732 205-5000

(G-5040)
BASISTA FURNITURE INC
Also Called: Warehouse
5340 Brookpark Rd (44134-1044)
PHONE..............................216 398-5900
Stanley Basista, *Branch Mgr*
EMP: 30
SALES (corp-wide): 8.9MM **Privately Held**
WEB: www.basista.com
SIC: 4225 General warehousing & storage
PA: Basista Furniture, Inc.
5277 State Rd
Cleveland OH 44134
216 635-1200

(G-5041)
BATCH LABS INC
9655 Sweet Valley Dr # 1 (44125-4270)
PHONE..............................216 901-9366
Jennie Zamberlan, *CEO*
Martin Hlavaty, *Human Resources*
EMP: 54
SALES (est): 992.5K **Privately Held**
SIC: 7371 Computer software development & applications

(G-5042)
BATTLE BULLYING HOTLINE INC
3185 Warren Rd (44111-1153)
PHONE..............................216 731-1976
Michael Prandich, *President*
EMP: 75
SALES (est): 233K **Privately Held**
SIC: 8322 Hotline

(G-5043)
BAY VILLAGE CITY SCHOOL DST
Also Called: Glenview Cntr For Chld Cr & Lr
28727 Wolf Rd (44140-1351)
PHONE..............................440 617-7330
Barbara Manning, *Director*
EMP: 35
SALES (corp-wide): 37.1MM **Privately Held**
SIC: 8211 8351 Public elementary school; child day care services
PA: Bay Village City School District
377 Dover Center Rd
Cleveland OH 44140
440 617-7300

(G-5044)
BAYLESS PATHMARK INC
19250 Bagley Rd Ste 101 (44130-3348)
PHONE..............................440 274-2494
Benjamin Tanseco, *CEO*
EMP: 34
SALES (est): 3MM **Privately Held**
SIC: 8071 8734 Pathological laboratory; testing laboratories

(G-5045)
BDI INC (PA)
Also Called: Baring Distributors
8000 Hub Pkwy (44125-5731)
PHONE..............................216 642-9100
Frank L Bystricky, *CEO*
Mike Fryz, *Principal*
Bud Thayer, *Vice Pres*
▲ EMP: 188
SALES (est): 346.5MM **Privately Held**
WEB: www.bdi.com
SIC: 1389 Oil sampling service for oil companies

(G-5046)
BDO USA LLP
1422 Euclid Ave Ste 1500 (44115-2068)
PHONE..............................216 325-1700
Ross Vozar, *Director*
EMP: 52
SALES (corp-wide): 940.4MM **Privately Held**
SIC: 8721 Certified public accountant
PA: Bdo Usa, Llp
330 N Wabash Ave Ste 3200
Chicago IL 60611
312 240-1236

(G-5047)
BEACHWOOD CITY SCHOOLS
23757 Commerce Park (44122-5825)
PHONE..............................216 464-6609
Paul Williams, *Superintendent*
EMP: 40
SQ FT: 13,600
SALES (corp-wide): 43.3MM **Privately Held**
SIC: 4151 School buses
PA: Beachwood City Schools
24601 Fairmount Blvd
Cleveland OH 44122
216 464-2600

(G-5048)
BEARING DISTRIBUTORS INC (HQ)
Also Called: Bdi-USA
8000 Hub Pkwy (44125-5788)
P.O. Box 5931, Troy MI (48007-5931)
PHONE..............................216 642-9100
Carl G James, *President*
John Ruth, *COO*
Steve Kieffer, *Vice Pres*
Bud Thayer, *Vice Pres*
Dan Maisonville, *CFO*
◆ EMP: 200 EST: 1935
SQ FT: 150,000
SALES (est): 544.9MM
SALES (corp-wide): 549.3MM **Privately Held**
WEB: www.bdi-usa.com
SIC: 5085 Bearings; gears; power transmission equipment & apparatus
PA: Forge Industries, Inc.
4450 Market St
Youngstown OH 44512
330 782-8301

(G-5049)
BECK CENTER FOR ARTS
17801 Detroit Ave (44107-3499)
PHONE....................................216 521-2540
Lucinda Einhouse, *CEO*
Frederick B Unger, *Chairman*
Dena Adler, *Development*
William J Backus Jr, *Treasurer*
Jerry McThersom, *Finance*
EMP: 127
SQ FT: 60,000
SALES: 3.8MM **Privately Held**
WEB: www.beckcenter.org
SIC: 7922 Performing arts center production

(G-5050)
BECK COMPANY
10701 Broadway Ave (44125-1650)
P.O. Box 25469 (44125-0469)
PHONE....................................216 883-0909
Mark Beck, *President*
EMP: 35 EST: 1983
SQ FT: 20,000
SALES (est): 4.1MM **Privately Held**
WEB: www.engineeredroofing.com
SIC: 1761 Roofing contractor; sheet metalwork

(G-5051)
BEECHMONT INC
Also Called: Beechmont Country Club
29600 Chagrin Blvd (44122-4620)
PHONE....................................216 831-9100
Doug Foote, *Principal*
EMP: 100
SQ FT: 40,000
SALES: 5.2MM **Privately Held**
WEB: www.beechmontcc.com
SIC: 7997 Country club, membership

(G-5052)
BELLWETHER ENTP RE CAPITL LLC (PA)
1360 E 9th St Ste 300 (44114-1730)
PHONE....................................216 820-4500
Ned Huffman, *CEO*
Michael Gruss, *President*
Deborah Rogan, *Exec VP*
Marty Clancy, *Senior VP*
David S Davenpoert, *Senior VP*
EMP: 34 EST: 2008
SQ FT: 7,000
SALES (est): 15.2MM **Privately Held**
SIC: 6531 Real estate agent, commercial

(G-5053)
BELMORE LEASING CO LLC
Also Called: Candlewood Park Healthcare Ctr
1835 Belmore Rd (44112-4301)
PHONE....................................216 268-3600
Stephen L Rosedale, *Mng Member*
Charles R Stoltz,
Ronald S Wilheim,
EMP: 156
SQ FT: 28,000
SALES (est): 4.4MM **Privately Held**
SIC: 8051 Skilled nursing care facilities

(G-5054)
BENEVENTO ENTERPRISES INC
Also Called: Herbst Electric Company
1384 E 26th St (44114-4039)
PHONE....................................216 621-5890
John R Benevento, *President*
Duke Benevento, *President*
Kenneth Maher, *President*
Frank Polanski, *Purch Agent*
Deborah Benevento, *Treasurer*
EMP: 65 EST: 1946
SQ FT: 6,000
SALES (est): 12.8MM **Privately Held**
WEB: www.herbstelectric.com
SIC: 1731 General electrical contractor

(G-5055)
BENJAMIN ROSE INSTITUTE
850 Euclid Ave Ste 1100 (44114-3313)
PHONE....................................216 791-8000
Carole Johnson, *Principal*
EMP: 88
SALES (corp-wide): 9.4MM **Privately Held**
SIC: 8733 Noncommercial research organizations

PA: Benjamin Rose Institute
11890 Fairhill Rd
Cleveland OH 44120
216 791-8000

(G-5056)
BENJAMIN ROSE INSTITUTE
Also Called: Margret Wagner House
2373 Euclid Heights Blvd 2f (44106-2716)
PHONE....................................216 791-3580
Richard Browdie, *CEO*
Beth Sipple, *Director*
Crystal Wallace, *Asst Director*
EMP: 53
SQ FT: 27,326
SALES (corp-wide): 9.4MM **Privately Held**
SIC: 8361 8741 8322 Rest home, with health care incidental; management services; individual & family services
PA: Benjamin Rose Institute
11890 Fairhill Rd
Cleveland OH 44120
216 791-8000

(G-5057)
BENJAMIN ROSE INSTITUTE (PA)
11890 Fairhill Rd (44120-1000)
PHONE....................................216 791-8000
Richard Browdie, *President*
Frank Cardinale, *CFO*
Jeanne Hoban, *Corp Comm Staff*
Bert Rahl, *Director*
Mary Dziedzicki, *Admin Sec*
EMP: 80 EST: 1908
SQ FT: 31,000
SALES: 9.4MM **Privately Held**
SIC: 8082 8322 Home health care services; individual & family services

(G-5058)
BEST CUTS INC
Also Called: Signature Salon
7541 W Ridgewood Dr (44129)
PHONE....................................440 884-6300
Andre Duval, *Manager*
EMP: 30
SALES (corp-wide): 12.3MM **Privately Held**
SIC: 7231 Unisex hair salons
PA: Best Cuts, Inc.
3626 Mayfield Rd
Cleveland OH 44118
216 382-2600

(G-5059)
BEST REWARD CREDIT UNION
Also Called: PARMAUTO FEDERAL CREDIT UNION
5681 Smith Rd (44142-2030)
PHONE....................................216 367-8000
Susan Madden, *President*
Pam Akers, *President*
Stephen Halas, *Exec VP*
Sandy Sauvey, *Vice Pres*
Jennifer Cole, *Marketing Staff*
EMP: 32
SQ FT: 2,800
SALES: 3.5MM **Privately Held**
WEB: www.vantagefcu.com
SIC: 6061 6163 Federal credit unions; loan brokers

(G-5060)
BETHLEHEM LUTHERAN CH PARMA
7500 State Rd (44134-6199)
PHONE....................................440 845-2230
Robert Green, *Pastor*
EMP: 30
SQ FT: 8,579
SALES (est): 949.6K **Privately Held**
SIC: 8661 8351 Lutheran Church; child day care services

(G-5061)
BEVERAGE DISTRIBUTORS INC
3800 King Ave (44114-3703)
PHONE....................................216 431-1600
James V Conway, *President*
Marci Austin, *Sales Associate*
Sarah Hong, *Manager*
Geoff Lentz, *Director*
▲ EMP: 150
SQ FT: 125,000

SALES (est): 72.9MM **Privately Held**
WEB: www.beveragedist.com
SIC: 5181 Beer & other fermented malt liquors

(G-5062)
BEYOND 2000 REALTY INC
18332 Bagley Rd (44130-3411)
PHONE....................................440 842-7200
Mark Snyder, *President*
EMP: 50
SALES (est): 2.7MM **Privately Held**
WEB: www.beyond2000realty.com
SIC: 6531 Real estate agent, residential

(G-5063)
BLOOD COURIER INC
3965 W 130th St (44111-5103)
P.O. Box 110634 (44111-0634)
PHONE....................................216 251-3050
James T Mahony Jr, *President*
Mary Mahony, *Corp Secy*
Ken Kerns, *Manager*
EMP: 38
SQ FT: 5,000
SALES (est): 2.6MM **Privately Held**
WEB: www.bloodcourier.com
SIC: 4212 4731 Delivery service, vehicular; freight forwarding

(G-5064)
BLUE RIBBON MEATS INC
3316 W 67th Pl (44102-5243)
PHONE....................................216 631-8850
Albert J Radis, *President*
June Altschuld, *Principal*
Mary Cain, *Principal*
John Forrester, *Principal*
Paul Radis, *Corp Secy*
EMP: 100 EST: 1952
SQ FT: 8,400
SALES (est): 57.6MM **Privately Held**
SIC: 5147 5142 Meats, fresh; meat, frozen; packaged

(G-5065)
BLUE TECH SMART SOLUTIONS LLC
5885 Grant Ave (44105-5607)
PHONE....................................216 271-4800
Paul Hanna, *President*
EMP: 47 EST: 2013
SALES (est): 7.6MM **Privately Held**
SIC: 5045 Computers, peripherals & software
PA: Blue Technologies, Inc.
5885 Grant Ave
Cleveland OH 44105

(G-5066)
BLUE TECHNOLOGIES INC (PA)
5885 Grant Ave (44105-5607)
P.O. Box 31475 (44131-0475)
PHONE....................................216 271-4800
Paul Hanna, *President*
David Morrell, *Vice Pres*
William Nelson, *Vice Pres*
David Vitaz, *CFO*
Keith Stump, *Treasurer*
EMP: 107
SQ FT: 36,000
SALES: 26.5MM **Privately Held**
WEB: www.btohio.com
SIC: 5044 Copying equipment

(G-5067)
BLUE WATER CHAMBER ORCHESTRA
3631 Perkins Ave Apt 4cn (44114-4707)
PHONE....................................440 781-6215
Carlton R Woods, *Administration*
EMP: 44 EST: 2017
SALES (est): 229.4K **Privately Held**
SIC: 7929 Orchestras or bands

(G-5068)
BONEZZI SWTZER POLITO HUPP LPA (PA)
1300 E 9th St Ste 1950 (44114-1503)
PHONE....................................216 875-2767
William Bonezzi, *President*
John Polito, *Vice Pres*
Donald Switzer, *Vice Pres*
Patrick Murphy, *Treasurer*
Steven Hupp, *Admin Sec*

EMP: 35
SQ FT: 11,000
SALES (est): 6.1MM **Privately Held**
WEB: www.bsmplaw.com
SIC: 8111 Criminal law; specialized law offices, attorneys

(G-5069)
BOSTWICK DESIGN PARTNR INC
2729 Prospect Ave E (44115-2605)
PHONE....................................216 621-7900
Robert Bostwick, *President*
Michael Zambo, *Project Mgr*
Chris Kidd, *Info Tech Dir*
Robert L Bostwick, *Director*
Robert Godshall, *Executive*
EMP: 32
SQ FT: 12,500
SALES (est): 5.1MM **Privately Held**
WEB: www.cgbarch.com
SIC: 8712 Architectural engineering

(G-5070)
BOULEVARD MOTEL CORP
Also Called: Comfort Inn
17550 Rosbough Blvd (44130-2580)
PHONE....................................440 234-3131
Lindsey Stoneman, *Branch Mgr*
EMP: 30
SQ FT: 21,973
SALES (corp-wide): 198.1MM **Privately Held**
WEB: www.hotspringsclarion.com
SIC: 7011 Hotel, franchised
HQ: Boulevard Motel Corp
10750 Columbia Pike # 300
Silver Spring MD 20901

(G-5071)
BOY SCUTS AMER - LK ERIE CNCIL
2241 Woodland Ave (44115-3214)
PHONE....................................216 861-6060
Marc Ryan, *Principal*
John Cadwallader, *Exec Dir*
EMP: 30
SQ FT: 20,000
SALES: 3.8MM **Privately Held**
SIC: 8641 Boy Scout organization

(G-5072)
BOYAS EXCAVATING INC (PA)
11311 Rockside Rd (44125-6208)
PHONE....................................216 524-3620
Lea Boyas Morabito, *President*
Michael Boyas, *President*
Joseph J Berdis, *Owner*
Stacey Asimou, *Treasurer*
Marjorie Boyas, *Admin Sec*
EMP: 37
SQ FT: 6,000
SALES (est): 8.6MM **Privately Held**
WEB: www.boyas.com
SIC: 1795 1542 1794 1799 Wrecking & demolition work; commercial & office building contractors; excavation work; shoring & underpinning work

(G-5073)
BRAEVIEW MANOR INC
20611 Euclid Ave (44117-1592)
PHONE....................................216 486-9300
A John Bartholemew, *President*
Kimberly Armstrong, *Principal*
Ray Lin Walsh, *Accounting Mgr*
Natalya Myaskovsky, *Office Mgr*
Stephanie Mills, *Nursing Dir*
EMP: 190 EST: 1964
SQ FT: 160,000
SALES (est): 4.4MM **Privately Held**
SIC: 8051 8052 Convalescent home with continuous nursing care; intermediate care facilities

(G-5074)
BRANDMUSCLE INC (HQ)
1100 Superior Ave E # 500 (44114-2530)
PHONE....................................216 464-4342
Philip Alexander, *CEO*
Dan Hickox, *President*
Dave Wilson, *President*
Robert Bernstein, *Exec VP*
Tracy Parker, *Exec VP*
EMP: 150
SQ FT: 24,000

▲ = Import ▼=Export
◆ =Import/Export

SALES (est): 39.3MM
SALES (corp-wide): 2B **Privately Held**
WEB: www.brandmuscle.com
SIC: 7373 8742 Systems software development services; marketing consulting services
PA: Riverside Partners L.L.C.
45 Rockefeller Plz # 400
New York NY 10111
212 265-6575

(G-5075)
BRAVO WELLNESS LLC (PA)
20445 Emerald Pkwy # 400 (44135-6010)
PHONE..................................216 658-9500
Jim Pshock, *CEO*
Chris Yessayan, *President*
Mikhail Kumo, *Exec VP*
Cheryl Tidwell, *Exec VP*
Cory Jones, *VP Bus Dvlpt*
EMP: 116
SQ FT: 7,000
SALES: 22.5MM **Privately Held**
SIC: 8748 8741 Employee programs administration; administrative management

(G-5076)
BRENNAN & ASSOCIATES INC
1550 E 33rd St (44114-4322)
PHONE..................................216 391-4822
David J Masciarelli, *President*
Bill Call, *Principal*
William D Call Jr, *Corp Secy*
Frederick Johnston, *Vice Pres*
Kathleen Oconnor, *Admin Asst*
EMP: 28
SQ FT: 6,000
SALES (est): 4.5MM **Privately Held**
WEB: www.brennanhvac.com
SIC: 1711 Warm air heating & air conditioning contractor

(G-5077)
BRENNAN INDUSTRIES INC (PA)
Also Called: B I
6701 Cochran Rd (44139-3997)
PHONE..................................440 248-1880
David D Carr, *CEO*
David M Carr, *President*
Michael Donahoe, *General Mgr*
Dwayne Potts, *General Mgr*
Dave Weeden, *General Mgr*
▲ EMP: 26
SQ FT: 24,000
SALES (est): 40.1MM **Privately Held**
WEB: www.brennaninc.com
SIC: 5085 Valves, pistons & fittings

(G-5078)
BRENTLEY INSTITUTE INC
3143 W 33rd St Ste 2 (44109-1552)
P.O. Box 20724 (44120-7724)
PHONE..................................216 225-0087
Toney Foreman, *President*
EMP: 34
SALES: 350K **Privately Held**
WEB: www.brentleyonline.com
SIC: 7382 8742 Security systems services; industry specialist consultants

(G-5079)
BRIDGEWAY INC (PA)
2202 Prame Ave (44109-1626)
PHONE..................................216 688-4114
Ralph Fee, *Director*
EMP: 278 EST: 1972
SQ FT: 50,000
SALES (est): 2.9MM **Privately Held**
WEB: www.employmentalliance.org
SIC: 8322 8093 Social service center; general counseling services; alcoholism counseling, nontreatment; offender rehabilitation agency; specialty outpatient clinics

(G-5080)
BRINKS INCORPORATED
1422 Superior Ave E (44114-2904)
PHONE..................................216 621-7493
Justo Rodriguez, *Manager*
EMP: 85
SQ FT: 18,105
SALES (corp-wide): 3.4B **Publicly Held**
WEB: www.brinksinc.com
SIC: 7381 Armored car services

HQ: Brink's, Incorporated
1801 Bayberry Ct Ste 400
Richmond VA 23226
804 289-9600

(G-5081)
BRITESKIES LLC
2658 Scranton Rd Ste 3 (44113-5115)
PHONE..................................216 369-3600
Michael Berlin, *Mng Member*
William Onion,
EMP: 25
SALES (est): 1.4MM **Privately Held**
SIC: 7371 Computer software development

(G-5082)
BRITTON-GALLAGHER & ASSOC INC
1375 E 9th St Fl 30 (44114-1797)
PHONE..................................216 658-7100
Bruce H Ball, *Ch of Bd*
Jeremy Bryant, *President*
John L Hazen, *President*
Terry Dragan, *Principal*
Jeremy A Bryant, *Senior VP*
EMP: 60
SQ FT: 15,000
SALES (est): 21.6MM **Privately Held**
WEB: www.britton-gallagher.com
SIC: 6411 Insurance agents

(G-5083)
BROADVOX LLC (HQ)
75 Erieview Plz Fl 4 (44114-1839)
PHONE..................................216 373-4600
Fritz Hendricks, *President*
Michael Donahue, *CFO*
Craig Olson, *Architect*
John Hanna, *CIO*
EMP: 45
SALES (est): 41.3MM
SALES (corp-wide): 223.1MM **Privately Held**
WEB: www.broadvox.net
SIC: 4813 ;
PA: Onvoy, Llc
10300 6th Ave N
Plymouth MN 55441
763 230-2036

(G-5084)
BROADVUE MOTORS INC
Also Called: Ganley Lincoln Middleburg Hts
6930 Pearl Rd (44130-7832)
PHONE..................................440 845-6000
Kenneth Ganley, *President*
Lois Ganley, *Vice Pres*
David Robinson, *Treasurer*
Ronald Courey, *Asst Treas*
Russel W Harris, *Admin Sec*
EMP: 70
SQ FT: 26,191
SALES (est): 25.9MM **Privately Held**
SIC: 5511 5012 Automobiles, new & used; automobiles

(G-5085)
BROKAW INC
1213 W 6th St (44113-1339)
PHONE..................................216 241-8003
Bill Brokaw, *Principal*
EMP: 35
SQ FT: 11,300
SALES (est): 8.9MM **Privately Held**
WEB: www.brokaw.com
SIC: 7311 Advertising consultant

(G-5086)
BROOK BEECH
3737 Lander Rd (44124-5712)
PHONE..................................216 831-2255
Mario Tonti, *President*
Bari E Goggins, *Chairman*
Lavisa Bell, *Assistant VP*
Valerie Dowery, *Assistant VP*
Nicole Roettger, *Assistant VP*
EMP: 200 EST: 1852
SQ FT: 30,000
SALES: 21.2MM **Privately Held**
WEB: www.beechbrook.org
SIC: 8322 Child related social services; adoption services; outreach program; family counseling services

(G-5087)
BROOKDALE SENIOR LIVING INC
3151 Mayfield Rd (44118-1757)
PHONE..................................216 321-6331
Linda Delozier, *Branch Mgr*
EMP: 36
SALES (corp-wide): 4.5B **Publicly Held**
SIC: 8051 Skilled nursing care facilities
PA: Brookdale Senior Living
111 Westwood Pl Ste 400
Brentwood TN 37027
615 221-2250

(G-5088)
BROOKPARK FREEWAY LANES LLC
12859 Brookpark Rd (44130-1159)
PHONE..................................216 267-2150
Glen Gable,
Dave Patz,
EMP: 30 EST: 1997
SALES (est): 1.5MM **Privately Held**
SIC: 7933 Ten pin center

(G-5089)
BROOKS & STAFFORD CO
55 Public Sq Ste 1650 (44113-1972)
PHONE..................................216 696-3000
Neil Corrigan, *President*
John Kunze, *Vice Pres*
Brooks Stafford, *Agent*
EMP: 39
SQ FT: 11,000
SALES (est): 6.8MM **Privately Held**
WEB: www.brooks-stafford.com
SIC: 6411 Insurance agents

(G-5090)
BROUSE MCDOWELL LPA
600 Superior Ave E # 1600 (44114-2604)
PHONE..................................216 830-6830
Craig Marvinney, *Partner*
Linda L Bluso, *Branch Mgr*
EMP: 29
SALES (corp-wide): 23.3MM **Privately Held**
SIC: 8111 General practice law office
PA: Brouse Mcdowell, Lpa
388 S Main St Ste 500
Akron OH
330 535-5711

(G-5091)
BROWN AND MARGOLIUS CO LPA
55 Public Sq Ste 1100 (44113-1901)
PHONE..................................216 621-2034
Marsha Margolius, *President*
EMP: 50
SALES (est): 3.2MM **Privately Held**
SIC: 8111 General practice law office

(G-5092)
BROWN GIBBONS LANG & CO LLC (PA)
1 Cleveland Ctr (44114)
PHONE..................................216 241-2800
Anthony Delfre, *Managing Dir*
Vince Pappalardo, *Managing Dir*
Andrew K Petry, *Managing Dir*
John Riddle, *Managing Dir*
Chris Stai, *Managing Dir*
EMP: 40
SQ FT: 13,000
SALES (est): 17MM **Privately Held**
WEB: www.bglco.com
SIC: 6211 Investment bankers

(G-5093)
BROWN GIBBONS LANG LTD PTRSHIP
1111 Superior Ave E # 900 (44114-2522)
PHONE..................................216 241-2800
Michael Gibbons, *President*
EMP: 30
SALES (est): 2MM **Privately Held**
SIC: 7519 Utility trailer rental

(G-5094)
BROWN WD GENERAL AGENCY INC
Also Called: Northwestern Mutl Fincl Netwrk
950 Main Ave Ste 600 (44113-7207)
PHONE..................................216 241-5840
William D Brown, *President*
EMP: 75
SALES (est): 12.5MM **Privately Held**
SIC: 6411 6282 Life insurance agents; investment advice

(G-5095)
BRUNSWICK COMPANIES (PA)
5309 Transportation Blvd (44125-5333)
PHONE..................................330 864-8800
Todd Stein, *President*
Michelle Hirsch, *Senior VP*
Donna Schroeder, *Senior VP*
Michelle Stein, *Vice Pres*
Stuart Weinstein, *CFO*
▲ EMP: 57
SALES (est): 17.1MM **Privately Held**
WEB: www.brunswickcompany.com
SIC: 6411 Insurance agents

(G-5096)
BRYANT ELIZA VILLAGE
7201 Wade Park Ave (44103-2765)
PHONE..................................216 361-6141
Harvey Shankman, *President*
Odessa Fields, *Accountant*
Rhonda Roberts, *Nursing Mgr*
Jeanna Davis, *Director*
Evelyn Smith, *Director*
EMP: 255
SQ FT: 50,450
SALES: 14.1MM **Privately Held**
SIC: 8322 8051 Outreach program; skilled nursing care facilities

(G-5097)
BSL - APPLIED LASER TECH LLC (PA)
Also Called: A L T
4560 Johnston Pkwy (44128-2953)
PHONE..................................216 663-8181
Judy Harshman, *President*
Dov Nisman, *General Mgr*
EMP: 50
SQ FT: 20,000
SALES (est): 22.3MM **Privately Held**
WEB: www.altconnect.com
SIC: 5045 7378 Printers, computer; computer maintenance & repair

(G-5098)
BUCKEYE HOMECARE SERVICES INC
14077 Cedar Rd Ste 103 (44118-3332)
PHONE..................................216 321-9300
Ashfaq Ahmed, *Principal*
Farzana Ahmed, *Principal*
Nitesh Patel, *Administration*
EMP: 75
SALES (est): 101.8K **Privately Held**
SIC: 8082 Home health care services

(G-5099)
BUCKINGHAM DLTTLE BRROUGHS LLC
Also Called: Buckingham Doolittle Burroughs
1375 E 9th St Ste 1700 (44114-1790)
PHONE..................................216 621-5300
David M Abromowitz, *Partner*
Joseph L Ackerman, *Partner*
Ronald C Allan, *Partner*
Ralph D Amiet, *Partner*
Steven A Armatas, *Partner*
EMP: 62
SALES (corp-wide): 40.6MM **Privately Held**
SIC: 8111 General practice law office
PA: Buckingham, Doolittle & Burroughs, Llc
3800 Embassy Pkwy
Akron OH 44333
330 376-5300

(G-5100)
BUDDIES INC (PA)
Also Called: A J'S Body Shop
3888 Pearl Rd (44109-3159)
P.O. Box 33022 (44133-0022)
PHONE..................................216 642-3362
James Dillinger, *President*

Alvin J Alvarez, *Admin Sec*
EMP: 30
SQ FT: 4,800
SALES (est): 1.2MM **Privately Held**
WEB: www.buddies.com
SIC: 7532 7549 Body shop, automotive; interior repair services; undercoating/rust-proofing cars

(G-5101)
BUDGET RENT A CAR SYSTEM INC
Also Called: Budget Rent-A-Car
19719 Maplewood Ave (44135)
PHONE.................................216 267-2080
Harry Baker, *Manager*
EMP: 80
SALES (corp-wide): 9.1B **Publicly Held**
WEB: www.blackdogventures.com
SIC: 7514 Rent-a-car service
HQ: Budget Rent A Car System, Inc.
　6 Sylvan Way Ste 1
　Parsippany NJ 07054
　973 496-3500

(G-5102)
BUILDERS EXCHANGE INC (PA)
Also Called: BX OHIO
9555 Rockside Rd Ste 300 (44125-6282)
PHONE.................................216 393-6300
Ashley Grandetti, *Branch Mgr*
Melissa Alley, *Manager*
Ashley Myers, *Manager*
Heather Szarka, *Manager*
Gregg Mazurek, *Exec Dir*
EMP: 36
SQ FT: 10,000
SALES: 4MM **Privately Held**
WEB: www.bxcleve.com
SIC: 8611 Contractors' association

(G-5103)
BURKSHIRE CONSTRUCTION COMPANY
6033 State Rd (44134-2869)
P.O. Box 347248 (44134-7248)
PHONE.................................440 885-9700
Anne M Burkey, *President*
EMP: 30
SALES (est): 3.3MM **Privately Held**
SIC: 1541 1542 Industrial buildings, new construction; nonresidential construction; commercial & office building, new construction; institutional building construction

(G-5104)
BURTON CAROL MANAGEMENT (PA)
Also Called: B C M
4832 Richmond Rd Ste 200 (44128-5993)
PHONE.................................216 464-5130
Robert G Risman, *CEO*
Joy Anzalone, *COO*
Joseph W Kincaid, *Vice Pres*
John Petryshin, *Vice Pres*
Marcia Hayward, *Opers Staff*
EMP: 40
SALES (est): 7.6MM **Privately Held**
SIC: 6513 Apartment building operators

(G-5105)
BUSINESS AIRCRAFT GROUP INC (PA)
Also Called: Bussines Air Craft Center
2301 N Marginal Rd (44114-3708)
PHONE.................................216 348-1415
Mike Hoyle, *President*
EMP: 60
SQ FT: 25,000
SALES (est): 7.4MM **Privately Held**
WEB: www.businessaircraftgroup.com
SIC: 4522 Flying charter service

(G-5106)
BUSINESS RESEARCH SERVICES
26600 Renaissance Pkwy # 150 (44128-5791)
PHONE.................................216 831-5200
Ronald J Mayher, *President*
Trudy M Mayher, *Corp Secy*
EMP: 25

SALES (est): 1.9MM **Privately Held**
SIC: 8732 Business research service; market analysis or research

(G-5107)
BUSINESS STATIONERY LLC
4944 Commerce Pkwy (44128-5908)
PHONE.................................216 514-1192
Brad Wolf, *President*
Lee Brantley, *Vice Pres*
Patrick Cowan, *Plant Mgr*
Patrick Cowlen, *Opers Mgr*
Mark Cupach, *Sls & Mktg Exec*
EMP: 85
SALES (est): 35.7MM
SALES (corp-wide): 259.3MM **Privately Held**
WEB: www.bsiprint.com
SIC: 5112 Stationery
HQ: Identity Group Holdings Llc
　1480 Gould Dr
　Cookeville TN 38506
　931 432-4000

(G-5108)
BUY BELOW RETAIL INC
23600 Mercantile Rd Ste G (44122-5949)
PHONE.................................216 292-7805
Benjamin Woomer, *President*
EMP: 45 **EST:** 2000
SALES (est): 3.4MM **Privately Held**
WEB: www.factorydirectltd.com
SIC: 5199 General merchandise, non-durable

(G-5109)
C & J CONTRACTORS INC
866 Addison Rd (44103-1608)
P.O. Box 874, Willoughby (44096-0874)
PHONE.................................216 391-5700
James Crawford, *President*
Craig Crawford, *Vice Pres*
Robert Crawford, *VP Sales*
Alicia R Wigand, *Admin Sec*
EMP: 25
SQ FT: 87,120
SALES: 2.8MM **Privately Held**
WEB: www.cjcontractorsinc.com
SIC: 1795 1794 Demolition, buildings & other structures; excavation work

(G-5110)
C C MITCHELL SUPPLY COMPANY
3001 E Royalton Rd (44147-2894)
PHONE.................................440 526-2040
Jerome Mitchell, *Ch of Bd*
Stu Kaine, *Sales Staff*
Eric Schniegenberg, *Marketing Staff*
EMP: 35
SQ FT: 48,000
SALES (est): 11.6MM **Privately Held**
WEB: www.mtndew.com
SIC: 5064 Electrical appliances, major

(G-5111)
C-AUTO GLASS INC
Also Called: Pure Led Solutions
2500 Brookpark Rd # 111 (44134-1400)
PHONE.................................216 351-2193
Joeseph Tieber, *President*
Eileen Joyce, *Admin Sec*
▲ **EMP:** 29
SALES (est): 4.7MM **Privately Held**
SIC: 7536 Automotive glass replacement shops

(G-5112)
CABLE TV SERVICES INC
6400 Kolthoff Dr (44142-1313)
PHONE.................................440 816-0033
Jay Geib, *President*
Dan Geib, *Corp Secy*
EMP: 50
SALES (est): 5MM **Privately Held**
SIC: 1731 Cable television installation

(G-5113)
CALABRESEM RACEK & MARKOS INC
1110 Euclid Ave Ste 300 (44115-1626)
PHONE.................................216 696-5442
Richard G Racek, *President*
Steve Calabrese, *Exec VP*
David Fortunato, *Exec VP*
Eric Calabrese, *Treasurer*

Marcie Gilmore, *Marketing Staff*
EMP: 25
SQ FT: 10,000
SALES (est): 3.3MM **Privately Held**
WEB: www.crmonline.com
SIC: 6531 8748 Appraiser, real estate; real estate brokers & agents; real estate managers; business consulting

(G-5114)
CALFEE HALTER & GRISWOLD LLP (PA)
1405 E 6th St Ste 1 (44114-1601)
PHONE.................................216 831-2732
Amy Flanigan, *President*
Debra Hale, *President*
Judi Krahn, *President*
Kathleen Kunes, *President*
Nancy Malinowski, *President*
EMP: 358
SALES (est): 49.3MM **Privately Held**
SIC: 8111 Legal Services Office

(G-5115)
CALVERT WIRE & CABLE CORP (DH)
17909 Cleve Pkwy Ste 180 (44142)
PHONE.................................216 433-7600
Lorraine Nunez, *President*
Howard Hawn, *Accounting Mgr*
◆ **EMP:** 38
SQ FT: 12,000
SALES (est): 29.5MM **Publicly Held**
WEB: www.calvert-wire.com
SIC: 4899 5063 Data communication services; wire & cable
HQ: Communications Supply Corp
　200 E Lies Rd
　Carol Stream IL 60188
　630 221-6400

(G-5116)
CAMGEN LTD
1621 Euclid Ave Ste 220-3 (44115-2114)
P.O. Box 13141, Akron (44334-8541)
PHONE.................................330 204-8636
William Genkin,
EMP: 55
SALES (est): 1.2MM **Privately Held**
SIC: 7371 Computer software development & applications

(G-5117)
CAMPUSEAI INC
1111 Superior Ave E # 310 (44114-2540)
PHONE.................................216 589-9626
Surya Pratap, *Project Mgr*
Alma Chopra, *VP Human Res*
Mark Stevens, *Manager*
Naresh K Bishnoi, *Consultant*
Kyle Stevens, *Consultant*
EMP: 120
SALES (est): 16.7MM **Privately Held**
SIC: 7371 Software programming applications

(G-5118)
CANAL ROAD PARTNERS
5585 Canal Rd (44125-4874)
PHONE.................................216 447-0814
Jeffrey Wallis, *Partner*
Jim Allega, *Partner*
John Allega, *Partner*
EMP: 30
SALES (est): 1.7MM **Privately Held**
SIC: 6512 Nonresidential building operators

(G-5119)
CANTERBURY GOLF CLUB INC
22000 S Woodland Rd (44122-3061)
PHONE.................................216 561-1914
Michael Kernicki, *General Mgr*
Edward Kloboves, *Controller*
Ed Kloboves, *Executive*
EMP: 80
SQ FT: 50,000
SALES: 3.9MM **Privately Held**
SIC: 7997 5812 Golf club, membership; eating places

(G-5120)
CAPITAL PROPERTIES MGT LTD
12929 Shaker Blvd (44120-2034)
PHONE.................................216 991-3057
David J Goodman, *Partner*

EMP: 30
SALES (est): 3.7MM **Privately Held**
WEB: www.cpm-ltd.com
SIC: 6531 Real estate managers

(G-5121)
CAR WASH
5195 Northfield Rd (44146-1130)
PHONE.................................216 662-6289
Russell Patel, *President*
Rusell Patel, *President*
EMP: 25
SQ FT: 5,700
SALES (est): 780.5K **Privately Held**
SIC: 7542 Washing & polishing, automotive

(G-5122)
CARDINAL HEALTH 200 LLC
Also Called: Cardinal Health Medical
5260 Naiman Pkwy (44139-1006)
PHONE.................................440 349-1247
Mark Howard, *Branch Mgr*
EMP: 35
SQ FT: 5,000
SALES (corp-wide): 136.8B **Publicly Held**
WEB: www.allegiancehealth.com
SIC: 5047 Medical & hospital equipment
HQ: Cardinal Health 200, Llc
　3651 Birchwood Dr
　Waukegan IL 60085

(G-5123)
CARDIOLOGIST
6525 Powers Blvd 301 (44129-5461)
PHONE.................................440 882-0075
Richard Ader, *Principal*
Connie Klein, *Practice Mgr*
EMP: 75
SALES (est): 1.1MM **Privately Held**
SIC: 8011 Offices & clinics of medical doctors

(G-5124)
CARDIOVASCULAR CLINIC INC
6525 Powers Blvd Rm 301 (44129-5461)
PHONE.................................440 882-0075
Richard S Ader MD, *President*
Christine Zirafi MD, *Corp Secy*
Connie Clein, *Office Mgr*
Connie Klein, *Office Mgr*
James Sechler, *Cardiovascular*
EMP: 70
SALES (est): 8.9MM **Privately Held**
SIC: 8011 Cardiologist & cardio-vascular specialist

(G-5125)
CARDIOVASCULAR MEDICINE ASSOC
7255 Old Oak Blvd C208 (44130-3329)
PHONE.................................440 816-2708
Trilok C Sharma MD, *President*
Sabino Velloze MD, *Vice Pres*
EMP: 30
SALES (est): 4MM **Privately Held**
SIC: 8011 Cardiologist & cardio-vascular specialist

(G-5126)
CARESOURCE MANAGEMENT GROUP CO
5900 Landerbrook Dr # 300 (44124-4020)
PHONE.................................216 839-1001
Mikka George, *Accountant*
Glen Sigel, *Manager*
EMP: 755 **Privately Held**
SIC: 6324 Health maintenance organization (HMO), insurance only
PA: Caresource Management Group Co.
　230 N Main St
　Dayton OH 45402

(G-5127)
CARGILL INCORPORATED
2400 Ships Channel (44113-2673)
P.O. Box 6920 (44101-1920)
PHONE.................................216 651-7200
Bob Soupko, *Branch Mgr*
EMP: 205
SALES (corp-wide): 114.7B **Privately Held**
WEB: www.cargill.com
SIC: 1479 2899 Salt (common) mining; chemical preparations

PA: Cargill, Incorporated
15407 Mcginty Rd W
Wayzata MN 55391
952 742-7575

(G-5128)
CARNEGIE CAPITAL ASSET MGT LLC
Also Called: Carnegie Investment Counsel
30300 Chagrin Blvd (44124-5725)
PHONE..................................216 595-1349
Winifred Coleman, *Vice Pres*
Richard Alt, *Ch Invest Ofcr*
Paul McCollum, *Portfolio Mgr*
Doug Pease, *Portfolio Mgr*
Gwen Graham, *Client Mgr*
EMP: 44
SALES (est): 138.1K **Privately Held**
SIC: 6282 Investment advice

(G-5129)
CARRIE CERINO RESTAURANTS INC
8922 Ridge Rd (44133-1869)
PHONE..................................440 237-3434
Carmen Cerino, *President*
Michael Cerino, *Corp Secy*
Dominic Cerino III, *Vice Pres*
EMP: 115
SQ FT: 30,000
SALES (est): 4.6MM **Privately Held**
WEB: www.carriecerinos.com
SIC: 5812 5813 7299 Italian restaurant; American restaurant; cocktail lounge; banquet hall facilities

(G-5130)
CASE WESTERN RESERVE UNIV
Also Called: Shipping & Receiving Dept
2232 Circle Dr (44106-2629)
PHONE..................................216 368-2560
Art Hardee, *Branch Mgr*
Elisse Cortez, *Asst Director*
EMP: 25
SALES (corp-wide): 1B **Privately Held**
WEB: www.cwru.edu
SIC: 7331 8221 Mailing service; university
PA: Case Western Reserve University
10900 Euclid Ave
Cleveland OH 44106
216 368-2000

(G-5131)
CATHOLIC ASSOCIATION OF THE DI (PA)
10000 Miles Ave (44105-6130)
P.O. Box 605310 (44105-0310)
PHONE..................................216 641-7575
Robert Winnicki, *CFO*
Andrej Lah, *Director*
EMP: 100
SALES (est): 22.2MM **Privately Held**
SIC: 6553 Cemetery subdividers & developers

(G-5132)
CATHOLIC CHARITIES CORPORATION
Also Called: Catholic Charities Svc Cuyah
7800 Detroit Ave (44102-2814)
PHONE..................................216 939-3713
Edward Carter, *Director*
Evelyn Santos, *Director*
Roz Dowdell, *Admin Asst*
EMP: 30 **Privately Held**
WEB: www.catholic-action.org
SIC: 8399 8322 Fund raising organization, non-fee basis; general counseling services
PA: Catholic Charities Corporation
7911 Detroit Ave
Cleveland OH 44102

(G-5133)
CATHOLIC CHARITIES CORPORATION
Also Called: Deporres, Martin Emrgncy Asst
1264 E 123rd St (44108-4002)
PHONE..................................216 268-4006
Marsha Blanks, *Principal*
EMP: 35 **Privately Held**
WEB: www.catholic-action.org
SIC: 8399 8322 Fund raising organization, non-fee basis; individual & family services

PA: Catholic Charities Corporation
7911 Detroit Ave
Cleveland OH 44102

(G-5134)
CATHOLIC CHARITIES CORPORATION (PA)
Also Called: CATHOLIC CHARITIES DIOCESE OF
7911 Detroit Ave (44102-2815)
PHONE..................................216 334-2900
Patrick Gareau, *President*
Maureen Dee, *General Mgr*
Patricia Holian, *COO*
Tracee Ingram, *COO*
Michael Haggerty, *Vice Pres*
EMP: 50
SALES: 51MM **Privately Held**
WEB: www.catholic-action.org
SIC: 8399 Fund raising organization, non-fee basis

(G-5135)
CATHOLIC DIOCESE OF CLEVELAND
Also Called: Holy Cross Cemetary
14609 Brookpark Rd (44142-1709)
PHONE..................................216 267-2850
Sharon Merzina, *Manager*
EMP: 40
SALES (corp-wide): 79.9MM **Privately Held**
WEB: www.oce-ocs.org
SIC: 6553 Cemetery subdividers & developers
PA: Catholic Diocese Of Cleveland
1404 E 9th St Ste 201
Cleveland OH 44114
216 696-6525

(G-5136)
CAVALIERS HOLDINGS LLC (PA)
Also Called: Quicken Loans Arena
1 Center Ct (44115-4001)
PHONE..................................216 420-2000
Brooks Neal, *Partner*
Antony Bonavita, *Vice Pres*
Matt Haltuch, *Production*
Ben Penman, *Accountant*
Dan Gilbert, *Broker*
EMP: 134
SALES (est): 87.3MM **Privately Held**
WEB: www.thegarena.com
SIC: 7941 6512 Basketball club; nonresidential building operators

(G-5137)
CAVALIERS OPERATING CO LLC
Also Called: Q, The
1 Center Ct (44115-4001)
PHONE..................................216 420-2000
Len Komorski, *CEO*
Alberta Lee, *Vice Pres*
Bob Pollard, *Facilities Dir*
Ray Deemer, *Engineer*
Robert Cole, *Accountant*
EMP: 1300
SALES (est): 48.6MM
SALES (corp-wide): 87.3MM **Privately Held**
SIC: 7941 Sports field or stadium operator, promoting sports events
PA: Cavaliers Holdings, Llc
1 Center Ct
Cleveland OH 44115
216 420-2000

(G-5138)
CAVITCH FAMILO & DURKIN CO LPA
1300 E 9th St (44114-1501)
PHONE..................................216 621-7860
Harvey L Furtkin, *Partner*
Michael C Cohen, *Partner*
Alex Goetsch,
EMP: 40
SQ FT: 16,500
SALES (est): 5.3MM **Privately Held**
WEB: www.cfdf.com
SIC: 8111 General practice law office

(G-5139)
CBIZ INC (PA)
6050 Oak Tree Blvd # 500 (44131-6951)
PHONE..................................216 447-9000
Steven L Gerard, *Ch of Bd*
Rick L Burdick, *Vice Ch Bd*
Jerry Grisko, *President*
Michael P Kouzelos, *President*
Chris Spurio, *President*
EMP: 148
SALES: 922MM **Publicly Held**
WEB: www.cbizinc.com
SIC: 8742 7389 7363 Management consulting services; financial services; employee leasing service

(G-5140)
CBIZ OPERATIONS INC (HQ)
6050 Oaktee Blvd Ste 500 (44131)
PHONE..................................216 447-9000
Jerry Grisko, *CEO*
EMP: 55
SALES (est): 4MM **Publicly Held**
WEB: www.cbizinc.com
SIC: 7379 7371 8748 Computer related consulting services; custom computer programming services; business consulting

(G-5141)
CBIZ RISK & ADVISORY SVCS LLC
6050 Oak Tree Blvd (44131-6927)
PHONE..................................216 447-9000
Brian Gregory, *President*
Terri Bur, *Exec VP*
Matthew J Morelli, *Exec VP*
Ware H Grove, *Vice Pres*
Bruce J Kowalski, *Vice Pres*
EMP: 32
SALES (est): 476.7K **Publicly Held**
SIC: 8748 Business consulting
HQ: Cbiz Operations, Inc.
6050 Oaktee Blvd Ste 500
Cleveland OH 44131

(G-5142)
CBRE INC
950 Main Ave Ste 200 (44113-7203)
PHONE..................................216 687-1800
Kevin Malinowski, *Vice Pres*
David Browning, *Manager*
Terry D Kaufman, *Manager*
Jennifer Priest, *Manager*
Peter Miller, *Associate*
EMP: 45
SALES (corp-wide): 21.3B **Publicly Held**
SIC: 6531 Real estate agent, commercial
HQ: Cbre, Inc.
400 S Hope St Ste 25
Los Angeles CA 90071
213 613-3333

(G-5143)
CBRE HEERY INC
1660 W 2nd St (44113-1454)
PHONE..................................216 781-1313
John R May, *Manager*
EMP: 25
SALES (corp-wide): 21.3B **Publicly Held**
WEB: www.hlm-heery.com
SIC: 8711 8712 8741 Engineering services; architectural services; management services
HQ: Cbre Heery, Inc.
999 Peachtree St Ne # 300
Atlanta GA 30309
404 881-9880

(G-5144)
CBS RADIO INC
1041 Huron Rd E (44115-1706)
PHONE..................................216 861-0100
Walter Tiburski, *Branch Mgr*
Dan Vloedman, *Info Tech Dir*
EMP: 25
SALES (corp-wide): 1.4B **Publicly Held**
WEB: www.infinityradio.com
SIC: 4832 Radio broadcasting stations
HQ: Cbs Radio Inc.
345 Hudson St Fl 10
New York NY 10014
212 314-9200

(G-5145)
CEFARATTI INVESTIGATION & PRCS
Also Called: Cefaratti Group
4608 Saint Clair Ave (44103-1206)
PHONE..................................216 696-1161
Arther Cefaratti, *President*
Robert Adelman, *Managing Prtnr*
Paul Cefaratti, *Vice Pres*
Kim Fleming, *Financial Exec*
Arthur Cefaratti, *Manager*
EMP: 25
SALES (est): 711.9K **Privately Held**
WEB: www.cefgroup.com
SIC: 7381 Detective agency

(G-5146)
CELEBRITY SECURITY INC
3408 West Blvd (44111-1232)
PHONE..................................216 671-6425
Paul Jurcisin, *President*
Jim Morrison, *Vice Pres*
EMP: 50
SALES (est): 920K **Privately Held**
SIC: 7381 8748 Detective/Armored Car Services Business Consulting Services

(G-5147)
CELLCO PARTNERSHIP
Also Called: Verizon
5945 Mayfield Rd (44124-2902)
PHONE..................................440 646-9625
Jim Sankey, *Branch Mgr*
EMP: 25
SALES (corp-wide): 130.8B **Publicly Held**
SIC: 4812 5999 Cellular telephone services; mobile telephones & equipment
HQ: Cellco Partnership
1 Verizon Way
Basking Ridge NJ 07920

(G-5148)
CENTER FOR COMMUNITY SOLUTIONS
1501 Euclid Ave Ste 311 (44115-2108)
PHONE..................................216 781-2944
Roslyn Kaleal, *Office Admin*
Gregory L Brown, *Exec Dir*
Sheila Lettsome, *Executive Asst*
Loren Anthes, *Fellow*
EMP: 30
SQ FT: 17,500
SALES: 2.9MM **Privately Held**
SIC: 8399 Advocacy group

(G-5149)
CENTER FOR FAMILIES & CHILDREN
5955 Ridge Rd (44129-3936)
PHONE..................................440 888-0300
Betty Rossi, *Director*
EMP: 25
SALES (corp-wide): 26MM **Privately Held**
SIC: 8322 General counseling services
PA: Center For Families & Children, Inc
4500 Euclid Ave
Cleveland OH 44103
216 432-7200

(G-5150)
CENTER FOR FAMILIES & CHILDREN (PA)
4500 Euclid Ave (44103-3736)
PHONE..................................216 432-7200
Lee Fisher, *President*
Sharon Sobol Jordan, *Principal*
Elizabeth Newman, *COO*
Judith Z Peters, *Exec VP*
Dennis Anderson, *Vice Pres*
EMP: 65
SQ FT: 23,000
SALES (est): 26MM **Privately Held**
SIC: 8322 Child related social services

(G-5151)
CENTER FOR FAMILIES & CHILDREN
3929 Rocky River Dr (44111-4153)
PHONE..................................216 252-5800
Charlie Bango, *Manager*
Olga Rosado, *Manager*
Nathan Rhea, *Supervisor*

GEOGRAPHIC

Heather Roberts, *Supervisor*
EMP: 25
SALES (corp-wide): 26MM **Privately Held**
SIC: 8322 8093 Family counseling services; mental health clinic, outpatient
PA: Center For Families & Children, Inc
4500 Euclid Ave
Cleveland OH 44103
216 432-7200

(G-5152)
CENTER FOR HEALTH AFFAIRS
Also Called: Greater Cleveland Hosp Assn
1226 Huron Rd E (44115-1789)
PHONE..............................800 362-2628
William T Ryan, *President*
EMP: 78 **EST:** 1997
SALES: 1MM **Privately Held**
SIC: 8062 8699 8742 General medical & surgical hospitals; athletic organizations; management consulting services

(G-5153)
CENTRAL CADILLAC LIMITED
Also Called: Central Cadillac-Hummer
2801 Carnegie Ave (44115-2628)
PHONE..............................216 861-5800
Frank H Porter Jr, *President*
EMP: 83
SQ FT: 40,000
SALES (est): 8.4MM **Privately Held**
WEB: www.centralcadillac.com
SIC: 7538 5521 5511 General automotive repair shops; used car dealers; automobiles, new & used

(G-5154)
CENTRAL HOSPITAL SERVICES INC
Also Called: CHAMPS MANAGEMENT SERVICES
1226 Huron Rd E Ste 2 (44115-1702)
PHONE..............................216 696-6900
Bill Ryan, *President*
Phil Mazanec, *COO*
Laura Gronowski, *Vice Pres*
John Piazza, *Vice Pres*
EMP: 55
SQ FT: 18,000
SALES: 7MM **Privately Held**
SIC: 8621 Medical field-related associations

(G-5155)
CENTRAL HUMMR EAST
25975 Central Pkwy (44122-7308)
PHONE..............................216 514-2700
Scott Newman, *Manager*
EMP: 30
SALES: 1MM **Privately Held**
SIC: 5012 Automobiles

(G-5156)
CENTURA INC
Also Called: Centura X-Ray
4381 Renaissance Pkwy (44128-5759)
PHONE..............................216 593-0226
Douglas Brook, *President*
Mary Luzi, *Principal*
John T Mulligan, *Principal*
Mark Hale, *CFO*
EMP: 40
SQ FT: 16,500
SALES (est): 10.2MM **Privately Held**
WEB: www.centuraxray.com
SIC: 5047 Medical equipment & supplies; X-ray machines & tubes

(G-5157)
CENTURY 21 TRAMMELL ODONNELL
7087 Pearl Rd (44130-4940)
PHONE..............................440 888-6800
Bruce Trammell, *Partner*
Janet O Donnell, *Partner*
EMP: 70
SQ FT: 4,700
SALES (est): 3MM **Privately Held**
SIC: 6531 Real estate agent, residential

(G-5158)
CENTURY EQUIPMENT INC
26565 Miles Rd Ste 200 (44128-5998)
PHONE..............................216 292-6911
Ron Smallwick, *Branch Mgr*

EMP: 37
SALES (corp-wide): 41.7MM **Privately Held**
WEB: www.centuryequip.com
SIC: 5083 5088 Mowers, power; lawn machinery & equipment; garden machinery & equipment; irrigation equipment; golf carts
PA: Century Equipment, Inc.
5959 Angola Rd
Toledo OH 43615
419 865-7400

(G-5159)
CENTURY FEDERAL CREDIT UNION
10701 East Blvd (44106-1702)
PHONE..............................216 535-3600
Adrew Dickson, *Manager*
EMP: 30
SALES (corp-wide): 11.5MM **Privately Held**
WEB: www.centuryfederalcreditunion.com
SIC: 6061 Federal credit unions
PA: Century Federal Credit Union Inc
1240 E 9th St Ste 719
Cleveland OH
216 535-3200

(G-5160)
CENTURY LINES INC
3184 E 79th St (44104-4325)
P.O. Box 27469 (44127-0469)
PHONE..............................216 271-0700
Robert O Rucker, *President*
Mike Trent, *Vice Pres*
Marilyn Rucker, *Admin Sec*
EMP: 50 **EST:** 1973
SQ FT: 150,000
SALES (est): 6.7MM **Privately Held**
SIC: 4212 4213 Local trucking, without storage; trucking, except local

(G-5161)
CETEK LTD
6779 Engle Rd Ste A (44130-7926)
PHONE..............................216 362-3900
Derek Scott, *CEO*
EMP: 30
SALES (est): 2.1MM **Privately Held**
SIC: 2851 8711 Lacquers, varnishes, enamels & other coatings; heating & ventilation engineering
PA: Integrated Global Services, Inc.
7600 Whitepine Rd
North Chesterfield VA 23237

(G-5162)
CEVA FREIGHT LLC
Also Called: Ceva Ocean Line
18601 Cleveland Pkwy Dr (44135-3231)
PHONE..............................216 898-6765
Ken Towers, *Manager*
EMP: 45
SALES (corp-wide): 20.8MM **Privately Held**
WEB: www.tntlogistics.com
SIC: 4731 Freight forwarding
HQ: Ceva Freight, Llc
15350 Vickery Dr
Houston TX 77032

(G-5163)
CGI TECHNOLOGIES SOLUTIONS INC
1001 Lakeside Ave E # 800 (44114-1158)
PHONE..............................216 687-1480
Jeff Lawson, *President*
Renee Jones, *Facilities Mgr*
Sophia Youngbauer, *HR Admin*
Richard Schmitz, *Manager*
Jeff Hirsch, *Info Tech Dir*
EMP: 150
SALES (corp-wide): 8.6B **Privately Held**
SIC: 7379 Computer related consulting services
HQ: Cgi Technologies And Solutions Inc.
11325 Random Hills Rd
Fairfax VA 22030
703 267-8000

(G-5164)
CH ROBINSON FREIGHT SVCS LTD
Also Called: Phoenix International Frt Svcs
7261 Engle Rd Ste 400 (44130-3479)
PHONE..............................440 234-7811
Michelle Yancy, *Principal*
EMP: 50
SALES (corp-wide): 16.6B **Publicly Held**
WEB: www.phoenixintl.com
SIC: 4731 Freight forwarding
HQ: C.H. Robinson Freight Services, Ltd.
1501 N Mittel Blvd Ste A
Wood Dale IL 60191
630 766-4445

(G-5165)
CHA CONSULTING INC
1501 N Marginal Rd # 200 (44114-3760)
PHONE..............................216 443-1700
William Barley, *Vice Pres*
EMP: 115
SALES (corp-wide): 186.4MM **Privately Held**
SIC: 8711 8712 Consulting engineer; architectural services
PA: Cha Consulting, Inc.
575 Broadway Ste 301
Albany NY 12207
518 453-4500

(G-5166)
CHAL-RON LLC
Also Called: Jubilee Academy
15751 Lake Shore Blvd (44110-1020)
P.O. Box 37214, Maple Heights (44137-0214)
PHONE..............................216 383-9050
Chalfonte Smith,
Arrian Smith,
Marche Smith,
EMP: 25
SALES (est): 1.1MM **Privately Held**
SIC: 8351 Child day care services

(G-5167)
CHANDLER PRODUCTS LLC
1491 Chardon Rd (44117-1598)
PHONE..............................216 481-4400
Ron Kiter, *Manager*
EMP: 31
SALES (est): 4.8MM
SALES (corp-wide): 70MM **Privately Held**
SIC: 5085 Fasteners, industrial: nuts, bolts, screws, etc.
HQ: Elgin Fastener Group, Llc
10217 Brecksville Rd # 101
Brecksville OH 44141

(G-5168)
CHANGE HLTHCARE OPERATIONS LLC
2060 E 9th St (44115-1313)
PHONE..............................216 589-5878
Aji Fabi, *Branch Mgr*
EMP: 37
SALES (corp-wide): 208.3B **Publicly Held**
SIC: 7374 Data processing service
HQ: Change Healthcare Operations, Llc
3055 Lebanon Pike # 1000
Nashville TN 37214

(G-5169)
CHARLES RVER LABS CLVELAND INC
14656 Neo Pkwy (44128-3156)
PHONE..............................216 332-1665
Emily Hickey, *President*
David Smith, *Treasurer*
Luke Armstrong, *Director*
Jessica Brimecombe, *Director*
Antonio E Lacerda, *Director*
EMP: 55 **EST:** 2007
SQ FT: 27,000
SALES (est): 8.1MM
SALES (corp-wide): 2.2B **Publicly Held**
WEB: www.chantest.com
SIC: 8731 Commercial physical research
HQ: Charles River Laboratories, Inc.
251 Ballardvale St
Wilmington MA 01887
781 222-6000

(G-5170)
CHARLES SCHWAB CORPORATION
24737 Cedar Rd (44124-3786)
PHONE..............................216 291-9333
Jeffrey L Hurst, *Principal*
Mike Myers, *Client Mgr*
EMP: 26
SALES (corp-wide): 10.9B **Publicly Held**
SIC: 6211 Brokers, security
PA: The Charles Schwab Corporation
211 Main St Fl 17
San Francisco CA 94105
415 667-7000

(G-5171)
CHARTWELL GROUP LLC (PA)
1350 Euclid Ave Ste 700 (44115-1889)
PHONE..............................216 360-0009
Michael Berland, *Managing Dir*
Gordon Greene, *Managing Dir*
Robert Biggar, *Mng Member*
William Nice,
David Wagner,
EMP: 25
SQ FT: 4,500
SALES: 3.5MM **Privately Held**
SIC: 6531 8742 Real estate brokers & agents; real estate consultant

(G-5172)
CHATTREE AND ASSOCIATES INC
Also Called: Community Behavioral Hlth Ctr
3355 Richmond Rd Ste 225 (44122-4180)
PHONE..............................216 831-1494
Arun Chattree, *President*
Luan Hutchinson, *Vice Pres*
EMP: 87
SALES: 3.5MM **Privately Held**
SIC: 8742 Hospital & health services consultant

(G-5173)
CHEMICAL SOLVENTS INC (PA)
3751 Jennings Rd (44109-2889)
PHONE..............................216 741-9310
Edward Pavlish, *Ch of Bd*
Thos A Mason, *Principal*
E H Pavlish, *Principal*
Patricia Pavlish, *Corp Secy*
Blaine Davidson, *Vice Pres*
▲ **EMP:** 45 **EST:** 1970
SQ FT: 30,000
SALES: 112.5MM **Privately Held**
WEB: www.chemicalsolvents.com
SIC: 5169 7349 3471 2992 Detergents & soaps, except specialty cleaning; specialty cleaning & sanitation preparations; chemical cleaning services; cleaning & descaling metal products; oils & greases, blending & compounding

(G-5174)
CHEMICAL SOLVENTS INC
1010 Denison Ave (44109-2853)
P.O. Box 931705 (44193-1813)
PHONE..............................216 741-9310
Dan Reynolds, *Manager*
EMP: 65
SALES (est): 6.4MM
SALES (corp-wide): 112.5MM **Privately Held**
WEB: www.chemicalsolvents.com
SIC: 5169 Industrial chemicals; specialty cleaning & sanitation preparations
PA: Chemical Solvents, Inc.
3751 Jennings Rd
Cleveland OH 44109
216 741-9310

(G-5175)
CHICAGO TITLE INSURANCE CO
1111 Superior Ave E # 600 (44114-2541)
PHONE..............................216 241-6045
Shelley Maggard, *Manager*
Mark Cook, *Manager*
Jay West, *Information Mgr*
Samantha Babcock, *Executive*
Dave Mader, *Executive*
EMP: 50
SALES (corp-wide): 7.5B **Publicly Held**
SIC: 6361 Title insurance

HQ: Chicago Title Insurance Company
601 Riverside Ave
Jacksonville FL 32204

(G-5176)
CHIEFTAIN TRUCKING & EXCAV INC
3926 Valley Rd Ste 300 (44109-3058)
PHONE..................................216 485-8034
Eileen Martin, *President*
Betty Martin, *President*
Brian Murphy, *Project Mgr*
Pat Tomazic, *Controller*
Patrick Tomazic, *Controller*
EMP: 35
SQ FT: 17,500
SALES: 8MM **Privately Held**
SIC: 1794 4231 Excavation & grading; building construction; trucking terminal facilities

(G-5177)
CHILD CARE RESOURCE CENTER (PA)
Also Called: Starting Point
4600 Euclid Ave Ste 500 (44103-3761)
PHONE..................................216 575-0061
Bilie Osbourne, *Director*
EMP: 33
SALES (est): 9.9MM **Privately Held**
SIC: 8351 Child day care services

(G-5178)
CHILDRENS AID SOCIETY
10427 Detroit Ave (44102-1694)
PHONE..................................216 521-6511
Lawrence S Waldman, *Owner*
EMP: 50
SALES (est): 1.5MM **Privately Held**
SIC: 8049 Clinical psychologist

(G-5179)
CINEMARK USA INC
Also Called: Cinemark At Valley View
6001 Canal Rd (44125-4232)
PHONE..................................216 447-8820
Melissa Truhn, *Manager*
EMP: 110 **Publicly Held**
SIC: 7832 Motion picture theaters, except drive-in
HQ: Cinemark Usa, Inc.
3900 Dallas Pkwy Ste 500
Plano TX 75093
972 665-1000

(G-5180)
CINTAS CORPORATION NO 2
1 Andrews Cir (44141-3250)
PHONE..................................440 838-8611
Lisa Coone, *Manager*
EMP: 57
SQ FT: 110,970
SALES (corp-wide): 6.4B **Publicly Held**
WEB: www.cintas-corp.com
SIC: 7389 Document storage service
HQ: Cintas Corporation No. 2
6800 Cintas Blvd
Mason OH 45040

(G-5181)
CIPRIANO PAINTING
27387 Hollywood Dr (44145-5356)
PHONE..................................440 892-1827
Mike Cipriano, *Owner*
EMP: 25
SALES (est): 731.1K **Privately Held**
SIC: 1721 Residential painting

(G-5182)
CIRCLE HEALTH SERVICES
12201 Euclid Ave (44106-4310)
PHONE..................................216 721-4010
Maryaitta Elston, *Psychologist*
Danny Williams, *Exec Dir*
Fatima Warren, *Associate Dir*
Tim Dennis, *Administration*
Hallie Arrigon, *Nurse Practr*
EMP: 44
SQ FT: 28,000
SALES: 5.3MM **Privately Held**
WEB: www.thefreeclinic.org
SIC: 8322 Individual & family services

(G-5183)
CITIGROUP GLOBAL MARKETS INC
Also Called: Smith Barney
2035 Crocker Rd Ste 201 (44145-2194)
PHONE..................................440 617-2000
EMP: 25
SALES (corp-wide): 92.5B **Publicly Held**
SIC: 6211 Securities Brokers/Dealers
HQ: Citigroup Global Markets Inc.
388 Greenwich St Fl 18
New York NY 10013
212 816-6000

(G-5184)
CITIZENS CAPITAL MARKETS INC
200 Public Sq Ste 3750 (44114-2321)
PHONE..................................216 589-0900
Ralph M Della Ratta, *General Mgr*
EMP: 28
SALES (corp-wide): 7.3B **Publicly Held**
SIC: 6141 Personal credit institutions
HQ: Citizens Capital Markets, Inc.
28 State St Fl 13
Boston MA 02109
617 725-5636

(G-5185)
CITY ARCHITECTURE INC
3636 Euclid Ave Fl 3 (44115-2539)
PHONE..................................216 881-2444
Paul Volpe, *President*
Mark Dodds, *Corp Secy*
Ryan Grass, *Project Mgr*
Christophe Auvil, *Architect*
Christine Perry, *Manager*
EMP: 30
SQ FT: 9,000
SALES (est): 3.7MM **Privately Held**
WEB: www.cityarch.com
SIC: 8712 Architectural services

(G-5186)
CITY LIFE INC (PA)
Also Called: Sammy's
1382 W 9th St Ste 310 (44113-1231)
PHONE..................................216 523-5899
Denise M Fugo, *President*
Ralph Diorio, *COO*
EMP: 40
SQ FT: 14,550
SALES (est): 12.1MM **Privately Held**
WEB: www.sammys.com
SIC: 5812 5813 7299 American restaurant; caterers; cocktail lounge; banquet hall facilities

(G-5187)
CITY MISSION (PA)
5310 Carnegie Ave (44103-4360)
PHONE..................................216 431-3510
Mark Charvat, *Finance Dir*
Joshua Foote, *Marketing Staff*
Deborah Phillips, *Manager*
Johnny Braden, *Info Tech Mgr*
Richard Trickel, *Exec Dir*
EMP: 65 EST: 1910
SALES (est): 6.3MM **Privately Held**
WEB: www.thecitymission.org
SIC: 8322 8361 Rehabilitation services; rehabilitation center, residential: health care incidental

(G-5188)
CITY OF BROOK PARK
Also Called: Brook Park Recreation Center
17400 Holland Rd (44142-3524)
PHONE..................................216 433-1545
Gary Marken, *Director*
EMP: 35 **Privately Held**
WEB: www.cityofbrookpark.com
SIC: 7999 Recreation center
PA: City Of Brook Park
6161 Engle Rd
Cleveland OH 44142
216 433-1533

(G-5189)
CITY OF CLEVELAND
Also Called: Public Safety
1701 Lakeside Ave E (44114-1118)
PHONE..................................216 664-2555
George Chaloupka, *Commander*
Edward Eckart, *Mfg Staff*

EMP: 325 **Privately Held**
SIC: 4119 9229 Ambulance service; emergency management office, government;
PA: City Of Cleveland
601 Lakeside Ave E Rm 210
Cleveland OH 44114
216 664-2000

(G-5190)
CITY OF CLEVELAND
Also Called: Cleveland Emergency Med Svc
1701 Lakeside Ave E (44114-1118)
PHONE..................................216 664-2555
Edward Eckart, *Commissioner*
EMP: 325 **Privately Held**
SIC: 4119 Ambulance service
PA: City Of Cleveland
601 Lakeside Ave E Rm 210
Cleveland OH 44114
216 664-2000

(G-5191)
CITY OF CLEVELAND
Public Services Dept
955 Clague Rd (44145-1504)
PHONE..................................216 664-3121
Mark Petre, *Manager*
Rich Patt, *Exec Dir*
EMP: 42 **Privately Held**
SIC: 4941 9511 Water supply; air, water & solid waste management;
PA: City Of Cleveland
601 Lakeside Ave E Rm 210
Cleveland OH 44114
216 664-2000

(G-5192)
CITY OF CLEVELAND
Division Information Tech Svcs
205 W Saint Clair Ave # 4 (44113-1503)
PHONE..................................216 664-2941
Doug Davis, *Branch Mgr*
EMP: 40 **Privately Held**
SIC: 7376 Computer facilities management
PA: City Of Cleveland
601 Lakeside Ave E Rm 210
Cleveland OH 44114
216 664-2000

(G-5193)
CITY OF CLEVELAND
Public Works, Dept of
500 Lkeside Ave Ground Fl (44114)
PHONE..................................216 621-4231
EMP: 47 **Privately Held**
SIC: 6512 9512 Nonresidential Building Operator
PA: City Of Cleveland
601 Lakeside Ave E Rm 210
Cleveland OH 44114
216 664-2000

(G-5194)
CITY OF CLEVELAND
Also Called: Finance Dept
205 W Saint Clair Ave # 4 (44113-1503)
PHONE..................................216 664-2430
Doug Divish, *Commissioner*
EMP: 60 **Privately Held**
SIC: 7374 9199 Data processing & preparation; general government administration;
PA: City Of Cleveland
601 Lakeside Ave E Rm 210
Cleveland OH 44114
216 664-2000

(G-5195)
CITY OF CLEVELAND
Also Called: Finance Dept
601 Lakeside Ave E Rm 128 (44114-1065)
PHONE..................................216 664-2620
Tiffany White Johnson, *Manager*
EMP: 25 **Privately Held**
SIC: 7389 9311 Purchasing service; finance, taxation & monetary policy;
PA: City Of Cleveland
601 Lakeside Ave E Rm 210
Cleveland OH 44114
216 664-2000

(G-5196)
CITY OF CLEVELAND
Also Called: Parks Recreation & Prpts Dept
21400 Chagrin Blvd (44122-5308)
PHONE..................................216 348-7210

David R Mitchell, *Manager*
EMP: 35
SQ FT: 856 **Privately Held**
SIC: 6553 9512 Cemetery subdividers & developers; land, mineral & wildlife conservation;
PA: City Of Cleveland
601 Lakeside Ave E Rm 210
Cleveland OH 44114
216 664-2000

(G-5197)
CITY OF CLEVELAND
Also Called: Fire Station
3765 Pearl Rd (44109-2752)
PHONE..................................216 664-6800
Kevin Gerrity, *Principal*
EMP: 72 **Privately Held**
SIC: 9224 7922 Fire department, not including volunteer; ; theatrical producers & services
PA: City Of Cleveland
601 Lakeside Ave E Rm 210
Cleveland OH 44114
216 664-2000

(G-5198)
CITY OF CLEVELAND
Also Called: Department of Public Utilities
1300 Lakeside Ave E (44114-1135)
PHONE..................................216 664-3922
Jim Mager, *Branch Mgr*
EMP: 32 **Privately Held**
SIC: 7389 Patrol of electric transmission or gas lines
PA: City Of Cleveland
601 Lakeside Ave E Rm 210
Cleveland OH 44114
216 664-2000

(G-5199)
CITY OF CLEVELAND HEIGHTS
Recycling Department
14200 Superior Rd (44118-1748)
PHONE..................................216 691-7300
Tony Torres, *Manager*
EMP: 35 **Privately Held**
WEB: www.clevelandheights.com
SIC: 4953 Recycling, waste materials
PA: City Of Cleveland Heights
40 Severance Cir
Cleveland Heights OH 44118
216 291-4444

(G-5200)
CITY OF EUCLID
Also Called: Streets & Sewer Departments
25500 Lakeland Blvd (44132-2633)
PHONE..................................216 289-2800
Steve Marco, *Manager*
EMP: 40 **Privately Held**
WEB: www.cityofeuclid.com
SIC: 1611 9111 Highway & street maintenance; executive offices
PA: City Of Euclid
585 E 222nd St
Cleveland OH 44123
216 289-2700

(G-5201)
CITY OF GARFIELD HEIGHTS
Also Called: Service Garage
13600 Mccracken Rd (44125-1976)
PHONE..................................216 475-1107
Mark Sikon, *Manager*
EMP: 35 **Privately Held**
WEB: www.garfieldhts.org
SIC: 7521 Parking garage
PA: City Of Garfield Heights
5407 Turney Rd
Cleveland OH 44125
216 475-1100

(G-5202)
CITY OF HIGHLAND HEIGHTS
Senior Assistance
5827 Highland Rd (44143-2017)
PHONE..................................440 461-2441
Mary Velota, *Director*
EMP: 55 **Privately Held**
SIC: 8322 Geriatric social service
PA: City Of Highland Heights
5827 Highland Rd
Cleveland OH 44143
440 461-2440

GEOGRAPHIC

(G-5203)
CITY OF INDEPENDENCE
Also Called: Recreation Dept
6363 Selig Blvd (44131-4926)
PHONE..................................216 524-3262
Tom Walchanowicz, *Director*
EMP: 37 **Privately Held**
SIC: 7999 Recreation services
PA: City Of Independence
6800 Brecksville Rd
Independence OH 44131
216 524-4131

(G-5204)
CITY OF INDEPENDENCE
Also Called: Civic Center
6363 Selig Blvd (44131-4926)
PHONE..................................216 524-7373
Natalie Buc, *Director*
EMP: 40
SQ FT: 8,463 **Privately Held**
WEB: www.independenceohio.org
SIC: 8322 Community center
PA: City Of Independence
6800 Brecksville Rd
Independence OH 44131
216 524-4131

(G-5205)
CITY OF LAKEWOOD
Also Called: Div of Refuse and Recycling
12920 Berea Rd (44111-1626)
PHONE..................................216 252-4322
Chris Perry, *General Mgr*
EMP: 30
SQ FT: 28,810 **Privately Held**
SIC: 4953 9511 Refuse systems; water
control & quality agency, government
PA: City Of Lakewood
12650 Detroit Ave
Lakewood OH 44107
216 521-7580

(G-5206)
CITY OF LAKEWOOD
Also Called: Lakewood Community Care
Center
2019 Woodward Ave (44107-5635)
PHONE..................................216 226-0080
Stephanie McMahan, *Principal*
Jeanne E Halladay, *Branch Mgr*
EMP: 37 **Privately Held**
SIC: 8351 Child day care services
PA: City Of Lakewood
12650 Detroit Ave
Lakewood OH 44107
216 521-7580

(G-5207)
CITY OF LAKEWOOD
Also Called: Lakewood Police Dept
12650 Detroit Ave (44107-2832)
PHONE..................................216 529-6170
Gary Sprague, *Commander*
Daniel Clark, *Chief*
EMP: 110 **Privately Held**
SIC: 9221 8111 ; legal services
PA: City Of Lakewood
12650 Detroit Ave
Lakewood OH 44107
216 521-7580

(G-5208)
CITY OF LAKEWOOD
Also Called: Municipal Garage
12920 Berea Rd (44111-1626)
PHONE..................................216 941-1116
Larry Slanick, *Manager*
EMP: 55 **Privately Held**
SIC: 7521 Automobile parking
PA: City Of Lakewood
12650 Detroit Ave
Lakewood OH 44107
216 521-7580

(G-5209)
CITY OF LAKEWOOD
16024 Madison Ave (44107-5616)
PHONE..................................216 521-1288
Paulette McMoneguel, *Director*
EMP: 31 **Privately Held**
SIC: 4119 Local passenger transportation
PA: City Of Lakewood
12650 Detroit Ave
Lakewood OH 44107
216 521-7580

(G-5210)
CITY OF NORTH ROYALTON
Also Called: Street and Service Department
11545 Royalton Rd (44133-4458)
PHONE..................................440 582-3002
Skip Mayor, *Branch Mgr*
EMP: 40 **Privately Held**
WEB: www.northroyalton.org
SIC: 1611 Highway & street maintenance
PA: City Of North Royalton
14600 State Rd
North Royalton OH 44133
440 237-5686

(G-5211)
CITY OF PARMA
Also Called: Parma Service Garage
5680 Chevrolet Blvd (44130-1404)
PHONE..................................440 885-8983
Jack Sparks, *General Mgr*
EMP: 100
SQ FT: 41,762 **Privately Held**
WEB: www.parmajustice.net
SIC: 7521 Parking garage
PA: Parma City Of (Inc)
6611 Ridge Rd
Cleveland OH 44129
440 885-8000

(G-5212)
CITY OF PARMA
Also Called: Ridgewood Golf Course
6505 Ridge Rd (44129-5528)
PHONE..................................440 885-8876
Howard Murphy, *Manager*
EMP: 50
SQ FT: 9,468 **Privately Held**
WEB: www.parmajustice.net
SIC: 7992 7997 Public golf courses; golf
club, membership
PA: Parma City Of (Inc)
6611 Ridge Rd
Cleveland OH 44129
440 885-8000

(G-5213)
CITY OF PARMA
Senior Center
7001 W Ridgewood Dr (44129-6922)
PHONE..................................440 888-4514
EMP: 28 **Privately Held**
WEB: www.parmajustice.net
SIC: 8322 Senior citizens' center or association
PA: Parma City Of (Inc)
6611 Ridge Rd
Cleveland OH 44129
440 885-8000

(G-5214)
CITY OF ROCKY RIVER
Also Called: Hamilton Ice Arena
21018 Hilliard Blvd (44116-3312)
PHONE..................................440 356-5656
Mike Patterson, *Manager*
EMP: 26 **Privately Held**
WEB: www.rrcity.com
SIC: 7999 Recreation center
PA: City Of Rocky River
21012 Hilliard Blvd
Rocky River OH 44116
440 331-0600

(G-5215)
CITY OF ROCKY RIVER
21012 Hilliard Blvd (44116-3312)
PHONE..................................440 356-5630
Dave Winterich, *Commissioner*
EMP: 50 **Privately Held**
WEB: www.rrcity.com
SIC: 8999 Personal services
PA: City Of Rocky River
21012 Hilliard Blvd
Rocky River OH 44116
440 331-0600

(G-5216)
CITY OF SOUTH EUCLID
Also Called: Victory Pool
1352 Victory Dr (44121-3629)
PHONE..................................216 291-3902
Peter Titas, *Manager*
EMP: 31 **Privately Held**
WEB: www.cityofsoutheuclid.com
SIC: 7999 Swimming pool, non-membership

PA: City Of South Euclid
1349 S Green Rd
South Euclid OH 44121
216 381-1214

(G-5217)
CITY OF WARRENSVILLE HEIGHTS
Also Called: Service Dept
19700 Miles Rd (44128-4116)
PHONE..................................216 587-1230
Wesley Haynes, *Chief*
Albert C Williams, *Manager*
Deborah Hutton, *Council Mbr*
EMP: 30 **Privately Held**
SIC: 8399 Social service information exchange
PA: City Of Warrensville Heights
4301 Warrensville Ctr Rd
Warrensville Heights OH 44128
216 587-6500

(G-5218)
CITY VIEW NURSING & REHAB LLC
Also Called: Cityview Nrsing Rhbltation Ctr
6606 Carnegie Ave (44103-4622)
PHONE..................................216 361-1414
Stephen L Rosedale, *President*
Charles R Stoltz, *Exec VP*
Ronald S Wilheim, *Exec VP*
Kevin Kilbane, *Administration*
EMP: 225
SQ FT: 41,000
SALES: 9.1MM **Privately Held**
SIC: 8051 Convalescent home with continuous nursing care

(G-5219)
CIULLA SMITH & DALE LLP (PA)
6364 Pearl Rd Ste 4 (44130-3063)
PHONE..................................440 884-2036
Joseph Ciulla, *Partner*
Ted L Hlavka, *Partner*
Dennis R Horan, *Partner*
Robert A Huttner, *Partner*
Robert Mc Minn, *Partner*
EMP: 28
SQ FT: 5,500
SALES (est): 4.1MM **Privately Held**
SIC: 8721 Certified public accountant

(G-5220)
CIUNI & PANICHI INC
25201 Chagrin Blvd # 200 (44122-5683)
PHONE..................................216 831-7171
Charles Ciunini, *Managing Prtnr*
Vincent Panichi, *Senior Partner*
Jay A Bagdasarian, *Partner*
James Komos, *Partner*
David A Linscott, *Partner*
EMP: 60
SQ FT: 20,000
SALES (est): 5.7MM **Privately Held**
WEB: www.cp-advisors.com
SIC: 8721 Certified public accountant

(G-5221)
CLARK SCHAEFER HACKETT & CO
600 Superior Ave E # 1300 (44114-2614)
PHONE..................................216 672-5252
Carl Coburn, *President*
EMP: 50
SALES (corp-wide): 37.2MM **Privately Held**
SIC: 8721 Certified public accountant
PA: Clark, Schaefer, Hackett & Co.
1 E 4th St Ste 1200
Cincinnati OH 45202
513 241-3111

(G-5222)
CLEAN HARBORS ENVMTL SVCS INC
Also Called: Milestone
2900 Broadway Ave (44115)
PHONE..................................216 429-2402
Clayton Burtif, *Manager*
EMP: 80
SQ FT: 14,616
SALES (corp-wide): 3.3B **Publicly Held**
SIC: 4953 Hazardous waste collection & disposal

HQ: Clean Harbors Environmental Services, Inc.
42 Longwater Dr
Norwell MA 02061
781 792-5000

(G-5223)
CLEAN HARBORS ENVMTL SVCS INC
2930 Independence Rd (44115-3616)
PHONE..................................216 429-2401
Brian Overmyer, *Manager*
Michael Petkozich, *Manager*
EMP: 78
SALES (corp-wide): 3.3B **Publicly Held**
SIC: 4953 Hazardous waste collection & disposal
HQ: Clean Harbors Environmental Services, Inc.
42 Longwater Dr
Norwell MA 02061
781 792-5000

(G-5224)
CLEARVIEW CLEANING CONTRACTORS
2140 Hamilton Ave (44114-1173)
P.O. Box 93631 (44101-5631)
PHONE..................................216 621-6688
Richard Matonis, *President*
EMP: 40
SALES (est): 1.4MM **Privately Held**
SIC: 7349 Window cleaning

(G-5225)
CLEVELAN CLINIC HLTH SYS W REG
5555 Transportation Blvd (44125-5371)
PHONE..................................216 518-3444
William Wick, *Branch Mgr*
EMP: 411
SALES (corp-wide): 8.9B **Privately Held**
SIC: 8741 Hospital management
HQ: Cleveland Clinic Health System-Western Region
18101 Lorain Ave
Cleveland OH 44111
216 476-7000

(G-5226)
CLEVELAN CLINIC HLTH SYS W REG (HQ)
18101 Lorain Ave (44111-5612)
PHONE..................................216 476-7000
Fred M Degrandis, *CEO*
Scott Pecka, *Business Mgr*
John Olach, *Project Mgr*
Perlita Cerilo, *Opers Staff*
Michelle Rigsby, *Human Res Mgr*
EMP: 2800
SQ FT: 327,000
SALES (est): 108.1MM
SALES (corp-wide): 8.9B **Privately Held**
SIC: 8741 Hospital management
PA: The Cleveland Clinic Foundation
9500 Euclid Ave
Cleveland OH 44195
216 636-8335

(G-5227)
CLEVELAN CLINIC HLTH SYS W REG
Also Called: Hassler Medical Center
18200 Lorain Ave (44111-5605)
PHONE..................................216 476-7606
Timothy Spiro, *Med Doctor*
Stevens Flynn, *Director*
EMP: 40
SALES (corp-wide): 8.9B **Privately Held**
SIC: 8741 8011 Hospital management;
general & family practice, physician/surgeon
HQ: Cleveland Clinic Health System-Western Region
18101 Lorain Ave
Cleveland OH 44111
216 476-7000

(G-5228)
CLEVELAN CLINIC HLTH SYS W REG
15531 Lorain Ave (44111-5539)
PHONE..................................216 476-7007
EMP: 63

SALES (corp-wide): 6.4B **Privately Held**
SIC: 8741 8011 Management Services
Medical Doctor's Office
HQ: Cleveland Clinic Health System-Western Region
18101 Lorain Ave
Cleveland OH 44111
216 476-7000

(G-5229)
CLEVELAND ALL BREED TRNING CLB
210 Hayes Dr Ste B (44131-1094)
PHONE..................216 398-1118
Debbie Sacerich, *Principal*
EMP: 100
SALES (est): 1MM **Privately Held**
WEB: www.cabtc.org
SIC: 0752 Training services, pet & animal specialties (not horses)

(G-5230)
CLEVELAND AMERICA SCORES
3631 Perkins Ave Ste 2ce (44114-4701)
PHONE..................216 881-7988
D Pence-Meyenberg, *Exec Dir*
Debra Pence-Meyenberg, *Exec Dir*
EMP: 35
SALES: 579.8K **Privately Held**
SIC: 8699 Charitable organization

(G-5231)
CLEVELAND AUTO LIVERY INC
Also Called: A A Angelone
10802 Cedar Ave (44106-3032)
PHONE..................216 421-1101
Peter T Angelone, *President*
EMP: 25
SQ FT: 7,200
SALES: 1.2MM **Privately Held**
SIC: 4119 Limousine rental, with driver

(G-5232)
CLEVELAND BOTANICAL GARDEN (PA)
11030 East Blvd (44106-1706)
PHONE..................216 721-1600
Natalie A Ronayne, *President*
Robert Rensel, *CFO*
Julia E S Grant, *Treasurer*
Natalie Ronayne, *Exec Dir*
Mark Druckenbrod, *Director*
EMP: 30
SQ FT: 125,000
SALES: 4MM **Privately Held**
WEB: www.cbgarden.org
SIC: 8641 Civic associations

(G-5233)
CLEVELAND CHILD CARE INC (PA)
3274 W 58th St Fl 1 (44102-5681)
PHONE..................216 631-3211
Gil Janke, *President*
William Mldasi, *Treasurer*
Patricia Jelinek, *Exec Dir*
EMP: 38
SQ FT: 5,000
SALES: 444.9K **Privately Held**
SIC: 8351 Child day care services

(G-5234)
CLEVELAND CHRISTIAN HOME INC
4614 Prospect Ave Ste 240 (44103-4365)
PHONE..................216 671-0977
James M McCafferty, *CEO*
Katharine Johnson Vinciquerra, *Development*
Steve Letsky, *CFO*
EMP: 112
SALES: 6.7MM **Privately Held**
SIC: 8322 8331 8361 Social service center; job training & vocational rehabilitation services; residential care

(G-5235)
CLEVELAND CLINIC COLE EYE INST
9500 Euclid Ave (44195-0001)
PHONE..................216 444-4508
Toby Cosgrove, *CEO*
Jonathan Boyd, *Urology*
EMP: 26

SALES (est): 5.6MM **Privately Held**
SIC: 8011 Clinic, operated by physicians

(G-5236)
CLEVELAND CLINIC FOUNDATION (PA)
Also Called: CLEVELAND CLINIC HEALTH SYSTEM
9500 Euclid Ave (44195-0002)
PHONE..................216 636-8335
Delos M Cosgrove, *CEO*
Brian Donley, *CEO*
Janet Gulley, *President*
Peter Studer, *Publisher*
Mary Kander, *General Mgr*
▲ **EMP:** 4708
SALES: 8.9B **Privately Held**
SIC: 8062 8011 8741 General medical & surgical hospitals; medical centers; management services

(G-5237)
CLEVELAND CLINIC FOUNDATION
Also Called: Council of Child & Adoles
9500 Euclid Ave Ste P57 (44195-0002)
PHONE..................216 444-2820
Tom Schiltz, *Branch Mgr*
Jack T Andrish, *Med Doctor*
Frank Aucremanne, *Exec Dir*
Georgina Rodgers, *Director*
EMP: 82
SALES (corp-wide): 8.9B **Privately Held**
SIC: 6733 8062 Trusts; general medical & surgical hospitals
PA: The Cleveland Clinic Foundation
9500 Euclid Ave
Cleveland OH 44195
216 636-8335

(G-5238)
CLEVELAND CLINIC FOUNDATION
Also Called: Alcohol and Drug Recovery Ctr
9500 Euclid Ave P-47 (44195-0002)
PHONE..................216 445-8585
Rita Hanuschock, *Manager*
Diane Zimmerman, *Admin Sec*
EMP: 30
SALES (corp-wide): 8.9B **Privately Held**
SIC: 6733 Trusts
PA: The Cleveland Clinic Foundation
9500 Euclid Ave
Cleveland OH 44195
216 636-8335

(G-5239)
CLEVELAND CLINIC FOUNDATION
Also Called: Cleveland Clnic HSP Fincl Dept
9500 Euclid Ave (44195-0002)
P.O. Box 931058 (44193-1384)
PHONE..................216 444-5000
Anne Robakowski, *Project Mgr*
Megan McConnell, *Research*
Matthew H Sutliff, *Manager*
Angela P Kiska, *Director*
Frank Lauderman, *Administration*
EMP: 300
SALES (corp-wide): 8.9B **Privately Held**
SIC: 6733 7389 Trusts; financial services
PA: The Cleveland Clinic Foundation
9500 Euclid Ave
Cleveland OH 44195
216 636-8335

(G-5240)
CLEVELAND CLINIC FOUNDATION
2111 E 96th St (44106-2917)
PHONE..................800 223-2273
EMP: 2554
SALES (corp-wide): 8.9B **Privately Held**
SIC: 8062 General medical & surgical hospitals
PA: The Cleveland Clinic Foundation
9500 Euclid Ave
Cleveland OH 44195
216 636-8335

(G-5241)
CLEVELAND CLINIC FOUNDATION
10300 Carnegie Ave (44106)
PHONE..................216 444-5755

EMP: 2554
SALES (corp-wide): 8.9B **Privately Held**
SIC: 8062 General medical & surgical hospitals
PA: The Cleveland Clinic Foundation
9500 Euclid Ave
Cleveland OH 44195
216 636-8335

(G-5242)
CLEVELAND CLINIC FOUNDATION
Also Called: Cleveland Clnic Lyndhrst Cmpus
1950 Richmond Rd (44124-3719)
PHONE..................216 448-4325
Maria Tejada, *Project Mgr*
Scott Simmons, *Human Resources*
Michael Novak, *Manager*
Scarlet Soriano, *Director*
EMP: 300
SALES (corp-wide): 8.9B **Privately Held**
SIC: 8011 Medical centers; primary care medical clinic
PA: The Cleveland Clinic Foundation
9500 Euclid Ave
Cleveland OH 44195
216 636-8335

(G-5243)
CLEVELAND CLINIC FOUNDATION
6801 Brecksville Rd # 10 (44131-5058)
PHONE..................216 444-2200
Beth Viscomi, *CEO*
James Soukup, *Pharmacist*
Michelle Bruno, *Nursing Mgr*
Mike Berk, *Manager*
Jennifer Devecchio, *Manager*
EMP: 85
SALES (corp-wide): 8.9B **Privately Held**
SIC: 6733 Trusts
PA: The Cleveland Clinic Foundation
9500 Euclid Ave
Cleveland OH 44195
216 636-8335

(G-5244)
CLEVELAND CLINIC FOUNDATION
Also Called: Cleveland Clinic Coordinating
9500 Euclid Ave (44195-0002)
PHONE..................216 445-6439
EMP: 85
SALES (corp-wide): 6.4B **Privately Held**
SIC: 6733 Trust Management
PA: The Cleveland Clinic Foundation
9500 Euclid Ave
Cleveland OH 44195
216 636-8335

(G-5245)
CLEVELAND CLINIC FOUNDATION
Also Called: Cleveland Clinic Innovations
10000 Cedar Ave Ste 6 (44106-2119)
PHONE..................216 444-5757
Gary Fingerhut, *Exec Dir*
EMP: 85
SALES (corp-wide): 8.9B **Privately Held**
SIC: 8062 General medical & surgical hospitals
PA: The Cleveland Clinic Foundation
9500 Euclid Ave
Cleveland OH 44195
216 636-8335

(G-5246)
CLEVELAND CLINIC FOUNDATION
9500 Euclid Ave (44195-0002)
PHONE..................216 444-2200
Doug Lippus, *Project Mgr*
David Hines, *Opers Staff*
Meghan O'Hanlon, *Buyer*
Caroline Androjna, *Research*
Babal Jha, *Research*
EMP: 3544
SALES (corp-wide): 8.9B **Privately Held**
SIC: 8062 General medical & surgical hospitals
PA: The Cleveland Clinic Foundation
9500 Euclid Ave
Cleveland OH 44195
216 636-8335

(G-5247)
CLEVELAND CLINIC HEALTH SYSTEM
Also Called: Hillcrest Hospital
6780 Mayfield Rd (44124-2203)
PHONE..................440 449-4500
Ross Federico, *Human Res Dir*
Kathy Young, *Pharmacist*
Samuel V Calabrese, *Director*
Glen Levy, *Administration*
EMP: 45
SALES (corp-wide): 8.9B **Privately Held**
SIC: 8062 General medical & surgical hospitals
HQ: Cleveland Clinic Health System-East Region
6803 Mayfield Rd Ste 500
Cleveland OH 44124
440 312-6010

(G-5248)
CLEVELAND CLINIC HEALTH SYSTEM
Also Called: Euclid Hospital
18901 Lake Shore Blvd (44119-1078)
PHONE..................216 692-7555
Paula Florack, *Pharmacist*
Warren Rock, *Mng Officer*
EMP: 25
SALES (corp-wide): 8.9B **Privately Held**
SIC: 8062 General medical & surgical hospitals
HQ: Cleveland Clinic Health System-East Region
6803 Mayfield Rd Ste 500
Cleveland OH 44124
440 312-6010

(G-5249)
CLEVELAND CLINIC LERNER COLLEG
9500 Euclid Ave (44195-0001)
PHONE..................216 445-3853
Jacqueline Whatley, *Principal*
EMP: 99
SALES: 500K **Privately Held**
SIC: 8062 8221 Hospital, medical school affiliation; colleges universities & professional schools

(G-5250)
CLEVELAND CORPORATE SVCS INC
2929 Clarkson Rd (44118-2810)
PHONE..................216 397-1492
Gregory Peck, *President*
EMP: 106
SQ FT: 32,000
SALES: 41.3MM **Privately Held**
WEB: www.teachsmart.org
SIC: 5999 7389 Audio-visual equipment & supplies; audio-visual equipment & supply rental

(G-5251)
CLEVELAND CROWNE PLAZA AIRPORT
7230 Engle Rd (44130-3427)
PHONE..................440 243-4040
EMP: 41
SALES (est): 1MM **Privately Held**
SIC: 7011 5812 Hotels; eating places

(G-5252)
CLEVELAND EAST HOTEL LLC
Also Called: Marriott
26300 Harvard Rd (44122-6146)
PHONE..................216 378-9191
Kenny Didier, *Manager*
EMP: 99
SQ FT: 64,509
SALES (est): 8.6MM **Privately Held**
SIC: 7011 Hotels & motels

(G-5253)
CLEVELAND EXPRESS TRCKG CO INC
3091 Rockefeller Ave (44115-3611)
PHONE..................216 348-0922
John Lamb, *Ch of Bd*
Jeff Darkow, *COO*
Jeb Black, *Vice Pres*
Andy Ilcin, *Chief Mktg Ofcr*
Nick Loparo, *Marketing Staff*

EMP: 75
SQ FT: 20,000
SALES: 4.8MM **Privately Held**
WEB: www.cetruck.com
SIC: 4214 4213 Local trucking with storage; trucking, except local

(G-5254)
CLEVELAND F E S CENTER
10701 East Blvd (44106-1702)
PHONE.................................216 231-3257
Paul P Pechkan, *CEO*
Dennis Johnson, *Engineer*
Mary Buckett, *Corp Comm Staff*
Betty Dunger, *Analyst*
Lisa Lombardo,
EMP: 75
SALES (est): 3.7MM **Privately Held**
SIC: 8731 Commercial physical research

(G-5255)
CLEVELAND FOUNDATION
1422 Euclid Ave Ste 1300 (44115-2063)
PHONE.................................216 861-3810
Ronald B Richard, *CEO*
Sally Gries, *Ch of Bd*
James A Ratner, *Principal*
Charles P Bolton, *Chairman*
Robert E Eckardt, *Exec VP*
EMP: 75
SQ FT: 26,000
SALES: 87.1MM **Privately Held**
SIC: 6732 Charitable trust management; educational trust management

(G-5256)
CLEVELAND GLASS BLOCK INC (PA)
Also Called: Mid America Glass Block
4566 E 71st St (44105-5604)
PHONE.................................216 531-6363
Michael Foti, *President*
Frank Foti, *Corp Secy*
▼ EMP: 46
SQ FT: 15,500
SALES (est): 11.7MM **Privately Held**
WEB: www.clevelandglassblock.com
SIC: 5231 5039 Glass; glass construction materials

(G-5257)
CLEVELAND HEALTH NETWORK (PA)
6000 W Creek Rd Ste 10 (44131-2139)
PHONE.................................216 986-1100
Martin Hauser, *President*
Dennis Pijor, *Administration*
EMP: 35
SALES (est): 2.5MM **Privately Held**
WEB: www.chnetwork.com
SIC: 8621 8741 Health association; management services

(G-5258)
CLEVELAND HEARTLAB INC
6701 Carnegie Ave Ste 500 (44103-4639)
PHONE.................................866 358-9828
Jake Orville, *President*
Darren Hudach, *COO*
Deborah H Sun, *Vice Pres*
Pam Gornall, *CFO*
Marc Penn, *Officer*
▼ EMP: 100
SQ FT: 38,000
SALES (est): 13.3MM
SALES (corp-wide): 7.5B **Publicly Held**
SIC: 8071 Medical laboratories
PA: Quest Diagnostics Incorporated
500 Plaza Dr Ste G
Secaucus NJ 07094
973 520-2700

(G-5259)
CLEVELAND HEIGHTS HIGHSCHOOL
Also Called: Cleveland Heights Gospel Choir
3638 Mount Laurel Rd (44121-1329)
PHONE.................................216 691-5452
Sandra Dixon, *Director*
EMP: 25 EST: 2010
SALES (est): 130.5K **Privately Held**
SIC: 8641 Singing society

(G-5260)
CLEVELAND HTS TIGERS YOUTH SPO
3686 Berkeley Rd (44118-1970)
PHONE.................................216 906-4168
Michael Payne, *President*
Branella Basit, *Vice Pres*
Cedric Marshall, *Vice Pres*
EMP: 40 EST: 2014
SALES (est): 538.5K **Privately Held**
SIC: 7997 Membership sports & recreation clubs

(G-5261)
CLEVELAND HUNGARIAN HERITG SOC
Also Called: CLEVELAND HUNGARIAN HERITAGE M
1301 E 9th St Ste 2400 (44114-1888)
P.O. Box 24134 (44124-0134)
PHONE.................................216 523-3900
Andrea Meszaros, *President*
Otto Friedrich, *Exec Dir*
EMP: 50
SALES: 111.9K **Privately Held**
SIC: 8412 Museum

(G-5262)
CLEVELAND INDIANS BASEBALL COM (PA)
2401 Ontario St (44115-4003)
PHONE.................................216 420-4487
Paul J Dolan, *CEO*
Mark Shapiro, *President*
Lawrence J Dolan, *Owner*
Chris Antonetti, *Exec VP*
Valerie Arcuri, *Vice Pres*
EMP: 100
SQ FT: 4,000
SALES (est): 17.8MM **Privately Held**
SIC: 7941 Baseball club, professional & semi-professional

(G-5263)
CLEVELAND JEWISH FEDERATION
25701 Science Park Dr (44122-7302)
PHONE.................................216 593-2900
Erika B Rudin-Luria, *President*
Paul Feinberg, *Counsel*
Barry Reis, *Senior VP*
Shelley Marcus, *Assistant VP*
Tami Caplan, *VP Opers*
EMP: 130
SQ FT: 20,000
SALES (est): 101.7MM **Privately Held**
WEB: www.jcfcleve.net
SIC: 8399 Fund raising organization, non-fee basis

(G-5264)
CLEVELAND JOB CORPS CENTER
13421 Coit Rd (44110-2269)
PHONE.................................216 541-2500
Ramon Serrato, *President*
Tom Fitzwater, *Principal*
EMP: 160
SALES (est): 13MM **Privately Held**
SIC: 7361 Employment agencies

(G-5265)
CLEVELAND MARBLE MOSAIC CO (PA)
4595 Hinckley Indus Pkwy (44109-6099)
PHONE.................................216 749-2840
Robert J Zavagno Jr, *President*
Jim Small, *Regional Mgr*
Raymond L Zavagno, *Vice Pres*
Howard Patterson, *CFO*
Gale Chrostowski, *Controller*
▲ EMP: 246
SQ FT: 26,800
SALES (est): 31.7MM **Privately Held**
WEB: www.clevelandmarble.com
SIC: 1743 1741 Marble installation, interior; tile installation, ceramic; terrazzo work; marble masonry, exterior construction; stone masonry

(G-5266)
CLEVELAND METRO BAR ASSN
1301 E 9th St (44114-1804)
PHONE.................................216 696-3525

Larkin Chenault, *President*
Kari Burns, *Counsel*
Alla Leydiker, *CFO*
James Smolinski, *Manager*
L Chenault, *Exec Dir*
EMP: 30
SALES: 3MM **Privately Held**
SIC: 8111 Legal services

(G-5267)
CLEVELAND METROPARKS
Also Called: Cleveland Metroparks Zoo
3900 Wildlife Way (44109-3132)
PHONE.................................216 661-6500
Gayle Albers, *Manager*
Edith Ricchiuto, *Manager*
Steve Taylor, *Director*
EMP: 110
SALES (corp-wide): 57.3MM **Privately Held**
WEB: www.clemetparks.com
SIC: 8422 7299 Botanical garden; banquet hall facilities
PA: Cleveland Metroparks
4101 Fulton Pkwy
Cleveland OH 44144
216 635-3200

(G-5268)
CLEVELAND METROPARKS
4600 Valley Pkwy (44126-2853)
PHONE.................................440 331-5530
EMP: 60
SALES (corp-wide): 57.3MM **Privately Held**
SIC: 7999 Recreation services
PA: Cleveland Metroparks
4101 Fulton Pkwy
Cleveland OH 44144
216 635-3200

(G-5269)
CLEVELAND METROPARKS (PA)
4101 Fulton Pkwy (44144-1923)
PHONE.................................216 635-3200
Brian Zimmerman, *CEO*
Debra K Berry, *Vice Pres*
David Whitehead, *Vice Pres*
Weldon Maples, *Opers Staff*
Becky Eicher, *Purchasing*
EMP: 292
SQ FT: 9,000
SALES (est): 57.3MM **Privately Held**
WEB: www.clemetparks.com
SIC: 7999 Recreation services

(G-5270)
CLEVELAND METROPARKS
Also Called: Rainforest At Zoo
3900 Wildlife Way (44109-3132)
PHONE.................................216 661-6500
Steve Taylor, *Director*
EMP: 110
SALES (corp-wide): 57.3MM **Privately Held**
WEB: www.clemetparks.com
SIC: 8422 Arboreta & botanical or zoological gardens
PA: Cleveland Metroparks
4101 Fulton Pkwy
Cleveland OH 44144
216 635-3200

(G-5271)
CLEVELAND METROPARKS
Also Called: Shawnee Hills Golf Course
18753 Egbert Rd (44146-4239)
PHONE.................................440 232-7184
Linda Janson, *Manager*
EMP: 60
SQ FT: 5,488
SALES (corp-wide): 57.3MM **Privately Held**
WEB: www.clemetparks.com
SIC: 7992 Public golf courses
PA: Cleveland Metroparks
4101 Fulton Pkwy
Cleveland OH 44144
216 635-3200

(G-5272)
CLEVELAND METROPARKS
Also Called: Big Mat Golf Course
4811 Valley Pkwy (44126-2846)
PHONE.................................440 331-1070
Mike Raby, *Principal*

EMP: 38
SALES (corp-wide): 57.3MM **Privately Held**
SIC: 7992 Public golf courses
PA: Cleveland Metroparks
4101 Fulton Pkwy
Cleveland OH 44144
216 635-3200

(G-5273)
CLEVELAND MUNICIPAL SCHOOL DST
Also Called: Ridge Road Depot
3832 Ridge Rd (44144-1112)
PHONE.................................216 634-7005
Mark Cegelski, *Branch Mgr*
EMP: 300
SALES (corp-wide): 854.1MM **Privately Held**
WEB: www.cmsdnet.net
SIC: 4151 School buses
PA: Cleveland Municipal School District
1111 Superior Ave E # 1800
Cleveland OH 44114
216 838-0000

(G-5274)
CLEVELAND MUNICIPAL SCHOOL DST
Also Called: Lake Center Depot
870 E 79th St (44103-1820)
PHONE.................................216 432-4600
Mark Cegelski, *Branch Mgr*
EMP: 360
SALES (corp-wide): 854.1MM **Privately Held**
WEB: www.cmsdnet.net
SIC: 4151 School buses
PA: Cleveland Municipal School District
1111 Superior Ave E # 1800
Cleveland OH 44114
216 838-0000

(G-5275)
CLEVELAND MUNICIPAL SCHOOL DST
Also Called: Rhodes Hs-Sch of Leadership
5100 Biddulph Ave (44144-3802)
PHONE.................................216 459-4200
Charlene Hilliard, *Principal*
Kathleen Freilino, *Principal*
Brian K Evans, *Assistant*
EMP: 85
SALES (corp-wide): 854.1MM **Privately Held**
WEB: www.cmsdnet.net
SIC: 8641 8222 8211 Environmental protection organization; technical institute; professional schools; public adult education school
PA: Cleveland Municipal School District
1111 Superior Ave E # 1800
Cleveland OH 44114
216 838-0000

(G-5276)
CLEVELAND MUNICIPAL SCHOOL DST (PA)
Also Called: CLEVELAND METROPOLITAN SCHOOL
1111 Superior Ave E # 1800 (44114-2500)
PHONE.................................216 838-0000
Eric Gordon, *CEO*
Denise W Link, *Ch of Bd*
Lisa Spraggins, *Partner*
Patrick Zohn, *COO*
Dale Laux, *Asst Supt*
EMP: 350 EST: 2012
SQ FT: 70,000
SALES: 854.1MM **Privately Held**
WEB: www.cmsdnet.net
SIC: 8211 8399 Public elementary & secondary schools; advocacy group

(G-5277)
CLEVELAND MUNICIPAL SCHOOL DST
Also Called: New Tech West High School
11801 Worthington Ave (44111-5064)
PHONE.................................216 838-8700
Shaunamichelle Leonard, *Principal*
EMP: 32

SALES (corp-wide): 854.1MM **Privately
Held**
SIC: 8211 8399 Public elementary & sec-
ondary schools; advocacy group
PA: Cleveland Municipal School District
1111 Superior Ave E # 1800
Cleveland OH 44114
216 838-0000

(G-5278)
CLEVELAND MUNICIPAL
SCHOOL DST
Also Called: Children's Aid Society
10427 Detroit Ave (44102-1645)
PHONE..............................216 521-6511
Jennifer Blumhagen, *CEO*
EMP: 75
SQ FT: 44,926
SALES (corp-wide): 854.1MM **Privately
Held**
WEB: www.cmsdnet.net
SIC: 8322 Children's aid society
PA: Cleveland Municipal School District
1111 Superior Ave E # 1800
Cleveland OH 44114
216 838-0000

(G-5279)
CLEVELAND MUNICIPAL
SCHOOL DST
Also Called: Jones Home, The
3518 W 25th St (44109-1951)
PHONE..............................216 459-9818
Harriet Freeman, *Branch Mgr*
EMP: 150
SALES (corp-wide): 854.1MM **Privately
Held**
WEB: www.cmsdnet.net
SIC: 8361 Residential care
PA: Cleveland Municipal School District
1111 Superior Ave E # 1800
Cleveland OH 44114
216 838-0000

(G-5280)
CLEVELAND MUS SCHL
SETTLEMENT
11125 Magnolia Dr (44106-1813)
PHONE..............................216 421-5806
Charles D Lawrence, *President*
Norman Wells, *Controller*
Gabe Pollack, *Manager*
John Sharpe, *Director*
Alfredo Guerrieri, *Program Dir*
EMP: 220
SQ FT: 800,000
SALES (est): 5MM **Privately Held**
WEB: www.thecmss.org
SIC: 8299 8351 7911 Art school, except
commercial; child day care services;
dance studios, schools & halls

(G-5281)
CLEVELAND PRETERM
12000 Shaker Blvd (44120-1922)
PHONE..............................216 991-4577
Chrisse France, *Exec Dir*
EMP: 40
SQ FT: 15,000
SALES: 4.7MM **Privately Held**
WEB: www.preterm.org
SIC: 8093 8011 Abortion clinic; birth con-
trol clinic; offices & clinics of medical doc-
tors

(G-5282)
CLEVELAND RACQUET CLUB
INC
29825 Chagrin Blvd (44124-5797)
PHONE..............................216 831-2155
Michael Schumann, *President*
George Champman, *Vice Pres*
Oliver Emerson, *Treasurer*
Troy Budgen, *Director*
Joe Russell, *Director*
EMP: 75 EST: 1968
SQ FT: 50,000
SALES: 4.6MM **Privately Held**
WEB: www.clevelandracquet.com
SIC: 7997 5812 Tennis club, membership;
swimming club, membership; squash
club, membership; racquetball club, mem-
bership; eating places

(G-5283)
CLEVELAND REAL ESTATE
PARTNERS
1801 E 9th St Ste 1700 (44114-3187)
PHONE..............................216 623-1600
Thomas W Adler, *Ch of Bd*
Eric Friedman, *Principal*
Caryn Hilfer, *Executive Asst*
Peter L Galvin, *Admin Sec*
EMP: 30
SQ FT: 3,000
SALES (est): 1.2MM **Privately Held**
SIC: 6531 Real estate managers

(G-5284)
CLEVELAND RESEARCH
COMPANY LLC
1375 E 9th St Ste 2700 (44114-1795)
PHONE..............................216 649-7250
Omar Aleem, *Partner*
Doug Amy, *Partner*
Joe Calvello, *Partner*
Michael S Henry, *Partner*
Chris Hodson, *Partner*
EMP: 34
SALES (est): 9.7MM **Privately Held**
SIC: 6282 Investment research

(G-5285)
CLEVELAND REST OPER LTD
PARTNR
6000 Fredom Sq Dr Ste 280 (44131)
PHONE..............................216 328-1121
John Climaco, *Partner*
Mike Climaco, *Partner*
Ross Farro, *General Ptnr*
EMP: 180
SALES (est): 2.1MM **Privately Held**
SIC: 5812 6794 Eating places; patent
owners & lessors

(G-5286)
CLEVELAND S HOSPITALITY
LLC
Also Called: Doubletree Hotel
6200 Quarry Ln (44131-2218)
PHONE..............................216 447-1300
Jock Litras, *General Mgr*
EMP: 49
SQ FT: 59,489
SALES (est): 4MM **Privately Held**
SIC: 7011 Hotels & motels

(G-5287)
CLEVELAND SKATING CLUB
2500 Kemper Rd (44120-1299)
PHONE..............................216 791-2800
Mike Sullivan,
EMP: 125
SQ FT: 60,000
SALES: 4MM **Privately Held**
WEB: www.clevelandskatingclub.org
SIC: 7997 Country club, membership

(G-5288)
CLEVELAND SOC FOR THE
BLIND
Also Called: CLEVELAND SIGHT CENTER
1909 E 101st St (44106-4110)
P.O. Box 1988 (44106-0188)
PHONE..............................216 791-8118
Andrew L Sikorovsky, *Chairman*
Gary W Poth, *Treasurer*
Stephen Friedman, *Exec Dir*
EMP: 140
SQ FT: 100,000
SALES: 12.2MM **Privately Held**
SIC: 8322 5441 Association for the handi-
capped; rehabilitation services; confec-
tionery produced for direct sale on the
premises

(G-5289)
CLEVELAND STATE UNIVERSITY
Computer Science Information
1860 E 18th St Rm 344 (44114-3602)
PHONE..............................216 687-3786
Santos Misra, *Director*
EMP: 25
SALES (corp-wide): 204.4MM **Privately
Held**
WEB: www.csuohio.edu
SIC: 7374 8221 Data processing & prepa-
ration; university

PA: Cleveland State University
2121 Euclid Ave
Cleveland OH 44115
216 687-2000

(G-5290)
CLEVELAND SYSCO INC (HQ)
4747 Grayton Rd (44135-2300)
P.O. Box 94570 (44101-4570)
PHONE..............................216 201-3000
Bill Delaney, *CEO*
Chuck Staes, *Senior VP*
Mark Kleiman, *VP Sales*
Marc Canterbury, *Manager*
Jeff Moore, *Software Dev*
EMP: 640
SQ FT: 990
SALES (est): 232.4MM
SALES (corp-wide): 58.7B **Publicly Held**
WEB: www.syscocleveland.com
SIC: 5149 Specialty food items
PA: Sysco Corporation
1390 Enclave Pkwy
Houston TX 77077
281 584-1390

(G-5291)
CLEVELAND TANK & SUPPLY
INC
6560 Juniata Ave (44103-1614)
PHONE..............................216 771-8265
Jack Sattler, *President*
EMP: 28
SQ FT: 10,000
SALES (est): 12.3MM **Privately Held**
WEB: www.clevelandtank.com
SIC: 5084 Tanks, storage

(G-5292)
CLEVELAND TEACHERS UNION
INC
1228 Euclid Ave Ste 1100 (44115-1846)
PHONE..............................216 861-7676
Richard Decolibus, *President*
EMP: 40
SQ FT: 20,000
SALES: 3.4MM **Privately Held**
SIC: 8631 8111 Labor union; legal serv-
ices

(G-5293)
CLEVELAND THERMAL LLC
1921 Hamilton Ave (44114-1112)
PHONE..............................216 241-3636
Marc G Divis, *President*
Donald J Hoffman, *Chairman*
James R Kavalec, *Vice Pres*
Chris Hare, *Opers Staff*
Linda S Atkins, *CFO*
EMP: 46
SQ FT: 4,000
SALES (est): 10.3MM **Privately Held**
WEB: www.clevelandthermal.com
SIC: 4961 Steam supply systems, includ-
ing geothermal

(G-5294)
CLEVELAND TREATMENT
CENTER (PA)
1127 Carnegie Ave (44115-2805)
PHONE..............................216 861-4246
Len Collins, *Director*
EMP: 29 EST: 1970
SQ FT: 12,000
SALES: 1.9MM **Privately Held**
SIC: 8093 Rehabilitation center, outpatient
treatment

(G-5295)
CLEVELAND VA MEDICAL
RESEARCH
10701 East Blvd (44106-1702)
PHONE..............................216 791-2300
Marion Yowler, *Opers Mgr*
Gail Burns, *Exec Dir*
Greg Zimina, *Radiology Dir*
EMP: 25
SALES: 1.7MM **Privately Held**
SIC: 8733 Medical research

(G-5296)
CLEVELAND WATER
DEPARTMENT
5953 Deering Ave (44130-2306)
PHONE..............................216 664-3168

Dick Kmetz, *Principal*
Brian Finks, *Manager*
Bernardo Garcia, *Commissioner*
Kenitha Sturdivant, *Info Tech Dir*
B Withers, *Director*
EMP: 1200
SALES (est): 76.7MM **Privately Held**
SIC: 4941 Water supply

(G-5297)
CLEVELAND WORKS RAILWAY
CO
3175 Independence Rd (44105-1045)
PHONE..............................216 429-7267
Ted Shank, *Manager*
EMP: 78
SALES (est): 3.2MM **Privately Held**
SIC: 4011 Railroads, line-haul operating

(G-5298)
CLEVELAND YACHTING CLUB
INC
200 Yacht Club Dr (44116-1736)
PHONE..............................440 333-1155
Diane May, *Controller*
Ann Swift, *Manager*
EMP: 60
SQ FT: 25,000
SALES: 2.9MM **Privately Held**
WEB: www.cycrr.org
SIC: 7997 Yacht club, membership

(G-5299)
CLEVELAND-CLIFFS INC (PA)
200 Public Sq Ste 3300 (44114-2315)
PHONE..............................216 694-5700
Lourenco Goncalves, *Ch of Bd*
Clifford T Smith, *COO*
Terry G Fedor, *Exec VP*
Maurice D Harapiak, *Exec VP*
Terrence R Mee, *Exec VP*
EMP: 76
SALES: 2.3B **Publicly Held**
WEB: www.cliffsnaturalresources.com
SIC: 1011 Iron ore mining; iron ore pelletiz-
ing

(G-5300)
CLEVELND CLNC HLTH SYSTM
EAST
Also Called: Huron School of Nursing
13951 Terrace Rd (44112)
PHONE..............................216 761-3300
Kathleen Mitchell, *President*
EMP: 25
SALES (corp-wide): 8.9B **Privately Held**
SIC: 8641 Youth organizations
HQ: Cleveland Clinic Health System-East
Region
6803 Mayfield Rd Ste 500
Cleveland OH 44124
440 312-6010

(G-5301)
CLEVELND MUSEUM OF
NATURAL HIS
1 Wade Oval Dr (44106-1701)
PHONE..............................216 231-4600
Sonia Winner, *President*
Doughlas Stelzer, *CFO*
Bonnie Cummings, *Director*
▲ EMP: 90
SQ FT: 225,000
SALES: 24.2MM **Privately Held**
WEB: www.cmnh.org
SIC: 8412 Museum

(G-5302)
CLIFFS CLEVELAND
FOUNDATION
1100 Superior Ave E # 1500 (44114-2530)
PHONE..............................216 694-5700
John Brinzo, *Principal*
EMP: 42
SALES: 3MM **Privately Held**
SIC: 8699 Charitable organization

(G-5303)
CLIFFS MINNESOTA MINERALS
CO
1100 Superior Ave E (44114-2530)
PHONE..............................216 694-5700
W R Calfee, *President*
EMP: 511

SQ FT: 65,000
SALES (est): 9.1MM
SALES (corp-wide): 2.3B **Publicly Held**
SIC: **1011** 4931 Iron ore mining; electric &
other services combined
PA: Cleveland-Cliffs Inc.
200 Public Sq Ste 3300
Cleveland OH 44114
216 694-5700

(G-5304)
CLIFFS RESOURCES INC (HQ)
200 Public Sq Ste 200 # 200 (44114-2301)
PHONE....................................216 694-5700
J S Brinzo, *CEO*
James A Trethewey, *President*
Cynthia B Bezik, *CFO*
EMP: 160
SQ FT: 65,000
SALES (est): 20.5MM
SALES (corp-wide): 2.3B **Publicly Held**
SIC: **4011** Railroads, line-haul operating
PA: Cleveland-Cliffs Inc.
200 Public Sq Ste 3300
Cleveland OH 44114
216 694-5700

(G-5305)
CLIMACO LEFKWTZ PECA WLCOX & (PA)
55 Public Sq Ste 1950 (44113-1972)
PHONE....................................216 621-8484
John R Climaco, *Partner*
Cheryl Allen, *Legal Staff*
Colleen M Bonk, *Assistant*
EMP: 100 EST: 1971
SQ FT: 40,000
SALES (est): 8.7MM **Privately Held**
WEB: www.climacolaw.com
SIC: **8111** General practice law office

(G-5306)
CLINIC CARE INC
Also Called: Cleveland Clinic Guesthouse
9601 Euclid Ave (44106)
PHONE....................................216 707-4200
Kathy Gransford, *Manager*
EMP: 52
SALES (corp-wide): 18.5MM **Privately Held**
SIC: **7011** Hotels & motels
PA: Clinic Care Inc.
6100 W Creek Rd Ste 25
Cleveland OH 44131
216 986-2680

(G-5307)
CLOUDROUTE LLC
59 Alpha Park (44143-2202)
PHONE....................................216 373-4601
Andre Temnorod, *President*
Matthew Sharp, *Partner*
Eugene Blumin, *CFO*
Christopher Shaffer, *Sales Staff*
EMP: 25
SALES (est): 1MM **Privately Held**
SIC: **7371** Computer software development

(G-5308)
CLOVERLEAF BOWLING CENTER INC
Also Called: Cloverleaf Lanes
5619 Brecksville Rd (44131-1510)
PHONE....................................216 524-4833
Joan Spehar, *President*
Michael Copalian, *Corp Secy*
EMP: 34
SQ FT: 45,000
SALES (est): 1.1MM **Privately Held**
WEB: www.bowlcloverleaflanes.com
SIC: **7933** 7999 Ten pin center; billiard parlor

(G-5309)
CLUBCORP USA INC
Also Called: Shoreby Club
40 Shoreby Dr (44108-1191)
PHONE....................................216 851-2582
Kellner Mary Ros, *Chief Engr*
Jan Harcourt, *Corp Comm Staff*
Wendy Harley-Campbell, *Corp Comm Staff*
Randy Owoc, *Manager*
EMP: 30
SQ FT: 10,368

SALES (corp-wide): 477MM **Privately Held**
WEB: www.remington-gc.com
SIC: **7997** Country club, membership
HQ: Clubcorp Usa, Inc.
3030 Lyndon B Johnson Fwy
Dallas TX 75234
972 243-6191

(G-5310)
CLUBHOUSE PUB N GRUB
Also Called: Clubhouse, The
6365 Pearl Rd (44130-3077)
PHONE....................................440 884-2582
Roberta House Peschock, *President*
Charles Belsito, *Corp Secy*
EMP: 25
SALES (est): 900K **Privately Held**
WEB: www.cbdecorating.com
SIC: **1721** 1742 5812 5813 Wallcovering contractors; drywall; eating places; drinking places

(G-5311)
COLEMAN SPOHN CORPORATION (PA)
1775 E 45th St (44103-2318)
PHONE....................................216 431-8070
Lonzo Coleman, *President*
David Kause, *Vice Pres*
Charlie Coleman, *Project Mgr*
Anthony Payne, *Safety Mgr*
Terry Bumgarner, *Purchasing*
EMP: 30
SQ FT: 12,000
SALES (est): 8.8MM **Privately Held**
WEB: www.colemanspohn.com
SIC: **1711** Mechanical contractor

(G-5312)
COLLEGE NOW GRTER CLVELAND INC (PA)
50 Public Sq (44113-2202)
PHONE....................................216 241-5587
Lee Friedman, *President*
EMP: 55
SALES: 13.1MM **Privately Held**
SIC: **8322** General counseling services

(G-5313)
COLORTONE AUDIO VISUAL (PA)
Also Called: Colortone Staging & Rentals
5401 Naiman Pkwy Ste A (44139-1023)
PHONE....................................216 928-1530
Robert E Leon, *President*
Karen N Leon, *Vice Pres*
Matt Rowe, *Opers Mgr*
Ed Rezny, *Opers Staff*
Michael Marcel, *Manager*
EMP: 32
SQ FT: 7,900
SALES (est): 4.5MM **Privately Held**
SIC: **7359** Audio-visual equipment & supply rental

(G-5314)
COLUMBIA GAS OF OHIO INC
7080 Fry Rd (44130-2513)
PHONE....................................440 891-2458
Paul Fackler, *Area Mgr*
Doug Nusbaum, *Sales Dir*
EMP: 100
SALES (corp-wide): 5.1B **Publicly Held**
WEB: www.meterrepairshop.com
SIC: **4924** Natural gas distribution
HQ: Columbia Gas Of Ohio, Inc.
290 W Nationwide Blvd # 114
Columbus OH 43215
614 460-6000

(G-5315)
COMCAST SPOTLIGHT INC
Also Called: Adelphia
3300 Lakeside Ave E (44114-3751)
PHONE....................................216 575-8016
Larry Drake, *Branch Mgr*
EMP: 300
SALES (corp-wide): 94.5B **Publicly Held**
WEB: www.cablecomcast.com
SIC: **4841** Cable television services
HQ: Comcast Spotlight
55 W 46th St Fl 33
New York NY 10036
212 907-8641

(G-5316)
COMEX NORTH AMERICA INC (HQ)
Also Called: Comex Group
101 W Prospect Ave # 1020 (44115-1093)
PHONE....................................303 307-2100
Christopher Connor, *CEO*
Leon Cohen, *President*
Julie Zamski, *City Mgr*
◆ EMP: 90
SQ FT: 2,900
SALES (est): 204.4MM
SALES (corp-wide): 17.5B **Publicly Held**
WEB: www.professionalpaintinc.com
SIC: **2851** 8742 5198 5231 Paints & paint additives; paints, waterproof; paints: oil or alkyd vehicle or water thinned; corporation organizing; paints; paint brushes, rollers, sprayers; wallcoverings; paint; paint brushes, rollers, sprayers & other supplies; wallcoverings
PA: The Sherwin-Williams Company
101 W Prospect Ave # 1020
Cleveland OH 44115
216 566-2000

(G-5317)
COMFORT HEALTHCARE
8310 Detroit Ave (44102-1806)
PHONE....................................216 281-9999
Kirill Simakovsky, *Owner*
Vavitaly Kucsay, *Co-Owner*
EMP: 50
SALES (est): 870.3K **Privately Held**
SIC: **8082** Home health care services

(G-5318)
COMMERCIAL ELECTRIC PDTS CORP (PA)
1821 E 40th St (44103-3503)
PHONE....................................216 241-2886
Roger Meyer, *President*
Russ Arslanian, *General Mgr*
Kenneth Culp, *Vice Pres*
Char Page, *Sales Staff*
Scott Sacerich, *Sales Staff*
EMP: 44 EST: 1927
SQ FT: 15,000
SALES (est): 25.7MM **Privately Held**
WEB: www.commercialelectric.com
SIC: **5085** 3661 3824 1731 Power transmission equipment & apparatus; telephones & telephone apparatus; telegraph & related apparatus; mechanical & electromechanical counters & devices; general electrical contractor; industrial equipment services; electrical equipment & supplies

(G-5319)
COMMERCIAL TRAFFIC COMPANY (PA)
Also Called: C T Logistics
12487 Plaza Dr (44130-1084)
PHONE....................................216 267-2000
Jack Miner, *CEO*
Allan J Miner, *President*
Debra Rose, *Purch Dir*
Patrick Cahill, *Finance*
Michelle Bizorik, *Manager*
EMP: 170
SQ FT: 16,000
SALES (est): 41.8MM **Privately Held**
WEB: www.freitrater.com
SIC: **4731** Transportation agents & brokers

(G-5320)
COMMERCIAL TRAFFIC COMPANY
Also Called: C T Logistics
12487 Plaza Dr (44130-1084)
PHONE....................................216 267-2000
Robert Dibello, *General Mgr*
EMP: 70
SALES (corp-wide): 41.8MM **Privately Held**
WEB: www.freitrater.com
SIC: **4731** Transportation agents & brokers
PA: The Commercial Traffic Company
12487 Plaza Dr
Cleveland OH 44130
216 267-2000

(G-5321)
COMMONWEALTH FINANCIAL SVCS (PA)
26451 Curtiss Wright Pkwy (44143-4410)
PHONE....................................440 449-7709
Frank Kolbe, *President*
Armand Cosenza Jr, *Corp Secy*
John Catalano, *Accountant*
Caitlyn Feeney, *Accountant*
Sean Williams, *Shareholder*
EMP: 25
SQ FT: 6,000
SALES (est): 4.3MM **Privately Held**
SIC: **6163** Mortgage brokers arranging for loans, using money of others

(G-5322)
COMMONWEALTH HOTELS LLC
Also Called: Embassy Suites
5800 Rockside Woods Blvd (44131-2346)
PHONE....................................216 524-5814
Bob Grossman, *Branch Mgr*
EMP: 66
SALES (corp-wide): 92.4MM **Privately Held**
WEB: www.commonwealth-hotels.com
SIC: **7011** Hotels & motels
PA: Commonwealth Hotels, Llc
100 E Rivercenter Blvd # 1050
Covington KY 41011
859 392-2264

(G-5323)
COMMUNITY ACTION AGAINST ADDIC
5209 Euclid Ave (44103-3703)
PHONE....................................216 881-0765
Ronald Winbush, *Director*
EMP: 35
SQ FT: 24,000
SALES (est): 5.8MM **Privately Held**
SIC: **8093** Drug clinic, outpatient

(G-5324)
COMMUNITY ASSESMENT AND TREATM (PA)
8411 Broadway Ave (44105-3932)
PHONE....................................216 441-0200
Paul M Gerace, *Project Mgr*
William G Malenich, *CFO*
Tom Wengerd, *CFO*
Riva Colvin, *Program Mgr*
William Maddox, *Program Mgr*
EMP: 64
SQ FT: 19,000
SALES (est): 7.4MM **Privately Held**
WEB: www.communityassessment.com
SIC: **8093** Specialty outpatient clinics

(G-5325)
COMMUNITY DIALYSIS CENTER
Also Called: Center For Dialysis Care
11717 Euclid Ave (44106-4350)
PHONE....................................216 295-7000
Diane Wish, *Branch Mgr*
EMP: 30 **Privately Held**
WEB: www.curvesohio.com
SIC: **8092** Kidney dialysis centers
PA: Community Dialysis Center
18720 Chagrin Blvd
Shaker Heights OH 44122

(G-5326)
COMMUNITY DIALYSIS CENTER
Also Called: Center For Dialysis Care
11717 Euclid Ave (44106-4350)
P.O. Box 12220 (44112-0220)
PHONE....................................216 229-6170
Alan Zarach, *Technical Mgr*
Brenda Krzywicki, *Controller*
Dee Conway, *Accounting Mgr*
Gabrielle Hall, *Human Resources*
Lisa Hogan, *Med Doctor*
EMP: 125 EST: 1974
SQ FT: 25,000
SALES: 69.3MM **Privately Held**
SIC: **8092** Kidney dialysis centers

(G-5327)
COMMUNITY RE-ENTRY INC
4515 Superior Ave (44103-1215)
PHONE....................................216 696-2717
Charles See, *Director*
EMP: 40

SALES: 919.1K **Privately Held**
WEB: www.reentrymediaoutreach.org
SIC: 8399 Social change association

(G-5328)
COMMUNITY SRGL SPLY TOMS RVR
14500 Broadway Ave (44125-1960)
PHONE..................................216 475-8440
Michael Fried, *Branch Mgr*
EMP: 126
SALES (corp-wide): 176.7MM **Privately Held**
SIC: 5047 Surgical equipment & supplies
PA: Community Surgical Supply Of Toms River Inc
1390 Rte 37 W
Toms River NJ 08755
732 349-2990

(G-5329)
COMPANY INC
4125 Payne Ave (44103-2324)
PHONE..................................216 431-2334
James Zadd, *President*
Steven Vitas, *Vice Pres*
EMP: 25 EST: 1979
SQ FT: 4,000
SALES (est): 3.3MM **Privately Held**
SIC: 1752 Floor laying & floor work

(G-5330)
COMPASS SELF STORAGE LLC (PA)
Also Called: Moore Self Storage
20445 Emerald Pkwy (44135-6009)
PHONE..................................216 458-0670
Todd Amsdell, *President*
Shawn Madison, *District Mgr*
Mike Laubecher, *Area Mgr*
Rhianna Wallen, *Mktg Coord*
EMP: 36
SQ FT: 784
SALES (est): 6.1MM **Privately Held**
SIC: 4225 Warehousing, self-storage

(G-5331)
COMPLIANT HEALTHCARE TECH LLC (PA)
Also Called: C H T
7123 Pearl Rd Ste 305 (44130-4944)
PHONE..................................216 255-9607
John Zbozien, *Vice Pres*
Dave Boehne, *Accounts Mgr*
Keith Kassouf, *Sales Staff*
Jason Di Marco, *Mng Member*
Scot Wederquist,
EMP: 25
SQ FT: 8,200
SALES: 7.5MM **Privately Held**
SIC: 7389 3826 Gas system conversion; gas testing apparatus

(G-5332)
COMPOSITE TECH AMER INC
25201 Chagrin Blvd # 360 (44122-5600)
PHONE..................................330 562-5201
Bassem A Mansour, *Principal*
EMP: 41
SALES (est): 1.2MM
SALES (corp-wide): 2.9B **Privately Held**
SIC: 8748 Business consulting
HQ: Custom Pultrusions, Inc.
1331 S Chillicothe Rd
Aurora OH 44202

(G-5333)
CONCORDIA CARE
2373 Euclid Heights Blvd (44106-2776)
PHONE..................................216 791-3580
Janis Fraehnrich, *President*
Cynthia Dougherty, *Director*
EMP: 62
SQ FT: 17,000
SALES (est): 12.5MM **Privately Held**
SIC: 8322 Geriatric social service

(G-5334)
CONRADS TIRE SERVICE INC (PA)
Also Called: Conrad's Total Car Care
14577 Lorain Ave (44111-3156)
P.O. Box 110584 (44111-0584)
PHONE..................................216 941-3333
John Turk, *President*

EMP: 35
SQ FT: 10,000
SALES (est): 43.6MM **Privately Held**
WEB: www.econrads.com
SIC: 7538 5531 5014 General automotive repair shops; automotive tires; automotive accessories; automobile tires & tubes

(G-5335)
CONSOLDATED GRAPHICS GROUP INC
Also Called: Consolidated Solutions
1614 E 40th St (44103-2319)
PHONE..................................216 881-9191
Terry Hartman, *CEO*
Kenneth A Lanci, *Ch of Bd*
Matt Reville, *COO*
Matthew Reville, *COO*
Stephen Henn, *Vice Pres*
▲ EMP: 140
SQ FT: 75,000
SALES: 25MM **Privately Held**
SIC: 2752 2759 7331 2791 Commercial printing, offset; commercial printing; direct mail advertising services; typesetting; bookbinding & related work

(G-5336)
CONSORTIUM FOR HLTHY & IMMUNZD
Also Called: CHIC
10840 Barrington Blvd (44130-4407)
PHONE..................................216 201-2001
Cindy Modie, *Director*
EMP: 99
SALES: 22.7K **Privately Held**
SIC: 8621 Health association

(G-5337)
CONSTANT AVIATION LLC
355 Richmond Rd (44143-4405)
PHONE..................................216 261-7119
Mike Rossi,
EMP: 50 **Privately Held**
SIC: 7699 Aircraft & heavy equipment repair services
PA: Constant Aviation, Llc
18601 Cleveland Pkwy Dr 1b
Cleveland OH 44135

(G-5338)
CONSTANT AVIATION LLC (PA)
18601 Cleveland Pkwy Dr 1b (44135-3267)
PHONE..................................800 440-9004
Stephen Maiden, *President*
Dave Bowman, *Vice Pres*
Kevin Dillon, *Vice Pres*
Pat Flaherty, *CFO*
EMP: 200
SALES (est): 45.4MM **Privately Held**
SIC: 7363 4581 Pilot service, aviation; aircraft maintenance & repair services

(G-5339)
CONSTRUCTION RESOURCES INC
33900 Station St (44139-2995)
PHONE..................................440 248-9800
Bud Griffith, *President*
EMP: 36
SALES (est): 2.8MM **Privately Held**
WEB: www.constres.com
SIC: 8748 Systems engineering consultant, ex. computer or professional

(G-5340)
CONSULATE MANAGEMENT CO LLC
Also Called: Mt Royal Villa Care Center
13900 Bennett Rd (44133-3808)
PHONE..................................440 237-7966
Doug Pearson, *Manager*
EMP: 60
SALES (corp-wide): 580.2MM **Privately Held**
WEB: www.tandemhealthcare.com
SIC: 8051 8052 Skilled nursing care facilities; intermediate care facilities
PA: Consulate Management Company, Llc
800 Concourse Pkwy S
Maitland FL 32751
407 571-1550

(G-5341)
CONSUMER CREDIT COUNSELING SER (PA)
1228 Euclid Ave Ste 390 (44115-1800)
PHONE..................................800 254-4100
Jay Seaton, *President*
EMP: 35
SQ FT: 1,700
SALES: 2.1MM **Privately Held**
SIC: 8742 Financial consultant

(G-5342)
CONTAINERPORT GROUP INC (HQ)
1340 Depot St Fl 2 (44116-1741)
PHONE..................................440 333-1330
Frederick Hunger, *CEO*
Richard C Coleman, *President*
Russell A Graef, *President*
Jeff Horton, *General Mgr*
Rob Movshin, *General Mgr*
EMP: 57
SQ FT: 14,000
SALES (est): 149.3MM
SALES (corp-wide): 274.1MM **Privately Held**
WEB: www.containerport.com
SIC: 4731 Brokers, shipping
PA: World Shipping, Inc.
1340 Depot St Ste 200
Cleveland OH 44116
440 356-7676

(G-5343)
CONTAINERPORT GROUP INC
5155 Warner Rd (44125-1124)
PHONE..................................216 341-4800
Brian Barry, *Manager*
EMP: 30
SALES (corp-wide): 274.1MM **Privately Held**
WEB: www.containerport.com
SIC: 4225 4214 4213 General warehousing; local trucking with storage; trucking, except local
HQ: Containerport Group, Inc.
1340 Depot St Fl 2
Cleveland OH 44116
440 333-1330

(G-5344)
CONTINENTAL PRODUCTS COMPANY
2926 Chester Ave (44114-4414)
PHONE..................................216 531-0710
Mary Ann Strebeck, *CEO*
EMP: 26
SALES (est): 3.2MM
SALES (corp-wide): 8.7MM **Privately Held**
WEB: www.paintdoc.com
SIC: 2851 5198 2891 Paints & paint additives; stains: varnish, oil or wax; putty; paints, varnishes & supplies; adhesives & sealants
PA: The Continental Products Company
2926 Chester Ave
Cleveland OH 44114
216 383-3932

(G-5345)
CONTRACT TRANSPORT SERVICES
3223 Perkins Ave (44114-4629)
PHONE..................................216 524-8435
William Madachik, *President*
EMP: 26
SALES (est): 1.7MM **Privately Held**
SIC: 4119 Local passenger transportation

(G-5346)
CONTROLSOFT INC
5387 Avion Park Dr (44143-1916)
PHONE..................................440 443-3900
Tien LI Chia, *President*
Matt Petras, *Project Engr*
Paul Botzman, *Sales Staff*
EMP: 50
SALES (est): 4.2MM **Privately Held**
WEB: www.controlsoftinc.com
SIC: 8748 Systems engineering consultant, ex. computer or professional

(G-5347)
CONVENTION & VISTORS BUREAU OF (PA)
Also Called: Convention & Visitors Bureau
50 Public Sq Ste 3100 (44113-2242)
PHONE..................................216 875-6603
Dennis Roche, *President*
EMP: 33
SQ FT: 7,200
SALES (est): 8MM **Privately Held**
WEB: www.travelcleveland.com
SIC: 7389 Convention & show services; tourist information bureau

(G-5348)
COOPERATE SCREENING SERVICES
16530 Commerce Ct Ste 1 (44130-6316)
PHONE..................................440 816-0500
Dennis E Drellishak, *President*
Sandra Drellishak, *Corp Secy*
EMP: 30
SALES (est): 330.3K **Privately Held**
SIC: 7381 Private investigator

(G-5349)
CORAL COMPANY (PA)
13219 Shaker Sq (44120-2314)
PHONE..................................216 932-8822
Peter Rubin, *President*
EMP: 37
SQ FT: 4,000
SALES (est): 23.3MM **Privately Held**
SIC: 6552 Land subdividers & developers, commercial

(G-5350)
CORPORATE FLOORS INC
15901 Mccracken Rd (44128-3224)
PHONE..................................216 475-3232
Scott Reese, *President*
Kimberly Reese, *Admin Sec*
EMP: 40
SALES (est): 5.5MM **Privately Held**
SIC: 1752 Access flooring system installation

(G-5351)
CORPORATE SCREENING SVCS INC (PA)
16530 Commerce Ct Ste 3 (44130-6316)
P.O. Box 361219 (44136-0021)
PHONE..................................440 816-0500
Dennis E Drellishak, *CEO*
Greg Dubecky, *President*
Sandra Drellishak, *Corp Secy*
Todd Feher, *Vice Pres*
Jessica Fellers, *Accounting Mgr*
EMP: 63
SQ FT: 12,900
SALES (est): 8.9MM **Privately Held**
WEB: www.corporatescreening.com
SIC: 7381 Private investigator

(G-5352)
CORPORATE WNGS - CLEVELAND LLC
355 Richmond Rd Ste A (44143-4404)
PHONE..................................216 261-9000
Elizabeth Ricci, *CEO*
Mark Gully, *VP Opers*
Beth Lovey, *Opers Mgr*
Robert Sullivan, *VP Human Res*
Todd Davidson, *Info Tech Dir*
EMP: 30
SALES (est): 4.1MM **Privately Held**
SIC: 4581 Airport control tower operation, except government

(G-5353)
COUNCIL FOR ECONOMIC OPPORT
14209 Euclid Ave (44112-3809)
PHONE..................................216 541-7878
EMP: 59
SALES (corp-wide): 36.6MM **Privately Held**
SIC: 8399 Antipoverty board
PA: Council For Economic Opportunities In Greater Cleveland
1801 Superior Ave E Fl 4
Cleveland OH 44114
216 696-9077

(G-5354)
COUNCIL FOR ECONOMIC OPPORT
14402 Puritas Ave (44135-2800)
PHONE.................................216 476-3201
Kelly Demarco, *Branch Mgr*
EMP: 79
SALES (corp-wide): 36.6MM **Privately Held**
SIC: 8699 Charitable organization
PA: Council For Economic Opportunities In Greater Cleveland
1801 Superior Ave E Fl 4
Cleveland OH 44114
216 696-9077

(G-5355)
COUNCIL FOR ECONOMIC OPPORT (PA)
Also Called: Ceogc
1801 Superior Ave E Fl 4 (44114-2135)
PHONE.................................216 696-9077
Jacklyn Chisholm, *President*
Deborah Armstong, *CFO*
Evelyn Rice, *Director*
EMP: 100
SQ FT: 26,000
SALES: 36.6MM **Privately Held**
WEB: www.ceogc.org
SIC: 8399 8322 8351 Antipoverty board; individual & family services; child day care services

(G-5356)
COUNCIL FOR ECONOMIC OPPORT
Also Called: Carl B Stokes Head Start Ctr
1883 Torbenson Dr (44112-1308)
PHONE.................................216 692-4010
Sonya Dean, *Supervisor*
EMP: 35
SQ FT: 67,962
SALES (corp-wide): 36.6MM **Privately Held**
WEB: www.ceogc.org
SIC: 8399 Antipoverty board
PA: Council For Economic Opportunities In Greater Cleveland
1801 Superior Ave E Fl 4
Cleveland OH 44114
216 696-9077

(G-5357)
COUNCIL FOR ECONOMIC OPPORT
Also Called: William Patrick Day
2421 Cmnty College Ave (44115-3118)
PHONE.................................216 736-2934
Grover Crayton, *Principal*
EMP: 177
SALES (corp-wide): 36.6MM **Privately Held**
WEB: www.ceogc.org
SIC: 8351 Head start center, except in conjunction with school
PA: Council For Economic Opportunities In Greater Cleveland
1801 Superior Ave E Fl 4
Cleveland OH 44114
216 696-9077

(G-5358)
COUNCIL OF ECNMC OPPRTNTS OF G
Also Called: Willard Head Start Day Care
2220 W 95th St (44102-3762)
PHONE.................................216 651-5154
Leynnore Walker, *Administration*
EMP: 36
SALES (est): 679.3K **Privately Held**
SIC: 8351 Head start center, except in conjunction with school

(G-5359)
COUNTRY CLUB INC
2825 Lander Rd (44124-4899)
PHONE.................................216 831-9200
Robert C Josey, *CEO*
EMP: 110
SQ FT: 112,000
SALES: 10.6MM **Privately Held**
WEB: www.thecountryclub.com
SIC: 7997 Country club, membership

(G-5360)
COUNTS CONTAINER CORPORATION
5137 W 161st St (44142-1604)
PHONE.................................216 433-4336
Roby Kountz, *President*
Vern Heiskell, *Principal*
Kimberly Kountz, *Treasurer*
Maxine Stegman, *Office Admin*
EMP: 25
SQ FT: 20,000
SALES: 5MM **Privately Held**
WEB: www.countscontainer.com
SIC: 4953 Recycling, waste materials

(G-5361)
COUNTY OF CUYAHOGA
Also Called: Alcohol/Drug Outpatient T
310 W Lkeside Ave Ste 500 (44113)
PHONE.................................216 443-7035
Maria Nemec, *Manager*
EMP: 25 **Privately Held**
SIC: 8093 9431 Substance abuse clinics (outpatient); public health agency administration, government
PA: County Of Cuyahoga
1215 W 3rd St
Cleveland OH 44113
216 443-7022

(G-5362)
COUNTY OF CUYAHOGA
Also Called: Maple Heights Atc
14775 Broadway Ave (44137-1103)
PHONE.................................216 475-7066
David Gillespie, *Manager*
EMP: 70
SQ FT: 42,389 **Privately Held**
SIC: 8331 9229 Vocational rehabilitation agency;
PA: County Of Cuyahoga
1215 W 3rd St
Cleveland OH 44113
216 443-7022

(G-5363)
COUNTY OF CUYAHOGA
Also Called: Coroner's Office
11001 Cedar Ave Ste 400 (44106-3043)
PHONE.................................216 721-5610
Elizabeth Balraj, *Manager*
EMP: 80
SQ FT: 720 **Privately Held**
SIC: 8049 9431 ;
PA: County Of Cuyahoga
1215 W 3rd St
Cleveland OH 44113
216 443-7022

(G-5364)
COUNTY OF CUYAHOGA
Also Called: Department Information Tech
2079 E 9th St Fl 6 (44115-1302)
PHONE.................................216 443-8011
Scot Rourke, *Branch Mgr*
Gerry Mc Clamy, *Manager*
EMP: 142
SQ FT: 2,332 **Privately Held**
SIC: 7374 9431 Data processing service; health statistics center, government
PA: County Of Cuyahoga
1215 W 3rd St
Cleveland OH 44113
216 443-7022

(G-5365)
COUNTY OF CUYAHOGA
Also Called: Child Support Enforcement Agcy
1640 Superior Ave E (44114-2908)
P.O. Box 93318 (44101-5318)
PHONE.................................216 443-5100
Cassondra McArthuour, *Manager*
EMP: 50
SQ FT: 44,726 **Privately Held**
SIC: 9441 8322 ; child guidance agency
PA: County Of Cuyahoga
1215 W 3rd St
Cleveland OH 44113
216 443-7022

(G-5366)
COUNTY OF CUYAHOGA
Also Called: Central Services Department
2079 E 9th St (44115-1302)
PHONE.................................216 443-6954
Jay Ross, *Manager*

Cecily Meacher, *Admin Sec*
EMP: 650
SQ FT: 35,640 **Privately Held**
SIC: 7349 9431 Building maintenance services; health statistics center, government
PA: County Of Cuyahoga
1215 W 3rd St
Cleveland OH 44113
216 443-7022

(G-5367)
COUNTY OF CUYAHOGA
Also Called: Cuyahoga County Board of Menta
1275 Lakeside Ave E (44114-1129)
PHONE.................................216 241-8230
Marie Barni, *General Mgr*
Terry Ryan, *Superintendent*
John McLaughlin, *Human Res Dir*
Michael Donzella, *Branch Mgr*
Carey Kleinschmidt, *Supervisor*
EMP: 200 **Privately Held**
SIC: 8361 9431 Home for the mentally retarded; mental health agency administration, government
PA: County Of Cuyahoga
1215 W 3rd St
Cleveland OH 44113
216 443-7022

(G-5368)
COUNTY OF CUYAHOGA
Also Called: Activity Training
13231 Euclid Ave (44112-4523)
PHONE.................................216 681-4433
Albert Trefeny, *Manager*
Vicki Rice, *Manager*
EMP: 75 **Privately Held**
SIC: 9441 8322 ; individual & family services
PA: County Of Cuyahoga
1215 W 3rd St
Cleveland OH 44113
216 443-7022

(G-5369)
COUNTY OF CUYAHOGA
Also Called: County Administrator's Office
1219 Ontario St Rm 304 (44113-1601)
PHONE.................................216 443-7181
Lee A Trotter, *Administration*
EMP: 300 **Privately Held**
SIC: 8741 Administrative management
PA: County Of Cuyahoga
1215 W 3rd St
Cleveland OH 44113
216 443-7022

(G-5370)
COUNTY OF CUYAHOGA
Also Called: Department Children Services
3955 Euclid Ave Rm 344e (44115-2505)
PHONE.................................216 432-2621
James Mc Cafferty, *Manager*
EMP: 650 **Privately Held**
SIC: 8322 9431 Child related social services; child health program administration, government
PA: County Of Cuyahoga
1215 W 3rd St
Cleveland OH 44113
216 443-7022

(G-5371)
COUNTY OF CUYAHOGA
Also Called: Youth Services
1276 W 3rd St Ste 319 (44113-1512)
PHONE.................................216 443-7265
Steven Terry, *Branch Mgr*
EMP: 65 **Privately Held**
SIC: 9441 8641 Administration of social & human resources; youth organizations
PA: County Of Cuyahoga
1215 W 3rd St
Cleveland OH 44113
216 443-7022

(G-5372)
COURTYARD BY MARRIOTT
3695 Orange Pl (44122-4401)
PHONE.................................216 765-1900
Graham Herscham, *President*
EMP: 30 **EST:** 2008
SALES (est): 1.4MM **Privately Held**
SIC: 7011 Hotels & motels

(G-5373)
COURTYARD MANAGEMENT CORP
5051 W Creek Rd (44131-2165)
PHONE.................................216 901-9988
Scott Arra, *Branch Mgr*
EMP: 50
SALES (corp-wide): 20.7B **Publicly Held**
SIC: 7011 Hotels
HQ: Courtyard Management Corporation
10400 Fernwood Rd
Bethesda MD 20817

(G-5374)
COX CABLE CLEVELAND AREA INC
12221 Plaza Dr (44130-1072)
PHONE.................................216 676-8300
Ron Hammaker, *President*
EMP: 121
SALES (est): 6.6MM
SALES (corp-wide): 32.5B **Privately Held**
WEB: www.coxenterprises.com
SIC: 4841 Cable television services
PA: Cox Enterprises, Inc.
6205 Pachtree Dunwoody Rd
Atlanta GA 30328
678 645-0000

(G-5375)
CRAWFORD & COMPANY
7271 Engle Rd Ste 303 (44130-8404)
PHONE.................................440 243-8710
Joseph M Weber, *Branch Mgr*
EMP: 36
SQ FT: 2,700
SALES (corp-wide): 1.1B **Publicly Held**
WEB: www.crawfordandcompany.com
SIC: 6411 Insurance adjusters
PA: Crawford & Company
5335 Triangle Pkwy Ofc C
Peachtree Corners GA 30092
404 300-1000

(G-5376)
CREATIVE PLAYROOM (PA)
Also Called: Solon Crtive Plyroom Mntessori
16574 Broadway Ave (44137-2602)
PHONE.................................216 475-6464
Joan Wenk, *President*
EMP: 100
SQ FT: 12,000
SALES (est): 999K **Privately Held**
SIC: 8351 Montessori child development center

(G-5377)
CREDIT FIRST NATIONAL ASSN
Also Called: C F N A
6275 Eastland Rd (44142-1301)
P.O. Box 81315 (44181-0315)
PHONE.................................216 362-5300
Dean S Miller, *President*
Alan K Meier, *Finance Dir*
Lori Caldwell, *Manager*
Abbie Jones, *Manager*
Diane Hendricks, *Supervisor*
EMP: 300
SALES: 35MM
SALES (corp-wide): 32.4B **Privately Held**
SIC: 7389 Financial services
HQ: Bridgestone Americas Tire Operations, Llc
200 4th Ave S Ste 100
Nashville TN 37201
615 937-1000

(G-5378)
CREMATION SERVICE INC (PA)
1612 Leonard St (44113-2418)
PHONE.................................216 861-2334
Robert J Inman, *President*
Marilyn Nixon, *Vice Pres*
EMP: 46
SQ FT: 600
SALES (est): 2.2MM **Privately Held**
SIC: 7261 4119 Crematory; local passenger transportation

(G-5379)
CREMATION SERVICE INC
Also Called: Inman Nationwide Shipping
1605 Merwin Ave (44113-2421)
PHONE.................................216 621-6222
Robert J Inman, *Branch Mgr*

EMP: 26
SALES (corp-wide): 2.2MM **Privately
Held**
SIC: 7261 Funeral service & crematories
PA: Cremation Service Inc
1612 Leonard St
Cleveland OH 44113
216 861-2334

(G-5380)
**CRESTMONT CADILLAC
CORPORATION (PA)**
26000 Chagrin Blvd (44122-4298)
PHONE..................................216 831-5300
Jay Park, *President*
Tom Schrader, *Business Mgr*
Mario Bennici, *Parts Mgr*
Michael Gutowitz, *Sales Mgr*
Paul Guy, *Sales Staff*
EMP: 40
SQ FT: 45,000
SALES (est): 34.2MM **Privately Held**
WEB: www.crestmontcadillac.com
SIC: 5511 7538 Automobiles, new & used;
general automotive repair shops

(G-5381)
CRESTWOOD MGMT LLC
23550 Commerce Park # 5000
(44122-5862)
PHONE..................................440 484-2400
Marcel Dovier,
EMP: 75
SALES (est): 5.5MM **Privately Held**
SIC: 8741 Management services

(G-5382)
CROWE LLP
600 Superior Ave E # 902 (44114-2614)
PHONE..................................216 623-7500
Mike Varney, *Partner*
Greg McClure, *Branch Mgr*
EMP: 37
SALES (corp-wide): 883.5MM **Privately
Held**
SIC: 8721 Certified public accountant
PA: Crowe Llp
225 W Wacker Dr Ste 2600
Chicago IL 60606
312 899-7000

(G-5383)
CROWNE GROUP LLC (PA)
127 Public Sq Ste 5110 (44114-1313)
PHONE..................................216 589-0198
Robert Henderson, *Mng Member*
EMP: 65
SALES (est): 830.8MM **Privately Held**
SIC: 3559 8711 Degreasing machines, au-
tomotive & industrial; industrial engineers

(G-5384)
CSA AMERICA INC
Also Called: Csa International Services
8501 E Pleasant Valley Rd (44131-5516)
PHONE..................................216 524-4990
Randall Luecke, *Vice Pres*
Terry Nagy, *Opers Mgr*
Lisa Eberman, *Sales Staff*
EMP: 100
SALES (corp-wide): 253.6MM **Privately
Held**
SIC: 8734 Testing laboratories
HQ: Csa America Standards, Inc.
8501 E Pleasant Valley Rd
Independence OH 44131
216 524-4990

(G-5385)
CSL PLASMA INC
Also Called: Z L B
3204 W 25th St (44109-1641)
PHONE..................................216 398-0440
Doug Pearbeck, *Manager*
Joanne Farley, *Asst Mgr*
EMP: 60 **Privately Held**
WEB: www.zlbplasma.com
SIC: 8099 Blood bank
HQ: Csl Plasma Inc.
900 Broken Sound Pkwy Nw # 4
Boca Raton FL 33487
561 981-3700

(G-5386)
**CSU/CAREER SERVICES
CENTER**
2121 Euclid Ave (44115-2214)
PHONE..................................216 687-2233
Paul Klein, *Director*
EMP: 30
SALES (est): 1.6MM **Privately Held**
WEB: www.nhlink.net
SIC: 7361 Employment agencies

(G-5387)
CT LOGISTICS INC
12487 Plaza Dr (44130-1056)
PHONE..................................216 267-1636
Allan Miner, *President*
Patrick Cahill, *CFO*
EMP: 150
SQ FT: 1,000
SALES (est): 6.2MM **Privately Held**
SIC: 4789 7371 Pipeline terminal facilities,
independently operated; computer soft-
ware development

(G-5388)
CTRAC INC
2222 W 110th St (44102-3512)
PHONE..................................440 572-1000
Susan Williamson, *President*
Gary A Seitz, *Exec VP*
EMP: 50 EST: 1972
SQ FT: 15,000
SALES (est): 7.2MM
SALES (corp-wide): 7.8MM **Privately
Held**
WEB: www.ctrac.com
SIC: 7331 7374 Mailing service; data pro-
cessing service; data entry service
PA: Pierry, Inc.
557 Grand St
Redwood City CA 94062
800 860-7953

(G-5389)
**CUMMINGS AND DAVIS FNRL
HM INC**
Also Called: Service Corporation Intl
13201 Euclid Ave (44112-4523)
PHONE..................................216 541-1111
Wallace D Davis, *President*
Evelyn B Davis, *Corp Secy*
EMP: 25
SQ FT: 45,000
SALES (est): 1.7MM **Privately Held**
SIC: 7261 Funeral home

(G-5390)
**CURRENT LIGHTING
SOLUTIONS LLC (HQ)**
1975 Noble Rd Ste 338e (44112-1719)
P.O. Box 5000, Schenectady NY (12301-
5000)
PHONE..................................800 435-4448
Maryrose Sylvester, *President*
Agostino Renna, *President*
Steve Germain, *Engineer*
◆ EMP: 42
SQ FT: 20,890
SALES (est): 26.5MM
SALES (corp-wide): 78.3MM **Privately
Held**
WEB: www.gelcore.com
SIC: 3648 5063 Lighting equipment; light-
ing fixtures
PA: Current Lighting Holdco, Inc.
745 Atlantic Ave
Boston MA 02111
216 956-7734

(G-5391)
**CUSTOM FABRICATORS INC
(PA)**
1621 E 41st St (44103-2305)
PHONE..................................216 831-2266
Anne T Powers, *Principal*
Harold Fallon, *Principal*
Shirley A Garmon, *Principal*
Wendy Feldman, *Corp Secy*
Gary Feldman, *Vice Pres*
◆ EMP: 40 EST: 1956
SQ FT: 3,000
SALES (est): 15.6MM **Privately Held**
WEB: www.customfabricators.net
SIC: 5021 1799 Public building furniture;
office furniture installation

(G-5392)
**CUSTOM HALTHCARE
PROFFESIONAL**
5001 Mayfield Rd Ste 210 (44124-2609)
PHONE..................................216 381-1010
Paul Kloppman, *President*
EMP: 30
SALES (est): 1.6MM **Privately Held**
SIC: 7361 Placement agencies

(G-5393)
CUYAHOGA COUNTY
Also Called: Department Senior Adult S
1701 E 12th St Ste 11 (44114-3237)
PHONE..................................216 420-6750
Susan E Axelrod, *Manager*
EMP: 62 **Privately Held**
SIC: 9441 8322 Administration of social &
human resources; senior citizens' center
or association
PA: County Of Cuyahoga
1215 W 3rd St
Cleveland OH 44113
216 443-7022

(G-5394)
CUYAHOGA COUNTY
Also Called: Parma Adult Training Center
12660 Plaza Dr (44130-1046)
PHONE..................................216 265-3030
Karen Fifelski, *Manager*
EMP: 60 **Privately Held**
SIC: 8331 9411 Sheltered workshop;
PA: County Of Cuyahoga
1215 W 3rd St
Cleveland OH 44113
216 443-7022

(G-5395)
CUYAHOGA COUNTY
Also Called: Children and Family Services
3955 Euclid Ave (44115-2505)
PHONE..................................216 431-4500
William Denihan, *Branch Mgr*
EMP: 650 **Privately Held**
SIC: 8322 9441 Individual & family serv-
ices;
PA: County Of Cuyahoga
1215 W 3rd St
Cleveland OH 44113
216 443-7022

(G-5396)
CUYAHOGA COUNTY
Also Called: Cuyahoga County Dept Pub
Works
2079 E 9th St (44115-1302)
PHONE..................................216 348-3800
Robert C Klaiber, *Principal*
Dottie Sievers, *Technology*
EMP: 640 **Privately Held**
SIC: 8711 9532 Engineering services;
PA: County Of Cuyahoga
1215 W 3rd St
Cleveland OH 44113
216 443-7022

(G-5397)
CUYAHOGA COUNTY
Also Called: Marriage License Bureau
1 W Lakeside Ave Ste 146 (44113-1023)
PHONE..................................216 443-8920
EMP: 62 **Privately Held**
SIC: 9441 7299 Administration of social &
human resources; marriage bureau
PA: County Of Cuyahoga
1215 W 3rd St
Cleveland OH 44113
216 443-7022

(G-5398)
**CUYAHOGA COUNTY
CONVENTION FAC**
Also Called: SMG AGENT FOR CLEVELAND
CONVEN
1 Saint Clair Ave Ne (44114-1251)
PHONE..................................216 928-1600
Matt Carroll, *President*
Mark Leahy, *General Mgr*
Steve Wells, *Finance*
EMP: 75
SALES (est): 57.6MM **Privately Held**
SIC: 8744 Facilities support services

(G-5399)
**CUYAHOGA COUNTY SANI
ENGRG SVC**
6100 W Canal Rd (44125-3330)
PHONE..................................216 443-8211
David Reines, *Director*
EMP: 105
SALES (est): 7.6MM **Privately Held**
SIC: 4959 Sanitary services

(G-5400)
**CUYAHOGA MARKETING
SERVICE**
Also Called: Great Day Tours Chrtr Bus Svc
375 Treeworth Blvd (44147-2985)
PHONE..................................440 526-5350
Allen Kinney, *President*
Phyllis Ann Kinney, *Treasurer*
Doris Kinney, *Admin Sec*
EMP: 40
SQ FT: 3,000
SALES (est): 2.3MM **Privately Held**
WEB: www.greatdaytours.com
SIC: 4141 4142 Local bus charter service;
bus charter service, except local

(G-5401)
**CWM ENVRONMENTAL
CLEVELAND LLC**
4450 Johnston Pkwy Ste B (44128-2956)
PHONE..................................216 663-0808
David Kohl, *Mng Member*
EMP: 30
SQ FT: 15,000
SALES (est): 3.6MM
SALES (corp-wide): 8.3MM **Privately
Held**
WEB: www.precisionanalytical.com
SIC: 7389 Water softener service
PA: Cwm Environmental, Inc.
101 Parkview Drive Ext
Kittanning PA 16201
724 545-2827

(G-5402)
**CYPRESS COMMUNICATIONS
INC (DH)**
75 Erieview Plz Fl 4 (44114-1839)
PHONE..................................404 965-7248
Stephen L Schilling, *President*
Ray Johnson, *President*
Frank M Grillo, *Exec VP*
Jorge L Rosado, *Exec VP*
John A Harwood, *Vice Pres*
EMP: 125
SQ FT: 64,952
SALES (est): 41.3MM
SALES (corp-wide): 223.1MM **Privately
Held**
WEB: www.cypresscom.net
SIC: 8741 4813 Management services;
telephone communication, except radio;
local & long distance telephone communi-
cations
HQ: Broadvox, Llc
75 Erieview Plz Fl 4
Cleveland OH 44114
216 373-4600

(G-5403)
**DAKOTA SOFTWARE
CORPORATION (PA)**
1375 Euclid Ave Ste 500 (44115-1808)
PHONE..................................216 765-7100
Reginald C Shiverick, *President*
Darrin Fleming, *Partner*
Chuck Schmermund, *Business Mgr*
Larry Taylor, *Engineer*
Nick Lay, *Finance*
EMP: 61
SALES (est): 7.7MM **Privately Held**
WEB: www.dakotasoft.com
SIC: 7372 Prepackaged software

(G-5404)
DAN-RAY CONSTRUCTION LLC
4500 Lee Rd Ste 207 (44128-2959)
P.O. Box 221095, Beachwood (44122-
0993)
PHONE..................................216 518-8484
Paul R Jenkins, *Principal*
Ralph Birdsong, *Principal*
Clem Jackson, *Principal*
Tim Jenkins, *Principal*
Steve Rogers, *Principal*

G
E
O
G
R
A
P
H
I
C

EMP: 25
SQ FT: 1,000
SALES (est): 2MM **Privately Held**
SIC: 8748 Business consulting

(G-5405)
DASH SERVICES LLC
3100 E 45th St (44127-1088)
PHONE....................216 273-9133
Elizabeth Smith, *Vice Pres*
Charles Powell,
EMP: 62
SALES: 6.8MM **Privately Held**
SIC: 4731 Foreign freight forwarding

(G-5406)
DATAVANTAGE CORPORATION (DH)
Also Called: Micros Retail
30500 Bruce Industrial Pk (44139-3970)
PHONE....................440 498-4414
Marvin Lader, *CEO*
John E Gularson, *President*
Jeremy Grunzweig, *COO*
Bob Walters, *Senior VP*
EMP: 270
SQ FT: 56,400
SALES: 32MM
SALES (corp-wide): 39.8B **Publicly Held**
SIC: 5734 5045 8748 7371 Computer & software stores; computers, peripherals & software; business consulting; custom computer programming services
HQ: Micros Systems, Inc.
   7031 Columbia Gateway Dr # 1
   Columbia MD 21046
   443 285-6000

(G-5407)
DAVEY TREE EXPERT COMPANY
Also Called: Davey Tree & Lawn Care
7625 Bond St (44139-5350)
PHONE....................440 439-4770
Ken Cloutier, *Manager*
EMP: 25
SALES (corp-wide): 1B **Privately Held**
SIC: 0782 0783 Lawn services; ornamental shrub & tree services
PA: The Davey Tree Expert Company
   1500 N Mantua St
   Kent OH 44240
   330 673-9511

(G-5408)
DAVID FRANCIS CORPORATION (PA)
Also Called: Electronic Merchant Systems
250 W Huron Rd Ste 300 (44113-1451)
PHONE....................216 524-0900
James Weiland, *Ch of Bd*
Dan Neistadt, *President*
Ed Graham, *Exec VP*
Margaret S Weiland, *Treasurer*
Eric Marquardt, *Controller*
EMP: 110
SQ FT: 23,400
SALES (est): 30.2MM **Privately Held**
WEB: www.emscorporate.com
SIC: 7359 5044 Business machine & electronic equipment rental services; office equipment

(G-5409)
DAVIS YOUNG A LEGAL PROF ASSN (PA)
600 Superior Ave E # 1200 (44114-2614)
PHONE....................216 348-1700
Martin J Murphy, *Vice Pres*
Paul D Eklund, *Admin Sec*
EMP: 50
SQ FT: 12,000
SALES (est): 3.9MM **Privately Held**
WEB: www.dyyoungstown.com
SIC: 8111 General practice law office; general practice attorney, lawyer

(G-5410)
DAVITA HEALTHCARE PARTNERS INC
7901 Detroit Ave (44102-2828)
PHONE....................216 961-6498
Gayle Nemecek, *Branch Mgr*
EMP: 27 **Publicly Held**
SIC: 8092 Kidney dialysis centers

PA: Davita Inc.
   2000 16th St
   Denver CO 80202

(G-5411)
DAVITA INC
Also Called: Davita 1620
7360 Engle Rd (44130-3429)
PHONE....................440 891-5645
Anthony Marflak, *Project Mgr*
Davita Smith, *Branch Mgr*
EMP: 27 **Publicly Held**
SIC: 8092 Kidney dialysis centers
PA: Davita Inc.
   2000 16th St
   Denver CO 80202

(G-5412)
DAYTON HEIDELBERG DISTRG CO
9101 E Pleasant Vly (44131-5504)
PHONE....................216 520-2626
Randy Cook, *General Mgr*
Daniel Greathouse, *Branch Mgr*
EMP: 170
SALES (corp-wide): 369.4MM **Privately Held**
SIC: 5181 Beer & other fermented malt liquors
PA: Dayton Heidelberg Distributing Co.
   3601 Dryden Rd
   Moraine OH 45439
   937 222-8692

(G-5413)
DEALER TIRE LLC (PA)
7012 Euclid Ave (44103-4014)
PHONE....................216 432-0088
Doug Goodman, *Warehouse Mgr*
Ken Hummel, *Warehouse Mgr*
Douglas Orfield, *Warehouse Mgr*
Eric Stives, *Opers Staff*
Steven Moyer, *Buyer*
◆ **EMP:** 450 **EST:** 2000
SQ FT: 50,000
SALES (est): 2.1B **Privately Held**
SIC: 5014 Tires & tubes

(G-5414)
DECKER EQUIPMENT COMPANY INC
Also Called: Decker Forklifts
9601 Granger Rd (44125-5350)
PHONE....................866 252-4395
Andrew C Decker, *President*
▼ **EMP:** 28
SALES (est): 8.4MM **Privately Held**
SIC: 5084 Materials handling machinery

(G-5415)
DELOITTE & TOUCHE LLP
127 Public Sq Ste 3300 (44114-1303)
PHONE....................216 589-1300
Patrick Mullen, *Partner*
Jeffrey A Aukerman, *Partner*
Michael J O Brien, *Partner*
Joesph A Buccilli, *Partner*
Michael J Deering, *Partner*
EMP: 250
SALES (corp-wide): 6.2B **Privately Held**
WEB: www.deloitte.com
SIC: 8721 8742 Certified public accountant; management consulting services
HQ: Deloitte & Touche Llp
   30 Rockefeller Plz # 4350
   New York NY 10112
   212 492-4000

(G-5416)
DELTA AIR LINES INC
Also Called: Delta Airlines
5300 Riverside Dr Ste 11 (44135-3146)
PHONE....................216 265-2400
Pat Jones, *Manager*
EMP: 30
SALES (corp-wide): 44.4B **Publicly Held**
WEB: www.delta.com
SIC: 4729 Transportation ticket offices
PA: Delta Air Lines, Inc.
   1030 Delta Blvd
   Atlanta GA 30354
   404 715-2600

(G-5417)
DEPENDABLE PAINTING CO
4403 Superior Ave (44103-1135)
PHONE....................216 431-4470
Cindy Friedmann, *President*
Donald K Hansen, *Exec VP*
EMP: 50 **EST:** 1928
SQ FT: 20,000
SALES (est): 4.7MM **Privately Held**
WEB: www.dependableptg.com
SIC: 1721 Exterior commercial painting contractor; commercial wallcovering contractor

(G-5418)
DETROIT DOVER ANIMALS HOSPITAL
27366 Detroit Rd (44145-2298)
PHONE....................440 871-5220
David Snavely, *President*
Loretta Dennis MD, *President*
Don Grath, *Treasurer*
Clyde Rhein, *Admin Sec*
EMP: 30
SQ FT: 10,000
SALES (est): 1MM **Privately Held**
SIC: 0742 Animal hospital services, pets & other animal specialties

(G-5419)
DETROIT ROYALTY INCORPORATED
1100 Superior Ave E Fl 10 (44114-2530)
PHONE....................216 771-5700
David Demuth, *Branch Mgr*
EMP: 65
SALES (corp-wide): 75.6MM **Privately Held**
WEB: www.donerus.com
SIC: 7311 Advertising agencies
PA: Detroit Royalty, Incorporated
   25900 Northwestern Hwy
   Southfield MI 48075
   248 354-9700

(G-5420)
DIALAMERICA MARKETING INC
7271 Engle Rd Ste 400 (44130-8404)
PHONE....................440 234-4410
Sylvia Freeman, *Program Mgr*
Jerry Banchek, *Director*
EMP: 125
SALES (corp-wide): 395.1MM **Privately Held**
WEB: www.dialupamerica.net
SIC: 7389 Telemarketing services
PA: Dialamerica Marketing, Inc.
   960 Macarthur Blvd
   Mahwah NJ 07430
   201 327-0200

(G-5421)
DIAMOND METALS DIST INC
4635 W 160th St (44135-2629)
PHONE....................216 898-7900
Michael Marrapese, *President*
David Palisin, *Treasurer*
EMP: 30
SALES (est): 12.1MM **Privately Held**
WEB: www.diamondmetals.com
SIC: 5051 Metals service centers & offices

(G-5422)
DIGIKNOW INC
3615 Superior Ave E 4404a (44114-4139)
PHONE....................888 482-4455
King Hill, *President*
John Katila, *Vice Pres*
Harvey Scholnick, *Vice Pres*
Ian Verschuren, *Vice Pres*
Cathy Rivera, *Treasurer*
EMP: 43
SQ FT: 22,500
SALES (est): 2.7MM
SALES (corp-wide): 22.3MM **Privately Held**
WEB: www.digiknow.com
SIC: 7371 Custom computer programming services
PA: Marcus Thomas, Llc.
   4781 Richmond Rd
   Cleveland OH 44128
   216 292-4700

(G-5423)
DINN HOCHMAN AND POTTER LLC
5910 Landerbrook Dr # 200 (44124-6500)
PHONE....................440 446-1100
David B Hochman, *Managing Prtnr*
Betsy Grincius, *Office Admin*
Irwin Dinn,
Tracey Stockton,
Toni Barni,
EMP: 25
SALES (est): 3.1MM **Privately Held**
WEB: www.dhplaw.com
SIC: 8111 General practice attorney, lawyer

(G-5424)
DIRECT IMPORT HOME DECOR INC (PA)
Also Called: Cabinet and Granite Direct
4979 W 130th St (44135-5139)
PHONE....................216 898-9758
Eddie Ni, *President*
Fannie Chen, *General Mgr*
Eric Cheung, *Vice Pres*
Ed Pena, *Sales Staff*
Stephanie Walkos, *Office Admin*
▲ **EMP:** 32
SQ FT: 50,000
SALES (est): 10.4MM **Privately Held**
SIC: 5032 5031 Granite building stone; kitchen cabinets

(G-5425)
DIRECTCONNECTGROUP LTD
Also Called: D C G
5501 Cass Ave (44102-2121)
PHONE....................216 281-2866
Robert A Durham, *Partner*
Brad Clarke, *Partner*
Scott L Durham, *Partner*
Tammy Peniston, *Partner*
James E Pinkin, *Partner*
EMP: 525
SALES (est): 34.2MM **Privately Held**
WEB: www.dcgrp.com
SIC: 2752 7331 Commercial printing, lithographic; mailing service

(G-5426)
DISANTO COMPANIES
1960 Caronia Dr (44124-3919)
PHONE....................440 442-0600
Carolyn Disanto, *Treasurer*
EMP: 30
SALES: 150K **Privately Held**
SIC: 0782 Landscape contractors

(G-5427)
DISKCOPY DUPLICATION SERVICES
107 Alpha Park (44143-2224)
PHONE....................440 460-0800
Sheldon Rubin, *President*
Shannon Klee, *Vice Pres*
Darrel Rubin, *Vice Pres*
EMP: 26
SQ FT: 10,500
SALES: 4.1MM **Privately Held**
SIC: 7371 Computer software development

(G-5428)
DISTILLATA COMPANY (PA)
1608 E 24th St (44114-4212)
P.O. Box 93845 (44101-5845)
PHONE....................216 771-2900
William E Schroeder, *President*
Dalphine Axline, *Principal*
R M Egan, *Principal*
J C Little, *Principal*
Herbert Buckman, *Corp Secy*
EMP: 70 **EST:** 1897
SQ FT: 100,000
SALES (est): 15.9MM **Privately Held**
WEB: www.distillata.com
SIC: 2899 5149 Distilled water; mineral or spring water bottling

(G-5429)
DISTTECH LLC
8101 Union Ave (44105-1560)
PHONE....................800 321-3143
John Manfredi, *Manager*
EMP: 100

SQ FT: 1,749
SALES (corp-wide): 2.4B **Privately Held**
WEB: www.disttech.com
SIC: **4231** 4213 4212 Trucking terminal facilities; trucking, except local; local trucking, without storage
HQ: Disttech, Llc
4366 Mount Pleasant St Nw
North Canton OH 44720
330 491-0474

(G-5430)
DIVERSIFIED LABOR SUPPORT LLC
7050 Engle Rd Ste 101 (44130-8406)
P.O. Box 42242, Brookpark (44142-0242)
PHONE....................................440 234-3090
EMP: 482
SQ FT: 2,769
SALES: 4.4MM **Privately Held**
SIC: **7363** Help Supply Services

(G-5431)
DIX & EATON INCORPORATED
200 Public Sq Ste 3900 (44114-2322)
PHONE....................................216 241-0405
Chas Withers, *CEO*
Lisa Rose, *President*
Kris Dorsey, *Senior VP*
Amy McGahan, *Senior VP*
Ann Lentz, *Vice Pres*
EMP: 50
SQ FT: 23,000
SALES (est): 12MM **Privately Held**
WEB: www.dix-eaton.com
SIC: **8743** 7311 Public relations & publicity; advertising agencies

(G-5432)
DJ NEFF ENTERPRISES INC
Also Called: Neff and Associates
6405 York Rd (44130-3052)
PHONE....................................440 884-3100
Dan Neff, *President*
EMP: 35
SALES (est): 2.5MM **Privately Held**
WEB: www.neff-assoc.com
SIC: **8711** 8713 Civil engineering; surveying services

(G-5433)
DLR GROUP INC
Also Called: Westlake Reed Leskosky
1422 Euclid Ave Ste 300 (44115-1912)
PHONE....................................216 522-1350
EMP: 60
SALES (corp-wide): 109.7MM **Privately Held**
SIC: **8711** 8712 Engineering services; architectural services
HQ: Dlr Group Inc.
6457 Frances St Ste 200
Omaha NE 68106
216 522-1350

(G-5434)
DMD MANAGEMENT INC (PA)
Also Called: Legacy Health Services
12380 Plaza Dr (44130-1043)
PHONE....................................216 898-8399
Bruce Daskal, *CEO*
Jim Taylor, *COO*
Harold Shachter, *Vice Pres*
Barry Stump, *CFO*
Larry Dancziger, *Treasurer*
EMP: 50
SQ FT: 28,360
SALES (est): 105.4MM **Privately Held**
SIC: **8741** Nursing & personal care facility management

(G-5435)
DMD MANAGEMENT INC
12504 Cedar Rd (44106-3217)
PHONE....................................216 371-3600
Bruce Daskal, *Branch Mgr*
EMP: 590 **Privately Held**
SIC: **8322** 8051 Adult day care center; skilled nursing care facilities
PA: Dmd Management, Inc.
12380 Plaza Dr
Cleveland OH 44130

(G-5436)
DOLLAR PARADISE (PA)
Also Called: United Discount
1240 E 55th St (44103-1029)
PHONE....................................216 432-0421
Amin Alsoussou, *President*
EMP: 27
SALES (est): 8.6MM **Privately Held**
SIC: **5199** 5331 Gifts & novelties; variety stores

(G-5437)
DOMINO FOODS INC
Also Called: Domino Sugar
2075 E 65th St (44103-4630)
PHONE....................................216 432-3222
Darrell Lubinsky, *Vice Pres*
Jeffrey Bender, *Branch Mgr*
EMP: 70
SALES (corp-wide): 2B **Privately Held**
WEB: www.dominospecialtyingredients.com
SIC: **2099** 7389 Sugar; packaging & labeling services
HQ: Domino Foods Inc.
99 Wood Ave S Ste 901
Iselin NJ 08830
732 590-1173

(G-5438)
DON BOSCO COMMUNITY CENTER INC
Also Called: Bosco Centre For Senior
1763 Wickford Rd (44112-1207)
PHONE....................................816 421-3160
Nick Fcielzo, *Director*
EMP: 25
SALES (corp-wide): 2.2MM **Privately Held**
SIC: **8322** Community center
PA: The Don Bosco Community Center Inc
580 Campbell St
Kansas City MO 64106
816 421-3160

(G-5439)
DONLEN INC (HQ)
8905 Lake Ave (44102-6315)
PHONE....................................216 961-6767
Donald Strang, *President*
EMP: 75
SALES (est): 2.1MM
SALES (corp-wide): 15.5MM **Privately Held**
SIC: **7011** Hotels & motels
PA: Strang Corporation
8905 Lake Ave Fl 1
Cleveland OH 44102
216 961-6767

(G-5440)
DONLEYS INC (PA)
5430 Warner Rd (44125-1140)
PHONE....................................216 524-6800
Terrance K Donley, *Ch of Bd*
Malcolm M Donley, *President*
Joshua Brown, *Superintendent*
John Clark, *Superintendent*
Kirk Jones, *Superintendent*
EMP: 141 EST: 1941
SQ FT: 44,000
SALES (est): 140.2MM **Privately Held**
WEB: www.donleyinc.com
SIC: **1542** Commercial & office building, new construction

(G-5441)
DONS BROOKLYN CHEVROLET INC
4941 Pearl Rd (44109-5184)
PHONE....................................216 741-1500
Donald Petruzzi, *President*
EMP: 45
SQ FT: 31,920
SALES: 13.3MM **Privately Held**
WEB: www.donsbrooklyn.com
SIC: **5511** 5012 Automobiles, new & used; automobiles & other motor vehicles

(G-5442)
DORSKY HODGSON + PARTNERS INC (PA)
Also Called: Dorsky Hodgson Parrish Yue
23240 Chagrin Blvd # 300 (44122-5405)
PHONE....................................216 464-8600
William Dorsky, *Ch of Bd*
Corneila Hodgeson, *President*
Charles A Cohen, *Principal*
James M Friedman, *Principal*
Geoffrey J Porter, *Principal*
EMP: 60
SALES (est): 10.3MM **Privately Held**
WEB: www.dorskyhodgson.com
SIC: **8712** Architectural engineering

(G-5443)
DORTRONIC SERVICE INC (PA)
Also Called: Action Door
201 E Granger Rd (44131-6728)
PHONE....................................216 739-3667
Michelle Lorello-Zoocki, *CEO*
Michael Wittwer, *President*
Dino Mastanuono, *Vice Pres*
Dave Cavasini, *Treasurer*
Dino Mastanuono, *VP Sales*
EMP: 50
SQ FT: 25,000
SALES (est): 18.9MM **Privately Held**
SIC: **1751** 7699 5031 Garage door, installation or erection; door & window repair; doors

(G-5444)
DOUGLASS & ASSOCIATES CO LPA
4725 Grayton Rd (44135-2307)
PHONE....................................216 362-7777
David Douglass, *Managing Prtnr*
Sean Berney, *Vice Pres*
EMP: 28 EST: 1983
SALES (est): 1.9MM **Privately Held**
WEB: www.douglasslaw.com
SIC: **8111** General practice attorney, lawyer

(G-5445)
DOVETAIL CONSTRUCTION CO INC (PA)
Also Called: Dovetail Solar and Wind
26055 Emery Rd Ste G (44128-6211)
P.O. Box 23038, Chagrin Falls (44023-0038)
PHONE....................................740 592-1800
Alan R Frasz, *President*
Matthew Bennett, *Vice Pres*
Tom Taylor, *Manager*
EMP: 27
SQ FT: 7,200
SALES (est): 5.6MM **Privately Held**
WEB: www.dovetailsolar.com
SIC: **1731** 1711 Electric power systems contractors; solar energy contractor

(G-5446)
DRS HILL & THOMAS CO
Also Called: Eastside Mri
2785 Som Center Rd (44194-0001)
PHONE....................................440 944-8887
EMP: 25
SALES (corp-wide): 11.4MM **Privately Held**
SIC: **8011** 8071 Medical Doctor's Office Medical Laboratory
PA: Drs Hill & Thomas Co
4853 Galaxy Pkwy Ste I
Cleveland OH 44128
216 831-9786

(G-5447)
DUANE MORRIS LLP
1614 E 40th St Fl 3 (44103-2319)
PHONE....................................202 577-3075
Duane Morris, *Branch Mgr*
EMP: 36
SALES (corp-wide): 300MM **Privately Held**
SIC: **8111** General practice attorney, lawyer
PA: Duane Morris Llp
30 S 17th St Fl 5
Philadelphia PA 19103
215 979-1000

(G-5448)
DUCTS INC
883 Addison Rd (44103-1607)
PHONE....................................216 391-2400
Patricia Sickle Mc Elroy, *CEO*
John E Sickle Jr, *President*
Charlotte Sickle, *Chairman*
James Sickle, *Vice Pres*
EMP: 50
SQ FT: 30,000
SALES (est): 3.1MM **Privately Held**
SIC: **1761** 3444 Sheet metalwork; sheet metalwork

(G-5449)
DUNBAR ARMORED INC
5505 Cloverleaf Pkwy (44125-4814)
PHONE....................................216 642-5700
Jeff Johansen, *President*
Art Schossow, *Vice Pres*
Chad Tylicki, *Branch Mgr*
David Spring, *Manager*
EMP: 50
SALES (corp-wide): 3.4B **Publicly Held**
WEB: www.dunbararmored.com
SIC: **7381** Armored car services
HQ: Dunbar Armored, Inc.
50 Schilling Rd
Hunt Valley MD 21031
410 584-9800

(G-5450)
DWELLWORKS LLC (PA)
Also Called: Rss
1317 Euclid Ave (44115-1819)
PHONE....................................216 682-4200
Bob Rosing, *CEO*
Gene Novak, *Mng Member*
Susan Lasalla,
Eugene Novak,
EMP: 99
SQ FT: 11,000
SALES (est): 26.7MM **Privately Held**
SIC: **7389** Relocation service

(G-5451)
DWORKEN & BERNSTEIN CO LPA (PA)
Also Called: Dworken and Bernstein
1468 W 9th St Ste 135 (44113-1220)
PHONE....................................216 861-4211
David M Dworken, *President*
Howard W Bernstein, *Vice Pres*
Marvin F Dworken, *Treasurer*
Daniel Williams, *Associate*
EMP: 43
SQ FT: 2,000
SALES (est): 5.7MM **Privately Held**
WEB: www.dworken-bernstein.com
SIC: **8111** General practice attorney, lawyer; general practice law office

(G-5452)
DWORKIN INC (PA)
Also Called: Dworkin Trucking
5400 Harvard Ave (44105-4899)
PHONE....................................216 271-5318
Jack E Hankison, *Principal*
Jake Dworkin, *Principal*
Otto L Hankison, *Principal*
EMP: 50 EST: 1939
SQ FT: 15,000
SALES (est): 8MM **Privately Held**
WEB: www.dworkin.com
SIC: **4213** Contract haulers

(G-5453)
E F BOYD & SON INC (PA)
Also Called: Boyd Funeral Home
2165 E 89th St (44106-3420)
PHONE....................................216 791-0770
William F Boyd II, *President*
Marcella Cox, *Vice Pres*
Marina Grant, *Vice Pres*
Helen Floyd, *Receptionist*
Charlie Harris, *Assistant*
EMP: 34
SQ FT: 20,000
SALES (est): 3.6MM **Privately Held**
SIC: **7261** Funeral home

(G-5454)
EAB TRUCK SERVICE
7951 Granger Rd (44125-4826)
PHONE....................................216 525-0020
Darryl Fife, *CEO*
Ed Woods, *General Mgr*
Don Jones, *Vice Pres*
Dennis Myers, *Vice Pres*
Ed Adair, *Manager*
EMP: 64
SALES (est): 5MM **Privately Held**
WEB: www.trksvc.com
SIC: **4231** Trucking terminal facilities

(G-5455)
EARLY CHILDHOOD ENRICHMENT CTR
19824 Sussex Rd Rm 178 (44122-4917)
PHONE..................................216 991-9761
Lynne Prange, *Director*
Michelle Block, *Asst Director*
EMP: 25
SALES: 2.8MM **Privately Held**
SIC: 8351 Preschool center

(G-5456)
EAST END NEIGHBORHOOD HSE ASSN
2749 Woodhill Rd (44104-3660)
PHONE..................................216 791-9378
Clarence Williams, *Case Mgr*
Paul Hill Jr, *Director*
Denise Draper, *Program Dir*
Atunyese Herron, *Officer*
EMP: 43
SQ FT: 50,000
SALES (est): 2.4MM **Privately Held**
WEB: www.ritesofpassage.org
SIC: 8322 8351 Social service center;
youth center; senior citizens' center or association; child day care services

(G-5457)
EAST OHIO GAS COMPANY (HQ)
Also Called: Dominion Energy Ohio
1201 E 55th St (44103-1081)
PHONE..................................800 362-7557
Tom D Newland, *President*
Anne E Bomar, *Senior VP*
Brian Brakeman, *Vice Pres*
B C Klink Sr, *Vice Pres*
Ron Kovach, *Vice Pres*
EMP: 1051
SQ FT: 121,000
SALES (est): 2.2B
SALES (corp-wide): 13.3B **Publicly Held**
SIC: 4924 Natural gas distribution
PA: Dominion Energy, Inc.
120 Tredegar St
Richmond VA 23219
804 819-2000

(G-5458)
EAST OHIO GAS COMPANY
Also Called: Dominion Energy Ohio
21200 Miles Rd (44128-4502)
PHONE..................................216 736-6959
Bill Armstrong, *Manager*
EMP: 50
SQ FT: 37,452
SALES (corp-wide): 13.3B **Publicly Held**
SIC: 4924 Natural gas distribution
HQ: The East Ohio Gas Company
1201 E 55th St
Cleveland OH 44103
800 362-7557

(G-5459)
EASTERN STAR HM OF CYHOGA CNTY
2114 Noble Rd (44112-1725)
PHONE..................................216 761-0170
Jim Eckerle, *Administration*
EMP: 100
SQ FT: 15,000
SALES: 196.1K **Privately Held**
SIC: 8052 8051 Intermediate care facilities; skilled nursing care facilities

(G-5460)
EASTSIDE LANDSCAPING INC
572 Trebisky Rd (44143-2862)
P.O. Box 21801 (44121-0801)
PHONE..................................216 381-0070
Ned Cultrona, *President*
Jim Freireich, *Vice Pres*
Gary Henry, *Manager*
EMP: 25
SALES (est): 1.7MM **Privately Held**
WEB: www.eastsidelandscaping.com
SIC: 0781 Landscape services

(G-5461)
EASY2 TECHNOLOGIES INC
Also Called: Easy 2 Technologies
1111 Chester Ave (44114-3545)
PHONE..................................216 479-0482
Ethan Cohen, *CEO*
Matt Walsh, *President*

Carl Persson, *Vice Pres*
George Koenig, *VP Sales*
EMP: 30
SQ FT: 9,400
SALES (est): 2.6MM
SALES (corp-wide): 9.9MM **Privately Held**
WEB: www.easy2.com
SIC: 7373 Systems software development services
HQ: Answers Corporation
6665 Delmar Blvd Ste 3000
Saint Louis MO 63130

(G-5462)
EATON CORPORATION
Eaton Family Credit Union
333 Babbitt Rd Ste 100 (44123-1636)
PHONE..................................216 920-2000
Michael Losneck, *Branch Mgr*
EMP: 260 **Privately Held**
WEB: www.eaton.com
SIC: 3714 5084 Hydraulic fluid power pumps for auto steering mechanism; hydraulic systems equipment & supplies
HQ: Eaton Corporation
1000 Eaton Blvd
Cleveland OH 44122
440 523-5000

(G-5463)
EATON CORPORATION
P.O. Box 818031 (44181-8031)
PHONE..................................888 402-1915
EMP: 37 **Privately Held**
SIC: 5063 Electrical apparatus & equipment
HQ: Eaton Corporation
1000 Eaton Blvd
Cleveland OH 44122
440 523-5000

(G-5464)
EBSO INC
Also Called: Administrative Service Cons
3301 E Royalton Rd Ste 1 (44147-2835)
PHONE..................................440 262-1133
Lisa Messer, *Branch Mgr*
Lynn Bletsh, *Info Tech Dir*
EMP: 30
SALES (corp-wide): 9.2MM **Privately Held**
SIC: 6324 Hospital & medical service plans
PA: Ebso Inc.
7020 N Pt Wshngton Rd 2
Glendale WI 53217
414 410-1802

(G-5465)
ECLIPSE CO LLC
23209 Miles Rd (44128-5465)
PHONE..................................440 552-9400
Yvette Jones, *Mng Member*
Jennifer Agresta,
Tom Agresta,
EMP: 50
SQ FT: 700
SALES (est): 4.1MM **Privately Held**
SIC: 8741 Construction management

(G-5466)
ECONOMY PROD VEGETABLE CO INC (PA)
4000 Orange Ave Unit 38 (44115-3563)
PHONE..................................216 431-2800
Jack Jakobovitch, *President*
Hershel Weiser, *Sales Staff*
EMP: 30
SQ FT: 70,000
SALES (est): 18.9MM **Privately Held**
SIC: 5148 Fruits, fresh; vegetables, fresh

(G-5467)
EDUCATION LOAN SERVICING CORP
Also Called: Xpress Loan Servicing
1500 W 3rd St Ste 125 (44113-1422)
PHONE..................................216 706-8130
David H Harmon, *President*
Douglas L Feist, *Exec VP*
Perry D Moore, *Exec VP*
James G Clark, *CFO*
Jerry McFadden, *CFO*
EMP: 99
SQ FT: 20,000

SALES (est): 11.9MM **Privately Held**
WEB: www.educationloanservicingcorporation.com
SIC: 6141 Personal credit institutions

(G-5468)
EDWARD HOWARD & CO (PA)
1100 Superior Ave E # 1600 (44114-2530)
PHONE..................................216 781-2400
Kathleen A Obert, *Ch of Bd*
Wayne R Hill, *President*
Mark Grieves, *Exec VP*
Nora C Jacobs, *Exec VP*
Donald C Hohmeier, *CFO*
EMP: 43
SALES (est): 3.3MM **Privately Held**
SIC: 8743 7336 Public relations & publicity; graphic arts & related design

(G-5469)
EIGHTH DAY SOUND SYSTEMS INC
5450 Avion Park Dr (44143-1919)
PHONE..................................440 995-2647
Tom Arko, *President*
Jack Boessneck, *Exec VP*
Alan Herschman, *Vice Pres*
Cw Alkire, *Project Mgr*
Jordan Kolenc, *Project Mgr*
▲ EMP: 27
SQ FT: 27,500
SALES (est): 7.7MM **Privately Held**
WEB: www.8thdaysound.com
SIC: 1731 Sound equipment specialization

(G-5470)
ELDERCARE SERVICES INST LLC
11890 Fairhill Rd (44120-1053)
PHONE..................................216 791-8000
Frank Cardinale, *CFO*
EMP: 85 EST: 2006
SALES (est): 752.5K **Privately Held**
SIC: 8082 Home health care services

(G-5471)
ELECTRA SOUND INC
10779 Brookpark Rd Ste A (44130-1164)
PHONE..................................216 433-1050
Charles Masa, *President*
EMP: 125
SALES (est): 3.2MM
SALES (corp-wide): 31MM **Privately Held**
WEB: www.electrasound.com
SIC: 7622 7382 Television repair shop; security systems services
PA: Electra Sound, Inc.
5260 Commerce Pkwy W
Parma OH 44130
216 433-9600

(G-5472)
ELEMENT MTRLS TCHNLGY HNTNGTN
Also Called: Stork Herron Cleveland
5405 E Schaaf Rd (44131-1337)
PHONE..................................216 643-1208
EMP: 50
SALES (corp-wide): 135.5MM **Privately Held**
SIC: 8734 Testing Laboratory
HQ: Element Materials Technology Huntington Beach Inc.
15062 Bolsa Chica St
Huntington Beach CA 92649
714 933-2070

(G-5473)
EMERALD DEV ECNOMIC NETWRK INC
Also Called: Eden
7812 Madison Ave (44102-4056)
PHONE..................................216 961-9690
Wayne Harris, *Engineer*
Irene Collins, *CFO*
Christopher West, *Finance*
Frank Koncz, *Property Mgr*
Emma Barcelona, *Manager*
EMP: 51
SQ FT: 17,000
SALES: 27.6MM **Privately Held**
WEB: www.edeninc.org
SIC: 6513 Apartment building operators

(G-5474)
EMERGENCY MEDICAL SVCS BILLING
1701 Lakeside Ave E (44114-1118)
PHONE..................................216 664-2598
Nicole Carlton, *Principal*
EMP: 40 EST: 2010
SALES (est): 71.2K **Privately Held**
SIC: 8721 9199 Billing & bookkeeping service; supply agency, government

(G-5475)
EMERITUS CORPORATION
Also Called: Emeritus At Brookside Estates
15435 Bagley Rd Ste 1 (44130-4827)
PHONE..................................440 201-9200
Chris Belford, *Principal*
EMP: 60
SALES (corp-wide): 4.5B **Publicly Held**
WEB: www.emeraldestatesslc.com
SIC: 8051 Skilled nursing care facilities
HQ: Emeritus Corporation
3131 Elliott Ave Ste 500
Milwaukee WI 53214

(G-5476)
EMERY LEASING CO LLC
Also Called: SUBURBAN PAVILION NURSING AND
20265 Emery Rd (44128-4122)
PHONE..................................216 475-8880
David W Trimble, *CPA*
Stephen L Rosedale, *Mng Member*
EMP: 270
SALES (est): 11.4MM **Privately Held**
SIC: 8051 Convalescent home with continuous nursing care

(G-5477)
EMPIRE BRASS CO
Also Called: American Brass
5000 Superior Ave (44103-1238)
PHONE..................................216 431-6565
Robert Mc Connville, *President*
▲ EMP: 50
SALES (est): 6.8MM **Privately Held**
WEB: www.empirebrassfaucets.com
SIC: 5074 3432 3364 Plumbing fittings & supplies; plumbing fixture fittings & trim; nonferrous die-castings except aluminum

(G-5478)
EMS RAMS YOUTH DEV GROUP INC
Also Called: E.M.s Rams Youth Football Team
1536 E 85th St (44106-3764)
PHONE..................................216 282-4688
Heyward R Prude III, *CEO*
EMP: 30
SALES: 70.7K **Privately Held**
WEB: www.emsrams.org
SIC: 8641 Civic social & fraternal associations

(G-5479)
ENERGY MGT SPECIALISTS INC
Also Called: Ems
15800 Industrial Pkwy (44135-3320)
PHONE..................................216 676-9045
Alan J Guzik, *President*
Benj Guzik, *Project Engr*
Kristine Guzik, *VP Sales*
EMP: 30
SQ FT: 8,800
SALES (est): 5.3MM **Privately Held**
WEB: www.energyman.com
SIC: 1711 Mechanical contractor

(G-5480)
ENGINEERED CON STRUCTURES CORP
14510 Broadway Ave (44125-1960)
PHONE..................................216 520-2000
Donald J Mayer, *President*
Richard M Mayer, *Vice Pres*
EMP: 30
SALES (est): 4.2MM **Privately Held**
WEB: www.lakesideconstruction.com
SIC: 1771 Concrete work

(G-5481)
ENGINEERING DESIGN AND TESTING
Also Called: Ebnt
P.O. Box 30160 (44130-0160)
PHONE..................440 239-0362
Kim A Jur PHD, *President*
Mark Rusell, *Chief Engr*
EMP: 100
SALES (est): 331.7K **Privately Held**
SIC: 8711 Consulting engineer

(G-5482)
ENPROTECH INDUSTRIAL TECH LLC (DH)
4259 E 49th St (44125-1001)
PHONE..................216 883-3220
Pedro Garcia, *Mng Member*
Ben Handshue, *Sr Project Mgr*
▲ **EMP:** 210
SQ FT: 96,000
SALES: 75MM
SALES (corp-wide): 51.7B **Privately Held**
WEB: www.itochu.com
SIC: 3547 3365 3599 8711 Rolling mill machinery; machinery castings, aluminum; custom machinery; engineering services; electrical repair shops
HQ: Enprotech Corp.
4259 E 49th St
Cleveland OH 44125
216 206-0080

(G-5483)
ENRICHMENT CENTER OF WISHING W (PA)
14574 Ridge Rd (44133-4940)
PHONE..................440 237-5000
Johanne Wigton, *President*
EMP: 80
SQ FT: 11,000
SALES (est): 1.8MM **Privately Held**
SIC: 8351 Preschool center

(G-5484)
ENTRYPOINT CONSULTING LLC
600 Superior Ave E # 1300 (44114-2654)
PHONE..................216 674-9070
Peter Martin, *President*
Robert Waldrop, *Vice Pres*
Mario Mancini, *Director*
Nichalas A Canitano,
David Moore,
EMP: 55
SQ FT: 1,500
SALES (est): 5.9MM **Privately Held**
WEB: www.entrypointconsulting.com
SIC: 7379

(G-5485)
ENVIROTEST SYSTEMS CORP
13000 York Delta Dr (44133-3521)
PHONE..................330 963-4464
F Miller, *Branch Mgr*
EMP: 34
SQ FT: 7,672 **Privately Held**
WEB: www.il.etest.com
SIC: 7549 Emissions testing without repairs, automotive
HQ: Envirotest Systems Corp.
7 Kripes Rd
East Granby CT 06026

(G-5486)
ENVIROTEST SYSTEMS CORP
Also Called: Ohio E-Check
24770 Sperry Dr (44145-1531)
PHONE..................330 963-4464
EMP: 34
SQ FT: 7,651 **Privately Held**
WEB: www.il.etest.com
SIC: 7549 Emissions testing without repairs, automotive
HQ: Envirotest Systems Corp.
7 Kripes Rd
East Granby CT 06026

(G-5487)
ENVISION WASTE SERVICES LLC
4451 Renaissance Pkwy (44128-5754)
PHONE..................216 831-1818
Steven M Viny, *CEO*
Clayton A Minder, *CFO*
Clayton Minder, *CFO*

Alice Soeder, *Office Mgr*
EMP: 93
SQ FT: 4,000
SALES (est): 13.1MM **Privately Held**
SIC: 4953 Recycling, waste materials

(G-5488)
EQUIPMENT MANUFACTURERS INTL
Also Called: E M I
16151 Puritas Ave (44135-2617)
P.O. Box 94725 (44101-4725)
PHONE..................216 651-6700
Jerry Senk, *Principal*
John Zelli, *Engineer*
R T Mackin, *Treasurer*
Jim Mudri, *Finance Mgr*
Dave Bowman, *Sales Engr*
▲ **EMP:** 30
SQ FT: 65,000
SALES: 10MM **Privately Held**
WEB: www.emi-inc.com
SIC: 3559 5084 Foundry machinery & equipment; industrial machinery & equipment

(G-5489)
EQUITY RESIDENTIAL PROPERTIES
Also Called: Reserve Square Apts
1701 E 12th St Ste 35 (44114-3237)
PHONE..................216 861-2700
Sandy Gorie, *General Mgr*
Ray Ratermann, *Manager*
EMP: 50
SQ FT: 1,709,000
SALES (est): 3.1MM **Privately Held**
WEB: www.thekanddgroup.com
SIC: 6513 6512 Apartment building operators; commercial & industrial building operation

(G-5490)
ERNST & YOUNG LLP
Also Called: Ey
950 Main Ave Ste 1800 (44113-7214)
PHONE..................216 861-5000
Christopher W Smith, *Manager*
Terence Kennedy, *Manager*
Michael Pugh, *Manager*
Benjamin Basinski, *Consultant*
Tim Patrick, *Senior Mgr*
EMP: 65
SALES (corp-wide): 4.3B **Privately Held**
WEB: www.ey.com
SIC: 8721 Certified public accountant
PA: Ernst & Young Llp
5 Times Sq Fl Conlv1
New York NY 10036
212 773-3000

(G-5491)
ERNST & YOUNG LLP
Also Called: Ey
1660 W 2nd St Ste 200 (44113-1446)
PHONE..................216 583-1823
Michelle Settecase, *Principal*
EMP: 228
SALES (corp-wide): 4.3B **Privately Held**
SIC: 8721 Certified public accountant
PA: Ernst & Young Llp
5 Times Sq Fl Conlv1
New York NY 10036
212 773-3000

(G-5492)
ETHNIC VOICE OF AMERICA
4606 Bruening Dr (44134-4640)
PHONE..................440 845-0922
Irene K Smirnov, *President*
EMP: 30 **EST:** 1996
SALES: 0 **Privately Held**
WEB: www.ethnic-voice.com
SIC: 8699 Personal interest organization

(G-5493)
EUCLID INDUS MAINT CLG CONTRS
1561 E 40th St (44103-2301)
PHONE..................216 361-0288
Carol Presser, *President*
EMP: 150
SQ FT: 5,000

SALES (est): 4.1MM **Privately Held**
SIC: 7349 1799 Janitorial service, contract basis; window cleaning; sandblasting of building exteriors

(G-5494)
EUCLID SC TRANSPORTATION
393 Babbitt Rd (44123-1645)
PHONE..................216 797-7600
Dan Dodson, *Principal*
Laura Tomba, *Teacher*
EMP: 65
SALES (est): 1.7MM **Privately Held**
SIC: 4789 Transportation services

(G-5495)
EURO USA INC (PA)
4481 Johnston Pkwy (44128-2952)
PHONE..................216 714-0500
Joseph D O'Donnell, *President*
Nancy A Farmer, *President*
Jerry L Marshaw Jr, *Principal*
Terry Comer, *Vice Pres*
Frank Fox, *Opers Mgr*
▲ **EMP:** 100
SQ FT: 75,000
SALES (est): 69MM **Privately Held**
SIC: 5149 Specialty food items

(G-5496)
EVENTIONS LTD
14925 Shaker Blvd (44120-1647)
PHONE..................216 952-9898
Randy Dauchot, *Managing Prtnr*
Stephanie Eisele, *Partner*
EMP: 32
SALES: 70K **Privately Held**
WEB: www.eventions.net
SIC: 7299 7389 Party planning service; business services

(G-5497)
EVERGREEN COOPERATIVE LDRY INC
540 E 105th St Ste 206 (44108-4310)
PHONE..................216 268-3548
Cecil Lee, *CEO*
EMP: 40
SQ FT: 15,000
SALES (est): 1.1MM **Privately Held**
SIC: 7211 Power laundries, family & commercial

(G-5498)
EVERYONE COUNTS INC
50 Public Sq Ste 200 (44113-2226)
PHONE..................858 427-4673
Bill Kuncz, *CEO*
James Simmons, *Vice Pres*
David Wallick, *Project Mgr*
Judson Neer, *Engineer*
Brandon Johnson, *Sales Staff*
EMP: 70
SALES (est): 700K
SALES (corp-wide): 800K **Privately Held**
SIC: 7371 Computer software development
PA: Votem Corp.
50 Public Sq Ste 200
Cleveland OH 44113
216 930-4300

(G-5499)
EXCELAS LLC
387 Golfview Ln Ste 200 (44143-4417)
PHONE..................440 442-7310
Jean C Bourgeois, *Principal*
Sharon Ezzone, *Manager*
Kim Henchar, *Officer*
Joshua Sherkel, *Officer*
Patty Strohmeier, *Executive Asst*
EMP: 40
SALES (est): 2.2MM **Privately Held**
SIC: 8099 Medical services organization

(G-5500)
EXEL GLOBAL LOGISTICS INC
21500 Aerospace Pkwy (44142-1071)
PHONE..................440 243-5900
Bill Krabec, *Branch Mgr*
EMP: 70
SALES (corp-wide): 70.4B **Privately Held**
WEB: www.exelgloballogistics.com
SIC: 4731 Freight forwarding

HQ: Exel Global Logistics Inc.
22879 Glenn Dr Ste 100
Sterling VA 20164
703 350-1298

(G-5501)
EXPEDITORS INTL WASH INC
18029 Cleveland Pkwy Dr (44135-3247)
PHONE..................440 243-9900
Robert Gierszal, *Manager*
EMP: 80
SALES (corp-wide): 8.1B **Publicly Held**
WEB: www.expd.com
SIC: 4731 Foreign freight forwarding
PA: Expeditors International Of Washington, Inc.
1015 3rd Ave Fl 12
Seattle WA 98104
206 674-3400

(G-5502)
EXPERT CRANE INC
5755 Grant Ave (44105-5605)
PHONE..................216 451-9900
James C Doty, *President*
Rebecca Doty, *Vice Pres*
Carl Dell, *VP Opers*
Brian Doles, *Purchasing*
Tempest Doty, *Manager*
EMP: 47
SQ FT: 15,000
SALES (est): 22.2MM **Privately Held**
WEB: www.expertcrane.com
SIC: 3536 7699 1796 5084 Hoists, cranes & monorails; industrial machinery & equipment repair; machinery installation; cranes, industrial

(G-5503)
EXPLORYS INC
1111 Superior Ave E # 2600 (44114-2560)
PHONE..................216 767-4700
Stephen McHale, *CEO*
Charles Lougheed, *President*
Thomas Chickerella, *COO*
Aaron Cornell, *CFO*
EMP: 54
SALES (est): 12.7MM
SALES (corp-wide): 79.5B **Publicly Held**
SIC: 7372 Prepackaged software
PA: International Business Machines Corporation
1 New Orchard Rd Ste 1 # 1
Armonk NY 10504
914 499-1900

(G-5504)
FABRIZI TRUCKING & PAV CO INC (PA)
20389 1st Ave (44130-2433)
PHONE..................330 483-3291
Emilio Fabrizi Jr, *President*
Maria Fearer, *Exec VP*
Patricia A Fabrizi, *Treasurer*
Wes Moloney, *Credit Mgr*
Cindy Turk, *Human Res Dir*
EMP: 160 **EST:** 1949
SQ FT: 5,000
SALES (est): 33.8MM **Privately Held**
SIC: 1623 1611 Water & sewer line construction; highway & street paving contractor

(G-5505)
FAIRMOUNT MONTESSORI ASSN
Also Called: RUFFING MONTESSORI SCHOOL
3380 Fairmount Blvd (44118-4214)
PHONE..................216 321-7571
Debra Mitchell, *Finance*
Gordon Maas, *Director*
EMP: 44
SQ FT: 22,250
SALES: 5.3MM **Privately Held**
WEB: www.ruffingeast.org
SIC: 8351 8211 Montessori child development center; private elementary & secondary schools

(G-5506)
FAIRVIEW EYE CENTER INC
21375 Lorain Rd (44126-2122)
PHONE..................440 333-3060
Dr Louis P Caravella, *President*
Jeff Terbeck, *Vice Pres*

Mary Becka, *Administration*
EMP: 45
SQ FT: 5,000
SALES (est): 5.2MM **Privately Held**
WEB: www.fairvieweyecenter.com
SIC: 8011 Ophthalmologist

(G-5507)
FAIRVIEW HLTH SYS FDERAL CR UN
18101 Lorain Ave (44111-5612)
PHONE..................216 476-7000
K Gopal, *Owner*
EMP: 1115
SALES (est): 1.1MM
SALES (corp-wide): 8.9B **Privately Held**
SIC: 6061 Federal credit unions
HQ: Fairview Hospital
18101 Lorain Ave
Cleveland OH 44111
216 476-7000

(G-5508)
FAIRVIEW HOSPITAL (HQ)
Also Called: Fairview West Physician Center
18101 Lorain Ave (44111-5612)
PHONE..................216 476-7000
Toby Cosgrove, *CEO*
Louis Caravella MD, *President*
Delos Cosgrove, *President*
Adam Miller, *Business Mgr*
Jeffrey A Leimgruber,
EMP: 35
SQ FT: 327,000
SALES: 474.3MM
SALES (corp-wide): 8.9B **Privately Held**
SIC: 8062 8011 General medical & surgical hospitals; offices & clinics of medical doctors
PA: The Cleveland Clinic Foundation
9500 Euclid Ave
Cleveland OH 44195
216 636-8335

(G-5509)
FAMICOS FOUNDATION
1325 Ansel Rd (44106-1079)
PHONE..................216 791-6476
Richard Weaver, *Ch of Bd*
Peter Lee, *Vice Ch Bd*
Michael Griffen, *Treasurer*
John Anoliefo, *Exec Dir*
Rev Robert Marva, *Admin Sec*
EMP: 29
SALES: 7.4MM **Privately Held**
WEB: www.famicos.org
SIC: 8399 Community development groups

(G-5510)
FAMILY PHYSICIANS ASSOCIATES (PA)
5187 Mayfield Rd Ste 102 (44124-2467)
PHONE..................440 442-3866
Terrence Isakov, *President*
EMP: 50
SQ FT: 14,179
SALES (est): 5.4MM **Privately Held**
WEB: www.southernrain.net
SIC: 8011 Physicians

(G-5511)
FAMOUS ENTERPRISES INC
11200 Madison Ave (44102-2323)
PHONE..................216 529-1010
Steve Wisman, *Manager*
EMP: 50 **Privately Held**
WEB: www.jfgood.com
SIC: 5251 5075 Hardware; warm air heating equipment & supplies
PA: Famous Enterprises, Inc.
2620 Ridgewood Rd Ste 200
Akron OH 44313

(G-5512)
FANTON LOGISTICS INC (PA)
10801 Broadway Ave (44125-1653)
PHONE..................216 341-2400
Mycola Kachaluba, *President*
EMP: 52
SQ FT: 3,700
SALES: 7.6MM **Privately Held**
SIC: 4213 Trucking, except local

(G-5513)
FARM HOUSE FOOD DISTRS INC
9000 Woodland Ave (44104-3225)
PHONE..................216 791-6948
Daniel Simon, *President*
Meryl Simon, *Treasurer*
Matthew Armstrong, *Controller*
EMP: 25 **EST:** 1974
SQ FT: 10,000
SALES (est): 3.4MM **Privately Held**
WEB: www.farmhousefish.com
SIC: 5411 5146 Supermarkets, independent; fish & seafoods

(G-5514)
FARROW CLEANERS CO (PA)
Also Called: Guild Custom Drapery
3788 Lee Rd (44128-1464)
PHONE..................216 561-2355
Jack Grimaldi, *President*
Salvatore P Grimaldi, *Vice Pres*
EMP: 39 **EST:** 1948
SQ FT: 8,000
SALES (est): 2.8MM **Privately Held**
SIC: 7217 5714 5713 7216 Carpet & rug cleaning plant; draperies; carpets; drycleaning plants, except rugs; curtain cleaning & repair; repairing fire damage, single-family houses; renovation, remodeling & repairs: industrial buildings

(G-5515)
FASHION ARCHITECTURAL DESIGNS
Also Called: Fashion Wallcoverings
4005 Carnegie Ave (44103-4334)
PHONE..................216 432-1600
Louis Roesch, *Ch of Bd*
Joseph Olivier, *President*
Dorothy Roesch, *Corp Secy*
EMP: 90 **EST:** 1959
SQ FT: 92,500
SALES (est): 11.2MM **Privately Held**
WEB: www.fashionwallcoverings.com
SIC: 5198 Wallcoverings

(G-5516)
FASTBALL SPT PRODUCTIONS LLC
Also Called: Sportstime Ohio
1333 Lakeside Ave E (44114-1134)
PHONE..................440 746-8000
F McGillicuedy, *General Mgr*
Francois McGillicuedy, *General Mgr*
EMP: 35
SALES (est): 1.2MM
SALES (corp-wide): 89.8B **Publicly Held**
SIC: 7812 Motion picture & video production
HQ: Twenty-First Century Fox, Inc.
1211 Avenue Of The Americ
New York NY 10036
212 852-7000

(G-5517)
FATHOM SEO LLC (PA)
Also Called: Fathom Online Marketing
8200 Sweet Valley Dr (44125-4267)
PHONE..................216 525-0510
Elizabeth Lynch, *Vice Pres*
Rob Ament, *VP Opers*
Sean Wenger, *VP Mfg*
Kris Scaffide, *Accounting Mgr*
Joe Kneale, *Marketing Staff*
EMP: 68
SALES (est): 24.5MM **Privately Held**
WEB: www.fathomseo.com
SIC: 8742 Marketing consulting services

(G-5518)
FAY SHARPE LLP
The Halle Bldg 1228e (44115)
PHONE..................216 363-9000
Roseanne Giuliani, *Partner*
Patrick Roche, *Managing Prtnr*
Joseph D Dreher, *Partner*
Steven Haas, *Partner*
Richard M Klein, *Partner*
EMP: 94
SQ FT: 40,000
SALES (est): 13.2MM **Privately Held**
WEB: www.faysharpe.com
SIC: 8111 General practice law office

(G-5519)
FC CONTINENTAL LANDLORD LLC
50 Public Sq Ste 1360 (44113-2233)
PHONE..................216 621-6060
Forest City Residential Group, *Mng Member*
Fc Continental Master Tenant L,
EMP: 2917
SQ FT: 2,500
SALES: 5MM
SALES (corp-wide): 80.4MM **Privately Held**
SIC: 6531 Real estate agents & managers
HQ: Forest City Enterprises, L.P.
127 Public Sq Ste 3200
Cleveland OH 44114
216 621-6060

(G-5520)
FEDELI GROUP INC
5005 Rockside Rd Ste 500 (44131-2184)
P.O. Box 318003 (44131-8003)
PHONE..................216 328-8080
Umberto Fedeli, *CEO*
David Graf, *Controller*
Daniela Dinwiddie, *Director*
Mary Gonsowski, *Advisor*
EMP: 90 **EST:** 1975
SQ FT: 25,000
SALES (est): 35.8MM **Privately Held**
WEB: www.thefedeligroup.com
SIC: 6411 Insurance agents; property & casualty insurance agent

(G-5521)
FEDERAL INSURANCE COMPANY
Also Called: Chubb
1375 E 9th St Ste 1960 (44114-1724)
PHONE..................216 687-1700
Jessica M Jung, *Manager*
EMP: 35
SALES (corp-wide): 29B **Privately Held**
WEB: www.federalinsurancecompany.com
SIC: 6411 Insurance agents, brokers & service
HQ: Federal Insurance Company
202 N Illinois St # 2600
Indianapolis IN 46204
908 903-2000

(G-5522)
FEDERAL MACHINERY & EQP CO (PA)
Also Called: Federal Equipment Company
8200 Bessemer Ave (44127-1837)
PHONE..................800 652-2466
Larry Kadis, *CEO*
Michael Kadis, *President*
Morris I Goldsmithn, *Principal*
Matt Hicks, *COO*
Adam Covitt, *Vice Pres*
◆ **EMP:** 33 **EST:** 1957
SQ FT: 350,000
SALES (est): 15MM **Privately Held**
WEB: www.fedequip.com
SIC: 5084 Materials handling machinery

(G-5523)
FEDERAL RSRVE BNK OF CLEVELAND (HQ)
1455 E 6th St (44114-2517)
P.O. Box 6387 (44101-1387)
PHONE..................216 579-2000
Sandra Pianalto, *CEO*
Alfred M Rankin Jr, *Ch of Bd*
John P Surma, *Ch of Bd*
John Lytell, *President*
Michael Vangelos, *President*
EMP: 760 **EST:** 1914
SALES (est): 4.3MM **Privately Held**
WEB: www.clevelandfed.com
SIC: 6011 Federal reserve banks
PA: Board Of Governors Of The Federal Reserve System
20th St Cnsttution Ave Nw
Washington DC 20551
202 452-3000

(G-5524)
FEDEX CORPORATION
17831 Englewood Dr (44130-3452)
PHONE..................440 234-0315
EMP: 34

SALES (corp-wide): 47.4B **Publicly Held**
SIC: 4513 Air Courier Services
PA: Fedex Corporation
942 Shady Grove Rd S
Memphis TN 38120
901 818-7500

(G-5525)
FERRALLOY INC
28001 Ranney Pkwy (44145-1159)
PHONE..................440 250-1900
William Habansky Jr, *President*
Sherri Habansky, *Corp Secy*
▲ **EMP:** 27
SQ FT: 15,000
SALES (est): 10.3MM **Privately Held**
WEB: www.ferralloy.com
SIC: 5051 3599 Castings, rough: iron or steel; machine shop, jobbing & repair

(G-5526)
FINANCIAL PLNNERS OF CLEVELAND
Also Called: Nca Financial Planners
6095 Parkland Blvd # 210 (44124-6139)
PHONE..................440 473-1115
Kevin Myeroff, *President*
Bob Casarona, *Vice Pres*
Amy Smith, *Vice Pres*
Leslie Globits, *Ch Invest Ofcr*
Amanda Ballantyne, *Financial Analy*
EMP: 28
SQ FT: 3,000
SALES (est): 4.8MM **Privately Held**
WEB: www.ncafinancial.com
SIC: 6282 6411 Investment advisory service; pension & retirement plan consultants

(G-5527)
FIREFIGHTERS CMNTY CR UN INC
2300 Saint Clair Ave Ne (44114-4049)
PHONE..................216 621-4644
William Deighton, *Ch of Bd*
Lyn Ruggeri, *COO*
John Carrick, *CFO*
Sandy Ananewich, *Loan Officer*
Terrence Corrigan, *Loan Officer*
EMP: 28
SALES (corp-wide): 9.5MM **Privately Held**
SIC: 6062 6163 State credit unions, not federally chartered; loan brokers
PA: Firefighters Community Credit Union, Inc.
4664 E 71st St
Cleveland OH 44125
216 621-4644

(G-5528)
FIRST AMERICAN EQUITY LN SVCS (DH)
1100 Superior Ave E # 3 (44114-2530)
PHONE..................800 221-8683
Michael B Hopkins, *President*
John Baumbick, *Counsel*
Michael Cullen, *Senior VP*
Sean Conway, *CFO*
EMP: 200
SQ FT: 37,736
SALES: 70MM **Publicly Held**
WEB: www.faequity.com
SIC: 6361 Real estate title insurance
HQ: First American Title Insurance Company
1 First American Way
Santa Ana CA 92707
800 854-3643

(G-5529)
FIRST AMERICAN TITLE INSUR CO
1100 Superior Ave E # 200 (44114-2518)
PHONE..................216 241-1278
Stephen Vogt, *Branch Mgr*
EMP: 27 **Publicly Held**
SIC: 6361 Real estate title insurance
HQ: First American Title Insurance Company
1 First American Way
Santa Ana CA 92707
800 854-3643

▲ = Import ▼=Export
◆ =Import/Export

(G-5530)
FIRST BAPTIST DAY CARE CENTER
Also Called: Childrens Ctr of Frst Bptst Ch
3630 Fairmount Blvd (44118-4341)
PHONE..................216 371-9394
Jane Pernicone, *Director*
EMP: 31
SALES (est): 951.5K **Privately Held**
SIC: 8351 Child day care services

(G-5531)
FIRST CHOICE MEDICAL STAFFING
1457 W 117th St (44107-5101)
PHONE..................216 521-2222
Ed Newton, *Principal*
EMP: 152
SALES (corp-wide): 4.6MM **Privately Held**
SIC: 8059 Nursing home, except skilled & intermediate care facility
PA: First Choice Medical Staffing Of Ohio, Inc.
1457 W 117th St
Cleveland OH 44107
216 521-2222

(G-5532)
FIRST CHOICE MEDICAL STAFFING (PA)
1457 W 117th St (44107-5101)
PHONE..................216 521-2222
Charles Slone, *President*
Karen V D, *Medical Dir*
EMP: 425
SALES: 4.6MM **Privately Held**
SIC: 7361 Employment agencies

(G-5533)
FIRST CLASS LIMOS INC
31525 Aurora Rd Ste 5 (44139-2763)
PHONE..................440 248-1114
Jimmy Michalek, *President*
EMP: 25
SALES (est): 636K **Privately Held**
WEB: www.firstclasslimos.net
SIC: 4119 Limousine rental, with driver

(G-5534)
FIRST FEDERAL CREDIT CONTROL
Also Called: Interntnal Spcial Adit Systems
24700 Chagrin Blvd # 205 (44122-5630)
PHONE..................216 360-2000
Norm Shafran, *President*
Brian Himmel, *Vice Pres*
Angel Shingary, *Vice Pres*
Ian Shafran, *Sales Executive*
Jill Joseph, *Manager*
EMP: 40
SQ FT: 6,300
SALES (est): 2.8MM **Privately Held**
SIC: 7322 Collection agency, except real estate

(G-5535)
FIRST FINCL TITLE AGCY OF OHIO
1500 W 3rd St Ste 400 (44113-1438)
PHONE..................216 664-1920
David Kreisman, *President*
EMP: 28
SALES (est): 1.1MM **Privately Held**
SIC: 6541 Title & trust companies

(G-5536)
FIRST INTERSTATE PROPERTIES
25333 Cedar Rd Ste 300 (44124-3763)
PHONE..................216 381-2900
Mitchell Schneider, *President*
John Grafton, *Manager*
Diane Kotowski, *Director*
Steve Pickett, *Director*
Heather Corrigan, *Admin Sec*
EMP: 40
SQ FT: 2,400
SALES (est): 5.5MM **Privately Held**
WEB: www.first-interstate.com
SIC: 6512 Shopping center, property operation only

(G-5537)
FIRST OHIO BANC & LENDING INC
6100 Rckside Woods Blvd N (44131-2366)
PHONE..................216 642-8900
Kirk Doskocil, *President*
EMP: 280
SALES (est): 32.8MM **Privately Held**
SIC: 6162 Mortgage bankers & correspondents

(G-5538)
FIRSTAT NURSING SERVICES
21825 Chagrin Blvd # 300 (44122-5359)
PHONE..................216 295-1500
David Skoglunb, *Owner*
EMP: 100
SALES (est): 2.6MM **Privately Held**
WEB: www.firstat.cc
SIC: 7361 7363 Nurses' registry; help supply services

(G-5539)
FIRSTENERGY NUCLEAR OPER CO
Also Called: Beta Lab & Technical Svcs
6670 Beta Dr (44143-2352)
PHONE..................440 604-9836
Pete Cena, *President*
EMP: 75 **Publicly Held**
SIC: 8731 8734 Commercial research laboratory; testing laboratories
HQ: Firstenergy Nuclear Operating Company
76 S Main St Bsmt
Akron OH 44308
800 646-0400

(G-5540)
FIT TECHNOLOGIES LLC
1375 Euclid Ave Ste 310 (44115-1808)
PHONE..................216 583-5000
Micki Tubbs, *CEO*
Michelle Tomallo, *President*
EMP: 48
SALES (est): 11.1MM **Privately Held**
WEB: www.schoolone.com
SIC: 7379

(G-5541)
FIVE SEASONS SPT CNTRY CLB INC
28105 Clemens Rd (44145-1100)
PHONE..................440 899-4555
Fax: 440 892-3376
EMP: 100 **Privately Held**
SIC: 7997 Membership Sport/Recreation Club
HQ: Five Seasons Sports Country Club, Inc.
100 E Rivercenter Blvd # 1100
Covington KY 41011

(G-5542)
FLACK STEEL LLC (PA)
Also Called: Flack Global Metals
425 W Lkeside Ave Ste 200 (44113)
PHONE..................216 456-0700
Jeremy Flack, *President*
Ben Bucci, *President*
Greg Underwood, *Exec VP*
John Lascola, *Vice Pres*
Brittany Damico, *Project Mgr*
▲ **EMP:** 25 EST: 2010
SALES (est): 103.7MM **Privately Held**
SIC: 5051 Steel

(G-5543)
FLASH SEATS LLC (PA)
1 Center Ct (44115-4001)
PHONE..................216 420-2000
Samuel Gerace, *President*
EMP: 28
SALES (est): 3.1MM **Privately Held**
SIC: 7999 Concession operator

(G-5544)
FLAVIK VILLAGE DEVELOPMENT
5620 Broadway Ave Rm 200 (44127-1754)
PHONE..................216 429-1182
Peter Gentile, *President*
William Woods, *Vice Pres*
Christine Smetna, *Treasurer*
Anthony Brancatelli, *Exec Dir*
Sr Ann Solma, *Admin Sec*
EMP: 30 EST: 1981
SQ FT: 4,500
SALES (est): 2MM **Privately Held**
WEB: www.slavicvillage.org
SIC: 8748 Urban planning & consulting services

(G-5545)
FLEXECO INCORPORATED
Also Called: Flex Spas Cleveland
2600 Hamilton Ave (44114-3756)
PHONE..................216 812-3304
Cleve Rudolph, *Branch Mgr*
EMP: 35
SALES (corp-wide): 5.1MM **Privately Held**
WEB: www.flexbaths.com
SIC: 7991 Health club; exercise facilities; spas
PA: Flexeco Incorporated
2600 Hamilton Ave
Cleveland OH 44114
216 812-3371

(G-5546)
FLEXNOVA INC
6100 Oak Tree Blvd (44131-2544)
PHONE..................216 288-6961
Steve Rossi, *President*
EMP: 30
SQ FT: 1,000
SALES (est): 2MM **Privately Held**
SIC: 7372 Prepackaged software

(G-5547)
FLIGHT OPTIONS LLC (HQ)
26180 Curtiss Wright Pkwy (44143-1453)
PHONE..................216 261-3500
Kenn Ricci, *CEO*
Ernest Royal, *General Mgr*
Gary Taylor, *Business Mgr*
Michael Scheerringa, *COO*
Jim P Miller, *Exec VP*
EMP: 240
SQ FT: 119,000
SALES (est): 49.3MM
SALES (corp-wide): 71.5MM **Privately Held**
WEB: www.flightoptions.com
SIC: 7359 Aircraft rental
PA: Directional Capital Llc
355 Richmond Rd
Richmond Heights OH 44143
216 261-3000

(G-5548)
FLIGHT SERVICES & SYSTEMS INC (PA)
5005 Rockside Rd Ste 940 (44131-6829)
PHONE..................216 328-0090
Robert Weitzel, *CEO*
Phil Armstrong, *Exec VP*
Sarah Collier, *Director*
Joe Fatula, *Director*
EMP: 94
SALES (est): 103.1MM **Privately Held**
SIC: 7389 Safety inspection service

(G-5549)
FLOW POLYMERS LLC
12819 Coit Rd (44108-1614)
PHONE..................216 249-4900
Mike Ivany, *President*
Martin Eble, *CFO*
EMP: 105
SALES (est): 59.8MM
SALES (corp-wide): 40.4MM **Privately Held**
WEB: www.flowpolymers.com
SIC: 5169 Chemicals & allied products
PA: Polymer Solutions Group Finance, Llc
100 Park Ave Fl 31
New York NY 10017
212 771-1717

(G-5550)
FNB CORPORATION
413 Northfield Rd (44146-2202)
PHONE..................440 439-2200
Robert Toth, *Branch Mgr*
EMP: 44
SALES (corp-wide): 1.4B **Publicly Held**
SIC: 6021 National commercial banks

PA: F.N.B. Corporation
1 N Shore Ctr 12 Fdral St
Pittsburgh PA 15212
800 555-5455

(G-5551)
FOR WOMEN LIKE ME INC
8800 Woodland Ave (44104-3221)
PHONE..................407 848-7339
Arline Burks, *CEO*
EMP: 42
SALES (corp-wide): 53MM **Privately Held**
SIC: 7812 Television film production
PA: For Women Like Me, Inc.
46 Shopping Center Ste 155
Chagrin Falls OH 44022
407 848-7339

(G-5552)
FOREST CITY COMMERCIAL MGT INC (DH)
50 Public Sq Ste 1200 (44113-2204)
PHONE..................216 621-6060
Samuel Miller, *Ch of Bd*
Albert Ratner, *Ch of Bd*
Charles Ratner, *President*
Mark Gerteis, *Vice Pres*
Linda Kane, *Vice Pres*
EMP: 250
SALES (est): 35.2MM
SALES (corp-wide): 80.4MM **Privately Held**
SIC: 6531 Real estate managers
HQ: Forest City Properties, Llc
127 Public Sq Ste 3100
Cleveland OH 44114
216 621-6060

(G-5553)
FOREST CITY ENTERPRISES LP (DH)
127 Public Sq Ste 3200 (44114-1229)
PHONE..................216 621-6060
David J Larue, *President*
James A Ratner, *Chairman*
Duane F Bishop Jr, *COO*
Charles D Obert, *Exec VP*
Brian J Ratner, *Exec VP*
▲ **EMP:** 350
SALES (est): 782.5MM
SALES (corp-wide): 80.4MM **Privately Held**
WEB: www.fceinc.com
SIC: 6512 6513 6552 Nonresidential building operators; commercial & industrial building operation; shopping center, property operation only; apartment building operators; subdividers & developers
HQ: Forest City Realty Trust, Inc.
127 Public Sq Ste 3100
Cleveland OH 44114
216 621-6060

(G-5554)
FOREST CITY ENTERPRISES LP
Also Called: Cascade Crossing
3454 Main St (44113)
PHONE..................216 416-3756
John Neely, *Manager*
EMP: 28
SALES (corp-wide): 80.4MM **Privately Held**
WEB: www.fceinc.com
SIC: 6512 Nonresidential building operators
HQ: Forest City Enterprises, L.P.
127 Public Sq Ste 3200
Cleveland OH 44114
216 621-6060

(G-5555)
FOREST CITY ENTERPRISES LP
Also Called: Independence Place II
9233 Independence Blvd # 114 (44130-4781)
PHONE..................440 888-8664
George Gorman, *Branch Mgr*
EMP: 28
SALES (corp-wide): 80.4MM **Privately Held**
SIC: 6512 Nonresidential building operators

HQ: Forest City Enterprises, L.P.
127 Public Sq Ste 3200
Cleveland OH 44114
216 621-6060

(G-5556)
FOREST CITY ENTERPRISES LP
Also Called: Parmatown South
6880 Ridge Rd (44129-5627)
PHONE..................................216 416-3780
EMP: 28
SQ FT: 3,998
SALES (corp-wide): 911.9MM **Privately Held**
SIC: 6512 Nonresidential Building Operator
HQ: Forest City Enterprises, L.P.
50 Public Sq Ste 1100
Cleveland OH 44114
216 621-6060

(G-5557)
FOREST CITY ENTERPRISES LP
Also Called: Aberdeen Business Park
50 Public Sq Ste 1050 (44113-2269)
PHONE..................................216 416-3766
Samuel Miller, *Manager*
EMP: 100
SALES (corp-wide): 80.4MM **Privately Held**
WEB: www.fceinc.com
SIC: 6512 Nonresidential building operators
HQ: Forest City Enterprises, L.P.
127 Public Sq Ste 3200
Cleveland OH 44114
216 621-6060

(G-5558)
FOREST CITY ENTERPRISES LP
127 Public Sq Ste 3100 (44114-1228)
PHONE..................................216 621-6060
Ron Ratner, *Manager*
EMP: 70
SALES (corp-wide): 80.4MM **Privately Held**
WEB: www.fceinc.com
SIC: 8742 Management consulting services
HQ: Forest City Enterprises, L.P.
127 Public Sq Ste 3200
Cleveland OH 44114
216 621-6060

(G-5559)
FOREST CITY PROPERTIES LLC (DH)
127 Public Sq Ste 3100 (44114-1228)
PHONE..................................216 621-6060
David La Rue, *CEO*
Charles Ratner, *Ch of Bd*
James Ratner, *Exec VP*
Ketan Patel, *Admin Sec*
EMP: 130
SALES (est): 66MM
SALES (corp-wide): 80.4MM **Privately Held**
SIC: 6512 6513 Shopping center, property operation only; commercial & industrial building operation; apartment hotel operation
HQ: Forest City Enterprises, L.P.
127 Public Sq Ste 3200
Cleveland OH 44114
216 621-6060

(G-5560)
FOREST CITY REALTY TRUST INC (HQ)
127 Public Sq Ste 3100 (44114-1228)
PHONE..................................216 621-6060
Ketan K Patel, *President*
Charles D Obert, *CFO*
EMP: 38
SALES: 911.9MM
SALES (corp-wide): 80.4MM **Privately Held**
SIC: 6798 Real estate investment trusts
PA: Antlia Holdings Llc
250 Vesey St Fl 15
New York NY 10281
212 417-7000

(G-5561)
FOREST CITY RESIDENTIAL DEV (DH)
1170 Trml Twr 50 Pub Sq 1170 Terminal Tower (44113)
PHONE..................................216 621-6060
Ronald A Ratner, *Ch of Bd*
Edward Pelavin, *Vice Pres*
Albert B Ratner, *Vice Pres*
Samuel H Miller, *Treasurer*
Thomas G Smith, *Admin Sec*
EMP: 50 **EST:** 1955
SALES (est): 14.1MM
SALES (corp-wide): 80.4MM **Privately Held**
SIC: 1522 1542 6163 Apartment building construction; condominium construction; specialized public building contractors; mortgage brokers arranging for loans, using money of others
HQ: Forest City Enterprises, L.P.
127 Public Sq Ste 3200
Cleveland OH 44114
216 621-6060

(G-5562)
FOREST CITY WASHINGTON LLC (DH)
127 Public Sq Ste 3200 (44114-1229)
PHONE..................................261 621-6060
David J Larue, *President*
Duane F Bishop, *Vice Pres*
Peter Calkins, *Vice Pres*
James W Finnerty, *Vice Pres*
Mark Gerteis, *Vice Pres*
EMP: 28
SALES (est): 10MM
SALES (corp-wide): 80.4MM **Privately Held**
SIC: 6552 Land subdividers & developers, commercial; land subdividers & developers, residential
HQ: Forest City Properties, Llc
127 Public Sq Ste 3100
Cleveland OH 44114
216 621-6060

(G-5563)
FOREST CY RESIDENTIAL MGT INC (DH)
50 Public Sq Ste 1200 (44113-2204)
PHONE..................................216 621-6060
Ron Ratner, *CEO*
Charles A Ratner, *CEO*
James J Prohaska, *Exec VP*
John D Brocklehurst, *Vice Pres*
Nancy McCann, *Vice Pres*
EMP: 120
SQ FT: 25,000
SALES (est): 49.6MM
SALES (corp-wide): 80.4MM **Privately Held**
SIC: 6531 6552 Real estate managers; subdividers & developers
HQ: Forest City Enterprises, L.P.
127 Public Sq Ste 3200
Cleveland OH 44114
216 621-6060

(G-5564)
FORT AUSTIN LTD PARTNERSHIP
Also Called: Westlake Village
28550 Westlake Village Dr (44145-7608)
PHONE..................................440 892-4200
Jeanne Barnard, *Director*
EMP: 240 **Privately Held**
SIC: 6513 8052 Retirement hotel operation; intermediate care facilities
PA: Fort Austin Limited Partnership
111 Westwood Pl Ste 200
Brentwood TN 37027

(G-5565)
FOSBEL INC (HQ)
Also Called: Cetek
6779 Engle Rd Ste A (44130-7926)
PHONE..................................216 362-3900
Derek Scott, *President*
Kathlene Stevens, *CFO*
◆ **EMP:** 120

SALES (est): 25.4MM
SALES (corp-wide): 24.3MM **Privately Held**
SIC: 7629 7692 Electrical repair shops; welding repair
PA: Fosbel Holding, Inc.
20600 Sheldon Rd
Cleveland OH 44142
216 362-3900

(G-5566)
FOSBEL HOLDING INC (PA)
20600 Sheldon Rd (44142-1319)
PHONE..................................216 362-3900
Derek Scott, *President*
Kathleen Stevens, *CFO*
EMP: 30
SALES (est): 24.3MM **Privately Held**
SIC: 7692 Investment holding companies, except banks

(G-5567)
FOSECO MANAGEMENT INC
20200 Sheldon Rd (44142-1315)
PHONE..................................440 826-4548
EMP: 300
SALES (est): 4.9MM **Privately Held**
SIC: 8741 Mgt Services

(G-5568)
FOX TELEVISION STATIONS INC
Also Called: Fox 8
5800 S Marginal Rd (44103-1040)
PHONE..................................216 431-8888
Mike Renda, *Branch Mgr*
Greg Easterly, *Manager*
EMP: 250
SALES (corp-wide): 89.8B **Publicly Held**
WEB: www.foxtv.com
SIC: 7812 4833 Motion picture production & distribution, television; television broadcasting stations
HQ: Fox Television Stations, Inc.
1999 S Bundy Dr
Los Angeles CA 90025
310 584-2000

(G-5569)
FPT CLEVELAND LLC (DH)
Also Called: Ferrous Processing and Trading
8550 Aetna Rd (44105-1607)
PHONE..................................216 441-3800
Andrew M Luntz, *President*
James Prokes, *Vice Pres*
Yale Levin,
▲ **EMP:** 115
SALES (est): 31.6MM
SALES (corp-wide): 1.8B **Privately Held**
SIC: 4953 5051 5093 3341 Recycling, waste materials; iron & steel (ferrous) products; ferrous metal scrap & waste; secondary nonferrous metals
HQ: Ferrous Processing And Trading Company
3400 E Lafayette St
Detroit MI 48207
313 567-9710

(G-5570)
FRAMECO INC
9005 Bank St (44125-3425)
PHONE..................................216 433-7080
Kevin Wyman, *President*
Jean Wyman, *President*
Reginald Wyman, *CFO*
Lynn Wyman, *Finance Mgr*
EMP: 35
SALES (est): 4.5MM **Privately Held**
SIC: 1791 Precast concrete structural framing or panels, placing of

(G-5571)
FRANCISCAN SISTERS OF CHICAGO
Also Called: Mount Alverna Home
6765 State Rd (44134-4581)
PHONE..................................440 843-7800
Patrick Walsh, *Manager*
Emily Keeran, *Director*
Marylou Fleck, *Hlthcr Dir*
Judy Sabo, *Exec Sec*
EMP: 250
SALES (corp-wide): 56.7MM **Privately Held**
SIC: 8051 Skilled nursing care facilities

PA: Franciscan Sisters Of Chicago
11500 Theresa Dr
Lemont IL 60439
708 647-6500

(G-5572)
FRANCK AND FRIC INCORPORATED
7919 Old Rockside Rd (44131-2300)
P.O. Box 31148 (44131-0148)
PHONE..................................216 524-4451
Donald R Skala Sr, *President*
Stacey Carson, *Assistant VP*
David R Skala, *Vice Pres*
Donald C Skala Jr, *Treasurer*
EMP: 51
SQ FT: 20,000
SALES (est): 7.2MM **Privately Held**
SIC: 1711 1761 3441 3444 Ventilation & duct work contractor; warm air heating & air conditioning contractor; sheet metalwork; fabricated structural metal; sheet metalwork

(G-5573)
FRANK NOVAK & SONS INC
Also Called: Flooring Specialties Div
23940 Miles Rd (44128-5425)
PHONE..................................216 475-2495
Gayle Pinchot, *President*
Nick Bukovecky, *Division Mgr*
Allen J Pinchot, *Vice Pres*
Brad Pinchot, *Vice Pres*
Mark Pinchot, *Vice Pres*
EMP: 100
SQ FT: 12,000
SALES (est): 12MM **Privately Held**
WEB: www.franknovak.com
SIC: 1721 1752 1742 Interior commercial painting contractor; exterior commercial painting contractor; wood floor installation & refinishing; acoustical & ceiling work

(G-5574)
FRANKLIN BLVD NURSING HM INC
Also Called: Franklin Plaza
3600 Franklin Blvd (44113-2831)
PHONE..................................216 651-1600
Bruce Daskal, *President*
David Farkas, *Vice Pres*
Larry Dancziger, *Treasurer*
Harold Schachter, *Admin Sec*
EMP: 220 **EST:** 1948
SQ FT: 26,000
SALES (est): 9.3MM **Privately Held**
WEB: www.hueyproductions.com
SIC: 8051 Extended care facility

(G-5575)
FRANTZ WARD LLP
200 Public Sq Ste 3020 (44114-1230)
PHONE..................................216 515-1660
Gina Gennaro, *President*
Carrie Grieco, *President*
Lisa Lindhurst, *President*
Michael J Frantz, *Managing Prtnr*
Keith A Ashmus, *Partner*
EMP: 115
SQ FT: 27,000
SALES (est): 21.2MM **Privately Held**
WEB: www.franzward.com
SIC: 8111 Specialized law offices, attorneys

(G-5576)
FREDERICKS WINE & DINE
22005 Emery Rd (44128-4609)
PHONE..................................216 581-5299
Frederick Parks, *Principal*
EMP: 43 **EST:** 2010
SALES (est): 1.2MM **Privately Held**
SIC: 5182 5812 Brandy & brandy spirits; caterers

(G-5577)
FREEDONIA PUBLISHING LLC
767 Beta Dr (44143-2379)
PHONE..................................440 684-9600
Jeffrey Weiss, *CEO*
Ellen Klepac, *Editor*
Jean Nadeau, *Editor*
Chris Staneluis, *Business Mgr*
Jennifer Tobin, *Human Res Mgr*
EMP: 100
SQ FT: 11,000

▲ = Import ▼=Export
◆ =Import/Export

SALES (est): 9.6MM
SALES (corp-wide): 33.6MM **Privately Held**
WEB: www.freedoniagroup.com
SIC: 8732 Market analysis or research
PA: Marketresearch.Com, Inc.
11200 Rockville Pike # 504
Rockville MD 20852
240 747-3000

(G-5578)
FRESENIUS MED CARE HLDINGS INC
14670 Snow Rd (44142-2461)
PHONE...................................216 267-1451
Lori Shelby, *Manager*
EMP: 30
SALES (corp-wide): 18.9B **Privately Held**
SIC: 8092 Kidney dialysis centers
HQ: Fresenius Medical Care Holdings, Inc.
920 Winter St
Waltham MA 02451

(G-5579)
FRIEDBERG MEYERS ROMAN
28601 Chagrin Blvd # 500 (44122-4556)
PHONE...................................216 831-0042
Anne L Meyers, *President*
Russell O'Rourke, *Partner*
Carolyn Blake, *Counsel*
Janice Isakoff, *Counsel*
Machelle Larkin, *Marketing Staff*
EMP: 41
SQ FT: 7,700
SALES: 6MM **Privately Held**
SIC: 8111 General practice attorney, lawyer

(G-5580)
FRIEDMAN DOMIANO SMITH CO LPA
55 Public Sq Ste 1055 (44113-1901)
PHONE...................................216 621-0070
Jeffrey Friedman, *President*
Joseph Domiano, *Treasurer*
David Smith, *Admin Sec*
EMP: 30
SQ FT: 12,500
SALES (est): 3.4MM **Privately Held**
SIC: 8111 General practice attorney, lawyer

(G-5581)
FRIEND TO FRIEND PROGRAM
4515 Superior Ave (44103-1215)
PHONE...................................216 861-1838
Stephen Messner, *Manager*
EMP: 33
SALES (est): 388.3K **Privately Held**
SIC: 8322 General counseling services

(G-5582)
FRIENDLY INN SETTLEMENT HOUSE
2386 Unwin Rd (44104-1099)
PHONE...................................216 431-7656
Richgina Jeff, *Exec Dir*
Richgina Jeff-Carter, *Director*
EMP: 39
SALES: 1.8MM **Privately Held**
SIC: 8322 Neighborhood center

(G-5583)
FRITO-LAY NORTH AMERICA INC
4580 Hinckley Indus Pkwy (44109-6010)
PHONE...................................216 491-4000
Chris Patterson, *Manager*
Michelle Dematteis, *Assistant*
EMP: 150
SQ FT: 65,936
SALES (corp-wide): 64.6B **Publicly Held**
WEB: www.fritolay.com
SIC: 5145 5149 Snack foods; groceries & related products
HQ: Frito-Lay North America, Inc.
7701 Legacy Dr
Plano TX 75024

(G-5584)
FX DIGITAL MEDIA INC (PA)
1600 E 23rs St Rs (44114)
PHONE...................................216 241-4040
John Gadd, *CEO*
Columbus Woodruff, *President*

Nora Lane, *Marketing Staff*
Nikki Woodruff, *Shareholder*
EMP: 35
SQ FT: 15,000
SALES (est): 4MM **Privately Held**
WEB: www.hotcards.com
SIC: 7336 2754 Commercial art & graphic design; color printing, gravure

(G-5585)
G & S METAL PRODUCTS CO INC
26840 Fargo Ave (44146-1339)
PHONE...................................216 831-2388
Mark Schwartz, *Branch Mgr*
EMP: 135
SQ FT: 145,964
SALES (corp-wide): 90.9MM **Privately Held**
WEB: www.gsmetal.com
SIC: 4225 General warehousing & storage
PA: G & S Metal Products Co., Inc.
3330 E 79th St
Cleveland OH 44127
216 441-0700

(G-5586)
G J GOUDREAU & CO (PA)
Also Called: Goudreau Management
9701 Brookpark Rd Ste 200 (44129-6824)
PHONE...................................216 351-5233
George J Goudreau Jr, *President*
EMP: 28
SQ FT: 12,500
SALES (est): 6.3MM **Privately Held**
SIC: 1522 1542 6531 7349 Apartment building construction; commercial & office building, new construction; real estate managers; building maintenance, except repairs

(G-5587)
G J GOUDREAU OPERATING CO
9701 Brookpark Rd Ste 200 (44129-6824)
PHONE...................................216 741-7524
G J Goudreau Jr, *Partner*
A G Homza, *CFO*
EMP: 30
SQ FT: 10,000
SALES (est): 1.4MM **Privately Held**
SIC: 6513 Apartment building operators

(G-5588)
G ROBERT TONEY & ASSOC INC (PA)
Also Called: National Liquidators
5401 N Marginal Rd (44114-3925)
PHONE...................................216 391-1900
Matthew J Amata, *President*
Shane Hunt, *Vice Pres*
Frank Kups, *Vice Pres*
Jane S Toney, *Vice Pres*
▼ EMP: 50
SQ FT: 6,500
SALES (est): 5.4MM **Privately Held**
WEB: www.nationalyachtsales.com
SIC: 7389 Repossession service; auctioneers, fee basis; yacht brokers

(G-5589)
GALAXY BALLOONS INCORPORATED
11750 Berea Rd Ste 3 (44111-1603)
P.O. Box 698, Lakewood (44107-0998)
PHONE...................................216 476-3360
Terry Brizz, *President*
Alex Kovarik, *Purch Mgr*
▲ EMP: 130
SQ FT: 50,000
SALES (est): 21.1MM **Privately Held**
WEB: www.galaxyballoon.com
SIC: 2752 7336 5092 5199 Commercial printing, offset; silk screen design; balloons, novelty; advertising specialties; signs & advertising specialties; sporting & athletic goods

(G-5590)
GALLAGHER BENEFIT SERVICES INC
1100 Superior Ave E # 1700 (44114-2521)
PHONE...................................216 623-2600
Mark Alder, *President*
EMP: 30

SALES (est): 5.8MM **Privately Held**
WEB: www.herbruckalder.com
SIC: 6411 Insurance information & consulting services

(G-5591)
GALLAGHER SHARP
1501 Euclid Ave Fl 7 (44115-2131)
PHONE...................................216 241-5310
Todd Haemmerle, *Partner*
Thomas E Dover, *Partner*
Robert H Eddy, *Partner*
Patrick Foy, *Partner*
Forrest A Norman, *Partner*
EMP: 110
SALES (est): 18.3MM **Privately Held**
SIC: 8111 General practice attorney, lawyer

(G-5592)
GARLAND/DBS INC
3800 E 91st St (44105-2103)
PHONE...................................216 641-7500
Dave Sokol, *President*
Melvin Chrostowski, *Vice Pres*
Richard Debacco, *Vice Pres*
Dan Healy, *Plant Mgr*
Chuck Ripepi, *CFO*
EMP: 250
SALES: 157.1MM
SALES (corp-wide): 378.6MM **Privately Held**
WEB: www.garlandco.com
SIC: 2952 6512 8712 Roofing materials; roofing felts, cements or coatings; coating compounds, tar; commercial & industrial building operation; architectural services
HQ: The Garland Company Inc
3800 E 91st St
Cleveland OH 44105
216 641-7500

(G-5593)
GASTRNTRLOGY ASSOC CLVLAND INC (PA)
3700 Park East Dr Ste 100 (44122-4339)
PHONE...................................216 593-7700
James Andrassy, *CEO*
Mario D Kamionkowski, *President*
Michael H Frankel, *Vice Pres*
Jack S Lissauer, *Treasurer*
Eric Shapiro, *Med Doctor*
EMP: 44
SQ FT: 1,500
SALES (est): 7.6MM **Privately Held**
SIC: 8011 Gastronomist

(G-5594)
GATEWAY ELECTRIC INCORPORATED
4450 Johnston Pkwy Ste A (44128-2956)
PHONE...................................216 518-5500
Rajinder Singh, *President*
Vernon Krieger, *Superintendent*
Satwant Singh, *Corp Secy*
Brenda Smith, *Controller*
Jane Mantz, *Manager*
EMP: 110
SQ FT: 5,000
SALES (est): 16.2MM **Privately Held**
SIC: 1731 General electrical contractor

(G-5595)
GATEWAY HEALTH CARE CENTER
3 Gateway (44119-2447)
PHONE...................................216 486-4949
Kathy Nemeth, *Nursing Dir*
Nancy Sugarman, *Administration*
EMP: 140
SQ FT: 42,177
SALES (est): 8.6MM **Privately Held**
SIC: 8051 8052 Skilled nursing care facilities; intermediate care facilities

(G-5596)
GATEWAY PRODUCTS RECYCLING INC (PA)
Also Called: Gateway Recycling
4223 E 49th St (44125-1001)
PHONE...................................216 341-8777
Tom Sustersic, *President*
Cindy Sustersic, *Treasurer*
EMP: 44
SQ FT: 24,000

SALES: 20MM **Privately Held**
WEB: www.gatewayrecycle.com
SIC: 4953 5084 Recycling, waste materials; recycling machinery & equipment

(G-5597)
GC NEIGHBORHOOD CTRS ASSOC INC
Also Called: Neighborhood Centers
1814 E 40th St Ste 4d (44103-3530)
PHONE...................................216 298-4440
Stanley Miller, *Exec Dir*
EMP: 247 EST: 1948
SALES: 1.4MM **Privately Held**
SIC: 8399 Neighborhood development group

(G-5598)
GCA SERVICES GROUP INC (HQ)
1350 Euclid Ave Ste 1500 (44115-1832)
PHONE...................................800 422-8760
Robert Norton, *President*
Eric Hudgens, *President*
Lamar Anderson, *General Mgr*
Lisa Mattes, *General Mgr*
Hector Aguilar, *Regional Mgr*
EMP: 60
SQ FT: 17,000
SALES (est): 1.2B
SALES (corp-wide): 6.4B **Publicly Held**
WEB: www.gcaservices.com
SIC: 7349 Janitorial service, contract basis
PA: Abm Industries Incorporated
1 Liberty Plz Fl 7
New York NY 10006
212 297-0200

(G-5599)
GCHA
1226 Huron Rd E (44115-1702)
PHONE...................................216 696-6900
Bill Ryan, *CEO*
EMP: 70
SALES: 2.1MM **Privately Held**
SIC: 8741 Hospital management

(G-5600)
GE REUTER STOKES
4710 Elizabeth Ln (44144-3244)
PHONE...................................216 749-6332
Al Lada, *Owner*
EMP: 100
SALES (est): 90.3K **Privately Held**
SIC: 8399 Social services

(G-5601)
GEARITY EARLY CHILD CARE CTR
Also Called: Stepping Stones Child Care
2323 Wrenford Rd (44118-3902)
PHONE...................................216 371-7356
Sherry Miller, *Principal*
EMP: 45
SALES (est): 868.6K **Privately Held**
SIC: 8351 Child day care services

(G-5602)
GENE PTACEK SON FIRE EQP INC (PA)
Also Called: G P S Fire Equipment
7310 Associate Ave (44144-1101)
PHONE...................................216 651-8300
Mary Jane Ptacek, *President*
Gene Ptacek Jr, *Vice Pres*
Sandy Kepich, *Accountant*
Wade Watts, *Sales Staff*
Brian Craft, *Manager*
EMP: 35
SQ FT: 15,000
SALES (est): 10.2MM **Privately Held**
WEB: www.gpsfire.com
SIC: 5099 5999 5063 1731 Fire extinguishers; alcoholic beverage making equipment & supplies; fire alarm systems; fire detection & burglar alarm systems specialization; fire alarm maintenance & monitoring

(G-5603)
GENERAL ELECTRIC COMPANY
4477 E 49th St (44125-1097)
PHONE...................................216 883-1000
Donald Mysliwiec, *Enginr/R&D Mgr*
EMP: 100

SQ FT: 12,000
SALES (corp-wide): 121.6B **Publicly Held**
SIC: 7629 3621 3613 3612 Electrical repair shops; motors & generators; switchgear & switchboard apparatus; transformers, except electric; power transmission equipment; pumps & pumping equipment
PA: General Electric Company
　41 Farnsworth St
　Boston MA 02210
　617 443-3000

(G-5604)
GENERAL PEST CONTROL COMPANY
3561 W 105th St (44111-3897)
PHONE...............................216 252-7140
John H Gedeon Jr, *President*
Ruth Gedeon, *Corp Secy*
EMP: 35 EST: 1949
SQ FT: 5,000
SALES (est): 2.7MM **Privately Held**
SIC: 7342 Pest control in structures

(G-5605)
GENOMONCOLOGY LLC
1375 E 9th St Ste 1120 (44114-1753)
PHONE...............................216 496-4216
Manuel J Glynias, *CEO*
Ian Maurer, *Vice Pres*
Baiju Parikh, *Vice Pres*
Victor Peroni, *CFO*
David Lasecki, *Ch Credit Ofcr*
EMP: 30
SALES (est): 2.7MM **Privately Held**
SIC: 7371 Computer software systems analysis & design, custom

(G-5606)
GIA USA INC
4701 Richmond Rd (44128-5949)
PHONE...............................216 831-8678
Gino Zavarrella Jr, *CEO*
Joseph Fabetese, *President*
Karen Miller, *Principal*
Lorri Parenti, *Exec VP*
EMP: 38
SALES (est): 2.8MM **Privately Held**
SIC: 5099 Crystal goods

(G-5607)
GIDEON
4122 Superior Ave (44103-1130)
PHONE...............................800 395-6014
Osmon Wright, *Principal*
EMP: 58
SALES (est): 619.4K **Privately Held**
SIC: 6531 Real estate agents & managers

(G-5608)
GILLMORE SECURITY SYSTEMS INC
Also Called: Honeywell Authorized Dealer
26165 Broadway Ave (44146-6512)
PHONE...............................440 232-1000
Alan H Gillmore III, *President*
EMP: 40
SQ FT: 6,000
SALES (est): 8.4MM **Privately Held**
SIC: 1731 7382 Fire detection & burglar alarm systems specialization; fire alarm maintenance & monitoring; burglar alarm maintenance & monitoring

(G-5609)
GIRL SCOUTS NORTH EAST OHIO
4019 Prospect Ave (44103-4317)
PHONE...............................216 481-1313
Kim Klima, *Branch Mgr*
EMP: 71 **Privately Held**
SIC: 8641 Girl Scout organization
PA: Girl Scouts Of North East Ohio
　1 Girl Scout Way
　Macedonia OH 44056

(G-5610)
GLIDDEN HOUSE ASSOCIATES LTD
Also Called: Glidden House Inn
1901 Ford Dr (44106-3923)
PHONE...............................216 231-8900
Joseph Shafran, *Managing Prtnr*

Thomas Farinacci, *General Mgr*
EMP: 30
SALES (est): 2.5MM **Privately Held**
WEB: www.gliddenhouse.com
SIC: 7011 Hotels

(G-5611)
GLORIA GADMACK DO
Also Called: Premier Physicians
17800 Shaker Blvd (44120-1748)
PHONE...............................216 363-2353
Gloria Gadmack, *Partner*
Mary Kalamasz, *Office Mgr*
Mark Berkowitz, *Med Doctor*
Bryan Loos, *Med Doctor*
Beth Rehor, *Manager*
EMP: 150 EST: 1991
SALES (est): 2.3MM **Privately Held**
SIC: 8071 Medical laboratories

(G-5612)
GMS MANAGEMENT CO INC (PA)
Also Called: Gms Realty
4645 Richmond Rd Ste 101 (44128-5917)
PHONE...............................216 766-6000
Susan Graines, *President*
Patty Stegh, *Admin Sec*
EMP: 45
SQ FT: 12,000
SALES (est): 3.6MM **Privately Held**
SIC: 6513 6512 Apartment building operators; commercial & industrial building operation

(G-5613)
GOLDBERG COMPANIES INC
Also Called: Clarkwood Granada Apartments
4440 Granada Blvd Apt 1 (44128-6018)
PHONE...............................216 475-2600
Melvin Tucker, *Manager*
EMP: 25
SALES (corp-wide): 19.2MM **Privately Held**
WEB: www.goldbergcompanies.com
SIC: 6512 6513 Commercial & industrial building operation; apartment building operators
PA: Goldberg Companies, Inc.
　25101 Chagrin Blvd # 300
　Beachwood OH 44122
　216 831-6100

(G-5614)
GOODRICH GNNETT NGHBORHOOD CTR
Also Called: Goodrich Gannett Headstart
1400 E 55th St (44103-1304)
PHONE...............................216 432-1717
Dave Gunning, *President*
Stuart Bryan, *Vice Pres*
William D Pattie, *Treasurer*
Allison Wallace, *Director*
Judith Varn, *Admin Sec*
EMP: 48
SALES (est): 1MM **Privately Held**
WEB: www.ggnc.org
SIC: 8322 7999 Family service agency; social service center; recreation services

(G-5615)
GOODWILL IDSTRS GRTR CLVLND L
12650 Rockside Rd (44125-4525)
PHONE...............................216 581-6320
EMP: 31
SALES (corp-wide): 27.6MM **Privately Held**
SIC: 8331 Vocational rehabilitation agency
PA: Goodwill Industries Of Greater Cleveland And East Central Ohio, Inc.
　408 9th St Sw
　Canton OH 44707
　330 454-9461

(G-5616)
GORDON FOOD SERVICE INC
Also Called: G F S Marketplace
7575 Granger Rd (44125-4818)
PHONE...............................216 573-4900
Zscoot Schnieter, *Manager*
EMP: 50

SALES (corp-wide): 13B **Privately Held**
WEB: www.gfs.com
SIC: 5149 5142 Groceries & related products; packaged frozen goods
PA: Gordon Food Service, Inc.
　1300 Gezon Pkwy Sw
　Wyoming MI 49509
　888 437-3663

(G-5617)
GORJANC COMFORT SERVICES INC
Also Called: Gorjanc Mechanical
42 Alpha Park (44143-2208)
PHONE...............................440 449-4411
John Gorjanc, *President*
Phillip Gorjanc, *Vice Pres*
Gregory Gorjanc, *Treasurer*
Paul Hamilton, *Controller*
Phil Gorjanc, *Marketing Mgr*
EMP: 34
SQ FT: 3,400
SALES (est): 5.2MM **Privately Held**
SIC: 1711 1731 Warm air heating & air conditioning contractor; general electrical contractor

(G-5618)
GOVERNORS VILLAGE LLC
Also Called: Governor's Village Assisted Li
280 N Cmmons Blvd Apt 101 (44143)
PHONE...............................440 449-8788
Christopher Randall, *Mng Member*
Michelle Gorman, *Exec Dir*
Lloyd R Chapman,
Charles E Randall,
EMP: 45
SQ FT: 33,800
SALES (est): 2.3MM **Privately Held**
SIC: 8051 Extended care facility

(G-5619)
GRACE HOSPICE LLC
Also Called: Grace Hospice of Middleburg
16600 W Sprague Rd Ste 35 (44130-6318)
PHONE...............................440 826-0350
Michael E Smith, *CEO*
EMP: 140 **Privately Held**
SIC: 8361 Geriatric residential care
PA: Grace Hospice, Llc
　500 Kirts Blvd Ste 250
　Troy MI 48084

(G-5620)
GRACE HOSPITAL
18101 Lorain Ave (44111-5612)
PHONE...............................216 476-2704
David Pelini, *Principal*
Mary Chentnik, *VP Human Res*
EMP: 60
SALES (corp-wide): 17.4MM **Privately Held**
SIC: 8062 General medical & surgical hospitals
PA: Grace Hospital
　2307 W 14th St
　Cleveland OH 44113
　216 687-1500

(G-5621)
GRAFFITI INC
3200 Carnegie Ave (44115-2635)
PHONE...............................216 881-5550
Russ Beller, *Controller*
EMP: 70
SALES (est): 2.2MM **Privately Held**
SIC: 7336 Commercial art & graphic design

(G-5622)
GRANGE MUTUAL CASUALTY COMPANY
Also Called: Grange Mutual Casualty Co 601
7271 Engle Rd Ste 400 (44130-8404)
P.O. Box 182087, Columbus (43218-2087)
PHONE...............................614 337-4400
Brian Crisp, *Manager*
EMP: 30
SALES (corp-wide): 992.5MM **Privately Held**
SIC: 6411 Insurance claim processing, except medical
PA: Grange Mutual Casualty Company
　671 S High St
　Columbus OH 43206
　614 445-2900

(G-5623)
GRANT THORNTON LLP
1375 E 9th St Ste 1500 (44114-1718)
PHONE...............................216 771-1400
Dan Zittnan, *Manager*
Gino Scipione, *Manager*
EMP: 110
SALES (corp-wide): 65MM **Privately Held**
WEB: www.gt.com
SIC: 8721 Certified public accountant
HQ: Grant Thornton Llp
　171 N Clark St Ste 200
　Chicago IL 60601
　312 856-0200

(G-5624)
GRAY MEDIA GROUP INC
Also Called: W O I O
1717 E 12th St (44114-3246)
PHONE...............................216 367-7300
Bill Applegate, *Vice Pres*
Jim Stunek, *Engineer*
EMP: 225
SALES (corp-wide): 1B **Publicly Held**
WEB: www.kwwl.com
SIC: 4833 Television broadcasting stations
HQ: Gray Media Group, Inc.
　201 Monroe St Fl 20
　Montgomery AL 36104

(G-5625)
GRAYBAR ELECTRIC COMPANY INC
6161 Halle Dr (44125-4613)
PHONE...............................216 573-6144
Gerard Musbach, *Sales/Mktg Mgr*
EMP: 45
SQ FT: 41,949
SALES (corp-wide): 7.2B **Privately Held**
WEB: www.graybar.com
SIC: 5063 5065 Electrical supplies; electronic parts & equipment
PA: Graybar Electric Company, Inc.
　34 N Meramec Ave
　Saint Louis MO 63105
　314 573-9200

(G-5626)
GREAT LAKES CONTRACTORS LLC
1234 West Blvd (44102-1602)
PHONE...............................216 631-7777
Arunas Nasvytis, *Mng Member*
EMP: 25
SALES: 555K **Privately Held**
SIC: 1542 1522 Commercial & office building contractors; residential construction

(G-5627)
GREAT LAKES GROUP
Also Called: Great Lakes Towing
4500 Division Ave (44102-2228)
PHONE...............................216 621-4854
Sheldon Guren, *Ch of Bd*
Ronald Rasmus, *President*
George Sogar, *Vice Pres*
EMP: 120
SQ FT: 6,000
SALES (est): 21.3MM **Privately Held**
SIC: 3731 4492 Shipbuilding & repairing; marine towing services

(G-5628)
GREAT LAKES MANAGEMENT INC (PA)
2700 E 40th St Ste 1 (44115-3501)
PHONE...............................216 883-6500
Margaret Ruebensaal, *President*
Charles M Ruebensaal Jr, *Treasurer*
David Biasio, *Admin Sec*
David Di Biasio, *Admin Sec*
EMP: 35
SALES (est): 2.3MM **Privately Held**
SIC: 6512 3822 Nonresidential building operators; switches, thermostatic

(G-5629)
GREAT LAKES MUSEUM OF SCIENCE
Also Called: Great Lakes Science Center
601 Erieside Ave (44114-1021)
PHONE...............................216 694-2000
Kirsten Ellenbogen, *CEO*
Kirsten M Ellenbogen, *CEO*

Linda Abrams-Silver, *President*
Richard Coyne, *President*
Gary Oatey, *Chairman*
▲ **EMP:** 145
SALES: 7.4MM **Privately Held**
WEB: www.glsc.org
SIC: 8412 Museum

(G-5630)
GREAT LAKES PUBLISHING COMPANY (PA)
Also Called: Cleveland Magazine
1422 Euclid Ave Ste 730 (44115-2001)
PHONE................................216 771-2833
Lute Harmon Jr, *Ch of Bd*
Steve Gleydura, *Vice Pres*
Susan Harmon, *Vice Pres*
George Sedlak, *CFO*
Sarah Desmond, *Director*
EMP: 75
SQ FT: 19,000
SALES (est): 9.2MM **Privately Held**
WEB: www.clevelandmagazine.com
SIC: 2721 7374 Magazines: publishing only, not printed on site; computer graphics service

(G-5631)
GREAT LAKES WATER TREATMENT
4949 Galaxy Pkwy Ste Q (44128-5959)
PHONE................................216 464-8292
Abe Bahhage, *President*
Jim McGreal, *Vice Pres*
EMP: 32
SQ FT: 3,000
SALES (est): 3.6MM **Privately Held**
SIC: 5999 5084 Water purification equipment; industrial machinery & equipment

(G-5632)
GREAT SOUTHERN VIDEO INC
Also Called: Great Expectations
4511 Rockside Rd Ste 210 (44131-2157)
PHONE................................216 642-8855
John Mereggi, *Owner*
EMP: 30 **Privately Held**
WEB: www.greatexpectationsdfw.com
SIC: 7299 Dating service
PA: Great Southern Video, Inc
14180 Dallas Pkwy Ste 100
Dallas TX 75254

(G-5633)
GREATER CLEVELAND
Also Called: E & C Div
1240 W 6th St Fl 6 (44113-1302)
PHONE................................216 566-5107
Sheryl King Benford, *Manager*
EMP: 2200
SQ FT: 17,000
SALES (corp-wide): 48.4MM **Privately Held**
WEB: www.riderta.com
SIC: 4111 Passenger rail transportation; local railway passenger operation
PA: Greater Cleveland Regional Transit Authority
1240 W 6th St
Cleveland OH 44113
216 566-5100

(G-5634)
GREATER CLEVELAND AUTO AUCTION
5801 Engle Rd (44142-1598)
PHONE................................216 433-7777
Patrick A Morsillo, *President*
Thomas Coury, *Corp Secy*
Michael Morsillo, *Vice Pres*
EMP: 55
SQ FT: 22,500
SALES (est): 6.6MM **Privately Held**
WEB: www.gcaacars.com
SIC: 5012 Automobile auction

(G-5635)
GREATER CLEVELAND FOOD BNK INC
15500 S Waterloo Rd (44110-3800)
PHONE................................216 738-2265
Kristin Warzocha, *President*
Anthony Rego, *Vice Chairman*
John Corlett, *Trustee*
John Cymanski, *Trustee*

Anita Gray, *Trustee*
EMP: 130
SQ FT: 125,000
SALES: 92.2MM **Privately Held**
WEB: www.clevelandfoodbank.com
SIC: 8399 8322 Community development groups; individual & family services

(G-5636)
GREATER CLEVELAND HOSP ASSN
1226 Huron Rd E Ste 2 (44115-1702)
PHONE................................216 696-6900
C Wayne Rice, *President*
Richard Fox, *CFO*
EMP: 83
SQ FT: 30,000
SALES (est): 941.1K **Privately Held**
SIC: 8621 Medical field-related associations

(G-5637)
GREATER CLEVELAND PARTNERSHIP (PA)
Also Called: CLEVELAND DEVELOPMENT FOUNDATI
1240 Huron Rd E Ste 300 (44115-1722)
PHONE................................216 621-3300
William Christopher, *Ch of Bd*
Joe Roman, *President*
John Kropf, *Principal*
Vette Ittu, *Exec VP*
Carol Caruso, *Senior VP*
EMP: 95
SQ FT: 45,000
SALES: 46.5K **Privately Held**
WEB: www.cose.com
SIC: 8611 Chamber of Commerce

(G-5638)
GREATER CLEVELAND REGIONAL
1240 W 6th St (44113-1302)
PHONE................................216 575-3932
Joseph A Calabrese, *Branch Mgr*
EMP: 88
SALES (corp-wide): 48.4MM **Privately Held**
SIC: 4111 Local & suburban transit
PA: Greater Cleveland Regional Transit Authority
1240 W 6th St
Cleveland OH 44113
216 566-5100

(G-5639)
GREATER CLEVELAND REGIONAL
Paratransit
4601 Euclid Ave (44103-3737)
PHONE................................216 781-1110
Sylvester Williams, *Principal*
EMP: 110
SALES (corp-wide): 48.4MM **Privately Held**
WEB: www.riderta.com
SIC: 4119 Local passenger transportation
PA: Greater Cleveland Regional Transit Authority
1240 W 6th St
Cleveland OH 44113
216 566-5100

(G-5640)
GREATER CLVLAND HALTHCARE ASSN
Also Called: GCHA
1226 Huron Rd E (44115-1702)
PHONE................................216 696-6900
William Ryan, *President*
Mark Melvin, *CFO*
EMP: 99
SALES: 2.4MM **Privately Held**
SIC: 8611 8099 Trade associations; health & allied services

(G-5641)
GREENBRIER SENIOR LIVING CMNTY
Also Called: Greenbriar Retirement Center
6455 Pearl Rd (44130-2984)
PHONE................................440 888-5900
Terri Plush, *Manager*
EMP: 240

SALES (est): 2.1MM
SALES (corp-wide): 5MM **Privately Held**
SIC: 8051 8069 Convalescent home with continuous nursing care; specialty hospitals, except psychiatric
PA: Senior Greenbrier Living Community
2 Berea Cmns Ste 1
Berea OH 44017
440 888-5900

(G-5642)
GREENBRIER SENIOR LIVING CMNTY
Also Called: Greenbrier Retirement Cmnty
6457 Pearl Rd (44130-2936)
PHONE................................440 888-0400
Debbie Smith, *Manager*
EMP: 68
SALES (corp-wide): 5MM **Privately Held**
SIC: 8361 8051 Residential care; skilled nursing care facilities
PA: Senior Greenbrier Living Community
2 Berea Cmns Ste 1
Berea OH 44017
440 888-5900

(G-5643)
GREENS OF LYNDHURST THE INC
Also Called: The Fountain On The Greens
1555 Brainard Rd Apt 305 (44124-6201)
PHONE................................440 460-1000
Liz Gay, *Administration*
EMP: 120
SALES (est): 3.5MM **Privately Held**
WEB: www.greenscommunities.com
SIC: 8051 8052 Skilled nursing care facilities; intermediate care facilities

(G-5644)
GROOVERYDE CLE
1120 Chester Ave (44114-3546)
PHONE................................323 595-1701
Zosimo Maximo,
EMP: 25
SALES (est): 97K **Privately Held**
SIC: 7991 Physical fitness facilities

(G-5645)
GROUPCLE LLC
12500 Berea Rd (44111-1618)
PHONE................................216 251-9641
Dave Ticchione, *Managing Dir*
David Ticchione, *Mng Member*
Andrew Bacher,
David Gabe,
EMP: 30
SQ FT: 90,000
SALES (est): 6MM **Privately Held**
SIC: 7319 Display advertising service

(G-5646)
GUND SPORTS MARKETING LLC
100 Gateway Plz (44115-4002)
PHONE................................216 420-2000
Gordon Gund, *Ch of Bd*
EMP: 25
SALES (est): 2.4MM **Privately Held**
SIC: 8742 Marketing consulting services

(G-5647)
GUNTON CORPORATION (PA)
Also Called: Pella Window & Door
26150 Richmond Rd (44146-1438)
PHONE................................216 831-2420
Mark Mead, *President*
Robert J Gunton, *Co-COB*
William E Gunton, *Co-COB*
Joe Bobnar, *VP Opers*
Reggie Stacy, *Treasurer*
EMP: 180
SQ FT: 90,000
SALES (est): 81.2MM **Privately Held**
WEB: www.guntonpella.com
SIC: 5031 Windows; doors; metal doors, sash & trim

(G-5648)
GUST GALLUCCI CO
Also Called: Imperial Foods
6610 Euclid Ave (44103-3912)
PHONE................................216 881-0045
Ray Gallucci Jr, *President*
Joan A Skok, *Corp Secy*

Kevin Balaban, *Vice Pres*
Carol Kotora, *Vice Pres*
Marc Kotora, *Vice Pres*
▲ **EMP:** 25
SQ FT: 42,000
SALES (est): 4.1MM **Privately Held**
WEB: www.gustgallucci.com
SIC: 5149 5499 Groceries & related products; gourmet food stores

(G-5649)
GYMNASTIC WORLD INC
6630 Harris Rd (44147-2960)
PHONE................................440 526-2970
Ron Ganim, *President*
Greg Ganim, *Vice Pres*
Joan Ganim, *Admin Sec*
EMP: 36 **EST:** 1976
SALES (est): 1.8MM **Privately Held**
WEB: www.gymworldohio.com
SIC: 7999 5699 5136 5137 Gymnastic instruction, non-membership; sports apparel; sportswear, men's & boys'; sportswear, women's & children's

(G-5650)
H A M LANDSCAPING INC
4667 Northfield Rd (44128-4508)
PHONE................................216 663-6666
Herrick Mann, *President*
Lisa Mann, *Vice Pres*
Joseph Wise, *Vice Pres*
EMP: 25 **EST:** 1971
SQ FT: 5,000
SALES: 1MM **Privately Held**
WEB: www.hamlandscaping.com
SIC: 0781 4959 0782 Landscape services; snowplowing; lawn & garden services

(G-5651)
H LEFF ELECTRIC COMPANY (PA)
4700 Spring Rd (44131-1027)
PHONE................................216 325-0941
Jim Bracken, *CEO*
Bruce E Leff, *President*
Sanford Leff Jr, *Exec VP*
David Comodeca, *Purch Agent*
John Stephan, *Finance Mgr*
EMP: 107
SQ FT: 60,000
SALES (est): 107.5MM **Privately Held**
WEB: www.leffelectric.com
SIC: 5063 Electrical supplies

(G-5652)
H T V INDUSTRIES INC
30195 Chagrin Blvd 310n (44124-5763)
PHONE................................216 514-0060
Daniel Harrington, *Ch of Bd*
Pat Johnson, *Controller*
EMP: 100
SALES (est): 7.3MM **Privately Held**
SIC: 8742 Management consulting services

(G-5653)
H&R BLOCK INC
Also Called: H & R Block
2068 W 25th St (44113-4114)
PHONE................................216 861-1185
Marion Gross, *Manager*
EMP: 25
SALES (corp-wide): 3.1B **Publicly Held**
WEB: www.hrblock.com
SIC: 7291 Tax return preparation services
PA: H&R Block, Inc.
1 H&R Block Way
Kansas City MO 64105
816 854-3000

(G-5654)
HABITAT FOR HUMANITY
2110 W 110th St (44102-3510)
PHONE................................216 429-1299
Jeffrey Bowen, *Principal*
EMP: 34
SALES (est): 2.6MM **Privately Held**
SIC: 8399 Community development groups

(G-5655)
HAHMOOESER & PARKS
200 Public Sq Ste 2000 (44114-2316)
PHONE................................330 864-5550
Mark Watkins, *Partner*

Erik Gum, *Partner*
Scott Oldham, *Partner*
EMP: 30
SQ FT: 7,600
SALES (est): 1.8MM **Privately Held**
SIC: 8111 General practice law office

(G-5656)
HAHN LOESER & PARKS LLP (PA)
200 Public Sq Ste 2800 (44114-2303)
PHONE...............................216 621-0150
Stanley Gorom, *Partner*
Dale Hunt, *Partner*
Stephen J Knerly Jr, *Partner*
N Herschel Koblenz, *Partner*
Sean Medina, *Partner*
EMP: 172
SQ FT: 83,400
SALES (est): 37.1MM **Privately Held**
WEB: www.hahnloeser.com
SIC: 8111 General practice law office

(G-5657)
HAJOCA CORPORATION
Also Called: Welker-Mckee Div
6606 Granger Rd (44131-1429)
PHONE...............................216 447-0050
Gene Strine, *Manager*
EMP: 50
SALES (corp-wide): 2.4B **Privately Held**
WEB: www.hajoca.com
SIC: 5074 Plumbing fittings & supplies
PA: Hajoca Corporation
2001 Joshua Rd
Lafayette Hill PA 19444
610 649-1430

(G-5658)
HALLMARK MANAGEMENT ASSOCIATES (PA)
1821 Noble Rd Ofc C (44112-1670)
PHONE...............................216 681-0080
Leon R Hogg, *President*
Wilmer Cooks, *Vice Pres*
Roger Saffold, *Treasurer*
EMP: 39
SQ FT: 4,500
SALES (est): 3.4MM **Privately Held**
SIC: 6531 Real estate managers

(G-5659)
HANNA COMMERCIAL LLC
Also Called: Hanna Commercial Real Estate
1350 Euclid Ave Ste 700 (44115-1889)
PHONE...............................216 861-7200
Mac Biggar Jr, *President*
Mark Abood, *Managing Dir*
David Wagner, *Managing Dir*
Michael Clegg, *Vice Pres*
Joseph Ditchman, *Vice Pres*
EMP: 65 EST: 2016
SALES (est): 2.7MM **Privately Held**
SIC: 8742 Real estate consultant

(G-5660)
HANS TRUCK AND TRLR REPR INC
Also Called: Hans' Freightliner Cleveland
14520 Broadway Ave (44125-1960)
PHONE...............................216 581-0046
Hans Dabernig, *President*
Ilse Dabernig, *Treasurer*
Chris Tench, *Admin Sec*
EMP: 45
SQ FT: 20,000
SALES (est): 8.6MM **Privately Held**
WEB: www.hansfreightliner.com
SIC: 7539 4173 7699 5511 Trailer repair; maintenance facilities, buses; construction equipment repair; trucks, tractors & trailers: new & used

(G-5661)
HARLEY-DVIDSON DLR SYSTEMS INC
9885 Rockside Rd Ste 100 (44125-6200)
PHONE...............................216 573-1393
Dennis Stapleton, *President*
Robert Maurer, *Vice Pres*
EMP: 78
SQ FT: 20,000

SALES (est): 12.1MM
SALES (corp-wide): 5.7B **Publicly Held**
WEB: www.harley-davidson.com
SIC: 5734 7371 Computer & software stores; custom computer programming services
PA: Harley-Davidson, Inc.
3700 W Juneau Ave
Milwaukee WI 53208
414 342-4680

(G-5662)
HARRINGTON ELECTRIC COMPANY
3800 Perkins Ave (44114-4635)
PHONE...............................216 361-5101
Thomas A Morgan, *President*
Jerry Yeamans, *President*
James B Morgan Jr, *Exec VP*
Gary Laidman, *VP Opers*
Nader Ghassemi, *Project Mgr*
EMP: 70
SQ FT: 18,500
SALES (est): 14.3MM **Privately Held**
WEB: www.harringtonelectric.com
SIC: 1731 General electrical contractor; communications specialization

(G-5663)
HARRY ROCK & COMPANY
8550 Aetna Rd (44105-1607)
PHONE...............................330 644-3748
James Eubank, *General Mgr*
EMP: 30
SQ FT: 5,000
SALES (est): 3.4MM **Privately Held**
SIC: 5093 Ferrous metal scrap & waste; nonferrous metals scrap

(G-5664)
HARTFORD FIRE INSURANCE CO
7100 E Pleasant Valley Rd # 200 (44131-5544)
PHONE...............................216 447-1000
Fred Hammond, *Branch Mgr*
John Rodman, *Manager*
Barbara Gaglione, *Agent*
Baker E Niles,
EMP: 135 **Publicly Held**
WEB: www.hartfordinvestmentscanada.com
SIC: 6411 Insurance agents
HQ: Hartford Fire Insurance Company
1 Hartford Plz
Hartford CT 06115
860 547-5000

(G-5665)
HARVEST FACILITY HOLDINGS LP
Also Called: Pearl Crossing
19205 Pearl Rd Ofc (44136-6902)
PHONE...............................440 268-9555
Robert Kobak, *Branch Mgr*
EMP: 30 **Privately Held**
WEB: www.holidaytouch.com
SIC: 6513 Retirement hotel operation
HQ: Harvest Facility Holdings Lp
5885 Meadows Rd Ste 500
Lake Oswego OR 97035
503 370-7070

(G-5666)
HATTENBACH COMPANY (PA)
5309 Hamilton Ave (44114-3909)
PHONE...............................216 881-5200
Cathy Hattenbach, *President*
Joseph G Berick, *Principal*
Dennis Bruckman, *Vice Pres*
John Heinert, *CFO*
EMP: 65 EST: 1944
SQ FT: 50,000
SALES (est): 15MM **Privately Held**
WEB: www.hattenbach.com
SIC: 1711 5078 2541 2434 Refrigeration contractor; commercial refrigeration equipment; cabinets, except refrigerated: show, display, etc.: wood; wood kitchen cabinets

(G-5667)
HAVEN FINANCIAL ENTERPRISE
675 Alpha Dr Ste E (44143-2139)
PHONE...............................800 265-2401

EMP: 27
SALES (est): 176.5K **Privately Held**
SIC: 6211 7389 Security Broker/Dealer Business Services At Non-Commercial Site

(G-5668)
HAWKINS & CO LPA LTD
Also Called: Edward C Hawkins & Co Limited
1267 W 9th St Ste 500 (44113-1064)
PHONE...............................216 861-1365
Ann Hawkins, *President*
EMP: 25 EST: 1976
SALES (est): 2.7MM **Privately Held**
SIC: 8111 General practice attorney, lawyer

(G-5669)
HCA HOLDINGS INC
Also Called: The Surgery Center
19250 Bagley Rd Ste 100 (44130-3348)
PHONE...............................440 826-3240
Barbara Paris Draves, *Manager*
EMP: 82
SQ FT: 13,000 **Publicly Held**
SIC: 8093 Specialty outpatient clinics
HQ: Hca Inc.
1 Park Plz
Nashville TN 37203
615 344-9551

(G-5670)
HCR MANORCARE MED SVCS FLA LLC
Also Called: Manorcare Hlth Svcs Rcky River
4102 Rocky River Dr (44135-1139)
PHONE...............................216 251-3300
Brian Karstetter, *Administration*
EMP: 220
SQ FT: 22,000
SALES (corp-wide): 2.4B **Publicly Held**
WEB: www.manorcare.com
SIC: 8051 Convalescent home with continuous nursing care
HQ: Hcr Manorcare Medical Services Of Florida, Llc
333 N Summit St Ste 100
Toledo OH 43604
419 252-5500

(G-5671)
HCR MANORCARE MED SVCS FLA LLC
Also Called: Manorcare Hlth Svcs-Mayfield H
6757 Mayfield Rd (44124-2236)
PHONE...............................440 473-0090
Jennifer Mann, *Administration*
EMP: 100
SQ FT: 27,730
SALES (corp-wide): 2.4B **Publicly Held**
WEB: www.manorcare.com
SIC: 8051 Convalescent home with continuous nursing care
HQ: Hcr Manorcare Medical Services Of Florida, Llc
333 N Summit St Ste 100
Toledo OH 43604
419 252-5500

(G-5672)
HCR MANORCARE MED SVCS FLA LLC
Also Called: Manorcare Hlth Svcs Lakeshore
16101 Euclid Beach Blvd (44110-1175)
PHONE...............................216 486-2300
Melissa Campbell, *Branch Mgr*
EMP: 135
SQ FT: 30,000
SALES (corp-wide): 2.4B **Publicly Held**
WEB: www.manorcare.com
SIC: 8051 Convalescent home with continuous nursing care
HQ: Hcr Manorcare Medical Services Of Florida, Llc
333 N Summit St Ste 100
Toledo OH 43604
419 252-5500

(G-5673)
HEALTHCARE WALTON GROUP LLC
Also Called: Walton Manor Health Care Ctr
19859 Alexander Rd (44146-5345)
PHONE...............................440 439-4433
George S Repchick, *President*

William I Weisberg, *Vice Pres*
Sarah Depompei, *Contract Law*
EMP: 235
SALES (est): 53K
SALES (corp-wide): 157.7MM **Privately Held**
SIC: 8051 Skilled nursing care facilities
PA: Saber Healthcare Group, L.L.C.
26691 Richmond Rd Frnt
Bedford OH 44146
216 292-5706

(G-5674)
HEALTHCOMP INC
Also Called: Champs
1226 Huron Rd E Ste 2 (44115-1702)
PHONE...............................216 696-6900
Bill Ryan, *President*
Philip C Mazanec, *COO*
EMP: 55
SALES (est): 5.2MM **Privately Held**
SIC: 8742 Hospital & health services consultant

(G-5675)
HEALTHSPAN INTEGRATED CARE
Also Called: Kaiser Foundation Health Plan
12301 Snow Rd (44130-1002)
PHONE...............................216 362-2000
Amy Kramer, *Pharmacist*
Carol Dsouza, *Med Doctor*
Geoffrey D Moebius, *Manager*
Frederick G Schmieder, *Podiatrist*
Nabil Chehade, *Urology*
EMP: 60
SALES (corp-wide): 4.7B **Privately Held**
SIC: 6324 Hospital & medical service plans
HQ: Healthspan Integrated Care
1001 Lakeside Ave E # 1200
Cleveland OH 44114
216 621-5600

(G-5676)
HEALTHSPAN INTEGRATED CARE
Also Called: Kaiser Foundation Health Plan
3733 Park East Dr (44122-4338)
PHONE...............................216 524-7377
Dr Mark Binstock, *Director*
EMP: 45
SALES (corp-wide): 4.7B **Privately Held**
SIC: 6324 Hospital & medical service plans
HQ: Healthspan Integrated Care
1001 Lakeside Ave E # 1200
Cleveland OH 44114
216 621-5600

(G-5677)
HEALTHSPAN INTEGRATED CARE (HQ)
1001 Lakeside Ave E # 1200 (44114-1172)
P.O. Box 5316 (44101-0316)
PHONE...............................216 621-5600
Kenneth Page, *CEO*
George Halverson, *CEO*
Patricia D Kennedy-Scott, *President*
Thomas Revis, *CFO*
Denise Swanm, *Exec Sec*
EMP: 250
SALES: 435MM
SALES (corp-wide): 4.7B **Privately Held**
SIC: 6324 Hospital & medical service plans
PA: Mercy Health
1701 Mercy Health Pl
Cincinnati OH 45237
513 639-2800

(G-5678)
HEALTHSPAN INTEGRATED CARE
Also Called: Kaiser Foundation Health Plan
17406 Royalton Rd (44136-5151)
PHONE...............................440 572-1000
EMP: 32
SALES (corp-wide): 4.7B **Privately Held**
SIC: 6324 Hospital/Medical Service Plan
HQ: Healthspan Integrated Care
1001 Lakeside Ave E # 1200
Cleveland OH 44114
216 621-5600

(G-5679)
HEARTHSTONE UTILITIES INC (HQ)
Also Called: Gas Natural Inc.
1375 E 9th St Ste 3100 (44114-1797)
PHONE....................................440 974-3770
Gregory J Osborne, *President*
Kevin J Degenstein, *COO*
James Sprague, *CFO*
Christopher J Hubbert, *Admin Sec*
EMP: 65 EST: 1909
SQ FT: 5,300
SALES: 99.4MM **Privately Held**
WEB: www.ewst.com
SIC: 4924 4911 5172 5984 Natural gas
distribution; distribution, electric power;
gases, liquefied petroleum (propane);
propane gas, bottled
PA: Fr Bison Holdings, Inc.
1375 E 9th St Ste 3100
Cleveland OH 44114
440 974-3770

(G-5680)
HEERY INTERNATIONAL INC
5445 West Blvd (44137-2656)
PHONE....................................216 510-4701
EMP: 31
SALES (corp-wide): 15B **Privately Held**
SIC: 8712 Architectural Services
HQ: Heery International, Inc.
999 Peachtree St Ne # 300
Atlanta GA 30309
404 881-9880

(G-5681)
HEIDTMAN STEEL PRODUCTS INC
4600 Heidtman Pkwy (44105-1023)
PHONE....................................216 641-6995
David Cooley, *Manager*
EMP: 99
SALES (corp-wide): 296.3MM **Privately Held**
WEB: www.heidtman.com
SIC: 5051 Steel
HQ: Heidtman Steel Products, Inc.
2401 Front St
Toledo OH 43605
419 691-4646

(G-5682)
HEIGHTS EMERGENCY FOOD CENTER
3663 Mayfield Rd (44121-1733)
PHONE....................................216 381-0707
Hazel Haffner, *Director*
EMP: 80
SALES: 81.4K **Privately Held**
SIC: 8699 5411 Food co-operative; grocery stores

(G-5683)
HELP FOUNDATION INC
Also Called: Nottingham Home
17702 Nottingham Rd (44119-2946)
PHONE....................................216 486-5258
Peggy Congdon, *Director*
EMP: 48
SALES (corp-wide): 8.3MM **Privately Held**
SIC: 8361 Group foster home
PA: Help Foundation, Inc
26900 Euclid Ave
Euclid OH 44132
216 432-4810

(G-5684)
HENRY CALL INC
308 Pines St Ste 100 (44135)
PHONE....................................216 433-5609
Clarence Sneed, *Manager*
EMP: 125 **Privately Held**
SIC: 8744 7371 8742 Base maintenance
(providing personnel on continuing basis);
computer software development; management consulting services
PA: Call Henry Inc
1425 Chaffee Dr Ste 4
Titusville FL 32780

(G-5685)
HENRY SCHEIN INC
30600 Aurora Rd Ste 110 (44139-2761)
PHONE....................................440 349-0891

Henry Schein, *President*
Wade Hinds, *Sales Staff*
Bob Lavigna, *Sales Staff*
EMP: 37
SALES (corp-wide): 13.2B **Publicly Held**
SIC: 5047 Dental equipment & supplies
PA: Henry Schein, Inc.
135 Duryea Rd
Melville NY 11747
631 843-5500

(G-5686)
HERNANDO ZEGARRA
3401 Entp Pkwy Ste 300 (44122)
PHONE....................................216 831-5700
Hernando Zegarra, *Owner*
EMP: 50
SALES (est): 1.2MM **Privately Held**
SIC: 8011 Physical medicine,
physician/surgeon

(G-5687)
HERTZ CLVLAND 600 SUPERIOR LLC
600 Superior Ave E # 100 (44114-2614)
PHONE....................................310 584-8108
Gary Horwitz, *President*
EMP: 50 EST: 2015
SALES (est): 2.4MM **Privately Held**
SIC: 6519 Real property lessors

(G-5688)
HERTZ CORPORATION
19025 Maplewood Ave (44135-2445)
PHONE....................................216 267-8900
Lois Stironek, *Purch Agent*
Steve McCraw, *Manager*
EMP: 88
SALES (corp-wide): 8.8B **Publicly Held**
WEB: www.hertz.com
SIC: 7514 Rent-a-car service
HQ: The Hertz Corporation
8501 Williams Rd
Estero FL 33928
239 301-7000

(G-5689)
HILL SIDE PLAZA
Also Called: Hillside Plaza
18220 Euclid Ave (44112-1013)
PHONE....................................216 486-6300
David Farkas, *Vice Pres*
Paul Sobel, *Administration*
Bob Jones, *Admin Sec*
EMP: 55
SQ FT: 14,000
SALES (est): 1.9MM **Privately Held**
SIC: 8051 8052 Convalescent home with
continuous nursing care; intermediate
care facilities

(G-5690)
HILLBROOK CLUB INC
17200 S Woodland Rd (44120-1882)
PHONE....................................440 247-4940
Ernest Mishne, *Principal*
EMP: 30
SQ FT: 8,000
SALES (est): 326.5K **Privately Held**
SIC: 7997 5812 Country club, membership; swimming club, membership; tennis
club, membership; American restaurant

(G-5691)
HILLCREST EGG & CHEESE CO (PA)
Also Called: Hillcrest Foodservice
2735 E 40th St (44115-3510)
PHONE....................................216 361-4625
Armin Abraham, *President*
Mark Kobak, *President*
David Abraham, *Vice Pres*
Joe Abraham, *Vice Pres*
Paul Gilman, *Vice Pres*
EMP: 99 EST: 1974
SQ FT: 95,000
SALES (est): 110MM **Privately Held**
SIC: 5143 5142 5147 5144 Dairy products, except dried or canned; packaged
frozen goods; meats, fresh; eggs; canned
goods: fruit, vegetables, seafood, meats,
etc.; fruits, fresh; vegetables, fresh

(G-5692)
HILLCREST HOSPITAL AUXILIARY
6780 Mayfield Rd (44124-2294)
PHONE....................................440 449-4500
Harold M Chattman, *Director*
Gerald B Chattman, *Director*
Gloria D Higgs, *Director*
EMP: 51
SQ FT: 750
SALES: 13.8K **Privately Held**
SIC: 8062 General medical & surgical hospitals

(G-5693)
HILLTOP VILLAGE
25900 Euclid Ave Ofc (44132-2751)
PHONE....................................216 261-8383
Audrey Keppler, *Director*
EMP: 50
SALES (est): 3MM **Privately Held**
WEB: www.hilltopvillage.com
SIC: 6513 Retirement hotel operation

(G-5694)
HIT PORTFOLIO I MISC TRS LLC
Also Called: Hyatt Hotel
420 Superior Ave E (44114-1208)
PHONE....................................216 575-1234
Tim Meyer, *General Mgr*
EMP: 200
SALES (corp-wide): 4.4B **Publicly Held**
WEB: www.hyatt.com
SIC: 7011 5812 Hotels; eating places
HQ: Hyatt Corporation
150 N Riverside Plz
Chicago IL 60606
312 750-1234

(G-5695)
HITCHCOCK CENTER FOR WOMEN INC
Also Called: HCFW
1227 Ansel Rd (44108-3323)
PHONE....................................216 421-0662
Stephen Monto, *President*
Sharon Brettas, *Vice Pres*
Tony Kuhel, *Treasurer*
Melvin Haynes, *Info Tech Dir*
Rochena Hall, *Info Tech Mgr*
EMP: 45
SQ FT: 20,000
SALES: 2.2MM **Privately Held**
WEB: www.hcfw.org
SIC: 8361 8093 Rehabilitation center, residential: health care incidental; alcohol
clinic, outpatient; drug clinic, outpatient

(G-5696)
HKM DRECT MKT CMMNICATIONS INC (PA)
Also Called: H K M
5501 Cass Ave (44102-2121)
PHONE....................................216 651-9500
Rob Durham, *President*
Scott Durham, *COO*
EMP: 135
SQ FT: 86,000
SALES (est): 55.8MM **Privately Held**
WEB: www.hkmdirectmarket.com
SIC: 2752 7375 2791 2759 Commercial
printing, lithographic; information retrieval
services; typesetting; commercial printing;
mailing service

(G-5697)
HNTB CORPORATION
1100 Superior Ave E # 1701 (44114-2518)
PHONE....................................216 522-1140
Anthony Yacobucci, *Branch Mgr*
EMP: 41
SALES (corp-wide): 48.1MM **Privately Held**
WEB: www.hntb.com
SIC: 8711 Consulting engineer
HQ: Hntb Corporation
715 Kirk Dr
Kansas City MO 64105
816 472-1201

(G-5698)
HOBE LCAS CRTIF PUB ACCNTANTS
4807 Rockside Rd Ste 510 (44131-2161)
PHONE....................................216 524-7167

David Hobe, *Principal*
Francis G Bonning Jr, *Principal*
Jerry Lucas, *Principal*
Floyd Trouten, *Principal*
EMP: 31
SALES (est): 2.5MM **Privately Held**
WEB: www.hobe.com
SIC: 8721 Certified public accountant

(G-5699)
HODELL-NATCO INDUSTRIES INC (PA)
Also Called: Locktooth Division
7825 Hub Pkwy (44125-5710)
PHONE....................................773 472-2305
Otto Reidl, *CEO*
Kevin Reidl, *President*
Ryan Causey, *General Mgr*
Dave Crowl, *General Mgr*
Ken Lyman, *General Mgr*
▲ EMP: 40
SQ FT: 101,000
SALES (est): 33.7MM **Privately Held**
WEB: www.hodell-natco.com
SIC: 5072 Bolts; nuts (hardware); screws

(G-5700)
HOME DEPOT USA INC
Also Called: Home Depot, The
10800 Brookpark Rd (44130-1119)
PHONE....................................216 676-9969
Louis Zager, *Manager*
EMP: 200
SALES (corp-wide): 108.2B **Publicly Held**
WEB: www.homerentalsdepot.com
SIC: 5211 7359 Home centers; tool rental
HQ: Home Depot U.S.A., Inc.
2455 Paces Ferry Ave
Atlanta GA 30339

(G-5701)
HOME DEPOT USA INC
Also Called: Home Depot, The
11901 Berea Rd (44111-1606)
PHONE....................................216 251-3091
Kennett Johansson, *Manager*
EMP: 150
SALES (corp-wide): 108.2B **Publicly Held**
WEB: www.homerentalsdepot.com
SIC: 5211 7359 Home centers; tool rental
HQ: Home Depot U.S.A., Inc.
2455 Paces Ferry Ave
Atlanta GA 30339

(G-5702)
HONEYWELL INTERNATIONAL INC
925 Keynote Cir Ste 100 (44131-1869)
PHONE....................................216 459-6053
Mark Gilger, *Branch Mgr*
EMP: 80
SALES (corp-wide): 41.8B **Publicly Held**
WEB: www.honeywell.com
SIC: 5075 7623 7699 4961 Warm air
heating & air conditioning; refrigeration
service & repair; boiler & heating repair
services; steam & air-conditioning supply
PA: Honeywell International Inc.
115 Tabor Rd
Morris Plains NJ 07950
973 455-2000

(G-5703)
HOPKIN ARPRT LMSINE SHTTLE SVC
Also Called: Hopkin S Airport Limosine Svc
1315 Brookpark Rd (44109-5829)
PHONE....................................216 267-8282
Mary Goebel, *President*
EMP: 30
SALES (est): 418.6K **Privately Held**
SIC: 4119 Limousine rental, with driver

(G-5704)
HOPKINS AIRPORT LIMOUSINE SVC (PA)
Also Called: Hopkins Transportation Svcs
13315 Brookpark Rd (44142-1822)
PHONE....................................216 267-8810
Tom Goebel, *President*
Mike Goebel, *Corp Secy*
Chris Goebel, *Vice Pres*
Jack Goebel, *Vice Pres*

G
E
O
G
R
A
P
H
I
C

James Goebel, *Vice Pres*
EMP: 200
SQ FT: 1,000
SALES: 4.5MM **Privately Held**
WEB: www.gohopkins.com
SIC: 4119 Limousine rental, with driver

(G-5705)
HOPKINS PARTNERS
Also Called: Sheraton Airport Hotel
5300 Riverside Dr Ste 30 (44135-3145)
PHONE....................................216 267-1500
David McArdle, *Partner*
Kerry Chelm, *Partner*
Richard Watson, *Partner*
EMP: 180
SALES (est): 9.4MM **Privately Held**
WEB: www.hopkinspartners.com
SIC: 7011 Resort hotel

(G-5706)
HORIZON FREIGHT SYSTEM INC (PA)
8777 Rockside Rd (44125-6112)
PHONE....................................216 341-7410
David Ferrante, *President*
Ron Bailey, *Business Mgr*
James Gifford, *Vice Pres*
Billie Russell, *Vice Pres*
Janet Fraley, *Safety Mgr*
EMP: 50
SQ FT: 15,000
SALES (est): 38.9MM **Privately Held**
WEB: www.horizonfreightsyste.com
SIC: 4213 Trucking, except local

(G-5707)
HORIZON MID ATLANTIC INC
Also Called: Trx Great Plains, Inc.
8777 Rockside Rd (44125-6112)
PHONE....................................800 480-6829
David Ferrante, *President*
James Gifford, *Vice Pres*
Robert A Bosak, *CFO*
EMP: 75
SALES (est): 2.1MM
SALES (corp-wide): 38.9MM **Privately Held**
SIC: 4213 Trucking, except local
PA: Horizon Freight System, Inc.
8777 Rockside Rd
Cleveland OH 44125
216 341-7410

(G-5708)
HORIZON SOUTH INC
Also Called: Horizon Freight
8777 Rockside Rd (44125-6112)
PHONE....................................800 480-6829
David Ferrante, *CEO*
Robert A Bosak, *CFO*
EMP: 78 EST: 2012
SALES (est): 5MM
SALES (corp-wide): 38.9MM **Privately Held**
SIC: 4213 Trucking, except local
PA: Horizon Freight System, Inc.
8777 Rockside Rd
Cleveland OH 44125
216 341-7410

(G-5709)
HORSESHOE CLEVELAND MGT LLC
Also Called: Jack Entertainment
100 Public Sq Ste 100 # 100 (44113-2208)
PHONE....................................216 297-4777
Maila Aganon,
EMP: 45 EST: 2010
SALES (est): 2.7MM **Privately Held**
SIC: 7011 Casino hotel

(G-5710)
HOSPICE OF OHIO LLC (PA)
Also Called: Harbor Light Hospice
677 Alpha Dr Ste H (44143-2165)
PHONE....................................440 286-2500
Brian Crum, *Sales Executive*
Gina Covelli,
Frank Rosenbaum,
EMP: 90
SALES: 14.3MM **Privately Held**
WEB: www.hospiceofohio.com
SIC: 8052 Intermediate Care Facility

(G-5711)
HOSPICE OF THE WESTERN RESERVE
4670 Richmond Rd Ste 200 (44128-6411)
PHONE....................................800 707-8921
Angie Conyards, *Principal*
Patricia Kilfoyle, *Director*
EMP: 60
SALES (corp-wide): 97.5MM **Privately Held**
SIC: 8082 Visiting nurse service
PA: Hospice Of The Western Reserve, Inc
17876 Saint Clair Ave
Cleveland OH 44110
216 383-2222

(G-5712)
HOSPICE OF THE WESTERN RESERVE (PA)
17876 Saint Clair Ave (44110-2602)
PHONE....................................216 383-2222
William E Finn, *CEO*
Jane Van Bergen, *Sls & Mktg Exec*
John E Harvan Jr, *CFO*
John Harvan, *CFO*
Linnea Fox, *Financial Analy*
EMP: 130
SQ FT: 60,000
SALES: 97.5MM **Privately Held**
SIC: 8052 Personal care facility

(G-5713)
HOSPICE OF THE WESTERN RESERVE
17876 Saint Clair Ave (44110-2602)
PHONE....................................800 707-8922
Laura Martin, *Sr Corp Ofcr*
Mary Kay Tyler, *Manager*
EMP: 60
SALES (corp-wide): 89.8MM **Privately Held**
SIC: 8052 Personal care facility
PA: Hospice Of The Western Reserve, Inc
17876 Saint Clair Ave
Cleveland OH 44110
216 383-2222

(G-5714)
HOSPICE OF THE WESTERN RESERVE
22730 Fairview Center Dr # 100 (44126-3614)
PHONE....................................216 227-9048
Nancy Miller, *Branch Mgr*
EMP: 115
SALES (corp-wide): 97.5MM **Privately Held**
SIC: 8082 Home health care services
PA: Hospice Of The Western Reserve, Inc
17876 Saint Clair Ave
Cleveland OH 44110
216 383-2222

(G-5715)
HOTEL 1100 CARNEGIE OPCO L P
Also Called: Hilton Grdn Inn Clvland Dwntwn
1100 Carnegie Ave (44115-2806)
P.O. Box 91126 (44101-3126)
PHONE....................................216 658-6400
Harvey Schach, *General Ptnr*
EMP: 66 EST: 1999
SALES (est): 8.3MM **Privately Held**
SIC: 7011 Hotels

(G-5716)
HOWARD HANNA SMYTHE CRAMER (HQ)
6000 Parkland Blvd (44124-6120)
PHONE....................................216 447-4477
Lucius B Mc Kelvey, *Ch of Bd*
David C Paul, *President*
Alan C Chandler, *Senior VP*
EMP: 250 EST: 1972
SQ FT: 16,500
SALES (est): 17.3MM
SALES (corp-wide): 73.7MM **Privately Held**
WEB: www.smythecramer.com
SIC: 6531 Real estate agent, residential
PA: Hanna Holdings, Inc.
1090 Freeport Rd Ste 1a
Pittsburgh PA 15238
412 967-9000

(G-5717)
HOWARD HANNA SMYTHE CRAMER
Also Called: Howard Hannah Smythe Cramer
27115 Knickerbocker Rd (44140-2345)
PHONE....................................440 835-2800
Kathy Miller, *Manager*
EMP: 45
SQ FT: 2,975
SALES (corp-wide): 73.7MM **Privately Held**
WEB: www.smythecramer.com
SIC: 6531 Real estate brokers & agents
HQ: Howard Hanna Smythe Cramer
6000 Parkland Blvd
Cleveland OH 44124
216 447-4477

(G-5718)
HOWARD HANNA SMYTHE CRAMER
Also Called: Smythe Cramer Reltrs
6240 Som Center Rd # 100 (44139-2950)
PHONE....................................440 248-3380
Barbara Jayme, *Manager*
EMP: 35
SALES (corp-wide): 72.1MM **Privately Held**
WEB: www.smythecramer.com
SIC: 6531 Real estate brokers & agents
HQ: Howard Hanna Smythe Cramer
6000 Parkland Blvd
Cleveland OH 44124
216 447-4477

(G-5719)
HOWARD HANNA SMYTHE CRAMER
8949 Brecksville Rd (44141-2301)
PHONE....................................440 526-1800
Ric Leavenworth, *Manager*
EMP: 35
SALES (corp-wide): 72.1MM **Privately Held**
WEB: www.smythecramer.com
SIC: 6531 Real estate brokers & agents
HQ: Howard Hanna Smythe Cramer
6000 Parkland Blvd
Cleveland OH 44124
216 447-4477

(G-5720)
HOWARD WERSHBALE & CO (PA)
23240 Chagrin Blvd # 700 (44122-5450)
PHONE....................................216 831-1200
Harvey Wershbale, *CEO*
Stanley J Olejarski, *President*
John Fleischer, *Shareholder*
Mel Howard, *Shareholder*
William Kutschbach, *Shareholder*
EMP: 75
SQ FT: 3,374
SALES (est): 12.3MM **Privately Held**
SIC: 8721 Certified public accountant

(G-5721)
HP MANUFACTURING COMPANY INC (PA)
Also Called: House of Plastics
3705 Carnegie Ave (44115-2750)
PHONE....................................216 361-6500
John R Melchiorre, *President*
Elmer Krizek, *Principal*
Paul Glozer, *QC Mgr*
EMP: 63
SQ FT: 110,000
SALES (est): 10.2MM **Privately Held**
WEB: www.hpmanufacturing.com
SIC: 3089 5162 3993 3082 Plastic processing; plastics sheets & rods; signs & advertising specialties; unsupported plastics profile shapes; partitions & fixtures, except wood

(G-5722)
HUNTER REALTY INC
Also Called: Coldwell Banker
25101 Chagrin Blvd # 170 (44122-5688)
PHONE....................................216 831-2911
Edwin Dolinski, *President*
Dave Bocchieri, *Asst Broker*
Barbara Glick, *Real Est Agnt*
EMP: 30

SALES (corp-wide): 2.6MM **Privately Held**
WEB: www.cbhunter.com
SIC: 6531 Real estate agent, residential
PA: Hunter Realty Inc
24600 Detroit Rd Ste 240
Westlake OH 44145
440 892-7040

(G-5723)
HUNTINGTON INSURANCE INC
925 Euclid Ave Ste 550 (44115-1405)
PHONE....................................216 206-1787
Biagio Impala, *Vice Pres*
EMP: 37
SALES (corp-wide): 5.2B **Publicly Held**
WEB: www.skyinsure.com
SIC: 6411 Insurance agents, brokers & service
HQ: Huntington Insurance, Inc.
519 Madison Ave
Toledo OH 43604
419 720-7900

(G-5724)
HUNTINGTON NATIONAL BANK
101 W Prospect Ave (44115-1093)
PHONE....................................216 621-1717
David Janus, *CEO*
EMP: 50
SQ FT: 800
SALES (corp-wide): 5.2B **Publicly Held**
SIC: 6029 Commercial banks
HQ: The Huntington National Bank
17 S High St Fl 1
Columbus OH 43215
614 480-4293

(G-5725)
HUNTINGTON NATIONAL BANK
Also Called: Home Mortgage
905 Euclid Ave (44115-1401)
P.O. Box 5065 (44101-0065)
PHONE....................................216 515-6401
Eddie Strattonbey, *Manager*
EMP: 38
SALES (corp-wide): 5.2B **Publicly Held**
WEB: www.huntingtonnationalbank.com
SIC: 6029 6021 Commercial banks; national trust companies with deposits, commercial
HQ: The Huntington National Bank
17 S High St Fl 1
Columbus OH 43215
614 480-4293

(G-5726)
HUNTLEIGH USA CORPORATION
11147 Barrington Blvd (44130-4414)
P.O. Box 81333 (44181-0333)
PHONE....................................216 265-3707
Greg Conwell, *Manager*
EMP: 300
SALES (corp-wide): 298.2MM **Privately Held**
WEB: www.huntleighusa.com
SIC: 4581 Aircraft servicing & repairing
HQ: Huntleigh Usa Corporation
545 E John Carpenter Fwy
Irving TX

(G-5727)
HWH ARCHTCTS-NGNRS-PLNNERS INC
600 Superior Ave E # 1100 (44114-2614)
PHONE....................................216 875-4000
Joseph J Matts, *President*
Peter P Jancar, *Chairman*
David Lehmer, *Exec VP*
Robert McCullough, *Exec VP*
Terry Angle, *Vice Pres*
EMP: 80
SQ FT: 20,000
SALES (est): 9.6MM **Privately Held**
WEB: www.hwhaep.com
SIC: 8711 8712 0781 Consulting engineer; architectural services; landscape counseling & planning

(G-5728)
HY-GRADE CORPORATION (PA)
3993 E 93rd St (44105-4052)
PHONE....................................216 341-7711
Michael Pemberton, *President*
EMP: 35

▲ = Import ▼=Export
◆ =Import/Export

SQ FT: 25,000
SALES (est): 9.1MM **Privately Held**
WEB: www.upm.com
SIC: 5032 2952 2951 Asphalt mixture; asphalt felts & coatings; asphalt paving mixtures & blocks

(G-5729)
HYATT LEGAL PLANS INC
1111 Superior Ave E # 800 (44114-2541)
PHONE.................................216 241-0022
William H Brooks, *President*
Andrew Kohn, *Vice Pres*
Mike Penzner, *CFO*
EMP: 96
SQ FT: 20,000
SALES (est): 25.5MM
SALES (corp-wide): 67.9B **Publicly Held**
WEB: www.legalplans.com
SIC: 6411 Insurance brokers; advisory services, insurance; information bureaus, insurance; policyholders' consulting service
HQ: Metropolitan Life Insurance Company (Inc)
501 Us Highway 22
Bridgewater NJ 08807
908 253-1000

(G-5730)
HYLANT GROUP INC
Also Called: Hylant Group of Cleveland
6000 Fredom Sq Dr Ste 400 (44131)
P.O. Box 31807 (44131-0807)
PHONE.................................216 447-1050
Nick Milanich, *Vice Pres*
Carter Davies, *Client Mgr*
John Gallagher, *Branch Mgr*
EMP: 82
SALES (corp-wide): 129.8MM **Privately Held**
WEB: www.hylant.com
SIC: 6411 Insurance agents
PA: Hylant Group, Inc.
811 Madison Ave Fl 11
Toledo OH 43604
419 255-1020

(G-5731)
I & M J GROSS COMPANY (PA)
Also Called: Gross Builders
14300 Ridge Rd Ste 100 (44133-4936)
PHONE.................................440 237-1681
Gary Gross, *President*
Chris Sheely, *Regional Mgr*
Scott Cable, *Business Mgr*
Harley Gross, *Vice Pres*
Aaron Gross, *Project Mgr*
EMP: 35 EST: 1916
SQ FT: 9,425
SALES (est): 84.6MM **Privately Held**
WEB: www.grossbuilders.com
SIC: 1522 Multi-family dwellings, new construction

(G-5732)
I-X CENTER CORPORATION
Also Called: International Exposition Ctr
6200 Riverside Dr (44135-3189)
PHONE.................................216 265-2675
Brad Gentille, *President*
Robert Peterson, *President*
EMP: 125 EST: 1975
SQ FT: 2,000,000
SALES (est): 20.7MM
SALES (corp-wide): 516.8MM **Privately Held**
WEB: www.ixcenter.com
SIC: 7389 5812 6512 Convention & show services; eating places; nonresidential building operators
PA: Park Corporation
6200 Riverside Dr
Cleveland OH 44135
216 267-4870

(G-5733)
ICX CORPORATION (DH)
2 Summit Park Dr Ste 105 (44131-2558)
PHONE.................................330 656-3611
Mark Marinik, *President*
Michael Babbitt, *Senior VP*
Gerald F Bender, *Senior VP*
Robert Rowland, *Senior VP*
James T Lovins, *CFO*
EMP: 50

SALES (est): 9.6MM
SALES (corp-wide): 7.3B **Publicly Held**
WEB: www.icxcorp.com
SIC: 6021 National Commercial Bank
HQ: Citizens Bank, National Association
1 Citizens Plz Ste 1 # 1
Providence RI 02903
401 282-7000

(G-5734)
IDEASTREAM (PA)
Also Called: Wviz/Pbs Hd
1375 Euclid Ave (44115-1826)
PHONE.................................216 916-6100
Jerry F Wareham, *CEO*
Larry Pollock, *Chairman*
Denise Hallman, *COO*
Sylvia Strobel, *COO*
Jeff Carlton, *Opers Mgr*
▲ EMP: 130
SQ FT: 70,000
SALES: 24.3MM **Privately Held**
WEB: www.ideastream.com
SIC: 4833 Television broadcasting stations

(G-5735)
IEH AUTO PARTS LLC
Also Called: Kovachy Auto Parts
4565 Hinckley Indus Pkwy (44109-6009)
PHONE.................................216 351-2560
Chuck Reimel, *Manager*
EMP: 30
SALES (corp-wide): 11.7B **Publicly Held**
SIC: 4225 General warehousing & storage
HQ: Ieh Auto Parts Llc
1155 Roberts Blvd Nw # 175
Kennesaw GA 30144
770 701-5000

(G-5736)
IHEARTCOMMUNICATIONS INC
Also Called: Wmvx Radio
6200 Oak Tree Blvd Fl 4 (44131-6933)
PHONE.................................216 520-2600
Allen Colon, *Managing Dir*
Mike Kenney, *Principal*
Jim Meltzer, *Vice Pres*
Rachel Oettinger, *Project Mgr*
Mark Manolio, *Engineer*
EMP: 200 **Publicly Held**
SIC: 4832 4833 Radio broadcasting stations; television broadcasting stations
HQ: Iheartcommunications, Inc.
20880 Stone Oak Pkwy
San Antonio TX 78258
210 822-2828

(G-5737)
IHEARTCOMMUNICATIONS INC
Also Called: Wmji-FM
310 W Lakeside Ave Fl 6 (44113-1021)
PHONE.................................216 409-9673
Rick Weinkauf, *Manager*
EMP: 43 **Publicly Held**
SIC: 4832 Radio broadcasting stations
HQ: Iheartcommunications, Inc.
20880 Stone Oak Pkwy
San Antonio TX 78258
210 822-2828

(G-5738)
ILS TECHNOLOGY LLC
6065 Parkland Blvd (44124-6119)
PHONE.................................800 695-8650
Fred Yentz, *President*
EMP: 30
SQ FT: 41,000
SALES (est): 2.6MM
SALES (corp-wide): 1.6B **Publicly Held**
WEB: www.pkoh.com.cn
SIC: 7371 Computer software development
HQ: Park-Ohio Industries, Inc.
6065 Parkland Blvd Ste 1
Cleveland OH 44124
440 947-2000

(G-5739)
IMAGE CONSULTING SERVICES INC (PA)
1775 Donwell Dr (44121-3780)
PHONE.................................440 951-9919
Amy G O'Dea, *President*
Amy O'Dea, *President*
Patrick W O'Dea, *Vice Pres*

EMP: 25
SALES (est): 3.8MM **Privately Held**
SIC: 8748 Business consulting

(G-5740)
IMPACT CERAMICS LLC
17000 Saint Clair Ave # 3 (44110-2535)
PHONE.................................440 554-3624
Matthew Mullarkey,
EMP: 50
SALES (est): 2.6MM **Privately Held**
SIC: 8742 Manufacturing management consultant

(G-5741)
INCENTISOFT SOLUTIONS LLC
20445 Emerald Pkwy # 400 (44135-6010)
PHONE.................................877 562-4461
James Pshock, *CEO*
EMP: 69
SALES (est): 2.9MM
SALES (corp-wide): 22.5MM **Privately Held**
SIC: 8742 8748 Administrative services consultant; employee programs administration
PA: Bravo Wellness, Llc
20445 Emerald Pkwy # 400
Cleveland OH 44135
216 658-9500

(G-5742)
INDEPENDENCE BANK
4401 Rockside Rd (44131-2146)
P.O. Box 318048 (44131-8048)
PHONE.................................216 447-1444
Christopher W Mack, *Ch of Bd*
Russell G Fortlage, *Vice Pres*
Albert E Wainio, *Vice Pres*
Dennis A Williams, *Vice Pres*
Michael J Occhionaro, *Admin Sec*
EMP: 30
SALES: 6.4MM
SALES (corp-wide): 7.1MM **Privately Held**
SIC: 6022 State commercial banks
PA: Independence Bancorp
4401 Rockside Rd
Cleveland OH 44131
216 447-1444

(G-5743)
INDEPENDENCE ONCOLOGY
6100 W Creek Rd Ste 16 (44131-2133)
PHONE.................................216 524-7979
Nanat Rock, *Owner*
EMP: 30
SALES (est): 818.4K **Privately Held**
WEB: www.independence-ohio.com
SIC: 8011 Oncologist

(G-5744)
INDEPENDENCE TRAVEL
5000 Rockside Rd Ste 240 (44131-2141)
PHONE.................................216 447-9950
Corinne Smith, *Owner*
EMP: 25
SALES (est): 2.2MM **Privately Held**
SIC: 4724 Tourist agency arranging transport, lodging & car rental

(G-5745)
INDEPENDENT HOTEL PARTNERS LLC
Also Called: Shereton Hotel Independance
5300 Rockside Rd (44131-2118)
PHONE.................................216 524-0700
Jennifer Pulver, *Marketing Staff*
Ernie Malas, *Mng Member*
EMP: 75
SQ FT: 300,000
SALES (est): 4.6MM **Privately Held**
SIC: 7011 Hotels

(G-5746)
INDEPNDENCE OFFICE BUS SUP INC
Also Called: Independence Business Supply
4550 Hinckley Indus Pkwy (44109-6010)
PHONE.................................216 398-8880
Steven Gordon, *President*
Tony Angelo, *Vice Pres*
Pat Bova, *Vice Pres*
James Connelly, *Vice Pres*
Ken Cramer, *Vice Pres*
EMP: 55

SQ FT: 10,250
SALES (est): 38.4MM **Privately Held**
WEB: www.ibuyibs.com
SIC: 5021 5112 Furniture; office supplies; furniture stores

(G-5747)
INDUSTRIAL ENERGY SYSTEMS INC
15828 Industrial Pkwy # 3 (44135-3349)
PHONE.................................216 267-9590
Michael Dragics, *President*
EMP: 45
SQ FT: 9,500
SALES (est): 6.2MM **Privately Held**
SIC: 1761 Roofing contractor; sheet metalwork

(G-5748)
INDUSTRIAL ORIGAMI INC
6755 Engle Rd Ste A (44130-7947)
PHONE.................................440 260-0000
V Gerry Corrigan, *President*
Zach Koekemoer, *CFO*
EMP: 29
SALES (est): 3.2MM **Privately Held**
SIC: 8711 Industrial engineers

(G-5749)
INERTIAL AIRLINE SERVICES INC
Also Called: Inertial Aerospace Services
375 Alpha Park (44143-2237)
PHONE.................................440 995-6555
Eric Mendelson, *President*
Terri Moorfield, *General Mgr*
C Jeff Willams, *Vice Pres*
Nicholas Wright, *Vice Pres*
Teodor Molcut, *Engineer*
EMP: 33
SALES (est): 5.8MM **Publicly Held**
SIC: 7699 Nautical & navigational instrument repair
HQ: Heico Aerospace Holdings Corp.
3000 Taft St
Hollywood FL 33021
954 987-4000

(G-5750)
INFOACCESSNET LLC
8801 E Pleasant Valley Rd (44131-5510)
PHONE.................................216 328-0100
Daniel Andrew, *Mng Member*
EMP: 31
SQ FT: 25,000
SALES (est): 3.1MM
SALES (corp-wide): 90MM **Privately Held**
WEB: www.infoaccess.net
SIC: 7372 Business oriented computer software
HQ: Corcentric Collective Business System Corp.
7927 Jones Branch Dr # 3200
Mc Lean VA 22102
703 790-7272

(G-5751)
INFORMA BUSINESS MEDIA INC
1100 Superior Ave E # 800 (44114-2530)
PHONE.................................216 696-7000
EMP: 27
SALES (corp-wide): 2.3B **Privately Held**
SIC: 7299 Information services, consumer
HQ: Informa Business Media, Inc.
605 3rd Ave
New York NY 10158
212 204-4200

(G-5752)
INFOSTORE LLC
1200 E Granger Rd (44131-1234)
P.O. Box 1150, Grove City (43123-6150)
PHONE.................................216 749-4636
Bill Berry, *Manager*
Toby O'Brian,
Mike James,
Roy Radigan,
EMP: 30
SALES (est): 5MM **Privately Held**
SIC: 4226 Document & office records storage

GEOGRAPHIC

(G-5753)
INFOTELECOM HOLDINGS LLC (PA)
Also Called: Broadvox
75 Erieview Plz Fl 4 (44114-1839)
PHONE...............................216 373-4811
Eugene Blumin,
Alex Bederman,
Andre Temnorod,
EMP: 400
SALES (est): 23.1MM Privately Held
SIC: 4813 7373 ; ; computer system selling services

(G-5754)
INNER CITY NURSING HOME
Also Called: Fairfax Health Care Center
9014 Cedar Ave (44106-2932)
PHONE...............................216 795-1363
Melvin Pye Jr, President
Ethel Pye, Vice Pres
John Dugard, Manager
Henry Edwards, Officer
EMP: 130
SQ FT: 10,000
SALES (est): 5.6MM Privately Held
WEB: www.fairfaxplace.com
SIC: 8052 Personal care facility

(G-5755)
INNER-SPACE CLEANING CORP
6151 Wilson Mills Rd # 240 (44143-2134)
PHONE...............................440 646-0701
Bill Spigoutz, President
EMP: 125
SALES (est): 3.9MM Privately Held
SIC: 7699 Cleaning services

(G-5756)
INTEGER HOLDINGS CORPORATION
1771 E 30th St (44114-4407)
PHONE...............................216 937-2800
EMP: 50
SALES (corp-wide): 1.3B Publicly Held
SIC: 8732 Commercial Nonphysical Research
PA: Integer Holdings Corporation
2595 Dallas Pkwy Ste 310
Frisco TX 75024
214 618-5243

(G-5757)
INTEGRATED CC LLC
Also Called: Holiday Inn
8650 Euclid Ave (44106-2034)
PHONE...............................216 707-4132
John T Murphy, Mng Member
Michael Ciuni, Director
EMP: 50 EST: 2014
SALES (est): 898.6K Privately Held
SIC: 7011 Hotels

(G-5758)
INTEGRATED POWER SERVICES LLC
Also Called: Monarch
5325 W 130th St (44130-1034)
PHONE...............................216 433-7808
Bridgette Gullatta, President
EMP: 27
SALES (corp-wide): 924.8MM Privately Held
SIC: 7694 Armature rewinding shops
HQ: Integrated Power Services Llc
3 Independence Pt Ste 100
Greenville SC 29615

(G-5759)
INTELLINET CORPORATION (PA)
1111 Chester Ave Ste 200 (44114-3516)
PHONE...............................216 289-4100
Richard E Taton, CEO
Ronald J Taton, President
John O'Donnell, Vice Pres
John Odonnell, Vice Pres
Kenneth Maurer, Engineer
EMP: 70
SQ FT: 4,000
SALES (est): 10.5MM Privately Held
WEB: www.intellinetcorp.com
SIC: 4813 ;

(G-5760)
INTERCNTNNTAL HT GROUP RSURCES
8800 Euclid Ave (44106-2038)
PHONE...............................216 707-4300
Pablo Criado, Manager
EMP: 74 Privately Held
WEB: www.intercontinentalhotel.com
SIC: 7011 Hotels
HQ: Intercontinental Hotels Group Resources, Inc.
3 Ravinia Dr Ste 100
Atlanta GA 30346
770 604-5000

(G-5761)
INTERCONTINENTAL HOTELS GROUP
9801 Carnegie Ave (44106-2100)
PHONE...............................216 707-4100
Flo M Hunt, Human Res Dir
Rob Austin, Manager
EMP: 50 Privately Held
SIC: 7011 Hotels
HQ: Intercontinental Hotels Group Resources, Inc.
3 Ravinia Dr Ste 100
Atlanta GA 30346
770 604-5000

(G-5762)
INTERNATIONAL MANAGEMENT GROUP (HQ)
1360 E 9th St Ste 100 (44114-1782)
PHONE...............................216 522-1200
Ian Todd, President
Adair Mattingly, Partner
Libby McCormick, Partner
Jared Bell, General Mgr
Andrew Kossoff, General Mgr
◆ EMP: 289
SALES (est): 22.2MM
SALES (corp-wide): 55MM Privately Held
WEB: www.imgworld.com
SIC: 7941 7999 7922 Manager of individual professional athletes; sports instruction, schools & camps; theatrical producers & services
PA: William Morris Endeavor Entertainment, Llc
11 Madison Ave Fl 18
New York NY 10010
212 586-5100

(G-5763)
INTERNATIONAL MDSG CORP (DH)
1360 E 9th St Ste 100 (44114-1730)
PHONE...............................216 522-1200
Mark H Mc Cormack, President
Peter Kuhn, CFO
Arthur J La Fave Jr, CFO
EMP: 325 EST: 1967
SQ FT: 15,000
SALES (est): 12.6MM
SALES (corp-wide): 55MM Privately Held
SIC: 7941 7999 Manager of individual professional athletes; sports instruction, schools & camps
HQ: International Management Group (Overseas), Llc
1360 E 9th St Ste 100
Cleveland OH 44114
216 522-1200

(G-5764)
INTERNATIONAL UNION UNITED AU
Also Called: U A W Region 2 Headquarters
5000 Rockside Rd Ste 300 (44131-2178)
PHONE...............................216 447-6080
Warren Davis, Director
EMP: 30
SALES (corp-wide): 237.6MM Privately Held
SIC: 8631 Labor union
PA: International Union, United Automobile, Aerospace And Agricultural Implement Workers Of Am
8000 E Jefferson Ave
Detroit MI 48214
313 926-5000

(G-5765)
INTERSTATE DIESEL SERVICE INC (PA)
Also Called: American Diesel, Inc.
5300 Lakeside Ave E (44114-3916)
PHONE...............................216 881-0015
Alfred J Buescher, CEO
Ann Buescher, President
Brad Buescher, COO
◆ EMP: 325 EST: 1947
SQ FT: 70,000
SALES (est): 62.6MM Privately Held
WEB: www.interstate-mcbee.com
SIC: 5013 3714 Automotive engines & engine parts; fuel systems & parts, motor vehicle; fuel pumps, motor vehicle

(G-5766)
INTL EUROPA SALON & SPA
24700 Chagrin Blvd # 101 (44122-5630)
PHONE...............................216 292-6969
Tanya Sigal, Owner
EMP: 30
SALES (est): 440K Privately Held
SIC: 7231 Beauty shops

(G-5767)
ISLANDER COMPANY
Also Called: Islander Apartments
7711 Normandie Blvd (44130-6522)
PHONE...............................440 243-0593
Moses Krislov, Partner
EMP: 40
SQ FT: 13,448
SALES (est): 2.6MM Privately Held
SIC: 6513 6512 Apartment hotel operation; commercial & industrial building operation

(G-5768)
IVORY SERVICES INC
2122 Saint Clair Ave Ne (44114-4047)
P.O. Box 181082 (44118-7082)
PHONE...............................216 344-3094
Ivory Brooks, President
EMP: 27
SALES: 700K Privately Held
SIC: 7349 Janitorial service, contract basis

(G-5769)
J A A INTERIOR & COML CNSTR
3615 Superior Ave E 3103h (44114-4138)
PHONE...............................216 431-7633
John Berry, Owner
EMP: 36
SALES: 900K Privately Held
SIC: 1521 Single-family housing construction

(G-5770)
J AND S TOOL INCORPORATED
15330 Brookpark Rd (44135-3355)
PHONE...............................216 676-8330
Vernon Justice, President
Donald Justice, Vice Pres
EMP: 36
SQ FT: 10,000
SALES: 2MM Privately Held
SIC: 3542 5084 3544 3541 Machine tools, metal forming type; machine tools & accessories; special dies, tools, jigs & fixtures; machine tools, metal cutting type; saw blades & handsaws; hand & edge tools

(G-5771)
J G MARTIN INC
4159 Lee Rd (44128-2462)
PHONE...............................216 491-1584
John Martin, Principal
EMP: 66
SALES (est): 4.1MM Privately Held
WEB: www.jgmartin.com
SIC: 8742 Management consulting services

(G-5772)
J R JOHNSON ENGINEERING INC
6673 Eastland Rd (44130-2423)
PHONE...............................440 234-9972
James R Johnson, President
Ken Lewis, Vice Pres
Raymond Esser, Project Mgr
Gustavo Ramirez, Engineer

Larry Reeves, Engineer
EMP: 40
SQ FT: 10,000
SALES (est): 2.7MM Privately Held
WEB: www.jrjohnsonengr.com
SIC: 8711 Consulting engineer

(G-5773)
J T ADAMS CO
Also Called: Tensile Tsting Mtllurgical Lab
4520 Willow Pkwy (44125-1042)
PHONE...............................216 641-3290
Tim Adams, President
Tracey Waugaman, Treasurer
Bree Movens, Marketing Staff
William Loewenthal, Manager
Sj Arsenault, Admin Sec
EMP: 30 EST: 1956
SQ FT: 30,000
SALES (est): 5.6MM Privately Held
WEB: www.tensile.com
SIC: 8734 Metallurgical testing laboratory

(G-5774)
J V JANITORIAL SERVICES INC
1230 E Schaaf Rd Ste 1 (44131-1399)
PHONE...............................216 749-1150
Joseph N Vocaire Sr, President
EMP: 25
SQ FT: 6,600
SALES (est): 1.3MM Privately Held
WEB: www.jvjanitorial.com
SIC: 7349 Janitorial service, contract basis

(G-5775)
JACK THISTLEDOWN RACINO LLC (PA)
21501 Emery Rd (44128-4513)
PHONE...............................216 662-8600
Mark Miller, President
Mark Dunkeson, COO
Glen Tomaszewski, Senior VP
Van Baltz, Vice Pres
Bill Hyde, Vice Pres
EMP: 44
SALES (est): 3.8MM Privately Held
SIC: 7993 Gambling establishments operating coin-operated machines

(G-5776)
JACKSON KOHRMAN & PLL KRANTZ
1375 E 9th St Fl 29 (44114-1797)
PHONE...............................216 696-8700
Jessica B Rescina, President
Rachel Stewart, President
Lori Walter, President
Marc C Krantz, Partner
Steven Bersticker, Partner
EMP: 60 EST: 1968
SQ FT: 20,000
SALES (est): 9.1MM Privately Held
WEB: www.kjk.com
SIC: 8111 General practice law office

(G-5777)
JACOB REAL ESTATE SERVICES
127 Public Sq Ste 2828 (44114-1227)
PHONE...............................216 687-0500
Tom Kroth, General Mgr
Richard Kopek, Vice Pres
EMP: 30
SALES (est): 2.3MM Privately Held
SIC: 7349 6531 Building maintenance services; real estate agents & managers

(G-5778)
JAGI CLVELAND INDEPENDENCE LLC
Also Called: Holiday Inn
6001 Rockside Rd (44131-2209)
PHONE...............................216 524-8050
Tom Hibsman, General Mgr
Lynette Slama, Manager
EMP: 180
SQ FT: 81,713
SALES (est): 8.6MM Privately Held
SIC: 7011 Hotels & motels

(G-5779)
JAMES AIR CARGO INC
6519 Eastland Rd Ste 6 (44142-1347)
P.O. Box 81852 (44181-0852)
PHONE...............................440 243-9095

James T Goff, *President*
EMP: 26
SQ FT: 10,000
SALES: 2MM **Privately Held**
WEB: www.jamesaircargo.com
SIC: 4212 4581 Delivery service, vehicular; air freight handling at airports

(G-5780)
JANIK LLP (PA)
9200 S Hills Blvd Ste 300 (44147-3524)
PHONE.................................440 838-7600
Scott Cerny, *Office Mgr*
Steven Janik, *Mng Member*
Kevin Zakiewicz, *Manager*
Michael Salopek, *Info Tech Mgr*
Della Sisson, *Legal Staff*
EMP: 52
SQ FT: 8,000
SALES (est): 8.9MM **Privately Held**
WEB: www.janiklaw.com
SIC: 8111 General practice law office

(G-5781)
JANITORIAL SERVICES INC
4830 E 49th St (44125-1014)
PHONE.................................216 341-8601
Ronald J Martinez Sr, *President*
Ronald J Martinez Jr, *Vice Pres*
EMP: 325
SQ FT: 6,000
SALES (est): 13.3MM **Privately Held**
WEB: www.jsijanitorial.com
SIC: 7349 Janitorial service, contract basis

(G-5782)
JAVITCH BLOCK LLC (PA)
1100 Superior Ave E Fl 19 (44114-2521)
PHONE.................................216 623-0000
Kelly Volckening, *Accountant*
Bruce A Block, *Mng Member*
Joel Rathbone, *Mng Member*
Robert Ahlstrom, *Manager*
Dionne Bailey, *Manager*
EMP: 220
SQ FT: 54,000
SALES (est): 58.1MM **Privately Held**
WEB: www.jber.com
SIC: 8111 General practice law office

(G-5783)
JAY BLUE COMMUNICATIONS
7500 Associate Ave (44144-1105)
PHONE.................................216 661-2828
John Houlihan, *Owner*
Wayne Davis, *Project Mgr*
Donald Schwark, *Project Mgr*
EMP: 25
SALES (est): 3.4MM **Privately Held**
SIC: 4899 Data communication services

(G-5784)
JBK GROUP INC (PA)
Also Called: Event Source
6001 Towpath Dr (44125-4221)
PHONE.................................216 901-0000
John Bibbo, *President*
Bryan Bibbo, *Vice Pres*
Patrick Kennedy, *Info Tech Mgr*
Suzanne Chandler, *Executive*
Candace Conner, *Executive*
EMP: 45
SQ FT: 57,530
SALES (est): 12.3MM **Privately Held**
WEB: www.eventsource.net
SIC: 7353 7359 Heavy construction equipment rental; equipment rental & leasing

(G-5785)
JBO HOLDING COMPANY
Also Called: Oswald Companies
1100 Superior Ave E # 1500 (44114-2530)
PHONE.................................216 367-8787
Marc S Byrnes, *Ch of Bd*
Jeffery Phillips, *Vice Pres*
Bill Fisher, *Marketing Staff*
Joann Cole, *Manager*
Brendan Salk, *Admin Asst*
EMP: 180
SQ FT: 30,000 **Privately Held**
SIC: 6719 Personal holding companies, except banks

(G-5786)
JDD INC (PA)
3615 Superior Ave E 3104a (44114-4138)
PHONE.................................216 464-8855
James Vaughan Jr, *President*
EMP: 36 **EST:** 1994
SALES: 10MM **Privately Held**
SIC: 7349 Janitorial service, contract basis

(G-5787)
JEFFERSON MEDICAL CO
950 Main Ave Ste 500 (44113-7206)
PHONE.................................216 443-9000
L Erb, *Principal*
EMP: 40
SALES (est): 894.8K **Privately Held**
SIC: 8111 Legal services

(G-5788)
**JENNINGS ELIZA HOME INC
(HQ)**
10603 Detroit Ave (44102-1647)
PHONE.................................216 226-0282
Deborah Hiller, *CEO*
Jim Rogerson, *COO*
Joan Lampe, *CFO*
EMP: 210
SQ FT: 60,000
SALES (est): 8.6MM **Privately Held**
WEB: www.elizajen.org
SIC: 8051 8052 Convalescent home with continuous nursing care; intermediate care facilities

(G-5789)
**JENNINGS CTR FOR OLDER
ADULTS**
Also Called: Jennings Hall Nursing Facility
10204 Granger Rd 232 (44125-3106)
PHONE.................................216 581-2900
Martha M Kutik, *President*
Allison Salopeck, *COO*
Richard Zak, *CFO*
Denise Smudla, *Human Res Dir*
Debbie Carver, *Director*
EMP: 375
SQ FT: 120,000
SALES: 19.2MM **Privately Held**
WEB: www.jenningscenter.org
SIC: 8059 8051 8052 Nursing home, except skilled & intermediate care facility; skilled nursing care facilities; intermediate care facilities

(G-5790)
JERGENS INC (PA)
Also Called: Tooling Components Division
15700 S Waterloo Rd (44110-3898)
PHONE.................................216 486-5540
Jack H Schron Jr, *President*
W Wesley Howard III, *CFO*
Tim Easton, *Natl Sales Mgr*
Mary Delaney, *Marketing Mgr*
Mark Kish, *Manager*
▲ **EMP:** 195 **EST:** 1942
SQ FT: 104,000
SALES (est): 63MM **Privately Held**
WEB: www.jergensinc.com
SIC: 3443 3452 5084 3545 Fabricated plate work (boiler shop); bolts, nuts, rivets & washers; machine tools & accessories; drill bushings (drilling jig); precision measuring tools; jigs & fixtures

(G-5791)
**JERSEY CENTRAL PWR & LIGHT
CO**
Also Called: Firstenergy
6800 S Marginal Rd (44103-1047)
PHONE.................................216 432-6330
EMP: 65
SALES (corp-wide): 15B **Publicly Held**
SIC: 4911 Electric Services
HQ: Jersey Central Power & Light Company
76 S Main St
Akron OH 44308
800 736-3402

(G-5792)
**JERSEY CENTRAL PWR & LIGHT
CO**
Also Called: Firstenergy
2423 Payne Ave (44114-4428)
PHONE.................................216 479-1132

Rick Louse, *Branch Mgr*
Terry Perona, *Admin Sec*
EMP: 67 **Publicly Held**
WEB: www.jersey-central-power-light.monmouth.n
SIC: 4911 Distribution, electric power
HQ: Jersey Central Power & Light Company
76 S Main St
Akron OH 44308
800 736-3402

(G-5793)
JES FOODS INC (PA)
4733 Broadway Ave (44127-1007)
PHONE.................................216 883-8987
Elaine R Freed, *President*
William Freed, *Exec VP*
Jerry Mc Donald, *Vice Pres*
Rebecca Thomas, *Accountant*
EMP: 32
SQ FT: 7,000
SALES (est): 20.6MM **Privately Held**
WEB: www.jesfoods.com
SIC: 5148 Vegetables; vegetables, fresh

(G-5794)
**JETRO CASH AND CARRY
ENTPS LLC**
Also Called: Restaurant Depot
6150 Halle Dr (44125-4614)
PHONE.................................216 525-0101
Dan Nicholas, *Manager*
EMP: 100 **Privately Held**
WEB: www.jetro.com
SIC: 5147 5194 5141 5181 Meats, fresh; tobacco & tobacco products; groceries, general line; beer & other fermented malt liquors; packaged frozen goods
HQ: Jetro Cash And Carry Enterprises, Llc
1524 132nd St
College Point NY 11356
718 939-6400

(G-5795)
**JEWISH FAMILY SERVICES
ASSOCIA (PA)**
Also Called: JEWISH COMMUNITY CARE AT HOME
3659 Green Rd Ste 322 (44122-5715)
PHONE.................................216 292-3999
Robert Shakno, *President*
Arline Adams, *Business Mgr*
Lynn Wasserman, *Business Mgr*
Patrick Sidley, *CFO*
Lluvia Rodriguez, *Bookkeeper*
EMP: 500
SQ FT: 16,000
SALES: 25.7MM **Privately Held**
WEB: www.jfsa-cleveland.org
SIC: 8322 Family service agency

(G-5796)
**JEWISH FAMILY SERVICES
ASSOCIA**
Also Called: Professional Services
24075 Commerce Park # 105
(44122-5846)
PHONE.................................216 292-3999
Jessica Rosenblitt, *Manager*
Kathy Levine, *Director*
Michael Schultz, *Director*
Jaime Lowy, *Associate Dir*
EMP: 40
SQ FT: 9,900
SALES (corp-wide): 25.7MM **Privately
Held**
WEB: www.jfsa-cleveland.org
SIC: 8322 Social service center
PA: Jewish Family Service Association Of
Cleveland, Ohio
3659 Green Rd Ste 322
Cleveland OH 44122
216 292-3999

(G-5797)
JMA HEALTHCARE LLC
Also Called: Oak Park Health Care Center
24579 Broadway Ave (44146-0632)
PHONE.................................440 439-7976
Lisa Berkowitz, *Principal*
EMP: 125 **EST:** 1990
SQ FT: 33,000
SALES (est): 2.2MM **Privately Held**
SIC: 8051 Convalescent home with continuous nursing care

(G-5798)
JOBAR ENTERPRISE INC
3361 E 147th St (44120-4133)
P.O. Box 20264 (44120-0264)
PHONE.................................216 561-5184
Barbara McMahn, *President*
EMP: 25
SALES: 110K **Privately Held**
SIC: 6531 Real estate agents & managers

(G-5799)
JOHN H KAPPUS CO (PA)
Also Called: Kappus Company
4755 W 150th St (44135-3329)
PHONE.................................216 367-6677
Fred Kappus, *CEO*
John Kappus, *President*
John Zalenka, *COO*
Michael J Marcis, *CFO*
Ryan Huffman, *Mng Member*
EMP: 49
SALES (est): 21.1MM **Privately Held**
WEB: www.kappuscompany.com
SIC: 5046 Restaurant equipment & supplies

(G-5800)
**JOHN RBRTS HAIR STUDIO SPA
INC (PA)**
673 Alpha Dr Ste F (44143-2140)
PHONE.................................216 839-1430
John R Di Julius III, *President*
EMP: 73
SQ FT: 7,000
SALES (est): 4MM **Privately Held**
SIC: 7231 Hairdressers

(G-5801)
**JOHNSON MIRMIRAN
THOMPSON INC**
959 W Saint Clair Ave # 300 (44113-1298)
PHONE.................................614 714-0270
James Prevost, *Vice Pres*
EMP: 70
SALES (corp-wide): 259.1MM **Privately
Held**
SIC: 8711 Civil engineering
PA: Johnson, Mirmiran & Thompson, Inc.
40 Wight Ave
Hunt Valley MD 21030
410 329-3100

(G-5802)
**JONATHON R JOHNSON &
ASSOC**
1489 Rydalmount Rd (44118-1347)
PHONE.................................216 932-6529
Johnathon R Johnson, *Principal*
EMP: 25
SALES (est): 1.1MM **Privately Held**
SIC: 8742 Management consulting services

(G-5803)
**JONES DAY LIMITED
PARTNERSHIP (PA)**
901 Lakeside Ave E Ste 2 (44114-1190)
PHONE.................................216 586-3939
Jones Day, *Partner*
Brett P Barragate, *Partner*
Dennis Barsky, *Partner*
Patrick Belville, *Partner*
Erin L Burke, *Partner*
EMP: 900
SQ FT: 300,000
SALES (est): 833.4MM **Privately Held**
SIC: 8111 General practice law office

(G-5804)
**JOSHEN PAPER & PACKAGING
CO (PA)**
5800 Grant Ave (44105-5608)
PHONE.................................216 441-5600
Michelle Reiner, *CEO*
Bob Reiner, *President*
Elliot M Kaufman, *Principal*
John Caldwell, *Vice Pres*
Don Morgenroth, *Vice Pres*
◆ **EMP:** 140
SQ FT: 180,000

SALES (est): 326.1MM **Privately Held**
WEB: www.joshen.com
SIC: 5113 5169 Bags, paper & disposable plastic; cups, disposable plastic & paper; boxes & containers; sanitation preparations

(G-5805)
JPMORGAN CHASE BANK NAT ASSN
5332 Mayfield Rd (44124-2452)
PHONE..................................440 442-7800
Jonathan Willie, *Branch Mgr*
EMP: 26
SALES (corp-wide): 131.4B **Publicly Held**
SIC: 6021 National commercial banks
HQ: Jpmorgan Chase Bank, National Association
1111 Polaris Pkwy
Columbus OH 43240
614 436-3055

(G-5806)
JPMORGAN CHASE BANK NAT ASSN
1300 E 9th St Fl 13 (44114-1501)
PHONE..................................216 781-4437
Pete Van Allsburg, *Assistant VP*
Richard Landel, *Manager*
EMP: 32
SALES (corp-wide): 131.4B **Publicly Held**
WEB: www.chase.com
SIC: 6022 State commercial banks
HQ: Jpmorgan Chase Bank, National Association
1111 Polaris Pkwy
Columbus OH 43240
614 436-3055

(G-5807)
JTC CONTRACTING INC
Also Called: Jtc Office Services
7635 Hub Pkwy Ste C (44125-5741)
PHONE..................................216 635-0745
Kathleen Morris, *President*
Kathy Morris, *General Mgr*
Ty Morris, *Opers Mgr*
Ken Morris, *Treasurer*
EMP: 40 EST: 1993
SALES (est): 4.8MM **Privately Held**
WEB: www.jtcinstall.com
SIC: 1799 Office furniture installation

(G-5808)
JUDSON (PA)
Also Called: JUDSON UNIVERSITY CIRCLE
2181 Ambleside Dr Apt 411 (44106-7604)
PHONE..................................216 791-2004
Hong Chae, *CEO*
Cynthia Dunn, *President*
James Carnovale, *Senior VP*
Bill Fehrenbach, *Vice Pres*
Steve Wincek, *Maintenance Dir*
EMP: 80
SQ FT: 800,000
SALES: 23.7MM **Privately Held**
WEB: www.judsonretirement.com
SIC: 8059 6513 8052 Domiciliary care; personal care home, with health care; retirement hotel operation; intermediate care facilities

(G-5809)
JUDSON
Also Called: Judson Manor
1890 E 107th St (44106-2235)
PHONE..................................216 791-2555
Julie Anderson, *Vice Pres*
EMP: 80
SALES (est): 4.8MM
SALES (corp-wide): 23.7MM **Privately Held**
WEB: www.judsonretirement.com
SIC: 8361 Residential care
PA: Judson
2181 Ambleside Dr Apt 411
Cleveland OH 44106
216 791-2004

(G-5810)
JZE ELECTRIC INC (PA)
Also Called: Hilliard Electric
6800 Eastland Rd (44130-2426)
PHONE..................................440 243-7600

Mike O'Hara, *President*
EMP: 16
SALES (est): 9.9MM **Privately Held**
WEB: www.hilliardelectric.com
SIC: 1731 General electrical contractor

(G-5811)
K M & M
9715 Clinton Rd (44144-1031)
P.O. Box 360379, Strongsville (44136-0036)
PHONE..................................216 651-3333
Robert Kassouf, *Managing Prtnr*
EMP: 150
SQ FT: 10,000
SALES (est): 6.2MM **Privately Held**
SIC: 1622 Tunnel construction

(G-5812)
KANGAROO POUCH DAYCARE INC
488 Leverett Ln (44143-3722)
PHONE..................................440 473-4725
Teresa Fragomeni, *President*
EMP: 25
SALES (est): 397.3K **Privately Held**
SIC: 8351 Child day care services

(G-5813)
KAPLAN TRUCKING COMPANY (PA)
8777 Rockside Rd (44125-6112)
PHONE..................................216 341-3322
David Ferrante, *President*
James B Gifford, *Vice Pres*
John Wynne, *VP Opers*
Linda Chluda, *Safety Mgr*
Eric Hoffman, *Opers Mgr*
EMP: 75 EST: 1934
SQ FT: 30,000
SALES (est): 56.1MM **Privately Held**
SIC: 4213 Contract haulers

(G-5814)
KAPTON CAULKING & BUILDING
6500 Harris Rd (44147-2978)
PHONE..................................440 526-0670
Joseph H Anton, *President*
Mildred B Anton, *Corp Secy*
John S Anton, *Vice Pres*
EMP: 38
SQ FT: 4,000
SALES: 2MM **Privately Held**
SIC: 1741 1799 Tuckpointing or restoration; waterproofing; caulking (construction)

(G-5815)
KARAMU HOUSE INC (PA)
Also Called: KARAMU THEATRE
2355 E 89th St (44106-3403)
PHONE..................................216 795-7070
Nathaniel Jackson, *Facilities Mgr*
Gerry McClamy, *Director*
Aseelah Shareef, *Director*
EMP: 31 EST: 1919
SQ FT: 50,000
SALES: 1.8MM **Privately Held**
SIC: 8399 Community development groups

(G-5816)
KARPINSKI ENGINEERING INC (PA)
3135 Euclid Ave Ste 200 (44115-2524)
PHONE..................................216 391-3700
Jim Cicero, *President*
James T Cicero, *Principal*
Matt Morgan, *Engineer*
Erica Lesch, *Admin Asst*
Lee Hodkey, *Administration*
EMP: 60
SQ FT: 14,000
SALES (est): 10.4MM **Privately Held**
SIC: 8711 Electrical or electronic engineering; mechanical engineering

(G-5817)
KAUFMAN CONTAINER COMPANY (PA)
1000 Keystone Pkwy # 100 (44135-5119)
P.O. Box 35902 (44135-0902)
PHONE..................................216 898-2000
Roger Seid, *CEO*
Ken Slater, *President*

Charles Borowiak, *Vice Pres*
Roderick Cywinski, *Vice Pres*
Jeffery Gross, *Vice Pres*
▲ EMP: 128 EST: 1910
SQ FT: 180,000
SALES (est): 81.9MM **Privately Held**
SIC: 5085 2759 Commercial containers; plastic bottles; glass bottles; screen printing; labels & seals; printing

(G-5818)
KEGLER BROWN HL RITTER CO LPA
600 Superior Ave E # 2500 (44114-2600)
PHONE..................................216 586-6650
Jim Sammon, *President*
EMP: 70
SALES (est): 2.4MM
SALES (corp-wide): 30.5MM **Privately Held**
SIC: 8111 General practice attorney, lawyer
PA: Kegler, Brown, Hill & Ritter Co Lpa
65 E State St Ste 1800
Columbus OH 43215
614 462-5400

(G-5819)
KEITHLEY INSTRUMENTS INTL CORP
28775 Aurora Rd (44139-1891)
PHONE..................................440 248-0400
Joseph P Keithley, *President*
Ron Molder, *Treasurer*
EMP: 450
SQ FT: 200,000
SALES (est): 38.8MM
SALES (corp-wide): 6.4B **Publicly Held**
WEB: www.keithley.com
SIC: 5065 3825 Electronic parts & equipment; test equipment for electronic & electric measurement
HQ: Keithley Instruments, Llc
28775 Aurora Rd
Solon OH 44139
440 248-0400

(G-5820)
KELLEY & FERRARO LLP
950 Main Ave Ste 1300 (44113-7210)
PHONE..................................216 575-0777
James L Ferraro, *Partner*
Anthony Gallucci, *Partner*
John M Murphy, *Partner*
Thomas M Wilson, *Partner*
Jack Ruddy, *Marketing Staff*
EMP: 60
SALES (est): 7.7MM **Privately Held**
WEB: www.kelley-ferraro.com
SIC: 8111 General practice attorney, lawyer

(G-5821)
KELLEY STEEL ERECTORS INC (PA)
7220 Division St (44146-5406)
PHONE..................................440 232-1573
Dan Gold, *CEO*
Michael Kelley, *President*
Bob Hurley, *COO*
Jim Diver, *VP Opers*
Nancy Thompson, *Safety Dir*
EMP: 64
SQ FT: 150,000
SALES (est): 38.4MM **Privately Held**
SIC: 1791 7353 Structural steel erection; cranes & aerial lift equipment, rental or leasing

(G-5822)
KELLISON & CO (PA)
4925 Galaxy Pkwy Ste U (44128-5961)
PHONE..................................216 464-5160
Kevin Ellison, *Owner*
EMP: 59
SALES (est): 12.5MM **Privately Held**
WEB: www.kellison.com
SIC: 6411 Insurance brokers

(G-5823)
KENDIS & ASSOCIATES CO LPA
614 W Superior Ave # 1500 (44113-1334)
PHONE..................................216 579-1818
Toll Free:..................................888 -
James D Kendis, *President*

Robert D Kendis, *Corp Secy*
Mary Herbert, *Accountant*
Carl J Stanek,
EMP: 25
SALES (est): 2.5MM **Privately Held**
SIC: 8111 General practice law office

(G-5824)
KENNEDY MINT INC
Also Called: Kennedy Graphics
12102 Pearl Rd Rear (44136-3398)
PHONE..................................440 572-3222
Renato Montorsi, *President*
Theresa Montorsi, *Vice Pres*
George Berk, *Director*
EMP: 55
SQ FT: 60,000
SALES (est): 8.4MM **Privately Held**
WEB: www.kennedysg.com
SIC: 2653 2752 7538 Corrugated boxes, partitions, display items, sheets & pad; offset & photolithographic printing; general automotive repair shops

(G-5825)
KEY CAREER PLACE
2415 Woodland Ave (44115-3239)
PHONE..................................216 987-3029
Jeri Sue Thorton, *President*
EMP: 100
SALES (est): 1MM **Privately Held**
WEB: www.keycareerplace.com
SIC: 8222 7361 8299 Community college; employment agencies; schools & educational service

(G-5826)
KEYBANC CAPITAL MARKETS INC (HQ)
Also Called: McDonald Finanacial Group
127 Public Sq (44114-1217)
PHONE..................................800 553-2240
Douglas Preiser, *CEO*
Randy Paine, *President*
Matt Bevenour, *Managing Dir*
Ray Carso, *Managing Dir*
Jeff Geuther, *Managing Dir*
EMP: 400
SQ FT: 70,000
SALES (est): 300.6MM
SALES (corp-wide): 7.3B **Publicly Held**
WEB: www.keybanccm.com
SIC: 6021 6211 National commercial banks; security brokers & dealers
PA: Keycorp
127 Public Sq
Cleveland OH 44114
216 689-3000

(G-5827)
KEYBANK NATIONAL ASSOCIATION (HQ)
127 Public Sq Ste 5600 (44114-1226)
P.O. Box 92986 (44194-2986)
PHONE..................................800 539-2968
R B Heisler, *CEO*
Patrick Auletta, *President*
Mark R Danahy, *President*
Kevin Fowler, *President*
Jon Ogden, *President*
EMP: 500
SALES: 6.4B
SALES (corp-wide): 7.3B **Publicly Held**
WEB: www.keybank.com
SIC: 6021 6022 6159 National commercial banks; state commercial banks; automobile finance leasing
PA: Keycorp
127 Public Sq
Cleveland OH 44114
216 689-3000

(G-5828)
KEYBANK NATIONAL ASSOCIATION
100 Public Sq Ste 600 (44113-2207)
P.O. Box 94768 (44101-4768)
PHONE..................................216 689-8481
Lara Deleone, *Senior VP*
Lee Ann Habinak, *Vice Pres*
William Isley, *Vice Pres*
Janet Thiel, *Vice Pres*
Sean Flinn, *Engineer*
EMP: 46
SALES (corp-wide): 7.3B **Publicly Held**
SIC: 6021 National commercial banks

HQ: Keybank National Association
127 Public Sq Ste 5600
Cleveland OH 44114
800 539-2968

(G-5829)
KEYBANK NATIONAL ASSOCIATION
Key Education Resources
4910 Tiedeman Rd (44144-2338)
PHONE...................................216 813-0000
EMP: 130
SALES (corp-wide): 4.5B **Publicly Held**
SIC: 6411 Insurance Educational Services
HQ: Keybank National Association
127 Public Sq Ste 5600
Cleveland OH 44114
800 539-2968

(G-5830)
KINDERCARE EDUCATION LLC
Also Called: Children's World Learning Cent
679 Alpha Dr (44143-2152)
PHONE...................................440 442-3360
Sherri Wallace, *Director*
Erin Porter, *Director*
EMP: 30
SALES (corp-wide): 1.2B **Privately Held**
WEB: www.knowledgelearning.com
SIC: 8351 Group day care center
PA: Kindercare Education Llc
650 Ne Holladay St # 1400
Portland OR 97232
503 872-1300

(G-5831)
KINDERCARE LEARNING CTRS LLC
Also Called: Kindercare Child Care Network
5684 Mayfield Rd (44124-2916)
PHONE...................................440 442-8067
Melanie Baisden, *Director*
EMP: 26
SALES (corp-wide): 1.2B **Privately Held**
WEB: www.kindercare.com
SIC: 8351 Group day care center
HQ: Kindercare Learning Centers, Llc
650 Ne Holladay St # 1400
Portland OR 97232
503 872-1300

(G-5832)
KINGSBURY TOWER I LTD
8925 Hough Ave (44106-5700)
PHONE...................................216 795-3950
EMP: 99 EST: 2012
SALES (est): 2.7MM **Privately Held**
SIC: 6513 Apartment Building Operator

(G-5833)
KINNECT
1427 E 36th St Ste 4203f (44114-4170)
PHONE...................................216 692-1161
Mike Kenney, *Exec Dir*
John Cunningham, *Director*
Shannon Deinhart, *Director*
EMP: 30
SALES: 218.3K **Privately Held**
SIC: 8322 Child related social services

(G-5834)
KNALL BEVERAGE INC
4550 Tiedeman Rd Ste 1 (44144-2394)
PHONE...................................216 252-2500
Robert Knall, *CEO*
Michael A Knall, *Vice Pres*
▲ EMP: 65
SQ FT: 65,000
SALES (est): 9.8MM **Privately Held**
WEB: www.knallbev.com
SIC: 5181 5149 Beer & other fermented
malt liquors; ale; beverages, except cof-
fee & tea; mineral or spring water bottling

(G-5835)
KOINONIA HOMES INC
6161 Oak Tree Blvd # 400 (44131-2581)
PHONE...................................216 588-8777
William E Tumney, *Principal*
James C Maher, *Principal*
Dineen B Terstage, *Principal*
Cory Pearson, *Info Tech Dir*
Kia Wourms, *Recruiter*
EMP: 500
SALES: 25.2MM **Privately Held**
SIC: 8699 Charitable organization

(G-5836)
KOINONIA HOMES INC
Also Called: Brooklyn House
4248 W 35th St (44109-3108)
PHONE...................................216 351-5361
Dave Baund, *Branch Mgr*
EMP: 63
SALES (corp-wide): 5.5MM **Privately Held**
SIC: 8059 Rest home, with health care
PA: Koinonia Homes Inc
6797 Stearns Rd
North Olmsted OH 44070
216 588-8777

(G-5837)
KOLBUS AMERICA INC (HQ)
812 Huron Rd E Ste 750 (44115-1126)
PHONE...................................216 931-5100
Robert Shafer, *President*
Kelly Adams, *Area Mgr*
Charlie Carlevarini, *VP Finance*
Ruth Wilson, *Human Res Mgr*
Arthur Crawley, *Administration*
▲ EMP: 33
SQ FT: 22,000
SALES (est): 11MM
SALES (corp-wide): 136MM **Privately Held**
SIC: 5084 Industrial machinery & equip-
ment
PA: Kolbus Gmbh & Co. Kg
Osnabrucker Str. 77
Rahden 32369
577 171-0

(G-5838)
KOLLANDER WORLD TRAVEL INC
761 E 200th St (44119-3082)
PHONE...................................216 692-1000
Maya Kollander, *CEO*
August Kollander, *Ch of Bd*
Michael Benz, *President*
Tony Petkovsek, *Vice Pres*
Joseph Tomsick, *Vice Pres*
EMP: 30
SQ FT: 4,200
SALES (est): 4.2MM **Privately Held**
WEB: www.kollander-travel.com
SIC: 4724 Tourist agency arranging trans-
port, lodging & car rental

(G-5839)
KONE INC
6670 W Snowville Rd Ste 7 (44141-4300)
PHONE...................................330 762-8886
David Lytle, *President*
EMP: 25
SALES (corp-wide): 732.3MM **Privately Held**
WEB: www.us.kone.com
SIC: 7699 Elevators: inspection, service &
repair
HQ: Kone Inc.
4225 Naperville Rd # 400
Lisle IL 60532
630 577-1650

(G-5840)
KONICA MINOLTA BUSINESS SOLUTI
2 Summit Park Dr Ste 450 (44131-2586)
PHONE...................................910 990-5837
John Fabinak, *Branch Mgr*
EMP: 35
SQ FT: 12,000
SALES (corp-wide): 9.6B **Privately Held**
WEB: www.konicabt.com
SIC: 5044 Photocopy machines
HQ: Konica Minolta Business Solutions
U.S.A., Inc.
100 Williams Dr
Ramsey NJ 07446
201 825-4000

(G-5841)
KPMG LLP
1375 E 9th St Ste 2600 (44114-1796)
PHONE...................................216 696-9100
Robert Raaf, *Manager*
Sphr K Koutris, *Manager*
James Mylen, *Director*
EMP: 168

SALES (corp-wide): 3.8B **Privately Held**
SIC: 8721 Certified public accountant
PA: Kpmg Llp
1676 Intl Dr Ste 1200
Mclean VA 22102
703 286-8000

(G-5842)
L B & B ASSOCIATES INC
555 E 88th St (44108-1068)
PHONE...................................216 451-2672
Rachel M Rakes, *Branch Mgr*
EMP: 42 **Privately Held**
SIC: 8744 Facilities support services
PA: L B & B Associates Inc.
9891 Broken Land Pkwy # 400
Columbia MD 21046

(G-5843)
L O M INC
1370 Ontario St Ste 2000 (44113-1812)
PHONE...................................216 363-6009
Charles R Laurie, *President*
William T Doyle, *Vice Pres*
Patrick J Gannon, *Vice Pres*
Daniel J Ryan, *Treasurer*
Michael Flament, *Admin Sec*
EMP: 35
SQ FT: 20,000
SALES (est): 2.3MM **Privately Held**
SIC: 6531 Real estate managers

(G-5844)
LA VILLA CNFERENCE BANQUET CTR
11500 Brookpark Rd (44130-1133)
PHONE...................................216 265-9305
Ali Faraj, *President*
EMP: 25
SALES (est): 565.2K **Privately Held**
SIC: 7299 Banquet hall facilities

(G-5845)
LABELLE HMHEALTH CARE SVCS LLC
5500 Ridge Rd Ste 138 (44129-2367)
PHONE...................................440 842-3005
Sally Njume-Tatsing, *President*
EMP: 64
SALES (corp-wide): 2.4MM **Privately Held**
SIC: 8082 Home health care services
PA: Labelle Homehealth Care Services Llc
1653 Brice Rd
Reynoldsburg OH 43068
614 367-0881

(G-5846)
LABORATORY CORPORATION AMERICA
6789 Ridge Rd Ste 210 (44129-5635)
PHONE...................................440 884-1591
Tammy Rose, *Branch Mgr*
EMP: 25 **Publicly Held**
WEB: www.labcorp.com
SIC: 8071 Testing laboratories
HQ: Laboratory Corporation Of America
358 S Main St Ste 458
Burlington NC 27215
336 229-1127

(G-5847)
LABORATORY CORPORATION AMERICA
2525 E Royalton Rd Ste 3 (44147-2842)
PHONE...................................440 838-0404
Barbara Stone, *General Mgr*
EMP: 43 **Publicly Held**
WEB: www.labcorp.com
SIC: 8071 Blood analysis laboratory
HQ: Laboratory Corporation Of America
358 S Main St Ste 458
Burlington NC 27215
336 229-1127

(G-5848)
LAKE SIDE BUILDING MAINTENANCE
200 Public Sq (44114-2316)
PHONE...................................216 589-9900
Palmer Roy, *Manager*
EMP: 30
SALES (est): 304K **Privately Held**
SIC: 7349 Building maintenance services

(G-5849)
LAKESIDE SUPPLY CO
3000 W 117th St (44111-1667)
PHONE...................................216 941-6800
Ken Mathews, *President*
Brian Driscoll, *Vice Pres*
John Joseph Mathews, *Vice Pres*
John Mathews, *Vice Pres*
Steve Driscoll, *Purch Mgr*
EMP: 39 EST: 1932
SQ FT: 35,000
SALES (est): 31.3MM **Privately Held**
WEB: www.lakesidesupply.com
SIC: 5074 5075 5085 Plumbing fittings &
supplies; warm air heating equipment &
supplies; valves & fittings

(G-5850)
LAKEWOOD ACCEPTANCE CORP
15200 Lorain Ave (44111-5531)
PHONE...................................216 658-1234
Robert M Fairchild, *President*
Derre Buike, *Vice Pres*
EMP: 25
SALES (est): 2.4MM **Privately Held**
SIC: 6153 Financing of dealers by motor
vehicle manufacturers organ.

(G-5851)
LAKEWOOD COUNTRY CLUB COMPANY
2613 Bradley Rd (44145-1799)
PHONE...................................440 871-0400
Brian Pizzimenti, *General Mgr*
Dan Draeger, *Manager*
EMP: 75
SQ FT: 24,952
SALES: 5.9MM **Privately Held**
SIC: 7997 Country club, membership

(G-5852)
LAKEWOOD HOSPITAL ASSOCIATION
1450 Belle Ave (44107-4211)
PHONE...................................216 228-5437
Mary Jo Schwartz, *Personnel*
Mary Jo Swartz, *Manager*
EMP: 25
SALES (corp-wide): 8.9B **Privately Held**
SIC: 8062 8011 General medical & surgi-
cal hospitals; offices & clinics of medical
doctors
HQ: Lakewood Hospital Association
14519 Detroit Ave
Lakewood OH 44107
216 529-7160

(G-5853)
LAMAR ADVERTISING COMPANY
12222 Plaza Dr (44130-1058)
PHONE...................................216 676-4321
Tim Gerity, *Manager*
William Platko, *Manager*
EMP: 40
SQ FT: 4,879 **Publicly Held**
WEB: www.clearchanneloutdoor.com
SIC: 7312 Outdoor advertising services
PA: Lamar Advertising Company
5321 Corporate Blvd
Baton Rouge LA 70808

(G-5854)
LANCER INSURANCE COMPANY
6095 Parkland Blvd # 310 (44124-6140)
PHONE...................................440 473-1634
Paul Burn, *Vice Pres*
Maria Finucan, *Underwriter*
Pier Langmack, *Administration*
EMP: 50 **Privately Held**
WEB: www.mopslicenseins.com
SIC: 6331 Fire, marine & casualty insur-
ance
HQ: Lancer Insurance Company
370 W Park Ave
Long Beach NY 11561

(G-5855)
LARCHWOOD HEALTH GROUP LLC
Also Called: Larchwood Village Independent
4110 Rcky Rver Dr Ste 251 (44135)
PHONE...................................216 941-6100

Paul Dennis, *Partner*
Associated Estates, *General Ptnr*
Estate of Morris Fine, *General Ptnr*
Jeffrey Friedman, *General Ptnr*
Mark Milstein, *General Ptnr*
EMP: 35
SQ FT: 24,784
SALES (est): 2.4MM **Privately Held**
SIC: 8361 8051 Residential care; skilled
nursing care facilities

(G-5856)
LASSITER CORPORATION
Also Called: Financial Bookkeeping Service
3700 Kelley Ave (44114-4533)
PHONE................................216 391-4800
Frank Arstone, *President*
EMP: 50
SQ FT: 4,000
SALES (est): 1.9MM **Privately Held**
SIC: 8721 6282 Accounting, auditing &
bookkeeping; investment advice

(G-5857)
LAUREL SCHOOL (PA)
1 Lyman Cir (44122-2199)
PHONE................................216 464-1441
Heather Ettinger, *President*
Ann Klotz, *Principal*
Mary Pellerano, *Facilities Dir*
Sharon Stusek, *Accounting Mgr*
Allison Grant, *Human Res Mgr*
EMP: 104
SQ FT: 70,000
SALES: 19.9MM **Privately Held**
SIC: 8351 8211 Preschool center; private
combined elementary & secondary school

(G-5858)
**LAWRENCE INDUSTRIES INC
(PA)**
4500 Lee Rd Ste 120 (44128-2959)
PHONE................................216 518-7000
Lawrence A Kopittke Sr, *President*
Arthur Kopittke, *Vice Pres*
Richard L Kopittke, *Vice Pres*
◆ **EMP:** 151
SQ FT: 160,000
SALES (est): 17.2MM **Privately Held**
WEB: www.hudsonsupply.com
SIC: 3599 3541 7699 5084 Machine
shop, jobbing & repair; sawing & cutoff
machines (metalworking machinery); tool
repair services; metalworking tools (such
as drills, taps, dies, files); machine tools &
metalworking machinery; industrial sup-
plies; abrasive products

(G-5859)
LE NAILS (PA)
1144 Southpark Ctr (44136-9326)
PHONE................................440 846-1866
Luu Tran, *Owner*
Jackie Volfe, *Owner*
EMP: 46
SALES (est): 601.9K **Privately Held**
SIC: 7231 Manicurist, pedicurist

(G-5860)
LEFCO WORTHINGTON LLC
18451 Euclid Ave (44112-1016)
PHONE................................216 432-4422
Larry E Fulton,
EMP: 31
SQ FT: 30,000
SALES (est): 6.2MM **Privately Held**
WEB: www.lefcoindustries.com
SIC: 4783 2441 4226 Packing & crating;
boxes, wood; special warehousing & stor-
age

(G-5861)
**LEGACY VILLAGE HOSPITALITY
LLC**
Also Called: Hyatt Place Cleveland/
24665 Cedar Rd (44124-3789)
PHONE................................216 382-3350
Dena St Clair, *General Mgr*
EMP: 99
SALES (est): 301.3K **Privately Held**
SIC: 7011 Hotels

(G-5862)
**LEGACY VILLAGE
MANAGEMENT OFF**
25333 Cedar Rd Ste 303 (44124-3788)
PHONE................................216 382-3871
Diane Kotowski, *Owner*
EMP: 30
SALES (est): 3.1MM **Privately Held**
SIC: 8741 Management services

(G-5863)
**LEGAL AID SOCIETY OF
CLEVELAND (PA)**
1223 W 6th St Fl 4 (44113-1354)
PHONE................................216 861-5500
Tom Mlakar, *Vice Pres*
Bettina Kaplan, *Finance*
Colleen Cotter, *Exec Dir*
EMP: 60
SQ FT: 25,200
SALES: 7.3MM **Privately Held**
SIC: 8111 Legal aid service

(G-5864)
LEGNDARY CLEANERS LLC
1215 W 10th St Apt 1003 (44113-1285)
PHONE................................216 374-1205
Donnie Burton, *Director*
EMP: 35 **EST:** 2011
SALES (est): 1.5MM **Privately Held**
SIC: 4581 Aircraft cleaning & janitorial
service

(G-5865)
LESCO INC (HQ)
1385 E 36th St (44114-4114)
PHONE................................216 706-9250
J Martin Erbaugh, *Ch of Bd*
Jeffrey L Rutherford, *President*
Vincent C Fornes, *Principal*
James I Fitzgibbon, *Principal*
Louise Lang, *Principal*
▼ **EMP:** 220 **EST:** 1962
SQ FT: 38,643
SALES (est): 193.7MM
SALES (corp-wide): 37.3B **Publicly Held**
WEB: www.lesco.com
SIC: 5191 5083 5261 Grass seed; lawn
machinery & equipment; mowers, power;
nurseries; lawn & garden equipment; lawn
& garden supplies
PA: Deere & Company
1 John Deere Pl
Moline IL 61265
309 765-8000

(G-5866)
LIBERTY EMS SERVICES LLC
1294 W 70th St (44102-2018)
PHONE................................216 630-6626
Heinrich Kitiss, *Partner*
Susan Rushworth,
EMP: 50
SALES (est): 562.1K **Privately Held**
SIC: 4119 Ambulance service

(G-5867)
**LIBERTY FORD SOUTHWEST
INC**
6600 Pearl Rd (44130-3808)
PHONE................................440 888-2600
James Herrick, *President*
EMP: 60
SALES (est): 18.7MM **Privately Held**
SIC: 5511 5012 Automobiles, new & used;
trucks, commercial

(G-5868)
LIFEBANC
4775 Richmond Rd (44128-5919)
PHONE................................216 752-5433
Barbara Welker, *Finance*
James Bartlebaugh, *Human Res Dir*
Tom Krempa, *Info Tech Dir*
Steve Sharish, *Prgrmr*
Gordon Bowen, *Exec Dir*
EMP: 81
SQ FT: 2,100
SALES: 31.8MM **Privately Held**
WEB: www.lifebanc.org
SIC: 8099 Organ bank

(G-5869)
LIGHT OF HEARTS VILLA
283 Union St Ofc (44146-4500)
PHONE................................440 232-1991
Sister Christine Rody, *Principal*
Ida Stanley, *Mktg Dir*
Beth Hickle, *Exec Dir*
Sister Helen T Scasny, *Director*
Dennis Giangiacomo, *Director*
EMP: 70
SALES: 3.9MM **Privately Held**
SIC: 8322 8052 Emergency shelters; in-
termediate care facilities

(G-5870)
**LILLIAN AND BETTY RATNER
SCHL**
27575 Shaker Blvd (44124-5002)
PHONE................................216 464-0033
Sam Chestnut, *Headmaster*
Michael Griffith, *Headmaster*
EMP: 40
SQ FT: 32,248
SALES: 2.5MM **Privately Held**
SIC: 8211 8351 Private elementary
school; Montessori child development
center

(G-5871)
**LINCOLN MOVING & STORAGE
CO**
8686 Brookpark Rd (44129-6808)
PHONE................................216 741-5500
Toll Free:................................888 -
Lawrence H Roush, *President*
Jim Morris, *General Mgr*
Eugene Dietrich, *Vice Pres*
Edith Roush, *Treasurer*
Sharon Dietrich, *Admin Sec*
EMP: 70 **EST:** 1976
SQ FT: 60,000
SALES (est): 7.8MM **Privately Held**
WEB: www.lincolnstorage.com
SIC: 1799 4213 4214 Office furniture in-
stallation; trucking, except local; local
trucking with storage

(G-5872)
**LINKING EMPLOYMENT
ABILITIES (PA)**
Also Called: LEAP
2545 Lorain Ave (44113-3412)
PHONE................................216 696-2716
Melanie Hogan, *Exec Dir*
David Reichert, *Exec Dir*
EMP: 36
SQ FT: 9,000
SALES (est): 2.3MM **Privately Held**
WEB: www.leapinfo.org
SIC: 8331 Job counseling

(G-5873)
**LINSALATA CAPITAL PARTNERS
FUN**
5900 Landerbrook Dr # 280 (44124-4020)
PHONE................................440 684-1400
Frank Linsalata, *Partner*
EMP: 204
SALES (est): 14MM **Privately Held**
SIC: 6211 Brokers, security; dealers, secu-
rity

(G-5874)
**LITTLE BARK VIEW LIMITED
(PA)**
8111 Rockside Rd Ste 200 (44125-6135)
PHONE................................216 520-1250
Terry A Gardner, *Partner*
Andrew R Bailey, *Exec VP*
Catherine Harris, *Vice Pres*
Domenic Vitanza, *Purch Mgr*
Bradley Carroll, *Accountant*
EMP: 30
SQ FT: 5,480
SALES (est): 9.3MM **Privately Held**
SIC: 6513 Apartment building operators

(G-5875)
LITTLER MENDELSON PC
1100 Superior Ave E Fl 20 (44114-2518)
PHONE................................216 696-7600
Bradley Scherman, *Branch Mgr*
EMP: 80

SALES (corp-wide): 342.9MM **Privately
Held**
SIC: 8111 General practice law office
PA: Littler Mendelson, P.C.
333 Bush St Fl 34
San Francisco CA 94104
415 433-1940

(G-5876)
LIVING MATTERS LLC
13613 Caine Ave (44105-6335)
P.O. Box 25771 (44125-0771)
PHONE................................866 587-8074
Charlea Brown, *CEO*
EMP: 35
SALES (est): 401.4K **Privately Held**
SIC: 7349 7342 Building & office cleaning
services; building cleaning service; office
cleaning or charring; rest room cleaning
service

(G-5877)
LLP ZIEGLER METZGER
1111 Superior Ave E # 1000 (44114-2568)
PHONE................................216 781-5470
Robert Metzger, *Managing Prtnr*
Stephen M Darlington, *Partner*
Paul Klaug, *Partner*
Richard Spotz Jr, *Partner*
William L Spring, *Partner*
EMP: 40
SALES (est): 4.6MM **Privately Held**
SIC: 8111 General practice attorney,
lawyer

(G-5878)
LOCAL 18 IUOE (PA)
3515 Prospect Ave E Fl 1 (44115-2661)
PHONE................................216 432-3131
Patrick L Sink, *Manager*
EMP: 25
SALES: 20.6MM **Privately Held**
SIC: 8631 Labor unions & similar labor or-
ganizations

(G-5879)
LOGAN CLUTCH CORPORATION
Also Called: Lc
28855 Ranney Pkwy (44145-1173)
PHONE................................440 808-4258
Madelon Logan, *CEO*
William A Logan, *President*
Elyse Logan, *Vice Pres*
▲ **EMP:** 30
SQ FT: 33,000
SALES (est): 8.1MM **Privately Held**
WEB: www.loganclutch.com
SIC: 3568 5085 Clutches, except vehicu-
lar; industrial supplies

(G-5880)
**LONGWOOD PHASE ONE
ASSOC LP**
Also Called: Arbor Park Village
3750 Fleming Ave (44115-3741)
PHONE................................561 998-0700
Dennis H Blackinton, *Partner*
EMP: 30
SALES (est): 1MM **Privately Held**
SIC: 6531 Real estate agents & managers

(G-5881)
LOUIS STOKES HEAD START
4075 E 173rd St (44128-1700)
PHONE................................216 295-0854
Brenda Vann, *Manager*
EMP: 30
SALES (est): 686.9K **Privately Held**
SIC: 8351 Head start center, except in con-
junction with school

(G-5882)
LOWES HOME CENTERS LLC
7327 Northcliff Ave (44144-3249)
PHONE................................216 351-4723
Mike Hoffmeier, *Branch Mgr*
EMP: 150
SALES (corp-wide): 68.6B **Publicly Held**
SIC: 5211 5031 5722 5064 Lumber &
other building materials; building materi-
als, exterior; building materials, interior;
household appliance stores; electrical ap-
pliances, television & radio

HQ: Lowe's Home Centers, Llc
1605 Curtis Bridge Rd
Wilkesboro NC 28697
336 658-4000

(G-5883)
LQ MANAGEMENT LLC
Also Called: La Quinta Inn
6161 Quarry Ln (44131-2203)
PHONE...............................216 447-1133
Virginia Klamut, *Branch Mgr*
EMP: 25
SALES (corp-wide): 1.8B **Publicly Held**
WEB: www.neubayern.net
SIC: 7011 Hotels
HQ: Lq Management L.L.C.
909 Hidden Rdg Ste 600
Irving TX 75038
214 492-6600

(G-5884)
LQ MANAGEMENT LLC
Also Called: La Quinta Inn
4222 W 150th St (44135-1308)
PHONE...............................216 251-8500
Greg Shields, *Manager*
EMP: 30
SALES (corp-wide): 1.8B **Publicly Held**
WEB: www.neubayern.net
SIC: 7011 Hotels
HQ: Lq Management L.L.C.
909 Hidden Rdg Ste 600
Irving TX 75038
214 492-6600

(G-5885)
LTD PRODUCTIONS LLC
9904 S Highland Ave (44125-5914)
PHONE...............................440 688-1905
Douglas Jones, *Principal*
EMP: 54
SALES (est): 681.1K **Privately Held**
SIC: 7389 Developing & laboratory services, motion picture

(G-5886)
LU-JEAN FENG CLINIC LLC
31200 Pinetree Rd (44124-5928)
PHONE...............................216 831-7007
Lu Jean Feng, *Ltd Ptnr*
Christine George, *Vice Pres*
Quinn Walko, *Opers-Prdtn-Mfg*
Gary Williams, *Controller*
Dori Savron, *Director*
EMP: 30
SALES (est): 4.4MM **Privately Held**
SIC: 8011 Plastic surgeon

(G-5887)
LUCAS PRECISION LLC
13020 Saint Clair Ave (44108-2033)
PHONE...............................216 451-5588
Jiri Ferenc, *President*
Paul Mandelbaum, *Vice Pres*
Rodney Zimmerman, *Sales Mgr*
JD Correa, *Accounts Mgr*
Jim Gray, *Accounts Mgr*
▲ EMP: 25 EST: 2014
SALES (est): 4.3MM **Privately Held**
SIC: 7699 Industrial machinery & equipment repair

(G-5888)
LUCIEN REALTY
18630 Detroit Ave (44107-3202)
PHONE...............................440 331-8500
Ron Lucien, *Owner*
John Lucien, *Co-Owner*
Andy Tabor, *Real Est Agnt*
EMP: 60
SALES (est): 1.6MM **Privately Held**
SIC: 6531 Real estate agent, residential

(G-5889)
LUTHERAN HOME
2116 Dover Center Rd (44145-3154)
PHONE...............................440 871-0090
Charles H Rinne, *CEO*
Carolyn Nyikes, *CFO*
Nancy Marks, *Asst Controller*
Mary Davies, *Director*
William E Seefeld, *Director*
EMP: 280
SQ FT: 120,000

SALES: 16.8K **Privately Held**
WEB: www.lutheran-home.org
SIC: 8052 8051 Intermediate care facilities; skilled nursing care facilities

(G-5890)
LUTHERAN METROPOLITAN MINISTRY
Also Called: Homeless Center
2100 Lakeside Ave E (44114-1126)
P.O. Box 201443 (44120-8107)
PHONE...............................216 658-4638
Sue Cynatus, *CFO*
Michael Sering, *Director*
EMP: 180
SALES: 950K **Privately Held**
SIC: 8399 Community development groups

(G-5891)
M & M WINTERGREENS INC
3728 Fulton Rd (44109-2379)
P.O. Box 34179 (44134-0879)
PHONE...............................216 398-1288
Michael Boost, *President*
Mary L Boost, *Vice Pres*
Shannon M Kurt, *Vice Pres*
EMP: 53
SQ FT: 48,000
SALES: 1.6MM **Privately Held**
WEB: www.wintergreens.com
SIC: 5199 Gifts & novelties

(G-5892)
MACDONALD MOTT LLC
18013 Cleveland Pkwy Dr # 200
(44135-3235)
PHONE...............................216 535-3640
Michael Vitale, *Vice Pres*
Zachary Cline, *Project Mgr*
Frank Frandina, *Project Mgr*
Donald Wotring, *Engineer*
Mike McCarthy, *Office Mgr*
EMP: 25
SALES (corp-wide): 507.4MM **Privately Held**
SIC: 8711 Sanitary engineers; consulting engineer
HQ: Macdonald Mott Llc
12647 Alcosta Blvd
San Ramon CA 94583

(G-5893)
MACE PERSONAL DEF & SEC INC (HQ)
4400 Carnegie Ave (44103-4342)
PHONE...............................440 424-5321
Carl Smith, *CFO*
◆ EMP: 30
SQ FT: 30,000
SALES (est): 5.1MM
SALES (corp-wide): 28.3MM **Publicly Held**
SIC: 3999 5065 Self-defense sprays; security control equipment & systems
PA: Mace Security International, Inc.
4400 Carnegie Ave
Cleveland OH 44103
440 424-5321

(G-5894)
MAGOLIUS MARGOLIUS & ASSOC LPA
55 Public Sq Ste 1100 (44113-1901)
PHONE...............................216 621-2034
Andrew Margolius, *Owner*
EMP: 60
SALES (est): 5.8MM **Privately Held**
SIC: 8111 General practice attorney, lawyer

(G-5895)
MAHALLS 20 LANES
13200 Madison Ave (44107-4813)
PHONE...............................216 521-3280
Thomas J Mahall, *President*
Sue Shestina, *Manager*
EMP: 45
SQ FT: 16,000
SALES (est): 1.8MM **Privately Held**
WEB: www.mahalls.com
SIC: 7933 5813 Ten pin center; tavern (drinking places)

(G-5896)
MAI CAPITAL MANAGEMENT LLC
1360 E 9th St Ste 1100 (44114-1717)
PHONE...............................216 920-4800
Roberta Lemmo, *Managing Dir*
Gerald Gray, *Portfolio Mgr*
Jeff Stark, *Portfolio Mgr*
Richard J Buoncore, *Mng Member*
Bill Collins, *Director*
EMP: 95
SQ FT: 25,500
SALES: 22.5MM **Privately Held**
SIC: 6282 Investment advisory service

(G-5897)
MAI CAPITAL MANAGEMENT LLC
1360 E 9th St Ste 1100 (44114-1717)
PHONE...............................216 920-4913
Scott Roulston, *Principal*
EMP: 42
SALES (est): 6.7MM **Privately Held**
SIC: 6211 Security brokers & dealers

(G-5898)
MAIN SAIL LLC
20820 Chagrin Blvd # 102 (44122-5323)
PHONE...............................216 472-5100
D Brian Conley, *Managing Prtnr*
Ken Conley, *Partner*
Scott Harris, *Partner*
Robert Mackinley, *Partner*
Rodger Cahn, *CFO*
EMP: 70
SQ FT: 5,000
SALES (est): 12.8MM **Privately Held**
SIC: 7379 ; computer related consulting services

(G-5899)
MAINTHIA TECHNOLOGIES INC
Also Called: MTI
21000 Brookpark Rd (44135-3127)
PHONE...............................216 433-2198
Hemant Mainthia, *President*
EMP: 80
SALES (est): 6.5MM **Privately Held**
SIC: 1531 Operative builders
PA: Mainthia Technologies, Inc.
7055 Engle Rd Ste 502
Cleveland OH 44130

(G-5900)
MAJASTAN GROUP LLC
Also Called: Visiting Angels
12200 Fairhill Rd B201 (44120-1058)
PHONE...............................216 231-6400
Kevin Johnson, *CEO*
Connie Johnson, *Director*
EMP: 80
SALES (est): 1.8MM **Privately Held**
SIC: 8082 Home health care services

(G-5901)
MAJESTIC STEEL PROPERTIES INC
31099 Chagrin Blvd # 150 (44124-5930)
PHONE...............................440 786-2666
Todd Leebow, *President*
Matthew Leebow, *Principal*
George Reider, *Vice Pres*
Susan Suvak, *Treasurer*
Christopher Meyer, *Admin Sec*
EMP: 100 EST: 2012
SALES (est): 2.4MM **Privately Held**
SIC: 6512 Commercial & industrial building operation

(G-5902)
MAJESTIC STEEL USA INC (PA)
Also Called: Majestic Steel Service
31099 Chagrin Blvd # 150 (44124-5930)
PHONE...............................440 786-2666
Todd Leebow, *President*
Jonathan Leebow, *Exec VP*
Matthew Leebow, *Exec VP*
Mike Garrett, *Vice Pres*
Susan Suvak, *CFO*
▲ EMP: 186
SQ FT: 450,000
SALES (est): 166.6MM **Privately Held**
WEB: www.majesticsteel.com
SIC: 5051 Sheets, metal; structural shapes, iron or steel

(G-5903)
MALLEYS CANDIES INC
Also Called: Malley's Chocolates
13400 Brookpark Rd (44135-5145)
PHONE...............................216 529-6262
Patrick Malley, *Manager*
EMP: 25
SQ FT: 1,960
SALES (corp-wide): 53.5MM **Privately Held**
WEB: www.malleys.com
SIC: 2066 4225 5441 2064 Chocolate & cocoa products; general warehousing & storage; candy, nut & confectionery stores; candy & other confectionery products
PA: Malley's Candies
1685 Victoria Ave
Lakewood OH 44107
216 362-8700

(G-5904)
MALONEY + NOVOTNY LLC (PA)
1111 Superior Ave E # 700 (44114-2540)
PHONE...............................216 363-0100
Matthew Maloney, *Mng Member*
Peter J Chudyk,
Chris Felice,
Diane Gallagher,
Timothy Novotny,
EMP: 82 EST: 1930
SQ FT: 33,241
SALES (est): 18.3MM **Privately Held**
SIC: 8721 Certified public accountant

(G-5905)
MANNION & GRAY CO LPA
1375 E 9th St Ste 1600 (44114-1752)
PHONE...............................216 344-9422
Thomas P Mannion, *Principal*
EMP: 29
SALES (est): 4.5MM **Privately Held**
SIC: 8111 General practice law office

(G-5906)
MARC GLASSMAN INC
Also Called: Marc's Distribution Center
19101 Snow Rd (44142-1416)
PHONE...............................216 265-7700
Jim How, *Manager*
EMP: 200
SALES (corp-wide): 1.1B **Privately Held**
WEB: www.marcs.com
SIC: 4225 General warehousing & storage
PA: Marc Glassman, Inc.
5841 W 130th St
Cleveland OH 44130
216 265-7700

(G-5907)
MARCUS THOMAS LLC (PA)
4781 Richmond Rd (44128-5919)
PHONE...............................216 292-4700
Jim Nash, *President*
Mark Bachmann,
Joseph J Blaha,
Beth Hallisy,
Joanne Kim,
EMP: 94
SQ FT: 26,000
SALES (est): 22.3MM **Privately Held**
WEB: www.marcusthomasad.com
SIC: 7311 Advertising consultant

(G-5908)
MARIOS INTERNATIONAL SPA & HT
7155 W Pleasant Valley Rd (44129-6747)
PHONE...............................440 845-7373
Bonnie Kadelski, *Branch Mgr*
EMP: 25
SQ FT: 2,842
SALES (est): 234.7K
SALES (corp-wide): 2.2MM **Privately Held**
SIC: 7231 Hairdressers
PA: Mario's International Spa & Hotel, Inc
34 N Chillicothe Rd
Aurora OH 44202
330 562-5141

(G-5909)
MARKOWITZ ROSENBERG ASSOC DRS
5850 Landerbrook Dr # 100 (44124-4067)
PHONE.................................440 646-2200
Stuart Markowitz, *President*
Kristen Johnson, *Manager*
EMP: 26
SALES (est): 2.1MM **Privately Held**
SIC: 8011 Internal medicine, physician/surgeon

(G-5910)
MARLIN MECHANICAL LLC
6600 Grant Ave (44105-5624)
PHONE.................................800 669-2645
Robert M Ambrose,
EMP: 25
SQ FT: 12,500
SALES (est): 2.8MM
SALES (corp-wide): 78.3MM **Privately Held**
WEB: www.marlinmech.com
SIC: 1711 Mechanical contractor
PA: Columbia National Group, Inc.
　6600 Grant Ave
　Cleveland OH 44105
　216 883-4972

(G-5911)
MARRIOTT HOTEL SERVICES INC
4277 W 150th St (44135-1310)
PHONE.................................216 252-5333
Greg Huber, *General Mgr*
Christy Horner, *Manager*
EMP: 150
SALES (corp-wide): 20.7B **Publicly Held**
SIC: 7011 5812 5947 5813 Hotels; eating places; gift, novelty & souvenir shop; drinking places
HQ: Marriott Hotel Services, Inc.
　10400 Fernwood Rd
　Bethesda MD 20817

(G-5912)
MARRIOTT INTERNATIONAL INC
127 Public Sq Fl 1 (44114-1216)
PHONE.................................216 696-9200
Bob Megazzini, *Manager*
EMP: 300
SALES (corp-wide): 20.7B **Publicly Held**
SIC: 7011 Hotels & motels
PA: Marriott International, Inc.
　10400 Fernwood Rd
　Bethesda MD 20817
　301 380-3000

(G-5913)
MARS ELECTRIC COMPANY (PA)
6655 Beta Dr Ste 200 (44143-2380)
PHONE.................................440 946-2250
Mark Doris, *President*
Steve Funk, *Business Mgr*
David Rathbun, *Project Mgr*
Brandon Light, *Warehouse Mgr*
Michael Doris, *Opers Staff*
EMP: 65
SQ FT: 43,000
SALES (est): 52.6MM **Privately Held**
WEB: www.mars-electric.com
SIC: 5063 5719 Electrical supplies; lighting fixtures; lighting fixtures

(G-5914)
MARSH USA INC
200 Public Sq Ste 3760 (44114-2321)
PHONE.................................216 937-1700
Claudia Kundrod, *President*
Leonard Gray, *Principal*
Charles Becker, *Sales/Mktg Mgr*
Jim Henderson, *Info Tech Mgr*
EMP: 300
SALES (corp-wide): 14.9B **Publicly Held**
WEB: www.marsh.com
SIC: 6411 Insurance brokers
HQ: Marsh Usa Inc.
　1166 Ave Of The Americas
　New York NY 10036
　212 345-6000

(G-5915)
MARSH USA INC
200 Public Sq Ste 900 (44114-2312)
PHONE.................................216 830-8000
EMP: 64
SALES (corp-wide): 14B **Publicly Held**
SIC: 6411 Insurance Agent/Broker
HQ: Marsh Usa Inc.
　1166 Ave Of The Americas
　New York NY 10036
　212 345-6000

(G-5916)
MARSOL APARTMENTS
6503 1/2 Marsol Rd (44124-3599)
PHONE.................................440 449-5800
Alvin Krenzler, *Partner*
Aron Drost, *Partner*
Charles Lawrence, *Partner*
Michael Link, *Partner*
Andrew Rosenfeld, *Partner*
EMP: 40
SQ FT: 12,000
SALES: 5.9MM **Privately Held**
SIC: 6513 Apartment building operators

(G-5917)
MARTENS DONALD & SONS (PA)
Also Called: Donald Martens Sons
10830 Brookpark Rd (44130-1119)
PHONE.................................216 265-4211
Dean Martens, *Owner*
Kevin Nolan, *General Mgr*
Donald A Martens Jr, *Vice Pres*
Michelle Martens, *Vice Pres*
Maureen Mino, *Human Res Dir*
EMP: 70
SQ FT: 7,410
SALES (est): 19.5MM **Privately Held**
SIC: 4119 Ambulance Service

(G-5918)
MARVEL CONSULTANTS (PA)
28601 Chagrin Blvd # 210 (44122-4546)
PHONE.................................216 292-2855
John M Sowers, *President*
Amy Bluso, *Opers Staff*
David Goldie, *Director*
Linda L Sowers, *Admin Sec*
Laura Oriani, *Recruiter*
EMP: 32
SQ FT: 5,000
SALES (est): 2.1MM **Privately Held**
SIC: 7361 Executive placement

(G-5919)
MARYMOUNT HEALTH CARE SYSTEMS
Also Called: CLEVELAND CLINIC HEALTH SYSTEM
13900 Mccracken Rd (44125)
PHONE.................................216 332-1100
Peggy Matthews, *Administration*
EMP: 30
SQ FT: 411,000
SALES: 2MM
SALES (corp-wide): 8.9B **Privately Held**
WEB: www.marymountplace.com
SIC: 8059 8741 Convalescent home; hospital management
PA: The Cleveland Clinic Foundation
　9500 Euclid Ave
　Cleveland OH 44195
　216 636-8335

(G-5920)
MARYMOUNT HOSPITAL INC (HQ)
9500 Euclid Ave (44195-0001)
PHONE.................................216 581-0500
David Kilarski, *CEO*
▲ EMP: 445
SQ FT: 411,000
SALES: 149.5MM
SALES (corp-wide): 8.9B **Privately Held**
SIC: 8062 8063 8051 8082 General medical & surgical hospitals; psychiatric hospitals; skilled nursing care facilities; home health care services
PA: The Cleveland Clinic Foundation
　9500 Euclid Ave
　Cleveland OH 44195
　216 636-8335

(G-5921)
MASON STEEL ERECTING INC
7500 Northfield Rd (44146-6110)
PHONE.................................440 439-1040
Leonard N Polster, *Partner*
Keith Polster, *Partner*
EMP: 40
SQ FT: 40,000
SALES (est): 2.3MM **Privately Held**
SIC: 1791 Structural steel erection

(G-5922)
MASSACHUSETTS MUTL LF INSUR CO
Also Called: Blue Chip, The
1660 W 2nd St Ste 850 (44113-1419)
PHONE.................................216 592-7359
Robert Fichter, *Sales Mgr*
Jeffrey Gale, *Branch Mgr*
Brenda James, *Case Mgr*
Amy Ryan, *Assistant*
EMP: 45
SALES (corp-wide): 16.7B **Privately Held**
WEB: www.massmutual.com
SIC: 6311 Life insurance
PA: Massachusetts Mutual Life Insurance Company
　1295 State St
　Springfield MA 01111
　413 788-8411

(G-5923)
MATT CONSTRUCTION SERVICES
6600 Grant Ave (44105-5624)
PHONE.................................216 641-0030
David Miller, *Ch of Bd*
Stephen F Ruscher, *Vice Pres*
EMP: 75
SQ FT: 13,000
SALES: 7MM
SALES (corp-wide): 78.3MM **Privately Held**
SIC: 1541 Renovation, remodeling & repairs: industrial buildings
PA: Columbia National Group, Inc.
　6600 Grant Ave
　Cleveland OH 44105
　216 883-4972

(G-5924)
MAYFIELD SAND RIDGE CLUB
1545 Sheridan Rd (44121-4023)
PHONE.................................216 381-0826
Robert McCreary III, *President*
Bonnie Milo, *Accountant*
Mike Sarris, *Assistant*
EMP: 90
SQ FT: 50,000
SALES: 8.4MM **Privately Held**
SIC: 7997 5941 5813 5812 Country club, membership; sporting goods & bicycle shops; drinking places; eating places

(G-5925)
MAZANEC RASKIN & RYDER CO LPA (PA)
Also Called: Mazanec Raskin & Ryder
34305 Solon Rd Ste 100 (44139-2660)
PHONE.................................440 248-7906
Todd M Raskin, *President*
Joseph Nicholas Jr, *Managing Prtnr*
Stanley S Keller, *Partner*
Walter H Krohngold, *Partner*
Thomas S Mazanec, *Vice Pres*
EMP: 70
SALES (est): 10.8MM **Privately Held**
WEB: www.mrrlaw.com
SIC: 8111 General practice attorney, lawyer

(G-5926)
MAZZELLA HOLDING COMPANY INC (PA)
Also Called: Mazella Companies
21000 Aerospace Pkwy (44142-1072)
PHONE.................................513 772-4466
Tony Mazzella, *CEO*
Kenneth Wright, *General Mgr*
James J Mazzella, *Vice Pres*
Mark Shubel, *Vice Pres*
Trevor Shubel, *Opers Mgr*
EMP: 62

SALES (est): 121.7MM **Privately Held**
SIC: 5051 5085 5088 5072 Rope, wire (not insulated); industrial supplies; marine supplies; builders' hardware

(G-5927)
MC CORMACK ADVISORS INTL
1360 E 9th St Ste 100 (44114-1730)
PHONE.................................216 522-1200
Rodney I Woods, *CEO*
Raymond G Banta, *CFO*
Gerald Gray, *Administration*
EMP: 47
SALES (est): 3.6MM **Privately Held**
SIC: 6282 Investment counselors

(G-5928)
MC MEECHAN CONSTRUCTION CO
17633 S Miles Rd (44128-3900)
PHONE.................................216 581-9373
Richard Mc Meechan, *President*
John Mc Meechan, *Vice Pres*
Gary Fetsko, *Manager*
EMP: 40
SQ FT: 5,000
SALES (est): 2.8MM **Privately Held**
WEB: www.mcmeechan.com
SIC: 1542 1541 Commercial & office buildings, renovation & repair; renovation, remodeling & repairs: industrial buildings

(G-5929)
MC PHILLIPS PLBG HTG & AC CO
Also Called: Honeywell Authorized Dealer
16115 Waterloo Rd (44110-1665)
PHONE.................................216 481-1400
Thomas P Mc Phillips III, *President*
EMP: 35
SQ FT: 8,000
SALES (est): 4.5MM **Privately Held**
SIC: 1711 1731 Plumbing contractors; mechanical contractor; warm air heating & air conditioning contractor; boiler maintenance contractor; energy management controls

(G-5930)
MCBEE SUPPLY CORPORATION
Also Called: Interstate-Mcbee
5300 Lakeside Ave E (44114-3916)
PHONE.................................216 881-0015
Ann Buescher, *President*
Brad Buescher, *Principal*
▲ EMP: 100 EST: 1958
SQ FT: 65,000
SALES (est): 29.2MM **Privately Held**
SIC: 5013 Automotive supplies & parts

(G-5931)
MCDONALD HOPKINS LLC (PA)
600 Superior Ave E # 2100 (44114-2690)
PHONE.................................216 348-5400
David Movius, *Ch of Bd*
Edward G Quinlisk, *Ch of Bd*
Michael P Witzke, *Ch of Bd*
Sharon Hach, *President*
Lori Kruszynski, *President*
EMP: 175 EST: 1933
SQ FT: 80,000
SALES (est): 44.6MM **Privately Held**
WEB: www.mcdonaldhopkins.com
SIC: 8111 General practice law office

(G-5932)
MCGOWAN & COMPANY INC (PA)
Also Called: McGowan Program Administrators
20595 Lorain Rd Ste 300 (44126-2062)
PHONE.................................800 545-1538
Thomas B Mc Gowan IV, *President*
Michael Palm, *Manager*
EMP: 89 EST: 1954
SQ FT: 48,000
SALES (est): 45.5MM **Privately Held**
WEB: www.mcgowanpersonal.com
SIC: 6411 Property & casualty insurance agent

(G-5933)
MCGREGOR SENIOR IND HSING
14900 Private Dr (44112-3470)
PHONE.................................216 851-8200

Robertson Hilton, *Principal*
EMP: 99
SQ FT: 96,040
SALES: 319.8K **Privately Held**
SIC: 8051 Skilled nursing care facilities

(G-5934)
MCI COMMUNICATIONS SVCS INC
Also Called: Verizon Business
21000 Brookpark Rd (44135-3127)
PHONE....................216 265-9953
David Fleming, *Branch Mgr*
EMP: 450
SALES (corp-wide): 130.8B **Publicly Held**
SIC: 4813 Long distance telephone communications
HQ: Mci Communications Services, Inc.
22001 Loudoun County Pkwy
Ashburn VA 20147
703 886-5600

(G-5935)
MCKINSEY & COMPANY INC
950 Main Ave Ste 1200 (44113-7209)
PHONE....................216 274-4000
Steve Schwarzwaelder, *Manager*
John Warner, *Manager*
EMP: 45
SQ FT: 3,000
SALES (corp-wide): 2.4B **Privately Held**
WEB: www.mckinsey.com
SIC: 8742 Business consultant
PA: Mckinsey & Company, Inc.
55 E 52nd St Fl 16
New York NY 10055
212 446-7000

(G-5936)
MCKINSEY & COMPANY INC
950 Main Ave Ste 1200 (44113-7209)
PHONE....................216 274-4000
Stefan Knupfer, *Manager*
EMP: 55
SALES (corp-wide): 2.4B **Privately Held**
WEB: www.mckinsey.com
SIC: 8742 Management consulting services
PA: Mckinsey & Company, Inc.
55 E 52nd St Fl 16
New York NY 10055
212 446-7000

(G-5937)
MCM GENERAL PROPERTIES LTD
13829 Euclid Ave (44112-4203)
PHONE....................216 851-8000
T Lichko, *Owner*
EMP: 25
SALES (est): 1.4MM **Privately Held**
SIC: 6512 Nonresidential building operators

(G-5938)
MCTECH CORP (PA)
8100 Grand Ave Ste 100 (44104-3164)
P.O. Box 5270 (44101-0270)
PHONE....................216 391-7700
Mark F Perkins, *President*
Lisa Cifani, *Corp Secy*
EMP: 40
SALES: 32.7MM **Privately Held**
WEB: www.mctech360.com
SIC: 1541 Industrial buildings & warehouses

(G-5939)
MEADEN & MOORE LLP (PA)
1375 E 9th St Ste 1800 (44114-2523)
PHONE....................216 241-3272
James P Carulas, *President*
Larry J Holland, *President*
David E Daywalt, *Vice Pres*
Theodore C Hocevar, *Vice Pres*
William Smith, *Vice Pres*
EMP: 90
SQ FT: 27,000
SALES (est): 36.2MM **Privately Held**
WEB: www.meadenmoore.com
SIC: 8721 Certified public accountant

(G-5940)
MED -CENTER/MED PARTNERS
Also Called: Med Center
34055 Solon Rd Ste 106 (44139-2600)
PHONE....................440 349-6400
Walter Offenhartz MD, *President*
Mariam Offenhartz, *Corp Secy*
Jeffery Folkman, *Vice Pres*
Susan Gerard, *Systems Staff*
EMP: 25
SQ FT: 2,525
SALES: 1.3MM **Privately Held**
SIC: 8011 Freestanding emergency medical center; general & family practice, physician/surgeon; occupational & industrial specialist, physician/surgeon; allergist

(G-5941)
MEDICAL ARTS PHYSICIAN CENTER
Also Called: St Vincent Medical Group
2475 E 22nd St Ste 120 (44115-3221)
PHONE....................216 431-1500
Stephanie Houston, *Principal*
Elueze Emmanuel I, *Med Doctor*
EMP: 60 **EST:** 2010
SALES (est): 123.3K **Privately Held**
SIC: 8099 8011 Health & allied services; physicians' office, including specialists

(G-5942)
MEDICAL CENTER CO (INC)
Also Called: McCo
2250 Circle Dr (44106-2664)
PHONE....................216 368-4256
Michael B Heise, *President*
Anne Roberts, *Business Mgr*
Todd Gadawski, *Vice Pres*
Scott Wilson, *Asst Treas*
EMP: 31
SQ FT: 112,000
SALES: 40.4MM **Privately Held**
SIC: 4961 4931 4941 Steam & air-conditioning supply; electric & other services combined; water supply

(G-5943)
MEDICAL MUTUAL OF OHIO (PA)
Also Called: Consumers Life Insurance Co
2060 E 9th St Frnt Ste (44115-1355)
PHONE....................216 687-7000
Rick A Chiricosta, *CEO*
Gardner Abbott, *Principal*
Et Al, *Principal*
John S Garber, *Principal*
Carter Kissell, *Principal*
EMP: 1400
SQ FT: 381,000
SALES (est): 1.2B **Privately Held**
WEB: www.medmutual.com
SIC: 6324 Dental insurance

(G-5944)
MEDLINK OF OHIO INC (DH)
20600 Chagrin Blvd # 290 (44122-5327)
PHONE....................216 751-5900
Stuart R Russell, *President*
Donald G Foster, *Admin Sec*
EMP: 400
SQ FT: 1,200
SALES (est): 8.8MM
SALES (corp-wide): 1.8B **Publicly Held**
SIC: 8049 8082 Nurses, registered & practical; home health care services
HQ: Almost Family, Inc.
9510 Ormsby Station Rd # 300
Louisville KY 40223
502 891-1000

(G-5945)
MEDPORT INC
8104 Madison Ave (44102-2725)
P.O. Box 25277 (44125-0277)
PHONE....................216 244-6832
Jay Reinholz, *President*
EMP: 54
SQ FT: 12,000
SALES (est): 4.6MM **Privately Held**
SIC: 7363 Medical help service

(G-5946)
MEDSEARCH STAFFING SVCS INC (PA)
16600 W Sprague Rd # 190 (44130-6318)
PHONE....................440 243-6363
Ralph E Steeber, *CEO*
Judith Steeber, *President*
EMP: 30
SQ FT: 2,400
SALES (est): 1.3MM **Privately Held**
WEB: www.medsearchonline.com
SIC: 7363 Labor resource services

(G-5947)
MEGA TECHWAY INC
760 Beta Dr Ste F (44143-2334)
PHONE....................440 605-0700
Richard Sadler, *President*
Teodoro Fragoso, *Vice Pres*
Steven Turchik, *Project Mgr*
Betty Ramirez, *Purch Mgr*
Ernesto Sarmiento, *Engineer*
EMP: 125
SQ FT: 3,500
SALES (est): 72.5MM **Privately Held**
WEB: www.megatechway.com
SIC: 5065 Electronic parts & equipment

(G-5948)
MEHLER AND HAGESTROM INC (PA)
Also Called: Mehler & Hagestrom
1660 W 2nd St Ste 780 (44113-1455)
PHONE....................216 621-4984
Edward Mehler, *President*
Pamela Greenfield, *Vice Pres*
EMP: 40
SQ FT: 6,000
SALES (est): 3.8MM **Privately Held**
WEB: www.mandh.com
SIC: 7338 Court reporting service

(G-5949)
MEI HOTELS INCORPORATED
1375 E 9th St Ste 2800 (44114-1795)
PHONE....................216 589-0441
David Moyar, *CEO*
Leandra James, *General Mgr*
Bert Moyar, *Chairman*
Dale Pelletier, *COO*
Gretchen Roberts, *Purchasing*
EMP: 250 **EST:** 1998
SALES (est): 18.1MM **Privately Held**
WEB: www.meihotels.com
SIC: 8741 6512 Hotel or motel management; commercial & industrial building operation

(G-5950)
MELAMED RILEY ADVERTISING LLC
1375 Euclid Ave Ste 410 (44115-1838)
PHONE....................216 241-2141
John Butler, *Partner*
Darla Dackiewicz, *Vice Pres*
Sarah Melamed,
Chuck Hurley,
Rick Riley,
EMP: 25
SQ FT: 8,000
SALES (est): 4.5MM **Privately Held**
WEB: www.mradvertising.com
SIC: 7311 Advertising consultant

(G-5951)
MELO INTERNATIONAL INC
3700 Kelley Ave (44114-4533)
PHONE....................440 519-0526
Rondee Kamins, *CEO*
EMP: 350
SALES (est): 9.8MM **Privately Held**
SIC: 8742 Retail trade consultant

(G-5952)
MENORAH PARK CENTER FOR SENIO (PA)
27100 Cedar Rd (44122-1156)
PHONE....................216 831-6500
Ira Kaplan, *President*
Enid Roseinberg, *President*
Art Kitch, *General Mgr*
Steve Saneda, *Business Mgr*
Amy Morgenstern, *Trustee*
EMP: 920
SQ FT: 242,000
SALES: 71.1MM **Privately Held**
WEB: www.menorahpark.org
SIC: 8051 6513 8322 Skilled nursing care facilities; apartment building operators; outreach program

(G-5953)
MENTAL HEALTH SERVICES (PA)
Also Called: Frontline Service
1744 Payne Ave (44114-2910)
PHONE....................216 623-6555
Nicole Eggert, *Program Mgr*
Susan Lisw-S, *Program Mgr*
Steve Friedman, *Exec Dir*
Katie Paul, *Executive Asst*
Kimberly Johnston, *Social Worker*
EMP: 38
SQ FT: 7,500
SALES: 24.4MM **Privately Held**
SIC: 8093 Mental health clinic, outpatient

(G-5954)
MENZIES AVIATION (TEXAS) INC
5921 Cargo Rd (44135-3111)
P.O. Box 81145 (44181-0145)
PHONE....................216 362-6565
Paul Yagel, *Branch Mgr*
EMP: 50
SALES (corp-wide): 3.2B **Privately Held**
WEB: www.asig.com
SIC: 4581 Airports, flying fields & services
HQ: Menzies Aviation (Texas), Inc.
4900 Diplomacy Rd
Fort Worth TX 76155
469 281-8200

(G-5955)
MERIT LEASING CO LLC
Also Called: Grande Pointe Healthcare Cmnty
3 Merit Dr (44143-1457)
PHONE....................216 261-9592
Stephen L Rosedale, *Chairman*
Charles R Stoltz, *CPA*
Jen Stitt, *Office Mgr*
Ruthie Boris, *Director*
Tyne Esarey, *Director*
EMP: 180
SQ FT: 62,000
SALES (est): 5.4MM **Privately Held**
SIC: 8051 Skilled nursing care facilities

(G-5956)
MERITECH INC
4577 Hinckley Indus Pkwy (44109-6009)
PHONE....................216 459-8333
Dennis Bednar, *President*
Mary Ann Bednar, *Vice Pres*
John Defranco, *Manager*
Rob Montgomery, *Technology*
Bill Beiter, *Assistant*
EMP: 98
SQ FT: 30,000
SALES (est): 55.1MM **Privately Held**
SIC: 5044 Copying equipment

(G-5957)
MERLE-HOLDEN ENTERPRISES INC (PA)
Also Called: Illusion Unlimited
5715 Broadview Rd (44134-1601)
PHONE....................216 661-6887
Dennis Millard, *President*
Tom Reid, *Vice Pres*
EMP: 25
SQ FT: 3,000
SALES: 1.2MM **Privately Held**
WEB: www.illusionunlimited.com
SIC: 7231 Unisex hair salons

(G-5958)
MERRICK HOUSE (PA)
Also Called: MERRICK HOUSE CLARK/FULTON
1050 Starkweather Ave (44113-4455)
PHONE....................216 771-5077
Michelle Curry, *Exec Dir*
Tiffany Ashley, *Director*
Lovie Freeman, *Admin Asst*
Patricia Cronin, *Assistant*
EMP: 30
SQ FT: 10,940
SALES: 1.1MM **Privately Held**
WEB: www.mhsettlement.org
SIC: 8322 8351 Community center; child day care services

GEOGRAPHIC

(G-5959)
MERRILL LYNCH PIERCE FENNER
1375 E 9th St Ste 1400 (44114-1747)
PHONE....................216 363-6500
Jean Shank, *Assistant VP*
Adam Schoesler, *Vice Pres*
Dean Ducato, *Investment Ofcr*
Paul Lehrman, *Investment Ofcr*
Craig Leone, *Investment Ofcr*
EMP: 165
SALES (corp-wide): 110.5B **Publicly Held**
WEB: www.merlyn.com
SIC: 6211 6282 Security brokers & dealers; investment advice
HQ: Merrill Lynch, Pierce, Fenner & Smith Incorporated
111 8th Ave
New York NY 10011
800 637-7455

(G-5960)
MERRILL LYNCH PIERCE FENNER
30195 Chagrin Blvd # 120 (44124-5776)
PHONE....................216 292-8000
Edward Grimpe, *Manager*
Kenneth Otstot, *Manager*
Martin R Berwitt, *Agent*
EMP: 40
SALES (corp-wide): 110.5B **Publicly Held**
WEB: www.merlyn.com
SIC: 6211 Security brokers & dealers
HQ: Merrill Lynch, Pierce, Fenner & Smith Incorporated
111 8th Ave
New York NY 10011
800 637-7455

(G-5961)
MET-CHEM INC
837 E 79th St (44103-1807)
PHONE....................216 881-7900
Walter Senney, *President*
Jeff Kubiak, *VP Sales*
Dick Martin, *Info Tech Dir*
▲ EMP: 45
SQ FT: 25,000
SALES (est): 14.6MM **Privately Held**
SIC: 5084 Industrial machinery & equipment

(G-5962)
METAL FRAMING ENTERPRISES LLC
Also Called: Frameco
9005 Bank St (44125-3425)
PHONE....................216 433-7080
Neville McAlman, *President*
Kevin Wyman, *Engineer*
EMP: 29
SQ FT: 3,300
SALES (est): 6MM **Privately Held**
WEB: www.framecoframing.com
SIC: 1751 Framing contractor

(G-5963)
METCALF & EDDY INC
1375 E 9th St Ste 2801 (44114-1739)
PHONE....................216 910-2000
Debra Gay, *Manager*
EMP: 27
SALES (corp-wide): 20.1B **Publicly Held**
WEB: www.m-e.aecom.com
SIC: 8711 Professional engineer
HQ: Metcalf & Eddy, Inc.
1 Federal St Ste 800
Boston MA 02110
781 246-5200

(G-5964)
METRO HEALTH DENTAL ASSOCIATES
2500 Metrohealth Dr (44109-1900)
PHONE....................216 778-4982
Terry White, *CEO*
Kathy Blessinger, *General Mgr*
Walter Jones, *Senior VP*
John Zigman, *Research*
Joseph Immler, *Business Anlyst*
EMP: 25
SALES (est): 4.5MM **Privately Held**
SIC: 8021 Offices & clinics of dentists

(G-5965)
METROHEALTH DEPT OF DENTISTRY
2500 Metrohealth Dr (44109-1900)
PHONE....................216 778-4739
John Sideris, *President*
EMP: 25
SALES (est): 501.7K **Privately Held**
SIC: 8021 Dental clinic

(G-5966)
METROHEALTH SYSTEM
Also Called: Metrohealth West Park Hlth Ctr
3838 W 150th St (44111-5805)
PHONE....................216 957-5000
Thomas Ginley, *Principal*
Ann Marie Slice, *Nutritionist*
EMP: 26
SALES (corp-wide): 1B **Privately Held**
SIC: 8093 8099 9221 Specialty outpatient clinics; medical rescue squad; police protection
PA: The Metrohealth System
2500 Metrohealth Dr
Cleveland OH 44109
216 398-6000

(G-5967)
METROHEALTH SYSTEM (PA)
2500 Metrohealth Dr (44109-1900)
PHONE....................216 398-6000
Thomas McDonald, *Ch of Bd*
Howard Gottesman, *Managing Dir*
SL Werner, *Managing Dir*
Linda Lavelle, *Business Mgr*
Daniel K Lewis, *COO*
EMP: 4000
SQ FT: 1,860,000
SALES: 1B **Privately Held**
SIC: 8062 Hospital, affiliated with AMA residency

(G-5968)
METROHEALTH SYSTEM
Also Called: Metrohealth Buckeye Health Ctr
2816 E 116th St (44120-2111)
PHONE....................216 957-4000
Anthony Minnillo, *Manager*
E Harry Walker, *Director*
EMP: 150
SALES (corp-wide): 1B **Privately Held**
SIC: 8062 4119 Hospital, affiliated with AMA residency; ambulance service
PA: The Metrohealth System
2500 Metrohealth Dr
Cleveland OH 44109
216 398-6000

(G-5969)
METROHEALTH SYSTEM
Also Called: Department of Ob/Gyn
2500 Metrohealth Dr (44109-1900)
PHONE....................216 778-8446
Brian Mercer, *Med Doctor*
Susan Boyle, *Admin Sec*
EMP: 100
SALES (corp-wide): 1B **Privately Held**
SIC: 8011 8093 Obstetrician; gynecologist; rehabilitation center, outpatient treatment
PA: The Metrohealth System
2500 Metrohealth Dr
Cleveland OH 44109
216 398-6000

(G-5970)
METROHEALTH SYSTEM
Also Called: Metrohealth Broadway Hlth Ctr
6835 Broadway Ave (44105-1313)
PHONE....................216 957-1500
Anne C Sowell, *Branch Mgr*
Rebecca Lowenthal, *Family Practiti*
EMP: 26
SALES (corp-wide): 1B **Privately Held**
SIC: 8062 8021 General medical & surgical hospitals; offices & clinics of dentists
PA: The Metrohealth System
2500 Metrohealth Dr
Cleveland OH 44109
216 398-6000

(G-5971)
METROHEALTH SYSTEM
2500 Metrohealth Dr (44109-1900)
PHONE....................216 778-3867
EMP: 26

SALES (corp-wide): 1B Privately Held
SIC: 4119 6324 8069 Ambulance service; hospital & medical service plans; children's hospital
PA: The Metrohealth System
2500 Metrohealth Dr
Cleveland OH 44109
216 398-6000

(G-5972)
METROHEALTH SYSTEM
4229 Pearl Rd (44109-4218)
PHONE....................216 957-2100
Amy Delp, *QA Dir*
Rob Kubasak, *Branch Mgr*
Patricia Campbell, *Med Doctor*
Paul Aboukhaled, *Manager*
Ronda Heitz, *Supervisor*
EMP: 210
SALES (corp-wide): 1B **Privately Held**
SIC: 8069 0783 Cancer hospital; surgery services, ornamental tree
PA: The Metrohealth System
2500 Metrohealth Dr
Cleveland OH 44109
216 398-6000

(G-5973)
METROPOLITAN SECURITY SVCS INC
Also Called: Walden Security
801 W Superior Ave (44113-1829)
PHONE....................216 298-4076
EMP: 877 **Privately Held**
SIC: 7381 Security guard service
PA: Metropolitan Security Services, Inc.
100 E 10th St Ste 400
Chattanooga TN 37402

(G-5974)
MFBUSINESS GROUP
Also Called: Fontaine Bleu'
14037 Puritas Ave (44135-2841)
Rural Route 5214 Thomas St, Maple Heights (44137)
PHONE....................216 510-0717
Manuel Isler-Freeman, *Director*
Donnell Isler-Freeman, *Director*
EMP: 30
SALES (est): 890.3K **Privately Held**
SIC: 8741 Business management

(G-5975)
MICELI DAIRY PRODUCTS CO (PA)
2721 E 90th St (44104-3396)
PHONE....................216 791-6222
Joseph D Miceli, *CEO*
John J Miceli Jr, *Exec VP*
Joseph Lograsso, *Vice Pres*
Charles Surace, *Vice Pres*
Rosemary Surace, *Treasurer*
▲ EMP: 90
SQ FT: 25,000
SALES (est): 74.4MM **Privately Held**
SIC: 2022 0241 Natural cheese; milk production

(G-5976)
MICHAEL BAKER INTL INC
1111 Superior Ave E # 2300 (44114-2568)
PHONE....................412 269-6300
Steven Collar, *Manager*
EMP: 30
SALES (corp-wide): 592.9MM **Privately Held**
WEB: www.reedfarmstead.com
SIC: 8711 8741 Civil engineering; management services
HQ: Baker Michael International Inc
500 Grant St Ste 5400
Pittsburgh PA 15219
412 269-6300

(G-5977)
MICHAEL CHRISTOPHER SALON INC
6255 Wilson Mills Rd (44143-2106)
PHONE....................440 449-0999
Marianne Nicolli, *President*
Darren Nicolli, *Vice Pres*
EMP: 25
SALES (est): 947.8K **Privately Held**
WEB: www.michaelchristophersalon.com
SIC: 7231 Unisex hair salons

(G-5978)
MICHAELS BAKERY INC
Also Called: Michael's Bakery & Deli
4478 Broadview Rd (44109-4372)
PHONE....................216 351-7530
Michael Mitterholzer, *President*
Becky Mitterholzer, *Corp Secy*
EMP: 27
SQ FT: 4,800
SALES (est): 1MM **Privately Held**
SIC: 5461 5149 5411 Bakeries; bakery products; delicatessens

(G-5979)
MICRO ELECTRONICS INC
1349 Som Center Rd (44124-2103)
PHONE....................440 449-7000
Chris Tripodo, *Manager*
EMP: 150
SALES (corp-wide): 3.6B **Privately Held**
WEB: www.microcenter.com
SIC: 5734 5045 Personal computers; computer peripheral equipment
PA: Micro Electronics, Inc.
4119 Leap Rd
Hilliard OH 43026
614 850-3000

(G-5980)
MICROSOFT CORPORATION
6050 Oak Tree Blvd # 300 (44131-6929)
PHONE....................216 986-1440
Kerry Duncan, *Accounts Mgr*
Chris Caster, *Manager*
EMP: 50
SALES (corp-wide): 110.3B **Publicly Held**
WEB: www.microsoft.com
SIC: 7372 Application computer software
PA: Microsoft Corporation
1 Microsoft Way
Redmond WA 98052
425 882-8080

(G-5981)
MID AMERICA TRUCKING COMPANY
Also Called: Anthony Allega
5585 Canal Rd (44125-4874)
PHONE....................216 447-0814
John Allega, *President*
James Allega, *Vice Pres*
Joseph Allega, *Vice Pres*
EMP: 25 EST: 1979
SQ FT: 15,000
SALES (est): 3.4MM **Privately Held**
SIC: 4212 Local trucking, without storage

(G-5982)
MID-AMERICA STEEL CORP
Also Called: Mid-America Stainless
20900 Saint Clair Ave (44117-1020)
PHONE....................800 282-3466
John Ratica, *Sales Staff*
Jim Cash, *Pub Rel Dir*
Elliot M Kaufman, *Incorporator*
EMP: 50
SQ FT: 120,000
SALES (est): 58.4MM **Privately Held**
SIC: 5051 3469 3316 3312 Steel; sheets, metal; metal stampings; cold finishing of steel shapes; blast furnaces & steel mills

(G-5983)
MIDDOUGH INC (PA)
1901 E 13th St Ste 400 (44114-3542)
PHONE....................216 367-6000
Ronald Ledin, *President*
Joseph S Cardile, *Senior VP*
Charles Dietz, *Senior VP*
George Hlavacs, *Vice Pres*
Sam Khalilieh, *Vice Pres*
EMP: 390
SQ FT: 120,000
SALES (est): 141.5MM **Privately Held**
SIC: 8711 8712 Consulting engineer; architectural engineering

(G-5984)
MIDFITZ INC
Also Called: Berman Moving & Storage
23800 Corbin Dr (44128-5454)
PHONE....................216 663-8816
Brad Robbins, *CEO*
Marcy Robbins, *President*
Doug Phillips, *Controller*

Dan Kovacs, *Director*
Heidi Pitts, *Executive*
EMP: 25 **EST:** 1912
SQ FT: 40,000
SALES (est): 5.4MM **Privately Held**
WEB: www.bermanmovers.com
SIC: 4213 4214 Household goods transport; household goods moving & storage, local

(G-5985)
MIDLAND CONTRACTING INC
7239 Free Ave (44146-5427)
PHONE................................440 439-4571
Keith Patterson, *President*
EMP: 25 **EST:** 1982
SQ FT: 1,200
SALES (est): 372.1K **Privately Held**
SIC: 1542 Commercial & office building, new construction

(G-5986)
MIDLAND TITLE SECURITY INC (DH)
Also Called: First Amrcn Ttle Midland Title
1111 Superior Ave E # 700 (44114-2540)
PHONE................................216 241-6045
James Stipanovich, *President*
Diane Davies, *Manager*
Shawn Neel, *Officer*
EMP: 100
SALES (est): 72.9MM **Publicly Held**
WEB: www.lancotitle.com
SIC: 6361 Real estate title insurance
HQ: First American Title Insurance Company
1 First American Way
Santa Ana CA 92707
800 854-3643

(G-5987)
MIDPARK ANIMAL HOSPITAL
6611 Smith Rd (44130-2699)
PHONE................................216 362-6622
Art Anton, *President*
EMP: 25
SQ FT: 3,000
SALES (est): 746.8K
SALES (corp-wide): 2.5B **Privately Held**
WEB: www.vcawoodlands.com
SIC: 0742 Animal hospital services, pets & other animal specialties
HQ: Vca Inc.
12401 W Olympic Blvd
Los Angeles CA 90064
310 571-6500

(G-5988)
MIDWAY DELIVERY SERVICE
4699 Commerce Ave (44103-3517)
PHONE................................216 391-0700
Moses Groves, *Owner*
EMP: 33
SQ FT: 3,000
SALES (est): 2MM **Privately Held**
SIC: 4212 Delivery service, vehicular

(G-5989)
MIDWEST CURTAINWALLS INC
5171 Grant Ave (44125-1031)
PHONE................................216 641-7900
Donald F Kelly Jr, *President*
Lisa Smith, *Mktg Dir*
EMP: 80
SQ FT: 55,000
SALES (est): 18.5MM
SALES (corp-wide): 11.6MM **Privately Held**
WEB: www.midwestcurtainwalls.com
SIC: 3449 3442 1751 Curtain wall, metal; curtain walls for buildings, steel; window & door frames; window & door (prefabricated) installation
PA: Innovest Global, Inc.
8834 Mayfield Rd Ste A
Chesterland OH 44026
216 815-1122

(G-5990)
MIDWEST EQUIPMENT CO
9800 Broadway Ave (44125-1639)
PHONE................................216 441-1400
Joseph Manos, *Ch of Bd*
Mike Ricchino, *President*
EMP: 25
SQ FT: 26,000

SALES (est): 4.8MM **Privately Held**
WEB: www.midwestcranerental.com
SIC: 7353 Cranes & aerial lift equipment, rental or leasing

(G-5991)
MILES ALLOY INC
13800 Miles Ave (44105-5594)
PHONE................................216 245-8893
Michael Shubert, *President*
EMP: 30
SQ FT: 30,000
SALES (est): 5.9MM **Privately Held**
SIC: 4953 Recycling, waste materials

(G-5992)
MILES CLEANING SERVICES INC
Also Called: Coit
23580 Miles Rd (44128-5433)
PHONE................................330 633-8562
Harvey Siegel, *President*
Teresa Fryer, *General Mgr*
Adrian Siegal, *Corp Secy*
Rick Schaffer, *Manager*
EMP: 55 **EST:** 1934
SQ FT: 22,000
SALES: 6MM **Privately Held**
WEB: www.cleveland.coit.com
SIC: 7216 7217 Cleaning & dyeing, except rugs; curtain cleaning & repair; carpet & furniture cleaning on location; upholstery cleaning on customer premises

(G-5993)
MILLCRAFT GROUP LLC (PA)
Also Called: Deltacraft
6800 Grant Ave (44105-5628)
PHONE................................216 441-5500
Kay Mlakar, *Ch of Bd*
Katherine Mlakar, *Ch of Bd*
Travis Mlakar, *President*
Frank Kohl, *Division Mgr*
Lisa Pryor, *Division Mgr*
▲ **EMP:** 75
SQ FT: 90,000
SALES (est): 430.1MM **Privately Held**
WEB: www.deltacraft.com
SIC: 5111 5113 2679 Printing paper; industrial & personal service paper; paper products, converted

(G-5994)
MILLCRAFT PAPER COMPANY (HQ)
6800 Grant Ave (44105-5628)
PHONE................................216 441-5505
Travis Mlakar, *President*
Charles Mlakar, *President*
Mike Davoran, *Vice Pres*
Eric Michel, *Vice Pres*
John Orlando, *Vice Pres*
▲ **EMP:** 151
SQ FT: 90,000
SALES (est): 430.1MM **Privately Held**
WEB: www.millcraft.com
SIC: 5111 5113 Printing paper; industrial & personal service paper

(G-5995)
MILLCRAFT PAPER COMPANY
Also Called: Cleveland Division
6800 Grant Ave (44105-5628)
PHONE................................216 441-5500
Sid Greenwood, *Branch Mgr*
EMP: 45 **Privately Held**
WEB: www.millcraft.com
SIC: 5111 5113 Printing paper; industrial & personal service paper
HQ: The Millcraft Paper Company
6800 Grant Ave
Cleveland OH 44105
216 441-5505

(G-5996)
MILLENNIA HOUSING MGT LTD (PA)
127 Public Sq Ste 1300 (44114-1310)
PHONE................................216 520-1250
Frank Sinito, *CEO*
Alan Weckerly, *General Mgr*
Staci Couch, *Regional Mgr*
Gloria Lankin, *Regional Mgr*
John McGinty, *CFO*
EMP: 45

SALES (est): 271.9MM **Privately Held**
SIC: 6513 6531 Apartment building operators; rental agent, real estate

(G-5997)
MILLERS RENTAL AND SLS CO INC
5410 Warner Rd (44125-1100)
PHONE................................216 642-1447
Kenneth Waback, *Purchasing*
Ric Miller, *Branch Mgr*
Chuck Lewis, *Manager*
EMP: 30
SALES (est): 1.5MM
SALES (corp-wide): 23.9MM **Privately Held**
SIC: 7359 Equipment rental & leasing
PA: Miller's Rental And Sales Company Incorporated
2023 Romig Rd
Akron OH 44320
330 753-8600

(G-5998)
MINISTERIAL DAY CARE-HEADSTART (PA)
Also Called: Ministerial Dare Care
7020 Superior Ave (44103-2638)
PHONE................................216 881-6924
Verneda Bentley, *Principal*
EMP: 30 **EST:** 1970
SQ FT: 15,000
SALES: 1MM **Privately Held**
SIC: 8351 8741 Group day care center; management services

(G-5999)
MINUTE MEN INC (PA)
Also Called: Minute Men of FL
3740 Carnegie Ave Ste 201 (44115-2756)
PHONE................................216 426-2225
Samuel Lucarelli, *President*
Sam Lucarelli, *Principal*
Jason Lucarelli, *Vice Pres*
EMP: 60
SQ FT: 5,000
SALES (est): 26.4MM **Privately Held**
WEB: www.minutemeninc.com
SIC: 7363 Temporary help service

(G-6000)
MIRACLE SPIRTL RETRST ORGNSIZN
11609 Wade Park Ave (44106-4403)
PHONE................................216 324-4287
Delilah Bell Fowler, *Director*
EMP: 25
SALES: 5K **Privately Held**
SIC: 8322 Individual & family services

(G-6001)
MIRIFEX SYSTEMS LLC (PA)
4577 Hinckley Indus Pkwy (44109-6009)
PHONE................................440 891-1210
James Meder, *CIO*
William Nemeth,
Frank Desimone, *Administration*
Chris Brinkman,
Dennis Langdon,
EMP: 200
SALES (est): 11.5MM **Privately Held**
WEB: www.mirifex.com
SIC: 7371 7375 Computer software development; remote data base information retrieval

(G-6002)
MJR-CONSTRUCTION CO
Also Called: Mrivera Construction
3101 W 25th St Ste 100 (44109-1646)
PHONE................................216 523-8050
Mark Rivera, *President*
EMP: 25
SQ FT: 3,000
SALES (est): 3MM **Privately Held**
SIC: 1751 Carpentry work

(G-6003)
MOBILITY REVOLUTION LLC
6753 Engle Rd Ste A (44130-7935)
PHONE................................909 980-2259
Evan Smiedt, *CEO*
Bradley Smiedt, *Mng Member*
▲ **EMP:** 25 **EST:** 2011

SALES (est): 2.2MM **Privately Held**
SIC: 5047 Medical equipment & supplies

(G-6004)
MODERN BUILDERS SUPPLY INC
4549 Industrial Pkwy (44135-4541)
PHONE................................216 273-3605
Bryan Blasko, *Manager*
EMP: 30
SQ FT: 53,842
SALES (corp-wide): 347.7MM **Privately Held**
WEB: www.polaristechnologies.com
SIC: 5033 5211 Siding, except wood; lumber & other building materials
PA: Modern Builders Supply, Inc.
3500 Phillips Ave
Toledo OH 43608
419 241-3961

(G-6005)
MODULAR SYSTEMS TECHNICIANS
15708 Industrial Pkwy (44135-3318)
PHONE................................216 459-2630
Kirk Meurer, *President*
Francesca Meurer, *Vice Pres*
Angela Easa, *Admin Sec*
EMP: 30
SQ FT: 2,500
SALES: 460.9K **Privately Held**
WEB: www.modsystech.com
SIC: 1799 Office furniture installation

(G-6006)
MONARCH ELECTRIC SERVICE CO (DH)
5325 W 130th St (44130-1034)
PHONE................................216 433-7800
John Zuleger, *CEO*
George E Roller, *CEO*
Tim Jeans, *Chairman*
Richard Mintern, *COO*
Brad Roller, *Vice Pres*
◆ **EMP:** 80 **EST:** 1958
SQ FT: 55,000
SALES (est): 17.2MM
SALES (corp-wide): 924.8MM **Privately Held**
WEB: www.monarch-electric.com
SIC: 7699 5063 Industrial machinery & equipment repair; electrical apparatus & equipment

(G-6007)
MONARCH STEEL COMPANY INC
4650 Johnston Pkwy (44128-3219)
PHONE................................216 587-8000
Josh Kaufman, *CEO*
Robert L Meyer, *President*
Phil Stidham, *Plant Mgr*
Nino Frostino, *Materials Mgr*
Otis Friday, *Transportation*
▲ **EMP:** 40 **EST:** 1934
SQ FT: 118,000
SALES (est): 43.6MM
SALES (corp-wide): 24.9MM **Privately Held**
WEB: www.monarchsteel.com
SIC: 5051 5049 3353 Steel; precision tools; coils; sheet aluminum
PA: American Consolidated Industries, Inc.
4650 Johnston Pkwy
Cleveland OH 44128
216 587-8000

(G-6008)
MONTESSORI HIGH SCHOOL ASSN
Also Called: MHS
2254 Tudor Dr (44106-3210)
PHONE................................216 421-3033
David Kahn, *Exec Dir*
Carrie Barnabei, *Director*
EMP: 26
SALES: 6.5MM **Privately Held**
SIC: 8351 Child Day Care Services

(G-6009)
MORGAN SERVICES INC
Also Called: Morgan Uniforms & Linen Rental
2013 Columbus Rd (44113-3553)
PHONE................................216 241-3107

GEOGRAPHIC

Larry Cooper, *General Mgr*
Curtis Smith, *Maint Spvr*
Chris Radford, *Manager*
EMP: 150
SQ FT: 15,000
SALES (corp-wide): 38.6MM **Privately Held**
WEB: www.morganservices.com
SIC: 7213 7218 Linen supply; industrial uniform supply
PA: Morgan Services, Inc.
323 N Michigan Ave
Chicago IL 60601
312 346-3181

(G-6010)
MORGAN STANLEY
1301 E 9th St Ste 3100 (44114-1831)
PHONE................................216 523-3000
Richard Radke, *Manager*
EMP: 50
SQ FT: 1,500
SALES (corp-wide): 40.1B **Publicly Held**
SIC: 6211 Stock brokers & dealers
PA: Morgan Stanley
1585 Broadway
New York NY 10036
212 761-4000

(G-6011)
MORGAN STNLEY SMITH BARNEY LLC
31099 Chagrin Blvd Fl 3 (44124-5959)
PHONE................................216 360-4900
Tom Russ, *Branch Mgr*
EMP: 50
SALES (corp-wide): 40.1B **Publicly Held**
SIC: 6211 Stock brokers & dealers
HQ: Morgan Stanley Smith Barney, Llc
2000 Westchester Ave
Purchase NY 10577

(G-6012)
MORTGAGE INFORMATION SERVICES (PA)
4877 Galaxy Pkwy Ste I (44128-5952)
PHONE................................216 514-7480
Leonard R Stein-Sapir, *Ch of Bd*
Schorr Brian, *Vice Pres*
Dawn Podobnik, *Vice Pres*
Dawn Wolf, *Vice Pres*
Todd Rossman, *CFO*
EMP: 60
SALES (est): 134.5MM **Privately Held**
SIC: 6361 6531 Title insurance; appraiser, real estate

(G-6013)
MORTGAGE NOW INC (PA)
9700 Rockside Rd Ste 295 (44125-6267)
PHONE................................800 245-1050
James Marchese, *President*
Michael Perry, *Vice Pres*
Scott Marinelli, *Director*
EMP: 38 **EST:** 1997
SQ FT: 6,800
SALES (est): 26.2MM **Privately Held**
WEB: www.mtgnow.com
SIC: 6162 Mortgage bankers

(G-6014)
MOTI CORPORATION
Also Called: Ramada Inn
22115 Brookpark Rd (44126-3121)
P.O. Box 688, New York NY (10150-0688)
PHONE................................440 734-4500
EMP: 45
SQ FT: 85,000
SALES (est): 2.3MM **Privately Held**
SIC: 7011 Hotels And Motels

(G-6015)
MOUNTAIN LAUREL ASSURANCE CO
6300 Wilson Mills Rd (44143-2109)
PHONE................................440 461-5000
EMP: 178
SALES: 223.5MM
SALES (corp-wide): 31.9B **Publicly Held**
SIC: 6331 Automobile insurance
HQ: Progressive Direct Holdings, Inc.
6300 Wilson Mills Rd
Cleveland OH 44143

(G-6016)
MOYAL AND PETROFF MD
730 Som Center Rd Ste 230 (44143-2362)
PHONE................................440 461-6477
Roman Petroff MD, *Owner*
EMP: 25
SALES (est): 1.5MM **Privately Held**
SIC: 8011 Internal medicine, physician/surgeon

(G-6017)
MPLX TERMINALS LLC
10439 Brecksville Rd (44141-3339)
PHONE................................440 526-4653
Keith Gigliotti, *Manager*
EMP: 50
SALES (corp-wide): 6.4B **Publicly Held**
WEB: www.mapllc.com
SIC: 5172 Gasoline
HQ: Mplx Terminals Llc
200 E Hardin St
Findlay OH

(G-6018)
MPW CONTAINER MANAGEMENT CORP
4848 W 130th St (44135-5163)
PHONE................................216 362-8400
Monte R Black, *CEO*
EMP: 66
SALES (est): 3.7MM
SALES (corp-wide): 208.7MM **Privately Held**
SIC: 7699 Industrial equipment cleaning
HQ: Mpw Industrial Services, Inc.
9711 Lancaster Rd
Hebron OH 43025
800 827-8790

(G-6019)
MRN LIMITED PARTNERSHIP
629 Euclid Ave Fl 2 (44114-3007)
P.O. Box 14100 (44114-0100)
PHONE................................216 589-5631
Richard Maron, *Partner*
Judith Eigenfeld, *Partner*
David Minah, *General Mgr*
Rebecca Harper, *Hum Res Coord*
EMP: 29
SALES (est): 3.7MM **Privately Held**
WEB: www.east4thstreet.com
SIC: 6513 Apartment building operators

(G-6020)
MRN-NEWGAR HOTEL LTD
Also Called: Holiday Inn
629 Euclid Ave Lbby 1 (44114-3008)
PHONE................................216 443-1000
Thomas W Adler, *CEO*
EMP: 48
SALES: 3.3MM **Privately Held**
SIC: 7011 Hotels & motels

(G-6021)
MS CONSULTANTS INC
600 Superior Ave E # 1300 (44114-2654)
PHONE................................216 522-1926
Denis Yurkovich, *Branch Mgr*
Jeremy Gaston, *Director*
EMP: 39
SALES (corp-wide): 43.8MM **Privately Held**
SIC: 8711 Consulting engineer
PA: Ms Consultants, Inc
333 E Federal St
Youngstown OH 44503
330 744-5321

(G-6022)
MSI INTERNATIONAL LLC
6100 Oak Tree Blvd # 200 (44131-2544)
PHONE................................330 869-6459
William C Allio,
EMP: 32
SQ FT: 4,000
SALES (est): 1.8MM **Privately Held**
SIC: 7371 Computer software development

(G-6023)
MULTI CNTRY SEC SLUTIONS GROUP
3459 W 117th St (44111-3580)
PHONE................................216 973-0291
Timothy Williams, *Owner*

EMP: 35
SALES: 950K **Privately Held**
SIC: 1799 Special trade contractors

(G-6024)
MULTI-FUND INC (PA)
9700 Rockside Rd Ste 100 (44125-6268)
PHONE................................216 750-2331
Paul Montigny, *President*
Stuart Montigny, *Admin Sec*
EMP: 28
SQ FT: 6,500
SALES: 3.5MM **Privately Held**
SIC: 6163 Mortgage brokers arranging for loans, using money of others

(G-6025)
MURAL & SON INC
11340 Brookpark Rd (44130-1129)
PHONE................................216 267-3322
Robert W Mural, *President*
David Simon, *Vice Pres*
Sandra Simon, *Treasurer*
EMP: 25
SQ FT: 5,000
SALES (est): 2.1MM **Privately Held**
SIC: 1741 1799 1541 1542 Foundation building; waterproofing; renovation, remodeling & repairs: industrial buildings; commercial & office buildings, renovation & repair; general remodeling, single-family houses

(G-6026)
MURTECH CONSULTING LLC
4700 Rockside Rd Ste 310 (44131-2171)
PHONE................................216 328-8580
Ailish Murphy, *Mng Member*
EMP: 95 **EST:** 2000
SQ FT: 1,600
SALES (est): 11.9MM **Privately Held**
WEB: www.murtechconsulting.com
SIC: 8742 7361 General management consultant; employment agencies

(G-6027)
MUSEUM CNTMPRARY ART CLEVELAND
Also Called: Moca Cleveland
11400 Euclid Ave (44106-3926)
PHONE................................216 421-8671
Colleen Kelly, *Sr Corp Ofcr*
Kory Dakin, *Production*
Desiree Kellers, *Buyer*
Grace Garver, *CFO*
Arthur Henke, *Manager*
▲ **EMP:** 27 **EST:** 1968
SQ FT: 34,000
SALES: 3.4MM **Privately Held**
SIC: 8412 Museum

(G-6028)
MUSICAL ARTS ASSOCIATION (PA)
Also Called: Cleveland Orchestra, The
11001 Euclid Ave (44106-1796)
PHONE................................216 231-7300
Cleveland Miami, *Managing Dir*
Lynn Cameron, *Manager*
Julie Weiner, *Manager*
Abby Mitchell, *Senior Mgr*
Gary Hanson, *Exec Dir*
▲ **EMP:** 190 **EST:** 1925
SQ FT: 125,000
SALES: 54.5MM **Privately Held**
WEB: www.clevelandorchestra.com
SIC: 7929 6512 Symphony orchestras; orchestras or bands; auditorium & hall operation

(G-6029)
MUSSUN SALES INC (PA)
3419 Carnegie Ave (44115-2638)
PHONE................................216 431-5088
Geoffrey L Andres, *President*
Fred O Burkhalter, *Principal*
Robert F Hesser, *Principal*
Jim Nowak, *Purch Agent*
Michelle Shoemaker, *Buyer*
EMP: 44 **EST:** 1951
SQ FT: 45,000
SALES (est): 20.7MM **Privately Held**
WEB: www.mussun.com
SIC: 5074 Plumbing & hydronic heating supplies

(G-6030)
MUTUAL HEALTH SERVICES COMPANY
Also Called: Mutual Holding Company
2060 E 9th St (44115-1313)
PHONE................................216 687-7000
John Burry Jr, *CEO*
James W Harless, *President*
Kent Clapp, *Treasurer*
Joya Newman, *Manager*
Jerome Rogers, *Admin Sec*
EMP: 85
SQ FT: 18,600
SALES (est): 10MM
SALES (corp-wide): 1.2B **Privately Held**
SIC: 8099 Medical services organization
HQ: Medical Mutual Services, Llc
17800 Royalton Rd
Strongsville OH 44136
440 878-4800

(G-6031)
MYOCARE NURSING HOME INC
Also Called: West Park Healthcare
24300 Sperry Dr (44145-1565)
PHONE................................216 252-7555
Elias J Coury, *President*
Norman A Fox Jr, *Corp Secy*
EMP: 135
SQ FT: 44,000
SALES: 5MM **Privately Held**
SIC: 8051 Skilled nursing care facilities

(G-6032)
MZF INC
Also Called: Studio Mz Hair Design
27629 Chagrin Blvd 101b (44122-4477)
PHONE................................216 464-3910
Tracy Fish, *President*
Susan Bell, *Vice Pres*
EMP: 35
SQ FT: 3,000
SALES (est): 1.1MM **Privately Held**
SIC: 7231 Beauty shops

(G-6033)
N C B INTERNATIONAL DEPARTMENT
23000 Millcreek Blvd # 7350 (44122-5720)
PHONE................................216 488-7990
Laraine Sharp, *Administration*
EMP: 60
SALES (est): 4.4MM **Privately Held**
SIC: 6159 Intermediate investment banks

(G-6034)
NACCO INDUSTRIES INC (PA)
5875 Landerbrook Dr # 220 (44124-6511)
PHONE................................440 229-5151
Alfred M Rankin Jr, *Ch of Bd*
J C Butler Jr, *President*
Fernando Urquidi, *Business Mgr*
Elizabeth I Loveman, *Vice Pres*
John D Neumann, *Vice Pres*
EMP: 39
SALES: 104.7MM **Publicly Held**
SIC: 3634 1221 5719 3631 Electric household cooking appliances; toasters, electric: household; irons, electric: household; coffee makers, electric: household; surface mining, lignite; kitchenware; cookware, except aluminum; household cooking equipment; microwave ovens, including portable: household

(G-6035)
NANAELES DAY CARE INC
3685 Lee Rd (44120-5108)
PHONE................................216 991-6139
Denise Zama, *President*
Ella Witherspoon, *Principal*
EMP: 50
SALES (est): 588.3K **Privately Held**
SIC: 8351 Child day care services

(G-6036)
NAS RCRTMENT CMMUNICATIONS LLC (HQ)
Also Called: N A S
9700 Rockside Rd Ste 170 (44125-6267)
PHONE................................216 478-0300
Philip Ridolfi, *CEO*
Matthew Adam, *President*
Matt Adam, *Exec VP*
Patty Van Leer, *Exec VP*

▲ = Import ▼=Export
◆ =Import/Export

EMP: 102
SALES (est): 16.9MM
SALES (corp-wide): 37.7MM **Privately Held**
WEB: www.nasrecruitment.com
SIC: 7311 8748 Advertising consultant; communications consulting
PA: Stone-Goff Partners, Llc
900 3rd Ave
New York NY 10022
212 308-2058

(G-6037)
NATIONAL BENEVOLENT ASSOCIATIO
Also Called: Cleveland Christian Home
4614 Prospect Ave Ste 240 (44103-4365)
PHONE.....................................216 476-0333
David Lundeen, *CEO*
EMP: 60
SQ FT: 36,548
SALES (corp-wide): 17.4MM **Privately Held**
WEB: www.cchome.org
SIC: 8351 8361 Child day care services; residential care
PA: The National Benevolent Association Of The Christian Church
733 Union Blvd 300
Saint Louis MO 63108
314 993-9000

(G-6038)
NATIONAL CAR MART III INC
9255 Brookpark Rd (44129-6822)
PHONE.....................................216 398-2228
William Wise, *President*
David Venable, *Vice Pres*
Marge Eger, *Manager*
▼ EMP: 35
SQ FT: 30,000
SALES (est): 8.1MM **Privately Held**
WEB: www.nationalcarmart.com
SIC: 5012 Automobiles & other motor vehicles

(G-6039)
NATIONAL CITY CMNTY DEV CORP
1900 E 9th St (44114-3404)
PHONE.....................................216 575-2000
Danny Cameran, *President*
Michael Rie,
Joseph G Schneider,
EMP: 250
SALES (est): 12.3MM
SALES (corp-wide): 19.9B **Publicly Held**
WEB: www.pnc.com
SIC: 8742 Planning consultant
PA: The Pnc Financial Services Group Inc
300 5th Ave
Pittsburgh PA 15222
412 762-2000

(G-6040)
NATIONAL CONCESSION COMPANY
4582 Willow Pkwy (44125-1046)
PHONE.....................................216 881-9911
Tuck Axelrod, *President*
Christopher Axelrod, *Vice Pres*
EMP: 35
SQ FT: 7,500
SALES (est): 3MM **Privately Held**
WEB: www.nationalconcession.com
SIC: 7999 Concession operator; amusement concession

(G-6041)
NATIONAL CONTINENTAL INSUR CO
6300 Wilson Mills Rd (44143-2109)
PHONE.....................................631 320-2405
S Patricia Griffith, *CEO*
EMP: 440
SALES: 12.1MM
SALES (corp-wide): 31.9B **Publicly Held**
SIC: 6331 Fire, marine & casualty insurance
HQ: Progressive Commercial Holdings, Inc.
6300 Wilson Mills Rd
Cleveland OH 44143

(G-6042)
NATIONAL DENTEX LLC
Also Called: Salem Dental Laboratory
3873 Rocky River Dr (44111-4112)
PHONE.....................................216 671-0577
David Brown, *Manager*
EMP: 39
SALES (corp-wide): 151.4MM **Privately Held**
WEB: www.nationaldentex.com
SIC: 8072 Crown & bridge production
HQ: National Dentex, Llc
11601 Kew Gardens Ave # 200
Palm Beach Gardens FL 33410
561 537-8300

(G-6043)
NATIONAL ELECTRO-COATINGS INC
Also Called: National Office
15655 Brookpark Rd (44142-1619)
PHONE.....................................216 898-0080
Gregory R Schneider, *CEO*
Richard Corl, *President*
Robert W Schneider, *Chairman*
Greg Hurst, *Plant Mgr*
Katie Saliba, *Accounts Mgr*
▲ EMP: 90
SQ FT: 175,000
SALES (est): 20MM **Privately Held**
WEB: www.natoffice.com
SIC: 2522 2521 1721 Office furniture, except wood; wood office furniture; painting & paper hanging

(G-6044)
NATIONAL ENGRG & CONTG CO
Also Called: Netco
50 Public Sq Ste 2175 (44113-2252)
PHONE.....................................440 238-3331
Walter Gratz, *CEO*
Clarke Wilson, *Vice Pres*
Anthony Martin, *Treasurer*
EMP: 700 EST: 1933
SQ FT: 50,000
SALES (est): 88MM
SALES (corp-wide): 9.1B **Privately Held**
SIC: 1622 1623 Bridge construction; highway construction, elevated; sewer line construction; pumping station construction
HQ: Balfour Beatty, Llc
1011 Centre Rd Ste 322
Wilmington DE 19805
302 573-3873

(G-6045)
NATIONAL GENERAL INSURANCE
Also Called: Ngic
800 Superior Ave E (44114-2613)
PHONE.....................................212 380-9462
Kevin Bailey, *Principal*
Jimmy Hernandez, *Agent*
EMP: 500
SALES (corp-wide): 135.5MM **Privately Held**
SIC: 6411 Insurance agents; insurance agents & brokers
PA: National General Insurance
59 Maiden Ln Fl 38
New York NY 10038
212 380-9477

(G-6046)
NATIONAL HERITG ACADEMIES INC
Also Called: Apex Academy
16005 Terrace Rd (44112-2001)
PHONE.....................................216 451-1725
Michael Bean, *Branch Mgr*
EMP: 54 **Privately Held**
SIC: 8741 Management services
PA: National Heritage Academies, Inc.
3850 Broadmoor Ave Se # 201
Grand Rapids MI 49512

(G-6047)
NATIONAL LABOR RELATIONS BOARD
Also Called: Region 8
1240 E 9th St Ste 1695 (44199-9930)
PHONE.....................................216 522-3716
Fax: 216 522-2418
EMP: 46 **Publicly Held**

SIC: 8111 Legal Services Office
HQ: National Labor Relations Board
1015 Half St Se
Washington DC 20003
202 273-3884

(G-6048)
NATIONAL MENTOR INC
9800 Rockside Rd Ste 800 (44125-6265)
PHONE.....................................216 525-1885
Lisa Clark, *Manager*
EMP: 25
SALES (corp-wide): 310.7MM **Privately Held**
SIC: 8361 Residential care
HQ: National Mentor, Inc.
313 Congress St Fl 5
Boston MA 02210
617 790-4800

(G-6049)
NATIONAL TESTING LABORATORIES (PA)
6571 Wilson Mills Rd # 3 (44143-3439)
PHONE.....................................440 449-2525
Robert Gelbach, *President*
Thomas Zimmerman, *VP Finance*
Steve Tischler, *Director*
EMP: 37
SQ FT: 3,500
SALES (est): 5.8MM **Privately Held**
WEB: www.quasintl.com
SIC: 8734 Water testing laboratory

(G-6050)
NATIONAL WEATHER SERVICE
5301 W Hngr Fdral Fclties (44135)
PHONE.....................................216 265-2370
William Comeaux, *Principal*
EMP: 28 **Publicly Held**
SIC: 8999 9611 Weather forecasting; administration of general economic programs;
HQ: National Weather Service
1325 E West Hwy
Silver Spring MD 20910

(G-6051)
NBW INC
4556 Industrial Pkwy (44135-4542)
PHONE.....................................216 377-1700
Burgess J Holt, *Chairman*
Thomas Graves, *Vice Pres*
Buck L Holt, *Treasurer*
Todd Holt, *Admin Sec*
EMP: 48
SQ FT: 25,000
SALES (est): 15MM **Privately Held**
WEB: www.nbwinc.com
SIC: 1711 1796 7699 3443 Boiler setting contractor; installing building equipment; boiler & heating repair services; fabricated plate work (boiler shop)

(G-6052)
NCS INCORPORATED
729 Miner Rd (44143-2117)
PHONE.....................................440 684-9455
Mary B Cowan, *President*
Deloras Cowan, *Vice Pres*
EMP: 68
SALES (est): 7.6MM **Privately Held**
SIC: 7322 Collection agency, except real estate

(G-6053)
NEIGHBORHOOD HEALTH CARE INC (PA)
Also Called: Neighborhood Family Practice
4115 Bridge Ave 300 (44113-3304)
PHONE.....................................216 281-8945
Jean Polster, *CEO*
Laurel Domanski, *Vice Pres*
Peggy Keating, *Vice Pres*
Daniel Gauntner, *CFO*
Jim Massey, *CFO*
EMP: 36
SALES: 11.4MM **Privately Held**
WEB: www.neighborhoodfamilypractice.com
SIC: 8011 General & family practice, physician/surgeon

(G-6054)
NEIGHBORHOOD PROGRESS INC (PA)
Also Called: N P I
11327 Shaker Blvd Ste 500 (44104-3863)
PHONE.....................................216 830-2770
Joe Ratner, *President*
Steve Strnisha, *Principal*
Kandis Williams, *Vice Pres*
Jenny Swanson, *Accountant*
Sheri Dozier, *Director*
EMP: 26
SALES: 1.8MM **Privately Held**
SIC: 8399 Community action agency; neighborhood development group

(G-6055)
NEO-PET LLC
1894 E 123rd St Apt 1 (44106-1942)
PHONE.....................................440 893-9949
Carla Miraldi, *Mng Member*
Vito Salvo, *Mng Member*
Floro Miraldi,
Lee Adler,
EMP: 30
SALES (est): 2.6MM **Privately Held**
WEB: www.neopet.com
SIC: 7363 Medical help service

(G-6056)
NEPTUNE PLUMBING & HEATING CO
23860 Miles Rd Ste G (44128-5464)
PHONE.....................................216 475-9100
Scott Wallenstein, *President*
Pat Looby, *Project Mgr*
Adam Wallenstein, *Director*
EMP: 80
SQ FT: 8,000
SALES (est): 14MM **Privately Held**
WEB: www.neptuneplumbing.net
SIC: 1711 Plumbing contractors; warm air heating & air conditioning contractor

(G-6057)
NERONE & SONS INC
19501 S Miles Rd Ste 1 (44128-4261)
PHONE.....................................216 662-2235
Ton Nerone, *President*
Rick Nerone Sr, *President*
Tom Nerone, *President*
Richard Nerone, *Corp Secy*
Rick Nerone Jr, *Corp Secy*
EMP: 50 EST: 1955
SQ FT: 28,500
SALES: 17MM **Privately Held**
WEB: www.nerone.biz
SIC: 1623 1611 Sewer line construction; water main construction; general contractor, highway & street construction

(G-6058)
NETEAM SYSTEMS LLC
1111 Superior Ave E # 1111 (44114-2522)
PHONE.....................................330 523-5100
Michael Wyss, *Ch of Bd*
Patrick Aulizia, *President*
William Cannon, *COO*
Robert Lapmarado, *Sales Mgr*
EMP: 40
SQ FT: 10,000
SALES: 12.3MM **Privately Held**
SIC: 5065 8711 Telephone equipment; engineering services

(G-6059)
NEW AGE LOGISTICS LLC
Also Called: New Age Container
7120 Krick Rd Ste 1b (44146-4444)
PHONE.....................................440 439-0846
Fran Szymkowski, *Cust Mgr*
Jerry Peters, *Mng Member*
Doug Sopko, *Supervisor*
EMP: 32
SALES (corp-wide): 12.7MM **Privately Held**
SIC: 4225 General warehousing & storage
PA: New Age Logistics, Llc
360 Highland Rd E Unit 2
Macedonia OH 44056
330 468-0734

GEOGRAPHIC

(G-6060)
NEW AVENUES TO
INDEPENDENCE (PA)
17608 Euclid Ave (44112-1216)
PHONE...................................216 481-1907
Tom Lewins, President
Donnamarie Berardinelli, Project Mgr
Lou Baga, Controller
Jennifer Woods, Manager
David Carr, CIO
EMP: 100
SQ FT: 30,000
SALES: 14.6MM Privately Held
WEB: www.newavenues.net
SIC: 8361 Home for the mentally retarded;
home for the physically handicapped

(G-6061)
NEW AVENUES TO
INDEPENDENCE
12131 Bennington Ave (44135-3729)
PHONE...................................216 671-8224
EMP: 26
SALES (corp-wide): 14.6MM Privately
Held
SIC: 8361 Residential Care Services
PA: New Avenues To Independence Inc
17608 Euclid Ave
Cleveland OH 44112
216 481-1907

(G-6062)
NEW DIRECTIONS INC
30800 Chagrin Blvd (44124-5925)
PHONE...................................216 591-0324
Michael Matoney, CEO
Laura Gest, Controller
Kristine Frankenberry, Director
EMP: 55
SQ FT: 19,000
SALES: 3.8MM Privately Held
WEB: www.newdirect.org
SIC: 8361 Rehabilitation center, residen-
tial: health care incidental

(G-6063)
NEW YORK COMMUNITY BANK
5767 Broadview Rd (44134-1681)
PHONE...................................216 741-7333
Kelly Rusthn, Manager
EMP: 31 Publicly Held
WEB: www.amtrustinvest.com
SIC: 6035 Federal savings & loan associa-
tions
HQ: New York Community Bank
615 Merrick Ave
Westbury NY 11590
516 203-0010

(G-6064)
NEW YORK COMMUNITY BANK
Also Called: Ohio Savings Bank
1801 E 9th St (44114-3107)
PHONE...................................216 736-3480
Zhongcai Zhang, Vice Pres
Robert Gillespie, Human Res Dir
Robert Goldberg, Branch Mgr
Grant Adamson, Manager
Kathleen Crowley, Manager
EMP: 874 Publicly Held
SIC: 6035 Federal savings & loan associa-
tions
HQ: New York Community Bank
615 Merrick Ave
Westbury NY 11590
516 203-0010

(G-6065)
NEWMARK & COMPANY RE INC
Also Called: Newmark Grubb Knight Frank
1350 Euclid Ave Ste 300 (44115-1833)
PHONE...................................216 453-3000
David Hooper, Manager
EMP: 35
SALES (corp-wide): 2B Publicly Held
SIC: 6531 6799 Real estate agents &
managers; investors
HQ: Newmark & Company Real Estate, Inc.
125 Park Ave
New York NY 10017
212 372-2000

(G-6066)
NEXSTEP HEALTHCARE LLC
673 Alpha Dr Ste G (44143-2140)
PHONE...................................216 797-4040
Michelle Haines, COO
Gary Knouff, CFO
Jerry Cangelosi, Mng Member
EMP: 150
SQ FT: 4,200
SALES (est): 6.8MM Privately Held
WEB: www.nexstephc.com
SIC: 8049 8741 Physical therapist; man-
agement services

(G-6067)
NEXUS ENGINEERING GROUP
LLC (PA)
1422 Euclid Ave Ste 1400 (44115-2015)
PHONE...................................216 404-7867
Jeffrey O Herzog, President
Marianne C Corrao, Exec VP
Ron Justiniani, Project Engr
EMP: 44
SALES (est): 12MM Privately Held
SIC: 8711 Consulting engineer

(G-6068)
NF II CLEVELAND OP CO LLC
Also Called: Residence Inn Cleveland Dwn-
twn
527 Prospect Ave E (44115-1113)
PHONE...................................216 443-9043
Steven Rudolph, General Mgr
EMP: 40
SQ FT: 700,000
SALES: 7MM Privately Held
SIC: 7011 Hotel, franchised

(G-6069)
NICOLA GUDBRANSON &
COOPER LLC
25 W Prospect Ave # 1400 (44115-1048)
PHONE...................................216 621-7227
Michael Cicero, President
James L Juliano Jr, Partner
Megan Mehalko, Partner
Gloria Merritt, Office Mgr
Laura Murray, Technology
EMP: 34
SQ FT: 6,000
SALES: 2.5MM Privately Held
WEB: www.nicola.com
SIC: 8111 General practice attorney,
lawyer

(G-6070)
NIEDERST MANAGEMENT LTD
(PA)
Also Called: NM Residential
21400 Lorain Rd (44126-2125)
PHONE...................................440 331-8800
Michael Niederst,
EMP: 53
SQ FT: 4,600
SALES: 32.2MM Privately Held
WEB: www.niederstmanagement.com
SIC: 8741 Management services

(G-6071)
NORFOLK SOUTHERN
CORPORATION
6409 Clark Ave (44102-5301)
PHONE...................................216 362-6087
EMP: 43
SALES (corp-wide): 11.4B Publicly Held
SIC: 4011 Railroads, line-haul operating
PA: Norfolk Southern Corporation
3 Commercial Pl Ste 1a
Norfolk VA 23510
757 629-2680

(G-6072)
NORFOLK SOUTHERN
CORPORATION
4860 W 150th St (44135-3302)
PHONE...................................216 362-6087
Joseph Giuliano, Manager
EMP: 43
SALES (corp-wide): 11.4B Publicly Held
WEB: www.nscorp.com
SIC: 4011 Railroads, line-haul operating

PA: Norfolk Southern Corporation
3 Commercial Pl Ste 1a
Norfolk VA 23510
757 629-2680

(G-6073)
NORMAN NOBLE INC
6120 Parkland Blvd # 306 (44124-6129)
PHONE...................................216 761-2133
Daniel Haddock, Branch Mgr
EMP: 190
SALES (corp-wide): 125.3MM Privately
Held
WEB: www.nnoble.com
SIC: 3599 7692 Machine shop, jobbing &
repair; welding repair
PA: Norman Noble, Inc.
5507 Avion Park Dr
Highland Heights OH 44143
216 761-5387

(G-6074)
NORRIS BROTHERS CO INC
2138 Davenport Ave (44114-3724)
PHONE...................................216 771-2233
Bernard E Weir Jr, President
Kenneth McBride, President
Catherine McBride, Corp Secy
EMP: 120 EST: 1867
SQ FT: 60,000
SALES (est): 16.5MM Privately Held
WEB: www.norrisbr.com
SIC: 1796 1541 7699 1771 Machinery in-
stallation; industrial buildings, new con-
struction; boiler repair shop; concrete
work

(G-6075)
NORTH CENTRAL SALES INC
528 E 200th St (44119-1569)
PHONE...................................216 481-2418
Thomas R Shankal, President
Karen Shenkal, Vice Pres
EMP: 26
SALES (est): 4.2MM Privately Held
WEB: www.northcentralsales.com
SIC: 5087 Beauty parlor equipment & sup-
plies

(G-6076)
NORTH COAST CONCRETE INC
6061 Carey Dr (44125-4259)
PHONE...................................216 642-1114
Robert Dalrymple, President
Linda A Dalrymple, Admin Sec
EMP: 30
SQ FT: 5,000
SALES (est): 3.6MM Privately Held
WEB: www.northcoastconcrete.com
SIC: 1771 Concrete pumping

(G-6077)
NORTH ELECTRIC INC
12117 Bennington Ave # 200 (44135-3729)
PHONE...................................216 331-4141
Jose Rivera, President
EMP: 40 EST: 1996
SALES (est): 4.4MM Privately Held
SIC: 1731 Electrical work

(G-6078)
NORTH OHIO HEART CENTER
INC
Also Called: Ohio Medical Group
7255 Old Oak Blvd C408 (44130-3331)
PHONE...................................440 414-9500
Qarab Syed MD, Director
EMP: 47
SALES (corp-wide): 13.5MM Privately
Held
SIC: 8011 Cardiologist & cardio-vascular
specialist
PA: North Ohio Heart Center, Inc
3600 Kolbe Rd Ste 127
Lorain OH 44053
440 204-4000

(G-6079)
NORTH PARK RETIREMENT
CMNTY (PA)
Also Called: Sovereign Healthcare
14801 Holland Rd Lbby (44142-3080)
PHONE...................................216 267-0555
John Coury Jr, President
Theresa Ammons, Nursing Dir
EMP: 50

SALES (est): 3.8MM Privately Held
SIC: 8059 Rest home, with health care

(G-6080)
NORTH RANDALL VILLAGE (PA)
21937 Miles Rd Side (44128-4775)
PHONE...................................216 663-1112
David Smith, Mayor
EMP: 82
SQ FT: 6,000
SALES (est): 8.9MM Privately Held
WEB: www.northrandall.com
SIC: 8741 Office management

(G-6081)
NORTHAST OHIO RGONAL
SEWER DST (PA)
3900 Euclid Ave (44115-2506)
PHONE...................................216 881-6600
Darnell Brown, President
Robert Bonnett, Superintendent
Tamar Gontovnik, Counsel
Ronald D Sulik, Vice Pres
Robin Rupe, Project Mgr
EMP: 120
SQ FT: 85,000
SALES: 343.8MM Privately Held
SIC: 4941 Water supply

(G-6082)
NORTHAST OHIO RGONAL
SEWER DST
Also Called: Southrly Wstwater Trtmnt Plant
6000 Canal Rd (44125-1026)
PHONE...................................216 641-3200
Lowell Eisnaugle, Manager
Thomas Seiter, Manager
EMP: 151
SQ FT: 9,916
SALES (corp-wide): 343.8MM Privately
Held
SIC: 4959 4952 Sanitary services; sewer-
age systems
PA: Northeast Ohio Regional Sewer District
3900 Euclid Ave
Cleveland OH 44115
216 881-6600

(G-6083)
NORTHAST OHIO RGONAL
SEWER DST
Also Called: Westerly Wstwater Trtmnt Plant
5800 Cleveland Mem Shr (44102-2122)
PHONE...................................216 961-2187
Andrew Rossiter, Superintendent
Ken Wilson, Manager
Alexander Render, Technician
Nolan Carver, Maintence Staff
EMP: 59
SALES (corp-wide): 343.8MM Privately
Held
SIC: 8711 Civil engineering
PA: Northeast Ohio Regional Sewer District
3900 Euclid Ave
Cleveland OH 44115
216 881-6600

(G-6084)
NORTHAST OHIO RGONAL
SEWER DST
Also Called: Amsc
4747 E 49th St (44125-1011)
PHONE...................................216 641-6000
Frank Foley, Superintendent
Tim Weber, Principal
Nancy Custard, Business Mgr
John Gonzalez, Corp Comm Staff
Bob Gow, Branch Mgr
EMP: 122
SALES (corp-wide): 343.8MM Privately
Held
SIC: 4952 8734 Sewerage systems; test-
ing laboratories
PA: Northeast Ohio Regional Sewer District
3900 Euclid Ave
Cleveland OH 44115
216 881-6600

(G-6085)
NORTHAST OHIO RGONAL
SEWER DST
Also Called: Southerly Waste Water Plant
14021 Lake Shore Blvd (44110-1932)
PHONE...................................216 531-4892
Raymond Weeden, Branch Mgr

EMP: 53
SQ FT: 3,383
SALES (corp-wide): 343.8MM Privately Held
SIC: 4952 Sewerage systems
PA: Northeast Ohio Regional Sewer District
3900 Euclid Ave
Cleveland OH 44115
216 881-6600

(G-6086)
NORTHAST OHIO TRNCHING SVC INC
17900 Miles Rd (44128-3400)
PHONE.................................216 663-6006
George J Gorup, President
EMP: 35
SQ FT: 14,422
SALES (est): 5MM Privately Held
SIC: 1794 Excavation & grading, building construction

(G-6087)
NORTHCOAST DUPLICATING INC
7850 Hub Pkwy (44125-5711)
PHONE.................................216 573-6681
Sunantan Kumar, President
Ineka Kumar, Vice Pres
EMP: 130
SQ FT: 7,500
SALES (est): 8.3MM
SALES (corp-wide): 37B Privately Held
WEB: www.northcoastduplicating.com
SIC: 5044 7378 Duplicating machines; computer maintenance & repair
HQ: Topac U.S.A., Inc.
25530 Commercentre Dr
Lake Forest CA 92630

(G-6088)
NORTHEAST LUBRICANTS LTD (PA)
4500 Renaissance Pkwy (44128-5702)
PHONE.................................216 478-0507
Dan McCollum, Controller
Thomas Arcoria, Mng Member
EMP: 143
SALES: 25MM Privately Held
SIC: 5172 Lubricating oils & greases

(G-6089)
NORTHEAST OH NEIGHBORHOOD HEAL
Also Called: Hough Health Center
8300 Hough Ave (44103-4247)
PHONE.................................216 231-7700
EMP: 50
SALES (corp-wide): 25.8MM Privately Held
SIC: 8099 Medical services organization
PA: Northeast Ohio Neighborhood Health Services, Inc.
4800 Payne Ave
Cleveland OH 44103
216 231-7700

(G-6090)
NORTHEAST OH NEIGHBORHOOD HEAL (PA)
4800 Payne Ave (44103-2443)
PHONE.................................216 231-7700
Willie S Austin, President
Karen Butler, COO
Perry Murdock, Human Res Dir
Al Barker, Info Tech Mgr
Lynn Johnson, Director
EMP: 125
SQ FT: 67,000
SALES: 25.8MM Privately Held
SIC: 8099 8071 8011 5912 Medical services organization; medical laboratories; offices & clinics of medical doctors; drug stores & proprietary stores

(G-6091)
NORTHEAST OHIO AREAWIDE
Also Called: Noaca
1299 Superior Ave E (44114-3204)
PHONE.................................216 621-3055
William M Grace, Chairman
Howard Maier, Exec Dir
EMP: 45

SALES: 5.8MM Privately Held
WEB: www.mpo.noaca.org
SIC: 8748 Urban planning & consulting services

(G-6092)
NORTHEAST OHIO CHAPTER NATNL (PA)
6155 Rockside Rd Ste 202 (44131-2217)
PHONE.................................216 696-8220
Janet L Kramer, President
Beth Robertson, Vice Pres
Lois Walter, Vice Pres
EMP: 25 EST: 1953
SALES (est): 939.4K Privately Held
SIC: 8322 Association for the handicapped

(G-6093)
NORTHEAST OHIO ELECTRIC LLC (PA)
Also Called: Doan Pyramid Electric
5069 Corbin Dr (44128-5413)
PHONE.................................216 587-9510
Mike Forlani, Mng Member
Karen Zamlen, Manager
Raymond Ditomas, CIO
Lenny Heisler,
Douglas K Sesnowitz,
▼ EMP: 440
SALES (est): 55.1MM Privately Held
SIC: 1731 General electrical contractor

(G-6094)
NORTHEAST PROJECTIONS INC
Also Called: N P I Audio Video Solutions
8600 Sweet Valley Dr (44125-4212)
PHONE.................................216 514-5023
Joe Thompson, President
Tracy L Thompson, Principal
Ted Van Hyning, Principal
EMP: 25
SQ FT: 4,400
SALES (est): 5MM Privately Held
WEB: www.npiav.com
SIC: 7359 Audio-visual equipment & supply rental

(G-6095)
NORTHEAST SCENE INC
Also Called: Scene Magazine
737 Bolivar Rd (44115-1246)
PHONE.................................216 241-7550
Richard Kabat, President
Desiree Bourgeois, Publisher
Keith Rathbun, Corp Secy
EMP: 48
SQ FT: 5,300
SALES (est): 4.3MM Privately Held
SIC: 2721 7336 2711 Periodicals: publishing only; graphic arts & related design; newspapers

(G-6096)
NORTHERN FROZEN FOODS INC
Also Called: Northern Haserot
21500 Alexander Rd (44146-5511)
PHONE.................................440 439-0600
Douglas Kern, President
Bruce Kern, Corp Secy
Richard C Speicher, Vice Pres
Brad Morgan, Marketing Staff
EMP: 200
SQ FT: 105,000
SALES (est): 209.7MM Privately Held
WEB: www.northernhaserot.com
SIC: 5142 5149 5147 Packaged frozen goods; canned goods: fruit, vegetables, seafood, meats, etc.; meats, fresh

(G-6097)
NORTHERN MANAGEMENT & LEASING
5231 Engle Rd (44142-1531)
PHONE.................................216 676-4600
Todd Armanini, President
Marlene Sutowski, Treasurer
EMP: 70
SALES (est): 2MM Privately Held
SIC: 7513 Truck rental & leasing, no drivers

(G-6098)
NORTHWESTERLY LTD
Also Called: Northwesterly Assisted Living
1341 Marlowe Ave (44107-2654)
PHONE.................................216 228-2266
Jean Rosenthal, Administration
Kristen Montague, Administration
EMP: 30
SQ FT: 200
SALES (est): 1.5MM
SALES (corp-wide): 6MM Privately Held
WEB: www.northwesterly.com
SIC: 6513 Retirement hotel operation
PA: Kandu Capital, Llc
260 E Brown St Ste 315
Birmingham MI 48009
248 642-2914

(G-6099)
NORTHWIND INDUSTRIES INC
15500 Commerce Park Dr (44142-2013)
PHONE.................................216 433-0666
Garry Patla, President
Christine Klukan, Vice Pres
EMP: 27
SQ FT: 2,000
SALES (est): 3.4MM Privately Held
SIC: 3599 7692 3469 3444 Machine shop, jobbing & repair; grinding castings for the trade; welding repair; metal stampings; sheet metalwork; fabricated structural metal; metal heat treating

(G-6100)
NOTRE DAME ACADEMY APARTMENTS
1325 Ansel Rd (44106-1079)
PHONE.................................216 707-1590
Joseph Weiss Jr, President
EMP: 30
SALES: 430.3K Privately Held
SIC: 6513 Apartment building operators

(G-6101)
NOTTINGHAM-SPIRK DES
2200 Overlook Rd (44106-2326)
PHONE.................................216 800-5782
John Nottingham, President
John Spirk, President
EMP: 50
SQ FT: 8,000
SALES (est): 8.9MM Privately Held
WEB: www.ns-design.com
SIC: 7336 8711 Package design; designing: ship, boat, machine & product; mechanical engineering

(G-6102)
NRP CONTRACTORS LLC (HQ)
1228 Euclid Ave Fl 4 (44115-1834)
PHONE.................................216 475-8900
J David Heller, Mng Member
T R Bailey,
Alan Scott,
EMP: 40
SQ FT: 15,000
SALES (est): 62.9MM Privately Held
SIC: 1521 1522 Single-family housing construction; hotel/motel & multi-family home construction
PA: The Nrp Group Llc
1228 Euclid Ave Ste 400
Cleveland OH 44115
216 475-8900

(G-6103)
NRP GROUP LLC (PA)
1228 Euclid Ave Ste 400 (44115-1831)
PHONE.................................216 475-8900
JD Crow, Asst Supt
Johnson Bazzel, Vice Pres
David J Heller, Mng Member
Rick Bailey,
EMP: 60
SALES (est): 62.9MM Privately Held
SIC: 1521 General remodeling, single-family houses

(G-6104)
NRP HOLDINGS LLC
5309 Transportation Blvd (44125-5333)
PHONE.................................216 475-8900
J David Heller, Mng Member
T R Bailey,
Alan Scott,
EMP: 150

SALES: 100MM Privately Held
SIC: 1531 Townhouse developers

(G-6105)
NSL ANALYTICAL SERVICES INC (PA)
4450 Cranwood Pkwy (44128-4004)
PHONE.................................216 438-5200
Lawrence Somrack, President
Steve Dusek, Facilities Mgr
Melissa Gorris, Marketing Staff
EMP: 55
SQ FT: 30,877
SALES (est): 21MM Privately Held
WEB: www.nslanalytical.com
SIC: 8734 Testing laboratories

(G-6106)
NU-DI PRODUCTS CO INC
Also Called: Nu-Di Corporation
12730 Triskett Rd (44111-2529)
PHONE.................................216 251-9070
Kenneth Bihn, President
Tim Bihn, Vice Pres
Michael Cupach, Buyer
Charles Novicky, Maintence Staff
EMP: 85
SQ FT: 38,000
SALES (est): 15.7MM Privately Held
WEB: www.nu-di.com
SIC: 3825 5013 Engine electrical test equipment; testing equipment, electrical: automotive

(G-6107)
NURENBERG PLEVIN HELLER
600 Superior Ave E # 1200 (44114-2654)
PHONE.................................440 423-0750
Leon M Plevin, President
Marshall I Nurenberg, Vice Pres
Maurice L Heller, Treasurer
John J McCarthy, Admin Sec
Andrew P Krembs,
EMP: 64 EST: 1926
SQ FT: 28,000
SALES (est): 8.2MM Privately Held
WEB: www.nphm.com
SIC: 8111 General practice law office

(G-6108)
NYMAN CONSTRUCTION CO
23209 Miles Rd Fl 2 (44128-5467)
PHONE.................................216 475-7800
Michael Nyman, President
Ken Murphy, Vice Pres
Brian Miller, Manager
EMP: 30
SQ FT: 16,000
SALES (est): 10.7MM Privately Held
SIC: 1541 1542 Industrial buildings & warehouses; nonresidential construction

(G-6109)
OAKWOOD HEALTH CARE SVCS INC
Also Called: Grande Oaks & Grande Pavillion
24579 Broadway Ave (44146-6338)
PHONE.................................440 439-7976
Aaron Handler, President
EMP: 150
SQ FT: 5,000
SALES (est): 5.3MM Privately Held
SIC: 8059 Nursing home, except skilled & intermediate care facility

(G-6110)
OATEY SUPPLY CHAIN SVCS INC (HQ)
Also Called: Oatey Company
20600 Emerald Pkwy (44135-6022)
PHONE.................................216 267-7100
John H McMillan, CEO
Gary Oatey, Ch of Bd
Eric Hull, Director
▲ EMP: 200
SQ FT: 165,000
SALES (est): 99.6MM
SALES (corp-wide): 470MM Privately Held
WEB: www.oateyscs.com
SIC: 3444 5074 Metal roofing & roof drainage equipment; plumbing & hydronic heating supplies

GEOGRAPHIC

PA: Oatey Co.
20600 Emerald Pkwy
Cleveland OH 44135
800 203-1155

(G-6111)
OATEY SUPPLY CHAIN SVCS INC
Also Called: Oatey Distribution Center
4565 Industrial Pkwy (44135-4541)
PHONE..................................216 267-7100
John Dettorre, *Manager*
EMP: 50
SALES (corp-wide): 470MM Privately Held
WEB: www.oateyscs.com
SIC: 4225 Warehousing, self-storage
HQ: Oatey Supply Chain Services, Inc.
20600 Emerald Pkwy
Cleveland OH 44135
216 267-7100

(G-6112)
OFFICE DEPOT INC
9880 Sweet Valley Dr # 2 (44125-4268)
PHONE..................................800 463-3768
Rannigan Walsh, *Branch Mgr*
EMP: 29
SALES (corp-wide): 11B Publicly Held
WEB: www.officedepot.com
SIC: 5943 5044 5045 Office forms & supplies; office equipment; computers, peripherals & software; computers
PA: Office Depot, Inc.
6600 N Military Trl
Boca Raton FL 33496
561 438-4800

(G-6113)
OFFICE FURNITURE RESOURCES INC
Also Called: S. Rose Company
1213 Prospect Ave E (44115-1258)
PHONE..................................216 781-8200
Richard Rose, *Ch of Bd*
Clark Rose, *President*
Paul Johanni, *COO*
Gary Herwald, *Vice Pres*
Howard Rose, *Treasurer*
EMP: 36
SQ FT: 30,000
SALES (est): 15.1MM
SALES (corp-wide): 68.9MM Privately Held
WEB: www.srose.com
SIC: 5021 Office furniture
PA: River City Furniture, Llc
6454 Centre Park Dr
West Chester OH 45069
513 612-7303

(G-6114)
OHIO AEROSPACE INSTITUTE (PA)
Also Called: O A I
22800 Cedar Point Rd (44142-1012)
PHONE..................................440 962-3000
Salvatore Miraglia, *Ch of Bd*
Michael Heil, *President*
Jake Breland, *Vice Pres*
Tony H Smith, *Vice Pres*
EMP: 56
SQ FT: 70,000
SALES: 16.3MM Privately Held
SIC: 8733 Noncommercial research organizations

(G-6115)
OHIO BELL TELEPHONE COMPANY (DH)
Also Called: AT&T Ohio
45 Erieview Plz (44114-1801)
PHONE..................................216 822-3439
Jolie Lagrange-Johnson, *Manager*
EMP: 869
SQ FT: 100,000
SALES (est): 651.9MM
SALES (corp-wide): 170.7B Publicly Held
SIC: 4813 8721 Telephone Communications Accounting/Audit/Bookkpg
HQ: AT&T Teleholdings, Inc.
30 S Wacker Dr Fl 34
Chicago IL 60606
800 288-2020

(G-6116)
OHIO BLOW PIPE COMPANY (PA)
446 E 131st St (44108-1684)
PHONE..................................216 681-7379
Edward Fakeris, *President*
William Roberts, *Vice Pres*
Lisa Kern, *CFO*
EMP: 33
SQ FT: 45,000
SALES (est): 24.2MM Privately Held
WEB: www.obpairsystems.com
SIC: 8711 3564 3444 Engineering services; blowers & fans; sheet metalwork

(G-6117)
OHIO BUSINESS MACHINES LLC (PA)
Also Called: O B M
1111 Superior Ave E # 105 (44114-2522)
PHONE..................................216 485-2000
Salvatore J Spagnola,
EMP: 25
SALES (est): 46.5MM Privately Held
SIC: 5044 7629 5734 Office equipment; business machine repair, electric; computer & software stores

(G-6118)
OHIO CATHOLIC FEDERAL CR UN (PA)
13623 Rockside Rd (44125-5173)
PHONE..................................216 663-6800
Stephen Halas, *CEO*
Joseph Zaite, *President*
Stephanie Thomas, *Opers Mgr*
Brian Mooney, *CFO*
John Hartman, *Treasurer*
EMP: 43
SALES: 6.3MM Privately Held
WEB: www.ohiocatholicfederalcreditunion.com
SIC: 6061 Federal credit unions

(G-6119)
OHIO CITIZEN ACTION (PA)
614 W Superior Ave # 1200 (44113-1386)
PHONE..................................216 861-5200
Alexandra Buchanan, *Exec Dir*
EMP: 50 EST: 1976
SALES: 955K Privately Held
WEB: www.ohiocitizenaction.org
SIC: 8399 Community action agency

(G-6120)
OHIO HEALTH CHOICE INC (DH)
6000 Parkland Blvd # 100 (44124-6120)
P.O. Box 2090, Akron (44309-2090)
PHONE..................................800 554-0027
Bryan Kennedy, *President*
Michael Rutherford, *Exec VP*
Lisa Vieront, *Accounts Exec*
EMP: 58
SQ FT: 8,100
SALES (est): 10.4MM
SALES (corp-wide): 1B Privately Held
SIC: 6324 Group hospitalization plans

(G-6121)
OHIO NEWS NETWORK
3001 Euclid Ave (44115-2516)
PHONE..................................216 367-7493
Michael Fiorello, *Vice Pres*
EMP: 70
SALES (est): 925.5K Privately Held
WEB: www.ohionewsnetwork.com
SIC: 4833 Television broadcasting stations

(G-6122)
OHIO PAVING GROUP LLC
4873 Osborn Rd (44128-3139)
PHONE..................................216 475-1700
Brock Evans, *Mng Member*
EMP: 25
SALES (est): 1.7MM Privately Held
SIC: 1771 Concrete work

(G-6123)
OHIO REAL TITLE AGENCY LLC (PA)
1213 Prospect Ave E # 200 (44115-1260)
PHONE..................................216 373-9900
Donald McFadden, *Principal*
Dean Talaganis, *Opers Mgr*
Richard Neff, *Sales Staff*

Karen Mann, *Banking Exec*
EMP: 30
SALES (est): 7.4MM Privately Held
SIC: 6361 Real estate title insurance

(G-6124)
OHIO TECHNICAL COLLEGE INC
Powersport Institute PSI
1374 E 51st St (44103-1269)
PHONE..................................216 881-1700
Bernie Thompson, *Principal*
EMP: 195
SALES (est): 21.2MM Privately Held
SIC: 8733 Noncommercial research organizations
PA: Ohio Technical College, Inc.
1374 E 51st St
Cleveland OH 44103
216 361-0983

(G-6125)
OHIO TRANSPORT INC
Also Called: Cincinnati
3750 Valley Rd Ste A (44109-3095)
PHONE..................................216 741-8000
Gregory F Tavrell, *President*
William Hill, *Vice Pres*
EMP: 25
SQ FT: 21,000
SALES (est): 3MM Privately Held
SIC: 4731 Truck transportation brokers

(G-6126)
OHIOGUIDESTONE
Also Called: Pro Kids & Families Program
3500 Carnegie Ave (44115-2641)
PHONE..................................440 260-8900
Thomas Copper, *Vice Pres*
EMP: 200
SALES (corp-wide): 62.8MM Privately Held
WEB: www.bchfs.org
SIC: 8322 Social service center
PA: Ohioguidestone
434 Eastland Rd
Berea OH 44017
440 234-2006

(G-6127)
OLD DOMINION FREIGHT LINE INC
8055 Old Granger Rd (44125-4852)
PHONE..................................216 641-5566
Jack Amato, *Manager*
EMP: 34
SALES (corp-wide): 4B Publicly Held
WEB: www.odfl.com
SIC: 4213 Contract haulers
PA: Old Dominion Freight Line Inc
500 Old Dominion Way
Thomasville NC 27360
336 889-5000

(G-6128)
OLD TIME POTTERY INC
7011 W 130th St Ste 1 (44130-7889)
PHONE..................................440 842-1244
Jack H Peterson, *Branch Mgr*
EMP: 82
SALES (corp-wide): 691.2MM Privately Held
WEB: www.oldtimepottery.com
SIC: 5999 5023 Art, picture frames & decorations; home furnishings
PA: Old Time Pottery, Llc
480 River Rock Blvd
Murfreesboro TN 37128
615 890-6060

(G-6129)
OLYMPIC STEEL INC (PA)
22901 Millcreek Blvd # 650 (44122-5732)
PHONE..................................216 292-3800
Richard T Marabito, *CEO*
Donald McNeeley, *President*
David A Wolfort, *President*
Andrew S Greiff, *COO*
Andrew F Wolfort, *Vice Pres*
EMP: 58
SQ FT: 127,000
SALES: 1.3B Publicly Held
WEB: www.olysteel.com
SIC: 5051 Steel; pipe & tubing, steel; iron or steel flat products

(G-6130)
OLYMPIC STEEL INC
5092 Richmond Rd (44146-1329)
PHONE..................................216 292-3800
Ray Walker, *Vice Pres*
EMP: 100
SALES (corp-wide): 1.3B Publicly Held
WEB: www.olysteel.com
SIC: 5051 Steel
PA: Olympic Steel, Inc.
22901 Millcreek Blvd # 650
Cleveland OH 44122
216 292-3800

(G-6131)
OMNI INTERGLOBAL INC
600 Superior Ave E # 1300 (44114-2654)
PHONE..................................216 239-3833
James B Abrams, *Principal*
EMP: 50 EST: 2015
SQ FT: 2,500
SALES (est): 2.1MM Privately Held
SIC: 4731 Domestic freight forwarding

(G-6132)
ONCODIAGNOSTIC LABORATORY INC
812 Huron Rd E Ste 520 (44115-1126)
P.O. Box 117, Bolton MA (01740-0117)
PHONE..................................216 861-5846
Joseph Galang, *CEO*
Cirilo F Galang MD, *President*
Jennifer J Perry, *Business Mgr*
Chanho H Park MD, *Admin Sec*
EMP: 40
SQ FT: 3,000
SALES (est): 1.9MM Privately Held
WEB: www.oncodiagnostic.com
SIC: 8071 Pathological laboratory
PA: Predictive Biosciences, Inc.
128 Spring St 400 Level B
Lexington MA 02421

(G-6133)
ONE SKY FLIGHT LLC
26180 Curtiss Wright Pkwy (44143-1453)
PHONE..................................877 703-2348
Michael Silvestro, *CEO*
Kenneth Ricci, *Chairman*
Michael Rossi, *CFO*
EMP: 860
SALES (est): 2.1MM
SALES (corp-wide): 61.7MM Privately Held
SIC: 4522 Flying charter service; non-scheduled charter services
PA: Flight Options, Inc.
26180 Curtiss Wright Pkwy
Richmond Heights OH 44143
216 261-3880

(G-6134)
ONE SOURCE TECHNOLOGY LLC
Also Called: Asurint
1111 Superior Ave E # 2000 (44114-2522)
PHONE..................................216 420-1700
Gregg Gay, *CEO*
Todd Pierce, *Partner*
Connie Clore, *COO*
Steve Palek, *Exec VP*
Joe Dose, *Project Mgr*
EMP: 50
SQ FT: 7,000
SALES (est): 10.5MM Privately Held
SIC: 7375 Data base information retrieval

(G-6135)
ONE WAY EXPRESS INCORPORATED
380 Solon Rd Ste 5 (44146-3809)
PHONE..................................440 439-9182
Cynthia Jackson, *President*
Richard Jackson, *Vice Pres*
Cindy Pavkov, *Office Admin*
EMP: 40
SQ FT: 2,500
SALES (est): 5.1MM Privately Held
WEB: www.onewayexpress.com
SIC: 4212 4213 Local trucking, without storage; trucking, except local

▲ = Import ▼=Export
◆ =Import/Export

(G-6136)
ONX USA LLC (DH)
5910 Landerbrook Dr # 250 (44124-6508)
PHONE..............................440 569-2300
Mike Cox, *CEO*
Bart Foster, *Ch of Bd*
Paul Khawaja, *President*
Wayne Kiphart, *President*
Andrew Tweedie, *Mfg Mgr*
EMP: 75
SQ FT: 20,000
SALES (est): 78.4MM
SALES (corp-wide): 1.3B **Publicly Held**
SIC: 7379 7372 Computer related consulting services; business oriented computer software
HQ: Onx Holdings Llc
221 E 4th St
Cincinnati OH 45202
866 587-2287

(G-6137)
ONYX CREATIVE INC (PA)
Also Called: Herschman Architects
25001 Emery Rd Ste 400 (44128-5627)
PHONE..............................216 223-3200
Mike Crislip, *President*
Carole Sanderson, *Corp Secy*
Jennifer Dort, *Project Mgr*
Matthew Emerson, *Project Mgr*
Patrick Fox, *Project Mgr*
EMP: 90
SQ FT: 20,000
SALES: 17.5MM **Privately Held**
SIC: 8711 8712 7389 Engineering services; architectural engineering; interior design services

(G-6138)
OPTIMA 777 LLC
Also Called: Westin Cleveland
777 Saint Clair Ave Ne (44114-1711)
PHONE..............................216 771-7700
Alan Feuerman,
Mark Anderson,
EMP: 49
SALES (est): 4.2MM **Privately Held**
SIC: 7011 Hotels & motels

(G-6139)
OPTIONS FLIGHT SUPPORT INC
26180 Curtiss Wright Pkwy (44143-1453)
PHONE..............................216 261-3500
Michael Scheerringa, *CEO*
Mark Brody, *CFO*
EMP: 160 EST: 1993
SALES (est): 14.2MM
SALES (corp-wide): 61.7MM **Privately Held**
SIC: 5599 4522 Aircraft dealers; air transportation, nonscheduled
PA: Flight Options, Inc.
26180 Curtiss Wright Pkwy
Richmond Heights OH 44143
216 261-3880

(G-6140)
OR COLAN ASSOCIATES LLC
22710 Fairview Center Dr # 150
(44126-3621)
PHONE..............................440 827-6116
Eric Kirk, *Manager*
EMP: 49
SALES (corp-wide): 16MM **Privately Held**
SIC: 8742 Management consulting services
PA: O.R. Colan Associates, Llc
7005 Shannon Willow Rd # 100
Charlotte NC 28226
704 529-3115

(G-6141)
ORBIT INDUSTRIES INC (PA)
6840 Lake Abrams Dr (44130-3455)
PHONE..............................440 243-3311
Robert Aleksandrovic, *President*
EMP: 54 EST: 1965
SQ FT: 70,000
SALES (est): 8MM **Privately Held**
WEB: www.orbitndt.com
SIC: 7389 Industrial & commercial equipment inspection service

(G-6142)
ORCA HOUSE
1905 E 89th St (44106-2007)
PHONE..............................216 231-3772
Rochena Crosby, *Director*
EMP: 40
SQ FT: 24,030
SALES: 1.5MM **Privately Held**
WEB: www.orcahouse.org
SIC: 8093 Alcohol clinic, outpatient; rehabilitation center, outpatient treatment

(G-6143)
ORIANA HOUSE INC
3540 Croton Ave (44115-3212)
PHONE..............................216 361-9655
EMP: 182
SALES (corp-wide): 48.4MM **Privately Held**
SIC: 8069 Specialty Hospital
PA: Oriana House, Inc.
885 E Buchtel Ave
Akron OH 44305
330 535-8116

(G-6144)
ORION CARE SERVICES LLC
18810 Harvard Ave (44122-6848)
PHONE..............................216 752-3600
Sally Schwartz, *President*
Abram Schwartz, *Vice Pres*
Keith Yoder, *CFO*
Chris Ayewoh, *Administration*
EMP: 250
SALES (est): 3.7MM **Privately Held**
SIC: 8051 8052 Skilled nursing care facilities; intermediate care facilities

(G-6145)
OSBORN ENGINEERING COMPANY (PA)
1100 Superior Ave E # 300 (44114-2530)
PHONE..............................216 861-2020
E P Baxendale, *President*
Don P Archiable, *Exec VP*
L V Hooper, *Vice Pres*
Lee Hooper, *Vice Pres*
Doug Lancashire, *Vice Pres*
EMP: 90
SALES (est): 18.7MM **Privately Held**
WEB: www.osborn-eng.com
SIC: 8711 8712 Consulting engineer; architectural engineering

(G-6146)
OSTENDORF-MORRIS PROPERTIES
1100 Superior Ave E # 800 (44114-2530)
PHONE..............................216 861-7200
Bill West, *President*
Mike Clegg, *Partner*
EMP: 80
SALES (est): 7.4MM **Privately Held**
SIC: 6552 Land subdividers & developers, commercial

(G-6147)
OTIS ELEVATOR COMPANY
9800 Rockside Rd Ste 1200 (44125-6270)
PHONE..............................216 573-2333
Gordy Sell, *Manager*
EMP: 73
SALES (corp-wide): 66.5B **Publicly Held**
WEB: www.otis.com
SIC: 7699 1796 3534 Elevators: inspection, service & repair; elevator installation & conversion; elevators & equipment
HQ: Otis Elevator Company
1 Carrier Pl
Farmington CT 06032
860 674-3000

(G-6148)
OUTREACH PROFESSIONAL SVCS INC
Also Called: St. Vincent Medical Group
2351 E 22nd St (44115-3111)
PHONE..............................216 472-4094
David F Perse, *President*
Beverly Lozar, *COO*
Vincent Farinacci, *Director*
Emily Woods, *Associate*
EMP: 90
SQ FT: 3,700

SALES (est): 8.7MM
SALES (corp-wide): 142.3MM **Privately Held**
WEB: www.cpnmd.com
SIC: 8741 Office management
PA: St. Vincent Charity Medical Center
2351 E 22nd St
Cleveland OH 44115
216 861-6200

(G-6149)
OVATIONS
2000 Prospect Ave E (44115-2318)
PHONE..............................216 687-9292
Wes Westley, *President*
EMP: 40
SALES (est): 2.1MM **Privately Held**
SIC: 7922 Concert management service

(G-6150)
OVERLOOK HOUSE
2187 Overlook Rd (44106-2323)
P.O. Box 161070, Rocky River (44116-7070)
PHONE..............................216 795-3550
Diana Henn, *Administration*
EMP: 28
SQ FT: 20,000
SALES: 262.2K **Privately Held**
WEB: www.overlookhouse.org
SIC: 8059 8661 Nursing home, except skilled & intermediate care facility; religious organizations

(G-6151)
OWNERS MANAGEMENT
Also Called: Trans Con Buildings
25250 Rockside Rd Ste 1 (44146-1839)
PHONE..............................440 439-3800
Fred Rzepka, *President*
EMP: 40
SALES (est): 1MM **Privately Held**
WEB: www.ownerslive.com
SIC: 8641 Condominium association

(G-6152)
OXCYON INC
17520 Engle Lake Dr Ste 1 (44130-8360)
PHONE..............................440 239-3345
Samuel Keller, *CEO*
John Hunter, *Vice Pres*
James Venus, *Vice Pres*
Cheryl Meier, *Opers Dir*
Joe Frey, *Prdtn Mgr*
EMP: 42
SQ FT: 15,000
SALES (est): 5.4MM **Privately Held**
WEB: www.oxcyon.com
SIC: 4813

(G-6153)
OZANNE CONSTRUCTION CO INC
1635 E 25th St (44114-4214)
PHONE..............................216 696-2876
Leroy Ozanne, *Ch of Bd*
Dominic L Ozanne, *President*
Robert E Fitzgerald, *Vice Pres*
Fred Rodgers, *Vice Pres*
EMP: 40
SQ FT: 4,000
SALES (est): 16.3MM **Privately Held**
WEB: www.ozanne.com
SIC: 1542 Commercial & office building, new construction

(G-6154)
P C VPA
16600 W Sprague Rd Ste 80 (44130-6318)
PHONE..............................440 826-0500
Rebecca R Reyes, *Family Practiti*
EMP: 43 **Privately Held**
SIC: 8099 Medical services organization
PA: P C Vpa
500 Kirts Blvd Ste 200
Troy MI 48084

(G-6155)
P JS HAIR STYLING SHOPPE
20400 Lorain Rd (44126-3516)
PHONE..............................440 333-1244
Peter J Holick, *Owner*
EMP: 25
SALES (est): 146K **Privately Held**
SIC: 7231 Hairdressers

(G-6156)
P-AMERICAS LLC
4561 Industrial Pkwy (44135-4541)
PHONE..............................216 252-7377
Andy Connelly, *Principal*
Dennis Stanley, *Manager*
EMP: 60
SQ FT: 17,043
SALES (corp-wide): 64.6B **Publicly Held**
SIC: 5149 5499 Soft drinks; beverage stores
HQ: P-Americas Llc
1 Pepsi Way
Somers NY 10589
336 896-5740

(G-6157)
PAINTERS DISTRICT COUNCIL 6
8257 Dow Cir (44136-1761)
PHONE..............................440 239-4575
Jim Nagy, *Accountant*
George Boots, *Training Dir*
Dana Clark, *Asst Director*
Carly Sell, *Admin Sec*
Annette Danczak, *Admin Asst*
EMP: 29
SALES: 5.5MM **Privately Held**
SIC: 8631 Trade union

(G-6158)
PALADIN PROTECTIVE SYSTEMS INC
Also Called: Paladin Professional Sound
7680 Hub Pkwy (44125-5707)
PHONE..............................216 441-6500
Calvin Corsi, *President*
Jeffrey L Kocian, *Principal*
Kevin Corsi, *Vice Pres*
Daniel Akins, *Project Mgr*
Nancy Peck, *Purchasing*
EMP: 50
SQ FT: 11,800
SALES (est): 20.6MM **Privately Held**
WEB: www.paladinps.com
SIC: 1731 Fire detection & burglar alarm systems specialization; closed circuit television installation; access control systems specialization; sound equipment specialization

(G-6159)
PALLADIUM HEALTHCARE LLC
16910 Harvard Ave (44128-2210)
PHONE..............................216 644-4383
Lawanna Porter, *CEO*
Rose Radovanic, *CFO*
Kenneth Porter, *Director*
EMP: 200
SALES (est): 2.6MM **Privately Held**
SIC: 8082 Home health care services

(G-6160)
PARAGON CONSULTING INC
5900 Landerbrook Dr # 205 (44124-4020)
PHONE..............................440 684-3101
Carmen Tulino, *President*
Larry Koester, *Principal*
Mark Atwood, *Vice Pres*
Ray Modic, *Shareholder*
EMP: 30
SQ FT: 3,800
SALES (est): 5MM **Privately Held**
WEB: www.paragon-inc.com
SIC: 8742 General management consultant

(G-6161)
PARAGON TEC INC
3740 Carnegie Ave Ste 302 (44115-2756)
PHONE..............................216 361-5555
Gail Dolman-Smith, *President*
Dan Lawson, *VP Opers*
Gail Dolmansmith, *Manager*
Maurice Reynolds, *Coordinator*
EMP: 76
SALES (est): 4.4MM **Privately Held**
WEB: www.paragon-tec.com
SIC: 8742 General management consultant

(G-6162)
PARAN MANAGEMENT COMPANY LTD
2720 Van Aken Blvd # 200 (44120-2271)
PHONE..............................216 921-5663

Joseph Shafran,
Mark Zielinski,
EMP: 47 **EST:** 1975
SQ FT: 3,500
SALES (est): 5.7MM **Privately Held**
WEB: www.paranmgt.com
SIC: 6531 Real estate managers

(G-6163)
PARK CORPORATION (PA)
6200 Riverside Dr (44135-3132)
P.O. Box 8678, South Charleston WV
(25303-0678)
PHONE................................216 267-4870
Raymond P Park, *Ch of Bd*
Daniel K Park, *President*
Ricky L Bertrem, *Vice Pres*
Shelva J Davis, *Vice Pres*
Kelly C Park, *Vice Pres*
◆ **EMP:** 300
SQ FT: 2,500,000
SALES (est): 568.1MM **Privately Held**
WEB: www.parkcorp.com
SIC: 3547 1711 3443 5084 Rolling mill
machinery; boiler maintenance contractor;
mechanical contractor; boilers: industrial,
power, or marine; industrial machinery &
equipment; commercial & industrial build-
ing operation; exposition operation

(G-6164)
**PARK CREEK RTIREMENT
CMNTY INC**
10064 N Church Dr (44130-4066)
PHONE................................440 842-5100
John D Spielbuger, *President*
Jessica Rowland, *Admin Sec*
Linda Fgoice, *Administration*
EMP: 30
SQ FT: 40,000
SALES (est): 1.1MM **Privately Held**
SIC: 8052 Intermediate care facilities

(G-6165)
PARK HOTELS & RESORTS INC
Also Called: Hilton
6200 Quarry Ln (44131-2218)
PHONE................................216 447-0020
Jock Litras, *General Mgr*
EMP: 120
SALES (corp-wide): 2.7B **Publicly Held**
WEB: www.esirvine.com
SIC: 7011 Hotels
PA: Park Hotels & Resorts Inc.
1775 Tysons Blvd Fl 7
Tysons VA 22102
571 302-5757

(G-6166)
PARK HOTELS & RESORTS INC
Also Called: Hilton
3663 Park East Dr (44122-4315)
PHONE................................216 464-5950
Robert W Boykin, *General Mgr*
EMP: 300
SALES (corp-wide): 2.7B **Publicly Held**
WEB: www.esirvine.com
SIC: 7011 5813 5812 Hotels; drinking
places; eating places
PA: Park Hotels & Resorts Inc.
1775 Tysons Blvd Fl 7
Tysons VA 22102
571 302-5757

(G-6167)
PARK N FLY INC
19000 Snow Rd (44142-1412)
PHONE................................404 264-1000
Judy Behrend, *Branch Mgr*
Susan Brenders, *Manager*
Steven Dossa, *Manager*
Allen Ng, *Asst Mgr*
EMP: 30
SALES (corp-wide): 70.9MM **Privately
Held**
WEB: www.parkholding.com
SIC: 7521 Parking lots
HQ: Park 'n Fly, Inc.
2060 Mount Paran Rd Nw # 207
Atlanta GA 30327
404 264-1000

(G-6168)
**PARK PLACE MANAGEMENT
INC**
Also Called: Park Place Airport Parking
18975 Snow Rd (44142-1411)
P.O. Box 81376 (44181-0376)
PHONE................................216 362-1080
William Maloof, *President*
Walter J Himmelman, *CFO*
Shannon Saiko, *Manager*
EMP: 45
SQ FT: 2,000
SALES (est): 1.7MM **Privately Held**
SIC: 7521 Parking lots

(G-6169)
**PARK PLACE TECHNOLOGIES
LLC**
5910 Landerbrook Dr # 300 (44124-6500)
PHONE................................603 617-7123
James Stevens, *Manager*
Jean Hackathorn, *Manager*
EMP: 34 **Privately Held**
SIC: 7378 Computer maintenance & repair
PA: Park Place Technologies, Llc
5910 Landerbrook Dr # 300
Mayfield Heights OH 44124

(G-6170)
**PARKER-HANNIFIN
CORPORATION**
Parker Service Center
6035 Parkland Blvd (44124-4186)
PHONE................................216 896-3000
Sherroll Manning, *Senior Buyer*
Tom Boyer, *Manager*
EMP: 30
SALES (corp-wide): 12B **Publicly Held**
WEB: www.parker.com
SIC: 5084 Industrial machinery & equip-
ment
PA: Parker-Hannifin Corporation
6035 Parkland Blvd
Cleveland OH 44124
216 896-3000

(G-6171)
**PARKER-HANNIFIN
CORPORATION**
Motion & Control Training Div
6035 Parkland Blvd (44124-4186)
PHONE................................216 531-3000
Joe Bocian, *Branch Mgr*
EMP: 600
SALES (corp-wide): 12B **Publicly Held**
WEB: www.parker.com
SIC: 4225 3823 3714 General Ware-
house/Storage Mfg Process Control In-
struments Mfg Motor Vehicle
Parts/Accessories
PA: Parker-Hannifin Corporation
6035 Parkland Blvd
Cleveland OH 44124
216 896-3000

(G-6172)
**PARKER-HANNIFIN INTL CORP
(HQ)**
6035 Parkland Blvd (44124-4186)
PHONE................................216 896-3000
Donald Washkewic, *President*
Timothy K Pistell, *Treasurer*
Leomdruno Bruno, *Controller*
EMP: 450
SALES (est): 36.5MM
SALES (corp-wide): 14.3B **Publicly Held**
SIC: 8741 Administrative management
PA: Parker-Hannifin Corporation
6035 Parkland Blvd
Cleveland OH 44124
216 896-3000

(G-6173)
**PARKING COMPANY AMERICA
INC**
Also Called: Airport Pass Park
18899 Snow Rd (44142-1409)
PHONE................................216 265-0500
Lew Bodee, *Branch Mgr*
Marie Cunningham, *Manager*
Missy Kim, *Manager*
EMP: 30

SALES (corp-wide): 94.4MM **Privately
Held**
WEB: www.airportfastparkandshuttle.com
SIC: 7521 Parking garage
PA: Parking Company Of America, Inc.
250 W Court St Ste 200e
Cincinnati OH 45202
513 241-0415

(G-6174)
**PARKWOOD CORPORATION
(PA)**
1000 Lakeside Ave E (44114-1117)
PHONE................................216 875-6500
Morton L Mandel, *Ch of Bd*
Jack N Mandel, *Ch of Bd*
Thomas Mandel, *Vice Ch Bd*
Joseph C Mandel, *Chairman*
James R Fox, *Vice Pres*
EMP: 42
SQ FT: 13,680
SALES (est): 10.3MM **Privately Held**
WEB: www.parkwd.com
SIC: 6282 Investment advisory service

(G-6175)
PARMA CARE CENTER INC
Also Called: PARMA CARE NURSING AND
REHABIL
5553 Broadview Rd (44134-1604)
PHONE................................216 661-6800
Mike Flank, *President*
Eitan Flank, *Owner*
David Farkas, *Vice Pres*
Brian Choleran, *Controller*
Louis Schonfeld, *Administration*
EMP: 125
SQ FT: 55,000
SALES (est): 7.9MM **Privately Held**
WEB: www.parmacarecenter.com
SIC: 8052 8051 Intermediate care facili-
ties; skilled nursing care facilities

(G-6176)
**PARMA CLINIC CANCER
CENTER**
Also Called: Parma Communirty Hospital
6525 Parma Blvd Fl 2 Flr 2 (44129)
PHONE................................440 743-4747
Gerald Burma, *Med Doctor*
Kim Monaco, *Manager*
EMP: 25
SALES (est): 1MM **Privately Held**
SIC: 8069 Cancer hospital

(G-6177)
PARTNERS OF CITY VIEW LLC
Also Called: City View Nrsing Rhabilitation
6606 Carnegie Ave (44103-4622)
PHONE................................216 361-1414
Kevin Kilbane, *Director*
EMP: 150
SQ FT: 24,676
SALES (est): 5.7MM **Privately Held**
SIC: 8059 Nursing home, except skilled &
intermediate care facility

(G-6178)
PARTNERSHIP LLC
29077 Clemens Rd (44145-1135)
PHONE................................440 471-8310
John J Finucane Jr, *President*
Chad Reusch, *Area Mgr*
Laura Schramm, *Opers Mgr*
Brian Ferancy, *VP Sales*
Jennifer Hammersmith, *Cust Mgr*
EMP: 45
SALES (est): 7.7MM
SALES (corp-wide): 30MM **Privately
Held**
SIC: 4213 Less-than-truckload (LTL) trans-
port
PA: National Association Of College Stores,
Inc.
500 E Lorain St
Oberlin OH 44074
440 775-7777

(G-6179)
**PASSION TO HEAL
HEALTHCARE**
4228 W 58th St (44144-1713)
PHONE................................216 849-0180
Jacques Pollard, *Owner*
EMP: 25

SALES (est): 118.5K **Privately Held**
SIC: 8082 Home health care services

(G-6180)
**PAT YOUNG SERVICE CO INC
(PA)**
6100 Hillcrest Dr (44125-4622)
PHONE................................216 447-8550
Derek W Young, *President*
Eugene Resovsky, *Vice Pres*
Kirk Young, *Vice Pres*
Fran Young, *Treasurer*
Ernest Mansour, *Admin Sec*
▲ **EMP:** 49
SQ FT: 35,000
SALES (est): 54MM **Privately Held**
WEB: www.pysfederated.com
SIC: 5531 5013 Automotive parts; auto-
motive supplies & parts

(G-6181)
PATH ROBOTICS INC
1768 E 25th St (44114-4418)
PHONE................................330 808-2788
Kenneth Lonsberry, *President*
EMP: 25
SALES (est): 524.1K **Privately Held**
SIC: 7371 Computer software systems
analysis & design, custom

(G-6182)
PATHWAY HOUSE LLC
15539 Saranac Rd (44110-2458)
PHONE................................872 223-9797
James T Hemphil,
EMP: 30
SALES (corp-wide): 240K **Privately Held**
SIC: 7389 Telephone services
PA: Pathway House Llc
3126 W 101st St
Cleveland OH 44111
872 223-9797

(G-6183)
PAUL A ERTEL
Also Called: Nautica Queen
1153 Main Ave (44113-2324)
PHONE................................216 696-8888
Paul A Ertel, *Owner*
Colleen Grey, *Sales Mgr*
EMP: 65
SQ FT: 1,000
SALES (est): 1.5MM **Privately Held**
WEB: www.nauticaqueen.com
SIC: 5812 5813 7999 American restau-
rant; cocktail lounge; beach & water
sports equipment rental & services

(G-6184)
PAYCOR INC
4500 Rockside Rd Ste 320 (44131-2170)
PHONE................................216 447-7913
Michael Yaquinto, *Branch Mgr*
EMP: 27
SALES (corp-wide): 105.2MM **Privately
Held**
SIC: 8721 Payroll accounting service
PA: Paycor, Inc.
4811 Montgomery Rd
Cincinnati OH 45212
513 381-0505

(G-6185)
PCM SALES INC
8200 Sweet Valley Dr # 108 (44125-4267)
PHONE................................501 342-1000
John Strauss, *Senior VP*
John Carsuo, *Manager*
EMP: 35
SALES (corp-wide): 2.1B **Publicly Held**
WEB: www.sarcom.com
SIC: 5045 Computers
HQ: Pcm Sales, Inc.
1940 E Mariposa Ave
El Segundo CA 90245
310 354-5600

(G-6186)
PCS COST
1360 E 9th St Ste 910 (44114-1719)
PHONE................................216 771-1090
Robert Strickland, *Principal*
EMP: 43
SALES: 950K **Privately Held**
SIC: 8742 Management consulting serv-
ices

(G-6187)
PEARNE & GORDON LLP
Also Called: Pearne Gordon McCoy & Granger
1801 E 9th St Ste 1200 (44114-3108)
PHONE...................................216 579-1700
David B Deioma, *Partner*
Richard Dickinson, *Partner*
James M Moore, *Partner*
John P Murtaugh, *Partner*
Carl Rankin, *Partner*
EMP: 50
SQ FT: 6,000
SALES (est): 7.8MM **Privately Held**
WEB: www.pearnegordon.com
SIC: 8111 General practice law office; patent solicitor

(G-6188)
PEASE & ASSOCIATES LLC (PA)
1422 Euclid Ave Ste 801 (44115-1902)
PHONE...................................216 348-9600
Joseph Pease, *President*
Lindsay Arcuri, *Accountant*
Lauren Burzanko, *Accountant*
Tiffany Idiaquez, *Accountant*
Carly Roberts, *Accountant*
EMP: 49
SALES (est): 6.4MM **Privately Held**
WEB: www.peasecpa.com
SIC: 8721 Accounting services, except auditing

(G-6189)
PEDIATRIC SERVICES INC (PA)
6707 Powers Blvd Ste 203 (44129-5494)
PHONE...................................440 845-1500
Daniel Hostetler MD, *President*
Joann Hempel, *Director*
EMP: 38 EST: 1969
SQ FT: 4,000
SALES (est): 4.2MM **Privately Held**
WEB: www.pediatricservices.com
SIC: 8011 Pediatrician

(G-6190)
PEITRO PROPERTIES LTD PARTNR
Also Called: Comfort Inn
6191 Quarry Ln (44131-2203)
PHONE...................................216 328-7777
Teresa Shaley, *Managing Prtnr*
Peter Maisano, *Partner*
EMP: 30
SQ FT: 1,000
SALES (est): 1.5MM **Privately Held**
SIC: 7011 Hotels & motels

(G-6191)
PEL LLC
4666 Manufacturing Ave (44135-2638)
PHONE...................................216 267-5775
Michael Sotak, *President*
Jeff Simon, *Finance Dir*
Maureen Palka, *Sales Mgr*
Sara Lutz, *Manager*
Sarah Kramer, *Supervisor*
EMP: 38
SQ FT: 45,000
SALES (est): 14.6MM **Privately Held**
WEB: www.pelsupply.com
SIC: 5047 Artificial limbs; orthopedic equipment & supplies

(G-6192)
PENSKE LOGISTICS LLC
7600 First Pl (44146-6700)
PHONE...................................440 232-5811
Dan Florig,
EMP: 70
SALES (corp-wide): 2.6B **Privately Held**
WEB: www.penskelogistics.com
SIC: 7513 Truck leasing, without drivers
HQ: Penske Logistics Llc
2675 Morgantown Rd
Reading PA 19607
610 775-6000

(G-6193)
PEPPER PIKE CLUB COMPANY INC
Also Called: PEPPER PIKE GOLF CLUB
2800 Som Center Rd (44124-4924)
PHONE...................................216 831-9400
Dwayne Collins, *President*
Linda Wasco, *Controller*
EMP: 75
SQ FT: 10,000
SALES: 4.1MM **Privately Held**
SIC: 7997 8699 Golf club, membership; charitable organization

(G-6194)
PERCEPTIS LLC
1250 Old River Rd Ste 300 (44113-1244)
PHONE...................................216 458-4122
William Bradfield,
EMP: 150
SQ FT: 3,500
SALES (est): 9.8MM **Privately Held**
WEB: www.perceptis.net
SIC: 7379

(G-6195)
PERK COMPANY INC (PA)
8100 Grand Ave Ste 300 (44104-3164)
PHONE...................................216 391-1444
Charles Perkins, *President*
Anthony Cifani, *Corp Secy*
Joseph Cifani, *Vice Pres*
EMP: 45
SQ FT: 15,000
SALES (est): 13.2MM **Privately Held**
WEB: www.perkcompany.com
SIC: 1611 General contractor, highway & street construction; concrete construction: roads, highways, sidewalks, etc.

(G-6196)
PERMANENT GEN ASRN CORP OHIO
9700 Rockside Rd (44125-6268)
PHONE...................................216 986-3000
Steven Mason, *Ch of Bd*
Randy P Parker, *President*
David Hettinger, *Senior VP*
Brian Donovan, *Vice Pres*
EMP: 45
SQ FT: 15,000
SALES (est): 11.6MM
SALES (corp-wide): 10.3B **Privately Held**
WEB: www.pgac.com
SIC: 6331 Fire, marine & casualty insurance & carriers
HQ: Permanent General Companies, Inc.
2636 Elm Hill Pike # 510
Nashville TN 37214
615 242-1961

(G-6197)
PERSONAL TOUCH HM CARE IPA INC
4500 Rockside Rd Ste 460 (44131-6822)
PHONE...................................216 986-0885
EMP: 200
SALES (corp-wide): 363MM **Privately Held**
SIC: 8082 Home Health Care
PA: Personal Touch Home Care Ipa, Inc.
1985 Marcus Ave Ste 202
New Hyde Park NY 11042
718 468-4747

(G-6198)
PERSONALIZED DATA CORPORATION
Also Called: Personalized Data Entry & Word
26155 Euclid Ave Uppr (44132-3366)
PHONE...................................216 289-2200
Anthony Ruque, *President*
James Horne, *Vice Pres*
EMP: 40 EST: 1967
SQ FT: 2,100
SALES (est): 2.3MM **Privately Held**
WEB: www.personalizeddata.com
SIC: 7374 5734 Tabulating service; data punch service; data processing service; computer peripheral equipment

(G-6199)
PERSPECTUS ARCHITECTURE LLC (PA)
13212 Shaker Sq Ste 204 (44120-2398)
PHONE...................................216 752-1800
Mike Lipowski, *Principal*
John Walkosak, *Project Dir*
Mary Seifert, *Accounts Mgr*
William Ayars, *Mng Member*
Marlene Fscher, *Manager*
EMP: 40

SALES: 9MM **Privately Held**
SIC: 8712 Architectural engineering

(G-6200)
PETE BAUR BUICK GMC INC (PA)
14000 Pearl Rd (44136-8706)
PHONE...................................440 238-5600
Daniel E Baur, *President*
Henry J Baur, *Vice Pres*
EMP: 36
SQ FT: 26,000
SALES (est): 23.7MM **Privately Held**
WEB: www.petebaurpontiac.com
SIC: 5511 5531 7549 Automobiles, new & used; automobile & truck equipment & parts; automotive maintenance services

(G-6201)
PETERJ BRODHEAD
1001 Lakeside Ave E (44114-1158)
PHONE...................................216 696-3232
Peter Brodhead, *Partner*
EMP: 30
SALES (est): 1.1MM **Privately Held**
SIC: 8111 General practice attorney, lawyer

(G-6202)
PETROS HOMES INC
10474 Broadview Rd (44147-3225)
PHONE...................................440 546-9000
Sam Petros, *CEO*
Gary Naim, *President*
Chad Enders, *Opers Mgr*
Tricia Soltesz, *Manager*
Mandie Abraham, *Executive*
EMP: 50
SQ FT: 9,216
SALES (est): 9.3MM **Privately Held**
WEB: www.petroshomes.com
SIC: 1521 6531 New construction, single-family houses; real estate agents & managers

(G-6203)
PHILIPS MEDICAL SYSTEMS CLEVEL (HQ)
Also Called: Medical Imaging Equipment
595 Miner Rd (44143-2131)
PHONE...................................440 247-2652
David A Dripchak, *CEO*
Jerry C Cirino, *Exec VP*
William J Cull Sr, *Vice Pres*
Robert Blankenship, *CFO*
◆ EMP: 500
SQ FT: 495,000
SALES (est): 739.7MM
SALES (corp-wide): 20.9B **Privately Held**
SIC: 3844 5047 5137 3842 X-ray apparatus & tubes; X-ray film & supplies; instruments, surgical & medical; hospital gowns, women's & children's; surgical appliances & supplies; laboratory apparatus & furniture; electrical equipment & supplies
PA: Koninklijke Philips N.V.
High Tech Campus 5
Eindhoven 5656
402 791-111

(G-6204)
PHILLIS WHEATLEY
Also Called: Kohler Day Care
4450 Cedar Ave Ste 1 (44103-4453)
PHONE...................................216 391-4443
Thomas Harrington, *Chairman*
Jacquelyn Bradshaw, *Exec Dir*
EMP: 25
SALES: 377.1K **Privately Held**
SIC: 8322 8299 Neighborhood center; adult day care center; music school

(G-6205)
PHOENIX RESIDENTIAL CENTERS
6465 Pearl Rd Ste 1 (44130-2979)
PHONE...................................440 887-6097
Gary Toth, *Branch Mgr*
EMP: 87
SQ FT: 5,845
SALES (corp-wide): 3.2MM **Privately Held**
WEB: www.phoenixresidential.com
SIC: 6513 Apartment building operators

PA: Phoenix Residential Centers Inc.
1954 Hubbard Rd Ste 1
Madison OH 44057
440 428-9082

(G-6206)
PHOENIX STEEL SERVICE INC
4679 Johnston Pkwy (44128-3221)
PHONE...................................216 332-0600
Stuart Eisner, *President*
EMP: 26
SQ FT: 102,000
SALES (est): 25.5MM **Privately Held**
WEB: www.phoenixsteelservice.com
SIC: 5051 Steel

(G-6207)
PHYCAL INC
51 Alpha Park (44143-2202)
PHONE...................................440 460-2477
J Kevin Berner, *President*
Robert B Polak, *Chairman*
Richard Sayre, *CTO*
EMP: 25
SALES (est): 1.7MM **Privately Held**
WEB: www.directcarbonenergy.com
SIC: 8731 Commercial Physical Research

(G-6208)
PHYLLIS WHEATLEY ASSN DEV
Also Called: Phillis Wheatley Association
4450 Cedar Ave Ste 1 (44103-4453)
PHONE...................................216 391-4443
Fax: 216 391-4543
EMP: 25
SQ FT: 1,504
SALES (est): 301.9K **Privately Held**
SIC: 8051 8399 Skilled Nursing Care Facility Social Services

(G-6209)
PHYSICIAN STAFFING INC
Also Called: Martin Healthcare Group, The
30575 Bnbridge Rd Ste 200 (44139)
PHONE...................................440 542-5000
John S Martin III, *CEO*
Anthony Bernardo, *President*
John S Martin IV, *COO*
Ryan A Carletti, *Opers Staff*
Jennifer Hayes, *CFO*
EMP: 365
SQ FT: 10,000
SALES (est): 23.5MM
SALES (corp-wide): 6.3MM **Privately Held**
WEB: www.physicianstaffing.com
SIC: 7363 Medical help service
PA: Hospitalists Now, Inc.
7500 Rialto Blvd 1-140
Austin TX 78735
512 730-3053

(G-6210)
PHYSICIANS AMBULANCE SVC INC (PA)
Also Called: Physicians Medical Trnspt Team
4495 Cranwood Pkwy (44128-4003)
PHONE...................................216 332-1667
Ron Hess, *President*
Terry Finnerty, *Vice Pres*
Jason Hess, *Vice Pres*
Scott Wildenheim, *Opers Staff*
Jaime Jordan, *Director*
EMP: 42
SALES (est): 8.5MM **Privately Held**
WEB: www.physiciansambulance.com
SIC: 4119 Ambulance & Ambulate Services

(G-6211)
PINATA FOODS INC
Also Called: Festa Food Company
3590 W 58th St (44102-5663)
PHONE...................................216 281-8811
Timothy Fagan, *President*
EMP: 30
SQ FT: 32,000
SALES (est): 14.9MM **Privately Held**
WEB: www.festafood.com
SIC: 5142 Packaged frozen goods

(G-6212)
PINS & NEEDLES INC (PA)
7300 Pearl Rd (44130-4807)
PHONE...................................440 243-6400
Jim Brostek, *President*
Janice M Brostek, *Corp Secy*

Janice Brostek, *Vice Pres*
EMP: 30
SALES (est): 5.9MM **Privately Held**
WEB: www.pinsandneedles.com
SIC: 5722 7219 5949 Sewing machines; garment making, alteration & repair; knitting goods & supplies

(G-6213)
PIONEER CLDDING GLZING SYSTEMS
2550 Brookpark Rd (44134-1407)
PHONE..............................216 816-4242
Michael Robinson, *Branch Mgr*
EMP: 35
SALES (corp-wide): 56.9MM **Privately Held**
SIC: 1793 1741 3448 Glass & glazing work; masonry & other stonework; prefabricated metal components
PA: Pioneer Cladding And Glazing Systems
　　4074 Bethany Rd
　　Mason OH 45040
　　513 583-5925

(G-6214)
PIRHL CONTRACTORS LLC
800 W Saint Clair Ave 4 (44113-1266)
PHONE..............................216 378-9690
David Burg, *Principal*
John Tarnowski, *CFO*
David Uram,
EMP: 28
SALES (est): 4.1MM
SALES (corp-wide): 36.5MM **Privately Held**
SIC: 1521 Single-family housing construction
PA: Pirhl, Llc
　　800 W Saint Clair Ave 4
　　Cleveland OH 44113
　　216 378-9690

(G-6215)
PITT-OHIO EXPRESS LLC
15225 Industrial Pkwy (44135-3307)
PHONE..............................216 433-9000
Mike Todd, *Opers-Prdtn-Mfg*
Cheryl Groff, *Executive*
EMP: 300
SALES (corp-wide): 457MM **Privately Held**
SIC: 4231 4213 4212 Trucking terminal facilities; trucking, except local; local trucking, without storage
PA: Pitt-Ohio Express, Llc
　　15 27th St
　　Pittsburgh PA 15222
　　412 232-3015

(G-6216)
PLANTSCAPING INC
Also Called: Blooms By Plantscaping
1865 E 40th St (44103-3552)
PHONE..............................216 367-1200
Nancy Silverman, *President*
Todd Silverman, *Vice Pres*
EMP: 60
SQ FT: 31,800
SALES (est): 4.2MM **Privately Held**
WEB: www.plantscaping.com
SIC: 5193 Plants, potted

(G-6217)
PLAYHOUSE SQUARE FOUNDATION
Also Called: Crowne Plaza Cleveland
1260 Euclid Ave (44115-1837)
PHONE..............................216 615-7500
Brian Malone, *General Mgr*
Amanda Strieter, *General Mgr*
EMP: 175 **Privately Held**
WEB: www.wyndham.com
SIC: 7011 5812 Hotels; eating places
PA: Playhouse Square Foundation
　　1501 Euclid Ave Ste 200
　　Cleveland OH 44115

(G-6218)
PLAYHOUSE SQUARE FOUNDATION (PA)
1501 Euclid Ave Ste 200 (44115-2108)
PHONE..............................216 771-4444
Art J Falco, *President*
Tom Einhouse, *Vice Pres*

Patricia Gaul, *Vice Pres*
Michelle Stewart, *Vice Pres*
Allen Wiant, *Vice Pres*
EMP: 72
SALES (est): 77.7MM **Privately Held**
SIC: 7922 Entertainment promotion; amateur theatrical company

(G-6219)
PLAYHOUSE SQUARE HOLDG CO LLC (PA)
Also Called: Prop Shop
1501 Euclid Ave Ste 200 (44115-2108)
PHONE..............................216 771-4444
Patti Gaul, *CEO*
Art J Falco, *President*
Rosemary Burless, *President*
Tom Einhouse, *Vice Pres*
Autumn Kiser, *Vice Pres*
EMP: 150
SQ FT: 10,000
SALES: 225.8K **Privately Held**
SIC: 8399 7922 Fund raising organization, non-fee basis; performing arts center production

(G-6220)
PLEASANT LAKE APARTMENTS LTD
10129 S Lake Blvd (44130-7552)
PHONE..............................440 845-2694
Edward Marotta, *Branch Mgr*
EMP: 25
SALES (est): 1MM **Privately Held**
SIC: 6513 Apartment building operators

(G-6221)
PLEASANT LAKE NURSING HOME
Also Called: Pleasant Lake Villa
7260 Ridge Rd (44129-6636)
PHONE..............................440 842-2273
Alex Daskal, *President*
Bruce Daskal, *Corp Secy*
David Farkas, *Vice Pres*
Harold Schachter, *Vice Pres*
Kelly Wright, *Administration*
EMP: 350
SQ FT: 65,000
SALES (est): 15MM **Privately Held**
SIC: 8051 8052 Skilled nursing care facilities; intermediate care facilities

(G-6222)
PORTER WRGHT MORRIS ARTHUR LLP
950 Main Ave Ste 500 (44113-7206)
PHONE..............................216 443-2506
Hugh McKay, *Partner*
James Conroy,
Ezio A Listati,
Shawna Rosner,
David Lewis, *Sr Associate*
EMP: 75
SALES (corp-wide): 83MM **Privately Held**
SIC: 8111 General practice law office
PA: Porter, Wright, Morris & Arthur Llp
　　41 S High St Ste 2900
　　Columbus OH 43215
　　614 227-2000

(G-6223)
POSITIVE EDUCATION PROGRAM
Also Called: Hopewell Day Treatment Center
11500 Franklin Blvd (44102-2335)
PHONE..............................216 227-2730
Stephen Sheppard, *Director*
EMP: 40
SQ FT: 6,764
SALES (corp-wide): 43.6MM **Privately Held**
WEB: www.pepcleve.org
SIC: 8211 8322 Specialty education; self-help organization
PA: Positive Education Program Inc
　　3100 Euclid Ave
　　Cleveland OH 44115
　　216 361-4400

(G-6224)
POSITIVE EDUCATION PROGRAM
Also Called: West Shore Day Treatment Ctr
4320 W 220th St (44126-1818)
PHONE..............................440 471-8200
Ken Seiman,
EMP: 40
SALES (corp-wide): 43.6MM **Privately Held**
WEB: www.pepcleve.org
SIC: 8211 8093 Specialty education; specialty outpatient clinics
PA: Positive Education Program Inc
　　3100 Euclid Ave
　　Cleveland OH 44115
　　216 361-4400

(G-6225)
PRECIOUS ANGELS LRNG CTR INC
Also Called: Precious Angels Child Care I
5574 Pearl Rd (44129-2541)
PHONE..............................440 886-1919
Kristen Little, *Principal*
EMP: 40
SALES (est): 501.6K **Privately Held**
SIC: 8351 Child day care services

(G-6226)
PRECISION WELDING CORPORATION
7900 Exchange St (44125-3334)
P.O. Box 25548 (44125-0548)
PHONE..............................216 524-6110
Dennis Nader, *President*
Randy Nader, *Vice Pres*
EMP: 32
SQ FT: 26,000
SALES (est): 4.5MM **Privately Held**
SIC: 7692 3444 3441 Welding repair; sheet metalwork; fabricated structural metal

(G-6227)
PREDICTIVE SERVICE LLC (PA)
25200 Chagrin Blvd # 300 (44122-5684)
PHONE..............................866 772-6770
Ralph Delisio, *Exec VP*
Rachel Kingsley, *Accounting Mgr*
Roseanne Mawn, *Accounts Mgr*
Michelle Weaver, *Accounts Mgr*
Rachel Bolton, *Accounts Exec*
EMP: 51
SQ FT: 16,000
SALES (est): 20.1MM **Privately Held**
WEB: www.pscorp.com
SIC: 7389 Industrial & commercial equipment inspection service

(G-6228)
PREEMPTIVE SOLUTIONS LLC
767 Beta Dr (44143-2379)
PHONE..............................440 443-7200
Gabriel Torok, *CEO*
Paul Ruflin, *President*
Andy Forsyth, *Vice Pres*
Mark Fagerholm, *CFO*
EMP: 30
SQ FT: 4,000
SALES (est): 3.8MM **Privately Held**
WEB: www.preemptive.com
SIC: 7372 Application computer software

(G-6229)
PREFERRED ACQUISITION CO LLC (PA)
4871 Neo Pkwy (44128-3101)
PHONE..............................216 587-0957
Craig S Hartman, *CEO*
Brian Miller, *Vice Pres*
Susan Tubbs, *CFO*
Deborah Abbott, *Controller*
Justin Valenta, *Mng Member*
EMP: 60
SQ FT: 14,000
SALES (est): 9.2MM **Privately Held**
SIC: 1752 1721 Floor laying & floor work; commercial painting

(G-6230)
PREFERRED CAPITAL LENDING INC
200 Public Sq Ste 160 (44114-2398)
PHONE..............................216 472-1391
Brian T Garelli, *Branch Mgr*
EMP: 26
SALES (corp-wide): 8MM **Privately Held**
SIC: 6153 Working capital financing
PA: Preferred Capital Lending, Inc.
　　368 W Huron St Ste 200n
　　Chicago IL 60654
　　312 212-5000

(G-6231)
PREFERRED ROOFING OHIO INC
4871 Neo Pkwy (44128-3101)
PHONE..............................216 587-0957
Thomas M Miller, *President*
Craig Sibbio, *Vice Pres*
Daniel Engle, *VP Opers*
Heidi Berg, *Office Mgr*
Deborah Abbott, *Admin Sec*
EMP: 35
SALES (est): 3.4MM **Privately Held**
WEB: www.roofinghelp.com
SIC: 1761 Roofing contractor

(G-6232)
PREFERRED ROOFING SERVICES LLC
4871 Neo Pkwy (44128-3101)
PHONE..............................216 587-0957
Craig Hartman, *Mng Member*
Stacey Romano, *Administration*
Brian Miller,
EMP: 35
SQ FT: 10,000
SALES (est): 1.9MM **Privately Held**
WEB: www.preferredcleveland.com
SIC: 1761 Roofing contractor

(G-6233)
PREMIER TRUCK PARTS INC
5800 W Canal Rd (44125-3341)
PHONE..............................216 642-5000
Claude Humberson, *President*
Joey Lojek, *Corp Secy*
Brent Humberson, *Vice Pres*
EMP: 40
SQ FT: 17,000
SALES (est): 7.6MM **Privately Held**
SIC: 5531 5013 7513 Truck equipment & parts; truck parts & accessories; truck rental, without drivers

(G-6234)
PREMIER TRUCK SLS & RENTL INC
7700 Wall St (44125-3324)
PHONE..............................800 825-1255
Joey Lojek, *President*
Claude Humberson, *Corp Secy*
Brent Humberson, *Vice Pres*
▼ **EMP:** 35
SQ FT: 17,000
SALES (est): 7MM **Privately Held**
WEB: www.premiertrucksales.com
SIC: 5521 7513 Trucks, tractors & trailers: used; truck rental & leasing, no drivers

(G-6235)
PRICEWATERHOUSECOOPERS LLP
200 Public Sq Fl 18 (44114-2310)
PHONE..............................216 875-3000
James E Wilcosky, *Partner*
Richard P Stovsky, *Manager*
Kazi Islam, *Manager*
T Kane, *Manager*
Paul Ramos, *Manager*
EMP: 300
SALES (corp-wide): 7.8B **Privately Held**
WEB: www.pwcglobal.com
SIC: 8721 Certified public accountant
PA: Pricewaterhousecoopers Llp
　　300 Madison Ave Fl 24
　　New York NY 10017
　　646 471-4000

(G-6236)
PRIME TIME ENTERPRISES INC
Also Called: Prime Time Delivery & Whse
6410 Eastland Rd Ste A (44142-1306)
P.O. Box 811144 (44181-1144)
PHONE.....................................440 891-8855
Dave Reichbaum, *President*
Lisa Levis, *President*
EMP: 35
SQ FT: 20,000
SALES (est): 5.1MM **Privately Held**
SIC: 4215 4225 4513 Courier services,
except by air; general warehousing &
storage; air courier services

(G-6237)
PRIVATE PRACTICE NURSES INC
403 Cary Jay Blvd (44143-1727)
PHONE.....................................216 481-1305
Lisa Ashcroft, *President*
Susan Ashcroft, *Corp Secy*
EMP: 35
SALES (est): 1.5MM **Privately Held**
WEB: www.privatepracticenurses.com
SIC: 7361 Nurses' registry

(G-6238)
PRO ED COMMUNICATIONS INC
25101 Chagrin Blvd # 230 (44122-5688)
PHONE.....................................216 595-7919
Marta Brookes, *President*
Mary Rofael, *Exec VP*
Greg Connel, *Vice Pres*
Jeff Riegel, *Vice Pres*
Allen McCrodden, *Supervisor*
EMP: 35
SQ FT: 4,000
SALES (est): 4.1MM **Privately Held**
WEB: www.proedcom.com
SIC: 8748 Communications consulting

(G-6239)
PROFESSIONAL SERVICE INDS INC
Also Called: PSI Testing and Engineering
5555 Canal Rd (44125-4874)
PHONE.....................................216 447-1335
Chris Lopez, *Branch Mgr*
Wessam Mekhael, *Department Mgr*
Paul Bowyer, *Manager*
Jeanette Dezelan, *Receptionist*
EMP: 70
SALES (corp-wide): 3.6B **Privately Held**
SIC: 8711 Consulting engineer
HQ: Professional Service Industries, Inc.
545 E Algonquin Rd
Arlington Heights IL 60005
630 691-1490

(G-6240)
PROFIT RECOVERY OF OHIO
Also Called: Basista & Associates
16510 Webster Rd (44130-5464)
PHONE.....................................440 243-1743
Amil E Basista, *Owner*
EMP: 115
SALES: 1.9MM **Privately Held**
SIC: 4813

(G-6241)
PROGRESIVE SPCLTY INS AGCY INC
Also Called: Progressive Insurance
6300 Wilson Mills Rd (44143-2109)
PHONE.....................................440 461-5000
EMP: 101
SALES (est): 1.7MM
SALES (corp-wide): 31.9B **Publicly Held**
SIC: 6411 Insurance agents & brokers
HQ: Progressive Direct Holdings, Inc.
6300 Wilson Mills Rd
Cleveland OH 44143

(G-6242)
PROGRESSIVE ADVANCED INSUR CO
Also Called: PROGRESSIVE INSURANCE
6300 Wilson Mills Rd (44143-2109)
PHONE.....................................440 461-5000
EMP: 133
SALES: 440.3MM
SALES (corp-wide): 31.9B **Publicly Held**
SIC: 6331 Fire, marine & casualty insur-
ance

HQ: Progressive Direct Holdings, Inc.
6300 Wilson Mills Rd
Cleveland OH 44143

(G-6243)
PROGRESSIVE CASUALTY INSUR CO
Also Called: Progressive Insurance
651 Beta Dr 150 (44143-2318)
PHONE.....................................440 683-8164
Jim Kaiser, *Manager*
EMP: 30
SQ FT: 77,059
SALES (corp-wide): 31.9B **Publicly Held**
WEB: www.progressinsurance.com
SIC: 6331 6411 Fire, marine & casualty in-
surance; insurance agents & brokers
HQ: Progressive Casualty Insurance Com-
pany
6300 Wilson Mills Rd .
Mayfield Village OH 44143
440 461-5000

(G-6244)
PROGRESSIVE CASUALTY INSUR CO
Progressive Insurance
747 Alpha Dr Ste A21 (44143-2124)
PHONE.....................................440 603-4033
Bob Flerchinger, *Manager*
Sirish Anne, *Manager*
Neil Miklovic, *Manager*
EMP: 100
SALES (corp-wide): 31.9B **Publicly Held**
WEB: www.progressinsurance.com
SIC: 6331 6321 Automobile insurance; ac-
cident insurance carriers
HQ: Progressive Casualty Insurance Com-
pany
6300 Wilson Mills Rd
Mayfield Village OH 44143
440 461-5000

(G-6245)
PROGRESSIVE CHOICE INSUR CO
Also Called: PROGRESSIVE INSURANCE
6300 Wilson Mills Rd (44143-2109)
PHONE.....................................440 461-5000
Steven A Broz, *President*
EMP: 355
SALES (est): 123MM
SALES (corp-wide): 31.9B **Publicly Held**
SIC: 6331 Fire, marine & casualty insur-
ance
HQ: Progressive Direct Holdings, Inc.
6300 Wilson Mills Rd
Cleveland OH 44143

(G-6246)
PROGRESSIVE CORPORATION
Also Called: Progressive Insurance
600 Mills Rd (44101)
P.O. Box 6807 (44101-1807)
PHONE.....................................800 925-2886
John Raguz, *Payroll Mgr*
EMP: 517
SALES (corp-wide): 31.9B **Publicly Held**
SIC: 6411 Insurance agents & brokers
PA: The Progressive Corporation
6300 Wilson Mills Rd
Mayfield Village OH 44143
440 461-5000

(G-6247)
PROGRESSIVE CORPORATION
Also Called: Progressive Insurance
300 N Commons Blvd (44143-1589)
PHONE.....................................440 461-5000
Diane Zuercher, *Project Mgr*
Laura Land, *QC Mgr*
Carolyn Bowman, *Engineer*
Pat Bemer, *Human Res Dir*
Lori Skiljan, *Human Resources*
EMP: 301
SALES (corp-wide): 31.9B **Publicly Held**
SIC: 6351 6331 Credit & other financial re-
sponsibility insurance; property damage
insurance
PA: The Progressive Corporation
6300 Wilson Mills Rd
Mayfield Village OH 44143
440 461-5000

(G-6248)
PROGRESSIVE EXPRESS INSUR CO
Also Called: PROGRESSIVE INSURANCE
6300 Wilson Mills Rd (44143-2109)
PHONE.....................................440 461-5000
Susan Patricia Griffith, *CEO*
S Patricia Griffith, *President*
EMP: 586
SALES: 55MM
SALES (corp-wide): 31.9B **Publicly Held**
SIC: 6331 Automobile insurance
HQ: Progressive Commercial Holdings, Inc.
6300 Wilson Mills Rd
Cleveland OH 44143

(G-6249)
PROGRESSIVE FREEDOM INSUR CO
Also Called: PROGRESSIVE INSURANCE
6300 Wilson Mills Rd (44143-2109)
PHONE.....................................440 461-5000
S Patricia Griffith, *CEO*
EMP: 133
SALES (est): 12.5MM
SALES (corp-wide): 31.9B **Publicly Held**
SIC: 6331 Fire, marine & casualty insur-
ance
HQ: Progressive Direct Holdings, Inc.
6300 Wilson Mills Rd
Cleveland OH 44143

(G-6250)
PROGRESSIVE GRDN STATE INSUR
Also Called: PROGRESSIVE INSURANCE
6300 Wilson Mills Rd (44143-2109)
PHONE.....................................440 461-5000
EMP: 178 **EST:** 2005
SALES: 67.8MM
SALES (corp-wide): 31.9B **Publicly Held**
SIC: 6331 Automobile insurance
HQ: Progressive Direct Holdings, Inc.
6300 Wilson Mills Rd
Cleveland OH 44143

(G-6251)
PROGRESSIVE NORTHWESTERN INSUR
Also Called: PROGRESSIVE INSURANCE
6300 Wilson Mills Rd (44143-2109)
PHONE.....................................440 461-5000
S Patricia Griffith, *President*
Stephen Peterson, *Treasurer*
Dane Shrallow, *Admin Sec*
Margaret Burke, *Legal Staff*
EMP: 25
SQ FT: 3,500
SALES: 1.8B
SALES (corp-wide): 31.9B **Publicly Held**
SIC: 6331 Fire, marine & casualty insur-
ance
HQ: Drive Insurance Holdings, Inc.
6300 Wilson Mills Rd
Cleveland OH 44143

(G-6252)
PROGRESSIVE PALOVERDE INSUR CO
Also Called: Progressive Insurance
6300 Wilson Mills Rd (44143-2109)
PHONE.....................................440 461-5000
EMP: 151
SALES: 34.3MM
SALES (corp-wide): 31.9B **Publicly Held**
SIC: 6331 Fire, marine & casualty insur-
ance
HQ: Progressive Direct Holdings, Inc.
6300 Wilson Mills Rd
Cleveland OH 44143

(G-6253)
PROGRESSIVE PARK LLC
Also Called: University Park Nursing Home
5553 Broadview Rd (44134-1604)
PHONE.....................................330 434-4514
Jennifer Conley,
EMP: 110
SALES (est): 5.2MM **Privately Held**
WEB: www.universityparknursing.com
SIC: 8051 Skilled Nursing Care Facility

(G-6254)
PROGRESSIVE PREMIER INSURANCE
Also Called: PROGRESSIVE INSURANCE
6300 Wilson Mills Rd W33 (44143-2109)
PHONE.....................................440 461-5000
S Patricia Griffith, *CEO*
EMP: 178
SALES: 220.1MM
SALES (corp-wide): 31.9B **Publicly Held**
SIC: 6411 Insurance agents & brokers
HQ: Progressive Direct Holdings, Inc.
6300 Wilson Mills Rd
Cleveland OH 44143

(G-6255)
PROGRESSIVE RSC INC
Also Called: Progressive Insurance
6300 Wilson Mills Rd (44143-2109)
PHONE.....................................440 461-5000
S Patricia Griffith, *CEO*
EMP: 129
SALES (est): 9.2MM
SALES (corp-wide): 31.9B **Publicly Held**
SIC: 6331 Fire, marine & casualty insur-
ance
PA: The Progressive Corporation
6300 Wilson Mills Rd
Mayfield Village OH 44143
440 461-5000

(G-6256)
PROGRESSIVE SELECT INSUR CO
Also Called: PROGRESSIVE INSURANCE
6300 Wilson Mills Rd (44143-2109)
PHONE.....................................440 461-5000
James R Haas, *Principal*
EMP: 311
SALES: 220.9MM
SALES (corp-wide): 31.9B **Publicly Held**
SIC: 6331 Automobile insurance
HQ: Progressive Direct Holdings, Inc.
6300 Wilson Mills Rd
Cleveland OH 44143

(G-6257)
PROGRESSIVE UNIVERSAL INSUR CO
Also Called: Progressive Insurance
6300 Wilson Mills Rd (44143-2109)
PHONE.....................................440 461-5000
S Patricia Griffith, *CEO*
Susan Patricia Griffith, *CEO*
Bob Hein, *Finance Mgr*
David Schneider, *Admin Sec*
EMP: 196
SALES (est): 181.3K
SALES (corp-wide): 31.9B **Publicly Held**
SIC: 6331 Fire, marine & casualty insur-
ance
HQ: Progressive Direct Holdings, Inc.
6300 Wilson Mills Rd
Cleveland OH 44143

(G-6258)
PROGRESSIVE VEHICLE SERVICE CO
Also Called: Progressive Insurance
6300 Wilson Mills Rd (44143-2109)
PHONE.....................................440 461-5000
S Patricia Griffith, *CEO*
EMP: 129
SALES (est): 9.2MM
SALES (corp-wide): 31.9B **Publicly Held**
SIC: 6331 Automobile insurance
PA: The Progressive Corporation
6300 Wilson Mills Rd
Mayfield Village OH 44143
440 461-5000

(G-6259)
PROGRESSIVE WEST INSURANCE CO
Also Called: PROGRESSIVE INSURANCE
6300 Wilson Mills Rd (44143-2109)
PHONE.....................................440 446-5100
Kanik Varma, *CEO*
Mark Niehaus, *President*
Jan Dolohanty, *Assistant VP*
Jan Kusner, *Asst Treas*
Kathleen Scerny, *Asst Sec*
EMP: 400
SQ FT: 750

SALES: 32.7MM
SALES (corp-wide): 31.9B **Publicly Held**
SIC: 6331 Automobile insurance
HQ: Drive Insurance Holdings, Inc.
6300 Wilson Mills Rd
Cleveland OH 44143

(G-6260)
PROJECT PACKAGING INC
Also Called: P P I
17877 Saint Clair Ave # 6 (44110-2636)
PHONE..................................216 451-7878
Ken Franklin, *President*
EMP: 50
SQ FT: 132,000
SALES (est): 3MM **Privately Held**
SIC: 7389 Packaging & labeling services

(G-6261)
PROTEM HOMECARE LLC
3535 Lee Rd (44120-5122)
PHONE..................................216 663-8188
Ada Nworie,
EMP: 27
SALES (est): 2.5MM **Privately Held**
SIC: 8082 Home health care services

(G-6262)
PROTIVITI INC
1001 Lakeside Ave E (44114-1158)
PHONE..................................216 696-6010
Shannon Scopano, *Branch Mgr*
EMP: 48
SALES (corp-wide): 5.8B **Publicly Held**
SIC: 8721 8742 Auditing services; industry
specialist consultants
HQ: Protiviti Inc.
2884 Sand Hill Rd Ste 200
Menlo Park CA 94025
650 234-6000

(G-6263)
PROVIDENCE HOUSE INC
Also Called: CRISIS NURSERY
2050 W 32nd St (44113-4018)
PHONE..................................216 651-5982
Natalie Leek-Nelson, *President*
Stacy Schiemann, *Prgrmr*
EMP: 37
SQ FT: 5,000
SALES (est): 2.4MM **Privately Held**
SIC: 8322 8361 Child related social serv-
ices; residential care

(G-6264)
**PRUDENTIAL INSUR CO OF
AMER**
5875 Landerbrook Dr # 110 (44124-4069)
PHONE..................................440 684-4409
Mark Pietsch, *Manager*
EMP: 40
SALES (corp-wide): 62.9B **Publicly Held**
SIC: 6411 Insurance agents, brokers &
service
HQ: The Prudential Insurance Company Of
America
751 Broad St
Newark NJ 07102
973 802-6000

(G-6265)
PS LIFESTYLE LLC
Also Called: Salon PS
55 Public Sq Ste 1180 (44113-1901)
PHONE..................................440 600-1595
John J Polatz, *CEO*
Theresa Doolittle, *District Mgr*
Alisha Gilliam, *District Mgr*
Shelley Kondas, *Exec VP*
Brett McMillan, *Exec VP*
EMP: 800
SQ FT: 4,000
SALES: 12MM **Privately Held**
SIC: 7231 Unisex hair salons; hairdressers

(G-6266)
PSC METALS INC
4250 E 68th Berdelle (44105)
PHONE..................................216 341-3400
Dustin Busser, *Branch Mgr*
EMP: 42
SQ FT: 3,384
SALES (corp-wide): 11.7B **Publicly Held**
WEB: www.pscmetals.com
SIC: 5093 Metal scrap & waste materials

HQ: Psc Metals, Llc
5875 Landerbrook Dr # 200
Mayfield Heights OH 44124
440 753-5400

(G-6267)
PTC HOLDINGS INC
1422 Euclid Ave Ste 1130 (44115-2065)
PHONE..................................216 771-6960
Rocco Guarnaccia, *CEO*
Joe Maceda, *President*
EMP: 285
SALES (est): 234.6K **Publicly Held**
SIC: 6099 Clearinghouse associations,
bank or check
PA: Lpl Financial Holdings Inc.
75 State St Ste 2401
Boston MA 02109

(G-6268)
PUBCO CORPORATION (PA)
3830 Kelley Ave (44114-4534)
PHONE..................................216 881-5300
William Dillingham, *President*
Stephen R Kalette, *Vice Pres*
Robert Turnbull, *Vice Pres*
Maria Szubski, *CFO*
◆ **EMP:** 85
SQ FT: 312,000
SALES (est): 94.9MM **Privately Held**
SIC: 3531 6512 3955 Construction ma-
chinery; nonresidential building operators;
carbon paper & inked ribbons

(G-6269)
**QUALITY CONTROL
INSPECTION (PA)**
40 Tarbell Ave (44146-3615)
PHONE..................................440 359-1900
Rick Capone, *President*
Chris Liotta, *Technology*
Harold Miller, *Data Proc Staff*
Ron Baker, *Administration*
EMP: 60
SALES (est): 11MM **Privately Held**
WEB: www.qcigroup.com
SIC: 7389 8741 Building inspection serv-
ice; construction management

(G-6270)
QUICKEN LOANS INC
100 Public Sq Ste 400 (44113-2207)
PHONE..................................216 586-8900
Christopher Mahnen, *President*
EMP: 33
SALES (corp-wide): 1.6B **Privately Held**
SIC: 6162 Mortgage bankers
HQ: Quicken Loans Inc.
1050 Woodward Ave
Detroit MI 48226
800 251-9080

(G-6271)
**R AND G ENTERPRISES OF
OHIO**
9213 Harrow Dr (44129-1734)
PHONE..................................440 845-6870
Rita Assour, *President*
EMP: 30
SALES (est): 1.6MM **Privately Held**
SIC: 5092 Toys & games

(G-6272)
**R B C APOLLO EQUITY
PARTNERS (DH)**
600 Superior Ave E # 2300 (44114-2612)
PHONE..................................216 875-2626
Kathy Beuck, *Asst Controller*
Thomas Rini,
Lawrence Brattain,
Jack Griffith,
Bryant Wensinger,
EMP: 36
SQ FT: 5,000
SALES (est): 6.5MM
SALES (corp-wide): 21.4B **Privately Held**
WEB: www.apollohousing.com
SIC: 6211 Investment bankers
HQ: Rbc Capital Markets Corporation
60 S 6th St Ste 700
Minneapolis MN 55402
612 371-2711

(G-6273)
R D D INC (PA)
Also Called: Power Direct
4719 Blythin Rd (44125-1209)
PHONE..................................216 781-5858
Daniel Delfino, *President*
Mindy Delfino, *Vice Pres*
EMP: 120
SQ FT: 15,000
SALES (est): 16.4MM **Privately Held**
WEB: www.power-direct.com
SIC: 7389 8742 Telemarketing services;
marketing consulting services

(G-6274)
R SQUARE INC
6100 Oak Tree Blvd # 200 (44131-2544)
PHONE..................................216 328-2077
Ravi Velu, *President*
EMP: 25
SQ FT: 1,500
SALES (est): 832.8K **Privately Held**
SIC: 7379 Computer related consulting
services

(G-6275)
R-CAP SECURITY LLC
7800 Superior Ave (44103-2858)
P.O. Box 10167 (44110-0167)
PHONE..................................216 761-6355
Charlotte Perkins,
EMP: 120
SALES: 3.8MM **Privately Held**
SIC: 7381 Security guard service

(G-6276)
RA STAFF COMPANY INC
Also Called: Staffco-Campisano
16500 W Sprague Rd (44130-6315)
PHONE..................................440 891-9900
Larry McHale, *President*
Heather Kantor, *Office Mgr*
Frank Campisano, *Manager*
Marianne Laine, *Manager*
EMP: 25
SQ FT: 10,000
SALES (est): 3MM **Privately Held**
WEB: www.rastaffco.com
SIC: 8743 Sales promotion

(G-6277)
RADIO SEAWAY INC
Also Called: Radio Station Wclv
1375 Euclid Ave Ste 450 (44115-1839)
PHONE..................................216 916-6100
Robert D Conrad, *President*
Rich Marschner, *General Mgr*
Annie Bartlett, *Vice Pres*
Wiley Cornell, *Vice Pres*
Bill Oconnell, *Vice Pres*
EMP: 36 **EST:** 1962
SALES: 3MM **Privately Held**
WEB: www.wclv.com
SIC: 4832 7929 Radio broadcasting sta-
tions; entertainers & entertainment groups

(G-6278)
**RADISSON HOTEL CLEVELAND
GTWY**
Also Called: Radisson Inn
651 Huron Rd E (44115-1116)
PHONE..................................216 377-9000
Donna White, *Director*
EMP: 70
SALES (est): 2.1MM **Privately Held**
WEB: www.uctonline.org
SIC: 7011 Hotels & motels

(G-6279)
RADIX WIRE CO (PA)
Also Called: Radix Wire Company, The
26000 Lakeland Blvd (44132-2638)
PHONE..................................216 731-9191
Keith D Nootbaar, *President*
Jim Schaefer, *President*
Marylou Vermerris, *Chairman*
Brain Bukovec, *Vice Pres*
EMP: 60 **EST:** 1944
SQ FT: 14,000
SALES (est): 21.5MM **Privately Held**
WEB: www.radix-wire.com
SIC: 3357 5051 Nonferrous wiredrawing &
insulating; cable, wire

(G-6280)
RAE-ANN ENTERPRISES INC
Also Called: Rae-Ann Suburban
27310 W Oviatt Rd (44140-2139)
P.O. Box 40175 (44140-0175)
PHONE..................................440 249-5092
Ray Griffiths, *Vice Pres*
EMP: 55
SALES (est): 3.3MM **Privately Held**
SIC: 8059 Convalescent home

(G-6281)
RAE-ANN HOLDINGS INC
Also Called: Rae-Suburban
29505 Detroit Rd (44145-1932)
PHONE..................................440 871-5181
John Brutvan, *Purch Dir*
John Griffith, *Manager*
Chris Meinke, *Administration*
EMP: 99
SALES (corp-wide): 36.6MM **Privately
Held**
SIC: 8059 8051 Nursing home, except
skilled & intermediate care facility; skilled
nursing care facilities
PA: Rae-Ann Holdings, Inc.
27310 W Oviatt Rd
Bay Village OH 44140
440 835-3004

(G-6282)
RAEANN INC (PA)
Also Called: Rae-Ann Center
P.O. Box 40175, Bay Village (44140-0175)
PHONE..................................440 871-5181
John Griffiths, *President*
Ray Griffiths, *President*
Mary Ann Griffiths, *Vice Pres*
Susan Griffiths, *Vice Pres*
Lee Mokry, *Controller*
EMP: 25
SQ FT: 2,000
SALES (est): 6.2MM **Privately Held**
SIC: 8051 Skilled nursing care facilities

(G-6283)
RAHIM INC
Also Called: R N R Consulting
1111 Superior Ave E # 1330 (44114-2522)
PHONE..................................216 621-8977
Abhijit Verekar, *CEO*
EMP: 29
SALES (est): 2.7MM **Privately Held**
WEB: www.rnrconsulting.com
SIC: 8742 Management consulting serv-
ices

(G-6284)
**RAKESH RANJAN MD & ASSOC
INC (PA)**
Also Called: Charak Ctr For Hlth & Wellness
12395 Mccracken Rd Ste A (44125-2946)
PHONE..................................216 375-9897
Ranjan Rakesh, *President*
EMP: 25
SQ FT: 20,000
SALES (est): 19.1MM **Privately Held**
SIC: 8011 Psychiatrist

(G-6285)
**RAMOS TRUCKING
CORPORATION**
2890 W 3rd St (44113-2516)
PHONE..................................216 781-0770
Don Bugen, *President*
EMP: 25
SQ FT: 1,500
SALES (est): 1MM **Privately Held**
SIC: 4212 Local trucking, without storage

(G-6286)
RATHBONE GROUP LLC
1100 Superior Ave E # 1850 (44114-2544)
PHONE..................................800 870-5521
Joel Rathbone, *CEO*
Jason Sullivan,
Jennie Smith-Howard, *Sr Associate*
EMP: 63
SALES (est): 4.6MM **Privately Held**
SIC: 8111 General practice law office

(G-6287)
RAY FOGG BUILDING METHODS INC
981 Keynote Cir Ste 15 (44131-1842)
PHONE....................216 351-7976
Raymon B Fogg Jr, *President*
Michael Merle, *President*
Richard Neiden, *Vice Pres*
Virginia Fogg, *Admin Sec*
EMP: 25 EST: 1959
SQ FT: 5,700
SALES (est): 11.5MM **Privately Held**
SIC: **1541** 1542 Industrial buildings, new construction; commercial & office building, new construction

(G-6288)
RDL ARCHITECTS INC
16102 Chagrin Blvd # 200 (44120-3708)
PHONE....................216 752-4300
Ronald Lloyd, *President*
Harold Dempsey, *Project Mgr*
Bob Reighard, *Design Engr*
Haley Lloyd, *Director*
Mark Poltorek, *Director*
EMP: 38
SALES (est): 2.6MM **Privately Held**
SIC: **8712** 7389 Architectural services; interior design services

(G-6289)
REAL AMERICA INC
24555 Lake Shore Blvd (44123-1226)
PHONE....................216 261-1177
Edward Gudenas, *President*
EMP: 301
SALES (est): 17.8MM **Privately Held**
SIC: **5039** 7033 Prefabricated buildings; campgrounds

(G-6290)
REAL ESTATE CAPITAL FUND LLC
Also Called: Taragon Advisors
20820 Chagrin Blvd # 300 (44122-5323)
PHONE....................216 491-3990
Terence Sullivan,
EMP: 25
SALES (est): 1.4MM **Privately Held**
SIC: **6531** 8742 Real estate brokers & agents; financial consultant

(G-6291)
REBIZ LLC
1925 Saint Clair Ave Ne (44114-2028)
PHONE....................844 467-3249
Jumaid Hasan, *Mng Member*
EMP: 50 EST: 2014
SALES (est): 55.4K **Privately Held**
SIC: **7372** 7374 Business oriented computer software; optical scanning data service

(G-6292)
RECOVERY RESOURCES (PA)
3950 Chester Ave (44114-4625)
PHONE....................216 431-4131
Debora Rodriguez, *President*
Charlotte Rerko, *COO*
William Morgan, *CFO*
Ayme McCain, *Manager*
Jason Joyce, *Director*
EMP: 48
SQ FT: 6,800
SALES: 13.8MM **Privately Held**
SIC: **8093** Mental health clinic, outpatient

(G-6293)
RECOVERY RESOURCES
4269 Pearl Rd Ste 300 (44109-4232)
PHONE....................216 431-4131
Gordon Hewitt, *Branch Mgr*
EMP: 65
SALES (corp-wide): 12.5MM **Privately Held**
SIC: **8093** Substance abuse clinics (outpatient)
PA: Recovery Resources
    3950 Chester Ave
    Cleveland OH 44114
    216 431-4131

(G-6294)
RED ROOF INNS INC
29595 Clemens Rd (44145-1056)
PHONE....................440 892-7920
EMP: 28 **Privately Held**
WEB: www.redroof.com
SIC: **7011** Hotels & motels
HQ: Red Roof Inns, Inc.
    7815 Walton Pkwy
    New Albany OH 43054
    614 744-2600

(G-6295)
RED ROOF INNS INC
17555 Bagley Rd (44130-2551)
PHONE....................440 243-5166
EMP: 26 **Privately Held**
WEB: www.redroof.com
SIC: **7011** Hotels & motels
HQ: Red Roof Inns, Inc.
    7815 Walton Pkwy
    New Albany OH 43054
    614 744-2600

(G-6296)
REGAL CARPET CENTER INC
Also Called: Regal Carpet Co
5411 Northfield Rd (44146-1187)
PHONE....................216 475-1844
Marvin Kinstlinger, *President*
Les Kinsley, *Treasurer*
Howard Kinstlinger, *Admin Sec*
EMP: 29
SQ FT: 15,000
SALES (est): 6.3MM **Privately Held**
SIC: **5713** 5023 1752 Carpets; carpets; floor laying & floor work

(G-6297)
REGAL CINEMAS INC
18348 Bagley Rd (44130-3411)
PHONE....................440 891-9845
John Deluca, *Manager*
EMP: 35 **Privately Held**
WEB: www.regalcinemas.com
SIC: **7832** Movie Theater
HQ: Regal Cinemas, Inc.
    101 E Blount Ave Ste 100
    Knoxville TN 37920
    865 922-1123

(G-6298)
REID ASSET MANAGEMENT COMPANY
Also Called: Predict Technologies Div
9555 Rockside Rd Ste 350 (44125-6283)
PHONE....................216 642-3223
Donald F Kautzman, *Principal*
EMP: 40
SALES (est): 1.6MM
SALES (corp-wide): 9.9MM **Privately Held**
WEB: www.magnusequipment.com
SIC: **7389** 8734 3826 5084 Industrial & commercial equipment inspection service; testing laboratories; analytical instruments; industrial machinery & equipment
PA: Reid Asset Management Company
    9555 Rockside Rd Ste 350
    Cleveland OH 44125
    216 642-3223

(G-6299)
REILLY SWEEPING INC
120350 Hannan Pkwy (44146)
PHONE....................440 786-8400
Patrick Reilly, *President*
Michael Reilly, *Vice Pres*
Sean Reilly, *Admin Sec*
EMP: 30
SALES (est): 5.3MM
SALES (corp-wide): 172.4MM **Privately Held**
SIC: **4959** Sweeping service: road, airport, parking lot, etc.
PA: Sweep America Intermediate Holdings, Llc
    4141 Rockside Rd Ste 210
    Seven Hills OH 44131
    216 777-2750

(G-6300)
RELENTLESS RECOVERY INC
1898 Scranton Rd Uppr (44113-2434)
PHONE....................216 621-8333
David Ziebro, *President*

Amy Osterling, *Vice Pres*
Danielle Crump, *Admin Asst*
EMP: 60
SALES (est): 20.2MM **Privately Held**
SIC: **6153** Credit card services, central agency collection

(G-6301)
RELIABILITY FIRST CORPORATION
3 Summit Park Dr Ste 600 (44131-6900)
PHONE....................216 503-0600
Timothy R Gallagher, *President*
Raymond J Palmieri, *Vice Pres*
Jack Ispvan, *Treasurer*
Larry Bugh, *Admin Sec*
EMP: 30
SALES: 19.2MM **Privately Held**
WEB: www.rfirst.org
SIC: **4911** Transmission, electric power

(G-6302)
RELMEC MECHANICAL LLC
4975 Hamilton Ave (44114-3906)
PHONE....................216 391-1030
Sharon Lunato, *CEO*
Layne Kendig, *President*
Jerry Mikus, *Vice Pres*
J Patrick O'Brien, *Vice Pres*
Matt Dean, *Project Mgr*
EMP: 180
SALES (est): 27.7MM **Privately Held**
SIC: **1711** Mechanical contractor

(G-6303)
REMELT SOURCES INCORPORATED (PA)
27151 Tungsten Rd (44132-2940)
PHONE....................216 289-4555
David Drage, *CEO*
Brendan Drage, *President*
George Knapp, *Exec VP*
Steve Sikkenga, *Vice Pres*
Steve Sprowls, *Plant Mgr*
◆ EMP: 45
SQ FT: 30,000
SALES (est): 40.5MM **Privately Held**
WEB: www.remeltsources.com
SIC: **5051** Steel

(G-6304)
REMINGER CO LPA (PA)
101 W Prospect Ave # 1400 (44115-1074)
PHONE....................216 687-1311
Stephen Walters, *President*
William Meadows, *Vice Pres*
Donald Moracz, *Vice Pres*
Nick Satullo, *Treasurer*
Heather Kelling, *Admin Sec*
EMP: 175 EST: 1958
SQ FT: 64,000
SALES (est): 52.2MM **Privately Held**
WEB: www.reminger.com
SIC: **8111** Specialized law offices, attorneys

(G-6305)
RENAISSANCE HOTEL OPERATING CO
24 Public Sq Fl 1 (44113-2222)
PHONE....................216 696-5600
Jerry McGauley, *Branch Mgr*
EMP: 650
SALES (corp-wide): 20.7B **Publicly Held**
WEB: www.renaissancehotel.com
SIC: **7011** 7389 Hotels; office facilities & secretarial service rental
HQ: Renaissance Hotel Operating Company, Inc
    10400 Fernwood Rd
    Bethesda MD 20817
    301 380-3000

(G-6306)
RENNER OTTO BOISELLE & SKLAR
1621 Euclid Ave Ste 1900 (44115-2191)
PHONE....................216 621-1113
Armand Boiselle, *Senior Partner*
John Renner, *Senior Partner*
Warren Sklar, *Senior Partner*
Donald Otto, *Partner*
Paul Steffes, *Engineer*
EMP: 35 EST: 1900

SALES (est): 3.8MM **Privately Held**
WEB: www.rennerotto.com
SIC: **8111** General practice law office

(G-6307)
RENOVO NEURAL INC
10000 Cedar Ave (44106-2119)
PHONE....................216 445-4202
Satish Medicetty, *President*
Caroline Lego, *Research*
Chris Ryan, *Exec Dir*
Bruce Trapp, *Officer*
EMP: 29
SQ FT: 4,000
SALES: 3MM **Privately Held**
SIC: **8731** Biotechnical research, commercial
PA: Renovo Biosciences Inc
    10000 Cedar Ave
    Cleveland OH 44106
    216 445-4252

(G-6308)
RENTAL CONCEPTS INC (PA)
Also Called: Fleet Response
6450 Rockside Woods Blvd (44131-2237)
PHONE....................216 525-3870
Ronald E Mawaka, *CEO*
Myron S Zadony, *President*
R Michael O'Neal, *Principal*
Scott Mawaka, *Chairman*
Claude E Nolty, *Admin Sec*
EMP: 50
SQ FT: 11,000
SALES (est): 10.5MM **Privately Held**
WEB: www.fleetresponse.com
SIC: **7514** Rent-a-car service

(G-6309)
REPRO ACQUISITION COMPANY LLC
Also Called: Reprocenter, The
25001 Rockwell Dr (44117-1239)
PHONE....................216 738-3800
Ronald Smith, *Sales Executive*
▲ EMP: 40
SQ FT: 32,000
SALES (est): 4.7MM **Privately Held**
WEB: www.reprocntr.com
SIC: **2752** 7375 2789 Commercial printing, offset; information retrieval services; bookbinding & related work

(G-6310)
REPUBLIC SERVICES INC
8123 Jones Rd (44105-2046)
PHONE....................216 741-4013
EMP: 34
SALES (corp-wide): 8.7B **Publicly Held**
SIC: **4953** Refuse System
PA: Republic Services, Inc.
    18500 N Allied Way # 100
    Phoenix AZ 85054
    480 627-2700

(G-6311)
REPUBLIC SERVICES INC
8123 Jones Rd (44105-2046)
PHONE....................216 741-4013
Allen Marino, *Manager*
Matthew Mucha, *Manager*
EMP: 100
SALES (corp-wide): 10B **Publicly Held**
WEB: www.republicservices.com
SIC: **4953** Refuse collection & disposal services
PA: Republic Services, Inc.
    18500 N Allied Way # 100
    Phoenix AZ 85054
    480 627-2700

(G-6312)
RESEARCH ASSOCIATES INC (PA)
Also Called: R A I
27999 Clemens Rd Frnt (44145-1182)
PHONE....................440 892-1000
Kevin P Prendergast, *President*
Art Sommer, *Vice Pres*
Arthur L Sommer, *Vice Pres*
Shirley Kopp, *Purch Agent*
Donna Ogle, *CFO*
EMP: 70
SQ FT: 10,800

(PA)=Parent Co (HQ)=Headquarters (DH)=Div Headquarters
✪ = New Business established in last 2 years

SALES (est): 2.8MM **Privately Held**
WEB: www.raiglobal.com
SIC: 7299 Information services, consumer

(G-6313)
RESERS FINE FOODS INC
Also Called: Sidaris Italian Foods
1921 E 119th St (44106-1903)
PHONE...........................216 231-7112
Mardy Gilnut, *Manager*
EMP: 30
SQ FT: 22,726
SALES (corp-wide): 1.7B **Privately Held**
SIC: 1541 Food products manufacturing or
packing plant construction
PA: Reser's Fine Foods, Inc.
15570 Sw Jenkins Rd
Beaverton OR 97006
503 643-6431

(G-6314)
RESERVES NETWORK INC (PA)
22021 Brookpark Rd # 220 (44126-3100)
PHONE...........................440 779-1400
Neil Stallard, *CEO*
Donald L Stallard, *Ch of Bd*
Nicholas Stallard, *CFO*
EMP: 30
SQ FT: 32,000
SALES (est): 28MM **Privately Held**
WEB: www.trnstaffing.com
SIC: 7363 7361 Temporary help service;
placement agencies

(G-6315)
RESOURCE TITLE AGENCY INC (PA)
7100 E Pleasant Vly # 100 (44131-5545)
PHONE...........................216 520-0050
Leslie Rennell, *President*
Richard Rennell, *Chairman*
Andrew Rennell, *Exec VP*
Raymond Bailey, *CFO*
Nancy Shear, *Sales Staff*
EMP: 87
SQ FT: 24,933
SALES (est): 21.2MM **Privately Held**
WEB: www.resourcetitle.com
SIC: 6361 6531 Real estate title insur-
ance; escrow agent, real estate

(G-6316)
RESTAURANT DEPOT LLC
6150 Halle Dr (44125-4614)
PHONE...........................216 525-0101
Oaura, *Branch Mgr*
EMP: 25 **Privately Held**
SIC: 5141 4225 Groceries, general line;
general warehousing & storage
HQ: Restaurant Depot, Llc
1524 132nd St
College Point NY 11356

(G-6317)
REVENUE ASSISTANCE CORPORATION
Also Called: Revenue Group
3711 Chester Ave (44114-4623)
P.O. Box 93983 (44101-5983)
PHONE...........................216 763-2100
Trey Sheehan, *President*
Michael Sheehan, *Vice Pres*
Stephanie Elliott, *Manager*
Reza Gheitantschi, *Director*
Brittney Johnson,
EMP: 200
SALES (est): 25MM **Privately Held**
WEB: www.revenuegroup.com
SIC: 7322 Collection agency, except real
estate

(G-6318)
REXEL USA INC
Also Called: Gexpro
5605 Granger Rd (44131-1213)
PHONE...........................216 778-6400
Scott Geraghty, *Manager*
EMP: 30
SALES (corp-wide): 2.2MM **Privately Held**
SIC: 5063 Electrical supplies
HQ: Rexel Usa, Inc.
14951 Dallas Pkwy
Dallas TX 75254

(G-6319)
RICCO ENTERPRISES INCORPORATED
6010 Fleet Ave Frnt Ste (44105-3498)
PHONE...........................216 883-7775
EMP: 28 **EST:** 1969
SALES (est): 1.4MM **Privately Held**
SIC: 6512 8741 Nonresidential Building
Operator Management Services

(G-6320)
RICHARD E JACOBS GROUP LLC
25425 Center Ridge Rd (44145-4122)
PHONE...........................440 871-4800
Judson E Smith, *CEO*
Richard Jacobs, *Partner*
Thomas Schmitz, *COO*
James F Eppele, *Exec VP*
William R Hansen, *Exec VP*
EMP: 50
SQ FT: 120,000
SALES (est): 5.7MM **Privately Held**
WEB: www.richardejacobsgroup.com
SIC: 6512 Nonresidential building opera-
tors

(G-6321)
RICHARD L BOWEN & ASSOC INC (PA)
13000 Shaker Blvd Ste 1 (44120-2098)
PHONE...........................216 491-9300
Richard L Bowen, *President*
Carol Padvorac, *Vice Pres*
Wayne Welker, *Engineer*
Gavin Smith, *Director*
Peggy Burke, *Admin Asst*
EMP: 73
SQ FT: 18,000
SALES (est): 14.7MM **Privately Held**
SIC: 8712 8741 8711 Architectural engi-
neering; construction management; civil
engineering

(G-6322)
RICHARD R JENCEN & ASSOCIATES
2850 Euclid Ave (44115-2414)
PHONE...........................216 781-0131
Jerry Rothenberg, *Partner*
E R Kanuer, *Partner*
E R Knauer, *Partner*
Nick Zalany, *Partner*
Amber Price, *Project Mgr*
EMP: 25
SALES (est): 3.4MM **Privately Held**
WEB: www.jencen.com
SIC: 8712 Architectural services

(G-6323)
RICHARD TOMM MD
Also Called: Tomm, Richard MD
1611 S Green Rd Ste 213 (44121-4138)
PHONE...........................216 297-3060
Michael Sheahan, *President*
Charlene Sapola, *Manager*
EMP: 65 **EST:** 1971
SQ FT: 8,200
SALES (est): 3.7MM **Privately Held**
SIC: 8011 General & family practice, physi-
cian/surgeon

(G-6324)
RICOH USA INC
Also Called: Nightrider Overnite Copy Svc
1360 E 9th St Bsmt 1 (44114-1779)
PHONE...........................216 574-9111
Michael Perkins, *Manager*
Mike Perkins, *Manager*
EMP: 80
SALES (corp-wide): 19.3B **Privately Held**
WEB: www.ikon.com
SIC: 5044 Office equipment
HQ: Ricoh Usa, Inc.
70 Valley Stream Pkwy
Malvern PA 19355
610 296-8000

(G-6325)
RIDGE PLEASANT VALLEY INC (PA)
Also Called: Pleasantview Nursing Home
7377 Ridge Rd (44129-6602)
PHONE...........................440 845-0200

Ester Daskal, *Vice Pres*
Irimie Borzea, *Director*
Kris Leonard, *Director*
Thomas Mandat, *Director*
Sarah Stack, *Director*
EMP: 190
SQ FT: 60,000
SALES (est): 10.6MM **Privately Held**
SIC: 8051 8052 Extended care facility; in-
termediate care facilities

(G-6326)
RIDGEPARK MEDICAL ASSOCIATES
7575 Northcliff Ave # 307 (44144-3267)
PHONE...........................216 749-8256
Bruce Resnik, *President*
Keith Koepke, *Med Doctor*
Terence Witham, *Psychiatry*
EMP: 30
SALES (est): 2.9MM **Privately Held**
SIC: 8071 Blood analysis laboratory

(G-6327)
RIPCHO STUDIO
7630 Lorain Ave (44102-4297)
PHONE...........................216 631-0664
Bill Ripcho, *Owner*
Jennie Vannewhouse, *Admin Asst*
Josh Jasko, *Graphic Designe*
Phil Hicks, *Analyst*
EMP: 45 **EST:** 1941
SQ FT: 20,000
SALES (est): 2.5MM **Privately Held**
WEB: www.ripchostudio.com
SIC: 7221 Photographer, still or video

(G-6328)
RIVER RECYCLING ENTPS LTD (PA)
4195 Bradley Rd (44109-3779)
PHONE...........................216 459-2100
William A Grodin, *President*
Kenneth Behrens, *Corp Secy*
James A Grodin, *Vice Pres*
▼ **EMP:** 26 **EST:** 1920
SQ FT: 76,000
SALES (est): 45MM **Privately Held**
WEB: www.rivershell.com
SIC: 5093 Ferrous metal scrap & waste

(G-6329)
RIVERSIDE DRIVES INC
Also Called: Riverside Drives Disc
4509 W 160th St (44135-2627)
P.O. Box 35166 (44135-0166)
PHONE...........................216 362-1211
Bernard Dillemuth, *President*
Kathleen Dillemuth, *Corp Secy*
David Dillemuth, *Vice Pres*
Kathy Straka, *Purchasing*
Vic Pringle, *Sales Engr*
▼ **EMP:** 28
SQ FT: 7,500
SALES (est): 19.8MM **Privately Held**
WEB: www.riversidedrives.com
SIC: 5063 3699 Power transmission
equipment, electric; electrical equipment
& supplies

(G-6330)
RIVERSIDECOMPANYCOM
Also Called: Riverside Company, The
50 Public Sq Ste 2900 (44113-2284)
PHONE...........................216 344-1040
Stewart Kohl, *CEO*
Charlie Rial, *Principal*
Timothy Tengea, *Engineer*
Rahul Mohan, *Finance Mgr*
Heather Dawson, *Manager*
EMP: 45
SALES (corp-wide): 1.9MM **Privately Held**
WEB: www.riversidecompany.com
SIC: 6211 Investment bankers
PA: Riversidecompany.Com
45 Rockefeller Plz
New York NY 10111
212 265-6575

(G-6331)
RMS AQUACULTURE INC (PA)
6629 Engle Rd Ste 108 (44130-7943)
PHONE...........................216 433-1340
Steven Zarzeczny, *President*
Mike Daversa, *Vice Pres*

Robert Knyszek, *Treasurer*
Sung Ho Shin, *Admin Sec*
EMP: 35
SALES (est): 3.6MM **Privately Held**
WEB: www.rmsaquaculture.com
SIC: 5999 0742 Tropical fish; veterinary
services, specialties

(G-6332)
ROBERT HALF INTERNATIONAL INC
Rhi Consulting
1001 Lakeside E 1320a (44114-1142)
PHONE...........................216 621-4253
Nancy Ramirez, *Manager*
EMP: 40
SALES (corp-wide): 5.8B **Publicly Held**
WEB: www.rhii.com
SIC: 7361 Employment agencies
PA: Robert Half International Inc.
2884 Sand Hill Rd Ste 200
Menlo Park CA 94025
650 234-6000

(G-6333)
ROBERT L STARK ENTERPRISES INC
1350 W 3rd St (44113-1806)
PHONE...........................216 292-0242
Robert L Stark, *President*
Steven Rubin, *COO*
Ezra Stark, *COO*
Raymond Weiss Jr, *CFO*
Mary Gregorich, *Controller*
EMP: 50
SQ FT: 11,000
SALES (est): 13.8MM **Privately Held**
SIC: 6552 Land subdividers & developers,
commercial

(G-6334)
ROBERT W BAIRD & CO INC
200 Public Sq Ste 1650 (44114-2301)
PHONE...........................216 737-7330
Brian Kurtz, *Branch Mgr*
Joseph Kraft, *Manager*
Steve Milvet, *Manager*
Michael Roethler, *Manager*
Kevin Alberty, *Advisor*
EMP: 25
SALES (corp-wide): 871.3MM **Privately Held**
WEB: www.rwbaird.com
SIC: 6211 Brokers, security
HQ: Robert W. Baird & Co. Incorporated
777 E Wisconsin Ave Fl 29
Milwaukee WI 53202
414 765-3500

(G-6335)
ROBERT WILEY MD INC
Also Called: Cleveland Eye Clinic
2740 Carnegie Ave (44115-2627)
PHONE...........................216 621-3211
Robert G Wiley MD, *President*
Thomas Chester Od, *Principal*
Chelsea Froats, *Research*
Shamik Bafna, *Director*
Heather Hendrock, *Assistant*
EMP: 25
SQ FT: 1,000
SALES (est): 2.5MM **Privately Held**
WEB: www.clevelandeyeclinic.com
SIC: 8011 Ophthalmologist

(G-6336)
ROCK AND ROLL OF FAME AND MUSE
1100 Rock And Roll Blvd (44114-1023)
PHONE...........▲...........216 781-7625
Greg Harris, *CEO*
Frank Suloivan, *Chairman*
Jann Wenner, *Chairman*
Caprice Bragg, *Vice Pres*
Karen Herman, *Vice Pres*
EMP: 100
SQ FT: 150,000
SALES (est): 36.4MM **Privately Held**
WEB: www.rockhall.com
SIC: 8412 7922 Museum; theatrical pro-
ducers & services

▲ = Import ▼=Export
◆ =Import/Export

(G-6337)
ROCKWOOD EQUITY PARTNERS LLC (PA)
3201 Entp Pkwy Ste 370 (44122)
PHONE....................216 342-1760
Owen M Colligan,
Brett Keith,
EMP: 41
SALES (est): 15.5MM Privately Held
SIC: 6726 Investment offices

(G-6338)
ROETZEL AND ANDRESS A LEGAL P
1375 E 9th St Fl 10 (44114-1788)
PHONE....................216 623-0150
John J Schriner Jr, Principal
EMP: 50
SALES (corp-wide): 53.4MM Privately Held
WEB: www.ralaw.com
SIC: 8111 General practice law office
PA: Roetzel And Andress, A Legal Professional Association
222 S Main St Ste 400
Akron OH 44308
330 376-2700

(G-6339)
ROSBY BROTHERS INC
Also Called: Rosby Brothers Grnhse & Grnhse
42 E Schaaf Rd (44131-1202)
PHONE....................216 351-0850
Michael P Rosby, President
EMP: 30
SQ FT: 60,000
SALES (est): 1.1MM Privately Held
SIC: 5992 0181 Flowers, fresh; plants, potted; ornamental nursery products

(G-6340)
ROSE MARY JOHANNA GRASSELL (PA)
Also Called: Cedar House
2346 W 14th St (44113-3613)
PHONE....................216 481-4823
A M Pilla Dd, Principal
EMP: 113
SALES (est): 2.9MM Privately Held
SIC: 8361 8052 Rehabilitation center, residential: health care incidental; intermediate care facilities

(G-6341)
ROSE PROPERTIES INC
Also Called: Rose Metal Industries
1536 E 43rd St (44103-2310)
PHONE....................216 881-6000
Robert Rose, President
Kara Aberts, General Mgr
Joe Schirra, Materials Mgr
Bryan Bridgett, Controller
Kurt Rose, Manager
EMP: 50
SQ FT: 10,000
SALES (est): 1.9MM Privately Held
SIC: 6512 Commercial & industrial building operation

(G-6342)
ROULSTON & COMPANY INC (PA)
Also Called: Fairport Asset Management
1350 Euclid Ave Ste 400 (44115-1847)
PHONE....................216 431-3000
Scott D Roulston, President
EMP: 46
SQ FT: 37,500
SALES (est): 5.5MM Privately Held
SIC: 6282 Investment advisory service

(G-6343)
ROULSTON RESEARCH CORP
1350 Euclid Ave Ste 400 (44115-1847)
PHONE....................216 431-3000
Scott D Roulston, President
EMP: 30
SQ FT: 35,000
SALES (est): 1.5MM
SALES (corp-wide): 5.5MM Privately Held
WEB: www.roulston.com
SIC: 6799 Commodity contract pool operators

PA: Roulston & Company, Inc.
1350 Euclid Ave Ste 400
Cleveland OH 44115
216 431-3000

(G-6344)
ROYAL APPLIANCE MFG CO (HQ)
Also Called: TTI Floor Care North America
7005 Cochran Rd (44139-4303)
PHONE....................440 996-2000
Chris Gurreri, President
Dave Brickner, Vice Pres
Richard C Farone, Vice Pres
Kevin Terry, Research
Tony Cannon, Engineer
◆ EMP: 250 EST: 1905
SQ FT: 458,000
SALES (est): 341.4MM
SALES (corp-wide): 6B Privately Held
WEB: www.dirtdevil.com
SIC: 5064 Vacuum cleaners, household
PA: Techtronic Industries Company Limited
29/F Kowloon Commerce Ctr Twr 2
Kwai Chung NT
240 268-88

(G-6345)
ROYAL MANOR HEALTH CARE INC (PA)
18810 Harvard Ave (44122-6848)
PHONE....................216 752-3600
Abraham Schwartz, President
Sally Schwartz, Treasurer
EMP: 50
SALES (est): 6.3MM Privately Held
SIC: 8051 8052 Skilled nursing facilities; intermediate care facilities

(G-6346)
ROYAL OAK NRSING RHBLTTION CTR
Also Called: Royal Manor Homes
6973 Pearl Rd (44130-7831)
PHONE....................440 884-9191
Margaret Halas, Director
EMP: 100
SALES (est): 4.7MM Privately Held
SIC: 8051 Convalescent home with continuous nursing care

(G-6347)
ROYALTON FINANCIAL GROUP
Also Called: Gaydosh Associates
13374 Ridge Rd Ste 1 (44133-3803)
PHONE....................440 582-3020
Edward Gaydosh, President
James E Gaydosh, Vice Pres
Ed Gaydosh, Manager
EMP: 30
SQ FT: 11,000
SALES (est): 2.3MM Privately Held
SIC: 8742 6411 Financial consultant; insurance agents, brokers & service

(G-6348)
RPC ELECTRONICS INC
Silicon Turnkey Express
749 Miner Rd Ste 4 (44143-2137)
PHONE....................877 522-7927
Art Czarnitzki, Sales Staff
Ira Dryer, Branch Mgr
EMP: 31
SALES (corp-wide): 24.9MM Privately Held
WEB: www.rpcelectronics.com
SIC: 5064 Electrical appliances, television & radio
PA: Rpc Electronics, Inc.
749 Miner Rd
Highland Heights OH 44143
440 461-4700

(G-6349)
RSM US LLP
1001 Lakeside Ave E # 200 (44114-1158)
PHONE....................216 523-1900
Donna Sciarappa, Partner
Penelope A Vitantonio, Sales Executive
John Balick, Branch Mgr
Loraine A Kalic, Director
Christine S Klaiber, Director
EMP: 125
SALES (corp-wide): 2.1B Privately Held
SIC: 8721 Certified public accountant

PA: Rsm Us Llp
1 S Wacker Dr Ste 800
Chicago IL 60606
312 384-6000

(G-6350)
RUSSELL WEISMAN JR MD
11100 Euclid Ave (44106-1716)
PHONE....................216 844-3127
Russell Jr Weisman, Owner
Lashawn Lovelady, Accountant
Gary Balog, Technology
Seth Eisengart,
Stacie Cole, Admin Sec
EMP: 130
SALES (est): 17.8MM Privately Held
SIC: 8011 Physicians' office, including specialists

(G-6351)
RWK SERVICES INC (PA)
Also Called: Ductbreeze
4700 Rockside Rd Ste 330 (44131-2151)
PHONE....................440 526-2144
William Wachs, President
Kerri Wachs, Shareholder
EMP: 29
SQ FT: 2,000
SALES: 2.8MM Privately Held
WEB: www.rwkservices.com
SIC: 7349 Janitorial service, contract basis; cleaning service, industrial or commercial

(G-6352)
RX HOME HEALTH CARE INC (PA)
2020 Carnegie Ave Ste 2 (44115-2338)
PHONE....................216 295-0056
Lemma Getacheu, President
Hirut Mengesha, Office Mgr
EMP: 60
SALES (est): 2MM Privately Held
SIC: 8082 Home health care services

(G-6353)
RYDER TRUCK RENTAL INC
11250 Brookpark Rd (44130-1178)
PHONE....................216 433-4700
James Yarwood, Manager
EMP: 150
SQ FT: 15,240
SALES (corp-wide): 8.4B Publicly Held
SIC: 7513 Truck rental, without drivers
HQ: Ryder Truck Rental, Inc.
11690 Nw 105th St
Medley FL 33178
305 500-3726

(G-6354)
S & S INC
21300 Saint Clair Ave (44117-1024)
PHONE....................216 383-1880
Paul Nared, President
Nancy Kunes, Vice Pres
Jack Armstrong, Sales Staff
Erin Dodson, Sales Staff
Richard Soltis, Sales Staff
EMP: 25 EST: 1953
SQ FT: 17,000
SALES: 10.8MM Privately Held
WEB: www.sspackaging.com
SIC: 5199 5084 7699 Packaging materials; packaging machinery & equipment; industrial machinery & equipment repair

(G-6355)
S B MORABITO TRUCKING INC
3560 E 55th St (44105-1126)
PHONE....................216 441-3070
Sebastian Morabito Jr, President
Tony Morabito, Vice Pres
EMP: 100 EST: 1956
SQ FT: 20,000
SALES (est): 12MM Privately Held
WEB: www.sbmtruck.com
SIC: 4212 Local trucking, without storage

(G-6356)
S R RESTAURANT CORP
Also Called: Rascal House Pizza
1836 Euclid Ave Ste 800 (44115-2234)
PHONE....................216 781-6784
Mike Frangos, President
Fouly Frangos, Vice Pres
EMP: 50

SQ FT: 25,000
SALES (est): 2.4MM Privately Held
WEB: www.srrestaurant.com
SIC: 8641 Bars & restaurants, members only

(G-6357)
S S KEMP & COMPANY (HQ)
Also Called: Trimark Ss Kemp
4567 Willow Pkwy (44125-1052)
PHONE....................216 271-7062
Mark Fishman, President
Howard Fishman, Chairman
Steven Fishman, Vice Pres
EMP: 136
SQ FT: 70,000
SALES (est): 94.2MM
SALES (corp-wide): 1B Privately Held
WEB: www.sskemp.com
SIC: 5046 Commercial cooking & food service equipment
PA: Trimark Usa, Llc
505 Collins St
Attleboro MA 02703
508 399-2400

(G-6358)
S&P DATA OHIO LLC
1500 W 3rd St Ste 130 (44113-1447)
PHONE....................216 965-0018
Dan Plashkes, CEO
Daniel Bemis, President
Samirah Graham, Manager
Lino Di Julio, Officer
EMP: 400
SALES (est): 39.4MM Privately Held
SIC: 7389 Telemarketing services

(G-6359)
SABRY HOSPITAL
Also Called: Fairview Hospital
18101 Lorain Ave (44111-5612)
PHONE....................216 476-7052
Sabry Ayad, Chairman
EMP: 25 EST: 1970
SALES (est): 713.4K Privately Held
SIC: 8011 Anesthesiologist

(G-6360)
SAFEGARD BCKGRUND SCREENING LLC
3711 Chester Ave (44114-4623)
PHONE....................216 370-7345
Lana Iklodi, Opers Mgr
Neil J Adelman,
EMP: 200
SALES (est): 5.1MM Privately Held
SIC: 7361 Employment agencies

(G-6361)
SAFEGUARD PROPERTIES LLC (HQ)
7887 Safeguard Cir (44125-5742)
PHONE....................216 739-2900
Alan Jaffa, CEO
Robert Klein, Ch of Bd
Jennifer Jozity, Assoc VP
Tod Burkert, VP Bus Dvlpt
Gregory Robinson, CFO
EMP: 800
SQ FT: 33,600
SALES (est): 188.6MM
SALES (corp-wide): 217.9MM Privately Held
SIC: 8741 7382 7381 Management services; security systems services; detective & armored car services
PA: Safeguard Properties Management, Llc
7887 Hub Pkwy
Cleveland OH 44125
216 739-2900

(G-6362)
SAFEGUARD PROPERTIES MGT LLC (PA)
7887 Hub Pkwy (44125)
PHONE....................216 739-2900
Alan Jaffa, CEO
Jennifer Anspach, Manager
Scott Heller, Manager
Jeremy Williams, Manager
Stacie Hauswirth, Technology
EMP: 700

SALES (est): 217.9MM **Privately Held**
SIC: **1522** Remodeling, multi-family dwellings

(G-6363)
SAFELITE FULFILLMENT INC
Also Called: Safelite Autoglass
6050 Towpath Dr Ste A (44125-4276)
PHONE.................................216 475-7781
Randy George, *Manager*
EMP: 35
SALES (corp-wide): 2.6MM **Privately Held**
WEB: www.belronus.com
SIC: **7536 4225** Automotive glass replacement shops; general warehousing & storage
HQ: Safelite Fulfillment, Inc.
7400 Safelite Way
Columbus OH 43235
614 210-9000

(G-6364)
SAINT FRANCIS DE SALES CHURCH
3434 George Ave (44134-2904)
PHONE.................................440 884-2319
Rev Robert L Hoban, *Pastor*
EMP: 32
SALES (est): 754.9K **Privately Held**
SIC: **8661 6061** Catholic Church; federal credit unions

(G-6365)
SALEM MEDIA GROUP INC
Also Called: W F H M - F M 95.5
4 Summit Park Dr Ste 150 (44131-6921)
PHONE.................................216 901-0921
Tim Vaughan, *Sales Mgr*
Mark Jaycox, *Manager*
EMP: 100
SALES (corp-wide): 262.7MM **Publicly Held**
WEB: www.srnradio.com
SIC: **4832** Radio broadcasting stations
PA: Salem Media Group, Inc.
4880 Santa Rosa Rd
Camarillo CA 93012
805 987-0400

(G-6366)
SALS HEATING AND COOLING INC
11701 Royalton Rd (44133-4210)
PHONE.................................216 676-4949
Salvatore C Sidoti, *President*
Elaine Sidoti, *Vice Pres*
EMP: 25
SQ FT: 6,435
SALES (est): 5.8MM **Privately Held**
SIC: **1711** Warm air heating & air conditioning contractor; heating & air conditioning contractors

(G-6367)
SALVAGEDATA RECOVERY LLC (PA)
43 Alpha Park (44143-2202)
PHONE.................................914 600-2434
Ralph Pierre, *President*
EMP: 30
SQ FT: 6,000
SALES (est): 2.9MM **Privately Held**
WEB: www.salvagedata.com
SIC: **7375** Information retrieval services

(G-6368)
SALVATION ARMY
2507 E 22nd St (44115-3202)
P.O. Box 5847 (44101-0847)
PHONE.................................216 861-8185
Ricardo Fernandez, *Manager*
EMP: 85
SQ FT: 28,928
SALES (corp-wide): 4.3B **Privately Held**
WEB: www.salvationarmy-usaeast.org
SIC: **8661 8641 8322** Religious organizations; civic social & fraternal associations; individual & family services
HQ: The Salvation Army
440 W Nyack Rd Ofc
West Nyack NY 10994
845 620-7200

(G-6369)
SAM-TOM INC
Also Called: Royce Security Services
3740 Euclid Ave Ste 102 (44115-2228)
PHONE.................................216 426-7752
Joseph W Conley, *President*
EMP: 200
SQ FT: 2,000
SALES (est): 3.3MM **Privately Held**
SIC: **7381** Security guard service

(G-6370)
SAMSEL ROPE & MARINE SUPPLY CO (PA)
Also Called: Samsel Supply Company
1285 Old River Rd Uppr (44113-1279)
PHONE.................................216 241-0333
Kathleen A Petrick, *President*
Larry E Nauth, *Principal*
Grace F Wilcox, *Principal*
Rosemary Woidke, *Principal*
F Michael Samsel, *Exec VP*
▲ EMP: 33
SQ FT: 100,000
SALES (est): 4.4MM **Privately Held**
WEB: www.samselsupply.com
SIC: **2394 5051 4959 5085** Canvas & related products; rope, wire (not insulated); miscellaneous nonferrous products; environmental cleanup services; industrial supplies; industrial tools; manufactured hardware (general); narrow fabric mills

(G-6371)
SANICO INC
7601 First Pl Ste 12 (44146-6702)
PHONE.................................440 439-5686
Michael T Pallaise, *President*
M Terry Pallaise, *President*
EMP: 70
SQ FT: 2,000
SALES (est): 3.5MM **Privately Held**
WEB: www.saniko.com.pl
SIC: **6512** Nonresidential building operators

(G-6372)
SAW SERVICE AND SUPPLY COMPANY
11925 Zelis Rd (44135-4692)
PHONE.................................216 252-5600
Robert Belock, *President*
Linda Belock, *Asst Sec*
▲ EMP: 50 EST: 1953
SQ FT: 30,000
SALES (est): 21.6MM **Privately Held**
WEB: www.sawservicesupply.com
SIC: **5072 7699** Power tools & accessories; power tool repair

(G-6373)
SAXON HOUSE CONDO
3167 Linden Rd (44116-4170)
PHONE.................................440 333-8675
Dorothy O'Nill, *President*
EMP: 65
SALES (est): 529.8K **Privately Held**
SIC: **8641** Condominium association

(G-6374)
SCHINDLER ELEVATOR CORPORATION
Also Called: Millar Elevator Service
1100 E 55th St (44103-1027)
PHONE.................................216 391-8600
Gerald Plezner, *Manager*
EMP: 60
SALES (corp-wide): 10.9B **Privately Held**
WEB: www.us.schindler.com
SIC: **7699** Elevators: inspection, service & repair
HQ: Schindler Elevator Corporation
20 Whippany Rd
Morristown NJ 07960
973 397-6500

(G-6375)
SCHINDLER ELEVATOR CORPORATION
18013 Clvlnd Pkw Dr 140 (44135)
PHONE.................................216 370-9524
Miggy Torres, *Sales Staff*
Jeff Davis, *Manager*
EMP: 100

SALES (corp-wide): 10.9B **Privately Held**
WEB: www.us.schindler.com
SIC: **7699** Elevators: inspection, service & repair
HQ: Schindler Elevator Corporation
20 Whippany Rd
Morristown NJ 07960
973 397-6500

(G-6376)
SCHOMER GLAUS PYLE
Also Called: Gpd Group
5595 Transportation Blvd (44125-5379)
PHONE.................................216 518-5544
David Martin, *Design Engr Mgr*
Jacque Gorman, *Engineer*
John Sullivan, *Engineer*
Joseph Ciuni, *Branch Mgr*
Ed Franks, *Manager*
EMP: 50
SALES (corp-wide): 93.9MM **Privately Held**
SIC: **8711 8712** Civil engineering; architectural services
PA: Glaus, Pyle, Schomer, Burns & Dehaven, Inc.
520 S Main St Ste 2531
Akron OH 44311
330 572-2100

(G-6377)
SCHUSTERS GREENHOUSE LTD
9165 Columbia Rd (44138-2426)
PHONE.................................440 235-2440
David Schuster, *Partner*
EMP: 25
SALES (est): 1.9MM **Privately Held**
WEB: www.schustersgreenhouse.com
SIC: **0181** Bedding plants, growing of; flowers: grown under cover (e.g. greenhouse production); foliage, growing of

(G-6378)
SCHWEIZER DIPPLE INC
7227 Division St (44146-5405)
PHONE.................................440 786-8090
Michael J Kelley, *President*
Dennis Clark, *Exec VP*
Dennis J Clark, *Vice Pres*
James G Dwyer, *Vice Pres*
Peter A McGrogan, *Vice Pres*
EMP: 55
SQ FT: 27,000
SALES (est): 11.7MM
SALES (corp-wide): 38.4MM **Privately Held**
WEB: www.schweizer-dipple.com
SIC: **1711 3496 3444 3443** Mechanical contractor; process piping contractor; plumbing contractors; warm air heating & air conditioning contractor; miscellaneous fabricated wire products; sheet metalwork; fabricated plate work (boiler shop)
PA: Kelley Steel Erectors, Inc.
7220 Division St
Cleveland OH 44146
440 232-1573

(G-6379)
SCOTT FETZER COMPANY
Adalet
4801 W 150th St (44135-3301)
PHONE.................................216 267-9000
Fred Lemke, *Sales Staff*
EMP: 150
SALES (corp-wide): 225.3B **Publicly Held**
WEB: www.adalet.com
SIC: **5063 3469 3357 3613** Wire & cable; metal stampings; nonferrous wiredrawing & insulating; control panels, electric; metal housings, enclosures, casings & other containers
HQ: The Scott Fetzer Company
28800 Clemens Rd
Westlake OH 44145
440 892-3000

(G-6380)
SCOTT FETZER FINANCIAL GROUP
Also Called: Scott Fetzer Co
28800 Clemens Rd (44145-1197)
PHONE.................................440 892-3000
Ken Semelberger, *CEO*
EMP: 40

SALES (est): 3.9MM
SALES (corp-wide): 225.3B **Publicly Held**
WEB: www.scottfetzer.com
SIC: **6153** Short-term business credit
HQ: The Scott Fetzer Company
28800 Clemens Rd
Westlake OH 44145
440 892-3000

(G-6381)
SCRAP YARD LLC
Also Called: Cleveland Scrap
15000 Miles Ave (44128-2370)
PHONE.................................216 271-5825
Allen Youngman, *President*
Jacobe Youngman, *Vice Pres*
EMP: 25
SALES (est): 2.7MM **Privately Held**
SIC: **5093** Metal scrap & waste materials

(G-6382)
SCRIBES & SCRBBLR CHLD DEV CTR
14101 Uhlin Dr (44130-5604)
PHONE.................................440 884-5437
Dennis Cox, *President*
Carol Cox, *Vice Pres*
EMP: 34
SQ FT: 31,000
SALES (est): 1MM **Privately Held**
SIC: **8351 7032** Nursery school; summer camp, except day & sports instructional

(G-6383)
SEAGATE HOSPITALITY GROUP LLC
Also Called: Holiday Inn
4181 W 150th St (44135-1303)
PHONE.................................216 252-7700
Todd Middleton, *Branch Mgr*
EMP: 25
SALES (corp-wide): 13.4MM **Privately Held**
SIC: **7011 5812** Hotels; eating places
PA: Seagate Hospitality Group, Llc
400 Linden Oaks Ste 120
Rochester NY 14625
585 419-4000

(G-6384)
SEAMANS SERVICES
Also Called: Cleaveland Seaman's Service
1050 W 3rd St (44114-1002)
PHONE.................................216 621-4107
Al Oberst, *President*
Homer Cook, *Vice Pres*
Donald Bisesi, *Treasurer*
EMP: 30
SALES (est): 577.4K **Privately Held**
SIC: **8322** Individual & family services

(G-6385)
SEARS ROEBUCK AND CO
Also Called: Sears Credit Central
13200 Smith Rd (44130-7856)
PHONE.................................440 845-0120
EMP: 230
SALES (corp-wide): 16.7B **Publicly Held**
SIC: **6153** Credit Card Service
HQ: Sears, Roebuck And Co.
3333 Beverly Rd
Hoffman Estates IL 60179
847 286-2500

(G-6386)
SEARS ROEBUCK AND CO
Also Called: Sears Auto Center
17271 Southpark Ctr (44136-9311)
PHONE.................................440 846-3595
EMP: 150
SALES (corp-wide): 16.7B **Publicly Held**
SIC: **7549** Automotive Services
HQ: Sears, Roebuck And Co.
3333 Beverly Rd
Hoffman Estates IL 60179
847 286-2500

(G-6387)
SECURESTATE LLC
23340 Miles Rd (44128-5491)
PHONE.................................216 927-0115
Ken Stasiak, *CEO*
Stephen Marchewitz, *President*
Brian Telesz, *Managing Dir*
Sue Satink, *CFO*

▲ = Import ▼=Export
◆ =Import/Export

Doreen Huggett, *Accounts Mgr*
EMP: 28 **EST:** 2001
SQ FT: 5,500
SALES (est): 5.1MM **Privately Held**
WEB: www.securestate.net
SIC: 7382 Security systems services

(G-6388)
SECURITAS SEC SVCS USA INC
3747 Euclid Ave (44115-2501)
PHONE..................................216 431-3139
Cynthia Pacyga, *Branch Mgr*
EMP: 182
SALES (corp-wide): 10.9B **Privately Held**
SIC: 7381 Security guard service
HQ: Securitas Security Services Usa, Inc.
    9 Campus Dr
    Parsippany NJ 07054
    973 267-5300

(G-6389)
SECURITAS SEC SVCS USA INC
Also Called: East Coast Region
12000 Snow Rd Ste 5 (44130-9314)
PHONE..................................440 887-6800
Scott Fry, *Branch Mgr*
EMP: 630
SALES (corp-wide): 10.9B **Privately Held**
WEB: www.securitasinc.com
SIC: 7381 Security guard service
HQ: Securitas Security Services Usa, Inc.
    9 Campus Dr
    Parsippany NJ 07054
    973 267-5300

(G-6390)
SECURITAS SEC SVCS USA INC
Also Called: Shared Services
9885 Rockside Rd Ste 155 (44125-6272)
PHONE..................................216 503-2021
Nick Riggs, *President*
Laura Svasta, *Branch Mgr*
EMP: 116
SALES (corp-wide): 10.9B **Privately Held**
WEB: www.securitasinc.com
SIC: 7381 Security guard service
HQ: Securitas Security Services Usa, Inc.
    9 Campus Dr
    Parsippany NJ 07054
    973 267-5300

(G-6391)
SEDLAK MANAGEMENT CONSULTANTS
22901 Millcreek Blvd # 600 (44122-5724)
PHONE..................................216 206-4700
Jeffrey B Graves, *President*
Joseph A Sedlak, *Chairman*
Ned N Sedlak, *Exec VP*
Jeff Mueller, *Vice Pres*
Patrick S Sedlak, *Vice Pres*
EMP: 32 **EST:** 1958
SQ FT: 18,500
SALES (est): 6.1MM **Privately Held**
WEB: www.jasedlak.com
SIC: 8742 7374 Planning consultant; industrial consultant; automation & robotics consultant; management information systems consultant; data processing & preparation

(G-6392)
SEELEY SVDGE EBERT GOURASH LPA
26600 Detroit Rd Fl 3 (44145-2395)
PHONE..................................216 566-8200
Gregory Seeley, *Partner*
Gary Ebert, *Partner*
Daniel Gourash, *Partner*
Patrick J McIntyre, *Partner*
Keith Savidge, *Partner*
EMP: 30
SQ FT: 15,200
SALES (est): 4.7MM **Privately Held**
WEB: www.sse-law.com
SIC: 8111 General practice attorney, lawyer

(G-6393)
SELECT HOTELS GROUP LLC
Also Called: Hyatt Pl Clveland/Independence
6025 Jefferson Dr (44131-2145)
PHONE..................................216 328-1060
Kevin Hastings, *Branch Mgr*
Barbara Yeater, *Manager*
EMP: 50

SALES (corp-wide): 4.4B **Publicly Held**
WEB: www.amerisuites.com
SIC: 7011 Hotels
HQ: Select Hotels Group, L.L.C.
    71 S Wacker Dr
    Chicago IL 60606
    312 750-1234

(G-6394)
SELECT MEDICAL CORPORATION
Also Called: Select Specialty Hospital
11900 Fairhill Rd Ste 100 (44120-1063)
PHONE..................................216 983-8030
EMP: 218
SALES (corp-wide): 3.7B **Publicly Held**
SIC: 8062 General medical & surgical hospitals
HQ: Select Medical Corporation
    4714 Gettysburg Rd
    Mechanicsburg PA 17055
    717 972-1100

(G-6395)
SELF-FUNDED PLANS INC (PA)
1432 Hamilton Ave (44114-1146)
PHONE..................................216 566-1455
Donna B Luby, *President*
John Haines, *Vice Pres*
Marsha A Phillips, *Vice Pres*
Donald Messinger, *Admin Sec*
EMP: 45 **EST:** 1980
SQ FT: 25,000
SALES (est): 12.6MM **Privately Held**
WEB: www.sfpi.com
SIC: 6411 Insurance agents

(G-6396)
SELMAN & COMPANY (PA)
6110 Parkland Blvd (44124-4187)
PHONE..................................440 646-9336
David Selman, *President*
John L Selman, *Chairman*
Cheryl M Ahmad, *Vice Pres*
Elizabeth M Boettcher, *Vice Pres*
Elizabeth Boettcher, *Vice Pres*
EMP: 75
SQ FT: 26,000
SALES (est): 33.1MM **Privately Held**
WEB: www.sel-co.com
SIC: 6411 Insurance agents

(G-6397)
SENIOR OUTREACH SERVICES
Also Called: S.O.S.
2390 E 79th St (44104-2161)
P.O. Box 606177 (44106-0677)
PHONE..................................216 421-6900
Ken Strother, *President*
Delores Lynch, *Director*
EMP: 50
SQ FT: 3,000
SALES: 1.2MM **Privately Held**
SIC: 8322 4119 Old age assistance; meal delivery program; local passenger transportation

(G-6398)
SERVICE CORPS RETIRED EXECS
Also Called: S C O R E
1350 Euclid Ave Ste 216 (44115-1815)
PHONE..................................216 522-4194
Anita Khayat, *Branch Mgr*
EMP: 50
SALES (corp-wide): 13.1MM **Privately Held**
WEB: www.score199.mv.com
SIC: 8611 Business associations
PA: Service Corps Of Retired Executives Association
    1175 Herndon Pkwy Ste 900
    Herndon VA 20170
    703 487-3612

(G-6399)
SERVICE KING HOLDINGS LLC
Also Called: Service King Cllision Repr Ctr
15703 Puritas Ave (44135-2609)
PHONE..................................216 362-1600
EMP: 100
SALES (corp-wide): 347.9MM **Privately Held**
SIC: 7532 Body shop, automotive

PA: Service King Holdings, Llc
    2375 N Glenville Dr
    Richardson TX 75082
    972 960-7595

(G-6400)
SERVISAIR LLC (DH)
Also Called: Global Ground
5851 Cargo Rd (44135-3111)
P.O. Box 811150 (44181-1150)
PHONE..................................216 267-9910
Michael J Hancock, *President*
Douglas Mc Connell, *Exec VP*
Timothy R Archer, *Senior VP*
Wes A Bement, *Senior VP*
Michael A Albanese, *Vice Pres*
EMP: 200
SQ FT: 10,000
SALES (est): 25.7MM
SALES (corp-wide): 1.1MM **Privately Held**
SIC: 4581 Airport terminal services
HQ: Servisair Usa & Carribean
    6065 Nw 18th St Bldg 716d
    Miami FL 33126
    305 262-4059

(G-6401)
SHAIAS PARKING INC
812 Huron Rd E Ste 701 (44115-1165)
PHONE..................................216 621-0328
Victor Shaia, *President*
EMP: 25
SQ FT: 1,000
SALES (est): 842.9K **Privately Held**
SIC: 7521 Parking lots

(G-6402)
SHAKER HOUSE
3700 Northfield Rd Ste 3 (44122-5240)
PHONE..................................216 991-6000
Robert Nash, *Mayor*
Craig Koslan, *Vice Pres*
EMP: 70
SQ FT: 7,897
SALES (est): 800K **Privately Held**
SIC: 7011 6513 Hotels; apartment building operators

(G-6403)
SHAKER VALLEY FOODS INC
3304 W 67th Pl (44102-5243)
PHONE..................................216 961-8600
Dean Comber, *President*
Jeff Koutris, *Purch Mgr*
Jim Comber, *Technology*
EMP: 40
SQ FT: 30,000
SALES (est): 21.6MM **Privately Held**
WEB: www.shakervalleyfoods.com
SIC: 5141 2011 Food brokers; meat packing plants

(G-6404)
SHAPIRO SHAPIRO & SHAPIRO
Also Called: Kahan & Kahan
4469 Renaissance Pkwy (44128-5754)
PHONE..................................216 927-2030
Alan Shapiro, *President*
EMP: 25
SALES (est): 2.1MM **Privately Held**
SIC: 8111 General practice attorney, lawyer

(G-6405)
SHIPPERS CONSOLIDATED DIST
Also Called: Shippers Cartage & Dist
1840 Carter Rd (44113-2402)
PHONE..................................216 579-9303
Robert Mangini, *President*
Charles H Glazer, *Corp Secy*
EMP: 41 **EST:** 1980
SQ FT: 25,000
SALES (est): 4.7MM **Privately Held**
SIC: 4214 4213 Local trucking with storage; trucking, except local

(G-6406)
SHOREBY CLUB INC
40 Shoreby Dr (44108-1191)
PHONE..................................216 851-2587
Chris Mancusho, *General Mgr*
Chris Mancuso, *Personnel*
Erin Petre, *Manager*
EMP: 60

SALES: 2.8MM **Privately Held**
SIC: 8699 5812 Personal interest organization; restaurant, family: independent

(G-6407)
SIEGFRIED GROUP LLP
600 Superior Ave E (44114-2614)
PHONE..................................216 522-1910
Brian Seidner, *Manager*
EMP: 34
SALES (corp-wide): 170MM **Privately Held**
SIC: 8721 Certified public accountant
PA: The Siegfried Group Llp
    1201 N Market St Ste 700
    Wilmington DE 19801
    302 984-1800

(G-6408)
SIEVERS SECURITY SYSTEMS INC (PA)
18210 Saint Clair Ave (44110-2626)
PHONE..................................216 383-1234
Michael Sievers, *President*
James Sievers, *Vice Pres*
Amy Sievers, *Treasurer*
Rob Sievers, *Admin Sec*
EMP: 30
SQ FT: 4,000
SALES (est): 3.6MM **Privately Held**
WEB: www.sieverssecurity.com
SIC: 7382 Security systems services

(G-6409)
SIGNAL PRODUCTIONS INC
1267 W 9th St (44113-1064)
P.O. Box 26, Grafton (44044-0026)
PHONE..................................323 382-0000
Tyler Davidson, *Principal*
EMP: 50
SALES (est): 965.4K **Privately Held**
SIC: 7819 Services allied to motion pictures

(G-6410)
SINGLETON HEALTH CARE CENTER
1867 E 82nd St (44103-4263)
PHONE..................................216 231-0076
Garth Ireland, *President*
Joseph Ireland, *Owner*
Channa Ireland, *Vice Pres*
Mary Ireland, *Vice Pres*
EMP: 50 **EST:** 1960
SQ FT: 15,000
SALES: 3.8MM **Privately Held**
SIC: 8052 8051 Personal care facility; skilled nursing care facilities

(G-6411)
SKODA MINOTTI HOLDINGS LLC (PA)
Also Called: Mayfield Village
6685 Beta Dr (44143-2320)
PHONE..................................440 449-6800
Gregory J Skoda, *Ch of Bd*
Michael Minotti, *President*
Patrick Carney, *Vice Pres*
Robert E Coode, *Vice Pres*
Kenneth Haffey, *Vice Pres*
EMP: 27
SQ FT: 25,939
SALES (est): 18.6MM **Privately Held**
WEB: www.skodaminotti.com
SIC: 7291 Tax return preparation services

(G-6412)
SKYE DEVELOPMENT COMPANY LLC
25001 Emery Rd Ste 420 (44128-5626)
PHONE..................................216 223-0160
EMP: 30
SALES (est): 1.9MM **Privately Held**
SIC: 6531 Real Estate Agent/Manager

(G-6413)
SKYLIGHT FINANCIAL GROUP LLC (PA)
2012 W 25th St Ste 900 (44113-4124)
PHONE..................................216 621-5680
Cathy Prather, *Agent*
Joseph Paulsey, *Info Tech Dir*
E John Brzytwa,
Bailey Conner, *Executive Asst*
Corbin Blackburn, *Advisor*

GEOGRAPHIC

EMP: 34
SALES (est): 3.2MM Privately Held
SIC: 8742 Financial consultant

(G-6414)
SKYLINE CLVLAND RNAISSANCE LLC
Also Called: Renaissance Cleveland Hotel
24 Public Sq (44113-2213)
PHONE...............................216 696-5600
Michael Snegd, President
Patricia Barrett, Human Res Dir
Louisa Yeung, Administration
EMP: 99 EST: 2015
SQ FT: 873,000
SALES (est): 485.2K Privately Held
SIC: 7011 Hotels

(G-6415)
SLAVIC VILLAGE DEVELOPMENT
5620 Broadway Ave Uppr (44127-1762)
PHONE...............................216 429-1182
Christopher Alvarado, Principal
Michael Geregach, Principal
Jim Oryl, Safety Mgr
Andrew Kinney, Marketing Mgr
Anthony Brancatelli, Exec Dir
EMP: 28
SALES: 1.8MM Privately Held
SIC: 6552 Land subdividers & developers, commercial

(G-6416)
SLAWSON EQUIPMENT CO INC
7851 Freeway Cir (44130-6308)
PHONE...............................216 391-7263
Thomas H Mc Clave, President
Gary L Mc Clave, Corp Secy
Gary McClave, CFO
EMP: 38
SQ FT: 10,500
SALES: 7MM Privately Held
SIC: 5075 Warm air heating equipment & supplies; ventilating equipment & supplies; air conditioning equipment, except room units

(G-6417)
SLOVENE HOME FOR THE AGED
18621 Neff Rd (44119-3018)
PHONE...............................216 486-0268
Jeffrey Saf, Administration
EMP: 190
SQ FT: 77,000
SALES: 11.6MM Privately Held
SIC: 8051 Skilled nursing care facilities

(G-6418)
SM DOUBLE TREE HOTEL LAKE
Also Called: Doubletree Hotel
1111 Lakeside Ave E (44114-1130)
PHONE...............................216 241-5100
Ozie Ross, Accounting Mgr
Leonard Clifton, Manager
Josh Fleming, Manager
Billie Jones, Manager
Jackie Angel, Director
EMP: 33
SALES (est): 1.9MM Privately Held
SIC: 7011 Hotels & motels

(G-6419)
SOGETI USA LLC
6055 Rockside Woods # 170 (44131-2301)
PHONE...............................216 654-2230
Melinda White, Principal
Navin Goel, Manager
Robert Winn, Manager
EMP: 30
SALES (corp-wide): 355MM Privately Held
WEB: www.sogeti-usa.com
SIC: 7379
HQ: Sogeti Usa Llc
10100 Innovation Dr # 200
Miamisburg OH 45342
937 291-8100

(G-6420)
SOLIDARITY HEALTH NETWORK INC
4853 Galaxy Pkwy Ste K (44128-5939)
PHONE...............................216 831-1220
Anne Glorioso, Principal

Vince Palumbo, Sales Staff
Alexandra Granakis, Manager
Jeneen Cipullo, Admin Asst
EMP: 29
SQ FT: 4,500
SALES (est): 1.9MM Privately Held
SIC: 8399 Health systems agency

(G-6421)
SORBIR INC (PA)
Also Called: Marshall Ford Leasing
6200 Mayfield Rd (44124-3203)
P.O. Box 241355 (44124-8355)
PHONE...............................440 449-1000
Larry Elk, President
George Ducas, Treasurer
Jerry Sorkin, Admin Sec
EMP: 63
SQ FT: 40,000
SALES (est): 5.4MM Privately Held
SIC: 7515 5511 Passenger car leasing; automobiles, new & used

(G-6422)
SOUTH E HARLEY DAVIDSON SLS CO (PA)
Also Called: Southeast Golf Cars
23105 Aurora Rd (44146-1703)
PHONE...............................440 439-5300
Paul Meyers Sr, CEO
Paul Meyers Jr, President
Dave Baumgardner, General Mgr
Linda Russell, Controller
Jane Hook, Mktg Dir
EMP: 48
SQ FT: 20,000
SALES (est): 33MM Privately Held
WEB: www.southeastpolaris.com
SIC: 5571 7999 Motorcycle dealers; golf cart, power, rental

(G-6423)
SOUTH E HARLEY DAVIDSON SLS CO
Also Called: Southeast Golf Cars
23165 Aurora Rd (44146-1703)
PHONE...............................440 439-3013
Paul Meyres, Manager
EMP: 45
SALES (corp-wide): 33MM Privately Held
WEB: www.southeastpolaris.com
SIC: 4225 General warehousing
PA: South East Harley Davidson Sales Co.
23105 Aurora Rd
Cleveland OH 44146
440 439-5300

(G-6424)
SOUTH SHORE CABLE CNSTR INC
6400 Kolthoff Dr (44142-1310)
PHONE...............................440 816-0033
Daniel Geib, President
James Stack, Vice Pres
Bill Sunderman, Project Mgr
Chris Yeager, Project Mgr
Jay Geib, Treasurer
EMP: 70
SALES (est): 13.4MM Privately Held
SIC: 1623 Cable laying construction

(G-6425)
SOUTH TRANSPORTATION
5044 Mayfield Rd (44124-2605)
PHONE...............................216 691-2040
Chester Young, Principal
EMP: 50
SALES (est): 654.2K Privately Held
SIC: 4111 Local & suburban transit

(G-6426)
SOUTHWEST ASSOCIATES
Also Called: Century Oak Care Center
7250 Old Oak Blvd (44130-3341)
PHONE...............................440 243-7888
David Crisafi, Owner
Stewart Bossel, Partner
Frank Crisafi, Partner
Danial Rocker, Partner
Senior H Ohio, General Ptnr
EMP: 120
SQ FT: 48,000

SALES (est): 9.7MM Privately Held
SIC: 6512 Commercial & industrial building operation

(G-6427)
SOUTHWEST CLEVELAND SLEEP CTR (PA)
18100 Jefferson Park Rd # 103 (44130-8458)
PHONE...............................440 239-7533
Nazima Ahmed, President
Mansoor Ahmed, Vice Pres
EMP: 25 EST: 2000
SALES (est): 837.1K Privately Held
SIC: 8011 Pulmonary specialist, physician/surgeon; specialized medical practitioners, except internal

(G-6428)
SOUTHWEST CMNTY HLTH SYSTEMS
Also Called: Southwest General Hospital
18697 Bagley Rd (44130-3417)
PHONE...............................440 816-8000
Thomas A Selden, President
Vasu Pandrangi, Chairman
James Bastian, Treasurer
Benjamin Tancinco, Pathologist
Mark Pangersis, Technology
EMP: 1982
SQ FT: 567,121
SALES (est): 14.7K Privately Held
SIC: 8062 General medical & surgical hospitals

(G-6429)
SOUTHWEST FAMILY PHYSICIANS
7225 Old Oak Blvd A210 (44130-3339)
PHONE...............................440 816-2750
David Lash, President
Steven Tymcio, Vice Pres
EMP: 48 EST: 1975
SQ FT: 10,000
SALES (est): 5.3MM Privately Held
WEB: www.southwestfamilyphysicians.com
SIC: 8011 Physicians' office, including specialists; general & family practice, physician/surgeon

(G-6430)
SOUTHWEST GENERAL HEALTH CTR
Also Called: Lifeworks At Southwest General
7390 Old Oak Blvd (44130-3328)
PHONE...............................440 816-4202
Karen Siegel, Manager
Cara Padin, Director
EMP: 65
SALES (corp-wide): 363.2MM Privately Held
SIC: 8062 7991 General medical & surgical hospitals; health club
PA: Southwest General Health Center
18697 Bagley Rd
Cleveland OH 44130
440 816-8000

(G-6431)
SOUTHWEST GENERAL HEALTH CTR
Also Called: Southwest General Health Ctr
18697 Oak Vw (44130)
PHONE...............................440 816-8200
Cory Shaw, Pharmacist
Phillip Kuntz, Director
EMP: 70
SQ FT: 83,892
SALES (corp-wide): 363.2MM Privately Held
SIC: 8062 8069 General medical & surgical hospitals; drug addiction rehabilitation hospital
PA: Southwest General Health Center
18697 Bagley Rd
Cleveland OH 44130
440 816-8000

(G-6432)
SOUTHWEST GENERAL HEALTH CTR (PA)
18697 Bagley Rd (44130-3417)
PHONE...............................440 816-8000
L Jon Schurmeier, President
Albert Matyas, Vice Pres

Karen Green, Purch Mgr
Dana Hardy, Purch Agent
Kathleen Zazzara, Purch Agent
EMP: 2400
SQ FT: 150,000
SALES: 363.2MM Privately Held
SIC: 8062 General medical & surgical hospitals

(G-6433)
SOUTHWEST GENERAL HEALTH CTR
Also Called: Home Hlth Svcs Southwest Hosp
17951 Jefferson Park Rd (44130-8439)
PHONE...............................440 816-8005
Debbie Borowski, Director
EMP: 40
SALES (corp-wide): 363.2MM Privately Held
SIC: 8062 General medical & surgical hospitals
PA: Southwest General Health Center
18697 Bagley Rd
Cleveland OH 44130
440 816-8000

(G-6434)
SOUTHWEST INTERNAL MEDICINE
7255 Old Oak Blvd C209 (44130-3329)
PHONE...............................440 816-2777
James D Wismar, Principal
Kamesh Gundataneni MD, Internal Med
EMP: 25
SALES (est): 2MM Privately Held
WEB: www.southwestinternalmedicine.com
SIC: 8062 General medical & surgical hospitals

(G-6435)
SOUTHWEST UROLOGY LLC (PA)
Also Called: Southwest Urlogy Wmen Cnnctons
6900 Pearl Rd Ste 200 (44130-3640)
PHONE...............................440 845-0900
Claudio Zanin, CEO
Michael Barkoukis MD, President
Arturo Bossa MD, Principal
Laurence Dervasi MD, Principal
Tim Sildor MD, Principal
EMP: 40
SQ FT: 6,000
SALES (est): 5.8MM Privately Held
SIC: 8071 8011 Medical laboratories; pathologist; urologist

(G-6436)
SP PLUS CORPORATION
Also Called: Standard Parking
9500 Euclid Ave Wb1 (44195-0001)
PHONE...............................216 444-2255
Harold McMann, Branch Mgr
EMP: 90
SALES (corp-wide): 1.4B Publicly Held
SIC: 7521 Parking lots
PA: Sp Plus Corporation
200 E Randolph St # 7700
Chicago IL 60601
312 274-2000

(G-6437)
SP PLUS CORPORATION
1301 E 9th St Ste 1050 (44114-1888)
PHONE...............................216 687-0141
Bob Kohler, Regional Mgr
Tom Svoboda, Accountant
EMP: 50
SALES (corp-wide): 1.4B Publicly Held
SIC: 7521 Parking garage
PA: Sp Plus Corporation
200 E Randolph St # 7700
Chicago IL 60601
312 274-2000

(G-6438)
SP PLUS CORPORATION
5300 Riverside Dr (44135-3130)
PHONE...............................216 267-7275
Dennis McAndrew, General Mgr
EMP: 60
SALES (corp-wide): 1.4B Publicly Held
SIC: 7521 Parking lots

PA: Sp Plus Corporation
200 E Randolph St # 7700
Chicago IL 60601
312 274-2000

(G-6439)
SP PLUS CORPORATION
5300 Riverside Dr (44135-3130)
PHONE..................................216 267-5030
Dennis McAndrew, *General Mgr*
EMP: 70
SALES (corp-wide): 1.4B **Publicly Held**
SIC: 7521 Parking lots
PA: Sp Plus Corporation
200 E Randolph St # 7700
Chicago IL 60601
312 274-2000

(G-6440)
SPANGENBERG SHIBLEY LIBER LLP
Also Called: Spangenberg Law Firm
1001 Lakeside Ave E # 1700 (44114-1158)
PHONE..................................216 215-7445
Dennis Lansdowne, *Partner*
William Hawal, *Partner*
Justin Madden, *Partner*
Peter H Weinberger, *Partner*
EMP: 32 **EST:** 1959
SALES (est): 5.1MM **Privately Held**
WEB: www.spanglaw.com
SIC: 8111 General practice law office

(G-6441)
SPANISH AMERICAN COMMITTEE (PA)
4407 Lorain Ave Fl 1 (44113-3779)
PHONE..................................216 961-2100
Efrain Colon, *President*
Ramonita Vargas, *Principal*
Jazmin Torres, *Corp Comm Staff*
Elizabeth Leon, *Case Mgr*
Gladys Ortiz, *Education*
EMP: 26
SQ FT: 12,500
SALES: 854.5K **Privately Held**
WEB: www.spanishamerican.org
SIC: 8322 8331 8351 Social service center; job training services; head start center, except in conjunction with school

(G-6442)
SPARKBASE INC
3615 Superior Ave E 4403d (44114-4139)
PHONE..................................216 867-0877
Douglas Hardman, *CEO*
Geoffry Hardman, *President*
EMP: 50
SQ FT: 6,800
SALES (est): 4.7MM **Privately Held**
SIC: 7389 Financial services

(G-6443)
SPECIALTY HOSP CLEVELAND INC
Also Called: Kindred Hosp - Clveland - Gtwy
2351 E 22nd St Fl 7 (44115-3111)
PHONE..................................216 592-2830
Rothgerber L Arthur, *Senior VP*
Papouras Despina, *Manager*
EMP: 98
SALES (est): 4.3MM
SALES (corp-wide): 6B **Privately Held**
SIC: 8062 General medical & surgical hospitals
HQ: Kindred Healthcare, Llc
680 S 4th St
Louisville KY 40202
502 596-7300

(G-6444)
SPECIALTY STEEL CO INC
18250 Miles Rd (44128-3439)
P.O. Box 28152 (44128-0152)
PHONE..................................800 321-8500
Theodore Cohen Jr, *President*
Ronald De Camp, *Manager*
EMP: 40
SQ FT: 48,000
SALES (est): 6.2MM **Privately Held**
WEB: www.specialtysteel.com
SIC: 5051 Steel

(G-6445)
SPECTRUM SUPPORTIVE SERVICES
Also Called: Spectrum Supportive Services
4269 Pearl Rd Ste 300 (44109-4232)
PHONE..................................216 875-0460
Stephen S Morse, *Exec Dir*
EMP: 50
SALES (corp-wide): 897K **Privately Held**
WEB: www.spectrumsupport.org
SIC: 8331 8322 Vocational rehabilitation agency; association for the handicapped
PA: Spectrum Of Supportive Services
2900 Detroit Ave Fl 3
Cleveland OH 44113
216 939-2075

(G-6446)
SPEEDEON DATA LLC
5875 Landerbrook Dr # 130 (44124-4069)
PHONE..................................440 264-2100
Joshua Shale, *COO*
Linda Montgomery, *CFO*
Marc Jerauld, *Officer*
Gerard Daher,
EMP: 26
SQ FT: 2,148
SALES (est): 3.7MM **Privately Held**
SIC: 7374 7379 Data processing service; computer data escrow service

(G-6447)
ST AUGUSTINE TOWERS
7821 Lake Ave Apt 304 (44102-6400)
PHONE..................................216 634-7444
Anita Newsham, *Principal*
Nancy Minerd, *Manager*
Anita Gerriasch, *Director*
EMP: 30
SALES: 1.9MM **Privately Held**
SIC: 8082 Home health care services

(G-6448)
ST CLAIR AUTO BODY
Also Called: St Clair Auto Body Shop
13608 Saint Clair Ave (44110-3547)
PHONE..................................216 531-7300
Norman Kirchner, *President*
EMP: 25 **EST:** 1967
SQ FT: 15,000
SALES (est): 4.3MM **Privately Held**
SIC: 7532 Body shop, automotive; paint shop, automotive

(G-6449)
ST REGIS INVESTMENT LLC
8111 Rockside Rd (44125-6129)
PHONE..................................216 520-1250
Frank Sinito,
EMP: 99 **EST:** 2015
SALES (est): 1.9MM **Privately Held**
SIC: 6513 Apartment building operators

(G-6450)
ST VINCENT CHARITY MED CTR (PA)
2351 E 22nd St (44115-3111)
PHONE..................................216 861-6200
Melvin G Pye Jr, *Ch of Bd*
David F Perse MD, *President*
Joan Ross, *COO*
Beverly Lozar, *Vice Pres*
Deborah Christopher, *Purch Agent*
EMP: 903
SQ FT: 200,000
SALES: 142.3MM **Privately Held**
WEB: www.cccmhb.org
SIC: 8062 General medical & surgical hospitals

(G-6451)
STANTEC ARCH & ENGRG PC
3700 Park East Dr Ste 200 (44122-4339)
PHONE..................................216 454-2150
Lori Van Dermark, *Marketing Staff*
Amy Strasheim, *Branch Mgr*
EMP: 25
SALES (corp-wide): 4B **Privately Held**
SIC: 8711 8712 Engineering services; architectural services
HQ: Stantec Architecture And Engineering P.C.
311 Summer St
Boston MA 02210

(G-6452)
STANTEC ARCHITECTURE INC
1300 E 9th St Ste 1100 (44114-1506)
PHONE..................................216 621-2407
EMP: 53
SALES (corp-wide): 4B **Privately Held**
SIC: 8712 Architectural Services
HQ: Stantec Architecture Inc.
224 S Michigan Ave # 1400
Chicago IL 60604
336 714-7413

(G-6453)
STANTEC ARCHITECTURE INC
1001 Lakeside Ave E # 1600 (44114-1158)
PHONE..................................216 454-2150
Lori Van Dermark, *Marketing Staff*
Michael Carter, *Branch Mgr*
EMP: 25
SALES (corp-wide): 4B **Privately Held**
WEB: www.burthill.com
SIC: 8712 8711 Architectural services; engineering services
HQ: Stantec Architecture Inc.
224 S Michigan Ave # 1400
Chicago IL 60604
336 714-7413

(G-6454)
STANTEC CONSULTING SVCS INC
3700 Park East Dr Ste 200 (44122-4339)
PHONE..................................216 454-2150
EMP: 25
SALES (corp-wide): 4B **Privately Held**
SIC: 8712 8711 Architectural Services Engineering Services
HQ: Stantec Consulting Services Inc.
475 5th Ave Fl 12
New York NY 10017
212 352-5160

(G-6455)
STANTEC CONSULTING SVCS INC
1001 Lakeside Ave E # 1600 (44114-1158)
PHONE..................................216 621-2407
Sven Wiberg, *Branch Mgr*
Anthony Green, *Architect*
EMP: 44
SALES (est): 4B **Privately Held**
WEB: www.mw.com
SIC: 8711 Consulting engineer
HQ: Stantec Consulting Services Inc.
475 5th Ave Fl 12
New York NY 10017
212 352-5160

(G-6456)
STATE FARM MUTL AUTO INSUR CO
Also Called: State Farm Insurance
2700 W 25th St (44113-4710)
PHONE..................................216 621-3723
Andriann Dumar, *Manager*
Dick McClement, *Manager*
EMP: 72
SALES (corp-wide): 39.5B **Privately Held**
WEB: www.statefarm.com
SIC: 6411 Insurance agents & brokers
PA: State Farm Mutual Automobile Insurance Company
1 State Farm Plz
Bloomington IL 61710
309 766-2311

(G-6457)
STATE FARM MUTL AUTO INSUR CO
Also Called: State Farm Insurance
2245 Warrensville Ctr Rd (44118-3145)
PHONE..................................216 321-1422
Linda Myers, *Branch Mgr*
Linda Meyers, *Agent*
EMP: 72
SALES (corp-wide): 39.5B **Privately Held**
WEB: www.statefarm.com
SIC: 6411 Insurance agents & brokers
PA: State Farm Mutual Automobile Insurance Company
1 State Farm Plz
Bloomington IL 61710
309 766-2311

(G-6458)
STATE INDUSTRIAL PRODUCTS CORP (PA)
Also Called: State Chemical Manufacturing
5915 Landerbrook Dr # 300 (44124-4039)
PHONE..................................877 747-6986
Harold Uhrman, *President*
Robert M San Julian, *President*
William Barnett, *Corp Secy*
Brian Limbert, *COO*
Dan Prugar, *CFO*
▼ **EMP:** 300 **EST:** 1911
SQ FT: 240,000
SALES: 107.9MM **Privately Held**
WEB: www.stateindustrial.com
SIC: 2841 5072 2842 2992 Soap: granulated, liquid, cake, flaked or chip; bolts, nuts & screws; specialty cleaning, polishes & sanitation goods; degreasing solvent; disinfectants, household or industrial plant; lubricating oils & greases; asphalt felts & coatings; chemical preparations

(G-6459)
STATE INDUSTRIAL PRODUCTS CORP
Also Called: U Z Engineered Products Co
12420 Plaza Dr (44130-1057)
PHONE..................................216 861-6363
Dave Debord, *Branch Mgr*
EMP: 200
SALES (corp-wide): 107.9MM **Privately Held**
WEB: www.stateindustrial.com
SIC: 5085 Fasteners, industrial: nuts, bolts, screws, etc.
PA: State Industrial Products Corporation
5915 Landerbrook Dr # 300
Cleveland OH 44124
877 747-6986

(G-6460)
STATE-WIDE EXPRESS INC
5231 Engle Rd (44142-1531)
PHONE..................................216 676-4600
Tom Armanini, *President*
Dean Armanini, *Vice Pres*
Dino Armani, *Marketing Mgr*
EMP: 63
SQ FT: 25,000
SALES (est): 6.9MM **Privately Held**
SIC: 4214 4213 4212 Local trucking with storage; trucking, except local; local trucking, without storage

(G-6461)
STEEL WAREHOUSE CLEVELAND LLC (DH)
3193 Independence Rd (44105-1045)
PHONE..................................888 225-3760
Jake Budzielek, *Plant Mgr*
Marc Stephens, *Engineer*
Rick Kings, *Controller*
Hugh Garvey, *Mng Member*
Dave Glacken, *Clerk*
EMP: 31
SALES (est): 29.2MM **Privately Held**
SIC: 5051 Steel
HQ: Steel Warehouse Company Llc
2722 Tucker Dr
South Bend IN 46619
574 236-5100

(G-6462)
STEEL WAREHOUSE COMPANY LLC
Also Called: Steel Warehouse Ohio
4700 Heidtman Pkwy (44105-1026)
PHONE..................................216 206-2800
Jake Budzielek, *Branch Mgr*
EMP: 30 **Privately Held**
SIC: 5051 Steel
HQ: Steel Warehouse Company Llc
2722 Tucker Dr
South Bend IN 46619
574 236-5100

(G-6463)
STEEL WAREHOUSE OF OHIO LLC
4700 Heidtman Pkwy (44105-1026)
PHONE..................................888 225-3760
Dave Lerman, *CEO*
Mike Lerman, *President*
Bill Lerman, *Vice Pres*

Marc Lerman, *Vice Pres*
Jake Budzielek, *Plant Mgr*
EMP: 60
SALES (est): 13.5MM **Privately Held**
SIC: 5051 Steel
PA: Lerman Holding Co. Inc.
2722 Tucker Dr
South Bend IN 46619

(G-6464)
STEIN INC
1034 Holmden Ave (44109-1836)
PHONE................................216 883-4277
Dave Bilez, *General Mgr*
EMP: 75
SALES (corp-wide): 83.5MM **Privately Held**
SIC: 1791 Structural steel erection
PA: Stein, Inc.
1929 E Royalton Rd Ste C
Cleveland OH 44147
440 526-9301

(G-6465)
STELLA MARIS INC
Also Called: Stella Mris Detoxification Ctr
1320 Washington Ave (44113-2333)
PHONE................................216 781-0550
Roselyn Price, *Finance Dir*
Margaret Roche, *Director*
Karen Ferrell, *Nurse*
EMP: 30
SQ FT: 15,000
SALES: 3.2MM **Privately Held**
SIC: 8069 Substance abuse hospitals

(G-6466)
STEPHEN A RUDOLPH INC
1611 S Green Rd Ste 260 (44121-4192)
PHONE................................216 381-1367
Stephen A Rudolph MD, *President*
EMP: 35
SALES (est): 1MM **Privately Held**
SIC: 8011 Internal medicine, physician/surgeon

(G-6467)
STEPSTONE GROUP REAL ESTATE LP
127 Public Sq Ste 5050 (44114-1246)
PHONE................................216 522-0330
EMP: 30
SALES (corp-wide): 1.5MM **Privately Held**
SIC: 8742 6282 Real estate consultant; investment advice
PA: Stepstone Group Real Estate Lp
885 3rd Ave Fl 14
New York NY 10022
212 351-6100

(G-6468)
STERN ADVERTISING INC (PA)
950 Main Ave Ste 700 (44113-7208)
PHONE................................216 331-5827
Freda Royed, *CEO*
William J Stern, *President*
Kathryn Hanley, *Principal*
Joseph H Persky, *Principal*
Jeff Thomas, *Vice Pres*
EMP: 50
SQ FT: 15,000
SALES (est): 10.9MM **Privately Held**
SIC: 7311 Advertising consultant

(G-6469)
STONE GARDENS
27090 Cedar Rd (44122-8108)
PHONE................................216 292-0070
Ross Wilkoff, *Administration*
EMP: 75
SALES (est): 3.5MM **Privately Held**
SIC: 8361 Residential care

(G-6470)
STONEWOOD RESIDENTIAL INC (PA)
6320 Smith Rd (44142-3711)
P.O. Box 42155 (44142-0155)
PHONE................................216 267-9777
Bill Stacho, *President*
Beverly Krug, *Manager*
Lynn Urbanski, *Director*
EMP: 25
SQ FT: 5,800

SALES (est): 2MM **Privately Held**
SIC: 8361 Residential care for the handicapped

(G-6471)
STOUT RISIUS ROSS LLC
600 Superior Ave E # 1700 (44114-2622)
PHONE................................216 685-5000
Greg O'Hara, *Managing Dir*
Jason Maracco, *Branch Mgr*
EMP: 25 **Privately Held**
SIC: 8748 Business consulting
PA: Stout Risius Ross, Llc
1 S Wacker Dr Lbby 38
Chicago IL 60606

(G-6472)
STRANG CORPORATION (PA)
Also Called: Don's Lighthouse Inn
8905 Lake Ave Fl 1 (44102-6319)
PHONE................................216 961-6767
Donald W Strang Jr, *Ch of Bd*
Donald W Strang III, *President*
Chris Mattiola, *District Mgr*
David Strang, *Vice Pres*
Peter Strang, *Vice Pres*
EMP: 50
SQ FT: 20,000
SALES (est): 15.5MM **Privately Held**
SIC: 7011 Hotels & motels

(G-6473)
STREAMLINK SOFTWARE INC (PA)
812 Huron Rd E Ste 550 (44115-1143)
PHONE................................216 377-5500
Adam Roth, *President*
EMP: 25 **EST:** 2013
SALES (est): 3.6MM **Privately Held**
SIC: 7371 Computer software development

(G-6474)
SUMMERS ACQUISITION CORP (DH)
Also Called: Summers Rubber Company
12555 Berea Rd (44111-1619)
PHONE................................216 941-7700
Mike Summers, *President*
William M Summers, *Chairman*
Eugene Mayo, *Vice Pres*
Gene Mayo, *Vice Pres*
Sam Petillo, *Vice Pres*
▲ **EMP:** 26
SQ FT: 63,000
SALES (est): 22.3MM
SALES (corp-wide): 3.1B **Privately Held**
WEB: www.summersrubber.com
SIC: 5085 3429 Rubber goods, mechanical; manufactured hardware (general)
HQ: Hampton Rubber Company
1669 W Pembroke Ave
Hampton VA 23661
757 722-9818

(G-6475)
SUMMIT ASSOCIATES INC
Also Called: Holiday Inn
3750 Orange Pl (44122-4404)
PHONE................................216 831-3300
Ken Hiller, *Manager*
EMP: 100
SALES (corp-wide): 39.8K **Privately Held**
WEB: www.sairealestate.com
SIC: 7011 5813 5812 Hotels & motels; drinking places; eating places
PA: Summit Associates Inc
Raritan Plz 1 Raritan Ctr St Raritan Pla
Edison NJ 08837
732 225-2900

(G-6476)
SUMMIT HOTEL TRS 144 LLC
Also Called: Residence Inn By Marriott
527 Prospect Ave E (44115-1113)
PHONE................................216 443-9043
Tracy Sauers, *Principal*
Christopher Eng, *Principal*
EMP: 48
SALES (est): 180.6K **Privately Held**
SIC: 7011 Hotels & motels

(G-6477)
SUNBELT RENTALS INC
13800 Brookpark Rd (44135-5149)
PHONE................................216 362-0300
Tim Tausch, *District Mgr*
Robert Rogers, *Branch Mgr*
EMP: 30
SALES (corp-wide): 5.2B **Privately Held**
WEB: www.sunbeltrentals.com
SIC: 7353 7359 Heavy construction equipment rental; equipment rental & leasing
HQ: Sunbelt Rentals, Inc.
2341 Deerfield Dr
Fort Mill SC 29715
803 578-5811

(G-6478)
SUNRISE LAND CO (DH)
1250 Trml Twr 50 Pub Sq 1250 Terminal Tower (44113)
PHONE................................216 621-6060
Robert Monchein, *President*
Layton Mc Cown, *Controller*
EMP: 39
SALES (est): 3MM
SALES (corp-wide): 80.4MM **Privately Held**
SIC: 6552 Land subdividers & developers, commercial; land subdividers & developers, residential
HQ: Forest City Enterprises, L.P.
127 Public Sq Ste 3200
Cleveland OH 44114
216 621-6060

(G-6479)
SUNRISE SENIOR LIVING INC
Also Called: Sunrise At Shaker Heights
16333 Chagrin Blvd (44120-3711)
PHONE................................216 751-0930
Vesta Jones, *Exec Dir*
EMP: 100
SALES (corp-wide): 4.7B **Publicly Held**
WEB: www.sunrise.com
SIC: 8051 Skilled nursing care facilities
HQ: Sunrise Senior Living, Llc
7902 Westpark Dr
Mc Lean VA 22102

(G-6480)
SUNRISE SENIOR LIVING LLC
Also Called: Sunrise At Parma
7766 Broadview Rd (44134-6743)
PHONE................................216 447-8909
Rima Hanson, *Manager*
EMP: 50
SQ FT: 20,703
SALES (corp-wide): 4.7B **Publicly Held**
WEB: www.sunrise.com
SIC: 8051 8361 Skilled nursing care facilities; residential care
HQ: Sunrise Senior Living, Llc
7902 Westpark Dr
Mc Lean VA 22102

(G-6481)
SUNSET MNOR HLTHCARE GROUP INC
Also Called: Crawford Manor Healthcare Ctr
1802 Crawford Rd (44106-2030)
PHONE................................216 795-5710
Sarah Depompei, *Assistant*
EMP: 36
SALES (corp-wide): 1.8MM **Privately Held**
SIC: 8051 Skilled nursing care facilities
PA: Sunset Manor Healthcare Group, Inc.
26691 Richmond Rd
Bedford Heights OH 44146
216 292-5706

(G-6482)
SUPERIOR APARTMENTS
1850 Superior Ave E 102a (44114-2130)
PHONE................................216 861-6405
Joseph Weiss, *President*
EMP: 30
SALES (est): 641.4K **Privately Held**
WEB: www.superioapartments.net
SIC: 6513 Apartment building operators

(G-6483)
SUPERIOR PRODUCTS LLC
Also Called: Sp Medical
3786 Ridge Rd (44144-1127)
PHONE................................216 651-9400

Tomas Sarrel, *President*
Donald L Mottinger, *President*
Tim Austin, *Managing Dir*
Louise Egofske, *CFO*
Tim Giesse, *Admin Sec*
◆ **EMP:** 80 **EST:** 1961
SALES (est): 17.8MM **Privately Held**
WEB: www.superiorprod.com
SIC: 3451 3494 5085 3492 Screw machine products; valves & pipe fittings; industrial fittings; fluid power valves & hose fittings

(G-6484)
SUPERIOR PRODUCTS LLC
3786 Ridge Rd (44144-1127)
PHONE................................216 651-9400
Donald L Mottinger, *President*
Tim Austin, *Managing Dir*
Gregory K Gens, *CFO*
Tim Giesse, *Admin Sec*
EMP: 65
SQ FT: 75,000
SALES (est): 8.5MM
SALES (corp-wide): 145.8MM **Privately Held**
SIC: 3494 5085 3492 Valves & pipe fittings; industrial fittings; fluid power valves & hose fittings
HQ: Superior Holding, Llc
3786 Ridge Rd
Cleveland OH 44144
216 651-9400

(G-6485)
SUPPLY TECHNOLOGIES LLC (HQ)
Also Called: I L S
6065 Parkland Blvd Ste 2 (44124-6146)
P.O. Box 248199 (44124-8199)
PHONE................................440 947-2100
Michael L Justice, *President*
Brad Hudson, *Vice Pres*
Tom Blevins, *Opers Mgr*
Mike Nixon, *Opers Mgr*
Jim Rabb, *Opers Staff*
▲ **EMP:** 150 **EST:** 1998
SQ FT: 7,000
SALES (est): 43.2MM
SALES (corp-wide): 1.6B **Publicly Held**
WEB: www.deloscrew.com
SIC: 5085 3452 3469 Fasteners, industrial: nuts, bolts, screws, etc.; bolts, nuts, rivets & washers; screws, metal; nuts, metal; stamping metal for the trade
PA: Park-Ohio Holdings Corp.
6065 Parkland Blvd Ste 1
Cleveland OH 44124
440 947-2000

(G-6486)
SUPPORT TO AT RISK TEENS
Also Called: Start
4515 Superior Ave (44103-1215)
PHONE................................216 696-5507
Mark Brauer, *Exec Dir*
EMP: 40
SALES (est): 2.6MM **Privately Held**
WEB: www.lmmyouth.org
SIC: 8322 Social service center

(G-6487)
SUPREME COURT UNITED STATES
Also Called: US Probation Office
801 W Superior Ave 20-100 (44113-1833)
PHONE................................216 357-7300
Greg Johnson, *Branch Mgr*
EMP: 27 **Publicly Held**
SIC: 8322 9211 Probation office; courts;
HQ: Supreme Court, United States
1 1st St Ne
Washington DC 20543
202 479-3000

(G-6488)
SURGERY CTR AN OHIO LTD PARTNR
Also Called: Surgery Center, The
19250 Bagley Rd (44130-3347)
PHONE................................440 826-3240
Barbara Draves, *Partner*
EMP: 60
SALES (est): 7.9MM
SALES (corp-wide): 18.3B **Publicly Held**
SIC: 8011 Surgeon

HQ: United Surgical Partners International, Inc.
15305 Dallas Pkwy # 1600
Addison TX 75001
972 713-3500

(G-6489)
SWA INC
Also Called: Century Oak Care Center
7250 Old Oak Blvd (44130-3341)
PHONE..............................440 243-7888
Stewart Bossel, *President*
EMP: 116
SQ FT: 48,000
SALES (est): 2.9MM **Privately Held**
WEB: www.centuryoakcarecenter.com
SIC: 8051 Skilled nursing care facilities

(G-6490)
SWEENEY ROBERT E CO LPA
55 Public Sq Ste 1500 (44113-1998)
PHONE..............................216 696-0606
Robert E Sweeney, *President*
Patricia Sorcek, *Business Mgr*
Kevin E McDermott,
William A Sweeney,
EMP: 48
SQ FT: 10,000
SALES (est): 3.6MM **Privately Held**
SIC: 8111 General practice law office

(G-6491)
SYSTEM SEALS INC (HQ)
9505 Midwest Ave (44125-2421)
PHONE..............................440 735-0200
Arnold V Engelbrechten, *President*
▲ EMP: 60
SQ FT: 10,000
SALES (est): 8.4MM
SALES (corp-wide): 319.4K **Privately Held**
WEB: www.systemseals.com
SIC: 3953 5084 Embossing seals & hand stamps; hydraulic systems equipment & supplies

(G-6492)
T & F SYSTEMS INC
1599 E 40th St (44103-2389)
PHONE..............................216 881-3525
Brian Stenger, *President*
EMP: 100
SQ FT: 14,000
SALES: 8MM **Privately Held**
SIC: 1761 Roofing/Siding Contractor

(G-6493)
T AND J TRNSTNAL HM FOR DSBLED
17635 Parkmount Ave (44135-4119)
PHONE..............................216 703-4673
Tajuansha Moton, *Principal*
EMP: 25
SALES (est): 141K **Privately Held**
SIC: 8399 Advocacy group

(G-6494)
T J NEFF HOLDINGS INC
Also Called: Neff & Associates
6405 York Rd (44130-3052)
PHONE..............................440 884-3100
Daniel Neff, *President*
Daniel J Neff, *President*
Mike Denallo, *Engineer*
Stefan Kloss, *Engineer*
Steven Metcalf, *Manager*
EMP: 40
SALES (est): 4.2MM **Privately Held**
SIC: 8711 8713 Civil engineering; consulting engineer; surveying services

(G-6495)
T L C LANDSCAPING INC
Also Called: Park Place Nursery
38000 Aurora Rd (44139-4619)
PHONE..............................440 248-4852
Gary S Stanek, *President*
Kathy Stanek, *Admin Sec*
EMP: 47
SQ FT: 5,000
SALES (est): 1.4MM **Privately Held**
SIC: 0782 4959 Landscape contractors; snowplowing

(G-6496)
T W I INTERNATIONAL INC (DH)
24460 Aurora Rd (44146-1728)
PHONE..............................440 439-1830
Armond Waxman, *Ch of Bd*
Melvin Waxman, *President*
Mark Wester, *Finance Dir*
EMP: 110
SQ FT: 21,000
SALES (est): 7.3MM
SALES (corp-wide): 100MM **Privately Held**
SIC: 7389 Packaging & labeling services

(G-6497)
TAFT STETTINIUS HOLLISTER LLP
200 Public Sq Ste 3500 (44114-2317)
PHONE..............................216 241-3141
Stephen M O'Bryan, *Managing Prtnr*
Bruce Gaynor, *Partner*
Jack Guthman, *Partner*
Elizabeth Stanton, *Partner*
Theresa Vella, *Partner*
EMP: 74
SALES (corp-wide): 104.2MM **Privately Held**
SIC: 8111 General practice law office
PA: Taft Stettinius & Hollister Llp
425 Walnut St Ste 1800
Cincinnati OH 45202
513 381-2838

(G-6498)
TANOS SALON
24225 Chagrin Blvd (44122-5516)
PHONE..............................216 831-7880
Leonard Cosentino, *Owner*
Elaine Kausman, *Admin Sec*
EMP: 35
SALES (est): 316.5K **Privately Held**
SIC: 7231 Beauty shops

(G-6499)
TARGET AUTO BODY INC
5005 Carnegie Ave (44103-4353)
PHONE..............................216 391-1942
Misun Pak, *President*
EMP: 25
SALES (est): 917K **Privately Held**
SIC: 7532 Body shop, automotive

(G-6500)
TAUSSIG CANCER CENTER
Also Called: Cleveland Clinic
10201 Carnegie Ave (44106-2130)
PHONE..............................866 223-8100
Talitha Howse, *Research*
Sandy Hathaway, *Accountant*
Gerrie Smith, *Admin Sec*
Marcia Miller, *Analyst*
Linda McLellan, *Social Worker*
EMP: 26
SALES (est): 1.4MM **Privately Held**
SIC: 8062 General medical & surgical hospitals

(G-6501)
TAYLOR MADE GRAPHICS
7921 Hollenbeck Cir (44129-6214)
PHONE..............................440 882-6318
James Keserich, *Owner*
Danette Keserich, *Co-Owner*
EMP: 27
SALES (est): 1.1MM **Privately Held**
SIC: 7336 Graphic arts & related design

(G-6502)
TAYLOR MURTIS HUMAN SVCS SYS
12395 Mccracken Rd (44125-2967)
PHONE..............................216 283-4400
Ella Thomas, *Director*
EMP: 132
SALES (corp-wide): 25.1MM **Privately Held**
SIC: 8099 Blood related health services
PA: Murtis Taylor Human Services System
13422 Kinsman Rd
Cleveland OH 44120
216 283-4400

(G-6503)
TAYLOR MURTIS HUMAN SVCS SYS (PA)
13422 Kinsman Rd (44120-4410)
PHONE..............................216 283-4400
Lovell J Custard, *CEO*
Muqit Sabur, *Chairman*
John Chan, *Senior VP*
Ella Thomas, *Project Dir*
Annetta L Fisher, *Treasurer*
EMP: 70
SQ FT: 35,000
SALES: 25.1MM **Privately Held**
SIC: 8093 8322 Mental health clinic, outpatient; community center; social service center; child related social services; emergency social services

(G-6504)
TAYLOR MURTIS HUMAN SVCS SYS
3167 Fulton Rd (44109-1465)
PHONE..............................216 281-7192
Murtis Taylor, *Owner*
EMP: 66
SALES (corp-wide): 25.1MM **Privately Held**
SIC: 8322 8093 Community center; mental health clinic, outpatient
PA: Murtis Taylor Human Services System
13422 Kinsman Rd
Cleveland OH 44120
216 283-4400

(G-6505)
TAYLOR MURTIS HUMAN SVCS SYS
16005 Terrace Rd (44112-2001)
PHONE..............................216 283-4400
EMP: 82
SALES (corp-wide): 25.1MM **Privately Held**
SIC: 8093 8322 Mental health clinic, outpatient; social service center
PA: Murtis Taylor Human Services System
13422 Kinsman Rd
Cleveland OH 44120
216 283-4400

(G-6506)
TEAM INDUSTRIAL SERVICES INC
5901 Harper Rd (44139-1834)
PHONE..............................440 498-9494
Chuck Avis, *Branch Mgr*
EMP: 32
SALES (corp-wide): 1.2B **Publicly Held**
SIC: 7699 Industrial equipment services
HQ: Team Industrial Services, Inc.
13131 Dairy Ashford Rd # 600
Sugar Land TX 77478
281 388-5525

(G-6507)
TEAM NEO
1111 Superior Ave E # 1600 (44114-2552)
PHONE..............................216 363-5400
Bill Koehler, *CEO*
Bernardine Van Kessel, *Director*
EMP: 26
SALES: 4.7MM **Privately Held**
SIC: 8748 8699 Economic consultant; charitable organization

(G-6508)
TECH MAHINDRA (AMERICAS) INC
200 W Prospect Ave (44113-1432)
PHONE..............................216 912-2002
Sudhakar Shetty, *Branch Mgr*
EMP: 80
SALES (corp-wide): 4.7B **Privately Held**
SIC: 7371 Custom computer programming services
HQ: Tech Mahindra (Americas) Inc.
4965 Preston Park Blvd # 500
Plano TX 75093

(G-6509)
TELEMESSAGING SERVICES INC
Also Called: Tasco Inc Ohio
7441 W Ridgewood Dr # 130 (44129-5544)
PHONE..............................440 845-5400
Jerri Habbyshaw, *Branch Mgr*
EMP: 25
SALES (corp-wide): 9.1MM **Privately Held**
WEB: www.tascoteleserve.com
SIC: 7389 Telephone answering service
PA: Telemessaging Services Inc
6600 York Rd Ste 203
Baltimore MD 21212
410 377-3000

(G-6510)
TEN THUSAND VILLAGES CLEVELAND
12425 Cedar Rd (44106-3155)
P.O. Box 18193 (44118-0193)
PHONE..............................216 575-1058
EMP: 25
SALES: 139.7K **Privately Held**
SIC: 5023 Whol Homefurnishings

(G-6511)
TENABLE PROTECTIVE SVCS INC (PA)
2423 Payne Ave (44114-4428)
PHONE..............................216 361-0002
Peter Miragliotta, *CEO*
Francis Crish, *President*
Todd Andersen, *Counsel*
Paul Moviel, *Opers Staff*
Jerry Prather, *Opers Staff*
EMP: 2835
SQ FT: 12,000
SALES (est): 85.3MM **Privately Held**
WEB: www.ac-products.com
SIC: 7381 Security guard service; private investigator

(G-6512)
TENDON MANUFACTURING INC
20805 Aurora Rd (44146-1005)
PHONE..............................216 663-3200
Gregory F Tench, *President*
Michael J Gordon, *Corp Secy*
Thomas Tench, *Sls & Mktg Exec*
Nancy Ryzner, *Finance Mgr*
Kathy Thomas, *Office Mgr*
EMP: 46
SQ FT: 36,000
SALES (est): 9.4MM **Privately Held**
WEB: www.tendon.com
SIC: 3599 3479 1761 7692 Machine shop, jobbing & repair; painting of metal products; sheet metalwork; welding repair; sheet metalwork; automotive & apparel trimmings

(G-6513)
TERENCE ISAKOV MD
Also Called: Family Physicans Associates
5187 Mayfield Rd Ste 102 (44124-2467)
PHONE..............................440 449-1014
Terence Isakov MD, *Partner*
EMP: 55
SALES (est): 2.3MM **Privately Held**
SIC: 8011 General & family practice, physician/surgeon

(G-6514)
TERMINIX INTL CO LTD PARTNR
5350 Transportation Blvd (44125-5327)
PHONE..............................216 518-1091
Ron Trebec, *Manager*
EMP: 29
SALES (corp-wide): 1.9B **Publicly Held**
SIC: 7342 Pest control services
HQ: The Terminix International Company Limited Partnership
150 Peabody Pl
Memphis TN 38103
901 766-1400

(G-6515)
TERRACE CONSTRUCTION CO INC
3965 Pearl Rd (44109-3103)
PHONE..............................216 739-3170
Jeffrey Nock, *Owner*
Mark Edzma, *Vice Pres*
EMP: 55
SQ FT: 7,500

SALES (est): 14.8MM **Privately Held**
WEB: www.terraceconstruction.com
SIC: **1623** Underground utilities contractor; water main construction; sewer line construction

(G-6516)
TERRY J REPPA & ASSOCIATES
7029 Pearl Rd Ste 350 (44130-4979)
PHONE.....................................440 888-8533
Terry Reppa, *President*
EMP: 26
SALES (est): 1.8MM **Privately Held**
SIC: **8742 8721** Consulting And Billing Service

(G-6517)
TESAR INDUSTRIAL CONTRS INC (PA)
3920 Jennings Rd (44109-2860)
PHONE.....................................216 741-8008
James Tesar Jr, *President*
Sharon Tesar, *Vice Pres*
EMP: 29 EST: 1920
SQ FT: 20,000
SALES (est): 8.6MM **Privately Held**
WEB: www.tesarindustrialcontractors.com
SIC: **1796 4212 4213** Machinery installation; heavy machinery transport, local; heavy machinery transport

(G-6518)
TH MARTIN INC
8500 Brookpark Rd (44129-6806)
PHONE.....................................216 741-2020
Thomas H Martin, *President*
Michael Martin, *Vice Pres*
Ryan Pepper, *Project Mgr*
Tony Salamone, *Foreman/Supr*
Bonnie M Felice, *Controller*
EMP: 100
SQ FT: 66,000
SALES (est): 24.8MM **Privately Held**
SIC: **1711** Ventilation & duct work contractor

(G-6519)
THE ANTER BROTHERS COMPANY (PA)
Also Called: Davis Tobacco Co
12501 Elmwood Ave (44111-5909)
PHONE.....................................216 252-4555
Richard G Anter, *President*
Victor M Anter Jr, *Vice Pres*
George M Anter, *Treasurer*
Lester T Tolt, *Asst Sec*
EMP: 48
SQ FT: 100,000
SALES (est): 6.1MM **Privately Held**
SIC: **5194 5145** Whol Tobacco Products Whol Confectionery

(G-6520)
THE CLEVELAND-CLIFFS IRON CO
1100 Superior Ave E # 1500 (44114-2530)
PHONE.....................................216 694-5700
J A Carrabba, *CEO*
D S Gallagher, *President*
W R Calfee, *Exec VP*
Laurie Brlas, *CFO*
EMP: 176
SQ FT: 40,000
SALES (est): 14.1MM
SALES (corp-wide): 2.3B **Publicly Held**
SIC: **1011** Iron ore mining; iron ore beneficiating
PA: Cleveland-Cliffs Inc.
    200 Public Sq Ste 3300
    Cleveland OH 44114
    216 694-5700

(G-6521)
THERMAL TREATMENT CENTER INC (HQ)
Also Called: Nettleton Steel Treating Div
1101 E 55th St (44103-1026)
PHONE.....................................216 881-8100
Carmen Paponitti, *President*
Jack Luck, *Vice Pres*
Louise Profughi, *Treasurer*
EMP: 35 EST: 1945
SQ FT: 85,000

SALES (est): 7.1MM
SALES (corp-wide): 9.4MM **Privately Held**
WEB: www.htg.cc
SIC: **3398 8711** Metal heat treating; engineering services
PA: Hi Tecmetal Group, Inc.
    1101 E 55th St
    Cleveland OH 44103
    216 881-8100

(G-6522)
THIRD FEDERAL SAVINGS (HQ)
7007 Broadway Ave (44105-1490)
PHONE.....................................800 844-7333
Marc A Stefanski, *Ch of Bd*
Judie Johnson, *General Mgr*
Snow Mendelsohn, *Regional Mgr*
Michelle Hay, *Business Mgr*
John P Ringenbach, *COO*
EMP: 300 EST: 1938
SALES: 430.3MM
SALES (corp-wide): 894.9MM **Publicly Held**
SIC: **6035** Federal savings & loan associations
PA: Third Federal Savings
    103 Foulk Rd Ste 101
    Wilmington DE 19803
    302 661-2009

(G-6523)
THIRD FEDERAL SAVINGS
5950 Ridge Rd (44129-3998)
PHONE.....................................440 885-4900
Donna Walraph, *Manager*
EMP: 26
SALES (corp-wide): 894.9MM **Publicly Held**
SIC: **6162** Mortgage bankers & correspondents
HQ: Third Federal Savings And Loan Association Of Cleveland
    7007 Broadway Ave
    Cleveland OH 44105
    800 844-7333

(G-6524)
THIRD FEDERAL SAVINGS
Also Called: Third Federal Savings & Loan
6849 Pearl Rd (44130-3616)
PHONE.....................................440 843-6300
Sandy Long, *Manager*
EMP: 26
SALES (corp-wide): 894.9MM **Publicly Held**
SIC: **6035** Federal savings & loan associations
HQ: Third Federal Savings And Loan Association Of Cleveland
    7007 Broadway Ave
    Cleveland OH 44105
    800 844-7333

(G-6525)
THISTLEDOWN INC
Also Called: Thistledown Racetrack
21501 Emery Rd (44128-4556)
PHONE.....................................216 662-8600
Fax: 216 662-5339
EMP: 200
SQ FT: 340,000
SALES (est): 13.3MM **Privately Held**
SIC: **7948** Racing Or Track Operation

(G-6526)
THOMPSON HINE LLP (PA)
127 Public Sq (44114-1217)
PHONE.....................................216 566-5500
Kip T Bollin, *President*
Deborah Z Read, *Managing Prtnr*
Michael L Hardy, *Partner*
James B Aronoff, *Partner*
April M Boise, *Partner*
EMP: 370
SQ FT: 145,000
SALES (est): 176.3MM **Privately Held**
WEB: www.thompsonhine.com
SIC: **8111** General practice law office

(G-6527)
THREE VILLAGE CONDOMINIUM
5150 Three Village Dr (44124-3772)
PHONE.....................................440 461-1483
V S Sagal, *President*
Harrison Fuerst, *President*

EMP: 37
SQ FT: 261,000
SALES (est): 1MM **Privately Held**
SIC: **8641** Condominium association

(G-6528)
THRIFTY RENT-A-CAR SYSTEM INC
Also Called: Thrifty Car Rental
7701 Day Dr (44129-5604)
PHONE.....................................440 842-1660
Joseph E Cappy, *Ch of Bd*
EMP: 30
SALES (corp-wide): 8.8B **Publicly Held**
SIC: **7514** Rent-a-car service
HQ: Thrifty Rent-A-Car System, Inc.
    8501 Williams Rd
    Estero FL 33928
    239 301-7000

(G-6529)
THYSSENKRUPP MATERIALS NA INC
Ken-Mac Metals
17901 Englewood Dr (44130-3454)
PHONE.....................................440 234-7500
Victoria Brolund, *Sales Staff*
Timothy Yost, *Branch Mgr*
Gary Halterman, *Manager*
EMP: 202
SALES (corp-wide): 39.8B **Privately Held**
SIC: **5051** Nonferrous metal sheets, bars, rods, etc.; aluminum bars, rods, ingots, sheets, pipes, plates, etc.
HQ: Thyssenkrupp Materials Na, Inc.
    22355 W 11 Mile Rd
    Southfield MI 48033
    248 233-5600

(G-6530)
TILDEN MINING COMPANY LC (HQ)
200 Public Sq Ste 3300 (44114-2315)
PHONE.....................................216 694-5700
Lourenco Goncalves, *President*
P Kelly Tompkins, *COO*
Terry Fedor, *Exec VP*
Maurice Harapiak, *Exec VP*
Terrence Mee, *Exec VP*
EMP: 580
SALES (est): 346.6MM
SALES (corp-wide): 2.3B **Publicly Held**
SIC: **1011** Iron ore mining; iron ore pelletizing; iron ore beneficiating
PA: Cleveland-Cliffs Inc.
    200 Public Sq Ste 3300
    Cleveland OH 44114
    216 694-5700

(G-6531)
TOLEDO INNS INC
Also Called: Crowne Plaza Cleveland Airport
7230 Engle Rd (44130-3427)
PHONE.....................................440 243-4040
J B Patel, *Principal*
EMP: 32
SQ FT: 61,845
SALES (est): 3.5MM **Privately Held**
SIC: **7011** Hotels

(G-6532)
TOM PAIGE CATERING COMPANY
2275 E 55th St (44103-4452)
PHONE.....................................216 431-4236
Thomas E Paige, *President*
Ryan Strickland, *Vice Pres*
EMP: 35
SQ FT: 92,000
SALES (est): 4.1MM **Privately Held**
SIC: **8322** Meal delivery program

(G-6533)
TOSHIBA AMER BUS SOLUTIONS INC
7850 Hub Pkwy (44125-5711)
PHONE.....................................216 642-7555
Gary Miller, *Branch Mgr*
EMP: 37

SALES (corp-wide): 37B **Privately Held**
WEB: www.levenstein.com
SIC: **5999 7629** Business machines & equipment; facsimile equipment; photocopy machines; telephone equipment & systems; business machine repair, electric
HQ: Toshiba America Business Solutions, Inc.
    25530 Commercentre Dr
    Lake Forest CA 92630
    949 462-6000

(G-6534)
TOTAL TRANSPORTATION TRCKG INC
Also Called: R J W
5755 Granger Rd Ste 400 (44131-1456)
PHONE.....................................216 398-6090
Jeffrey Wenham, *President*
Ed Tovey, *Vice Pres*
EMP: 25
SQ FT: 6,000
SALES (est): 1.7MM **Privately Held**
SIC: **4789** Cabs, horse drawn: for hire

(G-6535)
TOTAL WHOLESALE INC
Also Called: Seaway Cash N Carry
3900 Woodland Ave (44115-3411)
PHONE.....................................216 361-5757
Ali Faraj, *President*
EMP: 30
SQ FT: 1,000
SALES (est): 10.3MM **Privately Held**
WEB: www.seawaycashncarry.com
SIC: **5141** Food brokers

(G-6536)
TOURS OF BLACK HERITAGE INC
Also Called: Tobh
8800 Woodland Ave (44104-3221)
PHONE.....................................440 247-2737
Arline Burks, *CEO*
Dakota Gant, *President*
EMP: 63
SQ FT: 5,000
SALES (est): 2.5MM **Privately Held**
SIC: **4725** Tour Operator

(G-6537)
TOWARDS EMPLOYMENT INC
1255 Euclid Ave Ste 300 (44115-1807)
PHONE.....................................216 696-5750
Jill Rizika, *Exec Dir*
EMP: 40
SQ FT: 12,500
SALES: 5.6MM **Privately Held**
WEB: www.towardsemployment.org
SIC: **8641** Civic social & fraternal associations

(G-6538)
TRAFFTECH INC
7000 Hubbard Ave (44127-1419)
PHONE.....................................216 361-8808
William J Porter, *President*
Carol Porter, *Vice Pres*
Kim Mc Peak, *Admin Sec*
EMP: 50
SQ FT: 55,000
SALES (est): 7.6MM **Privately Held**
SIC: **1611** General contractor, highway & street construction

(G-6539)
TRANE INC
Also Called: Trane Cleveland
9555 Rockside Rd Ste 350 (44125-6283)
PHONE.....................................440 946-7823
EMP: 30 **Privately Held**
SIC: **1711** Warm air heating & air conditioning contractor; refrigeration contractor
HQ: Trane Inc.
    1 Centennial Ave Ste 101
    Piscataway NJ 08854
    732 652-7100

(G-6540)
TRANSCON BUILDERS INC (PA)
25250 Rockside Rd Ste 2 (44146-1839)
PHONE.....................................440 439-3400
Peter Rzepka, *Ch of Bd*
Fred Rzepka, *President*
Lawrence Apple, *Vice Pres*

Stanley Freeman, *Vice Pres*
EMP: 30
SQ FT: 14,000
SALES (est): 38.4MM **Privately Held**
WEB: www.transconbuilders.com
SIC: 6513 1522 Apartment building operators; residential construction

(G-6541)
TRANSCORE ITS LLC
Also Called: Trans Core
6930 Engle Rd Ste Y (44130-8459)
PHONE..................................440 243-2222
Edward L Brisann Sr, *Manager*
EMP: 25
SALES (corp-wide): 5.1B **Publicly Held**
SIC: 8711 Engineering services
HQ: Transcore Its, Llc
   3721 Tecport Dr Ste 102
   Harrisburg PA 17111
   717 561-5869

(G-6542)
TRANSDIGM GROUP INCORPORATED (PA)
1301 E 9th St Ste 3000 (44114-1871)
PHONE..................................216 706-2960
W Nicholas Howley, *Ch of Bd*
Kevin Stein, *President*
Jorge L Valladares III, *COO*
Bernt G Iversen II, *Exec VP*
Jorge Valladares, *Exec VP*
EMP: 136
SQ FT: 20,100
SALES: 3.8B **Publicly Held**
WEB: www.transdigm.com
SIC: 3728 5088 Aircraft parts & equipment; aircraft equipment & supplies

(G-6543)
TRANSPORT SERVICES INC (PA)
10499 Royalton Rd (44133-4432)
PHONE..................................440 582-4900
Adam Therrien, *President*
Albert Therrien, *Chairman*
Tom Soggs, *Vice Pres*
Patricia Therrien, *Vice Pres*
Mike Collins, *CFO*
EMP: 63
SQ FT: 20,000
SALES (est): 21.4MM **Privately Held**
WEB: www.transportservices.net
SIC: 5013 7519 7539 Trailer parts & accessories; trailer rental; trailer repair

(G-6544)
TRANSPORTATION UNLIMITED INC (PA)
3740 Carnegie Ave Ste 101 (44115-2756)
PHONE..................................216 426-0088
Samuel Lucarelli, *President*
Jason Lucarelli, *Corp Secy*
Michael Panzarelli, *Vice Pres*
EMP: 1450 EST: 1974
SQ FT: 40,000
SALES (est): 52.8MM **Privately Held**
SIC: 7363 4213 4212 Truck driver services; trucking, except local; local trucking, without storage

(G-6545)
TRANSYSTEMS CORPORATION
1100 Superior Ave E # 1000 (44114-2520)
PHONE..................................216 861-1780
Tracy Engle, *Branch Mgr*
EMP: 30
SALES (corp-wide): 144.2MM **Privately Held**
SIC: 8711 Consulting engineer
PA: Transystems Corporation
   2400 Pershing Rd Ste 400
   Kansas City MO 64108
   816 329-8700

(G-6546)
TRAVELERS PROPERTY CSLTY CORP
Also Called: Travelers Insurance
6150 Oak Tree Blvd # 400 (44131-6917)
PHONE..................................216 643-2100
Paul Nebraska, *Manager*
Frank Hager, *Manager*
EMP: 110

SALES (corp-wide): 30.2B **Publicly Held**
WEB: www.travelerspc.com
SIC: 6411 Insurance agents
HQ: Travelers Property Casualty Corp.
   1 Tower Sq 8ms
   Hartford CT 06183

(G-6547)
TRI ZOB INC
Also Called: West Park Animal Hospital
4117 Rocky River Dr (44135-1107)
PHONE..................................216 252-4500
Borys Pakush, *President*
EMP: 30
SALES (est): 1.4MM **Privately Held**
WEB: www.westparkanimalhospital.com
SIC: 0742 Animal hospital services, pets & other animal specialties

(G-6548)
TRIAD ENGINEERING & CONTG CO (PA)
9715 Clinton Rd (44144-1031)
PHONE..................................440 786-1000
Clifford J Kassouf, *President*
Ernest P Mansour, *Principal*
Philip Kassouf, *Treasurer*
Paul Kassouf, *Admin Sec*
EMP: 30
SQ FT: 5,600
SALES (est): 13.2MM **Privately Held**
WEB: www.triad-engineering.com
SIC: 8711 Engineering services

(G-6549)
TRIMARK USA LLC
Trimark S S Kemp
4567 Willow Pkwy (44125-1041)
PHONE..................................216 271-7700
Tomwine Claw, *Manager*
EMP: 100
SALES (corp-wide): 1B **Privately Held**
SIC: 5046 Restaurant equipment & supplies
PA: Trimark Usa, Llc
   505 Collins St
   Attleboro MA 02703
   508 399-2400

(G-6550)
TROLLEY TOURS OF CLEVELAND
Also Called: Lolly The Trolley
1790 Columbus Rd (44113-2412)
P.O. Box 91658 (44101-3658)
PHONE..................................216 771-4484
Sherrill Paul, *President*
Peter Paul, *Treasurer*
EMP: 40
SQ FT: 12,000
SALES (est): 4.6MM **Privately Held**
WEB: www.lollytrolley.com
SIC: 4725 Tours, conducted

(G-6551)
TRX GREAT PLAINS INC
6600 Bessemer Ave (44127-1804)
PHONE..................................855 259-9259
EMP: 75 EST: 2010
SALES (est): 6.2MM **Privately Held**
SIC: 4731 Freight Transportation Arrangement

(G-6552)
TSS ACQUISITION COMPANY (HQ)
Also Called: TSS Technologies
25101 Chagrin Blvd D (44122-5643)
PHONE..................................513 772-7000
Marc Drapp, *CEO*
EMP: 100
SQ FT: 93,600
SALES: 21MM
SALES (corp-wide): 226.8MM **Privately Held**
SIC: 7549 Automotive customizing services, non-factory basis; automotive maintenance services
PA: Resilience Capital Partners Llc
   25101 Chagrin Blvd # 350
   Cleveland OH 44122
   216 292-0200

(G-6553)
TUCKER ELLIS LLP
950 Main Ave Ste 1100 (44113-7213)
PHONE..................................720 897-4400
Frederick Wich, *Branch Mgr*
EMP: 95
SALES (est): 3.6MM
SALES (corp-wide): 49.1MM **Privately Held**
SIC: 8111 General practice attorney, lawyer
PA: Tucker Ellis Llp
   950 Main Ave Ste 1100
   Cleveland OH 44113
   216 592-5000

(G-6554)
TUCKER ELLIS LLP (PA)
950 Main Ave Ste 1100 (44113-7213)
PHONE..................................216 592-5000
Robert Tucker, *Partner*
Stephen Ellis, *Partner*
Kim West, *Partner*
Arthur Bernstein, *COO*
Ann Caresani, *Counsel*
EMP: 201
SQ FT: 100,000
SALES (est): 49.1MM **Privately Held**
WEB: www.tuckerellis.com
SIC: 8111 General practice attorney, lawyer

(G-6555)
TUDOR ARMS MSTR SUBTENANT LLC
Also Called: Doubletree By Hilton
10660 Carnegie Ave (44106-3019)
P.O. Box 14100 (44114-0100)
PHONE..................................216 696-6611
Piyaporn Pongpeerapat, *Controller*
David Minah, *Manager*
Jori Maron,
EMP: 100
SALES (est): 3MM **Privately Held**
SIC: 8741 Hotel or motel management

(G-6556)
TURNER CONSTRUCTION COMPANY
1422 Euclid Ave Ste 1400 (44115-2015)
PHONE..................................216 522-1180
Jeffery V Abke, *Project Mgr*
Mark Dent, *Branch Mgr*
EMP: 50
SALES (corp-wide): 579.6MM **Privately Held**
WEB: www.tcco.com
SIC: 1542 Commercial & office building, new construction
HQ: Turner Construction Company Inc
   375 Hudson St Fl 6
   New York NY 10014
   212 229-6000

(G-6557)
U S ASSOCIATES REALTY INC
4700 Rockside Rd Ste 150 (44131-2171)
PHONE..................................216 663-3400
Al Dailide, *President*
Susan Dailide, *Admin Sec*
EMP: 25 EST: 1973
SALES (est): 440K **Privately Held**
WEB: www.usassoc.com
SIC: 6531 Real estate brokers & agents

(G-6558)
U S LABORATORIES INC
33095 Bainbridge Rd (44139-2834)
PHONE..................................440 248-1223
Ratanjit S Sondhe, *President*
EMP: 30
SQ FT: 60,000
SALES (est): 1.7MM
SALES (corp-wide): 85.9B **Publicly Held**
SIC: 8731 Chemical laboratory, except testing
HQ: The Dow Chemical Company
   2211 H H Dow Way
   Midland MI 48642
   989 636-1000

(G-6559)
U S TITLE AGENCY INC
1213 Prospect Ave E # 400 (44115-1260)
PHONE..................................216 621-1424

Gerald Goldberg, *President*
William Boukalik, *COO*
Michael Gerome, *Senior VP*
Robert Levine, *Senior VP*
EMP: 33
SALES (est): 13.2MM **Privately Held**
SIC: 6361 6531 Real estate title insurance; real estate agents & managers

(G-6560)
UBS FINANCIAL SERVICES INC
2000 Auburn Dr Ste 100 (44122-4328)
PHONE..................................216 831-3400
John Minnillo, *Manager*
John Ryan, *Advisor*
EMP: 50
SALES (corp-wide): 29.4B **Privately Held**
SIC: 6211 Stock brokers & dealers
HQ: Ubs Financial Services Inc.
   1285 Ave Of The Americas
   New York NY 10019
   212 713-2000

(G-6561)
UHHS/CSAHS - CUYAHOGA INC
6935 Treeline Dr Ste J (44141-3375)
PHONE..................................440 746-3401
John Rusnaczyk, *President*
EMP: 70
SALES: 14.3MM **Privately Held**
SIC: 7389 Financial services

(G-6562)
UHMG DEPARTMENT OF UROLOGIST (PA)
11100 Euclid Ave (44106-1716)
PHONE..................................216 844-3009
Firouz Daneshgari, *President*
Brad Calabrese, *General Mgr*
Alan Wiggers, *Med Doctor*
Sherri White, *Manager*
James Persky, *Surgeon*
EMP: 42
SQ FT: 2,500
SALES (est): 4.3MM **Privately Held**
SIC: 8011 Urologist

(G-6563)
ULMER & BERNE LLP (PA)
Also Called: Ulmer & Berne Illinois
1660 W 2nd St Ste 1100 (44113-1406)
PHONE..................................216 583-7000
Jeffrey S Dunlap, *Ch of Bd*
John J Haggerty, *Ch of Bd*
Richard T Hamilton, *Ch of Bd*
Richard G Hardy, *Ch of Bd*
Peter A Rome, *Ch of Bd*
EMP: 284
SQ FT: 65,000
SALES (est): 85.9MM **Privately Held**
SIC: 8111 General practice law office

(G-6564)
UNION CLUB COMPANY
1211 Euclid Ave (44115-1865)
PHONE..................................216 621-4230
John Wheeler, *President*
Lawrence McFadden, *General Mgr*
John Sherwood, *Vice Pres*
Mary Laughlin, *Treasurer*
Nancy Zaroogian, *Sales Mgr*
EMP: 75
SQ FT: 75,000
SALES (est): 3.7MM **Privately Held**
WEB: www.unionclub.com
SIC: 8641 5813 5812 Social club, membership; drinking places; eating places

(G-6565)
UNITED AGENCIES INC
1422 Euclid Ave Ste 510 (44115-1901)
PHONE..................................216 696-8044
John Boyle III, *President*
Tim Bowman, *Vice Pres*
Suzanne Eggli, *Vice Pres*
Susan Minner, *Broker*
Luis Jaramillo, *Accounts Mgr*
EMP: 30
SALES (est): 7.2MM **Privately Held**
SIC: 6411 Insurance agents

(G-6566)
UNITED AIRLINES INC
Also Called: Continental Airlines
5970 Cargo Rd (44135-3110)
PHONE..................................216 501-4700

Connie Mutch, *Human Res Mgr*
Tom Braun, *Manager*
EMP: 167
SALES (corp-wide): 41.3B **Publicly Held**
WEB: www.continental.com
SIC: 4512 Air passenger carrier, scheduled
HQ: United Airlines, Inc.
     233 S Wacker Dr Ste 710
     Chicago IL 60606
     872 825-4000

(G-6567)
UNITED ATMTC HTNG SPPLY OF CLV (PA)
Also Called: United Electric Motor Repair
2125 Superior Ave E (44114-2101)
PHONE...................................216 621-5571
Michael Morris, *President*
Lionel Meister, *Vice Pres*
Elizabeth Morris, *Treasurer*
Joan Meister, *Admin Sec*
EMP: 40
SQ FT: 50,000
SALES (est): 5.5MM **Privately Held**
SIC: 5074 5075 Heating equipment (hydronic); air conditioning equipment, except room units

(G-6568)
UNITED CEREBRAL PALSY (PA)
10011 Euclid Ave (44106-4701)
PHONE...................................216 791-8363
Patricia S Otter, *President*
Trish Rooney, *Director*
Randy Simmons, *Administration*
EMP: 235 **EST:** 1950
SQ FT: 40,000
SALES: 10.4MM **Privately Held**
SIC: 8361 8331 Rehabilitation center, residential: health care incidental; vocational rehabilitation agency

(G-6569)
UNITED CEREBRAL PALSY
Also Called: Edendale House
1374 Edendale St (44121-1627)
PHONE...................................216 381-9993
Diane Mc Kenna, *Branch Mgr*
EMP: 60
SALES (corp-wide): 10.4MM **Privately Held**
SIC: 8361 8052 8059 Rehabilitation center, residential: health care incidental; intermediate care facilities; home for the mentally retarded, exc. skilled or intermediate
PA: United Cerebral Palsy Association Of Greater Cleveland, Inc.
     10011 Euclid Ave
     Cleveland OH 44106
     216 791-8363

(G-6570)
UNITED CONSUMER FINCL SVCS CO
865 Bassett Rd (44145-1142)
PHONE...................................440 835-3230
Cliff Hooley, *CEO*
Bill Francis, *President*
Scott Wolf, *President*
William Ciszczon, *Vice Pres*
EMP: 200
SQ FT: 27,000
SALES: 44.9MM
SALES (corp-wide): 225.3B **Publicly Held**
SIC: 6141 Consumer finance companies
HQ: The Scott Fetzer Company
     28800 Clemens Rd
     Westlake OH 44145
     440 892-3000

(G-6571)
UNITED FD COML WKRS LOCAL 880 (PA)
2828 Euclid Ave (44115-2455)
PHONE...................................216 241-5930
Thomas H Robertson, *President*
Robert W Grauvogl, *Admin Sec*
EMP: 43
SQ FT: 30,000
SALES (est): 4.2MM **Privately Held**
SIC: 8631 6512 Labor union; commercial & industrial building operation

(G-6572)
UNITED GARAGE & SERVICE CORP (PA)
2069 W 3rd St (44113-2502)
PHONE...................................216 623-1550
EMP: 60
SQ FT: 10,000
SALES (est): 15.2MM **Privately Held**
SIC: 4121 7539 Taxicab Service & Repairs Taxicabs

(G-6573)
UNITED HEALTHCARE OHIO INC
1001 Lkeside Ave Ste 1000 (44114)
PHONE...................................216 694-4080
Lisa Chapman-Smith, *CEO*
Marvin Gossett, *Technical Mgr*
Thomas Sullivan, *Exec Dir*
Chelsey Berstler, *Director*
EMP: 80
SALES (corp-wide): 226.2B **Publicly Held**
WEB: www.uhc.com
SIC: 6324 Group hospitalization plans
HQ: United Healthcare Of Ohio, Inc.
     9200 Worthington Rd
     Columbus OH 43085
     614 410-7000

(G-6574)
UNITED LABOR AGENCY INC
737 Bolivar Rd Ste 3000 (44115-1233)
PHONE...................................216 664-3446
D Megenhardt, *Exec Dir*
David Megenhardt, *Exec Dir*
EMP: 115
SQ FT: 20,000
SALES: 9.2MM **Privately Held**
WEB: www.ula-ohio.org
SIC: 8399 Community development groups

(G-6575)
UNITED OMAHA LIFE INSURANCE CO
6060 Rockside Woods # 330 (44131-7303)
PHONE...................................216 573-6900
Neil Chonofski, *Manager*
Richard Doyle, *Manager*
EMP: 25
SALES (corp-wide): 8.7B **Privately Held**
SIC: 6311 Life insurance carriers
HQ: United Of Omaha Life Insurance Company
     Mutual Of Omaha Plaza
     Omaha NE 68175
     402 342-7600

(G-6576)
UNITED PARCEL SERVICE INC
Also Called: UPS
17940 Englewood Dr (44130-3463)
PHONE...................................440 826-2591
Oscar Vasquez, *Manager*
Tania Renko, *Manager*
EMP: 400
SALES (corp-wide): 71.8B **Publicly Held**
WEB: www.ups.com
SIC: 4215 Parcel delivery, vehicular
PA: United Parcel Service, Inc.
     55 Glenlake Pkwy
     Atlanta GA 30328
     404 828-6000

(G-6577)
UNITED PARCEL SERVICE INC OH
Also Called: UPS
4300 E 68th St (44105-5797)
PHONE...................................800 742-5877
EMP: 158
SALES (corp-wide): 71.8B **Publicly Held**
SIC: 4215 Parcel delivery, vehicular; package delivery, vehicular
HQ: United Parcel Service, Inc. (Oh)
     55 Glenlake Pkwy
     Atlanta GA 30328
     404 828-6000

(G-6578)
UNITED PARCEL SERVICE INC OH
Also Called: UPS
18685 Sheldon Rd (44130-2471)
PHONE...................................216 676-4560
EMP: 316

SALES (corp-wide): 71.8B **Publicly Held**
SIC: 7389 Mailing & messenger services
HQ: United Parcel Service, Inc. (Oh)
     55 Glenlake Pkwy
     Atlanta GA 30328
     404 828-6000

(G-6579)
UNITED STATES CARGO & COURIER
Also Called: U S Cargo
4735 W 150th St Ste D (44135-3300)
PHONE...................................216 325-0483
Tim Pullman, *Branch Mgr*
EMP: 30
SALES (corp-wide): 11.1MM **Privately Held**
WEB: www.usccs.com
SIC: 4215 4513 Courier services, except by air; air courier services
HQ: United States Cargo & Courier Service Incorporated
     900 Williams Ave
     Columbus OH
     614 552-2746

(G-6580)
UNITED WAY GREATER CLEVELAND (PA)
1331 Euclid Ave (44115-1819)
PHONE...................................216 436-2100
William Kitson, *CEO*
Sylvia Cash, *Vice Pres*
Dan Mansoor, *Vice Pres*
Michael E Headen, *CFO*
Tom Casterline, *VP Finance*
EMP: 121
SQ FT: 90,000
SALES: 39.8MM **Privately Held**
WEB: www.uws.org
SIC: 8399 United Fund councils; fund raising organization, non-fee basis

(G-6581)
UNIVERSAL GRINDING CORPORATION
1234 W 78th St (44102-1914)
PHONE...................................216 631-9410
Donald R Toth, *President*
Kevin Decaire, *Corp Secy*
Nancy Toth, *Vice Pres*
▼ **EMP:** 49
SQ FT: 86,000
SALES: 7MM **Privately Held**
WEB: www.universalgrinding.com
SIC: 7389 Grinding, precision: commercial or industrial

(G-6582)
UNIVERSAL OIL INC
265 Jefferson Ave (44113-2594)
PHONE...................................216 771-4300
John J Purcell, *President*
Scott Fox, *COO*
Steven Cala, *Controller*
EMP: 30
SQ FT: 25,000
SALES (est): 30.9MM **Privately Held**
WEB: www.universaloil.com
SIC: 5171 2992 Petroleum bulk stations; lubricating oils

(G-6583)
UNIVERSAL STEEL COMPANY
6600 Grant Ave (44105-5692)
PHONE...................................216 883-4972
Richard W Williams, *President*
David P Miller, *Chairman*
Tom Vinci, *COO*
William B Bourne, *Treasurer*
Stephen F Ruscher, *Treasurer*
▲ **EMP:** 100
SQ FT: 200,000
SALES (est): 28MM
SALES (corp-wide): 78.3MM **Privately Held**
WEB: www.univsteel.com
SIC: 3444 5051 Sheet metalwork; steel
PA: Columbia National Group, Inc.
     6600 Grant Ave
     Cleveland OH 44105
     216 883-4972

(G-6584)
UNIVERSITIES SPACE RES ASSN
Also Called: National Center For Space Expl
10900 Euclid Ave (44106-1712)
PHONE...................................216 368-0750
Iwan Alexander, *Director*
EMP: 40
SALES (corp-wide): 115.8MM **Privately Held**
SIC: 8733 Scientific research agency
PA: Universities Space Research Association
     7178 Columbia Gateway Dr
     Columbia MD 21046
     410 730-2656

(G-6585)
UNIVERSITY ANESTHESIOLOGISTS
11100 Euclid Ave Ste 2517 (44106-1716)
PHONE...................................216 844-3777
David Rapkin, *Med Doctor*
David Wallace, *Med Doctor*
Cindy Patrzyk, *Administration*
EMP: 50
SALES (est): 4.5MM **Privately Held**
SIC: 8011 Anesthesiologist

(G-6586)
UNIVERSITY CIRCLE INCORPORATED (PA)
Also Called: UCI
10831 Magnolia Dr (44106-1887)
PHONE...................................216 791-3900
Christopher Ronayne, *President*
Jim Walton, *Vice Pres*
Daniel J Stahura, *CFO*
David Razum, *Comms Mgr*
Diane Hansson, *Manager*
EMP: 30
SQ FT: 10,000
SALES: 11.3MM **Privately Held**
SIC: 6531 Real estate agents & managers

(G-6587)
UNIVERSITY HOSPITALS
Also Called: U H Ahuja Medical Center
3999 Richmond Rd (44122-6046)
PHONE...................................216 593-5500
Vanessa Sowell, *Human Res Dir*
Susan Juris, *Branch Mgr*
EMP: 500
SALES (corp-wide): 580MM **Privately Held**
SIC: 8062 General medical & surgical hospitals
PA: University Hospitals Health System, Inc.
     3605 Warrensville Ctr Rd
     Shaker Heights OH 44122
     216 767-8900

(G-6588)
UNIVERSITY HOSPITALS
2915 Ludlow Rd (44120-2308)
P.O. Box 202625, Shaker Heights (44120-8127)
PHONE...................................216 536-3020
Charles Sullivan, *Principal*
EMP: 35 **EST:** 2015
SALES (est): 3.7MM **Privately Held**
SIC: 8062 General medical & surgical hospitals

(G-6589)
UNIVERSITY HOSPITALS
12200 Fairhill Rd Frnt (44120-1058)
PHONE...................................216 844-6400
Bill Ditirro, *Manager*
EMP: 40
SALES (corp-wide): 580MM **Privately Held**
SIC: 8062 General medical & surgical hospitals
PA: University Hospitals Health System, Inc.
     3605 Warrensville Ctr Rd
     Shaker Heights OH 44122
     216 767-8900

▲ = Import ▼=Export
◆ =Import/Export

(G-6590)
UNIVERSITY HOSPITALS
Also Called: Ireland Cancer Center
11100 Euclid Ave Wrn5065 (44106-1716)
PHONE..216 844-8797
Dr Danton Gerson, *Branch Mgr*
Mary Wright, *Exec Sec*
EMP: 85
SALES (corp-wide): 580MM **Privately Held**
SIC: 8733 8011 8741 Medical research; offices & clinics of medical doctors; management services
PA: University Hospitals Health System, Inc.
3605 Warrensville Ctr Rd
Shaker Heights OH 44122
216 767-8900

(G-6591)
UNIVERSITY HOSPITALS
Healthmatch
11001 Euclid Ave (44106-1713)
PHONE..216 767-8500
Bruce Wilkinfield, *Partner*
Baruch Kleinman, *Engineer*
EMP: 25
SALES (corp-wide): 580MM **Privately Held**
SIC: 8062 General medical & surgical hospitals
PA: University Hospitals Health System, Inc.
3605 Warrensville Ctr Rd
Shaker Heights OH 44122
216 767-8900

(G-6592)
UNIVERSITY HOSPITALS CLEVELAND
Also Called: Research Institute Univ Hosp
11100 Euclid Ave (44106-1716)
PHONE..216 844-1000
Tom Zenty, *President*
Amy Knott, *Division Mgr*
Kim Bixenstine, *Vice Pres*
Brent Carson, *Vice Pres*
Chenguttai Manohar, *Vice Pres*
EMP: 656
SALES (corp-wide): 580MM **Privately Held**
SIC: 8062 General medical & surgical hospitals
HQ: University Hospitals Of Cleveland
11100 Euclid Ave
Cleveland OH 44106
216 844-1000

(G-6593)
UNIVERSITY HOSPITALS CLEVELAND (HQ)
11100 Euclid Ave (44106-1716)
PHONE..216 844-1000
Thomas Zenty, *President*
Brian Albright, *Purch Agent*
Thomas Leskovec, *Research*
Bradley Bond, *Sales Staff*
Akansha Agrawal, *Med Doctor*
▲ EMP: 7000
SALES (est): 256.7MM
SALES (corp-wide): 580MM **Privately Held**
SIC: 8062 8069 General medical & surgical hospitals; specialty hospitals, except psychiatric
PA: University Hospitals Health System, Inc.
3605 Warrensville Ctr Rd
Shaker Heights OH 44122
216 767-8900

(G-6594)
UNIVERSITY HOSPITALS CLEVELAND
4510 Richmond Rd (44128-5757)
PHONE..216 844-4663
Mary Havannah, *Manager*
EMP: 70
SALES (corp-wide): 580MM **Privately Held**
SIC: 8062 8082 General medical & surgical hospitals; home health care services

HQ: University Hospitals Of Cleveland
11100 Euclid Ave
Cleveland OH 44106
216 844-1000

(G-6595)
UNIVERSITY HOSPITALS CLEVELAND
Rainbow Babies and Chld Hosp
11100 Euclid Ave (44106-1716)
PHONE..216 844-3528
Gary Weimer, *Senior VP*
Michelle Carter, *Manager*
Joyce Deptola, *Director*
Tim Kirchmeir, *Director*
EMP: 25
SALES (corp-wide): 580MM **Privately Held**
SIC: 8062 8741 General medical & surgical hospitals; management services
HQ: University Hospitals Of Cleveland
11100 Euclid Ave
Cleveland OH 44106
216 844-1000

(G-6596)
UNIVERSITY HOSPITALS HE
4510 Richmond Rd (44128-5757)
PHONE..216 844-4663
Mary Havannah, *Principal*
Becky Ivcic, *CFO*
Ralph Portzer, *Manager*
EMP: 350
SALES (est): 3MM
SALES (corp-wide): 580MM **Privately Held**
SIC: 8082 Home health care services
PA: University Hospitals Health System, Inc.
3605 Warrensville Ctr Rd
Shaker Heights OH 44122
216 767-8900

(G-6597)
UNIVERSITY HOSPITALS HEALTH SY
11100 Euclid Ave (44106-1716)
PHONE..216 844-4663
Thomas F Zenty III, *CEO*
EMP: 28
SALES (est): 269.9MM **Privately Held**
SIC: 8062 General medical & surgical hospitals

(G-6598)
UNIVERSITY MANOR HEALTHCARE
Also Called: UNIVERSITY MANOR HEALTH CARE CENTER
2186 Ambleside Dr (44106-4620)
PHONE..216 721-1400
George S Repchick, *President*
William I Weisberg, *Vice Pres*
Sarah Depompei, *Assistant*
EMP: 171 EST: 2002
SALES: 10.4MM
SALES (corp-wide): 157.7MM **Privately Held**
SIC: 8051 Skilled nursing care facilities
PA: Saber Healthcare Group, L.L.C.
26691 Richmond Rd Frnt
Bedford OH 44146
216 292-5706

(G-6599)
UNIVERSITY MANOR HLTH CARE CTR
2186 Ambleside Dr (44106-4620)
PHONE..216 721-1400
Suzanne Fromson, *President*
Patricia Weisberg, *Corp Secy*
Milton Fromson, *Shareholder*
EMP: 240
SALES (est): 7.4MM **Privately Held**
SIC: 8051 8052 Skilled nursing care facilities; intermediate care facilities

(G-6600)
UNIVERSITY OPHTHALMOLOGY ASSOC
1611 S Green Rd Ste 306c (44121-4192)
PHONE..216 382-8022
William Annable, *President*
Ronald Price MD, *Office Mgr*
EMP: 25

SALES (est): 2.3MM **Privately Held**
SIC: 8011 Ophthalmologist

(G-6601)
UNIVERSITY ORTHPEDIC ASSOC INC (PA)
Also Called: University Hospital
11100 Euclid Ave Ste 3001 (44106-1716)
PHONE..216 844-1000
Fred C Rothstein, *President*
Heidi Gartland, *Vice Pres*
Stephen Previs, *Research*
Paul Macdonald, *Engineer*
Michelle Puchowicz, *Engineer*
EMP: 25 EST: 1969
SQ FT: 2,300
SALES (est): 34.4MM **Privately Held**
SIC: 8011 Orthopedic physician

(G-6602)
UNIVERSITY RDLGSTS OF CLVELAND
Also Called: Cleveland University
2485 Euclid Ave (44115)
PHONE..216 844-1700
John Haaga, *Principal*
Adonis K Hijaz, *Urology*
EMP: 52 EST: 1976
SALES (est): 3.1MM **Privately Held**
SIC: 8011 Radiologist

(G-6603)
UNIVERSITY SETTLEMENT INC (PA)
4800 Broadway Ave (44127-1071)
PHONE..216 641-8948
Tracey Mason, *Director*
EMP: 40
SQ FT: 8,525
SALES (est): 2.4MM **Privately Held**
WEB: www.universitysettlement.net
SIC: 8399 Community development groups

(G-6604)
UNIVERSITY SUBURBAN HEALTH CTR (PA)
1611 S Green Rd Ste A61 (44121-4100)
PHONE..216 382-8920
John L Naylor Jr, *Principal*
Chuck Abbey, *Exec Dir*
EMP: 200
SQ FT: 27,500
SALES: 9.2MM **Privately Held**
SIC: 8011 Medical centers; ambulatory surgical center

(G-6605)
UNIVERSITY SURGEONS INC
11100 Euclid Ave 7002 (44106-1716)
PHONE..216 844-3021
Thomas Stellato, *President*
Cathy Korponic, *Office Mgr*
EMP: 25
SALES (est): 990.9K **Privately Held**
SIC: 8062 General medical & surgical hospitals

(G-6606)
URBAN LEAGU OF GREATER CLEVLND
2930 Prospect Ave E (44115-2608)
PHONE..216 622-0999
Myron F Robinson, *President*
Gregory Johnson, *COO*
Frank Usowell, *Vice Pres*
Tim Haas, *CFO*
EMP: 28
SQ FT: 1,800
SALES: 1.4MM **Privately Held**
WEB: www.ulcleveland.org
SIC: 8641 Civic associations

(G-6607)
URBAN ONE INC
Also Called: Wzak
6555 Carnegie Ave (44103-4637)
PHONE..216 579-1111
Eddiie Harreol, *Owner*
EMP: 52
SALES (corp-wide): 439.1MM **Publicly Held**
WEB: www.radio-one.com
SIC: 4832 Radio broadcasting stations

PA: Urban One, Inc.
1010 Wayne Ave Fl 14
Silver Spring MD 20910
301 429-3200

(G-6608)
URBAN ONE INC
Also Called: Were-AM
1041 Huron Rd E (44115-1706)
PHONE..216 861-0100
Tom Hershel, *General Mgr*
EMP: 70
SQ FT: 10,000
SALES (corp-wide): 439.1MM **Publicly Held**
WEB: www.radio-one.com
SIC: 4832 Radio broadcasting stations
PA: Urban One, Inc.
1010 Wayne Ave Fl 14
Silver Spring MD 20910
301 429-3200

(G-6609)
URS GROUP INC
1300 E 9th St Ste 500 (44114-1503)
PHONE..216 622-2300
Jeff Toney, *Engineer*
William Laubscher, *Branch Mgr*
Mary Sax, *Executive*
Mary Znidarsic, *Executive*
EMP: 100
SALES (corp-wide): 20.1B **Publicly Held**
SIC: 8711 Engineering services
HQ: Urs Group, Inc.
300 S Grand Ave Ste 1100
Los Angeles CA 90071
213 593-8000

(G-6610)
US COMMUNICATIONS AND ELC INC
4933 Neo Pkwy (44128-3103)
PHONE..440 519-0880
Patricia Connole, *CEO*
James Connole, *President*
Robert Williams, *Vice Pres*
Tony Wulk, *Vice Pres*
Tom Kaufhold, *Project Mgr*
EMP: 85
SQ FT: 50,000
SALES: 15MM **Privately Held**
WEB: www.uscande.com
SIC: 1731 Communications specialization

(G-6611)
USA PARKING SYSTEMS INC
1325 Carnegie Ave Frnt (44115-2836)
PHONE..216 621-9255
Lou Frangos, *President*
Pedro Chevalier, *Vice Pres*
Ashlee Brunello, *Human Res Mgr*
EMP: 80
SQ FT: 2,500
SALES (est): 4MM **Privately Held**
WEB: www.usaparking.com
SIC: 7521 Parking garage

(G-6612)
USF HOLLAND LLC
Also Called: USFreightways
10720 Memphis Ave (44144-2057)
PHONE..216 941-4340
Mike Dzura, *Human Res Mgr*
Joe Goodall, *Manager*
EMP: 150
SQ FT: 51,207
SALES (corp-wide): 5B **Publicly Held**
WEB: www.usfc.com
SIC: 4731 4213 4212 Freight forwarding; trucking, except local; local trucking, without storage
HQ: Usf Holland Llc
700 S Waverly Rd
Holland MI 49423
616 395-5000

(G-6613)
USHC PHYSICIANS INC
1611 S Green Rd Ste 260 (44121-4192)
PHONE..216 382-2036
Dr Steven Rudolph, *President*
J Dennis Morton, *President*
EMP: 25
SALES (est): 1.5MM **Privately Held**
SIC: 8011 Internal medicine, physician/surgeon

(G-6614)
UTILICON CORPORATION
6140 Parkland Blvd (44124-6142)
PHONE.............................216 391-8500
Kenneth Lavan, *President*
Ken Lavan, *Executive*
EMP: 50
SALES (est): 11.6MM **Privately Held**
WEB: www.utiliconcorp.com
SIC: 1623 Underground utilities contractor

(G-6615)
VAHALLA COMPANY INC
Also Called: Environmental Engineering Cons
3257 E 139th St (44120-3971)
P.O. Box 201607 (44120-8110)
PHONE.............................216 326-2245
Joseph H Daniels Jr, *President*
Jasper Day, *Director*
Kennar Hairston, *Director*
EMP: 35 EST: 1993
SQ FT: 2,500
SALES: 100K **Privately Held**
WEB: www.vahalla.com
SIC: 8748 Environmental consultant

(G-6616)
VALLEJO COMPANY
1340 E 38th St (44114-3829)
PHONE.............................216 741-3933
Katharine Yaroshak, *President*
EMP: 26
SALES: 6.2MM **Privately Held**
SIC: 4212 1623 Local trucking, without
storage; oil & gas pipeline construction;
sewer line construction

(G-6617)
VALLEY FORD TRUCK INC (PA)
Also Called: Valley Sterling of Cleveland
5715 Canal Rd (44125-3494)
PHONE.............................216 524-2400
Brian O'Donnell, *President*
Michelle Steibner, *Corp Secy*
Audrey Coffin, *Human Res Mgr*
David Krankowski, *Accounts Mgr*
Cheryl McDaniel, *Sales Staff*
◆ EMP: 68 EST: 1964
SQ FT: 15,000
SALES: 125MM **Privately Held**
WEB: www.valley2.com
SIC: 5013 5511 5521 5531 Truck parts &
accessories; automobiles, new & used;
trucks, tractors & trailers: used; truck
equipment & parts; automobiles & other
motor vehicles

(G-6618)
VALLEY RIDING
Also Called: ROCKY RIVER RIDING
19901 Puritas Ave (44135-1095)
PHONE.............................216 267-2525
Margaret Macelhany, *President*
Martha Costello, *Vice Pres*
Jeanette Swisher, *Treasurer*
EMP: 25
SALES: 671.5K **Privately Held**
WEB: www.valleyriding.com
SIC: 7999 Riding stable

(G-6619)
VALLEY VIEW FIRE DEPT
6899 Hathaway Rd (44125-4705)
PHONE.............................216 524-7200
Michael Tyna, *Finance Mgr*
Thomas Koscielski, *Manager*
EMP: 27
SALES (est): 2.5MM **Privately Held**
WEB: www.valleyview.net
SIC: 1542 Fire station construction

(G-6620)
VAND CORP
1301 E 9th St Ste 1900 (44114-1862)
PHONE.............................216 481-3788
Fax: 216 481-3066
EMP: 26
SALES (est): 2.1MM **Privately Held**
SIC: 8742 Management Consulting Serv-
ices

(G-6621)
VANDRA BROS CONSTRUCTION INC
24629 Broadway Ave (44146-6340)
PHONE.............................440 232-3030
Anthony Melarango, *President*
Peter Melarango, *Vice Pres*
Victor Melarango, *Treasurer*
Bruno Melarango, *Admin Sec*
EMP: 25
SQ FT: 10,000
SALES (est): 4.3MM **Privately Held**
SIC: 1771 Concrete work

(G-6622)
VEDISCOVERY LLC
Also Called: Visual Evidence/E-Discovery
1382 W 9th St Ste 400 (44113-1231)
PHONE.............................216 241-3443
Ronald Copfer, *CEO*
Daniel Copfer, *President*
Manfred Troibner,
EMP: 26
SQ FT: 6,000
SALES (est): 2MM **Privately Held**
SIC: 7371 7374 8742 Custom computer
programming services; data processing &
preparation; management consulting
services

(G-6623)
VERITIV OPERATING COMPANY
Also Called: Xpedx
9797 Sweet Valley Dr (44125-4241)
PHONE.............................216 901-5700
James Yamsek, *Purch Mgr*
Michael Doerrr, *Branch Mgr*
Robert Stelma, *Manager*
EMP: 100
SALES (corp-wide): 8.7B **Publicly Held**
WEB: www.internationalpaper.com
SIC: 5084 Processing & packaging equip-
ment; printing trades machinery, equip-
ment & supplies
HQ: Veritiv Operating Company
1000 Abernathy Rd
Atlanta GA 30328
770 391-8200

(G-6624)
VETERANS FGN WARS POST 2850
3296 W 61st St (44102-5614)
PHONE.............................216 631-2585
George Dennison, *Principal*
EMP: 100
SQ FT: 6,215
SALES: 57.4K **Privately Held**
SIC: 8641 Veterans' organization

(G-6625)
VETERANS HEALTH ADMINISTRATION
Also Called: Louis Stokes Cleveland Vamc
10701 East Blvd (44106-1702)
PHONE.............................216 791-3800
William Montague, *Director*
J Barry Hylton,
EMP: 3200 **Publicly Held**
WEB: www.veterans-ru.org
SIC: 8011 9451 Medical centers;
HQ: Veterans Health Administration
810 Vermont Ave Nw
Washington DC 20420

(G-6626)
VETERANS HEALTH ADMINISTRATION
Also Called: McCafferty Community Based
4242 Lorain Ave (44113-3715)
PHONE.............................216 939-0699
Jodell Howard, *Admin Asst*
Ingrid-Jane V Barcelona, *Nurse Practr*
EMP: 264 **Publicly Held**
WEB: www.veterans-ru.org
SIC: 8011 9451 Clinic, operated by physi-
cians; psychiatric clinic;
HQ: Veterans Health Administration
810 Vermont Ave Nw
Washington DC 20420

(G-6627)
VGS INC
2239 E 55th St (44103-4451)
PHONE.............................216 431-7800

Robert Comben Jr, *President*
James Huduk, *Vice Pres*
Mick Latkovich, *Vice Pres*
Donald E Carlton, *CFO*
James Hudak, *Sales Staff*
EMP: 200
SQ FT: 36,000
SALES: 5MM **Privately Held**
SIC: 8331 2326 2311 Job training & voca-
tional rehabilitation services; work uni-
forms; military uniforms, men's & youths':
purchased materials

(G-6628)
VICTORY WHITE METAL COMPANY (PA)
6100 Roland Ave (44127-1399)
PHONE.............................216 271-1400
Alex J Stanwick, *President*
Jennifer Sturman, *Admin Sec*
▲ EMP: 60 EST: 1920
SQ FT: 60,000
SALES (est): 30.8MM **Privately Held**
WEB: www.vwmc.com
SIC: 5085 3356 Valves & fittings; solder;
wire, bar, acid core, & rosin core; lead &
zinc; tin

(G-6629)
VICTORY WHITE METAL COMPANY
3027 E 55th St (44127-1275)
PHONE.............................216 271-1400
Tim Hess, *Manager*
EMP: 25
SQ FT: 50,000
SALES (corp-wide): 30.8MM **Privately
Held**
WEB: www.vwmc.com
SIC: 3341 4941 4225 Lead smelting & re-
fining (secondary); water supply; general
warehousing & storage
PA: The Victory White Metal Company
6100 Roland Ave
Cleveland OH 44127
216 271-1400

(G-6630)
VIKING EXPLOSIVES LLC
25800 Science Park Dr (44122-7339)
PHONE.............................218 263-8845
Bob Prittinen, *Manager*
EMP: 28
SALES (corp-wide): 22.6MM **Privately
Held**
SIC: 5169 2892 Explosives; explosives
HQ: Viking Explosives Llc
25800 Science Park Dr # 300
Cleveland OH
216 464-2400

(G-6631)
VILLAGE OF CUYAHOGA HEIGHTS (PA)
4863 E 71st St Frnt (44125-1080)
PHONE.............................216 641-7020
Barbara Biro, *Principal*
Jack Bacci, *Mayor*
EMP: 117 **Privately Held**
WEB: www.cuyahogaheights.com
SIC: 9111 8641 City & town managers' of-
fices; ; civic social & fraternal associations

(G-6632)
VILLAGE OF VALLEY VIEW
6848 Hathaway Rd (44125-4767)
PHONE.............................216 524-6511
Randall Westfall, *Mayor*
EMP: 150 **Privately Held**
SIC: 8741 Administrative management
PA: Village Of Valley View
6848 Hathaway Rd
Cleveland OH 44125
216 524-6511

(G-6633)
VILLAGE TRANSPORT CORP
6300 Wilson Mills Rd (44143-2109)
PHONE.............................440 461-5000
EMP: 131
SALES (est): 1.4MM
SALES (corp-wide): 31.9B **Publicly Held**
SIC: 4789 Transportation services

PA: The Progressive Corporation
6300 Wilson Mills Rd
Mayfield Village OH 44143
440 461-5000

(G-6634)
VISCONSI COMPANIES LTD
30050 Chagrin Blvd # 360 (44124-5716)
PHONE.............................216 464-5550
Dominic Visconsi Jr, *CEO*
Anthoni Visconsi II, *CEO*
Barry Fader, *Senior VP*
Michael Olsen, *Vice Pres*
Alan Prince, *CFO*
EMP: 30
SQ FT: 8,000
SALES (est): 5MM **Privately Held**
SIC: 6552 6531 Land subdividers & devel-
opers, commercial; real estate agents &
managers

(G-6635)
VISCONSI MANAGEMENT INC
Also Called: Visconsi Company
30050 Chagrin Blvd # 360 (44124-5716)
PHONE.............................216 464-5550
Dominic A Visconsi, *CEO*
Anthoni Visconsi II, *Co-CEO*
EMP: 30
SALES (est): 35.2K **Privately Held**
WEB: www.visconsi.com
SIC: 6512 Commercial & industrial building
operation

(G-6636)
VISITING NRSE ASSN OF MID-OHIO
Also Called: VNA
2500 E 22nd St (44115-3204)
PHONE.............................216 931-1300
Claire Zangerle, *CEO*
Holly Coughlin, *General Mgr*
Karen Hagerman, *Human Res Mgr*
Melissa Heileman, *Manager*
Sylvia Stevenson, *Manager*
EMP: 32
SALES: 1.6MM **Privately Held**
SIC: 8082 Visiting nurse service

(G-6637)
VITALYST
3615 Superior Ave E 4406a (44114-4139)
PHONE.............................216 201-9070
Kevin P Walters, *Branch Mgr*
EMP: 75 **Privately Held**
SIC: 7379 Computer related consulting
services
PA: Vitalyst, Llc
1 Bala Plz Ste 434
Bala Cynwyd PA 19004

(G-6638)
VITRAN EXPRESS INC
5300 Crayton Ave (44104-2832)
PHONE.............................216 426-8584
Rich Huffman, *Manager*
EMP: 100
SQ FT: 25,271
SALES (corp-wide): 109.4MM **Privately
Held**
SIC: 4213 Contract haulers
PA: Vitran Express, Inc.
12225 Stephens Rd
Warren MI 48089
317 803-4000

(G-6639)
VOCATIONAL GUIDANCE SERVICES (PA)
2239 E 55th St (44103-4451)
PHONE.............................216 431-7800
Robert E Comben Jr, *CEO*
Susie M Barragate, *President*
Tavi Gargano, *General Mgr*
Mick Latkovich, *General Mgr*
Et Al, *Principal*
EMP: 608
SQ FT: 130,931
SALES: 10.7MM **Privately Held**
SIC: 8331 Community service employment
training program

(G-6640)
VOCATIONAL SERVICES INC
2239 E 55th St (44103-4451)
PHONE.............................216 431-8085

▲ = Import ▼=Export
◆ =Import/Export

Robert Comben, *President*
Donald E Carlson, *CFO*
Donald Carlson, *Treasurer*
EMP: 150
SQ FT: 17,541
SALES: 1.2MM **Privately Held**
SIC: 2391 2511 8331 Curtains &
draperies; wood household furniture; job
training & vocational rehabilitation serv-
ices

(G-6641)
VOCON DESIGN INC (PA)
3142 Prospect Ave E (44115-2612)
PHONE...............................216 588-0800
Debbie Donley, *President*
David M Douglass, *Principal*
Debbie McCann, *Vice Pres*
Paul G Voinovich, *Vice Pres*
Paul M Voinovich, *Vice Pres*
EMP: 65
SQ FT: 17,000
SALES (est): 18.4MM **Privately Held**
WEB: www.vocon.com
SIC: 7389 Interior design services

(G-6642)
**VOLUNTERS OF AMER
GREATER OHIO**
775 E 152nd St (44110-2304)
PHONE...............................216 541-9000
EMP: 75
SALES (corp-wide): 10.7MM **Privately
Held**
SIC: 8322 Social service center
PA: Volunteers Of America Ohio & Indiana
1776 E Broad St Frnt
Columbus OH 43203
614 253-6100

(G-6643)
**VORYS SATER SEYMOUR
PEASE LLP**
200 Public Sq Ste 1400 (44114-2327)
PHONE...............................216 479-6100
F Daniel Balmert, *Partner*
Daniel Balmert,
Chas J French III,
John W Read,
EMP: 50
SALES (corp-wide): 133.4MM **Privately
Held**
SIC: 8111 General practice law office
PA: Vorys, Sater, Seymour And Pease Llp
52 E Gay St
Columbus OH 43215
614 464-6400

(G-6644)
W B MASON CO INC
12985 Snow Rd (44130-1006)
PHONE...............................216 267-5000
Richard C Voigt, *Branch Mgr*
EMP: 53
SALES (corp-wide): 773MM **Privately
Held**
SIC: 5112 5044 5021 Stationery & office
supplies; office equipment; office furniture
PA: W. B. Mason Co., Inc.
59 Center St
Brockton MA 02301
781 794-8800

(G-6645)
W R G INC
Also Called: Buckeye Metals
3961 Pearl Rd (44109-3103)
PHONE...............................216 351-8494
Mike Rauch, *President*
Mildred Neumann, *Principal*
Nathan R Simon, *Principal*
Sandra L Sotos, *Principal*
Robert Rauch, *Vice Pres*
EMP: 25
SQ FT: 121,500
SALES (est): 12.3MM **Privately Held**
SIC: 5093 3341 Nonferrous metals scrap;
secondary nonferrous metals

(G-6646)
W W WILLIAMS COMPANY LLC
Also Called: Guaranteed Truck Service
4545 Industrial Pkwy (44135-4541)
PHONE...............................216 252-9977
Bryan Pratt, *Branch Mgr*
EMP: 25

SQ FT: 12,000
SALES (corp-wide): 4.8B **Privately Held**
SIC: 7538 General truck repair
HQ: The W W Williams Company Llc
5025 Bradenton Ave # 130
Dublin OH 43017
614 228-5000

(G-6647)
**WABUSH MINES CLIFFS MINING
CO**
200 Public Sq Ste 3300 (44114-2315)
PHONE...............................216 694-5700
Terrance Taridei, *CFO*
John Tuomi, *Mng Member*
EMP: 800
SALES (est): 15.8MM
SALES (corp-wide): 2.3B **Publicly Held**
SIC: 1011 Iron ore mining; iron ore pelletiz-
ing; iron ore beneficiating
PA: Cleveland-Cliffs Inc.
200 Public Sq Ste 3300
Cleveland OH 44114
216 694-5700

(G-6648)
WADE TRIM
1100 Superior Ave E # 1710 (44114-2518)
PHONE...............................216 363-0300
J Howard Flower, *President*
Kenneth A Tyrpak, *Corp Secy*
David Dipietro, *COO*
Richard J Allar, *Vice Pres*
Wendy Sherrill, *Mktg Dir*
EMP: 35
SQ FT: 17,000
SALES (est): 3.6MM **Privately Held**
SIC: 8711 8713 Civil engineering; survey-
ing services

(G-6649)
**WAELZHOLZ NORTH AMERICA
LLC**
5221 W 164th St (44142-1507)
PHONE...............................216 267-5500
David Zenker, *Vice Pres*
Frank Kluwe, *Mng Member*
▲ **EMP:** 25 **EST:** 1953
SQ FT: 45,000
SALES (est): 13.4MM
SALES (corp-wide): 730.8MM **Privately
Held**
SIC: 5051 Steel
PA: C.D. Walzholz Gmbh & Co. Kg
Feldmuhlenstr. 55
Hagen 58093
233 196-40

(G-6650)
WALTER HAVERFIELD LLP (PA)
1301 E 9th St Ste 3500 (44114-1821)
PHONE...............................216 781-1212
Karen Waldron, *President*
Ralph Cascarilla, *Managing Prtnr*
Douglas N Barr, *Partner*
Darrell A Clay, *Partner*
Michael A Cyphert, *Partner*
EMP: 100 **EST:** 1932
SQ FT: 24,500
SALES (est): 18.4MM **Privately Held**
WEB: www.walterhav.com
SIC: 8111 General practice attorney,
lawyer

(G-6651)
WALTHALL LLP (PA)
6300 Rockside Rd Ste 100 (44131-2221)
PHONE...............................216 573-2330
Richard T Lash CPA, *Partner*
Charles P Battiato Jr CPA, *Partner*
Richard H Cause CPA, *Partner*
Daniel B Holben CPA, *Partner*
Judith A Mondry CPA, *Partner*
EMP: 45
SQ FT: 10,000
SALES (est): 7.3MM **Privately Held**
WEB: www.walthall.com
SIC: 8721 Certified public accountant

(G-6652)
**WALTON MANOR HEALTH CARE
CTR**
19859 Alexander Rd (44146-5345)
PHONE...............................440 439-4433
Morton J Weisberg, *President*

Tiffany Hexter, *Purchasing*
Susan Waters, *Human Res Mgr*
Debbie Pequignot, *Hlthcr Dir*
Roland Cunningham, *Maintence Staff*
EMP: 125
SQ FT: 55,299
SALES (est): 6MM **Privately Held**
SIC: 8051 Convalescent home with contin-
uous nursing care

(G-6653)
**WARNER DENNEHEY
MARSHALL**
127 Public Sq Ste 3510 (44114-1250)
PHONE...............................216 912-3787
EMP: 54
SALES (corp-wide): 153.4MM **Privately
Held**
SIC: 8111 General practice law office
PA: Marshall Dennehey Warner Coleman &
Goggin P.C.
2000 Market St Ste 2300
Philadelphia PA 19103
215 575-2600

(G-6654)
WARRENTON COPPER LLC
1240 Marquette St (44114-3920)
PHONE...............................636 456-3488
◆ **EMP:** 50
SQ FT: 100,000
SALES (est): 3.5MM **Privately Held**
SIC: 1021 Copper Ore Mining
PA: Compagnie Americaine De Fer &
Metaux Inc, La
9100 Boul Henri-Bourassa E
Montreal-Est QC H1E 2
514 494-2000

(G-6655)
WATERWORKS AMERICA INC
Also Called: Waterworks Crystals
5005 Rckside Rd Crwn Cn 6f Crown Centre
(44131)
PHONE...............................440 526-4815
Bruce S Wirtanen, *President*
Gary Palinkas, *Vice Pres*
Susan Peters, *Vice Pres*
Barry Stevens, *VP Sales*
Byron Krantz, *Admin Sec*
EMP: 247
SQ FT: 160,000
SALES (est): 27.8MM **Privately Held**
WEB: www.1water.com
SIC: 5191 Chemicals, agricultural

(G-6656)
**WAXMAN CONSUMER PDTS
GROUP INC (HQ)**
24455 Aurora Rd (44146-1727)
PHONE...............................440 439-1830
Lawrence Waxman, *President*
Armond Waxman, *Chairman*
Melvin Waxman, *Chairman*
John Holzheimer, *Vice Pres*
Mark Wester, *Vice Pres*
▲ **EMP:** 75
SQ FT: 9,000
SALES (est): 39.2MM
SALES (corp-wide): 100MM **Privately
Held**
WEB: www.waxmancpgvendor.com
SIC: 5072 5074 Casters & glides; furniture
hardware; plumbing & hydronic heating
supplies
PA: Waxman Industries, Inc.
24460 Aurora Rd
Cleveland OH 44146
440 439-1830

(G-6657)
WAXMAN INDUSTRIES INC (PA)
24460 Aurora Rd (44146-1794)
PHONE...............................440 439-1830
Armond Waxman, *Ch of Bd*
Melvin Waxman, *Ch of Bd*
Larry Waxman, *President*
Laurence Waxman, *President*
Robert Feldman, *Senior VP*
◆ **EMP:** 110 **EST:** 1962
SQ FT: 21,000

SALES: 100MM **Privately Held**
WEB: www.waxmanind.com
SIC: 5072 5074 3494 3491 Hardware;
plumbing & hydronic heating supplies;
valves & pipe fittings; industrial valves;
plumbing fixture fittings & trim

(G-6658)
**WEGMAN HESSLER
VANDERBURG**
6055 Rockside Woods Blvd # 200
(44131-2302)
PHONE...............................216 642-3342
David J Hessler, *President*
Stephanie Lankhorst, *Counsel*
Peter A Hessler, *Treasurer*
Peter Hessler, *General Counsel*
Keith Vanderburg, *Admin Sec*
EMP: 60
SALES (est): 6.8MM **Privately Held**
WEB: www.wegmanlaw.com
SIC: 8111 General practice attorney,
lawyer

(G-6659)
WEINER KEITH D CO L P A INC
Also Called: Keith D Weiner & Assoc Lpa
75 Public Sq Ste 600 (44113-2079)
PHONE...............................216 771-6500
Keith D Weiner, *President*
Evelyn Schonberg, *Corp Secy*
Brad Hanson, *Manager*
Vicki Depould, *Legal Staff*
EMP: 45
SALES: 1MM **Privately Held**
WEB: www.weinerlaw.com
SIC: 8111 General practice attorney,
lawyer

(G-6660)
**WELCH PACKAGING GROUP
INC**
6090 Hillcres Dr (44125)
PHONE...............................216 447-9800
Steve Kevern, *Manager*
EMP: 60
SALES (corp-wide): 546.3MM **Privately
Held**
SIC: 5199 Packaging materials
PA: Welch Packaging Group, Inc.
1020 Herman St
Elkhart IN 46516
574 295-2460

(G-6661)
**WELLS FARGO CLEARING SVCS
LLC**
Also Called: Wells Fargo Advisors
30100 Chagrin Blvd # 200 (44124-5722)
PHONE...............................216 378-2722
Steven Berman, *Vice Pres*
Wellborn Jack, *Vice Pres*
Jeffrey Swartzentruber, *Vice Pres*
Marc Silbiger,
Hank Spain, *Advisor*
EMP: 40
SALES (corp-wide): 101B **Publicly Held**
WEB: www.wachoviasec.com
SIC: 6211 Security brokers & dealers
HQ: Wells Fargo Clearing Services, Llc
1 N Jefferson Ave Fl 7
Saint Louis MO 63103
314 955-3000

(G-6662)
**WELLS FARGO CLEARING SVCS
LLC**
Also Called: Wells Fargo Advisors
950 Main Ave Ste 300 (44113-7204)
PHONE...............................216 574-7300
Thomas Freeman, *Vice Pres*
Marc Silbiger, *Manager*
Eric Nilson, *Director*
EMP: 62
SALES (corp-wide): 101B **Publicly Held**
WEB: www.wachoviasec.com
SIC: 6211 6221 Stock brokers & dealers;
commodity contracts brokers, dealers
HQ: Wells Fargo Clearing Services, Llc
1 N Jefferson Ave Fl 7
Saint Louis MO 63103
314 955-3000

(G-6663)
**WELTMAN WEINBERG & REIS
CO LPA (PA)**
Also Called: WW&r
323 W Lkeside Ave Ste 200 (44113)
PHONE..................................216 685-1000
Robert B Weltman, *President*
Alan Weinberg, *Managing Prtnr*
Michael Dougherty, *Partner*
Theresa Fortunato, *Partner*
Terrence Heffernan, *Partner*
EMP: 170 EST: 1951
SQ FT: 36,412
SALES (est): 151.3MM **Privately Held**
SIC: 8111 General practice law office; general practice attorney, lawyer

(G-6664)
**WELTMAN WEINBERG & REIS
CO LPA**
981 Keynote Cir (44131-1871)
PHONE..................................216 459-8633
EMP: 110
SALES (corp-wide): 151.3MM **Privately
Held**
SIC: 8111 General practice law office
PA: Weltman, Weinberg & Reis Co., L.P.A.
323 W Lkeside Ave Ste 200
Cleveland OH 44113
216 685-1000

(G-6665)
WESCO DISTRIBUTION INC
4741 Hinckley Indus Pkwy (44109-6004)
PHONE..................................216 741-0441
Vincent Lutman, *Opers Mgr*
Sharon Batsch, *Sales Staff*
Terry Mason, *Sales Associate*
Mike Clark, *Sales Executive*
Chad Marrison, *Manager*
EMP: 27 **Publicly Held**
SIC: 5063 5085 Electrical supplies; industrial supplies
HQ: Wesco Distribution, Inc.
225 W Station Square Dr # 700
Pittsburgh PA 15219

(G-6666)
**WEST DENISON BASEBALL
LEAGUE**
3556 W 105th St (44111-3838)
P.O. Box 44483 (44144-0483)
PHONE..................................216 251-5790
Ralph J Lukich, *Principal*
Mike Balina, *Vice Pres*
John Deighton, *Treasurer*
EMP: 40
SQ FT: 2,692
SALES: 20.2K **Privately Held**
SIC: 7997 Outdoor field clubs

(G-6667)
**WEST SHORE CHILD CARE
CENTER**
20401 Hilliard Blvd (44116-3506)
PHONE..................................440 333-2040
Karen O'Hagan, *Director*
EMP: 30
SALES (est): 844K **Privately Held**
WEB: www.wschildcare.org
SIC: 8351 Child day care services

(G-6668)
**WEST SIDE CARDIOLOGY
ASSOC**
Also Called: Cumberford & Watts
20455 Lorain Rd Fl 2 (44126-3530)
PHONE..................................440 333-8600
Marcello Mellino, *President*
Thomas Comerford, *Vice Pres*
EMP: 30
SALES (est): 1.3MM **Privately Held**
WEB: www.wscardiology.com
SIC: 8011 Cardiologist & cardio-vascular
specialist

(G-6669)
**WEST SIDE CARDIOLOGY
ASSOC**
20455 Lorain Rd Fl 2 (44126-3530)
PHONE..................................440 333-8600
Marcel Malino MD, *Chairman*
EMP: 40
SQ FT: 6,400

SALES (est): 2.6MM **Privately Held**
SIC: 8011 Cardiologist & cardio-vascular
specialist

(G-6670)
WEST SIDE COMMUNITY HOUSE
9300 Lorain Ave (44102-4725)
PHONE..................................216 771-7297
Dawn Kolograf, *Exec Dir*
Yvette Medina, *Director*
Rachelle Milner, *Director*
Terry Weber, *Director*
EMP: 35
SQ FT: 4,620
SALES: 1.6MM **Privately Held**
WEB: www.wschouse.org
SIC: 8322 Social service center

(G-6671)
**WEST SIDE ECUMENICAL
MINISTRY (PA)**
Also Called: W S E M
5209 Detroit Ave (44102-2224)
PHONE..................................216 325-9369
Phil Buck, *Exec Dir*
EMP: 130
SQ FT: 29,075
SALES (est): 9MM **Privately Held**
SIC: 8322 8661 Individual & family services; religious organizations

(G-6672)
**WESTERN MANAGEMENT INC
(PA)**
14577 Lorain Ave (44111-3156)
PHONE..................................216 941-3333
John Turk, *President*
Thomas M Cawley, *Principal*
Eric George Turk, *Principal*
EMP: 45
SQ FT: 10,000
SALES (est): 8.2MM **Privately Held**
SIC: 8741 Management services

(G-6673)
**WESTERN RESERVE AREA
AGENCY (PA)**
Also Called: WRAAA
1700 E 13th St Ste 114 (44114-3285)
PHONE..................................216 621-0303
E Douglas Beach, *CEO*
Christopher Hall, *Finance*
Chris Demagistris, *Manager*
Heather Witherite, *Consultant*
Teresa Allerton, *Social Worker*
EMP: 235
SALES: 66.2MM **Privately Held**
SIC: 8322 8082 Senior citizens' center or
association; home health care services

(G-6674)
**WESTERN RESERVE AREA
AGENCY**
Also Called: Passport
1700 E 13th St Ste 114 (44114-3285)
PHONE..................................216 621-0303
Ron Hill, *Director*
EMP: 30
SALES (est): 460.9K **Privately Held**
SIC: 8322 Senior citizens' center or association
PA: Western Reserve Area Agency On
Aging
1700 E 13th St Ste 114
Cleveland OH 44114

(G-6675)
**WESTERN RESERVE
HISTORICAL SOC (PA)**
Also Called: HALE FARM & VILLAGE
10825 East Blvd (44106-1777)
PHONE..................................216 721-5722
Gainor B Davis, *CEO*
Kelly Falcone, *Vice Pres*
Mary Thoburn, *CFO*
Susan Hall, *Mktg Dir*
Ann Sindelar, *Supervisor*
EMP: 60
SALES: 7.4MM **Privately Held**
SIC: 8412 8231 Historical society; museum; specialized libraries

(G-6676)
**WESTERN RESERVE INTERIORS
INC**
7777 Exchange St Ste 7 (44125-3337)
PHONE..................................216 447-1081
Leslie S Cooke, *President*
Tom Cooke, *Vice Pres*
Jo Ann Castelli, *Treasurer*
Kevin Allar, *Manager*
Bruce Cooke, *Executive*
EMP: 30
SQ FT: 25,000
SALES (est): 4.3MM **Privately Held**
WEB: www.wri-net.com
SIC: 1742 Plastering, plain or ornamental;
drywall; acoustical & ceiling work

(G-6677)
WESTLAKE CAB SERVICE
2069 W 3rd St (44113-2502)
PHONE..................................440 331-5000
Arthur McBride, *President*
Edward Mc Bride, *Principal*
EMP: 80
SQ FT: 14,984
SALES (est): 3.5MM **Privately Held**
SIC: 4121 Taxicabs

(G-6678)
WESTLAKE VILLAGE INC
28550 Westlake Village Dr (44145-7608)
PHONE..................................440 892-4200
Jeanne Barnard, *President*
Patrick Payne, *Exec Dir*
EMP: 130
SQ FT: 125,000
SALES: 6.9MM
SALES (corp-wide): 4.5B **Publicly Held**
WEB: www.westlakevillage.com
SIC: 6513 Retirement hotel operation
HQ: American Retirement Corporation
111 Westwood Pl Ste 200
Brentwood TN 37027
615 221-2250

(G-6679)
WESTON INC (PA)
Also Called: Property 3
4760 Richmond Rd Ste 200 (44128-5979)
PHONE..................................440 349-9000
Ann S Asher, *President*
Dave Caretti, *Facilities Mgr*
Joe Soltesz, *Controller*
Tom Flaherty, *Manager*
Wayne Nuhfer, *Info Tech Mgr*
EMP: 29
SALES (est): 26.1MM **Privately Held**
WEB: www.weston.com
SIC: 6512 6541 Commercial & industrial
building operation; title search companies

(G-6680)
WFTS
W E W S - TV
3001 Euclid Ave (44115-2516)
PHONE..................................216 431-5555
Eliot Case, *Branch Mgr*
EMP: 200
SQ FT: 10,000
SALES (corp-wide): 2.9B **Publicly Held**
WEB: www.diytv.com
SIC: 4833 Television broadcasting stations
HQ: Wfts
4045 N Himes Ave
Tampa FL 33607
813 354-2800

(G-6681)
**WHITING-TURNER
CONTRACTING CO**
5875 Landerbrook Dr # 100 (44124-6513)
PHONE..................................440 449-9200
Frank Miller, *Superintendent*
Jeff Maeder, *Vice Pres*
Jason Gebhardt, *Project Mgr*
Joan Hoyer, *Office Mgr*
EMP: 70
SALES (corp-wide): 6.1B **Privately Held**
WEB: www.whiting-turner.com
SIC: 1541 1542 1629 Industrial buildings
& warehouses; nonresidential construction; industrial plant construction

PA: The Whiting-Turner Contracting Company
300 E Joppa Rd Ste 800
Baltimore MD 21286
410 821-1100

(G-6682)
**WHOLE HEALTH MANAGEMENT
INC (DH)**
1375 E 9th St Ste 2500 (44114-1743)
PHONE..................................216 921-8601
James J Hummer, *President*
Randy Twyman, *CFO*
Randall Twyman, *Treasurer*
Chuck Siemon, *CIO*
EMP: 40
SQ FT: 5,000
SALES (est): 18.4MM
SALES (corp-wide): 131.5B **Publicly
Held**
WEB: www.wholehealthnet.com
SIC: 8011 Medical Doctor's Office
HQ: Walgreen Co.
200 Wilmot Rd
Deerfield IL 60015
847 315-2500

(G-6683)
WILDWOOD YACHT CLUB INC
P.O. Box 19001 (44119-0001)
PHONE..................................216 531-9052
Stan Powski, *President*
EMP: 83
SALES (est): 38.8K **Privately Held**
SIC: 7997 Yacht club, membership

(G-6684)
WINDY HILL LTD INC (PA)
Also Called: Transworld News
3700 Kelley Ave (44114-4533)
PHONE..................................216 391-4800
Joel Kaminsky, *President*
Jeffrey Gross, *Admin Sec*
EMP: 75
SQ FT: 55,000
SALES (est): 19.9MM **Privately Held**
SIC: 5192 5099 Magazines; video cassettes, accessories & supplies

(G-6685)
WINSTON PRODUCTS LLC
30339 Diamond Pkwy # 105 (44139-5473)
PHONE..................................440 478-1418
Winston Breeden, *CEO*
Scott Jared, *President*
Bob Schmidt, *General Mgr*
Melissa Mirt, *Purch Mgr*
Kris Ramer, *VP Sales*
▲ EMP: 100
SQ FT: 115,000
SALES (est): 36.5MM **Privately Held**
SIC: 3556 5013 Food products machinery;
automotive supplies

(G-6686)
WIRELESS CENTER INC (PA)
1925 Saint Clair Ave Ne (44114-2028)
PHONE..................................216 503-3777
Azam Kazmi, *Principal*
Dave Phillips, *District Mgr*
Tariq Khan, *Vice Pres*
Joseph Kim, *Store Mgr*
Doug George, *Sales Dir*
EMP: 300
SQ FT: 10,000
SALES (est): 28MM **Privately Held**
SIC: 4812 Cellular telephone services

(G-6687)
WKYC-TV INC
Also Called: W K Y C Channel 3
1333 Lakeside Ave E (44114-1159)
PHONE..................................216 344-3300
Brooke Spectorsky, *President*
Mary Dreis, *Accounts Exec*
Janet Forrai, *Executive*
EMP: 220
SALES (est): 22.6MM
SALES (corp-wide): 2.2B **Publicly Held**
WEB: www.wkyc.com
SIC: 4833 Television broadcasting stations
PA: Tegna Inc.
8350 Broad St Ste 2000
Tysons VA 22102
703 873-6600

▲ = Import ▼=Export
◆ =Import/Export

(G-6688)
WONG MARGARET W ASSOC CO LPA (PA)
3150 Chester Ave (44114-4617)
PHONE................................313 527-9989
Margaret W Wong, *President*
Kathy Hill, *General Mgr*
Gordon H Landefeld, *Marketing Mgr*
Marykay Covington, *Technology*
Michelle A Rahija, *Associate*
EMP: 35
SALES (est): 4.4MM Privately Held
WEB: www.imwong.com
SIC: 8111 General practice law office

(G-6689)
WORLD AUTO PARTS INC
1240 Carnegie Ave (44115-2808)
PHONE................................216 781-8418
Michael Maloof, *President*
Michael D Maloof, *President*
Daniel Maloof, *Vice Pres*
EMP: 28 EST: 1979
SQ FT: 100,000
SALES (est): 3.8MM Privately Held
SIC: 5013 Automotive supplies & parts

(G-6690)
WORLD SHIPPING INC (PA)
1340 Depot St Ste 200 (44116-1741)
PHONE................................440 356-7676
Frederick M Hunger, *President*
Dennis Mahoney, *Vice Pres*
John E Hunger, *CFO*
Lisa McCaffrey, *Agent*
Jackie Csiszar, *Business Dir*
EMP: 30
SQ FT: 15,000
SALES (est): 274.1MM Privately Held
WEB: www.worldshipping.com
SIC: 4213 4731 Trucking, except local;
agents, shipping

(G-6691)
WRIGHT CENTER
Also Called: Wright Surgery Center
1611 S Green Rd Ste 124 (44121-4121)
PHONE................................216 382-1868
Cassy Schilero, *Director*
EMP: 45
SALES (est): 3.9MM Privately Held
WEB: www.wrightcenter.com
SIC: 8062 General medical & surgical hospitals

(G-6692)
WTB INC
Also Called: M&J Fox Investments
815 Superior Ave E (44114-2706)
PHONE................................216 298-1895
Matthew Fox, *President*
Jennifer Fox, *Vice Pres*
Ceda Sherman, *CFO*
EMP: 26
SQ FT: 1,200
SALES (est): 3MM Privately Held
SIC: 8748 7389 Business consulting;

(G-6693)
WTW DELAWARE HOLDINGS LLC
Also Called: Willis Towers Watson
1001 Lakeside Ave E (44114-1158)
PHONE................................216 937-4000
EMP: 145 Privately Held
WEB: www.watsonwyatt.com
SIC: 8742 8999 7371 7361 Compensation & benefits planning consultant;
human resource consulting services; actuarial consultant; computer software systems analysis & design, custom;
computer software development; employment agencies
HQ: Wtw Delaware Holdings Llc
800 N Glebe Rd
Arlington VA 22203

(G-6694)
WUNDERLICH SECURITIES INC
5885 Landerbrook Dr # 304 (44124-4045)
PHONE................................440 646-1400
EMP: 30 Publicly Held
SIC: 6211 Security brokers & dealers

HQ: Wunderlich Securities, Inc.
40 S Main St Ste 1800
Memphis TN 38103
901 251-1330

(G-6695)
WYSE ADVERTISING INC (PA)
668 Euclid Ave Ste 100 (44114-3024)
PHONE................................216 696-2424
Michael Marino, *CEO*
Sharyn F Hinman, *Senior VP*
David N Jankowski, *Senior VP*
Margaret Weitzel, *CFO*
EMP: 98
SQ FT: 56,000
SALES (est): 12.6MM Privately Held
WEB: www.wyseadvertising.com
SIC: 7311 Advertising consultant

(G-6696)
X-RAY INDUSTRIES INC
Also Called: Xri Testing
5403 E Schaaf Rd (44131-1337)
PHONE................................216 642-0100
Robert Henchar, *Med Doctor*
Bob Hensher, *Manager*
Bob Henchar, *Manager*
Ron Lezon, *Lab Dir*
EMP: 25
SALES (corp-wide): 30.9MM Privately Held
SIC: 8071 8734 X-ray laboratory, including dental; testing laboratories
PA: X-Ray Industries, Inc.
1961 Thunderbird
Troy MI 48084
248 362-2242

(G-6697)
XEROX CORPORATION
6000 Fredom Sq Dr Ste 100 (44131)
PHONE................................216 642-7806
EMP: 100
SALES (corp-wide): 10.2B Publicly Held
SIC: 5044 7699 7378 5045 Whol Office
Equipment Repair Services Computer
Maint/Repair Whol Computer/Peripheral
PA: Xerox Corporation
201 Merritt 7
Norwalk CT 06851
203 968-3000

(G-6698)
XO COMMUNICATIONS LLC
3 Summit Park Dr Ste 250 (44131-2598)
PHONE................................216 619-3200
Chris Ryan, *Branch Mgr*
EMP: 40
SALES (corp-wide): 130.8B Publicly Held
SIC: 4813 Long distance telephone communications
HQ: Xo Communications, Llc
13865 Sunrise Valley Dr
Herndon VA 20171
703 547-2000

(G-6699)
YORK BUILDING MAINTENANCE INC
4748 Broadview Rd (44109-4668)
PHONE................................216 398-8100
Fax: 216 398-8102
EMP: 120 EST: 1981
SQ FT: 3,200
SALES (est): 2.5MM Privately Held
SIC: 7349 Building Maintenance Svc

(G-6700)
YORK RISK SERVICES GROUP INC
16560 Commerce Ct Ste 100 (44130-6305)
P.O. Box 183188, Columbus (43218-3188)
PHONE................................440 863-2500
Tom McArthur, *Owner*
EMP: 27
SALES (corp-wide): 2.3B Privately Held
SIC: 6411 Insurance claim adjusters, not employed by insurance company
HQ: York Risk Services Group, Inc.
1 Upper Pond
Parsippany NJ 07054
973 404-1200

(G-6701)
YORK RITE
13512 Kinsman Rd (44120-4412)
PHONE................................216 751-1417
Clerence Foxhall, *President*
EMP: 26
SQ FT: 8,646
SALES (est): 1.3MM Privately Held
WEB: www.yorkrite.com
SIC: 8641 Civic social & fraternal associations

(G-6702)
YOUNG MNS CHRSTN ASSN CLVELAND
Also Called: YMCA West Park
15501 Lorain Ave (44111-5539)
PHONE................................216 941-4654
Christine Vidal, *Director*
Noelle Gwin, *Executive*
EMP: 25
SALES (corp-wide): 29.2MM Privately Held
SIC: 8641 8322 7997 Youth organizations; individual & family services; membership sports & recreation clubs
PA: Young Men's Christian Association Of Cleveland
1801 Superior Ave E # 130
Cleveland OH 44114
216 781-1337

(G-6703)
YOUNG MNS CHRSTN ASSN CLVELAND
631 Babbitt Rd (44123-2025)
PHONE................................216 731-7454
John Reid, *Director*
EMP: 40
SQ FT: 17,240
SALES (corp-wide): 29.2MM Privately Held
SIC: 8641 7991 8351 7032 Youth organizations; physical fitness facilities; child day care services; youth camps; individual & family services
PA: Young Men's Christian Association Of Cleveland
1801 Superior Ave E # 130
Cleveland OH 44114
216 781-1337

(G-6704)
YOUNG MNS CHRSTN ASSN CLVELAND
Also Called: Hillcrest Ymca-Adrian
5000 Mayfield Rd (44124-2605)
PHONE................................216 382-4300
Jane Martin, *Director*
EMP: 60
SQ FT: 17,286
SALES (corp-wide): 29.2MM Privately Held
SIC: 8641 7997 7991 Youth organizations; membership sports & recreation clubs; physical fitness facilities
PA: Young Men's Christian Association Of Cleveland
1801 Superior Ave E # 130
Cleveland OH 44114
216 781-1337

(G-6705)
YOUNG WOMENS CHRISTIAN ASSOCI (PA)
Also Called: YWCA of Cleveland
4019 Prospect Ave (44103-4317)
PHONE................................216 881-6878
Margaret Mitchell, *President*
Teresa Sanders, *Vice Pres*
Carol Lyles, *Transportation*
Cynthia Harrigan, *Manager*
Barbara Danforth, *Exec Dir*
EMP: 42
SQ FT: 24,000
SALES (est): 3.1MM Privately Held
SIC: 8641 7991 8351 7032 Youth organizations; physical fitness facilities; child day care services; youth camps; individual & family services

(G-6706)
YOUTH OPPORTUNITIES UNLIMITED
1361 Euclid Ave (44115-1819)
PHONE................................216 566-5445
Carol Rizchun, *President*
Craig Dorn, *Vice Pres*
Pam Macer, *Vice Pres*
Lisa Theis, *Opers Staff*
Maggie Simak, *Controller*
EMP: 40
SQ FT: 4,000
SALES: 10.4MM Privately Held
WEB: www.youthopportunities.org
SIC: 7361 Placement agencies

(G-6707)
Z A F INC
Also Called: Markfrank Hair Salons
2165 S Green Rd (44121-3313)
P.O. Box 605, Gates Mills (44040-0605)
PHONE................................216 291-1234
Frank Alvarez, *President*
EMP: 30
SQ FT: 2,000
SALES (est): 560.1K Privately Held
WEB: www.markfrank.com
SIC: 7231 Unisex hair salons; manicurist, pedicurist

(G-6708)
ZAREMBA GROUP INCORPORATED
14600 Detroit Ave # 1500 (44107-4299)
PHONE................................216 221-6600
Walter Zaremba Jr, *President*
Robert Steadley, *Vice Pres*
EMP: 48
SALES (est): 2.9MM Privately Held
SIC: 6552 8111 6531 Land subdividers & developers, commercial; legal services; real estate managers; real estate agent, commercial

(G-6709)
ZAREMBA LLC
14600 Detroit Ave # 1500 (44107-4299)
PHONE................................216 221-6600
Realty I Limite, *Partner*
Realty I Limited, *Partner*
Eastlake Retail Investment Lim, *Ltd Ptnr*
Joseph Urbancic, *Mng Member*
EMP: 100
SQ FT: 20,000
SALES (est): 6.3MM Privately Held
SIC: 6512 6531 Shopping center, property operation only; real estate brokers & agents

(G-6710)
ZASHIN & RICH CO LPA (PA)
950 Main Ave Fl 4 (44113-7215)
PHONE................................216 696-4441
Andrew Zashin, *President*
Cindy Hetman, *Legal Staff*
Tammy Rhodes, *Legal Staff*
Amy Keating,
AMI Patel,
EMP: 35
SALES (est): 3.9MM Privately Held
WEB: www.zrlaw.com
SIC: 8111 Labor & employment law

(G-6711)
ZAVARELLA BROTHERS CNSTR CO
5381 Erie St Ste B (44146-1739)
P.O. Box 46983, Bedford Heights (44146-0983)
PHONE................................440 232-2243
Dan Zaverella, *President*
Nicholas Zavarella, *President*
Daniel Zavarella, *Vice Pres*
Dennis Fiorilli, *Project Mgr*
Chuck Zavarella, *Admin Sec*
EMP: 50
SQ FT: 1,000
SALES (est): 4.1MM Privately Held
SIC: 1741 Bricklaying

(G-6712)
ZENITH SYSTEMS LLC (PA)
5055 Corbin Dr (44128-5462)
PHONE................................216 587-9510
David Weiland, *President*

G
E
O
G
R
A
P
H
I
C

Robert Heiser, *General Mgr*
Greg Ropple, *Superintendent*
Micheal Joyce, *Exec VP*
Michael Colosimo, *Vice Pres*
EMP: 500
SALES (est): 158.5MM **Privately Held**
SIC: 1731 Communications specialization

(G-6713)
ZEP INC
Zep Manufacturing
6777 Engle Rd Ste A (44130-7953)
PHONE..................................440 239-1580
Scott Ward, *Manager*
EMP: 37
SALES (corp-wide): 1B **Privately Held**
SIC: 5169 Whol Chemicals
HQ: Zep Inc.
3330 Cumberland Blvd Se # 700
Atlanta GA 30339
877 428-9937

(G-6714)
ZUCKER BUILDING COMPANY
Also Called: State Chemical
5915 Landerbrook Dr # 300 (44124-4039)
PHONE..................................216 861-7114
Harold Uhrman, *President*
Malcolm Zucker, *Principal*
EMP: 58
SQ FT: 240,000
SALES (est): 5.4MM **Privately Held**
WEB: www.statechemical.com
SIC: 6512 Commercial & industrial building
operation

Cleveland Heights
Cuyahoga County

(G-6715)
CENTER FOR FAMILIES & CHILDREN
Rapp Art Center
1941 S Taylor Rd Ste 225 (44118-2103)
PHONE..................................216 932-9497
Pamela Bradford, *Manager*
EMP: 25
SALES (corp-wide): 26MM **Privately Held**
SIC: 8322 Individual & family services
PA: Center For Families & Children, Inc
4500 Euclid Ave
Cleveland OH 44103
216 432-7200

(G-6716)
CITY OF CLEVELAND HEIGHTS
Community Relations Service
40 Severance Cir (44118-1501)
PHONE..................................216 291-2323
Susanna O'Neal, *Director*
EMP: 30 **Privately Held**
WEB: www.clevelandheights.com
SIC: 8743 Public relations services
PA: City Of Cleveland Heights
40 Severance Cir
Cleveland Heights OH 44118
216 291-4444

(G-6717)
CITY OF CLEVELAND HEIGHTS
Water Dept
40 Severance Cir (44118-1501)
PHONE..................................216 291-5995
Dennis Zentarski, *Principal*
Collette Clinkscale, *Director*
EMP: 35 **Privately Held**
WEB: www.clevelandheights.com
SIC: 4941 Water supply
PA: City Of Cleveland Heights
40 Severance Cir
Cleveland Heights OH 44118
216 291-4444

(G-6718)
HEIGHTS LAUNDRY & DRY CLEANING (PA)
1863 Coventry Rd (44118-1610)
PHONE..................................216 932-9666
Manning Dishler, *President*
Arlene Dishler, *Vice Pres*
EMP: 32
SQ FT: 3,000

SALES (est): 990.8K **Privately Held**
SIC: 7211 7216 Power laundries, family &
commercial; drycleaning plants, except
rugs

(G-6719)
HOME DEPOT USA INC
Also Called: Home Depot, The
3460 Mayfield Rd (44118-1405)
PHONE..................................216 297-1303
Timothy E McCarthy, *Manager*
EMP: 150
SALES (corp-wide): 108.2B **Publicly Held**
WEB: www.homerentalsdepot.com
SIC: 5211 7359 Home centers; tool rental
HQ: Home Depot U.S.A., Inc.
2455 Paces Ferry Ave
Atlanta GA 30339

(G-6720)
JEWISH EDCATN CTR OF CLEVELAND
2030 S Taylor Rd (44118-2605)
PHONE..................................216 371-0446
Yossi Israeli, *Info Tech Dir*
Ilya Kligman, *Technology*
Seymour Kopelowitz, *Exec Dir*
Judith Schiller, *Director*
Elana Cohen, *Executive Asst*
EMP: 75
SQ FT: 20,000
SALES (est): 5.8MM **Privately Held**
SIC: 8399 Council for social agency

(G-6721)
KAISER FOUNDATION HOSPITALS
Also Called: Cleveland Heights Medical Ctr
10 Severance Cir (44118-1533)
PHONE..................................800 524-7777
EMP: 593
SALES (corp-wide): 93B **Privately Held**
SIC: 8011 Medical centers
HQ: Kaiser Foundation Hospitals Inc
1 Kaiser Plz
Oakland CA 94612
510 271-6611

(G-6722)
REALTY CORPORATION OF AMERICA
3048 Meadowbrook Blvd (44118-2842)
PHONE..................................216 522-0020
Fax: 216 522-0033
EMP: 46
SQ FT: 50,000
SALES: 5MM **Privately Held**
SIC: 6162 Mortgage Banker/Correspondent

(G-6723)
REILLY PAINTING CO
1899 S Taylor Rd (44118-2160)
PHONE..................................216 371-8160
Michael Reilly, *President*
Fiona Reilly, *Vice Pres*
EMP: 30
SQ FT: 8,063
SALES (est): 2.5MM **Privately Held**
SIC: 1721 1761 Exterior residential painting contractor; interior residential painting contractor; exterior commercial painting contractor; interior commercial painting contractor; roofing, siding & sheet metal work

---

Cleves
Hamilton County

(G-6724)
ALUMINA RLING CSTM IR WRKS INC
Also Called: ALUMINA RAILING PRODUCTS
8301 Strimple Rd (45002-9778)
PHONE..................................513 353-1116
Terry Bunnell, *President*
Kimberly Bunnell, *Admin Sec*
EMP: 25 **EST:** 1994
SQ FT: 27,000

SALES: 3.3MM **Privately Held**
WEB: www.aluminarailing.com
SIC: 1799 Fence construction

(G-6725)
BANTA ELECTRICAL CONTRS INC
5701 Hamilton Cleves Rd (45002-9504)
P.O. Box 377, Miamitown (45041-0377)
PHONE..................................513 353-4446
Gale F Banta, *President*
Ed Ginter, *Vice Pres*
Mr Stephen Banta, *Project Mgr*
Bill Monterosso, *Project Mgr*
Martin Grider, *Manager*
EMP: 100
SQ FT: 12,000
SALES (est): 15MM **Privately Held**
WEB: www.bantaelectric.com
SIC: 1731 General electrical contractor

(G-6726)
CINCINNATI ASPHALT CORPORATION
7959 Harrison Ave (45002-9203)
P.O. Box 757, Harrison (45030-0757)
PHONE..................................513 367-0250
Joey Madden, *President*
Joe Durham, *Vice Pres*
Shane Gardner, *Vice Pres*
EMP: 52
SQ FT: 7,000
SALES: 11.4MM **Privately Held**
SIC: 1611 1794 1771 Concrete construction: roads, highways, sidewalks, etc.; excavation work; concrete work; blacktop (asphalt) work

(G-6727)
DAY PRECISION WALL INC
5715 Hamilton Cleves Rd (45002-9504)
PHONE..................................513 353-2999
Jim Day, *President*
Joseph H Day, *Vice Pres*
Larry Day, *Vice Pres*
Sam Hirst, *Treasurer*
EMP: 30
SALES (est): 2.6MM **Privately Held**
SIC: 1771 Foundation & footing contractor

(G-6728)
EQUIPMENT MAINTENANCE INC (PA)
Also Called: Equipment Maintenance & Repair
5885 Hamilton Cleves Rd (45002-9529)
PHONE..................................513 353-3518
Don Holden, *President*
EMP: 34
SQ FT: 22,000
SALES (est): 2.5MM **Privately Held**
SIC: 7699 5261 5082 Aircraft & heavy equipment repair services; general household repair services; lawn & garden equipment; construction & mining machinery

(G-6729)
KATHMAN ELECTRIC CO INC
8969 Harrison Pike (45002-9757)
PHONE..................................513 353-3365
Raymond E Kathman, *President*
Thomas Kathman, *Vice Pres*
Gary Kathman, *Admin Sec*
EMP: 45
SQ FT: 3,000
SALES (est): 5.3MM **Privately Held**
SIC: 1731 General electrical contractor

(G-6730)
KEN NEYER PLUMBING INC
4895 Hamilton Cleves Rd (45002-9752)
PHONE..................................513 353-3311
James Neyer, *President*
Ken Neyer Jr, *Vice Pres*
Janet Neyer, *Treasurer*
Cheryl Tucker, *Finance Mgr*
Rodney Deffinger, *Manager*
EMP: 150 **EST:** 1972
SQ FT: 2,500
SALES (est): 32.8MM **Privately Held**
WEB: www.neyerplumbing.com
SIC: 1711 Plumbing contractors

(G-6731)
KINDERTOWN EDUCATIONAL CENTERS (PA)
Also Called: Biederman Educational Centers
8720 Bridgetown Rd (45002-1328)
PHONE..................................859 344-8802
Stewart J Biederman, *President*
Amy Early, *Director*
Cheryl Lawrence, *Director*
Amy Morgan, *Director*
EMP: 48
SALES (est): 1.4MM **Privately Held**
WEB:
www.biedermaneducationalcenters.com
SIC: 8351 Group day care center

(G-6732)
LARRY SMITH CONTRACTORS INC
Also Called: Larry Smith Plumbing
5737 Dry Fork Rd (45002-9730)
PHONE..................................513 367-0218
Larry Smith, *President*
Marvin Smith, *Vice Pres*
Matthew Young, *Vice Pres*
EMP: 50
SQ FT: 4,000
SALES (est): 8.8MM **Privately Held**
SIC: 1623 Sewer line construction; water main construction

(G-6733)
MATTLIN CONSTRUCTION INC
5835 Hamilton Cleves Rd (45002-9529)
PHONE..................................513 598-5402
C David Mattlin, *President*
David M Mattlin, *Vice Pres*
Tammy Mattlin, *Sales Executive*
Tim Mattlin, *Admin Sec*
EMP: 30
SALES (est): 7MM **Privately Held**
WEB: www.mattlinconstruction.net
SIC: 1542 1771 Commercial & office buildings, renovation & repair; concrete work

(G-6734)
REIS TRUCKING INC
10080 Valley Junction Rd (45002-9406)
PHONE..................................513 353-1960
Paul A Reis, *President*
Lois Reis, *Admin Sec*
EMP: 28
SQ FT: 7,000
SALES: 6.8MM **Privately Held**
WEB: www.reistrucking.com
SIC: 4212 Local trucking, without storage

(G-6735)
USI INC
9585 Cilley Rd (45002-9702)
PHONE..................................513 954-4561
Jodi Noble, *President*
Jon Greg Martin, *Principal*
Mark Westrich, *Vice Pres*
EMP: 32
SALES (est): 2.9MM **Privately Held**
SIC: 1731 General electrical contractor

(G-6736)
WM KRAMER AND SONS INC
Also Called: W K S
9171 Harrison Pike # 12 (45002-9076)
PHONE..................................513 353-1142
Steven M Kramer, *President*
Greg Terhar, *Superintendent*
Bruce Kramer, *Vice Pres*
Doug Kramer, *Vice Pres*
Kevin Kramer, *Vice Pres*
EMP: 75
SQ FT: 22,357
SALES (est): 11.8MM **Privately Held**
WEB: www.kramerroofing.com
SIC: 1761 Roofing contractor; sheet metal work

Clinton
Summit County

(G-6737)
RESIDNTIAL COML RNOVATIONS INC
7686 S Clvland Mssllon Rd (44216-8912)
PHONE...................................330 815-1476
EMP: 50
SALES (est): 3.8MM **Privately Held**
SIC: 1521 1522 1542 1761 Single-Family House Cnst Residential Construction Nonresidential Cnstn Roofing/Siding Contr

Clyde
Sandusky County

(G-6738)
ARBORS AT CLIDE ASSSTED LIVING
Also Called: Abror Health Care
700 Coulson St (43410-2065)
PHONE...................................419 547-7746
Ramonda Stahl, *Director*
Ramonda Weiker, *Director*
EMP: 25
SALES (est): 860.6K **Privately Held**
SIC: 8052 Intermediate care facilities

(G-6739)
ASTORIA PLACE OF CLYDE LLC
Also Called: HERITAGE VILLAGE OF CLYDE
700 Helen St (43410-2051)
PHONE...................................419 547-9595
Jason Dipasqua, *COO*
Eric Hutchins, *Administration*
EMP: 70 EST: 2014
SALES: 4.7MM **Privately Held**
SIC: 8051 Skilled nursing care facilities

(G-6740)
BAKER BNNGSON RLTY AUCTIONEERS
1570 W Mcpherson Hwy (43410-1012)
PHONE...................................419 547-7777
Bill Baker, *Partner*
Ken Bonnigson, *Partner*
Teri Meyer, *Office Mgr*
EMP: 25
SALES (est): 1.4MM **Privately Held**
WEB: www.bakerbonnigson.com
SIC: 6519 6531 7359 7389 Real property lessors; appraiser, real estate; tent & tarpaulin rental; auctioneers, fee basis

(G-6741)
CHANEY ROOFING MAINTENANCE
Also Called: C R M
7040 State Route 101 N (43410-9636)
PHONE...................................419 639-2761
Shawn Chaney, *President*
Gary S Chaney, *Chairman*
EMP: 30
SQ FT: 50,000
SALES: 4MM **Privately Held**
WEB: www.chaney-roofing.com
SIC: 1761 1542 Roofing contractor; commercial & office building, new construction

(G-6742)
CLYDE-FINDLAY AREA CR UN INC (PA)
1455 W Mcpherson Hwy (43410-1009)
PHONE...................................419 547-7781
Paul Howard, *President*
Scott Hicks, *President*
Kenneth Cobb, *Treasurer*
EMP: 28
SQ FT: 12,416
SALES: 4.1MM **Privately Held**
WEB: www.cfacu.com
SIC: 6061 6163 Federal credit unions; loan brokers

(G-6743)
FULTZ & SON INC
Also Called: FSI Disposal
100 S Main St (43410-1633)
PHONE...................................419 547-9365
Larry F Fultz, *President*
Audra Albright, *Admin Sec*
EMP: 28 EST: 1952
SQ FT: 22,000
SALES (est): 3.8MM **Privately Held**
WEB: www.fsidisposal.com
SIC: 4212 4953 Garbage collection & transport, no disposal; recycling, waste materials

(G-6744)
HMSHOST CORPORATION
Also Called: Marriott
888 N County Road 260 (43410-8514)
PHONE...................................419 547-8667
EMP: 125 **Privately Held**
SIC: 7011 8741 6531 Hotel/Motel Operation Management Services Real Estate Agent/Manager
HQ: Hmshost Corporation
6905 Rockledge Dr 1f
Bethesda MD 20817

(G-6745)
HOSPICE OF MEMORIAL HOSPITA L
430 S Main St (43410-2142)
PHONE...................................419 334-6626
Anne Shelley, *Director*
EMP: 30
SALES (est): 252.2K **Privately Held**
SIC: 8082 Home health care services

(G-6746)
J B HUNT TRANSPORT INC
600 N Woodland Ave (43410-1054)
PHONE...................................419 547-2777
Tracey Walker, *Branch Mgr*
EMP: 166
SALES (corp-wide): 8.6B **Publicly Held**
SIC: 4213 Trucking, except local
HQ: J. B. Hunt Transport, Inc.
615 J B Hunt Corporate Dr
Lowell AR 72745
479 820-0000

(G-6747)
KF CONSTRUCTION AND EXCVTG LLC
220 Norwest St (43410-2162)
PHONE...................................419 547-7555
Michelle Bishop, *President*
EMP: 25
SALES: 950K **Privately Held**
SIC: 1521 New construction, single-family houses

(G-6748)
MEMORIAL HOSPITAL
Memorial Home Health & Hospice
430 S Main St (43410-2142)
PHONE...................................419 547-6419
Anne Shelley, *Director*
EMP: 40
SALES (corp-wide): 67.8MM **Privately Held**
SIC: 8062 8082 General medical & surgical hospitals; home health care services
PA: Memorial Hospital
715 S Taft Ave
Fremont OH 43420
419 334-6657

(G-6749)
PENSKE LOGISTICS LLC
600 N Woodland Ave (43410-1054)
PHONE...................................419 547-2615
Matt Barrown, *Manager*
EMP: 42
SALES (corp-wide): 2.6B **Privately Held**
WEB: www.penskelogistics.com
SIC: 7389 Field warehousing
HQ: Penske Logistics Llc
2675 Morgantown Rd
Reading PA 19607
610 775-6000

(G-6750)
POLYCHEM CORPORATION
Also Called: Evergreen Plastics
202 Watertower Dr (43410-2154)
PHONE...................................419 547-1400
Mark Jeckering, *General Mgr*
EMP: 75 **Privately Held**
SIC: 3052 4953 Plastic belting; recycling, waste materials
HQ: Polychem Corporation
6277 Heisley Rd
Mentor OH 44060
440 357-1500

(G-6751)
ROCKWELL SPRINGS TROUT CLUB (PA)
1581 County Road 310 (43410-9733)
PHONE...................................419 684-7971
Toni Borchardt, *Principal*
Kevin Ramsey, *Admin Sec*
Jeff Smith, *Asst Sec*
EMP: 41
SQ FT: 4,000
SALES: 1MM **Privately Held**
SIC: 7032 7041 5812 Fishing camp; lodging house, organization; eating places

(G-6752)
SANDCO INDUSTRIES
567 Premier Dr (43410-2157)
PHONE...................................419 334-9090
Donald Nalley, *Director*
EMP: 130
SALES: 1.4MM **Privately Held**
WEB: www.sanmrdd.org
SIC: 8331 Sheltered workshop

(G-6753)
SPADER FREIGHT CARRIERS INC
1134 E Mcpherson Hwy (43410-9802)
P.O. Box 246 (43410-0246)
PHONE...................................419 547-1117
David Spader, *President*
David L Spader, *President*
Steve Spader, *Vice Pres*
Tom Spader, *Admin Sec*
EMP: 62
SQ FT: 58,000
SALES: 8.9MM **Privately Held**
SIC: 4213 Trucking, except local

(G-6754)
SPADER FREIGHT SERVICES INC (PA)
Also Called: S F S
1134 E Mcpherson Hwy (43410-9802)
P.O. Box 246 (43410-0246)
PHONE...................................419 547-1117
David Spader, *President*
Steve Spader, *Vice Pres*
Steve Schwiebert, *Safety Dir*
Adam Powell, *Manager*
Tom Spader, *Admin Sec*
EMP: 60
SQ FT: 60,000
SALES (est): 6.8MM **Privately Held**
WEB: www.spaderfreight.com
SIC: 4213 Contract haulers

(G-6755)
WHIRLPOOL CORPORATION
1081 W Mcpherson Hwy (43410-1001)
PHONE...................................419 547-2610
Joe Lafave, *Senior Engr*
Tom Borro, *Manager*
EMP: 125
SALES (corp-wide): 21B **Publicly Held**
WEB: www.whirlpoolcorp.com
SIC: 4225 General warehousing
PA: Whirlpool Corporation
2000 N M 63
Benton Harbor MI 49022
269 923-5000

Coal Grove
Lawrence County

(G-6756)
TRI-STATE INDUSTRIES INC
606 Carlton Davidson Ln (45638-2926)
PHONE...................................740 532-0406
Paul Mollett, *Director*
EMP: 175
SQ FT: 30,000
SALES: 1.4MM **Privately Held**
SIC: 8331 Sheltered workshop

Coldwater
Mercer County

(G-6757)
COUNTY OF MERCER
Also Called: Coldwater Ems
510 W Main St (45828-1607)
PHONE...................................419 678-8071
Kevin Sanning, *Chief*
EMP: 25 **Privately Held**
WEB: www.mercercountyohio.org
SIC: 8322 Emergency social services
PA: County Of Mercer
220 W Livingston St A201
Celina OH 45822
419 586-3178

(G-6758)
HCF OF BRIARWOOD INC
Also Called: Briarwood Mano
100 Don Desch Dr D (45828-1583)
PHONE...................................419 678-2311
Dean Nuff, *QC Dir*
Kirsten Fennig, *Hum Res Coord*
Janelle Dhulte, *Marketing Staff*
Janel Schulte, *Marketing Staff*
Shanna Holland, *Exec Dir*
EMP: 224
SALES (est): 5.2MM
SALES (corp-wide): 154.8MM **Privately Held**
WEB: www.hcfinc.com
SIC: 8051 Extended care facility
PA: Hcf Management, Inc.
1100 Shawnee Rd
Lima OH 45805
419 999-2010

(G-6759)
HOSPICE OF DARKE COUNTY INC
Also Called: State of Heart HM Hlth Hospice
230 W Main St (45828-1703)
PHONE...................................419 678-4808
Tammy Fox, *Director*
EMP: 25 **Privately Held**
WEB: www.stateoftheheartcare.org
SIC: 8093 7361 Specialty outpatient clinics; employment agencies
PA: Hospice Of Darke County, Inc.
1350 N Broadway St
Greenville OH 45331

(G-6760)
KENN-FELD GROUP LLC (PA)
5228 State Route 118 (45828-9702)
PHONE...................................419 678-2375
Tom Burenga, *Managing Prtnr*
Dan Lefeld, *Store Mgr*
Bruce C Kennedy, *Mng Member*
EMP: 31
SALES (est): 29.5MM **Privately Held**
SIC: 5083 Farm & garden machinery

(G-6761)
LEFELD IMPLEMENT INC (PA)
Also Called: John Deere Authorized Dealer
5228 State Route 118 (45828-9702)
PHONE...................................419 678-2375
Steve Layfield, *President*
Judy Marbaugh, *Corp Secy*
Dan Lefeld, *Vice Pres*
Michael Lefeld, *Vice Pres*
Paul J Lefeld Jr, *Vice Pres*
▲ EMP: 28
SQ FT: 40,000

SALES (est): 5.2MM **Privately Held**
SIC: **5999** 5082 Farm machinery; farm
equipment & supplies; construction &
mining machinery

(G-6762)
**LEFELD WELDING & STL SUPS
INC (PA)**
Also Called: Lefeld Supplies Rental
600 N 2nd St (45828-9777)
PHONE.................................419 678-2397
Stanley E Lefeld, *CEO*
Gary Lefeld, *President*
Stan Lefeld, *General Mgr*
Roy Kremer, *Purchasing*
Marge Lefeld, *Controller*
▲ EMP: 43 EST: 1953
SQ FT: 10,400
SALES (est): 25.1MM **Privately Held**
WEB: www.lefeld.com
SIC: **5084** 7353 1799 3441 Welding ma-
chinery & equipment; heavy construction
equipment rental; welding on site; fabri-
cated structural metal

(G-6763)
**MERCER CNTY JOINT
TOWNSHP HOSP**
Also Called: Mercer County Community Hosp
800 W Main St (45828-1613)
PHONE.................................419 678-2341
EMP: 342
SALES (corp-wide): 54.5MM **Privately
Held**
SIC: **8062** General medical & surgical hos-
pitals
PA: Mercer County Joint Township Commu-
nity Hospital
800 W Main St
Coldwater OH 45828
419 678-2341

(G-6764)
PAX STEEL PRODUCTS INC
104 E Vine St (45828-1246)
PHONE.................................419 678-1481
Bill Kramer, *President*
EMP: 50
SALES (est): 3MM **Privately Held**
SIC: **5083** Farm & garden machinery

(G-6765)
**THE PEOPLES BANK CO INC
(PA)**
112 W Main St 114 (45828-1701)
P.O. Box 110 (45828-0110)
PHONE.................................419 678-2385
Jack A Hartings, *President*
Jeff Wolters, *Credit Staff*
EMP: 29 EST: 1905
SQ FT: 8,000
SALES: 17.7MM **Privately Held**
SIC: **6022** 8721 State trust companies ac-
cepting deposits, commercial; accounting,
auditing & bookkeeping

(G-6766)
THE PEOPLES BANK CO INC
112 W Main St (45828-1701)
P.O. Box 110 (45828-0110)
PHONE.................................419 678-2385
Jack Hartings, *Manager*
EMP: 30
SALES (corp-wide): 17.7MM **Privately
Held**
SIC: **6022** State commercial banks
PA: The Peoples Bank Co Inc
112 W Main St 114
Coldwater OH 45828
419 678-2385

(G-6767)
VILLAGE OF COLDWATER
Also Called: Tax Department
610 W Sycamore St (45828-1662)
PHONE.................................419 678-2685
Eric Thomas, *Manager*
EMP: 80 **Privately Held**
WEB: www.villageofcoldwater.com
SIC: **7291** 9111 Tax return preparation
services; city & town managers' offices
PA: Village Of Coldwater
610 W Sycamore St
Coldwater OH 45828
419 678-4881

(G-6768)
OHIO STATE PARKS INC
Also Called: Hueston Woods Lodge,
5201 Lodge Rd (45003-9038)
PHONE.................................513 664-3504
Susan Chapin, *Sales Staff*
Tom Arvan, *Manager*
EMP: 60
SALES (est): 3MM **Privately Held**
WEB: www.hwpaintball.com
SIC: **7011** 7992 5813 5812 Vacation
lodges; public golf courses; drinking
places; eating places

(G-6769)
AMERI-LINE INC
27060 Royalton Rd (44028-9048)
P.O. Box 965 (44028-0965)
PHONE.................................440 316-4500
Joseph Michetti, *President*
Gregory Romanovich, *Corp Secy*
Jerome Santivasci, *Vice Pres*
EMP: 30
SQ FT: 12,000
SALES: 2.7MM **Privately Held**
WEB: www.ameri-line.com
SIC: **4213** 4731 Contract haulers; truck
transportation brokers

(G-6770)
CAMILLUS VILLA INC
10515 East River Rd (44028-9541)
PHONE.................................440 236-5091
Bruce A Schirhart, *President*
EMP: 90
SQ FT: 18,000
SALES (est): 4.1MM **Privately Held**
SIC: **8051** Skilled nursing care facilities

(G-6771)
CENTRAL COMMAND INC
33891 Henwell Rd (44028-9150)
PHONE.................................330 723-2062
Keith Peer, *President*
EMP: 25
SQ FT: 4,000
SALES (est): 2.1MM **Privately Held**
WEB: www.centralcommand.com
SIC: **7374** Data processing & preparation

(G-6772)
CLEVELAND PICK-A-PART INC
12420 Station Rd (44028-9501)
PHONE.................................440 236-5031
Richard Fragnoli, *President*
Rebecca Fragnoli, *Principal*
Brian Fragnoli, *Vice Pres*
EMP: 32
SQ FT: 10,000
SALES (est): 950K **Privately Held**
WEB: www.clevelandpickapart.com
SIC: **7549** Automotive maintenance serv-
ices

(G-6773)
**COLUMBIA HILLS COUNTRY
CLB INC**
16200 East River Rd (44028-9485)
PHONE.................................440 236-5051
Michael Weinhardt, *President*
Karsen Eckweiler, *Manager*
Jon Standen, *Executive*
EMP: 25
SQ FT: 43,000
SALES (est): 1.4MM **Privately Held**
WEB: www.columbiahills.org
SIC: **7997** Country club, membership

(G-6774)
DORLON GOLF CLUB
18000 Station Rd (44028-8726)
PHONE.................................440 236-8234
Debra Lontor, *Owner*
EMP: 25

SQ FT: 2,500
SALES (est): 768.4K **Privately Held**
WEB: www.dorlon.com
SIC: **7992** Public golf courses

(G-6775)
**EMERALD WOODS GOLF
COURSE**
11464 Clarke Rd (44028-9231)
PHONE.................................440 236-8940
Richard McCoain, *President*
EMP: 25
SQ FT: 1,500
SALES (est): 1MM **Privately Held**
WEB: www.emeraldwoodsgc.com
SIC: **7992** 5941 Public golf courses; sport-
ing goods & bicycle shops

(G-6776)
J D S LEASING INC
27230 Royalton Rd (44028-9159)
PHONE.................................440 236-6575
Scott Mihu, *President*
EMP: 33
SALES (est): 1.5MM **Privately Held**
WEB: www.jdstrucking.com
SIC: **7538** Truck engine repair, except in-
dustrial

(G-6777)
**M & B TRUCKING EXPRESS
CORP**
27457 Royalton Rd (44028-9159)
P.O. Box 395 (44028-0395)
PHONE.................................440 236-8820
Michael A Bagi, *President*
Deborah Hawley, *Treasurer*
Malissa Ware,
EMP: 26
SQ FT: 1,500
SALES (est): 1MM **Privately Held**
SIC: **4213** Trucking, except local

(G-6778)
MASLYK LANDSCAPING INC
12289 Eaton Commerce Pkwy # 2
(44028-9208)
PHONE.................................440 748-3635
Alan Maslyk, *President*
EMP: 30
SALES (est): 2.1MM **Privately Held**
SIC: **0781** Landscape services

(G-6779)
MORTONS LAWN SERVICE INC
Also Called: Morton Landscape Dev Co
11564 Station Rd (44028-9501)
P.O. Box 967 (44028-0967)
PHONE.................................440 236-3550
Barry J Morton, *President*
EMP: 50 EST: 1981
SQ FT: 3,000
SALES (est): 3.7MM **Privately Held**
WEB: www.mortonslandscaping.com
SIC: **0781** 0782 Landscape services; fertil-
izing services, lawn

(G-6780)
**TOTAL RHABILITATION
SPECIALIST**
23050 Louise Ln (44028-9474)
PHONE.................................440 236-8527
Ray Bilecky, *Principal*
David Chhoransky, *Principal*
Mizzy Chhoransky, *Principal*
EMP: 50
SALES (est): 479.9K **Privately Held**
SIC: **8049** Physical therapist

(G-6781)
BUCKEYE COMPONENTS LLC
1340 State Route 14 (44408-9648)
PHONE.................................330 482-5163
Robert Holmes,
EMP: 30
SQ FT: 8,000
SALES (est): 2.8MM **Privately Held**
SIC: **5031** 2439 Lumber, plywood & mill-
work; trusses, wooden roof

(G-6782)
C TUCKER COPE & ASSOC INC
170 Duquesne St (44408-1637)
PHONE.................................330 482-4472
Charles T Cope, *President*
Linda Cope, *Vice Pres*
EMP: 42
SALES (est): 11.9MM **Privately Held**
WEB: www.ctcope.com
SIC: **1611** 1542 1541 Concrete construc-
tion: roads, highways, sidewalks, etc.;
commercial & office building, new con-
struction; industrial buildings, new con-
struction

(G-6783)
**CHRISTIAN HEARTLAND
SCHOOL**
28 Pittsburgh St (44408-1310)
PHONE.................................330 482-2331
Dallas Lehman, *Principal*
Patricia Hall, *Treasurer*
Eric Hosler, *Administration*
Claudia Bell, *Teacher*
Cindy Russo, *Teacher*
EMP: 103
SALES: 2.2MM **Privately Held**
SIC: **8211** 8351 Private elementary & sec-
ondary schools; preschool center

(G-6784)
**COLUMBIANA BOILER
COMPANY LLC**
200 W Railroad St (44408-1281)
PHONE.................................330 482-3373
Michael J Sherwin, *President*
Wayne Good, *Vice Pres*
Chuck Gorby, *Vice Pres*
Gerianne Klepfer, *CFO*
Tina Cousins, *Asst Mgr*
◆ EMP: 45 EST: 1894
SQ FT: 50,000
SALES: 9.5MM
SALES (corp-wide): 4.3MM **Privately
Held**
SIC: **1791** 3443 Storage tanks, metal:
erection; process vessels, industrial:
metal plate
PA: Columbiana Holding Co Inc
200 W Railroad St
Columbiana OH 44408
330 482-3373

(G-6785)
**COLUMBIANA SERVICE
COMPANY LLC**
Also Called: Reichard Industries, LLC
338 S Main St (44408-1509)
PHONE.................................330 482-5511
James Hawkins,
EMP: 65
SALES: 2MM **Privately Held**
SIC: **7363** Employee leasing service

(G-6786)
D & V TRUCKING INC
12803 Clmbana Canfield Rd (44408-9769)
PHONE.................................330 482-9440
Danny W Fowler Jr, *President*
EMP: 50
SQ FT: 20,000
SALES (est): 6.3MM **Privately Held**
SIC: **4212** Dump truck haulage

(G-6787)
DAS DUTCH VILLAGE INN
150 E State Route 14 (44408-8425)
PHONE.................................330 482-5050
Ralph Witmer, *Partner*
Raymond Horst, *Partner*
David Stryffeler, *General Mgr*
Jacqueline Smith, *Chief Mktg Ofcr*
Rose Conrad, *Marketing Mgr*
EMP: 63 EST: 2001
SQ FT: 3,400
SALES (est): 3.1MM **Privately Held**
WEB: www.dasdutchvillage.com
SIC: **7011** Vacation lodges

(G-6788)
**FOUR WHEEL DRIVE
HARDWARE LLC**
Also Called: 4wd
44488 State Route 14 (44408-9540)
PHONE.................................330 482-4733

George Adler, *CEO*
Eb Peters, *President*
◆ **EMP:** 155
SQ FT: 53,000
SALES (est): 31.3MM
SALES (corp-wide): 131.4B **Publicly Held**
WEB: www.performanceproduct.net
SIC: 5013 5531 Automotive supplies & parts; automotive parts; automotive accessories
HQ: Transamerican Dissolution Company, Llc
400 W Artesia Blvd
Compton CA 90220
310 900-5500

(G-6789)
MACO CONSTRUCTION SERVICES
170 Duquesne St (44408-1637)
PHONE..................................330 482-4472
Linda Cope, *President*
C Tucker Cope, *Corp Secy*
EMP: 35
SQ FT: 1,500
SALES (est): 4.3MM **Privately Held**
SIC: 1541 1611 Steel building construction; concrete construction: roads, highways, sidewalks, etc.

(G-6790)
MCMASTER FARMS
345 Old Fourteen Rd (44408-9493)
PHONE..................................330 482-2913
David McMaster, *Owner*
Jon Jesse McMaster, *Partner*
EMP: 69
SALES (est): 4.6MM **Privately Held**
SIC: 0161 0134 0119 Corn farm, sweet; pumpkin farm; Irish potatoes; feeder grains

(G-6791)
R & L TRANSFER INC
1320 Springfield Rd (44408)
PHONE..................................330 482-5800
Timothy Oswald, *Manager*
EMP: 200 **Privately Held**
WEB: www.robertsarena.com
SIC: 4213 4212 Trucking, except local; local trucking, without storage
HQ: R & L Transfer, Inc.
600 Gilliam Rd
Wilmington OH 45177
937 382-1494

(G-6792)
STG COMMUNICATION SERVICES INC
1401 Wardingsley Ave (44408-9756)
PHONE..................................330 482-0500
Mark Muzzane, *President*
Brien Meals, *Project Mgr*
Bob Wright, *Opers Staff*
Teri Kechler, *Finance*
Sharon McDevitt, *Office Mgr*
EMP: 35
SALES (est): 4.3MM **Privately Held**
SIC: 8999 Communication services

(G-6793)
STG COMMUNICATION SERVICES INC
1401 Wardingsley Ave (44408-9756)
PHONE..................................330 482-0500
Mark Muccana, *President*
M Scott Strong, *Vice Pres*
EMP: 25
SQ FT: 10,000
SALES (est): 4.2MM **Privately Held**
WEB: www.stgcom.com
SIC: 1623 Transmitting tower (telecommunication) construction

(G-6794)
U S A CONCRETE SPECIALISTS
145 Nulf Dr (44408-9730)
PHONE..................................330 482-9150
Joseph L Rich, *President*
EMP: 30
SALES (est): 1.8MM **Privately Held**
SIC: 1771 Concrete work

(G-6795)
WINDSOR HOUSE INC
Also Called: Parkside Health Care Center
930 E Park Ave (44408-1452)
PHONE..................................330 482-1375
Wendy Dickson, *Human Res Dir*
Jennifer Connely, *Manager*
EMP: 100
SALES (corp-wide): 14.1MM **Privately Held**
SIC: 8051 Skilled nursing care facilities
PA: Windsor House, Inc.
101 W Liberty St
Girard OH
330 545-1550

(G-6796)
WINDSOR HOUSE INC
Also Called: Northeastern Ohio Alzheimer Ctr
1899 W Garfield Rd (44408-9785)
PHONE..................................330 549-9259
Kim Guarnieri, *Principal*
EMP: 125
SALES (corp-wide): 14.1MM **Privately Held**
SIC: 8051 8052 Skilled nursing care facilities; intermediate care facilities
PA: Windsor House, Inc.
101 W Liberty St
Girard OH
330 545-1550

Columbus
Delaware County

(G-6797)
3SG PLUS LLC
8415 Pulsar Pl Ste 100 (43240-4032)
PHONE..................................614 652-0019
Nanda Nair, *President*
Jason Fair, *Production*
Erick Lobao, *Manager*
Jeffrey Wiedl, *CTO*
EMP: 37
SQ FT: 20,000
SALES (est): 1.2MM **Privately Held**
SIC: 8742 7299 Management information systems consultant; personal document & information services

(G-6798)
ADENA COMMERCIAL LLC
Also Called: Colliers International
8800 Lyra Dr Ste 650 (43240-2107)
PHONE..................................614 436-9800
Richard B Schuen, *CEO*
Michael R Linder, *Senior VP*
EMP: 40
SQ FT: 7,500
SALES (est): 7MM
SALES (corp-wide): 2.2B **Privately Held**
WEB: www.adenarealty.com
SIC: 6531 Real estate agent, commercial
HQ: Colliers International Property Consultants Inc.
601 Union St Ste 3320
Seattle WA 98101
206 695-4200

(G-6799)
ANTHEM INSURANCE COMPANIES INC
Also Called: Blue Cross
8940 Lyra Dr (43240-2162)
P.O. Box 182361 (43218-2361)
PHONE..................................614 438-3542
Joe Bobey, *Branch Mgr*
Thomas Sandercock, *Manager*
EMP: 81
SALES (corp-wide): 92.1B **Publicly Held**
WEB: www.anthem-inc.com
SIC: 6324 Hospital & medical service plans
HQ: Anthem Insurance Companies, Inc.
220 Virginia Ave
Indianapolis IN 46204
317 488-6000

(G-6800)
BANC ONE SERVICES CORPORATION (HQ)
1111 Polaris Pkwy Ste B3 (43240-2031)
P.O. Box 710638 (43271-0001)
PHONE..................................614 248-5800
Neil Williams, *Senior VP*
EMP: 2855
SALES (est): 156.1MM
SALES (corp-wide): 131.4B **Publicly Held**
WEB: www.bancone.com
SIC: 7389 Financial services
PA: Jpmorgan Chase & Co.
383 Madison Ave
New York NY 10179
212 270-6000

(G-6801)
BANKERS LIFE & CASUALTY CO
8740 Orion Pl Ste 204 (43240-4063)
PHONE..................................614 987-0590
Sandy Harned, *Sales Staff*
John M Kwasnik, *Manager*
William McKinney, *Agent*
EMP: 37
SALES (corp-wide): 4.3B **Publicly Held**
WEB: www.bankerslife.com
SIC: 6311 Life insurance
HQ: Bankers Life & Casualty Co
111 E Wacker Dr Ste 2100
Chicago IL 60601
312 396-6000

(G-6802)
CAPITAL LIGHTING INC
901 Polaris Pkwy (43240-2035)
PHONE..................................614 841-1200
Larry W King, *President*
David L Winks, *Vice Pres*
Ann Landis, *Warehouse Mgr*
Jeff Santille, *Warehouse Mgr*
Keith Shuck, *Sales Staff*
▲ **EMP:** 60
SQ FT: 32,000
SALES (est): 39.3MM **Privately Held**
WEB: www.capitallightinginc.com
SIC: 5063 5719 Lighting fixtures; lighting, lamps & accessories

(G-6803)
CENTER FOR DAGNSTC IMAGING INC
2141 Polaris Pkwy (43240-2022)
PHONE..................................614 841-0800
EMP: 114 **Privately Held**
SIC: 8011 Radiologist
PA: Center For Diagnostic Imaging, Inc.
5775 Wayzata Blvd Ste 400
Minneapolis MN 55416

(G-6804)
CENTURY 21-JOE WALKER & ASSOC
Also Called: Century 21 - North Office
8800 Lyra Dr Ste 600 (43240-2120)
PHONE..................................614 899-1400
Joseph Walker, *President*
Charity Walker, *Vice Pres*
EMP: 40
SALES: 3.5MM **Privately Held**
WEB: www.maxcopeland.com
SIC: 6531 Real estate agent, residential

(G-6805)
CGI TECHNOLOGIES SOLUTIONS INC
2000 Polaris Pkwy (43240-2108)
PHONE..................................614 880-2200
Joyce Clause, *Branch Mgr*
EMP: 56
SALES (corp-wide): 8.6B **Privately Held**
SIC: 7379 Computer related consulting services
HQ: Cgi Technologies And Solutions Inc.
11325 Random Hills Rd
Fairfax VA 22030
703 267-8000

(G-6806)
CHANGES HAIR DESIGNERS INC
Also Called: Changes Salon & Day Spa
2054 Polaris Pkwy (43240-2007)
PHONE..................................614 846-6666
William Reichert, *President*
Sonya Pellegrini, *Manager*
EMP: 25
SQ FT: 3,200
SALES (est): 713.5K **Privately Held**
WEB: www.changessalon.com
SIC: 7991 7231 Spas; beauty shops

(G-6807)
CHASE EQUIPMENT FINANCE INC (HQ)
1111 Polaris Pkwy Ste A3 (43240-2031)
PHONE..................................800 678-2601
Clif H Gottwals, *CEO*
Gary S Gage, *Vice Pres*
EMP: 230
SQ FT: 43,000
SALES (est): 64.4MM
SALES (corp-wide): 131.4B **Publicly Held**
SIC: 6021 National commercial banks
PA: Jpmorgan Chase & Co.
383 Madison Ave
New York NY 10179
212 270-6000

(G-6808)
CHASE EQUIPMENT FINANCE INC
1111 Polaris Pkwy Ste A3 (43240-2031)
PHONE..................................614 213-2246
Portfolio Service, *Manager*
EMP: 212
SALES (corp-wide): 131.4B **Publicly Held**
SIC: 6021 National commercial banks
HQ: Chase Equipment Finance, Inc.
1111 Polaris Pkwy Ste A3
Columbus OH 43240
800 678-2601

(G-6809)
COLUMBUS FINANCIAL GR
8425 Pulsar Pl Ste 450 (43240-2008)
PHONE..................................614 785-5100
Paul J Vineis, *Principal*
Barbara De Francisco, *Administration*
EMP: 25
SALES (est): 5.1MM **Privately Held**
SIC: 6311 Life insurance

(G-6810)
CORPORATE ONE FEDERAL CR UN (PA)
8700 Orion Pl (43240-2078)
P.O. Box 2770 (43216-2770)
PHONE..................................614 825-9314
Lee C Butke, *CEO*
Melissa Ashley, *Exec VP*
Tammy Cantrell, *Exec VP*
Joseph Ghammashi, *Exec VP*
Jim Horlacher, *Exec VP*
EMP: 98
SQ FT: 35,000
SALES (est): 23.5MM **Privately Held**
SIC: 6061 Federal credit unions

(G-6811)
CRANEL INCORPORATED (PA)
Also Called: Cranel Imaging
8999 Gemini Pkwy Ste A (43240-2250)
PHONE..................................614 431-8000
Craig Wallace, *President*
James Wallace, *Chairman*
Leslie Duff, *Vice Pres*
Joseph Jackson, *Vice Pres*
Scott Slack, *Vice Pres*
EMP: 100
SQ FT: 65,000
SALES (est): 52.5MM **Privately Held**
WEB: www.adexisstorage.com
SIC: 5045 Computer peripheral equipment

(G-6812)
DUGAN & MEYERS CONSTRUCTION CO
8740 Orion Pl Ste 220 (43240-4063)
PHONE..................................614 257-7430
Jeffery Kelly, *President*
Lincoln Ketterer, *Vice Pres*
Jeffrey Kelly, *Treasurer*
Jerome E Meyers, *Admin Sec*
EMP: 40
SQ FT: 2,500

SALES (est): 4.4MM
SALES (corp-wide): 103.1MM **Privately Held**
WEB: www.dugan-meyers.com
SIC: 1541 1542 Industrial buildings, new construction; commercial & office building, new construction
HQ: Dugan & Meyers Construction Co
　　11110 Kenwood Rd
　　Blue Ash OH 45242
　　513 891-4300

(G-6813)
GOOD NIGHT MEDICAL OHIO LLC
8999 Gemini Pkwy Ste A (43240-2250)
PHONE..................................614 384-7433
Alan Rudy, *CEO*
Larry Pliskin, *Senior VP*
EMP: 30
SALES (est): 1.2MM **Privately Held**
SIC: 8099 Medical services organization

(G-6814)
HILTON GRDN INN CLMBUS POLARIS
8535 Lyra Dr (43240-2026)
PHONE..................................614 846-8884
Dan Fox, *Principal*
EMP: 25
SALES (est): 1.4MM **Privately Held**
SIC: 7011 Hotels

(G-6815)
HILTON POLARIS
Also Called: Hilton Columbus Polaris
8700 Lyra Dr (43240-2103)
PHONE..................................614 885-1600
Jamie Johnson, *Principal*
EMP: 47 **EST:** 2008
SALES (est): 3.5MM **Privately Held**
SIC: 7011 Hotels

(G-6816)
HTP INC
8720 Orion Pl Ste 300 (43240-2111)
PHONE..................................614 885-1272
Ray Shealy, *CEO*
Dennis Swartzlander, *Ch of Bd*
Fred Richards, *Vice Pres*
EMP: 42
SQ FT: 13,968
SALES: 5.5MM **Privately Held**
WEB: www.htp-inc.com
SIC: 8999 Communication services

(G-6817)
JOSEPH WALKER INC
Also Called: Century 21
8800 Lyra Dr Ste 600 (43240-2120)
PHONE..................................614 895-3840
Joseph Walker, *President*
EMP: 50
SQ FT: 3,050
SALES (est): 2MM **Privately Held**
WEB: www.plcox.com
SIC: 6531 Real estate agent, residential

(G-6818)
JPMORGAN CHASE BANK NAT ASSN (HQ)
1111 Polaris Pkwy (43240-2050)
PHONE..................................614 436-3055
James Dimon, *Ch of Bd*
Sean Friedman, *President*
David Lawton, *Principal*
Jeffrey Imes, *Vice Pres*
Kenneth Johnson, *Vice Pres*
◆ **EMP:** 1800
SALES: 81.8MM
SALES (corp-wide): 131.4B **Publicly Held**
WEB: www.chase.com
SIC: 6022 6099 6799 6211 State commercial banks; travelers' checks issuance; safe deposit companies; real estate investors, except property operators; investment bankers; mortgage bankers; credit card service
PA: Jpmorgan Chase & Co.
　　383 Madison Ave
　　New York NY 10179
　　212 270-6000

(G-6819)
JPMORGAN HIGH YIELD FUND
1111 Polaris Pkwy (43240-2031)
PHONE..................................614 248-7017
Toni Demsky, *Manager*
EMP: 36
SALES (est): 255K
SALES (corp-wide): 131.4B **Publicly Held**
SIC: 6722 Money market mutual funds
HQ: Jpmorgan Investment Advisors Inc.
　　1111 Polaris Pkwy
　　Columbus OH 43240

(G-6820)
JPMORGAN INV ADVISORS INC (HQ)
1111 Polaris Pkwy (43240-2031)
P.O. Box 711235 (43271-0001)
PHONE..................................614 248-5800
David J Kundert, *President*
Tracie Stamm, *Vice Pres*
April Wilson, *Vice Pres*
Ley Sip, *Manager*
EMP: 550
SQ FT: 50,000
SALES (est): 96.4MM
SALES (corp-wide): 131.4B **Publicly Held**
SIC: 6282 Investment advisory service
PA: Jpmorgan Chase & Co.
　　383 Madison Ave
　　New York NY 10179
　　212 270-6000

(G-6821)
KARPINSKI ENGINEERING INC
8800 Lyra Dr Ste 530 (43240-2100)
PHONE..................................614 430-9820
Ken Borah, *Vice Pres*
EMP: 30
SALES (est): 1.9MM
SALES (corp-wide): 10.4MM **Privately Held**
SIC: 8711 Mechanical engineering; consulting engineer
PA: Karpinski Engineering, Inc.
　　3135 Euclid Ave Ste 200
　　Cleveland OH 44115
　　216 391-3700

(G-6822)
LOWES HOME CENTERS LLC
1465 Polaris Pkwy (43240-6002)
PHONE..................................614 433-9957
Chad Pratt, *Branch Mgr*
EMP: 150
SALES (corp-wide): 68.6B **Publicly Held**
SIC: 5211 5031 5722 5064 Home centers; building materials, exterior; building materials, interior; household appliance stores; electrical appliances, television & radio
HQ: Lowe's Home Centers, Llc
　　1605 Curtis Bridge Rd
　　Wilkesboro NC 28697
　　336 658-4000

(G-6823)
MANTA MEDIA INC
8760 Orion Pl Ste 200 (43240-2109)
PHONE..................................888 875-5833
John Swanciger, *CEO*
George Troutman, *CFO*
Dario Ambrosini, *Chief Mktg Ofcr*
Jonathan Flaugher, *Marketing Staff*
Eva Zielinski, *Marketing Staff*
EMP: 48
SQ FT: 5,000
SALES (est): 7.5MM **Privately Held**
WEB: www.ecnext.com
SIC: 7313 Printed media advertising representatives

(G-6824)
MERRILL LYNCH PIERCE FENNER
8425 Pulsar Pl Ste 200 (43240-4048)
PHONE..................................614 825-0350
Jeffrey Swartz, *Vice Pres*
Leonard Barbe, *Investment Ofcr*
Jeff Daniels, *Investment Ofcr*
Patti Schultz, *Investment Ofcr*
Larry Tyree, *Manager*
EMP: 40

SALES (corp-wide): 110.5B **Publicly Held**
WEB: www.merlyn.com
SIC: 6211 Security brokers & dealers
HQ: Merrill Lynch, Pierce, Fenner & Smith Incorporated
　　111 8th Ave
　　New York NY 10011
　　800 637-7455

(G-6825)
MICROSOFT CORPORATION
8800 Lyra Dr Ste 400 (43240-2100)
PHONE..................................614 719-5900
Marrida Davis, *General Mgr*
EMP: 45
SALES (corp-wide): 110.3B **Publicly Held**
WEB: www.microsoft.com
SIC: 7372 Application computer software
PA: Microsoft Corporation
　　1 Microsoft Way
　　Redmond WA 98052
　　425 882-8080

(G-6826)
NEWCOME CORP
Also Called: Newcome Electronic Systems
9005 Antares Ave (43240-2012)
P.O. Box 12247 (43212-0247)
PHONE..................................614 848-5688
Timothy W Newcome, *President*
EMP: 40
SQ FT: 8,500
SALES (est): 4.7MM **Privately Held**
WEB: www.newcome.com
SIC: 1731 Fiber optic cable installation; voice, data & video wiring contractor; computer installation

(G-6827)
OHIO BAR TITLE INSURANCE CO
8740 Orion Pl Ste 310 (43240-4063)
PHONE..................................614 310-8098
James Stipanovich, *Ch of Bd*
James M Nussbaum Jr, *COO*
W F Tom Burch Jr, *Senior VP*
Thomas R Jacklitch, *Senior VP*
Greg Holtz, *Vice Pres*
EMP: 52
SQ FT: 9,000
SALES (est): 570.5K **Privately Held**
WEB: www.ohiobartitle.com
SIC: 6361 Real estate title insurance

(G-6828)
OHIO FARMERS INSURANCE COMPANY
Also Called: Westfield Group
2000 Polaris Pkwy Ste 202 (43240-2006)
PHONE..................................614 848-6174
Keith Gilliam, *Manager*
Jennifer Stjohn, *Manager*
EMP: 75
SALES (corp-wide): 1.7B **Privately Held**
WEB: www.westfieldgrp.com
SIC: 6411 Property & casualty insurance agent
PA: Ohio Farmers Insurance Company
　　1 Park Cir
　　Westfield Center OH 44251
　　800 243-0210

(G-6829)
PACIFIC HERITG INN POLARIS LLC
9090 Lyra Dr (43240-2116)
PHONE..................................614 880-9080
Rachel Marchant, *Mng Member*
Juliann Beatty,
EMP: 50
SQ FT: 100,000
SALES (est): 757.5K **Privately Held**
SIC: 7011 Inns

(G-6830)
POLARIS TOWNE CENTER LLC
1500 Polaris Pkwy # 3000 (43240-2126)
PHONE..................................614 456-0123
Richard Hunt,
Richard Hunt,
EMP: 30

SALES (est): 967K
SALES (corp-wide): 843.4MM **Publicly Held**
WEB: www.glimcher.com
SIC: 6512 Nonresidential building operators
PA: Washington Prime Group Inc.
　　180 E Broad St Fl 21
　　Columbus OH 43215
　　614 621-9000

(G-6831)
PRIME AE GROUP INC
8415 Pulsar Pl Ste 300 (43240-4032)
PHONE..................................614 839-0250
Kumar Buvanendaran, *President*
Karen Curran, *Administration*
EMP: 82 **Privately Held**
SIC: 8711 8712 Civil engineering; architectural engineering
PA: Prime Ae Group, Inc.
　　5521 Res Pk Dr Ste 300
　　Baltimore MD 21228

(G-6832)
RANDSTAD TECHNOLOGIES LLC
8415 Pulsar Pl Ste 110 (43240-4032)
PHONE..................................614 436-0961
Reanna Lancaster, *Branch Mgr*
EMP: 72
SALES (corp-wide): 27.2B **Privately Held**
SIC: 7361 Employment agencies
HQ: Randstad Technologies, Llc
　　150 Presidential Way # 300
　　Woburn MA 01801
　　781 938-1910

(G-6833)
RIGHT AT HOME LLC
8828 Commerce Loop Dr (43240-2121)
PHONE..................................614 734-1110
Kathy Noble,
EMP: 30
SALES (est): 562.1K **Privately Held**
SIC: 8082 Home health care services

(G-6834)
ROCKFORD HOMES INC (PA)
999 Polaris Pkwy Ste 200 (43240-2051)
PHONE..................................614 785-0015
Robert E Yoakam Sr, *CEO*
Robert Yoakam Jr, *President*
Don Wick, *Vice Pres*
Rita Yoakam, *Treasurer*
EMP: 62
SALES (est): 15.8MM **Privately Held**
WEB: www.rockfordhomes.net
SIC: 1521 1522 6552 New construction, single-family houses; residential construction; subdividers & developers

(G-6835)
SEARS ROEBUCK AND CO
1280 Polaris Pkwy (43240-2036)
PHONE..................................614 797-2095
Michael Ladd, *Manager*
EMP: 116
SALES (corp-wide): 16.7B **Publicly Held**
SIC: 7549 Automotive maintenance services
HQ: Sears, Roebuck And Co.
　　3333 Beverly Rd
　　Hoffman Estates IL 60179
　　847 286-2500

(G-6836)
SEQUENT INC (PA)
Also Called: SEQUENT INFORMATION SOLUTIONS
8415 Pulsar Pl Ste 200 (43240-4032)
PHONE..................................614 436-5880
Bill Hutter, *CEO*
Joseph W Cole, *President*
Leigh Chaffin, *Payroll Mgr*
Barb Torchia, *Payroll Mgr*
Regina Risner, *Manager*
EMP: 85
SQ FT: 12,000
SALES: 10.9MM **Privately Held**
WEB: www.sequent.com
SIC: 7363 8748 Employee leasing service; employee programs administration

(G-6837)
VENTECH SOLUTIONS INC (PA)
8425 Pulsar Pl Ste 300 (43240-2079)
PHONE.....................614 757-1167
Herb Jones, *CEO*
Ravi Kunduru, *Chairman*
Randy Fogle, *CFO*
Harsh Trivedi, *Senior Mgr*
Jamie Shipman, *Technical Staff*
▼ EMP: 85
SQ FT: 14,000
SALES: 118MM **Privately Held**
WEB: www.ventechsolutions.com
SIC: 7371 7373 7379 Custom computer
programming services; systems engineer-
ing, computer related; systems integration
services; computer related maintenance
services

(G-6838)
WESTERN & SOUTHERN LF
INSUR CO
8425 Pulsar Pl Ste 310 (43240-4041)
PHONE.....................614 898-1066
Terry Garner, *Manager*
EMP: 27 **Privately Held**
SIC: 6411 Life insurance agents
HQ: The Western & Southern Life Insur-
ance Company
400 Broadway St
Cincinnati OH 45202
513 629-1800

(G-6839)
WESTFIELD SERVICES INC (PA)
2000 Polaris Pkwy Ste 202 (43240-2006)
P.O. Box 1690 (43216-1690)
PHONE.....................614 796-7700
Jon Park, *CEO*
Brian Bowerman, *Vice Pres*
EMP: 28 EST: 1998
SALES (est): 6.2MM **Privately Held**
WEB: www.westfieldservices.com
SIC: 6411 Property & casualty insurance
agent

Columbus
Franklin County

(G-6840)
1522 HESS STREET LLC
1522 Hess St (43212-2642)
PHONE.....................614 291-6876
Jeffery Brown, *President*
EMP: 35
SALES (est): 2.6MM **Privately Held**
SIC: 1521 General remodeling, single-fam-
ily houses

(G-6841)
1ST ADVANCED EMS LLC
723 N James Rd (43219-1839)
PHONE.....................614 348-9991
Lucy Kimkhe, *Financial Exec*
Yuri Fish, *Mng Member*
Mike Moore, *Manager*
EMP: 78
SALES (est): 2.9MM **Privately Held**
SIC: 4119 Ambulance service

(G-6842)
5 STAR HOTEL MANAGEMENT
IV LP
Also Called: Residence Inn By Marriott
6191 Quarter Horse Dr (43229-2568)
PHONE.....................614 431-1819
Stephanie Martin, *Principal*
EMP: 80
SALES (est): 1.8MM **Privately Held**
SIC: 7011 Hotels & motels

(G-6843)
50 S FRONT LLC
Also Called: Doubletree Suites by Hilton
50 S Front St (43215-4129)
PHONE.....................614 224-4600
EMP: 66
SALES (est): 3.3MM **Privately Held**
SIC: 7011 Hotels

(G-6844)
6TH CIRCUIT COURT
Also Called: US Probation Office
85 Marconi Blvd Rm 546 (43215-2835)
PHONE.....................614 719-3100
Linda Wilmouth, *Manager*
EMP: 34 **Publicly Held**
WEB: www.mied.uscourts.gov
SIC: 8322 Probation office
HQ: 6th Circuit Court
601 W Broadway Bsmt
Louisville KY 40202
502 625-3800

(G-6845)
845 YARD STREET LLC (PA)
375 N Front St Ste 200 (43215-2258)
PHONE.....................614 857-2330
Brian Ellis,
EMP: 60
SALES (est): 3.2MM **Privately Held**
SIC: 6798 Realty investment trusts

(G-6846)
A B INDUSTRIAL COATINGS
212 N Grant Ave (43215-2642)
PHONE.....................614 228-0383
EMP: 35
SALES (est): 1MM **Privately Held**
SIC: 1721 Painting/Paper Hanging Con-
tractor

(G-6847)
A BETTER CHOICE CHILD CARE
LLC
2572 Cleveland Ave (43211-1679)
PHONE.....................614 268-8503
Jama Farrah, *Branch Mgr*
EMP: 25
SALES (est): 434.3K **Privately Held**
SIC: 8322 Child related social services

(G-6848)
A T V INC
2047 Leonard Ave (43219-2277)
PHONE.....................614 252-5060
Paul Vellani, *President*
EMP: 115
SQ FT: 7,325
SALES: 3.9MM **Privately Held**
SIC: 4141 Local bus charter service

(G-6849)
A&R LOGISTICS INC
1230 Harmon Ave (43223-3307)
PHONE.....................614 444-4111
James Bedeker, *Manager*
EMP: 70
SALES (corp-wide): 247.6MM **Privately**
Held
WEB: www.arpdsi.com
SIC: 4213 Contract haulers
PA: A&R Logistics, Inc.
600 N Hurstbourne Pkwy # 110
Louisville KY 40222
815 941-5200

(G-6850)
A-1 NURSING CARE INC
2500 Corp Exchange Dr # 220
(43231-7601)
PHONE.....................614 268-3800
Naresh Patel, *President*
EMP: 200
SQ FT: 22,000
SALES (est): 11.3MM **Privately Held**
SIC: 7361 8082 Nurses' registry; home
health care services

(G-6851)
ABBOTT LABORATORIES
Also Called: Abbott Nutrition
585 Cleveland Ave (43211-1755)
P.O. Box 16546 (43216-6546)
PHONE.....................614 624-3191
Chuck Mundy, *Principal*
Ed Govekar, *Manager*
EMP: 550
SQ FT: 378,500
SALES (corp-wide): 30.5B **Publicly Held**
WEB: www.abbott.com
SIC: 8099 2834 2087 2086 Nutrition
services; pharmaceutical preparations;
flavoring extracts & syrups; bottled &
canned soft drinks; canned specialties
PA: Abbott Laboratories
100 Abbott Park Rd
Abbott Park IL 60064
224 667-6100

(G-6852)
ABF FREIGHT SYSTEM INC
1720 Joyce Ave (43219-1026)
P.O. Box 24666 (43224-0666)
PHONE.....................614 294-3537
Patrick Petit, *Sales Mgr*
Rich Desantis, *Manager*
EMP: 45
SALES (corp-wide): 3B **Publicly Held**
WEB: www.abfs.com
SIC: 4213 Contract haulers
HQ: Abf Freight System, Inc.
3801 Old Greenwood Rd
Fort Smith AR 72903
479 785-8700

(G-6853)
ABLE COMPANY LTD
PARTNERSHIP (PA)
Also Called: Able Roofing
4777 Westerville Rd (43231-6042)
PHONE.....................614 444-7663
Paul Demboski, *President*
Steven K Weyl,
EMP: 57
SQ FT: 23,000
SALES (est): 21.6MM **Privately Held**
SIC: 1761 1741 Roofing contractor; chim-
ney construction & maintenance

(G-6854)
ABLE ROOFING LLC
4777 Westerville Rd (43231-6042)
PHONE.....................614 444-7663
Paul Demboski, *Branch Mgr*
EMP: 50
SALES (corp-wide): 21.6MM **Privately**
Held
SIC: 1761 Roofing contractor
PA: Able Company Limited Partnership
4777 Westerville Rd
Columbus OH 43231
614 444-7663

(G-6855)
ABOVE & BEYOND
CAREGIVERS LLC
2862 Johnstown Rd (43219-1793)
PHONE.....................614 478-1700
Crystal L Sillah,
Elisee Ndenga,
EMP: 28
SALES (est): 772.1K **Privately Held**
SIC: 8082 4119 Home health care serv-
ices; local passenger transportation

(G-6856)
ABSOLUTE CARE
MANAGEMENT LLC (PA)
4618 Sawmill Rd (43220-2247)
PHONE.....................614 846-8053
Mark King, *CEO*
EMP: 35
SALES (est): 1.5MM **Privately Held**
WEB: www.absolutecarecompany.com
SIC: 8322 Individual & family services

(G-6857)
ACADEMIC SUPPORT SERVICES
LLC
Also Called: Janitorial Support Services
2958 Blossom Ave (43231-2925)
PHONE.....................740 274-6138
Audra Johnson, *Mng Member*
EMP: 31
SALES: 350K **Privately Held**
SIC: 8299 7349 Tutoring school; janitorial
service, contract basis

(G-6858)
ACADEMY KIDS LEARNING CTR
INC
289 Woodland Ave (43203-1747)
PHONE.....................614 258-5437
David R Weaver, *President*
Carol Burns, *Director*
Annett Howell, *Administration*
EMP: 30
SALES (est): 884K **Privately Held**
SIC: 8351 Preschool center

(G-6859)
ACCELERATED MOVING & STOR
INC
4001 Refugee Rd Ste 2 (43232-5187)
PHONE.....................614 836-1007
Todd G Wilson, *President*
Sherman Willis, *Assistant VP*
James Willis, *Vice Pres*
Michelle Kinnett, *Admin Asst*
EMP: 25
SQ FT: 11,000
SALES (est): 2.3MM **Privately Held**
SIC: 4214 4213 4212 Furniture moving &
storage, local; household goods transport;
moving services

(G-6860)
ACCENT DRAPERY CO INC
Also Called: Accent Drapery Supply Co
1180 Goodale Blvd (43212-3793)
PHONE.....................614 488-0741
Patrick Casbarro, *President*
Brian Whiteside, *Vice Pres*
Pat Casbarro, *Info Tech Mgr*
EMP: 27
SQ FT: 19,500
SALES (est): 4.1MM **Privately Held**
SIC: 5714 5023 2391 Draperies;
draperies; curtains & draperies

(G-6861)
ACCENTURE LLP
400 W Nationwide Blvd # 100
(43215-2377)
PHONE.....................614 629-2000
James Struntz, *Managing Prtnr*
Gregg Bourdo, *Corp Comm Staff*
John Hrusovsky, *Branch Mgr*
Richard Wyant, *Consultant*
Eric Matz, *Director*
EMP: 215 **Privately Held**
WEB: www.wavesecurities.com
SIC: 8742 8748 Business consultant; busi-
ness consulting
HQ: Accenture Llp
161 N Clark St Ste 1100
Chicago IL 60601
312 693-0161

(G-6862)
ACCESS OHIO
99 N Brice Rd Ste 360 (43213-6525)
PHONE.....................614 367-7700
Danielle Forsman, *Branch Mgr*
EMP: 31
SALES (corp-wide): 5.7MM **Privately**
Held
SIC: 8093 8031 8011 Mental health clinic,
outpatient; offices & clinics of osteopathic
physicians; clinic, operated by physicians
PA: Access Ohio
899 E Broad St Ste 150
Columbus OH 43205
614 985-3112

(G-6863)
ACCURATE INVENTORY AND C
Also Called: Quantum Services
4284 N High St Fl 1 (43214-2695)
PHONE.....................800 777-9414
Ray Crook Jr, *President*
Pam Hoyt, *Office Mgr*
Mark Flynn, *CTO*
EMP: 355 EST: 1971
SQ FT: 11,600
SALES (est): 26.4MM **Privately Held**
WEB: www.quantum.com
SIC: 7389 8742 Inventory computing serv-
ice; business consultant

(G-6864)
ACE BUILDING MAINTENANCE
LLC
2565 Mccutcheon Rd (43219-3337)
P.O. Box 24190 (43224-0190)
PHONE.....................614 471-2223
Raymond Doughty, *Supervisor*
Ruby J Doughty,
EMP: 37
SALES: 217K **Privately Held**
WEB: www.acebuildmaint.com
SIC: 7349 Building cleaning service; build-
ing maintenance, except repairs

G E O G R A P H I C

(G-6865)
ACLOCHE LLC (PA)
Also Called: Academy Medical Staffing Svcs
1800 Watermark Dr Ste 430 (43215-1397)
PHONE..................................888 608-0889
Kim Shoemaker, *CEO*
Georgia Ruch, *Founder*
Betty Lou Ruch, *Founder*
Toni Good, *Purch Agent*
Stacey Wibbeler, *Accounting Mgr*
EMP: 33
SQ FT: 12,000
SALES (est): 13.4MM **Privately Held**
WEB: www.acloche.com
SIC: 7363 8742 Temporary help service;
human resource consulting services

(G-6866)
ACOCK ASSOC ARCHITECTS LLC
383 N Front St Ste 1 (43215-2251)
PHONE..................................614 228-1586
Jack Maki, *Principal*
Leonard Whitley, *Project Mgr*
Mikey Perone, *Accountant*
George Acock, *Mng Member*
EMP: 25
SQ FT: 30,000
SALES: 4.8MM **Privately Held**
SIC: 8712 Architectural engineering

(G-6867)
ACORN DISTRIBUTORS INC
5310 Crosswind Dr (43228-3600)
PHONE..................................614 294-6444
Jennifer Rosenberg, *President*
Mary Beth Warner, *General Mgr*
Jim Long, *Purchasing*
Stephanie Garrett, *HR Admin*
Craig Cottingham, *Sales Mgr*
EMP: 40 **EST:** 2010
SQ FT: 100,000
SALES (est): 11.8MM **Privately Held**
SIC: 5113 5087 5046 Disposable plates,
cups, napkins & eating utensils; towels,
paper; napkins, paper; janitors' supplies;
commercial equipment

(G-6868)
ACTION FOR CHILDREN INC (PA)
78 Jefferson Ave (43215-3860)
PHONE..................................614 224-0222
Rhonda Fraas, *President*
Diane Bennett, *Exec Dir*
EMP: 38
SALES (est): 3.7MM **Privately Held**
WEB: www.actionforchildren.com
SIC: 7299 8351 8322 Information serv-
ices, consumer; child day care services;
individual & family services

(G-6869)
AD FARROW LLC (PA)
491 W Broad St (43215-2755)
PHONE..................................614 228-6353
Lisa Wallace, *Controller*
Bill Patton, *Sales Staff*
Paul Collins, *Manager*
Robert B Althoff,
EMP: 50 **EST:** 1912
SQ FT: 82,500
SALES (est): 11.3MM **Privately Held**
WEB: www.adfarrow.com
SIC: 5571 7699 Motorcycles; motorcycle
repair service

(G-6870)
AD INVESTMENTS LLC
375 N Front St Ste 200 (43215-2258)
PHONE..................................614 857-2340
Brian Ellis, *CEO*
EMP: 50
SALES: 2.6MM
SALES (corp-wide): 13.2B **Privately Held**
SIC: 6512 Commercial & industrial building
operation
HQ: Nationwide Realty Investors, Ltd.
375 N Front St Ste 200
Columbus OH 43215
614 857-2330

(G-6871)
ADEPT MARKETING OUTSOURCED LLC
855 Grandview Ave Ste 140 (43215-1189)
PHONE..................................614 452-4011
Sara Kear, *Vice Pres*
Gail Sech, *Vice Pres*
Marie Werhan, *Accounts Exec*
Justin Spring, *Mng Member*
Danielle Walton,
EMP: 35
SALES (est): 314K **Privately Held**
SIC: 8742 Marketing consulting services

(G-6872)
ADMINISTRATIVE SVCS OHIO DEPT
Also Called: Office of Procurement Services
4200 Surface Rd (43228-1313)
PHONE..................................614 466-5090
Wayne McCulty, *Principal*
EMP: 70 **Privately Held**
SIC: 7299 Consumer purchasing services
HQ: Ohio Department Of Administrative
Services
30 E Broad St
Columbus OH 43215

(G-6873)
ADVANCE HOME CARE LLC (PA)
1191 S James Rd Ste D (43227-1800)
PHONE..................................614 436-3611
Saed Mohamed, *CEO*
Abdillahi Yusuf, *President*
Idil Abdukadir, *Principal*
EMP: 80
SQ FT: 2,000
SALES (est): 1.6MM **Privately Held**
SIC: 8082 Home health care services

(G-6874)
ADVANCED FACILITIES MAINT CORP (PA)
6171 Huntley Rd Ste G (43229-1079)
P.O. Box 91171 (43209-7171)
PHONE..................................614 389-3495
Ross Pappas, *President*
EMP: 34
SQ FT: 10,000
SALES (est): 6.9MM **Privately Held**
SIC: 7349 Building maintenance services

(G-6875)
ADVANTAGE AEROTECH INC
Also Called: Alliance Advantage
1400 Hollybrier Dr # 121 (43230-8472)
PHONE..................................614 759-8329
EMP: 40
SALES (est): 3.1MM **Privately Held**
SIC: 8733 8711 Noncommercial Research
Organization Engineering Services

(G-6876)
ADVOCATE SOLUTIONS LLC
762 S Pearl St (43206-2032)
PHONE..................................614 444-5144
Peter McGeoch, *Partner*
Lynn Farley, *Office Mgr*
Jeff Jarvis, *Director*
Dwaine Gould,
Frank Carchedi,
EMP: 50
SQ FT: 5,300
SALES (est): 3.2MM **Privately Held**
WEB: www.gcrltd.com
SIC: 8742 Business consultant

(G-6877)
AEP ENERGY PARTNERS INC
1 Riverside Plz (43215-2355)
PHONE..................................614 716-1000
Nicholas K Akins, *CEO*
Robert P Powers, *Exec VP*
Paul Vegliante, *Exec VP*
Lana L Hillebrand, *Senior VP*
Mark Hagan, *Maint Spvr*
EMP: 50
SALES (est): 21.9MM **Privately Held**
SIC: 4911 Electric services

(G-6878)
AEP ENERGY SERVICES INC
155 W Nationwide Blvd (43215-2570)
PHONE..................................614 583-2900
Melissa Neal, *Partner*

Stephan T Haynes, *Vice Pres*
Mark Becker, *Engineer*
Jamie Jankowski, *Director*
EMP: 260
SALES (est): 4MM
SALES (corp-wide): 16.2B **Publicly Held**
WEB: www.aep.com
SIC: 4911 Electric services
PA: American Electric Power Company, Inc.
1 Riverside Plz Fl # 1
Columbus OH 43215
614 716-1000

(G-6879)
AEP GENERATING COMPANY (HQ)
Also Called: Aegco
1 Riverside Plz Ste 1600 (43215-2355)
PHONE..................................614 223-1000
Nick Akins, *CEO*
E L Draper Jr, *President*
Mark A Gray, *Vice Pres*
Alice Bonning, *Analyst*
EMP: 1800
SALES: 564MM
SALES (corp-wide): 16.2B **Publicly Held**
WEB: www.aepmedia1.com
SIC: 4911 Generation, electric power
PA: American Electric Power Company, Inc.
1 Riverside Plz Fl # 1
Columbus OH 43215
614 716-1000

(G-6880)
AEP POWER MARKETING INC (HQ)
Also Called: America Electric Power Texas
1 Riverside Plz Fl 1 # 1 (43215-2355)
PHONE..................................614 716-1000
Michael Morris, *President*
Barbara Belville, *Counsel*
Mark Menezes, *Manager*
Nalini Selvaraj, *Manager*
Richard Hartman, *Info Tech Mgr*
EMP: 2000
SALES (est): 94.7MM
SALES (corp-wide): 16.2B **Publicly Held**
SIC: 4911 Electric services
PA: American Electric Power Company, Inc.
1 Riverside Plz Fl 1 # 1
Columbus OH 43215
614 716-1000

(G-6881)
AETNA BUILDING MAINTENANCE INC (DH)
Also Called: Aetna Integrated Services
646 Parsons Ave (43206-1435)
PHONE..................................614 476-1818
Paul Greenland, *President*
Darick Brown, *President*
Sean Letwat, *Opers Staff*
Robert Perlman, *Opers Staff*
David Hazlett, *Manager*
EMP: 354 **EST:** 1959
SQ FT: 12,000
SALES (est): 67.6MM
SALES (corp-wide): 29.6MM **Privately Held**
WEB: www.aetnabuilding.com
SIC: 7349 1711 1731 Janitorial service,
contract basis; window cleaning; plumb-
ing, heating, air-conditioning contractors;
electrical work
HQ: Atalian Global Services, Inc.
417 5th Ave
New York NY 10016
212 251-7846

(G-6882)
AFLAC INCORPORATED
30 Northwoods Blvd # 100 (43235-4716)
PHONE..................................614 410-1696
Robert Hare, *Branch Mgr*
EMP: 102
SALES (corp-wide): 21.7B **Publicly Held**
SIC: 6411 Insurance agents, brokers &
service
PA: Aflac Incorporated
1932 Wynnton Rd
Columbus GA 31999
706 323-3431

(G-6883)
AGEE CLYMER MTCHLL & PRTMAN (PA)
226 N 5th St Ste 501 (43215-2718)
PHONE..................................614 221-3318
James G Clymer, *Principal*
Russell Canestraro, *Principal*
Joffre Laret, *Principal*
Greg Mitchell, *Principal*
Mary Hahn, *Payroll Mgr*
EMP: 30
SALES (est): 3.7MM **Privately Held**
WEB: www.ageeclymer.com
SIC: 8111 General practice law office; gen-
eral practice attorney, lawyer

(G-6884)
AGGRESSIVE MECHANICAL INC
638 Greenlawn Ave (43223-2635)
PHONE..................................614 443-3280
Kevin Hall, *President*
Dan Bosworth, *Vice Pres*
John Mills, *Treasurer*
Russell Cochenour, *Admin Sec*
EMP: 25
SQ FT: 8,600
SALES (est): 5.7MM **Privately Held**
SIC: 1711 Heating & air conditioning con-
tractors

(G-6885)
AGRI COMMUNICATORS INC
Also Called: Ohio's Country Journal
1625 Bethel Rd Ste 203 (43220-2071)
PHONE..................................614 273-0465
Bart Johnson, *President*
Marilyn Johnson, *Corp Secy*
EMP: 25
SQ FT: 4,000
SALES (est): 2.2MM **Privately Held**
WEB: www.ocj.com
SIC: 7313 2721 Radio, television, pub-
lisher representatives; periodicals: pub-
lishing only

(G-6886)
AIRNET SYSTEMS INC (PA)
7250 Star Check Dr (43217-1025)
PHONE..................................614 409-4900
Joan C Makley, *Owner*
Jeffery B Harris, *COO*
Larry M Glasscock Jr, *Senior VP*
Greig Lake, *Vice Pres*
Craig A Leach, *Vice Pres*
EMP: 174
SALES (est): 132.2MM **Privately Held**
WEB: www.airnet.com
SIC: 4731 4522 Freight transportation
arrangement; air cargo carriers, non-
scheduled

(G-6887)
AIRPORT CORE HOTEL LLC (PA)
Also Called: Embassy Suites Columbus Arprt
2886 Airport Dr (43219-2240)
PHONE..................................614 536-0500
Michael Cooney, *General Mgr*
EMP: 150 **EST:** 2009
SALES (est): 7.8MM **Privately Held**
SIC: 7011 Hotels

(G-6888)
AIRTRON LP
3021 International St (43228-4635)
PHONE..................................614 274-2345
Bill Duecker, *Manager*
Rosie Crago,
EMP: 80 **Privately Held**
SIC: 1711 5075 Warm air heating & air
conditioning contractor; warm air heating
& air conditioning
HQ: Airtron, Inc.
9260 Marketpl Dr
Miamisburg OH 45342
937 898-0826

(G-6889)
AKSM/GENESIS MEDICAL SVCS INC
100 W 3rd Ave Ste 350 (43201-7205)
PHONE..................................614 447-0281
Ann Stevens, *President*
EMP: 25

SALES: 950K **Privately Held**
SIC: 8099 Medical services organization

(G-6890)
AKZO NOBEL COATINGS INC
1313 Windsor Ave (43211-2851)
P.O. Box 489 (43216-0489)
PHONE.................................614 294-3361
John Wolff, *Manager*
EMP: 200
SALES (corp-wide): 11.3B **Privately Held**
WEB: www.nam.sikkens.com
SIC: 2851 8734 Paints & allied products;
testing laboratories
HQ: Akzo Nobel Coatings Inc.
8220 Mohawk Dr
Strongsville OH 44136
440 297-5100

(G-6891)
ALL CRANE RENTAL CORP (PA)
683 Oakland Park Ave (43224-3936)
PHONE.................................614 261-1800
Michael C Liptak Jr, *President*
Mike Flanders, *General Mgr*
Stephanie Reynolds, *General Mgr*
Larry Liptak, *Vice Pres*
Kevin Flack, *Human Resources*
EMP: 60
SQ FT: 46,000
SALES (est): 10.8MM **Privately Held**
SIC: 7353 Cranes & aerial lift equipment,
rental or leasing

(G-6892)
ALLEN GARDINER DEROBERTS
777 Goodale Blvd Ste 200 (43212-3862)
PHONE.................................614 221-1500
Andrew Gardiner,
Stu Allen,
Jim Deroberts,
Paul Schnoover,
Bill C Shimp,
EMP: 37
SQ FT: 14,000
SALES (est): 6.8MM **Privately Held**
WEB: www.allengardiner.co.za
SIC: 6411 Insurance agents

(G-6893)
**ALLEN KHNLE STOVALL
NEUMAN LLP**
Also Called: Aksn
17 S High St Ste 1220 (43215-3441)
PHONE.................................614 221-8500
Thomas R Allen, *Managing Prtnr*
Rick L Ashton, *Partner*
J Matthew Fisher, *Partner*
Kenton L Kuehnle, *Partner*
Todd Neuman, *Partner*
EMP: 30
SALES (est): 1MM **Privately Held**
SIC: 8111 General practice attorney,
lawyer

(G-6894)
**ALLIANCE DATA SYSTEMS
CORP**
3075 Loyalty Cir (43219-3673)
P.O. Box 31262 (43219)
PHONE.................................614 729-4000
Michael J Galeano, *Counsel*
Sheryl McKenzie, *Vice Pres*
Eileen Ouellette, *Vice Pres*
Brian Showalter, *Opers Mgr*
Doug Westmill, *Engineer*
EMP: 263 **Publicly Held**
WEB: www.alliancedatasystems.com
SIC: 7374 Data processing service
PA: Alliance Data Systems Corporation
7500 Dallas Pkwy Ste 700
Plano TX 75024

(G-6895)
**ALLIED BUILDING PRODUCTS
CORP**
1055 Kinnear Rd (43212-1150)
PHONE.................................614 488-0717
Todd Mitchell, *Sales Mgr*
Rick Miller, *Manager*
EMP: 30
SALES (corp-wide): 4.3B **Publicly Held**
WEB: www.alliedbuilding.com
SIC: 5033 Roofing & siding materials

HQ: Allied Building Products Corp.
15 E Union Ave
East Rutherford NJ 07073
201 507-8400

(G-6896)
**ALLIED COMMUNICATIONS
CORP (PA)**
Also Called: Georgesville
755 Georgesville Rd (43228-2826)
PHONE.................................614 275-2075
Roberto Nueberger, *Principal*
EMP: 28
SALES (est): 10.9MM **Privately Held**
SIC: 4899 Data communication services

(G-6897)
**ALLIED FABRICATING & WLDG
CO**
5699 Chantry Dr (43232-4799)
PHONE.................................614 751-6664
Thomas Caminiti, *CEO*
Jack Burgoon, *President*
Joseph Caminiti, *President*
Raymond Cunningham, *Vice Pres*
Gary Arthurs, *Plant Mgr*
EMP: 34
SQ FT: 30,000
SALES (est): 7.4MM **Privately Held**
WEB: www.afaw.net
SIC: 3444 7692 3535 3441 Sheet metal
specialties, not stamped; welding repair;
conveyors & conveying equipment; fabri-
cated structural metal; rubber & plastics
hose & beltings

(G-6898)
ALLIED INTERSTATE LLC
P.O. Box 561534
PHONE.................................715 386-1810
EMP: 65
SALES (corp-wide): 1B **Privately Held**
SIC: 7322 Adjustment/Collection Services
HQ: Allied Interstate, Llc
12755 Hwy 55 Ste 300
Plymouth MN 55441
973 630-5720

(G-6899)
ALLPRO PARKING OHIO LLC
431 E Broad St (43215-4004)
PHONE.................................614 221-9696
Richard A Serra, *CEO*
EMP: 30
SALES (est): 402.5K
SALES (corp-wide): 25.1MM **Privately
Held**
SIC: 7521 Automobile parking
PA: Allpro Parking, Llc
465 Washington St Ste 100
Buffalo NY 14203
716 849-7275

(G-6900)
ALMOST FAMILY INC
Also Called: Home Care By Blackstone
445 Hutchinson Ave (43235-5677)
PHONE.................................614 457-1900
Jennifer Lockard, *Branch Mgr*
EMP: 26
SALES (corp-wide): 1.8B **Publicly Held**
SIC: 8082 Home health care services
HQ: Almost Family, Inc.
9510 Ormsby Station Rd # 300
Louisville KY 40223
502 891-1000

(G-6901)
ALPHA CHI OMEGA
103 E 15th Ave (43201-1601)
PHONE.................................614 291-3871
Lesley King, *President*
EMP: 38
SQ FT: 10,268
SALES (est): 1MM **Privately Held**
SIC: 7041 Fraternities & sororities

(G-6902)
ALPHA EPSILON PHI
200 E 17th Ave (43201-1535)
PHONE.................................614 294-5243
Rachel Campbell, *President*
Ashley Peterson, *Vice Pres*
Jessica Zuckerman, *Treasurer*
Daniele Lewis, *Admin Sec*
EMP: 46 EST: 2001

SALES: 88.8K **Privately Held**
SIC: 7041 Sorority residential house; fraternities & sororities

(G-6903)
**ALPHA GROUP OF DELAWARE
INC**
85 Marconi Blvd (43215-2823)
PHONE.................................614 222-1855
EMP: 51
SALES (corp-wide): 3.6MM **Privately
Held**
SIC: 8331 9111 Job Training/Related
Services Executive Office
PA: The Alpha Group Of Delaware Inc
1000 Alpha Dr
Delaware OH 43015
740 368-5810

(G-6904)
ALPINE INSULATION I LLC
495 S High St Ste 50 (43215-5689)
PHONE.................................614 221-3399
Jeffrey W Edwards, *President*
Jay P Elliott, *COO*
Michael T Miller, *CFO*
Todd R Fry,
EMP: 3675
SALES (est): 36.3MM
SALES (corp-wide): 1.3B **Publicly Held**
SIC: 5033 5211 Insulation materials; insu-
lation material, building
PA: Installed Building Products, Inc.
495 S High St Ste 50
Columbus OH 43215
614 221-3399

(G-6905)
ALRO STEEL CORPORATION
555 Hilliard Rome Rd (43228-9265)
PHONE.................................614 878-7271
Steve White, *Manager*
Tim Castle, *Manager*
EMP: 40
SALES (corp-wide): 1.9B **Privately Held**
WEB: www.alro.com
SIC: 5051 5085 5162 3444 Steel; alu-
minum bars, rods, ingots, sheets, pipes,
plates, etc.; nonferrous metal sheets,
bars, rods, etc.; industrial supplies; plas-
tics materials; sheet metalwork
PA: Alro Steel Corporation
3100 E High St
Jackson MI 49203
517 787-5500

(G-6906)
ALTIMATE CARE LLC (PA)
5869 Cleveland Ave (43231-2859)
PHONE.................................614 794-9600
Ninell Drankwalter, *Owner*
EMP: 32
SALES: 12.4MM **Privately Held**
SIC: 8082 Home health care services

(G-6907)
ALVIS INC
Also Called: Alvis House
844 Bryden Rd (43205-1728)
PHONE.................................614 252-1788
Wendy Saez, *Manager*
Jeneen Peloquin, *Data Proc Dir*
EMP: 108
SALES (corp-wide): 22.3MM **Privately
Held**
WEB: www.alvishouse.org
SIC: 8361 Halfway group home, persons
with social or personal problems
PA: Alvis, Inc.
2100 Stella Ct
Columbus OH 43215
614 252-8402

(G-6908)
AMANDACARE INC
Also Called: Amandacare Home Health
2101 S Hamilton Rd # 212 (43232-4143)
PHONE.................................614 884-8880
Paulene Crocco, *CEO*
Beverly Schaffer, *Vice Pres*
EMP: 120 EST: 1996
SALES (est): 3MM **Privately Held**
WEB: www.amandacare.com
SIC: 8082 Home health care services

(G-6909)
AMBER HOME CARE LLC
2800 Corp Exchange Dr # 100
(43231-7661)
PHONE.................................614 523-0668
Douglas S Speelman,
Jason Huxley,
EMP: 30
SALES (est): 1MM **Privately Held**
SIC: 8082 Visiting nurse service

(G-6910)
AMC ENTERTAINMENT INC
6360 Busch Blvd (43229-1805)
PHONE.................................614 846-6575
Michael Reid, *Branch Mgr*
EMP: 45
SALES (corp-wide): 7.3MM **Publicly Held**
WEB: www.amctheatres.com
SIC: 7832 Motion picture theaters, except
drive-in
HQ: Amc Entertainment Inc.
11500 Ash St
Leawood KS 66211
913 213-2000

(G-6911)
AMC ENTERTAINMENT INC
275 Easton Town Ctr (43219-6077)
PHONE.................................614 428-5716
Stephanie McClullan, *Manager*
EMP: 30
SALES (corp-wide): 7.3MM **Publicly Held**
WEB: www.amctheatres.com
SIC: 7832 Motion picture theaters, except
drive-in
HQ: Amc Entertainment Inc.
11500 Ash St
Leawood KS 66211
913 213-2000

(G-6912)
AMC ENTERTAINMENT INC
777 Kinnear Rd (43212-1441)
PHONE.................................614 429-0100
John Swaney, *Manager*
EMP: 27
SALES (corp-wide): 7.3MM **Publicly Held**
WEB: www.amctheatres.com
SIC: 7832 Exhibitors, itinerant: motion pic-
ture
HQ: Amc Entertainment Inc.
11500 Ash St
Leawood KS 66211
913 213-2000

(G-6913)
**AMERICAN BOTTLING
COMPANY**
Also Called: 7 Up / R C/Canada Dry Btlg Co
950 Stelzer Rd (43219-3740)
PHONE.................................614 237-4201
Mike Stall, *Branch Mgr*
EMP: 100 **Publicly Held**
WEB: www.cs-americas.com
SIC: 2086 5149 Soft drinks: packaged in
cans, bottles, etc.; groceries & related
products
HQ: The American Bottling Company
5301 Legacy Dr
Plano TX 75024

(G-6914)
**AMERICAN CHEM SOC FDERAL
CR UN**
2540 Olentangy River Rd (43202-1505)
PHONE.................................614 447-3675
Gregory A Kidwell, *CEO*
EMP: 1669
SALES (est): 484K **Privately Held**
SIC: 6061 Federal credit unions

(G-6915)
**AMERICAN COMMERCE
INSURANCE CO (DH)**
3590 Twin Creeks Dr (43204-1628)
PHONE.................................614 272-6951
Greg Clark, *Vice Pres*
Lisa Celona, *Business Anlyst*
Ganesh Perumal, *Applctn Conslt*
EMP: 191
SQ FT: 39,000

SALES: 193.7MM
SALES (corp-wide): 200.2K **Privately Held**
WEB: www.acilink.com
SIC: 6331 6351 Automobile insurance; property damage insurance; liability insurance
HQ: The Commerce Insurance Company
211 Main St
Webster MA 01570
508 943-9000

(G-6916)
AMERICAN ELECTRIC POWER CO INC
5900 Refugee Rd (43232-4727)
PHONE..................................614 856-2750
Daniel Cox, *Principal*
Tim Galecki, *Manager*
EMP: 30
SALES (corp-wide): 16.2B **Publicly Held**
SIC: 4911 Electric services
PA: American Electric Power Company, Inc.
1 Riverside Plz Fl 1 # 1
Columbus OH 43215
614 716-1000

(G-6917)
AMERICAN ELECTRIC POWER CO INC
Also Called: Columbus Southern Power Co
1759 W Mound St (43223-1813)
PHONE..................................614 351-3715
Doug Ickes, *General Mgr*
Scott Krueger, *Area Spvr*
EMP: 75
SALES (corp-wide): 16.2B **Publicly Held**
SIC: 4911 Distribution, electric power
PA: American Electric Power Company, Inc.
1 Riverside Plz Fl 1 # 1
Columbus OH 43215
614 716-1000

(G-6918)
AMERICAN ELECTRIC POWER CO INC
Also Called: AEP Pro Serv Rso
1 Riverside Plz Ste 1600 (43215-2355)
PHONE..................................614 716-1000
David Bnks, *President*
John Powers, *President*
Jeffrey D Cross, *Manager*
EMP: 30
SALES (corp-wide): 16.2B **Publicly Held**
SIC: 1731 General electrical contractor
PA: American Electric Power Company, Inc.
1 Riverside Plz Fl 1 # 1
Columbus OH 43215
614 716-1000

(G-6919)
AMERICAN ELECTRIC PWR SVC CORP (HQ)
1 Riverside Plz Fl 1 # 1 (43215-2373)
P.O. Box 16631 (43216-6631)
PHONE..................................614 716-1000
Nicholas K Akins, *Ch of Bd*
Johnathan Powers, *President*
Ronnie Young, *Managing Dir*
David Canter, *Business Mgr*
Heather Geiger, *Counsel*
▲ EMP: 500 EST: 1937
SQ FT: 800,000
SALES: 1.3B
SALES (corp-wide): 16.2B **Publicly Held**
WEB: www.myenviroassistant.com
SIC: 4911 8711 8713 8721 Distribution, electric power; engineering services; surveying services; accounting services, except auditing; auditing services; billing & bookkeeping service
PA: American Electric Power Company, Inc.
1 Riverside Plz Fl 1 # 1
Columbus OH 43215
614 716-1000

(G-6920)
AMERICAN ELECTRIC PWR SVC CORP
Also Called: AEP Service
825 Tech Center Dr (43230-6653)
PHONE..................................614 582-1742
Ben Mehraban, *Project Mgr*
Steve Boyd, *Engineer*
Ted Everman, *Engineer*

Matthew Gauss, *Engineer*
Travis Wheeler, *Design Engr*
EMP: 29
SALES (corp-wide): 16.2B **Publicly Held**
SIC: 4911 Electric services
HQ: American Electric Power Service Corporation
1 Riverside Plz Fl 1 # 1
Columbus OH 43215
614 716-1000

(G-6921)
AMERICAN FIDELITY ASSURANCE CO
90 Northwoods Blvd Ste B (43235-4719)
PHONE..................................800 437-1011
James Gray, *President*
EMP: 1000 **Privately Held**
WEB: www.afadvantage.com
SIC: 6411 Insurance agents
HQ: American Fidelity Assurance Company
9000 Cameron Pkwy
Oklahoma City OK 73114
405 523-2000

(G-6922)
AMERICAN HEALTH NETWORK INC
2500 Corp Exchange Dr # 100 (43231-7601)
PHONE..................................614 794-4500
Kim Rittenhouse, *Manager*
EMP: 27
SALES (corp-wide): 226.2B **Publicly Held**
SIC: 8011 Offices & clinics of medical doctors
HQ: American Health Network, Inc.
10689 N Pennsylvna St # 200
Indianapolis IN 46280

(G-6923)
AMERICAN HEART ASSOCIATION INC
5455 N High St (43214-1127)
P.O. Box 163549 (43216-3549)
PHONE..................................614 848-6676
Charles Romane, *Branch Mgr*
Alieen Meyer, *Exec Dir*
Charles C Tweel, *Director*
Bryce Morrice, *Admin Sec*
EMP: 50
SALES (corp-wide): 780.2MM **Privately Held**
WEB: www.americanheart.org
SIC: 8621 Professional membership organizations
PA: American Heart Association, Inc.
7272 Greenville Ave
Dallas TX 75231
214 373-6300

(G-6924)
AMERICAN HLTH NETWRK OHIO LLC (HQ)
2500 Corporate Exchange D (43231-7601)
PHONE..................................614 794-4500
Ben Park, *CEO*
EMP: 80
SALES (est): 229.2MM
SALES (corp-wide): 226.2B **Publicly Held**
SIC: 8011 Offices & clinics of medical doctors
PA: Unitedhealth Group Incorporated
9900 Bren Rd E Ste 300w
Minnetonka MN 55343
952 936-1300

(G-6925)
AMERICAN HOME HEALTH CARE INC
Also Called: American Medical Equipment
861 Taylor Rd Unit I (43230-6275)
PHONE..................................614 237-1133
Brad Yakam, *President*
Tushar Shah, *Vice Pres*
Stewart Brownstein, *Accounts Mgr*
EMP: 30
SQ FT: 6,500
SALES (est): 9.4MM **Privately Held**
WEB: www.ame-medical.com
SIC: 7352 5999 5047 Medical equipment rental; medical apparatus & supplies; hospital equipment & furniture

(G-6926)
AMERICAN INSTITUTE RESEARCH
41 S High St Ste 2425 (43215-6148)
PHONE..................................614 221-8717
Terry Salinger, *Branch Mgr*
EMP: 329
SALES (corp-wide): 474MM **Privately Held**
SIC: 8733 Noncommercial social research organization
PA: American Institutes For Research In The Behavioral Sciences
1000 Thmas Jfferson St Nw
Washington DC 20007
202 403-5000

(G-6927)
AMERICAN INSTITUTE RESEARCH
820 Freeway Dr N (43229-5440)
PHONE..................................614 310-8982
EMP: 329
SALES (corp-wide): 474MM **Privately Held**
SIC: 8733 Research institute
PA: American Institutes For Research In The Behavioral Sciences
1000 Thmas Jfferson St Nw
Washington DC 20007
202 403-5000

(G-6928)
AMERICAN KIDNEY STONE MGT LTD (PA)
Also Called: Aksm
100 W 3rd Ave Ste 350 (43201-7205)
PHONE..................................800 637-5188
Henry Wise II, *Chairman*
Bruce Campbell, *Regional Mgr*
Alice Blankenship, *Counsel*
Ted Amland, *Vice Pres*
Alan Buergenthal, *Vice Pres*
EMP: 30
SQ FT: 11,000
SALES (est): 15.6MM **Privately Held**
WEB: www.aksm.com
SIC: 8093 Specialty outpatient clinics

(G-6929)
AMERICAN LINEHAUL CORPORATION
1860 Williams Rd (43207-5113)
PHONE..................................614 409-8568
Scott Scheurell, *President*
EMP: 27
SALES (corp-wide): 29.9MM **Privately Held**
SIC: 4789 Cargo loading & unloading services
PA: American Linehaul Corporation
99 Mount Bethel Rd
Warren NJ 07059
973 589-0101

(G-6930)
AMERICAN MECHANICAL GROUP INC
Also Called: Honeywell Authorized Dealer
5729 Westbourne Ave (43213-1449)
PHONE..................................614 575-3720
Brian Yockey, *President*
Michelle Culp, *Executive*
Kyle Murray, *Technician*
EMP: 32
SALES (est): 6.5MM **Privately Held**
WEB: www.american-mech.com
SIC: 1711 Warm air heating & air conditioning contractor

(G-6931)
AMERICAN MUNICIPAL POWER INC
Also Called: AMP-Ohio
1111 Schrock Rd Ste 100 (43229-1155)
PHONE..................................614 540-1111
Jon Bisher, *Ch of Bd*
Marc Gerken, *President*
John Bentine, *Senior VP*
Bobby Little, *Senior VP*
Pam Sullivan, *Senior VP*
◆ EMP: 229
SQ FT: 100,000

SALES: 1.1B **Privately Held**
WEB: www.amppartners.org
SIC: 4911 Generation, electric power

(G-6932)
AMERICAN NATIONAL RED CROSS
Also Called: American Red Cross
1 W Nationwide Blvd (43215-2752)
PHONE..................................800 448-3543
EMP: 39
SALES (corp-wide): 2.5B **Privately Held**
SIC: 8322 Emergency social services
PA: The American National Red Cross
430 17th St Nw
Washington DC 20006
202 737-8300

(G-6933)
AMERICAN NATIONAL RED CROSS
Also Called: American Natl Red CRS-Bld Svcs
4327 Equity Dr (43228-3842)
PHONE..................................614 334-0425
EMP: 49
SALES (corp-wide): 2.5B **Privately Held**
SIC: 8099 Blood donor station
PA: The American National Red Cross
430 17th St Nw
Washington DC 20006
202 737-8300

(G-6934)
AMERICAN PRECAST REFRACTORIES
2700 Scioto Pkwy (43221-4657)
PHONE..................................614 876-8416
John Turner, *President*
Suzanne T Deffet, *Vice Pres*
EMP: 275
SALES (est): 13MM
SALES (corp-wide): 149.2MM **Privately Held**
WEB: www.amprecast.com
SIC: 1611 Concrete construction: roads, highways, sidewalks, etc.; surfacing & paving
PA: Allied Mineral Products, Inc.
2700 Scioto Pkwy
Columbus OH 43221
614 876-0244

(G-6935)
AMERICAN RED CROSS OF GRTR COL (PA)
995 E Broad St (43205-1339)
PHONE..................................614 253-7981
Michael Carroll, *CEO*
Mark Whitman, *Sls & Mktg Exec*
Mary E Wissel, *Med Doctor*
Rita Barnes, *Manager*
EMP: 50
SQ FT: 80,000
SALES (est): 5.6MM **Privately Held**
WEB: www.redcrosscolumbus.org
SIC: 8322 Social service center

(G-6936)
AMERICAN REPROGRAPHICS CO LLC
Also Called: ARC
1159 Dublin Rd (43215-1874)
PHONE..................................614 224-5149
Gerald Schueller, *Branch Mgr*
Tim Werking, *Manager*
EMP: 25
SALES (corp-wide): 400.7MM **Publicly Held**
WEB: www.e-arc.com
SIC: 7334 Blueprinting service
HQ: American Reprographics Company, L.L.C.
1981 N Broadway Ste 385
Walnut Creek CA 94596
925 949-5100

(G-6937)
AMERICAN RESIDENTIAL SVCS LLC
Also Called: Rescue Rooter of Columbus
3050 Switzer Ave (43219-2316)
PHONE..................................888 762-7752
Jason Norris, *General Mgr*
Ralph Fumo, *Sales Executive*

EMP: 50
SQ FT: 18,000
SALES (corp-wide): 2.4B Privately Held
WEB: www.ars.com
SIC: 1711 Plumbing contractors
PA: American Residential Services Llc
965 Ridge Lake Blvd # 201
Memphis TN 38120
901 271-9700

(G-6938)
AMERICAN SOCIETY FOR NONDSTCTV
1711 Arlingate Ln (43228-4116)
P.O. Box 28518 (43228-0518)
PHONE..........................614 274-6003
Haley Cowans, *Editor*
Arnold Bereson, *Exec Dir*
EMP: 47
SQ FT: 18,000
SALES: 8.6MM Privately Held
WEB: www.asnt.net
SIC: 8621 Medical field-related associations

(G-6939)
AMERICAN SVCS & PROTECTION LLC
2572 Oakstone Dr 8 (43231-7614)
PHONE..........................614 884-0177
Aaron Harper, *President*
Lovell Harper, *Vice Pres*
Philana Harper, *Finance*
Shawn Harper,
EMP: 80
SALES (est): 898.1K Privately Held
SIC: 7382 7381 Security systems services; guard services

(G-6940)
AMERICAS FLOOR SOURCE LLC (PA)
3442 Millennium Ct (43219-5551)
PHONE..........................614 808-3915
John Caragliano, *Division Mgr*
Ron Rieger, *Regional Mgr*
Gina Hoffer, *Exec VP*
Cary Jerris, *Vice Pres*
Peter Hill, *Opers Mgr*
▲ **EMP:** 58
SQ FT: 50,000
SALES: 65MM Privately Held
WEB: www.americasfloorsource.com
SIC: 5713 5023 Carpets; floor coverings

(G-6941)
AMERISOURCE HEALTH SVCS LLC
Also Called: American Health Packaging
2550 John Glenn Ave Ste A (43217-1188)
PHONE..........................614 492-8177
Rick Knight, *President*
Greg Hamilton, *Vice Pres*
Bob Kavanaugh, *Vice Pres*
Robert Kavanaugh, *Vice Pres*
John Swartz, *Vice Pres*
EMP: 89
SQ FT: 153,000
SALES (est): 22.3MM
SALES (corp-wide): 167.9B Publicly Held
WEB: www.healthpack.com
SIC: 2064 4783 Cough drops, except pharmaceutical preparations; packing goods for shipping
HQ: Amerisourcebergen Drug Corporation
1300 Morris Dr Ste 100
Chesterbrook PA 19087
610 727-7000

(G-6942)
AMERISOURCEBERGEN CORPORATION
1200 E 5th Ave (43219-2410)
P.O. Box 870, Worthington (43085-0870)
PHONE..........................610 727-7000
Gary Van Dyke, *Sales Mgr*
Jeff Spencer, *Director*
EMP: 200
SALES (corp-wide): 167.9B Publicly Held
WEB: www.amerisourcebergen.net
SIC: 5122 Pharmaceuticals

PA: Amerisourcebergen Corporation
1300 Morris Dr Ste 100
Chesterbrook PA 19087
610 727-7000

(G-6943)
AMETHYST INC
455 E Mound St (43215-5595)
PHONE..........................614 242-1284
Lois Hochstetler, *Exec Dir*
EMP: 55
SALES: 4.1MM Privately Held
WEB: www.amethyst-inc.org
SIC: 8322 8093 Alcoholism counseling, nontreatment; drug clinic, outpatient

(G-6944)
AMF BOWLING CENTERS INC
4825 Sawmill Rd (43235-7266)
PHONE..........................614 889-0880
Melvin Harrington, *Manager*
EMP: 50
SALES (corp-wide): 323MM Privately Held
WEB: www.kidsports.org
SIC: 7933 Ten pin center
HQ: Amf Bowling Centers, Inc.
7313 Bell Creek Rd
Mechanicsville VA 23111

(G-6945)
AMUSEMENTS OF AMERICA INC
717 E 17th Ave (43211-2494)
PHONE..........................614 297-8863
Karen Salas, *Branch Mgr*
EMP: 190
SALES (corp-wide): 7.6MM Privately Held
SIC: 7999 Carnival operation
PA: Amusements Of America Inc
24 Federal Rd
Monroe Township NJ 08831
305 258-2020

(G-6946)
ANDERSON ALUMINUM CORPORATION
Also Called: Anderson Properties
2816 Morse Rd (43231-6034)
PHONE..........................614 476-4877
Helena Anderson, *President*
Bradley Anderson, *Vice Pres*
Nestor Perez, *Project Mgr*
George Deniro, *Opers Mgr*
Mike Daniel, *Opers Staff*
EMP: 70 **EST:** 1980
SQ FT: 70,000
SALES (est): 17.8MM Privately Held
SIC: 1793 Glass & glazing work

(G-6947)
ANDERSON GLASS CO INC
2816 Morse Rd (43231-6094)
PHONE..........................614 476-4877
Bradley Anderson, *President*
Helena Anderson, *Vice Pres*
Judy Mullen, *Office Mgr*
EMP: 30 **EST:** 1949
SQ FT: 32,000
SALES: 4MM Privately Held
WEB: www.andersonglassco.com
SIC: 5039 3231 3229 Exterior flat glass: plate or window; interior flat glass: plate or window; products of purchased glass; pressed & blown glass

(G-6948)
ANDREW DISTRIBUTION INC
509 Industry Dr (43204-6242)
PHONE..........................614 824-3123
Mario Malek, *Principal*
EMP: 305 Privately Held
SIC: 5099 Brass goods
PA: Andrew Distribution, Inc.
2000 Anson Dr
Melrose Park IL 60160

(G-6949)
ANESTHESIOLOGY CONSULTANT INC
111 S Grant Ave (43215-4701)
PHONE..........................614 566-9983
Michael Romanelli Do, *President*
Z Chad Nguyen, *Anesthesiology*
EMP: 30

SALES (est): 4.5MM Privately Held
SIC: 8062 General medical & surgical hospitals

(G-6950)
ANIMAL CARE UNLIMITED INC
2665 Billingsley Rd (43235-1904)
PHONE..........................614 766-2317
Donald Burton Dvm, *President*
EMP: 29
SALES (est): 2.2MM Privately Held
WEB: www.animalcareunlimited.com
SIC: 0742 0752 Veterinarian, animal specialties; animal hospital services, pets & other animal specialties; boarding services, kennels

(G-6951)
ANSPACH MEEKS ELLENBERGER LLP
175 S 3rd St Ste 285 (43215-5188)
PHONE..........................614 745-8350
Bob Anspach, *Branch Mgr*
EMP: 28
SALES (corp-wide): 9.1MM Privately Held
SIC: 8111 General practice attorney, lawyer
PA: Anspach Meeks Ellenberger Llp
300 Madison Ave Ste 1600
Toledo OH 43604
419 447-6181

(G-6952)
AON CONSULTING INC
445 Hutchinson Ave # 900 (43235-8619)
PHONE..........................614 436-8100
EMP: 27
SQ FT: 1,500
SALES (corp-wide): 10B Privately Held
WEB: www.radford.com
SIC: 6411 Insurance brokers
HQ: Aon Consulting, Inc.
200 E Randolph St Ll3
Chicago IL 60601
312 381-1000

(G-6953)
AON CONSULTING INC
355 E Campus View Blvd (43235-5616)
PHONE..........................614 847-4670
EMP: 61
SALES (corp-wide): 10B Privately Held
SIC: 6411 Insurance brokers
HQ: Aon Consulting, Inc.
200 E Randolph St Ll3
Chicago IL 60601
312 381-1000

(G-6954)
AP23 SPORTS COMPLEX LLC
775 Georgesville Rd (43228-2826)
PHONE..........................614 452-0760
Derrick Pryor,
EMP: 27
SQ FT: 204,000
SALES (est): 260.8K Privately Held
SIC: 7941 Sports clubs, managers & promoters

(G-6955)
APCO ALUMINUM AWNING CO
815 Michigan Ave (43215-1161)
PHONE..........................614 334-2726
Mark Mason, *Owner*
EMP: 38
SALES: 9MM Privately Held
SIC: 1799 Awning installation

(G-6956)
APCO INDUSTRIES INC
Also Called: Apco Window & Door Company
777 Michigan Ave (43215-1177)
PHONE..........................614 224-2345
Bill Clarken Jr, *President*
William M Clarkin, *President*
Warren C Gifford, *President*
Mark M Mason, *President*
Joe Lieonart, *Vice Pres*
EMP: 100 **EST:** 1962
SQ FT: 52,000

SALES (est): 21.3MM Privately Held
WEB: www.apco.com
SIC: 1761 5033 5039 5031 Gutter & downspout contractor; siding contractor; siding, except wood; eaves troughing, parts & supplies; doors; general remodeling, single-family houses; home centers

(G-6957)
APELLES LLC
3700 Corp Dr 2f Ste 240 2 F (43231)
PHONE..........................614 899-7322
Michael Fitzmartin,
EMP: 30
SALES (est): 4.4MM Privately Held
WEB: www.apelles.com
SIC: 7322 Collection agency, except real estate

(G-6958)
APPALACHIAN POWER COMPANY (HQ)
1 Riverside Plz (43215-2355)
PHONE..........................614 716-1000
Nicholas K Akins, *Ch of Bd*
Jeffery Lafleur, *Vice Pres*
Frank Pifer, *Vice Pres*
Brian X Tierney, *CFO*
Louis Prete, *Supervisor*
▲ **EMP:** 170 **EST:** 1926
SALES: 2.9B
SALES (corp-wide): 16.2B Publicly Held
SIC: 4911 Distribution, electric power
PA: American Electric Power Company, Inc.
1 Riverside Plz Fl 1 # 1
Columbus OH 43215
614 716-1000

(G-6959)
APPLIED RESEARCH ASSOC INC
Also Called: Berriehill
1330 Kinnear Rd (43212-1166)
PHONE..........................937 435-1016
EMP: 30
SALES (corp-wide): 251.4MM Privately Held
SIC: 8731 Commercial physical research
PA: Applied Research Associates, Inc.
4300 San Mateo Blvd Ne
Albuquerque NM 87110
505 883-3636

(G-6960)
APRIA HEALTHCARE LLC
4060 Business Park Dr A (43204-5047)
PHONE..........................614 351-5920
Christopher Bell, *Branch Mgr*
EMP: 36 Privately Held
WEB: www.apria.com
SIC: 7352 Medical equipment rental
HQ: Apria Healthcare Llc
26220 Enterprise Ct
Lake Forest CA 92630
949 639-2000

(G-6961)
AQUARIUS MARINE LLC
250 N Hartford Ave (43222-1100)
Po Box 1267
PHONE..........................614 875-8200
Colin McBride, *General Mgr*
Colin A McBride,
EMP: 25
SALES (est): 3MM Privately Held
SIC: 1629 Marine construction

(G-6962)
ARAMARK UNF & CAREER AP LLC
1900 Progress Ave (43207-1727)
PHONE..........................614 445-8341
Bert Murray, *Project Engr*
Joe Carrothers, *Manager*
Rob Keim, *Executive*
EMP: 250 Publicly Held
WEB: www.aramark-uniform.com
SIC: 7218 7213 Industrial launderers; uniform supply
HQ: Aramark Uniform & Career Apparel, Llc
115 N First St Ste 203
Burbank CA 91502
818 973-3700

GEOGRAPHIC

(G-6963)
ARBORS EAST LLC
5500 E Broad St (43213-1497)
PHONE..................................614 575-9003
Stacy Duncan, *Administration*
EMP: 100
SALES (est): 5.2MM **Privately Held**
WEB: www.extendicarehealth.com
SIC: 8052 8051 Intermediate care facilities; skilled nursing care facilities

(G-6964)
ARC INDUSTRIES
INCORPORATED O (PA)
2780 Airport Dr (43219-2289)
PHONE..................................614 479-2500
Geraldine C Nasse, *Principal*
EMP: 143
SQ FT: 8,976
SALES: 11.1MM **Privately Held**
WEB: www.arcind.com
SIC: 8331 Sheltered workshop

(G-6965)
ARC INDUSTRIES
INCORPORATED O
Also Called: ARC Industries North
6633 Doubletree Ave (43229-1156)
PHONE..................................614 436-4800
Nan Burns, *Director*
EMP: 300
SALES (corp-wide): 11.1MM **Privately Held**
WEB: www.arcind.com
SIC: 8331 Sheltered workshop
PA: Arc Industries, Incorporated, Of Franklin County, Ohio
2780 Airport Dr
Columbus OH 43219
614 479-2500

(G-6966)
ARC INDUSTRIES
INCORPORATED O
Also Called: ARC Industreis East
909 Taylor Station Rd (43230-6655)
PHONE..................................614 864-2406
John Dixon, *Opers Staff*
Clarice Pavlick, *Manager*
EMP: 300
SALES (corp-wide): 11.1MM **Privately Held**
WEB: www.arcind.com
PA: Arc Industries, Incorporated, Of Franklin County, Ohio
2780 Airport Dr
Columbus OH 43219
614 479-2500

(G-6967)
ARC INDUSTRIES
INCORPORATED O
Also Called: ARC Industries West
250 W Dodridge St (43202-1599)
PHONE..................................614 267-1207
Janet Montgomery, *Director*
EMP: 65
SALES (corp-wide): 11.1MM **Privately Held**
WEB: www.arcind.com
SIC: 8331 Sheltered workshop
PA: Arc Industries, Incorporated, Of Franklin County, Ohio
2780 Airport Dr
Columbus OH 43219
614 479-2500

(G-6968)
ARCHITCTURAL CON
SOLUTIONS INC
1997 Harmon Ave (43223-3828)
P.O. Box 1056, Grove City (43123-6056)
PHONE..................................614 940-5399
Brian Snyder, *President*
Andre Bondurant, *Principal*
Patrick Donahue, *Vice Pres*
EMP: 25
SALES (est): 1.9MM **Privately Held**
SIC: 1771 Patio construction, concrete

(G-6969)
ARLEDGE CONSTRUCTION INC
(PA)
2460 Performance Way (43207-2857)
PHONE..................................614 732-4258
Craig Arledge, *President*
Craig Stover, *Manager*
EMP: 41
SALES: 5MM **Privately Held**
SIC: 1771 Foundation & footing contractor

(G-6970)
ARLINGTON CONTACT LENS
SVC INC (DH)
Also Called: AC Lens
4265 Diplomacy Dr (43228-3834)
PHONE..................................614 921-9894
Peter Clarkson, *President*
Phillip Dietrich, *Vice Pres*
Christine Vakaleris, *Vice Pres*
▲ EMP: 47
SQ FT: 21,000
SALES (est): 4.8MM
SALES (corp-wide): 1.5B **Publicly Held**
WEB: www.aclens.com
SIC: 5995 8011 Contact lenses, prescription; offices & clinics of medical doctors
HQ: National Vision, Inc.
2435 Commerce Ave # 2200
Duluth GA 30096
770 822-3600

(G-6971)
ARLINGTON TOWING INC
Also Called: Camcar Towing
2354 Wood Ave (43221-3520)
PHONE..................................614 488-2006
Mike Davis, *President*
EMP: 30
SALES (est): 1.3MM **Privately Held**
SIC: 7549 Towing service, automotive

(G-6972)
ARTHUR G JAMES CANCE
460 W 10th Ave (43210-1240)
PHONE..................................614 293-4878
David E Schuller, *Director*
EMP: 700
SALES: 2.2MM
SALES (corp-wide): 5.8B **Privately Held**
WEB: www.jamesline.com
SIC: 8733 8731 8069 Medical research; commercial physical research; specialty hospitals, except psychiatric
PA: The Ohio State University
Student Acade Servi Bldg
Columbus OH 43210
614 292-6446

(G-6973)
ARTHUR G JAMES CANCER
HOSPITAL
300 W 10th Ave (43210-1280)
PHONE..................................614 293-3300
Jan A Rupert, *Principal*
Jill Hannah, *Human Res Dir*
Shannon Thompson, *Director*
Karl Haglund, *Oncology*
EMP: 27
SALES: 332.6K **Privately Held**
SIC: 8069 Cancer hospital

(G-6974)
ARTISTIC DANCE ENTERPRISES
Also Called: Dublin Dance Center
2665 Farmers Dr (43235-2767)
PHONE..................................614 761-2882
Teresa Crye, *President*
EMP: 25
SQ FT: 7,000
SALES (est): 984.5K **Privately Held**
WEB: www.dublindance.com
SIC: 7911 5621 5632 Children's dancing school; boutiques; dancewear

(G-6975)
ARVIND SAGAR INC
Also Called: Homewood Suites
2880 Airport Dr (43219-2240)
PHONE..................................614 428-8800
Arvind Sagar, *Owner*
EMP: 25
SALES (est): 1.5MM **Privately Held**
WEB: www.arvindsagar.com
SIC: 7011 Hotels & motels

(G-6976)
ASC GROUP INC (PA)
800 Freeway Dr N Ste 101 (43229-5447)
PHONE..................................614 268-2514
Shaune M Skinner, *President*
Elsie Immel Blei, *Vice Pres*
EMP: 32
SQ FT: 10,000
SALES: 4MM **Privately Held**
WEB: www.ascgroup.net
SIC: 8713 8712 8731 8733 Surveying services; architectural services; environmental research; archeological expeditions; earth science services

(G-6977)
ASHLAND LLC
Also Called: Ashland Performance Materials
802 Harmon Ave (43223-2410)
PHONE..................................614 232-8510
Paul W Chellgren, *Ch of Bd*
Sandra Derthick, *Relations*
EMP: 75
SQ FT: 19,378
SALES (corp-wide): 3.7B **Publicly Held**
WEB: www.ashland.com
SIC: 5169 Alkalines & chlorine
HQ: Ashland Llc
50 E Rivercenter Blvd # 1600
Covington KY 41011
859 815-3333

(G-6978)
ASHLAND LLC
Ashland Distribution
3849 Fisher Rd (43228-1015)
PHONE..................................614 276-6144
Larry B Clark, *Branch Mgr*
EMP: 30
SQ FT: 4,656
SALES (corp-wide): 3.7B **Publicly Held**
WEB: www.ashland.com
SIC: 5169 Alkalines & chlorine
HQ: Ashland Llc
50 E Rivercenter Blvd # 1600
Covington KY 41011
859 815-3333

(G-6979)
ASPEN COMMUNITY LIVING
2021 E Dublin Granville R (43229-3552)
PHONE..................................614 880-6000
Martha Clifford, *Manager*
EMP: 104
SALES (corp-wide): 151.2MM **Privately Held**
SIC: 7363 7361 Help supply services; employment agencies
HQ: Aspen Nursing Services, Inc.
2360 Edgerton St
Little Canada MN 55117
651 415-1444

(G-6980)
ASPLUNDH CONSTRUCTION
CORP
481 Schrock Rd (43229-1027)
PHONE..................................614 532-5224
Jarrod Wachter, *Branch Mgr*
EMP: 180
SALES (corp-wide): 4.5B **Privately Held**
SIC: 1521 Single-family housing construction
HQ: Asplundh Construction, Corp.
93 Sills Rd
Yaphank NY 11980
631 205-9340

(G-6981)
ASSISTNCE IN MKTG
COLUMBUS INC
1 Easton Oval Ste 100 (43219-6062)
PHONE..................................614 583-2100
Carl Iseman, *President*
EMP: 28
SALES: 1.2MM **Privately Held**
SIC: 8732 Market analysis or research

(G-6982)
ASSOC DVLPMTLY DISABLED
Also Called: Dahlberg Learning Center
1915 E Cooke Rd (43224-2266)
PHONE..................................614 447-0606
Bernice Hagler-Cody, *Director*
EMP: 30

SQ FT: 22,213
SALES (corp-wide): 17.2MM **Privately Held**
WEB: www.add1.com
SIC: 8361 8351 Home for the mentally handicapped; preschool center
PA: Association For The Developmentally Disabled
769 Brooksedge Blvd
Westerville OH 43081
614 486-4361

(G-6983)
ASSOCIATED MATERIALS LLC
Also Called: Alside Supply Center
640 Dearborn Park Ln (43085-5701)
PHONE..................................614 985-4611
Dan Dreyman, *Branch Mgr*
Michael Gerken, *Manager*
EMP: 25 **Privately Held**
WEB: www.associatedmaterials.com
SIC: 5033 Roofing & siding materials
HQ: Associated Materials, Llc
3773 State Rd
Cuyahoga Falls OH 44223
330 929-1811

(G-6984)
ASSOCIATED PRESS
1103 Schrock Rd Ste 300 (43229-1179)
PHONE..................................614 885-3444
Eva Parziale, *Manager*
EMP: 25
SALES (corp-wide): 510.1MM **Privately Held**
WEB: www.apme.com
SIC: 7383 News reporting services for newspapers & periodicals
PA: The Associated Press
200 Liberty St Fl 19
New York NY 10281
212 621-1500

(G-6985)
ASTORIA PLACE COLUMBUS
LLC
Also Called: Columbus Rhbilitation Subacute
44 S Souder Ave (43222-1539)
PHONE..................................614 228-5900
Matthew Macklin, *Mng Member*
Joseph Brandman, *Manager*
Yehudit Goldberg, *Manager*
Michael Nudell, *Manager*
EMP: 99 EST: 2014
SQ FT: 52,000
SALES: 8.6MM **Privately Held**
SIC: 8051 Mental retardation hospital

(G-6986)
ASTUTE INC (PA)
Also Called: Astute Solutions
4400 Easton Cmns (43219-6226)
PHONE..................................614 508-6100
Ray Carey, *CEO*
Richard Jones, *Senior VP*
Scott Williams, *Senior VP*
John D'Andrea, *CFO*
Liz Shaver, *Manager*
EMP: 49
SQ FT: 12,230
SALES (est): 14.2MM **Privately Held**
WEB: www.astutesolutions.com
SIC: 7371 Computer software development

(G-6987)
ASYMMETRIC TECHNOLOGIES
LLC
1395 Grandview Ave Ste 3 (43212-2859)
PHONE..................................614 725-5310
Brian J Borkowski, *Managing Dir*
Cress Clanton, *Director*
EMP: 35
SQ FT: 2,000
SALES: 3.9MM **Privately Held**
SIC: 8731 Biological research

(G-6988)
AT T BROADBAND & INTERN
P.O. Box 182552 (43218-2552)
PHONE..................................614 839-4271
EMP: 25
SALES (est): 2.4MM **Privately Held**
SIC: 4813

(G-6989)
AT&T CORP
3419 Indianola Ave (43214-4129)
PHONE.................................614 223-6513
Ed Humeidan, *Branch Mgr*
EMP: 69
SALES (corp-wide): 170.7B **Publicly Held**
SIC: 4813 Telephone communication, except radio
HQ: At&T Corp.
1 At&T Way
Bedminster NJ 07921
800 403-3302

(G-6990)
AT&T CORP
150 E Gay St Ste 4a (43215-3130)
PHONE.................................614 223-8236
Connie Browning, *President*
Cari Walters, *Assistant VP*
Dustin Howell, *Sales Associate*
Jaymee Nemec, *Sales Executive*
Lois Gardner, *Manager*
EMP: 1000
SALES (corp-wide): 170.7B **Publicly Held**
WEB: www.att.com
SIC: 7629 4813 2741 Telecommunication equipment repair (except telephones); telephone communication, except radio; miscellaneous publishing
HQ: At&T Corp.
1 At&T Way
Bedminster NJ 07921
800 403-3302

(G-6991)
AT&T CORP
2583 S Hamilton Rd (43232-4964)
PHONE.................................614 575-3044
Dorothy Tanner, *Branch Mgr*
EMP: 97
SALES (corp-wide): 170.7B **Publicly Held**
SIC: 4812 Cellular telephone services
HQ: At&T Corp.
1 At&T Way
Bedminster NJ 07921
800 403-3302

(G-6992)
AT&T CORP
1649 Georgesville Sq Dr (43228-3689)
PHONE.................................614 851-2400
Demond Chambliss, *Branch Mgr*
EMP: 97
SALES (corp-wide): 170.7B **Publicly Held**
SIC: 4812 Cellular telephone services
HQ: At&T Corp.
1 At&T Way
Bedminster NJ 07921
800 403-3302

(G-6993)
AT&T CORP
4300 Appian Way (43230-1446)
PHONE.................................614 337-3902
EMP: 69
SALES (corp-wide): 170.7B **Publicly Held**
WEB: www.att.com
SIC: 4813 Telephone communication, except radio
HQ: At&T Corp.
1 At&T Way
Bedminster NJ 07921
800 403-3302

(G-6994)
AT&T MOBILITY LLC
1555 Olentangy River Rd (43212-1495)
PHONE.................................614 291-2500
Craig Dieckhoner, *Vice Pres*
Nate Linn, *Opers Staff*
James Carson, *Sales Staff*
John Jude, *Manager*
EMP: 26
SALES (corp-wide): 170.7B **Publicly Held**
WEB: www.cingular.com
SIC: 4812 4813 Cellular telephone services; telephone communication, except radio

HQ: At&T Mobility Llc
1025 Lenox Park Blvd Ne
Brookhaven GA 30319
800 331-0500

(G-6995)
ATLAPAC CORP
2901 E 4th Ave Ste 5 (43219-2896)
PHONE.................................614 252-2121
James R Staeck, *President*
Mike Mc Coy, *CFO*
▲ EMP: 70 EST: 1964
SQ FT: 50,000
SALES (est): 12.1MM **Privately Held**
WEB: www.atlapaccorp.com
SIC: 2673 5113 Plastic bags: made from purchased materials; cellophane bags, unprinted: made from purchased materials; bags, paper & disposable plastic

(G-6996)
ATLAS ADVISORS LLC
1795 S High St (43207-1865)
PHONE.................................888 282-0873
Ken Szymborski, *CFO*
Anthony Abner, *Mng Member*
Rick Abner, *Officer*
EMP: 35
SALES (est): 3.3MM **Privately Held**
SIC: 8742 Management consulting services

(G-6997)
ATLAS CAPITAL SERVICES INC (PA)
Also Called: Atlas Butler Heating & Cooling
4849 Evanswood Dr (43229-6206)
PHONE.................................614 294-7373
Mark Swepston, *President*
George Hoskins, *Vice Pres*
James Smith, *Project Mgr*
Larry J Winner, *CFO*
EMP: 80
SQ FT: 16,000
SALES (est): 21.9MM **Privately Held**
WEB: www.atlasbutler.com
SIC: 1711 Warm air heating & air conditioning contractor; heating & air conditioning contractors

(G-6998)
ATLAS CONSTRUCTION COMPANY
4672 Friendship Dr (43230-4302)
PHONE.................................614 475-4705
Steven Testa, *President*
Richard Testa, *Vice Pres*
EMP: 60
SQ FT: 4,000
SALES (est): 7.8MM **Privately Held**
SIC: 1771 Concrete Contractor

(G-6999)
ATLAS HOME MOVING & STORAGE
1570 Integrity Dr E (43209-2704)
PHONE.................................614 445-8831
Jack Herring, *Owner*
Dave Woodhouse, *General Mgr*
EMP: 50
SALES (est): 2MM **Privately Held**
SIC: 4214 Local trucking with storage

(G-7000)
ATLAS INDUSTRIAL CONTRS LLC (HQ)
5275 Sinclair Rd (43229-5042)
PHONE.................................614 841-4500
George Ghanem, *President*
Jeff Forgey, *Division Mgr*
Dallas Gerwig, *Division Mgr*
Rich Wine, *Division Mgr*
Blue McDonald, *Vice Pres*
EMP: 300 EST: 1923
SQ FT: 20,000
SALES: 140.1MM **Privately Held**
WEB: www.atlascos.com
SIC: 1731 3498 1796 Electrical work; fabricated pipe & fittings; machine moving & rigging

(G-7001)
AUBURN DAIRY PRODUCTS INC
2200 Cardigan Ave (43215-1092)
PHONE.................................614 488-2536

Douglas A Smith, *President*
Martin Lavine, *Vice Pres*
Thomas G Michaelides, *Treasurer*
G Frederick Smith, *Admin Sec*
EMP: 31
SQ FT: 10,300
SALES (est): 3.8MM
SALES (corp-wide): 47.5MM **Privately Held**
SIC: 2026 5143 Whipped topping, except frozen or dry mix; dairy products, except dried or canned
PA: Instantwhip Foods, Inc.
2200 Cardigan Ave
Columbus OH 43215
614 488-2536

(G-7002)
AUSSIEFIT I LLC
5929 E Main St (43213-3353)
PHONE.................................614 755-4400
Geoff Dyer, *CEO*
EMP: 30
SQ FT: 28,700
SALES (est): 839.2K
SALES (corp-wide): 1MM **Privately Held**
SIC: 7991 Physical fitness clubs with training equipment
PA: I Aussiefit
497 1st St W
Saint Petersburg FL 33715
727 393-9484

(G-7003)
AUSTIN FOAM PLASTICS INC
Also Called: A F P Ohio
2200 International St (43228-4630)
PHONE.................................614 921-0824
Dan Berona, *Manager*
EMP: 25
SALES (corp-wide): 4.7B **Publicly Held**
WEB: www.austinfoam.com
SIC: 3086 7336 Insulation or cushioning material, foamed plastic; package design
HQ: Austin Foam Plastics, Inc.
2933 A W Grimes Blvd
Pflugerville TX 78660
512 251-6300

(G-7004)
AUTO BODY NORTH INC (PA)
Also Called: Auto Body Mill Run
8675 N High St (43235-1003)
P.O. Box 720, Worthington (43085-0720)
PHONE.................................614 436-3700
Thomas Carpenter, *President*
Darryl Patterson, *President*
William L Denney, *Exec VP*
Robert Vance, *Vice Pres*
Ron Betz, *Manager*
EMP: 70
SQ FT: 1,800
SALES (est): 5.8MM **Privately Held**
WEB: www.autobodyofcolumbus.com
SIC: 7532 Collision shops, automotive; body shop, automotive

(G-7005)
AUTOMOTIVE DISTRIBUTORS CO INC (PA)
Also Called: Automotive Distributors Whse
2981 Morse Rd (43231-6098)
PHONE.................................614 476-1315
Robert I Yeoman, *President*
Frank Schmidt, *Vice Pres*
Jim Ballweg, *Opers Mgr*
Matt Dorr, *Sales Staff*
Lonnie Allan, *Manager*
EMP: 65
SQ FT: 70,000
SALES: 132.8MM **Privately Held**
WEB: www.adw1.com
SIC: 5013 Automotive supplies & parts

(G-7006)
AVNET INC
Also Called: Avnet Computers
2800 Corp Exchange Dr # 160 (43231-7661)
PHONE.................................614 865-1400
Gary Brady, *Branch Mgr*
Craig Shoemaker, *Manager*
EMP: 26
SALES (corp-wide): 19B **Publicly Held**
WEB: www.avnet.com
SIC: 5065 Semiconductor devices

PA: Avnet, Inc.
2211 S 47th St
Phoenix AZ 85034
480 643-2000

(G-7007)
AXA ADVISORS LLC
7965 N High St Ste 140 (43235-8404)
PHONE.................................614 985-3015
Christopher Polle, *Principal*
Tracy Drew, *Advisor*
EMP: 120
SALES (corp-wide): 1MM **Publicly Held**
WEB: www.axacs.com
SIC: 6211 Mutual funds, selling by independent salesperson
HQ: Axa Advisors, Llc
1290 Ave Of Amrcs Fl Cnc1
New York NY 10104
212 554-1234

(G-7008)
AXIA CONSULTING INC
1391 W 5th Ave Ste 320 (43212-2902)
PHONE.................................614 675-4050
Brian Pellot, *Human Resources*
Paul Grove, *Mng Member*
Paul D Grove, *Manager*
Eric Laus, *Consultant*
Tony Kopyar, *Director*
EMP: 65
SALES: 24.9MM **Privately Held**
WEB: www.axiaconsulting.net
SIC: 7373 Systems integration services

(G-7009)
B & B PLASTICS RECYCLERS INC
3300 Lockbourne Rd (43207-3917)
PHONE.................................614 409-2880
Maria Carreon, *Branch Mgr*
EMP: 109
SALES (corp-wide): 128.9MM **Privately Held**
SIC: 4953 Recycling, waste materials
PA: B & B Plastics Recyclers, Inc.
3040 N Locust Ave
Rialto CA 92377
909 829-3606

(G-7010)
BABBAGE-SIMMEL & ASSOC INC
Also Called: Babbage Simmel
2780 Airport Dr Ste 160 (43219-2291)
PHONE.................................614 481-6555
Houshang Maani, *Ch of Bd*
Louis Maani, *President*
EMP: 39
SALES (est): 3.3MM **Privately Held**
WEB: www.babsim.com
SIC: 8243 8743 Operator training, computer; public relations services

(G-7011)
BAILEY & LONG INC
Also Called: Goddard School
101 E Town St Ste 115 (43215-5247)
PHONE.................................614 937-9435
Malvin Long, *President*
Meredith C Bailey, *CFO*
EMP: 25
SALES (est): 549.6K **Privately Held**
SIC: 8351 Preschool center

(G-7012)
BAILEY ASSOCIATES
6836 Caine Rd (43235-4290)
PHONE.................................614 760-7752
Rudy Bailey, *Owner*
EMP: 110
SALES: 3.2MM **Privately Held**
SIC: 8741 Financial management for business

(G-7013)
BAILEY CAVALIERI LLC (PA)
10 W Broad St Ste 2100 (43215-3455)
PHONE.................................614 221-3258
Michael Mahoney, *Managing Dir*
Joan Parrish, *Manager*
Michael P Mahoney, *Director*
Donna Williams, *Administration*
Michael Goodstein,
EMP: 86
SQ FT: 45,000

SALES (est): 13.1MM **Privately Held**
SIC: 8111 General practice attorney, lawyer

(G-7014)
BAKER & HOSTETLER LLP
65 E State St Ste 2100 (43215-4213)
PHONE.....................................614 228-1541
Fax: 614 462-2616
EMP: 123
SALES (corp-wide): 316.3MM **Privately Held**
SIC: 8111 Legal Services Office
PA: Baker & Hostetler Llp
    127 Public Sq Ste 2000
    Cleveland OH 44114
    216 621-0200

(G-7015)
BALL BOUNCE AND SPORT INC
3275 Alum Creek Dr (43207-3460)
PHONE.....................................614 662-5381
Shaun Davis, *Branch Mgr*
EMP: 30
SALES (est): 1.4MM
SALES (corp-wide): 195.8MM **Privately Held**
SIC: 5092 Toys & hobby goods & supplies
PA: Ball, Bounce And Sport, Inc.
    1 Hedstrom Dr
    Ashland OH 44805
    419 289-9310

(G-7016)
BALLET METROPOLITAN INC
Also Called: BALLETMET COLUMBUS
322 Mount Vernon Ave (43215-2131)
PHONE.....................................614 229-4860
Sue Porter, *Exec Dir*
EMP: 150
SQ FT: 35,000
SALES (est): 7MM **Privately Held**
WEB: www.balletmet.org
SIC: 7922 7911 Ballet production; professional dancing school

(G-7017)
BARCUS COMPANY INC
1601 Bethel Rd Ste 100 (43220-2006)
PHONE.....................................614 451-9000
Philip Barcus, *President*
Lisa Moorhead, *General Mgr*
EMP: 50
SQ FT: 10,000
SALES (est): 4.3MM **Privately Held**
WEB: www.barcuscompany.com
SIC: 6513 6512 Apartment building operators; commercial & industrial building operation

(G-7018)
BARKAN & NEFF CO LPA (PA)
250 E Broad St Fl 10 (43215-3708)
PHONE.....................................614 221-4221
Frank J Neff, *President*
Sanford Meizlish, *Managing Prtnr*
Bob Derose, *Senior Partner*
Eileen Goodin, *Principal*
C R Canestraro,
EMP: 40
SQ FT: 15,000
SALES (est): 13.9MM **Privately Held**
WEB: www.bnhmlaw.com
SIC: 8111 General practice law office

(G-7019)
BARR ENGINEERING INCORPORATED (PA)
Also Called: National Engrg Archtctral Svcs
2800 Corp Exchange Dr # 240 (43231-7628)
PHONE.....................................614 714-0299
Jawdat Siddiqi, *President*
Enoch Chipukaizer, *Principal*
Robin Lamb, *Principal*
Jessica Cave, *Accountant*
EMP: 35
SQ FT: 1,500
SALES (est): 9.4MM **Privately Held**
SIC: 8711 8713 8734 1799 Civil engineering; surveying services; testing laboratories; core drilling & cutting; nonmetallic minerals development & test boring

(G-7020)
BATTELLE MEMORIAL INSTITUTE (PA)
505 King Ave (43201-2681)
PHONE.....................................614 424-6424
Lewis Von Thaer, *CEO*
John Welch, *Ch of Bd*
Martin Inglis, *Exec VP*
Russell Austin, *Senior VP*
Michael Janus, *Vice Pres*
▲ EMP: 4712 EST: 1925
SQ FT: 3,810
SALES (est): 2.5B **Privately Held**
WEB: www.battelle.org
SIC: 8731 8699 Commercial physical research; medical research, commercial; environmental research; electronic research; charitable organization

(G-7021)
BAY STATE GAS COMPANY
200 Civic Center Dr (43215-7510)
PHONE.....................................614 460-4292
Tony Amurgis, *Vice Pres*
Steven Jablonski, *Branch Mgr*
EMP: 273
SALES (corp-wide): 5.1B **Publicly Held**
WEB: www.baystategas.com
SIC: 4924 Natural gas distribution
HQ: Bay State Gas Company
    4 Technology Dr
    Westborough MA 01581
    508 836-7000

(G-7022)
BBS PROFESSIONAL CORPORATION (DH)
1103 Schrock Rd Ste 400 (43229-1179)
PHONE.....................................614 888-3100
Edward O Vance, *Ch of Bd*
Paul R Schlegel, *President*
Donald F Cuthbert, *Vice Pres*
EMP: 49
SQ FT: 19,000
SALES (est): 4.2MM
SALES (corp-wide): 10B **Publicly Held**
SIC: 8711 Consulting engineer
HQ: Ch2m Hill, Inc.
    9191 S Jamaica St
    Englewood CO 80112
    303 771-0900

(G-7023)
BDO USA LLP
300 Spruce St Ste 100 (43215-1173)
PHONE.....................................614 488-3126
Mike Voinovich, *Managing Prtnr*
EMP: 45
SALES (corp-wide): 940.4MM **Privately Held**
SIC: 8721 Certified public accountant
PA: Bdo Usa, Llp
    330 N Wabash Ave Ste 3200
    Chicago IL 60611
    312 240-1236

(G-7024)
BEECHWOLD VETERINARY HOSPITAL (PA)
4590 Indianola Ave (43214-2248)
PHONE.....................................614 268-8666
Stephen D Wenger, *President*
Marilyn A Schwab, *Principal*
Bruce Wenger, *Principal*
Ed Winderl, *Corp Secy*
Robert Hanson, *Vice Pres*
EMP: 40
SQ FT: 6,000
SALES (est): 3.9MM **Privately Held**
WEB: www.beechwoldvet.vetsuite.com
SIC: 0742 Animal hospital services, pets & other animal specialties

(G-7025)
BEHAL SAMPSON DIETZ INC
990 W 3rd Ave (43212-3127)
PHONE.....................................614 464-1933
Thomas Sampson, *CEO*
John Behal, *Principal*
Keith De Voe III, *Principal*
James F Dietz, *Treasurer*
James Dietz, *Treasurer*
EMP: 25
SQ FT: 9,500

SALES (est): 4.4MM **Privately Held**
WEB: www.bsdarchitects.com
SIC: 1521 8712 1542 1522 General remodeling, single-family houses; architectural services; nonresidential construction; residential construction

(G-7026)
BELCAN CORPORATION
Also Called: Belcan Staffing Solutions
519 S High St (43215-5602)
PHONE.....................................614 224-6080
EMP: 749
SALES (corp-wide): 813.3MM **Privately Held**
SIC: 7363 Engineering help service
PA: Belcan, Llc
    10200 Anderson Way
    Blue Ash OH 45242
    513 891-0972

(G-7027)
BENESCH FRIEDLANDER COPLAN &
41 S High St Ste 2600 (43215-6164)
PHONE.....................................614 223-9300
David Paragas, *Partner*
N Victor Goodman, *Partner*
EMP: 50
SALES (corp-wide): 57.2MM **Privately Held**
SIC: 8111 General practice attorney, lawyer
PA: Benesch, Friedlander, Coplan & Aronoff Llp
    200 Public Sq Ste 2300
    Cleveland OH 44114
    216 363-4500

(G-7028)
BERARDI + PARTNERS
1398 Goodale Blvd (43212-3720)
PHONE.....................................614 221-1110
George Berardi, *Partner*
Christopher Bruzzese, *Partner*
Brehmlarry Brehm, *Engineer*
Dan Mayer, *Director*
EMP: 25
SQ FT: 9,000
SALES (est): 4.2MM **Privately Held**
WEB: www.bpiarch.com
SIC: 8712 Architectural engineering

(G-7029)
BERTEC CORPORATION
6171 Huntley Rd Ste J (43229-1047)
PHONE.....................................614 543-0962
Necip Berme, *President*
Scott Barnes, *General Mgr*
Murat Berme, *COO*
Mark Burkhart, *Opers Staff*
Jeff S Sobotka, *Purch Mgr*
EMP: 27
SQ FT: 12,000
SALES (est): 5.2MM **Privately Held**
WEB: www.bertec.com
SIC: 8711 Consulting engineer; mechanical engineering

(G-7030)
BEST WESTERN COLUMBUS N HOTEL
Also Called: Best Western Columbus North
888 E Dublin Granville Rd (43229-2416)
PHONE.....................................614 888-8230
Shawn Chang, *General Mgr*
EMP: 40
SALES: 1.4MM **Privately Held**
SIC: 6512 7991 7011 5813 Nonresidential building operators; physical fitness facilities; hotels & motels; drinking places; eating places

(G-7031)
BESTTRANSPORTCOM INC
1103 Schrock Rd Ste 100 (43229-1179)
PHONE.....................................614 888-2378
Michael Dolan, *President*
Scott Cummans, *Vice Pres*
Denisa Cellar, *Engineer*
Pete Scolieri, *Sales Staff*
Randy Combs, *Manager*
EMP: 30
SALES (est): 4.7MM **Privately Held**
WEB: www.besttransport.com
SIC: 7372 Prepackaged software

(G-7032)
BETH-EL AGAPE CHRISTIAN CENTER
840 Mansfield Ave (43219-2453)
PHONE.....................................614 445-0674
Benita Farve, *President*
Quanta Brown, *Corp Secy*
Rowena Bryant, *Admin Sec*
EMP: 25
SALES (est): 161.7K **Privately Held**
SIC: 8322 Outreach program

(G-7033)
BEYOND THE HORIZONS HOME HEALT
2645 Fairwood Ave (43207-2729)
PHONE.....................................608 630-0617
William Reynolds, *Principal*
Julius Myricks, *Principal*
EMP: 25
SALES (est): 194.8K **Privately Held**
SIC: 8082 Home health care services

(G-7034)
BIG BROTH AND BIG SISTE OF CEN (PA)
Also Called: MENTORING CENTER FOR CENTRAL O
1855 E Dbln Grnvl Rd Fl 1 Flr 1 (43229)
PHONE.....................................614 839-2447
Heather Campbell, *CEO*
Douglas Peterman Jr, *Chairman*
Dave Schirner, *Vice Pres*
Denise McConnell, *Treasurer*
Edward Cohn, *Director*
EMP: 50
SQ FT: 11,000
SALES: 4.5MM **Privately Held**
WEB: www.bbbscolumbus.org
SIC: 8322 7033 Helping hand service (Big Brother, etc.); campgrounds

(G-7035)
BIG LOTS STORES INC (HQ)
4900 E Dblin Granville Rd (43081-7651)
PHONE.....................................614 278-6800
Bruce Thorn, *President*
Lisa Bachmann, *COO*
Mike Schlonsky, *Exec VP*
Steve Haffer, *Senior VP*
Rocky Robins, *Senior VP*
▲ EMP: 800
SALES: 5.3B
SALES (corp-wide): 5.2B **Publicly Held**
WEB: www.biglots.com
SIC: 5331 5021 5044 Variety stores; furniture; office equipment
PA: Big Lots, Inc.
    4900 E Dblin Granville Rd
    Columbus OH 43081
    614 278-6800

(G-7036)
BIG RED ROOSTER (HQ)
121 Thurman Ave (43206-2656)
PHONE.....................................614 255-0200
Martin J Beck, *CEO*
Vicki Eickelberger, *President*
Don Hasulak, *President*
Stephen Jay, *President*
Staci Mandrell, *President*
EMP: 49
SALES (est): 15MM
SALES (corp-wide): 16.3B **Publicly Held**
SIC: 8712 8748 7371 Architectural services; industrial development planning; computer software systems analysis & design, custom
PA: Jones Lang Lasalle Incorporated
    200 E Randolph St # 4300
    Chicago IL 60601
    312 782-5800

(G-7037)
BIG WESTERN OPERATING CO INC
Also Called: Big Western Lanes
500 Georgesville Rd (43228-2421)
PHONE.....................................614 274-1169
Paul Cusmano, *President*
EMP: 25
SQ FT: 45,000
SALES (est): 500.6K **Privately Held**
SIC: 7933 Ten pin center

(G-7038)
BIMBO BAKERIES USA INC
1020 Claycraft Rd Ste D (43230-6684)
PHONE....................................614 868-7565
Dave Melaragno, *Manager*
EMP: 30 **Privately Held**
WEB: www.gwbakeries.com
SIC: 5149 Bakery products
HQ: Bimbo Bakeries Usa, Inc
    255 Business Center Dr # 200
    Horsham PA 19044
    215 347-5500

(G-7039)
BIO-BLOOD COMPONENTS INC
1393 N High St (43201-2459)
PHONE....................................614 294-3183
Jane Hancock, *Manager*
EMP: 30
SALES (corp-wide): 18.6MM **Privately Held**
SIC: 8099 2836 Blood bank; biological products, except diagnostic
PA: Bio-Blood Components, Inc.
    5700 Pleasant View Rd
    Memphis TN 38134
    901 384-6250

(G-7040)
BIO-MDCAL APPLCATIONS OHIO INC
Also Called: Fresenius Kidney Care Olentang
758 Communications Pkwy (43214-1948)
PHONE....................................614 538-1060
Mary Garber, *Principal*
Michelle Smallwood, *Principal*
EMP: 25 EST: 2017
SALES (est): 157.2K **Privately Held**
SIC: 8092 Kidney dialysis centers

(G-7041)
BIO-MDCAL APPLCATIONS OHIO INC
Also Called: Fresenius Med Care Cntl Ohio E
4039 E Broad St (43213-1136)
PHONE....................................614 338-8202
Jim Barsanti, *Manager*
EMP: 25
SALES (corp-wide): 18.9B **Privately Held**
WEB: www.fresenius.org
SIC: 8092 Kidney dialysis centers
HQ: Bio-Medical Applications Of Ohio, Inc.
    920 Winter St
    Waltham MA 02451

(G-7042)
BKG HOLDINGS LLC
Also Called: Bartha Audio Visual
600 N Cassady Ave Ofc (43219-2790)
PHONE....................................614 252-7455
Dan Bashore, *Managing Dir*
Wayne Perry, *Prdtn Mgr*
David Watts, *Warehouse Mgr*
Michelle Broidy, *Production*
Thomas B Gabbert, *Mng Member*
EMP: 45
SQ FT: 48,115
SALES (est): 7.3MM **Privately Held**
WEB: www.bartha.com
SIC: 7812 7359 Audio-visual program production; audio-visual equipment & supply rental

(G-7043)
BKG SERVICES INC
3948 Townsfair Way # 230 (43219-6096)
P.O. Box 307352 (43230-7352)
PHONE....................................614 476-1800
Benjamin Harper, *President*
EMP: 30
SQ FT: 500
SALES (est): 882.2K **Privately Held**
WEB: www.bkgservices.com
SIC: 7349 Janitorial service, contract basis

(G-7044)
BLACK & VEATCH CORPORATION
4449 Easton Way Ste 150 (43219-7002)
PHONE....................................614 473-0921
Pat Roman, *Manager*
EMP: 30
SALES (corp-wide): 3.3B **Privately Held**
WEB: www.bv.com
SIC: 8711 Consulting engineer

HQ: Black & Veatch Corporation
    11401 Lamar Ave
    Overland Park KS 66211
    913 458-2000

(G-7045)
BLACK SAPPHIRE C COLUMBUS UNIV
Also Called: Springhill Suites
1421 Olentangy River Rd (43212-1449)
PHONE....................................614 297-9912
Alan Schreiber, *General Mgr*
Dena St Clair, *Asst Director*
EMP: 100
SALES (est): 2.2MM **Privately Held**
SIC: 7011 Hotels & motels

(G-7046)
BLACKBURNS FABRICATION INC
2467 Jackson Pike (43223-3846)
PHONE....................................614 875-0784
Mark A Blackburn, *President*
Edsel L Blackburn Sr, *Vice Pres*
Steve Bosak, *Sales Associate*
Carolyn Blackburn, *Admin Sec*
Kim Green, *Admin Sec*
EMP: 30
SQ FT: 50,000
SALES (est): 9.2MM **Privately Held**
WEB: www.blackburnsfab.com
SIC: 3441 5051 Fabricated structural metal; structural shapes, iron or steel

(G-7047)
BLASTMASTER HOLDINGS USA LLC
Also Called: Blastone International
4510 Bridgeway Ave (43219-1891)
PHONE....................................877 725-2781
Timothy D Gooden,
Andrew Gooden,
James Gooden,
◆ EMP: 100
SQ FT: 56,000
SALES (est): 60.5MM **Privately Held**
SIC: 5084 Industrial machinery & equipment

(G-7048)
BLOOD SERVICES CENTL OHIO REG (PA)
995 E Broad St (43205-1322)
PHONE....................................614 253-7981
Ambrose Ng, *CEO*
Kurt Anders, *Finance*
Rita Barns, *MIS Mgr*
David Gabriel, *Administration*
EMP: 200
SQ FT: 80,000
SALES (est): 2.8MM **Privately Held**
SIC: 8099 Blood related health services

(G-7049)
BMI FEDERAL CREDIT UNION (PA)
760 Kinnear Rd Frnt (43212-1487)
P.O. Box 3670, Dublin (43016-0340)
PHONE....................................614 298-8527
Sharon Custer, *President*
EMP: 70
SQ FT: 18,000
SALES: 13.5MM **Privately Held**
WEB: www.bmifcu.com
SIC: 6061 Federal credit unions

(G-7050)
BNAI BRITH HILLEL FDN AT OSU
46 E 16th Ave (43201-1615)
PHONE....................................614 294-4797
Aaron Shocket, *President*
EMP: 36
SALES (est): 1.1MM **Privately Held**
SIC: 8661 8611 Religious organizations; community affairs & services

(G-7051)
BOB SUMEREL TIRE CO INC
2807 International St (43228-4616)
PHONE....................................614 527-9700
Timothy Hooker, *Manager*
EMP: 32

SALES (corp-wide): 89.7MM **Privately Held**
WEB: www.bobsumereltire.com
SIC: 5014 5015 7534 Tires & tubes; batteries, used: automotive; tire retreading & repair shops
PA: Bob Sumerel Tire Co., Inc.
    1257 Cox Ave
    Erlanger KY 41018
    859 283-2700

(G-7052)
BOBB AUTOMOTIVE INC
Also Called: Bobb Suzuki
4639 W Broad St (43228-1610)
P.O. Box 28148 (43228-0148)
PHONE....................................614 853-3000
Jeff May, *President*
Thomas O'Ryan, *Vice Pres*
Cindy Blagg, *Human Res Mgr*
Mac Levins, *Sales Staff*
Cheryl Walters, *Sales Staff*
EMP: 50
SQ FT: 15,000
SALES (est): 69.2MM **Privately Held**
WEB: www.fetrucks.com
SIC: 5511 7515 5012 Automobiles, new & used; passenger car leasing; automobiles & other motor vehicles

(G-7053)
BONDED CHEMICALS INC (HQ)
Also Called: Chemgroup
2645 Charter St (43228-4605)
PHONE....................................614 777-9240
Marty Wehr, *President*
Sue Wiford, *Corp Secy*
Chris Davis, *Manager*
Mike Davis, *Manager*
Brett McMillen, *Manager*
▲ EMP: 30
SALES (est): 39.5MM
SALES (corp-wide): 131MM **Privately Held**
WEB: www.chemgroup.com
SIC: 5169 Sanitation preparations; industrial chemicals
PA: Chemgroup, Inc
    2600 Thunderhawk Ct
    Dayton OH 45414
    937 898-5566

(G-7054)
BORDNER AND ASSOCIATES INC (PA)
Also Called: Laser Reproductions
950 Taylor Station Rd E (43230-6670)
PHONE....................................614 552-6905
Paul Gerald Bordner II, *President*
Shirley Bordner, *Exec VP*
Bret Douglas Bordner, *Vice Pres*
Lisa Mannon, *Shareholder*
▲ EMP: 40
SQ FT: 8,000
SALES (est): 9.3MM **Privately Held**
WEB: www.laserrepro.com
SIC: 5085 Industrial supplies

(G-7055)
BOWEN ENGINEERING CORPORATION
22 E Gay St Ste 700 (43215-3173)
PHONE....................................614 536-0273
EMP: 148
SALES (corp-wide): 349.9MM **Privately Held**
SIC: 8711 Engineering services
PA: Bowen Engineering Corporation
    8802 N Meridian St Ste X
    Indianapolis IN 46260
    219 661-9770

(G-7056)
BOYS & GIRLS CLUB OF COLUMBUS
1108 City Park Ave # 301 (43206-3686)
PHONE....................................614 221-8830
Drew Dimaccio, *President*
EMP: 46
SQ FT: 22,000
SALES: 2.5MM **Privately Held**
SIC: 8641 Youth organizations

(G-7057)
BP-LS-PT CO
5275 Sinclair Rd (43229-5042)
PHONE....................................614 841-4500
Peter C Taub, *President*
Randy Goddard, *Vice Pres*
EMP: 95
SALES (est): 4.4MM **Privately Held**
SIC: 1731 General electrical contractor

(G-7058)
BPM REALTY INC
195 N Grant Ave Fl 2a (43215-2855)
PHONE....................................614 221-6811
Frederick W Ziegler, *Ch of Bd*
John M Ziegler, *President*
EMP: 27
SQ FT: 43,000
SALES (est): 3MM **Privately Held**
WEB: www.buckeyepm.com
SIC: 7331 2752 Mailing service; commercial printing, offset

(G-7059)
BRADY WARE & SCHOENFELD INC
4249 Easton Way Ste 100 (43219-6170)
PHONE....................................614 885-7407
EMP: 65
SALES (corp-wide): 14.6MM **Privately Held**
SIC: 8721 Accounting/Auditing /Bookkeeping
PA: Brady, Ware & Schoenfeld, Inc.
    3601 Rigby Rd Ste 400
    Miamisburg OH 45342
    937 223-5247

(G-7060)
BRADY WARE & SCHOENFELD INC
Also Called: Brady Ware
4249 Easton Way Ste 175 (43219-6186)
PHONE....................................614 825-6277
Bob Reynolds, *Branch Mgr*
EMP: 65
SALES (corp-wide): 15.6MM **Privately Held**
SIC: 8721 Certified public accountant
PA: Brady, Ware & Schoenfeld, Inc.
    3601 Rigby Rd Ste 400
    Miamisburg OH 45342
    937 223-5247

(G-7061)
BREATHING ASSOCIATION
1520 Old Henderson Rd # 201 (43220-3639)
PHONE....................................614 457-4570
Krystal Conner, *Manager*
Marie E Collart, *Exec Dir*
EMP: 27 EST: 1906
SQ FT: 1,800
SALES: 2MM **Privately Held**
SIC: 8621 Medical field-related associations

(G-7062)
BRIAR-GATE REALTY INC
1675 W Mound St (43223-1809)
P.O. Box 1150, Grove City (43123-6150)
PHONE....................................614 299-2121
EMP: 27
SALES (corp-wide): 22MM **Privately Held**
SIC: 4225 General warehousing & storage
PA: Briar-Gate Realty, Inc.
    3827 Brookham Dr
    Grove City OH 43123
    614 299-2121

(G-7063)
BRICKER & ECKLER LLP (PA)
100 S 3rd St Ste B (43215-4291)
PHONE....................................614 227-2300
Richard C Simpson, *Partner*
Rebecca Princehorn, *Partner*
Rosemarie Delsignore, *Vice Pres*
David Hasman, *Litigation*
Jerry O Allen,
EMP: 311 EST: 1997
SQ FT: 100,000

SALES (est): 51.9MM **Privately Held**
WEB: www.counselfor.net
SIC: 8111 General practice law office; general practice attorney, lawyer

(G-7064)
BRIGHT HORIZONS CHLD CTRS LLC
Also Called: Bright Horizons Battelle
835 Thomas Ln (43214-3905)
PHONE...............................614 754-7023
Rebecca Komarov, *Director*
EMP: 40
SALES (corp-wide): 1.9B **Publicly Held**
SIC: 8351 Group day care center
HQ: Bright Horizons Children's Centers Llc
200 Talcott Ave
Watertown MA 02472
617 673-8000

(G-7065)
BRIGHT HORIZONS CHLD CTRS LLC
111 S Grant Ave (43215-4701)
PHONE...............................614 566-9322
Karen Hughes, *Manager*
EMP: 27
SALES (corp-wide): 1.9B **Publicly Held**
WEB: www.atlantaga.ncr.com
SIC: 8351 Group day care center
HQ: Bright Horizons Children's Centers Llc
200 Talcott Ave
Watertown MA 02472
617 673-8000

(G-7066)
BRIGHT HORIZONS CHLD CTRS LLC
277 E Town St (43215-4627)
PHONE...............................614 227-0550
Catherine Edgar, *Director*
EMP: 28
SALES (corp-wide): 1.9B **Publicly Held**
WEB: www.atlantaga.ncr.com
SIC: 8748 Business consulting
HQ: Bright Horizons Children's Centers Llc
200 Talcott Ave
Watertown MA 02472
617 673-8000

(G-7067)
BRIGHT HORIZONS CHLD CTRS LLC
835 Thomas Ln (43214-3905)
PHONE...............................614 566-4847
Lori Ritter, *Manager*
EMP: 27
SALES (corp-wide): 1.9B **Publicly Held**
WEB: www.atlantaga.ncr.com
SIC: 8351 Child day care services
HQ: Bright Horizons Children's Centers Llc
200 Talcott Ave
Watertown MA 02472
617 673-8000

(G-7068)
BRIGHTVIEW LANDSCAPE SVCS INC
3001 Innis Rd (43224-3741)
PHONE...............................614 801-1712
Maria Sanbuco, *Sales Executive*
EMP: 38
SALES (corp-wide): 2.8B **Publicly Held**
SIC: 0781 Landscape services
HQ: Brightview Landscape Services, Inc.
24151 Ventura Blvd
Calabasas CA 91302
818 223-8500

(G-7069)
BRIGHTVIEW LANDSCAPE SVCS INC
3001 Innis Rd (43224-3741)
PHONE...............................614 478-2085
Joel Korte, *Manager*
EMP: 56
SQ FT: 845
SALES (corp-wide): 2.8B **Publicly Held**
SIC: 0781 Landscape services
HQ: Brightview Landscape Services, Inc.
24151 Ventura Blvd
Calabasas CA 91302
818 223-8500

(G-7070)
BRIGHTVIEW LANDSCAPE SVCS INC
3001 Innis Rd (43224-3741)
PHONE...............................740 369-4800
Eric Klopfer, *Accounts Mgr*
EMP: 56
SALES (corp-wide): 2.8B **Publicly Held**
SIC: 0781 Landscape services
HQ: Brightview Landscape Services, Inc.
24151 Ventura Blvd
Calabasas CA 91302
818 223-8500

(G-7071)
BRIGHTVIEW LANDSCAPES LLC
2323 Performance Way (43207-2858)
PHONE...............................301 987-9200
Joe Pistininzi, *Principal*
EMP: 36
SALES (corp-wide): 2.8B **Publicly Held**
SIC: 0781 Landscape services
HQ: Brightview Landscapes, Llc
401 Plymouth Rd Ste 500
Plymouth Meeting PA 19462
484 567-7204

(G-7072)
BRIGHTVIEW LANDSCAPES LLC
2240 Harper Rd (43204-3410)
PHONE...............................614 276-5500
Jeff Rupp, *Principal*
Mark Kubasak, *Accounts Mgr*
EMP: 56
SALES (corp-wide): 2.8B **Publicly Held**
SIC: 0781 Landscape services
HQ: Brightview Landscapes, Llc
401 Plymouth Rd Ste 500
Plymouth Meeting PA 19462
484 567-7204

(G-7073)
BRINKS INCORPORATED
1362 Essex Ave (43211-2632)
PHONE...............................614 291-1268
David Bramkamp, *Manager*
Debbie Stanton, *Executive*
EMP: 42
SALES (corp-wide): 3.4B **Publicly Held**
WEB: www.brinksinc.com
SIC: 7381 Armored car services
HQ: Brink's, Incorporated
1801 Bayberry Ct Ste 400
Richmond VA 23226
804 289-9600

(G-7074)
BRINKS INCORPORATED
506 E Starr Ave (43201-3618)
PHONE...............................614 291-0624
Charles Redmond, *Principal*
EMP: 42
SALES (corp-wide): 3.4B **Publicly Held**
SIC: 7381 Armored car services
HQ: Brink's, Incorporated
1801 Bayberry Ct Ste 400
Richmond VA 23226
804 289-9600

(G-7075)
BROAD & JAMES INC
Also Called: Broad & James Towing
3502 E 7th Ave (43219-1735)
PHONE...............................614 231-8697
Tim Shriner, *President*
Jim Shriner, *Vice Pres*
EMP: 30 EST: 1973
SQ FT: 2,500
SALES (est): 3.9MM **Privately Held**
SIC: 7549 7539 Towing service, automotive; automotive repair shops

(G-7076)
BROAD STREET HOTEL ASSOC LP
Also Called: Ramada Inn East - Airport
4801 E Broad St (43213-1356)
PHONE...............................614 861-0321
Kevork Toroyian, *Partner*
Patrick Barrett, *Partner*
Barkev Kayajian, *Partner*
Bill Nikolis, *Partner*
EMP: 60

SQ FT: 15,000
SALES (est): 1.7MM **Privately Held**
WEB: www.endlessresin.com
SIC: 7011 7991 5813 5812 Hotels; physical fitness facilities; drinking places; eating places

(G-7077)
BROADSPIRE SERVICES INC
445 Hutchinson Ave # 550 (43235-5677)
PHONE...............................614 436-8990
Michael Carney, *General Mgr*
EMP: 25
SALES (corp-wide): 1.1B **Publicly Held**
WEB: www.choosebroadspire.com
SIC: 6331 8099 Workers' compensation insurance; medical services organization
HQ: Broadspire Services Inc
1391 Nw 136th Ave
Sunrise FL 33323
954 452-4000

(G-7078)
BROADVIEW NH LLC
5151 N Hamilton Rd (43230-1313)
PHONE...............................614 337-1066
Mordecai Rosenberg, *President*
Lisa Schwartz, *Principal*
Ronald Swartz, *Principal*
Dawn Woznak, *Opers Staff*
Katie Cape, *Marketing Staff*
EMP: 99
SALES (est): 574.4K **Privately Held**
SIC: 8051 Skilled nursing care facilities

(G-7079)
BROOK WILLOW CHRSTN CMMUNITIES
Also Called: Willow Brook Christian Home
55 Lazelle Rd (43235-1402)
PHONE...............................614 885-3300
David Chappell, *Administration*
EMP: 65
SALES (corp-wide): 4.2MM **Privately Held**
WEB: www.willow-brook.org
SIC: 8052 8051 Intermediate care facilities; skilled nursing care facilities
PA: Willow Brook Christian Communities, Inc
100 Delaware Xing W
Delaware OH 43015
740 369-0048

(G-7080)
BROOKDALE LVING CMMUNITIES INC
Also Called: Brookdale Living Cmnty Ohio
3500 Trillium Xing (43235-7991)
PHONE...............................614 734-1000
Debbie Castle, *Manager*
EMP: 100
SALES (corp-wide): 4.5B **Publicly Held**
WEB: www.parkplace-spokane.com
SIC: 8361 Residential care
HQ: Brookdale Living Communities, Inc.
515 N State St Ste 1750
Chicago IL 60654

(G-7081)
BROOKSIDE GOLF & CNTRY CLB CO
2770 W Dblin Granville Rd (43235-2785)
PHONE...............................614 889-2581
James Rowlette, *President*
Joseph T Furko III, *General Mgr*
EMP: 150 EST: 1927
SQ FT: 75,000
SALES: 5.3MM **Privately Held**
WEB: www.brooksidegcc.com
SIC: 7997 Country club, membership; golf club, membership

(G-7082)
BROWN AND CALDWELL
445 Hutchinson Ave # 540 (43235-8631)
PHONE...............................614 410-6144
Tim Block, *Manager*
Michael O'Shaughnessy, *Administration*
EMP: 32
SALES (corp-wide): 540.3MM **Privately Held**
SIC: 8711 Professional engineer; consulting engineer

PA: Brown And Caldwell
201 N Civic Dr Ste 115
Walnut Creek CA 94596
925 937-9010

(G-7083)
BRUSH CONTRACTORS INC
5000 Transamerica Dr (43228-9335)
P.O. Box 3213, Dublin (43016-0098)
PHONE...............................614 850-8500
Stephen Brush, *President*
EMP: 65
SQ FT: 10,500
SALES (est): 8.2MM **Privately Held**
WEB: www.brushcontractors.com
SIC: 1731 Lighting contractor

(G-7084)
BUCKEYE ASSN SCHL ADMNSTRATORS
8050 N High St Ste 150 (43235-6486)
PHONE...............................614 846-4080
Kathy Lowery, *Principal*
Dr Jerry Klenke, *Director*
EMP: 25
SALES: 3MM **Privately Held**
SIC: 8621 Education & teacher association

(G-7085)
BUCKEYE BOXES INC
601 N Hague Ave (43204-1498)
PHONE...............................614 274-8484
EMP: 30
SALES (est): 1.8MM
SALES (corp-wide): 56.9MM **Privately Held**
SIC: 5113 2653 Industrial & personal service paper; corrugated & solid fiber boxes
PA: Buckeye Boxes, Inc.
601 N Hague Ave
Columbus OH 43204
614 274-8484

(G-7086)
BUCKEYE CMNTY EIGHTY ONE LP
Also Called: Williams Street Apartments
3021 E Dblin Granville Rd (43231-4031)
PHONE...............................614 942-2020
Brenda Jacques, *General Ptnr*
Steven Boone, *Ltd Ptnr*
EMP: 37
SALES (est): 559.1K **Privately Held**
SIC: 6513 Apartment building operators

(G-7087)
BUCKEYE CMNTY HOPE FOUNDATION (PA)
3021 E Dblin Grndville Rd (43231)
PHONE...............................614 942-2014
Steve J Boone, *President*
Ian Maute, *Vice Pres*
Carlisa Stewart, *Vice Pres*
Jody McRainey, *Director*
Jennifer Schorr, *Director*
EMP: 100
SQ FT: 5,000
SALES: 26.4MM **Privately Held**
SIC: 1521 Single-family housing construction

(G-7088)
BUCKEYE CMNTY TWENTY SIX LP
Also Called: Montpelier Gardens
3021 E Dblin Granville Rd (43231-4031)
PHONE...............................614 942-2020
Steven Boone, *President*
EMP: 30
SALES (est): 925.2K **Privately Held**
SIC: 6531 Real estate agents & managers

(G-7089)
BUCKEYE POWER INC (PA)
Also Called: Ohio Rural Electric Coops
6677 Busch Blvd (43229-1101)
PHONE...............................614 781-0573
Steven Nelson, *Ch of Bd*
Anthony J Ahern, *President*
Bobby Daniel, *Vice Pres*
Thomas Alban, *Director*
James Walker Jr, *Director*
EMP: 28
SQ FT: 36,000

SALES: 708.2MM **Privately Held**
WEB: www.buckeyepower.com
SIC: **8611** 4911 Business Association
Electric Services

(G-7090)
BUCKEYE RANCH INC
Also Called: Permanent Family Solutions
697 E Broad St (43215-3948)
PHONE....................................614 384-7700
Steve Richard, *Branch Mgr*
EMP: 55
SALES (corp-wide): 44.4MM **Privately Held**
SIC: **8361** Home for the emotionally disturbed; halfway group home, persons with social or personal problems; halfway home for delinquents & offenders; juvenile correctional home
PA: The Buckeye Ranch Inc
5665 Hoover Rd
Grove City OH 43123
614 875-2371

(G-7091)
BUCKEYE TRUCK EQUIPMENT INC
Also Called: Buckeye Body and Equipment
939 E Starr Ave (43201-3042)
P.O. Box 1150 (43216-1150)
PHONE....................................614 299-1136
Fred Bongiovanni, *President*
Jeff Massey, *General Mgr*
Jeffrey Massey, *Vice Pres*
Roger Clark, *Opers Mgr*
Doug Callahan, *Treasurer*
EMP: 34
SQ FT: 55,000
SALES: 9MM **Privately Held**
SIC: **5012** Truck bodies

(G-7092)
BUCKNER AND SONS MASONRY INC
2300 Sullivant Ave (43204-3133)
PHONE....................................614 279-9777
Otis Jerome Buckner, *President*
Otis Buckner, *President*
Bailene Buckner, *Corp Secy*
Otis Lee Buckner, *Director*
EMP: 30
SQ FT: 3,200
SALES: 4MM **Privately Held**
SIC: **1741** Masonry & other stonework

(G-7093)
BUDENHEIM USA INC
855 Grandview Ave Ste 120 (43215-2884)
PHONE....................................614 345-2400
Douglas Lim, *Ch of Bd*
Harold Schaub, *President*
Jerry Cohen, *President*
Becca Beck, *General Mgr*
Silke John, *General Mgr*
◆ EMP: 25 EST: 1955
SALES: 18.8MM
SALES (corp-wide): 222.7MM **Privately Held**
WEB: www.gallard.com
SIC: **5169** Industrial chemicals; food additives & preservatives
PA: Chemische Fabrik Budenheim Kg
Rheinstr. 27
Budenheim 55257
613 989-0

(G-7094)
BUDROS RUHLIN & ROE INC
1801 Watermark Dr Ste 300 (43215-7088)
PHONE....................................614 481-6900
James L Budros, *President*
Daniel Roe, *Principal*
Peggy Ruhlin, *Principal*
John Schuman, *Principal*
Janice Dreher, *Admin Asst*
EMP: 39
SALES: 3.3MM **Privately Held**
WEB: www.b-r-r.com
SIC: **8742** Financial consultant

(G-7095)
BUILDER SERVICES GROUP INC
Also Called: Gale Insulation
2365 Scioto Harper Dr (43204-3495)
PHONE....................................614 263-9378
EMP: 70
SALES (corp-wide): 2.3B **Publicly Held**
WEB: www.galeind.com
SIC: **1742** Insulation, buildings
HQ: Builder Services Group, Inc.
475 N Williamson Blvd
Daytona Beach FL 32114
386 304-2222

(G-7096)
BUILDERS TRASH SERVICE
1575 Harmon Ave (43223-3316)
PHONE....................................614 444-7060
Mike Neri, *Owner*
EMP: 25
SALES (est): 2.5MM **Privately Held**
WEB: www.builderstrash.com
SIC: **4953** Refuse collection & disposal services

(G-7097)
BULKMATIC TRANSPORT COMPANY
2271 Williams Rd (43207-5121)
PHONE....................................614 497-2372
Mickey Hancock, *Branch Mgr*
EMP: 30
SALES (corp-wide): 369.5MM **Privately Held**
SIC: **4213** Contract haulers
PA: Bulkmatic Transport Company Inc
2001 N Cline Ave
Griffith IN 46319
800 535-8505

(G-7098)
BURGESS & NIPLE INC (PA)
5085 Reed Rd (43220-2513)
PHONE....................................502 254-2344
Ronald R Schultz, *CEO*
Kenneth R Davis Jr, *President*
EMP: 275
SQ FT: 60,000
SALES (est): 122.1MM **Privately Held**
WEB: www.burgessniple.com
SIC: **8711** 8712 Consulting engineer; architectural engineering

(G-7099)
BURGESS & NIPLE-HEAPY LLC
5085 Reed Rd (43220-2513)
PHONE....................................614 459-2050
Robert Draper,
Karen Anderson,
EMP: 99
SALES (est): 1.8MM **Privately Held**
SIC: **8711** 8712 7389 Consulting engineer; architectural services;

(G-7100)
BUTLER ANIMAL HEALTH SUP LLC
Also Called: Henry Schein Animal Health
3820 Twin Creeks Dr (43204-5000)
PHONE....................................614 718-2000
Tiffany Swetz, *Sales Staff*
Kevin Eilerman, *Manager*
Mark Axelrod, *Manager*
Joshua Coates, *Manager*
Terri Parker, *Manager*
EMP: 37
SALES (corp-wide): 13.2B **Publicly Held**
SIC: **5122** Biologicals & allied products
HQ: Butler Animal Health Supply Llc
400 Metro Pl N Ste 100
Dublin OH 43017
614 761-9095

(G-7101)
BUTLER CINCIONE AND DICUCCIO
556 E Town St 100 (43215-3337)
PHONE....................................614 221-3151
Gerald N Dicaccio, *Partner*
Alphonse P Cincione, *Partner*
N Gerald Dicuccio, *Partner*
David Barnhardt, *Principal*
Matthew P Cincione, *Associate*
EMP: 30

SQ FT: 10,000
SALES: 2.9MM **Privately Held**
WEB: www.bcdlaws.com
SIC: **8111** General practice attorney, lawyer

(G-7102)
C A E C INC
Also Called: Columbus Car Audio & ACC
2975 Morse Rd Ste A (43231-6051)
PHONE....................................614 337-1091
Todd Hays, *President*
Danielle Hays, *Admin Sec*
EMP: 38
SQ FT: 14,000
SALES (est): 5.4MM **Privately Held**
SIC: **5731** 5065 Sound equipment, automotive; sound equipment, electronic

(G-7103)
C M LIMITED
5255 Sinclair Rd (43229-5042)
PHONE....................................614 888-4567
Max Brown, *President*
Herbert Cook Jr, *Principal*
EMP: 50
SQ FT: 60,000
SALES (est): 1.7MM **Privately Held**
SIC: **6512** Commercial & industrial building operation

(G-7104)
C T CORPORATION SYSTEM
Also Called: C T Columbus
4400 Easton Cmns Ste 300 (43219-6226)
PHONE....................................614 473-9749
Ann Roberson, *Manager*
EMP: 50
SALES (corp-wide): 5.2B **Privately Held**
WEB: www.ctadvantage.com
SIC: **8111** Corporate, partnership & business law
HQ: C T Corporation System
28 Liberty St 26
New York NY 10005
212 894-8940

(G-7105)
C V PERRY & CO (PA)
370 S 5th St (43215-5408)
P.O. Box 20405 (43220-0405)
PHONE....................................614 221-4131
Brian Vain, *President*
EMP: 47
SQ FT: 3,500
SALES (est): 4.2MM **Privately Held**
WEB: www.cvperry.com
SIC: **1521** 6552 6531 New construction, single-family houses; land subdividers & developers, commercial; real estate brokers & agents

(G-7106)
CALFEE HALTER & GRISWOLD LLP
41 S High St Ste 1200 (43215-3465)
PHONE....................................614 621-1500
Karen Scurlock, *Branch Mgr*
EMP: 25
SALES (corp-wide): 49.3MM **Privately Held**
SIC: **8111** General practice attorney, lawyer
PA: Calfee, Halter & Griswold Llp
1405 E 6th St Ste 1
Cleveland OH 44114
216 831-2732

(G-7107)
CALFEE HALGERR GRISWOLD LLC
41 S High St Ste 1200 (43215-3465)
PHONE....................................614 621-7003
Brent Ballard,
EMP: 25 EST: 2010
SALES (est): 772.3K **Privately Held**
SIC: **8111** General practice attorney, lawyer

(G-7108)
CAMERON MITCHELL REST LLC (PA)
Also Called: Ocean Prime
390 W Nationwide Blvd # 300 (43215-2337)
PHONE....................................614 621-3663
David Miller, *President*
Cameron Mitchell,
EMP: 46
SQ FT: 7,800
SALES: 112.7MM **Privately Held**
WEB: www.cameronmitchell.com
SIC: **8741** 5812 Restaurant management; eating places

(G-7109)
CAMP PINECLIFF INC
277 S Cassingham Rd (43209-1804)
PHONE....................................614 236-5698
EMP: 100
SALES (est): 1.6MM **Privately Held**
SIC: **7032** 8661 Sporting And Recreational Camps, Nsk

(G-7110)
CANNELL GRAPHICS LLC
1465 Northwest Blvd (43212-3062)
PHONE....................................614 781-9760
Biz Phil Ferguson, *General Mgr*
Nicole Dobson, *Principal*
Pete Lauer, *Production*
Marcus McElas, *Manager*
EMP: 25
SALES (est): 3.4MM **Privately Held**
WEB: www.cannellgraphics.com
SIC: **7334** 5199 Blueprinting service; art goods

(G-7111)
CANYON MEDICAL CENTER INC
5969 E Broad St Ste 200 (43213-1546)
PHONE....................................614 864-6010
Stephen D Shell MD, *President*
Robert Hershfield MD, *Bd of Directors*
EMP: 40 EST: 1976
SQ FT: 18,000
SALES (est): 5.9MM **Privately Held**
WEB: www.canyonmc.com
SIC: **8011** Internal medicine, physician/surgeon

(G-7112)
CAPITAL FIRE PROTECTION CO (PA)
3360 Valleyview Dr (43204-1296)
PHONE....................................614 279-9448
William P Jolley, *President*
Christian Bradford, *President*
Steve Stump, *Principal*
John C Falk Sr, *Co-President*
Mark E Hunnell, *Vice Pres*
EMP: 42 EST: 1963
SQ FT: 20,000
SALES (est): 9.9MM **Privately Held**
WEB: www.capfire.com
SIC: **1799** Coating, caulking & weather, water & fireproofing

(G-7113)
CAPITAL TRANSPORTATION INC
1170 N Cassady Ave (43219-2232)
PHONE....................................614 258-0400
Richard M Crockett, *President*
David Evans, *Project Mgr*
EMP: 104
SQ FT: 70,000
SALES (est): 4MM **Privately Held**
SIC: **4119** Limousine rental, with driver

(G-7114)
CAPITAL WHOLESALE DRUG COMPANY
Also Called: Capital Drug
873 Williams Ave (43212)
PHONE....................................614 297-8225
George D Richards, *Ch of Bd*
George K Richards, *President*
Daniel G Macleod, *Principal*
Edgar P Stocker, *Principal*
Linda R Franklin, *Corp Secy*
EMP: 55
SQ FT: 45,000

SALES (est): 44.1MM **Privately Held**
SIC: 5122 Pharmaceuticals; druggists' sundries

(G-7115)
CAPITOL CITY CARDIOLOGY INC (PA)
5825 Westbourne Ave (43213-1459)
PHONE..................................614 464-0884
Charles Noble MD, *President*
Raj Patel MD, *Shareholder*
Ruben Sheares MD, *Shareholder*
EMP: 40
SQ FT: 3,000
SALES (est): 5.5MM **Privately Held**
WEB: www.capitolcitycardiology.com
SIC: 8011 Cardiologist & cardio-vascular specialist

(G-7116)
CAPITOL EXPRESS ENTPS INC (PA)
Also Called: Cisco Capitol Express
3815 Twin Creeks Dr (43204-5005)
P.O. Box 462, Hilliard (43026-0462)
PHONE..................................614 279-2819
Kennon Wissinger, *President*
Linda Cose, *Vice Pres*
EMP: 60
SQ FT: 6,000
SALES: 5.5MM **Privately Held**
SIC: 4212 Delivery service, vehicular

(G-7117)
CAPITOL TUNNELING INC
2216 Refugee Rd (43207-2800)
PHONE..................................614 444-0255
Kyle Lucas, *President*
Matt Jutte, *Project Mgr*
Christine Harris, *Accounting Mgr*
EMP: 30
SQ FT: 1,200
SALES (est): 7.4MM **Privately Held**
SIC: 1623 Underground utilities contractor

(G-7118)
CARCORP INC
Also Called: Dennis Mitsubishi
2900 Morse Rd (43231-6036)
P.O. Box 29365 (43229-0365)
PHONE..................................877 857-2801
Keith Dennis, *President*
Aaron Masterson, *Vice Pres*
Aaron Casto, *Director*
Jim Tigyer, *Director*
▼ EMP: 146
SQ FT: 12,000
SALES (est): 68.8MM **Privately Held**
SIC: 5511 5521 7515 5571 Automobiles, new & used; used car dealers; passenger car leasing; motorcycle dealers

(G-7119)
CARDINAL BUILDERS INC
4409 E Main St (43213-3061)
PHONE..................................614 237-1000
Tim Coady, *President*
Tim Kane, *Shareholder*
EMP: 25 EST: 1965
SQ FT: 22,000
SALES: 6.5MM **Privately Held**
WEB: www.cardinalbuilders.com
SIC: 3541 1521 1522 1799 Machine tool replacement & repair parts, metal cutting types; general remodeling, single-family houses; patio & deck construction & repair; hotel/motel & multi-family home renovation & remodeling; kitchen & bathroom remodeling; siding contractor; roofing contractor

(G-7120)
CARDINAL HEALTH INC
2215 Citygate Dr Ste D (43219-3589)
PHONE..................................614 473-0786
EMP: 200
SALES (corp-wide): 129.9B **Publicly Held**
SIC: 8099 Health/Allied Services
PA: Cardinal Health, Inc.
　　7000 Cardinal Pl
　　Dublin OH 43017
　　614 757-5000

(G-7121)
CARDINAL HEALTH INC
2088 West Case Rd Ste 110 (43235-2540)
PHONE..................................614 757-7690
EMP: 74
SALES (corp-wide): 136.8B **Publicly Held**
SIC: 5122 Pharmaceuticals
PA: Cardinal Health, Inc.
　　7000 Cardinal Pl
　　Dublin OH 43017
　　614 757-5000

(G-7122)
CARDINAL HEALTH 200 LLC
1548 Mcgaw Rd (43207)
PHONE..................................614 491-0050
Mario Lombardi, *Manager*
EMP: 150
SQ FT: 18,750
SALES (corp-wide): 136.8B **Publicly Held**
WEB: www.allegiancehealth.com
SIC: 5047 Medical equipment & supplies
HQ: Cardinal Health 200, Llc
　　3651 Birchwood Dr
　　Waukegan IL 60085

(G-7123)
CARDINAL HEALTHCARE
P.O. Box 183005 (43218-3005)
PHONE..................................954 202-1883
EMP: 30
SALES (est): 860K **Privately Held**
SIC: 8099 Health & allied services

(G-7124)
CARDINAL ORTHOPAEDIC GROUP INC
170 Taylor Station Rd (43213-4491)
PHONE..................................614 759-1186
Dale Ingram, *President*
EMP: 33
SQ FT: 16,000
SALES (est): 3.2MM **Privately Held**
SIC: 8011 Physicians' office, including specialists

(G-7125)
CARDIO THORACIC SURGERY
410 W 10th Ave (43210-1240)
PHONE..................................614 293-4509
Benjamin Sun, *Director*
EMP: 40
SALES (est): 1.1MM **Privately Held**
SIC: 8011 Offices & clinics of medical doctors

(G-7126)
CAREER PARTNERS INTL LLC (PA)
20 S 3rd St Ste 210 (43215-4206)
PHONE..................................919 401-4260
Terry Gillis, *Vice Ch Bd*
Doug Matthews, *President*
Karen Romeo, *Senior VP*
Sue Rowley, *Senior VP*
EMP: 1600 EST: 1987
SALES (est): 80.2MM **Privately Held**
WEB: www.cpiworld.com
SIC: 8742 General management consultant

(G-7127)
CARFAGNAS INCORPORATED
Also Called: Carfagna's Cleve Meats
1405 E Dblin Granville Rd (43229-3357)
PHONE..................................614 846-6340
Edward Carfagna, *CEO*
Dino Carfagna, *President*
Cecilia Carfagna, *Vice Pres*
Sam Carfagna, *Treasurer*
Julie Riley, *Financial Exec*
EMP: 50
SQ FT: 9,000
SALES (est): 6.4MM **Privately Held**
WEB: www.carfagnas.com
SIC: 5411 5147 Grocery stores, independent; meats & meat products

(G-7128)
CARLILE PATCHEN & MURPHY LLP (PA)
366 E Broad St (43215-3819)
PHONE..................................614 228-6135

Ricky Hollenbaugh, *Partner*
Michael Igo, *Partner*
James R Moats, *Partner*
Kathy Benjamin, *Counsel*
Bobbie O'Keefe, *Counsel*
EMP: 90
SQ FT: 24,000
SALES (est): 12.7MM **Privately Held**
WEB: www.cpmlaw.com
SIC: 8111 General practice attorney, lawyer

(G-7129)
CARLISLE HOTELS INC
Also Called: Hampton Inn
5625 Trabue Rd (43228-9567)
PHONE..................................614 851-5599
Bikha Patel, *Branch Mgr*
EMP: 47
SALES (corp-wide): 145.5MM **Privately Held**
WEB: www.cheapaccommodation.com
SIC: 7011 Hotels & motels
HQ: Carlisle Hotels, Inc.
　　119 S Main St Ste 800
　　Memphis TN 38103
　　901 526-5000

(G-7130)
CARPENTER LIPPS & LELAND LLP (PA)
280 N High St Ste 1300 (43215-7515)
PHONE..................................614 365-4100
Michael H Carpenter, *Managing Prtnr*
David A Beck, *Counsel*
Jeffrey A Lipps,
Phyllis Sneed, *Legal Staff*
Karla Lebeau, *Assistant*
EMP: 50
SALES (est): 8.3MM **Privately Held**
WEB: www.carpenterlipps.com
SIC: 8111 General practice law office

(G-7131)
CARRIER INDUSTRIES INC
1700 Georgesville Rd (43228-3620)
PHONE..................................614 851-6363
Myron P Shevell, *Branch Mgr*
EMP: 394
SALES (corp-wide): 30.1MM **Privately Held**
SIC: 4213 4212 Trucking Operator-Nonlocal Local Trucking Operator
PA: Carrier Industries, Inc.
　　1-71 North Ave E
　　Elizabeth NJ

(G-7132)
CASKEY CLEANING CO
Also Called: Caskey Cleaners
47 W Gates St (43206-3441)
PHONE..................................614 443-7448
Lloyd Hill, *Principal*
EMP: 67
SQ FT: 50,000
SALES (est): 2.3MM **Privately Held**
SIC: 7216 Cleaning & dyeing, except rugs

(G-7133)
CASLEO CORPORATION
Also Called: Global Meals
2741 E 4th Ave (43219-2824)
PHONE..................................614 252-6508
Nataliya Krylova, *CEO*
Olga Silvnyak, *President*
EMP: 48
SALES: 8.5MM **Privately Held**
SIC: 8322 Meal delivery program

(G-7134)
CASS INFORMATION SYSTEMS INC
2644 Kirkwood Hyw Newark (43218)
PHONE..................................614 839-4503
Kathy Callanan, *Branch Mgr*
EMP: 40
SALES (corp-wide): 152MM **Publicly Held**
SIC: 4813 Telephone communication, except radio
PA: Cass Information Systems, Inc.
　　12444 Powerscort Dr # 550
　　Saint Louis MO 63131
　　314 506-5500

(G-7135)
CASS INFORMATION SYSTEMS INC
Also Called: Cass Logistics
2675 Corporate Exchange (43231-1662)
P.O. Box 182447 (43218-2447)
PHONE..................................614 766-2277
Jeff Nini, *Vice Pres*
Harold Ellis, *Opers Mgr*
Monique Winston, *Human Res Mgr*
Lani Wollam, *Accounts Mgr*
Susan Kimble, *Consultant*
EMP: 131
SALES (corp-wide): 152MM **Publicly Held**
WEB: www.cassinfo.com
SIC: 7389 Personal service agents, brokers & bureaus
PA: Cass Information Systems, Inc.
　　12444 Powerscort Dr # 550
　　Saint Louis MO 63131
　　314 506-5500

(G-7136)
CASSADY VLG APRTMENTS OHIO LLC
3089 Cassady Village Trl (43219-3501)
PHONE..................................216 520-1250
EMP: 99
SALES (est): 789.1K **Privately Held**
SIC: 6513 Apartment building operators

(G-7137)
CASTO COMMUNITIES CNSTR LTD
191 W Nationwide Blvd # 200 (43215-2568)
PHONE..................................614 228-8545
Don M Casto, *Branch Mgr*
EMP: 382
SALES (corp-wide): 21MM **Privately Held**
SIC: 6512 Commercial & industrial building operation
PA: Casto Communities Construction Limited
　　191 W Nationwide Blvd # 200
　　Columbus OH 43215
　　614 228-5331

(G-7138)
CATHOLIC DIOCESE OF COLUMBUS
Also Called: Bishop Ready High School
707 Salisbury Rd (43204-2449)
PHONE..................................614 276-5263
Celene Seamen, *Principal*
Zenia Strickland, *Director*
Jennifer Gramlich, *Admin Sec*
Ben Hilsheimer, *Teacher*
Jeri Rod, *Assistant*
EMP: 55
SALES (corp-wide): 6.3MM **Privately Held**
WEB: www.colscss.org
SIC: 8211 7929 Catholic elementary & secondary schools; entertainers & entertainment groups
PA: Catholic Diocese Of Columbus
　　198 E Broad St
　　Columbus OH 43215
　　614 224-2251

(G-7139)
CATHOLIC DIOCESE OF COLUMBUS
197 E Gay St Ste 1 (43215-3229)
PHONE..................................614 221-5891
Don Wisler, *President*
EMP: 35
SALES (corp-wide): 6.3MM **Privately Held**
WEB: www.colscss.org
SIC: 8322 Social service center
PA: Catholic Diocese Of Columbus
　　198 E Broad St
　　Columbus OH 43215
　　614 224-2251

(G-7140)
CATHOLIC SOCIAL SERVICES INC
197 E Gay St (43215-3229)
PHONE..................................614 221-5891

Rachel Lustig, *President*
Hannah Haines, *Manager*
Barbara McKenzie, *Director*
Ramona Reyes, *Director*
Debbie Hilliard, *Program Dir*
EMP: 85
SALES: 5.6MM **Privately Held**
SIC: 8322 Social service center

(G-7141)
CBC COMPANIES INC
1691 Nw Professional Plz (43220-3866)
PHONE.................................614 222-4343
Robert Cornett, *Engineer*
Mike Frabott, *Manager*
David McMullin, *Technology*
Audrey Clark, *Database Admin*
Bryan Kloss, *Administration*
EMP: 30
SQ FT: 19,560
SALES (corp-wide): 246.2MM **Privately Held**
SIC: 7323 Credit reporting services
PA: Cbc Companies, Inc.
250 E Broad St Fl 21
Columbus OH 43215
614 222-4343

(G-7142)
CBC COMPANIES INC
1651 Nw Professional Plz (43220-3866)
PHONE.................................614 538-6100
Jonathon Price, *Vice Pres*
Jonathan Price, *Manager*
Houangvilay Chinda, *Director*
Roger Sponseller, *Director*
EMP: 80
SALES (corp-wide): 246.2MM **Privately Held**
SIC: 7323 7374 Credit bureau & agency; data processing & preparation
PA: Cbc Companies, Inc.
250 E Broad St Fl 21
Columbus OH 43215
614 222-4343

(G-7143)
CBCINNOVIS INTERNATIONAL INC (HQ)
250 E Broad St Fl 21 (43215-3770)
PHONE.................................614 222-4343
Jonathan Price, *President*
Keith Kotowicz, *Vice Pres*
Dirk Cantrell, *Treasurer*
Christopher Richard, *Human Res Mgr*
Glenn Fitzgerald, *Sales Mgr*
EMP: 37
SALES (est): 9.6MM
SALES (corp-wide): 246.2MM **Privately Held**
SIC: 7323 Credit bureau & agency
PA: Cbc Companies, Inc.
250 E Broad St Fl 21
Columbus OH 43215
614 222-4343

(G-7144)
CBRE INC
200 Civic Center Dr Fl 14 (43215-4177)
PHONE.................................614 438-5488
Barbara Frost, *Architect*
Rob Click, *Manager*
EMP: 80
SALES (corp-wide): 21.3B **Publicly Held**
SIC: 6531 Real estate agent, commercial
HQ: Cbre, Inc.
400 S Hope St Ste 25
Los Angeles CA 90071
213 613-3333

(G-7145)
CD1025
Also Called: Wwcd
1036 S Front St (43206-3402)
PHONE.................................614 221-9923
Randy Malloy, *President*
Leslie Edwards, *Sales Staff*
Andrea Marcus, *Marketing Staff*
Tina Coleman, *Manager*
Mark Jaworski, *Manager*
EMP: 25
SALES: 106.5K **Privately Held**
SIC: 4832 Radio broadcasting stations

(G-7146)
CDC MANAGEMENT CO
4949 Freeway Dr E (43229-5401)
PHONE.................................614 781-0216
Paul Jenkins Jr, *President*
Cindy Axthelm, *VP Opers*
Jim Stahl, *Finance Mgr*
EMP: 250
SQ FT: 24,019
SALES (est): 12MM **Privately Held**
SIC: 8741 5181 Management services; beer & ale

(G-7147)
CDM SMITH INC
445 Hutchinson Ave # 820 (43235-8633)
PHONE.................................614 847-8340
Rusty Neff, *Vice Pres*
Trent Branson, *Project Mgr*
Lynne Hughes, *Admin Asst*
EMP: 33
SALES (corp-wide): 1.1B **Privately Held**
WEB: www.cdm.com
SIC: 8748 Environmental consultant
PA: Cdm Smith Inc
75 State St Ste 701
Boston MA 02109
617 452-6000

(G-7148)
CELLCO PARTNERSHIP
Also Called: Verizon
2180 Henderson Rd (43220-2320)
PHONE.................................614 459-7200
Mike Demko, *Branch Mgr*
EMP: 25
SALES (corp-wide): 130.8B **Publicly Held**
SIC: 4812 5999 Cellular telephone services; mobile telephones & equipment
HQ: Cellco Partnership
1 Verizon Way
Basking Ridge NJ 07920

(G-7149)
CELLULAR SALES KNOXVILLE INC
Also Called: Verizon Wreless Authorized Ret
5976 E Main St (43213-3378)
PHONE.................................614 322-9975
EMP: 44 **Privately Held**
SIC: 4812 Cellular telephone services
PA: Cellular Sales Of Knoxville, Inc.
9040 Executive Park Dr
Knoxville TN 37923

(G-7150)
CENTENNIAL PRSRVTION GROUP LLC
600 N Cassady Ave Ste D (43219-2789)
PHONE.................................614 238-0730
Matt Wolf, *CEO*
Susan Martinez, *Administration*
EMP: 38
SALES: 4MM **Privately Held**
SIC: 1741 Masonry & other stonework

(G-7151)
CENTER FOR COGNITIVE AND BEH (PA)
Also Called: Kevin D Arnold
4624 Sawmill Rd (43220-2247)
PHONE.................................614 459-4490
Kevin D Arnold, *President*
Kevin Arnold, *Director*
EMP: 30
SALES (est): 2.1MM **Privately Held**
WEB: www.ccbtcolumbus.com
SIC: 8049 Clinical psychologist

(G-7152)
CENTER FOR COGNITV BEHAV PSYCH
4624 Sawmill Rd (43220-2247)
PHONE.................................614 459-4490
Sarah Shearer, *Council Mbr*
EMP: 30 EST: 2015
SALES (est): 52K **Privately Held**
SIC: 8322 Individual & family services

(G-7153)
CENTER FOR EATING DISORDERS
Also Called: CENTER FOR BALANCED LIVING, TH
8001 Ravines Edge Ct # 201 (43235-5423)
PHONE.................................614 896-8222
Kelly Trautner, *President*
Cheryl Ryland, *CFO*
Lori Johnson, *Executive*
EMP: 42
SALES: 2.9MM **Privately Held**
SIC: 8052 8731 Home for the mentally retarded; with health care; medical research, commercial

(G-7154)
CENTER OF VOCTNL ALTRNTVS MNTL (PA)
Also Called: Cova
3770 N High St (43214-3525)
PHONE.................................614 294-7117
Judy Braun, *President*
EMP: 63
SQ FT: 3,500
SALES: 3MM **Privately Held**
SIC: 8331 Vocational rehabilitation agency

(G-7155)
CENTRAL CMNTY HSE OF COLUMBUS (PA)
1150 E Main St (43205-1902)
P.O. Box 7047 (43205-0047)
PHONE.................................614 253-7267
Tammy Hall, *Finance Dir*
Pamela McCarthy, *Director*
Lix Hughes-Weaver, *Director*
EMP: 40
SQ FT: 1,500
SALES: 1.1MM **Privately Held**
SIC: 8322 Social service center

(G-7156)
CENTRAL OH AREA AGENCY ON AGNG
Also Called: Passport
3776 S High St (43207-4012)
PHONE.................................614 645-7250
Amy Slocum, *Manager*
Cindy Farson, *Director*
EMP: 150
SALES (est): 7.4MM **Privately Held**
WEB: www.coaaa.org
SIC: 8322 Senior citizens' center or association

(G-7157)
CENTRAL OHIO BUILDING CO INC
Also Called: Thor Construction
3756 Agler Rd (43219-3699)
PHONE.................................614 475-6392
Otis Wilbur Ronk, *President*
Jay Watkins, *President*
Sol Morton Isaac, *Principal*
C F O'Brien, *Principal*
William N Postlewaite, *Principal*
EMP: 35
SQ FT: 2,000
SALES (est): 11.1MM **Privately Held**
SIC: 1542 1541 Institutional building construction; industrial buildings, new construction

(G-7158)
CENTRAL OHIO HOSPITALISTS
3525 Olentangy River Rd # 4330 (43214-3937)
PHONE.................................614 255-6900
Joseph A Mack, *President*
Nicholas Nelson, *Treasurer*
EMP: 39 EST: 2000
SALES (est): 2.2MM **Privately Held**
SIC: 7363 Medical help service

(G-7159)
CENTRAL OHIO MEDICAL TEXTILES
Also Called: COMTEX
575 Harmon Ave (43223-2449)
PHONE.................................614 453-9274
Ken Boock, *Chairman*
Myles Noel, *COO*
Becky Davis, *CFO*

Theresa Jones, *Assistant*
EMP: 150
SQ FT: 100,000
SALES: 23.4MM **Privately Held**
WEB: www.comtex.com
SIC: 7219 Laundry, except power & coin-operated

(G-7160)
CENTRAL OHIO NUTRITION CENTER (PA)
Also Called: Conci
648 Taylor Rd (43230-3202)
PHONE.................................614 864-7225
Edward Baltes, *Principal*
Judy Loper MD, *Principal*
J T Broyles MD, *Vice Pres*
Richard A Lutes MD, *Vice Pres*
Robert K May MD, *Vice Pres*
EMP: 35
SQ FT: 2,500
SALES (est): 3MM **Privately Held**
WEB: www.buddywhite.com
SIC: 8049 Nutritionist

(G-7161)
CENTRAL OHIO POISON CENTER
Also Called: Childrens Hospital
700 Childrens Dr (43205-2664)
PHONE.................................800 222-1222
Fax: 614 221-2672
EMP: 30 EST: 1958
SQ FT: 19,950
SALES (est): 1.6MM **Privately Held**
WEB: www.copeds.org
SIC: 8099 Health/Allied Services

(G-7162)
CENTRAL OHIO PRIMARY CARE
770 Jasonway Ave Ste G2 (43214-4333)
PHONE.................................614 459-3687
Drexdal Pratt, *Branch Mgr*
David Neiger, *Med Doctor*
EMP: 37 **Privately Held**
SIC: 8011 General & family practice, physician/surgeon
PA: Central Ohio Primary Care Physicians, Inc.
570 Polaris Pkwy Ste 250
Westerville OH 43082

(G-7163)
CENTRAL OHIO PRIMARY CARE
4885 Olentangy River Rd # 2 (43214-1952)
PHONE.................................614 451-1551
EMP: 48 **Privately Held**
SIC: 8011 General & family practice, physician/surgeon
PA: Central Ohio Primary Care Physicians, Inc.
570 Polaris Pkwy Ste 250
Westerville OH 43082

(G-7164)
CENTRAL OHIO PRIMARY CARE
4885 Olentangy River Rd (43214-1952)
PHONE.................................614 268-6555
John W Wulf MD, *CEO*
Pallavi Mandiga, *Family Practiti*
EMP: 48 **Privately Held**
SIC: 8049 Acupuncturist
PA: Central Ohio Primary Care Physicians, Inc.
570 Polaris Pkwy Ste 250
Westerville OH 43082

(G-7165)
CENTRAL OHIO PRIMARY CARE
Also Called: Capital City Medical Assoc
2489 Stelzer Rd 101 (43219-4007)
PHONE.................................614 473-1300
Sheryl Moyer, *Manager*
EMP: 30 **Privately Held**
WEB: www.copcp.com
SIC: 8011 General & family practice, physician/surgeon
PA: Central Ohio Primary Care Physicians, Inc.
570 Polaris Pkwy Ste 250
Westerville OH 43082

(G-7166)
CENTRAL OHIO PRIMARY CARE
3535 Olentangy River Rd (43214-3908)
PHONE.................................614 268-8164

Jonathan Matthew Enlow, *Principal*
Dave Condon, *Med Doctor*
Donald Deep, *Med Doctor*
Eric Hard, *Internal Med*
Svetlana Novak, *Internal Med*
EMP: 90 **Privately Held**
SIC: 8011 General & family practice, physician/surgeon
PA: Central Ohio Primary Care Physicians, Inc.
570 Polaris Pkwy Ste 250
Westerville OH 43082

(G-7167)
CENTRAL OHIO PRIMARY CARE
4030 Henderson Rd (43220-2287)
PHONE.................................614 442-7550
John Leff, *Med Doctor*
Alan Steginsky, *Med Doctor*
Lisa Mewhort, *Internal Med*
EMP: 35 **Privately Held**
SIC: 8049 8011 Acupuncturist; offices & clinics of medical doctors
PA: Central Ohio Primary Care Physicians, Inc.
570 Polaris Pkwy Ste 250
Westerville OH 43082

(G-7168)
CENTRAL OHIO SURGICAL ASSOC (PA)
750 Mount Carmel Mall # 380
(43222-1589)
PHONE.................................614 222-8000
Jeff Turner, *President*
Pam Abraham, *Office Mgr*
Dr Ghalib A Hannun, *Med Doctor*
EMP: 31
SQ FT: 4,000
SALES (est): 4.6MM **Privately Held**
WEB: www.midohiosurgical.com
SIC: 8011 Cardiologist & cardio-vascular specialist; surgeon

(G-7169)
CENTRAL OHIO TRANSIT AUTHORITY
1333 Fields Ave (43201-2908)
PHONE.................................614 275-5800
Doug Moore, *Branch Mgr*
EMP: 133
SALES (corp-wide): 84.8MM **Privately Held**
SIC: 4111 Bus line operations
PA: Central Ohio Transit Authority
33 N High St
Columbus OH 43215
614 275-5800

(G-7170)
CENTRAL OHIO TRANSIT AUTHORITY (PA)
Also Called: Cota
33 N High St (43215-3076)
PHONE.................................614 275-5800
W Curtis Stitt, *President*
Melissa Segreti, *General Mgr*
Doug Moore, *Vice Pres*
Timothy Smith, *Facilities Dir*
Jon Hancock, *Facilities Mgr*
EMP: 600
SQ FT: 390,000
SALES (est): 84.8MM **Privately Held**
WEB: www.cota.com
SIC: 4111 Bus line operations

(G-7171)
CERTIFIED OIL INC
949 King Ave (43212-2662)
P.O. Box 182439 (43218-2439)
PHONE.................................614 421-7500
Peter Lacaillade, *President*
Carol Dillard, *Shareholder*
EMP: 100
SQ FT: 24,500
SALES (est): 5.6MM
SALES (corp-wide): 51.5MM **Privately Held**
SIC: 4212 Petroleum haulage, local
PA: Certified Oil Corporation
949 King Ave
Columbus OH 43212
614 421-7500

(G-7172)
CEVA LOGISTICS US INC
Also Called: Eagle USA Airfreight
2727 London Groveport Rd (43207)
PHONE.................................614 482-5107
Larry Savage, *Manager*
EMP: 50
SALES (corp-wide): 20.8MM **Privately Held**
WEB: www.tntlogistics.com
SIC: 4731 Freight forwarding
HQ: Ceva Logistics U.S., Inc.
15350 Vickery Dr
Houston TX 77032
281 618-3100

(G-7173)
CGI TECHNOLOGIES SOLUTIONS INC
88 E Broad St Ste 1425 (43215-3506)
PHONE.................................614 228-2245
Nola Haug, *Manager*
Galen Bock, *Technical Staff*
EMP: 56
SALES (corp-wide): 8.6B **Privately Held**
SIC: 7379 Computer related consulting services
HQ: Cgi Technologies And Solutions Inc.
11325 Random Hills Rd
Fairfax VA 22030
703 267-8000

(G-7174)
CH RELTY IV/CLMBUS PARTNERS LP
Also Called: Doubletree Columbus Hotel
175 Hutchinson Ave (43235-1413)
PHONE.................................614 885-3334
Dan Ouellette, *Manager*
EMP: 100
SQ FT: 44,962 **Privately Held**
SIC: 7011 6512 5813 5812 Hotels; nonresidential building operators; drinking places; eating places
PA: Ch Realty Iv/Columbus Partners, L.P.
3819 Maple Ave
Dallas TX 75219

(G-7175)
CH ROBINSON COMPANY INC
Also Called: C.H. Robinson 123
800 Yard St Ste 200 (43212-3882)
PHONE.................................614 933-5100
Scott Norris, *General Mgr*
EMP: 35
SALES (corp-wide): 16.6B **Publicly Held**
SIC: 4731 Freight transportation arrangement
HQ: C.H. Robinson Company Inc.
14701 Charlson Rd Ste 900
Eden Prairie MN 55347

(G-7176)
CH2M HILL INC
2 Easton Oval Ste 125 (43219-6042)
PHONE.................................614 888-3100
Tim Coleman, *General Mgr*
Gary Long, *Project Mgr*
Nicole McQueary, *Safety Mgr*
B Casey, *Branch Mgr*
Don Fisher, *Info Tech Mgr*
EMP: 41
SALES (corp-wide): 14.9B **Publicly Held**
SIC: 8711 Consulting engineer
HQ: Ch2m Hill, Inc.
9191 S Jamaica St
Englewood CO 80112
303 771-0900

(G-7177)
CHAD DOWNING
Also Called: Point Plus Personnel
679 Rose Way (43230-5806)
PHONE.................................614 532-5127
Chad Downing, *Owner*
EMP: 25
SALES (est): 1MM **Privately Held**
SIC: 7361 Executive placement

(G-7178)
CHAMPAIGN RESIDENTIAL SERVICES
1350 W 5th Ave Ste 230 (43212-2907)
PHONE.................................614 481-5550
Dan Johnson, *Exec Dir*

EMP: 35 **EST:** 1976
SALES (est): 840.1K **Privately Held**
SIC: 8322 Social services for the handicapped

(G-7179)
CHANGE HEALTHCARE TECH ENABLED
Also Called: Midwest Physicians
3535 Olentangy River Rd (43214-3908)
PHONE.................................614 566-5861
Nancy Buel, *Director*
John Burnett,
EMP: 64
SALES (corp-wide): 208.3B **Publicly Held**
SIC: 8641 8062 Civic social & fraternal associations; general medical & surgical hospitals
HQ: Change Healthcare Technology Enabled Services, Llc
5995 Windward Pkwy
Alpharetta GA 30005
770 237-4300

(G-7180)
CHASE MANHATTAN MORTGAGE CORP
200 E Campus View Blvd # 3 (43235-4678)
PHONE.................................614 422-7982
Caidy Patricia, *Branch Mgr*
EMP: 108
SALES (corp-wide): 131.4B **Publicly Held**
SIC: 6162 Mortgage bankers
HQ: Chase Manhattan Mortgage Corp
343 Thornall St Ste 7
Edison NJ 08837
732 205-0600

(G-7181)
CHASE MANHATTAN MORTGAGE CORP
3415 Vision Dr (43219-6009)
PHONE.................................614 422-6900
Beverly Berry, *Branch Mgr*
EMP: 3000
SALES (corp-wide): 131.4B **Publicly Held**
SIC: 6162 Mortgage bankers & correspondents
HQ: Chase Manhattan Mortgage Corp
343 Thornall St Ste 7
Edison NJ 08837
732 205-0600

(G-7182)
CHESROWN OLDSMOBILE GMC INC
Also Called: Chessrown Kia Town
4675 Karl Rd (43229-6456)
P.O. Box 160, Delaware (43015-0160)
PHONE.................................614 846-3040
Jim Gill, *President*
Ryan Meeks, *Finance Mgr*
Cindy Whitaker, *Cust Mgr*
Robert Adkins, *Sales Staff*
Virgil Schnell, *Consultant*
EMP: 45
SQ FT: 55,000
SALES (est): 10.3MM **Privately Held**
WEB: www.chesrown.com
SIC: 5511 7532 7515 5531 Automobiles, new & used; pickups, new & used; top & body repair & paint shops; passenger car leasing; automotive & home supply stores; used car dealers

(G-7183)
CHESTNUT HILL MANAGEMENT CO
Also Called: Inn At Chestnut Hill, The
5055 Thompson Rd (43230-6336)
PHONE.................................614 855-3700
Don Alspach, *President*
David Alspach, *Vice Pres*
Kim Waits, *Exec Dir*
EMP: 90
SALES (est): 2.6MM **Privately Held**
SIC: 8082 Home health care services

(G-7184)
CHICN FIXINS INC
2041 Pine Needle Ct (43232-2664)
PHONE.................................614 929-8431

Deric Butler, *CEO*
EMP: 35
SQ FT: 1,500
SALES (est): 547.3K **Privately Held**
SIC: 0251 Broiler, fryer & roaster chickens

(G-7185)
CHILD DVLPMNT CNCL OF FRNKLN (PA)
1077 Lexington Ave (43201-2936)
PHONE.................................614 221-1709
Mattie James, *President*
Debbie Eiland, *Area Mgr*
Dave Proctor, *Area Mgr*
Brenda Rivers, *Senior VP*
Marlita Bartlett, *Vice Pres*
EMP: 60
SALES: 27MM **Privately Held**
SIC: 8351 Head start center, except in conjunction with school

(G-7186)
CHILD DVLPMNT CNCL OF FRNKLN
Also Called: Cdc Capital Park Head St Ctr
2150 Agler Rd (43224-4523)
PHONE.................................614 416-5178
Carlene Ibenegbu, *Branch Mgr*
EMP: 30
SALES (corp-wide): 27MM **Privately Held**
SIC: 8351 Head start center, except in conjunction with school
PA: The Child Development Council Of Franklin County
1077 Lexington Ave
Columbus OH 43201
614 221-1709

(G-7187)
CHILDREN FIRST INC
Also Called: Children First Day Care
77 S High St Fl 7 (43215-6108)
PHONE.................................614 466-0945
Deanna Kropf, *Director*
EMP: 30
SQ FT: 9,000
SALES: 1MM **Privately Held**
SIC: 8351 Group day care center

(G-7188)
CHILDRENS HOMECARE SERVICES
455 E Mound St (43215-5595)
PHONE.................................614 355-1100
Terry Laurila, *Manager*
Heidi Drake, *Director*
EMP: 150
SQ FT: 7,000
SALES (est): 2.5MM
SALES (corp-wide): 2.3B **Privately Held**
SIC: 8082 8322 Home health care services; individual & family services
PA: Nationwide Children's Hospital
700 Childrens Dr
Columbus OH 43205
614 722-2000

(G-7189)
CHILDRENS HOSPITAL FOUNDATION
700 Childrens Dr (43205-2664)
P.O. Box 16810 (43216-6810)
PHONE.................................614 355-0888
James Digan, *President*
Timothy Robinson, *Vice Pres*
Kevin Welch, *Vice Pres*
Denise Zabawski, *Vice Pres*
Sheri Sanford, *Purchasing*
EMP: 31
SALES (est): 3.8MM **Privately Held**
SIC: 8399 Fund raising organization, nonfee basis

(G-7190)
CHILDRENS HUNGER ALLIANCE (PA)
1105 Schrock Rd Ste 505 (43229-1181)
PHONE.................................614 341-7700
Judy Mobley, *President*
Stella Marshall, *Regional Mgr*
Erin Flynn, *Senior VP*
Charlie Kozlesky, *Senior VP*
John Kimmel, *Vice Pres*
EMP: 40

SQ FT: 5,900
SALES: 11.6MM **Privately Held**
SIC: 8322 8399 Social service center; advocacy group

(G-7191)
CHILDRENS SURGERY CENTER INC
700 Childrens Dr (43205-2666)
PHONE..................................614 722-2920
D Alan Tingley, *Administration*
EMP: 60
SQ FT: 25,000
SALES (est): 3.2MM **Privately Held**
SIC: 8011 Ambulatory surgical center

(G-7192)
CHILLER LLC
3600 Chiller Ln (43219-6026)
PHONE..................................614 475-7575
Andy Deyo, *President*
Pam Morlan, *Executive*
EMP: 50
SALES (corp-wide): 12.8MM **Privately Held**
WEB: www.chiller.com
SIC: 7999 Ice skating rink operation
PA: Chiller Llc
7001 Dublin Park Dr
Dublin OH 43016
614 764-1000

(G-7193)
CHOICE RECOVERY INC
1550 Old Henderson Rd S100 (43220-3662)
PHONE..................................614 358-9900
Chad Silverstein, *President*
Steve Reiss, *Vice Pres*
Allison Avner, *VP Sales*
Erin Sullivan, *Consultant*
EMP: 65
SALES: 15MM **Privately Held**
SIC: 7322 Collection agency, except real estate

(G-7194)
CHOICES FOR VCTIMS DOM VOLENCE
770 E Main St (43205-1715)
PHONE..................................614 258-6080
EMP: 60
SQ FT: 2,200
SALES: 1.1MM **Privately Held**
SIC: 8361 8322 Residential Care Services Individual/Family Services

(G-7195)
CHRISTIAN MISSIONARY ALLIANCE
Also Called: Sunshine Nursery School
3750 Henderson Rd (43220-2236)
PHONE..................................614 457-4085
Jennifer Rupert, *Director*
EMP: 27
SALES (corp-wide): 51.9MM **Privately Held**
WEB: www.fac-columbus.org
SIC: 8351 Child day care services
PA: The Christian Missionary Alliance
8595 Explorer Dr
Colorado Springs CO 80920
719 599-5999

(G-7196)
CHRISTIAN WORTHINGTON VLG INC
165 Highbluffs Blvd (43235-1484)
PHONE..................................614 846-6076
Richardson Randy, *Director*
EMP: 31
SALES: 4MM **Privately Held**
SIC: 8051 Skilled nursing care facilities

(G-7197)
CHRISTOPHER C KAEDING
2050 Kenny Rd Ste 3100 (43221-3502)
PHONE..................................614 293-3600
Christopher Kaeding, *Partner*
Dr Grant Jones, *Partner*
EMP: 50
SALES (est): 1.2MM **Privately Held**
SIC: 8011 Physicians' office, including specialists

(G-7198)
CHUTE GERDEMAN INC
455 S Ludlow St (43215-5647)
PHONE..................................614 469-1001
Brian Shafley, *CEO*
Jay Highland, *COO*
Wendy Johnson, *COO*
George Nauman, *Exec VP*
Elle C Gerdeman, *Vice Pres*
EMP: 64
SQ FT: 19,000
SALES (est): 9.1MM
SALES (corp-wide): 9.5MM **Privately Held**
WEB: www.chutegerdeman.com
SIC: 7389 8712 Interior designer; architectural services
PA: Foote, Cone & Belding, Inc.
875 N Michigan Ave # 1850
Chicago IL 60611
312 425-5626

(G-7199)
CINEMARK USA INC
Also Called: Cinemark Carriage Pl Movies 12
2570 Bethel Rd (43220-2225)
PHONE..................................614 538-0403
Christa Sexton, *Manager*
EMP: 30 **Publicly Held**
SIC: 7832 Motion picture theaters, except drive-in
HQ: Cinemark Usa, Inc.
3900 Dallas Pkwy Ste 500
Plano TX 75093
972 665-1000

(G-7200)
CINEMARK USA INC
Also Called: Cinemark Movies 10
5275 Westpointe Plaza Dr (43228-9131)
PHONE..................................614 529-8547
Kevin Smith, *Manager*
EMP: 25 **Publicly Held**
SIC: 7832 Motion picture theaters, except drive-in
HQ: Cinemark Usa, Inc.
3900 Dallas Pkwy Ste 500
Plano TX 75093
972 665-1000

(G-7201)
CINTAS CORPORATION NO 2
1300 Boltonfield St (43228-3696)
P.O. Box 28246 (43228-0246)
PHONE..................................614 878-7313
John Borak, *Branch Mgr*
EMP: 98
SALES (corp-wide): 6.4B **Publicly Held**
WEB: www.cintas-corp.com
SIC: 7213 7218 Uniform supply; industrial launderers
HQ: Cintas Corporation No. 2
6800 Cintas Blvd
Mason OH 45040

(G-7202)
CIRCLE BUILDING SERVICES INC
742 Harmon Ave (43223-2450)
P.O. Box 1473 (43216-1473)
PHONE..................................614 228-6090
Daniel M Litzinger, *President*
Jos Stein, *Accounts Mgr*
EMP: 90
SALES (est): 2.8MM **Privately Held**
WEB: www.circlebuildingservices.com
SIC: 7349 Building cleaning service; janitorial service, contract basis

(G-7203)
CIRCLE S TRANSPORT INC
1008 Arcaro Dr (43230-3855)
PHONE..................................614 207-2184
Edward Saraniero, *President*
Lorna Basham, *Admin Asst*
EMP: 45
SALES (est): 5.7MM **Privately Held**
SIC: 4213 4212 Trucking, except local; local trucking, without storage

(G-7204)
CITICORP CREDIT SERVICES INC
1500 Boltonfield St (43228-3669)
PHONE..................................212 559-1000

Ken Vanderoef, *Manager*
EMP: 303
SALES (corp-wide): 72.8B **Publicly Held**
SIC: 7389 Credit card service
HQ: Citicorp Credit Services, Inc.
One Court Square 25th Flr
Long Island City NY 11120
718 248-3192

(G-7205)
CITY OF COLUMBUS
Also Called: Public Utlties-Electricity Div
3500 Indianola Ave (43214-3702)
PHONE..................................614 645-7627
Ray Lorello, *Engineer*
Jeffery Hubbard, *Administration*
EMP: 120
SQ FT: 6,176 **Privately Held**
WEB: www.cityofcolumbus.org
SIC: 4931 9631 Electric & other services combined;
PA: City Of Columbus
90 W Broad St Rm B33
Columbus OH 43215
614 645-7671

(G-7206)
CITY OF COLUMBUS
Also Called: Dept of Public Utilities
910 Dublin Rd Ste 4050 (43215-1169)
PHONE..................................614 645-7490
Pamela Davis, *Purchasing*
Danella Pettenski, *Branch Mgr*
Thomas Finnegan, *Manager*
Heather Truesdell, *Supervisor*
Greg Davis, *Officer*
EMP: 35 **Privately Held**
SIC: 4941 Water supply
PA: City Of Columbus
90 W Broad St Rm B33
Columbus OH 43215
614 645-7671

(G-7207)
CITY OF COLUMBUS
Also Called: Health Dept
3433 Agler Rd Ste 2800 (43219-3389)
PHONE..................................614 645-1600
Kate Ondra, *Administration*
EMP: 25 **Privately Held**
WEB: www.cityofcolumbus.org
SIC: 8011 9431 General & family practice, physician/surgeon; administration of public health programs;
PA: City Of Columbus
90 W Broad St Rm B33
Columbus OH 43215
614 645-7671

(G-7208)
CITY OF COLUMBUS
Also Called: Health Dept
1875 Morse Rd 235 (43229-6603)
PHONE..................................614 645-3072
EMP: 55 **Privately Held**
WEB: www.cityofcolumbus.org
SIC: 8399 9431 Fund raising organization, non-fee basis; administration of public health programs;
PA: City Of Columbus
90 W Broad St Rm B33
Columbus OH 43215
614 645-7671

(G-7209)
CITY OF COLUMBUS
Also Called: Health, Dept Of- Admin
240 Parsons Ave (43215-5331)
PHONE..................................614 645-7417
Alyssa Dorsey, *Manager*
Joseph Duffy, *Manager*
Teresa Long, *Director*
Christopher Long, *Officer*
Mysheika W Roberts, *Internal Med*
EMP: 100 **Privately Held**
WEB: www.cityofcolumbus.org
SIC: 8399 9431 Health & welfare council;
PA: City Of Columbus
90 W Broad St Rm B33
Columbus OH 43215
614 645-7671

(G-7210)
CITY OF COLUMBUS
910 Dublin Rd (43215-1169)
PHONE..................................614 645-8270

Chuck Turner, *Manager*
EMP: 69 **Privately Held**
WEB: www.cityofcolumbus.org
SIC: 9532 4941 ; water supply
PA: City Of Columbus
90 W Broad St Rm B33
Columbus OH 43215
614 645-7671

(G-7211)
CITY OF COLUMBUS
Also Called: City Attorney
375 S High St Fl 7 (43215-4520)
PHONE..................................614 645-6624
Lara Baker, *Branch Mgr*
EMP: 40 **Privately Held**
WEB: www.cityofcolumbus.org
SIC: 8111 9222 Legal services;
PA: City Of Columbus
90 W Broad St Rm B33
Columbus OH 43215
614 645-7671

(G-7212)
CITY OF COLUMBUS
Also Called: Public Utilities- Water Div
940 Dublin Rd (43215-1169)
PHONE..................................614 645-8297
Scott Lockhart, *Opers Mgr*
Tom Camden, *Branch Mgr*
EMP: 35 **Privately Held**
WEB: www.cityofcolumbus.org
SIC: 4941 9511 Water supply; air, water & solid waste management;
PA: City Of Columbus
90 W Broad St Rm B33
Columbus OH 43215
614 645-7671

(G-7213)
CITY OF WHITEHALL
Also Called: Whitehall Division of Fire
390 S Yearling Rd (43213-1876)
PHONE..................................614 237-5478
Tim Tilton, *Chief*
EMP: 44 **Privately Held**
WEB: www.cityofwhitehall.com
SIC: 9224 8011 ; offices & clinics of medical doctors
PA: City Of Whitehall
360 S Yearling Rd
Columbus OH 43213
614 237-8613

(G-7214)
CITYNET OHIO LLC
343 N Front St Ste 400 (43215-2266)
PHONE..................................614 364-7881
James Martin, *Mng Member*
EMP: 30
SALES (est): 1.4MM **Privately Held**
SIC: 7372 Prepackaged software

(G-7215)
CJ MAHAN CONSTRUCTION CO LLC (PA)
250 N Hartford Ave (43222-1100)
PHONE..................................614 277-4545
Gary Yancer, *Project Mgr*
Douglas R McCrea, *Mng Member*
C Jeffrey Mahan, *Mng Member*
EMP: 99
SALES (est): 53.3MM **Privately Held**
SIC: 1622 Bridge, tunnel & elevated highway

(G-7216)
CLAIRE DE LEIGH CORP
Also Called: Figlio Wood Fired Pizza
3712 Riverside Dr (43221-1134)
PHONE..................................614 459-6575
Peter Ganis, *President*
EMP: 50
SALES (est): 1.4MM **Privately Held**
SIC: 5812 5813 7011 Pizza restaurants; drinking places; hotels & motels

(G-7217)
CLAPROOD ROMAN J CO
242 N Grant Ave (43215-2642)
PHONE..................................614 221-5515
Floyd R Claprood Sr, *President*
F Raymond Claprood Jr, *Treasurer*
EMP: 30 EST: 1939
SQ FT: 25,000

SALES (est): 3.8MM **Privately Held**
SIC: 5193 Flowers, fresh; florists' supplies

(G-7218)
CLAREMONT RETIREMENT VILLAGE
7041 Bent Tree Blvd (43235-3916)
PHONE..................................614 761-2011
Clare Kilar, *Partner*
EMP: 70
SALES (est): 4.4MM **Privately Held**
SIC: 6513 Retirement hotel operation

(G-7219)
CLARK SCHAEFER HACKETT & CO
4449 Easton Way Ste 400 (43219-7002)
PHONE..................................614 885-2208
Edward Walsh, *Managing Prtnr*
Edwad V Walsh, *Partner*
Herb Lemaster, *Exec VP*
Michelle Argueta, *Manager*
Paula Bedford, *Manager*
EMP: 87
SALES (corp-wide): 37.2MM **Privately Held**
WEB: www.cshco.com
SIC: 8721 Certified public accountant
PA: Clark, Schaefer, Hackett & Co.
1 E 4th St Ste 1200
Cincinnati OH 45202
513 241-3111

(G-7220)
CLASSIC DENTAL LABS INC
1252 S High St (43206-3446)
P.O. Box 6276 (43206-0276)
PHONE..................................614 443-0328
Fax: 614 443-7311
EMP: 34 EST: 1980
SALES (est): 2.2MM **Privately Held**
SIC: 8072 Dental Laboratory

(G-7221)
CLASSIC PAPERING & PAINTING
1061 Goodale Blvd (43212-3830)
PHONE..................................614 221-0505
Jeff Clifton, *President*
Stacia Clifton, *Human Resources*
EMP: 28
SALES (est): 1.9MM **Privately Held**
WEB:
www.classicpaperingandpainting.com
SIC: 1721 Residential painting

(G-7222)
CLEAN INNOVATIONS (PA)
Also Called: Columbus Jan Healthnet Svcs
575 E 11th Ave (43211-2605)
P.O. Box 11399 (43211-0399)
PHONE..................................614 299-1187
Howard Cohen, *President*
Annette Cohen, *Corp Secy*
Susan Cohen Ungar, *Vice Pres*
Bill Daniels, *Accounts Exec*
Bruce Lange, *Sales Staff*
EMP: 27
SQ FT: 26,000
SALES (est): 10.1MM **Privately Held**
WEB: www.cjs.net
SIC: 5087 Janitors' supplies; cleaning & maintenance equipment & supplies

(G-7223)
CLEVELAND CLINIC FOUNDATION
Also Called: Cleveland Clinic Star Imaging
921 Jasonway Ave (43214-2352)
PHONE..................................614 451-0489
Kristen Gilmore, *Manager*
EMP: 85
SALES (corp-wide): 8.9B **Privately Held**
SIC: 6733 Trusts
PA: The Cleveland Clinic Foundation
9500 Euclid Ave
Cleveland OH 44195
216 636-8335

(G-7224)
CLEVELAND CONSTRUCTION COMMUNI INC
6399 Broughton Ave (43213-1690)
PHONE..................................740 927-9000
Richard G Small, *Principal*
EMP: 30

SALES (corp-wide): 400.6MM **Privately Held**
SIC: 1542 1742 1752 Commercial & office building contractors; commercial & office building, new construction; commercial & office buildings, renovation & repair; specialized public building contractors; plastering, plain or ornamental; drywall; insulation, buildings; acoustical & ceiling work; floor laying & floor work
PA: Cleveland Construction, Inc.
8620 Tyler Blvd
Mentor OH 44060
440 255-8000

(G-7225)
CLEVELAND GLASS BLOCK INC
Also Called: Columbus Glass Block
3091 E 14th Ave (43219-2356)
PHONE..................................614 252-5888
John Krulcik, *Manager*
EMP: 25
SALES (corp-wide): 11.7MM **Privately Held**
WEB: www.clevelandglassblock.com
SIC: 5231 5039 Glass; glass construction materials
PA: Cleveland Glass Block, Inc.
4566 E 71st St
Cleveland OH 44105
216 531-6363

(G-7226)
CLIME LEASING CO LLC
Also Called: Columbus Healthcare Center
4301 Clime Rd N (43228-3403)
PHONE..................................614 276-4400
Cody Brown, *Mng Member*
Stephen Rosedale,
EMP: 99
SALES (est): 3.9MM
SALES (corp-wide): 125.8MM **Privately Held**
SIC: 8051 Skilled nursing care facilities
HQ: Health Care Facility Management, Llc
4700 Ashwood Dr Ste 200
Blue Ash OH 45241

(G-7227)
CLINIC5
1466 Northwest Blvd (43212-3063)
PHONE..................................614 598-9960
Xavier Salvatorino, *Mng Member*
Winston Vandesol,
EMP: 25 EST: 2010
SALES (est): 166.9K **Privately Held**
SIC: 8099 Health & allied services

(G-7228)
CLINICAL SPECIALTIES INC
Also Called: C S I
7654 Crosswoods Dr (43235-4621)
PHONE..................................614 659-6580
Kevin Cunningham, *Branch Mgr*
EMP: 116
SALES (corp-wide): 20.1MM **Privately Held**
SIC: 5047 Medical & hospital equipment
PA: Clinical Specialties, Inc.
6955 Treeline Dr Ste A
Brecksville OH 44141
888 873-7888

(G-7229)
CLINTON-CARVELL INC
Also Called: Crystal Crystal Carpet Care
1131 Harrisburg Pike (43223-2835)
PHONE..................................614 351-8858
Darryl C Reed, *President*
EMP: 30
SQ FT: 2,000
SALES (est): 2.2MM **Privately Held**
WEB: www.clintoncarvell.com
SIC: 8734 7349 8748 Testing laboratories; office cleaning or charring; environmental consultant

(G-7230)
CLINTONVILLE BEECHWOLD COMMUNI (PA)
Also Called: CRC
3222 N High St (43202-1114)
PHONE..................................614 268-3539
John H Hamilton, *President*
Phillip Moots, *Vice Pres*

Judith Jones, *Treasurer*
William Owen, *Director*
Nora Huber, *Admin Sec*
EMP: 30
SQ FT: 4,000
SALES (est): 1.6MM **Privately Held**
SIC: 8322 Community center

(G-7231)
CLINTONVILLE COMMUNITY MKT
Also Called: Clintonville Community Market
85 E Gay St Ste 1000 (43215-3118)
PHONE..................................614 261-3663
Karen Hansen, *General Mgr*
EMP: 30
SALES (est): 1.8MM **Privately Held**
WEB: www.communitymarket.org
SIC: 5149 5812 Natural & organic foods; eating places

(G-7232)
CLK MULTI-FAMILY MGT LLC
Also Called: Spring Creek Apts
5811 Spring Run Dr (43229-2890)
PHONE..................................614 891-0011
EMP: 104
SALES (corp-wide): 26.4MM **Privately Held**
SIC: 8741 Management services
PA: Clk Multi-Family Management, Llc
5545 Murray Ave Fl 3
Memphis TN 38119
901 435-9300

(G-7233)
CLM PALLET RECYCLING INC
4311 Janitrol Rd Ste 150 (43228-1389)
PHONE..................................614 272-5761
Steve Foor, *Branch Mgr*
EMP: 93
SALES (corp-wide): 39MM **Privately Held**
SIC: 4953 Recycling, waste materials
PA: Clm Pallet Recycling, Inc.
3103 W 1000 N
Fortville IN 46040
317 485-4080

(G-7234)
CLOSEOUT DISTRIBUTION INC (HQ)
4900 E Dblin Granville Rd (43081-7651)
PHONE..................................614 278-6800
Michael J Potter, *CEO*
Jared A Poff, *Treasurer*
▲ EMP: 600
SALES (est): 199.4MM
SALES (corp-wide): 5.2B **Publicly Held**
SIC: 5092 Toys & games
PA: Big Lots, Inc.
4900 E Dblin Granville Rd
Columbus OH 43081
614 278-6800

(G-7235)
CME FEDERAL CREDIT UNION (PA)
150 E Mound St Ste 100 (43215-7428)
PHONE..................................614 224-4388
Audrey Havranek, *Principal*
EMP: 28
SALES: 11MM **Privately Held**
SIC: 6062 State credit unions, not federally chartered

(G-7236)
CMP I COLUMBUS II OWNER LLC
Also Called: Courtyard Columbus Worthington
7411 Vantage Dr (43235-1415)
PHONE..................................614 436-7070
Judy Lynam, *Manager*
EMP: 32
SALES (est): 552.8K
SALES (corp-wide): 50.6MM **Privately Held**
SIC: 7011 Hotels
PA: Cmp I Owner-T, Llc
399 Park Ave Fl 18
New York NY 10022
212 547-2609

(G-7237)
CMP I OWNER-T LLC
7411 Vantage Dr (43235-1415)
PHONE..................................614 436-7070
Judy Lynam, *Branch Mgr*
EMP: 32
SALES (corp-wide): 50.6MM **Privately Held**
SIC: 8741 Hotel or motel management
PA: Cmp I Owner-T, Llc
399 Park Ave Fl 18
New York NY 10022
212 547-2609

(G-7238)
COAXIAL COMMUNICATIONS OF SOUT (PA)
700 Ackerman Rd Ste 280 (43202-1559)
PHONE..................................513 797-4400
Dennis J Mc Gillicuddy, *Ch of Bd*
W Edward Wood, *President*
D Steven Mc Voy, *Exec VP*
Art Loescher, *Vice Pres*
Tom Wilson, *CFO*
EMP: 55 EST: 1985
SALES: 15.4MM **Privately Held**
SIC: 4841 Cable television services

(G-7239)
COBA/SELECT SIRES INC (PA)
1224 Alton Darby Creek Rd (43228-9792)
PHONE..................................614 878-5333
Duane Logan, *President*
Kim M House, *CFO*
Chris Lahmers, *Marketing Staff*
Jim Ray, *Manager*
Brad Unrau, *Manager*
EMP: 100
SQ FT: 15,000
SALES: 22.1MM **Privately Held**
WEB: www.cobaselect.com
SIC: 0752 Artificial insemination services, animal specialties

(G-7240)
CODE ONE COMMUNICATIONS INC
2785 Castlewood Rd (43209-3140)
PHONE..................................614 338-0321
F Leon Wilson, *CEO*
EMP: 26
SALES: 38MM **Privately Held**
WEB: www.blackagenda.com
SIC: 8743 Public relations services

(G-7241)
COFFMAN FAMILY PARTNERSHIP
5435 Nelsonia Pl (43213-3532)
PHONE..................................614 864-5400
Tean Coffman, *Owner*
EMP: 50
SALES: 4MM **Privately Held**
SIC: 6531 Real estate leasing & rentals

(G-7242)
COILPLUS INC
Coilplus Berwick
5677 Alshire Rd (43232-4703)
PHONE..................................614 866-1338
R Terry Harrold, *Division Pres*
EMP: 51
SALES (corp-wide): 71B **Privately Held**
SIC: 5051 Steel
HQ: Coilplus, Inc.
6250 N River Rd Ste 6050
Rosemont IL 60018
847 384-3000

(G-7243)
COLDLINER EXPRESS INC
4921 Vulcan Ave (43228-9573)
P.O. Box 28767 (43228-0767)
PHONE..................................614 570-0836
Marci S Hinton, *President*
Douglas Abel, *Principal*
EMP: 100
SQ FT: 5,000
SALES: 18.2MM **Privately Held**
SIC: 4789 Cargo loading & unloading services

(G-7244)
COLHOC LIMITED PARTNERSHIP
Also Called: Columbus Blue Jackets
200 W Nationwide Blvd (43215-2561)
PHONE...................................614 246-4625
Craig L Leipold, *Owner*
Larry Hoepfner, *Exec VP*
T J Lamendola, *CFO*
▲ EMP: 150 EST: 1998
SALES (est) 18.7MM **Privately Held**
WEB: www.bluejackets.com
SIC: 7941 Ice hockey club

(G-7245)
COLLECTIONS ACQUISITION CO LLC
2 Easton Oval Ste 350 (43219-6193)
PHONE...................................614 944-5788
Brad West, *Senior VP*
Steven Balachovic, *Mng Member*
Lex Crosett, *CTO*
EMP: 125
SALES (est): 8.8MM **Privately Held**
SIC: 7389 Financial services

(G-7246)
COLLECTOR WELLS INTL INC
6360 Huntley Rd (43229-1008)
PHONE...................................614 888-6263
Sam Stowe, *President*
Andrew Smith, *Corp Secy*
James French, *Vice Pres*
Henry Hunt, *Vice Pres*
Mark Nilges, *Vice Pres*
EMP: 30
SALES (est): 5.7MM
SALES (corp-wide): 2.9B **Publicly Held**
WEB: www.collectorwellsint.com
SIC: 1781 Water well drilling
HQ: Layne Christensen Company
1800 Hughes Landing Blvd
The Woodlands TX 77380
281 475-2600

(G-7247)
COLUMBIA ENERGY GROUP
200 Civic Center Dr (43215-7510)
PHONE...................................614 460-4683
Robert Skaggs Jr, *President*
Robert Skaggs, *President*
Gary W Pottorff, *Vice Pres*
EMP: 2100
SALES (est): 341.3MM
SALES (corp-wide): 5.1B **Publicly Held**
WEB: www.nisource.com
SIC: 4922 1311 1731 Natural gas transmission; crude petroleum production; electric power systems contractors
PA: Nisource Inc.
801 E 86th Ave
Merrillville IN 46410
877 647-5990

(G-7248)
COLUMBIA GAS OF OHIO INC (HQ)
290 W Nationwide Blvd # 114
(43215-1082)
P.O. Box 117 (43216-0117)
PHONE...................................614 460-6000
Jack Partridge, *President*
Dick James, *President*
Devit Vajda, *Treasurer*
Ms Jaime Hartenback, *Accountant*
EMP: 30 EST: 1951
SQ FT: 50,000
SALES: 908.1MM
SALES (corp-wide): 5.1B **Publicly Held**
WEB: www.meterrepairshop.com
SIC: 4924 Natural gas distribution
PA: Nisource Inc.
801 E 86th Ave
Merrillville IN 46410
877 647-5990

(G-7249)
COLUMBIA GAS OF OHIO INC
290 W Nationwide Blvd (43215-4157)
P.O. Box 2318 (43216-2318)
PHONE...................................614 481-1000
Gary Schuler, *Principal*
EMP: 250

SALES (corp-wide): 5.1B **Publicly Held**
WEB: www.meterrepairshop.com
SIC: 4924 Natural gas distribution
HQ: Columbia Gas Of Ohio, Inc.
290 W Nationwide Blvd # 114
Columbus OH 43215
614 460-6000

(G-7250)
COLUMBIA GAS TRANSMISSION LLC (DH)
200 Cizzic Ctr Dr (43216)
PHONE...................................614 460-6000
Glen L Kettering, *President*
Mc S Hall, *Manager*
Melissa Gibson, *Technology*
EMP: 50 EST: 1969
SALES (est): 679.9MM
SALES (corp-wide): 10.5B **Privately Held**
SIC: 4922 Pipelines, natural gas; storage, natural gas
HQ: Columbia Pipeline Group, Inc.
5151 San Felipe St
Houston TX 77056
713 386-3701

(G-7251)
COLUMBIA GAS TRANSMISSION LLC
Also Called: Columbia Energy
290 W Nationwide Blvd # 114
(43215-4157)
PHONE...................................614 460-4704
EMP: 40
SALES (corp-wide): 10.5B **Privately Held**
SIC: 4922 Natural gas transmission
HQ: Columbia Gas Transmission, Llc
200 Cizzic Ctr Dr
Columbus OH 43216
614 460-6000

(G-7252)
COLUMBS/WORTHINGTON HTG AC INC
Also Called: Columbus/Worthington Htg & AC
6363 Fiesta Dr (43235-5202)
PHONE...................................614 771-5381
Jeff Ford, *President*
George Petty, *CFO*
EMP: 45
SQ FT: 22,400
SALES (est): 7.3MM
SALES (corp-wide): 2.4B **Privately Held**
WEB: www.columbusmechanical.com
SIC: 1711 7623 7699 Warm air heating & air conditioning contractor; air conditioning repair; boiler & heating repair services
PA: American Residential Services Llc
965 Ridge Lake Blvd # 201
Memphis TN 38120
901 271-9700

(G-7253)
COLUMBUS AIRPORT LTD PARTNR
Also Called: Columbus Airport Marriott
1375 N Cassady Ave (43219-1524)
PHONE...................................614 475-7551
Janet Rhodes, *Principal*
EMP: 160
SQ FT: 220,000
SALES (est): 7.6MM **Privately Held**
SIC: 7011 5813 5812 Hotels; drinking places; eating places

(G-7254)
COLUMBUS ALZHEIMERS CARE CTR
700 Jasonway Ave (43214-2458)
PHONE...................................614 459-7050
Tonia Hoak, *Exec Dir*
Monica Wiess, *Administration*
Donna Lane,
EMP: 125
SQ FT: 41,654
SALES: 8.4MM **Privately Held**
SIC: 8059 8051 Nursing home, except skilled & intermediate care facility; skilled nursing care facilities

(G-7255)
COLUMBUS AREA
899 E Broad St Ste 100 (43205-1156)
PHONE...................................614 251-6561
Bailey Janie, *CEO*

EMP: 65
SALES (corp-wide): 14.5MM **Privately Held**
SIC: 8093 8051 Specialty Outpatient Clinic Skilled Nursing Care Facility
PA: Columbus Area Integrated Health Services, Inc.
1515 E Broad St
Columbus OH 43205
614 252-0711

(G-7256)
COLUMBUS AREA INC
Also Called: Pathways Center
1515 E Broad St (43205-1550)
PHONE...................................614 252-0711
Janie Bailey, *President*
EMP: 50
SALES (corp-wide): 14.5MM **Privately Held**
WEB: www.columbus-area.com
SIC: 8093 Mental health clinic, outpatient
PA: Columbus Area Integrated Health Services, Inc.
1515 E Broad St
Columbus OH 43205
614 252-0711

(G-7257)
COLUMBUS AREA INTEGRATED HEALT (PA)
Also Called: Columbus Area Community
1515 E Broad St (43205-1550)
PHONE...................................614 252-0711
Anthony L Penn, *President*
Cassandra A Ellis, *CFO*
Beverly Perry, *Manager*
Janie Bailey, *Exec Dir*
Dr Arthur Rose, *Director*
EMP: 80
SQ FT: 80,000
SALES: 14.5MM **Privately Held**
WEB: www.columbus-area.com
SIC: 8093 8052 Mental health clinic, outpatient; drug clinic, outpatient; intermediate care facilities; home for the mentally retarded, with health care

(G-7258)
COLUMBUS ARTHRITIS CENTER INC
1211 Dublin Rd (43215-1077)
P.O. Box 2097, Westerville (43086-2097)
PHONE...................................614 486-5200
Sterling W Hedrick MD, *President*
Sheryl Osborne, *Finance Mgr*
Sarah Williams, *Human Res Mgr*
Jennifer Richardson, *Med Doctor*
Kevin Schlessel, *Med Doctor*
EMP: 25
SALES (est): 5.3MM **Privately Held**
WEB: www.columbusarthritis.com
SIC: 8011 Rheumatology specialist, physician/surgeon

(G-7259)
COLUMBUS ASSOCIATION FOR THE P (PA)
Also Called: Capa
55 E State St (43215-4203)
PHONE...................................614 469-1045
William B Conner Jr, *President*
Michael Petrecca, *Vice Chairman*
Stephanie E Green, *Treasurer*
Barbara B Lach, *Admin Sec*
▲ EMP: 1065
SALES: 5.9MM **Privately Held**
SIC: 7922 Legitimate live theater producers

(G-7260)
COLUMBUS ASSOCIATION FOR THE P
39 E State St (43215-4203)
PHONE...................................614 469-0939
William Conner, *Director*
EMP: 90
SALES (corp-wide): 5.9MM **Privately Held**
SIC: 7922 7929 Legitimate live theater producers; entertainers & entertainment groups

PA: The Columbus Association For The Performing Arts
55 E State St
Columbus OH 43215
614 469-1045

(G-7261)
COLUMBUS BAR ASSOCIATION
175 S 3rd St Ste 1100 (43215-5197)
PHONE...................................614 221-4112
Alex Lagusch, *Director*
Eric Becker,
John Cassidy,
Mary Duffey,
Jeffrey Lindemann,
EMP: 32
SALES: 2.9MM **Privately Held**
SIC: 8621 Bar association

(G-7262)
COLUMBUS BEHAVIORAL HEALTH LLC (PA)
Also Called: Sun Behavioral Columbus
900 E Dublin Granville Rd (43229-2452)
PHONE...................................732 747-1800
Mark Creamer, *Director*
EMP: 25 EST: 2014
SALES (est): 4.1MM **Privately Held**
SIC: 8082 Home health care services

(G-7263)
COLUMBUS BRIDE
34 S 3rd St (43215-4201)
PHONE...................................614 888-4567
Ray Tatrocki, *General Mgr*
Randy Beyer, *Controller*
EMP: 60
SQ FT: 1,000
SALES (est): 4.4MM **Privately Held**
WEB: www.columbusalive.com
SIC: 2721 7389 Magazines: publishing only, not printed on site; convention & show services

(G-7264)
COLUMBUS CARDIOLOGY CONS INC
85 Mcnaughten Rd Ste 300 (43213-5112)
PHONE...................................614 224-2281
Karen Kane, *Manager*
EMP: 150 **Privately Held**
SIC: 8011 Cardiologist & cardio-vascular specialist
PA: Columbus Cardiology Consultants, Inc.
745 W State St Ste 750
Columbus OH 43222

(G-7265)
COLUMBUS CARDIOLOGY CONS INC (PA)
745 W State St Ste 750 (43222-1515)
PHONE...................................614 224-2281
F Kevin Hackett, *President*
EMP: 220
SQ FT: 20,000
SALES (est): 14.2MM **Privately Held**
SIC: 8011 Cardiologist & cardio-vascular specialist

(G-7266)
COLUMBUS CHRISTIAN CENTER INC (PA)
Also Called: Faith Christian Accademy
2300 N Cassady Ave (43219-1508)
P.O. Box 24009 (43224-0009)
PHONE...................................614 416-9673
David C Forbes, *Pastor*
EMP: 40
SALES (est): 2.4MM **Privately Held**
SIC: 8661 8351 Non-denominational church; child day care services

(G-7267)
COLUMBUS CITY TRNSP DIV
1800 E 17th Ave (43219-1007)
PHONE...................................614 645-3182
Henry Gusman, *Director*
EMP: 150
SALES (est): 9.7MM **Privately Held**
SIC: 1542 Nonresidential construction

(G-7268)
COLUMBUS CLUB CO
181 E Broad St (43215-3788)
PHONE...................................614 224-4131

Steve Landerman, *President*
EMP: 30
SQ FT: 5,000
SALES (est): 1.8MM **Privately Held**
WEB: www.columbusclub.com
SIC: 7997 Membership sports & recreation clubs

(G-7269)
COLUMBUS COAL & LIME CO (PA)
Also Called: Granville Builders Supply
1150 Sullivant Ave (43223-1427)
P.O. Box 23156 (43223-0156)
PHONE...................................614 224-9241
Katherine N Gatterdam, *CEO*
John Niermeyer, *Ch of Bd*
Rich Gatterdam, *President*
E L Humphreys, *Principal*
Carl H Niermeyer, *Principal*
EMP: 30
SQ FT: 20,000
SALES (est): 11.9MM **Privately Held**
WEB: www.columbuscoal.com
SIC: 5032 5211 Sand, construction; brick

(G-7270)
COLUMBUS COL-WELD CORPORATION
1515 Harrisburg Pike (43223-3609)
P.O. Box 23097 (43223-0097)
PHONE...................................614 276-5303
Charles Stump, *President*
Maynard Stump, *Vice Pres*
John W Stump, *Treasurer*
Roger Stump, *Admin Sec*
EMP: 40 EST: 1944
SQ FT: 40,000
SALES (est): 2.2MM **Privately Held**
SIC: 7538 Engine repair, except diesel: automotive

(G-7271)
COLUMBUS CONCORD LTD PARTNR
Also Called: Courtyard By Marriott
35 W Spring St (43215-2215)
PHONE...................................614 228-3200
Bob Micklash, *CEO*
Anne Turpin, *General Mgr*
Dan Peterson, *Manager*
EMP: 70
SALES (est): 2.7MM **Privately Held**
SIC: 7011 Hotels & motels

(G-7272)
COLUMBUS COUNTRY CLUB
4831 E Broad St (43213-1390)
PHONE...................................614 861-0800
Mark Collins, *President*
Jay Frank, *General Mgr*
Amanda Greenwood, *Sales Dir*
Jim Creighton, *Director*
EMP: 30
SQ FT: 14,000
SALES (est): 4.7MM **Privately Held**
WEB: www.columbuscc.com
SIC: 7997 7991 5941 5813 Country club, membership; physical fitness facilities; sporting goods & bicycle shops; drinking places; eating places

(G-7273)
COLUMBUS CTR FOR HUMN SVCS INC (PA)
Also Called: Cchs Johnstown Home
540 Industrial Mile Rd (43228-2413)
PHONE...................................614 641-2904
Rebecca Sharp, *CEO*
David McCarty, *President*
Brent Garland, *Vice Pres*
S Brewster Randall, *Director*
EMP: 145
SQ FT: 32,000
SALES: 7.7MM **Privately Held**
SIC: 8059 Home for the mentally retarded, exc. skilled or intermediate

(G-7274)
COLUMBUS DAY CARE CENTER
3389 Westerville Rd (43224-3052)
PHONE...................................614 269-8980
Iman Ali, *Director*
EMP: 27 EST: 2010

SALES (est): 407.4K **Privately Held**
SIC: 8351 Child day care services

(G-7275)
COLUMBUS DISTRIBUTING COMPANY (PA)
Also Called: Delmar Distributing
4949 Freeway Dr E (43229-5479)
PHONE...................................614 846-1000
Paul A Jenkins Jr, *Ch of Bd*
Barbara Jenkins, *Vice Ch Bd*
Paul Jenkins Jr, *President*
▲ EMP: 275
SQ FT: 130,000
SALES (est): 96.7MM **Privately Held**
WEB: www.delmardistributing.com
SIC: 5181 Beer & other fermented malt liquors

(G-7276)
COLUMBUS DRYWALL & INSULATION
876 N 19th St (43219-2417)
PHONE...................................614 257-0257
Steve Ostrander, *President*
EMP: 65 EST: 1969
SQ FT: 28,000
SALES (est): 3MM **Privately Held**
WEB: www.columbusinsulation.com
SIC: 1742 1521 Drywall; insulation, buildings; acoustical & ceiling work; single-family housing construction

(G-7277)
COLUMBUS DRYWALL INC
Also Called: Columbus Drywall Installation
876 N 19th St (43219-2417)
PHONE...................................614 257-0257
Steve Ostrander, *President*
Darvis Ostrander, *Vice Pres*
EMP: 50
SQ FT: 20,000
SALES (est): 3.3MM **Privately Held**
WEB: www.columbusdrywall.com
SIC: 1742 1521 Drywall; single-family housing construction

(G-7278)
COLUMBUS EASTON HOTEL LLC
Also Called: Marriott
3999 Easton Loop W (43219-6152)
PHONE...................................614 414-1000
Brad Gester, *General Mgr*
EMP: 35
SALES (est): 1.1MM **Privately Held**
SIC: 7011 Hotels & motels

(G-7279)
COLUMBUS EASTON HOTEL LLC (PA)
Also Called: Hilton Columbus At Easton
3900 Chagrin Dr Fl 7 (43219-7100)
PHONE...................................614 414-5000
Janetta Tischer, *Principal*
EMP: 89
SALES (est): 11.8MM **Privately Held**
SIC: 7011 Hotels

(G-7280)
COLUMBUS EASTON HOTEL LLC
3900 Morse Xing (43219-6081)
PHONE...................................614 383-2005
Mort Olshan, *Branch Mgr*
EMP: 40
SALES (corp-wide): 11.8MM **Privately Held**
SIC: 7011 Hotels
PA: Columbus Easton Hotel Llc
3900 Chagrin Dr Fl 7
Columbus OH 43219
614 414-5000

(G-7281)
COLUMBUS EQUIPMENT COMPANY (PA)
Also Called: Kubota Authorized Dealer
2323 Performance Way (43207-2473)
PHONE...................................614 437-0352
Josh Stivison, *President*
Ray Frase, *General Mgr*
Chris Taylor, *COO*
Tim Albright, *Vice Pres*

Ernie Potter, *Vice Pres*
▼ EMP: 43 EST: 1951
SQ FT: 12,000
SALES (est): 84.2MM **Privately Held**
WEB: www.colsequipment.com
SIC: 5082 7353 General construction machinery & equipment; heavy construction equipment rental

(G-7282)
COLUMBUS EQUIPMENT COMPANY
2323 Performance Way (43207-2473)
PHONE...................................614 443-6541
Albert Allen, *Branch Mgr*
EMP: 45
SALES (corp-wide): 84.2MM **Privately Held**
WEB: www.colsequipment.com
SIC: 5082 7353 General construction machinery & equipment; heavy construction equipment rental
PA: The Columbus Equipment Company
2323 Performance Way
Columbus OH 43207
614 437-0352

(G-7283)
COLUMBUS FOUNDATION
1234 E Broad St (43205-1453)
PHONE...................................614 251-4000
Douglas Kridler, *President*
Kelley Griesmer, *Senior VP*
Raymond Biddiscombe, *Vice Pres*
Tamera Durrence, *Vice Pres*
Carol Harmon, *Vice Pres*
EMP: 45
SQ FT: 20,000
SALES (est): 3.7MM **Privately Held**
SIC: 8641 Civic social & fraternal associations

(G-7284)
COLUMBUS GREEN CABS INC (PA)
Also Called: Yellow Cabs
1989 Camaro Ave (43207-1716)
PHONE...................................614 444-4444
Jeff Kates, *President*
Jeff R Glassman, *Vice Pres*
EMP: 40 EST: 1928
SQ FT: 26,000
SALES (est): 4.8MM **Privately Held**
SIC: 4121 Taxicabs

(G-7285)
COLUMBUS GSTRNTRLOGY GROUP INC
3820 Olentangy River Rd (43214-5403)
PHONE...................................614 457-1213
Richard A Edgin, *President*
EMP: 60
SQ FT: 3,545
SALES (est): 3MM **Privately Held**
SIC: 8011 Gastronomist

(G-7286)
COLUMBUS HEATING & VENT CO
182 N Yale Ave (43222-1127)
PHONE...................................614 274-1177
Charles R Gulley, *President*
Greogy Yoak, *President*
Michael Blythe, *Corp Secy*
Mikel Plythe, *Admin Sec*
EMP: 135 EST: 1874
SALES (est): 23.6MM **Privately Held**
WEB: www.columbusheat.com
SIC: 1711 3585 Warm air heating & air conditioning contractor; ventilation & duct work contractor; furnaces, warm air: electric

(G-7287)
COLUMBUS HOSPITALITY
775 Yard St Ste 180 (43212-3857)
PHONE...................................614 461-2648
EMP: 30
SALES (est): 3.9MM **Privately Held**
SIC: 7011 Hotel/Motel Operation

(G-7288)
COLUMBUS HOTEL PARTNERSHIP LLC
Also Called: Embassy Suites Columbus
2700 Corporate Exch Dr (43231-1690)
PHONE...................................614 890-8600
Alpesh Patel,
EMP: 85
SALES (est): 333.9K **Privately Held**
SIC: 7011 Resort hotel, franchised

(G-7289)
COLUMBUS HOUSING PARTNR INC
Also Called: C.H.P.
3443 Agler Rd Ste 200 (43219-3385)
PHONE...................................614 221-8889
Bruce Luecke, *President*
Valorie Schwarzmann, *CFO*
EMP: 58
SQ FT: 10,000
SALES: 5.9MM **Privately Held**
SIC: 6552 Land subdividers & developers, residential

(G-7290)
COLUMBUS JEWISH FEDERATION
1175 College Ave (43209-2827)
PHONE...................................614 237-7686
Marsha Hurowitz, *President*
Hal Lewis, *President*
Mitchell J Orlik, *Vice Pres*
Donald Kelly, *CFO*
Randy Arndt, *Treasurer*
EMP: 30
SQ FT: 15,000
SALES: 5.4MM **Privately Held**
SIC: 8399 Fund raising organization, non-fee basis

(G-7291)
COLUMBUS LANDMARKS FOUNDATION
57 Jefferson Ave Fl 1 (43215-3866)
PHONE...................................614 221-0227
Kathy M Kane, *Exec Dir*
Becky West, *Exec Dir*
Ed Lentz, *Director*
EMP: 26 EST: 1977
SALES: 165.9K **Privately Held**
WEB: www.columbuslandmarks.org
SIC: 8699 8399 Automobile owners' association; historical club; advocacy group

(G-7292)
COLUMBUS LEASING LLC
Also Called: Crowne Plaza Columbus North
6500 Doubletree Ave (43229-1111)
PHONE...................................614 885-1885
Daniel Ouellette,
EMP: 99
SALES (est): 6.4MM **Privately Held**
SIC: 7011 Hotels

(G-7293)
COLUMBUS MAENNERCHOR
Also Called: GERMAN SINGING SOCIETY
976 S High St (43206-2524)
PHONE...................................614 444-3531
Rene V Blaha, *President*
EMP: 35
SQ FT: 4,000
SALES: 225.8K **Privately Held**
WEB: www.maennerchor.com
SIC: 8641 Community membership club

(G-7294)
COLUMBUS MED ASSN FOUNDATION
1390 Dublin Rd (43215-1009)
PHONE...................................614 240-7420
Phil Cass, *Director*
EMP: 30
SALES: 2.2MM **Privately Held**
SIC: 8621 Medical field-related associations

(G-7295)
COLUMBUS MED PARTNERS LLC
758 Communications Pkwy (43214-1948)
PHONE...................................614 538-1060
Mary Garber, *Principal*

Michelle Smallwood, *Principal*
EMP: 25
SALES (est): 177.9K **Privately Held**
SIC: 8092 Kidney dialysis centers

(G-7296)
COLUMBUS MEDICAL ASSOCIATION
1390 Dublin Rd (43215-1009)
PHONE....................614 240-7410
Phillip Cass, *CEO*
Gerald Penn, *President*
Penny James, *Receptionist*
EMP: 30
SQ FT: 12,432
SALES: 414.2K **Privately Held**
SIC: 8621 Health association; medical field-related associations

(G-7297)
COLUMBUS METRO FEDERAL CR UN
4000 E Broad St (43213-1140)
P.O. Box 13240 (43213-0240)
PHONE....................614 239-0210
Tim Ritchey, *Principal*
EMP: 28
SALES (corp-wide): 7MM **Privately Held**
SIC: 6111 6211 Federal & federally sponsored credit agencies; security brokers & dealers
PA: Columbus Metro Federal Credit Union (Inc)
   4000 E Broad St
   Columbus OH 43213
   614 239-0210

(G-7298)
COLUMBUS METRO FEDERAL CR UN (PA)
4000 E Broad St (43213-1140)
P.O. Box 13240 (43213-0240)
PHONE....................614 239-0210
Tim Richey, *President*
Pam Dixon, *Accountant*
Jim Downey, *Manager*
Tim Ford, *Manager*
Tony Southall, *Director*
EMP: 33
SQ FT: 20,503
SALES: 7MM **Privately Held**
SIC: 6111 6163 Federal & federally sponsored credit agencies; loan brokers

(G-7299)
COLUMBUS MONTESSORI EDUCATION
979 S James Rd (43227-1071)
PHONE....................614 231-3790
Peggy Fein, *Director*
EMP: 40
SQ FT: 26,369
SALES: 2.8MM **Privately Held**
WEB: www.columbusmontessori.org
SIC: 8351 8299 Educational service, nondegree granting; continuing educ.; Montessori child development center

(G-7300)
COLUMBUS MUNICIPAL EMPLOYEES (PA)
365 S 4th St (43215-5422)
PHONE....................614 224-8890
Jim Riederer, *President*
Crystal Gatchel, *Assistant VP*
Tracy Cera, *CFO*
Clark Will, *Controller*
Eric Chandler, *Officer*
EMP: 31
SQ FT: 5,000
SALES: 9.6MM **Privately Held**
SIC: 6061 Federal credit unions

(G-7301)
COLUMBUS MUSEUM OF ART
480 E Broad St (43215-3886)
PHONE....................614 221-6801
F C Sessions Et Al, *Principal*
W G Deshler, *Principal*
P W Huntington, *Principal*
David Leach, *Facilities Dir*
Rod Bouc, *Opers Staff*
▲ **EMP:** 100
SQ FT: 89,000

SALES: 14.8MM **Privately Held**
WEB: www.cmaohio.org
SIC: 8412 5812 Art gallery; eating places

(G-7302)
COLUMBUS NEIGHBORHOOD HEALTH C
1905 Parsons Ave (43207-1933)
PHONE....................614 445-0685
EMP: 118
SALES (corp-wide): 31.7MM **Privately Held**
SIC: 8011 Clinic, operated by physicians
PA: Columbus Neighborhood Health Center, Inc.
   2780 Airport Dr Ste 100
   Columbus OH 43219
   614 645-5500

(G-7303)
COLUMBUS OBSTTRCANS GYNCLGISTS (PA)
Also Called: Columbus Obgyn
750 Mount Carmel Mall # 100 (43222-1553)
PHONE....................614 434-2400
Ralph R Ballenger MD, *President*
Mark Vanmeter, *COO*
R D Blose MD, *Vice Pres*
Charles A Caranna MD, *Vice Pres*
Larry A Simon MD, *Treasurer*
EMP: 41
SQ FT: 2,850
SALES (est): 11MM **Privately Held**
SIC: 8011 Obstetrician; gynecologist

(G-7304)
COLUMBUS ONCOLOGY ASSOC INC
Also Called: Columbus Onclogy Hmtlogy Assoc
810 Jasonway Ave Ste A (43214-4359)
PHONE....................614 442-3130
Peter Kourlas, *President*
Christopher George, *Vice Pres*
John Kuebler, *Vice Pres*
Thomas Sweeney, *Treasurer*
Scott Blair, *Admin Sec*
▲ **EMP:** 51
SQ FT: 23,000
SALES (est): 5.6MM **Privately Held**
WEB: www.coainc.net
SIC: 8011 Hematologist; oncologist

(G-7305)
COLUMBUS PUBLIC SCHOOL DST
Also Called: Columbus Pub Schl Vhcl Maint
889 E 17th Ave (43211-2492)
PHONE....................614 365-5263
Nick Brown, *Maint Spvr*
Phil Downs, *Manager*
EMP: 200
SALES (corp-wide): 1B **Privately Held**
WEB: www.siebertschool.com
SIC: 5013 Automotive servicing equipment
PA: Columbus Public School District
   270 E State St Fl 3
   Columbus OH 43215
   614 365-5000

(G-7306)
COLUMBUS PUBLIC SCHOOL DST
Also Called: Cassady Alternative Elementary
2500 N Cassady Ave (43219-1514)
PHONE....................614 365-5456
Natasha Shaefer, *Principal*
EMP: 40
SALES (corp-wide): 1B **Privately Held**
WEB: www.siebertschool.com
SIC: 8211 8351 Public elementary school; preschool center
PA: Columbus Public School District
   270 E State St Fl 3
   Columbus OH 43215
   614 365-5000

(G-7307)
COLUMBUS PUBLIC SCHOOL DST
Also Called: Cols Boe Custodial Services
889 E 17th Ave (43211-2492)
PHONE....................614 365-5043
Chuck Holler, *Manager*

EMP: 500
SALES (corp-wide): 1B **Privately Held**
WEB: www.siebertschool.com
SIC: 7349 Building maintenance services
PA: Columbus Public School District
   270 E State St Fl 3
   Columbus OH 43215
   614 365-5000

(G-7308)
COLUMBUS PUBLIC SCHOOL DST
Also Called: Food Service
450 E Fulton St (43215-5527)
PHONE....................614 365-5000
Dudley Hawkey, *Director*
EMP: 40
SALES (corp-wide): 1B **Privately Held**
WEB: www.siebertschool.com
SIC: 8742 Restaurant & food services consultants
PA: Columbus Public School District
   270 E State St Fl 3
   Columbus OH 43215
   614 365-5000

(G-7309)
COLUMBUS PUBLIC SCHOOL DST
Also Called: Columbus Schl Dst Bus Compound
4001 Appian Way (43230-1469)
PHONE....................614 365-6542
Greg McCandless, *Manager*
EMP: 158
SALES (corp-wide): 1B **Privately Held**
WEB: www.siebertschool.com
SIC: 4111 Bus transportation
PA: Columbus Public School District
   270 E State St Fl 3
   Columbus OH 43215
   614 365-5000

(G-7310)
COLUMBUS REGIONAL AIRPORT AUTH
4760 E 5th Ave Ste G (43219-1877)
PHONE....................614 239-4000
Bill Burford, *Supervisor*
Christopher Baughman, *Officer*
EMP: 31 **Privately Held**
SIC: 4581 Airport
PA: Columbus Regional Airport Authority
   4600 Intl Gtwy Ste 2
   Columbus OH 43219

(G-7311)
COLUMBUS REGIONAL AIRPORT AUTH (PA)
Also Called: John Glenn Columbus Intl Arprt
4600 Intl Gtwy Ste 2 (43219)
PHONE....................614 239-4015
Elaine Roberts, *President*
Joshua Burger, *Senior VP*
Brian Sarkis, *Vice Pres*
Kristina Baker, *Project Mgr*
Bart Powell, *Project Mgr*
EMP: 320
SQ FT: 821,795
SALES: 88.1MM **Privately Held**
WEB: www.columbusairports.com
SIC: 4581 Airport

(G-7312)
COLUMBUS SAI MOTORS LLC
Also Called: Hatifield Hyundai
1400 Auto Mall Dr (43228-3657)
PHONE....................614 851-3273
Keith Daniels, *President*
Bud C Hatfield, *Principal*
Scott Smith, *COO*
Jacob Watson, *Parts Mgr*
Jeff Warrington, *Sales Mgr*
EMP: 50
SQ FT: 24,000
SALES (est): 6.5MM
SALES (corp-wide): 9.9B **Publicly Held**
SIC: 7538 5511 7515 5521 General automotive repair shops; automobiles, new & used; passenger car leasing; used car dealers
PA: Sonic Automotive, Inc.
   4401 Colwick Rd
   Charlotte NC 28211
   704 566-2400

(G-7313)
COLUMBUS SERUM COMPANY (DH)
2025 S High St (43207-2426)
PHONE....................614 444-5211
Robert Peterson, *President*
Bruce A Peterson, *Vice Pres*
Bruce Peterson, *Vice Pres*
EMP: 138 **EST:** 1922
SQ FT: 30,000
SALES (est): 47.7MM
SALES (corp-wide): 5.4B **Publicly Held**
WEB: www.milburnequine.com
SIC: 5122 5199 Whol Drugs/Sundries Whol Nondurable Goods
HQ: Patterson Veterinary Supply, Inc.
   137 Barnum Rd
   Devens MA 01434
   978 353-6000

(G-7314)
COLUMBUS SOUTHERN POWER CO (HQ)
1 Riverside Plz (43215-2355)
PHONE....................614 716-1000
Michael G Morris, *Ch of Bd*
Joseph Hamrock, *President*
Holly K Koeppel, *Exec VP*
Brian X Tierney, *CFO*
Nicholas K Akins, *Director*
EMP: 57
SALES (est): 16.8MM
SALES (corp-wide): 16.2B **Publicly Held**
SIC: 4911 Distribution, electric power
PA: American Electric Power Company, Inc.
   1 Riverside Plz Fl 1 # 1
   Columbus OH 43215
   614 716-1000

(G-7315)
COLUMBUS SPEECH & HEARING CTR
510 E North Broadway St (43214-4114)
PHONE....................614 263-5151
James O Dye, *President*
Karen Deeter, *Director*
Rachel Milligan, *Director*
EMP: 79
SQ FT: 40,000
SALES (est): 4.1MM **Privately Held**
SIC: 8322 Social services for the handicapped

(G-7316)
COLUMBUS SQUARE BOWLING PALACE
5707 Forest Hills Blvd (43231-2990)
PHONE....................614 895-1122
William H Hadler, *President*
William N Hadler, *Vice Pres*
EMP: 48
SALES (est): 1.9MM **Privately Held**
WEB: www.palacelanes.com
SIC: 7933 5813 Ten pin center; cocktail lounge

(G-7317)
COLUMBUS STEEL ERECTORS INC
1700 Walcutt Rd (43228-9612)
PHONE....................614 876-5050
Lisa Runyon, *CEO*
Shawn Runyon, *President*
EMP: 25
SALES (est): 3.9MM **Privately Held**
WEB: www.columbussteelerectors.com
SIC: 1791 Iron work, structural

(G-7318)
COLUMBUS SYMPHONY ORCHESTRA
55 E State St Fl 5 (43215-4203)
PHONE....................614 228-9600
Chad Wintton, *CFO*
Kathy Karnap, *Marketing Mgr*
Devon Broderick, *Manager*
Pavana Stetzik, *Manager*
David Davis, *Info Tech Dir*
EMP: 85
SALES: 19.6MM **Privately Held**
WEB: www.columbussymphony.com
SIC: 7929 Orchestras or bands

(G-7319)
COLUMBUS TEAM SOCCER LLC (PA)
Also Called: Columbus Crew, The
1 Black And Gold Blvd (43211-2091)
PHONE................................614 447-1301
Mark McCullers,
▲ EMP: 40
SALES (est): 4.9MM Privately Held
SIC: 7941 Soccer club

(G-7320)
COLUMBUS URBAN LEAGUE INC
788 Mount Vernon Ave (43203-1408)
PHONE................................614 257-6300
Stephanie Hightower, President
Gready Pettigrew, Principal
EMP: 50
SQ FT: 25,000
SALES: 5.3MM Privately Held
WEB: www.cul.org
SIC: 8399 Community development groups

(G-7321)
COLUMBUS WORTHINGTON HOSPITALI
Also Called: Double Tree
175 Hutchinson Ave (43235-1413)
PHONE................................614 885-3334
Daniel Ouellette, Manager
Sattish Duggal,
EMP: 85 EST: 2013
SALES (est): 5.8MM Privately Held
SIC: 7011 Hotel, franchised

(G-7322)
COLUMBUS-RNA-DAVITA LLC
Also Called: Columbus Dialysis
226 Graceland Blvd (43214-1532)
PHONE................................614 985-1732
Zach King, Director
EMP: 25 Publicly Held
WEB: www.us.gambro.com
SIC: 8092 Kidney dialysis centers
HQ: Columbus-Rna-Davita, Llc
601 Hawaii St
El Segundo CA 90245

(G-7323)
COMBINED INSURANCE CO AMER
150 E Campus View Blvd # 230
(43235-6610)
PHONE................................614 210-6209
Domic Pallante, Manager
EMP: 85
SQ FT: 2,000
SALES (corp-wide): 29B Privately Held
SIC: 6411 Insurance agents; education services, insurance
HQ: Combined Insurance Company Of America
8750 W Bryn Mawr Ave
Chicago IL 60631
800 225-4500

(G-7324)
COMENITY SERVICING LLC
3095 Loyalty Cir (43219-3673)
PHONE................................614 729-4000
EMP: 137
SALES (est): 466.7K Publicly Held
SIC: 7389 Advertising, promotional & trade show services
HQ: Ads Alliance Data Systems, Inc.
7500 Dallas Pkwy Ste 700
Plano TX 75024
214 494-3000

(G-7325)
COMFORT INNS
1213 E Dblin Granville Rd (43229-3301)
PHONE................................614 885-4084
Dehesh Patle, General Mgr
Gagan Dada, Manager
EMP: 25
SALES (est): 854.2K Privately Held
SIC: 7011 Hotels & motels

(G-7326)
COMMERCIAL DEBT CUNSELING CORP
445 Hutchinson Ave # 500 (43235-5677)
PHONE................................614 848-9800
Kenneth Monnett, President
Lora J Columbro, Admin Sec
EMP: 75
SQ FT: 40,000
SALES (est): 7.6MM Privately Held
WEB: www.amerassist.com
SIC: 8742 Financial consultant

(G-7327)
COMMERCIAL PARTS & SER
5033 Transamerica Dr (43228-9381)
PHONE................................614 221-0057
Steve Weigel, Branch Mgr
EMP: 55
SALES (corp-wide): 17.9MM Privately Held
WEB: www.cpsohio.com
SIC: 5087 Restaurant supplies
PA: Commercial Parts & Service Of Cincinnati, Ohio, Inc.
10671 Techwoods Cir Ste 1
Blue Ash OH 45242
513 984-1900

(G-7328)
COMMUNITIES IN SCHOOLS
6500 Busch Blvd Ste 105 (43229-1738)
PHONE................................614 268-2472
Sarah Neikirk, Exec Dir
EMP: 54
SALES: 1.1MM Privately Held
WEB: www.ciskids.org
SIC: 8641 Youth organizations

(G-7329)
COMMUNITY CRIME PATROL
248 E 11th Ave (43201-2255)
PHONE................................614 247-1765
Ellen Moore, Executive
Kevin Widmer, Asst Director
EMP: 40
SALES: 614.3K Privately Held
SIC: 7381 Protective services, guard

(G-7330)
COMMUNITY DEV FOR ALL PEOPLE
946 Parsons Ave (43206-2346)
P.O. Box 6063 (43206-0063)
PHONE................................614 445-7342
David Cofer, Managing Dir
John Edgar, Exec Dir
EMP: 28
SALES: 2.9MM Privately Held
SIC: 8699 Charitable organization

(G-7331)
COMMUNITY EMRGCY MED SVCS OHIO
Also Called: Medcare Ambulance
3699 Paragon Dr (43228-9751)
PHONE................................614 751-6651
Phil Koster, Director
EMP: 120
SALES (est): 3MM Privately Held
SIC: 4119 Ambulance service

(G-7332)
COMMUNITY HSING NETWRK DEV CO
1680 Watermark Dr (43215-1034)
PHONE................................614 487-6700
Susan Weaver, CEO
Anthony Penn, COO
Don Hollenack, CFO
EMP: 125
SALES: 15.1MM Privately Held
WEB: www.chninc.org
SIC: 8361 Home for the mentally handicapped

(G-7333)
COMMUNITY LIVING EXPERIENCES
2939 Donnylane Blvd (43235-3228)
PHONE................................614 588-0320
William H Campbell, President
Becky Campbell, CFO
Nancy Cooper, Controller
Renee Chandler, Human Resources
Becky Kerns, Director
EMP: 30
SALES (est): 2.6MM Privately Held
SIC: 8361 Home for the mentally handicapped

(G-7334)
COMMUNITY PRPTS OHIO III LLC
Also Called: Cpo3
42 N 17th St (43203-1801)
PHONE................................614 253-0984
Michelle Hert, Principal
Isabel Toth,
EMP: 55
SALES: 515K Privately Held
SIC: 6513 Apartment building operators

(G-7335)
COMMUNITY PRPTS OHIO MGT SVCS
Also Called: Cpo Managment Services
910 E Broad St (43205-1150)
PHONE................................614 253-0984
Isabel Toth, President
Chad Ketler, Vice Pres
Sharon Griffith, CFO
Sarah J French, Marketing Staff
EMP: 55
SALES (est): 6.4MM Privately Held
SIC: 6513 Apartment building operators
PA: City Of Columbus
90 W Broad St Rm B33
Columbus OH 43215
614 645-7671

(G-7336)
COMMUNITY REFUGEE & IMMIGRATION
1925 E Dublin Granville R (43229-3517)
PHONE................................614 235-5747
Angela Plummer, Train & Dev Mgr
Dahir Adan, Case Mgr
Karin Blythe, Program Mgr
Abdulcadir Giama, Manager
Marcus Gorman, Supervisor
EMP: 75 EST: 1995
SALES: 4.1MM Privately Held
WEB: www.cris-ohio.com
SIC: 8322 Refugee service

(G-7337)
COMMUNITY SHELTER BOARD
355 E Campus View Blvd # 250
(43235-5680)
PHONE................................614 221-9195
Michelle Hertigae, Exec Dir
Janet Bridges, Director
EMP: 25
SALES: 27.1MM Privately Held
WEB: www.csb.org
SIC: 8621 Professional membership organizations

(G-7338)
COMMUNITY SRGL SPLY TOMS RVR
3823 Twin Creeks Dr (43204-5005)
PHONE................................614 307-2975
Andy Tyler, Branch Mgr
EMP: 126
SALES (corp-wide): 176.7MM Privately Held
SIC: 5047 Medical equipment & supplies
PA: Community Surgical Supply Of Toms River Inc
1390 Rte 37 W
Toms River NJ 08755
732 349-2990

(G-7339)
COMPASS PROFESSIONAL SVCS LLC
175 S 3rd St Ste 200 (43215-5194)
PHONE................................216 705-2233
Anthony Montville,
EMP: 75
SALES (est): 1MM Privately Held
SIC: 7361 Employment agencies

(G-7340)
COMPDRUG (PA)
Also Called: YOUTH TO YOUTH
547 E 11th Ave (43211-2603)
PHONE................................614 224-4506
Robert E Sweet, President
Dustin Mets, Exec VP
Ronald L Pogue, Senior VP
Mark Sellers, Vice Pres
EMP: 60
SQ FT: 15,000
SALES: 15.5MM Privately Held
WEB: www.compdrug.org
SIC: 8322 8361 General counseling services; rehabilitation center, residential: health care incidental

(G-7341)
COMPETITOR SWIM PRODUCTS INC
Also Called: Great American Woodies
5310 Career Ct (43213)
P.O. Box 12160 (43212-0160)
PHONE................................800 888-7946
Brad Underwood, President
Alan Sprague, CFO
EMP: 85
SQ FT: 60,000
SALES (est): 20.2MM Privately Held
WEB: www.richeyind.com
SIC: 5091 Swimming pools, equipment & supplies

(G-7342)
COMPLETE GENERAL CNSTR CO (PA)
1221 E 5th Ave (43219-2493)
PHONE................................614 258-9515
Lee Guzzo, Ch of Bd
Gildo Guzzo Jr, President
Jim George, Vice Pres
Fred Lawson, Vice Pres
John Mc Kinley, Vice Pres
EMP: 150
SQ FT: 6,000
SALES (est): 64.3MM Privately Held
WEB: www.completegeneral.com
SIC: 1622 Bridge construction; highway construction, elevated

(G-7343)
COMPREHENSIVE SERVICES INC
1555 Bethel Rd (43220-2003)
PHONE................................614 442-0664
Richard C Davis, President
Susan Blacock, Partner
Jan Brewer, Partner
Louisa Celebrese, Partner
Edward Dagenfield, Partner
EMP: 30
SQ FT: 8,800
SALES (est): 1.9MM Privately Held
WEB: www.comprehensive-services.us
SIC: 8322 General counseling services

(G-7344)
COMPRODUCTS INC (PA)
Also Called: B & C COMMUNICATIONS
1740 Harmon Ave Ste F (43223-3355)
PHONE................................614 276-5552
Thomas Harb, CEO
Leland Haydon, President
Steven Stauch, Vice Pres
Bob Lash, Sales Mgr
Jesse Stanley, Sales Staff
EMP: 84
SQ FT: 12,000
SALES: 12.9MM Privately Held
SIC: 5065 7622 Radio parts & accessories; radio receiving & transmitting tubes; radio repair & installation

(G-7345)
COMPUTER HELPER PUBLISHING
450 Beecher Rd (43230-1797)
P.O. Box 30191, Gahanna (43230-0191)
PHONE................................614 939-9094
Mel Wygant, President
EMP: 25
SQ FT: 3,300

SALES (est): 4.1MM **Privately Held**
SIC: 5045 7371 5734 Computer software;
custom computer programming services;
computer & software stores

(G-7346)
COMRESOURCE INC
1159 Dublin Rd Ste 200 (43215-1874)
PHONE......................................614 221-6348
Gary L Potts, *President*
Richard C Hannon Jr, *Principal*
Danny Puckett, *Engineer*
Kristen Dyer, *Applctn Conslt*
Levi Smith, *Administration*
EMP: 45
SQ FT: 3,500
SALES (est): 9.7MM **Privately Held**
WEB: www.comresource.com
SIC: 7379

(G-7347)
COMTECH GLOBAL INC
355 E Campus View Blvd # 195
(43235-8624)
PHONE......................................614 796-1148
Sridhar Nannapaneni, *President*
EMP: 72
SQ FT: 3,000
SALES (est): 8.2MM **Privately Held**
WEB: www.comtech-global.com
SIC: 7371 Computer software develop-
ment

(G-7348)
CONGRESSIONAL BANK
Also Called: American Federal Bank
4343 Easton Cmns Ste 150 (43219-6237)
PHONE......................................614 441-9230
Dan Snyder, *Manager*
EMP: 50 **Privately Held**
SIC: 6021 National commercial banks
HQ: Congressional Bank
6701 Democracy Blvd # 400
Bethesda MD 20817
301 299-8810

(G-7349)
CONNAISSANCE CONSULTING LLC
4071 Easton Way (43219-6087)
PHONE......................................614 289-5200
Jeffrey Lussenhop, *CEO*
Harold Williams, *President*
Steven A Minick, *COO*
Tim Bosco, *CFO*
EMP: 113
SQ FT: 4,000
SALES (est): 3.5MM **Privately Held**
SIC: 8748 Business consulting

(G-7350)
CONNOR EVANS HAFENSTEIN LLP
2000 Henderson Rd Ste 460 (43220-2466)
PHONE......................................614 464-2025
Daniel D Connor, *Managing Prtnr*
Robert Behal, *Partner*
EMP: 25 EST: 1970
SQ FT: 8,500
SALES (est): 2.6MM **Privately Held**
WEB: www.connorbehal.com
SIC: 8111 General practice attorney,
lawyer

(G-7351)
CONSOLIDATED ELEC DISTRS INC
C E D
2101 S High St (43207-2428)
PHONE......................................614 445-8871
Jim Bemiller, *Warehouse Mgr*
John Allen, *Sales Staff*
Logan Jones, *Sales Staff*
Shawn Miller, *Sales Staff*
Sean Oneil, *Sales Staff*
EMP: 50
SALES (corp-wide): 1.9B **Privately Held**
SIC: 5063 Electrical supplies
PA: Consolidated Electrical Distributors,
Inc.
1920 Westridge Dr
Irving TX 75038
972 582-5300

(G-7352)
CONSTRUCTION LABOR CONTRS LLC
Also Called: CLC
6155 Huntley Rd Ste G (43229-1096)
PHONE......................................614 932-9937
Steve Dorsey, *General Mgr*
M Columbus, *Executive*
EMP: 100 **Privately Held**
WEB:
www.constructionlaborcontractors.com
SIC: 7361 Labor contractors (employment
agency)
HQ: Construction Labor Contractors, Llc
9760 Shepard Rd
Macedonia OH 44056
330 247-1080

(G-7353)
CONSTRUCTION ONE INC
Also Called: Construction First
101 E Town St Ste 401 (43215-5247)
PHONE......................................614 961-1140
William A Moberger, *President*
Paul Heatherly, *Superintendent*
Tim Hovda, *Superintendent*
Vince Wardle, *Superintendent*
Robert C Moberger, *Corp Secy*
EMP: 30
SQ FT: 7,500
SALES (est): 28.9MM **Privately Held**
SIC: 1542 Commercial & office building,
new construction

(G-7354)
CONSTRUCTION SYSTEMS INC (PA)
2865 E 14th Ave (43219-2301)
PHONE......................................614 252-0708
JD Flaherty Jr, *President*
Andrew Poczik, *Exec VP*
Tim Faherty, *Vice Pres*
Andy Poczik, *Vice Pres*
Ted Roshon, *Vice Pres*
EMP: 68
SQ FT: 4,500
SALES (est): 19.4MM **Privately Held**
WEB: www.consysohio.com
SIC: 1742 Drywall; acoustical & ceiling
work; plastering, plain or ornamental

(G-7355)
CONTAINERPORT GROUP INC
Also Called: Cpg
2400 Creekway Dr (43207-3431)
PHONE......................................440 333-1330
Glenn Fehribach, *Senior VP*
Ioana Sgondea, *Accountant*
Keith Fulk, *Branch Mgr*
Jim Pospishil, *Manager*
Andy Distler, *Supervisor*
EMP: 40
SALES (corp-wide): 274.1MM **Privately Held**
WEB: www.containerport.com
SIC: 4783 4212 4213 Containerization of
goods for shipping; light haulage &
cartage, local; trucking, except local
HQ: Containerport Group, Inc.
1340 Depot St Fl 2
Cleveland OH 44116
440 333-1330

(G-7356)
CONTINENTAL BUILDING COMPANY
150 E Broad St Ste 610 (43215-3628)
PHONE......................................614 221-1800
Todd Alexander, *CEO*
EMP: 75
SALES (est): 1.9MM **Privately Held**
SIC: 1541 Industrial buildings & ware-
houses

(G-7357)
CONTINENTAL BUSINESS SERVICES
Also Called: Continental Mewthod Solutions
41 S Grant Ave Fl 2 (43215-3979)
PHONE......................................614 224-4534
Beau Hamer, *President*
Wendell R Kessler, *Corp Secy*
EMP: 30 EST: 1967
SQ FT: 5,000

SALES (est): 1.2MM **Privately Held**
SIC: 7389 Telephone answering service

(G-7358)
CONTINENTAL OFFICE FURN CORP (PA)
Also Called: Continntal Office Environments
5061 Freeway Dr E (43229-5401)
PHONE......................................614 262-5010
Ira Sharfin, *CEO*
Franklin Kass, *Ch of Bd*
John Lucks Jr, *Ch of Bd*
Kyle Johnson, *President*
Nick Magoto, *Exec VP*
◆ EMP: 150 EST: 1941
SQ FT: 70,000
SALES (est): 110MM **Privately Held**
WEB: www.continentaloffice.com
SIC: 5021 1752 Office furniture; wood
floor installation & refinishing

(G-7359)
CONTINENTAL OFFICE FURN CORP
Continental Office Moves
5063 Freeway Dr E (43229-5401)
PHONE......................................614 781-0080
Tim Conrad, *Manager*
EMP: 50
SALES (corp-wide): 110MM **Privately Held**
WEB: www.continentaloffice.com
SIC: 4212 Moving services
PA: Continental Office Furniture Corpora-
tion
5061 Freeway Dr E
Columbus OH 43229
614 262-5010

(G-7360)
CONTINENTAL PROPERTIES
150 E Broad St Ste 700 (43215-3610)
P.O. Box 712 (43216-0712)
PHONE......................................614 221-1800
Franklin Kass, *Managing Prtnr*
John Lucks Jr, *Partner*
EMP: 300
SALES (est): 21.8MM **Privately Held**
WEB: www.continental-communities.com
SIC: 6512 Commercial & industrial building
operation

(G-7361)
CONTINENTAL RE COMPANIES (PA)
150 E Broad St Ste 200 (43215-3644)
PHONE......................................614 221-1800
Franklin Kass, *Ch of Bd*
John Lucks Jr, *Vice Pres*
James Conway, *CFO*
EMP: 140
SALES (est): 100.7MM **Privately Held**
WEB: www.continental-realestate.com
SIC: 1542 1541 Commercial & office build-
ing, new construction; industrial buildings
& warehouses

(G-7362)
CONTINENTAL REALTY LTD
180 E Broad St Ste 1708 (43215-3727)
PHONE......................................614 221-6260
Angel Robbins, *Manager*
EMP: 29 **Privately Held**
SIC: 6531 Real estate brokers & agents
PA: Continental Realty Ltd
150 E Gay St
Columbus OH 43215

(G-7363)
CONTINENTAL/OLENTANGY HT LLC
1421 Olentangy River Rd (43212-1449)
PHONE......................................614 297-9912
Dena Heinlein, *Director*
EMP: 99
SALES (est): 894.5K **Privately Held**
SIC: 7011 Hotels & motels

(G-7364)
CONTINNTAL MSSAGE SOLUTION INC
Also Called: CMS Customer Solutions
41 S Grant Ave Fl 2 (43215-3979)
PHONE......................................614 224-4534
Beau A Hamer, *President*

EMP: 65
SALES (est): 7.4MM **Privately Held**
SIC: 8741 7299 Circuit management for
motion picture theaters; personal document & information services

(G-7365)
CONTRACT LUMBER INC
200 Schofield Dr (43213-3803)
PHONE......................................614 751-1109
EMP: 60
SALES (corp-wide): 76.6MM **Privately Held**
SIC: 7349 5211 5031 2421 Building
maintenance services; lumber & other
building materials; lumber: rough, dressed
& finished; lumber: rough, sawed or
planed
PA: Contract Lumber, Inc.
3245 Hazelton Etna Rd Sw
Pataskala OH 43062
740 964-3147

(G-7366)
CONTRACT SWEEPERS & EQP CO (PA)
2137 Parkwood Ave (43219-1145)
PHONE......................................614 221-7441
Charles F Glander, *CEO*
Gerald Kesselring, *President*
Robert E Fultz, *Principal*
John C Hartranft, *Principal*
Mark Dusseau, *Vice Pres*
EMP: 50 EST: 1960
SQ FT: 10,000
SALES (est): 58.8MM **Privately Held**
WEB: www.sweepers.com
SIC: 4959 5084 Sweeping service: road,
airport, parking lot, etc.; snowplowing;
cleaning equipment, high pressure, sand
or steam

(G-7367)
COPART INC
1680 Williams Rd (43207-5111)
PHONE......................................614 497-1590
Richard Hulker, *Manager*
EMP: 30
SALES (corp-wide): 1.8B **Publicly Held**
WEB: www.copart.com
SIC: 5012 Automobile auction
PA: Copart, Inc.
14185 Dallas Pkwy Ste 300
Dallas TX 75254
972 391-5000

(G-7368)
COPC HOSPITALS
3555 Olentangy River Rd (43214-3912)
PHONE......................................614 268-8164
Timothy Fallon, *President*
EMP: 27 EST: 2011
SALES (est): 1.9MM **Privately Held**
SIC: 8062 General medical & surgical hos-
pitals

(G-7369)
CORI CARE INC
1060 Kingsmill Pkwy (43229-1143)
PHONE......................................614 848-4357
Candace Allegra, *President*
Jacki Frost, *Admin Asst*
EMP: 55
SALES (est): 2MM **Privately Held**
SIC: 8082 Home health care services

(G-7370)
CORK INC
2006 Kenton St (43205-1655)
PHONE......................................614 253-8400
Charles Blauman, *President*
EMP: 50
SALES (est): 2.7MM **Privately Held**
SIC: 1521 Single-Family House Construc-
tion

(G-7371)
CORPORATE CLEANING INC
781 Northwest Blvd # 103 (43212-3858)
PHONE......................................614 203-6051
Crystal Hughey, *CEO*
Eugene Hughey, *COO*
EMP: 33 EST: 2010

SALES (est): 1.3MM **Privately Held**
SIC: 7699 7349 7342 1542 Cleaning services; building & office cleaning services; building cleaning service; rest room cleaning service; commercial & office building, new construction

(G-7372)
CORPORATE ENVIRONMENTS OF OHIO
Also Called: C E O
2899 Morse Rd (43231-6033)
PHONE...................................614 358-3375
Fax: 614 358-8732
EMP: 43
SQ FT: 33,000
SALES (est): 3.9MM **Privately Held**
SIC: 5712 1799 Office Furniture

(G-7373)
CORPORATE EXCHANGE HOTEL ASSOC
Also Called: Embassy Suites
2700 Corporate Exch Dr (43231-1690)
PHONE...................................614 890-8600
Kendal Clay, *General Ptnr*
EMP: 150
SALES (est): 6.5MM **Privately Held**
SIC: 7011 5812 5813 Hotels; eating places; cocktail lounge

(G-7374)
CORPORATE FIN ASSOC OF CLUMBUS
671 Camden Yard Ct (43235-3492)
PHONE...................................614 457-9219
Charles E Washbush, *President*
EMP: 100
SQ FT: 750
SALES (est): 100MM **Privately Held**
SIC: 8742 7389 6211 Business consultant; brokers, business: buying & selling business enterprises; security brokers & dealers

(G-7375)
CORROSION FLUID PRODUCTS CORP (DH)
3000 E 14th Ave (43219-2355)
PHONE...................................248 478-0100
Joseph V Andronaco, *CEO*
Joseph P Andronaco, *President*
▲ EMP: 30
SQ FT: 28,500
SALES (est): 57.5MM
SALES (corp-wide): 3B **Publicly Held**
WEB: www.corrosionfluid.com
SIC: 5084 5074 Pumps & pumping equipment; pipes & fittings, plastic; plumbing & heating valves
HQ: Fcx Performance, Inc
3000 E 14th Ave
Columbus OH 43219
614 324-6050

(G-7376)
COS EXPRESS INC
3616 Fisher Rd (43228-1012)
PHONE...................................614 276-9000
Charles J Casey Jr, *President*
Ed Weisenberger, *Vice Pres*
EMP: 99
SQ FT: 5,460
SALES (est): 8.3MM **Privately Held**
SIC: 4731 Freight transportation arrangement

(G-7377)
COSMIC CONCEPTS LTD
399 E Main St Ste 140 (43215-5384)
PHONE...................................614 228-1104
Corey Black, *Division Mgr*
John Riddle, *Branch Mgr*
Jennifer Shaw, *Manager*
Kirk Taylor, *Manager*
Megan Mitchell, *Executive Asst*
EMP: 92
SALES (corp-wide): 46MM **Privately Held**
SIC: 8742 Marketing consulting services
PA: Cosmic Concepts, Ltd.
318 Clubhouse Rd
Hunt Valley MD 21031
410 825-8500

(G-7378)
COSTUME SPECIALISTS INC (PA)
211 N 5th St Ste 100 (43215-2603)
PHONE...................................614 464-2115
Wendy C Goldstein, *President*
Greg Manger, *Sales Staff*
Tracy Liberatore, *Admin Asst*
EMP: 36
SQ FT: 34,500
SALES (est): 3.1MM **Privately Held**
WEB: www.cospec.com
SIC: 2389 7299 Theatrical costumes; costume rental

(G-7379)
COTT SYSTEMS INC
2800 Corp Exchange Dr # 300 (43231-1678)
PHONE...................................614 847-4405
Deborah A Ball, *CEO*
Karen L Bailey, *Exec VP*
Jodie Bare, *Vice Pres*
Drew Sheppared, *Vice Pres*
Ron Swords, *Facilities Mgr*
EMP: 77
SQ FT: 20,000
SALES (est): 16.4MM **Privately Held**
WEB: www.cottsystems.com
SIC: 7373 7371 2789 Computer integrated systems design; computer software development & applications; beveling of cards

(G-7380)
COUNTRYSIDE ELECTRIC INC
2920 Switzer Ave (43219-2372)
PHONE...................................614 478-7960
Glen Lehman, *President*
Vicki Lehman, *Corp Secy*
EMP: 25
SALES (est): 4MM **Privately Held**
WEB: www.countrysideelectricinc.com
SIC: 1731 General electrical contractor

(G-7381)
COURTYARD MANAGEMENT CORP
Also Called: Courtyard By Marriott
2901 Airport Dr (43219-2299)
PHONE...................................614 475-8530
Mark Laport, *Manager*
EMP: 50
SALES (corp-wide): 20.7B **Publicly Held**
SIC: 7011 Hotels & motels
HQ: Courtyard Management Corporation
10400 Fernwood Rd
Bethesda MD 20817

(G-7382)
COVENANT HOME HEALTH CARE LLC
5212 W Broad St Ste J (43228-1670)
PHONE...................................614 465-2017
Zina Ali, *Managing Prtnr*
Zeinab A Ali, *Mng Member*
EMP: 30
SALES (est): 654.9K **Privately Held**
SIC: 8082 Home health care services

(G-7383)
COVENANT TRANSPORT INC
3825 Aries Brook Dr (43207-4696)
PHONE...................................423 821-1212
EMP: 71 **Publicly Held**
WEB: www.covenanttransport.com
SIC: 4213 Trucking, except local
HQ: Covenant Transport, Inc.
400 Birmingham Hwy
Chattanooga TN 37419
423 821-1212

(G-7384)
CRABBE BROWN & JAMES LLP (PA)
500 S Front St Ste 1200 (43215-7631)
PHONE...................................614 229-4587
Larry James, *CEO*
Luis M Alcade,
EMP: 50
SALES (est): 7.9MM **Privately Held**
SIC: 8111 Legal Services Office

(G-7385)
CRAWFORD MECHANICAL SVCS INC
3445 Morse Rd (43231-6183)
PHONE...................................614 478-9424
William T Crawford, *President*
Suzette Crawford, *Vice Pres*
Bill Blake, *Project Mgr*
Priscilla Rhoads, *Controller*
EMP: 70
SALES (est): 15.6MM **Privately Held**
WEB: www.crawfordmech.com
SIC: 1711 Plumbing contractors

(G-7386)
CREATIVE LIVING INC
150 W 10th Ave (43201-2093)
PHONE...................................614 421-1131
Todd D Ackerman, *President*
John Lepley, *Trustee*
Ron Mains, *Treasurer*
Marilyn Frank, *Exec Dir*
Jody Orsine Geiger, *Admin Sec*
EMP: 29 EST: 1969
SQ FT: 10,000
SALES: 380.2K **Privately Held**
WEB: www.creative-living.com
SIC: 6513 Retirement hotel operation

(G-7387)
CREATIVE LIVING HOUSING CORP
150 W 10th Ave Ofc (43201-7015)
PHONE...................................614 421-1226
Anne Nagey, *President*
Robert Overs, *Director*
EMP: 25
SQ FT: 10,000
SALES: 414.9K **Privately Held**
SIC: 6513 Apartment building operators

(G-7388)
CREDIT BUR COLLECTN SVCS INC (HQ)
Also Called: Cbcs
236 E Town St (43215-4631)
PHONE...................................614 223-0688
Larry Ebert, *President*
Dirk Cantrell, *Corp Secy*
Christina Barnoli, *Human Res Mgr*
EMP: 50
SQ FT: 60,000
SALES (est): 20MM
SALES (corp-wide): 246.2MM **Privately Held**
SIC: 7322 Collection agency, except real estate
PA: Cbc Companies, Inc.
250 E Broad St Fl 21
Columbus OH 43215
614 222-4343

(G-7389)
CREEKSIDE II LLC
Also Called: Pizzuti
2 Miranova Pl Ste 100 (43215-7003)
PHONE...................................614 280-4000
Ronald Pizzuti, *CEO*
EMP: 45 EST: 1973
SALES (est): 2.4MM **Privately Held**
WEB: www.pizzuti.com
SIC: 6552 Land subdividers & developers, commercial

(G-7390)
CRESTLINE HOTELS & RESORTS LLC
7490 Vantage Dr (43235-1416)
PHONE...................................614 846-4355
Liz Buxton, *Manager*
EMP: 34
SALES (corp-wide): 49.8MM **Privately Held**
SIC: 8741 Hotel or motel management
PA: Crestline Hotels & Resorts, Llc
3950 University Dr # 301
Fairfax VA 22030
571 529-6100

(G-7391)
CRETE CARRIER CORPORATION
5400 Crosswind Dr (43228-3778)
PHONE...................................614 853-4500

Scott Clay, *Manager*
EMP: 150
SALES (corp-wide): 1.1B **Privately Held**
SIC: 4213 Refrigerated products transport
PA: Crete Carrier Corporation
400 Nw 56th St
Lincoln NE 68528
800 998-4095

(G-7392)
CREW SOCCER STADIUM LLC
1 Black And Gold Blvd (43211-2091)
PHONE...................................614 447-2739
Andy Louthnane, *President*
Mark McCullers, *President*
EMP: 50
SALES (est): 3.2MM **Privately Held**
SIC: 7941 Soccer club

(G-7393)
CRITICAL CARE TRANSPORT INC
2936 E 14th Ave (43219-2304)
P.O. Box 360912 (43236-0912)
PHONE...................................614 775-0564
William Staton, *President*
Christian Staton, *Principal*
James Samuell, *Director*
EMP: 60
SALES (est): 2.5MM **Privately Held**
WEB: www.criticalcaretransport.net
SIC: 4119 Ambulance service

(G-7394)
CRITTENTON FAMILY SERVICES
1414 E Broad St (43205-1505)
PHONE...................................614 251-0103
Steve Votow, *Director*
EMP: 35
SQ FT: 3,500
SALES: 7.1MM **Privately Held**
SIC: 8322 Youth center

(G-7395)
CROSSCHX INC
99 E Main St (43215-5115)
PHONE...................................800 501-3161
Sean Lane, *CEO*
Brad Mascho, *President*
Bubba Fox, *COO*
Carlton Fox, *COO*
Ian Gall, *Engineer*
▲ EMP: 73
SQ FT: 5,500
SALES (est): 4.4MM **Privately Held**
SIC: 7371 Computer software development & applications

(G-7396)
CROWE LLP
155 W Nationwide Blvd # 500 (43215-2570)
PHONE...................................614 469-0001
Michael Giammalvo, *Partner*
Bill Watts, *Partner*
Joseph Santucci, *Principal*
Benjamin Hackett, *Finance Mgr*
Valerie Winkler, *Accountant*
EMP: 126
SQ FT: 6,600
SALES (corp-wide): 883.5MM **Privately Held**
SIC: 8721 Certified public accountant
PA: Crowe Llp
225 W Wacker Dr Ste 2600
Chicago IL 60606
312 899-7000

(G-7397)
CROWN DIELECTRIC INDS INC
Also Called: Crown Auto Top Mfg Co
830 W Broad St (43222-1421)
PHONE...................................614 224-5161
Anthony Gurvis, *President*
Andrew M Kauffman, *Principal*
EMP: 105 EST: 1931
SQ FT: 2,000
SALES (est): 6.9MM **Privately Held**
SIC: 2394 2399 2273 5013 Convertible tops, canvas or boat: from purchased materials; seat covers, automobile; automobile floor coverings, except rubber or plastic; automotive supplies & parts; automotive parts

(G-7398)
CRP CONTRACTING
4477 E 5th Ave (43219-1817)
PHONE....................................614 338-8501
James Head, *Partner*
Paul Ondera, *Partner*
EMP: 60
SALES (est): 1.5MM **Privately Held**
SIC: 1611 Airport runway construction

(G-7399)
CS HOTELS LIMITED PARTNERSHIP
Also Called: Courtyard Columbus West
2350 Westbelt Dr (43228-3822)
PHONE....................................614 771-8999
EMP: 75 **Privately Held**
SIC: 7011 Hotels And Motels, Nsk
PA: Cs Hotels Limited Partnership
740 Centre View Blvd
Crestview Hills KY 41017

(G-7400)
CSC DISTRIBUTION INC (HQ)
4900 E Dblin Granville Rd (43081-7651)
PHONE....................................614 278-6800
Michael J Potter, *President*
▲ **EMP:** 25
SALES (est): 140.9MM
SALES (corp-wide): 5.2B **Publicly Held**
SIC: 5092 Toys & games
PA: Big Lots, Inc.
4900 E Dblin Granville Rd
Columbus OH 43081
614 278-6800

(G-7401)
CSL PLASMA INC
2650 N High St (43202-2520)
PHONE....................................614 267-4982
Carmen Fannin, *Branch Mgr*
Angie Funk, *Manager*
Mark Leach, *Assistant*
EMP: 100
SQ FT: 3,000 **Privately Held**
WEB: www.zlbplasma.com
SIC: 8099 Plasmapherous center; blood bank
HQ: Csl Plasma Inc.
900 Broken Sound Pkwy Nw # 4
Boca Raton FL 33487
561 981-3700

(G-7402)
CSX CORPORATION
2600 Parsons Ave (43207-2972)
PHONE....................................614 242-3932
EMP: 1000
SALES (corp-wide): 12.2B **Publicly Held**
SIC: 4789 Pipeline terminal facilities, independently operated
PA: Csx Corporation
500 Water St Fl 15
Jacksonville FL 32202
904 359-3200

(G-7403)
CTD INVESTMENTS LLC (PA)
630 E Broad St (43215-3999)
PHONE....................................614 570-9949
Richard L Gerhardt II,
Stephanie Jandik,
William Lewis,
EMP: 50
SQ FT: 6,000
SALES: 20MM **Privately Held**
SIC: 6799 5999 Investors; electronic parts & equipment

(G-7404)
CTL ENGINEERING INC (PA)
2860 Fisher Rd (43204-3538)
P.O. Box 44548 (43204-0548)
PHONE....................................614 276-8123
C K Satyapriya, *CEO*
David Breitfeller, *Vice Pres*
Ali Jamshidi, *CFO*
Donald S Pierce, *Branch Mgr*
Bipender Jindal, *Admin Sec*
EMP: 120
SQ FT: 35,000

SALES: 36.1MM **Privately Held**
WEB: www.ctleng.com
SIC: 8711 8731 8734 8713 Consulting engineer; commercial physical research; metallurgical testing laboratory; product testing laboratory, safety or performance; forensic laboratory; surveying services

(G-7405)
D & D INVESTMENT CO
Also Called: Columbus Cold Storage
3080 Valleyview Dr (43204-2011)
PHONE....................................614 272-6567
Donald Dick, *Partner*
Daniel Dick, *Partner*
EMP: 50
SALES (est): 3.3MM **Privately Held**
SIC: 4225 4222 5169 5999 General warehousing & storage; warehousing, cold storage or refrigerated; dry ice; ice

(G-7406)
D & J MASTER CLEAN INC
Also Called: Master Clean Carpet & Uphlstry
680 Dearborn Park Ln (43085-5701)
PHONE....................................614 847-1181
Don Kessler, *CEO*
Theresa Kessler, *General Mgr*
Stephanie Kessler, *Corp Secy*
Van Wilcox, *Vice Pres*
Joe Wooster, *Vice Pres*
EMP: 100
SQ FT: 15,000
SALES (est): 7.6MM **Privately Held**
SIC: 7217 7349 Carpet & upholstery cleaning on customer premises; janitorial service, contract basis

(G-7407)
D & S PROPERTIES
Also Called: S & W Properties
854 E Broad St (43205-1110)
PHONE....................................614 224-6663
David L Fisher, *Partner*
Suzanne P Fisher, *Partner*
EMP: 28
SQ FT: 900
SALES: 3.7MM **Privately Held**
SIC: 6513 Apartment hotel operation

(G-7408)
D H I COOPERATIVE INC
1224 Alton Darby Creek Rd A (43228-9813)
P.O. Box 28168 (43228-0168)
PHONE....................................614 545-0460
Tony Broering, *President*
Brian Winters, *General Mgr*
Cathy Strong, *Accounting Mgr*
EMP: 65 EST: 1969
SQ FT: 7,200
SALES (est): 6.1MM **Privately Held**
WEB: www.dhiohio.com
SIC: 0762 Farm management services

(G-7409)
D L A TRAINING CENTER
3990 E Broad St Bldg 11 (43213-1152)
PHONE....................................614 692-5986
Kathleen Tuskas, *Director*
EMP: 100 EST: 1999
SALES (est): 4.5MM **Privately Held**
SIC: 8742 Training & development consultant

(G-7410)
D M I DISTRIBUTION INC
6150 Huntley Rd Ste A (43229-1000)
PHONE....................................765 584-3234
Ray Waudby, *Warehouse Mgr*
Roger Stewart, *Manager*
EMP: 35 **Privately Held**
WEB: www.dmidistribution.com
SIC: 4225 5084 General warehousing & storage; brewery products manufacturing machinery, commercial
PA: D M I Distribution, Inc.
990 Industrial Park Dr
Winchester IN 47394

(G-7411)
DAILY SERVICES LLC (PA)
1110 Morse Rd Ste B1 (43229-6325)
PHONE....................................614 431-5100
Ryan Cote, *President*
Rick Fazzina, *CFO*

Ryan Mason, *Mng Member*
EMP: 250
SQ FT: 2,000
SALES (est): 22.3MM **Privately Held**
SIC: 7361 Executive placement

(G-7412)
DAN TOBIN PONTIAC BUICK GMC
Also Called: Tobin, Dan Pontiac
2539 Billingsley Rd (43235-5975)
PHONE....................................614 889-6300
Daniel L Tobin, *CEO*
Craig Sims, *Business Mgr*
Adam Cottrill, *Finance Mgr*
Keith Chambers, *Sales Mgr*
Marc Cox, *Sales Mgr*
EMP: 85
SQ FT: 40,000
SALES (est): 34.4MM **Privately Held**
WEB: www.dantobin.com
SIC: 5511 7538 7532 5521 Automobiles, new & used; general automotive repair shops; top & body repair & paint shops; used car dealers

(G-7413)
DANA & PARISER ATTYS
495 E Mound St (43215-5596)
PHONE....................................614 253-1010
David Pariser, *Owner*
EMP: 40
SALES (est): 4.1MM **Privately Held**
WEB: www.dplawyers.com
SIC: 8111 General practice attorney, lawyer

(G-7414)
DANCOR INC
2155 Dublin Rd (43228-9668)
PHONE....................................614 340-2155
Dan Fronk, *CEO*
Melissa Tassie, *Vice Pres*
Nick Malagreca, *Sales Mgr*
Neil Patel, *Info Tech Mgr*
Ryan Connor, *Technology*
EMP: 35
SQ FT: 20,000
SALES (est): 4.9MM **Privately Held**
WEB: www.dancorinc.com
SIC: 8748 Business consulting

(G-7415)
DANIEL LOGISTICS INC
426 Mccormick Blvd (43213-1525)
PHONE....................................614 367-9442
Ellen Cathers, *President*
Mick Bolon, *General Mgr*
Gay Cathers, *Corp Secy*
Seth Lingo, *Facilities Mgr*
EMP: 75
SQ FT: 14,000
SALES (est): 4.7MM **Privately Held**
WEB: www.daniellogistics.com
SIC: 4225 General warehousing

(G-7416)
DANITE HOLDINGS LTD
Also Called: Danite Sign Co
1640 Harmon Ave (43223-3321)
PHONE....................................614 444-3333
Tim McCord, *President*
C William Klausman, *Partner*
James Detty, *Project Mgr*
Jill Waddell, *Sales Executive*
Noah Brown, *Manager*
EMP: 50
SQ FT: 33,500
SALES (est): 8.1MM **Privately Held**
WEB: www.danitesign.com
SIC: 3993 1799 Electric signs; neon signs; sign installation & maintenance

(G-7417)
DAR PLUMBING
Also Called: D A R Plumbing
2230 Refugee Rd (43207-2843)
P.O. Box 7791 (43207-0791)
PHONE....................................614 445-8243
Don Hughes, *Owner*
EMP: 27
SQ FT: 1,500
SALES (est): 2.3MM **Privately Held**
SIC: 1711 Plumbing contractors

(G-7418)
DAVEY TREE EXPERT COMPANY
3567 Westerville Rd (43224)
PHONE....................................330 673-9511
James Serdy, *Branch Mgr*
Keary Doon, *Manager*
EMP: 60
SALES (corp-wide): 1B **Privately Held**
SIC: 0783 Ornamental shrub & tree services
PA: The Davey Tree Expert Company
1500 N Mantua St
Kent OH 44240
330 673-9511

(G-7419)
DAVEY TREE EXPERT COMPANY
Also Called: Davey Tree and Lawn Care
3603 Westerville Rd (43224-2538)
PHONE....................................614 471-4144
Tom Bowman, *Manager*
EMP: 55
SQ FT: 1,445
SALES (corp-wide): 1B **Privately Held**
SIC: 0782 0783 Landscape contractors; ornamental shrub & tree services
PA: The Davey Tree Expert Company
1500 N Mantua St
Kent OH 44240
330 673-9511

(G-7420)
DAWSON RESOURCES (PA)
Also Called: Dawson Personnel Systems
1114 Dublin Rd (43215-1039)
PHONE....................................614 255-1400
Michael Linton, *President*
Christopher Decapua, *Principal*
David Decapua, *Principal*
Phillip Freeman, *Senior VP*
EMP: 45
SQ FT: 5,000
SALES (est): 38.4MM **Privately Held**
WEB: www.dawsonworks.com
SIC: 7361 7363 Placement agencies; temporary help service; employee leasing service; office help supply service

(G-7421)
DAWSON RESOURCES
Also Called: Dawson Personnel
4184 W Broad St (43228-1671)
PHONE....................................614 274-8900
Maurine Kenneley, *Branch Mgr*
EMP: 386
SALES (corp-wide): 38.4MM **Privately Held**
WEB: www.dawsonworks.com
SIC: 7361 Employment agencies
PA: Dawson Resources
1114 Dublin Rd
Columbus OH 43215
614 255-1400

(G-7422)
DAYTON FREIGHT LINES INC
1406 Blatt Blvd (43230-6627)
PHONE....................................614 860-1080
Grey Armstrong, *Manager*
EMP: 30
SALES (corp-wide): 971MM **Privately Held**
SIC: 4213 Trucking, except local
PA: Dayton Freight Lines, Inc.
6450 Poe Ave Ste 311
Dayton OH 45414
937 264-4060

(G-7423)
DAYTON HEIDELBERG DISTRG CO
3801 Parkwest Dr (43228-1457)
PHONE....................................614 308-0400
Greg Maurer, *Branch Mgr*
EMP: 200
SALES (corp-wide): 369.4MM **Privately Held**
SIC: 5182 5181 Wine; beer & ale
PA: Dayton Heidelberg Distributing Co.
3601 Dryden Rd
Moraine OH 45439
937 222-8692

(G-7424)
DB&P LOGISTICS INC
3544 Watkins Rd (43232-5544)
P.O. Box 32335 (43232-0335)
PHONE...............................614 491-4035
Danie Barke, *Principal*
EMP: 30
SALES (est): 1.5MM **Privately Held**
WEB: www.pemberton-inc.com
SIC: 7011 Hotels

(G-7425)
DDR CORP
445 Hutchinson Ave # 800 (43235-5677)
PHONE...............................614 785-6445
Steve Eroskey, *Principal*
EMP: 50
SALES (corp-wide): 707.2MM **Privately Held**
WEB: www.ddrc.com
SIC: 6798 Real estate investment trusts
PA: Site Centers Corp.
　3300 Enterprise Pkwy
　Beachwood OH 44122
　216 755-5500

(G-7426)
DEARTH MANAGEMENT COMPANY (PA)
Also Called: Morning View Care Center
134 Northwoods Blvd Ste C (43235-4727)
P.O. Box 10, Marengo (43334-0010)
PHONE...............................614 847-1070
Glen H Dearth, *Administration*
EMP: 217
SQ FT: 10,000
SALES (est): 12.3MM **Privately Held**
WEB: www.schoenbrunnhealthcare.com
SIC: 8052 8741 Personal care facility; management services

(G-7427)
DEDICATED TECHNOLOGIES INC
175 S 3rd St Ste 200 (43215-5194)
PHONE...............................614 460-3200
Jeffrey P Dalton, *President*
Patricia Lickliter, *Vice Pres*
Kevin Kinlin, *Project Mgr*
Shadyne Nunley, *Project Mgr*
Jessica Berridge, *Business Anlyst*
EMP: 82
SQ FT: 7,000
SALES (est): 8.6MM **Privately Held**
WEB: www.dedicatedtech.com
SIC: 8742 7361 8748 Industry specialist consultants; placement agencies; business consulting

(G-7428)
DEFENSE FIN & ACCOUNTING SVC
3990 E Broad St (43213-1152)
PHONE...............................410 436-9740
Paul Fincato, *Principal*
EMP: 50
SALES (est): 10.4MM **Privately Held**
SIC: 8721 Accounting, auditing & bookkeeping

(G-7429)
DEFENSE FIN & ACCOUNTING SVC
Also Called: West Entitlement Operations
3990 E Broad St (43213-1152)
PHONE...............................614 693-6700
Johnathan Witter, *Director*
EMP: 2900 **Publicly Held**
WEB: www.osd.pentagon.mil
SIC: 8721 9711 Accounting services, except auditing; national security;
HQ: Defense Finance & Accounting Service
　8899 E 56th St
　Indianapolis IN 46249

(G-7430)
DEFENSE INFO SYSTEMS AGCY
Also Called: D I S A D E C C Columbus
3990 E Broad St Bldg 20c (43213-1152)
PHONE...............................614 692-4433
Michael Robertson, *Director*
EMP: 153 **Publicly Held**
WEB: www.scott.disa.mil
SIC: 6411 Insurance agents, brokers & service

HQ: Defense Information Systems Agency
　6910 Cooper Rd
　Fort Meade MD 20755

(G-7431)
DEL MONTE FRESH PRODUCE NA INC
2200 Westbelt Dr (43228-3820)
PHONE...............................614 527-7398
Andrew Pschesang, *Manager*
EMP: 30 **Privately Held**
SIC: 5148 Fruits, fresh
HQ: Del Monte Fresh Produce N.A., Inc.
　241 Sevilla Ave
　Coral Gables FL 33134
　305 520-8400

(G-7432)
DELILLE OXYGEN COMPANY (PA)
772 Marion Rd (43207-2595)
P.O. Box 7809 (43207-0809)
PHONE...............................614 444-1177
Joseph R Smith, *Ch of Bd*
Tom Smith, *President*
Richard F Carlile, *Principal*
Jim Smith, *Vice Pres*
Tim Hefner, *Sales Staff*
EMP: 30
SQ FT: 20,000
SALES (est): 19.8MM **Privately Held**
WEB: www.delille.com
SIC: 2813 5085 Acetylene; welding supplies

(G-7433)
DELOITTE & TOUCHE LLP
180 E Broad St Ste 1400 (43215-3611)
PHONE...............................614 221-1000
John McEwan, *Branch Mgr*
EMP: 250
SALES (corp-wide): 6.2B **Privately Held**
WEB: www.deloitte.com
SIC: 8721 Accounting services, except auditing; certified public accountant
HQ: Deloitte & Touche Llp
　30 Rockefeller Plz # 4350
　New York NY 10112
　212 492-4000

(G-7434)
DELTA AIR LINES INC
Also Called: Delta Airlines
4600 Intl Gtwy Ste 6 (43219)
PHONE...............................614 239-4440
Felix Sciuloi, *General Mgr*
EMP: 53
SALES (corp-wide): 44.4B **Publicly Held**
WEB: www.delta.com
SIC: 4512 Air passenger carrier, scheduled
PA: Delta Air Lines, Inc.
　1030 Delta Blvd
　Atlanta GA 30354
　404 715-2600

(G-7435)
DENT MAGIC
4629 Poth Rd (43213-1329)
PHONE...............................614 864-3368
David Bradley Miller, *Owner*
EMP: 26
SALES (est): 729.8K **Privately Held**
SIC: 7532 Body shop, automotive

(G-7436)
DENTAL FACILITY
Also Called: Dental Agent
305 W 12th Ave Rm 1159 (43210-1267)
PHONE...............................614 292-1472
Paul Casamassimo, *President*
EMP: 50
SALES (est): 9MM **Privately Held**
WEB: www.dentalfacility.com
SIC: 8021 Dentists' office

(G-7437)
DEPUY PAVING INC
1850 Mckinley Ave (43222-1004)
PHONE...............................614 272-0256
Clyde Depuy, *President*
Laura Depuy, *Vice Pres*
EMP: 25
SQ FT: 6,400
SALES (est): 3.2MM **Privately Held**
SIC: 1771 Blacktop (asphalt) work

(G-7438)
DESIGN CENTRAL INC
6464 Presidential Gtwy (43231-7673)
PHONE...............................614 890-0202
Rainer Teufel, *Chairman*
Diana Juratovac, *Vice Pres*
Jay Perkins, *Vice Pres*
EMP: 35
SQ FT: 13,000
SALES (est): 3.9MM **Privately Held**
WEB: www.design-central.com
SIC: 7389 Design, commercial & industrial

(G-7439)
DEVCARE SOLUTIONS LTD
131 N High St Ste 640 (43215-3079)
PHONE...............................614 221-2277
Janaki Thiru, *President*
Ramkumar Regupathy, *Bus Dvlpt Dir*
EMP: 47
SQ FT: 600
SALES (est): 7.3MM **Privately Held**
SIC: 8748 7371 7373 Systems engineering consultant, ex. computer or professional; custom computer programming services; systems engineering, computer related; office computer automation systems integration

(G-7440)
DEVELPMNTAL DSBLTIES OHIO DEPT
Also Called: Youngstown Developmental Ctr
30 E Broad St Fl 8 (43215-3414)
PHONE...............................330 544-2231
Cynthia Renner, *Superintendent*
Pat Negro, *Director*
EMP: 245 **Privately Held**
SIC: 8361 9431 Home for the mentally retarded;
HQ: Ohio Department Of Developmental Disabilities
　30 E Broad St Fl 13
　Columbus OH 43215

(G-7441)
DEVELPMNTAL DSBLTIES OHIO DEPT
Also Called: Columbus Developmental Center
1601 W Broad St (43222-1054)
PHONE...............................614 272-0509
Charles Flowers, *Manager*
EMP: 350 **Privately Held**
SIC: 8063 8052 9431 Psychiatric hospitals; intermediate care facilities;
HQ: Ohio Department Of Developmental Disabilities
　30 E Broad St Fl 13
　Columbus OH 43215

(G-7442)
DEVELPMNTAL DSBLTIES OHIO DEPT
Also Called: Montgomery Developmental Ctr
30 E Broad St Fl 8 (43215-3414)
PHONE...............................937 233-8108
Greg Darling, *Superintendent*
EMP: 200 **Privately Held**
SIC: 8322 9431 Individual/Family Services Administrative Public Health Programs
HQ: Ohio Department Of Developmental Disabilities
　30 E Broad St Fl 13
　Columbus OH 43215

(G-7443)
DEVRY UNIVERSITY INC
1350 Alum Creek Dr (43209-2705)
PHONE...............................614 251-6969
Scarlett Howery, *President*
EMP: 225
SQ FT: 92,000
SALES (corp-wide): 350.9MM **Privately Held**
WEB: www.devryuniversity.com
SIC: 8742 8221 Human resource consulting services; university
HQ: Devry University, Inc.
　3005 Highland Pkwy # 700
　Downers Grove IL 60515
　630 515-7700

(G-7444)
DIAMOND HILL CAPITAL MGT INC
325 John H Mcconnell Blvd (43215-2672)
PHONE...............................614 255-3333
Ric Dillon, *President*
Lisa M Wesolek, *COO*
Richard Snowdon, *Vice Pres*
Harsh Acharya, *Research*
Tyler Ventura, *Research*
EMP: 45
SALES (est): 9MM **Publicly Held**
SIC: 6282 Investment advisory service
PA: Diamond Hill Investment Group, Inc.
　325 John H Mcconnell Blvd # 200
　Columbus OH 43215

(G-7445)
DIAMOND HILL FUNDS
325 John H Mcconnell Blvd # 200 (43215-2677)
PHONE...............................614 255-3333
Roderick Dillon, *Partner*
EMP: 30
SQ FT: 8,000
SALES (est): 4.1MM **Privately Held**
SIC: 6282 Investment advisory service

(G-7446)
DIGICO IMAGING INC
Also Called: DCI
3487 E Fulton St (43227-1126)
PHONE...............................614 239-5200
Ira Nutis, *President*
Steve Spain, *Vice Pres*
Cindy Adams, *Project Mgr*
Michael Eyer, *Prdtn Mgr*
Tred Rowland, *CIO*
▲ **EMP:** 75 **EST:** 1997
SQ FT: 14,454
SALES (est): 12.4MM
SALES (corp-wide): 86.5MM **Privately Held**
WEB: www.digicoimaging.com
SIC: 7384 Photofinishing laboratory
PA: Nutis Press, Inc.
　3540 E Fulton St
　Columbus OH 43227
　614 237-8626

(G-7447)
DIRECTIONS FOR YOUTH FAMILIES
657 S Ohio Ave (43205-2743)
PHONE...............................614 258-8043
John Cervi, *Program Dir*
EMP: 34
SALES (corp-wide): 7.4MM **Privately Held**
SIC: 8322 Youth center
PA: Directions For Youth & Families Inc
　1515 Indianola Ave
　Columbus OH 43201
　614 294-2661

(G-7448)
DIRECTIONS FOR YOUTH FAMILIES
3840 Kimberly Pkwy N (43232-4232)
PHONE...............................614 694-0203
EMP: 27
SALES (corp-wide): 7.4MM **Privately Held**
SIC: 8322 Youth center
PA: Directions For Youth & Families Inc
　1515 Indianola Ave
　Columbus OH 43201
　614 294-2661

(G-7449)
DIRECTIONS FOR YOUTH FAMILIES (PA)
1515 Indianola Ave (43201-2118)
PHONE...............................614 294-2661
Duane Casares, *CEO*
Patricia Lassiter, *Marketing Staff*
James Ramage, *Program Mgr*
Gary Smith, *Program Mgr*
Alvin Parker, *Manager*
EMP: 50
SQ FT: 1,000
SALES: 7.4MM **Privately Held**
WEB: www.directionsforyouth.org
SIC: 8322 General counseling services

2019 Harris Ohio
Services Directory

▲ = Import ▼=Export
◆ =Import/Export

(G-7450)
DISPATCH CONSUMER SERVICES (HQ)
Also Called: Dispatch Color Press
5300 Crosswind Dr (43228-3600)
PHONE....................................740 548-5555
John Curtain, President
Clyde C Bourne, VP Sales
Floyd V Jones, Director
EMP: 30
SQ FT: 63,000
SALES (est): 5.4MM
SALES (corp-wide): 651.9MM Privately Held
SIC: 7319 Distribution of advertising material or sample services
PA: The Dispatch Printing Company
62 E Broad St
Columbus OH 43215
614 461-5000

(G-7451)
DISPATCH PRINTING COMPANY (PA)
Also Called: Columbus Dispatch, The
62 E Broad St (43215-3503)
PHONE....................................614 461-5000
Michael J Fiorile, CEO
John F Wolfe, Ch of Bd
Joseph Y Gallo, President
J H Peterson Et Al, Principal
Joseph J Gill, Principal
EMP: 600
SQ FT: 200,000
SALES (est): 651.9MM Privately Held
WEB: www.columbusdispatch.com
SIC: 4833 Television broadcasting stations

(G-7452)
DISPATCH PRODUCTIONS INC
770 Twin Rivers Dr (43215-1127)
PHONE....................................614 460-3700
Michael Fiorile, President
Tom Greece Dorn, General Mgr
John Butte, Vice Pres
EMP: 80
SALES (est): 3.1MM
SALES (corp-wide): 651.9MM Privately Held
WEB: www.dispatchbroadcast.com
SIC: 8999 Radio & television announcing
PA: The Dispatch Printing Company
62 E Broad St
Columbus OH 43215
614 461-5000

(G-7453)
DIST-TRANS INC
1580 Williams Rd (43207-5183)
PHONE....................................614 497-1660
John E Ness, President
Noel Johnson, General Mgr
Robert E Ness, Chairman
Theodore Waltz, Corp Secy
John Ness, Vice Pres
EMP: 110 EST: 1978
SQ FT: 50,000
SALES (est): 244.1K
SALES (corp-wide): 266.3K Privately Held
SIC: 4213 Trucking, except local
PA: Jebren, Inc
1580 Williams Rd
Columbus OH 43207
614 497-1660

(G-7454)
DIVERSIFIED HEALTH MANAGEMENT
3569 Refugee Rd Ste C (43232-9306)
PHONE....................................614 338-8888
Alex Thommasathit, CEO
Alexander Phommasathit, Administration
EMP: 26 EST: 2013
SALES (est): 1.2MM Privately Held
SIC: 8082 Home health care services

(G-7455)
DIVERSITY SEARCH GROUP LLC
2550 Corp Exchange Dr # 15 (43231-1660)
PHONE....................................614 352-2988
Teresa Sherald, CEO
EMP: 273

SALES (est): 14.5MM Privately Held
WEB: www.diversitysearchgroup.com
SIC: 7361 Executive placement

(G-7456)
DIVINE HEALTHCARE SERVICES LLC
2374 E Dublin Granvl Rd (43229-3507)
PHONE....................................614 899-6767
Sheillah Sowah, Owner
EMP: 50
SALES (est): 302.7K Privately Held
SIC: 8099 Health & allied services

(G-7457)
DIVISION DRNKING GROUND WATERS
Also Called: Ddhew
50 W Town St Ste 700 (43215-4173)
PHONE....................................614 644-2752
Mike Baker, Chief
Chris Korleski, Director
EMP: 65
SALES (est): 418.3K Privately Held
SIC: 8641 1711 Environmental protection organization; plumbing, heating, air-conditioning contractors

(G-7458)
DIVISION OF GEOLOGICAL SURVEY
2045 Morse Rd Bldg C (43229-6693)
PHONE....................................614 265-6576
Michael Angle, Principal
Thomas Serenko, Chief
EMP: 30 EST: 2010
SALES (est): 108.9K Privately Held
SIC: 8713 Surveying services

(G-7459)
DLZ AMERICAN DRILLING INC
6121 Huntley Rd (43229-1003)
PHONE....................................614 888-0040
James May, Treasurer
EMP: 26
SALES (est): 1.3MM
SALES (corp-wide): 93MM Privately Held
SIC: 8711 Consulting engineer
PA: Dlz Corporation
6121 Huntley Rd
Columbus OH 43229
614 888-0040

(G-7460)
DLZ CONSTRUCTION SERVICES INC
6121 Huntley Rd (43229-1003)
PHONE....................................614 888-0040
Vikram Rajadhyaksha, CEO
EMP: 48
SQ FT: 80,000
SALES: 10MM
SALES (corp-wide): 93MM Privately Held
SIC: 8711 Engineering services
HQ: Dlz National, Inc.
6121 Huntley Rd
Columbus OH 43229

(G-7461)
DLZ NATIONAL INC (HQ)
6121 Huntley Rd (43229-1003)
PHONE....................................614 888-0040
Vikram Rajadhyaksha, CEO
Ram V Rajadhyaksha, Info Tech Dir
EMP: 25
SQ FT: 80,000
SALES (est): 13.5MM
SALES (corp-wide): 93MM Privately Held
WEB: www.dlznational.com
SIC: 8711 Consulting engineer
PA: Dlz Corporation
6121 Huntley Rd
Columbus OH 43229
614 888-0040

(G-7462)
DLZ OHIO INC (HQ)
6121 Huntley Rd (43229-1003)
PHONE....................................614 888-0040
A James Siebert, President
Vikram Rajadhyaksha, Chairman
P V Rajadhyaksha, COO

David Cutlip, Vice Pres
John Sprouse, Engineer
EMP: 200
SQ FT: 45,000
SALES (est): 24.6MM
SALES (corp-wide): 93MM Privately Held
SIC: 8711 1382 8712 8713 Consulting engineer; civil engineering; geophysical exploration, oil & gas field; architectural services; surveying services
PA: Dlz Corporation
6121 Huntley Rd
Columbus OH 43229
614 888-0040

(G-7463)
DNO INC
3650 E 5th Ave (43219-1805)
PHONE....................................614 231-3601
Anthony Dinovo, President
Carol Dinovo, Vice Pres
EMP: 80
SQ FT: 10,000
SALES: 24MM Privately Held
WEB: www.dnoinc.com
SIC: 2099 5148 Salads, fresh or refrigerated; fruits, fresh

(G-7464)
DOCTORS OHIOHEALTH CORPORATION (HQ)
Also Called: Doctors Hospital North
5100 W Broad St (43228-1607)
PHONE....................................614 544-5424
David Blom, CEO
Michael Bernstein, Senior VP
Steve Garlock, Senior VP
Cheryl Herbert, Senior VP
Ed Cotter, Vice Pres
EMP: 100
SQ FT: 270,000
SALES (est): 389.5MM
SALES (corp-wide): 4B Privately Held
SIC: 8062 8011 Hospital, medical school affiliated with residency; medical insurance plan
PA: Ohiohealth Corporation
180 E Broad St
Columbus OH 43215
614 788-8860

(G-7465)
DOCUMENT SOLUTIONS OHIO LLC
Also Called: Document Solutions Group
100 E Campus View Blvd # 105 (43235-4647)
PHONE....................................614 846-2400
Jeff Lacy,
Mitch Brown,
Michael Tutko Jr,
EMP: 45
SQ FT: 3,500
SALES (est): 3.8MM Privately Held
SIC: 5044 Copying equipment

(G-7466)
DONALD BOWEN AND ASSOC DDS
2575 W Broad St Unit 3 (43204-3333)
PHONE....................................614 274-0454
Donald Bowen, Owner
EMP: 45
SALES (est): 828.5K Privately Held
SIC: 8021 Dentists' office

(G-7467)
DOOLEY HEATING AND AC LLC
2010 Zettler Rd (43232-3834)
PHONE....................................614 278-9944
Brian Dooley, Mng Member
EMP: 31
SALES (est): 3MM Privately Held
WEB: www.dooleyheating.com
SIC: 1711 Warm air heating & air conditioning contractor

(G-7468)
DOUBLE Z CONSTRUCTION COMPANY
2550 Harrison Rd (43204-3510)
PHONE....................................614 274-9334
David Guzzo, President
Larry Lyons, Vice Pres

John T Stinson, Vice Pres
Vince Guzzo, Chief Engr
Vincent M Guzzo, Chief Engr
EMP: 60
SQ FT: 6,500
SALES (est): 14.2MM Privately Held
SIC: 1611 Highway & street construction

(G-7469)
DOVE BUILDING SERVICES INC
1691 Cleveland Ave (43211-2558)
PHONE....................................614 299-4700
Vernon L Gibson, President
EMP: 70 EST: 1977
SQ FT: 2,500
SALES (est): 2.9MM Privately Held
SIC: 7349 Janitorial service, contract basis

(G-7470)
DRS PAUL BOYLES & KENNEDY
Also Called: Paul, Elaine MD
3545 Olentangy River Rd (43214-3907)
PHONE....................................614 734-3347
Elaine Paul, President
EMP: 35
SALES (est): 714.9K Privately Held
SIC: 8011 Gynecologist

(G-7471)
DRURY HOTELS COMPANY LLC
Also Called: Drury Inn & Suites Clmbus Conv
88 E Nationwide Blvd (43215-2576)
PHONE....................................614 221-7008
Scott Bosak, Manager
EMP: 31
SALES (corp-wide): 397.7MM Privately Held
WEB: www.druryhotels.com
SIC: 7011 Hotels
PA: Drury Hotels Company, Llc
721 Emerson Rd Ste 400
Saint Louis MO 63141
314 429-2255

(G-7472)
DRY IT RITE LLC
Also Called: Rite Way Restoration
4330 Groves Rd (43232-4103)
PHONE....................................614 295-8135
John Phillippi,
EMP: 29
SALES: 2.5MM Privately Held
SIC: 1521 General remodeling, single-family houses

(G-7473)
DUANE MORRIS LLP
200 N High St (43215-2416)
PHONE....................................937 424-7086
Kathleen Deland, Branch Mgr
EMP: 36
SALES (corp-wide): 300MM Privately Held
SIC: 8111 General practice attorney, lawyer
PA: Duane Morris Llp
30 S 17th St Fl 5
Philadelphia PA 19103
215 979-1000

(G-7474)
DUBLIN CLEANERS INC (PA)
6845 Caine Rd (43235-4234)
PHONE....................................614 764-9934
Gregory J Butler, President
Ryan Brown, Manager
EMP: 55
SQ FT: 12,000
SALES (est): 2.6MM Privately Held
WEB: www.dublincleaners.com
SIC: 7216 Cleaning & dyeing, except rugs

(G-7475)
DUMMEN GROUP (HQ)
250 S High St Ste 650 (43215-4630)
PHONE....................................614 850-9551
Frank Magnusson, CFO
Alejandro Chacon, Manager
▲ EMP: 25
SALES: 884.5K
SALES (corp-wide): 39MM Privately Held
WEB: www.ecke.com
SIC: 0181 5193 Flowers grown in field nurseries; flowers & florists' supplies

GEOGRAPHIC

PA: Dummen Na, Inc.
250 S High St Ste 650
Columbus OH 43215
614 850-9551

(G-7476)
DUMMEN NA INC (PA)
Also Called: Ecke Ranch
250 S High St Ste 650 (43215-4630)
PHONE...........................614 850-9551
Paul Ecke, Ch of Bd
▲ EMP: 57
SQ FT: 1,500,000
SALES (est): 39MM Privately Held
SIC: 0181 Flowers grown in field nurseries

(G-7477)
DUNBAR ARMORED INC
2300 Citygate Dr Unit B (43219-3665)
PHONE...........................614 475-1969
Matthew Lytle, Manager
EMP: 35
SALES (corp-wide): 3.4B Publicly Held
WEB: www.dunbararmored.com
SIC: 7381 Armored car services
HQ: Dunbar Armored, Inc.
50 Schilling Rd
Hunt Valley MD 21031
410 584-9800

(G-7478)
DURABLE SLATE CO (PA)
Also Called: Durable Slate Company, The
3933 Groves Rd (43232-4138)
PHONE...........................614 299-5522
Michael Chan, CEO
John Chan, Vice Pres
Ed Delong, Shareholder
▲ EMP: 70
SQ FT: 14,000
SALES (est): 21.5MM Privately Held
WEB: www.durableslate.com
SIC: 1761 Roofing contractor; roof repair;
sheet metalwork

(G-7479)
DUTYS TOWING
Also Called: Duty's Towing & Auto Service
3288 E Broad St (43213-1006)
PHONE...........................614 252-3336
EMP: 30
SALES (est): 1.1MM Privately Held
SIC: 7549 Automotive Towing Service

(G-7480)
DYNALECTRIC COMPANY
1762 Dividend Dr (43228-3845)
PHONE...........................614 529-7500
Brad Baker, Manager
EMP: 35
SALES (corp-wide): 8.1B Publicly Held
WEB: www.dyna-fl.com
SIC: 1731 General electrical contractor
HQ: Dynalectric Company
22930 Shaw Rd Ste 100
Dulles VA 20166
703 288-2866

(G-7481)
DYNAMITE TECHNOLOGIES
LLC (PA)
274 Marconi Blvd Ste 300 (43215-2363)
PHONE...........................614 538-0095
Matt Dopkiss, Managing Prtnr
Heather Tutt, Controller
Kylie Hammons, Accounts Mgr
Steve Funk, Marketing Staff
Matthew Dopkiss, Mng Member
EMP: 80
SALES (est): 9.9MM Privately Held
SIC: 7371 Custom computer programming
services

(G-7482)
DYNAMIX ENGINEERING LTD
855 Grandview Ave Ste 300 (43215-1193)
PHONE...........................614 443-1178
Eugene Griffin, Partner
Todd Mace, Partner
Stuart Hill, Project Mgr
Adam Grubb, Engineer
Alexander Hume, Engineer
EMP: 55
SQ FT: 10,000

SALES (est): 8.9MM Privately Held
WEB: www.dynamix-ltd.com
SIC: 8711 Civil engineering

(G-7483)
DYNOTEC INC
2931 E Dublin Granv Rd (43231)
PHONE...........................614 880-7320
Tobias A Iloka, President
Mike Welch, Vice Pres
Alphonso Kolliesuah, Engineer
Vicky Henry, CFO
Jack Fravel, Accountant
EMP: 40
SQ FT: 1,000
SALES: 5MM Privately Held
SIC: 8711 Civil engineering; consulting engineer

(G-7484)
E M COLUMBUS LLC
Also Called: Eastland Mall
2740 Eastland Mall Ste B (43232-4959)
PHONE...........................614 861-3232
Holly Dozer, General Mgr
Herb Glimcher, Mng Member
EMP: 33
SALES (est): 1.8MM
SALES (corp-wide): 3.1MM Privately Held
WEB: www.shopeastland-oh.com
SIC: 6531 Real estate managers
PA: Glimcher Realty Trust
2740 Eastland Mall Ste B
Columbus OH 43232
614 861-3232

(G-7485)
E P FERRIS & ASSOCIATES INC
880 King Ave (43212-2654)
PHONE...........................614 299-2999
Edward P Ferris, President
Kay Ferris, Admin Sec
EMP: 25
SALES (est): 2.6MM Privately Held
WEB: www.epferris.com
SIC: 8711 8713 Civil engineering; surveying services

(G-7486)
E RETAILING ASSOCIATES LLC
Also Called: Customized Girl
2282 Westbrooke Dr (43228-9416)
PHONE...........................614 300-5785
Cindy Terapak, Cust Mgr
Taj Schaffnit, Mng Member
Marty Laroche, CTO
Jeff Benzenberg, Director
Kurt J Schmalz,
EMP: 64
SALES (est): 8.6MM Privately Held
WEB: www.customisegirl.com
SIC: 8748 5961 2253 Business consulting; ; T-shirts & tops, knit

(G-7487)
E WYNN INC
Also Called: Columbus Window Cleaning Co
1851 S High St (43207-2372)
P.O. Box 2201 (43216-2201)
PHONE...........................614 444-5288
Lynn Elliott, President
Neil Schultz, President
James Waddy, Sales Executive
Rezella Fraley, Manager
EMP: 30
SQ FT: 7,000
SALES (est): 1.2MM Privately Held
WEB: www.columbuswindowcleaning.com
SIC: 7349 Window cleaning; building
cleaning service

(G-7488)
EARLY CHILDHOOD LEARNING
COMMU
4141 Rudy Rd (43214-2943)
PHONE...........................614 451-6418
Becky Love, Director
Sally Harrington, Deputy Dir
EMP: 65
SALES (est): 701K Privately Held
SIC: 8351 Child day care services

(G-7489)
EASTERN HORIZON INC
Also Called: Urban Express Transportation
1640 E 5th Ave (43219-2554)
PHONE...........................614 253-7000
Qeis M Atieh, President
EMP: 45
SQ FT: 3,000
SALES (est): 1.6MM Privately Held
WEB: www.urbanexpress.biz
SIC: 4119 Limousine rental, with driver

(G-7490)
EASTLAND CRANE SERVICE
INC
Also Called: Eastland Crane & Towing
2190 S Hamilton Rd (43232-4487)
PHONE...........................614 868-9750
Robert M Marshall, President
Brenda Marshall, Corp Secy
EMP: 25
SQ FT: 1,500
SALES (est): 4.5MM Privately Held
SIC: 7353 7549 Cranes & aerial lift equipment, rental or leasing; towing service, automotive

(G-7491)
EASTLAND LANES INC
2666 Old Courtright Rd (43232-2603)
P.O. Box 735, Morgantown WV (26507-0735)
PHONE...........................614 868-9866
Steve Lorenze Jr, President
Jack Keener, Corp Secy
Ginger Lorenze, Vice Pres
Carol Clemens, Manager
EMP: 50
SQ FT: 62,000
SALES (est): 1.5MM Privately Held
WEB: www.eastlandlanes.com
SIC: 7933 Ten pin center

(G-7492)
EASTON TOWN CENTER II LLC
Also Called: Steiner Associates
160 Easton Town Ctr (43219-6074)
PHONE...........................614 416-7000
Roxanne Nally, Marketing Staff
Kristin Scott, Marketing Staff
EMP: 60
SALES (est): 2.7MM Privately Held
SIC: 6512 Shopping center, property operation only

(G-7493)
EASTON TOWN CENTER LLC
Also Called: Easton Town Center Guest Svcs
4016 Townsfair Way # 201 (43219-6083)
PHONE...........................614 337-2560
Yaromir Steiner, Mng Member
Eddie Bauer,
EMP: 175
SQ FT: 10,000
SALES (est): 14.5MM Privately Held
WEB: www.eastontowncenter.com
SIC: 6512 Shopping center, regional
(300,000 - 1,000,000 sq ft)

(G-7494)
EASTWAY SUPPLIES INC
1561 Alum Creek Dr (43209-2780)
PHONE...........................614 252-3650
Gary M Glanzman, President
Jason Burton, CFO
Vanessa Glanzman, Admin Sec
EMP: 40 EST: 1971
SQ FT: 10,000
SALES (est): 33.7MM Privately Held
WEB: www.eastwaysupplies.com
SIC: 5074 Plumbing fittings & supplies

(G-7495)
EATON CORPORATION
Also Called: Ledger 6031
P.O. Box 182175 (43218-2175)
PHONE...........................614 839-4387
EMP: 25 Privately Held
SIC: 5063 Electrical apparatus & equipment
HQ: Eaton Corporation
1000 Eaton Blvd
Cleveland OH 44122
440 523-5000

(G-7496)
EBUYS INC (DH)
Also Called: Shoemetro
810 Dsw Dr (43219-1828)
PHONE...........................858 831-0839
David Tam Duong, CEO
EMP: 50
SQ FT: 8,700
SALES (est): 51.5MM
SALES (corp-wide): 3.1B Publicly Held
WEB: www.shoemetro.com
SIC: 5139 Shoes
HQ: Dsw Shoe Warehouse, Inc.
4314 E 5th Ave
Columbus OH 43219
614 237-7100

(G-7497)
ECHO RESIDENTIAL SUPPORT
6500 Busch Blvd Ste 215 (43229-6708)
PHONE...........................614 210-0944
Brad Kurash, CEO
Thomas Scarce, President
Jovita Lark, Director
EMP: 35
SALES (est): 1.3MM Privately Held
WEB: www.ehos.org
SIC: 8361 Home for the mentally handicapped

(G-7498)
ECHO-TAPE LLC
651 Dearborn Park Ln (43085)
PHONE...........................614 892-3246
Scott Taylor,
EMP: 25
SALES (est): 2.1MM Privately Held
SIC: 7379 Computer related maintenance
services

(G-7499)
ECOMMERCE LLC
1774 Dividend Dr (43228-3845)
PHONE...........................800 861-9394
Fathi Said, CEO
Kevin Nelson, Technical Staff
EMP: 99 EST: 2010
SALES (est): 4.6MM Privately Held
SIC: 7375 Data base information retrieval

(G-7500)
ECONOMIC & CMNTY DEV INST
INC
Also Called: ECDI
1655 Old Leonard Ave (43219-2541)
PHONE...........................614 559-0104
Inna Kinney, President
Sharelle Buyer, Controller
Tim Kehoe, Portfolio Mgr
Lauren Smith, Manager
Carrie Rosenfelt, Exec Dir
EMP: 41
SALES: 7.5MM Privately Held
SIC: 8399 Community development groups

(G-7501)
EDISON EQUIPMENT (PA)
Also Called: EE
2225 Mckinley Ave (43204-3484)
PHONE...........................614 883-5710
Paul Collini, President
Brad Burbacher, Sales Associate
EMP: 36
SQ FT: 20,000
SALES (est): 14.1MM Privately Held
WEB: www.edisonequipment.com
SIC: 5063 Whol Electrical Equipment

(G-7502)
EDISON WELDING INSTITUTE
INC (PA)
Also Called: Buffalo Mfg Works BMW
1250 Arthur E Adams Dr (43221-3585)
PHONE...........................614 688-5000
Henry Cialone, CEO
Edward W Ungar, Principal
Phil Weisenbach, COO
Mark Matson, Vice Pres
Constance Reichert, Project Mgr
EMP: 145
SQ FT: 135,000
SALES: 33.7MM Privately Held
WEB: www.ewi.org
SIC: 8731 Commercial physical research

▲ = Import ▼=Export
◆ =Import/Export

(G-7503)
EDMOND HOTEL INVESTORS LLC
24 E Lincoln St (43215-1586)
PHONE..................................614 891-2900
Robyn Asher, *CFO*
Scott Somerville,
EMP: 65
SALES (est): 260.2K **Privately Held**
SIC: 7011 Hotels & motels

(G-7504)
EDUCATIONAL SOLUTIONS CO
1155 Highland St (43201-3277)
PHONE..................................614 989-4588
Robert Stephens, *Exec Dir*
Estella Stephens, *Director*
EMP: 75
SALES (est): 2.6MM **Privately Held**
SIC: 8748 Business consulting

(G-7505)
EDWARDS MOONEY & MOSES
Also Called: Edwards Mooney & Moses of Ohio
1320 Mckinley Ave Ste B (43222-1155)
PHONE..................................614 351-1439
Randall Hall, *Officer*
EMP: 80
SALES (est): 4.5MM
SALES (corp-wide): 1.3B **Publicly Held**
WEB: www.ibpteam.com
SIC: 1742 Insulation, buildings
HQ: Installed Building Products Llc
    495 S High St Ste 50
    Columbus OH 43215
    614 221-3399

(G-7506)
EDWARDS CREATIVE LEARNING CTR
3858 Alum Creek Dr Ste A (43207-5135)
PHONE..................................614 492-8977
Shirley Atkins, *Owner*
EMP: 30
SALES (est): 628.3K **Privately Held**
SIC: 8351 Group day care center

(G-7507)
EDWARDS ELECTRICAL & MECH
685 Grandview Ave (43215-1119)
PHONE..................................614 485-2003
Matt Snyder, *Branch Mgr*
EMP: 40 **Privately Held**
WEB: www.edwards-elec.com
SIC: 2752 1711 Commercial printing, lithographic; mechanical contractor
HQ: Edwards Electrical & Mechanical Inc
    2350 N Shadeland Ave
    Indianapolis IN 46219
    317 543-3460

(G-7508)
EDWARDS LAND COMPANY
495 S High St Ste 150 (43215-5695)
PHONE..................................614 241-2070
Charlie Driscoll, *Chairman*
Charles Driscoll, *Chairman*
EMP: 27
SALES (est): 3MM
SALES (corp-wide): 14.9MM **Privately Held**
SIC: 6552 Subdividers & developers
PA: The Edwards Industries Inc
    495 S High St Ste 150
    Columbus OH 43215
    614 241-2070

(G-7509)
EFCO CORP
Also Called: Economy Forms
3900 Zane Trace Dr (43228-3833)
PHONE..................................614 876-1226
Jim Davis, *Manager*
Jim Grubb, *Manager*
EMP: 26
SALES (corp-wide): 256.4MM **Privately Held**
SIC: 5051 7353 4225 3444 Steel; heavy construction equipment rental; general warehousing; concrete forms, sheet metal; miscellaneous fabricated wire products; fabricated plate work (boiler shop)

HQ: Efco Corp
    1800 Ne Broadway Ave
    Des Moines IA 50313
    515 266-1141

(G-7510)
EFFICIENT ELECTRIC CORP
4800 Groves Rd (43232-4165)
PHONE..................................614 552-0200
Ken Havice, *President*
Jim Ruisinger, *Corp Secy*
EMP: 33
SQ FT: 15,000
SALES (est): 6MM **Privately Held**
WEB: www.efficient-electric.com
SIC: 1731 General electrical contractor

(G-7511)
ELFORD INC
Also Called: Elford Construction Services
1220 Dublin Rd (43215-1008)
PHONE..................................614 488-4000
James W Smith, *CEO*
Jeffrey Copeland, *Ch of Bd*
Michael Fitzpatrick, *President*
Eric Bull, *Exec VP*
Randy Petitt, *Exec VP*
EMP: 200
SQ FT: 54,000
SALES (est): 135.7MM **Privately Held**
WEB: www.elford.com
SIC: 1542 1541 8741 Commercial & office building, new construction; institutional building construction; industrial buildings, new construction; construction management

(G-7512)
ELITE HOME REMODELING INC
6295a Busch Blvd Ste A (43229-1801)
PHONE..................................614 785-6700
Robert S Harmon, *President*
Susan B Harmon, *Admin Sec*
EMP: 35
SQ FT: 2,500
SALES (est): 3.5MM **Privately Held**
SIC: 1521 Single-family housing construction

(G-7513)
EMCOR FCLITIES SVCS N AMER INC
280 N High St Ste 1700 (43215-7511)
PHONE..................................614 430-5078
Matthew Seguin, *Manager*
EMP: 90
SALES (corp-wide): 8.1B **Publicly Held**
SIC: 1711 Heating systems repair & maintenance
HQ: Emcor Facilities Services Of North America, Inc.
    306 Northern Ave Ste 5
    Boston MA

(G-7514)
EMERGENCY SERVICES INC
2323 W 5th Ave Ste 220 (43204-4899)
PHONE..................................614 224-6420
Alen Gora, *President*
Michael Glueckert, *Med Doctor*
Kim Mayo-Bailey, *Recruiter*
Angie Castle, *Physician Asst*
Chelli Richmond, *Physician Asst*
EMP: 45 EST: 1972
SALES (est): 53.3K **Privately Held**
SIC: 8011 Offices & clinics of medical doctors

(G-7515)
ENERVISE INCORPORATED
6663 Huntley Rd Ste K (43229-1038)
PHONE..................................614 885-9800
Brenda Burnette, *Manager*
Rebecca Marischen, *Manager*
EMP: 50
SALES (est): 4.7MM
SALES (corp-wide): 40.9MM **Privately Held**
WEB: www.engineeringexcellence.com
SIC: 1711 Mechanical contractor
PA: Enervise Incorporated
    4360 Glendale Milford Rd
    Blue Ash OH 45242
    513 761-6000

(G-7516)
ENGAGED HEALTH CARE BUS SVCS
Also Called: Ppmc
4619 Kenny Rd Ste 100 (43220-2779)
PHONE..................................614 457-8180
Samuel J Kiehl III, *President*
Gary W Beauchamp, *President*
Craig A Adkins, *Vice Pres*
Jay W Eckersley, *Vice Pres*
Steve Nagle, *Vice Pres*
EMP: 50 EST: 1980
SQ FT: 10,000
SALES (est): 2.5MM **Privately Held**
WEB: www.ppmc.net
SIC: 8099 8742 Blood related health services; business consultant

(G-7517)
ENHANCED HOME HEALTH CARE LLC
700 Morse Rd Ste 206 (43214-1879)
PHONE..................................614 433-7266
Sadia Y Abdi, *Principal*
EMP: 80
SALES (est): 966.7K **Privately Held**
SIC: 8082 Visiting nurse service

(G-7518)
ENHANCED SOFTWARE INC
Also Called: Vsync
625 E North Broadway St (43214-4133)
PHONE..................................877 805-8388
James C McAllister, *CEO*
Bill Knapp, *President*
EMP: 25
SQ FT: 7,000
SALES (est): 2.8MM **Privately Held**
WEB: www.vsync.com
SIC: 5045 Computer software

(G-7519)
ENTRUST SOLUTIONS LLC
Also Called: Entrust Healthcare
20 S 3rd St Ste 210 (43215-4206)
PHONE..................................614 504-4900
Christopher Assif, *Mng Member*
EMP: 30
SALES: 3MM **Privately Held**
SIC: 7379 Computer related consulting services

(G-7520)
ENVIRO IT LLC
Also Called: Accurate It Services
3854 Fisher Rd (43228-1016)
PHONE..................................614 453-0709
Scott Weigand, *COO*
Sergey Zeleny, *Purch Mgr*
Michael Yankelevich, *Mng Member*
Shaun Taylor, *Manager*
Peter Digravio, *Admin Asst*
EMP: 30
SALES (est): 3.8MM **Privately Held**
WEB: www.accurateit.com
SIC: 7379 5065 ; modems, computer

(G-7521)
ENVIRONMENT CONTROL OF GREATER
2218 Dividend Dr (43228-3808)
PHONE..................................614 868-9788
Jonathan Hanks, *President*
Wendy Hanks, *Corp Secy*
Sean Frazier, *Opers Staff*
EMP: 80
SQ FT: 6,849
SALES (est): 4.8MM **Privately Held**
SIC: 4959 7349 Environmental cleanup services; building maintenance services

(G-7522)
ENVIRONMENTAL SYSTEMS RESEARCH
Also Called: Esri
1085 Beecher Xing N Ste A (43230-4563)
PHONE..................................614 933-8698
Steven Kenzie, *Manager*
EMP: 76
SALES (corp-wide): 1B **Privately Held**
WEB: www.esri.com
SIC: 5045 Computer software

PA: Environmental Systems Research Institute, Inc.
    380 New York St
    Redlands CA 92373
    909 793-2853

(G-7523)
ENVOY AIR INC
Also Called: AMR Eagle
4100 E 5th Ave (43219-1802)
PHONE..................................614 231-4391
EMP: 54
SALES (corp-wide): 44.5B **Publicly Held**
SIC: 4512 Air passenger carrier, scheduled
HQ: Envoy Air Inc.
    4301 Regent Blvd
    Irving TX 75063
    972 374-5200

(G-7524)
EQUITABLE MORTGAGE CORPORATION (PA)
3530 Snouffer Rd Ste 100 (43235-2702)
PHONE..................................614 764-1232
Bruce Calabrese, *President*
Steve Stasuilewicz, *Exec VP*
Richard Cercone, *Vice Pres*
John Stamolis, *Vice Pres*
Lynda D Calabrese, *Admin Sec*
EMP: 25
SQ FT: 21,500
SALES: 5.5MM **Privately Held**
WEB: www.eqfin.com
SIC: 6162 Mortgage bankers & correspondents

(G-7525)
EQUITAS HEALTH INC
Also Called: Columbus Alpha Bldg
889 E Long St (43203-1854)
PHONE..................................614 926-4132
Randle Moore, *Branch Mgr*
EMP: 49
SALES (corp-wide): 23.4MM **Privately Held**
SIC: 8093 Mental health clinic, outpatient
PA: Equitas Health, Inc.
    4400 N High St Ste 300
    Columbus OH 43214
    614 299-2437

(G-7526)
EQUITAS HEALTH INC
Also Called: King-Lincoln Medical Center
750 E Long St Ste 3000 (43203-1874)
PHONE..................................614 340-6700
EMP: 62
SALES (corp-wide): 23.4MM **Privately Held**
SIC: 8011 Medical centers
PA: Equitas Health, Inc.
    4400 N High St Ste 300
    Columbus OH 43214
    614 299-2437

(G-7527)
EQUITAS HEALTH INC (PA)
4400 N High St Ste 300 (43214-2635)
PHONE..................................614 299-2437
William Hardy, *CEO*
Peggy Anderson, *COO*
Carole Anderson, *Sr Corp Ofcr*
Fikru Nigusse, *CFO*
Aaron Clark, *Manager*
EMP: 84
SQ FT: 10,000
SALES (est): 23.4MM **Privately Held**
WEB: www.catf.net
SIC: 8322 8093 8011 8049 Individual & family services; mental health clinic, outpatient; primary care medical clinic; specialized medical practitioners, except internal; nurses & other medical assistants; specialized dental practitioners

(G-7528)
ERIE INSURANCE EXCHANGE
445 Hutchinson Ave (43235-5677)
PHONE..................................614 430-8530
EMP: 65
SALES (corp-wide): 373.8MM **Privately Held**
SIC: 6411 Insurance agents, brokers & service

PA: Erie Insurance Exchange
100 Erie Insurance Pl
Erie PA 16530
800 458-0811

(G-7529)
ERIE INSURANCE EXCHANGE
445 Hutchinson Ave # 350 (43235-5677)
P.O. Box 23, Worthington (43085-0023)
PHONE.................................614 436-0224
Paul Miller, *Manager*
EMP: 110
SQ FT: 5,000
SALES (corp-wide): 373.8MM **Privately Held**
WEB: www.erie-insurance.com
SIC: 6331 Reciprocal interinsurance exchanges: fire, marine, casualty
PA: Erie Insurance Exchange
100 Erie Insurance Pl
Erie PA 16530
800 458-0811

(G-7530)
ERNEST FRITSCH
6245 Sunderland Dr (43229-1977)
PHONE.................................614 436-5995
EMP: 50
SALES (est): 4.7MM **Privately Held**
SIC: 1542 Nonresidential Construction

(G-7531)
ERNST & YOUNG LLP
Also Called: Ey
800 Yard St Ste 200 (43212-3882)
PHONE.................................614 224-5678
Craig Marshall, *Managing Prtnr*
Daniel Eck, *Broker*
Brad Durst, *Senior Mgr*
EMP: 170
SALES (corp-wide): 4.3B **Privately Held**
WEB: www.ey.com
SIC: 8721 8742 Certified public accountant; auditing services; business consultant; management information systems consultant
PA: Ernst & Young Llp
5 Times Sq Fl Conlv1
New York NY 10036
212 773-3000

(G-7532)
ESC AND COMPANY INC
2000 Toronado Blvd A (43207-1755)
PHONE.................................614 794-0568
Emil S Colucci, *President*
Matt Colucci, *Vice Pres*
Melissa Colucci, *Vice Pres*
▲ **EMP:** 30
SALES (est): 7.2MM **Privately Held**
WEB: www.esctradingcompany.com
SIC: 5199 Gifts & novelties

(G-7533)
ESCAPE ENTERPRISES INC
Also Called: Steak Escape
222 Neilston St (43215-2636)
PHONE.................................614 224-0300
Mark Turner, *Principal*
Kennard Smith, *Chairman*
EMP: 35
SQ FT: 10,000
SALES (est): 1.9MM **Privately Held**
WEB: www.steakescape.com
SIC: 5812 6794 Fast food restaurants & stands; franchises, selling or licensing

(G-7534)
ESSENDANT CO
1634 Westbelt Dr (43228-3810)
PHONE.................................614 876-7774
Mike Huettel, *President*
Michael Martin, *Manager*
Frank Phillips, *Manager*
Mike McHale, *Maintence Staff*
EMP: 100
SQ FT: 126,000
SALES (corp-wide): 5B **Privately Held**
WEB: www.ussco.com
SIC: 5112 5044 Office supplies; office equipment
HQ: Essendant Co.
1 Parkway North Blvd # 100
Deerfield IL 60015
847 627-7000

(G-7535)
ESSENTIALPROFILE1CORP
735 N Wilson Rd (43204-1463)
PHONE.................................614 805-4794
John Harris, *Principal*
EMP: 80
SALES: 350K **Privately Held**
SIC: 7349 Cleaning service, industrial or commercial

(G-7536)
ESSEX HEALTHCARE CORPORATION (PA)
2780 Airport Dr Ste 400 (43219-2289)
PHONE.................................614 416-0600
Don Finney, *President*
Francis J Crosby, *President*
Sue Malone, *Vice Pres*
Keith Yoder, *CFO*
EMP: 30
SQ FT: 15,000
SALES (est): 41.3MM **Privately Held**
WEB: www.atriumliving centers.com
SIC: 6531 Real estate agents & managers

(G-7537)
ESSILOR LABORATORIES AMER INC
Also Called: Top Network
3671 Interchange Rd (43204-1499)
PHONE.................................614 274-0840
Don Lepore, *Manager*
EMP: 50
SALES (corp-wide): 283.5MM **Privately Held**
WEB: www.crizal.com
SIC: 3851 5049 Eyeglasses, lenses & frames; optical goods
HQ: Essilor Laboratories Of America, Inc.
13515 N Stemmons Fwy
Dallas TX 75234
972 241-4141

(G-7538)
ESTES EXPRESS LINES INC
1009 Frank Rd (43223-3858)
PHONE.................................614 275-6000
Tom Siefert, *Manager*
Annette Weiner, *Executive*
EMP: 105
SQ FT: 4,331
SALES (corp-wide): 2.7B **Privately Held**
WEB: www.estes-express.com
SIC: 4213 Less-than-truckload (LTL) transport
PA: Estes Express Lines, Inc.
3901 W Broad St
Richmond VA 23230
804 353-1900

(G-7539)
ETRANSMEDIA TECHNOLOGY INC
1111 Schrock Rd Ste 200 (43229-1155)
PHONE.................................724 743-5960
Vikram Agrawal, *Branch Mgr*
EMP: 40
SALES (corp-wide): 68.5MM **Privately Held**
SIC: 7389 5734 Personal service agents, brokers & bureaus; software, business & non-game
HQ: Etransmedia Technology, Inc.
385 Jordan Rd
Troy NY 12180
518 283-5418

(G-7540)
EVANS ADHESIVE CORPORATION (HQ)
925 Old Henderson Rd (43220-3779)
PHONE.................................614 451-2665
C Russell Thompson, *President*
Wilbur J Liddil, *Senior VP*
Gene Hollo, *Vice Pres*
Steve Overby, *Plant Mgr*
David Jarvis, *Opers Staff*
EMP: 27
SALES: 24MM
SALES (corp-wide): 42.1MM **Privately Held**
SIC: 2891 5085 Adhesives; abrasives & adhesives

PA: Meridian Adhesives Group Llc
100 Park Ave Fl 31
New York NY 10017
212 771-1717

(G-7541)
EXCEL DECORATORS INC
3910 Groves Rd Ste A (43232-4162)
PHONE.................................614 522-0056
Sonja Winscott, *Branch Mgr*
EMP: 128
SALES (corp-wide): 7.4MM **Privately Held**
SIC: 7299 Party planning service
PA: Excel Decorators Inc
3748 Kentucky Ave
Indianapolis IN 46221
317 856-1300

(G-7542)
EXCEL TRUCKING LLC
1000 Frank Rd (43223-3859)
PHONE.................................614 826-1988
Abdulla Abdi, *CEO*
EMP: 25 **EST:** 2011
SQ FT: 900
SALES: 13MM **Privately Held**
SIC: 4213 Trucking, except local

(G-7543)
EXECUTIVES AGENCIES
30 E Broad St Fl 26 (43215-3414)
PHONE.................................614 466-2980
Mathew Lamtke, *Exec Dir*
Peter Thomas, *Deputy Dir*
EMP: 35
SALES (est): 1.4MM **Privately Held**
SIC: 8111 Legal services

(G-7544)
EXEL FREIGHT CONNECT INC
Also Called: Dhl Transport Brokerage
226 N 5th St Ste 21 (43215-2656)
P.O. Box 15850 (43215-0850)
PHONE.................................855 393-5378
Brian Malinowski, *Director*
EMP: 68 **EST:** 2014
SALES (est): 18MM
SALES (corp-wide): 70.4B **Privately Held**
SIC: 4731 Freight forwarding
HQ: Exel Inc.
570 Polaris Pkwy
Westerville OH 43082
614 865-8500

(G-7545)
EXEL GLOBAL LOGISTICS INC
2144a John Glenn Ave (43217-1154)
PHONE.................................614 409-4500
Roger Richard, *Branch Mgr*
EMP: 25
SALES (corp-wide): 70.4B **Privately Held**
WEB: www.exelgloballogistics.com
SIC: 4731 Domestic freight forwarding
HQ: Exel Global Logistics, Inc.
22879 Glenn Dr Ste 100
Sterling VA 20164
703 350-1298

(G-7546)
EXPERIS FINANCE US LLC
175 S 3rd St Ste 375 (43215-6196)
PHONE.................................614 223-2300
Rich Grunenwald, *Branch Mgr*
EMP: 63 **Publicly Held**
SIC: 8721 Accounting, auditing & bookkeeping
HQ: Experis Finance Us, Llc
100 W Manpower Pl
Milwaukee WI 53212

(G-7547)
EXPERIS US INC
175 S 3rd St Ste 375 (43215-6196)
PHONE.................................614 223-2300
Sisi Nguyen, *Branch Mgr*
EMP: 36 **Publicly Held**
SIC: 7361 Executive placement
HQ: Experis Us, Inc.
100 W Manpower Pl
Milwaukee WI 53212

(G-7548)
EXPONENTIA US INC
424 Beecher Rd Ste A (43230-3510)
PHONE.................................614 944-5103

Giri Suvramani, *President*
Gira Suvramani, *President*
EMP: 30
SQ FT: 5,200
SALES: 4.8MM **Privately Held**
SIC: 7372 Publishers' computer software

(G-7549)
EXXCEL PROJECT MANAGEMENT LLC
328 Civic Center Dr (43215-5087)
PHONE.................................614 621-4500
F Douglas Reardon, *President*
Douglas Kaiser, *Vice Pres*
Cliff Aiken, *Ch Invest Ofcr*
Eric Olson, *Manager*
Lindsay Hodge, *Director*
EMP: 28
SQ FT: 10,000
SALES (est): 13.9MM **Privately Held**
WEB: www.exxcel.com
SIC: 1542 1541 Commercial & office building, new construction; industrial buildings, new construction

(G-7550)
EYE SURGERY CENTER OHIO INC (PA)
Also Called: Arena Eye Surgeons
262 Neil Ave Ste 320 (43215-4624)
PHONE.................................614 228-3937
Peter Utrata, *Principal*
Lisa Russell, *Corp Comm Staff*
Robert P Bennett, *Med Doctor*
Mary Delong, *Administration*
Kelly Kidd, *Ophthalmic Tech*
EMP: 25
SQ FT: 2,200
SALES (est): 4.7MM **Privately Held**
WEB: www.eyesurgerycenterofohio.com
SIC: 3841 8011 Eye examining instruments & apparatus; offices & clinics of medical doctors

(G-7551)
F S T EXPRESS INC
1727 Georgesville Rd (43228-3619)
PHONE.................................614 529-7900
Arthur J Decrane, *President*
David S Kent, *CFO*
EMP: 80
SQ FT: 12,000
SALES (est): 10.7MM
SALES (corp-wide): 77.1MM **Privately Held**
WEB: www.fstfst.com
SIC: 4213 Contract haulers
PA: Fst Logistics, Inc.
1727 Georgesville Rd
Columbus OH 43228
614 529-7900

(G-7552)
FAHLGREN INC (PA)
4030 Easton Sta Ste 300 (43219-7012)
PHONE.................................614 383-1500
Neil Mortine, *President*
Aaron Brown, *Senior VP*
Marcia Chocinsky, *Vice Pres*
Peter Craig, *Vice Pres*
Jude Divierte, *Vice Pres*
EMP: 40
SALES: 23MM **Privately Held**
WEB: www.fahlgren.com
SIC: 7311 Advertising consultant

(G-7553)
FAHLGREN INC
4030 Easton Sta Ste 300 (43219-7012)
PHONE.................................614 383-1500
Steve Drongowski, *CEO*
EMP: 60
SALES (corp-wide): 23MM **Privately Held**
WEB: www.fahlgren.com
SIC: 7311 8742 Advertising consultant; marketing consulting services; public relations & publicity
PA: Fahlgren, Inc.
4030 Easton Sta Ste 300
Columbus OH 43219
614 383-1500

▲ = Import ▼=Export
◆ =Import/Export

(G-7554)
FAIRFIELD INN STES CLMBUS ARPRT
4300 International Gtwy (43219-1749)
PHONE.................................614 237-2100
Stephen Schwartz, *CEO*
EMP: 30
SALES (est): 1MM **Privately Held**
SIC: 7011 Hotels & motels

(G-7555)
FAIRFIELD INN
3031 Olentangy River Rd (43202-1572)
PHONE.................................614 267-1111
Frank Stnichols, *Principal*
EMP: 80
SALES (est): 2.3MM **Privately Held**
SIC: 7011 Hotels & motels

(G-7556)
FAIRWAY INDEPENDENT MRTG CORP
4215 Worth Ave Ste 220 (43219-1546)
PHONE.................................614 930-6552
EMP: 35 **Privately Held**
SIC: 6162 Mortgage bankers & correspondents
PA: Fairway Independent Mortgage Corporation
4750 S Biltmore Ln
Madison WI 53718

(G-7557)
FAITH MISSION INC (HQ)
245 N Grant Ave (43215-2641)
PHONE.................................614 224-6617
John Dickey, *Exec Dir*
Susan Villilo, *Exec Dir*
EMP: 50
SQ FT: 20,000
SALES: 8.1MM
SALES (corp-wide): 49.2MM **Privately Held**
SIC: 8322 Emergency shelters
PA: Lutheran Social Services Of Central Ohio
500 W Wilson Bridge Rd
Worthington OH 43085
419 289-3523

(G-7558)
FAITH MISSION INC
245 N Grant Ave (43215-2641)
PHONE.................................614 224-6617
Ereuss Preuss, *Director*
EMP: 45
SQ FT: 15,708
SALES (corp-wide): 49.2MM **Privately Held**
SIC: 8322 Social service center
HQ: Faith Mission, Inc
245 N Grant Ave
Columbus OH 43215
614 224-6617

(G-7559)
FAMILY HEALTH CARE CENTER INC
Also Called: Linden Medical Center
2800 W Broad St Ste B (43204-2600)
PHONE.................................614 274-4171
Michelle Washington, *President*
EMP: 43
SQ FT: 1,200
SALES (est): 2.3MM **Privately Held**
SIC: 8011 General & family practice, physician/surgeon

(G-7560)
FAMILY PHYSICIANS OF GAHANNA
725 Buckles Ct N (43230-5316)
PHONE.................................614 471-9654
Michael Baehr, *Partner*
Joseph Lutz, *Partner*
Maria Sammarco, *Partner*
Evan Stathulis, *Partner*
John Tyznik, *Partner*
EMP: 30
SALES (est): 2.7MM **Privately Held**
WEB: www.fpoginc.com
SIC: 8011 General & family practice, physician/surgeon

(G-7561)
FARBER CORPORATION
Also Called: Honeywell Authorized Dealer
800 E 12th Ave (43211-2670)
PHONE.................................614 294-1626
Edward A Farber, *President*
Tim Farber, *Vice Pres*
Michael Klingler, *Vice Pres*
Sandra B Farber, *Treasurer*
Michael Klinger, *Manager*
▲ **EMP:** 30
SQ FT: 12,000
SALES (est): 7.5MM **Privately Held**
WEB: www.farbercorp.com
SIC: 1711 Mechanical contractor

(G-7562)
FARMERS GROUP INC
Also Called: Farmers Insurance
7400 Safelite Way (43235-5086)
PHONE.................................614 766-6005
Robert Fuller, *Branch Mgr*
EMP: 30
SALES (corp-wide): 65.1B **Privately Held**
WEB: www.farmers.com
SIC: 6411 Insurance agents, brokers & service
HQ: Farmers Group, Inc.
6301 Owensmouth Ave
Woodland Hills CA 91367
323 932-3200

(G-7563)
FARMERS GROUP INC
Also Called: Farmers Insurance
2545 Farmers Dr Ste 440 (43235-2705)
P.O. Box 268994, Oklahoma City OK (73126-8994)
PHONE.................................614 799-3200
Craig Miller, *Manager*
EMP: 40
SALES (corp-wide): 65.1B **Privately Held**
WEB: www.farmers.com
SIC: 6411 Insurance agents, brokers & service
HQ: Farmers Group, Inc.
6301 Owensmouth Ave
Woodland Hills CA 91367
323 932-3200

(G-7564)
FARMERS INSURANCE OF COLUMBUS (DH)
7400 Skyline Dr E (43235-2706)
P.O. Box 2910, Shawnee Mission KS (66201-1310)
PHONE.................................614 799-3200
Annette K Schons-Thompson, *President*
Martin D Feinstein, *Vice Pres*
John H Lynch, *Vice Pres*
Russell L Powers, *Vice Pres*
Warren B Tucker, *Vice Pres*
EMP: 400
SQ FT: 350,000
SALES (est): 48.9MM
SALES (corp-wide): 65.1B **Privately Held**
SIC: 6411 Insurance agents, brokers & service
HQ: Farmers Insurance Exchange
6301 Owensmouth Ave # 300
Woodland Hills CA 91367
323 932-3200

(G-7565)
FATHOM SEO LLC
1465 Northwest Blvd (43212-3062)
PHONE.................................614 291-8456
Phil Kopp, *Sales Staff*
Christopher Lowry, *Branch Mgr*
James Ketchaver, *Director*
EMP: 72
SALES (corp-wide): 24.5MM **Privately Held**
SIC: 8742 Marketing consulting services
PA: Fathom Seo, Llc
8200 Sweet Valley Dr
Cleveland OH 44125
216 525-0510

(G-7566)
FAVRET COMPANY
Also Called: Favret Heating & Cooling
1296 Dublin Rd (43215-1008)
PHONE.................................614 488-5211
William Favret, *CEO*
Mark Favret, *President*
Philip Favret, *Vice Pres*
Jim Chesbrough, *Sales Staff*
Matthew Favret, *Info Tech Mgr*
EMP: 63
SQ FT: 20,000
SALES (est): 10.9MM **Privately Held**
WEB: www.favret.com
SIC: 1711 Warm air heating & air conditioning contractor; plumbing contractors

(G-7567)
FCX PERFORMANCE INC (HQ)
Also Called: Jh Instruments
3000 E 14th Ave (43219-2355)
PHONE.................................614 324-6050
Thomas Cox, *CEO*
Jeff Caswell, *President*
Russell S Frazee, *COO*
Tim Cancila, *Division VP*
Chris Hill, *Exec VP*
▲ **EMP:** 40
SQ FT: 44,000
SALES (est): 338MM
SALES (corp-wide): 3B **Publicly Held**
WEB: www.fcxperformance.com
SIC: 5084 5085 3494 Instruments & control equipment; industrial supplies; valves & fittings; valves & pipe fittings
PA: Applied Industrial Technologies, Inc.
1 Applied Plz
Cleveland OH 44115
216 426-4000

(G-7568)
FEDERAL EXPRESS CORPORATION
Also Called: Fedex
7066 Cargo Rd (43217-1346)
PHONE.................................614 492-6106
EMP: 300
SALES (corp-wide): 47.4B **Publicly Held**
SIC: 4513 4512 4522 4215 Air And Ground Cargo Carrier/Warehouse
HQ: Federal Express Corporation
3610 Hacks Cross Rd
Memphis TN 38125
901 369-3600

(G-7569)
FEDERAL EXPRESS CORPORATION
Also Called: Fedex
2424 Citygate Dr (43219-3590)
PHONE.................................800 463-3339
Curt Zimbric, *Manager*
EMP: 109
SALES (corp-wide): 65.4B **Publicly Held**
WEB: www.federalexpress.com
SIC: 4513 Package delivery, private air
HQ: Federal Express Corporation
3610 Hacks Cross Rd
Memphis TN 38125
901 369-3600

(G-7570)
FEDERAL EXPRESS CORPORATION
Also Called: Fedex
2850 International St (43228-4612)
PHONE.................................800 463-3339
EMP: 109
SALES (corp-wide): 65.4B **Publicly Held**
WEB: www.federalexpress.com
SIC: 4513 Package delivery, private air
HQ: Federal Express Corporation
3610 Hacks Cross Rd
Memphis TN 38125
901 369-3600

(G-7571)
FEDEX GROUND PACKAGE SYS INC
4600 Poth Rd (43213-1328)
PHONE.................................800 463-3339
Chris V Esche, *Manager*
EMP: 146
SALES (corp-wide): 65.4B **Publicly Held**
SIC: 4213 Contract haulers
HQ: Fedex Ground Package System, Inc.
1000 Fed Ex Dr
Coraopolis PA 15108
800 463-3339

(G-7572)
FEDEX OFFICE & PRINT SVCS INC
180 N High St (43215-2403)
PHONE.................................614 621-1100
EMP: 32
SALES (corp-wide): 65.4B **Publicly Held**
WEB: www.kinkos.com
SIC: 7334 2791 Photocopying & duplicating services; typesetting
HQ: Fedex Office And Print Services, Inc.
7900 Legacy Dr
Plano TX 75024
800 463-3339

(G-7573)
FEINKNOPF MACIOCE SCHAPPA ARC
995 W 3rd Ave (43212-3109)
PHONE.................................614 297-1020
Joseph F Schappa, *President*
Rhonda Hillis, *Vice Pres*
David A Youse, *Vice Pres*
George Pack, *Project Mgr*
John Risteter, *Sr Project Mgr*
EMP: 25 EST: 1928
SQ FT: 7,000
SALES (est): 3.7MM **Privately Held**
WEB: www.fmsarchitects.com
SIC: 8712 Architectural engineering

(G-7574)
FHC ENTERPRISES LLC
Also Called: Government Resource Partners
5489 Blue Ash Rd (43229-3630)
PHONE.................................614 271-3513
Mike Cieply, *Director*
Jim Cieply,
EMP: 34
SQ FT: 1,400
SALES: 375K **Privately Held**
SIC: 7379 Computer related maintenance services

(G-7575)
FIFTH AVENUE LUMBER CO (HQ)
Also Called: Lumber Craft
479 E 5th Ave (43201-2876)
P.O. Box 8098 (43201-0098)
PHONE.................................614 294-0068
Wilbur C Strait Jr, *CEO*
William A Cady, *President*
Craig Mitchell, *Marketing Staff*
Todd Buxton, *Manager*
Chuck Stewart, *Manager*
EMP: 90
SQ FT: 8,000
SALES (est): 13MM
SALES (corp-wide): 39.1MM **Privately Held**
WEB: www.straitandlamp.com
SIC: 5211 5031 Lumber products; lumber, plywood & millwork
PA: The Strait & Lamp Lumber Company Incorporated
269 National Rd Se
Hebron OH 43025
740 928-4501

(G-7576)
FIFTH THIRD BNK OF COLUMBUS OH
21 E State St Fl 4 (43215-4208)
PHONE.................................614 744-7553
Jordan Miller, *President*
EMP: 900
SALES (est): 395.9MM
SALES (corp-wide): 7.9B **Publicly Held**
WEB: www.53.com
SIC: 6022 State trust companies accepting deposits, commercial
PA: Fifth Third Bancorp
38 Fountain Square Plz
Cincinnati OH 45202
800 972-3030

(G-7577)
FINE LINE GRAPHICS CORP (PA)
1481 Goodale Blvd (43212-3402)
P.O. Box 163370 (43216-3370)
PHONE.................................614 486-0276
James Basch, *President*
Mark Carro, *Principal*
Gregory Davis, *Vice Pres*

Allie Davis, *VP Human Res*
Greg Davis, *VP Sales*
▲ EMP: 151
SQ FT: 42,000
SALES (est): 39MM Privately Held
SIC: 2752 7331 Lithographic Commercial
　Printing Direct Mail Advertising Services

(G-7578)
FINISHMASTER INC
Also Called: Autobody Supply Company
212 N Grant Ave (43215-2642)
PHONE......................................614 228-4328
James Volpe, *Branch Mgr*
EMP: 68
SALES (corp-wide): 1.4B Privately Held
SIC: 3563 5013 5198 Air & gas compres-
　sors including vacuum pumps; automotive
　supplies; paints, varnishes & supplies;
　paints; lacquers; enamels
HQ: Finishmaster, Inc.
　115 W Washington St Fl 7
　Indianapolis IN 46204
　317 237-3678

(G-7579)
FIRM HAHN LAW
Also Called: Hahn Loeser & Parks
65 E State St Ste 1400 (43215-4209)
PHONE......................................614 221-0240
Arland Stein, *Partner*
Aaron Schu, *Associate*
EMP: 25 EST: 2008
SALES (est): 1.7MM Privately Held
SIC: 8111 General practice law office

(G-7580)
FIRST ACCEPTANCE
CORPORATION
895 S Hamilton Rd (43213-3069)
PHONE......................................614 237-9700
Joanne Wein, *Principal*
EMP: 27
SALES (corp-wide): 347.5MM Publicly
Held
SIC: 6411 Insurance agents
PA: First Acceptance Corporation
　3813 Green Hills Vlg Dr
　Nashville TN 37215
　615 844-2800

(G-7581)
FIRST ACCEPTANCE
CORPORATION
3497 Parsons Ave (43207-3883)
PHONE......................................614 492-1446
Donna Jones, *Manager*
EMP: 27
SALES (corp-wide): 347.5MM Publicly
Held
SIC: 6411 Insurance agents, brokers &
　service
PA: First Acceptance Corporation
　3813 Green Hills Vlg Dr
　Nashville TN 37215
　615 844-2800

(G-7582)
FIRST ACCEPTANCE
CORPORATION
4898 W Broad St (43228-1602)
PHONE......................................614 853-3344
Ken Hollister, *Principal*
EMP: 36
SALES (corp-wide): 347.5MM Publicly
Held
SIC: 6411 Insurance agents, brokers &
　service
PA: First Acceptance Corporation
　3813 Green Hills Vlg Dr
　Nashville TN 37215
　615 844-2800

(G-7583)
FIRST COMMUNITY CHURCH
(PA)
1320 Cambridge Blvd (43212-3200)
PHONE......................................614 488-0681
Ruth Decker, *Ch of Bd*
Richard Wing, *Minister*
Cynthia Harsany, *Finance*
Michael Barber, *Mktg Dir*
James Long, *Relg Ldr*
EMP: 48
SQ FT: 56,796

SALES (est): 4.7MM Privately Held
SIC: 8661 8351 Community church; child
　day care services

(G-7584)
FIRST COMMUNITY CHURCH
Also Called: Mary Evans Childcare Center
3777 Dublin Rd (43221-4915)
PHONE......................................614 488-0681
Jamy Zambito, *Director*
EMP: 26
SQ FT: 17,424
SALES (corp-wide): 4.7MM Privately
Held
SIC: 8661 8351 Community church; child
　day care services
PA: The First Community Church
　1320 Cambridge Blvd
　Columbus OH 43212
　614 488-0681

(G-7585)
FIRST COMMUNITY VILLAGE
Also Called: NATIONAL CHURCH RESI-
DENCES FIRST COMMUNITY VILLAGE
1800 Riverside Dr Ofc (43212-1819)
PHONE......................................614 324-4455
Tanya Kim Hahn, *President*
Harold G Edwards, *Principal*
Jane Nash, *Principal*
Edward D Schorr Jr, *Principal*
Diane Tomlinson, *Senior VP*
EMP: 300 EST: 1963
SQ FT: 1,269
SALES: 24.7MM
SALES (corp-wide): 38.2MM Privately
Held
WEB: www.firstcommunityvillage.org
SIC: 8082 8051 8059 8322 Home health
　care services; skilled nursing care facili-
　ties; nursing home, except skilled & inter-
　mediate care facility; outreach program;
　geriatric residential care
PA: National Church Residences
　2335 N Bank Dr
　Columbus OH 43220
　614 451-2151

(G-7586)
FIRST HOTEL ASSOCIATES LP
Also Called: Westin Hotel
310 S High St (43215-4508)
PHONE......................................614 228-3800
Steve Dietrich, *Controller*
EMP: 100
SALES (est): 2.7MM Privately Held
SIC: 7011 5813 5812 Hotels; drinking
　places; eating places

(G-7587)
FIRST MERCHANTS BANK
2130 Tremont Ctr (43221-3110)
PHONE......................................614 486-9000
EMP: 30
SALES (corp-wide): 484.4MM Publicly
Held
SIC: 6029 6163 Commercial banks; loan
　brokers
HQ: First Merchants Bank
　189 W Market St
　Wabash IN 46992
　260 563-4116

(G-7588)
FISHEL COMPANY (PA)
Also Called: Fishel Technologies
1366 Dublin Rd (43215-1093)
PHONE......................................614 274-8100
John E Phillips, *President*
Bob Laprath, *Division Mgr*
Tracy Pate, *Division Mgr*
Diane F Keeler, *Chairman*
Eric Smith, *Vice Chairman*
EMP: 60
SQ FT: 22,000
SALES: 434.8MM Privately Held
WEB: www.fishelco.com
SIC: 1623 1731 8711 Telephone & com-
　munication line construction; electric
　power line construction; cable television
　line construction; gas main construction;
　general electrical contractor; engineering
　services

(G-7589)
FISHEL COMPANY
1600 Walcutt Rd (43228-9394)
PHONE......................................614 850-9012
Ryan Homberger, *Project Mgr*
Patty Rounds, *Accounts Mgr*
Scott Homberger, *Manager*
Bob Brownlee, *Manager*
EMP: 130
SALES (corp-wide): 434.8MM Privately
Held
WEB: www.fishelco.com
SIC: 1623 Underground utilities contractor
PA: The Fishel Company
　1366 Dublin Rd
　Columbus OH 43215
　614 274-8100

(G-7590)
FISHEL COMPANY
Johnson Brothers Construction
1600 Walcutt Rd (43228-9394)
PHONE......................................614 850-4400
Jason Montgomery, *Engineer*
Ed Evans, *Manager*
EMP: 65
SALES (corp-wide): 434.8MM Privately
Held
WEB: www.fishelco.com
SIC: 1623 8711 1731 3612 Telephone &
　communication line construction; electric
　power line construction; cable television
　line construction; gas main construction;
　engineering services; electrical work;
　transformers, except electric
PA: The Fishel Company
　1366 Dublin Rd
　Columbus OH 43215
　614 274-8100

(G-7591)
FITCH INC (DH)
585 Suth Front St Ste 300 (43215)
PHONE......................................614 885-3453
Simon Bolton, *CEO*
Dan Stanek, *Partner*
Kevin Doherty, *General Mgr*
Vicky Leavitt, *Managing Dir*
Rick Redpath, *Managing Dir*
EMP: 60 EST: 1960
SQ FT: 40,000
SALES (est): 12.8MM
SALES (corp-wide): 20.1B Privately Held
SIC: 7336 Graphic arts & related design
HQ: Wpp Clapton Square, Llc
　100 Park Ave Fl 4
　New York NY 10017
　212 632-2200

(G-7592)
FIVE STAR SENIOR LIVING INC
Also Called: Forum At Knightsbridge
4590 Knightsbridge Blvd (43214-4327)
PHONE......................................614 451-6793
Rebecca Converse, *Exec Dir*
Gary Sontag, *Program Dir*
EMP: 63 Publicly Held
WEB: www.fivestarqualitycare.com
SIC: 8051 Skilled nursing care facilities
PA: Five Star Senior Living Inc.
　400 Centre St
　Newton MA 02458

(G-7593)
FIXARI FAMILY DENTAL INC (PA)
4241 Kimberly Pkwy (43232-7225)
PHONE......................................614 866-7445
Mark Fixari, *President*
Shane Fixari, *Vice Pres*
Leigha Morrison, *Mktg Dir*
EMP: 30
SQ FT: 2,700
SALES (est): 4.1MM Privately Held
SIC: 8021 Dentists' office

(G-7594)
FLAIRSOFT LTD (PA)
7720 Rivers Edge Dr Ste 2 (43235-1361)
PHONE......................................614 888-0700
Dheeraj Kulshrestha, *Partner*
EMP: 25
SALES: 9.5MM Privately Held
SIC: 7371 Computer software develop-
　ment

(G-7595)
FLEETWOOD MANAGEMENT
INC
1675 Old Henderson Rd (43220-3644)
PHONE......................................614 538-1277
Robert J Beggs, *President*
Joseph E Scruggs, *Vice Pres*
Juli A Difolco, *CFO*
EMP: 40 EST: 1996
SQ FT: 2,850
SALES (est): 2.2MM Privately Held
SIC: 6531 Real estate managers

(G-7596)
FLIGHT EXPRESS INC (HQ)
7250 Star Check Dr (43217-1025)
PHONE......................................305 379-8686
Pat Hawk, *President*
Stephen Howery, *Treasurer*
EMP: 80
SALES (est): 13.9MM
SALES (corp-wide): 461MM Privately
Held
SIC: 4512 Air cargo carrier, scheduled
PA: Bayside Capital, Inc.
　1450 Brickell Ave Fl 31
　Miami FL 33131
　305 379-8686

(G-7597)
FLODRAULIC GROUP
INCORPORATED
765 N Hague Ave (43204-1424)
PHONE......................................614 276-8141
Henrietta Blair, *Branch Mgr*
EMP: 25
SALES (corp-wide): 2.5B Privately Held
WEB: www.flodraulicgroup.com
SIC: 5085 Industrial supplies
PA: Flodraulic Group Incorporated
　3539 N 700 W
　Greenfield IN 46140
　317 890-3700

(G-7598)
FLOWER FACTORY INC
4395 Clime Rd (43228-3406)
PHONE......................................614 275-6220
Bruce Mann, *Manager*
EMP: 60
SALES (corp-wide): 140.6MM Privately
Held
SIC: 5199 5193 5092 Gifts & novelties;
　general merchandise, non-durable; artifi-
　cial flowers; arts & crafts equipment &
　supplies
PA: Flower Factory, Inc.
　5655 Whipple Ave Nw
　North Canton OH 44720
　330 494-7978

(G-7599)
FMW RRI OPCO LLC (PA)
Also Called: Red Roof Inn
605 S Front St Ste 150 (43215-5809)
PHONE......................................614 744-2659
James G Glasgow Jr, *President*
EMP: 36
SALES (est): 8.9MM Privately Held
SIC: 7011 Inns

(G-7600)
FOOD FOR GOOD THOUGHT
INC
4185 N High St (43214-3011)
PHONE......................................614 447-0424
Audrey Todd, *President*
Sarah Duplessis, *Program Dir*
EMP: 30
SALES: 186.2K Privately Held
SIC: 8331 Vocational rehabilitation agency

(G-7601)
FOOD SAFETY NET SERVICES
LTD
4130 Fisher Rd (43228-1022)
PHONE......................................614 274-2070
Steve Palmer, *Branch Mgr*
EMP: 35
SALES (corp-wide): 32.3MM Privately
Held
SIC: 8734 Food testing service

PA: Food Safety Net Services, Ltd.
199 W Rhapsody Dr
San Antonio TX 78216
888 525-9788

(G-7602)
FORTUNE BRANDS WINDOWS INC (DH)
Also Called: Simonton Windows
3948 Townsfair Way # 200 (43219-6095)
PHONE....................................614 532-3500
Mark Savan, *President*
Matthew C Lenz, *Treasurer*
Angela M Pla, *Admin Sec*
▲ **EMP:** 110
SALES (est): 57.3MM
SALES (corp-wide): 2B **Publicly Held**
WEB: www.simontonwindows.com
SIC: 1751 5211 Window & door installation & erection; window & door (prefabricated) installation; door & window products
HQ: Ply Gem Industries, Inc.
5020 Weston Pkwy Ste 400
Cary NC 27513
919 677-3900

(G-7603)
FRANKLIN CNTY BD COMMISSIONERS
Also Called: County Engineers Office
970 Dublin Rd (43215-1169)
PHONE....................................614 462-3030
Dean Ringle, *Principal*
Amy Lowe, *Comms Dir*
Andrea Lossick, *Corp Comm Staff*
Michael Phelps, *Manager*
Teal Slike, *MIS Mgr*
EMP: 180
SQ FT: 8,040
SALES (corp-wide): 1.2B **Privately Held**
SIC: 1611 9111 Highway & street construction; county supervisors' & executives' offices
PA: Franklin County Board Of Commissioners
373 S High St Fl 26
Columbus OH 43215
614 525-3322

(G-7604)
FRANKLIN CNTY BD COMMISSIONERS (PA)
373 S High St Fl 26 (43215-4591)
PHONE....................................614 525-3322
Marilyn Brown, *Commissioner*
Catherine Richards, *Contractor*
EMP: 46
SALES: 1.2B **Privately Held**
SIC: 7389

(G-7605)
FRANKLIN CNTY BD COMMISSIONERS
Franklin County Chld Svcs Bd
855 W Mound St (43223-2208)
PHONE....................................614 275-2571
Chip Spinning, *Director*
EMP: 200
SALES (corp-wide): 1.2B **Privately Held**
SIC: 8322 Children's aid society; adoption services
PA: Franklin County Board Of Commissioners
373 S High St Fl 26
Columbus OH 43215
614 525-3322

(G-7606)
FRANKLIN CNTY BD COMMISSIONERS
Franklin County Facility MGT
373 S High St Fl 2 (43215-4591)
PHONE....................................614 462-3800
Maryann Barnhart, *Director*
EMP: 250
SALES (corp-wide): 1.2B **Privately Held**
SIC: 8744 Facilities support services
PA: Franklin County Board Of Commissioners
373 S High St Fl 26
Columbus OH 43215
614 525-3322

(G-7607)
FRANKLIN CNTY BD COMMISSIONERS
Also Called: Child Support Enforcement Agcy
80 E Fulton St (43215-5128)
PHONE....................................614 462-3275
Joe Pilat, *Director*
EMP: 300
SALES (corp-wide): 1.2B **Privately Held**
SIC: 8322 Child related social services
PA: Franklin County Board Of Commissioners
373 S High St Fl 26
Columbus OH 43215
614 525-3322

(G-7608)
FRANKLIN CNTY BD COMMISSIONERS
Also Called: Juvenile Detention Center
399 S Front St (43215-5389)
PHONE....................................614 462-3429
Kathryn Lias, *Principal*
EMP: 30
SALES (corp-wide): 1.2B **Privately Held**
SIC: 8361 Juvenile correctional facilities
PA: Franklin County Board Of Commissioners
373 S High St Fl 26
Columbus OH 43215
614 525-3322

(G-7609)
FRANKLIN CNTY BD COMMISSIONERS
Also Called: Franklin County Childrens Svcs
4071 E Main St (43213-2952)
PHONE....................................614 229-7100
Chip Spinning, *Director*
EMP: 500
SALES (corp-wide): 1.2B **Privately Held**
SIC: 8322 Child related social services
PA: Franklin County Board Of Commissioners
373 S High St Fl 26
Columbus OH 43215
614 525-3322

(G-7610)
FRANKLIN CNTY BD COMMISSIONERS
Also Called: Franklin County Pub Defender
373 S High St Fl 12 (43215-4591)
PHONE....................................614 462-3194
Judith M Stevenson, *Manager*
EMP: 145
SALES (corp-wide): 1.2B **Privately Held**
SIC: 8111 Legal services
PA: Franklin County Board Of Commissioners
373 S High St Fl 26
Columbus OH 43215
614 525-3322

(G-7611)
FRANKLIN CNTY BD COMMISSIONERS
1731 Alum Creek Dr (43207-1708)
PHONE....................................614 462-4360
Patricia Sphar, *President*
EMP: 33
SALES (corp-wide): 1.2B **Privately Held**
SIC: 8699 Animal humane society
PA: Franklin County Board Of Commissioners
373 S High St Fl 26
Columbus OH 43215
614 525-3322

(G-7612)
FRANKLIN CNTY CRT COMMON PLEAS
Division of Domestic Relations
373 S High St Fl 6 (43215-4591)
PHONE....................................614 525-5775
Dana Preisse,
EMP: 30 **Privately Held**
SIC: 7363 Domestic help service

(G-7613)
FRANKLIN COMMUNICATIONS INC
Also Called: W S N Y F M Sunny 95
4401 Carriage Hill Ln (43220-3837)
PHONE....................................614 451-2191
Alan Goodman, *President*
EMP: 100
SALES (est): 6.2MM **Privately Held**
WEB: www.columbusradiogroup.com
SIC: 4832 Radio broadcasting stations

(G-7614)
FRANKLIN COMMUNICATIONS INC
Also Called: Wsny FM
4401 Carriage Hill Ln (43220-3837)
PHONE....................................614 459-9769
Edward K Christian, *CEO*
Alan Goodman, *President*
EMP: 65
SQ FT: 10,000
SALES (est): 2.1MM **Publicly Held**
WEB: www.sagacommunications.com
SIC: 4832 2711 Radio broadcasting stations; newspapers
HQ: Saga Communications Of New England, Inc.
73 Kercheval Ave Ste 201
Grosse Pointe Farms MI 48236
313 886-7070

(G-7615)
FRANKLIN COMMUNITY BASE CORREC
1745 Alum Creek Dr (43207-1708)
PHONE....................................614 525-4600
Gayle Dittmer, *Principal*
Jacki Dickinson,
Ricky Hodge, *Clerk*
EMP: 75
SALES (est): 2.1MM **Privately Held**
WEB: www.fccourts.org
SIC: 8744 Correctional facility

(G-7616)
FRANKLIN COUNTY ADAMH BOARD
447 E Broad St (43215-3822)
PHONE....................................614 224-1057
David Royer, *CEO*
EMP: 50
SALES (est): 932.8K **Privately Held**
SIC: 8099 Health & allied services

(G-7617)
FRANKLIN COUNTY HISTORICAL SOC
Also Called: Cosi
333 W Broad St (43215-2738)
PHONE....................................614 228-2674
David Chesebrough, *CEO*
Bernie Ostrowski, *Partner*
Kimberly Pratt, *Principal*
Rick Dodsworth, *VP Admin*
◆ **EMP:** 124
SQ FT: 200,000
SALES (est): 16.9MM **Privately Held**
WEB: www.mail.cosi.org
SIC: 8412 Museum

(G-7618)
FRANKLIN IMAGING LLC (PA)
500 Schrock Rd (43229-1028)
PHONE....................................614 885-6894
Emily Williamson,
Joe Williamson,
EMP: 30
SQ FT: 14,400
SALES (est): 6.2MM **Privately Held**
WEB: www.franklinimaging.com
SIC: 7334 5044 5049 Blueprinting service; blueprinting equipment; engineers' equipment & supplies

(G-7619)
FRANKLIN SHCP INC
Also Called: Crown Pointe Care Center
1850 Crown Park Ct (43235-2400)
PHONE....................................440 614-0160
Brian Colleran, *President*
EMP: 99

SALES: 6.6MM **Privately Held**
SIC: 8051 Convalescent home with continuous nursing care

(G-7620)
FRANKLIN SPECIALTY TRNSPT INC (HQ)
2040 Atlas St (43228-9645)
PHONE....................................614 529-7900
Arthur J Decrane, *CEO*
Steve Brooks, *Exec VP*
Richard Sydney, *CFO*
EMP: 26
SQ FT: 42,000
SALES: 21MM
SALES (corp-wide): 77.1MM **Privately Held**
WEB: www.fstfst.com
SIC: 4213 Less-than-truckload (LTL) transport; refrigerated products transport
PA: Fst Logistics, Inc.
1727 Georgesville Rd
Columbus OH 43228
614 529-7900

(G-7621)
FRATERNAL ORDER OF POLICE OF O (PA)
222 E Town St Fl 1e (43215-4611)
PHONE....................................614 224-5700
Jay McDonald, *President*
Mark Drum, *Treasurer*
Gwen Callender,
Kay Cremeans,
Mike Piotrowski,
EMP: 30
SQ FT: 6,500
SALES: 1.1MM **Privately Held**
SIC: 8641 Fraternal associations

(G-7622)
FREEDOM SPECIALTY INSURANCE CO (DH)
Also Called: NATIONWIDE E&S/SPECIALTY
1 W Nationwide Blvd (43215-2752)
P.O. Box 182171 (43218-2171)
PHONE....................................614 249-1545
Chris Watson, *President*
▲ **EMP:** 202 **EST:** 1976
SQ FT: 96,000
SALES (est): 4.8MM
SALES (corp-wide): 13.2B **Privately Held**
WEB: www.atlanticinsurancecompany.com
SIC: 6411 Insurance agents
HQ: Scottsdale Insurance Company
8877 N Gainey Center Dr
Scottsdale AZ 85258
480 365-4000

(G-7623)
FREELAND CONTRACTING CO
2100 Integrity Dr S (43209-2752)
PHONE....................................614 443-2718
James R Fry, *President*
Brenda Fry, *Vice Pres*
EMP: 32
SQ FT: 19,200
SALES (est): 8.9MM **Privately Held**
SIC: 1711 Plumbing contractors

(G-7624)
FRESENIUS MED CARE HLDINGS INC
Also Called: Liberty Dlysis Md-Mrica Dlysis
2355 S Hamilton Rd (43232-4305)
PHONE....................................800 881-5101
EMP: 30
SALES (corp-wide): 18.9B **Privately Held**
SIC: 8092 Kidney dialysis centers
HQ: Fresenius Medical Care Holdings, Inc.
920 Winter St
Waltham MA 02451

(G-7625)
FRESHEALTH LLC
3650 E 5th Ave (43219-1805)
PHONE....................................614 231-3601
James Griffin, *CFO*
Alex Dinovo, *Mng Member*
EMP: 80
SALES (est): 1.1MM **Privately Held**
SIC: 0723 Fruit crops market preparation services

(G-7626)
FRIEDMAN MANAGEMENT COMPANY
50 W Broad St Ste 200 (43215-3301)
PHONE...................................614 224-2424
Andrew Rausthe, Branch Mgr
EMP: 57 Privately Held
SIC: 6512 Property operation, retail establishment
PA: Friedman Management Company
34975 W 12 Mile Rd # 100
Farmington Hills MI 48331

(G-7627)
FRIENDS OF ART FOR CULTURAL
Also Called: F A C E
191 Melyers Ct (43235-6418)
PHONE...................................614 888-9929
Caffan T Willis, Vice Pres
EMP: 25
SALES: 84K Privately Held
SIC: 8641 Youth organizations

(G-7628)
FRIENDSHIP VLG OF CLUMBUS OHIO
5757 Ponderosa Dr (43231-3102)
PHONE...................................614 890-8287
Amanda Trzcinski, Principal
Eric Heinzer, Marketing Staff
Jennifer Sanchez, Executive
EMP: 92
SALES (corp-wide): 16.8MM Privately Held
SIC: 8051 Convalescent home with continuous nursing care
PA: Friendship Village Of Columbus Ohio, Inc
5800 Frest Hills Blvd Ofc
Columbus OH 43231
614 890-8282

(G-7629)
FRIENDSHIP VLG OF CLUMBUS OHIO (PA)
5800 Frest Hills Blvd Ofc (43231)
PHONE...................................614 890-8282
Chris Harbert, Opers Staff
Thomas Miller, Exec Dir
Lisa Burkhart, Exec Dir
Nancy Semones, Receptionist
EMP: 205
SQ FT: 265,000
SALES: 16.8MM Privately Held
WEB: www.friendshipvillageoh.com
SIC: 8361 8051 Home for the aged; skilled nursing care facilities

(G-7630)
FRITZ-RUMER-COOKE CO INC
635 E Woodrow Ave (43207-2030)
PHONE...................................614 444-8844
Clement C Cooke, President
Gordon Webster, General Mgr
Karen Cooke, Vice Pres
EMP: 35 EST: 1879
SQ FT: 1,500
SALES (est): 10.3MM Privately Held
SIC: 1629 Railroad & railway roadbed construction

(G-7631)
FROST BROWN TODD LLC
1 Columbus Ste 2300 10 W (43215)
PHONE...................................614 464-1211
Thomas V Willams, Branch Mgr
Carol Dunn, Executive
Wanda Hoffman, Admin Sec
Jennifer Rini, Admin Sec
Linda Schengeli, Admin Sec
EMP: 38
SALES (corp-wide): 138MM Privately Held
WEB: www.fbtextra.com
SIC: 8111 General practice attorney, lawyer
PA: Frost Brown Todd Llc
3300 Grt Amrcn Towe 301e
Cincinnati OH 45202
513 651-6800

(G-7632)
FTM ASSOCIATES LLC
150 E Campus View Blvd (43235-4648)
PHONE...................................614 846-1834
David B Friedman,
EMP: 80
SQ FT: 134,000
SALES (est): 2.4MM Privately Held
SIC: 6513 Apartment building operators

(G-7633)
FUJIYAMA INTERNATIONAL INC
5755 Cleveland Ave (43231-2831)
PHONE...................................614 891-2224
Bill Marcum, President
Myung Kim, Vice Pres
EMP: 30
SALES: 1.5MM Privately Held
SIC: 6531 Real estate agents & managers

(G-7634)
FUNNY BONE COMEDY CLUB & CAFE
145 Easton Town Ctr (43219-6075)
PHONE...................................614 471-5653
Dave Stroupe, Owner
EMP: 35
SALES (est): 794.8K Privately Held
WEB: www.gofunnybone.com
SIC: 7922 Theatrical producers & services

(G-7635)
FURNITURE BANK CENTRAL OHIO
Also Called: FURNITURE WITH A HEART
118 S Yale Ave (43222-1369)
PHONE...................................614 272-9544
James C Stein, President
Steve Votaw, President
John Vidosh, Director
EMP: 25
SQ FT: 1,820
SALES: 4.5MM Privately Held
WEB: www.mapfurniturebank.org
SIC: 8322 Social service center

(G-7636)
FUTURE POLY TECH INC (PA)
2215 Citygate Dr Ste D (43219-3589)
PHONE...................................614 942-1209
Ron Anderko, President
EMP: 30
SALES (est): 3.5MM Privately Held
SIC: 7389 Packaging & labeling services

(G-7637)
G & G CONCRETE CNSTR LLC
2849 Switzer Ave (43219-2313)
PHONE...................................614 475-4151
Mikel Giammarco,
EMP: 32
SALES (est): 1.1MM Privately Held
SIC: 1521 Single-family housing construction

(G-7638)
G III REITTER WALLS LLC
1759 Old Leonard Ave (43219-2561)
PHONE...................................614 545-4444
Dave Reitter,
EMP: 27 EST: 2013
SALES: 2MM Privately Held
SIC: 1522 1542 Residential construction; nonresidential construction

(G-7639)
G MECHANICAL INC
6635 Singletree Dr (43229-1120)
PHONE...................................614 844-6750
Christopher Giannetto, President
EMP: 42
SALES: 7.5MM Privately Held
SIC: 1711 Mechanical contractor

(G-7640)
G STEPHENS INC
1175 Dublin Rd Ste 2 (43215-1252)
PHONE...................................614 227-0304
Glenn Stephens, Branch Mgr
EMP: 65 Privately Held
SIC: 8741 Construction management
PA: G. Stephens, Inc.
133 N Summit St
Akron OH 44304

(G-7641)
G-COR AUTOMOTIVE CORP (PA)
2100 Refugee Rd (43207-2841)
PHONE...................................614 443-6735
Stanley Greenblott, President
Donald L Feinstein, Principal
Kenny Greenblott, Vice Pres
▼ EMP: 45
SQ FT: 250,000
SALES (est): 27.6MM Privately Held
SIC: 5013 5015 5093 Automotive supplies & parts; automotive parts & supplies, used; metal scrap & waste materials

(G-7642)
G4S SECURE SOLUTIONS USA INC
Also Called: Wackenhut
2211 Lake Club Dr Ste 105 (43232-3204)
PHONE...................................614 322-5100
Graham Gibson, Branch Mgr
EMP: 150 Privately Held
SIC: 7381 Security guard service
HQ: G4s Secure Solutions (Usa) Inc.
1395 University Blvd
Jupiter FL 33458
561 622-5656

(G-7643)
GAHANNA HEALTH CARE CENTER
Also Called: Rocky Creek Hlth Rhabilitation
121 James Rd (43230-2825)
PHONE...................................614 475-7222
Brian Colleran, President
EMP: 50
SALES (est): 1.1MM Privately Held
SIC: 8051 Skilled nursing care facilities

(G-7644)
GAHANNA-JEFFERSON PUB SCHL DST
Also Called: Bus Transportation Department
782 Science Blvd (43230-6641)
PHONE...................................614 751-7581
Robert McCafferty, Principal
EMP: 60
SALES (corp-wide): 99.9MM Privately Held
SIC: 4151 School buses
PA: Gahanna-Jefferson Public School District
160 S Hamilton Rd
Gahanna OH 43230
614 471-7065

(G-7645)
GALLAGHER GAMS PRYOR TALLAN
471 E Broad St Fl 19 (43215-3864)
PHONE...................................614 228-5151
Laurie Duckworth, President
James R Gallagher, Partner
Brian Gallagher, Partner
Mark H Gams, Partner
Barry Littrell, Partner
EMP: 26
SALES (est): 3.8MM Privately Held
WEB: www.ggptl.com
SIC: 8111 General practice law office; general practice attorney, lawyer

(G-7646)
GARDA CL GREAT LAKES INC
Also Called: At Systems
201 Schofield Dr (43213-3831)
PHONE...................................614 863-4044
Ron Drener, Manager
EMP: 30 Privately Held
WEB: www.gocashlink.com
SIC: 7381 Armored car services
HQ: Garda Cl Great Lakes, Inc.
201 Schofield Dr
Columbus OH 43213
561 939-7000

(G-7647)
GARDA CL GREAT LAKES INC (DH)
Also Called: United Armored Services
201 Schofield Dr (43213-3831)
PHONE...................................561 939-7000
Stephan Cretier, President
Tim Henry, President

Chris W Jamroz, President
Thomas Devico, Finance
Jack Deml, Empl Rel Dir
EMP: 400 EST: 1971
SQ FT: 60,000
SALES (est): 20.4MM Privately Held
SIC: 7381 7389 7359 Armored car services; packaging & labeling services; equipment rental & leasing

(G-7648)
GARDNER INC (PA)
3641 Interchange Rd (43204-1499)
PHONE...................................614 456-4000
John F Finn, CEO
James P Finn, Vice Pres
Michael L Finn, Vice Pres
John T Finn, CFO
EMP: 222
SQ FT: 204,000
SALES (est): 56.2MM Privately Held
SIC: 6512 5084 Nonresidential building operators; engines, gasoline

(G-7649)
GARDNER-CONNELL LLC
3641 Interchange Rd (43204-1499)
PHONE...................................614 456-4000
Bill Shamon, Branch Mgr
EMP: 37 Privately Held
SIC: 5191 5083 Farm supplies; farm & garden machinery
PA: Gardner-Connell, Llc
125 Constitution Blvd
Franklin MA 02038

(G-7650)
GARLAND GROUP INC
Also Called: Buckeye Real Estate
48 E 15th Ave Frnt (43201-1679)
P.O. Box 8310 (43201-0310)
PHONE...................................614 294-4411
Wayne Garland, President
Lorie Garland, Vice Pres
Robert Hendershot, Treasurer
EMP: 50 EST: 1975
SQ FT: 7,300
SALES (est): 5.6MM Privately Held
WEB: www.buckeyere.com
SIC: 6513 1522 6531 Apartment building operators; remodeling, multi-family dwellings; real estate brokers & agents

(G-7651)
GBQ CONSULTING LLC
230 West St Ste 700 (43215-2663)
PHONE...................................614 221-1120
Darci Congrove, CEO
Cara Hounshell,
EMP: 53 EST: 2005
SALES (est): 440.7K
SALES (corp-wide): 20.7MM Privately Held
SIC: 8742 Management consulting services
PA: Gbq Holdings, Llc
230 West St Ste 700
Columbus OH 43215
614 221-1120

(G-7652)
GBQ HOLDINGS LLC (PA)
230 West St Ste 700 (43215-2663)
PHONE...................................614 221-1120
Darci Congrove, Principal
Nancy Bretas, Admin Asst
Paul Anderson,
James Bechtel,
Mark Laplace,
EMP: 47 EST: 2012
SQ FT: 39,178
SALES (est): 20.7MM Privately Held
SIC: 8721 Certified public accountant

(G-7653)
GENERAL PARTS INC
Also Called: Carquest Auto Parts
2825 Silver Dr (43211-1052)
PHONE...................................614 267-5197
Kendra Reiss, Branch Mgr
EMP: 25
SALES (corp-wide): 9.3B Publicly Held
WEB: www.carquest.com
SIC: 5013 5531 Automotive supplies; automotive parts

HQ: General Parts, Inc.
2635 E Millbrook Rd Ste C
Raleigh NC 27604
919 573-3000

(G-7654)
GENERAL SERVICES CLEANING CO
8111 Blind Brook Ct (43235-1203)
P.O. Box 1052, Powell (43065-1052)
PHONE..............................614 840-0562
Brad Kilgore, *President*
Becky Kilgore, *Vice Pres*
EMP: 30
SQ FT: 3,000
SALES (est): 1MM Privately Held
SIC: 7349 Janitorial service, contract basis

(G-7655)
GENERAL THEMING CONTRS LLC
Also Called: GTC Artist With Machines
3750 Courtright Ct (43227-2253)
PHONE..............................614 252-6342
Richard D Rogovin, *Principal*
April Andrick, *Director*
Kim Schanzenbach,
Rich Witherspoon,
EMP: 105
SQ FT: 60,000
SALES (est): 17.9MM Privately Held
WEB: www.theming.net
SIC: 7389 7336 2759 2396 Sign painting & lettering shop; commercial art & graphic design; commercial printing; automotive & apparel trimmings

(G-7656)
GENERATION HEALTH CORP
Also Called: Broadview Health Center
5151 N Hamilton Rd (43230-1313)
PHONE..............................614 337-1066
George R Powell, *President*
Renee M Hott, *Vice Pres*
Kelly C McGee, *Treasurer*
Edward Powell Jr, *Admin Sec*
EMP: 130
SQ FT: 57,946
SALES (est): 7.9MM Privately Held
WEB: www.broadviewhealth.com
SIC: 8051 Skilled nursing care facilities

(G-7657)
GENESIS CORP
Also Called: Genesis 10
4449 Easton Way (43219-6093)
PHONE..............................614 934-1211
Kim Murgas, *Branch Mgr*
EMP: 35
SALES (corp-wide): 179.7MM Privately Held
SIC: 7379 8742 Computer related consulting services; management consulting services
PA: Genesis Corp.
950 3rd Ave Ste 900
New York NY 10022
212 688-5522

(G-7658)
GEO BYERS SONS HOLDING INC
Also Called: Hertz
4185 E 5th Ave (43219-1813)
PHONE..............................614 239-1084
Blaine Byers, *Manager*
EMP: 30
SALES (corp-wide): 191.9MM Privately Held
SIC: 7514 7513 Rent-a-car service; truck rental, without drivers
PA: Geo. Byers Sons Holding, Inc.
427 S Hamilton Rd
Columbus OH 43213
614 228-5111

(G-7659)
GEORGE J IGEL & CO INC
2040 Alum Creek Dr (43207-1714)
PHONE..............................614 445-8421
Brad Swallie, *Superintendent*
Louis Smoot Sr, *Principal*
George Ige, *Vice Pres*
Brian Van Deventer, *Vice Pres*
Ronald L Wallace, *Vice Pres*

EMP: 892 EST: 1911
SQ FT: 50,000
SALES (est): 158.5MM Privately Held
WEB: www.igelco.com
SIC: 1794 1623 6552 Excavation & grading, building construction; sewer line construction; water main construction; subdividers & developers

(G-7660)
GEORGE KUHN ENTERPRISES INC
Also Called: A J Asphalt Maintenance & Pav
2200 Mckinley Ave (43204-3417)
PHONE..............................614 481-8838
Margaret Kuhn, *CEO*
James Kuhn, *President*
Kevin George, *Vice Pres*
EMP: 50
SQ FT: 8,000
SALES (est): 5.5MM Privately Held
SIC: 1771 1611 Blacktop (asphalt) work; highway & street maintenance

(G-7661)
GEORGE W MC CLOY
921 Chatham Ln Ste 302 (43221-2482)
PHONE..............................614 457-6233
George W Mc Cloy, *Owner*
EMP: 70
SQ FT: 53,000
SALES (est): 7.3MM Privately Held
SIC: 6411 6163 Insurance agents & brokers; loan brokers

(G-7662)
GEOTEX CONSTRUCTION SVCS INC
1025 Stimmel Rd (43223-2911)
P.O. Box 16331 (43216-6331)
PHONE..............................614 444-5690
Richard Clark, *President*
James W Jordan, *Principal*
Pete Kelley, *Vice Pres*
EMP: 50
SQ FT: 6,000
SALES (est): 9.2MM Privately Held
SIC: 1623 1794 Underground utilities contractor; excavation & grading, building construction

(G-7663)
GERLACH JOHN J CENTER FOR SEN
Also Called: Ohio Health
180 E Broad St Fl 34 (43215-3707)
PHONE..............................614 566-5858
Michelle Stokes, *Director*
EMP: 30
SALES (est): 751.6K Privately Held
SIC: 8322 Senior citizens' center or association

(G-7664)
GERMAIN FORD LLC
7250 Sawmill Rd (43235-1942)
PHONE..............................614 889-7777
Randy Hellmann, *Parts Mgr*
Shane Kitts, *Finance Mgr*
Melissa McDowell, *Personnel*
Christopher Andreas, *Sales Staff*
John Carl, *Sales Staff*
EMP: 135
SQ FT: 41,000
SALES (est): 46.6MM Privately Held
SIC: 5511 7539 Automobiles, new & used; automotive repair shops

(G-7665)
GERMAIN ON SCARBOROUGH LLC
Also Called: Germain Toyota
5711 Scarborough Blvd (43232-4748)
PHONE..............................614 868-0300
Todd Mathews, *Mktg Dir*
Steve Germain, *Manager*
Sandy Mintier, *Manager*
EMP: 150
SALES (corp-wide): 146.3MM Privately Held
WEB: www.germainbmw.com
SIC: 5511 7538 5531 7515 Automobiles, new & used; general automotive repair shops; automotive & home supply stores; passenger car leasing

PA: Germain On Scarborough, Llc
4250 Morse Xing
Columbus OH 43219
239 592-5550

(G-7666)
GETHSEMANE LUTHERAN CHURCH
35 E Stanton Ave (43214-1198)
PHONE..............................614 885-4319
Karen Asmus-Alsnauer, *Pastor*
Diane Gutgesell, *Admin Sec*
EMP: 25
SQ FT: 10,000
SALES (est): 795.6K Privately Held
SIC: 8661 8351 Lutheran Church; child day care services

(G-7667)
GFS CHEMICALS INC
800 Mckinley Ave (43222-1107)
PHONE..............................740 881-5501
EMP: 52
SALES (corp-wide): 23.6MM Privately Held
SIC: 5169 Chemicals & allied products
PA: Gfs Chemicals, Inc.
3041 Home Rd
Powell OH 43065
740 881-5501

(G-7668)
GILBANE BUILDING COMPANY
145 E Rich St Fl 4 (43215-5253)
PHONE..............................614 948-4000
Walt McKelvey, *Branch Mgr*
EMP: 30
SALES (corp-wide): 4.9B Privately Held
WEB: www.gilbaneco.com
SIC: 8741 1542 Construction management; nonresidential construction
HQ: Gilbane Building Company
7 Jackson Walkway Ste 2
Providence RI 02903
401 456-5800

(G-7669)
GIRL SCOUTS OF THE US AMER
Girl Scouts Ohio's Heartland
1700 Watermark Dr (43215-1097)
PHONE..............................614 487-8101
Tammy Wharton, *CEO*
EMP: 102
SALES (corp-wide): 92.4MM Privately Held
SIC: 8641 Girl Scout organization
PA: Girl Scouts Of The United States Of America
420 Fifth Ave 37th St Fl G
New York NY 10018
212 852-8000

(G-7670)
GIRL SCUTS OHIOS HEARTLAND INC (PA)
1700 Watermark Dr (43215-1097)
PHONE..............................614 340-8820
Tammy Wharton, *CEO*
EMP: 93
SALES: 7.9MM Privately Held
SIC: 8641 Girl Scout organization

(G-7671)
GLADDEN COMMUNITY HOUSE
183 Hawkes Ave (43223-1533)
P.O. Box 23030 (43223-0030)
PHONE..............................614 221-7801
Joy Chivers, *President*
Kevin Ballard, *Vice Pres*
Mardi Ciriaco, *Vice Pres*
EMP: 30
SQ FT: 40,000
SALES: 1.9MM Privately Held
SIC: 8322 Neighborhood center

(G-7672)
GLAVAN & ACCOCIATES ARCHITECTS
107 S High St Ste 200 (43215-3492)
PHONE..............................614 205-4060
Jeffrey L Glavan, *President*
Jay Edward Feher, *Vice Pres*
EMP: 30
SQ FT: 10,000

SALES: 2.7MM Privately Held
WEB: www.glavan.com
SIC: 8712 Architectural services

(G-7673)
GLEN WESLEY INC
Also Called: WESLEY RIDGE
5155 N High St (43214-1694)
PHONE..............................614 888-7492
Margaret Carmany, *CEO*
Africa Thomas, *Principal*
Tina Cassady, *Principal*
Lauren Croman, *Principal*
Charles Leader III, *Vice Pres*
EMP: 100 EST: 1967
SQ FT: 279,000
SALES: 20.4MM Privately Held
WEB: www.glenwesley.com
SIC: 8051 6513 8361 Skilled nursing care facilities; apartment building operators; retirement hotel operation; geriatric residential care; home for the aged; rehabilitation center, residential: health care incidental

(G-7674)
GLIMCHER REALTY TRUST (PA)
Also Called: Eastland Mall
2740 Eastland Mall Ste B (43232-4959)
PHONE..............................614 861-3232
Michael Tlimcher, *President*
EMP: 33
SALES (est): 3.1MM Privately Held
SIC: 6512 Shopping center, community (100,000 - 300,000 sq ft); shopping center, property operation only

(G-7675)
GODMAN GUILD (PA)
303 E 6th Ave (43201-2888)
PHONE..............................614 294-5476
Erin Fay, *General Mgr*
Greta Rzymek, *Senior VP*
Linda Silva, *Senior VP*
Janis Dean, *Opers Staff*
Ikhlas Asadi, *Supervisor*
EMP: 30
SALES: 4.2MM Privately Held
WEB: www.godmanguild.org
SIC: 8322 Social service center; community center

(G-7676)
GOLD STAR INSULATION L P
495 S High St (43215-5689)
PHONE..............................614 221-3241
Pam Hanson, *Admin Sec*
EMP: 40
SALES: 5MM Privately Held
SIC: 1542 1521 Commercial & office building, new construction; new construction, single-family houses

(G-7677)
GOLDEN ENDINGS GOLDEN RET RESC
1043 Elmwood Ave (43212-3255)
PHONE..............................614 486-0773
Kay Hirsch, *President*
EMP: 50
SALES: 79.5K Privately Held
SIC: 6732 Trusts: educational, religious, etc.

(G-7678)
GOLDEN LIVING LLC
Also Called: Beverly
1425 Yorkland Rd (43232-1686)
PHONE..............................614 861-6666
Robert Brooks, *Exec Dir*
EMP: 110
SALES (corp-wide): 7.4MM Privately Held
SIC: 8059 8052 8051 Convalescent home; intermediate care facilities; skilled nursing care facilities
PA: Golden Living Llc
5220 Tennyson Pkwy # 400
Plano TX 75024
972 372-6300

(G-7679)
GOODWILL INDS CENTL OHIO INC (PA)
Also Called: GOODWILL COLUMBUS
1331 Edgehill Rd (43212-3123)
PHONE..............................614 294-5181

Marjory Pizzuti, *President*
Holly Gross, *President*
Anthony Hartley, *COO*
Hartley Anthony, *Vice Pres*
Michael Goldbeck, *Vice Pres*
EMP: 275
SQ FT: 185,000
SALES: 48.1MM **Privately Held**
SIC: 8331 5399 Job training services; vocational rehabilitation agency; surplus & salvage goods

(G-7680)
GOODWILL INDS CENTL OHIO INC
Also Called: Working Community Services
890 N Hague Ave (43204-2174)
PHONE..........................614 274-5296
Timmy Hughes, *Manager*
EMP: 50
SALES (corp-wide): 48.1MM **Privately Held**
SIC: 8331 Job training services
PA: Goodwill Industries Of Central Ohio, Inc.
1331 Edgehill Rd
Columbus OH 43212
614 294-5181

(G-7681)
GOSH ENTERPRISES INC (PA)
Also Called: Charley's Steakery
2500 Farmers Dr 140 (43235-5706)
PHONE..........................614 923-4700
Charley Shin, *President*
Bob Wright, *President*
Jefferson Dayne, *Project Mgr*
Ed Kim, *Purchasing*
Candra Alisiswanto, *CFO*
EMP: 42
SQ FT: 4,000
SALES (est): 14.6MM **Privately Held**
SIC: 5812 6794 Grills (eating places); franchises, selling or licensing

(G-7682)
GOWDY PARTNERS LLC
1533 Lake Shore Dr Ste 50 (43204-3897)
PHONE..........................614 488-4424
Conrad Wisinger, *Principal*
EMP: 32
SALES (est): 2.7MM **Privately Held**
SIC: 1542 Commercial & office building, new construction

(G-7683)
GRAF AND SONS INC
Also Called: Overhead Door Company
2300 International St (43228-4621)
PHONE..........................614 481-2020
Dean Monnin, *President*
EMP: 30
SQ FT: 30,000
SALES (est): 3.9MM **Privately Held**
WEB: www.grafsons.com
SIC: 1751 5031 Garage door, installation or erection; doors, garage; doors

(G-7684)
GRANDVIEW FAMILY PRACTICE
1550 W 5th Ave Lowr (43212-2474)
PHONE..........................740 258-9267
Dr Charles May, *President*
EMP: 25
SQ FT: 4,000
SALES (est): 2.6MM **Privately Held**
SIC: 8031 8011 Offices & clinics of osteopathic physicians; general & family practice, physician/surgeon

(G-7685)
GRANGE INDEMNITY INSURANCE CO
Also Called: Grange Mutual Casualty Company
671 S High St (43206-1066)
P.O. Box 1218 (43216-1218)
PHONE..........................614 445-2900
Tom Welch, *President*
Martin J Dinehart, *Vice Pres*
David T Roark, *Vice Pres*
Randall J Montelone, *Treasurer*
EMP: 52
SQ FT: 9,500

SALES (est): 14.4MM
SALES (corp-wide): 992.5MM **Privately Held**
SIC: 6411 Insurance agents
PA: Grange Mutual Casualty Company
671 S High St
Columbus OH 43206
614 445-2900

(G-7686)
GRANGE LIFE INSURANCE COMPANY
671 S High St (43206-1066)
PHONE..........................800 445-3030
Thomas Welch, *CEO*
Brandon Karg, *Manager*
EMP: 32 **EST:** 2014
SALES (est): 17MM **Privately Held**
SIC: 6411 Insurance agents, brokers & service

(G-7687)
GRANGE MUTUAL CASUALTY COMPANY (PA)
Also Called: Grange Insurance Companies
671 S High St (43206-1049)
P.O. Box 1218 (43216-1218)
PHONE..........................614 445-2900
Tom Welch, *CEO*
David Berentz, *President*
John R Delucia, *President*
Scott Drab, *President*
Gary Irvine, *President*
EMP: 850
SQ FT: 212,000
SALES (est): 992.5MM **Privately Held**
SIC: 6331 Automobile insurance; fire, marine & casualty insurance: mutual

(G-7688)
GRAYBAR ELECTRIC COMPANY INC
1200 Kinnear Rd (43212-1154)
PHONE..........................614 486-4391
Eric Winigman, *Sales Staff*
Harodl Yarborough, *Sales Staff*
Rick Dannhausen, *Branch Mgr*
EMP: 44
SALES (corp-wide): 7.2B **Privately Held**
WEB: www.graybar.com
SIC: 5063 Electrical supplies
PA: Graybar Electric Company, Inc.
34 N Meramec Ave
Saint Louis MO 63105
314 573-9200

(G-7689)
GREAT NTHRN CNSULTING SVCS INC (PA)
200 E Campus View Blvd # 200 (43235-4678)
PHONE..........................614 890-9999
James C Deboard, *Principal*
Jeffrey Jones, *CFO*
Anna Mary Abel, *Administration*
EMP: 40
SQ FT: 4,000
SALES (est): 8.5MM **Privately Held**
WEB: www.gnorth.com
SIC: 7379 ; computer related consulting services

(G-7690)
GREAT VALUE STORAGE
5301 Tamarack Cir E (43229-4501)
PHONE..........................614 848-8420
EMP: 33
SALES (corp-wide): 33.8MM **Privately Held**
SIC: 4226 4225 Household goods & furniture storage; general warehousing & storage
PA: Great Value Storage
401 Congress Ave Fl 33
Austin TX 78701
512 327-3300

(G-7691)
GREATER CLUMBUS CONVENTION CTR
400 N High St Fl 4 (43215-2078)
PHONE..........................614 827-2500
Craig Liston, *General Mgr*
Art McAndew, *Manager*
EMP: 189 **EST:** 1974

SALES (est): 20.2MM **Privately Held**
SIC: 6512 Commercial & industrial building operation

(G-7692)
GREATER COLUMBUS CHMBR COMMRCE
Also Called: Greater Clmbus Chmber Commerce
150 S Front St Ste 220 (43215-7107)
PHONE..........................614 221-1321
Ty Marsh, *President*
Sally A Jackson, *President*
EMP: 40
SQ FT: 23,000
SALES (est): 3.2MM **Privately Held**
WEB: www.columbus.org
SIC: 8611 Chamber of Commerce

(G-7693)
GREATER COLUMBUS REGIONAL
285 E State St Ste 170 (43215-4322)
PHONE..........................614 228-9114
Kris Stelzer, *Director*
DH Ventures
EMP: 70
SALES (est): 1.6MM **Privately Held**
SIC: 8092 Kidney dialysis centers

(G-7694)
GREATR COLUMBUS CONVENTN & VIS (PA)
Also Called: Gccvb
277 W Nationwide Blvd (43215-2853)
PHONE..........................614 221-6623
Paul Astleford, *President*
Michelle Ford, *Editor*
Jodi Beekman, *Vice Pres*
Angela Hammond, *Natl Sales Mgr*
Brian Ross, *VP Sales*
EMP: 38
SQ FT: 17,000
SALES: 15.1MM **Privately Held**
WEB: www.experiencecolumbus.com
SIC: 7389 Tourist information bureau

(G-7695)
GREEN LAWN CEMETERY ASSN
1000 Greenlawn Ave (43223-2618)
PHONE..........................614 444-1123
Linda Burkey, *General Mgr*
Joesph Glandon, *Manager*
EMP: 25 **EST:** 1848
SALES: 698K **Privately Held**
WEB: www.greenlawncolumbus.org
SIC: 6553 Cemetery association

(G-7696)
GREENSCAPES LANDSCAPE COMPANY
Also Called: Greenscapes Landscape Arch
4220 Winchester Pike (43232-5612)
PHONE..........................614 837-1869
William A Gerhardt, *President*
John Loos, *Project Mgr*
Tom Kuhn, *Sales Executive*
Bill Gerhardt, *Office Mgr*
EMP: 70
SQ FT: 3,000
SALES (est): 9.2MM **Privately Held**
SIC: 0782 0781 4959 Landscape contractors; landscape architects; snowplowing

(G-7697)
GREYHOUND LINES INC
111 E Town St Ste 100 (43215-5153)
PHONE..........................614 221-0577
Dole Butterball, *Branch Mgr*
EMP: 40
SALES (corp-wide): 8.9B **Privately Held**
SIC: 4142 4131 Bus charter service, except local; intercity & rural bus transportation
HQ: Greyhound Lines, Inc.
350 N Saint Paul St # 300
Dallas TX 75201
214 849-8000

(G-7698)
GTE INTERNET
6816 Lauffer Rd (43231-1623)
PHONE..........................614 508-6000
Scott Klabunde, *Owner*
EMP: 70

SALES (est): 1.2MM **Privately Held**
SIC: 8011 Offices & clinics of medical doctors

(G-7699)
GUARDIAN BUSINESS SERVICES
3948 Townsfair Way # 220 (43219-6095)
PHONE..........................614 416-6090
Rick Wayman, *CEO*
Dale Bring, *President*
EMP: 25
SALES (est): 1MM **Privately Held**
SIC: 6411 Insurance agents, brokers & service

(G-7700)
GUARDIAN CARE SERVICES
665 E Dublin Granville Rd # 330 (43229-3334)
PHONE..........................614 436-8500
Sean Smar, *Owner*
Tamika Smar, *Co-Owner*
EMP: 30
SALES: 400K **Privately Held**
SIC: 7349 Building cleaning service

(G-7701)
GUARDIAN ELDER CARE COLUMBUS
2425 Kimberly Pkwy E (43232-4271)
PHONE..........................614 868-9306
Brian Rendos, *CFO*
Brian Bosak, *Accounting Mgr*
EMP: 73 **EST:** 2016
SALES (est): 336.1K **Privately Held**
SIC: 8059 Nursing & personal care

(G-7702)
GUARDIAN ENTERPRISE GROUP INC
3948 Townsfair Way # 220 (43219-6095)
P.O. Box 1497, Westerville (43086-1497)
PHONE..........................614 416-6080
Richard Schilg, *President*
EMP: 42
SALES (est): 5.8MM
SALES (corp-wide): 5.9MM **Privately Held**
WEB: www.guardianstudios.com
SIC: 7311 Advertising consultant
PA: Guardian Vision International, Inc.
3948 Townsfair Way # 220
Columbus OH 43219
614 416-6080

(G-7703)
GUARDIAN WATER & POWER INC (PA)
1160 Goodale Blvd (43212-3728)
PHONE..........................614 291-3141
Harry Apostolos, *President*
Patricia Apostolos, *Treasurer*
Sean Dicks, *Natl Sales Mgr*
Chris Apostolos, *Regl Sales Mgr*
George Gagnon, *Manager*
EMP: 60
SQ FT: 8,000
SALES (est): 7.1MM **Privately Held**
WEB: www.guardianwp.com
SIC: 7389 7322 Meter readers, remote; adjustment & collection services

(G-7704)
GUDENKAUF CORPORATION (PA)
2679 Mckinley Ave (43204-3898)
PHONE..........................614 488-1776
Jeffrey Gudenkauf, *President*
Sandy Potterton, *President*
Bill Adkins, *Regional Mgr*
Susan Gudenkauf, *Vice Pres*
Sanford Potterton, *Vice Pres*
EMP: 140 **EST:** 1977
SQ FT: 10,000
SALES (est): 43.2MM **Privately Held**
WEB: www.gudenkauf.com
SIC: 1623 Telephone & communication line construction; underground utilities contractor; gas main construction

(G-7705)
GUTKNECHT CONSTRUCTION COMPANY
2280 Citygate Dr (43219-3588)
PHONE..................................614 532-5410
Ben Lindsay, *Vice Pres*
Jamie Weisent, *Vice Pres*
Tom Beddow, *Project Mgr*
Josh Larsen, *Project Mgr*
Jerry McClaskey, *Warehouse Mgr*
EMP: 44
SQ FT: 7,500
SALES (est): 21.1MM **Privately Held**
WEB: www.gutknecht.com
SIC: 1542 Commercial & office building, new construction; commercial & office buildings, renovation & repair

(G-7706)
H & M PATCH COMPANY
Also Called: Gooseberry Patch
2500 Farmers Dr 110 (43235-5706)
PHONE..................................614 339-8950
Shelby V Hutchins, *CEO*
Vickie Hutchins, *Principal*
Joann Martin, *Principal*
Cindy Watson, *Accounts Mgr*
Jen Licon-Conner, *Manager*
▲ **EMP:** 70
SQ FT: 52,000
SALES (est): 9.2MM **Privately Held**
WEB: www.gooseberrypatch.com
SIC: 5961 5192 5947 Gift items, mail order; books; gift shop

(G-7707)
H & M PLUMBING CO
4015 Alum Creek Dr (43207-5161)
PHONE..................................614 491-4880
Doug Houchard, *President*
William Severns, *Vice Pres*
EMP: 40
SQ FT: 6,000
SALES (est): 4.8MM **Privately Held**
SIC: 1711 Plumbing contractors

(G-7708)
HABITAT FOR HUMANITY-MIDOHIO (PA)
6665 Busch Blvd (43229-1767)
PHONE..................................614 422-4828
E J Thomas, *CEO*
Deb Light, *Vice Pres*
Mike Cosgrove, *CFO*
Julie Byers, *Accountant*
Al Finnical, *Manager*
EMP: 47
SALES (est): 7.3MM **Privately Held**
SIC: 1522 Residential construction; individual & family services

(G-7709)
HADLER REALTY COMPANY
Also Called: Hadler Company
2000 Henderson Rd Ste 500 (43220-2496)
PHONE..................................614 457-6650
William N Hadler, *Owner*
EMP: 42 **EST:** 1945
SQ FT: 5,500
SALES (est): 6.2MM **Privately Held**
SIC: 6531 Real estate agent, commercial; real estate managers

(G-7710)
HADLER-ZIMMERMAN INC
2000 Henderson Rd Ste 500 (43220-2497)
PHONE..................................614 457-6650
William H Hadler, *CEO*
George Hadler, *President*
EMP: 25
SQ FT: 7,500
SALES (est): 1.6MM **Privately Held**
SIC: 6512 Commercial & industrial building operation

(G-7711)
HALLMARK HOME MORTGAGE LLC
7965 N High St Ste 100 (43235-8402)
PHONE..................................614 568-1960
Jack Ammons, *Branch Mgr*
EMP: 30 **Privately Held**
SIC: 6162 Mortgage bankers

PA: Hallmark Home Mortgage, Llc
7421 Coldwater Rd
Fort Wayne IN 46825

(G-7712)
HAMILTON HOMECARE INC
Also Called: Hamilton Healthcare
309 S 4th St (43215-5428)
PHONE..................................614 221-0022
Lisa Hamilton, *President*
EMP: 35
SALES (est): 1.6MM **Privately Held**
SIC: 8082 Home health care services

(G-7713)
HAMILTON-PARKER COMPANY (PA)
1865 Leonard Ave (43219-4500)
PHONE..................................614 358-7800
Adam Lewin, *President*
Michelle Brokaw, *Purchasing*
Connie Tuckerman, *Treasurer*
Erica Kuhn, *Accounting Mgr*
Laura Harper, *Human Res Mgr*
▲ **EMP:** 88
SQ FT: 50,000
SALES (est): 43.8MM **Privately Held**
WEB: www.hamiltonparker.com
SIC: 5075 5032 5031 5211 Warm air heating & air conditioning; brick, stone & related material; lumber, plywood & millwork; brick

(G-7714)
HANDSON CENTRAL OHIO INC
1105 Schrock Rd Ste 107 (43229-1174)
PHONE..................................614 221-2255
Marilee Chinnici-Zuercher, *President*
Marilee Zuercher, *President*
Joseph J Patrick Jr, *Vice Pres*
Joseph Schulte, *Research*
Bridget Wolf, *CFO*
EMP: 50
SALES (est): 2.3MM **Privately Held**
WEB: www.firstlink.org
SIC: 8322 8331 Social service center; job training & vocational rehabilitation services

(G-7715)
HANLIN-RAINALDI CONSTRUCTION
6610 Singletree Dr (43229-1121)
PHONE..................................614 436-4204
Grant L Douglass, *Ch of Bd*
Marty Romine, *Superintendent*
Ed Rainaldi, *Vice Pres*
Sean Suttle, *Vice Pres*
Matt Rupp, *Project Mgr*
EMP: 34
SQ FT: 6,000
SALES (est): 9.3MM **Privately Held**
WEB: www.hanlinrainaldi.com
SIC: 1542 Commercial & office building, new construction

(G-7716)
HANSON CONCRETE PRODUCTS OHIO
Also Called: Hanson Pipe & Products
1500 Haul Rd (43207-1888)
PHONE..................................614 443-4846
Terry Feather, *Manager*
EMP: 35 **Privately Held**
SIC: 1771 3441 3272 Concrete Contractor Structural Metal Fabrication Mfg Concrete Products

(G-7717)
HARDLINES DESIGN COMPANY (PA)
4608 Indianola Ave Ste D (43214-2287)
PHONE..................................614 784-8733
Charissa W Durst, *President*
Mej Stokes, *Office Mgr*
EMP: 25
SQ FT: 7,000
SALES (est): 3.2MM **Privately Held**
WEB: www.hardlinesdesign.com
SIC: 8712 Architectural engineering

(G-7718)
HAWA INCORPORATED (PA)
980 Old Henderson Rd C (43220-3723)
PHONE..................................614 451-1711

Douglas S Coffey, *President*
Chris A Pore, *Exec VP*
Neb Heminger, *Vice Pres*
Jeff Ortman, *Vice Pres*
Michelle Hughes, *Manager*
EMP: 29 **EST:** 1954
SQ FT: 10,000
SALES: 7.5MM **Privately Held**
SIC: 8711 Consulting engineer; mechanical engineering; industrial engineers; electrical or electronic engineering

(G-7719)
HAYDOCY AUTOMOTIVE INC
Also Called: Haydocy Automotors
3895 W Broad St (43228-1444)
P.O. Box 28125 (43228-0125)
PHONE..................................614 279-8880
Chris Haydocy, *President*
Rita Fitch, *Corp Secy*
Dan Lynch, *Sales Mgr*
Bobb Park, *Sales Mgr*
EMP: 60
SALES (est): 7.8MM **Privately Held**
WEB: www.haydocy.com
SIC: 7538 5511 7532 5531 General automotive repair shops; automobiles, new & used; pickups, new & used; vans, new & used; top & body repair & paint shops; automotive & home supply stores; automobiles & other motor vehicles

(G-7720)
HAYWARD DISTRIBUTING CO (PA)
4061 Perimeter Dr (43228-1048)
PHONE..................................614 272-5953
John M Budde, *Ch of Bd*
Ronald L Monroe, *President*
Mark Roberts, *Opers Mgr*
Greg Clouse, *Sales Dir*
Michael Fink, *Sales Mgr*
▲ **EMP:** 35 **EST:** 1947
SQ FT: 36,000
SALES (est): 35.2MM **Privately Held**
WEB: www.haydist.com
SIC: 5083 5023 Lawn machinery & equipment; garden machinery & equipment; grills, barbecue

(G-7721)
HBI PAYMENTS LTD
Also Called: Purepay
3 Easton Oval Ste 210 (43219-6011)
PHONE..................................614 944-5788
John Cullen, *Partner*
Brad West, *Partner*
EMP: 75
SALES (est): 5.1MM **Privately Held**
SIC: 6211 Investment firm, general brokerage

(G-7722)
HDR ENGINEERING INC
2800 Corp Exchange Dr # 100 (43231-7661)
PHONE..................................614 839-5770
Matt Selhorst, *Manager*
EMP: 41
SALES (corp-wide): 1.7B **Privately Held**
SIC: 8742 8711 Management consulting services; engineering services
HQ: Hdr Engineering, Inc.
1917 S 67th St
Omaha NE 68106
402 399-1000

(G-7723)
HEAD INC
4477 E 5th Ave (43219-1817)
PHONE..................................614 338-8501
Middleton E Head Jr, *Ch of Bd*
James M Head, *President*
Jim Head, *President*
John Boyce, *General Mgr*
Kevin Gallagher, *General Mgr*
EMP: 50
SQ FT: 6,000
SALES (est): 24.7MM **Privately Held**
WEB: www.headinc.com
SIC: 1541 1542 Industrial buildings, new construction; institutional building construction

(G-7724)
HEALTH CARE DATAWORKS INC
4215 Worth Ave Ste 320 (43219-1546)
PHONE..................................614 255-5400
Charles Birmingham, *CEO*
Charles Birminghan, *CEO*
Jason Buskirk, *COO*
Jessica V Gerken, *Vice Pres*
Michael Ostrander, *Vice Pres*
EMP: 62
SQ FT: 13,000
SALES (est): 7.8MM
SALES (corp-wide): 63.4MM **Privately Held**
SIC: 7371 Computer software development
PA: Health Catalyst, Inc.
3165 E Millrock Dr # 400
Salt Lake City UT 84121
801 708-6800

(G-7725)
HEALTH CARE RTREMENT CORP AMER
Also Called: Heartland - Victorian Village
920 Thurber Dr W (43215-1247)
PHONE..................................614 464-2273
Gretchen Mangone, *Branch Mgr*
Janice Berridge, *Manager*
EMP: 100
SQ FT: 31,974
SALES (corp-wide): 2.4B **Publicly Held**
WEB: www.hrc-manorcare.com
SIC: 8051 Convalescent home with continuous nursing care
HQ: Health Care And Retirement Corporation Of America
333 N Summit St Ste 103
Toledo OH 43604
419 252-5500

(G-7726)
HEALTHCARE AND SOCIAL
Also Called: Ohio Health Care Employees
1395 Dublin Rd (43215-1086)
PHONE..................................614 461-1199
Tom Woodruff, *Principal*
Delores Brantley, *Vice Pres*
Larry Daniels, *Vice Pres*
Renee Hamrick, *Vice Pres*
Cheryl Hill, *Vice Pres*
EMP: 33
SALES (est): 1.1MM **Privately Held**
SIC: 8631 Labor union

(G-7727)
HEALTHY LIFE HM HEALTHCARE LLC
5454 Cleveland Ave # 201 (43231-4021)
PHONE..................................614 865-3368
Peter Arhin, *Mng Member*
EMP: 30
SALES (est): 139.7K **Privately Held**
SIC: 8082 Home health care services

(G-7728)
HEART OHIO FAMILY HEALTH CTRS
882 S Hamilton Rd (43213-3003)
PHONE..................................614 235-5555
Maggie Bornhorst, *Project Mgr*
Kylie Noble, *Project Mgr*
Christopher Penrod, *CFO*
Danielle Reed, *Manager*
John B Sandman, *Exec Dir*
EMP: 31
SQ FT: 2,925
SALES (est): 4.7MM **Privately Held**
SIC: 8011 Clinic, operated by physicians

(G-7729)
HEART SPECIALISTS OF OHIO
3650 Olentangy River Rd # 300 (43214-3464)
P.O. Box 59, Plain City (43064-0059)
PHONE..................................614 538-0527
Timothy Obarski, *President*
Dr Michael R Jennings, *President*
Dr Lawrence Murcko, *Corp Secy*
Dr Debbra Debates, *Vice Pres*
Dr Tim Obarski, *Vice Pres*
EMP: 25

SALES (est): 3.5MM **Privately Held**
WEB: www.heartspecialistsofohio.com
SIC: 8011 Medical Doctor's Office

(G-7730)
HEARTBEAT INTERNATIONAL INC
5000 Arlington Centre Blv (43220-3083)
PHONE..................................614 885-7577
Margaret H Hartshorn, *President*
Jor-El Godsey, *President*
Susan Hart, *President*
Jennifer Minor, *Editor*
Gary Thome, *Treasurer*
EMP: 45
SALES: 4.7MM **Privately Held**
WEB: www.heartbeatinternational.org
SIC: 8661 8322 Religious organizations; adoption services

(G-7731)
HEARTLAND HOME CARE LLC
Also Called: Heartland Home Health Care
6500 Busch Blvd Ste 210 (43229-1738)
PHONE..................................614 433-0423
Susan Abbott, *Branch Mgr*
EMP: 50
SALES (corp-wide): 2.4B **Publicly Held**
SIC: 8082 Home health care services
HQ: Heartland Home Care, Llc
333 N Summit St Ste 100
Toledo OH 43604

(G-7732)
HEARTLAND HOSPICE SERVICES LLC
Also Called: Heartland HM Hlth Care Hospice
6500 Busch Blvd Ste 210 (43229-1738)
PHONE..................................614 433-0423
Chrissy Goelz, *Branch Mgr*
EMP: 98
SALES (corp-wide): 2.4B **Publicly Held**
SIC: 8082 Home health care services
HQ: Heartland Hospice Services, Llc
333 N Summit St
Toledo OH 43604

(G-7733)
HEARTLAND PETROLEUM LLC (PA)
4001 E 5th Ave (43219-1812)
PHONE..................................614 441-4001
William C Snedegar, *CEO*
Cheri Puckett, *Office Mgr*
EMP: 41
SQ FT: 9,400
SALES (est): 15.9MM **Privately Held**
WEB: www.heartland-petroleum.com
SIC: 5172 Fuel oil

(G-7734)
HEIDELBERG DISTRIBUTING CO
3801 Parkwest Dr (43228-1457)
PHONE..................................614 308-0400
Greg Maurer, *Exec VP*
Jerry Ervin, *Sales Mgr*
Dan Diem, *Manager*
Mike Ross, *Manager*
EMP: 28
SALES (est): 10.9MM **Privately Held**
SIC: 5181 Beer & other fermented malt liquors

(G-7735)
HEINZERLING FOUNDATION (PA)
Also Called: Heinzerling Mem Foundation
1800 Heinzerling Dr (43223-3642)
PHONE..................................614 272-8888
N Christan Raseld, *Manager*
Dennis Sites, *Manager*
Robert Heninzerli, *Exec Dir*
EMP: 250
SQ FT: 67,000
SALES: 25.1MM **Privately Held**
SIC: 8059 8052 Home for the mentally retarded, exc. skilled or intermediate; intermediate care facilities

(G-7736)
HEINZERLING FOUNDATION
Also Called: Heinzerling Developmental Ctr
1755 Heinzerling Dr (43223-3672)
PHONE..................................614 272-2000
Bob Heinzerling, *Director*

EMP: 550
SQ FT: 40,300
SALES (corp-wide): 25.1MM **Privately Held**
SIC: 8059 8361 Home for the mentally retarded, exc. skilled or intermediate; residential care
PA: Heinzerling Foundation
1800 Heinzerling Dr
Columbus OH 43223
614 272-8888

(G-7737)
HEISER STAFFING SERVICES LLC
330 W Spring St Ste 205 (43215-7300)
PHONE..................................614 800-4188
Karla Heiser, *Mng Member*
EMP: 33 EST: 2014
SALES: 354K **Privately Held**
SIC: 7363 Temporary help service

(G-7738)
HELMSMAN MANAGEMENT SVCS LLC
700 Taylor Rd Ste 220 (43230-3318)
P.O. Box 307230, Gahanna (43230-7230)
PHONE..................................614 478-8282
Michael Topin, *Branch Mgr*
EMP: 85
SALES (corp-wide): 38.3B **Privately Held**
SIC: 8741 Management services
HQ: Helmsman Management Services Llc
175 Berkeley St
Boston MA 02116
857 224-1970

(G-7739)
HENDERSON ROAD REST SYSTEMS (PA)
Also Called: Hyde Park Grille
1615 Old Henderson Rd (43220-3617)
PHONE..................................614 442-3310
Joseph Soccone, *President*
Richard Hauck, *Vice Pres*
EMP: 40
SQ FT: 6,516
SALES (est): 1MM **Privately Held**
SIC: 5812 4119 7542 American restaurant; limousine rental, with driver; carwashes

(G-7740)
HER INC
Also Called: Her Real Living
583 1/2 S 3rd St (43215)
PHONE..................................614 240-7400
Louise Potter, *Manager*
EMP: 25
SQ FT: 993
SALES (corp-wide): 14.3MM **Privately Held**
WEB: www.eassent.com
SIC: 6531 Real estate agent, residential
PA: Her, Inc
4261 Morse Rd
Columbus OH 43230
614 221-7400

(G-7741)
HER INC (PA)
4261 Morse Rd (43230-1522)
PHONE..................................614 221-7400
George W Smith, *CEO*
Harley E Rouda Sr, *Ch of Bd*
Harley E Rouda Jr, *President*
Geri Van Lent, *Senior VP*
Robert E Zellar, *Senior VP*
EMP: 27
SQ FT: 9,800
SALES (est): 14.3MM **Privately Held**
WEB: www.eassent.com
SIC: 6531 Real estate agent, residential

(G-7742)
HER INC
Also Called: H E R Realtors
2815 E Main St (43209-2520)
P.O. Box 9957 (43209-0957)
PHONE..................................614 239-7400
Kathy Landry, *Manager*
EMP: 40

SALES (corp-wide): 14.3MM **Privately Held**
WEB: www.eassent.com
SIC: 6531 Real estate brokers & agents
PA: Her, Inc
4261 Morse Rd
Columbus OH 43230
614 221-7400

(G-7743)
HER INC
Also Called: H E R Realtors
4680 W Broad St (43228-1611)
PHONE..................................614 878-4734
Art Travis, *Manager*
EMP: 25
SALES (corp-wide): 14.3MM **Privately Held**
WEB: www.eassent.com
SIC: 6531 Real estate brokers & agents
PA: Her, Inc
4261 Morse Rd
Columbus OH 43230
614 221-7400

(G-7744)
HERITAGE DAY HEALTH CENTERS (HQ)
Also Called: NATIONAL CHURCH RESIDENCES CENTER FOR SENIOR HEALTH
2335 N Bank Dr (43220-5423)
PHONE..................................614 451-2151
Tanya Kim Hahn, *President*
EMP: 35
SQ FT: 4,200
SALES: 4.7MM
SALES (corp-wide): 38.2MM **Privately Held**
SIC: 8082 Home health care services
PA: National Church Residences
2335 N Bank Dr
Columbus OH 43220
614 451-2151

(G-7745)
HERITAGE MARBLE OF OHIO INC
Also Called: Heritage Marbles
7086 Huntley Rd (43229-1022)
PHONE..................................614 436-1464
Gene Daniels, *President*
EMP: 25
SQ FT: 22,000
SALES (est): 1.9MM **Privately Held**
WEB: www.heritagemarble.com
SIC: 3281 1411 Marble, building: cut & shaped; dimension stone

(G-7746)
HIDDEN LAKE CONDOMINIUMS
Also Called: Real Property Management
1363 Lake Shore Dr (43204-3640)
PHONE..................................614 488-1131
Dwight Penn, *CEO*
Brent Vanoss, *Administration*
EMP: 85
SALES (est): 2.1MM **Privately Held**
SIC: 6531 Real Estate Agent/Manager

(G-7747)
HIGHBANKS CARE CENTER LLC
111 Lazelle Rd (43235-1419)
PHONE..................................614 888-2021
Brian Colleran, *Mng Member*
Roxanne Cannon, *Director*
Richard A Schloss,
EMP: 62
SALES: 4.2MM **Privately Held**
WEB: www.highbanks-care.net
SIC: 8051 Convalescent home with continuous nursing care

(G-7748)
HIGHLAND RELIEF ORGANIZATION
2761 Regaldo Dr (43219-8131)
PHONE..................................614 843-5152
Farah Elmi, *President*
EMP: 40
SALES (est): 126.4K **Privately Held**
SIC: 8641 Civic social & fraternal associations

(G-7749)
HILL BARTH & KING LLC
Also Called: Hbk CPA & Consultants
226 N 5th St Ste 500 (43215-2784)
PHONE..................................614 228-4000
Paul Ritchui, *Manager*
EMP: 71
SALES (corp-wide): 49.7MM **Privately Held**
SIC: 8721 Certified public accountant
PA: Hill, Barth & King Llc
6603 Summit Dr
Canfield OH 44406
330 758-8613

(G-7750)
HILL MANOR 1 INC
3244 Southfield Dr E (43207-3341)
PHONE..................................740 972-3227
Fannie Mills, *President*
EMP: 36
SQ FT: 2,994
SALES (est): 418.5K **Privately Held**
SIC: 8361 8093 Residential care; rehabilitation center, outpatient treatment

(G-7751)
HILTON GARDEN INN
3232 Olentangy River Rd (43202-1519)
PHONE..................................614 263-7200
John Businger, *Manager*
EMP: 80
SALES (est): 2.2MM **Privately Held**
SIC: 7011 Hotels & motels

(G-7752)
HILTON GRDN INN COLUMBUS ARPRT
4265 Sawyer Rd (43219-3812)
PHONE..................................614 231-2869
Paul Malcolm, *General Mgr*
EMP: 80
SALES (est): 2.5MM **Privately Held**
SIC: 7011 Hotels

(G-7753)
HIT PORTFOLIO I MISC TRS LLC
Also Called: Hyatt On Capitol Square
75 E State St (43215-4203)
PHONE..................................614 228-1234
Bruce Flyer, *General Mgr*
Karen Theis, *Branch Mgr*
EMP: 200
SALES (corp-wide): 4.4B **Publicly Held**
WEB: www.hyatt.com
SIC: 6512 7011 5812 5813 Nonresidential building operators; hotels; eating places; drinking places
HQ: Hyatt Corporation
150 N Riverside Plz
Chicago IL 60606
312 750-1234

(G-7754)
HIT PORTFOLIO I TRS LLC
Also Called: Hyatt Pl Columbus Worthington
7490 Vantage Dr (43235-1416)
PHONE..................................614 846-4355
Sarah Hughes, *Sales Staff*
Bo Hagood, *Branch Mgr*
EMP: 25
SALES (corp-wide): 49.8MM **Privately Held**
SIC: 7011 Hotels
HQ: Hit Portfolio I Trs, Llc
106 York Rd
Jenkintown PA

(G-7755)
HIT SWN TRS LLC
Also Called: Courtyard Columbus Downtown
35 W Spring St (43215-2215)
PHONE..................................614 228-3200
Anne Turpin, *Manager*
EMP: 30
SALES (corp-wide): 621MM **Privately Held**
SIC: 7011 Hotels
HQ: Hit Swn Trs, Llc
450 Park Ave Ste 14
New York NY 10022
212 415-6500

▲ = Import ▼=Export
◆ =Import/Export

(G-7756)
HITE PARTS EXCHANGE INC
2235 Mckinley Ave (43204-3400)
PHONE..............................614 272-5115
Thomas A Blake, *President*
Chris Allred, *Sales Staff*
Dona Blake, *Admin Sec*
EMP: 30
SQ FT: 14,000
SALES (est): 4.7MM **Privately Held**
WEB: www.hiteparts.com
SIC: 5013 3714 3625 3594 Automotive
supplies & parts; pumps, oil & gas;
clutches; motor vehicle engines & parts;
clutches, motor vehicle; relays & industrial
controls; fluid power pumps & motors;
carburetors, pistons, rings, valves; power
transmission equipment

(G-7757)
HOCKADEN & ASSOCIATES INC
883 N Cassady Ave (43219-2203)
PHONE..............................614 252-0993
Gurgun Muharrem, *President*
Mark Schroeder, *Vice Pres*
Kurt Ziessler, *Project Engr*
EMP: 40
SALES (est): 3.8MM **Privately Held**
WEB: www.hockaden.com
SIC: 8711 Civil engineering

(G-7758)
HOGAN SERVICES INC
1500 Obetz Rd (43207-4477)
PHONE..............................614 491-8402
Ronnie Hogan, *Production*
Max Baker, *Branch Mgr*
EMP: 30
SALES (est): 732.5K
SALES (corp-wide): 13.3MM **Privately
Held**
SIC: 4789 Pipeline terminal facilities, inde-
pendently operated
PA: Hogan Services, Inc
2150 Schuetz Rd Ste 210
Saint Louis MO 63146
314 421-6000

(G-7759)
HOLIDAY INN EXPRESS
3045 Olentangy River Rd (43202-1516)
PHONE..............................614 447-1212
Jagdeep Singh,
EMP: 25
SALES (est): 1.1MM **Privately Held**
SIC: 7011 Hotels & motels

(G-7760)
HOLIDAY LANES INC
4589 E Broad St (43213-3852)
PHONE..............................614 861-1600
Rick Kennedy, *President*
Joseph E Ducey, *Principal*
Helen P Price, *Principal*
William E Shirk, *Principal*
EMP: 42 EST: 1956
SQ FT: 50,000
SALES (est): 1.4MM **Privately Held**
SIC: 7933 5813 5812 Ten pin center;
cocktail lounge; snack bar

(G-7761)
HOLLAND ROOFING INC
Also Called: Holland Roofing of Columbus
3494 E 7th Ave (43219-1735)
PHONE..............................614 430-3724
Clayton Marshall, *Principal*
EMP: 40
SALES (corp-wide): 47.8MM **Privately
Held**
WEB: www.pondliners.com
SIC: 1761 Roofing contractor
PA: Holland Roofing, Inc.
7450 Industrial Rd
Florence KY 41042
859 525-0887

(G-7762)
HOME DEPOT USA INC
Also Called: Home Depot, The
6333 Cleveland Ave (43231-1617)
PHONE..............................614 523-0600
Jason Gage, *Manager*
EMP: 150

SALES (corp-wide): 108.2B **Publicly
Held**
WEB: www.homerentalsdepot.com
SIC: 5211 7359 Home centers; tool rental
HQ: Home Depot U.S.A., Inc.
2455 Paces Ferry Ave
Atlanta GA 30339

(G-7763)
HOME DEPOT USA INC
Also Called: Home Depot, The
100 S Grener Ave (43228-1922)
PHONE..............................614 878-9150
Dan Hernan, *Manager*
EMP: 150
SALES (corp-wide): 108.2B **Publicly
Held**
WEB: www.homerentalsdepot.com
SIC: 5211 7359 Home centers; tool rental
HQ: Home Depot U.S.A., Inc.
2455 Paces Ferry Ave
Atlanta GA 30339

(G-7764)
HOME DEPOT USA INC
Also Called: Home Depot, The
5200 N Hamilton Rd (43230-1316)
PHONE..............................614 939-5036
Chuck Fry, *Manager*
EMP: 120
SALES (corp-wide): 108.2B **Publicly
Held**
WEB: www.homerentalsdepot.com
SIC: 5211 7359 Home centers; tool rental
HQ: Home Depot U.S.A., Inc.
2455 Paces Ferry Ave
Atlanta GA 30339

(G-7765)
**HOMELESS FAMILIES
FOUNDATION**
33 N Grubb St (43215-2748)
PHONE..............................614 461-9427
Jim Hopkins, *Chairman*
Adrian Corbet, *Exec Dir*
EMP: 25
SALES (est): 2.4MM **Privately Held**
SIC: 8322 Social service center

(G-7766)
HOMES AMERICA INC
83 E Stanton Ave (43214-1110)
PHONE..............................614 848-8551
David Jones, *Manager*
EMP: 28
SALES (corp-wide): 17.3MM **Privately
Held**
SIC: 1521 Single-family housing construc-
tion
PA: Homes America Inc
4604 Dundas Dr
Greensboro NC

(G-7767)
HOMETOWN IMPROVEMENT CO
1430 Halfhill Way (43207-4494)
PHONE..............................614 846-1060
Richard Hatfield, *Owner*
EMP: 25
SALES: 35MM **Privately Held**
SIC: 1521 General remodeling, single-fam-
ily houses

(G-7768)
HOMETOWN URGENT CARE
4400 N High St Ste 101 (43214-2635)
PHONE..............................614 263-4400
Wendy Melick, *Branch Mgr*
EMP: 148
SALES (corp-wide): 73.2MM **Privately
Held**
SIC: 8011 Medical centers
PA: Hometown Urgent Care
2400 Corp Exchange Dr # 102
Columbus OH 43231
614 505-7633

(G-7769)
HOMETOWN URGENT CARE
2880 Stelzer Rd (43219-3133)
PHONE..............................614 472-2880
George Thomas, *Branch Mgr*
EMP: 123
SALES (corp-wide): 73.2MM **Privately
Held**
SIC: 8011 Primary care medical clinic

PA: Hometown Urgent Care
2400 Corp Exchange Dr # 102
Columbus OH 43231
614 505-7633

(G-7770)
HOMETOWN URGENT CARE
4300 Clime Rd Ste 110 (43228-6491)
PHONE..............................614 272-1100
Bill Stricker, *Branch Mgr*
EMP: 123
SALES (corp-wide): 73.2MM **Privately
Held**
SIC: 8011 Medical centers
PA: Hometown Urgent Care
2400 Corp Exchange Dr # 102
Columbus OH 43231
614 505-7633

(G-7771)
**HOMEWOOD CORPORATION
(PA)**
2700 E Dublin Granville R (43231-4089)
PHONE..............................614 898-7200
John H Bain, *CEO*
George Anthony Skestos, *President*
Robert Story, *Info Tech Dir*
EMP: 120
SQ FT: 20,000
SALES (est): 44.4MM **Privately Held**
WEB: www.homewood-homes.com
SIC: 1522 Apartment building construction

(G-7772)
**HONEYWELL INTERNATIONAL
INC**
2080 Arlingate Ln (43228-4112)
PHONE..............................614 717-2270
Ronald Vogt,
EMP: 50
SALES (corp-wide): 41.8B **Publicly Held**
WEB: www.honeywell.com
SIC: 5075 5065 7382 Warm air heating &
air conditioning; security control equip-
ment & systems; security systems serv-
ices
PA: Honeywell International Inc.
115 Tabor Rd
Morris Plains NJ 07950
973 455-2000

(G-7773)
**HORIZON HM HLTH CARE AGCY
LLC**
3035 W Broad St Ste 102 (43204-2653)
PHONE..............................614 279-2933
Ibrahim Osman, *Mng Member*
EMP: 40
SALES (est): 256.1K **Privately Held**
SIC: 8082 Home health care services

(G-7774)
HOTEL 50 S FRONT OPCO L P
Also Called: Doubletree Columbus
50 S Front St (43215-4129)
PHONE..............................614 885-3334
Dan Ouellette, *Manager*
EMP: 100
SALES (est): 275.5K **Privately Held**
SIC: 7011 6512 5813 5812 Hotels & mo-
tels; nonresidential building operators;
drinking places; eating places

(G-7775)
HOTEL 50 S FRONT OPCO LP
50 S Front St (43215-4129)
PHONE..............................614 228-4600
Jan Hando, *Controller*
Raymond Schulte, *Manager*
EMP: 85
SALES (est): 250.9K **Privately Held**
SIC: 7011 Resort hotel

(G-7776)
HOTEL 75 E STATE OPCO L P
Also Called: Sheraton Columbus
75 E State St (43215-4203)
PHONE..............................614 365-4500
David Buddemeyer, *President*
Teresa Tompkins, *Marketing Staff*
Mandy Berryman, *Manager*
Lynda Ciminello, *Manager*
EMP: 48
SALES (est): 4.1MM **Privately Held**
SIC: 7011 Hotels

(G-7777)
HUCKLEBERRY HOUSE
1421 Hamlet St (43201-2599)
PHONE..............................614 294-5553
Tom Meers, *Partner*
Rebecca Westerfelt, *Director*
EMP: 60 EST: 1970
SQ FT: 9,000
SALES: 3.2MM **Privately Held**
WEB: www.huckhouse.org
SIC: 8322 Crisis center; children's aid soci-
ety; emergency shelters

(G-7778)
**HUGHES & KNOLLMAN
CONSTRUCTION**
4601 E 5th Ave (43219-1819)
P.O. Box 20372 (43220-0372)
PHONE..............................614 237-6167
EMP: 55
SALES (est): 5MM **Privately Held**
SIC: 1542 1742 Nonresidential Construc-
tion Drywall/Insulating Contractor

(G-7779)
**HUNTINGTON AUTO TRUST
2015-1**
Huntington Ctr 41 S High (43287-0001)
PHONE..............................302 636-5401
EMP: 186
SALES (est): 51.3K
SALES (corp-wide): 5.2B **Publicly Held**
SIC: 6733 Trusts
PA: Huntington Bancshares Incorporated
41 S High St
Columbus OH 43215
614 480-8300

(G-7780)
**HUNTINGTON AUTO TRUST
2016-1**
41 S High St (43215-6170)
PHONE..............................302 636-5401
EMP: 134
SALES (est): 76.6K
SALES (corp-wide): 5.2B **Publicly Held**
SIC: 6733 Trusts
PA: Huntington Bancshares Incorporated
41 S High St
Columbus OH 43215
614 480-8300

(G-7781)
**HUNTINGTON BANCSHARES
INC (PA)**
41 S High St (43215-6170)
PHONE..............................614 480-8300
Stephen D Steinour, *Ch of Bd*
Leslie Garvin, *General Mgr*
Deborah Strick, *Business Mgr*
Tiffany D Scurti-Swain, *Counsel*
Daniel Neumeyer, *Sr Exec VP*
EMP: 154
SALES: 5.2B **Publicly Held**
WEB: www.huntington.com
SIC: 6021 National commercial banks

(G-7782)
HUNTINGTON CAPITAL I
41 S High St (43215-6170)
PHONE..............................614 480-4038
EMP: 111
SALES (est): 206K
SALES (corp-wide): 5.2B **Publicly Held**
SIC: 6029 Commercial banks
PA: Huntington Bancshares Incorporated
41 S High St
Columbus OH 43215
614 480-8300

(G-7783)
HUNTINGTON INSURANCE INC
7 Easton Oval (43219-6010)
PHONE..............................614 480-3800
Candi Moore, *Principal*
Chris McCoy, *Software Engr*
EMP: 37
SALES (corp-wide): 5.2B **Publicly Held**
SIC: 6411 6211 Insurance agents; security
brokers & dealers
HQ: Huntington Insurance, Inc.
519 Madison Ave
Toledo OH 43604
419 720-7900

(G-7784)
HUNTINGTON INSURANCE INC
37 W Broad St Ste 1100 (43215-4159)
PHONE...................................614 899-8500
Steven M Weiler, *Senior VP*
Brian Hinton, *Vice Pres*
Mary Sullivan, *Vice Pres*
Ashley Bauer, *Marketing Staff*
Tom Weissling, *Manager*
EMP: 100
SALES (corp-wide): 5.2B **Publicly Held**
WEB: www.skyinsure.com
SIC: 6411 Insurance agents
HQ: Huntington Insurance, Inc.
    519 Madison Ave
    Toledo OH 43604
    419 720-7900

(G-7785)
HUNTINGTON NATIONAL BANK
4078 Powell Ave (43213-2321)
PHONE...................................614 480-0067
Jenne Roboerts, *Principal*
EMP: 100
SALES (corp-wide): 5.2B **Publicly Held**
SIC: 6099 Check clearing services
HQ: The Huntington National Bank
    17 S High St Fl 1
    Columbus OH 43215
    614 480-4293

(G-7786)
HUNTINGTON NATIONAL BANK (PA)
17 S High St Fl 1 (43215-3413)
PHONE...................................614 480-4293
EMP: 27
SALES (est): 1.5MM **Privately Held**
SIC: 6029 Commercial Banks, Not Chartered

(G-7787)
HUNTINGTON NATIONAL BANK (HQ)
17 S High St Fl 1 (43215-3413)
PHONE...................................614 480-4293
Stephen D Steinour, *President*
Renee Csuhran, *President*
William C Shivers, *President*
Paul Heller, *COO*
Richard A Cheap, *Exec VP*
▲ EMP: 300
SQ FT: 190,000
SALES: 4.5B
SALES (corp-wide): 5.2B **Publicly Held**
WEB: www.huntingtonnationalbank.com
SIC: 6029 Commercial banks
PA: Huntington Bancshares Incorporated
    41 S High St
    Columbus OH 43215
    614 480-8300

(G-7788)
HUNTINGTON NATIONAL BANK
2361 Morse Rd (43229-5856)
PHONE...................................614 480-8300
EMP: 54
SALES (corp-wide): 4.7B **Publicly Held**
SIC: 6021 National Commercial Bank
HQ: The Huntington National Bank
    17 S High St Fl 1
    Columbus OH 43215
    614 480-4293

(G-7789)
HUNTINGTON TECHNOLOGY FINANCE
37 W Broad St (43215-4132)
PHONE...................................614 480-5169
EMP: 223
SALES (est): 226.6K
SALES (corp-wide): 5.2B **Publicly Held**
SIC: 6021 National commercial banks
PA: Huntington Bancshares Incorporated
    41 S High St
    Columbus OH 43215
    614 480-8300

(G-7790)
HY-TEK MATERIAL HANDLING INC (PA)
2222 Rickenbacker Pkwy W (43217-5002)
PHONE...................................614 497-2500
Samuel Grooms, *President*
Mark Bruner, *Vice Pres*

Donnie Johnson, *Vice Pres*
David Tumbas, *CFO*
Brian Schepman, *Admin Sec*
▲ EMP: 76
SQ FT: 55,000
SALES (est): 81.4MM **Privately Held**
WEB: www.hy-tek.net
SIC: 5084 5013 7538 7513 Materials handling machinery; conveyor systems; lift trucks & parts; truck parts & accessories; truck engine repair, except industrial; truck rental, without drivers; machinery installation

(G-7791)
HYATT CORPORATION
Also Called: Hyatt Hotel
350 N High St (43215-2006)
PHONE...................................614 463-1234
Stephen Stewart, *General Mgr*
Charles Lutrick, *Controller*
Jennifer Pringle, *Sales Mgr*
Kevin McCarty, *Supervisor*
EMP: 300
SALES (corp-wide): 4.4B **Publicly Held**
WEB: www.hyatt.com
SIC: 7011 5813 5812 Hotel, franchised; bar (drinking places); diner
HQ: Hyatt Corporation
    150 N Riverside Plz
    Chicago IL 60606
    312 750-1234

(G-7792)
HYATT REGENCY COLUMBUS
350 N High St (43215-2006)
PHONE...................................614 463-1234
Hyatt Columbus Corp, *General Ptnr*
Charles Lutrick, *Controller*
EMP: 325
SALES (est): 13.4MM **Privately Held**
SIC: 7011 Hotels

(G-7793)
HYPERLOGISTICS GROUP INC (PA)
9301 Intermodal Ct N (43217-6101)
PHONE...................................614 497-0800
Seatta K Layland, *President*
James Brooks, *Warehouse Mgr*
Sandi Conti, *Accountant*
Amy Barnes, *Director*
Geoff Manack,
EMP: 40 EST: 1973
SALES (est): 9.1MM **Privately Held**
SIC: 4225 General warehousing

(G-7794)
I H SCHLEZINGER INC
Also Called: Schlezinger Metals
1041 Joyce Ave (43219-2448)
P.O. Box 83624 (43203-0624)
PHONE...................................614 252-1188
Kenneth Cohen, *President*
Jack Joseph, *Vice Pres*
John Miller, *Vice Pres*
Donald Zulanch, *Vice Pres*
Robert Joseph, *Treasurer*
EMP: 42
SQ FT: 9,000
SALES (est): 13.6MM **Privately Held**
WEB: www.ihschlezinger.com
SIC: 3341 5093 Secondary nonferrous metals; ferrous metal scrap & waste

(G-7795)
I VRABLE INC
Also Called: Heritage Manor Skilled Nursing
3248 Henderson Rd (43220-7337)
PHONE...................................614 545-5500
Allan Vrable, *President*
James Merrill, *CFO*
EMP: 133
SALES: 7MM **Privately Held**
SIC: 8051 Skilled nursing care facilities
PA: Vrable Healthcare, Inc.
    3248 Henderson Rd
    Columbus OH 43220

(G-7796)
I-FORCE LLC
Also Called: Iforce
1110 Morse Rd Ste 200 (43229-6325)
PHONE...................................614 431-5100
Ryan Mason, *Mng Member*
EMP: 150

SALES (est): 182.4K **Privately Held**
SIC: 7361 Employment agencies

(G-7797)
IACOVETTA BUILDERS INC
2525 Fisher Rd (43204-3533)
PHONE...................................614 272-6464
Eugene Iacovetta, *President*
EMP: 50
SQ FT: 1,200
SALES (est): 3.3MM **Privately Held**
SIC: 1522 6513 Multi-family dwelling construction; apartment building operators

(G-7798)
ICE MILLER LLP
250 West St Ste 700 (43215-7509)
PHONE...................................614 462-2700
Joanne Pastwa, *President*
Tonya Toops, *President*
Marita Clarke, *Marketing Staff*
John Daniels, *Branch Mgr*
EMP: 100
SALES (corp-wide): 105MM **Privately Held**
SIC: 8111 General practice law office
PA: Ice Miller Llp
    1 American Sq Ste 2900
    Indianapolis IN 46282
    317 236-2100

(G-7799)
IHEARTCOMMUNICATIONS INC
92.3 Wcol FM
2323 W 5th Ave Ste 200 (43204-4988)
PHONE...................................614 486-6101
Tom Thon, *General Mgr*
Brian Dytko, *General Mgr*
Rhonda Everhart, *Asst Controller*
EMP: 100 **Publicly Held**
SIC: 4832 Radio broadcasting stations
HQ: Iheartcommunications, Inc.
    20880 Stone Oak Pkwy
    San Antonio TX 78258
    210 822-2828

(G-7800)
IHG MANAGEMENT (MARYLAND) LLC
Also Called: Crowne Plaza Columbus Downtown
33 E Nationwide Blvd (43215-2512)
PHONE...................................614 461-4100
Juan Laginia, *Branch Mgr*
EMP: 145 **Privately Held**
SIC: 7011 Hotels
HQ: Maryland Llc Ihg Management
    8844 Columbia 100 Pkwy
    Columbia MD 21045

(G-7801)
ILLINOIS & MIDLAND RR INC (HQ)
4349 Easton Way Ste 110 (43219-6114)
PHONE...................................217 670-1242
Spencer D White, *President*
EMP: 67
SALES (est): 8.7MM
SALES (corp-wide): 2.3B **Publicly Held**
SIC: 4011 Railroads, line-haul operating
PA: Genesee & Wyoming Inc.
    20 West Ave
    Darien CT 06820
    203 202-8900

(G-7802)
IMPACT COMMUNITY ACTION
700 Bryden Rd Fl 2 (43215-4839)
PHONE...................................614 252-2799
Robert E Chilton, *CEO*
Anita Maldonado, *Vice Pres*
McLain Davis, *Project Mgr*
Charline Jordan, *QC Mgr*
Sue Petersen, *CFO*
EMP: 75
SALES: 7MM **Privately Held**
SIC: 8322 Community center

(G-7803)
IMPACT FULFILLMENT SVCS LLC
2035 Innis Rd (43224-3646)
PHONE...................................614 262-8911
EMP: 120

SALES (corp-wide): 98.7MM **Privately Held**
SIC: 4225 4783 General warehousing; packing & crating
PA: Impact Fulfillment Services, Llc
    1601 Anthony Rd
    Burlington NC 27215
    336 227-1130

(G-7804)
IMPROVE IT HOME REMODELING (PA)
4580 Bridgeway Ave B (43219-1891)
PHONE...................................614 297-5121
Seth Cammeyer, *President*
Brian Leader, *Vice Pres*
Anthony Baird, *Controller*
EMP: 145
SQ FT: 14,000
SALES: 12MM **Privately Held**
SIC: 1521 General remodeling, single-family houses

(G-7805)
IN HIS PRSENCE MINISTRIES INTL
Also Called: INPREM HOLISTIC COMMUNITY RESO
5757 Karl Rd (43229-3603)
PHONE...................................614 516-1812
Alex-Eric Clottey, *Pastor*
Alex-Eric Abrokwa-Clottey, *Pastor*
Angela Gibbs, *Admin Asst*
Pranklina Sowah, *Assistant*
EMP: 25
SALES: 4.4K **Privately Held**
SIC: 8661 8611 Non-denominational church; community affairs & services

(G-7806)
INC/BALLEW A HEAD JOINT VENTR
4477 E 5th Ave (43219-1817)
PHONE...................................614 338-5801
James Head, *Partner*
Paul Ondera, *Vice Pres*
EMP: 55
SALES (est): 1.7MM **Privately Held**
SIC: 6531 Real estate leasing & rentals

(G-7807)
INDIANA MICHIGAN POWER COMPANY (HQ)
Also Called: AEP
1 Riverside Plz (43215-2355)
PHONE...................................614 716-1000
Nicholas K Akins, *Ch of Bd*
Paul Chodak III, *President*
Ed Ehler, *Vice Pres*
Thomas A Kratt, *Vice Pres*
Marc E Lewis, *Vice Pres*
EMP: 128 EST: 1907
SALES: 2.3B
SALES (corp-wide): 16.2B **Publicly Held**
SIC: 4911 Distribution, electric power
PA: American Electric Power Company, Inc.
    1 Riverside Plz Fl 1 # 1
    Columbus OH 43215
    614 716-1000

(G-7808)
INDUS AIRPORT HOTEL II LLC
Also Called: Hampton Inn
4280 International Gtwy (43219-1747)
PHONE...................................614 235-0717
Janet Boissy, *Principal*
Matthew Shier, *Principal*
EMP: 55
SALES (est): 195.3K **Privately Held**
SIC: 7011 Hotels & motels

(G-7809)
INDUS AIRPORT HOTELS I LLC
Also Called: Hilton Grdn Inn Columbus Arprt
4265 Sawyer Rd (43219-3812)
PHONE...................................614 231-2869
Janet Boissy, *Principal*
Matthew Shier, *Principal*
EMP: 55 EST: 2016
SALES (est): 430.9K **Privately Held**
SIC: 7011 Inns

(G-7810)

INDUS NEWARK HOTEL LLC
Also Called: Doubletree By Hilton Newark
4265 Sawyer Rd (43219-3812)
PHONE..............................740 322-6455
Janet Boissy, *Principal*
Matthew Shier, *Principal*
EMP: 65
SALES (est): 215K **Privately Held**
SIC: 7011 Hotels

(G-7811)

INDUS TRADE & TECHNOLOGY LLC (PA)
Also Called: Stone Mart
2249 Westbrooke Dr Bldg H (43228-9643)
PHONE..............................614 527-0257
Surendra Kankriya, *Mng Member*
Surendra Kentkerya, *Mng Member*
▲ EMP: 26
SQ FT: 5,000
SALES: 17.5MM **Privately Held**
SIC: 5032 Granite building stone

(G-7812)

INDUSTRIAL AIR CENTERS INC
Also Called: Columbus Air Center
2840 Fisher Rd Ste E (43204-3559)
PHONE..............................614 274-9171
George Burch, *President*
EMP: 50 **Privately Held**
WEB: www.iacserv.com
SIC: 5084 Compressors, except air conditioning
PA: Industrial Air Centers Inc.
731 E Market St
Jeffersonville IN 47130

(G-7813)

INDUSTRIAL FINANCIAL SVCS INC
Also Called: A1a Highway & Construction Eqp
3001 Bethel Rd Ste 108 (43220-2285)
PHONE..............................614 777-0000
Carmen Grace, *President*
EMP: 25 EST: 1998
SQ FT: 3,000
SALES: 2MM **Privately Held**
WEB: www.ifslease.com
SIC: 5084 Industrial machinery & equipment

(G-7814)

INDUSTRY INSIGHTS INC
6235 Emerald Pkwy (43235)
P.O. Box 4330, Dublin (43016-0708)
PHONE..............................614 389-2100
Thomas J Noon, *Ch of Bd*
Stephen Kretzer, *Vice Pres*
Shawn Six, *Vice Pres*
EMP: 25
SQ FT: 3,500
SALES: 2.2MM **Privately Held**
WEB: www.industryinsights.com
SIC: 8742 Business consultant

(G-7815)

INFOQUEST INFORMATION SERVICES
2000 Henderson Rd Ste 300 (43220-2453)
PHONE..............................614 761-3003
John Hughes, *President*
EMP: 25
SALES (est): 5MM **Privately Held**
SIC: 6411 Insurance claim processing, except medical

(G-7816)

INFOR (US) INC
2800 Corp Exchange Dr # 350
(43231-7661)
PHONE..............................678 319-8000
EMP: 350
SALES (corp-wide): 3.1B **Privately Held**
SIC: 7373 7371 Systems software development services; computer system selling services; custom computer programming services
HQ: Infor (Us), Inc.
13560 Morris Rd Ste 4100
Alpharetta GA 30004
678 319-8000

(G-7817)

INFORMATION CONTROL CO LLC
Also Called: Clutch Interactive
2500 Corporate Exch Dr (43231-7665)
PHONE..............................614 523-3070
Steven Glaser, *CEO*
Blane Walter, *Ch of Bd*
Kelly Gratz, *President*
Dave Dieterle, *Vice Pres*
Donald Jackson, *Vice Pres*
EMP: 500
SQ FT: 35,000
SALES: 66.4MM **Privately Held**
WEB: www.iccohio.com
SIC: 7379

(G-7818)

INGLESIDE INVESTMENTS INC
Also Called: Ww CD Radio
1036 S Front St (43206-3402)
PHONE..............................614 221-1025
Roger Vaughan, *President*
EMP: 35
SALES (est): 1.6MM **Privately Held**
WEB: www.cd101.com
SIC: 4832 8742 Radio broadcasting stations; new business start-up consultant

(G-7819)

INLAND PRODUCTS INC (PA)
599 Frank Rd (43223-3813)
PHONE..............................614 443-3425
Gary H Baas, *President*
Jerry Phillips, *Vice Pres*
EMP: 25
SQ FT: 40,000
SALES (est): 5.5MM **Privately Held**
SIC: 2077 5159 Grease rendering, inedible; tallow rendering, inedible; bone meal, except as animal feed; meat meal & tankage, except as animal feed; hides

(G-7820)

INNOVATIVE ARCHITECTURAL
Also Called: Iap Government Services Group
2740 Airport Dr Ste 300 (43219-2295)
PHONE..............................614 416-0614
Thomas G Banks, *CEO*
Jennifer Schneider, *Senior VP*
EMP: 25
SQ FT: 5,000
SALES: 19.9MM **Privately Held**
WEB: www.iaparchitectural.com
SIC: 8741 Construction management

(G-7821)

INNOVEL SOLUTIONS INC
Also Called: Sears
5330 Crosswind Dr (43228-3600)
PHONE..............................614 878-2092
Tom Dardis, *Manager*
EMP: 99
SALES (corp-wide): 16.7B **Publicly Held**
WEB: www.slslogistics.com+%22sears+logistics+servi
SIC: 4731 Agents, shipping
HQ: Innovel Solutions, Inc.
3333 Beverly Rd
Hoffman Estates IL 60179
847 286-2500

(G-7822)

INNOVEL SOLUTIONS INC
Also Called: Sears
4100 Lockbourne Industria (43207-4377)
PHONE..............................614 492-5304
John Mannella, *Manager*
EMP: 600
SALES (corp-wide): 16.7B **Publicly Held**
WEB: www.slslogistics.com+%22sears+logistics+servi
SIC: 4731 Agents, shipping
HQ: Innovel Solutions, Inc.
3333 Beverly Rd
Hoffman Estates IL 60179
847 286-2500

(G-7823)

INNOVIS DATA SOLUTIONS INC
250 E Broad St (43215-3708)
PHONE..............................614 222-4343
Jonathan H Price, *President*
Dirk Cantrell, *Vice Pres*
Keith Kotrowicsz, *Treasurer*
Allison Lemaster, *Sales Staff*
Rob Cornett, *Prgrmr*
EMP: 35 EST: 1999
SALES (est): 4.4MM
SALES (corp-wide): 246.2MM **Privately Held**
WEB: www.innovis.com
SIC: 7323 Credit bureau & agency
PA: Cbc Companies, Inc.
250 E Broad St Fl 21
Columbus OH 43215
614 222-4343

(G-7824)

INQUIRY SYSTEMS INC
1195 Goodale Blvd (43212-3730)
PHONE..............................614 464-3800
Carey Hindall, *President*
Kathy Hindall, *Vice Pres*
EMP: 30
SQ FT: 14,000
SALES: 529.2K **Privately Held**
WEB: www.inquirysys.com
SIC: 8742 4783 7311 7389 Marketing consulting services; packing goods for shipping; advertising agencies; subscription fulfillment services: magazine, newspaper, etc.

(G-7825)

INSIGHT COMMUNICATIONS OF CO
Also Called: Insight Ohio
3770 E Livingston Ave (43227-2280)
PHONE..............................614 236-1200
Dan Mannino,
Pat Elztroth,
EMP: 200 EST: 1998
SALES (est): 5.6MM **Privately Held**
SIC: 4841 1731 Cable television services; electrical work

(G-7826)

INSIGHT DIRECT USA INC
375 N Front St (43215-2232)
PHONE..............................614 456-0423
Jason Steiner, *Counsel*
Bethany Howell, *Auditor*
Tom Montes, *Branch Mgr*
Jason Williams, *Practice Mgr*
Joseph Collier, *Supervisor*
EMP: 60 **Publicly Held**
SIC: 5045 Computer software
HQ: Insight Direct Usa, Inc.
6820 S Harl Ave
Tempe AZ 85283
480 333-3000

(G-7827)

INSTALLED BUILDING PDTS II LLC
Also Called: Insulation Northwest
495 S High St Ste 50 (43215-5689)
PHONE..............................626 812-6070
Pamela Henson, *Partner*
EMP: 97
SALES (est): 8.4MM
SALES (corp-wide): 1.3B **Publicly Held**
SIC: 1742 Insulation, buildings
PA: Installed Building Products, Inc.
495 S High St Ste 50
Columbus OH 43215
614 221-3399

(G-7828)

INSTALLED BUILDING PDTS INC (PA)
Also Called: IBP
495 S High St Ste 50 (43215-5689)
PHONE..............................614 221-3399
Vikas Verma, *CEO*
Jeffrey W Edwards, *Ch of Bd*
W Jeffrey Hire, *President*
R Scott Jenkins, *President*
Matthew J Momper, *President*
EMP: 151
SALES: 1.3B **Publicly Held**
SIC: 1522 5033 5211 Residential construction; insulation materials; insulation material, building

(G-7829)

INSTALLED BUILDING PDTS LLC
Also Called: IBP Columbus
1320 Mckinley Ave Ste A (43222-1155)
PHONE..............................614 308-9900
Mark Lomax, *Branch Mgr*
EMP: 27
SALES (corp-wide): 1.3B **Publicly Held**
SIC: 1742 Insulation, buildings
HQ: Installed Building Products Llc
495 S High St Ste 50
Columbus OH 43215
614 221-3399

(G-7830)

INSTITUTE FOR HUMAN SERVICES (PA)
1706 E Broad St (43203-2039)
PHONE..............................614 251-6000
Ronald C Hughes, *Director*
EMP: 28
SALES: 7MM **Privately Held**
SIC: 8742 Human resource consulting services

(G-7831)

INSURANCE INTERMEDIARIES INC
280 N High St Ste 300 (43215-2535)
PHONE..............................614 846-1111
David S Schmidt, *President*
Duane Knauer, *President*
Larry Bobb, *Vice Pres*
EMP: 65
SQ FT: 14,000
SALES (est): 8.1MM
SALES (corp-wide): 13.2B **Privately Held**
WEB: www.nirassn.com
SIC: 6411 Insurance brokers
PA: Nationwide Mutual Insurance Company
1 Nationwide Plz
Columbus OH 43215
614 249-7111

(G-7832)

INTER HEALT CARE OF CAMBR ZANE (PA)
Also Called: INTERIM SERVICES
960 Checkrein Ave Ste A (43229-1107)
PHONE..............................614 436-9404
Michael W Hartshorn, *President*
Harold A Salo, *President*
Tom Kirker, *Principal*
Linda Martin, *Principal*
Thomas Di Marco, *Corp Secy*
EMP: 29
SQ FT: 7,500
SALES: 13.9MM **Privately Held**
SIC: 8082 Home health care services

(G-7833)

INTERBAKE FOODS LLC
1740 Joyce Ave (43219-1026)
PHONE..............................614 294-4931
Raymond Baxter, *President*
EMP: 128
SALES (corp-wide): 37.8B **Privately Held**
WEB: www.interbake.com
SIC: 5149 Bakery products
HQ: Interbake Foods Llc
3951 Westerre Pkwy # 200
Henrico VA 23233
804 755-7107

(G-7834)

INTERBAKE FOODS LLC
Norse Dairy Systems
1700 E 17th Ave (43219-1005)
P.O. Box 1869 (43216-1869)
PHONE..............................614 294-4931
Scott Fullbright, *Vice Pres*
EMP: 600
SALES (corp-wide): 37.8B **Privately Held**
WEB: www.interbake.com
SIC: 5149 Bakery products
HQ: Interbake Foods Llc
3951 Westerre Pkwy # 200
Henrico VA 23233
804 755-7107

(G-7835)

INTERIOR SUPPLY CINCINNATI LLC
481 E 11th Ave (43211-2601)
PHONE..............................614 424-6611
Robert Pickard, *President*
Timothy Flynn,
EMP: 30
SALES (est): 3.6MM **Privately Held**
SIC: 7389 Interior design services

(G-7836)
INTERNAL MDCINE CONS OF CLMBUS
104 N Murray Hill Rd (43228-1524)
PHONE.................................614 878-6413
Robert A Palma, *President*
Peter Pema, *Vice Pres*
Jeffrey Kaufman, *Treasurer*
Thomas E Wanko, *Admin Sec*
EMP: 30
SQ FT: 5,000
SALES (est): 2.1MM **Privately Held**
SIC: 8031 8011 Offices & clinics of osteo-pathic physicians; internal medicine, physician/surgeon

(G-7837)
INTERNATIONAL MASONRY INC
135 Spruce St (43215-1623)
P.O. Box 1598 (43216-1598)
PHONE.................................614 469-8338
John C Casey, *Chairman*
Mitchell Casey, *Corp Secy*
Brian Casey, *Vice Pres*
Douglas Casey, *Vice Pres*
Eric J Casey, *Vice Pres*
EMP: 90
SQ FT: 7,500
SALES (est): 7.7MM **Privately Held**
WEB: www.imi-smc.com
SIC: 1741 Bricklaying

(G-7838)
INTERNATIONAL UN ELEV CONSTRS
Also Called: International Union Elvtor Cns
23 W 2nd Ave Ste C (43201-3406)
PHONE.................................614 291-5859
John Neil Rouse III, *Manager*
EMP: 122
SALES (corp-wide): 11.9MM **Privately Held**
SIC: 8641 Civic associations
PA: International Union Of Elevator Constructors
7154 Columbia Gateway Dr
Columbia MD 21046
410 953-6150

(G-7839)
INTERSTATE TRUCKWAY INC
5440 Renner Rd (43228-8941)
PHONE.................................614 771-1220
Willy Walraven, *Branch Mgr*
EMP: 32 **Privately Held**
WEB: www.itdsdedicated.com
SIC: 3799 5012 Trailers & trailer equip-ment; automobiles & other motor vehicles
PA: Interstate Truckway Inc
1755 Dreman Ave
Cincinnati OH 45223

(G-7840)
INTERTEK TESTING SVCS NA INC
Also Called: Etl
1717 Arlingate Ln (43228-4116)
PHONE.................................614 279-8090
Jennifer Chandler, *Vice Pres*
Terry Lansing, *Opers Mgr*
Andy Gbur, *Manager*
Bob Gray, *Manager*
Beth Mobley,
EMP: 40
SALES (corp-wide): 3.6B **Privately Held**
WEB: www.intertektestingservices.com
SIC: 8734 Testing laboratories
HQ: Intertek Testing Services Na, Inc.
3933 Us Route 11
Cortland NY 13045
607 753-6711

(G-7841)
IQ INNOVATIONS LLC
580 N 4th St Ste 560 (43215-2158)
PHONE.................................614 222-0882
Zita Hunt, *CEO*
William Lager,
EMP: 33
SALES (est): 6MM **Privately Held**
SIC: 7371 8299 Computer software devel-opment; educational services

(G-7842)
IRON MOUNTAIN INFO MGT LLC
4848 Evanswood Dr (43229-6207)
PHONE.................................614 840-9321
John Furgus, *Manager*
EMP: 38
SALES (corp-wide): 4.2B **Publicly Held**
SIC: 4226 Document & office records stor-age
HQ: Iron Mountain Information Manage-ment, Llc
1 Federal St
Boston MA 02110
800 899-4766

(G-7843)
IRTH SOLUTIONS INC (PA)
5009 Horizons Dr Ste 100 (43220-5284)
PHONE.................................614 459-2328
Jason Adams, *CEO*
G Brent Bishop, *President*
EMP: 29
SQ FT: 12,100
SALES (est): 8.6MM **Privately Held**
WEB: www.irth.com
SIC: 7371 Computer software develop-ment

(G-7844)
ISAAC BRANT LEDMAN TEETOR LLP
2 Miranova Pl Ste 700 (43215-3742)
PHONE.................................614 221-2121
Angela Reed, *President*
Tim Miller, *Managing Prtnr*
Dennis Newman, *Partner*
Donald Anspaugh, *Partner*
Charles Brant, *Partner*
EMP: 70
SALES (est): 7.4MM **Privately Held**
WEB: www.isaacbrant.com
SIC: 8111 General practice law office

(G-7845)
ISAAC WILES BURKHOLDER & TEETO
2 Miranova Pl Ste 700 (43215-5098)
PHONE.................................614 221-5216
Steve Teetor, *Partner*
Isaac Wiles, *Principal*
James Palmer, *Info Tech Mgr*
Robert E Sander, *Administration*
David Jennings, *Education*
EMP: 51
SALES (est): 8MM **Privately Held**
SIC: 8111 General practice law office

(G-7846)
ISABELLE RIDGWAY CARE CTR INC
1520 Hawthorne Ave (43203-1762)
PHONE.................................614 252-4931
Patricia Mullins, *CEO*
John Atala, *CFO*
Darrell E Elliott, *Treasurer*
Teresa Travis, *Hlthcr Dir*
Veronica Cooney, *Records Dir*
EMP: 140 EST: 1912
SQ FT: 70,400
SALES (est): 6.9MM **Privately Held**
WEB: www.isabelleridgway.com
SIC: 8051 8052 Convalescent home with continuous nursing care; intermediate care facilities

(G-7847)
ISLAND HOSPITALITY MGT LLC
Also Called: Columbus-Gatehouse Inn
2084 S Hamilton Rd (43232-4302)
PHONE.................................614 864-8844
Bryan Zeitlin, *Branch Mgr*
EMP: 25
SALES (corp-wide): 814.6MM **Privately Held**
WEB: www.napleshamptoninn.com
SIC: 8742 7991 7011 Management con-sulting services; physical fitness facilities; hotels
PA: Island Hospitality Management, Llc
222 Lakeview Ave Ste 200
West Palm Beach FL 33401
561 832-6132

(G-7848)
ITICKETSCOM
700 Taylor Rd Ste 210 (43230-3318)
PHONE.................................614 410-4140
EMP: 25 EST: 2013
SALES (est): 313.4K **Privately Held**
SIC: 7999 Ticket sales office for sporting events, contract

(G-7849)
J & J CARRIERS LLC
2572 Cleveland Ave Ste 5 (43211-1679)
PHONE.................................614 447-2615
Charmaine Kimble, *Partner*
April L Boykins, *Partner*
Jerry B Boykins, *Partner*
Jason D Kimble, *Partner*
EMP: 50
SQ FT: 1,000
SALES (est): 2.6MM **Privately Held**
SIC: 4213 Contract haulers

(G-7850)
J K ENTERPRISES INC
Also Called: A & J Asphalt
2200 Mckinley Ave (43204-3417)
PHONE.................................614 481-8838
James Kuhn, *President*
EMP: 55
SALES (est): 5.4MM **Privately Held**
SIC: 1771 1611 Blacktop (asphalt) work; highway & street maintenance

(G-7851)
J S P A INC
2717 Burnaby Dr (43209-3200)
PHONE.................................407 957-6664
Joel Slaven, *President*
EMP: 40 EST: 1997
SALES (est): 418.7K **Privately Held**
WEB: www.jspa.com
SIC: 7929 Entertainers & entertainment groups

(G-7852)
JACK CONIE & SONS CORP
Also Called: Conie Construction Company
1340 Windsor Ave (43211-2852)
PHONE.................................614 291-5931
Richard P Conie, *Ch of Bd*
Michael C Conie, *President*
Carol Conie, *Treasurer*
Joseph A Connie, *Shareholder*
EMP: 75 EST: 1971
SQ FT: 10,000
SALES (est): 15.8MM **Privately Held**
SIC: 1623 1629 Sewer line construction; water main construction; earthmoving contractor

(G-7853)
JAMES POWERS
340 E Town St Ste 8700 (43215-4660)
PHONE.................................614 566-9397
James Powers, *Med Doctor*
EMP: 25
SALES (est): 61K **Privately Held**
SIC: 8322 Rehabilitation services

(G-7854)
JAVITCH BLOCK LLC
140 E Town St Ste 1250 (43215-4268)
PHONE.................................216 623-0000
Bruce A Block, *Branch Mgr*
EMP: 87
SALES (corp-wide): 58.1MM **Privately Held**
SIC: 8111 General practice attorney, lawyer
PA: Javitch Block Llc
1100 Superior Ave E Fl 19
Cleveland OH 44114
216 623-0000

(G-7855)
JB HUNT TRANSPORT SVCS INC
5435 Crosswind Dr (43228-3654)
PHONE.................................614 335-6681
EMP: 1721
SALES (corp-wide): 8.6B **Publicly Held**
SIC: 4213 4731 Trucking, except local; freight transportation arrangement
PA: J. B. Hunt Transport Services, Inc.
615 Jb Hunt Corp Dr
Lowell AR 72745
479 820-0000

(G-7856)
JDEL INC
200 W Nationwide Blvd # 1 (43215-2561)
PHONE.................................614 436-2418
EMP: 25
SQ FT: 4,500
SALES (est): 2MM
SALES (corp-wide): 96MM **Privately Held**
SIC: 6211 Security Broker/Dealer
PA: Jmac Inc.
200 W Nationwide Blvd # 1
Columbus OH 43215
614 436-2418

(G-7857)
JETSELECT LLC (PA)
4130 E 5th Ave (43219-1802)
PHONE.................................614 338-4380
Robert Austin, *CEO*
John Adams, *Accountant*
Gina Ziessler, *Technology*
Nathan Batty, *Director*
Harvey Mosher, *Asst Director*
EMP: 54
SALES (est): 15.1MM **Privately Held**
WEB: www.jetselect.net
SIC: 4522 Flying charter service

(G-7858)
JEWISH FAMILY SERVICES
1070 College Ave Ste A (43209-2489)
PHONE.................................614 231-1890
Karen Mozenter, *COO*
Garett Ray, *Manager*
Carol Shkolnik, *Manager*
Tim Snodgrass, *Consultant*
Chuck Wheiden, *Director*
EMP: 60
SALES: 3.4MM **Privately Held**
WEB: www.jfscolumbus.org
SIC: 8322 8331 Social service center; family (marriage) counseling; settlement house; vocational rehabilitation agency

(G-7859)
JIM KEIM FORD
Also Called: Keim, Jim Ford Sales
5575 Keim Cir (43228-7328)
PHONE.................................614 888-3333
James Keim, *President*
L D Pellissier III, *Corp Secy*
Nancy Joseph, *Controller*
Michael Phillips, *Sales Staff*
Jerry Stierhoff, *Sales Staff*
EMP: 100 EST: 1922
SQ FT: 40,000
SALES (est): 42.4MM **Privately Held**
SIC: 5511 7538 5521 Automobiles, new & used; pickups, new & used; general auto-motive repair shops; used car dealers

(G-7860)
JOBSOHIO
41 S High St (43215-6170)
PHONE.................................614 224-6446
J P Nauseef, *President*
Elyse Salisbury, *President*
Valentina Isakina, *Managing Dir*
Glenn Richardson, *Managing Dir*
Matt Cybulski, *Project Mgr*
EMP: 90
SALES (est): 156.1MM **Privately Held**
SIC: 8732 Business economic service

(G-7861)
JOHN A BECKER CO
Also Called: Becker Electric Supply
3825 Business Park Dr (43204-5007)
PHONE.................................614 272-8800
James Becker, *General Mgr*
EMP: 38
SALES (corp-wide): 219.3MM **Privately Held**
WEB: www.beckerelectric.com
SIC: 5063 1731 Electrical supplies; electri-cal work
PA: The John A Becker Co
1341 E 4th St
Dayton OH 45402
937 226-1341

(G-7862)
JOHNSON & FISCHER INC
Also Called: J F Painting Co
5303 Trabue Rd (43228-9783)
PHONE..................................614 276-8868
Robert J Johnson, *President*
EMP: 45
SQ FT: 3,000
SALES (est): 4.3MM **Privately Held**
WEB: www.jfpaintingcompany.com
SIC: 1721 Commercial painting; industrial painting

(G-7863)
JOHNSON MIRMIRAN THOMPSON INC
Also Called: Barr & Prevost, A Jmt Division
2800 Corp Exchange Dr # 250
(43231-7661)
PHONE..................................614 714-0270
Jack Moeller, *President*
Andrew Barr, *Manager*
EMP: 86
SALES (corp-wide): 259.1MM **Privately Held**
SIC: 8711 8712 8742 4785 Civil engineering; architectural engineering; management engineering; highway bridge operation
PA: Johnson, Mirmiran & Thompson, Inc.
40 Wight Ave
Hunt Valley MD 21030
410 329-3100

(G-7864)
JOHNSON MIRMIRAN THOMPSON INC
Also Called: Jmt
2800 Corp Exchange Dr (43231-7661)
PHONE..................................614 714-0270
EMP: 30
SALES (corp-wide): 124.8MM **Privately Held**
SIC: 8711 Engineering Services
PA: Johnson, Mirmiran & Thompson, Inc.
72 Loveton Cir
Sparks MD 21030
410 329-3100

(G-7865)
JOLLY TOTS TOO INC
5511 N Hamilton Rd (43230-1321)
PHONE..................................614 471-0688
Brenda Warnock, *President*
EMP: 33
SALES (est): 1MM **Privately Held**
SIC: 8351 Group day care center

(G-7866)
JONES DAY LIMITED PARTNERSHIP
325 John H Mcconnell Blvd # 600
(43215-2672)
P.O. Box 165017 (43216)
PHONE..................................614 469-3939
Morris Jackson, *Librarian*
Fordham Huffman, *Manager*
Nancy Clark, *Manager*
Brian Hannan, *Manager*
Robin A Ruf, *Office Admin*
EMP: 200
SALES (corp-wide): 833.4MM **Privately Held**
SIC: 8111 General practice attorney, lawyer
PA: Jones Day Limited Partnership
901 Lakeside Ave E Ste 2
Cleveland OH 44114
216 586-3939

(G-7867)
JONES LAW GROUP LLC
513 E Rich St Ste 100 (43215-5376)
PHONE..................................614 545-9998
Eric Jones, *Principal*
EMP: 25
SALES (est): 372K **Privately Held**
SIC: 8111 General practice law office

(G-7868)
JONES TRUCK & SPRING REPR INC
350 Frank Rd (43207-2423)
PHONE..................................614 443-4619
John Richard Jones, *President*

Jack E Fink, *Vice Pres*
EMP: 70 EST: 1978
SQ FT: 12,000
SALES (est): 6.6MM **Privately Held**
WEB: www.jonesspring.com
SIC: 7539 Trailer repair

(G-7869)
JOSHUA INVESTMENT COMPANY INC
Also Called: Joshua Homes
3065 Mcctcheon Crssing Dr (43219-5054)
PHONE..................................614 428-5555
Eric Schottenstein, *President*
▲ EMP: 45
SALES (est): 4.1MM **Privately Held**
WEB: www.joshuahomes.com
SIC: 1521 New construction, single-family houses

(G-7870)
JPMORGAN CHASE BANK NAT ASSN
4000 Morse Xing (43219-6037)
PHONE..................................614 476-1910
EMP: 26
SALES (corp-wide): 131.4B **Publicly Held**
SIC: 6021 National commercial banks
HQ: Jpmorgan Chase Bank, National Association
1111 Polaris Pkwy
Columbus OH 43240
614 436-3055

(G-7871)
JPMORGAN CHASE BANK NAT ASSN
3415 Vision Dr (43219-6009)
PHONE..................................216 781-2127
John Barth, *Vice Pres*
Clinton Sampson, *Manager*
EMP: 26
SALES (corp-wide): 131.4B **Publicly Held**
WEB: www.chase.com
SIC: 6022 State commercial banks
HQ: Jpmorgan Chase Bank, National Association
1111 Polaris Pkwy
Columbus OH 43240
614 436-3055

(G-7872)
JPMORGAN CHASE BANK NAT ASSN
100 E Broad St Ste 2460 (43215-3618)
PHONE..................................614 248-5391
Bob Skea, *COO*
David Lauer, *Mfg Staff*
EMP: 26
SALES (corp-wide): 131.4B **Publicly Held**
SIC: 6022 State commercial banks
HQ: Jpmorgan Chase Bank, National Association
1111 Polaris Pkwy
Columbus OH 43240
614 436-3055

(G-7873)
JPMORGAN CHASE BANK NAT ASSN
Also Called: Chase HM Mrtgages Florence Off
3415 Vision Dr (43219-6009)
PHONE..................................843 679-3653
Sharon Hardee, *Principal*
Michael Lichwa, *Assistant VP*
Lauren Hammons, *Vice Pres*
Jake Meyers, *Vice Pres*
Rita Volpe, *Vice Pres*
EMP: 400
SALES (corp-wide): 131.4B **Publicly Held**
SIC: 6029 Commercial banks
HQ: Jpmorgan Chase Bank, National Association
1111 Polaris Pkwy
Columbus OH 43240
614 436-3055

(G-7874)
JPMORGAN CHASE BANK NAT ASSN
1199 Corrugated Way (43201-2901)
PHONE..................................614 248-2083
Lori Walkowiak, *Branch Mgr*
EMP: 26
SALES (corp-wide): 131.4B **Publicly Held**
WEB: www.chase.com
SIC: 6022 State commercial banks
HQ: Jpmorgan Chase Bank, National Association
1111 Polaris Pkwy
Columbus OH 43240
614 436-3055

(G-7875)
JUICE TECHNOLOGIES INC
Also Called: Plug Smart
350 E 1st Ave Ste 210 (43201-3792)
PHONE..................................800 518-5576
Richard Housh, *CEO*
Dave Zehala, *President*
Rich Housh, *General Mgr*
Tom Martin, *COO*
Duane Dickey, *Vice Pres*
EMP: 27 EST: 2008
SALES: 6.3MM **Privately Held**
SIC: 8748 7389 8734 8741 Business consulting; ; product certification, safety or performance; management services; mechanical engineering

(G-7876)
JULIAN SPEER CO
Also Called: Speer Mechanical
5255 Sinclair Rd (43229-5042)
PHONE..................................614 261-6331
Dennis Shuman, *President*
John Harper, *Vice Pres*
Michael A Shuman, *Vice Pres*
Dale Witte, *Vice Pres*
EMP: 55 EST: 1957
SALES (est): 6.4MM
SALES (corp-wide): 41.2MM **Privately Held**
WEB: www.speermechanical.com
SIC: 1711 Mechanical contractor
PA: Speer Industries Incorporated
5255 Sinclair Rd
Columbus OH 43229
614 261-6331

(G-7877)
JUMPLINECOM INC
5000 Arlngton Centre Blvd (43220-3075)
PHONE..................................614 859-1170
Rick Barber, *President*
Marc Hardgrove, *Treasurer*
Jason Beyke, *Director*
Robert Kaufman, *Admin Sec*
EMP: 26 EST: 1997
SQ FT: 4,500
SALES (est): 3MM **Privately Held**
WEB: www.jumpline.com
SIC: 4813

(G-7878)
JURUS STANLEY R ATTY AT LAW
Also Called: Jurus Law Office
1375 Dublin Rd (43215-1074)
PHONE..................................614 486-0297
Stanley R Jurus, *Owner*
John R Workman,
EMP: 29
SALES (est): 2.7MM **Privately Held**
SIC: 8111 Labor & employment law

(G-7879)
JUST IN TIME CARE INC
Also Called: Just In Time Care Services
5320 E Main St Ste 200 (43213-2567)
PHONE..................................614 985-3555
Dr David Orgen, *President*
Dr David Rex Orgen, *President*
Sarah Orgen, *Vice Pres*
EMP: 30 EST: 2007
SALES: 1MM **Privately Held**
SIC: 8059 8049 Personal care home, with health care; speech therapist

(G-7880)
KARE A LOT
1030 King Ave (43212-2609)
PHONE..................................614 298-8933
Milagros Neuman, *President*
EMP: 30 EST: 1984
SALES (est): 966.4K **Privately Held**
SIC: 8351 Group day care center

(G-7881)
KARE A LOT INFNT TDDLR DEV CTR
Also Called: Kare A Lot Child Care Center
3164 Riverside Dr (43221-2540)
PHONE..................................614 481-7532
Milagros Neuman, *CEO*
EMP: 28
SQ FT: 2,700
SALES (est): 1.1MM **Privately Held**
SIC: 8351 Group day care center

(G-7882)
KARL HC LLC
Also Called: Villa Angela Care Center
5700 Karl Rd (43229-3602)
PHONE..................................614 846-5420
James Griffiths, *Mng Member*
Dianna Bozek, *Mng Member*
Brian Colleran, *Mng Member*
EMP: 350
SQ FT: 102,000
SALES: 16.1MM **Privately Held**
WEB: www.villa-angela.net
SIC: 8051 Skilled nursing care facilities

(G-7883)
KARLSBERGER COMPANIES (PA)
99 E Main St (43215-5115)
P.O. Box 340130 (43234-0130)
PHONE..................................614 461-9500
Michael Tyne, *Ch of Bd*
Richard Barger, *COO*
William O Anderson, *CFO*
EMP: 105 EST: 1927
SQ FT: 32,000
SALES (est): 10.9MM **Privately Held**
SIC: 8712 8742 7389 Architectural services; planning consultant; hospital & health services consultant; interior decorating

(G-7884)
KARRINGTON OPERATING CO INC (DH)
919 Old Henderson Rd (43220-3722)
PHONE..................................614 324-5951
Richard R Slager, *Ch of Bd*
Pete Klisares, *President*
Richard J Clark, *COO*
Robin Holderman, *Exec VP*
Stephen Lewis, *Senior VP*
EMP: 55
SQ FT: 14,000
SALES (est): 10.7MM
SALES (corp-wide): 4.7B **Publicly Held**
WEB: www.karrington.com
SIC: 8059 Personal care home, with health care

(G-7885)
KASTLE TECHNOLOGIES CO LLC
185-H Huntley Rd (43229)
PHONE..................................614 433-9860
Dennis Quebe, *CEO*
EMP: 25
SALES (corp-wide): 66.4MM **Privately Held**
SIC: 1731 General electrical contractor
HQ: Kastle Technologies Co., Llc
100 Cart Path Dr
Monroe OH 45050
513 360-2901

(G-7886)
KEGLER BROWN HL RITTER CO LPA (PA)
65 E State St Ste 1800 (43215-4294)
PHONE..................................614 462-5400
Michael E Zatezalo, *Managing Prtnr*
Michael Zatezalo, *Managing Dir*
Christopher Allwein, *Counsel*
Ralph Breitfeller, *Counsel*

Anthonio C Fiore, *Counsel*
EMP: 142
SQ FT: 51,000
SALES (est): 30.5MM **Privately Held**
WEB: www.keglerbrown.com
SIC: 8111 General practice attorney, lawyer

(G-7887)
KELLER GROUP LIMITED
Also Called: Keller Farms Landscape & Nurs
3909 Groves Rd (43232-4138)
PHONE..................................614 866-9551
Melonie Westhoven, *Info Tech Mgr*
Bernard W Fleming,
EMP: 36
SQ FT: 11,400
SALES (est): 4.1MM **Privately Held**
WEB: www.kellerfarmslandscaping.com
SIC: 0782 Landscape contractors; lawn care services

(G-7888)
KELLER WILLIAMS CLASSIC PRO
1510 W Lane Ave (43221-3960)
PHONE..................................614 451-8500
Susan Parrish,
Chip Parrish, *Real Est Agnt*
EMP: 75
SALES (est): 3MM **Privately Held**
WEB:
www.kellerwilliamsclassicproperties.yourkwoff
SIC: 6531 Real estate agent, residential

(G-7889)
KEMBA FINANCIAL CREDIT UN INC
4311 N High St (43214-2609)
PHONE..................................614 235-2395
Gerald Guy, *CEO*
EMP: 78
SALES (corp-wide): 46.4MM **Privately Held**
SIC: 6282 Investment advice
PA: Kemba Financial Credit Union, Inc,
555 Officenter Pl Ste 100
Gahanna OH 43230
614 235-2395

(G-7890)
KEMBA FINANCIAL CREDIT UNION
4220 E Broad St (43213-1216)
P.O. Box 307370 (43230-7370)
PHONE..................................614 235-2395
Jerry Guy, *CEO*
EMP: 69
SQ FT: 1,200
SALES (est): 7.2MM **Privately Held**
SIC: 6062 State credit unions, not federally chartered

(G-7891)
KENDALL HOLDINGS LTD (PA)
Also Called: Phpk Technologies
2111 Builders Pl (43204-4886)
PHONE..................................614 486-4750
Richard Coleman, *Partner*
Ken Krienbrink, *Vice Pres*
Terry Deerfoot, *Mfg Mgr*
Steve Willming, *Design Engr*
Tim Savely, *Marketing Mgr*
▲ **EMP:** 45
SQ FT: 60,000
SALES (est): 10.8MM **Privately Held**
SIC: 3443 8711 Fabricated plate work (boiler shop); engineering services

(G-7892)
KENDRICK-MOLLENAUER PNTG CO
1099 Stimmel Rd (43223-2911)
PHONE..................................614 443-7037
Howard Kendrick, *President*
Rose M Kendrick, *Corp Secy*
James W Kendrick Jr, *Vice Pres*
Jerry Sahr, *Vice Pres*
EMP: 35 **EST:** 1970
SALES (est): 3.4MM **Privately Held**
SIC: 1721 Residential painting; commercial painting

(G-7893)
KENNETHS HAIR SALONS & DAY SP (PA)
Also Called: Kenneth's Design Group
5151 Reed Rd Ste 250b (43220-2594)
PHONE..................................614 457-7712
Kenneth Anders, *President*
Kathy Masters, *Marketing Staff*
Emily Harrison, *Manager*
Christian Holcomb, *Manager*
Steve McElheny, *Manager*
EMP: 310
SQ FT: 46,000
SALES (est): 11.5MM **Privately Held**
WEB: www.kenneths.com
SIC: 7231 5999 Toiletries, cosmetics & perfumes; hair dressing school

(G-7894)
KENOSHA BEEF INTERNATIONAL LTD
Birchwood Meats & Provisions
1821 Dividend Dr (43228-3848)
PHONE..................................614 771-1330
Ken Fudy, *Principal*
Daniel Kesicki, *Plant Mgr*
Troy Maynard, *Opers Staff*
Marty Roberts, *Chief Mktg Ofcr*
Koenia Siebers, *Manager*
EMP: 107
SQ FT: 10,000
SALES (est): 16.1MM
SALES (corp-wide): 187.4MM **Privately Held**
WEB: www.bwfoods.com
SIC: 5147 2013 Meats, fresh; sausages & other prepared meats
PA: Kenosha Beef International, Ltd.
3111 152nd Ave
Kenosha WI 53144
800 541-1684

(G-7895)
KENSINGTON PLACE INC
1001 Parkview Blvd (43219-2270)
PHONE..................................614 252-5276
Larry Crowell, *President*
Phil Helser, *CFO*
Penny Smith, *Director*
EMP: 26
SALES (est): 829K **Privately Held**
SIC: 6513 Retirement hotel operation

(G-7896)
KENT PLACE HOUSING
Also Called: Buckeye Community Forty Four
1414 Gault St (43205-2933)
PHONE..................................614 942-2020
Steve Boone, *Partner*
Trenda Cooper, *Clerk*
EMP: 99
SQ FT: 1,445
SALES (est): 2MM **Privately Held**
SIC: 6514 Dwelling operators, except apartments

(G-7897)
KEVIN KENNEDY ASSOCIATES INC
275 Outerbelt St (43213-1529)
PHONE..................................317 536-7000
Sharon Kennedy, *CEO*
Randy Clarksean, *President*
Tom Weisgerber, *President*
EMP: 37
SALES (est): 3.8MM **Privately Held**
WEB: www.kkai.com
SIC: 8711 Consulting engineer

(G-7898)
KEY BLUE PRINTS INC (PA)
Also Called: Key Color
195 E Livingston Ave (43215-5793)
PHONE..................................614 228-3285
David M Key III, *President*
Brian Hunnicutt, *Managing Dir*
Mark J Koster, *Managing Dir*
Mark R Lasek, *Managing Dir*
Raymond J Lemanski, *Managing Dir*
▲ **EMP:** 54
SQ FT: 18,000
SALES (est): 30.9MM **Privately Held**
WEB: www.key-evidence.com
SIC: 5049 7334 Drafting supplies; blue-printing service

(G-7899)
KEYSTONE FREIGHT CORP
2545 Parsons Ave (43207-2974)
PHONE..................................614 542-0320
John Dietz, *Branch Mgr*
EMP: 30
SQ FT: 8,772
SALES (corp-wide): 264MM **Privately Held**
SIC: 4213 Trucking, except local
HQ: Keystone Freight Corp.
611 Us Highway 46 W # 301
Hasbrouck Heights NJ 07604
201 330-1900

(G-7900)
KFORCE INC
200 E Campus View Blvd # 225
(43235-6619)
PHONE..................................614 436-4027
EMP: 30
SALES (corp-wide): 1.3B **Publicly Held**
SIC: 7361 Staffing Services
PA: Kforce Inc.
1001 E Palm Ave
Tampa FL 33605
813 552-5000

(G-7901)
KIDDIE WEST PEDIATRIC CENTER
4766 W Broad St (43228-1613)
PHONE..................................614 276-7733
Carl R Backes Do, *President*
EMP: 30
SALES (est): 3.2MM **Privately Held**
SIC: 8011 Pediatrician

(G-7902)
KIDNEY CENTER OF BEXLEY LLC
1151 College Ave (43209-2827)
PHONE..................................614 231-2200
EMP: 93
SALES: 19.4MM **Publicly Held**
SIC: 8092 Kidney dialysis centers
PA: American Renal Associates Holdings, Inc.
500 Cummings Ctr Ste 6550
Beverly MA 01915

(G-7903)
KIDS WORLD
2812 Morse Rd (43231-6034)
PHONE..................................614 473-9229
Yna Ness, *President*
EMP: 25
SALES (est): 576.1K **Privately Held**
SIC: 8351 Group day care center

(G-7904)
KINDERCARE LEARNING CTRS LLC
Also Called: Mount Carmel Kindercare
5959 E Broad St (43213-1501)
PHONE..................................614 759-6622
Laquanta Austin, *Director*
EMP: 30
SALES (corp-wide): 1.2B **Privately Held**
WEB: www.kindercare.com
SIC: 8351 Group day care center
HQ: Kindercare Learning Centers, Llc
650 Ne Holladay St # 1400
Portland OR 97232
503 872-1300

(G-7905)
KINDRED NURSING CENTERS E LLC
Also Called: Kindred Transitional Care
2770 Clime Rd (43223-3626)
PHONE..................................614 276-8222
Dawn Lewis, *Manager*
EMP: 100
SALES (corp-wide): 6B **Privately Held**
WEB: www.salemhaven.com
SIC: 8051 Convalescent home with continuous nursing care
HQ: Kindred Nursing Centers East, L.L.C.
680 S 4th St
Louisville KY 40202
502 596-7300

(G-7906)
KING BUSINESS INTERIORS INC
1400 Goodale Blvd Ste 102 (43212-3777)
PHONE..................................614 430-0020
Darla J King, *President*
David R King, *Vice Pres*
Dave King, *CFO*
Diane Flinders, *VP Sales*
Tony Casey, *Accounts Mgr*
EMP: 36
SQ FT: 10,000
SALES (est): 32.2MM **Privately Held**
WEB: www.kbiinc.com
SIC: 5021 Office furniture

(G-7907)
KING MEMORY LLC
380 Morrison Rd Ste A (43213-1430)
PHONE..................................614 418-6044
Darryl Tanner, *CEO*
▲ **EMP:** 25
SQ FT: 3,700
SALES (est): 6.2MM **Privately Held**
SIC: 5045 Computers, peripherals & software

(G-7908)
KING TUT LOGISTICS LLC
Also Called: Cleopatra Trucking
3600 Enterprise Ave (43228-1047)
PHONE..................................614 538-0509
Jesse Brown, *Mng Member*
Mark Gabriel,
Maged Tadros,
Michael G Wessa,
EMP: 50
SALES (est): 6.1MM **Privately Held**
SIC: 4214 4225 7389 Local Trucking-With Storage General Warehouse/Storage Business Services

(G-7909)
KLARNA INC
629 N High St Ste 300 (43215-2025)
PHONE..................................614 615-4705
Brian Billingsley, *CEO*
Kristi Barbosky, *Partner*
Jason Bozarth, *Opers Mgr*
Melissa Donohue, *Manager*
Michael Rouse, *Officer*
EMP: 37
SQ FT: 3,300
SALES (est): 9.9MM
SALES (corp-wide): 535MM **Privately Held**
SIC: 6099 Electronic funds transfer network, including switching
HQ: Klarna Bank Ab
Sveavagen 46
Stockholm 111 3
812 012-000

(G-7910)
KLEAN A KAR INC (PA)
3383 S High St (43207-3624)
PHONE..................................614 221-3145
Dennis Ramsey, *President*
Doug Ramsey, *Vice Pres*
Dan Ramsey, *Treasurer*
EMP: 45
SALES (est): 2.3MM **Privately Held**
WEB: www.kleanakar.com
SIC: 7542 Washing & polishing, automotive

(G-7911)
KLINGBEIL MANAGEMENT GROUP CO (PA)
21 W Broad St Fl 10 (43215-4172)
PHONE..................................614 220-8900
James D Klingbeil, *President*
EMP: 30
SALES (est): 2.6MM **Privately Held**
SIC: 6531 1522 8742 8721 Real estate managers; remodeling, multi-family dwellings; administrative services consultant; accounting services, except auditing

(G-7912)
KLINGBEIL MULTIFAMILTY FUND IV
21 W Broad St Fl 11 (43215-4100)
PHONE..................................415 398-0106
Paul Rose, *Branch Mgr*

EMP: 100
SALES (corp-wide): 33.2MM **Privately Held**
WEB: www.kcmapts.com
SIC: 6513 Apartment building operators
PA: Klingbeil Multifamilty Fund Iv
200 California St Ste 300
San Francisco CA 94111
415 398-3590

(G-7913)
KM2 SOLUTIONS LLC
Also Called: Technology Hub
2400 Corp Exchange Dr # 120
(43231-7606)
PHONE..................................610 213-1408
EMP: 374
SALES (corp-wide): 41.3MM **Privately Held**
SIC: 8742 Financial consultant
PA: Km2 Solutions, Llc
100 Park Ave Rm 1600
New York NY 10017
404 848-8886

(G-7914)
KMI INC
5025 Arlington Centre Blv (43220-2959)
PHONE..................................614 326-6304
Mark Colasante, Principal
Joel Copeland, COO
Eric Blevins, Engineer
Greg Wasylik, Manager
Nathan Faulkner, Administration
EMP: 38 EST: 2010
SQ FT: 10,000
SALES (est): 1.4MM **Privately Held**
SIC: 7371 Computer software development & applications

(G-7915)
KNAPP VETERINARY HOSPITAL INC
596 Oakland Park Ave (43214-4199)
PHONE..................................614 267-3124
Paul H Knapp Dvm, President
Robert Knapp, Vice Pres
John C Munsell, Vice Pres
EMP: 29 EST: 1945
SQ FT: 5,000
SALES (est): 2.1MM **Privately Held**
SIC: 0742 Animal hospital services, pets & other animal specialties

(G-7916)
KNIGHT TRANSPORTATION INC
4275 Westward Ave (43228-1045)
PHONE..................................614 308-4900
Dan Kutter, Branch Mgr
EMP: 78
SALES (corp-wide): 5.3B **Publicly Held**
SIC: 4213 4212 Heavy hauling; local trucking, without storage
HQ: Knight Transportation, Inc.
20002 N 19th Ave
Phoenix AZ 85027
602 269-2000

(G-7917)
KNIGHT-SWIFT TRNSP HLDINGS INC
4141 Parkwest Dr (43228-1400)
PHONE..................................614 274-5204
Dale Cooley, General Mgr
Patricia Rooney, Human Res Dir
Michael Click, Manager
Mike Click, Manager
EMP: 75
SQ FT: 1,364
SALES (corp-wide): 5.3B **Publicly Held**
SIC: 4213 Contract haulers
PA: Knight-Swift Transportation Holdings Inc.
2200 S 75th Ave
Phoenix AZ 85043
602 269-9700

(G-7918)
KNOLLMAN CONSTRUCTION LLC
4601 E 5th Ave (43219-1819)
P.O. Box 20372 (43220-0372)
PHONE..................................614 841-0130
Trey Knollman,
EMP: 200

SALES (est): 10.6MM **Privately Held**
WEB: www.knollmanconstruction.com
SIC: 1742 Drywall

(G-7919)
KNOWLEDGE MGT INTERACTIVE INC
Also Called: K M I
330 W Spring St Ste 320 (43215-7305)
PHONE..................................614 224-0664
Mark Colasante, CEO
Joel Copeland, COO
Dawn Devillers, Prdtn Mgr
Tanya Zarnitsa, QC Mgr
Eric Blevins, Engineer
EMP: 35
SQ FT: 6,800
SALES (est): 5.1MM **Privately Held**
WEB: www.kmionline.com
SIC: 7371 Computer software development

(G-7920)
KOHR ROYER GRIFFITH DEV CO LLC
1480 Dublin Rd (43215-1068)
PHONE..................................614 228-2471
Richard L Royer, CEO
EMP: 47
SQ FT: 4,500
SALES (est): 1.9MM **Privately Held**
SIC: 6512 Commercial & industrial building operation

(G-7921)
KONKUS MARBLE & GRANITE INC
3737 Zane Trace Dr (43228-3854)
PHONE..................................614 876-4000
Marc Konkus, President
Mark Frost, General Mgr
Annie Konkus, Vice Pres
Lynn Cannon, Accounting Mgr
Robert Pancott, Sales Staff
▲ EMP: 140
SQ FT: 99,000
SALES: 19MM **Privately Held**
WEB: www.konkusmarbleandgranite.com
SIC: 5032 Marble building stone; granite building stone

(G-7922)
KOORSEN FIRE & SECURITY INC
727 Manor Park Dr (43228-9522)
PHONE..................................614 878-2228
Dale Underwood, Branch Mgr
George Hinkle, Manager
EMP: 45
SALES (corp-wide): 244.8MM **Privately Held**
WEB: www.koorsen.com
SIC: 7382 Security systems services
PA: Koorsen Fire & Security, Inc.
2719 N Arlington Ave
Indianapolis IN 46218
317 542-1800

(G-7923)
KOORSEN FIRE & SECURITY INC
727 Manor Park Dr (43228-9522)
PHONE..................................614 878-2228
Fred Hillma, Branch Mgr
EMP: 25
SALES (corp-wide): 244.8MM **Privately Held**
SIC: 5099 Fire extinguishers; lifesaving & survival equipment (non-medical)
PA: Koorsen Fire & Security, Inc.
2719 N Arlington Ave
Indianapolis IN 46218
317 542-1800

(G-7924)
KORMAN CONSTRUCTION CORP
3695 Interchange Rd (43204-1499)
PHONE..................................614 274-2170
Young Bok Lee, President
EMP: 30
SQ FT: 10,560
SALES (est): 4.1MM **Privately Held**
SIC: 1761 1799 Roofing contractor; kitchen & bathroom remodeling

(G-7925)
KPMG LLP
191 W Nationwide Blvd # 500
(43215-2575)
PHONE..................................614 249-2300
Harold I Zeidman, Partner
Todd Babione, Managing Dir
Cassie Crandell, Sales Mgr
Phillip Smith, Branch Mgr
Samuel Jones, Manager
EMP: 160
SALES (corp-wide): 3.8B **Privately Held**
SIC: 8721 Accounting services, except auditing; certified public accountant
PA: Kpmg Llp
1676 Intl Dr Ste 1200
Mclean VA 22102
703 286-8000

(G-7926)
KREBER GRAPHICS INC (PA)
2580 Westbelt Dr (43228-3827)
PHONE..................................614 529-5701
Jim Kreber, CEO
Todd Alexander, Exec VP
Jeremy Gufstason, Vice Pres
Troy Machamer, VP Opers
Tony Cline, Production
EMP: 90
SQ FT: 86,000
SALES (est): 19MM **Privately Held**
WEB: www.kreber.com
SIC: 7311 Advertising consultant

(G-7927)
KRIEGER FORD INC (PA)
1800 Morse Rd (43229-6691)
PHONE..................................614 888-3320
G Douglas Krieger, President
Harold Samour, Business Mgr
Brent Ferguson, Corp Secy
John Jeffrey Krieger, Vice Pres
William Coultas, Store Mgr
▲ EMP: 160 EST: 1965
SQ FT: 50,000
SALES (est): 69.2MM **Privately Held**
SIC: 5511 7515 7538 7513 Automobiles, new & used; passenger car leasing; general automotive repair shops; truck rental & leasing, no drivers

(G-7928)
KROGER CO
850 S Hamilton Rd (43213-3000)
PHONE..................................614 759-2745
Lou Gilliam, Manager
EMP: 173
SALES (corp-wide): 121.1B **Publicly Held**
WEB: www.kroger.com
SIC: 5411 5141 5912 Supermarkets, chain; supermarkets, 66,000-99,000 square feet; convenience stores, chain; groceries, general line; drug stores & proprietary stores
PA: The Kroger Co
1014 Vine St Ste 1000
Cincinnati OH 45202
513 762-4000

(G-7929)
KROGER REFILL CENTER
2270 Rickenbacker Pkwy W (43217-5002)
PHONE..................................614 333-5017
Marette Parry, CEO
EMP: 50
SALES (est): 3.6MM **Privately Held**
SIC: 8742 Human resource consulting services

(G-7930)
KST SECURITY INC
727 Manor Park Dr (43228-9522)
PHONE..................................614 878-2228
Constance A Morgan, Administration
EMP: 38 **Privately Held**
SIC: 7382 Security systems services
PA: Kst Security, Inc.
6121 E 30th St
Indianapolis IN 46219

(G-7931)
KUSAN INC
Also Called: Quality Air Heating and AC
4060 Indianola Ave (43214-3160)
PHONE..................................614 262-1818

Thomas Kusan, President
Nick Kusan, Vice Pres
EMP: 27
SQ FT: 5,000
SALES (est): 4.5MM **Privately Held**
WEB: www.qualityairandheat.com
SIC: 1711 Warm air heating & air conditioning contractor

(G-7932)
L & W SUPPLY CORPORATION
1150 Mckinley Ave (43222-1113)
PHONE..................................614 276-6391
Jon Tribbie, Manager
EMP: 25
SALES (corp-wide): 438.1MM **Privately Held**
WEB: www.lwsupply.com
SIC: 5032 Drywall materials
HQ: L & W Supply Corporation
300 S Riverside Plz # 200
Chicago IL 60606
312 606-4000

(G-7933)
L BRANDS SERVICE COMPANY LLC
Also Called: Limited Services Corporation
3 Limited Pkwy (43230-1467)
PHONE..................................614 415-7000
Leslie H Wexner, Ch of Bd
Dona Maturo, Manager
EMP: 94
SALES (est): 4.7MM
SALES (corp-wide): 13.2B **Publicly Held**
WEB: www.limited.com
SIC: 6512 8743 Nonresidential building operators; public relations services
PA: L Brands, Inc.
3 Limited Pkwy
Columbus OH 43230
614 415-7000

(G-7934)
L BRANDS STORE DSIGN CNSTR INC
Also Called: Limited
3 Ltd Pkwy (43230)
PHONE..................................614 415-7000
Gene Torcha, President
Rick Felice, Vice Pres
Josie Harris, Purch Agent
Timothy Faber, Treasurer
▲ EMP: 230
SALES (est): 108.2MM
SALES (corp-wide): 13.2B **Publicly Held**
WEB: www.limited.com
SIC: 1542 Commercial & office building, new construction
PA: L Brands, Inc.
3 Limited Pkwy
Columbus OH 43230
614 415-7000

(G-7935)
L J NAVY TRUCKING COMPANY
2365 Performance Way (43207-2858)
PHONE..................................614 754-8929
Thad Blatt, President
Carolyn Blatt, Corp Secy
EMP: 25
SALES (est): 4.5MM **Privately Held**
SIC: 4213 Trucking, except local

(G-7936)
L JACK RUSCILLI
Also Called: Ruscilli Investment Co
2041 Arlingate Ln (43228-4113)
PHONE..................................614 876-9484
L Jack Ruscilli, Owner
Chuck Wiseman, Opers Mgr
Doug Garey, Manager
EMP: 50
SALES (est): 3MM **Privately Held**
SIC: 1542 Nonresidential construction

(G-7937)
L V TRUCKING INC
Also Called: L V Trckng
2440 Harrison Rd (43204-3508)
PHONE..................................614 275-4994
Brad Moore, President
L Vince Moore, Vice Pres
Neil Hever, Opers Mgr
Cheryl Criss, Mktg Dir
Lorri Baker, Manager

EMP: 41
SQ FT: 3,000
SALES (est): 6.2MM **Privately Held**
WEB: www.lvtrucking.com
SIC: 4213　4212　Contract haulers; local trucking, without storage

(G-7938)
L3 AVIATION PRODUCTS INC
Also Called: Goodrich Avionics
1105 Schrock Rd Ste 800 (43229-1154)
PHONE.................................614 825-2001
Billie Stevens, *Manager*
EMP: 60
SALES (corp-wide): 10.2B **Publicly Held**
SIC: 3812　8711　Aircraft flight instruments; gyroscopes; automatic pilots, aircraft; radar systems & equipment; engineering services
HQ: L3 Aviation Products, Inc.
　　5353 52nd St Se
　　Grand Rapids MI 49512
　　616 949-6600

(G-7939)
LA-Z-BOY INCORPORATED
4228 Easton Gateway Dr (43219-1543)
PHONE.................................614 478-0898
EMP: 203
SALES (corp-wide): 1.5B **Publicly Held**
SIC: 5021　Furniture
PA: La-Z-Boy Incorporated
　　1 Lazboy Dr
　　Monroe MI 48162
　　734 242-1444

(G-7940)
LABORATORY CORPORATION AMERICA
941 E Johnstown Rd (43230-1851)
PHONE.................................614 475-7852
James Duff, *Principal*
EMP: 25 **Publicly Held**
SIC: 8071　Blood analysis laboratory
HQ: Laboratory Corporation Of America
　　358 S Main St Ste 458
　　Burlington NC 27215
　　336 229-1127

(G-7941)
LABORATORY CORPORATION AMERICA
5888 Cleveland Ave (43231-2860)
PHONE.................................614 882-6278
Angela Myers, *Branch Mgr*
Michael Longstreth, *Technician*
EMP: 25 **Publicly Held**
SIC: 8071　Testing laboratories
HQ: Laboratory Corporation Of America
　　358 S Main St Ste 458
　　Burlington NC 27215
　　336 229-1127

(G-7942)
LADAN LEARNING CENTER
6028 Cleveland Ave (43231-2230)
PHONE.................................614 426-4306
Hibo Omar, *Owner*
EMP: 35
SALES (est): 124.7K **Privately Held**
SIC: 8351　Child day care services

(G-7943)
LADERA HEALTHCARE COMPANY
1661 Old Henderson Rd (43220-3644)
PHONE.................................614 459-1313
Ralph Hazelbaker, *Partner*
Diane Haemmerly, *Partner*
John Haemmerly, *Partner*
Billie Hazelbaker, *Partner*
EMP: 30
SALES (est): 1.6MM **Privately Held**
SIC: 6512　Nonresidential building operators

(G-7944)
LAKEFRONT LINES INC
Also Called: Lakefront Trailways
3152 E 17th Ave (43219-2353)
P.O. Box 360556 (43236-0556)
PHONE.................................614 476-1113
Christopher McCrady, *Branch Mgr*
EMP: 25

SALES (corp-wide): 4.5B **Privately Held**
WEB: www.lakefrontlines.com
SIC: 4119　4142　Local passenger transportation; bus charter service, except local
HQ: Lakefront Lines, Inc.
　　13315 Brookpark Rd
　　Brookpark OH 44142
　　216 267-8810

(G-7945)
LANCASTER COMMERCIAL PDTS LLC
2353 Westbrooke Dr (43228-9557)
P.O. Box 870, Worthington (43085-0870)
PHONE.................................740 286-5081
Kenneth Evans, *President*
◆ EMP: 34
SALES (est): 15.7MM **Privately Held**
SIC: 5085　3089　Whol Industrial Supplies Mfg Plastic Products

(G-7946)
LANCASTER POLLARD & CO LLC (HQ)
65 E State St Ste 1600 (43215-4237)
PHONE.................................614 224-8800
Thomas Green, *CEO*
T B Pollard, *Vice Chairman*
Grant T Goodman, *Vice Pres*
Tanya Hahn, *Vice Pres*
Matt Sherman, *Vice Pres*
EMP: 25
SALES (est): 11.7MM **Privately Held**
WEB: www.lancasterpollard.com
SIC: 6211　Investment bankers

(G-7947)
LANCASTER POLLARD MRTG CO LLC (PA)
65 E State St Ste 1600 (43215-4237)
PHONE.................................614 224-8800
Thomas R Green, *CEO*
Timothy J Dobyns, *Exec VP*
Kevin J Beerman, *CFO*
EMP: 70
SALES (est): 43.6MM **Privately Held**
SIC: 6159　6162　6282　Intermediate investment banks; mortgage bankers; investment advisory service

(G-7948)
LANCE A1 CLEANING SERVICES LLC
342 Hanton Way (43213-4430)
PHONE.................................614 370-0550
Lance Owens,
EMP: 100
SALES (est): 44K **Privately Held**
SIC: 7699　Cleaning services

(G-7949)
LANE ALTON & HORST LLC
2 Miranova Pl Ste 220 (43215-7050)
PHONE.................................614 228-6885
Kortnee Hardin, *President*
Joseph Gerling, *Managing Prtnr*
Joseph A Gerling,
Rick E Marsh,
Mary B McBride,
EMP: 45
SQ FT: 24,000
SALES: 304.2K **Privately Held**
WEB: www.lah4law.com
SIC: 8111　General practice law office

(G-7950)
LANE AVIATION CORPORATION
4389 International Gtwy # 228 (43219-3819)
P.O. Box 360420 (43236-0420)
PHONE.................................614 237-3747
Donna L Earl, *CEO*
Brad Primm, *President*
Steve Evans, *Vice Pres*
Steve Lawson, *Sales Staff*
Dave Rousselle, *Info Tech Dir*
EMP: 130 EST: 1935
SQ FT: 172,000

SALES (est): 48.1MM **Privately Held**
WEB: www.laneaviation.com
SIC: 5599　4581　4522　4512　Aircraft, self-propelled; aircraft instruments, equipment or parts; aircraft servicing & repairing; air passenger carriers, nonscheduled; air transportation, scheduled

(G-7951)
LANG STONE COMPANY INC (PA)
4099 E 5th Ave (43219-1812)
P.O. Box 360747 (43236-0747)
PHONE.................................614 235-4099
E Dean Coffman, *President*
Joan First, *VP Admin*
Joann Coffman, *Vice Pres*
▲ EMP: 55 EST: 1856
SQ FT: 10,000
SALES (est): 20.3MM **Privately Held**
WEB: www.langstone.com
SIC: 5032　5211　3281　3272　Building stone; marble building stone; granite building stone; lumber & other building materials; masonry materials & supplies; cut stone & stone products; concrete products; crushed & broken limestone

(G-7952)
LAPHAM-HICKEY STEEL CORP
753 Marion Rd (43207-2554)
PHONE.................................614 443-4881
Mike Salmons, *Plant Mgr*
George Keel, *Safety Mgr*
Joni Fritz, *Sales Staff*
Eric Sattler, *Manager*
EMP: 25
SQ FT: 110,000
SALES (corp-wide): 279.5MM **Privately Held**
WEB: www.lapham-hickey.com
SIC: 5051　3443　3441　3398　Steel; fabricated plate work (boiler shop); fabricated structural metal; metal heat treating; blast furnaces & steel mills
PA: Lapham-Hickey Steel Corp.
　　5500 W 73rd St
　　Chicago IL 60638
　　708 496-6111

(G-7953)
LARRIMER & LARRIMER LLC
165 N High St (43215-2486)
PHONE.................................419 222-6266
Darla Kaikis, *Branch Mgr*
EMP: 28
SALES (corp-wide): 5.8MM **Privately Held**
SIC: 8111　Labor & employment law
PA: Larrimer & Larrimer, Llc
　　165 N High St Fl 3
　　Columbus OH 43215
　　614 221-7548

(G-7954)
LARRIMER & LARRIMER LLC (PA)
165 N High St Fl 3 (43215-2486)
PHONE.................................614 221-7548
Gavin R Larrimer, *Partner*
Terrence W Larrimer, *Partner*
EMP: 50 EST: 1960
SQ FT: 7,500
SALES (est): 5.8MM **Privately Held**
WEB: www.larrimer.com
SIC: 8111　General practice law office

(G-7955)
LASTING IMPRESSIONS EVENT
Also Called: Lasting Imprssions Event Rentl
5080 Sinclair Rd Ste 200 (43229-5412)
PHONE.................................614 252-5400
James P Fritz, *President*
J P Fritz, *President*
Melissa Ellison, *Manager*
EMP: 78
SQ FT: 105,000
SALES: 3.5MM **Privately Held**
WEB: www.lirents.net
SIC: 7359　Dishes, silverware, tables & banquet accessories rental

(G-7956)
LATORRE CONCRETE CNSTR INC
850 N Cassady Ave (43219-2298)
PHONE.................................614 257-1401
Mark Latorre, *President*
Anthony Latorre, *Admin Sec*
EMP: 25
SQ FT: 11,000
SALES: 2MM **Privately Held**
WEB: www.latorreconcrete.com
SIC: 1771　Concrete work

(G-7957)
LAW OFFCES RBERT A SCHRGER LPA
81 S 5th St Ste 400 (43215-4323)
PHONE.................................614 824-5731
Robert A Schuerger, *President*
EMP: 30
SQ FT: 13,500
SALES (est): 3.7MM **Privately Held**
SIC: 8111　General practice law office

(G-7958)
LAWHON AND ASSOCIATES INC (PA)
1441 King Ave (43212-2108)
PHONE.................................614 481-8600
Susan Daniels, *President*
Karrie Bontrager, *Exec VP*
Richard Isaly, *CFO*
Michele Glinsky, *Human Res Mgr*
Jordan Mederer, *Department Mgr*
EMP: 38
SQ FT: 16,300
SALES (est): 5.4MM **Privately Held**
WEB: www.lawhon-assoc.com
SIC: 8748　Environmental consultant

(G-7959)
LAWRENCE M SHELL DDS
Also Called: Dental Associates
2862 E Main St Ste A (43209-3709)
PHONE.................................614 235-3444
Lawrence M Shell DDS, *Owner*
Cheryl Devore, *Admin Sec*
EMP: 27
SQ FT: 5,000
SALES (est): 1.3MM **Privately Held**
WEB: www.dentalassociatesbexley.com
SIC: 8021　Dentists' office

(G-7960)
LBI STARBUCKS DC 3
3 Limited Pkwy (43230-1467)
PHONE.................................614 415-6363
Edward Razek, *Principal*
EMP: 230
SALES (est): 13MM **Privately Held**
SIC: 8041　Offices & clinics of chiropractors

(G-7961)
LEADER PROMOTIONS INC (PA)
Also Called: Leaderpromos.com
790 E Johnstown Rd (43230-2116)
PHONE.................................614 416-6565
Stephanie Leader, *CEO*
Kevin Clark, *Opers Mgr*
Kathy Weible, *CFO*
Amber Brown, *Controller*
David Broxterman, *Accountant*
▲ EMP: 80
SQ FT: 14,000
SALES (est): 42.5MM **Privately Held**
WEB: www.leaderpromos.com
SIC: 5199　Advertising specialties

(G-7962)
LEGACY COMMERCIAL FLOORING LTD (PA)
Also Called: Legacy Commercial Finishes
800 Morrison Rd (43230-6643)
PHONE.................................614 476-1043
Tony Nixon, *President*
George Holinga, *Vice Pres*
EMP: 251
SQ FT: 6,500
SALES (est): 22.4MM **Privately Held**
WEB: www.legacycommercialflooring.com
SIC: 1752　Carpet laying

(G-7963)
LEGACY FREEDOM TREATMENT CTR
751 Northwest Blvd # 200 (43212-1977)
PHONE..............................614 741-2100
Alli Becker, *CEO*
Alli Beckerm, *CEO*
EMP: 50 EST: 2015
SALES (est): 344.8K **Privately Held**
SIC: 8093 Substance abuse clinics (outpatient)

(G-7964)
LEGAL AID SOCIETY OF COLUMBUS (PA)
1108 City Park Ave # 100 (43206-3583)
PHONE..............................614 737-0139
Thomas Weeks, *Director*
EMP: 68
SALES: 5.7MM **Privately Held**
SIC: 8111 Legal aid service

(G-7965)
LEIDOS INC
4449 Easton Way Ste 150 (43219-7002)
PHONE..............................858 826-6000
John Jumper, *CEO*
Christopher Brewster, *Manager*
EMP: 350
SALES (corp-wide): 10.1B **Publicly Held**
WEB: www.saic.com
SIC: 8731 Commercial physical research
HQ: Leidos, Inc.
11951 Freedom Dr Ste 500
Reston VA 20190
571 526-6000

(G-7966)
LEO YANNENOFF JEWISH COMMUNITY (PA)
1125 College Ave (43209-7802)
PHONE..............................614 231-2731
Louise Young, *CFO*
Sharon Sadlowski, *Accounting Mgr*
Carol Folkerth, *Exec Dir*
Nikki Henry, *Director*
Kaley Rosenthal, *Director*
EMP: 137
SQ FT: 106,000
SALES: 10.2MM **Privately Held**
WEB: www.columbusjcc.org
SIC: 8641 8699 7999 8351 Social club, membership; recreation association; charitable organization; day camp; preschool center

(G-7967)
LEVY & ASSOCIATES LLC
4645 Executive Dr (43220-3601)
PHONE..............................614 898-5200
Yale Levy, *CEO*
EMP: 47
SQ FT: 12,000
SALES (est): 5.9MM **Privately Held**
SIC: 8111 General practice attorney, lawyer

(G-7968)
LEWIS & MICHAEL MVG & STOR CO
845 Harrisburg Pike (43223-2526)
PHONE..............................614 275-2997
Charles M Lewis, *President*
David M Lewis, *Vice Pres*
William E Lewis, *Vice Pres*
EMP: 45
SQ FT: 50,000
SALES (est): 3.4MM
SALES (corp-wide): 8MM **Privately Held**
WEB: www.atlaslm.com
SIC: 4214 Local trucking with storage
PA: Lewis & Michael, Inc.
1827 Woodman Dr
Dayton OH 45420
937 252-6683

(G-7969)
LEXTANT CORPORATION
250 S High St Ste 600 (43215-4622)
PHONE..............................614 228-9711
Chris Rockwell, *President*
Craig Kavicky, *Vice Pres*
Spencer Murrell, *Vice Pres*
Mark Palmer, *Vice Pres*
Sheila Zwelling, *Research*

EMP: 48 EST: 2000
SALES (est): 2MM **Privately Held**
WEB: www.lextant.com
SIC: 8748 Business consulting

(G-7970)
LIBERTY COMM SFTWR SLTIONS INC
Also Called: Newfound Technologies
1050 Kingsmill Pkwy (43229-1143)
PHONE..............................614 318-5000
Padmanbhan Sathyanarayana, *CEO*
Gary Olander, *Principal*
Shalini Sathyanarayana, *Director*
Ronald Kester, *Administration*
EMP: 25
SQ FT: 8,300
SALES (est): 2.3MM **Privately Held**
WEB: www.nfti.com
SIC: 7371 Computer software development

(G-7971)
LIBERTY MORTGAGE COMPANY INC
473 E Rich St (43215-5300)
P.O. Box 918, Powell (43065-0918)
PHONE..............................614 224-4000
Karen Richmond, *President*
Stephone Beason, *Loan Officer*
John Vlahos, *Director*
Mary Fallieros, *Admin Sec*
EMP: 49
SQ FT: 4,500
SALES (est): 7.8MM **Privately Held**
SIC: 6162 Mortgage bankers & correspondents

(G-7972)
LIFE CARE CENTERS AMERICA INC
Also Called: Mayfare Village
3000 Bethel Rd (43220-2262)
PHONE..............................614 889-6320
Julie Klein, *Manager*
EMP: 100
SALES (corp-wide): 119.8MM **Privately Held**
SIC: 8051 Convalescent home with continuous nursing care
PA: Life Care Centers Of America, Inc.
3570 Keith St Nw
Cleveland TN 37312
423 472-9585

(G-7973)
LIFE TIME INC
Also Called: Lifetime Fitness
3900 Easton Sta (43219-6064)
PHONE..............................614 428-6000
Rob Zwelling, *Manager*
Landon Pheneger, *Manager*
EMP: 250
SALES (corp-wide): 773.5MM **Privately Held**
WEB: www.ltfcorporatewellness.com
SIC: 7991 7299 Health club; personal appearance services
HQ: Life Time, Inc.
2902 Corporate Pl
Chanhassen MN 55317

(G-7974)
LIFECARE ALLIANCE
Also Called: Meals On Wheels
1699 W Mound St (43223-1855)
PHONE..............................614 278-3130
Charles W Gehring, *CEO*
Robert Click, *President*
Joseph W Cole II, *Chairman*
John Gregory, *Senior VP*
Andrea Albanese Denning, *Vice Pres*
EMP: 210
SQ FT: 33,000
SALES (est): 12.6MM **Privately Held**
WEB: www.lifecarealliance.org
SIC: 8082 Home health care services

(G-7975)
LIFECARE MEDICAL SERVICES
3065 E 14th Ave (43219-2356)
PHONE..............................614 258-2545
EMP: 30
SALES (est): 910K **Privately Held**
SIC: 4119 Local Passenger Transportation

(G-7976)
LIFESTYLE COMMUNITIES LTD (PA)
230 West St Ste 200 (43215-2655)
PHONE..............................614 918-2000
Michael J Deasecentis Jr, *Partner*
Michael J Deasecentis Sr, *Partner*
Alexis Webb, *General Mgr*
Dan Powers, *Vice Pres*
Guy Skoy, *Vice Pres*
EMP: 53
SQ FT: 40,000
SALES (est): 21.8MM **Privately Held**
SIC: 1522 Multi-family dwellings, new construction

(G-7977)
LIMBACH COMPANY LLC
851 Williams Ave (43212)
PHONE..............................614 299-2175
William Meadows, *Branch Mgr*
EMP: 28 **Privately Held**
SIC: 1711 Warm air heating & air conditioning contractor; plumbing contractors
HQ: Limbach Company Llc
1251 Waterfront Pl # 201
Pittsburgh PA 15222
412 359-2173

(G-7978)
LIMBACH COMPANY LLC
822 Cleveland Ave (43201-3612)
PHONE..............................614 299-2175
Nick Covert, *Foreman/Supr*
Jay Sharp, *Branch Mgr*
EMP: 110 **Privately Held**
SIC: 1711 Mechanical contractor
HQ: Limbach Company Llc
1251 Waterfront Pl # 201
Pittsburgh PA 15222
412 359-2173

(G-7979)
LIMITLESS SOLUTIONS INC
600 Claycraft Rd (43230-5328)
PHONE..............................614 577-1550
Tom Kuhnash, *President*
EMP: 25
SALES (est): 2MM **Privately Held**
WEB: www.limitless-solutions.net
SIC: 7389 Personal service agents, brokers & bureaus

(G-7980)
LINCOLN FINCL ADVISORS CORP
7650 Rivers Edge Dr # 200 (43235-1342)
PHONE..............................614 888-6516
Terry Sanders, *Financial Exec*
Jamie Allmon, *Manager*
John Schatz, *Director*
Adam Weingartner, *Executive*
EMP: 100
SALES (corp-wide): 16.4B **Publicly Held**
SIC: 8742 Financial consultant
HQ: Lincoln Financial Advisors Corporation
1300 S Clinton St
Fort Wayne IN 46802
800 237-3813

(G-7981)
LINDSEY ACCURA INC
Also Called: Hbl Automotive
5880 Scarborough Blvd (43232-4746)
PHONE..............................800 980-8199
Burt Lindsey, *President*
Kim Blackman, *Executive*
EMP: 45
SALES (est): 7MM **Privately Held**
SIC: 5511 7538 5599 Automobiles, new & used; general automotive repair shops; automotive dealers

(G-7982)
LIQUI-BOX CORPORATION
480 Schrock Rd Ste G (43229-1092)
PHONE..............................614 888-9280
Doug Schwartz, *Controller*
EMP: 25
SQ FT: 29,848
SALES (corp-wide): 377.1MM **Privately Held**
WEB: www.liquibox.com
SIC: 5199 Packaging materials

PA: Liqui-Box Corporation
901 E Byrd St Ste 1105
Richmond VA 23219
804 325-1400

(G-7983)
LIQUI-BOX INTERNATIONAL INC
480 Schrock Rd Ste G (43229-1092)
PHONE..............................614 888-9280
Stewart Grave, *President*
EMP: 100
SQ FT: 63,000
SALES (corp-wide): 377.1MM **Privately Held**
WEB: www.liquibox.com
SIC: 6719 Investment holding companies, except banks
PA: Liqui-Box Corporation
901 E Byrd St Ste 1105
Richmond VA 23219
804 325-1400

(G-7984)
LITHKO RESTORATION TECH LLC
1059 Cable Ave (43222-1201)
PHONE..............................614 221-0711
Scott Rees, *Branch Mgr*
EMP: 40
SALES (est): 2.2MM
SALES (corp-wide): 23.1MM **Privately Held**
SIC: 1771 Concrete repair
PA: Lithko Restoration Technologies, Llc
990 N Main St
Monroe OH 45050
513 863-5500

(G-7985)
LITTLE DRMERS BIG BLIEVERS LLC
870 Michigan Ave (43215-1109)
PHONE..............................614 824-4666
Sarah Delay, *Director*
EMP: 31
SALES (est): 235.8K **Privately Held**
SIC: 8351 Group day care center

(G-7986)
LIVE TECHNOLOGIES LLC
3445 Millennium Ct (43219-5550)
PHONE..............................614 278-7777
Michael L Ranney Jr, *President*
Shawn D Loevenguth, *Vice Pres*
David Vuppo, *Vice Pres*
Thomas Marks, *CFO*
Erin Fielschott, *Accounts Mgr*
EMP: 100
SALES (est): 19MM **Privately Held**
SIC: 1731 5099 7359 7819 Sound equipment specialization; lighting contractor; video & audio equipment; audio-visual equipment & supply rental; sound (effects & music production), motion picture
PA: Live Technologies Holdings, Inc.
3445 Millennium Ct
Columbus OH 43219
614 278-7777

(G-7987)
LOEB ELECTRIC COMPANY (PA)
Also Called: Unistrut-Columbus
1800 E 5th Ave Ste A (43219-2592)
PHONE..............................614 294-6351
Charles A Loeb, *President*
Debbie Coffmon, *General Mgr*
M J Walsh, *Principal*
Lon Smith, *Vice Pres*
Stephanie Pierce, *Project Mgr*
▲ EMP: 95 EST: 1911
SQ FT: 220,000
SALES (est): 182.5MM **Privately Held**
WEB: www.loebelectric.com
SIC: 5063 Electrical supplies; lighting fixtures; circuit breakers; wire & cable

(G-7988)
LONGTERM LODGING INC
Also Called: Abaco Rhblttion Nursing Fcilty
721 S Souder Ave (43223)
PHONE..............................614 224-0614
Mary Rhinehart, *President*
EMP: 106
SQ FT: 30,000

SALES (est): 6.4MM **Privately Held**
WEB: www.wecarehealthfacility.com
SIC: 8051 Skilled nursing care facilities

(G-7989)
LOTH INC
Also Called: T W Ruff
855 Grandview Ave Ste 2 (43215-1102)
PHONE..................................614 487-4000
Jason Walaler, *General Mgr*
EMP: 55
SALES (corp-wide): 58.2MM **Privately Held**
WEB: www.lothmbi.com
SIC: 5021 5712 Office furniture; office furniture
PA: Loth, Inc.
　　3574 E Kemper Rd
　　Cincinnati OH 45241
　　513 554-4900

(G-7990)
LOWES HOME CENTERS LLC
1675 Georgesville Sq Dr (43228-3689)
PHONE..................................614 853-6200
Billy Houghton, *Manager*
EMP: 175
SALES (corp-wide): 68.6B **Publicly Held**
SIC: 5211 5031 5722 5064 Home centers; building materials, exterior; building materials, interior; household appliance stores; electrical appliances, television & radio
HQ: Lowe's Home Centers, Llc
　　1605 Curtis Bridge Rd
　　Wilkesboro NC 28697
　　336 658-4000

(G-7991)
LOWES HOME CENTERS LLC
3616 E Broad St (43213-1154)
PHONE..................................614 238-2601
Jason Cressy, *Manager*
EMP: 150
SALES (corp-wide): 68.6B **Publicly Held**
SIC: 5211 5031 5722 5064 Home centers; building materials, exterior; building materials, interior; household appliance stores; electrical appliances, television & radio
HQ: Lowe's Home Centers, Llc
　　1605 Curtis Bridge Rd
　　Wilkesboro NC 28697
　　336 658-4000

(G-7992)
LOWES HOME CENTERS LLC
3899 S High St (43207-4013)
PHONE..................................614 497-6170
Jason Altemose, *Branch Mgr*
EMP: 150
SALES (corp-wide): 68.6B **Publicly Held**
SIC: 5211 5031 5722 5064 Home centers; building materials, exterior; building materials, interior; household appliance stores; electrical appliances, television & radio
HQ: Lowe's Home Centers, Llc
　　1605 Curtis Bridge Rd
　　Wilkesboro NC 28697
　　336 658-4000

(G-7993)
LOWES HOME CENTERS LLC
2345 Silver Dr (43211-1050)
PHONE..................................614 447-2851
Ed Wuthrich, *Manager*
EMP: 150
SALES (corp-wide): 68.6B **Publicly Held**
SIC: 5211 5031 5722 5064 Home centers; building materials, exterior; building materials, interior; household appliance stores; electrical appliances, television & radio
HQ: Lowe's Home Centers, Llc
　　1605 Curtis Bridge Rd
　　Wilkesboro NC 28697
　　336 658-4000

(G-7994)
LOWES HOME CENTERS LLC
4141 Morse Xing (43219-6015)
PHONE..................................614 476-7100
Mike Cuellar, *Branch Mgr*
EMP: 150

SALES (corp-wide): 68.6B **Publicly Held**
SIC: 5211 5031 5722 5064 Home centers; building materials, exterior; building materials, interior; household appliance stores; electrical appliances, television & radio
HQ: Lowe's Home Centers, Llc
　　1605 Curtis Bridge Rd
　　Wilkesboro NC 28697
　　336 658-4000

(G-7995)
LSI ADL TECHONOLOGY LLC
2727 Scioto Pkwy (43221-4658)
PHONE..................................614 345-9040
Kevin Kelly, *President*
Dave Feeney, *COO*
Craig Miller, *Vice Pres*
Nick Klein, *Engineer*
Melinda Kelly, *Treasurer*
EMP: 45
SQ FT: 56,000
SALES (est): 10.7MM **Privately Held**
WEB: www.adltech.com
SIC: 8711 Designing: ship, boat, machine & product

(G-7996)
LTI INC
3445 Millennium Ct (43219-5550)
PHONE..................................614 278-7777
Michael L Ranney Jr, *President*
Shawn Loevenguth, *Vice Pres*
Ted Karl, *Project Mgr*
Tracey Adams, *Accounts Exec*
Grant Ripp, *Sales Staff*
EMP: 70
SQ FT: 35,000
SALES (est): 3.2MM **Privately Held**
WEB: www.livetechnologiesinc.com
SIC: 6799 Commodity investors

(G-7997)
LUMENANCE LLC (PA)
4449 Easton Way Fl 2 (43219-7005)
PHONE..................................319 541-6811
Theordore J Messerly,
Mark Luo,
EMP: 30
SALES (est): 2.5MM **Privately Held**
SIC: 8748 Systems analysis & engineering consulting services

(G-7998)
LUPER NEIDENTAL & LOGAN A LEG
1160 Dublin Rd Ste 400 (43215-1052)
PHONE..................................614 221-7663
Frederick M Luper, *President*
William B Logan Jr, *Vice Pres*
K Wallace Neidenthal, *Vice Pres*
Jack L Stewart, *Vice Pres*
Henry P Wickham Jr, *Vice Pres*
EMP: 45
SQ FT: 20,000
SALES (est): 5.9MM **Privately Held**
WEB: www.lnlattorneys.com
SIC: 8111 General practice law office

(G-7999)
LUSK & HARKIN LTD
Also Called: Lusk Hrkin Architects Planners
35 N 4th St Fl 5 (43215-3625)
PHONE..................................614 221-3707
Michael Lusk, *Partner*
James L Harkin, *Partner*
Steve McCoppin, *Partner*
James Harkin, *Principal*
EMP: 26
SQ FT: 5,000
SALES (est): 2.2MM **Privately Held**
WEB: www.luskharkin.com
SIC: 8712 Architectural engineering

(G-8000)
LUTHERAN SENIOR CITY INC (HQ)
Also Called: Lutheran Village Courtyard
935 N Cassady Ave (43219-2283)
PHONE..................................614 228-5200
Larry Crowell, *President*
Rev Thomas Hudson, *Chairman*
Phil Helser, *CFO*
EMP: 299
SQ FT: 121,000

SALES: 13.2MM
SALES (corp-wide): 49.2MM **Privately Held**
SIC: 8051 Convalescent home with continuous nursing care
PA: Lutheran Social Services Of Central Ohio
　　500 W Wilson Bridge Rd
　　Worthington OH 43085
　　419 289-3523

(G-8001)
LYONS DOUGHTY & VELDHUIS PC
471 E Broad St Fl 12 (43215-3806)
PHONE..................................614 229-3888
EMP: 35 **Privately Held**
SIC: 8111 General practice law office; debt collection law
PA: Lyons, Doughty & Veldhuis Pc
　　136 Gaither Dr Ste 100
　　Mount Laurel NJ 08054

(G-8002)
M & A DISTRIBUTING CO INC
871 Michigan Ave (43215-1108)
PHONE..................................614 294-3555
John M Antonucci, *Branch Mgr*
EMP: 98
SALES (corp-wide): 53.7MM **Privately Held**
SIC: 5182 Wine & distilled beverages
PA: M. & A. Distributing Co., Inc.
　　31031 Diamond Pkwy
　　Solon OH 44139
　　440 703-4580

(G-8003)
M J S HOLDING
Also Called: Instanceworkplace
226 N 5th St (43215-2656)
PHONE..................................614 410-2512
EMP: 25 **Privately Held**
SIC: 6719 Holding Company

(G-8004)
M P DORY CO
2001 Integrity Dr S (43209-2729)
PHONE..................................614 444-2138
Thomas Kuhn, *President*
Jeff Kuhn, *Corp Secy*
Michele Brown, *Assistant*
EMP: 80
SQ FT: 11,000 *
SALES (est): 14.7MM **Privately Held**
SIC: 1611 Guardrail construction, highways; highway & street sign installation

(G-8005)
M/I FINANCIAL LLC (HQ)
3 Easton Oval Ste 340 (43219-6011)
PHONE..................................614 418-8650
Paul Rosen, *President*
Derek Klutch, *COO*
Kate Elmquist, *Vice Pres*
Philip G Creek, *CFO*
Susan Depuy, *Admin Asst*
EMP: 53
SALES (est): 26.3MM
SALES (corp-wide): 2.2B **Publicly Held**
SIC: 6162 Mortgage brokers, using own money
PA: M/I Homes, Inc.
　　3 Easton Oval Ste 500
　　Columbus OH 43219
　　614 418-8000

(G-8006)
M/I HOMES INC (PA)
3 Easton Oval Ste 500 (43219-6011)
PHONE..................................614 418-8000
Robert H Schottenstein, *Ch of Bd*
Todd Miller, *Vice Pres*
Rick Stevens, *Vice Pres*
Tom Brick, *Purch Mgr*
Phillip G Creek, *CFO*
EMP: 290 **EST:** 1973
SQ FT: 85,000
SALES: 2.2B **Publicly Held**
WEB: www.mihomes.com
SIC: 1531 6162 Speculative builder, single-family houses; townhouse developers; mortgage bankers & correspondents

(G-8007)
M/I HOMES OF AUSTIN LLC
3 Easton Oval Ste 500 (43219-6011)
PHONE..................................614 418-8000
Irving Schottenstein, *Principal*
Tanya Szolnok, *Supervisor*
EMP: 47
SALES (est): 3.1MM
SALES (corp-wide): 2.2B **Publicly Held**
SIC: 1531 Operative builders
PA: M/I Homes, Inc.
　　3 Easton Oval Ste 500
　　Columbus OH 43219
　　614 418-8000

(G-8008)
MAGIC INDUSTRIES INC
Also Called: Dent Magic
4651 Poth Rd (43213-1396)
PHONE..................................614 759-8422
David B Miller, *President*
Derrick C Osborne, *Vice Pres*
Roy Gelin, *Manager*
EMP: 50
SQ FT: 6,000
SALES (est): 7.2MM **Privately Held**
SIC: 7532 5999 Body shop, automotive; mobile telephones & equipment

(G-8009)
MAGNETIC SPRINGS WATER COMPANY (PA)
1917 Joyce Ave (43219-1029)
P.O. Box 182076 (43218-2076)
PHONE..................................614 421-1780
Jeffrey Allison, *President*
James E Allison, *Chairman*
Beverly Allison, *Corp Secy*
Sherry Allison, *Vice Pres*
EMP: 70 **EST:** 1973
SQ FT: 100,000
SALES (est): 69.6MM **Privately Held**
WEB: www.magneticsprings.com
SIC: 5149 5499 Mineral or spring water bottling; water: distilled mineral or spring

(G-8010)
MAGUIRE & SCHNEIDER LLP
1650 Lake Shore Dr # 150 (43204-4942)
PHONE..................................614 224-1222
Patrick Maguire, *Partner*
Paul Schneider, *Partner*
Julie Thompson, *Vice Pres*
Gayna Strachota, *Receptionist*
EMP: 30
SALES (est): 4.9MM **Privately Held**
WEB: www.maguire-schneider.com
SIC: 8111 General practice attorney, lawyer; general practice law office

(G-8011)
MAJIDZADEH ENTERPRISES INC (PA)
Also Called: Resource International
6350 Presidential Gtwy (43231-7653)
PHONE..................................614 823-4949
Farah Majidzadeh, *Ch of Bd*
Kamran Majidzadeh, *President*
Steve Johnson, *Vice Pres*
Dominic Maxwell, *CFO*
Jeffrey Engram, *Exec Dir*
EMP: 50
SALES (est): 29.3MM **Privately Held**
WEB: www.smpscolumbus.org
SIC: 8711 Consulting engineer

(G-8012)
MANAGEMENT RECRUITERS INTL INC
Also Called: Management Recruiters Intl
800 E Broad St (43205-1015)
PHONE..................................614 252-6200
John Zambito, *Sales/Mktg Mgr*
EMP: 40
SALES (corp-wide): 864.3MM **Privately Held**
WEB: www.mrwg.com
SIC: 7361 Executive placement
HQ: Management Recruiters International, Inc.
　　1735 Market St Ste 200
　　Philadelphia PA 19103
　　800 875-4000

(G-8013)
MANLEY DEAS & KOCHALSKI LLC (PA)
1555 Lake Shore Dr (43204-3825)
P.O. Box 165028 (43216-5028)
PHONE..............................614 220-5611
Brian T Deas, *Mng Member*
Edward M Kochalski,
EMP: 62
SALES (est): 32.4MM **Privately Held**
SIC: 8111 General practice law office

(G-8014)
MAPSYS INC (PA)
Also Called: MAP SYSTEMS AND SOLUTIONS
920 Michigan Ave (43215-1165)
PHONE..............................614 255-7258
Steve Bernard, *President*
Paul Neal, *Corp Secy*
Jim Heiberger, *Vice Pres*
Terry Payne, *Vice Pres*
Scott Abrams, *Engineer*
EMP: 40
SQ FT: 6,000
SALES: 19.3MM **Privately Held**
WEB: www.mapsysinc.com
SIC: 7372 7371 5045 Business oriented computer software; custom computer programming services; computers, peripherals & software

(G-8015)
MARATHON PETROLEUM COMPANY LP
Lincoln Village Sta (43228)
PHONE..............................614 274-1125
J F Grant, *District Mgr*
EMP: 25 **Publicly Held**
WEB: www.mapllc.com
SIC: 5172 Gasoline
HQ: Marathon Petroleum Company Lp
539 S Main St
Findlay OH 45840

(G-8016)
MARCUS HOTELS INC
Also Called: Westin Columbus
310 S High St (43215-4508)
PHONE..............................614 228-3800
Tom Baker, *Manager*
Carol Keene, *Admin Asst*
EMP: 43
SALES (corp-wide): 707.1MM **Publicly Held**
SIC: 7011 Hotels
HQ: Marcus Hotels Inc
100 E Wisconsin Ave
Milwaukee WI 53202

(G-8017)
MARCUS MLLCHAP RE INV SVCS INC
230 West St Ste 100 (43215-2391)
PHONE..............................614 360-9800
Nandy Hart, *Branch Mgr*
EMP: 30
SALES (corp-wide): 814.8MM **Publicly Held**
SIC: 6531 Real estate agent, commercial
HQ: Marcus & Millichap Real Estate Investment Services, Inc.
23975 Park Sorrento # 400
Calabasas CA 91302

(G-8018)
MARCUS THEATRES CORPORATION
Also Called: Crosswoods Ultrascreen Cinema
200 Hutchinson Ave (43235-4687)
PHONE..............................614 436-9818
Tim Burn, *Branch Mgr*
EMP: 100
SALES (corp-wide): 707.1MM **Publicly Held**
SIC: 7832 5813 5812 Motion picture theaters, except drive-in; tavern (drinking places); fast food restaurants & stands
HQ: Marcus Theatres Corporation
100 E Wisconsin Ave
Milwaukee WI 53202
414 905-1500

(G-8019)
MARFO COMPANY (PA)
Also Called: Trading Corp of America
799 N Hague Ave (43204-1424)
PHONE..............................614 276-3352
Bill Giovanello, *CEO*
Cheryl Beery, *President*
Crystal Kordes, *Traffic Mgr*
Carla Jay, *Buyer*
Alan Johnson, *CFO*
EMP: 100
SQ FT: 41,000
SALES (est): 21.9MM **Privately Held**
WEB: www.marsala.com
SIC: 5094 3911 Jewelry; jewelry apparel

(G-8020)
MARION ROAD ENTERPRISES
Also Called: Wasserstom Disrtributing Ofc
477 S Front St (43215-5625)
PHONE..............................614 228-6525
Reid Wasserstrom, *Partner*
EMP: 200
SQ FT: 250,000
SALES (est): 5.6MM **Privately Held**
SIC: 6512 Nonresidential building operators

(G-8021)
MARKETING RESULTS LTD
3985 Groves Rd (43232-4138)
PHONE..............................614 575-9300
Brady Churches, *Principal*
Karen Waldmann, *Vice Pres*
Jerry Sommers,
◆ **EMP:** 25
SQ FT: 130,000
SALES (est): 21.1MM **Privately Held**
SIC: 5023 Home furnishings

(G-8022)
MARRIOTT INTERNATIONAL INC
695 Taylor Rd (43230-6203)
PHONE..............................614 861-1400
EMP: 173
SALES (corp-wide): 20.7B **Publicly Held**
SIC: 7011 Hotels & motels
PA: Marriott International, Inc.
10400 Fernwood Rd
Bethesda MD 20817
301 380-3000

(G-8023)
MARRIOTT INTERNATIONAL INC
50 N 3rd St (43215-3510)
PHONE..............................614 228-5050
Gerie Lonbarob, *Manager*
EMP: 275
SALES (corp-wide): 20.7B **Publicly Held**
SIC: 7011 Hotels & motels
PA: Marriott International, Inc.
10400 Fernwood Rd
Bethesda MD 20817
301 380-3000

(G-8024)
MARRIOTT INTERNATIONAL INC
7411 Vantage Dr (43235-1415)
PHONE..............................614 436-7070
Shane Ewald, *General Mgr*
EMP: 30
SALES (corp-wide): 20.7B **Publicly Held**
SIC: 7011 Hotels & motels
PA: Marriott International, Inc.
10400 Fernwood Rd
Bethesda MD 20817
301 380-3000

(G-8025)
MARRIOTT INTERNATIONAL INC
2901 Airport Dr (43219-2299)
PHONE..............................614 475-8530
Becky Krieger, *Manager*
EMP: 167
SALES (corp-wide): 20.7B **Publicly Held**
SIC: 7011 Hotels & motels
PA: Marriott International, Inc.
10400 Fernwood Rd
Bethesda MD 20817
301 380-3000

(G-8026)
MARRIOTT INTERNATIONAL INC
Also Called: Residence Inn By Marriott
2084 S Hamilton Rd (43232-4302)
PHONE..............................614 864-8844
Rob Kennedy, *Branch Mgr*
EMP: 167
SALES (corp-wide): 20.7B **Publicly Held**
SIC: 7011 Hotels & motels
PA: Marriott International, Inc.
10400 Fernwood Rd
Bethesda MD 20817
301 380-3000

(G-8027)
MARRIOTT INTERNATIONAL INC
Also Called: Residence Inn By Marriott
36 E Gay St (43215-3108)
PHONE..............................614 222-2610
Joey Guiyab, *Branch Mgr*
EMP: 167
SALES (corp-wide): 20.7B **Publicly Held**
SIC: 7011 Hotels & motels
PA: Marriott International, Inc.
10400 Fernwood Rd
Bethesda MD 20817
301 380-3000

(G-8028)
MARRIOTT INTERNATIONAL INC
Also Called: Residence Inn By Marriott
7300 Huntington Park Dr (43235-5718)
PHONE..............................614 885-0799
Tim Whitehead, *General Mgr*
EMP: 40
SALES (corp-wide): 20.7B **Publicly Held**
SIC: 7011 Hotels & motels
PA: Marriott International, Inc.
10400 Fernwood Rd
Bethesda MD 20817
301 380-3000

(G-8029)
MARSH USA INC
325 John H Mcconnell Blvd # 350 (43215-7644)
PHONE..............................614 227-6200
Vivica Wall, *Vice Pres*
Kyle Ewart, *Facilities Mgr*
Tom Hayden, *Branch Mgr*
EMP: 64
SALES (corp-wide): 14.9B **Publicly Held**
WEB: www.marsh.com
SIC: 6411 Insurance brokers
HQ: Marsh Usa Inc.
1166 Ave Of The Americas
New York NY 10036
212 345-6000

(G-8030)
MARSHALL INFORMATION SVCS LLC
Also Called: Primary Solutions
6665 Busch Blvd (43229-1767)
PHONE..............................614 430-0355
EMP: 31 **EST:** 1999
SALES (est): 3.6MM **Privately Held**
SIC: 7371 Custom Computer Programing

(G-8031)
MARTIN CARPET CLEANING COMPANY
795 S Wall St (43206-1995)
PHONE..............................614 443-4655
John Martin, *Ch of Bd*
Brent Martin, *Vice Pres*
Chad Martin, *Vice Pres*
EMP: 28
SQ FT: 8,030
SALES (est): 2.1MM **Privately Held**
SIC: 7217 Carpet & rug cleaning plant; upholstery cleaning on customer premises

(G-8032)
MARYHAVEN INC (PA)
1791 Alum Creek Dr (43207-1757)
PHONE..............................614 449-1530
Shawn Holts, *CEO*
Tonya Mabra, *Supervisor*
Joyce F Clark, *Executive*
EMP: 275 **EST:** 1959

SQ FT: 100,000
SALES: 21.9MM **Privately Held**
WEB: www.maryhaven.com
SIC: 8069 Alcoholism rehabilitation hospital; drug addiction rehabilitation hospital

(G-8033)
MAS INTERNATIONAL MKTG LLC
3498 Derbyshire Dr Apt C (43224-5009)
PHONE..............................614 446-2003
Mohamed Salad, *Mng Member*
EMP: 100 **EST:** 2016
SALES (est): 1.3MM **Privately Held**
SIC: 5963 8742 Direct sales, telemarketing; marketing consulting services

(G-8034)
MAST INDUSTRIES INC (DH)
Also Called: L Brands
2 Limited Pkwy (43230-1445)
PHONE..............................614 415-7000
Leslie H Wexner, *CEO*
James M Schwartz, *President*
Stuart Burgdoerfer, *Vice Pres*
▲ **EMP:** 125
SALES (est): 394.4MM
SALES (corp-wide): 13.2B **Publicly Held**
WEB: www.mast.com
SIC: 5137 5136 Women's & children's clothing; men's & boys' clothing

(G-8035)
MAST LOGISTICS SERVICES INC
2 Limited Pkwy (43230-1445)
PHONE..............................614 415-7500
Bruce Mosier, *President*
Nicole Virden, *Manager*
▲ **EMP:** 150
SALES (est): 172.7MM
SALES (corp-wide): 13.2B **Publicly Held**
WEB: www.ldsltd.com
SIC: 5113 Shipping supplies
PA: L Brands, Inc.
3 Limited Pkwy
Columbus OH 43230
614 415-7000

(G-8036)
MAST TECHNOLOGY SERVICES INC
Also Called: Limited Technology Svcs Inc
3 Limited Pkwy (43230-1467)
PHONE..............................614 415-7000
Jon Ricker, *President*
Pamela Rice, *Vice Pres*
EMP: 800
SALES (est): 80.2MM
SALES (corp-wide): 13.2B **Publicly Held**
WEB: www.limited.com
SIC: 7374 Data processing & preparation
PA: L Brands, Inc.
3 Limited Pkwy
Columbus OH 43230
614 415-7000

(G-8037)
MATERN OHIO MANAGEMENT INC
Also Called: Maternohio Management Services
1241 Dublin Rd Ste 200 (43215-7062)
PHONE..............................614 457-7660
Christophe M Copeland MD, *President*
EMP: 65
SALES (est): 4.3MM **Privately Held**
WEB: www.maternohio.com
SIC: 8011 Clinic, operated by physicians

(G-8038)
MATERNOHIO CLINICAL ASSOICATES
1241 Dublin Rd Ste 102 (43215-7048)
PHONE..............................614 457-7660
Dan Shemenski, *Principal*
EMP: 25
SALES (est): 2.3MM **Privately Held**
SIC: 8071 Medical laboratories

(G-8039)
MATRIX MEDIA SERVICES INC
463 E Town St Ste 200 (43215-4706)
PHONE..............................614 228-2200
Charles Mc Crimmon, *President*

Marty Blanton, *Production*
Ashley Griffith, *Buyer*
Jeremy Mitchell, *Sales Mgr*
Emily Beringer, *Accounts Mgr*
EMP: 30
SQ FT: 15,000
SALES (est): 7.9MM **Privately Held**
WEB: www.matrixmediaservices.com
SIC: 7311 7312 Advertising consultant;
outdoor advertising services; billboard advertising

(G-8040)
MATVEST INC
Also Called: Bermex
1380 Dublin Rd Ste 200 (43215-1025)
PHONE...........................614 487-8720
Mark Everly, *General Mgr*
Chris Covey, *Branch Mgr*
Raymond Tackett, *Manager*
EMP: 30
SALES (corp-wide): 12MM **Privately Held**
WEB: www.bermexinc.com
SIC: 3545 7389 Machine tool accessories;
meter readers, remote
PA: Matvest, Inc.
37244 S Groesbeck Hwy A
Clinton Township MI 48036
586 461-2051

(G-8041)
MAYFAIR NURSING CARE CENTERS
Also Called: MAYFAIR VILLAGE
3000 Bethel Rd (43220-2262)
PHONE...........................614 889-6320
J Edwin Farmer, *President*
EMP: 100
SQ FT: 10,000
SALES: 8.6MM **Privately Held**
SIC: 8051 Convalescent home with continuous nursing care

(G-8042)
MC CLOY FINANCIAL SERVICES
Also Called: New Enland Life Ins Co
921 Chatham Ln Ste 300 (43221-2418)
PHONE...........................614 457-6233
George W McCloy, *President*
Jeffrey Logan, *General Ptnr*
Teresa Rusell, *Marketing Staff*
Jeff Logan, *Council Mbr*
EMP: 65
SQ FT: 21,000
SALES: 2.5MM **Privately Held**
WEB: www.columbusoh.nef.com
SIC: 6211 6411 8742 Security brokers &
dealers; insurance agents; financial consultant

(G-8043)
MCDANIELS CNSTR CORP INC
1069 Woodland Ave (43219-2177)
PHONE...........................614 252-5852
Dan Moncrief III, *CEO*
Eric Girard, *President*
Rob Laveck, *Superintendent*
Brian Davis, *Project Mgr*
Chris Leonard, *Project Mgr*
EMP: 60
SQ FT: 12,000
SALES (est): 15.8MM **Privately Held**
WEB: www.mcdanielsconstruction.com
SIC: 1611 8741 General contractor, highway & street construction; construction management

(G-8044)
MCDONALDS CORPORATION
2600 Corporate Exch Dr (43231-7683)
PHONE...........................614 682-1128
EMP: 38
SALES (corp-wide): 25.4B **Publicly Held**
SIC: 5812 6794 Operates & Franchises
Restaurants
PA: Mcdonald's Corporation
1 Mcdonalds Dr
Oak Brook IL 60607
630 623-3000

(G-8045)
MCGILL AIRCLEAN LLC
1777 Refugee Rd (43207-2119)
PHONE...........................614 829-1200
James D McGill, *President*

Paul R Hess, *Mng Member*
Jerry Childress,
◆ EMP: 70 **EST:** 2004
SQ FT: 15,000
SALES (est): 18.2MM
SALES (corp-wide): 67.7MM **Privately Held**
WEB: www.mcgillairclean.com
SIC: 3564 1796 Precipitators, electrostatic; pollution control equipment installation
HQ: United Mcgill Corporation
1 Mission Park
Groveport OH 43125
614 829-1200

(G-8046)
MCNAUGHTON-MCKAY ELC OHIO INC (HQ)
Also Called: McNaughton-Mckay Electric Ohio
2255 Citygate Dr (43219-3567)
P.O. Box 849 (43216-0849)
PHONE...........................614 476-2800
Donald D Slominski Jr, *CEO*
William Parsons, *General Mgr*
Michael G Mimnaugh, *Corp Secy*
Richard M Dahlstrom, *Exec VP*
John R McNaughton III, *Exec VP*
▲ EMP: 70 **EST:** 1996
SQ FT: 65,000
SALES (est): 101.2MM
SALES (corp-wide): 822.5MM **Privately Held**
WEB: www.mc.mc.com
SIC: 5063 Electrical supplies
PA: Mcnaughton-Mckay Electric Co.
1357 E Lincoln Ave
Madison Heights MI 48071
248 399-7500

(G-8047)
MCR SERVICES INC
638 E 5th Ave (43201-2965)
PHONE...........................614 421-0860
Wade F Hungerford, *President*
Scott Gallagher, *Vice Pres*
EMP: 32
SQ FT: 14,000
SALES (est): 13.8MM **Privately Held**
WEB: www.mcrservices.com
SIC: 1542 Commercial & office building,
new construction

(G-8048)
MEACHAM & APEL ARCHITECTS INC
Also Called: MA Architects
775 Yard St Ste 325 (43212-3890)
PHONE...........................614 764-0407
Mark Daniels, *President*
Jim Mitchell, *Exec VP*
Ken Cleaver, *Project Mgr*
Seth Oakley, *Project Mgr*
Denise Orr, *Accountant*
EMP: 65
SQ FT: 18,000
SALES: 4.5MM **Privately Held**
WEB: www.meachamapel.com
SIC: 8712 Architectural engineering

(G-8049)
MEADOWBROOK MEAT COMPANY INC
M B M
4300 Diplomacy Dr (43228-3804)
PHONE...........................614 771-9660
Al Monsaw, *Manager*
EMP: 220
SQ FT: 80,000
SALES (corp-wide): 225.3B **Publicly Held**
WEB: www.mbmlc.com
SIC: 5147 5141 Meats & meat products;
groceries, general line
HQ: Meadowbrook Meat Company, Inc.
2641 Meadowbrook Rd
Rocky Mount NC 27801
252 985-7200

(G-8050)
MED CLEAN
5725 Westbourne Ave (43213-1449)
PHONE...........................614 207-3317
Anthony Christopher, *Owner*
EMP: 107

SQ FT: 14,000
SALES: 7.2MM **Privately Held**
SIC: 7699 Cleaning services

(G-8051)
MED RIDE EMS
2741 E 4th Ave (43219-2824)
P.O. Box 30754, Gahanna (43230-0754)
PHONE...........................614 747-9744
Ibrahim Y Halloway, *CEO*
Abe Halloway, *CEO*
Robert Oros, *Director*
EMP: 55
SQ FT: 12,000
SALES: 2MM **Privately Held**
SIC: 4119 Ambulance service

(G-8052)
MEDIA ADVERTISING CONS LLC
1629 Anchor Dr W (43207-1506)
PHONE...........................614 615-1398
Tyrone Flowers,
EMP: 25
SALES (est): 463.1K **Privately Held**
SIC: 5199 Advertising specialties

(G-8053)
MEDICAL MUTUAL OF OHIO
10 W Broad St Ste 1400 (43215-3469)
PHONE...........................614 621-4585
Janet Keslar, *Accounts Exec*
Mike Broderick, *Sales Staff*
John Stofa, *Manager*
Pj Apostle, *Network Enginr*
EMP: 35
SALES (corp-wide): 1.2B **Privately Held**
SIC: 8011 Medical insurance plan
PA: Medical Mutual Of Ohio
2060 E 9th St Frnt Ste
Cleveland OH 44115
216 687-7000

(G-8054)
MEDIGISTICS INC (PA)
1111 Schrock Rd Ste 200 (43229-1155)
PHONE...........................614 430-5700
Susan Long, *President*
Roger Broome, *Vice Pres*
Don Kyle, *Vice Pres*
Michael Poling, *Vice Pres*
Gary Broughman, *Treasurer*
EMP: 65
SQ FT: 30,000
SALES (est): 9MM **Privately Held**
SIC: 7389 8721 Charge account service;
accounting, auditing & bookkeeping

(G-8055)
MEDONE HOSPITAL PHYSICIANS
3525 Olentangy River Rd (43214-3937)
PHONE...........................314 255-6900
Christine C Quilling, *Principal*
EMP: 34
SALES (est): 2.5MM **Privately Held**
SIC: 8062 General medical & surgical hospitals

(G-8056)
MENARD INC
6800 E Broad St (43213-1515)
PHONE...........................614 501-1654
Scott Sirsich, *President*
EMP: 208
SALES (corp-wide): 12.5B **Privately Held**
SIC: 7299 Home improvement & renovation contractor agency
PA: Menard, Inc.
5101 Menard Dr
Eau Claire WI 54703
715 876-5911

(G-8057)
MENTAL HEALTH AND ADDI SERV
Also Called: Twin Vly Behavioral Healthcare
2200 W Broad St (43223-1297)
PHONE...........................614 752-0333
Richard Freeland, *Branch Mgr*
Missy McGarvey, *MIS Dir*
EMP: 51 **Privately Held**
SIC: 8063 9431 Psychiatric hospitals;
mental health agency administration, government;

HQ: Ohio Department Of Mental Health
And Addiction Services
30 E Broad St Fl 8
Columbus OH 43215

(G-8058)
MENTAL HEALTH AND ADDI SERV
Also Called: Twin Vly Behavioral Hlth Care
2200 W Broad St (43223-1297)
PHONE...........................614 752-0333
Bob Short, *Branch Mgr*
EMP: 190 **Privately Held**
SIC: 8062 9431 8093 General medical &
surgical hospitals; administration of public
health programs; ; mental health clinic,
outpatient
HQ: Ohio Department Of Mental Health
And Addiction Services
30 E Broad St Fl 8
Columbus OH 43215

(G-8059)
MERRILL LYNCH PIERCE FENNER
65 E State St Ste 2600 (43215-4254)
PHONE...........................614 225-3152
Christopher Boyd, *Investment Ofcr*
Michael Elsner, *Investment Ofcr*
Kelly Kashmiry, *Investment Ofcr*
Kelly Willmer, *Investment Ofcr*
Milt Leeman, *Manager*
EMP: 60
SALES (corp-wide): 110.5B **Publicly Held**
WEB: www.ml.com
SIC: 6211 Security brokers & dealers
HQ: Merrill Lynch, Pierce, Fenner & Smith
Incorporated
111 8th Ave
New York NY 10011
800 637-7455

(G-8060)
MERRILL LYNCH PIERCE FENNER
2 Easton Oval Ste 100 (43219-6036)
PHONE...........................614 475-2798
Alan Beymer, *Investment Ofcr*
Thomas Puleri, *Investment Ofcr*
Kelly O'Connor, *Manager*
Anthony Mabry, *Executive*
Scott Mann, *Executive*
EMP: 48
SALES (corp-wide): 110.5B **Publicly Held**
WEB: www.merlyn.com
SIC: 6211 Security brokers & dealers
HQ: Merrill Lynch, Pierce, Fenner & Smith
Incorporated
111 8th Ave
New York NY 10011
800 637-7455

(G-8061)
MERRILL LYNCH PIERCE FENNER
4661 Sawmill Rd Ste 200 (43220-6123)
PHONE...........................614 225-3000
Nelson Heinrichs, *Vice Pres*
Jim Schaine, *Exec Dir*
Debbie Lance, *Advisor*
EMP: 90
SALES (corp-wide): 110.5B **Publicly Held**
WEB: www.merlyn.com
SIC: 6211 8742 6282 Security brokers &
dealers; financial consultant; investment
advice
HQ: Merrill Lynch, Pierce, Fenner & Smith
Incorporated
111 8th Ave
New York NY 10011
800 637-7455

(G-8062)
MESSER CONSTRUCTION CO
3705 Business Park Dr (43204-5007)
PHONE...........................614 275-0141
Jason Brett, *Regional Mgr*
James R Hess, *Vice Pres*
Mike Malone, *Vice Pres*
Chris Malinowski, *Accounts Mgr*
Erin Thompson, *Director*
EMP: 100

SALES (corp-wide): 1B **Privately Held**
WEB: www.messer.com
SIC: **1542** Commercial & office building, new construction
PA: Messer Construction Co.
643 W Court St
Cincinnati OH 45203
513 242-1541

(G-8063)
METAMATERIA PARTNERS LLC
1275 Kinnear Rd (43212-1180)
PHONE..............................614 340-1690
J Richard Schorr, *Partner*
EMP: 27
SQ FT: 3,000
SALES (est): 1.6MM **Privately Held**
WEB: www.metamateria.com
SIC: **8711** Consulting engineer

(G-8064)
METRO SAFETY AND SECURITY LLC
5785 Emporium Sq (43231-2802)
PHONE..............................614 792-2770
Jeff Clark, *Mng Member*
EMP: 65
SQ FT: 3,000
SALES: 1.4MM **Privately Held**
SIC: **7381 7382** Protective services, guard; security guard service; fire alarm maintenance & monitoring

(G-8065)
MEYERS + ASSOCIATES ARCH LLC
232 N 3rd St Ste 300 (43215-2786)
PHONE..............................614 221-9433
Christopher P Meyers,
EMP: 28
SALES (est): 59.6K **Privately Held**
SIC: **8712** Architectural services

(G-8066)
MGF SOURCING US LLC (HQ)
4200 Regent St Ste 205 (43219-6229)
PHONE..............................614 904-3300
James Schwartz, *CEO*
Dan Bloch, *President*
Jennie Wilson, *CFO*
▲ EMP: 60
SQ FT: 16,000
SALES (est): 1.1B **Privately Held**
SIC: **5137 5136** Women's & children's clothing; men's & boys' clothing

(G-8067)
MICHAEL A GARCIA SALON
2440 E Main St (43209-2441)
PHONE..............................614 235-1605
Michael Garcia, *Owner*
Leslie Garcia, *Co-Owner*
EMP: 30
SALES (est): 635.8K **Privately Held**
SIC: **7231** Hairdressers

(G-8068)
MICHAEL BAKER INTL INC
250 West St Ste 420 (43215-7527)
PHONE..............................614 418-1773
Bill Arrighi, *Branch Mgr*
EMP: 239
SALES (corp-wide): 592.9MM **Privately Held**
WEB: www.michaelbaker.com
SIC: **8711** Engineering Services
HQ: Baker Michael International Inc
500 Grant St Ste 5400
Pittsburgh PA 15219
412 269-6300

(G-8069)
MICRO CENTER ONLINE INC
747 Bethel Rd (43214-1901)
P.O. Box 1143, Hilliard (43026-6143)
PHONE..............................614 326-8500
R Dale Brown, *CEO*
John F Baker, *Ch of Bd*
T James Koehler, *CFO*
EMP: 150
SALES (est): 12.1MM
SALES (corp-wide): 3.6B **Privately Held**
SIC: **5045 5734** Computer peripheral equipment; personal computers

PA: Micro Electronics, Inc.
4119 Leap Rd
Hilliard OH 43026
614 850-3000

(G-8070)
MICRO ELECTRONICS INC
Also Called: Micro Center Computer Educatn
747 Bethel Rd (43214-1901)
PHONE..............................614 326-8500
Chuck Gammello, *Manager*
EMP: 75
SALES (corp-wide): 3.6B **Privately Held**
SIC: **5045** Computers, peripherals & software
PA: Micro Electronics, Inc.
4119 Leap Rd
Hilliard OH 43026
614 850-3000

(G-8071)
MICRO ELECTRONICS INC
Also Called: Microcenter DC
2701 Charter St Ste B (43228-4639)
PHONE..............................614 334-1430
Steve Lancaster, *Manager*
EMP: 80
SALES (corp-wide): 3.6B **Privately Held**
WEB: www.microcenter.com
SIC: **5045 5734 4225** Computer peripheral equipment; computer & software stores; general warehousing & storage
PA: Micro Electronics, Inc.
4119 Leap Rd
Hilliard OH 43026
614 850-3000

(G-8072)
MICROWAVE LEASING SERVICES LLC
Also Called: M L S
2860 Fisher Rd (43204-3538)
PHONE..............................614 308-5433
C K Satyapriyam,
John Werner,
EMP: 30
SQ FT: 37,000
SALES (est): 7.2MM
SALES (corp-wide): 36.1MM **Privately Held**
WEB: www.ctleng.com
SIC: **1623** Communication line & transmission tower construction
PA: Ctl Engineering, Inc.
2860 Fisher Rd
Columbus OH 43204
614 276-8123

(G-8073)
MID OHIO EMERGENCY SVCS LLC
3525 Olentangy Blvd # 4330 (43214)
PHONE..............................614 566-5070
Jennifer Bailey, *Principal*
Tom Nolan, *COO*
EMP: 25
SALES (est): 1.1MM **Privately Held**
SIC: **8999** Services

(G-8074)
MID-AMERICAN CLG CONTRS INC
1046 King Ave (43212-2609)
PHONE..............................614 291-7170
Tony Cordoso, *Manager*
Susan Smetanko, *Manager*
EMP: 200 **Privately Held**
WEB: www.corporatesupportinc.com
SIC: **7349** Janitorial service, contract basis
PA: Mid-American Cleaning Contractors, Inc.
447 N Elizabeth St
Lima OH 45801

(G-8075)
MID-OHIO AIR CONDITIONING
456 E 5th Ave (43201-2971)
P.O. Box 8397 (43201-0397)
PHONE..............................614 291-4664
Rod Burkett, *President*
Karen York, *Info Tech Mgr*
Matt Trubee, *Admin Sec*
Matthew Trubee, *Admin Sec*
EMP: 34
SQ FT: 16,000

SALES (est): 7MM **Privately Held**
WEB: www.midohioac.com
SIC: **7623** Air conditioning repair

(G-8076)
MID-OHIO ELECTRIC CO
1170 Mckinley Ave (43222-1113)
PHONE..............................614 274-8000
Cynthia Langhirt, *President*
Bruce A Langhirt, *Vice Pres*
Vince Langhirt, *Vice Pres*
Bret Law, *Accountant*
Bob Calkins, *Sales Staff*
EMP: 26
SQ FT: 13,800
SALES (est): 5.8MM **Privately Held**
WEB: www.mid-ohioelectric.com
SIC: **7694 5063 7629 8711** Electric motor repair; motors, electric; circuit board repair; generator repair; electrical or electronic engineering

(G-8077)
MID-OHIO REGIONAL PLG COMM (PA)
111 Liberty St Ste 100 (43215-5850)
PHONE..............................614 228-2663
Marilyn Brown, *Chairman*
William Murdock, *Exec VP*
Susan Tsen, *Finance Dir*
Chester R Jourdan Jr, *Exec Dir*
Matt Greeson, *Admin Sec*
EMP: 56
SALES: 10.2MM **Privately Held**
WEB: www.morpc.org
SIC: **8611** Business associations

(G-8078)
MID-STATE BOLT AND NUT CO INC (PA)
1575 Alum Creek Dr (43209-2712)
PHONE..............................614 253-8631
David R Broehm, *President*
Stephen English, *Vice Pres*
Curt McCullough, *Vice Pres*
William C McCullough, *Vice Pres*
David A Breault, *Treasurer*
▲ EMP: 43 EST: 1946
SQ FT: 85,000
SALES (est): 30.3MM **Privately Held**
WEB: www.msbolt.com
SIC: **5085 5072** Fasteners, industrial: nuts, bolts, screws, etc.; bolts

(G-8079)
MIDOHIO CRDIOLGY VASCULAR CONS (PA)
3705 Olentangy River Rd # 100 (43214-3467)
PHONE..............................614 262-6772
Anthony T Chapekis, *President*
EMP: 125
SQ FT: 42,000
SALES (est): 8.6MM **Privately Held**
WEB: www.mocvc.com
SIC: **8011** Cardiologist & cardio-vascular specialist

(G-8080)
MIDWEST ALLERGY ASSOCIATES (PA)
Also Called: Bullock, Jos D MD
8080 Ravines Edge Ct # 100 (43235-5424)
PHONE..............................614 846-5944
Joseph D Bullock MD, *Vice Pres*
Lori Knisley, *Manager*
EMP: 25
SQ FT: 9,600
SALES (est): 7MM **Privately Held**
SIC: **8011** Physicians' office, including specialists; allergist

(G-8081)
MIDWEST FRESH FOODS INC
38 N Glenwood Ave (43222-1206)
PHONE..............................614 469-1492
Charles Giller, *President*
Stan Hunt, *Vice Pres*
Rich Anthony, *QC Mgr*
John Pottkotter, *Accounting Mgr*
Kate Giller, *Sales Staff*
EMP: 35
SQ FT: 7,000

SALES (est): 24.6MM **Privately Held**
WEB: www.midwestfresh.com
SIC: **5148** Fruits, fresh; vegetables, fresh

(G-8082)
MIDWEST MOTOR SUPPLY CO (PA)
Also Called: Kimball Midwest
4800 Roberts Rd (43228-9791)
P.O. Box 2470 (43216-2470)
PHONE..............................800 233-1294
Patrick J McCurdy Jr, *President*
A Glenn McClelland, *Principal*
Charles McCurdy, *Vice Pres*
David McCurdy, *Vice Pres*
Ed McCurdy, *Vice Pres*
▲ EMP: 200
SQ FT: 85,000
SALES (est): 147.9MM **Privately Held**
WEB: www.kimballmidwest.com
SIC: **3965 3399 8742** Fasteners; metal fasteners; materials mgmt. (purchasing, handling, inventory) consultant

(G-8083)
MIDWEST PHYSCANS ANSTHSIA SVCS
5151 Reed Rd Ste 225c (43220-2553)
PHONE..............................614 884-0641
Daniel Hiestand, *President*
Dustin Arnold, *Anesthesiology*
Kelly Clark, *Anesthesiology*
Angela Denoble, *Anesthesiology*
Deanna Dipillo, *Anesthesiology*
EMP: 98
SALES (est): 13.6MM **Privately Held**
SIC: **8011** Anesthesiologist

(G-8084)
MIDWEST ROOFING & FURNACE CO
Also Called: Midwest Heating & Cooling
646 S Nelson Rd (43205-2599)
PHONE..............................614 252-5241
H Terry Hoover, *President*
Donna Hoover, *President*
Leon C Hoover, *Corp Secy*
EMP: 25
SQ FT: 9,000
SALES (est): 3.2MM **Privately Held**
SIC: **1711 1761 1521 1542** Warm air heating & air conditioning contractor; roofing contractor; sheet metalwork; general remodeling, single-family houses; commercial & office building, new construction

(G-8085)
MILE INC
Also Called: Lions Den
1144 Alum Creek Dr (43209-2701)
PHONE..............................614 252-6724
EMP: 123 **Privately Held**
SIC: **7841** Video tape rental
PA: Mile Inc
110 E Wilson Bridge Rd # 100
Worthington OH 43085

(G-8086)
MILES-MCCLELLAN CNSTR CO INC (PA)
2100 Builders Pl (43204-4885)
PHONE..............................614 487-7744
Lonnie Miles, *CEO*
Matthew Q McClellan, *President*
Dave McIntosh, *Vice Pres*
Mike Rodriguez, *Vice Pres*
Ted Tinkler, *Vice Pres*
EMP: 28
SQ FT: 19,000
SALES (est): 31.6MM **Privately Held**
WEB: www.miles-mcclellan.com
SIC: **1542 1541** Industrial buildings, new construction; renovation, remodeling & repairs: industrial buildings; commercial & office building, new construction; commercial & office buildings, renovation & repair

(G-8087)
MILLCRAFT PAPER COMPANY
Also Called: Columbus Division
4311 Janitrol Rd Ste 600 (43228-1389)
PHONE..............................614 675-4800
Eric Michel, *Branch Mgr*
J R Dobbins, *Administration*

EMP: 28　Privately Held
WEB: www.millcraft.com
SIC: 5111 5113 Printing paper; industrial & personal service paper
HQ: The Millcraft Paper Company
　6800 Grant Ave
　Cleveland OH 44105
　216 441-5505

(G-8088)
MIMRX CO INC
Also Called: Scrip Pharmacy
2787 Charter St　(43228-4607)
PHONE..............................614 850-6672
Rich Friedman, *President*
Al Corfera, *Vice Pres*
EMP: 500
SALES (est): 37MM　Privately Held
SIC: 5122 Druggists' sundries

(G-8089)
MINAMYER RESIDENTIAL MR/DD SVC
967 Worthington Woods Loo　(43085)
PHONE..............................614 802-0190
Darla Minamyer, *President*
Dean Minamyer, *Vice Pres*
EMP: 33
SALES (est): 1.4MM　Privately Held
SIC: 8059 Home for the mentally retarded, exc. skilled or intermediate

(G-8090)
MIRCALE HEALTH CARE
3245 E Livingston Ave # 108　(43227-1943)
PHONE..............................614 237-7702
Tedila Zacchaues, *Partner*
Karen Woosley, *Office Mgr*
Cathy Comer, *Director*
EMP: 200
SALES (est): 3MM　Privately Held
WEB:
www.miraclehealthcarecolumbus.com
SIC: 8082 Home health care services

(G-8091)
MISPACE INC
5954 Rockland Ct　(43221)
PHONE..............................614 626-2602
Aleta Baird, *CEO*
EMP: 30　EST: 2009
SQ FT: 800
SALES (est): 556K　Privately Held
SIC: 7699 Cleaning services

(G-8092)
MJ BAUMANN CO INC
Also Called: M J Baumann
6400 Broughton Ave　(43213-1524)
PHONE..............................614 759-7100
Lawrence Irwin, *President*
Bob A Irwin, *Executive*
EMP: 67
SQ FT: 7,200
SALES (est): 8.7MM　Privately Held
SIC: 1711 Plumbing contractors

(G-8093)
MKSK INC
462 S Ludlow St　(43215-5647)
PHONE..............................614 621-2796
Brian Kinzelman, *CEO*
Timothy Schmalenberger, *President*
Mark Kline, *Vice Pres*
Christopher Hostettler, *CFO*
Thomas Porto, *Administration*
EMP: 81
SALES (est): 717.3K　Privately Held
SIC: 0781 Landscape architects

(G-8094)
MODLICH STONEWORKS INC
Also Called: Modlich Stone Works
2255 Harper Rd　(43204-3411)
PHONE..............................614 276-2848
Linus Modlich, *President*
Mark Modlich, *Corp Secy*
Chris Modlich, *Vice Pres*
Chris Di Rienzo, *Project Mgr*
Rob Estep, *Opers Mgr*
▲ EMP: 25
SQ FT: 15,000
SALES (est): 4.6MM　Privately Held
SIC: 5211 1799 Counter tops; counter top installation

(G-8095)
MOHUN HEALTH CARE CENTER
Also Called: MOHUN HEALTH CARE CENTER GIFT
2320 Airport Dr　(43219-2059)
PHONE..............................614 416-6132
Katherine Baker, *Director*
Angie Schwart, *Director*
Sister Jacqueline Baum, *Administration*
EMP: 35
SALES (est): 6.4MM　Privately Held
SIC: 8059 5947 Nursing home, except skilled & intermediate care facility; greeting cards; novelties

(G-8096)
MOLINA HEALTHCARE INC
Also Called: Molina Healthcare of Ohio
3000 Corp Exchange Dr # 100　(43231-7689)
PHONE..............................800 642-4168
Kathy Mancini, *Branch Mgr*
Mark Downs, *Manager*
Takeysha Cheney, *Director*
Virginia P Fuentes, *Director*
EMP: 651
SALES (corp-wide): 18.8B　Publicly Held
SIC: 6324 Hospital & medical service plans
PA: Molina Healthcare, Inc.
　200 Oceangate Ste 100
　Long Beach CA 90802
　562 435-3666

(G-8097)
MONESI TRUCKING & EQP REPR INC
1715 Atlas St　(43228-9648)
PHONE..............................614 921-9183
Donald Monesi, *President*
Marlene Monesi, *Vice Pres*
EMP: 40
SQ FT: 5,000
SALES (est): 5.2MM　Privately Held
SIC: 4212 Dump truck haulage

(G-8098)
MONRO INC
2869 E Main St　(43209-3715)
PHONE..............................614 235-3684
EMP: 30
SALES (corp-wide): 1.1B　Publicly Held
SIC: 7539 Brake repair, automotive
PA: Monro, Inc.
　200 Holleder Pkwy
　Rochester NY 14615
　585 647-6400

(G-8099)
MONRO INC
Also Called: Monro Muffler Brake
4570 W Broad St　(43228-1644)
PHONE..............................614 360-3883
EMP: 61
SALES (corp-wide): 1.1B　Publicly Held
SIC: 7533 Muffler shop, sale or repair & installation
PA: Monro, Inc.
　200 Holleder Pkwy
　Rochester NY 14615
　585 647-6400

(G-8100)
MOODY NAT CY DT CLUMBUS MT LLC
Also Called: Courtyard By Mrt Clmbs Dwntwn
35 W Spring St　(43215-2215)
PHONE..............................614 228-3200
Ann Turpin, *General Mgr*
EMP: 65
SALES (est): 2.1MM　Privately Held
SIC: 7011 Hotels

(G-8101)
MOODY-NOLAN INC (PA)
300 Spruce St Ste 300 # 300　(43215-1175)
PHONE..............................614 461-4664
Curtis J Moody, *CEO*
John William Miller, *Principal*
Paul F Pryor, *Principal*
Larry Pointer, *Business Mgr*
Yanitza Brongers-Marrer, *Vice Pres*
EMP: 115
SQ FT: 77,000

SALES (est): 33.3MM　Privately Held
WEB: www.moodynolan.com
SIC: 8712 8711 Architectural engineering; engineering services

(G-8102)
MORGAN STANLEY
4449 Easton Way Ste 300　(43219-7001)
PHONE..............................614 473-2086
Beth Caravati, *Office Mgr*
EMP: 72
SALES (est): 2.4MM　Privately Held
SIC: 6282 6211 Investment advice; stock brokers & dealers

(G-8103)
MORGAN STANLEY & CO LLC
41 S High St Ste 2700　(43215-6104)
PHONE..............................614 228-0600
Andy Crunpins, *Branch Mgr*
EMP: 50
SALES (corp-wide): 40.1B　Publicly Held
WEB: www.msvp.com
SIC: 6211 Investment firm, general brokerage
HQ: Morgan Stanley & Co. Llc
　1585 Broadway
　New York NY 10036
　212 761-4000

(G-8104)
MOTEL 6 OPERATING LP
7474 N High St　(43235-1446)
PHONE..............................614 431-2525
Jim Hanson, *Branch Mgr*
EMP: 50
SQ FT: 8,160
SALES (corp-wide): 608.6MM　Privately Held
WEB: www.motel6.com
SIC: 7011 Motels
HQ: Motel 6 Operating L.P.
　4001 Intl Pkwy Ste 500
　Carrollton TX 75007
　972 360-9000

(G-8105)
MOTORISTS COML MUTL INSUR CO (PA)
Also Called: MOTORISTS INSURANCE GROUP
471 E Broad St Bsmt　(43215-3852)
PHONE..............................614 225-8211
John J Bishop, *Ch of Bd*
David L Kaufman, *President*
Susan E Haack, *CFO*
EMP: 32
SQ FT: 300,000
SALES: 111.9MM　Privately Held
SIC: 6331 Fire, marine & casualty insurance: mutual

(G-8106)
MOTORISTS LIFE INSURANCE CO
Also Called: MOTORISTS INSURANCE GROUP
471 E Broad St Ste 200　(43215-3842)
PHONE..............................614 225-8211
David Kaufman, *CEO*
John Bishop, *Ch of Bd*
Michael Agan, *President*
Susan Haack, *CFO*
Anne King, *Admin Sec*
EMP: 48
SQ FT: 5,000
SALES: 180.6MM
SALES (corp-wide): 352.1MM　Privately Held
SIC: 6311 Life insurance
PA: Motorists Mutual Insurance Company
　471 E Broad St Ste 200
　Columbus OH 43215
　614 225-8211

(G-8107)
MOTORISTS MUTUAL INSURANCE CO (PA)
Also Called: MOTORISTS INSURANCE GROUP
471 E Broad St Ste 200　(43215-3805)
PHONE..............................614 225-8211
David Kaufman, *CEO*
Gregory Burton, *Ch of Bd*
Michael J Agan, *President*

Larry Conner, *President*
Thomas Obrokta Jr, *President*
EMP: 550
SQ FT: 300,000
SALES: 352.1MM　Privately Held
SIC: 6331 Fire, marine & casualty insurance: mutual; automobile insurance; property damage insurance; burglary & theft insurance

(G-8108)
MOTORISTS MUTUAL INSURANCE CO
Also Called: Motorists Life Ins Co
471 E Broad St Bsmt　(43215-3882)
P.O. Box 750306, Dayton　(45475-0306)
PHONE..............................937 435-5540
Brent Morrison, *Branch Mgr*
EMP: 30
SALES (corp-wide): 352.1MM　Privately Held
SIC: 6331 6411 Fire, marine & casualty insurance: mutual; insurance agents, brokers & service
PA: Motorists Mutual Insurance Company
　471 E Broad St Ste 200
　Columbus OH 43215
　614 225-8211

(G-8109)
MOUNT CARMEL E DIALYSIS CLNC
Also Called: Fersenius Medical Center
85 Mcnaughten Rd　(43213-2174)
PHONE..............................614 322-0433
Natasha Shaas, *Office Mgr*
Dottie Camiscione, *Director*
EMP: 30
SALES (est): 764.9K　Privately Held
SIC: 8092 Kidney dialysis centers

(G-8110)
MOUNT CARMEL EAST HOSPITAL
6001 E Broad St　(43213-1570)
PHONE..............................614 234-6000
Joseph Calvaruso, *CEO*
Denise Minor, *Opers Staff*
Laura Mangia, *Human Resources*
Jenni Wai, *Pharmacist*
Thomas Brady, *Med Doctor*
EMP: 1100
SALES (est): 144.8MM
SALES (corp-wide): 18.3B　Privately Held
WEB: www.mountcarmelhealth.com
SIC: 8062 General medical & surgical hospitals
HQ: Niagara Health Corporation
　6150 E Broad St
　Columbus OH 43213
　614 898-4000

(G-8111)
MOUNT CARMEL HEALTH (DH)
793 W State St　(43222-1551)
PHONE..............................614 234-5000
Marcia Ladue, *Principal*
Elezabeth M Young, *Obstetrician*
Dale St Arnold, *Director*
Kevin V Ware, *Psychiatry*
EMP: 1600　EST: 1886
SQ FT: 17,236
SALES (est): 304.1MM
SALES (corp-wide): 18.3B　Privately Held
SIC: 8062 Hospital, professional nursing school
HQ: Niagara Health Corporation
　6150 E Broad St
　Columbus OH 43213
　614 898-4000

(G-8112)
MOUNT CARMEL HEALTH
730 W Rich St　(43222-1620)
PHONE..............................614 234-8170
Lisa Wallschlaeger, *Project Mgr*
Dave Yoder, *Branch Mgr*
EMP: 110
SQ FT: 3,036
SALES (corp-wide): 18.3B　Privately Held
SIC: 8322 Senior citizens' center or association
HQ: Mount Carmel Health
　793 W State St
　Columbus OH 43222
　614 234-5000

(G-8113)
MOUNT CARMEL HEALTH SYSTEM (HQ)
6150 E Broad St (43213-1574)
PHONE..................614 234-6000
Claus Von Zychlin, CEO
Douglas H Stine, President
Christine Aucreman, Vice Pres
David Cozier, Vice Pres
Lyn Flanagan, Vice Pres
EMP: 800
SALES: 1.9B
SALES (corp-wide): 18.3B Privately Held
SIC: 8062 General medical & surgical hospitals
PA: Trinity Health Corporation
20555 Victor Pkwy
Livonia MI 48152
734 343-1000

(G-8114)
MOUNT CARMEL IMAGING & THERAPY
Also Called: Horizons Imaging & Therapy Ctr
5969 E Broad St Ste 100 (43213-1546)
PHONE..................614 234-8080
Roger Stile, Exec Dir
EMP: 35
SQ FT: 15,000
SALES (est): 2.6MM Privately Held
SIC: 8071 X-ray laboratory, including dental

(G-8115)
MOUNT CRMEL HOSPICE EVRGRN CTR
1144 Dublin Rd (43215-1039)
PHONE..................614 234-0200
Lorie Yosick, Director
EMP: 67
SALES: 6MM Privately Held
SIC: 8099 8082 Medical services organization; home health care services

(G-8116)
MOWERYS COLLISION INC
155 Phillipi Rd (43228-1383)
PHONE..................614 274-6072
Richard Mowery, President
Jerome Mitchell, Vice Pres
Paula Mowery, Admin Sec
EMP: 27
SQ FT: 20,000
SALES: 2MM Privately Held
SIC: 7532 Body shop, automotive

(G-8117)
MRAP LLC
Also Called: Market Ready Services
1721 Westbelt Dr (43228-3811)
PHONE..................614 545-3190
Jeffrey Wilkins, CEO
Jason Bowling, Division Mgr
EMP: 50
SALES (est): 4.9MM Privately Held
SIC: 1799 1721 7349 6531 Exterior cleaning, including sandblasting; exterior residential painting contractor; interior residential painting contractor; building maintenance services; building cleaning service; buying agent, real estate; real estate agent, residential; selling agent, real estate

(G-8118)
MS CONSULTANTS INC
2221 Schrock Rd (43229-1547)
PHONE..................614 898-7100
Thomas E Mozier, President
Donald Killmeyer, Transptn Dir
Tom Martin, Project Mgr
Scott Leiter, Technical Mgr
Justin Kerns, Engineer
EMP: 105
SALES (corp-wide): 43.8MM Privately Held
WEB: www.moshsolutions.com
SIC: 8711 Consulting engineer
PA: Ms Consultants, Inc
333 E Federal St
Youngstown OH 44503
330 744-5321

(G-8119)
MSA GROUP INC
Also Called: Crown Logistics
2839 Charter St (43228-4607)
P.O. Box 20405 (43220-0405)
PHONE..................614 334-0400
Jeff Hoover, CEO
James Carmody Jr, COO
EMP: 300
SQ FT: 40,000
SALES: 6MM Privately Held
SIC: 5087 5122 Beauty parlor equipment & supplies; drugs & drug proprietaries

(G-8120)
MUETZEL PLUMBING & HEATING CO
1661 Kenny Rd (43212-2264)
P.O. Box 12489 (43212-0489)
PHONE..................614 299-7700
John R Muetzel, President
Thomas C Muetzel, Vice Pres
Susie Lewis, Purch Agent
Robert Muetzel, Treasurer
Dan Muetzel, Manager
EMP: 52 EST: 1967
SQ FT: 16,000
SALES: 11.2MM Privately Held
WEB: www.muetzel.com
SIC: 1711 Plumbing contractors; hydronics heating contractor; warm air heating & air conditioning contractor; process piping contractor

(G-8121)
MULTICON BUILDERS INC (PA)
495 S High St Ste 150 (43215-5695)
PHONE..................614 241-2070
Charles P Driscoll, President
Peter H Edwards, Chairman
Douglas A Hill, CFO
Tom Markworth, Admin Sec
EMP: 30
SQ FT: 3,000
SALES (est): 3.1MM Privately Held
SIC: 6552 1542 Land subdividers & developers, commercial; commercial & office building contractors

(G-8122)
MULTICON BUILDERS INC
Also Called: Multicon Construction
503 S High St (43215-5660)
PHONE..................614 463-1142
Peter H Edward, Ch of Bd
EMP: 27
SALES (corp-wide): 3.1MM Privately Held
SIC: 6552 1542 Land subdividers & developers, commercial; commercial & office building contractors
PA: Multicon Builders Inc
495 S High St Ste 150
Columbus OH 43215
614 241-2070

(G-8123)
MULTICON CONSTRUCTION CO
Also Called: Eclipse Real Estate Group
1320 Mckinley Ave Ste C (43222-1155)
PHONE..................614 351-2683
Randy Bosscawen, President
EMP: 25
SALES (est): 3.6MM Privately Held
WEB: www.multiconconstruction.com
SIC: 1531 Operative builders

(G-8124)
MUNICH REINSURANCE AMERICA INC
471 E Broad St Fl 17 (43215-3842)
PHONE..................614 221-7123
Richard Schultz, Manager
EMP: 26
SALES (corp-wide): 15.6B Privately Held
SIC: 6331 Fire, marine & casualty insurance & carriers
HQ: Munich Reinsurance America, Inc.
555 College Rd E
Princeton NJ 08540
609 243-4200

(G-8125)
MYERS/SCHMALENBERGER INC (PA)
Also Called: M S I Design
462 S Ludlow St (43215-5647)
PHONE..................614 621-2796
Tim Schmalenberger, President
Keith Myers, Principal
Chris Hostettler, CFO
Tom Porto, Controller
EMP: 38
SALES (est): 3.2MM Privately Held
WEB: www.msidesign.com
SIC: 0781 Landscape counseling & planning

(G-8126)
N WASSERSTROM & SONS INC (HQ)
Also Called: Wasserstrom Marketing Division
2300 Lockbourne Rd (43207-6111)
PHONE..................614 228-5550
William Wasserstrom, President
John H Mc Cormick, Senior VP
Reid Wasserstrom, Admin Sec
◆ EMP: 250
SQ FT: 175,000
SALES (est): 119.1MM
SALES (corp-wide): 824.5MM Privately Held
SIC: 3556 5046 3444 Food products machinery; restaurant equipment & supplies; sheet metalwork
PA: The Wasserstrom Company
4500 E Broad St
Columbus OH 43213
614 228-6525

(G-8127)
NAS VENTURES
4477 E 5th Ave (43219-1817)
PHONE..................614 338-8501
James Head, Partner
Paul Ondera, Partner
EMP: 60
SALES (est): 1.5MM Privately Held
SIC: 1611 Airport runway construction

(G-8128)
NATIONAL AFFRDBL HSING TR INC (PA)
2245 N Bank Dr Ste 200 (43220-5422)
PHONE..................614 451-9929
James A Bowman, President
Jennifer Armstrong, Manager
EMP: 35
SQ FT: 800
SALES: 6.4MM Privately Held
SIC: 8399 Community development groups; fund raising organization, non-fee basis

(G-8129)
NATIONAL BOARD OF BOILER (PA)
1055 Crupper Ave (43229-1108)
PHONE..................614 888-8320
Michael A Mess, Principal
Judy Longhenry, Facilities Mgr
Tim Gardner, Manager
Robert McLaughlin, Senior Engr
Kimberly Edlund, Manager
EMP: 61
SQ FT: 5,000
SALES: 18.6MM Privately Held
SIC: 7389 Inspection & testing services

(G-8130)
NATIONAL CHURCH RESIDENCES (PA)
2335 N Bank Dr (43220-5423)
PHONE..................614 451-2151
Mark Ricketts, President
Tim Slemmer, President
Kellie Jones, General Mgr
Jerry B Kuyoth, COO
Teresa D Allton, Vice Pres
EMP: 193
SQ FT: 20,000
SALES: 38.2MM Privately Held
SIC: 6513 8051 8059 6531 Apartment building operators; apartment hotel operation; retirement hotel operation; skilled nursing care facilities; convalescent home with continuous nursing care; convalescent home; nursing home, except skilled & intermediate care facility; real estate agents & managers

(G-8131)
NATIONAL ELECTRIC COIL INC (PA)
Also Called: N E C Columbus
800 King Ave (43212-2644)
P.O. Box 370 (43216-0370)
PHONE..................614 488-1151
Robert Barton, CEO
Athena Amaxas, Principal
Danial Bucklew, Vice Pres
Stephen I Jeney, Vice Pres
Steve McMahon, Plant Mgr
◆ EMP: 300
SQ FT: 500,000
SALES (est): 77.4MM Privately Held
WEB: www.national-electric-coil.com
SIC: 7694 Electric motor repair

(G-8132)
NATIONAL GUARD OHIO
Also Called: Air National Guard Med Clinic
7370 Minuteman Way (43217-1161)
PHONE..................614 492-3166
Bob Schraft, Manager
EMP: 86 Privately Held
WEB: www.ohionationalguard.com
SIC: 9711 8011 National Guard; ; offices & clinics of medical doctors
HQ: Ohio National Guard
2825 W Dblin Granville Rd
Columbus OH 43235

(G-8133)
NATIONAL HIGHWAY EQUIPMENT CO
971 Old Henderson Rd (43220-3722)
P.O. Box 20262 (43220-0262)
PHONE..................614 459-4900
William S Dutcher, President
Greg Buckey, Vice Pres
EMP: 61
SALES (est): 9.9MM Privately Held
WEB: www.nationalhighwayexpress.com
SIC: 4212 4213 Local trucking, without storage; trucking, except local

(G-8134)
NATIONAL HOUSING CORPORATION (PA)
45 N 4th St Ste 200 (43215-3602)
PHONE..................614 481-8106
H Burkley Showe, President
Showe Builders, Principal
Betty Hays, Principal
Andrew Showe, Vice Pres
Hugh B Showe II, Vice Pres
EMP: 40 EST: 1963
SQ FT: 5,000
SALES (est): 96MM Privately Held
WEB: www.nationalhousingcorp.com
SIC: 1522 1542 1531 Apartment building construction; commercial & office building, new construction; apartment building operators

(G-8135)
NATIONAL HOUSING TR LTD PARTNR
Also Called: Nht
2335 N Bank Dr (43220-5423)
PHONE..................614 451-9929
James Bowman, President
Lori Little, Director
EMP: 45
SQ FT: 800
SALES: 6.1MM Privately Held
SIC: 6726 Management investment funds, closed-end

(G-8136)
NATIONAL REALTY SERVICES INC (HQ)
2261 Sandover Rd (43220-2919)
PHONE..................614 798-0971
Ronald E Scherer, Ch of Bd

Ronald A Huff, *President*
David B Thompson, *Treasurer*
EMP: 25
SQ FT: 8,000
SALES (est): 2MM
SALES (corp-wide): 4.3MM **Privately Held**
WEB: www.nationalrsi.com
SIC: 6531 Real estate brokers & agents; real estate managers; real estate leasing & rentals
PA: National/Rs Inc
        5131 Post Rd
        Dublin OH
        614 798-0971

(G-8137)
NATIONAL RENTAL (US) INC
Also Called: National Rent A Car
4600 International Gtwy (43219-1779)
PHONE...................................614 239-3270
Natilie Martin, *Manager*
EMP: 30
SALES (corp-wide): 4.9B **Privately Held**
WEB: www.specialtyrentals.com
SIC: 7514 Rent-a-car service
HQ: National Rental (Us) Llc
        14002 E 21st St Ste 1500
        Tulsa OK 74134

(G-8138)
NATIONAL RGSTRY EMRGNCY MDCL
Also Called: National Registry-Emergency
6610 Busch Blvd (43229-1740)
P.O. Box 29233 (43229-0233)
PHONE...................................614 888-4484
Mark Terry, *Treasurer*
Lindsey Durham, *Controller*
Sherry Mason, *Manager*
Doug Ehlert, *Software Dev*
Severo Rodriguez, *Exec Dir*
EMP: 35
SALES: 15.6MM **Privately Held**
SIC: 8732 8011 Market analysis, business & economic research; offices & clinics of medical doctors

(G-8139)
NATIONAL YOUTH ADVOCATE PROGRA (PA)
1801 Watermark Dr Ste 200 (43215-7088)
PHONE...................................614 487-8758
Marvena Twigg, *President*
Wellington Chimbwanda, *Exec VP*
Michelle Corry, *Vice Pres*
Dru Whitaker, *Officer*
EMP: 42
SALES: 53.3MM **Privately Held**
WEB: www.iyaf.org
SIC: 8322 8399 Individual & family services; adoption services; child related social services; family service agency; advocacy group

(G-8140)
NATIONAL YOUTH ADVOCATE PROGRA
Also Called: Nyap - Care Management
1303 E Main St (43205-2047)
PHONE...................................614 252-6927
Jen Tala, *Director*
EMP: 85
SALES (corp-wide): 53.3MM **Privately Held**
WEB: www.iyaf.org
SIC: 8322 Individual & family services; child related social services; adoption services; family service agency
PA: National Youth Advocate Program, Inc.
        1801 Watermark Dr Ste 200
        Columbus OH 43215
        614 487-8758

(G-8141)
NATIONS TITLE AGENCY OF OHIO (HQ)
3700 Corporate Dr Ste 200 (43231-4996)
PHONE...................................614 839-3848
Robert Berryman, *President*
EMP: 25
SALES (est): 2.5MM
SALES (corp-wide): 50MM **Privately Held**
SIC: 6411

PA: Nations Holding Company
        5370 W 95th St
        Prairie Village KS 66207
        913 383-8185

(G-8142)
NATIONSTAR MORTGAGE LLC
150 E Campus View Blvd (43235-4648)
PHONE...................................614 985-9500
EMP: 87 **Publicly Held**
SIC: 6162 6163 Mortgage bankers; loan brokers
HQ: Nationstar Mortgage Llc
        8950 Cypress Waters Blvd
        Coppell TX 75019
        469 549-2000

(G-8143)
NATIONWIDE CHILDRENS HOSPITAL
Also Called: Short and Sweet
700 Childrens Dr (43205-2639)
PHONE...................................614 722-2700
Roy Lucas, *Finance*
EMP: 200
SALES (corp-wide): 2.3B **Privately Held**
SIC: 8069 8731 8071 8399 Children's hospital; commercial physical research; medical laboratories; fund raising organization, non-fee basis
PA: Nationwide Children's Hospital
        700 Childrens Dr
        Columbus OH 43205
        614 722-2000

(G-8144)
NATIONWIDE CHILDRENS HOSPITAL
Also Called: Caniano Bsner Pdiatrics Clinic
555 S 18th St Ste 6g (43205-2654)
PHONE...................................614 722-5750
Thomas Hansen, *CEO*
Sarah Obrien, *Oncology*
EMP: 473
SALES (corp-wide): 2.3B **Privately Held**
SIC: 8062 General medical & surgical hospitals
PA: Nationwide Children's Hospital
        700 Childrens Dr
        Columbus OH 43205
        614 722-2000

(G-8145)
NATIONWIDE CHILDRENS HOSPITAL (PA)
700 Childrens Dr (43205-2639)
PHONE...................................614 722-2000
Steve Allen, *CEO*
Alpa Patel, *Managing Dir*
Michelle Miller, *Chief*
Rick Miller, *COO*
Karen Heiser, *Vice Pres*
◆ **EMP:** 12000
SQ FT: 1,324,000
SALES: 2.3B **Privately Held**
SIC: 8062 General medical & surgical hospitals

(G-8146)
NATIONWIDE CHILDRENS HOSPITAL
Also Called: Wexner Research Institute
700 Childrens Dr (43205-2639)
PHONE...................................614 722-2000
Kristin Roberts, *Research*
Andrew Shonk, *Research*
Laura Novotny, *Med Doctor*
Anthony Villella, *Med Doctor*
Brenda Van Dyke, *Technology*
EMP: 3000
SALES (corp-wide): 2.3B **Privately Held**
SIC: 8069 8733 Children's hospital; research institute
PA: Nationwide Children's Hospital
        700 Childrens Dr
        Columbus OH 43205
        614 722-2000

(G-8147)
NATIONWIDE CHILDRENS HOSPITAL
Also Called: Columbus Childrens Hospital
655 E Livingston Ave (43205-2618)
PHONE...................................614 722-8200
Kelly Kelleher, *Vice Pres*

Karen Days, *Branch Mgr*
Tracy Burris, *Manager*
Gina Howard, *Manager*
Pamella Pyles, *Supervisor*
EMP: 473
SALES (corp-wide): 2.3B **Privately Held**
SIC: 8069 8399 Children's hospital; advocacy group
PA: Nationwide Children's Hospital
        700 Childrens Dr
        Columbus OH 43205
        614 722-2000

(G-8148)
NATIONWIDE CHILDRENS HOSPITAL
3433 Agler Rd Ste 1400 (43219-3388)
PHONE...................................614 355-0802
Steve Allen, *Branch Mgr*
EMP: 830
SALES (corp-wide): 2.3B **Privately Held**
SIC: 8069 Children's hospital
PA: Nationwide Children's Hospital
        700 Childrens Dr
        Columbus OH 43205
        614 722-2000

(G-8149)
NATIONWIDE CHILDRENS HOSPITAL
Also Called: Close To Home Health Care Ctr
6435 E Broad St (43213-1507)
PHONE...................................614 355-8100
Steve Allen, *Branch Mgr*
Jodie Bookman, *Manager*
Michael Keeley, *Analyst*
EMP: 473
SALES (corp-wide): 2.3B **Privately Held**
SIC: 8062 General medical & surgical hospitals
PA: Nationwide Children's Hospital
        700 Childrens Dr
        Columbus OH 43205
        614 722-2000

(G-8150)
NATIONWIDE CHILDRENS HOSPITAL
1125 E Main St (43205-1931)
PHONE...................................614 355-9200
Steve Allen, *Branch Mgr*
EMP: 473
SALES (corp-wide): 2.3B **Privately Held**
SIC: 8069 Children's hospital
PA: Nationwide Children's Hospital
        700 Childrens Dr
        Columbus OH 43205
        614 722-2000

(G-8151)
NATIONWIDE CHILDRENS HOSPITAL
Also Called: Childrens Hosp Guidance Ctrs
495 E Main St (43215-5349)
PHONE...................................614 355-8000
Jennifer Reese, *Psychologist*
Elise Berlan, *Med Doctor*
Steve Gysan, *Database Admin*
Linda Wolf, *Director*
Regina Dewitt, *Admin Asst*
EMP: 473
SALES (corp-wide): 2.3B **Privately Held**
SIC: 8069 8093 Children's hospital; mental health clinic, outpatient
PA: Nationwide Children's Hospital
        700 Childrens Dr
        Columbus OH 43205
        614 722-2000

(G-8152)
NATIONWIDE CORPORATION (HQ)
1 Nationwide Plz (43215-2226)
PHONE...................................614 249-7111
Steve Rasmussen, *CEO*
Cathy Ellwood, *President*
Damon R McFerson, *President*
Brian O'Dell, *President*
John Trucco, *President*
◆ **EMP:** 27 **EST:** 1947
SQ FT: 9,500

SALES (est): 16.8B
SALES (corp-wide): 13.2B **Privately Held**
WEB: www.nationwide.com
SIC: 6411 6321 Insurance agents, brokers & service; accident insurance carriers; health insurance carriers
PA: Nationwide Mutual Insurance Company
        1 Nationwide Plz
        Columbus OH 43215
        614 249-7111

(G-8153)
NATIONWIDE ENERGY PARTNERS LLC
230 West St Ste 150 (43215-2785)
PHONE...................................614 918-2031
Dan Lhota, *President*
Robert Davis, *CFO*
Rick Eurich, *Controller*
Adam C Collins, *Accounts Mgr*
Nicholas Whitt, *Programmer Anys*
EMP: 36
SALES (est): 4.5MM **Privately Held**
WEB: www.nationwideenergypartners.com
SIC: 1731 8748 Electrical work; energy conservation consultant

(G-8154)
NATIONWIDE FIN INST DIS AGENCY
1 Nationwide Plz 2-0501 (43215-2226)
PHONE...................................614 249-6825
Mark R Thresher, *CEO*
David L Giertz, *President*
Richard Karas, *President*
EMP: 60
SQ FT: 10,000
SALES (est): 6.9MM
SALES (corp-wide): 13.2B **Privately Held**
SIC: 6211 Mutual funds, selling by independent salesperson
HQ: Nationwide Corporation
        1 Nationwide Plz
        Columbus OH 43215
        614 249-7111

(G-8155)
NATIONWIDE FINANCIAL SVCS INC (DH)
1 Nationwide Plz (43215-2226)
P.O. Box 182049 (43218-2049)
PHONE...................................614 249-7111
Mark R Thresher, *President*
Vince Antonucci, *President*
Keith D Bernard, *President*
Cortez Crosby, *President*
Patrick Gill, *President*
EMP: 105
SQ FT: 898,000
SALES (est): 15.9B
SALES (corp-wide): 13.2B **Privately Held**
WEB: www.nationwidefinancial.com
SIC: 6311 6411 8742 Life insurance; pension & retirement plan consultants; life insurance agents; advisory services, insurance; banking & finance consultant
HQ: Nationwide Corporation
        1 Nationwide Plz
        Columbus OH 43215
        614 249-7111

(G-8156)
NATIONWIDE GENERAL INSUR CO
1 W Nationwide Blvd # 100 (43215-2752)
P.O. Box 182171 (43218-2171)
PHONE...................................614 249-7111
Harold Weihl, *Ch of Bd*
Dimon Richard Mc Frson, *President*
Richard D Crabtree, *President*
Dimon Richard Mc Ferson, *President*
Brenda L Ross-Mathes, *President*
EMP: 75
SQ FT: 10,000
SALES (est): 9.4MM
SALES (corp-wide): 13.2B **Privately Held**
WEB: www.nirassn.com
SIC: 6311 6331 7389 8741 Life insurance; fire, marine & casualty insurance; financial services; administrative management
PA: Nationwide Mutual Insurance Company
        1 Nationwide Plz
        Columbus OH 43215
        614 249-7111

▲ = Import ▼=Export
◆ =Import/Export

(G-8157)
NATIONWIDE INV SVCS CORP
2 Nationwide Plz (43215-2534)
PHONE....................................614 249-7111
Duane Meek, *President*
EMP: 75
SALES (est): 12.2MM
SALES (corp-wide): 13.2B **Privately Held**
WEB: www.nationwideinsurance.com
SIC: 6211 Security brokers & dealers
HQ: Nationwide Life Insurance Company
1 Nationwide Plz
Columbus OH 43215
877 669-6877

(G-8158)
NATIONWIDE LIFE INSUR CO AMER
P.O. Box 182928 (43218-2928)
PHONE....................................800 688-5177
Gary D McMahan, *President*
James G Potter Jr, *Exec VP*
Joan Tucker, *Exec VP*
Sarah Coxe Lange, *Senior VP*
Jim Benson, *Vice Pres*
EMP: 1500 EST: 1865
SQ FT: 110,000
SALES (est): 211.1MM
SALES (corp-wide): 13.2B **Privately Held**
SIC: 6411 6211 6719 Insurance agents;
brokers, security; investment holding
companies, except banks
HQ: Nationwide Financial Services, Inc.
1 Nationwide Plz
Columbus OH 43215

(G-8159)
NATIONWIDE MUTL FIRE INSUR CO (HQ)
1 W Nationwide Blvd # 100 (43215-2752)
P.O. Box 182171 (43218-2171)
PHONE....................................614 249-7111
Dimon R Mc Ferson, *Ch of Bd*
Richard D Crabtree, *President*
Gordon E Mc Cutchan, *Exec VP*
Robert J Woodward Jr, *Exec VP*
Robert A Oakley, *CFO*
EMP: 30
SALES: 4.2B
SALES (corp-wide): 13.2B **Privately Held**
SIC: 6411 Insurance agents
PA: Nationwide Mutual Insurance Company
1 Nationwide Plz
Columbus OH 43215
614 249-7111

(G-8160)
NATIONWIDE MUTUAL INSURANCE CO (PA)
1 Nationwide Plz (43215-2226)
P.O. Box 182171 (43218-2171)
PHONE....................................614 249-7111
Steve Rasmussen, *CEO*
Anne Arvia, *President*
Erik Bennett, *President*
Larry Hilsheimer, *President*
Angie Klett, *President*
◆ EMP: 3695
SQ FT: 1,328,797
SALES: 13.2B **Privately Held**
WEB: www.nirassn.com
SIC: 6331 6311 6321 6531 Fire, marine
& casualty insurance: mutual; property
damage insurance; automobile insurance;
life insurance carriers; accident insurance
carriers; health insurance carriers; real
estate agents & managers

(G-8161)
NATIONWIDE RLTY INVESTORS LTD (HQ)
Also Called: N R I
375 N Front St Ste 200 (43215-2258)
PHONE....................................614 857-2330
Brian Ellis, *Managing Prtnr*
EMP: 32
SALES (est): 7.5MM
SALES (corp-wide): 13.2B **Privately Held**
SIC: 6552 Subdividers & developers
PA: Nationwide Mutual Insurance Company
1 Nationwide Plz
Columbus OH 43215
614 249-7111

(G-8162)
NATURAL RESOURCES OHIO DEPT
Also Called: Division of Engineering
2045 Morse Rd Bldg C (43229-6693)
PHONE....................................614 265-6948
Steve Manila, *Chief*
EMP: 40 **Privately Held**
WEB: www.ohiostateparks.com
SIC: 9512 9199 8711 Land, mineral &
wildlife conservation; ; ; civil engineering
HQ: Ohio Department Of Natural Re-
sources
2045 Morse Rd Bldg D-3
Columbus OH 43229

(G-8163)
NATURAL RESOURCES OHIO DEPT
Also Called: Odnr Computer Communication
1894 Fountain Square Ct (43224-1360)
PHONE....................................614 265-6852
Greg Mountz, *Manager*
EMP: 39 **Privately Held**
WEB: www.ohiostateparks.com
SIC: 7379 9512 8731 7373 Computer re-
lated consulting services; land, mineral &
wildlife conservation; ; commercial physi-
cal research; computer integrated sys-
tems design
HQ: Ohio Department Of Natural Re-
sources
2045 Morse Rd Bldg D-3
Columbus OH 43229

(G-8164)
NAVIGTOR MGT PRTNERS LTD LBLTY
1400 Goodale Blvd Ste 100 (43212-3777)
PHONE....................................614 796-0090
David K Schoettmer, *Senior Partner*
Kelly REO, *Vice Pres*
Richard Walega, *Vice Pres*
Casey Cramer, *Opers Staff*
Heather Bodak, *CFO*
EMP: 43
SQ FT: 3,500
SALES: 38.6MM **Privately Held**
WEB: www.navmp.com
SIC: 7379 8742 Computer related consult-
ing services; management consulting
services

(G-8165)
NBBJ LLC (PA)
Also Called: NBBJ Construction Services
250 S High St Ste 300 (43215-4629)
PHONE....................................206 223-5026
A J Montero,
Ryan Hullinger,
EMP: 700
SALES: 23.1MM **Privately Held**
WEB: www.nbbj.com
SIC: 8712 Architectural engineering

(G-8166)
NCR AT HOME HEALTH & WELLNESS
2335 N Bank Dr (43220-5423)
PHONE....................................614 451-2151
Teresa Allton, *President*
Mike Miller, *Accountant*
Noah Moore, *Exec Dir*
EMP: 75
SALES: 595.3K
SALES (corp-wide): 38.2MM **Privately Held**
SIC: 8082 Home health care services
PA: National Church Residences
2335 N Bank Dr
Columbus OH 43220
614 451-2151

(G-8167)
NCS HEALTHCARE OF OHIO LLC
Also Called: Omnicare of Central Ohio
2305 Westbrooke Dr Bldg C (43228-9644)
P.O. Box 520, Hilliard (43026-0520)
PHONE....................................614 534-0400
Stefan Stewart, *Branch Mgr*
EMP: 49
SALES (corp-wide): 194.5B **Publicly Held**
SIC: 5122 Pharmaceuticals

HQ: Ncs Healthcare Of Ohio, Llc
201 E 4th St Ste 900
Cincinnati OH 45202

(G-8168)
NEACE ASSOC INSUR AGCY OF OHIO
285 Cozzins St (43215-2334)
PHONE....................................614 224-0772
Jeff Kurz, *Manager*
EMP: 48
SALES (est): 2.6MM **Privately Held**
WEB: www.neacelukens.com
SIC: 6411 Insurance agents
PA: Neace & Associates Insurance Agency
Of Ohio, Inc
5905 E Galbraith Rd
Cincinnati OH 45236

(G-8169)
NEIGHBORHOOD HOUSE (PA)
1000 Atcheson St (43203-1353)
P.O. Box 555, Blacklick (43004-0555)
PHONE....................................614 252-4941
Fax: 614 252-7919
EMP: 51
SQ FT: 30,000
SALES: 1.8MM **Privately Held**
SIC: 8351 8093 8322 Child Day Care
Services Individual/Family Svcs Specialty
Outpatient Fac

(G-8170)
NEST TENDERS LIMITED
Also Called: Two Men & A Truck
5083 Westerville Rd (43231-4909)
PHONE....................................614 901-1570
Gail Kelley, *President*
John Kelley, *Vice Pres*
Stephanie Clarey, *Sales Staff*
Steve Barton, *Manager*
EMP: 100
SQ FT: 22,000
SALES (est): 10.1MM **Privately Held**
SIC: 4212 Moving services

(G-8171)
NETCARE CORPORATION (PA)
Also Called: NETCARE ACCESS
199 S Cent Ave (43223)
PHONE....................................614 274-9500
A King Stumpp, *President*
P G Baynes, *Principal*
J A Bonham, *Principal*
W Brannon, *Principal*
W Colwell, *Principal*
EMP: 100
SQ FT: 30,000
SALES: 16.1MM **Privately Held**
SIC: 8093 Mental health clinic, outpatient

(G-8172)
NETCARE CORPORATION
199 S Central Ave (43223-1301)
PHONE....................................614 274-9500
Diane Durkim, *Branch Mgr*
EMP: 40
SALES (corp-wide): 16.1MM **Privately Held**
SIC: 8049 Psychologist, psychotherapist &
hypnotist
PA: Netcare Corporation
199 S Cent Ave
Columbus OH 43223
614 274-9500

(G-8173)
NETJETS ASSN SHRED ARCFT PLOTS
Also Called: Njasap
2740 Airport Dr Ste 330 (43219-2286)
PHONE....................................614 532-0555
John Malmborg, *President*
EMP: 75
SALES (est): 5.1MM **Privately Held**
SIC: 7363 Pilot service, aviation

(G-8174)
NETJETS INC (HQ)
4111 Bridgeway Ave (43219-1882)
PHONE....................................614 239-5500
Adam Johnson, *CEO*
Bill Noe, *President*
Robert Molsbergen, *COO*
Colleen Nissl, *Senior VP*
Aaron Pinsker, *Senior VP*

EMP: 25
SALES: 3.8B
SALES (corp-wide): 225.3B **Publicly Held**
WEB: www.netjets.com
SIC: 4522 5088 7359 Flying charter serv-
ice; aircraft & parts; aircraft rental
PA: Berkshire Hathaway Inc.
3555 Farnam St Ste 1140
Omaha NE 68131
402 346-1400

(G-8175)
NETJETS INTERNATIONAL INC (DH)
4111 Bridgeway Ave (43219-1882)
PHONE....................................614 239-5500
Lesha Thorpe, *Treasurer*
EMP: 665 EST: 1995
SQ FT: 22,500
SALES (est): 36.1MM
SALES (corp-wide): 225.3B **Publicly Held**
SIC: 4522 Flying charter service
HQ: Netjets Inc.
4111 Bridgeway Ave
Columbus OH 43219
614 239-5500

(G-8176)
NETJETS LARGE AIRCRAFT INC
4111 Bridgeway Ave (43219-1882)
PHONE....................................614 239-4853
Michael Wargotz, *Principal*
EMP: 71
SALES (est): 5.2MM **Privately Held**
SIC: 4581 Aircraft maintenance & repair
services

(G-8177)
NETJETS SALES INC
4111 Bridgeway Ave (43219-1882)
P.O. Box 369099 (43236-9099)
PHONE....................................614 239-5500
Bill Noe, *President*
Jeff Hanna, *Vice Pres*
Chris White, *Vice Pres*
Lesha Thorpe, *Treasurer*
Greg Rapp, *Manager*
EMP: 200
SALES (est): 118.3MM
SALES (corp-wide): 225.3B **Publicly Held**
SIC: 5088 4522 Aircraft & parts; air trans-
portation, nonscheduled
HQ: Netjets Inc.
4111 Bridgeway Ave
Columbus OH 43219
614 239-5500

(G-8178)
NETWORK HOUSING 2005 INC
1680 Watermark Dr (43215-1034)
PHONE....................................614 487-6700
Susan E Weaver, *Exec Dir*
EMP: 99
SQ FT: 1,024
SALES: 129.4K **Privately Held**
SIC: 8361 Home for the mentally handi-
capped

(G-8179)
NETWORK RESTORATIONS II
Also Called: Nr2
129 E 7th Ave (43201-2589)
PHONE....................................614 253-0984
Michelle Hert, *Principal*
EMP: 55
SALES: 950K **Privately Held**
SIC: 6513 Apartment building operators

(G-8180)
NETWORK RESTORATIONS III LLC
Also Called: Nr3
910 E Broad St (43205-1150)
PHONE....................................614 253-0984
Michelle Hert,
EMP: 55
SALES: 950K **Privately Held**
SIC: 6513 Apartment building operators

(G-8181)
NEUROLOGICAL ASSOCIATES INC
931 Chatham Ln Ste 200 (43221-2486)
PHONE..................................614 544-4455
Jeff Ubank, *President*
J Alan Logeay, *COO*
Edward C Kosnik, *Treasurer*
Michele J Meagher, *Admin Sec*
J Allen Lougeay, *Administration*
EMP: 60
SALES (est): 5MM **Privately Held**
WEB: www.neuroassociates.com
SIC: 8011 Neurologist; surgeon

(G-8182)
NEUROSCIENCE CENTER INC
Also Called: Department of Neurology
1654 Upham Dr Fl 4 (43210-1250)
PHONE..................................614 293-8930
Jerry Mendell, *President*
EMP: 85
SALES (est): 2.5MM **Privately Held**
SIC: 8062 General medical & surgical hospitals

(G-8183)
NEW ALBANY CARE CENTER LLC
5691 Thompson Rd (43230-1345)
PHONE..................................614 855-8866
Melanie O'Neil, *Principal*
Mike Vanvoorhis, *Human Res Dir*
Daniel Clark, *Director*
Patrick Dineen, *Director*
Tosha McClendon, *Nursing Dir*
EMP: 125
SALES (est): 4.7MM **Privately Held**
SIC: 8051 Convalescent home with continuous nursing care

(G-8184)
NEW BGNNNGS ASSEMBLY OF GOD CH
492 Williams Rd (43207-5156)
PHONE..................................614 497-2658
Samuel J Kirk Jr, *President*
Margaret Kirk, *VP Mktg*
Charlotte Roff, *VP Mktg*
EMP: 25
SQ FT: 3,640
SALES: 180K **Privately Held**
SIC: 8661 8351 Assembly of God Church; child day care services

(G-8185)
NEW ENGLAND LIFE INSURANCE CO
Also Called: New England Securities
921 Chatham Ln Ste 300 (43221-2418)
PHONE..................................614 457-6233
Yolande Circosta, *Manager*
EMP: 50
SALES (corp-wide): 67.9B **Publicly Held**
WEB: www.thehoovercompanies.com
SIC: 6411 Insurance agents
HQ: The New England Life Insurance Company
501 Boylston St Ste 500
Boston MA 02116
617 578-2000

(G-8186)
NEW JERSEY AQUARIUM LLC
4016 Townsfair Way # 201 (43219-6083)
PHONE..................................614 414-7300
Yaromir Steiner, *Mng Member*
Sheri Kamer, *Manager*
EMP: 100
SALES (est): 2.2MM **Privately Held**
WEB: www.adventureaquarium.com
SIC: 7299 Banquet hall facilities

(G-8187)
NEWARK PARCEL SERVICE COMPANY
640 N Cassady Ave (43219-2721)
PHONE..................................614 253-3777
Patrick Sullivan, *President*
EMP: 33
SQ FT: 60,000

SALES (est): 7.3MM **Privately Held**
WEB: www.npsfrt.com
SIC: 4731 Freight transportation arrangement

(G-8188)
NEXSTAR BROADCASTING INC
Also Called: Wcmh
3165 Olentangy River Rd (43202-1518)
PHONE..................................614 263-4444
Jody Van Fossen, *Manager*
EMP: 151
SALES (corp-wide): 2.7B **Publicly Held**
WEB: www.media-general.com
SIC: 4833 Television broadcasting stations
HQ: Nexstar Broadcasting, Inc.
545 E John Carpenter Fwy # 700
Irving TX 75062
972 373-8800

(G-8189)
NIAGARA HEALTH CORPORATION (HQ)
6150 E Broad St (43213-1574)
PHONE..................................614 898-4000
Randall E Moore, *Principal*
Jessica Amendolare, *Marketing Mgr*
Brandi Pennington, *Marketing Mgr*
Jillian Buschman, *Manager*
Lora Miller, *Manager*
EMP: 200
SALES (est): 451MM
SALES (corp-wide): 18.3B **Privately Held**
WEB: www.mchs.com
SIC: 8741 8062 Hospital management; general medical & surgical hospitals
PA: Trinity Health Corporation
20555 Victor Pkwy
Livonia MI 48152
734 343-1000

(G-8190)
NISOURCE INC
290 W Nationwide Blvd (43215-2561)
PHONE..................................614 460-4878
Craig Homan, *Buyer*
Joseph M Siget Jr, *Auditing Mgr*
Stacye Nelson, *Branch Mgr*
Wanda Dixon, *Med Doctor*
Joe Ferry, *Manager*
EMP: 34
SALES (corp-wide): 5.1B **Publicly Held**
SIC: 4911 Electric services
PA: Nisource Inc.
801 E 86th Ave
Merrillville IN 46410
877 647-5990

(G-8191)
NJ EXECUTIVE SERVICES INC
4111 Bridgeway Ave (43219-1882)
PHONE..................................614 239-2996
Steve Ohl, *Administration*
EMP: 42
SALES (est): 4.6MM **Privately Held**
SIC: 5088 Aircraft equipment & supplies

(G-8192)
NL OF KY INC
Also Called: Neace Lukens
285 Cozzins St (43215-2334)
PHONE..................................614 224-0772
Jeff Kurz, *Manager*
EMP: 49 **Privately Held**
SIC: 6411 Insurance agents
HQ: Nl Of Ky, Inc.
2305 River Rd
Louisville KY 40206

(G-8193)
NORFOLK SOUTHERN CORPORATION
Also Called: Tarsec
3329 Thoroughbred Dr (43217-1200)
PHONE..................................614 251-2684
Steve Gray, *Principal*
EMP: 100
SALES (corp-wide): 11.4B **Publicly Held**
WEB: www.nscorp.com
SIC: 4011 Railroads, line-haul operating
PA: Norfolk Southern Corporation
3 Commercial Pl Ste 1a
Norfolk VA 23510
757 629-2680

(G-8194)
NORMAN JONES ENLOW & CO (PA)
226 N 5th St Ste 500 (43215-2784)
PHONE..................................614 228-4000
Fax: 614 228-4040
EMP: 40 **EST:** 1954
SALES (est): 6.8MM **Privately Held**
SIC: 8721 Accounting/Auditing/Bookkeeping

(G-8195)
NORSE DAIRY SYSTEMS INC
1700 E 17th Ave (43219-1005)
P.O. Box 1869 (43216-1869)
PHONE..................................614 294-4931
Ralph Denisco, *President*
Randy Harvey, *Vice Pres*
EMP: 201
SQ FT: 850
SALES (corp-wide): 37.8B **Privately Held**
SIC: 6719 3565 3556 2671 Investment holding companies, except banks; packaging machinery; food products machinery; ice cream manufacturing machinery; packaging paper & plastics film, coated & laminated; paperboard mills
PA: George Weston Limited
22 St Clair Ave E Suite 1901
Toronto ON M4T 2
416 922-2500

(G-8196)
NORTH AMERICAN BROADCASTING
Also Called: Wrkz
1458 Dublin Rd (43215-1010)
PHONE..................................614 481-7800
Matthew Minich, *President*
Bill Bowin, *Editor*
Nick Reed, *Treasurer*
Lori Whisman, *Accounts Exec*
Drew Schwartz, *Marketing Staff*
EMP: 60 **EST:** 1956
SQ FT: 11,000
SALES (est): 6.4MM **Privately Held**
WEB: www.nabco-inc.com
SIC: 4832 Radio broadcasting stations

(G-8197)
NORTH BROADWAY CHILDRENS CTR
48 E North Broadway St (43214-4112)
PHONE..................................614 262-6222
Rebecca McCoy, *Owner*
EMP: 40
SALES (est): 1.2MM **Privately Held**
SIC: 8351 Preschool center

(G-8198)
NORTH CNTL MNTAL HLTH SVCS INC (PA)
Also Called: NCC ASSOCIATES
1301 N High St (43201-2460)
PHONE..................................614 227-6865
Don Wood, *CEO*
John Hunter, *Vice Pres*
Joseph Niedzwidski, *CFO*
Sophy Kutemperor, *Case Mgr*
Diane Ruck, *MIS Dir*
EMP: 80
SQ FT: 21,500
SALES: 16.7MM **Privately Held**
SIC: 8093 8361 Mental health clinic, outpatient; alcohol clinic, outpatient; drug clinic, outpatient; rehabilitation center, outpatient treatment; residential care

(G-8199)
NORTH COMMUNITY COUNSELING CTR (PA)
4897 Karl Rd (43229-5147)
PHONE..................................614 846-2588
David Kittridge, *President*
Davis Kittridge, *President*
Courtney Cornell, *Pub Rel Mgr*
Michelle Meffley, *Director*
Sandy Wood, *Admin Asst*
EMP: 55
SQ FT: 3,500
SALES (est): 2.5MM **Privately Held**
SIC: 8093 Mental health clinic, outpatient

(G-8200)
NORTHERN AUTOMOTIVE INC (PA)
Also Called: Satum-West
8600 N High St (43235-1004)
PHONE..................................614 436-2001
Thomas Carpenter, *President*
William L Denney, *Exec VP*
Robert Vance, *Exec VP*
Robert Stoll, *Controller*
EMP: 50
SQ FT: 29,000
SALES (est): 32.5MM **Privately Held**
SIC: 5511 7538 5521 Automobiles, new & used; general automotive repair shops; used car dealers

(G-8201)
NORTHLAND BRDG FRANKLIN CNTY
Also Called: Bridge Counseling Center
4897 Karl Rd (43229-5147)
PHONE..................................614 846-2588
David Kittredge, *President*
EMP: 30
SQ FT: 4,158
SALES (est): 421.5K **Privately Held**
WEB: www.bridgecounselingcenter.com
SIC: 8322 General counseling services

(G-8202)
NORTHLAND HOTEL INC
Also Called: Super 8 Motel Columbus North
1078 E Dblin Granville Rd (43229-2503)
PHONE..................................614 885-1601
Ray Lin, *President*
EMP: 30
SALES (est): 1.6MM **Privately Held**
SIC: 7011 Hotels & motels

(G-8203)
NORTHPOINTE PLAZA
Also Called: Departmental Store
191 W Nationwide Blvd # 200 (43215-2568)
PHONE..................................614 744-2229
Nancy Novatney, *Manager*
EMP: 70
SALES (est): 2.1MM **Privately Held**
WEB: www.departmentalstore.com
SIC: 6531 Real estate agent, commercial

(G-8204)
NORTHPOINTE PROPERTY MGT LLC
3250 Henderson Rd Ste 103 (43220-2398)
PHONE..................................614 579-9712
Aniko Marcy, *Principal*
EMP: 197
SALES (est): 113.1K **Privately Held**
SIC: 7349 1799 Building maintenance services; exterior cleaning, including sandblasting; cleaning new buildings after construction; construction site cleanup

(G-8205)
NORTHWEST EYE SURGEONS INC (PA)
2250 N Bank Dr (43220-5420)
PHONE..................................614 451-7550
Robert Lembach, *President*
Todd Whitaker, *Med Doctor*
Michael Kayser,
EMP: 32
SALES (est): 6.6MM **Privately Held**
WEB: www.northwesteyesurgeons.com
SIC: 8011 Ophthalmologist

(G-8206)
NORTHWEST HTS TITLE AGCY LLC
4200 Regent St Ste 210 (43219-6229)
PHONE..................................614 451-6313
Beverly Harris, *Principal*
Elizabeth Davis, *Principal*
EMP: 25
SALES (est): 3.3MM **Privately Held**
SIC: 6361 Title insurance

(G-8207)
NORTHWEST MENTAL HEALTH SVCS
Also Called: Northwest Counseling Services
1560 Fishinger Rd Ste 100 (43221-2108)
PHONE..................................614 457-7876
Susan Hunt, *Human Res Dir*
Kay Sims, *MIS Dir*
A King Stumpp, *Exec Dir*
Mary Brett, *Exec Dir*
Hollie Goldberg, *Exec Dir*
EMP: 50
SALES: 772.5K **Privately Held**
WEB:
www.northwestcounselingservices.org
SIC: 8093 8322 Mental health clinic, out-
patient; individual & family services

(G-8208)
NORTHWEST SWIM CLUB INC
1064 Bethel Rd (43220-2610)
P.O. Box 20015 (43220-0015)
PHONE..................................614 442-8716
Dick Rabolb, *Director*
EMP: 40
SALES: 451.9K **Privately Held**
WEB: www.northwestswimclub.com
SIC: 7997 Swimming club, membership

(G-8209)
NORTHWESTERN MUTL LF INSUR CO
Also Called: Central Ohio Financial Group
800 Yard St Ste 300 (43212-3882)
PHONE..................................614 221-5287
Steve Shoulders, *Manager*
James Hayden, *Manager*
Bethany Thompson, *Tech/Comp Coord*
Brandon McIntyre, *Representative*
EMP: 48
SALES (corp-wide): 28.1B **Privately Held**
WEB: www.nmfn.com
SIC: 6311 Life insurance
PA: The Northwestern Mutual Life Insur-
ance Company
720 E Wisconsin Ave
Milwaukee WI 53202
414 271-1444

(G-8210)
NOVOTEC RECYCLING LLC (PA)
3960 Groves Rd (43232-4137)
PHONE..................................614 231-8326
Tom Bolon, *CEO*
David Robbins, *Controller*
Charlene White, *Human Res Mgr*
Mayling Inthisarn, *Admin Dir*
EMP: 30
SALES (est): 54.2MM **Privately Held**
SIC: 4953 8741 Recycling, waste materi-
als; management services

(G-8211)
NRT COMMERCIAL UTAH LLC
Also Called: Bexley
2288 E Main St (43209-2335)
PHONE..................................614 239-0808
Mark Kraus, *Manager*
EMP: 55 **Publicly Held**
WEB: www.nrtinc.com
SIC: 6531 Real estate agent, residential
HQ: Nrt Commercial Utah Llc
175 Park Ave
Madison NJ 07940

(G-8212)
NTK HOTEL GROUP II LLC
Also Called: Hampton Inn
501 N High St (43215-2008)
PHONE..................................614 559-2000
Maria Schroeder, *Manager*
David Patel,
EMP: 60
SALES (est): 4.1MM **Privately Held**
SIC: 7011 Hotels

(G-8213)
NUCON INTERNATIONAL INC
6800 Huntley Rd (43229)
PHONE..................................614 846-5710
Louis Kovach, *Branch Mgr*
EMP: 26

EMP: 50
SALES (est): 1.5MM
SALES (corp-wide): 9.1MM **Privately Held**
WEB: www.nucon-int.com
SIC: 8734 Testing laboratories
PA: Nucon International, Inc.
7000 Huntley Rd
Columbus OH 43229
614 846-5710

(G-8214)
NUETERRA HOLDINGS LLC
Also Called: Ohio Surgery Center
930 Bethel Rd (43214-1906)
PHONE..................................614 451-0500
Kim Esteph, *Manager*
EMP: 40
SALES (corp-wide): 46.4MM **Privately Held**
WEB: www.findlaysurgerycenter.com
SIC: 8011 Surgeon
PA: Nueterra Dc Holdings, Llc
11221 Roe Ave Ste 1a
Leawood KS 66211
913 387-0689

(G-8215)
NUGROWTH SOLUTIONS LLC (PA)
Also Called: Strategic Insurance Software
4181 Arlingate Plz (43228-4115)
PHONE..................................800 747-9273
Mandi Mellott, *Creative Dir*
Greg Tillar,
Alex Deak,
EMP: 31
SALES (est): 5.8MM **Privately Held**
SIC: 8743 8748 Sales promotion; busi-
ness consulting

(G-8216)
NUNN PRODUCTIONS LLC
341 S 3rd St 100-291 (43215-5463)
PHONE..................................614 695-5350
Bobby Nunn Jr,
EMP: 27
SALES: 950K **Privately Held**
SIC: 7822 Motion picture & tape distribu-
tion

(G-8217)
NURSES HEART MED STAFFING LLC
1100 Morse Rd Ste 104 (43229-1170)
PHONE..................................614 648-5111
James Teague, *Mng Member*
Rosaland Berenguer,
Vanessa Garnes,
EMP: 40 **EST:** 2013
SALES (est): 1.2MM **Privately Held**
SIC: 7361 Employment agencies

(G-8218)
NUTIS PRESS INC (PA)
Also Called: Printed Resources
3540 E Fulton St (43227-1100)
P.O. Box 27248 (43227-0248)
PHONE..................................614 237-8626
Ira Nutis, *President*
Gary Abrams, *President*
Joey Nutis, *Vice Pres*
Sam Nutis, *Vice Pres*
Todd Delman, *Design Engr*
▼ EMP: 193 **EST:** 1961
SQ FT: 95,000
SALES (est): 86.5MM **Privately Held**
WEB: www.nutispress.com
SIC: 5199 Advertising specialties

(G-8219)
NWD ARENA DISTRICT II LLC
375 N Front St Ste 200 (43215-2258)
PHONE..................................614 857-2330
Brian Ellis,
EMP: 50
SQ FT: 7,250
SALES: 1,000K **Privately Held**
SIC: 6531 Real estate leasing & rentals

(G-8220)
O S U FACULTY CLUB
Also Called: OHIO STATE UNIVERSITY FAC-
ULTY
181 S Oval Mall (43210-1325)
PHONE..................................614 292-2262
Goeffrey White, *General Mgr*

EMP: 50
SQ FT: 7,500
SALES: 2.3MM **Privately Held**
WEB: www.ohio-statefacultyclub.com
SIC: 8641 Community membership club;
social club, membership

(G-8221)
OAKLAND NURSERY INC (PA)
1156 Oakland Park Ave (43224-3317)
PHONE..................................614 268-3834
Paul S Reiner, *President*
John G Reiner, *Co-President*
Lisa Maxwell, *Controller*
Kathy Friedberg, *Marketing Staff*
Marge Bland, *Manager*
▲ EMP: 50
SQ FT: 5,000
SALES (est): 12.2MM **Privately Held**
WEB: www.oaklandnursery.com
SIC: 5261 0781 Nursery stock, seeds &
bulbs; lawnmowers & tractors; garden
supplies & tools; landscape services

(G-8222)
OAKLEAF VILLAGE LTD
5500 Karl Rd Apt 113 (43229-3664)
PHONE..................................614 431-1739
Michelle Spiert, *Office Mgr*
Don Courtright, *Manager*
Dawn Nero, *Manager*
EMP: 60
SQ FT: 110,000
SALES (est): 5.1MM **Privately Held**
WEB: www.oakleafvillage.com
SIC: 8361 Geriatric residential care

(G-8223)
OBETZ ANIMAL HOSPITAL
3999 Alum Creek Dr (43207-5136)
PHONE..................................614 491-5676
Alec Land, *President*
Rona Shapiro Dvm, *Partner*
EMP: 50
SQ FT: 5,000
SALES (est): 1.8MM **Privately Held**
WEB: www.obetzah.com
SIC: 0742 Veterinarian, animal specialties;
animal hospital services, pets & other ani-
mal specialties

(G-8224)
OCCUPATIONAL HEALTH LINK (PA)
445 Hutchinson Ave # 205 (43235-5677)
PHONE..................................614 885-0039
Karen Conger, *Partner*
Sandy Devery, *CFO*
Occupational Health Research I,
William L Newkirk,
EMP: 28
SQ FT: 8,500
SALES (est): 11.9MM **Privately Held**
WEB: www.oehpmco.com
SIC: 6331 8399 Workers' compensation
insurance; health systems agency

(G-8225)
ODW LOGISTICS INC (PA)
Also Called: O D W
400 W Nationwide Blvd # 200
(43215-2394)
PHONE..................................614 549-5000
Jason Poot, *President*
Eric Isakson, *General Mgr*
Scott Leonard, *General Mgr*
Robert E Ness, *Chairman*
Doug Might, *Business Mgr*
EMP: 300
SQ FT: 1,000,000
SALES (est): 166.7MM **Privately Held**
SIC: 4225 General warehousing & storage

(G-8226)
ODYSSEY CONSULTING SERVICES
2531 Oakstone Dr (43231-7612)
PHONE..................................614 523-4248
Mike McGovern, *President*
Kevin Martinez, *Assistant VP*
Diana McGovern, *Vice Pres*
Bonnie Harmor, *Director*
EMP: 110
SQ FT: 4,000

SALES (est): 5.5MM **Privately Held**
SIC: 7371 Computer software systems
analysis & design, custom

(G-8227)
OHIC INSURANCE COMPANY (HQ)
300 E Broad St Ste 450 (43215-3614)
PHONE..................................614 221-7777
Jerry Cassidy, *Ch of Bd*
Jim Daldyga, *Vice Pres*
Nancy Libke, *Vice Pres*
Darrell Rainum, *Vice Pres*
Steve Turover, *VP Finance*
EMP: 80
SALES: 8.9MM
SALES (corp-wide): 393.7MM **Privately Held**
WEB: www.ohic.com
SIC: 6331 6411 8742 Fire, marine & ca-
sualty insurance & carriers; insurance
claim adjusters, not employed by insur-
ance company; hospital & health services
consultant
PA: The Doctors' Company An Interinsur-
ance Exchange
185 Greenwood Rd
Napa CA 94558
707 226-0100

(G-8228)
OHIO ASSN PUB SCHL EMPLOYEES (PA)
Also Called: Oapse-Local 4
6805 Oak Creek Dr Ste 1 (43229-1501)
PHONE..................................614 890-4770
Robert Fantauzzo, *Consultant*
Joe Rugola, *Exec Dir*
Lloyd Rains, *Director*
Courtney Belcher, *Legal Staff*
Larry Malone, *Advisor*
EMP: 32
SQ FT: 18,000
SALES (est): 9.9MM **Privately Held**
SIC: 8631 Labor union

(G-8229)
OHIO ASSOCIATION OF FOODBANKS
101 E Town St Ste 540 (43215-5119)
PHONE..................................614 221-4336
Joree Jacobs, *Comms Dir*
Lisa Hamler Fugitt, *Exec Dir*
Lisa Hamler-Fuggit, *Exec Dir*
EMP: 32
SQ FT: 8,700
SALES: 28.5MM **Privately Held**
SIC: 8322 Social service center

(G-8230)
OHIO ASSOCIATION REALTORS INC
200 E Town St (43215-4608)
PHONE..................................614 228-6675
Robert E Fletcher, *CEO*
Robin Jennings, *VP Opers*
Denis Nowacki, *Treasurer*
Cherie Murray, *CTO*
Sample Sharon, *Director*
EMP: 25 **EST:** 1911
SQ FT: 15,168
SALES: 5.3MM **Privately Held**
WEB: www.ohiorealtor.com
SIC: 8611 2721 Trade associations; trade
journals; publishing & printing

(G-8231)
OHIO AUTOMOBILE CLUB
Also Called: AAA Car Care Plus
2400 Sobeck Rd (43232-3801)
PHONE..................................614 559-0000
Mark Boyer, *Manager*
EMP: 30
SQ FT: 18,200
SALES (corp-wide): 59.9MM **Privately Held**
SIC: 7538 General automotive repair
shops
PA: The Ohio Automobile Club
90 E Wilson Bridge Rd # 1
Worthington OH 43085
614 431-7901

G
E
O
G
R
A
P
H
I
C

(G-8232)
OHIO CHAMBER OF COMMERCE
34 S 3rd St Ste 100 (43215-4201)
P.O. Box 15159 (43215-0159)
PHONE..............................614 228-4201
Andrew E Doehrel, *President*
John E Schuster, *Vice Pres*
Linda Woggon, *Vice Pres*
EMP: 25
SALES: 4MM **Privately Held**
WEB: www.ohiochamber.com
SIC: 8611 Chamber of Commerce

(G-8233)
OHIO CON SAWING & DRLG INC
2935 E 14th Ave Ste 200 (43219-2364)
PHONE..............................614 252-1122
Tom Lenix, *Manager*
EMP: 25
SALES (corp-wide): 14.7MM **Privately
Held**
WEB: www.gp-radar.com
SIC: 1771 Concrete repair
PA: Ohio Concrete Sawing And Drilling, Inc.
　8534 Central Ave
　Sylvania OH 43560
　419 841-1330

(G-8234)
OHIO CONSUMERS COUNSEL
65 E State St Ste 700 (43215-3485)
PHONE..............................614 466-8574
Bruce Western, *Principal*
Dennis Stapleton, *Director*
Dorothy Leslie, *Bd of Directors*
EMP: 36 **EST:** 1976
SALES (est): 2.1MM **Privately Held**
SIC: 8999 9121 Information bureau; leg-
islative assembly

(G-8235)
**OHIO CUSTODIAL
MAINTENANCE**
Also Called: Ohio Custodial Management
1291 S High St (43206-3472)
PHONE..............................614 443-1232
John Tucker, *CEO*
Scott Tucker, *President*
Bill Weaver, *Project Mgr*
EMP: 120
SQ FT: 7,000
SALES (est): 2.6MM
SALES (corp-wide): 9.5MM **Privately
Held**
WEB: www.ohiocustodial.com
SIC: 7349 8742 Janitorial service, contract
basis; management consulting services
PA: Ohio Support Services Corp.
　1291 S High St
　Columbus OH 43206
　614 443-0291

(G-8236)
OHIO DEPARTMENT OF AGING
246 N High St Fl 1 (43215-3363)
PHONE..............................614 466-5500
Cathy McNamara, *Accounting Mgr*
Barbara Riley, *Director*
EMP: 100
SQ FT: 35,000
SALES (est): 4.9MM **Privately Held**
SIC: 8361 9441 Home for the aged; old
soldiers' home; administration of social &
manpower programs;
HQ: Executive Office State Of Ohio
　30 E Broad St
　Columbus OH 43215

(G-8237)
**OHIO DEPARTMENT OF
COMMERCE**
Division of Securities
77 S High St Fl 22 (43215-6108)
PHONE..............................614 644-7381
Joe Bishop, *Commissioner*
EMP: 39 **Privately Held**
SIC: 6211 9311 Security brokers & deal-
ers;
HQ: Department Of Commerce Ohio
　6606 Tussing Rd
　Reynoldsburg OH 43068

(G-8238)
**OHIO DEPARTMENT OF
COMMERCE**
Division Fincl Institutions
77 S High St Fl 21 (43215-6108)
PHONE..............................614 728-8400
Charles Dolezal, *Superintendent*
EMP: 115 **Privately Held**
SIC: 8611 9611 Business associations;
HQ: Department Of Commerce Ohio
　6606 Tussing Rd
　Reynoldsburg OH 43068

(G-8239)
OHIO DEPARTMENT OF HEALTH
Also Called: Wic
3850 Sullivant Ave # 102 (43228-4327)
PHONE..............................614 645-3621
EMP: 269 **Privately Held**
SIC: 8322 Individual & family services
HQ: Department Of Health Ohio
　246 N High St
　Columbus OH 43215

(G-8240)
OHIO DEPARTMENT OF HEALTH
Also Called: Bureau Information & Support
246 N High St (43215-2406)
P.O. Box 118 (43216-0118)
PHONE..............................614 466-1521
Nick Baird, *Director*
EMP: 200 **Privately Held**
WEB: www.jchealth.com
SIC: 8621 9431 Health association; ad-
ministration of public health programs;
HQ: Department Of Health Ohio
　246 N High St
　Columbus OH 43215

(G-8241)
OHIO DEPARTMENT OF HEALTH
Also Called: Rehabilitation Services
400 E Campus View Blvd (43235-4685)
PHONE..............................614 438-1255
John Connelly, *Director*
EMP: 800 **Privately Held**
WEB: www.jchealth.com
SIC: 8322 9431 Rehabilitation services;
administration of public health programs;
HQ: Department Of Health Ohio
　246 N High St
　Columbus OH 43215

(G-8242)
**OHIO DEPARTMENT
TRANSPORTATION**
Also Called: Material Management
1600 W Broad St (43223-1202)
PHONE..............................614 275-1324
James Beasley, *Director*
EMP: 65 **Privately Held**
SIC: 8734 9621 Automobile proving &
testing ground;
HQ: Ohio Department Of Transportation
　1980 W Broad St
　Columbus OH 43223

(G-8243)
**OHIO DEPARTMENT VETERANS
SVCS**
77 S High St Fl 7 (43215-6108)
PHONE..............................614 644-0898
Michael Liptay, *Controller*
Thomas Moe, *Director*
EMP: 800
SALES: 199.2K **Privately Held**
WEB: www.governor.ohio.gov
SIC: 8051 Skilled nursing care facilities
HQ: Executive Office State Of Ohio
　30 E Broad St
　Columbus OH 43215

(G-8244)
**OHIO DEPARTMENT YOUTH
SERVICES**
Also Called: Freedom Center
51 N High St Fl 5 (43215-3008)
PHONE..............................740 881-3337
Joyce Bednerek, *Superintendent*
EMP: 30 **Privately Held**
SIC: 9431 8069 Public health agency ad-
ministration, government; ; substance
abuse hospitals

HQ: Department Of Youth Service, Ohio
　30 W Spring St Fl 5
　Columbus OH 43215

(G-8245)
**OHIO DEPT AMVET SVC
FOUNDATION (PA)**
1395 E Dublin Granville R (43229-3314)
PHONE..............................614 431-6990
Donald Limer, *President*
Jane Brown, *Admin Sec*
EMP: 75
SQ FT: 3,024
SALES (est): 1.3MM **Privately Held**
WEB: www.ohamvets.org
SIC: 8641 Veterans' organization

(G-8246)
**OHIO DEPT OF JOB & FMLY
SVCS**
Also Called: Bureau Labor Market Info
4300 Kimberly Pkwy N (43232-8296)
PHONE..............................614 752-9494
Keith Ewald, *Director*
EMP: 50 **Privately Held**
WEB: www.job.com
SIC: 8331 9441 Community service em-
ployment training program;
HQ: The Ohio Department Of Job And
　Family Services
　30 E Broad St Fl 32
　Columbus OH 43215

(G-8247)
**OHIO DEPT OF JOB & FMLY
SVCS**
Also Called: Office For Children Fmly Svcs
255 E Main St Fl 3 (43215-5222)
PHONE..............................614 466-1213
Rick Smith, *Manager*
EMP: 120 **Privately Held**
WEB: www.job.com
SIC: 8351 9441 8322 Child day care
services; administration of social & man-
power programs; ; individual & family
services
HQ: The Ohio Department Of Job And
　Family Services
　30 E Broad St Fl 32
　Columbus OH 43215

(G-8248)
**OHIO DEPT RHBILITATION
CORECTN**
Also Called: Parole & Community Services
770 W Broad St (43222-1419)
PHONE..............................614 274-9000
Jannet Morman, *Chief*
EMP: 300 **Privately Held**
SIC: 8322 9223 Parole office; correctional
institutions;
HQ: Ohio Department Of Rehabilitation And
　Correction
　770 W Broad St
　Columbus OH 43222

(G-8249)
**OHIO DISABILITY RIGHTS LAW
POL**
Also Called: DISABILLITY RIGHTS OHIO
200 Civic Center Dr (43215-7510)
PHONE..............................614 466-7264
Michael Kirkman, *Exec Dir*
EMP: 45 **EST:** 2012
SALES (est): 4.4MM **Privately Held**
SIC: 8111 Legal services

(G-8250)
OHIO EDUCATION ASSOCIATION
Also Called: E-Tech Ohio Commision
2470 North Star Rd (43221-3405)
PHONE..............................614 485-6000
Kate BR, *Manager*
EMP: 60
SALES (corp-wide): 58.5MM **Privately
Held**
SIC: 8631 Labor union
PA: Ohio Education Association Inc
　225 E Broad St Fl 2
　Columbus OH 43215
　614 228-4526

(G-8251)
**OHIO EDUCATION ASSOCIATION
(PA)**
225 E Broad St Fl 2 (43215-3709)
P.O. Box 2550 (43216-2550)
PHONE..............................614 228-4526
Patricia F Brooks, *President*
Jim Timlin, *Treasurer*
Larry Wicks, *Exec Dir*
Patricia Murdock, *Director*
Linda Fiely, *General Counsel*
EMP: 60
SQ FT: 5,734
SALES: 58.5MM **Privately Held**
SIC: 8631 Labor union

(G-8252)
OHIO EQUITIES LLC
6210 Busch Blvd (43229-1804)
PHONE..............................614 207-1805
EMP: 40
SALES (corp-wide): 14.6MM **Privately
Held**
SIC: 8742 Real estate consultant
PA: Ohio Equities, Llc
　605 S Front St Ste 200
　Columbus OH 43215
　614 224-2400

(G-8253)
OHIO EQUITIES LLC
Also Called: Nai Ohio Equities, Realtors
17 S High St Ste 799 (43215-3450)
PHONE..............................614 469-0058
Lynne Raduege, *Manager*
EMP: 66
SALES (corp-wide): 14.6MM **Privately
Held**
WEB: www.ohioequities.com
SIC: 6531 Real estate agent, commercial
PA: Ohio Equities, Llc
　605 S Front St Ste 200
　Columbus OH 43215
　614 224-2400

(G-8254)
OHIO EQUITY FUND INC
88 E Broad St Ste 1800 (43215-3526)
PHONE..............................614 469-1797
Hal Keller, *President*
EMP: 26
SALES (est): 2.1MM **Privately Held**
SIC: 6163 Loan brokers
PA: Ohio Capital Corporation For Housing
　88 E Broad St Ste 1800
　Columbus OH 43215
　614 224-8446

(G-8255)
OHIO EXPOSITION CENTER
717 E 17th Ave (43211-2494)
PHONE..............................614 644-4000
Virgil Strickler, *CEO*
Birgil Strickler, *General Mgr*
EMP: 75
SALES (est): 3.1MM **Privately Held**
SIC: 7999 Exposition operation

(G-8256)
OHIO EXTERMINATING CO INC
1347 N High St (43201-2497)
PHONE..............................614 294-6311
Thomas Christman, *President*
Brooke Christman, *Manager*
EMP: 30
SQ FT: 10,000
SALES (est): 2.1MM **Privately Held**
WEB: www.ohioexterminating.com
SIC: 7342 Termite control; pest control in
structures

(G-8257)
OHIO FAIR PLAN UNDWRT ASSN
2500 Corp Exchange Dr # 250
(43231-8616)
PHONE..............................614 839-6446
Norman E Beal, *Partner*
David Culler, *Partner*
David Engleson, *Partner*
Ellen Leslie, *Partner*
Ta Brininger, *Vice Pres*
EMP: 38 **EST:** 1968
SALES (est): 15.9MM **Privately Held**
WEB: www.ohiofairplan.com
SIC: 6331 Property damage insurance

(G-8258)
OHIO FARM BUR FEDERATION INC (PA)
Also Called: Our Ohio Communications
280 N High St Fl 6 (43215-2594)
P.O. Box 182383 (43218-2383)
PHONE.................................614 249-2400
Frank Burkett, *President*
Steve Hirsch, *President*
Lynn Snyder, *Editor*
Roger Baker, *Trustee*
Adam Sharp, *Exec VP*
EMP: 55
SQ FT: 12,700
SALES (est): 11.9MM **Privately Held**
WEB: www.ohioapples.com
SIC: 8611 Business associations

(G-8259)
OHIO GSTROENTEROLOGY GROUP INC
815 W Broad St Ste 220 (43222-1478)
PHONE.................................614 221-8355
Edward Brand, *Branch Mgr*
David Sabol, *Gastroenterlgy*
EMP: 28 **Privately Held**
SIC: 8011 Cardiologist & cardio-vascular specialist; gastronomist
PA: Ohio Gastroenterology Group, Inc.
3400 Olentangy River Rd
Columbus OH 43202

(G-8260)
OHIO GSTROENTEROLOGY GROUP INC
85 Mcnaughten Rd Ste 320 (43213-5111)
PHONE.................................614 754-5500
Edward Brand, *Principal*
Seth Hoffman, *Med Doctor*
Michael Taxier, *Med Doctor*
Victor Jochem, *Gastroenterlgy*
EMP: 33 **Privately Held**
SIC: 8011 Gastronomist
PA: Ohio Gastroenterology Group, Inc.
3400 Olentangy River Rd
Columbus OH 43202

(G-8261)
OHIO GSTROENTEROLOGY GROUP INC (PA)
3400 Olentangy River Rd (43202-1523)
PHONE.................................614 754-5500
Thomas Ransbottom, *President*
Frank J Chapman, *COO*
Megan Dana, *Opers Staff*
Heather Foisset, *Human Res Mgr*
May Meeks, *Office Mgr*
EMP: 69
SALES (est): 16.5MM **Privately Held**
WEB: www.ohiogastro.com
SIC: 8011 Gastronomist

(G-8262)
OHIO HEALTH COUNCIL
155 E Broad St Ste 301 (43215-3640)
PHONE.................................614 221-7614
John Callender, *Ch of Bd*
Amy Andres, *Vice Pres*
EMP: 70
SALES (est): 11.2K **Privately Held**
SIC: 8621 Health association

(G-8263)
OHIO HEALTH GROUP LLC
155 E Broad St Ste 1700 (43215-3673)
PHONE.................................614 566-0010
Tom Thompson,
EMP: 40
SQ FT: 36,000
SALES (est): 5.2MM **Privately Held**
WEB: www.ohiohealthgroup.com
SIC: 8011 Medical insurance associations

(G-8264)
OHIO HEATING & AC INC
1465 Clara St (43211-2623)
P.O. Box 91203 (43209-7203)
PHONE.................................614 863-6666
Sam Goldstein Norman, *President*
Ken Scott, *Project Mgr*
Tom Sefchick, *Project Mgr*
Jamie Gary,
EMP: 26

SALES (est): 10.4MM **Privately Held**
SIC: 1711 Warm air heating & air conditioning contractor; plumbing contractors

(G-8265)
OHIO HISTORICAL SOCIETY (PA)
Also Called: OHIO HISTORY CONNECTION
800 E 17th Ave (43211-2497)
PHONE.................................614 297-2300
Glenda S Greenwood, *President*
Ronald J Ungvarsky, *Vice Pres*
Andy Hite, *Site Mgr*
Tim Jordan, *Site Mgr*
Tom Kindell, *Engineer*
EMP: 200 EST: 1885
SQ FT: 50,000
SALES (est): 21MM **Privately Held**
WEB: www.ohiotimelessadventures.com
SIC: 8412 Museum

(G-8266)
OHIO HOSPITAL ASSOCIATION
155 E Broad St Ste 301 (43215-3640)
PHONE.................................614 221-7614
James R Castle, *President*
Mike Abrams, *President*
Amy Andres, *General Mgr*
Ryan Biles, *Exec VP*
Ronald D Wade Sr, *Exec VP*
EMP: 62 EST: 1935
SQ FT: 9,000
SALES: 17MM **Privately Held**
SIC: 8621 Health association

(G-8267)
OHIO HOSPITAL FOR PSYCHIATRY
880 Greenlawn Ave (43223-2616)
PHONE.................................877 762-9026
Marcia Berch, *CEO*
EMP: 50
SALES (est): 7MM **Publicly Held**
SIC: 8063 Psychiatric Hospital
HQ: Behavioral Centers Of America, Llc
830 Crescent Centre Dr # 610
Franklin TN 37067
615 292-9514

(G-8268)
OHIO HOUSING FINANCE AGENCY
Also Called: Ohfa
57 E Main St Fl 3 (43215-5115)
PHONE.................................614 466-7970
Blaine Brockman, *CEO*
Douglas A Garver, *Exec Dir*
Arlyne Alston, *Director*
Barbara J Creech, *Director*
Guy Ford, *Director*
EMP: 340
SALES (est): 32.9MM **Privately Held**
SIC: 8748 Urban planning & consulting services

(G-8269)
OHIO INDEMNITY COMPANY
250 E Broad St Fl 7 (43215-3708)
PHONE.................................614 228-1601
John Sokol, *Ch of Bd*
Sally Cress, *Corp Secy*
Daniel J Stephan, *Senior VP*
Stephen J Toth, *Vice Pres*
EMP: 25
SQ FT: 12,000
SALES (est): 12.5MM
SALES (corp-wide): 46.1MM **Privately Held**
WEB: www.ohioindemnity.com
SIC: 6331 6411 Automobile insurance; property damage insurance; insurance agents, brokers & service
PA: Bancinsurance Corporation
250 E Broad St Fl 7
Columbus OH 43215
614 220-5200

(G-8270)
OHIO LEGAL RIGHTS SERVICE
50 W Broad St Ste 1400 (43215-3301)
PHONE.................................614 466-7264
Paula Jones, *CFO*
Michael Kirkman, *Exec Dir*
EMP: 47
SQ FT: 17,694

SALES (est): 1.6MM **Privately Held**
WEB: www.governor.ohio.gov
SIC: 8399 Advocacy group
HQ: Executive Office State Of Ohio
30 E Broad St
Columbus OH 43215

(G-8271)
OHIO LIVING
Also Called: Westminster Thurber
645 Neil Ave Ofc (43215-1624)
PHONE.................................614 224-1651
Lovely Belfance, *Director*
EMP: 300
SQ FT: 8,728 **Privately Held**
WEB: www.nwo.oprs.org
SIC: 6513 8051 8052 Apartment Building Operator Skilled Nursing Care Facility Intermediate Care Facility
PA: Ohio Living
1001 Kingsmill Pkwy
Columbus OH 43229

(G-8272)
OHIO LIVING (PA)
1001 Kingsmill Pkwy (43229-1129)
PHONE.................................614 888-7800
Laurence Gumina, *CEO*
Robert Stillman, *CFO*
EMP: 50
SQ FT: 12,000
SALES: 228.2MM **Privately Held**
WEB: www.oprs.org
SIC: 8361 Rest home, with health care incidental

(G-8273)
OHIO MACHINERY CO
Ohio Cat
5252 Walcutt Ct (43228-9641)
PHONE.................................614 878-2287
Dan McManamon, *CFO*
Craig Curtis, *Sales Mgr*
Ed Buerger, *Sales Staff*
Jeff Van Linge, *Sales Staff*
Keith Musgrave, *Sales Associate*
EMP: 300
SALES (corp-wide): 222.7MM **Privately Held**
WEB: www.enginesnow.com
SIC: 5082 General construction machinery & equipment
PA: Ohio Machinery Co.
3993 E Royalton Rd
Broadview Heights OH 44147
440 526-6200

(G-8274)
OHIO MEDICAL TRNSP INC (PA)
Also Called: Medflight of Ohio
2827 W Dblin Granville Rd (43235-2712)
PHONE.................................614 791-4400
Rod Crane, *President*
Charles E Ansley, *CFO*
John Lindaman, *CFO*
Thomas E Allenstein, *Ch Credit Ofcr*
Sara Craig, *Human Resources*
EMP: 80
SALES: 45.1MM **Privately Held**
WEB: www.medflight.com
SIC: 4522 4119 Ambulance services, air; ambulance service

(G-8275)
OHIO NEWS NETWORK
Also Called: Ohio News Network, The
770 Twin Rivers Dr (43215-1127)
PHONE.................................614 460-3700
Tom Greidorn, *General Mgr*
EMP: 80
SALES (est): 3.7MM **Privately Held**
WEB: www.onnnews.com
SIC: 7383 2711 4841 News syndicates; newspapers; cable & other pay television services

(G-8276)
OHIO OPERATING ENGINEERS APPRN
1184 Dublin Rd (43215-7004)
PHONE.................................614 487-6531
Don Black, *Principal*
EMP: 30
SALES (est): 3.4MM **Privately Held**
SIC: 8631 Labor union

(G-8277)
OHIO ORTHPD SURGERY INST LLC
4605 Sawmill Rd (43220-2246)
PHONE.................................614 827-8777
A S C Group Lc, *Mng Member*
William Fitz MD,
EMP: 30
SALES: 400K **Privately Held**
WEB: www.ohio-ortho-surg.com
SIC: 8011 Orthopedic physician

(G-8278)
OHIO OSTEOPATHIC HOSPITAL ASSN
52 W 3rd Ave (43201)
P.O. Box 8130 (43201-0130)
PHONE.................................614 299-2107
Jon F Wills, *Principal*
EMP: 26
SALES: 78.4K **Privately Held**
SIC: 8062 General medical & surgical hospitals

(G-8279)
OHIO POWER COMPANY (HQ)
Also Called: AEP
1 Riverside Plz (43215-2355)
PHONE.................................614 716-1000
Nicholas K Akins, *Ch of Bd*
Brian X Tierney, *CFO*
Joseph M Buonaiuto,
EMP: 170
SALES: 3B
SALES (corp-wide): 16.2B **Publicly Held**
SIC: 4911 Electric services; distribution, electric power; generation, electric power; transmission, electric power
PA: American Electric Power Company, Inc.
1 Riverside Plz Fl 1 # 1
Columbus OH 43215
614 716-1000

(G-8280)
OHIO PRESBT RETIREMENT SVCS
Also Called: Westminster Thurber Community
717 Neil Ave (43215-1609)
PHONE.................................614 228-8888
Leslie Belfance, *Exec Dir*
EMP: 174 **Privately Held**
SIC: 8049 Acupuncturist
PA: Ohio Living
1001 Kingsmill Pkwy
Columbus OH 43229

(G-8281)
OHIO PRESBYTERIAN RTR SVCS
Also Called: OPRS FOUNDATION
1001 Kingsmill Pkwy (43229-1129)
PHONE.................................614 888-7800
Thomas G Hofmann, *President*
Sandy Simpson, *Vice Pres*
Sue Welty, *Vice Pres*
EMP: 38
SALES: 11.6MM **Privately Held**
SIC: 7389 Fund raising organizations

(G-8282)
OHIO PUB EMPLYEES RTREMENT SYS
277 E Town St (43215-4627)
PHONE.................................614 228-8471
Sharon Downs, *Principal*
Cinthia Sledz, *Chairman*
Blake W Sherry, *COO*
Jenny Starr, *CFO*
Brad Sturm, *Portfolio Mgr*
EMP: 468
SQ FT: 145,404
SALES (est): 326.2MM **Privately Held**
WEB: www.opers.org
SIC: 6371 9441 Pension funds; administration of social & manpower programs;
HQ: Executive Office State Of Ohio
30 E Broad St
Columbus OH 43215

(G-8283)
OHIO RURAL ELECTRIC COOPS INC
Also Called: Country Living
6677 Busch Blvd (43229-1101)
PHONE.................................614 846-5757
Anthony J Ahern, *President*
EMP: 25 **EST:** 1941
SALES: 6MM **Privately Held**
SIC: 8611 5063 Trade associations; electrical apparatus & equipment; electrical supplies

(G-8284)
OHIO SCHOOL BOARDS ASSOCIATION
8050 N High St Ste 100 (43235-6481)
PHONE.................................614 540-4000
Rick Lewis, *Exec Dir*
▲ **EMP:** 48 **EST:** 1955
SALES: 8.6MM **Privately Held**
SIC: 8699 Animal humane society

(G-8285)
OHIO SCHOOL PSYCHOLOGISTS ASSN
4449 Easton Way Fl 2offi (43219-6093)
PHONE.................................614 414-5980
Cheryl Vandenburg, *Principal*
EMP: 44
SALES: 309.4K **Privately Held**
WEB: www.ospaonline.org
SIC: 8211 8621 Elementary & secondary schools; professional membership organizations

(G-8286)
OHIO SENIOR HOME HLTH CARE LLC
6004 Cleveland Ave (43231-2230)
PHONE.................................614 470-6070
Saeed Ali, *CEO*
Nada Mohamed,
EMP: 80 **EST:** 2015
SALES (est): 326.8K **Privately Held**
SIC: 8082 Home health care services

(G-8287)
OHIO SOC OF CRTIF PUB ACCNTNTS
Also Called: OHIO SOCEITY OF CPAS
4249 Easton Way Ste 150 (43219-6163)
P.O. Box 1810, Dublin (43017-7810)
PHONE.................................614 764-2727
Scott Wiley, *President*
Laura Hay, *COO*
Boyd Search, *Vice Pres*
Jan Johnson, *Accountant*
Gary Hunt, *Comms Mgr*
EMP: 53
SQ FT: 13,500
SALES: 9MM **Privately Held**
SIC: 8621 Accounting association

(G-8288)
OHIO STATE BAR ASSOCIATION
Also Called: Ohio Cle Institute
1700 Lake Shore Dr (43204-4895)
PHONE.................................614 487-2050
Denny Ramey, *Exec Dir*
Gail Buttrick, *Receptionist*
EMP: 37
SQ FT: 13,338
SALES (est): 6.7MM **Privately Held**
SIC: 8111 Legal services

(G-8289)
OHIO STATE BAR ASSOCIATION
1700 Lake Shore Dr (43204-4895)
P.O. Box 16562 (43216-6562)
PHONE.................................614 487-2050
Keith Ashman, *President*
Reginal Jackson, *Vice Pres*
Denny Ramey, *Exec Dir*
Tammy Savage, *Director*
Rick Banister, *Asst Director*
EMP: 55
SALES: 10.8MM **Privately Held**
WEB: www.ohiostatebarassociation.com
SIC: 8621 Bar association

(G-8290)
OHIO STATE UNIV ALUMNI ASSN
Also Called: ALUMNI ASSOCIATION, THE
2200 Olentangy River Rd (43210-1035)
PHONE.................................614 292-2200
Archie Griffin, *President*
EMP: 60 **EST:** 1910
SQ FT: 9,600
SALES: 11.4MM **Privately Held**
WEB: www.ohiostatealumni.org
SIC: 8641 8661 Alumni association; religious organizations

(G-8291)
OHIO STATE UNIV WEXNER MED CTR
369 Grenadine Way (43235-5742)
PHONE.................................614 293-2663
Corey Beals, *Surgeon*
EMP: 135
SALES (corp-wide): 5.8B **Privately Held**
SIC: 8011 Medical centers
HQ: The Ohio State University Wexner Medical Center
410 W 10th Ave
Columbus OH 43210
614 293-8000

(G-8292)
OHIO STATE UNIV WEXNER MED CTR (HQ)
410 W 10th Ave (43210-1240)
PHONE.................................614 293-8000
Michael V Drake, *President*
Chris Heckler, *Project Mgr*
Denny Sweet, *Human Res Dir*
Erin W Sommer, *Marketing Staff*
Erin M Bontrager, *Manager*
EMP: 1000 **EST:** 1910
SALES: 3.1B
SALES (corp-wide): 5.8B **Privately Held**
SIC: 8062 General medical & surgical hospitals
PA: The Ohio State University Student Acade Servi Bldg
Columbus OH 43210
614 292-6446

(G-8293)
OHIO STATE UNIV WEXNER MED CTR
Also Called: Otolaryngology Department
1492 E Broad St (43205-1546)
PHONE.................................614 366-3687
Michelle Schnurr, *Branch Mgr*
Curt Brown, *Officer*
EMP: 188
SALES (corp-wide): 5.8B **Privately Held**
SIC: 8062 General medical & surgical hospitals
HQ: The Ohio State University Wexner Medical Center
410 W 10th Ave
Columbus OH 43210
614 293-8000

(G-8294)
OHIO STATE UNIV WEXNER MED CTR
Also Called: Division of Gastroenterology
410 W 10th Ave (43210-1240)
PHONE.................................614 293-6255
Darwin L Conwell, *Director*
EMP: 574
SALES (corp-wide): 5.8B **Privately Held**
WEB: www.ohio-state.edu
SIC: 8011 8221 Cardiologist & cardio-vascular specialist; university
HQ: The Ohio State University Wexner Medical Center
410 W 10th Ave
Columbus OH 43210
614 293-8000

(G-8295)
OHIO STATE UNIVERSITY
Also Called: Dodd Hall Inptent Rhbilitation
480 Medical Center Dr (43210-1229)
PHONE.................................614 366-3692
Martin Joyce, *CFO*
Mark Larmore, *CFO*
Janelle Janowiecki, *Nursing Mgr*
Jessica Macdonald, *Psychologist*
EMP: 547

SALES (corp-wide): 5.8B **Privately Held**
SIC: 8011 8049 8322 Medical centers; physical therapist; rehabilitation services
PA: The Ohio State University Student Acade Servi Bldg
Columbus OH 43210
614 292-6446

(G-8296)
OHIO STATE UNIVERSITY
Also Called: Schottenstein Center, The
555 Borror Dr (43210-1187)
PHONE.................................614 688-3939
Joe Odoguardi, *Finance Dir*
EMP: 730
SALES (corp-wide): 5.8B **Privately Held**
WEB: www.ohio-state.edu
SIC: 6512 8221 Property operation, auditoriums & theaters; university
PA: The Ohio State University Student Acade Servi Bldg
Columbus OH 43210
614 292-6446

(G-8297)
OHIO STATE UNIVERSITY
Also Called: Internal Medicine
410 W 10th Ave Rm 205 (43210-1240)
PHONE.................................614 293-8045
Robert McKenney, *Assistant VP*
Daisy Sinha, *Project Mgr*
Lynne Miller, *Research*
Karna Anthony, *Accounting Mgr*
Heather Berger, *Accountant*
EMP: 574
SALES (corp-wide): 5.8B **Privately Held**
SIC: 8011 Internal medicine, physician/surgeon
PA: The Ohio State University Student Acade Servi Bldg
Columbus OH 43210
614 292-6446

(G-8298)
OHIO STATE UNIVERSITY
Also Called: Osu Cnter For Wllness Prvntion
2050 Kenny Rd Ste 1010 (43221-3502)
PHONE.................................614 293-2800
Trish Neal, *Director*
EMP: 40
SALES (corp-wide): 5.8B **Privately Held**
WEB: www.ohio-state.edu
SIC: 7991 8221 Physical fitness facilities; university
PA: The Ohio State University Student Acade Servi Bldg
Columbus OH 43210
614 292-6446

(G-8299)
OHIO STATE UNIVERSITY
Also Called: College of Dentistry
305 W 12th Ave (43210-1267)
PHONE.................................614 292-5578
Gordon Gee, *President*
EMP: 60
SALES (corp-wide): 5.8B **Privately Held**
WEB: www.ohio-state.edu
SIC: 8021 8221 Prosthodontist; university
PA: The Ohio State University Student Acade Servi Bldg
Columbus OH 43210
614 292-6446

(G-8300)
OHIO STATE UNIVERSITY
University Hospitals East
300 W 10th Ave (43210-1280)
PHONE.................................614 257-3000
Robert Salmen, *Financial Exec*
Thoma Spackman, *Branch Mgr*
Jane Poulson, *Manager*
Ben Leonard, *Food Svc Dir*
EMP: 800
SALES (corp-wide): 5.8B **Privately Held**
WEB: www.ohio-state.edu
SIC: 8062 8093 8049 8011 General medical & surgical hospitals; rehabilitation center, outpatient treatment; physical therapist; oncologist
PA: The Ohio State University Student Acade Servi Bldg
Columbus OH 43210
614 292-6446

(G-8301)
OHIO STATE UNIVERSITY
Also Called: Medohio Family Care Center
1615 Fishinger Rd (43221-2103)
PHONE.................................614 293-7417
William Padamadan, *Principal*
EMP: 574
SQ FT: 1,677
SALES (corp-wide): 5.8B **Privately Held**
WEB: www.ohio-state.edu
SIC: 8011 8221 Cardiologist & cardio-vascular specialist; university
PA: The Ohio State University Student Acade Servi Bldg
Columbus OH 43210
614 292-6446

(G-8302)
OHIO STATE UNIVERSITY
Also Called: Medical Center
480 W 9th Ave (43210-1245)
PHONE.................................614 293-8750
Robert Vanecko, *Branch Mgr*
Daniel Clinchot, *Med Doctor*
EMP: 188
SALES (corp-wide): 5.8B **Privately Held**
SIC: 8062 8221 General medical & surgical hospitals; university
PA: The Ohio State University Student Acade Servi Bldg
Columbus OH 43210
614 292-6446

(G-8303)
OHIO STATE UNIVERSITY
Also Called: Glaucoma Consultants
915 Olentangy River Rd (43212-3153)
PHONE.................................614 293-8116
Paul Weber,
EMP: 523
SALES (corp-wide): 5.8B **Privately Held**
SIC: 8011 Ophthalmologist
PA: The Ohio State University Student Acade Servi Bldg
Columbus OH 43210
614 292-6446

(G-8304)
OHIO STATE UNIVERSITY
Also Called: Department of Human Nutrition
350 Campbell Hl (43210)
PHONE.................................614 292-5504
James Kinder, *Chairman*
EMP: 50
SALES (corp-wide): 5.8B **Privately Held**
WEB: www.ohio-state.edu
SIC: 8099 8221 Nutrition services; university
PA: The Ohio State University Student Acade Servi Bldg
Columbus OH 43210
614 292-6446

(G-8305)
OHIO STATE UNIVERSITY
Also Called: College Engineering/Aerospace
2300 West Case Rd (43235-7531)
PHONE.................................614 292-5491
MO Samimy, *Director*
EMP: 75
SALES (corp-wide): 5.8B **Privately Held**
WEB: www.ohio-state.edu
SIC: 8221 8732 University; educational research
PA: The Ohio State University Student Acade Servi Bldg
Columbus OH 43210
614 292-6446

(G-8306)
OHIO STATE UNIVERSITY
Also Called: Osu Industrial Welding Sy
1248 Arthur E Adams Dr (43221-3560)
PHONE.................................614 292-4139
Richard A Miller, *Chairman*
EMP: 32
SALES (corp-wide): 5.8B **Privately Held**
WEB: www.ohio-state.edu
SIC: 7692 8221 Welding repair; university
PA: The Ohio State University Student Acade Servi Bldg
Columbus OH 43210
614 292-6446

(G-8307)
OHIO STATE UNIVERSITY
Also Called: Osu Value City Arena
555 Borror Dr Ste 1030 (43210-1187)
PHONE................................614 292-2624
Michael Gatto, *Director*
EMP: 37
SALES (corp-wide): 5.8B **Privately Held**
WEB: www.ohio-state.edu
SIC: 7941 8221 Sports field or stadium operator, promoting sports events; university
PA: The Ohio State University
Student Acade Servi Bldg
Columbus OH 43210
614 292-6446

(G-8308)
OHIO STATE UNIVERSITY
Also Called: Mershon Center For Education
1501 Neil Ave (43201-2602)
PHONE................................614 292-1681
Richard Harman, *Director*
EMP: 70
SALES (corp-wide): 5.8B **Privately Held**
WEB: www.ohio-state.edu
SIC: 8733 8221 Noncommercial research organizations; university
PA: The Ohio State University
Student Acade Servi Bldg
Columbus OH 43210
614 292-6446

(G-8309)
OHIO STATE UNIVERSITY
Also Called: Medical Center
1375 Perry St (43201-3177)
P.O. Box 183111 (43218-3111)
PHONE................................614 293-3860
Phil Skinner, *Director*
Robin Wharton, *Professor*
EMP: 5249
SALES (corp-wide): 5.8B **Privately Held**
WEB: www.ohio-state.edu
SIC: 8011 8221 Medical centers; university
PA: The Ohio State University
Student Acade Servi Bldg
Columbus OH 43210
614 292-6446

(G-8310)
OHIO STATE UNIVERSITY
Also Called: Blackwell Inn, The
2110 Tuttle Park Pl (43210-1137)
PHONE................................614 247-4000
Eric Adelman, *General Mgr*
EMP: 26
SALES (corp-wide): 5.8B **Privately Held**
WEB: www.ohio-state.edu
SIC: 7011 8221 Hotels; university
PA: The Ohio State University
Student Acade Servi Bldg
Columbus OH 43210
614 292-6446

(G-8311)
OHIO STATE UNIVERSITY
Also Called: Ohio State Univ Child Care
725 Ackerman Rd (43202-1502)
PHONE................................614 292-4453
Maggie Sommers, *Director*
EMP: 75
SALES (corp-wide): 5.8B **Privately Held**
WEB: www.ohio-state.edu
SIC: 8351 8221 Child day care services; colleges universities & professional schools
PA: The Ohio State University
Student Acade Servi Bldg
Columbus OH 43210
614 292-6446

(G-8312)
OHIO STATE UNIVERSITY
Also Called: Wosu Am-FM TV
2400 Olentangy River Rd (43210-1027)
PHONE................................614 292-4510
Tom Rieland, *General Mgr*
Mary Alice Akins, *Finance*
EMP: 120
SALES (corp-wide): 5.8B **Privately Held**
WEB: www.ohio-state.edu
SIC: 4832 4833 Radio broadcasting stations; television translator station

PA: The Ohio State University
Student Acade Servi Bldg
Columbus OH 43210
614 292-6446

(G-8313)
OHIO STATE UNIVERSITY
Also Called: University Tech Service
1121 Kinnear Rd Bldg E (43212)
PHONE................................614 292-4843
Eileen Strider, *Principal*
EMP: 250
SALES (corp-wide): 5.8B **Privately Held**
WEB: www.ohio-state.edu
SIC: 8221 7379 University; computer related consulting services
PA: The Ohio State University
Student Acade Servi Bldg
Columbus OH 43210
614 292-6446

(G-8314)
OHIO STATE UNIVERSITY
Also Called: Veterans ADM Out Ptient Clinic
420 N James Rd (43219-1834)
PHONE................................614 257-5200
Bernard F Williams, *Manager*
EMP: 52
SALES (corp-wide): 5.8B **Privately Held**
WEB: www.ohio-state.edu
SIC: 8099 8221 Blood related health services; university
PA: The Ohio State University
Student Acade Servi Bldg
Columbus OH 43210
614 292-6446

(G-8315)
OHIO STATE UNIVERSITY
Also Called: Accounts Payable Department
901 Woody Hayes Dr (43210-4013)
PHONE................................614 292-6831
Ronald Holland, *Manager*
EMP: 35
SALES (corp-wide): 5.8B **Privately Held**
WEB: www.ohio-state.edu
SIC: 8721 Accounting services, except auditing
PA: The Ohio State University
Student Acade Servi Bldg
Columbus OH 43210
614 292-6446

(G-8316)
OHIO STATE UNIVERSITY
Also Called: Center Ed/Train Employmnt
1900 Kenny Rd (43210-1016)
PHONE................................614 292-4353
Ray D Ryan, *Exec Dir*
EMP: 75
SALES (corp-wide): 5.8B **Privately Held**
WEB: www.ohio-state.edu
SIC: 8732 8331 Educational research; job training services
PA: The Ohio State University
Student Acade Servi Bldg
Columbus OH 43210
614 292-6446

(G-8317)
OHIO STATE UNIVERSITY
Also Called: Osu Obgyn
395 W 12th Ave (43210-1267)
PHONE................................614 293-4997
Cheryl N Wall, *Principal*
Larry Copeland, *Chairman*
Bassel Shneker, *Neurology*
Mary Pat Bartoszek, *Nurse Practr*
EMP: 50
SALES (corp-wide): 5.8B **Privately Held**
WEB: www.ohio-state.edu
SIC: 8011 8221 Obstetrician; university
PA: The Ohio State University
Student Acade Servi Bldg
Columbus OH 43210
614 292-6446

(G-8318)
OHIO STATE UNIVERSITY
Also Called: Osu Personnel
2130 Neil Ave (43210-1296)
PHONE................................614 293-2494
William E Kerwan, *President*
EMP: 600

(G-8319)
OHIO STATE UNIVERSITY
Also Called: O S U Telephone Service
320 W 8th Ave (43201-2331)
PHONE................................614 292-7788
Bob Corben, *Director*
EMP: 75
SALES (corp-wide): 5.8B **Privately Held**
WEB: www.ohio-state.edu
SIC: 8331 8221 Manpower training; university
PA: The Ohio State University
Student Acade Servi Bldg
Columbus OH 43210
614 292-6446

(G-8320)
OHIO STATE UNIVERSITY
Also Called: Center For Human Resource RES
921 Chatham Ln Ste 100 (43221-2418)
PHONE................................614 442-7300
Randell Olson, *Director*
EMP: 60
SALES (corp-wide): 5.8B **Privately Held**
WEB: www.ohio-state.edu
SIC: 8732 8221 Economic research; university
PA: The Ohio State University
Student Acade Servi Bldg
Columbus OH 43210
614 292-6446

(G-8321)
OHIO STATE UNIVERSITY
Also Called: Infectious Diseases Department
N.1135 Doan Hl (43210)
PHONE................................614 293-8732
Robert J Fass, *Director*
EMP: 40
SALES (corp-wide): 5.8B **Privately Held**
WEB: www.ohio-state.edu
SIC: 8011 8221 Infectious disease specialist, physician/surgeon; university
PA: The Ohio State University
Student Acade Servi Bldg
Columbus OH 43210
614 292-6446

(G-8322)
OHIO STATE UNIVERSITY
Also Called: Communiction/Journalism
3007 Derby Rd (43221-2607)
PHONE................................614 292-6291
Don Dell, *Principal*
EMP: 36
SALES (corp-wide): 5.8B **Privately Held**
WEB: www.ohio-state.edu
SIC: 4813 8221 Telephone communication, except radio; university
PA: The Ohio State University
Student Acade Servi Bldg
Columbus OH 43210
614 292-6446

(G-8323)
OHIO STATE UNIVERSITY
Also Called: Osu Medical Staff ADM
410 W 10th Ave Rm 130 (43210-1240)
PHONE................................614 293-8158
Andrew Thomas, *Director*
EMP: 35
SALES (corp-wide): 5.8B **Privately Held**
WEB: www.ohio-state.edu
SIC: 8062 8221 Hospital, medical school affiliation; university
PA: The Ohio State University
Student Acade Servi Bldg
Columbus OH 43210
614 292-6446

(G-8324)
OHIO STATE UNIVERSITY
Also Called: Student Wilce Health Center
1875 Millikin Rd Fl 3 (43210-2200)
PHONE................................614 292-0110

Ted W Grace, *Director*
EMP: 100
SALES (corp-wide): 5.8B **Privately Held**
WEB: www.ohio-state.edu
SIC: 8099 8221 Health screening service; university
PA: The Ohio State University
Student Acade Servi Bldg
Columbus OH 43210
614 292-6446

(G-8325)
OHIO STATE UNIVERSITY
Also Called: Osu Dept Psychology
Ps Pschology Rm 225 St Rm 2 (43210)
PHONE................................614 292-6741
Dr Gifford Weary, *Chairman*
EMP: 60
SALES (corp-wide): 5.8B **Privately Held**
WEB: www.ohio-state.edu
SIC: 8049 8221 Clinical psychologist; university
PA: The Ohio State University
Student Acade Servi Bldg
Columbus OH 43210
614 292-6446

(G-8326)
OHIO STATE UNIVERSITY
Oral and Maxillofacial Surgery
305 W 12th Ave Ste 2131 (43210-1267)
P.O. Box 907, Hilliard (43026-0907)
PHONE................................614 292-5144
Dr Gregory Ness, *Director*
EMP: 27
SALES (corp-wide): 5.8B **Privately Held**
WEB: www.ohio-state.edu
SIC: 8021 8221 Dental surgeon; maxillofacial specialist; university
PA: The Ohio State University
Student Acade Servi Bldg
Columbus OH 43210
614 292-6446

(G-8327)
OHIO STATE UNIVERSITY
Also Called: Osu-Infectious Diseases
456 W 10th Ave Rm 4725 (43210-1240)
PHONE................................614 293-8732
EMP: 37
SALES (corp-wide): 5.8B **Privately Held**
WEB: www.ohio-state.edu
SIC: 4959 8221 Disease control; university
PA: The Ohio State University
Student Acade Servi Bldg
Columbus OH 43210
614 292-6446

(G-8328)
OHIO STATE UNIVERSITY
Also Called: Medical Center
410 W 10th Ave (43210-1240)
PHONE................................614 293-8588
Carl Story, *Manager*
EMP: 40
SALES (corp-wide): 5.8B **Privately Held**
WEB: www.ohio-state.edu
SIC: 5047 8221 Medical & hospital equipment; university
PA: The Ohio State University
Student Acade Servi Bldg
Columbus OH 43210
614 292-6446

(G-8329)
OHIO STATE UNIVERSITY
Also Called: School Edctl Policy Leadership
29 W Woodruff Ave Ofc 121 (43210-1116)
PHONE................................614 688-5721
Robert Lawson, *Director*
EMP: 50
SALES (corp-wide): 5.8B **Privately Held**
WEB: www.ohio-state.edu
SIC: 8221 8641 University; educator's association
PA: The Ohio State University
Student Acade Servi Bldg
Columbus OH 43210
614 292-6446

(G-8330)
OHIO STATE UNIVERSITY
University Hospital
650 Ackerman Rd Ste 135 (43202-4500)
PHONE................................614 293-3737

Beth Necamp, *Principal*
Ron Kibbe, *Asst Director*
EMP: 40
SALES (corp-wide): 5.8B **Privately Held**
WEB: www.ohio-state.edu
SIC: 8743 8221 Public relations services; university
PA: The Ohio State University
Student Acade Servi Bldg
Columbus OH 43210
614 292-6446

(G-8331)
OHIO STATE UNIVERSITY
Also Called: Nuclear Reactor Laboratory
1298 Kinnear Rd (43212-1154)
PHONE....................614 688-8220
Thomas E Blue, *Director*
EMP: 101
SALES (corp-wide): 5.8B **Privately Held**
SIC: 8731 Chemical laboratory, except testing
PA: The Ohio State University
Student Acade Servi Bldg
Columbus OH 43210
614 292-6446

(G-8332)
OHIO STATE UNIVERSITY
Also Called: Transportation Department
2578 Kenny Rd (43210-1038)
PHONE....................614 292-6122
Steve Basinger, *Director*
EMP: 35
SALES (corp-wide): 5.8B **Privately Held**
WEB: www.ohio-state.edu
SIC: 4789 8221 Cargo loading & unloading services; university
PA: The Ohio State University
Student Acade Servi Bldg
Columbus OH 43210
614 292-6446

(G-8333)
OHIO STATE UNIVERSITY
Also Called: Fawcett Center For Tomorrow
2400 Olentangy River Rd (43210-1027)
PHONE....................614 292-3238
Diane Whitbeck, *Principal*
EMP: 300
SALES (corp-wide): 5.8B **Privately Held**
WEB: www.ohio-state.edu
SIC: 8221 7991 7011 5813 Colleges universities & professional schools; physical fitness facilities; hotels & motels; drinking places; eating places
PA: The Ohio State University
Student Acade Servi Bldg
Columbus OH 43210
614 292-6446

(G-8334)
OHIO STATE UNIVERSITY
Also Called: Ohio State Univ Vtrnarian Hosp
601 Vernon Tharp St (43210-4007)
PHONE....................614 292-6661
Dr Richard M Bednarski, *Director*
EMP: 150
SALES (corp-wide): 5.8B **Privately Held**
WEB: www.ohio-state.edu
SIC: 0742 8221 Animal hospital services, pets & other animal specialties; university
PA: The Ohio State University
Student Acade Servi Bldg
Columbus OH 43210
614 292-6446

(G-8335)
OHIO STATE UNIVERSITY
Osu Center Automotive Research
930 Kinnear Rd (43212-1443)
PHONE....................614 292-5990
David Cooke, *Manager*
EMP: 149
SALES (corp-wide): 5.8B **Privately Held**
WEB: www.ohio-state.edu
SIC: 8733 8221 Research institute; university
PA: The Ohio State University
Student Acade Servi Bldg
Columbus OH 43210
614 292-6446

(G-8336)
OHIO STATE UNIVERSITY
Also Called: Delta Theta Sigma Fraternity
80 E 13th Ave (43201-1808)
PHONE....................614 294-2635
Austin Kirk, *President*
EMP: 25
SALES (corp-wide): 5.8B **Privately Held**
WEB: www.ohio-state.edu
SIC: 7041 8221 Fraternities & sororities; university
PA: The Ohio State University
Student Acade Servi Bldg
Columbus OH 43210
614 292-6446

(G-8337)
OHIO STATE UNIVERSITY
Also Called: Speech Language Hearing Clinic
1070 Carmack Rd (43210-1002)
PHONE....................614 292-6251
Gail Whitelaw, *Director*
EMP: 188
SALES (corp-wide): 5.8B **Privately Held**
WEB: www.ohio-state.edu
SIC: 8062 8221 Hospital, medical school affiliation; colleges universities & professional schools
PA: The Ohio State University
Student Acade Servi Bldg
Columbus OH 43210
614 292-6446

(G-8338)
OHIO STATE UNIVERSITY
Also Called: Oarnet
1224 Kinnear Rd (43212-1154)
PHONE....................614 728-8100
Douglas Gale, *Director*
EMP: 45
SALES (corp-wide): 5.8B **Privately Held**
WEB: www.ohio-state.edu
SIC: 7373 8742 Computer integrated systems design; management consulting services
PA: The Ohio State University
Student Acade Servi Bldg
Columbus OH 43210
614 292-6446

(G-8339)
OHIO STATE UNIVERSITY
Also Called: Ohio State Univ Spt Mdcine Ctr
2050 Kenny Rd Fl 3 (43221-3502)
PHONE....................614 293-2222
Terry Hazucha, *Principal*
EMP: 60
SALES (corp-wide): 5.8B **Privately Held**
WEB: www.ohio-state.edu
SIC: 8011 8221 Sports medicine specialist, physician; university
PA: The Ohio State University
Student Acade Servi Bldg
Columbus OH 43210
614 292-6446

(G-8340)
OHIO STATE UNIVERSITY
Also Called: Dept of Surgery
410 W 10th Ave Fl 7 (43210-1240)
PHONE....................614 293-8133
Christopher Ellison, *Chairman*
Mark W Arnold, *Professor*
EMP: 350
SALES (corp-wide): 5.8B **Privately Held**
WEB: www.ohio-state.edu
SIC: 8011 8221 Physicians' office, including specialists; university
PA: The Ohio State University
Student Acade Servi Bldg
Columbus OH 43210
614 292-6446

(G-8341)
OHIO STATE UNIVERSITY
Also Called: Nat'l Rglartory RES Institue
1080 Carmack Rd (43210-1002)
PHONE....................614 292-9404
EMP: 30
SALES (corp-wide): 5.1B **Privately Held**
SIC: 8732 8221 Commercial Nonphysical Research College/University
PA: The Ohio State University
Student Acade Servi Bldg
Columbus OH 43210
614 292-6446

(G-8342)
OHIO STATE UNIVERSITY
Also Called: James Cancer Center
300 W 10th Ave 924 (43210-1280)
PHONE....................614 293-5066
Stephen Povoski, *Branch Mgr*
Jennifer Carlson, *Director*
Tina Latimer, *Admin Dir*
Kathleen Terry, *Asst Director*
Harry Evans, *Analyst*
EMP: 574
SALES (corp-wide): 5.8B **Privately Held**
SIC: 8011 8221 Oncologist; university
PA: The Ohio State University
Student Acade Servi Bldg
Columbus OH 43210
614 292-6446

(G-8343)
OHIO STATE UNIVERSITY
Also Called: Medical Records Department
410 W 10th Ave Rm 140 (43210-1240)
PHONE....................614 293-8419
Liz Curtis, *Director*
EMP: 35
SALES (corp-wide): 5.8B **Privately Held**
WEB: www.ohio-state.edu
SIC: 8062 8221 General medical & surgical hospitals; university
PA: The Ohio State University
Student Acade Servi Bldg
Columbus OH 43210
614 292-6446

(G-8344)
OHIO STATE UNIVERSITY
Also Called: Osu Faculty Practice
305 W 12th Ave (43210-1267)
PHONE....................614 292-1472
Kelly Shader DDS, *Director*
EMP: 62
SALES (corp-wide): 5.8B **Privately Held**
WEB: www.ohio-state.edu
SIC: 8021 8221 Prosthodontist; university
PA: The Ohio State University
Student Acade Servi Bldg
Columbus OH 43210
614 292-6446

(G-8345)
OHIO STATE UNIVERSITY
Also Called: Surgical Oncology Division
N924 Doan Hall 410 W 10 (43210)
PHONE....................614 293-8196
Ben Walters, *Opers Staff*
Amy Gellegani, *VP Mktg*
Linda Montler, *Marketing Staff*
Valerie Wright, *Manager*
William Farrar, *Director*
EMP: 35
SALES (corp-wide): 5.8B **Privately Held**
WEB: www.ohio-state.edu
SIC: 8062 8221 General medical & surgical hospitals; university
PA: The Ohio State University
Student Acade Servi Bldg
Columbus OH 43210
614 292-6446

(G-8346)
OHIO STATE UNIVERSITY
Also Called: Medical Center Security
450 W 10th Ave (43210-1240)
PHONE....................614 293-8333
Spero Vasila, *Director*
EMP: 47
SALES (corp-wide): 5.8B **Privately Held**
WEB: www.ohio-state.edu
SIC: 8062 8221 General medical & surgical hospitals; colleges universities & professional schools
PA: The Ohio State University
Student Acade Servi Bldg
Columbus OH 43210
614 292-6446

(G-8347)
OHIO STATE UNIVERSITY
Also Called: Osu Hospitals
450 W 10th Ave (43210-1240)
PHONE....................614 293-8000
Peter Geier, *CEO*
Joseph Yu, *Radiology Dir*
EMP: 1000

SALES (corp-wide): 5.8B **Privately Held**
WEB: www.ohio-state.edu
SIC: 8062 8221 General medical & surgical hospitals; university
PA: The Ohio State University
Student Acade Servi Bldg
Columbus OH 43210
614 292-6446

(G-8348)
OHIO STATE UNIVERSITY
Also Called: Osu Division of Pulmonary
2050 Kenny Rd Ste 2200 (43221-3502)
PHONE....................614 293-4925
Carl V Leier, *Med Doctor*
Tim Mazik, *Administration*
EMP: 50
SALES (corp-wide): 5.8B **Privately Held**
WEB: www.ohio-state.edu
SIC: 8069 8221 Specialty hospitals, except psychiatric; university
PA: The Ohio State University
Student Acade Servi Bldg
Columbus OH 43210
614 292-6446

(G-8349)
OHIO STATE UNIVERSITY
915 Olentangy River Rd (43212-3153)
PHONE....................614 293-8074
Mark Inman, *Branch Mgr*
EMP: 52
SALES (corp-wide): 5.8B **Privately Held**
SIC: 8099 Medical services organization
PA: The Ohio State University
Student Acade Servi Bldg
Columbus OH 43210
614 292-6446

(G-8350)
OHIO STATE UNIVERSITY
305 W 12th Ave (43210-1267)
PHONE....................614 292-2751
Dean Henry Fields, *Manager*
EMP: 100
SALES (corp-wide): 5.8B **Privately Held**
WEB: www.ohio-state.edu
SIC: 8021 8221 Offices & clinics of dentists; university
PA: The Ohio State University
Student Acade Servi Bldg
Columbus OH 43210
614 292-6446

(G-8351)
OHIO STATE UNIVERSITY
Also Called: Department of Internal Med Div
473 W 12th Ave (43210-1252)
PHONE....................614 293-4967
Patricia Caldwell, *Med Doctor*
John Larry, *Med Doctor*
Angie Crespin, *Manager*
Philip Binkley, *Professor*
EMP: 574
SALES (corp-wide): 5.8B **Privately Held**
SIC: 8011 Cardiologist & cardio-vascular specialist
PA: The Ohio State University
Student Acade Servi Bldg
Columbus OH 43210
614 292-6446

(G-8352)
OHIO STATE UNIVERSITY
Also Called: Facilities Operation and Dev
2003 Millikin Rd Rm 150 (43210-1243)
PHONE....................614 292-6158
Mellisa Belleney, *Vice Pres*
EMP: 2000
SALES (corp-wide): 5.8B **Privately Held**
WEB: www.ohio-state.edu
SIC: 7629 7349 Electronic equipment repair; cleaning service, industrial or commercial
PA: The Ohio State University
Student Acade Servi Bldg
Columbus OH 43210
614 292-6446

(G-8353)
OHIO SUPPORT SERVICES CORP (PA)
1291 S High St (43206-3445)
PHONE....................614 443-0291
John W Tucker, *CEO*
Scott Tucker, *President*

EMP: 36
SQ FT: 7,000
SALES (est): 9.5MM **Privately Held**
WEB: www.ohiosupport.com
SIC: 7381 Security guard service

(G-8354)
OHIO SURGERY CENTER LTD
930 Bethel Rd (43214-1906)
PHONE................................614 451-0500
Jeffrey Hiltbrand, *Partner*
EMP: 60
SQ FT: 17,000
SALES (est): 7.9MM **Privately Held**
SIC: 8011 Ambulatory surgical center

(G-8355)
OHIO TCTCAL ENFRCMENT SVCS LLC
6100 Channingway Blvd (43232-2910)
PHONE................................614 989-9485
Jessica Walters, *Mng Member*
Rondal Davis,
Carl A Dunn,
EMP: 53
SQ FT: 800
SALES (est): 557K **Privately Held**
SIC: 7381 7382 Guard services; security systems services

(G-8356)
OHIO TECHNICAL SERVICES INC
1949 Camaro Ave (43207-1716)
PHONE................................614 372-0829
Brian Hatfield, *President*
William Lawhon, *President*
EMP: 43
SQ FT: 11,000
SALES (est): 12.2MM **Privately Held**
WEB: www.ohiotechserv.com
SIC: 1542 Commercial & office building contractors

(G-8357)
OHIO TRANSMISSION CORPORATION (HQ)
Also Called: Otp Industrial Solutions
1900 Jetway Blvd (43219-1681)
PHONE................................614 342-6247
Philip Derrow, *CEO*
David D Derrow, *Chairman*
Kurt Lang, *Exec VP*
Joe Beyer, *Vice Pres*
Kevin Kammer, *Vice Pres*
◆ EMP: 110 EST: 1963
SQ FT: 40,000
SALES (est): 493.1MM **Privately Held**
WEB: www.otpnet.com
SIC: 5085 5084 Power transmission equipment & apparatus; bearings; materials handling machinery

(G-8358)
OHIO TRANSMISSION CORPORATION
Also Called: Air Technologies
1900 Jetway Blvd (43219-1681)
PHONE................................614 342-6247
Kurt Lang, *Branch Mgr*
EMP: 33 **Privately Held**
WEB: www.otpnet.com
SIC: 7537 Automotive transmission repair shops
HQ: Ohio Transmission Corporation
    1900 Jetway Blvd
    Columbus OH 43219
    614 342-6247

(G-8359)
OHIOHEALTH CORPORATION
Also Called: Community Medicine
3595 Olentangy River Rd (43214-3440)
PHONE................................614 566-5456
John Boswell, *Manager*
EMP: 108
SALES (corp-wide): 4B **Privately Held**
WEB: www.ohiohealth.com
SIC: 8062 General medical & surgical hospitals
PA: Ohiohealth Corporation
    180 E Broad St
    Columbus OH 43215
    614 788-8860

(G-8360)
OHIOHEALTH CORPORATION
180 E Broad St (43215-3707)
P.O. Box 8 (43216-0008)
PHONE................................614 566-2124
David Blom, *Branch Mgr*
Michael Akers, *Manager*
Stephen Noftz, *Manager*
Stefani Moreland, *Supervisor*
Barbara Alenik, *Director*
EMP: 107
SALES (corp-wide): 4B **Privately Held**
SIC: 8062 General medical & surgical hospitals
PA: Ohiohealth Corporation
    180 E Broad St
    Columbus OH 43215
    614 788-8860

(G-8361)
OHIOHEALTH CORPORATION
3333 Chippewa St (43204-1654)
PHONE................................614 566-3500
Mary Jo McEllroy, *Branch Mgr*
EMP: 65
SALES (corp-wide): 4B **Privately Held**
WEB: www.ohiohealth.com
SIC: 8742 Hospital & health services consultant
PA: Ohiohealth Corporation
    180 E Broad St
    Columbus OH 43215
    614 788-8860

(G-8362)
OHIOHEALTH CORPORATION (PA)
180 E Broad St (43215-3707)
PHONE................................614 788-8860
David Blom, *President*
Earl Barnes, *Principal*
Michael W Louge, *COO*
Robert P Millen, *COO*
Michael S Bernstein, *Senior VP*
EMP: 1500
SALES: 4B **Privately Held**
WEB: www.ohiohealth.com
SIC: 8062 8082 8051 General medical & surgical hospitals; home health care services; convalescent home with continuous nursing care; extended care facility

(G-8363)
OHIOHEALTH CORPORATION
Also Called: Distrubution Center
2601 Silver Dr (43211-1056)
PHONE................................614 566-5977
Thomas Sherrin, *Director*
EMP: 60
SALES (corp-wide): 4B **Privately Held**
WEB: www.ohiohealth.com
SIC: 8062 General medical & surgical hospitals
PA: Ohiohealth Corporation
    180 E Broad St
    Columbus OH 43215
    614 788-8860

(G-8364)
OHIOHEALTH CORPORATION
Also Called: Grant Hospital
111 S Grant Ave (43215-4701)
PHONE................................614 566-9000
Bruce Hagen, *President*
Joni Ballou, *Business Mgr*
Amy Imm, *Vice Pres*
Douglas Knutson, *Vice Pres*
Anita Laterro, *Vice Pres*
EMP: 108
SALES (corp-wide): 4B **Privately Held**
WEB: www.ohiohealth.com
SIC: 8062 General medical & surgical hospitals
PA: Ohiohealth Corporation
    180 E Broad St
    Columbus OH 43215
    614 788-8860

(G-8365)
OHIOHEALTH CORPORATION
755 Thomas Ln (43214-3903)
PHONE................................614 566-4800
Sally Robinson, *General Mgr*
EMP: 200

(G-8366)
OHIOHEALTH CORPORATION
697 Thomas Ln (43214-3931)
PHONE................................614 566-5414
Sarah Grafner, *Engineer*
Gabrielle Stepter, *Med Doctor*
Henry Szabo, *Manager*
Edward T Bope, *Director*
EMP: 30
SALES (corp-wide): 4B **Privately Held**
WEB: www.ohiohealth.com
SIC: 8062 Hospital, medical school affiliated with residency
PA: Ohiohealth Corporation
    180 E Broad St
    Columbus OH 43215
    614 788-8860

(G-8367)
OHIOHEALTH RESEARCH INSTITUTE
3545 Olentangy River Rd # 328 (43214-3907)
PHONE................................614 566-4297
Jennifer Griggs, *Manager*
John Niles, *Director*
Christine Hotz, *Administration*
EMP: 40
SALES (est): 1.6MM **Privately Held**
SIC: 8062 General medical & surgical hospitals

(G-8368)
OHIOHLTH RVERSIDE METHDST HOSP
3535 Olentangy River Rd (43214-3908)
PHONE................................614 566-5000
Brian D Jepson, *President*
Steve Markovitch, *Senior VP*
James Lowder, *Technical Mgr*
Kathryn Schneider, *Nursing Mgr*
Mark Brownell, *Med Doctor*
EMP: 944 EST: 1884
SQ FT: 327,886
SALES (est): 1.2B **Privately Held**
SIC: 8062 General medical & surgical hospitals

(G-8369)
OLD DOMINION FREIGHT LINE INC
2885 Alum Creek Dr (43207-2818)
PHONE................................614 491-3903
Bill Pressler, *Manager*
EMP: 260
SALES (corp-wide): 4B **Publicly Held**
WEB: www.odfl.com
SIC: 4213 Less-than-truckload (LTL) transport
PA: Old Dominion Freight Line Inc
    500 Old Dominion Way
    Thomasville NC 27360
    336 889-5000

(G-8370)
OLD TIME POTTERY INC
2200 Morse Rd (43229-5821)
PHONE................................614 337-1258
David Sidall, *Manager*
EMP: 80
SALES (corp-wide): 691.2MM **Privately Held**
WEB: www.oldtimepottery.com
SIC: 5999 5023 Art, picture frames & decorations; home furnishings
PA: Old Time Pottery, Llc
    480 River Rock Blvd
    Murfreesboro TN 37128
    615 890-6060

(G-8371)
OLENTANGY VILLAGE ASSOCIATES
Also Called: Olentangy Village Apartments
2907 N High St (43202-1101)
PHONE................................614 515-4680

John W Kessler, *Partner*
Kerry Wintrich, *General Mgr*
Jeremy Smith, *Controller*
Michelle Fairchild, *Marketing Mgr*
EMP: 40
SQ FT: 2,100
SALES (est): 3.3MM **Privately Held**
WEB: www.olentanyvillage.com
SIC: 6513 6512 Apartment hotel operation; commercial & industrial building operation

(G-8372)
OLOGIE LLC
447 E Main St Ste 122 (43215-5661)
PHONE................................614 221-1107
Bill Faust, *Managing Prtnr*
Patricia Taylor, *Project Mgr*
Susan Cahall, *Accountant*
Jeremy Bensman, *Accounts Mgr*
Dawn Marinacci, *Mktg Dir*
EMP: 51
SALES: 12.1MM **Privately Held**
WEB: www.ologie.com
SIC: 8742 Marketing consulting services

(G-8373)
OLSHAN HOTEL MANAGEMENT INC
Also Called: Residence Inn By Marriott
3999 Easton Loop W (43219-6152)
PHONE................................614 414-1000
Tonya Thomas, *General Mgr*
Michael Gouzie, *Branch Mgr*
EMP: 36
SALES (corp-wide): 13.9MM **Privately Held**
WEB: www.hiltoncolumbus.com
SIC: 7011 Hotels & motels
HQ: Olshan Hotel Management, Inc.
    560 S Collier Blvd
    Marco Island FL 34145

(G-8374)
OLSHAN HOTEL MANAGEMENT INC
Also Called: Courtyard Easton
3900 Morse Xing (43219-6081)
PHONE................................614 416-8000
Brad Jester, *Manager*
EMP: 25
SALES (corp-wide): 13.9MM **Privately Held**
WEB: www.hiltoncolumbus.com
SIC: 7011 Resort hotel
HQ: Olshan Hotel Management, Inc.
    560 S Collier Blvd
    Marco Island FL 34145

(G-8375)
OPEN ARMS HEALTH SYSTEMS LLC
868 Freeway Dr N (43229-5420)
PHONE................................614 385-8354
Christopher Allison, *CEO*
Natalie Bartholomew, *Director*
EMP: 31
SALES (est): 1.9MM **Privately Held**
SIC: 8082 Home health care services

(G-8376)
OPEN ONLINE LLC (PA)
Also Called: Openonline
1650 Lake Shore Dr # 350 (43204-4978)
PHONE................................614 481-6999
Nick Vanoff, *CEO*
Richard Henderson, *COO*
EMP: 31
SQ FT: 4,100
SALES (est): 4.6MM **Privately Held**
SIC: 7323 Credit reporting services

(G-8377)
OPERS LEGAL DEPT
277 E Town St (43215-4642)
PHONE................................614 227-0550
Cinthia Sledz, *Principal*
EMP: 29
SALES (est): 4.4MM **Privately Held**
SIC: 8111 Legal services

(G-8378)

OPHTHLMIC SRGEONS CONS OF OHIO

262 Neil Ave Ste 430　(43215-7312)
PHONE............................614 221-7464
John Burns, *President*
Alice Epitropoulos, *Principal*
Jill Foster MD, *Principal*
David M Lehmann, *Principal*
Dr N Douglas Baker, *Treasurer*
EMP: 38
SQ FT: 14,000
SALES (est): 5.3MM　Privately Held
WEB: www.ohioeyesurgeons.com
SIC: 8011　Ophthalmologist

(G-8379)

OPPORTUNITIES FOR OHIOANS (DH)

150 E Campus View Blvd　(43235-4648)
PHONE............................614 438-1200
Christina Wendell, *Counsel*
Therese Dyer, *CFO*
Janine Salloum Ashanin, *Human Resources*
Brad Reynolds, *Commissioner*
Tim Nguyen, *CIO*
EMP: 31
SALES (est): 8.5MM　Privately Held
WEB: www.rsc.ohio.gov
SIC: 8322　Social services for the handicapped; rehabilitation services

(G-8380)

OPTIMUM TECHNOLOGY INC (PA)

Also Called: Oti
100 E Campus View Blvd # 380　(43235-4702)
PHONE............................614 785-1110
Jagdish M Davda, *President*
Frank Xavier, *Vice Pres*
Satyen S Hombali, *Director*
Savitha Narayan, *Director*
EMP: 29
SQ FT: 6,581
SALES: 8.8MM　Privately Held
SIC: 7379

(G-8381)

OPTION CARE INFUSION SVCS INC

7654 Crosswoods Dr　(43235-4621)
PHONE............................614 431-6453
Nancy Creadon, *Manager*
EMP: 30
SALES (corp-wide): 1.4B　Privately Held
SIC: 8082　Home health care services
HQ: Option Care Infusion Services, Inc.
　　3000 Lakeside Dr Ste 300n
　　Bannockburn IL 60015
　　312 940-2500

(G-8382)

OPTION LINE

665 E Dublin Granville Rd # 290　(43229-3245)
PHONE............................614 586-1380
EMP: 30
SALES (est): 412.3K　Privately Held
SIC: 8322　Individual/Family Services

(G-8383)

ORANGE BARREL MEDIA LLC

250 N Hartford Ave　(43222-1100)
PHONE............................614 294-4898
Peter Scantland, *Principal*
Adam Borchers, *CFO*
Chad Truitt, *Asst Controller*
Lauren Stephens, *Executive*
Danielle Williamson, *Executive*
EMP: 25
SALES (est): 2.5MM　Privately Held
WEB: www.orangebarrelmedia.com
SIC: 3993　7312　Signs & advertising specialties; outdoor advertising services

(G-8384)

ORCHARD HILTZ & MCCLIMENT INC

580 N 4th St Ste 610　(43215-2157)
PHONE............................614 418-0600
Gerry Bird, *Chairman*
EMP: 65

SALES (est): 3.4MM
SALES (corp-wide): 47.4MM　Privately Held
SIC: 8712　Architectural engineering
PA: Orchard, Hiltz & Mccliment, Inc.
　　34000 Plymouth Rd
　　Livonia MI 48150
　　734 522-6711

(G-8385)

ORDER OF UNITE COMMERCIAL TRA (PA)

Also Called: FRATERNAL INSURANCE
1801 Watermark Dr Ste 100　(43215-7088)
P.O. Box 159019　(43215-8619)
PHONE............................614 487-9680
Ron Hunt, *CEO*
Ron Ives, *Vice Pres*
Martha Tate Horn, *Treasurer*
Mindy Van Order, *Accountant*
EMP: 58　EST: 1888
SQ FT: 33,000
SALES: 18.4MM　Privately Held
SIC: 8641　Fraternal associations

(G-8386)

ORKIN LLC

Also Called: Orkin Pest Control 561
6230 Huntley Rd　(43229-1006)
PHONE............................614 888-5811
Bob Toledo, *Branch Mgr*
EMP: 30
SALES (corp-wide): 1.8B　Publicly Held
WEB: www.orkin.com
SIC: 7342　Exterminating & fumigating
HQ: Orkin, Llc
　　2170 Piedmont Rd Ne
　　Atlanta GA 30324
　　404 888-2000

(G-8387)

ORTHONEURO

4420 Refugee Rd　(43232-4416)
PHONE............................614 890-6555
EMP: 65
SALES (corp-wide): 25.1MM　Privately Held
SIC: 8011　8049　Offices And Clinics Of Medical Doctors, N
PA: Orthoneuro
　　70 S Cleveland Ave
　　Westerville OH 43081
　　614 839-3203

(G-8388)

ORTHONEURO

Also Called: Christopher D Cannell
1313 Olentangy River Rd　(43212-3120)
PHONE............................614 890-6555
Charles Cure, *President*
Gene Steffen, *Finance*
Steven Nash, *Neurology*
EMP: 100
SALES (corp-wide): 21.2MM　Privately Held
SIC: 8011　Neurologist; orthopedic physician
PA: Orthoneuro
　　70 S Cleveland Ave
　　Westerville OH 43081
　　614 890-6555

(G-8389)

ORTHOPEDIC ONE INC

4605 Sawmill Rd　(43220-2246)
PHONE............................614 827-8700
Tom Ellis, *President*
EMP: 90　Privately Held
SIC: 8011　Orthopedic physician; surgeon
PA: Orthopedic One, Inc.
　　170 Taylor Station Rd
　　Columbus OH 43213

(G-8390)

ORTHOPEDIC ONE INC (PA)

Also Called: Cardinal Orthopaedic Institute
170 Taylor Station Rd　(43213-4491)
PHONE............................614 545-7900
Dale Ingram, *CEO*
EMP: 58
SALES (est): 2.3MM　Privately Held
SIC: 8011　Orthopedic physician

(G-8391)

OSU EMERGENCY MEDICINE LLC

700 Ackerman Rd Ste 270　(43202-1553)
PHONE............................614 947-3700
Tammie Adkins, *Principal*
Douglas Rund,
EMP: 99
SALES (est): 4.2MM
SALES (corp-wide): 5.8B　Privately Held
SIC: 8011　Medical centers
HQ: Ohio State University Physicians, Inc.
　　700 Ackerman Rd Ste 600
　　Columbus OH 43202

(G-8392)

OSU NEPHROLOGY MEDICAL CTR

410 W 10th Ave　(43210-1240)
PHONE............................614 293-8300
Brad Rovin, *Director*
EMP: 25　EST: 1939
SALES (est): 2.3MM　Privately Held
SIC: 8062　8299　General medical & surgical hospitals; educational services

(G-8393)

OSU ORTHODONTIC CLINIC

2010 901 Woody Hayes Dr　(43210)
PHONE............................614 292-1058
Henry Fields, *Ch of Bd*
EMP: 32
SALES (est): 498.2K　Privately Held
SIC: 8021　Orthodontist

(G-8394)

OSU PATHOLOGY SERVICES LLC

1645 Neil Ave　(43210-1218)
PHONE............................614 247-6461
Daniel Sedmak, *Mng Member*
Sanford Barsky,
Amy Giwirtz,
EMP: 99
SALES (est): 4.1MM
SALES (corp-wide): 5.8B　Privately Held
SIC: 8071　Pathological laboratory
HQ: Ohio State University Physicians, Inc.
　　700 Ackerman Rd Ste 600
　　Columbus OH 43202

(G-8395)

OSU PHYSICAL MEDICINE LLC

480 Medical Center Dr # 1036　(43210-1229)
PHONE............................614 366-6398
William S Pease MD, *President*
Joyce Martin, *CFO*
EMP: 25
SALES: 950K
SALES (corp-wide): 5.8B　Privately Held
SIC: 8011　Medical centers
HQ: Ohio State University Physicians, Inc.
　　700 Ackerman Rd Ste 600
　　Columbus OH 43202

(G-8396)

OSU PSYCHIATRY LLC

700 Ackerman Rd Ste 600　(43202-1559)
PHONE............................614 794-1818
Vanessa Armentrout, *Controller*
Radu Saveanu, *Exec Dir*
EMP: 31
SALES: 950K
SALES (corp-wide): 5.8B　Privately Held
SIC: 8011　Psychiatric clinic
HQ: Ohio State University Physicians, Inc.
　　700 Ackerman Rd Ste 600
　　Columbus OH 43202

(G-8397)

OSU RADIOLOGY LLC

395 W 12th Ave　(43210-1267)
PHONE............................614 293-8315
Kevin Crofoot, *Business Mgr*
EMP: 32
SALES (est): 1.1MM
SALES (corp-wide): 5.8B　Privately Held
SIC: 8011　Radiologist
HQ: Ohio State University Physicians, Inc.
　　700 Ackerman Rd Ste 600
　　Columbus OH 43202

(G-8398)

OSU SPT MDCINE PHYSICANS INC

2835 Fred Taylor Dr　(43202-1552)
PHONE............................614 293-3600
Chris Kaeding, *Principal*
Jennifer Carter, *Sports Medicine*
EMP: 33　EST: 1994
SALES (est): 2.5MM　Privately Held
SIC: 8011　Sports medicine specialist, physician; orthopedic physician

(G-8399)

OSU SURGERY LLC

Genrl Srgry Dept OH State Univ
915 Olentangy River Rd # 2100　(43212-3154)
PHONE............................614 293-8116
Scott Melvin, *Branch Mgr*
EMP: 50
SQ FT: 3,000
SALES (corp-wide): 25MM　Privately Held
SIC: 8011　Surgeon
PA: Osu Surgery, Llc
　　700 Ackerman Rd Ste 350
　　Columbus OH 43202
　　614 261-1141

(G-8400)

OSU SURGERY LLC (PA)

700 Ackerman Rd Ste 350　(43202-1583)
PHONE............................614 261-1141
Chris Kaiser, *CFO*
E C Ellison MD,
Robert L Rubert MD,
EMP: 150
SQ FT: 6,700
SALES: 25MM　Privately Held
SIC: 8011　Surgeon

(G-8401)

OSUP COMMUNITY OUTREACH LLC

700 Ackerman Rd Ste 600　(43202-1559)
PHONE............................614 685-1542
Alisa A Schueneman,
EMP: 30
SALES (est): 1.3MM　Privately Held
SIC: 8011　Physicians' office, including specialists

(G-8402)

OTIS ELEVATOR COMPANY

777 Dearbom Park Ln L　(43085-5716)
PHONE............................614 777-6500
Tim Collins, *Manager*
EMP: 50
SALES (corp-wide): 66.5B　Publicly Held
WEB: www.otis.com
SIC: 5084　7699　Elevators; elevators: inspection, service & repair
HQ: Otis Elevator Company
　　1 Carrier Pl
　　Farmington CT 06032
　　860 674-3000

(G-8403)

OTP HOLDING LLC

Also Called: Advanced Industrial Products
1900 Jetway Blvd　(43219-1681)
PHONE............................614 342-6123
Rob Webb, *Mng Member*
EMP: 50　EST: 2014
SALES (est): 13.2MM　Privately Held
SIC: 5085　Industrial fittings
HQ: Ohio Transmission Corporation
　　1900 Jetway Blvd
　　Columbus OH 43219
　　614 342-6247

(G-8404)

OUR LADY OF BETHLEHEM SCHOOLS

4567 Olentangy River Rd　(43214-2499)
PHONE............................614 459-8285
Marilyn Dono, *Principal*
Lauren Don, *Marketing Staff*
EMP: 30
SALES (est): 1.3MM　Privately Held
WEB: www.cdeducation.org
SIC: 8211　8661　8351　Catholic elementary & secondary schools; Catholic Church; child day care services

(G-8405)
P & D TRANSPORTATION INC
Also Called: Putnam Logistics
4274 Groves Rd (43232-4103)
PHONE....................................614 577-1130
Earl Taylor, *Manager*
EMP: 30
SALES (corp-wide): 21.3MM **Privately Held**
SIC: 4213 4212 Trucking, except local; local trucking, without storage
PA: P & D Transportation, Inc.
1705 Moxahala Ave
Zanesville OH 43701
740 454-1221

(G-8406)
P C C REFRIGERATED EX INC
Also Called: PCC Transportation
2365 Performance Way (43207-2858)
PHONE....................................614 754-8929
Robert Perry Jr, *President*
EMP: 30
SQ FT: 5,000
SALES (est): 8.2MM **Privately Held**
SIC: 4213 Refrigerated products transport

(G-8407)
P E MILLER & ASSOC
1341 S Hamilton Rd (43227-1304)
P.O. Box 1898, Buckeye Lake (43008-1898)
PHONE....................................614 231-4743
Petty Miller, *President*
EMP: 80
SIC: 8082 7361 Home Health Care Services Employment Agency

(G-8408)
P E MILLER & ASSOCIATES INC
1341 S Hamilton Rd (43227-1304)
P.O. Box 1898, Buckeye Lake (43008-1898)
PHONE....................................614 231-4743
Peggy E Miller, *President*
Charles Miller, *Vice Pres*
Jonathan Miller, *Treasurer*
Harriette Blaskis, *Admin Sec*
Harriet Hill, *Admin Sec*
EMP: 100
SALES (est): 3.1MM **Privately Held**
SIC: 7363 8082 Help Supply Services Home Health Care Services

(G-8409)
PACHE MANAGEMENT COMPANY INC
5026 Dierker Rd Ofc (43220-5278)
PHONE....................................614 451-5919
Paul C Herreid, *CEO*
Dorrit Herreid, *Vice Pres*
EMP: 50
SQ FT: 1,000
SALES (est): 2.9MM **Privately Held**
WEB: www.pachemgmt.com
SIC: 6531 Real estate managers

(G-8410)
PACTIV LLC
2120 Westbelt Dr (43228-3820)
P.O. Box 28147 (43228)
PHONE....................................614 771-5400
Joe Deal, *Opers Mgr*
Lynn Morgan, *Purch Agent*
EMP: 240
SALES (corp-wide): 1MM **Privately Held**
WEB: www.pactiv.com
SIC: 2631 7389 Paperboard mills; packaging & labeling services
HQ: Pactiv Llc
1900 W Field Ct
Lake Forest IL 60045
847 482-2000

(G-8411)
PACTIV LLC
1999 Dividend Dr (43228-3849)
PHONE....................................614 777-4019
See Berger, *Manager*
EMP: 200
SALES (corp-wide): 1MM **Privately Held**
WEB: www.pactiv.com
SIC: 5199 Packaging materials

HQ: Pactiv Llc
1900 W Field Ct
Lake Forest IL 60045
847 482-2000

(G-8412)
PAGETECH LTD
951 Robinwood Ave Ste F (43213-6707)
P.O. Box 9870 (43209-0870)
PHONE....................................614 238-0518
John W Page,
EMP: 60
SQ FT: 10,000
SALES (est): 3.2MM **Privately Held**
SIC: 7812 Audio-visual program production

(G-8413)
PAIN CONTROL CONSULTANTS INC
1680 Watermark Dr 100 (43215-1034)
PHONE....................................614 430-5727
W David Leak, *President*
EMP: 30
SQ FT: 12,000
SALES (est): 1.6MM **Privately Held**
SIC: 8011 Offices & clinics of medical doctors

(G-8414)
PAIN NET INC
99 N Brice Rd Ste 270 (43213-6525)
PHONE....................................614 481-5960
W David Leak, *President*
EMP: 54
SQ FT: 25,000
SALES (est): 4.6MM **Privately Held**
SIC: 8011 8621 Offices & clinics of medical doctors; professional membership organizations

(G-8415)
PALMER VOLKEMA THOMAS INC
140 E Town St Ste 1100 (43215-5183)
PHONE....................................614 221-4400
Elizabeth Burkett, *President*
Robert Gray Palmer, *Partner*
Craig Scott, *Partner*
Warner R Thomas, *Partner*
Daniel R Volkema, *Partner*
EMP: 25
SALES (est): 2.5MM **Privately Held**
WEB: www.vt-law.com
SIC: 8111 General practice law office

(G-8416)
PALMER-DONAVIN MFG CO (PA)
3210 Centerpoint Dr (43212)
P.O. Box 2109 (43216-2109)
PHONE....................................800 652-1234
Robert J Woodward Jr, *Ch of Bd*
Ronald Calhoun, *President*
Eric Belke, *Vice Pres*
Robert J McCollow, *Vice Pres*
David Zimmerman, *Vice Pres*
▲ EMP: 129
SQ FT: 73,000
SALES (est): 242MM **Privately Held**
WEB: www.palmerdonavin.com
SIC: 5033 Roofing & siding materials

(G-8417)
PALMETTO CONSTRUCTION SVCS LLC
892 Scott St (43222-1233)
PHONE....................................614 503-7150
Don Evans, *Project Mgr*
Jerry Diodore, *Mng Member*
Catherine Mohler, *Manager*
Casey Cusack,
EMP: 36
SQ FT: 15,000
SALES: 22MM **Privately Held**
SIC: 1541 1542 Industrial buildings, new construction; commercial & office building contractors

(G-8418)
PANACEA PRODUCTS CORPORATION (PA)
Also Called: J-Mak Industries
2711 International St (43228-4604)
PHONE....................................614 850-7000
Frank A Paniccia, *President*
Louis Calderone, *Principal*

Fred Pagura, *Principal*
Jim Fancelli, *Vice Pres*
Gregg Paniccia, *Vice Pres*
◆ EMP: 40
SALES (est): 45.2MM **Privately Held**
WEB: www.panac.com
SIC: 5051 2542 3496 Metals service centers & offices; partitions & fixtures, except wood; shelving, office & store: except wood; miscellaneous fabricated wire products; shelving, made from purchased wire

(G-8419)
PAPPAS LEAH
41 S High St Fl 12 (43215-3406)
PHONE....................................614 621-7007
Leah Pappas, *Owner*
EMP: 25
SALES (est): 646.2K **Privately Held**
SIC: 8111 Legal services

(G-8420)
PARK NATIONAL BANK
140 E Town St Ste 1400 (43215-5114)
PHONE....................................614 228-0063
Ralph Root, *Branch Mgr*
EMP: 25
SALES (corp-wide): 411.9MM **Publicly Held**
WEB: www.parknationalbank.com
SIC: 6021 National commercial banks
HQ: The Park National Bank
50 N 3rd St
Newark OH 43055
740 349-8451

(G-8421)
PARKER-HANNIFIN CORPORATION
Also Called: Tube Fittings Division
3885 Gateway Blvd (43228-9723)
PHONE....................................614 279-7070
Wendy Moore, *Safety Mgr*
Richard Gulley, *Sales Mgr*
William Bowman, *Branch Mgr*
Joe Pfister, *Manager*
Todd Ulshafer, *Technical Staff*
EMP: 120
SALES (corp-wide): 14.3B **Publicly Held**
WEB: www.parker.com
SIC: 3494 5074 Pipe fittings; plumbing fittings & supplies
PA: Parker-Hannifin Corporation
6035 Parkland Blvd
Cleveland OH 44124
216 896-3000

(G-8422)
PARKING SOLUTIONS INC (HQ)
Also Called: Parking Sltions For Healthcare
353 W Nationwide Blvd (43215-2311)
P.O. Box 906, New Albany (43054-0906)
PHONE....................................614 469-7000
Aaron D Shocket, *President*
EMP: 600
SALES (est): 21.7MM
SALES (corp-wide): 566.6MM **Privately Held**
WEB: www.parkingsolutionsinc.com
SIC: 7299 Valet parking
PA: Towne Park, Llc
1 Park Pl Ste 200
Annapolis MD 21401
410 267-6111

(G-8423)
PARKOPS COLUMBUS LLC
56 E Long St (43215-2911)
PHONE....................................877 499-9155
Joe Furnl, *Mng Member*
EMP: 500
SALES: 7.5MM **Privately Held**
SIC: 8741 Management services

(G-8424)
PARMAN GROUP INC (PA)
4501 Hilton Corporate Dr (43232-4154)
P.O. Box 360687 (43236-0687)
PHONE....................................513 673-0077
Jamie L Parman, *President*
EMP: 50
SQ FT: 22,000
SALES (est): 2.6MM **Privately Held**
SIC: 8742 Compensation & benefits planning consultant

(G-8425)
PATIENT ACCOUNT MGT SVCS LLC
950 Taylor Station Rd I (43230-6670)
PHONE....................................614 575-0044
Jess Ellerdrock, *Manager*
EMP: 25
SALES (est): 1MM
SALES (corp-wide): 208.3B **Publicly Held**
WEB: www.per-se.com
SIC: 8742 Hospital & health services consultant
HQ: Change Healthcare Technologies, Llc
5995 Windward Pkwy
Alpharetta GA 30005

(G-8426)
PATRICK MAHONEY
Also Called: Physical Thrapy Consulting Svc
1223 Neil Ave (43201-3119)
PHONE....................................614 292-5766
Patrick Mahoney, *Owner*
Dena J Gost, *Psychiatry*
EMP: 40
SALES (est): 2MM **Privately Held**
WEB: www.patrickmahoney.com
SIC: 8742 Personnel management consultant

(G-8427)
PAUL PETERSON COMPANY (PA)
950 Dublin Rd (43215-1169)
P.O. Box 1510 (43216-1510)
PHONE....................................614 486-4375
Paul Peterson Jr, *CEO*
Parr Peterson, *President*
Andrew J White Jr, *Principal*
Richard L Miller, *Principal*
Grant S Richards, *Principal*
EMP: 47
SALES (est): 13.7MM **Privately Held**
WEB: www.ppco.net
SIC: 1611 1799 3669 5084 Guardrail construction; highways; highway & street sign installation; waterproofing; traffic signals, electric; safety equipment; work zone traffic equipment (flags, cones, barrels, etc.)

(G-8428)
PAUL PETERSON SAFETY DIV INC
950 Dublin Rd (43215-1169)
P.O. Box 1510 (43216-1510)
PHONE....................................614 486-4375
Paul Peterson Jr, *President*
Colette Peterson, *Corp Secy*
Gary Boylan, *Vice Pres*
Parr Peterson, *Vice Pres*
EMP: 30
SQ FT: 3,800
SALES (est): 180.7K
SALES (corp-wide): 13.7MM **Privately Held**
WEB: www.ppco.net
SIC: 3993 5999 7359 Signs, not made in custom sign painting shops; safety supplies & equipment; work zone traffic equipment (flags, cones, barrels, etc.)
PA: The Paul Peterson Company
950 Dublin Rd
Columbus OH 43215
614 486-4375

(G-8429)
PAUL WERTH ASSOCIATES INC (PA)
10 N High St Ste 300 (43215-3497)
PHONE....................................614 224-8114
Sandra W Harbrecht, *President*
Carl West, *CFO*
Margaret Werth, *Treasurer*
EMP: 28
SALES: 5.8MM **Privately Held**
WEB: www.paulwerth.com
SIC: 8743 7319 Public relations & publicity; transit advertising services

(G-8430)
PCA-CORRECTIONS LLC
Also Called: Choice Pharmacy Services
4014 Venture Ct (43228-9600)
PHONE....................................614 297-8244

GEOGRAPHIC

Connie O'Connell, *Branch Mgr*
EMP: 50
SALES (est): 5.4MM **Privately Held**
SIC: 5122 Pharmaceuticals
PA: Pca-Corrections, Llc
　　2701 Chestnut Station Ct
　　Louisville KY 40299

(G-8431)
PEABODY LANDSCAPE CNSTR INC
Also Called: Peabody Landscape Group
2253 Dublin Rd (43228-9629)
PHONE......................614 488-2877
David G Peabody, *President*
Mary Muszynski, *Controller*
Dave Smith, *Sales Staff*
Jonathan Murray, *Manager*
Justina Stevens, *Administration*
EMP: 64
SQ FT: 2,000
SALES (est): 11.4MM **Privately Held**
WEB: www.peabodylandscape.com
SIC: 0782 Landscape contractors

(G-8432)
PEARL INTERACTIVE NETWORK INC
1103 Schrock Rd Ste 109 (43229-1177)
PHONE......................614 258-2943
Merry Korn, *CEO*
Diane Schrimpf, *Vice Pres*
David Logan, *CFO*
Melissa Metzger, *Director*
Cari Moisan, *Executive Asst*
EMP: 350
SALES (est): 21.3MM **Privately Held**
WEB: www.pearlinter.org
SIC: 7361 4813 Employment agencies; voice telephone communications

(G-8433)
PECO II INC
7060 Huntley Rd (43229-1082)
PHONE......................614 431-0694
Rich Powell, *Opers Mgr*
EMP: 55
SALES (corp-wide): 121.6B **Publicly Held**
WEB: www.peco2.com
SIC: 3661 8711 7372 3822 Telephone & telegraph apparatus; engineering services; prepackaged software; auto controls regulating residntl & coml environmt & applncs; relays & industrial controls
HQ: Peco Ii, Inc.
　　601 Shiloh Rd
　　Plano TX 75074
　　972 284-8449

(G-8434)
PEDERSEN INSULATION COMPANY
2901 Johnstown Rd (43219-1719)
P.O. Box 30744 (43230-0744)
PHONE......................614 471-3788
Gregory Pedersen, *President*
Jared Goodsite, *Vice Pres*
Valerie Pedersen, *Admin Sec*
EMP: 40 **EST:** 1963
SQ FT: 7,200
SALES (est): 4.8MM **Privately Held**
SIC: 1742 1799 Insulation, buildings; asbestos removal & encapsulation

(G-8435)
PEDIATRIC ASSOCIATES INC (PA)
1021 Country Club Rd A (43213-2484)
PHONE......................614 501-7337
Malcolm Robbins MD, *President*
William Fernald MD, *Corp Secy*
Sandra Boyle MD, *Vice Pres*
Anne Croft MD, *Vice Pres*
Tracy Hale, *Human Resources*
EMP: 44
SQ FT: 3,000
SALES (est): 9.5MM **Privately Held**
SIC: 8011 Pediatrician

(G-8436)
PENSKE TRUCK LEASING CO LP
2470 Westbelt Dr (43228-3825)
PHONE......................614 658-0000

Scott Stankovich, *Sales Staff*
Dennis Day, *Manager*
EMP: 50
SQ FT: 22,480
SALES (corp-wide): 2.6B **Privately Held**
WEB: www.pensketruckleasing.com
SIC: 7513 Truck leasing, without drivers
PA: Penske Truck Leasing Co., L.P.
　　2675 Morgantown Rd
　　Reading PA 19607
　　610 775-6000

(G-8437)
PEOPLE TO MY SITE LLC
Also Called: People To Site
580 N 4th St Ste 500 (43215-2158)
PHONE......................614 452-8179
Tood Swicker, *Mng Member*
EMP: 49
SALES (est): 5.9MM **Privately Held**
WEB: www.i16y.net
SIC: 7311 Advertising agencies

(G-8438)
PEP BOYS - MANNY MOE & JACK
2830 S Hamilton Rd (43232-4906)
PHONE......................614 864-2092
Greg Miller, *Manager*
EMP: 30
SQ FT: 22,400
SALES (corp-wide): 11.7B **Publicly Held**
SIC: 5531 7538 Automotive parts; general automotive repair shops
HQ: Pep Boys - Manny, Moe & Jack Of Delaware, Inc
　　3111 W Allegheny Ave
　　Philadelphia PA 19132

(G-8439)
PERKFECT DESIGN SOLUTIONS
308 E 9th Ave (43201-2207)
PHONE......................614 778-3560
Bert Perkins III, *Principal*
EMP: 25
SALES (est): 1.2MM **Privately Held**
SIC: 8712 Architectural services

(G-8440)
PERRY CONTRACT SERVICES INC
2319 Scioto Harper Dr (43204-3495)
PHONE......................614 274-4350
Anthony Perry, *President*
Liz Perry, *General Mgr*
EMP: 60
SALES (est): 1.5MM **Privately Held**
SIC: 7349 Janitorial service, contract basis; window cleaning

(G-8441)
PERSONAL SERVICE INSURANCE CO
2760 Airport Dr Ste 130 (43219-2294)
P.O. Box 105021, Atlanta GA (30348-5021)
PHONE......................800 282-9416
William Lockhorn, *President*
EMP: 380
SQ FT: 10,000
SALES (est): 89MM **Privately Held**
WEB: www.personalserviceinsurance.com
SIC: 6331 Property damage insurance; fire, marine & casualty insurance & carriers; automobile insurance

(G-8442)
PERSONAL TOUCH HM CARE IPA INC
454 E Main St Ste 227 (43215-5372)
PHONE......................614 227-6952
Patti Malm, *Manager*
EMP: 51
SALES (corp-wide): 363MM **Privately Held**
WEB: www.pthomecare.com
SIC: 8082 Home health care services
PA: Personal Touch Home Care Ipa, Inc.
　　1985 Marcus Ave Ste 202
　　New Hyde Park NY 11042
　　718 468-4747

(G-8443)
PETSMART INC
3713 Easton Market (43219-6023)
PHONE......................614 418-9389

Craig Samet, *Manager*
EMP: 55
SALES (corp-wide): 12.1B **Privately Held**
WEB: www.petsmart.com
SIC: 5999 0752 0742 Pet food; pet supplies; grooming services, pet & animal specialties; veterinary services, specialties
HQ: Petsmart, Inc.
　　19601 N 27th Ave
　　Phoenix AZ 85027
　　623 580-6100

(G-8444)
PHANTOM TECHNICAL SERVICES INC
111 Outerbelt St (43213-1548)
PHONE......................614 868-9920
William A Yates Jr, *President*
EMP: 30
SQ FT: 7,500
SALES (est): 2MM **Privately Held**
WEB: www.phantomtechnical.com
SIC: 8711 Electrical or electronic engineering; mechanical engineering

(G-8445)
PHINNEY INDUSTRIAL ROOFING
700 Hadley Dr (43228-1030)
PHONE......................614 308-9000
Mike Phinney, *President*
Kathey Phinney, *Vice Pres*
Thad Nelson, *Project Mgr*
▼ **EMP:** 65
SQ FT: 20,000
SALES (est): 16.1MM **Privately Held**
WEB: www.phinneyindustrial.com
SIC: 1761 Roofing contractor; sheet metal work

(G-8446)
PIERCE CLEANERS INC
5205 N High St (43214-1201)
P.O. Box 14371 (43214-0371)
PHONE......................614 888-4225
Robert Pierce, *President*
Diane Landauer, *Treasurer*
EMP: 29
SALES (est): 1.4MM **Privately Held**
SIC: 7216 Drycleaning collecting & distributing agency

(G-8447)
PILOT DOGS INCORPORATED
625 W Town St (43215-4496)
PHONE......................614 221-6367
James G Langford, *Vice Pres*
Ben Zox, *Treasurer*
J Jay Gray, *Exec Dir*
J Gray, *Exec Dir*
Pam Miller, *Director*
EMP: 26
SQ FT: 7,000
SALES: 2.5MM **Privately Held**
WEB: www.pilotdogs.org
SIC: 8399 Health systems agency

(G-8448)
PIONEER NORTH AMERICA INC
Also Called: Pioneer Communications America
2161 Dividend Dr (43228-3805)
PHONE......................614 771-1050
EMP: 45
SALES (corp-wide): 3.4B **Privately Held**
SIC: 4841 Cable/Pay Television Service
HQ: Pioneer North America, Inc.
　　2050 W 190th St Ste 100
　　Torrance CA 90504
　　310 952-2000

(G-8449)
PIZZUTI BUILDERS LLC
2 Miranova Pl Ste 800 (43215-3719)
PHONE......................614 280-4000
Ronald Pizzuti,
Richard Daley,
EMP: 40
SQ FT: 16,000
SALES (est): 2.5MM **Privately Held**
SIC: 6552 Subdividers & developers

(G-8450)
PIZZUTI INC (PA)
629 N High St 500 (43215-2025)
PHONE......................614 280-4000

Ronald A Pizzuti, *CEO*
Joel S Pizzuti, *President*
James S Russell, *COO*
Michael A Chivini, *Exec VP*
Jim Russell, *Exec VP*
EMP: 50
SQ FT: 12,000
SALES (est): 49.1MM **Privately Held**
WEB: www.twomiranovaplace.com
SIC: 6552 6531 Subdividers & developers; real estate managers; rental agent, real estate

(G-8451)
PLANES MVG & STOR CO COLUMBUS
2000 Dividend Dr (43228-3847)
PHONE......................614 777-9090
John J Planes, *CEO*
John Sabatalo, *President*
Jim Reed, *Warehouse Mgr*
Raymond Gundrum, *Treasurer*
Mark Geis, *Controller*
EMP: 51
SQ FT: 75,000
SALES: 10.1MM **Privately Held**
SIC: 4213 4214 Household goods transport; local trucking with storage

(G-8452)
PLANNED PRENTHOOD GREATER OHIO (PA)
206 E State St (43215-4311)
PHONE......................614 224-2235
Stephanie Kight, *CEO*
Lillian Williams, *Principal*
EMP: 30
SALES: 20.7MM **Privately Held**
SIC: 8093 Family planning clinic

(G-8453)
PLATINUM PRESTIGE PROPERTY
4120 Beechbank Rd (43213-2378)
PHONE......................614 705-2251
Delmar Williams, *Principal*
K E Williams, *Principal*
Kchina Williams, *Principal*
Kvontae Williams, *Principal*
EMP: 26
SALES (est): 421.5K **Privately Held**
SIC: 7389

(G-8454)
PLAYTIME PRESCHOOL LLC
1030 Alum Creek Dr (43209-2701)
PHONE......................614 975-1005
Elisabeth Lawson, *Mng Member*
Kelly Lawson,
EMP: 25
SQ FT: 10,000
SALES: 1.2MM **Privately Held**
SIC: 8351 Preschool center

(G-8455)
PLAZA PROPERTIES INC (PA)
Also Called: Bexley Plaza Apartments
3016 Maryland Ave (43209-1591)
P.O. Box 9601 (43209-0601)
PHONE......................614 237-3726
Larry Ruben, *Ch of Bd*
Bernard R Ruben, *Ch of Bd*
Lawrence G Ruben, *President*
Florine C Ruben, *Vice Pres*
Erica Brown, *Human Resources*
EMP: 50
SQ FT: 5,000
SALES (est): 11.3MM **Privately Held**
WEB: www.plazaproperties.com
SIC: 6513 6531 Apartment building operators; real estate managers

(G-8456)
POTTERY BARN INC
3945 Easton Square Pl W H-1 (43219-6072)
PHONE......................614 478-3154
Jean Gilbert, *General Mgr*
EMP: 25
SALES (corp-wide): 5.6B **Publicly Held**
WEB: www.potterybarn.com
SIC: 5719 5023 Kitchenware; kitchenware

▲ = Import ▼=Export
◆ =Import/Export

HQ: Pottery Barn, Inc.
3250 Van Ness Ave
San Francisco CA 94109
415 421-7900

(G-8457)
POWER DISTRIBUTORS LLC (PA)
Also Called: Central Power Systems
3700 Paragon Dr (43228-9750)
PHONE.....................614 876-3533
Matthew Finn, *President*
Tim Snell, *Manager*
▲ EMP: 92
SALES (est): 108.6MM Privately Held
SIC: 5084 3524 Engines & parts, air-cooled; lawn & garden equipment; lawn & garden tractors & equipment

(G-8458)
PREMIER BROADCASTING CO INC
Also Called: Massey's Pizza
5310 E Main St Ste 101 (43213-2598)
PHONE.....................614 866-0700
David Pallone, *President*
James Pallone, *Corp Secy*
EMP: 35
SQ FT: 1,200
SALES: 4MM Privately Held
SIC: 5812 6794 Pizza restaurants; franchises, selling or licensing

(G-8459)
PREMIERFIRST HOME HEALTH CARE
3033 Sullivant Ave (43204-2424)
PHONE.....................614 443-3110
Tim Smith, *Administration*
EMP: 35
SQ FT: 1,200
SALES (est): 1.3MM Privately Held
SIC: 8082 Home health care services

(G-8460)
PREVENT BLINDNESS - OHIO
1500 W 3rd Ave Ste 200 (43212-2817)
PHONE.....................614 464-2020
Sherill K Williams, *President*
EMP: 26
SQ FT: 4,016
SALES: 1.9MM Privately Held
SIC: 8399 Health systems agency

(G-8461)
PRICEWATERHOUSECOOPERS LLP
41 S High St Ste 25 (43215-6113)
PHONE.....................614 225-8700
Carrie L Clay, *Partner*
Jim Robbins, *Branch Mgr*
Jessica Blosser, *Manager*
Jesse Claypool, *Associate*
EMP: 200
SALES (corp-wide): 7.8B Privately Held
WEB: www.pwcglobal.com
SIC: 8721 Certified public accountant
PA: Pricewaterhousecoopers Llp
300 Madison Ave Fl 24
New York NY 10017
646 471-4000

(G-8462)
PRIMATECH INC (PA)
50 Northwoods Blvd Ste A (43235-4717)
PHONE.....................614 841-9800
Paul Baybutt, *President*
Daniel J Pissini, *Vice Pres*
Steven Baybutt, *Opers Mgr*
Shawn Ansbro, *Engineer*
EMP: 30
SQ FT: 3,500
SALES: 3.8MM Privately Held
WEB: www.primatech.com
SIC: 8748 7371 8711 Systems engineering consultant, ex. computer or professional; computer software systems analysis & design, custom; professional engineer

(G-8463)
PRIORITY DESIGNS INC
100 S Hamilton Rd (43213-2013)
PHONE.....................614 337-9979
Paul Kolada, *President*

Lois Kolada, *Corp Secy*
Ryan Crisp, *COO*
Laura Alexander, *Engineer*
Don Meves, *Engineer*
EMP: 55
SQ FT: 55,000
SALES (est): 6.9MM Privately Held
WEB: www.prioritydesigns.com
SIC: 7389 Design, commercial & industrial

(G-8464)
PRN NURSE INC
Also Called: Health Care Personnel
6161 Radekin Rd (43232-2921)
PHONE.....................614 864-9292
Sandra K Shane, *President*
EMP: 300
SALES: 3.1MM Privately Held
SIC: 7363 7361 Medical help service; employment agencies

(G-8465)
PRO-TOUCH INC
721 N Rose Ave (43219-2522)
PHONE.....................614 586-0303
Nancy Brugler, *CEO*
Douglas Brugler, *President*
EMP: 150
SQ FT: 6,500
SALES: 2.2MM Privately Held
WEB: www.pro-touchinc.com
SIC: 7349 5087 Janitorial service, contract basis; janitors' supplies

(G-8466)
PRO-TOW INC
1669 Harmon Ave (43223-3320)
PHONE.....................614 444-8697
James Whittredge, *President*
EMP: 25
SQ FT: 5,000
SALES (est): 2.2MM Privately Held
SIC: 7549 Towing services

(G-8467)
PROFESSIONAL DRIVERS GA INC
Also Called: Prodrivers
4251 Diplomacy Dr (43228-3803)
P.O. Box 102409, Atlanta GA (30368-2409)
PHONE.....................614 529-8282
Patricia Neoson, *Branch Mgr*
EMP: 31
SALES (corp-wide): 577.1MM Privately Held
SIC: 4212 Truck rental with drivers
HQ: Professional Drivers Of Georgia, Inc.
1040 Crown Pointe Pkwy
Atlanta GA 30338

(G-8468)
PROFESSIONAL INVESTIGATING (PA)
Also Called: Pica
551 S 3rd St (43215-5721)
PHONE.....................614 228-7422
Vince Volpi Jr, *CEO*
Vincent Volpi, *President*
Rudy Diaz, *COO*
Simon Cheetham, *Vice Pres*
Joseph Reisinger, *Vice Pres*
EMP: 100
SQ FT: 2,000
SALES (est): 3MM Privately Held
WEB: www.pica.net
SIC: 7381 Private investigator

(G-8469)
PROFESSIONAL MAINT OF COLUMBUS
541 Stimmel Rd (43223-2901)
PHONE.....................614 443-6528
Eldon L Hall, *Ch of Bd*
Dale Barnette, *President*
Eldon Hall Jr, *Vice Pres*
Robert L White, *Vice Pres*
EMP: 190
SQ FT: 9,500
SALES (est): 5.1MM Privately Held
SIC: 7349 Janitorial service, contract basis

(G-8470)
PROFESSIONAL SERVICE INDS INC
Also Called: Professional Service Inds
4960 Vulcan Ave Ste C (43228-9614)
PHONE.....................614 876-8000
Cathy Brandi, *Principal*
Charles Helm, *Principal*
Paul Hundley, *Business Mgr*
Matthew Decker, *Safety Mgr*
Michael Mazzoli, *Manager*
EMP: 25
SALES (corp-wide): 3.6B Privately Held
SIC: 8711 8734 Consulting engineer; testing laboratories
HQ: Professional Service Industries, Inc.
545 E Algonquin Rd
Arlington Heights IL 60005
630 691-1490

(G-8471)
PROFESSIONALS FOR WOMENS HLTH (PA)
921 Jasonway Ave Ste B (43214-2456)
PHONE.....................614 268-8800
Kevin Hacket MD, *Owner*
Kevin Hackett MD, *Owner*
Ann Wurst MD, *Co-Owner*
EMP: 35
SQ FT: 10,000
SALES (est): 6.5MM Privately Held
WEB: www.pwhealth.com
SIC: 8011 Gynecologist

(G-8472)
PROLOGUE RESEARCH INTL INC
580 N 4th St Ste 270 (43215-2158)
PHONE.....................614 324-1500
Tom Ludlam Jr, *President*
Kathleen Zajd, *Senior VP*
EMP: 60
SQ FT: 12,443
SALES (est): 3.8MM Publicly Held
WEB: www.procro.com
SIC: 8733 Medical research
HQ: Novella Clinical Inc.
1700 Perimeter Park Dr
Morrisville NC 27560
919 484-1921

(G-8473)
PROSPERITY CARE SERVICE
2021 Dublin Rd (43228)
PHONE.....................614 430-8626
Sallamadou Bangoura, *President*
EMP: 40
SALES (est): 1.1MM Privately Held
SIC: 8099 Medical services organization

(G-8474)
PROVIDENCE REES INC
2111 Builders Pl (43204-4886)
P.O. Box 12535 (43212-0535)
PHONE.....................614 833-6231
Leo Steger, *Corp Secy*
Billy Parsley, *Corp Secy*
Lee Nichols, *Production*
EMP: 35
SQ FT: 36,000
SALES: 4.7MM Privately Held
SIC: 3496 8711 Wire winding; engineering services

(G-8475)
PROVIDER PHYSICIANS INC
Also Called: Physician Providers North
6096 E Main St Ste 112 (43213-4302)
PHONE.....................614 755-3000
Dr Charles Block, *President*
Miller J Sullivan Jr, *Pediatrics*
EMP: 63
SALES (est): 3.3MM Privately Held
SIC: 8011 Surgeon; general & family practice, physician/surgeon

(G-8476)
PROVIDER SERVICES INC
Also Called: High Banks Care Centre
111 Lazelle Rd (43235-1419)
PHONE.....................614 888-2021
Aimee Palmer, *Manager*
Paula Bourne, *Administration*
EMP: 75

SALES (est): 1.7MM Privately Held
SIC: 8399 8059 Social change association; convalescent home

(G-8477)
PSC METALS INC
1283 Joyce Ave (43219-2134)
PHONE.....................614 299-4175
Kevin Ringle, *Manager*
EMP: 38
SALES (corp-wide): 11.7B Publicly Held
SIC: 5093 Metal scrap & waste materials
HQ: Psc Metals, Llc
5875 Landerbrook Dr # 200
Mayfield Heights OH 44124
440 753-5400

(G-8478)
PUBLIC SAFETY OHIO DEPARTMENT
Also Called: Licensing Section
1970 W Broad St (43223-1102)
P.O. Box 16520 (43216-6520)
PHONE.....................614 752-7600
James Chisman, *Branch Mgr*
EMP: 1100 Privately Held
SIC: 7299 9621 Personal document & information services; motor vehicle licensing & inspection office, government
HQ: Ohio Department Of Public Safety
1970 W Broad St Fl 5
Columbus OH 43223

(G-8479)
PUBLIC SERVICE COMPANY OKLA (HQ)
Also Called: AEP
1 Riverside Plz (43215-2355)
PHONE.....................614 716-1000
Nicholas K Akins, *CEO*
Tommy Slater, *Vice Pres*
Jason Pound, *Buyer*
Brian X Tierney, *CFO*
Lynn Becker, *Director*
EMP: 170
SALES: 1.5B
SALES (corp-wide): 16.2B Publicly Held
WEB: www.psoklahoma.com
SIC: 4911 Distribution, electric power
PA: American Electric Power Company, Inc.
1 Riverside Plz Fl 1 # 1
Columbus OH 43215
614 716-1000

(G-8480)
QUALITY ASSURED CLEANING INC
6407 Nicholas Dr (43235-5204)
P.O. Box 1250, Powell (43065-1250)
PHONE.....................614 798-1505
Eric Hassen, *Vice Pres*
EMP: 99
SALES (est): 4.1MM Privately Held
SIC: 7349 Janitorial service, contract basis

(G-8481)
QUANTUM HEALTH INC
7450 Huntington Park Dr (43235-5617)
PHONE.....................614 846-4318
Kara J Trott, *CEO*
Randy Gebhardt, *President*
Shannon Skaggs, *President*
Ryan Whiteleather, *President*
Amy Crowell, *Exec VP*
EMP: 99
SQ FT: 25,000
SALES (est): 13.8MM Privately Held
WEB: www.qh-quantum.com
SIC: 8082 Home health care services

(G-8482)
QUINCY MALL INC (PA)
191 W Nationwide Blvd # 200 (43215-2568)
PHONE.....................614 228-5331
Don M Casto III, *President*
Frank S Benson III, *Vice Pres*
EMP: 25
SQ FT: 1,500
SALES (est): 1.3MM Privately Held
WEB: www.cullprop.com
SIC: 6512 Shopping center, property operation only

(G-8483)
RACKSQUARED LLC
325 E Spring St (43215-2629)
PHONE..........................614 737-8812
Brad Wasserstrom, *President*
Brad Wasferstrom, *President*
Phil Smith, *COO*
Gary Mangelson, *CFO*
Carl Miller, *Director*
EMP: 28
SQ FT: 10,000
SALES: 3MM **Privately Held**
SIC: 7374 8742 Data processing & preparation; business consultant

(G-8484)
RADIOHIO INCORPORATED
Also Called: Wbns-AM Sports Radio 1460 Fan
605 S Front St Fl 3 (43215-5198)
PHONE..........................614 460-3850
John F Wolfe, *Ch of Bd*
Jeanine Porter, *Traffic Mgr*
Todd Pitt, *Sales Mgr*
Armando Di Bernardo, *Accounts Mgr*
Heather Labelle, *Sales Staff*
EMP: 75
SQ FT: 24,000
SALES (est): 6.5MM **Privately Held**
WEB: www.radiohio.com
SIC: 4832 Radio broadcasting stations

(G-8485)
RAINBOW EXPRESS INC (PA)
2000 S High St Fl 2 (43207-2425)
PHONE..........................614 444-5600
Bart A Snow, *President*
Kristen Snow, *Vice Pres*
EMP: 100
SQ FT: 35,000
SALES (est): 5.4MM **Privately Held**
WEB: www.rainbowexpressinc.com
SIC: 4212 4214 4213 Delivery service, vehicular; local trucking with storage; trucking, except local

(G-8486)
RAINBOW FLEA MARKET INC (PA)
Also Called: Livinginston Court Flea Market
865 King Ave (43212-2653)
PHONE..........................614 291-3133
Solly L Yassenoff, *President*
Karen Yassenoff, *Admin Sec*
EMP: 30
SQ FT: 5,000
SALES (est): 1.4MM **Privately Held**
SIC: 7389 Flea market

(G-8487)
RAINBOW LANES INC
Also Called: Rainbow Bowling Lanes
3224 S High St (43207-3695)
PHONE..........................614 491-7155
Bob McCracken, *President*
EMP: 30 EST: 1959
SQ FT: 45,000
SALES (est): 608K **Privately Held**
WEB: www.rainbowbowling.com
SIC: 7933 5813 Ten pin center; cocktail lounge

(G-8488)
RAMA INC
Also Called: Staybrdge Sites Columbus Arprt
2890 Airport Dr (43219-2240)
PHONE..........................614 473-9888
Bill Patel, *President*
EMP: 25
SALES (est): 1.8MM **Privately Held**
WEB: www.wm.staybridge.com
SIC: 7011 Hotel, franchised

(G-8489)
RANDOLPH AND ASSOCIATES RE
Also Called: Randolph & Assoc Real Estate
239 Buttonwood Ct (43230-6229)
PHONE..........................614 269-8418
Kevin Randolph, *President*
EMP: 30
SQ FT: 1,100
SALES (est): 1.6MM **Privately Held**
SIC: 6531 Real estate brokers & agents

(G-8490)
RAYMOND RECEPTON HOUSE
3860 Trabue Rd (43228-9559)
PHONE..........................614 276-6127
Stefanie Green, *Principal*
EMP: 30 EST: 2010
SALES (est): 297.2K **Privately Held**
SIC: 7299 Banquet hall facilities

(G-8491)
RBP ATLANTA LLC
4100 Regent St Ste G (43219-6160)
PHONE..........................614 246-2522
James Merkel,
EMP: 87 EST: 2011
SALES (est): 8.8MM
SALES (corp-wide): 48.8MM **Privately Held**
SIC: 8741 Hotel or motel management
PA: Rockbridge Capital, Llc
4100 Regent St Ste G
Columbus OH 43219
614 246-2400

(G-8492)
RCS ENTERPRISES INC
Also Called: Next Generation
139 W Johnstown Rd (43230-2700)
P.O. Box 30979 (43230-0979)
PHONE..........................614 337-8520
Larry Dempsey, *President*
EMP: 70
SALES (est): 2MM **Privately Held**
WEB: www.rpigraphic.com
SIC: 7349 Office cleaning or charring

(G-8493)
RCWC COL INC
Also Called: Bar 145
955 W 5th Ave Ste 7 (43212-2635)
PHONE..........................614 564-9344
Jeremy Fitzgerald, *President*
Johnny Runckel, *General Mgr*
EMP: 60
SALES (est): 653K **Privately Held**
SIC: 5812 7929 Eating places; entertainment service

(G-8494)
REAL ESTATE INVESTORS MGT INC (PA)
Also Called: Chimney Hill Apartments
4041 Roberts Rd (43228-9536)
PHONE..........................614 777-2444
Herm Gelliand, *President*
EMP: 25
SALES (est): 1.2MM **Privately Held**
SIC: 6513 Operator Of Apartment Buildings

(G-8495)
REAL LIVING TITLE AGENCY LTD (PA)
77 E Nationwide Blvd (43215-2512)
PHONE..........................614 459-7400
Dan Riley, *President*
EMP: 60
SALES (est): 24.2MM **Privately Held**
SIC: 6541 6531 Title search companies; escrow agent, real estate

(G-8496)
RECOVERY ONE LLC
3240 Henderson Rd Ste A (43220-2300)
PHONE..........................614 336-4207
Steve Jones, *Manager*
Shelly Kallon, *Manager*
Albert F Cameron III,
EMP: 67
SALES (est): 5.5MM **Privately Held**
SIC: 7322 8111 Collection agency, except real estate; legal services

(G-8497)
RED CAPITAL MARKETS LLC
10 W Broad St Ste 1800 (43215-3420)
PHONE..........................614 857-1400
James Croft, *CEO*
James Murphy, *President*
Andrew Steiner, *Vice Pres*
EMP: 234

SALES (est): 25.5MM
SALES (corp-wide): 19.9B **Publicly Held**
WEB: www.allegiantbank.com
SIC: 6211 Investment firm, general brokerage
HQ: Pnc Bank, National Association
222 Delaware Ave
Wilmington DE 19801
877 762-2000

(G-8498)
RED CAPITAL PARTNERS LLC (DH)
Also Called: Red Capital Advisors
10 W Broad St Fl 8 (43215-3418)
PHONE..........................614 857-1400
Ted Meylor, *CEO*
EMP: 75
SALES (est): 38.5MM
SALES (corp-wide): 26.8B **Privately Held**
WEB: www.redcapitalgroup.com
SIC: 6282 Investment advisory service
HQ: Red Capital Group Llc
10 W Broad St Fl 8
Columbus OH 43215
614 857-1400

(G-8499)
RED MORTGAGE CAPITAL LLC (DH)
10 W Broad St Ste 1800 (43215-3420)
PHONE..........................614 857-1400
Edward Meylor, *CEO*
Trent Brooks, *President*
Kathryn Burton Gray, *Director*
Scott Griffin, *Director*
Trever Smith, *Director*
EMP: 49
SALES (est): 34.7MM
SALES (corp-wide): 26.8B **Privately Held**
WEB: www.allegiantbank.com
SIC: 6162 Mortgage brokers, using own money
HQ: Red Capital Group Llc
10 W Broad St Fl 8
Columbus OH 43215
614 857-1400

(G-8500)
RED ROOF INNS INC
111 Nationwide Plz (43215)
PHONE..........................614 224-6539
Jeffrey Schwartz, *Manager*
EMP: 33 **Privately Held**
WEB: www.redroof.com
SIC: 7011 Hotels & motels
HQ: Red Roof Inns, Inc.
7815 Walton Pkwy
New Albany OH 43054
614 744-2600

(G-8501)
REFECTORY RESTAURANT INC
1092 Bethel Rd (43220-2610)
PHONE..........................614 451-9774
Kamal Boulos, *President*
EMP: 50
SQ FT: 10,000
SALES: 3.1MM **Privately Held**
WEB: www.therefectoryrestaurant.com
SIC: 5812 7299 French restaurant; banquet hall facilities

(G-8502)
REFRIGERATION SYSTEMS COMPANY (HQ)
1770 Genessee Ave (43211-1650)
PHONE..........................614 263-0913
Thomas A Leighty, *CEO*
Robert A Appleton, *President*
Yukari Niki, *Human Res Mgr*
EMP: 63 EST: 1961
SQ FT: 20,000
SALES (est): 7.5MM
SALES (corp-wide): 51.2MM **Privately Held**
WEB: www.rsc-gc.com
SIC: 7623 1541 Refrigeration repair service; food products manufacturing or packing plant construction
PA: Manweb Services, Inc.
11800 Exit 5 Pkwy Ste 106
Fishers IN 46037
317 863-0007

(G-8503)
REGAL CINEMAS INC
Also Called: Regal Entertainment Group
1800 Georgesville Sq (43228-3695)
PHONE..........................614 853-0850
Josh Dinan, *Manager*
EMP: 36 **Privately Held**
WEB: www.regalcinemas.com
SIC: 7832 Motion Picture Theater
HQ: Regal Cinemas, Inc.
101 E Blount Ave Ste 100
Knoxville TN 37920
865 922-1123

(G-8504)
REGAL HOSPITALITY LLC
Also Called: Sheraton Suites Columbus
201 Hutchinson Ave (43235-4689)
PHONE..........................614 436-0004
Elizabeth Procaccianti, *Manager*
EMP: 28
SALES (corp-wide): 2.3MM **Privately Held**
SIC: 8741 Hotel or motel management
PA: Regal Hospitality, Llc
400 Venture Dr Ste B
Lewis Center OH 43035
614 389-1916

(G-8505)
REGENCY LEASING CO LLC
Also Called: Regency Manor Rehab
2000 Regency Manor Cir (43207-1777)
PHONE..........................614 542-3100
Jay Hicks, *President*
Doug Rowe, *President*
EMP: 300
SALES (est): 10.8MM
SALES (corp-wide): 125.8MM **Privately Held**
WEB: www.communicarehealth.com
SIC: 8051 Skilled nursing care facilities
PA: Communicare Health Services, Inc.
4700 Ashwood Dr Ste 200
Blue Ash OH 45241
513 530-1654

(G-8506)
REGENSIS STNA TRAINING PROGRAM
415 E Mound St (43215-5532)
PHONE..........................614 849-0115
Mark Glover, *Owner*
EMP: 50 EST: 2008
SALES (est): 347.6K **Privately Held**
SIC: 8099 Health & allied services

(G-8507)
REHABLTATION CORECTN OHIO DEPT
Also Called: Columbus Regional Office
1030 Alum Creek Dr (43209-2701)
PHONE..........................614 752-0800
Kim Oats, *Administration*
EMP: 100 **Privately Held**
SIC: 8322 9223 Parole office; offender self-help agency;
HQ: Ohio Department Of Rehabilitation And Correction
770 W Broad St
Columbus OH 43222

(G-8508)
REITTER STUCCO INC
1100 King Ave (43212-2262)
PHONE..........................614 291-2212
Frederick J Reitter, *President*
John Spangler, *Superintendent*
John E Reitter, *Treasurer*
Jim Byerly, *Sales Staff*
Michele Yetzer, *Office Mgr*
EMP: 40
SQ FT: 30,000
SALES (est): 6.3MM **Privately Held**
WEB: www.reitterstucco.com
SIC: 1771 5072 Exterior concrete stucco contractor; hardware

(G-8509)
REITTER WALL SYSTEMS INC
1178 Joyce Ave (43219-2135)
PHONE..........................614 545-4444
R Gabe Reitter II, *President*
Brett Hoerig, *Vice Pres*
EMP: 54

SQ FT: 16,000
SALES (est): 4.6MM **Privately Held**
WEB: www.reitterwall.com
SIC: 1771 Exterior concrete stucco contractor

(G-8510)
RELAY GEAR LTD
3738 Paragon Dr (43228-9750)
PHONE..................................888 735-2943
Mark Betts, *Partner*
Duane Hickerson, *Partner*
Bob Southard, *Partner*
Derek Betts, *General Ptnr*
▲ **EMP:** 32
SQ FT: 25,000
SALES (est): 2.4MM **Privately Held**
WEB: www.relaygear.com
SIC: 5199 7389 Advertising specialties; advertising, promotional & trade show services

(G-8511)
RELIABLE APPL INSTALLATION INC
3755 Interchange Rd (43204-1485)
PHONE..................................614 817-1801
EMP: 38
SALES (corp-wide): 10.7MM **Privately Held**
SIC: 4212 Local trucking, without storage
PA: Reliable Appliance Installation, Inc.
      604 Office Pkwy
      Westerville OH 43082
      614 794-3307

(G-8512)
RELIABLE APPL INSTALLATION INC
3736 Paragon Dr (43228-9750)
PHONE..................................614 246-6840
Randy James, *Branch Mgr*
EMP: 36
SALES (corp-wide): 10.7MM **Privately Held**
SIC: 4212 Local trucking, without storage
PA: Reliable Appliance Installation, Inc.
      604 Office Pkwy
      Westerville OH 43082
      614 794-3307

(G-8513)
REMINGER CO LPA
65 E State St Ste 400 (43215-4213)
PHONE..................................614 228-1311
Ron Fresco, *Branch Mgr*
EMP: 67
SALES (corp-wide): 52.2MM **Privately Held**
WEB: www.reminger.com
SIC: 8111 General practice attorney, lawyer
PA: Reminger Co., L.P.A.
      101 W Prospect Ave # 1400
      Cleveland OH 44115
      216 687-1311

(G-8514)
RENIER CONSTRUCTION CORP
2164 Citygate Dr (43219-3556)
PHONE..................................614 866-4580
William R Heifner, *President*
Thomas Rice, *Vice Pres*
Robert Gibbs, *CFO*
EMP: 25
SQ FT: 8,500
SALES (est): 14.1MM **Privately Held**
WEB: www.renier.com
SIC: 1542 8741 Commercial & office building, new construction; construction management

(G-8515)
REPUBLIC SERVICES INC
933 Frank Rd (43223-3856)
PHONE..................................614 308-3000
Michael Davis, *Principal*
John Diiorio, *Sales Mgr*
Doug Murphy, *Manager*
EMP: 50
SALES (corp-wide): 10B **Publicly Held**
SIC: 4953 Rubbish collection & disposal
PA: Republic Services, Inc.
      18500 N Allied Way # 100
      Phoenix AZ 85054
      480 627-2700

(G-8516)
REPUBLIC SERVICES INC
933 Frank Rd (43223-3856)
PHONE..................................740 969-4487
Mike Varney, *Branch Mgr*
EMP: 60
SALES (corp-wide): 10B **Publicly Held**
WEB: www.republicservices.com
SIC: 4953 Refuse collection & disposal services
PA: Republic Services, Inc.
      18500 N Allied Way # 100
      Phoenix AZ 85054
      480 627-2700

(G-8517)
REPUBLICAN STATE CENTRAL EXECU
Also Called: Ohio Republican Party
211 S 5th St (43215-5203)
PHONE..................................614 228-2481
Robert Bennet, *Chairman*
Kaye Ayres, *Vice Chairman*
EMP: 30 **EST:** 1858
SALES: 50.2K **Privately Held**
WEB: www.ohiogop.org
SIC: 8651 Political campaign organization

(G-8518)
RESEARCH INSTITUTE AT NATION
700 Childrens Dr (43205-2664)
PHONE..................................614 722-2700
John Barnard, *President*
Sherwood L Fawcett, *Principal*
Robert Lazarus Jr, *Principal*
Janet E Porter, *Principal*
William Wise, *Principal*
EMP: 140
SQ FT: 106,000
SALES (est): 25MM
SALES (corp-wide): 2.3B **Privately Held**
SIC: 8062 8733 General medical & surgical hospitals; medical research
PA: Nationwide Children's Hospital
      700 Childrens Dr
      Columbus OH 43205
      614 722-2000

(G-8519)
RESIDENCE INN
Also Called: Residence Inn By Marriott
36 E Gay St (43215-3108)
PHONE..................................614 222-2610
Joey Guiyab, *Principal*
EMP: 40
SALES: 950K **Privately Held**
SIC: 7011 Hotels & motels

(G-8520)
RESIDENTIAL FINANCE CORP (PA)
1 Easton Oval Ste 400 (43219-6092)
PHONE..................................614 324-4700
David Stein, *President*
Michael Isaacs, *President*
Douglas Harris, *COO*
Barry Habib, *Vice Pres*
Jessica Manna, *Vice Pres*
EMP: 300
SQ FT: 36,000
SALES (est): 62.2MM **Privately Held**
WEB: www.myrfc.com
SIC: 6162 Mortgage Banker/Correspondent

(G-8521)
RESIDENTIAL ONE REALTY INC (PA)
Also Called: Prudential
8351 N High St Ste 150 (43235-1409)
PHONE..................................614 436-9830
Joanne Figge, *President*
EMP: 40
SQ FT: 4,500
SALES (est): 1.4MM **Privately Held**
SIC: 6531 Real estate agent, residential

(G-8522)
RESOURCE INTERACTIVE
250 S High St Ste 400 (43215-4622)
PHONE..................................614 621-2888
Nancy J Kramer, *CEO*
Kelly Moony, *President*
EMP: 41

SALES (est): 5.3MM **Privately Held**
SIC: 7389 7331 Advertising, promotional & trade show services; direct mail advertising services

(G-8523)
RESOURCE INTERNATIONAL INC (HQ)
Also Called: Rii
6350 Presidential Gtwy (43231-7653)
PHONE..................................614 823-4949
Kamran Majidzadeh, *CEO*
Farah B Majidzadeh, *CEO*
Sam Khorshidi, *President*
Marcia Lampman, *Vice Pres*
Mark Majidzadeh, *Vice Pres*
EMP: 120
SQ FT: 20,000
SALES (est): 29.3MM **Privately Held**
WEB: www.resourceinternational.com
SIC: 7371 8734 8713 1799 Custom computer programming services; testing laboratories; surveying services; spraying contractor, non-agricultural; consulting engineer; management services
PA: Majidzadeh Enterprises, Inc.
      6350 Presidential Gtwy
      Columbus OH 43231
      614 823-4949

(G-8524)
RESOURCE VENTURES LTD (HQ)
Also Called: Resource Interactive
250 S High St Ste 400 (43215-4622)
PHONE..................................614 621-2888
Kelly Mooney, *CEO*
Ramesh Rajan, *CFO*
Matthew Ammirati,
Janet Eads,
Deirdre Egan,
EMP: 81
SQ FT: 27,880
SALES (est): 45.4MM
SALES (corp-wide): 79.5B **Publicly Held**
WEB: www.resourceinteractive.com
SIC: 8742 Marketing consulting services
PA: International Business Machines Corporation
      1 New Orchard Rd Ste 1 # 1
      Armonk NY 10504
      914 499-1900

(G-8525)
RESTAURANT DEPOT LLC
270 N Wilson Rd (43204-6221)
PHONE..................................614 272-6670
Roy Pruitt, *Manager*
EMP: 50 **Privately Held**
SIC: 5046 Restaurant equipment & supplies
HQ: Restaurant Depot, Llc
      1524 132nd St
      College Point NY 11356

(G-8526)
RESTAURANT EQUIPPERS INC
Also Called: Warehouse
635 W Broad St (43215-2711)
PHONE..................................614 358-6622
Charlie Shaikov, *Manager*
EMP: 40
SALES (corp-wide): 45MM **Privately Held**
WEB: www.equippers.com
SIC: 4225 5046 General warehousing; commercial equipment
PA: Restaurant Equippers, Inc.
      635 W Broad St
      Columbus OH 43215
      800 235-3325

(G-8527)
RETAIL FORWARD INC
Also Called: Tns Retail Forward
2 Easton Oval Ste 500 (43219-6036)
PHONE..................................614 355-4000
Daniel Boehm, *President*
Al Meyers, *Vice Pres*
Paul Casper, *CFO*
EMP: 37
SQ FT: 10,500

SALES (est): 7.7MM
SALES (corp-wide): 20.1B **Privately Held**
WEB: www.retailforward.com
SIC: 8742 Planning consultant; marketing consulting services
HQ: Tns North America, Inc.
      175 Greenwich St Fl 16
      New York NY 10007
      212 991-6100

(G-8528)
RETINA GROUP INC (PA)
262 Neil Ave Ste 220 (43215-7310)
PHONE..................................614 464-3937
Jester Ribenour Do, *President*
E Mitchell Opremcakm, *Vice Pres*
Chet D Riedenour, *Treasurer*
Alan Rehmar, *Director*
EMP: 25
SQ FT: 20,000
SALES (est): 4MM **Privately Held**
WEB: www.theretinagroup.com
SIC: 8011 Ophthalmologist

(G-8529)
REV1 VENTURES
Also Called: Platform Lab
1275 Kinnear Rd (43212-1180)
PHONE..................................614 487-3700
Ted Ford, *President*
Kathleen Green, *President*
Parker Macdonell, *Managing Dir*
Wayne Embree, *Exec VP*
Mike Blackwell, *Vice Pres*
EMP: 25
SQ FT: 62,000
SALES (est): 7.7MM **Privately Held**
WEB: www.techcolumbus.org
SIC: 6799 8299 8741 8734 Venture capital companies; educational services; business management; testing laboratories

(G-8530)
RIDGEWOOD AT FRIENDSHIP VLG
5675 Ponderosa Dr Ofc (43231-6765)
PHONE..................................614 890-8285
Mick Feauto, *Principal*
Carol Gilbert, *Director*
EMP: 35 **EST:** 2001
SALES (est): 883.9K **Privately Held**
WEB: www.fvcolumbus.com
SIC: 8052 Intermediate care facilities

(G-8531)
RIGHTER CO INC
2424 Harrison Rd (43204-3508)
PHONE..................................614 272-9700
Bradley R Nadolson, *President*
Jerry Yantes, *Vice Pres*
Tracy Ferguson, *CFO*
Julie Klay, *Administration*
EMP: 45
SQ FT: 6,400
SALES: 15.2MM **Privately Held**
WEB: www.rightercompany.com
SIC: 1622 1542 Bridge construction; highway construction, elevated; tunnel construction; nonresidential construction

(G-8532)
RIGHTER CONSTRUCTION SVCS INC
Also Called: Piling & Shoring Services
2424 Harrison Rd (43204-3557)
PHONE..................................614 272-9700
Brad Nadolson, *CEO*
Bradley Nadolson, *President*
EMP: 50
SALES (est): 3.4MM **Privately Held**
SIC: 1622 1541 1542 1629 Bridge construction; highway construction, elevated; tunnel construction; industrial buildings & warehouses; nonresidential construction; pile driving contractor; dock construction; industrial plant construction

(G-8533)
RITE RUG CO
5465 N Hamilton Rd (43230-1319)
PHONE..................................614 478-3365
Joel Wood, *Manager*
EMP: 33

GEOGRAPHIC

SALES (corp-wide): 82.2MM **Privately Held**
SIC: 7389 5713 Interior design services; floor covering stores
PA: Rite Rug Co.
4450 Poth Rd Ste A
Columbus OH 43213
614 261-6060

(G-8534)
RIVER CONSULTING LLC (DH)
445 Hutchinson Ave # 740 (43235-5677)
PHONE....................614 797-2480
Gregory Dirfank, *President*
John Strayer, *Senior Partner*
Walter Martin, *Vice Pres*
Mike Patena, *Vice Pres*
Ron Bushar, *Project Mgr*
EMP: 85 **EST:** 1981
SQ FT: 16,000
SALES (est): 29.7MM **Publicly Held**
WEB: www.rci-columbus.com
SIC: 8711 Consulting engineer
HQ: Kinder Morgan Energy Partners, L.P.
1001 La St Ste 1000
Houston TX 77002
713 369-9000

(G-8535)
RIVER ROAD HOTEL CORP
Also Called: University Plz Ht Cnfrence Ctr
3110 Olentangy River Rd (43202)
PHONE....................614 267-7461
James L Nichols, *President*
Timothy Michael, *Corp Secy*
EMP: 50
SQ FT: 35,000
SALES (est): 1.7MM
SALES (corp-wide): 5.8B **Privately Held**
WEB: www.universityplazaosu.com
SIC: 5812 7011 5813 American restaurant; hotels; drinking places
PA: The Ohio State University
Student Acade Servi Bldg
Columbus OH 43210
614 292-6446

(G-8536)
RIVERSIDE NEPHROLOGY ASSOC INC
929 Jasonway Ave Ste A (43214-2464)
PHONE....................614 538-2250
Kevin Schroeder, *President*
Ronald Deandre Jr, *Vice Pres*
EMP: 25
SQ FT: 4,000
SALES (est): 4MM **Privately Held**
WEB: www.riversidenephrology.com
SIC: 8011 Nephrologist; physicians' office, including specialists

(G-8537)
RIVERSIDE RADIOLOGY AND (PA)
100 E Campus View Blvd # 100 (43235-4647)
PHONE....................614 340-7747
Marsha Flarghty, *President*
Mike Suddendorf, *Mktg Dir*
EMP: 145
SALES (est): 39.9MM **Privately Held**
WEB: www.riversiderad.com
SIC: 8011 Radiologist

(G-8538)
RIVERVIEW HOTEL LLC
Also Called: Hampton Inn
3160 Olentangy River Rd (43202-1517)
PHONE....................614 268-8700
Janet Boissy, *Owner*
Andrew Hann, *General Mgr*
EMP: 46
SQ FT: 106,000
SALES (est): 1.5MM **Privately Held**
SIC: 7011 Hotels & motels

(G-8539)
RLJ III - EM CLMBUS LESSEE LLC
Also Called: Embassy Suites Columbus
2700 Corporate Exch Dr (43231-1690)
PHONE....................614 890-8600
Don Gantt, *General Mgr*
Lacey McLachlan, *Sales Mgr*
Moly Curnutte, *Sales Staff*

EMP: 99
SALES (est): 4.4MM **Privately Held**
SIC: 7011 Hotels & motels

(G-8540)
RLJ MANAGEMENT CO INC (PA)
3021 E Dblin Granville Rd (43231-4031)
PHONE....................614 942-2020
Steve Boone, *President*
Denise Blair, *Area Mgr*
Bill Harvey, *Vice Pres*
Daniel Slane, *Treasurer*
Bobbi England, *Director*
EMP: 207
SQ FT: 5,200
SALES (est): 16.3MM **Privately Held**
WEB: www.rljmgmt.com
SIC: 6531 8721 Real estate managers; accounting services, except auditing

(G-8541)
ROBERT HALF INTERNATIONAL INC
277 W Nationwide Blvd (43215-2853)
PHONE....................614 221-8326
EMP: 93
SALES (corp-wide): 5.8B **Publicly Held**
SIC: 7361 Placement agencies
PA: Robert Half International Inc.
2884 Sand Hill Rd Ste 200
Menlo Park CA 94025
650 234-6000

(G-8542)
ROBERT HALF INTERNATIONAL INC
277 W Nationwide Blvd # 200 (43215-2853)
PHONE....................614 221-1544
Lami Beck, *Manager*
EMP: 91
SALES (corp-wide): 5.8B **Publicly Held**
WEB: www.rhii.com
SIC: 7361 Executive placement
PA: Robert Half International Inc.
2884 Sand Hill Rd Ste 200
Menlo Park CA 94025
650 234-6000

(G-8543)
ROBERT M NEFF INC
711 Stimmel Rd (43223-2905)
PHONE....................614 444-1562
Phillip Dante Berkhmeir, *Principal*
EMP: 64
SQ FT: 2,400
SALES (corp-wide): 9MM **Privately Held**
SIC: 4213 4215 4212 Contract haulers; courier services, except by air; mail carriers, contract
PA: Robert M Neff Inc
1955 James Pkwy
Heath OH 43056
740 928-4393

(G-8544)
ROCKBRIDGE CAPITAL LLC (PA)
4100 Regent St Ste G (43219-6160)
PHONE....................614 246-2400
James T Merkel, *CEO*
Marcos Casillas, *Managing Dir*
Ronald L Callentine, *Chairman*
Stephen C Denz, *Exec VP*
Kenneth J Krebs, *Exec VP*
EMP: 42
SQ FT: 7,000
SALES (est): 48.8MM **Privately Held**
WEB: www.rockbridgecapital.com
SIC: 6726 Investment offices

(G-8545)
ROEHRENBECK ELECTRIC INC
2525 English Rd (43207-2899)
PHONE....................614 443-9709
Richard Roehrenbeck, *President*
Ed Pouge, *Purchasing*
Nick Garner, *Engineer*
Carolyn Rogers, *Accounting Mgr*
EMP: 44 **EST:** 1964
SQ FT: 10,000
SALES (est): 7.7MM **Privately Held**
SIC: 1731 General electrical contractor

(G-8546)
ROETZEL AND ANDRESS A LEGAL P
41 S High St Fl 21 (43215-3406)
PHONE....................614 463-9489
Thomas Dillon, *Branch Mgr*
EMP: 40
SALES (corp-wide): 53.4MM **Privately Held**
WEB: www.ralaw.com
SIC: 8111 Corporate, partnership & business law
PA: Roetzel And Andress, A Legal Professional Association
222 S Main St Ste 400
Akron OH 44308
330 376-2700

(G-8547)
RON FOTH RETAIL INC
Also Called: Ron Foth Advertising
8100 N High St (43235-6475)
PHONE....................614 888-7771
Kay Foth, *President*
Mike Foth Jr, *Vice Pres*
Ron Foth Jr, *Vice Pres*
Kim Moore, *Vice Pres*
Debbie Fradette, *Buyer*
EMP: 55
SQ FT: 23,500
SALES (est): 13.5MM **Privately Held**
WEB: www.ronfoth.com
SIC: 7311 7812 Advertising consultant; audio-visual program production

(G-8548)
ROOFING SUPPLY GROUP LLC
1288 Essex Ave (43201-2928)
PHONE....................614 239-1111
Thomas Lecorchick, *Owner*
EMP: 29 **EST:** 2014
SALES (est): 6MM **Privately Held**
SIC: 5033 Roofing, siding & insulation

(G-8549)
ROOT INSURANCE COMPANY
80 E Rich St Fl 5 (43215-5249)
PHONE....................866 980-9431
Alex Timm, *CEO*
Cindy Powell, *CFO*
Dan Manges, *CTO*
EMP: 140
SALES: 4MM **Privately Held**
WEB: www.clubinsurance.com
SIC: 6411 Fire loss appraisal

(G-8550)
ROSE GRACIAS
Also Called: Hilton Homewood Suites
115 Hutchinson Ave 101-136 (43235-1413)
PHONE....................614 785-0001
Rose Gracias, *General Mgr*
Anna Toth, *Principal*
Greg Huss, *Manager*
EMP: 45
SALES (est): 1.2MM **Privately Held**
SIC: 7011 Hotels

(G-8551)
ROSE PRODUCTS AND SERVICES INC
545 Stimmel Rd (43223-2901)
PHONE....................614 443-7647
Robert Roth, *President*
EMP: 50 **EST:** 1926
SQ FT: 50,000
SALES (est): 7.9MM **Privately Held**
SIC: 5087 2842 Janitors' supplies; specialty cleaning preparations

(G-8552)
ROSEMARK PAPER INC (PA)
1845 Progress Ave (43207-1726)
PHONE....................614 443-0303
Robert A Rosenfeld, *President*
Howard Simons, *Vice Pres*
David Gurenberg, *Treasurer*
EMP: 98
SQ FT: 82,000
SALES (est): 13.2MM **Privately Held**
SIC: 5111 5199 Printing paper; packaging materials

(G-8553)
ROSEVILLE MOTOR EXPRESS INC
2720 Westbelt Dr (43228-3871)
PHONE....................614 921-2121
Bill Moore, *President*
EMP: 50
SALES (est): 2.4MM **Privately Held**
SIC: 4213 Automobiles, transport & delivery

(G-8554)
ROSSFORD GRTRIC CARE LTD PRTNR
Also Called: Heatherdowns Nursing Center
1661 Old Henderson Rd (43220-3644)
PHONE....................614 459-0445
Ralph E Hazelbaker, *Partner*
Heatherdown Health Care Corp, *General Ptnr*
Carol Campbell, *Ltd Ptnr*
EMP: 110
SALES (est): 5.6MM **Privately Held**
SIC: 8051 Skilled nursing care facilities

(G-8555)
ROTO-ROOTER SERVICES COMPANY
4480 Bridgeway Ave Ste B (43219-1886)
PHONE....................614 238-8006
Dennis Giffin, *Manager*
EMP: 40
SALES (corp-wide): 1.7B **Publicly Held**
SIC: 7699 Sewer cleaning & rodding
HQ: Roto-Rooter Services Company
255 E 5th St Ste 2500
Cincinnati OH 45202
513 762-6690

(G-8556)
ROYAL ELECTRIC CNSTR CORP
1250 Memory Ln N (43209-2749)
PHONE....................614 253-6600
Susan Ernst, *President*
Gregory Ernst, *Vice Pres*
EMP: 30 **EST:** 1973
SQ FT: 33,000
SALES (est): 6.1MM **Privately Held**
WEB: www.royalcorp.com
SIC: 1731 General electrical contractor

(G-8557)
ROYAL PAPER STOCK COMPANY INC (PA)
1300 Norton Rd (43228-3640)
PHONE....................614 851-4714
Michael Radtke, *President*
Richard Dahn, *Vice Pres*
John Daly, *CFO*
Martha Radke, *Treasurer*
Mickey Bowman, *Sales Staff*
EMP: 85
SQ FT: 80,000
SALES (est): 16.4MM **Privately Held**
WEB: www.royalpaperstock.com
SIC: 4953 Recycling, waste materials

(G-8558)
RSM US LLP
250 West St Ste 200 (43215-7538)
PHONE....................614 224-7722
William Petrus, *Manager*
Rex Larowe, *Info Tech Mgr*
EMP: 40
SALES (corp-wide): 2.1B **Privately Held**
SIC: 8721 Certified public accountant
PA: Rsm Us Llp
1 S Wacker Dr Ste 800
Chicago IL 60606
312 384-6000

(G-8559)
RTW INC
544 W Walnut St (43215-4480)
PHONE....................614 594-9217
Rod Warrix, *Principal*
EMP: 28
SALES (corp-wide): 1.5B **Publicly Held**
SIC: 6331 Assessment associations: fire, marine & casualty insurance
HQ: Rtw, Inc
15245 Lincoln St Se
Minerva OH 44657
952 893-0403

(G-8560)
RUSCILLI CONSTRUCTION CO INC (PA)
5000 Arlngtn Ctr Blvd # 300 (43220-3075)
PHONE..................................614 876-9484
Louis V Ruscilli, *CEO*
L Jack Ruscilli, *Ch of Bd*
Robert A Ruscilli Jr, *President*
Jeremy Crawford, *Superintendent*
Kenneth Marvin, *Superintendent*
EMP: 80
SQ FT: 35,000
SALES (est): 52.3MM **Privately Held**
WEB: www.ruscilli.com
SIC: 1541 8741 1542 Industrial buildings, new construction; warehouse construction; construction management; commercial & office building, new construction; school building construction; institutional building construction

(G-8561)
RUSH MOTOR SALES INC
Also Called: Rush Lincoln Mercury
2350 Morse Rd (43229-5801)
P.O. Box 29286 (43229-0286)
PHONE..................................614 471-9980
Carol Overfield, *Corp Secy*
Mark Rush, *Manager*
EMP: 40
SQ FT: 35,000
SALES (est): 8.9MM **Privately Held**
WEB: www.ronrushlm.com
SIC: 5511 7538 New & Used Cars

(G-8562)
RUSTYS TOWING SERVICE INC
4845 Obetz Reese Rd (43207-4831)
PHONE..................................614 491-6288
Russ Mc Quirt, *President*
EMP: 54
SQ FT: 1,200
SALES (est): 5.5MM **Privately Held**
SIC: 7549 Towing service, automotive; towing services

(G-8563)
RUTHERFORD FUNERAL HOME INC (PA)
2383 N High St (43202-2921)
PHONE..................................614 451-0593
William P Rutherford, *President*
Helen M Rutherford, *Admin Sec*
EMP: 29
SQ FT: 2,500
SALES (est): 2.7MM **Privately Held**
SIC: 7261 Funeral home; crematory

(G-8564)
RXP OHIO LLC
Also Called: Rxp Wireless
630 E Broad St (43215-3999)
P.O. Box 908, New Albany (43054-0908)
PHONE..................................614 937-2844
Stephanie Jandik, *Mng Member*
EMP: 80
SQ FT: 15,000
SALES (est): 732K **Privately Held**
SIC: 4813 Telephone communications broker

(G-8565)
RYBAC INC
407 E Livingston Ave (43215-5531)
PHONE..................................614 228-3578
Lawrence D Schaffer, *President*
EMP: 35
SALES (est): 1.6MM **Privately Held**
SIC: 6531 Real estate brokers & agents

(G-8566)
RYDER LAST MILE INC
1650 Watermark Dr Ste 100 (43215-1043)
PHONE..................................614 801-0621
Frank Gaura, *Vice Pres*
Mary Perez, *Opers Spvr*
John McCoy, *Manager*
Cathy Worster, *Manager*
EMP: 27
SALES (corp-wide): 8.4B **Publicly Held**
SIC: 4225 8742 General warehousing; transportation consultant

HQ: Ryder Last Mile, Inc.
7795 Walton Pkwy
New Albany OH 43054
866 711-3129

(G-8567)
RYDER TRUCK RENTAL INC
775 Schrock Rd (43229-1124)
P.O. Box 29623 (43229-0623)
PHONE..................................614 846-6780
Rick Lenkey, *Branch Mgr*
Jonathan Reed, *Business Dir*
EMP: 45
SALES (corp-wide): 8.4B **Publicly Held**
SIC: 7513 7519 Truck rental, without drivers; utility trailer rental
HQ: Ryder Truck Rental, Inc.
11690 Nw 105th St
Medley FL 33178
305 500-3726

(G-8568)
RYDER TRUCK RENTAL INC
2600 Westbelt Dr (43228-3829)
PHONE..................................614 876-0405
Michael Thompson, *Manager*
EMP: 30
SALES (corp-wide): 8.4B **Publicly Held**
SIC: 7513 Truck rental, without drivers
HQ: Ryder Truck Rental, Inc.
11690 Nw 105th St
Medley FL 33178
305 500-3726

(G-8569)
S & T TRUCK AND AUTO SVC INC
Also Called: Silvan Trucking Company Ohio
3150 Valleyview Dr Rm 8 (43204-2002)
PHONE..................................614 272-8163
Brent Greek, *President*
Stephen R Click, *Principal*
Glenda Purdy, *Vice Pres*
Jeremy Garrett, *Opers Mgr*
Steve Vincenc, *Manager*
EMP: 39
SQ FT: 8,000
SALES (est): 10.2MM **Privately Held**
SIC: 4213 Contract haulers

(G-8570)
S L KLABUNDE CORP (PA)
Also Called: Zimmer Ohio
893 N 4th St (43201-4151)
PHONE..................................614 508-6012
Scott L Klabunde, *President*
EMP: 35
SALES (est): 4.9MM **Privately Held**
SIC: 5047 Orthopedic equipment & supplies; artificial limbs

(G-8571)
SAFE AUTO INSURANCE COMPANY (HQ)
Also Called: S A
4 Easton Oval (43219-6010)
P.O. Box 182109 (43218-2109)
PHONE..................................614 231-0200
Ronald H Davies, *CEO*
Shawn M Flahive, *Principal*
Anne C Griffin, *Principal*
James A Yano, *Principal*
Greg Sutton, *CFO*
EMP: 258
SQ FT: 50,000
SALES (est): 678.8MM **Privately Held**
SIC: 6411 Insurance agents, brokers & service
PA: Safe Auto Insurance Group, Inc.
4 Easton Oval
Columbus OH 43219
614 231-0200

(G-8572)
SAFE AUTO INSURANCE GROUP INC (PA)
4 Easton Oval (43219-6010)
PHONE..................................614 231-0200
Ronald H Davies, *CEO*
ARI Deshe, *Ch of Bd*
Jon P Diamond, *Ch of Bd*
Jack H Coolidge, *Senior VP*
Jon L Trickey, *Senior VP*
EMP: 53
SQ FT: 45,000

SALES (est): 610.9MM **Privately Held**
SIC: 6331 6411 Automobile insurance; insurance agents, brokers & service

(G-8573)
SAFELITE FULFILLMENT INC
Also Called: Safelite Autoglass
760 Dearborn Park Ln (43085-5703)
PHONE..................................614 781-5449
Brenton Carr, *Branch Mgr*
Joel Marsh, *Manager*
EMP: 25
SALES (corp-wide): 2.6MM **Privately Held**
WEB: www.belronus.com
SIC: 7536 4225 Automotive glass replacement shops; general warehousing & storage
HQ: Safelite Fulfillment, Inc.
7400 Safelite Way
Columbus OH 43235
614 210-9000

(G-8574)
SAFELITE FULFILLMENT INC
Accounts Payable Department
7400 Safelite Way (43235-5086)
P.O. Box 182827 (43218-2827)
PHONE..................................614 210-9050
Kaleisha Johnson, *Principal*
EMP: 25
SALES (corp-wide): 2.6MM **Privately Held**
SIC: 7536 Automotive glass replacement shops
HQ: Safelite Fulfillment, Inc.
7400 Safelite Way
Columbus OH 43235
614 210-9000

(G-8575)
SAFELITE GLASS CORP (DH)
Also Called: Safelite Autoglass
7400 Safelite Way (43235-5086)
P.O. Box 182827 (43218-2827)
PHONE..................................614 210-9000
George T Haymaker Jr, *Ch of Bd*
Dan Wislon, *President*
Dan H Wilson, *President*
Sean Flynn, *District Mgr*
Steven Koos, *District Mgr*
▲ EMP: 700
SALES (est): 510.7MM
SALES (corp-wide): 2.6MM **Privately Held**
WEB: www.safelite.com
SIC: 7536 Automotive glass replacement shops
HQ: Safelite Group, Inc.
7400 Safelite Way
Columbus OH 43235
614 210-9000

(G-8576)
SAFELITE GROUP INC (HQ)
Also Called: Safelite Autoglass
7400 Safelite Way (43235-5086)
P.O. Box 182827 (43218-2827)
PHONE..................................614 210-9000
Thomas Feeney, *CEO*
Michelle Beiter, *President*
Paul Groves, *President*
Kerry Hurff, *President*
Brett Decker, *General Mgr*
▲ EMP: 1000
SALES (est): 930MM
SALES (corp-wide): 2.6MM **Privately Held**
WEB: www.safelitegroup.com
SIC: 7536 3231 6411 Automotive glass replacement shops; windshields, glass; made from purchased glass; insurance claim processing, except medical
PA: D'im Sa
Rue Guillaume Kroll 12
Luxembourg 1882
274 788-60

(G-8577)
SAFELITE SOLUTIONS LLC
7400 Safelite Way (43235-5086)
P.O. Box 182827 (43218-2827)
PHONE..................................614 210-9000
Dan Wislon, *President*
Douglas A Herron, *CFO*
EMP: 3500

SALES (est): 98.4MM
SALES (corp-wide): 2.6MM **Privately Held**
WEB: www.safelitegroup.com
SIC: 8742 Management consulting services
HQ: Safelite Group, Inc.
7400 Safelite Way
Columbus OH 43235
614 210-9000

(G-8578)
SAFETY SOLUTIONS INC (HQ)
6999 Huntley Rd Ste L (43229-1031)
PHONE..................................614 799-9900
David L Forsthoffer, *President*
Mike Boone, *Vice Pres*
John Perrin, *Vice Pres*
EMP: 72
SALES (est): 83.1MM
SALES (corp-wide): 11.2B **Publicly Held**
WEB: www.safetysolutions.com
SIC: 5084 5136 5139 Safety equipment; gloves, men's & boys'; shoes; boots
PA: W.W. Grainger, Inc.
100 Grainger Pkwy
Lake Forest IL 60045
847 535-1000

(G-8579)
SAFEWAY ELECTRIC COMPANY INC
1973 Lockbourne Rd (43207-1488)
PHONE..................................614 443-7672
Andy Untch, *President*
David Muncy, *Admin Sec*
EMP: 34
SQ FT: 22,000
SALES (est): 5.1MM **Privately Held**
SIC: 1731 General electrical contractor

(G-8580)
SAGA COMMUNICATIONS NENG INC
Also Called: Wsny Radio Station
4401 Carriage Hill Ln (43220-3837)
PHONE..................................614 451-2191
Alan Goodman, *Manager*
EMP: 80 **Publicly Held**
WEB: www.sagacommunications.com
SIC: 4832 Radio broadcasting stations
HQ: Saga Communications Of New England, Inc.
73 Kercheval Ave Ste 201
Grosse Pointe Farms MI 48236
313 886-7070

(G-8581)
SAGE SUSTAINABLE ELEC LLC (HQ)
2801 Charter St (43228-4607)
PHONE..................................844 472-4373
Robert Houghton, *CEO*
Jill Vaske, *President*
EMP: 25
SQ FT: 24,000
SALES: 13MM
SALES (corp-wide): 15.3MM **Privately Held**
SIC: 7629 Electronic equipment repair
PA: Hugo Neu Corporation
78 John Miller Way Ste 1
Kearny NJ 07032
646 467-6700

(G-8582)
SAIA MOTOR FREIGHT LINE LLC
1717 Krieger St (43228-3623)
PHONE..................................614 870-8778
Myles Hook, *Manager*
EMP: 80
SALES (corp-wide): 1.6B **Publicly Held**
WEB: www.saia.com
SIC: 4213 Contract haulers
HQ: Saia Motor Freight Line, Llc
11465 Johns Creek Pkwy # 400
Duluth GA 30097
770 232-5067

(G-8583)
SAINT CECILIA CHURCH
Also Called: St Cecilia School
440 Norton Rd (43228-7602)
PHONE..................................614 878-5353

Leo Connolly, *Pastor*
Trisha Jakubick, *Director*
Julie Beattie, *Admin Asst*
EMP: 42
SALES: 1MM **Privately Held**
SIC: 8211 8661 8351 Catholic elementary & secondary schools; religious organizations; preschool center

(G-8584)
SALLY BEAUTY SUPPLY LLC
Also Called: Sally Beauty Supply 9927
4309 Janitrol Rd (43228-1301)
PHONE..................................614 278-1691
Tracy Avdellas, *Human Res Mgr*
Tom Brown, *Director*
Mark Mendrygal, *Director*
EMP: 250 **Publicly Held**
WEB: www.sallybeauty.com
SIC: 4225 5087 General warehousing & storage; service establishment equipment
HQ: Sally Beauty Supply Llc
3001 Colorado Blvd
Denton TX 76210
940 898-7500

(G-8585)
SALO INC (PA)
Also Called: INTERIM HEALTHCARE
960 Checkrein Ave Ste A (43229-1107)
PHONE..................................614 436-9404
Kathleen Gilmartin, *CEO*
Michael Hartshorn, *Ch of Bd*
Max Hahnen, *Vice Pres*
Sonya Hinds, *Vice Pres*
Christine Oswald, *Vice Pres*
EMP: 95
SQ FT: 7,500
SALES: 19.8MM **Privately Held**
WEB: www.salo.com
SIC: 8082 Home health care services

(G-8586)
SALON COMMUNICATION SERVICES
Also Called: Jacob Neal Salon
650 N High St (43215-1547)
PHONE..................................614 233-8500
Jacob Neal, *President*
Jody Dierksheide, *Manager*
EMP: 26
SQ FT: 1,300
SALES (est): 809.6K **Privately Held**
WEB: www.jacobneal.com
SIC: 7231 Unisex hair salons

(G-8587)
SALVATION ARMY
966 E Main St (43205-2339)
PHONE..................................614 252-7171
Frank Kirk, *Principal*
EMP: 60
SALES (corp-wide): 4.3B **Privately Held**
WEB: www.salvationarmy-usaeast.org
SIC: 8322 8399 Multi-service center; advocacy group
HQ: The Salvation Army
440 W Nyack Rd Ofc
West Nyack NY 10994
845 620-7200

(G-8588)
SALVATION ARMY
1675 S High St (43207-1863)
P.O. Box 7827 (43207-0827)
PHONE..................................800 728-7825
Maj Dennis Gensler, *Manager*
EMP: 67
SALES (corp-wide): 4.3B **Privately Held**
WEB: www.salvationarmy-usaeast.org
SIC: 8322 8399 Multi-service center; community development groups
HQ: The Salvation Army
440 W Nyack Rd Ofc
West Nyack NY 10994
845 620-7200

(G-8589)
SAMKEL INC
Also Called: Children's Academy
100 Obetz Rd (43207-4031)
PHONE..................................614 491-3270
Ronald Sams, *President*
Barbara A Sams, *Corp Secy*
EMP: 50
SQ FT: 10,000

SALES (est): 2.1MM **Privately Held**
SIC: 8351 8211 Preschool center; group day care center; private elementary school

(G-8590)
SANDS DECKER CPS LLC (PA)
1495 Old Henderson Rd (43220-3613)
PHONE..................................614 459-6992
Glenn E Decker, *Principal*
Rick Cox, *Project Mgr*
Brenton McCuskey, *Engineer*
Sarah Stephens, *Mktg Coord*
J Scott Sands, *Mng Member*
EMP: 28
SQ FT: 1,000
SALES (est): 4.7MM **Privately Held**
WEB: www.sandsdecker.com
SIC: 8711 8713 Civil engineering; surveying services

(G-8591)
SANFILLIPO PRODUCE CO INC
Also Called: Sanfillipo Produce Company
4561 E 5th Ave Ste 1 (43219-1896)
PHONE..................................614 237-3300
James Sanfillipo, *CEO*
James S Sanfillipo III, *CEO*
EMP: 48
SALES (est): 16.9MM **Privately Held**
WEB: www.sanfillipoproduce.com
SIC: 5148 Fresh fruits & vegetables

(G-8592)
SAUER GROUP INC
1801 Lone Eagle St (43228-3647)
PHONE..................................614 853-2500
Charles D Steitz, *President*
Dennis Hartz, *VP Opers*
Terry Kilinay, *CFO*
EMP: 200 EST: 2007
SQ FT: 23,000
SALES (est): 48.2MM
SALES (corp-wide): 126.4MM **Privately Held**
SIC: 1711 Mechanical contractor
PA: Sauer Holdings, Inc.
30 51st St
Pittsburgh PA 15201
412 687-4100

(G-8593)
SAUER INCORPORATED
1801 Lone Eagle St (43228-3647)
PHONE..................................614 853-2500
Charles Steitz, *Branch Mgr*
EMP: 75
SALES (corp-wide): 126.4MM **Privately Held**
WEB: www.sauerinc.com
SIC: 1711 Mechanical contractor
HQ: Sauer Incorporated
30 51st St
Pittsburgh PA 15201
412 687-4100

(G-8594)
SAX 5TH AVE CAR WASH INC (PA)
Also Called: Sax Car Wash
1319 W 5th Ave (43212-2902)
PHONE..................................614 486-9093
Jeff Randolph, *President*
Bob Morgan, *President*
EMP: 25
SQ FT: 3,500
SALES (est): 1.9MM **Privately Held**
WEB: www.saxcarwash.com
SIC: 7542 Carwash

(G-8595)
SAYLES COMPANY LLC
Also Called: Miracle Method of Columbus
1575 Integrity Dr E (43209-2707)
PHONE..................................614 801-0432
Leo Sayles, *Mng Member*
Emily Sayles,
EMP: 25
SQ FT: 2,500
SALES: 3MM **Privately Held**
SIC: 1799 Bathtub refinishing

(G-8596)
SB CAPITAL ACQUISITIONS LLC
Also Called: Jc's 5 Star Outlet
4010 E 5th Ave (43219-1811)
PHONE..................................614 443-4080
Jay L Schottenstein, *Principal*
EMP: 1500 EST: 2011
SQ FT: 15,125
SALES: 353.4K **Privately Held**
SIC: 8742 Retail trade consultant
PA: Sb Capital Group Llc
4300 E 5th Ave
Columbus OH 43219

(G-8597)
SB CAPITAL GROUP LLC (PA)
Also Called: Retail 4 Less
4300 E 5th Ave (43219-1816)
PHONE..................................516 829-2400
Jay L Schottenstein, *Ch of Bd*
David Bernstein, *President*
John Duffy, *Controller*
Dathard Steele, *Controller*
Susan Levan, *Office Mgr*
EMP: 25
SQ FT: 325,000
SALES (est): 83.3MM **Privately Held**
WEB: www.sbcapitalgroup.com
SIC: 7389 Merchandise liquidators

(G-8598)
SCARBROUGH E TENNIS FITNES CTR
Also Called: Scarbrough E Tennis Fitnes CLB
5641 Alshire Rd (43232-4703)
PHONE..................................614 751-2597
Robert Weiler, *Partner*
Bob Kelly, *Partner*
Robert Hilborn, *Manager*
EMP: 50
SALES (est): 1.8MM **Privately Held**
SIC: 7997 Tennis club, membership

(G-8599)
SCHINDLER ELEVATOR CORPORATION
3607 Interchange Rd (43204-1499)
PHONE..................................614 573-2777
Betty Haddox, *Safety Mgr*
Sean Walsh, *Manager*
EMP: 45
SALES (corp-wide): 10.9B **Privately Held**
WEB: www.us.schindler.com
SIC: 7699 5084 1796 Elevators: inspection, service & repair; elevators; installing building equipment
HQ: Schindler Elevator Corporation
20 Whippany Rd
Morristown NJ 07960
973 397-6500

(G-8600)
SCHLEE MALT HOUSE CONDO ASSN
Also Called: Equip Estate Group
495 S High St Ste 10 (43215-5689)
PHONE..................................614 463-1999
Kim Ulle, *President*
EMP: 26 EST: 1989
SALES (est): 361.2K **Privately Held**
SIC: 8641 Fraternal associations

(G-8601)
SCHMID MECHANICAL CO
5255 Sinclair Rd (43229-5042)
PHONE..................................614 261-6331
Dennis Shuman, *President*
Dustin Fishburn, *Vice Pres*
Timothy Schmid, *Vice Pres*
Daniel Shuman, *Vice Pres*
EMP: 50
SALES (est): 683.6K
SALES (corp-wide): 41.2MM **Privately Held**
SIC: 1711 Mechanical contractor
PA: Speer Industries Incorporated
5255 Sinclair Rd
Columbus OH 43229
614 261-6331

(G-8602)
SCHNEIDER DOWNS & CO INC
65 E State St Ste 2000 (43215-4271)
PHONE..................................614 621-4060
Joe Patrick, *Manager*

EMP: 75
SALES (corp-wide): 41.1MM **Privately Held**
SIC: 8721 Certified public accountant
PA: Schneider Downs & Co., Inc.
1 Ppg Pl Ste 1700
Pittsburgh PA 15222
412 261-3644

(G-8603)
SCHODORF TRUCK BODY & EQP CO
885 Harmon Ave (43223-2411)
P.O. Box 23322 (43223-0322)
PHONE..................................614 228-6793
Joe Schodorf, *President*
Paul F Schodorf, *Vice Pres*
Mattday Schodorfwinches, *Parts Mgr*
Paul Schodorf, *VP Sales*
EMP: 40
SQ FT: 52,000
SALES (est): 10.3MM **Privately Held**
WEB: www.schodorftruck.com
SIC: 5012 3713 3211 Truck bodies; truck bodies (motor vehicles); flat glass

(G-8604)
SCHOMER GLAUS PYLE
Also Called: Gpd Group
1801 Watermark Dr Ste 210 (43215-1096)
PHONE..................................614 210-0751
Darrin Kotecki, *President*
Julie Shirk, *Administration*
EMP: 85
SALES (corp-wide): 93.9MM **Privately Held**
SIC: 8711 8712 Consulting engineer; architectural services
PA: Glaus, Pyle, Schomer, Burns & Dehaven, Inc.
520 S Main St Ste 2531
Akron OH 44311
330 572-2100

(G-8605)
SCHOOL CHOICE OHIO INC
88 E Broad St Ste 640 (43215-3506)
PHONE..................................614 223-1555
Kaleigh Frazier, *Corp Comm Staff*
Lois Graham, *Office Mgr*
Matt Cox, *Exec Dir*
Kaleigh Lemaster, *Exec Dir*
Daniel Talik, *Director*
EMP: 50
SALES: 457.4K **Privately Held**
SIC: 8699 Charitable organization

(G-8606)
SCHOOL EMPLOYEES RETIREMENT
300 E Broad St Ste 100 (43215-3747)
PHONE..................................614 222-5853
Deyetta Tharp, *Opers Staff*
Tim Fox, *Engineer*
Virginia Briszendine, *CFO*
Tracy Valentino, *CFO*
Phil Sisson, *Investment Ofcr*
EMP: 166
SQ FT: 197,980
SALES (est): 1.4B **Privately Held**
WEB: www.governor.ohio.gov
SIC: 6371 9441 Pension, health & welfare funds; administration of social & manpower programs
HQ: Executive Office State Of Ohio
30 E Broad St
Columbus OH 43215

(G-8607)
SCHOOLEY CALDWELL ASSOCIATES
300 Marconi Blvd Ste 100 (43215-2329)
PHONE..................................614 628-0300
Robert D Loversidge, *President*
Terence Sullivan, *General Mgr*
Jayne M Vandenburgh, *COO*
Vincent A Bednar, *Vice Pres*
Robert K Smith, *Vice Pres*
EMP: 55
SQ FT: 17,255
SALES (est): 6MM **Privately Held**
WEB: www.sca-ae.com
SIC: 8748 8711 8712 City planning; consulting engineer; architectural engineering

▲ = Import ▼=Export
◆ =Import/Export

(G-8608)
SCHOTTENSTEIN RE GROUP LLC
2 Easton Oval Ste 510 (43219-6013)
PHONE....................................614 418-8900
Brett Kaufman, *President*
Wes Smith, *President*
Deborah Wilson, *Vice Pres*
Darren Smith, *Supervisor*
George Harmanis, *Officer*
EMP: 38
SQ FT: 15,000
SALES (est): 5.9MM **Privately Held**
WEB: www.srealestateg.com
SIC: 6531 Real estate managers; real estate brokers & agents

(G-8609)
SCHOTTENSTEIN REALTY LLC
Also Called: Schottenstein Property Group
4300 E 5th Ave (43219-1816)
PHONE....................................614 445-8461
Beth Dreitler, *Counsel*
Dirk Greene, *Vice Pres*
Bill Kugel, *Vice Pres*
Dan Robinson, *Vice Pres*
Amy Romanowski, *Vice Pres*
EMP: 50
SALES (est): 4.8MM **Privately Held**
SIC: 6519 6512 Sub-lessors of real estate; shopping center, property operation only; shopping center, regional (300,000 - 1,000,000 sq ft); shopping center, neighborhood (30,000 - 100,000 sq ft)

(G-8610)
SCIENTIFIC FORMING TECH CORP (PA)
Also Called: Deform
2545 Farmers Dr Ste 200 (43235-3713)
PHONE....................................614 451-8330
Andy Tang, *President*
EMP: 29
SALES (est): 3.7MM **Privately Held**
WEB: www.deform.com
SIC: 7371 Computer software development

(G-8611)
SCIOTO DOWNS INC
6000 S High St (43207)
P.O. Box 7823 (43207-0823)
PHONE....................................614 295-4700
Edward T Ryan, *President*
Bill Gustafson, *Vice Pres*
Gene Kneisley, *Controller*
Sue Allen, *Payroll Mgr*
Kyle Coleman, *Manager*
EMP: 1000
SALES (est): 2.4MM
SALES (corp-wide): 2B **Publicly Held**
WEB: www.sciotodowns.com
SIC: 7948 Horse race track operation; harness horse racing
HQ: Mtr Gaming Group, Inc.
Hc 2 Box S
Chester WV 26034
304 387-8000

(G-8612)
SCIOTO PACKAGING INC
6969 Alum Creek Dr (43217-1244)
PHONE....................................614 491-1500
Dennis Hickox, *President*
Steve Burelison, *Admin Sec*
EMP: 50
SALES (est): 3.3MM **Privately Held**
WEB: www.sciotopackaging.com
SIC: 5199 Packaging materials

(G-8613)
SCOTT SCRIVEN & WAHOFF LLP
250 E Broad St Ste 900 (43215-3725)
PHONE....................................614 222-8686
Greg Scott, *Partner*
Timothy S Cowans,
Richard Goldberg,
Wanda T Lillis,
Julie C Martin,
EMP: 28
SALES (est): 3.4MM **Privately Held**
WEB: www.sswlaw.com
SIC: 8111 Labor & employment law

(G-8614)
SEA LTD (PA)
7001 Buffalo Pkwy (43229-1157)
PHONE....................................614 888-4160
Glenn Baker, *CEO*
Jason Baker, *CEO*
Robert K Rupp, *Principal*
Kirk Wolf, *Research*
Eric Baluch, *Engineer*
EMP: 100
SQ FT: 56,526
SALES (est): 65.2MM **Privately Held**
SIC: 8711 Consulting engineer

(G-8615)
SECURITY CHECK LLC (PA)
2 Easton Oval Ste 350 (43219-6193)
P.O. Box 1211, Oxford MS (38655-1211)
PHONE....................................614 944-5788
Dewitt Lovelace, *CFO*
John Lewis, *Mng Member*
William Alias Jr,
William Alias III,
EMP: 150
SQ FT: 6,000
SALES (est): 10.2MM **Privately Held**
WEB: www.security-check.net
SIC: 7389 7322 Check validation service; collection agency, except real estate

(G-8616)
SECURITY INVESTMENTS LLC
3681 Corporate Dr (43231-4965)
PHONE....................................614 441-4601
William Marks,
EMP: 65
SQ FT: 2,500
SALES: 2MM **Privately Held**
SIC: 7382 Protective devices, security

(G-8617)
SEG OF OHIO INC (PA)
Also Called: Steiner Associates
4016 Townsfair Way # 201 (43219-6083)
PHONE....................................614 414-7300
Yaromir Steiner, *CEO*
Barry Rosenberg, *President*
Beau Arnason, *Exec VP*
Patricia Curry, *Senior VP*
Scott Fox, *Vice Pres*
EMP: 35
SQ FT: 8,035
SALES (est): 60.2MM **Privately Held**
WEB: www.steiner.com
SIC: 6552 Subdividers & developers

(G-8618)
SELECT SPECIALTY HOSP COLUMBUS
1087 Dennison Ave (43201-3201)
PHONE....................................614 291-8467
Mary Burkett, *Branch Mgr*
EMP: 88
SALES (corp-wide): 3.7B **Publicly Held**
WEB: www.selectmedicalcorp.com
SIC: 8062 General medical & surgical hospitals
HQ: Select Specialty Hospital - Columbus, Inc.
4716 Old Gettysburg Rd
Mechanicsburg PA 17055
336 718-6300

(G-8619)
SELECT SPECLTY HOSPI-COLMBUS
410 W 10th Ave (43210-1240)
PHONE....................................614 293-6931
Michael T McGovern, *President*
Julie Crissinger, *Director*
Sherry Haberkern, *Pharmacy Dir*
EMP: 150
SALES (est): 5.1MM
SALES (corp-wide): 3.7B **Publicly Held**
WEB: www.selectmedicalcorp.com
SIC: 8062 General medical & surgical hospitals
HQ: Select Medical Corporation
4714 Gettysburg Rd
Mechanicsburg PA 17055
717 972-1100

(G-8620)
SEQUOIA PRO BOWL
5501 Sandalwood Blvd (43229-4476)
PHONE....................................614 885-7043
Tim Boss, *Owner*
EMP: 25
SQ FT: 32,000
SALES: 500K **Privately Held**
WEB: www.sequoiaprobowl.com
SIC: 7933 Ten pin center

(G-8621)
SERENITY CENTER INC
Also Called: Forest Hills Center
2841 E Dblin Granville Rd (43231-4037)
PHONE....................................614 891-1111
Cynthia Lawes, *President*
EMP: 110
SALES (est): 3.5MM **Privately Held**
SIC: 8059 Nursing home, except skilled & intermediate care facility

(G-8622)
SERVICE EXPERTS HTG & AC LLC
Also Called: Service Experts of Columbus
1751 Dividend Dr (43228-3899)
PHONE....................................614 859-6993
Rick Rogers, *Branch Mgr*
EMP: 30
SALES (corp-wide): 985.7MM **Privately Held**
SIC: 1711 Heating & air conditioning contractors
HQ: Service Experts Heating & Air Conditioning Llc
3820 American Dr Ste 200
Plano TX 75075
972 535-3800

(G-8623)
SERVICE PRONET INC
1535 Georgesville Rd (43228-3615)
PHONE....................................614 874-4300
Richard Deering, *President*
Andrew Deering, *Vice Pres*
Randy Hames, *Sales Mgr*
John Hames, *Manager*
James Rice, *Manager*
EMP: 35
SALES (est): 5MM **Privately Held**
WEB: www.theservicepro.net
SIC: 7374 7371 7389 Computer graphics service; computer software development & applications;

(G-8624)
SETIAWAN ASSOCIATES LLC
50 W Broad St Ste 1800 (43215-5910)
PHONE....................................614 285-5815
EMP: 25
SQ FT: 1,000
SALES (est): 738.4K **Privately Held**
SIC: 7359 Equipment Rental/Leasing

(G-8625)
SETTLE MUTER ELECTRIC LTD (PA)
Also Called: S M E
711 Claycraft Rd (43230-6631)
PHONE....................................614 866-7554
Mark Muter, *President*
Bill Muter, *Vice Pres*
Bryan Eckert, *Project Mgr*
Greg Howard, *Project Mgr*
Dana Penrod, *Project Mgr*
EMP: 113
SQ FT: 15,000
SALES (est): 28.4MM **Privately Held**
WEB: www.settlemuter.com
SIC: 1731 General electrical contractor

(G-8626)
SHADE TREE COOL LIVING LLC
6317 Busch Blvd (43229-1802)
PHONE....................................614 844-5990
Colin Leveque, *Mng Member*
▲ EMP: 25
SALES (est): 1.9MM **Privately Held**
SIC: 1521 Patio & deck construction & repair

(G-8627)
SHADOART PRODUCTIONS INC
Also Called: SHADOWBOX
503 S Front St Ste 260 (43215-5662)
PHONE....................................614 416-7625
Steven F Guyer, *President*
Stacie V Boord, *Corp Secy*
Julie A Klein, *Vice Pres*
EMP: 68
SALES: 3.7MM **Privately Held**
SIC: 7922 Theatrical companies

(G-8628)
SHAFFER DISTRIBUTING COMPANY (PA)
1100 W 3rd Ave (43212-3113)
P.O. Box 12427 (43212-0427)
PHONE....................................614 421-6800
Steven W Shaffer, *CEO*
William H Kraft, *President*
Paul T Westbrock, *Exec VP*
Charles Ropke, *Vice Pres*
Chuck Ropke, *Vice Pres*
▲ EMP: 58 EST: 1929
SQ FT: 63,000
SALES (est): 41.8MM **Privately Held**
WEB: www.shafferindy.com
SIC: 5087 Vending machines & supplies

(G-8629)
SHALOM HOUSE INC (HQ)
Also Called: HERITAGE HOUSE NURSING HOME
1135 College Ave (43209-7802)
PHONE....................................614 239-1999
David Rosen, *President*
Ruth Dodge, *Administration*
EMP: 35
SALES: 2.7MM
SALES (corp-wide): 12.1MM **Privately Held**
SIC: 8361 Residential care
PA: Wexner Heritage Village
1151 College Ave
Columbus OH 43209
614 231-4900

(G-8630)
SHAMROCK TAXI LTD
P.O. Box 360363 (43236-0363)
PHONE....................................614 263-8294
T Nagasi, *CEO*
EMP: 38
SALES (est): 698.8K **Privately Held**
SIC: 4121 Taxicabs

(G-8631)
SHEEDY PAVING INC
730 N Rose Ave (43219-2523)
PHONE....................................614 252-2111
James P Sheedy, *President*
Mark J Sheedy, *Vice Pres*
Michael Sheedy, *Vice Pres*
Alex Sheedy, *Mktg Dir*
Jean Sheedy, *Admin Sec*
EMP: 36 EST: 1941
SQ FT: 3,400
SALES (est): 5.9MM **Privately Held**
SIC: 1611 Surfacing & paving

(G-8632)
SHELLY AND SANDS INC
1515 Harmon Ave (43223-3309)
P.O. Box 2469 (43216-2469)
PHONE....................................614 444-5100
Doug Howell, *Branch Mgr*
EMP: 50
SALES (corp-wide): 276.3MM **Privately Held**
WEB: www.shellyandsands.com
SIC: 1611 1771 1542 Highway & street paving contractor; concrete work; nonresidential construction
PA: Shelly And Sands, Inc.
3570 S River Rd
Zanesville OH 43701
740 453-0721

(G-8633)
SHG WHITEHALL HOLDINGS LLC
Also Called: Manor At Whitehall, The
4805 Langley Ave (43213-6125)
PHONE....................................614 501-8271
George Repchick, *President*

William I Weisberg, *Vice Pres*
Sarah Depompei, *Assistant*
EMP: 120
SQ FT: 55,000
SALES: 11.5MM **Privately Held**
SIC: 8051 Convalescent home with continuous nursing care

(G-8634)
SHINING COMPANY LLC
3739 Wynds Dr (43232-4244)
PHONE....................614 588-4115
Wendell Hill, *President*
Tracie Moore, *Co-Owner*
EMP: 214
SQ FT: 1,200,000
SALES: 4MM **Privately Held**
SIC: 7349 0781 Building maintenance services; landscape services

(G-8635)
SHOEMAKER ELECTRIC COMPANY
Also Called: Shoemaker Industrial Solutions
831 Bonham Ave (43211-2999)
PHONE....................614 294-5626
Fred N Kletrovets, *President*
Derrick Crowe, *Engineer*
Teri Richardson, *Treasurer*
Betty Kletrovets, *Admin Sec*
▲ **EMP:** 29 **EST:** 1935
SQ FT: 16,000
SALES (est): 8.1MM **Privately Held**
WEB: www.shoemakerindustrial.com
SIC: 7694 5063 Electric motor repair; motors, electric

(G-8636)
SHOWE BUILDERS INC (HQ)
45 N 4th St (43215-3602)
PHONE....................614 481-8106
Hugh B Showe, *President*
David M Showe, *Vice Pres*
Hugh B Showe II, *Treasurer*
Kevin M Showe, *Admin Sec*
EMP: 26
SQ FT: 5,000
SALES (est): 7.2MM
SALES (corp-wide): 96MM **Privately Held**
SIC: 1522 Apartment building construction
PA: National Housing Corporation
45 N 4th St Ste 200
Columbus OH 43215
614 481-8106

(G-8637)
SHRADER TIRE & OIL INC
2021 Harmon Ave (43223-3828)
PHONE....................614 445-6601
EMP: 65
SALES (corp-wide): 69.9MM **Privately Held**
SIC: 5014 Tires & tubes
PA: Shrader Tire & Oil, Inc.
2045 W Sylvania Ave # 51
Toledo OH 43613
419 472-2128

(G-8638)
SIGMA CHI FRAT
260 E 15th Ave (43201-1902)
PHONE....................614 297-8783
Jeoff Korff, *President*
Todd Yarros, *President*
EMP: 50
SALES: 461.4K **Privately Held**
SIC: 8641 7041 University club; fraternities & sororities

(G-8639)
SIGNATURE CONTROL SYSTEMS LLC
Also Called: Signature Controls
2228 Citygate Dr (43219-3565)
PHONE....................614 864-2222
Toll Free:....................877 -
Tom Foster, *General Mgr*
John Bambey, *Vice Pres*
Thomas Foster, *Vice Pres*
Bryan Roche, *VP Opers*
Harold Smith, *Purchasing*
EMP: 50
SQ FT: 20,000

SALES (est): 16MM **Privately Held**
WEB: www.signaturecontrols.com
SIC: 5063 1799 Control & signal wire & cable, including coaxial; parking facility equipment installation

(G-8640)
SILLIKER LABORATORIES OHIO INC
2057 Builders Pl (43204-4886)
PHONE....................614 486-0150
Lori Benz, *Supervisor*
Amitha Miele, *Lab Dir*
EMP: 30
SQ FT: 4,700
SALES (est): 3.5MM
SALES (corp-wide): 7.5MM **Privately Held**
WEB: www.silliker.com
SIC: 8734 Food testing service
HQ: Silliker, Inc.
111 E Wacker Dr Ste 2300
Chicago IL 60601
312 938-5151

(G-8641)
SIMCO SUPPLY CO
Also Called: Simco Controls
3000 E 14th Ave (43219-2355)
PHONE....................614 253-1999
Charles M Simon, *President*
Don P Simon, *Vice Pres*
Julie Fields, *Controller*
EMP: 50
SQ FT: 50,000
SALES (est): 8.6MM **Privately Held**
WEB: www.simcosupply.com
SIC: 5084 Whol Industrial Equipment

(G-8642)
SIMON KNTON CNCIL BYSCUTS AMER (PA)
Also Called: BOY SCOUTS OF AMERICA
807 Kinnear Rd (43212-1490)
PHONE....................614 436-7200
E Linn Draper, *President*
Randy Larson, *Director*
EMP: 47
SQ FT: 20,000
SALES: 4.5MM **Privately Held**
WEB: www.skcbsa.org
SIC: 8641 Boy Scout organization

(G-8643)
SIMONE HEALTH MANAGEMENT INC
750 E Broad St Ste 300 (43205-1126)
PHONE....................614 224-1347
Viengkeo Vilay, *CEO*
EMP: 35 **EST:** 2011
SALES (est): 790.9K **Privately Held**
SIC: 8082 Home health care services

(G-8644)
SIMPLIFI ESO LLC
2 Miranova Pl Ste 500 (43215-7052)
PHONE....................614 635-8679
William Rowland, *CFO*
Kim Dibella, *Mng Member*
EMP: 120
SQ FT: 3,700
SALES (est): 8.8MM **Privately Held**
SIC: 8748 Employee programs administration

(G-8645)
SIMPSON STRONG-TIE COMPANY INC
2600 International St (43228-4617)
PHONE....................614 876-8060
Shane Vilasineekul, *Engineer*
Sharon Bott, *Human Res Dir*
Rick Reid, *Sales Staff*
Dave Williams, *Branch Mgr*
Jerry Gridley, *Manager*
EMP: 120
SALES (corp-wide): 1B **Publicly Held**
SIC: 5082 3643 3452 Construction & mining machinery; current-carrying wiring devices; bolts, nuts, rivets & washers
HQ: Simpson Strong-Tie Company Inc.
5956 W Las Positas Blvd
Pleasanton CA 94588
925 560-9000

(G-8646)
SINCLAIR MEDIA II INC
Also Called: Wwho TV
1261 Dublin Rd (43215-7000)
PHONE....................614 481-6666
Elen Daly, *Branch Mgr*
EMP: 110
SALES (corp-wide): 3B **Publicly Held**
SIC: 4833 Television broadcasting stations
HQ: Sinclair Media Ii, Inc
4990 Mobile Hwy
Pensacola FL 32506
850 456-3333

(G-8647)
SINCLAIR MEDIA II INC
Also Called: Wsyx and ABC 6
1261 Dublin Rd (43215-7000)
PHONE....................614 481-6666
Dan Mellon, *Manager*
EMP: 176
SQ FT: 31,942
SALES (corp-wide): 3B **Publicly Held**
WEB: www.kvbw.com
SIC: 4833 Television broadcasting stations
HQ: Sinclair Media Ii, Inc.
10706 Beaver Dam Rd
Hunt Valley MD 21030
513 641-4400

(G-8648)
SINCLAIR MEDIA II INC
1261 Dublin Rd (43215-7000)
PHONE....................614 481-6666
Dan Mellon, *Manager*
EMP: 55
SALES (corp-wide): 3B **Publicly Held**
WEB: www.weartv.com
SIC: 4833 Television broadcasting stations
HQ: Sinclair Media Ii, Inc
4990 Mobile Hwy
Pensacola FL 32506
850 456-3333

(G-8649)
SKINNER DIESEL SERVICES INC (PA)
Also Called: Commercial Radiator
2440 Lockbourne Rd (43207-2168)
PHONE....................614 491-8785
Mike L Skinner, *President*
EMP: 50
SQ FT: 12,000
SALES (est): 7.4MM **Privately Held**
WEB: www.quickwinch.com
SIC: 7538 7532 Diesel engine repair: automotive; truck engine repair, except industrial; body shop, trucks

(G-8650)
SKY FINANCIAL CAPITAL TR III
41 S High St (43215-6170)
PHONE....................614 480-3278
EMP: 134
SALES (est): 91.2K
SALES (corp-wide): 5.2B **Publicly Held**
SIC: 6733 Trusts
PA: Huntington Bancshares Incorporated
41 S High St
Columbus OH 43215
614 480-8300

(G-8651)
SKYLAND COLUMBUS LLC
Also Called: Paul Mitchell School Columbus
3000 Morse Rd (43231-6038)
PHONE....................614 478-0922
Tammy Marinis, *Director*
EMP: 26
SALES (est): 519.5K
SALES (corp-wide): 564.2K **Privately Held**
SIC: 7231 Cosmetology school
PA: Skyland Education Llc
10735 Ravenna Rd Ste 3
Twinsburg OH 44087
330 963-0119

(G-8652)
SLEEP CARE INC
985 Schrock Rd Ste 204 (43229-1139)
PHONE....................614 901-8989
Craig Pickerill, *President*
EMP: 42
SALES (est): 332.5K **Privately Held**
SIC: 8093 Biofeedback center

(G-8653)
SMART HARBOR LLC (PA)
Also Called: Shipyard, The
580 N 4th St Ste 500 (43215-2158)
PHONE....................800 295-4519
Stephen Howell, *Project Mgr*
Rob Simmons, *CFO*
Tiffanie Hiibner, *Ch Credit Ofcr*
David Sonderman, *Ch Credit Ofcr*
Gerald Kvortek, *Accountant*
EMP: 48 **EST:** 2005
SALES (est): 7.8MM **Privately Held**
SIC: 8742 Marketing consulting services

(G-8654)
SMG HOLDINGS INC
Also Called: Greater Clumbus Convention Ctr
400 N High St Fl 2 (43215-2096)
PHONE....................614 827-2500
John Page, *General Mgr*
Dittie Guise, *General Mgr*
EMP: 130
SALES (corp-wide): 23.7B **Privately Held**
WEB: www.smgworld.com
SIC: 8741 6512 Management services; nonresidential building operators
HQ: Smg Holdings, Llc
300 Cnshohckn State Rd # 450
Conshohocken PA 19428

(G-8655)
SMITH & ASSOCIATES EXCAVATING
2765 Drake Rd (43219-1603)
PHONE....................740 362-3355
Ken Belczak, *President*
EMP: 40 **EST:** 1976
SQ FT: 9,600
SALES (est): 6.2MM **Privately Held**
WEB: www.smithexc.com
SIC: 1794 Excavation & grading, building construction

(G-8656)
SMITH TANDY COMPANY
555 City Park Ave (43215-5737)
PHONE....................614 224-9255
Michael J Weisz, *Partner*
Edward Friedman, *Associate*
EMP: 25
SALES (est): 1.9MM **Privately Held**
WEB: www.smithtandy.com
SIC: 6513 Apartment building operators

(G-8657)
SMOOT CONSTRUCTION CO OHIO (HQ)
1907 Leonard Ave Ste 200 (43219-4506)
PHONE....................614 253-9000
Lewis R Smoot Sr, *CEO*
Mark Cain, *President*
Thomas J Fitzpatrick, *Principal*
Lewis R Smoot Jr, *Senior VP*
EMP: 50
SALES (est): 26.3MM
SALES (corp-wide): 52.9MM **Privately Held**
SIC: 8742 Construction project management consultant
PA: The Smoot Corporation
1907 Leonard Ave Ste 200
Columbus OH 43219
614 253-9000

(G-8658)
SONIC AUTOMOTIVE
Also Called: Toyota West
1500 Auto Mall Dr (43228-3660)
PHONE....................614 870-8200
Jeff Rachor, *Treasurer*
Richard Slusser, *Finance Mgr*
Don Marks, *Sales Mgr*
Asad Asghar, *Sales Staff*
Cory Doty, *Sales Staff*
EMP: 94
SALES (est): 32.7MM
SALES (corp-wide): 9.9B **Publicly Held**
SIC: 5511 7538 7515 5531 Automobiles, new & used; general automotive repair shops; passenger car leasing; automotive & home supply stores; used car dealers
PA: Sonic Automotive, Inc.
4401 Colwick Rd
Charlotte NC 28211
704 566-2400

G
E
O
G
R
A
P
H
I
C

(G-8659)
SONIC AUTOMOTIVE-1495 AUTOMALL
Also Called: Hatfield Lincoln Mercury
1495 Auto Mall Dr (43228-3658)
PHONE....................................614 317-4326
Scott Penn, *Manager*
Jay J Fraley, *Manager*
EMP: 30
SALES (est): 4MM
SALES (corp-wide): 9.9B **Publicly Held**
SIC: 5511 5561 5571 7532 Automobiles, new & used; travel trailers: automobile, new & used; motorcycle dealers; top & body repair & paint shops; passenger car leasing; used car dealers
PA: Sonic Automotive, Inc.
4401 Colwick Rd
Charlotte NC 28211
704 566-2400

(G-8660)
SOPHISTICATED SYSTEMS INC (PA)
2191 Citygate Dr (43219-3564)
PHONE....................................614 418-4600
Dwight Smith, *President*
Dwight E Smith, *President*
Jane L Borgelt, *CFO*
Chris Clark, *Technician*
EMP: 76
SQ FT: 10,000
SALES (est): 18.1MM **Privately Held**
WEB: www.ssicom.com
SIC: 7379 5045 Computer related consulting services; computers, peripherals & software

(G-8661)
SOUTHAST CMNTY MENTAL HLTH CTR (PA)
16 W Long St (43215-2815)
PHONE....................................614 225-0980
Steven Atwood, *CFO*
Melissa Miller, *Human Res Dir*
Pete Davis, *Technology*
William Lee, *Exec Dir*
Sandra Stephenson, *Exec Dir*
EMP: 250
SQ FT: 67,988
SALES (est): 12.5MM **Privately Held**
WEB: www.southeastinc.com
SIC: 8093 8361 8011 Mental health clinic, outpatient; substance abuse clinics (outpatient); residential care; offices & clinics of medical doctors

(G-8662)
SOUTHEAST CMNTY MENTAL HLTH CTR
1455 N 4th St (43207-1011)
PHONE....................................614 444-0800
Diane Sadler, *Branch Mgr*
Diana Sadler, *Director*
EMP: 40
SQ FT: 10,191
SALES (corp-wide): 12.5MM **Privately Held**
WEB: www.southeastinc.com
SIC: 8063 8322 8093 8069 Psychiatric hospitals; family counseling services; mental health clinic, outpatient; alcoholism rehabilitation hospital
PA: Southeast Community Mental Health Center Inc
16 W Long St
Columbus OH 43215
614 225-0980

(G-8663)
SOUTHAST CMNTY MENTAL HLTH CTR
Community Treatment
1705 S High St (43207-1864)
PHONE....................................614 445-6832
Don Strasser, *Associate Dir*
EMP: 40
SALES (corp-wide): 12.5MM **Privately Held**
WEB: www.southeastinc.com
SIC: 8093 8322 Mental health clinic, outpatient; telephone counseling service

PA: Southeast Community Mental Health Center Inc
16 W Long St
Columbus OH 43215
614 225-0980

(G-8664)
SOUTHERN GLZERS DSTRS OHIO LLC (HQ)
Also Called: Glazer's of Ohio
4800 Poth Rd (43213-1332)
PHONE....................................614 552-7900
Bennett Glazer, *President*
Mike Maxwell, *COO*
Scott Westerman, *Vice Pres*
Cliff Messenger, *Sales Staff*
Dan Tarpy, *Mktg Dir*
▲ EMP: 89
SQ FT: 100,000
SALES (est): 97.5MM
SALES (corp-wide): 7.2B **Privately Held**
SIC: 5181 5182 Beer & ale; wine
PA: Southern Glazer's Wine And Spirits, Llc
1600 Nw 163rd St
Miami FL 33169
305 625-4171

(G-8665)
SOUTHSIDE LEARNING & DEV CTR
280 Reeb Ave (43207-1936)
PHONE....................................614 444-1529
Roberta Bishop, *Director*
Amy Valentine, *Admin Asst*
EMP: 27
SALES: 1.7MM **Privately Held**
SIC: 8351 Preschool center

(G-8666)
SOUTHWESTERN ELECTRIC POWER CO (HQ)
Also Called: AEP
1 Riverside Plz (43215-2355)
PHONE....................................614 716-1000
Nicholas K Akins, *Ch of Bd*
Malcolm Smoak, *President*
Brian X Tierney, *CFO*
Kelly Currey, *Controller*
Joseph M Buonaiuto, *Controller*
EMP: 126
SALES: 1.8B
SALES (corp-wide): 16.2B **Publicly Held**
WEB: www.swepco.com
SIC: 4911 Generation, electric power; distribution, electric power; transmission, electric power
PA: American Electric Power Company, Inc.
1 Riverside Plz Fl 1 # 1
Columbus OH 43215
614 716-1000

(G-8667)
SOUTHWESTERN TILE AND MBL CO
1030 Cable Ave (43222-1202)
PHONE....................................614 464-1257
Vaughn Fowler Jr, *President*
Robert Fowler, *Vice Pres*
Judith Vest, *Admin Sec*
EMP: 30
SQ FT: 10,000
SALES: 2.6MM **Privately Held**
SIC: 1743 Tile installation, ceramic; marble installation, interior

(G-8668)
SPARTAN WHSE & DIST CO INC (PA)
Also Called: Spartan Logistics
4140 Lockbourne Rd (43207-4221)
PHONE....................................614 497-1777
Ed Harmon, *Ch of Bd*
Steve Harmon, *President*
Josh Ledford, *Vice Pres*
Elza Harman, *VP Opers*
Samantha Coil, *Controller*
▲ EMP: 85
SQ FT: 1,000,000
SALES (est): 59MM **Privately Held**
SIC: 4225 General warehousing

(G-8669)
SPECTRUM MGT HOLDG CO LLC
Also Called: Time Warner
3760 Interchange Rd (43204-4131)
PHONE....................................614 481-5408
Cindy Powell, *Opers Staff*
Gerald Capehart, *Manager*
Derrick Bohlin, *Manager*
EMP: 83
SALES (corp-wide): 43.6B **Publicly Held**
SIC: 4841 Cable television services
HQ: Spectrum Management Holding Company, Llc
400 Atlantic St
Stamford CT 06901
203 905-7801

(G-8670)
SPECTRUM MGT HOLDG CO LLC
Also Called: Time Warner
1015 Olentangy River Rd (43212-3148)
PHONE....................................614 344-4159
Rhonda Frost, *President*
Parker Goodson, *Director*
EMP: 50
SALES (corp-wide): 43.6B **Publicly Held**
SIC: 4841 Cable television services
HQ: Spectrum Management Holding Company, Llc
400 Atlantic St
Stamford CT 06901
203 905-7801

(G-8671)
SPEER INDUSTRIES INCORPORATED (PA)
Also Called: Speer Mechanical
5255 Sinclair Rd (43229-5042)
PHONE....................................614 261-6331
Samuel A Shuman, *Ch of Bd*
Tom Hangan, *President*
Dennis Shuman, *President*
Phil McEvoy, *COO*
Fred Bothwell, *Safety Dir*
EMP: 150
SQ FT: 60,000
SALES (est): 41.2MM **Privately Held**
SIC: 1711 Mechanical contractor; heating & air conditioning contractors

(G-8672)
SPILLMAN COMPANY
1701 Moler Rd (43207-1684)
P.O. Box 7847 (43207-0847)
PHONE....................................614 444-2184
Ted Coons, *CEO*
Don McNutt, *President*
Theodore W Coons, *Principal*
Lynn Coons, *Treasurer*
◆ EMP: 34 EST: 1948
SQ FT: 37,000
SALES: 7.9MM **Privately Held**
WEB: www.spillmanform.com
SIC: 1771 5084 3446 Concrete work; cement making machinery; architectural metalwork

(G-8673)
SPORTS MEDICINE GRANT INC (PA)
Also Called: Smgoa
323 E Town St Ste 100 (43215-4774)
PHONE....................................614 461-8174
Raymond J Tesner, *President*
EMP: 60
SQ FT: 8,600
SALES (est): 6.5MM **Privately Held**
WEB: www.smgoa.com
SIC: 8031 Offices & clinics of osteopathic physicians

(G-8674)
SPRAY A TREE INC
Also Called: S A T Landscaping
1585 Pemberton Dr (43221-1443)
PHONE....................................614 457-8257
Fortunato Merullo, *President*
Renee Merullo, *Vice Pres*
EMP: 25
SQ FT: 8,000
SALES (est): 1.9MM **Privately Held**
SIC: 0782 Landscape contractors

(G-8675)
SPRINT SPECTRUM LP
2367 S Hamilton Rd (43232-4305)
PHONE....................................614 575-5500
Mike Schull, *Branch Mgr*
EMP: 30
SALES (corp-wide): 85.9B **Publicly Held**
WEB: www.sprintpcs.com
SIC: 4813 4812 Local & long distance telephone communications; cellular telephone services
HQ: Sprint Spectrum L.P.
6800 Sprint Pkwy
Overland Park KS 66251

(G-8676)
SPRINT SPECTRUM LP
6614 Sawmill Rd (43235-4943)
PHONE....................................614 793-2500
David Starcher, *Manager*
EMP: 30
SALES (corp-wide): 85.9B **Publicly Held**
WEB: www.sprintpcs.com
SIC: 4813 Local & long distance telephone communications
HQ: Sprint Spectrum L.P.
6800 Sprint Pkwy
Overland Park KS 66251

(G-8677)
SPRINT SPECTRUM LP
3918 Townsfair Way (43219-6067)
PHONE....................................614 428-2300
Jeff Stalcup, *Manager*
EMP: 30
SALES (corp-wide): 85.9B **Publicly Held**
WEB: www.sprintpcs.com
SIC: 4813 4812 Local & long distance telephone communications; cellular telephone services
HQ: Sprint Spectrum L.P.
6800 Sprint Pkwy
Overland Park KS 66251

(G-8678)
SPRUCE BOUGH HOMES LLC
Also Called: Sbh I & II
18 E 3rd Ave (43201-3532)
PHONE....................................614 253-0984
Sarah French, *Principal*
EMP: 55
SALES: 944K **Privately Held**
SIC: 6513 Apartment building operators

(G-8679)
SSTH LLC
Also Called: Central Ohio Home Help Agency
739 S James Rd Ste 100 (43227-1098)
PHONE....................................614 884-0793
Tim Hanners,
EMP: 64
SQ FT: 1,800
SALES: 900K **Privately Held**
WEB: www.cohha.org
SIC: 8082 Visiting nurse service

(G-8680)
ST STEPHENS COMMUNITY HOUSE
Also Called: ST STEPHENS COMMUNITY SERVICE
1500 E 17th Ave (43219-1002)
PHONE....................................614 294-6347
Tim Kelly, *President*
Marilyn Mehaffie, *Vice Pres*
Ray Thomas, *Vice Pres*
Bruce Bennett, *CFO*
Kevin Barnett, *Treasurer*
EMP: 80
SQ FT: 41,000
SALES: 5.2MM **Privately Held**
WEB: www.saintstephensch.org
SIC: 8322 8351 Community center; child day care services

(G-8681)
ST VINCENT FAMILY CENTERS (PA)
1490 E Main St (43205-2140)
PHONE....................................614 252-0731
Anne Ransone, *President*
Debbie Elkins, *President*
John T Reed, *Vice Pres*
Cody Alspach, *Personnel Assit*
EMP: 180

SALES: 12.6MM **Privately Held**
SIC: 8322 8361 8093 Social service center; residential care for the handicapped; home for the mentally handicapped; specialty outpatient clinics

(G-8682)
STAID LOGIC LLC (PA)
595 E Broad St Ste 206 (43215-4043)
PHONE..........................309 807-0575
Kiran Basireddy, *CEO*
Meghana Penubolu, *President*
EMP: 35
SALES (est): 2.1MM **Privately Held**
SIC: 7379 7371 Computer related maintenance services; computer related consulting services; custom computer programming services

(G-8683)
STANTEC ARCH & ENGRG PC
1500 Lake Shore Dr # 100 (43204-3800)
PHONE..........................614 486-4383
Lori Van Dermark, *Marketing Staff*
Amy Strasheim, *Manager*
EMP: 25
SALES (corp-wide): 4B **Privately Held**
SIC: 8711 8712 Engineering services; architectural services
HQ: Stantec Architecture And Engineering
P.C.
311 Summer St
Boston MA 02210

(G-8684)
STANTEC CONSULTING SVCS INC
1500 Lake Shore Dr # 100 (43204-3800)
PHONE..........................614 486-4383
Lori Van Dermark, *Marketing Staff*
Matt Tin, *Manager*
EMP: 123
SALES (corp-wide): 4B **Privately Held**
WEB: www.fmsm.com
SIC: 8712 8711 Architectural services; engineering services
HQ: Stantec Consulting Services Inc.
475 5th Ave Fl 12
New York NY 10017
212 352-5160

(G-8685)
STAPLES INC
700 Taylor Rd Ste 100 (43230-3318)
PHONE..........................614 472-2014
Susie Petrak, *Branch Mgr*
EMP: 35 **Privately Held**
WEB: www.corporate-express.com
SIC: 5943 5021 Stationery stores; furniture
HQ: Staples, Inc.
500 Staples Dr
Framingham MA 01702
508 253-5000

(G-8686)
STAR HOUSE FOUNDATION
1220 Corrugated Way (43201-2902)
PHONE..........................614 826-5868
Ann Bischoff, *CEO*
Mark Batcheck, *COO*
EMP: 27 EST: 2016
SALES (est): 545.9K **Privately Held**
SIC: 8641 Civic social & fraternal associations

(G-8687)
STAR LEASING CO (PA)
4080 Business Park Dr (43204-5023)
PHONE..........................614 278-9999
Steve Jackson, *President*
Thomas C Copeland III, *Principal*
Jeffrey H Rosen, *Senior VP*
Jeffrey D Egle, *Vice Pres*
Michael Hensley, *Vice Pres*
EMP: 75
SALES (est): 52.7MM **Privately Held**
WEB: www.starleasing.com
SIC: 7513 7539 7549 Truck leasing, without drivers; truck rental, without drivers; towing services; automotive turbocharger & blower repair

(G-8688)
STAR PACKAGING INC
1796 Frebis Ave (43206-3729)
PHONE..........................614 564-9936
James R Tata, *President*
Kim Tata, *General Mgr*
Adam Frass, *Manager*
EMP: 32
SQ FT: 53,000
SALES (est): 13.8MM **Privately Held**
SIC: 5199 4783 Packaging materials; packing goods for shipping

(G-8689)
STARWOOD HOTELS & RESORTS
3030 Plaza Prpts Blvd (43219)
PHONE..........................614 345-9291
Laurie Hess, *Principal*
EMP: 195
SALES (corp-wide): 20.7B **Publicly Held**
SIC: 7011 Hotels & motels
HQ: Starwood Hotels & Resorts Worldwide,
Llc
1 Star Pt
Stamford CT 06902
203 964-6000

(G-8690)
STARWOOD HOTELS & RESORTS
888 E Dublin Granville Rd (43229-2416)
PHONE..........................614 888-8230
Steve Marangoni, *Manager*
EMP: 120
SALES (corp-wide): 20.7B **Publicly Held**
SIC: 7011 Hotels & motels
HQ: Starwood Hotels & Resorts Worldwide,
Llc
1 Star Pt
Stamford CT 06902
203 964-6000

(G-8691)
STATE AUTO FINANCIAL CORP (HQ)
Also Called: STATE AUTO INSURANCE
COMPANIES
518 E Broad St (43215-3901)
P.O. Box 182822 (43218-2822)
PHONE..........................614 464-5000
Michael E Larocco, *Ch of Bd*
Alita Burke, *President*
Tim Goeller, *Business Mgr*
Philip S Liechty, *Business Mgr*
Jason E Berkey, *Senior VP*
EMP: 51
SQ FT: 280,000
SALES: 1.2B
SALES (corp-wide): 1.5B **Publicly Held**
SIC: 6331 Fire, marine & casualty insurance
PA: State Automobile Mutual Insurance Co
Inc
518 E Broad St
Columbus OH 43215
833 724-3577

(G-8692)
STATE AUTOMOBILE MUTL INSUR CO (PA)
Also Called: State Auto Insurance Companies
518 E Broad St (43215-3901)
P.O. Box 182822 (43218-2822)
PHONE..........................833 724-3577
Mike Larocco, *Ch of Bd*
Bob Bachtell, *President*
Laurann Sage, *President*
John Bakkestuen, *Business Mgr*
David J Hosler, *Vice Pres*
EMP: 1500
SQ FT: 270,000
SALES (est): 1.5B **Publicly Held**
WEB: www.stfc.com
SIC: 6331 6411 6351 Fire, marine & casualty insurance & carriers; automobile insurance; insurance agents, brokers & service; surety insurance

(G-8693)
STATE OF OHIO
4200 Surface Rd (43228-1313)
PHONE..........................614 466-3455
Charles Wheeler, *Principal*
EMP: 94 **Privately Held**

SIC: 8742 Human resource consulting
services
PA: State Of Ohio
30 E Broad St Fl 40
Columbus OH 43215
614 466-3455

(G-8694)
STATE TCHERS RTREMENT SYS OHIO (HQ)
Also Called: Strs Ohio
275 E Broad St (43215-3703)
PHONE..........................614 227-4090
Robert Stein, *Chairman*
Corey Geog, *Top Exec*
Julie H Frazier, *Project Mgr*
Hope Rencher, *Project Mgr*
Heidi Spadaro, *Buyer*
EMP: 146
SQ FT: 176,000
SALES (est): 7.4B **Privately Held**
SIC: 6371 Pension funds
PA: State Of Ohio
30 E Broad St Fl 40
Columbus OH 43215
614 466-3455

(G-8695)
STATECO FINANCIAL SERVICES
518 E Broad St (43215-3901)
P.O. Box 182822 (43218-2822)
PHONE..........................614 464-5000
EMP: 200
SALES (est): 15.3MM
SALES (corp-wide): 1.5B **Publicly Held**
SIC: 6211 Investment Firm
HQ: State Auto Financial Corporation
518 E Broad St
Columbus OH 43215

(G-8696)
STAUFS COFFEE ROASTERS II INC (PA)
705 Hadley Dr (43228-1029)
PHONE..........................614 487-6050
Andy Tang, *CEO*
Mark J Swanson, *President*
William Strugis, *CFO*
Shawn Schulte, *Consultant*
EMP: 40
SQ FT: 4,400
SALES (est): 3.1MM **Privately Held**
WEB: www.staufs.com
SIC: 5499 5722 5149 5084 Gourmet food stores; coffee; tea; household appliance stores; coffee & tea; brewery products manufacturing machinery, commercial

(G-8697)
STERLING PAPER CO (HQ)
1845 Progress Ave (43207-1726)
PHONE..........................614 443-0303
Robert Rosenfeld, *President*
▲ **EMP:** 45
SALES (est): 103.6MM
SALES (corp-wide): 13.2MM **Privately Held**
SIC: 5111 5199 Printing paper; packaging materials
PA: Rosemark Paper, Inc.
1845 Progress Ave
Columbus OH 43207
614 443-0303

(G-8698)
STEVE SHAFFER
Also Called: Orkin
3905 Sullivant Ave (43228-4326)
PHONE..........................614 276-6355
Steve Shaffer, *Principal*
EMP: 30
SALES (est): 1MM **Privately Held**
SIC: 7342 Exterminating & fumigating

(G-8699)
STEVEN H BYERLY INC
Also Called: Steve Byerly Masonry
4890 Cleveland Ave (43231-4757)
P.O. Box 29133 (43229-0133)
PHONE..........................614 882-0092
Steve Byerly, *Owner*
EMP: 25
SALES (est): 1.4MM **Privately Held**
SIC: 1741 7699 Masonry & other stonework; cleaning services

(G-8700)
STILSON & ASSOCIATES INC
6121 Huntley Rd (43229-1003)
PHONE..........................614 847-0300
Vikram V Rajadhysha, *President*
Kevin M Bainter, *Vice Pres*
Manoj Sethi, *Vice Pres*
A J Siebert, *Vice Pres*
James G May, *CFO*
EMP: 40
SQ FT: 40,000
SALES (est): 3MM
SALES (corp-wide): 93MM **Privately Held**
SIC: 8712 8711 Architectural services; consulting engineer
PA: Dlz Corporation
6121 Huntley Rd
Columbus OH 43229
614 888-0040

(G-8701)
STONEHENGE CAPITAL COMPANY LLC
191 W Nationwide Blvd (43215-2568)
PHONE..........................614 246-2456
Thomas Adamak, *Branch Mgr*
EMP: 32
SALES (corp-wide): 1.8MM **Privately Held**
SIC: 6282 Investment advice
PA: Stonehenge Capital Company Llc
236 3rd St
Baton Rouge LA 70801
225 408-3000

(G-8702)
STONEHENGE FINCL HOLDINGS INC (PA)
191 W Nationwide Blvd # 600 (43215-2568)
PHONE..........................614 246-2500
David R Meuse, *President*
Ronald D Brooks, *Vice Pres*
Michael J Endres, *Vice Pres*
James Henson, *Vice Pres*
Brad L Pospichel, *Vice Pres*
EMP: 70
SQ FT: 17,000
SALES (est): 10.9MM **Privately Held**
WEB: www.stonehengepartners.com
SIC: 6722 Management investment, open-end

(G-8703)
STRADERS GARDEN CENTERS INC (PA)
Also Called: Strader's Green House
5350 Riverside Dr (43220-1700)
PHONE..........................614 889-1314
Jack D Strader, *President*
Ruth E Strader, *Corp Secy*
Mary Brennen, *Vice Pres*
▲ **EMP:** 125
SQ FT: 30,625
SALES: 10MM **Privately Held**
SIC: 5261 5193 Nurseries; plants, potted

(G-8704)
STRATEGIC RESEARCH GROUP INC
995 Goodale Blvd Ste 1 (43212-3865)
PHONE..........................614 220-8860
Kathleen Carr, *President*
EMP: 30 EST: 1999
SQ FT: 4,200
SALES (est): 4.9MM **Privately Held**
WEB: www.strategicresearchgroup.com
SIC: 6411 Research services, insurance

(G-8705)
STRAWSER CONSTRUCTION INC (HQ)
1392 Dublin Rd (43215-1009)
PHONE..........................614 276-5501
Pierre Peltier, *President*
Chris Anspaugh, *General Mgr*
Dave Kiser, *Vice Pres*
EMP: 32
SALES (est): 47.8MM **Privately Held**
SIC: 1522 Residential construction
PA: Barrett Industries Corp
1392 Dublin Rd
Columbus OH 43215
614 485-9168

(G-8706)
STRAWSER EQUIPMENT & LSG INC
1235 Stimmel Rd (43223-2915)
PHONE...................................614 444-2521
David Strawser, President
Kiendra Strawser, Admin Sec
EMP: 60
SQ FT: 50,000
SALES: 7MM **Privately Held**
SIC: 4212 Dump truck haulage

(G-8707)
STYLE-LINE INCORPORATED (PA)
Also Called: Chelsea House Fabrics
901 W 3rd Ave Ste A (43212-3131)
P.O. Box 2706 (43216-2706)
PHONE...................................614 291-0600
Laura R Prophater, President
William H Prophater, Vice Pres
EMP: 45
SQ FT: 54,000
SALES (est): 6MM **Privately Held**
SIC: 5023 5131 2391 1799 Venetian
blinds; vertical blinds; window shades;
window covering parts & accessories;
drapery material, woven; curtains, win-
dow; made from purchased materials;
drapery track installation

(G-8708)
SUCCESS KIDZ 24-HR ENRCHMT CTR
1800 Parsons Ave (43207-1929)
PHONE...................................614 419-2276
Wynter Kirkbride, Director
EMP: 30
SALES (est): 1.7MM **Privately Held**
SIC: 8351 Child day care services

(G-8709)
SUMMERFIELD HOMES LLC
27 Linwood Ave (43205-1512)
PHONE...................................614 253-0984
Michelle Hert, Principal
EMP: 55
SALES: 906K **Privately Held**
SIC: 6513 Apartment building operators

(G-8710)
SUMMIT FINANCIAL STRATEGIES
7965 N High St Ste 350 (43235-8446)
PHONE...................................614 885-1115
Samantha Maccia, President
Samantha M Macchia, COO
Liam J Hurley, Vice Pres
Brett Langer, Branch Mgr
Liam Ripeloux, Info Tech Dir
EMP: 30 EST: 1994
SALES (est): 2.6MM **Privately Held**
WEB: www.summitfin.com
SIC: 6282 Investment advisory service

(G-8711)
SUMTOTAL SYSTEMS LLC
100 E Campus View Blvd # 250
(43235-4682)
PHONE...................................352 264-2800
Bruce Duff, Senior VP
Joshua Roberts, Manager
Robert Thomas, Manager
Steven Fix, Technology
EMP: 218
SALES (corp-wide): 352.2K **Privately Held**
SIC: 7371 Computer software develop-
ment
HQ: Sumtotal Systems Llc
2850 Nw 43rd St Ste 150
Gainesville FL 32606
352 264-2800

(G-8712)
SUNRISE CONNECTICUT AVENUE ASS
Also Called: Forum At Knightsbridge
4590 Knightsbridge Blvd (43214-4327)
PHONE...................................614 451-6766
Beckey Converse, Director
Christina Lockhart, Director
Gary Sontaj, Director
Lurlie Sweet, Director

Chris Vehr, Food Svc Dir
EMP: 30
SQ FT: 4,000
SALES (corp-wide): 4.7B **Publicly Held**
SIC: 8051 Skilled nursing care facilities
HQ: Sunrise Connecticut Avenue Associa-
tion
5111 Connecticut Ave Nw
Washington DC 20008
202 966-8020

(G-8713)
SUPER LAUNDRY INC
Also Called: Ohio Laundry
2268 Westbrooke Dr (43228-9416)
PHONE...................................614 258-5147
Mitch Blatt, President
Thomas Duckworth, Regional Mgr
EMP: 25
SQ FT: 22,000
SALES (est): 2.1MM
SALES (corp-wide): 378.9MM **Privately Held**
SIC: 7215 Coin-operated laundries &
cleaning
HQ: Coinmach Laundry Corporation
1017 E Morehead St # 100
Charlotte NC 28204

(G-8714)
SUPERIOR GROUP
740 Waterman Ave (43215-1155)
PHONE...................................614 488-8035
Greg Stewart, CEO
Bryan Stewart, President
Buddy Brown, Superintendent
Suzanne Stewart, Exec VP
Ted Bader, Vice Pres
EMP: 180
SALES (est): 46.2MM **Privately Held**
WEB: www.electricalspecialists.com
SIC: 1731 Electrical work

(G-8715)
SUPPLY NETWORK INC
Viking Supply Net
2353 International St (43228-4622)
PHONE...................................614 527-5800
Johnette Wright, Credit Staff
Tommy Haberman, Sales Associate
Sandra Richter, Sales Associate
Gary Stumph, Branch Mgr
Ingrid Baack, Manager
EMP: 30
SQ FT: 15,800 **Privately Held**
WEB: www.vikingsupplynet.com
SIC: 1711 Sprinkler contractors
HQ: Supply Network, Inc.
210 Industrial Park Dr
Hastings MI 49058
269 945-9501

(G-8716)
SUPPLY TECH OF COLUMBUS LLC
5197 Trabue Rd (43228-9498)
PHONE...................................614 299-0184
Jeffrey Saley, Principal
EMP: 50 EST: 2012
SALES (est): 1.6MM **Privately Held**
SIC: 1731 Voice, data & video wiring con-
tractor

(G-8717)
SUPREME COURT UNITED STATES
Also Called: Federal Probation
85 Marconi Blvd Rm 546 (43215-2835)
PHONE...................................614 719-3107
Pat Crowley, Manager
EMP: 69 **Publicly Held**
WEB: www.supremecourtus.gov
SIC: 8322 Probation office
HQ: Supreme Court, United States
1 1st St Ne
Washington DC 20543
202 479-3000

(G-8718)
SUPREME COURT OF OHIO
Also Called: Court of Claims of Ohio
65 S Front St Fl 1 (43215-3431)
PHONE...................................614 387-9800
Miles Durfey, Clerk
EMP: 40 **Privately Held**
WEB: www.judicialstudies.com

SIC: 9199 6411 General government administration; ; insurance claim adjusters,
not employed by insurance company
HQ: The Supreme Court Of Ohio
65 S Front St Fl 1
Columbus OH 43215
614 387-9000

(G-8719)
SUPREME TOUCH HOME HEALTH SVCS
2547 W Broad St (43204-3324)
PHONE...................................614 783-1115
Gbolaga Akinboyede, President
Sefinat Akinboyede, Vice Pres
EMP: 98
SALES (est): 2.5MM **Privately Held**
SIC: 8082 Home health care services

(G-8720)
SURE HOME IMPROVMENTS LLC
6031 E Main St Ste 222 (43213-3356)
PHONE...................................614 586-0610
Joseph Schuer, Branch Mgr
EMP: 26 **Privately Held**
SIC: 1521 General remodeling, single-fam-
ily houses
PA: Sure Home Improvments, Llc
6031 E Main St
Columbus OH 43213

(G-8721)
SURGERY AND GYNECOLOGY INC (PA)
114r W 3rd Ave (43201-3211)
PHONE...................................614 294-1603
Judy Hutton, General Mgr
EMP: 25
SQ FT: 5,000
SALES (est): 1.1MM **Privately Held**
SIC: 8062 General medical & surgical hos-
pitals

(G-8722)
SVH HOLDINGS LLC
Also Called: Miracle Health Care
4322 N Hamilton Rd (43230-1710)
PHONE...................................844 560-7775
Suzanne Horn, COO
Verlin Horn, Administration
EMP: 99 EST: 2014
SQ FT: 1,900
SALES (est): 369.4K **Privately Held**
SIC: 8082 Home health care services

(G-8723)
SYGMA NETWORK INC
2400 Harrison Rd (43204-3508)
PHONE...................................614 771-3801
Sherrie Barrett, Human Resources
Bob Johnson, Branch Mgr
EMP: 117
SQ FT: 10,000
SALES (corp-wide): 58.7B **Publicly Held**
WEB: www.sygmanetwork.com
SIC: 5141 Food brokers
HQ: The Sygma Network Inc
5550 Blazer Pkwy Ste 300
Dublin OH 43017

(G-8724)
SYNORAN
2389 Bryden Rd (43209-2131)
PHONE...................................614 236-4014
William M Randle,
Mark Quinlan,
EMP: 30 EST: 2000
SQ FT: 10,000
SALES: 4.1MM **Privately Held**
WEB: www.synoran.com
SIC: 7371 Software programming applica-
tions

(G-8725)
SYSCO CENTRAL OHIO INC
2400 Harrison Rd (43204-3508)
P.O. Box 94570, Cleveland (44101-4570)
PHONE...................................614 272-0658
Debra Hamernick, President
EMP: 300
SQ FT: 308,000

SALES (est): 100.1MM
SALES (corp-wide): 58.7B **Publicly Held**
WEB: www.abbott.sysco.com
SIC: 5141 5142 Whol General Groceries
Whol Packaged Frozen Goods
PA: Sysco Corporation
1390 Enclave Pkwy
Houston TX 77077
281 584-1390

(G-8726)
T K EDWARDS LLC
782 N High St (43215-1430)
PHONE...................................614 406-8064
Don Roberts, General Ptnr
EMP: 38
SALES (est): 2.1MM **Privately Held**
SIC: 8741 Restaurant management

(G-8727)
T&L GLOBAL MANAGEMENT LLC
Also Called: Pro-Touch
1572 Lafayette Dr (43220-3867)
PHONE...................................614 586-0303
Liton K Bhowmick,
Liton Bhowmick,
Doug Brugler,
EMP: 86
SALES (est): 1.4MM **Privately Held**
SIC: 7349 5169 Janitorial service, contract
basis; chemicals & allied products

(G-8728)
TAFT STETTINIUS HOLLISTER LLP
65 E State St Ste 1000 (43215-4221)
PHONE...................................614 221-4000
David Johnson, Branch Mgr
Robert Clark,
EMP: 75
SALES (corp-wide): 104.2MM **Privately Held**
SIC: 8111 General practice law office
PA: Taft Stettinius & Hollister Llp
425 Walnut St Ste 1800
Cincinnati OH 45202
513 381-2838

(G-8729)
TAILORED MANAGEMENT SERVICES (PA)
1165 Dublin Rd (43215-1005)
PHONE...................................614 859-1500
Brad Beach, President
EMP: 85
SALES (est): 8.9MM **Privately Held**
SIC: 7361 Employment agencies

(G-8730)
TANGOE US INC
200 E Campus View Blvd (43235-4678)
PHONE...................................614 842-9918
EMP: 75
SALES (corp-wide): 395MM **Privately Held**
WEB: www.profitline.com
SIC: 8748 Telecommunications consultant
HQ: Tangoe Us, Inc.
1 Waterview Dr Ste 200
Shelton CT 06484
973 257-0300

(G-8731)
TARGET STORES INC
3720 Soldano Blvd (43228-1422)
PHONE...................................614 279-4224
Fax: 614 279-4224
EMP: 220
SALES (corp-wide): 69.5B **Publicly Held**
SIC: 5311 7384 5912 Department Store
Photofinishing Laboratory Ret Drugs/Sun-
dries
HQ: Target Stores, Inc.
1000 Nicollet Mall
Minneapolis MN 55403

(G-8732)
TARRIER FOODS CORP
2700 International St # 100 (43228-4640)
PHONE...................................614 876-8594
Timothy A Tarrier, President
Julia A Grooms, Principal
Ann Tarrier, Principal
EMP: 42

SQ FT: 54,000
SALES (est): 23.2MM **Privately Held**
WEB: www.tarrierfoods.com
SIC: 5149 5145 2099 Dried or canned
   foods; nuts, salted or roasted; candy;
   food preparations

(G-8733)
TAYLOR STN SURGICAL CTR LTD
275 Taylor Station Rd Ab (43213-2927)
PHONE....................................614 751-4466
Jane Ann Mead, *Opers Mgr*
Linda Meikle, *Director*
Mount Carmel Health System,
EMP: 60
SQ FT: 1,728
SALES (est): 9.9MM **Privately Held**
SIC: 8011 Surgeon

(G-8734)
TDS DOCUMENT MANAGEMENT LTD
Also Called: Shred It
161 Jackson St (43206-1124)
PHONE....................................614 367-9633
Shelley Barney, *Principal*
Daniel A Erhardt, *Accounts Mgr*
Thomas S Elsass, *Manager*
Thomas Elsass,
EMP: 28 EST: 1997
SALES (est): 4.2MM **Privately Held**
SIC: 7389 Document & office record de-
   struction

(G-8735)
TEAM MANAGEMENT INC
Also Called: T M I
2018 N 4th St (43201-1730)
PHONE....................................614 486-0864
Charles Belding, *President*
EMP: 150
SQ FT: 5,000
SALES (est): 7.3MM **Privately Held**
SIC: 7319 Display advertising service

(G-8736)
TEK-COLLECT INCORPORATED
871 Park St (43215-1441)
PHONE....................................614 299-2766
Nicole Buhr, *President*
Jon Ressler, *District Mgr*
Chet Groff, *COO*
Ron Douglas, *Vice Pres*
David Hughes, *Vice Pres*
EMP: 35
SQ FT: 5,500
SALES (est): 5.5MM **Privately Held**
WEB: www.tekcollect.com
SIC: 7322 Collection agency, except real
   estate

(G-8737)
TELHIO CREDIT UNION INC (PA)
96 N 4th St (43215-3163)
P.O. Box 1449 (43216-1449)
PHONE....................................614 221-3233
Leslie Bumgarner, *President*
Michael Marsh, *Business Mgr*
Karen Daniels, *Assistant VP*
Dave Ault, *Vice Pres*
Sheila Ponder, *Vice Pres*
EMP: 50
SQ FT: 24,000
SALES: 30.8MM **Privately Held**
WEB: www.telhio.org
SIC: 6061 Federal credit unions

(G-8738)
TELHIO CREDIT UNION INC
201 Outerbelt St (43213-1560)
PHONE....................................614 221-3233
Susan Tinnerello, *Manager*
EMP: 25
SALES (corp-wide): 30.8MM **Privately Held**
WEB: www.telhio.org
SIC: 6061 Federal credit unions
PA: Telhio Credit Union, Inc.
   96 N 4th St
   Columbus OH 43215
   614 221-3233

(G-8739)
TELLIGEN TECH INC
2740 Airport Dr Ste 190 (43219-2286)
PHONE....................................614 934-1554
Krishna Pandeswara, *President*
Ashwin Telligentechinc, *Info Tech Dir*
Rahul Telligentech, *Tech Recruiter*
EMP: 47 EST: 2012
SALES (est): 3.4MM **Privately Held**
SIC: 7373 7379 Systems engineering,
   computer related; office computer au-
   tomation systems integration; computer
   related consulting services;

(G-8740)
TERRAFIRM CONSTRUCTION LLC
250 N Hartford Ave (43222-1100)
PHONE....................................913 433-2998
Michael Coccia, *Treasurer*
Douglas McCrae,
EMP: 30 EST: 2014
SQ FT: 5,000
SALES (est): 3.4MM
SALES (corp-wide): 53.3MM **Privately Held**
SIC: 1799 Caulking (construction)
PA: C.J. Mahan Construction Company, Llc
   250 N Hartford Ave
   Columbus OH 43222
   614 277-4545

(G-8741)
TFH-EB INC
Also Called: Waterworks, The
550 Schrock Rd (43229-1062)
PHONE....................................614 253-7246
Thomas F Havens, *Ch of Bd*
David R Specht, *President*
Ellen Hardymon, *Corp Secy*
EMP: 80 EST: 1935
SQ FT: 25,000
SALES: 9.7MM **Privately Held**
WEB: www.thewaterworks.com
SIC: 7699 4212 1711 Sewer cleaning &
   rodding; hazardous waste transport;
   plumbing, heating, air-conditioning con-
   tractors

(G-8742)
THE COTTINGHAM PAPER CO
Also Called: Cottingham Party Savers
324 E 2nd Ave (43201-3624)
PHONE....................................614 294-6444
Richard S Cottingham, *President*
Craig Cottingham, *Vice Pres*
Mary Beth Willis, *CFO*
Ed Hilbert, *Sales Associate*
EMP: 45
SQ FT: 48,000
SALES (est): 5.6MM **Privately Held**
WEB: www.cottinghampaper.com
SIC: 5046 5113 5087 Restaurant equip-
   ment & supplies; industrial & personal
   service paper; janitors' supplies

(G-8743)
THE DAIMLER GROUP INC
1533 Lake Shore Dr (43204-3897)
PHONE....................................614 488-4424
Robert C Daimler, *Ch of Bd*
Conrad W Wisinger, *President*
Herman Ziegler, *COO*
Larry Wendling, *CFO*
EMP: 31
SQ FT: 7,000
SALES (est): 10.4MM **Privately Held**
WEB: www.daimlergroup.com
SIC: 6552 Land subdividers & developers,
   commercial; land subdividers & develop-
   ers, residential

(G-8744)
THE HUNTINGTON INVESTMENT CO (HQ)
41 S High St Fl 7 (43215-6116)
PHONE....................................614 480-3600
Michael Miroballi, *President*
Raymond Closz, *COO*
Jay O'Malley, *Vice Pres*
Jean Wing, *Sales Staff*
Cindy Husvar, *Supervisor*
EMP: 50
SQ FT: 110,000

SALES (est): 56.4MM
SALES (corp-wide): 5.2B **Publicly Held**
SIC: 6211 Brokers, security
PA: Huntington Bancshares Incorporated
   41 S High St
   Columbus OH 43215
   614 480-8300

(G-8745)
THIRTY-ONE GIFTS LLC (PA)
3425 Morse Xing (43219-6014)
PHONE....................................614 414-4300
Cynthia M Monroe, *CEO*
Sean Dunne, *Managing Dir*
Jason Compton, *Facilities Mgr*
Erin Brewer, *Opers Spvr*
Shana Martz, *Opers Spvr*
EMP: 1818
SQ FT: 1,000,000
SALES (est): 71.8MM **Privately Held**
SIC: 5947 4226 Gift shop; textile ware-
   housing

(G-8746)
THOMAS DOOR CONTROLS INC
4196 Indianola Ave (43214-2858)
PHONE....................................614 263-1756
Scott Thomas, *President*
George Claypool, *General Mgr*
Todd Sackett, *Vice Pres*
Dustin Bruggeman, *Project Mgr*
David Gregg, *Project Mgr*
▲ EMP: 36
SQ FT: 10,000
SALES: 19.8MM **Privately Held**
SIC: 5063 7699 Electrical apparatus &
   equipment; door & window repair

(G-8747)
THOMAS W RUFF AND COMPANY
Also Called: Office Furniture USA
855 Grandview Ave Ste 2 (43215-1102)
PHONE....................................800 828-0234
John V Johnson II, *President*
EMP: 260 EST: 2007
SALES (est): 21.8MM **Privately Held**
SIC: 5021 5712 Office & public building
   furniture; office furniture

(G-8748)
THOMPSON CAPRI LANES INC
5860 Roche Dr (43229-3208)
PHONE....................................614 888-3159
Daniel Thompson, *President*
EMP: 25
SQ FT: 12,500
SALES (est): 921.5K **Privately Held**
SIC: 7933 Ten pin center

(G-8749)
THOMPSON HINE LLP
10 W Broad St Ste 700 (43215-3476)
PHONE....................................614 469-3200
Bradley Vogel, *Chief*
David Benz, *Counsel*
Elizabeth Blattner, *Counsel*
Thomas Brigham, *Counsel*
Steven Davis, *Counsel*
EMP: 125
SALES (corp-wide): 162.4MM **Privately Held**
SIC: 8111 General practice attorney,
   lawyer
PA: Thompson Hine Llp
   127 Public Sq
   Cleveland OH 44114
   216 566-5500

(G-8750)
THOMPSON HINE LLP
41 S High St Ste 1700 (43215-6157)
PHONE....................................614 469-3200
Anthony White, *Branch Mgr*
Nick Seabolt, *Technology*
EMP: 123
SALES (corp-wide): 176.3MM **Privately Held**
SIC: 8111 General practice attorney,
   lawyer
PA: Thompson Hine Llp
   127 Public Sq
   Cleveland OH 44114
   216 566-5500

(G-8751)
THREE C BODY SHOP INC (PA)
2300 Briggs Rd (43223-3218)
PHONE....................................614 274-9700
Robert Juniper Jr, *President*
EMP: 65
SQ FT: 40,000
SALES (est): 7.8MM **Privately Held**
SIC: 7532 7539 Body shop, automotive;
   frame repair shops, automotive

(G-8752)
THREE C BODY SHOP INC
8321 N High St (43235-6459)
PHONE....................................614 885-0900
Juniper Bob, *General Mgr*
EMP: 35
SALES (corp-wide): 7.8MM **Privately Held**
SIC: 7532 Body shop, automotive
PA: Three C Body Shop Inc
   2300 Briggs Rd
   Columbus OH 43223
   614 274-9700

(G-8753)
THURNS BAKERY & DELI
541 S 3rd St (43215-5721)
PHONE....................................614 221-9246
Marilyn Plank, *President*
Bill Plank, *Vice Pres*
Chris Plank, *Vice Pres*
Dan Plank, *Vice Pres*
EMP: 25 EST: 1972
SQ FT: 2,100
SALES (est): 1.1MM **Privately Held**
SIC: 5461 5149 2051 Bakeries; bakery
   products; bread, cake & related products

(G-8754)
TIME WARNER CABLE ENTPS LLC
1600 Dublin Rd Fl 2 (43215-2098)
PHONE....................................614 255-6289
Rhonda Frost, *President*
EMP: 3000
SALES (corp-wide): 43.6B **Publicly Held**
SIC: 4841 Cable television services
HQ: Time Warner Cable Enterprises Llc
   400 Atlantic St Ste 6
   Stamford CT 06901

(G-8755)
TIME WARNER CABLE ENTPS LLC
1125 Chambers Rd (43212-1701)
PHONE....................................614 481-5072
John Uversagtz, *Manager*
EMP: 50
SQ FT: 11,813
SALES (corp-wide): 43.6B **Publicly Held**
SIC: 4841 Cable television services
HQ: Time Warner Cable Enterprises Llc
   400 Atlantic St Ste 6
   Stamford CT 06901

(G-8756)
TIME WARNER CABLE INC
Also Called: Insight Communications
3770 E Livingston Ave (43227-2246)
PHONE....................................614 236-1200
Jim Hires, *Manager*
EMP: 25
SALES (corp-wide): 43.6B **Publicly Held**
SIC: 4841 Cable television services
HQ: Spectrum Management Holding Com-
   pany, Llc
   400 Atlantic St
   Stamford CT 06901
   203 905-7801

(G-8757)
TIME WARNER CABLE INC
1980 Alum Creek Dr (43207-1792)
PHONE....................................614 481-5050
Pete Spicer, *Systems Mgr*
EMP: 60
SALES (corp-wide): 43.6B **Publicly Held**
WEB: www.rrbiznet.com
SIC: 4841 Cable television services
HQ: Spectrum Management Holding Com-
   pany, Llc
   400 Atlantic St
   Stamford CT 06901
   203 905-7801

(G-8758)
TIME WARNER CABLE INC
1266 Dublin Rd (43215-1008)
P.O. Box 2553 (43216-2553)
PHONE..............................614 481-5000
Rhonda Frost, *President*
EMP: 600
SALES (corp-wide): 43.6B **Publicly Held**
SIC: 4841 Cable television services
HQ: Spectrum Management Holding Company, Llc
400 Atlantic St
Stamford CT 06901
203 905-7801

(G-8759)
TITLE FIRST AGENCY INC (PA)
3650 Olentangy River Rd # 400
(43214-3654)
PHONE..............................614 224-9207
Sean Stoner, *President*
James Hewit, *President*
Tony Nauta, *Vice Pres*
Paul Thompson, *Vice Pres*
Tammy Leach, *Opers Staff*
EMP: 30 **EST:** 1956
SQ FT: 7,500
SALES (est): 37.5MM **Privately Held**
WEB: www.titlefirst.com
SIC: 6361 7375 Real estate title insurance; data base information retrieval

(G-8760)
TJM CLMBUS LLC TJM CLUMBUS LLC
6500 Doubletree Ave (43229-1111)
PHONE..............................614 885-1885
Steve Petrucelli, *General Mgr*
EMP: 99
SQ FT: 594,507
SALES (est): 1.3MM **Privately Held**
SIC: 8741 Hotel or motel management

(G-8761)
TNT EQUIPMENT COMPANY (PA)
6677 Broughton Ave (43213-1523)
PHONE..............................614 882-1549
Anthony J Valentine, *President*
Patrick Williams, *Regl Sales Mgr*
Ernie Bowman, *Sales Staff*
Joe Valentine, *Sales Staff*
Joel Baileys, *Marketing Staff*
EMP: 25
SQ FT: 7,000
SALES (est): 14.8MM **Privately Held**
WEB: www.tntequip.com
SIC: 5082 7353 7699 General construction machinery & equipment; heavy construction equipment rental; construction equipment repair

(G-8762)
TOM PROPERTIES LLC
777 Dearborn Park Ln A (43085-5716)
PHONE..............................614 781-0055
Kim Brown, *District Mgr*
EMP: 100
SQ FT: 5,000
SALES (est): 5.2MM **Privately Held**
WEB: www.tomproperties.com
SIC: 6531 Rental agent, real estate

(G-8763)
TOMMY BAHAMA GROUP INC
4185 The Strand (43219-6120)
PHONE..............................614 750-9668
EMP: 112
SALES (corp-wide): 1.1B **Publicly Held**
SIC: 7389 Apparel designers, commercial
HQ: Tommy Bahama Group, Inc.
400 Fairview Ave N # 488
Seattle WA 98109

(G-8764)
TOTH RENOVATION LLC
444 Siebert St (43206-2721)
PHONE..............................614 542-9683
EMP: 25
SALES (est): 3.1MM **Privately Held**
SIC: 1521 General remodeling, single-family houses

(G-8765)
TOWLIFT INC
1200 Milepost Dr (43228-9862)
PHONE..............................614 851-1001
Craig Reich, *Manager*
EMP: 70
SALES (corp-wide): 106.6MM **Privately Held**
SIC: 5084 7699 Lift trucks & parts; industrial equipment services
PA: Towlift, Inc.
1395 Valley Belt Rd
Brooklyn Heights OH 44131
216 749-6800

(G-8766)
TOWN INN CO LLC
Also Called: Holiday Inn
175 E Town St (43215-4609)
PHONE..............................614 221-3281
Gene Calloway, *Branch Mgr*
EMP: 79
SQ FT: 124,294
SALES (est): 1.4MM **Privately Held**
SIC: 7011 Hotels & motels
HQ: Town Inn Co Llc
3850 Bird Rd Ste 302
Miami FL 33146
614 221-3281

(G-8767)
TOWNHOMES MANAGEMENT INC
407 E Livingston Ave (43215-5587)
PHONE..............................614 228-3578
Lawrence D Schaffer, *President*
Darrell Spegal, *Vice Pres*
EMP: 29 **EST:** 1972
SQ FT: 1,500
SALES (est): 2.2MM **Privately Held**
WEB: www.ktohio.com
SIC: 6513 6531 Apartment building operators; real estate brokers & agents

(G-8768)
TP MECHANICAL CONTRACTORS INC
Also Called: T P McHncal Cntrs Svc Fbrction
2130 Franklin Rd (43209-2724)
PHONE..............................614 253-8556
Bill Riddle, *VP Opers*
Mike Kraner, *Foreman/Supr*
Tim Hoover, *Manager*
Rick Mercer, *Manager*
John Pennell, *Info Tech Dir*
EMP: 250
SALES (est): 24.6MM **Privately Held**
SIC: 1711 Mechanical contractor
PA: Tp Mechanical Contractors, Inc.
1500 Kemper Meadow Dr
Cincinnati OH 45240

(G-8769)
TPUSA INC
Also Called: Teleperformance USA
4335 Equity Dr (43228-3842)
PHONE..............................614 621-5512
Trevor Ferger, *Exec VP*
Jeffrey Torrence, *Manager*
Rob Wilson, *Prgrmr*
Jennifer Donaldson, *Recruiter*
EMP: 800
SALES (corp-wide): 123.7MM **Privately Held**
WEB: www.teleperformanceusa.com
SIC: 7389 Telemarketing services
HQ: Tpusa, Inc.
5295 S Commerce Dr # 600
Murray UT 84107
801 257-5800

(G-8770)
TRADER BUDS WESTSIDE DODGE
4000 W Broad St (43228-1449)
PHONE..............................614 272-0000
Nelson Bowers, *Vice Pres*
EMP: 85
SQ FT: 22,000
SALES: 77.6MM
SALES (corp-wide): 9.9B **Publicly Held**
WEB: www.traderbuds.com
SIC: 5511 7538 Automobiles, new & used; general automotive repair shops

PA: Sonic Automotive, Inc.
4401 Colwick Rd
Charlotte NC 28211
704 566-2400

(G-8771)
TRADESOURCE INC
1550 Old Henderson Rd (43220-3626)
PHONE..............................614 824-3883
EMP: 126 **Privately Held**
SIC: 7361 Labor contractors (employment agency)
PA: Tradesource, Inc.
205 Hallene Rd Unit 211
Warwick RI 02886

(G-8772)
TRADITIONS AT STYGLER ROAD
Also Called: National Ch Rsdnces Stygler Rd
167 N Stygler Rd (43230-2434)
PHONE..............................614 475-8778
Steve Bodkin, *President*
Lisa Crane, *Director*
Amy Haught, *Director*
Will Villasante, *Director*
EMP: 29 **EST:** 1994
SALES (est): 4.6MM
SALES (corp-wide): 38.2MM **Privately Held**
SIC: 8051 Skilled nursing care facilities
PA: National Church Residences
2335 N Bank Dr
Columbus OH 43220
614 451-2151

(G-8773)
TRANSAMERICA PREMIER LF INSUR
1335 Dublin Rd Ste 200c (43215-7008)
PHONE..............................614 488-5983
Raymond De Piro, *Branch Mgr*
EMP: 34
SALES (corp-wide): 593.2MM **Privately Held**
WEB: www.monlife.com
SIC: 6311 6321 Life insurance carriers; accident & health insurance
HQ: Transamerica Premier Life Insurance Company
4333 Edgewood Rd Ne
Cedar Rapids IA 52499
319 355-8511

(G-8774)
TRANSPORTATION OHIO DEPARTMENT
1600 W Broad St (43223-1202)
PHONE..............................614 275-1300
Jerry Wray, *Director*
EMP: 40 **Privately Held**
SIC: 9199 8734 ; automobile proving & testing ground
HQ: Ohio Department Of Transportation
1980 W Broad St
Columbus OH 43223

(G-8775)
TRANSYSTEMS CORPORATION
400 W Nationwide Blvd # 225
(43215-4373)
PHONE..............................614 433-7800
Aaron Grilliot, *Manager*
EMP: 25
SALES (corp-wide): 144.2MM **Privately Held**
SIC: 8711 Consulting engineer
PA: Transystems Corporation
2400 Pershing Rd Ste 400
Kansas City MO 64108
816 329-8700

(G-8776)
TRI MODAL SERVICE INC
2015 Walcutt Rd (43228-9575)
P.O. Box 109, Worthington (43085-0109)
PHONE..............................614 876-6325
Mark Stewart, *President*
John S Stewart, *Vice Pres*
Wilma S Stewart, *Treasurer*
Bernie Mauck, *Manager*
Richard Elliott, *Admin Sec*
EMP: 29
SQ FT: 2,500

SALES: 442.9K
SALES (corp-wide): 35.2MM **Privately Held**
WEB: www.trnj.com
SIC: 4214 Local trucking with storage
PA: Transinternational System, Inc.
130 E Wilson Bridge Rd # 150
Worthington OH 43085
614 891-4942

(G-8777)
TRIAD TRANSPORT INC
1484 Williams Rd (43207-5178)
P.O. Box 818, McAlester OK (74502-0818)
PHONE..............................614 491-9497
Jim Painter, *Branch Mgr*
EMP: 42
SALES (est): 1.8MM
SALES (corp-wide): 28MM **Privately Held**
WEB: www.triadtransport.com
SIC: 4213 4953 Trucking, except local; hazardous waste collection & disposal
PA: Triad Transport, Inc.
1630 Diesel Ave
Mcalester OK 74501
918 421-2429

(G-8778)
TRICONT TRUCKING COMPANY
2200 Westbelt Dr (43228-3820)
PHONE..............................614 527-7398
Jerry Baker, *General Mgr*
EMP: 181 **Privately Held**
SIC: 4212 Local trucking, without storage
HQ: Tricont Trucking Company
241 Sevilla Ave
Coral Gables FL 33134
305 520-8400

(G-8779)
TRIDENT USA HEALTH SVCS LLC
Also Called: Mobilex USA
6185 Huntley Rd Ste Q (43229-1094)
PHONE..............................614 888-2226
Rick Lang, *Manager*
EMP: 50 **Privately Held**
SIC: 8071 X-ray laboratory, including dental
PA: Trident Usa Health Services, Llc
930 Ridgebrook Rd Fl 3
Sparks MD 21152

(G-8780)
TRINITY CONTRACTING INC
4878 Mgnolia Blossom Blvd (43230-1025)
PHONE..............................614 905-4410
David Albrecht, *Principal*
EMP: 99
SALES (est): 3MM **Privately Held**
SIC: 1799 Special trade contractors

(G-8781)
TRINITY HEALTH CORPORATION
5700 Karl Rd (43229-3602)
PHONE..............................614 846-5420
James Griffith, *Director*
EMP: 350
SALES (corp-wide): 18.3B **Privately Held**
WEB: www.trinity-health.com
SIC: 8051 8092 8069 Skilled nursing care facilities; kidney dialysis centers; specialty hospitals, except psychiatric
PA: Trinity Health Corporation
20555 Victor Pkwy
Livonia MI 48152
734 343-1000

(G-8782)
TRINITY HEALTH GROUP LTD
827 Yard St (43212-3886)
PHONE..............................614 899-4830
John Chory, *Officer*
Robert Gesing,
EMP: 42
SQ FT: 70,000
SALES: 6.7MM **Privately Held**
WEB: www.trinityhealthgroup.com
SIC: 8712 Architectural services

(G-8783)
TRINITY HOME BUILDERS INC
2700 E Dublin Granville (43231-4094)
PHONE..............................614 889-7830
Jim Phieffer, *President*

Keith Pecinovski, *Principal*
Mark Vouis, *Vice Pres*
William Moorhead, *Treasurer*
Scott Esker, *Sales Staff*
EMP: 25
SALES (est): 3MM **Privately Held**
SIC: 1521 New construction, single-family houses

(G-8784)
TRIO LIMITED (PA)
Also Called: Equity Line Mortgage Company
2400 Corporate Exch Dr (43231-7605)
PHONE..............................614 898-5463
Dan Miller, *Partner*
Eric Bosley, *Senior Engr*
Ben Miller,
EMP: 35
SQ FT: 5,500
SALES (est): 2.7MM **Privately Held**
WEB: www.equitylinemortgage.com
SIC: 6163 Mortgage brokers arranging for loans, using money of others

(G-8785)
TRUBUILT CONSTRUCTION SVCS LLC
Also Called: Rezod
777 Harrison Dr (43204-3507)
PHONE..............................614 279-4800
Charles Dozer, *Mng Member*
EMP: 35
SALES (est): 2.8MM **Privately Held**
SIC: 1542 Commercial & office building, new construction

(G-8786)
TUCKER ELLIS LLP
175 S 3rd St Ste 520 (43215-7101)
PHONE..............................614 358-9717
Eric Weldele, *Manager*
EMP: 95
SALES (corp-wide): 49.1MM **Privately Held**
SIC: 8111 General practice attorney, lawyer
PA: Tucker Ellis Llp
   950 Main Ave Ste 1100
   Cleveland OH 44113
   216 592-5000

(G-8787)
TURN-KEY INDUSTRIAL SVCS LLC
820 Distribution Dr (43228-1004)
PHONE..............................614 274-1128
Gregory Less, *Mng Member*
EMP: 52
SQ FT: 10,000
SALES (est): 7.6MM **Privately Held**
SIC: 7692 3441 Automotive welding; building components, structural steel

(G-8788)
TURNER CONSTRUCTION COMPANY
262 Hanover St (43215-2332)
PHONE..............................614 984-3000
Joe Dziengelewski, *Superintendent*
Rik Labardi, *Vice Pres*
EMP: 75
SALES (corp-wide): 579.6MM **Privately Held**
WEB: www.tcco.com
SIC: 1542 Commercial & office building, new construction
HQ: Turner Construction Company Inc
   375 Hudson St Fl 6
   New York NY 10014
   212 229-6000

(G-8789)
TURNKEY NETWORK SOLUTIONS LLC
3450 Millikin Ct Ste A (43228-9378)
PHONE..............................614 876-9944
Michael Trudeau, *Branch Mgr*
EMP: 25
SALES (corp-wide): 1.2MM **Privately Held**
WEB: www.tkns.net
SIC: 8711 8748 Engineering services; telecommunications consultant

PA: Turnkey Network Solutions, Llc
   7020 Southbelt Dr Se
   Caledonia MI 49316
   616 455-9840

(G-8790)
TURTLES ENVMTL ABATEMENT CO
Also Called: Teac
5601 Little Ben Cir Apt B (43231-7105)
PHONE..............................614 603-9439
Nyesha Watson, *President*
EMP: 36
SALES (est): 495.1K **Privately Held**
SIC: 7389

(G-8791)
TWO MEN & A VACUUM LLC
81 S 4th St Ste 100 (43215-4355)
PHONE..............................614 300-7970
Cody Warren, *CEO*
EMP: 52
SALES: 700K **Privately Held**
SIC: 7349 7359 Cleaning service, industrial or commercial; home cleaning & maintenance equipment rental services

(G-8792)
U S A PLUMBING COMPANY
1425 Community Park Dr (43229-2258)
PHONE..............................614 882-6402
Fax: 614 882-5936
EMP: 27
SQ FT: 1,400
SALES (est): 1.7MM **Privately Held**
SIC: 1711 Plumbing Contractor

(G-8793)
UBS FINANCIAL SERVICES INC
41 S High St Ste 3300 (43215-6104)
PHONE..............................614 460-6559
EMP: 50
SALES (corp-wide): 28B **Privately Held**
SIC: 6211 Security Broker/Dealer
HQ: Ubs Financial Services Inc.
   1285 Ave Of The Americas
   New York NY 10019
   212 713-2000

(G-8794)
UBS FINANCIAL SERVICES INC
5025 Arlngtn Ctr Blvd # 120 (43220-2959)
PHONE..............................614 442-6240
Ken Dorsch, *Manager*
Susan Surtman, *Advisor*
EMP: 30
SALES (corp-wide): 29.4B **Privately Held**
SIC: 6211 Security brokers & dealers
HQ: Ubs Financial Services Inc.
   1285 Ave Of The Americas
   New York NY 10019
   212 713-2000

(G-8795)
UCT PROPERTY INC
1801 Watermark Dr Ste 100 (43215-7088)
PHONE..............................614 228-3276
Ron Hunt, *Vice Pres*
EMP: 40
SALES: 136.7K
SALES (corp-wide): 18.4MM **Privately Held**
SIC: 6411 Insurance agents & brokers
PA: The Order Of Unite Commercial Tra
   1801 Watermark Dr Ste 100
   Columbus OH 43215
   614 487-9680

(G-8796)
ULMER & BERNE LLP
65 E State St Ste 1100 (43215-4213)
PHONE..............................614 229-0000
Alexander Andrews, *Principal*
Rebecca B Swanson,
Brian E Linhart, *Associate*
EMP: 27
SALES (corp-wide): 85.9MM **Privately Held**
SIC: 8111 General practice attorney, lawyer
PA: Ulmer & Berne Llp
   1660 W 2nd St Ste 1100
   Cleveland OH 44113
   216 583-7000

(G-8797)
UNICO ALLOYS & METALS INC
Also Called: United Alloys and Metals
1177 Joyce Ave Ste B (43219-1900)
PHONE..............................614 299-0545
Dane Germuska, *President*
Frank Santorio, *Vice Pres*
John Churley, *Admin Sec*
◆ **EMP:** 76
SQ FT: 450,000
SALES (est): 33MM
SALES (corp-wide): 2.5B **Privately Held**
SIC: 5093 Ferrous metal scrap & waste; metal scrap & waste materials
HQ: Cronimet Ferroleg. Gmbh
   Sudbeckenstr. 22
   Karlsruhe 76189
   721 952-250

(G-8798)
UNICON INTERNATIONAL INC (PA)
241 Outerbelt St (43213-1529)
PHONE..............................614 861-7070
Peichen Jane Lee, *President*
David Lee, *General Mgr*
Sherman Lau, *Senior VP*
Li-Hung David Lee, *Vice Pres*
Michael McAlear, *Vice Pres*
EMP: 126
SQ FT: 10,000
SALES (est): 17.8MM **Privately Held**
WEB: www.unicon-intl.com
SIC: 7371 7379 Computer software systems analysis & design, custom; computer related consulting services

(G-8799)
UNION MORTGAGE SERVICES INC (PA)
Also Called: First Community Mortgage Svcs
1080 Fishinger Rd (43221-2302)
PHONE..............................614 457-4815
James P Simpson, *President*
W Matthew Baker, *Vice Pres*
EMP: 40
SQ FT: 1,200
SALES: 5MM **Privately Held**
SIC: 6163 Mortgage brokers arranging for loans, using money of others

(G-8800)
UNITED FOOD COMML WRKRS UN
Also Called: Ufcw Local 1059
4150 E Main St Fl 2 (43213-2953)
PHONE..............................614 235-3635
Rebecca A Berroyer, *President*
Jason Kaseman, *Comms Dir*
Julie Klein, *Office Mgr*
Tina Morgan, *Director*
EMP: 27
SQ FT: 3,700
SALES: 10.7MM **Privately Held**
WEB: www.ufcw1059.com
SIC: 8631 Labor union

(G-8801)
UNITED HEALTHCARE OHIO INC (DH)
9200 Worthington Rd (43085)
PHONE..............................614 410-7000
Tom Brady, *CEO*
G David Shafer, *President*
Thomas Sullivan, *COO*
Paula Conner, *Manager*
EMP: 350 **EST:** 1978
SQ FT: 72,000
SALES (est): 955.1MM
SALES (corp-wide): 226.2B **Publicly Held**
WEB: www.uhc.com
SIC: 6324 Group hospitalization plans; health maintenance organization (HMO), insurance only
HQ: United Healthcare Services Inc.
   9900 Bren Rd E Ste 300w
   Minnetonka MN 55343
   952 936-1300

(G-8802)
UNITED HOME HEALTH SERVICES
297 Woodland Ave (43203-1747)
PHONE..............................614 880-8686

David R Weaver, *President*
EMP: 85
SALES: 500K **Privately Held**
SIC: 8082 Home health care services

(G-8803)
UNITED MANAGEMENT INC (PA)
Also Called: Casto
250 Civic Center Dr (43215-5086)
PHONE..............................614 228-5331
Don M Casto III, *President*
Shannon Dixon, *President*
Brett Hutchens, *Partner*
Paul Lukeman, *Partner*
Frank S Benson Jr, *Principal*
EMP: 75 **EST:** 1955
SALES (est): 74.2MM **Privately Held**
WEB: www.castosoutheast.com
SIC: 6512 Shopping center, property operation only

(G-8804)
UNITED METHODIST CHILDRENS (PA)
Also Called: United Methodist Childrens HM
431 E Broad St (43215-4004)
PHONE..............................614 885-5020
David Kurtz, *CFO*
Sean Reilly, *Exec Dir*
Bill Brownson, *Director*
EMP: 130
SQ FT: 7,000
SALES (est): 3.9MM **Privately Held**
WEB: www.umchohio.org
SIC: 8361 8322 Home for the emotionally disturbed; group foster home; adoption services

(G-8805)
UNITED PARCEL SERVICE INC
Also Called: UPS
1711 Georgesville Rd (43228-3619)
PHONE..............................614 385-9100
Corey Thompson, *General Mgr*
Julia Manning, *Human Res Mgr*
John Cummins, *Branch Mgr*
EMP: 60
SALES (corp-wide): 71.8B **Publicly Held**
WEB: www.ups.com
SIC: 4513 Letter delivery, private air; package delivery, private air; parcel delivery, private air
PA: United Parcel Service, Inc.
   55 Glenlake Pkwy
   Atlanta GA 30328
   404 828-6000

(G-8806)
UNITED PARCEL SERVICE INC
Also Called: UPS
118 Graceland Blvd (43214-1530)
PHONE..............................614 431-0600
Vinu Patel, *Branch Mgr*
EMP: 38
SALES (corp-wide): 71.8B **Publicly Held**
WEB: www.ups.com
SIC: 4215 Package delivery, vehicular
PA: United Parcel Service, Inc.
   55 Glenlake Pkwy
   Atlanta GA 30328
   404 828-6000

(G-8807)
UNITED PARCEL SERVICE INC OH
Also Called: UPS
100 E Campus View Blvd # 300 (43235-8602)
PHONE..............................614 841-7159
EMP: 158
SALES (corp-wide): 71.8B **Publicly Held**
WEB: www.upsscs.com
SIC: 4215 Package delivery, vehicular; parcel delivery, vehicular
HQ: United Parcel Service, Inc. (Oh)
   55 Glenlake Pkwy
   Atlanta GA 30328
   404 828-6000

(G-8808)
UNITED PARCEL SERVICE INC OH
Also Called: UPS
5101 Trabue Rd (43228-9481)
PHONE..............................614 870-4111

EMP: 316
SALES (corp-wide): 71.8B **Publicly Held**
WEB: www.upsscs.com
SIC: 7389 Mailing & messenger services
HQ: United Parcel Service, Inc. (Oh)
55 Glenlake Pkwy
Atlanta GA 30328
404 828-6000

(G-8809)
UNITED PRODUCERS INC (PA)
8351 N High St Ste 250 (43235-1440)
PHONE..............................614 433-2150
Mike Bumgarner, *President*
Dennis Bolling, *President*
Bob Siegel, *Vice Pres*
Rich Majzik, *CFO*
Joe Werstak, *CFO*
EMP: 153
SALES (est): 114.1MM Privately Held
WEB: www.uproducers.com
SIC: 5154 Auctioning livestock; cattle

(G-8810)
UNITED STATES CARGO &
COURIER
2036 Williams Rd (43207-5117)
PHONE..............................614 449-2854
Alice Wassel, *Manager*
EMP: 45
SALES (corp-wide): 11.1MM **Privately**
Held
WEB: www.usccs.com
SIC: 4731 Freight transportation arrangement
HQ: United States Cargo & Courier Service
Incorporated
900 Williams Ave
Columbus OH
614 552-2746

(G-8811)
UNITED STATES TROTTING
ASSN
800 Michigan Ave (43215-1595)
PHONE..............................614 224-2291
Fred Noe, *Exec VP*
Deveau Zubrod, *Adv Dir*
David Carr, *Manager*
Igor Efremenkov, *Info Tech Mgr*
EMP: 78
SALES (corp-wide): 7.9MM **Privately**
Held
WEB: www.ustrotting.com
SIC: 8743 Public relations & publicity
PA: United States Trotting Association (Inc)
6130 S Sunbury Rd
Westerville OH 43081
614 224-2291

(G-8812)
UNITED STEELWORKERS
Also Called: Uswa
4467 Village Park Dr (43228-6430)
PHONE..............................614 272-8609
S Kidwell, *Branch Mgr*
EMP: 50
SALES (corp-wide): 4.9MM **Privately**
Held
WEB: www.uswa.org
SIC: 8631 Labor union
PA: United Steelworkers
60 Bolevard Of The Allies
Pittsburgh PA 15222
412 562-2400

(G-8813)
UNITED STTES BOWL
CONGRESS INC
643 S Hamilton Rd (43213-3176)
PHONE..............................614 237-3716
J E Dimond, *Branch Mgr*
EMP: 51
SALES (corp-wide): 32.9MM **Privately**
Held
SIC: 8699 Athletic organizations
PA: United States Bowling Congress, Inc.
621 Six Flags Dr
Arlington TX 76011
817 385-8200

(G-8814)
UNITED WAY CENTRAL OHIO
INC
360 S 3rd St (43215-5412)
PHONE..............................614 227-2700
Janet E Jackson, *President*
Helen Ninos, *COO*
Michael Robinson, *Assistant VP*
S Dianne Biggs, *Vice Pres*
Richard Carrick, *Vice Pres*
EMP: 78
SQ FT: 10,000
SALES: 53.3MM **Privately Held**
WEB: www.uwcentralohio.org
SIC: 8399 Fund raising organization, non-fee basis

(G-8815)
UNIVERSAL FABG CNSTR SVCS
INC
Also Called: UNI-Facs
1241 Mckinley Ave (43222-1114)
PHONE..............................614 274-1128
Steve Finkel, *President*
Robert Watts, *Treasurer*
▲ **EMP:** 86
SQ FT: 120,000
SALES (est): 25.1MM **Privately Held**
WEB: www.unifacs.com
SIC: 1541 3441 3599 1799 Renovation,
remodeling & repairs: industrial buildings;
building components, structural steel; ex-
pansion joints (structural shapes), iron or
steel; catapults; sandblasting of building
exteriors

(G-8816)
UNIVERSAL HEALTH CARE
SVCS INC
2873 Suwanee Rd (43224-4469)
PHONE..............................614 547-0282
Suliman Ahmed, *President*
Aden J Abu, *CFO*
EMP: 120
SQ FT: 3,600
SALES (est): 3.7MM **Privately Held**
SIC: 8082 Home health care services

(G-8817)
UNIVERSAL RECOVERY
SYSTEMS
Also Called: Stat Communications
5197 Trabue Rd (43228-9498)
PHONE..............................614 299-0184
Jeff Saley, *President*
Natalie Price, *Finance*
Elizabeth Rodriguez, *Office Mgr*
EMP: 54
SALES (est): 10.7MM **Privately Held**
SIC: 1623 1731 Cable laying construction;
fiber optic cable installation

(G-8818)
UNIVERSITY EYE SURGEONS
Also Called: Eye Physicians & Surgeons
456 W 10th Ave Ste 5241 (43210-1240)
PHONE..............................614 293-5635
Thomas Mauger, *Principal*
EMP: 150
SALES (est): 3.5MM **Privately Held**
SIC: 8011 Physicians' office, including specialists

(G-8819)
UNIVERSITY GYN&OB
CNSLTNTS INC (PA)
1654 Upham Dr Rm N500 (43210-1250)
PHONE..............................614 293-8697
L Copeland, *President*
M Landon, *Corp Secy*
Dan Pierce, *Administration*
EMP: 30
SALES (est): 1.2MM **Privately Held**
SIC: 8011 Gynecologist; obstetrician

(G-8820)
UNIVERSITY
OTOLARYNGOLOGISTS (PA)
Also Called: E N T
810 Mackenzie Dr (43220)
PHONE..............................614 273-2241
David E Schuller MD, *President*
David R Kelly MD, *Vice Pres*
EMP: 40 **EST:** 1964

SALES (est): 6MM **Privately Held**
WEB: www.excel-ent.com
SIC: 8011 5999 Ears, nose & throat spe-
cialist: physician/surgeon; hearing aids

(G-8821)
UNUM LIFE INSURANCE CO
AMER
445 Hutchinson Ave # 300 (43235-5677)
PHONE..............................614 807-2500
Sherry Thomas, *Sales Staff*
R G Peterson, *Manager*
EMP: 39 **Publicly Held**
WEB: www.benuckrainey.com
SIC: 6311 Life insurance
HQ: Unum Life Insurance Company Of
America
2211 Congress St
Portland ME 04122
207 575-2211

(G-8822)
UPGRADE HOMES
586 Blenheim Rd (43214-3264)
PHONE..............................614 975-8532
Jeff Trickett, *President*
EMP: 50
SALES (est): 1.6MM **Privately Held**
SIC: 1522 Residential construction

(G-8823)
UPH HOLDINGS LLC
Also Called: Marriott Columbus Univ Area
3100 Olentangy River Rd (43202-1517)
PHONE..............................614 447-9777
Dena St Clair, *Director*
EMP: 99
SALES (est): 533.8K **Privately Held**
SIC: 7011 Hotels & motels

(G-8824)
UPPER ARLINGTON CITY SCHL
DST
Also Called: School Age Child Care
4770 Burbank Dr (43220-2800)
PHONE..............................614 487-5133
Kathy Ficell, *Director*
EMP: 30
SALES (corp-wide): 59MM **Privately**
Held
SIC: 8211 8351 Public elementary school;
child day care services
PA: Upper Arlington City School District
1950 N Mallway Dr
Columbus OH 43221
614 487-5000

(G-8825)
UPPER ARLINGTON LUTHERAN
CH (PA)
2300 Lytham Rd (43220-4699)
PHONE..............................614 451-3736
Paul Uring, *Pastor*
EMP: 35
SALES (est): 1.9MM **Privately Held**
WEB: www.ualc.org
SIC: 8661 8351 Lutheran Church; pre-
school center

(G-8826)
UPPER ARLINGTON SURGERY
CENTER
2240 N Bank Dr (43220-5420)
PHONE..............................614 442-6515
Mary Ann Cooney, *President*
EMP: 48
SQ FT: 24,000
SALES (est): 3.4MM
SALES (corp-wide): 4B **Privately Held**
WEB: www.ohiohealth.com
SIC: 8093 Specialty outpatient clinics
PA: Ohiohealth Corporation
180 E Broad St
Columbus OH 43215
614 788-8860

(G-8827)
UPREACH LLC
4488 Mobile Dr (43220-3713)
PHONE..............................614 442-7702
Patrick Gourely, *Human Res Mgr*
Melissa Gourley, *Mng Member*
Beth Hunter, *Mng Member*
Pat Selbe, *Program Dir*
EMP: 300

SQ FT: 5,937
SALES (est): 5.8MM **Privately Held**
SIC: 8322 Social services for the handi-
capped

(G-8828)
URBAN ONE INC
Also Called: Wckx-FM
350 E 1st Ave Ste 100 (43201-3792)
PHONE..............................614 487-1444
Tara Berman, *Manager*
EMP: 40
SALES (corp-wide): 439.1MM **Publicly**
Held
WEB: www.radio-one.com
SIC: 4832 Radio broadcasting stations
PA: Urban One, Inc.
1010 Wayne Ave Fl 14
Silver Spring MD 20910
301 429-3200

(G-8829)
URBANCREST AFFRDBL HSING
LLC
3443 Agler Rd Ste 200 (43219-3385)
PHONE..............................614 228-3578
Amy Klaben, *President*
Carrie Hiatt, *Director*
EMP: 55
SALES (est): 1.8MM **Privately Held**
SIC: 6513 Apartment building operators

(G-8830)
UROLOGICAL ASSOCIATES INC
750 Mount Carmel Mall # 350
(43222-1553)
PHONE..............................614 221-5189
Stephen P Smith, *President*
R Daniel Bohl, *Treasurer*
EMP: 35 **EST:** 1948
SALES (est): 2.6MM **Privately Held**
SIC: 8011 Urologist

(G-8831)
URS GROUP INC
277 W Nationwide Blvd (43215-2853)
PHONE..............................614 464-4500
Kerry Hogan, *Vice Pres*
Jeff Kerr, *Project Mgr*
James R Linthicum, *Branch Mgr*
Robt J Holland, *Architect*
Harvey Harrison, *Sr Project Mgr*
EMP: 150
SALES (corp-wide): 20.1B **Publicly Held**
SIC: 8711 8712 Engineering services; ar-
chitectural services
HQ: Urs Group, Inc.
300 S Grand Ave Ste 1100
Los Angeles CA 90071
213 593-8000

(G-8832)
URS-SMITH GROUP VA IDIQ
JOINT
277 W Nationwide Blvd (43215-2853)
PHONE..............................614 464-4500
EMP: 50
SALES (est): 3.3MM **Privately Held**
SIC: 8711 Engineering Services

(G-8833)
US DENTAL CARE/M D
GELENDER
Also Called: U S Dental Care
949 E Livingston Ave (43205-2795)
PHONE..............................614 252-3181
Martin D Gelender DDS, *Owner*
EMP: 25 **EST:** 1962
SQ FT: 21,700
SALES (est): 1.6MM **Privately Held**
WEB: www.usdentalcare.com
SIC: 8021 Dentists' office

(G-8834)
US HOME CENTER LLC (PA)
Also Called: Owens Corning Basement Fin-
ishi
2050 Integrity Dr S (43209-2728)
PHONE..............................614 737-9000
Stephen Brookes, *President*
EMP: 27
SQ FT: 7,000

SALES (est): 2.6MM **Privately Held**
SIC: **8748** 1521 Business consulting; single-family home remodeling, additions & repairs

(G-8835)
US SECURITY HOLDINGS INC
1350 W 5th Ave Ste 300 (43212-2907)
PHONE....................................614 488-6110
EMP: 100
SALES (corp-wide): 301.8MM **Privately Held**
SIC: **7381** Security guard service
HQ: U.S. Security Holdings, Inc.
200 Mansell Ct E Ste 500
Roswell GA 30076
770 625-1400

(G-8836)
USF HOLLAND LLC
Also Called: USFreightways
4800 Journal St (43228-4611)
PHONE....................................614 529-9300
Joseph D Barnes, Opers Staff
J D Barnes, Manager
EMP: 250
SALES (corp-wide): 5B **Publicly Held**
WEB: www.usfc.com
SIC: **4213** 4212 Less-than-truckload (LTL) transport; local trucking, without storage
HQ: Usf Holland Llc
700 S Waverly Rd
Holland MI 49423
616 395-5000

(G-8837)
USI INSURANCE SERVICES NAT INC
580 N 4th St Ste 400 (43215-2153)
PHONE....................................614 228-5565
Michael Kelley, Vice Pres
Patty Woo, Branch Mgr
EMP: 43 **Privately Held**
SIC: **6411** Insurance agents
HQ: Usi Insurance Services National, Inc.
150 N Michigan Ave # 3900
Chicago IL 60601
866 294-2571

(G-8838)
UTICA NATIONAL INSURANCE GROUP
2600 Corp Exchange Dr # 200 (43231-1672)
PHONE....................................614 823-5300
Doug Randolph, Branch Mgr
EMP: 48
SALES (corp-wide): 932.2MM **Privately Held**
SIC: **6411** Insurance agents, brokers & service
HQ: Utica National Insurance Group
180 Genesee St
New Hartford NY 13413
315 734-2000

(G-8839)
V VRABLE INC
Also Called: Beeghly Oaks Skilled
3248 Henderson Rd Ste 104 (43220-7337)
PHONE....................................614 545-5500
Allan Vrable, President
James Merrill, CFO
Linda Vrable, Administration
EMP: 109
SQ FT: 56,000
SALES: 7.2MM **Privately Held**
SIC: **8051** Skilled nursing care facilities
PA: Vrable Healthcare, Inc.
3248 Henderson Rd
Columbus OH 43220

(G-8840)
VALLEY INTERIOR SYSTEMS INC
Also Called: Price Thrice Supply
3840 Fisher Rd (43228-1016)
PHONE....................................614 351-8440
Jim Melaragno, Manager
EMP: 150
SALES (corp-wide): 70.4MM **Privately Held**
SIC: **1742** Drywall; acoustical & ceiling work; plastering, plain or ornamental

PA: Valley Interior Systems, Inc.
2203 Fowler St
Cincinnati OH 45206
513 961-0400

(G-8841)
VALUE RECOVERY GROUP INC (PA)
919 Old Henderson Rd (43220-3722)
PHONE....................................614 324-5959
Barry Fromm, Ch of Bd
James Sisto, COO
Sharon Gorby, Senior VP
EMP: 30
SALES (est): 7.7MM **Privately Held**
WEB: www.valuerecovery.com
SIC: **8111** Debt collection law

(G-8842)
VAN DYNE-CROTTY CO (PA)
Also Called: Spirit Services Company
2150 Fairwood Ave (43207-1736)
PHONE....................................614 684-0048
Timothy F Crotty, CEO
Mike Crotty, President
Eugene A Mayl, Principal
R Frank Crotty, Chairman
Randy Hinton, Data Proc Exec
EMP: 25
SQ FT: 107,000
SALES (est): 35.9MM **Privately Held**
WEB: www.getspirit.com
SIC: **7218** 7213 7219 Industrial uniform supply; wiping towel supply; treated equipment supply: mats, rugs, mops, cloths, etc.; industrial clothing launderers; uniform supply; accessory & non-garment cleaning & repair; glove mending for individuals

(G-8843)
VAN DYNE-CROTTY CO
Also Called: Spirit Services Company
2150 Fairwood Ave (43207-1736)
P.O. Box 28506 (43228-0506)
PHONE....................................614 491-3903
Toll Free:............................877
Dennis Frermood, Branch Mgr
EMP: 150
SALES (corp-wide): 35.9MM **Privately Held**
WEB: www.getspirit.com
SIC: **7218** 7213 Industrial uniform supply; uniform supply
PA: Van Dyne-Crotty Co.
2150 Fairwood Ave
Columbus OH 43207
614 684-0048

(G-8844)
VANGUARD WINES LLC (PA)
1020 W 5th Ave (43212-2630)
PHONE....................................614 291-3493
Drew Neiman, CEO
Joan Braun, Sales Staff
Maureen Hunley, Marketing Staff
Kelly Derreberry, Office Mgr
Amanda Osterstock, Manager
▲ EMP: 80
SALES (est): 30.8MM **Privately Held**
WEB: www.vanguardwines.com
SIC: **5182** Wine

(G-8845)
VERTI INSURANCE COMPANY
3590 Twin Creeks Dr (43204-1628)
PHONE....................................844 448-3784
Marcos March, Branch Mgr
EMP: 60
SALES (corp-wide): 15.8MM **Privately Held**
SIC: **6331** Automobile insurance
PA: Verti Insurance Company
211 Main St
Webster MA 01570
844 448-3784

(G-8846)
VERTICAL ADVENTURES INC
Also Called: Training Center, The
6295 Busch Blvd Ste B (43229-1888)
PHONE....................................614 888-8393
Alexis M Roccos, CEO
Mattew Roberts, President
Martha Roberts, Treasurer
Carrie Roccos, Admin Sec

EMP: 70
SQ FT: 6,400
SALES (est): 366.3K **Privately Held**
WEB: www.verticaladventuresohio.com
SIC: **7997** 7999 Membership sports & recreation clubs; instruction schools, camps & services

(G-8847)
VERTIV CORPORATION (DH)
1050 Dearborn Dr (43085-1544)
P.O. Box 29186 (43229-0186)
PHONE....................................614 888-0246
Rob Johnson, CEO
Jason Forcier, Exec VP
David Fallon, CFO
◆ EMP: 1300
SQ FT: 330,000
SALES (est): 1.4B
SALES (corp-wide): 2.1B **Privately Held**
WEB: www.liebert.com
SIC: **3585** 3613 7629 Air conditioning equipment, complete; regulators, power; electronic equipment repair
HQ: Vertiv Group Corporation
1050 Dearborn Dr
Columbus OH 43085
614 888-0246

(G-8848)
VERTIV CORPORATION
6700 Huntley Rd Ste A (43229-1186)
P.O. Box 29186 (43229-0186)
PHONE....................................614 841-6104
Cathy Edly, Manager
EMP: 60
SALES (corp-wide): 322.9MM **Privately Held**
WEB: www.liebert.com
SIC: **7629** Electronic equipment repair
HQ: Vertiv Corporation
1050 Dearborn Dr
Columbus OH 43085
614 888-0246

(G-8849)
VETERANS HEALTH ADMINISTRATION
Also Called: Chalmers P Wylie VA
420 N James Rd (43219-1834)
PHONE....................................614 257-5524
Teri Mzozoyana, Manager
EMP: 250 **Publicly Held**
WEB: www.veterans-ru.org
SIC: **8011** 9451 Clinic, operated by physicians; psychiatric clinic;
HQ: Veterans Health Administration
810 Vermont Ave Nw
Washington DC 20420

(G-8850)
VIDEO DUPLICATION SERVICES INC (PA)
Also Called: Vds
3777 Busineoh Pk Dr Ste A (43204)
PHONE....................................614 871-3827
Peter A Stock, President
Christian Stock, Vice Pres
▲ EMP: 37
SQ FT: 47,000
SALES (est): 1.3MM **Privately Held**
SIC: **7812** Video tape production

(G-8851)
VILLA MILANO INC
Also Called: Villa Mlano Bnquet Cnfrnce Ctr
1630 Schrock Rd (43229-8220)
PHONE....................................614 882-2058
Joseph Milano Jr, President
Dina Milano, Treasurer
Tina Milano, Manager
EMP: 30 EST: 1982
SQ FT: 20,000
SALES (est): 1.5MM **Privately Held**
WEB: www.villamilano.com
SIC: **7299** Banquet hall facilities

(G-8852)
VINTAGE WINE DISTRIBUTOR INC
2277 Westbrooke Dr (43228-9368)
PHONE....................................614 876-2580
Bill Forbes, Sales/Mktg Mgr
Jay Valerio, Manager
EMP: 40

SALES (corp-wide): 21.2MM **Privately Held**
WEB: www.vintwine.com
SIC: **5182** Wine
PA: Vintage Wine Distributor, Inc.
6555 Davis Indus Pkwy
Solon OH 44139
440 248-1750

(G-8853)
VISION & VOCATIONAL SERVICES (PA)
1393 N High St (43201-2459)
P.O. Box 7, Ostrander (43061-0007)
PHONE....................................614 294-5571
Martin Gaudiose, Director
Mike Hanes, Director
Bob Turner, Director
EMP: 40 EST: 1940
SQ FT: 30,000
SALES: 989.7K **Privately Held**
WEB: www.visioncenter.org
SIC: **8331** Rehabilitation Center For The Blind

(G-8854)
VISION SERVICE PLAN
3400 Morris Xing (43219)
PHONE....................................614 471-7511
Roger Valine, Branch Mgr
EMP: 180
SALES (corp-wide): 3.2B **Privately Held**
WEB: www.vsp.com
SIC: **6411** Insurance agents
PA: Vision Service Plan
3333 Quality Dr
Rancho Cordova CA 95670
916 851-5000

(G-8855)
VISTA INDUSTRIAL PACKAGING LLC
Also Called: Vista Packaging & Logistics
4700 Fisher Rd (43228-9752)
PHONE....................................800 454-6117
Martha J Cahall,
J Matthew Cahall,
Kyle A Cahall,
Todd Hampton,
Jennifer Smith,
EMP: 65
SQ FT: 350,000
SALES (est): 25.5MM **Privately Held**
SIC: **4783** 7389 4226 2679 Packing & crating; inspection & testing services; special warehousing & storage; pressed fiber & molded pulp products except food products

(G-8856)
VISTACARE USA INC
540 Officenter Pl Ste 100 (43230-5332)
PHONE....................................614 975-3230
Gay Rogers, Branch Mgr
EMP: 35
SALES (corp-wide): 6B **Privately Held**
SIC: **8082** Home health care services
HQ: Vistacare Usa Inc
4800 N Scottsdale Rd # 5000
Scottsdale AZ 85251
480 648-4545

(G-8857)
VITRAN EXPRESS INC
5075 Krieger Ct (43228-3652)
PHONE....................................614 870-2255
John Swanson, Branch Mgr
EMP: 200
SALES (corp-wide): 109.4MM **Privately Held**
SIC: **4213** Trucking, except local
PA: Vitran Express, Inc.
12225 Stephens Rd
Warren MI 48089
317 803-4000

(G-8858)
VJP HOSPITALITY LTD
Also Called: Four Points By Sheritan
3030 Plaza Prpts Blvd (43219)
PHONE....................................614 475-8383
Paul Patel, General Ptnr
EMP: 25
SALES: 300K **Privately Held**
SIC: **7011** Hotels & motels

(G-8859)
VOLUNTEERS AMERICA OHIO & IND (PA)
1776 E Broad St Frnt (43203-1798)
PHONE..................................614 253-6100
Sherry Keyes-Hebron, *President*
EMP: 120 EST: 1904
SQ FT: 8,000
SALES (est): 10.7MM **Privately Held**
SIC: 8322 8361 5932 5521 Social service center; alcoholism counseling, non-treatment; home for destitute men & women; clothing, secondhand; furniture, secondhand; automobiles, used cars only

(G-8860)
VOLUNTERS OF AMER GREATER OHIO
4280 Macsway Ave (43232-4257)
PHONE..................................614 861-8551
Chris Westernburger, *Manager*
EMP: 36
SQ FT: 17,776
SALES (corp-wide): 10.7MM **Privately Held**
WEB: www.voa.org
SIC: 8322 Individual & family services
PA: Volunteers Of America Ohio & Indiana
1776 E Broad St Frnt
Columbus OH 43203
614 253-6100

(G-8861)
VOLUNTERS OF AMER GREATER OHIO
2335 N Bank Dr (43220-5423)
PHONE..................................614 372-3120
Dennis Kresak, *Manager*
EMP: 200
SALES (corp-wide): 10.7MM **Privately Held**
WEB: www.voa.org
SIC: 8322 Individual & family services
PA: Volunteers Of America Ohio & Indiana
1776 E Broad St Frnt
Columbus OH 43203
614 253-6100

(G-8862)
VOLUNTERS OF AMER GREATER OHIO
3620 Indianola Ave (43214-3758)
PHONE..................................614 263-9134
Ray Ramons, *Director*
EMP: 30
SALES (corp-wide): 10.7MM **Privately Held**
SIC: 8322 Social service center
PA: Volunteers Of America Ohio & Indiana
1776 E Broad St Frnt
Columbus OH 43203
614 253-6100

(G-8863)
VOYA FINANCIAL INC
7965 N High St (43235-8402)
PHONE..................................614 431-5000
EMP: 25
SALES (corp-wide): 8.5B **Publicly Held**
SIC: 6311 6411 Life insurance; insurance agents, brokers & service
PA: Voya Financial, Inc.
230 Park Ave Fl 14
New York NY 10169
212 309-8200

(G-8864)
VRABLE HEALTHCARE INC (PA)
3248 Henderson Rd (43220-7337)
PHONE..................................614 545-5500
Allan K Vrable, *President*
James P Merrill, *CFO*
Ann Blackman, *Manager*
EMP: 30
SALES: 39.5MM **Privately Held**
WEB: www.vrablehealthcare.com
SIC: 8051 Convalescent home with continuous nursing care

(G-8865)
VRABLE II INC
Also Called: Southern Hills Skilled
3248 Henderson Rd (43220-7337)
PHONE..................................614 545-5502
Allan K Vrable, *President*

Jim Merrill, *CFO*
EMP: 93
SQ FT: 40,000
SALES (est): 7.6MM **Privately Held**
SIC: 8051 Skilled nursing care facilities
PA: Vrable Healthcare, Inc.
3248 Henderson Rd
Columbus OH 43220

(G-8866)
VRABLE IV INC (HQ)
Also Called: Pembrooke Place Skilled
3248 Henderson Rd (43220-7337)
PHONE..................................614 545-5502
Allan Vrable, *President*
James Merrill, *CFO*
EMP: 89
SQ FT: 52,000
SALES: 7.2MM **Privately Held**
SIC: 8051 Skilled nursing care facilities

(G-8867)
W D TIRE WAREHOUSE INC (PA)
Also Called: Convenient Tire Service
3805 E Livingston Ave (43227-2359)
PHONE..................................614 461-8944
Doug Reed, *Principal*
Thomas J Brown Jr, *Principal*
Amy Reed, *Corp Secy*
▲ EMP: 32
SQ FT: 80,000
SALES (est): 51.3MM **Privately Held**
WEB: www.wdtire.net
SIC: 5014 Tires & tubes

(G-8868)
W F BOLIN COMPANY INC
4100 Fisher Rd (43228-1039)
PHONE..................................614 276-6397
Wilbur F Bolin Jr, *President*
William F Bolin, *Vice Pres*
EMP: 25
SQ FT: 4,500
SALES: 3MM **Privately Held**
SIC: 1721 Commercial painting; industrial painting

(G-8869)
WALGREEN CO
Also Called: Walgreens
3015 E Livingston Ave (43209-3047)
PHONE..................................614 236-8622
Ryan Serfin, *Branch Mgr*
EMP: 30
SALES (corp-wide): 131.5B **Publicly Held**
WEB: www.walgreens.com
SIC: 5912 7384 Drug stores; photofinishing laboratory
HQ: Walgreen Co.
200 Wilmot Rd
Deerfield IL 60015
847 315-2500

(G-8870)
WALKER NATIONAL INC
2195 Wright Brothers Ave (43217-1157)
PHONE..................................614 492-1614
Richard Longo, *President*
Deborah Krikorian, *CFO*
◆ EMP: 30
SALES (est): 6.6MM
SALES (corp-wide): 116.9MM **Privately Held**
WEB: www.walkernational.com
SIC: 3499 7699 Magnets, permanent; metallic; industrial equipment services
HQ: Walker Magnetics Group, Inc.
600 Day Hill Rd
Windsor CT 06095
508 853-3232

(G-8871)
WALLACE F ACKLEY CO (PA)
695 Kenwick Rd (43209-2592)
PHONE..................................614 231-3661
Gill Kirk, *Partner*
Stanford Ackley, *Principal*
Sandra Kirk, *Principal*
Kila Joseph, *Consultant*
EMP: 51 EST: 1922
SQ FT: 1,500
SALES (est): 4.4MM **Privately Held**
WEB: www.wallacefackleyco.com
SIC: 6513 Apartment building operators

(G-8872)
WALNUT HILLS PHYSICAL THERAPY
Also Called: Mount Carmel/Walnut Hills
5965 E Broad St Ste 390 (43213-1565)
PHONE..................................614 234-8000
Anna May Balmaseda, *President*
Laura Miller, *Principal*
Jean Waddell, *Vice Pres*
EMP: 28
SALES (est): 858.2K **Privately Held**
SIC: 8049 Physical therapist

(G-8873)
WALTEK INC
399 W State St (43215-4008)
PHONE..................................614 469-0156
EMP: 42
SALES (corp-wide): 10.6MM **Privately Held**
SIC: 1611 Highway/Street Construction
PA: Waltek Inc.
14310 Sunfish Lake Blvd
Ramsey MN 55303
763 427-3181

(G-8874)
WARD TRUCKING LLC
1601 Mckinley Ave (43222-1045)
PHONE..................................614 275-3800
Mike Stone, *Manager*
EMP: 45
SALES (corp-wide): 168.8MM **Privately Held**
SIC: 4213 Contract haulers
PA: Ward Trucking, Llc
1436 Ward Trucking Dr
Altoona PA 16602
814 944-0803

(G-8875)
WASHINGTON PRI (HQ)
Also Called: Glimcher Properties Ltd Partnr
180 E Broad St Fl 22 (43215-3714)
PHONE..................................614 621-9000
Herbert Glimcher, *Partner*
EMP: 102
SQ FT: 35,248
SALES (est): 26.8MM
SALES (corp-wide): 843.4MM **Publicly Held**
WEB: www.almedamall.com
SIC: 6512 Commercial & industrial building operation
PA: Washington Prime Group Inc.
180 E Broad St Fl 21
Columbus OH 43215
614 621-9000

(G-8876)
WASHINGTON PRIME GROUP LP (HQ)
180 E Broad St (43215-3707)
PHONE..................................614 621-9000
Louis G Conforti, *CEO*
Robert J Laikin, *Ch of Bd*
Bruce Goldsberry, *General Mgr*
Robert P Demchak, *Exec VP*
Robert Demchak, *Exec VP*
EMP: 940
SALES: 723.3MM
SALES (corp-wide): 843.4MM **Publicly Held**
SIC: 6798 Real estate investment trusts; realty investment trusts
PA: Washington Prime Group Inc.
180 E Broad St Fl 21
Columbus OH 43215
614 621-9000

(G-8877)
WASHINGTON PRIME GROUP INC (PA)
180 E Broad St Fl 21 (43215-3714)
PHONE..................................614 621-9000
Louis G Conforti, *CEO*
Robert J Laikin, *Ch of Bd*
Jeff Case, *General Mgr*
Barbara Roche, *General Mgr*
Douglas Snyder, *General Mgr*
EMP: 66
SALES: 843.4MM **Publicly Held**
SIC: 6512 6798 Property operation, retail establishment; realty investment trusts

(G-8878)
WASSERSTROM COMPANY (PA)
Also Called: National Smallwares
4500 E Broad St (43213-1360)
PHONE..................................614 228-6525
Rodney Wasserstrom, *President*
David A Tumen, *Principal*
Reid Wasserstrom, *Exec VP*
Dennis Blank, *CFO*
Alan Wasserstrom, *Treasurer*
◆ EMP: 395 EST: 1902
SQ FT: 250,000
SALES (est): 824.5MM **Privately Held**
WEB: www.wasserstrom.com
SIC: 5087 3566 5021 5046 Restaurant supplies; speed changers, drives & gears; office furniture; commercial cooking & food service equipment; office supplies; kitchenware

(G-8879)
WASSERSTROM COMPANY
Also Called: Wassarstrom Rest Sup Super Str
2777 Silver Dr (43211-1054)
PHONE..................................614 228-6525
Susan Coffman, *Manager*
EMP: 25
SALES (corp-wide): 824.5MM **Privately Held**
WEB: www.wasserstrom.com
SIC: 5149 Pizza supplies
PA: The Wasserstrom Company
4500 E Broad St
Columbus OH 43213
614 228-6525

(G-8880)
WASSERSTROM HOLDINGS INC
477 S Front St (43215-5625)
P.O. Box 182056 (43218-2056)
PHONE..................................614 228-6525
Rodney Wasserstrom, *Co-COB*
Alan Wasserstrom, *Co-COB*
EMP: 180 **Privately Held**
SIC: 6719 Investment holding companies, except banks

(G-8881)
WBNS TV INC
Also Called: Wnbs Channel 10 Weatherline
770 Twin Rivers Dr (43215-1159)
P.O. Box 1010 (43216-1010)
PHONE..................................614 460-3700
John F Wolfe, *Ch of Bd*
John Cardenas, *President*
Chris Walsh, *Editor*
Patty Williams, *Finance*
Jackie Armstrong, *Accounts Exec*
EMP: 220 EST: 1965
SQ FT: 40,000
SALES (est): 28.6MM **Privately Held**
WEB: www.wbns10tv.com
SIC: 4833 Television broadcasting stations

(G-8882)
WEBER PARTNERS LTD (PA)
Also Called: Weber Associates
775 Yard St Ste 350 (43212-3892)
PHONE..................................614 222-6806
Luke Smith, *President*
Tom Parry, *Partner*
Koichi Kiyohara, *Partner*
Andrew Leatherman, *Partner*
Brad Dresbach, *Vice Pres*
EMP: 30
SALES (est): 2.9MM **Privately Held**
SIC: 8742 Marketing consulting services

(G-8883)
WEILANDS FINE MEATS INC
Also Called: Weiland's Gourmet Market
3600 Indianola Ave (43214-3758)
PHONE..................................614 267-9910
John Williams, *President*
Tim Teegardin, *Vice Pres*
EMP: 47
SQ FT: 15,000
SALES (est): 4.2MM **Privately Held**
WEB: www.weilandsgourmetmarket.com
SIC: 5421 5411 5147 Meat & fish markets; delicatessens; meats & meat products

(G-8884)

WELCH PACKAGING GROUP INC

Also Called: Welch Packaging Columbus
4700 Alkire Rd (43228-3495)
PHONE.....................................614 870-2000
Tayler Darling, *Manager*
EMP: 110
SALES (corp-wide): 546.3MM **Privately Held**
SIC: 2621 7389 Wrapping & packaging papers; packaging & labeling services
PA: Welch Packaging Group, Inc.
1020 Herman St
Elkhart IN 46516
574 295-2460

(G-8885)

WELLS FARGO CLEARING SVCS LLC

Also Called: Wells Fargo Advisors
1 Easton Oval Ste 520 (43219-8033)
PHONE.....................................614 221-8371
Garrett Venetta, *Branch Mgr*
Cyrus McKinney, *Advisor*
EMP: 25
SALES (corp-wide): 101B **Publicly Held**
SIC: 6211 Stock brokers & dealers; bond dealers & brokers
HQ: Wells Fargo Clearing Services, Llc
1 N Jefferson Ave Fl 7
Saint Louis MO 63103
314 955-3000

(G-8886)

WENDT-BRISTOL HEALTH SERVICES (PA)

921 Jasonway Ave Ste B (43214-2456)
PHONE.....................................614 403-9966
Marvin D Kantor, *Ch of Bd*
Sheldon A Gold, *President*
EMP: 25 **EST:** 1966
SALES (est): 3.2MM **Privately Held**
SIC: 8093 Specialty outpatient clinics

(G-8887)

WENGER TEMPERATURE CONTROL

Also Called: Honeywell Authorized Dealer
2005 Progress Ave (43207-1759)
PHONE.....................................614 586-4016
Joseph E Wenger III, *President*
George Wenger, *Vice Pres*
EMP: 25 **EST:** 1977
SQ FT: 13,000
SALES (est): 3MM **Privately Held**
WEB: www.wengertempcontrol.com
SIC: 1711 1542 Heating & air conditioning contractors; refrigeration contractor; design & erection, combined: non-residential

(G-8888)

WESBANCO INC

2000 Henderson Rd Ste 100 (43220-2453)
PHONE.....................................614 208-7298
EMP: 40
SALES (corp-wide): 515.2MM **Publicly Held**
SIC: 6029 Commercial banks
PA: Wesbanco, Inc.
1 Bank Plz
Wheeling WV 26003
304 234-9000

(G-8889)

WEST ENTERPRISES INC

Also Called: Uniglobe Travel Designers
480 S 3rd St (43215-5702)
PHONE.....................................614 237-4488
Elizabeth Blount, *President*
Leonard Sandine, *Vice Pres*
Elizabeth McCormick, *Controller*
EMP: 44
SALES (est): 4.4MM **Privately Held**
SIC: 4724 Tourist agency arranging transport, lodging & car rental

(G-8890)

WESTMINSTER MANAGEMENT COMPANY

2731 Clime Rd (43223-3625)
PHONE.....................................614 274-5154
Thomas J Stewart, *President*
EMP: 108

SQ FT: 1,200
SALES (est): 5MM **Privately Held**
SIC: 8741 Nursing & personal care facility management

(G-8891)

WESTPATRICK CORP

250 N Hartford Ave 300 (43222-1100)
PHONE.....................................614 875-8200
Charles Jeffrey Mahan, *President*
Douglas R McCrae, *Partner*
Gary D Yancer, *Partner*
EMP: 40
SQ FT: 7,000
SALES (est): 10.2MM **Privately Held**
SIC: 1622 1611 Bridge construction; general contractor, highway & street construction

(G-8892)

WESTPOST COLUMBUS LLC

6500 Doubletree Ave (43229-1111)
PHONE.....................................614 885-1885
Daniel Ouellette, *Principal*
EMP: 99
SALES (est): 950K **Privately Held**
SIC: 7011 Hotels & motels

(G-8893)

WESTSIDE FAMILY PRACTICE INC

5206 Chaps Ct (43221-5706)
PHONE.....................................614 878-4541
EMP: 29
SALES (est): 2.3MM **Privately Held**
SIC: 8011 Family Practice

(G-8894)

WEXNER HERITAGE VILLAGE (PA)

Also Called: HERITAGE HOUSE NURSING HOME
1151 College Ave (43209-2827)
PHONE.....................................614 231-4900
Erin Keller, *Senior VP*
Chris Christian, *Vice Pres*
David Driver, *Vice Pres*
Cheryl Howard, *Vice Pres*
Thomas McDermott, *CFO*
EMP: 500
SQ FT: 224,000
SALES (est): 12.1MM **Privately Held**
SIC: 8052 8051 Intermediate care facilities; skilled nursing care facilities

(G-8895)

WHETSTONE CARE CENTER LLC

Also Called: Whetstone Center
3710 Olentangy River Rd (43214-3426)
PHONE.....................................614 457-1100
Michele Engelbach, *Principal*
EMP: 210
SQ FT: 62,000
SALES (corp-wide): 20.1MM **Privately Held**
WEB: www.macintoshcompany.com
SIC: 8051 8059 Convalescent home with continuous nursing care; convalescent home
PA: Whetstone Care Center Llc
3863 Trueman Ct
Hilliard OH 43026
614 345-9500

(G-8896)

WHITE CASTLE SYSTEM INC (PA)

555 W Goodale St (43215-1104)
P.O. Box 1498 (43216-1498)
PHONE.....................................614 228-5781
Edgar W Ingram III, *Ch of Bd*
Bette Everson, *President*
Elizabeth Ingram, *President*
David Rife, *President*
Laura Franson, *General Mgr*
◆ **EMP:** 275
SQ FT: 143,000
SALES (est): 613.7MM **Privately Held**
WEB: www.whitecastle.com
SIC: 5812 5142 2051 2013 Fast-food restaurant, chain; meat, frozen: packaged; bread, cake & related products; sausages & other prepared meats

(G-8897)

WHITE OAK INVESTMENTS INC

3730 Lockbourne Rd (43207-5133)
P.O. Box 182022 (43218-2022)
PHONE.....................................614 491-1000
Joseph C Bowman, *President*
Maureen Travis, *Human Res Dir*
Christina Carr, *Regl Sales Mgr*
Meaghan Blankenship, *Sales Staff*
Amanda Conn, *Sales Staff*
▲ **EMP:** 65
SQ FT: 65,000
SALES (est): 9.9MM **Privately Held**
WEB: www.cenres.com
SIC: 7389 Fund raising organizations

(G-8898)

WHITEHALL CITY SCHOOLS

Also Called: C Ray Wllams Erly Chldhood Ctr
4738 Kae Ave (43213-6100)
PHONE.....................................614 417-5680
Shirley Drakes, *Principal*
EMP: 40
SALES (corp-wide): 46.4MM **Privately Held**
WEB: www.whitehall.k12.oh.us
SIC: 8351 8211 Preschool center; kindergarten
PA: Whitehall City Schools
625 S Yearling Rd
Columbus OH 43213
614 417-5000

(G-8899)

WHITEHALL FRMENS BNVLENCE FUND

390 S Yearling Rd (43213-1876)
PHONE.....................................614 237-5478
Tim Tilton, *Chief*
EMP: 43
SALES (est): 321.3K **Privately Held**
SIC: 8641 Civic social & fraternal associations

(G-8900)

WICKERTREE TNNIS FTNES CLB LLC

5760 Maple Canyon Ave (43229-2894)
PHONE.....................................614 882-5724
Marvin Williams, *President*
Ravi Thenappan, *Mng Member*
EMP: 28
SQ FT: 60,000
SALES (est): 1.2MM **Privately Held**
WEB: www.wickertree.com
SIC: 7997 Tennis club, membership

(G-8901)

WIDEPINT INTGRTED SLTIONS CORP

8351 N High St Ste 200 (43235-1501)
PHONE.....................................614 410-1587
Todd McMillen, *Manager*
EMP: 45 **Publicly Held**
WEB: www.isysllc.com
SIC: 7371 Computer software development
HQ: Widepoint Integrated Solutions Corp.
11250 Waples
Fairfax VA 22030
703 349-5644

(G-8902)

WILES BOYLE BURKHOLDER &

Also Called: Wiles Doucher
2 Miranova Pl Ste 700 (43215-5098)
PHONE.....................................614 221-5216
James M Wiles, *Co-President*
Daniel Wiles, *Co-President*
Thomas E Boyle, *Corp Secy*
Peg Lowry, *Accounting Mgr*
EMP: 67
SQ FT: 25,000
SALES (est): 8.9MM **Privately Held**
SIC: 8111 General practice attorney, lawyer

(G-8903)

WILLGLO SERVICES INC

Also Called: Burge Service
995 Thurman Ave (43206-3133)
P.O. Box 77469 (43207-7469)
PHONE.....................................614 443-3020
William Burge, *President*
Gloria Burge, *Administration*

EMP: 50
SALES: 1.6MM **Privately Held**
SIC: 8052 Home for the mentally retarded, with health care

(G-8904)

WILLIAM I NOTZ

Also Called: Department of Statistics
1958 Neil Ave Rm 319 (43210-1247)
PHONE.....................................614 292-3154
William I Notz, *Principal*
Paul Brower, *Chairman*
EMP: 40
SALES (est): 2.4MM **Privately Held**
SIC: 8621 Professional standards review board

(G-8905)

WILLIAM SYDNEY DRUEN

85 E Deshler Ave (43206-2655)
PHONE.....................................614 444-7655
William Sydney Druen, *Owner*
EMP: 25
SALES (est): 1.1MM **Privately Held**
SIC: 8748 Business consulting

(G-8906)

WILLIAMS FREIGHT LOGISTICS

1893 Fiesta Ct Apt D (43229-6641)
PHONE.....................................614 333-9173
Delmar Williams, *CEO*
EMP: 25
SALES (est): 579K **Privately Held**
SIC: 4789 Transportation services

(G-8907)

WILLIS OF OHIO INC (DH)

775 Yard St Ste 200 (43212-3891)
PHONE.....................................614 457-7000
John Chaney, *CEO*
Peter Johnson, *Senior VP*
Donna Debly, *Vice Pres*
Alisa Long, *Vice Pres*
Barry Welch, *Vice Pres*
EMP: 25 **EST:** 1922
SALES (est): 10.5MM **Privately Held**
SIC: 6411 Insurance agents, brokers & service
HQ: Willis North America Inc.
200 Liberty St Fl 7
New York NY 10281
212 915-8888

(G-8908)

WILLO SECURITY INC

1989 W 5th Ave Ste 3 (43212-1912)
PHONE.....................................614 481-9456
Steven Alan, *Manager*
EMP: 143
SALES (corp-wide): 7.4MM **Privately Held**
WEB: www.willosecurity.com
SIC: 7381 Security guard service
PA: Willo Security, Inc.
38230 Glenn Ave
Willoughby OH 44094
440 953-9191

(G-8909)

WILSON ENTERPRISES INC

Also Called: Wilson's Turf
1600 Universal Rd (43207-1733)
PHONE.....................................614 444-8873
Richard B Wilson, *President*
Richard Wilson, *President*
Daniel Wilson, *Vice Pres*
Phil Paolini, *Treasurer*
EMP: 40
SQ FT: 4,000
SALES (est): 4.9MM **Privately Held**
WEB: www.wilsonsturf.com
SIC: 0782 Sodding contractor

(G-8910)

WINGLER CONSTRUCTION CORP

Also Called: One Stop Remodeling
771 S Hamilton Rd (43213-3001)
PHONE.....................................614 626-8546
Ronald E Wingler, *President*
EMP: 25
SQ FT: 13,000
SALES (est): 4MM **Privately Held**
SIC: 1521 1542 General remodeling, single-family houses; commercial & office buildings, renovation & repair

▲ = Import ▼=Export
◆ =Import/Export

(G-8911)
WM COLUMBUS HOTEL LLC
Also Called: Westin Columbus
310 S High St (43215-4508)
PHONE..................................614 228-3800
Mark Zettl, COO
Doug Denyer, CFO
Alisha Kalous, Human Resources
Nir Liebling, CIO
EMP: 250
SQ FT: 200,000
SALES (est): 13.3MM
SALES (corp-wide): 707.1MM Publicly
Held
SIC: 7011 Hotels
PA: The Marcus Corporation
100 E Wisconsin Ave # 1
Milwaukee WI 53202
414 905-1000

(G-8912)
WODA CONSTRUCTION INC
500 S Front St Fl 10 (43215-7628)
PHONE..................................614 396-3200
Jeffrey Woda, President
David Cooper Jr, Exec VP
EMP: 47
SQ FT: 3,000
SALES (est): 42.4MM Privately Held
WEB: www.wodagroup.com
SIC: 1522 1521 Apartment building con-
struction; new construction, single-family
houses
PA: Cooper Woda Companies Inc
500 S Front St Fl 10
Columbus OH 43215
614 396-3200

(G-8913)
**WOMEN PHYSICANS OF
OB/GYN INC (PA)**
3525 Olentangy River Rd # 6350
(43214-3937)
PHONE..................................614 734-3340
Elaine Paul, President
Rebecca Gallagher, Manager
EMP: 50
SALES (est): 3.1MM Privately Held
SIC: 8011 Gynecologist

(G-8914)
**WOODLAND ASSISTED LIVING
RESI**
Also Called: Woodlands of Columbus
5380 E Broad St Ofc (43213-3848)
PHONE..................................614 755-7591
Thomas J Smith,
Richard Osbourne,
EMP: 50
SALES (est): 2.5MM Privately Held
SIC: 8051 Skilled nursing care facilities

(G-8915)
WOOLPERT INC
1 Easton Oval Ste 400 (43219-6092)
PHONE..................................614 476-6000
Bridget Prosch, Branch Mgr
EMP: 50
SALES (corp-wide): 119.8MM Privately
Held
WEB: www.woolpert.com
SIC: 8711 Civil engineering
PA: Woolpert, Inc.
4454 Idea Center Blvd
Beavercreek OH 45430
937 461-5660

(G-8916)
**WORKERS COMPENSATION
OHIO BUR**
30 W Spring St (43215-2216)
PHONE..................................800 644-6292
Stephen Buehrer, Administration
EMP: 2300 Privately Held
SIC: 6411 Insurance agents, brokers &
service
HQ: Ohio Bureau Of Workers' Compensa-
tion
30 W Spring St Fl 2-29
Columbus OH 43215
800 644-6292

(G-8917)
**WORKERS COMPENSATION
OHIO BUR (DH)**
30 W Spring St Fl 2-29 (43215-2216)
PHONE..................................800 644-6292
Barbara Ingram, Manager
James Conrad, Administration
EMP: 1500
SALES (est): 2.4B Privately Held
SIC: 6331 9199 Workers' compensation
insurance; general government adminis-
tration

(G-8918)
**WORLY PLUMBING SUPPLY INC
(PA)**
400 Greenlawn Ave (43223-2611)
PHONE..................................614 445-1000
Jay Worly, President
Jeff Howell, COO
Jeff Worly, COO
Cindy Royce, Opers Staff
Judith Tompkins, Controller
EMP: 54 EST: 1952
SQ FT: 96,000
SALES (est): 54.6MM Privately Held
WEB: www.worly.com
SIC: 5074 Plumbing fittings & supplies;
heating equipment (hydronic)

(G-8919)
**WORTHNGTON STELPAC
SYSTEMS LLC (HQ)**
1205 Dearborn Dr (43085-4769)
PHONE..................................614 438-3205
Mark Russell, CEO
EMP: 250
SALES (est): 47.5MM
SALES (corp-wide): 3.5B Publicly Held
SIC: 3325 5051 Steel foundries; metals
service centers & offices
PA: Worthington Industries, Inc.
200 W Wlson Bridge Rd
Worthington OH 43085
614 438-3210

(G-8920)
**WRIGHT MATERIAL SOLUTIONS
LTD**
55 N Green St (43222-1220)
PHONE..................................614 530-6999
John Wright, CEO
EMP: 25
SQ FT: 5,000
SALES: 4MM Privately Held
SIC: 4212 Dump truck haulage

(G-8921)
WW GRAINGER INC
Also Called: Grainger 176
3640 Interchange Rd (43204-1434)
PHONE..................................614 276-5231
Rich Herron, Manager
EMP: 35
SALES (corp-wide): 11.2B Publicly Held
WEB: www.grainger.com
SIC: 5063 5084 5075 5078 Motors, electric; motor controls, starters & relays;
electric; power transmission equipment,
electric; generators; fans, industrial;
pumps & pumping equipment; compressors, except air conditioning; pneumatic
tools & equipment; warm air heating
equipment & supplies; air conditioning
equipment, except room units; refrigeration equipment & supplies; electric tools;
power tools & accessories; hand tools
PA: W.W. Grainger, Inc.
100 Grainger Pkwy
Lake Forest IL 60045
847 535-1000

(G-8922)
WYANDOTTE ATHLETIC CLUB
5198 Riding Club Ln (43213-3202)
PHONE..................................614 861-6303
Todd Decker, President
Bill Ward, General Mgr
EMP: 50
SALES (est): 2.2MM Privately Held
WEB: www.wyandotteathleticclub.com
SIC: 7991 Health club

(G-8923)
X F CONSTRUCTION SVCS INC
Also Called: X F Petroleum Equipment
1120 Claycraft Rd (43230-6640)
PHONE..................................614 575-2700
William R Patrick, President
James Fairchild, Vice Pres
Lucille Stallard, Vice Pres
Robert Patrick, Treasurer
Deborah K Smith, Admin Sec
EMP: 35
SQ FT: 20,000
SALES (est): 6MM Privately Held
SIC: 1731 1799 5172 General electrical
contractor; service station equipment in-
stallation, maintenance & repair; service
station supplies, petroleum

(G-8924)
XPO LOGISTICS FREIGHT INC
2625 Westbelt Dr (43228-3828)
PHONE..................................614 876-7100
Freda Hayner, Manager
EMP: 172
SQ FT: 6,460
SALES (corp-wide): 15.3B Publicly Held
WEB: www.con-way.com
SIC: 4231 4213 4212 Trucking terminal
facilities; trucking, except local; local
trucking, without storage
HQ: Xpo Logistics Freight, Inc.
2211 Old Earhart Rd # 100
Ann Arbor MI 48105
800 755-2728

(G-8925)
**YORK TEMPLE COUNTRY CLUB
INC**
Also Called: York Golf Club
7459 N High St (43235-1412)
PHONE..................................614 885-5459
Chuck Dahn, General Mgr
EMP: 40
SQ FT: 18,000
SALES: 1.9MM Privately Held
WEB: www.yorkgolfclub.com
SIC: 7997 5812 Country club, member-
ship; golf club, membership; eating places

(G-8926)
YORKLAND HEALTH CARE INC
Also Called: Yorkland Park Care Center
1425 Yorkland Rd (43232-1686)
PHONE..................................614 751-2525
Brian Colleran, President
EMP: 99
SQ FT: 2,561
SALES: 12.3MM Privately Held
WEB: www.yorkland-park.net
SIC: 8051 Skilled nursing care facilities

(G-8927)
**YOUNG MENS CHRISTIAN
ASSOC**
Also Called: YMCA
1640 Sandalwood Pl (43229-3640)
PHONE..................................614 885-4252
Neil Eichensehr, Facilities Dir
Chloe Viers, Director
Kathy Cook, Director
EMP: 170
SQ FT: 7,700
SALES (corp-wide): 44.9MM Privately
Held
WEB: www.ymca-columbus.com
SIC: 8641 8322 7032 7999 Youth organi-
zations; individual & family services;
sporting & recreational camps; recreation
center
PA: Young Men's Christian Association Of
Central Ohio
40 W Long St
Columbus OH 43215
614 389-4409

(G-8928)
**YOUNG MENS CHRISTIAN
ASSOC**
Also Called: Hilltop
2879 Valleyview Dr (43204-2010)
PHONE..................................614 276-8224
Cheryl Nielson, Branch Mgr
EMP: 100

SALES (corp-wide): 44.9MM Privately
Held
WEB: www.ymca-columbus.com
SIC: 8641 7999 8322 Youth organiza-
tions; recreation center; individual & fam-
ily services
PA: Young Men's Christian Association Of
Central Ohio
40 W Long St
Columbus OH 43215
614 389-4409

(G-8929)
**YOUNG MENS CHRISTIAN
ASSOC**
Also Called: YMCA
130 Woodland Ave (43203-1774)
PHONE..................................614 252-3166
Winifred Simpson, Director
EMP: 65
SALES (corp-wide): 44.9MM Privately
Held
WEB: www.ymca-columbus.com
SIC: 8641 7991 8351 7032 Youth organi-
zations; physical fitness facilities; child
day care services; youth camps; individ-
ual & family services
PA: Young Men's Christian Association Of
Central Ohio
40 W Long St
Columbus OH 43215
614 389-4409

(G-8930)
**YOUNG MENS CHRISTIAN
ASSOC**
Also Called: YMCA
600 Fox Ridge St (43228-2213)
PHONE..................................614 878-7269
Elana Lehihan, Director
EMP: 25
SALES (corp-wide): 44.9MM Privately
Held
WEB: www.ymca-columbus.com
SIC: 8641 7997 Youth organizations;
swimming club, membership
PA: Young Men's Christian Association Of
Central Ohio
40 W Long St
Columbus OH 43215
614 389-4409

(G-8931)
**YOUNG WOMENS CHRISTIAN
ASSN (PA)**
Also Called: YWCA
65 S 4th St (43215-4356)
PHONE..................................614 224-9121
Elfi Di Bella, President
Terri W Ifeduba, Vice Pres
Lee Wombles, Facilities Mgr
Joyce Swayne, Opers Staff
Valerie Henthorn, Accounting Mgr
EMP: 60
SQ FT: 100,880
SALES: 7.5MM Privately Held
SIC: 8641 7991 8351 7032 Youth organi-
zations; physical fitness facilities; child
day care services; youth camps; individ-
ual & family services

(G-8932)
YOUTH ADVOCATE SERVICES
825 Grandview Ave (43215-1123)
PHONE..................................614 258-9927
Sarah Cochey, CEO
Glenn Richard, CFO
Heather Gutierrez, Manager
Tracey Izzard, Exec Dir
Korlyn Davis, Director
EMP: 28
SQ FT: 10,500
SALES: 3.9MM Privately Held
WEB: www.youthad.org
SIC: 8322 Child related social services

(G-8933)
YRC INC
Also Called: Yellow Transportation
5400 Fisher Rd (43228-9771)
P.O. Box 28188 (43228)
PHONE..................................614 878-9281
Chuck Zinsmayer, Manager
EMP: 56
SQ FT: 6,800

SALES (corp-wide): 5B **Publicly Held**
WEB: www.roadway.com
SIC: 4231 4213 Trucking terminal facilities; trucking, except local
HQ: Yrc Inc.
　10990 Roe Ave
　Overland Park KS 66211
　913 696-6100

(G-8934)
Z PRODUCE CO INC
720 Harmon Ave (43223-2450)
PHONE.......................614 224-4373
Dean Zaglanis, *President*
Helen C Zaglanis, *Admin Sec*
EMP: 35
SQ FT: 28,000
SALES (est): 7.5MM **Privately Held**
WEB: www.zproduce.com
SIC: 5148 5149 5142 Banana ripening; fruits, fresh; potatoes, fresh; vegetables, fresh; canned goods: fruit, vegetables, seafood, meats, etc.; packaged frozen goods

(G-8935)
ZANER-BLOSER INC (HQ)
Also Called: Superkids Reading Program
1400 Goodale Blvd Ste 200 (43212-3777)
P.O. Box 16764 (43216-6764)
PHONE.......................614 486-0221
Lisa Carmona, *President*
Dawn Danneman, *Office Mgr*
EMP: 61
SQ FT: 15,000
SALES (est): 88.5MM
SALES (corp-wide): 216.2MM **Privately Held**
WEB: www.zaner-bloser.com
SIC: 5192 5049 8249 2731 Books; school supplies; correspondence school; book publishing
PA: Highlights For Children, Inc.
　1800 Watermark Dr
　Columbus OH 43215
　614 486-0631

(G-8936)
ZEIGER TIGGES & LITTLE LLP
41 S High St Ste 3500 (43215-6110)
PHONE.......................614 365-9900
Bradley T Ferrell, *Partner*
Marion H Little Jr, *Partner*
Stuart G Parsell, *Partner*
Steven W Tigges, *Partner*
John Zeiger, *General Ptnr*
EMP: 27
SQ FT: 16,000
SALES: 8MM **Privately Held**
WEB: www.litohio.com
SIC: 8111 General practice attorney, lawyer

(G-8937)
ZINK FOODSERVICE GROUP
Also Called: Zink Commercial
655 Dearborn Park Ln C (43085-5745)
PHONE.......................800 492-7400
Steve Castle, *President*
Tim Riordan, *President*
Jim Zink, *Managing Prtnr*
Mike McGuire, *Partner*
Bill Beshilas, *Vice Pres*
▲ **EMP:** 40
SALES: 22.1MM **Privately Held**
WEB: www.zinkmarketing.com
SIC: 5046 Restaurant equipment & supplies; commercial cooking & food service equipment

(G-8938)
ZIPLINE LOGISTICS LLC
2300 W 5th Ave (43215-1003)
PHONE.......................888 469-4754
Walter Lynch, *CEO*
Andrew Lynch, *President*
Pedro Martinez, *Accounting Mgr*
Matthew Dorow, *Sales Staff*
Ian Moy, *Sales Staff*
EMP: 54
SQ FT: 3,600
SALES (est): 12.2MM **Privately Held**
WEB: www.ziplinelogistics.com
SIC: 4731 Freight transportation arrangement

(G-8939)
ZUSMAN COMMUNITY HOSPICE
1151 College Ave (43209-2827)
PHONE.......................614 559-0350
Amy Kramer, *Info Tech Mgr*
April Mock, *Director*
EMP: 30 **EST:** 2007
SALES (est): 542.9K **Privately Held**
SIC: 8052 Personal care facility

Columbus Grove
Putnam County

(G-8940)
CARPE DIEM INDUSTRIES LLC (PA)
Also Called: Colonial Surface Solutions
4599 Campbell Rd (45830-9403)
PHONE.......................419 659-5639
Patricia Langhals, *President*
Darren Langhals, *Corp Secy*
EMP: 55
SQ FT: 750
SALES (est): 18.1MM **Privately Held**
WEB: www.colonialsurfacesolutions.com
SIC: 3479 3471 3398 1799 Painting of metal products; cleaning & descaling metal products; sand blasting of metal parts; tumbling (cleaning & polishing) of machine parts; metal heat treating; tempering of metal; coating of metal structures at construction site

(G-8941)
HALKER DRYWALL INC
Also Called: Halker Drywall & Plastering
21457 Road 15u (45830-9244)
PHONE.......................419 646-3679
Vickie Halker, *President*
Job Halker, *Corp Secy*
David Halker, *Vice Pres*
EMP: 45
SALES (est): 3.9MM **Privately Held**
WEB: www.halkerdrywall.com
SIC: 1742 Drywall; exterior insulation & finish (EIFS) applicator

(G-8942)
TOM LANGHALS
Also Called: Colonial Farms
4599 Campbell Rd (45830-9403)
PHONE.......................419 659-5629
Tom Langhals, *Owner*
Janice Langhals, *Co-Owner*
EMP: 30
SALES (est): 3.9MM **Privately Held**
SIC: 5084 0115 Cleaning equipment, high pressure, sand or steam; corn

Concord Township
Lake County

(G-8943)
KAISER FOUNDATION HOSPITALS
Also Called: Healthspan-Concord Med Offs
7536 Fredle Dr (44077-9406)
PHONE.......................440 350-3614
Amanda Currence, *Director*
EMP: 593
SALES (corp-wide): 93B **Privately Held**
SIC: 8011 Medical Doctor's Office
HQ: Kaiser Foundation Hospitals Inc
　1 Kaiser Plz
　Oakland CA 94612
　510 271-6611

(G-8944)
RANPAK CORP (PA)
7990 Auburn Rd (44077-9701)
P.O. Box 8004 (44077-8004)
PHONE.......................440 354-4445
Stephen A Kovach, *President*
Richard Zenoz, *Research*
Rob Pluijmen, *Engineer*
Hugo Van Ool, *Engineer*
Jeroen Van Oosterhout, *Mktg Dir*
▲ **EMP:** 110
SQ FT: 162,000

SALES (est): 142.3MM **Privately Held**
WEB: www.ranpak.com
SIC: 5113 Industrial & personal service paper

Concord Twp
Lake County

(G-8945)
GARDENLIFE INC
Also Called: Grimes Seeds
11335 Concord Hambden Rd (44077-9704)
PHONE.......................800 241-7333
Gary S Grimes, *Ch of Bd*
Rodney Ledrew, *Vice Pres*
EMP: 35
SQ FT: 9,000
SALES (est): 17.5MM **Privately Held**
WEB: www.grimeseeds.com
SIC: 5191 Seeds: field, garden & flower; garden supplies

(G-8946)
QH MANAGEMENT COMPANY LLC
Also Called: Quail Hollow Resort
11080 Concord Hambden Rd (44077-9704)
PHONE.......................440 497-1100
Mike Kelly,
EMP: 99
SALES: 1,000K **Privately Held**
SIC: 7011 Resort hotel

Conesville
Coshocton County

(G-8947)
AMERICAN ELECTRIC POWER CO INC
47201 County Road 273 (43811-9701)
PHONE.......................740 829-4129
Ronald Borton, *Production*
John McClain, *Production*
Bill Miller, *Electrical Engi*
Dan Lambert, *Manager*
Clarence Sidwell, *Manager*
EMP: 30
SALES (corp-wide): 16.2B **Publicly Held**
WEB: www.aep.com
SIC: 4911 Electric services
PA: American Electric Power Company, Inc.
　1 Riverside Plz Fl 1 # 1
　Columbus OH 43215
　614 716-1000

(G-8948)
COLUMBUS SOUTHERN POWER CO
47201 County Road 273 (43811-9701)
PHONE.......................740 829-2378
Dan Lambert, *Manager*
EMP: 100
SALES (corp-wide): 16.2B **Publicly Held**
SIC: 4911 Electric services
HQ: Columbus Southern Power Company
　1 Riverside Plz
　Columbus OH 43215
　614 716-1000

Conneaut
Ashtabula County

(G-8949)
ASHTABULA COUNTY COMMNTY ACTN
Also Called: Conneaut Senior Services
327 Mill St (44030-2439)
PHONE.......................440 593-6441
Persela Airhart, *Manager*
EMP: 100
SALES (corp-wide): 92.1K **Privately Held**
SIC: 8399 8322 Antipoverty board; senior citizens' center or association

PA: Ashtabula County Community Action Agency Properties Corporation
　6920 Austinburg Rd
　Ashtabula OH 44004
　440 997-1721

(G-8950)
ASHTABULA COUNTY RESIDENTIAL I (PA)
29 Parrish Rd (44030-1146)
PHONE.......................440 593-6404
Joy Groel, *Director*
EMP: 35
SQ FT: 1,000
SALES: 2.3MM **Privately Held**
SIC: 8361 Home for the mentally handicapped

(G-8951)
BESSEMER AND LAKE ERIE RR CO
Also Called: Pittsburgh & Conneaut Dock
950 Ford Ave (44030-1867)
P.O. Box 90 (44030-0090)
PHONE.......................440 593-1102
Robert S Rosati, *Branch Mgr*
EMP: 150
SALES (corp-wide): 10.2B **Privately Held**
SIC: 6519 Real property lessors
HQ: Bessemer And Lake Erie Railroad Company
　17641 Ashland Ave
　Homewood IL 60430
　708 206-6708

(G-8952)
BROWN MEMORIAL HOSPITAL
158 W Main Rd (44030-2039)
PHONE.......................440 593-1131
Robert David, *President*
Barbara Gurto, *Human Res Dir*
Kevin Kotnik, *Manager*
John Sullivan, *Manager*
Joanne Surbella, *Nursing Dir*
EMP: 300 **EST:** 1919
SQ FT: 97,000
SALES (est): 2.5MM
SALES (corp-wide): 580MM **Privately Held**
SIC: 8062 General medical & surgical hospitals
PA: University Hospitals Health System, Inc.
　3605 Warrensville Ctr Rd
　Shaker Heights OH 44122
　216 767-8900

(G-8953)
CONNEAUT TELEPHONE COMPANY
Also Called: Suite224 and Cablesuite541
224 State St (44030-2637)
P.O. Box 579 (44030-0579)
PHONE.......................440 593-7140
Ray Rapose, *Ch of Bd*
P Tom Picard, *General Mgr*
James Haney, *Vice Pres*
Jim Supplee, *Admin Sec*
EMP: 50 **EST:** 1897
SQ FT: 8,000
SALES (est): 12.6MM **Privately Held**
WEB: www.conneauttelephone.com
SIC: 4841 4813 Cable & other pay television services; local telephone communications

(G-8954)
ES3 MANAGEMENT INC
Also Called: Lake Pnte Rhbltion Nrsing Ctr
22 Parrish Rd (44030-1178)
PHONE.......................440 593-6266
Joyce M Humphrey, *President*
Robin L Hillier, *Shareholder*
EMP: 90
SALES (est): 2.5MM **Privately Held**
SIC: 8051 Skilled nursing care facilities

(G-8955)
MANAGEMENT & TRAINING CORP
Also Called: Lake Erie Correctional Fcilty
501 Thompson Rd (44030-8668)
P.O. Box 8000 (44030-8000)
PHONE.......................801 693-2600
Teresa Aramaki, *Vice Pres*

Rich Gansheihmer, *Branch Mgr*
R Gansheimer, *Manager*
EMP: 207
SALES (corp-wide): 667.6MM **Privately Held**
WEB: www.mtctrains.com
SIC: 8744 Correctional facility
PA: Management & Training Corporation
500 N Market Place Dr # 100
Centerville UT 84014
801 693-2600

(G-8956)
MERLENE ENTERPRISES INC
Also Called: Stanley Steemer
734 Harbor St (44030-1839)
PHONE..................................440 593-6771
Jeffrey Merlene, *Owner*
Rachael Merlene, *Treasurer*
EMP: 42
SALES: 173K **Privately Held**
SIC: 7217 Carpet & furniture cleaning on location

(G-8957)
ODD FELLOWS HALL
Also Called: Independent Order-Odd Fellows
253 Liberty St (44030-2705)
PHONE..................................440 599-7973
Harry Church, *Principal*
EMP: 45
SALES (est): 575.1K **Privately Held**
SIC: 8611 Business associations

(G-8958)
SHELDON HARRY E CALVARY CAMP
4411 Lake Rd (44030-1013)
PHONE..................................440 593-4381
Dave Allen, *President*
Tim Green, *Exec Dir*
EMP: 60
SALES: 400K **Privately Held**
WEB: www.calvarycamp.com
SIC: 7032 8661 Bible camp; religious organizations

(G-8959)
SUITE 224 INTERNET
224 State St (44030-2637)
PHONE..................................440 593-7113
Tom Ticard, *General Mgr*
Ken Johnson, *General Mgr*
Chris Siebeneck, *Info Tech Dir*
EMP: 30
SALES (est): 2.8MM **Privately Held**
WEB: www.suite224.com
SIC: 7373 4813 Computer integrated systems design;

(G-8960)
THE VILLA AT LAKE MGT CO
48 Parrish Rd Ofc (44030-1197)
PHONE..................................440 599-1999
Willa Hummer, *Director*
EMP: 65
SALES (est): 793.8K **Privately Held**
SIC: 8059 8052 Nursing home, except skilled & intermediate care facility; intermediate care facilities

Continental
Putnam County

(G-8961)
HOMIER & SONS INC (PA)
Also Called: Homier Implement Company
21133 State Route 613 (45831-8968)
P.O. Box 340 (45831-0340)
PHONE..................................419 596-3965
Raymond Homier, *President*
John Bibler, *Corp Secy*
Dan Homier, *Vice Pres*
Wilfred Homier, *Vice Pres*
EMP: 28
SQ FT: 18,000
SALES: 7MM **Privately Held**
SIC: 5083 Farm implements

Convoy
Van Wert County

(G-8962)
VANCREST LTD
Also Called: Vancrest of Convoy
510 E Tully St (45832-8876)
PHONE..................................419 749-2194
Denise Wehri, *Principal*
Jessica England, *Administration*
EMP: 123
SALES (corp-wide): 16.3MM **Privately Held**
SIC: 8051 Convalescent home with continuous nursing care
PA: Vancrest, Ltd.
120 W Main St Ste 200
Van Wert OH 45891
419 238-0715

Copley
Summit County

(G-8963)
BENEFIT SERVICES INC (PA)
3636 Copley Rd Ste 201 (44321-1602)
PHONE..................................330 666-0337
Connie Frazier, *President*
Jerry Newbauer, *COO*
Carolyn Esswein, *Sales Staff*
EMP: 100
SQ FT: 18,000
SALES (est): 28.9MM **Privately Held**
WEB: www.benefit-services.com
SIC: 6324 Health maintenance organization (HMO), insurance only

(G-8964)
CENTURION OF AKRON INC
1062 Jacoby Rd (44321-1711)
PHONE..................................330 645-6699
James Gebbie, *CEO*
Rich Gebbie, *President*
EMP: 85
SQ FT: 38,000
SALES (est): 3.6MM **Privately Held**
SIC: 7331 Mailing service

(G-8965)
COPLEY HEALTH CENTER INC
155 Heritage Woods Dr (44321-2791)
PHONE..................................330 666-0980
Alicia Holland, *Administration*
EMP: 170
SALES (corp-wide): 36.7MM **Privately Held**
WEB: www.copleyhealthcenter.com
SIC: 8051 Skilled nursing care facilities
PA: Copley Health Center Inc
155 Heritage Woods Dr
Copley OH 44321
330 666-0980

(G-8966)
DOMOKUR ARCHITECTS INC
4651 Medina Rd (44321-3130)
PHONE..................................330 666-7878
Michael Domokur, *President*
Dennis W Edwards, *Principal*
EMP: 25
SQ FT: 12,000
SALES (est): 5.1MM **Privately Held**
WEB: www.domokur.com
SIC: 8712 Architectural engineering

(G-8967)
KELLEY COMPANIES
Also Called: Northwestern Mutual Life
190 Montrose West Ave # 200 (44321-1372)
PHONE..................................330 668-6100
Donald E Kelley, *Owner*
EMP: 70
SALES (est): 3.4MM **Privately Held**
SIC: 8742 6311 6324 Financial consultant; life insurance; group hospitalization plans

(G-8968)
LEWIS LANDSCAPING INC
3606 Minor Rd (44321-2414)
PHONE..................................330 666-2655
Wilson Lewis, *Owner*
EMP: 40
SALES: 1.5MM **Privately Held**
SIC: 0782 Landscape contractors

(G-8969)
LORANTFFY CARE CENTER INC
2631 Copley Rd (44321-2198)
P.O. Box 4017 (44321-0017)
PHONE..................................330 666-2631
Elizabeth Domotor, *President*
Elizabeth Schmidt, *Administration*
EMP: 90
SQ FT: 19,000
SALES: 5MM **Privately Held**
SIC: 8051 Convalescent home with continuous nursing care

(G-8970)
MARRIOTT INTERNATIONAL INC
Also Called: Residence Inn By Marriott
120 Montrose West Ave (44321-1372)
PHONE..................................330 666-4811
Ray Merle, *Principal*
EMP: 50
SALES (corp-wide): 20.7B **Publicly Held**
SIC: 7011 Hotels & motels
PA: Marriott International, Inc.
10400 Fernwood Rd
Bethesda MD 20817
301 380-3000

(G-8971)
METROPLTAN VTERINARY MED GROUP
Also Called: Metropolitan Veterinary Hosp
1053 S Clvland Mssllon Rd (44321-1659)
PHONE..................................330 253-2544
Starr Earlenbaugh, *Purchasing*
Sheldon Padgett, *Med Doctor*
James M Sumner, *Director*
EMP: 25
SQ FT: 10,000
SALES (est): 1.7MM **Privately Held**
WEB: www.metropolitanvet.com
SIC: 0742 Veterinarian, animal specialties

(G-8972)
SALON WARE INC
1298 Centerview Cir (44321-1632)
PHONE..................................330 665-2244
Rod Hatch, *President*
Karen Hatch, *Corp Secy*
EMP: 38
SQ FT: 20,000
SALES (est): 6.1MM **Privately Held**
WEB: www.salonware.com
SIC: 5087 7231 Beauty parlor equipment & supplies; beauty shops

(G-8973)
SENIOR SELECT HOME HEALTH CARE
2830 Copley Rd 2 (44321-2142)
PHONE..................................330 665-4663
Jim Licitri, *President*
Brian Conners, *Finance*
EMP: 30
SALES (est): 1MM **Privately Held**
WEB: www.seniorselecthomecare.com
SIC: 8082 Home health care services

(G-8974)
SHELLS INC (PA)
1245 S Cleveland Massillo (44321-1680)
PHONE..................................330 808-5558
Henry C Bray Jr, *President*
Henry Bray Jr, *President*
John Edminister, *Vice Pres*
Julie Tremain, *Manager*
EMP: 75 **EST:** 1972
SQ FT: 85,000
SALES (est): 28.7MM **Privately Held**
WEB: www.shells.com
SIC: 5051 3543 Foundry products; industrial patterns

(G-8975)
SHETLERS SALES & SERVICE INC
Also Called: John Deere Authorized Dealer
3500 Copley Rd (44321-1609)
PHONE..................................330 760-3358
Leonard Shetler, *President*
EMP: 27
SQ FT: 9,760
SALES (est): 2.1MM **Privately Held**
SIC: 5261 5082 Lawnmowers & tractors; construction & mining machinery

(G-8976)
SUMNER HOME FOR THE AGED INC (PA)
Also Called: Sumner On Merriman
4327 Cobblestone Dr (44321-2930)
PHONE..................................330 666-2952
Ted Pappas, *CEO*
Robert D Wetter Jr, *Finance*
EMP: 199 **EST:** 1911
SQ FT: 25,000
SALES (est): 3.4MM **Privately Held**
WEB: www.sumnerhome.com
SIC: 8051 Skilled nursing care facilities

(G-8977)
SUMNER ON RIDGEWOOD
970 Sumner Pkwy (44321-1693)
PHONE..................................330 664-1360
Shane Gabis, *Principal*
EMP: 29 **EST:** 2009
SALES: 31.8MM **Privately Held**
SIC: 8059 Nursing & personal care

(G-8978)
TOWNSHIP OF COPLEY
Road Maintenance
1540 S Clvlnd Mssllon Rd (44321-1908)
PHONE..................................330 666-1853
Al James, *Manager*
EMP: 80 **Privately Held**
SIC: 1611 9111 Highway & street construction; mayors' offices
PA: Township Of Copley
1540 S Clvlnd Mssllon Rd
Copley OH 44321
330 666-1853

(G-8979)
VETERINARY RFRRL&EMER CTR OF
1321 Centerview Cir (44321-1627)
PHONE..................................330 665-4996
Rod Ferguson, *President*
James Voge, *Principal*
Shaun McWilliams, *Exec Dir*
EMP: 30
SALES (est): 2.2MM **Privately Held**
WEB: www.akronvet.com
SIC: 0742 8011 Animal hospital services, pets & other animal specialties; internal medicine, physician/surgeon

(G-8980)
WYNDHAM INTERNATIONAL INC
200 Montrose West Ave (44321-2788)
PHONE..................................330 666-9300
Chris Bitikofer, *General Mgr*
EMP: 46
SALES (corp-wide): 75MM **Privately Held**
WEB: www.wyndham.com
SIC: 7011 5813 5812 Hotels & motels; drinking places; eating places
HQ: Wyndham International, Inc
22 Sylvan Way
Parsippany NJ 07054
973 753-6000

(G-8981)
YRC INC
1275 Oh Ave (44321-1531)
PHONE..................................330 665-0274
Bill Gordon, *Branch Mgr*
EMP: 250
SALES (corp-wide): 5B **Publicly Held**
SIC: 4213 Contract haulers
HQ: Yrc Inc.
10990 Roe Ave
Overland Park KS 66211
913 696-6100

(G-8982)
YRC INC
Also Called: Yrc Ubc Cargo Claim Dept
1275 Oh Ave (44321-1531)
P.O. Box 7903, Overland Park KS (66207-0903)
PHONE................................913 344-5174
EMP: 35
SALES (corp-wide): 5B Publicly Held
SIC: 4731 Freight transportation arrangement
HQ: Yrc Inc.
　　10990 Roe Ave
　　Overland Park KS 66211
　　913 696-6100

Cortland
Trumbull County

(G-8983)
ARROWHEAD TRANSPORT CO
2555 Greenville Rd (44410-9648)
PHONE................................330 638-2900
Robert H Burn, President
EMP: 40
SQ FT: 3,000
SALES: 3MM Privately Held
SIC: 4212 5032 Light haulage & cartage, local; aggregate; gravel; sand, construction

(G-8984)
BOWERS INSURANCE AGENCY INC
339 N High St (44410-1022)
P.O. Box 280 (44410-0280)
PHONE................................330 638-6146
Ben Bowers, President
Matt Parise, Partner
Gene Francisco, Exec VP
Dina Hodnicky, Controller
Rob Hoy, Manager
EMP: 30
SQ FT: 4,100
SALES (est): 5.3MM
SALES (corp-wide): 117.2MM Publicly Held
WEB: www.thebowersagency.com
SIC: 6411 6211 Insurance agents; security brokers & dealers
HQ: Farmers National Bank
　　20 S Broad St
　　Canfield OH 44406
　　330 533-3341

(G-8985)
BURNETT POOLS INC (PA)
Also Called: Burnett Pools and Spas
2498 State Route 5 (44410-9339)
PHONE................................330 372-1725
Alan Burnett, President
Gary P Burnett, Vice Pres
Holly Hess, Treasurer
Myra May, Admin Sec
EMP: 40 EST: 1948
SQ FT: 8,400
SALES: 6MM Privately Held
WEB: www.burnettpoolsandspas.com
SIC: 5999 1799 5941 Swimming pool chemicals, equipment & supplies; swimming pool construction; pool & billiard tables

(G-8986)
CONTINENT HLTH CO CORTLAND LLC
Also Called: Concord Care Center Cortland
4250 Sodom Hutchings Rd (44410-9790)
PHONE................................330 637-7906
John Aldrich, Manager
Alexander Sherman,
EMP: 50
SALES (est): 1.8MM Privately Held
SIC: 8051 Skilled nursing care facilities

(G-8987)
CORTLAND HEALTHCARE GROUP INC
Also Called: Cortland Healthcare Center
369 N High St (44410-1022)
PHONE................................330 638-4015
Dale Sanders, Administration
Sarah Depompei, Assistant

EMP: 36
SALES (corp-wide): 996.4K Privately Held
SIC: 8051 Skilled nursing care facilities
PA: Cortland Healthcare Group, Inc.
　　26691 Richmond Rd
　　Bedford Heights OH 44146
　　216 292-5706

(G-8988)
J GILMORE DESIGN LIMITED
Also Called: Green Gate
3172 Niles Cortland Rd Ne (44410-1738)
P.O. Box 400 (44410-0400)
PHONE................................330 638-8224
James Gilmore, Principal
Sandra Gilmore,
EMP: 25
SQ FT: 8,600
SALES (est): 1.8MM Privately Held
SIC: 0782 Landscape contractors

(G-8989)
MARK THOMAS FORD INC
3098 State Route 5 (44410-9207)
PHONE................................330 638-1010
Tom Levak, President
Linda Helmuth, Office Mgr
Ed Ayers, Manager
James Turek, Manager
Curtis Stantial, CIO
EMP: 45
SQ FT: 27,700
SALES (est): 22.4MM Privately Held
SIC: 5511 7538 7532 5521 Automobiles, new & used; general automotive repair shops; top & body repair & paint shops; used car dealers

(G-8990)
MARYANN MCEOWEN
272 Wae Trl (44410-1642)
PHONE................................330 638-6385
Maryann McEowen, Owner
EMP: 80
SALES (est): 1.5MM Privately Held
SIC: 6531 Real estate agent, residential

(G-8991)
MILLER YOUNT PAVING INC
2295 Hagland Blackstub Rd (44410-9318)
PHONE................................330 372-4408
Herbert Cottrell, President
David A Grayson, Vice Pres
EMP: 35
SALES (est): 6.2MM Privately Held
SIC: 1794 1771 Excavation work; blacktop (asphalt) work; hotel/motel & multi-family home construction

(G-8992)
OHIO DEPARTMENT TRANSPORTATION
310 2nd St (44410-1539)
PHONE................................330 637-5951
Greg Solarz, General Mgr
EMP: 45 Privately Held
SIC: 7521 9621 Parking garage;
HQ: Ohio Department Of Transportation
　　1980 W Broad St
　　Columbus OH 43223

(G-8993)
OHIO LIVING
303 N Mecca St (44410-1074)
PHONE................................330 638-2420
EMP: 653 Privately Held
SIC: 6519 Real property lessors
PA: Ohio Living
　　1001 Kingsmill Pkwy
　　Columbus OH 43229

(G-8994)
THE CORTLAND SAV & BNKG CO (HQ)
Also Called: CORTLAND BANKS
194 W Main St (44410-1445)
P.O. Box 98 (44410-0098)
PHONE................................330 637-8040
James M Gasior, CEO
Lawrence A Fantauzzi, President
Tim Carney, Exec VP
Timothy Carney, Exec VP
Lance Morrison, Vice Pres
EMP: 100 EST: 1892
SQ FT: 22,000

SALES: 28.5MM
SALES (corp-wide): 33.4MM Publicly Held
WEB: www.cortland-banks.com
SIC: 6022 State trust companies accepting deposits, commercial
PA: Cortland Bancorp
　　194 W Main St
　　Cortland OH 44410
　　330 637-8040

(G-8995)
TRUMBULL-MAHONING MED GROUP
Also Called: Trumbll-Mhoning Med Group Phrm
2600 State Route 5 (44410-9393)
PHONE................................330 372-8800
Leonard Kanterman, Director
Andrew Marakas, Director
EMP: 84
SALES (est): 10.3MM Privately Held
SIC: 8011 5912 Medical centers; drug stores

(G-8996)
WIN TAMER CORPORATION
Also Called: Tamer Win Golf & Country Club
2940 Niles Cortland Rd Ne (44410-1734)
PHONE................................330 637-2881
Deborah A Rura, President
Charles D Winch, Vice Pres
EMP: 30
SQ FT: 4,400
SALES (est): 1.2MM Privately Held
SIC: 7992 Public golf courses

Coshocton
Coshocton County

(G-8997)
ALPHA NURSING HOMES INC
Also Called: Autumn Health Care
1991 Otsego Ave (43812-9370)
PHONE................................740 622-2074
Judy Moore, Branch Mgr
EMP: 100
SALES (est): 1.5MM
SALES (corp-wide): 3.1MM Privately Held
WEB: www.alphanursingservice.com
SIC: 8052 8059 Intermediate care facilities; nursing home, except skilled & intermediate care facility
PA: Alpha Nursing Homes, Inc
　　419 E Main St
　　Lancaster OH

(G-8998)
AMERICAN ELECTRIC POWER CO INC
405 Brewer Ln (43812-8965)
PHONE................................740 295-3070
Bret Berry, Supervisor
EMP: 33
SALES (corp-wide): 16.2B Publicly Held
SIC: 1731
PA: American Electric Power Company, Inc.
　　1 Riverside Plz Fl 1 # 1
　　Columbus OH 43215
　　614 716-1000

(G-8999)
BORAL RESOURCES LLC
48699 County Rd 275 (43812)
PHONE................................740 622-8042
Doug Rixters, Branch Mgr
EMP: 51 Privately Held
SIC: 5032 4953 8711 Cement; masons' materials; refuse systems; engineering services
HQ: Boral Resources, Llc
　　10701 S River Front Pkwy
　　South Jordan UT 84095
　　801 984-9400

(G-9000)
BPO ELKS OF USA
Also Called: Brotherhd Frtrnl Ordr
434 Chestnut St (43812-1134)
PHONE................................740 622-0794
Beverly Blair, Manager
EMP: 25

SQ FT: 4,500
SALES (est): 350.2K Privately Held
SIC: 8641 5812 5813 Fraternal associations; restaurant, lunch counter; bar (drinking places)

(G-9001)
CITY OF COSHOCTON
Also Called: Auditor's Office
760 Chestnut St Lbby (43812-1269)
PHONE................................740 622-1763
Timothy Turner, Mayor
EMP: 100
WEB: www.coshoctoncityhall.com
SIC: 8748 City planning
PA: City Of Coshocton
　　760 Chestnut St Lbby
　　Coshocton OH 43812
　　740 622-1763

(G-9002)
COLLEGE PARK INC
Also Called: College Park HM Hlth Care Plus
380 Browns Ln Ste 7 (43812-2075)
PHONE................................740 623-4607
Tim Postlewaite, President
EMP: 48
SALES (corp-wide): 3.9MM Privately Held
SIC: 8361 Geriatric residential care
PA: College Park, Inc
　　21990 Orchard St
　　West Lafayette OH
　　740 623-4612

(G-9003)
COLUMBUS & OHIO RIVER RR CO
47849 Papermill Rd (43812-9724)
PHONE................................740 622-8092
Jerry J Jacobson, CEO
Mike Connor, Vice Pres
Jerry Sattora, CFO
Denise Seal, Bookkeeper
EMP: 90
SALES (est): 5.4MM
SALES (corp-wide): 9.9MM Privately Held
SIC: 4011 Railroads, line-haul operating
PA: Summit View, Inc.
　　47849 Papermill Rd
　　Coshocton OH
　　740 622-8092

(G-9004)
COSHOCTON BOWLING CENTER
775 S 2nd St (43812-1979)
PHONE................................740 622-6332
Fax: 740 622-9336
EMP: 25
SALES (est): 874K Privately Held
SIC: 7933 5812 Bowling Center Eating Place

(G-9005)
COSHOCTON CNTY EMRGNCY MED SVC (HQ)
Also Called: Ccems
513 Chestnut St (43812-1210)
PHONE................................740 622-4294
Todd Shrower, Director
EMP: 50
SQ FT: 2,500
SALES (est): 3.1MM Privately Held
WEB: www.cc-ems.com
SIC: 4119 Ambulance service
PA: County of Coshocton
　　401 1/2 Main St
　　Coshocton OH 43812
　　740 622-1753

(G-9006)
COSHOCTON COUNTY HEAD START
3201 County Road 16 (43812-9123)
PHONE................................740 622-3667
Sheryl Hardesty, CFO
Suzy Lapp, CFO
Patricia Bachert, Director
EMP: 38
SALES: 2.5MM Privately Held
SIC: 8351 Head start center, except in conjunction with school

(G-9007)
COSHOCTON DRUG ALCOHOL COUNCIL
Also Called: Coshocton Bhvoral Hlth Cohices
610 Walnut St (43812-1655)
PHONE..............................740 622-0033
Beth Cormack, *Exec Dir*
EMP: 25
SALES: 925.5K **Privately Held**
SIC: 8322 Rehabilitation services

(G-9008)
COSHOCTON OPCO LLC
Also Called: Coshocton Healthcare and
100 S Whitewoman St (43812-1068)
PHONE..............................740 622-1220
Scott Burleyson,
EMP: 99
SALES (est): 2.2MM **Privately Held**
SIC: 8051 Skilled nursing care facilities

(G-9009)
COSHOCTON TRUCKING SOUTH INC
2702 S 6th St (43812-9776)
P.O. Box 1210 (43812-6210)
PHONE..............................740 622-1311
C James Woodie, *President*
Deanna Woodie, *Vice Pres*
EMP: 102
SALES (est): 11.2MM **Privately Held**
SIC: 4212 Dump truck haulage

(G-9010)
COSHOCTON VILLAGE INN SUITES
Also Called: Coshocton Village Inn & Suites
115 N Water St (43812-1004)
PHONE..............................740 622-9455
Jennifer Sigman, *General Mgr*
Megan Bradison, *Manager*
EMP: 25
SALES (est): 1MM **Privately Held**
SIC: 7011 7299 7991 Resort hotel; banquet hall facilities; physical fitness facilities

(G-9011)
COUNTY OF COSHOCTON
Also Called: County Engineer's Office
23194 County Road 621 (43812-8903)
PHONE..............................740 622-2135
Fred Wahtel, *Principal*
EMP: 30 **Privately Held**
SIC: 8711 Engineering services
PA: County Of Coshocton
401 1/2 Main St
Coshocton OH 43812
740 622-1753

(G-9012)
COUNTY OF COSHOCTON
Also Called: Child Support Agency
725 Pine St (43812-2318)
PHONE..............................740 622-1020
Melinda Fehrman, *Director*
EMP: 80 **Privately Held**
WEB: www.coshoctonlakepark.com
SIC: 8322 9111 Child related social services; county supervisors' & executives' offices
PA: County Of Coshocton
401 1/2 Main St
Coshocton OH 43812
740 622-1753

(G-9013)
COVINGTON SQUARE SENIOR APT
380 Browns Ln (43812-2073)
PHONE..............................740 623-4603
Tim Omlewey, *Owner*
EMP: 25
SALES (est): 203.4K **Privately Held**
SIC: 8082 Home health care services

(G-9014)
FAMILY PHYSICIANS OF COSHOCTON
440 Browns Ln (43812-2071)
PHONE..............................740 622-0332
Jerold A Meyer, *President*
EMP: 28
SQ FT: 2,400

SALES (est): 1.8MM **Privately Held**
SIC: 8011 General & family practice, physician/surgeon

(G-9015)
FRONTIER POWER COMPANY
770 S 2nd St (43812-1978)
P.O. Box 280 (43812-0280)
PHONE..............................740 622-6755
Robert E Wise, *President*
Steve Nelson, *General Mgr*
Blair Porteus, *Corp Secy*
Martin Daugherty, *Vice Pres*
John Powell, *Vice Pres*
EMP: 34
SQ FT: 8,000
SALES: 15.4MM **Privately Held**
WEB: www.frontier-power.com
SIC: 4911 Distribution, electric power

(G-9016)
HEALTH SERVICES COSHOCTON CNTY
230 S 4th St (43812-2019)
PHONE..............................740 622-7311
Barbara B Emmons, *Director*
EMP: 38
SALES: 259.7K **Privately Held**
SIC: 8082 Visiting nurse service

(G-9017)
HILSCHER-CLARKE ELECTRIC CO
572 S 3rd St (43812-2057)
PHONE..............................740 622-5557
Kellee Slack, *Project Mgr*
Ted Foster, *Manager*
EMP: 53
SALES (corp-wide): 48.2MM **Privately Held**
WEB: www.hilscher-clarke.com
SIC: 1731 General electrical contractor
PA: Hilscher-Clarke Electric Company
519 4th St Nw
Canton OH 44703
330 452-9806

(G-9018)
HOPEWELL INDUSTRIES INC (PA)
637 Chestnut St (43812-1212)
P.O. Box 4008, Newark (43058-4008)
PHONE..............................740 622-3563
Heather Kendall, *Principal*
Elaine Lipps, *Bookkeeper*
EMP: 70 EST: 1971
SQ FT: 14,000
SALES: 1.2MM **Privately Held**
WEB: www.hopewellind.org
SIC: 8331 7349 2789 0782 Sheltered workshop; building maintenance services; bookbinding & related work; lawn & garden services

(G-9019)
ITM MARKETING INC
Also Called: Intellitarget Marketing Svcs
470 Downtowner Plz (43812-1929)
PHONE..............................740 295-3575
Lawrence W Farrell, *President*
Bruce Collen, *CFO*
EMP: 124
SQ FT: 10,200
SALES (est): 16.8MM **Privately Held**
WEB: www.itmmarketing.com
SIC: 8742 Marketing consulting services

(G-9020)
JACOBS DWELLING NURSING HOME
25680 Bethlehem Township (43812)
PHONE..............................740 824-3635
Huldah Chestnut, *Administration*
Cynthia Trail, *Admin Sec*
Huldah Chesnut, *Administration*
EMP: 30
SALES (est): 294.5K **Privately Held**
WEB:
www.supremecouncilhouseofjacob.com
SIC: 8059 8051 Nursing home, except skilled & intermediate care facility; skilled nursing care facilities

(G-9021)
KNO-HO-CO- ASHLAND COMMUNITY A (PA)
120 N 4th St (43812-1504)
PHONE..............................740 622-9801
Michael Stephens, *CEO*
Donna Denning, *Director*
EMP: 180
SQ FT: 2,000
SALES: 9.9MM **Privately Held**
SIC: 8322 Social service center

(G-9022)
MCWANE INC
Clow Water Systems Company
2266 S 6th St (43812-8906)
P.O. Box 6001 (43812-6001)
PHONE..............................740 622-6651
Frank Eschleman, *President*
Jeff Otterstedt, *Vice Pres*
Terry Crozier, *Foreman/Supr*
Brandy Albert, *Purch Agent*
Adam Welsh, *Engineer*
EMP: 400
SALES (corp-wide): 1.3B **Privately Held**
WEB: www.mcwane.com
SIC: 3321 5085 5051 3444 Cast iron pipe & fittings; industrial supplies; pipe & tubing, steel; sheet metalwork; fabricated structural metal; blast furnaces & steel mills
PA: Mcwane, Inc.
2900 Highway 280 S # 300
Birmingham AL 35223
205 414-3100

(G-9023)
MUSKINGUM COACH COMPANY (PA)
Also Called: Eagle Rock Tours
1662 S 2nd St (43812-1950)
PHONE..............................740 622-2545
Deborah Brown, *President*
EMP: 26
SQ FT: 2,500
SALES (est): 4.6MM **Privately Held**
WEB: www.muskingumcoach.com
SIC: 4131 4724 Interstate bus line; travel agencies

(G-9024)
NOVELTY ADVERTISING CO INC
Also Called: Kenyon Co
1148 Walnut St (43812-1769)
P.O. Box 250 (43812-0250)
PHONE..............................740 622-3113
Gregory Coffman, *President*
James McConnel, *Vice Pres*
Casey Claxon, *Marketing Staff*
◆ EMP: 50 EST: 1895
SQ FT: 100,000
SALES (est): 9.6MM **Privately Held**
WEB: www.noveltyadv.com
SIC: 2752 5199 Calendars, lithographed; advertising specialties

(G-9025)
RESIDENTIAL HOME FOR THE DEVLP (PA)
925 Chestnut St (43812-1302)
P.O. Box 997 (43812-0997)
PHONE..............................740 622-9778
Rita Shaw, *President*
Marylin Shroyer, *President*
Rachel Murphy, *Manager*
Michael Dennis, *Exec Dir*
James Nelson, *Admin Sec*
EMP: 140
SQ FT: 1,200
SALES: 8.4MM **Privately Held**
WEB: www.reliabledist.com
SIC: 8361 Home for the mentally handicapped

(G-9026)
ROSCOE VILLAGE FOUNDATION
Also Called: Village Inn Restaurant
200 N Whitewoman St (43812-1059)
PHONE..............................740 622-2222
Joel Hampton, *CEO*
EMP: 60

SALES (corp-wide): 1MM **Privately Held**
WEB: www.roscoevillage.com
SIC: 5812 7299 5813 Restaurant, family: chain; banquet hall facilities; tavern (drinking places)
PA: Roscoe Village Foundation, Inc
600 N Whitewoman St
Coshocton OH 43812
740 622-7644

(G-9027)
SALO INC
232 Chestnut St (43812-1164)
PHONE..............................740 623-2331
EMP: 1299
SALES (corp-wide): 19.8MM **Privately Held**
SIC: 7363 Medical help service
PA: Salo, Inc.
960 Checkrein Ave Ste A
Columbus OH 43229
614 436-9404

(G-9028)
THOMPKINS CHILD ADLESCENT SVCS
1199 S 2nd St (43812-1920)
PHONE..............................740 622-4470
Charles Larrick, *Director*
EMP: 68
SALES (corp-wide): 4.9MM **Privately Held**
SIC: 8093 Mental health clinic, outpatient
PA: Thompkins Child And Adolescent Services
2845 Bell St
Zanesville OH 43701
740 454-0738

(G-9029)
THREE RIVERS ENERGY LLC
18137 County Road 271 (43812-9465)
PHONE..............................740 623-3035
Eamonn Byrne, *CEO*
EMP: 38
SALES (est): 5.7MM **Privately Held**
SIC: 4613 Refined petroleum pipelines

(G-9030)
UNITED STEELWORKERS
Also Called: Uswa
1048 S 6th St (43812-2804)
PHONE..............................740 622-8860
Don Freed, *Branch Mgr*
EMP: 44
SALES (corp-wide): 4.9MM **Privately Held**
WEB: www.uswa.org
SIC: 8631 Labor union
PA: United Steelworkers
60 Bolevard Of The Allies
Pittsburgh PA 15222
412 562-2400

(G-9031)
WINDSORWOOD PLACE INC
255 Browns Ln (43812-2063)
PHONE..............................740 623-4600
John Humersley, *President*
Stacy A Guilliams, *Administration*
EMP: 25
SALES (est): 905.4K **Privately Held**
SIC: 6513 8059 Retirement hotel operation; nursing & personal care

Coventry Township
Summit County

(G-9032)
AKRON AUTO AUCTION INC
2471 Ley Dr (44319-1100)
PHONE..............................330 724-7708
Jeff Bailey, *President*
Howard Campbell, *Vice Pres*
Gary Listed, *Treasurer*
EMP: 116
SQ FT: 2,000
SALES (est): 22.9MM **Privately Held**
WEB: www.akronautoauction.com
SIC: 5521 5012 Ret Used Automobiles Whol Autos/Motor Vehicles

GEOGRAPHIC

(G-9033)
BUCKEYE WASTE INDUSTRIES INC
2430 S Main St (44319-1154)
P.O. Box 1262, Cuyahoga Falls (44223-0262)
PHONE....................................330 645-9900
Gerry Konn, *President*
Diane Miller, *Corp Secy*
EMP: 25
SQ FT: 5,000
SALES (est): 4.5MM **Privately Held**
SIC: 4953 Refuse collection & disposal services

(G-9034)
FRED W ALBRECHT GROCERY CO
Also Called: Acme
3235 Manchester Rd Unit A (44319-1459)
PHONE....................................330 645-6222
Bernie King, *Branch Mgr*
Joe Lamb, *Manager*
EMP: 150
SALES (corp-wide): 419.7MM **Privately Held**
WEB: www.acmefreshmarket.com
SIC: 5912 5411 7384 5992 Drug stores & proprietary stores; grocery stores; photofinish laboratories; florists; eating places
PA: The Fred W Albrecht Grocery Company
2700 Gilchrist Rd Ste A
Akron OH 44305
330 733-2861

(G-9035)
HI-WAY DISTRIBUTING CORP AMER
3716 E State St (44203-4548)
PHONE....................................330 645-6633
Jeff Hornak, *President*
J L Miller, *Principal*
Joseph P Mueller, *Principal*
Dominic A Musitano Jr, *Principal*
Mark Hornak, *Admin Sec*
▲ EMP: 60
SQ FT: 48,000
SALES (est): 33.5MM **Privately Held**
WEB: www.hiwaydist.com
SIC: 5199 5731 General merchandise, non-durable; sound equipment, automotive

(G-9036)
INTERVAL BROTHERHOOD HOMES
Also Called: IBH
3445 S Main St (44319-3028)
PHONE....................................330 644-4095
Father Samuel Ciccolini, *Director*
EMP: 72
SQ FT: 1,626
SALES: 3.3MM **Privately Held**
WEB: www.ibh.org
SIC: 8361 8211 Rehabilitation center, residential; health care incidental; elementary & secondary schools

(G-9037)
K COMPANY INCORPORATED
Also Called: Honeywell Authorized Dealer
2234 S Arlington Rd (44319-1929)
PHONE....................................330 773-5125
Thomas Bauer, *CEO*
Christopher Martin, *President*
Thomas G Bauer, *Principal*
Jerry L Kriebel, *Principal*
Daniel Bauer, *Vice Pres*
EMP: 110
SQ FT: 43,000
SALES: 35MM **Privately Held**
SIC: 1711 Warm air heating & air conditioning contractor

(G-9038)
LAKES HEATING AND AC
Also Called: Honeywell Authorized Dealer
2476 N Turkeyfoot Rd (44319-1139)
PHONE....................................330 644-7811
Brian F Cuthbert, *President*
EMP: 25 EST: 1974
SQ FT: 2,500

SALES (est): 4.6MM **Privately Held**
WEB: www.lakeshtg.com
SIC: 1711 Warm air heating & air conditioning contractor

(G-9039)
NEW DIAMOND LINE CONT CORP
760 Killian Rd Ste B (44319-2560)
PHONE....................................330 644-9993
Barb Bishop, *President*
Glenn Witchey, *Manager*
◆ EMP: 30
SQ FT: 160,000
SALES (est): 5.2MM **Privately Held**
WEB: www.diamondline.com
SIC: 5193 Florists' supplies

(G-9040)
OHIO HICKORY HARVEST BRAND PRO
Also Called: Hickory Harvest Foods
90 Logan Pkwy (44319-1177)
PHONE....................................330 644-6266
Darlene Swiatkowski, *CEO*
Joseph Swiatkowski, *President*
Michael Swiatkowski, *Vice Pres*
EMP: 32 EST: 1972
SQ FT: 32,000
SALES: 17.7MM **Privately Held**
WEB: www.hickoryharvest.com
SIC: 5145 5149 2099 Nuts, salted or roasted; candy; fruits, dried; food preparations

(G-9041)
REM-OHIO INC
470 Portage Lakes Dr # 207 (44319-2290)
PHONE....................................330 644-9730
Neil Brendmoen, *Director*
EMP: 100
SALES (corp-wide): 2.8MM **Privately Held**
WEB: www.remohio.com
SIC: 8361 8721 Home for the mentally retarded; accounting, auditing & bookkeeping
PA: Rem-Ohio, Inc
6921 York Ave S
Minneapolis MN 55435
952 925-5067

(G-9042)
SCHOMER GLAUS PYLE
Also Called: Gpd Group
470 Portage Lakes Dr (44319-2290)
PHONE....................................330 645-2131
David B Granger, *President*
EMP: 63
SALES (corp-wide): 93.9MM **Privately Held**
SIC: 8711 Consulting engineer
PA: Glaus, Pyle, Schomer, Burns & Dehaven, Inc.
520 S Main St Ste 2531
Akron OH 44311
330 572-2100

(G-9043)
STANLEY STEMER OF AKRON CANTON
Also Called: C K M
76 Hanna Pkwy (44319-1165)
PHONE....................................330 785-5005
Craig Pucci, *President*
Kevin M Pucci, *Vice Pres*
Matt Reda, *Opers Staff*
Melvin Paul Pucci, *Treasurer*
EMP: 30
SQ FT: 3,000
SALES (est): 1.6MM **Privately Held**
SIC: 7217 7349 1799 Carpet & furniture cleaning on location; upholstery cleaning on customer premises; floor waxing; post-disaster renovations

(G-9044)
TERIK ROOFING INC
72 Hanna Pkwy (44319-1165)
PHONE....................................330 785-0060
Terry Clark, *President*
Eric Gelal, *Vice Pres*
EMP: 30
SQ FT: 4,000

SALES (est): 4.2MM **Privately Held**
WEB: www.terikroofing.com
SIC: 1761 Roofing contractor

Covington
Miami County

(G-9045)
APPLE FARM SERVICE INC (PA)
Also Called: Apple Farm Service Infc
10120 W Versailles Rd (45318-9618)
PHONE....................................937 526-4851
William Apple, *President*
Gary Schumacher, *General Mgr*
Linda Apple, *Corp Secy*
INA Pearl Apple, *Vice Pres*
EMP: 40
SQ FT: 16,875
SALES (est): 22.1MM **Privately Held**
WEB: www.applefarmservice.com
SIC: 5083 7699 Agricultural machinery; tractors, agricultural; farm implements; farm machinery repair; tractor repair

(G-9046)
BUFFALO JACKS
137 S High St (45318-1311)
PHONE....................................937 473-2524
Jack Maier, *Owner*
EMP: 25
SQ FT: 2,400
SALES (est): 701.6K **Privately Held**
SIC: 5812 7299 Family restaurants; American restaurant; banquet hall facilities

(G-9047)
LAVY CONCRETE CONSTRUCTION
7277 W Piqua Clayton Rd (45318-9698)
P.O. Box 9023, Dayton (45409-9023)
PHONE....................................937 606-4754
Terry Lavy, *President*
Jane Lavy, *Corp Secy*
EMP: 40
SQ FT: 14,000
SALES (est): 3.3MM **Privately Held**
WEB: www.lavyconcrete.com
SIC: 1771 Concrete work

(G-9048)
STAR-EX INC
1600 Mote Dr (45318-1213)
PHONE....................................937 473-2397
Lester Stacy, *President*
Kyla Manson, *Corp Secy*
Gary Manson, *Vice Pres*
EMP: 25
SQ FT: 2,000
SALES: 8MM **Privately Held**
SIC: 1794 Excavation work

(G-9049)
UVMC NURSING CARE INC
Also Called: Covington Care Center
75 Mote Dr (45318-1245)
PHONE....................................937 473-2075
Lisa Cecil, *Chf Purch Ofc*
Brenda Lewis, *Branch Mgr*
EMP: 103
SQ FT: 30,672
SALES (corp-wide): 20.3MM **Privately Held**
SIC: 8059 8069 8051 Nursing home, except skilled & intermediate care facility; specialty hospitals, except psychiatric; skilled nursing care facilities
PA: Uvmc Nursing Care, Inc.
3130 N County Road 25a
Troy OH 45373
937 440-4000

Creola
Vinton County

(G-9050)
AHOY TRANSPORT LLC
301 E Main St (45622)
PHONE....................................740 596-0536
Arretha Hoy, *Mng Member*
EMP: 28

SALES (est): 402.4K **Privately Held**
SIC: 4789 Cargo loading & unloading services

Crestline
Crawford County

(G-9051)
CONSULATE MANAGEMENT CO LLC
327 W Main St (44827-1434)
PHONE....................................419 683-3436
Susan Bacin, *CFO*
EMP: 596
SALES (corp-wide): 580.2MM **Privately Held**
SIC: 8741 Management services
PA: Consulate Management Company, Llc
800 Concourse Pkwy S
Maitland FL 32751
407 571-1550

(G-9052)
CONSULATE MANAGEMENT CO LLC
Also Called: Crestline Nursing Center
327 W Main St (44827-1434)
PHONE....................................419 683-3255
Joseph Conte, *Principal*
EMP: 106
SALES (corp-wide): 580.2MM **Privately Held**
SIC: 8051 Convalescent home with continuous nursing care
PA: Consulate Management Company, Llc
800 Concourse Pkwy S
Maitland FL 32751
407 571-1550

(G-9053)
CRESTLINE NURSING HOME INC
327 W Main St (44827-1488)
PHONE....................................419 683-3255
Brent Riefe, *Principal*
EMP: 50
SQ FT: 20,000
SALES (est): 1.8MM
SALES (corp-wide): 580.2MM **Privately Held**
WEB: www.tandemhealthcare.com
SIC: 8051 Skilled nursing care facilities
PA: Consulate Management Company, Llc
800 Concourse Pkwy S
Maitland FL 32751
407 571-1550

(G-9054)
EDGAR TRENT CNSTR CO LLC
1301 Freese Works Pl (44827)
PHONE....................................419 683-4939
Edgar Trent, *Owner*
EMP: 57 EST: 1994
SALES (est): 498K **Privately Held**
SIC: 1623 Cable laying construction

(G-9055)
GOLDEN HAWK INC
4594 Lincoln Hwy 30 (44827-9685)
PHONE....................................419 683-3304
Raymond Miller, *President*
EMP: 75 EST: 1976
SALES (est): 3.9MM **Privately Held**
SIC: 4212 Local trucking, without storage
PA: Golden Hawk Transportation Co.
4594 Lincoln Hwy
Crestline OH 44827

(G-9056)
GOLDEN HAWK TRANSPORTATION CO (PA)
4594 Lincoln Hwy (44827-9685)
PHONE....................................419 683-3304
Raymond Miller, *President*
Laina Vanbuskirk, *Director*
EMP: 70
SQ FT: 10,000
SALES (est): 9.2MM **Privately Held**
SIC: 4213 Heavy hauling; contract haulers

(G-9057)
MEDCENTRAL HEALTH SYSTEM
Also Called: Crestline Hospital
291 Heiser Ct (44827-1453)
PHONE.....................419 683-1040
Susan Brown, *CEO*
EMP: 120
SALES (corp-wide): 4B **Privately Held**
SIC: 8062 8093 8049 General medical &
surgical hospitals; rehabilitation center,
outpatient treatment; physical therapist
HQ: Medcentral Health System
335 Glessner Ave
Mansfield OH 44903
419 526-8000

(G-9058)
MOSIER INDUSTRIAL SERVICES
900 S Wiley St (44827-1766)
PHONE.....................419 683-4000
Rod Mosier, *Owner*
Dennis Hickman, *Project Mgr*
Bill Graaf, *Office Mgr*
EMP: 26
SALES: 3.5MM **Privately Held**
SIC: 1795 Wrecking & demolition work

(G-9059)
P-N-D COMMUNICATIONS INC
7900 Middletown Rd (44827-9795)
P.O. Box 956, Galion (44833-0956)
PHONE.....................419 683-1922
EMP: 25
SQ FT: 850
SALES: 1.3MM **Privately Held**
SIC: 5044 1799 Whol Office Equipment
Trade Contractor

(G-9060)
SUNRISE COOPERATIVE INC
Also Called: Crestline Agronomy
3000 W Bucyrus St (44827-1674)
PHONE.....................419 683-7340
Steve Niese, *Branch Mgr*
EMP: 27
SALES (corp-wide): 62MM **Privately
Held**
SIC: 5191 Farm supplies
PA: Sunrise Cooperative, Inc.
2025 W State St Ste A
Fremont OH 43420
419 332-6468

Creston
Wayne County

(G-9061)
HAWKINS MARKETS INC
Also Called: Hawks Nest Golf Club
2800 E Pleasant Home Rd (44217-9434)
PHONE.....................330 435-4611
Chris McCormick, *Manager*
EMP: 30
SALES (corp-wide): 1MM **Privately Held**
WEB: www.hawksnestgc.com
SIC: 7992 Public golf courses
PA: Hawkins Markets, Inc.
2033 Portage Rd
Wooster OH
330 262-4023

Cridersville
Auglaize County

(G-9062)
**CRIDERSVILLE HEALTH CARE
CTR**
Also Called: CRIDERSVILLE NURSING
HOME
603 E Main St Frnt (45806-2411)
PHONE.....................419 645-4468
Greg Costello, *Director*
EMP: 42 EST: 1961
SALES: 2.8MM **Privately Held**
SIC: 8052 8051 Intermediate care facili-
ties; skilled nursing care facilities

(G-9063)
**OTTERBEIN SNIOR LFSTYLE
CHICES**
Also Called: Otterbein Cridersville
100 Red Oak Dr (45806-9618)
PHONE.....................419 645-5114
Susan Chandler, *Exec Dir*
Jennifer Whitehead, *Executive*
EMP: 130
SQ FT: 50,000
SALES (corp-wide): 58.4MM **Privately
Held**
SIC: 8361 8051 Home for the aged; skilled
nursing care facilities
PA: Senior Otterbein Lifestyle Choices
585 N State Route 741
Lebanon OH 45036
513 933-5400

Crooksville
Perry County

(G-9064)
VALUE AUTO AUCTION LLC
3776 Hc 93 (43731)
PHONE.....................740 982-3030
Chris Fahey,
Robert J Fahey Jr,
EMP: 100
SALES (est): 4.2MM **Privately Held**
SIC: 5012 Automobile auction

Croton
Licking County

(G-9065)
OHIO FRESH EGGS LLC (PA)
11212 Croton Rd (43013)
PHONE.....................740 893-7200
Gary Bethel, *Mng Member*
▲ EMP: 250
SQ FT: 5,000
SALES (est): 25.9MM **Privately Held**
SIC: 5144 2015 Eggs; egg processing

Curtice
Ottawa County

(G-9066)
**NORTH COAST LIFT TRCK OHIO
LLC**
300 W Mill St (43412-7704)
P.O. Box 565, Mentor (44061-0565)
PHONE.....................419 836-2100
James R Gardner, *President*
Raymond W Layman, *Vice Pres*
EMP: 60
SALES (est): 1.3MM **Privately Held**
SIC: 5084 Lift trucks & parts

Cuyahoga Falls
Summit County

(G-9067)
**AJAX COMMERCIAL CLEANING
INC**
3566 State Rd Ste 5 (44223-2600)
P.O. Box 4031 (44223-4031)
PHONE.....................330 928-4543
William J Berger, *President*
Thomas Potts, *Sales Mgr*
EMP: 99
SALES: 950K **Privately Held**
WEB: www.ajaxcommercialcleaning.com
SIC: 7349 Cleaning service, industrial or
commercial; janitorial service, contract
basis

(G-9068)
AKRON ROUNDTABLE
P.O. Box 1051 (44223-0051)
PHONE.....................330 247-8682
Barbara Feld, *President*
Karen Talbott, *President*
Joan Lauck, *Principal*

EMP: 34 EST: 2010
SALES: 188.5K **Privately Held**
SIC: 8641 Civic associations

(G-9069)
ALRO STEEL CORPORATION
4787 State Rd (44223)
P.O. Box 3555 (44223-7555)
PHONE.....................330 929-4660
Todd Rumler, *Manager*
EMP: 40
SQ FT: 77,094
SALES (corp-wide): 1.9B **Privately Held**
WEB: www.alro.com
SIC: 5051 Steel
PA: Alro Steel Corporation
3100 E High St
Jackson MI 49203
517 787-5500

(G-9070)
**ASSOCIATED MATERIALS LLC
(DH)**
3773 State Rd (44223-2603)
P.O. Box 2010, Akron (44309-2010)
PHONE.....................330 929-1811
Erik D Ragatz, *Ch of Bd*
Brian C Strauss, *President*
William L Topper, *Exec VP*
Scott F Stephens, *CFO*
Dana A Schindler, *Chief Mktg Ofcr*
▲ EMP: 277
SQ FT: 63,000
SALES: 1.1B **Privately Held**
WEB: www.associatedmaterials.com
SIC: 3089 5033 5031 3442 Plastic hard-
ware & building products; siding, plastic;
windows, plastic; fences, gates & acces-
sories: plastic; roofing & siding materials;
siding, except wood; roofing, asphalt &
sheet metal; insulation materials; win-
dows; kitchen cabinets; metal doors, sash
& trim

(G-9071)
**ASSOCIATED MATERIALS
GROUP INC (PA)**
3773 State Rd (44223-2603)
PHONE.....................330 929-1811
Brian C Strauss, *President*
EMP: 41
SALES (est): 1.5B **Privately Held**
SIC: 3089 5033 5031 3442 Plastic hardware & building products; siding, plastic;
windows, plastic; fences, gates & accessories: plastic; roofing & siding materials;
siding, except wood; roofing, asphalt &
sheet metal; insulation materials; windows; kitchen cabinets; metal doors, sash
& trim

(G-9072)
**ASSOCIATED MTLS HOLDINGS
LLC**
3773 State Rd (44223-2603)
P.O. Box 2010, Akron (44309-2010)
PHONE.....................330 929-1811
Ira D Kleinman, *Ch of Bd*
Alex Amerio, *Engineer*
Bob Schindler, *VP Mktg*
Abby Kujawski, *Director*
EMP: 2000
SALES (est): 132.3MM **Privately Held**
SIC: 3089 5033 5031 5063 Plastic hard-
ware & building products; siding, plastic;
windows, plastic; fences, gates & acces-
sories: plastic; roofing & siding materials;
siding, except wood; roofing, asphalt &
sheet metal; insulation materials; win-
dows; kitchen cabinets; wire & cable;
metal doors, sash & trim
PA: Associated Materials Group, Inc.
3773 State Rd
Cuyahoga Falls OH 44223

(G-9073)
**BARRETT & ASSOCIATES INC
(PA)**
Also Called: B & A
1060 Graham Rd Ste C (44224-2960)
PHONE.....................330 928-2323
Gerald Barrett, *President*
Gary Roos, *Human Resources*
EMP: 42
SQ FT: 5,220

SALES (est): 3.9MM **Privately Held**
WEB: www.barrett-associates.com
SIC: 8742 Human resource consulting
services

(G-9074)
BECKER PUMPS CORPORATION
100 E Ascot Ln (44223-3768)
PHONE.....................330 928-9966
Dr Dorothee Becker, *President*
Jason Rathbun, *Managing Dir*
Steve Gilliam, *Area Mgr*
Mike Matijevich, *Area Mgr*
Paul Whitlock, *Area Mgr*
▲ EMP: 46
SQ FT: 33,400
SALES (est): 26.2MM **Privately Held**
WEB: www.beckerpumps.com
SIC: 5084 Compressors, except air condi-
tioning; pumps & pumping equipment

(G-9075)
**BRIDGESTONE RET
OPERATIONS LLC**
Also Called: Firestone
2761 State Rd (44223)
PHONE.....................330 929-3391
EMP: 30
SALES (corp-wide): 35.8B **Privately Held**
SIC: 5531 7539 Ret Auto/Home Supplies
Automotive Repair
HQ: Bridgestone Retail Operations, Llc
333 E Lake St Ste 300
Bloomingdale IL 60108
630 259-9000

(G-9076)
**CARDINAL RETIREMENT
VILLAGE**
171 Graham Rd (44223-1773)
PHONE.....................330 928-7888
Scott Phillips, *Partner*
Kim Richards, *Principal*
EMP: 30
SALES (est): 1.6MM **Privately Held**
SIC: 6513 8052 8361 Retirement hotel
operation; intermediate care facilities; res-
idential care

(G-9077)
CASCADE GROUP INC
Also Called: Cascade Audi
4149 State Rd (44223-2611)
PHONE.....................330 929-1861
Michelle Primm, *President*
Michael Primm, *Corp Secy*
Donald T Primm, *Vice Pres*
Patrick Primm, *Vice Pres*
Matt Rutherford, *Manager*
EMP: 50
SQ FT: 15,000
SALES (est): 14.7MM **Privately Held**
WEB: www.cascadeautogroup.com
SIC: 5511 7538 5531 5521 Automobiles,
new & used; general automotive repair
shops; automotive & home supply stores;
used car dealers

(G-9078)
**CHAPEL HL CHRSTN SCHL
ENDWMENT**
1090 Howe Ave (44221-5130)
PHONE.....................330 929-1901
Donald Lichi, *President*
Shelby Morgan, *President*
Sharon Ausdury, *Principal*
Kim Williams, *Business Mgr*
Everett Prentice, *Treasurer*
EMP: 60
SQ FT: 20,000
SALES (est): 2.1MM **Privately Held**
SIC: 7389 Fund raising organizations

(G-9079)
**CIRCLE PRIME
MANUFACTURING**
2114 Front St (44221-3220)
P.O. Box 112 (44222-0112)
PHONE.....................330 923-0019
James Mothersbaugh, *President*
Robert Mothersbaugh, *Vice Pres*
EMP: 27
SQ FT: 50,000

SALES (est): 5.1MM **Privately Held**
WEB: www.circleprime.com
SIC: **8731** 3672 3812 3663 Commercial physical research; printed circuit boards; antennas, radar or communications; radio broadcasting & communications equipment; electrical equipment & supplies; engineering services

(G-9080)
CITY OF CUYAHOGA FALLS
Also Called: Electric Services
2550 Bailey Rd (44221-2950)
PHONE....................................330 971-8000
Robert L Bye, *Superintendent*
EMP: 50 **Privately Held**
WEB: www.cfmunicourt.com
SIC: **4911** Distribution, electric power
PA: City Of Cuyahoga Falls
2310 2nd St
Cuyahoga Falls OH 44221
330 971-8230

(G-9081)
CITY OF CUYAHOGA FALLS
Also Called: Brookledge Golf Club
1621 Bailey Rd (44221-5209)
PHONE....................................330 971-8416
Steve Black, *President*
Vince Randazzo, *Manager*
EMP: 40 **Privately Held**
WEB: www.cfmunicourt.com
SIC: **7992** 9111 Public golf courses; mayors' offices
PA: City Of Cuyahoga Falls
2310 2nd St
Cuyahoga Falls OH 44221
330 971-8230

(G-9082)
CITY OF CUYAHOGA FALLS
Also Called: Water Department
2310 Second St (44221-2583)
PHONE....................................330 971-8130
John Christopher, *Manager*
EMP: 30 **Privately Held**
WEB: www.cfmunicourt.com
SIC: **4941** Water supply
PA: City Of Cuyahoga Falls
2310 2nd St
Cuyahoga Falls OH 44221
330 971-8230

(G-9083)
CITY OF CUYAHOGA FALLS
Also Called: Street Department
2560 Bailey Rd (44221-2950)
PHONE....................................330 971-8030
Charles J Mobak, *Manager*
EMP: 35 **Privately Held**
WEB: www.cfmunicourt.com
SIC: **1611** Highway & street construction
PA: City Of Cuyahoga Falls
2310 2nd St
Cuyahoga Falls OH 44221
330 971-8230

(G-9084)
COMMUNITY HOME CARE
1900 23rd St (44223-1404)
PHONE....................................330 971-7011
Fax: 330 971-7620
EMP: 30
SALES (est): 1.1MM **Privately Held**
SIC: **8082** 7361 Home Health Care Services Employment Agency

(G-9085)
DAVIS EYE CENTER
789 Graham Rd (44221-1045)
PHONE....................................330 923-5676
Charles H Davis, *Owner*
EMP: 50
SALES (est): 2.9MM **Privately Held**
SIC: **8031** 8011 Offices & clinics of osteopathic physicians; offices & clinics of medical doctors

(G-9086)
DENTRONIX INC
235 Ascot Pkwy (44223-3701)
PHONE....................................330 916-7300
Jerry Sullivan, *President*
Joseph Fasano, *Treasurer*
EMP: 50
SQ FT: 16,000

SALES: 5.5MM
SALES (corp-wide): 169,9MM **Privately Held**
WEB: www.dentronix.com
SIC: **3843** 5047 3842 3841 Orthodontic appliances; dental equipment & supplies; surgical appliances & supplies; surgical & medical instruments; analytical instruments; laboratory apparatus & furniture
HQ: Coltene/Whaledent Inc.
235 Ascot Pkwy
Cuyahoga Falls OH 44223
330 916-8800

(G-9087)
DIANE VISHNIA RN AND ASSOC
Also Called: Professional Nursing Service
2497 State Rd (44223-1503)
PHONE....................................330 929-1113
Diane Vishnia Rn, *President*
EMP: 100
SQ FT: 3,100
SALES (est): 1.7MM **Privately Held**
SIC: **8082** Visiting nurse service

(G-9088)
DOCUMENT TECH SYSTEMS LTD
Also Called: Dts
525 Portage Trail Ext W (44223-2541)
PHONE....................................330 928-5311
Pat Kelly, *Principal*
Mark Milosovic, *Sales Dir*
Jodi Wiff, *Manager*
EMP: 42
SQ FT: 2,700
SALES (est): 5.7MM **Privately Held**
WEB: www.dts-doc.com
SIC: **7373** Computer integrated systems design

(G-9089)
FALLS FAMILY PRACTICE INC (PA)
Also Called: Falls Dermatology
857 Graham Rd (44221-1170)
PHONE....................................330 923-9585
A Hugh McLaughlin, *President*
EMP: 40
SALES (est): 4.4MM **Privately Held**
WEB: www.fallsfamilypractice.com
SIC: **8011** General & family practice, physician/surgeon

(G-9090)
FALLS HEATING & COOLING INC
Also Called: Honeywell Authorized Dealer
461 Munroe Falls Ave (44221-3407)
PHONE....................................330 929-8777
Larry Burris, *President*
Marge Laria, *Treasurer*
Paul Burris, *Admin Sec*
EMP: 35
SQ FT: 4,069
SALES (est): 5.7MM **Privately Held**
SIC: **1711** Warm air heating & air conditioning contractor

(G-9091)
FALLS MOTOR CITY INC
Also Called: Falls Chrysler Jeep Dodge
4100 State Rd (44223-2612)
PHONE....................................330 929-3066
Paul Hrnchar, *President*
EMP: 50
SALES (est): 20.6MM **Privately Held**
SIC: **5511** 7514 Automobiles, new & used; rent-a-car service

(G-9092)
FALLS STAMPING & WELDING CO (PA)
2900 Vincent St (44221-1954)
P.O. Box 153 (44222-0153)
PHONE....................................330 928-1191
David Cesar, *CEO*
Rick Boettner, *Chairman*
Charlie Williams, *Plant Mgr*
Mic Kempt, *QC Mgr*
Jason Taft, *CFO*
EMP: 125 EST: 1919
SQ FT: 95,000

SALES (est): 39.7MM **Privately Held**
WEB: www.falls-stamping.com
SIC: **3465** 3469 3544 3711 Automotive stampings; stamping metal for the trade; special dies, tools, jigs & fixtures; chassis, motor vehicle; motor vehicle parts & accessories; welding repair

(G-9093)
FALLS SUPERSONIC CAR WASH INC
2720 2nd St (44221-2202)
PHONE....................................330 928-1657
Richard Sengpiel, *President*
Tim Sengpiel, *Vice Pres*
EMP: 25 EST: 1961
SQ FT: 4,160
SALES (est): 1MM **Privately Held**
SIC: **7542** Carwash, automatic

(G-9094)
FALLS VILLAGE RETIREMENT CMNTY
330 Broadway St E (44221-3312)
PHONE....................................330 945-9797
Micahel Francis, *Managing Dir*
Cheryl Herchenroeder, *Executive*
EMP: 100
SQ FT: 77,000
SALES (est): 6.2MM **Privately Held**
SIC: **8051** 8052 Convalescent home with continuous nursing care; intermediate care facilities

(G-9095)
FIFTH THIRD BANK
4070 Fishcreek Rd (44224-5402)
PHONE....................................330 686-0511
Andrew Karis, *Manager*
EMP: 64
SALES (corp-wide): 7.9B **Publicly Held**
WEB: www.53rd.com
SIC: **6022** State trust companies accepting deposits, commercial
HQ: The Fifth Third Bank
38 Fountain Square Plz
Cincinnati OH 45202
513 579-5203

(G-9096)
FLYTZ GYMNASTICS INC
Also Called: Flytz UAS Training Center
2900 State Rd Unit A (44223-1299)
PHONE....................................330 926-2900
John King, *President*
EMP: 25
SALES (est): 773.2K **Privately Held**
SIC: **7999** Gymnastic instruction, non-membership

(G-9097)
FRIENDS OF THE LIB CYAHOGA FLS
2015 3rd St (44221-3205)
PHONE....................................330 928-2117
Mary Ann Kenny, *President*
Robert Swedenborg, *Vice Pres*
Deborah Ziccardi, *Treasurer*
Wes Johnston, *Admin Sec*
EMP: 200
SALES: 5K **Privately Held**
SIC: **5942** 5192 Book stores; books, periodicals & newspapers

(G-9098)
GARDENS WESTERN RESERVE INC
45 Chart Rd (44223-2821)
PHONE....................................330 928-4500
Steve Tartaglione, *Maintenance Dir*
Rich Piekarski, *Branch Mgr*
EMP: 75
SALES (est): 1.9MM
SALES (corp-wide): 4.4MM **Privately Held**
SIC: **8361** Residential care
PA: Gardens Of Western Reserve, Inc.
9975 Greentree Pkwy
Streetsboro OH 44241
330 342-9100

(G-9099)
GENERAL ELECTRIC COMPANY
2914 Cedar Hill Rd (44223-1300)
PHONE....................................330 256-5331

EMP: 51
SALES (corp-wide): 121.6B **Publicly Held**
SIC: **1731** Electrical work
PA: General Electric Company
41 Farnsworth St
Boston MA 02210
617 443-3000

(G-9100)
HOME DEPOT USA INC
Also Called: Home Depot, The
325 Howe Ave (44221-4959)
PHONE....................................330 922-3448
Daniel Berend, *Manager*
EMP: 200
SALES (corp-wide): 108.2B **Publicly Held**
WEB: www.homerentalsdepot.com
SIC: **5211** 7359 Home centers; tool rental
HQ: Home Depot U.S.A., Inc.
2455 Paces Ferry Ave
Atlanta GA 30339

(G-9101)
ILLUMETEK CORP
121 E Ascot Ln (44223-3769)
P.O. Box 1147 (44223-0147)
PHONE....................................330 342-7582
James M Pulk, *President*
Roger Griffin, *Corp Secy*
J Anthe, *Vice Pres*
EMP: 26
SQ FT: 20,000
SALES (est): 6.5MM **Privately Held**
WEB: www.illumetek.com
SIC: **8741** Management services

(G-9102)
INTERNATIONAL FRAT OF DEL
2735 Elmwood St (44221-2307)
PHONE....................................330 922-5959
Carla Edwards, *Admin Sec*
EMP: 25
SALES (est): 166.5K **Privately Held**
SIC: **8641** University club

(G-9103)
J&J PRECISION MACHINE LTD
1474 Main St (44221-4927)
PHONE....................................330 923-5783
Hans R Leitner, *CEO*
Hans Leitner, *CEO*
EMP: 38
SALES (est): 7.1MM **Privately Held**
SIC: **3441** 7699 Building components, structural steel; industrial machinery & equipment repair

(G-9104)
JPMORGAN CHASE BANK NAT ASSN
2647 Bailey Rd (44221-2272)
PHONE....................................330 972-1905
Tim Bruzeski, *Principal*
EMP: 26
SALES (corp-wide): 131.4B **Publicly Held**
SIC: **6021** National commercial banks
HQ: Jpmorgan Chase Bank, National Association
1111 Polaris Pkwy
Columbus OH 43240
614 436-3055

(G-9105)
JULIUS ZORN INC
Also Called: Juzo
3690 Zorn Dr (44223-3580)
P.O. Box 1088 (44223-1088)
PHONE....................................330 923-4999
Anne Rose Zorn, *President*
Petra Zorn, *Vice Pres*
Uwe Schettler, *Treasurer*
Ray Gornik LI, *Controller*
Thomas Gross, *Natl Sales Mgr*
▲ EMP: 75
SQ FT: 30,000
SALES (est): 31.2MM
SALES (corp-wide): 100.8MM **Privately Held**
WEB: www.juzousa.com
SIC: **5047** 3842 Medical equipment & supplies; hosiery, support; supports: abdominal, ankle, arch, kneecap, etc.; socks, stump

PA: Julius Zorn Gmbh
Juliusplatz 1
Aichach 86551
825 190-10

(G-9106)
K H F INC
Also Called: Klassic Hardwood Flooring
3884 State Rd (44223-2606)
PHONE..................................330 928-0694
Thomas Kaser, *President*
EMP: 27
SALES (est): 2.7MM **Privately Held**
SIC: 1752 Wood floor installation & refinishing

(G-9107)
KARAM & SIMON REALTY INC
207 Portage Trail Ext W # 101
(44223-1297)
PHONE..................................330 929-0707
John G Simon, *Vice Pres*
Paul Simon, *Director*
EMP: 30
SALES (est): 2.4MM **Privately Held**
WEB: www.karamcompanies.com
SIC: 6531 Real estate agent, residential

(G-9108)
KEUCHEL & ASSOCIATES INC
Also Called: Spunfab
175 Muffin Ln (44223-3359)
PHONE..................................330 945-9455
Ken Keuchel, *President*
Herbert W Keuchel, *Principal*
Richard W Staehle, *Principal*
Herb Keuchel, *Shareholder*
◆ **EMP:** 50
SQ FT: 40,000
SALES (est): 7.8MM **Privately Held**
WEB: www.spunfab.com
SIC: 2241 8711 Narrow fabric mills; consulting engineer

(G-9109)
LINDEN INDUSTRIES INC
137 Ascot Pkwy (44223-3355)
PHONE..................................330 928-4064
Peter Tilgner, *President*
Ken Erwin, *Vice Pres*
Mike Cice, *Engineer*
Bob Hughey, *CFO*
Robert Hughey, *Controller*
EMP: 42
SQ FT: 26,000
SALES (est): 9.9MM **Privately Held**
WEB: www.lindenindustries.com
SIC: 3559 5084 Plastics working machinery; robots, molding & forming plastics; industrial machinery & equipment

(G-9110)
M C HAIR CONSULTANTS INC
833 Portage Trl (44221-3004)
PHONE..................................234 678-3987
Marcy Cona, *President*
Carol A Cogdeill, *Corp Secy*
Kathy Casper, *Vice Pres*
Sharon Roberson, *Admin Sec*
EMP: 40
SQ FT: 4,000
SALES (est): 1.7MM **Privately Held**
WEB: www.mchair.com
SIC: 7231 Cosmetology & personal hygiene salons

(G-9111)
MAPLEWOOD AT BATH CREEK LLC
Also Called: Maplewood At Cuyahoga Falls
190 W Bath Rd (44223-2516)
PHONE..................................234 208-9872
Gregory Smith,
EMP: 99
SALES (est): 362K **Privately Held**
SIC: 8059 Nursing home, except skilled & intermediate care facility

(G-9112)
MENORAH PARK CENTER FOR SENIO
Also Called: Summit Home Health Care Svcs
405 Tallmadge Rd Ste 1 (44221-3342)
PHONE..................................330 867-2143
Teresa Williams, *Manager*
Terry Williams, *Manager*

EMP: 54
SALES (corp-wide): 71.1MM **Privately Held**
WEB: www.menorahpark.org
SIC: 8082 Home health care services
PA: Menorah Park Center For Senior Living
Bet Moshav Zekenim Hadati
27100 Cedar Rd
Cleveland OH 44122
216 831-6500

(G-9113)
MICNAN INC (PA)
Also Called: Ace Mitchell Bowlers Mart
3365 Cavalier Trl (44224-4905)
P.O. Box 3168 (44223-0468)
PHONE..................................330 920-6200
David Grau, *President*
Mary E Limbach, *Principal*
Karen Grau, *Vice Pres*
▲ **EMP:** 50
SQ FT: 26,000
SALES (est): 41MM **Privately Held**
WEB: www.acemitchell.com
SIC: 5091 Bowling equipment

(G-9114)
MIDWAY BOWLING LANES INC
Also Called: Acne Bowling Supply
1925 20th St (44223-1966)
PHONE..................................330 762-7477
Richard Ray Stalnaker, *President*
Morris Laatsch, *Vice Pres*
EMP: 25
SALES: 1.3MM **Privately Held**
SIC: 7933 Bowling centers

(G-9115)
MILL POND FAMILY PHYSICIANS
265 Portage Trail Ext W (44223-3613)
PHONE..................................330 928-3111
Donald A Dahlen, *President*
Dawn Hubbard, *Assistant VP*
Dawn R Hubbard, *Med Doctor*
Ross Black, *Admin Sec*
EMP: 30
SALES (est): 1.9MM **Privately Held**
SIC: 8062 General medical & surgical hospitals

(G-9116)
OHIO RENAL CARE GROUP LLC
Also Called: Fresenius Kidney Care
320 Broadway St E (44221)
PHONE..................................330 928-4511
Mary Garber, *Manager*
EMP: 25
SALES (corp-wide): 18.9B **Privately Held**
SIC: 8092 Kidney dialysis centers
HQ: Ohio Renal Care Group, Llc
920 Winter St
Waltham MA 02451

(G-9117)
PETSMART INC
355 Howe Ave (44221-4900)
PHONE..................................330 922-4114
Richard Jacobs, *Manager*
EMP: 30
SALES (est): 12.1B **Privately Held**
WEB: www.petsmart.com
SIC: 5999 0752 Pet food; animal specialty services
HQ: Petsmart, Inc.
19601 N 27th Ave
Phoenix AZ 85027
623 580-6100

(G-9118)
PRC MEDICAL LLC (PA)
111 Stow Ave Ste 200 (44221-2560)
PHONE..................................330 493-9004
Harry Curley, *President*
EMP: 75
SQ FT: 10,000
SALES (est): 4.7MM **Privately Held**
WEB: www.prcontrol.com
SIC: 7322 Collection agency, except real estate

(G-9119)
PROSPECT MOLD & DIE COMPANY
1100 Main St (44221-4922)
PHONE..................................330 929-3311
Bruce W Wright, *CEO*

John D Wortman, *President*
Jeff Glick, *Vice Pres*
Walter Nagel, *Vice Pres*
▲ **EMP:** 100 **EST:** 1945
SQ FT: 100,000
SALES (est): 85.2MM **Privately Held**
WEB: www.prospectmold.com
SIC: 5084 3544 Industrial machinery & equipment; forms (molds), for foundry & plastics working machinery

(G-9120)
RIVERSIDE CMNTY URBAN REDEV
Also Called: Sheraton Suites Akron
1989 Front St (44221-3811)
PHONE..................................330 929-3000
Thomas J Dillon, *Ch of Bd*
Abe Moses, *President*
Eugene Fiocca, *Admin Sec*
EMP: 180
SQ FT: 255,000
SALES (est): 11.2MM **Privately Held**
WEB: www.sheratonakron.com
SIC: 5813 7011 5812 7299 Cocktail lounge; hotel, franchised; restaurant, family: independent; banquet hall facilities

(G-9121)
RON MARHOFER AUTOMALL INC
1260 Main St (44221-4923)
PHONE..................................330 835-6707
Mike Bell, *Sales Associate*
Ronald L Marhofer, *Branch Mgr*
Matt Siocum, *Manager*
Barb Smail, *Manager*
EMP: 253
SALES (corp-wide): 77.4MM **Privately Held**
SIC: 7532 5511 Body shop, automotive; automobiles, new & used
PA: Ron Marhofer Automall, Inc
1350 Main St
Cuyahoga Falls OH 44221
330 923-5059

(G-9122)
RON MARHOFER AUTOMALL INC (PA)
Also Called: Ron Marhofer Lincoln Mercury
1350 Main St (44221-4925)
PHONE..................................330 923-5059
Ron Marhofer, *President*
EMP: 50
SQ FT: 20,000
SALES (est): 77.4MM **Privately Held**
SIC: 5511 7538 7532 7515 Automobiles, new & used; general automotive repair shops; top & body repair & paint shops; passenger car leasing

(G-9123)
RV PROPERTIES LLC
Also Called: Carginal Retirement Village
171 Graham Rd (44223-1773)
PHONE..................................330 928-7888
W Scot Phillips, *President*
EMP: 40
SALES (est): 345.6K **Privately Held**
SIC: 6514 Residential building, four or fewer units: operation

(G-9124)
SOUNDTRACK PRINTING
1400 Sackett Ave (44223-2355)
PHONE..................................330 606-7117
Andrew Moore, *Owner*
EMP: 125
SALES (est): 3.8MM **Privately Held**
SIC: 5699 7389 T-shirts, custom printed;

(G-9125)
STATE VALLEY DENTAL CENTER
63 Graham Rd Ste 3 (44223-1294)
PHONE..................................330 920-8060
Christopher Nassif, *President*
EMP: 35
SQ FT: 3,800
SALES (est): 1.4MM **Privately Held**
SIC: 8021 8072 Dental clinic; dental laboratories

(G-9126)
SUMMA HEALTH
2345 4th St (44221-2573)
PHONE..................................330 926-0384
Jennifer L Eaton, *Director*
Jocelyn Davis, *Training Spec*
Kathryn Hausch,
Joan Hermann,
EMP: 498
SALES (corp-wide): 1B **Privately Held**
SIC: 8062 General medical & surgical hospitals
PA: Summa Health
525 E Market St
Akron OH 44304
330 375-3000

(G-9127)
SUMMIT ENVIRONMENTAL TECH INC (PA)
3310 Win St (44223-3790)
PHONE..................................330 253-8211
Mohamed Osman, *President*
Reza Tand, *Vice Pres*
Patti Alderson, *Project Mgr*
Christy Johnson, *Buyer*
Jackie Rasile, *Analyst*
EMP: 57
SQ FT: 20,000
SALES (est): 8.9MM **Privately Held**
SIC: 8734 Testing laboratories

(G-9128)
SUNRISE SENIOR LIVING LLC
Also Called: Sunrise of Cuyahoga Falls
1500 State Rd (44223-1302)
PHONE..................................330 929-8500
Bethany Hall, *Manager*
EMP: 60
SALES (corp-wide): 4.7B **Publicly Held**
WEB: www.sunrise.com
SIC: 8051 Skilled nursing care facilities
HQ: Sunrise Senior Living, Llc
7902 Westpark Dr
Mc Lean VA 22102

(G-9129)
TECHNICAL CONSTRUCTION SPC
Also Called: Ohio Pressure Grouting
3341 Cavalier Trl (44224-4905)
PHONE..................................330 929-1088
Edward R Sheeler, *President*
EMP: 25
SQ FT: 10,000
SALES (est): 2.6MM **Privately Held**
WEB: www.tcsdivisions.com
SIC: 1741 1771 8711 Tuckpointing or restoration; flooring contractor; foundation & footing contractor; structural engineering

(G-9130)
TESTA ENTERPRISES INC
2335 2nd St Ste A (44221-2529)
PHONE..................................330 926-9060
Paul Testa, *President*
Ryan Landi, *Vice Pres*
EMP: 35
SALES (est): 4.4MM **Privately Held**
SIC: 1541 Industrial buildings, new construction

(G-9131)
THAYER PWR COMM LINE CNSTR LLC
3432 State Rd (44223-3791)
PHONE..................................330 922-4950
Matt Luden, *Principal*
EMP: 56
SALES (corp-wide): 60.5MM **Privately Held**
SIC: 1623 Communication line & transmission tower construction
PA: Thayer Power & Communication Line Construction Company, Llc
12345 Worthington Rd Nw
Pataskala OH 43062
740 927-0021

(G-9132)
TRADITIONS AT BATH RD INC
Also Called: National Church
300 E Bath Rd (44223-2510)
PHONE..................................330 929-6272

Tom Slemmer, *President*
Betty Bramlett, *Comms Dir*
David Fox, *Director*
EMP: 140
SALES (est) 5.5MM **Privately Held**
SIC: 8051 8361 Skilled nursing care facilities; residential care

(G-9133)
TRILLIUM FAMILY SOLUTIONS INC
Also Called: FAMILY COUNSELING SERVICES OF
111 Stow Ave Ste 100 (44221-2560)
PHONE........................330 454-7066
Cathy Trubisay, *CEO*
EMP: 100
SALES: 2.4MM **Privately Held**
WEB: www.familyservicesinc.org
SIC: 8322 Family (marriage) counseling

(G-9134)
ULTRA TECH MACHINERY INC
297 Ascot Pkwy (44223-3701)
PHONE........................330 929-5544
Don Hagarty, *President*
Jim Hagarty, *Vice Pres*
Robert Hagarty, *Vice Pres*
Bruce Yuknavich, *Design Engr*
Debra Hoover, *Bookkeeper*
▲ **EMP:** 30
SQ FT: 11,000
SALES (est): 7.8MM **Privately Held**
WEB: www.utmachinery.com
SIC: 3599 7389 Machine shop, jobbing & repair; design, commercial & industrial

(G-9135)
UNITY HEALTH NETWORK LLC (PA)
3033 State Rd (44223-3614)
PHONE........................330 923-5899
Robert A Kent, *Principal*
Janelle Van Meter, *Assistant*
EMP: 51
SALES (est): 14.5MM **Privately Held**
SIC: 8099 Blood related health services

(G-9136)
VIP RESTORATION INC (PA)
Also Called: VIP Building Exteriors Contrs
650 Graham Rd Ste 106 (44221-1051)
PHONE........................216 426-9500
Rick Semersky, *President*
Bethany Friedlander, *COO*
Bethany Criscione, *Treasurer*
EMP: 25
SQ FT: 8,000
SALES (est): 17.3MM **Privately Held**
WEB: www.viprestoration.com
SIC: 1741 1542 Tuckpointing or restoration; commercial & office buildings, renovation & repair

(G-9137)
VISHNIA & ASSOCIATES INC
Also Called: Professional Nursing Service
2497 State Rd (44223-1503)
PHONE........................330 929-5512
Diane Vishnia, *President*
EMP: 75
SQ FT: 1,500
SALES (est): 1.7MM **Privately Held**
SIC: 8082 7361 Visiting nurse service; nurses' registry

(G-9138)
W B N X T V 55
2690 State Rd (44223-1644)
PHONE........................330 922-5500
Eddie Brown, *General Mgr*
Patty Armstrong, *Director*
Julie Wertheimer, *Admin Asst*
EMP: 50
SALES (est): 4.6MM **Privately Held**
SIC: 4833 Television broadcasting stations

(G-9139)
WALGREEN CO
Also Called: Walgreens
2645 State Rd (44223-1642)
PHONE........................330 928-5444
Monica Allebach, *Manager*
EMP: 25

SALES (corp-wide): 131.5B **Publicly Held**
WEB: www.walgreens.com
SIC: 5912 7384 Drug stores; photofinishing laboratory
HQ: Walgreen Co.
　　200 Wilmot Rd
　　Deerfield IL 60015
　　847 315-2500

(G-9140)
WINSTON BRDCSTG NETWRK INC (PA)
Also Called: Wbnx TV 55
2690 State Rd (44223-1644)
PHONE........................330 928-5711
Eddie Brown, *President*
Lori Bruch, *General Mgr*
Melissa Sullivan, *Accountant*
Cori McGowan, *Accounts Exec*
Lisa Kelly, *Commercial*
EMP: 50
SQ FT: 10,000
SALES (est): 41.7MM **Privately Held**
WEB: www.wbnx.com
SIC: 4833 Television broadcasting stations

(G-9141)
YOUNG MENS CHRISTIAN ASSOC
Also Called: YMCA Cuyahoga Falls Branch
544 Broad Blvd (44221-3836)
PHONE........................330 923-5223
Adam Clutts, *Exec Dir*
EMP: 60
SQ FT: 36,237
SALES (corp-wide): 16.8MM **Privately Held**
WEB: www.campynoah.com
SIC: 8641 7991 8351 7032 Youth organizations; physical fitness facilities; child day care services; youth camps; individual & family services
PA: The Young Men's Christian Association Of Akron Ohio
　　50 S Mn St Ste LI100
　　Akron OH 44308
　　330 376-1335

Cygnet
Wood County

(G-9142)
ALABAMA FARMERS COOP INC
Also Called: Bonnie Plant Farm
12419 Jerry City Rd (43413-9749)
PHONE........................419 655-2289
Tommy Paulk, *President*
EMP: 30
SALES (corp-wide): 12.7MM **Privately Held**
WEB: www.alafarm.com
SIC: 5191 Farm supplies
PA: Alabama Farmers Cooperative, Inc.
　　121 Somerville Rd Ne
　　Decatur AL 35601
　　256 353-6843

Dalton
Wayne County

(G-9143)
A PROVIDE CARE INC
Also Called: SHADY LAWN NURSING HOME
15028 Old Lincoln Way (44618-9731)
PHONE........................330 828-2278
David J Lipins, *President*
Reuven Dessler, *Corp Secy*
Nathan Levitansky, *VP Admin*
EMP: 150
SQ FT: 50,000
SALES: 6.5MM **Privately Held**
SIC: 8052 8051 Intermediate care facilities; skilled nursing care facilities

(G-9144)
DAS DUTCH KITCHEN INC
14278 Lincoln Way E (44618-9717)
PHONE........................330 683-0530
Larry Kannal, *President*
Donna Kannal, *Vice Pres*

Dennis Horst, *Controller*
EMP: 70
SQ FT: 9,000
SALES (est): 5MM **Privately Held**
WEB: www.dasdutch.com
SIC: 8741 Restaurant management

(G-9145)
GERBER FEED SERVICE INC
3094 Moser Rd (44618-9074)
P.O. Box 509 (44618-0509)
PHONE........................330 857-4421
Brad Gerber, *President*
Fae Gerber, *Vice Pres*
John Nussbaum, *Vice Pres*
Harley Gerber, *Treasurer*
Michelle Nussbaum, *Admin Sec*
EMP: 45
SQ FT: 250,000
SALES (est): 18.6MM **Privately Held**
SIC: 5191 Feed

(G-9146)
PETER GRAHAM DUNN INC
1417 Zuercher Rd (44618-9776)
PHONE........................330 816-0035
Peter G Dunn, *President*
Leanna Dunn, *Corp Secy*
▲ **EMP:** 50
SQ FT: 36,000
SALES: 9.3MM **Privately Held**
WEB: www.pgrahamdunn.com
SIC: 3499 5199 Novelties & giftware, including trophies; advertising specialties

(G-9147)
WENGER ASPHALT INC
Also Called: North Star Asphalt
26 N Cochran St (44618-9808)
PHONE........................330 837-4767
Howard J Wenger, *President*
EMP: 35
SQ FT: 6,000
SALES (est): 1.7MM **Privately Held**
SIC: 1771 Blacktop (asphalt) work

(G-9148)
WENGER EXCAVATING INC
26 N Cochran St (44618-9808)
P.O. Box 499 (44618-0499)
PHONE........................330 837-4767
Howard J Wenger, *President*
Clair Good, *Vice Pres*
Sandra Wenger, *Treasurer*
EMP: 45
SQ FT: 6,000
SALES (est): 6.1MM **Privately Held**
SIC: 1794 1623 Excavation & grading, building construction; sewer line construction; water main construction

---

Danville
Knox County

(G-9149)
CRST INTERNATIONAL INC
16559 Skyline Dr (43014-8620)
PHONE........................740 599-0008
Glenn Nyhart, *Branch Mgr*
EMP: 54
SALES (corp-wide): 2B **Privately Held**
SIC: 4213 Automobiles, transport & delivery
PA: Crst International, Inc.
　　201 1st St Se
　　Cedar Rapids IA 52401
　　319 396-4400

(G-9150)
CUDDY FARMS INC
15835 Danville Jelloway R (43014-9611)
PHONE........................740 599-7979
Sigrid Boersma, *Manager*
EMP: 36
SALES (corp-wide): 71.4MM **Privately Held**
WEB: www.cuddyfarms.com
SIC: 0254 Poultry hatcheries
HQ: Cuddy Farms, Inc.
　　2205 Blair Rd
　　Marshville NC
　　704 694-6501

(G-9151)
SELECT GENETICS LLC
15835 Dnville Jelloway Rd (43014)
P.O. Box 753, Willmar MN (56201-0753)
PHONE........................740 599-7979
Judy Goare, *Administration*
EMP: 42
SALES (corp-wide): 2.5B **Privately Held**
SIC: 0254 Chicken hatchery
HQ: Select Genetics, Llc
　　1800 Tech Dr Fl 2 Flr 2
　　Willmar MN 56201
　　320 235-8850

Dayton
Darke County

(G-9152)
POULTRY SERVICE ASSOCIATES
9317 Young Rd (45390-8620)
PHONE........................937 968-3339
Don Belt, *President*
EMP: 40
SALES (est): 1.9MM **Privately Held**
SIC: 0751 Poultry services

Dayton
Greene County

(G-9153)
1ST ADVNCE SEC INVSTGTIONS INC
1675 Woodman Dr (45432-3336)
P.O. Box 61128 (45406-9128)
PHONE........................937 210-9010
Darryl Johnson, *CEO*
EMP: 60
SALES: 1.2MM **Privately Held**
SIC: 7381 Security guard service; private investigator

(G-9154)
AFIT LS USAF
2950 Hobson Way (45433-7765)
PHONE........................937 255-3636
Billy Burt, *Principal*
EMP: 30 **EST:** 2011
SALES (est): 4MM **Privately Held**
SIC: 5192 Books

(G-9155)
AH STURGILL ROOFING INC
4358 Springfield St B (45431-1089)
PHONE........................937 254-2955
Allen H Sturgill, *President*
Jeremy Sturgill, *Principal*
EMP: 25
SALES (est): 3.5MM **Privately Held**
WEB: www.sturgillroofing.com
SIC: 1761 Roofing contractor

(G-9156)
AIR FORCE US DEPT OF
4225 Logistics Ave (45433-5769)
PHONE........................937 656-2354
EMP: 254 **Publicly Held**
SIC: 9711 7372 Air Force; business oriented computer software
HQ: United States Department Of The Air Force
　　1000 Air Force Pentagon
　　Washington DC 20330

(G-9157)
AIR FORCE US DEPT OF
Also Called: Naf Wright Patterson Afb
5215 Thurlow St 2 (45433-5547)
PHONE........................937 257-6068
Ron Canady, *Branch Mgr*
EMP: 99 **Publicly Held**
WEB: www.af.mil
SIC: 7041 9711 Lodging house, organization; Air Force
HQ: United States Department Of The Air Force
　　1000 Air Force Pentagon
　　Washington DC 20330

(G-9158)

AIR FRCE MUSEUM FOUNDATION INC
1100 Spaatz St Bldg 489 (45433-7102)
PHONE...................................937 258-1218
Tracy Clifton, *Purch Agent*
Kim Pierre, *Sales Mgr*
Bill Horner, *Manager*
Michael Imhoff, *Exec Dir*
Amy Callahan, *Admin Asst*
EMP: 40
SQ FT: 5,500
SALES: 5.9MM **Privately Held**
SIC: 8399 Fund raising organization, non-fee basis

(G-9159)

AMERICAN SALES INC
Also Called: A S I
1755 Spaulding Rd (45432-3727)
P.O. Box 1105 (45401-1105)
PHONE...................................937 253-9520
David Goldenberg, *President*
Judith Goldenberg, *Chairman*
David Drake, *Vice Pres*
David F Drake, *VP Sales*
Kathy Marshall, *Regl Sales Mgr*
EMP: 35 **EST:** 1908
SQ FT: 18,000
SALES (est): 1.4MM **Privately Held**
SIC: 7215 5087 Laundry, coin-operated; laundry equipment & supplies

(G-9160)

ARMY & AIR FORCE EXCHANGE SVC
Also Called: Wright Patterson Afb Lodging
2439 Schlatter Dr (45433-5519)
PHONE...................................937 257-2928
Mary Drury, *Branch Mgr*
EMP: 150 **Publicly Held**
WEB: www.aafes.com
SIC: 7011 9711 Hotels & motels; Air Force;
HQ: Army & Air Force Exchange Service
3911 S Walton Walker Blvd
Dallas TX 75236
214 312-2011

(G-9161)

ARMY & AIR FORCE EXCHANGE SVC
Also Called: Air Force Morale Welfare Rec
5215 Thurlow St Ste 2 (45433-5547)
PHONE...................................937 257-7736
Ronald Tarmelle, *Branch Mgr*
EMP: 900 **Publicly Held**
WEB: www.aafes.com
SIC: 7999 9711 Recreation services; Air Force
HQ: Army & Air Force Exchange Service
3911 S Walton Walker Blvd
Dallas TX 75236
214 312-2011

(G-9162)

BRINKS INCORPORATED
4395 Springfield St (45431-1077)
PHONE...................................937 253-9777
Glen Reno, *Manager*
Donna Justice, *Admin Sec*
EMP: 50
SALES (corp-wide): 3.4B **Publicly Held**
WEB: www.brinksinc.com
SIC: 7381 Armored car services
HQ: Brink's, Incorporated
1801 Bayberry Ct Ste 400
Richmond VA 23226
804 289-9600

(G-9163)

BUTT CONSTRUCTION COMPANY INC
3858 Germany Ln (45431-1607)
P.O. Box 31306 (45437-0306)
PHONE...................................937 426-1313
Bill Butt, *President*
Chuck Cheadle, *Planning*
EMP: 35 **EST:** 1927
SQ FT: 4,400
SALES (est): 13.8MM **Privately Held**
WEB: www.buttconstruction.com
SIC: 1542 1541 Institutional building construction; industrial buildings, new construction

(G-9164)

CDO TECHNOLOGIES INC (PA)
Also Called: C D O
5200 Sprngfeld St Ste 320 (45431)
PHONE...................................937 258-0022
Alphonso Wofford, *President*
Don Ertel, *Senior VP*
Greg Greening, *Vice Pres*
Kelvin Akles, *Director*
Grant Richardson, *Director*
EMP: 75
SQ FT: 6,000
SALES (est): 60.8MM **Privately Held**
WEB: www.cdotech.com
SIC: 7371 7373 Computer software systems analysis & design, custom; computer integrated systems design

(G-9165)

CHILDERS PHOTOGRAPHY
5616 Burkhardt Rd (45431-2202)
PHONE...................................937 256-0501
Charles Childers, *Owner*
EMP: 30
SQ FT: 1,800
SALES (est): 1.1MM **Privately Held**
WEB: www.childersphoto.com
SIC: 7221 7335 Photographer, still or video; photographic studio, commercial

(G-9166)

COMPUTER SCIENCES CORPORATION
2435 5th St Bldg 676 (45433-7802)
PHONE...................................937 904-5113
Donna Klecka, *Principal*
EMP: 50
SALES (corp-wide): 24.5B **Publicly Held**
WEB: www.csc.com
SIC: 7376 Computer facilities management
HQ: Computer Sciences Corporation
1775 Tysons Blvd Ste 1000
Tysons VA 22102
703 245-9675

(G-9167)

DAYTON INDUSTRIAL DRUM INC
1880 Radio Rd (45431-1035)
P.O. Box 172, Tipp City (45371-0172)
PHONE...................................937 253-8933
David Hussong, *President*
Ruth M Hussong, *Corp Secy*
Kylene Hussong, *Vice Pres*
EMP: 25
SQ FT: 25,000
SALES (est): 4.4MM **Privately Held**
WEB: www.daytonindustrialdrum.com
SIC: 7699 5085 5113 2673 Industrial equipment services; drums, new or reconditioned; industrial & personal service paper; bags: plastic, laminated & coated; fiber cans, drums & similar products

(G-9168)

DAYTON POWER AND LIGHT COMPANY (DH)
1065 Woodman Dr (45432-1423)
PHONE...................................937 331-4063
Andrew M Vesey, *Ch of Bd*
Tom Raga, *President*
H Ted Santo, *Vice Pres*
Mary Robinson, *Opers Spvr*
Craig L Jackson, *CFO*
EMP: 200 **EST:** 1911
SALES: 738.7MM
SALES (corp-wide): 10.7B **Publicly Held**
WEB: www.waytogo.com
SIC: 4911 4931 Generation, electric power; transmission, electric power; distribution, electric power; ; electric & other services combined
HQ: Dpl Inc.
1065 Woodman Dr
Dayton OH 45432
937 331-4063

(G-9169)

DEFENSE RESEARCH ASSOC INC
3915 Germany Ln Ste 102 (45431-1688)
PHONE...................................937 431-1644
Leroy E Anderson, *CEO*
Larry Janning, *Vice Pres*
Ray Trimmer, *Vice Pres*

Dale Cull, *Engineer*
Jeanette Anderson, *CFO*
EMP: 38
SQ FT: 15,000
SALES (est): 5.8MM **Privately Held**
WEB: www.dra-inc.net
SIC: 8731 Commercial physical research

(G-9170)

DPL INC (DH)
1065 Woodman Dr (45432-1438)
PHONE...................................937 331-4063
Phil Herrington, *President*
Derek Porter, *President*
Gregory S Campbell, *Vice Pres*
Timothy G Rice, *Vice Pres*
Jeff Hicks, *Project Mgr*
EMP: 32
SALES: 775.9MM
SALES (corp-wide): 10.7B **Publicly Held**
WEB: www.dpl.com
SIC: 4911 Generation, electric power; transmission, electric power; distribution, electric power
HQ: Aes Dpl Holdings, Llc
4300 Wilson Blvd
Arlington VA 22203
703 522-1315

(G-9171)

DUNCAN OIL CO (PA)
849 Factory Rd (45434-6134)
PHONE...................................937 426-5945
Roger McDaniel, *President*
Ryan McDaniel, *COO*
Kathryn McDaniel, *Opers Staff*
Anthony Antoni, *CFO*
Steven Heck, *CFO*
EMP: 28 **EST:** 1960
SQ FT: 5,000
SALES (est): 93.6MM **Privately Held**
WEB: www.duncan-oil.com
SIC: 5172 5411 5983 1542 Gasoline; fuel oil; convenience stores; fuel oil dealers; service station construction

(G-9172)

EAST DAYTON CHRISTIAN SCHOOL
999 Spinning Rd (45431-2847)
PHONE...................................937 252-5400
Stacey Auvil, *Principal*
Stan Ellingson, *Principal*
Rachelle Svoboda, *Business Mgr*
Cindy Hume, *Asst Supt*
Carol Veness, *Info Tech Dir*
EMP: 40
SALES (est): 1.9MM **Privately Held**
WEB: www.eastdaytonchristian.org
SIC: 8211 8351 Private combined elementary & secondary school; preschool center

(G-9173)

EVANHOE & ASSOCIATES INC
Also Called: Aidc Solutions
5089 Norman Blvd (45431-1224)
PHONE...................................937 235-2995
Charles E Evanhoe, *President*
Anita S Evanhoe, *Vice Pres*
Anita Evanhoe, *Vice Pres*
Bob Fudge, *Vice Pres*
Robert Fudge, *Vice Pres*
EMP: 50
SQ FT: 6,000
SALES (est): 7MM **Privately Held**
WEB: www.evanhoe.com
SIC: 7373 7371 7376 7379 Value-added resellers, computer systems; custom computer programming services; computer facilities management; ; computer maintenance & repair; computers, peripherals & software

(G-9174)

GROVE WALNUT COUNTRY CLUB INC
5050 Linden Ave (45432-1898)
PHONE...................................937 253-3109
Robert Reahling, *President*
EMP: 50 **EST:** 1935
SQ FT: 26,000
SALES: 1.6MM **Privately Held**
SIC: 7997 Country club, membership

(G-9175)

HEALTH CARE RTREMENT CORP AMER
Also Called: Heartland - Beavercreek
1974 N Fairfield Rd (45432)
PHONE...................................937 429-1106
Sherriann Wood, *Branch Mgr*
EMP: 145
SALES (corp-wide): 2.4B **Publicly Held**
WEB: www.hrc-manorcare.com
SIC: 8051 Convalescent home with continuous nursing care
HQ: Health Care And Retirement Corporation Of America
333 N Summit St Ste 103
Toledo OH 43604
419 252-5500

(G-9176)

HIDY MOTORS INC (PA)
Also Called: Hidy Honda
2300 Hller Drv Bevr Crk Beaver Creek (45434)
PHONE...................................937 426-9564
David Hidy, *President*
Rita Mayes, *CFO*
Rita Mays, *Office Mgr*
Chris Noland, *Manager*
EMP: 88
SQ FT: 33,000
SALES (est): 31.6MM **Privately Held**
WEB: www.hidyhonda.com
SIC: 5511 5012 7515 Automobiles, new & used; pickups, new & used; vans, new & used; automobiles & other motor vehicles; passenger car leasing

(G-9177)

HILTON GARDEN INN BEAVERCREEK
3498 Pentagon Park Blvd (45431)
PHONE...................................937 458-2650
Rob Hale, *Principal*
EMP: 80 **EST:** 2008
SALES (est): 2.2MM **Privately Held**
SIC: 7011 Hotels

(G-9178)

INFOCISION MANAGEMENT CORP
101 Woodman Dr (45431-1422)
PHONE...................................937 259-2400
Robert King, *Branch Mgr*
EMP: 182
SALES (corp-wide): 242.3MM **Privately Held**
SIC: 8741 Management services
PA: Infocision Management Corporation
325 Springside Dr
Akron OH 44333
330 668-1411

(G-9179)

INNOVATIVE TECHNOLOGIES CORP (PA)
Also Called: Itc
1020 Woodman Dr Ste 100 (45432-1410)
PHONE...................................937 252-2145
Ramesh K Mehan, *President*
Ramesh Mehan, *President*
Renee Mehan, *Vice Pres*
Shawn Irish, *VP Sales*
Karen Amrein, *Manager*
EMP: 70
SQ FT: 16,000
SALES (est): 11.1MM **Privately Held**
WEB: www.itc-1.com
SIC: 8742 7375 Management consulting services; information retrieval services

(G-9180)

LANDING GEAR TEST FACILITY
Also Called: Safety and Sustainment Branch
1981 5th St (45433-7202)
PHONE...................................937 255-5740
J Greer McClain, *Chief*
Martin Vogel, *Opers Staff*
EMP: 30
SQ FT: 60,000
SALES (est): 1.6MM **Privately Held**
SIC: 8734 Testing laboratories

(G-9181)
MECHANICAL SYSTEMS DAYTON INC
Also Called: Msd
4401 Springfield St (45431-1040)
PHONE....................................937 254-3235
Beverly Stewart, *CEO*
John Stewart, *Vice Pres*
Corey Hoke, *Project Mgr*
Rick Gilbert, *Engineer*
Sara Sowers, *Engineer*
EMP: 100 EST: 1984
SQ FT: 40,000
SALES (est): 30.7MM **Privately Held**
WEB: www.msdinc.net
SIC: 1711 Mechanical contractor

(G-9182)
NELSON FINANCIAL GROUP
Also Called: Successful Eductl Seminars
3195 Dayton Xenia Rd # 900 (45434-6390)
PHONE....................................513 686-7800
William Nelson, *CEO*
Phyllis Nelson, *President*
Ed Severt, *COO*
EMP: 25
SALES (est): 353.1K **Privately Held**
SIC: 7299 Personal financial services

(G-9183)
OHIO ASSN PUB SCHL EMPLOYEES
Also Called: Oapse
1675 Woodman Dr (45432-3336)
PHONE....................................937 253-5100
Karen Bosk, *Principal*
EMP: 55
SALES (corp-wide): 9.9MM **Privately Held**
SIC: 8631 Labor union
PA: Ohio Association Of Public School Employees
6805 Oak Creek Dr Ste 1
Columbus OH 43229
614 890-4770

(G-9184)
OHIO INSTITUTE OF CARDIAC CARE (PA)
Also Called: Oicc
2451 Patrick Blvd (45431-8497)
PHONE....................................937 322-1700
Salim O Dahdah MD, *President*
Cindy Dahdah, *Vice Pres*
EMP: 32
SALES (est): 11.6MM **Privately Held**
WEB: www.ohiohealthchoice.com
SIC: 8011 Cardiologist & cardio-vascular specialist

(G-9185)
P E SYSTEMS INC
5100 Sprngfeld St Ste 510 (45431)
PHONE....................................937 258-0141
Larry Bogemann, *Branch Mgr*
Robert Chapman, *Manager*
Leonard Gulley, *Database Admin*
EMP: 100 **Privately Held**
WEB: www.pesystems-ne.com
SIC: 8711 Consulting engineer
PA: P E Systems, Inc.
10201 Fairfax Blvd # 400
Fairfax VA 22030

(G-9186)
PAIN MANAGEMENT ASSOCIATES INC
Also Called: Dayton Outpatien Practice
1010 Woodman Dr Ste 100 (45432-1429)
PHONE....................................937 252-2000
Suresh Gupta, *President*
EMP: 30
SQ FT: 36,000
SALES (est): 953.7K
SALES (corp-wide): 287.4MM **Privately Held**
SIC: 8093 Specialty outpatient clinics
HQ: Team Health Holdings, Inc.
265 Brookview Centre Way
Knoxville TN 37919
865 693-1000

(G-9187)
SUPERIOR MECHANICAL SVCS INC
Also Called: Honeywell Authorized Dealer
3100 Plainfield Rd Ste C (45432-3725)
PHONE....................................937 259-0082
Steve Heidenreich, *President*
Mark Rath, *Vice Pres*
EMP: 26
SQ FT: 6,000
SALES (est): 4.4MM **Privately Held**
SIC: 1711 8711 Warm air heating & air conditioning contractor; ventilation & duct work contractor; mechanical contractor; engineering services

(G-9188)
UNISON INDUSTRIES LLC
2455 Dayton Xenia Rd (45434-7148)
PHONE....................................904 667-9904
Belinda Kidwell, *Manager*
Allen Glaug, *Manager*
EMP: 400
SALES (corp-wide): 121.6B **Publicly Held**
WEB: www.unisonindustries.com
SIC: 3728 4581 3714 3498 Aircraft parts & equipment; aircraft servicing & repairing; motor vehicle parts & accessories; fabricated pipe & fittings; steel pipe & tubes
HQ: Unison Industries, Llc
7575 Baymeadows Way
Jacksonville FL 32256
904 739-4000

(G-9189)
UNITED STATES DEPT OF NAVY
Also Called: Namru-Dayton
2624 Q St Bldg 851 Area B (45433)
PHONE....................................937 938-3926
Rees Lee, *President*
Nicholas Roberts, *Persnl Mgr*
EMP: 40 **Publicly Held**
SIC: 9711 8733 Navy; ; medical research
HQ: United States Department Of The Navy
1200 Navy Pentagon
Washington DC 20350

(G-9190)
US DEPT OF THE AIR FORCE
Also Called: Usaf-Medical Center
4881 Sug Mple Dr Bldg 830 (45433)
PHONE....................................937 257-0837
Gary Walker, *Branch Mgr*
EMP: 90 **Publicly Held**
WEB: www.af.mil
SIC: 8011 9711 Offices & clinics of medical doctors; Air Force;
HQ: United States Department Of The Air Force
1000 Air Force Pentagon
Washington DC 20330

(G-9191)
US DEPT OF THE AIR FORCE
2856 G St (45433-7400)
PHONE....................................937 255-5150
Richarard Stotts, *Director*
EMP: 391 **Publicly Held**
WEB: www.af.mil
SIC: 8733 9711 Medical research; Air Force;
HQ: United States Department Of The Air Force
1000 Air Force Pentagon
Washington DC 20330

(G-9192)
WRIGHT STATE UNIVERSITY
Also Called: Mini University
3640 Colonel Glenn Hwy (45435-0002)
PHONE....................................937 775-4070
Camy Scheffield, *Director*
Charlotta Taylor, *Associate Dir*
Allen Nagy, *Professor*
EMP: 30
SQ FT: 8,982
SALES (corp-wide): 230.3MM **Privately Held**
SIC: 8351 Child day care services
PA: Wright State University
3640 Colonel Glenn Hwy
Dayton OH 45435
937 775-3333

Dayton
Montgomery County

(G-9193)
10 WILMINGTON PLACE
10 Wilmington Ave (45420-1877)
PHONE....................................937 253-1010
Barry Humphries, *Owner*
EMP: 90
SQ FT: 300,000
SALES (est): 5.5MM **Privately Held**
WEB: www.10wilmingtonplace.com
SIC: 8051 8052 Skilled nursing care facilities; intermediate care facilities

(G-9194)
1ST ADVNCE SEC INVSTGTIONS INC
111 W 1st St Ste 101 (45402-1137)
P.O. Box 61128 (45406-9128)
PHONE....................................937 317-4433
Darryl Johnson, *President*
EMP: 49 EST: 2013
SALES (est): 281.9K **Privately Held**
SIC: 7381 8742 Guard services; training & development consultant

(G-9195)
5440 CHARLESGATE RD OPER LLC
Also Called: Rehab & Nursing Ctr Sprng Crk
5440 Charlesgate Rd (45424-1049)
PHONE....................................937 236-6707
Elizabeth Toohill, *Director*
EMP: 80
SALES (est): 2.2MM **Privately Held**
SIC: 8051 Skilled nursing care facilities

(G-9196)
6TH CIRCUIT COURT
Also Called: US Federal District Court
200 W 2nd St Ste 702 (45402-1472)
PHONE....................................614 719-3100
Tracey Whibb, *Officer*
EMP: 25 **Publicly Held**
WEB: www.mied.uscourts.gov
SIC: 9211 8322 Federal courts; ; probation office
HQ: 6th Circuit Court
601 W Broadway Bsmt
Louisville KY 40202
502 625-3800

(G-9197)
A & D DAYCARE AND LEARNING CTR
1049 Infirmary Rd (45417-5450)
PHONE....................................937 263-4447
Andrew Peterson, *President*
Dorothy Peterson, *Vice Pres*
EMP: 30
SALES (est): 1.1MM **Privately Held**
SIC: 8351 Preschool center

(G-9198)
A B S TEMPS INC
2770 Wilmington Pike (45419-2141)
PHONE....................................937 252-9888
Mike Nicks, *President*
EMP: 25
SALES (est): 1MM **Privately Held**
SIC: 7363 Temporary help service

(G-9199)
A PLUS EXPEDITING & LOGISTICS
2947 Boulder Ave (45414-4846)
P.O. Box 570 (45404-0570)
PHONE....................................937 424-0220
Billy E Back, *President*
EMP: 32
SALES (est): 5.2MM **Privately Held**
SIC: 4731 Freight transportation arrangement

(G-9200)
A TO Z GOLF MANAGMENT CO
Also Called: Rollandia Golf & Magic Castle
4990 Wilmington Pike (45440-2100)
PHONE....................................937 434-4911
Zachary Fink, *Owner*
EMP: 30
SALES (est): 1.3MM **Privately Held**
WEB: www.gorollandia.com
SIC: 7929 7992 Entertainment service; public golf courses

(G-9201)
AAA MIAMI VALLEY (PA)
Also Called: AAA Travel Agency
825 S Ludlow St (45402-2612)
P.O. Box 1801 (45401-1801)
PHONE....................................937 224-2896
Gus Geil, *Ch of Bd*
John E Horn, *Vice Ch Bd*
Raymond Keyton, *President*
James Moses, *CFO*
Witt Darner, *Treasurer*
EMP: 80 EST: 1920
SQ FT: 15,000
SALES (est): 28.9MM **Privately Held**
WEB: www.aaamiamivalley.com
SIC: 4724 8699 Travel agencies; automobile owners' association

(G-9202)
ABF FREIGHT SYSTEM INC
8051 Center Point 70 Blvd (45424-6374)
PHONE....................................937 236-2210
Nick Dinapoli, *President*
Greg Adams, *Opers Mgr*
Tim Magoto, *Sales/Mktg Mgr*
Dayna Sluterbeck, *Accounts Mgr*
EMP: 28
SALES (corp-wide): 3B **Publicly Held**
WEB: www.abfs.com
SIC: 4213 Contract haulers
HQ: Abf Freight System, Inc.
3801 Old Greenwood Rd
Fort Smith AR 72903
479 785-8700

(G-9203)
ABM PARKING SERVICES INC
40 N Main St Ste 1540 (45423-1043)
PHONE....................................937 461-2113
Alan Barnett, *Manager*
EMP: 30
SALES (corp-wide): 6.4B **Publicly Held**
WEB: www.meyers.net
SIC: 7521 Parking lots
HQ: Abm Parking Services, Inc.
1150 S Olive St Fl 19
Los Angeles CA 90015
213 284-7600

(G-9204)
ACCESS CLEANING SERVICE INC
5045 N Main St Ste 100 (45415-3637)
P.O. Box 5782 (45405-0782)
PHONE....................................937 276-2605
Spencer L Johnson, *President*
Cynthia Johnson, *Admin Sec*
EMP: 46
SQ FT: 1,600
SALES (est): 1.1MM **Privately Held**
SIC: 7349 Janitorial service, contract basis

(G-9205)
ACCESS HOME CARE LLC
2555 S Dixie Dr Ste 100 (45409-1532)
PHONE....................................937 224-9991
Michael Biggs, *Mng Member*
EMP: 40
SALES (est): 1.2MM **Privately Held**
SIC: 8059 4789 Personal care home, with health care; transportation services

(G-9206)
ACUREN INSPECTION INC
705 Albany St (45417-3460)
PHONE....................................937 228-9729
Jim Bailey, *President*
EMP: 52
SALES (corp-wide): 1.6B **Privately Held**
SIC: 1389 Testing, measuring, surveying & analysis services
HQ: Acuren Inspection, Inc.
30 Main St Ste 402
Danbury CT 06810
203 702-8740

(G-9207)
ACUREN INSPECTION INC
Also Called: Eastern Region Department
7333 Paragon Rd Ste 240 (45459-4157)
PHONE....................................937 228-9729

▲ = Import ▼=Export
◆ =Import/Export

Ricki Miller, *Branch Mgr*
EMP: 50
SALES (corp-wide): 1.6B **Privately Held**
SIC: 7389 Inspection & testing services
HQ: Acuren Inspection, Inc.
30 Main St Ste 402
Danbury CT 06810
203 702-8740

(G-9208)
ADAMS-ROBINSON
ENTERPRISES INC (PA)
Also Called: Adams Robinson Construction
2735 Needmore Rd (45414-4207)
PHONE..............................937 274-5318
Michael Adams, *CEO*
M Bradley Adams, *Vice Pres*
Patrick Ludwig, *Project Mgr*
Paul Russell, *Project Mgr*
Mark Guse, *Opers Staff*
EMP: 150
SQ FT: 10,324
SALES (est): 92.3MM **Privately Held**
SIC: 1623 Water, sewer & utility lines

(G-9209)
ADVANCE HOME CARE LLC
1250 W Dorothy Ln (45409-1317)
PHONE..............................937 723-6335
Karima Moudjud, *Branch Mgr*
EMP: 60
SALES (corp-wide): 1.6MM **Privately**
Held
SIC: 8082 Home health care services
PA: Advance Home Care Llc
1191 S James Rd Ste D
Columbus OH 43227
614 436-3611

(G-9210)
AECOM GLOBAL II LLC
7333 Paragon Rd Ste 175 (45459-4173)
PHONE..............................937 233-1230
Tim Koch, *Principal*
EMP: 35
SALES (corp-wide): 20.1B **Publicly Held**
WEB: www.wcc.com
SIC: 8711 Consulting engineer
HQ: Aecom Global Ii, Llc
1999 Avenue Of The Stars
Los Angeles CA 90067
213 593-8100

(G-9211)
AETNA BUILDING
MAINTENANCE INC
2044 Wayne Ave (45410-2140)
PHONE..............................866 238-6201
Hugh Bledle, *Manager*
EMP: 130
SALES (corp-wide): 29.6MM **Privately**
Held
WEB: www.aetnabuilding.com
SIC: 7349 Janitorial service, contract basis
HQ: Aetna Building Maintenance, Inc.
646 Parsons Ave
Columbus OH 43206
614 476-1818

(G-9212)
AHF OHIO INC
264 Wilmington Ave (45420-1989)
PHONE..............................937 256-4663
Rick Cordonnier, *Administration*
EMP: 89
SALES (corp-wide): 22.6MM **Privately**
Held
SIC: 8051 8361 Skilled nursing care facilities; residential care
PA: Ahf Ohio, Inc.
5920 Venture Dr Ste 100
Dublin OH 43017
614 760-7352

(G-9213)
ALCOHOL DRUG ADDCTION &
MENTAL
Also Called: Adamhs Bd For Montgomery
Cnty
409 E Monument Ave # 102 (45402-1482)
PHONE..............................937 443-0416
Helen Jones-Kelley, *CEO*
Jonathan Parks, *CFO*
Joseph Szoke, *Exec Dir*
Andrea Doolittle, *Director*

EMP: 30
SALES: 40MM **Privately Held**
WEB: www.adamhs.co.montgomery.oh.us
SIC: 8069 8093 Drug addiction rehabilitation hospital; mental health clinic, outpatient

(G-9214)
ALL ABOUT HOME CARE SVCS
LLC
1307 E 3rd St (45403-1816)
PHONE..............................937 222-2980
Patty L Shepherd,
EMP: 37
SALES (est): 256.3K **Privately Held**
SIC: 8082 Home health care services

(G-9215)
ALLIED BUILDERS INC (PA)
Also Called: Allied Fence Builders
1644 Kuntz Rd (45404-1234)
P.O. Box 94 (45404-0094)
PHONE..............................937 226-0311
Linda S Helton, *President*
Carol Gault, *General Mgr*
Bill Helton Jr, *Vice Pres*
EMP: 47
SQ FT: 25,500
SALES: 4.5MM **Privately Held**
WEB: www.allied-fence.com
SIC: 1799 Fence construction

(G-9216)
ALLIED SUPPLY COMPANY INC
(PA)
Also Called: Johnson Contrls Authorized Dlr
1100 E Monument Ave (45402-1343)
PHONE..............................937 224-9833
William V Homan, *Ch of Bd*
Thomas E Homan, *President*
J W Van De Grift, *Principal*
Debbie Beasley, *Purchasing*
Scott Gibbons, *Treasurer*
EMP: 40 **EST:** 1948
SQ FT: 65,000
SALES (est): 33.1MM **Privately Held**
WEB: www.alliedsupply.com
SIC: 5078 5075 5085 Refrigeration equipment & supplies; warm air heating equipment & supplies; air conditioning & ventilation equipment & supplies; mill supplies

(G-9217)
ALLIED WASTE SYSTEMS INC
Dempsey Waste Systems
1577 W River Rd (45417-6740)
PHONE..............................937 268-8110
Mark E Crowe, *Sales/Mktg Mgr*
EMP: 35
SQ FT: 25,000
SALES (corp-wide): 10B **Publicly Held**
SIC: 4953 Refuse collection & disposal services
HQ: Allied Waste Systems, Inc.
18500 N Allied Way # 100
Phoenix AZ 85054
480 627-2700

(G-9218)
ALLOYD INSULATION CO INC
5734 Webster St (45414-3521)
P.O. Box 13299 (45413-0299)
PHONE..............................937 890-7900
Thomas Wolfe, *President*
Martha Wolfe, *Vice Pres*
EMP: 25
SQ FT: 30,000
SALES (est): 3.1MM **Privately Held**
WEB: www.alloydco.com
SIC: 1742 Insulation, buildings

(G-9219)
ALPHA & OMEGA BLDG SVCS
INC (PA)
2843 Culver Ave Ste B (45429-3720)
PHONE..............................937 298-2125
James Baker, *President*
Cindy Landerer, *Treasurer*
EMP: 38
SQ FT: 7,000
SALES (est): 11.3MM **Privately Held**
WEB: www.aobuildingservices.com
SIC: 7349 Janitorial service, contract basis

(G-9220)
ALPHA MEDIA LLC
Also Called: Wing-FM
717 E David Rd (45429-5218)
PHONE..............................937 294-5858
John King, *General Mgr*
EMP: 40 **Privately Held**
SIC: 4832 Radio broadcasting stations
PA: Alpha Media Llc
1211 Sw 5th Ave Ste 600
Portland OR 97204

(G-9221)
ALRO STEEL CORPORATION
Also Called: Arlo Aluminum & Steel
821 Springfield St (45403-1252)
PHONE..............................937 253-6121
Tim Elliott, *Manager*
EMP: 40
SQ FT: 120,000
SALES (corp-wide): 1.9B **Privately Held**
WEB: www.alro.com
SIC: 5051 3441 3317 3316 Steel; fabricated structural metal; steel pipe & tubes; cold finishing of steel shapes; blast furnaces & steel mills
PA: Alro Steel Corporation
3100 E High St
Jackson MI 49203
517 787-5500

(G-9222)
ALTERNATE SLTIONS PRIVATE
DUTY (PA)
1251 E Dorothy Ln (45419-2106)
PHONE..............................937 298-1111
David Ganzsarto, *CEO*
Eric Masters, *Partner*
Chad Creech, *Opers Staff*
Steve Helton, *Controller*
EMP: 70
SALES (est): 1.8MM **Privately Held**
WEB: www.ashomecare.com
SIC: 8082 Home health care services

(G-9223)
ALTERNATE SOLUTIONS FIRST
LLC
1251 E Dorothy Ln (45419-2106)
PHONE..............................937 298-1111
Al Lefeld, *CFO*
David Ganszarto,
EMP: 200
SQ FT: 2,000
SALES: 1MM **Privately Held**
SIC: 8082 7361 Home health care services; nurses' registry

(G-9224)
ALTERNATE SOLUTIONS
HEALTHCARE
1050 Forrer Blvd (45420-1472)
PHONE..............................937 299-1111
David Ganszaro, *CEO*
Eric Masters, *Vice Pres*
BSN L Erickson Rn MN, *Manager*
EMP: 65
SALES (est): 3.8MM **Privately Held**
SIC: 7363 Temporary help service

(G-9225)
ALTICK & CORWIN CO LPA
1 S Main St Ste 1590 (45402-2035)
PHONE..............................937 223-1201
Marshal Ruchmann, *Principal*
Marshall D Ruchman, *Shareholder*
Dennis J Adkins, *Shareholder*
Deborah J Adler, *Shareholder*
Philip B Herron, *Shareholder*
EMP: 25
SQ FT: 15,750
SALES: 2.9MM **Privately Held**
WEB: www.altickcorwin.com
SIC: 8111 General practice attorney, lawyer

(G-9226)
AMERICAN CITY BUS
JOURNALS INC
Also Called: Dayton Business Journal
40 N Main St Ste 800 (45423-1053)
PHONE..............................937 528-4400
Caleb Stephens, *Editor*
Neil Arthur, *Manager*
Rick Titus, *Creative Dir*

EMP: 26
SALES (corp-wide): 1.4B **Privately Held**
SIC: 2711 7313 Newspapers: publishing only, not printed on site; newspaper advertising representative
HQ: American City Business Journals, Inc.
120 W Morehead St Ste 400
Charlotte NC 28202
704 973-1000

(G-9227)
AMERICAN FEDERATION OF
STATE
15 Gates St (45402-2917)
PHONE..............................937 461-9983
Marcia Knox, *Director*
EMP: 37
SALES: 100.9K **Privately Held**
SIC: 8631 Employees' association

(G-9228)
AMERICAN NURSING CARE INC
5335 Far Hills Ave # 103 (45429-2317)
PHONE..............................937 438-3844
Kitty Makley, *Branch Mgr*
EMP: 37 **Privately Held**
WEB: www.americannursingcare.com
SIC: 8051 8082 Skilled nursing care facilities; home health care services
HQ: American Nursing Care, Inc.
1700 Edison Dr Ste 300
Milford OH 45150
513 576-0262

(G-9229)
AMERICAN POWER LLC
1819 Troy St (45404-2400)
PHONE..............................937 235-0418
Adil Baguirov,
Islom Shakhbandarov,
EMP: 25 **EST:** 2013
SALES (est): 813.9K **Privately Held**
SIC: 4213 Trailer or container on flat car (TOFC/COFC); heavy machinery transport; refrigerated products transport; less-than-truckload (LTL) transport

(G-9230)
AMERICAN RED CROSS
370 W 1st St (45402-3006)
P.O. Box 517 (45401-0517)
PHONE..............................937 222-0124
Tom Foder, *CEO*
EMP: 50
SQ FT: 2,500
SALES (est): 3.6MM
SALES (corp-wide): 2.5B **Privately Held**
SIC: 8322 Individual & family services
PA: The American National Red Cross
430 17th St Nw
Washington DC 20006
202 737-8300

(G-9231)
AMERIPRO LOGISTICS LLC
6754 Stovali Dr (45424-7216)
PHONE..............................410 375-3469
Sevil Shakhmamov, *Principal*
EMP: 25 **EST:** 2010
SALES (est): 1.4MM **Privately Held**
SIC: 4789 Car loading

(G-9232)
AMF FACILITY SERVICES INC
844 Oakleaf Dr (45417-3544)
PHONE..............................800 991-2273
A Mark Fowler, *President*
EMP: 44
SALES: 3MM **Privately Held**
SIC: 7349 Building maintenance, except repairs

(G-9233)
AMG INC (PA)
Also Called: AMG-Eng
1497 Shoup Mill Rd (45414-3903)
PHONE..............................937 260-4646
Alberto G Mendez, *President*
Julieta Davis, *Vice Pres*
Scott Feller, *Vice Pres*
John Haas, *Vice Pres*
Maria C Mendez, *Treasurer*
EMP: 45
SQ FT: 26,796
SALES (est): 19.9MM **Privately Held**
SIC: 8711 Consulting engineer

(PA)=Parent Co (HQ)=Headquarters (DH)=Div Headquarters   2019 Harris Ohio
✪ = New Business established in last 2 years   Services Directory

379

GEOGRAPHIC

(G-9234)
ANESTHESIOLOGY SERVICES NETWRK
1 Wyoming St (45409-2722)
P.O. Box 632317, Cincinnati (45263-2317)
PHONE..................................937 208-6173
Charles Cardone, *President*
Mark Chambers, *Anesthesiology*
Jay Srour, *Anesthesiology*
EMP: 50 EST: 1996
SALES: 4.6MM **Privately Held**
WEB: www.asndayton.com
SIC: 8011 Anesthesiologist

(G-9235)
APPLIED RESEARCH ASSOC INC
7735 Paragon Rd (45459-4051)
PHONE..................................937 873-8166
Wally Zukauskas, *Manager*
EMP: 36
SALES (corp-wide): 251.4MM **Privately Held**
WEB: www.ara.com
SIC: 8731 8732 Commercial Physical Research Commercial Nonphysical Research
PA: Applied Research Associates, Inc.
    4300 San Mateo Blvd Ne
    Albuquerque NM 87110
    505 883-3636

(G-9236)
ARAMARK UNF & CAREER AP LLC
1200 Webster St (45404-1500)
P.O. Box 139 (45404-0139)
PHONE..................................937 223-6667
Jarrod Burch, *General Mgr*
Michelle Stout, *Site Mgr*
Sonya Crum, *Telecom Exec*
Mike Heyl, *Maintence Staff*
EMP: 100 **Publicly Held**
WEB: www.aramark-uniform.com
SIC: 7218 7213 7216 Industrial uniform supply; uniform supply; drycleaning plants, except rugs
HQ: Aramark Uniform & Career Apparel, Llc
    115 N First St Ste 203
    Burbank CA 91502
    818 973-3700

(G-9237)
ARC DOCUMENT SOLUTIONS INC
222 N Saint Clair St (45402-1230)
PHONE..................................937 277-7930
EMP: 27
SALES (corp-wide): 406.1MM **Publicly Held**
SIC: 7334 Photocopying Services
PA: Arc Document Solutions, Inc.
    1981 N Broadway Ste 385
    Walnut Creek CA 94583
    925 949-5100

(G-9238)
ARDENT TECHNOLOGIES INC
6234 Far Hills Ave (45459-1927)
PHONE..................................937 312-1345
Srinivas Appalaneni, *President*
EMP: 125
SALES (est): 12.8MM **Privately Held**
WEB: www.ardentinc.com
SIC: 8748 Business consulting

(G-9239)
AREA AGENCY ON AGING PLANNI
Also Called: Area Agency On Aging P S A 2
40 W 2nd St Ste 400 (45402-1873)
PHONE..................................800 258-7277
Doug McGarry, *Exec Dir*
EMP: 126
SALES: 44.7MM **Privately Held**
WEB: www.info4seniors.org
SIC: 8322 8082 Senior citizens' center or association; home health care services

(G-9240)
ARK FOUNDATION OF DAYTON
Also Called: ARKY BOOK STORE
2002 S Smithville Rd (45420-2804)
P.O. Box 20069 (45420-0069)
PHONE..................................937 256-2759
Ronnie E Cooper, *President*
EMP: 25
SALES: 30.9K **Privately Held**
WEB: www.arky.org
SIC: 8412 8661 Museum; religious organizations

(G-9241)
ASSOCIATED SPECIALISTS
7707 Paragon Rd Ste 101 (45459-4070)
PHONE..................................937 208-7272
Roger H Griffin MD, *President*
EMP: 25
SALES (est): 2.4MM **Privately Held**
SIC: 8011 Internal medicine, physician/surgeon

(G-9242)
ASSURED HEALTH CARE INC
Also Called: Assured Hlth Care HM Care Svcs
1250 W Dorothy Ln Ste 200 (45409-1317)
P.O. Box 143, Tipp City (45371-0143)
PHONE..................................937 294-2803
Fax: 937 294-4946
EMP: 32
SALES (est): 1MM **Privately Held**
SIC: 8082 7361 Home Health Care Services Employment Agency

(G-9243)
AUMAN MAHAN & FURRY A LEGAL
110 N Main St Ste 1000 (45402-3703)
PHONE..................................937 223-6003
Robert Dunlevey, *President*
Gary Auaman, *Vice Pres*
Gary Auman, *Vice Pres*
Stephen Watring, *Vice Pres*
Steve Watring, *Vice Pres*
EMP: 28
SALES (est): 3.7MM **Privately Held**
WEB: www.dmfdayton.com
SIC: 8111 General practice attorney, lawyer

(G-9244)
B AND D INVESTMENT PARTNERSHIP
Also Called: Danbarry Dollar Svr Cinema
7650 Waynetowne Blvd (45424-2000)
PHONE..................................937 233-6698
Tom Sanders, *General Mgr*
EMP: 25
SALES (corp-wide): 1.4MM **Privately Held**
WEB: www.danberrycinemas.com
SIC: 7832 Exhibitors, itinerant: motion picture
PA: B And D Investment Partnership
    8050 Hosbrook Rd Ste 203
    Cincinnati OH 45236
    513 784-1521

(G-9245)
BATHROOM ALTERNATIVES INC
Also Called: Bath Fitter
85 Westpark Rd (45459-4812)
PHONE..................................937 434-1984
Jason Haught, *President*
EMP: 30
SALES (est): 6.9MM **Privately Held**
SIC: 5211 1799 Bathroom fixtures, equipment & supplies; kitchen & bathroom remodeling

(G-9246)
BEAVERCREEK YMCA
111 W 1st St Ste 207 (45402-1154)
PHONE..................................937 426-9622
Karen Early, *Manager*
EMP: 90
SALES (est): 3MM **Privately Held**
SIC: 8351 8322 Child day care services; individual & family services

(G-9247)
BECKER CONSTRUCTION INC
525 Gargrave Rd (45449-5401)
PHONE..................................937 859-8308
Timothy J Becker, *President*
EMP: 30
SALES (est): 6.1MM **Privately Held**
SIC: 1542 Commercial & office building, new construction; commercial & office buildings, renovation & repair; institutional building construction

(G-9248)
BELCAN SVCS GROUP LTD PARTNR
Also Called: Belcan Staffing Services
832 S Ludlow St Ste 1 (45402-2651)
PHONE..................................937 586-5053
Erica King, *Branch Mgr*
EMP: 150
SALES (corp-wide): 813.3MM **Privately Held**
SIC: 7363 Temporary help service
HQ: Belcan Services Group Limited Partnership
    10200 Anderson Way
    Blue Ash OH 45242
    513 891-0972

(G-9249)
BELLAZIO SALON & DAY SPA
101 E Alex Bell Rd # 127 (45459-2779)
PHONE..................................937 432-6722
Eleanor Timmerman, *Owner*
EMP: 44 EST: 2000
SALES (est): 633.9K **Privately Held**
WEB: www.bellaziosalondayspa.com
SIC: 7991 Spas

(G-9250)
BIESER GREER & LANDIS LLP
6 N Main St Ste 400 (45402-1914)
PHONE..................................937 223-3277
Charles Shook, *Partner*
Irvin Bieser, *Partner*
David Greer, *Partner*
James Greer, *Partner*
John Haviland, *Partner*
EMP: 46
SALES (est): 5.8MM **Privately Held**
WEB: www.biesergreer.com
SIC: 8111 General practice attorney, lawyer

(G-9251)
BIG HILL REALTY CORP (PA)
Also Called: Federer Homes and Gardens RE
5580 Far Hills Ave (45429-2285)
PHONE..................................937 435-1177
William Ryan, *CEO*
Jeffrey Owens, *President*
George Long, *Vice Pres*
Jeff Owens, *Vice Pres*
EMP: 170
SQ FT: 3,500
SALES (est): 9.3MM **Privately Held**
WEB: www.bighillgmac.com
SIC: 6531 Real estate agent, residential

(G-9252)
BIGGER ROAD VETERINARY CLINIC (PA)
5655 Bigger Rd (45440-2714)
PHONE..................................937 435-3262
E Eugene Snyder Dvm, *President*
Christine Snyder, *Corp Secy*
Kelly Searles, *Practice Mgr*
Jesse Dorland, *Administration*
Nichole Olp, *Associate*
EMP: 35
SQ FT: 2,200
SALES (est): 2.1MM **Privately Held**
SIC: 0742 Animal hospital services, pets & other animal specialties; veterinarian, animal specialties

(G-9253)
BILLBACK SYSTEMS LLC
8000 Millers Farm Ln (45458-7310)
PHONE..................................937 433-1844
Andrew Moon,
David Alspach,
Larry Paule,
EMP: 25
SQ FT: 400
SALES (est): 2MM
SALES (corp-wide): 1MM **Privately Held**
WEB: www.billback.com
SIC: 7371 Computer software development
HQ: Espreon Pty Limited
    286 Sussex St
    Sydney NSW 2000

(G-9254)
BILTMORE APARTMENTS LTD
Also Called: Biltimore Towers
210 N Main St (45402-1234)
PHONE..................................937 461-9695
Jennifer Hardee, *Principal*
Leeann Morein, *Vice Pres*
Cheryl L Johnson, *Manager*
EMP: 99
SALES (est): 3.4MM **Publicly Held**
SIC: 6513 Apartment building operators
HQ: Aimco Properties, L.P.
    4582 S Ulster St Ste 1100
    Denver CO 80237

(G-9255)
BLADECUTTERS LAWN SERVICE INC
Also Called: Bladecutters Lawn and Ldscpg
5440 N Dixie Dr (45414-3947)
P.O. Box 403 (45405-0403)
PHONE..................................937 274-3861
John Scott, *President*
EMP: 25
SQ FT: 608
SALES: 626K **Privately Held**
WEB: www.bladecutters.com
SIC: 0782 5099 0781 4959 Lawn care services; firewood; landscape counseling & planning; snowplowing; top soil; wrecking & demolition work

(G-9256)
BOB SUMEREL TIRE CO INC
7711 Center Point 70 Blvd (45424-6368)
PHONE..................................937 235-0062
Dennis Lavoie, *Manager*
EMP: 25
SALES (corp-wide): 89.7MM **Privately Held**
WEB: www.bobsumereltire.com
SIC: 5531 7534 Automotive tires; tire retreading & repair shops
PA: Bob Sumerel Tire Co., Inc.
    1257 Cox Ave
    Erlanger KY 41018
    859 283-2700

(G-9257)
BOMBECK FAMILY LEARNING CENTER
941 Alberta St (45409-2806)
PHONE..................................937 229-2158
Ashley Smith, *Director*
Diana Smith, *Director*
Melissa Flanagan, *Asst Director*
EMP: 27
SALES (est): 351.8K **Privately Held**
SIC: 8351 Preschool center

(G-9258)
BONBRIGHT DISTRIBUTORS INC
1 Arena Park Dr (45417-4678)
PHONE..................................937 222-1001
H Brock Anderson, *President*
Richard B Pohl Jr, *Corp Secy*
John Dimario, *Vice Pres*
Jim Brown, *CFO*
Mark Brown, *Sales Mgr*
▲ EMP: 125
SQ FT: 70,000
SALES (est): 61.3MM **Privately Held**
WEB: www.bonbright.com
SIC: 5181 Beer & other fermented malt liquors

(G-9259)
BOOST TECHNOLOGIES LLC
Also Called: Shumsky Promotional
811 E 4th St (45402-2227)
PHONE..................................800 223-2203
Dawn Conway, *CEO*
Anita Emoff, *Chairman*
Jill Albers, *Exec Dir*
EMP: 74

SALES (est): 17.5MM **Privately Held**
SIC: 5199 Advertising specialties

(G-9260)
BOX 21 RESCUE SQUAD INC
100 E Helena St 120 (45404)
PHONE..................................937 223-2821
Karen Beavers, *President*
Ralph Wilhelm, *COO*
Bill Wentling, *Treasurer*
EMP: 50
SALES (est): 264K **Privately Held**
WEB: www.box21rescue.org
SIC: 8322 Family service agency

(G-9261)
BRIGHTVIEW LANDSCAPES LLC
38 Brandt St (45404)
PHONE..................................937 235-9595
Rich Martell, *Manager*
EMP: 36
SALES (corp-wide): 2.8B **Publicly Held**
SIC: 0782 Landscape contractors
HQ: Brightview Landscapes, Llc
401 Plymouth Rd Ste 500
Plymouth Meeting PA 19462
484 567-7204

(G-9262)
BRIXX ICE COMPANY
500 E 1st St (45402-1221)
PHONE..................................937 222-2257
Chris Bahi, *Owner*
EMP: 50
SALES (est): 794.1K **Privately Held**
WEB: www.brixxicecompany.com
SIC: 7941 Sports field or stadium operator,
promoting sports events

(G-9263)
BUCKEYE AMBULANCE LLC
1516 Nicholas Rd (45417-6713)
PHONE..................................937 435-1584
Dereck Pristas,
Donald Butts,
EMP: 70 EST: 2011
SQ FT: 12,000
SALES (est): 2.4MM **Privately Held**
SIC: 4119 Ambulance service

(G-9264)
BUCKEYE CHARTER SERVICE INC
Also Called: Buckeye Charters
8240 Expansion Way (45424-6382)
PHONE..................................937 879-3000
Jerry Biedenharn, *Principal*
Dale Stern, *Opers Mgr*
Lisa Pierce, *Office Mgr*
EMP: 30 **Privately Held**
WEB: www.buckeyecharterservice.com
SIC: 4142 Bus charter service, except local
PA: Buckeye Charter Service, Inc
1235 E Hanthorn Rd
Lima OH 45804

(G-9265)
BUCKEYE HOME HEALTH CARE (PA)
7700 Paragon Rd Ste A (45459-4081)
PHONE..................................937 291-3780
Tina Hardwick, *Principal*
Stacey Bennett, *Sales Associate*
Crystal Burst, *Manager*
Yolanda Bell, *Assistant*
EMP: 27
SALES (est): 10.4MM **Privately Held**
SIC: 8082 Home health care services

(G-9266)
BUCKEYE POOL INC
486 Windsor Park Dr (45459-4111)
P.O. Box 750548 (45475-0548)
PHONE..................................937 434-7916
Gary Aiken, *President*
Terry Blair, *General Mgr*
Chris Durbin, *Sales Mgr*
EMP: 25 EST: 1959
SQ FT: 3,200
SALES (est): 2.3MM **Privately Held**
SIC: 7389 1799 Swimming pool & hot tub
service & maintenance; swimming pool
construction

(G-9267)
BUCKEYE TRILS GIRL SCOUT CNCIL (PA)
450 Shoup Mill Rd (45415-3518)
PHONE..................................937 275-7601
Barbara Bonisas, *CEO*
EMP: 41
SQ FT: 40,000
SALES (est): 1.6MM **Privately Held**
WEB: www.btgirlscouts.org
SIC: 8641 Girl Scout organization

(G-9268)
BUDDE SHEET METAL WORKS INC (PA)
305 Leo St (45404-1083)
PHONE..................................937 224-0868
Thomas Budde, *President*
William R Budde Jr, *Corp Secy*
Stephen L Budde, *Vice Pres*
Angie Budde- Obrien, *Manager*
EMP: 39
SQ FT: 20,000
SALES (est): 7.4MM **Privately Held**
WEB: www.buddesheetmetal.com
SIC: 1761 3444 1711 Sheet metalwork;
sheet metalwork; plumbing, heating, air-
conditioning contractors

(G-9269)
BURD BROTHERS INC
1789 Stanley Ave (45404-1116)
PHONE..................................513 708-7787
Tyler Burdick, *Branch Mgr*
EMP: 33 **Privately Held**
SIC: 4731 Truck transportation brokers
PA: Burd Brothers, Inc.
4005 Borman Dr
Batavia OH 45103

(G-9270)
BURKHARDT SPRINGFIELD NEIGHBOR
735 Huffman Ave (45403-2651)
PHONE..................................937 252-7076
Lodia Furnas, *President*
Terry Middleton, *Vice Pres*
EMP: 40
SALES (est): 523.8K **Privately Held**
SIC: 8641 Civic social & fraternal associa-
tions

(G-9271)
BUSINESS FURNITURE LLC
8 N Main St (45402-1904)
PHONE..................................937 293-1010
Debra M Oakes, *Branch Mgr*
EMP: 50
SALES (corp-wide): 66.3MM **Privately Held**
SIC: 5021 7641 5023 Office furniture; fur-
niture repair & maintenance; carpets
PA: Business Furniture, Llc
8421 Bearing Dr Ste 200
Indianapolis IN 46268
317 216-4844

(G-9272)
CALIBER HOME LOANS INC
8534 Yankee St (45458-1888)
PHONE..................................937 435-5363
EMP: 39
SALES (corp-wide): 2.4B **Privately Held**
SIC: 6163 6141 Loan brokers; personal
credit institutions
PA: Caliber Home Loans, Inc.
1525 S Belt Line Rd
Coppell TX 75019
800 401-6587

(G-9273)
CALVIN LANIER
4003 Foxboro Dr (45416-1624)
PHONE..................................937 952-4221
Calvin Lanier, *Principal*
EMP: 25
SALES (est): 1MM **Privately Held**
SIC: 3423 7389 Plumbers' hand tools;

(G-9274)
CAPGEMINI AMERICA INC
Also Called: Sogeti
10100 Innvtion Dr Ste 200 (45459)
PHONE..................................678 427-6642
Adam Guediri, *Executive*

EMP: 300
SALES (corp-wide): 355MM **Privately Held**
SIC: 7379 Computer related consulting
services
HQ: Capgemini America, Inc.
79 5th Ave Fl 3
New York NY 10003
212 314-8000

(G-9275)
CAPITAL HEALTH SERVICES INC (PA)
5040 Philadelphia Dr (45415-3604)
PHONE..................................937 278-0404
Ken Bernsen, *CEO*
Joshua Huff, *Vice Pres*
Kara Bernsen, *Treasurer*
Pamela Cooke, *Director*
Sarah Manning, *Admin Sec*
EMP: 34
SALES (est): 6.3MM **Privately Held**
SIC: 8051 8059 Skilled nursing care facili-
ties; personal care home, with health care

(G-9276)
CAPRI BOWLING LANES INC
2727 S Dixie Dr (45409-1506)
PHONE..................................937 832-4000
Ernie Talos, *President*
Thomas Mantia, *Corp Secy*
Tim Janson, *IT/INT Sup*
EMP: 30 EST: 1959
SQ FT: 30,000
SALES (est): 871.5K **Privately Held**
SIC: 7933 5813 5812 Ten pin center;
cocktail lounge; eating places

(G-9277)
CARE ONE LLC
Also Called: Spring Creek Nursing Center
5440 Charlesgate Rd (45424-1049)
PHONE..................................937 236-6707
Karma Winburn, *Principal*
EMP: 160
SALES (corp-wide): 387.8MM **Privately Held**
SIC: 8051 Convalescent home with contin-
uous nursing care
PA: Care One, Llc
173 Bridge Plz N
Fort Lee NJ 07024
201 242-4000

(G-9278)
CARESOURCE MANAGEMENT GROUP CO (PA)
230 N Main St (45402-1263)
P.O. Box 8738 (45401-8738)
PHONE..................................937 224-3300
Pamela B Morris, *CEO*
Stephanie Humphrey, *Partner*
Bobby Jones, *COO*
Jason Bearden, *Vice Pres*
Mark Heitkamp, *Vice Pres*
EMP: 800
SALES: 1.4B **Privately Held**
WEB: www.caresource.com
SIC: 6321 Health insurance carriers

(G-9279)
CARESOURCE MANAGEMENT GROUP CO
230 N Main St (45402-1263)
PHONE..................................937 224-3300
Michael E Ervin, *Ch of Bd*
EMP: 40 **Privately Held**
SIC: 6321 Health insurance carriers
PA: Caresource Management Group Co.
230 N Main St
Dayton OH 45402

(G-9280)
CARLS BODY SHOP INC
Also Called: Carl's Body Shop & Towing
1120 Wayne Ave (45410-1406)
PHONE..................................937 253-5166
Matt Miller, *President*
Jill Oberschlake, *Manager*
Lee Miller, *Admin Sec*
EMP: 32
SQ FT: 10,000
SALES (est): 4.4MM **Privately Held**
WEB: www.carlsbodyshop.com
SIC: 7532 Body shop, automotive

(G-9281)
CARRIAGE INN OF TROTWOOD INC
Also Called: Shiloh Springs Care Center
5020 Philadelphia Dr (45415-3653)
PHONE..................................937 277-0505
Ken Bernsen, *President*
EMP: 100
SALES: 6MM **Privately Held**
SIC: 8051 Convalescent home with contin-
uous nursing care

(G-9282)
CARRIAGE INN RETIREMENT CMNTY
5040 Philadelphia Dr (45415-3604)
PHONE..................................937 278-0404
Joshua Huff, *Vice Pres*
Wayne Davis, *Administration*
EMP: 130
SALES (est): 5.8MM **Privately Held**
WEB: www.capitalhs.com
SIC: 8051 Convalescent home with contin-
uous nursing care

(G-9283)
CARRY TRANSPORT INC
5536 Brentlinger Dr (45414-3510)
PHONE..................................937 236-0026
Don Linder, *Branch Mgr*
EMP: 25 **Privately Held**
SIC: 4213 Contract haulers
PA: Carry Transport Inc
2630 Kindustry Park Rd
Keokuk IA 52632

(G-9284)
CASHLAND FINANCIAL SVCS INC (DH)
100 E 3rd St Ste 200 (45402-2128)
PHONE..................................937 253-7842
Steve McAllister, *President*
EMP: 40
SALES (est): 65.7MM
SALES (corp-wide): 1.7B **Publicly Held**
SIC: 6099 Check cashing agencies
HQ: Frontier Merger Sub Llc
1600 W 7th St
Fort Worth TX 76102
800 223-8738

(G-9285)
CASSANOS INC (PA)
Also Called: Cassano's Pizza & Subs
1700 E Stroop Rd (45429-5095)
PHONE..................................937 294-8400
Vic Cassano Jr, *Ch of Bd*
Chris Cassano, *Vice Pres*
Pat Dillon, *Maint Spvr*
Kent Warner, *Purchasing*
Janet Hurley, *Personnel*
EMP: 45 EST: 1949
SQ FT: 37,500
SALES (est): 14.3MM **Privately Held**
SIC: 5812 5149 6794 Pizzeria, chain;
sandwiches & submarines shop; baking
supplies; pizza supplies; franchises, sell-
ing or licensing

(G-9286)
CATALYST PAPER (USA) INC
7777 Wash Vlg Dr Ste 210 (45459-3995)
PHONE..................................937 528-3800
Linda McClinchy, *Vice Pres*
EMP: 50 **Privately Held**
SIC: 5111 Fine paper
HQ: Catalyst Paper (Usa) Inc.
2200 6th Ave Ste 800
Seattle WA 98121
206 838-2070

(G-9287)
CATHOLIC SOCIAL SVC MIAMI VLY (PA)
Also Called: Miami Valley Family Care Ctr
922 W Riverview Ave (45402-6424)
PHONE..................................937 223-7217
Andrea Skrlac, *Corp Comm Staff*
Ronald Eckerle Ex Dir, *Director*
Ron Dir, *Director*
Christie Linard, *Executive*
Kacie Pape,
EMP: 30

SALES: 19.6MM **Privately Held**
SIC: 8322 8351 Family service agency;
child guidance agency; adoption services;
child day care services

(G-9288)
CBC ENGINEERS & ASSOCIATES LTD (PA)
125 Westpark Rd (45459-4814) .
PHONE...................................937 428-6150
Alvin C Banner, *President*
EMP: 30
SALES (est): 4.3MM **Privately Held**
SIC: 8711 Consulting engineer

(G-9289)
CENTERVILLE CHILD DEVELOPMENT
8095 Garnet Dr (45458-2140)
PHONE...................................937 434-5949
Joseph Valentour, *Partner*
Catherine Valentour, *Partner*
EMP: 30
SQ FT: 4,700
SALES: 1MM **Privately Held**
SIC: 8351 Group day care center

(G-9290)
CENTRIC CONSULTING LLC (PA)
Also Called: Practical Solution
1215 Lyons Rd F (45458-1858)
PHONE...................................888 781-7567
Mike Brannan, *President*
Tj Felice, *Vice Pres*
Jennifer Sturm, *Opers Mgr*
Eileen Lynch, *Accounting Mgr*
Leann Ulrich, *Benefits Mgr*
EMP: 86
SQ FT: 1,000
SALES (est): 37.5MM **Privately Held**
WEB: www.centricconsulting.com
SIC: 8748 Systems engineering consult-
ant, ex. computer or professional

(G-9291)
CHAPEL ELECTRIC CO LLC
1985 Founders Dr (45420-4012)
PHONE...................................937 222-2290
Gregory P Ross, *President*
Dennis F Quebe, *Chairman*
Roger Van Der Horst, *Vice Pres*
Richard E Penewit, *Vice Pres*
EMP: 109
SQ FT: 40,000
SALES (est): 42.3MM
SALES (corp-wide): 66.4MM **Privately Held**
WEB: www.chapel.com
SIC: 1731 General electrical contractor
PA: Quebe Holdings, Inc.
1985 Founders Dr
Dayton OH 45420
937 222-2290

(G-9292)
CHAPEL-ROMANOFF TECH LLC
1985 Founders Dr (45420-4012)
PHONE...................................937 222-9840
Sam Warwar,
Gregory P Ross,
Dennis Severance,
Roger Vanderhorst,
EMP: 25
SQ FT: 40,000
SALES (est): 4.7MM
SALES (corp-wide): 66.4MM **Privately Held**
WEB: www.quebe.com
SIC: 1731 Telephone & telephone equip-
ment installation
PA: Quebe Holdings, Inc.
1985 Founders Dr
Dayton OH 45420
937 222-2290

(G-9293)
CHARLES F JERGENS CNSTR INC
1280 Brandt Pike (45404-2468)
PHONE...................................937 233-1830
Phillip Jergens, *President*
Charles F Jergens, *Vice Pres*
EMP: 30
SQ FT: 1,500

SALES: 6.8MM **Privately Held**
SIC: 1794 1795 Excavation work; wrecking & demolition work

(G-9294)
CHARLES JERGENS CONTRACTOR
1280 Brandt Pike (45404-2468)
PHONE...................................937 233-1830
Charles F Jergens, *President*
Patricia Jergens, *Vice Pres*
EMP: 40 EST: 1939
SQ FT: 1,500
SALES (est): 4.8MM **Privately Held**
SIC: 7353 1794 Heavy construction equip-
ment rental; excavation work

(G-9295)
CHEMICAL SERVICES INC
2600 Thunderhawk Ct (45414-3459)
PHONE...................................937 898-5566
Martin J Wehr, *President*
Matt Schneider, *Purch Mgr*
Sue Wiford, *Controller*
Barb Luebbers, *Sales Staff*
George Lueking, *Sales Executive*
EMP: 26
SQ FT: 40,000
SALES (est): 23.6MM
SALES (corp-wide): 131MM **Privately Held**
WEB: www.chemicalservices.com
SIC: 5169 Industrial chemicals
PA: Chemgroup, Inc
2600 Thunderhawk Ct
Dayton OH 45414
937 898-5566

(G-9296)
CHILDRENS HOME CARE DAYTON
18 Childrens Plz (45404-1867)
PHONE...................................937 641-4663
Susan Chandler, *Pharmacist*
Kendra Peters, *Pharmacist*
Susan Powell, *CTO*
Peggy Dolye, *Exec Dir*
Vickie Peoples, *Exec Dir*
EMP: 65
SALES: 8.2MM **Privately Held**
SIC: 7361 8082 Nurses' registry; home
health care services

(G-9297)
CHIMNEYS INN
767 Mmsburg Cnterville Rd (45459)
PHONE...................................937 567-7850
Philip Hayden, *President*
Matt Hayden, *General Mgr*
EMP: 25
SALES: 250K **Privately Held**
WEB: www.chimneysinn.com
SIC: 7011 Inns

(G-9298)
CHOICES IN COMMUNITY LIVING (PA)
1651 Needmore Rd Ste B (45414-3801)
PHONE...................................937 898-3655
W Thomas Weaver, *President*
EMP: 200
SQ FT: 2,000
SALES: 12.4MM **Privately Held**
WEB: www.choicesincl.com
SIC: 8361 8052 Home for the mentally re-
tarded; home for the mentally handi-
capped; intermediate care facilities

(G-9299)
CHRISTIAN TWIGS GYMNASTICS CLB
Also Called: Twigs Kids
1900 S Alex Rd (45449-5371)
P.O. Box 348, Miamisburg (45343-0348)
PHONE...................................937 866-8350
Bob Putman, *President*
EMP: 28
SQ FT: 9,400
SALES: 250K **Privately Held**
WEB: www.twigskids.com
SIC: 7999 Gymnastic instruction, non-
membership

(G-9300)
CHS OF BOWERSTON OPER CO INC
Also Called: Sunny Slope Nursing Home
5020 Philadelphia Dr (45415-3653)
PHONE...................................937 277-0505
Kenneth Bernsen, *President*
Kara Bernsen, *Shareholder*
Josh Huff, *Shareholder*
Sarah Manning, *Shareholder*
EMP: 60
SALES (est): 513.5K **Privately Held**
SIC: 8051 Skilled nursing care facilities

(G-9301)
CITY CASTERS
Also Called: Clear Channel
101 Pine St Ste 300 (45402-2948)
PHONE...................................937 224-1137
EMP: 50 EST: 2009
SALES (est): 2.6MM **Privately Held**
SIC: 4832 Radio Broadcast Station

(G-9302)
CITY OF CENTERVILLE
Also Called: Golf Course At Yankee Trace
10000 Yankee St (45458-3520)
PHONE...................................937 438-3585
Steve Shull, *Director*
EMP: 75 **Privately Held**
WEB: www.ci.centerville.oh.us
SIC: 5812 7299 Eating places; banquet
hall facilities
PA: City Of Centerville
100 W Spring Valley Pike
Dayton OH 45458
937 433-7151

(G-9303)
CITY OF DAYTON
Also Called: City Dayton Waste Collection
1010 Ottawa St Bldg 7 (45402-1317)
PHONE...................................937 333-4860
Tom Ritchie, *Manager*
EMP: 175 **Privately Held**
WEB: www.daytonconventioncenter.com
SIC: 4953 4212 Refuse systems; local
trucking, without storage
PA: City Of Dayton
101 W 3rd St
Dayton OH 45402
937 333-3333

(G-9304)
CITY OF DAYTON
Also Called: Water Department
320 W Monument Ave (45402-3017)
PHONE...................................937 333-3725
Greg Heft, *Project Mgr*
Ben Swain, *Engineer*
William Zilli, *Branch Mgr*
John Davis, *Supervisor*
Pete Hannah, *Administration*
EMP: 40
SQ FT: 14,000 **Privately Held**
WEB: www.daytonconventioncenter.com
SIC: 1623 4941 Water, sewer & utility
lines; water supply
PA: City Of Dayton
101 W 3rd St
Dayton OH 45402
937 333-3333

(G-9305)
CITY OF DAYTON
Also Called: Dayton Wastewater Trtmnt Plant
2800 Guthrie Rd Ste A (45417-6700)
PHONE...................................937 333-1837
Chris Clark, *Branch Mgr*
Phil Bennington, *Manager*
EMP: 72 **Privately Held**
WEB: www.daytonconventioncenter.com
SIC: 4952 Sewerage systems
PA: City Of Dayton
101 W 3rd St
Dayton OH 45402
937 333-3333

(G-9306)
CITY OF DAYTON
Also Called: Dayton City Water Department
3210 Chuck Wagner Ln (45414-4401)
PHONE...................................937 333-6070
George Crosby, *Manager*
EMP: 125 **Privately Held**
WEB: www.daytonconventioncenter.com

SIC: 4941 Water supply
PA: City Of Dayton
101 W 3rd St
Dayton OH 45402
937 333-3333

(G-9307)
CITY OF DAYTON
Also Called: City Dayton Water Distribution
945 Ottawa St (45402-1365)
PHONE...................................937 333-7138
Wayne Simpson, *Manager*
EMP: 95 **Privately Held**
WEB: www.daytonconventioncenter.com
SIC: 4971 Water distribution or supply sys-
tems for irrigation
PA: City Of Dayton
101 W 3rd St
Dayton OH 45402
937 333-3333

(G-9308)
CLEAN HRBORS ES INDUS SVCS INC
6151 Executive Blvd (45424-1440)
PHONE...................................937 425-0512
Tim Delph, *Sales Staff*
Mike Webb, *Branch Mgr*
EMP: 120
SALES (corp-wide): 3.3B **Publicly Held**
WEB: www.onyxindustrial.com
SIC: 4953 Hazardous waste collection &
disposal
HQ: Clean Harbors Es Industrial Services,
Inc.
4760 World Houston Pkwy # 100
Houston TX 77032
713 672-8004

(G-9309)
CLEAN WATER ENVIRONMENTAL LLC (PA)
300 Cherokee Dr (45417-8113)
P.O. Box 317, New Lebanon (45345-0317)
PHONE...................................937 268-6501
John Staton, *CEO*
Joyce Rivers, *Controller*
EMP: 50 EST: 2017
SALES (est): 3.9MM **Privately Held**
SIC: 4953 Recycling, waste materials

(G-9310)
CNI THL OPS LLC
Also Called: Courtyard Dayton
7087 Miller Ln (45414-2653)
PHONE...................................937 890-6112
Keon Marvasti, *Manager*
EMP: 30
SALES (corp-wide): 11.1MM **Privately Held**
WEB: www.daytonraiders.com
SIC: 7011 Hotels
PA: Cni Thl Ops, Llc
515 S Flower St Fl 44
Los Angeles CA

(G-9311)
COCA-COLA BOTTLING CO CNSLD
1000 Coca Cola Blvd (45424-6375)
PHONE...................................937 878-5000
Bob Tiootson, *Manager*
EMP: 95
SALES (corp-wide): 4.6B **Publicly Held**
WEB: www.colasic.net
SIC: 5149 2086 Soft drinks; carbonated
beverages, nonalcoholic: bottled &
canned
PA: Coca-Cola Consolidated, Inc.
4100 Coca Cola Plz # 100
Charlotte NC 28211
704 557-4400

(G-9312)
COLDWELL BNKR HRITG RLTORS LLC
8534 Yankee St Ste 1b (45458-1889)
PHONE...................................937 304-8500
Stephen Ericson, *Buyer*
Tom Bechtel, *Sales/Mktg Mgr*
EMP: 40
SALES (corp-wide): 6.5MM **Privately Held**
WEB: www.coldwellbankerdayton.com
SIC: 6531 Real estate agent, residential

PA: Coldwell Banker Heritage Realtors Llc
2000 Hewitt Ave
Dayton OH 45440
937 434-7600

(G-9313)
COLDWELL BNKR HRITG RLTORS LLC (PA)
2000 Hewitt Ave (45440-2917)
PHONE..................................937 434-7600
Kenneth Parrott,
Steve Erman,
EMP: 40 EST: 1967
SQ FT: 10,000
SALES (est): 6.5MM Privately Held
WEB: www.coldwellbankerdayton.com
SIC: 6531 6512 Real estate agent, residential; commercial & industrial building operation

(G-9314)
COMPTECH COMPUTER TECH INC
7777 Washington Village D (45459-3975)
PHONE..................................937 228-2667
Allan Stephen, CEO
EMP: 25
SQ FT: 1,200
SALES: 5.3MM Privately Held
SIC: 7379 Computer related consulting services

(G-9315)
COMPUNET CLINICAL LABS LLC
2508 Sandride Dr (45439)
PHONE..................................937 208-3555
Ed Doucette, Branch Mgr
EMP: 400
SALES (corp-wide): 17.2K Privately Held
SIC: 8071 Medical laboratories
HQ: Compunet Clinical Laboratories, Llc
2308 Sandridge Dr
Moraine OH 45439
937 296-0844

(G-9316)
CONCORD DAYTON HOTEL II LLC
Also Called: Dayton Marriott
1414 S Patterson Blvd (45409-2105)
PHONE..................................937 223-1000
Dena St Clair, Principal
Vicky Hensley, Controller
EMP: 99 EST: 2014
SALES (est): 4MM Privately Held
SIC: 5812 7011 American restaurant; hotels & motels

(G-9317)
CONNOR CONCEPTS INC
Also Called: Chop House Restaurant
7727 Washington Vlg Dr (45459-3954)
PHONE..................................937 291-1661
Jeff Roberts, Manager
EMP: 65 Privately Held
SIC: 5812 7299 American restaurant; banquet hall facilities
PA: Connor Concepts, Inc.
10911 Turkey Dr
Knoxville TN 37934

(G-9318)
COOLIDGE LAW
33 W 1st St Ste 600 (45402-1235)
PHONE..................................937 223-8177
Richard Schwartz, Partner
EMP: 68
SALES (est): 2.1MM Privately Held
SIC: 8111 General practice law office

(G-9319)
COOLIDGE WALL CO LPA (PA)
33 W 1st St Ste 600 (45402-1289)
PHONE..................................937 223-8177
J Stephen Herbert, President
EMP: 105
SQ FT: 30,000
SALES (est): 13.9MM Privately Held
SIC: 8111 General practice law office

(G-9320)
COPP SYSTEMS INC
Also Called: Copp Systems Integrator
123 S Keowee St (45402-2240)
PHONE..................................937 228-4188
Bill Defries, Principal
Daniel J Hilbert, Vice Pres
David Markham, Vice Pres
Rocale Bumpus, Opers Staff
Tim Glander, Opers Staff
EMP: 32
SQ FT: 12,000
SALES (est): 20.3MM Privately Held
SIC: 5065 1731 Intercommunication equipment, electronic; paging & signaling equipment; closed circuit television; sound equipment, electronic; electrical work

(G-9321)
CORBUS LLC (HQ)
1129 Miamisbrg Cntrvle Rd Ste (45449)
PHONE..................................937 226-7724
Vishal Soin, CEO
Rajesh K Soin, Ch of Bd
Paul Daloia, President
Jay Eisenmenger, Vice Pres
Patrick Sepate, Vice Pres
EMP: 80
SQ FT: 12,500
SALES (est): 87.2MM
SALES (corp-wide): 126.3MM Privately Held
WEB: www.corbus.com
SIC: 8748 8742 Business consulting; marketing consulting services
PA: Soin International, Llc
1129 Miamsbg Ctrvl Rd 1 Ste
Dayton OH 45449
937 427-7646

(G-9322)
CORNERSTONE CONTROLS INC
Dayton Precision Services
1440 Nicholas Rd (45417-6711)
PHONE..................................937 263-6429
Larry Seale, Director
EMP: 27
SALES (corp-wide): 34.6MM Privately Held
SIC: 5065 5085 Electronic parts & equipment; industrial supplies
PA: Cornerstone Controls, Inc.
7131 E Kemper Rd
Cincinnati OH 45249
513 489-2500

(G-9323)
COTTAGES OF CLAYTON
8212 N Main St (45415-1641)
PHONE..................................937 280-0300
Sarah Zerale, Administration
EMP: 45
SALES (est): 2.1MM Privately Held
SIC: 8082 Home health care services

(G-9324)
COUNTERTOP ALTERNATIVES INC
Also Called: Granite Transformations
2325 Woodman Dr (45420-1479)
PHONE..................................937 254-3334
Jayson Grothjan, President
EMP: 30
SALES (est): 2.8MM Privately Held
WEB: www.countertopalternatives.com
SIC: 1799 1751 Counter top installation; cabinet & finish carpentry

(G-9325)
COUNTY OF MONTGOMERY
Also Called: Sheriff's Office
345 W 2nd St (45422-6401)
PHONE..................................937 225-4192
Phil Plummer, Sheriff
EMP: 75 Privately Held
SIC: 9221 8399 Sheriffs' offices; community action agency
PA: County Of Montgomery
451 W 3rd St Fl 4
Dayton OH 45422
937 225-4000

(G-9326)
COUNTY OF MONTGOMERY
Also Called: Montgomery Cnty Children Svcs
3304 N Main St (45405-2709)
PHONE..................................937 224-5437
Mary Ann Nelson, Principal
EMP: 450 Privately Held
WEB: www.mcmrdd.org
SIC: 8322 Individual & family services
PA: County Of Montgomery
451 W 3rd St Fl 4
Dayton OH 45422
937 225-4000

(G-9327)
COUNTY OF MONTGOMERY
Also Called: Engineering Department
5625 Little Richmond Rd (45426-3219)
PHONE..................................937 854-4576
Jerry Crane, Foreman/Supr
Mark Hartung, Manager
EMP: 70
SQ FT: 5,000 Privately Held
WEB: www.mcmrdd.org
SIC: 8711 Engineering services
PA: County Of Montgomery
451 W 3rd St Fl 4
Dayton OH 45422
937 225-4000

(G-9328)
COUNTY OF MONTGOMERY
Also Called: Stillwater Center
8100 N Main St (45415-1702)
PHONE..................................937 264-0460
Michelle Pierce Mobley, Director
EMP: 251
SQ FT: 108,000 Privately Held
WEB: www.mcmrdd.org
SIC: 8051 8052 Mental retardation hospital; home for the mentally retarded, with health care
PA: County Of Montgomery
451 W 3rd St Fl 4
Dayton OH 45422
937 225-4000

(G-9329)
COUNTY OF MONTGOMERY
Also Called: Treasurers Office
451 W 3rd St Fl 2 (45422-0001)
P.O. Box 972 (45422)
PHONE..................................937 225-4010
Hugh Quill, Treasurer
Helen Kelly-Jones, Human Res Mgr
Stacy Murray, Assistant
EMP: 32 Privately Held
WEB: www.mcmrdd.org
SIC: 9111 8611 County supervisors' & executives' offices; business associations
PA: County Of Montgomery
451 W 3rd St Fl 4
Dayton OH 45422
937 225-4000

(G-9330)
COUNTY OF MONTGOMERY
Also Called: Montgomery County Dept of Job
1111 Edwin C Moses Blvd (45422-3600)
PHONE..................................937 225-4804
Kim Bridges, Principal
David Hess, Director
EMP: 300 Privately Held
WEB: www.mcmrdd.org
SIC: 8331 8322 Job training & vocational rehabilitation services; individual & family services
PA: County Of Montgomery
451 W 3rd St Fl 4
Dayton OH 45422
937 225-4000

(G-9331)
COUNTY OF MONTGOMERY
Also Called: Montgmery Cnty Prosecutors Off
301 W 3rd St Fl 5 (45402-1446)
P.O. Box 972 (45402)
PHONE..................................937 225-5623
George B Patricoff, Director
EMP: 200 Privately Held
WEB: www.mcmrdd.org
SIC: 8111 General practice attorney, lawyer

PA: County Of Montgomery
451 W 3rd St Fl 4
Dayton OH 45422
937 225-4000

(G-9332)
COUNTY OF MONTGOMERY
Also Called: Children Services
3501 Merrimac Ave (45405-2646)
PHONE..................................937 224-5437
Shannon Jones, Principal
EMP: 75 Privately Held
WEB: www.is-partner.com
SIC: 8322 Child related social services
PA: County Of Montgomery
451 W 3rd St Fl 4
Dayton OH 45422
937 225-4000

(G-9333)
COUNTY OF MONTGOMERY
Also Called: Management Information Svcs
41 N Perry St Rm 1 (45422-2000)
PHONE..................................937 496-3103
Joseph Pecquet, Manager
EMP: 300 Privately Held
WEB: www.mcmrdd.org
SIC: 7378 7371 Computer maintenance & repair; custom computer programming services
PA: County Of Montgomery
451 W 3rd St Fl 4
Dayton OH 45422
937 225-4000

(G-9334)
COUNTY OF MONTGOMERY
Also Called: Coroner
361 W 3rd St (45402-1418)
PHONE..................................937 225-4156
James Davis, Principal
Bryan Casto, Med Doctor
EMP: 34 Privately Held
WEB: www.mcmrdd.org
SIC: 8011 Pathologist
PA: County Of Montgomery
451 W 3rd St Fl 4
Dayton OH 45422
937 225-4000

(G-9335)
COURTYARD BY MARRIOTT DAYTON
2006 S Edwin C Moses Blvd (45417-4675)
PHONE..................................937 220-9060
Karen Younce, Principal
EMP: 25
SALES (est): 1.2MM Privately Held
SIC: 7011 Hotels

(G-9336)
COX COMMUNICATIONS INC
1611 S Main St (45409-2547)
PHONE..................................937 222-5700
David Dashewich, Vice Pres
Doug Franklin, Branch Mgr
EMP: 76
SALES (corp-wide): 32.5B Privately Held
SIC: 4813 Telephone communication, except radio
HQ: Cox Communications, Inc.
6205 B Pchtree Dunwody Ne
Atlanta GA 30328

(G-9337)
CREATIVE IMAGES COLLEGE OF B (PA)
Also Called: Creative Imges Inst Csmetology
7535 Poe Ave (45414-2557)
PHONE..................................937 478-7922
Nicholas Schindler, President
EMP: 30
SALES (est): 1.2MM Privately Held
SIC: 7231 Cosmetology school; beauty schools

(G-9338)
CREDIT BUR COLLECTN SVCS INC
Also Called: Cbcs
11 W Monument Ave Ste 200 (45402-1233)
PHONE..................................937 496-2577
Kevin Kastl, Principal
Kevin Castle, Manager
EMP: 35

SALES (corp-wide): 246.2MM **Privately Held**
SIC: 7322 Collection agency, except real estate
HQ: Credit Bureau Collection Services, Inc.
236 E Town St
Columbus OH 43215
614 223-0688

(G-9339)
CREDIT INFONET INC
Also Called: Cin Legal Data Services
4540 Honeywell Ct (45424-5760)
PHONE.................................866 218-1003
Dave Danielson, *CEO*
EMP: 25
SALES (est): 4.6MM
SALES (corp-wide): 23.5MM **Privately Held**
SIC: 7323 Credit reporting services
PA: Stretto
5 Peters Canyon Rd # 200
Irvine CA 92606
949 222-1212

(G-9340)
CROSWELL OF WILLIAMSBURG LLC
4828 Wolf Creek Pike (45417-9438)
PHONE.................................800 782-8747
John W Croswell, *Branch Mgr*
EMP: 65
SALES (corp-wide): 7MM **Privately Held**
SIC: 4142 Bus charter service, except local
PA: Croswell Of Williamsburg Llc
975 W Main St
Williamsburg OH 45176
513 724-2206

(G-9341)
CSA ANIMAL NUTRITION LLC
6640 Poe Ave Ste 225 (45414-2678)
PHONE.................................866 615-8084
Charles Schininger, *Mng Member*
EMP: 30
SQ FT: 11,000
SALES: 3MM **Privately Held**
SIC: 0752 Animal specialty services

(G-9342)
CSL PLASMA INC
850 N Main St (45405-4629)
PHONE.................................937 331-9186
Sashia Linder, *Branch Mgr*
EMP: 79 **Privately Held**
WEB: www.zlbplasma.com
SIC: 8099 Blood bank
HQ: Csl Plasma Inc.
900 Broken Sound Pkwy Nw # 4
Boca Raton FL 33487
561 981-3700

(G-9343)
DAHM BROTHERS COMPANY INC
743 Valley St (45404-1957)
PHONE.................................937 461-5627
Steve Dahm, *President*
Christopher Dahm, *President*
EMP: 25 EST: 1929
SQ FT: 4,500
SALES (est): 2.7MM **Privately Held**
SIC: 1761 Roofing contractor

(G-9344)
DAIKIN APPLIED AMERICAS INC
Also Called: Daikin Applied Parts Warehouse
2915 Needmore Rd (45414-4303)
PHONE.................................763 553-5009
Walt Moulton, *Branch Mgr*
EMP: 25
SALES (corp-wide): 21.5B **Privately Held**
SIC: 5075 4225 Warm air heating & air conditioning; general warehousing & storage
HQ: Daikin Applied Americas Inc.
13600 Industrial Pk Blvd
Minneapolis MN 55441
763 553-5330

(G-9345)
DAVID CAMPBELL
Also Called: Cold Well Banker Realty
2000 Hewitt Ave (45440-2917)
PHONE.................................937 266-7064
Ron Sweenmy, *Managing Prtnr*

Steve Arman, *Partner*
EMP: 25
SALES (est): 593.6K **Privately Held**
SIC: 6531 Real estate agent, residential

(G-9346)
DAVITA INC
Also Called: Davita Dialysis
5721 Bigger Rd (45440-2752)
PHONE.................................937 435-4030
David Howdyshell, *Administration*
EMP: 27 **Publicly Held**
SIC: 8092 Kidney dialysis centers
PA: Davita Inc.
2000 16th St
Denver CO 80202

(G-9347)
DAVUE OB-GYN ASSOCIATES INC (PA)
2200 Philadelphia Dr # 101 (45406-1840)
PHONE.................................937 277-8988
James Huey Jr, *President*
Druce J Bernie, *Vice Pres*
Stewart Weprin MD, *Treasurer*
EMP: 58 EST: 1947
SQ FT: 5,220
SALES (est): 1.6MM **Privately Held**
SIC: 8011 Obstetrician; gynecologist

(G-9348)
DAY AIR CREDIT UNION INC (PA)
3501 Wilmington Pike (45429-4840)
P.O. Box 292980 (45429-8980)
PHONE.................................937 643-2160
William J Burke, *President*
Don McCauley, *Chairman*
Paul Hauck, *Senior VP*
EMP: 43 EST: 1945
SQ FT: 16,000
SALES: 13.4MM **Privately Held**
WEB: www.dayair.com
SIC: 6061 Federal credit unions

(G-9349)
DAYBREAK INC (PA)
605 S Patterson Blvd (45402-2649)
PHONE.................................937 395-4600
Linda Kramer, *CEO*
Joanne Taylor, *Facilities Mgr*
Ginny Glass, *Supervisor*
Sarah Wildermuth, *Social Worker*
EMP: 48 EST: 1975
SQ FT: 53,681
SALES: 8.3MM **Privately Held**
WEB: www.daybreakdayton.org
SIC: 8399 Fund raising organization, non-fee basis

(G-9350)
DAYTON ANIMAL HOSPITAL ASSOC
Also Called: North Main Animal Clinic
8015 N Main St (45415-2250)
PHONE.................................937 890-4744
Beth S Weiseerger, *President*
EMP: 27
SQ FT: 4,920
SALES (est): 1.8MM **Privately Held**
SIC: 0742 0752 Animal hospital services, pets & other animal specialties; grooming services, pet & animal specialties

(G-9351)
DAYTON ANTHEM
Also Called: Well Point Anthem
1222 S Patterson Blvd # 4 (45402-2684)
PHONE.................................937 428-8000
Rich Gunza, *Director*
EMP: 60
SALES (est): 3.7MM **Privately Held**
SIC: 8621 Health association

(G-9352)
DAYTON APPLIANCE PARTS CO (PA)
122 Sears St (45402-1765)
PHONE.................................937 224-0487
Timothy Houtz, *President*
James C Houtz, *Vice Pres*
Hank Wolf, *Manager*
EMP: 35 EST: 1938
SQ FT: 15,000

SALES (est): 15.8MM **Privately Held**
WEB: www.partwizard.com
SIC: 5064 5722 Appliance parts, household; appliance parts

(G-9353)
DAYTON AREA CHAMBER COMMERCE
22 E 5th St Ste 200 (45402-2413)
PHONE.................................937 226-1444
Phil Parker, *President*
EMP: 28
SQ FT: 7,000
SALES: 2.2MM **Privately Held**
SIC: 8611 Chamber of Commerce

(G-9354)
DAYTON ART INSTITUTE
456 Belmonte Park N (45405-4700)
PHONE.................................937 223-5277
David Stacy, *CFO*
Alexander L Nyerges, *Director*
▲ EMP: 100
SQ FT: 105,000
SALES: 6.3MM **Privately Held**
WEB: www.daytonartinstitute.org
SIC: 8412 Museum

(G-9355)
DAYTON BAG & BURLAP CO (PA)
322 Davis Ave (45403-2900)
P.O. Box 8 (45401-0008)
PHONE.................................937 258-8000
Sam Lumby, *President*
Jeffery S Rutter, *COO*
Charlie Cretcher, *CFO*
Paul Johnston, *Manager*
Aaron Kohler, *Manager*
▲ EMP: 105 EST: 1910
SQ FT: 140,000
SALES (est): 41.2MM **Privately Held**
SIC: 5199 Burlap; dressed furs; baskets

(G-9356)
DAYTON CARDIOLOGY CONSULTANTS (PA)
Also Called: Dayton Crdiolgy Vascular Cons
1126 S Main St (45409-2616)
PHONE.................................937 223-3053
Raymond Pratt MD, *President*
EMP: 47
SQ FT: 10,000
SALES: 8MM **Privately Held**
WEB: www.daytoncardiology.com
SIC: 8011 Cardiologist & cardio-vascular specialist

(G-9357)
DAYTON CHILDRENS HOSPITAL
1 Childrens Plz (45404-1873)
PHONE.................................937 641-3376
Gary A Mueller, *Principal*
EMP: 30
SALES (est): 118.9K **Privately Held**
SIC: 8011 Internal medicine, physician/surgeon

(G-9358)
DAYTON CHILDRENS HOSPITAL (PA)
Also Called: Children's Medical Center
1 Childrens Plz (45404-1873)
PHONE.................................937 641-3000
Deborah Feldman, *CEO*
Vicki Giambrone, *General Mgr*
Karen Braun, *Business Mgr*
Matt Graybill Fache, *COO*
Lisa Coffey, *Vice Pres*
▲ EMP: 1000 EST: 1919
SQ FT: 345,000
SALES: 253.7MM **Privately Held**
SIC: 8069 Children's hospital

(G-9359)
DAYTON CITY PARKS GOLF MAINT
Also Called: Kittyhawk Golf Course
3383 Chuck Wagner Ln (45414-4402)
PHONE.................................937 333-3378
Tom Getts, *Superintendent*
Phillip Cline, *Superintendent*
Maria Oria, *Superintendent*
William Stutz, *Superintendent*
Kevin Moore, *Manager*

EMP: 30
SALES (est): 753.4K **Privately Held**
SIC: 0781 Landscape services

(G-9360)
DAYTON COUNTRY CLUB COMPANY
555 Kramer Rd (45419-3399)
PHONE.................................937 294-3352
Steven Gongola, *General Mgr*
Jeffrey Grant, *General Mgr*
EMP: 90
SALES: 3.8MM **Privately Held**
WEB: www.daytoncountryclub.com
SIC: 7997 Country club, membership

(G-9361)
DAYTON CVB
Also Called: Dayton Convention Visitors Bur
1 Chamber Plz Ste A (45402-2426)
PHONE.................................937 226-8211
Jacquelyn Powell, *President*
EMP: 40
SALES (est): 1.4MM **Privately Held**
SIC: 7389 Tourist information bureau

(G-9362)
DAYTON DIGITAL MEDIA INC
Also Called: Dayton Digital.com
2212 Patterson Rd (45420-3061)
PHONE.................................937 223-8335
Joseph Lutz, *Principal*
EMP: 50 EST: 1995
SALES (est): 1.9MM **Privately Held**
WEB: www.buyfireproducts.com
SIC: 7389 8742 Advertising, promotional & trade show services; training & development consultant

(G-9363)
DAYTON DMH INC
Also Called: Wood Glenn Nursing Center
3800 Summit Glen Dr (45449-3647)
PHONE.................................937 436-2273
Carmen Winburn, *Administration*
EMP: 170
SALES (corp-wide): 1.3MM **Privately Held**
SIC: 8051 Skilled nursing care facilities
PA: Dayton Dmh Inc
12348 High Bluff Dr # 100
San Diego CA 92130
858 350-4400

(G-9364)
DAYTON DOOR SALES INC (PA)
Also Called: Overhead Door Co of Dayton
1112 Springfield St (45403-1405)
P.O. Box 134 (45404-0134)
PHONE.................................937 253-9181
Kenneth F Monnin, *CEO*
Dean Monnin, *President*
Lawrence J Becker, *Vice Pres*
Terry Johnson, *Site Mgr*
Shawna Fuquea, *Credit Mgr*
EMP: 40
SQ FT: 8,800
SALES (est): 16.5MM **Privately Held**
WEB: www.daytondoorsales.com
SIC: 5211 7699 5031 1751 Garage doors, sale & installation; doors, wood or metal, except storm; doors, storm: wood or metal; windows, storm: wood or metal; garage door repair; door & window repair; doors, garage; doors; windows; window & door (prefabricated) installation

(G-9365)
DAYTON FOUNDATION INC
Also Called: DISABILITY FOUNDATION THE
40 N Main St Ste 500 (45423-1038)
PHONE.................................937 222-0410
Michael Parks, *Chairman*
Carol Hicks, *Pub Rel Staff*
Karen Simmons, *Admin Asst*
EMP: 30
SQ FT: 5,000
SALES: 4.3MM **Privately Held**
SIC: 8741 8733 8742 Management services; noncommercial research organizations; management consulting services

(G-9366)
DAYTON FREIGHT LINES INC
6265 Executive Blvd Ste A (45424-1400)
PHONE.................................937 236-4880

John McVey, *Vice Pres*
Derek Kirby, *Safety Dir*
Brian Gratch, *Manager*
EMP: 70
SALES (corp-wide): 971MM **Privately Held**
SIC: 4213 4731 4231 Less-than-truckload (LTL) transport; freight consolidation; trucking terminal facilities
PA: Dayton Freight Lines, Inc.
6450 Poe Ave Ste 311
Dayton OH 45414
937 264-4060

(G-9367)
DAYTON HEART CENTER INC (PA)
1530 Needmore Rd Ste 300 (45414-3980)
PHONE.................................937 277-4274
Davic Joffe, *President*
C David Joffe, *President*
Henry H Chong, *Partner*
Gary J Fishbein, *Partner*
Amit Goyal, *Partner*
EMP: 60
SQ FT: 38,000
SALES (est): 9.8MM **Privately Held**
SIC: 8011 Cardiologist & cardio-vascular specialist

(G-9368)
DAYTON HISTORY
Also Called: CARILLON HISTORICAL PARK
1000 Carillon Blvd (45409-2023)
PHONE.................................937 293-2841
Brady Kress, *CEO*
Eric Cluxton, *Chairman*
Alexandra Ollinger, *Treasurer*
Ginny Strausburg, *Admin Sec*
EMP: 125
SALES: 8.7MM **Privately Held**
SIC: 8412 7999 Museum; tourist attractions, amusement park concessions & rides

(G-9369)
DAYTON HOSPICE INCORPORATED (PA)
Also Called: Hospice Butler and Warren Cnty
324 Wilmington Ave (45420-1890)
PHONE.................................937 256-4490
Deborah Dailey, *President*
William H Macbeth, *Principal*
Jerry Durst, *CFO*
Susan Page, *Manager*
Chirag Patel, *Director*
EMP: 275
SQ FT: 85,000
SALES: 53.2MM **Privately Held**
WEB: www.hospicedayton.com
SIC: 8082 Home health care services

(G-9370)
DAYTON INTL PEACE MUSEUM
Also Called: Dayton Intl Peace Museum
208 W Monument Ave (45402-3015)
PHONE.................................937 227-3223
Steve Fryburg, *Director*
Michael Kalter, *Director*
Ralph Dull, *Author*
EMP: 50
SALES (est): 117.9K **Privately Held**
SIC: 8412 Museum

(G-9371)
DAYTON MAILING SERVICES INC
100 S Keowee St (45402-2241)
P.O. Box 2436 (45401-2436)
PHONE.................................937 222-5056
Christine Soward, *President*
Mark Kuns, *Accounts Exec*
Tom Cooper, *Manager*
Jason Reid, *Supervisor*
Natalie Bisnow, *Info Tech Mgr*
EMP: 30
SQ FT: 100,000
SALES (est): 9MM **Privately Held**
WEB: www.daytonmailing.com
SIC: 7331 2759 Mailing service; commercial printing

(G-9372)
DAYTON MEDICAL IMAGING
Also Called: U S Diagnostics
7901 Schatz Pointe Dr (45459-3826)
PHONE.................................937 439-0390
Jeffrey Cushman, *Med Doctor*
Jeffrey Sergent, *Manager*
Wilfredo J Suntay, *Radiology*
Michael Chune, *Urology*
EMP: 96
SQ FT: 3,372
SALES: 2MM **Privately Held**
SIC: 8011 8071 Radiologist; X-ray laboratory, including dental

(G-9373)
DAYTON NWBORN CARE SPCLSTS INC
1 Childrens Plz Rm 4085 (45404-1873)
PHONE.................................937 641-3329
Deborah Feldman, *President*
EMP: 502
SALES (est): 1.7MM **Publicly Held**
SIC: 8051 Skilled nursing care facilities
PA: Mednax, Inc.
1301 Concord Ter
Sunrise FL 33323

(G-9374)
DAYTON OSTEOPATHIC HOSPITAL (HQ)
Also Called: Grandview Hospital & Med Ctr
405 W Grand Ave (45405-7538)
PHONE.................................937 762-1629
Fred Manchur, *CEO*
Russell J Wetherell, *President*
Todd Anderson, *CFO*
Edward Mann, *Treasurer*
EMP: 1134 EST: 1926
SQ FT: 700,000
SALES (est): 118.5MM
SALES (corp-wide): 1.7B **Privately Held**
WEB: www.gvh-svh.org
SIC: 8062 General medical & surgical hospitals
PA: Kettering Adventist Healthcare
3535 Southern Blvd
Dayton OH 45429
937 298-4331

(G-9375)
DAYTON PERFORMING ARTS ALLIANCE
126 N Main St Ste 210 (45402-1766)
PHONE.................................937 224-3521
Wendy Campbell, *Chairman*
Peter Klosterman, *CFO*
Teri Warwick, *CFO*
Daniel Deitz, *Treasurer*
David Bukvic, *Marketing Staff*
EMP: 100 EST: 1933
SQ FT: 2,022
SALES: 4.7MM **Privately Held**
WEB: www.daytonphilharmonic.com
SIC: 7929 Symphony orchestras

(G-9376)
DAYTON PHYSICIANS LLC (PA)
6680 Poe Ave Ste 200 (45414-2855)
PHONE.................................937 280-8400
Dawn Koesters, *Opers Mgr*
James Moore, *Opers Mgr*
Jeffery Sergent, *Opers Mgr*
Yolanda Cleveland, *Purch Mgr*
Dan Miller, *Med Doctor*
EMP: 240
SQ FT: 5,000
SALES (est): 25.5MM **Privately Held**
SIC: 8011 Oncologist; general & family practice, physician/surgeon

(G-9377)
DAYTON PRIMARY & URGENT CARE
301 W 1st St Ste 100 (45402-3046)
PHONE.................................937 461-0800
Morris Brown, *President*
EMP: 28
SALES (est): 1.8MM **Privately Held**
SIC: 8011 Gastronomist

(G-9378)
DAYTON PROF BASBAL CLB LLC
Also Called: Dayton Dragons Baseball
220 N Patterson Blvd (45402-1279)
P.O. Box 2107 (45401-2107)
PHONE.................................937 228-2287
Robert Murphy, *President*
Eric Deutsch, *Exec VP*
EMP: 28
SALES (est): 2.7MM **Privately Held**
WEB: www.daytondragons.com
SIC: 7941 Baseball club, professional & semi-professional

(G-9379)
DAYTON PUBLIC SCHOOL DISTRICT
Also Called: Service Building
115 S Ludlow St (45402-1812)
PHONE.................................937 542-3000
Lori Ward, *Manager*
EMP: 80
SALES (corp-wide): 324.5MM **Privately Held**
WEB: www.dps.k12.oh.us
SIC: 4832 Educational
PA: Dayton Public School District
115 S Ludlow St
Dayton OH 45402
937 542-3000

(G-9380)
DAYTON REGIONAL DIALYSIS INC (PA)
8701 Old Troy Pike Ste 10 (45424-1053)
PHONE.................................937 898-5526
Lawrence W Klein, *President*
EMP: 33
SQ FT: 7,600
SALES (est): 1.1MM **Privately Held**
WEB: www.naod-drd.org
SIC: 8092 8011 Kidney Dialysis Centers Medical Doctor's Office

(G-9381)
DAYTON SOCIETY NATURAL HISTORY (PA)
Also Called: Boonshoft Museum of Discovery
2600 Deweese Pkwy (45414-5400)
PHONE.................................937 275-7431
Mark J Meister, *President*
Bethany Deines, *Vice Pres*
Doug Hull, *CFO*
Kristy Creel, *Manager*
Liz Fisher, *Manager*
▲ EMP: 80
SQ FT: 75
SALES (est): 4.2MM **Privately Held**
WEB: www.sunwatch.org
SIC: 8412 Museum

(G-9382)
DAYTON TORO MOTORCYCLE CLUB
1536 W 3rd St (45402-6717)
PHONE.................................937 723-9133
John Clork, *CEO*
Shawn Jones, *President*
Fox Rose, *President*
EMP: 51
SQ FT: 2,425
SALES (est): 1.9MM **Privately Held**
SIC: 7997 Membership sports & recreation clubs

(G-9383)
DAYTON URBAN LEAGUE (PA)
907 W 5th St (45402-8306)
PHONE.................................937 226-1513
Sheldon Mitchell, *President*
Clarence Ray III, *Vice Pres*
Willie F Walker, *Vice Pres*
Yvette R Fields, *Treasurer*
Leah Harger, *Admin Sec*
EMP: 25
SQ FT: 25,000
SALES: 3.8MM **Privately Held**
WEB: www.duleague.org
SIC: 8322 8331 Public welfare center; job training & vocational rehabilitation services

(G-9384)
DAYTON WALLS & CEILINGS INC
4328 Webster St (45414-4936)
P.O. Box 13561 (45413-0561)
PHONE.................................937 277-0531
Eric Peterson, *President*
Robert Coyle, *Exec VP*
John Peterson, *Vice Pres*
Randy Bindel, *Sr Project Mgr*
EMP: 82
SQ FT: 14,000
SALES: 11.4MM **Privately Held**
WEB: www.dwceiling.com
SIC: 1742 Drywall; acoustical & ceiling work

(G-9385)
DAYTON WINDUSTRIAL CO
137 E Helena St (45404-1052)
P.O. Box 931112, Atlanta GA (31193-1112)
PHONE.................................937 461-2603
Greg Jackson, *President*
John Grabeman, *Warehouse Mgr*
Brad Williams, *Sales Staff*
Jeremy Jackson, *Manager*
Debbie Moore, *Manager*
EMP: 30
SALES (est): 4MM
SALES (corp-wide): 4.9B **Privately Held**
WEB: www.daytonwindustrial.com
SIC: 5074 Plumbing & heating valves
PA: Winsupply Inc.
3110 Kettering Blvd
Moraine OH 45439
937 294-5331

(G-9386)
DELOITTE & TOUCHE LLP
220 E Monu Ave Ste 500 (45402)
PHONE.................................937 223-8821
Edward T Bentley, *Manager*
Rodney Berning, *Internal Med*
EMP: 100
SALES (corp-wide): 6.2B **Privately Held**
WEB: www.deloitte.com
SIC: 8721 8742 Certified public accountant; management consulting services
HQ: Deloitte & Touche Llp
30 Rockefeller Plz # 4350
New York NY 10112
212 492-4000

(G-9387)
DELOITTE CONSULTING LLP
711 E Monu Ave Ste 201 (45402)
PHONE.................................937 223-8821
Mark A Danis, *Principal*
EMP: 150
SALES (corp-wide): 6.2B **Privately Held**
WEB: www.dctoolset.com
SIC: 8742 8748 Management consulting services; business consulting
HQ: Deloitte Consulting Llp
30 Rockefeller Plz
New York NY 10112
212 492-4000

(G-9388)
DERMATLGISTS OF SOUTHWEST OHIO (PA)
5300 Far Hills Ave # 100 (45429-2381)
PHONE.................................937 435-2094
Stephen B Levitt MD, *President*
Thomas G Olsen, *Vice Pres*
EMP: 45
SQ FT: 3,000
SALES (est): 8.2MM **Privately Held**
WEB: www.dermswohio.com
SIC: 8011 Dermatologist

(G-9389)
DESIGN HOMES & DEVELOPMENT CO
Also Called: Dhdc
8534 Yankee St Ste A (45458-1889)
PHONE.................................937 438-3667
Shery Oakes, *President*
Scott Denlinger, *Manager*
Laura Sweney, *Manager*
Sharon Hackett, *Admin Asst*
Kari Knapke, *Associate*
EMP: 35

SALES (est): 6.6MM **Privately Held**
WEB: www.designhomesco.com
SIC: **8711** 1542 1521 6531 Civil engineering; commercial & office building contractors; single-family housing construction; real estate agents & managers

(G-9390)
DIALYSIS CENTER OF DAYTON EAST
1431 Business Center Ct (45410-3300)
PHONE..............................937 252-1867
Fax: 937 254-9312
EMP: 30
SALES (est): 1.2MM **Privately Held**
SIC: **8092** Dialysis Center

(G-9391)
DIGESTIVE SPECIALISTS INC
Also Called: Digestive Endoscopy Center
999 Brubaker Dr Ste 1 (45429-3505)
PHONE..............................937 534-7330
Ramesh Gandhi, *President*
Harold Fishman, *Vice Pres*
Cindy Klink, *Finance Mgr*
Linda Blazek, *Manager*
Linda Smith, *Executive*
▲ EMP: 30
SALES (est): 7.8MM **Privately Held**
SIC: **8011** Physicians' office, including specialists; gastronomist

(G-9392)
DIVERSCARE HEALTHCARE SVCS INC
6125 N Main St (45415-3110)
PHONE..............................937 278-8211
Loren Martin, *Branch Mgr*
EMP: 36
SALES (corp-wide): 563.4MM **Publicly Held**
SIC: **8322** 8051 Rehabilitation services; extended care facility
PA: Diversicare Healthcare Services, Inc.
1621 Galleria Blvd
Brentwood TN 37027
615 771-7575

(G-9393)
DOLING & ASSOCIATES DENTAL LAB
3318 Successful Way (45414-4318)
PHONE..............................937 254-0075
Ted Doling, *President*
Joe Wiener, *Vice Pres*
EMP: 25
SQ FT: 3,000
SALES (est): 2.4MM **Privately Held**
SIC: **3842** 8072 Surgical appliances & supplies; crown & bridge production

(G-9394)
DOMESTIC RELATIONS
301 W 3rd St Ste 500 (45402-1446)
PHONE..............................937 225-4063
Mike Howley, *Director*
EMP: 50
SALES (est): 2.5MM **Privately Held**
SIC: **8743** Public relations & publicity

(G-9395)
DRT HOLDINGS INC (PA)
618 Greenmount Blvd (45419-3271)
PHONE..............................937 298-7391
Gary Van Gundy, *President*
Sean McBermott, *Engineer*
John Penrod, *Engineer*
Joseph Zehenny, *CFO*
Greg Martin, *Admin Sec*
EMP: 60
SALES (est): 194.6MM **Privately Held**
SIC: **6719** 3599 3728 Investment holding companies, except banks; machine shop, jobbing & repair; aircraft parts & equipment

(G-9396)
DRURY HOTELS COMPANY LLC
Also Called: Drury Inn & Suites Dayton N
6616 Miller Ln (45414-2663)
PHONE..............................937 454-5200
Steven Patton, *Manager*
EMP: 39

SALES (corp-wide): 397.7MM **Privately Held**
WEB: www.druryhotels.com
SIC: **7011** Hotels
PA: Drury Hotels Company, Llc
721 Emerson Rd Ste 400
Saint Louis MO 63141
314 429-2255

(G-9397)
DUNSIANE SWIM CLUB
600 W Spring Valley Pike (45458-3617)
P.O. Box 41003 (45441-0003)
PHONE..............................937 433-7946
Rockne Morrissey, *Treasurer*
EMP: 31
SALES: 233.5K **Privately Held**
SIC: **7997** Swimming club, membership; tennis club, membership

(G-9398)
DUPONT INC
1515 Nicholas Rd (45417-6712)
PHONE..............................937 268-3411
Richard Russell, *Manager*
David Mueller, *Technology*
EMP: 55
SALES (est): 5.3MM **Privately Held**
SIC: **5169** Chemicals & allied products

(G-9399)
E-MEK TECHNOLOGIES LLC
7410 Webster St (45414-5816)
PHONE..............................937 424-3163
Larry Crossley, *President*
EMP: 60
SALES (est): 12.1MM **Privately Held**
SIC: **7379**

(G-9400)
EARLY EXPRESS SERVICES INC
Also Called: Early Express Mail Services
1333 E 2nd St (45403-1020)
P.O. Box 2422 (45401-2422)
PHONE..............................937 223-5801
Karen Sensel, *CEO*
Cindy Woodward, *President*
Beth Wright, *Accountant*
EMP: 39
SQ FT: 17,000
SALES (est): 5.7MM **Privately Held**
WEB: www.earlyexpress.com
SIC: **7331** 4212 7374 Mailing service; mailing list compilers; delivery service, vehicular; data processing service

(G-9401)
EARLY LEARNING TREE CHLD CTR (PA)
2332 N Main St (45405-3439)
PHONE..............................937 276-3221
Dorothy Pultz,
EMP: 55 EST: 1971
SQ FT: 7,200
SALES (est): 2.6MM **Privately Held**
SIC: **8351** Group day care center

(G-9402)
EARLY LEARNING TREE CHLD CTR
2332 N Main St (45405-3439)
PHONE..............................937 293-7907
Dorothy Pultz, *Owner*
EMP: 56
SALES (est): 3.3MM
SALES (corp-wide): 2.5MM **Privately Held**
SIC: **8741** 8351 Business management; preschool center
PA: Early Learning Tree Children's Center
2332 N Main St
Dayton OH 45405
937 276-3221

(G-9403)
EAST WAY BEHAVIORAL HLTH CARE
600 Wayne Ave (45410-1122)
PHONE..............................937 222-4900
Jonh Strahm, *President*
Bob Groskops, *Treasurer*
EMP: 200
SQ FT: 25,000

SALES: 63.9K
SALES (corp-wide): 20.3MM **Privately Held**
SIC: **8093** 8742 8249 Mental health clinic, outpatient; hospital & health services consultant; medical training services
PA: Eastway Corporation
600 Wayne Ave
Dayton OH 45410
937 496-2000

(G-9404)
EASTWAY CORPORATION (PA)
Also Called: EASTWAY BEHAVORIAL HEALTHCARE
600 Wayne Ave (45410-1199)
P.O. Box 983 (45401-0983)
PHONE..............................937 496-2000
John F Strahm, *CEO*
Resovsky Jody, *General Mgr*
Robert E Jaeger, *Principal*
R J Stubbs, *Principal*
Mary Louise Van Doren, *Principal*
EMP: 115 EST: 1957
SALES: 24.7MM **Privately Held**
SIC: **8063** 8322 Hospital for the mentally ill; individual & family services

(G-9405)
EASTWAY CORPORATION
Also Called: Eastco
600 Wayne Ave (45410-1199)
PHONE..............................937 531-7000
Joe Pesch, *Info Tech Mgr*
James Sherman, *Director*
EMP: 224
SQ FT: 9,100
SALES (corp-wide): 20.3MM **Privately Held**
SIC: **8063** 8093 Hospital for the mentally ill; specialty outpatient clinics
PA: Eastway Corporation
600 Wayne Ave
Dayton OH 45410
937 496-2000

(G-9406)
ECHOING HILLS VILLAGE INC
Also Called: Echoing Wood Residential Cntr
5455 Salem Bend Dr (45426-1609)
PHONE..............................937 854-5151
Rose Barber, *Manager*
Alice Byrd, *Clerk*
EMP: 60
SALES (corp-wide): 27MM **Privately Held**
WEB: www.echoinghillsvillage.org
SIC: **7032** 8051 Sporting & recreational camps; skilled nursing care facilities
PA: Echoing Hills Village, Inc.
36272 County Road 79
Warsaw OH 43844
740 327-2311

(G-9407)
ECHOING HILLS VILLAGE INC
Also Called: Echoing Valley
7040 Union Schoolhouse Rd (45424-5207)
PHONE..............................937 237-7881
Timothy Dotson, *Human Res Mgr*
Rose Barber, *Manager*
EMP: 50
SALES (corp-wide): 27MM **Privately Held**
WEB: www.echoinghillsvillage.org
SIC: **7032** 8059 Sporting & recreational camps; home for the mentally retarded, exc. skilled or intermediate
PA: Echoing Hills Village, Inc.
36272 County Road 79
Warsaw OH 43844
740 327-2311

(G-9408)
EDAPTIVE COMPUTING INC
1245 Lyons Rd Ste G (45458-1818)
PHONE..............................937 433-0477
Anju Chawla, *CEO*
Praveen Chawla, *President*
James Volters, *Vice Pres*
Brad Volters, *Project Mgr*
David Palmiter, *Software Dev*
EMP: 70
SQ FT: 10,000

SALES: 15MM **Privately Held**
WEB: www.edaptive.com
SIC: **7371** Computer software systems analysis & design, custom

(G-9409)
ELITE ISG
Also Called: Elite Investigations SEC Group
7825 N Dixie Dr Ste C (45414-2778)
PHONE..............................937 668-6858
Aw Powers, *Partner*
EMP: 35
SALES: 700K **Privately Held**
SIC: **7381** Security guard service

(G-9410)
ELIZABETH PLACE HOLDINGS LLC
1 Elizabeth Pl (45417-3445)
PHONE..............................323 300-3700
Troy Campbell,
Odet Mkrtchyan,
EMP: 30 EST: 2013
SALES (est): 3.4MM **Privately Held**
SIC: **8011** Physicians' office, including specialists

(G-9411)
ELIZABETHS NEW LIFE CENTER INC
Also Called: ELIZABETH'S NEW LIFE WOMEN'S C
2201 N Main St (45405-3528)
PHONE..............................937 226-7414
Rosemary Prier, *Opers Staff*
Terry Miller, *Human Res Dir*
Jennifer Ellis, *Manager*
Vivian Koob, *Exec Dir*
Kerry Braun, *Director*
EMP: 54
SALES: 2.8MM **Privately Held**
SIC: **8699** Charitable organization

(G-9412)
ELLIOTT TOOL TECHNOLOGIES LTD (PA)
1760 Tuttle Ave (45403-3428)
PHONE..............................937 253-6133
Joseph W Smith, *President*
Jason Triche, *Area Mgr*
Robert Columbus, *Vice Pres*
Tom Reynolds, *Mfg Mgr*
Dawn Luker, *Purchasing*
EMP: 68
SQ FT: 37,000
SALES (est): 16MM **Privately Held**
WEB: www.elliott-tool.com
SIC: **7359** 3542 5072 3541 Equipment rental & leasing; machine tools, metal forming type; hand tools; machine tools, metal cutting type; fabricated pipe & fittings

(G-9413)
ELLIPSE SOLUTIONS LLC
7917 Washington Woods Dr (45459-4026)
PHONE..............................937 312-1547
Kevin Davies, *Director*
EMP: 50
SALES (est): 2.5MM **Privately Held**
SIC: **8748** Systems engineering consultant, ex. computer or professional

(G-9414)
EMERGENCY MEDICINE SPECIALISTS
8280 Yankee St (45458-1806)
PHONE..............................937 438-8910
Richard Garrson, *President*
Jeffrey S Robinson, *Emerg Med Spec*
EMP: 56
SALES (est): 2MM **Privately Held**
SIC: **8011** Freestanding emergency medical center

(G-9415)
ENVIRNMENTAL ENGRG SYSTEMS INC
Also Called: Honeywell Authorized Dealer
17 Creston Ave (45404-1701)
PHONE..............................937 228-6492
Eric Miske, *President*
Jeredythe Miske, *Vice Pres*
Thomas J Miske, *Vice Pres*
Martin Stewart, *Vice Pres*

▲ = Import ▼=Export
◆ =Import/Export

Deborah Fin, *Finance Mgr*
EMP: 30
SQ FT: 10,000
SALES (est): 5.2MM **Privately Held**
WEB: www.envengsys.com
SIC: 1711 Mechanical contractor

(G-9416)
EQUITAS HEALTH INC
Also Called: Dayton Pharmacy
1222 S Patterson Blvd (45402-2684)
PHONE..............................937 424-1440
Matthew Insley, *Branch Mgr*
EMP: 37
SALES (corp-wide): 23.4MM **Privately Held**
SIC: 5122 Pharmaceuticals
PA: Equitas Health, Inc.
    4400 N High St Ste 300
    Columbus OH 43214
    614 299-2437

(G-9417)
ERIE CONSTRUCTION MID-WEST INC
Also Called: Erie Construction Co
3520 Sudachi Dr (45414-2435)
PHONE..............................937 898-4688
Jeff Block, *Manager*
EMP: 35
SALES (corp-wide): 50.6MM **Privately Held**
SIC: 1521 5211 1799 1761 General remodeling, single-family houses; door & window products; kitchen & bathroom remodeling; siding contractor
PA: Erie Construction Mid-West, Inc.
    4271 Monroe St
    Toledo OH 43606
    419 472-4200

(G-9418)
ESSEX AND ASSOCIATES INC
7501 Paragon Rd Ste 100 (45459-5319)
PHONE..............................937 432-1040
Wayne Essex, *President*
EMP: 30
SALES (est): 3MM **Privately Held**
SIC: 8721 Certified public accountant

(G-9419)
EVANGELICAL RETIREMENT
Also Called: Friendship Village of Dayton
5790 Denlinger Rd (45426-1838)
PHONE..............................937 837-5581
Rev Henry Gathagan, *President*
Rebecca Hamilton, *Nursing Dir*
EMP: 230 **EST:** 1972
SQ FT: 439,000
SALES (est): 19.6MM **Privately Held**
SIC: 6513 Retirement hotel operation

(G-9420)
EXCELLENCE IN MOTIVATION INC
6 N Main St Ste 370 (45402-1908)
PHONE..............................763 445-3000
Robert Miller, *President*
David Breedlove, *General Mgr*
Robert Sjostrom, *Opers Staff*
John Kernan, *CFO*
Richelle Taylor, *Marketing Staff*
EMP: 160
SALES (est): 15.1MM
SALES (corp-wide): 100MM **Privately Held**
WEB: www.eim-inc.com
SIC: 8748 8741 Business consulting; management services
PA: One10 Llc
    100 N 6th St Ste 700b
    Minneapolis MN 55403
    763 445-3000

(G-9421)
EXCLUSIVE HOMECARE SERVICES
4699 Salem Ave Ste 1 (45416-1724)
PHONE..............................937 236-6750
Sylvia Grubbs, *CEO*
EMP: 70
SALES (est): 962.9K **Privately Held**
SIC: 8082 Home health care services

(G-9422)
EXEL N AMERCN LOGISTICS INC
5522 Little Richmond Rd (45426-3218)
PHONE..............................937 854-7900
Robert Sutfin, *Opers Mgr*
Scott Marcus, *Manager*
EMP: 150
SALES (corp-wide): 70.4B **Privately Held**
SIC: 4222 Storage, frozen or refrigerated goods
HQ: Exel North American Logistics, Inc.
    570 Players Pkwy
    Westerville OH 43081
    800 272-1052

(G-9423)
EXPEDATA LLC
8073 Washington Vlg Dr (45458-1847)
PHONE..............................937 439-6767
Doug Patterson, *Mng Member*
EMP: 30
SALES (est): 3.1MM **Privately Held**
SIC: 7374 Data processing & preparation

(G-9424)
FACILITIES KAHN MANAGEMENT
121 Springboro Pike (45449-3639)
P.O. Box 253 (45401-0253)
PHONE..............................313 202-7607
EMP: 27
SALES (est): 1.4MM **Privately Held**
SIC: 8741 Management Services

(G-9425)
FAIRBORN SFTBALL OFFCIALS ASSN
8740 Cannondale Ln (45424-6460)
PHONE..............................937 902-9920
Sterling Kaimimoku, *President*
EMP: 40
SALES (est): 727.2K **Privately Held**
SIC: 4832 Sports

(G-9426)
FAR OAKS ORTHOPEDISTS INC
3737 Sthern Blvd Ste 2100 (45429)
PHONE..............................937 433-5309
Daniel J Dunaway MD, *Principal*
EMP: 29
SALES (est): 1.9MM
SALES (corp-wide): 6.5MM **Privately Held**
SIC: 8011 Sports medicine specialist; physician
PA: Far Oaks Orthopedists, Inc.
    6490 Centervl Bus Pkwy
    Dayton OH 45459
    937 433-5309

(G-9427)
FAR OAKS ORTHOPEDISTS INC (PA)
6490 Centervl Bus Pkwy (45459-2633)
PHONE..............................937 433-5309
Daniel Dunaway MD, *President*
Donald Ames MD, *Vice Pres*
Steven Klenhenz MD, *Vice Pres*
John Lochner MD, *Vice Pres*
Timothy Quinn MD, *Vice Pres*
EMP: 35
SQ FT: 10,600
SALES (est): 6.5MM **Privately Held**
SIC: 8011 Orthopedic physician

(G-9428)
FARUKI IRELAND & COX PLLC (PA)
500 Courthouse Plz 10 (45402-1122)
PHONE..............................937 227-3700
Teri Seabold, *President*
Charles J Faruki, *Partner*
John Kendall, *Director*
Christopher Hollon, *Associate*
EMP: 50
SALES (est): 6.1MM **Privately Held**
WEB: www.fgilaw.com
SIC: 8111 Corporate, partnership & business law

(G-9429)
FED/MATRIX A JOINT VENTURE LLC
249 Wayne Ave (45402-2939)
PHONE..............................863 665-6363
James Faulkner, *Managing Prtnr*
EMP: 25
SALES (corp-wide): 1MM **Privately Held**
SIC: 8712 8711 Architectural engineering; engineering services
PA: Fed/Matrix, A Joint Venture, Llc
    255 County Road 555 S
    Bartow FL 33830
    863 667-1491

(G-9430)
FEDEX FREIGHT INC
8101 Terminal Ln (45424-1457)
PHONE..............................937 233-4826
Fax: 937 233-4858
EMP: 120
SALES (corp-wide): 47.4B **Publicly Held**
SIC: 4213 Nonlocal Trucking Operator
HQ: Fedex Freight, Inc.
    2200 Forward Dr
    Harrison AR 72601
    870 741-9000

(G-9431)
FEDEX OFFICE & PRINT SVCS INC
1189 Mmsburg Cntrville Rd (45459)
PHONE..............................937 436-0677
EMP: 30
SALES (corp-wide): 47.4B **Publicly Held**
SIC: 7334 2791 2789 Photocopying Services Typesetting Services Bookbinding/Related Work
HQ: Fedex Office And Print Services, Inc.
    7900 Legacy Dr
    Dallas TX 75024
    214 550-7000

(G-9432)
FERGUSON CONSTRUCTION COMPANY
2201 Embury Park Rd (45414-5544)
PHONE..............................937 274-1173
James Champer, *Project Mgr*
Jay T Gearon, *Sales & Mktg St*
Tom Pleiman, *CFO*
Jay Grieshop, *Controller*
EMP: 70
SQ FT: 4,424
SALES (corp-wide): 111.4MM **Privately Held**
WEB: www.ferguson-construction.com
SIC: 1541 1542 Industrial buildings, new construction; nonresidential construction
PA: Ferguson Construction Company Inc
    2020 Wyeth Dr
    Guntersville AL 45365
    937 498-2381

(G-9433)
FERGUSON HILLS INC
Also Called: Caesar Creek Flea Market
7812 Mcewen Rd Ste 200 (45459-4069)
PHONE..............................513 539-4497
Louis Levin, *CEO*
Allen Levin, *Vice Pres*
EMP: 77
SQ FT: 3,000
SALES (est): 5.3MM **Privately Held**
WEB: www.levininc.com
SIC: 7389 Flea market

(G-9434)
FIRST COMMUNITY HLTH SVCS LLC
Also Called: Fchs
3634 Watertower Ln Ste 1 (45449-4000)
PHONE..............................937 247-0400
Selina Asamoah,
Yao Ayitey,
EMP: 50
SQ FT: 3,000
SALES: 1.5MM **Privately Held**
SIC: 8082 Home health care services

(G-9435)
FIRST DAY FINCL FEDERAL CR UN (PA)
1030 N Main St (45405-4212)
P.O. Box 407 (45405-0407)
PHONE..............................937 222-4546
Ben Roth, *President*
EMP: 30 **EST:** 1934
SQ FT: 6,000
SALES (est): 4.3MM **Privately Held**
SIC: 6061 6162 Federal credit unions; mortgage bankers & correspondents

(G-9436)
FIRST MENTAL RETARDATION CORP
2080 N Gettysburg Ave (45406-3562)
PHONE..............................937 262-3077
Janice Smith, *CEO*
EMP: 28
SALES: 17.9K **Privately Held**
SIC: 8361 Residential care

(G-9437)
FIRST SCHOOL CORP
7659 Mcewen Rd (45459-3907)
PHONE..............................937 433-3455
Mark Stone, *President*
EMP: 26 **EST:** 1971
SQ FT: 6,000
SALES (est): 794K **Privately Held**
SIC: 8351 8211 Preschool center; elementary & secondary schools

(G-9438)
FIRST STUDENT INC
4750 Sue Ann Blvd (45415-1167)
P.O. Box 49, Marysville (43040-0049)
PHONE..............................937 645-0201
Kim Scharf, *Manager*
EMP: 25
SALES (corp-wide): 8.9B **Privately Held**
WEB: www.leag.com
SIC: 4151 School buses
HQ: First Student, Inc.
    600 Vine St Ste 1400
    Cincinnati OH 45202

(G-9439)
FISHEL COMPANY
7651 Center Point 70 Blvd (45424-5193)
PHONE..............................937 233-2268
Tim Griffin, *Area Mgr*
Chris Sands, *Manager*
EMP: 110
SALES (corp-wide): 434.8MM **Privately Held**
WEB: www.fishelco.com
SIC: 1623 1794 Gas main construction; excavation work
PA: The Fishel Company
    1366 Dublin Rd
    Columbus OH 43215
    614 274-8100

(G-9440)
FIVE RIVERS HEALTH CENTERS (PA)
2261 Philadelphia Dr # 200 (45406-1814)
PHONE..............................937 734-6841
Gina McFarlane-El, *CEO*
Thomas Duncan, *President*
Ann Schuerman, *Principal*
David Bridge, *CFO*
EMP: 31
SALES: 15.9MM **Privately Held**
SIC: 8011 Clinic, operated by physicians

(G-9441)
FIVE SEASONS SPT CNTRY CLB INC
4242 Clyo Rd (45440-6101)
PHONE..............................937 848-9200
Bruce Stapleton, *Manager*
EMP: 100 **Privately Held**
WEB: www.fiveseasonsday.com
SIC: 7997 7941 Country club, membership; sports clubs, managers & promoters
HQ: Five Seasons Sports Country Club, Inc.
    100 E Rivercenter Blvd # 1100
    Covington KY 41011

(G-9442)
FLANAGAN LBERMAN HOFFMAN SWAIM
15 W 4th St Ste 100　(45402-2019)
PHONE..................................937 223-5200
Patrick A Flanagan, *Partner*
Thomas Angelo, *Partner*
Charles Geidner, *Partner*
Robert Goelz, *Partner*
David Grieshop, *Partner*
EMP: 45
SQ FT: 11,000
SALES (est): 5.2MM **Privately Held**
WEB: www.flhslaw.com
SIC: 8111　General practice attorney, lawyer

(G-9443)
FOODLINER INC
5560 Brentlinger Dr　(45414-3510)
PHONE..................................937 898-0075
Lowell Stepp, *Branch Mgr*
EMP: 34
SALES (corp-wide): 105.7MM **Privately Held**
SIC: 4213　Trucking, except local
PA: Foodliner, Inc.
　　2099 Southpark Ct Ste 1
　　Dubuque IA 52003
　　563 584-2670

(G-9444)
FOODLINER INC
5560 Brentlinger Dr　(45414-3510)
PHONE..................................563 451-1047
Lowell Stepp, *Manager*
EMP: 25
SALES (corp-wide): 105.7MM **Privately Held**
SIC: 4213　Contract haulers
PA: Foodliner, Inc.
　　2099 Southpark Ct Ste 1
　　Dubuque IA 52003
　　563 584-2670

(G-9445)
FORRER DEVELOPMENT LTD
7625 Paragon Rd Ste E　(45459-4063)
PHONE..................................937 431-6489
David Nianouris, *President*
EMP: 30
SQ FT: 100,000
SALES: 250K **Privately Held**
SIC: 6552　Land subdividers & developers, residential

(G-9446)
FOUNDATION FOR COMMUNIT (PA)
349 S Main St　(45402-2715)
PHONE..................................937 461-3450
David M Smith, *CEO*
Jodi L Minneman, *COO*
Diane L Wilson, *COO*
Kristine Belanger, *Vice Pres*
Trina Pearson, *Materials Mgr*
EMP: 250
SQ FT: 110,000
SALES: 0　**Privately Held**
SIC: 8099　Blood bank; organ bank

(G-9447)
FOX CLEANERS INC (PA)
4333 N Main St　(45405-5035)
PHONE..................................937 276-4171
John Roberts, *President*
EMP: 72
SQ FT: 30,000
SALES (est): 2.7MM **Privately Held**
SIC: 7216　7215　Drycleaning plants, except rugs; laundry, coin-operated

(G-9448)
FRANCISCAN AT ST LEONARD
8100 Clyo Rd　(45458-2720)
PHONE..................................937 433-0480
Mary Houston, *Manager*
Timothy Dressman, *Exec Dir*
Jack Harless, *Director*
Joe Thibodeau, *Director*
EMP: 360
SALES (est): 8.7MM **Privately Held**
WEB: www.stleonard.net
SIC: 8059　8052　Personal care home, with health care; intermediate care facilities

(G-9449)
FRANKLIN IRON & METAL CORP
1939 E 1st St　(45403-1131)
PHONE..................................937 253-8184
Jack Edelman, *President*
Debra Edelman, *Treasurer*
▲ EMP: 105
SQ FT: 60,000
SALES (est): 50.7MM **Privately Held**
SIC: 5093　3341　3312　Ferrous metal scrap & waste; secondary nonferrous metals; blast furnaces & steel mills

(G-9450)
FREEZE/ARNOLD A FREUND LEGAL (PA)
1 S Main St Ste 1800　(45402-2043)
PHONE..................................937 222-2424
Neil F Freund, *CEO*
Stephen V Freeze, *President*
Thomas B Bruns, *Vice Pres*
Wayne E Waite, *Treasurer*
John J Garvey Jr, *Admin Sec*
EMP: 90
SQ FT: 40,000
SALES (est): 18.4MM **Privately Held**
WEB: www.ffalaw.com
SIC: 8111　General practice attorney, lawyer

(G-9451)
FRITO-LAY NORTH AMERICA INC
49 Kelly Ave　(45404-1256)
PHONE..................................937 224-8716
John Dean, *Manager*
EMP: 42
SALES (corp-wide): 64.6B **Publicly Held**
WEB: www.fritolay.com
SIC: 5145　Snack foods
HQ: Frito-Lay North America, Inc.
　　7701 Legacy Dr
　　Plano TX 75024

(G-9452)
FRYMAN-KUCK GENERAL CONTRS INC
5150 Webster St　(45414-4228)
P.O. Box 13655　(45413-0655)
PHONE..................................937 274-2892
Paul Kuck, *President*
Kent Kuck, *Vice Pres*
Kurt Kuck, *Vice Pres*
Randy Kuck, *Vice Pres*
Amber Henderson, *Safety Dir*
EMP: 50　EST: 1945
SALES: 3.2MM **Privately Held**
WEB: www.fryman-kuck.com
SIC: 1542　1541　1629　1622　Commercial & office buildings, renovation & repair; commercial & office building, new construction; religious building construction; school building construction; renovation, remodeling & repairs; industrial buildings; industrial buildings, new construction; waste water & sewage treatment plant construction; highway construction, elevated; general contractor, highway & street construction

(G-9453)
FUTURA DESIGN SERVICE INC
6001 N Dixie Dr　(45414-4017)
PHONE..................................937 890-5252
Dennis Tresslar, *President*
EMP: 25
SQ FT: 6,500
SALES (est): 2.7MM **Privately Held**
SIC: 8711　Engineering services

(G-9454)
FUYAO GLASS AMERICA INC (HQ)
2801 W Stroop Rd　(45439)
PHONE..................................937 496-5777
Frank Welling, *President*
EMP: 228　EST: 2014
SALES (est): 172.4MM
SALES (corp-wide): 2.9B **Privately Held**
SIC: 3231　5013　Products of purchased glass; automobile glass
PA: Fuyao Glass Industry Group Co., Ltd.
　　Fuyao Industry Area
　　Fuqing　35030
　　591 853-8377

(G-9455)
G7 SERVICES INC
Also Called: ServiceMaster By Angler
1524 E 2nd St　(45403-1025)
PHONE..................................937 256-3473
Geoffrey Ganz, *President*
Mark Gerken, *Vice Pres*
EMP: 40
SALES (est): 1.5MM **Privately Held**
SIC: 7349　Building maintenance services

(G-9456)
GE AVIATION SYSTEMS LLC
111 River Park Dr　(45409-2109)
PHONE..................................937 474-9397
EMP: 99
SALES (est): 8MM **Privately Held**
SIC: 8711　Engineering Services

(G-9457)
GEM CITY WATERPROOFING
1424 Stanley Ave　(45404-1111)
PHONE..................................937 220-6800
Mike Ferraro, *Owner*
EMP: 30
SALES (est): 837K **Privately Held**
SIC: 1799　Waterproofing

(G-9458)
GENERAL ELECTRIC COMPANY
950 Forrer Blvd　(45420-1469)
P.O. Box 8726　(45401-8726)
PHONE..................................937 534-6920
Glen Marino, *Division Pres*
EMP: 1200
SALES (corp-wide): 121.6B **Publicly Held**
WEB: www.gecommercialfinance.com
SIC: 7389　6153　Packaging & labeling services; short-term business credit
PA: General Electric Company
　　41 Farnsworth St
　　Boston MA 02210
　　617 443-3000

(G-9459)
GENERAL ELECTRIC COMPANY
950 Forrer Blvd　(45420-1469)
PHONE..................................937 534-2000
Bill Ellingwood, *Manager*
EMP: 48
SALES (corp-wide): 121.6B **Publicly Held**
WEB: www.gecapital.com
SIC: 6153　Short-term business credit
PA: General Electric Company
　　41 Farnsworth St
　　Boston MA 02210
　　617 443-3000

(G-9460)
GERMAIN & CO INC
Also Called: Germane Solutions
10552 Success Ln Ste A　(45458-3664)
PHONE..................................937 885-5827
Art Boll, *CEO*
James Brown, *President*
Thomas Gentile, *Principal*
Bruce Deighton, *Vice Pres*
Matthew McCumber, *Vice Pres*
EMP: 25
SALES (est): 2MM **Privately Held**
SIC: 8742　Hospital & health services consultant

(G-9461)
GLOBAL GRAPHENE GROUP INC
1240 Mccook Ave　(45404-1059)
PHONE..................................937 331-9884
Bor Jang, *CEO*
Jennifer Smallwood, *Controller*
Aruna Zhamu, *CTO*
EMP: 40　EST: 2016　**Privately Held**
SIC: 6719　Investment holding companies, except banks

(G-9462)
GLOBAL GVRNMENT EDCATN SLTIONS
6450 Poe Ave Ste 200　(45414-2655)
PHONE..................................937 368-2308
Richard Leeds, *President*
Steve Goldschein, *Vice Pres*
Curt Rush, *Treasurer*
Shanda Deeter, *Accounts Mgr*
Jessica Gerlach, *Accounts Exec*
EMP: 70
SQ FT: 275,000
SALES: 36MM **Publicly Held**
WEB: www.globalgoved.com
SIC: 5045　Computer peripheral equipment
PA: Systemax Inc.
　　11 Harbor Park Dr
　　Port Washington NY 11050

(G-9463)
GMS INC
Also Called: United Building Materials
1509 Stanley Ave　(45404-1112)
PHONE..................................937 222-4444
Ray Zawadzki, *Vice Pres*
David Stawser, *Branch Mgr*
EMP: 30
SALES (corp-wide): 2.5B **Publicly Held**
SIC: 5211　5032　Lumber products; drywall materials
PA: Gms Inc.
　　100 Crescent Center Pkwy
　　Tucker GA 30084
　　800 392-4619

(G-9464)
GOODWILL ESTER SEALS MIAMI VLY (PA)
Also Called: EASTER SEAL
660 S Main St　(45402-2708)
PHONE..................................937 461-4800
Lance W Detrick, *President*
Denise Watts, *General Mgr*
Roger Baldridge, *District Mgr*
Kathy Rearick, *Vice Pres*
Rodney Perkins, *Opers Mgr*
EMP: 210
SQ FT: 105,000
SALES: 46.1MM **Privately Held**
WEB: www.ohiogoodwills.org
SIC: 8331　Vocational rehabilitation agency

(G-9465)
GOODWILL ESTER SEALS MIAMI VLY
Goodwill Inds of Miami Vly
660 S Main St　(45402-2708)
PHONE..................................937 461-4800
Amy Luttrell, *COO*
David Burrows, *Vice Pres*
Steve Couturier, *Director*
Kathy Trick, *Director*
EMP: 300
SALES (corp-wide): 46.1MM **Privately Held**
WEB: www.ohiogoodwills.org
SIC: 4225　General warehousing & storage
PA: Easter Goodwill Seals Miami Valley
　　660 S Main St
　　Dayton OH 45402
　　937 461-4800

(G-9466)
GOSIGER INC (PA)
108 Mcdonough St　(45402-2267)
P.O. Box 533　(45401-0533)
PHONE..................................937 228-5174
Peter G Haley, *Managing Prtnr*
John Haley, *Managing Prtnr*
Bill Dymond, *General Mgr*
Jane Haley, *Chairman*
Josh Collins, *Regional Mgr*
◆ EMP: 130
SQ FT: 60,000
SALES (est): 140.8MM **Privately Held**
WEB: www.gosiger.com
SIC: 5084　Machine tools & accessories

(G-9467)
GOSIGER INC
108 Mcdonough St　(45402-2267)
P.O. Box 533　(45401-0533)
PHONE..................................937 228-5174
Jerry Pressel, *Branch Mgr*
EMP: 100
SALES (corp-wide): 140.8MM **Privately Held**
WEB: www.gosiger.com
SIC: 5084　Machine tools & accessories
PA: Gosiger, Inc.
　　108 Mcdonough St
　　Dayton OH 45402
　　937 228-5174

(G-9468)
GRACEWORKS LUTHERAN SERVICES
Also Called: Bethany Village Linden
6443 Bethany Village Dr (45459-3571)
PHONE............................937 436-6850
John Brinkman, *Administration*
EMP: 500
SALES (corp-wide): 45.6MM **Privately Held**
SIC: 8082 Home health care services
PA: Graceworks Lutheran Services
6430 Inner Mission Way
Dayton OH 45459
937 433-2140

(G-9469)
GRACEWORKS LUTHERAN SERVICES (PA)
6430 Inner Mission Way (45459-7400)
PHONE............................937 433-2140
Willis O Serr II, *President*
Michael W Allen, *Vice Pres*
EMP: 550
SQ FT: 250,000
SALES: 45.6MM **Privately Held**
SIC: 8051 Skilled nursing care facilities

(G-9470)
GRACEWORKS LUTHERAN SERVICES
6430 Inner Mission Way (45459-7400)
PHONE............................937 433-2110
Michael Allen, *Branch Mgr*
EMP: 118
SALES (corp-wide): 45.6MM **Privately Held**
SIC: 8322 Individual & family services
PA: Graceworks Lutheran Services
6430 Inner Mission Way
Dayton OH 45459
937 433-2140

(G-9471)
GREATER DAYTON MVG & STOR CO
3516 Wright Way Rd Ste 2 (45424-5164)
PHONE............................937 235-0011
Ira Morgan, *President*
Orville Morgan Sr, *Chairman*
EMP: 50
SQ FT: 6,000
SALES (est): 5MM **Privately Held**
SIC: 4214 4213 4212 Household goods moving & storage, local; household goods transport; moving services

(G-9472)
GREATER DAYTON PUBLIC TV (PA)
Also Called: THINK TV
110 S Jefferson St (45402-2402)
PHONE............................937 220-1600
David M Fogarty, *President*
Sue Brinson, *Editor*
Kitty Lensman, *COO*
Mike Miller, *Financial Exec*
Diane Kroplin, *Manager*
EMP: 90
SQ FT: 24,500
SALES: 5MM **Privately Held**
SIC: 4833 Television broadcasting stations

(G-9473)
GREATER DAYTON SURGERY CTR LLC
1625 Delco Park Dr (45420-1391)
PHONE............................937 535-2200
Todd Evans, *Exec Dir*
Norbert Mertzman, *Director*
Larry Fischer, *Administration*
Atul Balwally,
Ronald Devore,
EMP: 35
SQ FT: 15,000
SALES (est): 6.3MM **Privately Held**
WEB: www.daytonsurgerycenter.com
SIC: 8011 Surgeon

(G-9474)
GREATER DYTON RGNAL TRNST AUTH (PA)
Also Called: R T A
4 S Main St Ste C (45402-2052)
PHONE............................937 425-8310
Mark Donaghy, *CEO*
Robert Ruzinsky, *General Mgr*
Joann Oliver, *Purch Agent*
Mary K Stanforth, *CFO*
Allison Ledford, *Human Res Dir*
EMP: 100
SALES: 8.5MM **Privately Held**
WEB: www.mvrta.org
SIC: 4111 Bus line operations

(G-9475)
GREATER DYTON RGNAL TRNST AUTH
Also Called: Recruiting Department
600 Cmpus 600 Lngworth St 600 Longworth (45401)
PHONE............................937 425-8400
EMP: 614
SALES (corp-wide): 8.5MM **Privately Held**
SIC: 7361 Employment agencies
PA: Greater Dayton Regional Transit Authority
4 S Main St Ste C
Dayton OH 45402
937 425-8310

(G-9476)
GREATER DYTON RGNAL TRNST AUTH
Also Called: Recruiting Department
600 Cmpus 600 Lngworth St 600 Longworth (45401)
PHONE............................937 425-8400
EMP: 614
SALES (corp-wide): 8.5MM **Privately Held**
SIC: 4131 Intercity & rural bus transportation
PA: Greater Dayton Regional Transit Authority
4 S Main St Ste C
Dayton OH 45402
937 425-8310

(G-9477)
GREENTREE GROUP INC (PA)
1360 Tech Ct Ste 100 (45430)
PHONE............................937 490-5500
Travis Greenwood, *CEO*
Samuel Greenwood, *Ch of Bd*
Rick Daprato, *Principal*
Tammy Whitaker, *Business Mgr*
Carolyn Greenwood, *CFO*
EMP: 65
SQ FT: 25,000
SALES (est): 19.3MM **Privately Held**
SIC: 7379 8742 Computer related maintenance services; management consulting services

(G-9478)
GS1 US INC
7887 Wash Vlg Dr Ste 300 (45459-3988)
PHONE............................609 620-0200
Laura Incorvia, *Human Resources*
Mandy Kaiser, *Supervisor*
Joe Gesior, *Admin Asst*
EMP: 60
SALES (corp-wide): 52.1MM **Privately Held**
WEB: www.uniformcodecouncil.com
SIC: 8611 Trade associations
PA: Gs1 Us, Inc.
300 Charles Ewing Blvd
Ewing NJ 08628
937 435-3870

(G-9479)
GYPC INC
Also Called: Marquette Group
475 Stonehaven Rd (45429-1645)
PHONE............................309 677-0405
Christopher F Cummings, *CEO*
Chris Cummings, *CEO*
Eric Webb, *President*
Theresa Lafontaine, *CFO*
EMP: 225

SALES (est): 60.4MM **Privately Held**
WEB: www.mqgroup.com
SIC: 7311 Advertising consultant

(G-9480)
H & R CONCRETE INC
9120 State Route 48 (45458-5127)
PHONE............................937 885-2910
Hershell Williams, *President*
Rick Williams, *Vice Pres*
Carol Ferrell, *Admin Sec*
EMP: 35
SQ FT: 480
SALES (est): 4.9MM **Privately Held**
SIC: 1771 1794 Concrete work; excavation work

(G-9481)
HADASSAH DAYTON CHAPTER
880 Fernshire Dr (45459-2310)
PHONE............................937 275-0227
Dena Briskin, *Principal*
EMP: 30 EST: 2003
SALES (est): 990K **Privately Held**
SIC: 8699 Charitable organization

(G-9482)
HAFENBRACK MKTG CMMNCTIONS INC
Also Called: Genessa Health Marketing
116 E 3rd St (45402-2130)
PHONE............................937 424-8950
Dave Hafenbrack, *President*
Hans Wagner, *Principal*
Elise Hafenbrack, *Vice Pres*
EMP: 26
SQ FT: 3,000
SALES (est): 2.3MM **Privately Held**
SIC: 8742 Marketing consulting services

(G-9483)
HAHN AUTOMOTIVE WAREHOUSE INC
Also Called: Genuine Auto Parts 864
32 Franklin St (45402-2633)
P.O. Box 2909 (45401-2909)
PHONE............................937 223-1068
Rick Bowman, *Sales Mgr*
Rob Zimmer, *Manager*
EMP: 30
SALES (corp-wide): 292.6MM **Privately Held**
WEB: www.iautoparts.com
SIC: 5013 5531 Automotive supplies & parts; automotive parts
PA: Hahn Automotive Warehouse, Inc.
415 W Main St
Rochester NY 14608
585 235-1595

(G-9484)
HAND CTR AT ORTHOPAEDIC INST
3205 Woodman Dr (45420-1143)
PHONE............................937 298-4417
Pam Hough, *Office Mgr*
Todd Evans, *Administration*
EMP: 60
SALES (est): 871.7K **Privately Held**
SIC: 8011 Orthopedic physician

(G-9485)
HANS ZWART MD & ASSOCIATES (PA)
1520 S Main St Ste 3 (45409-2643)
PHONE............................937 433-4183
Jeffrey K Hoffman, *President*
Jeffrey Hoffman MD, *President*
EMP: 40
SALES (est): 2MM **Privately Held**
WEB: www.mail2.erint.com
SIC: 8011 Medical Doctor's Office

(G-9486)
HARBORSIDE HEALTHCARE CORP
Also Called: Laurelwood, The
3797 Summit Glen Dr Frnt (45449-3663)
PHONE............................937 436-6155
Deborah Schott, *Branch Mgr*
EMP: 70 **Publicly Held**
WEB: www.harborsideuniversity.com
SIC: 8741 Hospital management; nursing & personal care facility management

HQ: Harborside Healthcare Corporation
5100 Sun Ave Ne
Albuquerque NM 87109

(G-9487)
HAVEN BHAVIORAL HEALTHCARE INC
1 Elizabeth Pl Ste A (45417-3445)
PHONE............................937 234-0100
EMP: 447 **Privately Held**
SIC: 8322 Senior citizens' center or association
PA: Haven Behavioral Healthcare, Inc.
3102 West End Ave # 1000
Nashville TN 37203

(G-9488)
HDI LTD
Also Called: Crowne Plaza Dayton
33 E 5th St (45402-2403)
PHONE............................937 224-0800
Don Bramer, *Partner*
EMP: 135
SALES (est): 5.9MM **Privately Held**
WEB: www.cpdayton.com
SIC: 7011 Hotels

(G-9489)
HEALING TOUCH HEALTHCARE
627 S Edwin C Moses Blvd 3l (45417-3461)
PHONE............................937 610-5555
Faisal M Ali, *Principal*
Fahad Ali, *Director*
EMP: 35
SALES (est): 1.4MM **Privately Held**
SIC: 8082 Home health care services

(G-9490)
HEALTH CARE RTREMENT CORP AMER
Also Called: Heartland of Kettering
3313 Wilmington Pike (45429-4023)
PHONE............................937 298-8084
Jennifer Woodward, *Administration*
EMP: 107
SQ FT: 26,152
SALES (corp-wide): 2.4B **Publicly Held**
WEB: www.hrc-manorcare.com
SIC: 8051 Skilled nursing care facilities
HQ: Health Care And Retirement Corporation Of America
333 N Summit St Ste 103
Toledo OH 43604
419 252-5500

(G-9491)
HEALTHSOUTH
1 Elizabeth Pl (45417-3445)
PHONE............................937 424-8200
John Pierson, *CEO*
EMP: 102
SALES (est): 7.8MM **Privately Held**
WEB: www.daytonrehab.com
SIC: 8069 Specialty hospitals, except psychiatric

(G-9492)
HEARTLAND HOSPICE SERVICES LLC
Also Called: Heartland HM Hlth Care Hospice
580 Lincoln Park Blvd # 320 (45429-3493)
PHONE............................937 299-6980
Stephanie Rich, *Administration*
EMP: 25
SALES (corp-wide): 2.4B **Publicly Held**
SIC: 8082 Home health care services
HQ: Heartland Hospice Services, Llc
333 N Summit St
Toledo OH 43604

(G-9493)
HEARTSPRING HOME HLTH CARE LLC
1251 E Dorothy Ln (45419-2106)
PHONE............................937 531-6920
EMP: 90
SALES (est): 2.4MM **Privately Held**
SIC: 8099 Health/Allied Services

(G-9494)
HEIDER CLEANERS INC
3720 Wilmington Pike (45429-4856)
PHONE............................937 298-6631
Joseph F Heider, *President*

Francis J Heider, *Exec VP*
Rita Heider, *Vice Pres*
Joan Rauch, *Admin Sec*
EMP: 26
SQ FT: 7,000
SALES (est): 1MM **Privately Held**
WEB: www.heidercleaners.com
SIC: 7216 Curtain cleaning & repair

(G-9495)
HEYMAN RALPH E ATTORNEY AT LAW
10 N Ludlow St (45402-1854)
PHONE...............................937 449-2820
Ralph E Heyman, *Partner*
Richard Chernasky, *Partner*
EMP: 60
SALES (est): 2.8MM **Privately Held**
SIC: 8111 General practice attorney, lawyer

(G-9496)
HIGH VOLTAGE MAINTENANCE CORP (DH)
Also Called: Vertiv
5100 Energy Dr (45414-3525)
P.O. Box 13059 (45413-0059)
PHONE...............................937 278-0811
Charles S Helldoerfer, *President*
Thomas E Nation, *Vice Pres*
EMP: 35 **EST:** 1966
SQ FT: 10,000
SALES (est): 25.7MM
SALES (corp-wide): 2.1B **Privately Held**
WEB: www.hvmcorp.com
SIC: 8734 8711 Testing laboratories; electrical or electronic engineering
HQ: Vertiv Group Corporation
1050 Dearborn Dr
Columbus OH 43085
614 888-0246

(G-9497)
HOLIDAY INN EXPRESS
5655 Wilmington Pike (45459-7102)
PHONE...............................937 424-5757
Angela Shockley, *Director*
EMP: 28
SALES (est): 1.3MM **Privately Held**
SIC: 7011 Hotels & motels

(G-9498)
HOME CARE NETWORK INC (PA)
190 E Spring Valley Pike A (45458-3803)
PHONE...............................937 435-1142
Betty Martin, *President*
Betty Adams, *Vice Pres*
Todd Tobe, *Info Tech Dir*
Carter Ledbetter, *Director*
Lisa D Priest, *Admin Asst*
EMP: 79
SALES (est): 21MM **Privately Held**
SIC: 8082 7361 Visiting nurse service; nurses' registry

(G-9499)
HOME DEPOT USA INC
Also Called: Home Depot, The
345 N Springboro Pike (45449-3644)
PHONE...............................937 312-9053
Darryl Sanders, *Manager*
EMP: 123
SALES (corp-wide): 108.2B **Publicly Held**
WEB: www.homerentalsdepot.com
SIC: 5211 7359 Home centers; tool rental
HQ: Home Depot U.S.A., Inc.
2455 Paces Ferry Ave
Atlanta GA 30339

(G-9500)
HOME DEPOT USA INC
Also Called: Home Depot, The
5860 Wilmington Pike (45459-7004)
PHONE...............................937 312-9076
Kelly Cassidy, *Manager*
EMP: 130
SALES (corp-wide): 108.2B **Publicly Held**
WEB: www.homerentalsdepot.com
SIC: 5211 7359 Home centers; tool rental
HQ: Home Depot U.S.A., Inc.
2455 Paces Ferry Ave
Atlanta GA 30339

(G-9501)
HOME DEPOT USA INC
Also Called: Home Depot, The
5200 Salem Ave Unit A (45426-1700)
PHONE...............................937 837-1551
Rick Goodrich, *President*
Julie Bradley, *Manager*
EMP: 100
SALES (corp-wide): 108.2B **Publicly Held**
WEB: www.homerentalsdepot.com
SIC: 5211 7359 Home centers; tool rental
HQ: Home Depot U.S.A., Inc.
2455 Paces Ferry Ave
Atlanta GA 30339

(G-9502)
HOME TOWN REALTORS LLC
9201 N Dixie Dr (45414-1862)
PHONE...............................937 890-9111
Keller Williams,
EMP: 75
SALES (est): 2.4MM **Privately Held**
SIC: 6531 Real estate agents & managers

(G-9503)
HOMEFULL
33 W 1st St Ste 100 (45402-1243)
PHONE...............................937 293-1945
Steve Cartright, *Principal*
Russell W Morgan, *Principal*
Karen M Shepler, *Principal*
Candace High, *CFO*
Tina Patterson, *Exec Dir*
EMP: 70
SALES (est): 3.9MM **Privately Held**
WEB: www.theotherplace.org
SIC: 8322 Emergency shelters

(G-9504)
HOMETOWN URGENT CARE
6210 Brandt Pike (45424-4019)
PHONE...............................937 236-8630
Lisa Kay, *Branch Mgr*
EMP: 173
SALES (corp-wide): 73.2MM **Privately Held**
SIC: 8011 Medical centers
PA: Hometown Urgent Care
2400 Corp Exchange Dr # 102
Columbus OH 43231
614 505-7633

(G-9505)
HORENSTEIN NICHO & BLUME A L
124 E 3rd St Fl 5 (45402-2186)
PHONE...............................937 224-7200
Steven V Hornstein, *Partner*
Gary Blumenthal, *Partner*
Bruce Nicholson, *Partner*
Wilbur S Lang, *Principal*
Bobbie Peed, *Info Tech Mgr*
EMP: 38
SALES (est): 4.4MM **Privately Held**
WEB: www.hnb-law.com
SIC: 8111 General practice law office; general practice attorney, lawyer

(G-9506)
HORIZON PAYROLL SERVICES INC
2700 Miamisburg Centervil (45459-3705)
P.O. Box 751053 (45475-1053)
PHONE...............................937 434-8244
Marilynne Saliwanchik, *President*
Alan Saliwanchik, *Vice Pres*
Stephanie Webster, *Opers Mgr*
Becky Sortman, *Tax Mgr*
Linda Smidl, *HR Admin*
EMP: 300
SQ FT: 3,000
SALES: 40MM **Privately Held**
WEB: www.gohorizon.com
SIC: 7371 5045 Custom computer programming services; computers, peripherals & software

(G-9507)
HOSS VALUE CARS & TRUCKS INC (PA)
Also Called: Voss Hyundai
766 Mmsburg Cnterville Rd (45459)
PHONE...............................937 428-2400
John E Voss, *President*

Jeff Tarzinski, *Sales Mgr*
Treva Littleton, *Administration*
EMP: 49
SALES (est): 12.2MM **Privately Held**
WEB: www.vosshyundai.com
SIC: 5511 7538 Automobiles, new & used; general automotive repair shops

(G-9508)
HUBER HEIGHTS YMCA
7251 Shull Rd (45424-1234)
PHONE...............................937 236-9622
Josh Sullenberger, *Principal*
Cindy Edwards, *Exec Dir*
EMP: 64
SALES (est): 709.9K **Privately Held**
SIC: 8641 7991 8351 7032 Youth organizations; physical fitness facilities; child day care services; youth camps; individual & family services

(G-9509)
HUBER INVESTMENT CORPORATION (PA)
5550 Huber Rd (45424-2099)
PHONE...............................937 233-1122
Charles H Huber, *President*
Terry Huber, *Vice Pres*
Rich Williams, *Admin Sec*
EMP: 50
SQ FT: 1,552
SALES (est): 4.3MM **Privately Held**
SIC: 6514 6513 Residential building, four or fewer units: operation; apartment building operators

(G-9510)
HUFFMAN HEALTH CARE INC
Also Called: Livingston Care Center
20 Livingston Ave (45403-2938)
PHONE...............................937 476-1000
Harold Sosna, *President*
EMP: 105
SALES: 5.7MM **Privately Held**
SIC: 8051 Skilled nursing care facilities

(G-9511)
IHEARTCOMMUNICATIONS INC
Also Called: Wize-AM
101 Pine St (45402-2948)
PHONE...............................937 224-1137
Lisa Rice, *President*
EMP: 50 **Publicly Held**
SIC: 4832 Radio broadcasting stations
HQ: Iheartcommunications, Inc.
20880 Stone Oak Pkwy
San Antonio TX 78258
210 822-2828

(G-9512)
IHEARTCOMMUNICATIONS INC
Also Called: Wxeg-FM
101 Pine St Ste 300 (45402-2948)
PHONE...............................937 224-1137
Nick Gnau, *Sales Mgr*
Robert Zuroweste, *Manager*
EMP: 150 **Publicly Held**
SIC: 4832 7313 Radio broadcasting stations; radio advertising representative
HQ: Iheartcommunications, Inc.
20880 Stone Oak Pkwy
San Antonio TX 78258
210 822-2828

(G-9513)
IMPACT SALES INC
2501 Neff Rd (45414-5001)
PHONE...............................937 274-1905
Carl Pennington, *Manager*
EMP: 95
SALES (corp-wide): 56.1MM **Privately Held**
SIC: 5141 Food brokers
PA: Impact Sales, Inc.
915 W Jefferson St Ste A
Boise ID 83702
208 343-5800

(G-9514)
INDUSTRIAL FIBERGLASS SPC INC
Also Called: Fiber Systems
521 Kiser St (45404-1641)
PHONE...............................937 222-9000
Theodore Morton, *Ch of Bd*
Diana Hall, *President*

Janice Morton, *Corp Secy*
Diana Partin, *Purchasing*
Rose Marie Wiliams, *Accounting Mgr*
EMP: 35 **EST:** 1978
SQ FT: 122,000
SALES (est): 5.9MM **Privately Held**
WEB: www.ifs-frp.com
SIC: 3229 1799 Glass fiber products; service station equipment installation, maintenance & repair

(G-9515)
INTEGRATED DATA SERVICES INC
111 Harries St Apt 202 (45402-1889)
PHONE...............................937 656-5496
Jerry W Murray, *Principal*
EMP: 57
SALES (corp-wide): 15.1MM **Privately Held**
SIC: 7374 Data processing service
PA: Integrated Data Services, Inc.
2141 Rosecrans Ave # 2050
El Segundo CA 90245
310 647-3439

(G-9516)
INTEGRATED SOLUTIONS AND
1430 Yankee Park Pl (45458-1829)
PHONE...............................513 826-1932
Clarence McGill, *President*
Vernice Taylor, *Vice Pres*
EMP: 27
SALES (est): 3.2MM **Privately Held**
WEB: www.iss-unlimited.com
SIC: 7379 8748 Computer related consulting services; business consulting

(G-9517)
INTEGRITY HOTEL GROUP
Also Called: Crowne Plaza Dayton Hotel
33 E 5th St (45402-2403)
PHONE...............................937 224-0800
Michael Larsen, *General Mgr*
Abdul Aziz Rupani, *Principal*
Emily Hobler, *Sales Staff*
EMP: 112
SALES: 950K **Privately Held**
SIC: 7011 Hotels

(G-9518)
INTERIM HEALTHCARE OF DAYTON
Also Called: Interim Services
30 W Rahn Rd Ste 2 (45429-2238)
PHONE...............................937 291-5330
Thomas J Dimarco, *President*
Craig Smith,
EMP: 299 **EST:** 1974
SQ FT: 2,500
SALES: 2.4MM
SALES (corp-wide): 19.8MM **Privately Held**
WEB: www.salo.com
SIC: 8082 Home health care services
PA: Salo, Inc.
960 Checkrein Ave Ste A
Columbus OH 43229
614 436-9404

(G-9519)
INTERNTIONAL MOLASSES CORP LTD
4744 Wolf Creek Pike (45417-9436)
PHONE...............................937 276-7980
Doug Harrison, *President*
▲ **EMP:** 30 **EST:** 2000
SALES (est): 9MM **Privately Held**
WEB: www.internationalmolasses.com
SIC: 5149 Molasses, industrial

(G-9520)
INTOWN SUITES MANAGEMENT INC
8981 Kingsridge Dr (45458-1624)
PHONE...............................937 433-9038
Tracey Rahe, *Manager*
EMP: 28 **Privately Held**
SIC: 6513 Apartment hotel operation
HQ: Intown Suites Management, Inc.
980 Hammond Dr Ste 1400
Atlanta GA 30328
800 769-1670

(G-9521)
IRONGATE INC
Also Called: Irongate Inc Realtors
4461 Far Hills Ave (45429-2405)
PHONE..........................937 298-6000
Pat Colman, *Manager*
Bob Wilson, *Manager*
Chip M Haak, *Real Est Agnt*
Michael Palmer, *Real Est Agnt*
EMP: 50
SALES (corp-wide): 12.9MM **Privately Held**
WEB: www.irongate-realtors.com
SIC: 6531 Real estate agents & managers
PA: Irongate, Inc
122 N Main St
Centerville OH 45459
937 433-3300

(G-9522)
IRONGATE INC
1353 Lyons Rd (45458-1822)
PHONE..........................937 432-3432
Steven Brown, *President*
Sydney Long, *Broker*
Patty Sonovick-Neeley, *Real Est Agnt*
EMP: 95
SALES (est): 3.4MM
SALES (corp-wide): 12.9MM **Privately Held**
WEB: www.irongate-realtors.com
SIC: 6531 Real estate brokers & agents
PA: Irongate, Inc
122 N Main St
Centerville OH 45459
937 433-3300

(G-9523)
JAMES L JACOBSON
40 N Main St Ste 2700 (45423-1005)
PHONE..........................937 223-1130
Andy Storar, *Principal*
EMP: 50
SALES (est): 1.2MM **Privately Held**
SIC: 8111 General practice attorney, lawyer

(G-9524)
JET EXPRESS INC (PA)
4518 Webster St (45414-4940)
PHONE..........................937 274-7033
Kevin Burch, *President*
Greg Atkinson, *Vice Pres*
Roger Atkinson Jr, *Vice Pres*
Amy Hogan, *Treasurer*
Archie Crawford, *Director*
EMP: 60
SQ FT: 36,000
SALES (est): 22.3MM **Privately Held**
WEB: www.jetexpressinc.com
SIC: 4212 4213 Local trucking, without storage; trucking, except local

(G-9525)
JEWISH FDRTION OF GRTER DAYTON
Also Called: Covenant House
4911 Covenant House Dr (45426-2007)
PHONE..........................937 837-2651
Arthur Cohn, *Manager*
EMP: 95
SALES (corp-wide): 4.9MM **Privately Held**
SIC: 8322 8051 Community center; skilled nursing care facilities
PA: Jewish Federation Of Greater Dayton, Inc
525 Versailles Dr
Dayton OH 45459
937 610-1555

(G-9526)
JOE AND JILL LEWIS INC
Also Called: J & J
716 N Broadway St (45402-6245)
P.O. Box 60183 (45406-0183)
PHONE..........................937 718-8829
Joseph W Lewis, *President*
EMP: 99
SALES: 100K **Privately Held**
SIC: 8331 Job training & vocational rehabilitation services

(G-9527)
JOHN A BECKER CO (PA)
Also Called: Becker Electric Supply
1341 E 4th St (45402-2235)
P.O. Box 247 (45401-0247)
PHONE..........................937 226-1341
Thomas J Becker, *CEO*
David Adkinson, *President*
James Becker, *Vice Pres*
Mark Covey, *Vice Pres*
James Dichito, *Vice Pres*
EMP: 62 EST: 1920
SQ FT: 65,000
SALES (est): 219.3MM **Privately Held**
WEB: www.beckerelectric.com
SIC: 5063 Electrical construction materials; electrical supplies; lighting fixtures; motor controls, starters & relays: electric

(G-9528)
JOHN O BOSTOCK JR
Also Called: Total Carpet & Cleaning Svc
5107 Midway Ave (45417-9068)
PHONE..........................937 263-8540
John O Bostock Jr, *Owner*
EMP: 28
SALES: 300K **Privately Held**
SIC: 7349 Building maintenance services

(G-9529)
JOSLIN DIABETES CENTER INC
1989 Miambrg Ctrvl Rd 2 Ste (45459)
PHONE..........................937 401-7575
Jannene Reibert, *Branch Mgr*
EMP: 25
SALES (corp-wide): 83.7MM **Privately Held**
SIC: 8011 Endocrinologist; diabetes specialist, physician/surgeon
PA: Joslin Diabetes Center, Inc.
1 Joslin Pl
Boston MA 02215
617 732-2400

(G-9530)
JPMORGAN CHASE BANK NAT ASSN
950 Forrer Blvd (45420-1469)
P.O. Box 8726 (45401-8726)
PHONE..........................937 534-8218
Jack Peltier, *Manager*
EMP: 1300
SALES (corp-wide): 131.4B **Publicly Held**
WEB: www.chase.com
SIC: 6021 National commercial banks
HQ: Jpmorgan Chase Bank, National Association
1111 Polaris Pkwy
Columbus OH 43240
614 436-3055

(G-9531)
JYG INNOVATIONS LLC
6450 Poe Ave Ste 103 (45414-2667)
PHONE..........................937 630-3858
Jacqueline Gamblin, *CEO*
EMP: 28
SQ FT: 3,000
SALES: 2.4MM **Privately Held**
SIC: 8742 8748 7371 7379 Management consulting services; systems engineering consultant, ex. computer or professional; custom computer programming services; computer related maintenance services; computer facilities management; clinic, operated by physicians

(G-9532)
KETTERING ADVENTIST HEALTHCARE
1079 W Stroop Rd (45429-1231)
PHONE..........................937 294-1658
Christine Annvandenburgh, *Branch Mgr*
EMP: 43
SALES (corp-wide): 1.7B **Privately Held**
SIC: 8062 General medical & surgical hospitals
PA: Kettering Adventist Healthcare
3535 Southern Blvd
Dayton OH 45429
937 298-4331

(G-9533)
KETTERING ADVENTIST HEALTHCARE
3965 Southern Blvd (45429-1229)
PHONE..........................937 298-4331
EMP: 59
SALES (corp-wide): 1.7B **Privately Held**
SIC: 8062 General medical & surgical hospitals
PA: Kettering Adventist Healthcare
3535 Southern Blvd
Dayton OH 45429
937 298-4331

(G-9534)
KETTERING ADVENTIST HEALTHCARE (PA)
Also Called: KETTERING HEALTH NETWORK
3535 Southern Blvd (45429-1221)
PHONE..........................937 298-4331
Roy Chew, *President*
Ladonna Laventure, *President*
Jeff Liette, *Partner*
Cathy Liesner, *Chief*
Russ Wethell, *Vice Pres*
EMP: 31
SQ FT: 500,000
SALES: 1.7B **Privately Held**
SIC: 8062 General medical & surgical hospitals

(G-9535)
KETTERING ANESTHESIA ASSOC INC
3533 Sthern Blvd Ste 5200 (45429)
PHONE..........................937 298-4331
Laurence J Holland, *President*
EMP: 94
SALES (est): 6.3MM **Privately Held**
SIC: 8011 Anesthesiologist

(G-9536)
KETTERING ANIMAL HOSPITAL INC
1600 Delco Park Dr (45420-1198)
PHONE..........................937 294-5211
Dennis A Kulasa, *President*
Dennis Kulasa, *President*
Dawn M Stiens, *Principal*
Alan Schulze, *Vice Pres*
EMP: 25
SALES (est): 2.1MM **Privately Held**
SIC: 0742 0752 Veterinarian, animal specialties; boarding services, kennels

(G-9537)
KETTERING CITY SCHOOL DISTRICT
Also Called: Kettering School Maintenance
2636 Wilmington Pike (45419-2455)
PHONE..........................937 297-1990
Tom Lee, *Manager*
EMP: 75
SALES (corp-wide): 118.1MM **Privately Held**
WEB: www.kettering.k12.oh.us
SIC: 8211 7349 Public elementary school; building maintenance services
PA: Kettering City School District
3750 Far Hills Ave
Dayton OH 45429
937 499-1400

(G-9538)
KETTERING CITY SCHOOL DISTRICT
Also Called: Transportation Dept
2640 Wilmington Pike (45419-2455)
PHONE..........................937 499-1770
Dan Girbin, *General Mgr*
EMP: 81
SALES (corp-wide): 118.1MM **Privately Held**
WEB: www.kettering.k12.oh.us
SIC: 8211 4789 Public elementary & secondary schools; cargo loading & unloading services
PA: Kettering City School District
3750 Far Hills Ave
Dayton OH 45429
937 499-1400

(G-9539)
KETTERING MEDICAL CENTER
Also Called: Kettering College Medical Art
3535 Southern Blvd (45429-1298)
PHONE..........................937 298-4331
Frank Perez, *CEO*
EMP: 50
SALES (corp-wide): 1.7B **Privately Held**
WEB: www.kmcfoundation.org
SIC: 8062 General medical & surgical hospitals
HQ: Kettering Medical Center
3535 Southern Blvd
Kettering OH 45429
937 298-4331

(G-9540)
KETTERING MEDICAL CENTER
Also Called: Kbec Sugarcreek Health Center
580 Lincoln Park Blvd # 200 (45429-3474)
PHONE..........................937 299-0099
Julie Hilman, *Branch Mgr*
EMP: 50
SALES (corp-wide): 1.7B **Privately Held**
WEB: www.kmcfoundation.org
SIC: 8062 General medical & surgical hospitals
HQ: Kettering Medical Center
3535 Southern Blvd
Kettering OH 45429
937 298-4331

(G-9541)
KETTERING MEDICAL CENTER
Also Called: Kettering Health Network
1251 E Dorothy Ln (45419-2106)
PHONE..........................937 384-8750
Christine Turner, *Director*
EMP: 30
SALES (corp-wide): 1.7B **Privately Held**
WEB: www.kmcfoundation.org
SIC: 8062 Hospital, professional nursing school
HQ: Kettering Medical Center
3535 Southern Blvd
Kettering OH 45429
937 298-4331

(G-9542)
KETTERING RECREATION CENTER
2900 Glengarry Dr (45420-1225)
PHONE..........................937 296-2587
Jim Garges, *President*
Ryan Davis, *Division Mgr*
Sonja Rom, *Principal*
Anna Breidenbach, *Program Mgr*
Jena Bosworth, *Manager*
EMP: 50
SALES (est): 1.4MM **Privately Held**
SIC: 8322 7999 7991 Senior citizens' center or association; amusement & recreation; physical fitness facilities

(G-9543)
KETTERING TENNIS CENTER
Also Called: Ktc Quell
4565 Gateway Cir (45440-1790)
PHONE..........................937 434-6602
Linda Heinz, *Owner*
EMP: 27
SALES (est): 622.9K **Privately Held**
WEB: www.ktcquail.com
SIC: 7997 Tennis club, membership

(G-9544)
KIG ENTERPRISES LLC
Also Called: Keaney Investment
1440 Nicholas Rd (45417-6711)
PHONE..........................937 263-6429
Linda Keaney, *CEO*
James Keaney, *President*
Brett Mitchell, *Accounts Mgr*
Eliza Wise, *Office Mgr*
Gary Ehlinger, *Manager*
EMP: 26
SQ FT: 20,000
SALES (est): 6MM **Privately Held**
SIC: 7699 Valve repair, industrial

GEOGRAPHIC

(G-9545)
KINDERCARE LEARNING CTRS INC
Also Called: Kindercare Center 1480
951 E Rahn Rd (45429-5927)
PHONE..............................937 435-2353
Sherlynn Mullen, *Director*
Jodi Sweeney, *Director*
EMP: 25
SALES (corp-wide): 1.2B **Privately Held**
WEB: www.kindercare.com
SIC: 8351 Group day care center
HQ: Kindercare Learning Centers, Llc
650 Ne Holladay St # 1400
Portland OR 97232
503 872-1300

(G-9546)
KINDRED HEALTHCARE INC
Also Called: Kindred Hospital
707 S Edwin C Moses Blvd (45417-3462)
PHONE..............................937 222-5963
Kim Lippke, *Controller*
Susan Davis, *Manager*
Bruce Moman, *Manager*
Antione Amos, *Director*
Richard Brown, *Radiology Dir*
EMP: 81
SALES (corp-wide): 6B **Privately Held**
SIC: 8062 8051 8011 General medical & surgical hospitals; skilled nursing care facilities; dispensary, operated by physicians
HQ: Kindred Healthcare, Llc
680 S 4th St
Louisville KY 40202
502 596-7300

(G-9547)
KINDRED HEALTHCARE INC
Also Called: Kindred Hospital-Dayton
601 S Edwin C Moses Blvd (45417-3424)
PHONE..............................937 222-5963
Christina Stover, *CEO*
EMP: 81
SALES (corp-wide): 6B **Privately Held**
WEB: www.kindredhealthcare.com
SIC: 8062 General medical & surgical hospitals
HQ: Kindred Healthcare, Llc
680 S 4th St
Louisville KY 40202
502 596-7300

(G-9548)
KING TREE LEASING CO LLC
Also Called: Riverside Nrsing Rhabilitation
1390 King Tree Dr (45405-1401)
PHONE..............................937 278-0723
Stephen Rosedale,
EMP: 99
SQ FT: 71,560
SALES (est): 10.1MM **Privately Held**
SIC: 8051 Convalescent home with continuous nursing care

(G-9549)
KNIGHTS OF COLUMBUS
6050 Dog Leg Rd (45415-2513)
PHONE..............................937 890-2971
John Grady, *Principal*
EMP: 50
SALES (corp-wide): 2.3B **Privately Held**
WEB: www.kofc.org
SIC: 8641 Fraternal associations
PA: Knights Of Columbus
1 Columbus Plz Ste 1700
New Haven CT 06510
203 752-4000

(G-9550)
KOHLER FOODS INC (PA)
Also Called: Kohler Catering
4572 Presidential Way (45429-5751)
PHONE..............................937 291-3600
Erwin Kohler Jr, *President*
Betty Kohler, *Corp Secy*
Craig Kohler, *Vice Pres*
Sue Delaney, *Sales Mgr*
Marcia West, *Sales Staff*
EMP: 50
SQ FT: 9,000
SALES (est): 3.6MM **Privately Held**
WEB: www.kohlercatering.net
SIC: 7299 5812 Banquet hall facilities; caterers

(G-9551)
KROGER CO
2917 W Alex Bell Rd (45459-1127)
PHONE..............................937 294-7210
Doug Palman, *Manager*
EMP: 187
SALES (corp-wide): 121.1B **Publicly Held**
WEB: www.kroger.com
SIC: 5411 7384 5912 Supermarkets, chain; photofinishing laboratory; drug stores
PA: The Kroger Co
1014 Vine St Ste 1000
Cincinnati OH 45202
513 762-4000

(G-9552)
KROGER CO
6480 Wilmington Pike (45459-7010)
PHONE..............................937 848-5990
Martin Crump, *Principal*
EMP: 100
SALES (corp-wide): 121.1B **Publicly Held**
WEB: www.kroger.com
SIC: 5411 5141 Supermarkets, chain; supermarkets, 66,000-99,000 square feet; convenience stores, chain; groceries, general line
PA: The Kroger Co
1014 Vine St Ste 1000
Cincinnati OH 45202
513 762-4000

(G-9553)
L R G INC
3795 Wyse Rd (45414-2540)
PHONE..............................937 890-0510
Brandon Shoup, *President*
Bruce Black, *Superintendent*
Heath Peters, *Vice Pres*
Roland Peters, *Vice Pres*
Wade Renicker, *VP Opers*
EMP: 53
SQ FT: 9,870
SALES: 55MM **Privately Held**
WEB: www.glrinc.net
SIC: 1542 1522 Commercial & office building contractors; residential construction

(G-9554)
LABORATORY OF DERMATOPATHOLOGY
7835 Paragon Rd (45459-4021)
PHONE..............................937 434-2351
Thomas G Olsen, *Principal*
EMP: 40
SQ FT: 3,000
SALES (est): 5.2MM **Privately Held**
SIC: 8071 Testing laboratories

(G-9555)
LAKESHORE DIALYSIS LLC
Also Called: Five Rivers Dialysis
4750 N Main St (45405-5021)
PHONE..............................937 278-0516
EMP: 33
SALES (est): 642.5K **Publicly Held**
SIC: 8092 Kidney Dialysis Centers
PA: Davita Inc.
2000 16th St
Denver CO 80202

(G-9556)
LAKEWOODS II LTD
980 Wilmington Ave (45420-1686)
PHONE..............................937 254-6141
Frank Sinito, *General Ptnr*
EMP: 99
SALES (est): 3MM **Privately Held**
SIC: 6513 Apartment building operators

(G-9557)
LANCO GLOBAL SYSTEMS INC
1430c Yankee Park Pl (45458-1829)
PHONE..............................937 660-8090
Venkat Kadiyala, *Branch Mgr*
EMP: 80
SALES (corp-wide): 10.1MM **Privately Held**
SIC: 7379
PA: Lanco Global Systems, Inc.
21515 Ridgetop Cir # 150
Sterling VA 20166
703 953-2157

(G-9558)
LAP TECHNOLOGY LLC
6101 Webster St (45414-3435)
PHONE..............................937 415-5794
Dilip Patel, *Mng Member*
Mike Patel,
Frank Penn,
EMP: 30
SALES (est): 2.5MM **Privately Held**
SIC: 7371 Computer software systems analysis & design, custom

(G-9559)
LASER HAIR REMOVAL CENTER
Also Called: Hair Removal Center of So
5300 Far Hills Ave # 250 (45429-2347)
PHONE..............................937 433-7536
Carla Miracle, *Manager*
EMP: 85 EST: 1999
SALES (est): 760K **Privately Held**
SIC: 8011 7231 Dermatologist; beauty shops

(G-9560)
LAURITO & LAURITO LLC
7550 Paragon Rd (45459-5317)
PHONE..............................937 743-4878
Jeffrey Laurito, *Mng Member*
Erin Laurito,
EMP: 35
SQ FT: 6,000
SALES (est): 3.7MM **Privately Held**
WEB: www.lauritolaw.com
SIC: 8111 General practice law office

(G-9561)
LEGRAND NORTH AMERICA LLC
Also Called: C2g
6500 Poe Ave (45414-2527)
PHONE..............................937 224-0639
Joe Cornwall, *Area Mgr*
Andrea McDermott, *Project Mgr*
April Mick, *Buyer*
Michael Leach, *Natl Sales Mgr*
Chad Studebaker, *Sales Mgr*
EMP: 420
SALES (corp-wide): 20.7MM **Privately Held**
SIC: 1731 5063 5045 3643 Communications specialization; cable conduit; computer peripheral equipment; current-carrying wiring devices; nonferrous wiredrawing & insulating
HQ: Legrand North America, Llc
60 Woodlawn St
West Hartford CT 06110
860 233-6251

(G-9562)
LEGRAND NORTH AMERICA LLC
1501 Webster St (45404-1559)
PHONE..............................937 224-0639
Geoffrey Hyman, *Principal*
Doug Saul, *Sales Staff*
EMP: 159
SALES (corp-wide): 20.7MM **Privately Held**
WEB: www.lastar.com
SIC: 1731 Communications specialization
HQ: Legrand North America, Llc
60 Woodlawn St
West Hartford CT 06110
860 233-6251

(G-9563)
LENZ INC
Also Called: Lenz Company
3301 Klepinger Rd (45406-1823)
P.O. Box 1044 (45401-1044)
PHONE..............................937 277-9364
Robert Wagner, *President*
Grace Campbell, *Human Resources*
Rick Brown, *Sales Staff*
Ken Whitson, *Sales Staff*
EMP: 50
SQ FT: 15,000
SALES (est): 6.5MM **Privately Held**
WEB: www.thelenz.com
SIC: 6531 3089 Real estate brokers & agents; fittings for pipe, plastic

(G-9564)
LEWIS & MICHAEL INC (PA)
1827 Woodman Dr (45420-2937)
P.O. Box 97 (45401-0097)
PHONE..............................937 252-6683
Charles M Lewis, *Ch of Bd*
David Lewis, *President*
EMP: 30 EST: 1941
SQ FT: 40,000
SALES: 8MM **Privately Held**
SIC: 4213 4214 4225 Household goods transport; household goods moving & storage, local; general warehousing

(G-9565)
LIFE CONNECTION OF OHIO INC
40 Wyoming St (45409-2721)
PHONE..............................937 223-8223
Michael Phillips, *CEO*
EMP: 36
SALES (est): 1MM **Privately Held**
SIC: 8099 Organ bank

(G-9566)
LIFESTGES SMRTAN CTR FOR WOMEN
Also Called: Lifestgs-Smrtan Ctrs For Women
2200 Philadelphia Dr # 101 (45406-1840)
PHONE..............................937 277-8988
Bruce Bernie, *Principal*
EMP: 50
SQ FT: 5,220
SALES (est): 2.4MM **Privately Held**
SIC: 8099 8011 Medical services organization; offices & clinics of medical doctors

(G-9567)
LIFETOUCH INC
3701 Wilmington Pike (45429-4844)
PHONE..............................937 298-6275
Kenneth Molz, *Site Mgr*
EMP: 33
SALES (corp-wide): 1.9B **Publicly Held**
SIC: 7221 Photographer, still or video
HQ: Lifetouch Inc.
11000 Viking Dr
Eden Prairie MN 55344
952 826-4000

(G-9568)
LINCOLN PARK ASSOCIATES II LP
Also Called: Lincoln Park Manor
694 Isaac Prugh Way (45429-3481)
PHONE..............................937 297-4300
Charles Osborn Jr, *Partner*
Miami Valley Hospital Extended, *General Ptnr*
Miami Valley Hospital, *Ltd Ptnr*
EMP: 130
SQ FT: 40,000
SALES: 7.4MM **Privately Held**
SIC: 8051 8059 8052 Convalescent home with continuous nursing care; nursing home, except skilled & intermediate care facility; intermediate care facilities

(G-9569)
LINK IQ LLC (PA)
125 Westpark Rd (45459-4814)
PHONE..............................859 983-6080
Andy Myers,
EMP: 25
SQ FT: 8,000
SALES (est): 3MM **Privately Held**
SIC: 4813 7379 ; computer related maintenance services

(G-9570)
LION GROUP INC (DH)
7200 Poe Ave Ste 400 (45414-2798)
PHONE..............................937 898-1949
Steve Schwartz, *CEO*
James Baker, *Opers Staff*
Spring Cutlip, *Purch Agent*
James Disanto, *Treasurer*
Richard Musick, *Treasurer*
EMP: 90
SQ FT: 3,700
SALES (est): 116.9MM **Privately Held**
SIC: 6719 Investment holding companies, except banks

HQ: Lion Protects B.V.
Industrieweg 5
Baarle Nassau 5111
135 076-800

(G-9571)
LION-VALLEN LTD
PARTNERSHIP (PA)
Also Called: L V I
7200 Poe Ave Ste 400 (45414-2798)
PHONE.............................937 898-1949
Stephen Schwartz, *Partner*
Terry Smith, *Senior VP*
Mark Boyed, *Vice Pres*
Dennis Dudek, *Vice Pres*
Alan Nash, *Vice Pres*
▼ EMP: 25
SALES (est): 54.2MM **Privately Held**
WEB: www.lionapparel.com
SIC: 5136 5137 Uniforms, men's & boys';
uniforms, women's & children's

(G-9572)
LOFINOS INC
Also Called: Lofino's Investment
6018 Wilmington Pike (45459-7006)
PHONE.............................937 431-1662
Michael D Lofino, *President*
Charles Lofino, *Chairman*
John Mantia, *Corp Secy*
EMP: 80
SQ FT: 45,000
SALES (est): 6.7MM **Privately Held**
WEB: www.lofinos.com
SIC: 5411 6512 Supermarkets, independ-
ent; shopping center, property operation
only

(G-9573)
LORENZ CORPORATION (PA)
Also Called: Show What You Know
501 E 3rd St (45402-2280)
P.O. Box 802 (45401-0802)
PHONE.............................937 228-6118
Reiff Lorenz, *Ch of Bd*
Tom Borchers, *Corp Secy*
▲ EMP: 78 EST: 1890
SQ FT: 55,000
SALES (est): 11.6MM **Privately Held**
WEB: www.lorenz.com
SIC: 2759 5049 2721 2741 Music sheet:
printing; school supplies; periodicals: pub-
lishing only; music, sheet: publishing only,
not printed on site

(G-9574)
LOWES HOME CENTERS LLC
8421 Old Troy Pike (45424-1029)
PHONE.............................937 235-2920
Benjamin Bolin, *Store Mgr*
Rob Kalp, *Manager*
EMP: 150
SALES (corp-wide): 68.6B **Publicly Held**
SIC: 5211 5031 5722 5064 Home cen-
ters; building materials, exterior; building
materials, interior; household appliance
stores; electrical appliances, television &
radio
HQ: Lowe's Home Centers, Llc
1605 Curtis Bridge Rd
Wilkesboro NC 28697
336 658-4000

(G-9575)
LOWES HOME CENTERS LLC
2900 Martins Dr (45449-3602)
PHONE.............................937 438-4900
Steve Dolan, *Manager*
EMP: 150
SALES (corp-wide): 68.6B **Publicly Held**
SIC: 5211 5031 5722 5064 Home cen-
ters; building materials, exterior; building
materials, interior; household appliance
stores; electrical appliances, television &
radio
HQ: Lowe's Home Centers, Llc
1605 Curtis Bridge Rd
Wilkesboro NC 28697
336 658-4000

(G-9576)
LOWES HOME CENTERS LLC
6300 Wilmington Pike (45459-7009)
PHONE.............................937 848-5600
Jim Dougherty, *Branch Mgr*
EMP: 165

SALES (corp-wide): 68.6B **Publicly Held**
SIC: 5211 5031 5722 5064 Home centers; building materials, exterior; building
materials, interior; household appliance
stores; electrical appliances, television &
radio
HQ: Lowe's Home Centers, Llc
1605 Curtis Bridge Rd
Wilkesboro NC 28697
336 658-4000

(G-9577)
LOWES HOME CENTERS LLC
5252 Salem Ave (45426-1702)
PHONE.............................937 854-8200
Michael Sturtz, *Office Mgr*
EMP: 150
SALES (corp-wide): 68.6B **Publicly Held**
SIC: 5211 5031 5722 5064 Lumber &
other building materials; building materi-
als, exterior; building materials, interior;
household appliance stores; electrical ap-
pliances, television & radio
HQ: Lowe's Home Centers, Llc
1605 Curtis Bridge Rd
Wilkesboro NC 28697
336 658-4000

(G-9578)
M & R ELECTRIC MOTOR SVC
INC
1516 E 5th St (45403-2397)
PHONE.............................937 222-6282
Charles Mader, *Corp Secy*
Ronald Mader, *Vice Pres*
Anthony Mader, *Vice Pres*
Craig Mader, *Treasurer*
EMP: 28 EST: 1949
SQ FT: 8,000
SALES: 4MM **Privately Held**
SIC: 5063 7694 Motors, electric; electric
motor repair

(G-9579)
M K MOORE & SONS INC
5150 Wagner Ford Rd (45414-3662)
P.O. Box 13149 (45413-0149)
PHONE.............................937 236-1812
Michael K Moore, *President*
Christoher Moore, *Vice Pres*
EMP: 30 EST: 1973
SQ FT: 10,000
SALES (est): 2.2MM **Privately Held**
SIC: 1799 1742 1711 Insulation of pipes
& boilers; insulation, buildings; plumbing,
heating, air-conditioning contractors

(G-9580)
MAGIC CASTLE INC
4990 Wilmington Pike (45440-2100)
PHONE.............................937 434-4911
Scott Callabouno, *President*
EMP: 30
SALES (est): 551.2K **Privately Held**
SIC: 7999 7993 Golf services & profes-
sionals; coin-operated amusement de-
vices

(G-9581)
MAIN LINE SUPPLY CO INC (PA)
300 N Findlay St (45403-1256)
PHONE.............................937 254-6910
Mike O'Brien, *CEO*
Tim Kroger, *President*
Steve Ireland, *Vice Pres*
◆ EMP: 40 EST: 1955
SQ FT: 70,000
SALES (est): 32.1MM **Privately Held**
WEB: www.mainlinesupply.com
SIC: 5085 Valves & fittings

(G-9582)
MALL REALTY INC
Also Called: Barnes Cope
862 Watertower Ln (45449-2413)
PHONE.............................937 866-3700
Barry Barnes, *President*
Lois Barnes, *Treasurer*
Tom Freeman, *Admin Sec*
EMP: 45
SQ FT: 6,000
SALES (est): 2.6MM **Privately Held**
SIC: 6531 Real estate agent, residential

(G-9583)
MANUFACTURING SERVICES
INTL
15 W Dorothy Ln (45429-1446)
PHONE.............................937 299-9922
William Hart, *Principal*
EMP: 25
SALES (est): 2.3MM **Privately Held**
SIC: 8711 Engineering services

(G-9584)
MARCA TERRACE WIDOWS
50 S Findlay St (45403-2023)
PHONE.............................937 252-1661
Mike Freeman, *Principal*
EMP: 80
SALES (est): 451K **Privately Held**
SIC: 8093 Rehabilitation center, outpatient
treatment

(G-9585)
MARSH & MCLENNAN AGENCY
LLC
409 E Monu Ave Ste 400 (45402)
PHONE.............................937 228-4135
Karen Harker, *Branch Mgr*
EMP: 125
SALES (corp-wide): 14.9B **Publicly Held**
SIC: 6411 Insurance brokers; property &
casualty insurance agent; life insurance
agents
HQ: Marsh & Mclennan Agency Llc
360 Hamilton Ave Ste 930
White Plains NY 10601

(G-9586)
MARSH BUILDING PRODUCTS
INC (PA)
2030 Winners Cir (45404-1130)
PHONE.............................937 222-3321
Ken Middleton, *President*
Mary C Gronefeld, *Principal*
Mike Middleton, *Vice Pres*
Tim Mac Veigh, *Financial Exec*
EMP: 25
SQ FT: 15,000
SALES (est): 22.7MM **Privately Held**
WEB: www.marshbuild.com
SIC: 5031 7699 5211 Building materials,
exterior; building materials, interior; door
& window repair; siding

(G-9587)
MARTIN CHEVROLET INC
8560 Troy Pike (45424-1031)
PHONE.............................937 849-1381
Cornelius Martin, *President*
EMP: 45
SQ FT: 50,000
SALES (est): 9.3MM **Privately Held**
SIC: 5511 7538 Ret New/Used Automo-
biles General Auto Repair

(G-9588)
MARY C ENTERPRISES INC (PA)
Also Called: Dots Market
2274 Patterson Rd (45420-3061)
PHONE.............................937 253-6169
Rob Bernhard, *President*
Frankie Davis, *Vice Pres*
Brad Medlin, *Manager*
EMP: 80
SQ FT: 18,000
SALES (est): 12.5MM **Privately Held**
WEB: www.dotsmarket.com
SIC: 5411 6099 5421 Supermarkets, in-
dependent; electronic funds transfer net-
work, including switching; meat markets,
including freezer provisioners

(G-9589)
MARY SCOTT NURSING HOME
INC
3109 Campus Dr (45406-4100)
PHONE.............................937 278-0761
Kenneth Crawford, *Exec Dir*
EMP: 98
SALES: 6.1MM
SALES (corp-wide): 7.5MM **Privately**
Held
WEB: www.msnc.org
SIC: 8052 Personal care facility

PA: Mary Scott Centers Inc
3109 Campus Dr
Dayton OH 45406
937 278-0761

(G-9590)
MAXWELL LIGHTNING
PROTECTION
621 Pond St (45402-1348)
PHONE.............................937 228-7250
Wayne S Maxwell, *President*
Lynn Busse, *Corp Secy*
Lee Maxwell, *Supervisor*
Caralee Fox, *Admin Sec*
David Busse,
EMP: 40
SQ FT: 7,200
SALES (est): 6.1MM **Privately Held**
WEB: www.maxwell-lp.com
SIC: 1799 Lightning conductor erection

(G-9591)
MBC CARDIOLOGIST INC
122 Wyoming St (45409-2731)
PHONE.............................937 223-4461
James M Pacenta MD, *Principal*
EMP: 55 EST: 2001
SALES (est): 1.3MM **Privately Held**
SIC: 8011 Offices & clinics of medical doc-
tors

(G-9592)
MBI SOLUTIONS INC
332 Congress Park Dr (45459-4133)
PHONE.............................937 619-4000
Paul Kolodzik MD, *CEO*
Steve Broughton, *President*
Tom Grile, *President*
Terry Heineman, *COO*
Bill Podell, *Vice Pres*
EMP: 112
SQ FT: 22,000
SALES (est): 7.8MM
SALES (corp-wide): 16.6MM **Privately**
Held
WEB: www.premierhcs.net
SIC: 8721 Billing & bookkeeping service
PA: Premier Health Care System, Inc.
332 Congress Park Dr
Dayton OH
937 312-3627

(G-9593)
MCAFEE HEATING & AC CO INC
Also Called: McAfee Air Duct Cleaning
4750 Hempstead Station Dr (45429-5164)
PHONE.............................937 438-1976
Gregory K McAfee, *President*
Naomi McAfee, *Vice Pres*
Candice Sally,
EMP: 45
SQ FT: 3,500
SALES (est): 8MM **Privately Held**
WEB: www.mcair.com
SIC: 1711 Warm air heating & air condi-
tioning contractor; heating & air condition-
ing contractors

(G-9594)
MCFARLAND TRUCK LINES INC
1844 Invention Dr (45426-2900)
PHONE.............................937 854-2200
Dennis Wells, *Branch Mgr*
EMP: 25
SALES (corp-wide): 12MM **Privately**
Held
SIC: 4213 Contract haulers
PA: Mcfarland Truck Lines, Inc.
1304 16th Ave Ne
Austin MN
507 437-6651

(G-9595)
MCH SERVICES INC
190 E Spring Valley Pike (45458-3803)
PHONE.............................260 432-9699
Melisa Roysdon, *Manager*
EMP: 118
SALES (corp-wide): 4.4MM **Privately**
Held
SIC: 8082 Home health care services
HQ: Mch Services Inc
108 Lundy Ln
Hattiesburg MS

(G-9596)
MCM ELECTRONICS INC
Also Called: M C M & One Com
650 Congress Park Dr (45459-4072)
PHONE...................................937 434-0031
Tom Marine, *Vice Pres*
Patty Berning, *Buyer*
Jeff Schillo, *Controller*
Mark Landers, *Accounts Mgr*
Jon Morgan, *Corp Comm Staff*
EMP: 60
SQ FT: 130,980
SALES (corp-wide): 19B **Publicly Held**
WEB: www.mcmelectronics.com
SIC: 5065 4225 Electronic parts; general
   warehousing
HQ: Mcm Electronics, Inc.
   650 Congress Park Dr
   Centerville OH 45459

(G-9597)
MECHANICAL CNSTR MANAGERS LLC (PA)
Also Called: RIECK SERVICES
5245 Wadsworth Rd (45414-3507)
P.O. Box 13565 (45413-0565)
PHONE...................................937 274-1987
Beth Moore, *Project Mgr*
Jim Cox, *Senior Engr*
Brian Clouse, *Accounts Mgr*
Wes Eversole, *Accounts Exec*
Tom Graham, *Manager*
EMP: 200 EST: 1949
SQ FT: 50,000
SALES: 31.7MM **Privately Held**
SIC: 1711 1761 Mechanical contractor;
   sheet metalwork; roofing contractor

(G-9598)
MED AMERICA HLTH SYSTEMS CORP (PA)
1 Wyoming St (45409-2722)
PHONE...................................937 223-6192
T G Breitenbach, *President*
Timothy Jackson, *CFO*
Dale Creech, *Admin Sec*
EMP: 4700
SQ FT: 1,000,000
SALES (est): 968.3MM **Privately Held**
SIC: 8062 8741 8082 General medical &
   surgical hospitals; management services;
   home health care services

(G-9599)
MED-PASS INCORPORATED
1 Reynolds Way (45430-1586)
PHONE...................................937 438-8884
Lisa Hanauer, *President*
Susan Spiegel, *Corp Secy*
Kim Buckingham, *Vice Pres*
Doug Harlow, *Vice Pres*
Valerie Hill, *Finance Mgr*
EMP: 40
SQ FT: 40,000
SALES (est): 9.3MM **Privately Held**
WEB: www.med-pass.com
SIC: 5112 8742 Computer & photocopying
   supplies; management consulting serv-
   ices

(G-9600)
MEDCATH INTERMEDIATE HOLDINGS
Also Called: Dayton Heart Hospital
707 S Edwin Moses Blvd (45408)
PHONE...................................937 221-8016
EMP: 370
SALES (corp-wide): 331MM **Privately
Held**
SIC: 8062 8069 General Hospital Spe-
   cialty Hospital
HQ: Medcath Intermediate Holdings Inc
   10720 Sikes Pl Ste 300
   Charlotte NC

(G-9601)
MEDICAL CENTER AT ELIZABETH PL
Also Called: McEp
1 Elizabeth Pl (45417-3445)
PHONE...................................937 223-6237
John Fleishman MD, *President*
Alex Rintoul, *Mng Member*
Karen Keller, *Director*
Donna Queen, *Lab Dir*

EMP: 120
SALES: 18.7MM **Privately Held**
SIC: 8062 General medical & surgical hos-
   pitals

(G-9602)
MEDICAL ONCLGY-HEMATOLOGY ASSN
3737 Sthern Blvd Ste 4200 (45429)
PHONE...................................937 223-2183
Basel Yanes, *President*
EMP: 25
SQ FT: 2,000
SALES (est): 2.4MM **Privately Held**
SIC: 8011 Hematologist

(G-9603)
MEDICINE MIDWEST LLC
Also Called: Primed At Congress Park
979 Congress Park Dr (45459-4009)
PHONE...................................937 435-8786
Leslie Schrager, *Manager*
EMP: 25
SALES (est): 774.7K
SALES (corp-wide): 1.5MM **Privately
Held**
SIC: 8043 Offices & clinics of podiatrists
PA: Medicine Midwest Llc
   4700 Smith Rd Ste A
   Cincinnati OH 45212
   513 533-1199

(G-9604)
MEDWORK LLC
Also Called: Medwork Occupational Hlth Care
7187 Tarryton Rd (45459-3448)
PHONE...................................937 449-0800
Dean Imbrogno, *President*
EMP: 58
SALES (est): 2.5MM **Privately Held**
SIC: 8049 Occupational therapist

(G-9605)
MEGACITY FIRE PROTECTION INC (PA)
8210 Expansion Way (45424-6382)
PHONE...................................937 335-0775
Larry Gagnon, *President*
Randy Carroll, *General Mgr*
Kathleen Gagnon, *Vice Pres*
Dale Shuster, *Opers Staff*
Jeff Barnes, *Manager*
EMP: 40 EST: 1970
SQ FT: 15,000
SALES (est): 5.8MM **Privately Held**
WEB: www.megacityfire.com
SIC: 7389 5085 1731 Fire extinguisher
   servicing; industrial supplies; fire detec-
   tion & burglar alarm systems specializa-
   tion

(G-9606)
MENDELSON ELECTRONICS CO INC
Also Called: Mendelson Liquidation Outlet
340 E 1st St (45402-1250)
PHONE...................................937 461-3525
Sanford Mendelson, *President*
Heather Mendelson, *Vice Pres*
Terry Pinsky, *Treasurer*
Harlan Mendelson, *Sales Executive*
Doris Theodald, *Manager*
EMP: 39
SQ FT: 517,000
SALES (est): 2.9MM **Privately Held**
WEB: www.meci.com
SIC: 5065 5999 Electronic parts; elec-
   tronic parts & equipment

(G-9607)
MENDELSON REALTY LTD
340 E 1st St (45402-1250)
PHONE...................................937 461-3525
Sanford Mendelson, *Partner*
EMP: 50
SALES (est): 3.2MM **Privately Held**
WEB: www.mendelsons.com
SIC: 6512 6531 Commercial & industrial
   building operation; real estate brokers &
   agents

(G-9608)
MERCHANTS SCRTY SRVC OF DAYTON
2015 Wayne Ave (45410-2134)
P.O. Box 432 (45409-0432)
PHONE...................................937 256-9373
James Houpt, *President*
Laura Strong, *Empl Rel Mgr*
EMP: 300
SQ FT: 1,500
SALES (est): 8.9MM **Privately Held**
WEB: www.merchantssecurity.com
SIC: 7381 Security guard service

(G-9609)
MESSER CONSTRUCTION CO
4801 Hempstead Station Dr A
(45429-5171)
PHONE...................................937 291-1300
Eric Wainscott, *Vice Pres*
C Allen Begley Jr, *Branch Mgr*
Ian Simpson, *Sr Project Mgr*
Terrel Washington, *Sr Project Mgr*
EMP: 100
SALES (corp-wide): 1B **Privately Held**
WEB: www.messer.com
SIC: 1541 Industrial buildings & ware-
   houses
PA: Messer Construction Co.
   643 W Court St
   Cincinnati OH 45203
   513 242-1541

(G-9610)
METLIFE AUTO HM INSUR AGCY INC (HQ)
9797 Springboro Pike (45448-0001)
PHONE...................................815 266-5301
Stephen Klingel, *Ch of Bd*
Howard Dalton, *Senior VP*
Andrew Douglass, *Senior VP*
Patrick Thiele, *CFO*
Donald Swanson, *Treasurer*
EMP: 700 EST: 1915
SQ FT: 180,000
SALES (est): 264.5MM
SALES (corp-wide): 67.9B **Publicly Held**
WEB: www.metlifeautoandhome.com
SIC: 6411 Insurance agents & brokers
PA: Metlife, Inc.
   200 Park Ave
   New York NY 10166
   212 578-9500

(G-9611)
MFH INC (PA)
Also Called: Media Group At Michael's, The
241 E Alex Bell Rd (45459-2706)
PHONE...................................937 435-4701
Michael Schuh Jr, *President*
Kathleen Lee, *General Mgr*
Kim Ash, *Sales Executive*
Mary Schuh, *Executive*
EMP: 33
SQ FT: 3,000
SALES: 3.5MM **Privately Held**
WEB: www.michaelssalons.com
SIC: 7231 7241 Beauty shops; barber
   shops

(G-9612)
MFH INC
Also Called: Michaels For Hair
241 E Alex Bell Rd (45459-2706)
PHONE...................................937 435-4701
Kathleen Lee, *Manager*
EMP: 100
SALES (corp-wide): 3.5MM **Privately
Held**
WEB: www.michaelssalons.com
SIC: 7231 Beauty shops
PA: Mfh, Inc.
   241 E Alex Bell Rd
   Dayton OH 45459
   937 435-4701

(G-9613)
MH EQUIPMENT COMPANY
Also Called: M H Equipment - Ohio
3000 Production Ct (45414-3514)
P.O. Box 13030 (45413-0030)
PHONE...................................937 890-6800
Doug Davis, *Parts Mgr*
Mitch Holland, *Sales Staff*
Ken Mauch, *Branch Mgr*

Shirley Neuhard, *Receptionist*
EMP: 50
SALES (corp-wide): 247.9MM **Privately
Held**
SIC: 5084 Materials handling machinery
HQ: Mh Equipment Company
   8901 N Industrial Rd
   Peoria IL 61615
   309 579-8020

(G-9614)
MIAMI CONSERVANCY DISTRICT (PA)
38 E Monument Ave (45402-1265)
PHONE...................................937 223-1271
Janet Bly, *General Mgr*
Bill Bogan, *Principal*
Noelle Novack, *Finance Asst*
Rhonda Snyder, *Office Mgr*
Mike Ekberg, *Manager*
EMP: 50
SQ FT: 8,500
SALES (est): 4MM **Privately Held**
SIC: 8999 Natural resource preservation
   service

(G-9615)
MIAMI VALLEY BEKINS INC
Also Called: Miami Valley Moving & Storage
5941 Milo Rd (45414-3415)
P.O. Box 13191 (45413-0191)
PHONE...................................937 278-4296
Sheila Westray, *President*
Michelle Scott, *Treasurer*
EMP: 25
SQ FT: 43,000
SALES (est): 2.3MM **Privately Held**
SIC: 4214 4213 Local trucking with stor-
   age; contract haulers

(G-9616)
MIAMI VALLEY BROADCASTING CORP
Also Called: Oldies 95
1611 S Main St (45409-2547)
PHONE...................................937 259-2111
Edrew Fichser, *President*
Karen Klimowicz, *VP Human Res*
Fantine Kerckaert, *Director*
James Hatcher, *Admin Sec*
EMP: 160
SQ FT: 54,000
SALES (est): 22.1MM
SALES (corp-wide): 32.5B **Privately Held**
SIC: 4832 Radio broadcasting stations
PA: Cox Enterprises, Inc.
   6205 Pachtree Dunwoody Rd
   Atlanta GA 30328
   678 645-0000

(G-9617)
MIAMI VALLEY COMMUNITY ACTION (PA)
Also Called: Mvcap
719 S Main St (45402-2709)
PHONE...................................937 222-1009
Cherish Cronmiller, *CEO*
Joyce E Price, *COO*
Stephen V Pipenger, *CFO*
EMP: 60 EST: 1964
SQ FT: 21,000
SALES: 13MM **Privately Held**
SIC: 8399 8322 6732 Community action
   agency; antipoverty board; individual &
   family services; trusts: educational, reli-
   gious, etc.

(G-9618)
MIAMI VALLEY GOLF CLUB (PA)
3311 Salem Ave (45406-2699)
PHONE...................................937 278-7381
Mel Cloud, *Manager*
EMP: 75 EST: 1919
SQ FT: 35,000
SALES: 1.7MM **Privately Held**
WEB: www.miamivalleygolfclub.com
SIC: 7992 Public golf courses

(G-9619)
MIAMI VALLEY HOSPITAL
Also Called: Miami Valley South Campus
2400 Miami Valley Dr (45459-4774)
PHONE...................................937 436-5200
Joanne Ringer, *Vice Pres*
EMP: 250

SALES (corp-wide): 968.3MM **Privately Held**
SIC: 8062 General medical & surgical hospitals
HQ: Miami Valley Hospital
1 Wyoming St
Dayton OH 45409
937 208-8000

(G-9620)
MIAMI VALLEY HOSPITAL (HQ)
1 Wyoming St (45409-2711)
PHONE....................................937 208-8000
Bobbie Gerhart, *President*
Mark Shaker, *President*
Barbara Johnson, *COO*
Makkie Clancy, *Vice Pres*
Lisa Bishop, *CFO*
EMP: 5000
SQ FT: 1,000,000
SALES: 809.9MM
SALES (corp-wide): 968.3MM **Privately Held**
WEB: www.mvafp.com
SIC: 8062 General medical & surgical hospitals
PA: Med America Health Systems Corporation
1 Wyoming St
Dayton OH 45409
937 223-6192

(G-9621)
MIAMI VALLEY HOSPITAL
Also Called: Child Care Center
28 Hill St (45409-2922)
PHONE....................................937 224-3916
Angela Collins, *Director*
EMP: 30
SQ FT: 1,068
SALES (corp-wide): 968.3MM **Privately Held**
WEB: www.mvafp.com
SIC: 8351 Child day care services
HQ: Miami Valley Hospital
1 Wyoming St
Dayton OH 45409
937 208-8000

(G-9622)
MIAMI VALLEY HOSPITALIST GROUP
30 E Apple St Ste 3300 (45409-2939)
PHONE....................................937 208-8394
Angela Black, *Principal*
EMP: 100
SALES (est): 616.5K **Privately Held**
SIC: 6324 Hospital & medical service plans

(G-9623)
MIAMI VALLEY HSING ASSN I INC
907 W 5th St (45402-8306)
PHONE....................................937 263-4449
Connie Isaac, *CEO*
Connie Isaacs, *CFO*
Dan Swan, *Director*
EMP: 44
SQ FT: 1,000
SALES: 48.7K **Privately Held**
SIC: 8052 Home for the mentally retarded, with health care

(G-9624)
MIAMI VALLEY MEMORY GRDNS ASSN (DH)
1639 E Lytle 5 Points Rd (45458-5203)
PHONE....................................937 885-7779
Lona Jones, *General Mgr*
David Carroll, *General Mgr*
EMP: 30
SALES (est): 5.2MM
SALES (corp-wide): 3.1B **Publicly Held**
SIC: 6553 0782 Cemetery association; lawn & garden services

(G-9625)
MIAMI VALLEY REGIONAL PLG COMM
10 N Ludlow St Ste 700 (45402-1855)
PHONE....................................937 223-6323
Tonya Lee, *General Mgr*
Paul Arnold, *Manager*
Brian Martin, *Exec Dir*
Donald R Spang, *Director*

Tashia Reese, *Receptionist Se*
EMP: 25
SQ FT: 11,000
SALES (est): 2.7MM **Privately Held**
WEB: www.mvrpc.org
SIC: 8748 Economic consultant; urban planning & consulting services

(G-9626)
MIAMI VALLEY SCHOOL
5151 Denise Dr (45429-1999)
PHONE....................................937 434-4444
Debbie Spiegel, *Ch of Bd*
Jay Scheurle, *Principal*
Peter B Benedict II, *Principal*
Jennifer Papadakis, *Comms Dir*
Sarah Jones, *Director*
EMP: 26
SALES (est): 7.1MM **Privately Held**
SIC: 8351 8211 Preschool center; elementary & secondary schools

(G-9627)
MIAMI VALLEY URGENT CARE
6229 Troy Pike (45424-3646)
PHONE....................................937 252-2000
Suresh Gupta, *President*
EMP: 30
SALES (est): 427.1K **Privately Held**
SIC: 8059 Rest home, with health care

(G-9628)
MIAMI VLY CHILD DEV CTRS INC (PA)
Also Called: Mvcdc
215 Horace St (45402-8318)
PHONE....................................937 226-5664
Marry Burn, *President*
Dayvenia Chesney, *COO*
William Hewitt, *COO*
Scott Siegfried, *QC Dir*
Glenn L Hewitt, *Manager*
EMP: 85 EST: 1964
SQ FT: 22,000
SALES: 32MM **Privately Held**
WEB: www.mvcdc.org
SIC: 8351 Head start center, except in conjunction with school

(G-9629)
MIAMI VLY CHILD DEV CTRS INC
Also Called: Miami View Head Start
215 Horace St (45402-8318)
PHONE....................................937 228-1644
Wilma Cade, *Manager*
EMP: 33
SALES (corp-wide): 32MM **Privately Held**
WEB: www.mvcdc.org
SIC: 8351 Head start center, except in conjunction with school
PA: Miami Valley Child Development Centers, Inc.
215 Horace St
Dayton OH 45402
937 226-5664

(G-9630)
MIAMI VLY HSING OPRTUNTIES INC (PA)
Also Called: MVHO
907 W 5th St (45402-8306)
PHONE....................................937 263-4449
Debbie Watts Robinson, *CEO*
Donna Everson, *COO*
EMP: 34
SQ FT: 1,000
SALES: 7.9MM **Privately Held**
SIC: 8361 Home for the mentally handicapped

(G-9631)
MID-AMERICAN CLG CONTRS INC
360 Gargrave Rd Ste E (45449-5405)
PHONE....................................937 859-6222
Nuesmeyer Kermit, *Branch Mgr*
EMP: 105 **Privately Held**
SIC: 7699 Cleaning services
PA: Mid-American Cleaning Contractors, Inc.
447 N Elizabeth St
Lima OH 45801

(G-9632)
MIDWEST BEHAVIORAL CARE LTD
3821 Little York Rd (45414-2409)
PHONE....................................937 454-0092
Steve Pearce, *Partner*
Phyllis Kuehnl-Walters, *Partner*
Debra Sowald, *Partner*
EMP: 25
SALES (est): 1.2MM **Privately Held**
SIC: 8093 8322 8049 Mental health clinic, outpatient; general counseling services; clinical psychologist

(G-9633)
MIDWEST IRON AND METAL CO
461 Homestead Ave (45417-3921)
P.O. Box 546 (45401-0546)
PHONE....................................937 222-5992
Joel Frydman, *CEO*
Farley Frydman, *President*
Bert Appel, *Principal*
Judy Griffith, *Principal*
Miriam Jacobs, *Principal*
EMP: 65
SQ FT: 150,000
SALES (est): 18.5MM **Privately Held**
SIC: 3341 5093 Secondary nonferrous metals; scrap & waste materials

(G-9634)
MIKE RENNIE
Also Called: Imagistics International
300 E Bus Way Ste 270 (45401)
PHONE....................................513 830-0020
Dan Baker, *Principal*
John Curtis, *Principal*
James Tucker, *Vice Pres*
Mike Rennie, *Manager*
EMP: 35
SALES (est): 1.5MM **Privately Held**
SIC: 7334 Photocopying & duplicating services

(G-9635)
MIKE-SELLS POTATO CHIP CO (HQ)
333 Leo St (45404-1080)
P.O. Box 115 (45404-0115)
PHONE....................................937 228-9400
D W Mikesell, *Principal*
Martha J Mikesell, *Principal*
Frank De Moss, *Mfg Staff*
Jennifer Terrell, *Purch Mgr*
Deanna Lewis, *Accountant*
EMP: 30
SQ FT: 95,000
SALES (est): 64MM
SALES (corp-wide): 65.7MM **Privately Held**
SIC: 2096 5145 Potato chips & other potato-based snacks; snack foods; pretzels; corn chips
PA: Mike-Sell's West Virginia, Inc.
333 Leo St
Dayton OH 45404
937 228-9400

(G-9636)
MILLCRAFT PAPER COMPANY
1200 Leo St (45404-1650)
PHONE....................................937 222-7829
Evan Baker, *Accounts Mgr*
Michael A McCaughey, *Branch Mgr*
EMP: 27
SQ FT: 6,600 **Privately Held**
SIC: 5111 5113 Fine paper; paper & products, wrapping or coarse; pressure sensitive tape
HQ: The Millcraft Paper Company
6800 Grant Ave
Cleveland OH 44105
216 441-5505

(G-9637)
MILLER-VALENTINE CONSTRUCTION
137 N Main St Ste 900 (45402-1846)
PHONE....................................937 293-0900
Bill Krul, *CEO*
Chris Knueven, *President*
David Settles, *Sr Project Mgr*
Dave Selby, *Manager*
Sharon Smethers, *Executive Asst*
EMP: 100

SQ FT: 25,000
SALES (est): 15.4MM **Privately Held**
SIC: 1541 1542 8011 Industrial buildings, new construction; nonresidential construction; commercial & office building, new construction; commercial & office buildings, renovation & repair; shopping center construction; medical centers

(G-9638)
MILLER-VLENTINE OPERATIONS INC (PA)
Also Called: Miller Valentine Group
137 N Main St Ste 900 (45402-1846)
PHONE....................................937 293-0900
Bill Krul, *CEO*
William Krul, *CEO*
Al Schneider, *Senior Partner*
William Schneider, *Senior Partner*
Larry Hedger, *Superintendent*
EMP: 35
SALES: 153MM **Privately Held**
SIC: 6552 6531 Subdividers & developers; real estate managers

(G-9639)
MILLER-VLENTINE OPERATIONS INC
Also Called: Miller Valentine Group
9435 Waterstone Blvd (45409)
PHONE....................................513 771-0900
Bill Krul, *Branch Mgr*
EMP: 510
SALES (corp-wide): 153MM **Privately Held**
SIC: 6552 6531 Subdividers & developers; real estate managers
PA: Miller-Valentine Operations, Inc.
137 N Main St Ste 900
Dayton OH 45402
937 293-0900

(G-9640)
MITOSIS LLC
116 N Jefferson St # 300 (45402-1399)
PHONE....................................937 557-3440
Tyler Back, *Mng Member*
EMP: 25
SALES (est): 55.4K **Privately Held**
SIC: 7336 7812 7371 Graphic arts & related design; video production; computer software development & applications

(G-9641)
MODERN BUILDERS SUPPLY INC
2627 Stanley Ave (45404-2732)
P.O. Box 155 (45404-0155)
PHONE....................................937 222-2627
Kerry Linsenbigler, *Site Mgr*
Richard Baindge, *Manager*
EMP: 31
SALES (corp-wide): 347.7MM **Privately Held**
WEB: www.polaristechnologies.com
SIC: 5033 Roofing & siding materials
PA: Modern Builders Supply, Inc.
3500 Phillips Ave
Toledo OH 43608
419 241-3961

(G-9642)
MONCO ENTERPRISES INC (PA)
700 Liberty Ln (45449-2135)
PHONE....................................937 461-0034
Phil Hartje, *General Mgr*
Dee Ann Yohe, *Vice Pres*
Alisha Hayes, *Manager*
Sarah Miller, *Manager*
Elvia Thomas, *Director*
EMP: 700
SQ FT: 50,000
SALES: 38.6K **Privately Held**
SIC: 8331 2789 Sheltered workshop; community service employment training program; bookbinding & related work

(G-9643)
MONTGOMERY IRON & PAPER CO INC
Also Called: Montgomery Paper Co Div
400 E 4th St (45402-2110)
PHONE....................................937 222-4059
Steven Jacobs, *President*
Victor Jacobs, *Vice Pres*

Charles Jacobs, *Director*
Claire Jacobs, *Director*
EMP: 64
SQ FT: 17,000
SALES (est): 12.9MM **Privately Held**
SIC: 4953 Recycling, waste materials

(G-9644)
MORAINE COUNTRY CLUB
4075 Southern Blvd Unit 1 (45429-1199)
PHONE..............................937 294-6200
Jack E King, *President*
Jack Proud, *President*
John Giering, *Treasurer*
Nancy Walton,
EMP: 35
SQ FT: 20,000
SALES: 5MM **Privately Held**
WEB: www.morainecountryclub.com
SIC: 7997 Country club, membership

(G-9645)
MORGAN SERVICES INC
817 Webster St (45404-1529)
PHONE..............................937 223-5241
Alan Hartzell, *Branch Mgr*
EMP: 90
SALES (corp-wide): 38.6MM **Privately Held**
SIC: 7213 Linen supply
PA: Morgan Services, Inc.
    323 N Michigan Ave
    Chicago IL 60601
    312 346-3181

(G-9646)
MOTO FRANCHISE CORPORATION (PA)
Also Called: Motophoto
7086 Corporate Way Ste 2 (45459-4298)
PHONE..............................937 291-1900
Harry D Loyle, *President*
Ron Mohney, *Vice Pres*
Joseph M O'Hara, *Vice Pres*
EMP: 32
SQ FT: 3,500
SALES (est): 10.1MM **Privately Held**
SIC: 6794 Franchises, selling or licensing

(G-9647)
MUHA CONSTRUCTION INC
Also Called: Midwest Painting
855 Congress Park Dr # 101 (45459-4096)
PHONE..............................937 435-0678
David J Muha, *President*
Chuck Albert, *Vice Pres*
Greg Beem, *Project Mgr*
EMP: 46
SQ FT: 40,000
SALES: 10MM **Privately Held**
WEB: www.muhaconstruction.com
SIC: 1721 1542 Commercial painting; commercial & office building contractors

(G-9648)
MULLINS INTERNATIONAL SLS CORP
2949 Valley Pike (45404-2609)
P.O. Box 24113 (45424-0113)
PHONE..............................937 233-4213
William R Mullins, *President*
Dennis D Mullins, *Vice Pres*
Richard F Mullins, *Vice Pres*
▲ **EMP:** 60 **EST:** 1972
SQ FT: 75,000
SALES: 1MM **Privately Held**
SIC: 5085 Rubber goods, mechanical

(G-9649)
MV LAND DEVELOPMENT COMPANY
Also Called: Valentine Group
137 N Main St Ste 900 (45402-1846)
PHONE..............................937 293-0900
Bill Krul, *CEO*
EMP: 450
SALES (est): 8.4MM **Privately Held**
SIC: 6531 Real estate agent, commercial

(G-9650)
MVHE INC (HQ)
110 N Main St Ste 370 (45402-3729)
PHONE..............................937 499-8211
Ken Prunier, *President*
David Sturgeon, *CFO*

Joseph Mendhall, *Director*
EMP: 40
SQ FT: 2,100
SALES: 24.8MM
SALES (corp-wide): 968.3MM **Privately Held**
SIC: 8099 8011 Medical services organization; offices & clinics of medical doctors
PA: Med America Health Systems Corporation
    1 Wyoming St
    Dayton OH 45409
    937 223-6192

(G-9651)
N C R EMPLOYEE BENEFIT ASSN
Also Called: NCR Country Club
4435 Dogwood Trl (45429-1239)
PHONE..............................937 299-3571
Steve Scarpino, *President*
Glenn Thompson, *Manager*
EMP: 150
SQ FT: 44,000
SALES (est): 10.4MM **Privately Held**
WEB: www.ncrcountryclub.com
SIC: 7997 7991 5812 Country club, membership; physical fitness facilities; eating places

(G-9652)
NASA-TRMI GROUP INC
7918 N Main St (45415-2328)
PHONE..............................937 387-6517
Deborah Young, *Principal*
EMP: 99
SQ FT: 1,000
SALES (est): 606K **Privately Held**
SIC: 7381 Guard services

(G-9653)
NATIONAL HERITG ACADEMIES INC
Also Called: Emerson Academy
501 Hickory St (45410-1232)
PHONE..............................937 223-2889
Alison Foreman, *Branch Mgr*
EMP: 54 **Privately Held**
SIC: 8741 Management services
PA: National Heritage Academies, Inc.
    3850 Broadmoor Ave Se # 201
    Grand Rapids MI 49512

(G-9654)
NATIONAL HERITG ACADEMIES INC
Also Called: Pathway School of Discovery
173 Avondale Dr (45404-2123)
PHONE..............................937 235-5498
Keith Colbert, *Branch Mgr*
EMP: 54 **Privately Held**
SIC: 8741 Management services
PA: National Heritage Academies, Inc.
    3850 Broadmoor Ave Se # 201
    Grand Rapids MI 49512

(G-9655)
NATIONAL HERITG ACADEMIES INC
Also Called: North Dayton School Discovery
3901 Turner Rd (45415-3654)
PHONE..............................937 278-6671
Ron Albino, *Branch Mgr*
EMP: 54 **Privately Held**
SIC: 8741 Management services
PA: National Heritage Academies, Inc.
    3850 Broadmoor Ave Se # 201
    Grand Rapids MI 49512

(G-9656)
NELSON TREE SERVICE INC (DH)
3300 Office Park Dr # 205 (45439-2394)
PHONE..............................937 294-1313
Lou Nekola, *President*
Jeff Jones, *Exec VP*
Tanya Gasperetti, *Engineer*
Bev Nelson, *Manager*
EMP: 35
SQ FT: 4,000
SALES (est): 19.9MM
SALES (corp-wide): 4.5B **Privately Held**
WEB: www.nelsontree.com
SIC: 0783 Tree trimming services for public utility lines

(G-9657)
NICHOLAS E DAVIS
Also Called: Taft Law
40 N Main St Ste 1700 (45423-1029)
PHONE..............................937 228-2838
Nicholas Davis, *Partner*
EMP: 48
SALES (est): 90.9K **Privately Held**
SIC: 8111 General practice law office

(G-9658)
NICKOLAS RSIDENTIAL TRTMNT CTR
5581 Dayton Liberty Rd (45417-5403)
PHONE..............................937 496-7100
Dedrick Howard, *Superintendent*
EMP: 33
SALES (est): 1.1MM **Privately Held**
SIC: 8361 Residential care for children

(G-9659)
NORMAN-SPENCER AGENCY INC (PA)
Also Called: Miami Valley Insurance Assoc
8075 Washington Vlg Dr (45458-1847)
PHONE..............................800 543-3248
Paul J Norman, *Ch of Bd*
Brian Norman, *President*
Sandy Welker, *Vice Pres*
EMP: 25
SQ FT: 9,000
SALES (est): 19.3MM **Privately Held**
SIC: 6411 Insurance agents

(G-9660)
NORTHWEST CHILD DEVELOPMENT AN
2823 Campus Dr (45406-4103)
PHONE..............................937 559-9565
Matthew C Boykin,
EMP: 40 **EST:** 2017
SALES (est): 141K **Privately Held**
SIC: 8351 Child day care services

(G-9661)
NVR INC
2094 Northwest Pkwy (45426-3200)
PHONE..............................937 529-7000
Kenneth Thomas, *Branch Mgr*
EMP: 122 **Publicly Held**
SIC: 1531 Operative builders
PA: Nvr, Inc.
    11700 Plaza America Dr # 500
    Reston VA 20190

(G-9662)
OAK CREEK TERRACE INC
2316 Springmill Rd (45440-2504)
PHONE..............................937 439-1454
Barry A Kohn, *President*
Samuel Boymel, *Chairman*
Harold J Sosna, *Vice Pres*
EMP: 101
SALES (est): 2.9MM **Privately Held**
WEB: www.oakcreekterrace.com
SIC: 8051 Convalescent home with continuous nursing care

(G-9663)
OAK CREEK UNITED CHURCH
5280 Bigger Rd (45440-2658)
PHONE..............................937 434-3941
Kim Leetch, *Director*
EMP: 30
SQ FT: 42,000
SALES (est): 587.9K **Privately Held**
SIC: 8661 8351 Church of Christ; child day care services

(G-9664)
OAKS OF WEST KETTERING INC
1150 W Dorothy Ln (45409-1305)
PHONE..............................937 293-1152
Kenneth J Bernsen, *Principal*
EMP: 118
SQ FT: 47,752
SALES: 9.2MM **Privately Held**
SIC: 8051 Skilled nursing care facilities

(G-9665)
OBERERS FLOWERS INC (PA)
1448 Troy St (45404-2725)
PHONE..............................937 223-1253

Richard A Oberer, *President*
Ann R Oberer, *Corp Secy*
Rhonda Oberer Dunn, *Vice Pres*
Randall Oberer, *Vice Pres*
Keith Fields, *Store Mgr*
▲ **EMP:** 32
SALES (est): 10.3MM **Privately Held**
WEB: www.oberers.com
SIC: 5992 5193 Flowers, fresh; flowers, fresh; florists' supplies

(G-9666)
OBSTETRICS & GYNECOLOGY S INC (PA)
3533 Sthern Blvd Ste 4600 (45429)
PHONE..............................937 296-0167
Art Altman, *President*
Emily Kimble, *Vice Pres*
Mary Adams, *Office Mgr*
EMP: 26
SALES (est): 2.7MM **Privately Held**
SIC: 8011 Obstetrician; gynecologist

(G-9667)
ODYSSEY HEALTHCARE INC
3085 Woodman Dr Ste 200 (45420-1193)
PHONE..............................937 298-2800
Donna Martz, *Branch Mgr*
EMP: 30
SALES (corp-wide): 6B **Privately Held**
SIC: 8093 Specialty outpatient clinics
HQ: Odyssey Healthcare, Inc.
    7801 Mesquite Bend Dr # 105
    Irving TX 75063

(G-9668)
OHIO DEPARTMENT OF HEALTH
1323 W 3rd St (45402-6714)
PHONE..............................937 285-6250
Barbara Nixon, *Branch Mgr*
EMP: 68 **Privately Held**
WEB: www.jchealth.com
SIC: 8322 9431 Individual & family services;
HQ: Department Of Health Ohio
    246 N High St
    Columbus OH 43215

(G-9669)
OHIO HOME HEALTH CARE INC
5050 Nebraska Ave Ste 5 (45424-6197)
PHONE..............................937 853-0271
Vickey Siegel, *President*
EMP: 40
SALES: 1MM **Privately Held**
SIC: 8082 Home Health Care Services

(G-9670)
OHIO IRRIGATION LAWN SPRINKLER (PA)
Also Called: O-Heil Irrigation
2109 E Social Row Rd (45458-4803)
PHONE..............................937 432-9911
Jeffrey W Heil, *President*
Justin Heil, *Vice Pres*
Jeff Heil, *Executive*
EMP: 25
SQ FT: 5,800
SALES (est): 4.4MM **Privately Held**
SIC: 1711 5083 4959 1629 Irrigation sprinkler system installation; lawn & garden machinery & equipment; snowplowing; drainage system construction

(G-9671)
OHIO PEDIATRICS INC
7200 Poe Ave Ste 201 (45414-2799)
PHONE..............................937 299-2339
Dee Speaks, *Manager*
EMP: 30
SALES (corp-wide): 7.5MM **Privately Held**
SIC: 8011 Pediatrician
PA: Ohio Pediatrics Inc
    1775 Delco Park Dr
    Dayton OH 45420
    937 299-2743

(G-9672)
OHIO PEDIATRICS INC (PA)
1775 Delco Park Dr (45420-1398)
PHONE..............................937 299-2743
James Bryant, *President*
EMP: 45
SALES (est): 7.5MM **Privately Held**
SIC: 8011 Pediatrician

▲ = Import ▼ =Export
◆ =Import/Export

(G-9673)
OHIO PRESBT RETIREMENT SVCS
6520 Poe Ave (45414-2792)
PHONE................................937 415-5666
EMP: 218 Privately Held
SIC: 8059 Convalescent home
PA: Ohio Living
1001 Kingsmill Pkwy
Columbus OH 43229

(G-9674)
OLD DOMINION FREIGHT LINE INC
3100 Transportation Rd (45404-2359)
PHONE................................937 235-1596
Jason Back, Manager
EMP: 48
SALES (corp-wide): 4B Publicly Held
WEB: www.odfl.com
SIC: 4213 Contract haulers
PA: Old Dominion Freight Line Inc
500 Old Dominion Way
Thomasville NC 27360
336 889-5000

(G-9675)
ONE LINCOLN PARK
590 Isaac Prugh Way (45429-3482)
PHONE................................937 298-0594
Miller Valentine, Partner
Charles A Osborn Jr, Partner
Miami Valley Hospital Extended, Ltd Ptnr
EMP: 100
SALES (est): 7MM Privately Held
WEB: www.lincolnparkseniors.com
SIC: 6513 6531 Retirement hotel operation; real estate agents & managers

(G-9676)
ONE10 LLC
130 W 2nd St Ste 500 (45402-1547)
PHONE................................763 445-3000
EMP: 80
SALES (corp-wide): 1.8B Privately Held
SIC: 8742 Management And Marketing Consulting Services
HQ: One10 Llc
100 N 6th St Ste 700b
Minneapolis MN 55403
763 445-3000

(G-9677)
ORBIT MOVERS & ERECTORS INC
1101 Negley Pl (45402-6258)
PHONE................................937 277-8080
James Arnett Jr, CEO
Jay Hahn, President
David Grayson, CFO
Donald Roberts, Admin Sec
EMP: 50
SQ FT: 125,000
SALES (est): 6.1MM
SALES (corp-wide): 15.9MM Privately Held
SIC: 1796 1791 Millwright; machine moving & rigging; iron work, structural
PA: Unitize Company, Inc.
1101 Negley Pl
Dayton OH 45402
937 277-2686

(G-9678)
ORTHOPEDIC ASSOCIATES DAYTON
7980 N Main St (45415-2328)
PHONE................................937 280-4988
Thomas Cook, Principal
Melinda Scott, Principal
Julie Shott, Principal
Lance Tigyer, Principal
Lisa Byers, Physician Asst
EMP: 25 EST: 2010
SALES (est): 3.1MM Privately Held
SIC: 8011 Orthopedic physician

(G-9679)
OSTERFELD CHAMPION SERVICE
121 Commerce Park Dr (45404-1213)
PHONE................................937 254-8437
Barbara Smith, CEO
Warren Smith, President
Fawnie Brown, Controller
EMP: 25
SALES (est): 5MM Privately Held
WEB: www.osterfeld.us
SIC: 1711 7699 7623 Mechanical contractor; boiler repair shop; air conditioning repair

(G-9680)
P & R COMMUNICATIONS SVC INC (PA)
Also Called: First Page
700 E 1st St (45402-1383)
PHONE................................937 222-0861
Steve Reeves, President
David Reeves, Vice Pres
Dan Marvin, Project Engr
Chris Hanes, Sales Mgr
Nikki Hanes, Manager
EMP: 45 EST: 1964
SQ FT: 30,000
SALES (est): 5.3MM Privately Held
WEB: www.prcdayton.com
SIC: 7622 5065 Radio repair shop; radio parts & accessories

(G-9681)
PACCAR LEASING CORPORATION
Also Called: PacLease
7740 Center Point 70 Blvd (45424-6367)
PHONE................................937 235-2589
Bill Evans, Branch Mgr
EMP: 25
SALES (corp-wide): 23.5B Publicly Held
WEB: www.glsayre.com
SIC: 7513 Truck leasing, without drivers
HQ: Paccar Leasing Corporation
777 106th Ave Ne
Bellevue WA 98004
425 468-7400

(G-9682)
PAE & ASSOCIATES INC
7925 Paragon Rd (45459-4019)
PHONE................................937 833-0013
John P Elder, President
Patrick A Elder, Chairman
Doug Mitchell, Vice Pres
Jay Willen, Vice Pres
Mary Thomas, Officer
EMP: 30
SQ FT: 5,700
SALES (est): 9.4MM Privately Held
WEB: www.paeassociates.com
SIC: 1629 Industrial plant construction

(G-9683)
PALMER TRUCKS INC
Also Called: Kenthworth of Dayton
7740 Center Point 70 Blvd (45424-6367)
PHONE................................937 235-3318
John Sidebottom, Branch Mgr
EMP: 30
SALES (corp-wide): 250.1MM Privately Held
WEB: www.palmertrucks.com
SIC: 7538 7532 5531 5511 General automotive repair shops; truck painting & lettering; truck equipment & parts; pickups, new & used
PA: Palmer Trucks, Inc.
2929 S Holt Rd
Indianapolis IN 46241
317 243-1668

(G-9684)
PANINI NORTH AMERICA INC
577 Congress Park Dr (45459-4036)
PHONE................................937 291-2195
Michael Pratt, CEO
Ugo Panini, President
Douglas L Roberts, President
Glen Devall, Business Mgr
Shawn Hilliard, Senior VP
▲ EMP: 37
SQ FT: 10,000
SALES (est): 17.5MM Privately Held
WEB: www.paninina.com
SIC: 5049 Bank equipment & supplies
PA: D21 Holding Spa
Via Po 39
Torino TO
011 817-6011

(G-9685)
PARADIGM INDUSTRIAL LLC
1345 Stanley Ave (45404-1015)
PHONE................................937 224-4415
Flem Messer, General Mgr
Ashley Webb, Principal
Greg Day, Opers Mgr
Shanna Bennett, Info Tech Mgr
EMP: 40
SQ FT: 14,000
SALES (est): 5.8MM Privately Held
WEB: www.paradigm-industrial.com
SIC: 7699 7363 Industrial machinery & equipment repair; employee leasing service

(G-9686)
PARK-N-GO INC
Also Called: Park-N-Go Airport Parking
2700 W National Rd (45414-1108)
P.O. Box 13542 (45413-0542)
PHONE................................937 890-7275
Brian West, President
EMP: 40
SALES (est): 2.2MM Privately Held
SIC: 4111 7521 4581 Airport transportation; parking garage; airport

(G-9687)
PARKS RECREATION DIVISION
455 Infirmary Rd (45417-8748)
PHONE................................937 496-7135
Kim Farrell, Principal
Allen Leab, Administration
EMP: 30
SALES: 100K Privately Held
SIC: 8641 Recreation association

(G-9688)
PATRICIA A DICKERSON MD
1299 E Alex Bell Rd (45459-2658)
PHONE................................937 436-1117
Patricia A Dickerson, Owner
EMP: 28
SALES (est): 1.1MM Privately Held
SIC: 8011 Dermatologist

(G-9689)
PAWS INN INC
8926 Kingsridge Dr (45458-1619)
PHONE................................937 435-1500
Raymond Fournier, President
Mandy Combs, Manager
EMP: 25
SALES (est): 769.3K Privately Held
WEB: www.pawsinnah.com
SIC: 0752 0742 Boarding services, kennels; grooming services, pet & animal specialties; veterinarian, animal specialties

(G-9690)
PEPSI-COLA METRO BTLG CO INC
526 Milburn Ave (45404-1678)
PHONE................................937 461-4664
Tim Trant, General Mgr
Jon Amrozowicz, Opers Mgr
Phillip Beach, Manager
Michael Sidenstick, Manager
EMP: 300
SQ FT: 115,000
SALES (corp-wide): 64.6B Publicly Held
WEB: www.joy-of-cola.com
SIC: 2086 5149 Soft drinks: packaged in cans, bottles, etc.; groceries & related products
HQ: Pepsi-Cola Metropolitan Bottling Company, Inc.
1111 Westchester Ave
White Plains NY 10604
914 767-6000

(G-9691)
PICKREL BROTHERS INC
901 S Perry St (45402-2589)
PHONE................................937 461-5960
Thomas Pickrel, President
Ted McGarry, General Mgr
James L Pickrel, Vice Pres
Michael Tangeman, Sales Staff
Jim Rohl, Manager
EMP: 50
SQ FT: 25,000

SALES (est): 33.4MM Privately Held
WEB: www.pickrelbros.com
SIC: 5074 Plumbing fittings & supplies

(G-9692)
PICKREL SCHAEFFER EBELING LPA
40 N Main St Ste 2700 (45423-2700)
PHONE................................937 223-1130
Paul Zimmer, President
Donald G Schweller, Counsel
Jon Rosmeyer, Admin Sec
Frank Macharoni, Administration
Samantha Naves, Legal Staff
EMP: 52
SQ FT: 16,000
SALES (est): 7.3MM Privately Held
WEB: www.pselaw.com
SIC: 8111 General practice law office; general practice attorney, lawyer

(G-9693)
PLACES INC
11 W Monument Ave Ste 700 (45402-1245)
PHONE................................937 461-4300
Dave Nuscher, Accounting Mgr
Kathy Nickell, Office Mgr
Barb Stokoe, Info Tech Mgr
Roy Craig, Exec Dir
EMP: 62
SALES (est): 3.6MM Privately Held
SIC: 8052 Home for the mentally retarded, with health care

(G-9694)
PLANNED PARENTHOOD ASSOCIATION (PA)
Also Called: Planned Prnthood of Grter Mami
224 N Wilkinson St (45402-3096)
PHONE................................937 226-0780
Noreen Willhelm, Acting CEO
EMP: 33
SQ FT: 14,000
SALES: 568K Privately Held
SIC: 8093 8322 Family planning clinic; individual & family services

(G-9695)
PLATINUM EXPRESS INC
2549 Stanley Ave (45404-2730)
PHONE................................937 235-9540
Mina Burba, President
EMP: 60 EST: 1999
SALES (est): 9MM Privately Held
SIC: 4213 Trucking, except local

(G-9696)
POELKING BOWLING CENTERS
8871 Kingsridge Dr (45458-1617)
PHONE................................937 435-3855
Joe Poelking, Owner
EMP: 25 EST: 1976
SALES (est): 880.6K Privately Held
SIC: 7933 Ten pin center

(G-9697)
POELKING LANES INC (PA)
1403 Wilmington Ave (45420-1542)
PHONE................................937 299-5573
Jon P Poelking, President
Jayson Poelking, General Mgr
Gisela Poelking, Managing Dir
Michael Poelking, Treasurer
EMP: 64 EST: 1951
SQ FT: 38,000
SALES (est): 4MM Privately Held
SIC: 7933 5813 Ten pin center; cocktail lounge

(G-9698)
POMEROY IT SOLUTIONS SLS INC
478 Windsor Park Dr (45459-4111)
PHONE................................937 439-9682
Chris Morgan, Manager
EMP: 32 Privately Held
SIC: 7373 Computer integrated systems design
HQ: Pomeroy It Solutions Sales Company, Inc.
1020 Petersburg Rd
Hebron KY 41048

(G-9699)
PORTER WRGHT MORRIS ARTHUR LLP
Also Called: Attorneys-At-Law
1 S Main St Ste 1600 (45402-2088)
P.O. Box 1805 (45401-1805)
PHONE..................................937 449-6810
R Bruce Snyder, *Managing Prtnr*
Brian D Hall, *Partner*
Molly Deverse, *Pastor*
David G Zimmerman, *Personnel*
Joanna Arnason, *Marketing Mgr*
EMP: 35
SQ FT: 25,500
SALES (corp-wide): 83MM **Privately Held**
SIC: 8111 General practice law office
PA: Porter, Wright, Morris & Arthur Llp
41 S High St Ste 2900
Columbus OH 43215
614 227-2000

(G-9700)
POSITIVE ELECTRIC INC
4738 Gateway Cir Ste C (45440-1724)
PHONE..................................937 428-0606
Guy Monnin, *President*
EMP: 50
SQ FT: 2,000
SALES: 8MM **Privately Held**
SIC: 1731 General electrical contractor

(G-9701)
POWER MANAGEMENT INC (PA)
420 Davis Ave (45403-2912)
PHONE..................................937 222-2909
Reece Powers, *President*
EMP: 28
SQ FT: 24,000
SALES (est): 2.8MM **Privately Held**
SIC: 6512 6513 2752 7331 Nonresidential building operators; apartment building operators; offset & photolithographic printing; mailing service; management consulting services; commercial nonphysical research

(G-9702)
PRECISION MTAL FABRICATION INC (PA)
191 Heid Ave (45404-1217)
PHONE..................................937 235-9261
Jim Hackenberger, *President*
John Limbing, *Corp Secy*
EMP: 52
SQ FT: 30,000
SALES (est): 7MM **Privately Held**
WEB: www.premetfab.com
SIC: 7692 3444 Welding repair; sheet metalwork

(G-9703)
PREMIER HEALTH GROUP LLC
110 N Main St Ste 350 (45402-3735)
PHONE..................................937 535-4100
James R Pancoast, *Principal*
Thomas M Duncan, *Senior VP*
Mary H Boosalis, *Vice Pres*
EMP: 38 EST: 2014
SALES (est): 13.1MM **Privately Held**
SIC: 8011 Offices & clinics of medical doctors

(G-9704)
PREMIER HEALTH PARTNERS (PA)
Also Called: MIAMI VALLEY
110 N Main St Ste 450 (45402-3712)
PHONE..................................937 499-9596
James R Pancoast, *President*
Sharon Rector, *Principal*
Mark Shaker, *Senior VP*
Mary H Boosalis, *Vice Pres*
William E Linesch, *Vice Pres*
EMP: 636
SALES: 17.2K **Privately Held**
SIC: 8082 Home health care services

(G-9705)
PREMIER HEALTH SPECIALISTS INC (HQ)
110 N Main St Ste 350 (45402-3735)
PHONE..................................937 223-4518

Thomas Thorton, *President*
EMP: 50
SALES (est): 10.5MM
SALES (corp-wide): 968.3MM **Privately Held**
WEB: www.mvcdayton.com
SIC: 8011 Surgeon
PA: Med America Health Systems Corporation
1 Wyoming St
Dayton OH 45409
937 223-6192

(G-9706)
PREMIER HEART ASSOCIATES INC
6251 Good Samaritan Way # 220 (45424-5464)
PHONE..................................937 832-2425
Steve Stratton, *Manager*
EMP: 30 EST: 2000
SALES (est): 3.3MM **Privately Held**
WEB: www.premierheartassociates.com
SIC: 8011 Cardiologist & cardio-vascular specialist

(G-9707)
PRIMARY CR NTWRK PRMR HLTH PRT
Also Called: Needmore Road Primary Care
1530 Needmore Rd Ste 200 (45414-3957)
PHONE..................................937 278-5854
Kenneth Prunier, *CEO*
EMP: 47
SALES (corp-wide): 33.7MM **Privately Held**
SIC: 8011 General & family practice, physician/surgeon
PA: Primary Care Network Of Premier Health Partners
110 N Main St Ste 350
Dayton OH 45402
937 226-7085

(G-9708)
PRIMARY CR NTWRK PRMR HLTH PRT
1222 S Patterson Blvd # 120 (45402-2684)
PHONE..................................937 208-9090
Heidi Buckingham, *Principal*
EMP: 55
SALES (corp-wide): 33.7MM **Privately Held**
SIC: 8011 General & family practice, physician/surgeon
PA: Primary Care Network Of Premier Health Partners
110 N Main St Ste 350
Dayton OH 45402
937 226-7085

(G-9709)
PRIMARY CR NTWRK PRMR HLTH PRT (PA)
Also Called: Samanritan Family Care
110 N Main St Ste 350 (45402-3735)
PHONE..................................937 226-7085
Ken Prunier, *President*
Dave Sturgeon, *CFO*
EMP: 55
SALES (est): 33.7MM **Privately Held**
SIC: 8011 General & family practice, physician/surgeon

(G-9710)
PRIMARY CR NTWRK PRMR HLTH PRT
Also Called: Perinatal Partners
2350 Miami Valley Dr # 410 (45459-4778)
PHONE..................................937 424-9800
Terri L Stuerman, *Vice Pres*
EMP: 55
SALES (corp-wide): 33.7MM **Privately Held**
SIC: 8011 Gynecologist
PA: Primary Care Network Of Premier Health Partners
110 N Main St Ste 350
Dayton OH 45402
937 226-7085

(G-9711)
PRIMARY DAYTON INNKEEPERS LLC
7701 Washington Vlg Dr (45459-3954)
PHONE..................................937 938-9550
Rob Hale, *Principal*
EMP: 27
SALES (est): 1.6MM **Privately Held**
SIC: 7011 Hotels

(G-9712)
PRIMED
979 Congress Park Dr (45459-4009)
PHONE..................................937 435-9013
Carrol H Estep, *Principal*
EMP: 25 EST: 2001
SALES (est): 739.7K **Privately Held**
SIC: 8011 General & family practice, physician/surgeon

(G-9713)
PRIMED PHYSICIANS
540 Lincoln Park Blvd # 390 (45429-6408)
PHONE..................................937 298-8058
John E Mauer MD, *Partner*
Malak Adib, *Partner*
Tamara Togliatti, *Partner*
EMP: 40
SALES (est): 4.6MM **Privately Held**
SIC: 8011 General & family practice, physician/surgeon

(G-9714)
PRIMED PREMIER INTEGRATED MED (PA)
Also Called: Primed Physicians
6520 Acro Ct (45459-2679)
PHONE..................................937 291-6893
Karen Davis, *Director*
EMP: 250
SALES (est): 14.9MM **Privately Held**
SIC: 8011 Medical Doctor's Office

(G-9715)
PRODUCE ONE INC
904 Woodley Rd (45403-1444)
PHONE..................................931 253-4749
Gary Pavlofsky, *President*
Jeanie Hargrove, *Vice Pres*
Ervin Pavlofsky, *Vice Pres*
Darrick Scott, *Opers Spvr*
Belinda Wright, *Human Res Dir*
EMP: 75
SQ FT: 14,000
SALES (est): 29.3MM **Privately Held**
WEB: www.produceone.com
SIC: 5148 5142 5147 5149 Fruits, fresh; vegetables, fresh; fish, frozen: packaged; meat, frozen: packaged; meats, fresh; canned goods: fruit, vegetables, seafood, meats, etc.
PA: Premier Produce Properties Ltd
4500 Willow Pkwy
Cleveland OH 44125
800 229-5517

(G-9716)
PRODUCTION DESIGN SERVICES INC (PA)
Also Called: Pdsi Technical Services
313 Mound St (45402-8370)
PHONE..................................937 866-3377
John H Schultz, *President*
Jeffrey R Schultz, *Vice Pres*
Pat Moore, *Plant Mgr*
Jeff Schultz, *Chief Engr*
James A Schultz, *CFO*
EMP: 80
SQ FT: 48,000
SALES (est): 24.9MM **Privately Held**
WEB: www.p-d-s-i.com
SIC: 3569 8711 7363 3823 Robots, assembly line: industrial & commercial; industrial engineers; mechanical engineering; temporary help service; industrial instrmnts msrmnt display/control process variable; machine tool accessories; special dies, tools, jigs & fixtures

(G-9717)
PRODUCTIVITY QULTY SYSTEMS INC (PA)
Also Called: PQ Systems
210b E Spring Valley Pike (45458-2653)
P.O. Box 750010 (45475-0010)
PHONE..................................937 885-2255
Michael J Cleary, *President*
Barbara Cleary, *Vice Pres*
EMP: 25
SQ FT: 20,000
SALES (est): 5.3MM **Privately Held**
WEB: www.pqsystems.com
SIC: 7371 5046 Computer software development; teaching machines, electronic; productivity improvement consultant

(G-9718)
PROFESSIONAL MAINT DAYTON
223 E Helena St (45404-1003)
PHONE..................................937 461-5259
John E Thompson, *President*
EMP: 85 EST: 1960
SQ FT: 3,000
SALES: 800K **Privately Held**
WEB: www.pmdayton.com
SIC: 7349 Janitorial service, contract basis

(G-9719)
PROFILE DIGITAL PRINTING LLC
5449 Marina Dr (45449-1833)
PHONE..................................937 866-4241
Terry Harmeyer, *General Mgr*
Tom Helmers, *Principal*
June Helmers,
EMP: 25
SALES (est): 4.1MM **Privately Held**
WEB: www.profiledpi.com
SIC: 7334 2759 2752 Blueprinting service; commercial printing; commercial printing, lithographic

(G-9720)
PROJECT C U R E INC
200 Daruma Pkwy (45439-7909)
PHONE..................................937 262-3500
Hasani Hayden, *Human Res Dir*
Renee Hicks, *Case Mgr*
Zel Skelton, *Director*
Sharon Conyers, *Director*
Herman Erving, *Deputy Dir*
EMP: 50
SQ FT: 14,280
SALES: 4.3MM **Privately Held**
WEB: www.projectcure.com
SIC: 8093 Substance abuse clinics (outpatient); alcohol clinic, outpatient; drug clinic, outpatient; rehabilitation center, outpatient treatment

(G-9721)
PROTECTIVE COATINGS INC
4321 Webster St (45414-4935)
PHONE..................................937 275-7711
Kevin Conley, *President*
Joe Conley, *Vice Pres*
Scott Jones, *Foreman/Supr*
Damon Halsey, *Program Mgr*
Dennis Mundt, *Info Tech Mgr*
EMP: 30
SQ FT: 4,000
SALES: 2.5MM **Privately Held**
WEB: www.protectivecoatings.com
SIC: 1721 1761 1752 1741 Interior commercial painting contractor; wallcovering contractors; roofing, siding & sheet metal work; floor laying & floor work; foundation building; industrial buildings & warehouses

(G-9722)
QUANEXUS INC
571 Congress Park Dr (45459-4036)
PHONE..................................937 885-7272
Jack Gerbs, *Principal*
Chris Elrod, *Marketing Staff*
EMP: 37
SALES (est): 7.4MM **Privately Held**
SIC: 4813 7379 Data telephone communications; voice telephone communications; computer related consulting services

(G-9723)
QUEBE HOLDINGS INC (PA)
Also Called: Chapel Electric Co.
1985 Founders Dr (45420-4012)
PHONE................................937 222-2290
Dennis F Quebe, *Ch of Bd*
Gregory P Ross, *President*
Richard E Penewit, *Vice Pres*
Richard Penewit, *Vice Pres*
Bob Shaffer, *Vice Pres*
EMP: 100
SQ FT: 40,000
SALES (est): 66.4MM **Privately Held**
WEB: www.quebe.com
SIC: 1731 Lighting contractor

(G-9724)
R L O INC (PA)
Also Called: Great Clips
466 Windsor Park Dr (45459-4111)
PHONE................................937 620-9998
Clara Osterhage, *President*
Raymond Osterhage, *Vice Pres*
EMP: 35
SALES (est): 749.6K **Privately Held**
SIC: 7231 Unisex hair salons

(G-9725)
RAHN DENTAL GROUP INC
5660 Far Hills Ave (45429-2206)
PHONE................................937 435-0324
Douglas Patton, *President*
Dr Paul Unverferth, *Vice Pres*
Dr Richard C Quinttus, *Admin Sec*
EMP: 32
SALES (est): 1.8MM **Privately Held**
SIC: 8021 Dentists' office

(G-9726)
RAM RESTORATION LLC
Also Called: Ram Resources
11125 Yankee St Ste A (45458-3698)
PHONE................................937 347-7418
Trish Jackson, *COO*
Doug Trent, *Project Mgr*
Randy Mount,
Regis Robbins,
Tom Weir,
EMP: 36
SQ FT: 2,500
SALES (est): 2.7MM **Privately Held**
SIC: 1799 1521 1522 Home/office interiors finishing, furnishing & remodeling; kitchen & bathroom remodeling; single-family home remodeling, additions & repairs; hotel/motel & multi-family home renovation & remodeling

(G-9727)
RDE SYSTEM CORPORATION
Also Called: Sonshine Commercial Cleaning
986 Windsor Ave (45402)
PHONE................................513 933-8000
Bob Espepp, *President*
EMP: 100
SALES (est): 1.5MM **Privately Held**
SIC: 7349 Janitorial service, contract basis

(G-9728)
REAL ART DESIGN GROUP INC (PA)
520 E 1st St (45402-1221)
PHONE................................937 223-9955
Christopher Wire, *President*
Betsy McFaddin, *Prdtn Mgr*
Tom Immen, *Accounts Exec*
Tom Davis, *Manager*
Casie Lord, *Manager*
EMP: 33
SQ FT: 25,000
SALES: 1.5MM **Privately Held**
WEB: www.realartusa.com
SIC: 7336 7311 Graphic arts & related design; advertising consultant

(G-9729)
REGENT SYSTEMS INC
Also Called: RSI
7590 Paragon Rd (45459-4065)
PHONE................................937 640-8010
Michael A Bernal, *CEO*
Wilma M Bernal, *Corp Secy*
Richard Nagel, *CFO*
EMP: 25
SQ FT: 8,000

SALES: 9.6MM **Privately Held**
WEB: www.regentsystems.com
SIC: 7379 8742 ; hospital & health services consultant

(G-9730)
RELIABLE CONTRACTORS INC
Also Called: Rave - Rlable Audio Video Elec
94 Compark Rd Ste 200 (45459-4853)
PHONE................................937 433-0262
Joe Ryan, *President*
Sam Durbin, *Project Mgr*
Matt Minor, *Project Mgr*
Dave White, *Department Mgr*
EMP: 60
SQ FT: 12,500
SALES (est): 12.4MM **Privately Held**
WEB: www.reliable-contractors.com
SIC: 1731 General electrical contractor

(G-9731)
RENTHOTEL DAYTON LLC
Also Called: Doubletree Hotel
11 S Ludlow St (45402-1810)
PHONE................................937 461-4700
Robert Holsten, *Principal*
C H Corp,
EMP: 95
SQ FT: 184,000
SALES (est): 2.3MM **Privately Held**
SIC: 7011 Hotels & motels

(G-9732)
RENTZ CORP (PA)
Also Called: Metropolitan Cleaners
759 Grants Trl (45459-3123)
PHONE................................937 434-2774
Richard J Rentz, *President*
Barbara Rentz, *Corp Secy*
EMP: 50
SALES (est): 1.7MM **Privately Held**
SIC: 7216 Drycleaning plants, except rugs

(G-9733)
REPUBLIC SERVICES INC
Also Called: Allied Waste Division
1577 W River Rd (45417-6740)
PHONE................................937 268-8110
Don Baer, *Branch Mgr*
EMP: 34
SALES (corp-wide): 10B **Publicly Held**
SIC: 4953 Refuse collection & disposal services
PA: Republic Services, Inc.
18500 N Allied Way # 100
Phoenix AZ 85054
480 627-2700

(G-9734)
RESIDENT HOME ASSOCIATION
3661 Salem Ave (45406-1661)
PHONE................................937 278-0791
Rhonda Rich, *Accountant*
Brenda Whitney, *Director*
EMP: 65
SQ FT: 4,582
SALES (est): 5.1MM **Privately Held**
SIC: 8621 Professional membership organizations

(G-9735)
RICHARD A BROOCK
10 N Ludlow St (45402-1854)
PHONE................................937 449-2840
Richard A Broock, *Principal*
EMP: 50
SALES (est): 1.9MM **Privately Held**
SIC: 8111 Corporate, partnership & business law

(G-9736)
RIVERVIEW HEALTH INSTITUTE
1 Elizabeth Pl (45417-3445)
PHONE................................937 222-5390
Ethan Fallang, *CEO*
Jonathan J Paley, *Surgeon*
EMP: 48
SALES (est): 10.6MM **Privately Held**
WEB: www.riverviewhealthinstitute.com
SIC: 8011 Medical centers

(G-9737)
RMS OF OHIO INC
5335 Far Hills Ave # 306 (45429-2317)
PHONE................................937 291-3622
Joseph Cozzolino, *President*

Briget Forsythe, *Director*
EMP: 55
SALES (est): 1.8MM **Privately Held**
SIC: 8082 Home health care services

(G-9738)
ROBERT HALF INTERNATIONAL INC
1 S Main St Ste 300 (45402-2065)
PHONE................................937 224-7376
Jill Crowe, *Manager*
EMP: 92
SALES (corp-wide): 5.8B **Publicly Held**
SIC: 7361 Executive placement
PA: Robert Half International Inc.
2884 Sand Hill Rd Ste 200
Menlo Park CA 94025
650 234-6000

(G-9739)
ROMITECH INC (PA)
2000 Composite Dr (45420-1493)
PHONE................................937 297-9529
Fax: 937 435-2430
EMP: 32
SQ FT: 45,000
SALES (est): 4.8MM **Privately Held**
SIC: 5999 8748 Ret Misc Merchandise
Business Consulting Services

(G-9740)
RUMPKE TRANSPORTATION CO LLC
Also Called: Rumpke Container Service
1932 E Monument Ave (45402-1359)
PHONE................................937 461-0004
Kyle Aughe, *Manager*
EMP: 38 **Privately Held**
SIC: 4953 7359 Refuse collection & disposal services; portable toilet rental
HQ: Rumpke Transportation Company, Llc
10795 Hughes Rd
Cincinnati OH 45251
513 851-0122

(G-9741)
RUSH EXPEDITING INC
2619 Needmore Rd (45414-4205)
PHONE................................937 885-0894
Jan E Parker, *President*
EMP: 30
SALES (est): 4MM **Privately Held**
SIC: 4729 Carpool/vanpool arrangement

(G-9742)
RUSH PACKAGE DELIVERY INC (PA)
Also Called: Rush Trnsp & Logistics
2619 Needmore Rd (45414-4205)
P.O. Box 2810 (45401-2810)
PHONE................................937 224-7874
Steve Parker, *CEO*
Ashley Parker, *President*
Jan Parker, *Principal*
EMP: 25
SQ FT: 5,500
SALES (est): 15.7MM **Privately Held**
WEB: www.rush-delivery.com
SIC: 4212 Delivery service, vehicular

(G-9743)
RUSH PACKAGE DELIVERY INC
Also Called: Rush Trnsp & Logistics
2619 Needmore Rd (45414-4205)
PHONE................................937 297-6182
Ron Hanyke, *General Mgr*
EMP: 80
SALES (corp-wide): 15.7MM **Privately Held**
WEB: www.rush-delivery.com
SIC: 4212 7389 Delivery service, vehicular; courier or messenger service
PA: Rush Package Delivery, Inc.
2619 Needmore Rd
Dayton OH 45414
937 224-7874

(G-9744)
RYDER TRUCK RENTAL INC
3580 Needmore Rd (45414-4316)
PHONE................................937 236-1650
Greg Stone, *General Mgr*
EMP: 40
SALES (corp-wide): 8.4B **Publicly Held**
SIC: 7513 Truck rental, without drivers

HQ: Ryder Truck Rental, Inc.
11690 Nw 105th St
Medley FL 33178
305 500-3726

(G-9745)
S & S MANAGEMENT INC
Also Called: Holiday Inn
5612 Merily Way (45424-2065)
PHONE................................937 235-2000
Brian McKenzie, *Manager*
EMP: 30
SALES (corp-wide): 6.9MM **Privately Held**
SIC: 7011 Hotels
PA: S & S Management Inc
550 Folkerth Ave 100
Sidney OH 45365
937 498-9645

(G-9746)
S&D/OSTERFELD MECH CONTRS INC
1101 Negley Pl (45402-6258)
PHONE................................937 277-1700
Jeff Arthur, *CEO*
James Arnett Jr, *CEO*
Lisa Schneider, *President*
Carl Crawford, *Vice Pres*
David Grayson, *CFO*
EMP: 50 EST: 1908
SQ FT: 125,000
SALES (est): 5.7MM
SALES (corp-wide): 15.9MM **Privately Held**
WEB: www.unitize.com
SIC: 1711 Plumbing contractors; heating & air conditioning contractors
PA: Unitize Company, Inc.
1101 Negley Pl
Dayton OH 45402
937 277-2686

(G-9747)
SALVATION ARMY
1000 N Keowee St (45404-1520)
P.O. Box 10007 (45402-7007)
PHONE................................937 528-5100
Thomas Depreis, *Branch Mgr*
EMP: 30
SALES (corp-wide): 4.3B **Privately Held**
WEB: www.salvationarmy-usaeast.org
SIC: 8322 8661 Family service agency; miscellaneous denomination church
HQ: The Salvation Army
440 W Nyack Rd Ofc
West Nyack NY 10994
845 620-7200

(G-9748)
SAMARITAN BEHAVIORAL HEALTH (DH)
601 Enid Ave (45429-5413)
PHONE................................937 276-8333
Sue McGatha, *CEO*
Marilyn Houser, *Vice Pres*
Janet Rogers, *Treasurer*
EMP: 26
SALES (est): 11.2MM **Privately Held**
SIC: 8093 Mental health clinic, outpatient
HQ: Samaritan Health Partners
2222 Philadelphia Dr
Dayton OH 45406
937 208-8400

(G-9749)
SAMARITAN HEALTH PARTNERS (HQ)
2222 Philadelphia Dr (45406-1813)
PHONE................................937 208-8400
K Douglas Deck, *President*
Thomas M Duncan, *CFO*
EMP: 2165
SQ FT: 1,000,000
SALES (est): 287.5MM **Privately Held**
SIC: 8062 General medical & surgical hospitals

(G-9750)
SAMPLE MACHINING INC
Also Called: Bitec
220 N Jersey St (45403-1220)
PHONE................................937 258-3338
Beverly Bleicher, *President*
Kevin Bleicher, *Vice Pres*

(PA)=Parent Co (HQ)=Headquarters (DH)=Div Headquarters

○ = New Business established in last 2 years

2019 Harris Ohio
Services Directory

399

David Calmes, *Mfg Mgr*
Chris Bell, *QC Mgr*
Larry Mullett, *Engineer*
EMP: 45
SQ FT: 19,000
SALES: 7MM **Privately Held**
WEB: www.bitecsmi.com
SIC: 3599 8734 Custom machinery; testing laboratories

(G-9751)
SANCTUARY AT WILMINGTON PLACE
264 Wilmington Ave (45420-1989)
PHONE................................937 256-4663
Robert Banasik, *President*
EMP: 60
SALES (est): 3.1MM **Privately Held**
SIC: 8051 Skilled nursing care facilities

(G-9752)
SATURN ELECTRIC INC
2628 Nordic Rd (45414-3424)
P.O. Box 13830 (45413-0830)
PHONE................................937 278-2580
Doug Kash, *President*
EMP: 50
SQ FT: 10,000
SALES (est): 10.3MM **Privately Held**
SIC: 1731 General electrical contractor

(G-9753)
SCOTT INDUSTRIAL SYSTEMS INC (PA)
4433 Interpoint Blvd (45424-5708)
P.O. Box 1387 (45401-1387)
PHONE................................937 233-8146
Randall Scott, *Ch of Bd*
Dave Baumann, *President*
Mark Bryan, *President*
Chuck Volpe, *President*
Greg Strickland, *Business Mgr*
EMP: 75
SQ FT: 63,000
SALES: 65.4MM **Privately Held**
WEB: www.scottindustrialsystems.com
SIC: 5084 Hydraulic systems equipment & supplies; pneumatic tools & equipment

(G-9754)
SCREEN WORKS INC (PA)
3970 Image Dr (45414-2524)
PHONE................................937 264-9111
Jeff Cottrell, *Principal*
EMP: 29
SQ FT: 42,000
SALES: 7MM **Privately Held**
WEB: www.screenworksinc.com
SIC: 7336 5199 7389 3993 Silk screen design; advertising specialties; embroidering of advertising on shirts, etc.; signs & advertising specialties; automotive & apparel trimmings

(G-9755)
SEBALY SHILLITO & DYER LPA (PA)
1900 Kettering Tower 40n (45423-1013)
PHONE................................937 222-2500
Jon M Sebaly, *Managing Prtnr*
Melissa Mills, *CFO*
James Dyer, *Shareholder*
Gale S Finley, *Shareholder*
Beverly Shillito, *Shareholder*
EMP: 48
SALES (est): 7.7MM **Privately Held**
SIC: 8111 General practice attorney, lawyer

(G-9756)
SECOND MENTAL RETARDATION
Also Called: First Mental Retardation
2080 N Gettysburg Ave (45406-3562)
PHONE................................937 262-3077
Janice Smith, *Exec Dir*
EMP: 30 **EST:** 1998
SALES: 47.5K **Privately Held**
SIC: 8361 Residential care

(G-9757)
SECURITAS SEC SVCS USA INC
Automotive Services Division
118 W 1st St (45402-1150)
PHONE................................937 224-7432

William Mangus, *Business Mgr*
Bill Mangus, *Sales Mgr*
Charles Baker, *Systems Staff*
EMP: 110
SALES (corp-wide): 10.9B **Privately Held**
SIC: 7381 Security guard service
HQ: Securitas Security Services Usa, Inc.
　9 Campus Dr
　Parsippany NJ 07054
　973 267-5300

(G-9758)
SELECT INDUSTRIES CORP
60 Heid Ave (45404-1216)
PHONE................................937 233-9191
Mike Ryan, *Principal*
EMP: 27
SALES (est): 16.5MM **Privately Held**
SIC: 5084 Industrial machinery & equipment

(G-9759)
SENIOR RESOURCE CONNECTION (PA)
Also Called: MEALS ON WHEELS
222 Salem Ave (45406-5805)
PHONE................................937 223-8246
Roger Davis, *Business Mgr*
Chuck Comp, *Vice Pres*
Lisa Garvic, *Human Res Dir*
Cristal Fillers, *Office Mgr*
Katherine Leger, *Case Mgr*
EMP: 195
SQ FT: 25,000
SALES: 7.3MM **Privately Held**
SIC: 8322 Senior citizens' center or association

(G-9760)
SERENITY HM HALTHCARE SVCS LLC
33 White Allen Ave (45405-4930)
PHONE................................937 222-0002
EMP: 80
SALES (est): 696.4K **Privately Held**
SIC: 8082 Home health care services

(G-9761)
SERVICE CENTER TITLE AGENCY
Also Called: Vantage Land Title
6718 Loop Rd (45459-2161)
PHONE................................937 312-3080
Andy Morgan, *President*
Collin Morgan, *Manager*
EMP: 27
SALES: 2.5MM **Privately Held**
SIC: 6361 Title insurance

(G-9762)
SFA ARCHITECTS INC
120 W 2nd St Ste 1800 (45402-1603)
PHONE................................937 281-0600
E Thomas Fernandez, *CEO*
Dave F Freeman, *General Mgr*
EMP: 36
SALES (est): 1.5MM **Privately Held**
SIC: 8712 Architectural engineering

(G-9763)
SHOOK CONSTRUCTION CO
Also Called: Building Group Division
4977 Northcutt Pl Ste 200 (45414-3839)
P.O. Box 138806 (45413-8806)
PHONE................................440 838-5400
EMP: 60
SQ FT: 4,000
SALES (corp-wide): 133.9MM **Privately Held**
SIC: 1629 1542 Heavy Construction Nonresidential Construction
PA: Shook Construction Co.
　2000 W Dorothy Ln
　Moraine OH 45439
　937 276-6666

(G-9764)
SHR MANAGEMENT RESOURCES CORP
2222 Philadelphia Dr (45406-1813)
PHONE................................937 274-1546
Doug Deck, *CEO*
John P Mason, *President*
Carolyn Harpel, *Treasurer*
EMP: 30

SALES (est): 711.3K **Privately Held**
SIC: 8093 5912 Specialty outpatient clinics; drug stores
HQ: Samaritan Health Partners
　2222 Philadelphia Dr
　Dayton OH 45406
　937 208-8400

(G-9765)
SHUMSKY ENTERPRISES INC (PA)
Also Called: Boost Technologies
811 E 4th St (45402-2227)
P.O. Box 36 (45401-0036)
PHONE................................937 223-2203
Anita Emoff, *CEO*
Michael J Emoff, *Ch of Bd*
William Diederich, *President*
Matt Toomb, *Vice Pres*
F James Donaghy, *Finance Dir*
▲ **EMP:** 66
SQ FT: 19,500
SALES (est): 32.9MM **Privately Held**
WEB: www.pointsdemo.com
SIC: 5199 Advertising specialties

(G-9766)
SIBCY CLINE INC
8353 Yankee St (45458-1809)
PHONE................................937 610-3404
Irma Wise, *Branch Mgr*
EMP: 42
SALES (corp-wide): 2.1B **Privately Held**
SIC: 6531 Real estate brokers & agents
PA: Sibcy Cline, Inc.
　8044 Montgomery Rd # 300
　Cincinnati OH 45236
　513 984-4100

(G-9767)
SIEBENTHALER COMPANY (PA)
Also Called: Siebenthaler's Garden Center
3001 Catalpa Dr (45405-1745)
PHONE................................937 427-4110
Jeff Siebenthaler, *President*
R Jeffrey Siebenthaler, *President*
Michael Fanning, *Vice Pres*
David C Ruppert, *Vice Pres*
EMP: 100 **EST:** 1870
SQ FT: 3,000
SALES (est): 5.7MM **Privately Held**
WEB: www.siebenthaler.com
SIC: 0782 5193 5261 Landscape contractors; nursery stock; nurseries & garden centers

(G-9768)
SIENA SPRINGS II
6217 N Main St (45415-3157)
PHONE................................513 639-2800
Laura Brown Wells, *Manager*
EMP: 28
SALES (est): 248.3K **Privately Held**
SIC: 6531 Real estate agents & managers

(G-9769)
SIGNATURE CONCRETE INC
517 Windsor Park Dr (45459-4112)
PHONE................................937 723-8435
Michael Leach, *President*
Jeffrey Mullins, *Vice Pres*
EMP: 26
SQ FT: 2,400
SALES (est): 4.4MM **Privately Held**
SIC: 1771 Concrete pumping

(G-9770)
SILVER SPRUCE HOLDING LLC
Also Called: Growthplay
3123 Res Blvd Ste 250 (45420)
PHONE................................937 259-1200
Dean Wright, *Opers Staff*
Bruce Sevy, *Manager*
EMP: 43
SALES (corp-wide): 5.8MM **Privately Held**
SIC: 8742 Management consulting services
PA: Silver Spruce Holding, Llc
　121 W Wacker Dr Ste 1750
　Chicago IL 60601
　312 281-6611

(G-9771)
SKATEWORLD INC (PA)
Also Called: Skateworld of Kettering
1601 E David Rd (45429-5709)
PHONE................................937 294-4032
Rick Corson, *President*
EMP: 25
SQ FT: 26,000
SALES (est): 1.7MM **Privately Held**
SIC: 7999 5812 Roller skating rink operation; skating instruction, ice or roller; fast-food restaurant, independent

(G-9772)
SMS TRANSPORT LLC
8235 Old Troy Pike 272 (45424-1025)
PHONE................................937 813-8897
Sevil Shakhmanov,
EMP: 25
SALES (est): 1.8MM **Privately Held**
SIC: 4213 4215 4731 Contract haulers; courier services, except by air; freight forwarding

(G-9773)
SOGETI USA LLC
6494 Centervl Bus Pkwy (45459-2633)
PHONE................................937 433-3334
Brian Hammond, *Vice Pres*
Jean-Pierre Petit, *VP Opers*
Benassis Jacques, *Project Dir*
Mike Blomer, *Senior Engr*
Marianne Linde, *Sls & Mktg Exec*
EMP: 56
SALES (corp-wide): 355MM **Privately Held**
SIC: 7379
HQ: Sogeti Usa Llc
　10100 Innovation Dr # 200
　Miamisburg OH 45342
　937 291-8100

(G-9774)
SONOCO PRTECTIVE SOLUTIONS INC
R P A Packaging Division
6061 Milo Rd (45414-3417)
PHONE................................937 890-7628
EMP: 35
SALES (corp-wide): 4.9B **Publicly Held**
SIC: 7389 Packing And Crating Service
HQ: Sonoco Protective Solutions, Inc.
　1 N 2nd St
　Hartsville SC 29550
　843 383-7000

(G-9775)
SOUTH COMMUNITY INC
Also Called: Youth Partial Hospitalization
2745 S Smthvlle Rd Ste 14 (45420)
PHONE................................937 252-0100
Melissa Buck, *Principal*
Rose Combs, *Finance Dir*
Anita Koerner, *Exec Dir*
Lisa Carter, *Director*
EMP: 45
SALES (corp-wide): 19.1MM **Privately Held**
SIC: 8093 Mental health clinic, outpatient
PA: South Community Inc.
　3095 Kettering Blvd Ste 1
　Moraine OH 45439
　937 293-8300

(G-9776)
SOUTH DAYTON ACUTE CARE CONS
33 W Rahn Rd (45429-2219)
PHONE................................937 433-8990
Robert L Barker, *President*
Dr Jeffrey Weinstein, *Corp Secy*
Dr George Crespo, *Vice Pres*
Dr Shachi Rattan, *Vice Pres*
Luann Miller, *Project Mgr*
EMP: 36
SQ FT: 10,000
SALES (est): 10MM **Privately Held**
WEB: www.sdacc.com
SIC: 8011 Physicians' office, including specialists

(G-9777)
SOUTH DYTON URLGCAL ASSCATIONS (PA)
10 Southmoor Cir Nw Ste 1 (45429-2444)
PHONE..................................937 294-1489
Juan M Palomar MD, *President*
Sammy Hemway MD, *Vice Pres*
Ralph M Cruz MD, *Treasurer*
Sharat C Kalvakota MD, *Admin Sec*
Raymond S Russell, *Urology*
EMP: 30 EST: 1975
SQ FT: 5,000
SALES (est): 2.5MM **Privately Held**
SIC: 8011 Urologist

(G-9778)
SOUTHERN EXPRESS LUBES INC
3781 Salem Ave (45406-1651)
PHONE..................................937 278-5807
Dwayne Mowen, *Manager*
EMP: 25 **Privately Held**
WEB: www.selubes.com
SIC: 7549 Lubrication service, automotive
PA: Southern Express Lubes, Inc.
8520 Conn Ave Ste 200
Chevy Chase MD

(G-9779)
SOUTHWEST OHIO ENT SPCLSTS INC (PA)
1222 S Patterson Blvd # 400 (45402-2642)
PHONE..................................937 496-2600
Hugh E Wall Jr, *Principal*
Robert B Matusoff, *Principal*
Nathan Soifer, *Principal*
Robert A Goldenberg, *Otolaryngology*
EMP: 29
SALES (est): 5.8MM **Privately Held**
SIC: 8011 Ears, nose & throat specialist:
physician/surgeon

(G-9780)
SOWDER CONCRETE CORPORATION
Also Called: Sowder Concrete Contractors
8510 N Dixie Dr (45414-2451)
PHONE..................................937 890-1633
Fax: 937 890-1648
EMP: 30
SQ FT: 5,000
SALES: 6.5MM **Privately Held**
SIC: 1771 Concrete Contractor

(G-9781)
SPACE MANAGEMENT INC
Also Called: Professional Building Maint
2109 S Smithville Rd (45420-2805)
PHONE..................................937 254-6622
Kevin Ray Findlay, *President*
EMP: 50
SQ FT: 5,000
SALES (est): 4MM **Privately Held**
SIC: 8744 Facilities support services

(G-9782)
SPEARS TRANSF & EXPEDITING INC
2637 Nordic Rd (45414-3423)
PHONE..................................937 275-2443
Mike Spears, *Branch Mgr*
EMP: 25
SALES (corp-wide): 8MM **Privately Held**
WEB: www.spearsexpedite.com
SIC: 4212 4214 Local trucking, without
storage; local trucking with storage
PA: Spears Transfer & Expediting, Inc.
303 Corporate Dr Ste 101b
Vandalia OH 45377
937 898-9700

(G-9783)
SPECTRUM MGT HOLDG CO LLC
Time Warner
275 Leo St (45404-1005)
PHONE..................................937 684-8891
Tim Cuss, *Branch Mgr*
EMP: 80
SALES (corp-wide): 43.6B **Publicly Held**
SIC: 4841 Cable television services

HQ: Spectrum Management Holding Company, Llc
400 Atlantic St
Stamford CT 06901
203 905-7801

(G-9784)
SPECTRUM MGT HOLDG CO LLC
Also Called: Time Warner
3691 Turner Rd (45415-3690)
PHONE..................................937 294-6800
Richard S Hutchinson, *Principal*
Lawrence Brugger, *Supervisor*
EMP: 83
SALES (corp-wide): 43.6B **Publicly Held**
SIC: 4841 Cable television services
HQ: Spectrum Management Holding Company, Llc
400 Atlantic St
Stamford CT 06901
203 905-7801

(G-9785)
SPRINGFIELD CARTAGE LLC
1546 Stanley Ave (45404-1113)
P.O. Box 1263 (45401-1263)
PHONE..................................937 222-2120
Nello Adducchio, *Mng Member*
EMP: 86
SALES: 13MM **Privately Held**
SIC: 4225 General warehousing & storage

(G-9786)
SPRINGHILLS LLC
Also Called: Spring Hills At Singing Woods
140 E Woodbury Dr (45415-2841)
PHONE..................................937 274-1400
John Steiner, *Principal*
EMP: 171
SALES (est): 3.9MM **Privately Held**
SIC: 8051 Convalescent home with continuous nursing care
PA: Springhills Llc
515 Plainfield Ave
Edison NJ 08817

(G-9787)
SPURLOCK TRUCK SERVICE
Also Called: Summit Towing
129 Lincoln Park Blvd (45429-2717)
PHONE..................................937 268-6100
Robert Spurlock, *President*
Dr Karen Garner, *Admin Sec*
EMP: 34 EST: 1927
SQ FT: 7,000
SALES: 1MM **Privately Held**
SIC: 7538 7549 General truck repair; towing service, automotive

(G-9788)
SSS CONSULTING INC
Also Called: H R Chally Group
3123 Res Blvd Ste 250 (45420)
PHONE..................................937 259-1200
Howard P Stevens, *Ch of Bd*
Gerald M Lerer, *President*
Christopher Holmes, *Vice Pres*
Sara C Stevens, *Vice Pres*
Howard Stevens, *CFO*
EMP: 35 EST: 1973
SQ FT: 15,000
SALES (est): 4.8MM **Privately Held**
WEB: www.chally.com
SIC: 8748 8732 8742 Testing services;
market analysis or research; management consulting services

(G-9789)
ST VINCENT DE PAUL SCL SVS
1133 S Edwin C Moses Blvd (45417-4094)
PHONE..................................937 222-7349
Christine Hampton, *Controller*
Leigh Sempeles, *Exec Dir*
EMP: 78
SALES (est): 4.3MM **Privately Held**
SIC: 8322 Individual & family services

(G-9790)
STARWIN INDUSTRIES LLC
Also Called: Starwin Industries, Inc.
3387 Woodman Dr (45429-4100)
PHONE..................................937 293-8568
Rick Little, *President*
John Whitaker, *General Mgr*
Mark Belt, *Mfg Spvr*

John Gevedon, *Sales Dir*
Michael Little, *Sales Staff*
EMP: 40
SQ FT: 30,000
SALES (est): 7.4MM
SALES (corp-wide): 911.5K **Privately Held**
WEB: www.starwin-ind.com
SIC: 3599 7372 Machine shop, jobbing &
repair; prepackaged software
PA: Eti Mission Controls, Llc
75 Holiday Dr
Englewood OH 45322
937 832-4200

(G-9791)
STATE FARM LIFE INSURANCE CO
Also Called: State Farm Insurance
1436 Needmore Rd (45414-3965)
PHONE..................................937 276-1900
Jim McGhee, *Manager*
EMP: 60
SALES (corp-wide): 39.5B **Privately Held**
WEB: www.davidvetch.com
SIC: 6411 Insurance agents & brokers
HQ: State Farm Life Insurance Company Inc
1 State Farm Plz
Bloomington IL 61701
309 766-2311

(G-9792)
STERLING LAND TITLE AGENCY
7016 Corporate Way Ste B (45459-4351)
PHONE..................................937 438-2000
Alex P Katona, *President*
EMP: 30
SQ FT: 12,500
SALES (est): 2MM **Privately Held**
SIC: 6541 Title & trust companies

(G-9793)
STEVE BROWN
1353 Lyons Rd (45458-1822)
PHONE..................................937 436-2700
Steve Brown, *Partner*
EMP: 60
SALES (est): 164.4K **Privately Held**
SIC: 6531 Real estate brokers & agents

(G-9794)
STONEMOR PARTNERS LP
Also Called: West Memory Gardens
6722 Hemple Rd (45439-6648)
PHONE..................................937 866-4135
Glenna Wall, *Principal*
EMP: 50
SALES (corp-wide): 316.1MM **Publicly Held**
WEB: www.stonemor.com
SIC: 6553 Cemetery subdividers & developers
PA: Stonemor Partners L.P.
3600 Horizon Blvd Ste 100
Trevose PA 19053
215 826-2800

(G-9795)
STOOPS FRGHTLNR-QLITY TRLR INC
Also Called: Stoops Freightliner of Dayton
7800 Center Point 70 Blvd (45424-6369)
PHONE..................................937 236-4092
Jeff Gast, *Manager*
EMP: 50
SALES (corp-wide): 542.1MM **Privately Held**
WEB: www.stoops.com
SIC: 5511 5531 7538 7539 Trucks, tractors & trailers: new & used; automotive parts; general truck repair; trailer repair; automobiles & other motor vehicles
HQ: Truck Country Of Indiana, Inc.
1851 W Thompson Rd
Indianapolis IN 46217
317 788-1533

(G-9796)
STRATACACHE INC (PA)
Also Called: Stratacache Products
2 Emmet St Ste 200 (45405)
PHONE..................................937 224-0485
Chris Riegel, *CEO*
Ken Boyle, *Senior VP*
Manish Kumar, *Senior VP*

Russell Young, *Senior VP*
John Rau, *Vice Pres*
▲ EMP: 110
SQ FT: 65,000
SALES (est): 66.8MM **Privately Held**
WEB: www.stratacache.com
SIC: 5734 4822 Software, business &
non-game; nonvocal message communications

(G-9797)
STUDEBAKER ELECTRIC COMPANY
8459 N Main St Ste 114 (45415-1382)
PHONE..................................937 890-9510
David L Studebaker, *CEO*
Phillip Lahrmer, *CFO*
EMP: 100
SQ FT: 1,600
SALES (est): 4.8MM **Privately Held**
WEB: www.studebakerelectric.com
SIC: 1731 General electrical contractor

(G-9798)
SUBURBAN VETERINARIAN CLINIC
102 E Spring Valley Pike (45458-3803)
PHONE..................................937 433-2160
Dan Lokai, *Owner*
EMP: 30
SQ FT: 6,200
SALES (est): 1.3MM **Privately Held**
SIC: 0742 Animal hospital services, pets &
other animal specialties; veterinarian, animal specialties

(G-9799)
SUMMIT SOLUTIONS INC
Also Called: Summit Quest
446 Windsor Park Dr (45459-4111)
PHONE..................................937 291-4333
Jeff S Lafave, *CEO*
Tom Schraer, *Transportation*
Aaron Lafave, *Consultant*
EMP: 40 EST: 1998
SALES (est): 4MM **Privately Held**
WEB: www.summitqwest.com
SIC: 8748 Business consulting

(G-9800)
SUMMITT OHIO LEASING CO LLC
Also Called: Wood Glen Alzheimers Community
3800 Summit Glen Dr (45449-3647)
PHONE..................................937 436-2273
Steve Rosedale, *CEO*
Stephen Rosedale,
EMP: 220
SALES (est): 7.1MM **Privately Held**
SIC: 8051 Convalescent home with continuous nursing care

(G-9801)
SUNRISE SENIOR LIVING INC
Also Called: Brighton Gardens Wash Township
6800 Paragon Rd Ofc (45459-3164)
PHONE..................................937 438-0054
Rose Marie Caldwell, *Manager*
Jenni Clark, *Executive*
EMP: 86
SALES (corp-wide): 4.7B **Publicly Held**
WEB: www.sunrise.com
SIC: 8051 Skilled nursing care facilities
HQ: Sunrise Senior Living, Llc
7902 Westpark Dr
Mc Lean VA 22102

(G-9802)
SUPERIOR DENTAL CARE INC
6683 Centervl Bus Pkwy (45459-2634)
PHONE..................................937 438-0283
Traci Harrell, *CEO*
Richard W Portune DDS, *President*
Douglas R Hoefling DDS, *Treasurer*
Anne Wassum, *Controller*
Anne Kessler, *Marketing Mgr*
EMP: 31
SQ FT: 7,878
SALES (est): 16.5MM **Privately Held**
WEB: www.superiordental.com
SIC: 6321 Health insurance carriers

(G-9803)
SWN COMMUNICATIONS INC
Also Called: One Call Now
6450 Poe Ave Ste 500 (45414-2648)
PHONE...................................877 698-3262
Shannon Bailey, *Senior VP*
EMP: 30
SALES (corp-wide): 1B **Privately Held**
SIC: 4813 Data telephone communications
HQ: Swn Communications Inc.
　500 Plaza Dr Ste 205
　Secaucus NJ 07094
　212 379-4900

(G-9804)
SYNERGY HOMECARE
Also Called: Synergy Homecare South Dayton
501 Windsor Park Dr (45459-4112)
PHONE...................................937 610-0555
Tim Homer, *Owner*
Mike Jones, *Opers Staff*
EMP: 95
SQ FT: 1,000
SALES (est): 100K **Privately Held**
SIC: 8082 Home health care services

(G-9805)
SYSTEMAX MANUFACTURING INC
6450 Poe Ave Ste 200 (45414-2655)
PHONE...................................937 368-2300
Curt Rush, *Admin Sec*
▲ EMP: 200
SQ FT: 185,000
SALES (est): 21MM **Publicly Held**
WEB: www.systemax.com
SIC: 5961 7373 3577 3571 Computers & peripheral equipment, mail order; systems integration services; computer peripheral equipment; electronic computers; computer peripheral equipment
PA: Systemax Inc.
　11 Harbor Park Dr
　Port Washington NY 11050

(G-9806)
TALMAGE N PORTER MD
979 Congress Park Dr (45459-4009)
PHONE...................................937 435-9013
Talmage Porter, *Principal*
EMP: 25 EST: 2001
SALES (est): 550K **Privately Held**
SIC: 8011 General & family practice, physician/surgeon

(G-9807)
TEAM RAHAL OF DAYTON INC (PA)
Also Called: Lexus of Dayton
8111 Yankee St (45458-1962)
PHONE...................................937 438-3800
John Higgins, *President*
Jeff Pizza, *General Mgr*
John Manning, *Parts Mgr*
Jim Harper, *Sales Staff*
John Plumer, *Sales Staff*
EMP: 30
SQ FT: 12,000
SALES (est): 12.3MM **Privately Held**
SIC: 5511 7515 Automobiles, new & used; passenger car leasing

(G-9808)
TEKNOL INC (PA)
Also Called: Rubber Seal Products
5751 Webster St (45414-3520)
P.O. Box 13387 (45413-0387)
PHONE...................................937 264-0190
Kent Von Behren, *President*
R Von Behren, *Shareholder*
▲ EMP: 57 EST: 1976
SQ FT: 60,000
SALES: 31MM **Privately Held**
WEB: www.rubber-seal.com
SIC: 2899 2891 5198 2851 Chemical preparations; sealants; paints, varnishes & supplies; paints & allied products

(G-9809)
TELAMON CORPORATION
600 N Irwin St (45403-1337)
PHONE...................................937 254-2004
Sean Quinn, *Owner*
EMP: 25

SALES (corp-wide): 497.5MM **Privately Held**
SIC: 7361 Employment agencies
PA: Telamon Corporation
　1000 E 116th St
　Carmel IN 46032
　317 818-6888

(G-9810)
THE FOODBANK INC
56 Armor Pl (45417-1187)
PHONE...................................937 461-0265
Burma Thomas, *CEO*
Michelle Riley, *CEO*
EMP: 29
SALES: 13.5MM **Privately Held**
SIC: 8322 Social service center

(G-9811)
THE FOR NATIONAL ASSOCIATION
4215 Breezewood Ave (45406-1313)
PHONE...................................937 470-1059
Jean Foward, *Branch Mgr*
EMP: 25
SALES (corp-wide): 27.6MM **Privately Held**
SIC: 8641 Social associations
PA: National Association For The Advancement Of Colored People
　4805 Mount Hope Dr
　Baltimore MD 21215
　410 580-5777

(G-9812)
THE MARIA-JOSEPH CENTER
4830 Salem Ave (45416-1716)
PHONE...................................937 278-2692
Sharon Thornton, *President*
EMP: 400
SQ FT: 500,000
SALES: 20.3MM **Privately Held**
WEB: www.mariajoseph.org
SIC: 8052 8051 Intermediate care facilities; skilled nursing care facilities
PA: Commonspirit Health
　198 Inverness Dr W
　Englewood CO 80112

(G-9813)
THINKTV NETWORK
110 S Jefferson St (45402-2402)
PHONE...................................937 220-1600
David Fogarty, *President*
EMP: 50
SALES (est): 1.7MM **Privately Held**
SIC: 4833 7313 Television broadcasting stations; television & radio time sales

(G-9814)
TIPHARAH GROUP CORP (PA)
Also Called: Tipharah Designs
252 Burgess Ave (45415-2630)
PHONE...................................937 430-6266
Deirdre Brown Postell, *President*
EMP: 168
SQ FT: 2,200
SALES (est): 3.8MM **Privately Held**
SIC: 8748 Business consulting

(G-9815)
TIPHARAH GROUP CORP
Also Called: Tipharah Hospitality
252 Burgess Ave (45415-2630)
PHONE...................................937 430-6266
Deirdre Postell, *President*
EMP: 152
SALES (corp-wide): 3.8MM **Privately Held**
SIC: 8748 Business consulting
PA: The Tipharah Group Corp
　252 Burgess Ave
　Dayton OH 45415
　937 430-6266

(G-9816)
TOP TIER SOCCER LLC
1268 Walnut Valley Ln (45458-9683)
PHONE...................................937 903-6114
Colin Jones, *Mng Member*
EMP: 29
SALES: 498K **Privately Held**
SIC: 5947 7389 Novelties;

(G-9817)
TOTAL RENAL CARE INC
Also Called: Linden Home Dialysis
1431 Business Center Ct (45410-3300)
PHONE...................................937 252-1867
Jim Hilger, *Branch Mgr*
EMP: 30 **Publicly Held**
SIC: 8092 Kidney dialysis centers
HQ: Total Renal Care, Inc.
　2000 16th St
　Denver CO 80202
　303 405-2100

(G-9818)
TOULA INDUSTRIES LTD LLC
1019 Valley Vista Way (45429-6139)
PHONE...................................937 689-1818
Martin Mershad, *President*
EMP: 150
SALES (est): 7.4MM **Privately Held**
SIC: 4412 Deep sea foreign transportation of freight

(G-9819)
TOYOTA INDUSTRIES N AMER INC
Also Called: Prolift Industrial Equipment
6254 Executive Blvd (45424-1423)
PHONE...................................937 237-0976
Stephen Ford, *Manager*
EMP: 27
SALES (corp-wide): 18.8B **Privately Held**
SIC: 5084 7699 Lift trucks & parts; industrial truck repair
HQ: Toyota Industries North America, Inc.
　3030 Barker Dr
　Columbus IN 47201
　812 341-3810

(G-9820)
TRAME MECHANICAL INC
Also Called: Honeywell Authorized Dealer
2721 Timber Ln (45414-4735)
P.O. Box 13596 (45413-0596)
PHONE...................................937 258-1000
Steve Walton, *CEO*
EMP: 25 EST: 1979
SQ FT: 9,000
SALES: 3.9MM **Privately Held**
WEB: www.trame.com
SIC: 1711 Mechanical contractor

(G-9821)
TRI-TECH ASSOCIATES INC
Also Called: Tri-Tech Engineering
1785 S Metro Pkwy (45459-2521)
PHONE...................................937 306-1630
Robert Thomson, *President*
Mark Stemmer, *Vice Pres*
Daniel Garman, *Project Mgr*
Roger Butler, *Engineer*
Andrew Kjellman, *Engineer*
EMP: 28
SQ FT: 14,000
SALES: 1MM **Privately Held**
WEB: www.tri-techceg.com
SIC: 8711 Consulting engineer

(G-9822)
TRIANGLE PRECISION INDUSTRIES
1650 Delco Park Dr (45420-1392)
PHONE...................................937 299-6776
Gerald D Schriml, *President*
Paul S Holzinger, *Vice Pres*
EMP: 57
SQ FT: 23,400
SALES (est): 10.2MM **Privately Held**
WEB: www.triangleprecision.com
SIC: 3599 7692 3446 3444 Machine shop, jobbing & repair; welding repair; architectural metalwork; sheet metalwork; fabricated plate work (boiler shop); fabricated structural metal

(G-9823)
TRIMBLE ENGINEERING & CNSTR
5475 Kellenburger Rd (45424-1013)
PHONE...................................937 233-8921
Madolyn Trimble, *Principal*
Kimberly Rife, *Manager*
▲ EMP: 31

SALES (est): 6.9MM **Privately Held**
SIC: 5712 7353 Office furniture; heavy construction equipment rental

(G-9824)
TRUGREEN LIMITED PARTNERSHIP
Also Called: Tru Green-Chemlawn
767 Liberty Ln (45449-2134)
PHONE...................................937 866-8399
Dan Brodbeck, *Manager*
EMP: 40
SALES (corp-wide): 3.4B **Privately Held**
SIC: 0782 Lawn care services
HQ: Trugreen Limited Partnership
　1790 Kirby Pkwy
　Memphis TN 38138
　901 251-4128

(G-9825)
TRUSTED HOMECARE SOLUTIONS
2324 Stanley Ave Ste 115 (45404-1202)
PHONE...................................937 506-7063
Viktoria E Peck, *Principal*
EMP: 25
SALES (est): 165.9K **Privately Held**
SIC: 8082 Home health care services

(G-9826)
TV MINORITY COMPANY INC
1700 E Monument Ave (45402-1364)
PHONE...................................937 226-1559
Dan Schreier, *General Mgr*
EMP: 50
SALES (corp-wide): 46.6MM **Privately Held**
WEB: www.ilgi.com
SIC: 4212 Local trucking, without storage
PA: T.V. Minority Company, Inc.
　9400 Pelham Rd
　Taylor MI 48180
　313 386-1048

(G-9827)
UBS FINANCIAL SERVICES INC
7887 Wash Vlg Dr Ste 100 (45459-3998)
PHONE...................................937 428-1300
Timothy Van Simaeys, *Principal*
David Scharff, *Advisor*
EMP: 25
SALES (corp-wide): 29.4B **Privately Held**
SIC: 6211 Security brokers & dealers
HQ: Ubs Financial Services Inc.
　1285 Ave Of The Americas
　New York NY 10019
　212 713-2000

(G-9828)
UFCW 75 REAL ESTATE CORP
7250 Poe Ave Ste 400 (45414-2698)
PHONE...................................937 677-0075
EMP: 60
SALES: 284.8K **Privately Held**
SIC: 6531 Real estate agents & managers

(G-9829)
UNION SAVINGS BANK
5651 Far Hills Ave (45429-2205)
PHONE...................................937 434-1254
Gary Smart, *Manager*
EMP: 60
SQ FT: 2,620
SALES (corp-wide): 142.7MM **Privately Held**
SIC: 6036 6035 Savings & loan associations, not federally chartered; federal savings banks
PA: Union Savings Bank
　8534 E Kemper Rd Fl 1
　Cincinnati OH 45249
　513 489-1955

(G-9830)
UNITED ART AND EDUCATION INC
799 Lyons Rd (45459-3980)
PHONE...................................800 322-3247
Justin Hunt, *Manager*
David Kirkwood, *Manager*
Kelly Warnen, *Director*
EMP: 48

SALES (corp-wide): 25MM **Privately Held**
SIC: **5999** 7389 5943 Artists' supplies & materials; laminating service; school supplies
PA: United Art And Education, Inc.
4413 Airport Expy
Fort Wayne IN 46809
260 478-1121

(G-9831)
UNITED FOOD AND COML WKRS
Also Called: Ufcw Local No. 75
7250 Poe Ave Ste 400 (45414-2698)
PHONE................................937 665-0075
Lennie Wyatt, *President*
EMP: 65
SQ FT: 1,500
SALES: 15.6MM **Privately Held**
SIC: **8631** Labor union

(G-9832)
UNITED REHABILITATION SERVICES
4710 Troy Pike (45424-5740)
PHONE................................937 233-1230
Kayla Bennett, *Accountant*
Ashley Crawford, *Corp Comm Staff*
Jeremy Nelson, *Manager*
Tracy Pohlabel, *Manager*
Patricia Wickham, *Manager*
EMP: 74
SQ FT: 37,000
SALES: 7.6MM **Privately Held**
SIC: **8399** 8351 8322 8093 United Fund councils; child day care services; individual & family services; rehabilitation center; outpatient treatment; speech pathologist; hearing aids

(G-9833)
UNITED TELEMANAGEMENT CORP
6450 Poe Ave Ste 401 (45414-2665)
PHONE................................937 454-1888
Terry L Henley, *CEO*
Don Campbell, *President*
Robert Gulledge, *COO*
James Hague, *CFO*
Barry Brooks, *Treasurer*
EMP: 25
SQ FT: 5,000
SALES (est): 3.2MM **Privately Held**
WEB: www.telelink-usa.com
SIC: **8741** Management services

(G-9834)
UNITED WAY OF THE GREATER DAYT (PA)
33 W 1st St Ste 500 (45402-1235)
P.O. Box 634625, Cincinnati (45263-4625)
PHONE................................937 225-3060
Tom Maultsby, *President*
Terri Leputa, *Vice Pres*
EMP: 35
SALES: 8.1MM **Privately Held**
SIC: **8399** 8322 United Fund councils; individual & family services

(G-9835)
UNIVERSAL 1 CREDIT UNION INC (PA)
1 River Park Dr (45409-2104)
P.O. Box 467 (45409-0467)
PHONE................................800 762-9555
Loren A Rush, *President*
Glenn Kershner, *Exec VP*
Steve Shore, *Exec VP*
Ann Parrish, *Treasurer*
Shannon Maloney, *Information Mgr*
EMP: 73 EST: 1937
SALES: 15.2MM **Privately Held**
WEB: www.universal1cu.biz
SIC: **6062** State credit unions, not federally chartered

(G-9836)
UNIVERSITY OF DAYTON
300 College Park Ave (45469-0002)
PHONE................................937 255-3141
Bernard Ploeger, *Branch Mgr*
EMP: 150

SALES (corp-wide): 521.5MM **Privately Held**
WEB: www.udayton.edu
SIC: **8742** 8221 Management consulting services; university
PA: The University Of Dayton
300 College Park Ave
Dayton OH 45469
937 229-2919

(G-9837)
UNIVERSITY OF DAYTON (PA)
300 College Park Ave (45469-0002)
PHONE................................937 229-2919
Dr Daniel J Curran, *President*
Phillip Chick, *President*
Todd Imwalle, *President*
David Schmidt, *President*
Cilla Shindell, *President*
▲ EMP: 2000
SQ FT: 25,000
SALES (est): 521.5MM **Privately Held**
WEB: www.udayton.edu
SIC: **8221** 8733 University; noncommercial research organizations

(G-9838)
UNIVERSITY OF DAYTON
Also Called: University Marketing
300 College Park Ave (45469-0002)
PHONE................................937 229-5432
Brian Mills, *Marketing Staff*
Mike Kurtz, *Manager*
EMP: 121
SALES (corp-wide): 521.5MM **Privately Held**
SIC: **7819** Services allied to motion pictures
PA: The University Of Dayton
300 College Park Ave
Dayton OH 45469
937 229-2919

(G-9839)
UNIVERSITY OF DAYTON
Also Called: University of Dyton Schl Engrg
300 College St (45402)
PHONE................................937 229-2113
Christopher Bruening, *Engineer*
Jeff Dennis, *Engineer*
Michael Merrill, *Engineer*
Andrew Thompson, *Engineer*
Ronnie Burrows, *Accountant*
EMP: 250
SALES (corp-wide): 521.5MM **Privately Held**
WEB: www.udayton.edu
SIC: **8733** 8221 Research institute; university
PA: The University Of Dayton
300 College Park Ave
Dayton OH 45469
937 229-2919

(G-9840)
UNIVERSITY OF DAYTON
Also Called: University Dayton RES Inst
711 E Monu Ave Ste 101 (45469-0001)
PHONE................................937 229-3822
Jon Borgwardt, *Purch Mgr*
Ruth Girouard, *Research*
Sirina Safriet, *Research*
Andrew Abbott, *Engineer*
Chris Buck, *Engineer*
EMP: 400
SALES (corp-wide): 521.5MM **Privately Held**
SIC: **8733** 8221 Research institute; university
PA: The University Of Dayton
300 College Park Ave
Dayton OH 45469
937 229-2919

(G-9841)
UNIVERSITY OF DAYTON
Also Called: Research Institute
1529 Brown St (45469-3401)
PHONE................................937 229-3913
Rachel Bryant, *Facilities Mgr*
Ken Soucy, *Manager*
Colleen Lampton Brill, *Exec Dir*
EMP: 150

SALES (corp-wide): 521.5MM **Privately Held**
WEB: www.udayton.edu
SIC: **8742** 8221 Management consulting services; university
PA: The University Of Dayton
300 College Park Ave
Dayton OH 45469
937 229-2919

(G-9842)
UNIVERSITY WOMENS HEALTHCARE
627 S Edwin C Moses Blvd (45417-3461)
PHONE................................937 208-2948
Mj Biery, *Director*
EMP: 42
SALES (est): 827.5K **Privately Held**
SIC: **8099** Medical services organization

(G-9843)
UPS GROUND FREIGHT INC
3730 Valley St (45424-5144)
PHONE................................937 236-4700
Scott Gettys, *Manager*
EMP: 50
SALES (corp-wide): 71.8B **Publicly Held**
WEB: www.overnite.com
SIC: **4213** 4212 Contract haulers; local trucking, without storage
HQ: Ups Ground Freight, Inc.
1000 Semmes Ave
Richmond VA 23224
866 372-5619

(G-9844)
US INSPECTION SERVICES INC (DH)
Also Called: Acuren Inspection
7333 Paragon Rd Ste 240 (45459-4157)
PHONE................................937 660-9879
Jim Bailey, *President*
Peter Scannell, *President*
EMP: 50
SQ FT: 18,000
SALES (est): 20.4MM
SALES (corp-wide): 1.6B **Privately Held**
SIC: **8734** Testing laboratories
HQ: Acuren Inspection, Inc.
30 Main St Ste 402
Danbury CT 06810
203 702-8740

(G-9845)
USF HOLLAND LLC
Also Called: USFreightways
2700 Valley Pike (45404-2695)
PHONE................................937 233-7600
Frank Blizzard, *Manager*
EMP: 150
SALES (corp-wide): 5B **Publicly Held**
WEB: www.usfc.com
SIC: **4212** 4213 Local trucking, without storage; trucking, except local
HQ: Usf Holland Llc
700 S Waverly Rd
Holland MI 49423
616 395-5000

(G-9846)
VALENTOUR EDUCATION INC
Also Called: Ccdc
8095 Garnet Dr (45458-2140)
PHONE................................937 434-5949
Kathy Valentour, *Exec Dir*
EMP: 35
SALES (est): 843.6K **Privately Held**
SIC: **8351** Preschool center

(G-9847)
VALLEY INTERIOR SYSTEMS INC
2760 Thunderhawk Ct (45414-3464)
PHONE................................937 890-7319
Terry Gyetvai, *Vice Pres*
Travis Henderson, *Foreman/Supr*
EMP: 50
SALES (corp-wide): 70.4MM **Privately Held**
SIC: **1742** Drywall; acoustical & ceiling work; plastering, plain or ornamental
PA: Valley Interior Systems, Inc.
2203 Fowler St
Cincinnati OH 45206
513 961-0400

(G-9848)
VAN HOWARDS LINES INC
Also Called: Morgan & Sons Moving & Storage
3516 Wright Way Rd Ste 2 (45424-5164)
PHONE................................937 235-0007
Orville Morgan Sr, *President*
Orville Morgan Jr, *Corp Secy*
Ira Morgan, *Vice Pres*
EMP: 47
SQ FT: 26,000
SALES: 1.7MM **Privately Held**
SIC: **4213** 4214 4212 Household goods transport; local trucking with storage; local trucking, without storage; furniture moving, local; without storage

(G-9849)
VANCE ROAD ENTERPRISES INC
1431 N Gettysburg Ave (45417-9517)
PHONE................................937 268-6953
Troy Peavy, *President*
EMP: 28
SALES (est): 5MM **Privately Held**
SIC: **4213** Trucking, except local

(G-9850)
VANDALIA BLACKTOP SEAL COATING
6740 Webster St (45414-2613)
PHONE................................937 454-0571
H David Brusman Jr, *President*
Tony Koehl, *Vice Pres*
Ron Cantrell, *Foreman/Supr*
Leon Davis, *Sales Staff*
EMP: 50
SQ FT: 2,000
SALES (est): 9.6MM **Privately Held**
WEB: www.vandaliablacktop.com
SIC: **1611** 1794 Highway & street paving contractor; excavation work

(G-9851)
VANGUARD IMAGING PARTNERS
6251 Good Samaritan Way # 140 (45424-5254)
PHONE................................937 236-4780
Scott Buchanen, *President*
EMP: 60
SALES (est): 2.9MM **Privately Held**
SIC: **8011** Radiologist

(G-9852)
VARTEK SERVICES INC
4770 Hempstead Station Dr A (45429-5125)
PHONE................................937 438-3550
Michael Hosford, *CEO*
Darlene Waite, *President*
Bill Flodder, *Project Mgr*
William Flodder, *Project Mgr*
David Campbell, *Engineer*
EMP: 35
SQ FT: 15,000
SALES (est): 6.9MM **Privately Held**
WEB: www.vartek.com
SIC: **8742** Management information systems consultant

(G-9853)
VERIZON WIRELESS INC
2799 Mmsburg Cntrville Rd (45459)
PHONE................................937 434-2355
Fax: 937 291-7759
EMP: 55
SALES (corp-wide): 125.9B **Publicly Held**
SIC: **4812** Radiotelephone Communication
HQ: Verizon Wireless, Inc.
1 Verizon Way
Basking Ridge NJ 07920

(G-9854)
VERNON F GLASER & ASSOCIATES
3085 Woodman Dr Ste 250 (45420-1181)
PHONE................................937 298-5536
Vernon F Glaser, *President*
Brandi Brooks, *Accounts Mgr*
EMP: 30
SQ FT: 8,500

SALES (est): 3.8MM **Privately Held**
SIC: 8742 8721 Hospital & health services consultant; accounting, auditing & bookkeeping

(G-9855)
VETERAN SECURITY PATROL CO
601 S E C Moses Blvd # 170 (45417-3424)
PHONE..............................937 222-7333
Roy Belcher, *Branch Mgr*
EMP: 40 **Privately Held**
WEB: www.veteransecurity.com
SIC: 7381 Detective & armored car services
PA: Veteran Security Patrol Co.
215 Taylor Ave
Bellevue KY 41073

(G-9856)
VETERANS AFFAIRS US DEPT
Also Called: Dayton V A Medical Center
4100 W 3rd St (45428-9000)
PHONE..............................937 268-6511
Jodi Cokl, *Branch Mgr*
Bharat Desai, *Pharmacist*
Denice Blunt, *Admin Asst*
Lori Quillen, *Diabetes*
EMP: 2000 **Publicly Held**
WEB: www.veterans-ru.org
SIC: 8011 9451 Medical centers; administration of veterans' affairs;
HQ: United States Dept Of Veterans Affairs
810 Vermont Ave Nw
Washington DC 20420
800 827-1000

(G-9857)
VIVIAL MEDIA LLC
3100 Res Blvd Ste 250 (45420)
PHONE..............................937 610-4100
Annie Laing, *Sales Staff*
Matthew Schreiber, *Business Dir*
Katelyn Mangione, *Analyst*
Robyn Rountree, *Recruiter*
EMP: 61
SALES (corp-wide): 31.3MM **Privately Held**
SIC: 7311 Advertising agencies
PA: Vivial Media Llc
160 Inverness Dr W # 250
Englewood CO 80112
303 867-1600

(G-9858)
VOCALINK INC
405 W 1st St Ste A (45402-3007)
PHONE..............................937 223-1415
Amelia Rodriguez, *President*
Christina Brownlee, *Mktg Dir*
EMP: 405
SALES (est): 3.5MM **Privately Held**
SIC: 7389 Translation services

(G-9859)
VOLVO BMW DYTON EVANS VOLKSWAG
Also Called: Evans Motor Works
7124 Poe Ave (45414-2546)
PHONE..............................937 890-6200
Jim Evans, *President*
Jims Evans, *President*
Ann Conrad, *Mktg Dir*
Aaron Forland, *Manager*
EMP: 50 **EST:** 2009
SALES (est): 2.1MM **Privately Held**
SIC: 5511 7538 Automobiles, new & used; general automotive repair shops

(G-9860)
VOSS AUTO NETWORK INC (PA)
Also Called: Hoss
766 Mmsburg Cnterville Rd (45459)
PHONE..............................937 428-2447
Chuck Belk, *President*
John Voss, *President*
Jeff Tarzinski, *General Mgr*
Teresa Haynes, *Principal*
Gregory Stout, *CFO*
EMP: 50
SQ FT: 45,288

SALES (est): 155.1MM **Privately Held**
WEB: www.vossauto.net
SIC: 5511 7538 7513 5521 Automobiles, new & used; general automotive repair shops; truck rental & leasing, no drivers; used car dealers; automobiles & other motor vehicles

(G-9861)
VOSS AUTO NETWORK INC
100 Loop Rd (45459-2142)
PHONE..............................937 433-1444
Greg Stout, *Vice Pres*
Greg Hill, *Sales Staff*
John Voss, *Manager*
Teresa Chandler, *Manager*
Karina Morgan, *Manager*
EMP: 450
SALES (corp-wide): 155.1MM **Privately Held**
WEB: www.vossauto.net
SIC: 7532 5521 Body shop, automotive; automobiles, used cars only
PA: Voss Auto Network, Inc.
766 Mmsburg Cnterville Rd
Dayton OH 45459
937 428-2447

(G-9862)
VOSS CHEVROLET INC
100 Loop Rd (45459-2197)
PHONE..............................937 428-2500
John E Voss, *President*
Douglas Brush, *Parts Mgr*
Scott Freels, *Parts Mgr*
Gregory Stout, *CFO*
David Blumenstock, *Finance Mgr*
EMP: 190
SQ FT: 55,000
SALES (est): 53.8MM **Privately Held**
SIC: 5511 5521 5012 Automobiles, new & used; used car dealers; automobiles & other motor vehicles

(G-9863)
VOSS DODGE (PA)
90 Loop Rd (45459-2140)
PHONE..............................937 435-7800
John E Voss, *President*
Mary Thomas, *Parts Mgr*
EMP: 50
SQ FT: 26,000
SALES (est): 7MM **Privately Held**
WEB: www.vossdodge.com
SIC: 5511 5521 5012 Automobiles, new & used; used car dealers; automobiles & other motor vehicles

(G-9864)
WALGREEN CO
Also Called: Walgreens
6485 Wilmington Pike (45459-7110)
PHONE..............................937 433-5314
Holly Kershner, *Pharmacist*
Cecil Perry, *Manager*
EMP: 40
SALES (corp-wide): 131.5B **Publicly Held**
WEB: www.walgreens.com
SIC: 5912 7384 Drug stores; photofinishing laboratory
HQ: Walgreen Co.
200 Wilmot Rd
Deerfield IL 60015
847 315-2500

(G-9865)
WALGREEN CO
Also Called: Walgreens
2600 S Smithville Rd (45420-2642)
PHONE..............................937 781-9561
Cristy Loebrich, *Manager*
EMP: 30
SALES (corp-wide): 131.5B **Publicly Held**
WEB: www.walgreens.com
SIC: 5912 7384 Drug stores; photofinishing laboratory
HQ: Walgreen Co.
200 Wilmot Rd
Deerfield IL 60015
847 315-2500

(G-9866)
WALGREEN CO
Also Called: Walgreens
2710 Salem Ave (45406-2730)
PHONE..............................937 277-6022
Bryan Astor, *Manager*
EMP: 25
SALES (corp-wide): 131.5B **Publicly Held**
WEB: www.walgreens.com
SIC: 5912 7384 Drug stores; photofinishing laboratory
HQ: Walgreen Co.
200 Wilmot Rd
Deerfield IL 60015
847 315-2500

(G-9867)
WASHINGTON MANOR INC (PA)
Also Called: Washington Manor Nursing Ctr
7300 Mcewen Rd (45459-3903)
PHONE..............................937 433-3441
Linda Kurke, *Owner*
EMP: 25
SQ FT: 52,000
SALES (est): 3.3MM **Privately Held**
WEB: www.libertynursingcenters.com
SIC: 8361 8052 8051 Geriatric residential care; intermediate care facilities; skilled nursing care facilities

(G-9868)
WASHINGTON TWNSHIP MNTGOMERY
Also Called: Washington Twnship Rcrtion Ctr
895 Mmsburg Cnterville Rd (45459)
PHONE..............................937 433-0130
David Paice, *Director*
Mark Metzger, *Director*
EMP: 125
SQ FT: 20,000 **Privately Held**
WEB: www.washingtontwp.org
SIC: 7999 7991 Recreation center; physical fitness facilities
PA: Washington Township, Montgomery County
8200 Mcewen Rd
Dayton OH 45458
937 435-2376

(G-9869)
WAYSIDE BODY SHOP INC (PA)
Also Called: Wayside Collision Center
6000 Executive Blvd Ste A (45424-1407)
PHONE..............................937 233-3182
Mark A Campbell Sr, *President*
Mark Campbell II, *Vice Pres*
EMP: 40
SQ FT: 12,000
SALES (est): 1.9MM **Privately Held**
WEB: www.waysidebodyshop.com
SIC: 7532 Body shop, automotive

(G-9870)
WEB YOGA INC
938 Senate Dr (45459-4017)
PHONE..............................937 428-0000
Vijay Vallabhaneni, *President*
Tamiko Lawton, *Manager*
Manohar Durgasi, *Technology*
Prasad Sirigineedi, *Technology*
EMP: 30
SQ FT: 2,400
SALES (est): 3.4MM **Privately Held**
WEB: www.webyoga.com
SIC: 7379 Computer related consulting services

(G-9871)
WEE CARE LEARNING CENTER
9675 N Dixie Dr (45414-1818)
PHONE..............................937 454-9363
Helene Gross, *Director*
EMP: 30
SALES (est): 192.5K **Privately Held**
SIC: 8351 Preschool center

(G-9872)
WELCH PACKAGING LLC
321 Hopeland St (45417-4027)
PHONE..............................937 223-3958
Scott Welch, *President*
EMP: 48
SALES (corp-wide): 546.3MM **Privately Held**
SIC: 5199 Packaging materials

HQ: Welch Packaging, Llc
1020 Herman St
Elkhart IN 46516
574 295-2460

(G-9873)
WENZLER DAYCARE LEARNING CTR
Also Called: Wenzler Daycare & Learning Ctr
4535 Presidential Way (45429-5752)
PHONE..............................937 435-8200
Brenda Wenzler, *President*
Benita Wenzler, *Vice Pres*
EMP: 30
SALES (est): 1.1MM **Privately Held**
SIC: 8351 Group day care center

(G-9874)
WESCO DISTRIBUTION INC
2080 Winners Cir (45404-1130)
P.O. Box 119 (45404-0119)
PHONE..............................937 228-9668
Bryan Roessner, *Sales Staff*
Robin Miller, *Sales Executive*
Mark Boytim, *Branch Mgr*
EMP: 25 **Publicly Held**
SIC: 5063 5085 Electrical apparatus & equipment; industrial supplies
HQ: Wesco Distribution, Inc.
225 W Station Square Dr # 700
Pittsburgh PA 15219

(G-9875)
WESLEY COMMUNITY CENTER INC
3730 Delphos Ave (45417-1647)
PHONE..............................937 263-3556
Harris Tay, *Exec Dir*
Harris K Tay, *Exec Dir*
EMP: 29
SALES (est): 997.6K **Privately Held**
SIC: 8641 Civic associations

(G-9876)
WESTCARE OHIO INC
Also Called: EAST END COMMUNITY SERVICES CO
624 Xenia Ave (45410-1826)
PHONE..............................937 259-1898
Danielle Weickert, *Safety Mgr*
Jan Lepore-Jentleson, *Exec Dir*
Stephanie Smith, *Exec Dir*
Kim Steinbrugge, *Exec Dir*
Doug Thompson, *Director*
EMP: 42
SQ FT: 3,706
SALES: 608.4K **Privately Held**
WEB: www.east-end.org
SIC: 8322 8399 Social service center; community development groups

(G-9877)
WESTMINSTER FINANCIAL COMPANY
125 N Wilkinson St (45402-1423)
PHONE..............................937 898-5010
Lawrence Miles, *CEO*
Louis Zone, *Finance Mgr*
EMP: 50
SALES (est): 9.1MM **Privately Held**
SIC: 6282 Investment advisory service

(G-9878)
WESTMNSTER FNCL SECURITIES INC
Also Called: Westminster Fincl Companies
40 N Main St Ste 2400 (45423-1057)
PHONE..............................937 898-5010
Miles Brazie, *CEO*
Lawrence Miles Brazie, *President*
Ken Warnick, *CFO*
Cecile Fahey, *Manager*
Jessica Trunck, *Manager*
EMP: 50
SQ FT: 10,000
SALES (est): 9MM **Privately Held**
WEB: www.westminsterfinancial.com
SIC: 6211 Brokers, security

(G-9879)
WHITE FAMILY COMPANIES INC
Also Called: White Allen Chevrolet
442 N Main St (45405-4923)
PHONE..............................937 222-3701
Howard Monk, *General Mgr*

▲ = Import ▼=Export
◆ =Import/Export

EMP: 160
SALES (corp-wide): 103.1MM **Privately Held**
WEB: www.whitecars.com
SIC: **5511** 7513 5012 Automobiles, new & used; truck rental & leasing, no drivers; automobiles & other motor vehicles
PA: The White Family Companies Inc
2 River Pl Ste 444
Dayton OH 45405
937 220-6394

(G-9880)
WIDOWS HOME OF DAYTON OHIO
50 S Findlay St (45403-2091)
PHONE.................................937 252-1661
Antonette Flohre, *President*
Everett Telljohann, *President*
Paul Heinrich, *Vice Pres*
Dale Heinz, *Treasurer*
Gloria Ross, *Admin Sec*
EMP: 70
SQ FT: 50,000
SALES (est): 6.1MM **Privately Held**
SIC: **8051** 8361 Skilled nursing care facilities; home for the aged

(G-9881)
WIGGINS CLG & CRPT SVC INC (PA)
4699 Salem Ave Ste 2 (45416-1724)
PHONE.................................937 279-9080
Jewel Wiggins, *President*
Brenda Wiggins, *Corp Secy*
EMP: 62
SQ FT: 2,400
SALES (est): 1.6MM **Privately Held**
WEB: www.wigginscleaning.com
SIC: **7349** 7217 Cleaning service, industrial or commercial; building cleaning service; carpet & furniture cleaning on location

(G-9882)
WILMER CUTLER PICK HALE DORR
Also Called: Wilmerhale
3139 Research Blvd (45420-4006)
PHONE.................................937 395-2100
Donna Smith, *Branch Mgr*
Chris Southern, *Manager*
Michaele Flesburg, *Administration*
Amanda L Major, *Sr Associate*
EMP: 270
SALES (corp-wide): 98.4MM **Privately Held**
SIC: **8111** Specialized law offices, attorneys
PA: Wilmer Cutler Pickering Hale And Dorr Llp
1875 Pennsylvania Ave Nw
Washington DC 20006
202 663-6000

(G-9883)
WISE SERVICES INC
1705 Guenther Rd (45417-9344)
P.O. Box 17159 (45417-0159)
PHONE.................................937 854-0281
David F Abney II, *President*
EMP: 45
SALES (est): 8.4MM **Privately Held**
SIC: **1542** Commercial & office building, new construction

(G-9884)
WOLF CREEK COMPANY INC (PA)
6051 Wolf Creek Pike (45426-2943)
PHONE.................................937 854-2694
Charles Knowles, *Ch of Bd*
Scott Knowles, *President*
Chris Knowles, *Vice Pres*
Bonnie Martin, *CFO*
▲ EMP: 67
SQ FT: 12,000
SALES (est): 52.4MM **Privately Held**
SIC: **5083** Irrigation equipment

(G-9885)
WOMENS CENTERS-DAYTON
359 Forest Ave Ste 106 (45405-4559)
PHONE.................................937 228-2222
Vivian Koob, *Principal*

EMP: 50 EST: 2010
SALES (est): 676.2K **Privately Held**
SIC: **8071** Ultrasound laboratory

(G-9886)
WOODY TREE MEDICS
Also Called: Tru-Gro Landscaping
4350 Delco Dell Rd (45429-1211)
PHONE.................................937 298-5316
William F Wesig, *President*
EMP: 25
SQ FT: 34,680
SALES (est): 795.1K **Privately Held**
SIC: **0782** 0783 Lawn & garden services; ornamental shrub & tree services

(G-9887)
WRIGHT BROTHERS AERO INC
Also Called: Logistics Department
3700 Mccall St (45417)
PHONE.................................937 454-8475
Kevin Keeley Jr, *Principal*
EMP: 25
SALES (corp-wide): 8.1MM **Privately Held**
SIC: **4212** Delivery service, vehicular
PA: Wright Brothers Aero, Inc.
3700 Mccauley Dr Ste C
Vandalia OH 45377
937 890-8900

(G-9888)
XPO LOGISTICS FREIGHT INC
3410 Stop 8 Rd (45414-3428)
PHONE.................................937 898-9808
John Crawley, *Manager*
EMP: 35
SQ FT: 18,920
SALES (corp-wide): 15.3B **Publicly Held**
WEB: www.con-way.com
SIC: **4213** Trucking, except local
HQ: Xpo Logistics Freight, Inc.
2211 Old Earhart Rd # 100
Ann Arbor MI 48105
800 755-2728

(G-9889)
YEARWOOD CORPORATION (PA)
Also Called: Carousel Beauty College
125 E 2nd St (45402-1701)
P.O. Box 750144 (45475-0144)
PHONE.................................937 223-3572
Donald Yearwood, *President*
EMP: 33
SQ FT: 5,000
SALES (est): 2MM **Privately Held**
WEB: www.carouselbeauty.com
SIC: **7231** Beauty Schools

(G-9890)
YODER INDUSTRIES INC (PA)
2520 Needmore Rd (45414-4204)
PHONE.................................937 278-5769
Ron Zeverka, *President*
Janet E Roush, *Principal*
Ron Veverka, *Principal*
J B Yoder, *Principal*
Charles W Slicer, *Chairman*
EMP: 110 EST: 1956
SQ FT: 32,000
SALES (est): 13MM **Privately Held**
WEB: www.yoderindustries.com
SIC: **3369** 3363 3365 3471 Nonferrous foundries; aluminum die-castings; aluminum foundries; plating & polishing; testing laboratories; nonferrous die-castings except aluminum

(G-9891)
YOUNG & ALEXANDER CO LPA (PA)
130 W 2nd St Ste 1500 (45402-1502)
PHONE.................................937 224-9291
Mark R Chilson, *President*
Steven Dean, *Vice Pres*
Jonathon Beck, *Shareholder*
Joanna Lenefonte, *Associate*
EMP: 53
SALES (est): 5MM **Privately Held**
SIC: **8111** General practice attorney, lawyer

(G-9892)
YOUNG MENS CHRISTIAN ASSOC (PA)
Also Called: YMCA of Greater Dayton
118 W 1st St Ste 300 (45402-1111)
PHONE.................................937 223-5201
Dale Brunner, *CEO*
Neal Pemberton, *Vice Pres*
Britney McClain, *Hum Res Coord*
EMP: 26 EST: 1882
SQ FT: 9,000
SALES: 26.1MM **Privately Held**
WEB: www.daytonymca.org
SIC: **8641** 7991 8351 7032 Youth organizations; physical fitness facilities; child day care services; youth camps; individual & family services

(G-9893)
YOUNG MENS CHRISTIAN ASSOC
Also Called: South Cmty Family YMCA Cdc
4545 Marshall Rd (45429-5716)
PHONE.................................937 312-1810
Kelley Ingram, *Engrg Dir*
Sara Nelson, *Director*
EMP: 25
SALES (corp-wide): 26.1MM **Privately Held**
WEB: www.daytonymca.org
SIC: **8641** 7991 8351 7032 Youth organizations; physical fitness facilities; child day care services; youth camps; individual & family services
PA: Young Men's Christian Association Of Greater Dayton
118 W 1st St Ste 300
Dayton OH 45402
937 223-5201

(G-9894)
YOUNG MENS CHRISTIAN ASSOC
Also Called: Beavercreek YMCA Sch's Out I
111 W 1st St Ste 207 (45402-1154)
PHONE.................................937 426-9622
Stacy Wentzell, *Director*
EMP: 80
SALES (corp-wide): 26.1MM **Privately Held**
WEB: www.daytonymca.org
SIC: **8641** 7997 Youth organizations; membership sports & recreation clubs
PA: Young Men's Christian Association Of Greater Dayton
118 W 1st St Ste 300
Dayton OH 45402
937 223-5201

(G-9895)
YOUNG MENS CHRISTIAN ASSOC
Also Called: YMCA Crayon Club Chld Care
316 N Wilkinson St (45402-3060)
PHONE.................................937 228-9622
Nancy Hudecek, *Director*
EMP: 40
SALES (corp-wide): 26.1MM **Privately Held**
WEB: www.daytonymca.org
SIC: **8641** 8351 7997 7991 Youth organizations; child day care services; membership sports & recreation clubs; physical fitness facilities; recreation center
PA: Young Men's Christian Association Of Greater Dayton
118 W 1st St Ste 300
Dayton OH 45402
937 223-5201

(G-9896)
YWCA DAYTON
141 W 3rd St (45402-1814)
PHONE.................................937 461-5550
Donna Audette, *CEO*
EMP: 79 EST: 1871
SQ FT: 100,000
SALES: 3.4MM **Privately Held**
SIC: **8641** 7991 8351 7032 Youth organizations; physical fitness facilities; child day care services; youth camps; individual & family services

(G-9897)
YWCA SHELTER & HOUSING NETWORK
141 W 3rd St (45402-1814)
PHONE.................................937 222-6333
Donna Audette, *CEO*
EMP: 30
SALES (est): 234.2K **Privately Held**
SIC: **8641** 7991 8351 7032 Youth organizations; physical fitness facilities; child day care services; youth camps; individual & family services

(G-9898)
ZIKS FAMILY PHARMACY 100
1130 W 3rd St (45402-6812)
PHONE.................................937 225-9350
Nnodum Iheme, *CEO*
Nnenna Iheme, *Vice Pres*
EMP: 30
SQ FT: 5,500
SALES (est): 5MM **Privately Held**
SIC: **5912** 5047 8082 Drug stores; medical & hospital equipment; home health care services

(G-9899)
ZIMMER ENTERPRISES INC (PA)
Also Called: Kettering Monogramming
911 Senate Dr (45459-4017)
PHONE.................................937 428-1057
Jeffrey Zimmer, *President*
Patricia M Zimmer, *Vice Pres*
▲ EMP: 25
SALES (est): 10.1MM **Privately Held**
WEB: www.pbj-sport.com
SIC: **5137** 2395 Women's & children's clothing; embroidery products, except schiffli machine

---

De Graff
Logan County

(G-9900)
SCHINDEWOLF EXPRESS INC
200 S Boggs St (43318-7905)
PHONE.................................937 585-5919
Suzie Schindewolf, *CEO*
Dan Schindewolf, *President*
Casey Schindewolf, *Corp Secy*
David Breneck, *Vice Pres*
Chad Shindewolf, *Vice Pres*
EMP: 52
SALES (est): 2.2MM **Privately Held**
SIC: **4213** 4212 Contract haulers; local trucking, without storage

---

Deerfield
Portage County

(G-9901)
ALLIANCE CRANE & RIGGING INC
Also Called: DIRTWORKS DRAINAGE
1370 Alliance Rd (44411-9792)
P.O. Box 338, Atwater (44201-0338)
PHONE.................................330 823-8823
Kurt Ryan Klingelhofer, *President*
Charles Klingelhofer, *Officer*
EMP: 28
SQ FT: 8,000
SALES (est): 898.1K **Privately Held**
SIC: **1794** Excavation & grading, building construction

(G-9902)
CHEVRON AE RESOURCES LLC
1823 State Route 14 (44411)
P.O. Box 160 (44411-0160)
PHONE.................................330 654-4343
EMP: 30
SALES (corp-wide): 129.9B **Publicly Held**
SIC: **1311** 1382 Crude Petroleum/Natural Gas Production Oil/Gas Exploration Services
HQ: Chevron Ae Resources Llc
1000 Commerce Dr Fl 4
Pittsburgh PA 15275
800 251-0171

(G-9903)
DEERFIELD FARMS
9041 State Route 224 (44411-8715)
P.O. Box 155 (44411-0155)
PHONE...................................330 584-4715
B William Wallbrown, *President*
John Wallbrown, *Vice Pres*
EMP: 32
SQ FT: 5,000
SALES (est): 2.4MM **Privately Held**
SIC: 0191 1799 1521 General farms, primarily crop; fence construction; patio & deck construction & repair

(G-9904)
DEERFIELD FARMS SERVICE INC (PA)
9041 State Route 224 (44411-8715)
P.O. Box 155 (44411-0155)
PHONE...................................330 584-4715
B William Wallbrown, *President*
Joan Wallbrown, *Corp Secy*
John Wallbrown, *Vice Pres*
Travis Wright, *Project Mgr*
Gary McQuiston, *Opers Staff*
EMP: 63
SQ FT: 25,000
SALES: 52MM **Privately Held**
WEB: www.deerfieldfarms.com
SIC: 5153 5191 4221 5083 Grain elevators; fertilizer & fertilizer materials; herbicides; animal feeds; grain elevator, storage only; agricultural machinery & equipment; grain elevators equipment & supplies

---

Defiance
Defiance County

(G-9905)
BROOKVIEW HEALTHCARE CTR
Also Called: Brookview Healthcare Center
214 Harding St (43512-1381)
PHONE...................................419 784-1014
Paul Dauerman, *President*
EMP: 90
SALES (est): 5MM **Privately Held**
WEB: www.brookview.com
SIC: 8059 8051 Convalescent home; skilled nursing care facilities

(G-9906)
CITY BEVERAGE COMPANY
8283 N State Route 66 (43512-6612)
P.O. Box 432 (43512-0432)
PHONE...................................419 782-7065
Thomas Sauer, *President*
Tim Sauer, *Vice Pres*
Mark Schelling, *Opers Mgr*
Corey Hale, *Sales Mgr*
Jim Huffmon, *Sales Mgr*
▲ **EMP:** 25 **EST:** 1960
SQ FT: 33,000
SALES (est): 5.8MM **Privately Held**
WEB: www.citybev.com
SIC: 5181 Beer & other fermented malt liquors

(G-9907)
CONSOLIDATED GRAIN & BARGE CO
Also Called: CGB -Defiance
11859 Krouse Rd (43512-8618)
PHONE...................................419 785-1941
EMP: 51 **Privately Held**
SIC: 5153 4221 Grains; grain elevator, storage only
HQ: Consolidated Grain & Barge Company
1127 Hwy 190 E Service Rd
Covington LA 70433
985 867-3500

(G-9908)
CREDIT ADJUSTMENTS INC (PA)
330 Florence St (43512-2512)
PHONE...................................419 782-3709
Jason Osborne, *Vice Pres*
Shelah Cheek, *Credit Mgr*
Lisa Bloomfield, *Admin Sec*
EMP: 81
SQ FT: 40,000
SALES: 11.1MM **Privately Held**
WEB: www.credit-adjustments.com
SIC: 7322 Collection agency, except real estate

(G-9909)
DEFIANCE CNTY BD COMMISSIONERS
Also Called: Defiance County Senior Center
140 E Broadway St (43512-1639)
PHONE...................................419 782-3233
Tina Hiler, *Director*
EMP: 26 **Privately Held**
SIC: 8322 Individual & family services
PA: Defiance County Board Of Commissioners
500 Court St Ste A
Defiance OH 43512
419 782-4761

(G-9910)
DEFIANCE FAMILY PHYSICIANS
1250 Ralston Ave Ste 104 (43512-5308)
PHONE...................................419 785-3281
Robert Barnett MD, *Partner*
EMP: 26 **EST:** 1982
SALES (est): 1.9MM **Privately Held**
SIC: 8011 General & family practice, physician/surgeon

(G-9911)
DEFIANCE HOSPITAL INC
Also Called: DEFIANCE REGIONAL MEDICAL CENTER
1200 Ralston Ave (43512-1396)
PHONE...................................419 782-6955
Tim Jakacki, *President*
Carl A Sixeas, *Principal*
Bernie Nawrocki, *CFO*
Carrie Miller, *HR Admin*
Lindsey Limbaugh, *Manager*
EMP: 359
SQ FT: 150,000
SALES: 63.5MM
SALES (corp-wide): 2.1B **Privately Held**
SIC: 8062 General Hospital
PA: Promedica Health Systems, Inc.
100 Madison Ave
Toledo OH 43604
567 585-7454

(G-9912)
ELLERBROCK HEATING & AC
13055 Dohoney Rd (43512-8716)
PHONE...................................419 782-1834
Scott Wagner, *President*
EMP: 25
SALES (est): 1.2MM **Privately Held**
SIC: 1711 Heating & air conditioning contractors

(G-9913)
FAUSTER-CAMERON INC (PA)
Also Called: Defiance Clinic
1400 E 2nd St (43512-2440)
PHONE...................................419 784-1414
Chad L Peter, *CEO*
Allen Gaspar, *Ch of Bd*
Nathan Fogt, *Corp Secy*
John Racciato, *Vice Pres*
EMP: 310
SQ FT: 101,908
SALES (est): 29.1MM **Privately Held**
WEB: www.defianceclinic.com
SIC: 8011 Medical centers

(G-9914)
FIRST FEDERAL BANK OF MIDWEST (HQ)
601 Clinton St Ste 1 (43512-2661)
P.O. Box 248 (43512-0248)
PHONE...................................419 782-5015
William J Small, *Ch of Bd*
Kimberly Carpenter, *President*
Vince Liuzzi, *President*
James L Rohrs, *President*
Gregory R Allen, *Exec VP*
EMP: 50
SQ FT: 10,000
SALES: 134.9MM **Publicly Held**
SIC: 6035 Federal savings & loan associations

(G-9915)
FITZENRIDER INC
827 Perry St (43512-2738)
PHONE...................................419 784-0828
John Jacob, *President*
Philip Fitzenrider, *Vice Pres*
EMP: 30 **EST:** 1955
SQ FT: 15,000
SALES (est): 6.2MM **Privately Held**
SIC: 1711 Warm air heating & air conditioning contractor; ventilation & duct work contractor; mechanical contractor

(G-9916)
FOUNTAIN CITY LEASING INC
2060 E 2nd St Ste 101 (43512-9208)
PHONE...................................419 785-3100
Sam Hornish, *President*
Jo Ellen Hornish, *Admin Sec*
EMP: 82
SQ FT: 14,000
SALES (est): 7.7MM **Privately Held**
SIC: 7513 Truck leasing, without drivers

(G-9917)
HUBBARD COMPANY
612 Clinton St (43512-2637)
P.O. Box 100 (43512-0100)
PHONE...................................419 784-4455
E Keith Hubbard, *Ch of Bd*
Thomas K Hubbard, *President*
Jean A Hubbard, *Treasurer*
Jean Hubbard, *Finance*
Dick Anderson, *Sales Staff*
EMP: 44
SQ FT: 20,000
SALES (est): 7.2MM **Privately Held**
WEB: www.hubbardcompany.com
SIC: 5943 5192 2752 2732 Office forms & supplies; books; commercial printing, offset; book printing; book publishing

(G-9918)
HUNTINGTON NATIONAL BANK
405 W 3rd St (43512-2136)
PHONE...................................419 782-5050
Robert Degler, *Manager*
EMP: 35
SALES (corp-wide): 5.2B **Publicly Held**
WEB: www.huntingtonnationalbank.com
SIC: 6029 6022 Commercial banks; state commercial banks
HQ: The Huntington National Bank
17 S High St Fl 1
Columbus OH 43215
614 480-4293

(G-9919)
IDEAL SETECH LLC
24862 Elliott Rd (43512-9217)
PHONE...................................419 782-5522
John McCarthey, *Branch Mgr*
EMP: 25
SALES (corp-wide): 270.1MM **Privately Held**
SIC: 8741 Management services
HQ: Ideal Setech, L.L.C.
2525 Clark St
Detroit MI 48209

(G-9920)
IHEARTCOMMUNICATIONS INC
2110 Radio Dr (43512-1977)
PHONE...................................419 782-9336
Bob Climanas, *Manager*
EMP: 61 **Publicly Held**
SIC: 4832 Radio broadcasting stations
HQ: Iheartcommunications, Inc.
20880 Stone Oak Pkwy
San Antonio TX 78258
210 822-2828

(G-9921)
JOHNS MANVILLE CORPORATION
600 Jackson Ave (43512-2769)
PHONE...................................419 784-7000
Jerry Henry, *Branch Mgr*
EMP: 54
SALES (corp-wide): 225.3B **Publicly Held**
SIC: 5033 5211 Roofing, siding & insulation; roofing material; insulation material, building
HQ: Johns Manville Corporation
717 17th St Ste 800
Denver CO 80202
303 978-2000

(G-9922)
KELLER LOGISTICS GROUP INC
24862 Elliott Rd Ste 101 (43512-9237)
PHONE...................................419 784-4805
Scott J Galbraith, *Branch Mgr*
EMP: 432 **Privately Held**
SIC: 4215 Courier services, except by air
PA: Keller Logistics Group, Inc.
24862 Elliott Rd Ste 101
Defiance OH 43512

(G-9923)
KELLER LOGISTICS GROUP INC (PA)
24862 Elliott Rd Ste 101 (43512-9237)
PHONE...................................866 276-9486
Bryan Keller, *CEO*
Dawn Nye, *Principal*
Nate Schaublin, *Principal*
Beth Woodbury, *Principal*
Aaron Keller, *Vice Pres*
EMP: 39
SALES (est): 48.9MM **Privately Held**
SIC: 4731 7389 4225 Freight transportation arrangement; packaging & labeling services; general warehousing & storage

(G-9924)
KELLER WAREHOUSING & DIST LLC
1160 Carpenter Rd (43512-1727)
PHONE...................................419 784-4805
EMP: 125
SQ FT: 7,000
SALES (est): 4.3MM **Privately Held**
SIC: 4225 General Warehouse/Storage

(G-9925)
LAUREL HEALTHCARE
Also Called: LAURRELS OF DEFIANCE
1701 Jefferson Ave (43512-3493)
PHONE...................................419 782-7879
Dennis G Sherman, *President*
Julie Vanzile, *Director*
Chuck Evans, *Food Svc Dir*
Susan Pasterz, *Executive*
EMP: 120
SALES (est): 10.6MM **Privately Held**
SIC: 8051 Convalescent home with continuous nursing care

(G-9926)
LOWES HOME CENTERS LLC
1831 N Clinton St (43512-8555)
PHONE...................................419 782-9000
Gail Post, *Branch Mgr*
EMP: 150
SALES (corp-wide): 68.6B **Publicly Held**
SIC: 5211 5031 5722 5064 Home centers; building materials, exterior; building materials, interior; household appliance stores; electrical appliances, television & radio
HQ: Lowe's Home Centers, Llc
1605 Curtis Bridge Rd
Wilkesboro NC 28697
336 658-4000

(G-9927)
MAUMEE VALLEY GUIDANCE CENTER (PA)
211 Biede Ave (43512-2497)
PHONE...................................419 782-8856
William Bierie, *Exec Dir*
EMP: 40
SQ FT: 6,000
SALES: 3.6MM **Privately Held**
SIC: 8093 Mental health clinic, outpatient

(G-9928)
MCDONALDS DESIGN & BUILD INC
101 Clinton St Ste 2200 (43512-2173)
PHONE...................................419 782-4191
Kevin R McDonald, *President*
Scott McDonald II, *Vice Pres*
Ann Westrick, *Treasurer*
EMP: 30
SQ FT: 3,500

▲ = Import ▼=Export
◆ =Import/Export

SALES (est): 5.5MM **Privately Held**
SIC: 1542 1541 Commercial & office building, new construction; industrial buildings, new construction

(G-9929)
MERCY HOSPITAL OF DEFIANCE
1400 E 2nd St (43512-2440)
PHONE...................................419 782-8444
Chad L Peter, *CEO*
EMP: 156
SALES: 29.2MM **Privately Held**
SIC: 8062 General medical & surgical hospitals

(G-9930)
METAL MANAGEMENT OHIO INC
Also Called: Simms Metal Management Ohio
27063 State Route 281 (43512-8963)
PHONE...................................419 782-7791
Tim Wiseman, *Plant Mgr*
Tim Weisman, *Plant Mgr*
EMP: 50 **Privately Held**
SIC: 4953 Recycling, waste materials
HQ: Metal Management Ohio, Inc.
3100 Lonyo St
Detroit MI 48209
313 841-1800

(G-9931)
MIDWEST CMNTY FEDERAL CR UN
1481 Deerwood Dr (43512-6738)
P.O. Box 608 (43512-0608)
PHONE...................................419 782-9856
Gina Medley, *President*
EMP: 30
SQ FT: 5,300
SALES: 3.5MM **Privately Held**
SIC: 6061 Federal credit unions

(G-9932)
NORTHWESTRN OH COMMUNITY ACTION (PA)
1933 E 2nd St (43512-2503)
PHONE...................................419 784-2150
Dean Genter, *President*
Rey Romero, *Supervisor*
Sally Gerken, *Technology*
Deborah Gerken, *Exec Dir*
Jennifer Burkhart, *Teacher*
EMP: 150
SQ FT: 8,000
SALES: 7.3MM **Privately Held**
WEB: www.nocac.org
SIC: 8399 8322 Community action agency; individual & family services

(G-9933)
OMNISOURCE LLC
880 Linden St (43512-2776)
PHONE...................................419 784-5669
John Lero, *Branch Mgr*
EMP: 30 **Publicly Held**
WEB: www.omnisource.com
SIC: 5093 Ferrous metal scrap & waste
HQ: Omnisource, Llc
7575 W Jefferson Blvd
Fort Wayne IN 46804
260 422-5541

(G-9934)
POSTEMA INSURANCE & INVESTMENT
2014 Baltimore St (43512-1918)
PHONE...................................419 782-2500
Dennis Postema, *Owner*
Paul Mallett, *Marketing Staff*
EMP: 30
SALES (est): 3.7MM **Privately Held**
SIC: 6411 Insurance agents

(G-9935)
PROMEDICA DEFIANCE REGIONAL
1200 Ralston Ave (43512-1396)
PHONE...................................419 783-6802
EMP: 33
SALES (est): 2.6MM **Privately Held**
SIC: 8062 General medical & surgical hospitals

(G-9936)
RELIANCE FINANCIAL SERVICES NA
401 Clinton St (43512-2632)
P.O. Box 467 (43512-0467)
PHONE...................................419 783-8007
Jeffrey D Sewell, *CEO*
Gregory Marquiss, *President*
EMP: 30
SALES (est): 1.1MM
SALES (corp-wide): 56.1MM **Publicly Held**
SIC: 7389 Financial services
HQ: The State Bank And Trust Company
401 Clinton St
Defiance OH 43512
419 783-8950

(G-9937)
RICHLAND CO & ASSOCIATES INC (PA)
101 Clinton St Ste 2200 (43512-2173)
PHONE...................................419 782-0141
Douglas A Mc Donald, *President*
Kevin R McDonald, *Vice Pres*
Ann Westrick, *Treasurer*
Brenda Mathewson, *Admin Sec*
EMP: 44
SQ FT: 3,500
SALES: 3MM **Privately Held**
SIC: 1761 Roofing contractor; sheet metalwork

(G-9938)
RURBANC DATA SERVICES INC
Also Called: Rdsi Banking Systems
7622 N State Route 66 (43512-6715)
PHONE...................................419 782-2530
Kurt Kratzer, *President*
Gwen Anderson, *Vice Pres*
Karen Oskey, *Vice Pres*
Gary Saxman, *CFO*
EMP: 60
SALES: 21.6MM
SALES (corp-wide): 56.1MM **Publicly Held**
WEB: www.rdsiweb.com
SIC: 7374 Data processing service
PA: Sb Financial Group, Inc.
401 Clinton St
Defiance OH 43512
419 783-8950

(G-9939)
SB FINANCIAL GROUP INC (PA)
401 Clinton St (43512-2632)
P.O. Box 467 (43512-0467)
PHONE...................................419 783-8950
Mark A Klein, *Ch of Bd*
Jonathan R Gathman, *Exec VP*
Anthony V Cosentino, *CFO*
Rita Kissner, *Bd of Directors*
EMP: 192
SALES: 56.1MM **Publicly Held**
WEB: www.rurban.net
SIC: 6022 State trust companies accepting deposits, commercial

(G-9940)
SERVICEMASTER OF DEFIANCE INC
1255 Carpenter Rd (43512-8505)
PHONE...................................419 784-5570
Richard F McCann, *President*
Richard F Mc Cann, *President*
Michael Mc Cann, *Corp Secy*
Pat McFarland, *Mktg Dir*
EMP: 100
SQ FT: 1,400
SALES (est): 3MM **Privately Held**
WEB: www.fortsm.com
SIC: 7349 6794 5087 Janitorial service, contract basis; franchises, selling or licensing; janitors' supplies

(G-9941)
STATE BANK AND TRUST COMPANY (HQ)
401 Clinton St (43512-2662)
P.O. Box 467 (43512-0467)
PHONE...................................419 783-8950
Mark A Klein, *CEO*
Steven D Vandemark, *Ch of Bd*
David Anderson, *President*
David Homoelle, *President*

Mark A Soukup, *President*
◆ **EMP:** 35
SQ FT: 10,000
SALES: 49MM
SALES (corp-wide): 56.1MM **Publicly Held**
SIC: 6022 6163 State trust companies accepting deposits, commercial; loan brokers
PA: Sb Financial Group, Inc.
401 Clinton St
Defiance OH 43512
419 783-8950

(G-9942)
STYKEMAIN PNTIAC-BUICK-GMC LTD (PA)
25124 Elliott Rd (43512-9003)
PHONE...................................419 784-5252
Ethan Stykemain, *Cust Mgr*
Jackson Mike, *Director*
James Stykemain,
Joseph Stykemain,
EMP: 100
SQ FT: 30,000
SALES (est): 28.7MM **Privately Held**
WEB: www.stykemain.com
SIC: 5511 5012 Automobiles, new & used; automobiles

(G-9943)
SUN HEALTHCARE GROUP INC
Also Called: Twin Rvers Care Rhbltation Ctr
395 Harding St (43512-1315)
PHONE...................................419 784-1450
Michael Adams, *Manager*
EMP: 130 **Publicly Held**
WEB: www.harborsidehealthcare.com
SIC: 8051 Skilled nursing care facilities
HQ: Sun Healthcare Group, Inc.
27442 Portola Pkwy # 200
Foothill Ranch CA 92610

(G-9944)
THOMAS E KELLER TRUCKING INC
24862 Elliott Rd (43512-9217)
PHONE...................................419 784-4805
Bryan Keller, *President*
Nate Schaublin, *COO*
Lori Adams, *Hum Res Coord*
Meredith Mickey, *Marketing Staff*
EMP: 110
SALES (est): 20.5MM **Privately Held**
SIC: 4213 Contract haulers

(G-9945)
UNITED PARCEL SERVICE INC OH
Also Called: UPS
820 Carpenter Rd (43512-1726)
PHONE...................................419 782-3552
Mike Kenneth, *Manager*
Jack Long, *Supervisor*
EMP: 70
SALES (corp-wide): 71.8B **Publicly Held**
WEB: www.martrac.com
SIC: 4215 4513 Package delivery, vehicular; air courier services
HQ: United Parcel Service, Inc. (Oh)
55 Glenlake Pkwy
Atlanta GA 30328
404 828-6000

(G-9946)
WERLOR INC
Also Called: Werlor Waste Control
1420 Ralston Ave (43512-1380)
PHONE...................................419 784-4285
Gerald Wertz, *President*
Judy Wertz, *Corp Secy*
Mark Hageman, *Vice Pres*
Tom Taylor, *Vice Pres*
Casey Wertz, *Vice Pres*
EMP: 40
SQ FT: 8,000
SALES (est): 5.5MM **Privately Held**
WEB: www.werlor.com
SIC: 4212 2875 Garbage collection & transport, no disposal; compost

(G-9947)
A L K INC
Also Called: Wintersong Village of Delaware
462 W Central Ave (43015-1405)
PHONE...................................740 369-8741
Charles Summers, *President*
Diane Summers, *Corp Secy*
EMP: 60
SQ FT: 14,000
SALES (est): 3.1MM **Privately Held**
SIC: 8051 Extended care facility

(G-9948)
ACI INDUSTRIES LTD (PA)
970 Pittsburgh Dr (43015-3872)
PHONE...................................740 368-4160
Ralph Paglieri, *Partner*
Scott H Fischer, *Partner*
Helen Harper, *Partner*
Shreelal Bhatter, *Vice Pres*
Helen Hraper, *Vice Pres*
◆ **EMP:** 50
SQ FT: 225,000
SALES: 3.8MM **Privately Held**
WEB: www.aci-industries.com
SIC: 3341 5093 3339 Secondary nonferrous metals; scrap & waste materials; primary nonferrous metals

(G-9949)
ACI INDUSTRIES CONVERTING LTD (HQ)
Also Called: J and J Sales
970 Pittsburgh Dr (43015-3872)
PHONE...................................740 368-4160
Mike Paglieri, *General Ptnr*
◆ **EMP:** 33
SQ FT: 232,000
SALES (est): 2.7MM
SALES (corp-wide): 3.8MM **Privately Held**
SIC: 2676 5113 Towels, napkins & tissue paper products; towels, paper
PA: Aci Industries, Ltd.
970 Pittsburgh Dr
Delaware OH 43015
740 368-4160

(G-9950)
ADVANCE STORES COMPANY INC
Advance Auto Parts
1675 Us Highway 42 S (43015-8285)
PHONE...................................740 369-4491
Chris Hagestad, *President*
Bob Scott, *Manager*
Jeff Monahan, *Data Proc Exec*
EMP: 125
SALES (corp-wide): 9.3B **Publicly Held**
SIC: 5013 Automotive supplies
HQ: Advance Stores Company Incorporated
5008 Airport Rd Nw
Roanoke VA 24012
540 362-4911

(G-9951)
ALPHA GROUP OF DELAWARE INC (PA)
1000 Alpha Dr (43015-8642)
PHONE...................................740 368-5810
Dave Nuscher, *CEO*
Joseph Leonard, *CEO*
Joe Leonard, *COO*
Lois Oswald, *Bookkeeper*
Curt Gwinn, *Finance*
EMP: 55
SALES: 5MM **Privately Held**
WEB: www.alphagroup.net
SIC: 8331 9111 Sheltered workshop; county supervisors' & executives' offices

(G-9952)
ALPHA GROUP OF DELAWARE INC
Also Called: Ergon
1000 Alpha Dr (43015-8642)
PHONE...................................740 368-5820
Laura Schick, *Manager*

Elliott Castello, *Director*
EMP: 47
SALES (corp-wide): 3.6MM Privately Held
WEB: www.alphagroup.net
SIC: 8331 9111 Job training & vocational rehabilitation services; county supervisors' & executives' offices
PA: The Alpha Group Of Delaware Inc
1000 Alpha Dr
Delaware OH 43015
740 368-5810

(G-9953)
ATLANTIC COASTAL TRUCKING
Also Called: Atlantic Triangle Trucking
222 E William St (43015-3282)
PHONE....................................201 438-6500
Peter Dykstra, *President*
Josephine Dykstra, *Corp Secy*
Mark Dykstra, *Vice Pres*
EMP: 110
SALES (est): 5.4MM Privately Held
WEB: www.act-tri.com
SIC: 4212 Local trucking, without storage

(G-9954)
AUTHENTIC FOOD LLC
Also Called: Corner Cafe
535 Sunbury Rd (43015-8656)
PHONE....................................740 369-0377
Dimitri Velalis, *Mng Member*
Maria Velalis, *Mng Member*
Tom Velalis,
EMP: 25
SQ FT: 2,560
SALES (est): 1.6MM Privately Held
SIC: 8741 Restaurant management

(G-9955)
BRIDGES TO INDEPENDENCE INC (PA)
61 W William St (43015-2338)
PHONE....................................740 362-1996
Chris Ritchie, *President*
Vickie Ritchie, *Finance*
Michelle Ferguson, *Office Admin*
Traci Pigg, *Director*
Lisa Clifford, *Associate Dir*
EMP: 125
SALES (est): 3.4MM Privately Held
WEB: www.bridgestoindependence.com
SIC: 8322 Social services for the handicapped

(G-9956)
BUNS OF DELAWARE INC
Also Called: Buns Restaurant & Bakery
14 W Winter St (43015-1919)
PHONE....................................740 363-2867
Vasili Konstantinidis, *President*
EMP: 40
SQ FT: 11,184
SALES (est): 1.1MM Privately Held
SIC: 5812 5461 7299 2051 Eating places; bakeries; banquet hall facilities; bread, cake & related products

(G-9957)
CARRIAGE TOWN CHRYSLER PLYMUTH
2815 Stratford Rd (43015-2951)
P.O. Box 420 (43015-0420)
PHONE....................................740 369-9611
James R Pancake Jr, *President*
Kim Bloom, *Vice Pres*
EMP: 70
SALES (est): 8.1MM Privately Held
SIC: 6411 Life insurance agents

(G-9958)
CENTRAL OHIO CONTRACTORS INC
888 Us Highway 42 N (43015-9014)
PHONE....................................740 369-7700
Joe Corwin, *Principal*
EMP: 70
SALES (corp-wide): 2.2MM Privately Held
SIC: 1522 4953 Residential construction; refuse collection & disposal services
PA: Central Ohio Contractors, Inc.
2879 Jackson Pike
Grove City OH 43123
614 539-2579

(G-9959)
CENTRAL OHIO MENTAL HEALTH CTR (PA)
250 S Henry St (43015-2978)
PHONE....................................740 368-7831
Neil Tolbert, *CFO*
Tom Sefcik, *Director*
EMP: 105
SQ FT: 6,000
SALES: 5.6MM Privately Held
SIC: 8093 Specialty Outpatient Clinic

(G-9960)
CITIGROUP INC
310 Greif Pkwy (43015)
PHONE....................................740 548-0594
Diane Matton, *Branch Mgr*
EMP: 380
SALES (corp-wide): 72.8B Publicly Held
WEB: www.citigroup.com
SIC: 7389 Telephone services
PA: Citigroup Inc.
388 Greenwich St
New York NY 10013
212 559-1000

(G-9961)
CONSOLIDATED ELECTRIC COOP
680 Sunbury Rd (43015-9555)
P.O. Box 630 (43015-0630)
PHONE....................................740 363-2641
Brian Newton, *President*
EMP: 43 EST: 1936
SQ FT: 19,000
SALES (est): 5.3MM Privately Held
SIC: 4911 Distribution, electric power

(G-9962)
COUNTY OF DELAWARE
50 Channing St (43015-2050)
P.O. Box 614, Lewis Center (43035-0614)
PHONE....................................740 833-2240
Chad Antel, *Manager*
EMP: 36 Privately Held
SIC: 1623 Water, sewer & utility lines
PA: County Of Delaware
101 N Sandusky St
Delaware OH 43015
740 368-1800

(G-9963)
COUNTY OF DELAWARE
Also Called: Delaware County Engineers
50 Channing St (43015-2050)
PHONE....................................740 833-2400
Chris Bauserman, *Manager*
EMP: 70 Privately Held
WEB: www.delawarecountysheriff.com
SIC: 8711 1611 Engineering services; highway & street construction
PA: County Of Delaware
101 N Sandusky St
Delaware OH 43015
740 368-1800

(G-9964)
COUNTY OF DELAWARE
Also Called: Delaware General Health Dst
1 W Winter St Fl 2 (43015-1918)
P.O. Box 570 (43015-0570)
PHONE....................................740 203-2040
Frances M Veverka, *President*
EMP: 70
SQ FT: 15,000
SALES (est): 6.4MM Privately Held
SIC: 8011 Clinic, operated by physicians

(G-9965)
CREATIVE FOUNDATIONS INC (PA)
57 N Sandusky St (43015-1925)
PHONE....................................740 362-5102
Michael Hite, *Marketing Staff*
David Robbins, *Exec Dir*
EMP: 54 EST: 2001
SQ FT: 6,000
SALES (est): 8MM Privately Held
SIC: 8322 Individual/Family Services

(G-9966)
DEL-CO WATER COMPANY INC (PA)
6658 Olentangy River Rd (43015-9211)
PHONE....................................740 548-7746

Timothy D McNamara, *President*
Kenneth Zarbaugh, *President*
Robert Jenkins, *Corp Secy*
Shane Clark, *Engineer*
Jeff Morrow, *Administration*
EMP: 75
SQ FT: 8,000
SALES: 27.5MM Privately Held
WEB: www.delcowater.com
SIC: 4941 Water supply

(G-9967)
DELAWARE CITY SCHOOL DISTRICT
Also Called: Delaware City School Garage
2462 Liberty Rd (43015-8810)
PHONE....................................740 363-5901
Larry Davis, *Director*
EMP: 30
SALES (corp-wide): 74MM Privately Held
WEB: www.dcs.k12.oh.us
SIC: 8211 7538 Public elementary school; general automotive repair shops
PA: Delaware City School District
74 W William St
Delaware OH 43015
740 833-1100

(G-9968)
DELAWARE COUNTY HISTORICAL SOC
2690 Stratford Rd (43015-2948)
PHONE....................................740 369-3831
Kris Thomas, *President*
EMP: 60
SQ FT: 2,244
SALES: 257.2K Privately Held
SIC: 8412 Museum

(G-9969)
DELAWARE GOLF CLUB INC
Also Called: Tnr Properties
3326 Columbus Pike (43015)
PHONE....................................740 362-2582
John Miller, *Director*
EMP: 40
SALES (est): 3MM Privately Held
SIC: 5941 7999 7299 Golf goods & equipment; golf services & professionals; golf driving range; wedding chapel, privately operated

(G-9970)
DELAWARE OPCO LLC
Also Called: ARBORS AT DELAWARE
2270 Warrensburg Rd (43015-1336)
PHONE....................................502 429-8062
Robert Norcross, *CEO*
EMP: 99 EST: 2014
SQ FT: 60,000
SALES: 6.5MM Privately Held
SIC: 8051 Skilled nursing care facilities

(G-9971)
DORNOCH GOLF CLUB INC
3329 Columbus Pike (43015-8963)
PHONE....................................740 369-0863
Fax: 614 457-3874
EMP: 25
SALES (est): 1.2MM Privately Held
SIC: 7997 Private Golf Club

(G-9972)
EDS TREE & TURF
Also Called: Maple Crest Builders
5801 S Section Line Rd (43015-9489)
PHONE....................................740 881-5800
Mark E Ross, *Owner*
Ed Ross, *Exec Dir*
EMP: 40
SQ FT: 5,500
SALES: 1MM Privately Held
SIC: 0782 Sodding contractor; seeding services, lawn

(G-9973)
EXCEL HEALTH SERVICES LLC
163 N Sandusky St Ste 201 (43015-1771)
PHONE....................................614 794-0006
Emiliah Oduah,
Lkenna Nzeogu,
EMP: 99
SALES (est): 3.6MM Privately Held
SIC: 8082 Visiting nurse service

(G-9974)
FIRST COMMONWEALTH BANK
100 Delaware Xing W (43015-7853)
PHONE....................................740 548-3340
Alfred Wise, *Branch Mgr*
EMP: 27
SALES (corp-wide): 380.8MM Publicly Held
SIC: 6021 National commercial banks
HQ: First Commonwealth Bank
601 Philadelphia St
Indiana PA 15701
724 349-7220

(G-9975)
FIRST COMMONWEALTH BANK
100 Willow Brook Way S (43015-3249)
PHONE....................................740 369-0048
David Eedwards, *Branch Mgr*
EMP: 27
SALES (corp-wide): 380.8MM Publicly Held
SIC: 6021 National commercial banks
HQ: First Commonwealth Bank
601 Philadelphia St
Indiana PA 15701
724 349-7220

(G-9976)
FIRSTENTERPRISES INC
2000 Nutter Farms Ln (43015-9195)
PHONE....................................740 369-5100
Mike Doyle, *Principal*
EMP: 389
SALES (corp-wide): 423.3MM Privately Held
SIC: 4213 Trucking, except local
PA: Firstenterprises, Inc.
202 Heritage Park Dr
Murfreesboro TN 37129
615 890-9229

(G-9977)
FLOYD BROWNE GROUP INC
Also Called: Floyd Brown Group
585 Sunbury Rd (43015-9795)
PHONE....................................740 363-6792
Daniel Whited, *Branch Mgr*
EMP: 50
SALES (corp-wide): 40MM Privately Held
SIC: 8748 Environmental consultant
HQ: Floyd Browne Group, Inc.
7965 N High St Ste 340
Columbus OH 43235
740 363-6792

(G-9978)
FOOR CONCRETE CO INC (PA)
5361 State Route 37 E (43015-9684)
PHONE....................................740 513-4346
Archie E Foor Jr, *President*
EMP: 55
SALES: 7.4MM Privately Held
WEB: www.foorconcrete.com
SIC: 1771 Concrete pumping

(G-9979)
FREDERICK C SMITH CLINIC INC
6 Lexington Blvd (43015-1047)
PHONE....................................740 363-9021
Linda Lowry, *Manager*
EMP: 50
SALES (corp-wide): 38MM Privately Held
WEB: www.marionareahealth.com
SIC: 8011 General & family practice, physician/surgeon
PA: Frederick C Smith Clinic Inc
1040 Delaware Ave
Marion OH 43302
740 383-7000

(G-9980)
GANZFAIR INVESTMENT INC
Also Called: Shamrock Golf Club
231 Clubhouse Dr (43015-8490)
PHONE....................................614 792-6630
Gary Bachinski, *President*
EMP: 25
SQ FT: 5,000
SALES: 1.4MM Privately Held
WEB: www.shamrockgc.com
SIC: 7992 7997 Public golf courses; membership sports & recreation clubs

(G-9981)
GLOBAL MALL UNLIMITED
1423 Missouri Ave (43015-2990)
PHONE..................................740 533-7203
EMP: 35
SALES: 950K Privately Held
SIC: 5045 Whol Computers/Peripherals

(G-9982)
GRADY MEMORIAL HOSPITAL (PA)
561 W Central Ave (43015-1489)
PHONE..................................740 615-1000
David Blom, CEO
Johnni Beckel, Senior VP
Lonnie Hicks, Opers Mgr
Valerie Ramsey, Purch Dir
William D Hammett, Med Doctor
EMP: 41
SQ FT: 124,740
SALES: 92MM Privately Held
SIC: 8062 General medical & surgical hospitals

(G-9983)
HEALTH WORKS MSO INC (PA)
561 W Central Ave (43015-1410)
PHONE..................................740 368-5366
Steven Garlock, President
EMP: 47
SALES (est): 1.5MM Privately Held
SIC: 8011 Medical Doctor's Office

(G-9984)
HELP LINE OF DLWARE MRROW CNTY
Also Called: HELPLINE
11 N Franklin St (43015-1913)
PHONE..................................740 369-3316
Leslie Baldwin, Financial Exec
Lauren Macdade, Program Mgr
Michelle Price, Manager
Susan Hanson, Exec Dir
Tiana Purvis, Exec Dir
EMP: 25
SQ FT: 3,187
SALES: 2.1MM Privately Held
SIC: 8322 Crisis intervention center; referral service for personal & social problems

(G-9985)
HENDERSON TRUCKING INC
124 Henderson Ct (43015-8479)
PHONE..................................740 369-6100
Jack Henderson, President
Joyce Henderson, Admin Sec
EMP: 40
SQ FT: 8,400
SALES (est): 4.9MM Privately Held
SIC: 4214 4212 Local trucking with storage; local trucking, without storage; dump truck haulage

(G-9986)
HOMELIFE COMPANIES INC (PA)
13 E Winter St (43015-1978)
PHONE..................................740 369-1297
Donald E Rankey Jr, President
Pamela Hertwig-Rankey, Shareholder
Donald Rankey, Admin Asst
EMP: 26
SQ FT: 12,000
SALES (est): 3.5MM Privately Held
SIC: 8742 6531 Real estate consultant; real estate agents & managers

(G-9987)
HOMETOWN URGENT CARE
1100 Sunbury Rd Ste 706 (43015-6040)
PHONE..................................740 363-3133
EMP: 99
SALES (corp-wide): 73.2MM Privately Held
SIC: 8049 8011 7291 Occupational therapist; medical centers; tax return preparation services
PA: Hometown Urgent Care
2400 Corp Exchange Dr # 102
Columbus OH 43231
614 505-7633

(G-9988)
INCUBIT LLC
40 N Sandusky St Ste 200 (43015-1973)
PHONE..................................740 362-1401
Dorian Wolter, CEO
Alicia Ward, Office Mgr
EMP: 100
SQ FT: 2,000
SALES: 15MM Privately Held
SIC: 8742 7371 Business consultant; computer software development

(G-9989)
INNO-PAK LLC (PA)
1932 Pittsburgh Dr (43015-3868)
PHONE..................................740 363-0090
Denny Tao, General Mgr
Adam Bechtold, Vice Pres
Gary Bechtold, Vice Pres
Nick Healey, Vice Pres
Brian Hughes, Vice Pres
▲ EMP: 43
SALES (est): 36.9MM Privately Held
SIC: 5199 Packaging materials

(G-9990)
JEGS AUTOMOTIVE INC (PA)
Also Called: Jeg's High-Performance Center
101 Jegs Pl (43015-9279)
PHONE..................................614 294-5050
Edward James Coughlin, President
Todd Iden, General Mgr
Wayne Perdue, General Mgr
Jeg Coughlin, Vice Pres
John Coughlin, Vice Pres
▲ EMP: 150
SQ FT: 200,000
SALES (est): 192.2MM Privately Held
SIC: 5013 5961 5531 Automotive supplies & parts; automotive supplies & equipment, mail order; automotive parts

(G-9991)
JENNINGS & ASSOCIATES
26 Northwood Dr (43015-1502)
PHONE..................................740 369-4426
Michael Jennings, Partner
EMP: 35
SALES (est): 2.3MM Privately Held
SIC: 8721 8748 7291 Accounting, auditing & bookkeeping; business consulting; tax return preparation services

(G-9992)
JPMORGAN CHASE BANK NAT ASSN
61 N Sandusky St (43015-1925)
P.O. Box 710573, Columbus (43271-0001)
PHONE..................................740 363-8032
Rhonda Uttam, Vice Pres
Mindy Hoffman, Manager
EMP: 800
SALES (corp-wide): 131.4B Publicly Held
WEB: www.firstusa.com
SIC: 6021 National commercial banks
HQ: Jpmorgan Chase Bank, National Association
1111 Polaris Pkwy
Columbus OH 43240
614 436-3055

(G-9993)
KHEMPCO BLDG SUP CO LTD PARTNR (PA)
Also Called: Arlington-Blaine Lumber Co
130 Johnson Dr (43015-8699)
PHONE..................................740 549-0465
Donny Bowman, Partner
Richard Robinson, Partner
James D Klingbeil Jr, General Ptnr
EMP: 100
SALES (est): 22.5MM Privately Held
SIC: 5031 5211 2439 2431 Lumber: rough, dressed & finished; building materials, exterior; building materials, interior; lumber & other building materials; trusses, except roof: laminated lumber; trusses, wooden roof; doors, wood; hardware

(G-9994)
KROGER CO
1840 Columbus Pike (43015-2728)
PHONE..................................740 363-4398
Brenda Young, Manager
EMP: 100
SALES (corp-wide): 121.1B Publicly Held
WEB: www.kroger.com
SIC: 5411 5141 Supermarkets, chain; supermarkets, 66,000-99,000 square feet; convenience stores, chain; groceries, general line
PA: The Kroger Co
1014 Vine St Ste 1000
Cincinnati OH 45202
513 762-4000

(G-9995)
LEVERING MANAGEMENT INC
Also Called: Delaware Court Health Care Ctr
4 New Market Dr (43015-2258)
PHONE..................................740 369-6400
William Levering, President
Jack Fling, Manager
Ken Levering, Administration
EMP: 85
SALES (est): 2.7MM
SALES (corp-wide): 27.7MM Privately Held
SIC: 8059 8052 8051 Nursing home, except skilled & intermediate care facility; intermediate care facilities; skilled nursing care facilities
PA: Levering Management, Inc.
201 N Main St
Mount Vernon OH 43050
740 397-3897

(G-9996)
LIBERTY CASTING COMPANY LLC
407 Curtis St (43015-2439)
P.O. Box 1368 (43015-8368)
PHONE..................................740 363-1941
Lonnie Buckner, Manager
EMP: 31
SALES (corp-wide): 51.5MM Privately Held
SIC: 7699 7692 5085 Cleaning services; welding repair; industrial supplies
PA: Liberty Casting Company Llc
550 Liberty Rd
Delaware OH 43015
740 363-1941

(G-9997)
NATIONAL LIME AND STONE CO
Also Called: National Lime Stone Clmbus Reg
2406 S Section Line Rd (43015-9518)
P.O. Box 537 (43015-0537)
PHONE..................................740 548-4206
Carolyn Coder, Office Mgr
Chad Doll, Manager
EMP: 40
SALES (corp-wide): 3.2B Privately Held
WEB: www.natlime.com
SIC: 1422 Crushed & broken limestone
PA: The National Lime And Stone Company
551 Lake Cascade Pkwy
Findlay OH 45840
419 422-4341

(G-9998)
NORTHPOINT SENIOR SERVICES LLC
Also Called: Arbors of Delaware
2270 Warrensburg Rd (43015-1336)
PHONE..................................740 369-9614
Bob Jablonfis, Manager
EMP: 100
SALES (corp-wide): 41.5MM Privately Held
WEB: www.extendicarehealth.com
SIC: 8051 8093 Skilled nursing care facilities; specialty outpatient clinics
PA: Senior Northpoint Services Llc
7400 New Lagrange 100
Louisville KY 40222
502 429-8062

(G-9999)
OHIO DEPARTMENT TRANSPORTATION
Also Called: District 6
400 E William St (43015-2138)
PHONE..................................740 363-1251
Michael C Flynn, Manager
EMP: 150
SQ FT: 71,438 Privately Held
SIC: 1611 9621 Highway & street maintenance;
HQ: Ohio Department Of Transportation
1980 W Broad St
Columbus OH 43223

(G-10000)
PIONEER HI-BRED INTL INC
59 Greif Pkwy Ste 200 (43015-2006)
P.O. Box 1000, Johnston IA (50131-9411)
PHONE..................................740 657-6120
Donna Dugas, Branch Mgr
EMP: 30
SALES (corp-wide): 85.9B Publicly Held
SIC: 5191 Seeds: field, garden & flower
HQ: Pioneer Hi-Bred International, Inc.
7100 Nw 62nd Ave
Johnston IA 50131
515 535-3200

(G-10001)
RADIOLOGY PHYSICIANS INC
3769 Columbus Pike # 220 (43015-7213)
PHONE..................................614 717-9840
Michael Gregg, Med Doctor
EMP: 29
SALES (est): 1.6MM Privately Held
SIC: 8011 Radiologist

(G-10002)
RECOVERY & PREVENTION RESOURCE
118 Stover Dr (43015-8601)
PHONE..................................740 369-6811
Tony Williams, CEO
EMP: 29
SQ FT: 20,000
SALES: 1.4MM Privately Held
SIC: 8093 Alcohol clinic, outpatient; drug clinic, outpatient

(G-10003)
REFLEKTIONS LTD
560 Sunbury Rd Ste 1 (43015-8692)
PHONE..................................614 560-6994
Justin B Livingston, Owner
Janet Fout, Partner
EMP: 30
SALES: 500K Privately Held
SIC: 8082 Home health care services

(G-10004)
RJW TRUCKING COMPANY LTD
Also Called: Henderson Trucking
124 Henderson Ct (43015-8479)
PHONE..................................740 363-5343
Jack Henderson, Mng Member
Shaun Henderson,
EMP: 25
SALES (est): 1.6MM Privately Held
SIC: 1442 4212 Construction sand & gravel; local trucking, without storage; dump truck haulage

(G-10005)
SARAH MOORE HLTH CARE CTR INC
Also Called: SARAH MOORE COMMUNITY
26 N Union St (43015-1922)
PHONE..................................740 362-9641
Ronald White, President
Thomas W Hess, Principal
EMP: 100
SQ FT: 30,000
SALES: 5.5MM Privately Held
SIC: 8059 8052 Nursing home, except skilled & intermediate care facility; intermediate care facilities

(G-10006)
SCHNEIDER NAT CARRIERS INC
600 London Rd (43015-3839)
PHONE..................................740 362-6910
Jerry Jackson, Manager
EMP: 30
SALES (corp-wide): 4.9B Publicly Held
SIC: 4731 4213 Truck transportation brokers; trucking, except local
HQ: Schneider National Carriers, Inc.
3101 Packerland Dr
Green Bay WI 54313
920 592-2000

(G-10007)
SKY CLIMBER TWR SOLUTIONS LLC
1800 Pittsburgh Dr (43015-3870)
PHONE....................740 203-3900
Thomas Warchol, General Mgr
EMP: 30
SQ FT: 10,000
SALES (est): 1.4MM Privately Held
SIC: 1623 Transmitting tower (telecommunication) construction

(G-10008)
SOURCEPOINT
800 Cheshire Rd (43015-6038)
PHONE....................740 363-6677
Robert Horrocks, Exec Dir
Kimberly Clewell, Director
Fara Waugh, Director
EMP: 90
SQ FT: 58,000
SALES: 10MM Privately Held
WEB: www.growingolder.org
SIC: 8322 Senior citizens' center or association

(G-10009)
THORSENS GREENHOUSE LLC
2069 Hyatts Rd (43015-9215)
PHONE....................740 363-5069
Doug Thorsen, Partner
▲ EMP: 35
SQ FT: 140,000
SALES: 3MM Privately Held
WEB: www.thorsensgreenhouse.com
SIC: 0181 5193 Flowers: grown under cover (e.g. greenhouse production); nursery stock

(G-10010)
TRUCCO CONSTRUCTION CO INC
3531 Airport Rd (43015-9467)
PHONE....................740 417-9010
Mark Trucco, CEO
Mitchell Trucco, President
Jon Pulcheon, Project Mgr
Dominic Trucco, Project Engr
Randy King, Technology
EMP: 130
SQ FT: 24,470
SALES: 65.9MM Privately Held
WEB: www.truccoconstruction.com
SIC: 1623 1771 1794 1611 Underground utilities contractor; concrete work; excavation & grading, building construction; highway & street construction

(G-10011)
TWOK GENERAL CO
Also Called: Two K General Company
19 Gruber St Ste B (43015-3750)
PHONE....................740 417-9195
William Morgan Jr, President
Gary Daubenspeck, Owner
EMP: 25
SQ FT: 2,500
SALES (est): 7.3MM Privately Held
WEB: www.2kgeneral.com
SIC: 1542 Commercial & office building, new construction; commercial & office buildings, renovation & repair

(G-10012)
U S XPRESS INC
2000 Nutter Farms Ln (43015-9195)
PHONE....................740 363-0700
Scott Cluff, Branch Mgr
EMP: 50 Publicly Held
SIC: 4213 Contract haulers
HQ: U. S. Xpress, Inc.
4080 Jenkins Rd
Chattanooga TN 37421
866 266-7270

(G-10013)
UNITED PARCEL SERVICE INC OH
Also Called: UPS
1675 Us Highway 42 S (43015-8285)
PHONE....................740 363-0636
Richard Gammons, Branch Mgr
Robert Marcum, Manager
EMP: 316

SALES (corp-wide): 71.8B Publicly Held
SIC: 7389 4731 4512 4215 Mailbox rental & related service; transportation agents & brokers; air cargo carrier, scheduled; courier services, except by air
HQ: United Parcel Service, Inc. (Oh)
55 Glenlake Pkwy
Atlanta GA 30328
404 828-6000

(G-10014)
V & P HYDRAULIC PRODUCTS LLC
1700 Pittsburgh Dr (43015-3869)
PHONE....................740 203-3600
Tom Greathouse, Production
Jeff Braumiller, Purchasing
Melanie Crane, Controller
Laura Scott, Controller
Glen Campbell, Accounts Mgr
EMP: 70
SQ FT: 45,000
SALES (est): 28.1MM Privately Held
WEB: www.vphyd.com
SIC: 5084 Hydraulic systems equipment & supplies

(G-10015)
WALGREEN CO
Also Called: Walgreens
19 London Rd (43015-2613)
PHONE....................740 368-9380
Sandera Jenamore, Manager
EMP: 30
SALES (corp-wide): 131.5B Publicly Held
WEB: www.walgreens.com
SIC: 5912 7384 Drug stores; photofinishing laboratory
HQ: Walgreen Co.
200 Wilmot Rd
Deerfield IL 60015
847 315-2500

(G-10016)
WILLOW BROOK CHRSTN CMMUNITIES (PA)
Also Called: WILLOW BROOK CHRISTIAN VILLAGE
100 Delaware Xing W (43015-7853)
PHONE....................740 369-0048
Larry Harris, CEO
Lauri Mosher, Purch Agent
EMP: 165
SQ FT: 21,780
SALES: 4.2MM Privately Held
WEB: www.willow-brook.org
SIC: 8052 8051 Intermediate care facilities; skilled nursing care facilities

(G-10017)
WOMEN HEALTH PARTNERS
Also Called: Smith Clinic
6 Lexington Blvd (43015-1047)
PHONE....................740 363-9021
David S Smith, Partner
Peter S D, Medical Dir
EMP: 50
SALES (est): 3.6MM Privately Held
SIC: 8011 Obstetrician; gynecologist

(G-10018)
ZNM WECARE CORPORATION
Also Called: Kiddie Academy
7166 Gooding Blvd (43015-7086)
PHONE....................740 548-2022
Mahmudur Rahman, President
Mahmudr Rahman, Principal
EMP: 26
SALES: 1.2MM Privately Held
SIC: 8351 Child day care services

Delphos
Allen County

(G-10019)
ALL TEMP REFRIGERATION INC
Also Called: Tdk Refrigeration Leasing
18996 State Route 66 (45833-9326)
PHONE....................419 692-5016
Keith Pohlman, President
EMP: 50
SQ FT: 11,900

SALES (est): 12.5MM Privately Held
WEB: www.alltemprefrigeration.org
SIC: 1711 7359 Refrigeration contractor; equipment rental & leasing

(G-10020)
BUNGE NORTH AMERICA FOUNDATION
234 S Jefferson St (45833-1820)
P.O. Box 485 (45833-0485)
PHONE....................419 692-6010
Tim Hodson, Opers-Prdtn-Mfg
EMP: 55 Privately Held
WEB: www.bungemarion.com
SIC: 5153 Grains
HQ: Bunge North America Foundation
1391 Timberlk Mnr Pkwy # 31
Chesterfield MO 63017
314 872-3030

(G-10021)
CITY OF DELPHOS
Also Called: Engineer Department
608 N Canal St (45833-2401)
PHONE....................419 695-4010
Gerald Neumeier, Principal
EMP: 50 Privately Held
SIC: 8711 Engineering services
PA: City Of Delphos
608 N Canal St
Delphos OH 45833
419 695-4010

(G-10022)
COMMUNITY HLTH PRFSSIONALS INC
1500 E 5th St (45833-9145)
PHONE....................419 695-8101
Amy Zalar, Manager
EMP: 32
SALES (corp-wide): 13.1MM Privately Held
SIC: 8082 Visiting nurse service
PA: Community Health Professionals, Inc.
1159 Westwood Dr
Van Wert OH 45891
419 238-9223

(G-10023)
D&D TRUCKING AND SERVICES INC
5191 Kill Rd (45833-9460)
PHONE....................419 692-3205
John Miller, CEO
Joyce Schimmoller, Admin Sec
EMP: 26 EST: 1996
SQ FT: 10,000
SALES: 2MM Privately Held
SIC: 4212 Local trucking, without storage

(G-10024)
DELPHOS AMBULATORY CARE CENTER
1800 E 5th St Ste 1 (45833-9180)
PHONE....................419 692-2662
Jim Reber, President
Sonya Selhorst, Manager
EMP: 35
SALES (est): 1.6MM Privately Held
SIC: 8062 General medical & surgical hospitals

(G-10025)
DOUBLE A TRAILER SALES INC (PA)
1750 E 5th St (45833-9138)
P.O. Box 129 (45833-0129)
PHONE....................419 692-7626
Mark A Wannemacher, President
Leann Blankemeyer, General Mgr
Dan Brickner, Vice Pres
Charles Wannemacher, Vice Pres
Leann Wannemacher, Vice Pres
▲ EMP: 29
SQ FT: 14,000
SALES (est): 10MM Privately Held
WEB: www.doubleatrailer.com
SIC: 5084 7539 Industrial machine parts; trailer repair

(G-10026)
FIRST FEDERAL BANK OF MIDWEST
230 E 2nd St (45833-1701)
PHONE....................419 695-1055
Cindy Metzger, Sales Executive
Becky Minnig, Manager
EMP: 40 Publicly Held
SIC: 6035 6162 6022 Federal savings & loan associations; mortgage bankers & correspondents; state commercial banks
HQ: First Federal Bank Of The Midwest
601 Clinton St Ste 1
Defiance OH 43512
419 782-5015

(G-10027)
FOR SPECIALIZED ALTERNATIVES (PA)
Also Called: S A F Y
10100 Elida Rd (45833-9056)
PHONE....................419 695-8010
Scott Spangler, President
Jim Sherman, Senior VP
Marc Bloomingdale, Vice Pres
Jane Wintz, Vice Pres
Norman Pfaadt, CFO
EMP: 85
SQ FT: 4,800
SALES: 7.4MM Privately Held
WEB: www.safy.org
SIC: 8322 Child related social services

(G-10028)
J W J INVESTMENTS INC
Also Called: Richland Manor
800 Ambrose Dr (45833-9146)
PHONE....................419 643-3161
William J Mc Clellan, President
Terri Schneider, Principal
Stephanie Theis, Principal
EMP: 112
SALES (est): 1.9MM
SALES (corp-wide): 2.6MM Privately Held
WEB: www.jwjinvestments.com
SIC: 8059 8051 Nursing home, except skilled & intermediate care facility; skilled nursing care facilities
PA: J W J Investments Inc
300 Cherry St
Genoa OH
419 855-7755

(G-10029)
K & M TIRE INC (PA)
965 Spencerville Rd (45833-2351)
P.O. Box 279 (45833-0279)
PHONE....................419 695-1061
Ken Langhals, President
Cheryl Gossard, Vice Pres
Mel Donnelly, Sales Mgr
Michael Mesker, Manager
▲ EMP: 130 EST: 1977
SQ FT: 150,000
SALES: 512.2MM Privately Held
SIC: 5014 Automobile tires & tubes

(G-10030)
K & M TIRE INC
502 N Main St (45833-1594)
PHONE....................419 695-1060
Ken Langholz, Owner
EMP: 29
SALES (corp-wide): 512.2MM Privately Held
SIC: 5014 Automobile tires & tubes
PA: K & M Tire, Inc.
965 Spencerville Rd
Delphos OH 45833
419 695-1061

(G-10031)
MENKE BROS CONSTRUCTION CO
24266 Road T (45833-9330)
P.O. Box 158, Fort Jennings (45844-0158)
PHONE....................419 286-2086
Craig Menke, President
Eugene P Menke, President
Matt Menke, Vice Pres
Thomas J Menke, Vice Pres
Connie Knott, Project Mgr
EMP: 40 EST: 1949
SQ FT: 4,500

SALES: 1MM Privately Held
SIC: 1771 1794 Foundation & footing contractor; excavation work

(G-10032)
PALMER-DONAVIN MFG CO
Lima Div
911 Spencerville Rd (45833-2351)
PHONE..............................419 692-5000
Jerry Miner, *Manager*
EMP: 35
SALES (corp-wide): 242MM **Privately Held**
WEB: www.palmerdonavin.com
SIC: 5039 5074 Prefabricated structures; heating equipment (hydronic)
PA: The Palmer-Donavin Manufacturing Company
3210 Centerpoint Dr
Columbus OH 43212
800 652-1234

(G-10033)
PHOENIX HOMES INC (PA)
238 N Main St (45833-1767)
PHONE..............................419 692-2421
Bruce Maag, *CEO*
EMP: 40
SALES (est): 991.1K **Privately Held**
WEB: www.phnxgroup.com
SIC: 8082 Home Health Care Services

(G-10034)
SARAH JANE LIVING CENTER LTD
328 W 2nd St (45833-1671)
PHONE..............................419 692-6618
Mick Murphy, *Administration*
EMP: 45
SALES: 2MM **Privately Held**
SIC: 8051 Convalescent home with continuous nursing care

(G-10035)
SPECIALIZED ALTERNATIVES FOR F (PA)
Also Called: SAFY
10100 Elida Rd (45833-9056)
PHONE..............................419 695-8010
Karen Niese, *Controller*
Charlene Boden, *Accountant*
Kim Page, *Accountant*
Kelli Bender, *Human Resources*
Martin Freeman, *Manager*
EMP: 40
SALES: 19.7MM **Privately Held**
SIC: 8322 Child related social services

(G-10036)
TOLEDO MOLDING & DIE INC
Also Called: Delphos Plant 2
24086 State Route 697 (45833-9203)
P.O. Box 393 (45833-0393)
PHONE..............................419 692-6022
Craig Norbeck, *Plant Mgr*
Brian Hohenbrink, *Engineer*
Robert Whitney, *Engineer*
Keith Riegle, *Manager*
Kathy Vorst, *Admin Asst*
EMP: 85
SALES (corp-wide): 309.9MM **Privately Held**
WEB: www.tmdinc.com
SIC: 5031 3714 Molding, all materials; motor vehicle parts & accessories
HQ: Toledo Molding & Die, Inc.
1429 Coining Dr
Toledo OH 43612
419 470-3950

(G-10037)
TRILOGY HEALTHCARE ALLEN LLC
800 Ambrose Dr (45833-9146)
PHONE..............................419 643-3161
Kathy Corbinn,
EMP: 76
SALES (est): 839.5K **Privately Held**
SIC: 8051 Skilled nursing care facilities

(G-10038)
VANCREST LTD
Also Called: Vancrest Healthcare Cntr
1425 E 5th St (45833-9142)
PHONE..............................419 695-2871

Cindy Langenkamp, *Manager*
Eric Burk, *Director*
Bob Kann, *Director*
Katie Schabbing, *Director*
Niki Wilhelm, *Nursing Dir*
EMP: 185
SQ FT: 1,306
SALES (corp-wide): 16.3MM **Privately Held**
WEB: www.vancrest.com
SIC: 8051 Convalescent home with continuous nursing care
PA: Vancrest, Ltd.
120 W Main St Ste 200
Van Wert OH 45891
419 238-0715

(G-10039)
VANCREST APTS
310 Elida Rd (45833-9134)
PHONE..............................419 695-7335
Rene Mueller, *Director*
EMP: 35
SALES (est): 494.9K **Privately Held**
SIC: 8051 Skilled nursing care facilities

Delta
Fulton County

(G-10040)
AECOM GLOBAL II LLC
605 Taylor St (43515-1045)
PHONE..............................419 774-9862
James Page, *Manager*
EMP: 93
SALES (corp-wide): 20.1B **Publicly Held**
SIC: 8748 Systems engineering consultant, ex. computer or professional
HQ: Aecom Global Ii, Llc
1999 Avenue Of The Stars
Los Angeles CA 90067
213 593-8100

(G-10041)
BEROSKE FARMS & GREENHOUSE INC
12647 County Road 5 (43515-9202)
PHONE..............................419 826-4547
Theodore Beroske, *President*
EMP: 50
SALES (est): 4.6MM **Privately Held**
WEB: www.beroskesgreenhouse.com
SIC: 0181 5193 Bedding plants, growing of; nursery stock

(G-10042)
EDW C LEVY CO
Also Called: Fullton Mill Services
6565 County Road 9 (43515-9449)
P.O. Box 86 (43515-0086)
PHONE..............................419 822-8286
Paul Ruffner, *Manager*
EMP: 30
SALES (corp-wide): 368.1MM **Privately Held**
WEB: www.edwclevy.com
SIC: 4212 3295 Dump truck haulage; minerals, ground or treated
PA: Edw. C. Levy Co.
9300 Dix
Dearborn MI 48120
313 429-2200

(G-10043)
FIRST FDRAL SVING LN ASSN DLTA (PA)
Also Called: FIRST FEDERAL SAVINGS AND LOAN
404 Main St (43515-1350)
PHONE..............................419 822-3131
James E Coe, *President*
John Brady, *Chairman*
Kerry Vandock, *CFO*
EMP: 48 **EST:** 1934
SQ FT: 10,000
SALES: 5.2MM **Privately Held**
WEB: www.firstfeddelta.com
SIC: 6035 Federal savings & loan associations

(G-10044)
FREE & ACCEPTED MASONS
317 Cherry Tree Ln (43515-9356)
PHONE..............................419 822-3736
Tim Churchill, *Admin Sec*
EMP: 80 **EST:** 1857
SALES (est): 697.6K **Privately Held**
SIC: 8699 Charitable organization

(G-10045)
INDUSTRIAL REPAIR & MFG INC (PA)
1140 E Main St Ste A (43515-9406)
PHONE..............................419 822-4232
Toll Free:..............................877 -
William H Toedter, *President*
Peggy J Toedter, *Vice Pres*
▲ **EMP:** 65
SQ FT: 48,000
SALES (est): 8.7MM **Privately Held**
SIC: 7699 7363 3443 Industrial machinery & equipment repair; truck driver services; containers, shipping (bombs, etc.); metal plate

(G-10046)
K & L TRUCKING INC
490 W Main St (43515-9490)
PHONE..............................419 822-3836
Greg A Stickley, *President*
Debra Stickley, *Admin Sec*
EMP: 25
SQ FT: 300
SALES (est): 4.8MM **Privately Held**
SIC: 4213 Contract haulers

(G-10047)
NATURE FRESH FARMS USA INC
9250 Us Highway 20a (43515-9441)
PHONE..............................419 330-5080
Peter Quiring, *President*
EMP: 36
SALES (est): 984.6K
SALES (corp-wide): 32.4MM **Privately Held**
SIC: 0182 Vegetable crops grown under cover
PA: Nature Fresh Farms Inc
634 Mersea Road 7
Leamington ON N8H 3
519 326-8603

(G-10048)
NRI GLOBAL INC
3401 Rodgers Rd (43515)
PHONE..............................905 790-2828
Sarah Couto-Viera, *Principal*
Saif Syed, *Art Dir*
EMP: 50 **EST:** 2010 **Privately Held**
SIC: 6719 Investment holding companies, except banks

Dennison
Tuscarawas County

(G-10049)
FIRST NATIONAL BNK OF DENNISON (HQ)
105 Grant St (44621-1247)
P.O. Box 31 (44621-0031)
PHONE..............................740 922-2532
Blair Hillyer, *President*
Larry J Mosher, *Exec VP*
Lawrence Mosher, *Exec VP*
R E Wise, *Vice Pres*
Polly Clark, *Opers Staff*
EMP: 40 **EST:** 1933
SQ FT: 6,200
SALES: 9.5MM
SALES (corp-wide): 8.7MM **Privately Held**
SIC: 6021 National commercial banks
PA: Fnb, Inc.
105 Grant St
Dennison OH 44621
740 922-2532

(G-10050)
FNB INC (PA)
105 Grant St (44621-1247)
P.O. Box 31 (44621-0031)
PHONE..............................740 922-2532
Blair Hillyer, *President*
Linda Clouse, *Vice Pres*
EMP: 30
SALES: 8.7MM **Privately Held**
SIC: 7389 Financial services

(G-10051)
IONNO PROPERTIES S CORP
Also Called: Tank Services Company
4412 Pleasant Vly Rd Se (44621-9038)
P.O. Box 71 (44621-0071)
PHONE..............................330 479-9267
John Ionno, *President*
Mike La Croix, *Vice Pres*
EMP: 45
SQ FT: 37,000
SALES (est): 5MM **Privately Held**
SIC: 1799 1721 Sandblasting of building exteriors; commercial painting

(G-10052)
M3 MIDSTREAM LLC
Also Called: Leesville Plant
8349 Azalea Rd Sw (44621-9100)
PHONE..............................740 431-4168
EMP: 28
SALES (corp-wide): 54.9MM **Privately Held**
SIC: 1311 Natural gas production
PA: M3 Midstream Llc
600 Travis St Ste 5600
Houston TX 77002
713 783-3000

(G-10053)
TRINITY HOSPITAL TWIN CITY
819 N 1st St (44621-1003)
PHONE..............................740 922-2800
Michael Zilm, *CEO*
Joseph J Mitchell, *President*
Lorna Morrow, *CFO*
EMP: 263
SQ FT: 52,127
SALES: 110.9K **Privately Held**
SIC: 8011 8062 Medical centers; hospital, AMA approved residency
HQ: Sylvania Franciscan Health
1715 Indian Wood Cir # 200
Maumee OH 43537
419 882-8373

(G-10054)
TUSCO GROCERS INC
30 S 4th St (44621-1412)
PHONE..............................740 922-8721
Gregory W Kimble, *CEO*
Jayn Devney, *President*
Mike Oberholzer, *Treasurer*
Fred Bollon, *Director*
Hudson Hillyer, *Admin Sec*
▼ **EMP:** 65
SQ FT: 259,000
SALES (est): 10.3MM
SALES (corp-wide): 281.2MM **Privately Held**
WEB: www.tuscogrocers.com
SIC: 5141 Groceries, general line
PA: Laurel Grocery Company Llc
129 Barbourville Rd
London KY 40744
606 878-6601

(G-10055)
TWIN CITY WATER AND SEWER DST
308 Grant St (44621-1218)
PHONE..............................740 922-1460
Donnie Fawcett, *Supt*
Rob Henry, *Asst Superint*
EMP: 26
SALES (est): 1.9MM **Privately Held**
SIC: 4941 Water supply

(G-10056)
UTICA EAST OHIO MIDSTREAM LLC
8349 Azalea Rd Sw (44621-9100)
PHONE..............................740 431-4168
EMP: 551

SALES (est): 4.6MM
SALES (corp-wide): 8.6B **Publicly Held**
SIC: 4922 Pipelines, natural gas
HQ: Utica Gas Services, L.L.C.
525 Central Park Dr # 1005
Oklahoma City OK 73105
877 413-1023

Deshler
Henry County

(G-10057)
EAST WATER LEASING CO LLC
Also Called: Communicare Health Services
620 E Water St (43516-1327)
PHONE...................................419 278-6921
Stephen L Rosedale, CEO
EMP: 99
SALES (est): 1.9MM **Privately Held**
SIC: 8051 Convalescent home with continuous nursing care

(G-10058)
HPJ INDUSTRIES INC
299 S Chestnut St (43516-1042)
PHONE...................................419 278-1000
Scott Rothweiler, President
EMP: 29
SALES (corp-wide): 14.1MM **Privately Held**
SIC: 4953 Recycling, waste materials
PA: Hpj Industries, Inc.
510 W Broadway St
North Baltimore OH 45872
419 278-1000

Dexter City
Noble County

(G-10059)
B&N COAL INC
38455 Marietta Rte (45727)
P.O. Box 100 (45727-0100)
PHONE...................................740 783-3575
Carl Baker, President
Bob Cunningham, Corp Secy
Roger Osborne, Vice Pres
EMP: 64 EST: 1962
SQ FT: 21,000
SALES: 18MM **Privately Held**
SIC: 1221 8711 Strip mining, bituminous; engineering services

(G-10060)
WARREN DRILLING CO INC
Also Called: Warren Trucking
305 Smithson St (45727-9749)
P.O. Box 103 (45727-0103)
PHONE...................................740 783-2775
Dan R Warren, President
Lewis D Warren, Principal
Paul H Warren, Principal
W T Warren, Principal
Randy C Warren, Vice Pres
EMP: 110 EST: 1939
SALES (est): 27.5MM **Privately Held**
WEB: www.warrendrilling.biz
SIC: 1381 Directional drilling oil & gas wells

Diamond
Portage County

(G-10061)
SDS EARTH MOVING INC
3966 Wayland Rd (44412-8737)
PHONE...................................330 358-2132
James W Sanders, President
EMP: 35
SALES: 8MM **Privately Held**
SIC: 4212 Moving services

Dillonvale
Jefferson County

(G-10062)
COLAIANNI CONSTRUCTION INC
2141 State Route 150 (43917-7889)
PHONE...................................740 769-2362
Vincent Colaianni, President
Mary Ann Colaianni, Corp Secy
EMP: 40
SALES (est): 8.6MM **Privately Held**
WEB: www.colaianniconst.com
SIC: 1542 Nonresidential construction

(G-10063)
COLERAIN VOLUNTEER FIRE CO
72555 Colerain Rd (43917)
PHONE...................................740 738-0735
Ty Wilson, President
Robert Finney, Treasurer
EMP: 32
SALES: 446K **Privately Held**
SIC: 7389 8049 Fire protection service other than forestry or public; paramedic

Dover
Tuscarawas County

(G-10064)
ADVENTURE HARLEY DAVIDSON
Also Called: H & M Harley Davidson
1465 State Route 39 Nw (44622-7336)
PHONE...................................330 343-2295
Larry Browning, CFO
Olga Bell, Human Res Dir
Dawn Buehler, Manager
Bill Whitmire, Manager
Steve Dulaney, Info Tech Mgr
EMP: 26
SQ FT: 14,000
SALES (est): 7.2MM **Privately Held**
WEB: www.hmhd.com
SIC: 5571 7699 Motorcycles; motorcycle repair service

(G-10065)
BARKETT FRUIT CO INC (PA)
Also Called: Farmer Smiths Market
1213 E 3rd St (44622-1227)
PHONE...................................330 364-6645
William Barkett, CEO
James Barkett, President
Thomas Barkett, Vice Pres
Ronald Barkett, Treasurer
EMP: 36
SQ FT: 20,000
SALES (est): 12.3MM **Privately Held**
WEB: www.barkettfruit.com
SIC: 5148 5143 5144 2099 Vegetables; fruits; dairy products, except dried or canned; eggs; salads, fresh or refrigerated

(G-10066)
BELDEN & BLAKE CORPORATION
1748 Saltwell Rd Nw (44622-7471)
PHONE...................................330 602-5551
Tim McConah, Branch Mgr
EMP: 30
SQ FT: 4,500 **Privately Held**
WEB: www.beldenblake.com
SIC: 1311 1389 4922 5082 Crude petroleum production; natural gas production; oil field services; natural gas transmission; oil field equipment; oil & gas exploration services
HQ: Belden & Blake Corporation
1001 Fannin St Ste 800
Houston TX 77002
713 659-3500

(G-10067)
BERNER TRUCKING INC
5885 Crown Rd Nw (44622-9610)
P.O. Box 660 (44622-0660)
PHONE...................................330 343-5812

James E Knisely, President
John M Berner, Vice Pres
Tim Goehring, Finance Mgr
Vic Kidder, Info Tech Dir
Adrienne M Berner, Admin Sec
EMP: 150
SQ FT: 22,500
SALES: 22MM **Privately Held**
WEB: www.bernertrucking.com
SIC: 4212 Dump truck haulage

(G-10068)
BUEHLER FOOD MARKETS INC
Also Called: Buehler 10
3000 N Wooster Ave (44622-9469)
PHONE...................................330 364-3079
Doug Wills, Manager
Melissa Steed, Cashier
EMP: 220
SALES (corp-wide): 443.4MM **Privately Held**
SIC: 5411 7384 5992 5912 Grocery stores, independent; photofinish laboratories; florists; drug stores & proprietary stores; eating places; gasoline service stations
HQ: Buehler Food Markets Incorporated
1401 Old Mansfield Rd
Wooster OH 44691
330 264-4355

(G-10069)
CHUCK NICHOLSON PNTC-GMC TRCKS
135 W Broadway St (44622-1916)
PHONE...................................330 343-7781
Charles Nicholson, President
Ron Garbrandt, President
Dan Kiethley, President
Jim Simo, CFO
Billie Nicholson, Treasurer
EMP: 40
SQ FT: 25,000
SALES (est): 12.5MM **Privately Held**
SIC: 5511 5521 5012 Automobiles, new & used; used car dealers; automobiles & other motor vehicles

(G-10070)
COMMUNITY MENTAL HEALTHCARE (PA)
201 Hospital Dr (44622-2058)
PHONE...................................330 343-1811
Gregg Martini, General Mgr
Cindy Hisrich, Human Res Mgr
Joseph Gavin PHD, Director
Coral Johnson, Clerk
EMP: 40 EST: 1969
SQ FT: 10,841
SALES: 5.1MM **Privately Held**
SIC: 8093 Mental health clinic, outpatient

(G-10071)
COUNTRY CLUB CENTER HOMES INC
Also Called: COUNTRY CLUB RETIREMENT CENTER
860 E Iron Ave (44622-2082)
PHONE...................................330 343-6351
Jeffrey Holland, President
John E Holland, Treasurer
Michael Hohman, Administration
EMP: 100
SALES: 5.9MM **Privately Held**
SIC: 8051 8059 8052 Convalescent home with continuous nursing care; convalescent home; intermediate care facilities

(G-10072)
DISCOUNT DRUG MART INC
3015 N Wooster Ave (44622-9491)
PHONE...................................330 343-7700
Mike Lantree, Manager
EMP: 30
SALES (corp-wide): 679.4MM **Privately Held**
WEB: www.discount-drugmart.com
SIC: 5912 7384 Drug stores; photofinishing laboratory
PA: Discount Drug Mart, Inc.
211 Commerce Dr
Medina OH 44256
330 725-2340

(G-10073)
DOVER CITY SCHOOLS
Also Called: New Dawn Child Care Center
865 1/2 E Iron Ave (44622-2099)
PHONE...................................330 343-8880
Sue Mathews, Director
EMP: 67
SALES (corp-wide): 35.8MM **Privately Held**
SIC: 8211 8351 Public elementary & secondary schools; child day care services
PA: Dover City Schools
219 W 6th St
Dover OH 44622
330 364-1906

(G-10074)
DOVER HYDRAULICS INC (PA)
Also Called: Dover Hydraulics South
2996 Progress St (44622-9639)
P.O. Box 2239 (44622-1000)
PHONE...................................330 364-1617
Robert D Sensel, President
Rich Engstrom, General Mgr
Eric Kinsey, Corp Secy
Bob Shively, VP Opers
Dane Thomas, Opers Mgr
▲ EMP: 79
SQ FT: 25,000
SALES (est): 15.8MM **Privately Held**
WEB: www.doverhydraulics.com
SIC: 7699 Hydraulic equipment repair

(G-10075)
DOVER NURSING CENTER
Also Called: Park Village Health Care Ctr
1525 N Crater Ave (44622-9558)
PHONE...................................330 364-4436
EMP: 81
SQ FT: 32,000
SALES (est): 4.8MM **Privately Held**
SIC: 8052 8051 Intermediate Care Facility Skilled Nursing Care Facility

(G-10076)
DOVER PHILA FEDERAL CREDIT UN (PA)
119 Filmore Ave (44622-2061)
PHONE...................................330 364-8874
Jack Dooling, President
Jason Garner, CFO
Megan Bender, Accountant
Kelsey McConaha, Marketing Staff
Wendy Slates, Marketing Staff
EMP: 40
SQ FT: 9,000
SALES: 11.2MM **Privately Held**
SIC: 6061 Federal credit unions

(G-10077)
FFD FINANCIAL CORPORATION (PA)
321 N Wooster Ave (44622-2949)
PHONE...................................330 364-7777
Trent B Troyer, President
Scott C Finnell, Exec VP
Kerr Egler-Whytsell, Vice Pres
Robert R Gerber, CFO
Stephenie Wilson, VP Human Res
EMP: 64
SALES (est): 11.7MM **Publicly Held**
WEB: www.onlinefirstfed.com
SIC: 6035 Federal savings & loan associations

(G-10078)
FLICKINGER PIPING COMPANY INC
439 S Tuscarawas Ave (44622-2360)
PHONE...................................330 364-4224
Joel D Flickinger, President
EMP: 25
SALES (est): 4.7MM **Privately Held**
SIC: 1711 Plumbing contractors

(G-10079)
GIANT EAGLE INC
515 Union Ave Ste 243 (44622-3000)
PHONE...................................330 364-5301
Jason Lanzer, Manager
EMP: 100
SALES (corp-wide): 6.9B **Privately Held**
SIC: 5411 5912 5193 Supermarkets; drug stores; flowers & florists' supplies

412   2019 Harris Ohio
Services Directory   ▲ = Import ▼=Export
◆ =Import/Export

PA: Giant Eagle, Inc.
101 Kappa Dr
Pittsburgh PA 15238
800 362-8899

(G-10080)
GREER STEEL COMPANY
1 Boat St (44622-2076)
P.O. Box 1900, Morgantown WV (26507-1900)
PHONE..................................330 343-8811
John R Raese, *President*
George Whalen, *VP Admin*
Mark Durisen, *Plant Supt*
Jamie Schmidt, *Engrg Dir*
James M Troy, *CFO*
◆ **EMP:** 150
SALES (est): 81.7MM
SALES (corp-wide): 132MM **Privately Held**
WEB: www.greerlimestone.com
SIC: 5051 Steel
PA: Greer Industries, Inc.
570 Canyon Rd
Morgantown WV 26508
304 296-2549

(G-10081)
HENNIS NURSING HOME
Also Called: HENNIS CARE CENTRE AT DOVER
1720 N Cross St (44622-1044)
PHONE..................................330 364-8849
Harry Hennis IL, *President*
Harry Hennis II, *President*
Harold Baker, *Manager*
Stephanie Hicks, *Manager*
Robin Miller, *Data Proc Staff*
EMP: 180
SALES: 11.8MM **Privately Held**
SIC: 8051 8052 Convalescent home with continuous nursing care; intermediate care facilities

(G-10082)
HORN ELECTRIC COMPANY
Also Called: Horn Engineering
608 S Tuscarawas Ave (44622-2346)
P.O. Box 493 (44622-0493)
PHONE..................................330 364-7784
Robert A Horn, *President*
Becky Horn, *Vice Pres*
EMP: 32 **EST:** 1953
SQ FT: 2,100
SALES (est): 3.2MM **Privately Held**
WEB: www.hornengineering.com
SIC: 8711 Consulting engineer

(G-10083)
HUNTINGTON NATIONAL BANK
232 W 3rd St Ste 207 (44622-2969)
P.O. Box 100 (44622-0100)
PHONE..................................330 343-6611
Katherine Fausnight, *Principal*
Lori James, *Administration*
EMP: 35
SALES (corp-wide): 5.2B **Publicly Held**
WEB: www.huntingtonnationalbank.com
SIC: 6029 6021 Commercial banks; national commercial banks
HQ: The Huntington National Bank
17 S High St Fl 1
Columbus OH 43215
614 480-4293

(G-10084)
KIMBLE RECYCL & DISPOSAL INC (PA)
Also Called: Ace Disposal
3596 State Route 39 Nw (44622-7232)
P.O. Box 448 (44622-0448)
PHONE..................................330 343-1226
Keith Kimble, *President*
Don Johnson, *Business Mgr*
Rick Kimble, *Corp Secy*
Eric Kimble, *Vice Pres*
Greg Kimble, *Vice Pres*
EMP: 121
SQ FT: 2,300
SALES (est): 129.9MM **Privately Held**
SIC: 4953 Garbage: collecting, destroying & processing; refuse collection & disposal services

(G-10085)
KNISELY INC
Also Called: Berner Trucking
5885 Crown Rd Nw (44622-9610)
P.O. Box 660 (44622-0660)
PHONE..................................330 343-5812
James E Knisely, *President*
EMP: 100
SQ FT: 22,500
SALES (est): 9.1MM **Privately Held**
WEB: www.knisely.com
SIC: 7389 5172 7513 Brokers' services; diesel fuel; truck leasing, without drivers

(G-10086)
L AND C SOFT SERVE INC
Also Called: Dover Softies
717 N Wooster Ave (44622-2866)
PHONE..................................330 364-3823
Cathy M Lawless, *President*
Luke Lawless, *Owner*
EMP: 25
SALES (est): 1.1MM **Privately Held**
SIC: 8742 Restaurant & food services consultants

(G-10087)
MARMON HIGHWAY TECH LLC
6332 Columbia Rd Nw (44622-7676)
P.O. Box 525 (44622-0525)
PHONE..................................330 878-5595
EMP: 40
SQ FT: 2,725
SALES (corp-wide): 210.8B **Publicly Held**
SIC: 7539 3714 Automotive Repair Mfg Motor Vehicle Parts/Accessories
HQ: Marmon Highway Technologies Llc
5915 Chalkville Rd 300
Birmingham AL 35235
205 508-2000

(G-10088)
METAL MASTERS INC
125 Williams Dr Nw (44622-7662)
PHONE..................................330 343-3515
Matthew Fox, *President*
Mary Lou Miller, *Treasurer*
Bret Kettlewell, *Controller*
EMP: 45
SALES (est): 7.7MM **Privately Held**
WEB: www.metal-masters.net
SIC: 1711 Warm air heating & air conditioning contractor

(G-10089)
MID-OHIO CONTRACTING INC
1817 Horns Ln Nw (44622-7314)
P.O. Box 708 (44622-0708)
PHONE..................................330 343-2925
EMP: 150 **EST:** 1981
SQ FT: 3,200
SALES (est): 27.8MM **Privately Held**
SIC: 1623 Oil & gas pipeline construction

(G-10090)
NEW DAWN HEALTH CARE INC
Also Called: New Dawn Retirement Community
865 E Iron Ave (44622-2099)
PHONE..................................330 343-5521
Daniel Hershberger, *President*
Harry Hershberger, *Vice Pres*
Perry Hershberger, *Vice Pres*
Sandy Stein, *QC Dir*
Sandra Hershberger, *Treasurer*
EMP: 187 **EST:** 1976
SQ FT: 73,000
SALES (est): 12MM **Privately Held**
WEB: www.new-dawn.net
SIC: 8051 8361 8351 8052 Skilled nursing care facilities; home for the aged; children's home; child day care services; intermediate care facilities

(G-10091)
NICK STRIMBU INC
303 Oxford St (44622-1976)
PHONE..................................330 448-4046
EMP: 79
SALES (corp-wide): 23.9MM **Privately Held**
SIC: 4213 Trucking, except local

PA: Nick Strimbu, Inc.
3500 Parkway Dr
Brookfield OH 44403
330 448-4046

(G-10092)
PACE SANKAR LANDSCAPING INC
Also Called: Pace-Sankar Landscaping
4005 Johnstown Rd Ne (44622-7562)
PHONE..................................330 343-0858
Michael Pace, *President*
Rick Charnock, *Financial Exec*
Beth Stoll, *Office Mgr*
EMP: 35
SALES (est): 2.4MM **Privately Held**
SIC: 0782 Landscape contractors

(G-10093)
PETERMAN PLUMBING AND HTG INC
525 W 15th St (44622-9711)
P.O. Box 278 (44622-0278)
PHONE..................................330 364-4497
Douglas L Peterman, *President*
Thomas Hisrich, *Vice Pres*
Natalie Peterman, *Mktg Dir*
EMP: 25
SQ FT: 14,000
SALES: 4.5MM **Privately Held**
SIC: 1711 Plumbing contractors; warm air heating & air conditioning contractor

(G-10094)
RANGE RSURCES - APPALACHIA LLC
1748 Saltwell Rd Nw (44622-7471)
PHONE..................................330 866-3301
Woody McDaniels, *Manager*
EMP: 41
SALES (corp-wide): 3.2B **Publicly Held**
WEB: www.gl-energy.com
SIC: 1382 Oil & gas exploration services
HQ: Range Resources - Appalachia, Llc.
3000 Town Center Blvd
Canonsburg PA 15317
724 743-6700

(G-10095)
RE/MAX EXPERTS REALTY
720 N Wooster Ave (44622-2871)
PHONE..................................330 364-7355
Kathy Pietro, *President*
Jennifer Hitchcock, *Partner*
EMP: 35
SQ FT: 2,000
SALES (est): 1.6MM **Privately Held**
SIC: 6531 Real estate agent, residential

(G-10096)
REPUBLICAN HEADQUARTERS
203 S Wooster Ave (44622-1942)
P.O. Box 542 (44622-0542)
PHONE..................................330 343-6131
Doug Wills, *President*
EMP: 40
SALES (est): 587.2K **Privately Held**
SIC: 8651 Political action committee

(G-10097)
RUSSELL HAWK ENTERPRISES INC
2198 Donald Dr (44622-7493)
PHONE..................................330 343-4612
Russell Hawk, *President*
Gary Hawk, *Vice Pres*
Wilma Hawk, *Vice Pres*
EMP: 35 **EST:** 1960
SQ FT: 4,000
SALES (est): 3.5MM **Privately Held**
SIC: 1623 Oil & gas pipeline construction

(G-10098)
SCHOENBRUNN LANDSCAPING INC
Also Called: Schoenbrunn Ldscp & Lawn Svc
1505 State Route 39 Nw (44622-7337)
PHONE..................................330 364-3688
Marty Kamban, *President*
Randy Kamban, *Vice Pres*
EMP: 30
SQ FT: 1,500

SALES (est): 3MM **Privately Held**
WEB: www.schoenbrunnlandscaping.com
SIC: 0781 0782 Landscape services; lawn services

(G-10099)
SMITH AMBULANCE SERVICE INC
214 W 3rd St (44622-2965)
PHONE..................................330 825-0205
Robert L Smith, *Branch Mgr*
EMP: 28 **Privately Held**
SIC: 4119 Ambulance service
PA: Smith Ambulance Service, Inc
214 W 3rd St
Dover OH 44622

(G-10100)
SMITH AMBULANCE SERVICE INC (PA)
214 W 3rd St (44622-2965)
PHONE..................................330 602-0050
Robert L Smith, *President*
Bob Stanley, *Human Res Dir*
Amy Hockenberry, *Manager*
EMP: 30
SALES (est): 6.1MM **Privately Held**
WEB: www.smithambulanceservice.com
SIC: 4119 Ambulance service

(G-10101)
SMITH CONCRETE CO (PA)
Also Called: Division of Selling Materials
2301 Progress St (44622-9641)
P.O. Box 356, Marietta (45750-0356)
PHONE..................................740 373-7441
Mike Murphy, *General Mgr*
Dick Wilson, *Manager*
EMP: 50 **EST:** 1922
SQ FT: 2,000
SALES (est): 5.6MM **Privately Held**
WEB: www.smithconcreteco.com
SIC: 3272 3273 1442 Dry mixture concrete; ready-mixed concrete; construction sand & gravel

(G-10102)
SPEEDIE AUTO SALVAGE LTD
6995 Eberhart Rd Nw (44622-7000)
PHONE..................................330 878-9961
Gregory Bender, *President*
Greg Bender, *President*
Matt Bender, *President*
EMP: 25
SQ FT: 2,178,000
SALES: 5MM **Privately Held**
WEB: www.speedieauto.com
SIC: 5015 Automotive supplies, used

(G-10103)
TEATER ORTHOPEDIC SURGEONS
Also Called: Dover Orthopedic Center
515 Union Ave Ste 167 (44622-3005)
PHONE..................................330 343-3335
Scott F Holder, *President*
James McQuillan, *Med Doctor*
Thomas L Teater, *Med Doctor*
EMP: 25
SQ FT: 4,879
SALES (est): 1.6MM **Privately Held**
SIC: 8011 Orthopedic physician

(G-10104)
TUSCARAWAS COUNTY COMMITTEE
Also Called: TUSCARAWAS COUNTY SENIOR CENTE
425 Prospect St (44622-2224)
PHONE..................................330 364-6611
Pam Ferrell, *Exec Dir*
Pam Serrelle, *Exec Dir*
EMP: 80
SALES: 2.2MM **Privately Held**
SIC: 8322 Senior citizens' center or association

(G-10105)
UNION COUNTRY CLUB
1000 N Bellevue Ave (44622-9457)
PHONE..................................330 343-5544
Jim Miller, *President*
Kate Morgan, *General Mgr*
Dave Garnett, *Accountant*
EMP: 40

SQ FT: 1,092
SALES: 1.4MM Privately Held
SIC: 7997 Country club, membership

(G-10106)
UNION HOSPITAL ASSOCIATION (HQ)
659 Boulevard St (44622-2077)
PHONE.................................330 343-3311
William W Harding, CEO
Cathy Corbett, President
David Brown, Ch Pathology
Stephen Sabo, Ch Radiology
Diana Boyd, Vice Pres
EMP: 55
SQ FT: 280,000
SALES: 107.7MM
SALES (corp-wide): 8.9B Privately Held
WEB: www.uhcareers.com
SIC: 8062 8011 General medical & surgical hospitals; offices & clinics of medical doctors
PA: The Cleveland Clinic Foundation
9500 Euclid Ave
Cleveland OH 44195
216 636-8335

(G-10107)
UNION HOSPITAL HOME HLTH CARE
659 Boulevard St (44622-2077)
PHONE.................................330 343-6909
Anne Phillips, Human Resources
Debra Albaugh, Exec Dir
EMP: 28
SALES (est): 474.9K Privately Held
SIC: 8082 Home health care services

Doylestown
Wayne County

(G-10108)
BEHEYDTS AUTO WRECKING
15475 Serfass Rd (44230)
PHONE.................................330 658-6109
Maxwell Beheydt, Owner
EMP: 50
SALES (est): 389.9K Privately Held
SIC: 7542 7389 5015 Carwashes; business services; motor vehicle parts, used

(G-10109)
CHIPPEWA GOLF CORP
Also Called: Chippewa Golf Club
12147 Shank Rd (44230-9707)
PHONE.................................330 658-2566
Kevin Larizza, President
EMP: 30
SQ FT: 4,800
SALES (est): 1.9MM Privately Held
WEB: www.chippewagolfclub.com
SIC: 7992 Public golf courses

(G-10110)
CHIPPEWA SCHOOL DISTRICT
Also Called: SC Chippewa Preschool
165 Brooklyn Ave (44230-1204)
PHONE.................................330 658-4868
Ronna Haer, Principal
EMP: 36
SALES (est): 647.4K
SALES (corp-wide): 20.3MM Privately Held
SIC: 8351 Preschool center
PA: Chippewa School District
56 N Portage St
Doylestown OH 44230
330 658-6700

(G-10111)
DOYLESTOWN COMMUNICATIONS
Also Called: Doylestown Cable TV
81 N Portage St (44230-1349)
PHONE.................................330 658-7000
Thomas Brockman, President
Sandra S Brockman, Vice Pres
EMP: 40
SQ FT: 4,400

SALES: 400K
SALES (corp-wide): 11.1MM Privately Held
WEB: www.doylestowncommunications.com
SIC: 4841 7375 Cable television services; on-line data base information retrieval
PA: Doylestown Telephone Company Inc
81 N Portage St
Doylestown OH 44230
330 658-2121

(G-10112)
DOYLESTOWN HEALTH CARE CENTER
95 Black Dr (44230-1300)
PHONE.................................330 658-1533
John J Masternick, President
Leo Grimes, Exec Dir
EMP: 105
SALES (est): 3MM Privately Held
SIC: 8051 8052 Convalescent home with continuous nursing care; intermediate care facilities

(G-10113)
DOYLESTOWN TELEPHONE COMPANY (PA)
Also Called: Doylestown Communications
81 N Portage St (44230-1349)
PHONE.................................330 658-2121
Tom Brockman, President
Sandra Brockman, Vice Pres
EMP: 38 EST: 1899
SQ FT: 4,400
SALES (est): 11.1MM Privately Held
WEB: www.neobright.net
SIC: 4813 Local telephone communications

(G-10114)
DOYLESTOWN TELEPHONE COMPANY
Also Called: Doylestown Cable
28 E Marion St (44230-1348)
PHONE.................................330 658-6666
Dennis Hartman, General Mgr
EMP: 40
SALES (corp-wide): 11.1MM Privately Held
WEB: www.neobright.net
SIC: 4813 4225 Local telephone communications; general warehousing
PA: Doylestown Telephone Company Inc
81 N Portage St
Doylestown OH 44230
330 658-2121

Dresden
Muskingum County

(G-10115)
AEP DRESDEN PLANT
9595 Mcglade School Rd (43821-9457)
PHONE.................................740 450-1964
EMP: 32 EST: 2007
SALES (est): 1.4MM Privately Held
SIC: 4931 Electric And Other Services Combined

(G-10116)
T/R RSDNTIAL CARE FCLITIES INC
507 Main St (43821-1110)
P.O. Box 693 (43821-0693)
PHONE.................................740 754-2600
Maura Mantell, CEO
EMP: 30
SQ FT: 6,000
SALES (est): 339K Privately Held
SIC: 8361 Home for the mentally handicapped

Dublin
Franklin County

(G-10117)
3SG CORPORATION
344 Cramer Creek Ct (43017-2585)
PHONE.................................614 309-3600

Adam Uhrig, Manager
EMP: 142
SALES (corp-wide): 14.3MM Privately Held
SIC: 5045 Computers, peripherals & software
PA: 3sg Corporation
344 Cramer Creek Ct
Dublin OH 43017
614 761-8394

(G-10118)
ACADIA SOLUTIONS INC
6751 Burnside Ln (43016-8015)
PHONE.................................614 505-6135
Frank Wang, President
Bence Toth, Vice Pres
EMP: 25
SALES (est): 2MM Privately Held
SIC: 7373 7371 8748 5065 Local area network (LAN) systems integrator; computer software development & applications; telecommunications consultant; telephone & telegraphic equipment

(G-10119)
ADVANCED PRGRM RESOURCES INC (PA)
Also Called: Touchmark
2715 Tuller Pkwy (43017-2310)
PHONE.................................614 761-9994
Danial Chacho, CEO
Larry Dado, President
Douglas Heagren, Treasurer
Jennifer Heagren, Director
EMP: 47
SQ FT: 5,100
SALES (est): 4.3MM Privately Held
SIC: 7379 7373 8742 7372 Computer related consulting services; systems integration services; management consulting services; application computer software; custom computer programming services

(G-10120)
AECOM GLOBAL II LLC
5550 Blazer Pkwy Ste 175 (43017-3495)
PHONE.................................614 726-3500
Frank Ambrosio, Branch Mgr
EMP: 268
SALES (corp-wide): 20.1B Publicly Held
SIC: 8712 Architectural engineering
HQ: Aecom Global Ii, Llc
1999 Avenue Of The Stars
Los Angeles CA 90067
213 593-8100

(G-10121)
AFFILIATED RESOURCE GROUP INC
5700 Perimeter Dr Ste H (43017-3247)
P.O. Box 491 (43017-0491)
PHONE.................................614 889-6555
Mike Moran, President
EMP: 51
SQ FT: 7,500
SALES (est): 4.2MM Privately Held
WEB: www.aresgrp.com
SIC: 7379 Computer related consulting services

(G-10122)
AHF OHIO INC
4880 Tuttle Rd (43017-7566)
PHONE.................................614 760-8870
Justin Moore, Administration
EMP: 97
SALES (corp-wide): 22.6MM Privately Held
SIC: 8051 8361 Skilled nursing care facilities; residential care
PA: Ahf Ohio, Inc.
5920 Venture Dr Ste 100
Dublin OH 43017
614 760-7352

(G-10123)
AHF/CENTRAL STATES INC
Also Called: Belcourt Terracenursing Home
5920 Venture Dr Ste 100 (43017-2236)
PHONE.................................615 383-3570
Brian Vermillion, Director
EMP: 62
SQ FT: 23,780

SALES (corp-wide): 11.6MM Privately Held
SIC: 8051 Skilled nursing care facilities
PA: Ahf/Central States, Inc.
249 W Mcmurray Rd
Canonsburg PA 15317
724 941-7150

(G-10124)
ALCATEL-LUCENT USA INC
5475 Rings Rd Ste 101 (43017-7564)
PHONE.................................614 860-2000
Linn Jones, Manager
EMP: 450
SALES (corp-wide): 27.3B Privately Held
WEB: www.lucent.com
SIC: 8731 Commercial physical research
HQ: Nokia Of America Corporation
600 Mountain Ave Ste 700
New Providence NJ 07974

(G-10125)
ALEXSON SERVICES INC
Also Called: Via Quest
525 Metro Pl N Ste 300 (43017-5320)
PHONE.................................614 889-5837
Richard Johnson, President
EMP: 37
SALES (est): 1.6MM Privately Held
SIC: 8322 Social services for the handicapped

(G-10126)
ALKON CORPORATION
6750 Crosby Ct (43016-7644)
PHONE.................................614 799-6650
Mark Marino, Branch Mgr
EMP: 35
SALES (corp-wide): 24.2MM Privately Held
WEB: www.alkoncorp.com
SIC: 3491 3082 5084 5085 Industrial valves; unsupported plastics profile shapes; industrial machinery & equipment; industrial supplies
PA: Alkon Corporation
728 Graham Dr
Fremont OH 43420
419 355-9111

(G-10127)
ALTERNATIVE CARE MGT SYSTEMS
Also Called: Alternative Care MGT Systs
4789 Rings Rd (43017-1513)
PHONE.................................614 761-0035
Fax: 614 761-0452
EMP: 25
SQ FT: 8,000
SALES (est): 21.4K
SALES (corp-wide): 42.8K Privately Held
SIC: 8742 6411 Management Consulting Services-Health Care
PA: Employee Benefit Management Corp
4789 Rings Rd
Dublin OH 43017
614 766-5800

(G-10128)
AMAXX INC
5975 Wilcox Pl Ste B (43016-8728)
PHONE.................................614 486-3481
Nicole Hall, Principal
Eric Hall, Vice Pres
EMP: 35
SALES (est): 5.7MM Privately Held
SIC: 7375 On-line data base information retrieval

(G-10129)
AMERICAN CANCER SOCIETY EAST
5555 Frantz Rd Frnt Frnt (43017-4184)
PHONE.................................888 227-6446
Gary Pincock, CEO
EMP: 262
SALES (corp-wide): 91.7MM Privately Held
SIC: 8733 Noncommercial research organizations
PA: American Cancer Society, East Central Division, Inc.
Sipe Ave Rr 422
Hershey PA 17033
717 533-6144

▲ = Import ▼=Export
◆ =Import/Export

(G-10130)
AMERICAN CLLEGE CRDLGY FNDTION
Also Called: Accf Accreditation
5600 Blazer Pkwy 320 (43017-3554)
PHONE.............................614 442-5950
Abe Joseph, *Branch Mgr*
EMP: 40
SALES (corp-wide): 113.9MM **Privately Held**
SIC: 8621 Medical field-related associations
PA: American College Of Cardiology Foundation
2400 N St Nw
Washington DC 20037
202 375-6000

(G-10131)
AMERICAN INSUR ADMINISTRATORS
5455 Rings Rd Ste 200 (43017-7529)
PHONE.............................614 486-5388
Jon Boes, *COO*
EMP: 30 EST: 2012
SALES (est): 4.5MM **Privately Held**
SIC: 6411 Insurance agents
PA: Usi, Inc.
200 Summit Lake Dr # 350
Valhalla NY 10595

(G-10132)
AMERICAN MULTI-CINEMA INC
Also Called: AMC
6700 Village Pkwy (43017-2073)
PHONE.............................614 889-0580
Stephanie McClullan, *General Mgr*
EMP: 50
SALES (corp-wide): 7.3MM **Publicly Held**
WEB: www.arrowheadtownecenter.com
SIC: 7832 Exhibitors, itinerant: motion picture
HQ: American Multi-Cinema, Inc.
1 Amc Way
Leawood KS 66211
913 213-2000

(G-10133)
AMERICAN MUTL SHARE INSUR CORP (PA)
Also Called: AMERICAN SHARE INSURANCE
5656 Frantz Rd (43017-2552)
PHONE.............................614 764-1900
Dennis R Adams, *President*
G Duane Welsh, *Vice Pres*
Curtis L Robson, *Treasurer*
Eva Chung, *Asst Controller*
Tahsin Imm, *Auditor*
EMP: 35
SQ FT: 10,000
SALES: 8.4MM **Privately Held**
WEB: www.americanshare.com
SIC: 6399 Deposit insurance

(G-10134)
AMERICAN SYSTEMS CNSULTING INC
Also Called: Asci
5777 Frantz Rd Ste 150 (43017-1885)
PHONE.............................614 282-7180
Cliff A Gallatin, *President*
Daryl L Mayfield, *Senior VP*
Patrick Gemperline, *Vice Pres*
EMP: 62
SQ FT: 29,000
SALES (est): 3.9MM **Privately Held**
WEB: www.asci.net
SIC: 7371 7379 Custom computer programming services; data processing consultant

(G-10135)
AMERIPRISE FINANCIAL SVCS INC
655 Metro Pl S Ste 450 (43017-3388)
PHONE.............................614 934-4057
Sandy Yinger, *Manager*
EMP: 45
SALES (corp-wide): 12.8B **Publicly Held**
WEB: www.amps.com
SIC: 8742 6282 Financial consultant; investment advice

HQ: Ameriprise Financial Services Inc.
707 2nd Ave S
Minneapolis MN 55402
612 671-2733

(G-10136)
AP/AIM DUBLIN SUITES TRS LLC
Also Called: Embassy Suites Columbus Dublin
5100 Upper Metro Pl (43017-3384)
PHONE.............................614 790-9000
Cheree Goodall, *Principal*
EMP: 99
SALES (est): 4MM **Privately Held**
SIC: 7011 Hotels

(G-10137)
ARLINGWORTH HOME HEALTH INC
6479 Reflections Dr # 100 (43017-2354)
PHONE.............................614 659-0961
Michael Legg, *Administration*
EMP: 40
SQ FT: 2,700
SALES (est): 1.1MM **Privately Held**
SIC: 8082 Home health care services

(G-10138)
ASHLAND LLC
5200 Blazer Pkwy (43017-3309)
P.O. Box 182586, Columbus (43218-2586)
PHONE.............................614 839-4503
Beth Moore, *Purchasing*
Bill Widger, *Accounts Mgr*
Brian Fruth, *Manager*
David Hatgas, *Director*
EMP: 153
SALES (corp-wide): 3.7B **Publicly Held**
SIC: 5169 Chemicals & allied products
HQ: Ashland Llc
50 E Rivercenter Blvd # 1600
Covington KY 41011
859 815-3333

(G-10139)
ASHLAND LLC
Also Called: Ashland Distribution
5200 Blazer Pkwy (43017-3309)
P.O. Box 2219, Columbus (43216-2219)
PHONE.............................614 790-3333
Sherri Nelson, *President*
Ted Harris, *Vice Pres*
Fred Good, *Vice Pres*
Frank Pettus, *Manager*
Antonio Tong, *Manager*
EMP: 150
SALES (corp-wide): 3.7B **Publicly Held**
WEB: www.ashland.com
SIC: 2899 5169 Chemical preparations; chemicals & allied products
HQ: Ashland Llc
50 E Rivercenter Blvd # 1600
Covington KY 41011
859 815-3333

(G-10140)
AT&T CORP
7497 Sawmill Rd (43016-9616)
PHONE.............................614 798-3898
Tisha Miller, *Manager*
EMP: 97
SALES (corp-wide): 170.7B **Publicly Held**
SIC: 4812 Cellular telephone services
HQ: At&t Corp.
1 At&t Way
Bedminster NJ 07921
800 403-3302

(G-10141)
AURORA IMAGING COMPANY
344 Cramer Creek Ct (43017-2585)
PHONE.............................614 761-1390
EMP: 35
SQ FT: 1,800
SALES (est): 1.1MM **Privately Held**
SIC: 7374 Document Imaging Services

(G-10142)
BBC&M ENGINEERING INC (PA)
6190 Enterprise Ct (43016-7297)
PHONE.............................614 793-2226
Stephen C Pasternack, *President*
Timothy A Van Echo, *Exec VP*
Ronald T Erb, *Vice Pres*

Daniel A Furgason, *Vice Pres*
Stephen L Loskota, *Vice Pres*
EMP: 65 EST: 1957
SQ FT: 25,000
SALES: 7.7MM **Privately Held**
WEB: www.bbcm.com
SIC: 8711 Consulting engineer

(G-10143)
BEECHWOLD VETERINARY HOSPITAL
Also Called: Riverside Veterinary Hospital
6924 Riverside Dr (43017-9519)
PHONE.............................614 766-1222
Dave McGuffin, *Manager*
EMP: 42
SQ FT: 1,509
SALES (corp-wide): 4.2MM **Privately Held**
WEB: www.beechwoldvet.vetsuite.com
SIC: 0742 Animal hospital services, pets & other animal specialties
PA: Beechwold Veterinary Hospital Inc
4590 Indianola Ave
Columbus OH 43214
614 268-8666

(G-10144)
BENCO DENTAL SUPPLY CO
4333 Tuller Rd Ste E (43017-5064)
PHONE.............................614 761-1053
Vickie Pfahler, *Manager*
EMP: 98
SALES (corp-wide): 621.9MM **Privately Held**
SIC: 5047 Dental equipment & supplies
PA: Benco Dental Supply Co.
295 Centerpoint Blvd
Pittston PA 18640
570 602-7781

(G-10145)
BENEFIT ADM AGCY LLC
5880 Venture Dr (43017-6140)
PHONE.............................614 791-1143
Courtlann Atkinson, *President*
EMP: 25
SALES (est): 1.7MM **Privately Held**
SIC: 6411 Insurance brokers

(G-10146)
BIOSORTIA PHARMACEUTICALS INC
4266 Tuller Rd (43017-5007)
PHONE.............................614 636-4850
Ross O Youngs, *President*
Haiyin He, *Vice Pres*
Guy T Carter, *CFO*
David Coho, *VP Sales*
Mike Rader, *Info Tech Dir*
EMP: 25
SALES (est): 2.6MM **Privately Held**
SIC: 8731 Biological research

(G-10147)
BMI FEDERAL CREDIT UNION
6165 Emerald Pkwy (43016-3248)
P.O. Box 3670 (43016-0340)
PHONE.............................614 707-4000
William Allender, *President*
Sharon Custer, *President*
EMP: 100 EST: 1934
SQ FT: 44,000
SALES: 15.1MM **Privately Held**
SIC: 6061 Federal credit unions

(G-10148)
BMW FINANCIAL SERVICES NA LLC
5515 Parkcenter Cir (43017-3584)
PHONE.............................614 718-6900
Brian Smith, *Project Mgr*
Bernard De Souza, *Sls & Mktg Exec*
Greg Finkey, *Sales Staff*
Jerry Morrow, *Marketing Staff*
Ashley Davis, *Case Mgr*
EMP: 150
SALES (corp-wide): 111.6B **Privately Held**
SIC: 6159 Automobile finance leasing
HQ: Bmw Financial Services Na, Llc
5550 Britton Pkwy
Hilliard OH 43026

(G-10149)
BOUND TREE MEDICAL LLC (HQ)
5000 Tuttle Crossing Blvd (43016-1534)
P.O. Box 8023 (43016-2023)
PHONE.............................614 760-5000
Bobbi Russell, *CEO*
Jimmy Greene, *Buyer*
Chris Bergeron, *Accounts Mgr*
Shawn Murphy, *Accounts Mgr*
Shannon Palma, *Accounts Mgr*
▲ EMP: 80
SQ FT: 30,000
SALES (est): 104.4MM **Privately Held**
WEB: www.boundtree.com
SIC: 5047 Medical equipment & supplies

(G-10150)
BRENTLINGER ENTERPRISES
Also Called: Midwestern Auto Group
6335 Perimeter Loop Rd (43017-3207)
PHONE.............................614 889-2571
Mark Brentlinger, *Partner*
Patrick Biles, *Opers Staff*
Richard Montgomery, *Sales Mgr*
Kevin Cobb, *Consultant*
Kira Adams, *Administration*
▲ EMP: 160
SQ FT: 100,000
SALES (est): 59.8MM **Privately Held**
WEB: www.magcars.com
SIC: 5511 7538 Automobiles, new & used; general automotive repair shops

(G-10151)
BROOKDALE SENIOR LIVING INC
7220 Muirfield Dr (43017-2862)
PHONE.............................614 336-3677
Heidi Strawn, *Office Mgr*
EMP: 42
SALES (corp-wide): 4.5B **Publicly Held**
SIC: 8051 Skilled nursing care facilities
PA: Brookdale Senior Living
111 Westwood Pl Ste 400
Brentwood TN 37027
615 221-2250

(G-10152)
BUCKEYE CHECK CASHING INC (HQ)
Also Called: First Virginia
6785 Bobcat Way Ste 200 (43016-1443)
PHONE.............................614 798-5900
Ted Saunders, *CEO*
Eric Austin, *President*
Kyle Hanson, *President*
Jerome Zingg, *Senior VP*
Lisa Vittorini, *Officer*
EMP: 200
SALES (est): 112.4MM **Privately Held**
WEB: www.buckeyecheckcashing.com
SIC: 6099 Check cashing agencies

(G-10153)
BUCKEYE DRMTLOGY DRMTHPHTHLOGY (PA)
5720 Blazer Pkwy (43017-3566)
PHONE.............................614 389-6331
Julio Cruz, *Principal*
Adam Hessel MD, *Principal*
Sandra Jones-Wu MD, *Principal*
Dean Hearne, *Dermatology*
EMP: 30
SALES (est): 3.6MM **Privately Held**
SIC: 8011 Dermatologist

(G-10154)
BUTLER ANIMAL HEALTH SUP LLC (DH)
Also Called: Henry Schein Animal Health
400 Metro Pl N Ste 100 (43017-3340)
PHONE.............................614 761-9095
Francis Dirksmeier, *President*
Matt Bridges, *Regional Mgr*
Dale Dye, *Regional Mgr*
Anthony Johnson, *Exec VP*
Ed Thomas, *Vice Pres*
◆ EMP: 170
SALES: 1.1B
SALES (corp-wide): 13.2B **Publicly Held**
SIC: 5047 5122 Veterinarians' equipment & supplies; biologicals & allied products

GEOGRAPHIC

HQ: Butler Animal Health Holding Company
Llc
400 Metro Pl N Ste 150
Dublin OH 43017
614 761-9095

(G-10155)
**BUTLER ANIMAL HLTH HOLDG
LLC (HQ)**
Also Called: Butler Animal Supply
400 Metro Pl N Ste 150 (43017-3392)
PHONE..............................614 761-9095
Hornsby Williams, *Purchasing*
Leslie Boesch, *Sales Staff*
Bobbie Riddle, *Sales Staff*
Kevin R Vasquez, *Mng Member*
Sheelah Jones, *Manager*
▼ EMP: 33
SALES (est): 1.1B
SALES (corp-wide): 13.2B **Publicly Held**
SIC: 5149 5047 5122 Pet foods; veteri-
narians' equipment & supplies; pharma-
ceuticals
PA: Henry Schein, Inc.
135 Duryea Rd
Melville NY 11747
631 843-5500

(G-10156)
CARDINAL HEALTH INC (PA)
7000 Cardinal Pl (43017-1091)
PHONE..............................614 757-5000
Michael C Kaufmann, *CEO*
Gregory B Kenny, *Ch of Bd*
Michele A M Holcomb, *Exec VP*
Patricia B Morrison, *Exec VP*
Martin Alires, *Vice Pres*
◆ EMP: 2800 EST: 1979
SALES: 136.8B **Publicly Held**
WEB: www.cardinal.com
SIC: 5122 5047 8741 3842 Pharmaceuti-
cals; blood plasma; druggists' sundries;
surgical equipment & supplies; hospital
equipment & supplies; management serv-
ices; surgical appliances & supplies

(G-10157)
**CARDINAL HEALTH 100 INC
(HQ)**
Also Called: Bindley Western Drug
7000 Cardinal Pl (43017-1091)
PHONE..............................614 757-5000
William E Bindley, *Ch of Bd*
Keith W Burks, *Exec VP*
Gregory S Beyerl, *Vice Pres*
Michael L Shinn, *Treasurer*
Seth B Harris, *Director*
EMP: 280
SQ FT: 70,000
SALES (est): 194.3MM
SALES (corp-wide): 136.8B **Publicly
Held**
WEB: www.bindley.com
SIC: 5122 5047 Drugs, proprietaries &
sundries; pharmaceuticals; cosmetics,
perfumes & hair products; druggists' sun-
dries; medical & hospital equipment
PA: Cardinal Health, Inc.
7000 Cardinal Pl
Dublin OH 43017
614 757-5000

(G-10158)
**CARDINAL HEALTH 201 INC
(HQ)**
7000 Cardinal Pl (43017-1091)
PHONE..............................614 757-5000
Lisa Ashby, *President*
EMP: 26
SALES (est): 51.9MM
SALES (corp-wide): 136.8B **Publicly
Held**
SIC: 5122 Drugs, proprietaries & sundries
PA: Cardinal Health, Inc.
7000 Cardinal Pl
Dublin OH 43017
614 757-5000

(G-10159)
**CARDINAL HEALTH 301 LLC
(HQ)**
Also Called: Pyxis Data Systems
7000 Cardinal Pl (43017-1091)
PHONE..............................614 757-5000
R Kerry Clark, *CEO*

Robert D Walter, *Ch of Bd*
Stephen S Thomas, *President*
▲ EMP: 600
SALES (est): 220.5MM
SALES (corp-wide): 136.8B **Publicly
Held**
SIC: 5047 Dental equipment & supplies
PA: Cardinal Health, Inc.
7000 Cardinal Pl
Dublin OH 43017
614 757-5000

(G-10160)
**CARE INFORMATION SYSTEMS
LLC**
5723 Dalymount Dr (43016-3234)
PHONE..............................614 496-4338
Krishna Char, *CEO*
EMP: 65
SALES: 750K **Privately Held**
SIC: 7371 Custom computer programming
services

(G-10161)
CAREWORKS OF OHIO INC (PA)
Also Called: Vocworks
5555 Glendon Ct Ste 300 (43016-3302)
P.O. Box 182726, Columbus (43218-2726)
PHONE..............................614 792-1085
William W Pfeiffer, *President*
Richard J Poach, *COO*
Tim James, *Senior VP*
Lori Finnerty, *Vice Pres*
Randy Kubacki, *Vice Pres*
EMP: 450
SQ FT: 85,000
SALES (est): 51.3MM **Privately Held**
WEB: www.careworks.com
SIC: 8059 7361 8741 6411 Personal care
home, with health care; employment
agencies; management services; insur-
ance agents, brokers & service

(G-10162)
CELLCO PARTNERSHIP
Also Called: Verizon
5165 Emerald Pkwy (43017-1063)
PHONE..............................614 560-2000
Dennis F Strigl, *President*
Anthony Yannone, *Director*
Amy Vollkommer, *Admin Sec*
EMP: 500
SALES (corp-wide): 130.8B **Publicly
Held**
SIC: 4812 Cellular telephone services
HQ: Cellco Partnership
1 Verizon Way
Basking Ridge NJ 07920

(G-10163)
CELLCO PARTNERSHIP
Also Called: Verizon Wireless
5520 Blazer Pkwy (43016-1525)
PHONE..............................614 793-8989
Marcy Geiger, *Branch Mgr*
EMP: 57
SALES (corp-wide): 130.8B **Publicly
Held**
SIC: 4812 Cellular telephone services
HQ: Cellco Partnership
1 Verizon Way
Basking Ridge NJ 07920

(G-10164)
CELLCO PARTNERSHIP
Also Called: Verizon
5035 Post Rd (43017-1115)
PHONE..............................614 793-8989
Walter Abood, *Branch Mgr*
EMP: 30
SALES (corp-wide): 130.8B **Publicly
Held**
SIC: 4812 5999 5731 Cellular telephone
services; telephone equipment & sys-
tems; radio, television & electronic stores
HQ: Cellco Partnership
1 Verizon Way
Basking Ridge NJ 07920

(G-10165)
CENTRAL OHIO ICE RINKS INC
7001 Dublin Park Dr (43016-8340)
PHONE..............................614 475-7575
Windy Herb, *President*
Greg Kirstein, *President*
EMP: 30

SQ FT: 70,000
SALES (est): 199.2K **Privately Held**
SIC: 7999 Ice skating rink operation

(G-10166)
**CENTRAL OHIO POURED
WALLS INC**
7627 Fishel Dr N (43016-8747)
PHONE..............................614 889-0505
Mark Del Col, *President*
Lena D Col, *Project Mgr*
EMP: 30
SQ FT: 6,000
SALES (est): 3MM **Privately Held**
SIC: 1771 Foundation & footing contractor

(G-10167)
CENTURYLINK INC
4650 Lakehurst Ct (43016-3252)
PHONE..............................614 215-4223
Robin Brannan, *Project Mgr*
Michelle Depompei, *Sales Staff*
Carlos Stuart, *Branch Mgr*
Robert Mulvaney, *Program Mgr*
Venkat Ashok, *Manager*
EMP: 3000
SALES (corp-wide): 23.4B **Publicly Held**
SIC: 4813 Local & long distance telephone
communications
PA: Centurylink, Inc.
100 Centurylink Dr
Monroe LA 71203
318 388-9000

(G-10168)
**CHAMPAIGN NATIONAL BANK
URBANA**
6400 Perimeter Loop Rd (43017-3205)
PHONE..............................614 798-1321
Brian Dupont, *Branch Mgr*
EMP: 30 **Privately Held**
WEB: www.champaignbank.com
SIC: 6021 National commercial banks
HQ: Champaign National Bank Of Urbana
601 Scioto St
Urbana OH 43078
937 653-1100

(G-10169)
**CHECKFREE SERVICES
CORPORATION**
Also Called: Fiserv
6000 Perimeter Dr (43017-3233)
PHONE..............................614 564-3000
Brian Forrest, *Business Anlyst*
Michael Kingery, *Business Anlyst*
Adam Fathauer, *Branch Mgr*
Pat McCabe, *Manager*
Gray Cleveland, *Info Tech Dir*
EMP: 1000
SALES (corp-wide): 5.8B **Publicly Held**
SIC: 7374 Data processing service
HQ: Checkfree Services Corporation
2900 Westside Pkwy
Alpharetta GA 30004
678 375-3000

(G-10170)
**CHECKSMART FINANCIAL
COMPANY (DH)**
6785 Bobcat Way Ste 200 (43016-1443)
PHONE..............................614 798-5900
Rob Grieser, *Principal*
EMP: 25
SALES (est): 78.3MM **Privately Held**
SIC: 6099 Check cashing agencies
HQ: Checksmart Financial Holdings Corp.
6785 Bobcat Way Ste 200
Dublin OH 43016
614 798-5900

(G-10171)
CHEMCOTE INC
Also Called: Cicar
7599 Fishel Dr N (43016-8818)
PHONE..............................614 792-2683
Frank Bucci, *President*
Joseph Bucci, *Vice Pres*
Drew Dimaccio, *Vice Pres*
Joe Sanderlin, *Vice Pres*
EMP: 120
SQ FT: 6,000
SALES (est): 29.8MM **Privately Held**
SIC: 1611 Highway & street paving con-
tractor; surfacing & paving

(G-10172)
**CHEMCOTE ROOFING
COMPANY**
7599 Fishel Dr N (43016-8818)
PHONE..............................614 792-2683
Frank Bucci, *President*
Drew Dimaccio, *Treasurer*
EMP: 70
SQ FT: 2,000
SALES (est): 6.3MM **Privately Held**
WEB: www.chemcote.com
SIC: 1761 Roofing contractor

(G-10173)
CHILLER LLC (PA)
7001 Dublin Park Dr (43016-8340)
PHONE..............................614 764-1000
Wendy Herb, *President*
David A Paitson, *Principal*
EMP: 75 EST: 1997
SQ FT: 76,000
SALES (est): 12.8MM **Privately Held**
WEB: www.chiller.com
SIC: 7999 Ice skating rink operation

(G-10174)
CISCO SYSTEMS INC
5400 Frantz Rd Ste 200 (43016-4147)
PHONE..............................614 764-4987
Bill Taylor, *Principal*
Jurgen Baucke, *Engineer*
Dana Daum, *Engineer*
Paul Wolfson, *Regl Sales Mgr*
Jim Capito, *Manager*
EMP: 98
SALES (corp-wide): 48B **Publicly Held**
WEB: www.cisco.com
SIC: 5045 Computer peripheral equipment
PA: Cisco Systems, Inc.
170 W Tasman Dr
San Jose CA 95134
408 526-4000

(G-10175)
CITY OF DUBLIN
Also Called: Division Streets & Utilities
6555 Shier Rings Rd (43016-8716)
PHONE..............................614 410-4750
Ron Burns, *Director*
EMP: 50
SQ FT: 3,052 **Privately Held**
SIC: 4911 Electric services
PA: City Of Dublin
5200 Emerald Pkwy
Dublin OH 43017
614 410-4400

(G-10176)
**CLOSE TO HOME HEALTH CARE
CTR**
Also Called: Children's Hospital Northwest
5675 Venture Dr (43017-2159)
PHONE..............................614 932-9013
Larry Long, *Director*
EMP: 50
SALES (est): 13MM **Privately Held**
SIC: 6324 Hospital & medical service plans

(G-10177)
CMP I COLUMBUS I OWNER LLC
Also Called: Courtyard Columbus Dublin
5175 Post Rd (43017-2125)
PHONE..............................614 764-9393
Christine Bowdle, *Facilities Dir*
Nichole Brinker, *Manager*
EMP: 37
SALES (est): 1.2MM
SALES (corp-wide): 50.6MM **Privately
Held**
SIC: 7011 Hotels
PA: Cmp I Owner-T, Llc
399 Park Ave Fl 18
New York NY 10022
212 547-2609

(G-10178)
CMP I OWNER-T LLC
5175 Post Rd (43017-2125)
PHONE..............................614 764-9393
Nichole Brinker, *Manager*
EMP: 37
SALES (corp-wide): 50.6MM **Privately
Held**
SIC: 8741 Hotel or motel management

PA: Cmp I Owner-T, Llc
399 Park Ave Fl 18
New York NY 10022
212 547-2609

(G-10179)
CNI THL OPS LLC
Also Called: Homewood Suites Dublin
5300 Parkcenter Ave (43017-7555)
PHONE..................................614 791-8675
Keon Marvasti, *Manager*
EMP: 26
SALES (corp-wide): 11.1MM **Privately Held**
WEB: www.daytonraiders.com
SIC: 7011 Hotels
PA: Cni Thl Ops, Llc
515 S Flower St Fl 44
Los Angeles CA

(G-10180)
COLONIAL LF ACCIDENT INSUR CO
5600 Blazer Pkwy Ste 300 (43017-7551)
PHONE..................................614 793-8622
Christopher McKee, *General Mgr*
EMP: 400 **Publicly Held**
SIC: 6311 Life insurance
HQ: Colonial Life & Accident Insurance
Company Inc
1200 Colonial Life Blvd W
Columbia SC 29210
803 798-7000

(G-10181)
COLUMBUS AAA CORP
Also Called: AAA Rental & Sales
2502 Starford Dr (43016-9247)
PHONE..................................614 889-2840
EMP: 25
SQ FT: 21,000
SALES (est): 2.6MM **Privately Held**
SIC: 7359 5712 Party Supply Rental & Ret
Furniture Store

(G-10182)
COLUMBUS SURGICAL CENTER LLP
5005 Parkcenter Ave (43017-3582)
PHONE..................................614 932-9503
Kim Heimlich, *Principal*
EMP: 50
SALES (est): 1.6MM **Privately Held**
SIC: 8011 8399 Ambulatory surgical center; social services

(G-10183)
COMMAND ALKON INCORPORATED
6750 Crosby Ct (43016-7644)
PHONE..................................614 799-0600
Randy Willaman, *Branch Mgr*
EMP: 60
SALES (corp-wide): 107.7MM **Privately Held**
WEB: www.commandalkon.com
SIC: 3823 7371 3625 Industrial process
measurement equipment; custom computer programming services; relays & industrial controls
PA: Command Alkon Incorporated
1800 Intl Pk Dr Ste 400
Birmingham AL 35243
205 879-3282

(G-10184)
COMMONWEALTH HOTELS LLC
Also Called: Embassy Suites
5100 Upper Metro Pl (43017-3384)
PHONE..................................614 790-9000
Lee Palaschak, *Branch Mgr*
EMP: 125
SALES (corp-wide): 92.4MM **Privately Held**
WEB: www.commonwealth-hotels.com
SIC: 7011 5813 5812 Hotels; drinking
places; eating places
PA: Commonwealth Hotels, Llc
100 E Rivercenter Blvd # 1050
Covington KY 41011
859 392-2264

(G-10185)
COMMUNITY CHOICE FINANCIAL INC (PA)
Also Called: EASY MONEY
6785 Bobcat Way Ste 200 (43016-1443)
PHONE..................................614 798-5900
William E Saunders Jr, *CEO*
Kyle Hanson, *President*
Ted Saunders, *Principal*
Robb Heitzman, *Director*
EMP: 51
SALES: 364MM **Privately Held**
SIC: 6099 Check cashing agencies

(G-10186)
COMPASS CONSTRUCTION INC
7670 Fishel Dr S (43016-8820)
PHONE..................................614 761-7800
Larry Mirgon, *President*
Guy Detrick, *Asst Supt*
Frank Reynolds, *Vice Pres*
EMP: 80
SQ FT: 14,400
SALES (est): 7.4MM **Privately Held**
WEB: www.compassconstruction.com
SIC: 1742 Drywall; acoustical & ceiling
work

(G-10187)
COMPMANAGEMENT INC (HQ)
6377 Emerald Pkwy (43016-3272)
P.O. Box 884 (43017-6884)
PHONE..................................614 376-5300
Stephen Brown, *CEO*
Cheryl Powers, *President*
Jonathan Wagner, *President*
Richard Kurth, *Exec VP*
Daniel Sullivan, *Senior VP*
EMP: 40
SALES (est): 211.9MM
SALES (corp-wide): 9.5B **Privately Held**
WEB: www.compmgt.com
SIC: 6411 Insurance agents, brokers &
service
PA: Sedgwick Cms Holdings, Inc.
1100 Ridgeway Loop Rd # 200
Memphis TN 38120
901 415-7400

(G-10188)
COMPMANAGEMENT HEALTH SYSTEMS
6377 Emerald Pkwy (43016-3272)
P.O. Box 1040 (43017-6040)
PHONE..................................614 766-5223
EMP: 100
SALES: 4.4MM
SALES (corp-wide): 3.4B **Privately Held**
SIC: 8748 Business Consulting Services
HQ: Compmanagement, Inc.
6377 Emerald Pkwy
Dublin OH 43016
614 376-5300

(G-10189)
CONSOLIDATED LEARNING CTRS INC
Also Called: Jelly Bean Junction Lrng Ctr
7100 Muirfield Dr Ste 200 (43017-3807)
PHONE..................................614 791-0050
Jeffry Roby, *CEO*
Bonnie Roby, *President*
Jessica Hoffman, *Vice Pres*
EMP: 115
SQ FT: 4,000
SALES (est): 2.5MM **Privately Held**
SIC: 8351 Child day care services

(G-10190)
COUNTRY CLUB AT MUIRFIELD VLG
Also Called: COUNTRY CLUB, THE
8715 Muirfield Dr (43017-9600)
PHONE..................................614 764-1714
Jim Hughes, *CEO*
John Blute, *General Mgr*
Alissa Klein, *Comms Dir*
D Mancini, *Manager*
Sean Fyffe, *Director*
EMP: 30
SQ FT: 35,000

SALES: 2.2MM **Privately Held**
WEB: www.tccmv.com
SIC: 7997 Country club, membership; golf
club, membership; swimming club, membership; tennis club, membership

(G-10191)
COVELLI ENTERPRISES INC
6693 Sawmill Rd (43017-9009)
PHONE..................................614 889-7802
EMP: 75
SALES (corp-wide): 384.2MM **Privately
Held**
SIC: 7389 Personal service agents, brokers & bureaus
PA: Covelli Enterprises, Inc.
3900 E Market St Ste 1
Warren OH 44484
330 856-3176

(G-10192)
CRAWFORD HOYING LTD
6640 Riverside Dr Ste 500 (43017-9534)
PHONE..................................614 335-2020
Chris Lanning, *President*
Brent D Crawford, *Chairman*
Robert C Hoying, *Chairman*
Mark Mayers, *COO*
Don Brokaw, *Vice Pres*
EMP: 215
SALES (est): 23.8MM **Privately Held**
SIC: 6531 Real estate agents & managers

(G-10193)
CRESTTEK LLC (PA)
565 Metro Pl S Ste 420 (43017-7321)
PHONE..................................248 602-2083
Madhu Naidu, *Mng Member*
Girish Gowda,
Walter Muccino,
EMP: 40
SQ FT: 2,800
SALES (est): 4MM **Privately Held**
SIC: 7549 Automotive customizing services, non-factory basis

(G-10194)
CUTLER REAL ESTATE INC
6375 Riverside Dr Ste 210 (43017-5241)
PHONE..................................614 339-4664
Doug Green, *General Mgr*
EMP: 45 EST: 2013
SALES (est): 218.9K **Privately Held**
SIC: 6531 6519 Real estate brokers &
agents; real property lessors

(G-10195)
CWB PROPERTY MANAGMENT INC (PA)
5775 Perimeter Dr Ste 290 (43017-3224)
PHONE..................................614 793-2244
William W Wolfe, *President*
Kenneth J Castrop, *Corp Secy*
Christopher D Conrath, *Vice Pres*
Marina Rabkin, *Accounting Mgr*
EMP: 30
SQ FT: 2,400
SALES (est): 2.6MM **Privately Held**
WEB: www.cwbpm.com
SIC: 6513 6514 7011 6531 Apartment
building operators; dwelling operators, except apartments; hotels & motels; real estate agents & managers

(G-10196)
DATALYSYS LLC
5200 Upper Metro Pl # 120 (43017-5314)
PHONE..................................614 495-0260
April Harris, *Partner*
Rajneesh Katarapu, *Manager*
Mayuri Sriram,
Raj Katarapu,
EMP: 40
SALES: 4MM **Privately Held**
SIC: 7379

(G-10197)
DEDICATED TECH SERVICES INC
545 Metro Pl S Ste 100 (43017-5353)
PHONE..................................614 309-0059
Patricia E Lickliter, *President*
EMP: 28
SQ FT: 2,300

SALES: 2.2MM **Privately Held**
SIC: 7371 7373 7376 7379 Computer
software development; local area network
(LAN) systems integrator; computer facilities management; computer related maintenance services; usher service;
management consulting services

(G-10198)
DELTA ENERGY LLC
545 Metro Pl S Ste 400 (43017-3386)
PHONE..................................614 761-3603
Justin McMaster, *President*
Fabrizio Puga, *Vice Pres*
Eric Cellar, *Manager*
Mitch Maynard, *Manager*
Sheri Tackett,
EMP: 45
SALES (est): 8.7MM **Privately Held**
WEB: www.deltaenergyllc.com
SIC: 4924 8742 Natural gas distribution;
management consulting services

(G-10199)
DEMARIUS CORPORATION
Also Called: Progressive Medical Intl
5000 Tuttle Crossing Blvd (43016-1534)
PHONE..................................760 957-5500
Marc Lawrence, *President*
▲ **EMP:** 40
SQ FT: 35,000
SALES (est): 6.5MM **Privately Held**
WEB: www.progressivemed.com
SIC: 5047 Medical equipment & supplies

(G-10200)
DIMENSION SERVICE CORPORATION
Also Called: D S C
5500 Frantz Rd Ste 100 (43017-3545)
P.O. Box 2082 (43017-7082)
PHONE..................................614 226-7455
Bradley Hunter, *President*
Al Stein, *COO*
Craig Andrew, *Vice Pres*
Kenny Halfpap, *Vice Pres*
Mike Murphy, *CFO*
EMP: 125
SQ FT: 25,000
SALES (est): 65.5MM **Privately Held**
WEB: www.dimensionservice.com
SIC: 6399 Warranty insurance, automobile

(G-10201)
DOCTORS CONSULTING SERVICE
200 Bradenton Ave (43017-3513)
PHONE..................................614 793-1980
Jerry Snively, *President*
Terrence Fickel, *Vice Pres*
EMP: 25
SQ FT: 4,120
SALES (est): 1.6MM **Privately Held**
SIC: 8721 Billing & bookkeeping service

(G-10202)
DOMINION HOMES INC (HQ)
4900 Tuttle Crossing Blvd (43016-1532)
P.O. Box 23404, Chagrin Falls (44023-0404)
PHONE..................................614 356-5000
Donn Borror, *Ch of Bd*
Jeffrey Croft, *President*
David S Borror, *Exec VP*
William G Cornely, *CFO*
EMP: 100
SALES (est): 66.9MM **Privately Held**
SIC: 1521 Single-family housing construction

(G-10203)
DRURY HOTELS COMPANY LLC
Also Called: Drury Inn & Suites Columbus NW
6170 Parkcenter Cir (43017-3583)
PHONE..................................614 798-8802
Jessica Baker, *Manager*
EMP: 28
SALES (corp-wide): 397.7MM **Privately Held**
WEB: www.druryhotels.com
SIC: 7011 Hotels
PA: Drury Hotels Company, Llc
721 Emerson Rd Ste 400
Saint Louis MO 63141
314 429-2255

(G-10204)
DUBLIN BUILDING SYSTEMS CO
6233 Avery Rd (43016-8788)
P.O. Box 370 (43017-0370)
PHONE..............................614 760-5831
Thomas W Irelan, *President*
Victor D Irelan, *Chairman*
Robert J Howe, *Vice Pres*
Richard W Irelan, *Vice Pres*
Scot Matthews, *Project Mgr*
EMP: 44
SQ FT: 5,000
SALES (est): 13.2MM **Privately Held**
WEB: www.dublinbuilding.com
SIC: 1791 1521 Structural steel erection;
single-family housing construction

(G-10205)
DUBLIN CITY SCHOOLS
6371 Shier Rings Rd (43016-9498)
PHONE..............................614 764-5926
Victor Dodds, *Director*
Andrea McCullough, *Teacher*
Mary A Petty, *Assistant*
EMP: 150
SALES (corp-wide): 245.6MM **Privately Held**
SIC: 4151 School buses
PA: Dublin City Schools
7030 Coffman Rd
Dublin OH 43017
614 764-5913

(G-10206)
DUBLIN FAMILY CARE INC
250 W Bridge St Ste 101 (43017-1172)
PHONE..............................614 761-2244
James J Barr MD, *President*
Dr Joseph Carducci, *Vice Pres*
EMP: 25
SALES (est): 3.4MM **Privately Held**
SIC: 8011 General & family practice, physician/surgeon

(G-10207)
DUBLIN GERIATRIC CARE CO LP
Also Called: Convalarium At Indian Run
6430 Post Rd (43016-1226)
PHONE..............................614 761-1188
Ralph E Hazelbaker, *Partner*
Dennison Health Ventures, *Partner*
Dublin Health Care Corp, *General Ptnr*
EMP: 50
SALES (est): 2.1MM **Privately Held**
SIC: 8059 8051 Convalescent home;
skilled nursing care facilities

(G-10208)
DUBLIN HOTEL LTD LIABILITY CO
Also Called: Columbus-Marriott NW
5605 Paul G Blazer Me (43017)
PHONE..............................513 891-1066
EMP: 125
SALES (est): 1.6MM **Privately Held**
SIC: 7011 Hotels & motels

(G-10209)
DUBLIN LATCHKEY INC
5970 Venture Dr Ste A (43017-2263)
PHONE..............................614 793-0871
Moreen Bruce, *Director*
Shirley Place, *Director*
Cris Williams, *Director*
EMP: 60
SALES: 2MM **Privately Held**
WEB: www.dublinlatchkey.com
SIC: 8351 Preschool center

(G-10210)
DUBLIN LEARNING ACADEMY
5900 Cromdale Dr (43017-8751)
PHONE..............................614 761-1800
Cathy Holbert, *President*
EMP: 25
SALES (est): 550.1K **Privately Held**
SIC: 8351 Preschool center

(G-10211)
DUBLIN MILLWORK CO INC
7575 Fishel Dr S (43016-8821)
PHONE..............................614 889-7776
Wilbur C Strait, *Ch of Bd*
Scott Evisol, *General Mgr*

Scott Ebersole, *Manager*
Andy Castle, *Executive*
EMP: 30 **EST:** 1981
SQ FT: 100,000
SALES (est): 4.5MM
SALES (corp-wide): 39.1MM **Privately Held**
WEB: www.dublinmillwork.com
SIC: 5031 2431 Trim, sheet metal; doors & windows; millwork
PA: The Strait & Lamp Lumber Company Incorporated
269 National Rd Se
Hebron OH 43025
740 928-4501

(G-10212)
DUKE REALTY CORPORATION
Also Called: Duke-Weeks Realty
6640 Riverside Dr Ste 320 (43017-0406)
PHONE..............................614 932-6000
Don Hunter, *President*
EMP: 75
SALES (corp-wide): 947.8MM **Privately Held**
WEB: www.dukereit.com
SIC: 6512 Commercial & industrial building operation
PA: Duke Realty Corporation
600 E 96th St Ste 100
Indianapolis IN 46240
317 808-6000

(G-10213)
ECI MACOLA/MAX LLC (DH)
5455 Rings Rd Ste 100 (43017-7519)
PHONE..............................978 539-6186
Lisa Wise, *General Mgr*
Mitchell Alcon,
Alex Braverman,
James A Workman,
EMP: 170
SQ FT: 30,000
SALES (est): 68MM
SALES (corp-wide): 216.4MM **Privately Held**
WEB: www.exactamerica.com
SIC: 7371 7372 5045 2759 Computer software development; prepackaged software; computer software; letterpress printing
HQ: Exact Holding B.V.
Molengraaffsingel 33
Delft 2629
157 115-000

(G-10214)
ECI MACOLA/MAX HOLDING LLC
Also Called: Eclipse Midco
5455 Rings Rd Ste 400 (43017-7531)
PHONE..............................614 410-2712
Ron Brooks, *CEO*
EMP: 30 **Privately Held**
SIC: 6719 Personal holding companies, except banks

(G-10215)
EDUCATION INNOVATIONS INTL LLC
655 Metro Pl S Ste 750 (43017-5306)
P.O. Box 266, Amlin (43002-0266)
PHONE..............................614 339-3676
Judy McCord, *CFO*
James E McCord,
EMP: 120
SQ FT: 75,000
SALES: 10MM **Privately Held**
SIC: 8741 Management services

(G-10216)
EMERALD PEDIATRICS
5695 Innovation Dr (43016-3312)
PHONE..............................614 932-5050
Donna Hickel, *Manager*
EMP: 35
SALES (est): 2.8MM **Privately Held**
WEB: www.emeraldpediatrics.com
SIC: 8011 Pediatrician

(G-10217)
EMPLOYEE BENEFIT MANAGEMENT (PA)
Also Called: Ebmc
4789 Rings Rd (43017-1772)
PHONE..............................614 766-5800
Tom Jack, *President*
Kenneth Patrick, *President*
James Armstrong, *CFO*
EMP: 34
SQ FT: 33,000
SALES: 42.8K **Privately Held**
SIC: 8748 6411 Employee programs administration; insurance agents, brokers & service

(G-10218)
EPCON CMMNTIES FRANCHISING INC
500 Stonehenge Pkwy (43017-7572)
PHONE..............................614 761-1010
Philip Fankhauser, *CEO*
Ed Bacome, *President*
EMP: 87
SQ FT: 10,000
SALES (est): 9.3MM **Privately Held**
WEB: www.epcongroup.com
SIC: 1531 6794 Condominium developers; franchises, selling or licensing

(G-10219)
EPCON COMMUNITIES INC
500 Stonehenge Pkwy (43017-7572)
PHONE..............................614 761-1010
Phil Fankhauser, *President*
Ed Bacome, *Vice Pres*
David P Blackmore, *CFO*
EMP: 70
SQ FT: 10,500
SALES (est): 26.9MM **Privately Held**
WEB: www.epconcommunities.com
SIC: 1531 Condominium developers

(G-10220)
ERP ANALYSTS INC
425 Metro Pl N Ste 510 (43017-7328)
PHONE..............................614 718-9222
Srikanth Gaddam, *President*
Ranjith K Reddy, *Business Mgr*
Dick Kelley, *Vice Pres*
Kenny Brady, *Manager*
Rachel Brown, *Manager*
EMP: 499
SALES: 75.1MM **Privately Held**
WEB: www.erpanalysts.com
SIC: 7371 Custom computer programming services

(G-10221)
EVERRIS NA INC (DH)
4950 Blazer Pkwy (43017-3305)
PHONE..............................614 726-7100
Ariana Cohen, *President*
◆ **EMP:** 37 **EST:** 1966
SQ FT: 73,000
SALES (est): 22.4MM **Privately Held**
WEB: www.everris.com
SIC: 1479 Fertilizer mineral mining; fertilizer mineral mining

(G-10222)
EXCESS SHARE INSURANCE CORP
Also Called: AMERICAN SHARE INSURANCE
5656 Frantz Rd (43017-2552)
PHONE..............................614 764-1900
Dennis Adams, *President*
Gerald D Welsh, *Corp Secy*
Curt Robson, *Treasurer*
EMP: 35
SQ FT: 10,000
SALES: 2.5MM
SALES (corp-wide): 8.4MM **Privately Held**
WEB: www.excessshare.com
SIC: 6399 Deposit insurance
PA: American Mutual Share Insurance Corporation
5656 Frantz Rd
Dublin OH 43017
614 764-1900

(G-10223)
F DOHMEN CO
F D C O Data Processing
7000 Cardinal Pl (43017-1091)
PHONE..............................614 757-5000
John Dohmen, *Principal*
EMP: 200
SALES (corp-wide): 131.4MM **Privately Held**
WEB: www.dohmen.com
SIC: 5122 Drugs & drug proprietaries
PA: The F Dohmen Co
215 N Water St Ste 300
Milwaukee WI 53202
866 336-1336

(G-10224)
FANNING/HOWEY ASSOCIATES INC
4930 Bradenton Ave # 200 (43017-7502)
PHONE..............................614 764-4661
Alan Esparza, *Manager*
EMP: 60
SALES (corp-wide): 37.5MM **Privately Held**
WEB: www.fhai.com
SIC: 8712 Architectural engineering
PA: Fanning/Howey Associates, Inc.
1200 Irmscher Blvd
Celina OH 45822
419 586-2292

(G-10225)
FANNING/HOWEY ASSOCIATES INC
4930 Bradenton Ave (43017-7599)
PHONE..............................919 831-1831
Wayne R Roberts, *Branch Mgr*
EMP: 60
SALES (corp-wide): 37.5MM **Privately Held**
SIC: 8712 Architectural services
PA: Fanning/Howey Associates, Inc.
1200 Irmscher Blvd
Celina OH 45822
419 586-2292

(G-10226)
FAST SWITCH LTD
4900 Blazer Pkwy (43017-3305)
P.O. Box 99 (43017-0099)
PHONE..............................614 336-1122
Mark Pukita, *CEO*
Kristin Buck, *Controller*
Ken Hamilton, *Accounts Mgr*
Tim Shea, *Accounts Mgr*
John Straubinger, *Accounts Mgr*
EMP: 300
SQ FT: 1,200
SALES: 51.1MM **Privately Held**
WEB: www.fastswitch.com
SIC: 7361 Executive placement

(G-10227)
FISERV INC
6000 Perimeter Dr (43017-3233)
PHONE..............................412 577-3326
Ken Kocis, *Sls & Mktg Exec*
Natalie Abel, *Manager*
John J Boucek, *Manager*
EMP: 79
SALES (corp-wide): 5.8B **Publicly Held**
WEB: www.fiserv.com
SIC: 7374 Data processing service
PA: Fiserv, Inc.
255 Fiserv Dr
Brookfield WI 53045
262 879-5000

(G-10228)
FISERV SOLUTIONS LLC
6000 Perimeter Dr (43017-3233)
PHONE..............................412 577-3000
EMP: 150
SALES (corp-wide): 5.8B **Publicly Held**
WEB: www.fiservdox.com
SIC: 7378 6282 Computer maintenance & repair; investment advice
HQ: Fiserv Solutions, Llc
255 Fiserv Dr
Brookfield WI 53045
262 879-5000

▲ = Import ▼=Export
◆ =Import/Export

(G-10229)
FLEX FUND INC
6125 Memorial Dr (43017-9000)
PHONE...................................614 766-7000
Robert S Meeder Jr, *President*
EMP: 45
SQ FT: 10,000
SALES (est): 2.9MM **Privately Held**
WEB: www.flexfunds.com
SIC: 6289 8721 Security transfer agents;
accounting services, except auditing

(G-10230)
FORESIGHT CORPORATION
655 Metro Pl S Ste 900 (43017-3398)
PHONE...................................614 791-1600
Robert Fisher, *President*
Douglas Spence, *Exec VP*
Mike Kennedy, *Purch Mgr*
Kristin Maxwell, *CFO*
Edward Hafner, *CTO*
EMP: 43
SALES (est): 2.3MM
SALES (corp-wide): 5.2B **Privately Held**
WEB: www.foresightcorp.com
SIC: 7371 Computer software develop-
ment & applications
HQ: Tibco Software Inc.
3307 Hillview Ave
Palo Alto CA 94304

(G-10231)
**FRANK GATES SERVICE
COMPANY (DH)**
Also Called: Avizent
5000 Bradenton Ave # 100 (43017-3520)
P.O. Box 182364, Columbus (43218-2364)
PHONE...................................614 793-8000
Daniel R Sullivan, *President*
Sandra Powell, *President*
Frank Gates, *Principal*
Madeleine Melancon, *Principal*
Harrison W Smith, *Principal*
EMP: 300
SQ FT: 66,000
SALES (est): 90MM
SALES (corp-wide): 2.3B **Privately Held**
WEB: www.fgsc.com
SIC: 8742 Compensation & benefits plan-
ning consultant
HQ: York Risk Services Group, Inc.
1 Upper Pond
Parsippany NJ 07054
973 404-1200

(G-10232)
**FRIENDSHIP VLG OF DUBLIN
OHIO**
6000 Riverside Dr Ofc Ofc (43017-5073)
PHONE...................................614 764-1600
John Schwarck, *CFO*
Don Paul, *Manager*
Beth Baker, *Director*
Tim Schneider, *Director*
Jessica Rieker, *Administration*
EMP: 250
SALES: 22.4MM **Privately Held**
WEB: www.fvdublin.org
SIC: 8059 8051 Rest home, with health
care; skilled nursing care facilities

(G-10233)
**GALLAGHER BASSETT
SERVICES**
545 Metro Pl S Ste 250 (43017-5310)
PHONE...................................614 764-7616
Richard Komparens, *Manager*
EMP: 35
SALES (corp-wide): 6.9B **Publicly Held**
WEB: www.atlantisad.com
SIC: 6411 Insurance agents & brokers
HQ: Gallagher Bassett Services, Inc.
2850 Golf Rd Ste 1000
Rolling Meadows IL 60008
630 773-3800

(G-10234)
GEMINI PROPERTIES
Also Called: G P M C
6470 Post Rd Ofc (43016-7206)
PHONE...................................614 764-2800
Ron Keller, *Director*
EMP: 50

SALES (corp-wide): 6.8MM **Privately
Held**
WEB: www.geminiproperties.com
SIC: 6513 Retirement hotel operation
PA: Gemini Properties
1516 S Boston Ave Ste 301
Tulsa OK 74119
918 592-4400

(G-10235)
GOLF CLUB OF DUBLIN LLC
5805 Eiterman Rd (43016-8004)
PHONE...................................614 792-3825
Tom Anderson,
EMP: 50
SALES (est): 1.6MM **Privately Held**
WEB: www.golfclubofdublin.net
SIC: 7992 Public golf courses

(G-10236)
GUILD ASSOCIATES INC (PA)
Also Called: Guild Biosciences
5750 Shier Rings Rd (43016-1234)
PHONE...................................614 798-8215
Dominic Dinovo, *President*
Dolores Dinovo, *Treasurer*
◆ EMP: 80
SQ FT: 53,000
SALES: 33MM **Privately Held**
SIC: 3559 8731 Chemical machinery &
equipment; chemical laboratory, except
testing; biotechnical research, commercial

(G-10237)
**HANOVER INSURANCE
COMPANY**
545 Metro Pl S Ste 380 (43017-5367)
PHONE...................................614 408-9000
Paula Leger, *Branch Mgr*
EMP: 75 **Publicly Held**
SIC: 6411 Insurance agents
HQ: The Hanover Insurance Company
440 Lincoln St
Worcester MA 01653
508 853-7200

(G-10238)
HARDAGE HOTELS I LLC
Also Called: Chase Suite Hotel
4130 Tuller Rd (43017-9502)
PHONE...................................614 766-7762
William Quigley, *Manager*
EMP: 30 **Privately Held**
WEB: www.woodfinsuitehotels.com
SIC: 7011 Hotel, franchised
PA: Hardage Hotels I, Llc
12555 High Bluff Dr # 330
San Diego CA 92130

(G-10239)
**HASLETT HEATING & COOLING
INC**
Also Called: Honeywell Authorized Dealer
7686 Fishel Dr N A (43016-8746)
PHONE...................................614 299-2133
Jeff Florer, *President*
Bruce Ames, *Vice Pres*
EMP: 38
SALES (est): 8.8MM **Privately Held**
WEB: www.haslettmechanical.com
SIC: 1711 Warm air heating & air condi-
tioning contractor

(G-10240)
HER INC
Also Called: H E R Realtors
5725 Perimeter Dr (43017-3216)
PHONE...................................614 889-7400
Dwight Everheart, *Manager*
EMP: 120
SALES (corp-wide): 14.3MM **Privately
Held**
WEB: www.eassent.com
SIC: 6531 Real estate agent, residential
PA: Her, Inc
4261 Morse Rd
Columbus OH 43230
614 221-7400

(G-10241)
**HERITAGE WRRANTY INSUR
RRG INC**
Also Called: Heritage Administration Svcs
400 Metro Pl N Ste 300 (43017-3377)
PHONE...................................800 753-5236

Haytham H Elzayn, *CEO*
Larry S Roseberry, *President*
Stephen E Goodrich, *Vice Pres*
Ronald L Uhing, *CFO*
Gary H Osborne, *Asst Treas*
EMP: 73 EST: 1998
SQ FT: 15,000
SALES (est): 19.7MM **Privately Held**
WEB: www.heritagewarranty.com
SIC: 6399 Warranty insurance, automobile

(G-10242)
HILL DISTRIBUTING COMPANY
5080 Tuttle Crossing Blvd # 325
(43016-3504)
PHONE...................................614 276-6533
Charles D Hill Jr, *Ch of Bd*
Cynthia Hill Conie, *President*
Christine Hill Wilson, *Vice Pres*
▲ EMP: 90
SQ FT: 50,400
SALES (est): 14.5MM **Privately Held**
WEB: www.hilldist.com
SIC: 5181 5149 Beer & other fermented
malt liquors; mineral or spring water bot-
tling

(G-10243)
HIT PORTFOLIO I HIL TRS LLC
Also Called: Hampton Inn Columbus Airport
3920 Tuller Rd (43017-5020)
PHONE...................................614 235-0717
Ken Morgan, *Manager*
EMP: 31
SALES (corp-wide): 621MM **Privately
Held**
SIC: 7011 Hotels
HQ: Hit Portfolio I Hil Trs, Llc
3950 University Dr # 301
Fairfax VA 22030
212 415-6500

(G-10244)
HOLO PUNDITS INC
425 Metro Pl N Ste 440 (43017-5325)
PHONE...................................614 707-5225
Vinod Dega, *CEO*
EMP: 50 EST: 2013
SALES: 20K **Privately Held**
SIC: 7371 Computer software writing serv-
ices

(G-10245)
HOTEL 2345 LLC
Also Called: Cloverleaf Suites
4130 Tuller Rd (43017-9502)
PHONE...................................614 766-7762
Ritesh Jariwala,
EMP: 30
SALES (est): 623.7K **Privately Held**
SIC: 7011 Inns

(G-10246)
HR BUTLER LLC
63 Corbins Mill Dr Ste A (43017-8314)
PHONE...................................614 923-2900
Thomas Hedge, *President*
EMP: 25 EST: 2000
SALES (est): 1.5MM **Privately Held**
SIC: 8721 8742 Payroll accounting serv-
ice; human resource consulting services

(G-10247)
HULL & ASSOCIATES INC (PA)
6397 Emerald Pkwy Ste 200 (43016-2231)
PHONE...................................614 793-8777
John H Hull, *Ch of Bd*
Craig A Kasper, *President*
David L Richards, *Vice Pres*
W Lance Turley, *Admin Sec*
EMP: 50
SQ FT: 9,180
SALES (est): 35.9MM **Privately Held**
WEB: www.hullinc.com
SIC: 8711 8748 Consulting engineer; envi-
ronmental consultant

(G-10248)
HUMANA INC
485 Metro Pl S Ste 410 (43017-5366)
PHONE...................................614 210-1038
Jane Hirsch, *Manager*
EMP: 41
SALES (corp-wide): 56.9B **Publicly Held**
SIC: 6324 Health maintenance organiza-
tion (HMO), insurance only

PA: Humana Inc.
500 W Main St 300
Louisville KY 40202
502 580-1000

(G-10249)
HUNTINGTON NATIONAL BANK
4300 Tuller Rd (43017-5008)
PHONE...................................614 336-4620
EMP: 100
SALES (corp-wide): 3.7B **Publicly Held**
SIC: 6099 Depository Banking Services
HQ: The Huntington National Bank
17 S High St Fl 1
Columbus OH 43215
614 480-4293

(G-10250)
**HUSKY MARKETING AND
SUPPLY CO**
Also Called: Husky Energy
5550 Blazer Pkwy Ste 200 (43017-3478)
PHONE...................................614 210-2300
Scott Howard, *General Mgr*
Rod Cundiff, *Business Mgr*
Jon Frueh, *Engineer*
Julie Quatman, *Engineer*
Harrison Thompson, *Marketing Staff*
EMP: 40
SALES: 191.6K
SALES (corp-wide): 14.8B **Privately Held**
SIC: 1321 1382 Natural gasoline produc-
tion; oil & gas exploration services
PA: Husky Energy Inc
707 8 Ave Sw
Calgary AB T2P 1
403 298-6111

(G-10251)
HYLANT GROUP INC
Also Called: Hylant Group of Columbus
565 Metro Pl S Ste 450 (43017-5386)
PHONE...................................614 932-1200
Craig Markos, *Manager*
EMP: 30
SALES (corp-wide): 129.8MM **Privately
Held**
WEB: www.hylant.com
SIC: 6411 Insurance agents
PA: Hylant Group, Inc.
811 Madison Ave Fl 11
Toledo OH 43604
419 255-1020

(G-10252)
HYLANT-MACLEAN INC
Also Called: Hylant Group
565 Metro Pl S Ste 450 (43017-5386)
PHONE...................................614 932-1200
Craig Markos, *President*
Steve Federer, *Vice Pres*
EMP: 43
SALES (est): 1.4MM **Privately Held**
SIC: 6411 Insurance agents

(G-10253)
IGS SOLAR LLC
6100 Emerald Pkwy (43016-3248)
PHONE...................................844 447-7652
Scott H White, *President*
EMP: 31 EST: 2014
SALES (est): 11.4MM **Privately Held**
SIC: 4911 Electric services

(G-10254)
INDECON SOLUTIONS LLC
655 Metro Pl S Ste 740 (43017-3356)
PHONE...................................614 799-1850
Edward Haas, *Manager*
EMP: 50
SALES (corp-wide): 46.7MM **Privately
Held**
WEB: www.indeconinc.com
SIC: 7371 7379 8748 Custom computer
programming services; data processing
consultant; systems engineering consult-
ant, ex. computer or professional
HQ: Indecon Solutions, Llc
115 W Washington St 1310s
Indianapolis IN 46204
317 634-9482

(G-10255)
INFOVERITY INC
5131 Post Rd Ste 220 (43017-2194)
PHONE...................................614 310-1709

G
E
O
G
R
A
P
H
I
C

Alison Minaglia, *Marketing Staff*
Mike Luthman, *Manager*
Nic Prellwitz, *Manager*
Turner Engle, *Consultant*
Justin Zaayer, *Consultant*
EMP: 40
SQ FT: 2,500
SALES: 1MM **Privately Held**
SIC: 8748 Business consulting

(G-10256)
INFOVISION 21 INC
6077 Frantz Rd Ste 105 (43017-3373)
PHONE...................614 761-8844
Bapaiah Koneru, *President*
EMP: 44 **EST:** 1996
SQ FT: 2,500
SALES: 5MM **Privately Held**
WEB: www.infovision21.com
SIC: 7374 7371 7379 Data processing &
preparation; computer software develop-
ment; computer related consulting serv-
ices

(G-10257)
**INTEGRA
CNCINNATI/COLUMBUS INC**
Also Called: Dublin
6241 Riverside Dr (43017-5068)
PHONE...................614 764-8040
Bruce Daubner, *President*
Gary Wright, *Director*
EMP: 30
SALES (est): 1.6MM **Privately Held**
SIC: 6531 Real estate agents & managers

(G-10258)
**INTERSTATE GAS SUPPLY INC
(PA)**
6100 Emerald Pkwy (43016-3248)
P.O. Box 9060 (43017-0960)
PHONE...................614 659-5000
Scott White, *President*
Jim Baich, *COO*
Doug Austin, *Exec VP*
Barb C Dodge, *Opers Staff*
Kerry Dlugosz, *Accountant*
EMP: 87
SQ FT: 100,000
SALES: 1.4B **Privately Held**
WEB: www.igsenergy.com
SIC: 1311 Natural gas production

(G-10259)
**JACKSON I-94 LTD
PARTNERSHIP**
Also Called: Rodeway Inn
6059 Frantz Rd Ste 205 (43017-3368)
PHONE...................614 793-2244
Earl Blinn, *Owner*
Castrop Wolfe, *General Ptnr*
EMP: 28
SQ FT: 2,400
SALES (est): 323K **Privately Held**
SIC: 7011 5812 Hotels & motels; eating
places

(G-10260)
**JOHNSON CNTRLS SEC
SLTIONS LLC**
6175 Shamrock Ct Ste S (43016-1224)
PHONE...................561 988-3600
Taylor Youtzy, *Manager*
EMP: 134 **Privately Held**
WEB: www.adt.com
SIC: 7382 Burglar alarm maintenance &
monitoring; fire alarm maintenance &
monitoring
HQ: Johnson Controls Security Solutions
Llc
6600 Congress Ave
Boca Raton FL 33487
561 264-2071

(G-10261)
JOHNSON CONTROLS
6175 Shamrock Ct Ste S (43016-1224)
PHONE...................614 717-9079
Mike Skunza, *Sales/Mktg Mgr*
EMP: 99 **Privately Held**
WEB: www.simplexgrinnell.com
SIC: 1711 Fire sprinkler system installation

HQ: Johnson Controls Fire Protection Lp
6600 Congress Ave
Boca Raton FL 33487
561 988-7200

(G-10262)
JUNIPER NETWORKS INC
545 Metro Pl S Ste 164 (43017-5316)
PHONE...................614 932-1432
Mike Isler, *Manager*
EMP: 72 **Publicly Held**
WEB: www.juniper.net
SIC: 7373 7372 Local area network (LAN)
systems integrator; prepackaged software
PA: Juniper Networks, Inc.
1133 Innovation Way
Sunnyvale CA 94089

(G-10263)
**KAPPA KAPPA GAMMA
FOUNDATION (PA)**
Also Called: Kappa Kappa Gamma Fraternity
6640 Riverside Dr Ste 200 (43017-9535)
PHONE...................614 228-6515
Maggie Sims Coons, *Exec Dir*
Joelle Folian, *Director*
Mary Wright, *Services*
EMP: 35
SALES: 6.5MM **Privately Held**
WEB: www.kappa.org
SIC: 8641 University club

(G-10264)
**KONICA MINOLTA BUSINESS
SOLUTI**
4700 Lakehurst Ct Ste 225 (43016-2255)
PHONE...................614 766-7800
Stan Dick, *Principal*
Rebecca Huston, *Project Mgr*
John Horn, *Accounts Exec*
Mark Matthews, *Accounts Exec*
Daniel Browning, *Manager*
EMP: 25
SALES (corp-wide): 9.6B **Privately Held**
WEB: www.konicabt.com
SIC: 5044 Photocopy machines
HQ: Konica Minolta Business Solutions
U.S.A., Inc.
100 Williams Dr
Ramsey NJ 07446
201 825-4000

(G-10265)
L JC HOME CARE LLC
Also Called: Firstlght HM Care Dblin Hliard
6543 Commerce Pkwy Ste D (43017-5299)
PHONE...................614 495-0276
Marianne E Christman, *Mng Member*
Lyndon Christman,
EMP: 95 **EST:** 2015
SALES (est): 103.1K **Privately Held**
SIC: 8059 Personal care home, with health
care

(G-10266)
**L&T TECHNOLOGY SERVICES
LTD**
5550 Blazer Pkwy Ste 125 (43017-3482)
PHONE...................732 688-4402
Feroz Reza, *Manager*
EMP: 50
SALES (corp-wide): 544K **Privately Held**
SIC: 8711 Acoustical engineering
PA: L&T Technology Services Limited
5th, Floor, West Block-li, L&T Knowl-
edge City (It/Ites) Sez
Vadodara GJ 39001
265 670-5000

(G-10267)
**LABORATORY CORPORATION
AMERICA**
5920 Wilcox Pl Ste F (43016-6802)
PHONE...................614 336-3993
Pam Oliver, *Branch Mgr*
Rick Chastain, *Manager*
Steve Beachy, *Maintence Staff*
EMP: 608
SQ FT: 82,000 **Publicly Held**
WEB: www.labcorp.com
SIC: 8071 8731 Testing laboratories; com-
mercial physical research

HQ: Laboratory Corporation Of America
358 S Main St Ste 458
Burlington NC 27215
336 229-1127

(G-10268)
LEADING EDJE LLC
5555 Perimeter Dr Ste 101 (43017-3219)
PHONE...................614 636-3353
Erica Krumlaus, *Branch Mgr*
EMP: 49
SALES (corp-wide): 8.2MM **Privately
Held**
SIC: 7379 Computer related consulting
services
PA: Leading Edje Llc
1491 Polaris Pkwy Ste 191
Columbus OH 43240
614 636-3353

(G-10269)
LEE & ASSOCIATES INC
Also Called: Lee & Associates - Columbus
5100 Prkcnter Ave Ste 100 (43017)
PHONE...................614 923-3300
Tim Kelton, *Principal*
EMP: 32 **Privately Held**
SIC: 6531 Real estate brokers & agents
PA: Lee & Associates Inc.
3200 E Camelback Rd # 100
Phoenix AZ 85018

(G-10270)
**LIBERTY VLG SENIOR
COMMUNITIES**
Also Called: Liberty Village Manor
4248 Tuller Rd Ste 201 (43017-5025)
PHONE...................614 889-5002
John M Haemmerle, *President*
EMP: 40
SALES (est): 558.8K **Privately Held**
SIC: 8059 Personal care home, with health
care

(G-10271)
LIFE TIME FITNESS INC
3825 Hard Rd (43016-8335)
PHONE...................952 229-7158
Rob Zwelling, *Principal*
EMP: 132
SALES (corp-wide): 773.5MM **Privately
Held**
SIC: 7991 Health club
HQ: Life Time, Inc.
2902 Corporate Pl
Chanhassen MN 55317

(G-10272)
LIGHTWELL INC (PA)
565 Metro Pl S Ste 220 (43017-5380)
PHONE...................614 310-2700
Michelle Abreu, *Ch of Bd*
Michelle Kerr, *Chairman*
Dennis Murphy, *Sales Staff*
Brian Klein, *Consultant*
Joe Spinosi, *Consultant*
EMP: 51
SQ FT: 7,500
SALES (est): 18.5MM **Privately Held**
WEB: www.oxford-consulting.com
SIC: 7379 ; computer related consulting
services

(G-10273)
LODGING FIRST LLC
94 N High St Ste 250 (43017-1110)
PHONE...................614 792-2770
Scott Somerville,
Jim Burkett,
Jim Petrone,
EMP: 50
SALES (est): 1MM **Privately Held**
WEB: www.flghospitality.com
SIC: 7021 Rooming & boarding houses

(G-10274)
LOGIC SOFT INC
Also Called: Www.logicsoftusa.com
5900 Sawmill Rd Ste 200 (43017-2588)
PHONE...................614 884-5544
Ketan Shah, *CEO*
Satish Barapatre, *President*
Harish Kukreja, *Exec VP*
EMP: 55
SQ FT: 3,000

SALES (est): 9.3MM **Privately Held**
SIC: 7371 Computer software systems
analysis & design, custom

(G-10275)
LOWES HOME CENTERS LLC
6555 Dublin Center Dr (43017-5016)
PHONE...................614 659-0530
Shane Thompson, *Manager*
EMP: 150
SALES (corp-wide): 68.6B **Publicly Held**
SIC: 5211 5031 5722 5064 Home cen-
ters; building materials, exterior; building
materials, interior; household appliance
stores; electrical appliances, television &
radio
HQ: Lowe's Home Centers, Llc
1605 Curtis Bridge Rd
Wilkesboro NC 28697
336 658-4000

(G-10276)
**MEDCO HEALTH SOLUTIONS
INC**
Also Called: Express Script
5151 Blazer Pkwy Ste B (43017-5405)
PHONE...................614 822-2000
William Kelly, *Manager*
Carolyn Weber, *Manager*
Amy Aldighere, *Director*
Edward Grix, *Director*
Christopher Mulier, *Director*
EMP: 800
SALES (corp-wide): 141.6B **Publicly
Held**
WEB: www.merck-medco.com
SIC: 5961 8742 Pharmaceuticals, mail
order; management consulting services
HQ: Medco Health Solutions, Inc.
100 Parsons Pond Dr
Franklin Lakes NJ 07417
201 269-3400

(G-10277)
**MEEDER ASSET MANAGEMENT
INC**
6125 Memor Dr (43017)
P.O. Box 7177 (43017-0777)
PHONE...................614 760-2112
Robert S Meeder Jr, *President*
Donald F Meeder, *Vice Pres*
EMP: 58
SQ FT: 10,000
SALES (est): 6.1MM **Privately Held**
WEB: www.meederadvisoryservices.com
SIC: 6282 Investment counselors

(G-10278)
**MERRILL LYNCH PIERCE
FENNER**
555 Metro Pl N Ste 550 (43017-5303)
PHONE...................614 798-4354
Robert Bishop, *Vice Pres*
David Morosky, *Manager*
Kimbrely Clellan, *Executive*
EMP: 25
SALES (corp-wide): 110.5B **Publicly
Held**
WEB: www.merlyn.com
SIC: 6211 Brokers, security
HQ: Merrill Lynch, Pierce, Fenner & Smith
Incorporated
111 8th Ave
New York NY 10011
800 637-7455

(G-10279)
METROPOLITAN LIFE INSUR CO
Also Called: MetLife
5600 Blazer Pkwy Ste 100 (43017-7525)
PHONE...................614 792-1463
EMP: 100
SALES (corp-wide): 62.3B **Publicly Held**
SIC: 6411 Ins Agnts And Brkrs
HQ: Metropolitan Life Insurance Company
(Inc)
501 Us Highway 22
Bridgewater NJ 08807
908 253-1000

(G-10280)
MICROMAN INC (PA)
Also Called: Telephony & Data Solutions
4393 Tuller Rd Ste A (43017-5106)
PHONE...................614 923-8000

Gina Hill, *General Mgr*
Bradford Mandell, *COO*
Frank Roberto, *Project Mgr*
Patty Baird, *Accounts Mgr*
Nikolay Kolev, *Sales Engr*
EMP: 42
SQ FT: 23,873
SALES: 15.8MM **Privately Held**
WEB: www.tel-dat.com
SIC: 7373 5734 Computer integrated systems design; computer peripheral equipment

(G-10281)
MITSUBSHI INTL FD INGRDNTS INC (DH)
5080 Tuttle Crossing Blvd (43016-3540)
PHONE 614 652-1111
Koji Shimizu, *President*
Gerry McKiernan, *Chairman*
Montgomery Emmanuel, *CFO*
Tonya Mast, *Accounts Mgr*
Patrick Leo, *Sales Staff*
▲ **EMP:** 35
SQ FT: 10,800
SALES (est): 121.5MM
SALES (corp-wide): 71B **Privately Held**
SIC: 5169 5122 Food additives & preservatives; vitamins & minerals
HQ: Mitsubishi Corporation (Americas)
655 3rd Ave
New York NY 10017
212 605-2000

(G-10282)
MORGAN STANLEY & CO LLC
545 Metro Pl S Ste 300 (43017-3385)
PHONE 614 798-3100
Michael Zid, *Branch Mgr*
EMP: 35
SALES (corp-wide): 40.1B **Publicly Held**
WEB: www.msvp.com
SIC: 6211 Security brokers & dealers
HQ: Morgan Stanley & Co. Llc
1585 Broadway
New York NY 10036
212 761-4000

(G-10283)
MUIRFIELD ASSOCIATION INC
8372 Muirfield Dr (43017-8590)
PHONE 614 889-0922
Warren Fishman, *President*
EMP: 30
SQ FT: 2,500
SALES (est): 1.1MM **Privately Held**
WEB: www.muirfieldassociation.com
SIC: 8641 Homeowners' association

(G-10284)
MUIRFIELD VILLAGE GOLF CLUB
Also Called: Memorial Tournament, The
5750 Memorial Dr (43017-9742)
PHONE 614 889-6700
Jack Nicklaus, *President*
Nicholas La Rocca, *General Mgr*
Kevin Kennebeck, *COO*
John G Hines, *Vice Pres*
John Jankovic, *CFO*
EMP: 50 **EST:** 1972
SQ FT: 40,000
SALES (est): 10.2MM **Privately Held**
WEB: www.muirfieldvillagegolfclub.com
SIC: 7997 Golf club, membership; country club, membership

(G-10285)
NATIONAL ADMINISTATIVE SVC LLC
400 Metro Pl N Ste 360 (43017-3318)
PHONE 614 358-3607
Haytham Elzayn,
EMP: 25
SQ FT: 10,000
SALES (est): 1.3MM **Privately Held**
SIC: 8742 Administrative services consultant

(G-10286)
NATIONAL CITY MORTGAGE
545 Metro Pl S Ste 100 (43017-5353)
PHONE 614 401-5030
George Maloof, *Vice Pres*
EMP: 32

SALES (est): 2.2MM **Privately Held**
SIC: 6021 National commercial banks

(G-10287)
NATIONWIDE RTRMNT SLTIONS INC (DH)
5900 Parkwood Pl (43016-1216)
P.O. Box 182171, Columbus (43218-2171)
PHONE 614 854-8300
Duane Meek, *President*
Chris Cole, *Manager*
Mark Farrell, *Agent*
EMP: 125
SQ FT: 7,000
SALES (est): 35.1MM
SALES (corp-wide): 13.2B **Privately Held**
WEB: www.pebscomo.com
SIC: 6371 8748 8742 6411 Pension funds; employee programs administration; management consulting services; insurance agents, brokers & service
HQ: Nationwide Corporation
1 Nationwide Plz
Columbus OH 43215
614 249-7111

(G-10288)
NESTLE USA INC
Also Called: Nestle Quality Assurance Ctr
6625 Eiterman Rd (43016-8727)
PHONE 614 526-5300
Les Smoot, *Manager*
EMP: 85
SALES (corp-wide): 90.8B **Privately Held**
WEB: www.nestleusa.com
SIC: 8734 Food testing service
HQ: Nestle Usa, Inc.
1812 N Moore St
Rosslyn VA 22209
818 549-6000

(G-10289)
NETWAVE CORPORATION
5910 Wilcox Pl Ste F (43016-6801)
PHONE 614 850-6300
Steve Hoffman, *President*
Mark Goodson, *Vice Pres*
EMP: 26
SQ FT: 13,000
SALES (est): 4.5MM **Privately Held**
WEB: www.netwavecorp.com
SIC: 7379 5045 Computer related consulting services; computers, peripherals & software

(G-10290)
NFGM INC
6465 Reflections Dr # 240 (43017-2355)
PHONE 800 236-2600
EMP: 89 **Privately Held**
SIC: 6162 Mortgage Banker/Correspondent
PA: Nfgm, Inc.
1801 Park 270 Dr Ste 240
Saint Louis MO 63146

(G-10291)
NIGHTINGALE HOME HEALTHCARE
Also Called: Aspire Home Healthcare of Ohio
5945 Wilcox Pl Ste C (43016-8713)
PHONE 614 408-0104
Dev A Brar MD, *Owner*
EMP: 38 **Privately Held**
SIC: 8082 Home health care services
PA: Nightingale Home Healthcare Inc
1036 S Rangeline Rd
Carmel IN 46032

(G-10292)
NORTHWODS CNSLTING PRTNERS INC
Also Called: Cabin In The Wood
5815 Wall St (43017-3264)
PHONE 614 781-7800
Gary Heinze, *President*
David Michael George, *President*
Chris Carlson, *COO*
Jon Petersen, *Vice Pres*
Gary Alan Heinze, *CFO*
EMP: 118
SQ FT: 4,000

SALES (est): 20.3MM **Privately Held**
WEB: www.teamnorthwoods.com
SIC: 7371 Computer software development

(G-10293)
NRT COMMERCIAL UTAH LLC
Also Called: Coldwell Banker
4535 W Dblin Granville Rd (43017-2081)
PHONE 614 889-0808
Sheri Cook, *President*
Jerry W White, *Exec VP*
Jill Siddle, *Sales Staff*
Susan Berg, *Sales Associate*
Shari Weber, *Sales Associate*
EMP: 28 **Publicly Held**
WEB: www.nrtinc.com
SIC: 6531 Real estate agent, residential
HQ: Nrt Commercial Utah Llc
175 Park Ave
Madison NJ 07940

(G-10294)
OAKLAND PK CNSERVATION CLB INC
3138 Strathaven Ct (43017-1913)
PHONE 614 989-8739
Steve Hiser, *Trustee*
Charles Hooker, *Treasurer*
EMP: 56
SALES (est): 69.1K **Privately Held**
SIC: 7997 Membership sports & recreation clubs

(G-10295)
OCLC INC (PA)
6565 Kilgour Pl (43017-3395)
PHONE 614 764-6000
David A Prichard, *President*
Pat Ring, *Principal*
Antonio Jose A Santana, *Regional Mgr*
William J Rozek, *Vice Pres*
Julie Presas, *General Counsel*
EMP: 860
SQ FT: 350,000
SALES (est): 208.3MM **Privately Held**
WEB: www.purl.com
SIC: 7375 On-line data base information retrieval

(G-10296)
OHIO ACADEMY OF SCIENCE
5930 Wilcox Pl Ste F (43016-6804)
P.O. Box 12519, Columbus (43212-0519)
PHONE 614 488-2228
Stephen McConoughey, *CEO*
Dr Richard Janson, *President*
Lynn Elfner, *Exec Dir*
Jaimie Crawford, *Administration*
EMP: 25 **EST:** 1891
SQ FT: 1,200
SALES: 1.7MM **Privately Held**
WEB: www.heartlandscience.org
SIC: 8211 8699 Academy; charitable organization

(G-10297)
OHIO HEALTHCARE FEDERAL CR UN (PA)
3955 W Dblin Granville Rd (43017-1435)
PHONE 614 737-6034
Christy Oconnell, *President*
EMP: 31
SALES (est): 3.6MM **Privately Held**
SIC: 6061 Federal credit unions

(G-10298)
OHIO STATE MEDICAL ASSOCIATION (PA)
Also Called: OSMA
5115 Prkcnter Ave Ste 200 (43017)
PHONE 614 527-6762
Richard R Ellison, *President*
Brent Mulgrew, *Exec Dir*
Krista Hazen, *Director*
Tim Maglione, *Director*
Rae Schnuerer, *Director*
EMP: 53 **EST:** 1904
SQ FT: 35,000
SALES: 6MM **Privately Held**
WEB: www.osma.org
SIC: 8621 Medical field-related associations

(G-10299)
OHIOHEALTH CORPORATION
Also Called: Dublin Methodist Hospital
7500 Hospital Dr (43016-8518)
PHONE 614 544-8000
Cheryl Herbert, *President*
Paul Duncan, *Manager*
Julie Wolfe, *Technology*
EMP: 500
SALES (corp-wide): 4B **Privately Held**
WEB: www.ohiohealth.com
SIC: 8062 General medical & surgical hospitals
PA: Ohiohealth Corporation
180 E Broad St
Columbus OH 43215
614 788-8860

(G-10300)
ORTHOPAEDIC & SPINE CENTER AT
6810 Perimeter Dr 200a (43016-8013)
PHONE 614 468-0300
Angelo Lamatrice, *Principal*
Maribel Gamble, *Practice Mgr*
Heather Gore,
Pamela Eckel, *Administration*
EMP: 28
SALES (est): 3.5MM **Privately Held**
WEB:
www.orthopaedicandspinecenter.com
SIC: 8011 Orthopedic physician

(G-10301)
OSU INTERNAL MEDICINE LLC (PA)
3900 Stoneridge Ln Ste B (43017-2289)
PHONE 614 293-0080
Earnest Mazzaferri MD, *President*
Earl Metz MD, *Vice Pres*
John Fromkes MD, *Treasurer*
Theresa Berner, *Senior Mgr*
Mark Barnhart,
EMP: 55
SQ FT: 17,500
SALES (est): 11.2MM **Privately Held**
SIC: 8741 Business management

(G-10302)
OXFORD BLAZER COMPANY INC
5700 Blazer Pkwy Ste B (43017-3665)
PHONE 614 792-2220
Rochelle Kiner, *Principal*
Christopher Black, *Principal*
EMP: 26
SQ FT: 85,263
SALES (est): 1.3MM **Privately Held**
SIC: 8351 6324 Preschool center; health maintenance organization (HMO), insurance only

(G-10303)
PACE ANALYTICAL SERVICES INC
4860 Blazer Pkwy (43017-3302)
PHONE 614 486-5421
Harry M Borg, *General Mgr*
EMP: 35
SALES (corp-wide): 65.2MM **Privately Held**
SIC: 8734 Testing laboratories
HQ: Pace Analytical Services, Llc
1800 Elm St Se
Minneapolis MN 55414

(G-10304)
PARALLEL TECHNOLOGIES INC
4868 Blazer Pkwy (43017-3302)
PHONE 614 798-9700
Joseph Redman, *President*
Martin B Jacobs, *Senior VP*
Jamie Baird, *Sales Executive*
Sarah Redman, *Executive*
EMP: 80
SQ FT: 8,500
SALES (est): 15.9MM **Privately Held**
WEB: www.paralleltech.com
SIC: 1623 7372 Telephone & communication line construction; business oriented computer software
PA: R C I Communications Inc
4868 Blazer Pkwy
Dublin OH

(G-10305)
PARKS DRILLING COMPANY (PA)
5745 Avery Rd (43016-8756)
PHONE...................................614 761-7707
Jim Parks, *CEO*
Danel Duff, *President*
Ronnie Golfman, *Superintendent*
David Bhornbeck, *Principal*
Trent Southworth, *Vice Pres*
EMP: 25 EST: 1971
SQ FT: 8,000
SALES (est): 7.5MM **Privately Held**
SIC: 1629 Caisson drilling

(G-10306)
PAYCHEX INC
5080 Tuttle Crossing Blvd # 450
(43016-3500)
PHONE...................................614 210-0400
Scott Muenzer, *Manager*
EMP: 83
SALES (corp-wide): 3.3B **Publicly Held**
WEB: www.paychex.com
SIC: 8721 Payroll accounting service
PA: Paychex, Inc.
    911 Panorama Trl S
    Rochester NY 14625
    585 385-6666

(G-10307)
PEPPER CNSTR CO OHIO LLC
495 Metro Pl S Ste 350 (43017-5399)
PHONE...................................614 793-4477
Paul Francois, *President*
Christopher Averill, *Exec VP*
J D Pepper, *Manager*
EMP: 40
SALES: 84.6MM
SALES (corp-wide): 1.1B **Privately Held**
SIC: 1542 1541 Commercial & office build-
ing, new construction; industrial buildings
& warehouses
HQ: Pepper Construction Group, Llc
    643 N Orleans St
    Chicago IL 60654
    312 266-4700

(G-10308)
PERIO INC (PA)
Also Called: Franklin Dental Manufacturing
6156 Wilcox Rd (43016-1265)
PHONE...................................614 791-1207
Tom Murray, *CEO*
Melanie Murray, *Corp Secy*
Don Buckingham, *Vice Pres*
John Price, *Vice Pres*
Chad Beining, *Accountant*
◆ EMP: 37
SQ FT: 14,000
SALES (est): 18.9MM **Privately Held**
WEB: www.barbasol.com
SIC: 5047 5087 8052 Dentists' profes-
sional supplies; beauty parlor equipment
& supplies; personal care facility

(G-10309)
POPPER & ASSOCIATES MSRP LLC
7153 Timberview Dr (43017-1017)
PHONE...................................614 798-8991
EMP: 50
SALES (est): 1.6MM **Privately Held**
SIC: 7331 7389 Direct Mail Advertising
Services Business Services At Non-Com-
mercial Site

(G-10310)
PRESIDIO INFRASTRUCTURE
5025 Bradenton Ave Ste B (43017-3506)
PHONE...................................614 381-1400
David Mowery, *Project Mgr*
Nicholas Thompson, *Engineer*
Michael Woltz, *Engineer*
Andrew Montes, *Mktg Coord*
Tom Montes, *Branch Mgr*
EMP: 36
SALES (corp-wide): 1.1B **Publicly Held**
SIC: 7373 Computer integrated systems
design
HQ: Presidio Infrastructure Solutions Llc
    6355 E Paris Ave Se
    Caledonia MI 49316
    616 871-1500

(G-10311)
PRIMARY CARE NURSING SERVICES
3140 Lilly Mar Ct (43017-5075)
PHONE...................................614 764-0960
Susan M Sharpe, *President*
Adrienne Beaty,
EMP: 52
SALES (est): 1.6MM **Privately Held**
WEB: www.pcnsohio.com
SIC: 8082 8011 Visiting nurse service; of-
fices & clinics of medical doctors

(G-10312)
PRIMERO HOME LOANS LLC
4725 Lakehurst Ct Ste 400 (43016-2251)
PHONE...................................877 959-2921
Robert Griffith, *CEO*
Brian Folwarezy, *Exec VP*
EMP: 80
SQ FT: 240,000
SALES: 20MM **Privately Held**
WEB: www.fearonfinancial.com
SIC: 6162 Mortgage bankers

(G-10313)
PSI SUPPLY CHAIN SOLUTIONS LLC
5050 Bradenton Ave (43017-3520)
P.O. Box 130 (43017-0130)
PHONE...................................614 389-4717
Stuart A Bishop, *Ch of Bd*
Michael P McCarrell, *President*
EMP: 25
SALES (est): 291.7K
SALES (corp-wide): 76.9MM **Privately
Held**
SIC: 8742 Hospital & health services con-
sultant
HQ: Pharmacy Systems, Inc.
    5050 Bradenton Ave
    Dublin OH
    614 766-0101

(G-10314)
QUALITY SUPPLY CHAIN CO-OP INC
1 Dave Thomas Blvd (43017-5452)
PHONE...................................614 764-3124
John Inwright, *President*
Ed Medlock, *Senior VP*
Amy Bertke, *Vice Pres*
Lorraine Green, *Vice Pres*
David Kourie, *Vice Pres*
EMP: 40
SALES (est): 5.1MM **Privately Held**
SIC: 8741 Business management

(G-10315)
QUEST SOFTWARE INC
Aeilita Div
6500 Emerald Pkwy Ste 400 (43016-6234)
PHONE...................................614 336-9223
Adam Hall, *Regl Sales Mgr*
Renee Chambers, *Sales Associate*
Ratmir Timashev, *Manager*
Erwin Bovens, *Manager*
Kelly Hardy, *Manager*
EMP: 70
SALES (corp-wide): 1.8B **Privately Held**
WEB: www.quest.com
SIC: 7372 Prepackaged software
HQ: Quest Software, Inc.
    4 Polaris Way
    Aliso Viejo CA 92656
    949 754-8000

(G-10316)
QWEST CORPORATION
4650 Lakehurst Ct Ste 100 (43016-3254)
PHONE...................................614 793-9258
Tom Wynne, *Branch Mgr*
EMP: 59
SALES (corp-wide): 23.4B **Publicly Held**
SIC: 4813 Telephone communication, ex-
cept radio
HQ: Qwest Corporation
    100 Centurylink Dr
    Monroe LA 71203
    318 388-9000

(G-10317)
RACAZA INTERNATIONAL LLC
555 N Metro Pls Ste 245 (43017)
PHONE...................................614 973-9266

Dyna Bala, *Principal*
Ila Mistry, *Principal*
Siva Bala, *Director*
EMP: 45 EST: 2010
SALES (est): 1.8MM **Privately Held**
SIC: 8711 Engineering services

(G-10318)
RANDALL MORTGAGE SERVICES (PA)
655 Metro Pl S Ste 600 (43017-3394)
PHONE...................................614 336-7948
Robert R Shepherd, *President*
Eric D Anderson, *Assistant VP*
Thomas A Clarkson, *Vice Pres*
EMP: 123
SALES (est): 18.1MM **Privately Held**
SIC: 6163 Mortgage brokers arranging for
loans, using money of others

(G-10319)
REA & ASSOCIATES INC
Also Called: Beall Rose Crtif Pub Accntants
5775 Perimeter Dr Ste 200 (43017-3224)
PHONE...................................614 889-8725
Leman G Beall, *Branch Mgr*
Andrea McLane, *Manager*
Chris Liebtag, *Director*
EMP: 33
SALES (corp-wide): 32.3MM **Privately
Held**
WEB: www.reacpa.com
SIC: 8721 Certified public accountant
PA: Rea & Associates, Inc.
    419 W High Ave
    New Philadelphia OH 44663
    330 339-6651

(G-10320)
REAL PROPERTY MANAGEMENT INC (PA)
5550 Blazer Pkwy Ste 175 (43017-3495)
PHONE...................................614 766-6500
Matt Steele, *President*
EMP: 36
SQ FT: 10,000
SALES (est): 7.5MM **Privately Held**
WEB: www.rpmanagement.com
SIC: 6531 8721 Real estate managers;
billing & bookkeeping service

(G-10321)
RESTAURANT FINANCE CORPORATION
4288 W Dblin Granville Rd (43017-1442)
PHONE...................................614 764-3100
Jack Schuessler, *CEO*
Gordon F Teeter, *Ch of Bd*
Frederick Reed, *CFO*
EMP: 100
SALES (est): 3.5MM
SALES (corp-wide): 1.5B **Publicly Held**
SIC: 7389 Financial services
HQ: Wendy's International, Llc
    1 Dave Thomas Blvd
    Dublin OH 43017

(G-10322)
RICH CRITES & DITTMER LLC
6400 Rverside Dr Ste D100 (43017)
PHONE...................................614 228-5822
Jeffrey A Rich,
Karol L Fox,
Mark H Gillis,
D Michael Crites,
Jeffrey A Dittmer,
EMP: 25
SQ FT: 7,700
SALES (est): 1.5MM **Privately Held**
WEB: www.richcrites.com
SIC: 8111 General practice attorney,
lawyer

(G-10323)
RIVERSIDE DRV ANIMAL CARE CTR
6924 Riverside Dr (43017-9519)
PHONE...................................614 414-2668
Becky Marsh, *Practice Mgr*
Jane Bock, *Administration*
David Abvp,
EMP: 50

SALES (est): 1.9MM **Privately Held**
SIC: 0742 Veterinarian, animal specialties;
animal hospital services, pets & other animal specialties

(G-10324)
ROBERT HALF INTERNATIONAL INC
Also Called: Officeteam
5550 Blazer Pkwy Ste 250 (43017-3481)
PHONE...................................614 602-0505
Krista Groves, *Branch Mgr*
EMP: 92
SALES (corp-wide): 5.8B **Publicly Held**
SIC: 7361 Labor contractors (employment
agency)
PA: Robert Half International Inc.
    2884 Sand Hill Rd Ste 200
    Menlo Park CA 94025
    650 234-6000

(G-10325)
ROTO GROUP LLC (PA)
7001 Discovery Blvd Fl 2 (43017-3261)
PHONE...................................614 760-8690
Joseph Wisne, *President*
Steve Langsdorf, *Vice Pres*
Janet Hurt, *CFO*
Neil Baker,
Allen Boerger,
EMP: 80
SQ FT: 60,000
SALES (est): 8.5MM **Privately Held**
WEB: www.rotostudio.com
SIC: 7999 Exhibition operation

(G-10326)
S&ME INC
6190 Enterprise Ct (43016-3293)
PHONE...................................614 793-2226
Stephen C Pasternack, *Branch Mgr*
EMP: 76 **Privately Held**
SIC: 8711 Consulting engineer
PA: S&Me, Inc.
    2724 Discovery Dr Ste 120
    Raleigh NC 27616

(G-10327)
SANCTUARY AT TUTTLE CROSSING
4880 Tuttle Rd (43017-7566)
PHONE...................................614 408-0182
Robert Banasik, *President*
EMP: 68
SALES (est): 3.3MM **Privately Held**
SIC: 8051 Skilled nursing care facilities

(G-10328)
SARNOVA INC (PA)
5000 Tuttle Crossing Blvd (43016-1534)
P.O. Box 8023 (43016-2023)
PHONE...................................614 760-5000
Dan Connors, *CEO*
Brian Laduke, *President*
Tom Metcalf, *President*
Jon Garrity, *Vice Pres*
Kathy Cunningham, *Buyer*
EMP: 80
SALES (est): 184.4MM **Privately Held**
SIC: 5999 5047 Medical apparatus & sup-
plies; medical equipment & supplies

(G-10329)
SB HOTEL LLC (PA)
Also Called: Ramada Inn
5775 Perimeter Dr Ste 290 (43017-3224)
PHONE...................................614 793-2244
Kenneth J Castrop, *Mng Member*
William W Wolfe,
EMP: 50
SQ FT: 100,000
SALES (est): 2.1MM **Privately Held**
WEB: www.hamptoninnsouthbend.com
SIC: 7011 5812 5813 Hotels & motels;
family restaurants; cocktail lounge

(G-10330)
SEARS ROEBUCK AND CO
4975 Tuttle Crossing Blvd (43016-1531)
PHONE...................................614 760-7195
EMP: 93
SALES (corp-wide): 16.7B **Publicly Held**
SIC: 7549 Automotive Services

HQ: Sears, Roebuck And Co.
3333 Beverly Rd
Hoffman Estates IL 60179
847 286-2500

(G-10331)
SEDGWICK CMS HOLDINGS INC
6377 Emerald Pkwy (43016-3272)
PHONE................................800 825-6755
Julie Kolibash, *Sales Staff*
Robert Bossart, *Branch Mgr*
EMP: 810
SALES (corp-wide): 9.5B Privately Held
SIC: 6411 Insurance agents
PA: Sedgwick Cms Holdings, Inc.
1100 Ridgeway Loop Rd # 200
Memphis TN 38120
901 415-7400

(G-10332)
SELECT HOTELS GROUP LLC
Also Called: Hyatt Place Columbus/Dublin
6161 Parkcenter Cir (43017-4701)
PHONE................................614 799-1913
Ryan Fisher, *Branch Mgr*
EMP: 25
SALES (corp-wide): 4.4B Publicly Held
WEB: www.amerisuites.com
SIC: 7011 7991 Hotels; physical fitness facilities
HQ: Select Hotels Group, L.L.C.
71 S Wacker Dr
Chicago IL 60606
312 750-1234

(G-10333)
SHEPHERD EXCAVATING INC
6295 Cosgray Rd (43016-8737)
PHONE................................614 889-1115
Jerry Semon, *President*
Robert Toombs, *Vice Pres*
Dianne Strunkenburg, *Controller*
Lisa Davidson, *Executive*
Melissa Chapman, *Receptionist*
EMP: 90
SQ FT: 4,000
SALES (est): 10.4MM Privately Held
SIC: 1771 Foundation & footing contractor

(G-10334)
SIGNATURE INC
5115 Prkcnter Ave Ste 200 (43017)
PHONE................................614 734-0010
Don Farrell, *President*
Steve Wolever, *COO*
Jeff Scholes, *CFO*
EMP: 250
SALES (est): 27.6MM Privately Held
WEB: www.signature-training.com
SIC: 8741 Management services

(G-10335)
SIMON PROPERTY GROUP
Also Called: Tuttle Crossing Associates
5043 Tuttle Crossing Blvd (43016-1511)
PHONE................................614 717-9300
Peter Cooper, *General Mgr*
EMP: 39 EST: 1995
SALES (est): 4MM Privately Held
SIC: 6512 Shopping center, property operation only

(G-10336)
SOLENIS LLC
5200 Blazer Pkwy (43017-3309)
PHONE................................614 336-1101
EMP: 40 EST: 2014
SALES (est): 12MM Privately Held
SIC: 8742 Management Consulting Services

(G-10337)
SONESTA INTL HOTELS CORP
435 Metro Pl S (43017-5315)
PHONE................................614 791-8554
EMP: 121
SALES (corp-wide): 213.9MM Privately Held
SIC: 7011 Hotels
PA: Sonesta International Hotels Corporation
255 Washington St Ste 270
Newton MA 02458
770 923-1775

(G-10338)
SOUTHEASTERN EQUIPMENT CO INC
6390 Shier Rings Rd (43016-5204)
P.O. Box 368 (43017-0368)
PHONE................................614 889-1073
Thomas Truck, *Opers-Prdtn-Mfg*
EMP: 156
SQ FT: 12,000 Privately Held
WEB: www.southeasternequip.com
SIC: 5082 General construction machinery & equipment
PA: Southeastern Equipment Company, Inc.
10874 E Pike Rd
Cambridge OH 43725

(G-10339)
SRINSOFT INC
7243 Sawmill Rd Ste 205 (43016-5016)
PHONE................................614 893-6535
Padma Hari, *President*
EMP: 29 EST: 2010
SALES (est): 3.2MM Privately Held
SIC: 7371 Computer software development

(G-10340)
STANDLEY LAW GROUP LLP
6300 Riverside Dr (43017-5043)
PHONE................................614 792-5555
Jeff Norris, *Partner*
EMP: 26
SQ FT: 7,000
SALES: 7MM Privately Held
WEB: www.standleyllp.com
SIC: 8111 Patent, trademark & copyright law

(G-10341)
STANLEY STEEMER INTL INC (PA)
Also Called: Stanley Steemer Carpet Cleaner
5800 Innovation Dr (43016-3271)
P.O. Box 8004 (43016-2004)
PHONE................................614 764-2007
Wesley C Bates, *CEO*
Jack A Bates, *President*
Justin Bates, *President*
Ron Cochran, *General Mgr*
Anthony Eonta, *General Mgr*
▲ EMP: 250
SQ FT: 55,000
SALES: 240MM Privately Held
WEB: www.stanley-steemer.com
SIC: 7217 3635 6794 5713 Carpet & furniture cleaning on location; upholstery cleaning on customer premises; household vacuum cleaners; franchises, selling or licensing; carpets

(G-10342)
STANLEY STEEMER INTL INC
Also Called: Stanley Steemer Carpet Clr 05
5500 Stanley Steemer Pkwy (43016-1210)
PHONE................................614 652-2241
Jeff Opencar, *General Mgr*
Eric Ford, *District Mgr*
Arnold Nunez, *Business Mgr*
Ralph Melvin, *Mfg Dir*
Warren Cousin, *Opers Mgr*
EMP: 50
SALES (corp-wide): 240MM Privately Held
WEB: www.stanley-steemer.com
SIC: 7217 Carpet & furniture cleaning on location
PA: Stanley Steemer International, Inc.
5800 Innovation Dr
Dublin OH 43016
614 764-2007

(G-10343)
STRATEGIC SYSTEMS INC
485 Metro Pl S Ste 270 (43017-7325)
PHONE................................614 717-4774
Jyothsna Vadada, *CEO*
Sankar Mangapuram, *CFO*
EMP: 116
SQ FT: 1,200
SALES (est): 17.4MM Privately Held
WEB: www.strategicsystems.com
SIC: 7379

(G-10344)
SUNNY DAY ACADEMY LLC (PA)
Also Called: SDA
255 Bradenton Ave (43017-2546)
PHONE................................614 718-1717
Sara Miller, *Mng Member*
EMP: 25 EST: 2010
SALES (est): 707.4K Privately Held
SIC: 8351 Group day care center

(G-10345)
SUNRISE SENIOR LIVING LLC
Also Called: Sunrise of Dublin
4175 Stoneridge Ln (43017-2080)
PHONE................................614 718-2062
EMP: 49
SALES (corp-wide): 4.7B Publicly Held
WEB: www.sunrise.com
SIC: 8361 Home for the aged
HQ: Sunrise Senior Living, Llc
7902 Westpark Dr
Mc Lean VA 22102

(G-10346)
SUPPORTCARE INC (PA)
Also Called: Supportcare Ohio
525 Metro Pl N Ste 350 (43017-5451)
PHONE................................614 889-5837
Richard Johnson, *President*
EMP: 35
SALES (est): 8.6MM Privately Held
SIC: 8082 Home health care services

(G-10347)
SUTPHEN CORPORATION (PA)
6450 Eiterman Rd (43016-8711)
P.O. Box 158, Amlin (43002-0158)
PHONE................................800 726-7030
Drew Sutphen, *President*
Thomas C Sutphen, *Chairman*
Julie S Phelps, *Vice Pres*
Greg Mallon, *CFO*
Robert M Sutphen, *Shareholder*
◆ EMP: 180
SQ FT: 90,000
SALES: 117.1MM Privately Held
WEB: www.sutpheneast.com
SIC: 3711 5087 Fire department vehicles (motor vehicles), assembly of; firefighting equipment

(G-10348)
SYGMA NETWORK INC
5550 Blazer Pkwy Ste 300 (43017-3478)
PHONE................................614 734-2500
Chet Minor, *Branch Mgr*
EMP: 320
SALES (corp-wide): 58.7B Publicly Held
WEB: www.sygmanetwork.com
SIC: 4225 General warehousing
HQ: The Sygma Network Inc
5550 Blazer Pkwy Ste 300
Dublin OH 43017

(G-10349)
SYGMA NETWORK INC (HQ)
5550 Blazer Pkwy Ste 300 (43017-3478)
P.O. Box 7327 (43017-0709)
PHONE................................614 734-2500
Thomas Russell, *CEO*
Steven Deasey, *President*
Bruce Harman, *President*
Mike Wren, *General Mgr*
Joseph A Sugar, *Chairman*
▲ EMP: 150
SQ FT: 30,000
SALES (est): 3.1B
SALES (corp-wide): 58.7B Publicly Held
WEB: www.sygmanetwork.com
SIC: 5149 Groceries & related products
PA: Sysco Corporation
1390 Enclave Pkwy
Houston TX 77077
281 584-1390

(G-10350)
SYNTERO INC (PA)
Also Called: DUBLIN COUNSELING CENTER
299 Cramer Creek Ct (43017-2586)
PHONE................................614 889-5722
Sharon Stine, *Manager*
Kim Vance, *Manager*
Wendy Vernon, *Info Tech Mgr*
Katherine Mihelich-Helms, *Director*
Kathleen Ritchey, *Director*

EMP: 45
SALES: 6.7MM Privately Held
WEB: www.dublincounselingcenter.org
SIC: 8093 8322 8069 Mental health clinic, outpatient; general counseling services; drug addiction rehabilitation hospital

(G-10351)
T & R PROPERTIES (PA)
Also Called: T & R Property Management
3895 Stoneridge Ln (43017-2152)
PHONE................................614 923-4000
P Ronald Sabatino, *President*
Tammy Potts, *Vice Pres*
Tamra L Potts, *CFO*
Lisa Durand, *Office Mgr*
Cathy Saporito, *Manager*
EMP: 30
SQ FT: 1,200
SALES (est): 16.4MM Privately Held
WEB: www.trprop.com
SIC: 6531 Real estate managers

(G-10352)
T-CETRA LLC
7240 Muirfield Dr Ste 200 (43017-2902)
PHONE................................877 956-2359
Amar Zedan, *President*
Steven Ascher, *Senior VP*
Olimpia Dawidowicz, *Finance*
Ghazwan Tarabishi, *VP Sales*
Tim Braskett, *Accounts Exec*
EMP: 27
SALES (est): 4MM Privately Held
SIC: 7371 Computer software development & applications

(G-10353)
TARTAN FIELDS GOLF CLUB LTD
8070 Tartan Fields Dr (43017-8780)
PHONE................................614 792-0900
Richard Burkardt, *General Mgr*
Joe Flynn, *General Mgr*
Mark Kelley, *General Mgr*
Phil Cassis, *Accountant*
Jim Russell, *Director*
EMP: 100
SALES (est): 7.1MM Privately Held
WEB: www.tartanfields.com
SIC: 7997 5941 5813 5812 Golf club, membership; sporting goods & bicycle shops; drinking places; eating places

(G-10354)
TEK SYSTEMS
5115 Prkcnter Ave Ste 170 (43017)
PHONE................................614 789-6200
Darren Yeager, *Principal*
EMP: 75
SALES (est): 228.4K Privately Held
SIC: 8742 Management information systems consultant

(G-10355)
TELECMMNCTONS STFFING SLUTIONS
Also Called: TSS Resources
8191 Glencree Pl (43016-9523)
PHONE................................614 799-9300
Ginny Berke, *President*
EMP: 25
SALES (est): 1.3MM Privately Held
SIC: 7361 Executive placement

(G-10356)
THE NATURE CONSERVANCY
Also Called: Ohio Field Office
6375 Riverside Dr Ste 100 (43017-5045)
PHONE................................614 717-2770
Marianne Gabel, *Ch of Bd*
Mark Schmaltz, *Opers Staff*
EMP: 30
SALES (corp-wide): 1.1B Privately Held
WEB: www.nature.org
SIC: 8641 Environmental protection organization
PA: The Nature Conservancy
4245 Fairfax Dr Ste 100
Arlington VA 22203
703 841-5300

(G-10357)
TRI-ANIM HEALTH SERVICES INC (HQ)
5000 Tuttle Crossing Blvd (43016-1534)
P.O. Box 8023 (43016-2023)
PHONE..............................614 760-5000
Jeff Prestel, *President*
Dale Clendon, *Principal*
Dan L Pister, *COO*
Eddie Avanessians, *CFO*
Jennifer Carter, *Credit Staff*
▲ EMP: 47
SQ FT: 38,600
SALES (est): 39.8MM **Privately Held**
WEB: www.trianim.com
SIC: 5047 Medical equipment & supplies

(G-10358)
UNITED SOFTWARE GROUP INC (PA)
565 Metro Pl S Ste 110 (43017-5380)
PHONE..............................614 791-3223
Anju Vallabhaneni, *CEO*
Susan Norton, *Vice Pres*
Aruna Vallabhaneni, *Vice Pres*
Swamy Jammula, *Accounts Mgr*
Rahul Singh, *Accounts Mgr*
EMP: 170
SQ FT: 600
SALES: 49.6MM **Privately Held**
SIC: 7379

(G-10359)
UNIVENTURE INC (PA)
Also Called: Univenture CD Packg & Systems
4266 Tuller Rd Ste 101 (43017-5007)
PHONE..............................937 645-4600
Ross O Youngs, *CEO*
Michele Cole, *President*
Larry George, *Vice Pres*
David Coho, *VP Sls/Mktg*
Jim Lowe, *Sales Mgr*
▲ EMP: 95
SQ FT: 100,000
SALES (est): 45.9MM **Privately Held**
WEB: www.univenture.com
SIC: 7389 7336 Packaging & labeling services; package design

(G-10360)
UNIVENTURE INC
4266 Tuller Rd Ste 101 (43017-5007)
PHONE..............................937 645-4600
Rick Nichols, *Manager*
EMP: 35
SALES (corp-wide): 45.9MM **Privately Held**
WEB: www.univenture.com
SIC: 7389 Packaging & labeling services
PA: Univenture, Inc.
4266 Tuller Rd Ste 101
Dublin OH 43017
937 645-4600

(G-10361)
URBAN OASSIS INC
Also Called: Spa At River Ridge Salon, The
5555 Wall St (43017-3244)
PHONE..............................614 766-9946
Peggi Fisher-Hanson, *President*
Steve Hilbert, *General Mgr*
Abbey Martini, *Mktg Dir*
Jackie Clark, *Art Dir*
Addison Owen, *Education*
EMP: 30
SALES (est): 701.7K **Privately Held**
SIC: 7231 Hairdressers

(G-10362)
VIAQUEST INC (PA)
525 Metro Pl N Ste 300 (43017-5320)
PHONE..............................614 889-5837
Richard Johnson, *President*
Janet Pell, *Admin Sec*
EMP: 38
SALES: 4.1MM **Privately Held**
WEB: www.viaquestinc.com
SIC: 8741 Business management

(G-10363)
VIAQUEST BEHAVIORAL HEALTH LLC (PA)
Also Called: Summit Quest Academy
525 Metro Pl N Ste 450 (43017-5321)
PHONE..............................614 339-0868

Richard Johnson, *President*
EMP: 33
SQ FT: 1,500
SALES (est): 8.9MM **Privately Held**
WEB: www.magcorp.com
SIC: 8082 Home health care services

(G-10364)
VIAQUEST HOME HEALTH LLC (HQ)
525 Metro Pl N (43017-5342)
PHONE..............................800 645-3267
Richard D Johnson,
EMP: 25 EST: 2005
SALES (est): 4.1MM **Privately Held**
SIC: 8059 Personal care home, with health care

(G-10365)
VIBO CONSTRUCTION INC
4140 Tuller Rd Ste 112 (43017-5013)
PHONE..............................614 210-6780
Tania Prespia, *President*
EMP: 35 EST: 2011
SQ FT: 2,500
SALES (est): 4MM **Privately Held**
SIC: 1521 Single-family housing construction

(G-10366)
VOC WORKS LTD
5555 Glendon Ct Ste 300 (43016-3302)
P.O. Box 182848, Columbus (43218-2848)
PHONE..............................614 760-3515
William Pfeiffer, *President*
L T Nichols, *Vice Pres*
Thomas R Brownlee,
EMP: 90
SALES (est): 1.6MM **Privately Held**
SIC: 8331 8741 Vocational rehabilitation agency; management services

(G-10367)
W T SPORTS INC
5288 Aryshire Dr (43017-9424)
PHONE..............................740 654-0035
Ed Thompson, *President*
EMP: 40
SQ FT: 17,000
SALES: 500K **Privately Held**
SIC: 7991 Physical fitness clubs with training equipment

(G-10368)
W W WILLIAMS COMPANY LLC (DH)
5025 Bradenton Ave # 130 (43017-3506)
PHONE..............................614 228-5000
John Simmons, *CEO*
Andy Gasser, *CFO*
Cynthia Piper, *Credit Mgr*
EMP: 60 EST: 2016
SALES (est): 219.2MM
SALES (corp-wide): 4.8B **Privately Held**
SIC: 7538 7537 Diesel engine repair: automotive; automotive transmission repair shops
HQ: Power Acquisition Llc
5025 Bradenton Ave # 130
Dublin OH 43017
614 228-5000

(G-10369)
WALGREEN CO
Also Called: Walgreens
6805 Hospital Dr (43016-8556)
PHONE..............................614 336-0431
Mike Strawser, *Manager*
EMP: 25
SALES (corp-wide): 131.5B **Publicly Held**
WEB: www.walgreens.com
SIC: 5912 7384 Drug stores; photofinishing laboratory
HQ: Walgreen Co.
200 Wilmot Rd
Deerfield IL 60015
847 315-2500

(G-10370)
WD PARTNERS INC
7007 Discovery Blvd (43017-3218)
PHONE..............................614 634-7000
Scott Hathaway, *Manager*
EMP: 35

SALES (corp-wide): 63.7MM **Privately Held**
SIC: 8712 Architectural services
PA: Wd Partners, Inc.
7007 Discovery Blvd
Dublin OH 43017
614 634-7000

(G-10371)
WEASTEC INCORPORATED
6195 Enterprise Ct (43016-3293)
PHONE..............................614 734-9645
Craig Miley, *Branch Mgr*
EMP: 42
SALES (corp-wide): 283.9MM **Privately Held**
SIC: 3711 8711 Automotive parts; engineering services
HQ: Weastec, Incorporated
1600 N High St
Hillsboro OH 45133
937 393-6800

(G-10372)
WELLS FARGO CLEARING SVCS LLC
Also Called: Wells Fargo Advisors
485 Metro Pl S Ste 300 (43017-1882)
PHONE..............................614 764-2040
Montford S Will,
Douglas Rose, *Advisor*
EMP: 25
SALES (corp-wide): 101B **Publicly Held**
WEB: www.wachoviasec.com
SIC: 6211 Stock brokers & dealers
HQ: Wells Fargo Clearing Services, Llc
1 N Jefferson Ave Fl 7
Saint Louis MO 63103
314 955-3000

(G-10373)
WELLS FARGO HOME MORTGAGE INC
485 Metro Pl S Ste 300 (43017-1882)
PHONE..............................614 781-8847
Toll Free:...........................877   -
Fax: 614 436-2744
EMP: 30
SALES (corp-wide): 90B **Publicly Held**
SIC: 6162 Mortgage Banker/Correspondent
HQ: Wells Fargo Home Mortgage Inc
1 Home Campus
Des Moines IA 50328
515 324-3707

(G-10374)
WENDYS COMPANY (PA)
1 Dave Thomas Blvd (43017-5452)
PHONE..............................614 764-3100
Nelson Peltz, *Ch of Bd*
Todd A Penegor, *President*
Erin Padula, *District Mgr*
Quinton Young, *District Mgr*
Robert D Wright, *COO*
◆ EMP: 475 EST: 1929
SQ FT: 324,025
SALES: 1.5B **Publicly Held**
WEB: www.wendysarbys.com
SIC: 5812 6794 Fast-food restaurant, chain; franchises, selling or licensing

(G-10375)
WENDYS RESTAURANTS LLC (HQ)
1 Dave Thomas Blvd (43017-5452)
PHONE..............................614 764-3100
Emil J Brolick, *President*
Emil Brolick, *President*
Steven B Graham, *Senior VP*
Todd Pengor, *CFO*
Katie Tanner, *Finance Other*
EMP: 120
SQ FT: 249,025
SALES (est): 1.2B
SALES (corp-wide): 1.5B **Publicly Held**
WEB: www.wendysarbys.com
SIC: 5812 6794 Fast-food restaurant, chain; franchises, selling or licensing
PA: The Wendy's Company
1 Dave Thomas Blvd
Dublin OH 43017
614 764-3100

(G-10376)
WINEGARDNER & HAMMONS INC
Also Called: Marriott
5605 Paul G Blzr Mmrl Pkw (43017)
PHONE..............................614 791-1000
Rich Byrd, *Manager*
EMP: 150
SALES (corp-wide): 84.3MM **Privately Held**
WEB: www.whihotels.com
SIC: 7011 Hotels & motels
PA: Req/Jqh Holdings, Inc.
4243 Hunt Rd Ste 2
Blue Ash OH 45242
513 891-1066

(G-10377)
XPO INTERMODAL INC (HQ)
5165 Emerald Pkwy 300 (43017-1063)
PHONE..............................614 923-1400
Daniel L Gardner, *CEO*
John T Hickerson, *Ch of Bd*
M Sean Fernandez, *President*
Larry Savage, *President*
Julie A Krehbiel, *Exec VP*
EMP: 80
SALES (est): 364.2MM
SALES (corp-wide): 15.3B **Publicly Held**
WEB: www.pacer-international.com
SIC: 4731 Freight transportation arrangement
PA: Xpo Logistics, Inc.
5 American Ln
Greenwich CT 06831
844 742-5976

(G-10378)
XPO INTERMODAL SOLUTIONS INC (DH)
Also Called: Pacer
5165 Emerald Pkwy (43017-1063)
PHONE..............................614 923-1400
Daniel W Avramovich, *President*
Charles Hoffman, *President*
Michael F Killea, *Exec VP*
James E Ward, *Exec VP*
Michael D Gordon, *Vice Pres*
EMP: 550
SQ FT: 107,000
SALES (est): 83MM
SALES (corp-wide): 15.3B **Publicly Held**
SIC: 4731 Agents, shipping
HQ: Xpo Intermodal, Inc.
5165 Emerald Pkwy 300
Dublin OH 43017
614 923-1400

(G-10379)
XPO STACKTRAIN LLC
Also Called: Pacer Stacktrain
5165 Emerald Pkwy (43017-1063)
PHONE..............................614 923-1400
Karen Beesinger, *Manager*
Barny Carter, *Systems Staff*
EMP: 32
SALES (corp-wide): 15.3B **Publicly Held**
WEB: www.pacerstack.com
SIC: 4731 Freight transportation arrangement
HQ: Xpo Stacktrain, Llc
5165 Emerald Pkwy
Dublin OH 43017
925 887-1400

(G-10380)
YORK RISK SERVICES GROUP INC
5555 Glendon Ct (43016-3304)
PHONE..............................866 391-9675
Layton McCallum, *Principal*
EMP: 250
SALES (corp-wide): 2.3B **Privately Held**
SIC: 6411 Insurance agents, brokers & service
HQ: York Risk Services Group, Inc.
1 Upper Pond
Parsippany NJ 07054
973 404-1200

Duncan Falls
Muskingum County

(G-10381)
DUNCAN FALLS ASSOC
Water St (43734)
PHONE..........................740 674-7105
Vernan Trout, *President*
EMP: 82
SALES (est): 2.7MM **Privately Held**
SIC: 8742 Management consulting services

Dundee
Tuscarawas County

(G-10382)
ALPINE STRUCTURES LLC
2675 Us Route 62 (44624-9235)
PHONE..........................330 359-5708
Moses Miller, *Mng Member*
Javan Miller, *Mng Member*
EMP: 25
SQ FT: 37,396
SALES (est): 5.8MM **Privately Held**
WEB: www.alpinestructures.com
SIC: 1542 Garage construction

(G-10383)
D C CURRY LUMBER COMPANY
17201 Dover Rd (44624-9445)
PHONE..........................330 264-5223
David Nally, *President*
Wayne Hochstetler, *Corp Secy*
Shayne Glass, *Controller*
EMP: 25
SQ FT: 19,600
SALES (est): 4.9MM **Privately Held**
SIC: 1522 5211 Residential construction; lumber & other building materials

Dunkirk
Hardin County

(G-10384)
BALL BOUNCE AND SPORT INC
Also Called: Diamond Plastics
211 W Geneva St (45836-1008)
PHONE..........................419 759-3838
EMP: 50
SALES (corp-wide): 148.6MM **Privately Held**
SIC: 5092 Whol Toys/Hobby Goods
PA: Ball, Bounce And Sport, Inc.
 1 Hedstrom Dr
 Ashland OH 44805
 419 759-3838

East Canton
Stark County

(G-10385)
AMERICAN LEGION
Also Called: American Legion Post 667
204 Wood St S (44730-1326)
PHONE..........................330 488-0119
Clifford F Tolston, *President*
EMP: 70
SALES (est): 373.5K **Privately Held**
SIC: 8641 Veterans' organization

(G-10386)
FTS INTERNATIONAL INC
1520 Wood Ave Se (44730-9591)
PHONE..........................330 754-2375
Richard Jelley, *Branch Mgr*
EMP: 628 **Publicly Held**
SIC: 1389 Measurement of well flow rates, oil & gas
PA: Fts International, Inc.
 777 Main St Ste 2900
 Fort Worth TX 76102

(G-10387)
KOCH KNIGHT LLC (DH)
5385 Orchardview Dr Se (44730-9568)
P.O. Box 30070 (44730-0070)
PHONE..........................330 488-1651
Mike Graeff, *President*
Mathew Phayer, *Vice Pres*
Teresa Falter, *Buyer*
Kevin Brooks,
◆ **EMP:** 80
SALES (est): 29.3MM
SALES (corp-wide): 42.4B **Privately Held**
WEB: www.kochknight.com
SIC: 2911 5172 5169 4922 Petroleum refining; petroleum products; chemicals & allied products; natural gas transmission; crude petroleum production; natural gas production; refinery, chemical processing & similar machinery
HQ: Koch-Glitsch, Lp
 4111 E 37th St N
 Wichita KS 67220
 316 828-5000

East Fultonham
Muskingum County

(G-10388)
CHESTERHILL STONE CO
Also Called: Shelly Materials
6305 Saltillo Rd (43735)
P.O. Box 28 (43735-0028)
PHONE..........................740 849-2338
Fax: 740 849-2599
EMP: 29
SALES (corp-wide): 9MM **Privately Held**
SIC: 1422 Limestone Quarry
PA: Chesterhill Stone Co
 773 E State Route 60 Ne
 Mcconnelsville OH

(G-10389)
COLUMBIA RECREATION ASSN
Also Called: Lake Isabella Recreation Assn
5960 Fourth St (43735)
P.O. Box 56 (43735-0056)
PHONE..........................740 849-2466
Alan Reed, *President*
Carl Border, *Principal*
Lou Willard, *Treasurer*
EMP: 35
SALES: 219.7K **Privately Held**
SIC: 7997 Hunting club, membership

East Liberty
Logan County

(G-10390)
CLARK TRUCKING INC (DH)
11590 Township Road 157 (43319)
PHONE..........................937 642-0335
Kaneo Meguro, *President*
John Jenkins, *Vice Pres*
Albert Wittkopp, *Vice Pres*
Edward Allison, *Treasurer*
EMP: 145 **EST:** 1954
SQ FT: 4,000
SALES (est): 13.4MM
SALES (corp-wide): 144.1B **Privately Held**
WEB: www.clarktrucking.com
SIC: 4214 4213 Local trucking with storage; contract haulers
HQ: Midwest Express Inc.
 11590 Township Road 298
 East Liberty OH 43319
 937 642-0335

(G-10391)
HONDA LOGISTICS NORTH AMER INC (DH)
11590 Township Road 298 (43319-9487)
PHONE..........................937 642-0335
Tamaki Hashimoto, *President*
Kristi Warren, *Supervisor*
EMP: 1338
SALES (est): 228.8MM
SALES (corp-wide): 144.1B **Privately Held**
SIC: 4226 Special warehousing & storage

HQ: Honda Logistics Inc.
 6, Ichibancho
 Chiyoda-Ku TKY 102-0
 353 571-041

(G-10392)
MIDWEST EXPRESS INC (DH)
11590 Township Road 298 (43319-9450)
PHONE..........................937 642-0335
Tamaki Hashimoto, *President*
Tadao Endo, *President*
Nichola Jordan, *COO*
Ed Allison, *Vice Pres*
Brian Blair, *Vice Pres*
EMP: 950
SQ FT: 1,833,902
SALES (est): 220.2MM
SALES (corp-wide): 144.1B **Privately Held**
SIC: 4226 Special warehousing & storage
HQ: Honda Logistics North America, Inc.
 11590 Township Road 298
 East Liberty OH 43319
 937 642-0335

(G-10393)
MPW INDUSTRIAL SERVICES INC
Also Called: Facility MGT & Support Svcs
11000 State Route 347 (43319-9470)
PHONE..........................937 644-0200
Duane Jolliff, *Manager*
Greg Armstrong, *Director*
EMP: 100
SALES (corp-wide): 208.7MM **Privately Held**
SIC: 7349 7363 Building Maintenance Services Help Supply Services
HQ: Mpw Industrial Services, Inc.
 9711 Lancaster Rd
 Hebron OH 43025
 800 827-8790

(G-10394)
NEX TRANSPORT INC
13900 State Route 287 (43319-9466)
PHONE..........................937 645-3761
Tosaki Watanabe, *President*
Fumio Moriyama, *President*
Toshiaki Watanabe, *President*
Tomie Mori, *Exec VP*
Teizo Kanda, *Vice Pres*
EMP: 220
SQ FT: 400,000
SALES: 39.3MM
SALES (corp-wide): 18.7B **Privately Held**
WEB: www.nextransport.com
SIC: 4226 Special warehousing & storage
HQ: Nippon Express U.S.A., Inc.
 2401 44th Rd Fl 14
 Long Island City NY 11101
 212 758-6100

East Liverpool
Columbiana County

(G-10395)
AARONS INC
16240 Dresden Ave Ste A (43920-8603)
PHONE..........................330 385-7201
Steven Harrington, *Branch Mgr*
EMP: 25
SALES (corp-wide): 3.8B **Publicly Held**
WEB: www.aaronrents.com
SIC: 7359 Home appliance, furniture & entertainment rental services
PA: Aaron's, Inc.
 400 Galleria Pkwy Se # 300
 Atlanta GA 30339
 678 402-3000

(G-10396)
ALSAN CORPORATION
Also Called: East Liverpool Motor Lodge
900 W 8th St (43920-2303)
PHONE..........................330 385-3636
Alfred C Gloeckner, *President*
EMP: 100 **EST:** 1980
SQ FT: 87,000

SALES (est): 2.7MM **Privately Held**
WEB: www.elmotorlodge.com
SIC: 5812 7011 7991 7231 Restaurant, family: independent; motels; spas; hairdressers

(G-10397)
ANKLE AND FOOT CARE CENTER (PA)
Also Called: Foot & Ankle Clinic
16844 Saint Clair Ave # 2 (43920-4278)
PHONE..........................330 385-2413
Lawrence Didomenico, *Partner*
Kenneth Emch, *Partner*
EMP: 25
SALES (est): 2.2MM **Privately Held**
SIC: 8043 Offices & clinics of podiatrists

(G-10398)
BLOSSOM HILL ELDERLY HOUSING L
100 Wilbert Ave (43920-4091)
PHONE..........................330 385-4310
Steve Boone, *Exec Dir*
EMP: 90
SALES (est): 2.4MM **Privately Held**
SIC: 6531 Real estate leasing & rentals

(G-10399)
CITY HOSPITAL ASSOCIATION
Also Called: EAST LIVERPOOL CITY HOSPITAL
425 W 5th St (43920-2405)
PHONE..........................330 385-7200
Kenneth J Cochran, *CEO*
Lee H Weisberger, *Principal*
Patrick Beaver, *Vice Pres*
Robert Blankenship, *Vice Pres*
Kyle Johnson, *Vice Pres*
EMP: 600
SQ FT: 226,660
SALES: 72.6MM **Privately Held**
SIC: 8062 General medical & surgical hospitals

(G-10400)
COMMUNITY ACTION COLUMBIANA CT
Also Called: Y M C A-Head Start
134 E 4th St (43920-3044)
PHONE..........................330 385-7251
Joyce Lapura, *Director*
EMP: 28
SALES (corp-wide): 18.4MM **Privately Held**
SIC: 7999 8641 Recreation center; youth organizations
PA: Community Action Agency Of Columbiana County, Inc.
 7880 Lincole Pl
 Lisbon OH 44432
 330 424-7221

(G-10401)
DUQUESNE LIGHT COMPANY
626 Saint Clair Ave (43920-3077)
PHONE..........................330 385-6103
EMP: 147 **Privately Held**
SIC: 4911 Electric services
HQ: Duquesne Light Company
 411 7th Ave 6-1
 Pittsburgh PA 15219
 412 393-6000

(G-10402)
EAST LIVERPOOL WATER DEPT
2220 Michigan Ave (43920-3638)
PHONE..........................330 385-8812
Keith Clark, *Superintendent*
Scott McNicol, *Superintendent*
EMP: 26
SALES (est): 3.4MM **Privately Held**
SIC: 4941 Water supply

(G-10403)
FARMERS NATIONAL BANK
16924 Saint Clair Ave (43920-4255)
P.O. Box 555, Canfield (44406-0555)
PHONE..........................330 385-9200
Kevin Helmick, *President*
EMP: 70
SALES (corp-wide): 117.2MM **Publicly Held**
SIC: 6021 National trust companies with deposits, commercial

GEOGRAPHIC

HQ: Farmers National Bank
20 S Broad St
Canfield OH 44406
330 533-3341

(G-10404)
HILL INTL TRCKS NA LLC (PA)
47866 Y And O Rd (43920-8724)
P.O. Box 2170 (43920-0170)
PHONE..................................330 386-6440
Mike Chronister, *Human Res Mgr*
David Dobbs, *Sales Staff*
Mark Donnadio, *Manager*
Wesley Householder, *Manager*
James Wood, *Technology*
▼ EMP: 100 EST: 1890
SQ FT: 30,000
SALES (est): 92.7MM **Privately Held**
WEB: www.hillinternationaltrucks.com
SIC: 5511 5531 7538 Trucks, tractors &
trailers: new & used; truck equipment &
parts; general automotive repair shops

(G-10405)
LIFETEAM EMS INC
Also Called: Lifeteam Ambulance Service
740 Dresden Ave Ste A (43920-4309)
P.O. Box 362 (43920-5362)
PHONE..................................330 386-9284
Raymond Strohacker, *CEO*
Kelly Betteridge, *President*
EMP: 42 EST: 1967
SQ FT: 15,000
SALES: 1.7MM **Privately Held**
WEB: www.lifeteamems.com
SIC: 4119 8049 Ambulance service; para-
medic

(G-10406)
**MARTIN ALTMEYER FUNERAL
HOME**
15872 Saint Clair Ave (43920-8984)
PHONE..................................330 385-3650
James Altmeyer Jr, *President*
EMP: 30
SQ FT: 4,358
SALES (est): 1.4MM **Privately Held**
SIC: 7261 Funeral home

(G-10407)
**MIKE PUSATERI EXCAVATING
INC**
16363 Saint Clair Ave (43920-9124)
P.O. Box 2136 (43920-0136)
PHONE..................................330 385-5221
Michael J Pusateri, *President*
James V Pusateri, *Vice Pres*
Michael Pusateri, *Treasurer*
Debra Smith, *Admin Sec*
EMP: 35
SQ FT: 4,800
SALES: 6.7MM **Privately Held**
SIC: 1794 Excavation work

(G-10408)
MURRAY LEASING INC
14778 E Liverpool Rd (43920-9712)
P.O. Box 2138 (43920-0138)
PHONE..................................330 386-4757
H B Murray, *President*
Betty Murray, *Vice Pres*
EMP: 125
SQ FT: 10,000
SALES (est): 6.6MM **Privately Held**
SIC: 7513 4213 4212 Truck leasing, with-
out drivers; trucking, except local; local
trucking, without storage

(G-10409)
**NENTWICK CONVALESCENT
HOME**
500 Selfridge St (43920-1997)
PHONE..................................330 385-5001
Rev John Nentwick, *President*
Mary Nentwick Tambellini, *Corp Secy*
Alfred Tambellini, *Vice Pres*
EMP: 105
SQ FT: 28,000
SALES (est): 4.4MM **Privately Held**
SIC: 8059 8051 Convalescent home;
skilled nursing care facilities

(G-10410)
**NORTH STAR CRITICAL CARE
LLC**
16356 State Route 267 (43920-3932)
P.O. Box 2011 (43920-0011)
PHONE..................................330 386-9110
Elio P Lerussi, *Mng Member*
Christine Lerussi,
EMP: 28
SALES (est): 810K **Privately Held**
SIC: 4119 Ambulance service

(G-10411)
OHIO MINORITY MEDICAL
517 Broadway St Ste 500 (43920-3167)
PHONE..................................513 400-5011
Michael Ward II, *President*
EMP: 50
SALES (est): 370K **Privately Held**
SIC: 8011 Offices & clinics of medical doc-
tors

(G-10412)
OHIO VALLEY HOME CARE LLC
425 W 5th St (43920-2405)
P.O. Box 80 (43920-5080)
PHONE..................................330 385-2333
Keith Richardson, *Principal*
Richard Adkins, *Admin Asst*
EMP: 34
SQ FT: 800
SALES (est): 285.8K **Privately Held**
SIC: 8082 Home health care services

(G-10413)
**OHIO VALLEY HOME HLTH SVCS
INC (PA)**
425 W 5th St (43920-2405)
PHONE..................................330 385-2333
Keith Richardson, *CEO*
Barbara Reed, *Treasurer*
Joseph Olenick, *Manager*
Richard Adkins, *Supervisor*
Janet McCoy, *Exec Dir*
EMP: 34
SQ FT: 1,500
SALES: 3.7MM **Privately Held**
WEB: www.ovhhs.com
SIC: 8082 Visiting nurse service

(G-10414)
OS HILL LEASING INC
47866 Y And O Rd (43920-8724)
P.O. Box 2170 (43920-0170)
PHONE..................................330 386-6440
Jack I Hill, *President*
Mike Fisher, *Corp Secy*
Gary Malonne, *Vice Pres*
EMP: 40
SQ FT: 30,000
SALES (est): 2.4MM
SALES (corp-wide): 92.7MM **Privately
Held**
WEB: www.hillinttrucks.com
SIC: 7513 Truck leasing, without drivers
PA: Hill International Trucks N.A., Llc
47866 Y And O Rd
East Liverpool OH 43920
330 386-6440

(G-10415)
P N P INC
Also Called: Chcc Home Health Care
48444 Bell School Rd (43920-9646)
PHONE..................................330 386-1231
Joseph Cilone, *President*
EMP: 100 EST: 2011
SQ FT: 144
SALES (est): 2.9MM
SALES (corp-wide): 3.6MM **Privately
Held**
SIC: 8099 Health screening service
PA: Jcth Holdings, Inc.
48444 Bell School Rd
East Liverpool OH 43920
330 386-1231

(G-10416)
**PRECESION FINNING BENDING
INC**
1250 Saint George St # 6 (43920-3400)
PHONE..................................330 382-9351
Mark Anderson, *President*
Jason Anderson, *Vice Pres*
EMP: 25

SQ FT: 70,000
SALES (est): 2MM **Privately Held**
SIC: 5051 Steel

(G-10417)
SH BELL COMPANY
2217 Michigan Ave (43920-3637)
PHONE..................................412 963-9910
Vince Monte, *Sales Staff*
Rusty Davis, *Manager*
Doris Thayer, *Director*
Chris McKenzie, *Assistant*
EMP: 37
SALES (corp-wide): 21.6MM **Privately
Held**
SIC: 3479 4226 4225 Aluminum coating
of metal products; special warehousing &
storage; general warehousing & storage
PA: S.H. Bell Company
644 Alpha Dr
Pittsburgh PA 15238
412 963-9910

(G-10418)
SOARING EAGLE INC
Also Called: Newbold Technologies
114 W 5th St (43920-2920)
PHONE..................................330 385-5579
Craig Newbold, *President*
Todd Alexander, *Vice Pres*
EMP: 30
SQ FT: 20,360
SALES (est): 5.4MM **Privately Held**
SIC: 7373 Systems software development
services

East Palestine
Columbiana County

(G-10419)
COVINGTON SNF INC
Also Called: COVINGTON SKILLED NURS-
ING AND
100 Covington Dr (44413-1007)
PHONE..................................330 426-2920
Timothy A Chesney, *Vice Pres*
Cayleigh Crook, *Office Mgr*
EMP: 30
SALES (est): 5.4MM **Privately Held**
SIC: 8051 Convalescent home with contin-
uous nursing care

(G-10420)
JASAR RECYCLING INC
183 Edgeworth Ave (44413-1554)
PHONE..................................864 233-5421
Ed McNee, *President*
Lynn Neely, *Controller*
Chris Toy, *Human Res Mgr*
Kelley Lester, *Natl Sales Mgr*
Maude Ciardi, *Admin Asst*
▼ EMP: 70
SQ FT: 240,000
SALES (est): 22.1MM **Privately Held**
WEB: www.jasarrecycling.com
SIC: 4953 Recycling, waste materials

(G-10421)
SMS GROUP INC
Also Called: SMS Technical Services
49560 State Route 14 (44413-9725)
PHONE..................................330 426-4126
Ken Heestend, *Branch Mgr*
Kenneth Heestand, *Director*
EMP: 35
SQ FT: 16,000
SALES (corp-wide): 96.1K **Privately Held**
SIC: 7699 Industrial machinery & equip-
ment repair
HQ: Sms Group Inc.
100 Sandusky St
Pittsburgh PA 15212
412 231-1200

(G-10422)
**THRESHOLD RESIDENTIAL
SVCS INC (PA)**
50 N Sumner St (44413-2044)
P.O. Box 466 (44413-0466)
PHONE..................................330 426-4553
John Hersh, *Ch of Bd*
Thomas Rice, *Exec Dir*
Bronwuyn Mechella, *Admin Sec*

EMP: 145 EST: 1975
SQ FT: 6,000
SALES (est): 4.8MM **Privately Held**
SIC: 8361 Home for the mentally retarded

East Sparta
Stark County

(G-10423)
MALAVITE EXCAVATING INC
5508 Ridge Ave Se (44626-9702)
PHONE..................................330 484-1274
Gust Malavite, *President*
Gust Malavite Jr, *Vice Pres*
Kevin Malavite, *Treasurer*
EMP: 25 EST: 1978
SQ FT: 10,000
SALES: 1MM **Privately Held**
SIC: 7353 Earth moving equipment, rental
or leasing

(G-10424)
**STANLEY MILLER
CONSTRUCTION CO**
2250 Howenstine Dr Se (44626-9538)
PHONE..................................330 484-2229
David S Miller, *President*
Steven Miller, *Vice Pres*
Terri Krupar, *Project Mgr*
Missy Coberly, *Admin Asst*
EMP: 25
SQ FT: 10,000
SALES (est): 8.9MM **Privately Held**
WEB: www.smillerconst.com
SIC: 1542 1541 Commercial & office build-
ing, new construction; commercial & of-
fice buildings, renovation & repair;
industrial buildings, new construction; ren-
ovation, remodeling & repairs: industrial
buildings

(G-10425)
WILLIAMS SUPER SERVICE INC
Also Called: Williams Toyota Lift
9462 Main Ave Se (44626-9583)
P.O. Box 359 (44626-0359)
PHONE..................................330 733-7750
Paul Williams, *President*
Jason Pratt, *Marketing Staff*
Jason Froman, *Vice Pres*
Nicholas Hough, *Manager*
Rod Lancaster, *Manager*
EMP: 27
SQ FT: 6,000
SALES (est): 5.4MM **Privately Held**
WEB: www.williamstoyotalift.com
SIC: 7699 5084 Industrial machinery &
equipment repair; lift trucks & parts

East Springfield
Jefferson County

(G-10426)
SPRING HILLS GOLF CLUB
99 Corder Dr (43925)
PHONE..................................740 543-3270
Charlie Corder Sr, *Principal*
EMP: 25
SALES (est): 452K **Privately Held**
SIC: 7999 Golf services & professionals

Eastlake
Lake County

(G-10427)
AVNET INC
Also Called: Avnet Computers
34201 Melinz Pkwy Unit D (44095-4018)
PHONE..................................440 479-3607
EMP: 27
SALES (corp-wide): 19B **Publicly Held**
SIC: 5065 Electronic parts
PA: Avnet, Inc.
2211 S 47th St
Phoenix AZ 85034
480 643-2000

(G-10428)
DISASTER RECONSTRUCTION INC
Also Called: Servicmaster By Disaster Recon
33851 Curtis Blvd Ste 202 (44095-4003)
PHONE...................................440 918-1523
Greg Dennison, *President*
EMP: 31
SQ FT: 3,000
SALES (est): 2.9MM **Privately Held**
SIC: 1521 1542 1799 General remodeling, single-family houses; commercial & office buildings, renovation & repair; post-disaster renovations

(G-10429)
EASTLAKE LODGING LLC
Also Called: Radisson Eastlake
35000 Curtis Blvd (44095-4019)
PHONE...................................440 953-8000
Mike Madonna, *General Mgr*
EMP: 50
SALES (est): 2.4MM
SALES (corp-wide): 6.8B **Publicly Held**
SIC: 7011 Bed & breakfast inn
HQ: Concord Hospitality Enterprises Company
11410 Common Oaks Dr
Raleigh NC 27614

(G-10430)
JOHN F GALLAGHER PLUMBING CO
36360 Lakeland Blvd (44095-5314)
PHONE...................................440 946-4256
Michael J Gallagher, *President*
John Gallagher II, *Shareholder*
Patrick F Gallagher, *Shareholder*
Thomas E Gallagher, *Shareholder*
EMP: 45
SQ FT: 10,000
SALES: 15.5MM **Privately Held**
WEB: www.jfgallagherco.com
SIC: 1711 1794 Mechanical contractor; plumbing contractors; warm air heating & air conditioning contractor; fire sprinkler system installation; excavation work

(G-10431)
MAJOR ELECTRONIX CORP
33801 Curtis Blvd Ste 110 (44095-4045)
PHONE...................................440 942-0054
William Rowell, *President*
J R Rowell, *Vice Pres*
Kristen Burkley, *Sales Staff*
Katie Wyatt, *Sales Staff*
▲ EMP: 25
SQ FT: 12,500
SALES (est): 7.1MM **Privately Held**
WEB: www.majorelectronix.com
SIC: 5065 5063 Electronic parts; electrical apparatus & equipment

(G-10432)
MILLENIUM CONTROL SYSTEMS LLC
34525 Melinz Pkwy Ste 205 (44095-4037)
PHONE...................................440 510-0050
Joel Conklin, *Vice Pres*
Patrick Gallagher,
Joseph Chuhran,
EMP: 37
SQ FT: 12,000
SALES (est): 12.1MM **Privately Held**
WEB: www.millenniumcontrols.com
SIC: 7373 Systems integration services

(G-10433)
NORTHERN OHIO PLUMBING CO
35601 Curtis Blvd Unit 1 (44095-4128)
PHONE...................................440 951-3370
James J Roddy, *President*
John Roddy Jr, *Corp Secy*
Roddy Frank, *Vice Pres*
Frank Roddy, *Vice Pres*
Mark Wilson, *Vice Pres*
EMP: 50
SQ FT: 12,000
SALES (est): 7MM **Privately Held**
SIC: 1711 Plumbing contractors

(G-10434)
SERVICE MASTER CO
Also Called: Service Mstr By Disaster Recon
33851 Curtis Blvd Ste 202 (44095-4003)
PHONE...................................330 864-7300
Fire Damage, *Manager*
EMP: 50
SALES (est): 109.3K **Privately Held**
SIC: 7349 Janitorial service, contract basis

(G-10435)
UNIVAR INC
Also Called: Southern Mill Creek Pdts Ohio
33851 Curtis Blvd Ste 208 (44095-4003)
PHONE...................................440 510-1259
Sam Hartwell, *Branch Mgr*
EMP: 40
SALES (corp-wide): 8.6B **Publicly Held**
SIC: 5169 Chemicals & allied products
PA: Univar Inc.
3075 Highland Pkwy # 200
Downers Grove IL 60515
331 777-6000

Eaton
Preble County

(G-10436)
ANCILLARY MEDICAL INVESTMENTS
Also Called: Gary's Prescription Pharmacy
125 Amelia Dr (45320-9508)
PHONE...................................937 456-5520
S Gary Pieratt, *President*
Bret Frence, *Principal*
EMP: 31
SQ FT: 6,000
SALES (est): 4.9MM **Privately Held**
SIC: 5912 7352 Drug stores; medical equipment rental

(G-10437)
AT&T SERVICES INC
1338 N Barron St (45320-1016)
PHONE...................................937 456-2330
Karen Williams, *Manager*
EMP: 168
SALES (corp-wide): 170.7B **Publicly Held**
SIC: 4813 4812 Local & long distance telephone communications; cellular telephone services
HQ: At&T Services, Inc.
208 S Akard St Ste 110
Dallas TX 75202
210 821-4105

(G-10438)
CITY OF EATON
Also Called: Eaton Fire Division
391 W Lexington Rd (45320)
P.O. Box 27 (45320-0027)
PHONE...................................937 456-5361
Brian Smith, *Branch Mgr*
EMP: 32 **Privately Held**
WEB: www.eatonmunicipalcourt.com
SIC: 9224 4119 Fire department, not including volunteer; ambulance service
PA: City Of Eaton
328 N Maple St
Eaton OH 45320
937 456-5310

(G-10439)
COLONIAL BANC CORP (PA)
110 W Main St (45320-1746)
P.O. Box 309 (45320-0309)
PHONE...................................937 456-5544
Joan Kreitzer, *President*
EMP: 36
SALES (est): 5.6MM **Privately Held**
WEB: www.enbbank.com
SIC: 6021 7291 National commercial banks; tax return preparation services

(G-10440)
COUNTY OF PREBLE
116 E Main St Ste B (45320-1763)
PHONE...................................937 456-2085
Dawna Simpson, *Branch Mgr*
EMP: 29 **Privately Held**
SIC: 8322 Probation office

PA: County Of Preble
101 E Main St
Eaton OH 45320
937 456-8143

(G-10441)
DAVITA INC
105 E Wash Jackson Rd (45320-9789)
PHONE...................................937 456-1174
Susan Dynes, *President*
EMP: 27 **Publicly Held**
SIC: 8092 Kidney dialysis centers
PA: Davita Inc.
2000 16th St
Denver CO 80202

(G-10442)
DAYTEP INC
1816 Alexander Rd (45320-9222)
PHONE...................................937 456-5860
Jayme M Day, *President*
James G Day, *Treasurer*
EMP: 35
SQ FT: 22,500
SALES: 6.4MM **Privately Held**
WEB: www.daytep.com
SIC: 1542 Commercial & office building, new construction

(G-10443)
DRAKE STATE AIR
3711 Ozias Rd (45320-9750)
PHONE...................................937 472-3740
Steve Christer, *CEO*
EMP: 50
SALES (est): 1.6MM **Privately Held**
SIC: 1711 Heating & air conditioning contractors

(G-10444)
DRAKE STATE AIR SYSTEMS INC
1417 E Main St (45320-2231)
PHONE...................................937 472-0640
Steve Chrismer, *President*
EMP: 26
SALES (est): 2.4MM **Privately Held**
WEB: www.drakecomfort.com
SIC: 1711 Warm air heating & air conditioning contractor

(G-10445)
EATON GARDENS REHABILITATION A
Also Called: Maple Gardens Rehab
515 S Maple St (45320-9413)
PHONE...................................937 456-5537
Robin Eck, *Manager*
Ephram Lahasky,
EMP: 85
SALES (est): 777.1K **Privately Held**
SIC: 8051 Skilled nursing care facilities

(G-10446)
GARYS PHARMACY INC
125 Amelia Dr (45320-9508)
PHONE...................................937 456-5777
Gary Pieratt, *President*
EMP: 31
SALES: 7MM **Privately Held**
SIC: 5912 5999 5947 5499 Drug stores; hospital equipment & supplies; greeting cards; health & dietetic food stores; hospital equipment & furniture; agents, shipping

(G-10447)
HEALTH CARE RTREMENT CORP AMER
Also Called: Heartland of Eaton
515 S Maple St (45320-9413)
PHONE...................................937 456-5537
Tom Nielander, *Manager*
EMP: 100
SALES (corp-wide): 2.4B **Publicly Held**
WEB: www.hrc-manorcare.com
SIC: 8051 Skilled nursing care facilities
HQ: Health Care And Retirement Corporation Of America
333 N Summit St Ste 103
Toledo OH 43604
419 252-5500

(G-10448)
KRAMER & KRAMER INC
Also Called: Kramer & Kramer Realtors
420 N Barron St (45320-1708)
P.O. Box 85 (45320-0085)
PHONE...................................937 456-1101
Horace J Kramer Sr, *President*
H John Kramer, *Vice Pres*
Debbie Kramer, *Treasurer*
Janet EBY, *Manager*
EMP: 30
SQ FT: 3,000
SALES (est): 2.1MM **Privately Held**
WEB: www.kramerauctions.com
SIC: 7389 6531 Auctioneers, fee basis; real estate brokers & agents

(G-10449)
L & M PRODUCTS INC
1407 N Barron St (45320-1017)
PHONE...................................937 456-7141
Ben Hollinger, *President*
EMP: 150
SQ FT: 14,000
SALES: 1.4MM **Privately Held**
SIC: 8331 Vocational rehabilitation agency

(G-10450)
LCNB NATIONAL BANK
110 W Main St (45320-1746)
PHONE...................................937 456-5544
Michele Kreitzer, *Officer*
Melanie Cottingim, *Executive*
EMP: 59
SALES (corp-wide): 65.6MM **Publicly Held**
SIC: 6021 National commercial banks
HQ: Lcnb National Bank
2 N Broadway St Lowr
Lebanon OH 45036
513 932-1414

(G-10451)
MARONDA HOMES INC FLORIDA
Also Called: Imperial Lumber
1050 S Barron St (45320-9387)
PHONE...................................937 472-3907
Larry Taylor, *Manager*
EMP: 100
SALES (corp-wide): 171.8MM **Privately Held**
WEB: www.maronda.com
SIC: 1521 New construction, single-family houses
HQ: Maronda Homes Inc Of Florida
11 Timberglen Dr
Imperial PA 15126
724 695-1200

(G-10452)
MEDPRO LLC
251 W Lexington Rd (45320-9282)
PHONE...................................937 336-5586
Gina Hatmaker, *CEO*
Patrick Caylor, *COO*
Ernest Hatmaker, *Officer*
EMP: 75
SALES (est): 980K **Privately Held**
SIC: 4119 Ambulance service

(G-10453)
MENTAL RTRDTION PREBLE CNTY BD (PA)
201 E Lexington Rd Ste A (45320-1578)
PHONE...................................937 456-5891
Diane Knupp, *Superintendent*
EMP: 60
SALES (est): 1.1MM **Privately Held**
SIC: 8051 8211 Mental retardation hospital; school for the retarded; public special education school

(G-10454)
MIAMI VALLEY COMMUNITY ACTION
308 Eaton Lewisburg Rd (45320-1105)
PHONE...................................937 456-2800
Rita Daily, *Director*
EMP: 45
SALES (corp-wide): 13MM **Privately Held**
SIC: 8322 Social service center

G E O G R A P H I C

PA: Miami Valley Community Action Partnership
719 S Main St
Dayton OH 45402
937 222-1009

(G-10455)
NAMI OF PREBLE COUNTY OHIO
800 E Saint Clair St (45320-2433)
PHONE....................................(937) 456-4947
Shelly Ratliff, *Director*
EMP: 50
SALES (est): 273.9K **Privately Held**
SIC: 8322 8699 Old age assistance; senior citizens' center or association; charitable organization

(G-10456)
OCTOBER ENTERPRISES INC
Also Called: Greenbriar Nursing Center, The
501 W Lexington Rd (45320-9274)
PHONE....................................937 456-9535
Paul De Palma, *President*
Viktorya Howard, *Marketing Staff*
Jennifer Besecker, *Admin Asst*
Chloe Robbins, *Administration*
EMP: 125
SQ FT: 27,660
SALES (est): 5.8MM **Privately Held**
WEB: www.greenbriarcampus.com
SIC: 8051 8052 Convalescent home with continuous nursing care; intermediate care facilities

(G-10457)
PARKER-HANNIFIN CORPORATION
Tube Fittings Division
725 N Beech St (45320-1499)
PHONE....................................937 456-5571
Jay Studer, *Mfg Mgr*
Dan Quinn, *Engineer*
Patricia Combs, *Cust Mgr*
William Bowman, *Branch Mgr*
Gary Clyburn, *Manager*
EMP: 400
SALES (corp-wide): 14.3B **Publicly Held**
WEB: www.parker.com
SIC: 3494 5074 3498 3492 Pipe fittings; couplings, except pressure & soil pipe; plumbing & heating valves; plumbing fittings & supplies; tube fabricating (contract bending & shaping); fluid power valves & hose fittings
PA: Parker-Hannifin Corporation
6035 Parkland Blvd
Cleveland OH 44124
216 896-3000

(G-10458)
PERSONAL TOUCH HM CARE IPA INC
Also Called: Health Force
302 Eaton Lewisburg Rd (45320-1105)
PHONE....................................937 456-4447
Susan Moore, *Director*
EMP: 40
SALES (corp-wide): 363MM **Privately Held**
WEB: www.pthomecare.com
SIC: 8082 7361 Visiting nurse service; nurses' registry
PA: Personal Touch Home Care Ipa, Inc.
1985 Marcus Ave Ste 202
New Hyde Park NY 11042
718 468-4747

(G-10459)
PREBLE COUNTY COUNCIL ON AGING
800 E Saint Clair St (45320-2433)
PHONE....................................937 456-4947
Shelley Ratliff, *Exec Dir*
Alice Mc Mann, *Director*
EMP: 25
SALES (est): 1.3MM **Privately Held**
SIC: 8322 Social worker

(G-10460)
PREBLE COUNTY GENERAL HLTH DST
Also Called: Erik Balster Hlth Commissioner
615 Hillcrest Dr (45320-8559)
PHONE....................................937 472-0087

Erik Balster, *Principal*
Sarah Hays, *Finance Dir*
Christine Maggard,
EMP: 28
SALES (est): 1.3MM **Privately Held**
SIC: 8011 Obstetrician

(G-10461)
REID PHYSICIAN ASSOCIATES INC
Also Called: Reid Physicians Associates
109b Wash Jackson Rd (45320-9793)
PHONE....................................937 456-4400
Joellen Tapalman, *Manager*
EMP: 488
SALES (corp-wide): 40MM **Privately Held**
SIC: 8011 General & family practice, physician/surgeon
PA: Reid Physician Associates, Inc.
1100 Reid Pkwy
Richmond IN 47374
765 983-3000

(G-10462)
TIME WARNER CABLE INC
419 S Barron St (45320-2401)
P.O. Box 348 (45320-0348)
PHONE....................................937 471-1572
Kathi Hollenbauga, *Manager*
EMP: 33
SQ FT: 2,500
SALES (corp-wide): 43.6B **Publicly Held**
SIC: 4841 Cable television services
HQ: Spectrum Management Holding Company, Llc
400 Atlantic St
Stamford CT 06901
203 905-7801

(G-10463)
TRINITY ACTION PARTNERSHIP
308 Eaton Lewisburg Rd (45320-1105)
PHONE....................................937 456-2800
John Dollenn, *CEO*
Joyce Price, *COO*
Steve Dipender, *CFO*
Rita Daily, *Director*
EMP: 50
SALES (est): 1.7MM **Privately Held**
WEB: www.cap-dayton.org
SIC: 8322 Meal delivery program

(G-10464)
UNITED PRODUCERS INC
617 S Franklin St (45320-9419)
PHONE....................................937 456-4161
Harry O'Call, *Manager*
EMP: 25
SALES (corp-wide): 114.1MM **Privately Held**
WEB: www.uproducers.com
SIC: 5154 Auctioning livestock
PA: United Producers, Inc.
8351 N High St Ste 250
Columbus OH 43235
614 433-2150

(G-10465)
VANCREST LTD
Also Called: Vancrest Healthcare Cntr Eaton
1600 Park Ave (45320-9674)
PHONE....................................937 456-3010
Brenda Newman, *Mktg Dir*
Mark Vosler, *Director*
Tracy Beare, *Nursing Dir*
Rosemary Dennis, *Nursing Dir*
Tina Deboo, *Records Dir*
EMP: 60
SALES (corp-wide): 16.3MM **Privately Held**
WEB: www.vancrest.com
SIC: 8051 Convalescent home with continuous nursing care
PA: Vancrest, Ltd.
120 W Main St Ste 200
Van Wert OH 45891
419 238-0715

Edgerton
Williams County

(G-10466)
ALL HEART HOME CARE LLC
143 N Michigan Ave (43517-9322)
P.O. Box 896 (43517-0896)
PHONE....................................419 298-0034
Kelly Wilhelm, *Mng Member*
EMP: 44
SALES (est): 158.2K **Privately Held**
SIC: 8082 Home health care services

(G-10467)
ANGELS VISITING
143 N Michigan Ave (43517-9322)
P.O. Box 896 (43517-0896)
PHONE....................................419 298-0034
Kelly Wilhelm, *Owner*
EMP: 60
SALES (est): 129.9K **Privately Held**
SIC: 8082 Home health care services

(G-10468)
MATERIAL SUPPLIERS INC
2444 State Route 49 (43517-9551)
P.O. Box 340 (43517-0340)
PHONE....................................419 298-2440
Gerry Weber, *President*
EMP: 30 EST: 1997
SALES (est): 2.5MM **Privately Held**
SIC: 4213 Trucking, except local

(G-10469)
PEREGRINE HEALTH SERVICES INC
Also Called: Park View Nursing Center
328 W Vine St (43517-9600)
PHONE....................................419 298-2321
Charlotte Stewart, *Marketing Staff*
Ed Fodrea, *Manager*
EMP: 100
SALES (corp-wide): 6.8MM **Privately Held**
WEB: www.nursinghomeinfo.org
SIC: 8099 Health screening service
PA: Peregrine Health Services, Inc.
1661 Old Henderson Rd
Columbus OH 43220
614 459-2656

Edon
Williams County

(G-10470)
AGRIDRY LLC
3460 Us Highway 20 (43518-9733)
P.O. Box 336 (43518-0336)
PHONE....................................419 459-4399
Eli P Troyer, *Mng Member*
EMP: 45
SALES (est): 10.7MM **Privately Held**
SIC: 3567 1541 Driers & redriers, industrial process; grain elevator construction

Elida
Allen County

(G-10471)
BOARD AMERCN TOWNSHIP TRUSTEES
102 Pioneer Rd (45807-1106)
PHONE....................................419 331-8651
G B Bowers, *President*
Paul Basinger, *Principal*
Darell Long, *Principal*
Larry Van Demark, *Principal*
Laurie Swick, *Treasurer*
EMP: 50
SALES (est): 4.4MM **Privately Held**
SIC: 4959 Road, airport & parking lot maintenance services

Elmore
Ottawa County

(G-10472)
CHIPMATIC TOOL & MACHINE INC
212 Ottawa St (43416-7710)
P.O. Box 87 (43416-0087)
PHONE....................................419 862-2737
Mike Detzel, *President*
Duane Glase, *Purch Agent*
Kim M Detzel, *Admin Sec*
Kim Detzel, *Admin Sec*
EMP: 67
SQ FT: 30,000
SALES (est): 10.4MM **Privately Held**
WEB: www.chipmatic.com
SIC: 3599 8711 7692 3544 Machine shop, jobbing & repair; mechanical engineering; welding repair; special dies, tools, jigs & fixtures

(G-10473)
INTERNATIONAL ORDR OF RNBOW FO
Also Called: Genoa Assembly 107
18706 W State Route 105 (43416-9525)
PHONE....................................419 862-3009
Brenda Roadarmel, *Director*
EMP: 30
SALES (est): 275.4K **Privately Held**
SIC: 8641 Civic associations

(G-10474)
ROTHERT FARM INC
1084 S Opfer Lentz Rd (43416-9789)
PHONE....................................419 467-0095
Trent Rothert, *President*
Susan Rohtert, *Treasurer*
EMP: 87
SALES (est): 7MM **Privately Held**
SIC: 0161 Cabbage farm

Elyria
Lorain County

(G-10475)
AA FIRE PROTECTION LLC
620 Sugar Ln (44035-6310)
PHONE....................................440 327-0060
Scott McMillen, *CEO*
EMP: 25
SALES (est): 2.2MM **Privately Held**
SIC: 7389 Fire protection service other than forestry or public

(G-10476)
ABBEWOOD LIMITED PARTNERSHIP
Also Called: The Abbewood
1210 Abbe Rd S Ofc (44035-7276)
PHONE....................................440 366-8980
Logan Sexton, *General Ptnr*
EMP: 27
SALES (est): 2.1MM **Privately Held**
SIC: 8361 Home for the aged

(G-10477)
ABRAHAM FORD LLC
Also Called: Elyria Ford
1115 E Broad St (44035-6305)
PHONE....................................440 233-7402
Nick Abraham, *President*
EMP: 30
SQ FT: 16,000
SALES (est): 2.5MM **Privately Held**
SIC: 7389 7538 5531 5521 Personal service agents, brokers & bureaus; general automotive repair shops; automotive & home supply stores; used car dealers

(G-10478)
AMERICAN HOOD SYSTEMS INC
177 Reaser Ct (44035-6285)
P.O. Box 1377 (44036-1377)
PHONE....................................440 365-4567
Michael Maynard, *President*
Daniel Reaser, *Principal*

EMP: 40
SQ FT: 40,000
SALES: 1MM Privately Held
WEB: www.americanhood.com
SIC: 5075 Ventilating equipment & supplies

(G-10479)
ARCH ABRAHAM SUSUKI LTD
Also Called: Arch Abraham Nissan & Susuki
1111 E Broad St (44035-6305)
PHONE..................................440 934-6001
Archie Abraham, Owner
EMP: 32
SQ FT: 9,600
SALES (est): 6.1MM Privately Held
SIC: 5511 7532 5521 Automobiles, new & used; top & body repair & paint shops; used car dealers

(G-10480)
ATLAS ELECTRICAL CONSTRUCTION
7974 Murray Ridge Rd (44035-2065)
P.O. Box 695 (44036-0695)
PHONE..................................440 323-5418
Pearl Myers, President
Rowena Myers, Corp Secy
Charles R Myers Jr, Vice Pres
EMP: 25
SQ FT: 5,700
SALES (est): 2.9MM Privately Held
SIC: 1731 General electrical contractor

(G-10481)
BELLMAN PLUMBING INC
7520 W Ridge Rd (44035-1960)
PHONE..................................440 324-4477
Robert Bellman, President
EMP: 28
SQ FT: 13,400
SALES (est): 3.5MM Privately Held
WEB: www.bellmanplumbing.com
SIC: 1711 Plumbing contractors

(G-10482)
BENDIX COML VHCL SYSTEMS LLC (DH)
901 Cleveland St (44035-4153)
P.O. Box 4016 (44036-2016)
PHONE..................................440 329-9000
Christian Fischer, President
Carlos Hungria, COO
Eugene Clair, Counsel
Claus Beyer, Vice Pres
Scott Burkhart, Vice Pres
◆ EMP: 350 EST: 1930
SALES (est): 1.1B
SALES (corp-wide): 711.6K Privately Held
SIC: 5013 8711 Automotive supplies & parts; engineering services
HQ: Knorr Brake Truck Systems Company
748 Starbuck Ave
Watertown NY 13601
315 786-5200

(G-10483)
BINDU ASSOCIATES LLC
Also Called: Country Suites By Carlson
645 Griswold Rd (44035-2394)
PHONE..................................440 324-0099
Kiran Patel, President
Sam Patel,
EMP: 25
SALES: 1MM Privately Held
SIC: 7011 Hotels & motels

(G-10484)
BRADY PLUMBING & HEATING INC
43191 N Ridge Rd (44035-1058)
PHONE..................................440 324-4261
Ken Brady, President
Loretta Brady, Vice Pres
EMP: 30
SALES (est): 2.2MM Privately Held
SIC: 1711 Plumbing contractors

(G-10485)
C&K TRUCKING LLC
41387 Schadden Rd (44035-2222)
PHONE..................................440 657-5249
EMP: 31 Privately Held
SIC: 4213 Contract haulers

PA: C&K Trucking, Llc
6205 W 101st St
Chicago Ridge IL 60415

(G-10486)
CELLCO PARTNERSHIP
Also Called: Verizon
1621 W River Rd N (44035-2715)
PHONE..................................440 324-9479
Joy Heldt, Manager
EMP: 30
SALES (corp-wide): 130.8B Publicly Held
SIC: 4812 Cellular telephone services
HQ: Cellco Partnership
1 Verizon Way
Basking Ridge NJ 07920

(G-10487)
CENTRO PROPERTIES GROUP LLC
3343 Midway Mall (44035-9003)
P.O. Box 7674, Merrifield VA (22116-7674)
PHONE..................................440 324-6610
Mark Bressler, Manager
EMP: 50
SALES (corp-wide): 2.2MM Privately Held
SIC: 5311 6512 Department stores; non-residential building operators
PA: Centro Properties Group Llc
1 Fayette St Ste 300
Conshohocken PA 19428
610 941-9304

(G-10488)
CHEMICAL BANK
111 Antioch Dr (44035-9104)
PHONE..................................440 323-7451
Matt Clark, Manager
EMP: 36
SALES (corp-wide): 924.5MM Publicly Held
SIC: 6035 Federal savings & loan associations
HQ: Chemical Bank
333 E Main St
Midland MI 48640
989 631-9200

(G-10489)
CITY OF ELYRIA
Also Called: Elyria Waste Water Plant
1194 Gulf Rd (44035-1752)
PHONE..................................440 366-2211
Gregory Worcester, Manager
EMP: 52 Privately Held
WEB: www.elyriahealth.com
SIC: 4953 Refuse systems
PA: City Of Elyria
131 Court St
Elyria OH 44035
440 326-1402

(G-10490)
CLEVELAND CLINIC FOUNDATION
303 Chestnut Commons Dr (44035-9607)
PHONE..................................440 366-9444
John Secrist, Branch Mgr
EMP: 85
SALES (corp-wide): 8.9B Privately Held
SIC: 6733 Trusts
PA: The Cleveland Clinic Foundation
9500 Euclid Ave
Cleveland OH 44195
216 636-8335

(G-10491)
COBOS INSURANCE CENTRE LLC
41436 Griswold Rd (44035-2324)
PHONE..................................440 324-3732
Roberto Cobos,
EMP: 25
SQ FT: 2,000
SALES (est): 3.6MM Privately Held
SIC: 6411 Insurance agents

(G-10492)
COMPREHENSIVE HEALTH CARE (HQ)
Also Called: Emh Regional Healthcare System
630 E River St (44035-5902)
PHONE..................................440 329-7500
Donald Sheldon, President
Daniel N Miller, Vice Pres
Gina Walker, Purch Agent
John Schneider, Technical Mgr
Gary Wharton, Controller
EMP: 1200
SQ FT: 450,000
SALES: 18.2MM
SALES (corp-wide): 580MM Privately Held
WEB: www.emh-healthcare.org
SIC: 8741 Hospital management
PA: University Hospitals Health System, Inc.
3605 Warrensville Ctr Rd
Shaker Heights OH 44122
216 767-8900

(G-10493)
CONSUMER FOODS
123 Gateway Blvd N (44035-4923)
PHONE..................................440 284-5972
Dennis Walter, President
EMP: 40
SALES (est): 254.7K Privately Held
SIC: 7542 Carwashes

(G-10494)
COUNTY OF LORAIN
Also Called: Lorain County Sani Engineers
247 Hadaway St (44035-7760)
PHONE..................................440 329-5584
Kenneth P Carney Sr, Principal
Peter Zwick, Engineer
EMP: 85 Privately Held
WEB: www.lcmhb.org
SIC: 4952 Sewerage systems
PA: County Of Lorain
226 Middle Ave
Elyria OH 44035
440 329-5201

(G-10495)
COUNTY OF LORAIN
Also Called: Lorain Cnty Brd Mntl Rtrdtn
1091 Infirmary Rd (44035-4804)
PHONE..................................440 329-3734
Amber Fisher PHD, Superintendent
EMP: 50 Privately Held
WEB: www.lcmhb.org
SIC: 8322 8361 Social service center; general counseling services; home for the mentally handicapped; home for the physically handicapped
PA: County Of Lorain
226 Middle Ave
Elyria OH 44035
440 329-5201

(G-10496)
COUNTY OF LORAIN
Also Called: Adult Probation Department
308 2nd St (44035-5506)
PHONE..................................440 326-4700
Bart Hobart, Director
EMP: 30 Privately Held
WEB: www.lcmhb.org
SIC: 8322 Probation office
PA: County Of Lorain
226 Middle Ave
Elyria OH 44035
440 329-5201

(G-10497)
COUNTY OF LORAIN
Also Called: Lorain County Engineers
247 Hadaway St (44035-7760)
PHONE..................................440 326-5884
Ken Carney, Manager
EMP: 29 Privately Held
WEB: www.lcmhb.org
SIC: 8711 Engineering services
PA: County Of Lorain
226 Middle Ave
Elyria OH 44035
440 329-5201

(G-10498)
COUNTY OF LORAIN
Also Called: Lorain Country Job & Fmly Svcs
42495 N Ridge Rd Ste A (44035-1045)
PHONE..................................440 284-1830
Jeff King, Branch Mgr
EMP: 100 Privately Held
SIC: 8322 Social service center
PA: County Of Lorain
226 Middle Ave
Elyria OH 44035
440 329-5201

(G-10499)
COUNTY OF LORAIN
Also Called: Drug and Alcohol
120 East Ave (44035-5652)
PHONE..................................440 989-4900
Vesta Warner, Director
EMP: 50 Privately Held
WEB: www.lcmhb.org
SIC: 8093 Alcohol clinic, outpatient
PA: County Of Lorain
226 Middle Ave
Elyria OH 44035
440 329-5201

(G-10500)
COUNTY OF LORAIN
Also Called: Lorain County Garage
42100 Russia Rd (44035-6813)
PHONE..................................440 326-5880
Mike Rodak, Superintendent
EMP: 55 Privately Held
WEB: www.lcmhb.org
SIC: 7538 General automotive repair shops
PA: County Of Lorain
226 Middle Ave
Elyria OH 44035
440 329-5201

(G-10501)
COUNTY OF LORAIN
Also Called: Lorain County Childrens Svcs
226 Middle Ave Fl 4 (44035-5629)
PHONE..................................440 329-5340
Dr Gary Crow, Director
Caroline McKinney, Social Worker
EMP: 140 Privately Held
WEB: www.lcmhb.org
SIC: 8322 8361 Adoption services; group foster home
PA: County Of Lorain
226 Middle Ave
Elyria OH 44035
440 329-5201

(G-10502)
DOT DIAMOND CORE DRILLING INC (PA)
780 Sugar Ln (44035-6312)
P.O. Box 683 (44036-0683)
PHONE..................................440 322-6466
Jeannie Nolan, President
David Dorst, General Mgr
Pat Nolan, Principal
Matt Nolan, Vice Pres
Ryan Nolan, Vice Pres
EMP: 37 EST: 1974
SQ FT: 7,200
SALES (est): 7.4MM Privately Held
WEB: www.dotdrilling.com
SIC: 1771 Concrete work

(G-10503)
DYNATECH SYSTEMS INC
161 Reaser Ct (44035-6285)
P.O. Box 1589 (44036-1589)
PHONE..................................440 365-1774
Sue A Everett, President
EMP: 25
SQ FT: 5,000
SALES (est): 3.3MM Privately Held
WEB: www.diamonddrillbit.com
SIC: 3425 5085 Saw blades & handsaws; industrial supplies

(G-10504)
EJQ HOME HEALTH CARE INC
800 Middle Ave (44035-5855)
PHONE..................................440 323-7004
Eva Boone, President
EMP: 75

SALES (est): 1.7MM **Privately Held**
WEB: www.ejqhomehealthcare.com
SIC: 8082 Visiting nurse service

(G-10505)
ELYRIA COUNTRY CLUB COMPANY
41625 Oberlin Elyria Rd (44035-7599)
PHONE.................................440 322-6391
Eric Toth, *Controller*
Kimberly Violo, *Manager*
EMP: 125
SQ FT: 19,892
SALES: 2.7MM **Privately Held**
SIC: 7997 Country club, membership

(G-10506)
ELYRIA FOUNDRY HOLDINGS LLC
120 Filbert St (44035-5357)
PHONE.................................440 322-4657
Bruce Smith,
EMP: 300 **Privately Held**
SIC: 6719 Investment holding companies, except banks

(G-10507)
ELYRIA-LORAIN BROADCASTING CO (HQ)
Also Called: Elts Broadcasting
538 Broad St 400 (44035-5508)
PHONE.................................440 322-3761
George Hudnutt, *President*
Philip Kelly, *Treasurer*
EMP: 50 EST: 1945
SQ FT: 3,000
SALES (est): 12.5MM
SALES (corp-wide): 27.9MM **Privately Held**
WEB: www.wnwv.com
SIC: 4832 Radio broadcasting stations
PA: Lorain County Printing & Publishing Co Inc
225 East Ave
Elyria OH
440 329-7000

(G-10508)
ELYRIA-LORAIN BROADCASTING CO
Also Called: Weol/Wnwv Radio
538 Broad St 400 (44035-5508)
PHONE.................................440 322-3761
Gary L Kneisley, *President*
EMP: 25
SALES (corp-wide): 27.9MM **Privately Held**
WEB: www.wnwv.com
SIC: 7319 Media buying service
HQ: Elyria-Lorain Broadcasting Company
538 Broad St 400
Elyria OH 44035
440 322-3761

(G-10509)
EMH REGIONAL HOMECARE AGENCY
90 E Broad St (44035-5521)
PHONE.................................440 329-7519
Don Sheldon, *President*
EMP: 30
SALES (est): 845K **Privately Held**
SIC: 8082 Home health care services

(G-10510)
EMPLOYMENT NETWORK
42495 N Ridge Rd (44035-1045)
PHONE.................................440 324-5244
Diana Mishlannau, *Manager*
Jan Rybarczyk, *Director*
EMP: 35
SALES (est): 1.2MM **Privately Held**
SIC: 7361 Placement agencies

(G-10511)
ENVELOPE MART OF NORTH E OHIO
Also Called: Em Print Group
1540 Lowell St (44035-4869)
PHONE.................................440 322-8862
Robert Thompson, *CEO*
Bradley Thompson, *President*
Andrew Thompson, *Vice Pres*
Brian Thompson, *Vice Pres*

Steve Burkey, *Finance Mgr*
EMP: 40
SQ FT: 80,000
SALES (est): 11.2MM **Privately Held**
WEB: www.envmart.com
SIC: 5112 Envelopes

(G-10512)
ENVELOPE MART OF OHIO INC
1540 Lowell St (44035-4869)
P.O. Box 808 (44036-0808)
PHONE.................................440 365-8177
Robert T Thompson, *President*
EMP: 50
SALES (est): 9MM **Privately Held**
SIC: 5112 2677 Envelopes; envelopes

(G-10513)
ENVIROTEST SYSTEMS CORP
128 Reaser Ct (44035-6285)
PHONE.................................330 963-4464
EMP: 34 **Privately Held**
WEB: www.il.etest.com
SIC: 7549 Emissions testing without repairs, automotive
HQ: Envirotest Systems Corp.
7 Kripes Rd
East Granby CT 06026

(G-10514)
GROSS PLUMBING INCORPORATED
Also Called: Gross Supply
6843 Lake Ave (44035-2149)
PHONE.................................440 324-9999
Daniel Gross, *President*
Chris Barnicle, *Vice Pres*
Edward J Gross, *Vice Pres*
Guy Gross, *Vice Pres*
Martha Taylor, *Treasurer*
EMP: 50 EST: 1956
SQ FT: 25,000
SALES (est): 10MM **Privately Held**
SIC: 1711 5999 Plumbing contractors; mechanical contractor; plumbing & heating supplies

(G-10515)
HOME DEPOT USA INC
Also Called: Home Depot, The
150 Market Dr (44035-2885)
PHONE.................................440 324-7222
James Meiden, *Manager*
EMP: 135
SALES (corp-wide): 108.2B **Publicly Held**
WEB: www.homerentalsdepot.com
SIC: 5211 7359 Home centers; tool rental
HQ: Home Depot U.S.A., Inc.
2455 Paces Ferry Ave
Atlanta GA 30339

(G-10516)
HORIZON EDUCATION CENTERS
233 Bond St (44035-3507)
PHONE.................................440 322-0288
Louise Reuter, *Branch Mgr*
EMP: 44
SALES (corp-wide): 6.1MM **Privately Held**
SIC: 8351 Preschool center
PA: Horizon Education Centers
29510 Lorain Rd
North Olmsted OH 44070
440 779-1930

(G-10517)
HORIZON EDUCATION CENTERS
Also Called: Allen Horizon Center
10347 Dewhurst Rd (44035-8403)
PHONE.................................440 458-5115
Donna Trent, *Branch Mgr*
EMP: 27
SALES (corp-wide): 6.1MM **Privately Held**
SIC: 8351 Child day care services
PA: Horizon Education Centers
29510 Lorain Rd
North Olmsted OH 44070
440 779-1930

(G-10518)
IMMACULATE INTERIORS
123 Brace Ave (44035-2659)
PHONE.................................440 324-9300
Russ Baldwin, *Owner*

EMP: 50
SALES (est): 1.8MM **Privately Held**
SIC: 1742 Acoustical & insulation work

(G-10519)
IMPACT MEDICAL MGT GROUP
1120 E Broad St (44035-6306)
P.O. Box 30 (44036-0030)
PHONE.................................440 365-7014
Kathy George, *President*
EMP: 35
SQ FT: 1,200
SALES (est): 2.3MM **Privately Held**
SIC: 8748 Business consulting

(G-10520)
JERSEY CENTRAL PWR & LIGHT CO
Also Called: Firstenergy
6326 Lake Ave (44035-1116)
PHONE.................................440 326-3222
Tony Alexander, *President*
EMP: 65 **Publicly Held**
WEB: www.jersey-central-power-light.monmouth.n
SIC: 4911 Generation, electric power
HQ: Jersey Central Power & Light Company
76 S Main St
Akron OH 44308
800 736-3402

(G-10521)
JOB CENTER LLC
2100 N Ridge Rd (44035-1241)
PHONE.................................440 499-1000
Julia Rodriguez, *Branch Mgr*
EMP: 33 **Privately Held**
SIC: 7361 Executive placement
PA: The Job Center Llc
11935 Mason Montgomery Rd
Cincinnati OH 45249

(G-10522)
KOKOSING CONSTRUCTION CO INC
1539 Lowell St (44035-4868)
PHONE.................................440 323-9346
Brian Burgett, *President*
EMP: 50
SQ FT: 12,440
SALES (est): 2.6MM **Privately Held**
SIC: 1629 1521 Heavy construction; single-family housing construction

(G-10523)
KS ASSOCIATES INC
260 Burns Rd Ste 100 (44035-1513)
PHONE.................................440 365-4730
Lynn Miggins, *President*
Mark Skellenger, *Vice Pres*
Nancy De Vielle, *Financial Exec*
EMP: 55
SALES (est): 8MM **Privately Held**
SIC: 8711 8713 Civil engineering; surveying services

(G-10524)
LIFE CARE CENTERS AMERICA INC
1212 Abbe Rd S (44035-7269)
PHONE.................................440 365-5200
Douglas McDermott, *Branch Mgr*
Douglas Mc Dermott, *Exec Dir*
Brianne Liederbach, *Records Dir*
EMP: 119
SALES (corp-wide): 119.8MM **Privately Held**
SIC: 8051 Convalescent home with continuous nursing care
PA: Life Care Centers Of America, Inc.
3570 Keith St Nw
Cleveland TN 37312
423 472-9585

(G-10525)
LIFECARE AMBULANCE INC
598 Cleveland St (44035)
PHONE.................................440 323-2527
Peter De La Porte, *Branch Mgr*
EMP: 53
SALES (corp-wide): 13MM **Privately Held**
SIC: 4119 Ambulance service

PA: Lifecare Ambulance Inc.
640 Cleveland St
Elyria OH 44035
440 323-6111

(G-10526)
LIFECARE AMBULANCE INC (PA)
Also Called: Lorain Lifecare Ambulance
640 Cleveland St (44035-4104)
P.O. Box 993 (44036-0993)
PHONE.................................440 323-6111
Peter De La Porte, *President*
Herbert De La Porte, *Vice Pres*
EMP: 25
SQ FT: 15,000
SALES (est): 13MM **Privately Held**
WEB: www.lifecareambulance.com
SIC: 4119 4111 Ambulance service; local & suburban transit

(G-10527)
LIFESHARE CMNTY BLOOD SVCS INC (PA)
105 Cleveland St Ste 101 (44035-6166)
PHONE.................................440 322-6159
Richard Cluck, *President*
Michael Dash, *Vice Pres*
EMP: 35
SQ FT: 10,000
SALES: 15.9MM **Privately Held**
SIC: 8099 Blood bank

(G-10528)
LIFESHARE COMMUNITY BLOOD SVCS
105 Cliffland St (44035)
PHONE.................................440 322-6573
Richard Cluck, *Manager*
EMP: 45
SALES (corp-wide): 15.9MM **Privately Held**
SIC: 8099 Blood bank
PA: Lifeshare Community Blood Services, Inc.
105 Cleveland St Ste 101
Elyria OH 44035
440 322-6159

(G-10529)
LODGING INDUSTRY INC
Also Called: Econo Lodge
523 Griswold Rd (44035-2306)
PHONE.................................440 324-3911
Scott Poldena, *Manager*
EMP: 25
SALES (corp-wide): 1.5MM **Privately Held**
SIC: 7011 Hotels & motels
PA: Lodging Industry Inc
910 Lorain Blvd Ste N
Elyria OH
440 323-9820

(G-10530)
LORAIN COUNTY BOARD
1091 Infirmary Rd (44035-4804)
PHONE.................................440 329-3734
Amber Fisher, *Superintendent*
Heather Gurchik, *Director*
EMP: 34
SALES (est): 700.6K **Privately Held**
SIC: 8093 8331 Mental health clinic, outpatient; sheltered workshop

(G-10531)
LOWES HOME CENTERS LLC
646 Midway Blvd (44035-2442)
PHONE.................................440 324-5004
Paul Fran, *Branch Mgr*
Thomas Kilroy, *Department Mgr*
EMP: 200
SALES (corp-wide): 68.6B **Publicly Held**
SIC: 5211 5031 5722 Home centers; building materials, exterior; building materials, interior; household appliance stores
HQ: Lowe's Home Centers, Llc
1605 Curtis Bridge Rd
Wilkesboro NC 28697
336 658-4000

(G-10532)
MAINTENANCE SYSTERMS OF N OHIO
42208 Albrecht Rd Ste 1 (44035-8925)
P.O. Box 1203 (44036-1203)
PHONE..................440 323-1291
Frank Rybarcyk Jr, *President*
EMP: 25
SQ FT: 5,200
SALES (est): 4.1MM **Privately Held**
WEB: www.maintenancesystemsco.com
SIC: 1611 1771 Surfacing & paving; highway & street maintenance; blacktop (asphalt) work

(G-10533)
MATCO PROPERTIES INC
823 Leona St (44035-2300)
PHONE..................440 366-5501
Jack Matia, *President*
EMP: 65
SQ FT: 50,000
SALES (est): 3.2MM **Privately Held**
SIC: 6512 Nonresidential building operators

(G-10534)
MATIA MOTORS INC
Also Called: Jack Matia Honda
823 Leona St (44035-2300)
PHONE..................440 365-7311
Jack Matia, *President*
Barbara Matia, *Vice Pres*
Gerald Draga, *Sales Mgr*
Phil Schultz, *Sales Associate*
Don Groff, *Associate*
EMP: 38
SQ FT: 10,000
SALES (est): 17MM **Privately Held**
WEB: www.jackmatia.com
SIC: 5511 7538 7532 5531 Automobiles, new & used; general automotive repair shops; top & body repair & paint shops; automotive & home supply stores

(G-10535)
MERCY HEALTH
1120 E Broad St Fl 2 (44035-6306)
PHONE..................440 336-2239
Edwin M Oley, *CEO*
EMP: 42
SALES (corp-wide): 4.7B **Privately Held**
SIC: 8011 Offices & clinics of medical doctors
PA: Mercy Health
1701 Mercy Health Pl
Cincinnati OH 45237
513 639-2800

(G-10536)
MERCY HEALTH
41201 Schadden Rd (44035-2249)
PHONE..................440 324-0400
EMP: 38
SALES (corp-wide): 4.7B **Privately Held**
SIC: 8099 8322 Medical services organization; general counseling services
PA: Mercy Health
1701 Mercy Health Pl
Cincinnati OH 45237
513 639-2800

(G-10537)
MIDWAY MALL MERCHANTS ASSOC
3343 Midway Mall (44035-9003)
PHONE..................440 244-1245
Mark Bressler, *Manager*
Suzy Davis, *Admin Sec*
Cindy Simms, *Admin Sec*
EMP: 50
SALES (est): 3.9MM **Privately Held**
SIC: 8743 Promotion service

(G-10538)
MIDWAY REALTY COMPANY
Also Called: Sommers Mobil Leasing
1800 Lorain Blvd (44035-2407)
P.O. Box 84 (44036-0084)
PHONE..................440 324-2404
Kenneth Sommer, *President*
Kent Sommer, *Vice Pres*
Ron Sommer, *Vice Pres*
Todd Sommer, *Vice Pres*
EMP: 45

SQ FT: 1,000
SALES (est): 2.2MM **Privately Held**
SIC: 6519 Real property lessors

(G-10539)
MOLLY MAID OF LORAIN COUNTY
753 Leona St (44035-2350)
PHONE..................440 327-0000
Craig P Zoladz, *President*
Molly Zoladz, *Vice Pres*
EMP: 30
SQ FT: 1,700
SALES (est): 720K **Privately Held**
SIC: 7349 Maid services, contract or fee basis

(G-10540)
MULTILINK INC
Also Called: Multifab
580 Ternes Ln (44035-6252)
PHONE..................440 366-6966
Steven Kaplan, *President*
Mike French, *Vice Pres*
Kathy Kaplan, *Vice Pres*
Steve Brown, *Engineer*
Sirisha Joish, *Accounts Exec*
▲ **EMP:** 140
SQ FT: 110,000
SALES (est): 147.4MM **Privately Held**
WEB: www.multilinkbroadband.com
SIC: 5063 3829 Wire & cable; cable testing machines

(G-10541)
MURRAY RIDGE PRODUCTION CENTER
1091 Infirmary Rd (44035-4804)
PHONE..................440 329-3734
Amber Fischer, *Superintendent*
Kimberly Rothgery, *Admin Sec*
EMP: 500
SQ FT: 100,000
SALES (est): 10MM **Privately Held**
WEB: www.mrpcinc.com
SIC: 8331 8322 Vocational rehabilitation agency; social services for the handicapped

(G-10542)
NC HHA INC
Also Called: Intrepid USA Healthcare Svcs
1170 E Broad St Ste 101 (44035-6351)
PHONE..................216 593-7750
Adrienne Adkins, *Principal*
Cecellia Callis, *Vice Pres*
EMP: 80
SALES (est): 1MM
SALES (corp-wide): 4B **Privately Held**
SIC: 8082 Home health care services
HQ: Intrepid U.S.A., Inc.
4055 Valley View Ln # 500
Dallas TX 75244
214 445-3750

(G-10543)
NELSON STUD WELDING INC
101 Liberty Ct (44035-2238)
PHONE..................440 250-9242
Doug Philips, *Branch Mgr*
EMP: 40
SALES (corp-wide): 3.4B **Privately Held**
SIC: 5084 Welding machinery & equipment
HQ: Nelson Stud Welding, Inc.
7900 W Ridge Rd
Elyria OH 44035
440 329-0400

(G-10544)
NOR CORP
Also Called: Northern Ohio Realty
10247 Dewhurst Rd Ste 101 (44035-8950)
PHONE..................440 366-0099
Lorene Albert, *President*
EMP: 28 **EST:** 1997
SALES (est): 1.3MM **Privately Held**
WEB: www.northernohiorealty.com
SIC: 6531 Real estate brokers & agents

(G-10545)
NORTH OHIO HEART CENTER INC
10325 Dewhurst Rd (44035-8403)
PHONE..................440 366-3600
Patricia Cathcart, *Branch Mgr*

EMP: 47
SALES (corp-wide): 13.5MM **Privately Held**
SIC: 8011 Cardiologist & cardio-vascular specialist
PA: North Ohio Heart Center, Inc
3600 Kolbe Rd Ste 127
Lorain OH 44053
440 204-4000

(G-10546)
NORTH OHIO HEART CENTER INC
125 E Broad St Ste 305 (44035-6447)
PHONE..................440 326-4120
Gary Ghome, *Manager*
EMP: 50
SALES (corp-wide): 13.5MM **Privately Held**
WEB: www.nohc.com
SIC: 8011 Cardiologist & cardio-vascular specialist
PA: North Ohio Heart Center, Inc
3600 Kolbe Rd Ste 127
Lorain OH 44053
440 204-4000

(G-10547)
NORTH SHORE DOOR CO INC
Also Called: Nsd
162 Edgewood St (44035-4006)
PHONE..................800 783-6112
Fax: 440 365-3514
EMP: 36
SQ FT: 9,000
SALES (est): 12.1MM **Privately Held**
SIC: 5031 Whol Lumber/Plywood/Millwork

(G-10548)
NORTHCUTT TRUCKING INC
40259 Butternut Ridge Rd (44035-7996)
P.O. Box 82 (44036-0082)
PHONE..................440 458-5139
Charles Northcutt, *President*
EMP: 40
SALES: 1.1MM **Privately Held**
SIC: 4212 Local trucking, without storage

(G-10549)
NORTHERN OHIO ROOFG SHTMTL INC
Also Called: Norfab
880 Infirmary Rd (44035-4884)
PHONE..................440 322-8262
David Phiel, *President*
Joseph A Blaszak, *Corp Secy*
EMP: 30
SQ FT: 12,000
SALES (est): 4.2MM **Privately Held**
WEB: www.northernohioroofing.com
SIC: 1761 Roofing contractor; sheet metal-work

(G-10550)
NORTHWEST LIMOUSINE INC
642 Sugar Ln Ste 207 (44035-6300)
P.O. Box 513 (44036-0513)
PHONE..................440 322-5804
Johnathan Squires, *President*
EMP: 33
SQ FT: 300,000
SALES (est): 840K **Privately Held**
SIC: 4119 Limousine rental, with driver

(G-10551)
OPEN DOOR CHRISTIAN SCHOOL
8287 W Ridge Rd (44035-4498)
PHONE..................440 322-6386
Tarrell Dunckel, *Principal*
Angie Lowe, *Principal*
Bonita Vereen, *Supervisor*
Denver Daniel, *Director*
Bill Dunston, *Athletic Dir*
EMP: 62
SQ FT: 42,000
SALES: 3.7MM **Privately Held**
WEB: www.odcs.org
SIC: 8211 8351 Private combined elementary & secondary school; private elementary school; private junior high school; private senior high school; preschool center

(G-10552)
PACIFIC MGT HOLDINGS LLC
Also Called: Pharmacy-Lite Packaging
250 Warden Ave (44035-2650)
P.O. Box 775 (44036-0775)
PHONE..................440 324-3339
Jack Brennan,
Ian Brennan,
▼ **EMP:** 30
SQ FT: 90,000
SALES (est): 12.7MM **Privately Held**
WEB: www.pharmacylite.com
SIC: 5199 Packaging materials

(G-10553)
PALM CREST EAST INC
Also Called: Palm Crest Nursing Homes
1251 East Ave (44035-7674)
PHONE..................440 322-0726
Sally Schwartz, *President*
Abraham Schwartz, *Corp Secy*
EMP: 40
SALES (est): 1.3MM **Privately Held**
SIC: 8052 Home for the mentally retarded, with health care
PA: Royal Manor Health Care Inc
18810 Harvard Ave
Cleveland OH 44122

(G-10554)
PEPSI-COLA METRO BTLG CO INC
925 Lorain Blvd (44035-2819)
PHONE..................440 323-5524
Mike Schonberg, *Branch Mgr*
EMP: 50
SALES (corp-wide): 64.6B **Publicly Held**
WEB: www.joy-of-cola.com
SIC: 4225 5149 General warehousing & storage; soft drinks
HQ: Pepsi-Cola Metropolitan Bottling Company, Inc.
1111 Westchester Ave
White Plains NY 10604
914 767-6000

(G-10555)
PLATINUM RESTORATION CONTRS
104 Reaser Ct (44035-6285)
PHONE..................440 327-0699
Michelle Brooks, *President*
EMP: 33 **EST:** 2010
SALES (est): 13.4MM **Privately Held**
SIC: 6331 Property damage insurance

(G-10556)
PLATINUM RESTORATION INC
104 Reaser Ct (44035-6285)
PHONE..................440 327-0699
Wayne Hudspath, *President*
Scott Danko, *General Mgr*
Matthew Benedict, *Business Mgr*
Michelle Brooks, *Vice Pres*
Randy Price, *Project Mgr*
EMP: 30
SQ FT: 5,000
SALES (est): 3.8MM **Privately Held**
SIC: 1741 1629 Tuckpointing or restoration; waste water & sewage treatment plant construction

(G-10557)
PURPLE MARLIN INC
Also Called: Maintenance Systems Nthm Ohio
42208 Albrecht Rd Ste 1 (44035-8925)
P.O. Box 1203 (44036-1203)
PHONE..................440 323-1291
Frank Rybarcyk, *President*
EMP: 25
SALES (est): 2.4MM **Privately Held**
SIC: 1799 Parking facility equipment & maintenance

(G-10558)
REGAL CINEMAS INC
Also Called: Cobblestone Square 20
5500 Abbe Rd (44035)
PHONE..................440 934-3356
Steve Flauto, *Branch Mgr*
EMP: 35 **Privately Held**
WEB: www.regalcinemas.com
SIC: 7832 Motion picture theaters, except drive-in

G E O G R A P H I C

HQ: Regal Cinemas, Inc.
101 E Blount Ave Ste 100
Knoxville TN 37920
865 922-1123

(G-10559)
REPUBLIC SERVICES INC
40195 Butternut Ridge Rd (44035-7903)
P.O. Box 4011 (44036-2011)
PHONE..............................440 458-5191
Keith Cordesman, Branch Mgr
EMP: 34
SALES (corp-wide): 10B Publicly Held
SIC: 4953 Refuse collection & disposal
services
PA: Republic Services, Inc.
18500 N Allied Way # 100
Phoenix AZ 85054
480 627-2700

(G-10560)
SANTANTONIO DIANA AND ASSOC
Also Called: Psychiatric Psychological Svcs
750 Abbe Rd S (44035-7246)
PHONE..............................440 323-5121
Diana Santantonio, Owner
Cindy Sabo, Manager
EMP: 25
SALES (est): 1.2MM Privately Held
WEB: www.psychandpsych.com
SIC: 8322 General counseling services

(G-10561)
SCHOOL EMPLOYEES LORAIN COUNTY
340 Griswold Rd (44035-2301)
PHONE..............................440 324-3400
Edward Enyedi, CEO
Brent Binkley, COO
Karen Akers, CFO
Shannon Boesel, Manager
EMP: 40
SALES: 4.1MM Privately Held
WEB: www.selccu.org
SIC: 6061 Federal credit unions

(G-10562)
SENSI CARE 3
1243 East Ave (44035-7674)
PHONE..............................440 323-6310
Wendy Morris, Director
EMP: 40
SALES (est): 795.1K Privately Held
SIC: 8051 8052 Convalescent home with
continuous nursing care; intermediate
care facilities

(G-10563)
SMINK ELECTRIC INC
215 Winckles St (44035-6129)
P.O. Box 1103 (44036-1103)
PHONE..............................440 322-5518
John Smink, President
Greg Smink, Vice Pres
Donna Smink, Accountant
EMP: 25
SQ FT: 2,200
SALES (est): 3.6MM Privately Held
WEB: www.sminkelectric.com
SIC: 1731 General electrical contractor

(G-10564)
SOUTH SHORE ELECTRIC INC
589 Ternes Ln (44035-6251)
P.O. Box 321 (44036-0321)
PHONE..............................440 366-6289
Paul Zielazienski, President
Kathryn Zielazienski, Corp Secy
Keith Buckley, Project Mgr
Karen M Hughes, Admin Sec
EMP: 40
SQ FT: 11,000
SALES (est): 7.2MM Privately Held
WEB: www.southshoreelectric.com
SIC: 1731 General electrical contractor

(G-10565)
SPORTS FACILITY ACOUSTICS INC
801 Bond St (44035-3318)
PHONE..............................440 323-1400
Chris Kysela, President
EMP: 35

SALES (est): 1.2MM Privately Held
SIC: 1742 Acoustical & ceiling work

(G-10566)
ST JUDE SOCIAL CONCERN HOT
636 Sycamore St (44035-4050)
PHONE..............................440 365-7971
Jean Koch, Principal
EMP: 80
SALES: 3K Privately Held
SIC: 8399 Social services

(G-10567)
TIME WARNER CABLE INC
578 Ternes Ln (44035-6252)
PHONE..............................440 366-0416
Chris Potts, Branch Mgr
EMP: 83
SALES (corp-wide): 43.6B Publicly Held
SIC: 4841 Cable television services
HQ: Spectrum Management Holding Com-
pany, Llc
400 Atlantic St
Stamford CT 06901
203 905-7801

(G-10568)
TRUGREEN LIMITED PARTNERSHIP
Also Called: Tru Green-Chemlawn
151 Keep Ct (44035-2214)
PHONE..............................440 540-4209
Matthew Rehlander, Branch Mgr
EMP: 70
SQ FT: 12,000
SALES (corp-wide): 3.4B Privately Held
SIC: 0782 Lawn care services
HQ: Trugreen Limited Partnership
1790 Kirby Pkwy
Memphis TN 38138
901 251-4128

(G-10569)
VANTAGE AGING
42495 N Ridge Rd (44035-1045)
PHONE..............................440 324-3588
Mary Ensman, Principal
Penny Holvey, Human Resources
EMP: 620
SALES (corp-wide): 13.1MM Privately
Held
SIC: 8322 Public welfare center
PA: Vantage Aging
2279 Romig Rd
Akron OH 44320
330 253-4597

(G-10570)
VOCATIONAL GUIDANCE SERVICES
Also Called: Vocational Services
359 Lowell St (44035-4935)
PHONE..............................440 322-1123
Lynn Merholz, Manager
EMP: 30
SALES (corp-wide): 10.7MM Privately
Held
SIC: 8331 Vocational training agency;
community service employment training
program; sheltered workshop; vocational
rehabilitation agency
PA: Vocational Guidance Services Inc
2239 E 55th St
Cleveland OH 44103
216 431-7800

(G-10571)
WEOL
Also Called: Lorraine Elyria Broadcasting
538 Broad St (44035-5508)
PHONE..............................440 236-9283
Gary Knisley, President
EMP: 50
SALES (est): 2.5MM Privately Held
WEB: www.weol.com
SIC: 4832 Radio broadcasting stations

(G-10572)
WESLEYAN SENIOR LIVING (PA)
Also Called: WESLEYAN VILLAGE
807 West Ave (44035-5893)
PHONE..............................440 284-9000
Michael Rogan, President
Kristen Jones, Director

EMP: 110
SALES: 21.2MM Privately Held
SIC: 8361 Residential care

(G-10573)
WESLEYAN VILLAGE
807 West Ave (44035-5898)
PHONE..............................440 284-9000
Michael Rogan, CEO
Leonard Budd, Chairman
Peter Duffield, CFO
Jennifer Piszczek, Director
EMP: 400 EST: 1923
SQ FT: 226,000
SALES: 273.9K
SALES (corp-wide): 21.2MM Privately
Held
WEB: www.villageliving.com
SIC: 8361 Home for the aged
PA: Senior Wesleyan Living
807 West Ave
Elyria OH 44035
440 284-9000

(G-10574)
WESTERN & SOUTHERN LF INSUR CO
347 Midway Blvd Ste 101 (44035-2496)
PHONE..............................440 324-2626
Paul Herman, Manager
EMP: 25 Privately Held
SIC: 6411 Life insurance agents
HQ: The Western & Southern Life Insur-
ance Company
400 Broadway St
Cincinnati OH 45202
513 629-1800

(G-10575)
WILLIAMS BROS BUILDERS INC
686 Sugar Ln (44035-6310)
PHONE..............................440 365-3261
Bart Williams, President
Jonathan R Traut, Treasurer
EMP: 30
SQ FT: 2,000
SALES (est): 6.1MM Privately Held
WEB: www.williamsbrothersbuilders.com
SIC: 1541 1542 Industrial buildings, new
construction; commercial & office building
contractors

(G-10576)
WISE CHOICES IN LEARNING LTD
352 Griswold Rd (44035-2301)
PHONE..............................440 324-6056
Karen Wise,
EMP: 27
SALES (est): 563.8K Privately Held
SIC: 8351 Group day care center

(G-10577)
ZONE TRANSPORTATION CO
41670 Schadden Rd (44035-2229)
P.O. Box 1379 (44036-1379)
PHONE..............................440 324-3544
Robert J Lehman Sr, President
EMP: 100
SQ FT: 55,000
SALES (est): 8.2MM Privately Held
SIC: 4213 4212 Trucking, except local;
local trucking, without storage

Englewood
Montgomery County

(G-10578)
ANALYTICAL PACE SERVICES LLC
25 Holiday Dr (45322-2706)
PHONE..............................937 832-8242
Brooke Chandler, Manager
EMP: 30
SALES (corp-wide): 65.2MM Privately
Held
SIC: 8734 Soil analysis; water testing labo-
ratory
HQ: Pace Analytical Services, Llc
1800 Elm St Se
Minneapolis MN 55414

(G-10579)
AVI-SPL EMPLOYEE
35 Rockridge Rd Ste B (45322-2738)
PHONE..............................937 836-4787
EMP: 45
SALES (corp-wide): 596.9MM Privately
Held
SIC: 4813 Telephone Communications
HQ: Avi-Spl Employee Emergency Relief
Fund, Inc.
6301 Benjamin Rd Ste 101
Tampa FL 33634
813 884-7168

(G-10580)
BROOKDALE SNIOR LVING CMMNTIES
350 Union Blvd (45322-2196)
PHONE..............................937 832-8500
Britney Jaco, Corp Comm Staff
Wendy Haines, Director
EMP: 30
SALES (corp-wide): 4.5B Publicly Held
WEB: www.assisted.com
SIC: 8059 Rest home, with health care
HQ: Brookdale Senior Living Communities,
Inc.
6737 W Wa St Ste 2300
Milwaukee WI 53214
414 918-5000

(G-10581)
CASTILIAN & CO
Also Called: Castilian Hair & Skin Center
848 Union Blvd (45322-2101)
PHONE..............................937 836-9671
Barbara E Crabtree, Owner
EMP: 25 EST: 1970
SALES (est): 621.9K Privately Held
SIC: 7231 Hairdressers

(G-10582)
CITY OF ENGLEWOOD
Also Called: Englewood, City of
333 W National Rd Ofc (45322-1495)
PHONE..............................937 836-2434
Vernon Brown, Superintendent
EMP: 50 Privately Held
SIC: 1623 Water, sewer & utility lines
PA: City Of Englewood
333 W National Rd Ofc
Englewood OH 45322
937 836-1732

(G-10583)
CREATIVE MICROSYSTEMS INC
Also Called: Civica CMI
52 Hillside Ct (45322-2745)
PHONE..............................937 836-4499
Lin Mallott, CEO
Missy Matherne, Purchasing
Arvind Kohli, Finance
David Swigart, Finance
Becky Chestnut, Human Resources
EMP: 80 EST: 1979
SQ FT: 14,400
SALES (est): 13.2MM Privately Held
WEB: www.creativemicrosystems.com
SIC: 7373 7372 Systems integration serv-
ices; prepackaged software

(G-10584)
DAYTON HOTELS LLC
Also Called: Best Western
20 Rockridge Rd (45322-2710)
PHONE..............................937 832-2222
Abhijit Vasani, CEO
EMP: 25
SALES (est): 1.5MM
SALES (corp-wide): 1.3MM Privately
Held
WEB: www.hamptoninndaytonnorth.com
SIC: 7011 Hotels & motels
PA: Indiana Motel Developers
2595 Eastwood Dr
Columbus IN 47203
812 372-1541

(G-10585)
DIXIE MANAGEMENT II INC
Also Called: Holiday Inn
10 Rockridge Rd (45322-2710)
PHONE..............................937 832-1234
Roy Smith, President
Todd Smith, Vice Pres
Virginia Steinbrugge, Bookkeeper

EMP: 90
SQ FT: 100,000
SALES (est): 2.6MM **Privately Held**
SIC: 7011 5812 Hotels & motels; eating places

(G-10586)
ENGLEWOOD SQUARE LTD
Also Called: Englewood Square Apartments
150 Chris Dr Apt 119 (45322-1117)
PHONE.................................937 836-4117
Leonard Gorsuch, *President*
Elizabeth Clark, *Manager*
EMP: 100
SALES (est): 3.3MM **Privately Held**
SIC: 6513 Apartment building operators

(G-10587)
GARBER ELECTRICAL CONTRS INC
Also Called: Garber Connect
100 Rockridge Rd (45322-2737)
PHONE.................................937 771-5202
Gary A Garber, *President*
John Killion, *Project Mgr*
Matt Murphy, *Foreman/Supr*
Terry Cool, *Sales Mgr*
Brett Garber, *Sales Mgr*
EMP: 60
SALES (est): 15.6MM **Privately Held**
SIC: 1731 General electrical contractor; electric power systems contractors

(G-10588)
GEM CITY UROLOGIST INC (PA)
9000 N Main St Ste 333 (45415-1185)
PHONE.................................937 832-8400
Ahmad Abouhossein MD, *Principal*
Jan Bernie MD, *Exec VP*
Howard B Abromowitz, *Treasurer*
EMP: 27
SALES (est): 2.2MM **Privately Held**
WEB: www.gemcityurology.com
SIC: 8011 Urologist

(G-10589)
GRACE BRETHREN VILLAGE INC
1010 Taywood Rd Ofc (45322-2415)
PHONE.................................937 836-4011
Mike Montgomery, *Administration*
EMP: 48
SALES (est): 2.9MM **Privately Held**
WEB: www.gbvillage.com
SIC: 8051 Convalescent home with continuous nursing care

(G-10590)
IDEAL IMAGE INC
115 Haas Dr (45322-2845)
PHONE.................................937 832-1660
Dale Paugh, *President*
Belinda Paugh, *Vice Pres*
J Belinda Paugh, *Treasurer*
Jenny Sutter, *Mktg Dir*
◆ EMP: 77
SQ FT: 40,000
SALES (est): 13.1MM **Privately Held**
WEB: www.idealimageinc.com
SIC: 7335 Photographic studio, commercial

(G-10591)
INNOVATIVE LOGISTICS GROUP INC
30 Lau Pkwy (45315-8777)
PHONE.................................937 832-9350
Brad Eib, *Branch Mgr*
EMP: 40
SALES (corp-wide): 10.5MM **Privately Held**
SIC: 4731 Domestic freight forwarding
HQ: Innovative Logistics Group, Inc.
9850 Pelham Rd
Taylor MI 48180

(G-10592)
KING KOLD INC
331 N Main St (45322-1333)
PHONE.................................937 836-2731
Douglas Smith, *President*
Robert L Smith, *Corp Secy*
EMP: 25
SQ FT: 5,210

SALES (est): 2.4MM **Privately Held**
SIC: 2038 2013 2011 5142 Frozen specialties; cooked meats from purchased meat; meat packing plants; fish, frozen: packaged

(G-10593)
LIBERTY NURSING CENTER
Also Called: Englewood Manor
425 Lauricella Ct (45322)
P.O. Box 340 (45322-0340)
PHONE.................................937 836-5143
Linda Black-Kurek, *President*
Linda Black Kurek, *President*
EMP: 34 EST: 1962
SALES (est): 3.1MM **Privately Held**
WEB: www.englewoodmanor.com
SIC: 8051 8052 Convalescent home with continuous nursing care; intermediate care facilities

(G-10594)
NORTHMONT SERVICE CENTER
7277 Hoke Rd (45315-8845)
PHONE.................................937 832-5050
Jason Watson, *Director*
John Blessing, *Director*
EMP: 100
SALES (est): 4.3MM **Privately Held**
SIC: 4151 School buses

(G-10595)
PARKVIEW MANOR INC (PA)
425 Lauricella Ct (45322)
PHONE.................................937 296-1550
James A Lauricella Sr, *President*
Lena M Lauricella, *Vice Pres*
EMP: 90 EST: 1997
SALES (est): 3.1MM **Privately Held**
SIC: 8052 8051 Intermediate care facilities; skilled nursing care facilities

(G-10596)
PEDIATRIC ASSOCIATES OF DAYTON (PA)
9000 N Main St Ste 332 (45415-1185)
PHONE.................................937 832-7337
Gary Youra, *President*
Richard Smith, *Vice Pres*
David Roer, *Treasurer*
EMP: 25
SQ FT: 2,600
SALES (est): 3.7MM **Privately Held**
SIC: 8011 Pediatrician

(G-10597)
POLYCOM INC
35 Rockridge Rd Ste A (45322-2767)
PHONE.................................937 245-1853
David Allen, *Branch Mgr*
EMP: 35
SALES (corp-wide): 856.9MM **Publicly Held**
WEB: www.polycom.com
SIC: 5065 Telephone equipment
HQ: Polycom, Inc.
345 Encinal St
Santa Cruz CA 95060
831 426-5858

(G-10598)
PREMIER HEART INC
9000 N Main St Ste 101 (45415-1184)
PHONE.................................937 832-2425
Ahmad Karim, *President*
EMP: 35
SALES (est): 2MM **Privately Held**
SIC: 8011 Cardiologist & cardio-vascular specialist

(G-10599)
PRISTINE SNIOR LVING ENGLEWOOD
425 Lauricella Ct (45322)
PHONE.................................937 836-5143
Jensen Glaze,
EMP: 200 EST: 2016
SALES (est): 9.7MM **Privately Held**
SIC: 8361 Home for the aged

(G-10600)
SAMARITAN N SURGERY CTR LTD
9000 N Main St (45415-1180)
PHONE.................................937 567-6100

David P Kelly, *Principal*
EMP: 34
SALES (est): 3.9MM **Privately Held**
SIC: 8062 General medical & surgical hospitals

(G-10601)
SUNRISE SENIOR LIVING LLC
95 W Wenger Rd (45322-2723)
PHONE.................................937 836-9617
Jennifer Tibbettgrady, *Branch Mgr*
EMP: 50
SALES (corp-wide): 4.7B **Publicly Held**
SIC: 8051 Skilled nursing care facilities
HQ: Sunrise Senior Living, Llc
7902 Westpark Dr
Mc Lean VA 22102

(G-10602)
SUNSET CARPET CLEANING
Also Called: E Z Cleaners
9 Beckenham Rd (45322-1262)
PHONE.................................937 836-5531
Bill Minnich, *President*
Fred Minnich, *Vice Pres*
EMP: 36
SQ FT: 5,100
SALES (est): 1.5MM **Privately Held**
WEB: www.sunsetcarpetcleaning.com
SIC: 7216 7217 Drycleaning plants, except rugs; carpet & upholstery cleaning

(G-10603)
TV MINORITY COMPANY INC
Dayton Origin Distribution Ctr
30 Lau Pkwy (45315-8777)
PHONE.................................937 832-9350
Brad Eib, *Branch Mgr*
EMP: 50
SALES (corp-wide): 46.6MM **Privately Held**
WEB: www.ilgi.com
SIC: 4731 8742 Freight forwarding; transportation consultant
PA: T.V. Minority Company, Inc.
9400 Pelham Rd
Taylor MI 48180
313 386-1048

(G-10604)
UPTOWN HAIR STUDIO INC
Also Called: Uptown Hair & Day Spa
390 W National Rd (45322-1401)
PHONE.................................937 832-2111
Linda S Harlamert, *President*
Theresa Bowers, *Vice Pres*
EMP: 35
SQ FT: 1,800
SALES (est): 859.5K **Privately Held**
SIC: 7991 7231 Spas; manicurist, pedicurist

(G-10605)
WEIFFENBACH MARBLE & TILE CO
150 Lau Pkwy (45315-8787)
PHONE.................................937 832-7055
Craig Lindsey, *President*
Jill Lindsey, *General Mgr*
Anne Lindsey, *Executive*
EMP: 40
SALES (est): 6.1MM **Privately Held**
SIC: 1752 Ceramic floor tile installation

(G-10606)
YOUNG MENS CHRISTIAN ASSOC
Also Called: Metropolitan YMCA
1200 W National Rd (45315-9504)
P.O. Box 38 (45322-0038)
PHONE.................................937 836-9622
April Turner, *Director*
EMP: 65
SALES (corp-wide): 26.1MM **Privately Held**
WEB: www.daytonymca.org
SIC: 8641 8661 7997 Community membership club; religious organizations; membership sports & recreation clubs
PA: Young Men's Christian Association Of Greater Dayton
118 W 1st St Ste 300
Dayton OH 45402
937 223-5201

(G-10607)
CONCRETE CORING COMPANY INC
400 E Main St (45323-1042)
P.O. Box 308 (45323-0308)
PHONE.................................937 864-7325
Terry D Holmes, *President*
EMP: 30
SQ FT: 1,996
SALES (est): 4.1MM **Privately Held**
SIC: 1771 Concrete work

(G-10608)
ENON FIREMANS ASSOCIATION
260 E Main St (45323-1054)
PHONE.................................937 864-7429
Maxine McKee, *President*
Don Ingram, *Treasurer*
EMP: 40 EST: 2001
SALES (est): 338.1K **Privately Held**
SIC: 8641 8611 Fraternal associations; business associations

(G-10609)
FIVE SEASONS LANDSCAPE MGT INC
9886 Mink St Sw Rear (43068-3812)
PHONE.................................740 964-2915
Bill Leidecker, *President*
Steve Woods, *Vice Pres*
John Josephson, *Controller*
Lacie Espenschied, *Human Res Mgr*
Josh Gilbert, *Accounts Mgr*
EMP: 100
SQ FT: 5,000
SALES (est): 7.5MM **Privately Held**
WEB: www.fiveseasonslandscape.com
SIC: 0781 Landscape services

(G-10610)
HARRIS & HEAVENER EXCAVATING
149 Humphries Dr (43068-6801)
PHONE.................................740 927-1423
Steven Heavener, *President*
Tom Evans, *Assistant VP*
Steve Corwin, *Project Mgr*
EMP: 28
SQ FT: 3,600
SALES (est): 5.1MM **Privately Held**
SIC: 1794 Excavation & grading, building construction

(G-10611)
MOO MOO NORTH HAMILTON LLC (PA)
Also Called: Moo Moo Carwash
13375 National Rd Sw D (43068-3388)
PHONE.................................614 751-9274
John Rousch, *Mng Member*
EMP: 51
SALES (est): 4.3MM **Privately Held**
SIC: 7542 Washing & polishing, automotive

(G-10612)
B & D CONCRETE FOOTERS INC
12897 National Rd Sw (43062-9281)
P.O. Box 400, Kirkersville (43033-0400)
PHONE.................................740 964-2294
Jason Deskins, *President*
EMP: 45
SALES (est): 4.8MM **Privately Held**
SIC: 1771 Concrete work

(G-10613)
BEST LIGHTING PRODUCTS INC (HQ)
1213 Etna Pkwy (43062-8041)
PHONE....................740 964-0063
Jeffrey S Katz, *CEO*
George Jue, *President*
▲ EMP: 55 EST: 1997
SQ FT: 60,000
SALES (est): 12.5MM
SALES (corp-wide): 284.4MM **Privately Held**
WEB: www.bestlighting.net
SIC: 3646 5063 Commercial indusl & institutional electric lighting fixtures; electrical apparatus & equipment
PA: Corinthian Capital Group, Llc
601 Lexington Ave Rm 5901
New York NY 10022
212 920-2300

(G-10614)
CUMBERLAND TRAIL GOLF CLB CRSE
8244 Columbia Rd Sw (43062-9290)
PHONE....................740 964-9336
Mike Tickett, *Principal*
EMP: 50
SALES (est): 1.6MM **Privately Held**
SIC: 7992 Public golf courses

(G-10615)
EXEL INC
127 Heritage Dr (43062-9805)
PHONE....................740 927-1762
EMP: 64
SALES (corp-wide): 70.4B **Privately Held**
SIC: 4225 General warehousing
HQ: Exel Inc.
570 Polaris Pkwy
Westerville OH 43082
614 865-8500

(G-10616)
K & W ROOFING INC
Also Called: K and W Roofing
8356 National Rd Sw (43062-8665)
PHONE....................740 927-3122
Bill Kilcoyne, *President*
Tricia Kilcoyne, *Corp Secy*
EMP: 25
SQ FT: 3,000
SALES: 4MM **Privately Held**
SIC: 1761 Roofing contractor

(G-10617)
MENLO LOGISTICS INC
107 Heritage Dr (43062-9805)
PHONE....................740 963-1154
Robert Bianco, *President*
EMP: 99 EST: 2015
SQ FT: 350,000
SALES (est): 5.2MM **Privately Held**
SIC: 4225 General warehousing & storage

(G-10618)
OHIO HIGH SCHOOL FOOTBALL COAC
138 Purple Finch Loop (43062-8974)
PHONE....................419 673-1286
Paul Farrah, *President*
Michael Mauk, *Treasurer*
Gerald Cooke, *Bd of Directors*
Mike Mauk, *Teacher*
EMP: 25
SALES: 125.7K **Privately Held**
SIC: 7941 Football club

(G-10619)
PROGRESSIVE FLOORING SVCS INC
100 Heritage Dr (43062-8042)
PHONE....................614 868-9005
Richard A South, *CEO*
Richard J South, *President*
Nino A Cervi, *Vice Pres*
Matthew Teets, *Project Mgr*
Irene Edginton, *Office Mgr*
EMP: 28
SQ FT: 45,300
SALES (est): 7MM **Privately Held**
WEB:
www.progressiveflooringservices.com
SIC: 1752 Carpet laying

(G-10620)
TEREX UTILITIES INC
Also Called: Columbus Division
110 Venture Dr (43062-9239)
PHONE....................614 444-7373
George Barr, *Branch Mgr*
EMP: 30
SALES (corp-wide): 5.1B **Publicly Held**
WEB: www.craneamerica.com
SIC: 7699 Industrial truck repair
HQ: Terex Utilities, Inc.
12805 Sw 77th Pl
Tigard OR 97223
503 620-0611

(G-10621)
WILLIAM D TAYLOR SR INC (PA)
Also Called: Jericho Investments Company
263 Trail E (43062-9680)
PHONE....................614 653-6683
William D Taylor, *Principal*
EMP: 51
SQ FT: 1,800
SALES (est): 3.4MM **Privately Held**
WEB: www.realmoments.net
SIC: 6163 6411 6282 Mortgage brokers arranging for loans, using money of others; insurance agents; investment advice

---

Euclid
Cuyahoga County

(G-10622)
A W S INC
Also Called: Euclid Adult Training Center
1490 E 191st St (44117-1321)
PHONE....................216 486-0600
Daisy Maleckar, *General Mgr*
EMP: 50
SALES (corp-wide): 7.8MM **Privately Held**
SIC: 8331 8322 Vocational rehabilitation agency; rehabilitation services
PA: A W S Inc
1275 Lakeside Ave E
Cleveland OH 44114
216 861-0250

(G-10623)
ASV SERVICES LLC
27801 Euclid Ave Ste 420 (44132-3547)
PHONE....................216 797-1701
EMP: 35
SALES (est): 458.5K **Privately Held**
SIC: 7521 4119 Automobile parking; local passenger transportation

(G-10624)
B H C SERVICES INC
Also Called: Brason's Willcare
26250 Euclid Ave Ste 901 (44132-3696)
PHONE....................216 289-5300
David Brason, *President*
Todd Brason, *Principal*
EMP: 2000
SALES: 11MM **Privately Held**
WEB: www.bhcservices.com
SIC: 8082 Visiting nurse service

(G-10625)
BP
Also Called: Aquasonic Car Wash
24310 Lakeland Blvd (44132-2658)
PHONE....................216 731-3826
John Attwood Jr, *President*
EMP: 40
SQ FT: 80,000
SALES (est): 427.9K **Privately Held**
SIC: 7542 5541 Carwashes; gasoline service stations

(G-10626)
BRACOR INC
Also Called: Willcare
26250 Euclid Ave Ste 901 (44132-3696)
PHONE....................216 289-5300
Edward Casey, *Manager*
EMP: 31
SALES (corp-wide): 1.8B **Publicly Held**
SIC: 8082 Visiting nurse service
HQ: Bracor, Inc.
346 Delaware Ave
Buffalo NY 14202
716 856-7500

(G-10627)
CONTAINERPORT GROUP INC
24881 Rockwell Dr (44117-1243)
PHONE....................216 692-3124
Stan Jurcevic, *Branch Mgr*
EMP: 55
SALES (corp-wide): 274.1MM **Privately Held**
SIC: 4212 4731 Draying, local: without storage; freight transportation arrangement
HQ: Containerport Group, Inc.
1340 Depot St Fl 2
Cleveland OH 44116
440 333-1330

(G-10628)
DAUGHERTY CONSTRUCTION INC
22460 Lakeland Blvd (44132-2655)
PHONE....................216 731-9444
Harold Daugherty, *President*
Hal Daugherty, *Executive*
EMP: 35
SQ FT: 6,600
SALES (est): 4.7MM **Privately Held**
SIC: 1761 1521 1542 5211 Roofing contractor; siding contractor; new construction, single-family houses; general remodeling, single-family houses; commercial & office buildings, renovation & repair; door & window products; siding

(G-10629)
DEACON 10
1353 E 260th St Ste 1 (44132-2818)
PHONE....................216 731-4000
Neal Alexander, *CEO*
Debra Fikaris, *Manager*
EMP: 99
SALES (est): 2.5MM **Privately Held**
SIC: 7381 Security guard service

(G-10630)
DEE JAY CLEANERS INC
878 E 222nd St (44123-3316)
PHONE....................216 731-7060
David Sabel, *President*
EMP: 25
SALES (est): 1.2MM **Privately Held**
WEB: www.jaydeecleaners.com
SIC: 7216 7211 Cleaning & dyeing, except rugs; power laundries, family & commercial

(G-10631)
EUCLID CITY SCHOOLS
Also Called: Service Center Warehouse
463 Babbitt Rd (44123-1640)
PHONE....................216 261-2900
Pat Blach, *Manager*
EMP: 70 **Privately Held**
WEB: www.euclid.k12.oh.us
SIC: 5049 School supplies
PA: Euclid City Schools
651 E 222nd St
Euclid OH 44123

(G-10632)
EUCLID HEAT TREATING CO
Also Called: E H T Company
1408 E 222nd St (44117-1108)
PHONE....................216 481-8444
John H Vanas, *President*
Dan Lipnicki, *Vice Pres*
EMP: 55 EST: 1946
SQ FT: 45,000
SALES (est): 14MM **Privately Held**
WEB: www.euclidheattreating.com
SIC: 3398 1711 Metal heat treating; plumbing, heating, air-conditioning contractors

(G-10633)
EUCLID HOSPITAL (HQ)
18901 Lake Shore Blvd (44119-1078)
PHONE....................216 531-9000
Tom Selden, *CEO*
Mark Froimson, *President*
Lauren Rock, *COO*
Bob Baker, *Manager*
Cheryl Pecon, *Exec Sec*
EMP: 67
SQ FT: 14,144
SALES: 110.3MM
SALES (corp-wide): 8.9B **Privately Held**
WEB: www.cchseast.org
SIC: 8062 General medical & surgical hospitals
PA: The Cleveland Clinic Foundation
9500 Euclid Ave
Cleveland OH 44195
216 636-8335

(G-10634)
EUCLID HOSPITAL
Also Called: Euclid Finance Division
18901 Lake Shore Blvd # 4 (44119-1078)
PHONE....................216 445-6440
Fax: 216 692-7524
EMP: 140
SALES (corp-wide): 8.4B **Privately Held**
SIC: 8721 Accounting/Auditing/Bookkeeping
HQ: Euclid Hospital
18901 Lake Shore Blvd
Euclid OH 44119
216 531-9000

(G-10635)
FIRST FRUITS CHILD DEV CTR I
21877 Euclid Ave (44117-1515)
P.O. Box 17438 (44117-0438)
PHONE....................216 862-4715
Chelsea Pernell, *President*
Chelsea T Pernell,
EMP: 30
SALES: 2MM **Privately Held**
SIC: 8351 Child day care services

(G-10636)
GATEWAY FAMILY HOUSE
1 Gateway (44119-2447)
PHONE....................216 531-5400
Paul Voniinovich, *Partner*
EMP: 40
SALES (est): 1.6MM **Privately Held**
SIC: 8051 Skilled nursing care facilities

(G-10637)
HELP FOUNDATION INC
27348 Oak Ct (44132-2114)
PHONE....................216 289-7710
EMP: 37
SALES (corp-wide): 8.3MM **Privately Held**
SIC: 8641 Civic social & fraternal associations
PA: Help Foundation, Inc
26900 Euclid Ave
Euclid OH 44132
216 432-4810

(G-10638)
HELP FOUNDATION INC (PA)
26900 Euclid Ave (44132-3404)
PHONE....................216 432-4810
Daniel J Rice, *CEO*
Nathan Kelly, *Trustee*
Lynn M Sargi, *Vice Pres*
Liz Linder, *Finance*
Angela Anderson, *Human Res Dir*
EMP: 51
SALES: 8.3MM **Privately Held**
SIC: 8741 Administrative management

(G-10639)
HGR INDUSTRIAL SURPLUS INC (PA)
Also Called: H G R
20001 Euclid Ave (44117-1480)
PHONE....................216 486-4567
Brian Krueger, *CEO*
Paul Betori, *President*
Jeff McLain, *Principal*
Dan Mooney, *Safety Mgr*
Jason Arnett, *Buyer*
▼ EMP: 47
SQ FT: 250,000
SALES (est): 31.6MM **Privately Held**
WEB: www.hgrindustrialsurplus.com
SIC: 5084 Materials handling machinery

▲ = Import ▼=Export
◆ =Import/Export

(G-10640)
HILLCREST AMBULANCE SVC INC
26420 Lakeland Blvd (44132-2642)
PHONE..................................216 797-4000
Edward Patriarca Sr, *President*
EMP: 180
SQ FT: 3,500
SALES (est): 5.4MM **Privately Held**
SIC: 4119 Ambulance service

(G-10641)
HOME CARE RELIEF INC
753 E 200th St (44119-2504)
PHONE..................................216 692-2270
Darlene Kennedy, *CEO*
EMP: 100
SALES (est): 1.8MM **Privately Held**
SIC: 8082 Home health care services

(G-10642)
HOME DEPOT USA INC
Also Called: Home Depot, The
877 E 200th St (44119-2515)
PHONE..................................216 692-2780
Ron Lockhart, *Manager*
EMP: 200
SALES (corp-wide): 108.2B **Publicly Held**
WEB: www.homerentalsdepot.com
SIC: 5211 7359 Home centers; tool rental
HQ: Home Depot U.S.A., Inc.
2455 Paces Ferry Ave
Atlanta GA 30339

(G-10643)
INDIAN HILLS SENIOR COMMUNITY
1541 E 191st St (44117-1330)
PHONE..................................216 486-7700
Juan Villanueva, *President*
EMP: 36
SQ FT: 7,000
SALES (est): 2MM **Privately Held**
SIC: 6513 Apartment building operators

(G-10644)
INDIAN HLLS HLTHCARE GROUP INC
Also Called: WILLOWS HEALTH & REHAB CENTER, THE
1500 E 191st St (44117-1398)
PHONE..................................216 486-8880
George S Repchick, *President*
William I Weisberg, *Vice Pres*
Sarah Depompei, *Assistant*
EMP: 2610
SALES: 6.8MM
SALES (corp-wide): 157.7MM **Privately Held**
SIC: 8051 8052 Skilled nursing care facilities; intermediate care facilities
PA: Saber Healthcare Group, L.L.C.
26691 Richmond Rd Frnt
Bedford OH 44146
216 292-5706

(G-10645)
INTEGRITY ENTERPRIZES (PA)
27801 Euclid Ave Ste 440 (44132-3547)
PHONE..................................216 289-8801
London Margerum, *Mng Member*
EMP: 50
SALES (est): 275K **Privately Held**
SIC: 7361 Employment Agency

(G-10646)
J RAYL TRANSPORT INC
Jrayl Drayage
24881 Rockwell Dr (44117-1243)
PHONE..................................330 940-1668
Stan Jurcevic, *Manager*
EMP: 25
SALES (corp-wide): 40.6MM **Privately Held**
SIC: 4731 Truck transportation brokers
PA: J. Rayl Transport, Inc.
1016 Triplett Blvd 1
Akron OH 44306
330 784-1134

(G-10647)
KITCHEN KATERING INC
Also Called: Manor, The
24111 Rockwell Dr (44117-1200)
PHONE..................................216 481-8080
Richard G Eberhard, *President*
EMP: 50 **EST:** 1961
SQ FT: 22,000
SALES (est): 2.3MM **Privately Held**
SIC: 7299 5812 Banquet hall facilities; caterers

(G-10648)
LIONS GATE SEC SOLUTIONS INC
Also Called: Lion's Gate Trning SEC Sltions
2073 E 221st St (44117-2103)
PHONE..................................440 539-8382
Charisse Montgomery, *President*
Richard Montgomery, *Vice Pres*
Joeseph Hodges, *Director*
EMP: 50
SALES (est): 705.2K **Privately Held**
SIC: 7389

(G-10649)
MULTICARE HOME HEALTH SERVICES
27691 Euclid Ave Ste B-1 (44132-3546)
PHONE..................................216 731-8900
Lorenza Henderson, *President*
EMP: 70
SALES (est): 2.7MM **Privately Held**
SIC: 8082 Home health care services

(G-10650)
NATIONAL HERITG ACADEMIES INC
Also Called: Pinnacle Academy
860 E 222nd St (44123-3317)
PHONE..................................216 731-0127
Jennifer Littlefield, *Branch Mgr*
EMP: 54 **Privately Held**
SIC: 8741 Management services
PA: National Heritage Academies, Inc.
3850 Broadmoor Ave Se # 201
Grand Rapids MI 49512

(G-10651)
OMNI PARK HEALTH CARE LLC
Also Called: Get Help Home
27801 Euclid Ave Ste 600 (44132-3548)
PHONE..................................216 289-8963
Terry Maynard, *Mng Member*
EMP: 115
SQ FT: 4,200
SALES (est): 4.8MM **Privately Held**
SIC: 8082 Home health care services

(G-10652)
PIONEER SOLUTIONS LLC
24800 Rockwell Dr (44117-1203)
PHONE..................................216 383-3400
David Juba, *Managing Dir*
Earl Lancaster, *Chief Engr*
Andrew Papcun, *Engineer*
Lynne Keller, *Office Mgr*
Joe Kaltenbach,
EMP: 30
SQ FT: 10,000
SALES (est): 4.6MM **Privately Held**
SIC: 8711 Consulting engineer

(G-10653)
POLLAK DISTRIBUTING CO INC
Also Called: Pollak Foods
1200 Babbitt Rd (44132-2704)
P.O. Box 17485 (44117-0485)
PHONE..................................216 851-9911
Arthur Pollak, *President*
Avrohom Pollak, *Purchasing*
Frank Pollak, *CFO*
Shlomo Pollak, *Mktg Dir*
EMP: 25
SQ FT: 45,000
SALES (est): 18.2MM **Privately Held**
WEB: www.pollakdist.com
SIC: 5141 5113 Groceries, general line; industrial & personal service paper

(G-10654)
R & A SPORTS INC
Also Called: Adler Team Sports
23780 Lakeland Blvd (44132-2615)
PHONE..................................216 289-2254
John Domo, *President*
Richard Domo, *Vice Pres*
Ruth Ann Domo, *Admin Sec*
EMP: 25
SQ FT: 16,000
SALES: 3.9MM **Privately Held**
SIC: 5091 5136 5137 2396 Sporting & recreation goods; sportswear, men's & boys'; sportswear, women's & children's; screen printing on fabric articles

(G-10655)
SABER HEALTHCARE GROUP LLC
Also Called: Willows Health and Rehab Ctr
1500 E 191st St (44117-1398)
PHONE..................................216 486-5736
Nick Gulich, *Administration*
EMP: 36
SALES (corp-wide): 157.7MM **Privately Held**
SIC: 8051 Skilled nursing care facilities
PA: Saber Healthcare Group, L.L.C.
26691 Richmond Rd Frnt
Bedford OH 44146
216 292-5706

(G-10656)
SISTERS OD SAINT JOSEPH OF SAI
Also Called: MOUNT ST JOSEPH NURSING HOME
21800 Chardon Rd (44117-2125)
PHONE..................................216 531-7426
SIS Paschal Yap, *Treasurer*
Mother M Raphael, *Administration*
Kathleen Bockanic, *Asst Admin*
Raphael Gregg, *Administration*
SIS Mary Raphael Gregg, *Administration*
EMP: 255
SQ FT: 90,000
SALES (est): 10.2MM **Privately Held**
SIC: 8051 Convalescent home with continuous nursing care

(G-10657)
STACK CONTAINER SERVICE INC
24881 Rockwell Dr (44117-1243)
P.O. Box 202, Chesterland (44026-0202)
PHONE..................................216 531-7555
Stan Jurcevic, *President*
John Jurcevic, *Exec VP*
Marko Bartulovic, *Vice Pres*
Anita Bartulovic, *Treasurer*
EMP: 55
SQ FT: 4,600
SALES (est): 6.2MM **Privately Held**
SIC: 4731 4212 Freight transportation arrangement; draying, local; without storage

(G-10658)
SUBURBAN MEDICAL LABORATORY
26300 Euclid Ave Ste 810 (44132-3708)
PHONE..................................330 929-7992
Sandra Fishel, *President*
Dr Mark Greenberg, *Director*
John Nehrer, *Admin Sec*
EMP: 120
SQ FT: 15,000
SALES (est): 2.5MM **Privately Held**
WEB: www.smlab.com
SIC: 8071 Testing laboratories

(G-10659)
THERMO-TEC INSULATION INC
1415 E 222nd St (44117-1107)
PHONE..................................216 663-3842
Margaret Scarl, *President*
Charles Scarl, *Vice Pres*
EMP: 25
SALES (est): 3.1MM **Privately Held**
SIC: 1742 Insulation, buildings

(G-10660)
UNIVERSITY MEDNET (PA)
18599 Lake Shore Blvd (44119-1093)
PHONE..................................216 383-0100
Seth Eisengart MD, *Ch of Bd*
Richard Hammond, *President*
Kenneth Spano MD, *Treasurer*
Arnold Rozensweig MD, *Admin Sec*
Delbert A Hoppes, *Family Practiti*
EMP: 300
SQ FT: 124,000
SALES (est): 10.4MM **Privately Held**
SIC: 8069 8082 5999 Specialty hospitals, except psychiatric; home health care services; medical apparatus & supplies

(G-10661)
ZAK ENTERPRISES LTD (PA)
Also Called: Clinical Health Laboratories
26250 Euclid Ave Ste 810 (44132-3718)
PHONE..................................216 261-9700
EMP: 75
SQ FT: 15,000
SALES (est): 3.4MM **Privately Held**
SIC: 8071 Medical Laboratory

Fairborn
Greene County

(G-10662)
ADVANCED MECHANICAL SVCS INC
Also Called: Honeywell Authorized Dealer
575 Sports St (45324-5138)
P.O. Box 68 (45324-0068)
PHONE..................................937 879-7426
William Burrowes, *President*
William D Parsons, *Principal*
▲ **EMP:** 32
SALES (est): 6.7MM **Privately Held**
SIC: 1711 Mechanical contractor

(G-10663)
AFFINITY SPECIALTY APPAREL INC (PA)
Also Called: Affinity Apparel
1202 E Dayton Yllow Spgs (45324-6326)
PHONE..................................866 548-8434
Robert McIntire, *President*
Bill Tucker, *CFO*
◆ **EMP:** 61
SALES (est): 18.9MM **Privately Held**
SIC: 5699 7389 Uniforms; textile & apparel services

(G-10664)
BRILLIGENT SOLUTIONS INC (PA)
1130 Channingway Dr (45324-9240)
PHONE..................................937 879-4148
David Geloneck, *President*
Doug Henry, *Vice Pres*
James Blair, *Engineer*
Aaron Burke, *Engineer*
Samuel Kuenneke, *Engineer*
EMP: 27
SQ FT: 7,400
SALES (est): 4MM **Privately Held**
SIC: 8711 8731 Consulting engineer; commercial physical research

(G-10665)
COMBS INTERIOR SPECIALTIES INC
475 W Funderburg Rd (45324-2359)
PHONE..................................937 879-2047
Marcus Combs, *President*
Gregg Inskeep, *Project Mgr*
Jaden Callahan, *Purchasing*
Chris McFadden, *Executive*
Byron Hubbard,
EMP: 75
SALES (est): 14.4MM **Privately Held**
SIC: 1542 1751 1521 Nonresidential construction; carpentry work; single-family housing construction

(G-10666)
COVENANT CARE OHIO INC
Wright Nursing Center
829 Yllow Sprng Frfeld Rd (45324)
PHONE..................................937 878-7046
Greg Nijack, *Administration*
EMP: 90 **Privately Held**
WEB: www.villageorgetown.com
SIC: 8052 8069 8051 Intermediate care facilities; specialty hospitals, except psychiatric; skilled nursing care facilities

---

(PA)=Parent Co (HQ)=Headquarters (DH)=Div Headquarters
✪ = New Business established in last 2 years

HQ: Covenant Care Ohio, Inc.
27071 Aliso Creek Rd # 100
Aliso Viejo CA 92656
949 349-1200

(G-10667)
CURTISS-WRIGHT CONTROLS
2600 Paramount Pl Ste 200 (45324-6816)
PHONE....................................937 252-5601
Cheryl Ullmer, *Buyer*
Boris Mikhaylenko, *Engineer*
Ron Taulton, *Branch Mgr*
Gorky Chin, *Manager*
Eric Freeman, *Info Tech Dir*
EMP: 50
SALES (corp-wide): 2.4B **Publicly Held**
SIC: 8711 8731 3769 3625 Consulting
engineer; commercial physical research;
guided missile & space vehicle parts &
auxiliary equipment; relays & industrial
controls
HQ: Curtiss-Wright Controls Electronic Sys-
tems, Inc.
28965 Avenue Penn
Santa Clarita CA 91355
661 702-1494

(G-10668)
DAVE MARSHALL INC (PA)
Also Called: Ziebart
1448 Kauffman Ave (45324-3108)
PHONE....................................937 878-9135
David Marshall, *President*
Susan Marshall, *Admin Sec*
EMP: 90
SALES (est): 5.5MM **Privately Held**
WEB: www.davemarshall.com
SIC: 7549 Undercoating/rustproofing cars

(G-10669)
DAVITA INC
1266 N Broad St (45324-5549)
PHONE....................................937 879-0433
Jeffrey Spears, *Administration*
EMP: 27 **Publicly Held**
SIC: 8092 Kidney dialysis centers
PA: Davita Inc.
2000 16th St
Denver CO 80202

(G-10670)
**DAYSPRING HEALTH CARE
CENTER**
8001 Dyton Springfield Rd (45324-1907)
PHONE....................................937 864-5800
Matt Walters, *President*
Barry Bortz, *Vice Pres*
EMP: 135 EST: 1998
SALES (est): 6.3MM
SALES (corp-wide): 97.1MM **Privately
Held**
SIC: 8051 8052 Skilled nursing care facili-
ties; intermediate care facilities
PA: Carespring Health Care Management,
Llc
390 Wards Corner Rd
Loveland OH 45140
513 943-4000

(G-10671)
DETMER & SONS INC (PA)
Also Called: Detmer & Sons Heating & AC
1170 Channingway Dr (45324-9240)
PHONE....................................937 879-2373
Frank Detmer Jr, *President*
Eric Detmer, *President*
Jim Streck, *Vice Pres*
EMP: 26
SQ FT: 3,000
SALES (est): 6.2MM **Privately Held**
WEB: www.detmersons.com
SIC: 1711 1761 Warm air heating & air
conditioning contractor; sheet metalwork

(G-10672)
FAIRBORN FISH
Also Called: Fairborn Fish Organization
101 Mann Ave (45324-5020)
P.O. Box 1484 (45324-1484)
PHONE....................................937 879-1313
Beth Player, *Principal*
EMP: 50
SALES (est): 182.7K **Privately Held**
SIC: 8322 Social service center

(G-10673)
**FAIRBORN ST LUKE UNTD
MTHDST**
Also Called: FAIRBORN PRE SCHOOL &
DAY CARE
100 N Broad St (45324-4804)
PHONE....................................937 878-5042
Mary Gale, *Director*
EMP: 25
SALES: 391.5K **Privately Held**
SIC: 8351 Preschool center

(G-10674)
FAIRBORN YMCA
Also Called: Young Mens Christn Assosiation
300 S Central Ave (45324-4721)
PHONE....................................937 754-9622
Larry Dryden, *Director*
Lori Setherolf, *Director*
EMP: 30 EST: 1949
SALES (est): 482.6K **Privately Held**
WEB: www.ymcaofgreenecounty.org
SIC: 8641 8322 Youth organizations;
youth center

(G-10675)
G&K SERVICES LLC
Also Called: Lion Uniform Group
1202 Dyton Yllow Sprng Rd (45324-6326)
PHONE....................................937 873-4500
EMP: 52
SALES (corp-wide): 6.4B **Publicly Held**
SIC: 7218 Industrial uniform supply
HQ: G&K Services, Llc
6800 Cintas Blvd
Mason OH 45040
952 912-5500

(G-10676)
I SUPPLY CO
1255 Spangler Rd (45324-9768)
P.O. Box 1739 (45324-7739)
PHONE....................................937 878-5240
Jerry Parisi, *CEO*
Gerald Parisi, *President*
Joe Parisi, *President*
Mario Parisi, *President*
Tim Detrick, *Vice Pres*
EMP: 175 EST: 1974
SQ FT: 109,000
SALES (est): 167.7MM **Privately Held**
WEB: www.isupplyco.com
SIC: 5087 5113 Janitors' supplies; indus-
trial & personal service paper; containers,
paper & disposable plastic

(G-10677)
K & R DISTRIBUTORS INC
Also Called: Aqua Falls Bottled Watrer
7606 Dayton Rd (45324-5944)
PHONE....................................937 864-5495
Bob Kennedy, *President*
EMP: 45
SALES (est): 3.1MM **Privately Held**
SIC: 5963 5961 7389 Bottled water deliv-
ery; cheese, mail order; coffee service

(G-10678)
**KETTERING ADVENTIST
HEALTHCARE**
1045 Channingway Dr (45324-9252)
PHONE....................................937 878-8644
EMP: 43
SALES (corp-wide): 1.7B **Privately Held**
SIC: 8062 General medical & surgical hos-
pitals
PA: Kettering Adventist Healthcare
3535 Southern Blvd
Dayton OH 45429
937 298-4331

(G-10679)
KLEIN ASSOCIATES INC
1750 Commerce Center Blvd (45324-6362)
PHONE....................................937 873-8166
Floyd D Reed, *President*
Dr Gary A Klein, *Chairman*
Dr Helen Klein, *Vice Pres*
EMP: 36
SQ FT: 9,800
SALES (est): 3.1MM **Privately Held**
SIC: 8732 Sociological Research Psychol-
ogists

(G-10680)
MANZANO DIALYSIS LLC
Also Called: Midwest Fairborn Dialysis
1266 N Broad St (45324-5549)
PHONE....................................937 879-0433
George Carghese, *Principal*
EMP: 48
SALES (est): 767.9K **Publicly Held**
SIC: 8092 Kidney dialysis centers
PA: Davita Inc.
2000 16th St
Denver CO 80202

(G-10681)
RITE RUG CO
2015 Commerce Center Blvd (45324-6335)
PHONE....................................937 318-9197
EMP: 33
SALES (corp-wide): 82.2MM **Privately
Held**
SIC: 5713 1752 Carpets; floor laying &
floor work
PA: Rite Rug Co.
4450 Poth Rd Ste A
Columbus OH 43213
614 261-6060

(G-10682)
**STICKELMAN SCHNEIDER
ASSOC LLC (HQ)**
1130 Channingway Dr (45324-9240)
PHONE....................................513 475-6000
Ronald Stickelman Jr,
Dirk Schneider,
Sarah Stickelman,
EMP: 35
SQ FT: 3,200
SALES (est): 2.1MM
SALES (corp-wide): 6MM **Privately Held**
WEB: www.stickelman.com
SIC: 6531 Appraiser, real estate
PA: Stickelman, Schneider & Association
Inc.
1130 Channingway Dr
Fairborn OH 45324
937 873-9900

(G-10683)
SUMMIT AT PARK HILLS LLC
2270 Park Hills Dr Ofc (45324-5900)
PHONE....................................317 462-8048
Todd Spittal,
EMP: 45
SALES (est): 1.6MM **Privately Held**
SIC: 8059 Nursing home, except skilled &
intermediate care facility

(G-10684)
UNITED CHURCH HOMES INC
Also Called: Patriot Ridge Community
789 Stoneybrook Trl (45324-6021)
PHONE....................................937 878-0262
Brian Allen, *Manager*
EMP: 110
SALES (corp-wide): 78.1MM **Privately
Held**
WEB: www.altenheimcommunity.org
SIC: 8052 8051 Intermediate care facili-
ties; skilled nursing care facilities
PA: United Church Homes Inc
170 E Center St
Marion OH 43302
740 382-4885

(G-10685)
**US BANK NATIONAL
ASSOCIATION**
Also Called: US Bank
1 W Main St (45324-4741)
PHONE....................................937 873-7845
Robert Carico, *Manager*
EMP: 100
SALES (corp-wide): 25.7B **Publicly Held**
WEB: www.firstar.com
SIC: 6021 National commercial banks
HQ: U.S. Bank National Association
425 Walnut St Fl 14
Cincinnati OH 45202
513 632-4234

(G-10686)
VALENTINE BUICK GMC INC
1105 N Central Ave (45324-5668)
P.O. Box 432 (45324-0432)
PHONE....................................937 878-7371

Dennis Valentine, *President*
Bette Green, *Treasurer*
Anthony Homan, *Sales Dir*
Roger Brown, *Sales Staff*
Ron Byrd, *Sales Staff*
EMP: 60
SALES (est): 17.8MM **Privately Held**
SIC: 5511 7538 Automobiles, new & used;
general automotive repair shops

(G-10687)
VISICON INC
Also Called: Hope Hotel & Conference Center
Area A Bldg 823 (45324)
PHONE....................................937 879-2696
David Meyers, *President*
Micki Witter, *General Mgr*
EMP: 100
SQ FT: 132,000
SALES (est): 849.6K **Privately Held**
SIC: 7011 Hotels

(G-10688)
**WASTE MANAGEMENT OHIO
INC**
1700 N Broad St (45324-9747)
P.O. Box 1799 (45324-7799)
PHONE....................................800 343-6047
Thomas Koogler, *Manager*
EMP: 100
SALES (corp-wide): 14.9B **Publicly Held**
SIC: 7359 4212 Portable toilet rental; local
trucking, without storage
HQ: Waste Management Of Ohio, Inc.
1700 N Broad St
Fairborn OH 45324

(G-10689)
**WASTE MANAGEMENT OHIO
INC (HQ)**
1700 N Broad St (45324-9747)
P.O. Box 4648, Carol Stream IL (60197-
4648)
PHONE....................................800 343-6047
Paul Pistono, *President*
Leana Hodges, *Human Res Mgr*
Thomas Koogler, *Manager*
EMP: 120
SALES (est): 43.2MM
SALES (corp-wide): 14.9B **Publicly Held**
WEB: www.wm.com
SIC: 4953 4212 Refuse collection & dis-
posal services; local trucking, without
storage
PA: Waste Management, Inc.
1001 Fannin St Ste 4000
Houston TX 77002
713 512-6200

(G-10690)
**WELLS & SONS JANITORIAL
SVC**
1877 S Maple Ave Ste 250 (45324-3487)
PHONE....................................937 878-4375
Kenneth Wells, *President*
Janet H Wells, *Corp Secy*
Edwin Wells, *Vice Pres*
James L Wells, *Vice Pres*
Rich Lutz, *Executive*
EMP: 42
SQ FT: 3,600
SALES: 869.4K **Privately Held**
SIC: 7349 Janitorial service, contract basis

Fairfield
Butler County

(G-10691)
AB MARKETING LLC
Also Called: Sphere, The
1211 Symmes Rd Apt B (45014-9501)
PHONE....................................513 385-6158
Darroll Alexander, *Mng Member*
EMP: 50
SALES: 500K **Privately Held**
SIC: 5091 Sporting & recreation goods

(G-10692)
AFC INDUSTRIES INC (PA)
Also Called: Advanced Fastener
3795 Port Union Rd (45014-2207)
PHONE....................................513 874-7456
Robert T Tomlinson, *President*

Mike Dusold, *General Mgr*
Steve Sullivan, *Exec VP*
Tom Riley, *VP Opers*
Curt Robertson, *VP Finance*
▲ **EMP:** 28
SQ FT: 27,000
SALES (est): 24.4MM **Privately Held**
WEB: www.pintech.com
SIC: 5085 Fasteners, industrial: nuts, bolts, screws, etc.

(G-10693)
AFFILIATES IN ORAL & MAXLOFCL (PA)
Also Called: Doctors Weaver Wallace Conley
5188 Winton Rd (45014-2900)
PHONE.............................513 829-8080
Dr David A Weaver, *Partner*
David Weaver, *Principal*
Timothy Conley, *Principal*
Douglas Wallace, *Principal*
EMP: 30
SQ FT: 7,000
SALES (est): 3.5MM **Privately Held**
SIC: 8069 8062 Specialty hospitals, except psychiatric; general medical & surgical hospitals

(G-10694)
ALBA MANUFACTURING INC
8950 Seward Rd (45011-9109)
PHONE.............................513 874-0551
Tom Moon, *President*
Thomas N Inderhees, *President*
Mike Kroger, *Vice Pres*
Mike Kees, *Purchasing*
EMP: 52
SQ FT: 67,000
SALES (est): 30.3MM **Privately Held**
WEB: www.albamfg.com
SIC: 3535 5084 3312 Conveyors & conveying equipment; conveyor systems; blast furnaces & steel mills

(G-10695)
ALEXSON SERVICES INC
Also Called: Fairfield Center
350 Kolb Dr (45014-5357)
PHONE.............................513 874-0423
Andrea Levenson, *CEO*
EMP: 263
SALES (est): 6.2MM
SALES (corp-wide): 4MM **Privately Held**
WEB: www.fairfieldcenter.com
SIC: 8361 8052 8051 Home for the mentally retarded; intermediate care facilities; skilled nursing care facilities
PA: Manor Home Ownership Of Facilities Inc
246 N Broadway
Geneva OH

(G-10696)
AREA WIDE PROTECTIVE INC
9500 Le Saint Dr (45014-2253)
PHONE.............................513 321-9889
Fax: 513 321-9891
EMP: 48
SALES (corp-wide): 111.4MM **Privately Held**
SIC: 3669 7381 7382 Mfg Communications Equip Detective/Armor Car Svcs Security System Svcs
HQ: Area Wide Protective, Inc.
826 Overholt Rd
Kent OH 44240
330 644-0655

(G-10697)
AURGROUP FINANCIAL CREDIT UN
8811 Holden Blvd (45014-2109)
PHONE.............................513 942-4422
Gareda Guecking, *President*
EMP: 63
SALES (est): 9.6MM **Privately Held**
SIC: 6061 Federal credit unions

(G-10698)
BANSAL CONSTRUCTION INC
3263 Homeward Way Ste A (45014-4237)
P.O. Box 132, West Chester (45071-0132)
PHONE.............................513 874-5410
Anurag Bansal, *President*
Ambrish K Bansal, *Vice Pres*
Faye Phillips, *Buyer*

EMP: 35
SQ FT: 5,000
SALES (est): 12.7MM **Privately Held**
SIC: 1731 1794 General electrical contractor; excavation work

(G-10699)
BELL MOVING AND STORAGE INC (PA)
4075 Port Union Rd (45014-2205)
PHONE.............................513 942-7500
Tamara Kissel, *President*
William Kissel, *Vice Pres*
EMP: 25
SQ FT: 25,000
SALES (est): 4.2MM **Privately Held**
WEB: www.bellmoving.com
SIC: 4214 4213 4212 Household goods moving & storage, local; trucking, except local; local trucking, without storage

(G-10700)
BRADCORP OHIO II LLC (PA)
Also Called: Hwz Contracting
3195 Profit Dr (45014-4234)
PHONE.............................513 671-3300
Bradley Hardig, *President*
EMP: 58
SALES (est): 24.8MM **Privately Held**
SIC: 1771 Concrete work

(G-10701)
BROCK & SONS INC
8731 N Gilmore Rd (45014-2105)
PHONE.............................513 874-4555
Linda Brock, *President*
Geoffrey Brock, *Treasurer*
EMP: 40 **EST:** 1937
SQ FT: 1,500
SALES (est): 6.9MM **Privately Held**
WEB: www.brockandsons.com
SIC: 1623 1611 Water main construction; sewer line construction; oil & gas pipeline construction; underground utilities contractor; general contractor, highway & street construction

(G-10702)
BUSAM FAIRFIELD LLC
Also Called: Busam Subaru/Suzuki
6195 Dixie Hwy (45014-4249)
PHONE.............................513 771-8100
Cathy L Tamm, *Controller*
Cathy Tamm, *Controller*
Greg Frye, *Consultant*
EMP: 27
SALES (est): 6.7MM **Privately Held**
SIC: 5511 7532 Automobiles, new & used; body shop, automotive

(G-10703)
BUTLER COUNTY BOARD OF DEVELOP
Also Called: Community Supports Services
441 Patterson Blvd (45014-2511)
PHONE.............................513 867-5913
Christina Hurr, *Superintendent*
EMP: 47
SALES (corp-wide): 5.9MM **Privately Held**
SIC: 8361 9111 8052 Home for the mentally retarded; county supervisors' & executives' offices; intermediate care facilities
PA: Butler County Board Of Developmental Disabilities
282 N Fair Ave Ste 1
Hamilton OH 45011
513 785-2815

(G-10704)
BYRON PRODUCTS INC
3781 Port Union Rd (45014-2207)
PHONE.............................513 870-9111
Mark Byron, *CEO*
Rick Henry, *President*
Don Vierling, *QC Mgr*
Mike Pavelka, *Department Mgr*
▲ **EMP:** 70
SQ FT: 44,000
SALES (est): 10.4MM **Privately Held**
WEB: www.byronproducts.com
SIC: 7692 Welding repair

(G-10705)
C & K INDUSTRIAL SERVICES INC
4980 Factory Dr (45014-1945)
PHONE.............................513 829-5353
Kirby Bolton, *Branch Mgr*
EMP: 40
SALES (corp-wide): 119.5MM **Privately Held**
SIC: 4959 Sweeping service: road, airport, parking lot, etc.
PA: C & K Industrial Services, Inc.
5617 E Schaaf Rd
Independence OH 44131
216 642-0055

(G-10706)
CALVARY INDUSTRIES INC (PA)
9233 Seward Rd (45014-5407)
PHONE.............................513 874-1113
John P Morelock Jr, *CEO*
Ivan Byers, *President*
Austin Morelock, *Business Mgr*
Thomas Rielage, *Vice Pres*
Les Paul, *Plant Mgr*
▲ **EMP:** 60
SQ FT: 100,000
SALES (est): 34.6MM **Privately Held**
WEB: www.calvaryindustries.com
SIC: 2819 5169 Industrial inorganic chemicals; chemicals & allied products

(G-10707)
CAPITAL SENIOR LIVING CORP
1400 Corydale Dr (45014-3361)
PHONE.............................513 829-6200
Sheryl Withrow, *Director*
EMP: 165
SALES (corp-wide): 460MM **Publicly Held**
SIC: 6513 Retirement hotel operation
PA: Capital Senior Living Corp
14160 Dallas Pkwy Ste 300
Dallas TX 75254
972 770-5600

(G-10708)
CHILDRENS HOSPITAL MEDICAL CTR
Also Called: Cincinatti Chld Hosp Med Ctr
3050 Mack Rd Ste 105 (45014-5375)
PHONE.............................513 636-6400
John Linser, *Branch Mgr*
Judy A Bush,
Michelle M Rodgers,
EMP: 30
SALES (corp-wide): 1.6B **Privately Held**
WEB: www.cincinnatichildrens.org
SIC: 8733 8071 Medical research; medical laboratories
PA: Children's Hospital Medical Center
3333 Burnet Ave
Cincinnati OH 45229
513 636-4200

(G-10709)
CINCINNATI CASUALTY COMPANY
6200 S Gilmore Rd (45014-5141)
P.O. Box 145496, Cincinnati (45250-5496)
PHONE.............................513 870-2000
James E Benoski, *Vice Ch Bd*
Larry Plum, *President*
Thomas A Joseph, *President*
Teresa L Cracas, *Counsel*
Robert B Morgan, *Senior VP*
EMP: 80 **EST:** 1973
SQ FT: 370,000
SALES (est): 34.4MM
SALES (corp-wide): 5.4B **Publicly Held**
WEB: www.cib-online.com
SIC: 6411 Insurance agents, brokers & service
HQ: Cincinnati Insurance Company
6200 S Gilmore Rd
Fairfield OH 45014
513 870-2000

(G-10710)
CINCINNATI FINANCIAL CORP (PA)
6200 S Gilmore Rd (45014-5141)
P.O. Box 145496, Cincinnati (45250-5496)
PHONE.............................513 870-2000
Kenneth W Stecher, *Ch of Bd*

Steven J Johnston, *President*
Terry Barrow, *Division Mgr*
Ken Kerby, *Superintendent*
Blake D Slater, *Exec VP*
EMP: 3262
SQ FT: 1,508,200
SALES: 5.4B **Publicly Held**
WEB: www.cinfin.com
SIC: 6311 6411 6211 7389 Life insurance carriers; property & casualty insurance agent; investment firm, general brokerage; financial services; fire, marine & casualty insurance & carriers

(G-10711)
CINCINNATI GYMNASTICS ACADEMY
3635 Woodridge Blvd (45014-8521)
PHONE.............................513 860-3082
Mary Lee Tracy, *President*
EMP: 50
SQ FT: 20,000
SALES: 194.3K **Privately Held**
WEB: www.cincinnatigymnastics.com
SIC: 7999 8661 Gymnastic instruction, non-membership; religious organizations

(G-10712)
CINCINNATI INDEMINTY CO
6200 S Gilmore Rd (45014-5141)
P.O. Box 145496, Cincinnati (45250-5496)
PHONE.............................513 870-2000
James E Benoski, *Vice Ch Bd*
John Schiff, *President*
Anthony Dunn, *President*
Philip Kramer, *President*
T F Elchynski, *Senior VP*
EMP: 600
SALES (est): 143.5MM
SALES (corp-wide): 5.4B **Publicly Held**
WEB: www.cib-online.com
SIC: 6331 Fire, marine & casualty insurance & carriers
HQ: Cincinnati Insurance Company
6200 S Gilmore Rd
Fairfield OH 45014
513 870-2000

(G-10713)
CINCINNATI LIFE INSURANCE CO
6200 S Gilmore Rd (45014-5141)
P.O. Box 145496, Cincinnati (45250-5496)
PHONE.............................513 870-2000
David M Popplewell, *President*
Teresa L Cracas, *Counsel*
Eric N Mathews, *Senior VP*
Theresa A Hoffer, *Vice Pres*
Kenneth W Stecher, *Treasurer*
EMP: 950
SQ FT: 383,000
SALES (est): 329.7MM
SALES (corp-wide): 5.4B **Publicly Held**
WEB: www.cib-online.com
SIC: 6311 Life insurance
HQ: Cincinnati Insurance Company
6200 S Gilmore Rd
Fairfield OH 45014
513 870-2000

(G-10714)
CLAYTON WEAVER TRUCKING INC
3043 Lelia Ln (45014-1204)
PHONE.............................513 896-6932
Clayton Weaver, *President*
Brenda Weaver, *Corp Secy*
Steve Bowden, *Manager*
EMP: 40
SQ FT: 864
SALES (est): 5.5MM **Privately Held**
SIC: 4213 4212 Trucking, except local; local trucking, without storage

(G-10715)
CPC LOGISTICS INC
Also Called: Pds
8695 Seward Rd (45011-9716)
PHONE.............................513 874-5787
Fax: 513 682-7555
EMP: 51 **EST:** 1972
SALES (est): 1.9MM **Privately Held**
SIC: 8742 7363 3674 Management Consulting Services Help Supply Services Mfg Semiconductors/Related Devices

G
E
O
G
R
A
P
H
I
C

(G-10716)
DAVITA INC
1210 Hicks Blvd (45014-1921)
PHONE................................513 939-1110
Tracie Metz, *Exec Dir*
Sarah Waits, *Administration*
EMP: 27 Publicly Held
SIC: 8092 Kidney dialysis centers
PA: Davita Inc.
2000 16th St
Denver CO 80202

(G-10717)
DEUFOL WORLDWIDE PACKAGING LLC
4380 Dixie Hwy (45014-1119)
PHONE................................414 967-8000
EMP: 54 EST: 2017
SALES (est): 1MM Privately Held
SIC: 4783 5113 Packing And Crating, Nsk

(G-10718)
DIALYSIS SPECIALISTS FAIRFIELD
4750 Dixie Hwy (45014-1848)
PHONE................................513 863-6331
Laura Nortman, *Manager*
EMP: 25
SALES (est): 890K Privately Held
SIC: 8092 Kidney dialysis centers

(G-10719)
DNA DIAGNOSTICS CENTER INC (HQ)
Also Called: Dna Technology Park
1 Ddc Way (45014-2281)
PHONE................................513 881-7800
Lori Tauber Marcus, *Ch of Bd*
Scott Cramer, *President*
Jerry Watkins, *COO*
Dan Leigh, *Vice Pres*
Robert Bosley, *CFO*
EMP: 168
SQ FT: 66,000
SALES (est): 22.2MM
SALES (corp-wide): 13.3MM Privately Held
WEB: www.paternite.com
SIC: 8071 Medical laboratories
PA: Gho Capital Partners Llp
44 Davies Street
London W1K 5
203 307-1600

(G-10720)
DYNAMIC MECHANICAL SYSTEMS
5623 Sigmon Way (45014-3946)
PHONE................................513 858-6722
Gregory P Dinkel, *President*
EMP: 30
SQ FT: 6,000
SALES (est): 2.1MM Privately Held
WEB: www.dynamicmechanical.com
SIC: 1731 1711 General electrical contractor; plumbing contractors; heating & air conditioning contractors

(G-10721)
EAGLE INDUSTRIES OHIO INC
Also Called: Allgood Home Improvements
275 Commercial Dr (45014-5565)
PHONE................................513 247-2900
Edward Grant, *President*
Dave Grant, *Regional Mgr*
Betty Grant,
EMP: 35 EST: 1995
SQ FT: 5,114
SALES (est): 5.5MM Privately Held
SIC: 7299 Home improvement & renovation contractor agency

(G-10722)
ELEMENT CINCINNATI
3701 Port Union Rd (45014-2200)
PHONE................................513 984-4112
Frank Worpenberg, *QC Mgr*
Crissy Zannoni, *Marketing Mgr*
April Renaker, *Office Mgr*
EMP: 39
SALES (est): 7.7MM Privately Held
SIC: 8734 Testing laboratories

(G-10723)
ELEMENT MTLS TECH CNCNNATI INC (PA)
3701 Port Union Rd (45014-2200)
PHONE................................513 771-2536
Charles Noall, *CEO*
Steven Etter, *CEO*
Michael Janssen, *General Mgr*
Phil Steele, *General Mgr*
Matthew Webb, *General Mgr*
EMP: 45
SQ FT: 11,000
SALES (est): 15.8MM Privately Held
WEB: www.mar-test.com
SIC: 8734 Testing laboratories

(G-10724)
EMBASSY HEALTHCARE INC
Also Called: Parkside Nrsing Rehabilitation
908 Symmes Rd (45014-1842)
PHONE................................513 868-6500
Aaron Handler, *President*
EMP: 64
SALES (est): 3.4MM Privately Held
SIC: 8051 Convalescent home with continuous nursing care

(G-10725)
ERIC BOEPPLER FMLY LTD PARTNR
Also Called: A Savannah Nite Limousine Svcs
9331 Seward Rd Ste A (45014-2272)
PHONE................................513 336-8108
Lynn Boeppler, *Partner*
Eric Boeppler, *General Ptnr*
EMP: 60
SALES (est): 571.9K Privately Held
SIC: 4119 Limousine rental, with driver

(G-10726)
ESJ CARRIER CORPORATION
3240 Production Dr (45014-4230)
P.O. Box 181060 (45018-1060)
PHONE................................513 728-7388
Eva Ambrose, *CEO*
Sandra Ambrose, *President*
Don McKinney, *Vice Pres*
Greg Maschinot, *Senior Mgr*
EMP: 40 EST: 1998
SALES (est): 13.8MM Privately Held
SIC: 4731 Truck transportation brokers

(G-10727)
FAIRFIELD TEMPO CLUB
8800 Holden Blvd (45014-2100)
PHONE................................513 863-2081
Carl Lampl, *Principal*
EMP: 28
SALES: 750.6K Privately Held
SIC: 7997 Membership sports & recreation clubs

(G-10728)
FEHR SERVICES LLC
6200 Pleasant Ave Ste 3 (45014-4671)
PHONE................................513 829-9333
Paul Fehring,
EMP: 38 EST: 1995
SQ FT: 1,100
SALES (est): 2.2MM Privately Held
WEB: www.drsbillinginc.com
SIC: 8721 Accounting services, except auditing

(G-10729)
FRANKS AUTO BODY SHOP INC
Also Called: Frank's Autobody Carstar
5264 Dixie Hwy (45014-3009)
PHONE................................513 829-8282
David Brinkman, *President*
EMP: 30 EST: 1970
SALES (est): 3MM Privately Held
SIC: 7532 Body shop, automotive

(G-10730)
GOZA DIALYSIS LLC
Also Called: Ross Dialysis
3825 Kraus Ln Ste S (45014-5867)
PHONE................................513 738-0276
James K Hilger,
EMP: 30
SALES (est): 302.8K Publicly Held
SIC: 8092 Kidney dialysis centers

PA: Davita Inc.
2000 16th St
Denver CO 80202

(G-10731)
GREAT AMERICAN INSURANCE CO
9450 Seward Rd (45014-5412)
P.O. Box 188060 (45018-8060)
PHONE................................513 603-2570
Robert Daniels, *Auditor*
Rick Weber, *Manager*
EMP: 75 Publicly Held
SIC: 6331 Fire, marine & casualty insurance
HQ: Great American Insurance Company
301 E 4th St Fl 8
Cincinnati OH 45202
513 369-5000

(G-10732)
GREAT MIAMI VALLEY YMCA
Also Called: Fairfield YMCA Pre-School
5220 Bibury Rd (45014-3665)
PHONE................................513 829-3091
Julia Brant, *Director*
EMP: 100
SALES (corp-wide): 13MM Privately Held
SIC: 8641 7991 8351 7032 Youth organizations; physical fitness facilities; child day care services; youth camps; individual & family services
PA: Great Miami Valley Ymca
105 N 2nd St
Hamilton OH 45011
513 887-0001

(G-10733)
HALCOMB CONCRETE CONSTRUCTION
1409 Veterans Dr (45014-1905)
PHONE................................513 829-3576
Richard Halcomb, *President*
EMP: 25
SQ FT: 2,500
SALES (est): 1.5MM Privately Held
SIC: 1771 Foundation & footing contractor

(G-10734)
HANOVER INSURANCE COMPANY
6061 Winton Rd (45014-4946)
PHONE................................513 829-4555
EMP: 75 Publicly Held
SIC: 6411 Insurance agents
HQ: The Hanover Insurance Company
440 Lincoln St
Worcester MA 01653
508 853-7200

(G-10735)
HERZIG-KRALL MEDICAL GROUP
5150 Sandy Ln (45014-2738)
PHONE................................513 896-9595
Edward Herzig, *President*
William Krall, *Vice Pres*
Ray Inders, *Manager*
Anthony Behler, *Admin Sec*
Vickie Kling, *Administration*
EMP: 40
SQ FT: 10,000
SALES (est): 2.9MM Privately Held
SIC: 8011 Offices & clinics of medical doctors

(G-10736)
HOGAN TRUCK LEASING INC
2001 Ddc Way (45014-2285)
PHONE................................513 454-3500
Jeff Buhraw, *Manager*
EMP: 35
SALES (corp-wide): 128.7MM Privately Held
SIC: 7513 7363 Truck rental & leasing, no drivers; truck driver services
PA: Hogan Truck Leasing, Inc.
2150 Schuetz Rd Ste 210
Saint Louis MO 63146
314 421-6000

(G-10737)
INTERCOASTAL TRNSP SYSTEMS
Also Called: Universial Transportation
5284 Winton Rd (45014-3912)
PHONE................................513 829-1287
Tom Burer, *President*
EMP: 60
SQ FT: 6,000
SALES (est): 2.8MM Privately Held
SIC: 4111 4119 Local & suburban transit; local passenger transportation

(G-10738)
INTERSTATE WAREHOUSING VA LLC
110 Distribution Dr (45014-4257)
PHONE................................513 874-6500
Paul Hanna, *General Mgr*
EMP: 80
SALES (corp-wide): 122.1MM Privately Held
WEB: www.tippmanngroup.com
SIC: 4222 4226 Warehousing, cold storage or refrigerated; special warehousing & storage
HQ: Interstate Warehousing Of Virginia, L.L.C.
9009 Coldwater Rd Ste 300
Fort Wayne IN 46825
260 490-3000

(G-10739)
JACO WATERPROOFING LLC
4350 Wade Mill Rd (45014-5853)
P.O. Box 865, Ross (45061-0865)
PHONE................................513 738-0084
Bill Sackenheim, *President*
Ron Smith, *Accounts Mgr*
Adam Tebbe, *Sales Staff*
Matt Sackenheim, *Manager*
Andrea Hartmann, *Admin Asst*
EMP: 27
SALES (est): 3.8MM Privately Held
WEB: www.appliedtechnologies.com
SIC: 1799 Waterproofing

(G-10740)
JTF CONSTRUCTION INC
4235 Muhlhauser Rd (45014-5450)
PHONE................................513 860-9835
Gregory W Fisher, *President*
EMP: 70
SQ FT: 6,900
SALES (est): 14MM Privately Held
SIC: 1521 Single-family housing construction

(G-10741)
JWF TECHNOLOGIES LLC (PA)
6820 Fairfield Bus Ctr (45014)
PHONE................................513 769-9611
Dominic Dipilla, *President*
Chris Torbeck, *Prdtn Mgr*
Scott Johnson, *QC Mgr*
Lisa Kreutz, *Controller*
Randy Buhl, *Accounts Mgr*
▲ **EMP: 26 EST:** 1998
SQ FT: 30,000
SALES (est): 13.5MM Privately Held
WEB: www.jwftechnologies.com
SIC: 5084 Hydraulic systems equipment & supplies

(G-10742)
KELLEY BROTHERS ROOFING INC
4905 Factory Dr (45014-1916)
PHONE................................513 829-7717
Robert Kelley, *President*
George Horton, *General Mgr*
Michael Kelley, *COO*
Steven Gebing, *Vice Pres*
John Newlon, *CFO*
EMP: 100 EST: 1978
SQ FT: 25,000
SALES (est): 22.8MM Privately Held
WEB: www.kbroof.com
SIC: 1761 Roofing contractor

(G-10743)
KENS BEVERAGE INC
3219 Homeward Way (45014-4237)
PHONE................................513 874-8200
Phil Morris, *Branch Mgr*

Michael Drumm, *Director*
EMP: 40
SALES (corp-wide): 53.2MM **Privately Held**
WEB: www.kensbeverage.com
SIC: 1799 7699 Food service equipment installation; restaurant equipment repair
PA: Ken's Beverage, Inc.
   10015 S Mandel St
   Plainfield IL 60585
   630 904-1555

(G-10744)
KINGS COVE AUTOMOTIVE LLC
Also Called: Performance Lexus
5726 Dixie Hwy (45014-4204)
PHONE.................................513 677-0177
Michael Dever, *Owner*
EMP: 60
SALES (est): 16.9MM **Privately Held**
SIC: 5511 6159 7539 Automobiles, new & used; automobile finance leasing; automotive repair shops

(G-10745)
KOCH MEAT CO INC
Also Called: Cooked Foods
4100 Port Union Rd (45014-2293)
PHONE.................................513 874-3500
Brian Reisen, *Manager*
EMP: 400
SALES (corp-wide): 2.1B **Privately Held**
SIC: 5142 5144 2015 Packaged frozen goods; poultry & poultry products; poultry slaughtering & processing
HQ: Koch Meat Co., Inc.
   1300 Higgins Rd Ste 100
   Park Ridge IL 60068
   847 384-8018

(G-10746)
LAKEFRONT LINES INC
Also Called: Lakefront Trailways
4991 Factory Dr (45014-1946)
P.O. Box 18613 (45018-0613)
PHONE.................................513 829-8290
Jerry Stedy, *Branch Mgr*
EMP: 80
SALES (corp-wide): 4.5B **Privately Held**
WEB: www.lakefrontlines.com
SIC: 4119 4141 Local passenger transportation; local bus charter service
HQ: Lakefront Lines, Inc.
   13315 Brookpark Rd
   Brookpark OH 44142
   216 267-8810

(G-10747)
LIBERTY MUTUAL INSURANCE CO
9450 Seward Rd (45014-5412)
PHONE.................................513 984-0550
Ross Hern, *Auditor*
David Elliott, *Underwriter*
Dan Noltte, *Manager*
Joan Gallina, *Manager*
Chad Scott, *Manager*
EMP: 70
SALES (corp-wide): 38.3B **Privately Held**
WEB: www.libertymutual.com
SIC: 6331 Fire, marine & casualty insurance
HQ: Liberty Mutual Insurance Company
   175 Berkeley St
   Boston MA 02116
   617 357-9500

(G-10748)
LOVELAND EXCAVATING INC
Also Called: Loveland Excavating and Paving
260 Osborne Dr (45014-2246)
PHONE.................................513 965-6600
Matthew J Brennan, *CEO*
Bryan Shepherd, *Vice Pres*
Mike Moeller, *Project Mgr*
Jeremy Redmon, *Project Mgr*
Sharon Rasnic, *Controller*
EMP: 45
SQ FT: 3,000
SALES (est): 7.4MM **Privately Held**
SIC: 1794 Excavation & grading, building construction
PA: Ohio Heavy Equipment Leasing, Llc
   9520 Le Saint Dr
   Fairfield OH 45014
   513 965-6600

(G-10749)
MARTIN LS DDS MS (PA)
Also Called: Martin Periodontics
1211 Nilles Rd (45014-2911)
PHONE.................................513 829-8999
L S Martin DDS Ms, *Owner*
EMP: 26
SALES (est): 1.1MM **Privately Held**
SIC: 8021 Periodontist

(G-10750)
MARTIN MARIETTA MATERIALS INC
Also Called: Fairfield Gravel
107 River Cir Bldg 1 (45014-2333)
PHONE.................................513 829-6446
Robert Lance, *Branch Mgr*
EMP: 50
SQ FT: 1,344 **Publicly Held**
WEB: www.martinmarietta.com
SIC: 5032 Aggregate
PA: Martin Marietta Materials Inc
   2710 Wycliff Rd
   Raleigh NC 27607

(G-10751)
MASTER-HALCO INC
620 Commerce Center Dr (45011-8664)
PHONE.................................513 869-7600
Paul Smith, *Manager*
EMP: 35
SALES (corp-wide): 51.7B **Privately Held**
WEB: www.fenceonline.com
SIC: 5051 3315 Steel; fence gates posts & fittings: steel
HQ: Master-Halco, Inc.
   3010 Lbj Fwy Ste 800
   Dallas TX 75234
   972 714-7300

(G-10752)
MCCLOY ENGINEERING LLC
Also Called: Accutek Testing Laboratory
3701 Port Union Rd (45014-2200)
PHONE.................................513 984-4112
John McCloy, *President*
Erin McCloy, *Sales Executive*
EMP: 45
SALES (est): 5.6MM
SALES (corp-wide): 222K **Privately Held**
WEB: www.accutektesting.com
SIC: 8734 Product testing laboratories
HQ: Element Materials Technology Huntington Beach Inc.
   15062 Bolsa Chica St
   Huntington Beach CA 92649
   714 892-1961

(G-10753)
MERCY HAMILTON HOSPITAL
3000 Mack Rd (45014-5335)
PHONE.................................513 603-8600
Dave Ferrell, *President*
EMP: 50
SALES: 231.3MM **Privately Held**
SIC: 8062 General medical & surgical hospitals

(G-10754)
MERCY HEALTH
2960 Mack Rd Ste 201 (45014-5300)
PHONE.................................513 829-1700
Vijay Rajan, *President*
EMP: 38
SALES (corp-wide): 4.7B **Privately Held**
SIC: 8011 Offices & clinics of medical doctors
PA: Mercy Health
   1701 Mercy Health Pl
   Cincinnati OH 45237
   513 639-2800

(G-10755)
MERCY HEALTH
3000 Mack Rd (45014-5335)
PHONE.................................513 870-7008
Dianne Raanz, *President*
EMP: 30
SQ FT: 13,800
SALES (corp-wide): 4.7B **Privately Held**
SIC: 8062 General medical & surgical hospitals
PA: Mercy Health
   1701 Mercy Health Pl
   Cincinnati OH 45237
   513 639-2800

(G-10756)
MERCY HEALTHPLEXM LLC
3050 Mack Rd Ste 210 (45014-5375)
PHONE.................................513 870-7101
Sean Slovenski, *Director*
EMP: 50
SALES (est): 1.2MM **Privately Held**
WEB: www.emercy.com
SIC: 8093 Specialty outpatient clinics

(G-10757)
MHC MEDICAL PRODUCTS LLC (PA)
8695 Seward Rd (45011-9716)
PHONE.................................877 358-4342
John Edmiston, *Vice Pres*
Joe Levenson, *Vice Pres*
James Light, *VP Bus Dvlpt*
Kevin J Moore, *CFO*
Mary Gentry, *Manager*
▲ **EMP:** 25
SALES (est): 10.4MM **Privately Held**
WEB: www.mastersinhealthcare.com
SIC: 5122 Pharmaceuticals

(G-10758)
MIDDLETOWN INNKEEPERS INC
Also Called: Hampton Inn Cinc Nw/Fairfield
430 Kolb Dr (45014-5361)
PHONE.................................513 942-3440
Har S Bharnagar, *President*
EMP: 40
SALES (est): 2.5MM **Privately Held**
SIC: 7011 Hotels & motels

(G-10759)
MULTICARE MANAGEMENT GROUP
Also Called: Parkside Nrsing Rhbltation Ctr
908 Symmes Rd (45014-1842)
PHONE.................................513 868-6500
Aaron B Handler, *President*
EMP: 105
SQ FT: 27,000
SALES: 950K **Privately Held**
WEB: www.communitymulticarecenter.com
SIC: 8051 Convalescent home with continuous nursing care

(G-10760)
NORM SHARLOTTE INC
Also Called: N. S. Farrington & Co.
300 Distribution Cir A (45014-2269)
PHONE.................................336 788-7705
John Erskine, *President*
Ken Farrington, *Vice Pres*
Earl Gardner, *Vice Pres*
Julia Farrington, *Admin Sec*
▲ **EMP:** 30
SALES (est): 8.8MM **Privately Held**
WEB: www.nsfarrington.com
SIC: 5087 Laundry & dry cleaning equipment & supplies

(G-10761)
NORTH STAR REALTY INCORPORATED
3501 Tylersville Rd Ste G (45011-8005)
PHONE.................................513 737-1700
Lonnie Lewis, *President*
EMP: 28
SALES: 585K **Privately Held**
SIC: 6531 Real estate brokers & agents

(G-10762)
OBSTETRICS & GYNECOLOGY ASSOC (PA)
3050 Mack Rd Ste 375 (45014-5378)
PHONE.................................513 221-3800
Lawrence Freeman, *Vice Pres*
Jerry A Goodman, *Vice Pres*
Stephen A Straubing, *Treasurer*
Amy Cole, *HR Admin*
Ian Foley, *Obstetrician*
EMP: 60
SALES (est): 10.2MM **Privately Held**
SIC: 8011 Physicians' office, including specialists; obstetrician; gynecologist

(G-10763)
OHIO CASUALTY INSURANCE CO (DH)
Also Called: Liberty Mutual
9450 Seward Rd (45014-5412)
PHONE.................................800 843-6446
Dan R Carmichael, *CEO*
Catherine Dooley, *President*
Debra K Crane, *Senior VP*
Ralph G Goode, *Senior VP*
John S Kellington, *Senior VP*
EMP: 1200
SQ FT: 3,379
SALES (est): 35.5MM
SALES (corp-wide): 38.3B **Privately Held**
WEB: www.oci.com
SIC: 6311 6331 Life insurance carriers; workers' compensation insurance
HQ: Liberty Mutual Insurance Company
   175 Berkeley St
   Boston MA 02116
   617 357-9500

(G-10764)
OHIO HEAVY EQUIPMENT LSG LLC (PA)
9520 Le Saint Dr (45014-2253)
PHONE.................................513 965-6600
Matthew Brennan, *Owner*
EMP: 30 **EST:** 2006
SALES (est): 7.4MM **Privately Held**
SIC: 1794 Excavation work

(G-10765)
ONE WAY FARM OF FAIRFIELD INC
Also Called: One Way Farm Children's Home
6131 E River Rd (45014-3241)
P.O. Box 18637 (45018-0637)
PHONE.................................513 829-3276
Jane Holmes, *President*
Ronda Croucher, *Marketing Staff*
Sabrina Smith, *Office Mgr*
Barbara Condo, *Exec Dir*
EMP: 35
SALES: 1.3MM **Privately Held**
WEB: www.onewayfarm.org
SIC: 8361 Children's boarding home

(G-10766)
OSBORNE TRUCKING COMPANY (PA)
325 Osborne Dr (45014-2250)
PHONE.................................513 874-2090
Brad Osborne, *President*
John Holmes, *Vice Pres*
Michael Heller, *VP Opers*
Brad Osbourne, *Sls & Mktg Exec*
Katie Martin, *Human Res Mgr*
EMP: 70
SQ FT: 510,000
SALES (est): 10.4MM **Privately Held**
WEB: www.osborneho.com
SIC: 4213 4225 General warehousing & storage

(G-10767)
OSF INTERNATIONAL INC
6320 S Gilmore Rd (45014-5125)
PHONE.................................513 942-6620
Chris Dussin, *Branch Mgr*
EMP: 56
SALES (corp-wide): 151.2MM **Privately Held**
SIC: 5149 Spaghetti
PA: Osf International, Inc.
   0715 Sw Bancroft St
   Portland OR 97239
   503 222-5375

(G-10768)
PAKMARK LLC
Also Called: Innomark Communications
420 Distribution Cir (45014-5473)
PHONE.................................513 285-1040
Megan Bair, *Production*
Neil Timmons, *Client Mgr*
Gary Boens, *Analyst*
Kyle Fitzgerald, *Analyst*
Bill Fair,
▼ **EMP:** 35
SQ FT: 20,000
SALES (est): 9.8MM **Privately Held**
SIC: 5199 Packaging materials

(G-10769)
PEDIATRIC ASSOC OF FAIRFIELD
5502 Dixie Hwy Ste A (45014-4297)
PHONE...................513 874-9460
Jean Janelle, *President*
Dr Robert Lerer, *Treasurer*
Dr Warren Webb, *Admin Sec*
EMP: 40
SQ FT: 8,200
SALES (est): 6.3MM **Privately Held**
WEB: www.pedsfairfield.com
SIC: 8011 Pediatrician

(G-10770)
PENNINGTON SEED INC
9530 Le Saint Dr (45014-2253)
PHONE...................513 642-8980
Grayson Godley, *Branch Mgr*
EMP: 93
SALES (corp-wide): 2.2B **Publicly Held**
SIC: 0181 Bulbs & seeds
HQ: Pennington Seed, Inc.
1280 Atlanta Hwy
Madison GA 30650
706 342-1234

(G-10771)
PREMIER CONSTRUCTION COMPANY
9361 Seward Rd (45014-5409)
PHONE...................513 874-2611
Jan Gilkey, *President*
EMP: 35
SQ FT: 10,000
SALES (est): 8.2MM **Privately Held**
SIC: 5031 1751 2452 Lumber: rough, dressed & finished; plywood; carpentry work; panels & sections, prefabricated, wood

(G-10772)
R B DEVELOPMENT COMPANY INC
5200 Camelot Dr (45014-4009)
P.O. Box 18040 (45018-0040)
PHONE...................513 829-8100
Didon Eldad, *President*
EMP: 300
SQ FT: 120,000
SALES (est): 16.6MM **Privately Held**
SIC: 1542 Shopping center construction

(G-10773)
RAY ST CLAIR ROOFING INC
3810 Port Union Rd (45014-2202)
PHONE...................513 874-1234
Raymond J St Clair, *President*
Kevin St Clair, *Vice Pres*
EMP: 35 **EST:** 1956
SQ FT: 7,000
SALES (est): 5MM **Privately Held**
WEB: www.raystclairroofing.com
SIC: 1761 1751 1741 Roofing contractor; siding contractor; window & door (prefabricated) installation; chimney construction & maintenance

(G-10774)
RIEMAN ARSZMAN CSTM DISTRS INC
9190 Seward Rd (45014-5406)
PHONE...................513 874-5444
Ken Rieman, *President*
Rebecca Rolfert, *Opers Mgr*
Tom Knodel, *Accounts Mgr*
Rob Saunders, *Accounts Mgr*
Brian Moseley, *Sales Staff*
EMP: 34
SQ FT: 15,000
SALES (est): 30.3MM **Privately Held**
SIC: 5064 Electrical appliances, major; dishwashers; refrigerators & freezers; washing machines

(G-10775)
RIVER CITY PHARMA
8695 Seward Rd (45011-9716)
PHONE...................513 870-1680
Danny Smith, *President*
Jason Smith, *Vice Pres*
EMP: 75
SALES (est): 5.7MM **Privately Held**
SIC: 2834 5122 Pharmaceutical preparations; pharmaceuticals

(G-10776)
ROBERT F ARROM MD INC
1020 Symmes Rd (45014-1844)
PHONE...................513 893-4107
Robert F Arrom MD, *Owner*
EMP: 30
SQ FT: 1,492
SALES (est): 2.2MM **Privately Held**
SIC: 8011 Offices & clinics of medical doctors

(G-10777)
SAFETY-KLEEN SYSTEMS INC
4120 Thunderbird Ln (45014-2235)
PHONE...................513 563-0931
Rich Goodwin, *Manager*
Gena Maras, *Admin Sec*
EMP: 30
SALES (corp-wide): 3.3B **Publicly Held**
SIC: 8748 Environmental consultant
HQ: Safety-Kleen Systems, Inc.
2600 N Central Expy # 400
Richardson TX 75080
972 265-2000

(G-10778)
SCHIFF JOHN J & THOMAS R & CO
Also Called: Schiff Agency
6200 S Gilmore Rd (45014-5141)
P.O. Box 145496, Cincinnati (45250-5496)
PHONE...................513 870-2580
John J Schiff Jr, *Ch of Bd*
Raymond E Broerman, *President*
Jeff Lutter, *General Mgr*
Scott Lindsay, *Vice Pres*
Mike Tiemeier, *Vice Pres*
EMP: 28
SALES (est): 4.8MM **Privately Held**
SIC: 6411 Property & casualty insurance agent; life insurance agents

(G-10779)
SHARPS VALET PARKING
Also Called: Sharp's Valet Parkg
843 Southwind Dr (45014-2755)
PHONE...................513 863-1777
Jeff Anders, *Owner*
EMP: 30 **EST:** 1978
SALES (est): 615.9K **Privately Held**
WEB: www.sharpsvalet.com
SIC: 7521 Automobile parking

(G-10780)
SHIP-PAQ INC
3845 Port Union Rd (45014-2208)
PHONE...................513 860-0700
James R Jarboe, *CEO*
Randy Jarboe, *President*
Kyle Jarboe, *Vice Pres*
Nancy L Jarboe, *Vice Pres*
▲ **EMP:** 34
SQ FT: 46,500
SALES (est): 10.4MM **Privately Held**
WEB: www.shippaq.com
SIC: 5199 Packaging materials

(G-10781)
SHRED-IT USA LLC
6838 Firfield Bus Ctr Dr (45014)
PHONE...................847 288-0377
Sean Wynn, *Branch Mgr*
EMP: 53
SALES (corp-wide): 3.4B **Publicly Held**
SIC: 7389 Document & office record destruction
HQ: Shred-It Usa Llc
6838 Firfield Bus Ctr Dr
Fairfield OH 45014
800 697-4733

(G-10782)
SHRED-IT USA LLC (HQ)
6838 Firfield Bus Ctr Dr (45014)
PHONE...................800 697-4733
Charles A Alutto, *President*
Brent Arnold, *COO*
Brenda Frank, *Vice Pres*
Dan Ginnetti, *CFO*
EMP: 36
SALES (est): 1B
SALES (corp-wide): 3.4B **Publicly Held**
SIC: 7389 Document & office record destruction

PA: Stericycle, Inc.
28161 N Keith Dr
Lake Forest IL 60045
847 367-5910

(G-10783)
SIBCY CLINE INC
600 Wessel Dr (45014-3600)
PHONE...................513 385-3330
Rob Stix, *Manager*
EMP: 45
SALES (corp-wide): 2.1B **Privately Held**
WEB: www.sibcycline.com
SIC: 6531 Real estate brokers & agents
PA: Sibcy Cline, Inc.
8044 Montgomery Rd # 300
Cincinnati OH 45236
513 984-4100

(G-10784)
SIBCY CLINE INC
600 Wessel Dr (45014-3600)
PHONE...................513 829-0044
Thomas Hasselbeck, *Manager*
EMP: 55
SALES (corp-wide): 2.1B **Privately Held**
WEB: www.sibcycline.com
SIC: 6531 Real estate brokers & agents
PA: Sibcy Cline, Inc.
8044 Montgomery Rd # 300
Cincinnati OH 45236
513 984-4100

(G-10785)
SKYLINE CHILI INC (PA)
4180 Thunderbird Ln (45014-2235)
PHONE...................513 874-1188
Kevin R Mc Donnell, *President*
Terry Donovan, *Exec VP*
Jim Konves, *Vice Pres*
Steve Gerwe, *Controller*
Sarah Lapham, *Marketing Mgr*
▲ **EMP:** 120 **EST:** 1949
SQ FT: 42,000
SALES (est): 60.8MM **Privately Held**
WEB: www.skylinechili.com
SIC: 5812 2038 6794 5149 Restaurant, family: chain; frozen specialties; franchises, selling or licensing; groceries & related products; dried or canned foods; canned goods: fruit, vegetables, seafood, meats, etc.; canned specialties

(G-10786)
SOUTHERN GLAZERS WINE AND SP
Also Called: Just Cheking Cash
4305 Muhlhauser Rd Ste 4 (45014-2265)
PHONE...................513 755-7082
John Roberts, *Manager*
Jeff McClanahan, *Manager*
EMP: 55
SALES (corp-wide): 7.2B **Privately Held**
WEB: www.glazer.com
SIC: 5182 Wine
HQ: Southern Glazer's Wine And Spirits Of Texas, Llc
2001 Diplomat Dr
Farmers Branch TX 75234
972 277-2000

(G-10787)
STEVEN L SAWDAI
6120 Pleasant Ave (45014-4623)
PHONE...................513 829-3830
Steven L Sawdai, *Partner*
EMP: 26
SALES (est): 388.5K **Privately Held**
SIC: 0742 Veterinarian, animal specialties

(G-10788)
SUNESIS ENVIRONMENTAL LLC
325 Commercial Dr (45014-5567)
PHONE...................513 326-6000
Richard E Jones Jr, *President*
Andrea Strunk, *Administration*
EMP: 92 **EST:** 2015
SALES (est): 2.8MM **Privately Held**
SIC: 1629 1795 1623 Dams, waterways, docks & other marine construction; earth-moving contractor; wrecking & demolition work; sewer line construction

(G-10789)
TERMINIX INTL CO LTD PARTNR
4305 Muhlhauser Rd Ste 2 (45014-2265)
PHONE...................513 942-6670
Kelvin Colter, *Manager*
EMP: 35
SALES (corp-wide): 1.9B **Publicly Held**
SIC: 7342 Pest control services
HQ: The Terminix International Company Limited Partnership
150 Peabody Pl
Memphis TN 38103
901 766-1400

(G-10790)
THERMAL SOLUTIONS INC
9491 Seward Rd (45014-5411)
PHONE...................513 742-2836
Tom Wiest, *President*
Mary C Guy, *Treasurer*
James Diersing, *Executive*
Russell Wiest, *Executive*
Jennifer L James, *Admin Sec*
EMP: 55
SQ FT: 2,100
SALES (est): 4.7MM **Privately Held**
SIC: 1742 Insulation, buildings

(G-10791)
TORIS STATION
Also Called: Fairfield Bnquet Convention Ctr
8657 N Gilmore Rd (45014-2104)
PHONE...................513 829-7815
Sam Minnielli, *Owner*
EMP: 30
SALES (est): 931.6K **Privately Held**
SIC: 7299 Banquet hall facilities

(G-10792)
TRI COUNTY ASSEMBLY OF GOD
7350 Dixie Hwy (45014-5597)
PHONE...................513 874-8575
Rev Brad H Rosenberg, *Pastor*
Rev Hugh H Rosenberg, *Pastor*
EMP: 35
SQ FT: 200,000
SALES (est): 2.1MM **Privately Held**
WEB: www.tcalife.com
SIC: 8661 8351 Assembly of God Church; preschool center

(G-10793)
TRI COUNTY EXTENDED CARE CTR
5200 Camelot Dr (45014-4009)
P.O. Box 18040 (45018-0040)
PHONE...................513 829-3555
Gidon Eltad, *CEO*
Samuel Boymel, *President*
Peggy Morris, *Vice Pres*
Rachel Boymel, *Treasurer*
EMP: 250
SQ FT: 120,000
SALES: 17.3MM **Privately Held**
WEB: www.tcecc.com
SIC: 8051 Extended care facility

(G-10794)
TRUGREEN LIMITED PARTNERSHIP
Also Called: Tru Green-Chemlawn
4041 Thunderbird Ln (45014-2232)
PHONE...................513 223-3707
Jeff Kozakiewicz, *General Mgr*
EMP: 40
SQ FT: 2,000
SALES (corp-wide): 3.4B **Privately Held**
SIC: 0782 Lawn care services
HQ: Trugreen Limited Partnership
1790 Kirby Pkwy
Memphis TN 38138
901 251-4128

(G-10795)
UNICUSTOM INC
3263 Homeward Way (45014-4237)
P.O. Box 74, West Chester (45071-0074)
PHONE...................513 874-9806
Avnish K Bansal, *President*
Veena Bansal, *Vice Pres*
EMP: 30
SQ FT: 7,000

SALES (est): 2.5MM **Privately Held**
SIC: 1731 1611 General electrical contractor; highway & street construction

(G-10796)
UNIVERSAL TRANSPORTATION SYSTE (PA)
Also Called: Uts
5284 Winton Rd (45014-3912)
PHONE.....................513 829-1287
Carolyn Burer,
EMP: 200
SQ FT: 1,200
SALES (est): 18.3MM **Privately Held**
WEB: www.utswct.com
SIC: 4111 8742 Local & suburban transit; transportation consultant

(G-10797)
US BRONCO SERVICES INC
280 Donald Dr (45014-3007)
P.O. Box 181418 (45018-1418)
PHONE.....................513 829-9880
Joseph Kulifay, *President*
EMP: 50
SALES (est): 2.3MM **Privately Held**
SIC: 7389 Meter readers, remote

(G-10798)
VERITIV OPERATING COMPANY
Also Called: International Paper
375 Distribution Cir (45014-5442)
PHONE.....................513 242-0800
Gary Burkert, *Branch Mgr*
EMP: 133
SALES (corp-wide): 8.7B **Publicly Held**
SIC: 5113 Industrial & personal service paper
HQ: Veritiv Operating Company
1000 Abernathy Rd
Atlanta GA 30328
770 391-8200

(G-10799)
VERITIV OPERATING COMPANY
Also Called: International Paper
6120 S Gilmore Rd (45014-5162)
PHONE.....................513 285-0999
Elizabeth Rhoden, *Program Mgr*
Jim Baumer, *Manager*
Joan Di Concilio, *Manager*
David V Reed, *Manager*
Tim Sullivan, *Manager*
EMP: 133
SALES (corp-wide): 8.7B **Publicly Held**
WEB: www.internationalpaper.com
SIC: 5113 Industrial & personal service paper
HQ: Veritiv Operating Company
1000 Abernathy Rd
Atlanta GA 30328
770 391-8200

(G-10800)
ZEBEC OF NORTH AMERICA INC
210 Donald Dr (45014-3007)
P.O. Box 181570 (45018-1570)
PHONE.....................513 829-5533
Ed Synder, *President*
Chris Snyder, *Vice Pres*
Scott Snyder, *Vice Pres*
▲ EMP: 35
SQ FT: 7,000
SALES (est): 3.6MM **Privately Held**
WEB: www.zebec.com
SIC: 3949 5091 Sporting & athletic goods; sporting & recreation goods

Fairfield Township
Butler County

(G-10801)
BETHESDA HOSPITAL INC
Also Called: Bethesda Butler Hospital
3125 Hamilton Mason Rd (45011-5307)
PHONE.....................513 894-8888
Greg Owens, *Medical Dir*
EMP: 28 **Privately Held**
SIC: 8062 General medical & surgical hospitals

HQ: Bethesda Hospital, Inc.
4750 Wesley Ave
Cincinnati OH 45212
513 569-6100

(G-10802)
BURCHWOOD CARE CENTER
Also Called: Hellandale Community
4070 Hamilton Mason Rd (45011-5414)
PHONE.....................513 868-3300
Brent Dixon, *Director*
Gregg Dixon, *Director*
Valerie Glen, *Director*
EMP: 50
SALES (est): 1.9MM **Privately Held**
SIC: 8051 Skilled nursing care facilities

(G-10803)
BUTLER COUNTY OF OHIO
Also Called: Butler County Care Facility
1800 Princeton Rd (45011-4742)
PHONE.....................513 887-3728
Charles Demidovich, *Director*
EMP: 180
SQ FT: 33,000 **Privately Held**
WEB: www.butlercountyclerk.org
SIC: 8052 9111 8322 8051 Intermediate care facilities; county supervisors' & executives' offices; individual & family services; skilled nursing care facilities
PA: Butler, County Of Ohio
315 High St Fl 6
Hamilton OH 45011
513 887-3278

(G-10804)
BUTLER CNTY ANCILLARY SVCS LLC (PA)
3035 Hamilton Mason Rd (45011-5544)
PHONE.....................513 454-1400
Robyn Finnegan, *Principal*
Ajay Mangal, *Principal*
Joyce Green, *Treasurer*
EMP: 35
SALES (est): 3.5MM **Privately Held**
WEB: www.docsgroup.com
SIC: 8062 General medical & surgical hospitals

(G-10805)
BUTLER COUNTY BD OF MENTAL RE
Liberty Center
5645 Liberty Fairfield Rd (45011-2251)
PHONE.....................513 785-2870
Sherry Dillon, *Manager*
EMP: 105
SALES (corp-wide): 5.9MM **Privately Held**
SIC: 8361 9111 8331 Home for the mentally retarded; county supervisors' & executives' offices; job training services
PA: Butler County Board Of Developmental Disabilities
282 N Fair Ave Ste 1
Hamilton OH 45011
513 785-2815

(G-10806)
CREEKSIDE GOLF LTD
Also Called: Walden Ponds Golf Club
6090 Golf Club Ln (45011-7816)
PHONE.....................513 785-2999
Ken Johnston, *General Mgr*
Jack Eifert, *Director*
EMP: 50
SALES (est): 2.6MM **Privately Held**
SIC: 7992 Public golf courses

(G-10807)
GLENWARD INC
Also Called: Glen Meadows
3472 Hamilton Mason Rd (45011-5437)
PHONE.....................513 863-3100
Glyndon Powell, *President*
Chuck Powell, *Administration*
EMP: 150
SQ FT: 4,000
SALES (est): 6.3MM **Privately Held**
WEB: www.glenmeadows.com
SIC: 8051 Skilled nursing care facilities

(G-10808)
GREAT MIAMI VALLEY YMCA
Also Called: East Butler County YMCA
6645 Morris Rd (45011-5417)
PHONE.....................513 892-9622
Cindy Koenig, *Branch Mgr*
EMP: 136
SALES (corp-wide): 13MM **Privately Held**
SIC: 8641 7991 8351 7032 Youth organizations; physical fitness facilities; child day care services; youth camps; individual & family services
PA: Great Miami Valley Ymca
105 N 2nd St
Hamilton OH 45011
513 887-0001

(G-10809)
HEALTH AND SAFETY SCIENCES LLC
3189 Princeton Rd (45011-5338)
PHONE.....................513 488-1952
Steve Ludwig, *Branch Mgr*
EMP: 38
SALES (corp-wide): 820K **Privately Held**
SIC: 8742 Management consulting services
PA: Health And Safety Sciences, Llc
3224 Winchester Ave
Ashland KY 41101
606 393-3036

(G-10810)
HOME DEPOT USA INC
Also Called: Home Depot, The
6562 Winford Ave (45011-0547)
PHONE.....................513 887-1450
Michael Yudt, *Manager*
EMP: 200
SALES (corp-wide): 108.2B **Publicly Held**
WEB: www.homerentalsdepot.com
SIC: 5211 7359 Home centers; tool rental
HQ: Home Depot U.S.A., Inc.
2455 Paces Ferry Ave
Atlanta GA 30339

(G-10811)
KERRINGTON HEALTH SYSTEMS INC
Also Called: Wellington Manor
2923 Hamilton Mason Rd (45011-5355)
PHONE.....................513 863-0360
Charles Powell, *Administration*
EMP: 150
SALES (est): 10MM **Privately Held**
SIC: 8741 Nursing & personal care facility management

(G-10812)
KINDERCARE EDUCATION LLC
Also Called: Kinder Care Learning Center
7939 Morris Rd (45011-7715)
PHONE.....................513 896-4769
Wendy Welch, *Director*
EMP: 25
SALES (corp-wide): 1.2B **Privately Held**
WEB: www.knowledgelearning.com
SIC: 8351 Group day care center
PA: Kindercare Education Llc
650 Ne Holladay St # 1400
Portland OR 97232
503 872-1300

(G-10813)
MENARD INC
2865 Princeton Rd (45011-5342)
PHONE.....................513 737-2204
EMP: 120
SALES (corp-wide): 12.5B **Privately Held**
SIC: 5211 1521 Home centers; single-family home remodeling, additions & repairs
PA: Menard, Inc.
5101 Menard Dr
Eau Claire WI 54703
715 876-5911

(G-10814)
ROBIDEN INC
Also Called: Red Squirrel
6059 Creekside Way (45011-7882)
PHONE.....................513 421-0000
Dennis Kurlas, *President*

EMP: 27
SALES (est): 878.9K **Privately Held**
SIC: 0782 Lawn & garden services

(G-10815)
TRANSITIONAL LIVING INC (HQ)
2052 Princeton Rd (45011-4746)
PHONE.....................513 863-6383
Mike Francis, *CFO*
Sheri Bartles, *Exec Dir*
David F Craft, *Exec Dir*
EMP: 65
SQ FT: 20,000
SALES: 3.4MM **Privately Held**
SIC: 8069 Alcoholism rehabilitation hospital
PA: Community Health Alliance
1020 Symmes Rd
Fairfield OH 45014
513 896-3458

Fairlawn
Summit County

(G-10816)
AKRON GEN EDWIN SHAW RHBLTTION
3600 W Market St Ste 102 (44333-4540)
PHONE.....................330 375-1300
EMP: 99
SALES (est): 4.1MM
SALES (corp-wide): 8.4B **Privately Held**
SIC: 8069 Specialty Hospital
HQ: Akron General Medical Center Inc
1 Akron General Ave
Akron OH 44307
330 344-6000

(G-10817)
BOBER MARKEY FEDOROVICH (PA)
Also Called: Bmf
3421 Ridgewood Rd Ste 300 (44333-3180)
PHONE.....................330 762-9785
Stanley M Bober, *President*
Richard C Fedorovich, *Managing Prtnr*
Jim Bowen, *Partner*
Robert Burak, *Partner*
Danielle J Kimmell, *Partner*
EMP: 69
SQ FT: 11,000
SALES (est): 12MM **Privately Held**
WEB: www.bmfadvisors.com
SIC: 8721 Certified public accountant

(G-10818)
CADNA RUBBER COMPANY INC
Also Called: Cadna Automotive
703 S Clvland Mssillon Rd (44333-3023)
PHONE.....................901 566-9090
Devin Hart, *CEO*
Tom Griffin, *CFO*
▲ EMP: 30
SQ FT: 50,000
SALES (est): 9.4MM
SALES (corp-wide): 50.8B **Privately Held**
WEB: www.cadna.com
SIC: 5013 Automotive engines & engine parts; automotive supplies & parts
HQ: Contitech Ag
Vahrenwalder Str. 9
Hannover 30165
511 938-02

(G-10819)
CHIMA TRAVEL BUREAU INC (PA)
55 Merz Blvd Unit B (44333-2895)
PHONE.....................330 867-4770
Craig P Chima, *President*
Derek Chima, *Vice Pres*
Lance Chima, *Vice Pres*
EMP: 29
SQ FT: 2,000
SALES (est): 5.8MM **Privately Held**
WEB: www.chimatravel.net
SIC: 4724 Tourist agency arranging transport, lodging & car rental

(G-10820)
CUTLER REAL ESTATE (PA)
2800 W Market St (44333-4007)
PHONE.....................330 836-9141

Jay Cutler, *President*
William H Marting, *President*
Dana E Gechoff, *Treasurer*
EMP: 177
SQ FT: 10,000
SALES (est): 6.9MM **Privately Held**
SIC: 6531 Real estate agent, residential

(G-10821)
DENTAL HEALTH SERVICES (PA)
110 N Miller Rd Ste 200 (44333-3787)
PHONE.............................330 864-9090
Franchesk Dearlo, *Owner*
Marvin D Cohen DDS, *Owner*
▲ **EMP:** 30
SALES (est): 2MM **Privately Held**
WEB: www.dentalhealthservicesinc.com
SIC: 8021 Dentists' office

(G-10822)
DIALAMERICA MARKETING INC
3090 W Market St Ste 210 (44333-3616)
PHONE.............................330 836-5293
Ted Herik, *Manager*
EMP: 180
SALES (corp-wide): 395.1MM **Privately Held**
WEB: www.dialupamerica.net
SIC: 7389 Telemarketing services; telephone services
PA: Dialamerica Marketing, Inc.
      960 Macarthur Blvd
      Mahwah NJ 07430
      201 327-0200

(G-10823)
E & L PREMIER CORPORATION
Also Called: Snelling
3250 W Market St Ste 102 (44333-3319)
PHONE.............................330 836-9901
Esther Gotschall, *President*
Sherry Samms, *Recruiter*
Amanda Steckel, *Recruiter*
EMP: 150
SQ FT: 7,703
SALES (est): 6.1MM **Privately Held**
SIC: 7363 7361 Temporary help service; employment agencies

(G-10824)
ELIOKEM INC (HQ)
175 Ghent Rd (44333-3330)
PHONE.............................330 734-1100
John F Malloy, *President*
Veronique Le Du, *Vice Pres*
Robert Smith, *Vice Pres*
▲ **EMP:** 85
SQ FT: 100,000
SALES (est): 20.9MM
SALES (corp-wide): 769.8MM **Publicly Held**
WEB: www.eliokem.com
SIC: 5169 Industrial chemicals
PA: Omnova Solutions Inc.
      25435 Harvard Rd
      Beachwood OH 44122
      216 682-7000

(G-10825)
EMERALD HEALTH NETWORK INC (HQ)
3320 W Market St 100 (44333-3306)
PHONE.............................216 479-2030
Peter Osner, *President*
EMP: 65
SQ FT: 26,000
SALES (est): 4.9MM **Privately Held**
WEB: www.emeraldhealth.com
SIC: 8742 Hospital & health services consultant

(G-10826)
FAIRLAWN ASSOCIATES LTD
Also Called: Hilton Akron Fairlawn
3180 W Market St (44333-3314)
PHONE.............................330 867-5000
Julie Costello, *Sales Mgr*
Rennick Andreoli, *Analyst*
EMP: 150
SQ FT: 250,000
SALES (est): 11.2MM **Privately Held**
SIC: 7011 5812 6519 6512 Inns; restaurant, family: chain; real property lessors; commercial & industrial building operation; drinking places

(G-10827)
FAIRLAWN OPCO LLC
Also Called: Arbors At Fairlawn
575 S Clvland Mssillon Rd (44333-3019)
PHONE.............................502 429-8062
Robert Norcross, *CEO*
Dannielle Sewell, *Lic Prac Nurse*
EMP: 99
SQ FT: 60,000
SALES (est): 6.4MM **Privately Held**
SIC: 8051 Extended care facility

(G-10828)
FAMILY DENTAL TEAM INC (PA)
620 Ridgewood Xing Ste K (44333-3531)
PHONE.............................330 733-7911
Mark Grucella, *Principal*
James George, *Fmly & Gen Dent*
EMP: 30
SQ FT: 4,000
SALES (est): 4.4MM **Privately Held**
SIC: 8021 Dentists' office

(G-10829)
FIRST CHOICE MED STAFF OF OHIO
3200 W Market St Ste 1 (44333-3315)
PHONE.............................330 867-1409
Cammy Davis, *Branch Mgr*
EMP: 25
SALES (corp-wide): 4.6MM **Privately Held**
SIC: 8099 Medical services organization
PA: First Choice Medical Staffing Of Ohio, Inc.
      1457 W 117th St
      Cleveland OH 44107
      216 521-2222

(G-10830)
FIRST COMMUNICATIONS LLC
3340 W Market St (44333-3381)
PHONE.............................330 835-2323
Jim Ducay, *Branch Mgr*
EMP: 29
SALES (corp-wide): 148.9MM **Privately Held**
SIC: 4813 Long distance telephone communications
PA: First Communications, Llc
      3340 W Market St
      Fairlawn OH 44333
      330 835-2323

(G-10831)
FIRST COMMUNICATIONS LLC (PA)
3340 W Market St (44333-3381)
PHONE.............................330 835-2323
Toll Free:.............................888
Raymond Hexamer, *CEO*
Margi Shaw, *President*
Mark Sollenberger, *CFO*
Nick Marema, *Accounts Exec*
Brent Stevens, *Accounts Exec*
▲ **EMP:** 85
SALES (est): 148.9MM **Privately Held**
SIC: 4813 Long distance telephone communications

(G-10832)
HOSPICE CARE OHIO (PA)
Also Called: Hospice Visiting Nurse Service
3358 Ridgewood Rd (44333-3118)
PHONE.............................330 665-1455
Karen Mullen, *President*
Tracey Nauer, *Director*
EMP: 26
SALES (est): 11.8MM **Privately Held**
SIC: 8082 Visiting nurse service

(G-10833)
INNOVAIRRE COMMUNICATIONS LLC
3200 W Market St Ste 302 (44333-3326)
PHONE.............................330 869-8500
Paul Noonan, *Managing Dir*
Tracy Maloy, *Director*
EMP: 56
SALES (corp-wide): 77.4MM **Privately Held**
SIC: 7389 Fund raising organizations

PA: Innovairre Communications, Llc
      2 Executive Campus # 200
      Cherry Hill NJ 08002
      856 663-2500

(G-10834)
INTERIM HALTHCARE COLUMBUS INC
Also Called: Interim Services
3040 W Market St Ste 1 (44333-3642)
PHONE.............................330 836-5571
Thomas J Dimarco, *President*
Jan Pike, *Manager*
Craig Smith,
EMP: 30
SALES (corp-wide): 19.8MM **Privately Held**
SIC: 8082 7361 7363 Home health care services; nurses' registry; medical help service
HQ: Interim Healthcare Of Columbus, Inc.
      784 Morrison Rd
      Gahanna OH 43230
      614 888-3130

(G-10835)
INTERNATIONAL DATA MGT INC (PA)
3200 W Market St Ste 302 (44333-3326)
PHONE.............................330 869-8500
Paul Noonan, *President*
Derrick Bell, *Vice Pres*
Chris Moore, *Vice Pres*
Andy Kepley, *Human Res Mgr*
Odreasha Bell, *Accounts Mgr*
EMP: 50
SQ FT: 24,000
SALES (est): 4.5MM **Privately Held**
WEB: www.idmi.com
SIC: 7374 Computer graphics service

(G-10836)
JERSEY CENTRAL PWR & LIGHT CO
Also Called: Firstenergy
395 Ghent Rd Rm 407 (44333-2678)
PHONE.............................330 315-6713
Brian Donahue, *Engineer*
Craig Truesdell, *VP Sales*
Doug Elliott, *Manager*
Rick Thayer, *Manager*
David Pinter, *Director*
EMP: 45 **Publicly Held**
WEB: www.jersey-central-power-light.monmouth.n
SIC: 4911 8742 4939 Electric services; management consulting services; combination utilities
HQ: Jersey Central Power & Light Company
      76 S Main St
      Akron OH 44308
      800 736-3402

(G-10837)
KAISER FOUNDATION HOSPITALS
Also Called: Fairlawn Medical Offices
4055 Embassy Pkwy Ste 110 (44333-1781)
PHONE.............................800 524-7377
EMP: 593
SALES (corp-wide): 93B **Privately Held**
SIC: 8011 Offices & clinics of medical doctors
HQ: Kaiser Foundation Hospitals Inc
      1 Kaiser Plz
      Oakland CA 94612
      510 271-6611

(G-10838)
KENNETH ZERRUSEN
Also Called: K and R
3412 W Market St (44333-3308)
PHONE.............................330 869-9007
Kenneth Zerrusen, *Principal*
Brandy Brewer, *Opers Staff*
Kevin Thompson, *Business Dir*
Amber Angelilli, *Admin Sec*
EMP: 70
SALES (est): 2MM **Privately Held**
SIC: 8111 General practice attorney, lawyer

(G-10839)
KLAIS AND COMPANY INC (PA)
3320 W Market St 100 (44333-3306)
PHONE.............................330 867-8443
Nancy Archibald, *Principal*
EMP: 37 **EST:** 1966
SALES (est): 5.3MM **Privately Held**
WEB: www.klais.com
SIC: 8748 Employee programs administration

(G-10840)
MET GROUP
2640 W Market St (44333-4202)
PHONE.............................330 864-1916
Dean Erickson, *President*
EMP: 36
SALES (est): 853.4K **Privately Held**
WEB: www.metgroup.com
SIC: 8093 Specialty outpatient clinics

(G-10841)
MIDWEST EMERGENCY SERVICES LLC
3585 Ridge Park Dr (44333-8203)
PHONE.............................586 294-2700
EMP: 45
SQ FT: 8,000
SALES (est): 2.3MM **Privately Held**
SIC: 8721 7361 Accounting/Auditing/Bookkeeping Employment Agency

(G-10842)
MONTROSE FORD INC (PA)
Also Called: MTA Leasing
3960 Medina Rd (44333-2495)
P.O. Box 5260, Akron (44334-0260)
PHONE.............................330 666-0711
Michael Thompson, *Ch of Bd*
Ryan Gassner, *General Mgr*
Brent Normando, *Business Mgr*
Chris Mills, *Vice Pres*
Joseph Stefanini, *Vice Pres*
EMP: 86 **EST:** 1980
SQ FT: 20,000
SALES (est): 94.7MM **Privately Held**
SIC: 5511 5521 7515 7513 Automobiles, new & used; used car dealers; passenger car leasing; truck rental & leasing, no drivers; general automotive repair shops; top & body repair & paint shops

(G-10843)
PREMIX HOLDING COMPANY
3637 Ridgewood Rd (44333-3123)
PHONE.............................330 666-3751
EMP: 320 **EST:** 2016
SALES (corp-wide): 34.5B **Privately Held**
SIC: 6719 Investment holding companies, except banks
HQ: Hpc Holdings, Llc
      3637 Ridgewood Rd
      Fairlawn OH 44333

(G-10844)
RISK INTERNATIONAL SVCS INC (HQ)
4055 Embassy Pkwy Ste 100 (44333-1781)
PHONE.............................216 255-3400
David O'Brien, *Ch of Bd*
Michael D Davis, *President*
Eric Krieg, *Managing Dir*
Douglas Talley, *Vice Pres*
Kirk Walsh, *Vice Pres*
EMP: 33
SALES (est): 6.8MM **Privately Held**
WEB: www.riskinternational.com
SIC: 8742 Management consulting services
PA: Risk International Holdings, Inc.
      4055 Embassy Pkwy Ste 100
      Fairlawn OH 44333
      216 255-3400

(G-10845)
RWDOP LLC
Also Called: Orchards of Ridgewood Livin
3558 Ridgewood Rd (44333-3122)
PHONE.............................330 666-3776
Charlie Ross, *Officer*
Adrin Chelzean, *Administration*
EMP: 160

SALES (est): 12.2MM **Privately Held**
SIC: 8051 Skilled nursing care facilities

(G-10846)
SAINT EDWARD HOUSING CORP
Also Called: Village At St Edward Ind Lving
3125 Smith Rd Ofc (44333-2671)
PHONE..................................330 668-2828
John Hennelly, *President*
EMP: 38
SALES (est): 1.9MM **Privately Held**
SIC: 6513 Retirement hotel operation

(G-10847)
SANCTUARY SOFTWARE STUDIO INC
3560 W Market St Ste 100 (44333-2660)
PHONE..................................330 666-9690
Michael J Terry, *President*
Stacy Simontom, *Director*
EMP: 28
SQ FT: 2,200
SALES: 2MM **Privately Held**
WEB: www.sancsoft.com
SIC: 7372 7371 Application computer software; computer software development

(G-10848)
SAND RUN SUPPORTS LLC
2695 Sand Run Pkwy (44333-3762)
PHONE..................................330 256-2127
Rich Willse,
EMP: 50
SALES (est): 463.7K **Privately Held**
WEB: www.sandrunsupports.com
SIC: 8082 Home health care services

(G-10849)
SEIBERT-KECK INSURANCE AGENCY (PA)
2950 W Market St Ste A (44333-3600)
PHONE..................................330 867-3140
Craig Hassinger, *President*
Johanne Williams, *COO*
David Critchfield, *Exec VP*
Shelley C White, *Assistant VP*
Cliff Baseler, *Vice Pres*
EMP: 38
SQ FT: 17,000
SALES (est): 13.3MM **Privately Held**
WEB: www.seibertkeck.com
SIC: 6411 Insurance agents; insurance brokers

(G-10850)
SENIOR INDEPENDENCE
Also Called: Rockynol
83 N Miller Rd Ste 101 (44333-3729)
PHONE..................................330 873-3468
Sheila Flannery, *Exec Dir*
Audrey M Coy, *Admin Asst*
EMP: 60
SALES (est): 3.4MM **Privately Held**
SIC: 8399 8082 Community development groups; home health care services

(G-10851)
ST EDWARD HOME
Also Called: VILLAGE AT SAINT EDWARD
3131 Smith Rd (44333-2697)
PHONE..................................330 668-2828
John J Hennelly, *President*
Elizabeth Weinhold, *CFO*
Melanie Gladden, *Accounting Mgr*
Megan Bright, *Director*
EMP: 200
SQ FT: 210,000
SALES: 15.4MM **Privately Held**
SIC: 8051 8361 Skilled nursing care facilities; residential care

(G-10852)
STOUFFER REALTY INC (PA)
130 N Miller Rd Ste A (44333-3728)
PHONE..................................330 835-4900
Gary D Stouffer, *President*
Quinnie Lane, *Sales Staff*
Michelle Miller, *Director*
Suzanne Casamento, *Admin Asst*
Robin Rohrich, *Real Est Agnt*
EMP: 47
SALES (est): 6.9MM **Privately Held**
WEB: www.stoufferrealty.com
SIC: 6531 Real estate brokers & agents

(G-10853)
SUMMIT ADVANTAGE LLC
3340 W Market St Ste 100 (44333-3381)
PHONE..................................330 835-2453
Jessica Newman, *President*
EMP: 75 EST: 2012
SALES (est): 4.1MM **Privately Held**
SIC: 7389 8741 Telemarketing services; telephone services; telephone answering service; office management

(G-10854)
VEYANCE INDUSTRIAL SVCS INC (PA)
703 S Clvland Mssillon Rd (44333-3023)
PHONE..................................307 682-7855
Hank Arnold, *General Mgr*
Bill Dixon, *General Mgr*
Bret Hall, *General Mgr*
Alison Boesch, *Principal*
Michael Hoying, *Business Mgr*
EMP: 233
SALES (est): 17.1MM **Privately Held**
SIC: 4212 Baggage transfer

(G-10855)
WELTY BUILDING COMPANY LTD (PA)
3421 Ridgewood Rd Ste 200 (44333-3165)
PHONE..................................330 867-2400
Donzell S Taylor, *President*
Bradley Ewing, *President*
Ed Paparone, *President*
Mike Melnyk, *General Mgr*
Scott Brady, *Superintendent*
EMP: 75
SQ FT: 2,400
SALES (est): 39MM **Privately Held**
SIC: 1542 Commercial & office building, new construction; commercial & office buildings, renovation & repair

(G-10856)
WEST MONTROSE PROPERTIES (PA)
2841 Riviera Dr Ste 300 (44333-3413)
PHONE..................................330 867-4013
Micheal Gallucci Jr, *Partner*
John Bresnahan, *Vice Pres*
EMP: 100
SQ FT: 5,000
SALES (est): 528.9K **Privately Held**
SIC: 7011 Hotel, franchised

Farmersville
Montgomery County

(G-10857)
FARMERSVILLE FIRE ASSN INC
Also Called: FARMERSVILLE FIRE DEPARTMENT
207 N Elm St (45325-1120)
PHONE..................................937 696-2863
Tom Wallace, *Chief*
Chisty Smith,
EMP: 27
SALES: 475.1K **Privately Held**
WEB: www.station67.com
SIC: 8641 Civic associations

Fayetteville
Brown County

(G-10858)
MEDIADVERTISER COMPANY
337 Lorelei Dr (45118-8498)
PHONE..................................513 651-0265
Tom Nelson, *President*
EMP: 28
SQ FT: 400
SALES: 2.5MM **Privately Held**
SIC: 8748 Communications consulting

Felicity
Clermont County

(G-10859)
FRANKLIN TOWNSHIP FIRE AND EMS
718 Market St (45120)
P.O. Box 58 (45120-0058)
PHONE..................................513 876-2996
Diane Seibert, *Manager*
Bradley Moore, *Asst Chief*
EMP: 25
SALES (est): 887.4K **Privately Held**
SIC: 4119 Ambulance service

Findlay
Hancock County

(G-10860)
1 AMAZING PLACE CO
207 E Foulke Ave (45840-3754)
PHONE..................................419 420-0424
Elizabeth A Manley, *President*
EMP: 34
SALES (est): 796.5K **Privately Held**
SIC: 8351 Preschool center

(G-10861)
631 SOUTH MAIN STREET DEV LLC
Also Called: Hancock Hotel
631 S Main St (45840-3127)
PHONE..................................419 423-0631
Rodney Nichols, *Mng Member*
Donald Malarky,
Kelly Niese,
Shane Pfleiderer,
Marland Turner,
EMP: 70
SALES (est): 557.4K **Publicly Held**
SIC: 7011 Hotels
PA: Marathon Petroleum Corporation
539 S Main St
Findlay OH 45840

(G-10862)
A B M INC
119 E Sandusky St (45840-4901)
PHONE..................................419 421-2292
Wayne Mitrick, *Manager*
EMP: 40 **Privately Held**
WEB: www.lakes-mortgage.com
SIC: 7349 Cleaning service, industrial or commercial
PA: A B M, Inc.
180 N Lasalle St Ste 1700
Chicago IL 60601

(G-10863)
ACT I TEMPORARIES FINDLAY INC
2017 Tiffin Ave (45840-9502)
PHONE..................................419 423-0713
Angela Robinson, *President*
William Robinson, *Principal*
EMP: 425
SQ FT: 750
SALES (est): 8.8MM **Privately Held**
SIC: 7363 Temporary help service

(G-10864)
AMERICAN ELECTRIC POWER CO INC
430 Emma St (45840-1736)
PHONE..................................419 420-3011
Louann Hampshire, *Branch Mgr*
EMP: 37
SALES (corp-wide): 16.2B **Publicly Held**
WEB: www.aep.com
SIC: 4911 Distribution, electric power
PA: American Electric Power Company, Inc.
1 Riverside Plz Fl 1 # 1
Columbus OH 43215
614 716-1000

(G-10865)
APPRAISAL RESEARCH CORPORATION (PA)
101 E Sandusky St Ste 408 (45840-3257)
P.O. Box 1002 (45839-1002)
PHONE..................................419 423-3582
Richard Hoffman, *President*
Janice A Hoffman, *Admin Sec*
EMP: 110 EST: 1978
SQ FT: 3,600
SALES (est): 6.9MM **Privately Held**
WEB: www.appraisalresearch.cc
SIC: 6531 Appraiser, real estate

(G-10866)
BACK IN BLACK CO
2100 Fostoria Ave (45840-8758)
P.O. Box 842 (45839-0842)
PHONE..................................419 425-5555
Rob Hayward, *President*
EMP: 40
SALES (est): 1.5MM **Privately Held**
SIC: 4212 Heavy machinery transport, local

(G-10867)
BASOL MAINTENANCE SERVICE INC
318 W Sundunsky St (45840)
P.O. Box 613 (45839-0613)
PHONE..................................419 422-0946
Judith A McMahon, *President*
Patricia Tisci, *Vice Pres*
Colleen Peterman, *Treasurer*
EMP: 60 EST: 1963
SQ FT: 25,000
SALES: 1.4MM **Privately Held**
SIC: 7349 Janitorial service, contract basis

(G-10868)
BIOLIFE PLASMA SERVICES LP
1789 E Melrose Ave (45840-4415)
PHONE..................................419 425-8680
Matt Walter, *Branch Mgr*
Matt Walters, *Manager*
EMP: 51
SALES (corp-wide): 15.1B **Privately Held**
WEB: www.bioliteplasma.com
SIC: 5122 8099 Blood plasma; plasmapherous center
HQ: Biolife Plasma Services L.P.
1200 Lakeside Dr
Bannockburn IL

(G-10869)
BIRCHAVEN VILLAGE
415 College St (45840-3619)
PHONE..................................419 424-3000
Robert Benson, *Principal*
EMP: 210
SALES (corp-wide): 11.6MM **Privately Held**
SIC: 8059 Convalescent home
PA: Birchaven Village
15100 Birchaven Ln Ofc C
Findlay OH 45840
419 424-3000

(G-10870)
BIRCHAVEN VILLAGE (PA)
15100 Birchaven Ln Ofc C (45840-9779)
P.O. Box 1425 (45839-1425)
PHONE..................................419 424-3000
Bridgett Mundy, *Vice Pres*
Deb Kriner, *Nursing Dir*
Tim Cooper, *Food Svc Dir*
Tim Storer, *Administration*
EMP: 300
SQ FT: 75,000
SALES (est): 11.6MM **Privately Held**
SIC: 8051 6514 Skilled nursing care facilities; dwelling operators, except apartments

(G-10871)
BLANCHARD VALLEY HEALTH SYSTEM (PA)
1900 S Main St (45840-1214)
PHONE..................................419 423-4500
Scott Malaney, *President*
Duane Jebbett, *Chairman*
Chris Keller, *Vice Pres*
Barbara Pasztor, *Vice Pres*
Tim Abbott, *Buyer*
EMP: 1196

SQ FT: 50,000
SALES: 32.5MM **Privately Held**
SIC: 8741 7349 Hospital management;
building maintenance, except repairs

(G-10872)
BLANCHARD VALLEY HEALTH SYSTEM
Also Called: Bridge Home Health & Hostice
15100 Birchaven Ln (45840-9773)
P.O. Box 1425 (45839-1425)
PHONE...............................419 424-3000
Robert Westphal, *President*
EMP: 70
SALES (corp-wide): 32.5MM **Privately Held**
SIC: 8741 7361 8082 Hospital management; nurses' registry; home health care services
PA: Blanchard Valley Health System
1900 S Main St
Findlay OH 45840
419 423-4500

(G-10873)
BLANCHARD VALLEY HOSPITAL
Also Called: Nearly New Shop
306 Lima Ave (45840-3042)
PHONE...............................419 423-4335
Dorthy Staley, *President*
EMP: 25
SALES (est): 625K **Privately Held**
WEB: www.blanchardvalleyhospital.com
SIC: 5932 8011 Used merchandise stores; general & family practice, physician/surgeon

(G-10874)
BLANCHARD VALLEY INDUSTRIES
318 W Main Cross St (45840-3315)
PHONE...............................419 422-6386
Mike Chiarelli, *CEO*
Dedra Estep, *Manager*
EMP: 80
SALES: 1.2MM **Privately Held**
SIC: 7361 Employment agencies

(G-10875)
BLANCHARD VALLEY MEDICAL ASSOC
200 W Pearl St (45840-1394)
PHONE...............................419 424-0380
Gary E Hirschfeld MD, *President*
Mary Ann Tucker, *Pharmacist*
Bruce Bouts, *Med Doctor*
Amy Hochstettler, *Technician*
Beth Wilhelm,
EMP: 90 EST: 1971
SQ FT: 14,000
SALES (est): 10MM **Privately Held**
WEB: www.bvma.com
SIC: 8011 Internal medicine, physician/surgeon

(G-10876)
BLANCHARD VLLY CRT CASE MNGMNT
Also Called: Blanchard Valley Center
318 W Main Cross St (45840-3315)
PHONE...............................419 422-6387
Kelli Grisham, *Superintendent*
EMP: 60
SALES (est): 2.6MM **Privately Held**
SIC: 8322 Individual & family services

(G-10877)
BLANCHARD VLY RESIDENTIAL CTR
Also Called: Blanchard Valley School
1705 E Main Cross St (45840-7064)
PHONE...............................419 422-6503
Jammy Bonifas, *Director*
EMP: 60
SALES (est): 2.7MM **Privately Held**
SIC: 8051 Mental retardation hospital

(G-10878)
BLANCHARD VLY RGIONAL HLTH CTR
1800 N Blanchard St # 121 (45840-4503)
PHONE...............................419 427-0809
Brenda Sciranka, *Branch Mgr*
EMP: 150

SALES (corp-wide): 32.5MM **Privately Held**
SIC: 8062 General medical & surgical hospitals
HQ: Blanchard Valley Regional Health Center
1900 S Main St
Findlay OH 45840
419 423-4500

(G-10879)
BLANCHARD VLY RGIONAL HLTH CTR (HQ)
Also Called: BLANCHARD VALLEY HOSPITAL
1900 S Main St (45840-1214)
PHONE...............................419 423-4500
John Bookmyer, *COO*
Ryan Kruse, *Vice Pres*
Amy Kidd, *Opers Staff*
Randy Schroeder, *Marketing Staff*
Sally Gockstetter, *Manager*
▲ EMP: 750
SQ FT: 50,000
SALES: 233.3MM
SALES (corp-wide): 32.5MM **Privately Held**
SIC: 8062 Hospital, affiliated with AMA residency
PA: Blanchard Valley Health System
1900 S Main St
Findlay OH 45840
419 423-4500

(G-10880)
BOB MILLER RIGGING INC
Also Called: Hrm Leasing
11758 Township Road 100 (45840-9730)
P.O. Box 1445 (45839-1445)
PHONE...............................419 422-7477
H Robert Miller, *President*
EMP: 27
SALES (est): 4.8MM **Privately Held**
SIC: 4212 Heavy machinery transport, local

(G-10881)
BOLOTIN LAW OFFICES
612 S Main St Ste 201 (45840-3153)
PHONE...............................419 424-9800
Toll Free:...............................888 -
EMP: 42
SALES (est): 1.3MM **Privately Held**
SIC: 8111 Legal Services Office

(G-10882)
BPREX PLASTIC PACKAGING INC
170 Stanford Pkwy (45840-1732)
PHONE...............................419 423-3271
John Lindy, *Manager*
EMP: 200 **Publicly Held**
SIC: 5162 Plastics products
HQ: Bprex Plastic Packaging Inc.
1 Seagate
Toledo OH 43604

(G-10883)
BROOKDALE SENIOR LIVING INC
Also Called: Grand Court, The
600 Fox Run Rd Ofc (45840-7403)
PHONE...............................419 422-8657
John P Rijos, *President*
Margaret Malloy, *Director*
EMP: 90
SALES (corp-wide): 4.5B **Publicly Held**
WEB: www.grandcourtlifestyles.com
SIC: 8051 Skilled nursing care facilities
PA: Brookdale Senior Living
111 Westwood Pl Ste 400
Brentwood TN 37027
615 221-2250

(G-10884)
BROOKDALE SNIOR LVING CMMNTIES
Also Called: Sterling House of Findlay
725 Fox Run Rd (45840-8403)
PHONE...............................419 423-4440
Robin Dilley, *Manager*
EMP: 35
SALES (corp-wide): 4.5B **Publicly Held**
WEB: www.assisted.com
SIC: 8059 Rest home, with health care

HQ: Brookdale Senior Living Communities, Inc.
6737 W Wa St Ste 2300
Milwaukee WI 53214
414 918-5000

(G-10885)
BULLDAWG HOLDINGS LLC (PA)
Also Called: Flag City Mack
151 Stanford Pkwy (45840-1731)
PHONE...............................419 423-3131
Alex B Clarke, *President*
Greg Jack, *Manager*
Jona Kleman, *Administration*
EMP: 49
SQ FT: 36,900
SALES: 20MM **Privately Held**
WEB: www.flagcitymack.com
SIC: 5012 5531 Truck tractors; truck equipment & parts

(G-10886)
CELLCO PARTNERSHIP
Also Called: Verizon
15073 E Us Route 224 (45840-7764)
PHONE...............................419 424-2351
Barry Alspth, *Branch Mgr*
EMP: 25
SALES (corp-wide): 130.8B **Publicly Held**
SIC: 4812 5999 Cellular telephone services; telephone equipment & systems
HQ: Cellco Partnership
1 Verizon Way
Basking Ridge NJ 07920

(G-10887)
CENTURY HEALTH INC (PA)
1918 N Main St (45840-3818)
PHONE...............................419 425-5050
Colleen Schlea, *CEO*
Carletta Capes, *Corp Secy*
Nida Rider, *Vice Pres*
EMP: 65
SQ FT: 11,700
SALES: 6MM **Privately Held**
SIC: 8093 Alcohol clinic, outpatient; drug clinic, outpatient

(G-10888)
CITY OF COMPASSION
1624 Tiffin Ave (45840-6852)
PHONE...............................419 422-7800
EMP: 51 **Privately Held**
SIC: 9111 8699 City & town managers' offices; charitable organization

(G-10889)
CITY OF FINDLAY
Also Called: Findlay Waste Water Treatment
1201 S River Rd (45840)
PHONE...............................419 424-7179
Randy Greeno, *Superintendent*
EMP: 33 **Privately Held**
SIC: 4952 Sewerage systems
PA: City Of Findlay
318 Dorney Plz Ste 313
Findlay OH 45840
419 424-7114

(G-10890)
COLUMBIA GAS OF OHIO INC
1800 Broad Ave (45840-2722)
P.O. Box 2318, Columbus (43216-2318)
PHONE...............................419 435-7725
H R Rowe, *Branch Mgr*
EMP: 50
SALES (corp-wide): 5.1B **Publicly Held**
WEB: www.meterrepairshop.com
SIC: 4924 Natural gas distribution
HQ: Columbia Gas Of Ohio, Inc.
290 W Nationwide Blvd # 114
Columbus OH 43215
614 460-6000

(G-10891)
COUNTY OF HANCOCK
Also Called: Blanchard Valley Industries
318 W Main Cross St (45840-3315)
PHONE...............................419 422-6387
Sheryl Cotter, *Manager*
EMP: 50 **Privately Held**
WEB: www.hancockparks.com

SIC: 8361 8331 Home for the physically handicapped; job training & vocational rehabilitation services
PA: County Of Hancock
300 S Main St
Findlay OH 45840
419 424-7015

(G-10892)
COUNTY OF HANCOCK
Also Called: Hancock County Home
7746 County Road 140 A (45840-1978)
PHONE...............................419 424-7050
EMP: 58 **Privately Held**
SIC: 8361 Residential Care Services
PA: County Of Hancock
300 S Main St
Findlay OH 45840
419 424-7015

(G-10893)
COUNTY OF HANCOCK
Also Called: Hancock County Engineer
1900 Lima Ave (45840-1439)
P.O. Box 828 (45839-0828)
PHONE...............................419 422-7433
Chris Long, *Director*
EMP: 34 **Privately Held**
WEB: www.hancockparks.com
SIC: 8711 4214 Structural engineering; local trucking with storage
PA: County Of Hancock
300 S Main St
Findlay OH 45840
419 424-7015

(G-10894)
COUNTY OF HANCOCK
Also Called: Hancock Park District
1424 E Main Cross St (45840-7006)
PHONE...............................419 425-7275
Kim Wickman, *Manager*
Gary Pruitt, *Director*
EMP: 25 **Privately Held**
WEB: www.hancockparks.com
SIC: 7999 9512 Recreation services; recreational program administration, government
PA: County Of Hancock
300 S Main St
Findlay OH 45840
419 424-7015

(G-10895)
DANBY PRODUCTS INC (DH)
1800 Production Dr (45840-5445)
P.O. Box 669 (45839-0669)
PHONE...............................419 425-8627
James Estill, *President*
Shauna Gamble, *COO*
Andrew Raymond, *CFO*
◆ EMP: 43
SQ FT: 155,948
SALES (est): 107.8MM
SALES (corp-wide): 1.2MM **Privately Held**
WEB: www.danbyproducts.com
SIC: 5064 Electrical appliances, major
HQ: Danby Products Limited
5070 Whitelaw Rd
Guelph ON N1H 6
519 837-0920

(G-10896)
DAVES RUNNING SHOP INC
1765 Tiffin Ave (45840-6833)
PHONE...............................567 525-4767
James D Mason, *Branch Mgr*
EMP: 25
SALES (corp-wide): 1.5MM **Privately Held**
SIC: 7999 5941 Sporting goods rental; sporting goods & bicycle shops
PA: Dave's Running Shop, Inc.
5700 Monroe St Unit 5702b
Sylvania OH 43560
419 882-8524

(G-10897)
DENTAL CENTER NORTHWEST OHIO
1800 N Blanchard St # 122 (45840-4509)
PHONE...............................419 422-7664
Maribel Ramero, *Manager*
EMP: 32

SALES (corp-wide): 5.2MM **Privately Held**
SIC: 8021 Dental clinic
PA: Dental Center Of Northwest Ohio
2138 Madison Ave
Toledo OH 43604
419 241-6215

(G-10898)
EBSO INC
Also Called: Administrative Service Cons
215 Stanford Pkwy (45840-1733)
PHONE..............................419 423-3823
Cori Guagenti, *Branch Mgr*
EMP: 39
SALES (corp-wide): 9.2MM **Privately Held**
SIC: 6324 6411 Hospital & medical service plans; insurance agents, brokers & service
PA: Ebso Inc.
7020 N Pt Wshngton Rd 2
Glendale WI 53217
414 410-1802

(G-10899)
FABCO INC
616 N Blanchard St (45840-5706)
PHONE..............................419 427-0872
Jon Ballinger, *President*
EMP: 60
SALES (corp-wide): 49.7MM **Privately Held**
SIC: 5082 Excavating machinery & equipment
HQ: Fabco, Inc.
616 N Blanchard St
Findlay OH 45840
419 421-4740

(G-10900)
FAMILY RSOURCE CTR NW OHIO INC
Also Called: Family Resource Centers
1941 Carlin St (45840-1460)
PHONE..............................419 422-8616
Tonnie Guagenta, *General Mgr*
Melissa Meyer, *Senior VP*
EMP: 30
SALES (corp-wide): 4.2MM **Privately Held**
WEB: www.frcohio.com
SIC: 8093 Mental health clinic, outpatient
PA: Family Resource Center Of Northwest Ohio, Inc.
530 S Main St
Lima OH 45804
419 222-1168

(G-10901)
FIELD & STREAM BOWHUNTERS
1023 Cypress Ave (45840-4726)
PHONE..............................419 423-9861
Harlod Spence, *President*
EMP: 80
SALES (est): 903.7K **Privately Held**
SIC: 7997 Gun & hunting clubs

(G-10902)
FINDLAY COUNTRY CLUB
1500 Country Club Dr (45840-6369)
PHONE..............................419 422-9263
James Price, *COO*
EMP: 40
SQ FT: 5,000
SALES: 2.8MM **Privately Held**
WEB: www.findlaycc.com
SIC: 7997 7991 5813 5812 Country club, membership; physical fitness facilities; drinking places; eating places

(G-10903)
FINDLAY IMPLEMENT CO (PA)
Also Called: John Deere Authorized Dealer
1640 Northridge Rd (45840-1902)
P.O. Box 824 (45839-0824)
PHONE..............................419 424-0471
Craig L Holmes, *CEO*
William Stall, *President*
EMP: 39
SQ FT: 30,000
SALES (est): 12.1MM **Privately Held**
WEB: www.findlay-imp.com
SIC: 5261 5082 Lawnmowers & tractors; construction & mining machinery

(G-10904)
FINDLAY INN & CONFERENCE CTR
200 E Main Cross St (45840-4819)
PHONE..............................419 422-5682
Ralph Russo, *Partner*
Todd McCracken, *General Mgr*
John Wengrow, *Sales Executive*
Bruce Schroder, *Manager*
Lolie Anez, *Executive*
EMP: 60
SALES (est): 4.4MM **Privately Held**
WEB: www.findlayinn.com
SIC: 7011 7299 6512 5812 Resort hotel; banquet hall facilities; nonresidential building operators; eating places

(G-10905)
FINDLAY PUBLISHING COMPANY
Also Called: Wfin AM
551 Lake Cascade Pkwy (45840-1388)
P.O. Box 1507 (45839-1507)
PHONE..............................419 422-4545
Sandra J Kozlevcar, *Manager*
EMP: 35
SALES (corp-wide): 14.3MM **Privately Held**
WEB: www.thecourier.com
SIC: 4832 Radio broadcasting stations
PA: Findlay Publishing Company, The (Inc)
701 W Sandusky St
Findlay OH
419 422-5151

(G-10906)
FINDLAY TRUCK LINE INC
106 W Front St (45840-3408)
P.O. Box 1362 (45839-1362)
PHONE..............................419 422-1945
Gregory J Cassidy, *President*
EMP: 86
SQ FT: 10,000
SALES (est): 7.2MM **Privately Held**
WEB: www.ftlco.com
SIC: 4212 Local trucking, without storage

(G-10907)
FINDLAY WOMENS CARE LLC (PA)
Also Called: Tiffin Womens Care
1917 S Main St (45840-1208)
PHONE..............................419 420-0904
Carmen Doty-Armstrong, *Mng Member*
EMP: 30
SALES (est): 3.2MM **Privately Held**
SIC: 8011 Gynecologist

(G-10908)
FINDLAY Y M C A CHILD DEV
231 E Lincoln St (45840-4940)
PHONE..............................419 422-3174
Vicki Montgomery, *Data Proc Exec*
Susan Stitnale, *Director*
Stewart Pelton, *Director*
EMP: 50
SALES (est): 741.6K **Privately Held**
SIC: 8641 7991 8351 7032 Youth organizations; physical fitness facilities; child day care services; youth camps; individual & family services

(G-10909)
FLEETMASTER EXPRESS INC
1531 Harvard Ave (45840-1738)
PHONE..............................419 420-1835
Paul Fricke, *Branch Mgr*
EMP: 70
SALES (corp-wide): 90.8MM **Privately Held**
SIC: 4213 Trucking, except local
PA: Fleetmaster Express, Incorporated
1814 Hollins Rd Ne Ste A
Roanoke VA 24012
540 344-8834

(G-10910)
FRIENDS SERVICE CO INC (PA)
Also Called: Friends Business Source
2300 Bright Rd (45840-5432)
PHONE..............................419 427-1704
Kenneth J Schroeder, *President*
Dale Alt, *President*
Betsy Hughes, *Vice Pres*
Peg Schroeder, *Human Res Dir*

Jennifer Dysinger, *Accounts Mgr*
EMP: 80
SQ FT: 65,000
SALES: 30MM **Privately Held**
WEB: www.friendsoffice.com
SIC: 5112 5021 5044 5087 Stationery & office supplies; furniture; office equipment; janitors' supplies; photolithographic printing

(G-10911)
G S WIRING SYSTEMS INC (HQ)
1801 Production Dr (45840-5446)
P.O. Box 1045 (45839-1045)
PHONE..............................419 423-7111
George Suzuki, *President*
Shinichi Inagaki, *President*
Yukinobu Ukai, *Treasurer*
Masami Kunimi, *Sales Mgr*
Joji Suzuki, *Admin Sec*
▲ **EMP:** 412
SQ FT: 72,000
SALES (est): 46MM
SALES (corp-wide): 250.2MM **Privately Held**
WEB: www.gswiring.com
SIC: 3714 5013 Automotive wiring harness sets; motor vehicle supplies & new parts
PA: G.S.Electech,Inc.
58-1, Hiroko, Yoshiwaracho
Toyota AIC 473-0
565 782-800

(G-10912)
GARNER TRUCKING INC
Also Called: Garner Transportation Group
9291 County Road 313 (45840-9005)
P.O. Box 1506 (45839-1506)
PHONE..............................419 422-5742
Jean Garner, *CEO*
Sherri Brumbaugh, *President*
Don Perkins, *Vice Pres*
Regina R Garner, *Incorporator*
Vernon E Garner, *Incorporator*
EMP: 136
SQ FT: 19,000
SALES: 20MM **Privately Held**
WEB: www.garnertrucking.com
SIC: 4213 4731 4212 Contract haulers; truck transportation brokers; local trucking, without storage

(G-10913)
GENE STEVENS AUTO & TRUCK CTR
Also Called: Gene Stevens Honda
1033 Bright Rd (45840-6978)
PHONE..............................419 429-2000
Gene Stevens, *President*
Scott Stevens, *Vice Pres*
Elaine Stevens, *Treasurer*
EMP: 50
SALES (est): 16.1MM **Privately Held**
WEB: www.genestevensauto.com
SIC: 5511 5521 5012 Automobiles, new & used; used car dealers; automobiles & other motor vehicles

(G-10914)
GRAHAM PACKG PLASTIC PDTS INC
170 Stanford Pkwy (45840-1732)
PHONE..............................419 423-3271
John Lindy, *Plant Mgr*
Nancy Cole, *Accountant*
Ken Flick, *Admin Mgr*
EMP: 200
SALES (est): 31.5MM
SALES (corp-wide): 1MM **Privately Held**
WEB: www.grahampackaging.com
SIC: 5199 Packaging materials
HQ: Graham Packaging Company, L.P.
700 Indian Springs Dr # 100
Lancaster PA 17601
717 849-8500

(G-10915)
H T I EXPRESS
110 Bentley Ct (45840-1779)
PHONE..............................419 423-9555
Jeff Hall, *President*
EMP: 26
SALES (est): 1.3MM **Privately Held**
SIC: 4212 Local trucking, without storage

(G-10916)
HANCO AMBULANCE INC
417 6th St (45840-5198)
PHONE..............................419 423-2912
Duane Donaldson, *President*
Rob Martin, *President*
Shirley Moore, *President*
EMP: 48
SQ FT: 4,200
SALES (est): 1.8MM **Privately Held**
WEB: www.hancoems.com
SIC: 4119 Ambulance service

(G-10917)
HANCOCK FEDERAL CREDIT UNION
1701 E Melrose Ave (45840-4415)
P.O. Box 1623 (45839-1623)
PHONE..............................419 420-0338
Joyce Mohr, *CEO*
Donna Litchle, *Principal*
Suzzette Boyd, *Senior VP*
John Holzwart, *Vice Pres*
Barbara Sidaway,
EMP: 25
SALES: 2.8MM **Privately Held**
WEB: www.hancockfcu.com
SIC: 6062 State credit unions, not federally chartered

(G-10918)
HANCOCK HARDIN WYANDOT PUTNAM (PA)
Also Called: Community Action Commission
122 Jefferson St (45840-4843)
P.O. Box 179 (45839-0179)
PHONE..............................419 423-3755
Dennis La Rocco, *Exec Dir*
Dave Salucci, *Deputy Dir*
EMP: 125 **EST:** 1965
SQ FT: 6,300
SALES (est): 8.7MM **Privately Held**
SIC: 8399 Community action agency

(G-10919)
HANCOCK JOB & FAMILY SERVICES
7814 County Road 140 (45840-1819)
PHONE..............................419 424-7022
Judy Wauford, *Administration*
EMP: 88
SALES (est): 1.1MM **Privately Held**
SIC: 8322 Child related social services

(G-10920)
HCF OF FINDLAY INC
Also Called: Fox Run Manor
11745 Township Road 145 (45840-1093)
PHONE..............................419 999-2010
Barbara Masella, *Vice Pres*
Lisa Williams, *Human Res Mgr*
Lisa Line, *Director*
EMP: 99
SALES (est): 1MM
SALES (corp-wide): 154.8MM **Privately Held**
SIC: 8059 Nursing home, except skilled & intermediate care facility
PA: Hcf Management, Inc.
1100 Shawnee Rd
Lima OH 45805
419 999-2010

(G-10921)
HCF OF FOX RUN INC
Also Called: Fox Run Manor
11745 Township Road 145 (45840-1093)
PHONE..............................419 424-0832
Sandy Patterson, *Exec Dir*
Shane Stewart, *Administration*
EMP: 99
SALES (est): 4MM
SALES (corp-wide): 154.8MM **Privately Held**
SIC: 8051 8059 Convalescent home with continuous nursing care; nursing home, except skilled & intermediate care facility
PA: Hcf Management, Inc.
1100 Shawnee Rd
Lima OH 45805
419 999-2010

(G-10922)
HELTON ENTERPRISES INC (PA)
151 Stanford Pkwy (45840-1731)
PHONE.................................419 423-4180
Charles D Walter, *Ch of Bd*
James Hoffman, *President*
Dan Campling, *Corp Secy*
EMP: 38
SQ FT: 39,600
SALES (est): 2.9MM **Privately Held**
SIC: 7513 5012 5531 Truck leasing, without drivers; truck tractors; trailers for trucks, new & used; truck equipment & parts

(G-10923)
HERCULES TIRE & RUBBER COMPANY
Also Called: Warehouse
14801 Township Rd 212 (45840)
PHONE.................................419 425-6400
Troy Farthing, *Manager*
EMP: 60
SALES (corp-wide): 5B **Privately Held**
WEB: www.herculestire.com
SIC: 5014 Tires & tubes
HQ: The Hercules Tire & Rubber Company
1995 Tiffin Ave Ste 205
Findlay OH 45840
419 425-6400

(G-10924)
HTI - HALL TRUCKING INC
110 Bentley Ct (45840-1779)
PHONE.................................419 423-9555
Jeffrey A Hall, *President*
Cassandra Hall, *Admin Sec*
EMP: 40
SALES (est): 6.2MM **Privately Held**
SIC: 4213 Trucking, except local

(G-10925)
HUNTINGTON INSURANCE INC
Also Called: Huntington Bank
236 S Main St (45840-3352)
PHONE.................................419 429-4627
Cynthy Wolke, *President*
Donald Bledsoe, *Broker*
Marcia Walton, *Branch Mgr*
EMP: 46
SALES (corp-wide): 5.2B **Publicly Held**
WEB: www.skyinsure.com
SIC: 6029 Commercial banks
HQ: Huntington Insurance, Inc.
519 Madison Ave
Toledo OH 43604
419 720-7900

(G-10926)
HYWAY TRUCKING COMPANY
10060 W Us Route 224 (45840-1914)
P.O. Box 416 (45839-0416)
PHONE.................................419 423-7145
Matt Lenhart, *President*
EMP: 100
SALES: 13.8MM **Privately Held**
WEB: www.hywaytrucking.com
SIC: 4213 4212 Contract haulers; local trucking, without storage

(G-10927)
INTER HEALT CARE OF NORTH OH I
Also Called: Interim Services
2129 Stephen Ave Ste 3 (45840)
PHONE.................................419 422-5328
Krista Finsto, *Manager*
EMP: 50
SALES (corp-wide): 19.8MM **Privately Held**
SIC: 8082 Home health care services
HQ: Interim Health Care Of Northwestern Ohio, Inc
3100 W Central Ave # 250
Toledo OH 43606

(G-10928)
JK-CO LLC
16960 E State Route 12 (45840-9744)
PHONE.................................419 422-5240
Joseph L Kurtz, *President*
C Leon Thornton, *Vice Pres*
Tony Butz, *Project Mgr*
Chuck Brothers, *Buyer*

Chad Vogel, *Project Engr*
▼ EMP: 45
SQ FT: 40,000
SALES (est): 11.7MM **Privately Held**
SIC: 3743 4789 Railroad car rebuilding; railroad car repair

(G-10929)
JPMORGAN CHASE BANK NAT ASSN
1971 Broad Ave (45840-2723)
PHONE.................................419 424-7570
Jeff Hire, *Branch Mgr*
EMP: 26
SALES (corp-wide): 131.4B **Publicly Held**
SIC: 6021 National commercial banks
HQ: Jpmorgan Chase Bank, National Association
1111 Polaris Pkwy
Columbus OH 43240
614 436-3055

(G-10930)
JPMORGAN CHASE BANK NAT ASSN
500 S Main St (45840-3230)
PHONE.................................419 424-7512
Anna Bretzing, *Manager*
EMP: 26
SALES (corp-wide): 131.4B **Publicly Held**
WEB: www.chase.com
SIC: 6021 National commercial banks
HQ: Jpmorgan Chase Bank, National Association
1111 Polaris Pkwy
Columbus OH 43240
614 436-3055

(G-10931)
JUDSON PALMER HOME CORP
2911 N Main St (45840-4099)
P.O. Box 119 (45839-0119)
PHONE.................................419 422-9656
Rebecca Rademacher, *Principal*
EMP: 25
SQ FT: 30,000
SALES: 1.3MM **Privately Held**
WEB: www.judsonpalmer.com
SIC: 8059 Rest home, with health care

(G-10932)
KRAMER ENTERPRISES INC (PA)
Also Called: City Laundry & Dry Cleaning Co
116 E Main Cross St (45840-4817)
PHONE.................................419 422-7924
Paul T Kramer, *President*
Carl P Kramer, *Principal*
Andrew Beach, *Vice Pres*
Phil Brown, *Manager*
Pamela E Kramer, *Admin Sec*
EMP: 70
SQ FT: 6,500
SALES (est): 9.6MM **Privately Held**
WEB: www.kramerenterprises.com
SIC: 7213 7216 Uniform supply; drycleaning plants, except rugs

(G-10933)
LARICHE SUBARU INC
Also Called: Lariche Chevrolet-Cadillac
215 E Main Cross St (45840-4818)
PHONE.................................419 422-1855
Lou Lariche, *President*
Scott Lariche, *Corp Secy*
John Lariche, *Vice Pres*
Cindy Mock, *Controller*
Clyde Geiser, *CPA*
EMP: 72
SQ FT: 25,000
SALES (est): 31.7MM **Privately Held**
WEB: www.larichechevrolet.com
SIC: 5511 5521 7515 7538 Automobiles, new & used; pickups, new & used; used car dealers; passenger car leasing; general automotive repair shops

(G-10934)
LEGACY NTRAL STONE SRFACES LLC
Also Called: Legacy Marble and Granite
229 Stanford Pkwy (45840-1733)
PHONE.................................419 420-7440

Traci Lee, *Business Mgr*
Craig Cook, *Project Mgr*
Kristi Frederick, *Project Mgr*
Randy Kubena, *Project Mgr*
Tina Reeves, *Project Mgr*
EMP: 40
SALES (est): 200K **Privately Held**
SIC: 1743 Marble installation, interior

(G-10935)
LOWES HOME CENTERS LLC
1077 Bright Rd (45840-6978)
PHONE.................................419 420-7531
Scott Adkins, *Store Mgr*
Mary Parkins, *Executive*
EMP: 150
SALES (corp-wide): 68.6B **Publicly Held**
SIC: 5211 5031 5722 5064 Home centers; building materials, exterior; building materials, interior; household appliance stores; electrical appliances, television & radio
HQ: Lowe's Home Centers, Llc
1605 Curtis Bridge Rd
Wilkesboro NC 28697
336 658-4000

(G-10936)
LUKE THEIS ENTERPRISES INC
Also Called: Luke Theis Contractors
14120 State Route 568 (45840-9428)
PHONE.................................419 422-2040
Luke Theis, *President*
EMP: 57
SALES: 122MM **Privately Held**
SIC: 1542 1541 1521 Nonresidential construction; industrial buildings & warehouses; new construction, single-family houses

(G-10937)
MANLEYS MANOR NURSING HOME INC
Also Called: Heritage, The
2820 Greenacre Dr (45840-4157)
PHONE.................................419 424-0402
L Don Manley, *President*
Karen Manley, *Corp Secy*
Dawn Harris, *Network Mgr*
EMP: 150
SQ FT: 1,200,000
SALES (est): 6.6MM **Privately Held**
SIC: 8051 6512 Convalescent home with continuing nursing care; commercial & industrial building operation

(G-10938)
MARATHON PETROLEUM CORPORATION (PA)
539 S Main St (45840-3229)
PHONE.................................419 422-2121
Gary R Heminger, *Ch of Bd*
Donald C Templin, *President*
Glenn M Plumby, *COO*
C Michael Palmer, *Senior VP*
Suzanne Gagle, *Vice Pres*
EMP: 277
SALES: 75.3B **Publicly Held**
SIC: 2911 5172 Petroleum refining; gasoline

(G-10939)
MARATHON PIPE LINE LLC (HQ)
539 S Main St Ste 7614 (45840-3229)
PHONE.................................419 422-2121
Gary R Heminger, *CEO*
Don P Bozell,
Kenneth J Hauck,
Craig O Pierson,
T L Shaw,
▲ EMP: 107
SQ FT: 25,000
SALES: 467.9MM **Publicly Held**
WEB: www.mapl.com
SIC: 4612 4613 Crude petroleum pipelines; refined petroleum pipelines

(G-10940)
MAY JIM AUTO SALES LLC
Also Called: Jim May Auto Sales & Svc Ctr
3690 Speedway Dr (45840-7246)
PHONE.................................419 422-9797
Jim May, *Managing Prtnr*
EMP: 25
SQ FT: 6,000

SALES (est): 4.4MM **Privately Held**
SIC: 5521 7538 Automobiles, used cars only; general automotive repair shops

(G-10941)
MCNAUGHTON-MCKAY ELC OHIO INC
1950 Industrial Dr (45840-5441)
PHONE.................................419 422-2984
Timothy J Krucki, *Principal*
EMP: 30
SQ FT: 35,000
SALES (corp-wide): 822.5MM **Privately Held**
WEB: www.mc.mc.com
SIC: 5063 Electrical supplies
HQ: Mcnaughton-Mckay Electric Company Of Ohio, Inc.
2255 Citygate Dr
Columbus OH 43219
614 476-2800

(G-10942)
MEDCORP INC
330 N Cory St (45840-3566)
PHONE.................................419 425-9700
Dick Bage, *Owner*
EMP: 198 **Privately Held**
SIC: 4119 8082 Ambulance service; home health care services
PA: Medcorp, Inc.
745 Medcorp Dr
Toledo OH 43608

(G-10943)
MELROSE REHAB LLC
2201 Jennifer Ln (45840-4472)
PHONE.................................419 424-9625
Dametri Coleman, *Principal*
Tom Lusk, *Principal*
EMP: 25
SALES (est): 292K **Privately Held**
SIC: 8093 Rehabilitation center, outpatient treatment

(G-10944)
MIAMI INDUSTRIAL TRUCKS INC
130 Stanford Pkwy (45840-1732)
PHONE.................................419 424-0042
Rob Gibson, *Opers Mgr*
Michael Wechta, *Manager*
John Shade, *Technical Staff*
EMP: 40
SALES (est): 3.4MM
SALES (corp-wide): 51.9MM **Privately Held**
WEB: www.mitlift.com
SIC: 5084 Materials handling machinery
PA: Miami Industrial Trucks, Inc.
2830 E River Rd
Moraine OH 45439
937 293-4194

(G-10945)
MID-AMERICAN CLG CONTRS INC
1648 Tiffin Ave (45840-6849)
PHONE.................................419 429-6222
John Whitaker, *Branch Mgr*
EMP: 117 **Privately Held**
SIC: 7349 Janitorial service, contract basis
PA: Mid-American Cleaning Contractors; Inc.
447 N Elizabeth St
Lima OH 45801

(G-10946)
MPLX LP (PA)
200 E Hardin St (45840-4963)
PHONE.................................419 421-2414
Gary R Heminger, *Ch of Bd*
Michael J Hennigan, *President*
Mplx GP LLC, *General Ptnr*
Timothy J Aydt, *Vice Pres*
EMP: 32 EST: 2012
SALES: 6.4B **Publicly Held**
SIC: 4612 4613 Crude petroleum pipelines; refined petroleum pipelines

(G-10947)
NAPOLEON WASH-N-FILL INC (PA)
Also Called: Flag City Auto Wash
339 E Main Cross St (45840-4820)
PHONE.................................419 422-7216
Randy Miller, *President*
Leo Snyder, *President*
Michael Snyder, *Vice Pres*
Chauncey Morse, *Treasurer*
EMP: 125
SALES (est): 2.8MM **Privately Held**
WEB: www.flagcityautowash.com
SIC: 7542 Washing & polishing, automotive

(G-10948)
NATIONAL LIME AND STONE CO
9860 County Road 313 (45840-9003)
P.O. Box 120 (45839-0120)
PHONE.................................419 423-3400
Tim Federici, *Sales Staff*
Denny Swick, *Branch Mgr*
EMP: 31
SALES (corp-wide): 3.2B **Privately Held**
WEB: www.natlime.com
SIC: 3273 1422 Ready-mixed concrete; crushed & broken limestone
PA: The National Lime And Stone Company
551 Lake Cascade Pkwy
Findlay OH 45840
419 422-4341

(G-10949)
NOAKES ROONEY RLTY & ASSOC CO
Also Called: ERA
2113 Tiffin Ave Ste 103 (45840-8516)
PHONE.................................419 423-4861
Greta Noakes, *President*
Gary Noakes, *Vice Pres*
EMP: 25
SQ FT: 2,500
SALES (est): 1.1MM **Privately Held**
WEB: www.noakesrooney.com
SIC: 6531 Real estate agent, residential

(G-10950)
NORTHWEST OHIO ORTHOPEDIC & SP
7595 County Road 236 (45840-8738)
PHONE.................................419 427-1984
James D Egleston, *President*
Michael Tremains, *Med Doctor*
Kim Smith, *Podiatrist*
Cara Wagner,
EMP: 110
SALES (est): 13.7MM **Privately Held**
SIC: 8069 Orthopedic hospital

(G-10951)
OHIO AUTOMOTIVE SUPPLY CO
525 W Main Cross St (45840-3370)
P.O. Box 209 (45839-0209)
PHONE.................................419 422-1655
Thomas E Winklejohn, *President*
J Theodore Winklejohn, *Vice Pres*
EMP: 29
SQ FT: 3,500
SALES (est): 6MM **Privately Held**
WEB: www.ohioautomotive.com
SIC: 5013 Truck parts & accessories; automotive supplies & parts; automotive supplies

(G-10952)
PETERBILT OF NORTHWEST OHIO
1330 Trenton Ave (45840-1924)
PHONE.................................419 423-3441
Alvin Daugherty, *CEO*
Rick Daugherty, *President*
Daryl Daugherty, *Treasurer*
EMP: 35
SQ FT: 30,000
SALES (est): 9.6MM **Privately Held**
WEB: www.peterbiltofnwohio.com
SIC: 5012 Truck tractors; trailers for trucks, new & used

(G-10953)
PETERMAN ASSOCIATES INC
3480 N Main St (45840-4207)
PHONE.................................419 722-9566
Nick Nigh, *President*

Tim Bechtol, *Internal Med*
EMP: 40
SQ FT: 2,400
SALES (est): 4.4MM **Privately Held**
WEB: www.petermanaes.com
SIC: 8711 8713 Consulting engineer; civil engineering; surveying services

(G-10954)
PLUMBLINE SOLUTIONS INC
Also Called: Solomon Cloud Solutions
1219 W Main Cross St # 101 (45840-0707)
PHONE.................................419 581-2963
Vern Strong, *CEO*
Gary Harpst, *Chairman*
Kim Parker, *Consultant*
Brian Binkley, *Software Dev*
Sandra Gibson, *Software Dev*
EMP: 50
SALES (est): 837.8K **Privately Held**
SIC: 7371 Computer software development

(G-10955)
PMC ACQUISITIONS INC
2040 Industrial Dr (45840-5443)
PHONE.................................419 429-0042
Duane Jebbett, *President*
EMP: 65 EST: 2014
SALES (est): 4.1MM **Privately Held**
SIC: 3081 6719 Plastic film & sheet; investment holding companies, except banks

(G-10956)
PRIDE TRANSPORTATION INC
611 Howard St (45840-2529)
PHONE.................................419 424-2145
Jonathan Ruehle, *President*
Jonathan E Ruehle, *President*
Sara Jones, *Corp Secy*
Tom Erdman, *Vice Pres*
Richard R Ruehle, *Vice Pres*
EMP: 32
SQ FT: 9,600
SALES (est): 5.4MM **Privately Held**
WEB: www.pridetransportation.com
SIC: 4731 4212 4213 Truck transportation brokers; local trucking, without storage; trucking, except local

(G-10957)
QUALITY LINES INC
2440 Bright Rd (45840-5436)
P.O. Box 904 (45839-0904)
PHONE.................................740 815-1165
Ronald Smith, *President*
EMP: 122
SQ FT: 6,000
SALES: 20MM **Privately Held**
WEB: www.qualitylines.com
SIC: 1623 7389 Pipeline construction;

(G-10958)
RIGHTTHING LLC (HQ)
Also Called: Rightthing, The
3401 Technology Dr (45840-9547)
PHONE.................................419 420-1830
Terry Terhark, *CEO*
EMP: 360
SQ FT: 43,000
SALES (est): 25MM
SALES (corp-wide): 13.3B **Publicly Held**
WEB: www.rightthinginc.com
SIC: 7361 Employment agencies
PA: Automatic Data Processing, Inc.
1 Adp Blvd Ste 1 # 1
Roseland NJ 07068
973 974-5000

(G-10959)
SIX DISCIPLINES LLC (PA)
1219 W Main Cross St # 205 (45840-0702)
PHONE.................................419 424-6647
Scott Boley, *Partner*
Gary Harpst, *Mng Member*
EMP: 47
SALES (est): 3.6MM **Privately Held**
WEB: www.sixdisciplines.com
SIC: 8748 Business consulting

(G-10960)
SOMETHING SPECIAL LRNG CTR INC
655 Fox Run Rd Ste J (45840-8401)
PHONE.................................419 422-1400

Kathleen Brandle, *Director*
EMP: 25
SALES (corp-wide): 2.9MM **Privately Held**
SIC: 8351 Child day care services
PA: Something Special Learning Center, Inc.
8251 Wterville Swanton Rd
Waterville OH 43566
419 878-4190

(G-10961)
SPECTRUM EYE CARE INC
15840 Medical Dr S Ste A (45840-7833)
PHONE.................................419 423-8665
Paul Armstrong, *President*
Jack G Hendershot Jr, *President*
Candice Hendershot, *Corp Secy*
EMP: 50
SQ FT: 2,000
SALES: 5.8MM **Privately Held**
SIC: 8011 Ophthalmologist

(G-10962)
ST CATHERINES CARE CTR FINDLAY
8455 County Road 140 (45840)
PHONE.................................419 422-3978
Albert E Jenkins III, *President*
EMP: 110
SQ FT: 8,500
SALES (est): 2MM **Privately Held**
SIC: 8051 Convalescent home with continuous nursing care

(G-10963)
STEARNS COMPANIES LLC
4404 Township Road 142 (45840-9607)
PHONE.................................419 422-0241
Erik Stearns,
EMP: 35
SALES (est): 1.1MM **Privately Held**
SIC: 7361 Labor contractors (employment agency)

(G-10964)
STONECO INC (DH)
1700 Fostoria Ave Ste 200 (45840-6218)
P.O. Box 865 (45839-0865)
PHONE.................................419 422-8854
John T Bearss, *President*
Don Weber, *Vice Pres*
Jack Zouhary, *Admin Sec*
EMP: 87
SQ FT: 34,000
SALES (est): 61.4MM
SALES (corp-wide): 29.7B **Privately Held**
WEB: www.stoneco.net
SIC: 2951 1411 Asphalt & asphaltic paving mixtures (not from refineries); limestone, dimension-quarrying
HQ: Shelly Company
80 Park Dr
Thornville OH 43076
740 246-6315

(G-10965)
STREACKER TRACTOR SALES INC
Also Called: Kubota Authorized Dealer
1218 Trenton Ave (45840-1922)
PHONE.................................419 422-6973
Joe Streacker, *Manager*
EMP: 25
SALES (corp-wide): 13.6MM **Privately Held**
WEB: www.streackertractor.com
SIC: 5999 5083 Farm equipment & supplies; farm & garden machinery
PA: Streacker Tractor Sales, Inc.
1400 N 5th St
Fremont OH 43420
419 334-9775

(G-10966)
SUNRISE SENIOR LIVING LLC
Also Called: Sunrise of Findlay
401 Lake Cascade Pkwy (45840-1378)
PHONE.................................419 425-3440
Charles Latta, *Exec Dir*
EMP: 45
SALES (corp-wide): 4.7B **Publicly Held**
WEB: www.sunrise.com
SIC: 8051 8361 Skilled nursing care facilities; residential care

HQ: Sunrise Senior Living, Llc
7902 Westpark Dr
Mc Lean VA 22102

(G-10967)
SWS ENVIRONMENTAL SERVICES
3820 Ventura Dr (45840-7200)
PHONE.................................254 629-1718
John Seifert, *Manager*
EMP: 32
SALES (corp-wide): 360.1MM **Publicly Held**
WEB: www.ecesi.com
SIC: 1794 1521 Excavation work; single-family housing construction
HQ: Southern Waste Services, Inc.
9204 Us Highway 287
Fort Worth TX 76131
850 234-8428

(G-10968)
T J D INDUSTRIAL CLG & MAINT
12340 Township Road 109 (45840-7685)
PHONE.................................419 425-5025
Timothy Durbin, *President*
Jeannie Durbin, *Corp Secy*
EMP: 30
SALES (est): 3.2MM **Privately Held**
SIC: 4959 Sweeping service: road, airport, parking lot, etc.

(G-10969)
TAYLOR CORPORATION
Also Called: Taylor House
1920 Breckenridge Rd # 110 (45840-8111)
PHONE.................................419 420-0790
Jamie Rush, *Director*
EMP: 25
SALES (est): 1.1MM **Privately Held**
SIC: 8322 Old age assistance

(G-10970)
TOUR DE FORCE INC
14601 County Road 212 # 1 (45840-7778)
P.O. Box 1262 (45839-1262)
PHONE.................................419 425-4800
Matt Hartman, *President*
Ryan Elliott, *Consultant*
Ann Fisher, *Consultant*
Jerry Waldman, *Consultant*
Tina Basinger, *Web Dvlpr*
EMP: 37
SALES (est): 7.1MM **Privately Held**
WEB: www.mrhtech.com
SIC: 7371 Computer software development

(G-10971)
TROY BUILT BUILDING LLC
1001 Fishlock Ave (45840-6427)
PHONE.................................419 425-1093
Troy Greer, *Mng Member*
EMP: 67
SALES (est): 4.2MM **Privately Held**
SIC: 1541 Industrial buildings, new construction

(G-10972)
UNITED PARCEL SERVICE INC OH
Also Called: UPS
1301 Commerce Pkwy (45840-1971)
PHONE.................................419 424-9494
EMP: 158
SALES (corp-wide): 71.8B **Publicly Held**
SIC: 4215 7521 Parcel delivery, vehicular; automobile storage garage
HQ: United Parcel Service, Inc. (Oh)
55 Glenlake Pkwy
Atlanta GA 30328
404 828-6000

(G-10973)
VCA ANIMAL HOSPITALS INC
Also Called: VCA Findlay Animal Hospital
2141 Bright Rd (45840-5433)
PHONE.................................419 423-7232
Annette Augsberger, *Branch Mgr*
EMP: 30
SALES (corp-wide): 2.5B **Privately Held**
SIC: 0742 Animal hospital services, pets & other animal specialties
HQ: Vca Animal Hospitals, Inc.
12401 W Olympic Blvd
Los Angeles CA 90064

(G-10974)
WARNER BUICK-NISSAN INC
Also Called: Warner Nissan
1060 County Road 95 (45840)
PHONE...............................419 423-7161
Larry R Warner, *President*
Chris Phillips, *Corp Secy*
Larry Warner, *Personnel*
Jason Deitrick, *Manager*
Bruce Herrig, *Director*
EMP: 42
SQ FT: 17,000
SALES (est): 16.7MM **Privately Held**
WEB: www.warnerbuicknissan.com
SIC: 5511 7538 7532 5521 Automobiles,
new & used; general automotive repair
shops; top & body repair & paint shops;
used car dealers; automobiles & other
motor vehicles

(G-10975)
WHIRLPOOL CORPORATION
4325 County Road 86 (45840-9327)
PHONE...............................419 423-6097
Rod Opelt, *Manager*
EMP: 60
SQ FT: 553,000
SALES (corp-wide): 21B **Publicly Held**
WEB: www.whirlpoolcorp.com
SIC: 5064 Washing machines
PA: Whirlpool Corporation
2000 N M 63
Benton Harbor MI 49022
269 923-5000

(G-10976)
WOLFF BROS SUPPLY INC
6000 Fostoria Ave (45840-9776)
PHONE...............................419 425-8511
Scott Ceol, *Sales Associate*
Pete Doyles, *Branch Mgr*
Carl Wohlford, *Manager*
EMP: 40
SALES (corp-wide): 114.4MM **Privately
Held**
SIC: 5074 5075 5063 Plumbing fittings &
supplies; air conditioning & ventilation
equipment & supplies; electrical appara-
tus & equipment
PA: Wolff Bros. Supply, Inc
6078 Wolff Rd
Medina OH 44256
330 725-3451

(G-10977)
**YOUNG MNS CHRISTN ASSN
FINDLAY (PA)**
Also Called: YMCA of Findlay
300 E Lincoln St (45840-4943)
PHONE...............................419 422-4424
Bent Finlay, *Exec Dir*
Deanna Haan, *Director*
Jennifer Treece, *Director*
EMP: 100
SQ FT: 70,000
SALES: 4.3MM **Privately Held**
SIC: 8641 7997 7991 Youth organiza-
tions; membership sports & recreation
clubs; physical fitness facilities

Flat Rock
Seneca County

(G-10978)
FLAT ROCK CARE CENTER
7353 County Rd 29 (44828)
PHONE...............................419 483-7330
Rev Nancy S Hull, *President*
Lois Binette, *Opers Mgr*
Rebecca Brandt, *Vice Pres*
Brianne Daniel, *Director*
Tami Cummings, *Human Res Dir*
EMP: 120
SALES: 4.1MM **Privately Held**
WEB: www.flatrockhomes.org
SIC: 8361 8741 Residential care for the
handicapped; management services

Flushing
Belmont County

(G-10979)
HILLANDALE FARMS INC
72165 Mrrstown Flshing Rd (43977-9706)
PHONE...............................740 968-3597
Orland Bethel, *President*
Gary Bethel, *Corp Secy*
EMP: 50
SALES (est): 11.9MM **Privately Held**
SIC: 5144 Eggs

(G-10980)
**JACK A HAMILTON & ASSOC
INC**
342 High St (43977-9750)
P.O. Box 471 (43977-0471)
PHONE...............................740 968-4947
Paul Hamilton, *CEO*
Rachel L Hamilton, *Corp Secy*
Ray L Luyster, *Vice Pres*
Ray Luyster, *Vice Pres*
Tina Marvin, *Admin Sec*
EMP: 31
SQ FT: 3,100
SALES (est): 2.8MM **Privately Held**
WEB: www.hamiltonandassoc.com
SIC: 8711 8713 Civil engineering; consult-
ing engineer; surveying services

(G-10981)
RES-CARE INC
41743 Mount Hope Rd (43977-9777)
PHONE...............................740 968-0181
EMP: 47
SALES (corp-wide): 23.7B **Privately Held**
SIC: 8052 Home for the mentally retarded,
with health care
HQ: Res-Care, Inc.
805 N Whittington Pkwy
Louisville KY 40222
502 394-2100

Forest
Hardin County

(G-10982)
WAMPUM HARDWARE CO
Also Called: Northern Ohio Explosives
17507 Township Road 50 (45843-9602)
P.O. Box 155 (45843-0155)
PHONE...............................419 273-2542
Gerald Davis, *President*
EMP: 39
SALES (corp-wide): 36.1MM **Privately
Held**
WEB: www.wampumhardware.com
SIC: 5169 Explosives
PA: Wampum Hardware Co.
636 Paden Rd
New Galilee PA 16141
724 336-4501

Fort Jennings
Putnam County

(G-10983)
**FORT JENNINGS STATE BANK
(PA)**
120 N Water St (45844-9657)
P.O. Box 186 (45844-0186)
PHONE...............................419 286-2527
Lawrence Schimmoler, *President*
EMP: 30 **EST:** 1918
SALES: 8MM **Privately Held**
WEB: www.fjsb.com
SIC: 6036 6022 State savings banks, not
federally chartered; state commercial
banks

(G-10984)
**NORTHWEST BLDG
RESOURCES INC (PA)**
23734 State Route 189 (45844-9510)
PHONE...............................419 286-5400
Mike Nichols, *President*

Steve Nichols, *Corp Secy*
Joe Nichols, *Vice Pres*
EMP: 30
SQ FT: 10,000
SALES (est): 11.9MM **Privately Held**
SIC: 5031 Building materials, exterior

Fort Loramie
Shelby County

(G-10985)
**DISTRIBUTION AND TRNSP SVC
INC (PA)**
401 S Main St (45845-8716)
PHONE...............................937 295-3343
Susan A Burke, *President*
James Burke, *Vice Pres*
EMP: 30
SQ FT: 60,000
SALES (est): 9.7MM **Privately Held**
SIC: 4214 4213 4512 4226 Local truck-
ing with storage; trucking, except local; air
transportation, scheduled; special ware-
housing & storage

(G-10986)
**WAYNE TRAIL TECHNOLOGIES
INC**
407 S Main St (45845-8716)
PHONE...............................937 295-2120
David M Knapke, *President*
Don Goldschmidt, *Buyer*
Dave Ruhenkamp, *Purchasing*
Ron Luthman, *Engineer*
Phil Deschner, *Project Engr*
EMP: 100 **EST:** 1962
SQ FT: 82,000
SALES (est): 30.8MM
SALES (corp-wide): 3B **Publicly Held**
WEB: www.waynetrail.com
SIC: 3728 3599 7692 3544 Aircraft parts
& equipment; tubing, flexible metallic; ma-
chine shop, jobbing & repair; welding re-
pair; special dies, tools, jigs & fixtures
PA: Lincoln Electric Holdings, Inc.
22801 Saint Clair Ave
Cleveland OH 44117
216 481-8100

Fort Recovery
Mercer County

(G-10987)
C W EGG PRODUCTS LLC
2360 Wabash Rd (45846-9586)
PHONE...............................419 375-5800
Jim Cooper, *Mng Member*
EMP: 50
SALES (est): 1.2MM **Privately Held**
SIC: 5144 Eggs

(G-10988)
CHEESEMAN LLC (HQ)
2200 State Route 119 (45846-9713)
P.O. Box 656 (45846-0656)
PHONE...............................419 375-4132
Ed Zumstein, *President*
Craig Watcke, *COO*
Doug Wall, *CFO*
Molly Watcke, *Sales Staff*
Janet Alden, *Manager*
EMP: 34
SALES (est): 52.2MM **Privately Held**
SIC: 4212 Local trucking, without storage
PA: Zumstein, Inc.
2200 State Route 119
Fort Recovery OH 45846
419 375-4132

(G-10989)
COOPER FARMS INC (PA)
2321 State Route 49 (45846-9501)
P.O. Box 339 (45846-0339)
PHONE...............................419 375-4116
James R Cooper, *President*
Brian Donley, *General Ptnr*
Jim Meeks, *General Ptnr*
Gary A Cooper, *Vice Pres*
Nick Decker, *Safety Mgr*
EMP: 100 **EST:** 1940
SQ FT: 38,000

SALES (est): 26.4MM **Privately Held**
WEB: www.cooperfarms.com
SIC: 2048 5191 Poultry feeds; feed

(G-10990)
**FORT RECOVERY EQUIPMENT
INC**
1201 Industrial Dr (45846-8046)
P.O. Box 646 (45846-0646)
PHONE...............................419 375-1006
Cyril G Le Fevre, *President*
Helen Le Fevere, *Vice Pres*
Greg Le Fevre, *Vice Pres*
◆ **EMP:** 50 **EST:** 1970
SQ FT: 30,000
SALES (est): 12.4MM **Privately Held**
WEB: www.fortrecoveryequipment.com
SIC: 5083 3523 Livestock equipment;
barn, silo, poultry, dairy & livestock ma-
chinery

(G-10991)
**FORT RECOVERY EQUITY INC
(PA)**
2351 Wabash Rd (45846-9586)
PHONE...............................419 375-4119
William Glass, *CEO*
Arnie Sumner, *President*
EMP: 165
SQ FT: 15,000
SALES (est): 18.6MM **Privately Held**
SIC: 2015 5153 Egg processing; grain ele-
vators

(G-10992)
HULL BROS INC
Also Called: Kubota Authorized Dealer
520 E Boundary St (45846-9795)
P.O. Box 634 (45846-0634)
PHONE...............................419 375-2827
Richard D Hull, *President*
Norman F Hull Jr, *Vice Pres*
EMP: 27
SQ FT: 30,000
SALES (est): 4MM **Privately Held**
SIC: 5999 5261 5722 5083 Farm equip-
ment & supplies; lawn & garden equip-
ment; household appliance stores; farm &
garden machinery

(G-10993)
**MIDWEST POULTRY SERVICES
LP**
Also Called: Sunny Side Farms
374 New Wston Ft Lrmie Rd (45846-9105)
PHONE...............................419 375-4417
EMP: 25
SQ FT: 35,000
SALES (corp-wide): 174.9MM **Privately
Held**
SIC: 0254 Poultry Hatchery
PA: Midwest Poultry Services, L.P.
9951 W State Road 25
Mentone IN 46539
574 353-7232

(G-10994)
V H COOPER & CO INC (HQ)
Also Called: Cooper Foods
2321 State Route 49 (45846-9501)
P.O. Box 339 (45846-0339)
PHONE...............................419 375-4116
James R Cooper, *President*
Gary A Cooper, *COO*
Neil Diller, *CFO*
Anada E Cooper, *Treasurer*
Dianne L Cooper, *Admin Sec*
EMP: 150
SQ FT: 4,400
SALES: 124MM
SALES (corp-wide): 256.7MM **Privately
Held**
WEB: www.cooperfoods.com
SIC: 0253 2015 2011 Turkeys & turkey
eggs; chicken slaughtering & processing;
pork products from pork slaughtered on
site; hams & picnics from meat slaugh-
tered on site
PA: Cooper Hatchery, Inc.
22348 Road 140
Oakwood OH 45873
419 594-3325

▲ = Import ▼ =Export
◆ =Import/Export

(G-10995)
WENDEL POULTRY SERVICE INC
1860 Union City Rd (45846-9316)
P.O. Box 267 (45846-0267)
PHONE...................................419 375-2439
Randall Wendel, *President*
Gary Wendel, *Vice Pres*
Pam Hicks, *Admin Sec*
EMP: 45
SALES (est): 3.3MM **Privately Held**
SIC: 4212 Live poultry haulage

Fostoria
Seneca County

(G-10996)
AVIATION MANUFACTURING CO INC
901 S Union St (44830-2561)
P.O. Box 1127 (44830-1127)
PHONE...................................419 435-7448
Richard W Norton Jr, *President*
EMP: 80 **EST:** 1996
SALES (est): 5.9MM **Privately Held**
SIC: 4581 Airports, flying fields & services

(G-10997)
BODIE ELECTRIC INC
1109 N Main St (44830-1979)
P.O. Box 1043 (44830-1043)
PHONE...................................419 435-3672
Marianne Bodie, *President*
R Scott Bodie, *President*
Pete Finch, *Vice Pres*
Scott Bodie, *Financial Exec*
EMP: 40
SQ FT: 8,200
SALES (est): 5.4MM **Privately Held**
WEB: www.bodieelectric.com
SIC: 1731 General electrical contractor

(G-10998)
BOWLING TRANSPORTATION INC (PA)
1827 Sandusky St (44830-2754)
PHONE...................................419 436-9590
Bill J Bowling, *President*
Don Bowling, *Vice Pres*
Jo Ann May, *Admin Sec*
EMP: 80
SQ FT: 4,250
SALES (est): 20MM **Privately Held**
WEB: www.bowtran.com
SIC: 4213 4212 Contract haulers; local trucking, without storage

(G-10999)
COUNTY OF SENECA
602 S Corporate Dr W (44830-9456)
PHONE...................................419 435-0729
Kathy Nye, *Manager*
EMP: 75 **Privately Held**
WEB: www.senecapros.org
SIC: 8331 Sheltered workshop
PA: County Of Seneca
111 Madison St
Tiffin OH 44883
419 447-4550

(G-11000)
FOSTORIA HOSPITAL ASSOCIATION (HQ)
Also Called: FOSTORIA COMMUNITY HOSPITAL
501 Van Buren St (44830-1534)
P.O. Box 907 (44830-0907)
PHONE...................................419 435-7734
Dan Schwanke, *President*
Peg Frankart, *Vice Pres*
EMP: 253
SQ FT: 68,000
SALES: 36.3MM
SALES (corp-wide): 2.1B **Privately Held**
WEB: www.grosenfeld.com
SIC: 8062 Hospital, affiliated with AMA residency
PA: Promedica Health Systems, Inc.
100 Madison Ave
Toledo OH 43604
567 585-7454

(G-11001)
FRUTH & CO (PA)
601 Parkway Dr Ste A (44830-1592)
P.O. Box 854 (44830-0854)
PHONE...................................419 435-8541
Ronald Brown,
Chris Chalsim,
David Miller,
Donald Yarris,
EMP: 28
SQ FT: 4,000
SALES (est): 1.9MM **Privately Held**
WEB: www.fruthpll.com
SIC: 8721 Certified public accountant

(G-11002)
GEARY FAMILY YMCA FOSTRIA
154 W Center St (44830-2201)
PHONE...................................419 435-6608
Eric Stinehelfer, *Director*
EMP: 45
SALES (est): 1.3MM **Privately Held**
WEB: www.gearyfamilyymca.org
SIC: 8641 8351 Recreation association; child day care services

(G-11003)
GOOD SHEPHERD HOME
725 Columbus Ave (44830-3255)
PHONE...................................419 937-1801
Chris Widman, *Director*
EMP: 145
SQ FT: 75,000
SALES: 12.7MM **Privately Held**
WEB: www.goodshepherdhome.com
SIC: 8052 8051 Intermediate care facilities; skilled nursing care facilities

(G-11004)
HANSON DISTRIBUTING CO INC
Also Called: Beerco Distributing Co
22116 Township Road 218 (44830-9612)
P.O. Box 590 (44830-0590)
PHONE...................................419 435-3214
Kris Clepper, *President*
Kris Klepper, *Vice Pres*
Mike Klepper, *Treasurer*
Robbie Maassel, *Office Mgr*
EMP: 75
SQ FT: 25,600
SALES (est): 20.2MM **Privately Held**
SIC: 5181 Ale; beer & other fermented malt liquors
PA: Superior Distributing Co Inc
22116 Township Road 218
Fostoria OH 44830
419 435-3214

(G-11005)
HCF MANAGEMENT INC
25 Christopher Dr (44830-3318)
PHONE...................................419 435-8112
Sandy Hatfield, *Human Res Dir*
Paula Kirkpatrick, *Branch Mgr*
EMP: 67
SALES (corp-wide): 154.8MM **Privately Held**
SIC: 8051 Skilled nursing care facilities
PA: Hcf Management, Inc.
1100 Shawnee Rd
Lima OH 45805
419 999-2010

(G-11006)
HOOSIER EXPRESS INC (PA)
1827 Sandusky St (44830-2754)
PHONE...................................419 436-9590
Bill J Bowling, *President*
Joann May, *Corp Secy*
EMP: 29
SALES (est): 1.6MM **Privately Held**
SIC: 4213 Contract haulers

(G-11007)
INDEPENDENCE CARE COMMUNITY
Also Called: Independence House
1000 Independence Ave (44830-9614)
PHONE...................................419 435-8505
Cheryl Buckland, *President*
Darlene Delarosa, *Principal*
Rick Gilbert, *Director*
Jason Mundy, *Director*
Aaron Rider, *Director*
EMP: 61
SQ FT: 40,000

SALES (est): 3.4MM **Privately Held**
WEB: www.independence-house.com
SIC: 8051 Skilled nursing care facilities

(G-11008)
LIFETOUCH INC
922 Springville Ave Ste B (44830-3285)
PHONE...................................419 435-2646
Chris Majoy, *Site Mgr*
Doug Smith, *Manager*
EMP: 50
SALES (corp-wide): 1.9B **Publicly Held**
WEB: www.lifetouch.com
SIC: 7221 Photographer, still or video
HQ: Lifetouch Inc.
11000 Viking Dr
Eden Prairie MN 55344
952 826-4000

(G-11009)
NORFOLK SOUTHERN CORPORATION
Also Called: Fostoria Mixing Center
3101 N Township Road 47 (44830-9381)
PHONE...................................419 436-2408
Tom Siler, *Manager*
EMP: 100
SALES (corp-wide): 11.4B **Publicly Held**
WEB: www.nscorp.com
SIC: 4011 Railroads, line-haul operating
PA: Norfolk Southern Corporation
3 Commercial Pl Ste 1a
Norfolk VA 23510
757 629-2680

(G-11010)
RES-CARE INC
Also Called: Dillon Group Homes
1016 Dillon Cir (44830-3395)
PHONE...................................419 435-6620
Denise Tucker, *Manager*
EMP: 48
SALES (corp-wide): 23.7B **Privately Held**
SIC: 8052 Home for the mentally retarded, with health care
HQ: Res-Care, Inc.
805 N Whittington Pkwy
Louisville KY 40222
502 394-2100

(G-11011)
ROPPE HOLDING COMPANY
Also Called: Roppe Distribution
1500 Sandusky St (44830-2753)
PHONE...................................419 435-9335
Angie Welly, *Branch Mgr*
EMP: 30
SALES (corp-wide): 189.7MM **Privately Held**
WEB: www.roppe.com
SIC: 4225 General warehousing & storage
PA: Roppe Holding Company
1602 N Union St
Fostoria OH 44830
419 435-8546

(G-11012)
SENECA RE ADS IND FOSTORIA DIV
602 S Corporate Dr W (44830-9456)
PHONE...................................419 435-0729
Laurie Fretz, *Principal*
Rodney Biggert, *Director*
EMP: 110 **EST:** 2010
SALES (est): 533.1K **Privately Held**
SIC: 8699 Charitable organization

(G-11013)
ST CATHERINES CARE CENTERS O
Also Called: St Catherine's Manor
25 Christopher Dr (44830-3399)
PHONE...................................419 435-8112
Jim Unverferth, *President*
EMP: 110
SQ FT: 34,000
SALES (est): 3.8MM **Privately Held**
SIC: 8051 Convalescent home with continuous nursing care

(G-11014)
VOCA OF OHIO
Also Called: Dillon R D
1021 Dillon Rd (44830-4604)
PHONE...................................419 435-5836

Robeta Walthour, *Director*
EMP: 45
SALES (est): 572K **Privately Held**
SIC: 8052 Home for the mentally retarded, with health care

(G-11015)
ZENDER ELECTRIC
966 Springville Ave (44830-3268)
P.O. Box 568 (44830-0568)
PHONE...................................419 436-1538
Buddy Zender, *Owner*
Joe Zender, *Administration*
EMP: 25
SQ FT: 3,000
SALES (est): 3.6MM **Privately Held**
SIC: 1731 7538 General electrical contractor; general automotive repair shops

Fowler
Trumbull County

(G-11016)
MEADOWBROOK MANOR OF HARTFORD
Also Called: Concord Health Center Hartford
3090 Five Pnts Hrtford Rd (44418-9726)
PHONE...................................330 772-5253
Debra Ifft, *President*
EMP: 66
SQ FT: 15,000
SALES (est): 2.7MM **Privately Held**
SIC: 8051 Convalescent home with continuous nursing care

(G-11017)
TOWNSHIP OF FOWLER (PA)
Also Called: Township Administration Office
4562 State Route 305 (44418-9749)
P.O. Box 174 (44418-0174)
PHONE...................................330 637-2653
Lynn M Michalec, *Principal*
Tom Carr, *Trustee*
Albert Crabbs, *Trustee*
Jeff Davis, *Trustee*
EMP: 52 **Privately Held**
SIC: 9111 9224 9221 6531 City & town managers' offices; fire department, not including volunteer; ; cemetery management service

Frankfort
Ross County

(G-11018)
DAVID W MILLIKEN (PA)
Also Called: Milliken's Dairy Cone
2 S Main St (45628-8018)
P.O. Box 427 (45628-0427)
PHONE...................................740 998-5023
David W Milliken, *Owner*
EMP: 30
SALES (est): 1.2MM **Privately Held**
SIC: 5812 1521 Ice cream, soft drink & soda fountain stands; ice cream stands or dairy bars; new construction, single-family houses; general remodeling, single-family houses

(G-11019)
VALLEY VIEW ALZHIMERS CARE CTR
3363 Ragged Ridge Rd (45628-9551)
PHONE...................................740 998-2948
Judith Heimerl-Brown, *President*
Marge Poyner, *Vice Pres*
Andrea Timson, *Office Mgr*
Tammy Robertson, *Admin Sec*
EMP: 60
SALES: 3.6MM **Privately Held**
WEB: www.valleyviewalz.com
SIC: 8059 8051 Rest home, with health care; skilled nursing care facilities

Franklin
Warren County

(G-11020)
3-D TECHNICAL SERVICES COMPANY
Also Called: 3-Dmed
255 Industrial Dr (45005-4429)
PHONE..........................937 746-2901
Robert Aumann, *President*
Jennifer Theriault, *Finance Mgr*
Becky Larson, *Sales Staff*
EMP: 25
SQ FT: 15,000
SALES (est): 3.1MM **Privately Held**
WEB: www.3-dtechnicalservices.com
SIC: 7389 2542 3999 Building scale models; design, commercial & industrial; partitions & fixtures, except wood; models, general, except toy

(G-11021)
ADESA CORPORATION LLC
4400 William C Good Blvd (45005-4438)
PHONE..........................937 746-5361
G Parker, *Branch Mgr*
EMP: 107 **Publicly Held**
SIC: 5012 Automobile auction
HQ: Adesa Corporation, Llc
13085 Hamilton Crossing B
Carmel IN 46032

(G-11022)
ASBUILT CONSTRUCTION LTD
29 Eagle Ct (45005-6322)
PHONE..........................937 550-4900
Martha Baldwin, *Partner*
EMP: 25
SQ FT: 3,500
SALES (est): 1.5MM **Privately Held**
SIC: 1522 Residential construction

(G-11023)
ATTENTN WEB ADMINISTRTR MARJON
3093 N State Route 741 (45005-9745)
PHONE..........................513 708-9888
EMP: 57 **Privately Held**
SIC: 9111 8748 Executive offices; business consulting

(G-11024)
BOBS MORAINE TRUCKING INC
8251 Claude Thomas Rd (45005-1412)
PHONE..........................937 746-8420
Rita Maschmeier, *President*
Bob Maschmeier, *Vice Pres*
Ron Maschmeier, *Opers Mgr*
Robert Maschmeier, *Treasurer*
EMP: 30
SQ FT: 15,000
SALES (est): 4MM **Privately Held**
WEB: www.bmtinc.us
SIC: 4213 Trucking, except local

(G-11025)
CARINGTON HEALTH SYSTEMS
Also Called: Franklin Ridge Care Facility
421 Mission Ln (45005-2327)
PHONE..........................937 743-2754
Sylvia Sipe, *Branch Mgr*
Richard Chamberlain, *Director*
Kim Sells, *Hlthcr Dir*
EMP: 130
SALES (corp-wide): 85.7MM **Privately Held**
SIC: 8051 8052 Convalescent home with continuous nursing care; intermediate care facilities
PA: Carington Health Systems
8200 Beckett Park Dr
Hamilton OH 45011
513 682-2700

(G-11026)
CENTIMARK CORPORATION
Also Called: Centimark Roofing Systems
319 Industrial Dr (45005-4431)
PHONE..........................937 704-9909
Mark Moore, *Sales/Mktg Mgr*
EMP: 30
SQ FT: 5,000

SALES (corp-wide): 670.5MM **Privately Held**
WEB: www.centimark.com
SIC: 1761 Roofing contractor
PA: Centimark Corporation
12 Grandview Cir
Canonsburg PA 15317
724 514-8700

(G-11027)
DAYTON HOSPICE INCORPORATED
5940 Long Meadow Dr (45005-9689)
PHONE..........................513 422-0300
Vicky Forrest, *Branch Mgr*
EMP: 225
SALES (corp-wide): 53.2MM **Privately Held**
SIC: 8082 Home health care services
PA: Hospice Of Dayton, Incorporated
324 Wilmington Ave
Dayton OH 45420
937 256-4490

(G-11028)
EAGLE EQUIPMENT CORPORATION
Also Called: Fluid Power Components
245 Industrial Dr (45005-4429)
PHONE..........................937 746-0510
Jeff Fronk, *President*
Chuck Docken, *Sales Staff*
EMP: 30
SQ FT: 7,000
SALES (corp-wide): 9.2MM **Privately Held**
WEB: www.eaglequip.com
SIC: 5085 Valves & fittings
PA: Eagle Equipment Corporation
666 Brooksedge Blvd
Westerville OH 43081
614 882-9200

(G-11029)
FRIENDLY NURSING HOME INC
4339 State Route 122 (45005-9762)
PHONE..........................937 855-2363
Barbara Lindsey, *President*
Tina Parker, *Admin Sec*
EMP: 40
SALES (est): 2.2MM **Privately Held**
SIC: 8051 Skilled nursing care facilities

(G-11030)
GREENPRO SERVICES INC
2969 Beal Rd (45005-4603)
PHONE..........................937 748-1559
Tod R Hernerson, *President*
Jeremy Anspach, *Division Mgr*
Betsey Click, *Vice Pres*
Miranda Dawn, *Manager*
EMP: 30
SQ FT: 1,000
SALES: 2.8MM **Privately Held**
SIC: 0781 Landscape services

(G-11031)
GREENSPACE ENTERPRISE TECH INC
8401 Claude Thomas Rd # 28 (45005-1497)
PHONE..........................888 309-8517
Jason Terry, *President*
EMP: 40 EST: 2014
SQ FT: 1,500
SALES (est): 914.1K **Privately Held**
SIC: 7389

(G-11032)
HENDERSON TURF FARM INC
2969 Beal Rd (45005-4603)
PHONE..........................937 748-1559
Marvin N Kolstein, *President*
Todd Henderson, *President*
Trent Gillam, *Division Mgr*
Reita C Henderson, *Principal*
Brandon Hunt, *Manager*
EMP: 40
SQ FT: 1,600
SALES (est): 5.7MM **Privately Held**
SIC: 0191 0181 0782 0711 General farms, primarily crop; sod farms; lawn services; fertilizer application services; local trucking, without storage

(G-11033)
JOINT EMERGENCY MED SVC INC
201 E 6th St (45005-2580)
P.O. Box 525 (45005-0525)
PHONE..........................937 746-3471
Andrew J Riddiough, *Chief*
Scott Fromeyer, *Officer*
Jesse Madde, *Asst Chief*
EMP: 47
SQ FT: 4,600
SALES: 572K **Privately Held**
SIC: 8099 8011 Medical services organization; freestanding emergency medical center

(G-11034)
KOEHLKE COMPONENTS INC
1201 Commerce Center Dr (45005-7206)
PHONE..........................937 435-5435
Tom Koehlke, *President*
Eric Jensen, *General Mgr*
Adam Koehlke, *Sales Mgr*
▲ EMP: 26
SQ FT: 10,000
SALES (est): 19.6MM **Privately Held**
WEB: www.koehlke.com
SIC: 5065 Electronic parts

(G-11035)
OHIO-KENTUCKY STEEL CORP
2001 Commerce Center Dr (45005-1478)
PHONE..........................937 743-4600
Christopher Fiora, *CEO*
Brian Baker, *Vice Pres*
EMP: 30 EST: 1974
SQ FT: 84,000
SALES: 3MM **Privately Held**
WEB: www.ohkysteel.com
SIC: 5051 Steel

(G-11036)
PATRICK STAFFING INC (PA)
1200 E 2nd St Ste B (45005-1974)
PHONE..........................937 743-5585
Joy Patrick, *President*
EMP: 35
SQ FT: 3,672
SALES (est): 2.8MM **Privately Held**
SIC: 7363 Manpower pools; temporary help service

(G-11037)
PEOPLES BANK NATIONAL ASSN
1400 E 2nd St (45005-1811)
PHONE..........................937 746-5733
EMP: 41
SALES (corp-wide): 208MM **Publicly Held**
SIC: 6021 National commercial banks
HQ: Peoples Bank
138 Putnam St
Marietta OH 45750
740 373-3155

(G-11038)
PRIMARY CR NTWRK PRMR HLTH PRT
8401 Claude Thomas Rd (45005-1497)
PHONE..........................937 743-5965
Jerome Yount, *Branch Mgr*
EMP: 34
SALES (corp-wide): 33.7MM **Privately Held**
SIC: 8011 Offices & clinics of medical doctors
PA: Primary Care Network Of Premier Health Partners
110 N Main St Ste 350
Dayton OH 45402
937 226-7085

(G-11039)
SIDE EFFECTS INC
259 Industrial Dr (45005-4429)
PHONE..........................937 704-9696
Bob Westerfield, *President*
Kylene Pippin, *President*
Kelli Adkins, *Project Mgr*
Elle Buell, *Project Mgr*
Brandon Castator, *Project Mgr*
EMP: 25

SALES (est): 3.3MM **Privately Held**
WEB: www.sideeffectsinc.com
SIC: 7389 Athletic equipment inspection service

(G-11040)
UNIFIRST CORPORATION
265 Industrial Dr (45005-4429)
PHONE..........................937 746-0531
Rodney Stebelton, *District Mgr*
John Leugers, *Branch Mgr*
EMP: 75
SQ FT: 38,000
SALES (corp-wide): 1.7B **Publicly Held**
WEB: www.unifirst.com
SIC: 7218 7213 Industrial uniform supply; uniform supply
PA: Unifirst Corporation
68 Jonspin Rd
Wilmington MA 01887
978 658-8888

(G-11041)
WALTER F STEPHENS JR INC
415 South Ave (45005-3647)
PHONE..........................937 746-0521
Ruth Ann Stephens, *Ch of Bd*
Carla Baker, *President*
Walter F Stephens Jr, *President*
Diane Stephens Maloney, *Corp Secy*
Patty Gleason, *Vice Pres*
EMP: 50
SQ FT: 45,000
SALES (est): 6.8MM **Privately Held**
SIC: 5999 2389 5122 5023 Police supply stores; uniforms & vestments; toiletries; toothbrushes, except electric; kitchenware; uniforms, men's & boys'; mattresses & foundations

Franklin Furnace
Scioto County

(G-11042)
BIG SANDY DISTRIBUTION INC (PA)
Also Called: Big Sandy Superstores
8375 Gallia Pike (45629-8989)
PHONE..........................740 574-2113
Rober Vanhoose III, *President*
Robert Van Hoose Jr, *Chairman*
Daniel Evans, *District Mgr*
Laura S Timberlake, *COO*
Derek Janey, *Opers Mgr*
EMP: 200
SQ FT: 150,000
SALES (est): 133.5MM **Privately Held**
SIC: 4225 General warehousing & storage

(G-11043)
BIG SANDY FURNITURE INC (HQ)
Also Called: Big Sandy Service Company
8375 Gallia Pike (45629-8989)
PHONE..........................740 574-2113
Robert W Vanhoose Jr, *Ch of Bd*
John C Stewart Jr, *President*
Zella Robinette, *Store Mgr*
Steve Vanhoose, *Purch Mgr*
Greg Sias, *Manager*
▲ EMP: 100
SQ FT: 250,000
SALES (est): 51.3MM **Privately Held**
WEB: www.bigsandyfurniture.com
SIC: 4225 5712 5995 5999 General warehousing & storage; furniture stores; optical goods stores; toiletries, cosmetics & perfumes; gas household appliances; electric household appliances, major

(G-11044)
FOUNTAINHEAD NURSING HOME INC
4734 Gallia Pike (45629-8600)
PHONE..........................740 354-9113
Jerry Ledingham, *President*
EMP: 34
SALES: 1MM **Privately Held**
SIC: 8051 Skilled nursing care facilities

▲ = Import ▼=Export
◆ =Import/Export

(G-11045)
G & J PEPSI-COLA BOTTLERS INC
Also Called: Pepsico
4587 Gallia Pike (45629-8777)
P.O. Box 299 (45629-0299)
PHONE..............................740 354-9191
Robert Ross, *Branch Mgr*
EMP: 350
SALES (corp-wide): 418.3MM **Privately Held**
WEB: www.gjpepsi.com
SIC: 2086 5149 Carbonated soft drinks, bottled & canned; groceries & related products
PA: G & J Pepsi-Cola Bottlers Inc
9435 Waterstone Blvd # 390
Cincinnati OH 45249
513 785-6060

(G-11046)
HAVERHILL COKE COMPANY LLC
Also Called: Sun Coke Energy
2446 Gallia Pike (45629-8837)
PHONE..............................740 355-9819
Steve Baker, *Vice Pres*
Dovie Majors,
▲ EMP: 65
SALES (est): 55.4MM
SALES (corp-wide): 1.4B **Publicly Held**
SIC: 5051 Steel
HQ: Suncoke Energy Partners, L.P.
1011 Warrenville Rd # 600
Lisle IL 60532
630 824-1000

(G-11047)
R & M DELIVERY
8375 Gallia Pike (45629-8989)
PHONE..............................740 574-2113
Robert W Meredith, *Partner*
Phillip Robinson, *Partner*
EMP: 25
SALES: 1.4MM **Privately Held**
SIC: 4212 Delivery service, vehicular

Frazeysburg
Muskingum County

(G-11048)
CALVARY CHRISTIAN CH OF OHIO
Also Called: Frazeysburg Restaurant & Bky
338 W 3rd St (43822-9785)
PHONE..............................740 828-9000
Rev Scott Egbert, *President*
Robert McGraw, *Vice Pres*
Mari Anne Holbrook, *Treasurer*
EMP: 40
SQ FT: 2,500
SALES: 55.4K **Privately Held**
SIC: 2051 8661 5541 0241 Bakery: wholesale or wholesale/retail combined; Christian & Reformed Church; filling stations, gasoline; milk production

(G-11049)
FRAZEYSBURG LIONS CLUB INC
12355 Scout Rd (43822-9713)
PHONE..............................740 828-2313
Dan Osborn, *Corp Secy*
EMP: 34
SALES (est): 304.9K **Privately Held**
SIC: 8699 Personal interest organization

(G-11050)
REM CORP
26 E 3rd St (43822-9651)
P.O. Box 3 (43822-0003)
PHONE..............................740 828-2601
Faith Oleary, *Manager*
EMP: 40
SALES (corp-wide): 3.1MM **Privately Held**
SIC: 8082 Home health care services
PA: Rem Corp.
265 S Pioneer Blvd
Springboro OH
800 990-0302

Fredericksburg
Wayne County

(G-11051)
IVAN WEAVER CONSTRUCTION CO (PA)
124 N Mill St (44627-9593)
P.O. Box 258 (44627-0258)
PHONE..............................330 695-3461
Ivan Weaver, *President*
Clara Weaver, *Corp Secy*
Allen Miller, *Manager*
EMP: 35 EST: 1964
SQ FT: 1,892
SALES (est): 10.1MM **Privately Held**
SIC: 1542 1521 Commercial & office building, new construction; new construction, single-family houses

Fredericktown
Knox County

(G-11052)
BURCH HYDRO INC
17860 Ankneytown Rd (43019-8065)
P.O. Box 230 (43019-0230)
PHONE..............................740 694-9146
Michael R Burch, *President*
Patricia A Burch, *Corp Secy*
EMP: 30
SALES (est): 5.9MM **Privately Held**
WEB: www.burchhydro.com
SIC: 4212 7699 Light haulage & cartage, local; machinery cleaning

(G-11053)
BURCH HYDRO TRUCKING INC
17860 Ankneytown Rd (43019-8065)
P.O. Box 230 (43019-0230)
PHONE..............................740 694-9146
Michael R Burch, *President*
Patricia A Burch, *Corp Secy*
EMP: 30
SQ FT: 3,200
SALES (est): 3.7MM **Privately Held**
SIC: 4212 Light haulage & cartage, local

(G-11054)
INTEGRITY KOKOSING PIPELINE SV
Also Called: Ikps
17531 Waterford Rd (43019-9561)
P.O. Box 226 (43019-0226)
PHONE..............................740 694-6315
Marsha Rinehart, *CEO*
Timothy Seibert, *President*
Adams Potes, *Manager*
EMP: 175 EST: 2012
SQ FT: 16,000
SALES (est): 64MM **Privately Held**
SIC: 4613 Gasoline pipelines (common carriers)

Freeport
Harrison County

(G-11055)
ROSEBUD MINING COMPANY
28490 Birmingham Rd (43973-9754)
PHONE..............................740 658-4217
EMP: 35
SALES (corp-wide): 605.3MM **Privately Held**
SIC: 1222 Bituminous coal-underground mining
PA: Rosebud Mining Company
301 Market St
Kittanning PA 16201
724 545-6222

Fremont
Sandusky County

(G-11056)
ADVANTAGE FORD LINCOLN MERCURY
885 Hagerty Dr (43420-9162)
P.O. Box 1167 (43420-8167)
PHONE..............................419 334-9751
Merlton Brandenburg, *President*
Herbert D Stump, *Vice Pres*
EMP: 40
SQ FT: 23,000
SALES (est): 15.3MM **Privately Held**
WEB: www.advantagefordlm.com
SIC: 5511 7538 7532 Automobiles, new & used; general automotive repair shops; top & body repair & paint shops

(G-11057)
ALFRED NICKLES BAKERY INC
721 White Rd (43420-1544)
PHONE..............................419 332-6418
David Owen, *Principal*
EMP: 29
SALES (corp-wide): 205MM **Privately Held**
WEB: www.nicklesbakery.com
SIC: 5149 Whol Groceries
PA: Alfred Nickles Bakery, Inc.
26 Main St N
Navarre OH 44662
330 879-5635

(G-11058)
ALKON CORPORATION (PA)
728 Graham Dr (43420-4073)
PHONE..............................419 355-9111
Mark Winter, *President*
Wayne Morroney, *President*
Mike Caron, *Vice Pres*
▲ EMP: 60
SQ FT: 40,000
SALES (est): 24.2MM **Privately Held**
WEB: www.alkoncorp.com
SIC: 3491 3082 5084 5085 Valves, nuclear; tubes, unsupported plastic; industrial machinery & equipment; pistons & valves; valves & fittings; fluid power valves & hose fittings

(G-11059)
BAUMAN CHRYSLER JEEP DODGE
2577 W State St (43420-1444)
P.O. Box 1127 (43420-8127)
PHONE..............................419 332-8291
Albert Bauman III, *President*
EMP: 34
SQ FT: 13,000
SALES (est): 9.9MM **Privately Held**
SIC: 5511 7532 Automobiles, new & used; body shop, automotive

(G-11060)
CARITAS INC
Also Called: PARKVIEW CARE CENTER
1406 Oak Harbor Rd (43420-1025)
PHONE..............................419 332-2589
Patrick Kriner, *President*
EMP: 46
SQ FT: 15,000
SALES: 2.5MM **Privately Held**
SIC: 8051 8361 Convalescent home with continuous nursing care; home for the aged

(G-11061)
CELLCO PARTNERSHIP
Also Called: Verizon
2140 Enterprise St Ste C (43420-8530)
PHONE..............................419 333-1009
Chris Webb, *Principal*
EMP: 71
SALES (corp-wide): 130.8B **Publicly Held**
SIC: 4812 5999 Cellular telephone services; telephone equipment & systems
HQ: Cellco Partnership
1 Verizon Way
Basking Ridge NJ 07920

(G-11062)
CERTIFIED POWER INC
Also Called: Toledo Driveline
1110 Napoleon St (43420-2328)
PHONE..............................419 355-1200
EMP: 79
SALES (corp-wide): 295.8MM **Privately Held**
SIC: 3714 7539 5013 Motor vehicle parts & accessories; automotive repair shops; automotive supplies & parts
PA: Certified Power, Inc.
970 Campus Dr
Mundelein IL 60060
847 573-3800

(G-11063)
COMMUNITY AND RURAL HLTH SVCS (PA)
Also Called: Community Health Services
2221 Hayes Ave (43420-2632)
PHONE..............................419 334-8943
J Liszak, *President*
Tyson Bouyack, *CFO*
Tiffany Tipple, *Human Res Dir*
Linda Thiel, *Marketing Staff*
Emily Brickner, *Supervisor*
EMP: 70
SQ FT: 28,000
SALES: 8.4MM **Privately Held**
SIC: 8099 Medical services organization

(G-11064)
COUNTY ENGINEERING OFFICE
2500 W State St (43420-1445)
PHONE..............................419 334-9731
Chad Fisher, *Superintendent*
James Moyer, *Director*
EMP: 34
SALES (est): 1.5MM **Privately Held**
SIC: 8711 7538 Civil engineering; general automotive repair shops

(G-11065)
COUNTY OF SANDUSKY
Also Called: School of Hope
1001 Castalia St (43420-4015)
PHONE..............................419 637-2243
Jayne Repp, *Principal*
EMP: 100 **Privately Held**
WEB: www.sanduskycohd.com
SIC: 8331 Sheltered workshop
PA: County Of Sandusky
622 Croghan St
Fremont OH 43420
419 334-6100

(G-11066)
COUNTY OF SANDUSKY
Also Called: Countyside Continuing Care
1865 Countryside Dr (43420-8748)
PHONE..............................419 334-2602
Linda Black-Kurek, *President*
Pat Kuzma, *Director*
EMP: 99
SALES (est): 1,000K **Privately Held**
SIC: 8051 Convalescent home with continuous nursing care

(G-11067)
CROGHAN COLONIAL BANK (HQ)
323 Croghan St (43420-3088)
P.O. Box C (43420-0557)
PHONE..............................419 332-7301
Kendall Rieman, *President*
John C Barrington, *Principal*
Ted L Hilty, *Principal*
J Phillip Keller, *Principal*
Don W Miller, *Principal*
EMP: 45
SQ FT: 39,500
SALES: 39.3MM **Publicly Held**
WEB: www.croghan.com
SIC: 6022 State trust companies accepting deposits, commercial

(G-11068)
CUSTOM SEAL INC
Also Called: Custom Seal Roofing
708 Graham Dr (43420-4073)
P.O. Box 1290 (43420-8290)
PHONE..............................419 334-1020
Steven Mayle, *President*
Robert L Mayle, *Vice Pres*

GEOGRAPHIC

Mike Keating, *Sales Staff*
John Cronin, *Executive*
Maribeth Pearson, *Admin Sec*
▼ **EMP:** 25
SQ FT: 10,000
SALES (est): 3.3MM **Privately Held**
WEB: www.customseal.com
SIC: 1761 Roofing contractor

(G-11069)
DAMSCHRODER ROOFING INC
2228 Hayes Ave Ste D (43420-2699)
PHONE..............................419 332-5000
Dana Howell, *President*
Jacob Pfotenhauer, *Project Mgr*
Mike Vodika, *Manager*
Tiffany Wood, *Administration*
EMP: 28
SALES: 4.7MM **Privately Held**
SIC: 1761 Roofing contractor

(G-11070)
DOEPKER GROUP INC
Also Called: Time Staffing
1303 W State St (43420-2016)
PHONE..............................419 355-1409
Jeffrey Doepker, *President*
Rita Crawford, *Admin Asst*
EMP: 27
SALES: 20MM **Privately Held**
SIC: 7363 Temporary help service

(G-11071)
EASTER SEALS METRO CHICAGO INC
Also Called: Easter Seal Northwestern Ohio
101 S Stone St (43420-2651)
PHONE..............................419 332-3016
Jennifer Lewis, *Manager*
EMP: 40
SALES (corp-wide): 40MM **Privately Held**
WEB: www.easterlsealsnwohio.org
SIC: 8322 Individual & family services
PA: Easter Seals Metropolitan Chicago, Inc.
　　1939 W 13th St Ste 300
　　Chicago IL 60608
　　312 491-4110

(G-11072)
FIRELANDS REGIONAL HEALTH SYS
Also Called: Firelnds Cnsling Recovery Svcs
675 Bartson Rd (43420-9672)
PHONE..............................419 332-5524
Dawn Kroh, *Superintendent*
EMP: 30
SALES (corp-wide): 280.7MM **Privately Held**
SIC: 8093 8069 8062 Mental health clinic, outpatient; drug addiction rehabilitation hospital; general medical & surgical hospitals
PA: Firelands Regional Health System
　　1111 Hayes Ave
　　Sandusky OH 44870
　　419 557-7400

(G-11073)
FIRST CHOICE PACKAGING INC (PA)
Also Called: First Choice Packg Solutions
1501 W State St (43420-1629)
PHONE..............................419 333-4100
Paul W Tomick, *President*
Frank Wolfinger, *Vice Pres*
▲ **EMP:** 150
SALES (est): 32.6MM **Privately Held**
WEB: www.firstchoicepackaging.com
SIC: 3089 7389 Thermoformed finished plastic products; packaging & labeling services

(G-11074)
FLEX TEMP EMPLOYMENT SERVICES
Also Called: Pagan
524 W State St (43420-2532)
PHONE..............................419 355-9675
Larry Aaron, *Manager*
EMP: 143
SALES (corp-wide): 5.8MM **Privately Held**
WEB: www.flextemp.com
SIC: 7363 Temporary help service

PA: Flex Temp Employment Services Inc
　　1514 E Farwell St Frnt
　　Sandusky OH 44870
　　419 625-3470

(G-11075)
FRATERNAL ORDER EAGLES INC
Also Called: Foe 712
2570 W State St (43420-1445)
PHONE..............................419 332-3961
James Hoffman, *President*
EMP: 27
SALES (corp-wide): 5.7MM **Privately Held**
WEB: www.fraternalorderofeagles.tribe.net
SIC: 8641 Fraternal associations
PA: Fraternal Order Of Eagles, Bryan Aerie
　　2233 Of Bryan, Ohio
　　221 S Walnut St
　　Bryan OH 43506
　　419 636-7812

(G-11076)
FREMONT FEDERAL CREDIT UNION (PA)
315 Croghan St (43420-3013)
P.O. Box 1208 (43420-8208)
PHONE..............................419 334-4434
Anthony Camilleri, *President*
Joseph Saalman, *Exec VP*
EMP: 115
SALES: 7.8MM **Privately Held**
WEB: www.fremontfcu.com
SIC: 6061 6163 Federal credit unions; loan brokers

(G-11077)
FREMONT LOGISTICS LLC
1301 Heinz Rd (43420-8584)
PHONE..............................419 333-0669
Scott Ellithorpe,
EMP: 100
SALES (est): 5MM
SALES (corp-wide): 25.9B **Privately Held**
WEB: www.es3.com
SIC: 4225 General warehousing & storage
HQ: Es3, Llc
　　6 Optical Ave
　　Keene NH 03431
　　603 354-6100

(G-11078)
GOODNIGHT INN INC
Also Called: Days Inn
3701 N State Route 53 (43420-9318)
PHONE..............................419 334-9551
Kerri Henry, *Manager*
EMP: 40
SALES (corp-wide): 5.3MM **Privately Held**
SIC: 7011 Hotels & motels
PA: Goodnight Inn, Inc.
　　11313 Us Highway 250 N
　　Milan OH 44846
　　419 626-3610

(G-11079)
GOODWILL INDUSTRIES OF ERIE
Also Called: Fremont Plant Operations
1597 Pontiac Ave (43420-9792)
PHONE..............................419 334-7566
T Burnsderter, *Branch Mgr*
EMP: 75
SALES (corp-wide): 8.9MM **Privately Held**
SIC: 8322 Individual & family services
PA: Goodwill Industries Of Erie, Huron, Ottawa And Sandusky Counties, Inc.
　　419 W Market St
　　Sandusky OH 44870
　　419 625-4744

(G-11080)
HOLIDAY INN EXPRESS
1501 Hospitality Ct (43420-8306)
PHONE..............................419 332-7700
Shanda McCluty, *General Mgr*
EMP: 50
SALES (est): 1MM **Privately Held**
SIC: 7011 Hotels & motels

(G-11081)
IN HOME HEALTH LLC
Also Called: Heartland HM Hlth Care Hospice
907 W State St Ste A (43420-2548)
PHONE..............................419 355-9209
Ann Wright, *Principal*
EMP: 38
SALES (corp-wide): 2.4B **Publicly Held**
SIC: 8082 Home health care services
HQ: In Home Health, Llc
　　333 N Summit St
　　Toledo OH 43604

(G-11082)
KELLER OCHS KOCH INC
Also Called: SCI
416 S Arch St (43420-2965)
PHONE..............................419 332-8288
John P Keller, *President*
Lawrence L Koch, *Vice Pres*
EMP: 30
SQ FT: 20,000
SALES: 800K
SALES (corp-wide): 3.1B **Publicly Held**
WEB: www.keller-ochs-kochfuneralhome.com
SIC: 7261 Funeral home
PA: Service Corporation International
　　1929 Allen Pkwy
　　Houston TX 77019
　　713 522-5141

(G-11083)
KINSWA DIALYSIS LLC
Also Called: Fremont Regional Dialysis
100 Pinnacle Dr (43420-7400)
PHONE..............................419 332-0310
James K Hilger,
EMP: 35
SALES (est): 790.6K **Publicly Held**
SIC: 8092 Kidney dialysis centers
PA: Davita Inc.
　　2000 16th St
　　Denver CO 80202

(G-11084)
LOWES HOME CENTERS LLC
1952 N State Route 53 (43420-8637)
PHONE..............................419 355-0221
Lori Thomas, *Branch Mgr*
EMP: 150
SALES (corp-wide): 68.6B **Publicly Held**
SIC: 5211 5031 5722 5064 Home centers; building materials, exterior; building materials, interior; household appliance stores; electrical appliances, television & radio
HQ: Lowe's Home Centers, Llc
　　1605 Curtis Bridge Rd
　　Wilkesboro NC 28697
　　336 658-4000

(G-11085)
MADISON MOTOR SERVICE INC
2921 W State St (43420-6600)
PHONE..............................419 332-0727
Richard Seitz, *President*
EMP: 31
SQ FT: 4,800
SALES (est): 2.7MM **Privately Held**
SIC: 7549 7538 Towing service, automotive; general automotive repair shops

(G-11086)
MEMORIAL HOSPITAL (PA)
Also Called: MEMORIAL HOSPITAL HEALTHLINK
715 S Taft Ave (43420-3296)
PHONE..............................419 334-6657
Pamella Jensen, *CEO*
John Al Gorman, *Principal*
EMP: 420 **EST:** 1915
SQ FT: 197,000
SALES: 67.8MM **Privately Held**
SIC: 8062 General medical & surgical hospitals

(G-11087)
MICHAEL BROTHERS INC
Also Called: Sycamore Hills Golf Club
3728 Hayes Ave (43420-9717)
PHONE..............................419 332-5716
Douglas A Michael, *President*
Douglas A Micaehl Jr, *President*
Tonny Michael, *Vice Pres*
Douglas Michael Sr, *Treasurer*

Wayne Michael, *Admin Sec*
EMP: 35
SQ FT: 5,000
SALES (est): 1.9MM **Privately Held**
SIC: 7992 Public golf courses

(G-11088)
MOTION CONTROLS ROBOTICS INC
1500 Walter Ave (43420-1449)
PHONE..............................419 334-5886
Scott D Lang, *President*
Tim Ellenberger, *Vice Pres*
EMP: 32
SQ FT: 57,000
SALES (est): 7.6MM **Privately Held**
WEB: www.motioncontrolsplus.com
SIC: 8742 Automation & robotics consultant

(G-11089)
OHIO DEPT OF JOB & FMLY SVCS
Also Called: Sandusky Cnty Job & Fmly Svcs
2511 Countryside Dr (43420-9016)
PHONE..............................419 334-3891
Peter Cantu, *Branch Mgr*
EMP: 28 **Privately Held**
WEB: www.job.com
SIC: 9441 7363 ; help supply services
HQ: The Ohio Department Of Job And Family Services
　　30 E Broad St Fl 32
　　Columbus OH 43215

(G-11090)
RK FAMILY INC
1800 E State St (43420-4000)
PHONE..............................419 355-8230
Tim Lodes, *Principal*
EMP: 256
SALES (corp-wide): 1.5B **Privately Held**
SIC: 5099 Firearms & ammunition, except sporting
PA: Rk Family, Inc.
　　4216 Dewitt Ave
　　Mattoon IL 61938
　　217 235-7102

(G-11091)
RTHRFORD B HAYES PRSDNTIAL CTR
Also Called: Rutherford Museums
Spiegel Grv (43420)
PHONE..............................419 332-2081
Kristina Smith, *Marketing Staff*
Mary L Halbeisen, *Information Mgr*
Christy Weininger, *Exec Dir*
Christie Weininger, *Exec Dir*
Christie M Weininger, *Exec Dir*
EMP: 43
SALES: 1.9MM **Privately Held**
SIC: 8231 8412 Libraries; museum

(G-11092)
SABROSKE ELECTRIC INC
115 Lincoln St (43420-2852)
PHONE..............................419 332-6444
Thomas P Decker, *President*
Eric Smart, *Vice Pres*
Linda E Decker, *Admin Sec*
EMP: 25 **EST:** 1930
SQ FT: 6,000
SALES: 2.4MM **Privately Held**
SIC: 1731 5063 General electrical contractor; electrical supplies

(G-11093)
SANDUSKY COUNTY ENGR & HWY GAR
2500 W State St (43420-1445)
PHONE..............................419 334-9731
James Moyer, *Principal*
Rich Randolph, *Design Engr*
EMP: 25
SALES (est): 2.2MM **Privately Held**
SIC: 8711 Consulting engineer

(G-11094)
SEAL AFTERMARKET PRODUCTS LLC
1110 Napoleon St (43420-2328)
PHONE..............................419 355-1200
Fred Burkhart, *Branch Mgr*
EMP: 65

SALES (est): 93.7K **Privately Held**
SIC: 5082 Construction & mining machinery
PA: Seal Aftermarket Products, Llc
2315 Sw 32nd Ave
Hollywood FL 33023

(G-11095)
SIERRA LOBO INC (PA)
102 Pinnacle Dr (43420-7400)
PHONE..................................419 332-7101
George A Satornino, *President*
Nabil Kattouah, *Vice Pres*
Daniel R Lowe, *Vice Pres*
EMP: 32
SALES (est): 92.2MM **Privately Held**
SIC: 8711 Consulting engineer

(G-11096)
SISTERS OF MERCY
Also Called: Sisters of Mercy Fremont, Ohio
1220 Tiffin St (43420-3562)
PHONE..................................419 332-8208
Janette Tahy, *Manager*
EMP: 35
SALES (corp-wide): 19.1MM **Privately Held**
SIC: 8361 Home for the aged
HQ: Sisters Of Mercy Of The Americas South Central Community, Inc
2335 Grandview Ave
Cincinnati OH
513 221-1800

(G-11097)
SPRINGLEAF FINCL HOLDINGS LLC
2200 Sean Dr Ste J (43420-9772)
PHONE..................................419 334-9748
EMP: 565
SALES (corp-wide): 2.3B **Privately Held**
SIC: 7389 Financial services
PA: Springleaf Financial Holdings, Llc
601 Nw 2nd St
Evansville IN 47708
800 961-5577

(G-11098)
STYLE CREST INC
605 Hagerty Dr (43420-9100)
P.O. Box A (43420-0555)
PHONE..................................419 332-7369
Steve Grine, *Manager*
EMP: 150
SALES (corp-wide): 173.7MM **Privately Held**
SIC: 5075 Warm air heating & air conditioning
HQ: Style Crest, Inc.
2450 Enterprise St
Fremont OH 43420
419 332-7369

(G-11099)
STYLE CREST INC (HQ)
2450 Enterprise St (43420-8553)
P.O. Box A (43420-0555)
PHONE..................................419 332-7369
Thomas Kern, *CEO*
Henry Valle, *President*
Phillip Burton, *Corp Secy*
William Goad, *Exec VP*
Bryan T Kern, *Exec VP*
◆ EMP: 277
SALES (est): 165.5MM
SALES (corp-wide): 173.7MM **Privately Held**
SIC: 3089 5075 5031 8361 Siding, plastic; warm air heating & air conditioning; building materials, exterior; building materials, interior; residential care
PA: Style Crest Enterprises, Inc.
2450 Enterprise St
Fremont OH 43420
419 355-8586

(G-11100)
STYLE CREST ENTERPRISES INC (PA)
2450 Enterprise St (43420-8553)
P.O. Box A (43420-0555)
PHONE..................................419 355-8586
Thomas L Kern, *CEO*
Henry Valle, *President*
Greg Risk, *General Mgr*
Phillip Burton, *Corp Secy*

Bryan T Kern, *Exec VP*
EMP: 70
SQ FT: 40,000
SALES (est): 173.7MM **Privately Held**
SIC: 3089 5075 Plastic hardware & building products; awnings, fiberglass & plastic combination; siding, plastic; warm air heating & air conditioning

(G-11101)
STYLE CREST TRANSPORT INC
2450 Enterprise St (43420-8553)
P.O. Box A (43420-0555)
PHONE..................................419 332-7369
Thomas L Kern, *CEO*
Henry Valle, *President*
Phillip Burton, *Corp Secy*
Bryan T Kern, *Exec VP*
Tyrone G Frantz, *CFO*
EMP: 51
SQ FT: 1,500
SALES (est): 4.7MM
SALES (corp-wide): 173.7MM **Privately Held**
SIC: 4213 4212 Trucking, except local; local trucking, without storage
PA: Style Crest Enterprises, Inc.
2450 Enterprise St
Fremont OH 43420
419 355-8586

(G-11102)
SUNRISE HOSPITALITY INC
Also Called: Hampton Inn
540 E County Road 89 (43420-9387)
PHONE..................................419 332-7650
Lori Reust, *Manager*
EMP: 69
SALES (corp-wide): 4MM **Privately Held**
SIC: 7011 Hotels
PA: Sunrise Hospitality, Inc.
27350 Lake View Dr
Perrysburg OH 43551
419 872-6161

(G-11103)
VOLUNTERS AMER CARE FACILITIES
Also Called: Bethesda Care Center
600 N Brush St (43420-1402)
PHONE..................................419 334-9521
Roger Wyman, *Exec Dir*
EMP: 110
SALES (corp-wide): 66.7MM **Privately Held**
SIC: 8051 Convalescent home with continuous nursing care
PA: Volunteers Of America Care Facilities
7530 Market Place Dr
Eden Prairie MN 55344
952 941-0305

(G-11104)
W S O S COMMUNITY A (PA)
Also Called: Great Lkes Cmnty Action Partnr
127 S Front St (43420-3021)
P.O. Box 590 (43420-0590)
PHONE..................................419 333-6068
Ruthann House, *CEO*
David Kipplen, *General Mgr*
David R Kipplen, *Vice Pres*
Jaime Munoz, *Controller*
Adrienne Fausey, *Human Res Dir*
EMP: 70
SQ FT: 17,000
SALES: 33MM **Privately Held**
WEB: www.wsos.org
SIC: 8351 8322 8331 Head start center, except in conjunction with school; individual & family services; job training services

(G-11105)
W S O S COMMUNITY A
Also Called: Fremont TMC Head Start
765 S Buchanan St (43420-4903)
PHONE..................................419 334-8511
Penny Moore, *Exec Dir*
Brenda Barton, *Director*
Kathy Morrison, *Director*
EMP: 60
SALES (corp-wide): 33MM **Privately Held**
SIC: 8351 8331 Head start center, except in conjunction with school; job training services

PA: W. S. O. S. Community Action Commission, Inc.
127 S Front St
Fremont OH 43420
419 333-6068

(G-11106)
WARNER MECHANICAL CORPORATION
1609 Dickinson St (43420-1119)
P.O. Box 747 (43420-0747)
PHONE..................................419 332-7116
Trent Bloomfield, *CEO*
James Krock, *President*
Kevin Reed, *Project Mgr*
EMP: 30 EST: 1946
SQ FT: 10,000
SALES (est): 7.3MM **Privately Held**
WEB: www.warnermech.com
SIC: 1711 Mechanical contractor

(G-11107)
WSOS CHILD DEVELOPMENT PROGRAM
Also Called: Wcdp
765 S Buchanan St (43420-4903)
PHONE..................................419 334-8511
Penny Moore, *Branch Mgr*
Kathy Morrison, *Director*
EMP: 45
SALES (est): 528.9K **Privately Held**
SIC: 8351 8661 Head start center, except in conjunction with school; Presbyterian Church

(G-11108)
YOUNG MENS CHRISTIAN ASSN
Also Called: YMCA
1000 North St (43420-1131)
PHONE..................................419 332-9622
Denise Reiter, *Exec Dir*
EMP: 50 EST: 1953
SALES (est): 1.1MM **Privately Held**
SIC: 8641 8322 7997 Youth organizations; individual & family services; membership sports & recreation clubs

Gahanna
Franklin County

(G-11109)
AMERICAN NATIONAL RED CROSS
Also Called: American Red Cross
337 Stoneridge Ln (43230-6783)
PHONE..................................614 473-3783
EMP: 39
SALES (corp-wide): 2.5B **Privately Held**
SIC: 8322 Emergency social services
PA: The American National Red Cross
430 17th St Nw
Washington DC 20006
202 737-8300

(G-11110)
ARROW GLOBL ASSET DSPSTION INC
Also Called: Retrobox.com
1120 Morrison Rd Ste A (43230-6646)
PHONE..................................614 328-4100
Dave Ryan, *Principal*
EMP: 70
SALES (corp-wide): 29.6B **Publicly Held**
WEB: www.intechra.com
SIC: 5045 Computers
HQ: Arrow Global Asset Disposition, Inc.
9101 Burnet Rd Ste 203
Austin TX 78758
800 378-6897

(G-11111)
CAPTIVE-AIRE SYSTEMS INC
850 Morrison Rd (43230-6643)
PHONE..................................614 777-7378
EMP: 27
SALES (corp-wide): 292.4MM **Privately Held**
SIC: 5722 5087 5046 Ret Household Appliances Whol Service Establishment Equipment Whol Commercial Equipment

PA: Captive-Aire Systems, Inc.
4641 Paragon Park Rd # 104
Raleigh NC 27616
919 882-2410

(G-11112)
CINEMARK USA INC
Also Called: Cinemark Stnrdge Plz Movies 16
323 Stoneridge Ln (43230-6783)
PHONE..................................614 471-7620
Scott Smith, *Manager*
EMP: 25 **Publicly Held**
SIC: 7832 Motion picture theaters, except drive-in
HQ: Cinemark Usa, Inc.
3900 Dallas Pkwy Ste 500
Plano TX 75093
972 665-1000

(G-11113)
COLUMBUS ASPHALT PAVING INC
1196 Technology Dr (43230-6607)
PHONE..................................614 759-9800
David J Power, *President*
Gary Pisano, *Opers Mgr*
John Power, *Manager*
EMP: 40 EST: 1975
SQ FT: 5,200
SALES (est): 8.9MM **Privately Held**
WEB: www.capasphalt.com
SIC: 1611 Highway & street paving contractor

(G-11114)
COLUMBUS OH-16 AIRPORT GAHANNA
Also Called: Springhill Suites
665 Taylor Rd (43230-6203)
PHONE..................................614 501-4770
Brian Moore, *Principal*
Greg Moundas, *Vice Pres*
EMP: 29
SALES (est): 2.1MM **Privately Held**
SIC: 7011 Hotels & motels

(G-11115)
CONSUMER CREDIT COUN (PA)
Also Called: APPRISEN
690 Taylor Rd Ste 110 (43230-3520)
PHONE..................................614 552-2222
Michael Kappas, *CEO*
Christopher Kallay, *CFO*
James Zeier, *CFO*
Campbell Rayfus, *Director*
EMP: 43
SQ FT: 50,000
SALES: 4.6MM **Privately Held**
WEB: www.cccservices.com
SIC: 7299 Debt counseling or adjustment service, individuals

(G-11116)
CUSTOM AC & HTG CO
Also Called: Honeywell Authorized Dealer
935 Claycraft Rd (43230-6650)
PHONE..................................614 552-4822
Patrick Halaiko, *President*
Leon Blalock, *COO*
Jeff Reed, *Vice Pres*
Jeffrey B Reed, *Sales Executive*
Steve Wistler, *Admin Sec*
EMP: 75
SQ FT: 7,500
SALES (est): 15.7MM **Privately Held**
WEB: www.customairco.com
SIC: 1711 Warm air heating & air conditioning contractor

(G-11117)
DEEMSYS INC (PA)
800 Cross Pointe Rd Afg (43230-6687)
PHONE..................................614 322-9928
Vijiayarani Benjamin, *Ch of Bd*
Jacob Benjamin, *President*
Dexter Benjamin, *Vice Pres*
EMP: 52
SQ FT: 5,100
SALES: 7.8MM **Privately Held**
WEB: www.deemsysinc.com
SIC: 8748 2741 7373 8299 Business consulting; ; systems software development services; educational service, non-degree granting: continuing educ.; computer software development & applications

(G-11118)
EQUITY CENTRAL LLC
81 Mill St Ste 300 (43230-1718)
PHONE................................614 861-7777
Colleen Martinelli, *Sales Associate*
Mekel Henderson,
EMP: 25
SQ FT: 1,300
SALES (est): 1.5MM **Privately Held**
WEB: www.equitycentralrealty.com
SIC: 6531 1521 1522 Real estate agent,
residential; single-family housing con-
struction; residential construction

(G-11119)
ESTATE INFORMATION SVCS
LLC
Also Called: Eis
670 Morrison Rd Ste 300 (43230-5324)
PHONE................................614 729-1700
J C Gunnell, *CEO*
Victoria Edwards, *Exec VP*
Victoria M Edwards, *Exec VP*
Michael Lame, *CFO*
Kip Randal, *CFO*
EMP: 70
SQ FT: 20,000
SALES (est): 9.5MM **Privately Held**
SIC: 7322 Collection agency, except real
estate

(G-11120)
FRESENIUS MEDICAL CARE
Also Called: Fresenius Kidney Care
991 E Johnstown Rd (43230-1851)
PHONE................................614 855-3677
Mary Garber, *Principal*
William Valle, *Principal*
EMP: 25
SALES (est): 451.5K **Privately Held**
SIC: 8011 Offices & clinics of medical doc-
tors

(G-11121)
FUN DAY EVENTS LLC
947 E Johnstown Rd # 163 (43230-1851)
PHONE................................740 549-9000
Michael Ross, *Manager*
EMP: 30
SQ FT: 10,000
SALES (est): 1.1MM **Privately Held**
WEB: www.fundayevents.com
SIC: 7299 Party planning service

(G-11122)
GAHANNA ANIMAL HOSPITAL
INC
144 W Johnstown Rd (43230-2773)
PHONE................................614 471-2201
John Worman Dvm, *President*
Julie Radabaugh, *Treasurer*
EMP: 50
SQ FT: 1,704
SALES (est): 1.8MM **Privately Held**
WEB: www.gahannaanimalhospital.com
SIC: 0742 Animal hospital services, pets &
other animal specialties

(G-11123)
GULF SOUTH MEDICAL SUPPLY
INC
915 Taylor Rd Unit A (43230-3292)
PHONE................................614 501-9080
Michael Evans, *Manager*
EMP: 40
SALES (corp-wide): 208.3B **Publicly**
Held
WEB: www.gsms.com
SIC: 5047 Medical equipment & supplies
HQ: Gulf South Medical Supply Inc
4345 Sthpint Blvd Ste 100
Jacksonville FL 32216
904 332-3000

(G-11124)
HEART CARE
765 N Hamilton Rd Ste 120 (43230-8707)
PHONE................................614 533-5000
Twilla Lee, *Manager*
Lora Siner, *Manager*
EMP: 51
SALES (est): 3.9MM **Privately Held**
SIC: 8011 Cardiologist & cardio-vascular
specialist

(G-11125)
HEARTLAND BANK (HQ)
850 N Hamilton Rd (43230-1757)
PHONE................................614 337-4600
G Scott McComb, *Ch of Bd*
Jay Eggspuehler, *Vice Ch Bd*
Tiney M Mc Comb, *President*
Paula Brutchey, *President*
Steve Hines, *COO*
EMP: 50 EST: 1988
SQ FT: 15,000
SALES: 40.6MM **Privately Held**
WEB: www.heartlandbank.com
SIC: 6022 State trust companies accepting
deposits, commercial

(G-11126)
IJUS LLC (PA)
Also Called: Innovative Joint Utility Svcs
690 Taylor Rd Ste 100 (43230-3520)
PHONE................................614 470-9882
William Schulze, *President*
EMP: 85
SQ FT: 15,000
SALES (est): 22.5MM **Privately Held**
WEB: www.ijus.net
SIC: 8711 Consulting engineer

(G-11127)
INTERIM HALTHCARE
COLUMBUS INC (HQ)
Also Called: Interim Services
784 Morrison Rd (43230-6642)
PHONE................................614 888-3130
Thomas J Dimarco, *President*
Michael W Hartshorn, *Principal*
Richard Nielsen, *Principal*
Craig Smith,
EMP: 30
SQ FT: 3,400
SALES: 20.2MM
SALES (corp-wide): 19.8MM **Privately**
Held
SIC: 7363 Temporary help service
PA: Salo, Inc.
960 Checkrein Ave Ste A
Columbus OH 43229
614 436-9404

(G-11128)
KINDERCARE EDUCATION LLC
Also Called: Childrens World Lrng Ctr 177
4885 Cherry Bottom Rd (43230-4535)
PHONE................................614 337-2035
EMP: 25
SALES (corp-wide): 1B **Privately Held**
SIC: 8351 Child Day Care Services
PA: Kindercare Education Llc
650 Ne Holladay St # 1400
Portland OR 97232
503 872-1300

(G-11129)
KONE INC
735 Cross Pointe Rd Ste G (43230-6786)
PHONE................................614 866-1751
Tony Crumley, *Manager*
EMP: 34
SALES (corp-wide): 732.3MM **Privately**
Held
WEB: www.us.kone.com
SIC: 7699 Elevators: inspection, service &
repair
HQ: Kone Inc.
4225 Naperville Rd # 400
Lisle IL 60532
630 577-1650

(G-11130)
LANDSEL TITLE AGENCY INC
(PA)
961 N Hamilton Rd Ste 100 (43230-1758)
PHONE................................614 337-1928
Randall L Craycraft, *President*
Lisa Tomba, *Controller*
Paul Wittenberg, *Accounts Mgr*
Britney Choina, *Accounts Exec*
Jon Lindahl, *Manager*
EMP: 45
SQ FT: 7,000
SALES: 3.5MM **Privately Held**
SIC: 6361 6541 Real estate title insur-
ance; title & trust companies

(G-11131)
LIBERTY MUTUAL INSURANCE
CO
630 Morrison Rd Ste 300 (43230-5318)
PHONE................................614 864-4100
Chingyee Lam, *Investment Ofcr*
Bryan Graham, *Manager*
EMP: 65
SALES (corp-wide): 38.3B **Privately Held**
WEB: www.libertymutual.com
SIC: 6331 Fire, marine & casualty insur-
ance
HQ: Liberty Mutual Insurance Company
175 Berkeley St
Boston MA 02116
617 357-9500

(G-11132)
LITTLE LAMBS CHILDRENS
CENTER
425 S Hamilton Rd (43230-3474)
PHONE................................614 471-9269
Stacy Barrett, *Principal*
EMP: 35
SALES: 972K **Privately Held**
SIC: 8351 Child day care services

(G-11133)
LIVING IN FAMILY
ENVIRONMENT
142 N High St (43230-3032)
P.O. Box 307416 (43230-7416)
PHONE................................614 475-5305
Mary Bill, *Manager*
EMP: 60 EST: 1997
SALES (est): 1.5MM **Privately Held**
SIC: 8322 Social service center

(G-11134)
MARK-L INC
Also Called: Mark-L Construction
1180 Claycraft Rd (43230-6640)
PHONE................................614 863-8832
Mark A Laivins Sr, *President*
Diana Dillinger, *Human Resources*
Dorothy Marcum, *Office Mgr*
EMP: 32
SQ FT: 8,000
SALES (est): 22.3MM **Privately Held**
WEB: www.mark-l.com
SIC: 1542 Commercial & office building,
new construction

(G-11135)
MAXIM HEALTHCARE SERVICES
INC
735 Taylor Rd (43230-6274)
PHONE................................614 986-3001
EMP: 94
SALES (corp-wide): 1.5B **Privately Held**
SIC: 7363 Medical help service
PA: Maxim Healthcare Services, Inc.
7227 Lee Deforest Dr
Columbia MD 21046
410 910-1500

(G-11136)
MPOWER INC
4643 Winery Way (43230-4232)
PHONE................................614 783-0478
Dejuante McKee, *President*
EMP: 30
SALES: 1.4MM **Privately Held**
SIC: 1542 Nonresidential construction

(G-11137)
NETJETS AVIATION INC
760 Morrison Rd Ste 250 (43230-6652)
PHONE................................614 239-5501
Pete Richards, *Manager*
EMP: 40
SALES (corp-wide): 225.3B **Publicly**
Held
SIC: 8741 Administrative management; of-
fice management
HQ: Netjets Aviation, Inc.
4111 Bridgeway Ave
Columbus OH 43219
614 239-5500

(G-11138)
ODYSSEY HEALTHCARE INC
Also Called: Odyssey Healthcare of Colum-
bus
540 Officenter Pl Ste 295 (43230-5323)
PHONE................................614 414-0500
Holly Franko, *General Mgr*
Stephanie Ward, *Accounts Exec*
EMP: 120
SALES (corp-wide): 6B **Privately Held**
SIC: 8082 Home health care services
HQ: Odyssey Healthcare, Inc.
7801 Mesquite Bend Dr # 105
Irving TX 75063

(G-11139)
OHIO PIA SERVICE
CORPORATION
600 Cross Pointe Rd (43230-6696)
PHONE................................614 552-8000
George Haenzel, *President*
Melody Cardenas, *Education*
EMP: 26
SALES (est): 3.3MM **Privately Held**
SIC: 6311 Life insurance

(G-11140)
PARKSIDE BEHAVIORAL
HEALTHCARE
349 Olde Ridenour Rd (43230-2528)
PHONE................................614 471-2552
EMP: 50
SALES (est): 2.2MM **Privately Held**
SIC: 8069 Specialty Hospital

(G-11141)
RELIANT CAPITAL SOLUTIONS
LLC
Also Called: Reliant Recovery Solutions
670 Cross Pointe Rd (43230-6862)
P.O. Box 30469, Columbus (43230-0469)
PHONE................................614 452-6100
David Shull, *CFO*
Margie Brickner,
EMP: 185
SQ FT: 20,000
SALES (est): 9.9MM **Privately Held**
WEB: www.reliantcapitalsolutions.com
SIC: 7322 Collection agency, except real
estate

(G-11142)
ROCKWOOD DRY CLEANERS
CORP
171 Granville St (43230-3005)
PHONE................................614 471-3700
Robert Rings, *President*
Justin Rings, *Vice Pres*
EMP: 28
SALES (est): 1.6MM **Privately Held**
SIC: 7216 Cleaning & dyeing, except rugs

(G-11143)
ROMANOFF ELECTRIC INC (PA)
1288 Research Rd (43230-6625)
PHONE................................614 755-4500
Matthew Romanoff, *President*
EMP: 128
SQ FT: 14,000
SALES (est): 61.9MM **Privately Held**
SIC: 1731 General electrical contractor

(G-11144)
SANDEL CORP
152 N High St (43230-3032)
P.O. Box 307262 (43230-7262)
PHONE................................614 475-5898
Walter P Sandel, *President*
Kathryn Sandel, *Treasurer*
EMP: 25
SQ FT: 2,000
SALES (est): 2.6MM **Privately Held**
SIC: 1742 Insulation, buildings

(G-11145)
SOLAR IMAGING LLC
825 Taylor Rd (43230-6235)
PHONE................................614 626-8536
Paul Hartong, *Prdtn Mgr*
Jeffrey B Burt, *Mng Member*
Stephanie Ryland, *Manager*
Sandra G Burt, *Admin Sec*
EMP: 40
SALES (est): 3.4MM **Privately Held**
SIC: 7384 Photofinishing laboratory

(G-11146)
STAR GROUP LTD
Also Called: Holiday Inn
460 Waterbury Ct (43230-3450)
PHONE..................................614 428-8678
Richard Chen,
EMP: 25
SALES (est): 2.2MM **Privately Held**
SIC: 7011 Hotels & motels

(G-11147)
STONE COFFMAN COMPANY LLC
6015 Taylor Rd (43230-3211)
PHONE..................................614 861-4668
Thomas Coffman,
Susan Coffman,
EMP: 25
SALES (est): 3.2MM **Privately Held**
WEB: www.coffmanstone.com
SIC: 5032 5211 Brick, stone & related material; masonry materials & supplies; paving stones

(G-11148)
SUNRISE MORTGAGE SERVICES INC
3596 Ringling Ln (43230-4609)
PHONE..................................614 989-5412
Richard Greer, *President*
EMP: 70
SALES (est): 5.2MM **Privately Held**
SIC: 6162 Mortgage bankers & correspondents

(G-11149)
SUNRISE SENIOR LIVING INC
Also Called: Sunrise of Gahanna
775 E Johnstown Rd (43230-2115)
PHONE..................................614 418-9775
Todd Gable, *Manager*
EMP: 35
SALES (corp-wide): 4.7B **Publicly Held**
WEB: www.sunrise.com
SIC: 8051 8361 Skilled nursing care facilities; residential care
HQ: Sunrise Senior Living, Llc
7902 Westpark Dr
Mc Lean VA 22102

(G-11150)
TERRACON CONSULTANTS INC
Also Called: Terracon Consultants N4
800 Morrison Rd (43230-6643)
PHONE..................................614 863-3113
Kevin Ernst, *Manager*
EMP: 35
SALES (corp-wide): 654.9MM **Privately Held**
SIC: 8711 8731 Consulting engineer; environmental research
HQ: Terracon Consultants, Inc.
10841 S Ridgeview Rd
Olathe KS 66061
913 599-6886

(G-11151)
WINN-SCAPES INC
Also Called: Winnscapes Inc/Schmidt Nurs Co
6079 Taylor Rd (43230-3211)
PHONE..................................614 866-9466
Richard Winnestaffer, *CEO*
Carl Morris Jr, *President*
Robert Parsons, *Sales Staff*
Mike Clapper, *Maintence Staff*
EMP: 51
SQ FT: 6,000
SALES (est): 4.7MM **Privately Held**
WEB: www.winnscapes.com
SIC: 0782 Landscape contractors

(G-11152)
YOUNG MENS CHRISTIAN ASSOC
Also Called: YMCA
555 Ymca Pl (43230-6851)
PHONE..................................614 416-9622
Chris Angelletta, *Manager*
EMP: 160

SALES (corp-wide): 44.9MM **Privately Held**
WEB: www.ymca-columbus.com
SIC: 8641 7991 8351 7032 Youth organizations; physical fitness facilities; child day care services; youth camps; individual & family services
PA: Young Men's Christian Association Of Central Ohio
40 W Long St
Columbus OH 43215
614 389-4409

Galena
Delaware County

(G-11153)
ACORN FARMS INC
7679 Worthington Rd B (43021-9412)
PHONE..................................614 891-9348
Paul Reiner, *President*
▲ **EMP:** 150
SQ FT: 3,200
SALES (est): 13MM **Privately Held**
WEB: www.acornfarms.com
SIC: 0181 Nursery stock, growing of

(G-11154)
AMERICAN GOLF CORPORATION
Also Called: Royal American Links Golf Club
3300 Miller Paul Rd (43021-9243)
PHONE..................................740 965-5122
Dave Philsburg, *Owner*
Jason Shelton, *Manager*
EMP: 46 **Publicly Held**
WEB: www.americangolf.com
SIC: 7997 7992 Golf club, membership; public golf courses
HQ: American Golf Corporation
909 N Pacific Coast Hwy
El Segundo CA 90245
310 664-4000

(G-11155)
B2B POWER PARTNERS
5647 Summer Blvd (43021-9003)
PHONE..................................614 309-6964
Craig Owens, *President*
EMP: 30
SALES (est): 844.3K **Privately Held**
SIC: 8748 Business consulting

(G-11156)
BIG RED LP
Also Called: Double Eagle Club
6025 Cheshire Rd (43021-9408)
PHONE..................................740 548-7799
John H McConnell, *Partner*
Bruce Ruhl, *General Mgr*
Beth Miller, *Manager*
Rick Mellen, *Executive*
EMP: 75
SQ FT: 5,731
SALES: 1.8MM **Privately Held**
SIC: 7997 Golf club, membership

(G-11157)
DIVISION 7 INC
Also Called: Division 7 Roofing
72 Holmes St (43021-9414)
P.O. Box 366 (43021-0366)
PHONE..................................740 965-1970
George W Reiss, *CEO*
John Kiesel, *President*
John C Seitzinger, *Vice Pres*
EMP: 40
SALES (est): 7.4MM **Privately Held**
SIC: 1761 7389 Roofing contractor; sheet metalwork; crane & aerial lift service

(G-11158)
FOXRIDGE FARMS CORP
7273 Cheshire Rd (43021-9409)
PHONE..................................740 965-1369
Kathy Dixon, *President*
EMP: 30
SALES (est): 599.6K **Privately Held**
WEB: www.foxridgefarms.com
SIC: 7999 0752 Riding stable; animal specialty services

(G-11159)
HEAT TTAL FCLTY SLUTIONS INC
5064 Red Bank Rd (43021-8603)
PHONE..................................740 965-3005
Ron Thomas, *President*
EMP: 30
SALES (est): 4.4MM **Privately Held**
SIC: 1711 7359 Heating & air conditioning contractors; sound & lighting equipment rental

(G-11160)
J R MEAD INDUSTRIAL CONTRS
6606 Lake Of The Woods Pt (43021-9616)
PHONE..................................614 891-4466
Joanie R Mead, *President*
James E Mead, *Vice Pres*
EMP: 50
SQ FT: 12,000
SALES (est): 3.4MM **Privately Held**
SIC: 1799 1796 Rigging & scaffolding; machinery dismantling

(G-11161)
LAKES COUNTRY CLUB INC
Also Called: Lakes Golf and Country Club
7129 Africa Rd (43021-9581)
PHONE..................................614 882-4167
Todd Ortlip, *President*
EMP: 150
SALES (est): 2.3MM **Privately Held**
WEB: www.lakescc.com
SIC: 7997 Golf club, membership

(G-11162)
LAZER KRAZE
6075 Braymoore Dr (43021-9093)
PHONE..................................513 339-1030
Robin Wilcox, *CEO*
Dave Wilcox, *Vice Pres*
EMP: 30
SALES: 110K **Privately Held**
SIC: 7996 Amusement parks

(G-11163)
PLANE DETAIL LLC
2720 S 3 Bs And K Rd (43021-9785)
PHONE..................................614 734-1201
Steve Rotermund, *President*
Stephen H Dodd, *Vice Pres*
EMP: 35
SALES (est): 4.2MM **Privately Held**
SIC: 4581 Aircraft cleaning & janitorial service

Galion
Crawford County

(G-11164)
A & G MANUFACTURING CO INC (PA)
Also Called: A G Mercury
280 Gelsanliter Rd (44833-2234)
P.O. Box 935 (44833-0935)
PHONE..................................419 468-7433
Arvin Shifley, *President*
Glen Shifley Sr, *Principal*
Doug Shifley, *CFO*
Carol Carder, *Regl Sales Mgr*
Glen E Shifley Jr, *Admin Sec*
▲ **EMP:** 40
SQ FT: 100,000
SALES (est): 10.4MM **Privately Held**
WEB: www.agmercury.com
SIC: 3599 7692 3446 3444 Machine shop, jobbing & repair; welding repair; architectural metalwork; sheet metalwork; fabricated plate work (boiler shop); fabricated structural metal

(G-11165)
A M COMMUNICATIONS LTD (PA)
5707 State Route 309 (44833-9541)
PHONE..................................419 528-3051
Alan Miller, *President*
Jim Jolly, *Opers Mgr*
Jeff Savnik, *Opers Mgr*
George Mathenia, *Production*
Kelly Weber, *Supervisor*
EMP: 59

SQ FT: 8,000
SALES (est): 22.2MM **Privately Held**
WEB: www.amcable.com
SIC: 8748 Communications consulting

(G-11166)
AVITA HEALTH SYSTEM
Also Called: Robert L Dawson M.D., James
955 Hosford Rd (44833-9325)
PHONE..................................419 468-7059
James H Wurm, *Partner*
EMP: 187
SALES (corp-wide): 444.6K **Privately Held**
SIC: 8011 Internal medicine, physician/surgeon
PA: Avita Health System
269 Portland Way S
Galion OH 44833
419 468-4841

(G-11167)
AVITA HEALTH SYSTEM (PA)
269 Portland Way S (44833-2312)
PHONE..................................419 468-4841
Jerry Morasko, *CEO*
EMP: 117
SALES: 444.6K **Privately Held**
SIC: 8011 Internal medicine, physician/surgeon

(G-11168)
BAILLIE LUMBER CO LP
3953 County Road 51 (44833)
PHONE..................................419 462-2000
Russel Jones, *Branch Mgr*
EMP: 40
SALES (corp-wide): 344.3MM **Privately Held**
SIC: 5031 2426 2421 Lumber: rough, dressed & finished; hardwood dimension & flooring mills; sawmills & planing mills, general
PA: Baillie Lumber Co., L.P.
4002 Legion Dr
Hamburg NY 14075
800 950-2850

(G-11169)
CRAWFORD CNTY SHARED HLTH SVCS
1220 N Market St (44833-1443)
P.O. Box 327 (44833-0327)
PHONE..................................419 468-7985
Bert Maglott, *Exec Dir*
EMP: 44
SALES: 4.2MM **Privately Held**
SIC: 8082 Home health care services

(G-11170)
FIRST FDRAL SAV LN ASSN GALION
140 N Columbus St (44833-1909)
PHONE..................................419 468-1518
Eric Geyer, *Principal*
EMP: 75
SALES (est): 5.8MM **Privately Held**
SIC: 6035 Federal savings & loan associations

(G-11171)
FIRST FEDERAL BANK OF OHIO (PA)
140 N Columbus St (44833-1909)
P.O. Box 957 (44833-0957)
PHONE..................................419 468-1518
David B Beach, *CEO*
Thomas Moore, *President*
Eric S Geyer, *Chairman*
David Schockman, *Vice Pres*
Rodney J Vose, *Vice Pres*
EMP: 60 **EST:** 1891
SQ FT: 12,000
SALES: 8.3MM **Privately Held**
WEB: www.firstfederalbankofohio.com
SIC: 6035 Federal savings & loan associations

(G-11172)
FLICK LUMBER CO INC
Also Called: Flick Packaging
340 S Columbus St (44833-2624)
P.O. Box 296 (44833-0296)
PHONE..................................419 468-6278
Gary G Flick, *President*

Erik Flick, *Vice Pres*
George Flick, *Vice Pres*
Kristi Stief, *Office Mgr*
EMP: 30
SQ FT: 35,200
SALES (est): 6.3MM **Privately Held**
WEB: www.flickpackaging.com
SIC: 4783 Packing goods for shipping; crating goods for shipping

(G-11173)
GALION COMMUNITY CENTER YMCA
500 Gill Ave (44833-1213)
PHONE................................419 468-7754
Terry Gribble, *CEO*
EMP: 25
SALES: 1.4MM **Privately Held**
SIC: 8641 7991 8351 7032 Youth organizations; physical fitness facilities; child day care services; youth camps; individual & family services

(G-11174)
GALION COMMUNITY HOSPITAL
269 Portland Way S (44833-2399)
PHONE................................419 468-4841
Lamar Wyse, *President*
Robert Melaragno, *CFO*
EMP: 465
SQ FT: 165,219
SALES: 106.5MM **Privately Held**
WEB: www.galionhospital.org
SIC: 8062 8051 Hospital, affiliated with AMA residency; skilled nursing care facilities

(G-11175)
GALION EAST OHIO I LP
1300 Harding Way E (44833-3063)
PHONE................................216 520-1250
Frank Sinito, *General Ptnr*
EMP: 99
SALES (est): 789.1K **Privately Held**
SIC: 6513 Apartment building operators

(G-11176)
GLEN-GERY CORPORATION
3785 Cardington Iberia Rd (44833)
PHONE................................419 468-4890
Joe Wishan, *Branch Mgr*
EMP: 78 **Privately Held**
WEB: www.glengerybrick.com
SIC: 5032 Brick, stone & related material
HQ: Glen-Gery Corporation
    1166 Spring St
    Reading PA 19610
    610 374-4011

(G-11177)
GMC EXCAVATION & TRUCKING
1859 Biddle Rd (44833-8962)
P.O. Box 203, Iberia (43325-0203)
PHONE................................419 468-0121
Steven J Beck, *Partner*
Mindy Beck, *Partner*
Lynn Dovenbarger, *Admin Sec*
EMP: 40
SALES (est): 3.2MM **Privately Held**
SIC: 4213 1794 4212 Trucking, except local; excavation work; local trucking, without storage

(G-11178)
GOUDY INTERNAL MEDICINE INC
Also Called: Goudy, James A II MD
270 Portland Way S Rear (44833-2395)
PHONE................................419 468-8323
James A Goudy II, *President*
EMP: 100
SALES (est): 2.5MM **Privately Held**
SIC: 8011 Internal medicine, physician/surgeon

(G-11179)
MILL CREEK NURSING
900 Wedgewood Cir (44833-8815)
PHONE................................419 468-4046
Brian Colleran, *President*
EMP: 50
SALES: 5.8MM **Privately Held**
SIC: 8051 Convalescent home with continuous nursing care

(G-11180)
OHIO HRTLAND CMNTY ACTION COMM
Also Called: Salvation Army
124 Buehler St (44833-2248)
PHONE................................419 468-5121
Frances Horton, *Manager*
EMP: 25
SALES (corp-wide): 10.4MM **Privately Held**
SIC: 8399 8322 Community action agency; individual & family services
PA: Ohio Heartland Community Action Commission
    372 E Center St
    Marion OH 43302
    740 387-1039

(G-11181)
OHIO TRANSMISSION CORPORATION
Otp Industrial Solutions
1311 Freese Works Pl (44833-9368)
P.O. Box 73278, Cleveland (44193-0002)
PHONE................................419 468-7866
David Falk, *Branch Mgr*
EMP: 25 **Privately Held**
SIC: 5084 5085 Pumps & pumping equipment; power transmission equipment & apparatus
HQ: Ohio Transmission Corporation
    1900 Jetway Blvd
    Columbus OH 43219
    614 342-6247

(G-11182)
STEELE DIALYSIS LLC
Also Called: Galion Dialysis
865 Harding Way W (44833-1637)
PHONE................................419 462-1028
James K Hilger,
EMP: 35 EST: 2013
SALES (est): 485.5K **Publicly Held**
SIC: 8092 Kidney dialysis centers
PA: Davita Inc.
    2000 16th St
    Denver CO 80202

(G-11183)
SURFSIDE MOTORS INC (PA)
Also Called: Craig Smith Auto Group
7459 State Route 309 (44833-9735)
P.O. Box 850 (44833-0850)
PHONE................................419 462-1746
Toll Free:................................866 -
Craig A Smith, *President*
Matt Wilson, *Parts Mgr*
Bonnie J Heston, *Admin Sec*
EMP: 50
SQ FT: 21,000
SALES (est): 16.8MM **Privately Held**
WEB: www.craigsmithrvcenter.com
SIC: 5511 5521 7538 7532 Automobiles, new & used; used car dealers; general automotive repair shops; top & body repair & paint shops; recreational vehicle dealers

(G-11184)
TSI INC
1263 State Route 598 (44833-9367)
P.O. Box 687 (44833-0687)
PHONE................................419 468-1855
George Dallas, *President*
Rita Masucci, *Vice Pres*
Bob Lynch, *Sales Executive*
EMP: 30
SALES (est): 3MM **Privately Held**
SIC: 8711 7373 Engineering services; computer integrated systems design

Gallipolis
Gallia County

(G-11185)
AREA AGENCY ON AGING DST 7 INC
Also Called: Galia County Council On Aging
1167 State Route 160 (45631-8407)
PHONE................................740 446-7000
Shirley Doff, *Branch Mgr*
EMP: 29

SALES (est): 866.6K
SALES (corp-wide): 61MM **Privately Held**
SIC: 8322 Senior citizens' center or association
PA: Area Agency On Aging District 7, Inc.
    160 Dorsey Dr
    Rio Grande OH 45674
    800 582-7277

(G-11186)
CITY OF GALLIPOLIS
Also Called: Gallipolis Municipal Pool
2501 Ohio Ave (45631-1656)
PHONE................................740 441-6003
Bradd Bostic, *Director*
EMP: 33 **Privately Held**
SIC: 7999 Swimming pool, non-membership
PA: City Of Gallipolis
    333 3rd Third Ave # 3
    Gallipolis OH 45631
    740 441-6003

(G-11187)
COUNTY OF GALLIA
Also Called: Gallia County Human Services
848 3rd Ave (45631-1625)
P.O. Box 339 (45631-0339)
PHONE................................740 446-3222
Kathy McCalla, *Director*
EMP: 55 **Privately Held**
SIC: 6371 9111 Pension, health & welfare funds; county supervisors' & executives' offices
PA: County Of Gallia
    18 Locust St Ste 1292
    Gallipolis OH 45631
    740 446-4612

(G-11188)
COUNTY OF GALLIA
Also Called: State Highway Dept Gallia
1107 State Route 160 (45631)
PHONE................................740 446-2665
Bob Howard, *Superintendent*
EMP: 32 **Privately Held**
SIC: 0782 9111 Highway lawn & garden maintenance services; county supervisors' & executives' offices
PA: County Of Gallia
    18 Locust St Ste 1292
    Gallipolis OH 45631
    740 446-4612

(G-11189)
COUNTY OF GALLIA
Also Called: Gallia County Engineer
1167 State Route 160 (45631-8407)
PHONE................................740 446-4009
Bret Boothe, *Engineer*
EMP: 29 **Privately Held**
SIC: 8711 Engineering services
PA: County Of Gallia
    18 Locust St Ste 1292
    Gallipolis OH 45631
    740 446-4612

(G-11190)
DEVELPMNTAL DSBLTIES OHIO DEPT
Also Called: Gallipolis Developmental Ctr
2500 Ohio Ave (45631-1656)
PHONE................................740 446-1642
Don Walker, *Branch Mgr*
EMP: 510 **Privately Held**
SIC: 8063 8052 9431 Psychiatric hospitals; intermediate care facilities;
HQ: Ohio Department Of Developmental Disabilities
    30 E Broad St Fl 13
    Columbus OH 43215

(G-11191)
FAMILY SENIOR CARE INC
859 3rd Ave (45631-1624)
PHONE................................740 441-1428
Teri Pearson, *Administration*
EMP: 27
SALES (est): 784.6K **Privately Held**
WEB: www.familyseniorcare.com
SIC: 8322 8082 Senior citizens' center or association; home health care services

(G-11192)
GALLCO INC
Also Called: GALLCO INDUSTRIES
77 Mill Creek Rd (45631-8423)
PHONE................................740 446-3775
Robert Burlile, *President*
Bernard Miehm, *Vice Pres*
Timothy Stout, *Director*
EMP: 55
SALES: 134.9K **Privately Held**
SIC: 8331 Sheltered workshop

(G-11193)
GALLIPOLIS AUTO AUCTION INC
286 Upper River Rd (45631-1839)
P.O. Box 421 (45631-0421)
PHONE................................740 446-1576
Bonnie Shelton, *President*
Don Shelton, *Corp Secy*
Roger Stover, *Manager*
EMP: 28
SQ FT: 10,000
SALES: 2.9MM **Privately Held**
SIC: 5012 Automobile auction

(G-11194)
GALLIPOLIS CARE LLC
Also Called: PRESTIGE HEALTHCARE
170 Pinecrest Dr (45631-1347)
PHONE................................740 446-7112
Melvin Rhinelander, *Ch of Bd*
Amanda Wray, *Administration*
EMP: 110
SALES: 6.8MM
SALES (corp-wide): 41.5MM **Privately Held**
SIC: 8051 Convalescent home with continuous nursing care
PA: Senior Northpoint Services Llc
    7400 New Lagrange 100
    Louisville KY 40222
    502 429-8062

(G-11195)
GALLIPOLIS HOSPITALITY INC
Also Called: Holiday Inn
577 State Route 7 N (45631-5921)
PHONE................................740 446-0090
Anthony Etnyre, *President*
Gary Kilgore, *General Mgr*
EMP: 40
SQ FT: 50,000
SALES (est): 1.2MM **Privately Held**
SIC: 7011 5813 5812 Hotels; drinking places; eating places

(G-11196)
HOLZER CLINIC LLC
100 Jackson Pike (45631-1560)
PHONE................................304 746-3701
Matt Johnson, *Branch Mgr*
EMP: 112
SALES (corp-wide): 323.8MM **Privately Held**
SIC: 8011 Clinic, operated by physicians
HQ: Holzer Clinic Llc
    90 Jackson Pike
    Gallipolis OH 45631
    740 446-5411

(G-11197)
HOLZER CLINIC LLC (HQ)
Also Called: Holzer Health Center
90 Jackson Pike (45631-1562)
PHONE................................740 446-5411
Christopher T Meyer, *CEO*
Craig Strafford, *President*
Michael J Zirille Do, *Osteopathy*
EMP: 566
SQ FT: 95,000
SALES (est): 78.6MM
SALES (corp-wide): 323.8MM **Privately Held**
WEB: www.holzerclinic.com
SIC: 8011 8741 Physicians' office, including specialists; management services
PA: Holzer Health System
    100 Jackson Pike
    Gallipolis OH 45631
    740 446-5060

(G-11198)
HOLZER CLINIC LLC
100 Jackson Pike (45631-1560)
PHONE................................304 744-2300
Marietta Babayev, *Branch Mgr*

EMP: 112
SALES (corp-wide): 323.8MM **Privately Held**
SIC: 8011 Physical medicine, physician/surgeon
HQ: Holzer Clinic Llc
90 Jackson Pike
Gallipolis OH 45631
740 446-5411

(G-11199)
HOLZER CLINIC LLC
Also Called: Holzer Hospital
90 Jackson Pike (45631-1562)
PHONE....................................740 446-5412
Lamar Wyfe, *CEO*
EMP: 43
SALES (corp-wide): 323.8MM **Privately Held**
WEB: www.holzerclinic.com
SIC: 8011 7991 Clinic, operated by physicians; health club
HQ: Holzer Clinic Llc
90 Jackson Pike
Gallipolis OH 45631
740 446-5411

(G-11200)
HOLZER HEALTH SYSTEM (PA)
Also Called: Holzer Cnsld Hlth Systems
100 Jackson Pike (45631-1560)
PHONE....................................740 446-5060
Brent Saundrs, *President*
Lisa Halley, *Vice Pres*
Linda Stanley, *Financial Analy*
EMP: 35
SALES: 323.8MM **Privately Held**
SIC: 8062 General medical & surgical hospitals

(G-11201)
HOLZER HOSPITAL FOUNDATION (HQ)
Also Called: Holzer Medical Center
100 Jackson Pike (45631-1560)
PHONE....................................740 446-5000
Christopher T Meyer, *CEO*
Brent A Saunders, *Ch of Bd*
Michael R Canady, *Chief Mktg Ofcr*
EMP: 898
SQ FT: 254,000
SALES: 154.4MM
SALES (corp-wide): 323.8MM **Privately Held**
WEB: www.holzer.org
SIC: 8062 General medical & surgical hospitals
PA: Holzer Health System
100 Jackson Pike
Gallipolis OH 45631
740 446-5060

(G-11202)
HOLZER HOSPITAL FOUNDATION
90 Jackson Pike (45631-1560)
PHONE....................................740 446-5000
Kenneth Coughenour, *Branch Mgr*
EMP: 457
SALES (corp-wide): 323.8MM **Privately Held**
SIC: 8062 General medical & surgical hospitals
HQ: Holzer Hospital Foundation Inc
100 Jackson Pike
Gallipolis OH 45631
740 446-5000

(G-11203)
LOCAL 911 UNITED MINE WORKERS
5102 State Route 218 (45631-8906)
PHONE....................................740 256-6083
Allen Wauth, *President*
Mike Dammeter, *Vice Pres*
Bryan Wood, *Treasurer*
EMP: 40
SALES (est): 1.9MM **Privately Held**
SIC: 8631 Labor unions & similar labor organizations

(G-11204)
MEDI HOME HEALTH AGENCY INC
Also Called: Medi Home Care
412 2nd Ave (45631-1130)
PHONE....................................740 441-1779
Diana Harless, *Manager*
EMP: 25
SALES (corp-wide): 180.5MM **Privately Held**
SIC: 8082 Home health care services
HQ: Medi Home Health Agency Inc
105 Main St
Steubenville OH 43953
740 266-3977

(G-11205)
MRM CONSTRUCTION INC
110 Bellomy Dr (45631-8998)
PHONE....................................740 388-0079
Patricia Luckeydoo, *CEO*
EMP: 25
SQ FT: 3,000
SALES (est): 2.9MM **Privately Held**
SIC: 1799 Construction site cleanup

(G-11206)
OHIO VALLEY BANK COMPANY
Also Called: Inside Foodland
236 2nd Ave (45631)
PHONE....................................740 446-2168
Julia Slone, *Branch Mgr*
EMP: 60 **Publicly Held**
WEB: www.ovbc.com
SIC: 6022 State trust companies accepting deposits, commercial
HQ: The Ohio Valley Bank Company
420 3rd Ave
Gallipolis OH 45631
740 446-2631

(G-11207)
OHIO VALLEY BANK COMPANY (HQ)
420 3rd Ave (45631-1135)
P.O. Box 240 (45631-0240)
PHONE....................................740 446-2631
Thomas E Wiseman, *President*
Jeffrey E Smith, *Chairman*
Katrinka V Hart, *Exec VP*
E Richard Mahan, *Exec VP*
Larry E Miller II, *Exec VP*
EMP: 188
SALES: 51.3MM **Publicly Held**
WEB: www.ovbc.com
SIC: 6022 State commercial banks

(G-11208)
OHIO VALLEY BANK COMPANY
100 Jackson Pike (45631-1560)
PHONE....................................740 446-1646
Rebecca Nesbitt, *Director*
EMP: 27 **Publicly Held**
SIC: 6022 State trust companies accepting deposits, commercial
HQ: The Ohio Valley Bank Company
420 3rd Ave
Gallipolis OH 45631
740 446-2631

(G-11209)
OHIO VALLEY BANK COMPANY
143 3rd Ave (45631-1023)
PHONE....................................740 446-2631
Lawrencene Miller, *Senior VP*
EMP: 27 **Publicly Held**
SIC: 6022 State commercial banks
HQ: The Ohio Valley Bank Company
420 3rd Ave
Gallipolis OH 45631
740 446-2631

(G-11210)
OHIO VALLEY HOME HEALTH INC (PA)
Also Called: FAMILY HOME HEALTH PLUS
1480 Jackson Pike (45631-2602)
P.O. Box 274 (45631-0274)
PHONE....................................740 441-1393
Don Corbin, *CEO*
Michael Valley, *President*
EMP: 74
SALES: 3.5MM **Privately Held**
SIC: 8082 Home health care services

(G-11211)
PIERCETON TRUCKING CO INC
4311 State Route 160 (45631-9814)
PHONE....................................740 446-0114
Flem Meade, *Manager*
EMP: 35
SALES (corp-wide): 4.8MM **Privately Held**
SIC: 4212 Local trucking, without storage
PA: Pierceton Trucking Co Inc
10322 N Troyer Rd
Laketon IN 46943
260 982-2175

(G-11212)
REPUBLIC SERVICES INC
97 Hubbard Ave (45631-1920)
PHONE....................................800 331-0988
EMP: 34
SALES (corp-wide): 10B **Publicly Held**
SIC: 4953 Refuse collection & disposal services
PA: Republic Services, Inc.
18500 N Allied Way # 100
Phoenix AZ 85054
480 627-2700

(G-11213)
RES-CARE INC
240 3rd Ave (45631-1026)
PHONE....................................740 446-7549
Colleen Houck, *Sales Executive*
Roberta Vangundy, *Manager*
EMP: 65
SALES (corp-wide): 23.7B **Privately Held**
WEB: www.rescare.com
SIC: 8052 Home for the mentally retarded, with health care
HQ: Res-Care, Inc.
805 N Whittington Pkwy
Louisville KY 40222
502 394-2100

(G-11214)
RICK EPLION PAVING
7159 State Route 7 S (45631-8925)
P.O. Box 712, Proctorville (45669-0712)
PHONE....................................740 446-3000
Rick Eplion, *Owner*
EMP: 25
SALES: 3MM **Privately Held**
SIC: 1611 Surfacing & paving

(G-11215)
THOMAS DO-IT CENTER INC (PA)
Also Called: Thomas Rental
176 Mccormick Rd (45631-8745)
PHONE....................................740 446-2002
Jim Thomas, *President*
Lee Cyrus, *President*
Jay Hall, *Principal*
Marlene Hall, *Vice Pres*
▲ EMP: 85
SQ FT: 85,000
SALES (est): 12.4MM **Privately Held**
SIC: 5251 7359 2439 5211 Hardware; builders' hardware; equipment rental & leasing; lawn & garden equipment rental; trusses, wooden roof; lumber products

(G-11216)
USF HOLLAND INC
Also Called: USFreightways
95 Holland Dr (45631-8241)
PHONE....................................740 441-1200
Andy Koziel, *Branch Mgr*
EMP: 75
SALES (corp-wide): 5B **Publicly Held**
WEB: www.usfc.com
SIC: 4213 4212 Less-than-truckload (LTL) transport; local trucking, without storage
HQ: Usf Holland Llc
700 S Waverly Rd
Holland MI 49423
616 395-5000

(G-11217)
WOODLAND CENTERS INC (PA)
3086 State Route 160 (45631-8409)
PHONE....................................740 446-5500
Louella M Stover, *CFO*
Adrienne Fitzsimmons, *Psychologist*
Legea McAvena, *Manager*
Regina Smith, *Manager*
Anna King, *Supervisor*

EMP: 90
SQ FT: 18,000
SALES: 5.6MM **Privately Held**
SIC: 8093 Mental health clinic, outpatient

Galloway
Franklin County

(G-11218)
ALDO PERAZA
308 Eastcreek Dr (43119-8914)
PHONE....................................614 804-0403
Aldo Peraza, *President*
EMP: 60
SALES (est): 97.1K **Privately Held**
SIC: 7363 Truck driver services

(G-11219)
DEDICATED NURSING ASSOC INC
5672 W Broad St (43119-8127)
PHONE....................................877 411-8350
EMP: 44 **Privately Held**
SIC: 7361 7363 8051 Nurses' registry; medical help service; skilled nursing care facilities
PA: Dedicated Nursing Associates, Inc.
6536 State Route 22
Delmont PA 15626

(G-11220)
HEALTH CARE LOGISTICS INC
6106 Bausch Rd (43119-9382)
PHONE....................................800 848-1633
Susan Egelhoff, *President*
Rick Kochensparger, *Facilities Mgr*
Diana Starkey, *Accounts Mgr*
EMP: 80
SALES (corp-wide): 56.4MM **Privately Held**
SIC: 4789 Pipeline terminal facilities, independently operated
PA: Health Care Logistics, Inc.
450 Town St
Circleville OH 43113
740 477-1686

(G-11221)
JPMORGAN CHASE BANK NAT ASSN
5684 W Broad St (43119-8127)
PHONE....................................614 853-2999
Alicia Jones, *Manager*
EMP: 26
SALES (corp-wide): 131.4B **Publicly Held**
WEB: www.chase.com
SIC: 6029 Commercial banks
HQ: Jpmorgan Chase Bank, National Association
1111 Polaris Pkwy
Columbus OH 43240
614 436-3055

(G-11222)
MENTAL MEMORIAL GOLF COURSE
6005 Alkire Rd (43119-9088)
PHONE....................................614 645-8453
Guy Amicon, *Principal*
EMP: 40
SALES (est): 498.3K **Privately Held**
SIC: 7992 Public golf courses

(G-11223)
MIKES TRUCKING LTD
570 Plain City Grgsvlle (43119)
PHONE....................................614 879-8808
Terri Roberts, *Office Mgr*
Mike Culbertson,
Mary Culbertson,
EMP: 35
SALES (est): 5.1MM **Privately Held**
WEB: www.mikestrucking.com
SIC: 4212 Dump truck haulage

Gambier
Knox County

(G-11224)
**HOCHSTEDLER
CONSTRUCTION LTD**
24761 Dennis Church Rd (43022-8706)
PHONE................................740 427-4880
Edward Hochstedler, *President*
Jeremy Hochstedler, *Vice Pres*
Matthew Hochstedler, *Vice Pres*
Paul Hochstedler, *Vice Pres*
EMP: 35
SALES (est): 3.2MM **Privately Held**
SIC: 1521 7389 Single-family housing
construction;

(G-11225)
KENYON COLLEGE
Also Called: Kenyon Inn
100 W Wegan St (43022)
P.O. Box 273 (43022-0273)
PHONE................................740 427-2202
Tristen Haas, *Manager*
Lisa Train, *Asst Director*
EMP: 30
SALES (corp-wide): 124.3MM **Privately
Held**
WEB: www.kenyon.edu
SIC: 7011 8221 Hotels & motels; college,
except junior
PA: Kenyon College
1 Kenyon College
Gambier OH 43022
740 427-5000

(G-11226)
SMALL SAND & GRAVEL INC
10229 Killduff Rd (43022-9657)
P.O. Box 617 (43022-0617)
PHONE................................740 427-3130
Michael W Small, *President*
William T Small, *Treasurer*
Carol Small, *Admin Sec*
EMP: 35
SALES (est): 8.6MM **Privately Held**
SIC: 1442 Sand mining; gravel mining

(G-11227)
SMALLS ASPHALT PAVING INC
10229 Killduff Rd (43022-9657)
P.O. Box 552 (43022-0552)
PHONE................................740 427-4096
Robert E Small, *President*
Michael Small, *Vice Pres*
William T Small, *Treasurer*
Carol Small, *Admin Sec*
EMP: 25
SALES (est): 2.5MM **Privately Held**
SIC: 1771 2951 1611 Blacktop (asphalt)
work; asphalt paving mixtures & blocks;
highway & street construction

Garfield Heights
Cuyahoga County

(G-11228)
CLOCKWORK LOGISTICS INC
4765 E 131st St (44105-7131)
PHONE................................216 587-5371
Frank Ilkanich Jr, *President*
Steve Toth, *VP Admin*
EMP: 47
SQ FT: 3,500
SALES (est): 5.4MM **Privately Held**
WEB: www.cwlog.com
SIC: 4215 Package delivery, vehicular

Garrettsville
Portage County

(G-11229)
COMMUNITY EMS DISTRICT
10804 Forest St (44231-1008)
PHONE................................330 527-4100
Christopher Sanchez, *Exec Dir*
EMP: 25 EST: 1981

SALES (est): 1MM **Privately Held**
SIC: 8322 Emergency social services

(G-11230)
SKYLANE LLC
Also Called: Sky Lane Drive-Thru
8311 Windham St (44231-9406)
PHONE................................330 527-9999
Aaron King,
Rob Murray,
Tracy Murray,
Brittain Paul,
Matthew Paul,
EMP: 26
SQ FT: 120,000
SALES (est): 875.2K **Privately Held**
SIC: 5812 7933 Restaurant, family: chain;
bowling centers

(G-11231)
SUGARBUSH GOLF INC
Also Called: Sugarbush Golf Club
11186 State Route 88 (44231-9601)
PHONE................................330 527-4202
Mike Koval, *President*
Lilian M Koval, *Corp Secy*
EMP: 30
SALES (est): 1.4MM **Privately Held**
WEB: www.sugarbushgolfclub.com
SIC: 7992 Public golf courses

(G-11232)
**TLC HEALTH WELLNESS &
FITNESS**
1 Memory Ln (44231-9443)
PHONE................................330 527-4852
Annette Andrews, *Owner*
EMP: 25
SALES (est): 395.8K **Privately Held**
SIC: 7991 Health club

Gates Mills
Cuyahoga County

(G-11233)
**ARBOR REHABILITATION &
HEALTCR**
45125 Fairmount Blvd (44040)
P.O. Box 99 (44040-0099)
PHONE................................440 423-0206
Robert Vadas, *President*
Phil Stitts, *VP Finance*
Allison Collins, *Technology*
Cindy Hudson, *Director*
EMP: 275
SALES: 7MM **Privately Held**
WEB: www.arborrehab.com
SIC: 8322 Rehabilitation services

(G-11234)
CHAGRIN VALLEY HUNT CLUB
7620 Old Mill Rd (44040-9700)
P.O. Box 159 (44040-0159)
PHONE................................440 423-4414
Fred Floyd, *President*
EMP: 40
SQ FT: 7,463
SALES: 2.1MM **Privately Held**
WEB: www.chagrinvalleyhunt.com
SIC: 7997 Country club, membership

Geneva
Ashtabula County

(G-11235)
599 W MAIN CORPORATION
Also Called: Homestead
599 W Main St (44041-1252)
PHONE................................440 466-5901
Jamie Miller, *President*
EMP: 50
SALES (est): 2.4MM **Privately Held**
SIC: 8052 Home for the mentally retarded,
with health care

(G-11236)
A2 SERVICES LLC
Also Called: Geneva Pipeline
4749 N Ridge Rd E (44041-8293)
PHONE................................440 466-6611

Llevelyn Rhone,
EMP: 60
SALES (est): 9.5MM **Privately Held**
WEB: www.genevapipeline.com
SIC: 1542 Nonresidential construction

(G-11237)
BUILDING TECHNICIANS CORP
4500 Clay St (44041-8107)
PHONE................................440 466-1651
Ellen Cumpston, *President*
Larry Cumpston, *Corp Secy*
EMP: 25 EST: 1976
SQ FT: 6,000
SALES (est): 3.5MM **Privately Held**
SIC: 1761 Roofing contractor

(G-11238)
**COMMUNITY IMPROVEMENT
CORP**
44 N Forest St (44041-1371)
PHONE................................440 466-4675
Jim Pearson, *Manager*
EMP: 50 EST: 2001
SALES: 50.1K **Privately Held**
SIC: 1521 General remodeling, single-fam-
ily houses

(G-11239)
**CONTINING HLTHCARE SLTIONS
INC**
Also Called: Esther Marie Nursing Home
60 West St (44041-9723)
PHONE................................440 466-1181
Susan Knowson, *Owner*
EMP: 100
SALES (corp-wide): 7.9MM **Privately
Held**
WEB: www.nursinghomemanagement.com
SIC: 8051 Skilled nursing care facilities
PA: Continuing Healthcare Solutions, Inc.
7261 Engle Rd Ste 200
Middleburg Heights OH 44130
216 772-1105

(G-11240)
FERRANTE WINE FARM INC
558 Rte 307 (44041)
PHONE................................440 466-8466
Nicholas Ferrante, *President*
Nicholas Ferrante, *President*
Pete Ferrante, *Managing Dir*
Mary Jo Ferrante, *Principal*
Peter Ferrante, *Principal*
EMP: 40
SQ FT: 3,023
SALES (est): 2.4MM **Privately Held**
WEB: www.ferrantewinery.com
SIC: 0172 2084 5812 Grapes; wines; eat-
ing places

(G-11241)
**GENEVA AREA CITY SCHOOL
DST**
Also Called: Bus Garage
75 North Ave E (44041-1154)
PHONE................................440 466-2684
Charlotte Lenard, *Admin Sec*
EMP: 42
SALES (corp-wide): 26.2MM **Privately
Held**
SIC: 4151 School buses
PA: Geneva Area City Schools
135 S Eagle St
Geneva OH 44041
440 466-4831

(G-11242)
GENEVA AREA RECREATIONAL
Also Called: Gareat Sports Complex
1822 S Broadway (44041)
PHONE................................440 466-1002
Ronald W Clutter, *Ch of Bd*
EMP: 25
SQ FT: 750,000
SALES: 9.5MM **Privately Held**
SIC: 7997 Membership sports & recreation
clubs

(G-11243)
HUNTER REALTY INC
Also Called: Coldwell Banker
385 S Broadway (44041-1808)
PHONE................................440 466-9177
William Drenik, *Manager*

EMP: 25
SALES (corp-wide): 2.6MM **Privately
Held**
WEB: www.cbhunter.com
SIC: 6531 Real estate agent, residential
PA: Hunter Realty Inc
24600 Detroit Rd Ste 240
Westlake OH 44145
440 892-7040

(G-11244)
**NEIGHBORHOOD LOGISTICS CO
INC**
Also Called: Truckmen
5449 Bishop Rd (44041-9600)
PHONE................................440 466-0020
Jeff Jenks, *CEO*
Bruce Fleischmann, *President*
Julie Lefelhoc, *Corp Secy*
David Jewell, *Director*
▲ EMP: 34
SQ FT: 110,000
SALES (est): 9.1MM **Privately Held**
WEB: www.truckmen.com
SIC: 4225 4214 4212 General warehous-
ing & storage; local trucking with storage;
local trucking, without storage

(G-11245)
RAEANN INC
Also Called: Rae-Ann Geneva Skld
Nrsng/Rehb
839 W Main St (44041-1218)
PHONE................................440 466-5733
Beth Cheney, *Pub Rel Dir*
John Griffiths, *Manager*
EMP: 80
SQ FT: 12,000
SALES (corp-wide): 6.2MM **Privately
Held**
SIC: 8052 8051 Intermediate care facili-
ties; skilled nursing care facilities
PA: Raeann Inc

Cleveland OH 44135
440 871-5181

(G-11246)
TEGAM INC (PA)
10 Tegam Way (44041-1144)
PHONE................................440 466-6100
Andrew Brush, *CEO*
Adam Fleder, *President*
EMP: 43
SQ FT: 28,600
SALES (est): 9.1MM **Privately Held**
WEB: www.tegam.com
SIC: 3829 7629 Measuring & controlling
devices; electrical measuring instrument
repair & calibration

(G-11247)
THIRD DIMENSION INC (PA)
633 Pleasant Ave (44041-1176)
PHONE................................877 926-3223
Jeanette De Jesus, *President*
Mike Kelly, *General Mgr*
Louis De Jesus, *Corp Secy*
Kyle Dejesus, *Opers Mgr*
Karim Nejdi, *Accounts Mgr*
EMP: 50
SQ FT: 180,000
SALES (est): 26.7MM **Privately Held**
WEB: www.dimensionthird.com
SIC: 7389 5199 7336 Packaging & label-
ing services; packaging materials; graphic
arts & related design

(G-11248)
**UHHS-MEMORIAL HOSP OF
GENEVA**
870 W Main St (44041-1219)
PHONE................................440 466-1141
Joel Elconin, *Vice Pres*
Lisa Exl, *Human Res Dir*
Stephanie Cleversy, *Manager*
John Baron, *Director*
Lori Boyce, *Director*
EMP: 183
SQ FT: 56,391
SALES (est): 10.6MM **Privately Held**
SIC: 8062 General medical & surgical hos-
pitals

(G-11249)
VECTOR SECURITY INC
50 E Main St (44041-1347)
PHONE..................................440 466-7233
Christine Longley, *Branch Mgr*
EMP: 32
SALES (corp-wide): 422.7MM **Privately Held**
SIC: 7382 1731 Burglar alarm maintenance & monitoring; fire detection & burglar alarm systems specialization
HQ: Vector Security Inc.
   2000 Ericsson Dr Ste 250
   Warrendale PA 15086
   724 741-2200

(G-11250)
WASTE MANAGEMENT OHIO INC
4339 Tuttle Rd (44041-9231)
PHONE..................................440 285-6767
Jan McCombs, *Branch Mgr*
EMP: 49
SALES (corp-wide): 14.9B **Publicly Held**
SIC: 4953 Refuse systems
HQ: Waste Management Of Ohio, Inc.
   1700 N Broad St
   Fairborn OH 45324

Genoa
Ottawa County

(G-11251)
ACCELERANT TECHNOLOGIES LLC
Also Called: Accelerant Solutions
2257 N Manor Dr (43430-9755)
PHONE..................................419 236-8768
Larry Sanders, *President*
Gary Wylie, *Vice Pres*
Tyler Ball, *CFO*
EMP: 58
SQ FT: 2,000
SALES: 20MM **Privately Held**
WEB: www.acceleranttech.com
SIC: 8999 8742 8711 Nuclear consultant; management consulting services; energy conservation engineering

(G-11252)
CIMARRON EXPRESS INC
21611 State Route 51 W (43430-1245)
P.O. Box 185 (43430-0185)
PHONE..................................419 855-7713
Glenn Grady, *President*
James Shepperd, *Senior VP*
Gale Johnson, *Vice Pres*
Mike Nopper, *Transptn Dir*
Denise Hoyles, *CFO*
EMP: 65
SQ FT: 800
SALES: 25MM **Privately Held**
WEB: www.cimarronexpress.com
SIC: 4213 Contract haulers; automobiles, transport & delivery

(G-11253)
FIRST FEDERAL BANK OF MIDWEST
22020 Main St (43430)
PHONE..................................419 855-8326
Jennifer Creager, *Branch Mgr*
EMP: 61 **Publicly Held**
SIC: 6035 Federal savings & loan associations
HQ: First Federal Bank Of The Midwest
   601 Clinton St Ste 1
   Defiance OH 43512
   419 782-5015

(G-11254)
GENBANC
801 Main St (43430-1637)
P.O. Box 98 (43430-0098)
PHONE..................................419 855-8381
Martin P Sutter, *President*
Margaret Haar, *Assistant VP*
Jean Holcombe, *Assistant VP*
Patricia Kelley, *Assistant VP*
Rochelle Wheeler, *Assistant VP*
EMP: 50 **Privately Held**
SIC: 6712 Bank holding companies

(G-11255)
GENOA BANKING COMPANY (PA)
801 Main St (43430-1637)
P.O. Box 98 (43430-0098)
PHONE..................................419 855-8381
Martin Sutter, *President*
Rob Burkholder, *President*
Ron Gladieux, *Chairman*
Kristinna Clauson, *Assistant VP*
Barbara Fleitz, *Assistant VP*
EMP: 29
SQ FT: 10,000
SALES: 15.5MM **Privately Held**
WEB: www.genoabank.com
SIC: 6022 State trust companies accepting deposits, commercial

(G-11256)
GENOA LEGION POST 324
302 West St (43430)
PHONE..................................419 855-7049
Virgil Roecker, *President*
EMP: 30
SALES (est): 290.4K **Privately Held**
WEB: www.genoavetshome.us
SIC: 8641 Veterans' organization

(G-11257)
JAMES RECKER
Also Called: Recker Brothers
1446 Ottawa Rd (43430-9502)
PHONE..................................419 837-5378
James Recker, *Owner*
Jack Recker, *Partner*
EMP: 25
SALES (est): 654.9K **Privately Held**
SIC: 0171 Strawberry farm

(G-11258)
MCCLELLAN MANAGEMENT INC
Also Called: Genoa Care Center
300 Cherry St (43430-1823)
PHONE..................................419 855-7755
William Mc Clellan, *President*
Wade Noftz, *Director*
Josh Mc Clellan, *Administration*
EMP: 124
SQ FT: 20,000
SALES (est): 2.5MM **Privately Held**
SIC: 8051 8052 Convalescent home with continuous nursing care; intermediate care facilities

(G-11259)
MIKE GEORGE EXCAVATING
24366 W Hellwig Rd (43430-9720)
PHONE..................................419 855-4147
Mike George, *Owner*
EMP: 35
SALES (est): 1.2MM **Privately Held**
SIC: 1794 Excavation work

Georgetown
Brown County

(G-11260)
ADAMS & BROWN COUNTIES ECONOMI (PA)
406 W Plum St (45121-1056)
PHONE..................................937 378-6041
Alvin M Norris, *Director*
EMP: 230 EST: 1965
SQ FT: 10,000
SALES: 10.4MM **Privately Held**
SIC: 8399 Community action agency

(G-11261)
BROWN CNTY BD MNTAL RTARDATION
325 W State St Ste A2 (45121-1262)
PHONE..................................937 378-4891
Theresa Armstrong, *Principal*
Lena Bradford, *Principal*
EMP: 35
SQ FT: 100,000
SALES: 131.9K **Privately Held**
SIC: 8331 3993 2396 Sheltered workshop; signs & advertising specialties; automotive & apparel trimmings

(G-11262)
BROWN CNTY SNIOR CTZEN COUNCIL
505 N Main St (45121-1029)
PHONE..................................937 378-6603
Sue Brooks, *Director*
Conney Taylor, *Administration*
EMP: 50
SALES: 1.1MM **Privately Held**
SIC: 8322 Senior citizens' center or association

(G-11263)
BROWN CO ED SERVICE CENTER
9231b Hamer Rd (45121-1527)
PHONE..................................937 378-6118
James D Fraizer, *Superintendent*
Robin Tore, *Principal*
Stephanie Wagoner, *Supervisor*
Mike Roades, *Education*
EMP: 100
SALES: 4.7MM **Privately Held**
WEB: www.brown.k12.oh.us
SIC: 8211 8741 Specialty education; management services

(G-11264)
BROWN COUNTY ASPHALT INC
11254 Hamer Rd (45121-8840)
PHONE..................................937 446-2481
Thomas Sawyer, *President*
Andrew Sawyers, *Vice Pres*
Duane Sawyers, *Vice Pres*
Joseph Sawyers, *Vice Pres*
Connie Sawyer, *Treasurer*
EMP: 25 EST: 1976
SALES (est): 2.8MM **Privately Held**
SIC: 1771 Blacktop (asphalt) work

(G-11265)
CAHALL BROS INC (PA)
Also Called: John Deere Authorized Dealer
896 S Main St (45121-8408)
PHONE..................................937 378-4439
Calvin H Cahall, *President*
Roland Cahall, *Corp Secy*
Kyle Cahall, *Vice Pres*
EMP: 25
SQ FT: 43,000
SALES (est): 7.1MM **Privately Held**
WEB: www.cahallbrosinc.com
SIC: 5083 Farm implements

(G-11266)
CHARLES D MCINTOSH TRCKG INC
669 E State St (45121-9323)
P.O. Box 21399 (45121-0399)
PHONE..................................937 378-3803
Donald Layman, *President*
EMP: 40 EST: 1967
SALES: 2MM **Privately Held**
SIC: 4212 Local trucking, without storage

(G-11267)
COUNTY OF BROWN
Also Called: Brown County Engineers Office
25 Veterans Blvd (45121-7417)
PHONE..................................937 378-6456
James Beasley, *Branch Mgr*
EMP: 35 **Privately Held**
WEB: www.browncohd.org
SIC: 8711 Engineering services
PA: Brown County
   800 Mount Orab Pike
   Georgetown OH 45121
   937 378-3956

(G-11268)
COUNTY OF BROWN
Also Called: Department of Human Services
775 Mount Orab Pike (45121-1123)
P.O. Box 21169 (45121-0169)
PHONE..................................937 378-6104
David M Sharp, *Branch Mgr*
EMP: 45 **Privately Held**
WEB: www.browncohd.org
SIC: 8322 9111 Public welfare center; county supervisors' & executives' offices
PA: Brown County
   800 Mount Orab Pike
   Georgetown OH 45121
   937 378-3956

(G-11269)
COVENANT CARE OHIO INC
Also Called: Villa Georgetown
8065 Dr Faul Rd (45121-8811)
PHONE..................................937 378-0188
Sandra Leedy, *Manager*
Mike Baker, *Director*
Janice Thompson, *Director*
Melissa Whisman, *Food Svc Dir*
EMP: 75 **Privately Held**
WEB: www.villageorgetown.com
SIC: 8051 Skilled nursing care facilities
HQ: Covenant Care Ohio, Inc.
   27071 Aliso Creek Rd # 100
   Aliso Viejo CA 92656
   949 349-1200

(G-11270)
DAVITA INC
458 Home St (45121-1408)
PHONE..................................615 341-6311
James Hilger, *Branch Mgr*
EMP: 26 **Publicly Held**
SIC: 8092 Kidney dialysis centers
PA: Davita Inc.
   2000 16th St
   Denver CO 80202

(G-11271)
GEORGETOWN LIFE SQUAD
301 S Main St Unit 1 (45121-1500)
P.O. Box 21184 (45121-0184)
PHONE..................................937 378-3082
Brian Dutlinger, *Director*
Anita McKenzie, *Admin Sec*
EMP: 30
SALES (est): 272.5K **Privately Held**
SIC: 4119 Ambulance service

(G-11272)
HEALTHSOURCE OF OHIO INC
Also Called: Southern Ohio Health
631 E State St (45121-1437)
PHONE..................................937 392-4381
Tammy Thackston, *Office Mgr*
EMP: 36
SALES (corp-wide): 47.8MM **Privately Held**
SIC: 8011 Pediatrician; internal medicine, physician/surgeon
PA: Healthsource Of Ohio, Inc.
   5400 Dupont Cir Ste A
   Milford OH 45150
   513 576-7700

(G-11273)
RELIABLE TRNSP SOLUTIONS LLC
Also Called: RTS
642 E State St (45121-9317)
P.O. Box 507, Amelia (45102-0507)
PHONE..................................937 378-2700
Ben Bird, *COO*
Lucas Brown,
Garry Fletcher,
EMP: 47
SQ FT: 5,000
SALES (est): 21.2MM **Privately Held**
SIC: 4731 Transportation agents & brokers

(G-11274)
RUMPKE WASTE INC
9427 Beyers Rd (45121-9301)
PHONE..................................937 378-4126
Ronda Yates, *Manager*
EMP: 55 **Privately Held**
SIC: 4953 4212 Refuse collection & disposal services; local trucking, without storage
HQ: Rumpke Waste, Inc.
   10795 Hughes Rd
   Cincinnati OH 45251
   513 851-0122

(G-11275)
SOUTHWEST HEALTHCARE OF BROWN
Also Called: Southwest Regional Medical Ctr
425 Home St (45121-1407)
P.O. Box 62609, Cincinnati (45262-0609)
PHONE..................................937 378-7800
Kathy Wolf, *Executive Asst*
EMP: 74 EST: 1952
SQ FT: 120,000

GEOGRAPHIC

SALES: 25.2MM **Privately Held**
SIC: 8062 General medical & surgical hospitals

Germantown
Montgomery County

(G-11276)
ASTORIA HEALTHCARE GROUP LLC
Also Called: ASTORIA HEALTH & REHAB CENTER
300 Astoria Rd (45327-1712)
PHONE.................................937 855-2363
George S Repchick, *President*
William I Weisberg, *Vice Pres*
EMP: 364
SALES: 3.6MM
SALES (corp-wide): 157.7MM **Privately Held**
SIC: 8051 Skilled nursing care facilities
PA: Saber Healthcare Group, L.L.C.
26691 Richmond Rd Frnt
Bedford OH 44146
216 292-5706

(G-11277)
SCHOOL TRANSPORTATION
59 Peffley St (45327-1021)
PHONE.................................937 855-3897
Rick Wharton, *General Mgr*
Sherry Parr, *Superintendent*
Frances Wagner, *Manager*
EMP: 50
SALES (est): 102K **Privately Held**
SIC: 4789 Transportation services

Gibsonburg
Sandusky County

(G-11278)
GIBSONBURG HEALTH LLC
Also Called: Windsor Lane Health Care
355 Windsor Ln (43431-1446)
PHONE.................................419 637-2104
Jack Hereth, *Mng Member*
Angela Ickes, *Food Svc Dir*
EMP: 110
SALES (est): 6MM **Privately Held**
SIC: 8051 Skilled nursing care facilities

(G-11279)
STOUT LORI CLEANING & SUCH
503 N Main St (43431-1113)
PHONE.................................419 637-7644
Lori Stout, *Owner*
EMP: 40
SALES (est): 717K **Privately Held**
SIC: 7349 7359 Building cleaning service; home cleaning & maintenance equipment rental services

(G-11280)
WESTFIELD ELECTRIC INC
2995 State Route 51 (43431-9710)
P.O. Box 93 (43431-0093)
PHONE.................................419 862-0078
Sheri M Busdeker, *CEO*
Thomas R Busdeker, *President*
Brian Freeman, *Vice Pres*
Mark Younker, *Project Mgr*
Monica Haney, *Admin Asst*
EMP: 35
SQ FT: 10,000
SALES (est): 5MM **Privately Held**
SIC: 1731 5063 General electrical contractor; electrical construction materials

Girard
Trumbull County

(G-11281)
AIM INTEGRATED LOGISTICS INC
Also Called: NationaLease
1500 Trumbull Ave (44420-3453)
PHONE.................................330 759-0438
Thomas J Fleming, *President*

EMP: 400
SALES (est): 46.8MM
SALES (corp-wide): 291.1MM **Privately Held**
WEB: www.aimnationalease.com
SIC: 4212 7513 8741 Truck rental with drivers; truck leasing, without drivers; management services
PA: Aim Leasing Company
1500 Trumbull Ave
Girard OH 44420
330 759-0438

(G-11282)
AIM LEASING COMPANY (PA)
Also Called: NationaLease
1500 Trumbull Ave (44420-3453)
PHONE.................................330 759-0438
Thomas Fleming, *President*
David Gurska, *President*
Colin Szitas, *Regional Mgr*
Rudy Corpus, *Business Mgr*
Hal Luebbe, *Business Mgr*
EMP: 60
SQ FT: 10,000
SALES (est): 291.1MM **Privately Held**
WEB: www.aimnationalease.com
SIC: 7513 7538 4212 5983 Truck leasing, without drivers; general truck repair; truck rental with drivers; fuel oil dealers

(G-11283)
BOARDMAN MEDICAL SUPPLY CO (HQ)
Also Called: Innovative Concept
300 N State St (44420-2595)
PHONE.................................330 545-6700
Felix S Savon, *President*
Robin S Ivany, *Vice Pres*
Christine E Savon, *Treasurer*
▲ EMP: 130
SQ FT: 3,400
SALES (est): 39.1MM **Privately Held**
WEB: www.boardmanmedicalsupply.com
SIC: 5999 7352 Hospital equipment & supplies; medical equipment rental
PA: Sateri Home Inc
7246 Ronjoy Pl
Youngstown OH 44512
330 758-8106

(G-11284)
CINTAS CORPORATION NO 2
1061 Trumbull Ave (44420-3484)
PHONE.................................440 746-7777
EMP: 88
SALES (corp-wide): 6.4B **Publicly Held**
SIC: 7218 Industrial uniform supply
HQ: Cintas Corporation No. 2
6800 Cintas Blvd
Mason OH 45040

(G-11285)
COMDOC INC
6790 Belmont Ave (44420-1306)
PHONE.................................330 539-4822
Syl Frazzini, *Manager*
EMP: 50
SALES (corp-wide): 9.8B **Publicly Held**
SIC: 5044 Photocopy machines
HQ: Comdoc, Inc.
3458 Massillon Rd
Uniontown OH 44685
330 896-2346

(G-11286)
CREEKSIDE GOLF DOME
1300 N State St (44420-3642)
PHONE.................................330 545-5000
Tonny Latell, *President*
Jim St George, *President*
Todd Lattell, *Principal*
Paul Latell, *Corp Secy*
EMP: 25
SALES (est): 704.9K **Privately Held**
WEB: www.creeksidegolfdome.com
SIC: 7999 Golf driving range; miniature golf course operation

(G-11287)
FIRE FOE CORP
999 Trumbull Ave (44420-3400)
PHONE.................................330 759-9834
Earnest A Nicholas, *President*
Thomas Spain, *Safety Dir*
Mary Nicholas, *Admin Sec*

EMP: 35
SQ FT: 18,000
SALES: 4.5MM **Privately Held**
WEB: www.firefoe.com
SIC: 3569 7699 Sprinkler systems, fire: automatic; fire control (military) equipment repair

(G-11288)
INDUSTRIAL INSUL COATINGS LLC
142 E 2nd St (44420-2905)
P.O. Box 154 (44420-0154)
PHONE.................................800 506-1399
Richard Marchese,
Edward Zajac,
John Zajac,
EMP: 28
SALES: 5.5MM **Privately Held**
SIC: 1742 7389 Insulation, buildings;

(G-11289)
INTERSTATE SHREDDING LLC
27 Furnace Ln (44420-3214)
P.O. Box 29 (44420-0029)
PHONE.................................330 545-5477
Gary Clayman, *Mng Member*
Michael Clayman,
▲ EMP: 40
SQ FT: 14,374
SALES (est): 9.1MM **Privately Held**
SIC: 4953 Recycling, waste materials

(G-11290)
JPMORGAN CHASE BANK NAT ASSN
43 W Liberty St (44420-2842)
PHONE.................................330 545-2551
Gene Tropf, *Manager*
EMP: 26
SALES (corp-wide): 131.4B **Publicly Held**
WEB: www.chase.com
SIC: 6021 National commercial banks
HQ: Jpmorgan Chase Bank, National Association
1111 Polaris Pkwy
Columbus OH 43240
614 436-3055

(G-11291)
JUNIOR ACHVMENT MHNING VLY INC
1601 Motor Inn Dr Ste 305 (44420-2483)
PHONE.................................330 539-5268
Michele Merkel, *President*
Brian Hoopes, *Chairman*
Kevin Murphy, *Admin Sec*
EMP: 30
SQ FT: 1,200
SALES: 424.7K **Privately Held**
SIC: 8641 Educator's association

(G-11292)
K & M CONTRACTING OHIO INC
5635 Sampson Dr (44420-3510)
P.O. Box 528, Vienna (44473-0528)
PHONE.................................330 759-1090
Kristenlynn Chizmar, *President*
EMP: 35
SQ FT: 2,200
SALES (est): 13.9MM **Privately Held**
SIC: 5082 General construction machinery & equipment

(G-11293)
KEYSTONE AUTOMOTIVE INDS INC
1282 Trumbull Ave Ste C (44420-3475)
PHONE.................................330 759-8019
Marty Grzybowski, *Manager*
EMP: 27
SALES (corp-wide): 11.8B **Publicly Held**
WEB: www.kool-vue.com
SIC: 5013 Automotive supplies & parts
HQ: Keystone Automotive Industries, Inc.
5846 Crossings Blvd
Antioch TN 37013
615 781-5200

(G-11294)
MAHONING COUNTRY CLUB INC
710 E Liberty St (44420-2310)
PHONE.................................330 545-2517
John Ezzo, *President*

Dave Ezzo, *Vice Pres*
Susan Sigulee, *Admin Sec*
EMP: 30
SQ FT: 50,000
SALES (est): 1.4MM **Privately Held**
WEB: www.mahoningcountryclub.com
SIC: 5812 7992 5941 Eating places; public golf courses; sporting goods & bicycle shops

(G-11295)
OHIO MACHINERY CO
Also Called: Caterpillar Authorized Dealer
1 Ohio Machinery Blvd (44420-3198)
PHONE.................................330 530-9010
Tim Brickner, *Sales Staff*
Bernice Tkach, *Sales Executive*
Tim Wagner, *Branch Mgr*
Glen Smith, *Manager*
Michael Nash, *Manager*
EMP: 50
SQ FT: 10,000
SALES (corp-wide): 222.7MM **Privately Held**
WEB: www.enginesnow.com
SIC: 7699 5082 7353 Construction equipment repair; general construction machinery & equipment; heavy construction equipment rental
PA: Ohio Machinery Co.
3993 E Royalton Rd
Broadview Heights OH 44147
440 526-6200

(G-11296)
OLD DOMINION FREIGHT LINE INC
1730 N State St (44420-1026)
PHONE.................................330 545-8628
Dave Robert, *Manager*
EMP: 48
SQ FT: 960
SALES (corp-wide): 4B **Publicly Held**
WEB: www.odfl.com
SIC: 4213 Less-than-truckload (LTL) transport
PA: Old Dominion Freight Line Inc
500 Old Dominion Way
Thomasville NC 27360
336 889-5000

(G-11297)
OMNI MANOR INC (PA)
101 W Liberty St (44420-2844)
PHONE.................................330 545-1550
John Masternick, *President*
Leo Grimes, *Vice Pres*
Kenneth James, *CFO*
Dorothy Masternick, *Treasurer*
Marci Craig, *Human Res Dir*
EMP: 200
SALES: 57.8K **Privately Held**
SIC: 8051 Convalescent home with continuous nursing care

(G-11298)
PRISMA INTEGRATION CORP
Also Called: Premier Integration
50 Harry St (44420-1709)
PHONE.................................330 545-8690
Richard Deeds, *Principal*
Dave Stierheim, *Electrical Engi*
Mark Cvetkovich, *Manager*
EMP: 29
SALES (est): 4.9MM **Privately Held**
SIC: 8711 Professional engineer

(G-11299)
RICKS HAIR CENTER
27 Churchill Rd (44420-1864)
PHONE.................................330 545-5120
Richard Calve, *Principal*
EMP: 25
SALES (est): 194.6K **Privately Held**
SIC: 7241 Barber shops

(G-11300)
SOFT TOUCH WOOD LLC
Also Called: Soft Tuch Furn Repr Rfinishing
1560 S State St (44420-3315)
PHONE.................................330 545-4204
Terry Chudakoff, *President*
Megan Vickers, *Vice Pres*
Tony Peluso, *Engineer*
Bob Leer, *Manager*
EMP: 40

SQ FT: 5,000
SALES (est): 2MM **Privately Held**
WEB: www.softtouchwood.com
SIC: **7641** 2531 Furniture refinishing; public building & related furniture

(G-11301)
STANDARD OIL COMPANY
Also Called: Dunkin' Donuts
2720 Salt Springs Rd (44420-3147)
PHONE..........................330 530-8049
Kenda Learn, *Manager*
EMP: 25
SALES (corp-wide): 240.2B **Privately Held**
WEB: www.crystal-enterprise.com
SIC: **5541** 7542 5411 5461 Filling stations, gasoline; carwash, automatic; convenience stores; bakeries
HQ: The Standard Oil Company
4101 Winfield Rd Ste 100
Warrenville IL 60555
630 836-5000

(G-11302)
UNITED PARCEL SERVICE INC OH
Also Called: UPS
800 Trumbull Ave (44420-3445)
PHONE..........................330 545-0177
Paul Hammond, *Manager*
Paul Saban, *Manager*
EMP: 209
SALES (corp-wide): 71.8B **Publicly Held**
WEB: www.upsscs.com
SIC: **4215** Parcel delivery, vehicular
HQ: United Parcel Service, Inc. (Oh)
55 Glenlake Pkwy
Atlanta GA 30328
404 828-6000

(G-11303)
UNIVERSAL DEVELOPMENT MGT INC (PA)
Also Called: Howard Johnson
1607 Motor Inn Dr Ste 1 (44420-2496)
PHONE..........................330 759-7017
Ronald R Anderson, *President*
Brian Anderson, *Exec VP*
Harold J Anderson, *Vice Pres*
EMP: 30 EST: 1973
SQ FT: 12,000
SALES (est): 8.9MM **Privately Held**
SIC: **6513** 1542 Apartment building operators; nonresidential construction

(G-11304)
VALLEY ELECTRICAL CNSLD INC
Also Called: Vec
977 Tibbetts Wick Rd (44420-1133)
PHONE..........................330 539-4044
Rex Ferry, *President*
Mary Ferry, *Corp Secy*
Brandon Davies, *COO*
Jeff Barber, *Exec VP*
Sharon Brown, *Exec VP*
EMP: 135
SQ FT: 17,200
SALES: 18.9MM **Privately Held**
WEB: www.vecohio.com
SIC: **1731** General electrical contractor

(G-11305)
VEC INC
977 Tibbetts Wick Rd (44420-1133)
PHONE..........................330 539-4044
Rex A Ferry, *President*
Keith Frederick, *Superintendent*
Jeff Barber, *Vice Pres*
Mark Waid, *Project Mgr*
Joe Wright, *Project Mgr*
EMP: 50 EST: 1965
SQ FT: 8,000
SALES: 71MM **Privately Held**
WEB: www.evetselectric.com
SIC: **1731** General electrical contractor

(G-11306)
YOUNGSTOWN WINDOW CLEANING CO
1057 Trumbull Ave Ste G (44420-3489)
PHONE..........................330 743-3880
Steven Altman, *President*
Sandra Altman, *President*

Carol Altmn, *Vice Pres*
EMP: 150
SQ FT: 12,000
SALES (est): 2.8MM **Privately Held**
SIC: **7349** Janitorial service, contract basis; window cleaning

Glandorf
Putnam County

(G-11307)
ST RITAS MEDICAL CENTER
Also Called: Catholic Health Partners
601 Us 224 (45848)
P.O. Box 100 (45848-0100)
PHONE..........................419 538-6288
Karen Zorst, *Manager*
EMP: 50
SALES (corp-wide): 4.7B **Privately Held**
SIC: **8062** General medical & surgical hospitals
HQ: Mercy Health - St. Rita's Medical Center, Llc
730 W Market St
Lima OH 45801
419 227-3361

Glenford
Perry County

(G-11308)
PIONEER SANDS LLC
Also Called: Glassrock Plant
2446 State Route 204 (43739)
PHONE..........................740 659-2241
Wayn Dailey, *Manager*
EMP: 40
SALES (corp-wide): 9.4B **Publicly Held**
SIC: **3295** 1446 Minerals, ground or treated; industrial sand
HQ: Pioneer Sands Llc
5205 N O Connor Blvd # 200
Irving TX 75039
972 444-9001

Glouster
Athens County

(G-11309)
HOCKING COLLEGE ADDC
19234 Taylor Ridge Rd (45732-9258)
PHONE..........................740 541-2221
Larry Sisson, *Owner*
EMP: 40
SALES (est): 245.6K **Privately Held**
SIC: **8322** Drug abuse counselor, nontreatment

(G-11310)
HOCKINGTHENSPERRY CMNTY ACTION (PA)
3 Cardaras Dr (45732-8011)
P.O. Box 220 (45732-0220)
PHONE..........................740 767-4500
Teresa Cline Scurlock, *Opers Staff*
Lisa Limo, *Opers-Prdtn-Mfg*
Scott Beatty, *Sales Staff*
Doug Stanley, *Exec Dir*
Douglas Stanley, *Exec Dir*
EMP: 200 EST: 1966
SQ FT: 7,400
SALES: 21.5MM **Privately Held**
SIC: **8399** 8331 8322 Community action agency; job training & vocational rehabilitation services; individual & family services

(G-11311)
U S ARMY CORPS OF ENGINEERS
23560 Jenkins Dam Rd (45732-9727)
PHONE..........................740 767-3527
EMP: 66 **Publicly Held**
SIC: **8711** Engineering Services
HQ: U S Army Corps Of Engineers
441 G Street Nw
Washington DC 20314
804 435-9362

Gnadenhutten
Tuscarawas County

(G-11312)
STOCKER SAND & GRAVEL CO (PA)
Rr 36 (44629)
PHONE..........................740 254-4635
Bill Stocker, *President*
Jeffrey Stocker, *President*
Thomas Stocker, *Corp Secy*
Bryan Stocker, *Vice Pres*
Shane Casimir, *Manager*
EMP: 30 EST: 1933
SQ FT: 3,000
SALES (est): 2.2MM **Privately Held**
SIC: **1442** 3271 Common sand mining; gravel mining; blocks, concrete or cinder: standard

Goshen
Clermont County

(G-11313)
NORTHERN PLUMBING SYSTEMS
1708 State Route 28 (45122-9754)
PHONE..........................513 831-5111
Timothy Moss,
Steward Moss Jr,
EMP: 31
SALES (est): 3.6MM **Privately Held**
SIC: **1711** Plumbing contractors

(G-11314)
PETERMAN
Also Called: School Bus Garage
6757 Linton Rd (45122-9402)
PHONE..........................513 722-2229
Janet Wilson, *Principal*
EMP: 40
SALES (est): 925.2K **Privately Held**
WEB: www.peterman.com
SIC: **4151** School buses

(G-11315)
SDR SERVICES LLC
2109 State Route 28 B (45122-9561)
PHONE..........................513 625-0695
Amber Stephens, *CEO*
Greg Pilot, *CFO*
EMP: 34
SALES (est): 1.4MM **Privately Held**
SIC: **7631** Jewelry repair services

Grafton
Lorain County

(G-11316)
CHEMICAL BANK
351 Main St (44044-1203)
PHONE..........................440 926-2191
Gretchan Francis, *Branch Mgr*
EMP: 39
SALES (corp-wide): 924.5MM **Publicly Held**
SIC: **6035** Federal savings & loan associations
HQ: Chemical Bank
333 E Main St
Midland MI 48640
989 631-9200

(G-11317)
JOSEPH RUSSO
Also Called: Eaton Tire & Auto Parts
12044 Island Rd (44044-9538)
PHONE..........................440 748-2690
Joseph Russo, *Owner*
EMP: 26
SQ FT: 30,000

SALES (est): 1.7MM **Privately Held**
WEB: www.josephrusso.com
SIC: **5531** 5013 5014 7538 Automotive parts; automotive tires; automotive supplies & parts; tires & tubes; general automotive repair shops

(G-11318)
M P & A FIBERS INC
1024 Commerce Dr (44044-1277)
PHONE..........................440 926-1074
Bill Crosby, *President*
EMP: 35
SALES (est): 1.1MM **Privately Held**
SIC: **7389** Packaging & labeling services

(G-11319)
PINE BROOK GOLF CLUB INC
11043 Durkee Rd (44044-9108)
PHONE..........................440 748-2939
EMP: 30
SQ FT: 4,800
SALES (est): 646.7K **Privately Held**
SIC: **7992** 5812 5941 Public Golf Course Catering Facilities Snack Bar And Pro Shop

(G-11320)
ROSS CONSOLIDATED CORP (PA)
36790 Giles Rd (44044-9125)
PHONE..........................440 748-5800
Maureen Cromling, *President*
EMP: 70
SQ FT: 3,008
SALES (est): 65.2MM **Privately Held**
SIC: **4953** 4212 8741 Incinerator operation; local trucking, without storage; management services

(G-11321)
ROSS INCINERATION SERVICES INC
36790 Giles Rd (44044-9125)
PHONE..........................440 366-2000
Arthur Hargate, *CEO*
Maureen M Cromling, *Ch of Bd*
James Larson, *President*
Pat Lawson, *Vice Pres*
Joe Ferritto, *Project Mgr*
▼ EMP: 115 EST: 1981
SALES (est): 29.1MM
SALES (corp-wide): 65.2MM **Privately Held**
SIC: **4953** Incinerator operation
PA: Ross Consolidated Corp
36790 Giles Rd
Grafton OH 44044
440 748-5800

(G-11322)
ROSS TRANSPORTATION SVCS INC
36790 Giles Rd (44044-9125)
PHONE..........................440 748-5900
William E Cromling II, *President*
Joe Calderoni, *Sales Staff*
EMP: 250 EST: 1981
SALES (est): 32.1MM
SALES (corp-wide): 65.2MM **Privately Held**
WEB: www.rosstransportation.com
SIC: **4213** Contract haulers
PA: Ross Consolidated Corp
36790 Giles Rd
Grafton OH 44044
440 748-5800

Grand Rapids
Wood County

(G-11323)
4 PAWS SAKE INC
13244 Neowash Rd (43522-9657)
PHONE..........................419 304-7139
Cindy Smith, *President*
Linda Boyle, *Vice Pres*
EMP: 50
SALES: 13.2K **Privately Held**
SIC: **0752** Grooming services, pet & animal specialties

(G-11324)
AE ELECTRIC INC
T483 County Road 1 (43522-9507)
P.O. Box 2744, Whitehouse (43571-0744)
PHONE.................................419 392-8468
Ken Bialecki, *President*
EMP: 25
SALES (est): 1.5MM **Privately Held**
SIC: 1731 Electrical work

(G-11325)
HALL NAZARETH INC
21211 W State Route 65 (43522-9818)
PHONE.................................419 832-2900
Robert Bettinger, *Admin Sec*
EMP: 100
SALES (est): 6.9MM **Privately Held**
WEB: www.nazarethhall.com
SIC: 6512 7299 Auditorium & hall operation; wedding chapel, privately operated

(G-11326)
HERTZFELD POULTRY FARMS INC
15799 Milton Rd (43522-9761)
PHONE.................................419 832-2070
Dave Hertzfeld, *Owner*
EMP: 80
SALES (est): 7.5MM
SALES (corp-wide): 6MM **Privately Held**
WEB: www.hpfeggs.com
SIC: 0191 0751 0119 General farms, primarily crop; poultry services; popcorn farm
PA: Hertzfeld Poultry Farms, Inc.
8525 Schadel Rd
Waterville OH

(G-11327)
KERR HOUSE INC
17777 Beaver St (43522-9496)
P.O. Box 363 (43522-0363)
PHONE.................................419 832-1733
Fax: 419 832-4303
EMP: 30
SQ FT: 10,000
SALES (est): 920K **Privately Held**
SIC: 7991 7231 Physical Fitness Facility Beauty Shop

(G-11328)
PIONEER HI-BRED INTL INC
15180 Henry Wood Rd (43522-9772)
PHONE.................................419 748-8051
Scott Millikan, *Manager*
EMP: 35
SQ FT: 6,000
SALES (corp-wide): 85.9B **Publicly Held**
WEB: www.pioneer.com
SIC: 5191 5153 2075 2041 Seeds: field, garden & flower; corn; soybeans; soybean oil mills; flour & other grain mill products
HQ: Pioneer Hi-Bred International, Inc.
7100 Nw 62nd Ave
Johnston IA 50131
515 535-3200

(G-11329)
RAPIDS NURSING HOMES INC
Also Called: Grand Rapids Care Center
24201 W 3rd St (43522-8702)
PHONE.................................216 292-5706
Robert Tebeau, *President*
Ernest Tebeau, *Corp Secy*
Ronald Tebeau, *Vice Pres*
EMP: 50
SALES (est): 2.1MM **Privately Held**
SIC: 8051 Skilled nursing care facilities

(G-11330)
SABER HEALTHCARE GROUP LLC
Also Called: Grand Rapids Care Center
24201 W 3rd St (43522-8702)
PHONE.................................419 484-1111
Natasha Bailey, *Administration*
EMP: 50
SALES (corp-wide): 157.7MM **Privately Held**
SIC: 8051 Skilled nursing care facilities
PA: Saber Healthcare Group, L.L.C.
26691 Richmond Rd Frnt
Bedford OH 44146
216 292-5706

Grand River
Lake County

(G-11331)
101 RIVER INC
Also Called: Grand River Seafood Supply
101 River St (44045-8212)
P.O. Box 120 (44045-0120)
PHONE.................................440 352-6343
Gerald Powell, *President*
Marilyn Merker, *Office Mgr*
Jerry Powell, *Executive*
EMP: 50
SQ FT: 7,000
SALES (est): 2MM **Privately Held**
WEB: www.101riverviews.com
SIC: 5812 5146 Steak & barbecue restaurants; fish & seafoods

(G-11332)
JED INDUSTRIES INC
320 River St (44045-8214)
P.O. Box 369 (44045-0369)
PHONE.................................440 639-9973
Donald Nye, *President*
EMP: 25
SQ FT: 27,000
SALES (est): 3.7MM **Privately Held**
WEB: www.jedindustries.com
SIC: 3599 5084 Machine & other job shop work; industrial machinery & equipment

(G-11333)
OSBORNE MATERIALS COMPANY (PA)
1 Williams St (44045-8253)
P.O. Box 248 (44045-0248)
PHONE.................................440 357-7026
Harold T Larned, *President*
Gary D Bradler, *President*
▼ **EMP:** 41
SQ FT: 2,500
SALES (est): 7.1MM **Privately Held**
SIC: 1442 Sand mining; gravel mining

Granville
Licking County

(G-11334)
BIG O REFUSE INC
1919 Lancaster Rd Ste B (43023-9417)
P.O. Box 625, New Lexington (43764-0625)
PHONE.................................740 344-7544
Sherman Adkins Sr, *President*
Ralph Adkins Sr, *Vice Pres*
EMP: 30
SALES (est): 5.1MM **Privately Held**
SIC: 4953 Rubbish collection & disposal; refuse collection & disposal services

(G-11335)
BUXTON INN INC
313 Broadway E (43023-1307)
PHONE.................................740 587-0001
Audrey V Orr, *Vice Pres*
Orville O Orr, *Manager*
EMP: 40
SQ FT: 20,000
SALES (est): 1.6MM **Privately Held**
WEB: www.buxtoninn.com
SIC: 5812 7011 Eating places; hotels

(G-11336)
CENTRAL OHIO GERIATRICS LLC
590 Newark Granville Rd (43023-1436)
PHONE.................................614 530-4077
John Weigand, *CEO*
EMP: 36 **EST:** 2009
SALES (est): 432.6K **Privately Held**
SIC: 8011 Primary care medical clinic

(G-11337)
CHESROWN OLDSMOBILE CADILLAC
Also Called: Chesrown Cadillac
371 Bryn Du Dr (43023-1512)
PHONE.................................740 366-7373
David T Chesrown, *President*
Janet Chesrown, *Corp Secy*
EMP: 25
SQ FT: 25,000
SALES (est): 6MM **Privately Held**
WEB: www.chesrownnewark.com
SIC: 5511 7549 Automobiles, new & used; high performance auto repair & service

(G-11338)
CLGT SOLUTIONS LLC
1670 Columbus Rd Ste C (43023-1232)
PHONE.................................740 920-4795
Frank Marois, *President*
Francis Marois, *Mng Member*
Ronnie Chaney,
Ann Graff,
Martin Graff,
EMP: 39
SQ FT: 150
SALES: 6MM **Privately Held**
WEB: www.clgtsolutions.com
SIC: 7389 8748 8742 Translation services; testing service, educational or personnel; management consulting services

(G-11339)
COUNTRY GARDENS
Also Called: Facklers
2326 Newark Granville Rd (43023-9290)
PHONE.................................740 522-8810
George Fackler, *CEO*
Danny Ghiloni, *Vice Pres*
EMP: 40
SALES (est): 837.8K **Privately Held**
SIC: 0781 Landscape services

(G-11340)
CRISPIN IRON & METAL CO LLC
190 Victoria Dr (43023-9106)
PHONE.................................740 616-6213
Todd Londot,
EMP: 25
SALES (est): 1.1MM **Privately Held**
SIC: 4953 Recycling, waste materials

(G-11341)
FACKLER COUNTRY GARDENS INC (PA)
Also Called: Kubota Authorized Dealer
2326 Newark Granville Rd (43023-9290)
PHONE.................................740 522-3128
George H Fackler III, *President*
Beth Jenkins, *Corp Secy*
Denny Ghiloni, *Vice Pres*
EMP: 40
SQ FT: 4,000
SALES (est): 5.5MM **Privately Held**
SIC: 5261 0782 5083 Garden supplies & tools; lawn care services; landscape contractors; farm & garden machinery

(G-11342)
GRANVILLE HOSPITALITY LLC
314 Broadway E (43023-1308)
PHONE.................................740 587-3333
Sean Mulryan, *General Mgr*
Linda Turk, *Sales Staff*
Chad Lavely, *Executive*
Anthony Beckerley,
Jerry Martin,
EMP: 80
SQ FT: 50,000
SALES (est): 3.3MM **Privately Held**
WEB: www.granvilleinn.com
SIC: 5812 7011 5813 Restaurant, family: independent; hotels; drinking places

(G-11343)
GRANVILLE MILLING CO (PA)
400 S Main St (43023-1470)
P.O. Box 393 (43023-0393)
PHONE.................................740 587-0221
Harold C Attebery, *Ch of Bd*
Phillip Watts, *President*
Francis Jane Eddy, *Principal*
John David Jones, *Principal*
Roderic M Jones, *Principal*
EMP: 30
SQ FT: 5,740
SALES (est): 5.1MM **Privately Held**
WEB: www.granvillemilling.com
SIC: 5999 5153 5191 Feed & farm supply; grains; farm supplies

(G-11344)
KENDAL AT GRANVILLE
2158 Columbus Rd (43023-1242)
PHONE.................................740 321-0400
Beth Waite, *Human Res Dir*
Douglas Helman, *Exec Dir*
Jennifer Weekly, *Executive*
Sandy Yeakley, *Receptionist*
EMP: 130 **EST:** 1999
SALES: 14.3MM **Privately Held**
WEB: www.kag.kendal.org
SIC: 8051 Skilled nursing care facilities

(G-11345)
LARRIMER & LARRIMER LLC
2000 Newark Granville Rd # 200 (43023-7009)
PHONE.................................740 366-0184
Terrence Larrimer, *Partner*
EMP: 25
SALES (corp-wide): 5.8MM **Privately Held**
SIC: 8111 Patent, trademark & copyright law
PA: Larrimer & Larrimer, Llc
165 N High St Fl 3
Columbus OH 43215
614 221-7548

(G-11346)
MID-OHIO MECHANICAL INC
1844 Lancaster Rd (43023-9411)
PHONE.................................740 587-3362
Neal Hartfield, *President*
EMP: 30
SALES (corp-wide): 8MM **Privately Held**
WEB: www.midohiomechanical.com
SIC: 1711 4225 Mechanical contractor; general warehousing & storage
PA: Mid-Ohio Mechanical Incorporated
1264 Weaver Dr
Granville OH 43023
740 587-3362

(G-11347)
OWENS CORNING SALES LLC
Owens Corning Science and Tech
2790 Columbus Rd (43023-1200)
PHONE.................................740 587-3562
Frank O'Brien Bernin, *Vice Pres*
EMP: 400 **Publicly Held**
WEB: www.owenscorning.com
SIC: 8731 2221 Commercial physical research; broadwoven fabric mills, manmade
HQ: Owens Corning Sales, Llc
1 Owens Corning Pkwy
Toledo OH 43659
419 248-8000

(G-11348)
UNIVERSAL VENEER SALES CORP
2825 Hallie Ln (43023-9256)
PHONE.................................740 522-2000
Dieter Heren, *CEO*
EMP: 50 **Privately Held**
SIC: 8743 Sales promotion
PA: Universal Veneer Sales Corporation
1776 Tamarack Rd
Newark OH 43055

(G-11349)
VARO ENGINEERS INC
2790 Columbus Rd (43023-1252)
PHONE.................................740 587-2228
Dane Cox, *Branch Mgr*
EMP: 35
SALES (corp-wide): 27.4MM **Privately Held**
WEB: www.varoeng.com
SIC: 8711 Consulting engineer
PA: Varo Engineers, Inc.
2751 Tuller Pkwy
Dublin OH 43017
614 459-0424

Green Springs
Seneca County

(G-11350)
ELMWOOD CENTER INC (PA)
Also Called: Elm Springs
441 N Broadway St (44836-9689)
PHONE....................................419 639-2581
Judy Blaha, *CEO*
Judy Downey, *CEO*
Kathy Hunt, *CEO*
Robin Hade, *Manager*
EMP: 67
SQ FT: 4,000
SALES (est): 9.2MM **Privately Held**
WEB: www.elmwoodassistedliving.com
SIC: 8052 Personal care facility

(G-11351)
ELMWOOD CENTER INC
Also Called: Elmwood At The Springs
401 N Broadway St (44836-9653)
PHONE....................................419 639-2626
Kathy Hunt, *Branch Mgr*
EMP: 60
SALES (corp-wide): 9.2MM **Privately Held**
SIC: 8051 Skilled nursing care facilities
PA: Elmwood Center Inc
441 N Broadway St
Green Springs OH 44836
419 639-2581

(G-11352)
ELMWOOD OF GREEN SPRINGS LTD
401 N Broadway St (44836-9653)
PHONE....................................419 639-2626
Kathy Hunt,
EMP: 99
SALES (est): 5.1MM **Privately Held**
SIC: 8062 General medical & surgical hospitals

(G-11353)
GREEN SPRINGS RESIDENTIAL LTD
430 N Broadway St (44836-9734)
PHONE....................................419 639-2581
Kathy Hunt, *President*
EMP: 250
SALES (est): 4.9MM **Privately Held**
SIC: 6531 Rental agent, real estate

(G-11354)
KENNETH G MYERS CNSTR CO INC
201 Smith St (44836-9669)
P.O. Box 37 (44836-0037)
PHONE....................................419 639-2051
Todd E Myers, *President*
Dan Willey, *Principal*
Butch Rowe, *Vice Pres*
Ron Rowe, *Vice Pres*
Ronald Rowe, *Vice Pres*
EMP: 100
SQ FT: 3,200
SALES (est): 15MM **Privately Held**
SIC: 1623 Telephone & communication line construction

(G-11355)
MILLER CABLE COMPANY
210 S Broadway St (44836-9635)
P.O. Box 68 (44836-0068)
PHONE....................................419 639-2091
Don W Miller, *Ch of Bd*
Jim Chamberlin, *President*
James Chamberlin Jr, *Vice Pres*
Jack Hartley, *Vice Pres*
John Hartley, *Vice Pres*
EMP: 62
SQ FT: 2,500
SALES: 17.5MM **Privately Held**
WEB: www.millercable.com
SIC: 1731 General electrical contractor

(G-11356)
W S O S COMMUNITY A
Also Called: Quilter Cvlian Cnsrvation Camp
1518 E County Road 113 (44836-9606)
P.O. Box 590, Fremont (43420-0590)
PHONE....................................419 639-2802
Tim Havice, *Branch Mgr*
EMP: 50
SALES (corp-wide): 33MM **Privately Held**
SIC: 8331 Job training services
PA: W. S. O. S. Community Action Commission, Inc.
127 S Front St
Fremont OH 43420
419 333-6068

(G-11357)
WYNN-REETH INC
Also Called: Remote Support Services
137 S Broadway St (44836-9319)
P.O. Box 785 (44836-0785)
PHONE....................................419 639-2094
Bruce Hunt, *President*
Destiny Pierce, *Case Mgr*
Adrian Smith, *Program Mgr*
Joy Sharp, *Manager*
Jarrod Hunt, *Director*
EMP: 50
SALES (est): 2.8MM **Privately Held**
WEB: www.wynn-reeth.com
SIC: 8361 Home for the mentally handicapped

Greenfield
Highland County

(G-11358)
ADENA HEALTH SYSTEM
Also Called: Adena Fmly Medicine-Greenfield
1075 N Washington St (45123-9780)
PHONE....................................937 981-9444
Keith Coleman, *Branch Mgr*
EMP: 213
SALES (corp-wide): 470.6MM **Privately Held**
SIC: 8062 Hospital, medical school affiliated with nursing & residency
PA: Adena Health System
272 Hospital Rd
Chillicothe OH 45601
740 779-7360

(G-11359)
COMMERCIAL CLEANING SOLUTIONS
10965 State Route 138 Sw (45123-8103)
PHONE....................................937 981-4870
Daniel Kinzer, *President*
EMP: 33
SALES (est): 606.7K **Privately Held**
SIC: 7349 Janitorial service, contract basis

(G-11360)
DALE ROSS TRUCKING INC
11408 State Route 41 S (45123)
PHONE....................................937 981-2168
Lee Ann Ross, *President*
Dale Ross, *Corp Secy*
EMP: 30
SQ FT: 7,200
SALES: 500K **Privately Held**
SIC: 4212 Dump truck haulage

(G-11361)
GREENFIELD AREA MEDICAL CTR
550 Mirabeau St (45123-1617)
PHONE....................................937 981-9400
Mark Shuter, *CEO*
Haley Teeters, *Supervisor*
Wilbur Bill Sever, *Surgeon*
Dave Olaker, *Asst Mgr*
Lee Anne Gabriel, *Director*
EMP: 100
SQ FT: 32,000
SALES: 13.7MM
SALES (corp-wide): 470.6MM **Privately Held**
WEB: www.adena.org
SIC: 8062 General medical & surgical hospitals

PA: Adena Health System
272 Hospital Rd
Chillicothe OH 45601
740 779-7360

(G-11362)
GREENFIELD PRODUCTS INC
1230 N Washington St (45123-9783)
P.O. Box 99 (45123-0099)
PHONE....................................937 981-2696
Ann Gessner Pence, *President*
Wesley Pence, *Vice Pres*
Tammy Wilson, *QC Mgr*
Steve McCoy, *Manager*
Gary Rhoads, *Technician*
▲ EMP: 51 EST: 1959
SQ FT: 12,000
SALES (est): 24.5MM **Privately Held**
WEB: www.greenfieldfinishing.com
SIC: 5088 Transportation equipment & supplies

(G-11363)
HEALTHSOURCE OF OHIO INC
Also Called: Greenfield Family Health Ctr
1075 N Washington St (45123-9780)
PHONE....................................937 981-7707
Mellisa Garland, *Manager*
EMP: 25
SALES (corp-wide): 47.8MM **Privately Held**
SIC: 8093 8011 8082 Specialty outpatient clinics; general & family practice, physician/surgeon; home health care services
PA: Healthsource Of Ohio, Inc.
5400 Dupont Cir Ste A
Milford OH 45150
513 576-7700

(G-11364)
MCMULLEN TRANSPORTATION LLC
11350 State Route 41 (45123-8562)
PHONE....................................937 981-4455
Jamey Popp,
EMP: 27
SQ FT: 7,680
SALES (est): 3MM **Privately Held**
SIC: 4213 Contract haulers

Greenville
Darke County

(G-11365)
ANDERSONS MARATHON ETHANOL LLC
5728 Sebring Warner Rd N (45331-9800)
PHONE....................................937 316-3700
Neill McKinstary, *President*
EMP: 40
SALES (est): 16.4MM **Publicly Held**
SIC: 5153 Grains
PA: Marathon Petroleum Corporation
539 S Main St
Findlay OH 45840

(G-11366)
BISTRO OFF BROADWAY
117 E 5th St (45331-1935)
PHONE....................................937 316-5000
CJ Jones, *Principal*
EMP: 35
SALES (est): 659.5K **Privately Held**
SIC: 5812 8741 Family restaurants; restaurant management

(G-11367)
BROOKDALE SENIOR LIVING COMMUN
Also Called: Sterling House of Greenville
1401 N Broadway St (45331-4300)
PHONE....................................937 548-6800
Ida Hecht, *Manager*
EMP: 40
SALES (corp-wide): 4.5B **Publicly Held**
WEB: www.assisted.com
SIC: 8059 8082 Rest home, with health care; home health care services
HQ: Brookdale Senior Living Communities, Inc.
6737 W Wa St Ste 2300
Milwaukee WI 53214
414 918-5000

(G-11368)
BROTHERS PUBLISHING CO LLC
Also Called: Early Bird, The
100 Washington Ave (45331-1515)
PHONE....................................937 548-3330
Ryan Berry, *Editor*
Louanna Gwinn, *Sales Staff*
Keith Foutz, *Mng Member*
Clinton Randall, *Webmaster*
EMP: 45
SALES (est): 2.7MM **Privately Held**
SIC: 2711 2791 7331 Newspapers: publishing only, not printed on site; typesetting; mailing list compilers

(G-11369)
CHAMBERS LEASING SYSTEMS
5187 Chld Hm Bradford Rd (45331)
PHONE....................................937 547-9777
Curt Betts, *Manager*
EMP: 45
SALES (est): 1.7MM **Privately Held**
SIC: 4213 Contract haulers

(G-11370)
CHN INC - ADULT DAY CARE
Also Called: Comprensive Health Network
5420 State Route 571 (45331-9606)
PHONE....................................937 548-0506
Nancy Zechar, *President*
Cynthia L Scott, *Vice Pres*
Cynthia Scott, *Director*
EMP: 35
SQ FT: 5,000
SALES: 5MM **Privately Held**
SIC: 8322 Adult day care center

(G-11371)
DARKE CNTY MENTAL HLTH CLINIC (PA)
212 E Main St (45331-1913)
P.O. Box 895 (45331-0895)
PHONE....................................937 548-1635
Ron Monroe, *Manager*
Lyn McArdle, *Exec Dir*
James Moore, *Exec Dir*
EMP: 27
SALES: 6.9K **Privately Held**
WEB: www.dcmhc.org
SIC: 8093 Mental health clinic, outpatient

(G-11372)
DARKE COUNTY SHERIFFS PATROL
5185 County Home Rd (45331-9753)
PHONE....................................937 548-3399
Toby Spencer, *Sheriff*
EMP: 75
SALES (est): 243.6K **Privately Held**
SIC: 7381 Protective services, guard

(G-11373)
DAVE KNAPP FORD LINCOLN INC (PA)
500 Wagner Ave (45331-2539)
PHONE....................................937 547-3000
David O Knapp, *President*
Charlie McFarland, *Sales Staff*
Vera Houpt, *Manager*
Bryan Knapp, *Manager*
Karen S Knapp, *Admin Sec*
EMP: 42
SALES (est): 18.4MM **Privately Held**
WEB: www.daveknappford.com
SIC: 5511 5531 5012 Automobiles, new & used; automotive & home supply stores; automobiles & other motor vehicles

(G-11374)
DAYTON PHYSICIANS LLC
1111 Sweitzer St Ste C (45331-1189)
PHONE....................................937 547-0563
Pilar Gonzalez-Monk, *Branch Mgr*
Cathryn Gibbs, *Analyst*
EMP: 182
SALES (corp-wide): 25.5MM **Privately Held**
SIC: 8011 Primary care medical clinic
PA: Dayton Physicians, Llc
6680 Poe Ave Ste 200
Dayton OH 45414
937 280-8400

(G-11375)
DICKMAN SUPPLY INC
1425 Sater St (45331-1672)
PHONE..................................937 492-6166
Brad Holzapfel, Sales Staff
Mark Winner, Manager
EMP: 25
SALES (est): 5.1MM
SALES (corp-wide): 114MM Privately
Held
WEB: www.electro-controls.com
SIC: 5063 5084 Electrical apparatus &
equipment; drilling bits; paper, sawmill &
woodworking machinery
PA: Dickman Supply, Inc.
1991 St Marys Ave
Sidney OH 45365
937 492-6166

(G-11376)
DREW AG-TRANSPORT INC
5450 Sebring Warner Rd (45331-8800)
PHONE..................................937 548-3200
Rod Drew, President
Cortnie Drew, CFO
EMP: 53
SALES (est): 8.8MM Privately Held
SIC: 4213 Contract haulers

(G-11377)
**FAMILY HLTH SVCS DRKE CNTY
INC (PA)**
5735 Meeker Rd (45331-1180)
PHONE..................................937 548-3806
Mitch Eiting, President
Michael Rieman, Vice Pres
Kent James, Treasurer
Ken Harshbarger, Med Doctor
Don Pohlman, Med Doctor
EMP: 120
SQ FT: 43,000
SALES (est): 23.7MM Privately Held
WEB: www.familyhealthwebsite.com
SIC: 8011 Clinic, operated by physicians;
primary care medical clinic

(G-11378)
GARBER AG FREIGHT INC
4667 Us Route 127 (45331-8806)
PHONE..................................937 548-8400
Ben Garber, President
Charles Garber, Exec VP
Jason Garber, Vice Pres
Ivan Garber, Admin Sec
EMP: 40
SALES (est): 4.6MM Privately Held
SIC: 4212 4213 Local trucking, without
storage; trucking, except local

(G-11379)
GEORGE KNICK
2637 Hllgrove Wdington Rd (45331-9417)
PHONE..................................937 548-2832
George Knick, Owner
EMP: 30
SALES (est): 1.4MM Privately Held
SIC: 0191 0161 General farms, primarily
crop; tomato farm

(G-11380)
**GRACE RESURRECTION
ASSOCIATION**
Also Called: Grace Resurrection Cmnty Ctr
Grace Rsrrction Cmnty Ctr (45331)
PHONE..................................937 548-2595
Peggy Follrod, Exec Dir
EMP: 26
SALES: 110.1K Privately Held
SIC: 8322 Social service center

(G-11381)
GREENVILLE FEDERAL
690 Wagner Ave (45331-2649)
PHONE..................................937 548-4158
Jeff Knisi, CEO
Susan Barker, Vice Pres
Betty Hartzell, Vice Pres
Susan Allread, CFO
EMP: 40
SQ FT: 11,000
SALES: 7.3MM
SALES (corp-wide): 6.8MM Privately
Held
SIC: 6035 Federal savings & loan associa-
tions

HQ: Greenville Federal Financial Corporation
690 Wagner Ave
Greenville OH 45331
937 548-4158

(G-11382)
**GREENVILLE NATIONAL
BANCORP (PA)**
446 S Bwy St (45331)
PHONE..................................937 548-1114
Steve Burns, President
Kent A James, Vice Pres
Douglas M Custenborder, Treasurer
EMP: 48
SQ FT: 7,500
SALES: 18.2MM Privately Held
SIC: 6712 Bank holding companies

(G-11383)
GREENVILLE NATIONAL BANK
446 S Broadway St (45331-1960)
P.O. Box 190 (45331-0190)
PHONE..................................937 548-1114
Steve Burns, Manager
EMP: 50
SALES (corp-wide): 18.2MM Privately
Held
WEB: www.greenvillenationalbank.com
SIC: 6021 National commercial banks
HQ: Greenville National Bank (Inc)
446 S Broadway St
Greenville OH

(G-11384)
**GREENVILLE TOWNSHIP
RESCUE**
Also Called: Rescue Squad
1401 Sater St (45331-1672)
P.O. Box 188 (45331-0188)
PHONE..................................937 548-9339
Mark Dotson, Principal
Steve Wenning, Chief
EMP: 30
SQ FT: 2,400
SALES (est): 810K Privately Held
SIC: 4119 Ambulance service

(G-11385)
**H & M PRECISION CONCRETE
LLC**
7805 Arcanum Bearsmill Rd (45331-9256)
PHONE..................................937 547-0012
Jason Haworth,
Todd Miller,
EMP: 32
SQ FT: 3,000
SALES: 4MM Privately Held
WEB: www.slabdocs.com
SIC: 1771 Concrete pumping

(G-11386)
**HEALTH CARE RTREMENT
CORP AMER**
Also Called: Heartland of Greenville
243 Marion Dr (45331-2613)
PHONE..................................937 548-3141
Kara Hoernemann, General Mgr
EMP: 115
SALES (corp-wide): 2.4B Publicly Held
WEB: www.hrc-manorcare.com
SIC: 8051 Skilled nursing care facilities
HQ: Health Care And Retirement Corpora-
tion Of America
333 N Summit St Ste 103
Toledo OH 43604
419 252-5500

(G-11387)
**HOSPICE OF DARKE COUNTY
INC (PA)**
Also Called: State of The Heart Hospice
1350 N Broadway St (45331-2461)
PHONE..................................937 548-2999
Megan Stull, Consultant
Ted Bauer, Exec Dir
Amy Pearson, Director
Sheri Arbuckle, Nursing Dir
EMP: 40
SQ FT: 5,000
SALES: 9MM Privately Held
WEB: www.stateoftheheartcare.org
SIC: 8052 Personal care facility

(G-11388)
KTM ENTERPRISES INC
Also Called: Janitorial Management Services
120 W 3rd St (45331-1409)
P.O. Box 896 (45331-0896)
PHONE..................................937 548-8357
Rick Lundy, President
Tj Richardson, Treasurer
EMP: 31
SALES (est): 591K Privately Held
SIC: 7349 Janitorial service, contract basis

(G-11389)
LOWES HOME CENTERS LLC
1550 Wagner Ave (45331-2892)
PHONE..................................937 547-2400
Gerald Carroll, Branch Mgr
Julia Crosby, Executive
EMP: 105
SALES (corp-wide): 68.6B Publicly Held
SIC: 5211 5031 5722 5064 Home cen-
ters; building materials, exterior; building
materials, interior; household appliance
stores; electrical appliances, television &
radio
HQ: Lowe's Home Centers, Llc
1605 Curtis Bridge Rd
Wilkesboro NC 28697
336 658-4000

(G-11390)
**MIAMI VALLEY COMMUNITY
ACTION**
Metropolitan Housing
1469 Sweitzer St (45331-1029)
PHONE..................................937 548-8143
Janey Christman, Director
EMP: 62
SALES (corp-wide): 13MM Privately
Held
SIC: 8322 Senior citizens' center or associ-
ation
PA: Miami Valley Community Action Part-
nership
719 S Main St
Dayton OH 45402
937 222-1009

(G-11391)
**OHIO DEPARTMENT
TRANSPORTATION**
Also Called: Hwy. Department
1144 Martin St (45331-9686)
PHONE..................................937 548-3015
Jeff Wetstone, Manager
EMP: 30 Privately Held
SIC: 1611 9621 Highway & street mainte-
nance;
HQ: Ohio Department Of Transportation
1980 W Broad St
Columbus OH 43223

(G-11392)
**REST HAVEN NURSING HOME
INC**
1096 N Ohio St (45331-2999)
PHONE..................................937 548-1138
Linelle Miller, Director
Michelle Bruns, Administration
Tara Rutschilling, Administration
EMP: 125
SQ FT: 20,000
SALES (est): 4.6MM Privately Held
SIC: 8052 8059 8051 Intermediate care
facilities; rest home, with health care;
skilled nursing care facilities

(G-11393)
RUMPKE WASTE INC
5474 Jaysville St John Rd (45331-9704)
PHONE..................................937 548-1939
Bruce Truman, Manager
EMP: 120 Privately Held
SIC: 4953 7359 4212 Recycling, waste
materials; equipment rental & leasing;
local trucking, without storage
HQ: Rumpke Waste, Inc.
10795 Hughes Rd
Cincinnati OH 45251
513 851-0122

(G-11394)
SALLY BEAUTY SUPPLY LLC
Also Called: Beauty Systems Group
5805 Jaysville St John Rd (45331-8342)
PHONE..................................937 548-7684
Tim Gibson, Manager
Holly Lawrence, Admin Asst
EMP: 220 Publicly Held
WEB: www.sallybeauty.com
SIC: 4225 5087 General warehousing &
storage; service establishment equipment
HQ: Sally Beauty Supply Llc
3001 Colorado Blvd
Denton TX 76210
940 898-7500

(G-11395)
SECOND NATIONAL BANK (HQ)
499 S Broadway St (45331-1961)
P.O. Box 130 (45331-0130)
PHONE..................................937 548-2122
John E Swallow, CEO
Marvin J Stammen, President
Ray Lear, Chairman
Steve Badgett, Exec VP
John Swallow, Senior VP
EMP: 40
SQ FT: 7,500
SALES (est): 3.4MM
SALES (corp-wide): 411.9MM Publicly
Held
WEB: www.secondnational.com
SIC: 6021 6163 National commercial
banks; loan brokers
PA: Park National Corporation
50 N 3rd St
Newark OH 43055
740 349-8451

(G-11396)
**SPIRIT MEDICAL TRANSPORT
LLC**
5484 S State Route 49 (45331-1032)
PHONE..................................937 548-2800
Cynthia Bruner, Human Resources
Sally Wilson, Human Resources
Dan Winner, Info Tech Mgr
Brian Hathaway,
EMP: 72
SALES (est): 3.4MM Privately Held
SIC: 4119 Ambulance service

(G-11397)
**TELECOM EXPERTISE INDS INC
(PA)**
Also Called: T X I
5879 Jysville St Johns Rd (45331-9398)
P.O. Box 67 (45331-0067)
PHONE..................................937 548-5254
Jack Born, President
Dave Pope, Vice Pres
David Pope, Vice Pres
Christopher Pope, Project Mgr
Imelda Pope, CFO
EMP: 100
SQ FT: 38,000
SALES (est): 12.6MM Privately Held
WEB: www.txiinc.com
SIC: 1731 8711 Communications special-
ization; engineering services

(G-11398)
**VALVOLINE INSTANT OIL
CHANGE**
661 Wagner Ave (45331-2648)
PHONE..................................937 548-0123
EMP: 190
SALES (corp-wide): 4.4MM Privately
Held
SIC: 7549 Automotive maintenance serv-
ices
PA: Valvoline Instant Oil Change Inc
7391 Bltmore Annplis Blvd
Glen Burnie MD 21061
410 760-5344

(G-11399)
**VILLAGE GREEN HEALTHCARE
CTR**
Also Called: Gade Nursing Home 2
405 Chestnut St (45331-1306)
PHONE..................................937 548-1993
Martha Gade, President
Cheryl Stump, Vice Pres
EMP: 70 EST: 1961

SALES (est): 2.3MM **Privately Held**
SIC: **8051** Convalescent home with continuous nursing care

(G-11400)
WAYNE HEALTHCARE (PA)
835 Sweitzer St (45331-1007)
PHONE.................................937 548-1141
Wayne Deschambeau, *President*
W H Matchett Et Al, *Principal*
S A Hawes, *Principal*
E G Husted, *Principal*
Michael Weinberg, *Pathologist*
EMP: **396** EST: 1920
SALES: **51MM Privately Held**
SIC: **8062** General medical & surgical hospitals

(G-11401)
WAYNE INDUSTRIES INC
5844 Jysville St Johns Rd (45331-9398)
PHONE.................................937 548-6025
Mary Brennan, *Director*
EMP: **45**
SALES: **291K Privately Held**
SIC: **7363** Temporary help service

Greenwich
Huron County

(G-11402)
JOHNSON BROS RUBBER CO INC
Also Called: Johnson Bros Greenwich
41 Center St (44837-1049)
PHONE.................................419 752-4814
Ken Bostic, *Manager*
EMP: **30**
SALES (corp-wide): **54.4MM Privately Held**
SIC: **5199 3743 3634 3545** Foams & rubber; railroad equipment; electric housewares & fans; machine tool accessories; gaskets, packing & sealing devices
PA: Johnson Bros. Rubber Co., Inc.
42 W Buckeye St
West Salem OH 44287
419 853-4122

Grove City
Franklin County

(G-11403)
ACE TRUCK BODY INC
1600 Thrailkill Rd (43123-9733)
P.O. Box 459 (43123-0459)
PHONE.................................614 871-3100
Gary L Leasure, *President*
Ruth Ross, *Principal*
Robert D Beitzel, *Chairman*
David R Peitzel, *Vice Pres*
Ken Maynard, *Parts Mgr*
EMP: **25**
SQ FT: 18,000
SALES: **10.4MM Privately Held**
WEB: www.acetruck.com
SIC: **5012 5013** Truck bodies; motor vehicle supplies & new parts

(G-11404)
AMERICAN AIR FURNACE COMPANY
Also Called: American Air Comfort Tech
3945 Brookham Dr (43123-9741)
PHONE.................................614 876-1702
Steve Sliemers, *President*
Michael Sliemers, *Vice Pres*
EMP: **63**
SQ FT: 24,000
SALES (est): **10.7MM Privately Held**
WEB: www.americanairheating.com
SIC: **1711** Heating systems repair & maintenance

(G-11405)
AMERICAN GOLF CORPORATION
Also Called: Oakhurst Country Club
3223 Norton Rd (43123-9695)
PHONE.................................310 664-4278
Shawn Logan, *Manager*
EMP: **35 Publicly Held**
SIC: **7997** Golf club, membership
HQ: American Golf Corporation
909 N Pacific Coast Hwy
El Segundo CA 90245
310 664-4000

(G-11406)
AMERICAN MULTI-CINEMA INC
4218 Buckeye Pkwy (43123-8377)
PHONE.................................614 801-9130
EMP: **61**
SALES (corp-wide): **7.3MM Publicly Held**
SIC: **7832** Exhibitors, itinerant: motion picture
HQ: American Multi-Cinema, Inc.
1 Amc Way
Leawood KS 66211
913 213-2000

(G-11407)
AT&T CORP
4108 Buckeye Pkwy (43123-8175)
P.O. Box 908 (43123-0908)
PHONE.................................614 539-0165
Wendy Stalcup, *Branch Mgr*
EMP: **97**
SALES (corp-wide): **170.7B Publicly Held**
WEB: www.cingular.com
SIC: **4812** Cellular telephone services
HQ: At&T Corp.
1 At&T Way
Bedminster NJ 07921
800 403-3302

(G-11408)
BIG RUN URGENT CARE CENTER
3000 Meadow Pond Ct # 200 (43123-9827)
PHONE.................................614 871-7130
M Smith MD, *Principal*
Janice Piscitelli, *Relations*
EMP: **30**
SALES (est): **947.9K Privately Held**
SIC: **8011** Medical centers

(G-11409)
BOSCH REXROTH CORPORATION
3940 Gantz Rd Ste F (43123-4845)
PHONE.................................614 527-7400
Ted Bojanowski, *President*
Douglas Knuth, *Sales Staff*
Glenn Hall, *Sales Executive*
EMP: **50**
SALES (corp-wide): **301.8MM Privately Held**
SIC: **5084** Hydraulic systems equipment & supplies
HQ: Bosch Rexroth Corporation
14001 S Lakes Dr
Charlotte NC 28273
704 583-4338

(G-11410)
BRIAR-GATE REALTY INC
Also Called: Fireproof Records Center
3655 Brookham Dr (43123-4852)
PHONE.................................614 299-2122
Michael James, *Manager*
EMP: **27**
SALES (corp-wide): **22MM Privately Held**
WEB: www.fireproof.com
SIC: **4226** Document & office records storage
PA: Briar-Gate Realty, Inc.
3827 Brookham Dr
Grove City OH 43123
614 299-2121

(G-11411)
BRIAR-GATE REALTY INC (PA)
Also Called: Fireproof Record Center
3827 Brookham Dr (43123-4827)
P.O. Box 1150 (43123-6150)
PHONE.................................614 299-2121
Michael James, *CEO*
Edward F James, *President*
C M Gibson, *Principal*
Sally R Gibson, *Principal*
Helen M Watkins, *Principal*
EMP: **66**

SQ FT: 80,000
SALES (est): **22MM Privately Held**
WEB: www.fireproof.com
SIC: **4226** Document & office records storage

(G-11412)
BROCON CONSTRUCTION INC
2120 Hardy Parkway St (43123-1240)
PHONE.................................614 871-7300
George Brobst, *President*
George M Brobst Jr, *President*
EMP: **45**
SALES (est): **14.6MM Privately Held**
WEB: www.brocon.net
SIC: **1542** Commercial & office building, new construction

(G-11413)
BROOKDALE SENIOR LIVING INC
1305 Lamplighter Dr (43123-8199)
PHONE.................................614 277-1200
EMP: **69**
SALES (corp-wide): **4.5B Publicly Held**
SIC: **8361** Residential care
PA: Brookdale Senior Living
111 Westwood Pl Ste 400
Brentwood TN 37027
615 221-2250

(G-11414)
BUCK EQUIPMENT INC
1720 Feddern Ave (43123-1206)
PHONE.................................614 539-3039
Dennis Hamilton, *CEO*
Jamie Odell, *Sales Executive*
▲ EMP: **35**
SQ FT: 60,000
SALES (est): **9.4MM Privately Held**
WEB: www.buckequipment.com
SIC: **3531 3743 3441 5088** Logging equipment; railroad equipment; fabricated structural metal; railroad equipment & supplies

(G-11415)
BUCKEYE DRMTLOGY DRMTHPHTHLOGY
1933 Ohio Dr (43123-4835)
PHONE.................................614 317-9630
Carlos Rodriguez, *Branch Mgr*
EMP: **25**
SALES (est): **1.7MM**
SALES (corp-wide): **3.6MM Privately Held**
SIC: **8011** Dermatologist
PA: Buckeye Dermatology & Dermathophathology Inc
5720 Blazer Pkwy
Dublin OH 43017
614 389-6331

(G-11416)
BUCKEYE RANCH INC (PA)
5665 Hoover Rd (43123-9280)
PHONE.................................614 875-2371
D Nicholas Rees, *CEO*
Stephen Richard, *President*
Richard Rieser, *President*
Roger Minner, *Vice Pres*
Gary Stammler, *Vice Pres*
EMP: **250** EST: 1961
SQ FT: 182,023
SALES: **44.4MM Privately Held**
SIC: **8361** Home for the emotionally disturbed; halfway group home, persons with social or personal problems; halfway home for delinquents & offenders; juvenile correctional home

(G-11417)
C H BRADSHAW CO
2004 Hendrix Dr (43123-1278)
PHONE.................................614 871-2087
Robert Slack, *President*
Jeanne Slack, *Vice Pres*
EMP: **27**
SQ FT: 22,000
SALES (est): **10.1MM Privately Held**
WEB: www.chbradshaw.com
SIC: **5084 7699** Petroleum industry machinery; tank repair

(G-11418)
CELLCO PARTNERSHIP
Also Called: Verizon Wireless
3043 Turnberry Ct (43123-1789)
PHONE.................................614 277-2900
EMP: **71**
SALES (corp-wide): **130.8B Publicly Held**
SIC: **4812** Cellular telephone services
HQ: Cellco Partnership
1 Verizon Way
Basking Ridge NJ 07920

(G-11419)
CENTRAL OHIO CONTRACTORS INC (PA)
2879 Jackson Pike (43123-9737)
PHONE.................................614 539-2579
Ralph D Loewendick, *President*
Luanne Sigman, *Corp Secy*
EMP: **70**
SALES: **2.2MM Privately Held**
WEB: www.coc-inc.com
SIC: **4953** Sanitary landfill operation

(G-11420)
CIRCLE S FARMS INC
Also Called: Fruits of The Earth
9015 London Groveport Rd (43123-8818)
PHONE.................................614 878-9462
Ethel Sullivan, *Principal*
EMP: **28**
SQ FT: 1,500
SALES (est): **1.1MM Privately Held**
SIC: **7999 5431 5148 5992** Festival operation; fruit & vegetable markets; fresh fruits & vegetables; flowers, fresh; general farms, primarily crop; groceries, general line

(G-11421)
COMPUTER SCIENCES CORPORATION
3940 Gantz Rd Ste F (43123-4845)
PHONE.................................614 801-2343
Charlene Stanley, *Director*
EMP: **145**
SALES (corp-wide): **24.5B Publicly Held**
WEB: www.csc.com
SIC: **7376** Computer facilities management
HQ: Computer Sciences Corporation
1775 Tysons Blvd Ste 1000
Tysons VA 22102
703 245-9675

(G-11422)
CONVERSE ELECTRIC INC
3783 Gantz Rd Ste A (43123-1892)
PHONE.................................614 808-4377
Jerry Converse, *President*
Chris Converse, *Vice Pres*
Bill Mount, *Vice Pres*
Dave Novontny, *Vice Pres*
Diane Lutsko, *Admin Sec*
EMP: **100**
SALES (est): **18.3MM Privately Held**
WEB: www.converseelectric.com
SIC: **1731** General electrical contractor

(G-11423)
COX AUTOMOTIVE INC
Also Called: Ohio Auto Auction
3905 Jackson Pike (43123-9731)
PHONE.................................614 871-2771
Debbie Mc Bride, *Sales Executive*
John Deck, *Manager*
EMP: **450**
SALES (corp-wide): **32.5B Privately Held**
WEB: www.manheim.com
SIC: **5012 5531** Automobile auction; automotive accessories
HQ: Cox Automotive, Inc.
6205-A Pchtree Dnwoody Rd
Atlanta GA 30328
404 843-5000

(G-11424)
DAKOTA GIRLS LLC
Also Called: Goddard School
2585 London Groveport Rd (43123-9035)
PHONE.................................614 801-2558
Kelly Vansyckle, *Owner*
Samantha Elliot,
EMP: **25**

SALES (est): 886.8K **Privately Held**
SIC: 8351 Preschool center

(G-11425)
DENIER ELECTRIC CO INC
4000 Gantz Rd Ste C (43123-4844)
PHONE.................................614 338-4664
Mike Kallmeyer, *Branch Mgr*
EMP: 50
SALES (corp-wide): 58.1MM **Privately Held**
SIC: 1731 General electrical contractor
PA: Denier Electric Co., Inc.
   10891 State Route 128
   Harrison OH 45030
   513 738-2641

(G-11426)
DISCOVER TRAINING INC
4882 Rheims Way (43123-7903)
PHONE.................................614 871-0010
Kristine H Kursinskis, *President*
EMP: 70
SALES: 3.5MM **Privately Held**
SIC: 7361 Employment agencies

(G-11427)
DOCTORS HOSPITAL HEALTH CENTER
Also Called: Doctors Hospital Fmly Practice
2030 Stringtown Rd Fl 3 (43123-3993)
PHONE.................................614 544-0101
William Burke, *Principal*
EMP: 35
SALES (est): 1.2MM **Privately Held**
WEB: www.doctorsfp.com
SIC: 8031 Offices & clinics of osteopathic physicians

(G-11428)
DRURY HOTELS COMPANY LLC
Also Called: Drury Inn & Suites Columbus S
4109 Parkway Centre Dr (43123-8095)
PHONE.................................614 798-8802
Sam Gregory, *Branch Mgr*
EMP: 30
SALES (corp-wide): 397.7MM **Privately Held**
WEB: www.druryhotels.com
SIC: 7011 Hotels
PA: Drury Hotels Company, Llc
   721 Emerson Rd Ste 400
   Saint Louis MO 63141
   314 429-2255

(G-11429)
DSI SYSTEMS INC
3650 Brookham Dr Ste K (43123-4929)
PHONE.................................614 871-1456
Traci Fusner, *Manager*
Donna Bocox, *Admin Sec*
▲ EMP: 30
SALES (est): 2.4MM **Privately Held**
SIC: 5065 Electronic parts & equipment

(G-11430)
ESEC CORPORATION
Also Called: Columbus Peterbilt
6240 Enterprise Pkwy (43123-9272)
PHONE.................................614 875-3732
Tim Darr, *Manager*
EMP: 29
SQ FT: 26,480
SALES: 2MM
SALES (corp-wide): 7MM **Privately Held**
SIC: 5084 5012 5531 Industrial machinery & equipment; trucks, commercial; truck equipment & parts
PA: Esec Corporation
   44 Victoria Rd
   Youngstown OH 44515
   330 799-1536

(G-11431)
FEDEX CORPORATION
3423 Southpark Pl (43123-4828)
PHONE.................................614 801-0953
EMP: 34
SALES (corp-wide): 47.4B **Publicly Held**
SIC: 4513 Courier Services
PA: Fedex Corporation
   942 Shady Grove Rd S
   Memphis TN 38120
   901 818-7500

(G-11432)
FEDEX GROUND PACKAGE SYS INC
6120 S Meadows Dr (43123-9298)
PHONE.................................800 463-3339
EMP: 500
SALES (corp-wide): 65.4B **Publicly Held**
SIC: 4213 4212 Contract haulers; local trucking, without storage
HQ: Fedex Ground Package System, Inc.
   1000 Fed Ex Dr
   Coraopolis PA 15108
   800 463-3339

(G-11433)
FEDEX SMARTPOST INC
2969 Lewis Centre Way (43123-1782)
PHONE.................................800 463-3339
EMP: 82
SALES (corp-wide): 65.4B **Publicly Held**
SIC: 4513 Air courier services
HQ: Fedex Smartpost, Inc.
   16555 W Rogers Dr
   New Berlin WI 53151
   800 463-3339

(G-11434)
FLOWERS FAMILY PRACTICE INC
3667 Marlane Dr (43123-8895)
PHONE.................................614 277-9631
Stephanie Flowers, *Owner*
EMP: 25
SALES (est): 1.3MM **Privately Held**
SIC: 8011 General & family practice, physician/surgeon

(G-11435)
FRESENIUS MEDICAL CARE VRO LLC
Also Called: Fresenius Med Care Grove Cy
3149 Farm Bank Way (43123-1258)
PHONE.................................614 875-2349
Mary Garber, *Manager*
Ron Kuerbitz,
EMP: 25
SALES (est): 715.4K **Privately Held**
SIC: 8092 Kidney dialysis centers

(G-11436)
GRAND AERIE OF THE FRATERNAL (PA)
1623 Gateway Cir (43123-9309)
PHONE.................................614 883-2200
Edgar L Bollenbacher, *Ch of Bd*
David Tice, *President*
Chris Lainas Jr, *Chairman*
Kristy Spires, *CFO*
Donald R Jim West, *Treasurer*
EMP: 42
SALES: 11MM **Privately Held**
WEB: www.foe.com
SIC: 8641 University club; fraternal associations

(G-11437)
GROVE CITY COMMUNITY CLUB
3397 Civic Pl (43123-3137)
P.O. Box 434 (43123-0434)
PHONE.................................614 875-6074
EMP: 45
SALES: 53.5K **Privately Held**
SIC: 8641 7997 Civic/Social Association Membership Sport/Recreation Club

(G-11438)
GROVE CY CHRSTN CHILD CARE CTR
4770 Hoover Rd (43123-8504)
PHONE.................................614 875-2551
Kellie Castle, *Principal*
Jessica Rose, *Principal*
Susan Feisert, *Director*
Susan Sienert, *Director*
EMP: 80
SALES (est): 1.5MM **Privately Held**
SIC: 8322 Child related social services

(G-11439)
H O C J INC
2135 Hardy Parkway St (43123-1213)
PHONE.................................614 539-4601
EMP: 31 **Privately Held**
SIC: 4213 Trucking, except local

PA: H O C J Inc
   323 Cash Memorial Blvd
   Forest Park GA 30297

(G-11440)
HAWKEYE HOTELS INC
Courtyard Columbus Grove City
1668 Buckeye Pl (43123-1519)
PHONE.................................614 782-8292
Dale Nysetvold, *Branch Mgr*
EMP: 32
SALES (corp-wide): 19.2MM **Privately Held**
SIC: 7011 Hotels
PA: Hawkeye Hotels Inc.
   2681 James St
   Coralville IA 52241
   319 752-7400

(G-11441)
HKT TELESERVICES INC (PA)
3400 Southpark Pl Ste F (43123-4857)
PHONE.................................614 652-6300
Andrew C Jacobs, *Ch of Bd*
Mark K Attinger, *President*
Scott P Lee, *Corp Secy*
Ken Cross, *Vice Pres*
Jeremy Johnston, *Vice Pres*
EMP: 175
SALES (est): 50MM **Privately Held**
WEB: www.influentinc.com
SIC: 7299 7389 Personal financial services; telemarketing services

(G-11442)
HOKUTO USA INC
2200 Southwest Blvd Ste F (43123-2854)
PHONE.................................614 782-6200
Robin Hughes, *CEO*
Yoshimasa Sekiguchi, *President*
EMP: 42
SALES: 14MM
SALES (corp-wide): 103.3MM **Privately Held**
SIC: 8711 Engineering services
PA: Hokuto Corporation
   155, Gonishicho
   Komaki AIC 485-0
   568 785-555

(G-11443)
INSTANTWHIP-COLUMBUS INC (HQ)
3855 Marlane Dr (43123-9224)
P.O. Box 249 (43123-0249)
PHONE.................................614 871-9447
Douglas A Smith, *President*
Tom G Michaelides, *Senior VP*
Vinson Lewis, *Vice Pres*
G Fredrick Smith, *Admin Sec*
EMP: 32
SQ FT: 10,300
SALES (est): 5.9MM
SALES (corp-wide): 47.5MM **Privately Held**
SIC: 2026 5143 2023 8741 Whipped topping, except frozen or dry mix; dairy products, except dried or canned; dietary supplements, dairy & non-dairy based; management services
PA: Instantwhip Foods, Inc.
   2200 Cardigan Ave
   Columbus OH 43215
   614 488-2536

(G-11444)
INTERSTATE CONSTRUCTION INC
3511 Farm Bank Way (43123-1970)
PHONE.................................614 539-1188
Dwight Kincaid, *President*
EMP: 25
SQ FT: 8,000
SALES (est): 5.6MM **Privately Held**
WEB: www.interstateconstruction.net
SIC: 1522 1542 Multi-family dwellings, new construction; remodeling, multi-family dwellings; commercial & office building, new construction; commercial & office buildings, renovation & repair

(G-11445)
KIRK WILLIAMS COMPANY INC
2734 Home Rd (43123-1701)
P.O. Box 189 (43123-0189)
PHONE.................................614 875-9023

James K Williams Jr, *President*
James K Williams III, *Corp Secy*
EMP: 80
SQ FT: 40,000
SALES (est): 31.3MM **Privately Held**
WEB: www.kirkwilliamsco.com
SIC: 1711 3564 3444 Mechanical contractor; warm air heating & air conditioning contractor; ventilation & duct work contractor; sheet metalwork; blowers & fans

(G-11446)
LA FORCE INC
3940 Gantz Rs Unit E (43123)
PHONE.................................614 875-2545
Tom Gaible, *Branch Mgr*
EMP: 100
SALES (corp-wide): 156.3MM **Privately Held**
SIC: 5072 Builders' hardware
PA: La Force, Inc.
   1060 W Mason St
   Green Bay WI 54303
   920 497-7100

(G-11447)
LENNOX INDUSTRIES INC
3750 Brookham Dr Ste A (43123-4850)
PHONE.................................614 871-3017
Mark Miltko, *Manager*
EMP: 35
SALES (corp-wide): 3.8B **Publicly Held**
WEB: www.davelennox.com
SIC: 5075 Warm air heating & air conditioning
HQ: Lennox Industries Inc.
   2100 Lake Park Blvd
   Richardson TX 75080
   972 497-5000

(G-11448)
LIBERTY TIRE RECYCLING LLC
3041 Jackson Pike (43123-9737)
PHONE.................................614 871-8097
Thomas Elder, *Cust Mgr*
Ed Kincaid, *Branch Mgr*
Rick Douglas, *Manager*
EMP: 26 **Privately Held**
SIC: 7534 Tire retreading & repair shops
HQ: Liberty Tire Recycling, Llc
   600 River Ave Ste 3
   Pittsburgh PA 15212
   412 562-1700

(G-11449)
LINEMASTER SERVICES LLC
5736 Buckeye Pkwy (43123-9177)
PHONE.................................614 507-9945
David T Ehrenberg II,
EMP: 28
SALES (est): 1.6MM **Privately Held**
SIC: 8999 Services

(G-11450)
LITTLE THEATER OFF BROADWAY
Also Called: L T O B
3981 Broadway (43123-2639)
P.O. Box 504 (43123-0504)
PHONE.................................614 875-3919
Cathy Hyghland, *President*
Jane Mixer, *Principal*
Ruby Callison, *Vice Pres*
James Schmitt, *Treasurer*
Rosemary Tulseln, *Admin Sec*
EMP: 30
SALES: 63.8K **Privately Held**
WEB: www.ltob.org
SIC: 7922 Legitimate live theater producers

(G-11451)
MARTIN MARIETTA MATERIALS INC
Also Called: Martin Marietta Aggregates
3300 Jackson Pike (43123-8875)
PHONE.................................614 871-6708
Mike Matoszkia, *Manager*
EMP: 40
SQ FT: 420 **Publicly Held**
WEB: www.martinmarietta.com
SIC: 5032 Aggregate
PA: Martin Marietta Materials Inc
   2710 Wycliff Rd
   Raleigh NC 27607

2019 Harris Ohio
Services Directory

▲ = Import ▼=Export
◆ =Import/Export

(G-11452)
MH EQUIPMENT COMPANY
2055 Hardy Parkway St (43123-1213)
PHONE..............................614 871-1571
Dennis Dmytryk, *Manager*
EMP: 35
SALES (corp-wide): 247.9MM **Privately Held**
SIC: 5084 Materials handling machinery
HQ: Mh Equipment Company
8901 N Industrial Rd
Peoria IL 61615
309 579-8020

(G-11453)
MID-OHIO FOODBANK
3960 Brookham Dr (43123-9741)
PHONE..............................614 317-9400
Mathew Habash, *President*
Kimberly Dorniden, *Principal*
Lyn Hang, *COO*
Bridget Decrane, *Vice Pres*
Marilyn Tomasi, *Vice Pres*
EMP: 118
SQ FT: 204,500
SALES: 95.3MM **Privately Held**
SIC: 8322 8699 Meal delivery program; athletic organizations; charitable organization

(G-11454)
MT CARMEL MEDICAL GROUP
3667 Marlane Dr (43123-8895)
PHONE..............................614 277-9631
Lisa Peterson, *Principal*
EMP: 35
SALES (est): 84.7K **Privately Held**
SIC: 8011 General & family practice, physician/surgeon

(G-11455)
MYERS MACHINERY MOVERS INC
2210 Hardy Parkway St (43123-1243)
PHONE..............................614 871-5052
Gary Myers, *President*
Butch Myers, *Vice Pres*
Stacie Cope, *Admin Sec*
EMP: 50
SQ FT: 10,000
SALES (est): 10MM **Privately Held**
WEB: www.myersmachinerymovers.com
SIC: 4213 1796 4212 Heavy machinery transport; machine moving & rigging; local trucking, without storage

(G-11456)
NATIONWIDE CORPORATION
3400 Southpark Pl Ste A (43123-4856)
PHONE..............................614 277-5103
Steve Schick, *Manager*
Brad McClain, *Manager*
Rob Allen, *Administration*
EMP: 350
SALES (corp-wide): 13.2B **Privately Held**
SIC: 6411 Insurance agents, brokers & service
HQ: Nationwide Corporation
1 Nationwide Plz
Columbus OH 43215
614 249-7111

(G-11457)
NATIONWIDE MUTUAL INSURANCE CO
3400 Southpark Pl Ste A (43123-4856)
PHONE..............................402 420-6153
Mike Pollard, *Manager*
EMP: 250
SALES (corp-wide): 13.2B **Privately Held**
WEB: www.nirassn.com
SIC: 6411 Insurance agents
PA: Nationwide Mutual Insurance Company
1 Nationwide Plz
Columbus OH 43215
614 249-7111

(G-11458)
NEXTEL COMMUNICATIONS INC
1727 Stringtown Rd (43123-9125)
PHONE..............................614 801-9267
Trent Burke, *Manager*
EMP: 60

SALES (corp-wide): 85.9B **Publicly Held**
WEB: www.nextel.com
SIC: 4812 Cellular telephone services
HQ: Nextel Communications, Inc.
12502 Sunrise Valley Dr
Reston VA 20191
703 433-4000

(G-11459)
NIPPON EXPRESS USA INC
3705 Urbancrest Indus Dr (43123-1772)
PHONE..............................614 801-5695
Hediki Takami, *Manager*
EMP: 60
SALES (corp-wide): 18.7B **Privately Held**
SIC: 4731 Freight forwarding
HQ: Nippon Express U.S.A., Inc.
2401 44th Rd Fl 14
Long Island City NY 11101
212 758-6100

(G-11460)
NURSE MEDICIAL HEALTHCARE SVCS
3421 Farm Bank Way (43123-1974)
P.O. Box 801 (43123-0801)
PHONE..............................614 801-1300
Johnnie Berry, *President*
EMP: 90 EST: 2009
SALES: 5MM **Privately Held**
SIC: 8082 Visiting nurse service

(G-11461)
OHIO AUTO DELIVERY INC
Also Called: Oad
1700 Feddern Ave (43123-1206)
P.O. Box 268 (43123-0268)
PHONE..............................614 277-1445
David Stynchula, *President*
Kevin M Loychik, *Vice Pres*
Valerie Stynchula, *Admin Sec*
EMP: 30
SQ FT: 6,000
SALES (est): 5MM **Privately Held**
WEB: www.ohioautodelivery.com
SIC: 4213 Trucking Operator-Nonlocal

(G-11462)
OHIO AUTOMOBILE CLUB
4750 Big Run South Rd B (43123-9692)
PHONE..............................614 277-1310
Natalie Nassie, *Branch Mgr*
EMP: 43
SALES (corp-wide): 59.9MM **Privately Held**
SIC: 7997 Membership sports & recreation clubs
PA: The Ohio Automobile Club
90 E Wilson Bridge Rd # 1
Worthington OH 43085
614 431-7901

(G-11463)
OHIO CITRUS JUICES INC
2201 Hardy Parkway St (43123-1219)
PHONE..............................614 539-0030
Les Clark, *President*
Steve Clark, *General Mgr*
Kevin Jones, *Business Mgr*
EMP: 30
SQ FT: 11,000
SALES (est): 5MM **Privately Held**
WEB: www.ohiocitrus.com
SIC: 5149 Juices

(G-11464)
PAVEMENT PROTECTORS INC
Also Called: M & D Blacktop Sealing
2020 Longwood Ave (43123-1218)
PHONE..............................614 875-9989
Steve Bernsdorf, *President*
Chad Bernsdorf, *Vice Pres*
Mark Nance, *Sales Mgr*
EMP: 27
SQ FT: 10,000
SALES (est): 4.6MM **Privately Held**
WEB: www.mdblacktop.com
SIC: 1771 Blacktop (asphalt) work

(G-11465)
PITT-OHIO EXPRESS LLC
2101 Hardy Parkway St (43123-1213)
PHONE..............................614 801-1064
Rich Hassit, *General Mgr*
Richard Hazelet, *Director*
EMP: 140

SALES (corp-wide): 457MM **Privately Held**
SIC: 4213 Heavy hauling
PA: Pitt-Ohio Express, Llc
15 27th St
Pittsburgh PA 15222
412 232-3015

(G-11466)
RR DONNELLEY & SONS COMPANY
Also Called: Wallace
3801 Gantz Rd Ste A (43123-4915)
PHONE..............................614 539-5527
Jeremy Liening, *Manager*
EMP: 25
SALES (corp-wide): 6.8B **Publicly Held**
WEB: www.rrdonnelley.com
SIC: 4225 General warehousing & storage
PA: R. R. Donnelley & Sons Company
35 W Wacker Dr Ste 3650
Chicago IL 60601
312 326-8000

(G-11467)
S G LOEWENDICK AND SONS INC
2877 Jackson Pike (43123-9737)
PHONE..............................614 539-2582
David Loewendick, *President*
Karl Loewendick, *Vice Pres*
EMP: 30
SQ FT: 25,000
SALES: 2.4MM **Privately Held**
SIC: 1795 Demolition, buildings & other structures

(G-11468)
SAFETY TODAY INC (HQ)
Also Called: Midwest Service Center
3287 Southwest Blvd (43123-2210)
PHONE..............................614 409-7200
Edward Gustafson, *Principal*
Anthony Spearing, *Vice Pres*
▲ EMP: 30 EST: 1946
SQ FT: 90,000
SALES (est): 20.9MM **Privately Held**
WEB: www.safetytoday.com
SIC: 5084 5047 5099 Safety equipment; instruments & control equipment; measuring & testing equipment, electrical; noise control equipment; industrial safety devices: first aid kits & masks; safety equipment & supplies; fire extinguishers; lifesaving & survival equipment (non-medical); reflective road markers

(G-11469)
SAXTON REAL ESTATE CO (PA)
3703 Broadway (43123-2201)
PHONE..............................614 875-2327
William E Saxton, *President*
Linda Clagg, *Real Est Agnt*
EMP: 60
SQ FT: 1,500
SALES (est): 4.7MM **Privately Held**
WEB: www.saxtonrealestate.com
SIC: 6531 Real estate agent, residential

(G-11470)
SECURITAS SEC SVCS USA INC
Also Called: East Central Region
2180 Southwest Blvd (43123-1893)
PHONE..............................614 871-6051
Jeremy Simpson, *Branch Mgr*
Wayne Bailey, *Manager*
Michael Hartsock, *Supervisor*
EMP: 116
SALES (corp-wide): 10.9B **Privately Held**
WEB: www.securitasinc.com
SIC: 7381 Security guard service
HQ: Securitas Security Services Usa, Inc.
9 Campus Dr
Parsippany NJ 07054
973 267-5300

(G-11471)
SOLID WASTE AUTH CENTL OHIO
Also Called: Swaco
4239 London Groveport Rd (43123-9522)
PHONE..............................614 871-5100
David J Bush, *Chairman*
Paul Koehler, *CFO*
Matt Reardon, *Manager*

Ronald J Mills, *Exec Dir*
EMP: 120
SQ FT: 7,500
SALES (est): 31.4MM **Privately Held**
SIC: 4953 Sanitary landfill operation

(G-11472)
SOUTH- WESTERN CITY SCHOOL DST
Also Called: South Western Head Start
4308 Haughn Rd (43123-3239)
PHONE..............................614 801-8438
Margie Bramel, *Director*
EMP: 70
SALES (corp-wide): 321.6MM **Privately Held**
WEB: www.swcs.k12.oh.us
SIC: 8351 Head start center, except in conjunction with school
PA: South- Western City School District
3805 Marlane Dr
Grove City OH 43123
614 801-3000

(G-11473)
SOUTHWESTERN OBSTETRICIANS & G
Also Called: Grogg, Terry W MD
4461 Broadway 200 (43123-3064)
PHONE..............................614 875-0444
Diane Fitter, *President*
EMP: 25
SALES (est): 1.4MM **Privately Held**
SIC: 8011 Gynecologist; obstetrician

(G-11474)
STATE OF OHIO
Also Called: Ohio Board of Cosmetology
1929 Gateway Cir (43123-9587)
PHONE..............................614 466-3834
C Logston, *Exec Dir*
EMP: 38 **Privately Held**
SIC: 8621 Professional membership organizations
PA: State Of Ohio
30 E Broad St Fl 40
Columbus OH 43215
614 466-3455

(G-11475)
SYNNEX CORPORATION
Also Called: Grove City-Doh
4001 Gantz Rd Ste A (43123-4833)
PHONE..............................614 539-6995
Ruby Ray Ezell, *Branch Mgr*
EMP: 25
SALES (corp-wide): 20B **Publicly Held**
WEB: www.newageinc.com
SIC: 4225 General warehousing
PA: Synnex Corporation
44201 Nobel Dr
Fremont CA 94538
510 656-3333

(G-11476)
T N C CONSTRUCTION INC
Also Called: T N C Recovery and Maintenance
6058 Winnebago St (43123-9076)
PHONE..............................614 554-5330
Terry Whitt, *President*
EMP: 28
SQ FT: 1,200
SALES: 750K **Privately Held**
SIC: 7349 Building maintenance services

(G-11477)
TMARZETTI COMPANY
Also Called: Marzetti Distribution Center
5800 N Meadows Dr (43123-8600)
PHONE..............................614 277-3577
Patrick Hopkins, *Warehouse Mgr*
Joyce Decker, *Purch Mgr*
Jake Dean, *Research*
Shelba Jackson, *Human Res Mgr*
Mark Norman, *Branch Mgr*
EMP: 122
SALES (corp-wide): 1.2B **Publicly Held**
SIC: 4225 2035 General warehousing & storage; pickles, sauces & salad dressings
HQ: T.Marzetti Company
380 Polaris Pkwy Ste 400
Westerville OH 43082
614 846-2232

(G-11478)
TOSOH AMERICA INC (HQ)
3600 Gantz Rd (43123-1895)
PHONE...................................614 539-8622
Jan Top, *President*
Dan Minard, *Supervisor*
▲ EMP: 350
SQ FT: 250,000
SALES (est): 215.4MM
SALES (corp-wide): 7.7B **Privately Held**
SIC: 5169 3564 5047 5052 Industrial
chemicals; blowers & fans; diagnostic
equipment, medical; coal & other minerals
& ores
PA: Tosoh Corporation
3-8-2, Shiba
Minato-Ku TKY 105-0
354 275-103

(G-11479)
VALMER LAND TITLE AGENCY
3383 Farm Bank Way (43123-1973)
PHONE...................................614 875-7001
Stephanie Pietrocini, *Branch Mgr*
EMP: 33
SALES (corp-wide): 20MM **Privately Held**
SIC: 6361 Real estate title insurance
PA: Valmer Land Title Agency
2227 State Route 256 B
Reynoldsburg OH 43068
614 860-0005

(G-11480)
VERITIV OPERATING COMPANY
3265 Southpark Pl (43123-4899)
PHONE...................................614 251-7100
Rhonda Yates, *Director*
EMP: 37
SALES (corp-wide): 8.7B **Publicly Held**
SIC: 5113 Industrial & personal service
paper
HQ: Veritiv Operating Company
1000 Abernathy Rd
Atlanta GA 30328
770 391-8200

(G-11481)
VOLUNTERS OF AMERICA CNTL OHIO
4026 Mcdowell Rd (43123-3942)
PHONE...................................614 801-1655
EMP: 75
SALES (corp-wide): 10.7MM **Privately Held**
SIC: 8322 Individual & family services
PA: Volunteers Of America Ohio & Indiana
1776 E Broad St Frnt
Columbus OH 43203
614 253-6100

(G-11482)
WALLICK PROPERTIES MIDWEST LLC
Also Called: Parkmead Apartments
4243 Farr Ct (43123-3951)
PHONE...................................614 539-9041
Cindy Byers, *Branch Mgr*
EMP: 113
SALES (corp-wide): 38.8MM **Privately Held**
SIC: 6531 Real estate managers
PA: Wallick Properties Midwest Llc
160 W Main St Ste 200
New Albany OH 43054
419 381-7477

(G-11483)
WATERBEDS N STUFF INC (PA)
Also Called: Beds N Stuff
3933 Brookham Dr (43123-9295)
PHONE...................................614 871-1171
Gerald Spero, *President*
▲ EMP: 35
SQ FT: 25,500
SALES (est): 19.1MM **Privately Held**
SIC: 5947 5712 5199 Gift shop; novelties;
waterbeds & accessories; gifts & novel-
ties

(G-11484)
WELSPUN USA INC
3901 Gantz Rd Ste A (43123-4914)
PHONE...................................614 945-5100
Devesh Shriv, *Branch Mgr*

EMP: 30
SALES (corp-wide): 191.9MM **Privately Held**
SIC: 5131 Textiles, woven
HQ: Welspun Usa, Inc.
295 Textile Bldg 5th Ave # 5
New York NY 10016
212 620-2000

(G-11485)
WELTMAN WEINBERG & REIS CO LPA
3705 Marlane Dr (43123-8895)
PHONE...................................614 801-2600
Allen Reis, *Branch Mgr*
Mary Gerlach, *Branch Mgr*
EMP: 132
SALES (corp-wide): 151.3MM **Privately Held**
SIC: 8111 General practice law office
PA: Weltman, Weinberg & Reis Co., L.P.A.
323 W Lkeside Ave Ste 200
Cleveland OH 44113
216 685-1000

(G-11486)
WESTERN & SOUTHERN LF INSUR CO
Also Called: Western-Southern Life Insur
1931 Ohio Dr (43123-4835)
PHONE...................................614 277-4800
Frank Runion, *District Mgr*
EMP: 40 **Privately Held**
SIC: 6311 Life insurance
HQ: The Western & Southern Life Insur-
ance Company
400 Broadway St
Cincinnati OH 45202
513 629-1800

(G-11487)
WHETSTONE CARE CENTER LLC
Also Called: Monterey Care Center
3929 Hoover Rd (43123-2853)
PHONE...................................614 875-7700
Bob Brooks, *Manager*
EMP: 210
SALES (corp-wide): 20.1MM **Privately Held**
WEB: www.macintoshcompany.com
SIC: 8051 8069 Convalescent home with
continuous nursing care; specialty hospi-
tals, except psychiatric
PA: Whetstone Care Center Llc
3863 Trueman Ct
Hilliard OH 43026
614 345-9500

(G-11488)
WHITE GLOVE EXECUTIVE SERVICES
2647 Bryan Cir (43123-3526)
PHONE...................................614 226-2553
Gary Holland, *President*
EMP: 25
SALES: 280K **Privately Held**
WEB: www.whiteglovemaintenance.com
SIC: 7349 Building maintenance services

(G-11489)
WOMENS CIVIC CLUB GROVE CITY
3881 Tamara Dr (43123-2864)
PHONE...................................614 871-0145
Carolyn Kromer, *President*
Rosemary Barkes, *President*
Carol Rorick, *Vice Pres*
Susan Norris, *Treasurer*
Ada Weygandt, *Admin Sec*
EMP: 40
SALES (est): 484.9K **Privately Held**
SIC: 8699 Charitable organization

(G-11490)
WOODLAND RUN EQUIN VET FACILTY
1474 Borror Rd (43123-8972)
PHONE...................................614 871-4919
Richard C Mather II, *Principal*
EMP: 25
SQ FT: 856
SALES (est): 1MM **Privately Held**
SIC: 0742 Veterinarian, animal specialties

(G-11491)
YOUNG MENS CHRISTIAN ASSOC
Also Called: Urban Craft
3600 Discovery Dr (43123-9482)
PHONE...................................614 871-9622
Kim Hodge, *Exec Dir*
Erica Hickox, *Director*
EMP: 180
SALES (corp-wide): 44.9MM **Privately Held**
WEB: www.ymca-columbus.com
SIC: 8641 7991 8351 7032 Youth organi-
zations; physical fitness facilities; child
day care services; youth camps; individ-
ual & family services
PA: Young Men's Christian Association Of
Central Ohio
40 W Long St
Columbus OH 43215
614 389-4409

Groveport
Franklin County

(G-11492)
AIRE-TECH INC
4681 Homer Ohio Ln (43125-9231)
PHONE...................................614 836-5670
Suzie Tamborelle, *President*
EMP: 30
SQ FT: 6,000
SALES: 3MM **Privately Held**
SIC: 1711 Warm air heating & air condi-
tioning contractor

(G-11493)
AMSTED INDUSTRIES INCORPORATED
Also Called: Griffin Wheel
3900 Bixby Rd (43125-9510)
PHONE...................................614 836-2323
Joe Cuske, *Plant Mgr*
EMP: 181
SALES (corp-wide): 2.4B **Privately Held**
SIC: 3321 5088 3743 3714 Railroad car
wheels & brake shoes, cast iron; railroad
equipment & supplies; railroad equip-
ment; motor vehicle parts & accessories
PA: Amsted Industries Incorporated
180 N Stetson Ave # 1800
Chicago IL 60601
312 645-1700

(G-11494)
ARC INDUSTRIES INCORPORATED O
Also Called: ARC Industries South
4395 Marketing Pl (43125-9556)
PHONE...................................614 836-0700
Dan Darling, *Human Res Dir*
Dan Espinoza, *Supervisor*
Sharon Evrard, *IT/INT Sup*
Kurt Smith, *Director*
EMP: 290
SALES (corp-wide): 11.1MM **Privately Held**
WEB: www.arcind.com
SIC: 8322 8331 Social services for the
handicapped; job training & vocational re-
habilitation services
PA: Arc Industries, Incorporated, Of
Franklin County, Ohio
2780 Airport Dr
Columbus OH 43219
614 479-2500

(G-11495)
ARC INDUSTRIES INCORPORATED O
Also Called: Bixby Living Skills Center
4200 Bixby Rd (43125-9509)
PHONE...................................614 836-6050
David Pisdale, *Manager*
Linda Monroe, *Director*
EMP: 50
SALES (corp-wide): 11.1MM **Privately Held**
WEB: www.arcind.com
SIC: 8399 Council for social agency

PA: Arc Industries, Incorporated, Of
Franklin County, Ohio
2780 Airport Dr
Columbus OH 43219
614 479-2500

(G-11496)
BLUE LINE DISTRIBUTION
Also Called: Blue Line Food Service
2250 Spiegel Dr Ste P (43125-9131)
PHONE...................................614 497-9610
Keith Jones, *Principal*
EMP: 41
SALES (est): 117.9MM **Privately Held**
SIC: 5141 Groceries, general line
HQ: Little Caesar Enterprises Inc
2211 Woodward Ave
Detroit MI 48201
313 983-6000

(G-11497)
BOARS HEAD PROVISIONS CO INC
2225 Spiegel Dr (43125-9036)
PHONE...................................614 662-5300
EMP: 301
SALES (corp-wide): 221.8MM **Privately Held**
SIC: 5147 Lard
PA: Boar's Head Provisions Co., Inc.
1819 Main St Ste 800
Sarasota FL 34236
941 955-0994

(G-11498)
C & R INC (PA)
5600 Clyde Moore Dr (43125-1081)
PHONE...................................614 497-1130
Ronald E Murphy, *President*
Phillip Lee Mc Kitrick, *Vice Pres*
Christina M Murphy, *Treasurer*
EMP: 47
SALES (est): 9.7MM **Privately Held**
WEB: www.crproducts.com
SIC: 3444 7692 3443 3312 Sheet metal
specialties, not stamped; welding repair;
fabricated plate work (boiler shop); blast
furnaces & steel mills

(G-11499)
CARDINAL HEALTH INC
5995 Commerce Center Dr (43125-1099)
PHONE...................................614 409-6770
Matthew Wig, *Opers Spvr*
Arnie Randall, *Director*
EMP: 34
SALES (est): 13.3MM **Privately Held**
SIC: 5122 Pharmaceuticals

(G-11500)
CEVA FREIGHT LLC
Also Called: Ceva Ocean Line
2727 London Groveport Rd (43125-9304)
PHONE...................................614 482-5100
Greg Russo, *Manager*
EMP: 75
SALES (corp-wide): 20.8MM **Privately Held**
WEB: www.tntlogistics.com
SIC: 4731 Domestic freight forwarding
HQ: Ceva Freight, Llc
15350 Vickery Dr
Houston TX 77032

(G-11501)
CEVA LOGISTICS LLC
2727 London Groveport Rd (43125-9304)
PHONE...................................614 482-5000
Robert Harper, *Branch Mgr*
EMP: 300
SALES (corp-wide): 20.8MM **Privately Held**
SIC: 4731 Freight forwarding
HQ: Ceva Logistics, Llc
15350 Vickery Dr
Houston TX 77032
281 618-3100

(G-11502)
COMMERCIAL WAREHOUSE & CARTAGE
6295 Commerce Center Dr (43125-1137)
PHONE...................................614 409-3901
EMP: 69

▲ = Import ▼=Export
◆ =Import/Export

SALES (corp-wide): 92.1MM **Privately Held**
SIC: **4225** General warehousing & storage
PA: Commercial Warehouse & Cartage Inc
3402 Meyer Rd
Fort Wayne IN 46803
260 426-7825

(G-11503)
CONCORD EXPRESS INC (HQ)
5905 Green Pointe Dr S D (43125-2007)
PHONE.................................718 656-7821
Joseph Chang, *Ch of Bd*
◆ EMP: 31
SQ FT: 100
SALES (est): 7.9MM
SALES (corp-wide): 3.8MM **Privately Held**
WEB: www.concordhk.com
SIC: **4731** Foreign freight forwarding
PA: Concord Express Limited
Rm 50-52 2/F Sino Indl Plaza
Kowloon Bay KLN
275 383-13

(G-11504)
CRAFT WHOLESALERS INC
Also Called: Craft Catalog
4600 S Hamilton Rd (43125-9636)
PHONE.................................740 964-6210
Tara Parker, *President*
David Parker, *Vice Pres*
Dawn Long, *Director*
Karen Piper, *Admin Sec*
▼ EMP: 108 EST: 1981
SQ FT: 50,000
SALES (est): 21.9MM **Privately Held**
WEB: www.craftwholesalers.com
SIC: **5092 5961** Arts & crafts equipment & supplies; arts & crafts equipment & supplies, mail order

(G-11505)
CUTHBERT GREENHOUSE INC (PA)
4900 Hendron Rd (43125-9506)
PHONE.................................614 836-3866
Wayne Cuthbert, *President*
David Cuthbert, *President*
Brett Cuthbert, *Corp Secy*
Grogery Cuthbert, *Vice Pres*
Ron Storm, *Sales Staff*
▲ EMP: 39
SQ FT: 518,000
SALES (est): 5MM **Privately Held**
WEB: www.cuthbertgreenhouse.com
SIC: **0181** Flowers: grown under cover (e.g. greenhouse production)

(G-11506)
DECKERS NURSERY INC
6239 Rager Rd (43125-9266)
PHONE.................................614 836-2130
Brian M Decker, *President*
Patricia D Decker, *Corp Secy*
EMP: 25
SQ FT: 10,000
SALES (est): 3.5MM **Privately Held**
WEB: www.deckersnursery.com
SIC: **0181** Nursery stock, growing of

(G-11507)
DHL SUPPLY CHAIN (USA)
6390 Commerce Ct (43125-1158)
PHONE.................................614 836-1265
EMP: 60
SALES (corp-wide): 70.4B **Privately Held**
SIC: **4731** Freight forwarding
HQ: Exel Inc.
570 Polaris Pkwy
Westerville OH 43082
614 865-8500

(G-11508)
DWYER CONCRETE LIFTING INC
5650 Groveport Rd (43125-1003)
PHONE.................................614 501-0998
Bryan Dwyer, *President*
Randy Bonhaus, *Executive*
EMP: 45
SALES (est): 1.4MM **Privately Held**
SIC: **1771** Concrete work

(G-11509)
EMERITUS CORPORATION
Also Called: Emeritus At Lakeview
4000 Lakeview Xing (43125-9059)
PHONE.................................614 836-5990
Jill Wallace, *Branch Mgr*
EMP: 43
SALES (corp-wide): 4.5B **Publicly Held**
SIC: **8052** Personal care facility
HQ: Emeritus Corporation
3131 Elliott Ave Ste 500
Milwaukee WI 53214

(G-11510)
ESSILOR OF AMERICA INC
2400 Spiegel Dr Ste A (43125-9132)
PHONE.................................614 492-0888
Dave Mann, *Facilities Mgr*
Robyn Taylor, *Human Res Mgr*
Den Lucas, *Manager*
Cindy McNeal, *Manager*
Mark Nicolia, *Analyst*
EMP: 250
SALES (corp-wide): 283.5MM **Privately Held**
WEB: www.essilor.com
SIC: **7389 4225** Personal service agents, brokers & bureaus; general warehousing & storage
HQ: Essilor Of America, Inc.
13555 N Stemmons Fwy
Dallas TX 75234
214 496-4000

(G-11511)
EXEL INC
Also Called: Exel Logistics
2829 Rohr Rd (43125-9305)
PHONE.................................614 662-9247
Chris Young, *Opers Spvr*
Regina McGraw, *Office Mgr*
Mark Spencer, *Director*
EMP: 300
SALES (corp-wide): 70.4B **Privately Held**
WEB: www.exel-logistics.com
SIC: **4731** Freight transportation arrangement
HQ: Exel Inc.
570 Polaris Pkwy
Westerville OH 43082
614 865-8500

(G-11512)
FAF INC
6800 Port Rd (43125-9109)
PHONE.................................800 496-4696
Mona Pritchard, *Principal*
Doug Smith, *Manager*
Mary Walker, *Manager*
EMP: 499
SALES (est): 31.8MM
SALES (corp-wide): 1.3B **Publicly Held**
SIC: **4731** Freight transportation arrangement
PA: Forward Air Corporation
1915 Snapps Ferry Rd L
Greeneville TN 37745
423 636-7000

(G-11513)
FARO SERVICES INC (PA)
7070 Pontius Rd (43125-7504)
PHONE.................................614 497-1700
Rich Ashton, *President*
Matthew Shaw, *Sales Mgr*
EMP: 200
SQ FT: 322,000
SALES (est): 94.6MM **Privately Held**
SIC: **4225 4731** General warehousing; freight transportation arrangement

(G-11514)
FUNAI SERVICE CORPORATION
2425 Spiegel Dr (43125-9278)
PHONE.................................614 409-2600
Takashi Miyamoto, *President*
▲ EMP: 25
SALES (est): 10MM **Privately Held**
SIC: **5065** Electronic parts

(G-11515)
HAGUE WATER CONDITIONING INC (PA)
4581 Homer Ohio Ln (43125-9082)
PHONE.................................614 482-8121
William Hague, *President*

Joyce Hague, *Corp Secy*
Jeff Hague, *Vice Pres*
Jeffrey Martin, *Prdtn Mgr*
Julie Daniel, *Office Mgr*
EMP: 26
SALES (est): 6.1MM **Privately Held**
SIC: **7389 5074** Water softener service; water softeners

(G-11516)
HD SUPPLY INC
6200 Commerce Center Dr (43125-1093)
PHONE.................................614 771-4849
Mike Phillips, *President*
EMP: 41 **Publicly Held**
SIC: **5031 5033** Building materials, exterior; building materials, interior; doors & windows; roofing, siding & insulation
HQ: Hd Supply, Inc.
3100 Cumberland Blvd Se # 1700
Atlanta GA 30339
770 852-9000

(G-11517)
HILL MANOR ENTERPRISES (PA)
Also Called: SHADY LANE CHILDREN'S HOME
5585 Morgan Ct (43125-9763)
P.O. Box 7128, Columbus (43205-0128)
PHONE.................................614 567-7134
Fannie Mills, *President*
EMP: 25
SALES: 891.2K **Privately Held**
SIC: **8361** Children's home; home for the mentally handicapped

(G-11518)
HOME CITY ICE COMPANY
4505 S Hamilton Rd (43125-9416)
PHONE.................................614 836-2877
Tony Bakes, *Branch Mgr*
EMP: 50
SQ FT: 12,000
SALES (corp-wide): 232.5MM **Privately Held**
WEB: www.homecityice.com
SIC: **5199 5999 2097** Ice, manufactured or natural; ice; manufactured ice
PA: The Home City Ice Company
6045 Bridgetown Rd Ste 1
Cincinnati OH 45248
513 574-1800

(G-11519)
HOMETOWN URGENT CARE
3813 S Hamilton Rd (43125-9330)
PHONE.................................614 835-0400
EMP: 123
SALES (corp-wide): 73.2MM **Privately Held**
SIC: **8011** Primary care medical clinic
PA: Hometown Urgent Care
2400 Corp Exchange Dr # 102
Columbus OH 43231
614 505-7633

(G-11520)
INNOVTIVE CRTIVE SOLUTIONS LLC
Also Called: I C S
5835 Green Pointe Dr S B (43125-2000)
PHONE.................................614 491-9638
Bob Pushay, *Mng Member*
EMP: 38
SALES (est): 1.2MM **Privately Held**
SIC: **2759 7336** Screen printing; commercial art & graphic design

(G-11521)
ISOMEDIX OPERATIONS INC
Also Called: Steris Isomedix
4405 Marketing Pl (43125-9556)
PHONE.................................614 836-5757
John M Schweers, *Principal*
EMP: 30
SQ FT: 2,197
SALES (corp-wide): 2.6B **Privately Held**
WEB: www.isomedix.com
SIC: **8734** Industrial sterilization service
HQ: Isomedix Operations Inc.
5960 Heisley Rd
Mentor OH 44060

(G-11522)
J C DIRECT MAIL INC
4241 Williams Rd (43125-9029)
PHONE.................................614 836-4848
Wayne Caltrider, *President*
EMP: 200
SQ FT: 76,736
SALES (est): 17MM **Privately Held**
WEB: www.wcnjcd.com
SIC: **7331** Mailing service

(G-11523)
JACOBSON WAREHOUSE COMPANY INC
Also Called: Xpo Logistics
2450 Spiegel Dr Ste H (43125-9120)
PHONE.................................614 409-0003
Judith Jacobsen, *Branch Mgr*
EMP: 26
SALES (corp-wide): 15.3B **Publicly Held**
SIC: **4225** General warehousing & storage
HQ: Jacobson Warehouse Company, Inc.
3811 Dixon St
Des Moines IA 50313
515 263-0854

(G-11524)
JACOBSON WAREHOUSE COMPANY INC
Also Called: Xpo Logistics
6600 Port Rd Ste 200 (43125-9129)
PHONE.................................614 497-6300
John Kettman, *Branch Mgr*
EMP: 80
SALES (corp-wide): 15.3B **Publicly Held**
WEB: www.jacobsonco.com
SIC: **4225** General warehousing & storage
HQ: Jacobson Warehouse Company, Inc.
3811 Dixon St
Des Moines IA 50313
515 263-0854

(G-11525)
K & M KLEENING SERVICE INC
4429 Professional Pkwy (43125-9228)
PHONE.................................614 737-3750
Morris Berkley, *President*
Carolyn Berkley, *Vice Pres*
Randall Parker, *Vice Pres*
Michelle White, *Admin Sec*
EMP: 62
SALES (est): 1.9MM **Privately Held**
SIC: **7349** Janitorial service, contract basis

(G-11526)
KRAFT ELECTRICAL CONTG INC
4407 Professional Pkwy (43125-9228)
PHONE.................................614 836-9300
EMP: 36
SALES (corp-wide): 13.4MM **Privately Held**
SIC: **4813 3699** Telephone communication, except radio; electrical equipment & supplies
PA: Kraft Electrical Contracting, Inc.
5710 Hillside Ave
Cincinnati OH 45233
513 467-0500

(G-11527)
NEW WORLD VAN LINES OHIO INC
4633 Homer Ohio Ln (43125-9231)
PHONE.................................614 836-5720
Michael M Marx, *President*
Richard Wilkus, *CFO*
EMP: 35
SALES (est): 2.5MM **Privately Held**
SIC: **4213** Household goods transport

(G-11528)
NIFCO AMERICA CORPORATION
Also Called: Groveport Warehouse
2435 Spiegel Dr (43125-9278)
PHONE.................................614 836-8733
John Deiker, *CFO*
EMP: 200
SALES (corp-wide): 2.5B **Privately Held**
SIC: **4225** General warehousing
HQ: Nifco America Corporation
8015 Dove Pkwy
Canal Winchester OH 43110
614 920-6800

(G-11529)
PETSMART INC
6499 Adelaide Ct (43125-9635)
PHONE.................................614 497-3001
San Juana Silos, *Branch Mgr*
Rusty Roof, *Manager*
EMP: 48
SALES (corp-wide): 12.1B **Privately Held**
WEB: www.petsmart.com
SIC: 5999 0752 General warehousing & storage
HQ: Petsmart, Inc.
19601 N 27th Ave
Phoenix AZ 85027
623 580-6100

(G-11530)
PRESORT AMERICA LTD
4227 Williams Rd (43125-9029)
PHONE.................................614 836-5120
Wayne Caltrider, *Partner*
EMP: 60
SALES (est): 4.7MM **Privately Held**
SIC: 7331 Mailing service

(G-11531)
PRESTIGE DELIVERY SYSTEMS LLC
4279 Directors Blvd (43125-9504)
PHONE.................................614 836-8980
Jeff Spocker, *Manager*
EMP: 30
SQ FT: 70,400
SALES (corp-wide): 144.7MM **Privately Held**
SIC: 4212 Delivery service, vehicular
HQ: Prestige Delivery Systems, Llc
1912 Woodford Rd
Vienna VA 22182
216 332-8000

(G-11532)
PRO HEALTH CARE SERVICES LTD
270 Main St Ste A (43125-1180)
P.O. Box 472 (43125-0472)
PHONE.................................614 856-9111
Marco A Quezada, *Partner*
Maria Delaluz-Munoz, *General Ptnr*
Claudia Sorrell, *Manager*
EMP: 50
SALES (est): 1.6MM **Privately Held**
SIC: 8082 Visiting nurse service

(G-11533)
RADIAL SOUTH LP
6360-6440 Port Rd (43125)
PHONE.................................678 584-4047
Steve Bolin, *Manager*
EMP: 200
SALES (corp-wide): 2.4B **Privately Held**
WEB: www.innotrac.com
SIC: 5045 4226 Computers, peripherals & software; special warehousing & storage
HQ: Radial South, L.P.
935 1st Ave
King Of Prussia PA 19406
610 491-7000

(G-11534)
RENTOKIL NORTH AMERICA INC
Also Called: Initial Tropical Plant Svcs
6300 Commerce Center Dr G (43125-1183)
PHONE.................................614 837-0099
Monica Desch, *Manager*
EMP: 35
SALES (corp-wide): 3.1B **Privately Held**
WEB: www.primescapeproducts.com
SIC: 5193 0781 Flowers & nursery stock; landscape services
HQ: Rentokil North America, Inc.
1125 Berkshire Blvd # 150
Wyomissing PA 19610
610 372-9700

(G-11535)
RICART FORD INC
Also Called: Ricart Automotive
4255 S Hamilton Rd (43125-9332)
PHONE.................................614 836-5321
Rhett C Ricart, *President*
Paul F Ricart Jr, *Vice Pres*
Rick Ricart, *Vice Pres*

Bradley Sells, *Prdtn Mgr*
Larry Mills, *Parts Mgr*
▲ EMP: 460 EST: 1953
SQ FT: 13,000
SALES (est): 71.8MM **Privately Held**
SIC: 5511 7538 Automobiles, new & used; general automotive repair shops

(G-11536)
S&P GLOBAL INC
6405 Commerce Ct (43125-1187)
PHONE.................................614 835-2444
EMP: 149
SALES (corp-wide): 6.2B **Publicly Held**
SIC: 6282 Investment advisory service
PA: S&P Global Inc.
55 Water St
New York NY 10041
212 438-1000

(G-11537)
SCHENKER INC
2842 Spiegel Dr (43125-9012)
PHONE.................................614 662-7217
Joyce Michles, *Manager*
EMP: 30
SALES (corp-wide): 23.3MM **Privately Held**
SIC: 4789 Pipeline terminal facilities, independently operated
HQ: Schenker, Inc.
1305 Executive Blvd # 200
Chesapeake VA 23320
757 821-3400

(G-11538)
SPRINGS WINDOW FASHIONS LLC
6295 Commerce Center Dr (43125-1137)
PHONE.................................614 492-6770
Mike Mehring, *Manager*
EMP: 66
SALES (corp-wide): 3.1B **Privately Held**
WEB: www.springs.com
SIC: 4225 General warehousing & storage
HQ: Springs Window Fashions, Llc
7549 Graber Rd
Middleton WI 53562
608 836-1011

(G-11539)
STEDMAN FLOOR CO INC
420 Lowery Ct (43125-9567)
P.O. Box 418 (43125-0418)
PHONE.................................614 836-3190
Richard Stedman, *President*
Wanda Stedman, *Admin Sec*
EMP: 30
SQ FT: 26,000
SALES: 4MM **Privately Held**
SIC: 1752 Carpet laying

(G-11540)
STRAND ASSOCIATES INC
4433 Professional Pkwy (43125-9228)
PHONE.................................614 835-0460
Richard Sanson, *Vice Pres*
EMP: 36
SALES (corp-wide): 55.2MM **Privately Held**
SIC: 8711 Consulting engineer
PA: Strand Associates, Inc.
910 W Wingra Dr
Madison WI 53715
608 251-4843

(G-11541)
TNT POWER WASH INC
Also Called: TNT Services
3220 Toy Rd (43125-9297)
PHONE.................................614 662-3110
Seth Bromberg, *President*
EMP: 26
SALES: 9.8MM **Privately Held**
SIC: 7349 Cleaning service, industrial or commercial

(G-11542)
TNT POWER WASH INC (PA)
Also Called: TNT Services
3220 Toy Rd (43125-9297)
PHONE.................................614 662-3110
Seth Bromberg, *President*
Terri Moore, *COO*
Sean Roche, *Opers Staff*
Angela Root, *Sales Mgr*

Ricky Martin, *Accounts Mgr*
EMP: 26
SALES: 9.8MM **Privately Held**
SIC: 7349 Cleaning service, industrial or commercial

(G-11543)
TRILOGY FULFILLMENT LLC
6600 Alum Creek Dr (43125-9420)
PHONE.................................614 491-0553
Charles Flannigan Jr,
EMP: 28
SALES (est): 70.3MM
SALES (corp-wide): 7.6B **Privately Held**
SIC: 8742 Distribution channels consultant
PA: Golden Gate Private Equity Incorporated
1 Embarcadero Ctr Fl 39
San Francisco CA 94111
415 983-2706

(G-11544)
TRUGREEN LIMITED PARTNERSHIP
Also Called: Tru Green-Chemlawn
4045 Lakeview Xing (43125-9039)
PHONE.................................614 610-4142
Tom Kiener, *Branch Mgr*
EMP: 45
SALES (corp-wide): 3.4B **Privately Held**
SIC: 0782 Lawn care services
HQ: Trugreen Limited Partnership
1790 Kirby Pkwy
Memphis TN 38138
901 251-4128

(G-11545)
UNION SUPPLY GROUP INC
Also Called: Food Express US
3321 Toy Rd (43125-9363)
PHONE.................................614 409-1444
Guy Steele, *COO*
EMP: 30 **Privately Held**
SIC: 5084 Industrial machinery & equipment
PA: Union Supply Group, Inc.
2301 E Pacifica Pl
Rancho Dominguez CA 90220

(G-11546)
UNITED MCGILL CORPORATION (HQ)
1 Mission Park (43125-1100)
PHONE.................................614 829-1200
James D McGill, *President*
Patrick Brooks, *QC Dir*
Jayne F McGill, *Admin Sec*
▲ EMP: 30 EST: 1951
SQ FT: 13,000
SALES (est): 67.7MM **Privately Held**
WEB: www.unitedmcgill.com
SIC: 3444 3564 5169 3567 Ducts, sheet metal; precipitators, electrostatic; air purification equipment; sealants; industrial furnaces & ovens; adhesives & sealants
PA: The Mcgill Corporation
1 Mission Park
Groveport OH 43125
614 829-1200

(G-11547)
USAVINYL LLC
Also Called: Weatherables
5795 Green Pointe Dr S (43125-1083)
PHONE.................................614 771-4805
Brad Halley,
◆ EMP: 26
SALES: 10MM **Privately Held**
SIC: 5211 5031 Fencing; building materials, exterior

(G-11548)
UTILITY TECHNOLOGIES INTL CORP
4700 Homer Ohio Ln (43125-9230)
PHONE.................................614 879-7624
Richard D Dickerson, *CEO*
Richard Dickerson, *CEO*
Hobart Griset, *President*
Rodney V Bennett, *Vice Pres*
Jason Julian, *Vice Pres*
EMP: 50
SALES (est): 9MM **Privately Held**
WEB: www.uti-corp.com
SIC: 8711 Consulting engineer

(G-11549)
VILLAGE OF GROVEPORT
655 Blacklick St (43125-1200)
PHONE.................................614 830-2060
Anthony Bales, *Branch Mgr*
EMP: 34 **Privately Held**
SIC: 8322 Senior citizens' center or association
PA: Village Of Groveport
655 Blacklick St
Groveport OH 43125
614 836-5301

(G-11550)
W C NATIONAL MAILING CORP
4241 Williams Rd (43125-9573)
PHONE.................................614 836-5703
Wayne Caltrider, *President*
EMP: 300
SQ FT: 30,000
SALES (est): 24.2MM **Privately Held**
SIC: 7331 Mailing service

(G-11551)
WAXMAN CONSUMER PDTS GROUP INC
5920 Green Pointe Dr S A (43125-1182)
PHONE.................................614 491-0500
Jeff Willey, *Manager*
EMP: 60
SALES (corp-wide): 100MM **Privately Held**
WEB: www.waxmancpgvendor.com
SIC: 5074 5072 Plumbing fittings & supplies; casters & glides; furniture hardware
HQ: Waxman Consumer Products Group Inc.
24455 Aurora Rd
Cleveland OH 44146

Hamden
Vinton County

(G-11552)
HUSTON NURSING HOME
38500 State Route 160 (45634-8805)
P.O. Box 327 (45634-0327)
PHONE.................................740 384-3485
Marjorie Houston, *President*
EMP: 90
SALES (est): 3.4MM **Privately Held**
SIC: 8051 Convalescent home with continuous nursing care

(G-11553)
SANDS HILL COAL HAULING CO INC (PA)
38701 State Route 160 (45634)
PHONE.................................740 384-4211
Alan Arthur, *President*
EMP: 142
SQ FT: 3,500
SALES (est): 7.2MM **Privately Held**
SIC: 1221 Strip mining, bituminous

Hamilton
Butler County

(G-11554)
ACPI SYSTEMS INC
3445 Hmlton New London Rd (45013-9459)
P.O. Box 368, Ross (45061-0368)
PHONE.................................513 738-3840
Laura L Meyer, *President*
James J Meyer, *Vice Pres*
Ken Brock, *Manager*
EMP: 45
SQ FT: 5,000
SALES (est): 13.5MM **Privately Held**
WEB: www.acpi-systems.com
SIC: 1731 8711 Electrical work; electrical or electronic engineering

(G-11555)
AIRGAS SAFETY INC
N Park Business (45011)
PHONE.................................513 942-1465
Hap Pfiefer, *Branch Mgr*
EMP: 50

SALES (corp-wide): 125.9MM **Privately Held**
WEB: www.airgas.com
SIC: 5169 Industrial gases
HQ: Airgas Safety, Inc.
  2501 Green Ln
  Levittown PA 19057

(G-11556)
ALAN WOODS TRUCKING INC
3592 Herman Rd (45013-9534)
PHONE...........................513 738-3314
Alan Woods, *President*
Mary Lou Woods, *Corp Secy*
Audra Woods, *Manager*
EMP: 28
SALES (est): 2.7MM **Privately Held**
SIC: 4212 Dump truck haulage

(G-11557)
APPLAUSE TALENT PRESENTATION
1525 Singer Ave (45011)
PHONE...........................513 844-6788
Mary Anne Weisbrod, *President*
EMP: 25 EST: 1988
SALES (est): 858.6K **Privately Held**
WEB: www.applausetalent.com
SIC: 7911 Dance hall services

(G-11558)
AUR GROUP FINANCIAL CREDIT UN
1401 Nw Washington Blvd (45013-1748)
PHONE...........................513 737-0508
Tim Boellner, *Branch Mgr*
EMP: 31
SALES (corp-wide): 39K **Privately Held**
SIC: 6061 6062 Federal credit unions; state credit unions
PA: Aurgroup Financial Credit Union, Inc.
  8811 Holden Blvd
  Fairfield OH 45014
  513 942-4422

(G-11559)
BOYS & GIRLS CLB HAMILTON INC (PA)
958 East Ave (45011-3809)
PHONE...........................513 893-0071
Mark Rentschler, *Vice Pres*
David Stitsinger, *Treasurer*
Karen Miller, *Exec Dir*
EMP: 30
SQ FT: 13,000
SALES: 553.6K **Privately Held**
SIC: 7997 Membership sports & recreation clubs

(G-11560)
BUILDER SERVICES GROUP INC
Also Called: Gale Insulation
28 Keisland Ct (45015)
PHONE...........................513 942-2204
Patrick Flanagan, *Division Mgr*
Russ Miller, *Branch Mgr*
EMP: 25
SALES (corp-wide): 2.3B **Publicly Held**
WEB: www.galeind.com
SIC: 1742 Insulation, buildings
HQ: Builder Services Group, Inc.
  475 N Williamson Blvd
  Daytona Beach FL 32114
  386 304-2222

(G-11561)
BUTLER COUNTY OF OHIO
Also Called: Clerk of Courts
315 High St Ste 550 (45011-6063)
PHONE...........................513 887-3282
Denise Davidson, *Officer*
EMP: 72 **Privately Held**
SIC: 9211 8111 9621 9199 Local courts; administrative & government law; motor vehicle licensing & inspection office, government; general government administration
PA: Butler, County Of Ohio
  315 High St Fl 6
  Hamilton OH 45011
  513 887-3278

(G-11562)
BUTLER COUNTY OF OHIO
Also Called: Auditors Office
130 High St Fl 4 (45011-2728)
PHONE...........................513 887-3154
Kay Roger, *Manager*
EMP: 90 **Privately Held**
WEB: www.butlercountyclerk.org
SIC: 6531 Auction, real estate
PA: Butler, County Of Ohio
  315 High St Fl 6
  Hamilton OH 45011
  513 887-3278

(G-11563)
BUTLER COUNTY OF OHIO
Also Called: Workforce One
4631 Dixie Hwy (45014-1845)
PHONE...........................513 785-6500
Donald Kell, *Supervisor*
EMP: 25 **Privately Held**
WEB: www.butlercountyclerk.org
SIC: 8331 Job counseling
PA: Butler, County Of Ohio
  315 High St Fl 6
  Hamilton OH 45011
  513 887-3278

(G-11564)
BUTLER BHAVIORAL HLTH SVCS INC (PA)
Also Called: Hamilton Counseling Center T/S
1502 University Blvd (45011-3335)
PHONE...........................513 896-7887
Kimball Stricklin, *CEO*
EMP: 28
SALES: 8.4MM **Privately Held**
SIC: 8093 Mental health clinic, outpatient

(G-11565)
BUTLER CNTY CMMTY HLTH CNSRTM
300 High St 4 (45011-6078)
PHONE...........................513 454-1460
Donald Reimer, *Director*
EMP: 65
SQ FT: 22,000
SALES: 9.7MM **Privately Held**
SIC: 8011 General & family practice, physician/surgeon

(G-11566)
BUTLER CNTY RGIONAL TRNST AUTH
Also Called: Bcrta
3045 Moser Ct (45011-5373)
PHONE...........................513 785-5237
Carla Oden, *Opers Mgr*
Robert Ruzinsky, *CFO*
Luke Morgan, *Manager*
Carla Lakatos, *Exec Dir*
EMP: 102
SALES (est): 3.8MM **Privately Held**
WEB: www.butlercountyclerk.org
SIC: 4111 Local & suburban transit

(G-11567)
BUTLER COUNTY BD OF MENTAL RE
Also Called: Janat Clemmons Center
282 N Fair Ave Ste 1 (45011-4252)
PHONE...........................513 785-2815
Mary May, *Principal*
Jessica Purkiser, *Supervisor*
Tanya Coffey, *Director*
EMP: 28
SALES (corp-wide): 5.9MM **Privately Held**
SIC: 8361 8351 Home for the mentally retarded; preschool center
PA: Butler County Board Of Developmental Disabilities
  282 N Fair Ave Ste 1
  Hamilton OH 45011
  513 785-2815

(G-11568)
BUTLER COUNTY EDUCTL SVC CTR
Also Called: Butler County Eductl Svcs Ctr
23 S Front St Fl 3 (45011-2819)
PHONE...........................513 737-2817
Kelly Hubbard, *Branch Mgr*
EMP: 35

SALES (corp-wide): 13.6MM **Privately Held**
SIC: 8351 Head start center, except in conjunction with school
PA: Butler County Educational Service Center
  400 N Erie Hwy Ste A
  Hamilton OH 45011
  513 887-3710

(G-11569)
BUTLER COUNTY OF OHIO
Also Called: Butler County Engineers Office
1921 Fairgrove Ave (45011-1965)
PHONE...........................513 867-5744
Greg Wilkens, *Manager*
Jerry Jackson, *Supervisor*
EMP: 75 **Privately Held**
WEB: www.butlercountyclerk.org
SIC: 8711 Engineering services
PA: Butler, County Of Ohio
  315 High St Fl 6
  Hamilton OH 45011
  513 887-3278

(G-11570)
BUTLER COUNTY OF OHIO
Also Called: Butler County Courts
315 High St Fl 5 (45011-6063)
PHONE...........................513 887-3090
Cindi Carpenter, *Principal*
EMP: 40 **Privately Held**
WEB: www.butlercountyclerk.org
SIC: 9211 8111 ; legal services
PA: Butler, County Of Ohio
  315 High St Fl 6
  Hamilton OH 45011
  513 887-3278

(G-11571)
BUTLER COUNTY OF OHIO
Also Called: Butler County Information Svcs
315 High St Fl 2 (45011-6097)
PHONE...........................513 887-3418
Greg Sullivan, *Director*
EMP: 30 **Privately Held**
WEB: www.butlercountyclerk.org
SIC: 7378 Computer maintenance & repair
PA: Butler, County Of Ohio
  315 High St Fl 6
  Hamilton OH 45011
  513 887-3278

(G-11572)
BUTLER PROCESSING INC
Also Called: Thompson Metals and Tubing
1326 Stephanie Dr (45013-6336)
P.O. Box 785 (45012-0785)
PHONE...........................513 874-1400
Kurt Robinson, *President*
Donald Ryan, *Vice Pres*
EMP: 50
SQ FT: 130,000
SALES (est): 6.5MM **Privately Held**
SIC: 5051 Steel

(G-11573)
CARINGTON HEALTH SYSTEMS (PA)
Also Called: Franklin Ridge Care Facility
8200 Beckett Park Dr (45011)
PHONE...........................513 682-2700
Glyndon Powell, *President*
Edward Byington, *Vice Pres*
EMP: 35
SALES (est): 85.7MM **Privately Held**
SIC: 8741 8051 Hospital management; nursing & personal care facility management; skilled nursing care facilities

(G-11574)
CENTERGRID LLC
101 Knightsbridge Dr (45011-3166)
PHONE...........................513 712-1212
Daniel Molina, *President*
Terri Hemmer, *Business Mgr*
Kevin Westendorf, *Vice Pres*
Lisa Rhoads, *Accounting Mgr*
Michael Callahan, *Manager*
EMP: 50
SALES (est): 123K **Privately Held**
SIC: 7371 Custom computer programming services

(G-11575)
CENTURY EQUIPMENT INC
8650 Bilstein Blvd (45015-2204)
P.O. Box 62148, Cincinnati (45262-0148)
PHONE...........................513 285-1800
Ed Etton, *Branch Mgr*
EMP: 35
SALES (corp-wide): 41.7MM **Privately Held**
WEB: www.centuryequip.com
SIC: 5083 5087 Mowers, power; service establishment equipment
PA: Century Equipment, Inc.
  5959 Angola Rd
  Toledo OH 43615
  419 865-7400

(G-11576)
CHACO CREDIT UNION INC (PA)
601 Park Ave (45013-3064)
PHONE...........................513 785-3500
Ronald Lang, *President*
Dan Daily, *Vice Pres*
Kurt Winkler, *Vice Pres*
Peggy Klinzing, *Opers Mgr*
Joel Kasfir, *Facilities Mgr*
EMP: 50 EST: 1938
SALES: 6.1MM **Privately Held**
WEB: www.chacocu.org
SIC: 6061 Federal credit unions

(G-11577)
CIMA INC
1010 Eaton Ave (45013-4640)
PHONE...........................513 382-8976
Tom Uhl, *President*
▲ EMP: 30
SALES (est): 4.8MM **Privately Held**
WEB: www.cima-kdt.com
SIC: 3561 7363 2449 Industrial pumps & parts; temporary help service; rectangular boxes & crates, wood

(G-11578)
CITY OF HAMILTON
Also Called: City Dept Streets and Sewers
2210 S Erie Hwy (45011-4128)
PHONE...........................513 785-7551
Bob Sutton, *Superintendent*
EMP: 31 **Privately Held**
WEB: www.ci.hamilton.oh.us
SIC: 4952 9621 Sewerage systems; transportation department: government, non-operating
PA: City Of Hamilton
  345 High St Fl 3
  Hamilton OH 45011
  513 785-7000

(G-11579)
CITY OF HAMILTON
Also Called: City of Hamilton Waste Water
2451 River Rd (45015-1432)
PHONE...........................513 868-5971
Thomas Hildebrand, *Manager*
EMP: 31 **Privately Held**
WEB: www.ci.hamilton.oh.us
SIC: 4952 Sewerage systems
PA: City Of Hamilton
  345 High St Fl 3
  Hamilton OH 45011
  513 785-7000

(G-11580)
CITY OF HAMILTON
Also Called: Municipal Power Plant
960 N 3rd St (45011-1515)
PHONE...........................513 785-7450
Daniel Moats, *Branch Mgr*
EMP: 63 **Privately Held**
WEB: www.ci.hamilton.oh.us
SIC: 4911 Generation, electric power
PA: City Of Hamilton
  345 High St Fl 3
  Hamilton OH 45011
  513 785-7000

(G-11581)
CLOSSMAN CATERING INCORPORATED
3725 Symmes Rd (45015-3305)
PHONE...........................513 942-7744
David Closky, *President*
Elizabeth Forman, *Vice Pres*
EMP: 40

SALES (est): 1.5MM **Privately Held**
SIC: 8322 Meal delivery program

(G-11582)
COLONIAL SENIOR SERVICES INC
Also Called: Berkeley Square Retirement Ctr
100 Berkley Dr (45013-1787)
PHONE.................................513 856-8600
Jim Mayer, *Branch Mgr*
EMP: 130 **Privately Held**
SIC: 8741 8211 8399 8351 Management services; kindergarten; fund raising organization, non-fee basis; preschool center
PA: Colonial Senior Services, Inc.
520 Eaton Ave
Hamilton OH 45013

(G-11583)
COLONIAL SENIOR SERVICES INC
Also Called: Westover Preparatory School
855 Stahlheber Rd (45013-1963)
PHONE.................................513 867-4006
Kathleen Jackman, *Director*
EMP: 130 **Privately Held**
SIC: 8741 8211 8351 Management services; kindergarten; preschool center
PA: Colonial Senior Services, Inc.
520 Eaton Ave
Hamilton OH 45013

(G-11584)
COLONIAL SENIOR SERVICES INC
Also Called: Westover Retirement Community
855 Stahlheber Rd (45013-1963)
PHONE.................................513 844-8004
David Mancuso, *Manager*
EMP: 130 **Privately Held**
SIC: 8741 Management services
PA: Colonial Senior Services, Inc.
520 Eaton Ave
Hamilton OH 45013

(G-11585)
COMMUNITY BEHAVIORAL HLTH INC
824 S Martin Luther King (45011-3216)
PHONE.................................513 887-8500
Mark Zoellner, *Branch Mgr*
EMP: 160
SALES (corp-wide): 11.9MM **Privately Held**
SIC: 8093 Substance abuse clinics (outpatient)
PA: Community Behavioral Health, Inc.
442 S 2nd St
Hamilton OH 45011
513 785-4783

(G-11586)
CONCORD HAMILTONIAN RVRFRNT HO
Also Called: Courtyard By Marriott
1 Riverfront Plz (45011-2712)
PHONE.................................513 896-6200
Carmam Johnson, *Principal*
Jamie Campbell, *Executive*
Mark G Laport,
EMP: 60
SALES (est): 1.9MM **Privately Held**
SIC: 7011 Hotels

(G-11587)
COOLANTS PLUS INC (PA)
Also Called: Starfire
2570 Van Hook Ave (45015-1582)
PHONE.................................513 892-4000
Kurt D Deimer, *President*
▲ **EMP:** 38
SQ FT: 9,000
SALES (est): 59.1MM **Privately Held**
WEB: www.coolantsplus.com
SIC: 5172 Fuel oil

(G-11588)
CREATIVE CENTER FOR CHILDREN
23 Court St (45011-2801)
PHONE 513 867-1118
Jennifer Dunkin, *Principal*

EMP: 45
SALES (est): 733.6K **Privately Held**
SIC: 8351 Child day care services

(G-11589)
DARANA HYBRID INC (PA)
345 High St Fl 5 (45011-6086)
PHONE.................................513 785-7540
Darryl Cuttell, *President*
Bart Tolleson, *Vice Pres*
Jeff Marcum, *CFO*
▲ **EMP:** 25
SQ FT: 20,000
SALES (est): 11.2MM **Privately Held**
SIC: 1731 General electrical contractor

(G-11590)
DIEBOLD NIXDORF INCORPORATED
8509 Bilstein Blvd (45015-2213)
PHONE.................................513 682-6216
John Pears, *Pub Rel Dir*
Greg Welsh, *Branch Mgr*
EMP: 75
SALES (corp-wide): 4.5B **Publicly Held**
WEB: www.diebold.com
SIC: 5049 1731 7378 Bank equipment & supplies; banking machine installation & service; computer maintenance & repair
PA: Diebold Nixdorf, Incorporated
5995 Mayfair Rd
North Canton OH 44720
330 490-4000

(G-11591)
DIVERSCARE HEALTHCARE SVCS INC
1302 Millville Ave (45013-3961)
PHONE.................................513 867-4100
EMP: 31
SALES (corp-wide): 563.4MM **Publicly Held**
SIC: 8099 Blood related health services
PA: Diversicare Healthcare Services, Inc.
1621 Galleria Blvd
Brentwood TN 37027
615 771-7575

(G-11592)
DON S CISLE CONTRACTOR INC (PA)
1714 Fairgrove Ave (45011-1962)
PHONE.................................513 867-1400
Don M Cisle, *President*
EMP: 65
SQ FT: 2,400
SALES (est): 4.5MM **Privately Held**
WEB: www.cisle.com
SIC: 1611 Highway/Street Construction

(G-11593)
ELLISON TECHNOLOGIES INC
5333 Muhlhauser Rd (45011-9349)
PHONE.................................310 323-2121
Art Seyler, *Branch Mgr*
EMP: 25
SALES (corp-wide): 45.9B **Privately Held**
WEB: www.ellisonmw.com
SIC: 5085 Industrial supplies
HQ: Ellison Technologies, Inc.
9912 Pioneer Blvd
Santa Fe Springs CA 90670
562 949-8311

(G-11594)
EMPLOYMENT RELATIONS BOARD
Southwest Regional Water Dst
3640 Old Oxford Rd (45013-9382)
PHONE.................................513 863-0828
Tom Yeager, *General Mgr*
EMP: 40 **Privately Held**
WEB: www.swwater.com
SIC: 4941 9199 Water supply; general government administration;
HQ: Employment Relations Board, Ohio State
65 E State St Ste 1200
Columbus OH 43215

(G-11595)
FLEXENTIAL CORP
5307 Muhlhauser Rd (45011-9349)
PHONE.................................513 645-2900
Ernest Leffler, *Branch Mgr*

EMP: 62
SALES (corp-wide): 251.7MM **Privately Held**
SIC: 8748 Systems engineering consultant, ex. computer or professional
HQ: Flexential Corp.
8809 Lenox Pointe Dr
Charlotte NC 28273

(G-11596)
FORT HAMILTON HOSP FOUNDATION
630 Eaton Ave (45013-2767)
PHONE.................................513 867-5492
EMP: 392
SALES (est): 686.7K
SALES (corp-wide): 1.7B **Privately Held**
SIC: 8399 Fund raising organization, non-fee basis
HQ: The Fort Hamilton Hospital
630 Eaton Ave
Hamilton OH 45013
513 867-2000

(G-11597)
FORT HAMILTON HOSPITAL (DH)
Also Called: CHARLES F KETTERING MEMORIAL H
630 Eaton Ave (45013-2767)
PHONE.................................513 867-2000
Paul Kolodzik, *COO*
Peter J King, *VP Finance*
Darrell Moore, *Hlthcr Dir*
Karen Wilson, *Radiology Dir*
Bob Weber, *Admin Sec*
EMP: 65 **EST:** 1925
SQ FT: 350,000
SALES: 122.6MM
SALES (corp-wide): 1.7B **Privately Held**
WEB: www.forthamiltonhospital.com
SIC: 8062 General medical & surgical hospitals
HQ: Kettering Medical Center
3535 Southern Blvd
Kettering OH 45429
937 298-4331

(G-11598)
FORT HMLTN-HGHES HLTHCARE CORP (PA)
630 Eaton Ave (45013-2767)
PHONE.................................513 867-2000
James A Kingsbury, *President*
EMP: 1135
SQ FT: 350,000
SALES (est): 14.7MM **Privately Held**
SIC: 8062 General medical & surgical hospitals

(G-11599)
FRESENIUS MED CARE BUTLER CTY
Also Called: Fresenius Kdney Care W Hmilton
890 Nw Washington Blvd (45013-1281)
PHONE.................................513 737-1415
Michelle Smallwood, *Branch Mgr*
EMP: 30
SALES (corp-wide): 944.2K **Privately Held**
SIC: 8092 Kidney dialysis centers
PA: Fresenius Medical Care Butler County, Llc
920 Winter St
Waltham MA 02451
781 699-4000

(G-11600)
GEMINI ADVERTISING ASSOCIATES
1637 Dixie Hwy (45011-4041)
PHONE.................................513 896-3541
Dave R Lippert, *President*
EMP: 65
SALES (est): 2.1MM **Privately Held**
WEB: www.hamiltoncaster.com
SIC: 5072 Hardware

(G-11601)
GOLDEN YEARS NURSING HOME INC
Also Called: Golden Years Health Care
2436 Old Oxford Rd (45013-9332)
PHONE.................................513 893-0471
Kyra Hornsby, *Administration*

EMP: 40
SQ FT: 15,000
SALES (est): 2.2MM
SALES (corp-wide): 85.7MM **Privately Held**
SIC: 8051 Extended care facility
PA: Carington Health Systems
8200 Beckett Park Dr
Hamilton OH 45011
513 682-2700

(G-11602)
GREAT MIAMI VALLEY YMCA (PA)
Also Called: FAIRFIELD YMCA
105 N 2nd St (45011-2701)
PHONE.................................513 887-0001
Daven W Fippon, *President*
EMP: 650
SQ FT: 60,000
SALES: 13MM **Privately Held**
SIC: 8641 7991 8351 7032 Youth organizations; physical fitness facilities; child day care services; youth camps; individual & family services

(G-11603)
GREAT MIAMI VALLEY YMCA
Also Called: YMCA Camp Campbell Gard
4803 Augspurger Rd (45011-9547)
PHONE.................................513 867-0600
Rick Taylor, *Branch Mgr*
EMP: 30
SALES (corp-wide): 13MM **Privately Held**
SIC: 8641 7033 Youth organizations; campsite
PA: Great Miami Valley Ymca
105 N 2nd St
Hamilton OH 45011
513 887-0001

(G-11604)
GREAT MIAMI VALLEY YMCA
Also Called: Central Hamilton YMCA
105 N 2nd St (45011-2701)
PHONE.................................513 887-0014
Angela Howard, *Branch Mgr*
EMP: 60
SALES (est): 199.8K
SALES (corp-wide): 13MM **Privately Held**
SIC: 8641 7991 8351 7032 Youth organizations; physical fitness facilities; child day care services; youth camps; individual & family services
PA: Great Miami Valley Ymca
105 N 2nd St
Hamilton OH 45011
513 887-0001

(G-11605)
GREAT MIAMI VALLEY YMCA
Also Called: Fitton Family YMCA
1307 Nw Washington Blvd (45013-1207)
PHONE.................................513 868-9622
Ron Thunderhouse, *Exec Dir*
EMP: 100
SALES (corp-wide): 13MM **Privately Held**
SIC: 8641 7991 8351 7032 Youth organizations; physical fitness facilities; child day care services; youth camps; individual & family services
PA: Great Miami Valley Ymca
105 N 2nd St
Hamilton OH 45011
513 887-0001

(G-11606)
H & R BLOCK INC
2304a Dixie Hwy (45015-1613)
PHONE.................................513 868-1818
Mike Wilson, *Branch Mgr*
EMP: 30
SALES (corp-wide): 3.1B **Publicly Held**
SIC: 7291 Tax return preparation services
PA: H&R Block, Inc.
1 H&R Block Way
Kansas City MO 64105
816 854-3000

(G-11607)
HAMILTON AUTOMOTIVE WAREHOUSE (PA)
Also Called: Savage Auto Supply Div
630 Maple Ave (45011-6001)
PHONE................................513 896-4100
Jared Licklitter, *General Mgr*
Mark Wessendorf, *Manager*
EMP: 75
SQ FT: 20,000
SALES (est): 15.1MM **Privately Held**
SIC: 5013 5531 Automotive supplies & parts; automotive parts

(G-11608)
HAMILTON PARKS CONSERVANCY
106 N 2nd St (45011-2702)
PHONE................................513 785-7055
William Timmer, *Director*
EMP: 28
SALES: 2.1MM **Privately Held**
SIC: 8742 Maintenance management consultant

(G-11609)
HAMILTON SCRAP PROCESSORS
134 Hensel Pl (45011-1508)
PHONE................................513 863-3474
Neil Cohen, *President*
Wilbur Cohen, *Corp Secy*
Kenneth Cohen, *Vice Pres*
EMP: 30
SQ FT: 140,000
SALES (est): 4MM **Privately Held**
SIC: 5093 Waste paper; metal scrap & waste materials; plastics scrap

(G-11610)
HOSPICE OF HAMILTON
1010 Eaton Ave (45013-4640)
PHONE................................513 895-1270
Janet Montgomery, *Chief Mktg Ofcr*
Donna Prickel, *Director*
EMP: 30
SALES (est): 735.2K **Privately Held**
SIC: 8052 Personal care facility

(G-11611)
IMFLUX INC
3550 Symmes Rd Ste 100 (45015-1498)
PHONE................................513 488-1017
Nathan Estruth, *CEO*
Dave Le Neveu, *CFO*
EMP: 32
SALES (est): 7.1MM
SALES (corp-wide): 66.8B **Publicly Held**
SIC: 7371 8741 Computer software development & applications; management services; business management
PA: The Procter & Gamble Company
1 Procter And Gamble Plz
Cincinnati OH 45202
513 983-1100

(G-11612)
INLOES MECHANICAL INC
Also Called: Inloes Heating and Cooling
157 N B St (45013-3102)
PHONE................................513 896-9499
Ryan Inloes, *President*
Richard A Inloes, *Vice Pres*
EMP: 28
SQ FT: 32,000
SALES: 5MM **Privately Held**
WEB: www.inloesheating.com
SIC: 1711 Warm air heating & air conditioning contractor

(G-11613)
INNOVATIVE ENRGY SOLUTIONS LLC
3680 Symmes Rd (45015-1380)
PHONE................................937 228-3044
Mark Putnam,
John Brofft,
EMP: 31
SALES (est): 11.6MM **Privately Held**
SIC: 5084 Controlling instruments & accessories

(G-11614)
INNOVTIVE LBLING SOLUTIONS INC
Also Called: I L S
4000 Hmlton Middletown Rd (45011-2263)
PHONE................................513 860-2457
Jay Dollries, *President*
Steve Wolf, *Vice Pres*
Jeanne Wolf, *Admin Sec*
▲ EMP: 65
SQ FT: 65,000
SALES (est): 22.3MM **Privately Held**
WEB: www.ilslabels.com
SIC: 5199 Packaging materials

(G-11615)
INTEGRATED POWER SERVICES LLC
2175a Schlichter Dr (45015-1482)
PHONE................................513 863-8816
Jason Reynolds, *Branch Mgr*
EMP: 28
SQ FT: 20,500
SALES (corp-wide): 924.8MM **Privately Held**
WEB: www.integratedps.com
SIC: 7694 Electric motor repair
HQ: Integrated Power Services Llc
3 Independence Pt Ste 100
Greenville SC 29615

(G-11616)
IRON MOUNTAIN INFO MGT LLC
3790 Symmes Rd (45015-1372)
PHONE................................513 942-7300
Sandy Freeman, *Manager*
EMP: 25
SALES (corp-wide): 4.2B **Publicly Held**
SIC: 4226 Document & office records storage
HQ: Iron Mountain Information Management, Llc
1 Federal St
Boston MA 02110
800 899-4766

(G-11617)
JEE FOODS
3371 Hamilton Cleves Rd (45013-9535)
PHONE................................513 917-1712
Michael Rivera, *CEO*
EMP: 25
SALES (est): 217K **Privately Held**
SIC: 4953 Recycling, waste materials

(G-11618)
JOSEPH T RYERSON & SON INC
Also Called: Ryerson Coil Processing
1108 Central Ave (45011-3823)
PHONE................................513 896-4600
Dave Winkler, *Branch Mgr*
EMP: 30 **Publicly Held**
SIC: 5051 Steel; iron & steel (ferrous) products; aluminum bars, rods, ingots, sheets, pipes, plates, etc.; nonferrous metal sheets, bars, rods, etc.
HQ: Joseph T. Ryerson & Son, Inc.
227 W Monroe St Fl 27
Chicago IL 60606
312 292-5000

(G-11619)
KAROPA INCORPORATE
Also Called: Comfort Keepers
3987 Hmiltn Mddltwn Rd (45011-2297)
P.O. Box 18156, Fairfield (45018-0156)
PHONE................................513 860-1616
Ron Rosenberg, *CEO*
Karen Rosenburg, *Vice Pres*
EMP: 45
SALES (est): 1.3MM **Privately Held**
SIC: 8082 Visiting nurse service

(G-11620)
KINGDOM KIDS INC
6106 Havenwood Ct (45011-7835)
PHONE................................513 851-6400
Fax: 513 851-3396
EMP: 32
SALES (est): 934.5K **Privately Held**
SIC: 8351 Daycare Center

(G-11621)
LAIRSON TRUCKING LLC
99 N Riverside Dr (45011-5741)
PHONE................................513 894-0452
Robert Lairson, *Partner*
Brenda Lairson, *Partner*
EMP: 25
SALES (est): 2MM **Privately Held**
SIC: 4212 Local trucking, without storage

(G-11622)
LARRY L MINGES
Also Called: Minges Drywall
4396 Wade Mill Rd (45014-5854)
PHONE................................513 738-4901
Larry L Minges, *Owner*
EMP: 25
SALES (est): 1MM **Privately Held**
SIC: 1742 Drywall

(G-11623)
LCD HOME HEALTH AGENCY LLC
Also Called: Lcd Nurse Aide Academy
6 S 2nd St Ste 409 (45011-2865)
PHONE................................513 497-0441
Lamonda Dye, *Mng Member*
EMP: 26
SQ FT: 1,500
SALES: 125K **Privately Held**
SIC: 8059 8249 Convalescent home; practical nursing school

(G-11624)
LIFESPAN INCORPORATED (PA)
1900 Fairgrove Ave (45011-1966)
PHONE................................513 868-3210
Cynthia Stever, *CEO*
Catherine Bidleman, *CFO*
Elizabeth Kelley, *Mktg Coord*
EMP: 74 EST: 1945
SQ FT: 21,000
SALES: 3.7MM **Privately Held**
WEB: www.lifespanohio.org
SIC: 8322 Family service agency; general counseling services

(G-11625)
LOWES HOME CENTERS LLC
1495 Main St (45013-1075)
PHONE................................513 737-3700
Jeff Orvechowski, *Manager*
EMP: 150
SALES (corp-wide): 68.6B **Publicly Held**
SIC: 5211 5031 5722 5064 Home centers; building materials, exterior; building materials, interior; household appliance stores; electrical appliances, television & radio
HQ: Lowe's Home Centers, Llc
1605 Curtis Bridge Rd
Wilkesboro NC 28697
336 658-4000

(G-11626)
M A FOLKES COMPANY INC
3095 Mcbride Ct (45011-5375)
P.O. Box 425 (45012-0425)
PHONE................................513 785-4200
Michael Folkes, *President*
Monica Robinson, *Executive*
EMP: 45
SQ FT: 200,000
SALES (est): 4.6MM **Privately Held**
WEB: www.mafolkes.com
SIC: 7389 4225 8741 Packaging & labeling services; general warehousing & storage; management services

(G-11627)
MATANDY STEEL & METAL PDTS LLC
Also Called: Matandy Steel Sales
1200 Central Ave (45011-3825)
P.O. Box 1186 (45012-1186)
PHONE................................513 844-2277
Andrew Schuster, *President*
Joanne Pfirman,
EMP: 100
SQ FT: 125,000
SALES (est): 32.1MM **Privately Held**
WEB: www.matandy.com
SIC: 4225 3312 3444 3399 General warehousing & storage; sheet or strip, steel, cold-rolled: own hot-rolled; studs & joists, sheet metal; nails: aluminum, brass or other nonferrous metal or wire

(G-11628)
MCCULLOUGH-HYDE MEM HOSP INC
1390 Eaton Ave (45013-1407)
PHONE................................513 863-2215
Peter Towne, *Owner*
EMP: 355
SALES (corp-wide): 55.4MM **Privately Held**
SIC: 8062 General medical & surgical hospitals
PA: The Mccullough-Hyde Memorial Hospital Incorporated
110 N Poplar St
Oxford OH 45056
513 523-2111

(G-11629)
MILLIKIN AND FITTON LAW FIRM (PA)
Also Called: Millikin & Fitton
232 High St (45011-2711)
P.O. Box 598 (45012-0598)
PHONE................................513 829-6700
John J Reister, *Partner*
John H Clemmons, *Partner*
Michael A Fulton, *Partner*
J S Irwin, *Partner*
William Keck, *Partner*
EMP: 28
SALES (est): 4.6MM **Privately Held**
WEB: www.mfitton.com
SIC: 8111 General practice law office

(G-11630)
MILLIS TRANSFER INC
1982 Jackson Rd (45011-9058)
PHONE................................513 863-0222
Randy Purkey, *Manager*
EMP: 25
SALES (corp-wide): 108.2MM **Privately Held**
WEB: www.millistransfer.com
SIC: 4213 Contract haulers
PA: Millis Transfer, Inc.
121 Gebhardt Rd
Black River Falls WI 54615
715 284-4384

(G-11631)
OHIO CASUALTY INSURANCE CO
136 N 3rd St (45011-2726)
PHONE................................513 867-3000
Jim Mc Goldrick, *Vice Pres*
Hal Goode, *Manager*
EMP: 148
SALES (corp-wide): 38.3B **Privately Held**
WEB: www.oci.com
SIC: 6331 Automobile insurance
HQ: The Ohio Casualty Insurance Company
9450 Seward Rd
Fairfield OH 45014
800 843-6446

(G-11632)
PERSONAL TOUCH HM CARE IPA INC
7924 Jessies Way Ste C (45011-1336)
PHONE................................513 868-2272
Jenny Justice, *Manager*
EMP: 150
SALES (corp-wide): 363MM **Privately Held**
WEB: www.pthomecare.com
SIC: 8082 Home health care services
PA: Personal Touch Home Care Ipa, Inc.
1985 Marcus Ave Ste 202
New Hyde Park NY 11042
718 468-4747

(G-11633)
PRESSLEY RIDGE FOUNDATION
734 Dayton St (45011-3460)
PHONE................................513 737-0400
Anna Robinson, *Manager*

EMP: 30 **Privately Held**
SIC: 8322 Individual & family services
PA: Pressley Ridge Foundation
    5500 Corporate Dr Ste 400
    Pittsburgh PA 15237

(G-11634)
R E WATSON INC
2728 Hamilton Cleves Rd (45013-9452)
P.O. Box 277, Ross (45061-0277)
PHONE..................................(513) 863-0070
Ronald E Watson, *President*
Michael Watson, *Vice Pres*
Janet Meyers, *Admin Sec*
EMP: 25 **EST:** 1964
SQ FT: 2,000
SALES: 5MM **Privately Held**
SIC: 4212 4213 Dump truck haulage;
    trucking, except local

(G-11635)
**RACK & BALLAUER EXCVTG CO
INC**
11321 Paddys Run Rd (45013-9403)
PHONE..................................513 738-7000
Larry Ballauer, *President*
Randy Rack, *Vice Pres*
Scot Rack, *Vice Pres*
EMP: 50
SQ FT: 4,000
SALES: 18.2MM **Privately Held**
SIC: 1794 Excavation work

(G-11636)
RAPIER ELECTRIC INC
4845 Augspurger Rd (45011-9547)
PHONE..................................513 868-9087
N Lynn Rapier, *President*
Lynn Rapier, *President*
Daniel Rapier, *Vice Pres*
EMP: 61
SQ FT: 2,100
SALES (est): 7.4MM **Privately Held**
SIC: 1731 General Electrical Contractor

(G-11637)
RESCARE OHIO INC
5099 Camelot Dr (45014-7423)
PHONE..................................513 829-8992
Melissa Moore, *Manager*
EMP: 70
SALES (corp-wide): 23.7B **Privately Held**
SIC: 8361 Self-help group home
HQ: Rescare Ohio Inc
    348 W Main St
    Williamsburg OH 45176

(G-11638)
**RESIDENCE AT KENSINGTON
PLACE**
Also Called: Residence At Huntington Court
350 Hancock Ave (45011-4448)
PHONE..................................513 863-4218
Larry Schindler, *Manager*
EMP: 125
SALES (corp-wide): 5.8MM **Privately
Held**
SIC: 8059 Nursing home, except skilled &
    intermediate care facility
PA: The Residence At Kensington Place
    751 Kensington St
    Middletown OH 45044
    513 424-3511

(G-11639)
RK FAMILY INC
1416 Main St (45013-1004)
PHONE..................................513 737-0436
David Pfeiffer, *Principal*
EMP: 255
SALES (corp-wide): 1.5B **Privately Held**
SIC: 5083 Farm equipment parts & sup-
    plies
PA: Rk Family, Inc.
    4216 Dewitt Ave
    Mattoon IL 61938
    217 235-7102

(G-11640)
**RUMPKE CNSLD COMPANIES
INC (PA)**
Also Called: Rumpke Waste and Recycl Svcs
3963 Kraus Ln (45014-5841)
PHONE..................................513 738-0800
William Rumpke Jr, *President*

Jeff Rumpke, *Vice Pres*
Todd Rumpke, *Vice Pres*
Phil Wehrman, *CFO*
EMP: 200
SQ FT: 25,000
SALES (est): 1.6B **Privately Held**
SIC: 4953 Recycling, waste materials

(G-11641)
SALVAGNINI AMERICA INC (DH)
27 Bicentennial Ct (45015-1382)
PHONE..................................513 874-8284
Eugenio Bassan, *CEO*
Vicente Undurraga, *Ch of Bd*
Doug Johnson, *Vice Pres*
▲ **EMP:** 40
SQ FT: 60,000
SALES (est): 34.6MM **Privately Held**
WEB: www.salvagnini.com
SIC: 5084 Machine tools & accessories;
    metalworking machinery
HQ: Salvagnini Italia Spa
    Via Ingegnere Guido Salvagnini 51
    Sarego VI 36040
    044 472-5111

(G-11642)
**SOJOURNER RECOVERY
SERVICES (PA)**
Also Called: Sojourner Home
294 N Fair Ave (45011-4222)
PHONE..................................513 868-7654
Scott Dehring, *CEO*
EMP: 80
SALES: 5.8MM **Privately Held**
WEB: www.sojournerrecovery.org
SIC: 8322 Alcoholism counseling, nontreat-
    ment

(G-11643)
STAARMANN CONCRETE INC
4316 Stahlheber Rd (45013-8912)
PHONE..................................513 756-9191
Joseph Staarmann, *President*
Lynn Staarmann, *Admin Sec*
EMP: 30
SALES (est): 1.6MM **Privately Held**
SIC: 1771 Concrete work

(G-11644)
STAHLHEBER & SONS INC
Also Called: Stahlheber Excavating
4205 Hamilton Eaton Rd (45011-9643)
PHONE..................................513 726-4446
Douglas W Stahlheber, *President*
Dave Long, *Vice Pres*
Chris Stahlheber, *Vice Pres*
Debra Stahlheber, *Admin Sec*
EMP: 28
SQ FT: 4,080
SALES: 1.4MM **Privately Held**
SIC: 1794 Excavation work

(G-11645)
SUNRISE SENIOR LIVING LLC
Also Called: Sunrise of Hamilton
896 Nw Washington Blvd (45013-1281)
PHONE..................................513 893-9000
Jamie Cianciolo, *Exec Dir*
EMP: 50
SALES (corp-wide): 4.7B **Publicly Held**
WEB: www.sunrise.com
SIC: 8051 Skilled nursing care facilities
HQ: Sunrise Senior Living, Llc
    7902 Westpark Dr
    Mc Lean VA 22102

(G-11646)
**TERRY ASPHALT MATERIALS
INC (DH)**
8600 Bilstein Blvd (45015-2204)
PHONE..................................513 874-6192
Dan Koeninger, *CEO*
Jim Monroe, *Terminal Mgr*
W Pierre Peltier, *Manager*
Ryan Terry, *Technical Staff*
Christopher Winter, *Administration*
EMP: 25
SALES (est): 38.3MM
SALES (corp-wide): 83.5MM **Privately
Held**
SIC: 5082 2952 Road construction &
    maintenance machinery; asphalt felts &
    coatings

HQ: Barrett Industries Corporation
    73 Headquarters Plz
    Morristown NJ 07960
    973 533-1001

(G-11647)
**THYSSENKRUPP BILSTEIN
AMER INC (HQ)**
8685 Bilstein Blvd (45015-2205)
PHONE..................................513 881-7600
Fabian Schmahl, *President*
Brian Driscoll, *Warehouse Mgr*
Vincent Elisan, *Engineer*
Sebastian Kaemper, *Engineer*
Jade O'Mara, *Engineer*
◆ **EMP:** 212
SQ FT: 115,000
SALES (est): 106.1MM
SALES (corp-wide): 39.8B **Privately Held**
SIC: 3714 5013 Shock absorbers, motor
    vehicle; springs, shock absorbers & struts
PA: Thyssenkrupp Ag
    Thyssenkrupp Allee 1
    Essen 45143
    201 844-0

(G-11648)
**THYSSENKRUPP BILSTEIN
AMER INC**
3033 Symmes Rd (45015)
PHONE..................................513 881-7600
Andrew Guthridge, *CFO*
EMP: 100
SALES (corp-wide): 39.8B **Privately Held**
SIC: 5014 Automobile tires & tubes
HQ: Thyssenkrupp Bilstein Of America, Inc.
    8685 Bilstein Blvd
    Hamilton OH 45015
    513 881-7600

(G-11649)
TRUTEAM LLC
Also Called: Gale Insulation
28 Kiesland Ct (45011-1374)
PHONE..................................513 942-2204
EMP: 25
SALES (corp-wide): 2.3B **Publicly Held**
SIC: 1742 Drywall/Insulating Contractor
HQ: Truteam, Llc
    260 Jimmy Ann Dr
    Daytona Beach FL

(G-11650)
**TWINBROOK HILLS BAPTIST
CHURCH**
40 Wrenwood Dr (45013-2499)
PHONE..................................513 863-3107
Richard Riddick, *Pastor*
EMP: 40
SALES (est): 899.6K **Privately Held**
WEB: www.twinbrook.net
SIC: 8661 8351 8211 Baptist Church; pre-
    school center; kindergarten; private com-
    bined elementary & secondary school;
    private junior high school; private senior
    high school

(G-11651)
**UNITED PARCEL SERVICE INC
OH**
Also Called: UPS
1951 Logan Ave (45015-1020)
PHONE..................................513 863-1681
Bryan Zelen, *Manager*
EMP: 72
SALES (corp-wide): 71.8B **Publicly Held**
WEB: www.upsscs.com
SIC: 4215 Parcel delivery, vehicular
HQ: United Parcel Service, Inc. (Oh)
    55 Glenlake Pkwy
    Atlanta GA 30328
    404 828-6000

(G-11652)
**UNITED PERFORMANCE
METALS INC (HQ)**
3475 Symmes Rd (45015-1363)
PHONE..................................513 860-6500
Tom Kennard, *President*
Craft O'Neal, *Chairman*
Greg Chase, *Vice Pres*
Jeffrey Liesch, *CFO*
◆ **EMP:** 141
SQ FT: 110,000

SALES (est): 109.7MM
SALES (corp-wide): 1.8B **Privately Held**
WEB: www.upmet.com
SIC: 5051 Steel
PA: O'neal Industries, Inc
    2311 Highland Ave S # 200
    Birmingham AL 35205
    205 721-2880

(G-11653)
UNIVAR USA INC
12 Standen Dr (45015-2208)
PHONE..................................513 870-4050
John Baird, *Branch Mgr*
EMP: 40
SALES (corp-wide): 8.6B **Publicly Held**
SIC: 5169 Industrial chemicals
HQ: Univar Usa Inc.
    3075 Highland Pkwy # 200
    Downers Grove IL 60515
    331 777-6000

(G-11654)
WATSON GRAVEL INC (PA)
2728 Hamilton Cleves Rd (45013-9452)
PHONE..................................513 863-0070
Ronald E Watson, *President*
Michael T Watson, *Vice Pres*
Janet L Meyers, *Treasurer*
Labreeska Stanifer, *Human Res Mgr*
Brian Bottoms, *Manager*
EMP: 55
SQ FT: 2,000
SALES (est): 10.6MM **Privately Held**
WEB: www.watsongravel.com
SIC: 1442 Gravel mining

(G-11655)
YWCA OF HAMILTON
Also Called: Y W C A
244 Dayton St (45011-1634)
PHONE..................................513 856-9800
Jane Rose, *President*
April Hamlin, *Education*
EMP: 29
SQ FT: 10,000
SALES: 954.8K **Privately Held**
SIC: 8641 7999 Youth organizations;
    recreation center

(G-11656)
ZARTRAN LLC
3035 Symmes Rd (45015-1330)
PHONE..................................513 870-4800
Donald Browning, *CEO*
EMP: 75
SALES (est): 3.9MM **Privately Held**
WEB: www.pierrefoods.com
SIC: 4213 Refrigerated products transport

Hammondsville
Jefferson County

(G-11657)
SALINE TOWNSHIP
Also Called: Emergency Medical Services
164 Main St (43930)
P.O. Box 177 (43930-0177)
PHONE..................................330 532-2195
Marsha Plunket, *Chief*
EMP: 28
SALES (est): 799.1K **Privately Held**
SIC: 8322 Emergency social services

Hanoverton
Columbiana County

(G-11658)
SPREAD EAGLE TAVERN INC
10150 Plymouth St (44423)
PHONE..................................330 223-1583
David Johnson, *President*
Mark Webb, *Admin Sec*
EMP: 40
SALES (est): 1.8MM
SALES (corp-wide): 34.5MM **Privately
Held**
WEB: www.spreadeagletavern.com
SIC: 7011 5812 Bed & breakfast inn; eat-
    ing places

PA: Summitville Tiles, Inc
15364 State Rte 644
Summitville OH 43962
330 223-1511

Harrison
Hamilton County

(G-11659)
3S INCORPORATED (HQ)
8686 Southwest Pkwy (45030-2109)
PHONE................................513 202-5070
Matthew M Euson, *President*
Joel Hernandez, *General Mgr*
Thomas Euson, *Vice Pres*
Simon Brakhage, *Project Mgr*
Doug Schmidt, *Manager*
EMP: 26
SQ FT: 10,000
SALES: 25.6MM
SALES (corp-wide): 3.7B **Privately Held**
SIC: 5099 Fire extinguishers
PA: Api Group Inc.
1100 Old Highway 8 Nw
Saint Paul MN 55112
651 636-4320

(G-11660)
ALTAQUIP LLC (DH)
100 Production Dr (45030-1477)
PHONE................................513 674-6464
Mike King, *Mng Member*
EMP: 50
SALES (est): 58.7MM
SALES (corp-wide): 225.3B **Publicly Held**
SIC: 7699 Lawn mower repair shop
HQ: The Scott Fetzer Company
28800 Clemens Rd
Westlake OH 44145
440 892-3000

(G-11661)
ARCHWAYS BROOKVILLE INC
375 Industrial Dr (45030-1483)
P.O. Box 218 (45030-0218)
PHONE................................513 367-2649
Robert Cummings, *President*
EMP: 60
SALES (est): 2.9MM **Privately Held**
SIC: 8721 Accounting, auditing & book-keeping

(G-11662)
BRIDGESTONE RET OPERATIONS LLC
Also Called: Michel Tires Plus 227925
10606 New Haven Rd (45030-2777)
PHONE................................513 367-7888
Cody George, *Manager*
EMP: 30
SALES (corp-wide): 32.4B **Privately Held**
WEB: www.tiresplus.com
SIC: 7534 Tire retreading & repair shops
HQ: Bridgestone Retail Operations, Llc
333 E Lake St Ste 300
Bloomingdale IL 60108
630 259-9000

(G-11663)
CINCINNATI EARLY LEARNING CTR
498 S State St (45030-1446)
PHONE................................513 367-2129
April Stewart, *Director*
EMP: 30
SALES (corp-wide): 5.3MM **Privately Held**
SIC: 8351 Preschool center
PA: Early Cincinnati Learning Center Inc
1301 E Mcmillan St
Cincinnati OH 45206
513 961-2690

(G-11664)
CIRCLING HILLS GOLF COURSE
10240 Carolina Trace Rd (45030-1604)
PHONE................................513 367-5858
John E Minges, *President*
Ed Minges, *Principal*
Gloria Minges, *Principal*
EMP: 40

SALES (est): 1.3MM **Privately Held**
WEB: www.circlinghills.com
SIC: 7992 5812 Public golf courses; eating places

(G-11665)
DENIER ELECTRIC CO INC (PA)
Also Called: Denier Technologies Div
10891 State Route 128 (45030-9236)
PHONE................................513 738-2641
Dennis J Denier, *CEO*
George D Roberts, *President*
Dave Eastabrooks, *Pastor*
Diane K Herbort, *Exec VP*
Mike King, *Vice Pres*
EMP: 215
SQ FT: 40,000
SALES: 58.1MM **Privately Held**
WEB: www.denier.com
SIC: 1731 General electrical contractor

(G-11666)
F & M MAFCO INC (PA)
9149 Dry Fork Rd (45030-1901)
P.O. Box 11013, Cincinnati (45211-0013)
PHONE................................513 367-2151
Daniel Mc Kenna, *President*
Pat Mc Kenna, *Exec VP*
Robert W Mc Kenna Jr, *Exec VP*
Patrick D McKenna, *Exec VP*
William Mc Kenna, *Vice Pres*
◆ **EMP:** 186
SQ FT: 85,000
SALES: 75.9MM **Privately Held**
WEB: www.fmmafco.com
SIC: 5085 5072 7353 5082 Welding supplies; hardware; heavy construction equipment rental; general construction machinery & equipment

(G-11667)
FAIRWAY INDEPENDENT MRTG CORP
1180 Stone Dr (45030-1658)
PHONE................................513 367-6344
EMP: 28 **Privately Held**
SIC: 6162 Mortgage bankers
PA: Fairway Independent Mortgage Corporation
4750 S Biltmore Ln
Madison WI 53718

(G-11668)
GREER & WHITEHEAD CNSTR INC
510 S State St Ste D (45030-1494)
PHONE................................513 202-1757
Steven Whitehead, *President*
Russell Whitehead, *General Mgr*
EMP: 35
SALES (est): 5.7MM **Privately Held**
SIC: 1711 1389 Mechanical contractor; building oil & gas well foundations on site

(G-11669)
HARRISON BUILDING AND LN ASSN (PA)
10490 New Haven Rd (45030-1657)
PHONE................................513 367-2015
Randall Grubbs, *President*
Ray Ferneding, *Vice Pres*
Robert Means, *Vice Pres*
Ferneding Ray, *CFO*
Jerry Heartmann, *CIO*
EMP: 28 **EST:** 1916
SALES: 7.6MM **Privately Held**
SIC: 6036 6035 Savings & loan associations, not federally chartered; federal savings & loan associations

(G-11670)
HUBERT COMPANY LLC (HQ)
9555 Dry Fork Rd (45030-1994)
PHONE................................513 367-8600
Mark Rudy, *President*
Chris Lewis, *General Mgr*
Rodger Reed, *General Mgr*
Tim Lansing, *Vice Pres*
Steve Martin, *Vice Pres*
◆ **EMP:** 306 **EST:** 1946
SQ FT: 453,000
SALES (est): 187.7MM **Privately Held**
SIC: 5046 Store fixtures; store equipment; display equipment, except refrigerated

(G-11671)
JAMES H ALVIS TRUCKING INC
Also Called: Alvis Lndcape Golf Curses Mtls
9570 State Route 128 (45030-9706)
P.O. Box 243, Miamitown (45041-0243)
PHONE................................513 623-8121
James H Alvis, *President*
EMP: 28
SQ FT: 84,000
SALES (est): 2.3MM **Privately Held**
SIC: 4212 Dump truck haulage

(G-11672)
K&K TECHNICAL GROUP INC
10053 Simonson Rd Ste 2 (45030-2194)
PHONE................................513 202-1300
James Kennedy, *President*
Lindsey Skeens, *Vice Pres*
Mindy Beeson, *Accounting Mgr*
EMP: 200
SQ FT: 200
SALES: 15MM **Privately Held**
WEB: www.kandktechnical.com
SIC: 8711 Engineering services

(G-11673)
M & S DRYWALL INC
10999 State Route 128 (45030-9237)
PHONE................................513 738-1510
Paul Spaulding, *President*
Terry Spaulding, *Vice Pres*
EMP: 26
SALES: 1.5MM **Privately Held**
SIC: 1742 Drywall

(G-11674)
MODERN DAY CONCRETE CNSTR
9773 Crosby Rd (45030-9707)
PHONE................................513 738-1026
Thomas Weisman, *President*
Frank Klosterman, *Chairman*
David Sellet, *Vice Pres*
Gail Evans, *Admin Sec*
EMP: 30 **EST:** 1964
SQ FT: 2,500
SALES (est): 3.8MM **Privately Held**
SIC: 1771 Concrete work

(G-11675)
NVR INC
9439 Tebbs Ct (45030-2822)
PHONE................................513 202-0323
EMP: 112
SALES (corp-wide): 5B **Publicly Held**
SIC: 1531 Operative Builders
PA: Nvr, Inc.
11700 Plaza America Dr # 500
Reston VA 20190
703 956-4000

(G-11676)
SCHERZINGER DRILLING INC
9629 State Route 128 (45030-9226)
P.O. Box 202, Miamitown (45041-0202)
PHONE................................513 738-2000
Kenneth E Scherzinger, *President*
Kathleen Scherzinger, *Vice Pres*
EMP: 25
SQ FT: 7,000
SALES: 6.5MM **Privately Held**
WEB: www.scherzingerdrilling.com
SIC: 1629 Caisson drilling; pier construction

(G-11677)
T J WILLIAMS ELECTRIC CO
7925 New Haven Rd (45030-9205)
P.O. Box 586, Miamitown (45041-0586)
PHONE................................513 738-5366
Joyce Meyer, *President*
Teresa Vogelsang, *Vice Pres*
Diane Vogelsang, *Manager*
EMP: 25
SQ FT: 6,000
SALES (est): 4.5MM **Privately Held**
SIC: 1731 General electrical contractor

(G-11678)
TAKKT AMERICA HOLDING INC (PA)
9555 Dry Fork Rd (45030-1906)
PHONE................................513 367-8600
C Bart Kohler, *Principal*
Jeff Shelton, *Treasurer*

Jennifer M Clements, *Admin Sec*
▲ **EMP:** 187
SQ FT: 576,715
SALES (est): 187.7MM **Privately Held**
SIC: 5046 Store fixtures; store equipment; display equipment, except refrigerated

(G-11679)
TRIUMPH ENERGY CORPORATION
9171 Dry Fork Rd (45030-1901)
PHONE................................513 367-9900
Gerry Francis, *President*
Ronald Wittekind, *Chairman*
EMP: 50
SQ FT: 14,500
SALES: 39.4MM
SALES (corp-wide): 82.1MM **Privately Held**
SIC: 5172 5541 Petroleum products; gasoline service stations
PA: Hawkstone Associates, Inc.
9171 Dry Fork Rd
Harrison OH
513 367-9900

(G-11680)
WAYNE/SCOTT FETZER COMPANY
Also Called: Wayne Water Systems
101 Production Dr (45030-1477)
PHONE................................800 237-0987
Duane Johnson, *President*
▲ **EMP:** 200
SQ FT: 160,000
SALES (est): 86MM
SALES (corp-wide): 225.3B **Publicly Held**
SIC: 3561 5074 Pumps, domestic: water or sump; water purification equipment
HQ: The Scott Fetzer Company
28800 Clemens Rd
Westlake OH 44145
440 892-3000

Harrod
Allen County

(G-11681)
R D JONES EXCAVATING INC
10225 Alger Rd (45850-9792)
P.O. Box 127 (45850-0127)
PHONE................................419 648-5870
Randy Jones, *President*
David Sehlhorst, *Project Mgr*
Dana Jones, *Admin Sec*
EMP: 50
SQ FT: 1,200
SALES (est): 13.4MM **Privately Held**
SIC: 1794 Excavation & grading, building construction

Hartville
Stark County

(G-11682)
AKA WIRELESS INC
Also Called: Z Wireless
882 W Maple St (44632-9088)
PHONE................................216 213-8040
EMP: 26 **Privately Held**
SIC: 5999 4812 Mobile telephones & equipment; cellular telephone services
HQ: Aka Wireless, Inc.
7505 S Louise Ave
Sioux Falls SD 57108
605 275-3733

(G-11683)
BRENCKLE FARMS INC
12434 Duquette Ave Ne (44632-9329)
PHONE................................330 877-4426
Thomas Brenckle, *President*
EMP: 30
SALES (est): 2.4MM **Privately Held**
SIC: 0161 Vegetables & melons

GEOGRAPHIC

(G-11684)
**CONGRESS LAKE CLUB
COMPANY**
1 East Dr Ne (44632-8890)
P.O. Box 370 (44632-0370)
PHONE...................................330 877-9318
Fred Zollinger III, *President*
EMP: 40 **EST:** 1896
SQ FT: 40,000
SALES: 3.4MM **Privately Held**
WEB: www.congresslakeclub.org
SIC: 7997 Golf club, membership

(G-11685)
ENERVEST LTD
125 State Route 43 (44632-9500)
PHONE...................................330 877-6747
EMP: 75 **Privately Held**
SIC: 1382 Oil & gas exploration services
PA: Enervest, Ltd.
  1001 Fannin St Ste 800
  Houston TX 77002

(G-11686)
GENTLEBROOK INC (PA)
880 Sunnyside St Sw (44632-9087)
PHONE...................................330 877-3694
Norman Wengerd, *CEO*
Mike Sleutz, *COO*
Marilyn Miller, *Admin Asst*
EMP: 220
SALES: 13.8MM **Privately Held**
SIC: 8361 8741 Home for the mentally re-
tarded; management services

(G-11687)
GFS LEASING INC
Also Called: Altercare Hartville
1420 Smith Kramer St Ne (44632-8730)
PHONE...................................330 877-2666
Chelle Sink, *Administration*
Paige Owen, *Administration*
EMP: 100
SALES (est): 1.5MM
SALES (corp-wide): 2.8MM **Privately
Held**
SIC: 8051 Convalescent home with contin-
uous nursing care
PA: Gfs Leasing Inc
  1463 Tallmadge Rd
  Kent OH 44240
  330 296-6415

(G-11688)
HARTVILLE HARDWARE INC
Also Called: John Deere Authorized Dealer
1315 Edison St Nw (44632-9046)
PHONE...................................330 877-4690
Howard Miller Jr, *President*
Wayne Miller, *Vice Pres*
Chris Wilson, *Financial Exec*
Susan Shea, *Human Resources*
Wayne Beachy, *Sales Staff*
▲ **EMP:** 210
SALES (est): 62.5MM **Privately Held**
WEB: www.hartvillehardware.com
SIC: 5251 5082 Hardware; construction &
mining machinery
PA: Hrm Enterprises, Inc.
  1015 Edison St Nw
  Hartville OH 44632
  330 877-9353

(G-11689)
**HEALTHSPAN INTEGRATED
CARE**
Also Called: Kaiser Foundation Health Plan
900 W Maple St (44632-9088)
PHONE...................................330 877-4018
Jim Innes, *Branch Mgr*
EMP: 29
SALES (corp-wide): 4.7B **Privately Held**
SIC: 6324 Hospital & medical service plans
HQ: Healthspan Integrated Care
  1001 Lakeside Ave E # 1200
  Cleveland OH 44114
  216 621-5600

(G-11690)
HERSH CONSTRUCTION INC
Also Called: Homes By John Hershberger
650 S Prospect Ave # 200 (44632-8904)
PHONE...................................330 877-1515
John Hershberger, *President*
EMP: 25

SQ FT: 20,000
SALES (est): 2.1MM **Privately Held**
SIC: 1521 New construction, single-family
houses

(G-11691)
HRM ENTERPRISES INC (PA)
Also Called: True Value
1015 Edison St Nw Ste 3 (44632-8510)
PHONE...................................330 877-9353
William J Howard, *President*
Wayne Miller, *Vice Pres*
Marion Coblentz, *Info Tech Mgr*
Scott McHale, *Info Tech Mgr*
Aaron Carey, *Technical Staff*
▲ **EMP:** 160
SQ FT: 85,000
SALES (est): 62.5MM **Privately Held**
WEB: www.hartvilletool.com
SIC: 5947 5812 7389 Gift shop; American
restaurant; flea market

(G-11692)
HUMANA INC
1289 Edison St Nw (44632-8942)
PHONE...................................330 877-5464
EMP: 43
SALES (corp-wide): 53.7B **Publicly Held**
SIC: 6324 Hospital/Medical Service Plan
PA: Humana Inc.
  500 W Main St Ste 300
  Louisville KY 40202
  502 580-1000

(G-11693)
K W ZELLERS & SON INC
13494 Duquette Ave Ne (44632-8820)
PHONE...................................330 877-9371
Jeffrey Zellers, *President*
Cecil Kene, *Vice Pres*
Kenneth Zellers Jr, *Treasurer*
Richard Zellers, *Shareholder*
EMP: 25
SQ FT: 20,000
SALES: 10MM **Privately Held**
SIC: 0181 Seeds, vegetable: growing of

(G-11694)
**LAKE LOCAL BOARD OF
EDUCATION**
13188 Kent Ave Ne (44632-9666)
PHONE...................................330 877-9383
Stella Loebmunson, *Owner*
EMP: 445
SALES (corp-wide): 16.3MM **Privately
Held**
SIC: 4789 Pipeline terminal facilities, inde-
pendently operated
PA: Lake Local Board Of Education
  436 King Church Ave Sw
  Uniontown OH 44685
  330 877-9383

(G-11695)
NILCO LLC (DH)
Also Called: Erie Lumber Co Division
1221 W Maple St Ste 100 (44632-8550)
PHONE...................................888 248-5151
Jim Smith, *CEO*
EMP: 35
SQ FT: 66,670
SALES (est): 73.7MM
SALES (corp-wide): 800MM **Privately
Held**
SIC: 5031 5251 Lumber: rough, dressed &
finished; building materials, exterior; hard-
ware
HQ: U.S. Lumber Group, Llc
  2160 Satellite Blvd # 450
  Duluth GA 30097
  678 474-4577

(G-11696)
OREILLY AUTOMOTIVE INC
1196 W Maple St (44632-9080)
PHONE...................................330 267-4383
Mike Hobbs, *President*
EMP: 39 **Publicly Held**
SIC: 7538 General automotive repair
shops
PA: O'reilly Automotive, Inc.
  233 S Patterson Ave
  Springfield MO 65802

(G-11697)
**SABLE CREEK GOLF COURSE
INC**
5942 Edison St Ne (44632-9175)
PHONE...................................330 877-9606
Robert Frase, *President*
Jeff Fraze, *Vice Pres*
Theresa Headley, *Admin Sec*
EMP: 35
SQ FT: 4,844
SALES (est): 2.1MM **Privately Held**
WEB: www.sablecreekgolf.com
SIC: 7992 Public golf courses

(G-11698)
SCHONER CHEVROLET INC
720 W Maple St (44632-8504)
P.O. Box 9 (44632-0009)
PHONE...................................330 877-6731
Mark E Hanlon, *President*
Dorothy Hanlon, *Corp Secy*
Joe Memmer, *Store Mgr*
Rick Borton, *Sales Mgr*
Dave Hite, *Manager*
EMP: 30 **EST:** 1936
SQ FT: 20,000
SALES (est): 10.9MM **Privately Held**
WEB: www.schonerchevrolet.com
SIC: 5511 7514 7538 7515 Automobiles,
new & used; pickups, new & used; vans,
new & used; rent-a-car service; general
automotive repair shops; passenger car
leasing; truck rental & leasing, no drivers;
used car dealers

(G-11699)
SOMMERS MARKET LLC (PA)
Also Called: Grocery Outlet Supermarket
214 Market Ave Sw (44632-8545)
PHONE...................................330 352-7470
Roland Sommers, *President*
David J Sommers, *Vice Pres*
Phil Weidler,
EMP: 56
SQ FT: 6,000
SALES: 3.5MM **Privately Held**
SIC: 5411 5141 Grocery stores, independ-
ent; groceries, general line

(G-11700)
**VIETNAM VETERANS AMERICA
INC**
874 Marigold St Nw (44632-9032)
P.O. Box 6018, Akron (44312-0018)
PHONE...................................330 877-6017
Lee Fisher, *President*
EMP: 26
SALES (corp-wide): 9.6MM **Privately
Held**
SIC: 8641 Veterans' organization
PA: Vietnam Veterans Of America, Inc.
  8719 Colesville Rd # 100
  Silver Spring MD 20910
  301 585-4000

Hayesville
Ashland County

(G-11701)
IMPRESSIVE PACKAGING INC
Also Called: Ipi
627 County Rd 30 A (44838)
P.O. Box 325 (44838-0325)
PHONE...................................419 368-6808
Wayne Willis, *President*
EMP: 33
SALES (est): 4.5MM **Privately Held**
WEB: www.impressivepackaging.com
SIC: 5199 5113 Packaging materials; cor-
rugated & solid fiber boxes

Heath
Licking County

(G-11702)
BIONETICS CORPORATION
813 Irving Wick Dr W (43056-1199)
PHONE...................................757 873-0900
W J Silvey, *Branch Mgr*
EMP: 25

SALES (corp-wide): 47.1MM **Privately
Held**
WEB: www.bionetics.com
SIC: 8732 8742 8734 Market analysis,
business & economic research; management consulting services; product testing
laboratory, safety or performance
PA: The Bionetics Corporation
  101 Production Dr Ste 100
  Yorktown VA 23693
  757 873-0900

(G-11703)
GLEMSURE REALTY TRUST
Also Called: Indian Mound Mall
771 S 30th St Ste 9001 (43056-1252)
PHONE...................................740 522-6620
John Guminski, *President*
EMP: 50
SALES (est): 2.1MM **Privately Held**
WEB: www.indianmoundmall.com
SIC: 6512 Shopping center, property oper-
ation only

(G-11704)
GUMMER WHOLESALE INC (PA)
1945 James Pkwy (43056-4000)
P.O. Box 2288 (43056-0288)
PHONE...................................740 928-0415
Chad Gummer, *President*
Lillian Gummer, *Corp Secy*
Michael Gummer, *Vice Pres*
Keith Myers, *Vice Pres*
Bill Yost, *Purchasing*
EMP: 67
SQ FT: 50,000
SALES (est): 45.8MM **Privately Held**
WEB: www.gummerwholesale.com
SIC: 5194 5145 5199 5141 Cigarettes;
candy; novelties, paper; groceries, gen-
eral line

(G-11705)
MISTRAS GROUP INC
1480 James Pkwy (43056-4018)
PHONE...................................740 788-9188
Mike Jones, *Branch Mgr*
Brian Frye, *Manager*
Russell Higgins, *Manager*
EMP: 35
SQ FT: 13,000 **Publicly Held**
SIC: 8734 Testing laboratories
PA: Mistras Group, Inc.
  195 Clarksville Rd Ste 2
  Princeton Junction NJ 08550

(G-11706)
MPLX TERMINALS LLC
840 Heath Rd (43056-1175)
PHONE...................................504 252-8064
EMP: 33
SALES (corp-wide): 6.4B **Publicly Held**
SIC: 5172 Gasoline
HQ: Mplx Terminals Llc
  200 E Hardin St
  Findlay OH

(G-11707)
NUWAY INCORPORATED
996 Thornwood Dr (43056-9333)
P.O. Box 498, Granville (43023-0498)
PHONE...................................740 587-2452
Dannette McInturff, *President*
Kody McInturff, *Vice Pres*
Kristopher McInturff, *Vice Pres*
Ashley McInturff, *Admin Sec*
EMP: 25
SQ FT: 1,600
SALES: 3.4MM **Privately Held**
SIC: 1794 Excavation & grading, building
construction

(G-11708)
ROBERTSON CNSTR SVCS INC
1801 Thornwood Dr (43056-9311)
PHONE...................................740 929-1000
Christian H Robertson, *President*
Clyde McIntire, *Project Mgr*
Dean Locher, *Opers Mgr*
Blake Swick, *Project Engr*
Michele Robertson, *Treasurer*
EMP: 100
SQ FT: 6,000
SALES (est): 45.2MM **Privately Held**
SIC: 1541 Industrial buildings & ware-
houses

▲ = Import ▼=Export
◆ =Import/Export

(G-11709)
SAMUEL STRAPPING SYSTEMS INC
1455 James Pkwy (43056-4007)
PHONE................................740 522-2500
Brad McConnell, *Production*
Matthew Taylor, *Controller*
Jay Jones, *Manager*
EMP: 100
SALES (corp-wide): 1.8B **Privately Held**
WEB: www.samuelstrapping.com
SIC: 3565 3089 5085 5084 Wrapping machines; plastic processing; industrial supplies; industrial machinery & equipment; packaging materials
HQ: Samuel, Son & Co. (Usa) Inc.
1401 Davey Rd Ste 300
Woodridge IL 60517
630 783-8900

Hebron
Licking County

(G-11710)
BAYER HERITAGE FEDERAL CR UN
1111 O Neill Dr (43025-9409)
PHONE................................740 929-2015
Andrew Bialy, *Controller*
Rod Herrick, *Manager*
EMP: 132
SALES (corp-wide): 14.1MM **Privately Held**
WEB: www.bayerefcu.com
SIC: 6061 Federal credit unions
PA: Bayer Heritage Federal Credit Union
17612 Energy Rd
Proctor WV 26055
304 455-4029

(G-11711)
CLEAN HARBORS ENVMTL SVCS INC
581 Milliken Dr (43025-9657)
PHONE................................740 929-3532
EMP: 43
SALES (corp-wide): 3.3B **Publicly Held**
SIC: 4953 Hazardous waste collection & disposal
HQ: Clean Harbors Environmental Services, Inc.
42 Longwater Dr
Norwell MA 02061
781 792-5000

(G-11712)
DDM-DIGITAL IMAGING DATA
Also Called: Ddm Direct of Ohio
190 Milliken Dr (43025-9657)
PHONE................................740 928-1110
Eill Hillard, *Branch Mgr*
EMP: 60
SALES (corp-wide): 6.8B **Publicly Held**
WEB: www.ddmdirect.com
SIC: 7331 Direct mail advertising services
HQ: Ddm-Digital Imaging, Data Processing And Mailing Services, L C
1223 William St
Buffalo NY 14206
716 893-8671

(G-11713)
EXEL INC
200 Arrowhead Blvd (43025-9466)
PHONE................................740 929-2113
John Wolfe, *General Mgr*
Giancarlo Delon, *Opers Mgr*
Jason Jones, *Opers Mgr*
Doug Linzinmeir, *Opers Mgr*
Jordan Bonifas, *Opers Spvr*
EMP: 70
SALES (corp-wide): 70.4B **Privately Held**
WEB: www.exel-logistics.com
SIC: 4731 Freight forwarding
HQ: Exel Inc.
570 Polaris Pkwy
Westerville OH 43082
614 865-8500

(G-11714)
HENDRICKSON INTERNATIONAL CORP
Also Called: Hendrickson Auxiliary Axles
277 N High St (43025-8008)
PHONE................................740 929-5600
Mike Keeler, *General Mgr*
Lisa Kirkingburg, *Accounting Dir*
EMP: 78
SALES (corp-wide): 916.4MM **Privately Held**
SIC: 3714 3493 3089 5084 Motor vehicle parts & accessories; steel springs, except wire; plastic containers, except foam; industrial machinery & equipment; truck & bus bodies
HQ: Hendrickson International Corporation
500 Park Blvd Ste 450
Itasca IL 60143
630 874-9700

(G-11715)
HERITAGE SPORTSWEAR INC (PA)
Also Called: Virginia T'S
102 Reliance Dr (43025-9204)
P.O. Box 760 (43025-0760)
PHONE................................740 928-7771
Michael Jurden, *President*
Cindy Hayes, *Sales Staff*
Dana Johnson, *Sales Staff*
Brianna Soley, *Sales Staff*
EMP: 75
SQ FT: 75,000
SALES (est): 167.4MM **Privately Held**
WEB: www.heritagesportswear.com
SIC: 5136 5137 Sportswear, men's & boys'; sportswear, women's & children's

(G-11716)
LEGEND SMELTING AND RECYCL INC (PA)
Also Called: L S R
717 Oneill Dr (43025)
PHONE................................740 928-0139
Randy Hess, *President*
Mark Sasko, *Vice Pres*
Paul Leary, *CFO*
▲ **EMP:** 60
SQ FT: 90,000
SALES (est): 24.1MM **Privately Held**
WEB: www.tarulli-tire.com
SIC: 5093 Nonferrous metals scrap

(G-11717)
MID STATE SYSTEMS INC
9455 Lancaster Rd (43025-9640)
P.O. Box 926 (43025-0926)
PHONE................................740 928-1115
Leon Zazworsky, *President*
Judy K Zazworsky, *Vice Pres*
EMP: 78
SQ FT: 11,500
SALES (est): 13.2MM **Privately Held**
WEB: www.midstatesystems.com
SIC: 4225 General warehousing & storage

(G-11718)
MPW INDUSTRIAL SERVICES INC (HQ)
9711 Lancaster Rd (43025-9764)
P.O. Box 10 (43025-0010)
PHONE................................800 827-8790
Monte Black, *CEO*
Shawn Foraker, *Sales Staff*
▲ **EMP:** 600 **EST:** 1972
SQ FT: 75,000
SALES (est): 208.7MM **Privately Held**
SIC: 7349 Cleaning service, industrial or commercial
PA: Mpw Industrial Services Group, Inc.
9711 Lancaster Rd
Hebron OH 43025
740 927-8790

(G-11719)
MPW INDUSTRIAL SVCS GROUP INC (PA)
9711 Lancaster Rd (43025-9764)
PHONE................................740 927-8790
Monte R Black, *CEO*
Jared Black, *President*
Jimmy Peck, *General Mgr*
Sean M Hutcheson, *Counsel*
Tyler Keathley, *Opers Mgr*

EMP: 86
SQ FT: 24,000
SALES (est): 208.7MM **Privately Held**
WEB: www.mpwgroup.com
SIC: 7349 8744 3589 Cleaning service, industrial or commercial; facilities support services; commercial cleaning equipment

(G-11720)
MPW INDUSTRIAL WATER SVCS INC
9711 Lancaster Rd (43025-9764)
P.O. Box 10 (43025-0010)
PHONE................................800 827-8790
Monte R Black, *President*
EMP: 176
SALES: 45MM
SALES (corp-wide): 208.7MM **Privately Held**
SIC: 4499 Water transportation cleaning services
HQ: Mpw Management Services Corp.
9711 Lancaster Rd
Hebron OH 43025

(G-11721)
NATIONAL GAS OIL CORP
120 O Neill Dr (43025-9680)
PHONE................................740 348-1243
Dave Detty, *Manager*
EMP: 50
SALES: 11.7MM **Privately Held**
SIC: 4924 Natural gas distribution

(G-11722)
NATIONAL HOT ROD ASSOCIATION
Also Called: National Trail Raceway
2650 National Rd Sw Ste B (43025-9639)
PHONE................................740 928-5706
Mike Fornataro, *General Mgr*
EMP: 139
SALES (corp-wide): 99.2MM **Privately Held**
WEB: www.nhra.com
SIC: 7948 8611 Dragstrip operation; business associations
PA: National Hot Rod Association
2035 E Financial Way
Glendora CA 91741
626 914-4761

(G-11723)
S R DOOR INC (PA)
Also Called: Seal-Rite Door
1120 O Neill Dr (43025-9409)
P.O. Box 2109, Columbus (43216-2109)
PHONE................................740 927-3558
Scott A Miller, *President*
Glen Miller, *Vice Pres*
EMP: 106 **EST:** 1980
SQ FT: 75,000
SALES (est): 15.9MM **Privately Held**
WEB: www.seal-ritedoor.com
SIC: 2431 3442 3211 5031 Doors, wood; windows & window parts & trim, wood; metal doors; construction glass; lumber, plywood & millwork

(G-11724)
SAFETY-KLEEN SYSTEMS INC
581 Milliken Dr (43025-9687)
PHONE................................740 929-3532
Steve Moyer, *Branch Mgr*
EMP: 61
SALES (corp-wide): 3.3B **Publicly Held**
SIC: 7389 4953 Solvents recovery service; refuse systems
HQ: Safety-Kleen Systems, Inc.
2600 N Central Expy # 400
Richardson TX 75080
972 265-2000

(G-11725)
TRUCKOMAT CORPORATION
Also Called: Iowa 80 Group
10707 Lancaster Rd Ste 37 (43025-9622)
P.O. Box 837 (43025-0837)
PHONE................................740 467-2818
Jeff Corley, *General Mgr*
EMP: 30
SALES (corp-wide): 374.4MM **Privately Held**
WEB: www.truckomat.com
SIC: 7542 5013 Truck wash; motor vehicle supplies & new parts

HQ: Truckomat Corporation
515 Sterling Dr
Walcott IA 52773
563 284-6965

Hicksville
Defiance County

(G-11726)
COMMUNITY MEMORIAL HOSPITAL (PA)
208 Columbus St (43526-1299)
PHONE................................419 542-6692
Mel Fahs, *CEO*
Chuck Bohlmann, *Senior VP*
Susan Hobeck, *CFO*
Melissa Phillips, *Case Mgr*
Amy Thornell, *Manager*
EMP: 119
SQ FT: 100,000
SALES: 24.6MM **Privately Held**
WEB: www.cmhosp.com
SIC: 8062 Hospital, affiliated with AMA residency

(G-11727)
FETTERS CONSTRUCTION INC
945 E High St (43526-1270)
PHONE................................419 542-0944
EMP: 120 **Privately Held**
SIC: 1521 Single-Family House Construction
PA: Fetters Construction, Inc.
5417 County Road 427
Auburn IN 46706

(G-11728)
HICKORY CREEK HEALTHCARE
Also Called: Creek At Hicksburg
401 Fountain St (43526-1337)
PHONE................................419 542-7795
Bill Langschiet, *Manager*
EMP: 60
SALES (corp-wide): 23.1MM **Privately Held**
SIC: 8051 Skilled nursing care facilities
PA: Hickory Creek Healthcare Foundation, Inc.
5555 Glenridge Connector # 650
Atlanta GA 30342
678 990-7262

(G-11729)
HICKSVILLE BANK INC (HQ)
144 E High St (43526-1163)
P.O. Box 283 (43526-0283)
PHONE................................419 542-7726
Anthony Primack, *President*
Larry Coburn, *President*
Lucy Hilbert, *Senior VP*
Greg Mohr, *Vice Pres*
Chad Yoder, *CFO*
EMP: 46
SQ FT: 5,000
SALES: 4.5MM **Privately Held**
WEB: www.thehicksvillebank.com
SIC: 6022 State trust companies accepting deposits, commercial

(G-11730)
NEMCO INC
Also Called: Nemco Food Equipment
301 Meuse Argonne St (43526-1169)
P.O. Box 305 (43526-0305)
PHONE................................419 542-7751
Kenny Moffatt, *CEO*
Stan Guillam, *President*
EMP: 70
SALES (est): 13MM **Privately Held**
SIC: 5046 Commercial cooking & food service equipment

(G-11731)
WHOLESALE HOUSE INC (PA)
Also Called: Twh
503 W High St (43526-1037)
P.O. Box 268 (43526-0268)
PHONE................................419 542-1315
Marcy Keesbury, *President*
Stephen D Height, *President*
Nick Vasu, *Purchasing*
Jason Wisecup, *Sales Staff*
Amy Stark, *Administration*

◆ **EMP:** 70
SQ FT: 74,000
SALES (est): 54.9MM **Privately Held**
WEB: www.twhouse.com
SIC: 5065 Electronic parts & equipment

Highland Heights
Cuyahoga County

(G-11732)
C & S ASSOCIATES INC
Also Called: National Lien Digest
729 Miner Rd (44143-2117)
P.O. Box 24101, Cleveland (44124-0101)
PHONE..........................440 461-9661
Mary B Cowan, *President*
Delores A Cowan, *President*
Cathleen M Cowan, *Principal*
Bernard J Cowan, *Exec VP*
Greg Powelson, *Vice Pres*
EMP: 50 **EST:** 1974
SQ FT: 9,000
SALES (est): 6.8MM **Privately Held**
SIC: 7322 2721 Collection agency, except
real estate; periodicals: publishing only

(G-11733)
ENESCO PROPERTIES LLC
Also Called: Things Remembered
5500 Avion Park Dr (44143-1911)
PHONE..........................440 473-2000
EMP: 1400 **Privately Held**
SIC: 7389 5947 Gift shop
HQ: Enesco Properties, Llc
225 Windsor Dr
Itasca IL 60143
630 875-5300

(G-11734)
HOME DEPOT USA INC
Also Called: Home Depot, The
6199 Wilson Mills Rd (44143-2101)
PHONE..........................440 684-1343
Rick Evans, *Manager*
EMP: 140
SALES (corp-wide): 108.2B **Publicly
Held**
WEB: www.homerentalsdepot.com
SIC: 5211 7359 Home centers; tool rental
HQ: Home Depot U.S.A., Inc.
2455 Paces Ferry Ave
Atlanta GA 30339

(G-11735)
PROVIDIAN MED FIELD SVC LLC
5335 Avion Park Dr Unit A (44143-1916)
PHONE..........................440 833-0460
Michael Skok, *President*
David Skok, *Vice Pres*
EMP: 26
SALES: 670K **Privately Held**
SIC: 7699 Hospital equipment repair services

(G-11736)
RPC ELECTRONICS INC (PA)
749 Miner Rd (44143-2145)
PHONE..........................440 461-4700
Lenord Applebaum, *President*
Robert Lyczkowski, *Vice Pres*
Ira Dryer, *CFO*
▲ **EMP:** 38
SALES (est): 24.9MM **Privately Held**
WEB: www.rpcelectronics.com
SIC: 5065 Electronic parts & equipment

Hilliard
Franklin County

(G-11737)
24 - SEVEN HOME HLTH CARE
LLC
5064 Edgeley Dr (43026-3410)
PHONE..........................614 794-0325
Ahmed M Guntane, *Mng Member*
EMP: 47 **EST:** 2010
SALES: 1.2MM **Privately Held**
SIC: 8099 Blood related health services

(G-11738)
A JACOBS INC
4410 Hansen Dr (43026-2461)
PHONE..........................614 774-6757
Andrew Jacobs, *President*
EMP: 26
SALES (est): 1.9MM **Privately Held**
SIC: 7363 Truck driver services

(G-11739)
ABILITY MATTERS LLC
6058 Heritage View Ct (43026-7614)
PHONE..........................614 214-9652
Kristyn Miller, *CEO*
EMP: 50
SALES (est): 202.9K **Privately Held**
SIC: 8059 8082 Personal care home, with
health care; home health care services

(G-11740)
ALL MY SONS MOVING &
STORGE OF
4401 Lyman Dr Ste D (43026-2201)
PHONE..........................614 405-7202
EMP: 29
SALES (est): 3.4MM **Privately Held**
SIC: 4212 Moving services

(G-11741)
AMERICAN REGENT INC
4150 Lyman Dr (43026)
PHONE..........................614 436-2222
Joseph Kenneth Keller, *CEO*
Robert Vultaggio, *Controller*
Linda Romaine, *Manager*
EMP: 100 **Privately Held**
WEB: www.pharmaforceinc.com
SIC: 2834 5122 Pharmaceutical preparations; pharmaceuticals
HQ: American Regent, Inc.
5 Ramsey Rd
Shirley NY 11967
631 924-4000

(G-11742)
APPLIANCE RECYCL CTRS
AMER INC
A R C A Ohio
3700 Parkway Ln Ste D&G (43026-1238)
PHONE..........................614 876-8771
Dan Chuhna, *Manager*
EMP: 100
SALES (corp-wide): 36.7MM **Publicly
Held**
WEB: www.arcainc.com
SIC: 5722 4953 Household appliance
stores; recycling, waste materials
PA: Appliance Recycling Centers Of America, Inc.
175 Jackson Ave N Ste 102
Hopkins MN 55343
952 930-9000

(G-11743)
ARCTIC EXPRESS INC
4277 Lyman Dr (43026-1227)
P.O. Box 129 (43026-0129)
PHONE..........................614 876-4008
Richard E Durst, *Ch of Bd*
Jay Durst, *Safety Dir*
Michael Ott, *Marketing Staff*
Charlene Bauer, *Manager*
Donna Manter, *Manager*
EMP: 111 **EST:** 1981
SQ FT: 12,100
SALES: 20.1MM **Privately Held**
WEB: www.arcticexpress.com
SIC: 4213 Contract haulers; refrigerated
products transport

(G-11744)
BANC CERTIFIED MERCH SVCS
LLC
5006 Cemetery Rd (43026-1640)
PHONE..........................614 850-2740
Ali Razi, *Mng Member*
EMP: 46 **EST:** 2000
SQ FT: 1,500
SALES (est): 3.4MM **Privately Held**
WEB: www.banccertified.net
SIC: 7389 Credit card service

(G-11745)
BARNETT ASSOCIATES INC
3455 Mill Run Dr Ste 100 (43026-9084)
PHONE..........................516 877-2860
Paul Barnett, *President*
Phyllis Kaufer, *Exec VP*
EMP: 80
SALES (est): 8.4MM **Privately Held**
WEB: www.barnettassociates.com
SIC: 7389 Legal & tax services

(G-11746)
BEHAVIORAL TREATMENTS
5275 Norwich St (43026-1424)
P.O. Box 430 (43026-0430)
PHONE..........................614 558-1968
William Jamison, *President*
EMP: 50
SALES (est): 627.6K **Privately Held**
SIC: 8322 Individual & family services

(G-11747)
BMW FINANCIAL SERVICES NA
LLC (DH)
Also Called: Alphera Financial Services
5550 Britton Pkwy (43026-7456)
PHONE..........................614 718-6900
Ed Robinson, *CEO*
Phil Masi, *General Mgr*
Emily Adams, *Vice Pres*
Chris Bennett, *Vice Pres*
Shaun Bugbee, *Vice Pres*
EMP: 45
SQ FT: 118,000
SALES (est): 514.9MM
SALES (corp-wide): 111.6B **Privately
Held**
SIC: 6159 Automobile finance leasing
HQ: Bmw Of North America, Llc
300 Chestnut Ridge Rd
Woodcliff Lake NJ 07677
201 307-4000

(G-11748)
BROOKSEDGE DAY CARE
CENTER
2185 Hilliard Rome Rd (43026-9068)
PHONE..........................614 529-0077
Carol Rezentes, *President*
Samuel Rezentes, *Vice Pres*
EMP: 30
SQ FT: 10,000
SALES (est): 682K **Privately Held**
SIC: 8351 Group day care center

(G-11749)
BRUNER CORPORATION (PA)
Also Called: Honeywell Authorized Dealer
3637 Lacon Rd (43026-1202)
PHONE..........................614 334-9000
Randy Sleeper, *CEO*
Mark Wenger, *President*
Alex Grant, *Business Mgr*
Mark Brown, *Vice Pres*
Mick Newman, *Vice Pres*
EMP: 175 **EST:** 1958
SQ FT: 4,200
SALES: 63MM **Privately Held**
WEB: www.brunercorp.com
SIC: 1711 Plumbing contractors; warm air
heating & air conditioning contractor

(G-11750)
BUCK AND SONS LDSCP SVC
INC
7147 Hayden Run Rd (43026-7792)
P.O. Box 1119 (43026-6119)
PHONE..........................614 876-5359
Charles William Buck, *CEO*
Steven A Buck, *President*
Mark Meyers, *Vice Pres*
Lisa Myers, *Office Mgr*
Joe Kaltenbach, *Manager*
EMP: 45 **EST:** 1972
SQ FT: 20,000
SALES (est): 2.6MM **Privately Held**
WEB: www.buckandsons.com
SIC: 0782 1711 Landscape contractors;
garden planting services; garden maintenance services; irrigation sprinkler system
installation

(G-11751)
BUCKHOLZ WALL SYSTEMS
LLC
Also Called: Buckholz Wall Systems
4160 Anson Dr (43026-2206)
P.O. Box 229, Galloway (43119-0229)
PHONE..........................614 870-1775
John Buckholz,
EMP: 50
SALES (est): 4.9MM **Privately Held**
SIC: 1771 1742 Stucco, gunite & grouting
contractors; insulation, buildings

(G-11752)
CACHE NEXT GENERATION
LLC
Also Called: C N G
3974 Brown Park Dr Ste D (43026-1168)
PHONE..........................614 850-9444
EMP: 98
SQ FT: 2,800
SALES (est): 3.9MM **Privately Held**
SIC: 7374 7379 Data Processing/Preparation Computer Related Services

(G-11753)
CARESOURCE MANAGEMENT
GROUP CO
3455 Mill Run Dr (43026-9078)
PHONE..........................614 221-3370
Carrol Beaufay, *Branch Mgr*
EMP: 40 **Privately Held**
SIC: 6321 Health insurance carriers
PA: Caresource Management Group Co.
230 N Main St
Dayton OH 45402

(G-11754)
CBIZ MED MGT
PROFESSIONALS INC
3455 Mill Run Dr Ste 450 (43026-9083)
PHONE..........................614 771-2222
Mark Hamon, *Manager*
EMP: 30
SALES (corp-wide): 137.5MM **Privately
Held**
WEB: www.llms.com
SIC: 8721 Billing & bookkeeping service
HQ: Cbiz Medical Management Professionals, Inc.
5959 Shallowford Rd # 575
Chattanooga TN 37421

(G-11755)
CINEMARK USA INC
Also Called: Cinemark Movies 12 At Mill Run
3773 Ridge Mill Dr (43026-9554)
PHONE..........................614 527-3773
EMP: 30
SALES (corp-wide): 2.9B **Publicly Held**
SIC: 7832 Motion Picture Theatre
HQ: Cinemark Usa, Inc.
3900 Dallas Pkwy Ste 500
Plano TX 75093
972 665-1000

(G-11756)
COBALT GROUP INC
Integralink
4635 Trueman Blvd Ste 100 (43026-2491)
PHONE..........................614 876-4013
EMP: 85
SALES (corp-wide): 11.6B **Publicly Held**
SIC: 7375 Information Retrieval Services
HQ: The Cobalt Group Inc
605 5th Ave S Ste 800
Seattle WA 98104

(G-11757)
CREDIT UNION OF OHIO INC
(PA)
5500 Britton Pkwy (43026-7456)
P.O. Box 165006, Columbus (43216-5006)
PHONE..........................614 487-6650
Susan Birkhimer, *CEO*
Tami Peyton, *Vice Pres*
Karen Rose, *Vice Pres*
Lisa Reynolds, *Accounting Mgr*
Tonya Keaton, *Loan Officer*
EMP: 30 **EST:** 1967
SQ FT: 10,000

SALES: 4.6MM **Privately Held**
WEB: www.cuofohio.org
SIC: 6062 State credit unions, not federally chartered

(G-11758)
CUMMINS BRIDGEWAY COLUMBUS LLC
4000 Lyman Dr (43026-1212)
PHONE....................614 771-1000
Bill Bergner,
EMP: 60
SALES (est): 7.4MM
SALES (corp-wide): 23.7B **Publicly Held**
WEB: www.bridgewaypower.com
SIC: 5084 Engines & parts, diesel; internal combustion engines
PA: Cummins Inc.
500 Jackson St
Columbus IN 47201
812 377-5000

(G-11759)
CUMMINS INC
4000 Lyman Dr (43026-1212)
PHONE....................614 771-1000
Greg Bowl, *Branch Mgr*
William Bergner, *Branch Mgr*
EMP: 25
SALES (corp-wide): 23.7B **Publicly Held**
WEB: www.bridgewaypower.com
SIC: 5084 7538 3519 Engines & parts, diesel; diesel engine repair: automotive; internal combustion engines
PA: Cummins Inc.
500 Jackson St
Columbus IN 47201
812 377-5000

(G-11760)
DFS CORPORATE SERVICES LLC
Also Called: Discover Card Services
3311 Mill Meadow Dr (43026-9088)
P.O. Box 3025, New Albany (43054-3025)
PHONE....................614 777-7020
Mike Devario, *Manager*
EMP: 300
SALES (corp-wide): 12.8B **Publicly Held**
WEB: www.discovercard.com
SIC: 7389 7322 Credit card service; adjustment & collection services
HQ: Dfs Corporate Services Llc
2500 Lake Cook Rd 2
Riverwoods IL 60015
224 405-0900

(G-11761)
DISH NETWORK CORPORATION
3315 Mill Meadow Dr (43026-9088)
PHONE....................614 534-2001
Randy Cox, *Manager*
Chris George, *Manager*
EMP: 52 **Publicly Held**
WEB: www.dishnetwork.com
SIC: 4841 Direct broadcast satellite services (DBS)
PA: Dish Network Corporation
9601 S Meridian Blvd
Englewood CO 80112

(G-11762)
DOCUMENT IMGING SPCIALISTS LLC
Also Called: Information Management Svcs
4460 Emmas Court Hilliard (43026)
P.O. Box 29230, Columbus (43229-0230)
PHONE....................614 868-9008
Michael Iadarola, *Mng Member*
Timothy Stephens,
EMP: 29
SQ FT: 3,700
SALES (est): 6.7MM **Privately Held**
SIC: 5044 7699 Office equipment; office equipment & accessory customizing

(G-11763)
E-CYCLE LLC
4105 Leap Rd (43026-1117)
PHONE....................614 832-7032
Christopher J Irion, *CEO*
Jen Myers, *COO*
Jennifer Myers, *COO*
Tony Jerig, *Vice Pres*
Dave Wine, *Opers Staff*

EMP: 55
SALES (est): 34MM **Privately Held**
WEB: www.e-cycle.com
SIC: 5065 Telephone & telegraphic equipment

(G-11764)
EASTER SEALS CENTER
3830 Trueman Ct (43026-2496)
PHONE....................614 228-5523
Pandora Shaw-Dupras, *CEO*
EMP: 99
SALES: 4.9MM
SALES (corp-wide): 73MM **Privately Held**
SIC: 8322 Social service center
PA: Easter Seals, Inc.
141 W Jackson Blvd 1400a
Chicago IL 60604
312 726-6200

(G-11765)
ECOPLUMBERS INC
4691 Northwest Pkwy (43026-1126)
PHONE....................614 299-9903
Michael Burnhart, *CFO*
Michael Barnhart, *CFO*
Braun Bocook, *Manager*
EMP: 34
SALES: 4MM **Privately Held**
SIC: 1711 Plumbing contractors

(G-11766)
EQUITY INC (PA)
Also Called: Equity Real Estate
4653 Trueman Blvd Ste 100 (43026-2490)
PHONE....................614 802-2900
Steve Wathen, *CEO*
James W Haring Jr, *COO*
Andy Johanni, *Exec VP*
Melanie B Wollenberg, *Exec VP*
Nathan Palmer, *Senior VP*
EMP: 48
SQ FT: 9,000
SALES (est): 35.9MM **Privately Held**
SIC: 1541 1542 6552 Industrial buildings, new construction; commercial & office building, new construction; subdividers & developers

(G-11767)
FERGUSON ENTERPRISES INC
Also Called: Ferguson 124
4363 Lyman Dr (43026-1266)
P.O. Box 211000, Columbus (43221-8000)
PHONE....................614 876-8555
Ron Sima, *Branch Mgr*
EMP: 25
SALES (corp-wide): 20.7B **Privately Held**
WEB: www.ferguson.com
SIC: 5074 5999 Plumbing fittings & supplies; heating equipment (hydronic); plumbing & heating supplies
HQ: Ferguson Enterprises, Inc.
12500 Jefferson Ave
Newport News VA 23602
757 874-7795

(G-11768)
GENERAL ELECTRIC COMPANY
3455 Mill Run Dr (43026-9078)
PHONE....................614 527-1078
EMP: 25
SALES (corp-wide): 123.6B **Publicly Held**
SIC: 1731 Electrical Contractor
PA: General Electric Company
41 Farnsworth St
Boston MA 02210
617 443-3000

(G-11769)
GLENMONT
4599 Avery Rd (43026-9786)
PHONE....................614 876-0084
Sara F Thorndike, *Principal*
Katherine Lundberg, *Director*
EMP: 39
SQ FT: 1,008
SALES: 5.2MM **Privately Held**
SIC: 8062 General medical & surgical hospitals

(G-11770)
GREAT DANE COLUMBUS INC
4080 Lyman Dr (43026-1287)
P.O. Box 9 (43026-0009)
PHONE....................614 876-0666
Henry T Skipper Jr, *President*
Donald L Ottney, *Vice Pres*
D J O'Connor, *Admin Sec*
William H Oliphant, *Asst Sec*
EMP: 45
SQ FT: 14,200
SALES (est): 18.9MM
SALES (corp-wide): 1.5B **Privately Held**
SIC: 5012 Trailers for trucks, new & used
HQ: Great Dane Llc
222 N Lasalle St Ste 920
Chicago IL 60601

(G-11771)
HAMILTON SAFE PRODUCTS CO INC
4770 Northwest Pkwy (43026-1131)
PHONE....................614 268-5530
Brad Hunter, *President*
Dale Peters, *Regional Mgr*
Eric De Bellis, *Vice Pres*
Fran Wooddrif, *Admin Sec*
EMP: 25
SQ FT: 13,500
SALES (est): 10.3MM **Privately Held**
SIC: 5049 Bank equipment & supplies

(G-11772)
HER INC
Also Called: H E R Realtors
3499 Main St (43026-1319)
PHONE....................614 771-7400
Sherol Saxton Mulligan, *Principal*
EMP: 40
SALES (corp-wide): 14.3MM **Privately Held**
WEB: www.eassent.com
SIC: 6531 Real estate agent, residential
PA: Her, Inc
4261 Morse Rd
Columbus OH 43230
614 221-7400

(G-11773)
HERITAGE GOLF CLUB LTD PARTNR
3525 Heritage Club Dr (43026-1313)
PHONE....................614 777-1690
Dan O'Brien, *Partner*
EMP: 100
SALES (est): 5.6MM
SALES (corp-wide): 477MM **Privately Held**
WEB: www.heritagegolfclub.com
SIC: 7992 5812 7997 5941 Public golf courses; eating places; membership sports & recreation clubs; sporting goods & bicycle shops
HQ: Clubcorp Holdings, Inc.
3030 Lbj Fwy Ste 600
Dallas TX 75234
972 243-6191

(G-11774)
HEYBURN DIALYSIS LLC
Also Called: Hilliard Station Dialysis
2447 Hilliard Rome Rd (43026-8194)
PHONE....................614 876-3610
James K Hilger, *Vice Pres*
EMP: 35
SALES (est): 446.5K **Publicly Held**
SIC: 8092 Kidney dialysis centers
PA: Davita Inc.
2000 16th St
Denver CO 80202

(G-11775)
HI-WAY PAVING INC
4343 Weaver Ct N (43026-1193)
P.O. Box 550 (43026-0550)
PHONE....................614 876-1700
Charles L Keith, *CEO*
James Taylor, *President*
Gail E Griffith, *Principal*
Brad Allison, *Exec VP*
Mark Lamonte, *CFO*
EMP: 100
SQ FT: 9,500

SALES (est): 41MM **Privately Held**
WEB: www.hiwaypaving.com
SIC: 1611 Concrete construction: roads, highways, sidewalks, etc.

(G-11776)
HOME DEPOT USA INC
Also Called: Home Depot, The
4101 Trueman Blvd (43026-2479)
PHONE....................614 876-5558
Wendy Ramjas, *Manager*
EMP: 150
SALES (corp-wide): 108.2B **Publicly Held**
WEB: www.homerentalsdepot.com
SIC: 5211 7359 Home centers; tool rental
HQ: Home Depot U.S.A., Inc.
2455 Paces Ferry Ave
Atlanta GA 30339

(G-11777)
INDUS HILLIARD HOTEL LLC
Also Called: Hampton Inn Stes Clmbus Hllard
3950 Lyman Dr (43026-1210)
PHONE....................614 334-1800
Janet Boissy, *Principal*
David Patel, *Principal*
EMP: 50
SALES (est): 344.9K **Privately Held**
SIC: 7011 Inns

(G-11778)
INLINER AMERICAN INC
4143 Weaver Ct S (43026-1119)
PHONE....................614 529-6440
Kathy Jarrell, *Manager*
EMP: 29
SALES (corp-wide): 2.9B **Publicly Held**
SIC: 1623 Water main construction; pipeline construction
HQ: Inliner American, Inc.
2601 W Lake Mary Blvd # 129
Lake Mary FL 32746
407 472-0014

(G-11779)
J M TOWNING INC
3690 Lacon Rd (43026-1223)
PHONE....................614 876-7335
EMP: 25
SALES (est): 1.5MM **Privately Held**
SIC: 4212 Local Trucking Operator

(G-11780)
JACOBS TELEPHONE CONTRS INC
3660 Parkway Ln Ste E (43026-1236)
PHONE....................614 527-8977
Shannon Brown, *Manager*
EMP: 26
SALES (corp-wide): 12.5MM **Privately Held**
SIC: 5999 7629 Telephone & communication equipment; telephone set repair
PA: Jacobs Telephone Contractors, Inc.
3831 Dayton Park Dr
Dayton OH 45414
937 233-9770

(G-11781)
JOHN ERAMO & SONS INC
3670 Lacon Rd (43026-1223)
PHONE....................614 777-0020
Anthony J Eramo, *President*
Rocco A Eramo, *Chairman*
John T Eramo, *Exec VP*
Brian R Eramo, *Vice Pres*
Micheal G Eramo, *Vice Pres*
EMP: 70 EST: 1966
SQ FT: 6,000
SALES (est): 14.1MM **Privately Held**
WEB: www.eramo.com
SIC: 1794 Excavation & grading, building construction

(G-11782)
K M T SERVICE
3786 Fishinger Blvd (43026-8549)
P.O. Box 606 (43026-0606)
PHONE....................614 777-7770
Karl Trajcevski, *Owner*
EMP: 29
SALES (est): 5.4MM **Privately Held**
SIC: 7622 Video repair

(G-11783)
LASERFLEX CORPORATION (HQ)
3649 Parkway Ln (43026-1214)
PHONE.....................614 850-9600
Ken Kinkopf, *President*
Mary Beth Hagerty, *Finance Mgr*
EMP: 62
SQ FT: 75,000
SALES (est): 25.4MM **Publicly Held**
WEB:
www.customlasercuttingservices.com
SIC: 7389 7699 7692 3599 Metal cutting
services; finishing services; industrial ma-
chinery & equipment repair; welding re-
pair; machine shop, jobbing & repair;
fabricated structural metal; metallizing of
fabrics

(G-11784)
LIGHTHOUSE MEDICAL STAFFING
Also Called: Ambassador Nursing
3970 Brown Park Dr Ste B (43026-1166)
PHONE.....................614 937-6259
James Burk, *CEO*
Greg Burk, *President*
EMP: 60
SQ FT: 1,000
SALES (est): 634.9K **Privately Held**
SIC: 8082 Home health care services

(G-11785)
LIN R ROGERS ELEC CONTRS INC
5050 Nike Dr Ste C (43026-7447)
PHONE.....................614 876-9336
Bobby Yeary, *Branch Mgr*
EMP: 333
SALES (est): 8.6MM
SALES (corp-wide): 131.4MM **Privately Held**
SIC: 1731 Electrical Contractor
PA: Lin R. Rogers Electrical Contractors,
Inc.
2050 Marconi Dr Ste 100
Alpharetta GA 30005
770 772-3400

(G-11786)
LOWES HOME CENTERS LLC
3600 Park Mill Run Dr (43026-8123)
PHONE.....................614 529-5900
Tom Worth, *Manager*
EMP: 150
SALES (corp-wide): 68.6B **Publicly Held**
SIC: 5211 5031 5722 5064 Home cen-
ters; building materials, exterior; building
materials, interior; household appliance
stores; electrical appliances, television &
radio
HQ: Lowe's Home Centers, Llc
1605 Curtis Bridge Rd
Wilkesboro NC 28697
336 658-4000

(G-11787)
MAKOY CENTER INC
5462 Center St (43026-1068)
PHONE.....................614 777-1211
George Yoakam, *President*
Clay Daniel, *General Mgr*
EMP: 35
SQ FT: 29,000
SALES (est): 1.4MM **Privately Held**
WEB: www.makoy.com
SIC: 7999 7299 6512 Recreation center;
banquet hall facilities; auditorium & hall
operation

(G-11788)
MATHESON TRI-GAS INC
4579 Sutphen Ct (43026-1224)
PHONE.....................614 771-1311
Melissa Diehl, *Manager*
EMP: 30 **Privately Held**
WEB: www.vngas.com
SIC: 5169 5084 Gases, compressed & liq-
uefied; welding machinery & equipment
HQ: Matheson Tri-Gas, Inc.
150 Allen Rd Ste 302
Basking Ridge NJ 07920
908 991-9200

(G-11789)
MAXIM TECHNOLOGIES INC
3960 Brown Park Dr Ste D (43026-1161)
PHONE.....................614 457-6325
Vijayalakshmi Chillakuru, *President*
Rajagopal Chillakuru, *COO*
EMP: 30
SALES: 3MM **Privately Held**
SIC: 7379 Computer related consulting
services

(G-11790)
MECHANICAL SUPPORT SVCS INC
4641 Northwest Pkwy (43026-1126)
P.O. Box 1475 (43026-6475)
PHONE.....................614 777-8808
Craig F Bateman, *President*
EMP: 25
SQ FT: 2,500
SALES: 1.8MM **Privately Held**
WEB:
www.mechanicalsupportservices.com
SIC: 8711 Mechanical engineering

(G-11791)
MERRY MOPPETS EARLY LEARNING
5075 Britton Pkwy (43026-9447)
PHONE.....................614 529-1730
Gary Estep, *President*
Mytle Estep, *Principal*
EMP: 35
SQ FT: 1,792
SALES (est): 744.9K **Privately Held**
WEB: www.merrymoppet.com
SIC: 8351 Preschool center

(G-11792)
METRO HEATING AND AC CO
Also Called: Metro Air
4731 Northwest Pkwy (43026-3102)
PHONE.....................614 777-1237
Frank J Tate Jr, *President*
EMP: 35
SQ FT: 5,000
SALES (est): 8MM **Privately Held**
SIC: 1711 Warm air heating & air condi-
tioning contractor; heating & air condition-
ing contractors

(G-11793)
METROPOLITAN ENVMTL SVCS INC
5055 Nike Dr (43026-9692)
PHONE.....................614 771-1881
Rick Gaffey, *President*
James Aman, *Corp Secy*
Erick Zeigler, *Vice Pres*
EMP: 90
SQ FT: 10,000
SALES (est): 6.9MM
SALES (corp-wide): 122.3MM **Privately Held**
WEB: www.metenviro.com
SIC: 7349 1794 1629 Cleaning service,
industrial or commercial; excavation work;
dredging contractor
PA: Carylon Corporation
2000 Palm Beach Lks
West Palm Beach FL 33409
561 323-4737

(G-11794)
MICRO CENTER INC
4119 Leap Rd (43026-1117)
PHONE.....................614 850-3000
Richard Mershad, *CEO*
EMP: 300
SALES (est): 17.4MM
SALES (corp-wide): 3.6B **Privately Held**
SIC: 5734 5045 Computer & software
stores; computers, peripherals & software
PA: Micro Electronics, Inc.
4119 Leap Rd
Hilliard OH 43026
614 850-3000

(G-11795)
MICRO ELECTRONICS INC (PA)
Also Called: Micro Center
4119 Leap Rd (43026-1117)
P.O. Box 910 (43026-0910)
PHONE.....................614 850-3000
Richard M Mershad, *President*

Peggy Wolfe, *COO*
John A Noble, *CFO*
Patrick Christie, *Sales Associate*
Sujan Ghimire, *Sales Associate*
▲ EMP: 400
SALES (est): 3.6B **Privately Held**
WEB: www.microcenter.com
SIC: 5045 5734 Computer peripheral
equipment; personal computers

(G-11796)
MICRO ELECTRONICS INC
Also Called: Micro Thinner
4055 Leap Rd (43026-1115)
P.O. Box 848 (43026-0848)
PHONE.....................614 850-3500
Jim Koehler, *Manager*
EMP: 79
SALES (corp-wide): 3.6B **Privately Held**
SIC: 5734 5045 Personal computers;
computer software & accessories; com-
puter peripheral equipment; computers &
accessories, personal & home entertain-
ment
PA: Micro Electronics, Inc.
4119 Leap Rd
Hilliard OH 43026
614 850-3000

(G-11797)
MICROANALYSIS SOCIETY INC
3405 Scioto Run Blvd (43026-3005)
PHONE.....................614 256-8063
Dan Kremser, *Treasurer*
EMP: 500
SALES (est): 3.3MM **Privately Held**
SIC: 8299 7389 Educational services;

(G-11798)
MILL RUN CARE CENTER LLC
Also Called: Mill Run Gardens & Care Center
3399 Mill Run Dr (43026-9078)
PHONE.....................614 527-3000
Laura Sandy, *Mng Member*
Maryanne Struck, *Manager*
EMP: 100
SALES (est): 4.7MM **Privately Held**
SIC: 8059 8052 8051 Nursing home, ex-
cept skilled & intermediate care facility; in-
termediate care facilities; skilled nursing
care facilities

(G-11799)
MILLER PIPELINE LLC
5000 Scioto Darby Rd (43026-1513)
PHONE.....................614 777-8377
Scott Miller, *Manager*
EMP: 300
SALES (corp-wide): 10.5B **Publicly Held**
WEB: www.millerpipeline.com
SIC: 1623 Pipeline construction
HQ: Miller Pipeline, Llc
8850 Crawfordsville Rd
Indianapolis IN 46234
317 293-0278

(G-11800)
MILLS/JAMES INC
Also Called: Mills James Productions
3545 Fishinger Blvd (43026-9550)
PHONE.....................614 777-9933
Cameron James, *CEO*
Ken Mills, *President*
Robert Dixon, *Editor*
Chip Houze, *Editor*
Jim Mahan, *Editor*
EMP: 130
SQ FT: 47,000
SALES (est): 21.3MM **Privately Held**
WEB: www.mjp.com
SIC: 7819 7812 Services allied to motion
pictures; motion picture production & dis-
tribution; video tape production

(G-11801)
NORWICH ELEMENTARY PTO
4454 Davidson Rd (43026-9647)
PHONE.....................614 921-6000
Abbe Kehler, *Principal*
EMP: 25
SALES: 53K **Privately Held**
SIC: 8641 Parent-teachers' association

(G-11802)
OHIO LAMINATING & BINDING INC
4364 Reynolds Dr (43026-1260)
PHONE.....................614 771-4868
Jim Ondecko, *President*
Jimmy R Ondecko, *Vice Pres*
▲ EMP: 40
SQ FT: 5,000
SALES (est): 3.3MM **Privately Held**
WEB: www.ohiolaminatingandbinding.com
SIC: 7389 2789 2672 Laminating service;
bookbinding & related work; coated &
laminated paper

(G-11803)
OHIO STATE HOME SERVICES INC
Everdry Waterproofing Columbus
4271 Weaver Ct N (43026-1132)
PHONE.....................614 850-5600
Ken Barnett, *Sales/Mktg Mgr*
Ken Barnette, *Manager*
EMP: 80
SQ FT: 1,700
SALES (corp-wide): 32.5MM **Privately Held**
WEB: www.ohiostatewaterproofing.com
SIC: 1799 1794 1741 Waterproofing; ex-
cavation & grading, building construction;
foundation building
PA: Ohio State Home Services, Inc.
365 Highland Rd E
Macedonia OH 44056
330 467-1055

(G-11804)
OPEN TEXT INC
3671 Ridge Mill Dr (43026-7752)
PHONE.....................614 658-3588
Anik Ganguly, *Manager*
Mike Nappi, *Manager*
EMP: 50
SALES (corp-wide): 2.8B **Privately Held**
SIC: 7372 Prepackaged software
HQ: Open Text Inc.
2950 S Delaware St
San Mateo CA 94403
650 645-3000

(G-11805)
PARKINS INCORPORATED
Also Called: Hampton Inn
3950 Lyman Dr (43026-1210)
PHONE.....................614 334-1800
Tarun Patel, *President*
Amanda Sparks, *Branch Mgr*
EMP: 27
SALES (est): 2.4MM **Privately Held**
SIC: 7011 Hotels & motels

(G-11806)
PMWI LLC
3177 Overbridge Dr (43026-8091)
PHONE.....................614 975-5004
Pavan Mehra, *Principal*
EMP: 99
SALES (est): 3.9MM **Privately Held**
SIC: 8711 7389 Engineering services;

(G-11807)
PREMIUM BEVERAGE SUPPLY LTD
3701 Lacon Rd (43026-1202)
PHONE.....................614 777-1007
Ron Wilson, *Owner*
▲ EMP: 38
SALES (est): 13.9MM **Privately Held**
WEB: www.premiumbeveragesupply.com
SIC: 5099 Wood & wood by-products

(G-11808)
PRUDENTIAL CALHOON CO REALTORS
3535 Fishinger Blvd # 100 (43026-7504)
PHONE.....................614 777-1000
Thomas F Calhoon II, *President*
Samuel Calhoon, *Vice Pres*
David Gill, *Broker*
Candice Bonfante, *Real Est Agnt*
Gretchen Bonnie, *Real Est Agnt*
EMP: 36
SALES (est): 2.8MM **Privately Held**
WEB: www.prucalhoonrealtors.com
SIC: 6531 Real estate agent, residential

(G-11809)
QUALITY LIFE PROVIDERS LLC
Also Called: Comfort Keepers
3974 Brown Park Dr Ste E (43026-1168)
PHONE..................................614 527-9999
Tina Murkowski, *Mng Member*
Bill Murkowski,
EMP: 25
SALES (est): 837.3K **Privately Held**
SIC: 8082 Visiting nurse service

(G-11810)
R & S HALLEY & CO INC
Also Called: Darby Creek Nursery
6368 Scioto Darby Rd (43026-9726)
PHONE..................................614 771-0388
Jeffrey Turnbull, *President*
Lucinda Turnbull, *Admin Sec*
EMP: 35
SALES (est): 2.2MM **Privately Held**
WEB: www.darbycreek.org
SIC: 0181 0782 Nursery stock, growing of;
landscape contractors

(G-11811)
RDP FOODSERVICE LTD
4200 Parkway Ct (43026-1200)
P.O. Box 14866, Columbus (43214-0866)
PHONE..................................614 261-5661
Mark Mizer, *President*
EMP: 72
SQ FT: 30,000
SALES (est): 67MM **Privately Held**
SIC: 5149 5087 Pizza supplies; restaurant
supplies

(G-11812)
REXEL USA INC
3670 Parkway Ln Ste A (43026-1237)
PHONE..................................614 771-7373
Gary L Martin, *Sales/Mktg Mgr*
EMP: 50
SQ FT: 36,000
SALES (corp-wide): 2.2MM **Privately
Held**
SIC: 5063 Electrical supplies
HQ: Rexel Usa, Inc.
14951 Dallas Pkwy
Dallas TX 75254

(G-11813)
RIEPENHOFF LANDSCAPE LTD
3872 Scoto Darby Creek Rd (43026-9702)
PHONE..................................614 876-4683
Steve Purcell, *President*
Ellen Purcell, *Vice Pres*
EMP: 25
SQ FT: 2,500
SALES (est): 1.5MM **Privately Held**
WEB: www.riepenhofflandscape.com
SIC: 0782 1629 Landscape contractors; ir-
rigation system construction

(G-11814)
SCIOTO-DARBY CONCRETE INC
4540 Edgewyn Ave (43026-1222)
PHONE..................................614 876-3114
David M Hamilton, *President*
EMP: 30
SQ FT: 20,000
SALES (est): 4.2MM **Privately Held**
WEB: www.sciotodarby.com
SIC: 1771 Concrete pumping

(G-11815)
SEDGWICK CMS HOLDINGS INC
3455 Mill Run Dr (43026-9078)
PHONE..................................614 658-0900
Mary Heyineman, *Manager*
Steve Jayne, *Manager*
Angela Popa, *Supervisor*
Itisha Anand, *Technology*
Ruvimbo Masara, *Technology*
EMP: 1295
SALES (corp-wide): 9.5B **Privately Held**
SIC: 6411 Insurance claim adjusters, not
employed by insurance company
PA: Sedgwick Cms Holdings, Inc.
1100 Ridgeway Loop Rd # 200
Memphis TN 38120
901 415-7400

(G-11816)
SPECTRUM MGT HOLDG CO LLC
3652 Main St (43026-1359)
PHONE..................................614 503-4153
EMP: 82
SALES (corp-wide): 43.6B **Publicly Held**
SIC: 4841 Cable television services
HQ: Spectrum Management Holding Com-
pany, Llc
400 Atlantic St
Stamford CT 06901
203 905-7801

(G-11817)
SPIRES MOTORS INC
Also Called: Buckeye Honda
3820 Parkway Ln (43026-1217)
P.O. Box 189, Lancaster (43130-0189)
PHONE..................................614 771-2345
Gerald J Spires, *President*
William B Schuck, *Principal*
Dennis E Spires, *Senior VP*
Tim Spires, *Vice Pres*
Bob Berus, *Parts Mgr*
EMP: 40
SQ FT: 10,000
SALES (est): 18.5MM **Privately Held**
WEB: www.buckeyehonda.com
SIC: 5511 7538 Automobiles, new & used;
general automotive repair shops

(G-11818)
STOVER TRANSPORTATION INC
3710 Lacon Rd (43026-1207)
P.O. Box 1328 (43026-6328)
PHONE..................................614 777-4184
Raymond Stover, *President*
Rynda Stover, *Corp Secy*
EMP: 25
SALES (est): 4.7MM **Privately Held**
WEB: www.stovertransportation.com
SIC: 4231 Trucking terminal facilities

(G-11819)
TALX CORPORATION
3455 Mill Run Dr (43026-9078)
PHONE..................................614 527-9404
Kathy Couglin, *Manager*
EMP: 42
SALES (corp-wide): 3.4B **Publicly Held**
WEB: www.talx.com
SIC: 7373 Systems software development
services
HQ: Talx Corporation
11432 Lackland Rd
Saint Louis MO 63146
314 214-7000

(G-11820)
TEAM RAHAL INC
Also Called: Rahal Land and Racing
4601 Lyman Dr (43026-1249)
PHONE..................................614 529-7000
Robert W Rahal, *President*
Steve Dickson, *General Mgr*
Brian Marks, *Vice Pres*
Dave Cline, *Purchasing*
Rob Trinkner, *Info Tech Mgr*
◆ **EMP:** 65
SQ FT: 30,000
SALES (est): 176.2K **Privately Held**
WEB: www.rahal.com
SIC: 7948 Motor vehicle racing & drivers;
race car drivers

(G-11821)
THOMAS AND KING INC
5561 Wstchster Woods Blvd (43026-7970)
PHONE..................................614 527-0571
Amy Lee, *Manager*
EMP: 101
SALES (corp-wide): 177.3MM **Privately
Held**
WEB: www.tandk.com
SIC: 8742 Restaurant & food services con-
sultants
PA: Thomas And King, Inc.
249 E Main St Ste 101
Lexington KY 40507
859 254-2180

(G-11822)
TODD A RUCK INC
5100 Harvest Meadow Ct (43026-9076)
P.O. Box 1327 (43026-6327)
PHONE..................................614 527-9927
Todd A Ruck, *President*
EMP: 31
SALES: 1.6MM **Privately Held**
SIC: 4212 Local trucking, without storage

(G-11823)
TRADITIONS AT MILL RUN
Also Called: National Ch Rsidences Mill Run
3550 Fishinger Blvd (43026-2100)
PHONE..................................614 771-0100
Tanya Kim Hahn, *CEO*
EMP: 60
SQ FT: 19,432
SALES: 3.7MM
SALES (corp-wide): 38.2MM **Privately
Held**
SIC: 8059 Nursing home, except skilled &
intermediate care facility
PA: National Church Residences
2335 N Bank Dr
Columbus OH 43220
614 451-2151

(G-11824)
TRUGREEN LIMITED PARTNERSHIP
Also Called: Tru Green-Chemlawn
5150 Nike Dr (43026-7448)
P.O. Box 1120 (43026-6120)
PHONE..................................614 527-7070
Joe Muller, *Manager*
EMP: 80
SALES (corp-wide): 3.4B **Privately Held**
SIC: 0782 Lawn care services
HQ: Trugreen Limited Partnership
1790 Kirby Pkwy
Memphis TN 38138
901 251-4128

(G-11825)
VARGO INC
3709 Parkway Ln (43026-1216)
PHONE..................................614 876-1163
Joseph Michael Vargo, *President*
Bart J Cera, *COO*
Carlos Ysasi, *Vice Pres*
Thanh Nguyen, *Engineer*
Ryan Thomas, *Engineer*
EMP: 40
SQ FT: 16,000
SALES (est): 72.1MM **Privately Held**
SIC: 5084 Conveyor systems

(G-11826)
VERIZON BUSINESS GLOBAL LLC
5000 Britton Pkwy (43026-9445)
PHONE..................................614 219-2317
EMP: 49
SALES (corp-wide): 130.8B **Publicly
Held**
WEB: www.mccmt.com
SIC: 4813 8721 4822 7375 Local & long
distance telephone communications; ac-
counting, auditing & bookkeeping; tele-
graph & other communications;
information retrieval services
HQ: Verizon Business Global Llc
22001 Loudoun County Pkwy
Ashburn VA 20147
703 886-5600

(G-11827)
VERIZON NEW YORK INC
5000 Britton Pkwy (43026-9445)
PHONE..................................614 301-2498
Janet Brumfield, *President*
Joseph Barbarita, *Branch Mgr*
Keith Dinucci, *Technology*
EMP: 25
SALES (corp-wide): 130.8B **Publicly
Held**
SIC: 4812 Cellular telephone services
HQ: Verizon New York Inc.
140 West St
New York NY 10007
212 395-1000

(G-11828)
W W WILLIAMS COMPANY LLC
Also Called: Williams Dtroit Diesel-Allison
3535 Parkway Ln (43026-1214)
PHONE..................................614 527-9400
Jason Milligan, *General Mgr*
EMP: 35
SALES (corp-wide): 4.8B **Privately Held**
WEB: www.wwwilliams.com
SIC: 7538 General truck repair
HQ: The W W Williams Company Llc
5025 Bradenton Ave # 130
Dublin OH 43017
614 228-5000

(G-11829)
W W WILLIAMS COMPANY LLC
Also Called: W W Wllams Company-Midwest
Div
3535 Parkway Ln (43026-1214)
PHONE..................................614 527-9400
Alan Gatlin, *President*
Andrea Douglass, *Principal*
L Ed McIntyre, *Manager*
EMP: 50
SALES (corp-wide): 4.8B **Privately Held**
WEB: www.williamsdistribution.com
SIC: 7538 General truck repair
HQ: The W W Williams Company Llc
5025 Bradenton Ave # 130
Dublin OH 43017
614 228-5000

(G-11830)
WHITE GORILLA CORPORATION
6218 Lampton Pond Dr (43026-7188)
PHONE..................................202 384-6486
Rondell Earvin, *Admin Sec*
EMP: 28
SALES (est): 103.3K **Privately Held**
SIC: 8699 Charitable organization

(G-11831)
YASHCO SYSTEMS INC
3974 Brown Park Dr (43026-1168)
PHONE..................................614 467-4600
Simren Datta, *President*
Pankaj Nagrath, *Sales Mgr*
Kalidasan Singaravelu, *Programmer Anys*
Manoj Mohan, *Recruiter*
EMP: 25
SALES (est): 2.2MM **Privately Held**
WEB: www.yashco.com
SIC: 8748 7371 Business consulting; cus-
tom computer programming services

(G-11832)
YOUNG MENS CHRISTIAN ASSOC
Also Called: YMCA
4515 Cosgray Rd (43026-7787)
PHONE..................................614 334-9622
William Oliver, *Branch Mgr*
Becky Ciminillo, *Exec Dir*
Valerie Baumann, *Director*
Heather Beaver, *Director*
Alison Horn, *Graphic Designe*
EMP: 175
SALES (corp-wide): 44.9MM **Privately
Held**
WEB: www.ymca-columbus.com
SIC: 8641 7991 8351 7032 Youth organi-
zations; physical fitness facilities; child
day care services; youth camps; individ-
ual & family services
PA: Young Men's Christian Association Of
Central Ohio
40 W Long St
Columbus OH 43215
614 389-4409

Hillsboro
Highland County

(G-11833)
CLASSIC REAL ESTATE CO
123 W Main St (45133-1452)
PHONE..................................937 393-3416
Joyce Fender, *President*
Jenny Cameron, *Owner*
EMP: 25
SQ FT: 1,800

(PA)=Parent Co (HQ)=Headquarters (DH)=Div Headquarters
✪ = New Business established in last 2 years

SALES (est): 1.5MM Privately Held
SIC: 6531 8742 Real estate agent, commercial; real estate agent, residential; real estate consultant

(G-11834)
CONGREGATE LIVING OF AMERICA
Also Called: Crestwood RDG Skilled Nursing
141 Willetsville Pike (45133-9476)
PHONE..................................937 393-6700
Ramona Stapleton, *Administration*
EMP: 50
SALES (corp-wide): 4MM Privately Held
SIC: 8052 8051 Intermediate care facilities; skilled nursing care facilities
PA: Congregate Living Of America, Inc
463 E Pike St
Morrow OH 45152
513 899-2801

(G-11835)
COUNTY OF HIGHLAND
Also Called: Child Sup Dept of Job & Family
1575 N High St Ste 100 (45133-8286)
P.O. Box 809 (45133-0809)
PHONE..................................937 393-4278
Nancy Wisecup, *Director*
EMP: 25 Privately Held
WEB: www.co.highland.oh.us
SIC: 8322 Individual & family services
PA: County Of Highland
1575 N High St Ste 200
Hillsboro OH 45133
937 393-1911

(G-11836)
CRESTVIEW RIDGE NURSING
141 Willetsville Pike (45133-9476)
PHONE..................................937 393-6700
Tracy Hughey, *Director*
Michael Harrison, *Administration*
Benjamin Parsons,
EMP: 50
SALES (est): 510.2K Privately Held
SIC: 8051 Convalescent home with continuous nursing care

(G-11837)
DENSO INTERNATIONAL AMER INC
Also Called: Weastec
1600 N High St (45133-8259)
PHONE..................................937 393-6800
Larry Akers, *Manager*
Nathan Roberts, *Prgrmr*
EMP: 500
SALES (corp-wide): 47.9B Privately Held
WEB: www.densocorp-na.com
SIC: 5013 Truck parts & accessories
HQ: Denso International America, Inc.
24777 Denso Dr
Southfield MI 48033
248 350-7500

(G-11838)
F R S CONNECTIONS
Also Called: Frs Counselling
149 Chillicothe Ave (45133-1533)
P.O. Box 823 (45133-0823)
PHONE..................................937 393-9662
Ellen Butcher, *Principal*
EMP: 40
SALES (est): 522.9K Privately Held
SIC: 8099 8093 8322 Medical services organization; mental health clinic, outpatient; general counseling services

(G-11839)
FIFTH THIRD BANK OF STHRN OH (HQ)
511 N High St (45133-1134)
PHONE..................................937 840-5353
Raymond Webb, *President*
EMP: 27
SQ FT: 18,000
SALES (est): 60.2MM
SALES (corp-wide): 7.9B Publicly Held
SIC: 6022 6162 State trust companies accepting deposits, commercial; mortgage bankers & correspondents
PA: Fifth Third Bancorp
38 Fountain Square Plz
Cincinnati OH 45202
800 972-3030

(G-11840)
FRS COUNSELING INC (PA)
104 Erin Ct (45133-8591)
P.O. Box 823 (45133-0823)
PHONE..................................937 393-0585
Joe Adray, *CEO*
Tom Tise, *CFO*
EMP: 30
SQ FT: 3,800
SALES (est): 6.2MM Privately Held
WEB: www.frshighland.org
SIC: 8093 8322 8069 Mental health clinic, outpatient; alcohol clinic, outpatient; detoxification center, outpatient; family counseling services; alcoholism rehabilitation hospital

(G-11841)
HEALTH CARE RTREMENT CORP AMER
Also Called: Heartland of Hillsboro
1141 Northview Dr (45133-8525)
PHONE..................................937 393-5766
Antonio Stewart, *Branch Mgr*
EMP: 95
SALES (corp-wide): 2.4B Publicly Held
WEB: www.hrc-manorcare.com
SIC: 8051 Convalescent home with continuous nursing care
HQ: Health Care And Retirement Corporation Of America
333 N Summit St Ste 103
Toledo OH 43604
419 252-5500

(G-11842)
HIGHLAND COUNTY FAMILY YMCA
201 Diamond Dr (45133-5398)
PHONE..................................937 840-9622
Terry Mull, *Director*
EMP: 30
SALES: 675.2K Privately Held
SIC: 8641 7991 8351 7032 Youth organizations; physical fitness facilities; child day care services; youth camps; individual & family services

(G-11843)
HIGHLAND COUNTY JOINT
Also Called: HIGHLAND DISTRICT HOSPITAL
1275 N High St (45133-8273)
PHONE..................................937 393-6100
Jim Baer, *CEO*
Thomas Degen, *Principal*
Paula Detterman, *Principal*
Larry Burns, *Vice Pres*
Karen Shadowens, *Vice Pres*
EMP: 400
SALES: 43.3MM Privately Held
SIC: 8062 Hospital, affiliated with AMA residency

(G-11844)
HIGHLAND COUNTY WATER CO INC (PA)
6686 Us Highway 50 (45133-7938)
P.O. Box 940 (45133-0940)
PHONE..................................937 393-4281
Larry Cockrell, *General Mgr*
EMP: 26
SQ FT: 28,000
SALES: 1.6MM Privately Held
SIC: 4941 Water supply

(G-11845)
HIGHLND CNTY COMMNTY ACTION OR (PA)
Also Called: Hccao
1487 N High St Ste 500 (45133-6812)
PHONE..................................937 393-3060
Fred Berry, *President*
Ruth Cutright, *General Mgr*
Richard Graves, *Corp Secy*
Greg Barr, *Vice Pres*
Rhonda Kidder, *Opers Mgr*
EMP: 35
SALES: 5.6MM Privately Held
WEB: www.hccao.com
SIC: 8322 Social service center

(G-11846)
HILLSBORO HEALTH CENTER INC
1108 Northview Dr Ste 1 (45133-1191)
PHONE..................................937 393-5781
Rene Hawthorne, *President*
Andrea McClain, *Practice Mgr*
EMP: 25
SALES (est): 1.8MM Privately Held
SIC: 8011 General & family practice, physician/surgeon

(G-11847)
HOME HELPERS
Also Called: Home Helpers and Direct Link
503 E Main St (45133-1585)
PHONE..................................937 393-8600
Janet Dean, *Owner*
EMP: 64
SALES (est): 423K Privately Held
SIC: 8082 Home health care services

(G-11848)
JERRY HAAG MOTORS INC
1475 N High St (45133-9473)
PHONE..................................937 402-2090
Steven R Haag, *President*
Theresa Luschek, *Office Mgr*
Mindy Sanders, *Technology*
EMP: 32 EST: 1953
SQ FT: 17,700
SALES (est): 12.7MM Privately Held
WEB: www.jerryhaagmotors.com
SIC: 5511 7538 5531 Automobiles, new & used; general automotive repair shops; automotive & home supply stores

(G-11849)
LAURELS OF HILLSBORO
Also Called: LOURIES OF HILLSBORO
175 Chillicothe Ave (45133-1533)
PHONE..................................937 393-1925
Kathy Moore, *VP Finance*
Kelley Condo, *Director*
Susan Baker, *Records Dir*
Lori Byron, *Administration*
EMP: 70 EST: 1970
SQ FT: 18,000
SALES: 8.2MM Privately Held
SIC: 8052 8051 Intermediate care facilities; skilled nursing care facilities
PA: Laurel Health Care Company Of North Worthington
8181 Worthington Rd
Westerville OH 43082

(G-11850)
LUCAS & CLARK FAMILY DENTISTRY
624 S High St (45133-1433)
P.O. Box 310 (45133-0310)
PHONE..................................937 393-3494
Lynne Lucas, *Vice Pres*
M Glenn Lucas DDS, *Director*
▲ **EMP: 25**
SQ FT: 3,000
SALES (est): 1.7MM Privately Held
SIC: 8021 Dentists' office

(G-11851)
MERCHANTS NATIONAL BANK (HQ)
100 N High St (45133-1152)
PHONE..................................937 393-1134
Don Fender, *Ch of Bd*
Paul Pence Jr, *President*
Scott J Hopf, *CFO*
EMP: 50
SALES: 31.5MM
SALES (corp-wide): 28.8MM Privately Held
SIC: 6021 National commercial banks
PA: Merchants Bancorp Inc
100 N High St
Hillsboro OH 45133
937 393-1993

(G-11852)
NATIONAL CONSUMER COOP BNK
139 S High St (45133-1442)
PHONE..................................937 393-4246
Jonathan Klugman, *Vice Pres*
Dami Odetola, *Vice Pres*
Michael J Merce, *Branch Mgr*

EMP: 27
SALES (corp-wide): 103.7MM Privately Held
SIC: 6099 Check clearing services
PA: National Consumer Cooperative Bank
1901 Penn Ave Nw Ste 300
Washington DC 20006
202 349-7444

(G-11853)
NATIONAL COOPERATIVE BANK NA (HQ)
Also Called: N C B-F S B
139 S High St Ste 1 (45133-1442)
PHONE..................................937 393-4246
Charles E Snyder, *President*
Steven Brookner, *President*
Chris Goettke, *Co-President*
Kathleen H Luzik, *COO*
Patrick N Connealy, *Exec VP*
EMP: 63 EST: 1890
SQ FT: 20,000
SALES (est): 81.1MM
SALES (corp-wide): 103.7MM Privately Held
SIC: 6111 National Consumer Cooperative Bank
PA: National Consumer Cooperative Bank
1901 Penn Ave Nw Ste 300
Washington DC 20006
202 349-7444

(G-11854)
PAS TECHNOLOGIES INC
214 Hobart Dr (45133-9487)
PHONE..................................937 840-1000
Joshua Ayers, *Engineer*
James Heiser, *Engineer*
Nathanael Young, *Engineer*
Mark Greene, *Manager*
Wayne Lowery, *Manager*
EMP: 100 Privately Held
WEB: www.pas-technologies.com
SIC: 3724 7699 Aircraft engines & engine parts; aircraft & heavy equipment repair services
HQ: Pas Technologies Inc.
1234 Atlantic Ave
North Kansas City MO 64116

(G-11855)
WESTERN & SOUTHERN LF INSUR CO
902 N High St Ste B (45133-8501)
PHONE..................................937 393-1969
Robert Miller, *Manager*
EMP: 25 Privately Held
SIC: 6411 Life insurance agents
HQ: The Western & Southern Life Insurance Company
400 Broadway St
Cincinnati OH 45202
513 629-1800

(G-11856)
XPO LOGISTICS FREIGHT INC
5215 Us Route 50 (45133-9166)
PHONE..................................937 364-2361
James New, *Manager*
EMP: 27
SALES (corp-wide): 15.3B Publicly Held
WEB: www.con-way.com
SIC: 4213 Trucking, except local
HQ: Xpo Logistics Freight, Inc.
2211 Old Earhart Rd # 100
Ann Arbor MI 48105
800 755-2728

Hinckley
Medina County

(G-11857)
ALDI INC
1319 W 130th St (44233-9500)
PHONE..................................330 273-7351
Thomas Behtz, *Vice Pres*
EMP: 80
SALES (corp-wide): 355.8K Privately Held
WEB: www.aldi.com
SIC: 5411 4225 Grocery stores, chain; general warehousing & storage

HQ: Aldi Inc.
1200 N Kirk Rd
Batavia IL 60510
630 879-8100

(G-11858)
BLACK HORSE CARRIERS INC
1319 W 130th St (44233-9500)
PHONE..................................330 225-2250
Roger Foulk, *Branch Mgr*
EMP: 125
SALES (corp-wide): 121.9MM **Privately Held**
SIC: 4213 Trucking, except local
PA: Black Horse Carriers Inc.
455 Kehoe Blvd Ste 105
Carol Stream IL 60188
630 690-8900

(G-11859)
ICON GOVERNMENT (HQ)
1265 Ridge Rd Ste A (44233-9801)
PHONE..................................330 278-2343
Victoria Tifft, *CEO*
Joseph Sgherza, *President*
Laurel Edelman, *Vice Pres*
Shannon Horel, *Vice Pres*
Quinten Tifft, *Vice Pres*
EMP: 356
SALES: 64.1MM **Privately Held**
WEB: www.clinicalrm.com
SIC: 8731 8732 Medical research, commercial; commercial nonphysical research

(G-11860)
PINE HILLS GOLF CLUB INC
433 W 130th St (44233-9566)
PHONE..................................330 225-4477
William Gertrack, *President*
Scott Forester, *Corp Secy*
EMP: 40 **EST:** 1955
SQ FT: 5,820
SALES (est): 2.2MM **Privately Held**
WEB: www.golfpinehills.net
SIC: 7992 Public golf courses

(G-11861)
UNIQUE HOME SOLUTIONS INC
1545 W 130th St Ste A2 (44233-9168)
PHONE..................................800 800-1971
John Hovey, *Human Res Mgr*
Bob Dillon, *Branch Mgr*
EMP: 25
SALES (corp-wide): 26.6MM **Privately Held**
SIC: 8748 Business consulting
PA: Unique Home Solutions, Inc.
5550 Progress Rd
Indianapolis IN 46241
317 337-9300

(G-11862)
VALLEAIRE GOLF CLUB INC
6969 Boston Rd (44233-9402)
PHONE..................................440 237-9191
Mike Burns, *General Mgr*
EMP: 50 **EST:** 1964
SALES (est): 2MM **Privately Held**
SIC: 7997 Golf club, membership

(G-11863)
VANS EXPRESS INC
222 Concord Ln (44233-9662)
P.O. Box 53 (44233-0053)
PHONE..................................216 224-5388
Gary Van Den Haute, *President*
Don Vandenhaute, *Vice Pres*
EMP: 26
SALES (est): 3.3MM **Privately Held**
SIC: 8748 Business consulting

Hiram
Portage County

(G-11864)
DURAMAX MARINE LLC
17990 Great Lakes Pkwy (44234-9681)
PHONE..................................440 834-5400
Richard Spangler, *President*
◆ **EMP:** 85
SQ FT: 65,000

SALES (est): 44.2MM **Privately Held**
WEB: www.duracooler.com
SIC: 5085 Industrial supplies

(G-11865)
GREAT LAKES CHEESE CO INC (PA)
17825 Great Lakes Pkwy (44234-9677)
P.O. Box 1806 (44234-1806)
PHONE..................................440 834-2500
Gary Vanic, *President*
Marcel Dasen, *Principal*
Hans Epprecht, *Principal*
Albert Z Meyers, *Principal*
John Epprecht, *Corp Secy*
◆ **EMP:** 500
SQ FT: 218,000
SALES (est): 1.6B **Privately Held**
WEB: www.greatlakescheese.com
SIC: 5143 2022 Cheese; natural cheese

Holgate
Henry County

(G-11866)
MERCY HEALTH
106 N Wilhelm St (43527-7734)
PHONE..................................419 264-5800
EMP: 43
SALES (corp-wide): 4.7B **Privately Held**
SIC: 8031 8011 Offices & clinics of osteopathic physicians; offices & clinics of medical doctors
PA: Mercy Health
1701 Mercy Health Pl
Cincinnati OH 45237
513 639-2800

(G-11867)
VANCREST HEALTH CARE CENTER
600 Joe E Brown Ave (43527-9803)
PHONE..................................419 264-0700
Mark White, *Principal*
Georgette Mekus, *Director*
Kim Ricker, *Records Dir*
Amber Merriman, *Administration*
EMP: 60
SALES (est): 1.9MM **Privately Held**
SIC: 8051 Skilled nursing care facilities

Holland
Lucas County

(G-11868)
3C TECHNOLOGIES INC
6834 Spring Valley Dr # 202 (43528-7864)
PHONE..................................419 868-8999
Dave Capur, *President*
Matt Bublick, *Exec VP*
EMP: 65
SQ FT: 9,000
SALES (est): 3MM **Privately Held**
WEB: www.3ctech.com
SIC: 8741 8299 Business management; educational services

(G-11869)
ALLIED PAVING INC
Also Called: Allied Paving Company
8406 Airport Hwy (43528-8638)
PHONE..................................419 666-3100
Thomas Buck, *President*
Louann Buck, *Vice Pres*
Heather Buck, *Manager*
EMP: 25
SQ FT: 3,000
SALES (est): 3.9MM **Privately Held**
WEB: www.alliedpavingcompany.com
SIC: 1611 1771 Highway & street paving contractor; driveway, parking lot & blacktop contractors

(G-11870)
ALTERNATIVE SERVICES INC
7710 Hill Ave (43528-7607)
PHONE..................................419 861-2121
Janice Porter, *President*
EMP: 35
SQ FT: 60,000

SALES (est): 2.2MM **Privately Held**
SIC: 7389 Packaging & labeling services

(G-11871)
ANNE GRADY CORPORATION
1645 Trade Rd (43528-8204)
PHONE..................................419 867-7501
David A Boston, *Exec Dir*
EMP: 50
SQ FT: 20,000
SALES (corp-wide): 17.4MM **Privately Held**
SIC: 8331 Job training & vocational rehabilitation services
PA: Anne Grady Corporation
1525 Eber Rd
Holland OH 43528
419 380-8985

(G-11872)
ANNE GRADY CORPORATION (PA)
1525 Eber Rd (43528-9616)
P.O. Box 1297 (43528-1297)
PHONE..................................419 380-8985
Velma Brown, *Human Res Mgr*
Chad Gamby, *Technology*
David Boston, *Exec Dir*
Roger Fortener, *Director*
EMP: 250
SQ FT: 70,000
SALES: 17.4MM **Privately Held**
WEB: www.annegrady.org
SIC: 8361 8052 Home for the mentally retarded; intermediate care facilities

(G-11873)
BLACK SWAMP STEEL INC
1761 Commerce Rd (43528-9789)
P.O. Box 1180 (43528-1180)
PHONE..................................419 867-8050
Dave Coronado, *President*
Steve Sieracke, *President*
Brad Carpenter, *Principal*
Jon West, *Principal*
EMP: 25 **EST:** 1991
SALES (est): 4.5MM **Privately Held**
SIC: 1791 Structural steel erection

(G-11874)
BLANCHARD TREE AND LAWN INC
1530 Kieswetter Rd (43528-8677)
P.O. Box 1100 (43528-1100)
PHONE..................................419 865-7071
James D Blanchard, *President*
EMP: 60 **EST:** 1958
SQ FT: 12,000
SALES (est): 2.4MM **Privately Held**
WEB: www.blanchardtree.com
SIC: 0783 0782 0781 0711 Ornamental shrub & tree services; mowing services, lawn; landscape services; fertilizer application services

(G-11875)
BRENNAN INDUSTRIAL TRUCK CO
Also Called: Brennan Equipment Services
6940 Hall St (43528-9485)
PHONE..................................419 867-6000
James H Brennan Jr, *President*
Thomas J Backoff, *Vice Pres*
EMP: 30 **EST:** 1957
SQ FT: 35,000
SALES (est): 18MM **Privately Held**
WEB: www.brennanindtrk.com
SIC: 5084 7359 Materials handling machinery; industrial truck rental

(G-11876)
BRENNAN-EBERLY TEAM SPORTS INC
6144 Merger Dr (43528-8438)
PHONE..................................419 865-8326
Robert Eberly, *President*
David Neely, *Administration*
EMP: 25
SQ FT: 8,500

SALES (est): 11.5MM
SALES (corp-wide): 2.1MM **Privately Held**
SIC: 5139 5136 5137 5091 Footwear, athletic; men's & boys' sportswear & work clothing; sportswear, men's & boys'; women's & children's sportswear & swimsuits; sportswear, women's & children's; athletic goods
PA: Asb Sports Acquisition, Inc.
1107 N Grant Ave
Odessa TX 79761
432 332-1568

(G-11877)
CARDINAL HEALTH 414 LLC
6156 Trust Dr Ste B (43528-7860)
PHONE..................................419 867-1077
Mike Smith, *Manager*
EMP: 29
SALES (corp-wide): 136.8B **Publicly Held**
WEB: www.syncor.com
SIC: 5122 Pharmaceuticals
HQ: Cardinal Health 414, Llc
7000 Cardinal Pl
Dublin OH 43017
614 757-5000

(G-11878)
CHILDRENS DISCOVERY CENTER
Also Called: Discovery Express Child Care
1640 Timber Wolf Dr (43528-8303)
PHONE..................................419 861-1060
Mona Taylor, *Director*
Lisa Hornyak, *Administration*
Cindi Taylor, *Administration*
EMP: 30
SQ FT: 10,829
SALES (corp-wide): 8MM **Privately Held**
WEB: www.discovery-express.com
SIC: 8351 Preschool center
PA: Childrens Discovery Center
6450 Weatherfield Ct 1a
Maumee OH 43537
419 867-8570

(G-11879)
COUNTY OF LUCAS
Also Called: Lucas County Engineer
1049 S Mccord Rd Bldg A (43528-7020)
PHONE..................................419 213-2892
Mark Drennen, *Financial Exec*
Keith G Earley, *Director*
EMP: 58 **Privately Held**
SIC: 8711 Engineering services
PA: County Of Lucas
1 Government Ctr Ste 600
Toledo OH 43604
419 213-4406

(G-11880)
CREATIVE PRODUCTS INC
Also Called: CPI
1430 Kieswetter Rd (43528-9785)
PHONE..................................419 866-5501
Marvin Smith, *President*
EMP: 33
SQ FT: 26,000
SALES (est): 2.2MM **Privately Held**
SIC: 5023 5211 2541 Kitchen tools & utensils; cabinets, kitchen; counter tops; wood partitions & fixtures

(G-11881)
DANA HEAVY VEHICLE SYSTEMS
Also Called: Dana Spicer Service Parts
6936 Airport Hwy (43528)
PHONE..................................419 866-3900
Jim Wojciehowski, *Manager*
James Tan, *Technology*
Gail Stolarski, *Software Dev*
EMP: 52 **Publicly Held**
SIC: 5013 Automotive supplies & parts
HQ: Dana Heavy Vehicle Systems Group, Llc
3939 Technology Dr
Maumee OH 43537

(G-11882)
DEVIRSIFIED MATERIAL HANDLING
Also Called: Interstate Lift Truck
8310 Airport Hwy (43528-8637)
PHONE..................................419 865-8025
Phil Graffy, *President*
▼ EMP: 26
SALES (est): 5.3MM Privately Held
SIC: 5084 Materials handling machinery

(G-11883)
DOUGLAS COMPANY (PA)
1716 Prrysburg Holland Rd (43528-9581)
PHONE..................................419 865-8600
Peter Douglas, *President*
Brian McCarthy, *Vice Pres*
David Reades, *Vice Pres*
David Bockbrader, *CFO*
Migdalia Accius, *Accountant*
EMP: 25 EST: 1976
SQ FT: 25,000
SALES (est): 25MM Privately Held
WEB: www.douglascompany.com
SIC: 1542 1522 Commercial & office building, new construction; hotel/motel & multi-family home construction

(G-11884)
DOUGLAS CONSTRUCTION COMPANY
Also Called: Design Services Cnstr Co
1716 Prrysburg Holland Rd (43528-9581)
PHONE..................................419 865-8600
Peter Douglas, *President*
David Bockbrader, *Treasurer*
EMP: 25
SQ FT: 7,000
SALES (est): 1.6MM Privately Held
SIC: 1522 1531 Multi-family dwellings, new construction; remodeling, multi-family dwellings; condominium developers

(G-11885)
DYNAMIC CURRENTS CORP
1761 Commerce Rd (43528-9789)
PHONE..................................419 861-2036
David P Coronado, *President*
Rachael M Mendoza, *Corp Secy*
EMP: 50
SALES (est): 3MM Privately Held
WEB: www.dynamiccurrents.com
SIC: 1731 Electrical work

(G-11886)
GLEASON CONSTRUCTION CO INC
540 S Centennial Rd (43528-8400)
PHONE..................................419 865-7480
James F Gleason, *President*
Carol S Gleason, *Admin Sec*
EMP: 60
SQ FT: 20,000
SALES (est): 7.7MM Privately Held
SIC: 1623 Underground utilities contractor

(G-11887)
HABITEC SECURITY INC (PA)
1545 Timber Wolf Dr (43528-9130)
P.O. Box 352497, Toledo (43635-2497)
PHONE..................................419 537-6768
Nancy Smythe, *CEO*
John Smythe, *President*
Donald Kraatz, *Opers Mgr*
Pat Ehrsam, *Opers Staff*
Kathy Vierling, *Human Res Mgr*
EMP: 85 EST: 1972
SQ FT: 9,000
SALES (est): 16.5MM Privately Held
WEB: www.habitecsecurity.com
SIC: 1731 Fire detection & burglar alarm systems specialization

(G-11888)
HAMILTON MANUFACTURING CORP
1026 Hamilton Dr (43528-8210)
PHONE..................................419 867-4858
Robin Ritz, *CEO*
Steve Alt, *President*
Bonnie Osborne, *Exec VP*
Laura Harris, *Treasurer*
▲ EMP: 45 EST: 1921
SQ FT: 32,000

SALES (est): 10.2MM Privately Held
WEB: www.hamiltonmfg.com
SIC: 3172 8711 Coin purses; designing; ship, boat, machine & product

(G-11889)
HRP CAPITAL INC
Also Called: PhyCor
6855 Spring Valley Dr # 120 (43528-8039)
PHONE..................................419 865-3111
Pat Montgomery, *Branch Mgr*
EMP: 26
SALES (corp-wide): 12.4MM Privately Held
SIC: 8741 8011 Nursing & personal care facility management; physicians' office, including specialists
PA: Hrp Capital, Inc.
    173 Bridge Plz N
    Fort Lee NJ 07024
    201 242-4938

(G-11890)
ITS TECHNOLOGIES INC (PA)
7060 Spring Meadows Dr W D (43528-8093)
PHONE..................................419 842-2100
Roger L Radeloff, *President*
Barrie Howell, *Treasurer*
Charles M Tarband, *Admin Sec*
Sarah Nadolny, *Tech Recruiter*
Tyler Steedman, *Tech Recruiter*
EMP: 100
SALES (est): 17MM Privately Held
SIC: 7363 7361 Temporary help service; employment agencies

(G-11891)
KEY REALTY LTD
130 Fountain Dr (43528-9061)
PHONE..................................419 270-7445
Phil Henderson,
EMP: 150 EST: 2008
SALES (est): 4MM Privately Held
SIC: 6531 Real estate agent, residential

(G-11892)
LAKE ERIE MED SURGICAL SUP INC
6920 Hall St (43528-9485)
P.O. Box 1267 (43528-1267)
PHONE..................................734 847-3847
Jeannie Sieren, *Branch Mgr*
EMP: 40
SALES (corp-wide): 16.4MM Privately Held
SIC: 5047 Medical & hospital equipment
PA: Lake Erie Medical & Surgical Supply, Inc.
    7560 Lewis Ave
    Temperance MI 48182
    734 847-3847

(G-11893)
LUTHERAN VILLAGE AT WOLF CREEK
Also Called: CREEKSIDE CONDOMINIUMS
2001 Prrysbrg Hllnd Ofc (43528-8001)
PHONE..................................419 861-2233
Mark Gavorski, *Principal*
Lorinda Schalk, *Vice Pres*
Amanda Karamol, *Chf Purch Ofc*
Sue Boyne, *Human Res Dir*
Bob Burns, *Director*
EMP: 160 EST: 1996
SQ FT: 113,154
SALES (est): 9.7MM Privately Held
WEB: www.creeksidecondominiums.com
SIC: 8059 8361 8052 8051 Rest home, with health care; residential care; intermediate care facilities; skilled nursing care facilities

(G-11894)
MAC QUEEN ORCHARDS INC
7605 Garden Rd (43528-8538)
PHONE..................................419 865-2916
Robert H Mac Queen, *President*
Bernice Mac Queen, *Vice Pres*
Robert Mac Queen II, *Treasurer*
Jeffery Mac Queen, *Officer*
Lynn Mac Queen, *Admin Sec*
EMP: 45

SALES (est): 1MM Privately Held
WEB: www.macqueenorchards.com
SIC: 0175 Apple orchard; peach orchard; pear orchard; plum orchard

(G-11895)
MARRIOTT INTERNATIONAL INC
Also Called: Courtyard By Marriott
1435 E Mall Dr (43528-9490)
PHONE..................................419 866-1001
Jamie Talberth, *Manager*
EMP: 167
SALES (corp-wide): 20.7B Publicly Held
SIC: 7011 Hotels & motels
PA: Marriott International, Inc.
    10400 Fernwood Rd
    Bethesda MD 20817
    301 380-3000

(G-11896)
MC CLURG & CREAMER INC
7450 Hill Ave (43528-8751)
PHONE..................................419 866-7080
Marshall Mc Clurg, *President*
Curt Creamer, *Vice Pres*
EMP: 26
SALES (est): 1.7MM Privately Held
WEB: www.mcclurg-creamer.com
SIC: 0781 0782 1711 4959 Landscape architects; lawn care services; irrigation sprinkler system installation; snowplowing

(G-11897)
MIDWEST CONTRACTING INC
1428 Albon Rd (43528-8683)
PHONE..................................419 866-4560
Aaron Koder, *President*
Chad Harr, *Superintendent*
Jennifer Koder, *Office Mgr*
Tom Dubois, *Sr Project Mgr*
Neil Raymond, *Sr Project Mgr*
EMP: 29 EST: 1996
SALES (est): 5.8MM Privately Held
SIC: 1542 Commercial & office building, new construction

(G-11898)
MIDWEST TAPE LLC
1417 Timber Wolf Dr (43528-8302)
P.O. Box 820 (43528-0820)
PHONE..................................419 868-9370
Sarah Helm, *Minister*
Jeff Patton, *Vice Pres*
Tim Holzemer, *Buyer*
Brian Maroszek, *Buyer*
John Weisenburger, *Purchasing*
▲ EMP: 330
SQ FT: 100,000
SALES (est): 95.1MM Privately Held
WEB: www.midwesttapes.com
SIC: 7822 5099 8741 7389 Video tapes, recorded; wholesale; motion picture distribution; video cassettes, accessories & supplies; administrative management; packaging & labeling services; ; data processing service

(G-11899)
MILLER FIREWORKS COMPANY INC (PA)
Also Called: Miller Fireworks Novelty
501 Glengary Rd (43528-9416)
PHONE..................................419 865-7329
John F Miller III, *President*
Jason Copeland, *Manager*
▲ EMP: 35
SQ FT: 2,520
SALES (est): 5.5MM Privately Held
WEB: www.millerfireworks.com
SIC: 5092 5999 Fireworks; fireworks

(G-11900)
NATIONAL COMPRESSOR SVCS LLC (PA)
10349 Industrial St (43528-9791)
P.O. Box 760 (43528-0760)
PHONE..................................419 868-4980
Brenda Sevenski, *Purch Mgr*
Erik E Babcock, *Mng Member*
EMP: 39
SQ FT: 60,000
SALES: 11MM Privately Held
SIC: 7699 Compressor repair

(G-11901)
NORTHWEST ELECTRICAL CONTG INC
1617 Shanrock Dr (43528-8368)
PHONE..................................419 865-4757
Jody Mc Collum, *President*
Nick Nemire, *Project Mgr*
Kathy McCollum, *Executive*
Kathy Mc Collum, *Admin Sec*
▲ EMP: 30
SQ FT: 8,800
SALES (est): 5.6MM Privately Held
WEB: www.nwelect.com
SIC: 1731 General electrical contractor

(G-11902)
NORTHWSTERN OHIO ADMNISTRATORS
7142 Nightingale Dr 1 (43528-7822)
P.O. Box 1330 (43528-1330)
PHONE..................................419 248-2401
Nick Madden, *President*
EMP: 25
SQ FT: 46,000
SALES (est): 3.9MM Privately Held
SIC: 6411 Insurance agents, brokers & service

(G-11903)
OCP CONTRACTORS INC (PA)
Also Called: O C P
1740 Commerce Rd (43528-9789)
PHONE..................................419 865-7168
Matthew Townsend, *President*
Sandy Gilday, *Business Mgr*
Pam Hepburn, *Vice Pres*
Matt Taylor, *Vice Pres*
Pam Breen, *Human Res Dir*
EMP: 25
SQ FT: 8,000
SALES: 58MM Privately Held
WEB: www.ocp-contractors.com
SIC: 1742 1751 1752 1743 Drywall; lightweight steel framing (metal stud) installation; floor laying & floor work; tile installation, ceramic; coating, caulking & weather, water & fireproofing

(G-11904)
OFFICE PRODUCTS TOLEDO INC
Also Called: M T Business Technologies
1205 Corporate Dr (43528-9590)
PHONE..................................419 865-7001
Susan Carl, *President*
Jack Jolley, *Sales Mgr*
Brian Mruzek, *Sales Mgr*
Shawn Glass, *Sales Staff*
EMP: 50
SALES (est): 17MM Privately Held
SIC: 5044 7359 Copying equipment; office machine rental, except computers

(G-11905)
PLASTIC TECHNOLOGIES INC (PA)
Also Called: Pti
1440 Timber Wolf Dr (43528-8301)
P.O. Box 964 (43528-0964)
PHONE..................................419 867-5400
Craig S Barrow, *President*
Tom Brady, *Chairman*
Elizabeth Brady, *Vice Pres*
Donald Miller, *Vice Pres*
Francis Schloss, *Vice Pres*
▲ EMP: 95
SQ FT: 46,000
SALES (est): 17.4MM Privately Held
WEB: www.plastictechnologies.com
SIC: 8734 8731 Product testing laboratory, safety or performance; commercial physical research

(G-11906)
R & F INC
Also Called: Allied Home Health Services
6228 Merger Dr (43528-9593)
PHONE..................................419 868-2909
Tom Leffler, *Manager*
EMP: 25

SALES (corp-wide): 13MM **Privately Held**
WEB: www.aprn1.com
SIC: **8049** 8051 8082 Physical therapist; skilled nursing care facilities; home health care services
PA: R & F Inc
1133 Corporate Dr Ste B
Holland OH 43528
419 882-9870

(G-11907)
R & R HVAC SYSTEMS
1650 Eber Rd Ste E (43528-9793)
PHONE..............................419 861-0266
EMP: 25
SALES (est): 2.2MM **Privately Held**
SIC: **1711** Heating & Air Conditioning Contractor

(G-11908)
R L KING INSURANCE AGENCY
7723 Airport Hwy Ste F (43528-7602)
P.O. Box 1265 (43528-1265)
PHONE..............................419 255-9947
Ronald L King, *President*
Bryan K Schira, *Vice Pres*
Brian King, *Consultant*
EMP: 25
SQ FT: 3,000
SALES (est): 5.4MM **Privately Held**
SIC: **6411** Insurance agents

(G-11909)
R P MARKETING PUBLIC RELATIONS
1500 Timber Wolf Dr (43528-9129)
PHONE..............................419 241-2221
Martha Vetter, *President*
Angie Coakley, *Director*
Jessica Lashley, *Director*
EMP: 30
SALES (est): 2.7MM **Privately Held**
SIC: **8742** 7389 Marketing consulting services; advertising, promotional & trade show services

(G-11910)
SAWYER STEEL ERECTORS INC
1761 Commerce Rd (43528-9789)
PHONE..............................419 867-8050
John Isola, *President*
EMP: 50
SALES (est): 3.1MM **Privately Held**
SIC: **1791** Structural steel erection

(G-11911)
SCHINDLER ELEVATOR CORPORATION
Millar Elevator Service
1530 Timber Wolf Dr (43528-9161)
P.O. Box 960 (43528-0960)
PHONE..............................419 867-5100
Louis Haefner, *General Mgr*
Cathie Teachout, *General Mgr*
Gary Hecklinger, *Buyer*
Vanessa Herrero, *Marketing Staff*
D Kornowa, *Marketing Staff*
EMP: 110
SQ FT: 2,000
SALES (corp-wide): 10.9B **Privately Held**
WEB: www.us.schindler.com
SIC: **7699** Elevators: inspection, service & repair
HQ: Schindler Elevator Corporation
20 Whippany Rd
Morristown NJ 07960
973 397-6500

(G-11912)
SCHINDLER ELEVATOR CORPORATION
1530 Timber Wolf Dr (43528-9161)
P.O. Box 960 (43528-0960)
PHONE..............................419 861-5900
Mark Kershner, *Manager*
Holly Byington, *Associate*
EMP: 26
SALES (corp-wide): 10.9B **Privately Held**
WEB: www.us.schindler.com
SIC: **3534** 7699 Elevators & equipment; escalators, passenger & freight; elevators: inspection, service & repair

HQ: Schindler Elevator Corporation
20 Whippany Rd
Morristown NJ 07960
973 397-6500

(G-11913)
SEAGATE OFFICE PRODUCTS INC
1044 Hamilton Dr (43528-8166)
PHONE..............................419 861-6161
Connie Leonardi, *President*
Steve Hamilton, *General Mgr*
Jackie Leonardi, *Accounts Mgr*
EMP: 25
SQ FT: 10,000
SALES (est): 9.9MM **Privately Held**
WEB: www.seagateop.com
SIC: **5112** 5021 Office supplies; office furniture

(G-11914)
SKYLINE CM PORTFOLIO LLC
Also Called: Courtyard Toledo Arprt Holland
1435 E Mall Dr (43528-9490)
PHONE..............................419 866-1001
Mona Rigdon, *Principal*
Vadim Shub, *Principal*
EMP: 30
SALES (est): 400.3K **Privately Held**
SIC: **7011** Hotels & motels

(G-11915)
SPONSELLER GROUP INC (PA)
1600 Timber Wolf Dr (43528-8303)
PHONE..............................419 861-3000
Keith Sponseller, *President*
Harold P Sponseller, *Chairman*
Kevin R Nevius, *Vice Pres*
David Nowak, *Vice Pres*
Mike Jacobs, *Project Mgr*
EMP: 44
SQ FT: 8,900
SALES (est): 8.7MM **Privately Held**
SIC: **8711** 3599 Consulting engineer; machine shop, jobbing & repair

(G-11916)
SPRING MEADOW EXTENDED CARE CE (PA)
1125 Clarion Ave (43528-8107)
PHONE..............................419 866-6124
John H Stone, *President*
Davida Tucker, *Director*
EMP: 63
SQ FT: 50,000
SALES (est): 1.4MM **Privately Held**
SIC: **8052** 8051 Intermediate care facilities; skilled nursing care facilities

(G-11917)
STONE OAK COUNTRY CLUB
100 Stone Oak Blvd (43528-9131)
PHONE..............................419 867-0969
Keith Olander, *President*
Beth Bazeley, *Sales Executive*
Julie Smith, *Manager*
EMP: 100
SQ FT: 25,517
SALES (est): 4.8MM **Privately Held**
SIC: **7997** Golf club, membership; country club, membership

(G-11918)
TEKNI-PLEX INC
Also Called: Global Technology Center
1445 Timber Wolf Dr (43528-8302)
PHONE..............................419 491-2399
Paul J Young, *CEO*
Phil Bourgeois, *Vice Pres*
Richard Rohrs, *Plant Mgr*
Edward McKinley, *Director*
Kimberly Neumeyer, *Executive Asst*
EMP: 28 EST: 1967
SALES (est): 6.1MM
SALES (corp-wide): 1.1B **Privately Held**
SIC: **2679** 7389 2672 Egg cartons, molded pulp: made from purchased material; packaging & labeling services; cloth lined paper: made from purchased paper
PA: Tekni-Plex, Inc.
460 E Swedesford Rd # 3000
Wayne PA 19087
484 690-1520

(G-11919)
TOLEDO CLINIC INC
6135 Trust Dr Ste 230 (43528-9360)
PHONE..............................419 865-3111
Robin Graham, *Branch Mgr*
EMP: 176
SALES (corp-wide): 118.9MM **Privately Held**
SIC: **8099** Blood related health services
PA: Toledo Clinic, Inc.
4235 Secor Rd
Toledo OH 43623
419 473-3561

(G-11920)
TOLEDO EDISON COMPANY
Also Called: Holland Operations Center
6099 Angola Rd (43528-9595)
PHONE..............................419 249-5364
Richard Reineck, *Accounts Mgr*
Trent Smith, *Manager*
EMP: 75
SQ FT: 92,928 **Publicly Held**
SIC: **4911** Distribution, electric power
HQ: The Toledo Edison Company
76 S Main St Bsmt
Akron OH 44308
800 447-3333

(G-11921)
TOTAL FLEET SOLUTIONS LLC
7050 Spring Meadows Dr W A (43528-7203)
PHONE..............................419 868-8853
Todd W Roberts, *Mng Member*
Chris Grubbs,
Brent Parent,
▲ EMP: 50 EST: 1995
SQ FT: 5,000
SALES (est): 40.7MM **Privately Held**
WEB: www.tfsglobal.com
SIC: **5084** Materials handling machinery

(G-11922)
TOYOTA INDUSTRIAL EQP DLR
Also Called: Dmh Toyota Lift
8310 Airport Hwy (43528-8637)
PHONE..............................419 865-8025
Philip Graffy, *President*
Ted Wente, *Vice Pres*
EMP: 25
SALES (est): 5.6MM **Privately Held**
SIC: **5084** Materials handling machinery

(G-11923)
UNION CNSTR WKRS HLTH PLAN
Also Called: NORTHWESTERN OHIO ADMINISTRATO
7142 Nightingale Dr Ste 1 (43528-7822)
P.O. Box 1330 (43528-1330)
PHONE..............................419 248-2401
Bill Topel, *Administration*
Richard Watkins, *Administration*
EMP: 25
SALES (est): 27.3MM **Privately Held**
WEB: www.nwoadm.com
SIC: **8631** Labor union

(G-11924)
VELOCITY GRTEST PHONE EVER INC
7130 Spring Meadows Dr W (43528-9296)
P.O. Box 1179 (43528-1179)
PHONE..............................419 868-9983
Gregory Kiley, *President*
Jennifer Murawski, *Human Res Dir*
Colleen Grogan, *Accounts Mgr*
Jennifer Emch, *Manager*
Rachael Freeman, *Manager*
EMP: 345
SALES (est): 157.5MM **Privately Held**
WEB: www.velocity.org
SIC: **7373** 4899 Computer system selling services; data communication services

(G-11925)
VINYL DESIGN CORPORATION
7856 Hill Ave (43528-9181)
PHONE..............................419 283-4009
Patrick J Trompeter, *President*
EMP: 29
SQ FT: 36,000

SALES (est): 5.4MM **Privately Held**
WEB: www.vinyldesigncorp.com
SIC: **3089** 5033 2452 Windows, plastic; siding, except wood; prefabricated wood buildings

(G-11926)
WAREHOUSE SERVICES GROUP LLC
6145 Merger Dr (43528-8430)
P.O. Box 965 (43528-0965)
PHONE..............................419 868-6400
Dan Kurz,
Mary Lou Anderson,
Craig Kurz,
George Kurz,
Kim Kurz,
EMP: 45
SQ FT: 70,000
SALES (est): 3.1MM **Privately Held**
SIC: **4225** General warehousing & storage

(G-11927)
YODER MACHINERY SALES COMPANY
1500 Holloway Rd (43528-9542)
P.O. Box 100 (43528-0100)
PHONE..............................419 865-5555
Timothy A Yoder, *President*
Timothy Yoder, *President*
Kory Yoder, *Vice Pres*
Ryan Yoder, *Vice Pres*
Terry Yoder, *Vice Pres*
EMP: 25
SQ FT: 106,000
SALES (est): 16.5MM **Privately Held**
WEB: www.yodermachinery.com
SIC: **5084** Machine tools & accessories

Holmesville
Holmes County

(G-11928)
ACTION COUPLING & EQP INC
8248 County Road 245 (44633-9724)
P.O. Box 99 (44633-0099)
PHONE..............................330 279-4242
Scott Eliot, *President*
▲ EMP: 80
SQ FT: 75,000
SALES (est): 19.4MM **Privately Held**
WEB: www.actiongolfcarts.com
SIC: **3569** 5087 3429 Firefighting apparatus & related equipment; firefighting equipment; manufactured hardware (general)

(G-11929)
COUNTY OF HOLMES
Also Called: Holmes County Home
7260 State Route 83 (44633-9749)
PHONE..............................330 279-2801
Leslee Mast, *Superintendent*
EMP: 32
SQ FT: 40,000 **Privately Held**
WEB: www.district1fire.com
SIC: **8361** 9111 Home for the mentally handicapped; county supervisors' & executives' offices
PA: County Of Holmes
2 Court St Ste 14
Millersburg OH 44654
330 674-1896

(G-11930)
HOLMES COUNTY BOARD OF DD
8001 Township Road 574 (44633-9751)
PHONE..............................330 674-8045
Scott F Brace, *Superintendent*
Marianne Madar, *Superintendent*
Curtis Goehring, *Treasurer*
EMP: 99
SALES (est): 2.6MM **Privately Held**
SIC: **8331** Job training & vocational rehabilitation services

(G-11931)
LYNN HOPE INDUSTRIES INC
Also Called: HOLMES COUNTY TRAINING CENTER
8001 Township Rd Ste 574 (44633)
PHONE..............................330 674-8045

Sherry Martin, *Director*
EMP: 75
SALES: 321.3K **Privately Held**
SIC: 8331 Sheltered workshop

(G-11932)
MILLER LOGGING INC
8373 State Route 83 (44633)
PHONE..................................330 279-4721
Roy A Miller Jr, *President*
Levi Miller, *Corp Secy*
Barbara Miller, *Vice Pres*
EMP: 28
SALES: 1.7MM **Privately Held**
SIC: 2421 1629 2411 Wood chips, produced at mill; land clearing contractor; logging

Homer
Licking County

(G-11933)
COLUMBIA GAS TRANSMISSION LLC
Also Called: Columbia Energy
1608 Homer Rd Nw (43027)
PHONE..................................740 892-2552
Rod Graham, *Manager*
EMP: 25
SALES (corp-wide): 10.5B **Privately Held**
SIC: 4922 Pipelines, natural gas
HQ: Columbia Gas Transmission, Llc
200 Cizzic Ctr Dr
Columbus OH 43216
614 460-6000

Hooven
Hamilton County

(G-11934)
BUSY BEE ELECTRIC INC
100 Washington St (45033-7600)
PHONE..................................513 353-3553
James R Oehlschlaeger, *President*
David Talbot, *Project Mgr*
Kathy Wiethe, *Treasurer*
Gary Buckhave, *Executive*
EMP: 25
SALES (est): 4.5MM **Privately Held**
WEB: www.busybeeelectric.com
SIC: 1731 General electrical contractor

(G-11935)
SEHLHORST EQUIPMENT SVCS INC
4450 Monroe Ave (45033-7640)
PHONE..................................513 353-9300
Douglas Sehlhorst, *President*
Mark Billman, *Vice Pres*
Daniel Sehlhorst Jr, *Vice Pres*
David Sehlhorst, *Vice Pres*
Anne Rosenfeldt, *Office Mgr*
EMP: 30
SQ FT: 5,000
SALES (est): 5.4MM **Privately Held**
SIC: 1794 Excavation & grading, building construction

Hopedale
Harrison County

(G-11936)
GABLES CARE CENTER INC
351 Lahm Dr (43976-9761)
PHONE..................................740 937-2900
Robert Huff, *President*
Lynn Huff, *Vice Pres*
EMP: 105
SQ FT: 26,000
SALES (est): 5.6MM **Privately Held**
SIC: 8051 Convalescent home with continuous nursing care

(G-11937)
HOPEDALE MINING LLC
86900 Sinfield Rd (43976)
P.O. Box 415 (43976-0415)
PHONE..................................740 937-2225

David G Zatezalo,
EMP: 40
SALES (est): 5.9MM **Privately Held**
SIC: 1081 Metal mining services

(G-11938)
WATER TRANSPORT LLC
100 Sammi Dr (43976-7713)
PHONE..................................740 937-2199
Michael Kuester, *Mng Member*
EMP: 50
SQ FT: 15,000
SALES: 5MM **Privately Held**
SIC: 4789 Cargo loading & unloading services

Howard
Knox County

(G-11939)
APPLE VLY PROPERTY OWNERS ASSN (PA)
113 Hasbrouck Cir (43028-9417)
PHONE..................................740 397-3311
John Hollback, *President*
Jackie Perrots, *President*
Richard Anderson, *Treasurer*
EMP: 25
SQ FT: 10,000
SALES: 2.4MM **Privately Held**
SIC: 8641 Homeowners' association

(G-11940)
PIONEER SANDS LLC
Also Called: Millwood Plant
26900 Coshocton Rd (43028-9216)
PHONE..................................740 599-7773
Steven Bell, *Manager*
EMP: 30
SALES (corp-wide): 9.4B **Publicly Held**
SIC: 3295 1446 1442 Minerals, ground or treated; industrial sand; construction sand & gravel
HQ: Pioneer Sands Llc
5205 N O Connor Blvd # 200
Irving TX 75039
972 444-9001

Hubbard
Trumbull County

(G-11941)
BLUE BEACON OF HUBBARD INC
7044 Truck World Blvd (44425-3253)
PHONE..................................330 534-4419
Charles Walker, *President*
EMP: 30 EST: 1979
SQ FT: 4,000
SALES (est): 372K **Privately Held**
SIC: 7542 Truck wash

(G-11942)
BLUE BEACON USA LP II
Also Called: Blue Beacon Truck Wash
7044 Truck World Blvd (44425-3253)
PHONE..................................330 534-4419
Bill Rigley, *Manager*
EMP: 37
SALES (corp-wide): 99MM **Privately Held**
WEB: www.bluebeacon.com
SIC: 7542 Truck wash
PA: Blue Beacon U.S.A., L.P. li
500 Graves Blvd
Salina KS 67401
785 825-2221

(G-11943)
CONNIE PARKS (PA)
Also Called: Biomedical Laboratory
4504 Logan Way Ste B (44425-3345)
PHONE..................................330 759-8334
Connie Parks, *Owner*
EMP: 40
SALES (est): 2.2MM **Privately Held**
WEB: www.metalworkinggroup.com
SIC: 8071 Testing laboratories

(G-11944)
DESALVO CONSTRUCTION COMPANY
1491 W Liberty St (44425-3310)
PHONE..................................330 759-8145
Joseph A Desalvo, *President*
Joseph K Desalvo, *Vice Pres*
Mark Dodd, *Vice Pres*
Sandra S Algoe, *Treasurer*
Sandra Algoe, *Treasurer*
EMP: 45
SQ FT: 12,320
SALES: 17.7MM **Privately Held**
SIC: 1541 1542 Industrial buildings, new construction; commercial & office building, new construction

(G-11945)
ERIE INSURANCE EXCHANGE
5676 Everett East Rd (44425-2826)
PHONE..................................330 568-1802
EMP: 62
SALES (corp-wide): 373.8MM **Privately Held**
WEB: www.erie-insurance.com
SIC: 6331 Reciprocal interinsurance exchanges: fire, marine, casualty
PA: Erie Insurance Exchange
100 Erie Insurance Pl
Erie PA 16530
800 458-0811

(G-11946)
GREENWOODS HUBBARD CHEVY-OLDS
Also Called: Greenwood's Oldsmobile
2635 N Main St (44425-3247)
P.O. Box 290 (44425-0290)
PHONE..................................330 568-4335
Greg Greenwood, *President*
Steve Rotunno, *Marketing Staff*
EMP: 35
SQ FT: 10,000
SALES (est): 6.6MM **Privately Held**
SIC: 5511 7538 7515 Automobiles, new & used; general automotive repair shops; passenger car leasing

(G-11947)
INDUSTRIAL AIR CONTROL INC
1276 Brookfield Rd (44425-3068)
P.O. Box 56 (44425-0056)
PHONE..................................330 772-6422
Elmer Takash, *President*
Mary Langley, *Corp Secy*
Robin Takash, *Assistant VP*
Jim Davidson, *Vice Pres*
EMP: 60
SQ FT: 6,000
SALES (est): 2.4MM **Privately Held**
SIC: 7349 7699 Cleaning service, industrial or commercial; industrial equipment cleaning

(G-11948)
LIBERTY STEEL PRODUCTS INC
7193 Masury Rd (44425-9756)
P.O. Box 175, North Jackson (44451-0175)
PHONE..................................330 534-7998
Bill McCullough, *Manager*
EMP: 200
SALES (corp-wide): 74MM **Privately Held**
SIC: 5051 Steel
PA: Liberty Steel Products, Inc.
11650 Mahoning Ave
North Jackson OH 44451
330 538-2236

(G-11949)
OHIO STEEL SHEET & PLATE INC
7845 Chestnut Ridge Rd (44425-9702)
P.O. Box 1146, Warren (44482-1146)
PHONE..................................800 827-2401
John Rebhan, *President*
Mike Link, *Vice Pres*
Eric Rebhan, *Vice Pres*
EMP: 45
SQ FT: 320,000

SALES (est): 12.9MM **Privately Held**
WEB: www.ohiosteelplate.com
SIC: 3312 5051 3444 Sheet or strip, steel, hot-rolled; plate, steel; metals service centers & offices; sheet metalwork

(G-11950)
S & B TRUCKING INC (PA)
3045 Gale Dr (44425-1012)
PHONE..................................614 554-4090
EMP: 26
SQ FT: 5,000
SALES (est): 4.3MM **Privately Held**
SIC: 7363 Help Supply Services

(G-11951)
W W WILLIAMS COMPANY LLC
7125 Masury Rd (44425-9756)
PHONE..................................330 534-1161
Alan Gatlin, *CEO*
L Ed McIntyre, *Branch Mgr*
EMP: 26
SALES (corp-wide): 4.8B **Privately Held**
WEB: www.williamsdistribution.com
SIC: 5084 Engines & parts, diesel
HQ: The W W Williams Company Llc
5025 Bradenton Ave # 130
Dublin OH 43017
614 228-5000

(G-11952)
YOUNGSTOWN-KENWORTH INC (PA)
Also Called: All-Line Truck Sales
7255 Hubbard Masury Rd (44425-9757)
PHONE..................................330 534-9761
Tomiel Mikes, *President*
Geraldine Mikes, *Principal*
Randall R Fiest, *Vice Pres*
Randall Fiest, *Vice Pres*
Dave Claypool, *Sales Staff*
EMP: 35
SQ FT: 14,900
SALES (est): 8.4MM **Privately Held**
WEB: www.youngstownkenworth.com
SIC: 5013 5012 7538 3713 Truck parts & accessories; trucks, commercial; general automotive repair shops; truck & bus bodies; industrial trucks & tractors

Huber Heights
Montgomery County

(G-11953)
CLARKE POWER SERVICES INC
6061 Executive Blvd (45424-1441)
PHONE..................................937 684-4402
Chris Hager, *Manager*
EMP: 34
SALES (corp-wide): 252.9MM **Privately Held**
SIC: 5084 Engines & parts, diesel
PA: Clarke Power Services, Inc.
3133 E Kemper Rd
Cincinnati OH 45241
513 771-2200

(G-11954)
ESTES EXPRESS LINES INC
6295 Executive Blvd (45424-1439)
PHONE..................................937 237-7536
Joe Ketring, *Branch Mgr*
EMP: 59
SALES (corp-wide): 2.7B **Privately Held**
SIC: 4213 Contract haulers
PA: Estes Express Lines, Inc.
3901 W Broad St
Richmond VA 23230
804 353-1900

(G-11955)
JAMES D EGBERT OPTOMETRIST (PA)
Also Called: Gemini Eye Care Center
6557 Brandt Pike (45424-3353)
PHONE..................................937 236-1770
James D Egbert, *President*
Anna R Egbert, *Corp Secy*
Dr Steven Connett, *Vice Pres*
William Hancock, *Administration*
EMP: 26

▲ = Import ▼=Export
◆ =Import/Export

SALES (est): 5.1MM **Privately Held**
WEB: www.geminieyecarecenters.com
SIC: 5995 8042 Contact lenses, prescription; offices & clinics of optometrists

(G-11956)
PENDSTER DIALYSIS LLC
Also Called: Huber Heights Dialysis
7769 Old Country Ct (45424-2097)
PHONE.................................937 237-0769
James K Hilger,
EMP: 26
SALES (est): 192.9K **Publicly Held**
SIC: 8092 Kidney dialysis centers
PA: Davita Inc.
2000 16th St
Denver CO 80202

(G-11957)
PETSMART INC
8281 Old Troy Pike (45424-1025)
PHONE.................................937 236-1335
Kami Mezcar, *Manager*
EMP: 30
SALES (corp-wide): 12.1B **Privately Held**
WEB: www.petsmart.com
SIC: 5999 0752 Pet food; animal specialty services
HQ: Petsmart, Inc.
19601 N 27th Ave
Phoenix AZ 85027
623 580-6100

(G-11958)
PRAIRIE FARMS DAIRY INC
5820 Executive Blvd (45424-1451)
PHONE.................................937 235-5930
Don Middlestetter, *Branch Mgr*
EMP: 63
SALES (corp-wide): 1.9B **Privately Held**
SIC: 5143 Dairy products, except dried or canned
PA: Prairie Farms Dairy, Inc.
3744 Staunton St
Edwardsville IL 62025
618 659-5700

(G-11959)
TRIDEC TECHNOLOGIES LLC
4764 Fishburg Rd Ste D (45424-5456)
PHONE.................................937 938-8160
Joe Smith, *Human Res Dir*
Leslie Godzik, *Office Mgr*
Debbie Butler, *Program Mgr*
Robert A Fritschie,
EMP: 25
SALES (est): 3.2MM **Privately Held**
SIC: 7371 Computer software systems analysis & design, custom

Hudson
Summit County

(G-11960)
A P O HOLDINGS INC (PA)
Also Called: A P O Pumps and Compressors
6607 Chittenden Rd (44236-2025)
PHONE.................................330 650-1330
Ted Mailey, *President*
Dave Murari, *Vice Pres*
EMP: 51
SALES (est): 47.6MM **Privately Held**
WEB: www.airpowerofohio.com
SIC: 5084 7699 Compressors, except air conditioning; compressor repair

(G-11961)
ADAPTIVE CORPORATION (PA)
118 W Streetsboro St # 221 (44236-2752)
PHONE.................................440 257-7460
Eric Doubell, *CEO*
Frank Thomas, *President*
Margie Ator, *CFO*
EMP: 46
SALES (est): 10MM **Privately Held**
SIC: 8711 Engineering services

(G-11962)
ALBERT GUARNIERI & CO
7481 Herrick Park Dr (44236-2367)
PHONE.................................330 794-9834
EMP: 56

SALES (corp-wide): 30MM **Privately Held**
SIC: 5194 5145 5141 Tobacco & tobacco products; confectionery; groceries, general line
PA: Albert Guarnieri & Co.
1133 E Market St
Warren OH 44483
330 394-5636

(G-11963)
ALLSTATE INSURANCE COMPANY
75 Milford Dr Ste 222 (44236-2778)
PHONE.................................330 650-2917
Tracy L Mc Kenica, *Principal*
Robert L McKenica, *Principal*
EMP: 30
SALES (est): 1.2MM **Privately Held**
SIC: 6411 6311 7389 Insurance agents; property & casualty insurance agent; life insurance; financial services

(G-11964)
ALLSTATE INSURANCE COMPANY
75 Executive Pkwy (44237-0002)
PHONE.................................330 656-6000
Doug Carpenter, *Manager*
EMP: 55 **Publicly Held**
WEB: www.allstate.com
SIC: 6411 Insurance agents, brokers & service
HQ: Allstate Insurance Company
2775 Sanders Rd
Northbrook IL 60062
847 402-5000

(G-11965)
ALPHA FREIGHT SYSTEMS INC
5876 Darrow Rd (44236-3864)
PHONE.................................800 394-9001
Paul Kithcart, *President*
EMP: 69
SQ FT: 10,000
SALES (est): 11.3MM
SALES (corp-wide): 2.2B **Publicly Held**
WEB: www.alphafreight.com
SIC: 4731 4213 Brokers, shipping; contract haulers
HQ: Ascent Global Logistics Holdings, Inc.
5876 Darrow Rd
Hudson OH 44236

(G-11966)
ALPHA TECHNOLOGIES SVCS LLC (DH)
6279 Hudson Crossing Pkwy (44236-4348)
PHONE.................................330 745-1641
Jeff Ward, *Buyer*
Ken Brown, *Mng Member*
Peter Boogaard, *Technology*
Darin Myers, *Technical Staff*
Barbara Davidson,
◆ EMP: 60
SALES (est): 25.2MM
SALES (corp-wide): 5.1B **Publicly Held**
SIC: 3823 8748 Industrial instrmnts msrmnt display/control process variable; testing services
HQ: Dynisco Instruments Llc
38 Forge Pkwy
Franklin MA 02038
508 541-9400

(G-11967)
ASCENT GLOBAL LOGISTICS HOLDIN (HQ)
Also Called: Group Transportation Svcs Inc
5876 Darrow Rd (44236-3864)
PHONE.................................800 689-6255
Michael Valentine, *President*
Paul Kithcart, *Vice Pres*
Brian Pollock, *Opers Staff*
Tom Drugan, *Associate*
EMP: 40
SQ FT: 24,780
SALES (est): 20.4MM
SALES (corp-wide): 2.2B **Publicly Held**
WEB: www.onestopshipping.com
SIC: 8742 Transportation consultant

PA: Roadrunner Transportation Systems, Inc.
1431 Opus Pl Ste 530
Downers Grove IL 60515
414 615-1500

(G-11968)
BROWN DERBY ROADHOUSE
72 N Main St Ste 208 (44236-2883)
PHONE.................................330 528-3227
Parris Girvas, *President*
Leo Carmelli, *Manager*
EMP: 46
SALES (est): 1.7MM **Privately Held**
SIC: 5812 7299 Steak restaurant; banquet hall facilities

(G-11969)
CELCO LTD
5600 Hudsn Indstl Pkwy (44236-5011)
PHONE.................................330 655-7000
Peter Spitalieri, *President*
EMP: 25
SALES (est): 1.1MM **Privately Held**
SIC: 7322 Collection agency, except real estate

(G-11970)
CHANGE HLTHCARE OPERATIONS LLC
300 Executive Pkwy W (44236-1690)
PHONE.................................330 405-0001
Kenneth Lucas, *Director*
EMP: 37
SALES (corp-wide): 208.3B **Publicly Held**
SIC: 7374 Data processing service
HQ: Change Healthcare Operations, Llc
3055 Lebanon Pike # 1000
Nashville TN 37214

(G-11971)
CHARLES L MACCALLUM MD INC
5778 Darrow Rd Ste D (44236-3808)
PHONE.................................330 655-2161
Charles L Maccallum MD, *President*
EMP: 25
SQ FT: 2,500
SALES (est): 878K **Privately Held**
SIC: 8011 Offices & clinics of medical doctors

(G-11972)
CHASE TRANSCRIPTIONS INC (PA)
1737 Georgetown Rd Ste G (44236-5013)
PHONE.................................330 650-0539
Michael C Geaney, *President*
Cynthia Boyle, *Supervisor*
EMP: 34
SQ FT: 4,000
SALES (est): 4.5MM **Privately Held**
WEB: www.chasetranscriptions.com
SIC: 7338 Secretarial & typing service; stenographic services

(G-11973)
CITY OF HUDSON VILLAGE
Also Called: Service Department
95 Owen Brown St (44236-2855)
PHONE.................................330 650-1052
Dan Worley, *Officer*
EMP: 55 **Privately Held**
WEB: www.ellsworthmeadows.com
SIC: 4911 Electric services
PA: City Of Hudson Village
115 Executive Pkwy # 400
Hudson OH 44236
330 650-1799

(G-11974)
COUNTRY CLUB OF HUDSON
2155 Middleton Rd (44236-1434)
P.O. Box 533 (44236-0533)
PHONE.................................330 650-1188
Karen Twedell, *Manager*
EMP: 45
SQ FT: 2,000
SALES: 2.4MM **Privately Held**
WEB: www.cchudson.com
SIC: 7997 5812 Country club, membership; eating places

(G-11975)
DOHNER LTD
Also Called: Dohner Landscaping
7738 Valley View Rd (44236-1247)
PHONE.................................330 814-4144
Christoper Dohner, *President*
EMP: 25 EST: 2011
SALES (est): 1.2MM **Privately Held**
SIC: 0782 Lawn care services

(G-11976)
DREW MEDICAL INC (PA)
75 Milford Dr Ste 201 (44236-2778)
PHONE.................................407 363-6700
Michael Dinkel, *President*
EMP: 30
SALES (est): 3.2MM **Privately Held**
SIC: 8071 Medical laboratories

(G-11977)
ESSENDANT CO
100 E Highland Rd (44236)
PHONE.................................330 650-9361
Dave Martin, *Manager*
EMP: 96
SALES (corp-wide): 5B **Privately Held**
WEB: www.ussco.com
SIC: 5112 Office supplies
HQ: Essendant Co.
1 Parkway North Blvd # 100
Deerfield IL 60015
847 627-7000

(G-11978)
FORTEC MEDICAL INC (PA)
6245 Hudson Crossing Pkwy (44236-4348)
PHONE.................................330 463-1265
Drew Forhan, *President*
John Voyzey, *President*
Mike Stickler, *Managing Dir*
Eileen Wachovec, *Asst Controller*
Joann Vosburgh, *Finance*
EMP: 30
SQ FT: 69,000
SALES (est): 14.7MM **Privately Held**
SIC: 7352 Medical equipment rental

(G-11979)
GEM EDWARDS INC
Also Called: Gemco Medical
5640 Hudson Indus Pkwy (44236-5011)
P.O. Box 429 (44236-0429)
PHONE.................................330 342-8300
Toni Edwards, *President*
Dee Edwards, *General Mgr*
George Edwards, *Exec VP*
Bill Baker, *Vice Pres*
David Draluck, *Vice Pres*
▲ EMP: 100
SQ FT: 80,000
SALES (est): 58.7MM **Privately Held**
SIC: 5122 5961 5999 5047 Medicinals & botanicals; patent medicines; pharmaceuticals; proprietary (patent) medicines; food, mail order; pharmaceuticals, mail order; alarm & safety equipment stores; incontinent care products; hospital equipment & furniture; medical equipment & supplies

(G-11980)
GIAMBRONE MASONRY INC
10000 Aurora Hudson Rd (44236-2520)
P.O. Box 810, Aurora (44202-0810)
PHONE.................................216 475-1200
David Giambrone, *President*
EMP: 80
SQ FT: 2,500
SALES (est): 5.4MM **Privately Held**
WEB: www.giambrone.com
SIC: 1741 Bricklaying

(G-11981)
HEALTH DESIGN PLUS INC
1755 Georgetown Rd (44236-4057)
PHONE.................................330 656-1072
Ruth Coleman, *CEO*
William Coleman, *President*
Noreen Sussman, *Vice Pres*
Sandra Pogozelski, *Opers Staff*
Pat Coen-Laird, *QC Mgr*
EMP: 92
SQ FT: 18,500

SALES (est): 35.2MM **Privately Held**
WEB: www.hdplus.com
SIC: 6411 Medical insurance claim processing, contract or fee basis

(G-11982)
HUDSON CITY ENGINEERING DEPT
115 Executive Pkwy # 400 (44236-1693)
PHONE..................330 342-1770
Cathy Clark, *Principal*
EMP: 28 **EST:** 2011
SALES (est): 2.2MM **Privately Held**
SIC: 8322 Community center

(G-11983)
HUDSON MONTESSORI ASSOCIATION
Also Called: HUDSON MONTESSORI SCHOOL
7545 Darrow Rd (44236-1305)
PHONE..................330 650-0424
Mat Virgil, *Principal*
Julia Brown, *Principal*
Peter Larrow, *Principal*
EMP: 40 **EST:** 1962
SALES: 3MM **Privately Held**
WEB: www.hudsonmontessori.org
SIC: 8351 8211 Preschool center; private elementary school

(G-11984)
HYDROGEOLOGIC INC
581 Boston Mills Rd # 600 (44236-1196)
PHONE..................330 463-3303
Peter S Huyakorn, *President*
EMP: 31
SALES (corp-wide): 67MM **Privately Held**
SIC: 8731 Environmental research
PA: Hydrogeologic, Inc.
11107 Sunset Hills Rd # 400
Reston VA 20190
703 478-5186

(G-11985)
INTEGRATED TELEHEALTH INC
Also Called: Global Telehealth Services
75 Milford Dr Ste 201 (44236-2778)
PHONE..................216 373-2221
Michael A Miller, *CEO*
Christopher T Beseda, *COO*
EMP: 25 **EST:** 2015
SQ FT: 2,800
SALES: 50K **Privately Held**
SIC: 7371 Computer software development

(G-11986)
J NAN ENTERPRISES LLC
Also Called: Goddard Schools
5601 Darrow Rd (44236-4087)
PHONE..................330 653-3766
Jeffery A Lutz, *Owner*
Nancy E Lutz, *Vice Pres*
EMP: 26
SQ FT: 8,000
SALES (est): 1.1MM **Privately Held**
SIC: 8351 Preschool center

(G-11987)
JE CARSTEN COMPANY (PA)
Also Called: Vita Pup
7481 Herrick Park Dr (44236-2367)
PHONE..................330 794-4440
J M Carsten, *President*
James E Carsten, *Corp Secy*
Peter Carsten, *Vice Pres*
EMP: 34
SALES (est): 4.9MM **Privately Held**
SIC: 5194 5145 Cigarettes; cigars; smoking tobacco; confectionery

(G-11988)
JO-ANN STORES HOLDINGS INC (PA)
Also Called: Jo-Ann Fabrics & Crafts
5555 Darrow Rd (44236-4054)
PHONE..................888 739-4120
Wade Miquelon, *President*
Erica Apfelbaum, *District Mgr*
Keith Morris, *District Mgr*
Robert Thrul, *District Mgr*
Jeff Csuy, *Senior VP*
EMP: 85

SALES (est): 2.7B **Privately Held**
SIC: 5949 6719 5945 Fabric stores piece goods; notions, including trim; patterns: sewing, knitting & needlework; sewing supplies; investment holding companies, except banks; hobby & craft supplies

(G-11989)
JPMORGAN CHASE BANK NAT ASSN
136 W Streetsboro St (44236-2746)
PHONE..................330 650-0476
Paula Gianinni, *Branch Mgr*
EMP: 26
SALES (corp-wide): 131.4B **Publicly Held**
SIC: 6029 Commercial banks
HQ: Jpmorgan Chase Bank, National Association
1111 Polaris Pkwy
Columbus OH 43240
614 436-3055

(G-11990)
KGK GARDENING DESIGN CORP
1975 Norton Rd (44236-4100)
PHONE..................330 656-1709
Kenneth Kuryla, *President*
Joyce Kuryla, *Vice Pres*
EMP: 40
SALES (est): 1.5MM **Privately Held**
SIC: 0782 Landscape contractors

(G-11991)
KINGS MEDICAL COMPANY
1920 Georgetown Rd A (44236-4060)
PHONE..................330 653-3968
Clark Labaski, *Controller*
EMP: 130
SALES (est): 12.7MM
SALES (corp-wide): 55MM **Privately Held**
WEB: www.kingsmedical.com
SIC: 8742 Banking & finance consultant; marketing consulting services
PA: King's Medical Group, Inc.
1920 Georgetown Rd A
Hudson OH 44236
330 528-1765

(G-11992)
KRISTIE WARNER
Also Called: Gavin Scott Salon & Spa
4960 Darrow Rd (44224-1406)
PHONE..................330 650-4450
Kristie Warner, *Owner*
EMP: 25
SALES (est): 575.9K **Privately Held**
SIC: 7231 7991 Manicurist, pedicurist; spas

(G-11993)
LAUREL LK RETIREMENT CMNTY INC
Also Called: CROWN CENTER
200 Laurel Lake Dr Rear (44236-9905)
PHONE..................330 650-0681
Michael Leslein, *CFO*
Lisa Mitchell, *Human Res Dir*
Donna Anderson, *Advt Staff*
David A Oster, *Exec Dir*
James Corrigan, *Director*
EMP: 350
SQ FT: 440,000
SALES: 851.4K **Privately Held**
SIC: 8361 8051 Rest home, with health care incidental; skilled nursing care facilities

(G-11994)
LEAFFILTER NORTH LLC (PA)
1595 Georgetown Rd Ste G (44236-4045)
PHONE..................330 655-7950
Michael Gori, *Vice Pres*
Don Wharton, *Vice Pres*
Matt Kaulig,
EMP: 108
SALES (est): 68MM **Privately Held**
SIC: 1761 Gutter & downspout contractor

(G-11995)
MERRILL LYNCH PIERCE FENNER
10 W Streetsboro St # 305 (44236-2850)
PHONE..................330 655-2312
Anastasia Kozer, *Manager*
EMP: 25
SALES (corp-wide): 110.5B **Publicly Held**
WEB: www.merlyn.com
SIC: 6029 Security brokers & dealers; financial consultant
HQ: Merrill Lynch, Pierce, Fenner & Smith Incorporated
111 8th Ave
New York NY 10011
800 637-7455

(G-11996)
MEYER DECORATIVE SURFACES USA (HQ)
Also Called: Mayer Laminates MA
300 Executive Pkwy W # 100 (44236-1690)
PHONE..................800 776-3900
David Sullivan, *President*
▲ **EMP:** 25
SQ FT: 25,000
SALES (est): 48.6MM
SALES (corp-wide): 215.9MM **Privately Held**
SIC: 5031 Building materials, interior
PA: Compagnie De Saint-Gobain ·
La Defense 3 Tour Les Miroirs
Courbevoie 92400
147 623-000

(G-11997)
MH LOGISTICS CORP
Also Called: M H Equipment
1892 Georgetown Rd (44236-4058)
PHONE..................330 425-2476
Mike Pinkus, *Sales Staff*
Harry Bruno, *Branch Mgr*
EMP: 30
SALES (corp-wide): 247.9MM **Privately Held**
WEB: www.mhlogistics.com
SIC: 5084 7359 Materials handling machinery; processing & packaging equipment; waste compactors; equipment rental & leasing
PA: M.H. Logistics Corp.
8901 N Industrial Rd
Peoria IL 61615
309 579-8020

(G-11998)
MILLENNIUM CPITL RECOVERY CORP
95 Executive Pkwy Ste 100 (44236-5400)
PHONE..................330 528-1450
Robert Bronchetti, *President*
Jayne Bronchetti, *Exec VP*
EMP: 40
SALES (est): 4.2MM **Privately Held**
WEB: www.automgmt.net
SIC: 7389 Repossession service

(G-11999)
NORANDEX BLDG MTLS DIST INC
Also Called: Norandex Building Mtls Dist
300 Executive Park (44236)
P.O. Box 860, Valley Forge PA (19482-0860)
PHONE..................330 656-8924
Glenn Knowlton, *President*
Rebecca Faulk, *Vice Pres*
EMP: 1000
SQ FT: 35,000
SALES (est): 13.3MM
SALES (corp-wide): 215.9MM **Privately Held**
WEB: www.norandex.com
SIC: 5033 5031 Siding, except wood; doors & windows
HQ: Saint-Gobain Corporation
20 Moores Rd
Malvern PA 19355

(G-12000)
NORTHWEST BANK
178 W Streetsboro St # 1 (44236-2754)
PHONE..................330 342-4018

Kevin Nelson, *Exec VP*
EMP: 300
SQ FT: 1,200
SALES (est): 6.7MM **Publicly Held**
WEB: www.morganbank.net
SIC: 6022 State commercial banks
PA: Northwest Bancshares, Inc.
100 Liberty St
Warren PA 16365

(G-12001)
PASCO INC
Also Called: G M A C Insurance Center
5600 Hudsn Indstl Pkwy (44236-3798)
PHONE..................330 650-0613
Peter Spitalieri, *President*
EMP: 300
SALES (est): 66.2MM **Privately Held**
SIC: 6411 7323 Insurance information & consulting services; credit reporting services

(G-12002)
PAYCHEX INC
100 E Hines Hill Rd (44236-1115)
PHONE..................330 342-0530
EMP: 123
SALES (corp-wide): 3.3B **Publicly Held**
SIC: 8721 Payroll accounting service
PA: Paychex, Inc.
911 Panorama Trl S
Rochester NY 14625
585 385-6666

(G-12003)
PETERMANN LTD
91 Owen Brown St (44236-2809)
PHONE..................330 653-3323
Kimberly Lane, *Manager*
EMP: 80
SALES (est): 1.4MM **Privately Held**
SIC: 4151 School buses
HQ: Petermann Ltd
8041 Hosbrook Rd Ste 330
Cincinnati OH 45236

(G-12004)
RESTORATION RESOURCES INC
Also Called: SERVPRO
1546 Georgetown Rd (44236-4067)
PHONE..................330 650-4486
Bruce Johnson, *President*
Terri Johnson, *Vice Pres*
EMP: 35
SQ FT: 2,700
SALES (est): 1.5MM **Privately Held**
WEB: www.restorationresources.com
SIC: 7349 Building maintenance services

(G-12005)
SETON CATHOLIC SCHOOL HUDSON
6923 Stow Rd (44236-3240)
PHONE..................330 342-4200
SIS M Damicone, *Principal*
Paula Worhatch, *Admin Sec*
EMP: 30
SQ FT: 20,624
SALES (est): 359.3K **Privately Held**
WEB: www.setoncatholicschool.org
SIC: 8211 8351 Private elementary & secondary schools; child day care services

(G-12006)
SHIELD SECURITY SERVICE
P.O. Box 1001 (44236-6201)
PHONE..................330 650-2001
Ray Hutchinson, *Owner*
Holly Stepnicki, *Co-Owner*
EMP: 25
SALES (est): 200K **Privately Held**
SIC: 7381 Security guard service

(G-12007)
STRUCTURAL BUILDING SYSTEMS
5802 Akron Cleveland Rd (44236-2010)
P.O. Box 463 (44236-0463)
PHONE..................330 656-9353
Paul Mills, *President*
EMP: 95
SALES (est): 7.1MM **Privately Held**
SIC: 1541 Industrial buildings & warehouses

▲ = Import ▼=Export
◆ =Import/Export

(G-12008)
T L C CHILD DEVELOPMENT CENTER
Also Called: Academy For Young Childrn
187 Ravenna St (44236-3466)
PHONE..................................330 655-2797
Alison Pfeister, *President*
EMP: 25
SQ FT: 7,262
SALES (est): 1.1MM **Privately Held**
WEB: www.onlinewithtlc.com
SIC: 8351 Preschool center; nursery school

(G-12009)
UBS FINANCIAL SERVICES INC
43 Village Way Ste 201 (44236-5383)
PHONE..................................330 655-8319
EMP: 43
SALES (corp-wide): 28B **Privately Held**
SIC: 7389 Financial services
HQ: Ubs Financial Services Inc.
1285 Ave Of The Americas
New York NY 10019
212 713-2000

(G-12010)
UNITY HEALTH NETWORK LLC
5655 Hudson Dr Ste 110 (44236-4454)
PHONE..................................330 655-3820
Laurie Swinehart, *Branch Mgr*
EMP: 34
SALES (corp-wide): 14.5MM **Privately Held**
SIC: 8099 Blood related health services
PA: Unity Health Network, Llc
3033 State Rd
Cuyahoga Falls OH 44223
330 923-5899

(G-12011)
VERITIV PUBG & PRINT MGT INC (DH)
Also Called: Uww
5700 Darrow Rd Ste 110 (44236-5026)
PHONE..................................330 650-5522
Mary A Laschinger, *CEO*
Allan Dragone, *CEO*
Matt Dawley, *President*
Mike Nash, *President*
Ken Flajs, *COO*
◆ EMP: 33
SALES (est): 221.5MM
SALES (corp-wide): 8.7B **Publicly Held**
SIC: 5111 7389 Fine paper; printing broker
HQ: Veritiv Operating Company
1000 Abernathy Rd
Atlanta GA 30328
770 391-8200

(G-12012)
WBC GROUP LLC (PA)
Also Called: Meyerpt
6333 Hudson Crossing Pkwy (44236-4346)
PHONE..................................866 528-2144
Ron Harrington, *CEO*
▲ EMP: 95
SQ FT: 50,000
SALES (est): 129.2MM **Privately Held**
WEB: www.indemed.com
SIC: 5122 5047 3843 Vitamins & minerals; pharmaceuticals; medical & hospital equipment; dental equipment & supplies

(G-12013)
WESTERN & SOUTHERN LF INSUR CO
85 Executive Pkwy Ste 200 (44236-1691)
PHONE..................................234 380-4525
Joseph Parker, *Manager*
Deanna May, *Officer*
EMP: 25 **Privately Held**
SIC: 6411 6311 Insurance agents; life insurance
HQ: The Western & Southern Life Insurance Company
400 Broadway St
Cincinnati OH 45202
513 629-1800

(G-12014)
WOLTERS KLUWER CLINICAL DRUG
1100 Terex Rd (44236-3771)
PHONE..................................330 650-6506
Denise Basow, *President*
David A Del Toro, *Vice Pres*
Mike Hofherr, *Vice Pres*
EMP: 65
SQ FT: 24,000
SALES (est): 11.2MM
SALES (corp-wide): 5.2B **Privately Held**
SIC: 2731 2791 7379 Books: publishing only; typesetting, computer controlled; computer related maintenance services
HQ: Wolters Kluwer Health, Inc.
2001 Market St Ste 5
Philadelphia PA 19103
215 521-8300

(G-12015)
WONDERWORKER INC
Also Called: Sky Zone Boston Heights
6217 Chittenden Rd (44236-2021)
PHONE..................................234 249-3030
Charles Hallis, *President*
Ivana Matyas, *Corp Secy*
EMP: 80
SQ FT: 24,000
SALES: 500K **Privately Held**
SIC: 7999 Trampoline operation

Huntsburg
Geauga County

(G-12016)
ARMS TRUCKING CO INC (PA)
14818 Mayfield Rd (44046-8770)
PHONE..................................800 362-1343
Howard W Bates, *President*
Rick Humphries, *Vice Pres*
David W Ronyak, *Vice Pres*
Brian Bates, *Treasurer*
Patricia Bates, *Admin Sec*
EMP: 40
SQ FT: 21,000
SALES (est): 9MM **Privately Held**
SIC: 4213 4214 Contract haulers; local trucking with storage

(G-12017)
BLOSSOM HILLS NURSING HOME
Also Called: Blossom Hill Care Center
12496 Princeton Rd (44046-9792)
P.O. Box 369 (44046-0369)
PHONE..................................440 635-5567
Donald Gray, *President*
George Ohman, *Corp Secy*
Charles Ohman, *Vice Pres*
Brad Baker, *Maint Spvr*
Theresa Weber, *Supervisor*
EMP: 85
SQ FT: 18,500
SALES (est): 3.7MM **Privately Held**
SIC: 8051 8052 Convalescent home with continuous nursing care; intermediate care facilities

(G-12018)
MAN GOLF OHIO LLC
14107 Mayfield Rd (44046-8722)
PHONE..................................440 635-5178
Robert Nance,
EMP: 35
SALES (est): 273.9K **Privately Held**
SIC: 7999 Golf services & professionals

Huron
Erie County

(G-12019)
AERIE FRTNRL ORDER EGLES 2875
2902 Cleveland Rd W (44839-1011)
P.O. Box 454 (44839-0454)
PHONE..................................419 433-4611
Jeff Widman, *President*
EMP: 35
SQ FT: 5,000
SALES (est): 325.1K **Privately Held**
SIC: 8641 University club; fraternal associations

(G-12020)
AMERICAN PUBLISHERS LLC
2401 Sawmill Pkwy Ste 10 (44839-2284)
PHONE..................................419 626-0623
Steven Ester, *President*
John P Loughlin, *Vice Pres*
John Rohan Jr, *Treasurer*
Catherine Bostron, *Admin Sec*
EMP: 100 EST: 1918
SQ FT: 25,000
SALES (est): 7MM
SALES (corp-wide): 6.4B **Privately Held**
WEB: www.ppsb.com
SIC: 7389 Telemarketing services
PA: The Hearst Corporation
300 W 57th St Fl 42
New York NY 10019
212 649-2000

(G-12021)
BARNES NURSERY INC (PA)
3511 Cleveland Rd W (44839-1025)
PHONE..................................800 421-8722
Robert Barnes, *President*
Jarret Barnes, *Vice Pres*
Steve Coughlin, *Buyer*
Julie Barnes, *Treasurer*
EMP: 49
SQ FT: 5,000
SALES (est): 6.9MM **Privately Held**
WEB: www.barnesnursery.com
SIC: 0782 0181 5261 Landscape contractors; nursery stock, growing of; garden supplies & tools

(G-12022)
CHEFS GARDEN INC
9009 Huron Avery Rd (44839-2448)
PHONE..................................419 433-4947
Barbara Jones, *President*
Robert N Jones, *COO*
Bob L Jones, *Vice Pres*
Lee Jones, *Treasurer*
Rebecca Lippus, *Accounting Mgr*
EMP: 130
SQ FT: 1,684
SALES: 10MM **Privately Held**
WEB: www.chefsgardeninc.com
SIC: 5148 Ready-to-eat meals, salads & sandwiches; fresh fruits & vegetables; fruits, fresh; vegetables, fresh; market garden

(G-12023)
CITY OF HURON
Water Department
417 Main St (44839-1652)
PHONE..................................419 433-5000
Ron Marsinick, *Principal*
EMP: 100 **Privately Held**
WEB: www.cityofhuron.org
SIC: 4941 Water supply
PA: City Of Huron
417 Main St
Huron OH 44839
419 433-5000

(G-12024)
COUNTY OF ERIE
Also Called: Erie County Care Facility
3916 Perkins Ave (44839-1059)
PHONE..................................419 627-8733
Jennifer Sherer, *Director*
Marian Hill, *Admin Director*
EMP: 155 **Privately Held**
WEB: www.gem.org
SIC: 8051 9111 Convalescent home with continuous nursing care; county supervisors' & executives' offices
PA: County Of Erie
2900 Columbus Ave
Sandusky OH 44870
419 627-7682

(G-12025)
HUMANTICS INNOVATIVE SOLUTIONS
900 Denton Dr (44839-8922)
PHONE..................................567 265-5200
EMP: 33 **Privately Held**
SIC: 8748 Business consulting
PA: Humanetics Innovative Solutions, Inc.
23300 Haggerty Rd
Farmington Hills MI 48335

(G-12026)
HURON CEMENT PRODUCTS COMPANY (PA)
Also Called: H & C Building Supplies
617 Main St (44839-2593)
PHONE..................................419 433-4161
John Caporini, *President*
EMP: 38 EST: 1914
SQ FT: 37,800
SALES (est): 9.4MM **Privately Held**
SIC: 5211 5032 3273 3546 Cement; sand & gravel; cement; gravel; ready-mixed concrete; power-driven handtools; concrete products; cement, hydraulic

(G-12027)
HURON HEALTH CARE CENTER INC
Also Called: Admirals Pnte Nrsing Rhblttion
1920 Cleveland Rd W (44839-1211)
PHONE..................................419 433-4990
Amy Donaldson, *Administration*
EMP: 125
SALES (est): 584.9MM **Privately Held**
SIC: 8051 Convalescent home with continuous nursing care

(G-12028)
NORTH POINT EDUCTL SVC CTR
Also Called: Erie Co Office of Ed
710 Cleveland Rd W (44839-1546)
PHONE..................................440 967-0904
Susan Peterson, *Principal*
EMP: 43
SALES (corp-wide): 12.2MM **Privately Held**
WEB: www.ehove.net
SIC: 8211 8052 9111 School for physically handicapped; home for the mentally retarded, with health care; county supervisors' & executives' offices
PA: North Point Educational Service Center
1210 E Bogart Rd
Sandusky OH 44870
419 627-3900

(G-12029)
SANDUSKY ROTARY CLUB CHARITABL
1722 Sandpiper Ct (44839-9134)
P.O. Box 717, Sandusky (44871-0717)
PHONE..................................419 625-1707
Cynthia Ball, *Principal*
EMP: 41
SALES: 69.7K **Privately Held**
SIC: 7997 Membership sports & recreation clubs

(G-12030)
SAW MILL CREEK LTD
Also Called: Lodge At Saw Mill Creek, The
400 Sawmill Creek Dr W (44839-2261)
PHONE..................................419 433-3800
Greg Hill, *Partner*
Tom Bleile, *Partner*
Tara Jones, *Marketing Mgr*
EMP: 150
SALES (est): 5.2MM **Privately Held**
WEB: www.sawmillcreek.com
SIC: 7011 6512 5813 5812 Hotels & motels; nonresidential building operators; drinking places; eating places; marinas

(G-12031)
SAWMILL CREEK RESORT LTD
400 Sawmill Creek Dr W (44839-2261)
PHONE..................................419 433-3800
Greg Hill, *President*
Jeff Oococo, *COO*
Jim Hill, *CFO*
Karen Wood, *Human Res Dir*
Sawmill Creek, *Webmaster*
EMP: 170
SALES (est): 6.5MM **Privately Held**
WEB: www.greatlakesresorts.com
SIC: 5812 7011 Eating places; resort hotel

(G-12032)
SAWMILL GREEK GOLF RACQUET CLB
Also Called: Sawmill Creek Golf Racquet CLB
300 Sawmill Creek Dr W (44839-2260)
PHONE..................................419 433-3789

GEOGRAPHIC

Chris Bleile, *Director*
EMP: 90
SALES (est): 1.8MM **Privately Held**
SIC: 7997 Golf club, membership

(G-12033)
SOUTH SHORE MARINE SERVICES
1611 Sawmill Pkwy (44839-2247)
P.O. Box 25 (44839-0025)
PHONE...............................419 433-5798
Thomas Mack, *President*
Norm Baur, *Opers Mgr*
Cory Frankboner, *Accountant*
Stephanie Payne, *Human Resources*
Scott Gilbert, *Sales Staff*
EMP: 35
SQ FT: 9,000
SALES (est): 6.1MM **Privately Held**
WEB: www.southshoremarine.com
SIC: 4499 5551 Boat cleaning; motor boat dealers

(G-12034)
VITAL RESOURCES INC
1119 Sheltered Brook Dr (44839-2824)
PHONE...............................440 614-5150
Charlene R Connell, *CEO*
Bruce Mihalick, *Vice Pres*
EMP: 25
SALES (est): 2.4MM **Privately Held**
SIC: 7379 Computer related consulting services

(G-12035)
WILKES & COMPANY INC
205 Sprowl Rd (44839-2635)
P.O. Box 98 (44839-0098)
PHONE...............................419 433-2325
Glen Ginesi, *President*
David Rengel, *Vice Pres*
EMP: 25 **EST:** 1912
SQ FT: 18,600
SALES (est): 5.7MM **Privately Held**
WEB: www.wilkesandcompany.com
SIC: 1711 Plumbing contractors; warm air heating & air conditioning contractor; mechanical contractor; process piping contractor

---

Independence
Cuyahoga County

(G-12036)
ACCEL PERFORMANCE GROUP LLC (DH)
6100 Oak Tree Blvd # 200 (44131-6914)
PHONE...............................216 658-6413
Robert Tobey, *CEO*
Robert Romanelli, *President*
Andrew Mazzarella, *CFO*
▲ **EMP:** 180
SQ FT: 200,000
SALES (est): 50.8MM
SALES (corp-wide): 109.9MM **Privately Held**
WEB: www.mrgasket.com
SIC: 3714 5013 3053 Motor vehicle parts & accessories; automotive supplies & parts; gaskets, packing & sealing devices
HQ: Msdp Group Llc
   1350 Pullman Dr Dr14
   El Paso TX 79936
   915 857-5200

(G-12037)
ACCURATE GROUP HOLDINGS INC (PA)
6000 Freedom Square Dr # 300 (44131-2547)
PHONE...............................216 520-1740
Paul Doman, *President*
Michael Lynch, *CFO*
EMP: 59
SALES (est): 28.7MM **Privately Held**
SIC: 6361 6411 Real estate title insurance;

(G-12038)
ACXIOM CORPORATION
5005 Rockside Rd Ste 600 (44131-6827)
PHONE...............................216 520-3181
Christina Basmagy, *COO*

EMP: 240
SALES (corp-wide): 9.7B **Publicly Held**
WEB: www.acxiom.com
SIC: 7375 On-line data base information retrieval
HQ: Acxiom Llc
   301 E Dave Ward Dr
   Conway AR 72032
   501 342-1000

(G-12039)
ACXIOM INFO SEC SVCS INC
6111 Oak Tree Blvd (44131-2589)
PHONE...............................216 685-7600
Fax: 216 615-7677
EMP: 350
SQ FT: 15,000
SALES (est): 21.8MM
SALES (corp-wide): 89.8MM **Privately Held**
SIC: 7389 Business Services
PA: Sterling Infosystems, Inc.
   1 State St Fl 24
   New York NY 10004
   800 899-2272

(G-12040)
AEROTEK INC
Also Called: Aerotek 58
5990 W Creek Rd Ste 150 (44131-2181)
PHONE...............................216 573-5520
Ken Sesco, *Principal*
EMP: 30
SALES (corp-wide): 12.3B **Privately Held**
WEB: www.searchhomesmn.com
SIC: 7363 Temporary help service
HQ: Aerotek, Inc.
   7301 Parkway Dr
   Hanover MD 21076
   410 694-5100

(G-12041)
AGILE GLOBAL SOLUTIONS INC
5755 Granger Rd Ste 610 (44131-1458)
PHONE...............................916 655-7745
EMP: 29
SALES (corp-wide): 5.2MM **Privately Held**
SIC: 7372 Business oriented computer software
PA: Agile Global Solutions, Inc.
   13405 Folsom Blvd Ste 515
   Folsom CA 95630
   916 353-1780

(G-12042)
AIRGAS USA LLC
6055 Rockside Woods (44131-2301)
PHONE...............................216 642-6600
EMP: 287
SALES (corp-wide): 125.9MM **Privately Held**
SIC: 5169 5084 5087 Compressed gas; industrial gases; industrial chemicals; welding machinery & equipment; safety equipment; janitors' supplies
HQ: Airgas Usa, Llc
   259 N Radnor Chester Rd # 100
   Radnor PA 19087
   610 687-5253

(G-12043)
ALLIANCE LEGAL SOLUTIONS LLC
Also Called: Major Legal Services
6161 Oak Tree Blvd # 300 (44131-2581)
PHONE...............................216 525-0100
Matt Lyon, *CFO*
EMP: 57
SQ FT: 2,000
SALES (est): 1.7MM **Privately Held**
SIC: 7361 Labor contractors (employment agency)

(G-12044)
ALLIANCE SOLUTIONS GROUP LLC (PA)
Also Called: Talentlaunch
6161 Oak Tree Blvd (44131-2516)
PHONE...............................216 503-1690
Aaron Grossman, *President*
Doug Dandurand, *President*
Matt Lyon, *CFO*
Kevin Cardiff, *Sales Mgr*

EMP: 39
SQ FT: 7,000
SALES (est): 5MM **Privately Held**
WEB: www.alliancestaffingsolutions.com
SIC: 7363 7361 Temporary help service; employment agencies

(G-12045)
AP/AIM INDPNDNCE SITES TRS LLC
Also Called: Embassy Suites
5800 Rckside Woods Blvd N (44131-2346)
PHONE...............................216 986-9900
Richard Somsak, *General Mgr*
Randy Torres,
EMP: 99
SALES (est): 950K **Privately Held**
SIC: 7011 Hotels & motels

(G-12046)
AREA TEMPS INC (PA)
4511 Rockside Rd Ste 190 (44131-2157)
PHONE...............................216 781-5350
Raymond Castelluccio, *CEO*
Kent Castelluccio, *President*
Connie Gramoy, *Controller*
Gail Enders, *Sales Mgr*
Karen Rosenhoffer, *Sales Mgr*
EMP: 40
SALES (est): 87.8MM **Privately Held**
WEB: www.areatemps.com
SIC: 7363 Temporary help service; office help supply service

(G-12047)
ARYSEN INC
Also Called: Dynamic Solution Associates
5005 Rockside Rd Ste 600 (44131-6827)
PHONE...............................440 230-4400
Richard Ken Hartman, *Managing Dir*
EMP: 57
SALES (est): 20MM **Privately Held**
WEB: www.dsasite.com
SIC: 8742 Business consultant

(G-12048)
AUTOMATIC DATA PROCESSING INC
Also Called: ADP
7007 E Pleasant Valley Rd (44131-5543)
PHONE...............................216 447-1980
David Miller, *District Mgr*
Meredith Parrilla, *District Mgr*
Gary Kudej, *Manager*
Kim Reinhardt, *Manager*
John Sciano, *IT/INT Sup*
EMP: 250
SQ FT: 20,000
SALES (corp-wide): 13.3B **Publicly Held**
SIC: 7374 Data processing service; computer processing services; data entry service
PA: Automatic Data Processing, Inc.
   1 Adp Blvd Ste 1 # 1
   Roseland NJ 07068
   973 974-5000

(G-12049)
BEAR COMMUNICATIONS INC
900 Resource Dr Ste 8 (44131-1884)
PHONE...............................216 642-1670
EMP: 35
SALES (corp-wide): 159.4MM **Privately Held**
SIC: 5065 Communication equipment
HQ: Bear Communications, Inc.
   4009 Dist Dr Ste 200
   Garland TX 75041

(G-12050)
BOBBY TRIPODI FOUNDATION INC (PA)
Also Called: CORNERSTONE OF HOPE BE-REAVEMEN
5905 Brecksville Rd (44131-1517)
P.O. Box 31555 (44131-0555)
PHONE...............................216 524-3787
Mark Tripodi, *Exec Dir*
EMP: 29
SALES: 1.9MM **Privately Held**
SIC: 8322 General counseling services

(G-12051)
BUTTERFLY INC
8200 E Pleasant Valley Rd (44131-5523)
PHONE...............................440 892-7777
Jim Eble, *President*
EMP: 30 **EST:** 2009
SALES (est): 4.4MM **Privately Held**
SIC: 4911 Electric services

(G-12052)
C & K INDUSTRIAL SERVICES INC (PA)
5617 E Schaaf Rd (44131-1334)
PHONE...............................216 642-0055
Arthur Karas, *President*
George Karas, *Vice Pres*
Matthew Fechter, *Project Mgr*
Sonjay Jones, *Project Mgr*
Cody Malkemus, *Project Mgr*
EMP: 100
SQ FT: 8,000
SALES (est): 119.5MM **Privately Held**
WEB: www.ckindustrial.com
SIC: 4959 7349 Sweeping service: road, airport, parking lot, etc.; building maintenance services

(G-12053)
CANON SOLUTIONS AMERICA INC
6100 Oak Tree Blvd (44131-2544)
PHONE...............................216 446-3830
Craig Palmer, *Branch Mgr*
EMP: 75
SALES (corp-wide): 35.1B **Privately Held**
SIC: 5044 Office equipment
HQ: Canon Solutions America, Inc.
   1 Canon Park
   Melville NY 11747
   631 330-5000

(G-12054)
CANON SOLUTIONS AMERICA INC
Also Called: Dps
6161 Oak Tree Blvd # 301 (44131-2516)
PHONE...............................216 750-2980
EMP: 27
SALES (corp-wide): 35.1B **Privately Held**
WEB: www.imagistics.com
SIC: 5112 Computer & photocopying supplies
HQ: Canon Solutions America, Inc.
   1 Canon Park
   Melville NY 11747
   631 330-5000

(G-12055)
CBIZ TECHNOLOGIES LLC
6050 Oak Tree Blvd (44131-6927)
PHONE...............................216 447-9000
Christine Artlip, *President*
Rhett Butler, *Managing Dir*
Tara Becker, *Area Mgr*
Todd Flessner, *Vice Pres*
Mary Jane McGrew, *Vice Pres*
EMP: 50
SQ FT: 6,000
SALES (est): 10MM **Publicly Held**
WEB: www.cbiztechnologies.com
SIC: 7379 ; computer related consulting services
PA: Cbiz, Inc.
   6050 Oak Tree Blvd # 500
   Cleveland OH 44131

(G-12056)
CELLCO PARTNERSHIP
Also Called: Verizon Wireless
6712 Rockside Rd (44131-2323)
PHONE...............................216 573-5880
Robert Moretti, *Manager*
EMP: 30
SALES (corp-wide): 130.8B **Publicly Held**
SIC: 4812 5999 Cellular telephone services; telephone equipment & systems
HQ: Cellco Partnership
   1 Verizon Way
   Basking Ridge NJ 07920

(G-12057)
CERTIFIED SEC SOLUTIONS INC (PA)
6050 Oak Tree Blvd (44131-6927)
PHONE..............................216 785-2986
Kevin Von Keyserling, *President*
John Cilli, *General Mgr*
Judah Aspler, *Vice Pres*
Jason Fiorotto, *Vice Pres*
Chris Hickman, *Vice Pres*
EMP: 50
SQ FT: 6,000
SALES (est): 10.3MM **Privately Held**
WEB: www.css-security.com
SIC: 7371 Computer software systems
analysis & design, custom

(G-12058)
CIGNA CORPORATION
3 Summit Park Dr Ste 250 (44131-2598)
PHONE..............................216 642-1700
Douglas Daubenspeck, *Branch Mgr*
Terri Kozmon, *Manager*
Andrea Poklar-Byrne, *Agent*
EMP: 226
SALES (corp-wide): 141.6B **Publicly Held**
SIC: 6311 Life insurance
HQ: Cigna Holding Company
900 Cottage Grove Rd
Bloomfield CT 06002
860 226-6000

(G-12059)
CLEVELAND ANESTHESIA GROUP
6701 Rockside Rd Ste 200 (44131-2316)
P.O. Box 94908, Cleveland (44101-4908)
PHONE..............................216 901-5706
John Bastulli, *President*
Keith Levendorf, *Treasurer*
Joyce Hardaway, *Med Doctor*
Robert Rogoff, *Med Doctor*
EMP: 42
SALES (est): 3.2MM **Privately Held**
SIC: 8011 Anesthesiologist

(G-12060)
CLEVELAND CLINIC COMMUNITY ONC
6100 W Creek Rd Ste 15 (44131-2133)
PHONE..............................216 447-9747
Kenneth Weiss, *Podiatrist*
Nanette Rock, *Director*
Colleen Binder, *Receptionist*
EMP: 35
SALES (est): 2.2MM **Privately Held**
SIC: 8011 Oncologist

(G-12061)
CLEVELAND CLINIC FOUNDATION
Also Called: Cleveland Clinic Health System
6801 Brecksville Rd # 10 (44131-5058)
PHONE..............................216 986-4000
Bertram Sue, *Branch Mgr*
Mary Hodgson, *Info Tech Dir*
EMP: 85
SALES (corp-wide): 8.9B **Privately Held**
SIC: 6733 Trusts
PA: The Cleveland Clinic Foundation
9500 Euclid Ave
Cleveland OH 44195
216 636-8335

(G-12062)
COOK PAVING AND CNSTR CO
4545 Spring Rd (44131-1023)
PHONE..............................216 267-7705
Linda Fletcher, *President*
Jim Matheos, *COO*
Michael Alex, *Vice Pres*
Keith L Rogers, *Admin Sec*
EMP: 50 EST: 1941
SQ FT: 12,000
SALES (est): 9.2MM **Privately Held**
SIC: 1623 8741 1795 1611 Sewer line
construction; underground utilities con-
tractor; construction management; wreck-
ing & demolition work; highway & street
construction; blacktop (asphalt) work

(G-12063)
COVIA HOLDINGS CORPORATION (HQ)
3 Summit Park Dr Ste 700 (44131-6901)
PHONE..............................440 214-3284
Richard A Navarre, *Ch of Bd*
Jenniffer D Deckard, *President*
Campbell J Jones, *COO*
Andrew D Eich, *CFO*
Gerald L Clancey, *Ch Credit Ofcr*
◆ EMP: 90
SALES: 1.8B
SALES (corp-wide): 136.2MM **Publicly Held**
WEB: www.unimin.com
SIC: 1446 1499 1422 1459 Silica mining;
quartz crystal (pure) mining; dolomite,
crushed & broken-quarrying; nepheline
syenite quarrying; steam railroads; con-
struction sand & gravel
PA: Scr - Sibelco
Plantin En Moretuslei 1a
Antwerpen 2018
322 366-11

(G-12064)
CSA AMRICA TSTG CRTFCATION LLC
8501 E Pleasant Valley Rd (44131-5516)
PHONE..............................216 524-4990
Raymond Varcho,
EMP: 340
SALES (est): 5.3MM **Privately Held**
SIC: 7389 Inspection & testing services

(G-12065)
DAVITA INC
4801 Acorn Dr Ste 1 (44131-2576)
PHONE..............................216 525-0990
Ted Vancs, *Mktg Dir*
Bob Badal, *Branch Mgr*
EMP: 27 **Publicly Held**
SIC: 8092 Kidney dialysis centers
PA: Davita Inc.
2000 16th St
Denver CO 80202

(G-12066)
DENTAL ONE INC
6200 Oak Tree Blvd # 220 (44131-6933)
PHONE..............................216 584-1000
Amy Bogle, *Opers Staff*
Jennifer Chlarson, *Opers Staff*
Amber Orton, *Opers Staff*
Alexa Raynor, *Opers Staff*
Rene Sullivan, *Opers Staff*
EMP: 50
SALES (corp-wide): 77.5MM **Privately Held**
SIC: 8742 8021 Business consultant; of-
fices & clinics of dentists; dentists' office
PA: Dental One, Inc.
7160 Dallas Pkwy Ste 400
Plano TX 75024
972 755-0800

(G-12067)
DIGERONIMO AGGREGATES LLC
6220 E Schaaf Rd (44131-1332)
PHONE..............................216 524-2950
Vic Digeronimo, *President*
Eric Dombrowski, *Technology*
EMP: 31
SALES (est): 8.8MM **Privately Held**
SIC: 5032 Aggregate

(G-12068)
DOUGLAS R DENNY
6480 Rckside Woods Blvd S (44131-2233)
PHONE..............................216 236-2400
Douglas Denny, *Principal*
EMP: 42
SALES (est): 831.6K **Privately Held**
SIC: 7389 Personal service agents, bro-
kers & bureaus

(G-12069)
EMC CORPORATION
6480 Rcksde Wds Blvd S # 330
(44131-2222)
PHONE..............................216 606-2000
Tom Weldon, *Manager*
Tony Emanuel, *Senior Mgr*
EMP: 39

SALES (corp-wide): 90.6B **Publicly Held**
WEB: www.emc.com
SIC: 3572 7372 Computer storage de-
vices; prepackaged software
HQ: Emc Corporation
176 South St
Hopkinton MA 01748
508 435-1000

(G-12070)
EMPLOYEESCREENIQ INC
Also Called: Background Information Svcs
6111 Oak Tree Blvd # 400 (44131-2585)
PHONE..............................216 514-2800
EMP: 80
SQ FT: 16,000
SALES (est): 7.9MM **Privately Held**
SIC: 7389 Business Services
PA: Sterling Infosystems, Inc.
1 State St Fl 24
New York NY 10004
800 899-2272

(G-12071)
ESC OF CUYAHOGA COUNTY
6393 Oak Tree Blvd # 300 (44131-6957)
PHONE..............................216 524-3000
Dr B Menderink, *Superintendent*
Dr Bob Menderink, *Superintendent*
EMP: 90
SALES (est): 707K **Privately Held**
SIC: 8331 Manpower training

(G-12072)
FAIRMOUNT MINERALS LLC
Also Called: Fairmount Santrol
3 Summit Park Dr Ste 700 (44131-6901)
PHONE..............................269 926-9450
Jennifer Deckard, *CEO*
EMP: 200
SALES (est): 988MM
SALES (corp-wide): 136.2MM **Publicly Held**
SIC: 1446 Industrial sand
HQ: Fairmount Santrol Inc.
3 Summit Park Dr Ste 700
Independence OH 44131
440 214-3200

(G-12073)
FARMERS GROUP INC
Also Called: Farmers Insurance
5990 W Creek Rd Ste 160 (44131-2181)
PHONE..............................216 750-4010
Larry Gallagher, *Manager*
EMP: 30
SALES (corp-wide): 65.1B **Privately Held**
WEB: www.farmers.com
SIC: 6411 Insurance agents, brokers &
service
HQ: Farmers Group, Inc.
6301 Owensmouth Ave
Woodland Hills CA 91367
323 932-3200

(G-12074)
FML RESIN LLC
3 Summit Park Dr Ste 700 (44131-6901)
PHONE..............................440 214-3200
Jenniffer D Deckard, *President*
EMP: 27
SALES (est): 847.3K **Privately Held**
SIC: 1442 Construction sand & gravel

(G-12075)
FOREMOST INSURANCE COMPANY
Also Called: Bristol West Casualty Insur Co
5990 W Creek Rd Ste 160 (44131-2181)
PHONE..............................216 674-7000
Frank Formichelli, *Branch Mgr*
EMP: 90
SALES (corp-wide): 65.1B **Privately Held**
SIC: 6331 Fire, marine & casualty insur-
ance
HQ: Foremost Insurance Company
5600 Beechtree Ln Se
Caledonia MI 49316
616 942-3000

(G-12076)
GALLERY HOLDINGS LLC
Also Called: Hr Plus
6111 Oak Tree Blvd (44131-2589)
PHONE..............................773 693-6220
EMP: 55
SQ FT: 10,500
SALES (est): 1.1MM
SALES (corp-wide): 89.8MM **Privately Held**
SIC: 7361 Employment Agency
PA: Sterling Infosystems, Inc.
1 State St Fl 24
New York NY 10004
800 899-2272

(G-12077)
GRAFTECH HOLDINGS INC
6100 Oak Tree Blvd # 300 (44131-6970)
PHONE..............................216 676-2000
Joel L Hawthorne, *CEO*
Bill McFadden, *General Mgr*
Erick R Asmussen, *Vice Pres*
John D Moran, *Vice Pres*
Vicki Vesel, *Safety Mgr*
EMP: 310
SALES (est): 757.5K
SALES (corp-wide): 8.5B **Publicly Held**
SIC: 1499 3624 Graphite mining; carbon &
graphite products
HQ: Graftech International Ltd.
982 Keynote Cir Ste 6
Brooklyn Heights OH 44131

(G-12078)
GREAT LAKES COLD LOGISTICS
Also Called: Coldstream Logistics
6548 Brecksville Rd (44131-4800)
PHONE..............................216 520-0930
Daniel Palus, *President*
Howard Schillinger, *Vice Pres*
EMP: 50
SALES (est): 2.1MM **Privately Held**
SIC: 4789 Cargo loading & unloading serv-
ices

(G-12079)
HEARTLAND HOSPICE SERVICES LLC
Also Called: Heartland HM Hlth Care Hospice
4807 Rockside Rd Ste 110 (44131-2140)
PHONE..............................216 901-1464
Diane Dawson, *Manager*
EMP: 100
SALES (corp-wide): 2.4B **Publicly Held**
SIC: 8082 Home health care services
HQ: Heartland Hospice Services, Llc
333 N Summit St
Toledo OH 43604

(G-12080)
HUMANA INC
6100 Oak Tree Blvd (44131-2544)
PHONE..............................216 328-2047
Larry Farmer, *Manager*
EMP: 41
SALES (corp-wide): 56.9B **Publicly Held**
SIC: 6324 Health maintenance organiza-
tion (HMO), insurance only
PA: Humana Inc.
500 W Main St Ste 300
Louisville KY 40202
502 580-1000

(G-12081)
IHS ENTERPRISE INC (PA)
Also Called: PWC International
5755 Granger Rd Ste 905 (44131-1461)
PHONE..............................216 588-9078
Ansir Junaid, *President*
Liaz Shah, *Vice Pres*
EMP: 150
SQ FT: 75,000
SALES (est): 11.9MM **Privately Held**
SIC: 4731 Domestic freight forwarding

(G-12082)
INDEPENDENCE EXCAVATING INC (PA)
5720 E Schaaf Rd (44131-1396)
PHONE..............................216 524-1700
Victor Digeronimo Sr, *CEO*
Victor Digeronimo Jr, *President*
Rick Digeronimo, *Vice Pres*

Rob D Digeronimo, *Vice Pres*
Brandon Meyer, *Project Mgr*
▲ **EMP:** 50
SQ FT: 35,000
SALES: 220.5MM **Privately Held**
WEB: www.indexc.com
SIC: 1629 1794 1611 1771 Land preparation construction; excavation work; general contractor, highway & street construction; concrete repair; demolition, buildings & other structures

(G-12083)
INDEPENDENCE LOCAL SCHOOLS
6111 Archwood Rd (44131-4901)
PHONE.................................216 642-5865
Robert Sykora, *Principal*
EMP: 29
SALES (est): 418.1K **Privately Held**
SIC: 8211 8351 Public elementary & secondary schools; child day care services
PA: Independence Local Schools
7733 Stone Rd
Independence OH 44131

(G-12084)
JAGI SPRINGHILL LLC
Also Called: Springhill Suites Independence
6060 Rockside Pl (44131-2225)
PHONE.................................216 264-4190
Michael Nanosky, *President*
EMP: 35
SALES (est): 242.5K **Privately Held**
SIC: 7011 Hotels

(G-12085)
KFORCE INC
3 Summit Park Dr Ste 550 (44131-6902)
PHONE.................................216 643-8141
Jeff Farrington, *Director*
EMP: 40
SALES (corp-wide): 1.4B **Publicly Held**
SIC: 7361 Executive placement
PA: Kforce Inc.
1001 E Palm Ave
Tampa FL 33605
813 552-5000

(G-12086)
KINGSLEY GATE PARTNERS LLC
6155 Rockside Rd Ste 203 (44131-2217)
PHONE.................................216 400-9880
EMP: 57
SALES (corp-wide): 4.6MM **Privately Held**
SIC: 8742 Management consulting services
PA: Kingsley Gate Partners, Llc
2711 Lbj Fwy Ste 850
Dallas TX 75234
972 726-5550

(G-12087)
LEGEND EQUITIES CORPORATION
5755 Granger Rd Ste 910 (44131-1461)
PHONE.................................216 741-3113
Todd Stout, *Manager*
EMP: 75
SIC: 7389 Personal service agents, brokers & bureaus
PA: Legend Equities Corporation
4600 E Park Dr Ste 300
West Palm Beach FL 33410

(G-12088)
LEVEL SEVEN
Also Called: S. B. Stone & Company
4807 Rockside Rd Ste 700 (44131-2159)
PHONE.................................216 524-9055
Stuart Taylor, *CEO*
Gina Drobnick, *COO*
Alysia Kaplan, *Project Mgr*
Larry Morris, *CFO*
Lisa Locklear, *Marketing Staff*
EMP: 75 **EST:** 2010
SALES (est): 8.6MM **Privately Held**
SIC: 8742 Management consulting services

(G-12089)
LEWIS P C JACKSON
6100 Oak Tree Blvd # 400 (44131-6944)
PHONE.................................216 750-0404
Jeffrey Keiper, *Owner*
Roland De, *Shareholder*
Stephen R Beiting, *Associate*
EMP: 36
SALES (corp-wide): 277.6MM **Privately Held**
SIC: 8111 General practice attorney, lawyer
PA: Lewis P C Jackson
1133 Weschester Ave
White Plains NY 10604
914 872-8060

(G-12090)
LIFE LINE SCREENING
6150 Oak Tree Blvd # 200 (44131-2569)
PHONE.................................216 581-6556
Colin Scully, *CEO*
Timothy Phillips, *Vice Pres*
EMP: 100
SALES (est): 9.8MM **Privately Held**
SIC: 8011 8062 Medical centers; general medical & surgical hospitals

(G-12091)
LIFE LINE SCREENING AMER LTD
6150 Oak Tree Blvd # 200 (44131-6917)
PHONE.................................216 581-6556
Mike Nicoletti, *Principal*
EMP: 206 **Privately Held**
SIC: 8099 Health screening service
PA: Life Line Screening Of America Ltd.
6150 Oak Tree Blvd
Independence OH 44131

(G-12092)
LIFE LINE SCREENING AMER LTD (PA)
6150 Oak Tree Blvd (44131-6917)
PHONE.................................216 581-6556
Sean Schultz, *CEO*
Andy Manganaro, *Principal*
Colin Scully, *Chairman*
Timothy Phillips, *Exec VP*
Eric Greenberg, *Vice Pres*
EMP: 150
SQ FT: 25,000
SALES (est): 45.2MM **Privately Held**
WEB: www.llsaz.com
SIC: 8099 Health screening service

(G-12093)
LIGHTHOUSE INSURANCE GROUP LLC (PA)
6100 Rockside Woods Blvd # 300
(44131-2340)
PHONE.................................216 503-2439
Jason Farro, *CEO*
Charles Farro, *Principal*
EMP: 80
SALES (est): 17.1MM **Privately Held**
SIC: 6411 Insurance agents

(G-12094)
LOCUM MEDICAL GROUP LLC
6100 Oak Tree Blvd (44131-2544)
PHONE.................................216 464-2125
Daniel Groth, *CEO*
Nancy Taber, *President*
Daniel Burg, *Exec VP*
Betsy Rader, *Senior VP*
Lisa Toth, *QC Mgr*
EMP: 55
SQ FT: 9,600
SALES (est): 2.7MM
SALES (corp-wide): 27.2B **Privately Held**
WEB: www.locummedical.com
SIC: 7363 Medical help service
HQ: Randstad Professionals Us, Llc
150 Presidential Way Fl 4
Woburn MA 01801

(G-12095)
LONGBOW RESEARCH LLC (PA)
6050 Oak Tree Blvd # 350 (44131-6931)
PHONE.................................216 986-0700
Anthony Deem, *Vice Pres*
Bob Wazevich, *Vice Pres*
Nikolay Todorov, *Research*

Rick Jamieson, *Sales Staff*
Lee Middlekauff, *Sales Staff*
EMP: 60
SQ FT: 15,000
SALES (est): 10.9MM **Privately Held**
SIC: 6282 Investment research

(G-12096)
M-A BUILDING AND MAINT CO
5515 Old Brecksville Rd (44131-1525)
PHONE.................................216 391-5577
Peter F Wamelink, *President*
Beverly Wamelink, *Corp Secy*
John Wamelink, *Vice Pres*
Scott Luthman, *Project Mgr*
Brian Vanatta, *Manager*
EMP: 25
SQ FT: 12,000
SALES (est): 7.2MM **Privately Held**
SIC: 1542 Nonresidential Construction

(G-12097)
MAXIM HEALTHCARE SERVICES INC
6155 Rockside Rd (44131-2200)
PHONE.................................216 606-3000
EMP: 80
SALES (corp-wide): 1.5B **Privately Held**
SIC: 7363 Medical help service
PA: Maxim Healthcare Services, Inc.
7227 Lee Deforest Dr
Columbia MD 21046
410 910-1500

(G-12098)
MMI-CPR LLC
7100 E Pleasant Valley Rd (44131-5544)
PHONE.................................216 674-0645
EMP: 50
SQ FT: 15,000
SALES (est): 2.7MM **Privately Held**
SIC: 7629 Electrical Repair

(G-12099)
MOLINA HEALTHCARE INC
Also Called: Molina Healthcare of Ohio
6161 Oak Tree Blvd (44131-2516)
PHONE.................................216 606-1400
EMP: 271
SALES (corp-wide): 18.8B **Publicly Held**
SIC: 8099 Childbirth preparation clinic
PA: Molina Healthcare, Inc.
200 Oceangate Ste 100
Long Beach CA 90802
562 435-3666

(G-12100)
MR ROOTER PLUMBING CORPORATION
8200 E Pleasant Valley Rd (44131-5523)
PHONE.................................419 625-4444
James Eble, *President*
▲ **EMP:** 50
SQ FT: 4,000
SALES (est): 10.6MM **Privately Held**
SIC: 7699 Sewer cleaning & rodding

(G-12101)
NATIONAL YLLOW PAGES MEDIA LLC
Also Called: Linkmedia 360
2 Summit Park Dr Ste 630 (44131-2565)
PHONE.................................216 447-9400
Dave Wolf, *Managing Prtnr*
Kurt Krejny, *Vice Pres*
Debbie Schuckert, *Accounts Exec*
Barra Terrigno, *Accounts Exec*
Joe Heney, *Marketing Mgr*
EMP: 50
SQ FT: 6,126
SALES (est): 8MM **Privately Held**
WEB: www.nypmedia.com
SIC: 7311 Advertising agencies

(G-12102)
NATIONS LENDING CORPORATION (PA)
Also Called: N L C
4 Summit Park Dr Ste 200 (44131-2583)
PHONE.................................440 842-4817
Jeremy E Sopko, *CEO*
George Chapin, *President*
Corey Caster, *Exec VP*
Frank Cimperman, *Vice Pres*
Mark Fantozzi, *Vice Pres*

EMP: 58
SQ FT: 8,500
SALES (est): 28.2MM **Privately Held**
SIC: 6162 6163 Mortgage bankers; mortgage brokers arranging for loans, using money of others

(G-12103)
NEW YORK LIFE INSURANCE CO
6100 Oak Tree Blvd # 300 (44131-6970)
PHONE.................................216 520-1345
Jerry Fish, *Managing Dir*
Gerry Fish, *Manager*
Serra Sandlin, *Officer*
EMP: 200
SALES (corp-wide): 18.3B **Privately Held**
WEB: www.newyorklife.com
SIC: 6411 Insurance agents & brokers
PA: New York Life Insurance Company
51 Madison Ave Bsmt 1b
New York NY 10010
212 576-7000

(G-12104)
NORTHAST SRGICAL ASSOC OF OHIO (PA)
6100 Rckside Woods Blvd N (44131-2366)
PHONE.................................216 643-2780
Keith Warner, *President*
Shukri Elkhariri,
Seung Kwon Lee,
Ivan Tewarson,
EMP: 43
SALES (est): 5.6MM **Privately Held**
SIC: 8011 Surgeon

(G-12105)
OHIO ALARM INC
Also Called: American Response Center
750 W Resource Dr Ste 200 (44131-1879)
PHONE.................................216 692-1204
James Osborne, *President*
Stan Nerderman, *Vice Pres*
Ron Price, *Vice Pres*
EMP: 30
SQ FT: 5,000
SALES (est): 1.6MM **Privately Held**
SIC: 5063 Alarm systems

(G-12106)
OLD RPBLIC TTLE NTHRN OHIO LLC
6480 Rckside Woods Blvd S (44131-2233)
PHONE.................................216 524-5700
Robert A Piazza,
EMP: 356
SALES (est): 82.1MM
SALES (corp-wide): 6B **Publicly Held**
SIC: 6411 6162 6211 Insurance agents, brokers & service; mortgage bankers; underwriters, security
HQ: Old Republic National Title Insurance Company
400 2nd Ave S
Minneapolis MN 55401
612 371-1111

(G-12107)
PFG VENTURES LP (PA)
Also Called: Proforma
8800 E Pleasant Valley Rd # 1
(44131-5558)
PHONE.................................216 520-8400
Brian Smith, *President*
Greg Muzzillo, *Principal*
Vera Muzzillo, *Co-CEO*
Tom Rizzi, *Senior VP*
EMP: 100
SQ FT: 30,000
SALES (est): 53.4MM **Privately Held**
WEB: www.proforma.com
SIC: 5112 Stationery & office supplies

(G-12108)
POLYMER ADDITIVES HOLDINGS INC (DH)
Also Called: Valtris
7500 E Pleasant Valley Rd (44131-5536)
PHONE.................................216 875-7200
Paul Angus, *President*
Anthony A Tamer, *President*
Steve Hughes, *Vice Pres*
Jay Xu, *Vice Pres*
Jim Mason, *VP Opers*

EMP: 200
SALES: 105MM **Privately Held**
SIC: 5169 2899 Chemicals & allied products; chemical preparations; fire retardant chemicals
HQ: H.I.G. Capital, Inc.
1450 Brickell Ave Fl 31
Miami FL 33131
305 379-2322

(G-12109)
PRECISION ENVIRONMENTAL CO (HQ)
5500 Old Brecksville Rd (44131-1508)
PHONE..................................216 642-6040
Tony Digeronimo, *President*
Thomas Zuchowski, *General Mgr*
John Savage, *Vice Pres*
George Pappas, *Project Dir*
Jim Bower, *Project Mgr*
EMP: 296
SALES (est): 29.4MM
SALES (corp-wide): 46.1MM **Privately Held**
WEB: www.precisionprocut.com
SIC: 1799 Asbestos removal & encapsulation; lead burning
PA: Integrated Solutions, Inc.
215 S Laura Ave
Wichita KS 67211
316 264-7050

(G-12110)
PRECISION METALFORMING ASSN (PA)
6363 Oak Tree Blvd (44131-2556)
PHONE..................................216 241-1482
William E Gaskin, *CEO*
Jody Fledderman, *Vice Ch Bd*
Roy Hardy, *President*
David C Klotz, *President*
Daniel E Ellashek, *Vice Pres*
▲ EMP: 41
SQ FT: 20,000
SALES: 6.3MM **Privately Held**
SIC: 8611 2731 Trade associations; book publishing

(G-12111)
RANDSTAD TECHNOLOGIES LLC
6100 Oak Tree Blvd # 110 (44131-2544)
PHONE..................................216 520-0206
Jeff Rosen, *Branch Mgr*
EMP: 66
SALES (corp-wide): 27.2B **Privately Held**
WEB: www.sapphire.com
SIC: 7361 Employment agencies
HQ: Randstad Technologies, Llc
150 Presidential Way # 300
Woburn MA 01801
781 938-1910

(G-12112)
REDWOOD LIVING INC
7510 E Pleasant Valley Rd (44131-5536)
PHONE..................................216 360-9441
David Conwill, *CEO*
Steven Kimmelman, *Ch of Bd*
Scott Jewell, *Regional Mgr*
John Lateulere, *Vice Pres*
Rose Mills, *Comms Dir*
EMP: 201
SALES (est): 2.3MM **Privately Held**
SIC: 8742 Management consulting services

(G-12113)
RESOURCE TITLE NAT AGCY INC
7100 E Pleasant Valley Rd # 100 (44131-5544)
PHONE..................................216 520-0050
Leslie C Rennell, *President*
Leslie Rennell, *General Mgr*
Anita Dembkowski, *Corp Secy*
Andrew W Rennell, *Vice Pres*
Richard J Rennell, *CFO*
EMP: 64
SQ FT: 9,000
SALES (est): 26.4MM **Privately Held**
SIC: 6361 6531 Real estate title insurance; escrow agent, real estate

(G-12114)
RGIS LLC
4500 Rockside Rd Ste 340 (44131-2170)
PHONE..................................216 447-1744
Richard Kaimer, *Branch Mgr*
EMP: 79
SALES (corp-wide): 6.8B **Publicly Held**
SIC: 7389 Inventory computing service
HQ: Rgis, Llc
2000 Taylor Rd
Auburn Hills MI 48326
248 651-2511

(G-12115)
ROCKSIDE HOSPITALITY LLC
Also Called: Crowne Plaza Clevenland
5300 Rockside Rd (44131-2118)
PHONE..................................216 524-0700
Joe Isernia, *General Mgr*
Gloria Maciak, *Controller*
Cathy Ruhling, *Sales Dir*
Barb Williams, *Sales Mgr*
Stephanie Irelan, *Director*
EMP: 81
SALES (est): 1MM **Privately Held**
SIC: 7011 Hotel, franchised

(G-12116)
ROE DENTAL LABORATORY INC
7165 E Pleasant Valley Rd (44131-5541)
PHONE..................................216 663-2233
Bruce Kowalski, *President*
Dana Banks, *Financial Exec*
Don Maddox, *Manager*
Michael Sims, *Supervisor*
Liz Goss, *Technical Staff*
EMP: 57 EST: 1930
SQ FT: 8,500
SALES: 6MM **Privately Held**
WEB: www.roedentallab.com
SIC: 8072 Crown & bridge production

(G-12117)
ROLTA ADVIZEX TECHNOLOGIES LLC (DH)
6480 S Rockside Woods (44131-2233)
PHONE..................................216 901-1818
Fred Traversi, *CEO*
Paul Rodwell, *Area Mgr*
Marc Sarazin, *Exec VP*
Don Aubert, *Vice Pres*
John Brier, *Vice Pres*
EMP: 39
SQ FT: 6,600
SALES (est): 186.1MM
SALES (corp-wide): 222.2MM **Privately Held**
WEB: www.advizex.com
SIC: 7373 Value-added resellers; computer systems; systems software development services

(G-12118)
ROSE COMMUNITY MANAGEMENT LLC (PA)
6000 Fredom Sq Dr Ste 500 (44131)
PHONE..................................917 542-3600
Angelo Pimpas, *President*
Mike Daly,
EMP: 195
SQ FT: 11,000
SALES: 5MM **Privately Held**
SIC: 6531 Real estate managers

(G-12119)
ROSS BRITTAIN SCHONBERG LPA
6480 Rckside Woods Blvd S (44131-2233)
PHONE..................................216 447-1551
Alan Ross, *President*
David Andrews, *Principal*
Patrick Harrington, *Principal*
Richard Walters, *Principal*
Lynn Schonberg, *Vice Pres*
EMP: 34
SQ FT: 11,257
SALES (est): 4.4MM **Privately Held**
WEB: www.rbslaw.com
SIC: 8111 Labor & employment law

(G-12120)
SIRVA INC
6200 Oak Tree Blvd # 300 (44131-6934)
PHONE..................................216 606-4000
Marie Henderson, *Branch Mgr*

EMP: 25
SALES (corp-wide): 2.1B **Privately Held**
SIC: 7389 Relocation service
PA: Sirva, Inc.
1 Parkview Plz
Oakbrook Terrace IL 60181
630 570-3047

(G-12121)
SIRVA MORTGAGE INC
6200 Oak Tree Blvd # 300 (44131-6934)
PHONE..................................800 531-3837
Paul Klemme, *President*
EMP: 76
SALES: 1.7MM
SALES (corp-wide): 2.1B **Privately Held**
WEB: www.sirvamortgage.com
SIC: 6162 Mortgage bankers
HQ: Cms Holding, Llc
700 Oakmont Ln
Westmont IL

(G-12122)
SIRVA RELOCATION LLC (DH)
Also Called: Sirva Worldwide Relocation Mvg
6200 Oak Tree Blvd # 300 (44131-6934)
PHONE..................................216 606-4000
Wes W Lucas, *CEO*
Deborah L Balli, *President*
Andrew P Coolidge, *COO*
Thomas Oberdorf, *CFO*
Douglas V Gathany, *Treasurer*
EMP: 385 EST: 1981
SALES (est): 71.8MM
SALES (corp-wide): 2.1B **Privately Held**
WEB: www.sirvarelocation.com
SIC: 7389 Relocation service
HQ: North American Van Lines, Inc.
101 E Wa Blvd Ste 1100
Fort Wayne IN 46802
800 348-3746

(G-12123)
SKILLSOFT CORPORATION
6645 Acres Dr (44131-4962)
PHONE..................................216 524-5200
Joe Garrison, *Branch Mgr*
EMP: 66
SALES (corp-wide): 352.2K **Privately Held**
SIC: 7372 Educational computer software
HQ: Skillsoft Corporation
300 Innovative Way # 201
Nashua NH 03062
603 324-3000

(G-12124)
SMITH PETER KALAIL CO LPA
6480 Rcksde Wds Blvd S # 300 (44131-2233)
PHONE..................................216 503-5055
Scott C Peters, *Managing Prtnr*
Karrie M Kalail, *Partner*
David Kane Smith, *Admin Sec*
EMP: 29 EST: 2001
SALES (est): 2.9MM **Privately Held**
WEB: www.ohioedlaw.com
SIC: 8111 Labor & employment law

(G-12125)
STERLING INFOSYSTEMS INC
Also Called: Occupational Hlth Safety Dept
4511 Rockside Rd (44131-2199)
PHONE..................................216 685-7600
Kurt Schwall, *Principal*
EMP: 27
SALES (corp-wide): 25MM **Privately Held**
SIC: 7381 7389 Private investigator; personal investigation service
PA: Sterling Infosystems, Inc.
1 State St Fl 24
New York NY 10004
800 899-2272

(G-12126)
SUPPORTCARE INC
4700 Rockside Rd Ste 100 (44131-2148)
PHONE..................................216 446-2650
Regan Eveland, *Administration*
EMP: 215 **Privately Held**
SIC: 8052 Home for the mentally retarded, with health care
PA: Supportcare, Inc.
525 Metro Pl N Ste 350
Dublin OH 43017

(G-12127)
SYMANTEC CORPORATION
6100 Oak Tree Blvd (44131-2544)
PHONE..................................216 643-6700
EMP: 70
SALES (corp-wide): 4.8B **Publicly Held**
SIC: 7372 Prepackaged software
PA: Symantec Corporation
350 Ellis St
Mountain View CA 94043
650 527-8000

(G-12128)
TALERIS CREDIT UNION INC
6111 Oak Tree Blvd # 110 (44131-2585)
P.O. Box 318072, Cleveland (44131-8072)
PHONE..................................216 739-2300
Robin D Thomas, *President*
James McKenzie, *Vice Pres*
Harley Hill, *CFO*
Ben Boggs, *Controller*
Rick Zimmerman, *Sales Dir*
EMP: 45
SALES: 2.6MM **Privately Held**
WEB: www.tcuohio.org
SIC: 6062 State credit unions

(G-12129)
TEKSYSTEMS INC
5990 W Creek Rd Ste 175 (44131-2191)
PHONE..................................216 606-3600
Chad Colombari, *Manager*
EMP: 30
SALES (corp-wide): 12.3B **Privately Held**
WEB: www.teksystems.com
SIC: 7379 Computer related consulting services
HQ: Teksystems, Inc.
7437 Race Rd
Hanover MD 21076

(G-12130)
THERAPY IN MOTION LLC
5000 Rockside Rd Ste 500 (44131-2178)
PHONE..................................216 459-2846
Neal Polan, *CEO*
Rudy Denius,
Deb Graziani,
Melodie Roach,
EMP: 190
SQ FT: 1,500
SALES (est): 6.4MM **Privately Held**
SIC: 8049 Occupational therapist; physical therapist; speech therapist

(G-12131)
THYSSENKRUPP MATERIALS NA INC
6050 Oak Tree Blvd # 110 (44131-6927)
PHONE..................................216 883-8100
Randy Pacelli, *Branch Mgr*
EMP: 87
SQ FT: 65,000
SALES (corp-wide): 39.8B **Privately Held**
SIC: 5051 3341 Steel; secondary nonferrous metals
HQ: Thyssenkrupp Materials Na, Inc.
22355 W 11 Mile Rd
Southfield MI 48033
248 233-5600

(G-12132)
TOYOTA MATERIAL HDLG OHIO INC (PA)
5667 E Schaaf Rd (44131-1305)
PHONE..................................216 328-0970
Brian Arnold, *General Mgr*
Daniel Hegler, *CFO*
Blaine Bobby, *Controller*
Sawsan Ganczak, *Human Res Mgr*
Tim Malone, *Accounts Mgr*
EMP: 98 EST: 2012
SALES (est): 38.8MM **Privately Held**
SIC: 5084 Lift trucks & parts; materials handling machinery

(G-12133)
TRANSAMERICA PREMIER LF INSUR
6480 Rockside Woods S 1 (44131-2233)
PHONE..................................216 524-1436
Florence Stan, *District Mgr*
EMP: 30

SALES (corp-wide): 593.2MM **Privately Held**
WEB: www.monlife.com
SIC: 6311 Life insurance
HQ: Transamerica Premier Life Insurance Company
4333 Edgewood Rd Ne
Cedar Rapids IA 52499
319 355-8511

(G-12134)
UNIFIRST CORPORATION
1450 E Granger Rd (44131-1207)
PHONE................................216 658-6900
Randy Thorton, *Principal*
Sanford Hejduk, *District Mgr*
EMP: 78
SALES (corp-wide): 1.7B **Publicly Held**
SIC: 7218 Industrial launderers
PA: Unifirst Corporation
68 Jonspin Rd
Wilmington MA 01887
978 658-8888

(G-12135)
UNITED STATES PROTECTIVE (PA)
Also Called: U S Protective Services
750 W Resource Dr Ste 200 (44131-1879)
PHONE................................216 475-8550
Theodore Cohen Jr, *President*
Gilda Cohen, *Corp Secy*
EMP: 50
SQ FT: 48,000
SALES (est): 8.2MM **Privately Held**
SIC: 7382 Burglar alarm maintenance & monitoring

(G-12136)
VERIFIED PERSON INC
4511 Rockside Rd Ste 400 (44131-2156)
PHONE................................901 767-6121
EMP: 41
SQ FT: 18,000
SALES (est): 2.5MM
SALES (corp-wide): 89.8MM **Privately Held**
SIC: 7363 Help Supply Services
PA: Sterling Infosystems, Inc.
1 State St Fl 24
New York NY 10004
800 899-2272

(G-12137)
VERITIV OPERATING COMPANY
Midwest Market Area
7575 E Pleasant Valley Rd # 200 (44131-5567)
PHONE................................216 573-7400
Steve Bartniski, *Sales/Mktg Mgr*
EMP: 35
SALES (corp-wide): 8.7B **Publicly Held**
WEB: www.unisourcelink.com
SIC: 5113 Industrial & personal service paper
HQ: Veritiv Operating Company
1000 Abernathy Rd
Atlanta GA 30328
770 391-8200

(G-12138)
VISITING NURSE ASSOCIATION
925 Keynote Cir Ste 300 (44131-1869)
PHONE................................216 931-1300
Joann Z Glick, *Chairman*
Althea Johnson, *Human Res Mgr*
Angela Golic,
EMP: 32
SALES: 0 **Privately Held**
SIC: 8621 Professional membership organizations

(G-12139)
VOX MOBILE
6100 Rockside Woods # 100 (44131-2355)
PHONE................................800 536-9030
Peter Paras, *CEO*
Gerald Hetrick, *COO*
Mark Cimino, *Vice Pres*
Zach Carman, *Project Mgr*
DEA Dobek, *Research*
EMP: 30

SALES (est): 6.6MM **Privately Held**
WEB: www.voxmobile.com
SIC: 4899 4813 Communication signal enhancement network system; telephone communication, except radio

(G-12140)
WELLINGTON GROUP LLC
6133 Rockside Rd Ste 205 (44131-2242)
PHONE................................216 525-2200
Dean Rossiter, *Manager*
EMP: 25
SALES (est): 2.2MM **Privately Held**
WEB: www.wellingtongroup.biz
SIC: 8742 Hospital & health services consultant

(G-12141)
WINE TRENDS INC
9101 E Pleasant Valley Rd (44131-5504)
PHONE................................216 520-2626
Daniel Greathouse, *Principal*
Craig Cracchiolo, *Marketing Staff*
▲ EMP: 50
SQ FT: 14,000
SALES (est): 9MM
SALES (corp-wide): 369.4MM **Privately Held**
WEB: www.winetrendsinc.com
SIC: 5182 Wine
PA: Dayton Heidelberg Distributing Co.
3601 Dryden Rd
Moraine OH 45439
937 222-8692

(G-12142)
X-S MERCHANDISE INC (PA)
7000 Granger Rd Ste 2 (44131-1462)
PHONE................................216 524-5620
Len Stern, *Ch of Bd*
David Robbins, *President*
Todd Stern, *President*
Bill Sample, *Vice Pres*
Rick Schwartz, *Vice Pres*
◆ EMP: 25
SQ FT: 65,000
SALES (est): 25.9MM **Privately Held**
WEB: www.xsmdse.com
SIC: 5199 General merchandise, non-durable

(G-12143)
ZURICH AMERICAN INSURANCE CO
5005 Rockside Rd Ste 200 (44131-6808)
PHONE................................216 328-9400
James Savage, *Accounts Exec*
Frank Hammers, *Branch Mgr*
Brian Held, *Manager*
EMP: 40
SALES (corp-wide): 65.1B **Privately Held**
WEB: www.zurichna.com
SIC: 6331 Fire, marine & casualty insurance
HQ: Zurich American Insurance Company
1299 Zurich Way
Schaumburg IL 60196
800 987-3373

Ironton
Lawrence County

(G-12144)
AHF OHIO INC
Also Called: Sanctuary At The Ohio Valley
2932 S 5th St (45638-2865)
PHONE................................740 532-6188
Mark Haemmerle, *President*
J Michael Haemmerle, *Treasurer*
Brian Eichenlaub, *Administration*
EMP: 68
SALES (corp-wide): 22.6MM **Privately Held**
SIC: 8051 Skilled nursing care facilities
PA: Ahf Ohio, Inc.
5920 Venture Dr Ste 100
Dublin OH 43017
614 760-7352

(G-12145)
BARTRAM & SONS GROCERIES
Also Called: Bartram Groceries
2407 S 6th St (45638-2632)
PHONE................................740 532-5216
Steve Bartram, *President*
Jane Mc Connell, *Corp Secy*
EMP: 40
SQ FT: 10,500
SALES: 300K **Privately Held**
SIC: 4225 General warehousing & storage

(G-12146)
BRAYMAN CONSTRUCTION CORP
505 S 3rd St (45638-1835)
PHONE................................740 237-0000
EMP: 40
SALES (corp-wide): 32.9MM **Privately Held**
SIC: 1521 Single-family housing construction
PA: Brayman Construction Corporation
1000 John Roebling Way
Saxonburg PA 16056
724 443-1533

(G-12147)
BRYANT HEALTH CENTER INC
Also Called: Sanctuary of The Ohio Valley
2932 S 5th St (45638-2865)
PHONE................................740 532-6188
Robert Banasik, *President*
Sue Capp, *Manager*
EMP: 136
SALES (est): 4.2MM
SALES (corp-wide): 9.1MM **Privately Held**
WEB: www.omnilife.net
SIC: 8059 8051 Nursing home, except skilled & intermediate care facility; skilled nursing care facilities
PA: Omnilife Health Care Systems, Inc.
50 W 5th Ave
Columbus OH 43201
614 299-3100

(G-12148)
BWC TRUCKING COMPANY INC
164 State Route 650 (45638-7919)
P.O. Box 267 (45638-0267)
PHONE................................740 532-5188
Randy Kelley, *President*
Kathy Kelley, *Corp Secy*
Beth Pugh, *Project Dir*
EMP: 50
SQ FT: 1,020
SALES (est): 10.9MM **Privately Held**
WEB: www.bwctrucking.com
SIC: 4212 Local trucking, without storage

(G-12149)
CARING HANDS HOME HEALTH CARE
2615 S 3rd St (45638-2759)
PHONE................................740 532-9020
Teresa Jenkins, *President*
George Jenkins, *Administration*
EMP: 25
SALES (est): 562.2K **Privately Held**
SIC: 8082 Visiting nurse service

(G-12150)
CLOSE TO HOME III
617 Center St (45638-1510)
PHONE................................740 534-1100
Charles Kunkel, *Owner*
Sharon Shartwig, *Co-Owner*
EMP: 30
SALES (est): 741.8K **Privately Held**
SIC: 8361 Residential care

(G-12151)
COAL GROVE LONG TERM CARE INC
Also Called: Sunset Nursing Center
813 1/2 Marion Pike (45638-3070)
PHONE................................740 532-0449
David Dixon, *Administration*
EMP: 60
SALES (est): 2.6MM **Privately Held**
WEB: www.sunsetnursingcare.com
SIC: 8051 Convalescent home with continuous nursing care

(G-12152)
FEECORP INDUSTRIAL SERVICES
1120 Wyanoke St (45638-2784)
P.O. Box 447, Pickerington (43147-0447)
PHONE................................740 533-1445
Karen Fee, *CEO*
EMP: 150
SALES (est): 1.2MM **Privately Held**
SIC: 7349 Building maintenance services

(G-12153)
FLAGSHIP SERVICES OF OHIO INC
82 Township Road 1331 (45638-8383)
PHONE................................740 533-1657
Keith Lewis, *President*
EMP: 55
SALES (est): 2.6MM **Privately Held**
SIC: 7538 General automotive repair shops

(G-12154)
HECLA WATER ASSOCIATION (PA)
3190 State Route 141 (45638-8486)
PHONE................................740 533-0526
Ray Howard, *CEO*
EMP: 41
SQ FT: 8,000
SALES: 6.9MM **Privately Held**
SIC: 4941 Water supply

(G-12155)
IRONTON AND LAWRENCE COUNTY (PA)
305 N 5th St (45638-1578)
PHONE................................740 532-3534
Ralph Kline, *General Mgr*
Carol Rideout, *Human Resources*
D R Gossett, *Exec Dir*
Cindy Anderson, *Director*
Alisha Boggs, *Director*
EMP: 260
SQ FT: 4,500
SALES: 26MM **Privately Held**
SIC: 4111 8099 8351 8331 Local & suburban transit; nutrition services; preschool center; job training & vocational rehabilitation services; primary care medical clinic; mental health clinic, outpatient

(G-12156)
IRONTON AND LAWRENCE COUNTY
Also Called: Family Guidance Center
1518 S 3rd St (45638-2140)
PHONE................................740 532-7855
Ruth Langer, *Branch Mgr*
EMP: 25
SALES (corp-wide): 26MM **Privately Held**
SIC: 8099 4111 Nutrition services; local & suburban transit
PA: Ironton And Lawrence County Area Community Action Organization
305 N 5th St
Ironton OH 45638
740 532-3534

(G-12157)
IZAAK WALTON LEAGUE AMERICA
1738 County Road 6 (45638-8563)
PHONE................................740 532-2342
Phillip Hardy, *President*
EMP: 30
SALES (corp-wide): 2.7MM **Privately Held**
SIC: 8641 Civic social & fraternal associations
PA: Izaak Walton League Of America
707 Conservation Ln # 210
Gaithersburg MD 20878
301 548-0150

(G-12158)
J & J GENERAL MAINTENANCE INC
2430 S 3rd St (45638-2637)
PHONE................................740 533-9729
Jackie Fields, *President*
Jeffery Fields, *Vice Pres*
Jeffrey Fields, *Vice Pres*

EMP: 30
SQ FT: 1,800
SALES: 11MM **Privately Held**
SIC: **1731** 1711 1794 1623 General electrical contractor; plumbing, heating, air-conditioning contractors; excavation & grading, building construction; water & sewer line construction; steel building construction

(G-12159)
JEFFREY W SMITH
411 Center St (45638-1506)
PHONE..................................740 532-9000
Jeffrey W Smith, *Principal*
EMP: 25
SALES (est): 1.7MM **Privately Held**
SIC: **8111** General practice attorney, lawyer

(G-12160)
JO LIN HEALTH CENTER INC
1050 Clinton St (45638-2876)
P.O. Box 329 (45638-0329)
PHONE..................................740 532-0860
Jo Linda Heaberlin, *President*
Richard Heaberlin, *Vice Pres*
Delores Jean Dalton, *Treasurer*
Delores Dalton, *Executive*
EMP: 215
SQ FT: 20,000
SALES: 10.1MM **Privately Held**
SIC: **8361** 8051 Rehabilitation center, residential: health care incidental; skilled nursing care facilities

(G-12161)
LAWRENCE CNTY HSTORICAL MUSEUM
506 S 6th St (45638-1825)
P.O. Box 73 (45638-0073)
PHONE..................................740 532-1222
Piggy Karfhner, *President*
Naumi Beer, *Vice Pres*
Patricia Ericson, *Treasurer*
Dibbie Rogers, *Admin Sec*
EMP: 50
SQ FT: 3,798
SALES (est): 777.7K **Privately Held**
SIC: **8412** 8111 Museum; legal services

(G-12162)
LUCAS BUILDING MAINENANCE LLC
323 Mastin Ave (45638-2432)
PHONE..................................740 479-1800
James R Lucas,
Kathy Hughes,
EMP: 740
SALES: 200K **Privately Held**
SIC: **7349** Building cleaning service

(G-12163)
MENDED REEDS HOME
803 Vernon St (45638-1645)
PHONE..................................740 533-1883
David Lambert, *Director*
EMP: 35
SALES (est): 890.4K **Privately Held**
SIC: **8361** Group foster home

(G-12164)
MI - DE - CON INC
3331 S 3rd St (45638-2863)
P.O. Box 4450 (45638-4450)
PHONE..................................740 532-2277
Michael L Floyd, *President*
Dennis L Salyers, *President*
EMP: 99 EST: 1999
SALES (est): 31.6MM **Privately Held**
SIC: **1542** Nonresidential construction

(G-12165)
PATRIOT EMERGENCY MED SVCS INC
2914 S 4th St (45638-2867)
P.O. Box 4434 (45638-4434)
PHONE..................................740 532-2222
Robert Blankenship, *Exec VP*
EMP: 30
SALES (est): 1MM **Privately Held**
WEB: www.patriotems.com
SIC: **4119** Ambulance service

(G-12166)
SHERMAN THOMPSON OH TC LP
275 N 3rd St (45638-1469)
PHONE..................................216 520-1250
Frank Sinito, *General Ptnr*
EMP: 99
SALES (est): 789.1K **Privately Held**
SIC: **6513** Apartment building operators

(G-12167)
WESBANCO INC
311 S 5th St (45638-1609)
PHONE..................................740 532-0263
Mary Cronacher, *Manager*
EMP: 40
SALES (corp-wide): 515.2MM **Publicly Held**
WEB: www.oakhillbanks.com
SIC: **6022** 6035 State commercial banks; federal savings banks
PA: Wesbanco, Inc.
  1 Bank Plz
  Wheeling WV 26003
  304 234-9000

Jackson
Jackson County

(G-12168)
A J STOCKMEISTER INC (PA)
702 E Main St (45640-2131)
P.O. Box 667 (45640-0667)
PHONE..................................740 286-2106
Alan Stockmeister, *Ch of Bd*
Tom Geiger, *President*
Seth Stockmeister, *Vice Pres*
Kay Howe, *CFO*
EMP: 30 EST: 1947
SQ FT: 5,000
SALES (est): 6.6MM **Privately Held**
SIC: **1711** Mechanical contractor

(G-12169)
BRENMAR CONSTRUCTION INC
900 Morton St (45640-1089)
PHONE..................................740 286-2151
Todd Ghearing, *President*
Andy Graham, *Corp Secy*
Tim Ousley, *Vice Pres*
EMP: 60
SQ FT: 5,000
SALES: 8MM **Privately Held**
WEB: www.brenmarconstruction.com
SIC: **1542** 3312 Commercial & office building contractors; structural shapes & pilings, steel

(G-12170)
CECIL I WALKER MACHINERY CO
Also Called: Walker Machinery and Lift
1477 Mayhew Rd (45640-9186)
P.O. Box 981 (45640-0981)
PHONE..................................740 286-7566
Bob Adkins, *Manager*
EMP: 25 **Privately Held**
WEB: www.walker-cat.com
SIC: **5084** 7699 5082 7353 Industrial machinery & equipment; industrial machinery & equipment repair; contractors' materials; heavy construction equipment rental
HQ: Cecil I. Walker Machinery Co.
  10001 Lyn Stn Rd Ky 40223
  Louisville KY 40223
  304 949-6400

(G-12171)
CHILD DEV CTR JACKSON CNTY
692 Pattonsville Rd (45640-9452)
P.O. Box 431 (45640-0431)
PHONE..................................740 286-3995
Sharon Hayes, *Office Mgr*
Marlene D Ray, *Exec Mgr*
EMP: 35
SQ FT: 4,000
SALES: 588.6K **Privately Held**
SIC: **8351** Group day care center

(G-12172)
COMMUNITY ACTION COMM PIKE CNT
Also Called: Valley View Health Center
14590 State Route 93 (45640-8977)
PHONE..................................740 286-2826
Cheryl Tackett, *Asst Director*
EMP: 50
SALES (corp-wide): 22.1MM **Privately Held**
SIC: **8322** Family service agency
PA: The Community Action Committee Of Pike County
  941 Market St
  Piketon OH 45661
  740 289-2371

(G-12173)
FAMILY ENTERTAINMENT SERVICES
780 Rock Run Rd (45640-8619)
PHONE..................................740 286-8587
Rosetta Johnson, *CEO*
David Ford, *Vice Pres*
Bryan Malott, *Vice Pres*
Thomas E Smith, *Treasurer*
EMP: 70
SQ FT: 2,500
SALES (est): 2.6MM **Privately Held**
SIC: **0781** 7349 1711 Landscape architects; janitorial service, contract basis; plumbing, heating, air-conditioning contractors

(G-12174)
HEALTH CARE RTREMENT CORP AMER
Also Called: Heartland of Jackson
8668 State Route 93 (45640-9728)
PHONE..................................740 286-5026
Bonnie McCain, *Administration*
EMP: 90
SALES (corp-wide): 2.4B **Publicly Held**
WEB: www.hrc-manorcare.com
SIC: **8051** Convalescent home with continuous nursing care
HQ: Health Care And Retirement Corporation Of America
  333 N Summit St Ste 103
  Toledo OH 43604
  419 252-5500

(G-12175)
HOLZER MEDICAL CTR - JACKSON
500 Burlington Rd (45640-9360)
PHONE..................................740 288-4625
Ross A Matlack, *President*
Rhonda Dailey, *Vice Pres*
EMP: 285
SALES: 28.8MM **Privately Held**
SIC: **8062** General medical & surgical hospitals

(G-12176)
HOSSER ASSISTED LIVING
101 Markham Dr (45640-8697)
PHONE..................................740 286-8785
Tim Hackworth, *Exec Dir*
Jami Gross, *Administration*
EMP: 40
SQ FT: 36,000
SALES (est): 890.3K **Privately Held**
SIC: **8051** Skilled nursing care facilities

(G-12177)
JACKSON COUNTY BOARD ON AGING (PA)
Also Called: JACKSON COUNTY SENIOR CITIZENS
25 E Mound St (45640-1223)
PHONE..................................740 286-2909
Anglea Harrisison, *Director*
Rose Henson, *Admin Sec*
EMP: 42
SALES: 977.2K **Privately Held**
SIC: **8322** Old age assistance; referral service for personal & social problems

(G-12178)
OHIO METAL PROCESSING INC
Also Called: Steelsummit Ohio
16064 Beaver Pike (45640-9659)
PHONE..................................740 286-6457

John Flick, *President*
Shigeki Tanaka, *Corp Secy*
Tom Prindle, *Purchasing*
Kay Howe, *CFO*
Amy Alvarez, *Sales Staff*
EMP: 48
SQ FT: 85,000
SALES (est): 54MM
SALES (corp-wide): 45.3B **Privately Held**
SIC: **5051** 7389 Metals service centers & offices; metal slitting & shearing
HQ: Sumitomo Corporation Of Americas
  300 Madison Ave Frnt 3
  New York NY 10017
  212 207-0700

(G-12179)
STOCKMEISTER ENTERPRISES INC
700 E Main St (45640-2131)
P.O. Box 684 (45640-0684)
PHONE..................................740 286-1619
Alan Stockmeister, *CEO*
EMP: 35
SQ FT: 5,300
SALES (est): 8.1MM **Privately Held**
SIC: **1542** Commercial & office building contractors

(G-12180)
TREPANIER DANIELS & TREPANIER
Also Called: A & A Truck Stop
80 Dixon Run Rd Ste 80 # 80 (45640-9511)
P.O. Box 966 (45640-0966)
PHONE..................................740 286-1288
Steve Trepanier, *President*
Alfred Daniels, *Corp Secy*
Sally Case, *Vice Pres*
EMP: 55
SALES (est): 9.6MM **Privately Held**
WEB: www.trepanierlambert.com
SIC: **5541** 5812 7538 5331 Truck stops; eating places; general automotive repair shops; variety stores

(G-12181)
UNITED CHURCH HOMES INC
Also Called: Four Winds Nursing Facility
215 Seth Ave (45640-9405)
PHONE..................................740 286-7551
John Evans, *Administration*
EMP: 78
SALES (corp-wide): 78.1MM **Privately Held**
WEB: www.altenheimcommunity.org
SIC: **8052** 8051 Intermediate care facilities; skilled nursing care facilities
PA: United Church Homes Inc
  170 E Center St
  Marion OH 43302
  740 382-4885

(G-12182)
WALMART INC
100 Walmart Dr (45640-8692)
PHONE..................................740 286-8203
Danny Tharpe, *Branch Mgr*
John Colbert, *Manager*
EMP: 450
SALES (corp-wide): 514.4B **Publicly Held**
WEB: www.walmartstores.com
SIC: **5311** 5411 5912 5048 Department stores, discount; supermarkets, hypermarket; drug stores & proprietary stores; ophthalmic goods
PA: Walmart Inc.
  702 Sw 8th St
  Bentonville AR 72716
  479 273-4000

Jackson Center
Shelby County

(G-12183)
EMI CORP (PA)
Also Called: E M I Plastic Equipment
801 W Pike St (45334-6037)
P.O. Box 590 (45334-0590)
PHONE..................................937 596-5511
James E Andraitis, *President*
Brad Wren, *Vice Pres*

Deb Hereld, *Purch Agent*
Linda Andraitis-Varljen, *Treasurer*
Kay Friders, *Controller*
▲ **EMP:** 85 **EST:** 1980
SQ FT: 80,000
SALES (est): 16.3MM **Privately Held**
WEB: www.emiplastics.com
SIC: 3544 5084 Special dies, tools, jigs &
fixtures; industrial machinery & equipment

(G-12184)
M E THEATERS INC
106 W Pike St (45334-6028)
P.O. Box 477 (45334-0477)
PHONE.....................937 596-6424
Rodney Miller, *President*
EMP: 26
SALES (est): 461.7K **Privately Held**
SIC: 7832 Motion picture theaters, except
drive-in

(G-12185)
RISING SUN EXPRESS LLC
1003 S Main St (45334-1123)
P.O. Box 610 (45334-0610)
PHONE.....................937 596-6167
Herman McBride, *Mng Member*
Barbara Howerton,
EMP: 90
SALES: 9.4MM **Privately Held**
SIC: 4213 4212 Trucking, except local;
local trucking, without storage

(G-12186)
RSE GROUP INC
Also Called: Rising Sun Express
1003 S Main St (45334-1123)
PHONE.....................937 596-6167
Lynn J McBride, *President*
Barb Howerton, *CFO*
EMP: 90
SALES: 9.4MM **Privately Held**
SIC: 6799 Venture capital companies

Jamestown
Greene County

(G-12187)
GREENEVIEW FOODS LLC
Also Called: Uhl's Jamestown Market
96 W Washington St (45335-2519)
PHONE.....................937 675-4161
Robert J Uhl, *President*
EMP: 30 **EST:** 2013
SALES (est): 5MM **Privately Held**
SIC: 5141 Groceries, general line

(G-12188)
**LIBERTY NRSING CTR OF
JMESTOWN**
4960 Old Us Route 35 E (45335-1712)
PHONE.....................937 675-3311
Linda Black-Kurck, *President*
Linda Blackkurck, *President*
EMP: 70
SALES: 3.9MM **Privately Held**
SIC: 8051 Convalescent home with contin-
uous nursing care

Jefferson
Ashtabula County

(G-12189)
**ASHTABULA COUNTY
COMMNTY ACTN**
32 E Jefferson St (44047-1112)
PHONE.....................440 576-6911
Diana Brook, *Manager*
EMP: 54
SALES (corp-wide): 92.1K **Privately Held**
SIC: 8399 8322 Antipoverty board; individ-
ual & family services
PA: Ashtabula County Community Action
Agency Properties Corporation
6920 Austinburg Rd
Ashtabula OH 44004
440 997-1721

(G-12190)
CENTERRA CO-OP
161 E Jefferson St (44047-1113)
PHONE.....................800 362-9598
Jim Reader, *Manager*
EMP: 28
SALES (corp-wide): 174.6MM **Privately
Held**
SIC: 5172 5261 2048 5191 Gases, lique-
fied petroleum (propane); fertilizer; bird
food, prepared; farm supplies
PA: Centerra Co-Op
813 Clark Ave
Ashland OH 44805
419 281-2153

(G-12191)
COUNTY OF ASHTABULA
Also Called: Ashtabula County Highway Dept
186 E Satin St (44047-1419)
PHONE.....................440 576-2816
Leroy McNeilly, *Engineer*
Timothy Martin, *Manager*
EMP: 50
SQ FT: 250 **Privately Held**
SIC: 1611 Highway & street maintenance
PA: County Of Ashtabula
25 W Jefferson St
Jefferson OH 44047

(G-12192)
SUNNY BORDER OHIO INC
3637 State Route 167 (44047-9463)
P.O. Box 483, Berlin CT (06037-0483)
PHONE.....................440 858-9660
Valerie Jo Hawkins, *President*
EMP: 60
SQ FT: 3,500
SALES (est): 1.6MM **Privately Held**
WEB: www.sunnyborderohio.com
SIC: 0181 0182 Flowers: grown under
cover (e.g. greenhouse production); food
crops grown under cover

Jeromesville
Ashland County

(G-12193)
**MOHICAN HILLS GOLF CLUB
INC**
25 County Road 1950 (44840-9627)
PHONE.....................419 368-4700
James A Markling Jr, *President*
David Markling, *Shareholder*
Thomas Markling, *Shareholder*
Janet Markling, *Admin Sec*
EMP: 30
SALES (est): 1MM **Privately Held**
SIC: 7992 Public Golf Course

(G-12194)
SCENIC RIDGE FRUIT FARMS
2031 State Route 89 (44840-9654)
PHONE.....................419 368-3353
James Kendel, *Owner*
Marion Bauman, *Owner*
EMP: 30
SALES (est): 551.5K **Privately Held**
SIC: 0175 Apple orchard

Johnstown
Licking County

(G-12195)
**ATRIUM APPAREL
CORPORATION**
188 Commerce Blvd (43031-9011)
PHONE.....................740 966-8200
Douglas Tu, *President*
Dave Hirsch, *Vice Pres*
Jason Tu, *CFO*
EMP: 65
SQ FT: 80,000
SALES (est): 7.4MM **Privately Held**
SIC: 7389 Apparel designers, commercial

(G-12196)
BIGMAR INC
9711 Sportsman Club Rd (43031-9141)
PHONE.....................740 966-5800

John Tramontana, *CEO*
John Tramontata, *CEO*
Cynthia R May, *President*
Bernard Kramer, *COO*
Massimo Pedrani, *Exec VP*
EMP: 50
SQ FT: 8,600
SALES (est): 3.7MM **Privately Held**
SIC: 2834 8111 Pharmaceutical prepara-
tions; legal services

(G-12197)
BLECKMANN USA LLC
188 Commerce Blvd Ste B (43031-9011)
PHONE.....................740 809-2645
EMP: 45
SALES (est): 4.5MM **Privately Held**
SIC: 4731 Freight transportation arrange-
ment

(G-12198)
**BON SECOURS HEALTH
SYSTEM**
8148 Windy Hollow Rd (43031-9515)
PHONE.....................740 966-3116
EMP: 46
SALES (corp-wide): 2.5B **Privately Held**
SIC: 8062 General Hospital
PA: Bon Secours Health System, Inc
1505 Marriottsville Rd
Marriottsville MD 21104
410 442-5511

(G-12199)
COUNTY OF LICKING
Also Called: Water & Sewer Department
395 W Jersey St (43031-1158)
P.O. Box 457 (43031-0457)
PHONE.....................740 967-5951
Michael Sharpe, *President*
Randy Ashbrook, *Manager*
EMP: 35 **Privately Held**
WEB: www.lcats.org
SIC: 4941 Water supply
PA: County Of Licking
20 S 2nd St
Newark OH 43055
740 670-5040

(G-12200)
HEIMERL FARMS LTD
3891 Mink St (43031-9529)
PHONE.....................740 967-0063
James Heimerl, *CEO*
Rachel Heimerl, *Office Mgr*
Brad Heimerl,
Matt Heimerl,
EMP: 40
SALES (est): 1MM **Privately Held**
SIC: 0191 General farms, primarily crop

(G-12201)
HILLANDALE FARMS TRNSP
10513 Croton Rd (43031-9105)
PHONE.....................740 893-2232
Jim Clark, *General Mgr*
EMP: 70
SALES (est): 5.9MM **Privately Held**
SIC: 4213 Trucking, except local

(G-12202)
OPCC LLC
Also Called: Country Club of Orange Park
243 Sunset Dr S (43031-1190)
PHONE.....................904 276-7660
Collen Armstrong,
EMP: 75
SALES (est): 1.2MM **Privately Held**
SIC: 7997 Membership Sport/Recreation
Club

(G-12203)
**SOHO DEVELOPMENT
COMPANY**
501 Cole Dr (43031-1088)
PHONE.....................614 207-3261
Braden Nida, *Manager*
EMP: 75
SALES (est): 2.1MM **Privately Held**
SIC: 6552 Subdividers & developers

(G-12204)
**TECHNICAL RUBBER COMPANY
INC (PA)**
Also Called: Tech International
200 E Coshocton St (43031-1083)
P.O. Box 486 (43031-0486)
PHONE.....................740 967-9015
Micheal Chambers, *CEO*
Dan Layne, *President*
Diane Kirkpatrick, *General Mgr*
Robert Overs, *COO*
Gary Armstrong, *Senior VP*
◆ **EMP:** 270
SQ FT: 10,000
SALES (est): 113.6MM **Privately Held**
WEB: www.techtirerepairs.com
SIC: 3011 5014 2891 Tire sundries or tire
repair materials; rubber; tire & tube repair
materials; sealing compounds, synthetic
rubber or plastic

(G-12205)
ZANDEX INC
Also Called: Northview Senior Living Center
267 N Main St (43031-1018)
PHONE.....................740 967-1111
Karen Baltzell, *Branch Mgr*
EMP: 70
SALES (corp-wide): 34MM **Privately
Held**
SIC: 8052 8051 Personal care facility;
skilled nursing care facilities
PA: Zandex, Inc.
1122 Taylor St
Zanesville OH 43701
740 454-1400

(G-12206)
**ZANDEX HEALTH CARE
CORPORATION**
Also Called: Northview Senior Living Center
267 N Main St (43031-1018)
PHONE.....................740 454-1400
Karen Baltzell, *Manager*
EMP: 70
SALES (corp-wide): 34MM **Privately
Held**
SIC: 8052 8059 Intermediate care facili-
ties; rest home, with health care
HQ: Zandex Health Care Corporation
1122 Taylor St
Zanesville OH 43701

Kalida
Putnam County

(G-12207)
**TRILOGY HEALTHCARE
PUTNAM LLC**
755 Ottawa St (45853)
P.O. Box 388 (45853-0388)
PHONE.....................419 532-2961
Randal J Bufford, *Mng Member*
Kevin Kidd, *Exec Dir*
EMP: 125 **EST:** 2005
SALES (est): 1.5MM
SALES (corp-wide): 149MM **Privately
Held**
SIC: 8051 Skilled nursing care facilities
PA: Trilogy Rehab Services, Llc
303 N Hurstbourne Pkwy # 200
Louisville KY 40222
800 335-1060

Kansas
Seneca County

(G-12208)
LAKOTA BUS GARAGE
5186 Sandusky Cty Rd 13 (44841)
PHONE.....................419 986-5558
Mike Eaglowski, *Superintendent*
EMP: 30 **EST:** 2001
SALES (est): 603.8K **Privately Held**
SIC: 7538 General automotive repair
shops

Kelleys Island
Erie County

(G-12209)
CAMP PATMOS INC
920 Monaghan Rd (43438-5502)
PHONE..................................419 746-2214
Ed Miller, *Exec Dir*
EMP: 50 **EST:** 1951
SALES (est): 760K **Privately Held**
WEB: www.camppatmos.com
SIC: 7032 Summer camp, except day &
sports instructional

Kensington
Columbiana County

(G-12210)
M3 MIDSTREAM LLC
Also Called: Kensington Plant
11543 Sr 644 (44427)
PHONE..................................330 223-2220
EMP: 28
SALES (corp-wide): 54.9MM **Privately
Held**
SIC: 1311 Natural gas production
PA: M3 Midstream Llc
600 Travis St Ste 5600
Houston TX 77002
713 783-3000

(G-12211)
PAULA JO MOORE
10990 Myers Rd (44427-9753)
PHONE..................................330 894-2910
Paula Moore, *Owner*
EMP: 30
SQ FT: 3,705
SALES (est): 540.8K **Privately Held**
SIC: 8082 Home health care services

Kent
Portage County

(G-12212)
1106 WEST MAIN INC
Also Called: Klaben Auto Group
1106 W Main St (44240-2008)
PHONE..................................330 673-2122
Richard Klaben, *President*
Michael Klaben, *Vice Pres*
Tim Assaf, *Treasurer*
Brian Franklin, *Finance Mgr*
Kimberly Devlin, *Finance*
EMP: 40
SQ FT: 10,000
SALES (est): 9MM **Privately Held**
SIC: 5511 7515 5012 Automobiles, new &
used; passenger car leasing; automobiles
& other motor vehicles

(G-12213)
ALPHAMICRON INC
1950 State Route 59 (44240-4112)
PHONE..................................330 676-0648
Bahman Taheriy, *President*
Tamas Kosa, *COO*
Thomas Kosa, *COO*
Ysabel Hoover, *Production*
Ludmila Sukhomlinova, *Director*
EMP: 40
SQ FT: 30,000
SALES (est): 5.5MM **Privately Held**
WEB: www.alphamicron.com
SIC: 8732 Research services, except laboratory

(G-12214)
**AMETEK TCHNICAL INDUS
PDTS INC (HQ)**
Also Called: Ametek Electromechanical
Group
100 E Erie St Ste 130 (44240-3587)
PHONE..................................330 677-3754
Todd Schlegel, *General Mgr*
Matt French, *Vice Pres*
Peter Smith, *CFO*
William D Burke, *Treasurer*

Kathryn E Sena, *Admin Sec*
EMP: 65 **EST:** 2009
SALES (est): 69MM
SALES (corp-wide): 4.8B **Publicly Held**
SIC: 3621 5063 3566 Motors, electric;
motors, electric; speed changers, drives &
gears
PA: Ametek, Inc.
1100 Cassatt Rd
Berwyn PA 19312
610 647-2121

(G-12215)
**AYSCO SECURITY
CONSULTANTS INC**
4075 Karg Industrial Pkwy B (44240-6485)
PHONE..................................330 733-8183
Eric Frasier, *CEO*
Rod Bragg, *Principal*
EMP: 32
SALES (est): 129.4K **Privately Held**
SIC: 3699 5065 Security devices; security
control equipment & systems

(G-12216)
CARE OF TREES INC
1500 N Mantua St (44240-2372)
PHONE..................................800 445-8733
Shelly, *Branch Mgr*
EMP: 45
SALES (corp-wide): 38MM **Privately
Held**
SIC: 0783 Surgery services, ornamental
tree
PA: The Care Of Trees Inc
2371 Foster Ave
Wheeling IL 60090
847 394-3903

(G-12217)
**CARTER-JONES COMPANIES
INC (PA)**
Also Called: DO IT BEST
601 Tallmadge Rd (44240-7331)
P.O. Box 5194 (44240-5194)
PHONE..................................330 673-6100
Neil Sackett, *President*
Jeffrey Donley, *CFO*
Brian Horning, *Controller*
Judy Lee, *Admin Sec*
EMP: 50
SQ FT: 60,000
SALES (est): 1.4B **Privately Held**
WEB: www.carterlumber.com
SIC: 5031 6552 5211 Lumber: rough,
dressed & finished; millwork; building materials, exterior; building materials, interior; subdividers & developers; millwork &
lumber

(G-12218)
**CARTER-JONES LUMBER
COMPANY (HQ)**
601 Tallmadge Rd (44240-7331)
PHONE..................................330 673-6100
Neil Sackett, *CEO*
Jeffrey S Donley, *CFO*
Judy Lee, *Admin Sec*
▲ **EMP:** 156 **EST:** 1934
SQ FT: 60,000
SALES (est): 358.8MM
SALES (corp-wide): 1.4B **Privately Held**
SIC: 5211 5031 Lumber products; lumber:
rough, dressed & finished
PA: Carter-Jones Companies, Inc.
601 Tallmadge Rd
Kent OH 44240
330 673-6100

(G-12219)
**CARTER-JONES LUMBER
COMPANY**
601 Tallmadge Rd (44240-7331)
PHONE..................................330 673-6000
EMP: 1575
SALES (corp-wide): 1.2B **Privately Held**
SIC: 5211 5031 Ret Lumber & Building
Materials Whol Lumber
HQ: The Carter-Jones Lumber Company
601 Tallmadge Rd
Kent OH 44240
330 673-6100

(G-12220)
**CHILDRENS HOSP MED CTR
AKRON**
1951 State Route 59 Ste A (44240-8128)
PHONE..................................330 676-1020
Carrie Gavriloff, *Principal*
Debbi Kilmer, *Nurse*
EMP: 40
SALES (corp-wide): 747.4MM **Privately
Held**
SIC: 8062 General medical & surgical hospitals
PA: Childrens Hospital Medical Center Of
Akron
1 Perkins Sq
Akron OH 44308
330 543-1000

(G-12221)
CITY OF AKRON
Also Called: Municipal Water Supply
1570 Ravenna Rd (44240-6111)
PHONE..................................330 678-0077
Jeff Bronowski, *Manager*
EMP: 40 **Privately Held**
SIC: 4941 Water supply
PA: City Of Akron
166 S High St Rm 502
Akron OH 44308
330 375-2720

(G-12222)
CITY OF KENT
Street & Sewer Maintenance
930 Overholt Rd (44240-7551)
PHONE..................................330 678-8105
Gene Roberts, *Director*
EMP: 60 **Privately Held**
SIC: 1611 4952 9111 Highway & street
maintenance; sewerage systems; executive offices
PA: City Of Kent
325 S Depeyster St
Kent OH 44240
330 676-4189

(G-12223)
**COLEMAN PROFESSIONAL
SVCS INC (PA)**
Also Called: Coleman Data Solutions
5982 Rhodes Rd (44240-8100)
PHONE..................................330 673-1347
Nelson Burns, *CEO*
Joe Vero, *Trustee*
Alison Miller, *Vice Pres*
Annette Petranic, *Opers Mgr*
Ken Alexander, *Mktg Dir*
EMP: 110
SALES (est): 51.3MM **Privately Held**
SIC: 8093 7349 7374 7371 Mental health
clinic, outpatient; rehabilitation center,
outpatient treatment; janitorial service,
contract basis; data entry service; custom
computer programming services; psychological consultant; offices & clinics of
medical doctors

(G-12224)
COMMAND CARPET
1976 Tallmadge Rd (44240-6808)
PHONE..................................330 673-7404
Michele Sibbio, *President*
John Sibbio, *Vice Pres*
EMP: 55
SALES (est): 5.5MM **Privately Held**
SIC: 5713 1752 Floor covering stores;
floor laying & floor work

(G-12225)
**DAVEY RESOURCE GROUP INC
(HQ)**
1500 N Mantua St (44240-2372)
PHONE..................................330 673-9511
Patrick Covey, *CEO*
Thea Sears, *Controller*
EMP: 85
SALES (est): 1.9MM
SALES (corp-wide): 1B **Privately Held**
SIC: 0783 Ornamental shrub & tree services
PA: The Davey Tree Expert Company
1500 N Mantua St
Kent OH 44240
330 673-9511

(G-12226)
**DAVEY TREE EXPERT
COMPANY (PA)**
1500 N Mantua St (44240-2399)
P.O. Box 5193 (44240-5193)
PHONE..................................330 673-9511
Karl J Warnke, *Ch of Bd*
William J Ginn, *Principal*
Douglas K Hall, *Principal*
Sandra W Harbrecht, *Principal*
John E Warfel, *Principal*
EMP: 175
SALES: 1B **Privately Held**
SIC: 0783 0782 0811 0181 Removal
services, bush & tree; lawn care services;
tree farm; nursery stock, growing of

(G-12227)
DAYTON FREIGHT LINES INC
280 Progress Blvd (44240-8015)
PHONE..................................330 346-0750
Robert Kantorowski, *Principal*
EMP: 35
SALES (corp-wide): 971MM **Privately
Held**
SIC: 4213 Contract haulers
PA: Dayton Freight Lines, Inc.
6450 Poe Ave Ste 311
Dayton OH 45414
937 264-4060

(G-12228)
DIAMOND HEAVY HAUL INC
123 N Water St Ste A (44240-2414)
PHONE..................................330 677-8061
Steven J Engel, *President*
Tonya Engel, *Vice Pres*
EMP: 25
SALES (est): 1.2MM **Privately Held**
SIC: 4213 Heavy hauling

(G-12229)
**DON WARTKO CONSTRUCTION
CO (PA)**
Also Called: Design Concrete Surfaces
975 Tallmadge Rd (44240-6474)
PHONE..................................330 673-5252
Thomas Wartko, *President*
David Wartko, *Vice Pres*
Mike Wartko, *Vice Pres*
Ron Wartko, *Vice Pres*
Doris Wartko, *Admin Sec*
EMP: 60
SQ FT: 15,000
SALES (est): 18.4MM **Privately Held**
SIC: 1623 1794 3732 Oil & gas line &
compressor station construction; sewer
line construction; water main construction;
excavation work; boat building & repairing

(G-12230)
EAST END WELDING COMPANY
357 Tallmadge Rd (44240-7201)
PHONE..................................330 677-6000
John E Susong, *President*
▲ **EMP:** 120 **EST:** 1967
SQ FT: 146,500
SALES (est): 36.4MM **Privately Held**
SIC: 3599 7692 Custom machinery; welding repair

(G-12231)
ENVIROTEST SYSTEMS CORP
1460t Fairchild Ave (44240-1818)
PHONE..................................330 963-4464
EMP: 34 **Privately Held**
WEB: www.il.etest.com
SIC: 7549 Emissions testing without repairs, automotive
HQ: Envirotest Systems Corp.
7 Kripes Rd
East Granby CT 06026

(G-12232)
**FAIRCHILD MD LEASING CO
LLC**
Also Called: Kent Healthcare Center
1290 Fairchild Ave (44240-1814)
PHONE..................................330 678-4912
Stephen Rosedale,
EMP: 150
SALES (est): 5.4MM **Privately Held**
SIC: 8051 Skilled nursing care facilities

(G-12233)
G & S TRANSFER INC
4055 Highway View Dr A (44240-8021)
PHONE..................................330 673-3899
Gary Begue, *President*
Shelly Begue, *Corp Secy*
EMP: 36
SALES (est): 3.8MM **Privately Held**
SIC: 4212 4213 Mail carriers, contract;
dump truck haulage; contract haulers

(G-12234)
GERMAN FAMILY SOCIETY INC
Also Called: GERMAN AMERICAN FAMILY
SOCIETY
3871 Ranfield Rd (44240-6760)
PHONE..................................330 678-8229
Joseph Geiser, *President*
Jim Armbrust, *Vice Pres*
Carl Townhauser, *Vice Pres*
Jim Resnick, *Treasurer*
Hilda Resnick, *Admin Sec*
EMP: 40
SALES: 585.5K **Privately Held**
WEB: www.germanfamilysociety.com
SIC: 7997 7299 Membership sports &
recreation clubs; banquet hall facilities

(G-12235)
GFS LEASING INC (PA)
Also Called: Altercare of Ravenna
1463 Tallmadge Rd (44240-6664)
PHONE..................................330 296-6415
Gerald F Schroer, *President*
EMP: 80
SQ FT: 23,000
SALES (est): 2.8MM **Privately Held**
SIC: 8051 Skilled nursing care facilities

(G-12236)
HOMETOWN BANK (PA)
142 N Water St (44240-2419)
P.O. Box 310 (44240-0006)
PHONE..................................330 673-9827
Timothy J McFarlane, *Chairman*
Brian Bialik, *Vice Pres*
Michael A Lewis, *Vice Pres*
Steve McDonald, *Vice Pres*
Patricia Buchanan, *Loan Officer*
EMP: 27 EST: 1898
SQ FT: 6,000
SALES: 8.6MM **Privately Held**
SIC: 6022 State commercial banks

(G-12237)
INDUSTRIAL TUBE AND STEEL CORP (PA)
4658 Crystal Pkwy (44240-8020)
P.O. Box 76054, Cleveland (44101-4203)
PHONE..................................330 474-5530
Dick Siess, *President*
Frederick H Gillen, *Principal*
H William Kranz Jr, *Principal*
Matthew Barnett, *Warehouse Mgr*
Dennis Thomas, *Warehouse Mgr*
▲ EMP: 35 EST: 1956
SQ FT: 30,000
SALES (est): 67.4MM **Privately Held**
SIC: 5051 Tubing, metal; bars, metal

(G-12238)
KAISER FOUNDATION HOSPITALS
Also Called: Kent Medical Offices
2500 State Route 59 (44240-7105)
PHONE..................................800 524-7377
EMP: 593
SALES (corp-wide): 93B **Privately Held**
SIC: 8011 Offices & clinics of medical doc-
tors
HQ: Kaiser Foundation Hospitals Inc
1 Kaiser Plz
Oakland CA 94612
510 271-6611

(G-12239)
KENT ADHESIVE PRODUCTS CO
Also Called: K A P C O
1000 Cherry St (44240-7501)
P.O. Box 626 (44240-0011)
PHONE..................................330 678-1626
Edward Small, *President*
Jenifer Codrea, *Vice Pres*
Philip M Zavracky, *Vice Pres*
Nate Foltz, *Purch Mgr*

Steve Smigel, *Controller*
▼ EMP: 80 EST: 1974
SQ FT: 100,000
SALES (est): 38.4MM **Privately Held**
WEB: www.kapco.com
SIC: 2679 2672 2675 7389 Paper products, converted; adhesive papers, labels
or tapes; from purchased material; tape,
pressure sensitive: made from purchased
materials; die-cut paper & board; laminating service; tape slitting

(G-12240)
KENT AUTOMOTIVE INC
Also Called: Kent Lincoln-Mercury Sales
1080 W Main St (44240-2006)
PHONE..................................330 678-5520
Bruce A Caudill, *President*
Heather Knapp, *Corp Secy*
Janet Caudill, *Vice Pres*
Joe Lipsett, *Sales Mgr*
Dave Shaner, *Sales Mgr*
EMP: 40
SALES: 32.9MM **Privately Held**
WEB: www.kentlm.com
SIC: 5511 5521 7538 7515 Automobiles,
new & used; used car dealers; general
automotive repair shops; passenger car
leasing; automotive & home supply stores

(G-12241)
KENT RIDGE AT GOLDEN POND LTD
5241 Sunnybrook Rd (44240-7383)
PHONE..................................330 677-4040
Sandy Warner, *Managing Prtnr*
EMP: 90
SALES (est): 2.8MM **Privately Held**
SIC: 8361 Home for the aged

(G-12242)
KENT STATE UNIVERSITY
Also Called: Procurement Payments
237 Schwartz Ste 237 (44242-0001)
P.O. Box 5190
PHONE..................................330 672-2607
Emily Hurmon, *Branch Mgr*
EMP: 79
SALES (corp-wide): 474.6MM **Privately Held**
WEB: www.kenteliv.kent.edu
SIC: 8221 8721 University; payroll ac-
counting service
PA: Kent State University
1500 Horning Rd
Kent OH 44242
330 672-3000

(G-12243)
KENT STATE UNIVERSITY
Also Called: Wksu FM Natl Public Radio
1613 E Summit St (44240-4684)
P.O. Box 5190 (44242-0001)
PHONE..................................330 672-3114
Al Bartholet, *Director*
EMP: 45
SALES (corp-wide): 474.6MM **Privately Held**
WEB: www.kenteliv.kent.edu
SIC: 4832 8221 Radio broadcasting sta-
tions; university
PA: Kent State University
1500 Horning Rd
Kent OH 44242
330 672-3000

(G-12244)
KLABEN FAMILY DODGE INC
1338 W Main St (44240-1940)
PHONE..................................330 673-9971
Michael G Klaben, *President*
Tim Assaf, *Corp Secy*
EMP: 50
SQ FT: 20,000
SALES (est): 8.6MM **Privately Held**
SIC: 5511 7538 7515 Automobiles, new &
used; trucks, tractors & trailers: new &
used; general automotive repair shops;
passenger car leasing

(G-12245)
KLABEN LEASING AND SALES INC
1338 W Main St (44240-1940)
PHONE..................................330 673-9971
Albert Klaben, *President*

EMP: 65 EST: 1990
SALES (est): 6.2MM **Privately Held**
SIC: 6159 Automobile finance leasing

(G-12246)
KLABEN LINCOLN FORD INC (PA)
Also Called: Klaben Auto Group
1089 W Main St (44240-2005)
PHONE..................................330 673-3139
Albert Klaben, *President*
Richard Klaben, *Vice Pres*
Steve Perkins, *Parts Mgr*
Christine Klaben, *Finance Mgr*
Andy Bellian, *Sales Mgr*
EMP: 81
SALES (est): 59.1MM **Privately Held**
WEB: www.klaben.com
SIC: 5511 7515 5012 Automobiles, new &
used; pickups, new & used; passenger
car leasing; automobiles & other motor
vehicles

(G-12247)
LOWES HOME CENTERS LLC
218 Nicholas Way (44240-8032)
PHONE..................................330 677-3040
Susan Sellf, *Branch Mgr*
EMP: 150
SALES (corp-wide): 68.6B **Publicly Held**
SIC: 5211 5031 5722 5064 Home cen-
ters; building materials, exterior; building
materials, interior; household appliance
stores; electrical appliances, television &
radio
HQ: Lowe's Home Centers, Llc
1605 Curtis Bridge Rd
Wilkesboro NC 28697
336 658-4000

(G-12248)
MAAG AUTOMATIK INC
Also Called: Maag Reduction Engineering
235 Progress Blvd (44240-8055)
PHONE..................................330 677-2225
EMP: 35
SALES (corp-wide): 6.9B **Publicly Held**
SIC: 3532 5084 Crushing, pulverizing &
screening equipment; pellet mills (mining
machinery); pulverizing machinery &
equipment
HQ: Maag Automatik, Inc.
9401 Southern Pine Blvd Q
Charlotte NC 28273

(G-12249)
MEDIA-COM INC
Also Called: Wnir/FM
2449 State Route 59 (44240)
P.O. Box 2170, Akron (44309-2170)
PHONE..................................330 673-2323
Richard M Klaus, *President*
Robert A Klaus, *Vice Pres*
William B Klaus, *Vice Pres*
Dan Hills, *Chief Engr*
Steve Stroup, *Accounts Exec*
EMP: 40
SQ FT: 4,200
SALES (est): 3.6MM **Privately Held**
WEB: www.wnir.com
SIC: 4832 Radio broadcasting stations

(G-12250)
NORTHAST OHIO EYE SURGEONS INC (PA)
2013 State Route 59 (44240-4113)
PHONE..................................330 678-0201
Lawrence E Lohman, *President*
Marc Jones, *Principal*
Matthew Willett, *Principal*
Katherine Hastings,
EMP: 26
SALES: 1.1MM **Privately Held**
WEB: www.neoes.net
SIC: 8011 Ophthalmologist

(G-12251)
NORTHASTERN EDUCTL TV OHIO INC
Also Called: Western Reserve Public Media
1750 W Campus Center Dr (44240-3820)
P.O. Box 5191 (44240-5191)
PHONE..................................330 677-4549
Trina Cutter, *President*
EMP: 30

SALES (corp-wide): 4.1MM **Privately Held**
SIC: 4833 Television broadcasting stations
PA: Northeastern Educational Television Of
Ohio, Inc.
1750 W Campus Center Dr
Kent OH
330 677-4549

(G-12252)
NVR INC
4034 Willow Way (44240-6888)
PHONE..................................440 584-4200
EMP: 33 **Publicly Held**
SIC: 1521 New construction, single-family
houses
PA: Nvr, Inc.
11700 Plaza America Dr # 500
Reston VA 20190

(G-12253)
PALESTINE CHLD RELIEF FUND
Also Called: Pcrf, The
1340 Morris Rd (44240-4518)
PHONE..................................330 678-2645
Steve Sosebee, *CEO*
Anna Hardy, *Finance Mgr*
Amanda Pudloski, *Admin Asst*
Maha Madani, *Social Worker*
EMP: 56
SALES: 7.9MM **Privately Held**
WEB: www.pcrf.net
SIC: 8099 Medical services organization

(G-12254)
PORTAGE AREA RGONAL TRNSP AUTH
Also Called: Parta
2000 Summit Rd (44240-7140)
PHONE..................................330 678-1287
Rick Bissler, *President*
Claudia Amrhein, *General Mgr*
John Drew Jr, *General Mgr*
Richard Brockett, *Trustee*
Bryan Trautman, *Opers Mgr*
EMP: 100
SQ FT: 41,905
SALES (est): 7.5MM **Privately Held**
WEB: www.partaonline.org
SIC: 4111 Local & suburban transit

(G-12255)
PROVINCE KENT OH LLC
609 S Lincoln St Ste F (44240-5366)
PHONE..................................330 673-3808
EMP: 30
SALES (est): 1.1MM **Privately Held**
SIC: 6513 Apartment Building Operator

(G-12256)
RAHF IV KENT LLC
1546 S Water St (44240-4464)
PHONE..................................216 621-6060
EMP: 50
SALES (est): 498.2K **Privately Held**
SIC: 6513 Apartment building operators

(G-12257)
ROBINSON HEALTH SYSTEM INC
Med Center One
1993 State Route 59 (44240-7609)
PHONE..................................330 297-0811
Jack Monda, *Director*
EMP: 30
SALES (corp-wide): 580MM **Privately Held**
SIC: 8062 General medical & surgical hos-
pitals
HQ: Robinson Health System, Inc.
6847 N Chestnut St
Ravenna OH 44266
330 297-0811

(G-12258)
SCHNELLER LLC
Polyplastex International
6019 Powdermill Rd (44240-7109)
PHONE..................................330 673-1299
Tom Spseisser, *Manager*
EMP: 75
SALES (corp-wide): 3.8B **Publicly Held**
WEB: www.schneller.com
SIC: 3083 8731 3728 Laminated plastic
sheets; commercial physical research;
aircraft parts & equipment

▲ = Import ▼=Export
◆ =Import/Export

HQ: Schneller Llc
6019 Powdermill Rd
Kent OH 44240
330 676-7183

(G-12259)
STOW-KENT ANIMAL HOSPITAL INC (PA)
4559 Kent Rd (44240-5298)
PHONE...................................330 673-0049
Thomas Albers Dvm, *President*
Carmella Albers, *Vice Pres*
EMP: 27
SALES (est): 2.5MM **Privately Held**
SIC: 0742 Animal hospital services, pets & other animal specialties; veterinarian, animal specialties

(G-12260)
STOW-KENT ANIMAL HOSPITAL INC
Also Called: Portage Animal Clinic
4148 State Route 43 (44240-6916)
PHONE...................................330 673-1002
EMP: 27
SALES (corp-wide): 2.5MM **Privately Held**
SIC: 0742 Animal hospital services, pets & other animal specialties
PA: Stow-Kent Animal Hospital Inc
4559 Kent Rd
Kent OH 44240
330 673-0049

(G-12261)
SYMCOX GRINDING & STEELE CO
825 Tallmadge Rd (44240-6463)
P.O. Box 156, Tallmadge (44278-0156)
PHONE...................................330 678-1080
Chuck Lewis, *President*
John Lewis, *Vice Pres*
Don Shaffer, *Treasurer*
Ron Lewis, *Admin Sec*
EMP: 32
SALES (est): 4.8MM **Privately Held**
SIC: 5051 Steel

(G-12262)
TALLMADGE ASPHALT & PAV CO INC
741 Tallmadge Rd (44240-7329)
PHONE...................................330 677-0000
Michael Sekulich, *President*
EMP: 60
SQ FT: 15,000
SALES (est): 9.9MM **Privately Held**
WEB: www.tallmadgeasphalt.com
SIC: 1771 Blacktop (asphalt) work

(G-12263)
TOWNHALL 2
Also Called: TOWNHALL 2 24 HOUR HELPLINE
155 N Water St (44240-2418)
PHONE...................................330 678-3006
Barbara Deakins, *Business Mgr*
Sue Whitehurst, *Exec Dir*
Robert Young, *Director*
Elizabeth Franczak, *Internal Med*
EMP: 50
SALES: 3.3MM **Privately Held**
WEB: www.townhall2.com
SIC: 8322 General counseling services

(G-12264)
U S DEVELOPMENT CORP (PA)
Also Called: Akro-Plastics
900 W Main St (44240-2285)
PHONE...................................330 673-6900
Jerold Ramsey, *President*
Fred Maurer, *Director*
EMP: 50
SQ FT: 185,000
SALES (est): 10.2MM **Privately Held**
WEB: www.rotomold.net
SIC: 3089 6512 Molding primary plastic; commercial & industrial building operation

(G-12265)
ULRICH PROFESSIONAL GROUP
401 Devon Pl Ste 215 (44240-6483)
PHONE...................................330 673-9501
Jack Monda, *President*

EMP: 25 EST: 1962
SALES (est): 1.1MM **Privately Held**
SIC: 8031 7361 Offices & clinics of osteopathic physicians; nurses' registry

(G-12266)
UNITY HEALTH NETWORK LLC
307 W Main St (44240-2400)
PHONE...................................330 678-7782
Robert A Kent Jr, *Administration*
EMP: 41
SALES (corp-wide): 14.5MM **Privately Held**
SIC: 8011 Internal medicine practitioners
PA: Unity Health Network, Llc
3033 State Rd
Cuyahoga Falls OH 44223
330 923-5899

(G-12267)
WALGREEN CO
Also Called: Walgreens
320 S Water St (44240-3528)
PHONE...................................330 677-5650
Andrew Dougt, *Manager*
EMP: 30
SALES (corp-wide): 131.5B **Publicly Held**
WEB: www.walgreens.com
SIC: 5912 7384 Drug stores; photofinishing laboratory
HQ: Walgreen Co.
200 Wilmot Rd
Deerfield IL 60015
847 315-2500

(G-12268)
WILBUR REALTY INC (PA)
Also Called: Century 21
548 S Water St (44240-3548)
P.O. Box 624 (44240-0011)
PHONE...................................330 673-5883
Steve Boyles, *President*
EMP: 40
SQ FT: 3,000
SALES (est): 2.2MM **Privately Held**
WEB: www.philmarch.com
SIC: 6531 Real estate agent, residential

(G-12269)
WINE-ART OF OHIO INC
Also Called: Carlson, L D Company
463 Portage Blvd (44240-7286)
PHONE...................................330 678-7733
Ronald Hartman, *CEO*
Laurence D Carlson, *Principal*
Ann Carst, *Principal*
Bruce B Laybourne, *Principal*
◆ EMP: 45
SQ FT: 40,000
SALES (est): 16.8MM **Privately Held**
WEB: www.ldcarlson.com
SIC: 5149 Wine makers' equipment & supplies

(G-12270)
YOUNG AND ASSOCIATES INC
121 E Main St (44240-2524)
P.O. Box 711 (44240-0013)
PHONE...................................330 678-0524
James Kleinfelter, *President*
Gary J Young, *Chairman*
Robert Whitehead, *Consultant*
EMP: 38
SQ FT: 2,500
SALES (est): 3.9MM **Privately Held**
WEB: www.younginc.com
SIC: 8742 Marketing consulting services; general management consultant

---

Kenton
Hardin County

(G-12271)
BKP AMBULANCE DISTRICT
439 S Main St (43326-1946)
PHONE...................................419 674-4574
Allen Barrett, *President*
Alan Long, *Principal*
Randy Scharf, *Vice Pres*
EMP: 30 EST: 1975
SALES: 786.7K **Privately Held**
SIC: 4119 Ambulance service

(G-12272)
BRIMS IMPORTS (PA)
Also Called: Brim's Imports Sales & Service
370 W Franklin St (43326-1711)
P.O. Box 471 (43326-0471)
PHONE...................................419 674-4137
Thomas E Brim, *Owner*
Ralph Brim, *Manager*
EMP: 42
SQ FT: 12,000
SALES (est): 5.6MM **Privately Held**
WEB: www.brimsimport.com
SIC: 5521 5093 Automobiles, used cars only; automotive wrecking for scrap

(G-12273)
CITY OF KENTON (PA)
111 W Franklin St (43326-1972)
PHONE...................................419 674-4850
Randy Manns, *Mayor*
EMP: 38 **Privately Held**
WEB: www.kentoncity.com
SIC: 9111 8611 Mayors' offices; business associations

(G-12274)
COUNTY OF HARDIN
Also Called: Hardin Cnty Dept Mntl Hlth Ret
705 N Ida St (43326-1060)
PHONE...................................419 674-4158
Mark Kieffer, *Principal*
EMP: 42 **Privately Held**
WEB: www.kenton.com
SIC: 8331 Vocational training agency
PA: County Of Hardin
1 Court House Sq Rm 100
Kenton OH 43326
419 674-2205

(G-12275)
FREEDOM ENTERPRISES INC
11441 County Road 75 (43326-9417)
PHONE...................................419 675-1192
James Michael Rose, *President*
Lavonna S Rose, *Admin Sec*
EMP: 27
SQ FT: 5,000
SALES: 3.2MM **Privately Held**
SIC: 4731 Truck transportation brokers

(G-12276)
HARCO INDUSTRIES INC
707 N Ida St (43326-1060)
PHONE...................................419 674-4159
David Schaub, *CEO*
Amy Newland, *Admin Sec*
EMP: 44
SQ FT: 7,000
SALES: 897.3K **Privately Held**
SIC: 8331 Sheltered workshop

(G-12277)
HARDIN CNTY CNCIL ON AGING INC
100 Memorial Dr (43326-2089)
PHONE...................................419 673-1102
Bette Bibler, *Director*
Sandra McKinley, *Bd of Directors*
Virginia Tice, *Bd of Directors*
EMP: 30
SALES: 1.3MM **Privately Held**
SIC: 8322 Senior citizens' center or association

(G-12278)
HARDIN COUNTY ENGINEER
1040 W Franklin St (43326-8852)
PHONE...................................419 673-2232
Michael Smith, *Engineer*
EMP: 35
SALES: 3MM **Privately Held**
SIC: 1611 Highway & street construction

(G-12279)
HARDIN COUNTY FAMILY YMCA
918 W Franklin St (43326-1720)
PHONE...................................419 673-6131
Shawn Galvin, *Director*
EMP: 48
SALES: 517.3K **Privately Held**
WEB: www.hardincoymca.com
SIC: 8641 7991 8351 7032 Youth organizations; physical fitness facilities; child day care services; youth camps; individual & family services

(G-12280)
HARDIN COUNTY HOME
Also Called: Hardin Hills Health Center
1211 W Lima St (43326-8846)
PHONE...................................419 673-0961
Debbie Lamb, *President*
Kathy Martino, *Executive*
Sara Reese, *Administration*
Mark Rogers, *Administration*
EMP: 71
SALES (est): 3.9MM **Privately Held**
WEB: www.hardinhills.org
SIC: 8059 Nursing home, except skilled & intermediate care facility

(G-12281)
HARDIN MEMORIAL HOSPITAL (HQ)
Also Called: Ohiohealth
921 E Franklin St (43326-2099)
PHONE...................................419 673-0761
David Blom, *CEO*
Mark Seckinger, *President*
Ron Snyder, *COO*
Michael W Louge, *Exec VP*
Chris Davis, *Pub Rel Dir*
EMP: 52
SQ FT: 91,678
SALES: 26MM
SALES (corp-wide): 4B **Privately Held**
WEB: www.hardinmemorialhospital.com
SIC: 8062 General medical & surgical hospitals
PA: Ohiohealth Corporation
180 E Broad St
Columbus OH 43215
614 788-8860

(G-12282)
HEALTH PARTNERS WESTERN OHIO
Also Called: Kenton Community Health Center
111 W Espy St (43326-2117)
PHONE...................................419 679-5994
Diane Russell, *Site Mgr*
Janis Allen, *Pharmacist*
Amy Brown, *Pharmacist*
Liza Frantz, *Director*
EMP: 30
SALES (corp-wide): 23.2MM **Privately Held**
SIC: 8099 Blood related health services
PA: Health Partners Of Western Ohio
441 E 8th St
Lima OH 45804
419 221-3072

(G-12283)
KENTON AUTO AND TRUCK WRECKING
Also Called: Kenton Motor Sales
13188 Us Highway 68 (43326-9302)
PHONE...................................419 673-8234
Franklin L Roof, *Owner*
EMP: 25
SQ FT: 1,200
SALES (est): 2MM **Privately Held**
SIC: 5093 5521 5013 Automotive wrecking for scrap; automobiles, used cars only; automotive supplies & parts

(G-12284)
MID-OHIO ENERGY COOPERATIVE
Also Called: Midohio Energy Cooperative
1210 W Lima St (43326-1798)
P.O. Box 224 (43326-0224)
PHONE...................................419 568-5321
John Metcalf, *President*
EMP: 28
SQ FT: 10,000
SALES: 21.1MM **Privately Held**
WEB: www.midohioenergy.com
SIC: 4911 Distribution, electric power

(G-12285)
MORTON BUILDINGS INC
Also Called: Morton Buildings Plant
14483 State Route 31 (43326-9055)
P.O. Box 223 (43326-0223)
PHONE...................................419 675-2311
Paul Hudson, *General Mgr*
Karen Baker, *Plant Mgr*
Marc Hale, *Engineer*

Garry Shirk, *Manager*
EMP: 70
SALES (corp-wide): 463.7MM **Privately Held**
SIC: 3448 5039 2452 Farm & utility buildings; prefabricated structures; prefabricated wood buildings
PA: Morton Buildings, Inc.
　　252 W Adams St
　　Morton IL 61550
　　800 447-7436

(G-12286)
PRECISION STRIP INC
190 Bales Rd (43326)
PHONE..............................419 674-4186
Don Bornhorst, *Branch Mgr*
EMP: 180
SALES (corp-wide): 11.5B **Publicly Held**
WEB: www.precision-strip.com
SIC: 4225 3341 General warehousing & storage; secondary nonferrous metals
HQ: Precision Strip Inc.
　　86 S Ohio St
　　Minster OH 45865
　　419 628-2343

(G-12287)
SCHNEIDER NATIONAL INC
808 Fontaine St (43326-2160)
PHONE..............................419 673-0254
EMP: 268
SALES (corp-wide): 4.9B **Publicly Held**
SIC: 4213 Trucking, except local
PA: Schneider National, Inc.
　　3101 Packerland Dr
　　Green Bay WI 54313
　　920 592-2000

(G-12288)
THE LIBERTY NAT BANKOF ADA
100 E Franklin St (43326-1924)
P.O. Box 234 (43326-0234)
PHONE..............................419 673-1217
William Carr, *CEO*
EMP: 25
SQ FT: 10,000
SALES (corp-wide): 13.5MM **Privately Held**
SIC: 6021 6022 National commercial banks; state commercial banks
PA: Liberty National Bankof Ada, The (Inc)
　　118 S Main St
　　Ada OH 45810
　　419 634-5015

(G-12289)
UNITED CHURCH RES OF KENTON
Also Called: CHAPEL HILL COMMUNITY
900 E Columbus St (43326-1758)
P.O. Box 1806, Marion (43301-1806)
PHONE..............................740 382-4885
Mark Seckinger, *President*
Brian Allen, *Assistant VP*
Robert Hart, *Vice Pres*
Ronald Beach, *CFO*
Cheryl Wickersham, *Treasurer*
EMP: 60
SQ FT: 28,000
SALES: 435.3K
SALES (corp-wide): 78.1MM **Privately Held**
WEB: www.altenheimcommunity.org
SIC: 6513 Apartment building operators
PA: United Church Homes Inc
　　170 E Center St
　　Marion OH 43302
　　740 382-4885

Kettering
Montgomery County

(G-12290)
ADVANCED MEDICAL EQUIPMENT INC (PA)
2655 S Dixie Dr (45409-1504)
PHONE..............................937 534-1080
Randy Willhelm, *Owner*
Andrew Willhelm, *Vice Pres*
Todd Wright, *Treasurer*
EMP: 37
SQ FT: 4,000

SALES (est) 9.1MM **Privately Held**
SIC: 5999 5047 Medical apparatus & supplies; medical equipment & supplies

(G-12291)
BASIN DIALYSIS LLC
Also Called: BUCKEYE DIALYSIS
3050 S Dixie Dr (45409-1516)
P.O. Box 2037, Tacoma WA (98401-2037)
PHONE..............................937 643-2337
James K Hilger,
Brenda Barrett, *Administration*
EMP: 48
SALES: 4MM **Publicly Held**
SIC: 8092 Kidney dialysis centers
PA: Davita Inc.
　　2000 16th St
　　Denver CO 80202

(G-12292)
EFIX COMPUTER REPAIR & SVC LLC
Also Called: It Services
1389 E Stroop Rd (45429-4925)
PHONE..............................937 985-4447
Edwin Kariuki, *Mng Member*
EMP: 45
SALES: 1MM **Privately Held**
SIC: 7378 Computer & data processing equipment repair/maintenance

(G-12293)
GENESIS RESCUE SYSTEMS
2780 Culver Ave (45429-3724)
PHONE..............................937 293-6240
Bill Halleran, *Regl Sales Mgr*
Marilou Beckley, *Office Mgr*
EMP: 50 **EST:** 2014
SALES (est): 7.3MM **Privately Held**
SIC: 5084 Hydraulic systems equipment & supplies

(G-12294)
KETTERING ADVENTIST HEALTHCARE
Also Called: Kettering Health Network
3533 Southern Blvd (45429-1264)
PHONE..............................937 298-3399
EMP: 61
SALES (corp-wide): 1.7B **Privately Held**
SIC: 8062 General medical & surgical hospitals
PA: Kettering Adventist Healthcare
　　3535 Southern Blvd
　　Dayton OH 45429
　　937 298-4331

(G-12295)
KETTERING MEDICAL CENTER (HQ)
Also Called: Charles F Kettering Mem Hosp
3535 Southern Blvd (45429-1298)
PHONE..............................937 298-4331
Jarrod McNaughton, *CEO*
Fred Manchur, *CEO*
Roy Chew, *President*
Terri Day, *President*
Walter Sackett, *President*
EMP: 37 **EST:** 1959
SQ FT: 500,000
SALES (est): 469MM
SALES (corp-wide): 1.7B **Privately Held**
WEB: www.kmcfoundation.org
SIC: 8062 Hospital, professional nursing school; hospital, medical school affiliated with nursing & residency
PA: Kettering Adventist Healthcare
　　3535 Southern Blvd
　　Dayton OH 45429
　　937 298-4331

(G-12296)
LADD DISTRIBUTION LLC (DH)
4849 Hempstead Station Dr (45429-5156)
PHONE..............................937 438-2646
Scott Leichtling, *Mng Member*
▲ **EMP:** 80
SQ FT: 48,000
SALES (est): 33.4MM
SALES (corp-wide): 13.1B **Privately Held**
SIC: 5065 Connectors, electronic
HQ: Te Connectivity Corporation
　　1050 Westlakes Dr
　　Berwyn PA 19312
　　610 893-9800

(G-12297)
MARXENT LABS LLC
3100 Res Blvd Ste 360 (45420)
PHONE..............................937 999-5005
Beck Desecker, *CEO*
Ryan Roche, *Design Engr*
Barry Desecker, *CTO*
Seth Cooper, *Director*
EMP: 78
SALES (est): 1.8MM **Privately Held**
SIC: 7371 Computer software development & applications

(G-12298)
OOVOO LLC
Also Called: Krush Technology
1700 S Patterson Blvd (45409-2140)
P.O. Box 340488, Dayton (45434-0488)
PHONE..............................917 515-2074
JP Nauses, *CEO*
EMP: 75
SALES (est): 4.1MM **Privately Held**
WEB: www.oovoo.com
SIC: 4899 Data communication services

(G-12299)
REYNOLDS AND REYNOLDS COMPANY (HQ)
1 Reynolds Way (45430-1586)
PHONE..............................937 485-2000
Bob Brockman, *CEO*
Monte Bion, *General Mgr*
Jeanne M Kirkland, *Principal*
David Hudson, *Business Mgr*
David Avery, *Exec VP*
EMP: 1000 **EST:** 1889
SQ FT: 60,000
SALES (est): 1.5B **Privately Held**
WEB: www.reyrey.com
SIC: 7373 6159 Computer integrated systems design; machinery & equipment finance leasing
PA: Universal Computer Systems, Inc.
　　6700 Hollister St
　　Houston TX 77040
　　713 718-1800

(G-12300)
STAMPER STAFFING LLC
2812 Purdue Dr (45420-3458)
PHONE..............................937 938-7010
Angela Perez,
Mary Stamper,
EMP: 49
SALES (est): 631K **Privately Held**
SIC: 7389 Placement agencies

(G-12301)
TOTAL RENAL CARE INC
Also Called: Home Dialysis of Dayton South
3030 S Dixie Dr (45409-1516)
PHONE..............................937 294-6711
James K Hilger,
EMP: 40
SQ FT: 14,095 **Publicly Held**
SIC: 8092 8011 Kidney dialysis centers; clinic, operated by physicians
HQ: Total Renal Care, Inc.
　　2000 16th St
　　Denver CO 80202
　　303 405-2100

(G-12302)
VAN BUREN DENTAL ASSOCIATES
1950 S Smithville Rd (45420-1446)
PHONE..............................937 253-9115
Michael C Dahm DDS, *Owner*
Michael Dahm, *Principal*
EMP: 30
SQ FT: 2,500
SALES (est): 1.5MM **Privately Held**
SIC: 8021 Dentists' office

(G-12303)
WALGREEN CO
Also Called: Walgreens
4497 Far Hills Ave (45429-2405)
PHONE..............................937 396-1358
John Fawer, *Manager*
EMP: 30

SALES (corp-wide): 131.5B **Publicly Held**
WEB: www.walgreens.com
SIC: 5912 7384 Drug stores; photofinishing laboratory
HQ: Walgreen Co.
　　200 Wilmot Rd
　　Deerfield IL 60015
　　847 315-2500

(G-12304)
WRIGHT STATE UNIVERSITY
Also Called: Cox Institute
3525 Southern Blvd (45429-1221)
PHONE..............................937 298-4331
Diane Myers, *Branch Mgr*
EMP: 45
SALES (corp-wide): 230.3MM **Privately Held**
WEB: www.wright.edu
SIC: 8733 8221 Medical research; university
PA: Wright State University
　　3640 Colonel Glenn Hwy
　　Dayton OH 45435
　　937 775-3333

Kidron
Wayne County

(G-12305)
CHRISTIAN SCHOOLS INC
Also Called: Central Christian School
3970 Kidron Rd (44636)
P.O. Box 9 (44636-0009)
PHONE..............................330 857-7311
Erin Maibach, *Manager*
Eugene Miller, *Director*
Bethany Nussbaum, *Director*
EMP: 55
SALES (est): 4.6MM **Privately Held**
SIC: 8211 8351 Private combined elementary & secondary school; private senior high school; preschool center

(G-12306)
JILCO INDUSTRIES INC (PA)
Also Called: Preferred Airparts
11234 Hackett Rd (44636)
P.O. Box 12 (44636-0012)
PHONE..............................330 698-0280
Ken Stoltzfus Jr, *President*
Brian Stoltzfus, *Corp Secy*
Colby Stoltfus, *Vice Pres*
Nate Berkey, *Sales Staff*
◆ **EMP:** 46
SQ FT: 78,000
SALES (est): 15.5MM **Privately Held**
WEB: www.preferredairparts.com
SIC: 5088 5599 4522 Aircraft & parts; aircraft instruments, equipment or parts; nonscheduled charter services

(G-12307)
KIDRON AUCTION INC
4885 Kidron Rd (44636)
PHONE..............................330 857-2641
John Sprunger, *President*
EMP: 50
SQ FT: 60,000
SALES (est): 2.5MM **Privately Held**
WEB: www.kidronauction.com
SIC: 7389 Auctioneers, fee basis

(G-12308)
KIDRON ELECTRIC INC
Also Called: Kidron Electric & Mech Contrs
5358 Kidron Rd (44636)
P.O. Box 248 (44636-0248)
PHONE..............................330 857-2871
Carrie Neuenschwander, *Principal*
Ken Neuenschwander, *Vice Pres*
David Daniels, *CFO*
Jon Baker, *Sales Staff*
Art Neuenschwander, *Sales Staff*
EMP: 30 **EST:** 1938
SQ FT: 50,000
SALES (est): 6.1MM **Privately Held**
WEB: www.kidronelectric.com
SIC: 1731 1711 General electrical contractor; warm air heating & air conditioning contractor; plumbing contractors

▲ = Import ▼=Export
◆ =Import/Export

(G-12309)
MILLER HOMES OF KIDRON LLC
6397 Kidron Rd (44636)
P.O. Box 212 (44636-0212)
PHONE..........................330 857-0161
Roy Miller, *Mng Member*
EMP: 26
SALES (est): 1.1MM **Privately Held**
SIC: 1521 New construction, single-family
houses

Killbuck
Holmes County

(G-12310)
**KILLBUCK SAVINGS BANK CO
INC (HQ)**
165 N Main St (44637-9795)
P.O. Box 407 (44637-0407)
PHONE..........................330 276-4881
Craig Lawhead, *President*
Vic Weaver, *Exec VP*
Marion Troyer, *Senior VP*
Lawrence Cardinal, *CFO*
Justin Smith, *Chief Mktg Ofcr*
EMP: 40
SQ FT: 12,000
SALES: 19.8MM **Publicly Held**
WEB: www.killbuckbank.com
SIC: 6022 State trust companies accepting
deposits, commercial

Kimbolton
Guernsey County

(G-12311)
CARDIDA CORPORATION (PA)
74978 Broadhead Rd (43749-9747)
PHONE..........................740 439-4359
Carl Larue, *President*
Bill La Rue, *Vice Pres*
Dan La Rue, *Admin Sec*
Karen Striff, *Administration*
EMP: 50
SALES: 2.6MM **Privately Held**
WEB: www.cardidaresortgroup.com
SIC: 7011 6552 Resort hotel; land subdi-
viders & developers, commercial

(G-12312)
SALT FORK RESORT CLUB INC
74978 Broadhead Rd (43749-9747)
PHONE..........................740 498-8116
Karl Larue, *President*
EMP: 1000
SALES: 1.8MM **Privately Held**
SIC: 7011 7997 Hotel/Motel Operation
Membership Sport/Recreation Club

Kings Mills
Warren County

(G-12313)
KINGS ISLAND COMPANY
6300 Kings Island Dr (45034)
PHONE..........................513 754-5700
Carl Lindner, *President*
Janet Richards, *Purchasing*
Mike Koontz, *Finance Dir*
Deborah Day, *Accounting Mgr*
Cindy Guenther, *Human Res Dir*
▲ EMP: 220
SALES (est): 23.7MM
SALES (corp-wide): 1.3B **Publicly Held**
SIC: 7996 Amusement parks
PA: Cedar Fair, L.P.
1 Cedar Point Dr
Sandusky OH 44870
419 626-0830

(G-12314)
KINGS ISLAND PARK LLC
6300 Kings Island Dr (45034)
P.O. Box 901 (45034-0901)
PHONE..........................513 754-5901
Craig Ross, *General Mgr*
Greg Scheid, *Branch Mgr*
EMP: 200

SALES (corp-wide): 1.3B **Publicly Held**
WEB: www.cedarfair.com
SIC: 7996 Theme park, amusement
HQ: Kings Island Park Llc
1 Cedar Point Dr
Sandusky OH 44870
419 626-0830

Kingston
Ross County

(G-12315)
**HAROLD TATMAN & SONS
ENTPS INC**
Also Called: Tatman, Harold & Sons
9171 State Route 180 (45644-9547)
P.O. Box 448, Adelphi (43101-0448)
PHONE..........................740 655-2880
Fax: 740 655-2887
EMP: 30 EST: 1963
SALES (est): 4.7MM **Privately Held**
SIC: 5199 Whol Nondurable Goods

(G-12316)
**KINGSTON NATIONAL BANK INC
(PA)**
2 N Main St (45644-9745)
P.O. Box 613 (45644-0613)
PHONE..........................740 642-2191
Phil Evans, *President*
Chris Kassner, *Assistant VP*
Ann Blake, *Vice Pres*
Lisa Wiseman, *Manager*
Lara Hauswirth, *Info Tech Mgr*
EMP: 36
SQ FT: 2,000
SALES: 11.7MM **Privately Held**
WEB: www.kingstonnationalbank.com
SIC: 6021 National commercial banks

Kinsman
Trumbull County

(G-12317)
**BAYLOFF STMPED PDTS
KNSMAN INC**
8091 State Route 5 (44428-9628)
PHONE..........................330 876-4511
Richard Bayer, *President*
Rufus S Day Jr, *Principal*
Dixon Morgan, *Principal*
M E Newcomer, *Principal*
Dan Moore, *Vice Pres*
EMP: 80
SQ FT: 115,000
SALES (est): 14.6MM **Privately Held**
SIC: 3469 7692 3444 3315 Stamping
metal for the trade; welding repair; sheet
metalwork; steel wire & related products

(G-12318)
BOYDS KINSMAN HOME INC
7929 State Route 5 (44428-9727)
P.O. Box 315 (44428-0315)
PHONE..........................330 876-5581
Paula Ruby, *Administration*
EMP: 39
SQ FT: 7,200
SALES: 2.9MM **Privately Held**
SIC: 8052 8059 Home for the mentally re-
tarded, with health care; home for the
mentally retarded, exc. skilled or interme-
diate

(G-12319)
PITMARK SERVICES INC
7925 State Route 5 (44428-9783)
P.O. Box 176 (44428-0176)
PHONE..........................330 876-2217
Anthony J Pitoscia, *Owner*
EMP: 50
SALES (est): 3.2MM **Privately Held**
SIC: 8742 Marketing consulting services

Kirkersville
Licking County

(G-12320)
**LIVIN CARE ALTER OF KIRKE
INC**
Also Called: Pine Kirk Nursing Home
205 E Main St (43033-7517)
P.O. Box 221 (43033-0221)
PHONE..........................740 927-3209
Thomas Rosser, *President*
Karen Rosser, *Principal*
EMP: 35
SALES (est): 1.5MM **Privately Held**
SIC: 8051 Skilled nursing care facilities

(G-12321)
LIVING CARE ALTERNATIVES
205 E Main St (43033-7517)
P.O. Box 223 (43033-0223)
PHONE..........................740 927-3209
Thomas Rosser, *Manager*
EMP: 35 **Privately Held**
SIC: 8051 Skilled nursing care facilities
PA: Living Care Alternatives
855 S Sunbury Rd
Westerville OH

Kirtland
Lake County

(G-12322)
LAKE METROPARKS
Also Called: Lake Farm Park
8800 Chardon Rd (44094-9520)
PHONE..........................440 256-2122
Lawrence Elswick, *Project Mgr*
Andrew Baker, *Manager*
Jen Irwin, *Manager*
Barbara Tokar, *Info Tech Mgr*
Paul Palagyi, *Exec Dir*
EMP: 80
SQ FT: 28,107
SALES (corp-wide): 20.9MM **Privately
Held**
WEB: www.lakemetroparks.com
SIC: 7999 Recreation services
PA: Lake Metroparks
11211 Spear Rd
Painesville OH 44077
440 639-7275

(G-12323)
MR EXCAVATOR INC
8616 Euclid Chardon Rd (44094-9586)
PHONE..........................440 256-2008
William A Flesher, *President*
Patricia Flesher, *Principal*
Tim Flesher, *Vice Pres*
Bob Flesher, *Chief Mktg Ofcr*
EMP: 85
SALES (est): 27.9MM **Privately Held**
WEB: www.mrexcavator.com
SIC: 1794 Excavation & grading, building
construction

La Rue
Marion County

(G-12324)
**STOFCHECK AMBULANCE SVC
INC (PA)**
220 S High St (43332-8881)
P.O. Box 333 (43332-0333)
PHONE..........................740 499-2200
Edward Stofcheck, *President*
Edward Stofcheck Sr, *President*
EMP: 30
SALES (est): 7MM **Privately Held**
SIC: 4119 Ambulance service

Lagrange
Lorain County

(G-12325)
MERCY HEALTH
105 Opportunity Way (44050-9018)
PHONE..........................440 355-4206
Cindi Keith, *Office Mgr*
EMP: 27
SALES (corp-wide): 4.7B **Privately Held**
SIC: 8062 General medical & surgical hos-
pitals
PA: Mercy Health
1701 Mercy Health Pl
Cincinnati OH 45237
513 639-2800

(G-12326)
**RURAL LORAIN COUNTY
WATER AUTH**
42401 State Route 303 (44050-9717)
P.O. Box 567 (44050-0567)
PHONE..........................440 355-5121
George Green, *President*
Andrew Provoznik, *Foreman/Supr*
Tim Mahoney, *Manager*
EMP: 60 EST: 1977
SALES: 15.5MM **Privately Held**
WEB: www.rlcwa.com
SIC: 4941 Water supply

(G-12327)
**WEST ROOFING SYSTEMS INC
(PA)**
121 Commerce Dr (44050-9491)
PHONE..........................800 356-5748
Jeff Johnson, *Prdtn Mgr*
Karen Swirs, *Manager*
▲ EMP: 39 EST: 1980
SQ FT: 10,700
SALES (est): 8.9MM **Privately Held**
WEB: www.westroofingsystems.com
SIC: 1761 1542 Roofing contractor; com-
mercial & office building, new construction

Lake Waynoka
Brown County

(G-12328)
**LAKE WYNOKA PRPRTY
OWNERS ASSN**
1 Waynoka Dr (45171-8728)
PHONE..........................937 446-3774
Vickie Johnson, *Principal*
EMP: 30
SQ FT: 1,100
SALES (est): 1.9MM **Privately Held**
WEB: www.lakewaynoka.com
SIC: 8641 Homeowners' association

Lakeside
Ottawa County

(G-12329)
LAKESIDE ASSOCIATION
236 Walnut Ave (43440-1400)
PHONE..........................419 798-4461
Shirley Stary, *Vice Pres*
Thomas Derby, *CFO*
Steve Koenig, *Manager*
Kevin Sibbring, *Exec Dir*
Robert Machovec Jr,
EMP: 30
SQ FT: 3,500
SALES: 11.5MM **Privately Held**
WEB: www.lakesideohio.com
SIC: 8621 Professional membership or-
ganizations

(G-12330)
**NORTH SHORE RETIREMENT
CMNTY**
Also Called: Otterbein North Shore
9400 E Northshore Blvd (43440-1337)
PHONE..........................419 798-8203
Lisa Hart, *Exec Dir*
Heather Jones, *Administration*

EMP: 45
SQ FT: 22,058
SALES: 1.4MM **Privately Held**
SIC: 8361 Home for the aged

Lakeside Marblehead
Ottawa County

(G-12331)
SOUTH BEACH RESORT
8620 E Bayshore Rd (43440-9719)
PHONE...................................419 798-4900
Kathy Kolar, *President*
EMP: 50
SALES (est): 1.6MM **Privately Held**
SIC: 7011 Motels

Lakeview
Logan County

(G-12332)
ACRUX INVESTIGATION
AGENCY (PA)
8823 Township Road 239 (43331-9321)
PHONE...................................937 842-5780
Alana Robinaugh, *Partner*
Deborah Proffrt, *Co-Owner*
EMP: 300
SALES: 9MM **Privately Held**
SIC: 7381 Detective agency; security
　guard service

Lakewood
Cuyahoga County

(G-12333)
12000 EDGEWATER DRIVE LLC
12000 Edgewater Dr (44107-1784)
PHONE...................................216 520-1250
Frank Sinito,
EMP: 99 **EST:** 2014
SALES (est): 954.8K **Privately Held**
SIC: 6513 Apartment building operators

(G-12334)
A-1 HEALTHCARE STAFFING
LLC
Also Called: Synergy Healthcare Systems
15644 Madison Ave (44107-5622)
PHONE...................................216 862-0906
Jennifer Fox,
EMP: 71
SALES (corp-wide): 6.5MM **Privately**
Held
SIC: 8011 7361 Offices & clinics of med-
　ical doctors; employment agencies
PA: A-1 Healthcare Staffing Llc
　2991 E 73rd St
　Cleveland OH 44104
　216 862-0906

(G-12335)
AMERIFIRST FINANCIAL CORP
14701 Detroit Ave Ste 750 (44107-4109)
PHONE...................................216 452-5120
EMP: 81
SALES (corp-wide): 172.5MM **Privately**
Held
SIC: 6162 Mortgage bankers & correspon-
　dents
PA: Amerifirst Financial Corporation
　950 Trade Centre Way # 400
　Portage MI 49002
　269 324-4240

(G-12336)
AREA TEMPS INC
14801 Detroit Ave (44107-3909)
PHONE...................................216 227-8200
Gail Enders, *Principal*
EMP: 1383
SALES (corp-wide): 87.8MM **Privately**
Held
SIC: 7363 Temporary help service
PA: Area Temps, Inc.
　4511 Rockside Rd Ste 190
　Independence OH 44131
　216 781-5350

(G-12337)
BROWNSTONE PRIVATE CHILD
CARE
18225 Sloane Ave (44107-3109)
PHONE...................................216 221-1470
Nancy Rafferty, *President*
Alice Mann, *Corp Secy*
Maggie Rafferty, *Director*
EMP: 35
SQ FT: 10,000
SALES (est): 1.7MM **Privately Held**
SIC: 8351 Preschool center

(G-12338)
CITY OF LAKEWOOD
Also Called: Senior Center West
16024 Madison Ave (44107-5616)
PHONE...................................216 521-1515
Paulette McMonagle, *Director*
EMP: 25 **Privately Held**
SIC: 8322 Senior citizens' center or associ-
　ation
PA: City Of Lakewood
　12650 Detroit Ave
　Lakewood OH 44107
　216 521-7580

(G-12339)
CORNUCOPIA INC
Also Called: Natures Bin
18120 Sloane Ave (44107-3108)
PHONE...................................216 521-4600
Nancy Cuttler, *Exec Dir*
Scott Duennes, *Exec Dir*
EMP: 36
SQ FT: 6,000
SALES: 2.4MM **Privately Held**
SIC: 8331 5499 Vocational rehabilitation
　agency; health foods

(G-12340)
CRESTMONT NURSING HOME N
CORP (PA)
Also Called: Crestmont North
13330 Detroit Ave (44107-2850)
PHONE...................................216 228-9550
Elias J Coury, *President*
Norman Fox, *Treasurer*
Eva Lefton, *Med Doctor*
Peter Chilton, *Technology*
EMP: 110
SALES (est): 7.9MM **Privately Held**
SIC: 8051 Convalescent home with contin-
　uous nursing care

(G-12341)
CRESTMONT NURSING HOME N
CORP
13330 Detroit Ave (44107-2850)
PHONE...................................216 228-9550
Wendy Tyler, *Administration*
EMP: 100
SQ FT: 24,209
SALES (corp-wide): 7.9MM **Privately**
Held
SIC: 8051 Convalescent home with contin-
　uous nursing care
PA: Crestmont Nursing Home North Corp.
　13330 Detroit Ave
　Lakewood OH 44107
　216 228-9550

(G-12342)
ETECH-SYSTEMS LLC
14600 Detroit Ave # 1500 (44107-4207)
PHONE...................................216 221-6600
Walter Zaremba, *CEO*
Gary Biales,
Robert Steadley,
Al Sulin,
Joseph J Urbancic,
EMP: 70
SQ FT: 12,000
SALES (est): 5.3MM **Privately Held**
SIC: 1542 1522 1521 Shopping center
　construction; apartment building construc-
　tion; new construction, single-family
　houses

(G-12343)
FIRST FDRAL SAV LN ASSN
LKWOOD (PA)
14806 Detroit Ave (44107-3910)
PHONE...................................216 221-7300
W Charles Geiger III, *Ch of Bd*

Timothy E Phillips, *President*
Judy Platek, *Assistant VP*
Jeffrey Bechtel, *Vice Pres*
Paul Capka, *Vice Pres*
EMP: 130
SQ FT: 12,000
SALES: 63MM **Privately Held**
WEB: www.ffl.net
SIC: 6035 Federal savings & loan associa-
　tions

(G-12344)
FORTUNEFAVORSTHE BOLD
LLC
11716 Detroit Ave (44107-3002)
PHONE...................................216 469-2845
Jennifer Ilgauskas, *President*
Mary Boyer, *Office Mgr*
EMP: 25
SQ FT: 6,980
SALES (est): 185.5K **Privately Held**
SIC: 8011 Offices & clinics of medical doc-
　tors

(G-12345)
HANSON SERVICES INC (PA)
17017 Madison Ave (44107-3501)
P.O. Box 771222, Cleveland (44107-0051)
PHONE...................................216 226-5425
Mary Ann Hanson, *President*
Kanchan Adhikary, *CFO*
Peggy Kilroy, *Human Resources*
Amy Johnston, *Mktg Dir*
Patty Murphy, *Marketing Staff*
EMP: 125 **EST:** 1996
SQ FT: 2,200
SALES (est): 8MM **Privately Held**
SIC: 8082 Visiting nurse service

(G-12346)
HEALTHSPAN INTEGRATED
CARE
Also Called: Kaiser Foundation Health Plan
14600 Detroit Ave Apt 700 (44107-4225)
PHONE...................................216 362-2277
Belva Denmark, *Director*
EMP: 25
SALES (corp-wide): 4.7B **Privately Held**
SIC: 6324 Hospital & medical service plans
HQ: Healthspan Integrated Care
　1001 Lakeside Ave E # 1200
　Cleveland OH 44114
　216 621-5600

(G-12347)
ICE LAND USA LAKEWOOD
14740 Lakewood Hts Blvd (44107-5901)
PHONE...................................216 529-1200
Patrick Krausman, *Manager*
EMP: 26
SALES (est): 381.4K **Privately Held**
SIC: 7999 Ice skating rink operation

(G-12348)
IMCD US LLC (HQ)
14725 Detroit Ave Ste 300 (44107-4124)
PHONE...................................216 228-8900
John L Mastrantoni, *President*
Bruce D Jarosz, *CFO*
David Carlin, *Sales Staff*
Erica Dziczek, *Technical Staff*
▲ **EMP:** 46
SALES (est): 259.9MM
SALES (corp-wide): 2.2B **Privately Held**
WEB: www.mfcachat.com
SIC: 5169 Chemicals & allied products
PA: Imcd N.V.
　Wilhelminaplein 32
　Rotterdam
　102 908-684

(G-12349)
KANSAS CITY HARDWOOD
CORP
17717 Hilliard Rd (44107-5332)
PHONE...................................913 621-1975
Dan Schneider, *President*
Robert Vogel, *Corp Secy*
John Hawkinson, *Vice Pres*
EMP: 28
SQ FT: 45,000
SALES (est): 6.3MM **Privately Held**
SIC: 5031 Hardboard

(G-12350)
L S C SERVICE CORP
14306 Detroit Ave Apt 237 (44107-4450)
PHONE...................................216 521-7260
Lawrence Faulhaber, *Director*
EMP: 35
SALES (est): 532.4K **Privately Held**
SIC: 6513 Apartment hotel operation

(G-12351)
LAKEWOOD CATHOLIC
ACADEMY
Also Called: Holy Family
14808 Lake Ave (44107-1352)
PHONE...................................216 521-4352
Charles P Battiato, *Partner*
Brian E Powers, *Partner*
Kathleen Ogrin, *Director*
EMP: 30 **Privately Held**
SIC: 8351 Child day care services
PA: Lakewood Catholic Academy
　14808 Lake Ave
　Lakewood OH 44107

(G-12352)
LAKEWOOD CITY SCHOOL
DISTRICT
Also Called: Winterhurst Ice Rink
14740 Lakewood Hts Blvd (44107-5901)
PHONE...................................216 529-4400
Tim Starks, *Manager*
EMP: 50
SALES (corp-wide): 117.8MM **Privately**
Held
SIC: 8211 7999 Public elementary & sec-
　ondary schools; ice skating rink operation
PA: Lakewood City School District
　1470 Warren Rd
　Cleveland OH 44107
　216 529-4092

(G-12353)
LAKEWOOD CLVELAND FMLY
MED CTR
16215 Madison Ave (44107-5618)
PHONE...................................216 227-2162
Robert T Colacarro, *Med Doctor*
Carl Culley MD, *Director*
Robert Colacarro, *Deputy Dir*
EMP: 25
SALES (est): 1.8MM **Privately Held**
SIC: 8011 Primary care medical clinic

(G-12354)
LAKEWOOD COMMUNITY CARE
CENTER
2019 Woodward Ave (44107-5635)
PHONE...................................216 226-0080
Pam Meade, *Exec Dir*
Gay Henrikson, *Director*
EMP: 30
SQ FT: 8,000
SALES: 639K **Privately Held**
SIC: 8351 Preschool center

(G-12355)
LAKEWOOD HEALTH CARE
CENTER
Also Called: Ennis Court
13315 Detroit Ave (44107-2849)
PHONE...................................216 226-3103
Patrice Campbell, *President*
Louis Klein, *Director*
EMP: 120
SQ FT: 20,000
SALES (est): 4.7MM **Privately Held**
SIC: 8051 Extended care facility

(G-12356)
LAKEWOOD HOSPITAL
ASSOCIATION (HQ)
14519 Detroit Ave (44107-4316)
PHONE...................................216 529-7160
Fred Degrandis, *CEO*
Mary Sauer, *Ch Nursing Ofcr*
Jack Gustin,
EMP: 530
SQ FT: 100,000
SALES: 94MM
SALES (corp-wide): 8.9B **Privately Held**
SIC: 8062 General Hospital

PA: The Cleveland Clinic Foundation
9500 Euclid Ave
Cleveland OH 44195
216 636-8335

(G-12357)
NEW YORK LIFE INSURANCE CO
14600 Detroit Ave Apt 900 (44107-4227)
PHONE..........................216 221-1100
George Hewlett, *Vice Pres*
Elizabeth Murphy, *Manager*
EMP: 60
SALES (corp-wide): 18.3B **Privately Held**
SIC: 6411 Insurance agents & brokers
PA: New York Life Insurance Company
51 Madison Ave Bsmt 1b
New York NY 10010
212 576-7000

(G-12358)
ON-CALL NURSING INC
15644 Madison Ave (44107-5622)
PHONE..........................216 577-8890
Jennifer Fox, *President*
EMP: 99
SALES (est): 613.8K **Privately Held**
SIC: 8059 8082 8052 Home for the mentally retarded, exc. skilled or intermediate; home health care services; visiting nurse service; personal care facility

(G-12359)
PALLET DISTRIBUTORS INC (PA)
Also Called: E-Pallet
14701 Detroit Ave Ste 610 (44107-4180)
PHONE..........................888 805-9670
Greg Fronk, *President*
Sandy Riedel, *Vice Pres*
EMP: 105
SQ FT: 3,500
SALES (est): 45.6MM **Privately Held**
SIC: 5031 5085 Pallets, wood; plastic pallets

(G-12360)
PRUDENTIAL LUCIEN REALTY
Also Called: Century 21
18630 Detroit Ave (44107-3202)
PHONE..........................216 226-4673
Ronald Lucien, *President*
Tim Cunningham, *Real Est Agnt*
EMP: 50
SALES (est): 3.1MM **Privately Held**
WEB: www.lucienrealty.com
SIC: 6531 Real estate agent, residential

(G-12361)
RAD-CON INC (PA)
Also Called: Entec International Systems
13001 Athens Ave Ste 300 (44107-6246)
PHONE..........................440 871-5720
David R Blackman, *President*
Christopher Messina, *President*
Michael McDonald, *Vice Pres*
Sean McGreer, *Vice Pres*
EMP: 26
SQ FT: 6,000
SALES (est): 10MM **Privately Held**
WEB: www.rad-con.com
SIC: 8711 3567 Engineering services; industrial furnaces & ovens

(G-12362)
ROUNDSTONE MANAGEMENT LTD
15422 Detroit Ave (44107-3830)
PHONE..........................440 617-0333
Mike Schroeder, *President*
Michael Schroeder, *President*
Matthew Monda, *COO*
Robert Pace, *Regl Sales Mgr*
Kelley Drumm, *Marketing Staff*
EMP: 32
SALES (est): 2.7MM **Privately Held**
SIC: 8741 Business management

(G-12363)
ST AUGUSTINE CORPORATION
1341 Nicholson Ave (44107-2735)
PHONE..........................216 939-7600
Patrick Gareau, *President*
EMP: 400
SQ FT: 256,593

SALES: 18MM **Privately Held**
SIC: 8741 8052 8051 Nursing & personal care facility management; intermediate care facilities; skilled nursing care facilities

(G-12364)
YOUNG MNS CHRSTN ASSN CLVELAND
Also Called: Lakewood Y
16915 Detroit Ave (44107-3620)
PHONE..........................216 521-8400
Gary Brick, *Director*
EMP: 39
SQ FT: 21,781
SALES (corp-wide): 29.2MM **Privately Held**
SIC: 8641 7991 8351 7032 Youth organizations; physical fitness facilities; child day care services; youth camps; individual & family services
PA: Young Men's Christian Association Of Cleveland
1801 Superior Ave E # 130
Cleveland OH 44114
216 781-1337

(G-12365)
ZARCAL ZANESVILLE LLC
14600 Detroit Ave # 1500 (44107-4207)
PHONE..........................216 226-2132
Edward Kiss, *Principal*
EMP: 60
SALES (est): 1.5MM **Privately Held**
SIC: 8741 Business management

(G-12366)
ZAREMBA GROUP LLC
14600 Detroit Ave (44107-4207)
PHONE..........................216 221-6600
David Zaremba, *CEO*
Alan J Bellis, *Project Mgr*
Gary Bialas, *Engineer*
Ed Kiss, *CFO*
Robert Steadley, *CFO*
EMP: 110 EST: 1997
SQ FT: 12,000
SALES (est): 18.5MM **Privately Held**
WEB: www.zarembagroup.com
SIC: 6552 8111 6531 Land subdividers & developers, commercial; legal services; real estate managers; real estate agent, commercial

(G-12367)
ZAREMBA ZANESVILLE LLC
14600 Detroit Ave # 1500 (44107-4207)
PHONE..........................216 221-6600
Robert F Steadley,
EMP: 50
SALES (est): 1.7MM **Privately Held**
SIC: 6531 Real estate agents & managers

Lancaster
Fairfield County

(G-12368)
ACCURATE MECHANICAL INC
566 Mill Park Dr (43130-7744)
PHONE..........................740 681-1332
EMP: 49
SALES (corp-wide): 26.3MM **Privately Held**
SIC: 5074 5063 3499 1711 Heating equipment (hydronic); electrical supplies; aerosol valves, metal; septic system construction
PA: Accurate Mechanical, Inc.
3001 River Rd
Chillicothe OH
740 775-5005

(G-12369)
ALLERGY & ASTHMA INC
2405 N Columbus St # 270 (43130-8185)
PHONE..........................740 654-8623
H C Nataraj, *Branch Mgr*
EMP: 28
SALES (corp-wide): 2.1MM **Privately Held**
SIC: 8011 Allergist

PA: Allergy & Asthma, Inc.
5965 E Broad St Ste 320
Columbus OH 43213
614 864-6649

(G-12370)
ALTERNACARE HOME HEALTH INC
1566 Monmouth Dr Ste 103 (43130-8048)
PHONE..........................740 689-1589
Diane Stuckey, *President*
Shawna Martens, *Principal*
EMP: 43
SQ FT: 2,421
SALES (est): 2.3MM **Privately Held**
WEB: www.alternacare.biz
SIC: 8082 Visiting nurse service

(G-12371)
ARBOR VIEW FAMILY MEDICINE INC
2405 N Columbus St # 200 (43130-8185)
PHONE..........................740 687-3386
David Scoggin, *Principal*
Stephanie Mesko, *Family Practiti*
EMP: 33 EST: 1997
SALES (est): 3.1MM **Privately Held**
WEB: www.avfm.org
SIC: 8071 Medical laboratories

(G-12372)
BOB-BOYD FORD INC (PA)
Also Called: Bobboyd Auto Family
2840 N Columbus St (43130-8128)
P.O. Box 767 (43130-0767)
PHONE..........................614 860-0606
Robert G Dawes, *President*
Michael D Bornstein, *Principal*
Mark Falls, *Principal*
Boyd Fackler, *Treasurer*
John Dillon, *Sales Staff*
EMP: 60 EST: 1946
SALES (est): 26.4MM **Privately Held**
WEB: www.bobboyd.com
SIC: 5511 7538 Automobiles, new & used; general automotive repair shops

(G-12373)
BROOKDALE SNIOR LVING CMMNTIES
Also Called: Sterling House of Lancaster
241 Whittier Dr S (43130-5717)
PHONE..........................740 681-9903
Michael Weeks, *Manager*
EMP: 28
SALES (corp-wide): 4.5B **Publicly Held**
WEB: www.assisted.com
SIC: 8059 Rest home, with health care
HQ: Brookdale Senior Living Communities, Inc.
6737 W Wa St Ste 2300
Milwaukee WI 53214
414 918-5000

(G-12374)
C M S ENTERPRISES INC (PA)
Also Called: ServiceMaster
664 S Columbus St (43130-4661)
PHONE..........................740 653-1940
Robert Marshall, *President*
EMP: 25
SQ FT: 8,000
SALES (est): 3.3MM **Privately Held**
SIC: 7349 1799 7217 Building maintenance services; post-disaster renovations; carpet & rug cleaning plant

(G-12375)
CARLETON REALTY INC
826 N Memorial Dr (43130-2567)
PHONE..........................740 653-5200
John Grady, *Sales Staff*
Renee Schmelzer, *Branch Mgr*
EMP: 47
SALES (corp-wide): 2.9MM **Privately Held**
SIC: 6531 Real estate agent, residential
PA: Carleton Realty Inc
580 W Schrock Rd
Westerville OH 43081
614 431-5700

(G-12376)
CARRIAGE COURT COMPANY INC
Also Called: Carriage Court Community
800 Becks Knob Rd Ofc (43130-8804)
PHONE..........................740 654-4422
Debbie Cook, *Manager*
EMP: 35 **Privately Held**
SIC: 8059 8361 8051 Personal care home, with health care; residential care; skilled nursing care facilities
PA: Carriage Court Company, Inc.
2041 Riverside Dr Ste 100
Columbus OH

(G-12377)
CELLCO PARTNERSHIP
Also Called: Verizon Wireless
1926 N Memorial Dr (43130-1665)
PHONE..........................740 652-9540
EMP: 71
SALES (corp-wide): 130.8B **Publicly Held**
SIC: 4812 Cellular telephone services
HQ: Cellco Partnership
1 Verizon Way
Basking Ridge NJ 07920

(G-12378)
CHEERS CHALET
Also Called: Cheers & Lakeside Chalet
1211 Coonpath Rd Nw (43130-8999)
PHONE..........................740 654-9036
Gary Krasnosky, *Partner*
EMP: 25
SALES (est): 1MM **Privately Held**
WEB: www.cheerschalet.com
SIC: 7299 5812 Banquet hall facilities; eating places

(G-12379)
CINTAS CORPORATION NO 2
2250 Commerce St (43130-9363)
PHONE..........................740 687-6230
Jason Hill, *General Mgr*
EMP: 50
SQ FT: 35,000
SALES (corp-wide): 6.4B **Publicly Held**
WEB: www.cintas-corp.com
SIC: 7213 Uniform supply
HQ: Cintas Corporation No. 2
6800 Cintas Blvd
Mason OH 45040

(G-12380)
CITY OF LANCASTER
Also Called: Lancaster Municipal Gas
1424 Campground Rd (43130-9503)
PHONE..........................740 687-6670
Michael R Pettit, *Superintendent*
Bill Burrows, *Superintendent*
Michael Pettit, *Manager*
Carrie Woody, *Admin Asst*
EMP: 25 **Privately Held**
WEB: www.ci.lancaster.oh.us
SIC: 1311 4924 Crude petroleum & natural gas; natural gas distribution
PA: City Of Lancaster
104 E Main St
Lancaster OH 43130
740 687-6617

(G-12381)
CLAYPOOL ELECTRIC INC
Also Called: Claypool Electrical Contg
1275 Lncstr Krkrsville Rd (43130-8969)
PHONE..........................740 653-5683
Charles Claypool, *CEO*
Greg Davis, *President*
Barbara Claypool, *Corp Secy*
Tucker Brady, *Treasurer*
David Arnett, *Manager*
EMP: 160 EST: 1955
SQ FT: 20,000
SALES (est): 31.3MM **Privately Held**
WEB: www.claypoolelectric.com
SIC: 1731 General electrical contractor

(G-12382)
CLOVVR LLC
1566 Monmouth Dr Ste 103 (43130-8048)
PHONE..........................740 653-2224
Hanad Duale,
EMP: 32
SALES (est): 248K **Privately Held**
SIC: 8082 Home health care services

(G-12383)
CMS BUSINESS SERVICES LLC
Also Called: Servicmster Coml Clg Advantage
416 N Mount Pleasant Ave (43130-3134)
PHONE....................................740 687-0577
Teresa Marshall, *Mng Member*
Dan Marshall, *Mng Member*
EMP: 80 EST: 2008
SALES: 1MM **Privately Held**
SIC: 7349 Janitorial service, contract basis

(G-12384)
COMMUNITY ACTION PROGRAM COMM (PA)
Also Called: LANCASTER-FAIRFIELD COMMUNITY
1743 E Main St (43130-9838)
P.O. Box 768 (43130-0768)
PHONE....................................740 653-1711
Kellie Ailes, *Exec Dir*
EMP: 174
SQ FT: 3,000
SALES: 7.9MM **Privately Held**
WEB: www.faircaa.org
SIC: 8322 Social service center

(G-12385)
COMMUNITY ASSISTED LIVING INC
500 N Pierce Ave (43130-2963)
PHONE....................................740 653-2575
Cynthia A Lamb, *President*
EMP: 50
SALES (est): 2.3MM **Privately Held**
SIC: 8361 Residential care

(G-12386)
CRESTVIEW MANOR NURSING HOME (PA)
Also Called: CRESTVIEW MANOR I
957 Becks Knob Rd (43130-8800)
PHONE....................................740 654-2634
Winfield S Eckert, *President*
Jo Ann Eckert, *Admin Sec*
EMP: 220
SQ FT: 52,000
SALES: 17.6MM **Privately Held**
SIC: 8051 6513 Extended care facility;
  apartment building operators

(G-12387)
CRESTVIEW MANOR NURSING HOME
Also Called: Crestview Manor II
925 Becks Knob Rd (43130-8800)
PHONE....................................740 654-2634
Winfield S Eckert, *President*
EMP: 110
SALES (corp-wide): 17MM **Privately Held**
SIC: 8051 Extended care facility
PA: Crestview Manor Nursing Home, Inc
  957 Becks Knob Rd
  Lancaster OH 43130
  740 654-2634

(G-12388)
DAGGER JOHNSTON MILLER (PA)
144 E Main St (43130-3712)
P.O. Box 667 (43130-0667)
PHONE....................................740 653-6464
Norman J Ogilvie, *Partner*
Mark Bibler, *Partner*
J Jay Hampson, *Partner*
Randy Happeney, *Partner*
Robert E Johnston, *Partner*
EMP: 35
SQ FT: 2,200
SALES (est): 4.5MM **Privately Held**
WEB: www.daggerlaw.com
SIC: 8111 General practice attorney,
  lawyer

(G-12389)
DISPATCH CONSUMER SERVICES
Also Called: Bag, The
3160 W Fair Ave (43130-9568)
PHONE....................................740 687-1893
Donna Holbrook, *Manager*
EMP: 70

SALES (corp-wide): 651.9MM **Privately Held**
SIC: 7319 Distribution of advertising material or sample services
HQ: Dispatch Consumer Services Inc
  5300 Crosswind Dr
  Columbus OH 43228
  740 548-5555

(G-12390)
DREW VENTURES INC (PA)
Also Called: Drew Shoe
252 Quarry Rd Se (43130-8054)
PHONE....................................740 653-4271
Dennis B Tishkoff, *Ch of Bd*
Marc Tishkoff, *President*
Marc Tishoff, *COO*
Paul Kilian, *Vice Pres*
Pete Struzzi, *CFO*
▲ EMP: 44 EST: 1875
SQ FT: 60,000
SALES (est): 13MM **Privately Held**
WEB: www.drewshoe.com
SIC: 5139 Shoes

(G-12391)
FAIRFIELD CNTY JOB & FMLY SVCS
239 W Main St (43130-3739)
PHONE....................................800 450-8845
Michael Orlando, *Principal*
Jamie Fauble, *Principal*
EMP: 99
SALES (est): 2.2MM **Privately Held**
WEB: www.fcjfs.org
SIC: 8399 Council for social agency

(G-12392)
FAIRFIELD COMMUNITY HEALTH CTR
Also Called: Fchc
1155 E Main St (43130-4056)
PHONE....................................740 277-6043
Clinton G Kuntz, *CEO*
Micheal Horn Berger, *CFO*
Lauree Althaus, *Manager*
EMP: 39
SQ FT: 5,000
SALES (est): 3.3MM **Privately Held**
SIC: 8082 Home health care services

(G-12393)
FAIRFIELD COUNTY
Also Called: Fairfield Cnty Chld Prtctd
239 W Main St (43130-3739)
PHONE....................................740 653-4060
Rich Bowlen, *Director*
EMP: 61 **Privately Held**
WEB: www.fairfieldmha.org
SIC: 8399 Council for social agency
PA: Fairfield County
  210 E Main St Rm 201
  Lancaster OH 43130
  740 652-7020

(G-12394)
FAIRFIELD DIAGNSTC IMAGING LLC
Also Called: Fairfield Medical Center
1241 River Valley Blvd (43130-1653)
PHONE....................................740 654-7559
Sky Gettys, *CEO*
Tamara Scott, *Med Doctor*
Wendy Melick, *Manager*
EMP: 25 EST: 1998
SALES (est): 1.1MM **Privately Held**
WEB: www.fairfielddiagnosticimaging.com
SIC: 8099 Physical examination & testing services

(G-12395)
FAIRFIELD FEDERAL SAV LN ASSN (PA)
111 E Main St (43130-3713)
P.O. Box 728 (43130-0728)
PHONE....................................740 653-3863
Ronald Keaton, *President*
Cathy Glenn, *Assistant VP*
Bev Stratton, *Assistant VP*
Bruce Baughman, *Vice Pres*
Sharon Drumm, *Vice Pres*
EMP: 50 EST: 1895
SQ FT: 22,500

SALES: 10.9MM **Privately Held**
WEB: www.fairfieldfederal.com
SIC: 6035 8111 Federal savings & loan
  associations; legal services

(G-12396)
FAIRFIELD HOMES INC (PA)
Also Called: Gorsuch Management
603 W Wheeling St (43130-3630)
P.O. Box 190 (43130-0190)
PHONE....................................740 653-3583
Leonard F Gorsuch, *CEO*
Michael Williams, *Project Mgr*
Ronald P Burson, *Treasurer*
Ronald Burson, *Treasurer*
Kathryn Iles, *Supervisor*
EMP: 30
SQ FT: 7,000
SALES (est): 20.4MM **Privately Held**
WEB: www.gorsuch-homes.com
SIC: 6531 1522 Real estate managers;
  multi-family dwelling construction

(G-12397)
FAIRFIELD HOMES INC (PA)
Also Called: Gorsuch Management
603 W Wheeling St (43130-3630)
PHONE....................................740 653-3583
Leonard F Gorsuch, *President*
Jackie Evans, *Controller*
EMP: 30
SALES (est): 2.1MM **Privately Held**
SIC: 6513 Apartment building operators

(G-12398)
FAIRFIELD INSUL & DRYWALL LLC
1655 Election House Rd Nw (43130-9059)
PHONE....................................740 654-8811
Paul Moentmann, *President*
EMP: 49
SQ FT: 10,000
SALES: 10K **Privately Held**
SIC: 1742 Acoustical & ceiling work

(G-12399)
FAIRFIELD MEDICAL CENTER (PA)
401 N Ewing St (43130-3371)
PHONE....................................740 687-8000
Sky Gettys, *CEO*
Pamela Starlin, *Safety Mgr*
Chuck Davis, *Buyer*
Jeff Solenbarger, *Buyer*
Kevin Effinger, *Accountant*
EMP: 2000 EST: 1914
SQ FT: 380,000
SALES (est): 283.9MM **Privately Held**
WEB: www.fmchealth.org
SIC: 8062 7352 5999 General medical &
  surgical hospitals; medical equipment
  rental; medical apparatus & supplies

(G-12400)
FAIRFIELD NATIONAL BANK (HQ)
143 W Main St (43130-3700)
P.O. Box 607 (43130-0607)
PHONE....................................740 653-7242
Stephen Wells, *President*
EMP: 50
SQ FT: 5,000
SALES (est): 4.7MM
SALES (corp-wide): 411.9MM **Publicly Held**
WEB: www.fairfieldnationalbank.com
SIC: 6021 National commercial banks
PA: Park National Corporation
  50 N 3rd St
  Newark OH 43055
  740 349-8451

(G-12401)
FAIRFLD CTR FOR DISABLTS & CER
681 E 6th Ave (43130-2602)
PHONE....................................740 653-1186
Edwin Payne, *Director*
EMP: 30
SQ FT: 10,000
SALES: 1.3MM **Privately Held**
WEB: www.fairfieldcenter.org
SIC: 8322 Individual & family services

(G-12402)
FAIRHOPE HOSPICE AND PALLIATIV
282 Sells Rd (43130-3461)
PHONE....................................740 654-7077
Denise Bauer, *CEO*
Joyce Cox, *Vice Pres*
Jared Bailey, *Finance*
Twylia Summers, *Director*
Ernie Doling, *Social Worker*
EMP: 100
SALES (est): 2.4MM **Privately Held**
WEB: www.hospicefairfieldco.org
SIC: 8051 8082 Skilled nursing care facilities; home health care services

(G-12403)
FAMILY YMCA OF LANCSTR&FAIRFLD
1180 E Locust St (43130-4044)
PHONE....................................740 277-7373
Mike Lieber, *Branch Mgr*
EMP: 63
SALES (corp-wide): 2.4MM **Privately Held**
SIC: 8641 7991 8351 7032 Youth organizations; physical fitness facilities; child day care services; youth camps; individual & family services
PA: Family Ymca Of Lancaster And Fairfield County
  465 W 6th Ave
  Lancaster OH 43130
  740 654-0616

(G-12404)
FAMILY YMCA OF LANCSTR&FAIRFLD (PA)
Also Called: ROBERT K FOX FAMILY WIDE
465 W 6th Ave (43130-2597)
PHONE....................................740 654-0616
Mike Lieber, *CEO*
Steve Murry, *CFO*
EMP: 110
SALES: 2.4MM **Privately Held**
WEB: www.ymcalancaster.com
SIC: 7991 7997 Physical fitness facilities; membership sports & recreation clubs

(G-12405)
FIRST MED URGENT & FMLY CTR
1201 River Valley Blvd (43130-1653)
PHONE....................................740 756-9238
Robert Dominguez, *President*
EMP: 26
SQ FT: 11,600
SALES (est): 2.4MM **Privately Held**
SIC: 8011 Urgent & Family Care Center

(G-12406)
GHP II LLC
2893 W Fair Ave (43130-8993)
P.O. Box 600 (43130-0600)
PHONE....................................740 681-6825
Tom Gilligan, *Manager*
EMP: 280
SQ FT: 1,300,000
SALES (corp-wide): 682.6MM **Privately Held**
WEB: www.anchorhocking.com
SIC: 5023 3231 China; glassware; products of purchased glass
HQ: Ghp Ii, Llc
  1115 W 5th Ave
  Lancaster OH 43130
  740 687-2500

(G-12407)
JONES COCHENOUR & CO INC (PA)
125 W Mulberry St (43130-3064)
PHONE....................................740 653-9581
David Jones, *President*
Dean Cochenour, *Vice Pres*
EMP: 50
SALES (est): 4.7MM **Privately Held**
WEB: www.jcccpa.com
SIC: 8721 Certified public accountant

▲ = Import ▼=Export
◆ =Import/Export

(G-12408)
KUMLER COLLISION INC
Also Called: Kumler Automotive
2313 E Main St (43130-9350)
PHONE..................................740 653-4301
Dean De Rolph, *President*
Scott Landis, *General Mgr*
Cathie De Rolph, *Vice Pres*
EMP: 34 **EST:** 1928
SQ FT: 24,000
SALES (est): 3.9MM **Privately Held**
WEB: www.kumlercollision.com
SIC: 7532 Body shop, automotive

(G-12409)
L AND M INVESTMENT CO
603 W Wheeling St (43130-3630)
P.O. Box 190 (43130-0190)
PHONE..................................740 653-3583
Leonard Gorsuch, *Principal*
EMP: 25
SQ FT: 7,000
SALES (est): 620.9K **Privately Held**
SIC: 6514 6512 Dwelling operators, ex-
cept apartments; commercial & industrial
building operation

(G-12410)
**LANCASTER BINGO COMPANY
INC (PA)**
Also Called: Lancaster Bingo Company
200 Quarry Rd Se (43130-9304)
P.O. Box 668 (43130-0668)
PHONE..................................740 681-4759
Mark A Sells, *Ch of Bd*
Jonathan Smith, *President*
Mitchell Shell, *Purch Mgr*
Tracey Friesner, *Buyer*
Beverly Blanchard, *Purchasing*
▲ **EMP:** 80
SQ FT: 2,700
SALES (est): 41.5MM **Privately Held**
WEB: www.lancasterbingo.com
SIC: 5092 Bingo games & supplies

(G-12411)
LANCASTER COUNTRY CLUB
3100 Country Club Rd Sw (43130-8937)
P.O. Box 1098 (43130-0818)
PHONE..................................740 654-3535
Jim Aranda, *Principal*
Richard Waibel,
EMP: 55 **EST:** 1909
SQ FT: 4,000
SALES (est): 3.1MM **Privately Held**
SIC: 7997 5941 5812 Swimming club,
membership; tennis club, membership;
golf club, membership; golf goods &
equipment; eating places

(G-12412)
LANCASTER HOST LLC
Also Called: Holiday Inn
1861 Riverway Dr (43130-1494)
PHONE..................................740 654-4445
Bill Curt,
EMP: 30
SALES (est): 1.2MM **Privately Held**
SIC: 7011 Hotels & motels

(G-12413)
LOWES HOME CENTERS LLC
2240 Lowes Dr (43130-5700)
PHONE..................................740 681-3464
Dave Taylor, *Manager*
EMP: 150
SALES (corp-wide): 68.6B **Publicly Held**
SIC: 5211 5031 5722 5064 Home cen-
ters; building materials, exterior; building
materials, interior; household appliance
stores; electrical appliances, television &
radio
HQ: Lowe's Home Centers, Llc
1605 Curtis Bridge Rd
Wilkesboro NC 28697
336 658-4000

(G-12414)
**MAIN STREET TERRACE CARE
CTR**
1318 E Main St (43130-4004)
PHONE..................................740 653-8767
Ed Telle, *President*
Peggy S Dupler, *Admin Sec*
EMP: 56

SQ FT: 5,182
SALES (est): 2.4MM **Privately Held**
SIC: 8052 8051 Intermediate care facili-
ties; skilled nursing care facilities

(G-12415)
**MCDERMOTT INTERNATIONAL
INC**
2600 E Main St (43130-8490)
PHONE..................................740 687-4292
Steve Shover, *Principal*
EMP: 171
SALES (corp-wide): 6.7B **Publicly Held**
SIC: 1629 Marine construction
PA: Mcdermott International, Inc.
757 N Eldridge Pkwy
Houston TX 77079
281 870-5000

(G-12416)
**MEALS ON WHEELS-OLDER
ADULT AL**
253 Boving Rd (43130-4240)
PHONE..................................740 681-5050
Phyllis Saylor, *Exec Dir*
EMP: 50
SQ FT: 6,600
SALES (est): 1.8MM **Privately Held**
SIC: 8322 Meal delivery program

(G-12417)
**MEDILL ELEMNTARY SCH OF
VOLNTR**
1160 Sheridan Dr (43130-1927)
PHONE..................................740 687-7352
EMP: 50
SALES (est): 461.5K **Privately Held**
SIC: 8211 8399 Elementary & secondary
schools; fund raising organization, non-
fee basis

(G-12418)
MICHA LTD
144 E Main St (43130-3712)
P.O. Box 667 (43130-0667)
PHONE..................................740 653-6464
Robert Johnston, *Partner*
EMP: 45
SALES (est): 2MM **Privately Held**
SIC: 8111 General practice attorney,
lawyer

(G-12419)
**MID-OHIO PSYCHLOGICAL
SVCS INC (PA)**
624 E Main St (43130-3903)
PHONE..................................740 687-0042
Kimberly Blair, *Exec Dir*
EMP: 92
SQ FT: 3,529
SALES: 3.5MM **Privately Held**
WEB: www.mopsohio.com
SIC: 8322 8093 General counseling serv-
ices; mental health clinic, outpatient

(G-12420)
**MULTI COUNTY JUVENILE DET
CTR**
923 Liberty Dr (43130-8045)
PHONE..................................740 652-1525
Dana Moore, *Superintendent*
Edgar A Penrod, *Principal*
EMP: 33
SALES (est): 2MM **Privately Held**
SIC: 8361 Juvenile correctional facilities

(G-12421)
**NEW HORIZON YOUTH FAMILY
CTR (PA)**
Also Called: Pickerngton Area Cunseling Ctr
1592 Granville Pike (43130-1076)
PHONE..................................740 687-0835
Anthony Motta, *CEO*
Patrick Fleming, *CFO*
EMP: 25
SALES: 4.6MM **Privately Held**
WEB: www.pickareacounseling.com
SIC: 8322 Family service agency

(G-12422)
NEW LIFE CHRISTIAN CENTER
2642 Clumbus Lancaster Rd (43130-8814)
P.O. Box 2239 (43130-5239)
PHONE..................................740 687-1572

Gary A Keller, *Pastor*
Amy Heston, *Director*
EMP: 27
SQ FT: 48,600
SALES (est): 846.4K **Privately Held**
SIC: 8661 8351 Pentecostal Church; child
day care services

(G-12423)
NL OF KY INC
Also Called: Hampson Insurance Agency
2680 Kull Rd (43130-7707)
P.O. Box 7, Baltimore (43105-0007)
PHONE..................................740 689-9876
Timothy D Hampson, *Branch Mgr*
EMP: 30 **Privately Held**
SIC: 6411 Insurance agents & brokers
HQ: Nl Of Ky, Inc.
2305 River Rd
Louisville KY 40206

(G-12424)
**OB GYN ASSOCIATES OF
LANCASTER**
1532 Wesley Way (43130-7642)
PHONE..................................740 653-5088
Laurel Santino MD, *President*
Debbie Leith, *Office Mgr*
EMP: 25
SALES (est): 1.4MM **Privately Held**
SIC: 8011 Physicians' office, including spe-
cialists; gynecologist

(G-12425)
PAYROLL SERVICES UNLIMITED
125 W Mulberry St (43130-3014)
PHONE..................................740 653-9581
Brian Long, *Partner*
EMP: 40
SALES (est): 1.3MM **Privately Held**
SIC: 8721 Payroll accounting service

(G-12426)
PRECISION PIPELINE SVCS LLC
10 Whiley Rd (43130-8147)
PHONE..................................740 652-1679
Matt Upp, *CFO*
EMP: 40 **Privately Held**
SIC: 1623 Underground utilities contractor

(G-12427)
**PRO-KLEEN INDUSTRIAL SVCS
INC**
Also Called: Porta-Kleen
1030 Mill Park Dr (43130-9576)
PHONE..................................740 689-1886
Monte Black, *Ch of Bd*
EMP: 45
SALES (est): 7.5MM **Privately Held**
WEB: www.portakleen.com
SIC: 7359 7699 5963 3088 Portable toi-
let rental; septic tank cleaning service;
bottled water delivery; tubs (bath, shower
& laundry), plastic

(G-12428)
PROLINE ELECTRIC INC
301 Cedar Hill Rd (43130-3641)
PHONE..................................740 687-4571
Mike Shafer, *President*
Michelle Hampson, *Manager*
EMP: 25
SALES (est): 600K **Privately Held**
SIC: 1731 General electrical contractor

(G-12429)
RECOVERY CENTER
201 S Columbus St (43130-4315)
PHONE..................................740 687-4500
Trisha Farrar, *Exec Dir*
EMP: 28
SQ FT: 12,500
SALES (est): 1.9MM **Privately Held**
SIC: 8699 8093 Charitable organization;
rehabilitation center, outpatient treatment

(G-12430)
RICKETTS EXCAVATING INC
230 Hamburg Rd Sw (43130-9040)
P.O. Box 912 (43130-0912)
PHONE..................................740 687-0338
Michael Ricketts, *President*
Harry H Ricketts, *Exec VP*
Della Ricketts, *Admin Sec*
EMP: 30 **EST:** 1951

SQ FT: 10,500
SALES (est): 4.2MM **Privately Held**
SIC: 1794 4212 Excavation & grading,
building construction; local trucking, without storage

(G-12431)
**RIVER VLY ORTHPDICS SPT
MDCINE (PA)**
Also Called: Ohio Orthopedic Center
2405 N Columbus St # 120 (43130-8185)
PHONE..................................740 687-3346
Stephen J Voto MD, *President*
EMP: 25
SALES (est): 3.6MM **Privately Held**
SIC: 8011 Orthopedic physician

(G-12432)
RIVERVIEW SURGERY CENTER
Also Called: River View Surgery Center
2401 N Columbus St (43130-8190)
PHONE..................................740 681-2700
Pamela Reed,
EMP: 45
SALES (est): 2.2MM **Privately Held**
SIC: 8011 Ambulatory surgical center

(G-12433)
SCHROER PROPERTIES INC
Also Called: Schroer Properties of Lanfair
1590 Chartwell St Ofc (43130-7843)
PHONE..................................740 687-5100
Sean Cleary, *Manager*
EMP: 90 **Privately Held**
SIC: 8051 Skilled nursing care facilities
PA: Schroer Properties, Inc
339 E Maple St
North Canton OH 44720

(G-12434)
**SERVICEMASTER BY SIDWELL
INC**
430 E Mulberry St (43130-3167)
PHONE..................................740 687-1077
Muriel S Sidwell, *President*
Todd George, *Vice Pres*
EMP: 28 **EST:** 1979
SQ FT: 3,200
SALES (est): 1MM **Privately Held**
SIC: 7349 Building maintenance services

(G-12435)
SLATERS INC
Also Called: Do It Best
1141 N Memorial Dr (43130-1749)
P.O. Box 489 (43130-0489)
PHONE..................................740 654-2204
Lou Ann Weisenstein, *President*
Jackie Pamston, *Co-Owner*
Steve Slater, *Vice Pres*
Nathan Weisenstein, *Technology*
EMP: 30 **EST:** 1947
SQ FT: 15,000
SALES (est): 3.6MM **Privately Held**
WEB: www.slatershardware.com
SIC: 5251 6513 Tools; apartment building
operators

(G-12436)
**SOUTH CENTRAL POWER
COMPANY (PA)**
2780 Coonpath Rd Ne (43130-9343)
P.O. Box 250 (43130-0250)
PHONE..................................740 653-4422
Rick Lemonds, *President*
James Evans, *Principal*
Mike Hummel, *Principal*
Richard Poling, *Principal*
Cathy Bitler, *Vice Pres*
▲ **EMP:** 235
SQ FT: 10,000
SALES: 282.1MM **Privately Held**
WEB: www.southcentralpower.com
SIC: 4911 Distribution, electric power

(G-12437)
**SPECTRUM MGT HOLDG CO
LLC**
Also Called: Time Warner
1315 Granville Pike Ne (43130-1034)
PHONE..................................740 772-7809
Todd Acker, *Manager*
EMP: 40
SALES (corp-wide): 43.6B **Publicly Held**
SIC: 4841 Cable television services

**G
E
O
G
R
A
P
H
I
C**

HQ: Spectrum Management Holding Company, Llc
400 Atlantic St
Stamford CT 06901
203 905-7801

(G-12438)
STANDING STONE NATIONAL BANK (PA)
137 W Wheeling St (43130-3708)
P.O. Box 2610 (43130-5610)
PHONE.....................................740 653-5115
Barry Ritchey, *President*
Betty Dennison, *Vice Pres*
Albert Horvath, *Vice Pres*
EMP: 50
SQ FT: 7,500
SALES: 4.7MM **Privately Held**
WEB: www.standingstonenationalbank.com
SIC: 6021 National commercial banks

(G-12439)
SUNBRIDGE CARE ENTERPRISES INC
Also Called: Homestead Care Rhblitation Ctr
1900 E Main St (43130-9302)
PHONE.....................................740 653-8630
David Perry, *Vice Pres*
Angela Mc Coy, *Branch Mgr*
EMP: 100 **Publicly Held**
SIC: 8051 Convalescent home with continuous nursing care
HQ: Sunbridge Care Enterprises, Inc.
5100 Sun Ave Ne
Albuquerque NM

(G-12440)
TAYLOR CHEVROLET INC
Also Called: Taylor Dealership
2510 N Memorial Dr (43130-1637)
P.O. Box 10 (43130-0010)
PHONE.....................................740 653-2091
Martin N Taylor, *President*
Milton Taylor Jr, *Vice Pres*
EMP: 150
SQ FT: 40,000
SALES: 42.9MM **Privately Held**
SIC: 5511 7538 7514 Automobiles, new & used; general automotive repair shops; passenger car rental

(G-12441)
TBN ACQUISITION LLC
Also Called: Hugh White Buick
2480 N Memorial Dr (43130-1637)
P.O. Box 10 (43130-0010)
PHONE.....................................740 653-2091
William Thagard, *Mng Member*
EMP: 100
SALES (est): 1.3MM **Privately Held**
SIC: 7389 5511 Automobile recovery service; automobiles, new & used

(G-12442)
TIKI BOWLING LANES INC
Also Called: Tiki Lounge & Restaurant
1521 Tiki Ln (43130-8793)
PHONE.....................................740 654-4513
James Shaner, *President*
EMP: 50
SALES (est): 2.4MM **Privately Held**
WEB: www.tikilanes.com
SIC: 7933 5812 Ten pin center; eating places

(G-12443)
V CLEW LLC
1201 River Valley Blvd (43130-1653)
PHONE.....................................740 687-2273
Paul Van Camp, *Principal*
EMP: 30
SALES (est): 327.4K **Privately Held**
SIC: 8051 Skilled nursing care facilities

(G-12444)
WESTERN & SOUTHERN LF INSUR CO
1583 Victor Rd Nw (43130-8039)
P.O. Box 648 (43130-0648)
PHONE.....................................740 653-3210
Greg Shaffer, *Manager*
EMP: 30 **Privately Held**
SIC: 6411 Life insurance agents

HQ: The Western & Southern Life Insurance Company
400 Broadway St
Cincinnati OH 45202
513 629-1800

(G-12445)
WINDSOR COMPANIES (PA)
1430 Collins Rd Nw (43130-8815)
PHONE.....................................740 653-8822
Thomas W Moore, *Partner*
Melvin L Moore, *Partner*
EMP: 33 EST: 1973
SQ FT: 2,200
SALES (est): 3.8MM **Privately Held**
WEB: www.thewindsorcompanies.com
SIC: 6552 Subdividers & developers

Lebanon
Warren County

(G-12446)
A 1 JANITORIAL CLEANING SVC
Also Called: ServiceMaster
939 Old 122 Rd (45036-8636)
P.O. Box 797 (45036-0797)
PHONE.....................................513 932-8003
Jimmy Collins, *President*
EMP: 50
SQ FT: 4,000
SALES: 750K **Privately Held**
SIC: 7349 Building maintenance services

(G-12447)
AAA ALLIED GROUP INC
Also Called: AAA Travel Agency
603 E Main St (45036-1915)
PHONE.....................................513 228-0866
James Pease, *Branch Mgr*
EMP: 78
SALES (corp-wide): 142.4MM **Privately Held**
SIC: 4481 Deep sea passenger transportation, except ferry
PA: Aaa Allied Group, Inc.
15 W Central Pkwy
Cincinnati OH 45202
513 762-3301

(G-12448)
ADDISONMCKEE INC (PA)
1637 Kingsview Dr (45036-8395)
PHONE.....................................513 228-7000
Jim Sabine, *CEO*
Lonnie McGrew, *Vice Pres*
Mike Burnett, *VP Mfg*
Claud Lessard, *CFO*
Nancy A McKee,
▲ EMP: 142
SQ FT: 78,000
SALES: 8MM **Privately Held**
WEB: www.addisonmckee.com
SIC: 3542 3599 5084 3549 Bending machines; machine shop, jobbing & repair; industrial machinery & equipment; metalworking machinery; rolling mill machinery; special dies, tools, jigs & fixtures

(G-12449)
ARMCO ASSOCIATION PARK
Also Called: Armco Park
1223 N State Route 741 (45036-9746)
PHONE.....................................513 695-3980
Tedd Wood, *President*
James Unglesby, *Vice Pres*
John Kraft, *Park Mgr*
EMP: 45 EST: 1956
SQ FT: 1,200
SALES: 29.8K **Privately Held**
WEB: www.armcopark.com
SIC: 7997 Membership sports & recreation clubs

(G-12450)
ASC OF CINCINNATI INC
4028 Binion Way (45036-9367)
P.O. Box 230, Alexandria KY (41001-0230)
PHONE.....................................513 886-7100
Steven Stortz, *President*
Stain Smith, *Vice Pres*
EMP: 34
SQ FT: 3,000

SALES: 2.7MM **Privately Held**
SIC: 4841 Cable & other pay television services

(G-12451)
BEST REALTY INC
645 Columbus Ave Ste A (45036-1605)
PHONE.....................................513 932-3948
Ralph Blanton, *Owner*
EMP: 25 EST: 2014
SALES (est): 111.7K **Privately Held**
SIC: 6531 Real estate brokers & agents

(G-12452)
BILL DELORD AUTOCENTER INC
Also Called: Pontiac Bill Delord Autocenter
917 Columbus Ave (45036-1401)
PHONE.....................................513 932-3000
William Delord, *President*
Jerry Perron, *General Mgr*
Julie Spencer, *Corp Secy*
Steve Butsch, *Finance Mgr*
EMP: 51
SQ FT: 21,500
SALES (est): 21.8MM **Privately Held**
WEB: www.billdelord.com
SIC: 5511 7538 Automobiles, new & used; pickups, new & used; vans, new & used; general automotive repair shops

(G-12453)
BOB PULTE CHEVROLET INC
909 Columbus Ave (45036-1401)
P.O. Box 814 (45036-0814)
PHONE.....................................513 932-0303
Robert Pulte, *President*
Dan Pulte, *President*
Jim Kleiser, *Sales Associate*
EMP: 36
SQ FT: 19,000
SALES (est): 14.5MM **Privately Held**
WEB: www.bobpulte.com
SIC: 5511 7515 5551 Automobiles, new & used; passenger car leasing; boat dealers

(G-12454)
CARL E OEDER SONS SAND & GRAV
1000 Mason Morrow Rd (45036-9271)
PHONE.....................................513 494-1555
Carl Edward Oeder, *President*
David Oeder, *Vice Pres*
Diane Browning, *Treasurer*
Verna Rae Oeder, *Admin Sec*
EMP: 30 EST: 1955
SQ FT: 23,600
SALES (est): 2.1MM **Privately Held**
WEB: www.oeder.com
SIC: 1442 4212 7538 Sand mining; gravel mining; dump truck haulage; truck engine repair, except industrial

(G-12455)
CO OPEN OPTIONS INC
19 N Mechanic St (45036-1801)
PHONE.....................................513 932-0724
Patricia Evans, *Owner*
Ben Vestal, *VP Sales*
EMP: 30
SALES: 1MM **Privately Held**
SIC: 8052 Personal care facility

(G-12456)
CONGER CONSTRUCTION GROUP INC
2020 Mckinley Blvd (45036-6425)
P.O. Box 1069 (45036-5069)
PHONE.....................................513 932-1206
Larry Conger, *President*
Joseph Litvin, *Principal*
Jacob Conger, *Exec VP*
Justin Conger, *Exec VP*
Mike Schulte, *Project Mgr*
EMP: 30
SQ FT: 12,000
SALES: 28MM **Privately Held**
WEB: www.gccontracting.com
SIC: 1542 Commercial & office building, new construction

(G-12457)
COUNTY OF WARREN
Also Called: Warren Co Human Services Dept
416 S East St Unit 1 (45036-2378)
PHONE.....................................513 695-1420
Doris Bishop, *Branch Mgr*
Duane Stansbury, *Manager*
Brenda Joseph, *Officer*
Joe Gambill, *Administration*
EMP: 40 **Privately Held**
SIC: 8322 Social service center
PA: County Of Warren
406 Justice Dr Rm 323
Lebanon OH 45036
513 695-1242

(G-12458)
COUNTY OF WARREN
Also Called: Warren County Park District
300 E Silver St Ste 5 (45036-1800)
PHONE.....................................513 695-1109
Larry Easterly, *Manager*
EMP: 30 **Privately Held**
SIC: 0782 Lawn care services
PA: County Of Warren
406 Justice Dr Rm 323
Lebanon OH 45036
513 695-1242

(G-12459)
COUNTY OF WARREN
Also Called: Warren County Wtr & Sewer Dept
406 Justice Dr Rm 323 (45036-2523)
P.O. Box 530 (45036-0530)
PHONE.....................................513 925-1377
Chris Brausch, *Manager*
EMP: 55
SQ FT: 1,940 **Privately Held**
SIC: 4941 4952 Water supply; sewerage systems
PA: County Of Warren
406 Justice Dr Rm 323
Lebanon OH 45036
513 695-1242

(G-12460)
DOMINION ENERGY TRANSM INC
1262 W State Route 122 (45036-9616)
P.O. Box 560 (45036-0560)
PHONE.....................................513 932-5793
Scott Ratcliff, *Manager*
EMP: 32
SALES (corp-wide): 13.3B **Publicly Held**
WEB: www.domres.com
SIC: 4922 Natural gas transmission
HQ: Dominion Energy Transmission, Inc.
120 Tredegar St
Richmond VA 23219
800 688-4673

(G-12461)
EASTGATE GRAPHICS LLC
611 Norgal Dr (45036-9275)
PHONE.....................................513 228-5522
Thomas Ludeke, *President*
EMP: 31
SALES (est): 5.5MM **Privately Held**
SIC: 5199 Packaging materials

(G-12462)
EASTSIDE NURSERY INC
2830 Greentree Rd (45036-9773)
PHONE.....................................513 934-1661
Cheryl Miyer, *Manager*
EMP: 50
SALES (est): 993.8K **Privately Held**
SIC: 0782 0781 Landscape contractors; landscape counseling & planning

(G-12463)
EQUIPMENT DEPOT OHIO INC
1000 Kingsview Dr (45036-9572)
PHONE.....................................513 934-2121
Tj Brinker, *General Mgr*
Jim Keller, *Accounts Mgr*
Evan Davies, *Sales Staff*
Ben Garner, *Marketing Staff*
Neil Williams, *Manager*
EMP: 45
SQ FT: 63,218
SALES (corp-wide): 1.8B **Privately Held**
WEB: www.portmanpeople.com
SIC: 5084 Materials handling machinery

HQ: Equipment Depot Ohio, Inc.
4331 Rossplain Dr
Blue Ash OH 45236
513 891-0600

(G-12464)
EQUIPMENT DEPOT OHIO INC
Cleaning Division
1000 Kingsview Dr (45036-9572)
PHONE......................................513 934-2121
Neil Williams, *General Mgr*
EMP: 35
SALES (corp-wide): 1.8B **Privately Held**
WEB: www.portmanpeople.com
SIC: 5084 7359 Processing & packaging
equipment; home cleaning & mainte-
nance equipment rental services
HQ: Equipment Depot Ohio, Inc.
4331 Rossplain Dr
Blue Ash OH 45236
513 891-0600

(G-12465)
FAMILY DENTISTRY INC (PA)
600 Mound Ct (45036-1994)
P.O. Box 467 (45036-0467)
PHONE......................................513 932-6991
David Haas DDS, *President*
David Robert Haas, *President*
Michael C Peters, *Treasurer*
EMP: 31 EST: 1975
SQ FT: 3,000
SALES (est): 2.6MM **Privately Held**
SIC: 8021 Dentists' office

(G-12466)
**GEORGE STEEL FABRICATING
INC**
1207 S Us Route 42 (45036-8198)
PHONE......................................513 932-2887
John George, *President*
Brad Frost, *Corp Secy*
Kevin Nickell, *Vice Pres*
Tom Bausmith, *Project Mgr*
Blake Berryman, *Project Mgr*
EMP: 35
SQ FT: 32,100
SALES (est): 7.1MM **Privately Held**
WEB: www.georgesteel.com
SIC: 7692 3441 3599 Welding repair; fab-
ricated structural metal; machine shop,
jobbing & repair

(G-12467)
GIDEONS INTERNATIONAL
8 Claridge Ct B (45036-2803)
P.O. Box 612 (45036-0612)
PHONE......................................513 932-2857
Robert F Amburgy, *Admin Sec*
EMP: 30
SALES (est): 394.4K **Privately Held**
SIC: 8699 Charitable organization

(G-12468)
GOLDEN LAMB
Also Called: Golden Lamb Rest Ht & Gift Sp
27 S Broadway St (45036-1705)
PHONE......................................513 932-5065
Bill Kilimnik, *General Mgr*
N Lee Comisar, *Chairman*
EMP: 125
SALES (est): 4MM **Privately Held**
SIC: 5812 5947 7011 Eating places; gift
shop; hotels

(G-12469)
**HEALTH CARE OPPORTUNITIES
INC (PA)**
Also Called: Cedars of Lebanon Nursing
Home
102 E Silver St (45036-1812)
PHONE......................................513 932-0300
Bernard Moscowitz, *President*
EMP: 50
SQ FT: 12,000
SALES (est): 2.1MM **Privately Held**
SIC: 8051 Skilled nursing care facilities

(G-12470)
**HEALTH CARE OPPORTUNITIES
INC**
Also Called: Lebanon Nursing Home
220 S Mechanic St (45036-2212)
PHONE......................................513 932-4861
Terri Moore, *Branch Mgr*

EMP: 50
SALES (corp-wide): 2.1MM **Privately
Held**
SIC: 8051 Skilled nursing care facilities
PA: Health Care Opportunities Inc
102 E Silver St
Lebanon OH 45036
513 932-0300

(G-12471)
**HENKLE-SCHUELER &
ASSOCIATES (PA)**
Also Called: Henkle Schueler Realtors
3000 Henkle Dr G (45036-9258)
PHONE......................................513 932-6070
Michael T Schueler, *President*
EMP: 35
SQ FT: 3,000
SALES (est): 5.5MM **Privately Held**
WEB: www.henkleschueler.com
SIC: 6531 6552 Real estate agent, resi-
dential; subdividers & developers

(G-12472)
**INDUSTRIAL VIBRATIONS CONS
(PA)**
Also Called: I V C
210 S West St (45036-2163)
PHONE......................................513 932-4678
Jeffrey Epperson, *Ch of Bd*
Jerry Matiyow, *President*
Pete Epperson, *President*
Peter Epperson, *President*
Pete Roy, *Regional Mgr*
EMP: 75
SQ FT: 12,000
SALES (est): 10.3MM **Privately Held**
WEB: www.ivctechnologies.com
SIC: 8748 Systems analysis & engineering
consulting services

(G-12473)
**INTERFAITH HOSPTLTY NTWRK
OF W**
Also Called: IHNWC
203 E Warren St (45036-1855)
PHONE......................................513 934-5250
Linda Rabolt, *Exec Dir*
EMP: 99
SALES (est): 518.9K **Privately Held**
SIC: 8322 Individual & family services

(G-12474)
**JIT PACKAGING CINCINNATI INC
(PA)**
Also Called: J I T
1550 Kingsview Dr (45036-8389)
PHONE......................................513 933-0250
Jeff Jones, *President*
EMP: 70
SALES (est): 20.4MM **Privately Held**
WEB: www.jitpackaging.net
SIC: 5199 Packaging materials

(G-12475)
**KINDRED NURSING CENTERS E
LLC**
Also Called: Kindred Nrsing Rhbltton- Lbnon
700 Monroe Rd (45036-1409)
PHONE......................................513 932-0105
Fax: 513 932-7232
EMP: 110
SALES (corp-wide): 7B **Publicly Held**
SIC: 8051 Skilled Nursing Care Facility
HQ: Kindred Nursing Centers East, L.L.C.
680 S 4th St
Louisville KY 40202
502 596-7300

(G-12476)
KINGSMASON PROPERTIES LTD
Also Called: Kings-Mason Properties,
3000 Henkle Dr Ste G (45036-9258)
PHONE......................................513 932-6010
Michael Schueler, *Managing Prtnr*
Ted Gilbert, *Manager*
EMP: 35
SALES (est): 2.2MM **Privately Held**
SIC: 6512 Shopping center, property oper-
ation only

(G-12477)
KWEEN INDUSTRIES INC
Also Called: King's Electric Services
2964 S State Route 42 (45036-8887)
P.O. Box 382 (45036-0382)
PHONE......................................513 932-2293
Kingsley M Wientge III, *President*
Kelly Wientge, *Admin Sec*
EMP: 50
SQ FT: 4,000
SALES (est): 11.2MM **Privately Held**
SIC: 1731 General electrical contractor

(G-12478)
LCNB NATIONAL BANK (HQ)
2 N Broadway St Lowr (45036-1795)
P.O. Box 59 (45036-0059)
PHONE......................................513 932-1414
Spencer S Cropper, *Ch of Bd*
Eric J Meilstrup, *President*
Ben Jackson, *Exec VP*
Matthew Layer, *Exec VP*
Leroy F McKay, *Exec VP*
EMP: 80
SALES: 55.3MM
SALES (corp-wide): 65.6MM **Publicly
Held**
WEB: www.lcnb.com
SIC: 6021 National commercial banks
PA: Lcnb Corp.
2 N Broadway St Lowr
Lebanon OH 45036
513 932-1414

(G-12479)
LEATHER GALLERY INC
50 Farnese Ct (45036-9601)
PHONE......................................513 312-1722
Curtis Jackson, *President*
Tammy Jackson, *Vice Pres*
▲ EMP: 30
SQ FT: 3,800
SALES (est): 2MM **Privately Held**
WEB: www.leather-gallery.com
SIC: 5948 5199 Leather goods, except
luggage & shoes; leather & cut stock

(G-12480)
**LEBANON CHRYSLER -
PLYMUTH INC**
Also Called: Sweeney Chrysler Dodge Jeep
518 W Main St (45036-2097)
PHONE......................................513 932-2717
Tim Sweeney, *President*
Brian Sweeney, *Vice Pres*
Zach Ferriman, *Parts Mgr*
EMP: 25 EST: 1976
SQ FT: 16,000
SALES (est): 8.9MM **Privately Held**
SIC: 5511 7538 7515 5531 Automobiles,
new & used; pickups, new & used; gen-
eral automotive repair shops; passenger
car leasing; automotive & home supply
stores; used car dealers

(G-12481)
**LEBANON NURSING & REHAB
CTR**
115 Oregonia Rd (45036-1983)
P.O. Box 376 (45036-0376)
PHONE......................................513 932-1121
Steve Feigenbaum, *Partner*
Leo Feigenbaum, *Partner*
EMP: 65
SALES: 40MM **Privately Held**
SIC: 8051 Skilled nursing care facilities

(G-12482)
**LEBANON PRESBYTERIAN
CHURCH**
123 N East St (45036-1881)
PHONE......................................513 932-0369
Peter Larson, *Pastor*
Randy Fannin, *Pastor Care Dir*
EMP: 30
SALES: 11.1K **Privately Held**
WEB: www.lebanonpresbyterian.org
SIC: 8661 8351 Presbyterian Church;
nursery school

(G-12483)
**MARATHON PETROLEUM
COMPANY LP**
999 W State Route 122 (45036-9615)
PHONE......................................513 932-6007

Joe Elsner, *Manager*
EMP: 34 **Publicly Held**
WEB: www.mapllc.com
SIC: 5172 Gasoline
HQ: Marathon Petroleum Company Lp
539 S Main St
Findlay OH 45840

(G-12484)
MASTERS DRUG COMPANY INC
Also Called: Masters Pharmaceutical
3600 Pharma Way (45036-9479)
PHONE......................................800 982-7922
Nick Loporcaro, *Principal*
EMP: 279
SALES (est): 11.9MM
SALES (corp-wide): 208.3B **Publicly
Held**
SIC: 5122 Pharmaceuticals
PA: Mckesson Corporation
1 Post St Fl 18
San Francisco CA 94104
415 983-8300

(G-12485)
**MIAMI VALLEY GAMING & RACG
LLC**
6000 W State Route 63 (45036-7900)
PHONE......................................513 934-7070
Domenic Mancini, *President*
EMP: 80
SALES (est): 7.7MM **Privately Held**
SIC: 7999 0971 Gambling & lottery serv-
ices; game services

(G-12486)
**MIAMI VLY FANDOM FOR
LITERACY**
Also Called: Mvfl
222 S Mechanic St (45036-2212)
PHONE......................................513 933-0452
Dan Ryan, *CEO*
EMP: 26
SALES (est): 477.5K **Privately Held**
WEB: www.mvfl.org
SIC: 8399 Advocacy group

(G-12487)
**NORTHSIDE BAPTST CHILD DEV
CTR**
Also Called: Northside Baptist Church
161 Miller Rd (45036-1233)
PHONE......................................513 932-5642
Jan Watson, *Pastor*
EMP: 26
SQ FT: 26,280
SALES (est): 615.5K **Privately Held**
WEB: www.northsideonline.net
SIC: 8351 Preschool center

(G-12488)
**OEDER CARL E SONS SAND &
GRAV**
1000 Mason Mrrow Mlgrv Rd (45036-9271)
PHONE......................................513 494-1238
Carl E Oeder, *President*
EMP: 35
SALES (est): 3.5MM **Privately Held**
SIC: 4213 1442 Trucking, except local;
construction sand & gravel

(G-12489)
ON-POWER INC
3525 Grant Ave Ste A (45036-6431)
PHONE......................................513 228-2100
Larry D Davis, *President*
Joe Back, *Purchasing*
Tim Quackenbush, *Electrical Engi*
Thomas Mergy, *CFO*
Tom Mergy, *CFO*
EMP: 32
SQ FT: 41,350
SALES: 8MM **Privately Held**
WEB: www.onpowerinc.com
SIC: 3511 8711 Gas turbines, mechanical
drive; consulting engineer

(G-12490)
OTTERBEIN HOMES
Also Called: Otterbein Snior Lfstyle Chices
580 N State Route 741 (45036-8839)
PHONE......................................513 933-5439
Jill Hreben, *President*
Ken Allen, *Principal*
Gary Horning, *Vice Pres*

Dani Jagucki, *Human Res Dir*
Geri Ricker, *Marketing Staff*
EMP: 60
SQ FT: 36,232
SALES: 105.5MM **Privately Held**
SIC: 8361 Home for the aged

(G-12491)
OTTERBEIN LEBANON
585 N State Route 741 (45036-8840)
PHONE....................513 933-5465
Richard A Mapes, *President*
Bob Dilgard, *Manager*
Sam Dotson, *Director*
EMP: 25
SALES: 21.5MM **Privately Held**
SIC: 8051 Skilled nursing care facilities

(G-12492)
OTTERBEIN SNIOR LFSTYLE CHICES (PA)
Also Called: OTTERBEIN ST MARY'S
585 N State Route 741 (45036-8840)
PHONE....................513 933-5400
Jill Hreben, *President*
Donald L Gilmore, *President*
George Phillips, *Pastor*
Tammy Cassidy, *Vice Pres*
J Christopher Green, *Vice Pres*
EMP: 400
SALES: 58.4MM **Privately Held**
SIC: 8361 8051 8052 1522 Home for the aged; skilled nursing care facilities; intermediate care facilities; residential construction

(G-12493)
PRODUCTION SERVICES UNLIMITED
Also Called: WARREN COUNTY OF PRODUCTION SE
575 Columbus Ave (45036-1603)
PHONE....................513 695-1658
Heather Moore, *Director*
EMP: 65 **EST:** 1969
SQ FT: 30,000
SALES: 962.8K **Privately Held**
SIC: 8331 Sheltered workshop

(G-12494)
QUANTUM METALS INC
3675 Taft Rd (45036-6424)
PHONE....................513 573-0144
Mark A Kolb, *President*
Cheryl Kolb, *Corp Secy*
◆ **EMP:** 40
SQ FT: 100,000
SALES (est): 22.9MM **Privately Held**
WEB: www.quantummetals.com
SIC: 5093 Nonferrous metals scrap

(G-12495)
RACEWAY FOODS INC
665 N Brdway Lbnon Rceway (45036)
P.O. Box 58 (45036-0058)
PHONE....................513 932-2457
Keith Nixon, *President*
EMP: 25
SALES (est): 830K **Privately Held**
SIC: 7948 Race track operation

(G-12496)
RDE SYSTEM CORP
Also Called: Sunshine Housekeeping
986 Winzig Ln (45036-8693)
PHONE....................513 933-8000
Bob Estepp, *President*
Donna Estepp, *Corp Secy*
Ruth Estepp, *Shareholder*
EMP: 140
SQ FT: 900
SALES (est): 10.6MM **Privately Held**
SIC: 5084 7349 5169 5087 Materials handling machinery; janitorial service, contract basis; chemicals & allied products; service establishment equipment

(G-12497)
REALM TECHNOLOGIES LLC
954 Greengate Dr (45036-7943)
PHONE....................513 297-3095
Melissa Bolton, *
EMP: 28
SALES: 980K **Privately Held**
SIC: 7378 Computer & data processing equipment repair/maintenance

(G-12498)
RK FAMILY INC
1879 Deerfield Rd (45036-8602)
PHONE....................513 934-0015
Tim F Lodes, *Principal*
EMP: 255
SALES (corp-wide): 1.5B **Privately Held**
SIC: 5099 Firearms & ammunition, except sporting
PA: Rk Family, Inc.
4216 Dewitt Ave
Mattoon IL 61938
217 235-7102

(G-12499)
SCHNEDER ELC BLDNGS AMRCAS INC
1770 Masn Mrrw Millgrv Rd (45036-9688)
PHONE....................513 398-9800
Bill Korn, *Branch Mgr*
Jeffrey Owens, *Manager*
EMP: 80
SALES (corp-wide): 355.8K **Privately Held**
SIC: 1731 3822 Electrical work; auto controls regulating residntl & coml environmt & applncs
HQ: Schneider Electric Buildings Americas, Inc.
1650 W Crosby Rd
Carrollton TX 75006
972 323-1111

(G-12500)
SHAKER RUN GOLF CLUB
1320 Golf Club Dr (45036-4069)
PHONE....................513 727-0007
Steve Lambert, *Owner*
Tyler Geswein, *Principal*
Patrick Piccioni, *Principal*
Ryan Gilley, *Director*
EMP: 52
SALES (est): 3.2MM **Privately Held**
SIC: 7992 Public golf courses

(G-12501)
SIBCY CLINE INC
Also Called: Sibcy, Cline Realtors
103 Oregonia Rd (45036-1983)
PHONE....................513 932-6334
Amy Davis, *Manager*
EMP: 80
SALES (corp-wide): 2.1B **Privately Held**
WEB: www.sibcycline.com
SIC: 6531 Real estate agent, residential
PA: Sibcy Cline, Inc.
8044 Montgomery Rd # 300
Cincinnati OH 45236
513 984-4100

(G-12502)
SIEMENS INDUSTRY INC
4170 Columbia Rd (45036-9588)
PHONE....................800 879-8079
Tony Telfer, *Manager*
EMP: 40
SALES (corp-wide): 95B **Privately Held**
WEB: www.sea.siemens.com
SIC: 7699 Industrial equipment services
HQ: Siemens Industry, Inc.
1000 Deerfield Pkwy
Buffalo Grove IL 60089
800 743-6367

(G-12503)
SITE WORX LLC
Also Called: Siteworx
3980 Turtlecreek Rd (45036-8643)
P.O. Box 767 (45036-0767)
PHONE....................513 229-0295
Matt Smith, *President*
Joe Smith, *Vice Pres*
Mike Smith, *Mng Member*
EMP: 95
SALES (est): 33.4MM **Privately Held**
SIC: 1542 Commercial & office building, new construction

(G-12504)
SOFTWARE SOLUTIONS INC (PA)
420 E Main St (45036-2234)
PHONE....................513 932-6667
John Rettig, *President*
Rick Fortman, *Vice Pres*

Kevin Nye, *Regl Sales Mgr*
Larry Hollingshead, *Manager*
Monica Scott, *Manager*
EMP: 32 **EST:** 1978
SQ FT: 12,200
SALES (est): 4.5MM **Privately Held**
WEB: www.elocalgovernment.com
SIC: 5045 7372 7373 Computer software; disk drives; application computer software; computer integrated systems design

(G-12505)
SOUTHERN OHIO GUN DISTRS INC
240 Harmon Ave (45036-8800)
PHONE....................513 932-8148
Phil Flannigan, *Branch Mgr*
EMP: 43
SALES (corp-wide): 6.7MM **Privately Held**
WEB: www.southernohiogun.com
SIC: 5099 Firearms, except sporting; ammunition, except sporting
PA: Southern Ohio Gun Distributors, Inc.
105 E Main St
Lebanon OH 45036
513 932-8148

(G-12506)
SPARTAN SUPPLY CO INC
942 Old 122 Rd (45036-8632)
PHONE....................513 932-6954
Tim Carpenter, *CEO*
Robert Hill, *Ch of Bd*
Joann Hill, *Corp Secy*
EMP: 40 **EST:** 1979
SQ FT: 50,000
SALES (est): 5MM **Privately Held**
WEB: www.spartanindustries.net
SIC: 7699 Pallet repair

(G-12507)
SUMMIT ENTERPRISES CONTG CORP
726 E Main St Ste F166 (45036-1900)
PHONE....................513 426-1623
Jerry Tarrab, *Ch of Bd*
EMP: 30
SALES (est): 273.5K **Privately Held**
SIC: 1761 Siding contractor

(G-12508)
SWEENEY TEAM INC
576 Mound Ct Ste A (45036-2090)
PHONE....................513 934-0700
Mike Walter, *Branch Mgr*
EMP: 25
SALES (est): 839.2K
SALES (corp-wide): 2.7MM **Privately Held**
SIC: 6531 Real estate agent, residential
PA: Sweeney Team, Inc.
1440 Main St
Cincinnati OH 45202
513 241-3400

(G-12509)
TALBERT HOUSE
Also Called: Community Correctional Center
5234 W State Route 63 (45036-8202)
PHONE....................513 933-9304
Jennifer Burnside, *Manager*
Scott McKay, *Manager*
Troy Newman, *Manager*
EMP: 55
SALES (corp-wide): 59.6MM **Privately Held**
WEB: www.talberthouse.org
SIC: 8322 Substance abuse counseling
PA: Talbert House
2600 Victory Pkwy
Cincinnati OH 45206
513 872-5863

(G-12510)
TEXAS EASTERN TRANSMISSION LP
1157 W State Route 122 (45036-9616)
PHONE....................513 932-1816
Larry D Moody, *Enginr/R&D Mgr*
Larry Moody, *Manager*
EMP: 33
SALES (corp-wide): 34.7B **Privately Held**
SIC: 4922 Natural gas transmission

HQ: Texas Eastern Transmission, Lp
5400 Westheimer Ct
Houston TX 77056
713 627-5400

(G-12511)
TRIPLE Q FOUNDATIONS CO INC
139 Harmon Ave (45036-9511)
PHONE....................513 932-3121
Darren Poore, *President*
Jeannie Szellinger, *Manager*
EMP: 35
SALES (est): 4.6MM **Privately Held**
SIC: 1771 Concrete work

(G-12512)
TWIN CEDARS SERVICES INC
935 Old Ralph 122 (45036)
PHONE....................513 932-0399
Jimmy Collins, *President*
Teresa Collins, *Vice Pres*
EMP: 71
SALES (est): 859.7K **Privately Held**
SIC: 7349 Janitorial service, contract basis

(G-12513)
VISIONS MATTER LLC
838 W State Route 122 (45036)
PHONE....................513 934-1934
Sandra Sebecke, *Principal*
Deidre Dyer, *Director*
EMP: 80
SALES (est): 1.7MM **Privately Held**
SIC: 8082 Home health care services

(G-12514)
WARREN COUNTY BOARD DEVLPMNTAL
42 Kings Way (45036-9593)
PHONE....................513 925-1813
Megan Manuel, *Superintendent*
Michele Swearingen, *CFO*
Amy Ledford, *Admin Sec*
Patrick Poteet, *Associate*
EMP: 25
SALES (est): 913.8K **Privately Held**
SIC: 8052 Home for the mentally retarded, with health care

(G-12515)
WARREN COUNTY COMMUNITY SVCS (PA)
Also Called: WCCS
570 N State Route 741 (45036-8839)
PHONE....................513 695-2100
Dr Charles Peckham, *President*
James Smith, *Controller*
Thomas Cox, *Nutritionist*
Tom Salzbrun, *Exec Dir*
Larry Sargeant, *Exec Dir*
EMP: 175 **EST:** 1966
SQ FT: 24,000
SALES: 9MM **Privately Held**
WEB: www.wccsinc.org
SIC: 8399 Antipoverty board

(G-12516)
YOUNG MENS CHRISTIAN
Also Called: Countryside YMCA Child Dev
1699 Deerfield Rd (45036-9215)
PHONE....................513 932-1424
Mike Carroll, *CEO*
Phil Breeding, *Maint Spvr*
Sandra Hamilton, *QA Dir*
Renee Lay, *Financial Exec*
Jenny Poling, *Exec Dir*
EMP: 300
SALES (corp-wide): 33.6MM **Privately Held**
WEB: www.cincinnatiymca.org
SIC: 8641 7991 8351 7032 Youth organizations; physical fitness facilities; child day care services; youth camps; individual & family services
PA: Young Mens Christian Association Of Greater Cincinnati
1105 Elm St
Cincinnati OH 45202
513 651-2100

▲ = Import ▼=Export
◆ =Import/Export

GEOGRAPHIC

Leetonia
Columbiana County

(G-12517)
2828 CLINTON INC (PA)
Also Called: Cleveland Vibrator Company
600 Cherry Fork Ave (44431-1279)
PHONE.....................................216 241-7157
Michael Valore, *CEO*
Jeffrey Chokel, *Ch of Bd*
Craig Macklin, *Vice Pres*
Glen Roberts, *Vice Pres*
Edilberto Colon, *Plant Mgr*
▲ EMP: 27 EST: 1922
SALES: 5.7MM **Privately Held**
WEB: www.clevelandvibrator.com
SIC: 5084 Industrial machinery & equipment

(G-12518)
ADVANTAGE TANK LINES INC
404 12 Pearl St (44431)
PHONE.....................................330 427-1010
Fax: 330 427-1012
EMP: 180
SALES (corp-wide): 26.3MM **Privately Held**
SIC: 4213 4212 Trucking Operator-Nonlocal Local Trucking Operator
PA: Advantage Tank Lines, Inc.
4366 Mount Pleasant St Nw
North Canton OH 44720
330 491-0474

(G-12519)
S&P GLOBAL INC
41438 Kings Ct (44431-8617)
PHONE.....................................330 482-9544
Nancy Marr, *Branch Mgr*
EMP: 148
SALES (corp-wide): 6.2B **Publicly Held**
SIC: 6282 Investment advisory service
PA: S&P Global Inc.
55 Water St
New York NY 10041
212 438-1000

Leipsic
Putnam County

(G-12520)
OTTERBEIN SNIOR LFSTYLE CHICES
Also Called: Oherbein Kpsic Rtirement Cmnty
901 E Main St (45856-9326)
PHONE.....................................419 943-4376
Jason McClellan, *Exec Dir*
EMP: 50
SALES (corp-wide): 58.4MM **Privately Held**
SIC: 8361 Home for the aged
PA: Senior Otterbein Lifestyle Choices
585 N State Route 741
Lebanon OH 45036
513 933-5400

(G-12521)
PGT TRUCKING INC
Also Called: C and D Truck Repairs
6302 Road 5 (45856-9761)
P.O. Box 107 (45856-0107)
PHONE.....................................419 943-3437
Charles Kitchen, *Manager*
EMP: 50
SALES (corp-wide): 151.4MM **Privately Held**
SIC: 4213 4212 7538 Contract haulers; local trucking, without storage; general truck repair
PA: Pgt Trucking, Inc.
4200 Industrial Blvd
Aliquippa PA 15001
724 728-3500

Lewis Center
Delaware County

(G-12522)
AMERICAN BUS SOLUTIONS INC
8850 Whitney Dr (43035-8297)
PHONE.....................................614 888-2227
Rajeev Kumar, *President*
Manisha Dixit, *Vice Pres*
Mark Heidkamp, *CFO*
Anissa Schisler, *Manager*
Lalu Chavan, *Prgrmr*
EMP: 58
SQ FT: 2,000
SALES: 17.5MM **Privately Held**
SIC: 7379 Computer related consulting services

(G-12523)
AMERICAN NATIONAL RED CROSS
Also Called: American Red Cross
1327 Cameron Ave (43035-9662)
PHONE.....................................614 436-3862
EMP: 39
SALES (corp-wide): 2.5B **Privately Held**
SIC: 8322 Emergency social services
PA: The American National Red Cross
430 17th St Nw
Washington DC 20006
202 737-8300

(G-12524)
ANIMAL HOSPITAL POLARIS LLC
8928 S Old State Rd (43035-8401)
PHONE.....................................614 888-4050
Brittani Sell,
EMP: 45
SALES (est): 2.6MM **Privately Held**
WEB: www.animalhospitalofpolaris.com
SIC: 0742 Animal hospital services, pets & other animal specialties

(G-12525)
AT&T CORP
8601 Columbus Pike (43035-9614)
PHONE.....................................740 549-4546
EMP: 82
SALES (corp-wide): 170.7B **Publicly Held**
SIC: 4812 Cellular telephone services
HQ: At&T Corp.
1 At&T Way
Bedminster NJ 07921
800 403-3302

(G-12526)
ATS CAROLINA INC
Also Called: Automation Tooling Systems
425 Enterprise Dr (43035-9424)
PHONE.....................................803 324-9300
Stew Wiatersprecher, *CEO*
▲ EMP: 63
SALES (est): 17.9MM
SALES (corp-wide): 769.5MM **Privately Held**
SIC: 7373 Systems integration services
PA: Ats Automation Tooling Systems Inc
730 Fountain St Suite 2b
Cambridge ON N3H 4
519 653-6500

(G-12527)
ATS SYSTEMS OREGON INC
425 Enterprise Dr (43035-9424)
PHONE.....................................541 738-0932
Anthony Caputo, *CEO*
Maria Perrella, *President*
Stewart McCvaig, *Admin Sec*
▲ EMP: 300
SQ FT: 85,000
SALES (est): 81.1MM
SALES (corp-wide): 769.5MM **Privately Held**
SIC: 3569 5084 Robots, assembly line: industrial & commercial; industrial machinery & equipment
PA: Ats Automation Tooling Systems Inc
730 Fountain St Suite 2b
Cambridge ON N3H 4
519 653-6500

(G-12528)
AUNTIES ATTIC
1550 Lewis Center Rd G (43035-8232)
PHONE.....................................740 548-5059
EMP: 35
SQ FT: 3,500
SALES (est): 1.5MM **Privately Held**
SIC: 2392 5199 Mfg Household Furnishings Whol Nondurable Goods

(G-12529)
BLENDON GARDENS INC
9590 S Old State Rd (43035-9492)
PHONE.....................................614 840-0500
Loren L Brelsford, *President*
Amy Mahler, *Office Mgr*
Brian Thornton, *Info Tech Mgr*
Deidra Ross, *Administration*
EMP: 26
SQ FT: 1,979
SALES (est): 3.6MM **Privately Held**
WEB: www.blendongardens.com
SIC: 0781 Landscape architects

(G-12530)
BOARD OF DELAWARE COUNTY
7991 Columbus Pike (43035-9611)
PHONE.....................................740 201-3600
Robert R Morgan, *Superintendent*
Anne Miller, *Corp Comm Staff*
Peggy Van Diest, *Director*
Deb Gibson, *Admin Asst*
Nicole Hardesty, *Admin Asst*
EMP: 82
SALES: 17.2MM **Privately Held**
SIC: 8322 Child related social services

(G-12531)
BOB WEBB BUILDERS INC
Also Called: Bob Webb Homes
7662 N Central Dr (43035-9400)
PHONE.....................................740 548-5577
Robert A Webb, *President*
Rebecca L Webb, *Treasurer*
Pete Taylor, *Admin Sec*
EMP: 30 EST: 1960
SQ FT: 5,000
SALES (est): 4.3MM **Privately Held**
SIC: 1521 New construction, single-family houses

(G-12532)
CENTRAL BEVERAGE GROUP LTD
Also Called: Superior Bev Group Centl Ohio
8133 Highfield Dr (43035-9673)
PHONE.....................................614 294-3555
John Antonucci, *Partner*
Scott Hall, *Purch Mgr*
Mike Scurria, *CFO*
Kelli Decker, *Controller*
▲ EMP: 140 EST: 1946
SQ FT: 116,000
SALES (est): 30.8MM **Privately Held**
SIC: 5181 Beer & other fermented malt liquors

(G-12533)
CHILLER LLC
8144 Highfield Dr (43035-9673)
PHONE.....................................740 549-0009
Jason Beebee, *Manager*
Carol Hall, *Director*
Denise Hughes, *Director*
Spanhel Martin, *Director*
Rob Schriner, *Director*
EMP: 40
SALES (corp-wide): 12.8MM **Privately Held**
SIC: 7999 Ice skating rink operation
PA: Chiller Llc
7001 Dublin Park Dr
Dublin OH 43016
614 764-1000

(G-12534)
COLUMBUS SAIL AND PWR SQUADRON
8492 Cotter St (43035-7139)
PHONE.....................................614 384-0245
Robert L Prior, *Commander*
Thresa Nadowlson, *Treasurer*
EMP: 250
SQ FT: 1,500
SALES: 35.2K **Privately Held**
SIC: 7997 Boating club, membership

(G-12535)
COUNTY OF DELAWARE
Also Called: Title Division
8647 Columbus Pike (43035-9616)
PHONE.....................................740 657-3945
Jan Antonoplis, *Clerk*
EMP: 26 **Privately Held**
WEB: www.delawarecountysheriff.com
SIC: 6541 Title abstract offices
PA: County Of Delaware
101 N Sandusky St
Delaware OH 43015
740 368-1800

(G-12536)
CULVER ART & FRAME CO
7890 N Central Dr (43035-9406)
P.O. Box 310 (43035-0310)
PHONE.....................................740 548-6868
Ronald D Lehman, *President*
Mark Lehman, *President*
David E Lehman, *Vice Pres*
▲ EMP: 40 EST: 1932
SQ FT: 42,000
SALES (est): 6.5MM **Privately Held**
WEB: www.culverframe.com
SIC: 5023 Frames & framing, picture & mirror

(G-12537)
D J- SEVE GROUP INC
Also Called: McDonald's
10030 Columbus Pike (43035-9414)
PHONE.....................................614 888-6600
Ron Severance, *President*
Shad Severance, *Vice Pres*
EMP: 42
SALES (est): 1.9MM **Privately Held**
SIC: 5812 8741 Fast-food restaurant, chain; restaurant management

(G-12538)
DEXXXON DIGITAL STORAGE INC
7611 Green Meadows Dr (43035-9445)
PHONE.....................................740 548-7179
Babak Sarshar, *Ch of Bd*
Simon N Garneau, *President*
Dave Burke, *Exec VP*
Leon Rijnbeek, *Treasurer*
Sassan Shafiee, *Admin Sec*
▲ EMP: 45
SQ FT: 60,000
SALES (est): 28.3MM **Privately Held**
SIC: 5112 7371 Computer & photocopying supplies; custom computer programming services
PA: Dexxon Groupe
79 Avenue Louis Roche
Gennevilliers 92230

(G-12539)
DIETARY SOLUTIONS INC
171 Green Meadows Dr S (43035-9458)
PHONE.....................................614 985-6567
Kay Lachi, *President*
EMP: 50
SALES (est): 1.2MM **Privately Held**
WEB: www.dietarysolutions.net
SIC: 8049 Dietician

(G-12540)
DIGITEK SOFTWARE INC
650 Radio Dr (43035-7111)
PHONE.....................................614 764-8875
Chetan Bhuta, *President*
Pankaj Oza, *General Mgr*
Art Andre, *Vice Pres*
Bharat Gandhi, *Vice Pres*
Tamana Nair, *Technology*
EMP: 40
SQ FT: 3,000
SALES (est): 5.6MM **Privately Held**
WEB: www.digiteksw.com
SIC: 7371 Computer software development

(G-12541)
DISPATCH PRINTING COMPANY
Also Called: Columbus Dispatch
7801 N Central Dr (43035-9407)
PHONE.....................................740 548-5331
Don Patton, *Branch Mgr*

EMP: 238
SALES (corp-wide): 651.9MM **Privately Held**
SIC: 2711 4833 Commercial printing & newspaper publishing combined; television broadcasting stations
PA: The Dispatch Printing Company
62 E Broad St
Columbus OH 43215
614 461-5000

(G-12542)
FIRST COMMONWEALTH BANK
110 Riverbend Ave (43035)
PHONE..................................740 657-7000
EMP: 166
SALES (corp-wide): 380.8MM **Publicly Held**
SIC: 6022 State trust companies accepting deposits, commercial
HQ: First Commonwealth Bank
601 Philadelphia St
Indiana PA 15701
724 349-7220

(G-12543)
GLEAMING SYSTEMS LLC
2417 Charoe St (43035-7290)
PHONE..................................614 348-7475
Pratik Shah, *CEO*
EMP: 30
SALES (est): 498.4K **Privately Held**
SIC: 8748 Systems engineering consultant, ex. computer or professional

(G-12544)
HE HARI INC (PA)
600 Enterprise Dr (43035-9432)
PHONE..................................614 846-6600
Naresh Patel, *Principal*
EMP: 90
SALES (est): 1.8MM **Privately Held**
SIC: 7011 Hotels & motels

(G-12545)
HOMEREACH INC
Also Called: Homereach Healthcare
7708 Green Meadows Dr D (43035-1116)
PHONE..................................614 566-0850
Ken Symanski, *Director*
EMP: 28
SALES (corp-wide): 4B **Privately Held**
WEB: www.homereach.net
SIC: 5047 Medical equipment & supplies
HQ: Homereach, Inc.
404 E Wilson Bridge Rd
Worthington OH 43085

(G-12546)
INDEPENDENT ORDER ODD FELLOWS
5230 Cypress Dr (43035-9028)
P.O. Box 333, Galena (43021-0333)
PHONE..................................740 548-5038
Lorraine Saunders, *Admin Sec*
EMP: 28
SALES (est): 261.9K **Privately Held**
SIC: 8641 Civic associations

(G-12547)
JPMORGAN CHASE BANK NAT ASSN
8681 Columbus Pike (43035-9617)
PHONE..................................740 657-8906
Michelle Mayberry, *Manager*
EMP: 26
SALES (corp-wide): 131.4B **Publicly Held**
WEB: www.chasebank.com
SIC: 6029 Commercial banks
HQ: Jpmorgan Chase Bank, National Association
1111 Polaris Pkwy
Columbus OH 43240
614 436-3055

(G-12548)
KINDERCARE LEARNING CTRS LLC
Also Called: Polaris Kindercare
96 Neverland Dr (43035-9151)
PHONE..................................740 549-0264
Deeann Goebel, *Branch Mgr*
EMP: 25

SALES (corp-wide): 1.2B **Privately Held**
WEB: www.kindercare.com
SIC: 8351 Group day care center
HQ: Kindercare Learning Centers, Llc
650 Ne Holladay St # 1400
Portland OR 97232
503 872-1300

(G-12549)
LEADER TECHNOLOGIES INC (PA)
674 Enterprise Dr (43035-9434)
P.O. Box 224 (43035-0224)
PHONE..................................614 890-1986
Michael T McKibben, *Ch of Bd*
James Sobwick, *COO*
Michael Mc Kibben, *Human Res Dir*
Deb Weckerly, *Director*
EMP: 30
SQ FT: 6,000
SALES (est): 3.3MM **Privately Held**
WEB: www.leader.com
SIC: 7371 Computer software development

(G-12550)
LUMENOMICS INC
Also Called: Inside Outfitters
8333 Green Meadows Dr N (43035-8496)
PHONE..................................614 798-3500
Carlee Swihart, *Vice Pres*
EMP: 46 **Privately Held**
SIC: 5023 2591 2221 2211 Draperies; venetian blinds; vertical blinds; window covering parts & accessories; drapery hardware & blinds & shades; window shades; draperies & drapery fabrics, man-made fiber & silk; draperies & drapery fabrics, cotton; shades, canvas: made from purchased materials
PA: Lumenomics, Inc.
500 Mercer St C2
Seattle WA 98109

(G-12551)
MEYERS LDSCP SVCS & NURS INC
6081 Columbus Pike (43035-9008)
P.O. Box 697 (43035-0697)
PHONE..................................614 210-1194
Michael Meyers, *President*
Charles Camphausen, *Vice Pres*
EMP: 45 **EST:** 1998
SQ FT: 2,400
SALES (est): 4.7MM **Privately Held**
SIC: 0781 Landscape services

(G-12552)
MULTI-PLASTICS INC (PA)
7770 N Central Dr (43035-9404)
PHONE..................................740 548-4894
John R Parsio, *President*
John Parsio Jr, *Exec VP*
Wesley Hall, *Vice Pres*
Steven Parsio, *Vice Pres*
Stephen Parsio, *VP Mfg*
◆ **EMP:** 55
SQ FT: 32,000
SALES (est): 198MM **Privately Held**
WEB: www.multi-plastics.com
SIC: 5162 Plastics film; plastics materials

(G-12553)
NATIONWIDE MUTUAL INSURANCE CO
9243 Columbus Pike (43035-8278)
PHONE..................................614 430-3047
Steve Falker, *Manager*
EMP: 35
SQ FT: 4,032
SALES (corp-wide): 13.2B **Privately Held**
WEB: www.nirassn.com
SIC: 6411 Insurance agents, brokers & service
PA: Nationwide Mutual Insurance Company
1 Nationwide Plz
Columbus OH 43215
614 249-7111

(G-12554)
NSB RETAIL SYSTEMS INC
400 Venture Dr (43035-9275)
PHONE..................................614 840-1421
Howard Stotland, *President*
Eric Eichensehr, *Vice Pres*

EMP: 90
SQ FT: 18,000
SALES: 7.9MM
SALES (corp-wide): 172.8K **Privately Held**
SIC: 7371 Computer Software Development
HQ: Nsb Retail Systems Limited
1 The Arena
Bracknell BERKS

(G-12555)
ON SITE INSTRUMENTS LLC
403 Venture Dr (43035-9519)
P.O. Box 290 (43035-0290)
PHONE..................................614 846-1900
Laurie Beckley, *Comptroller*
EMP: 50
SALES (est): 3.2MM **Privately Held**
WEB: www.on-siteinstruments.com
SIC: 8748 Environmental consultant

(G-12556)
ORBIT SYSTEMS INC
615 Carle Ave (43035-8294)
PHONE..................................614 504-8011
Amit Rateria, *President*
EMP: 40
SQ FT: 1,427
SALES (est): 2.4MM **Privately Held**
SIC: 8742 Business consultant

(G-12557)
PCM INC
Also Called: Pcm Logistics
8337 Green Meadows Dr N (43035-9451)
PHONE..................................614 854-1399
Paul Neiswinger, *Vice Pres*
Bob Bender, *Sales Staff*
Ellen N Marak, *Branch Mgr*
Pat Ellis, *Info Tech Dir*
EMP: 41
SALES (corp-wide): 2.1B **Publicly Held**
SIC: 8999 Artists & artists' studios
PA: Pcm, Inc.
1940 E Mariposa Ave
El Segundo CA 90245
310 354-5600

(G-12558)
PCM SALES INC
Also Called: Inacomp Computer Centers
8337 Green Meadows Dr N (43035-9451)
PHONE..................................740 548-2222
Anthony Rodriguez, *President*
Tonya Lee, *Business Mgr*
Theresa Vandavis, *Business Mgr*
Dave Raab, *Vice Pres*
Eric Keating, *Vice Pres*
EMP: 40
SALES (corp-wide): 2.1B **Publicly Held**
WEB: www.sarcom.com
SIC: 5045 Computers
HQ: Pcm Sales, Inc.
1940 E Mariposa Ave
El Segundo CA 90245
310 354-5600

(G-12559)
PF HOLDINGS LLC
8522 Cotter St (43035-7138)
PHONE..................................740 549-3558
Bob Patel, *President*
EMP: 90 **EST:** 2011
SQ FT: 1,500 **Privately Held**
SIC: 6719 Investment holding companies, except banks

(G-12560)
POLARIS AUTOMATION INC
Also Called: Electrical Design & Engrg Svcs
8333 Green Meadows Dr N A (43035-8497)
PHONE..................................614 431-0170
James D Cooke, *President*
Scott Cooke, *Principal*
Susan Cooke, *Corp Secy*
Tony Bickel, *Engineer*
Wally Hallas, *Engineer*
EMP: 51
SQ FT: 2,573
SALES (est): 4.7MM **Privately Held**
SIC: 7389 8711 Design, commercial & industrial; engineering services

(G-12561)
QUINTUS TECHNOLOGIES LLC
8270 Green Meadows Dr N (43035-9450)
PHONE..................................614 891-2732
Dennis Schwegel, *Manager*
Ed Williams,
EMP: 28
SALES (est): 3.7MM **Privately Held**
SIC: 7699 7389 3443 Industrial equipment services; industrial & commercial equipment inspection service; industrial vessels, tanks & containers

(G-12562)
SUPERIOR BEVERAGE GROUP LTD
8133 Highfield Dr (43035-9673)
PHONE..................................614 294-3555
Mike Scurria, *Vice Pres*
Brian Ahern, *Opers Mgr*
Aaron Jones, *Opers Mgr*
Kevin Lowrie, *Accounts Mgr*
Tucker Allen, *Sales Staff*
EMP: 57
SALES (corp-wide): 98.5MM **Privately Held**
SIC: 5149 5499 Beverages, except coffee & tea; beverage stores
PA: The Superior Beverage Group Ltd
31031 Diamond Pkwy
Solon OH 44139
440 703-4580

(G-12563)
TRIPLE T TRANSPORT INC (PA)
433 Lewis Center Rd (43035-9049)
P.O. Box 649 (43035-0649)
PHONE..................................740 657-3244
Darin Puppel, *President*
Terry McKenzie, *Vice Pres*
David Santisi, *Vice Pres*
Wade Amelung, *CFO*
April Morone, *Accounts Mgr*
EMP: 70
SQ FT: 12,000
SALES: 152.8MM **Privately Held**
WEB: www.triplettransport.com
SIC: 4731 Transportation agents & brokers

(G-12564)
TRUGREEN LIMITED PARTNERSHIP
Also Called: Tru Green-Chemlawn
461 Enterprise Dr (43035-9424)
P.O. Box 548, Westerville (43086-0548)
PHONE..................................614 285-3721
Al Carow, *Branch Mgr*
EMP: 103
SALES (corp-wide): 3.4B **Privately Held**
SIC: 0782 Lawn care services
HQ: Trugreen Limited Partnership
1790 Kirby Pkwy
Memphis TN 38138
901 251-4128

(G-12565)
V WESTAAR INC
6249 Westwick Pl (43035-8978)
PHONE..................................740 803-2803
Pam A Westerlund, *President*
Tom Westerlund, *Vice Pres*
EMP: 32
SALES (est): 1.9MM **Privately Held**
SIC: 8741 Restaurant management

(G-12566)
VAUGHN INDUSTRIES LLC
7749 Green Meadows Dr (43035-9445)
PHONE..................................740 548-7100
Kelli Kitzler, *Manager*
EMP: 25
SALES (est): 1.9MM
SALES (corp-wide): 158.5MM **Privately Held**
SIC: 1731 1711 General electrical contractor; mechanical contractor
PA: Vaughn Industries, Llc
1201 E Findlay St
Carey OH 43316
419 396-3900

▲ = Import ▼=Export
◆ =Import/Export

(G-12567)
XIGENT AUTOMATION SYSTEMS INC
8303 Green Meadows Dr N (43035-9451)
PHONE.....................740 548-3700
Joe Moreno, *President*
Brian Bleichrodt, *CFO*
David Hirth, *Admin Sec*
▲ EMP: 90
SQ FT: 78,000
SALES (est): 56.1MM **Privately Held**
WEB: www.xasinc.com
SIC: 5084 Industrial machinery & equipment

Lewisburg
Preble County

(G-12568)
IAMS COMPANY
6571 State Route 503 N (45338-6713)
P.O. Box 862 (45338)
PHONE.....................937 962-7782
Kurt Petry, *Manager*
EMP: 90
SQ FT: 35,000
SALES (corp-wide): 34.2B **Privately Held**
WEB: www.iams.com
SIC: 2047 5199 Dog food; pet supplies
HQ: The Iams Company
8700 S Masn Montgomery Rd
Mason OH 45040
800 675-3849

(G-12569)
JANUS HOTELS AND RESORTS INC
Also Called: Days Inn
6840 State Route 503 N (45338-9773)
PHONE.....................513 631-8500
Arun Patel, *Manager*
EMP: 25
SALES (corp-wide): 24MM **Privately Held**
WEB: www.bestwesterncambridge.com
SIC: 7011 Hotels & motels
PA: Janus Hotels And Resorts, Inc.
2300 Nw Corp Blvd Ste 232
Boca Raton FL 33431
561 997-2325

(G-12570)
M & L ELECTRIC INC
4439a New Market Banta Rd (45338-7747)
PHONE.....................937 833-5154
Don Myers, *President*
Mark Lehman, *Vice Pres*
Rebecca Myers, *Treasurer*
EMP: 25
SQ FT: 10,000
SALES (est): 2.9MM **Privately Held**
SIC: 1731 General electrical contractor

(G-12571)
NUTRITION TRNSP SVCS LLC
6531 State Route 503 N (45338-6713)
PHONE.....................937 962-2661
Mark A Poeschl, *COO*
Scott Rutgers, *Mng Member*
EMP: 250
SALES (est): 11.3MM
SALES (corp-wide): 114.7B **Privately Held**
WEB: www.vigortone.com
SIC: 4731 Freight forwarding
HQ: Provimi North America, Inc.
10 Collective Way
Brookville OH 45309
937 770-2400

Lewistown
Logan County

(G-12572)
MID-STATES PACKAGING INC
12163 State Route 274 (43333-9707)
PHONE.....................937 843-3243
Jeffrey C Davidson, *President*
Larry Winner, *Vice Pres*
EMP: 50

SQ FT: 80,000
SALES (est): 15MM **Privately Held**
SIC: 5199 Packaging materials

Lewisville
Monroe County

(G-12573)
BAKER & SONS EQUIPMENT CO
45381 State Route 145 (43754-9460)
PHONE.....................740 567-3317
James J Baker, *CEO*
Gregory S Baker, *President*
Mike Kuhn, *Manager*
EMP: 25
SQ FT: 18,000
SALES (est): 16MM **Privately Held**
WEB: www.bakerandsons.com
SIC: 5082 5083 Logging equipment & supplies; agricultural machinery & equipment

Lexington
Richland County

(G-12574)
MEADE CONSTRUCTION INC (PA)
Also Called: Meade Construction Company
13 N Mill St (44904-1200)
PHONE.....................740 694-5525
Andrew Meade, *CEO*
Chris Thornton, *Corp Secy*
Chris Mortimer, *Senior VP*
Philip Meade, *Vice Pres*
EMP: 30
SALES (est): 8.9MM **Privately Held**
WEB: www.meadeconstructioninc.com
SIC: 1761 Roofing contractor

Liberty Center
Henry County

(G-12575)
RUPP/ROSEBROCK INC
7464 County Road 424 (43532-9551)
PHONE.....................419 533-7999
Justin Groll, *President*
Jeffrey Smith, *Vice Pres*
Annette Miller, *Manager*
EMP: 25 EST: 1989
SALES: 8.8MM **Privately Held**
SIC: 1542 Commercial & office building contractors

(G-12576)
YOUTH SERVICES OHIO DEPARTMENT
Also Called: Maumee Youth Center
Township Rd 1 D U 469 (43532)
PHONE.....................419 875-6965
Nan Hoff, *Manager*
EMP: 145 **Privately Held**
SIC: 9223 8322 Prison, government; ; youth center
HQ: Department Of Youth Service, Ohio
30 W Spring St Fl 5
Columbus OH 43215

Liberty Township
Butler County

(G-12577)
AS LOGISTICS INC (DH)
Also Called: Amstan Logistics
7570 Bales St Ste 310 (45069-0003)
PHONE.....................513 863-4627
Jim Manfra, *President*
David Beckman, *Vice Pres*
Ken Hurley, *Accounting Mgr*
Michelle Brockmeier, *Accounts Mgr*
Robert Doerflein, *Cust Mgr*
◆ EMP: 70 EST: 1974
SQ FT: 28,000

SALES (est): 68.8MM
SALES (corp-wide): 15.6B **Privately Held**
WEB: www.amstan.com
SIC: 4213 Trucking, except local

(G-12578)
CAPANO & ASSOCIATES LLC
8312 Alpine Aster Ct (45044-1902)
PHONE.....................513 403-6000
Jeffrey Capano,
Cynthia Capano,
EMP: 49
SQ FT: 2,800
SALES: 15.5MM **Privately Held**
WEB: www.capanoandassociates.com/
SIC: 8331 8711 Skill training center; professional engineer

(G-12579)
CHESTER WEST YMCA
6703 Yankee Rd (45044-9130)
P.O. Box 692, West Chester (45071-0692)
PHONE.....................513 779-3917
John Schaller, *Director*
EMP: 25
SALES (est): 326.9K **Privately Held**
WEB: www.westchesterrunningclub.com
SIC: 8641 Youth organizations

(G-12580)
CHILDRENS HOSPITAL MEDICAL CTR
7777 Yankee Rd (45044-3500)
PHONE.....................513 803-9600
Keith McConnell, *Engineer*
Mark Mumford, *CFO*
Daniel Rechtin, *Director*
Victoria Dittrich,
EMP: 969
SALES (corp-wide): 1.6B **Privately Held**
SIC: 8062 8011 General medical & surgical hospitals; medical centers
PA: Children's Hospital Medical Center
3333 Burnet Ave
Cincinnati OH 45229
513 636-4200

(G-12581)
FOUR BRIDGES COUNTRY CLUB LTD
Also Called: Liberty Township
8300 Four Bridges Dr (45044-8489)
PHONE.....................513 759-4620
Ron Townsend, *Partner*
Mark Kelley, *General Mgr*
Amanda Cicchinelli, *Director*
Connie Rosenbloom,
EMP: 100
SALES (est): 5.8MM **Privately Held**
WEB: www.fourbridges.com
SIC: 7997 Country club, membership

(G-12582)
LAKOTA LOCAL SCHOOL DISTRICT
Also Called: Bus Garage
6947 Yankee Rd (45044-9719)
PHONE.....................513 777-2150
Doug Lantz, *Branch Mgr*
EMP: 230
SALES (corp-wide): 213.7MM **Privately Held**
SIC: 4151 4225 4173 School buses; general warehousing & storage; bus terminal & service facilities
PA: Lakota Local School District
5572 Princeton Rd
Liberty Twp OH 45011
513 874-5505

(G-12583)
LIBERTY CTR LODGING ASSOC LLC
Also Called: Liberty Center AC By Marriott
7505 Gibson St (45069-7517)
PHONE.....................608 833-4100
CJ Raymond, *Mng Member*
EMP: 30
SQ FT: 109,457
SALES (est): 359.5K **Privately Held**
SIC: 7011 Hotels

(G-12584)
ORTHOPEDIC ASSOCIATES
7117 Dutchland Pkwy (45044-9096)
PHONE.....................800 824-9861
EMP: 78 **Privately Held**
SIC: 8011 Orthopedic physician
PA: Orthopedic Associates Of Sw Ohio, Inc.
7677 Yankee St Ste 110
Centerville OH 45459

(G-12585)
SERVICES ON DECK INC (PA)
8263 Kyles Station Rd # 1 (45044-9573)
PHONE.....................513 759-2854
Daniel B Stoddard, *President*
EMP: 36
SQ FT: 5,000
SALES (est): 4MM **Privately Held**
SIC: 1521 Patio & deck construction & repair

Liberty Twp
Butler County

(G-12586)
HAMILTON LODGE 93 BENEVOLANT P
Also Called: ELKS B P O E
4444 Hmlton Middletown Rd (45011-2352)
PHONE.....................513 887-4384
Richard Sullivan, *President*
EMP: 25
SQ FT: 5,000
SALES: 1.1MM **Privately Held**
SIC: 8641 Fraternal associations

(G-12587)
INDIGO GROUP
4645 Stonehaven Dr (45011-6614)
PHONE.....................513 557-8794
EMP: 45
SALES: 1,000K **Privately Held**
SIC: 7371 Web Development And Consulting

(G-12588)
PHYSICIANS CHOICE INC
5130 Prnceton Glendale Rd (45011-2415)
PHONE.....................513 844-1608
Tammy Gebhart, *President*
Steven Gephart, *Treasurer*
EMP: 50 EST: 1997
SALES: 2MM **Privately Held**
WEB: www.physicianschoiceinc.com
SIC: 8082 Home health care services

(G-12589)
THE COLUMBIA OIL CO
4951 Hmlton Middletown Rd (45011-2370)
PHONE.....................513 868-8700
James W Megginson II, *President*
EMP: 70 EST: 1936
SALES (est): 19.6MM **Privately Held**
WEB: www.lykinscompanies.com
SIC: 5172 5983 Gasoline; fuel oil dealers

Lima
Allen County

(G-12590)
3 B VENTURES LLC
Also Called: 4 Seasons Car Wash
980 N Eastown Rd (45807-2273)
PHONE.....................419 236-9461
Kyle Benrogh, *Mng Member*
EMP: 25
SALES: 800K **Privately Held**
SIC: 7542 Washing & polishing, automotive

(G-12591)
AAA ALLIED GROUP INC
2115 Allentown Rd (45805-1749)
PHONE.....................419 228-1022
Marion Bicker, *Branch Mgr*
EMP: 35
SALES (corp-wide): 142.4MM **Privately Held**
SIC: 4724 Travel agencies

PA: Aaa Allied Group, Inc.
15 W Central Pkwy
Cincinnati OH 45202
513 762-3301

(G-12592)
ADO STAFFING INC
2100 Harding Hwy (45804-3443)
PHONE..........................419 222-8395
John Cavinee, *Branch Mgr*
EMP: 30
SALES (corp-wide): 27.9B **Privately Held**
WEB: www.adeccona.com
SIC: 7363 Temporary help service
HQ: Ado Staffing, Inc.
175 Broadhollow Rd
Melville NY 11747
631 844-7800

(G-12593)
AERCO SANDBLASTING COMPANY
429 N Jackson St (45801-4121)
PHONE..........................419 224-2464
Cynthia Wallace, *President*
Norma Miller, *Corp Secy*
Pearl Miller, *Vice Pres*
EMP: 35
SQ FT: 1,296
SALES: 5.1MM **Privately Held**
SIC: 1799 Sandblasting of building exteriors

(G-12594)
ALLEN CNTY REGIONAL TRNST AUTH
Also Called: R T A
200 E High St Ste 2a (45801-4465)
PHONE..........................419 222-2782
Patricia Stein, *Finance*
Lynn Cary, *Director*
EMP: 25
SQ FT: 200,000
SALES (est): 1.6MM **Privately Held**
WEB: www.acrta.com
SIC: 4111 Bus line operations

(G-12595)
ALLEN COUNTY EDUCTL SVC CTR
1920 Slabtown Rd (45801-3309)
PHONE..........................419 222-1836
Donald Smith, *Superintendent*
Teodosio Joe, *Teacher*
Krohn Mary, *Teacher*
Kim Nellis, *Education*
EMP: 91
SALES (est): 1.4MM **Privately Held**
SIC: 8299 8351 Educational services; preschool center

(G-12596)
ALLEN COUNTY RECYCLERS INC
Also Called: Allen County Refuse
541 S Central Ave (45804-1305)
P.O. Box 1264 (45802-1264)
PHONE..........................419 223-5010
Otis Roger Wright, *President*
EMP: 37
SQ FT: 5,500
SALES: 1.3MM **Privately Held**
SIC: 5093 Ferrous metal scrap & waste; bottles, waste; plastics scrap; waste paper

(G-12597)
ALLEN METRO HSING MGT DEV CORP
Also Called: Mat
600 S Main St (45804-1242)
PHONE..........................419 228-6065
Tiffany Wright, *Principal*
Anna Schnippel, *Exec Dir*
EMP: 27
SALES (est): 981K **Privately Held**
SIC: 6531 Real estate agents & managers

(G-12598)
ALLEN METROPOLITAN HSING AUTH
Also Called: Allen Metro Tenants Councel
600 S Main St (45804-1242)
PHONE..........................419 228-6065

Tiffany Wright, *General Mgr*
Kim Elwer, *Finance Mgr*
Anna Schnippel, *Exec Dir*
EMP: 35
SALES (est): 1.3MM **Privately Held**
WEB: www.allenmha.com
SIC: 6513 Apartment building operators

(G-12599)
ALLIED ENVIRONMENTAL SVCS INC
585 Liberty Commons Pkwy (45804-1829)
PHONE..........................419 227-4004
Kay E Rauch, *President*
Clyde R Rauch, *Vice Pres*
Chad Reynolds, *Sales Mgr*
Gary Gootee, *Manager*
Connie Stimmel, *Admin Asst*
EMP: 45
SQ FT: 5,000
SALES (est): 6.6MM **Privately Held**
WEB: www.allied-environmental.com
SIC: 8748 1799 Environmental consultant; asbestos removal & encapsulation

(G-12600)
AMERICAN ELECTRIC POWER CO INC
369 E Oconnor Ave (45801-2935)
PHONE..........................419 998-5106
Luersman Mike, *Principal*
Keith Kerner, *Supervisor*
EMP: 33
SALES (corp-wide): 16.2B **Publicly Held**
SIC: 4911 Electric services
PA: American Electric Power Company, Inc.
1 Riverside Plz Fl 1 # 1
Columbus OH 43215
614 716-1000

(G-12601)
AMERICAN NURSING CARE INC
658 W Market St Ste 200 (45801-5611)
PHONE..........................419 228-0888
Tracy Schramke, *Manager*
EMP: 100 **Privately Held**
WEB: www.americannursingcare.com
SIC: 8051 8082 Convalescent home with continuous nursing care; home health care services
HQ: American Nursing Care, Inc.
1700 Edison Dr Ste 300
Milford OH 45150
513 576-0262

(G-12602)
ASSISTED LIVING CONCEPTS LLC
Also Called: Amanda House
1070 Gloria Ave Ofc (45805-2967)
PHONE..........................419 224-6327
Janelle Miller, *Manager*
EMP: 35
SALES (corp-wide): 380.7MM **Privately Held**
WEB: www.assistedlivingconcepts.com
SIC: 8051 Skilled nursing care facilities
HQ: Assisted Living Concepts, Llc
330 N Wabash Ave Ste 3700
Chicago IL 60611

(G-12603)
AT&T MOBILITY LLC
2421 Elida Rd (45805-1203)
PHONE..........................419 516-0602
EMP: 26
SALES (corp-wide): 170.7B **Publicly Held**
SIC: 4812 Cellular telephone services
HQ: At&T Mobility Llc
1025 Lenox Park Blvd Ne
Brookhaven GA 30319
800 331-0500

(G-12604)
AUTO-OWNERS LIFE INSURANCE CO
2325 N Cole St (45801-2305)
P.O. Box 4570 (45802-4570)
PHONE..........................419 227-1452
Scott Wilder, *Manager*
Jim Kuhlman, *Manager*
EMP: 75

SALES (corp-wide): 2.4B **Privately Held**
WEB: www.sheratonlansing.com
SIC: 6411 Insurance agents; fire insurance underwriters' laboratories
HQ: Auto-Owners Life Insurance Company
6101 Anacapri Blvd
Lansing MI 48917

(G-12605)
BENJAMIN STEEL COMPANY INC
Also Called: Lima Division
3111 Saint Johns Rd (45804-4024)
PHONE..........................419 229-8045
Jerry Snyder, *Manager*
EMP: 40
SQ FT: 25,000
SALES (corp-wide): 86.5MM **Privately Held**
WEB: www.benjaminsteel.com
SIC: 5051 Steel
PA: Benjamin Steel Company, Inc.
777 Benjamin Dr
Springfield OH 45502
937 322-8600

(G-12606)
BEST ONE TIRE & SVC LIMA INC (PA)
701 E Hanthorn Rd (45804-3823)
PHONE..........................419 229-2380
David Mitchell, *President*
Sheila Mitchell, *Vice Pres*
▲ **EMP:** 45 **EST:** 1933
SQ FT: 100,000
SALES (est): 13.1MM **Privately Held**
WEB: www.eastertire.com
SIC: 7534 5531 5014 Tire recapping; automotive tires; truck tires & tubes

(G-12607)
BETTER BRAKE PARTS INC
915 Shawnee Rd (45805-3439)
PHONE..........................419 227-0685
Rosemarie Mikesell, *CEO*
Edwin F Mikesell, *CEO*
Damien Mikesell, *President*
Ronald Kimmel, *Vice Pres*
Mark Misell, *Vice Pres*
◆ **EMP:** 40 **EST:** 1981
SALES (est): 13.5MM **Privately Held**
WEB: www.betterbrake.com
SIC: 5013 Truck parts & accessories; automotive brakes

(G-12608)
BIOLIFE PLASMA SERVICES LP
4299 Elida Rd (45807-1551)
PHONE..........................419 224-0117
Deb Lauth, *Branch Mgr*
Jennifer Minnick, *Manager*
EMP: 33
SALES (corp-wide): 15.1B **Privately Held**
WEB: www.biolifeplasma.com
SIC: 8099 Blood bank
HQ: Biolife Plasma Services L.P.
1200 Lakeside Dr
Bannockburn IL

(G-12609)
BROOKSIDE HOLDINGS LLC
Also Called: Brookside Trucking
3211 S Dixie Hwy (45804-3759)
PHONE..........................419 224-7019
Tim Knotts, *Manager*
EMP: 30
SALES (corp-wide): 3.8MM **Privately Held**
SIC: 4212 Light haulage & cartage, local
PA: Brookside Holdings, Llc
8022 State Route 119
Maria Stein OH 45860
419 925-4457

(G-12610)
BUCKEYE CHARTER SERVICE INC (PA)
1235 E Hanthorn Rd (45804-3996)
P.O. Box 627 (45802-0627)
PHONE..........................419 222-2455
William Harnishfeger, *President*
Frank Harnishfeger, *Corp Secy*
EMP: 70

SALES (est): 4.1MM **Privately Held**
WEB: www.buckeyecharterservice.com
SIC: 4142 Bus charter service, except local

(G-12611)
CANCER NTWK OF W CENT
Also Called: CANCER NETWORK OF WEST CENTRAL
2615 Fort Amanda Rd (45804-3704)
PHONE..........................419 226-9085
Sheryl Darnell, *Director*
EMP: 30
SALES: 1.9MM **Privately Held**
WEB: www.cancernetwork.com
SIC: 8093 Rehabilitation center, outpatient treatment

(G-12612)
CITIZENS NAT BNK OF BLUFFTON
201 N Main St (45801-4432)
P.O. Box 990 (45802-0990)
PHONE..........................419 224-0400
Linda Houchin, *Manager*
EMP: 30 **Privately Held**
WEB: www.cnbohio.com
SIC: 6021 National commercial banks
HQ: The Citizens National Bank Of Bluffton
102 S Main St
Bluffton OH 45817
419 358-8040

(G-12613)
CITY OF LIMA
Streets & Traffic
900 S Collett St (45804-1005)
PHONE..........................419 221-5165
Saul Allen, *Director*
EMP: 50 **Privately Held**
WEB: www.cityhall.lima.oh.us
SIC: 9621 1611 ; highway & street paving contractor
PA: City Of Lima
50 Town Sq
Lima OH 45801
419 228-5462

(G-12614)
CITY OF LIMA
Sanitary Engineer
50 Town Sq Fl 3 (45801-4948)
P.O. Box 1198 (45802-1198)
PHONE..........................419 221-5294
David Burger, *Mayor*
EMP: 400 **Privately Held**
WEB: www.cityhall.lima.oh.us
SIC: 4959 Sanitary services
PA: City Of Lima
50 Town Sq
Lima OH 45801
419 228-5462

(G-12615)
CITY OF LIMA
Also Called: Utility Field Services
1405 Reservoir Rd (45804-2937)
PHONE..........................419 221-5175
Larry Huber, *Manager*
EMP: 30
SQ FT: 624 **Privately Held**
WEB: www.cityhall.lima.oh.us
SIC: 4952 Sewerage systems
PA: City Of Lima
50 Town Sq
Lima OH 45801
419 228-5462

(G-12616)
COLUMBIA PROPERTIES LIMA LLC
Also Called: Holiday Inn
1920 Roschman Ave (45804-3444)
PHONE..........................419 222-0004
Sharron Snider, *Sales Executive*
EMP: 80
SALES (est): 1.2MM **Privately Held**
SIC: 7011 Hotels & motels

(G-12617)
COMFORT KEEPERS
Also Called: Kin Care
1726 Allentown Rd (45805-1856)
PHONE..........................419 229-1031
Peggy J Kincaid, *President*
Walter Kincaid Jr, *Vice Pres*
EMP: 46

SALES (est): 1.4MM **Privately Held**
SIC: 8082 Visiting nurse service

(G-12618)
CONTINUED CARE INC
920 W Market St Ste 202 (45805-2774)
PHONE..................................419 222-2273
Francis Oruma, *President*
Rose Cookey-Aruma, *Vice Pres*
EMP: 25
SQ FT: 1,000
SALES (est): 1.4MM **Privately Held**
SIC: 8082 Home health care services

(G-12619)
CORA HEALTH SERVICES INC (PA)
Also Called: Cora Physical Therapy
1110 Shawnee St (45805-3529)
P.O. Box 150 (45802-0150)
PHONE..................................419 221-3004
Dennis R Smith, *President*
Justin A Borra, *COO*
Brad C Roush, *Exec VP*
Javier Othon, *Vice Pres*
Stephen R Krzyminski, *CFO*
▲ **EMP:** 40
SQ FT: 9,000
SALES (est): 35.8MM **Privately Held**
SIC: 8049 Physical therapist

(G-12620)
CORPORATE SUPPORT INC (PA)
750 Buckeye Rd (45804-1935)
PHONE..................................419 221-3838
Harold Breidenbach, *CEO*
Troy Breidenbach, *President*
Marc Finn, *Vice Pres*
William Schroeder, *Vice Pres*
John Whittaker, *Shareholder*
EMP: 50
SQ FT: 300,000
SALES (est): 9MM **Privately Held**
SIC: 7389 Packaging & labeling services

(G-12621)
COUNTY OF ALLEN
Also Called: Allen Metro Housinig Auth
600 S Main St (45804-1242)
PHONE..................................419 228-6065
Cindy Ring, *Director*
EMP: 25 **Privately Held**
WEB: www.allencountyohio.com
SIC: 6531 Housing authority operator
PA: County Of Allen
301 N Main St
Lima OH 45801
419 228-3700

(G-12622)
COUNTY OF ALLEN
Also Called: Allen County Health Care Ctr
3125 Ada Rd (45801-3328)
PHONE..................................419 221-1103
Jerome O'Neal, *Administration*
Jerome Neal, *Administration*
EMP: 110 **Privately Held**
WEB: www.allencountyohio.com
SIC: 8361 8051 Home for the aged; skilled
nursing care facilities
PA: County Of Allen
301 N Main St
Lima OH 45801
419 228-3700

(G-12623)
COUNTY OF ALLEN
Also Called: Information & Referral Center
1501 S Dixie Hwy (45804-1844)
P.O. Box 4506 (45802-4506)
PHONE..................................419 228-2120
Lynn Shock, *Director*
EMP: 150 **Privately Held**
WEB: www.allencountyohio.com
SIC: 8322 Social service center
PA: County Of Allen
301 N Main St
Lima OH 45801
419 228-3700

(G-12624)
COUNTY OF ALLEN
Also Called: Allen County Childrens Svcs Bd
123 W Spring St (45801-4833)
PHONE..................................419 227-8590

Mike Mullins, *Director*
EMP: 40 **Privately Held**
WEB: www.allencountyohio.com
SIC: 8322 Child related social services
PA: County Of Allen
301 N Main St
Lima OH 45801
419 228-3700

(G-12625)
COUNTY OF ALLEN
Also Called: Marimor Industries
2450 Ada Rd (45801-3342)
PHONE..................................419 221-1226
Angie Herzog, *Manager*
EMP: 50 **Privately Held**
WEB: www.allencountyohio.com
SIC: 8093 Mental health clinic, outpatient
PA: County Of Allen
301 N Main St
Lima OH 45801
419 228-3700

(G-12626)
COUNTY OF ALLEN
Also Called: Bureau of Support
608 W High St (45801-4706)
P.O. Box 1589 (45802-1589)
PHONE..................................419 996-7050
Daniel Cade, *Director*
EMP: 37
SQ FT: 3,424 **Privately Held**
WEB: www.allencountyohio.com
SIC: 8322 Child related social services
PA: County Of Allen
301 N Main St
Lima OH 45801
419 228-3700

(G-12627)
CSS PUBLISHING CO INC
5450 N Dixie Hwy (45807-9559)
PHONE..................................419 227-1818
Wesley T Runk, *President*
Patti Furr, *Vice Pres*
Elen Shockey, *Treasurer*
David Runk, *VP Sales*
EMP: 30
SQ FT: 50,000
SALES (est): 2.6MM **Privately Held**
WEB: www.csspub.com
SIC: 2731 5192 Books: publishing only;
books

(G-12628)
CSX CORPORATION
401 E Robb Ave (45801-2952)
PHONE..................................419 225-4121
Eric Osborn, *Principal*
EMP: 149
SALES (corp-wide): 12.2B **Publicly Held**
WEB: www.csx.com
SIC: 4011 Railroads, line-haul operating
PA: Csx Corporation
500 Water St Fl 15
Jacksonville FL 32202
904 359-3200

(G-12629)
CUSTOM STAFFING INC (PA)
505 W Market St (45801-4717)
P.O. Box 5275 (45802-5275)
PHONE..................................419 221-3097
Mike Simmons, *General Mgr*
EMP: 39
SALES (est): 6.5MM **Privately Held**
WEB: www.customstaffing-online.com
SIC: 7363 7361 Temporary help service;
employment agencies

(G-12630)
EAST OF CHICAGO PIZZA INC (PA)
121 W High St Fl 12 (45801-4349)
PHONE..................................419 225-7116
Anthony Collins, *President*
EMP: 28
SALES (est): 17.1MM **Privately Held**
SIC: 6794 5812 Franchises, selling or li-
censing; pizzeria, chain

(G-12631)
EDGEWOOD SKATE ARENA
2170 Edgewood Dr (45805-1147)
PHONE..................................419 331-0647
Betty Ray, *President*

Jerid Ray, *President*
EMP: 25
SQ FT: 24,000
SALES: 232.8K **Privately Held**
SIC: 7999 Roller skating rink operation

(G-12632)
ELDERLY DAY CARE CENTER
225 E High St (45801-4419)
PHONE..................................419 228-2688
Diane Bishope, *Exec Dir*
EMP: 25
SALES (est): 547.9K **Privately Held**
SIC: 8351 Child day care services

(G-12633)
ERIC W WARNOCK
Also Called: Whole Health Dentistry
230 N Eastown Rd (45807-2211)
PHONE..................................419 228-2233
Eric W Warnock, *Owner*
EMP: 30
SALES (est): 1.1MM **Privately Held**
WEB: www.wholehealthdentistry.com
SIC: 8021 Dentists' office

(G-12634)
EXEL INC
635 N Cool Rd (45801-9707)
PHONE..................................419 996-7703
EMP: 55
SALES (corp-wide): 70.4B **Privately Held**
SIC: 4225 General warehousing
HQ: Exel Inc.
570 Polaris Pkwy
Westerville OH 43082
614 865-8500

(G-12635)
EXEL INC
3875 Reservoir Rd (45801-3310)
PHONE..................................419 226-5500
Daniel King, *Manager*
EMP: 100
SALES (corp-wide): 70.4B **Privately Held**
WEB: www.exel-logistics.com
SIC: 4225 General warehousing
HQ: Exel Inc.
570 Polaris Pkwy
Westerville OH 43082
614 865-8500

(G-12636)
FAMILY BIRTH CENTER LIMA MEM
1001 Bellefontaine Ave (45804-2800)
PHONE..................................419 998-4570
Kathy Davis, *Director*
EMP: 35 **EST:** 1998
SALES (est): 410.9K **Privately Held**
SIC: 8099 Childbirth preparation clinic

(G-12637)
FAMILY RSOURCE CTR NW OHIO INC (PA)
Also Called: NORTHWEST FAMILY SERV-
ICES DDA
530 S Main St (45804-1240)
PHONE..................................419 222-1168
John Bindas, *President*
Mark Howe, *CFO*
Stephanie Carson, *Human Res Mgr*
Alicia Cook, *Case Mgr*
Laura Brickner, *Manager*
EMP: 50
SQ FT: 23,000
SALES: 4.2MM **Privately Held**
WEB: www.frcohio.com
SIC: 8093 Mental health clinic, outpatient;
drug clinic, outpatient; alcohol clinic, out-
patient

(G-12638)
FARMERS EQUIPMENT INC
6008 Elida Rd (45807-9453)
PHONE..................................419 339-7000
Todd Channel, *General Mgr*
EMP: 42
SALES (est): 1.1MM
SALES (corp-wide): 12MM **Privately Held**
SIC: 5083 Farm implements
PA: Farmers Equipment, Inc.
1749 E Us Highway 36 A
Urbana OH 43078
419 339-7000

(G-12639)
FAT JACKS PIZZA II INC (PA)
1806 N West St (45801-2631)
PHONE..................................419 227-1813
David Boyles, *President*
EMP: 25
SQ FT: 6,000
SALES: 2.1MM **Privately Held**
WEB: www.fatjackspizza.com
SIC: 5812 5813 7999 Pizzeria, independ-
ent; drinking places; lottery tickets, sale of

(G-12640)
FEDERAL EXPRESS CORPORATION
Also Called: Fedex
3499 Saint Johns Rd (45804-4018)
PHONE..................................800 463-3339
EMP: 27
SALES (corp-wide): 65.4B **Publicly Held**
WEB: www.federalexpress.com
SIC: 4513 Letter delivery, private air; pack-
age delivery, private air; parcel
delivery, private air
HQ: Federal Express Corporation
3610 Hacks Cross Rd
Memphis TN 38125
901 369-3600

(G-12641)
FEDEX FREIGHT CORPORATION
2335 Saint Johns Rd (45804-3862)
PHONE..................................800 521-3505
EMP: 39
SALES (corp-wide): 65.4B **Publicly Held**
SIC: 4213 4731 4215 Less-than-truckload
(LTL) transport; freight transportation
arrangement; courier services, except by
air
HQ: Fedex Freight Corporation
1715 Aaron Brenner Dr
Memphis TN 38120

(G-12642)
GENERAL AUDIT CORP
Also Called: Keybridge Medical Revenue
MGT
2348 Baton Rouge Ste A (45805-1167)
P.O. Box 1568 (45802-1568)
PHONE..................................419 993-2900
Scott G Koenig, *President*
Ned E Koenig, *Chairman*
N Jean Koenig, *Corp Secy*
Brandon Lee, *Vice Pres*
Brian Garver, *VP Sales*
EMP: 40
SQ FT: 6,300
SALES (est): 5.3MM **Privately Held**
SIC: 7322 8111 Collection agency, except
real estate; legal services

(G-12643)
GIRL SCUTS APPLESEED RIDGE INC
1870 W Robb Ave (45805-1535)
PHONE..................................419 225-4085
Jane Krites, *CEO*
EMP: 30
SQ FT: 1,404
SALES (est): 1.5MM **Privately Held**
SIC: 8641 8322 Girl Scout organization;
individual & family services

(G-12644)
GOLDEN LIVING LLC
Also Called: Beverly
599 S Shawnee St (45804-1461)
PHONE..................................419 227-2154
Peggy Stewart, *Manager*
EMP: 100
SALES (corp-wide): 7.4MM **Privately
Held**
SIC: 8059 8052 8051 Convalescent
home; intermediate care facilities; conva-
lescent home with continuous nursing
care
PA: Golden Living Llc
5220 Tennyson Pkwy # 400
Plano TX 75024
972 372-6300

GEOGRAPHIC

(G-12645)
GOODWILL INDUSTRIES OF LIMA (PA)
940 N Cable Rd Ste 1 (45805-1739)
PHONE....................................(419) 228-4821
Eugene Montycka, *President*
Amy Lutell, *President*
EMP: 86
SQ FT: 22,000
SALES (est): 2.6MM **Privately Held**
WEB: www.limagoodwill.org
SIC: 8331 Vocational rehabilitation agency

(G-12646)
GORDON FOOD SERVICE INC
Also Called: G F S Marketplace
3447 Elida Rd (45807-1627)
PHONE....................................(419) 225-8983
Dennis Clay, *Manager*
EMP: 25
SALES (corp-wide): 13B **Privately Held**
WEB: www.gfs.com
SIC: 5149 5142 Groceries & related products; packaged frozen goods
PA: Gordon Food Service, Inc.
1300 Gezon Pkwy Sw
Wyoming MI 49509
888 437-3663

(G-12647)
GRAND AERIE OF THE FRATERNAL
Also Called: Foe 370
800 W Robb Ave (45801-2760)
P.O. Box 1108 (45802-1108)
PHONE....................................(419) 227-1566
Ron Morris, *Branch Mgr*
EMP: 41
SALES (corp-wide): 11MM **Privately Held**
WEB: www.fraternalorderofeagles.tribe.net
SIC: 8641 Fraternal associations
PA: Grand Aerie Of The Fraternal Order Of Eagles
1623 Gateway Cir
Grove City OH 43123
614 883-2200

(G-12648)
GREENFIELD HTS OPER GROUP LLC
1318 Chestnut St (45804-2542)
PHONE....................................(312) 877-1153
Josiah Mathews,
EMP: 50 EST: 2017
SALES (est): 2.3MM **Privately Held**
SIC: 5122 Pharmaceuticals

(G-12649)
GUARDIAN ELDE
Also Called: Lost Creek Health C
804 S Mumaugh Rd (45804-3569)
PHONE....................................(419) 225-9040
Georgia Brumbrugh,
EMP: 95 EST: 2012
SALES (est): 2.4MM **Privately Held**
SIC: 8052 Intermediate care facilities

(G-12650)
GUARDSMARK LLC
209 N Main St Ste 4a (45801-4494)
PHONE....................................(419) 229-9300
Mark Morrissey, *Manager*
EMP: 45
SALES (corp-wide): 741.7MM **Privately Held**
WEB: www.guardsmark.com
SIC: 7381 Security guard service
HQ: Guardsmark, Llc
1551 N Tustin Ave Ste 650
Santa Ana CA 92705
714 619-9700

(G-12651)
HARTER VENTURES INC
Also Called: Lima-Allen County Paramedics
3623 S Buckskin Trl (45807-2168)
PHONE....................................(419) 224-4075
Brad Harter, *President*
EMP: 53
SQ FT: 8,000
SALES (est): 2.8MM **Privately Held**
SIC: 8099 4119 Medical rescue squad; ambulance service

(G-12652)
HCF MANAGEMENT INC (PA)
Also Called: Health Care Facilities
1100 Shawnee Rd (45805-3583)
PHONE....................................(419) 999-2010
Robert Wilson, *CEO*
Jim Unverferth, *President*
Steve Wilder, *Exec VP*
Robert Noft, *Vice Pres*
Fred J Rinehart, *Vice Pres*
EMP: 60
SQ FT: 15,000
SALES (est): 154.8MM **Privately Held**
WEB: www.hcfinc.com
SIC: 8051 6513 Convalescent home with continuous nursing care; apartment building operators

(G-12653)
HCF MANAGEMENT INC
Also Called: Shawnee Manor Nursing Home
2535 Fort Amanda Rd (45804-3728)
PHONE....................................(419) 999-2055
Amy Abbott, *Manager*
Kevin Kidd, *Director*
EMP: 175
SALES (corp-wide): 154.8MM **Privately Held**
WEB: www.hcfinc.com
SIC: 8361 8051 Geriatric residential care; skilled nursing care facilities
PA: Hcf Management, Inc.
1100 Shawnee Rd
Lima OH 45805
419 999-2010

(G-12654)
HCF OF LIMA INC
Also Called: Lima Manor
1100 Shawnee Rd (45805-3583)
PHONE....................................(419) 999-2010
EMP: 79
SALES (corp-wide): 7.4MM **Privately Held**
SIC: 8051 Skilled nursing care facilities
PA: Hcf Of Lima, Inc.
750 Brower Rd
Lima OH 45801
419 227-2611

(G-12655)
HCF OF SHAWNEE INC
Also Called: Shawnee Manor
2535 Fort Amanda Rd (45804-3728)
PHONE....................................(419) 999-2055
Kris Marker, *Managing Dir*
David Walsh, *Vice Pres*
Brenda Bruce, *Marketing Staff*
EMP: 99
SALES: 950K **Privately Held**
SIC: 8051 Convalescent home with continuous nursing care

(G-12656)
HEALTH PARTNERS WESTERN OHIO (PA)
Also Called: Lima Community Health Center
441 E 8th St (45804-2482)
PHONE....................................(419) 221-3072
Janis Sunderhaus, *Partner*
Leanne Kerschner, *Manager*
Brittney Raines, *Personnel Assit*
Amber McPheron, *Nurse*
Brenda Conrad, *Assistant*
EMP: 74
SALES: 23.2MM **Privately Held**
WEB: www.achp.biz
SIC: 8399 Health systems agency

(G-12657)
HEALTHPRO MEDICAL BILLING INC
4132 Elida Rd (45807-1548)
PHONE....................................(419) 223-2717
John Stiles, *President*
Dawn Fitch, *Finance*
Jaime Hale, *Human Res Mgr*
Cheri Brinkman, *Manager*
Nicole Jett, *Asst Mgr*
EMP: 55
SALES (est): 4.2MM **Privately Held**
WEB: www.healthpromedical.com
SIC: 8721 Billing & bookkeeping service

(G-12658)
HECTOR A BUCH JR MD
Also Called: Positions
750 W High St Ste 250 (45801-3959)
PHONE....................................(419) 227-7399
Hector Buch, *Principal*
EMP: 30 EST: 2001
SALES (est): 513.6K **Privately Held**
SIC: 8011 Internal medicine, physician/surgeon

(G-12659)
HERITAGE HEALTH CARE SERVICES
3748 Allentown Rd (45807-2140)
PHONE....................................(419) 222-2404
Pam Frese, *Manager*
EMP: 55
SALES (corp-wide): 9.8MM **Privately Held**
SIC: 8082 Home health care services
PA: Heritage Health Care Services
1745 Indian Wood Cir # 252
Maumee OH 43537
419 867-2002

(G-12660)
HR SERVICES INC
675 W Market St Ste 200 (45801-5619)
P.O. Box 1155 (45802-1155)
PHONE....................................(419) 224-2462
Robert Schulte, *President*
EMP: 25
SQ FT: 8,500
SALES (est): 1.2MM
SALES (corp-wide): 3.3B **Publicly Held**
WEB: www.mystaffingpro.com
SIC: 7363 7361 Employee leasing service; employment agencies
PA: Paychex, Inc.
911 Panorama Trl S
Rochester NY 14625
585 385-6666

(G-12661)
HUME SUPPLY INC
1359 E Hanthorn Rd (45804-3933)
PHONE....................................(419) 991-5751
Daven Stedke, *President*
John E Stedke, *Vice Pres*
Cory McMichael, *Project Mgr*
Janice Stedke, *Treasurer*
EMP: 42 EST: 1948
SQ FT: 15,000
SALES (est): 11.1MM **Privately Held**
WEB: www.humesupply.com
SIC: 1541 Industrial buildings, new construction

(G-12662)
HUNTINGTON NATIONAL BANK
Also Called: Home Mortgage
631 W Market St (45801-4603)
PHONE....................................(419) 226-8200
Rick Kortokrax, *Manager*
EMP: 50
SALES (corp-wide): 5.2B **Publicly Held**
WEB: www.huntingtonnationalbank.com
SIC: 6029 6162 6021 Commercial banks; mortgage bankers; national commercial banks
HQ: The Huntington National Bank
17 S High St Fl 1
Columbus OH 43215
614 480-4293

(G-12663)
I H S SERVICES INC
3225 W Elm St Ste D (45805-2520)
PHONE....................................(419) 224-8811
Janet Seward, *Director*
EMP: 40 **Privately Held**
SIC: 6531 Real estate managers
PA: I H S Services Inc
5888 Cleveland Ave # 201
Columbus OH 43231

(G-12664)
IHEARTCOMMUNICATIONS INC
Also Called: Clear Channel
667 W Market St (45801-4603)
PHONE....................................(419) 223-2060
Kim Field, *General Mgr*
EMP: 65 **Publicly Held**
SIC: 4832 2711 Radio broadcasting stations; newspapers

HQ: Iheartcommunications, Inc.
20880 Stone Oak Pkwy
San Antonio TX 78258
210 822-2828

(G-12665)
INDIANA & OHIO RAIL CORP
1750 N Sugar St (45801-3138)
PHONE....................................(419) 229-1010
Brad Urton, *Manager*
EMP: 25
SALES (corp-wide): 2.3B **Publicly Held**
SIC: 4011 Railroads, line-haul operating
HQ: The Indiana & Ohio Rail Corp
2856 Cypress Way
Cincinnati OH 45212
513 860-1000

(G-12666)
INTERDYNE CORPORATION
931 N Jefferson St (45801-4166)
PHONE....................................(419) 229-8192
Powell Prater, *President*
M D Basinger, *Principal*
Richard E Meredith, *Principal*
Bill Bresson, *Vice Pres*
Dan Lucke, *Vice Pres*
EMP: 35
SQ FT: 55,000
SALES (est): 9.7MM **Privately Held**
WEB: www.interdyne-transvac.com
SIC: 4959 8748 Environmental cleanup services; environmental consultant

(G-12667)
JACOBS CONSTRUCTORS INC
Also Called: Equipment Yard & Maint Div
1840 Buckeye Rd Gatew (45804-1830)
P.O. Box 5365 (45802-5365)
PHONE....................................(419) 226-1344
W Don Turner, *Manager*
EMP: 80
SALES (corp-wide): 14.9B **Publicly Held**
SIC: 1629 8711 Dams, waterways, docks & other marine construction; engineering services
HQ: Jacobs Constructors, Inc.
4949 Essen Ln
Baton Rouge LA 70809
225 769-7700

(G-12668)
K M CLEMENS DDS INC
Also Called: Butts, Charles L II DDS
2115 Allentown Rd Ste C (45805-1749)
PHONE....................................(419) 228-4036
Kenneth M Clemens, *President*
EMP: 25
SALES: 2MM **Privately Held**
SIC: 6799 Investors

(G-12669)
KIDNEY SERVICES W CENTL OHIO
750 W High St Ste 100 (45801-3959)
PHONE....................................(419) 227-0918
Dodi West, *CEO*
EMP: 50
SALES: 6.6MM **Privately Held**
SIC: 8092 Kidney dialysis centers

(G-12670)
KINDRED HOSPITAL CENTRAL OHIO
730 W Market St (45801-4602)
PHONE....................................(419) 526-0777
Vanessa Nelson, *CEO*
Joseph Rayman, *Safety Mgr*
EMP: 37
SALES (est): 4.4MM **Privately Held**
SIC: 8062 General medical & surgical hospitals

(G-12671)
KLEMAN SERVICES LLC
Also Called: ServiceMaster
2150 Baty Rd (45807-1957)
PHONE....................................(419) 339-0871
Michael C Kleman, *Mng Member*
EMP: 30
SQ FT: 7,500
SALES (est): 1MM **Privately Held**
SIC: 7349 Building maintenance services

▲ = Import ▼=Export
◆ =Import/Export

(G-12672)
LA KING TRUCKING INC
1516 Findlay Rd (45801-3110)
PHONE.....................................419 225-9039
Russell J King, *President*
Derrol R King, *Shareholder*
Kenneth E Lawrence, *Shareholder*
EMP: 40
SQ FT: 4,800
SALES (est): 4.3MM **Privately Held**
SIC: 4213 Contract haulers

(G-12673)
LACP ST RITAS MEDICAL CTR LLC
708 W Spring St (45801-4661)
PHONE.....................................419 324-4075
David Pohlman, *Coordinator*
EMP: 60
SALES (est): 829.2K **Privately Held**
SIC: 4119 Ambulance service

(G-12674)
LANES TRANSFER INC
Also Called: Lane's Moving & Storage
245 E Murphy St (45801-4172)
PHONE.....................................419 222-8692
Richard Lane, *President*
Brad A King, *Principal*
Janet Lane, *Vice Pres*
Tod Lane, *Manager*
EMP: 25
SQ FT: 20,000
SALES (est): 2.3MM **Privately Held**
SIC: 4214 Local trucking with storage

(G-12675)
LIMA AUTO MALL INC
Also Called: Lima Cdllac Pntiac Olds Nissan
2200 N Cable Rd (45807-1792)
P.O. Box 1649 (45802-1649)
PHONE.....................................419 993-6000
William C Timmermeister, *President*
Susan B Timmermeister, *Corp Secy*
Rodger L Mc Clain, *Vice Pres*
Ryan Swaney, *Sales Mgr*
Pamela Metcalf, *Manager*
EMP: 100 EST: 1921
SQ FT: 21,000
SALES (est): 39.8MM **Privately Held**
WEB: www.limaautomall.com
SIC: 5511 7538 7532 7515 Automobiles, new & used; general automotive repair shops; top & body repair & paint shops; passenger car leasing

(G-12676)
LIMA CITY SCHOOL DISTRICT
Also Called: Lima City School Central Svcs
600 E Wayne St (45801-4182)
PHONE.....................................419 996-3450
Tim Haller, *Principal*
EMP: 28
SALES (corp-wide): 52.7MM **Privately Held**
SIC: 8211 4151 7538 Public elementary school; school buses; general automotive repair shops
PA: Lima City School District
755 Saint Johns Ave
Lima OH 45804
419 996-3400

(G-12677)
LIMA CNVLSCENT HM FNDATION INC (PA)
1650 Allentown Rd (45805-1802)
PHONE.....................................419 227-5450
Sara Music, *Office Mgr*
Randy Cox, *Exec Dir*
EMP: 140
SQ FT: 41,886
SALES (est): 6.7MM **Privately Held**
WEB: www.limalochhaven.com
SIC: 8059 8051 Convalescent home; personal care home, with health care; skilled nursing care facilities

(G-12678)
LIMA COMMUNICATIONS CORP
Also Called: Wlio Television-Channel 35
1424 Rice Ave (45805-1949)
PHONE.....................................419 228-8835
Kevin Creamer, *President*
David E Plaugher, *Treasurer*
EMP: 75
SQ FT: 5,000
SALES (est): 11.1MM
SALES (corp-wide): 921.6MM **Privately Held**
WEB: www.wlio.com
SIC: 4833 Television broadcasting stations
PA: Block Communications, Inc.
405 Madison Ave Ste 2100
Toledo OH 43604
419 724-6212

(G-12679)
LIMA DENTAL ASSOC RISOLVATO LT
2115 Allentown Rd Ste C (45805-1749)
PHONE.....................................419 228-4036
Erik J Risolvato, *Principal*
Brenda Kimmett, *Dental Hygenist*
Carol Mohr, *Dental Hygenist*
EMP: 25
SALES (est): 2.1MM **Privately Held**
SIC: 8021 Offices & clinics of dentists

(G-12680)
LIMA FAMILY YMCA (PA)
345 S Elizabeth St (45801-4805)
PHONE.....................................419 223-6045
Clyde Raush, *Ch of Bd*
William Blewit, *President*
Terri Averesch, *Senior VP*
Chriss Martin, *Controller*
Michelle Marshall, *Human Resources*
EMP: 39 EST: 1888
SQ FT: 111,000
SALES (est): 3.8MM **Privately Held**
WEB: www.limaymca.net
SIC: 8641 8351 8322 7991 Civic associations; child day care services; individual & family services; physical fitness facilities

(G-12681)
LIMA MALL INC
2400 Elida Rd Ste 166 (45805-1233)
PHONE.....................................419 331-6255
Edward J Debartolo Sr, *Ch of Bd*
Simon Debartolo, *President*
Edward J Debartolo Jr, *President*
EMP: 30
SQ FT: 750,000
SALES (est): 1.8MM
SALES (corp-wide): 19.2MM **Privately Held**
WEB: www.shoprivercenter.com
SIC: 6512 Shopping center, property operation only
PA: Nid Corporation
15436 N Florida Ave # 200
Tampa FL 33613
813 908-8400

(G-12682)
LIMA MEDICAL SUPPLIES INC
770 W North St (45801-3923)
PHONE.....................................419 226-9581
Ron Drees, *Director*
EMP: 39 EST: 1964
SQ FT: 13,000
SALES (est): 330.1K
SALES (corp-wide): 4.7B **Privately Held**
SIC: 5047 Medical equipment & supplies
HQ: Mcauley Management Services, Inc.
730 W Market St
Lima OH 45801
419 226-9684

(G-12683)
LIMA MEMORIAL HOSPITAL (HQ)
Also Called: Lima Memorial Health System
1001 Bellefontaine Ave (45804-2899)
P.O. Box 932842, Cleveland (44193-0023)
PHONE.....................................419 228-3335
Michael Swick, *President*
Bob Armstrong, *Vice Pres*
Jeffrey Utz, *Finance*
Jeff Bogart, *IT/INT Sup*
Trevor Mumaugh, *IT/INT Sup*
EMP: 70
SALES: 180.1MM
SALES (corp-wide): 189.6MM **Privately Held**
SIC: 8062 General medical & surgical hospitals

(G-12684)
LIMA MEMORIAL JOINT OPER CO (PA)
1001 Belelfontaine Ave (45804)
P.O. Box 932842, Cleveland (44193-0023)
PHONE.....................................419 228-5165
Michael Swick, *President*
Eric Pohjala, *CFO*
EMP: 1500
SALES (est): 189.6MM **Privately Held**
SIC: 8062 General medical & surgical hospitals

(G-12685)
LIMA PATHOLOGY ASSOCIATES LABS (PA)
Also Called: Findlay Laboratory Services
415 W Market St Ste B (45801-4786)
PHONE.....................................419 226-9595
Joseph Sreenan, *President*
Anne M Gideon, *Treasurer*
EMP: 26
SQ FT: 3,200
SALES: 6MM **Privately Held**
WEB: www.limapathlabs.com
SIC: 8071 Pathological laboratory

(G-12686)
LIMA RADIO HOSPITAL INC (PA)
608 N Main St (45801-4010)
PHONE.....................................419 229-6010
Anthony W Depalma, *President*
EMP: 25
SQ FT: 2,000
SALES (est): 5.7MM **Privately Held**
WEB: www.jjbeads.com
SIC: 4812 Radio telephone communication

(G-12687)
LIMA SHEET METAL MACHINE & MFG
1001 Bowman Rd (45804-3409)
PHONE.....................................419 229-1161
Michael R Emerick, *President*
Ann Emerick, *Corp Secy*
Thomas Emerick, *Exec VP*
EMP: 31 EST: 1974
SQ FT: 26,250
SALES (est): 6.6MM **Privately Held**
WEB: www.limasheetmetal.com
SIC: 3589 3599 7349 7692 Commercial cooking & foodwarming equipment; machine shop, jobbing & repair; building maintenance, except repairs; welding repair; food products machinery; sheet metalwork

(G-12688)
LIMA SUPERIOR FEDERAL CR UN (PA)
4230 Elida Rd (45807-1550)
P.O. Box 1110 (45802-1110)
PHONE.....................................419 223-9746
Fax: 419 224-2803
EMP: 105
SQ FT: 5,200
SALES: 21.5MM **Privately Held**
SIC: 6061 Federal Credit Union

(G-12689)
LIPPINCOTT PLUMBING-HEATING AC
872 Saint Johns Ave (45804-1567)
PHONE.....................................419 222-0856
Michael Ray Lawrence, *President*
Rebecca Sue Lawrence, *Corp Secy*
Richard Michael Lyons, *Vice Pres*
EMP: 25
SQ FT: 2,000
SALES (est): 5MM **Privately Held**
SIC: 1731 1711 Electrical work; plumbing contractors

(G-12690)
LITTLE SQUIRT SPORTS PARK
1996 W Robb Ave (45805-1537)
P.O. Box 367587, Bonita Springs FL (34136-7587)
PHONE.....................................419 227-6200

Victoria Strickland, *President*
Norman Greber, *Owner*
EMP: 50 EST: 1994
SALES (est): 1.1MM **Privately Held**
SIC: 7996 Kiddie park

(G-12691)
LOST CREEK COUNTRY CLUB INC
2409 Lost Creek Blvd (45804-3221)
PHONE.....................................419 229-2026
Matt Holtsberry, *President*
EMP: 34
SQ FT: 10,000
SALES (est): 773.5K **Privately Held**
SIC: 7997 Golf club, membership; swimming club, membership

(G-12692)
LOST CREEK HEALTH CARE
Also Called: BRADYVIEW MANOR
804 S Mumaugh Rd (45804-3569)
PHONE.....................................419 225-9040
Jennifer Shugar, *President*
EMP: 465
SALES: 5.2MM **Privately Held**
SIC: 8051 Skilled nursing care facilities
PA: Guardian Elder Care, Llc
8796 Route 219
Brockway PA 15824

(G-12693)
LOWES HOME CENTERS LLC
2411 N Eastown Rd (45807-1618)
PHONE.....................................419 331-3598
Jason Carhorn, *Manager*
Anthony Adams, *Manager*
EMP: 150
SALES (corp-wide): 68.6B **Publicly Held**
SIC: 5211 5031 5722 5064 Home centers; building materials, exterior; building materials, interior; household appliance stores; electrical appliances, television & radio
HQ: Lowe's Home Centers, Llc
1605 Curtis Bridge Rd
Wilkesboro NC 28697
336 658-4000

(G-12694)
LUCKEY TRANSFER LLC
401 E Robb Ave (45801-2952)
PHONE.....................................800 435-4371
EMP: 91
SALES (corp-wide): 10.2MM **Privately Held**
SIC: 4213 Contract haulers
PA: Luckey Transfer, Llc
29988 N 00 East Rd
Streator IL 61364
815 672-2931

(G-12695)
LUKE IMMEDIATE CARE CENTER
Also Called: Luke Medical Center
825 W Market St Ste 205 (45805-2745)
PHONE.....................................419 227-2245
Jay W Martin, *President*
Silvia Kennis, *Treasurer*
EMP: 30
SQ FT: 4,100
SALES (est): 1.7MM **Privately Held**
SIC: 8011 Primary care medical clinic

(G-12696)
LUTHERAN SOCIAL
Also Called: Social Services of Allen, Augl
205 W Market St Ste 500 (45801-4868)
PHONE.....................................419 229-2222
Dr Mychail Scheramic, *Vice Pres*
EMP: 30
SALES (corp-wide): 2.1MM **Privately Held**
SIC: 8093 Mental health clinic, outpatient
PA: Lutheran Social Services
2149 Collingwood Blvd
Toledo OH 43620
419 243-9178

(G-12697)
M&W CONSTRUCTION ENTPS LLC
1201 Crestwood Dr (45805-1669)
PHONE.....................................419 227-2000

Steven W Roebuck, *President*
Brad Beining, *General Mgr*
EMP: 26
SALES (est): 4.7MM **Privately Held**
SIC: 1541 1542 1761 Industrial buildings & warehouses; nonresidential construction; roofing contractor

(G-12698)
MARIMOR INDUSTRIES INC
2450 Ada Rd (45801-3342)
PHONE..................................419 221-1226
Angela Herzog, *Exec Dir*
EMP: 200
SQ FT: 31,000
SALES: 3.9MM **Privately Held**
WEB: www.acbmrdd.org
SIC: 8331 Vocational rehabilitation agency

(G-12699)
MATHEWS JOSIAH
602 E 5th St (45804-2524)
PHONE..................................567 204-8818
EMP: 25
SALES (est): 430K **Privately Held**
SIC: 7349 Janitorial Service

(G-12700)
MAVERICK MEDIA (PA)
Also Called: Wege
57 Town Sq (45801-4950)
PHONE..................................419 331-1600
Gary Rozynek, *President*
EMP: 25
SALES (est): 2.7MM **Privately Held**
WEB: www.maverick-media.ws
SIC: 4832 7313 Radio broadcasting stations; radio, television, publisher representatives

(G-12701)
MERCY HEALTH
Also Called: St. Rita's Home Care
959 W North St (45805-2457)
PHONE..................................419 226-9064
EMP: 27
SALES (corp-wide): 4.7B **Privately Held**
SIC: 8069 Specialty hospitals, except psychiatric
PA: Mercy Health
1701 Mercy Health Pl
Cincinnati OH 45237
513 639-2800

(G-12702)
MERCY HEALTH - ST R (HQ)
Also Called: Putnam Cnty Amblatory Care Ctr
730 W Market St (45801-4602)
PHONE..................................419 227-3361
Steve Walter, *Ch of Bd*
John Renner, *CFO*
EMP: 1700 **EST:** 1970
SQ FT: 563,000
SALES: 427.6MM
SALES (corp-wide): 4.7B **Privately Held**
SIC: 8062 7352 General medical & surgical hospitals; medical equipment rental
PA: Mercy Health
1701 Mercy Health Pl
Cincinnati OH 45237
513 639-2800

(G-12703)
MID-AMERICAN CLG CONTRS INC (PA)
447 N Elizabeth St (45801-4336)
PHONE..................................419 229-3899
Harold Breidenbach, *CEO*
John Whittacker, *President*
Troy Breidenbach, *Treasurer*
Kermit Nuesmeyer, *Manager*
Robert Swann, *Director*
EMP: 100
SQ FT: 8,000
SALES (est): 19.8MM **Privately Held**
WEB: www.corporatesupportinc.com
SIC: 7349 Janitorial service, contract basis

(G-12704)
MISTRAS GROUP INC
3157 Harding Hwy Bldg (45804-2589)
PHONE..................................419 227-4100
EMP: 36 **Publicly Held**
SIC: 7389 Inspection & testing services

PA: Mistras Group, Inc.
195 Clarksville Rd Ste 2
Princeton Junction NJ 08550

(G-12705)
NELSON PACKAGING COMPANY INC
1801 Reservoir Rd (45804-3152)
PHONE..................................419 229-3471
Sharon Faza, *President*
Stephen L Becker, *Principal*
Issam Faza, *Corp Secy*
Barry Sprague, *QC Mgr*
Mary Maidon, *CFO*
EMP: 65 **EST:** 1980
SQ FT: 70,000
SALES (est): 10.4MM **Privately Held**
WEB: www.nelsonpackagingco.com
SIC: 7389 Packaging & labeling services

(G-12706)
NICHOLAS D STARR INC (PA)
Also Called: Master Maintenance Co
301 W Elm St (45801-4813)
P.O. Box 5092 (45802-5092)
PHONE..................................419 229-3192
Nicholas D Starr, *Owner*
Bob Riepenhoff, *Vice Pres*
Judy A Shrider, *Technology*
Wendy Flynn, *Admin Asst*
EMP: 120
SQ FT: 25,000
SALES (est): 6.1MM **Privately Held**
WEB: www.master-maintenance.com
SIC: 7349 Janitorial service, contract basis

(G-12707)
NORTHLAND LANES INC
721 N Cable Rd (45805-1738)
PHONE..................................419 224-1961
Andy Johnston, *President*
Ray Custer, *General Mgr*
Keith Callahan, *Treasurer*
EMP: 40
SQ FT: 10,000
SALES (est): 836.8K **Privately Held**
WEB: www.northlandlanes.com
SIC: 7933 5813 Ten pin center; tavern (drinking places)

(G-12708)
NORTHWESTERN OHIO SEC SYSTEMS (PA)
121 E High St (45801-4417)
P.O. Box 869 (45802-0869)
PHONE..................................419 227-1655
Trell Yocum, *President*
EMP: 32 **EST:** 1972
SQ FT: 36,000
SALES (est): 8.4MM **Privately Held**
SIC: 5999 1731 7382 Alarm signal systems; safety supplies & equipment; access control systems specialization; fire detection & burglar alarm systems specialization; security systems services; burglar alarm maintenance & monitoring; confinement surveillance systems maintenance & monitoring

(G-12709)
OB-GYN SPECIALISTS LIMA INC
Also Called: Ryan, Charles R MD Facog
830 W High St Ste 101 (45801-3968)
PHONE..................................419 227-0610
James L Kahn, *President*
Rita Myers, *Office Mgr*
William E Scherger, *Obstetrician*
Scott C Stallkamp, *Obstetrician*
Linda McGee, *Nursing Dir*
EMP: 30
SQ FT: 6,900
SALES (est): 1.2MM **Privately Held**
WEB: www.obgynspecialistsoflima.com
SIC: 8011 Gynecologist; obstetrician

(G-12710)
OFFICE CONCEPTS INC
Also Called: Office Concepts of Ohio
1064 W Market St (45805-2730)
PHONE..................................419 221-2679
Fax: 419 482-3265
EMP: 35
SALES (corp-wide): 5.5MM **Privately Held**
SIC: 5044 Whol Office Equipment

PA: Office Concepts, Inc.
5430 Distribution Dr
Fort Wayne IN 46809
260 484-0451

(G-12711)
OLD BARN OUT BACK INC
Also Called: Old Barn Out Back Restaurant
3175 W Elm St (45805-2516)
PHONE..................................419 999-3989
Peter J Williams, *President*
Melvin J Williams, *Vice Pres*
EMP: 60 **EST:** 1979
SQ FT: 20,000
SALES (est): 2.4MM **Privately Held**
SIC: 5812 7299 Restaurant, family: independent; banquet hall facilities

(G-12712)
OMNISOURCE LLC
1610 E 4th St (45804-2712)
PHONE..................................419 227-3411
Jake Yessenow, *Principal*
Todd Dilbone, *Branch Mgr*
EMP: 50
SQ FT: 15,000 **Publicly Held**
WEB: www.omnisource.com
SIC: 5093 Scrap & waste materials
HQ: Omnisource, Llc
7575 W Jefferson Blvd
Fort Wayne IN 46804
260 422-5541

(G-12713)
ORTHODONTIC ASSOCIATES LLC (PA)
Also Called: Fowler, Gary J DDS Ms
260 S Eastown Rd (45807-2200)
PHONE..................................419 229-8771
Thomas Ahman, *President*
EMP: 50
SALES (est): 3.1MM **Privately Held**
SIC: 8021 Orthodontist

(G-12714)
ORTHOPAEDIC INSTITUTE OHIO INC (PA)
801 Medical Dr Ste A (45804-4030)
PHONE..................................419 222-6622
John Duggan, *President*
Steven Calte, *Principal*
Nancy McMichael, *Principal*
Todd W Otto, *Principal*
Selvon St Clair, *Principal*
EMP: 100
SQ FT: 4,335
SALES (est): 11.9MM **Privately Held**
WEB: www.orthoohio.com
SIC: 8011 Orthopedic physician

(G-12715)
OTIS WRIGHT & SONS INC
1601 E 4th St (45804-2711)
PHONE..................................419 227-4400
O Roger Wright, *President*
EMP: 30 **EST:** 1940
SQ FT: 300,000
SALES (est): 2.4MM **Privately Held**
SIC: 4213 4212 Contract haulers; local trucking, without storage

(G-12716)
P-AMERICAS LLC
1750 Greely Chapel Rd (45804-4122)
PHONE..................................419 227-3541
Rob Rosser, *Manager*
EMP: 25
SALES (corp-wide): 64.6B **Publicly Held**
SIC: 5149 2086 Soft drinks; bottled & canned soft drinks
HQ: P-Americas Llc
1 Pepsi Way
Somers NY 10589
336 896-5740

(G-12717)
PAJKA EYE CENTER INC
855 W Market St Ste A (45805-2764)
P.O. Box 1692 (45802-1692)
PHONE..................................419 228-7432
John Pajka, *President*
EMP: 25
SALES (est): 2.4MM **Privately Held**
WEB: www.pajkaeyecenter.com
SIC: 8011 Ophthalmologist

(G-12718)
PAYCHEX INC
My Staffing Pro
675 W Market St (45801-4600)
PHONE..................................800 939-2462
Lara Soltren, *Human Resources*
Mike Mills, *Sales Staff*
Jamie Roof, *Branch Mgr*
Jennifer Brogee, *Manager*
EMP: 60
SALES (corp-wide): 3.3B **Publicly Held**
SIC: 8721 Payroll accounting service
PA: Paychex, Inc.
911 Panorama Trl S
Rochester NY 14625
585 385-6666

(G-12719)
PEDIATRICS OF LIMA INC
830 W High St Ste 102 (45801-3972)
PHONE..................................419 222-4045
Denise Schalk, *Office Mgr*
Cindy Beidelschies, *Manager*
Jaylene Ellerbrock, *Assistant*
EMP: 30
SQ FT: 3,000
SALES (est): 5.6MM **Privately Held**
SIC: 8011 Pediatrician

(G-12720)
PERRY PRO TECH INC (PA)
545 W Market St Lowr Lowr (45801-4792)
PHONE..................................419 228-1360
Barry Clark, *President*
Dave Krites, *General Mgr*
John Rees, *General Mgr*
Dave Utendorf, *Business Mgr*
David Zimerle, *Exec VP*
EMP: 80
SQ FT: 45,000
SALES (est): 59.6MM **Privately Held**
SIC: 5999 5044 7378 Typewriters & business machines; office equipment; computer maintenance & repair

(G-12721)
PGIM INC
Also Called: Prudential
2100 Harding Hwy Ste 4 (45804-3443)
PHONE..................................419 331-6604
J P Delano, *Branch Mgr*
EMP: 50
SALES (corp-wide): 62.9B **Publicly Held**
SIC: 6162 Mortgage bankers & correspondents
HQ: Pgim, Inc.
655 Broad St
Newark NJ 07102
973 802-3654

(G-12722)
PLUS MANAGEMENT SERVICES INC (PA)
2440 Baton Rouge Ofc C (45805-5105)
PHONE..................................419 225-9018
Jerome O'Neal, *President*
EMP: 112
SALES (est): 16MM **Privately Held**
SIC: 8742 8741 Hospital & health services consultant; management services

(G-12723)
POWELL COMPANY LTD (PA)
Also Called: Rightway Food Service
3255 Saint Johns Rd (45804-4022)
PHONE..................................419 228-3552
William Schroeder, *President*
Bev Bailey, *Purch Agent*
Todd Vandemark, *Buyer*
Ronald L Williams, *Purchasing*
Jeff Parsons, *Accountant*
EMP: 79 **EST:** 1995
SQ FT: 30,000
SALES (est): 59.3MM **Privately Held**
WEB: www.powellcompanyltd.com
SIC: 5149 5148 5142 5087 Canned goods: fruit, vegetables, seafood, meats, etc.; fruits, fresh; vegetables, fresh; fruits, frozen; vegetables, frozen; janitors' supplies; office supplies

(G-12724)
**PRIMROSE RTRMENT
CMMNITIES LLC**
3500 W Elm St (45807-2296)
PHONE...................................419 224-1200
Carla Dysert, *Exec Dir*
EMP: 40 **Privately Held**
SIC: 6513 Retirement hotel operation
PA: Primrose Retirement Communities Llc
815 N 2nd St
Aberdeen SD 57401

(G-12725)
QUALITY CARRIERS INC
1586 Findlay Rd (45801-3110)
PHONE...................................419 222-6800
Lenny Morgan, *President*
Mike Pence, *Terminal Mgr*
Lynn Pence, *Manager*
EMP: 25 **Privately Held**
WEB: www.qualitycarriers.com
SIC: 4213 Automobiles, transport & delivery
HQ: Quality Carriers, Inc.
1208 E Kennedy Blvd
Tampa FL 33602
800 282-2031

(G-12726)
**QUALITY ELECTRICAL & MECH
INC**
Also Called: Quality Mechanical Services
1190 E Kibby St (45804-1650)
PHONE...................................419 294-3591
Mark Kuss, *President*
EMP: 35
SQ FT: 2,000
SALES (est): 5.4MM **Privately Held**
SIC: 1711 1761 Warm air heating & air
conditioning contractor; sheet metalwork

(G-12727)
**QUALITY WLDG & FABRICATION
LLC**
4330 East Rd (45807-1535)
PHONE...................................419 225-6208
Ashley M Miller, *Principal*
EMP: 55
SALES (est): 76.2K **Privately Held**
SIC: 7692 Welding repair

(G-12728)
R & K GORBY LLC
Also Called: Howard Johnson Lima
1920 Roschman Ave (45804-3444)
PHONE...................................419 222-0004
Brittany Lee, *Info Tech Mgr*
Ron Gorby,
EMP: 44 EST: 1958
SALES (est): 2.5MM **Privately Held**
WEB: www.bvistmarys.com
SIC: 7011 Hotels

(G-12729)
REPUBLIC SERVICES INC
Also Called: Allied Waste Division
956 S Broadway St (45804-1125)
PHONE...................................567 712-6634
EMP: 34
SALES (corp-wide): 10B **Publicly Held**
SIC: 4953 Refuse systems
PA: Republic Services, Inc.
18500 N Allied Way # 100
Phoenix AZ 85054
480 627-2700

(G-12730)
**RESIDENTIAL MANAGEMENT
SYSTEMS**
1555 Allentown Rd (45805-2205)
PHONE...................................419 222-8806
Rose Childers, *COO*
Jennifer Gast, *Exec Dir*
EMP: 41
SALES (corp-wide): 4.5MM **Privately
Held**
SIC: 8361 Residential care for the handicapped
PA: Residential Management Systems, Inc
402 E Wilson Bridge Rd
Worthington OH 43085
614 880-6014

(G-12731)
**REYNOLDS ELECTRIC
COMPANY INC**
413 Flanders Ave (45801-4117)
PHONE...................................419 228-5448
Michael A Gossard, *President*
Gregory W Schade, *CFO*
EMP: 70 EST: 1936
SQ FT: 17,000
SALES (est): 4.9MM **Privately Held**
WEB: www.reynoldselectric.net
SIC: 1731 General electrical contractor

(G-12732)
RKPL INC
Also Called: National Staffing Alternative
216 N Elizabeth St (45801-4303)
P.O. Box 1155 (45802-1155)
PHONE...................................419 224-2121
Robert M Shulty, *President*
EMP: 100
SALES (est): 2.6MM **Privately Held**
SIC: 7361 7363 Employment agencies;
help supply services

(G-12733)
**ROEDER CARTAGE COMPANY
INC (PA)**
1979 N Dixie Hwy (45801-3253)
PHONE...................................419 221-1600
Calvin E Roeder, *CEO*
Mike Fay, *Maintence Staff*
EMP: 55
SQ FT: 21,000
SALES (est): 6.7MM **Privately Held**
SIC: 4213 Contract haulers

(G-12734)
**ROSCHMANS RESTAURANT
ADM**
Also Called: Hampton Inn
1933 Roschman Ave (45804-3496)
PHONE...................................419 225-8300
Robert Roschman, *President*
EMP: 30
SALES (est): 1.6MM **Privately Held**
SIC: 7011 Hotels & motels

(G-12735)
**RUSH TRUCK CENTERS OHIO
INC**
Also Called: Rush Truck Center, Lima
2655 Saint Johns Rd (45804-4006)
PHONE...................................419 224-6045
Todd Jordan, *Manager*
EMP: 40
SALES (corp-wide): 5.5B **Publicly Held**
SIC: 5012 7538 5531 5014 Automobiles
& other motor vehicles; general automotive repair shops; automotive & home
supply stores; tires & tubes; truck rental &
leasing, no drivers
HQ: Rush Truck Centers Of Ohio, Inc.
11775 Highway Dr
Cincinnati OH 45241
513 733-8500

(G-12736)
SCHAAF DRUGS LLC (PA)
Also Called: Heartlight Pharmacy Services
1331 N Cole St (45801-3415)
PHONE...................................419 879-4327
Eric H Schaaf, *Owner*
Sandy Gray, *Controller*
Angela Rhoades, *Cert Phar Tech*
James Kauchak, *Pharmacist*
Chris McClendon, *Director*
EMP: 40
SQ FT: 9,000
SALES: 4.4MM **Privately Held**
WEB: www.heartlightpharmacy.com
SIC: 5122 Pharmaceuticals

(G-12737)
SEARS ROEBUCK AND CO
2400 Elida Rd Ste 100 (45805-1299)
PHONE...................................419 226-4172
EMP: 93
SALES (corp-wide): 16.7B **Publicly Held**
SIC: 7549 Automotive services
HQ: Sears, Roebuck And Co.
3333 Beverly Rd
Hoffman Estates IL 60179
847 286-2500

(G-12738)
SENIOR CARE INC
2075 N Eastown Rd (45807-2067)
PHONE...................................419 516-4788
Suzanne Hollenbacher, *Principal*
EMP: 113 **Privately Held**
SIC: 8361 Residential care
PA: Senior Care, Inc.
700 N Hurstbourne Pkwy # 200
Louisville KY 40222

(G-12739)
**SEWER RODDING EQUIPMENT
CO**
Also Called: Sreco Flexible
3434 S Dixie Hwy (45804-3756)
PHONE...................................419 991-2065
Larry Drain, *Manager*
EMP: 30
SALES (corp-wide): 17.6MM **Privately
Held**
SIC: 5032 3546 3423 Sewer pipe, clay;
power-driven handtools; hand & edge
tools
PA: Sewer Rodding Equipment Co Inc
3217 Carter Ave
Marina Del Rey CA 90292
310 301-9009

(G-12740)
SHAWNEE COUNTRY CLUB
1700 Shawnee Rd (45805-3899)
PHONE...................................419 227-7177
Elliot Burke, *Manager*
EMP: 75 EST: 1904
SQ FT: 37,000
SALES: 2.2MM **Privately Held**
WEB: www.shawneecountryclub.com
SIC: 7997 5812 Country club, membership; eating places

(G-12741)
SIGN SOURCE USA INC
1700 S Dixie Hwy (45804-1834)
P.O. Box 776 (45802-0776)
PHONE...................................419 224-1130
Jeff Pisel, *President*
Sompahkoun Southibounnorath, *Vice Pres*
Grant Pisel, *Production*
Joe Pisel, *Purch Mgr*
Karen Hoblein, *Admin Sec*
EMP: 55
SALES (est): 25MM **Privately Held**
WEB: www.signsourceusa.com
SIC: 5085 3993 Signmaker equipment &
supplies; signs & advertising specialties

(G-12742)
**SPALLINGER MILLWRIGHT SVC
CO**
Also Called: Spall Autoc Syste / US Millwr
1155 E Hanthorn Rd (45804-3929)
PHONE...................................419 225-5830
Scott Spallinger, *President*
▲ EMP: 85
SQ FT: 80,000
SALES (est): 31.7MM **Privately Held**
WEB: www.spallinger.com
SIC: 3446 1796 Stairs, staircases, stair
treads: prefabricated metal; railings, prefabricated metal; machinery installation

(G-12743)
SPARKLE WASH OF LIMA
301 W Elm St (45801-4813)
P.O. Box 577 (45802-0577)
PHONE...................................419 224-9274
Nick Starr, *President*
Judy Shrider, *Manager*
EMP: 50
SALES (est): 1.1MM **Privately Held**
SIC: 7349 Chemical cleaning services

(G-12744)
SPARTANNASH COMPANY
Also Called: Lima Distribution Center
1100 Prosperity Rd (45801-3130)
P.O. Box 510 (45802-0510)
PHONE...................................419 228-3141
Bruce Brandfon, *Manager*
Scott Warris, *Manager*
Douglas Herr, *IT/INT Sup*
EMP: 350
SQ FT: 367,000

SALES (corp-wide): 8B **Publicly Held**
WEB: www.nashfinch.com
SIC: 5141 Food brokers
PA: Spartannash Company
850 76th St Sw
Byron Center MI 49315
616 878-2000

(G-12745)
SPARTANNASH COMPANY
1257 Neubrecht Rd (45801-3117)
PHONE...................................419 998-2562
Tina Fisher, *Marketing Staff*
Doug Herr, *Manager*
Mike Parish, *Manager*
EMP: 90
SALES (corp-wide): 8B **Publicly Held**
SIC: 5141 Groceries, general line
PA: Spartannash Company
850 76th St Sw
Byron Center MI 49315
616 878-2000

(G-12746)
**SPECIALIZED ALTERNATIVES
FOR F**
Also Called: Safy Behavioral Health of Lima
658 W Market St Ste 101 (45801-5604)
PHONE...................................419 222-1527
EMP: 156
SALES (corp-wide): 19.7MM **Privately
Held**
SIC: 8322 Child related social services;
adoption services; crisis intervention center; offender rehabilitation agency
PA: Specialized Alternatives For Families
And Youth Of Ohio, Inc.
10100 Elida Rd
Delphos OH 45833
419 695-8010

(G-12747)
SPHERION OF LIMA INC (PA)
216 N Elizabeth St (45801-4303)
P.O. Box 1155 (45802-1155)
PHONE...................................419 224-8367
Grace Schulte, *President*
Robert Schulte, *Vice Pres*
Brittany Holland, *Branch Mgr*
EMP: 4500
SQ FT: 4,400
SALES (est): 98.4MM **Privately Held**
WEB: www.spherion-schulte.com
SIC: 7363 Temporary help service

(G-12748)
**SPRINGVIEW MANOR NURSING
HOME**
883 W Spring St (45805-3228)
PHONE...................................419 227-3661
Josh McClellan, *Owner*
Joyce Hauenstein, *Director*
Jayna Fry, *Social Dir*
EMP: 25 EST: 1963
SQ FT: 20,000
SALES: 6.1MM **Privately Held**
SIC: 8051 Extended care facility

(G-12749)
ST RITAS MEDICAL CENTER
Also Called: Saint Rtas Bhavioral Hlth Svcs
730 W Market St (45801-4667)
PHONE...................................419 226-9067
Jim Reber, *President*
EMP: 50
SALES (corp-wide): 4.7B **Privately Held**
SIC: 8093 8063 Mental health clinic, outpatient; psychiatric hospitals
HQ: Mercy Health - St. Rita's Medical Center, Llc
730 W Market St
Lima OH 45801
419 227-3361

(G-12750)
ST RITAS MEDICAL CENTER
Also Called: New Vision Medical Labs
750 W High St Ste 400 (45801-2967)
PHONE...................................419 226-9229
Dr James Conley, *Principal*
EMP: 100
SALES (corp-wide): 4.7B **Privately Held**
SIC: 8071 Medical laboratories

HQ: Mercy Health - St. Rita's Medical Center, Llc
730 W Market St
Lima OH 45801
419 227-3361

(G-12751)
ST RITAS MEDICAL CENTER
Also Called: St Rita's Homecare
959 W North St (45805-2457)
PHONE...................................419 538-7025
Denice Cook, Director
EMP: 120
SALES (corp-wide): 4.7B Privately Held
SIC: 8082 7361 Home health care services; nurses' registry
HQ: Mercy Health - St. Rita's Medical Center, Llc
730 W Market St
Lima OH 45801
419 227-3361

(G-12752)
ST RITAS MEDICAL CENTER
Also Called: Putnam Cnty Amblatory Care Ctr
4357 Ottawa Rd (45801-1110)
PHONE...................................419 227-3361
Donna Konst, Director
EMP: 55
SALES (corp-wide): 4.7B Privately Held
SIC: 8011 Freestanding emergency medical center
HQ: Mercy Health - St. Rita's Medical Center, Llc
730 W Market St
Lima OH 45801
419 227-3361

(G-12753)
ST RITAS MEDICAL CENTER
967 Bellefontaine Ave # 201 (45804-2888)
PHONE...................................419 996-5895
Melvin Monroe, Manager
EMP: 50
SALES (corp-wide): 4.7B Privately Held
SIC: 8011 Medical centers
HQ: Mercy Health - St. Rita's Medical Center, Llc
730 W Market St
Lima OH 45801
419 227-3361

(G-12754)
STANLEY STEEMER INTL INC
1253 N Cole St (45801-3413)
P.O. Box 1431 (45802-1431)
PHONE...................................419 227-1212
Kris Nagley, Principal
EMP: 32
SALES (corp-wide): 240MM Privately Held
SIC: 7217 Carpet & furniture cleaning on location
PA: Stanley Steemer International, Inc.
5800 Innovation Dr
Dublin OH 43016
614 764-2007

(G-12755)
STERLING LODGING LLC
Also Called: Holiday Inn
803 S Leonard Ave (45804-3185)
PHONE...................................419 879-4000
Brad Will, General Mgr
Rob Hayes, Principal
Michele Hicks, Sales Mgr
Joan Knight, Asst Mgr
EMP: 45
SALES (est): 1.8MM Privately Held
SIC: 7011 Hotels & motels

(G-12756)
STOLLY INSURANCE AGENCY INC
Also Called: Stolly Financial Planning
1730 Allentown Rd (45805-1856)
P.O. Box 5067 (45802-5067)
PHONE...................................419 227-2570
Mark E Stolly, President
Janet K Wade, Corp Secy
Timothy J Stolly, Vice Pres
William R Stolly, Vice Pres
EMP: 27
SQ FT: 4,600
SALES (est): 7.7MM Privately Held
SIC: 6411 Insurance agents

(G-12757)
STOOPS OF LIMA INC
598 E Hanthorn Rd (45804-3822)
PHONE...................................419 228-4334
Jeffrey Stoops, CEO
John Frigge, CFO
EMP: 200 EST: 1983
SALES (est): 24MM Privately Held
SIC: 5012 5511 Trucks, commercial; trucks, tractors & trailers: new & used

(G-12758)
SWARTZ ENTERPRISES INC
Also Called: Swartz Contracting
2622 Baty Rd (45807-1511)
PHONE...................................419 331-1024
Paul Swartz, President
Carol Swartz, Treasurer
Linda Hirschfeld, Accounting Mgr
Tom Turner, Sales Staff
Blake Bartels, Business Dir
EMP: 25
SALES: 1.6MM Privately Held
SIC: 1542 1521 Commercial & office buildings, renovation & repair; general remodeling, single-family houses

(G-12759)
SWD CORPORATION
Also Called: SUPERIOR WHOLESALE DISTRIBUTOR
435 N Main St (45801-4314)
P.O. Box 340 (45802-0340)
PHONE...................................419 227-2436
Carl Berger Jr, President
Kenneth Simmers, Corp Secy
David L Cockerell, Exec VP
Sola Curtis, VP Opers
Jim Schweller, Buyer
EMP: 50 EST: 1884
SQ FT: 85,000
SALES: 47.4MM Privately Held
SIC: 5194 5142 Tobacco & tobacco products; packaged frozen goods

(G-12760)
T AND D INTERIORS INCORPORATED
3626 Allentown Rd (45807-2138)
PHONE...................................419 331-4372
Brad Selover, President
William Timothy Estes, President
Troy Selover, Project Mgr
Marsha Estes, Treasurer
Amy Hafer, Bookkeeper
EMP: 40
SQ FT: 14,800
SALES (est): 6.1MM Privately Held
SIC: 1742 1752 Acoustical & ceiling work; floor laying & floor work

(G-12761)
T J ELLIS ENTERPRISES INC (PA)
Also Called: Hardwood Wholesalers Exporters
1505 Neubrecht Rd (45801-3123)
PHONE...................................419 999-5026
Terry Ellis, President
Pam Ellis, Vice Pres
◆ EMP: 30
SQ FT: 3,000
SALES (est): 3.6MM Privately Held
SIC: 5031 Veneer; lumber: rough, dressed & finished

(G-12762)
TILTON CORPORATION
330 S Pine St (45804)
P.O. Box 839 (45802-0839)
PHONE...................................419 227-6421
Kevin Wiechart, President
Harry Coy, Treasurer
Gretchen Morin, Manager
Judy Tilton, Admin Sec
EMP: 125
SQ FT: 7,000
SALES (est): 13.1MM Privately Held
WEB: www.tiltonindustries.com
SIC: 1711 1761 3498 3444 Mechanical contractor; sheet metalwork; fabricated pipe & fittings; sheet metalwork; fabricated structural metal

PA: Tilton Industries, Inc.
330 S Pine St
Lima OH
419 227-6421

(G-12763)
TIME WARNER CABLE INC
3100 Elida Rd (45805-1218)
PHONE...................................419 331-1111
Marge Thompson, Branch Mgr
EMP: 83
SALES (corp-wide): 43.6B Publicly Held
SIC: 4841 Cable television services
HQ: Spectrum Management Holding Company, Llc
400 Atlantic St
Stamford CT 06901
203 905-7801

(G-12764)
TIMMERMAN JOHN P HEATING AC CO (PA)
Also Called: Honeywell Authorized Dealer
4563 Elida Rd (45807-1151)
PHONE...................................419 229-4015
Larry Esmonde, President
Darryl Sawmiller, General Mgr
Mike Theobalb, Principal
EMP: 35
SQ FT: 30,000
SALES (est): 5MM Privately Held
WEB: www.jptimmerman.com
SIC: 1711 1731 Warm air heating & air conditioning contractor; plumbing contractors; electrical work

(G-12765)
TOM AHL CHRYSLR-PLYMOUTH-DODGE
617 King Ave (45805-1793)
PHONE...................................419 227-0202
Thomas W Ahl, President
Andrea Ahl, Treasurer
EMP: 150
SQ FT: 4,000
SALES (est): 45MM Privately Held
SIC: 5511 7515 Automobiles, new & used; passenger car leasing

(G-12766)
TRACY REFRIGERATION INC
Also Called: Tracy Appliance
4064 Elida Rd (45807-1556)
PHONE...................................419 223-4786
Jeffrey K Tracy, President
Dennis Scott, Vice Pres
Rebecca Scott, Treasurer
EMP: 25 EST: 1952
SQ FT: 21,000
SALES (est): 4.3MM Privately Held
SIC: 5722 7699 Household appliance stores; household appliance repair services

(G-12767)
TRANS VAC INC
931 N Jefferson St (45801-4166)
PHONE...................................419 229-8192
Powell Prater, Ch of Bd
Brad Prater, President
Daniel Lucke, Vice Pres
Charlotte Prater, Treasurer
Lynn Bibler, Admin Sec
EMP: 30
SALES: 819K Privately Held
SIC: 4212 Hazardous waste transport

(G-12768)
TRIAD GROUP INC (PA)
855 W Market St Lowr (45805-2795)
PHONE...................................419 228-8800
Paul Shin, President
EMP: 55 EST: 1976
SQ FT: 4,800
SALES: 4MM Privately Held
WEB: www.medilabinc.com
SIC: 8071 Testing Laboratory

(G-12769)
TRISCO SYSTEMS INCORPORATED
2000 Baty Rd (45807-1955)
PHONE...................................419 339-9912
Steven W Walter, President
Brian U Walter, Vice Pres

Kelly Wuebker, Production
Jeremy Morris, Accounts Mgr
EMP: 130 EST: 1990
SQ FT: 15,000
SALES (est): 26.5MM Privately Held
WEB: www.triscosystems.com
SIC: 1541 1542 Renovation, remodeling & repairs: industrial buildings; commercial & office buildings, renovation & repair

(G-12770)
TRUCK COUNTRY INDIANA INC
598 E Hanthorn Rd (45804-3822)
PHONE...................................419 228-4334
Treavor Cole, General Mgr
EMP: 200
SALES (corp-wide): 542.1MM Privately Held
WEB: www.stoops.com
SIC: 5511 5012 Trucks, tractors & trailers: new & used; trucks, commercial
HQ: Truck Country Of Indiana, Inc.
1851 W Thompson Rd
Indianapolis IN 46217
317 788-1533

(G-12771)
TRUGREEN LIMITED PARTNERSHIP
Also Called: Tru Green-Chemlawn
2083 N Dixie Hwy (45801-3251)
P.O. Box 630 (45802-0630)
PHONE...................................419 516-4200
Tim Caloahan, Manager
EMP: 30
SQ FT: 2,500
SALES (corp-wide): 3.4B Privately Held
SIC: 0782 Lawn care services
HQ: Trugreen Limited Partnership
1790 Kirby Pkwy
Memphis TN 38138
901 251-4128

(G-12772)
UNITED PARCEL SERVICE INC OH
Also Called: UPS
801 Industry Ave (45804-4169)
PHONE...................................419 222-7399
John Smith, Manager
EMP: 90
SALES (corp-wide): 71.8B Publicly Held
WEB: www.upsscs.com
SIC: 4215 4513 Parcel delivery, vehicular; air courier services
HQ: United Parcel Service, Inc. (Oh)
55 Glenlake Pkwy
Atlanta GA 30328
404 828-6000

(G-12773)
UNITED TELEPHONE COMPANY OHIO
122 S Elizabeth St (45801-4802)
P.O. Box 2001, Cridersville (45806-0001)
PHONE...................................419 227-1660
James D Gadd, Manager
EMP: 300
SALES (corp-wide): 23.4B Publicly Held
SIC: 4813 Telephone communication, except radio
HQ: United Telephone Company Of Ohio
100 Centurylink Dr
Monroe LA 71203
318 388-9000

(G-12774)
VOLUNTERS AMER CARE FACILITIES
Also Called: Lost Creek Care Center
804 S Mumaugh Rd (45804-3569)
PHONE...................................419 225-9040
Shelley Kendick, Manager
EMP: 120
SALES (corp-wide): 66.7MM Privately Held
SIC: 8051 8052 Skilled nursing care facilities; intermediate care facilities
PA: Volunteers Of America Care Facilities
7530 Market Place Dr
Eden Prairie MN 55344
952 941-0305

(G-12775)
WANNEMACHER ENTERPRISES INC (PA)
Also Called: Wannemacher Truck Lines
400 E Hanthorn Rd (45804-2460)
PHONE...............................419 225-9060
Greg Wannemacher, *President*
Scott Cockerell, *Principal*
Randy Fetter, *Vice Pres*
Beth Nickles, *Vice Pres*
Andy Wannemacher, *Vice Pres*
EMP: 95
SQ FT: 1,000,450
SALES (est): 14.6MM **Privately Held**
WEB: www.wanntl.com
SIC: 4225 4213 General warehousing & storage; trucking, except local

(G-12776)
WASTE MANAGEMENT OHIO INC
Also Called: Waste Management of Lima
1550 E 4th St (45804-2710)
PHONE...............................419 221-3644
Ed Romatowski, *President*
Peggy McNett, *Human Resources*
EMP: 75
SQ FT: 1,340
SALES (corp-wide): 14.9B **Publicly Held**
SIC: 4953 Garbage: collecting, destroying & processing
HQ: Waste Management Of Ohio, Inc.
 1700 N Broad St
 Fairborn OH 45324

(G-12777)
WASTE MANAGEMENT OHIO INC
1550 E 4th St (45804-2710)
PHONE...............................419 221-2029
Ed Romatowski, *President*
EMP: 49
SALES (corp-wide): 14.9B **Publicly Held**
SIC: 4953 Refuse systems
HQ: Waste Management Of Ohio, Inc.
 1700 N Broad St
 Fairborn OH 45324

(G-12778)
WEST CENTRAL OHIO GROUP LTD
Also Called: Institute For Orthpdic Surgery
801 Medical Dr Ste B (45804-4030)
PHONE...............................419 224-7586
Mark G McDonald, *CEO*
Justin Waite, *Network Enginr*
EMP: 75 EST: 1998
SALES (est): 46.1MM **Privately Held**
SIC: 8011 Surgeon

(G-12779)
WEST CENTRAL OHIO INTERNET
Also Called: Wcoil
215 N Elizabeth St (45801-4302)
P.O. Box 5620 (45802-5620)
PHONE...............................419 229-2645
Toll Free:...............................888 -
Mike O'Connor, *President*
Barbara O'Connor, *Vice Pres*
Mark Figley, *Officer*
EMP: 27
SQ FT: 10,000
SALES (est): 5.4MM **Privately Held**
WEB: www.wcoil.com
SIC: 4813 ;

(G-12780)
WEST CENTRAL OHIO SURGERY & EN
770 W High St Ste 100 (45801-5900)
PHONE...............................419 226-8700
Cheryl Swenar,
EMP: 45 EST: 1998
SQ FT: 17,000
SALES: 1MM **Privately Held**
SIC: 8011 Ambulatory surgical center

(G-12781)
WEST OHIO CMNTY ACTION PARTNR
Also Called: Lacca
540 S Central Ave (45804-1306)
PHONE...............................419 227-2586

Jacqueline Fox, *CEO*
EMP: 116
SALES (est): 1.1MM **Privately Held**
SIC: 8322 Social service center
PA: West Ohio Community Action Partnership
 540 S Central Ave
 Lima OH 45804

(G-12782)
WEST OHIO CMNTY ACTION PARTNR (PA)
Also Called: HEAD START
540 S Central Ave (45804-1306)
PHONE...............................419 227-2586
Michelle Spradlin, *CFO*
Jacqueline Fox, *Exec Dir*
Kendra Roxo, *Admin Asst*
EMP: 160
SALES: 8.7MM **Privately Held**
SIC: 8399 8322 8351 Community action agency; individual & family services; child day care services

(G-12783)
WESTGATE LANES INCORPORATED
721 N Cable Rd (45805-1738)
PHONE...............................419 229-3845
Andy Johnston, *President*
Keith Callahan, *Corp Secy*
Wes Johnston, *Vice Pres*
EMP: 42 EST: 1958
SQ FT: 50,000
SALES: 2MM **Privately Held**
WEB: www.westgatelanes.com
SIC: 5812 7933 Cafeteria; bowling centers

(G-12784)
WIECHART ENTERPRISES INC
Also Called: All Service Glass Company
4511 Elida Rd (45807-1151)
PHONE...............................419 227-0027
Eric Wiechart, *President*
EMP: 30
SQ FT: 12,000
SALES (est): 8.6MM **Privately Held**
SIC: 7536 1793 Automotive glass replacement shops; glass & glazing work

(G-12785)
WRIGHT DISTRIBUTION CTRS INC
1000 E Hanthorn Rd (45804-3997)
P.O. Box 817 (45802-0817)
PHONE...............................419 227-7621
Donald E Wright, *President*
Emily Snyder, *General Mgr*
Dennis Perrin, *Opers Mgr*
Kyle Faulder, *Warehouse Mgr*
Kathleen Tomlinson, *Human Res Mgr*
EMP: 28
SQ FT: 300,000
SALES (est): 5.1MM **Privately Held**
WEB: www.wrightdistribution.com
SIC: 4225 4731 General warehousing; freight transportation arrangement

(G-12786)
WRIGHTWAY FD SVC REST SUP INC
3255 Saint Johns Rd (45804-4022)
PHONE...............................419 222-7911
Karen Wright, *Vice Pres*
Robert Balyeat, *Admin Sec*
EMP: 25 EST: 1952
SQ FT: 40,000
SALES (est): 4.5MM **Privately Held**
WEB: www.wrightwayfoods.com
SIC: 5141 Groceries, general line

(G-12787)
WZRX
667 W Market St (45801-4603)
PHONE...............................419 223-2060
Matt Bell, *District Mgr*
Todd Walker, *Director*
EMP: 30
SALES (est): 498.8K **Privately Held**
SIC: 4832 Radio broadcasting stations

(G-12788)
YOCUM REALTY COMPANY
421 S Cable Rd (45805-3111)
PHONE...............................419 222-3040

Timothy L Stanford, *President*
Paula Hillard, *Real Est Agnt*
John Mongelluzzo Jr, *Real Est Agnt*
Pamela Vickers, *Real Est Agnt*
EMP: 30
SQ FT: 2,240
SALES (est): 2.9MM **Privately Held**
WEB: www.yocumrealty.com
SIC: 6531 Real estate agent, residential

Lima
Auglaize County

(G-12789)
COMMUNITY HLTH PRFSSIONALS INC
Also Called: Helping Hands
3719 Shawnee Rd (45806-1618)
PHONE...............................419 991-1822
Claudia Crawfford, *Director*
EMP: 30
SALES (corp-wide): 13.1MM **Privately Held**
SIC: 8082 Visiting nurse service
PA: Community Health Professionals, Inc.
 1159 Westwood Dr
 Van Wert OH 45891
 419 238-9223

(G-12790)
LEARNING TREE CHILDCARE CTR
775 S Thayer Rd (45806-8205)
PHONE...............................419 229-5484
Shanda Cox, *Director*
Andrea Stout, *Director*
EMP: 27
SALES (est): 428.4K **Privately Held**
SIC: 8351 Preschool center

(G-12791)
OFFICE WORLD INC (PA)
Also Called: Virtual Pc's
3820 S Dixie Hwy (45806-1848)
PHONE...............................419 991-4694
Chuck Greeley, *President*
EMP: 41 EST: 1962
SQ FT: 20,000
SALES (est): 11.7MM **Privately Held**
SIC: 5045 5044 7374 5734 Computers; office equipment; copying equipment; data processing service; computer & software stores; radio & television repair; custom computer programming services

(G-12792)
REA & ASSOCIATES INC
2579 Shawnee Rd (45806-1409)
PHONE...............................419 331-1040
Dennis Gallant, *Partner*
EMP: 25
SALES (corp-wide): 32.3MM **Privately Held**
SIC: 8721 Certified public accountant
PA: Rea & Associates, Inc.
 419 W High Ave
 New Philadelphia OH 44663
 330 339-6651

(G-12793)
SHAWNEE WEEKDAY EARLY LRNG CTR
2600 Zurmehly Rd (45806-1424)
PHONE...............................419 991-4806
James Hile, *Ch of Bd*
J Ditto, *Director*
Cheryl Crites, *Administration*
J Leigh Ditto, *Administration*
EMP: 35 EST: 1969
SQ FT: 36,000
SALES (est): 1.4MM **Privately Held**
SIC: 6732 Trusts: educational, religious, etc.

(G-12794)
VIRTUAL TECHNOLOGIES GROUP (PA)
3820 S Dixie Hwy (45806-1848)
PHONE...............................419 991-4694
Mike Curtis, *Vice Pres*
EMP: 46
SQ FT: 14,000

SALES (est): 42.6MM **Privately Held**
SIC: 5045 5734 Computers; computer & software stores

Lisbon
Columbiana County

(G-12795)
ALBCO SALES INC (PA)
230 Maple St (44432-1274)
PHONE...............................330 424-9446
Joe Stafeld, *President*
Gary Staffeld, *President*
James Brewster, *Superintendent*
William Mullane Jr, *Treasurer*
Steve Meals, *Natl Sales Mgr*
EMP: 50
SQ FT: 1,000
SALES (est): 8.5MM **Privately Held**
WEB: www.albco.com
SIC: 5051 Steel

(G-12796)
COMMUNITY ACTION COLUMBIANA CT (PA)
7880 Lincole Pl (44432-8324)
PHONE...............................330 424-7221
Carol Bretz, *Exec Dir*
EMP: 64
SQ FT: 12,600
SALES: 18.4MM **Privately Held**
SIC: 8399 Social change association

(G-12797)
COMMUNITY EDUCATION CTRS INC
8473 County Home Rd (44432-9418)
PHONE...............................330 424-4065
Michael L Caltabiano, *Branch Mgr*
EMP: 374
SALES (corp-wide): 2.3B **Privately Held**
SIC: 8744 Correctional facility
HQ: Community Education Centers, Inc.
 621 Nw 53rd St Ste 700
 Boca Raton FL 33487
 973 226-2900

(G-12798)
COUNTY OF COLUMBIANA
Also Called: Community Action
7880 Lincole Pl (44432-8322)
PHONE...............................330 424-1386
Carol Bretz, *Manager*
EMP: 150 **Privately Held**
WEB: www.colcountysheriff.com
SIC: 8322 Individual & family services
PA: County Of Columbiana
 105 S Market St
 Lisbon OH 44432
 330 424-9511

(G-12799)
D W DICKEY AND SON INC (PA)
Also Called: D W Dickey
7896 Dickey Dr (44432-9391)
P.O. Box 189 (44432-0189)
PHONE...............................330 424-1441
Gary Neville, *President*
Timothy Dickey, *President*
David Dickey, *Vice Pres*
Janet Blosser, *Admin Sec*
EMP: 52
SALES (est): 62.6MM **Privately Held**
SIC: 5169 3273 5172 Explosives; ready-mixed concrete; fuel oil

(G-12800)
EMPLOYMENT DEVELOPMENT INC
8330 County Home Rd (44432-9418)
PHONE...............................330 424-7711
Phil Carter, *Director*
EMP: 250
SQ FT: 8,000
SALES: 1.6MM **Privately Held**
SIC: 8331 Sheltered workshop

GEOGRAPHIC

(G-12801)
FAMILY RECOVERY CENTER INC (PA)
964 N Market St (44432-9363)
P.O. Box 464 (44432-0464)
PHONE..........................330 424-1468
Ryan Hull, *Info Tech Mgr*
Maryann Theiss, *Exec Dir*
Eloise Traina, *Director*
Susan Albert, *Nursing Dir*
Jennifer Thorn, *Admin Asst*
EMP: 38
SQ FT: 4,800
SALES: 3.4MM **Privately Held**
SIC: 8093 Substance abuse clinics (outpatient); mental health clinic, outpatient

(G-12802)
GLOBAL-PAK INC (PA)
9636 Elkton Rd (44432-9575)
P.O. Box 89, Elkton (44415-0089)
PHONE..........................330 482-1993
Kevin Channell, *CEO*
James Foster, *President*
Brady Webster, *Sales Staff*
▲ EMP: 26 EST: 1998
SQ FT: 75,000
SALES: 10MM **Privately Held**
WEB: www.global-pak.com
SIC: 5199 Packaging materials

(G-12803)
LIONS CLUB INTERNATIONAL INC
Also Called: Lisbon Lions Club
38240 Industrial Park Rd (44432-8325)
P.O. Box 383 (44432-0383)
PHONE..........................330 424-3490
Daniel Webber, *President*
EMP: 35
SALES: 93.2K **Privately Held**
SIC: 8641 Civic associations

(G-12804)
MIKOUIS ENTERPRISE INC
Also Called: Sunrise Homes
38655 Saltwell Rd (44432-8348)
PHONE..........................330 424-1418
Jeannette Mikouis, *President*
Nick Mikouis, *Vice Pres*
EMP: 55
SALES: 840K **Privately Held**
WEB: www.sunrisehomes-oh.com
SIC: 8059 Nursing home, except skilled & intermediate care facility

(G-12805)
OPPORTUNITY HOMES INC
7891 State Route 45 (44432-9396)
P.O. Box 327 (44432-0327)
PHONE..........................330 424-1411
Jim King, *Exec Dir*
Carol Mc Gaffic, *Admin Sec*
EMP: 50
SQ FT: 10,000
SALES: 2.5MM **Privately Held**
SIC: 8361 Home for the mentally retarded

(G-12806)
VISTA CENTRE
100 Vista Dr (44432-1010)
PHONE..........................330 424-5852
Mary Rice, *President*
Jeff Anders, *Chf Purch Ofc*
Jan McKinley, *Technology*
Lisa Willis, *Nursing Dir*
Carrie Boso, *Records Dir*
EMP: 75
SALES (est): 3.5MM **Privately Held**
SIC: 8052 8051 Home for the mentally retarded, with health care; skilled nursing care facilities

Little Hocking
Washington County

(G-12807)
DSV SOLUTIONS LLC
251 Arrowhead Rd (45742-5394)
P.O. Box 452 (45742-0452)
PHONE..........................740 989-1200
Larry Hawkins, *Office Mgr*
EMP: 74

SALES (corp-wide): 12.1B **Privately Held**
SIC: 4731 Freight transportation arrangement
HQ: Dsv Solutions, Llc
1100 Laval Blvd Ste 100
Lawrenceville GA 30043
678 381-0553

Lockbourne
Franklin County

(G-12808)
AMERISOURCEBERGEN CORPORATION
6301 Lasalle Dr (43137-9280)
PHONE..........................614 497-3665
Frank Dicenso, *Director*
EMP: 100
SALES (corp-wide): 167.9B **Publicly Held**
SIC: 2834 5122 Pharmaceutical preparations; pharmaceuticals; druggists' sundries
PA: Amerisourcebergen Corporation
1300 Morris Dr Ste 100
Chesterbrook PA 19087
610 727-7000

(G-12809)
AMERISOURCEBERGEN DRUG CORP
Also Called: Columbus GF Division
6305 Lasalle Dr (43137-9280)
PHONE..........................614 409-0741
EMP: 66
SALES (corp-wide): 153.1B **Publicly Held**
SIC: 5122 Whol Drugs/Sundries
HQ: Amerisourcebergen Drug Corporation
1300 Morris Dr Ste 100
Chesterbrook PA 19087
610 727-7000

(G-12810)
CATHOLIC CEMETERIES
6440 S High St (43137-9207)
PHONE..........................614 491-2751
Rich Finn, *Director*
EMP: 30
SALES (est): 1.8MM **Privately Held**
SIC: 6553 Cemetery subdividers & developers

(G-12811)
CITY OF COLUMBUS
Also Called: Public Utilities- Water Div
6977 S High St (43137-9202)
PHONE..........................614 645-3248
Jeff Hall, *Opers Mgr*
Carry Estridge, *Manager*
EMP: 100 **Privately Held**
WEB: www.cityofcolumbus.org
SIC: 4952 9511 Sewerage systems; air, water & solid waste management;
PA: City Of Columbus
90 W Broad St Rm B33
Columbus OH 43215
614 645-7671

(G-12812)
DEALERS SUPPLY NORTH INC (HQ)
Also Called: Dsn
2315 Creekside Pkwy # 500 (43137-9313)
PHONE..........................614 274-6285
Kim R Holm, *President*
Ed Wiethe, *President*
▲ EMP: 30
SQ FT: 56,000
SALES (est): 14.1MM
SALES (corp-wide): 752.8MM **Privately Held**
WEB: www.dealersnorth.com
SIC: 5023 Carpets
PA: Mannington Mills Inc.
75 Mannington Mills Rd
Salem NJ 08079
856 935-3000

(G-12813)
DHL EXPRESS (USA) INC
2315 Creekside Pkwy (43137-9312)
PHONE..........................800 225-5345

Pmp Phelan, *Project Mgr*
Michael Parchem, *Opers Spvr*
Joan Bookheimer, *Accountant*
Bill Chen, *Financial Analy*
Shane Rhoades, *Manager*
EMP: 31
SALES (corp-wide): 70.4B **Privately Held**
SIC: 4513 Air courier services
HQ: Dhl Express (Usa), Inc.
1210 S Pine Island Rd
Plantation FL 33324
954 888-7000

(G-12814)
DHL SUPPLY CHAIN (USA)
2750 Creekside Pkwy (43137-9271)
PHONE..........................614 492-6614
Dorsey Hessler, *Branch Mgr*
EMP: 29
SALES (corp-wide): 70.4B **Privately Held**
WEB: www.exel-logistics.com
SIC: 4213 Trucking, except local
HQ: Exel Inc.
570 Polaris Pkwy
Westerville OH 43082
614 865-8500

(G-12815)
EXEL INC
Also Called: Dhl Supply Chain USA
2450 Creekside Pkwy (43137-7559)
PHONE..........................614 670-6473
Mark Smolik, *Officer*
EMP: 50 EST: 1983
SQ FT: 425,000
SALES (est): 1.5MM **Privately Held**
SIC: 4225 General warehousing & storage

(G-12816)
EXEL INC
Also Called: Dhl Solutions
4900 Creekside Pkwy (43137-7562)
PHONE..........................800 426-8434
Jeremiah Jensen, *Opers Spvr*
Paul Wills, *Finance Mgr*
Matt Brill, *Business Anlyst*
Mike Detty, *Branch Mgr*
EMP: 100
SALES (corp-wide): 70.4B **Privately Held**
SIC: 4731 Freight forwarding
HQ: Exel Inc.
570 Polaris Pkwy
Westerville OH 43082
614 865-8500

(G-12817)
EXPEDITORS INTL WASH INC
6054 Shook Rd Ste 100 (43137-9315)
PHONE..........................614 492-9840
Kelly Begley, *Manager*
EMP: 25
SALES (corp-wide): 8.1B **Publicly Held**
WEB: www.expd.com
SIC: 4731 Freight forwarding; foreign freight forwarding; domestic freight forwarding; customhouse brokers
PA: Expeditors International Of Washington, Inc.
1015 3rd Ave Fl 12
Seattle WA 98104
206 674-3400

(G-12818)
FEDEX SUP CHAIN DIST SYS INC
Also Called: Genco Atc
3795 Creekside Prk Way (43137)
PHONE..........................412 820-3700
EMP: 400
SALES (corp-wide): 65.4B **Publicly Held**
SIC: 4225 General warehousing & storage
HQ: Fedex Supply Chain Distribution System, Inc.
700 Cranberry Woods Dr
Cranberry Township PA 16066

(G-12819)
FEDEX SUPPLY CHAIN
Also Called: Genco
4555 Creekside Pkwy Ste A (43137-9287)
PHONE..........................614 491-1518
EMP: 250
SALES (corp-wide): 65.4B **Publicly Held**
SIC: 4731 Freight Transportation Arrangement

HQ: Fedex Supply Chain Distribution System, Inc.
700 Cranberry Woods Dr
Cranberry Township PA 16066

(G-12820)
INTELISOL INC
4555 Creekside Pkwy (43137-9287)
PHONE..........................614 409-0052
Charles Huggins, *Manager*
Lonnie Price, *Comp Tech*
EMP: 60
SALES (corp-wide): 5.2MM **Privately Held**
SIC: 7299 Personal shopping service
PA: Intelisol, Inc.
1001 Ne Loop 820 Ste 200
Fort Worth TX 76131
817 230-5000

(G-12821)
J A G BLACK GOLD MANAGEMENT CO
6301 S High St (43137-9723)
PHONE..........................614 565-3246
EMP: 61
SALES (corp-wide): 23.8MM **Privately Held**
SIC: 8741 Management services
PA: J A G Black Gold Management Co.
2560 London Groveport Rd
Groveport OH 43125
614 409-0290

(G-12822)
J P SAND & GRAVEL COMPANY
Also Called: Marble Cliff Block & Bldrs Sup
5911 Lockbourne Rd (43137-9256)
P.O. Box 2 (43137-0002)
PHONE..........................614 497-0083
Herbert Hartshorn, *Ch of Bd*
Richard A Roberts, *President*
Mike Craiglow, *Vice Pres*
Joann Roberts, *Treasurer*
EMP: 28 EST: 1925
SQ FT: 6,200
SALES (est): 3MM **Privately Held**
SIC: 3271 1442 Blocks, concrete or cinder: standard; construction sand mining; gravel mining

(G-12823)
NATIONAL LIME AND STONE CO
5911 Lockbourne Rd (43137-9256)
PHONE..........................614 497-0083
Martin Cudoc, *Plant Mgr*
Richard Roberts, *Branch Mgr*
EMP: 25
SQ FT: 4,032
SALES (corp-wide): 3.2B **Privately Held**
WEB: www.natlime.com
SIC: 3271 1442 Blocks, concrete or cinder: standard; construction sand mining; gravel mining
PA: The National Lime And Stone Company
551 Lake Cascade Pkwy
Findlay OH 45840
419 422-4341

(G-12824)
SCHENKER INC
2525 Rohr Rd Ste C (43137-9296)
PHONE..........................614 257-8365
EMP: 65
SALES (corp-wide): 23.3MM **Privately Held**
SIC: 5044 Microfilm equipment
HQ: Schenker, Inc.
1305 Executive Blvd # 200
Chesapeake VA 23320
757 821-3400

(G-12825)
STREAMLINE TECHNICAL SVCS LLC
4555 Creekside Pkwy (43137-9287)
PHONE..........................614 441-7448
EMP: 80
SALES (est): 37.2K **Privately Held**
SIC: 7389 Business services

▲ = Import ▼=Export
◆ =Import/Export

(G-12826)
YOUNG MENS CHRISTIAN ASSOC
Also Called: YMCA
1570 Rohr Rd (43137-9251)
PHONE......................614 491-0980
Kevin Pack, *Corp Comm Staff*
Heather Knoplesch, *Director*
Katrina Hacker, *Director*
EMP: 114
SQ FT: 864
SALES (corp-wide): 44.9MM **Privately Held**
WEB: www.ymca-columbus.com
SIC: 8641 Youth organizations
PA: Young Men's Christian Association Of Central Ohio
40 W Long St
Columbus OH 43215
614 389-4409

Lodi
Medina County

(G-12827)
LODI COMMUNITY HOSPITAL (PA)
225 Elyria St (44254-1096)
PHONE......................330 948-1222
Barb Fish, *Vice Pres*
Cindy Dennison, *CFO*
Tom Whelan, *Administration*
EMP: 130
SQ FT: 30,118
SALES: 16.5MM **Privately Held**
WEB: www.lodihospital.com
SIC: 8062 General medical & surgical hospitals

(G-12828)
MAPLE MOUNTAIN INDUSTRIES INC
312 Bank St (44254-1006)
PHONE......................330 948-2510
Aileen McDowell, *Principal*
EMP: 127 **Privately Held**
SIC: 5084 Industrial machinery & equipment
PA: Maple Mountain Industries Inc
1820 Mulligan Hill Rd
New Florence PA 15944

(G-12829)
TRAVELCENTERS OF AMERICA LLC
Also Called: Truckstops of America
Junction Of I 71 And I 76 (44254)
P.O. Box 125, Seville (44273-0125)
PHONE......................330 769-2053
Allan Buhite, *General Mgr*
EMP: 82 **Publicly Held**
WEB: www.iowa80group.com
SIC: 5541 5812 7011 5411 Gasoline service stations; eating places; hotels & motels; convenience stores, chain; general automotive repair shops; gift, novelty & souvenir shop
PA: Travelcenters Of America Llc
24601 Center Ridge Rd # 200
Westlake OH 44145

Logan
Hocking County

(G-12830)
ALCO INC
Also Called: U.S.t Environmental Contractor
36050 Smith Chapel Rd (43138-8855)
PHONE......................740 527-2991
Burbridge B Cook, *President*
Molly Cook, *Principal*
EMP: 25
SALES (est): 1.1MM **Privately Held**
SIC: 8744

(G-12831)
BAZELL OIL CO INC
14371 State Route 328 (43138-9449)
P.O. Box 2 (43138-0002)
PHONE......................740 385-5420
Joseph Michael Bazell, *President*
Donald D Poling, *Corp Secy*
EMP: 35
SQ FT: 7,500
SALES (est): 99.6MM **Privately Held**
WEB: www.bazellfuels.com
SIC: 5172 5983 Fuel oil; petroleum brokers; fuel oil dealers

(G-12832)
BRASS RING GOLF CLUB LTD
14405 Country Club Ln (43138-8638)
PHONE......................740 385-8966
Mike Bazell, *Owner*
Janet Bazell,
EMP: 30 EST: 1997
SALES (est): 867.2K **Privately Held**
WEB: www.brassringgolfclub.com
SIC: 7997 Golf club, membership

(G-12833)
CITIZENS BNK OF LOGAN OHIO INC (HQ)
188 W Main St (43138-1606)
P.O. Box 591 (43138-0591)
PHONE......................740 380-2561
Brayan K Starner, *President*
Doug Wells, *President*
Robert D Hammon, *Exec VP*
Alexander M Pavluck, *Assistant VP*
William Rose, *Assistant VP*
EMP: 48
SQ FT: 3,600
SALES: 9.3MM **Privately Held**
SIC: 6022 State commercial banks

(G-12834)
DARFUS
1135 W Hunter St (43138-1009)
PHONE......................740 380-1710
Jim Darfus, *Owner*
Melissa Frank, *Sales Associate*
Debbie Monger, *Sales Associate*
EMP: 50
SALES: 2MM **Privately Held**
WEB: www.darfus.com
SIC: 6519 6531 Real property lessors; real estate agents & managers

(G-12835)
FIRST COMMUNITY CHURCH
Also Called: Camp Akita
29746 Logan Horns Mill Rd (43138-9578)
PHONE......................740 385-3827
Mike Young, *Maintenance Dir*
Danita Wolfe, *Property Mgr*
Bill McComb, *Manager*
Andy Frick, *Director*
Scot Nicoll, *Director*
EMP: 26
SALES (corp-wide): 4.7MM **Privately Held**
SIC: 8661 7032 Community church; sporting & recreational camps
PA: The First Community Church
1320 Cambridge Blvd
Columbus OH 43212
614 488-0681

(G-12836)
HEALING HANDS HOME HEALTH LTD
30605 Stage Coach Rd (43138-8857)
PHONE......................740 385-0710
Jennifer Brown, *Owner*
EMP: 25
SALES: 680K **Privately Held**
SIC: 8082 Visiting nurse service

(G-12837)
HOCKING VALLEY COMMUNITY HO (PA)
601 State Route 664 N (43138-8541)
P.O. Box 966 (43138-0966)
PHONE......................740 380-8336
Julie Stuck, *CEO*
Leeann Helber, *President*
Julie Grow, *VP Finance*
Max M Haque, *Med Doctor*
Lori Linton, *Manager*
EMP: 380
SQ FT: 69,000
SALES: 131.2K **Privately Held**
WEB: www.hvch.org
SIC: 8062 Hospital, affiliated with AMA residency

(G-12838)
HOCKING VALLEY INDUSTRIES INC
1369 E Front St (43138-9031)
P.O. Box 64 (43138-0064)
PHONE......................740 385-2118
Karon Fisher, *Finance*
Janet Flanagan, *Manager*
Ron Spung, *Director*
EMP: 100
SQ FT: 12,000
SALES: 735.8K **Privately Held**
SIC: 8331 Sheltered workshop

(G-12839)
HOCKINGTHENSPERRY CMNTY ACTION
1005 C I C Dr (43138-9245)
PHONE......................740 385-6813
Dick Stevens, *Branch Mgr*
EMP: 30
SALES (est): 822.4K
SALES (corp-wide): 21.5MM **Privately Held**
SIC: 8322 Social service center
PA: Hocking.Athens.Perry Community Action
3 Cardaras Dr
Glouster OH 45732
740 767-4500

(G-12840)
HOPEWELL HEALTH CENTERS INC
460 E 2nd St (43138-1492)
PHONE......................740 385-8468
Kimberly Andrews, *Principal*
EMP: 140
SALES (corp-wide): 33.1MM **Privately Held**
SIC: 8093 Mental health clinic, outpatient
PA: Hopewell Health Centers, Inc.
1049 Western Ave
Chillicothe OH 45601
740 773-1006

(G-12841)
HOPEWELL HEALTH CENTERS INC
541 State Route 664 N C (43138-8541)
P.O. Box 1145 (43138-4145)
PHONE......................740 385-6594
Tom Odell, *Director*
EMP: 25
SALES (corp-wide): 33.1MM **Privately Held**
WEB: www.epilepsyservices.org
SIC: 8093 Mental health clinic, outpatient
PA: Hopewell Health Centers, Inc.
1049 Western Ave
Chillicothe OH 45601
740 773-1006

(G-12842)
INDIANA & OHIO CENTRAL RR
Also Called: Indiana & Ohio Rail
665 E Front St (43138-1719)
PHONE......................740 385-3127
Rail America, *Principal*
EMP: 120
SQ FT: 150
SALES (est): 3.9MM
SALES (corp-wide): 2.3B **Publicly Held**
SIC: 4011 Railroads, line-haul operating
HQ: The Indiana & Ohio Rail Corp
2856 Cypress Way
Cincinnati OH 45212
513 860-1000

(G-12843)
KILBARGER CONSTRUCTION INC
Also Called: C & L Supply
450 Gallagher Ave (43138-1893)
P.O. Box 946 (43138-0946)
PHONE......................740 385-6019
Edward Kilbarger, *CEO*
Anthony Kilbarger, *Vice Pres*
James E Kilbarger, *Vice Pres*
Tony Kilbarger, *Vice Pres*
Daniel Stohs, *Opers Mgr*
EMP: 120
SQ FT: 2,500
SALES (est): 23.2MM **Privately Held**
WEB: www.kilbarger.com
SIC: 1381 Drilling oil & gas wells

(G-12844)
KINDRED NURSING CENTERS E LLC
Also Called: Kindred Transitional Care
300 Arlington Ave (43138-1708)
PHONE......................502 596-7300
Jennifer Jones, *Med Doctor*
Cheryl Guyman, *Manager*
EMP: 135
SALES (corp-wide): 6B **Privately Held**
WEB: www.salemhaven.com
SIC: 8051 8093 Convalescent home with continuous nursing care; rehabilitation center, outpatient treatment
HQ: Kindred Nursing Centers East, L.L.C.
680 S 4th St
Louisville KY 40202
502 596-7300

(G-12845)
KIWANIS INTERNATIONAL INC
13519 Lakefront Dr (43138-8509)
P.O. Box 908 (43138-0908)
PHONE......................740 385-5887
Robert Lindsay, *Admin Sec*
EMP: 39
SALES (corp-wide): 23.6MM **Privately Held**
WEB: www.kfne.org
SIC: 8641 Civic associations
PA: Kiwanis International, Inc.
3636 Woodview Trce
Indianapolis IN 46268
317 875-8755

(G-12846)
LOGAN HEALTH CARE CENTER
300 Arlington Ave (43138-1797)
PHONE......................740 385-2155
Clay Enflen, *Administration*
EMP: 130
SALES: 2.9MM
SALES (corp-wide): 18.5MM **Privately Held**
SIC: 8051 Skilled nursing care facilities
PA: Midwest Geriatric Management, Llc
477 N Lindbergh Blvd # 310
Saint Louis MO 63141
314 631-3000

(G-12847)
LOGAN HEALTHCARE LEASING LLC
300 Arlington Ave (43138-1708)
PHONE......................216 367-1214
Eli Gunzburg, *Manager*
EMP: 99
SQ FT: 42,100
SALES (est): 356.7K **Privately Held**
SIC: 8051 Mental retardation hospital

(G-12848)
LOGAN-HOCKING SCHOOL DISTRICT
Also Called: Maintenance Department
13483 Mysville William Rd (43138-8971)
PHONE......................740 385-7844
Keith Brown, *Manager*
EMP: 45
SALES (corp-wide): 41.2MM **Privately Held**
SIC: 8211 7349 Public elementary school; school custodian, contract basis
PA: Logan-Hocking School District
2019 E Front St
Logan OH 43138
740 385-8517

(G-12849)
MENNEL MILLING COMPANY
Also Called: Mennel Milling Logan
1 W Front St (43138-1825)
PHONE......................740 385-6824
Larry Hawkins, *Branch Mgr*
EMP: 37

SALES (corp-wide): 119.2MM **Privately Held**
SIC: 5191 2041 Feed; flour mills, cereal (except feed)
PA: The Mennel Milling Company
319 S Vine St
Fostoria OH 44830
419 435-8151

(G-12850)
MENNEL MILLING COMPANY
Also Called: Mennel Milling Logan
1 W Front St (43138-1825)
PHONE..................................740 385-6824
EMP: 65
SALES (corp-wide): 119.2MM **Privately Held**
SIC: 2041 5191 Flour mills, cereal (except rice); feed
PA: The Mennel Milling Company
319 S Vine St
Fostoria OH 44830
419 435-8151

(G-12851)
NOTOWEEGA NATION INC
38494 Mysvlle Grendale Rd (43138)
PHONE..................................740 777-1480
Marshall Dancing Elk Lucas, *Director*
EMP: 99
SALES (est): 1.1MM **Privately Held**
SIC: 7389 Business services

(G-12852)
OSBURN ASSOCIATES INC (PA)
9383 Vanatta Rd (43138-8719)
P.O. Box 912 (43138-0912)
PHONE..................................740 385-5732
Harry Osburn, *Director*
Charles A Gerken, *Director*
Donna Osburn, *Director*
▲ EMP: 40
SQ FT: 39,360
SALES (est): 15.7MM **Privately Held**
WEB: www.osburnassociates.com
SIC: 3089 5063 Fittings for pipe, plastic; boxes & fittings, electrical

(G-12853)
SENECA STEEL ERECTORS INC (PA)
975 E Main St (43138-1743)
PHONE..................................740 385-0517
Dale Campbell, *President*
Kathie Campbell, *Corp Secy*
EMP: 30
SQ FT: 1,000
SALES (est): 6.9MM **Privately Held**
WEB: www.senecasteelerectors.com
SIC: 1791 Structural steel erection

(G-12854)
SOUTHSTERN OHIO RGIONAL FD CTR
1005 C I C Dr (43138-9245)
PHONE..................................740 385-6813
Dick Stevens, *Director*
EMP: 30 EST: 2000
SALES (est): 1.1MM **Privately Held**
SIC: 8322 Individual & family services

(G-12855)
TANSKY MOTORS INC (PA)
Also Called: Toyota of Logan
297 E Main St (43138-1399)
PHONE..................................650 322-7069
John Tansky, *President*
Marian Tansky, *Corp Secy*
EMP: 28
SQ FT: 10,000
SALES (est): 7.6MM **Privately Held**
SIC: 5511 7538 7532 7515 Automobiles, new & used; general automotive repair shops; top & body repair & paint shops; passenger car leasing; automotive & home supply stores; used car dealers

(G-12856)
TRI COUNTY NITE HUNTER ASSN CI
2940 Laurel Run Rd (43138)
PHONE..................................740 385-7341
Cyde Johnson, *President*
EMP: 40

SALES (est): 433.6K **Privately Held**
SIC: 7997 Hunting club, membership

(G-12857)
TRI-COUNTY COMMUNITY ACT
Also Called: Regional Food Program
1005 C I C Dr (43138-9245)
PHONE..................................740 385-6812
Richard Stevens, *Director*
EMP: 35
SALES (corp-wide): 3.6MM **Privately Held**
WEB: www.tricountycls.com
SIC: 8399 8322 Community action agency; individual & family services
PA: Tri-County Community Action Commission For Champaign, Logan And Shelby Counties
868 Amherst Dr
Urbana OH 43078
937 593-0034

London
Madison County

(G-12858)
AG-PRO OHIO LLC
Also Called: Agpro
1660 Us Highway 42 Ne (43140-9337)
PHONE..................................614 879-6620
EMP: 200
SALES (corp-wide): 232.6MM **Privately Held**
SIC: 5999 5083 Farm equipment & supplies; agricultural machinery & equipment
HQ: Ag-Pro Ohio, Llc
19595 Us Highway 84 E
Boston GA 31626
229 498-8833

(G-12859)
ARMALY LLC
Also Called: Armaly Brands
110 W 1st St (43140-1484)
PHONE..................................740 852-3621
Annmarie Armaly, *Treasurer*
▼ EMP: 40
SALES (est): 7.7MM
SALES (corp-wide): 8.2MM **Privately Held**
SIC: 3089 5199 3086 Floor coverings, plastic; sponges (animal); plastics foam products
PA: Armaly Sponge Company
1900 Easy St
Commerce Township MI 48390
248 669-2100

(G-12860)
BLUEBIRD RETIREMENT COMMUNITY
2260 State Route 56 Sw (43140-9380)
PHONE..................................740 845-1880
Jane Herman, *Exec Dir*
EMP: 30
SALES (est): 898.6K **Privately Held**
SIC: 8322 Old age assistance

(G-12861)
BUILDING SYSTEMS TRNSP CO
Also Called: B S T
460 E High St (43140-9303)
PHONE..................................740 852-9700
Jerry Alcott, *President*
David Beickman, *COO*
Brian Brady, *Vice Pres*
Bryan Robinson, *Manager*
EMP: 170
SQ FT: 95,000
SALES: 40MM **Privately Held**
WEB: www.bsttrucking.com
SIC: 4213 4212 4225 Trucking, except local; local trucking, without storage; general warehousing

(G-12862)
COUGHLIN CHEVROLET INC
255 Lafayette St (43140-9071)
P.O. Box 438 (43140-0438)
PHONE..................................740 852-1122
Tim Casey, *Business Mgr*
Todd Hardy, *Sales Mgr*
Ken McConnell, *Sales Mgr*

Mike Branham, *Sales Staff*
Ed Ramsey, *Sales Staff*
EMP: 40
SALES (corp-wide): 95.1MM **Privately Held**
WEB: www.coughlinford.com
SIC: 5511 7532 5521 5083 Automobiles, new & used; pickups, new & used; body shop, automotive; automobiles, used cars only; livestock equipment
PA: Coughlin Chevrolet, Inc.
9000 Broad St Sw
Pataskala OH 43062
740 964-9191

(G-12863)
COUNTY OF MADISON
Also Called: Madison County Engineer
825 Us Highway 42 Ne (43140-8512)
PHONE..................................740 852-9404
Jim Sabin, *Sheriff*
David Brand, *Manager*
EMP: 40 **Privately Held**
SIC: 8711 9111 Engineering services; county supervisors' & executives' offices
PA: County Of Madison
1 N Main St
London OH 43140
740 852-2972

(G-12864)
FORREST TRUCKING COMPANY (PA)
7 E 1st St (43140-1202)
P.O. Box 77, West Jefferson (43162-0077)
PHONE..................................614 879-7347
Donavon Forrest, *President*
Donovan Forrest, *President*
Donald Forrest, *Vice Pres*
Donna McVey, *Treasurer*
Caitlin Deluna, *Office Mgr*
EMP: 46 EST: 1948
SQ FT: 1,500
SALES (est): 5.5MM **Privately Held**
SIC: 4212 Local trucking, without storage

(G-12865)
LONDON HEALTH & REHAB CTR LLC
218 Elm St (43140-2130)
PHONE..................................740 852-3100
George S Repchick, *President*
William Weisberg, *Vice Pres*
Sarah Depompei, *Assistant*
EMP: 214
SALES: 5.9MM
SALES (corp-wide): 157.7MM **Privately Held**
SIC: 8099 Childbirth preparation clinic
PA: Saber Healthcare Group, L.L.C.
26691 Richmond Rd Frnt
Bedford OH 44146
216 292-5706

(G-12866)
LOVING CARE HOSPICE INC (PA)
56 S Oak St (43140-1024)
P.O. Box 445 (43140-0445)
PHONE..................................740 852-7755
Wendy Starr, *CEO*
Robbi Huddleston, *General Mgr*
Christina Kennedy, *CFO*
Robby Daily, *Manager*
EMP: 25
SALES: 2.9MM **Privately Held**
SIC: 8082 Home health care services

(G-12867)
MADISON CNTY LNDON CY HLTH DST
306 Lafayette St Ste B (43140-9392)
PHONE..................................740 852-3065
James Canney, *Superintendent*
Bridget Lane, *Finance*
Jennifer Michaelson, *Manager*
EMP: 25
SALES (est): 1.2MM **Privately Held**
SIC: 8099 Health & allied services

(G-12868)
MADISON FAMILY HEALTH CORP
210 N Main St (43140-1115)
PHONE..................................740 845-7000

Fred Kolb, *CEO*
Becky Rozell, *Officer*
EMP: 239
SALES (est): 938.9K
SALES (corp-wide): 47.3MM **Privately Held**
SIC: 8062 General medical & surgical hospitals
PA: Madison County Community Hospital
210 N Main St
London OH 43140
740 845-7000

(G-12869)
MADISON HOUSE INC
351 Keny Blvd (43140-8524)
PHONE..................................740 845-0145
Jane Herman, *Administration*
EMP: 50
SALES (est): 2.2MM **Privately Held**
SIC: 8361 Self-help group home

(G-12870)
MATCO INDUSTRIES INC
Also Called: MATCO SERVICES
204 Maple St (43140-1490)
P.O. Box 533 (43140-0533)
PHONE..................................740 852-7054
Van A Viney, *CEO*
Van Viney, *CEO*
Sharyn Koelling, *Director*
EMP: 28
SALES: 356.6K **Privately Held**
SIC: 8322 8331 Social services for the handicapped; job training & vocational rehabilitation services

(G-12871)
MENTAL HLTH SERV FOR CL & MAD
210 N Main St (43140-1115)
PHONE..................................740 852-6256
Keith Heinlein, *Controller*
Diana Padrutt, *Director*
EMP: 30
SALES (corp-wide): 12.5MM **Privately Held**
WEB: www.mhscc.com
SIC: 8063 8093 Hospital for the mentally ill; mental health clinic, outpatient
PA: Mental Health Services For Clark And Madison Counties, Inc.
474 N Yellow Springs St
Springfield OH 45504
937 399-9500

(G-12872)
PETERS MAIN STREET PHOTOGRAPHY (PA)
314 N Main St (43140-9339)
P.O. Box 587 (43140-0587)
PHONE..................................740 852-2731
Larry Peters, *President*
EMP: 28
SQ FT: 4,500
SALES (est): 1.6MM **Privately Held**
WEB: www.peters-photography.com
SIC: 7221 Photographer, still or video

(G-12873)
PRESBYTERIAN CHILD CENTER
211 Garfield Ave (43140-9203)
PHONE..................................740 852-3190
Cindy Cliffton, *Director*
Cindy Clifton, *Director*
EMP: 31
SALES (est): 855.2K **Privately Held**
SIC: 8351 Child day care services

(G-12874)
SABER HEALTHCARE GROUP LLC
Also Called: Arbors At London
218 Elm St (43140-2130)
PHONE..................................740 852-3100
Pam Degroodt, *Branch Mgr*
EMP: 449
SALES (corp-wide): 157.7MM **Privately Held**
WEB: www.extendicarehealth.com
SIC: 8051 Convalescent home with continuous nursing care

PA: Saber Healthcare Group, L.L.C.
26691 Richmond Rd Frnt
Bedford OH 44146
216 292-5706

(G-12875)
STAPLES INC
500 E High St (43140-9303)
PHONE....................740 845-5600
Arnold Ferayna, *Manager*
EMP: 40 **Privately Held**
SIC: 5943 5112 Stationery stores; stationery & office supplies
HQ: Staples, Inc.
500 Staples Dr
Framingham MA 01702
508 253-5000

(G-12876)
TRI GREEN INTERSTATE EQUIPMENT
1499 Us Highway 42 Ne (43140-1900)
PHONE....................614 879-7731
Richard Green, *President*
Connie Ballah, *Corp Secy*
Judy Green, *Vice Pres*
EMP: 30
SQ FT: 14,000
SALES (est): 2.5MM **Privately Held**
WEB: www.trigreeneq.com
SIC: 7389 5261 Auctioneers, fee basis; lawnmowers & tractors

Long Bottom
Meigs County

(G-12877)
BARBARA GHEENS PAINTING INC
50550 Rainbow Ridge Rd (45743-9001)
PHONE....................740 949-0405
Manuel Gheen, *President*
Daniel Gheen, *Vice Pres*
Michael Gheen, *Vice Pres*
Janine Gheen, *Admin Sec*
EMP: 25
SQ FT: 1,500
SALES (est): 3.5MM **Privately Held**
SIC: 1721 Exterior commercial painting contractor

Lorain
Lorain County

(G-12878)
ABSOLUTE MACHINE TOOLS INC (PA)
7420 Industrial Pkwy Dr (44053-2064)
PHONE....................440 839-9696
Steve Ortner, *President*
Jeffery Sturtevant, *General Mgr*
Dennis Tapper, *General Mgr*
Hayden Wellman, *Vice Pres*
Jason Bartosch, *Parts Mgr*
▲ **EMP:** 51
SQ FT: 18,000
SALES (est): 46.2MM **Privately Held**
SIC: 5084 Machine tools & accessories

(G-12879)
AMERICAN EAGLE MORTGAGE CO LLC (PA)
6145 Park Square Dr Ste 4 (44053-4147)
PHONE....................440 988-2900
John Schrenkel,
David Barry,
Diane Schrenkel,
EMP: 32 **EST:** 2000
SALES (est): 24.2MM **Privately Held**
SIC: 6162 Mortgage bankers & correspondents

(G-12880)
ANCHOR LODGE NURSING HOME INC
Also Called: SPRENGER HEALTH CARE SYSTEMS
3756 W Erie Ave Ofc (44053-1298)
PHONE....................440 244-2019
Scott Springer, *President*

Donel L Springer, *Vice Pres*
EMP: 150 **EST:** 1962
SQ FT: 20,000
SALES: 10.2MM
SALES (corp-wide): 13.2MM **Privately Held**
WEB: www.sprengerretirement.com
SIC: 8052 8051 Intermediate care facilities; skilled nursing care facilities
PA: Bluesky Healthcare Inc.
3885 Oberlin Ave
Lorain OH 44053
440 989-5200

(G-12881)
ANTHONY DAVID SALON & SPA
6401 S Broadway (44053-3955)
PHONE....................440 233-8570
Peggy S Sinibaldi, *President*
EMP: 26
SALES (est): 506.1K **Privately Held**
SIC: 7231 Hairdressers

(G-12882)
APPLEWOOD CENTERS INC
1865 N Ridge Rd E Ste A (44055-3359)
PHONE....................440 324-1300
Mary Munn, *Branch Mgr*
EMP: 45
SALES (corp-wide): 17.4MM **Privately Held**
SIC: 8322 Child related social services
PA: Applewood Centers, Inc.
10427 Detroit Ave
Cleveland OH 44102
216 696-6815

(G-12883)
AUTUMN AEGIS INC
Also Called: Assisted Living Apartments
1130 Tower Blvd Ste A (44052-5200)
PHONE....................440 282-6768
Anthony Sprenger, *President*
EMP: 85 **EST:** 1948
SALES (est): 2.7MM **Privately Held**
WEB: www.autumnaegis.com
SIC: 8051 Convalescent home with continuous nursing care
PA: Sprenger Enterprises, Inc.
2198 Gladstone Ct
Glendale Heights IL 60139

(G-12884)
BARB LINDEN
Also Called: Occupational Health Center
1800 Livingston Ave # 200 (44052-3781)
PHONE....................440 233-1068
Barbara Linden, *Principal*
EMP: 30
SALES (est): 744.9K **Privately Held**
SIC: 8011 Physical medicine, physician/surgeon

(G-12885)
BAY MECHANICAL & ELEC CORP
2221 W Park Dr (44053-1158)
PHONE....................440 282-6816
Terry Burns, *Ch of Bd*
Robin Newberry, *President*
Alan Fulkerson, *Opers Mgr*
Mary Lou Gross, *Controller*
Donald Reed, *Sr Project Mgr*
EMP: 51 **EST:** 1948
SQ FT: 22,000
SALES: 18MM **Privately Held**
WEB: www.baymec.com
SIC: 1711 1731 7389 Plumbing contractors; electrical work; crane & aerial lift service

(G-12886)
BERKEBILE RUSSELL & ASSOCIATES
1720 Cooper Foster Park R (44053-4200)
PHONE....................440 989-4480
Lawrence G Thorley MD, *President*
Stephen Ticich MD, *Admin Sec*
EMP: 26
SQ FT: 4,000
SALES (est): 3.1MM **Privately Held**
SIC: 8071 X-ray laboratory, including dental

(G-12887)
BRIAN-KYLES CONSTRUCTION INC
875 N Ridge Rd E (44055-3035)
PHONE....................440 242-0298
Douglas Maurer, *President*
EMP: 25
SALES (est): 3.1MM **Privately Held**
WEB: www.briankyles.com
SIC: 0782 1521 Landscape contractors; general remodeling, single-family houses

(G-12888)
BUCKEYE COMMUNITY BANK
105 Sheffield Ctr (44055-3134)
PHONE....................440 233-8800
Bruce E Stevens, *President*
Stephen C Wright, *Principal*
Sandi Dubell, *Senior VP*
Ben Norton, *Senior VP*
Linda O'Malley, *Senior VP*
EMP: 25
SQ FT: 10,000
SALES: 7.9MM **Privately Held**
WEB: www.buckeyebank.com
SIC: 6022 State commercial banks

(G-12889)
BURGE BUILDING CO INC
2626 Broadway (44052-4834)
P.O. Box 1352, Ormond Beach FL (32175-1352)
PHONE....................440 245-6871
Bruce Burge, *CEO*
Jeffry Watkins, *President*
Charlotte Burge, *Admin Sec*
EMP: 32
SQ FT: 3,600
SALES (est): 2.8MM **Privately Held**
SIC: 1521 1542 Residential Remodeling & Commercial Renovation

(G-12890)
CITY OF LORAIN
Also Called: Water Pollution Control
100 Alabama Ave (44052-2042)
PHONE....................440 288-0281
Alex Berki, *Maint Spvr*
EMP: 30 **Privately Held**
WEB: www.cityoflorain.org
SIC: 4941 Water supply
PA: Lorain, City Of (Inc)
200 W Erie Ave Ste 714
Lorain OH 44052
440 204-2090

(G-12891)
CITY OF LORAIN
Water Div
1106 W 1st St (44052-1434)
PHONE....................440 204-2500
Robert De Santis, *Director*
Mary Ivan-Garza, *Director*
Ron Russell, *Director*
EMP: 122 **Privately Held**
WEB: www.cityoflorain.org
SIC: 4941 4952 4939 Water supply; sewerage systems; combination utilities
PA: Lorain, City Of (Inc)
200 W Erie Ave Ste 714
Lorain OH 44052
440 204-2090

(G-12892)
CLEVELAND CLINIC FOUNDATION
Cleveland Clinic Hlth Systems
1142 W 37th St (44052-5115)
PHONE....................440 282-6669
EMP: 3544
SALES (corp-wide): 8.9B **Privately Held**
SIC: 8062 General Hospital
PA: The Cleveland Clinic Foundation
9500 Euclid Ave
Cleveland OH 44195
216 636-8335

(G-12893)
CLEVELAND CLINIC FOUNDATION
Also Called: Lorain Family Hlth & RES Ctrs
5700 Cooper Foster Park R (44053-4152)
PHONE....................440 988-5651
Floyd D Loop, *Branch Mgr*
EMP: 100

SALES (corp-wide): 8.9B **Privately Held**
SIC: 8093 8062 Specialty outpatient clinics; general medical & surgical hospitals
PA: The Cleveland Clinic Foundation
9500 Euclid Ave
Cleveland OH 44195
216 636-8335

(G-12894)
CLEVELAND CLINIC FOUNDATION
5800 Coper Foster Pk Rd W (44053-4131)
PHONE....................440 204-7800
Mandy White, *Med Doctor*
Blanca Gonzalez, *Manager*
EMP: 85
SALES (corp-wide): 8.9B **Privately Held**
SIC: 6733 Trusts
PA: The Cleveland Clinic Foundation
9500 Euclid Ave
Cleveland OH 44195
216 636-8335

(G-12895)
COMMUNITY HEALTH PARTNERS REGI (HQ)
3700 Kolbe Rd (44053-1611)
PHONE....................440 960-4000
Edwin M Oley, *President*
Cindy Dennison, *CFO*
EMP: 27
SALES: 197.5MM
SALES (corp-wide): 4.7B **Privately Held**
SIC: 8011 Medical centers
PA: Mercy Health
1701 Mercy Health Pl
Cincinnati OH 45237
513 639-2800

(G-12896)
COMMUNITY HEALTH PTNRS REG FOU (HQ)
3700 Kolbe Rd (44053-1611)
PHONE....................440 960-4000
Brian Lockwood, *President*
Heather Nickum, *Principal*
Everett Taylor, *Principal*
EMP: 1520
SALES: 4.4MM
SALES (corp-wide): 4.7B **Privately Held**
SIC: 8062 General medical & surgical hospitals
PA: Mercy Health
1701 Mercy Health Pl
Cincinnati OH 45237
513 639-2800

(G-12897)
COMMUNITY HLTH PTNR REG HLTH S
3700 Kolbe Rd (44053-1611)
PHONE....................440 960-4000
Fax: 440 960-4011
EMP: 2000
SALES: 31.6MM **Privately Held**
SIC: 8062 General Hospital

(G-12898)
COMPREHENSIVE LOGISTICS CO INC
5401 Baumhart Rd (44053-2078)
PHONE....................440 934-0870
Daryl Legg, *Branch Mgr*
EMP: 50 **Privately Held**
SIC: 4225 General warehousing & storage
PA: Comprehensive Logistics, Co., Inc.
4944 Belmont Ave Ste 202
Youngstown OH 44505

(G-12899)
CORNERSTONE MANAGED PRPTS LLC
2147 E 28th St (44055-1932)
PHONE....................440 263-7708
James E Dixon Jr, *Mng Member*
EMP: 30
SALES (est): 2.7MM **Privately Held**
SIC: 6512 Nonresidential building operators

(G-12900)
COUNTY OF LORAIN
Also Called: Loraine Cnty Bd Mntal Rtrdtion
4609 Meister Rd (44053-1530)
PHONE.................................440 282-3074
Amber Fisher, *Superintendent*
EMP: 28 **Privately Held**
WEB: www.lcmhb.org
SIC: 8361 8052 Home for the mentally re-
tarded; intermediate care facilities
PA: County Of Lorain
226 Middle Ave
Elyria OH 44035
440 329-5201

(G-12901)
**EASTER SEALS NOTHERN OHIO
INC**
2173 N Ridge Rd E Ste G (44055-3400)
PHONE.................................440 324-6600
Shiela Dunn, *President*
EMP: 185
SQ FT: 3,000
SALES (est): 2.9MM **Privately Held**
SIC: 8641 Civic associations

(G-12902)
ECHOING HILLS VILLAGE INC
Also Called: Echoing Lake Residential Home
3295 Leavitt Rd (44053-2203)
PHONE.................................440 989-1400
Standford Washington, *Manager*
EMP: 100
SALES (corp-wide): 27MM **Privately
Held**
WEB: www.echoinghillsvillage.org
SIC: 7032 8052 8051 Sporting & recre-
ational camps; intermediate care facilities;
skilled nursing care facilities
PA: Echoing Hills Village, Inc.
36272 County Road 79
Warsaw OH 43844
740 327-2311

(G-12903)
**ELECTRICAL CORP AMERICA
INC**
3807 W Erie Ave (44053-1239)
PHONE.................................440 245-3007
Mark Benco, *Manager*
EMP: 100
SALES (corp-wide): 76.2MM **Privately
Held**
WEB: www.ecahq.com
SIC: 1731 General electrical contractor
PA: Electrical Corporation Of America, Inc.
7320 Arlington Ave
Raytown MO 64133
816 737-3206

(G-12904)
**FIRST FDRAL SAV LN ASSN
LORAIN (PA)**
3721 Oberlin Ave (44053-2761)
PHONE.................................440 282-6188
John Malanski, *President*
Paul Czarney, *Vice Pres*
Cindy Mitchell, *Vice Pres*
Timothy Stursa, *Vice Pres*
Danielle Peffley, *Loan Officer*
EMP: 75
SQ FT: 28,000
SALES: 17MM **Privately Held**
WEB: www.firstfedlorain.com
SIC: 6035 Federal savings & loan associa-
tions

(G-12905)
GOODMAN BEVERAGE CO INC
Also Called: Heidelberg Distributing Lorain
5901 Baumhart Rd (44053-2012)
PHONE.................................440 787-2255
Kenneth H Goodman, *President*
Lawrence Z Goodman, *Vice Pres*
Michael Goodman, *Vice Pres*
Wendy Pickett, *Manager*
▲ EMP: 65
SQ FT: 75,000
SALES (est): 15.7MM **Privately Held**
SIC: 5181 5182 Beer & other fermented
malt liquors; ale; wine

(G-12906)
HEAD QUARTERS INC
Also Called: Head Qaurters Salon & Spa
6071 Middle Ridge Rd (44053-3948)
PHONE.................................440 233-8508
Ronald Bennett, *President*
EMP: 25
SALES (est): 641.6K **Privately Held**
WEB: www.hqoasis.com
SIC: 7231 7241 Beauty shops; barber
shops

(G-12907)
**HOSPICE OF THE WESTERN
RESERVE**
2173 N Ridge Rd E Ste H (44055-3400)
PHONE.................................440 787-2080
Jeff Zink, *Branch Mgr*
EMP: 30
SALES (corp-wide): 89.8MM **Privately
Held**
SIC: 8052 Personal care facility
PA: Hospice Of The Western Reserve, Inc
17876 Saint Clair Ave
Cleveland OH 44110
216 383-2222

(G-12908)
JIFFY PRODUCTS AMERICA INC
5401 Baumhart Rd Ste B (44053-2078)
PHONE.................................440 282-2818
Aarstein Knutson, *Ch of Bd*
Ornulf Sjursen, *Ch of Bd*
Daniel Schrodt, *President*
Stanton A Kessler, *Admin Sec*
◆ EMP: 30
SQ FT: 12,000
SALES (est): 20.9MM **Privately Held**
WEB: www.jiffyproducts.com
SIC: 5191 Farm supplies
HQ: Jiffy International As
Markens Gate 2a
Kristiansand S 4610
381 056-70

(G-12909)
**JPMORGAN CHASE BANK NAT
ASSN**
1882 E 29th St (44055-1806)
PHONE.................................440 277-1038
EMP: 34
SALES (corp-wide): 131.4B **Publicly
Held**
WEB: www.chase.com
SIC: 6029 Commercial banks
HQ: Jpmorgan Chase Bank, National Asso-
ciation
1111 Polaris Pkwy
Columbus OH 43240
614 436-3055

(G-12910)
**KOHLMYER SPORTING GOODS
INC**
Also Called: Kohlmyer Sports
5000 Grove Ave (44055-3659)
PHONE.................................440 277-8296
Mike Molnar, *President*
Richard Boesger, *Vice Pres*
Dale Hoffman, *Vice Pres*
▲ EMP: 40
SQ FT: 13,000
SALES (est): 3.9MM **Privately Held**
WEB: www.kohlmyer.com
SIC: 5941 5091 Sporting goods & bicycle
shops; sporting & recreation goods

(G-12911)
**KOLCZUN & KOLCZUN
ORTHOPEDICS**
Also Called: Cleveland Clinic
5800 Coper Foster Pk Rd W (44053-4134)
PHONE.................................440 985-3113
Michael Kolczun Jr, *President*
Donald Blanford, *Vice Pres*
EMP: 40
SQ FT: 11,000
SALES (corp-wide): 8.9B **Privately Held**
SIC: 8011 Orthopedic physician
PA: The Cleveland Clinic Foundation
9500 Euclid Ave
Cleveland OH 44195
216 636-8335

(G-12912)
LAKELAND GLASS CO (PA)
4994 Grove Ave (44055-3614)
PHONE.................................440 277-4527
Scott Kosman, *President*
EMP: 27
SQ FT: 40,000
SALES (est): 4.4MM **Privately Held**
WEB: www.lorainglass.com
SIC: 1793 Glass & glazing work

(G-12913)
LORAIN CITY SCHOOL DISTRICT
1930 W 19th St (44052-4014)
PHONE.................................440 233-2239
Karen Blazek, *Treasurer*
EMP: 29 **Privately Held**
SIC: 4832 Educational
PA: Lorain City School District
2601 Pole Ave
Lorain OH 44052

(G-12914)
**LORAIN CNTY BYS GIRLS CLB
INC (PA)**
4111 Pearl Ave (44055-2523)
PHONE.................................440 775-2582
Michael Conibear, *President*
EMP: 33 EST: 1997
SALES: 2.2MM **Privately Held**
SIC: 8641 Youth organizations

(G-12915)
**LORAIN CNTY ELDERLY HSING
CORP**
1600 Kansas Ave (44052-3366)
PHONE.................................440 288-1600
Barbara Hoover, *General Mgr*
Clark Hamlin, *CFO*
Homer A Virden, *Exec Dir*
Homer Virden, *Bd of Directors*
EMP: 99
SALES: 1.5MM **Privately Held**
SIC: 8748 Urban planning & consulting
services

(G-12916)
**LORAIN COUNTY ALCOHOL
AND DRUG**
305 W 20th St (44052-3726)
PHONE.................................440 246-0109
Sami Sfeir, *Owner*
EMP: 62
SALES (corp-wide): 7.2MM **Privately
Held**
SIC: 8093 Substance abuse clinics (outpa-
tient)
PA: Lorain County Alcohol And Drug Abuse
Services, Inc
2115 W Park Dr
Lorain OH 44053
440 989-4900

(G-12917)
**LORAIN COUNTY ALCOHOL
AND DRUG (PA)**
Also Called: L C A D A
2115 W Park Dr (44053-1138)
PHONE.................................440 989-4900
Dan Haight, *COO*
Tom Stuber, *Director*
Sharon Asimou, *Admin Asst*
EMP: 25
SQ FT: 6,000
SALES: 7.2MM **Privately Held**
WEB: www.lcada.com
SIC: 8069 8093 Drug addiction rehabilita-
tion hospital; rehabilitation center; outpa-
tient treatment

(G-12918)
**LORAIN COUNTY COMMUNITY
ACTION (PA)**
Also Called: Head Start Program
936 Broadway (44052-1950)
PHONE.................................440 245-2009
Carla Rodriguez, *Opers Mgr*
Chris Haney, *Finance*
Tracie Jackson, *Manager*
Adam Gill, *Technology*
William T Locke, *Exec Dir*
EMP: 25
SQ FT: 19,116

SALES: 9.5MM **Privately Held**
WEB: www.lccaa.net
SIC: 8399 Community action agency

(G-12919)
**LORAIN COUNTY COMMUNITY
ACTION**
Also Called: Lccaa-Hopkins Locke-Head Start
1050 Reid Ave (44052-1962)
PHONE.................................440 246-0480
Shauna Matelski, *Principal*
EMP: 30
SALES (est): 492.1K
SALES (corp-wide): 9.5MM **Privately
Held**
SIC: 8351 Head start center, except in con-
junction with school
PA: Lorain County Community Action
Agency, Inc.
936 Broadway
Lorain OH 44052
440 245-2009

(G-12920)
LORAIN GLASS CO INC
1865 N Ridge Rd E Ste E (44055-3360)
PHONE.................................440 277-6004
Eugene Sofranko, *Ch of Bd*
Kevin Sofranko, *President*
F J Stack, *Principal*
Jack Kosman, *Vice Pres*
Diane Kosman, *Treasurer*
EMP: 55 EST: 1924
SQ FT: 25,000
SALES (est): 7.9MM **Privately Held**
WEB: www.lorainglass.com
SIC: 1793 5231 Glass & glazing work;
glass

(G-12921)
**LORAIN LIFE CARE
AMBULANCE SVC**
109 W 23rd St (44052-4801)
PHONE.................................440 244-6467
Kim Mason, *Branch Mgr*
EMP: 65
SALES (est): 709.7K **Privately Held**
SIC: 4119 Ambulance service

(G-12922)
LORAIN NATIONAL BANK (HQ)
457 Broadway (44052-1769)
PHONE.................................440 244-6000
Dan Klimas, *CEO*
James R Herrick, *Ch of Bd*
James F Kidd, *Vice Ch Bd*
Kevin W Nelson, *COO*
Robert Cox, *Senior VP*
EMP: 125
SQ FT: 50,000
SALES: 55MM **Publicly Held**
SIC: 6021 National trust companies with
deposits, commercial

(G-12923)
LORAIN PARTY CENTER
Also Called: Bill & Don's Catering
5900 S Mayflower Dr (44053-4120)
PHONE.................................440 282-5599
Will Schuster, *Owner*
EMP: 37
SQ FT: 15,000
SALES: 300K **Privately Held**
SIC: 5812 7299 Caterers; banquet hall fa-
cilities

(G-12924)
LOWES HOME CENTERS LLC
7500 Oak Point Rd (44053-4149)
PHONE.................................440 985-5700
Dave Summers, *Branch Mgr*
Jeffrey Crabeels, *Manager*
EMP: 158
SALES (corp-wide): 68.6B **Publicly Held**
SIC: 5211 5031 5722 5064 Home cen-
ters; building materials, exterior; building
materials, interior; household appliance
stores; electrical appliances, television &
radio
HQ: Lowe's Home Centers, Llc
1605 Curtis Bridge Rd
Wilkesboro NC 28697
336 658-4000

▲ = Import ▼=Export
◆ =Import/Export

(G-12925)
LUCAS PLUMBING & HEATING INC
2125 W Park Dr (44053-1195)
PHONE....................................440 282-4567
Frank J Lucas, *President*
Bruce Mc Cartney, *Admin Sec*
EMP: 50
SQ FT: 9,800
SALES (est): 10.2MM **Privately Held**
SIC: 1711 Process piping contractor

(G-12926)
MERCY HEALTH
Also Called: Poison & Toxic Control Center
3700 Kolbe Rd (44053-1611)
PHONE....................................440 233-1000
Ed Oley, *Branch Mgr*
EMP: 4000
SALES (corp-wide): 4.7B **Privately Held**
SIC: 8322 8063 8062 Emergency social
services; psychiatric hospitals; general
medical & surgical hospitals
PA: Mercy Health
1701 Mercy Health Pl
Cincinnati OH 45237
513 639-2800

(G-12927)
MID-OHIO WINES INC
5901 Baumhart Rd (44053-2012)
PHONE....................................440 989-1011
Lawrence Goodman, *President*
Michael Goodman, *Vice Pres*
▲ EMP: 40
SQ FT: 35,000
SALES (est): 8.2MM **Privately Held**
SIC: 5182 Wine; liquor

(G-12928)
MPW INDUSTRIAL SERVICES INC
Also Called: Industrial Cleaning
1930 E 28th St (44055-1907)
PHONE....................................440 277-9072
Tom Webb, *Manager*
EMP: 40
SALES (corp-wide): 208.7MM **Privately Held**
SIC: 7349 Building cleaning service
HQ: Mpw Industrial Services, Inc.
9711 Lancaster Rd
Hebron OH 43025
800 827-8790

(G-12929)
NATIONAL BRONZE MTLS OHIO INC
Also Called: Aviva Metals
5311 W River Rd (44055-3735)
PHONE....................................440 277-1226
Michael Greathead, *President*
Norman M Lazarus, *Exec VP*
Jill Conyer, *Admin Sec*
▲ EMP: 27
SALES (est): 7.8MM **Privately Held**
SIC: 3366 3341 5051 Copper foundries;
secondary nonferrous metals; copper
PA: Metchem Anstalt
Feger Treuunternehmen Reg.
Vaduz
237 454-5

(G-12930)
NEW LIFE HOSPICE INC
Also Called: New Life Hospice Ctr St Joseph
3500 Kolbe Rd (44053-1632)
PHONE....................................440 934-1458
Tanya Anderson, *Manager*
EMP: 30
SALES (corp-wide): 4.7B **Privately Held**
SIC: 8082 8051 Home health care serv-
ices; skilled nursing care facilities
HQ: New Life Hospice Inc
3500 Kolbe Rd
Lorain OH 44053

(G-12931)
NEW LIFE HOSPICE INC (DH)
3500 Kolbe Rd (44053-1632)
PHONE....................................440 934-1458
Jon Hanson, *Director*
EMP: 60
SQ FT: 21,000

SALES (corp-wide): 4.7B **Privately Held**
SIC: 8082 8051 Home health care serv-
ices; skilled nursing care facilities
HQ: Community Health Partners Regional
Foundation
3700 Kolbe Rd
Lorain OH 44053
440 960-4000

(G-12932)
NORCARE ENTERPRISES INC (PA)
Also Called: NORTH CENTER, THE
6140 S Broadway (44053-3821)
PHONE....................................440 233-7232
Amy Denger, *CEO*
Bernadek Stchick, *CFO*
Betsey Kamm, *Director*
EMP: 289
SQ FT: 55,000
SALES (est): 2MM **Privately Held**
SIC: 8093 Mental health clinic, outpatient

(G-12933)
NORD CENTER
6140 S Broadway (44053-3891)
PHONE....................................440 233-7232
Amy Denger, *CEO*
William Richardson, *CFO*
Jane Cornwell, *Payroll Mgr*
Betsey Kamm, *Director*
Michael Rivera, *Maintence Staff*
EMP: 32
SALES: 13.2MM **Privately Held**
SIC: 8093 Mental health clinic, outpatient

(G-12934)
NORD CENTER ASSOCIATES INC (HQ)
Also Called: W.G. Nord Cmnty Mntal Hlth Ctr
6140 S Broadway (44053-3891)
PHONE....................................440 233-7232
Amy Denger, *CEO*
▲ EMP: 235
SQ FT: 46,371
SALES: 12.5MM
SALES (corp-wide): 635K **Privately Held**
SIC: 8093 Mental health clinic, outpatient
PA: Norcare Enterprises, Inc.
6140 S Broadway
Lorain OH 44053
440 233-7232

(G-12935)
NORD CENTER ASSOCIATES INC
Also Called: Nord Rehabilitation Center
3150 Clifton Ave (44055-1553)
PHONE....................................440 233-7232
Amy Denger, *Director*
EMP: 26
SALES (est): 1.4MM
SALES (corp-wide): 635K **Privately Held**
SIC: 8069 Specialty hospitals, except psy-
chiatric
HQ: Nord Center Associates Inc
6140 S Broadway
Lorain OH 44053
440 233-7232

(G-12936)
NORTH OHIO HEART CENTER
Also Called: John W. Schaeffer, M.d
3600 Kolbe Rd Ste 127 (44053-1652)
PHONE....................................440 204-4000
John W Schaeffer MD, *President*
EMP: 55
SQ FT: 2,000
SALES (est): 732.9K **Privately Held**
SIC: 8011 Cardiologist & cardio-vascular
specialist

(G-12937)
NORTH OHIO HEART CENTER INC (PA)
3600 Kolbe Rd Ste 127 (44053-1652)
PHONE....................................440 204-4000
John W Schaeffer, *President*
EMP: 50
SALES (est): 13.5MM **Privately Held**
WEB: www.nohc.com
SIC: 8011 Cardiologist & cardio-vascular
specialist

(G-12938)
PERKINS MOTOR SERVICE LTD (PA)
Also Called: Standard Welding & Lift Truck
1864 E 28th St (44055-1804)
PHONE....................................440 277-1256
Thomas L Shumaker,
EMP: 38
SQ FT: 10,200
SALES (est): 5.4MM **Privately Held**
SIC: 5013 5531 7692 7539 Truck parts &
accessories; automotive supplies & parts;
truck equipment & parts; automotive
parts; automotive welding; radiator repair
shop, automotive; brake repair, automo-
tive; automotive springs, rebuilding & re-
pair; hydraulic equipment repair

(G-12939)
R & J TRUCKING INC
5250 Baumhart Rd (44053-2046)
PHONE....................................440 960-1508
Glenn Parks, *Manager*
EMP: 52 **Privately Held**
WEB: www.rjtrucking.com
SIC: 4212 Dump truck haulage
HQ: R & J Trucking, Inc.
8063 Southern Blvd
Youngstown OH 44512
800 262-9365

(G-12940)
RDF TRUCKING CORPORATION
Also Called: RDF Logistics
7425 Industrial Pkwy Dr (44053-2064)
PHONE....................................440 282-9060
Rosario Boscarello, *President*
Dino Boscarello, *Vice Pres*
EMP: 70
SALES: 23MM **Privately Held**
SIC: 4213 Trucking, except local

(G-12941)
REBMAN RECREATION INC
5300 Oberlin Ave (44053-3438)
PHONE....................................440 282-6761
Richard Rebman, *President*
Mary Rebman, *Vice Pres*
Robert Rebman, *Vice Pres*
Dominic Rebman Jr, *Shareholder*
EMP: 25
SQ FT: 28,000
SALES (est): 743.2K **Privately Held**
SIC: 7933 Ten pin center

(G-12942)
S B S TRANSIT INC
Also Called: First Student
1800 Colorado Ave (44052-3280)
PHONE....................................440 288-2222
Kenneth Van Wagnen, *President*
EMP: 267
SALES (est): 10MM
SALES (corp-wide): 8.9B **Privately Held**
WEB: www.sbstransit.com
SIC: 4151 4142 4493 5551 School
buses; bus charter service, except local;
marinas; boat dealers; marine supplies;
marine supplies & equipment; local bus
charter service
PA: Firstgroup Plc
Exchequer House
Aberdeen AB24
122 465-0100

(G-12943)
SPECIALTY MEDICAL SERVICES
Also Called: Billing Services
221 W 8th St (44052-1817)
PHONE....................................440 245-8010
Walt Blackham, *President*
EMP: 25
SALES (est): 1.4MM **Privately Held**
SIC: 8721 Billing & bookkeeping service

(G-12944)
SPORTSMAN GUN & REEL CLUB INC
44165 Middle Ridge Rd (44053-3915)
PHONE....................................440 233-8287
Robert Sertgent, *President*
EMP: 150
SALES: 75.3K **Privately Held**
SIC: 7997 Gun club, membership

(G-12945)
SPRENGER ENTERPRISES INC
Also Called: Anchor Lodge
3756 W Erie Ave Apt 201 (44053-1291)
PHONE....................................440 244-2019
EMP: 669 **Privately Held**
SIC: 8051 Skilled nursing care facilities
PA: Sprenger Enterprises, Inc.
2198 Gladstone Ct
Glendale Heights IL 60139

(G-12946)
SUPERIOR MEDICAL CARE INC
5172 Leavitt Rd Ste B (44053-2385)
PHONE....................................440 282-7420
John Barb, *President*
Dr George Adams, *Vice Pres*
EMP: 25
SALES (est): 3.3MM **Privately Held**
SIC: 8011 8071 General & family practice,
physician/surgeon; medical laboratories

(G-12947)
TERMINAL READY-MIX INC
524 Colorado Ave (44052-2198)
PHONE....................................440 288-0181
Theresa Pelton, *President*
John Falbo, *Vice Pres*
Russ Rosso, *Plant Mgr*
Pete Falbo, *Treasurer*
Nora Lewis, *Bookkeeper*
▲ EMP: 45 EST: 1954
SQ FT: 1,000
SALES (est): 9.6MM **Privately Held**
WEB: www.falboconstruction.com
SIC: 3273 1611 Ready-mixed concrete;
highway & street paving contractor

(G-12948)
TRADEMARK GLOBAL LLC (HQ)
Also Called: Trademark Games
7951 W Erie Ave (44053-2093)
PHONE....................................440 960-6200
Daniel Sustar, *CEO*
Jim Sustar, *President*
Vince Tuttolomundo, *Business Mgr*
Paul Hervey, *Vice Pres*
Corinne Turner, *Opers Staff*
▲ EMP: 95
SQ FT: 300,000
SALES (est): 50.8MM **Privately Held**
WEB: www.5starwholesale.com
SIC: 5199 General merchandise, non-
durable
PA: Trademark Games Holdings, Llc
7951 W Erie Ave
Lorain OH 44053
440 960-6200

(G-12949)
UNITED STEELWORKERS
Also Called: Uswa
2501 Broadway (44052-4831)
PHONE....................................440 244-1358
Dash Sokol, *Branch Mgr*
EMP: 44
SALES (corp-wide): 4.9MM **Privately Held**
WEB: www.uswa.org
SIC: 8631 7361 Labor union; labor con-
tractors (employment agency)
PA: United Steelworkers
60 Bolevard Of The Allies
Pittsburgh PA 15222
412 562-2400

(G-12950)
VARCO LP
1807 E 28th St (44055-1803)
PHONE....................................440 277-8696
Randy Hamilton, *Branch Mgr*
EMP: 35
SALES (corp-wide): 8.4B **Publicly Held**
WEB: www.tuboscope.com
SIC: 1389 Running, cutting & pulling cas-
ings, tubes & rods
HQ: Varco, L.P.
2835 Holmes Rd
Houston TX 77051
713 799-5272

(G-12951)
VERTIV ENERGY SYSTEMS INC
1510 Kansas Ave (44052-3364)
PHONE....................................440 288-1122

Dennis Del Campo, *Vice Pres*
Dave Smith, *Opers Mgr*
Michael Neeley, *CFO*
Adam White, *Technical Staff*
◆ **EMP:** 800
SALES (est): 1.2MM
SALES (corp-wide): 2.1B **Privately Held**
SIC: 3661 3644 7629 Telephone & telegraph apparatus; noncurrent-carrying wiring services; telecommunication equipment repair (except telephones)
HQ: Vertiv Group Corporation
1050 Dearborn Dr
Columbus OH 43085
614 888-0246

Lore City
Guernsey County

(G-12952)
COUNTRYVIEW ASSISTANT LIVING
62825 County Home Rd (43755-9758)
PHONE..............................740 489-5351
Adrianne Paden, *Financial Exec*
Teresa Yakubik, *Corp Comm Staff*
Adrian Paden, *Director*
EMP: 26
SALES (est): 867.2K **Privately Held**
SIC: 8059 Rest home, with health care

(G-12953)
QES PRESSURE CONTROL LLC
64201 Wintergreen Rd (43755-9704)
PHONE..............................740 489-5721
Charles Jones, *Branch Mgr*
EMP: 25
SALES (corp-wide): 991.3MM **Privately Held**
SIC: 1381 Drilling oil & gas wells
HQ: Qes Pressure Control Llc
4500 Se 59th St
Oklahoma City OK 73135

Loudonville
Ashland County

(G-12954)
C E S CREDIT UNION INC
3030 State Route 3 (44842-9526)
PHONE..............................561 203-5443
Sandy Coffing, *Branch Mgr*
EMP: 25
SALES (corp-wide): 4MM **Privately Held**
SIC: 6062 State credit unions, not federally chartered
PA: C E S Credit Union, Inc.
1215 Yauger Rd
Mount Vernon OH 43050
740 397-1136

(G-12955)
COLONIAL MANOR HEALTH CARE CTR
747 S Mount Vernon Ave (44842-1416)
PHONE..............................419 994-4191
Jack Snowbarger, *President*
Linda Snowbarger, *Treasurer*
Linda O'Brien, *Dietician*
Rachel Cammuse, *Manager*
Connie Durbin, *Nursing Dir*
EMP: 110
SQ FT: 32,000
SALES (est): 5.3MM **Privately Held**
SIC: 8051 Skilled nursing care facilities

(G-12956)
H&H CUSTOM HOMES LLC
16573 State Route 3 (44842-9735)
P.O. Box 409 (44842-0409)
PHONE..............................419 994-4070
Eddie Troyer, *Mng Member*
EMP: 25
SQ FT: 2,000
SALES (est): 161K **Privately Held**
SIC: 1521 New construction, single-family houses

(G-12957)
JAC-LIN MANOR
695 S Mount Vernon Ave (44842-1414)
PHONE..............................419 994-5700
Bert Macqueen, *Director*
Bert McQueen, *Administration*
EMP: 70
SALES (est): 3.6MM **Privately Held**
SIC: 8093 Specialty Outpatient Clinic

(G-12958)
JO LYNN INC
Also Called: Gribble Foods
430 N Jefferson St (44842-1323)
PHONE..............................419 994-3204
Robert Gribble, *President*
Bonnie Gribble, *Vice Pres*
EMP: 75
SALES (est): 6MM **Privately Held**
SIC: 5411 7549 Supermarkets, chain; towing service, automotive

Louisville
Stark County

(G-12959)
ALTERCARE OF LOUISVILLE CENTER
7187 Saint Francis St (44641-9050)
PHONE..............................330 875-4224
Gerald Schroer, *President*
Gary Dubin, *Vice Pres*
Glenn Wickes, *Treasurer*
Kyle Blankenship, *Human Resources*
EMP: 107
SQ FT: 12,000
SALES (est): 4MM **Privately Held**
SIC: 8051 Skilled nursing care facilities

(G-12960)
AULTMAN HEALTH FOUNDATION
1925 Williamsburg Way Ne (44641-8781)
PHONE..............................330 875-6050
EMP: 397
SALES (corp-wide): 1.1MM **Privately Held**
SIC: 8049 Physical therapist
PA: Aultman Health Foundation
2600 6th St Sw
Canton OH 44710
330 452-9911

(G-12961)
CHAPMAN INDUSTRIAL CNSTR INC
3475 Rue Depaul St (44641-9134)
P.O. Box 356, Dover (44622-0356)
PHONE..............................330 343-1632
Michael Chapman, *President*
EMP: 80
SALES (est): 9.6MM **Privately Held**
SIC: 1541 Industrial buildings, new construction

(G-12962)
CITY OF LOUISVILLE (PA)
215 S Mill St (44641-1665)
PHONE..............................330 875-3321
Cynthia Kerchner, *Mayor*
Thomas Ault, *City Mgr*
EMP: 35 **EST:** 1834
SQ FT: 50,000 **Privately Held**
WEB: www.louisvilleohio.org
SIC: 9111 8611 City & town managers' offices; ; business associations

(G-12963)
CONCORDE THERAPY GROUP INC
513 E Main St (44641-1421)
PHONE..............................330 493-4210
Morgan Aster, *Branch Mgr*
EMP: 30
SALES (est): 402.7K **Privately Held**
SIC: 8049 Physiotherapist
PA: Concorde Therapy Group Inc
4645 Belpar St Nw
Canton OH 44718

(G-12964)
COON CAULKING & SEALANTS INC
Also Called: Coon Caulking & Restoration
7349 Ravenna Ave (44641-9788)
P.O. Box 259 (44641-0259)
PHONE..............................330 875-2100
Stephen Coon, *President*
Joseph Kreinbrink, *Vice Pres*
Carolyn M Buckridge, *Treasurer*
Jennifer Coon, *Admin Sec*
EMP: 60
SQ FT: 50,000
SALES (est): 8.7MM **Privately Held**
WEB: www.coonrestoration.com
SIC: 1799 Caulking (construction); waterproofing

(G-12965)
DISABLED AMERICAN VETERANS
128 Indiana Ave (44641-1102)
PHONE..............................330 875-5795
Denise Proffitt, *Treasurer*
EMP: 34
SALES (corp-wide): 137MM **Privately Held**
SIC: 8641 Veterans' organization
PA: Disabled American Veterans
3725 Alexandria Pike
Cold Spring KY 41076
859 441-7300

(G-12966)
ENVIROSCAPES
7727 Paris Ave (44641-9598)
PHONE..............................330 875-0768
Todd Pugh, *President*
Dave Lint, *Opers Staff*
Denise Bergert, *Human Resources*
Rhonda Patrick, *Sales Staff*
Matt Courtney, *Branch Mgr*
EMP: 50
SALES (est): 3.2MM **Privately Held**
SIC: 0782 Lawn care services; landscape contractors

(G-12967)
ESLICH WRECKING COMPANY
3525 Broadway Ave (44641-8902)
PHONE..............................330 488-8300
Richard Eslich, *CEO*
John Eslich, *President*
Elizabeth Eslich, *Admin Sec*
EMP: 50
SQ FT: 30,000
SALES (est): 7.8MM **Privately Held**
WEB: www.eslichwrecking.com
SIC: 1795 1794 Demolition, buildings & other structures; excavation work

(G-12968)
LOUISVILLE FRTERNAL ORDER OF E
306 W Main St (44641-1230)
PHONE..............................330 875-2113
David Fischer, *Admin Sec*
EMP: 27
SQ FT: 30,000
SALES (est): 568.3K **Privately Held**
SIC: 8641 5812 5813 Fraternal associations; restaurant, family: independent; bar (drinking places)

(G-12969)
O D MILLER ELECTRIC CO INC
1115 W Main St (44641-1109)
PHONE..............................330 875-1651
Robert Ickes, *President*
Dale Miller, *President*
Don Miller, *Vice Pres*
EMP: 28
SQ FT: 10,000
SALES (est): 3.4MM **Privately Held**
SIC: 1731 Electrical work

(G-12970)
OAKHILL MANOR CARE CENTER
4466 Lynnhaven Ave (44641-9513)
PHONE..............................330 875-5060
Ana Schaefer, *President*
EMP: 120
SALES (est): 5.1MM **Privately Held**
SIC: 8051 Skilled nursing care facilities

(G-12971)
PROGRESSIVE GREEN MEADOWS LLC
Also Called: Green Madows Hlth Wellness Ctr
7770 Columbus Rd (44641-9773)
PHONE..............................330 875-1456
Julie Esack, *Mng Member*
Julie Esackn, *Mng Member*
EMP: 180
SALES (est): 6.6MM **Privately Held**
WEB: www.progressivequalitycare.com
SIC: 8051 Convalescent home with continuous nursing care

(G-12972)
PROGRESSIVE QUALITY CARE INC
7770 Columbus Rd (44641-9773)
PHONE..............................330 875-7866
Daniel Shiller, *Branch Mgr*
EMP: 870
SALES (corp-wide): 64.7MM **Privately Held**
SIC: 7389 Personal service agents, brokers & bureaus
PA: Progressive Quality Care Inc
5553 Broadview Rd
Parma OH 44134
216 661-6800

(G-12973)
ROMAN CTHLIC DOCESE YOUNGSTOWN
Also Called: St Joseph Care Center
2308 Reno Dr (44641-9083)
PHONE..............................330 875-5562
John Banks, *Superintendent*
Leigh Nutial, *Office Mgr*
Nicole Cooper, *Director*
EMP: 160
SALES (corp-wide): 23.6MM **Privately Held**
WEB: www.stjosephmantua.com
SIC: 8361 8052 8051 Rest home, with health care incidental; intermediate care facilities; skilled nursing care facilities
PA: Roman Catholic Diocese Of Youngstown
144 W Wood St
Youngstown OH 44503
330 744-8451

(G-12974)
TODDS ENVIROSCAPES INC
7727 Paris Ave (44641-9598)
PHONE..............................330 875-0768
Todd E Pugh, *President*
John McBride, *Branch Mgr*
Bill McCroskeyr, *Manager*
Dustin Grigsby, *Supervisor*
EMP: 38 **EST:** 1987
SALES (est): 10.2MM **Privately Held**
WEB: www.enviroscapesgroup.com
SIC: 0782 Landscape contractors

(G-12975)
Y M C A CENTRAL STARK COUNTY
Also Called: Louisville YMCA
1421 S Nickelplate St (44641-2647)
PHONE..............................330 875-1611
Donna Kuehner, *Director*
EMP: 50
SALES (corp-wide): 16.5MM **Privately Held**
WEB: www.ymcastark.org
SIC: 8641 7991 8351 7032 Youth organizations; physical fitness facilities; child day care services; youth camps; individual & family services
PA: Y M C A Of Central Stark County
1201 30th St Nw Ste 200a
Canton OH 44709
330 491-9622

Loveland
Clermont County

(G-12976)
**ADVANCED GERIATRIC
EDUCATION &**
9823 Tulip Tree Ct (45140-5597)
PHONE..............................888 393-9799
Phyllis Atkinson,
EMP: 40
SALES (est): 690.9K
SALES (corp-wide): 13.8MM Privately
Held
SIC: 8361 Geriatric residential care
PA: Black Stone Of Cincinnati, Llc
4700 E Galbraith Rd Fl 3
Cincinnati OH 45236
513 924-1370

(G-12977)
AMS CONSTRUCTION INC (PA)
10670 Loveland Madeira Rd (45140-8964)
P.O. Box 42068, Cincinnati (45242-0068)
PHONE..............................513 794-0410
John K Stephenson, President
Brenda Stephenson, President
Karen Stephenson, Vice Pres
George Meyer, Sales Executive
EMP: 38
SALES (est): 24.4MM Privately Held
SIC: 1731 Electrical work

(G-12978)
AQUARIAN POOLS INC
631 Lveland Miamiville Rd (45140-6932)
PHONE..............................513 576-9771
Michael Iori, President
Linda Iori, Corp Secy
Becky Satutt, Manager
EMP: 25
SQ FT: 2,000
SALES (est): 3.6MM Privately Held
WEB: www.aquarianpools.com
SIC: 1799 Swimming pool construction

(G-12979)
BOY-KO MANAGEMENT INC
Also Called: Lodge Nursing & Rehab Center
9370 Union Cemetery Rd (45140-9577)
PHONE..............................513 677-4900
Richard J Friedmann, Vice Pres
Richard Friedmann, CFO
EMP: 50
SALES (est): 367.5K Privately Held
SIC: 8059 Convalescent home

(G-12980)
CANDO PHARMACEUTICAL
100 Commerce Dr (45140-7726)
PHONE..............................513 354-2694
Dennis Smith, Owner
EMP: 25
SALES (est): 663.1K
SALES (corp-wide): 10.4MM Privately
Held
WEB: www.mastersinhealthcare.com
SIC: 5047 Medical equipment & supplies
PA: Mhc Medical Products, Llc
8695 Seward Rd
Fairfield OH 45011
877 358-4342

(G-12981)
**CARESPRING HEALTH CARE
MGT LLC (PA)**
390 Wards Corner Rd (45140-6969)
PHONE..............................513 943-4000
Chris Chirumbolo, CEO
Debbie Berling, Vice Pres
Cathy Hamblen, Vice Pres
Kimberly Majick, Vice Pres
John Muller, Vice Pres
EMP: 40
SALES (est): 74.2MM Privately Held
SIC: 8741 8099 Hospital management;
nursing & personal care facility manage-
ment; blood related health services

(G-12982)
CINCINNATI DENTAL SERVICES
8944 Columbia Rd Ste 300 (45140-1173)
PHONE..............................513 774-8800
Fred White V, Officer

EMP: 45
SALES (corp-wide): 5.5MM Privately
Held
SIC: 8021 Dentists' office
PA: Cincinnati Dental Services Inc
121 E Mcmillan St
Cincinnati OH 45219
513 721-8888

(G-12983)
CINCINNATI VOICE AND DATA
136 Commerce Dr (45140-7726)
PHONE..............................513 683-4127
Jeffrey Black, President
Holly Black, Admin Sec
EMP: 100
SALES (est): 2.4MM Privately Held
SIC: 4899 7378 5065 1731 Communica-
tion signal enhancement network system;
computer maintenance & repair; elec-
tronic parts & equipment; electrical work

(G-12984)
COLLINS SALON INC
12125 N Lebanon Rd (45140-1824)
PHONE..............................513 683-1700
Donna Collins, Owner
EMP: 30
SALES (est): 584.3K Privately Held
WEB: www.collinssalons.com
SIC: 7231 Unisex hair salons

(G-12985)
**CRAPSEY & GILLIS
CONTRACTORS**
8887 Glendale Milford Rd (45140-8906)
PHONE..............................513 891-6333
Robert S Crapsey, President
Chris Gilles, Vice Pres
Christopher Gillis, Vice Pres
Tony Accurso, Project Mgr
James Nutter, Project Mgr
EMP: 35
SQ FT: 3,000
SALES (est): 4.3MM Privately Held
WEB: www.crapseyandgilles.com
SIC: 1521 1542 New construction, single-
family houses; commercial & office build-
ing, new construction

(G-12986)
CREEKSIDE LTD LLC
Also Called: Oasis Golf Club
902 Lveland Miamiville Rd (45140-6952)
PHONE..............................513 583-4977
Lew Rosenbloom, General Mgr
EMP: 70
SALES (est): 2.2MM Privately Held
SIC: 7992 Public golf courses
PA: Creekside, Ltd, Llc
1250 Springfield Pike # 400
Cincinnati OH 45215

(G-12987)
**CUSTOM CHEMICAL
SOLUTIONS**
167 Commerce Dr (45140-7727)
PHONE..............................800 291-1057
EMP: 45
SALES (est): 1.3MM Privately Held
SIC: 5169 Industrial chemicals

(G-12988)
**DANIEL MAURY
CONSTRUCTION CO**
8960 Glendale Milford Rd (45140-8908)
PHONE..............................513 984-4096
Joseph Bitzer, President
Maxine Bitzer, Vice Pres
EMP: 50 EST: 1951
SQ FT: 15,000
SALES (est): 1.8MM Privately Held
SIC: 6512 Commercial & industrial building
operation

(G-12989)
DECORATIVE PAVING COMPANY
39 Glendale Milford Rd (45140-8848)
PHONE..............................513 576-1222
Kevin Piers, President
EMP: 30
SALES (est): 6.5MM Privately Held
SIC: 1611 Highway & street paving con-
tractor; surfacing & paving

(G-12990)
**DEERFIELD CONSTRUCTION CO
INC (PA)**
8960 Glendale Milford Rd (45140-8900)
PHONE..............................513 984-4096
Joseph Bitzer, CEO
Steve Bitzer, President
Scott Bitzer, Vice Pres
John Stewart, CFO
Maxine Bitzer, Treasurer
EMP: 36
SQ FT: 15,000
SALES (est): 22.5MM Privately Held
WEB: www.deerfieldconstruction.com
SIC: 1542 1541 Commercial & office build-
ing, new construction; commercial & of-
fice buildings, renovation & repair;
restaurant construction; shopping center
construction; industrial buildings & ware-
houses; warehouse construction; renova-
tion, remodeling & repairs: industrial
buildings

(G-12991)
DILL-ELAM INC
Also Called: City Service
1461 State Route 28 (45140-8778)
PHONE..............................513 575-0017
Gary Dill, President
Steve Elam, Vice Pres
EMP: 48
SALES (est): 11.2MM Privately Held
SIC: 4213 4212 Trucking, except local;
local trucking, without storage

(G-12992)
**ELITE AMBULANCE SERVICE
LLC**
1451 State Route 28 Ste B (45140-8442)
PHONE..............................888 222-1356
Jeremy Woodward, Principal
Dillon Jacobs, Manager
Jeremy L Woodward,
EMP: 25
SALES (est): 438.9K Privately Held
SIC: 4119 Ambulance service

(G-12993)
EPIQ SYSTEMS INC
Also Called: Garretson Resolution Group
6281 Tri Ridge Blvd # 300 (45140-8345)
PHONE..............................513 794-0400
EMP: 200
SALES (corp-wide): 589.6MM Privately
Held
SIC: 8111 Bankruptcy law; debt collection
law; taxation law; corporate, partnership &
business law
HQ: Epiq Systems, Inc.
2 Ravinia Dr Ste 850
Atlanta GA 30346
913 621-9500

(G-12994)
**FISCHER PUMP & VALVE
COMPANY (PA)**
Also Called: Fischer Process Industries
155 Commerce Dr (45140-7727)
PHONE..............................513 583-4800
Ken Fischer, President
Ray Didonato, Vice Pres
▲ EMP: 38
SQ FT: 18,000
SALES (est): 33.1MM Privately Held
SIC: 5085 5084 Pistons & valves; pumps
& pumping equipment

(G-12995)
**GARRETYSON FRM
RESOLUTION GRP**
6281 Tri Ridge Blvd # 300 (45140-8345)
PHONE..............................513 794-0400
Shawn Kocher, CEO
Thomas Bagley,
David Johnston,
John Starcevich,
EMP: 180
SALES (est): 11.5MM Privately Held
SIC: 8742 Management consulting serv-
ices

(G-12996)
GL NAUSE CO INC
1971 Phoenix Dr (45140-9241)
PHONE..............................513 722-9500

Gregory L Nause, President
Jodie K Nause, Admin Sec
Jodie Nause, Admin Sec
EMP: 25
SQ FT: 30,000
SALES (est): 5.2MM Privately Held
WEB: www.glnause.com
SIC: 3441 3443 1791 7699 Building com-
ponents, structural steel; fabricated plate
work (boiler shop); structural steel erec-
tion; industrial equipment services; indus-
trial machinery & equipment repair;
architectural metalwork; sheet metalwork

(G-12997)
GODDARD SCHOOL
782 Lveland Miamiville Rd (45140-6933)
PHONE..............................513 697-9663
Sandy Joseph, Owner
EMP: 25
SALES (est): 491.5K Privately Held
SIC: 8351 Preschool center

(G-12998)
**HEARTLAND PAYMENT
SYSTEMS LLC**
3455 Steeplechase Ln (45140-3280)
PHONE..............................513 518-6125
EMP: 99
SALES (corp-wide): 3.3B Publicly Held
SIC: 7389 Credit card service
HQ: Heartland Payment Systems, Llc
10 Glenlake Pkwy Ste 324
Atlanta GA 30328
609 683-3831

(G-12999)
**HICKORY WOODS GOLF
COURSE INC**
1240 Hickory Woods Dr (45140-9488)
PHONE..............................513 575-3900
Dennis Acomb, President
EMP: 40
SALES (est): 1.6MM Privately Held
WEB: www.hickorywoods.com
SIC: 7992 Public golf courses

(G-13000)
I T E LLC
424 Wards Corner Rd # 300 (45140-6967)
PHONE..............................513 576-6200
Martha Mc Clain, Personnel Exec
George S Carper,
Daniel Lehr,
EMP: 60
SQ FT: 9,660
SALES (est): 9.2MM Privately Held
WEB: www.ite.com
SIC: 8711 8742 8732 Electrical or elec-
tronic engineering; management consult-
ing services; commercial nonphysical
research

(G-13001)
INTERNATIONAL PAPER COMPA
6283 Tri Ridge Blvd (45140-8318)
P.O. Box 62717, Cincinnati (45262-0717)
PHONE..............................513 248-6000
Michael Schumpp, Manager
EMP: 67
SALES (est): 17.7MM Privately Held
SIC: 8111 General practice attorney,
lawyer

(G-13002)
J DANIEL & COMPANY INC
1975 Phoenix Dr (45140-9241)
PHONE..............................513 575-3100
Price Jackson, President
John Tuerck, Safety Mgr
Robert Kearns, Treasurer
EMP: 90
SALES (est): 16.4MM
SALES (corp-wide): 208.3MM Privately
Held
WEB: www.jdanielco.com
SIC: 1623 Underground utilities contractor
PA: Danella Companies, Inc.
2290 Butler Pike
Plymouth Meeting PA 19462
610 828-6200

(G-13003)
J K MEURER CORP
33 Glendale Milford Rd (45140-8848)
PHONE..............................513 831-7500

GEOGRAPHIC

Jeffrey K Meurer, *President*
Mitch Meurer, *Vice Pres*
Kain Meurer, *Project Mgr*
Chad Miller, *Marketing Staff*
Mitchell Meurer, *Admin Sec*
EMP: 45
SQ FT: 3,500
SALES: 13.4MM **Privately Held**
SIC: 1611 Highway & street paving contractor

(G-13004)
KROSS ACQUISITION COMPANY LLC
10690 Loveland Madeira Rd (45140-8964)
PHONE................................513 554-0555
Robert D Miles,
EMP: 30
SALES (est): 4.5MM **Privately Held**
SIC: 8741 Business management

(G-13005)
L & I CUSTOM WALLS INC
10369 Cones Rd (45140-7211)
PHONE................................513 683-2045
Alvin Walker, *President*
Marjorie Walker, *Corp Secy*
Jack Walker, *Vice Pres*
EMP: 50
SQ FT: 1,200
SALES (est): 3.1MM **Privately Held**
SIC: 1771 Concrete work

(G-13006)
LIFE ENRICHING COMMUNITIES (PA)
6279 Tri Ridge Blvd # 320 (45140-8320)
PHONE................................513 719-3510
Jim Bowersox, *CFO*
Connie Kingsbury, *VP Mktg*
Diamond Crumpton-Scott, *Mktg Coord*
Nancy Hartman, *Manager*
Scott Jividen, *Manager*
EMP: 30
SALES: 50.7MM **Privately Held**
SIC: 8361 Home for the aged

(G-13007)
LODGE CARE CENTER INC
9370 Union Cemetery Rd (45140-9577)
PHONE................................513 683-9966
Barry A Kohn, *President*
Sam Boymel, *Vice Pres*
Amanda Plavsic, *Manager*
EMP: 164
SALES (est): 9.9MM **Privately Held**
WEB: www.lodgecarecenter.com
SIC: 8051 Convalescent home with continuous nursing care

(G-13008)
LOVELAND HEALTH CARE CENTER
501 N 2nd St (45140-6667)
PHONE................................513 605-6000
Steve Boymel, *President*
Tamara Bell, *Accountant*
Nicole Breving, *Human Res Dir*
Emmanuel Rivera, *Director*
Darci Schirmer, *Director*
EMP: 110 **EST:** 1979
SQ FT: 20,000
SALES (est): 6.4MM **Privately Held**
SIC: 8051 Convalescent home with continuous nursing care
PA: Central Accounting Systems
　　12500 Reed Hartman Hwy
　　Cincinnati OH 45241

(G-13009)
LOWRY CONTROLS INC
273 E Kemper Rd (45140-8627)
PHONE................................513 583-0182
Kelly Barry, *President*
Kelly Lowry, *President*
EMP: 27
SALES (est): 2.9MM **Privately Held**
WEB: www.lowrycontrols.com
SIC: 1731 General electrical contractor

(G-13010)
MARSH & MCLENNAN AGENCY LLC
6279 Tri Ridge Blvd # 400 (45140-8320)
PHONE................................513 248-4888

Chris Schwarz, *Accounts Exec*
Dave Eveleigh, *Sales Staff*
Debbie Joffe, *Marketing Staff*
Vicky Tuten, *Branch Mgr*
Bill Clasen, *Agent*
EMP: 27
SALES (corp-wide): 14.9B **Publicly Held**
SIC: 6411 Insurance brokers
HQ: Marsh & Mclennan Agency Llc
　　360 Hamilton Ave Ste 930
　　White Plains NY 10601

(G-13011)
MARSHALL & ASSOCIATES INC
1537 Durango Dr (45140-2129)
P.O. Box 498428, Cincinnati (45249-7428)
PHONE................................513 683-6396
Ronald Marshall, *President*
Betty Marshall, *Corp Secy*
Linda Hunter, *Vice Pres*
EMP: 28
SALES (est): 674K **Privately Held**
SIC: 7381 8111 Detective agency; security guard service; legal services

(G-13012)
MCCORMICK EQUIPMENT CO INC (PA)
112 Northeast Dr (45140-7144)
PHONE................................513 677-8888
R Peter Kimener, *President*
Bruce A Buckley, *CFO*
Dave Poissant, *VP Sales*
Anne Berigan, *Sales Staff*
Gary Murphy, *Sales Staff*
EMP: 33
SQ FT: 30,000
SALES (est): 41.5MM **Privately Held**
WEB: www.mccequip.com
SIC: 5084 Materials handling machinery

(G-13013)
MIKES CARWASH INC (PA)
100 Northeast Dr (45140-7144)
PHONE................................513 677-4700
Mike Dahm, *President*
Andrew Dowden, *COO*
Greg Reis, *Exec VP*
EMP: 250
SALES (est): 28.6MM **Privately Held**
SIC: 7542 Washing & polishing, automotive

(G-13014)
MMIC INC
6867 Obannon Blf (45140-6018)
PHONE................................513 697-0445
Beth McDonald, *President*
EMP: 75
SALES (est): 1.3MM **Privately Held**
SIC: 7699 Industrial machinery & equipment repair

(G-13015)
NESTLE USA INC
6279 Tri Ridge Blvd # 100 (45140-8396)
PHONE................................513 576-4930
Teresa Donley, *Branch Mgr*
EMP: 25
SALES (corp-wide): 90.8B **Privately Held**
WEB: www.nestleusa.com
SIC: 2064 5141 Candy & other confectionery products; groceries, general line
HQ: Nestle Usa, Inc.
　　1812 N Moore St
　　Rosslyn VA 22209
　　818 549-6000

(G-13016)
NURTUR HOLDINGS LLC (PA)
6279 Tri Ridge Blvd # 250 (45140-8301)
PHONE................................614 487-3033
Jefferson Dooley, *Manager*
Christopher Deluca,
EMP: 33
SALES (est): 4.5MM **Privately Held**
SIC: 7231 Cosmetology school

(G-13017)
NURTUR HOLDINGS LLC
6281 Try Rdge Blvd Ste 14 (45140)
PHONE................................513 576-9333
Patrick Thompson,
EMP: 150

SALES: 16MM **Privately Held**
SIC: 7231 Cosmetology school; cosmetology & personal hygiene salons

(G-13018)
OASIS TURF & TREE INC
8900 Glendl Milford Rd A4 (45140-8959)
PHONE................................513 697-9090
Robert A Reindl, *President*
Angela Reindl, *Vice Pres*
EMP: 25
SQ FT: 4,000
SALES (est): 3.5MM **Privately Held**
SIC: 0781 Landscape services

(G-13019)
OBANNON CREEK GOLF CLUB
6842 Oakland Rd (45140-9723)
PHONE................................513 683-5657
Marianne Fahms, *General Mgr*
EMP: 40
SQ FT: 17,000
SALES: 1.7MM **Privately Held**
SIC: 7997 5941 5813 5812 Golf club, membership; golf goods & equipment; bar (drinking places); grills (eating places)

(G-13020)
PARAMOUNT LAWN SERVICE INC
8900 Glendale Milford Rd A1 (45140-8959)
PHONE................................513 984-5200
Joseph Tekulve, *President*
Dennis Eppert, *Opers Mgr*
Sandra Dixon, *Office Mgr*
EMP: 25
SQ FT: 3,750
SALES: 2MM **Privately Held**
WEB: www.paramountlandscaping.com
SIC: 0782 4959 Landscape contractors; lawn services; snowplowing

(G-13021)
PRICE WOODS PRODUCTS INC
6507 Snider Rd (45140-9588)
PHONE................................513 722-1200
Dallas W Price, *Owner*
Theresa Price, *Vice Pres*
▼ **EMP:** 25
SALES: 3.3MM **Privately Held**
SIC: 5031 Lumber: rough, dressed & finished; veneer

(G-13022)
PROFESSIONAL TRANSIT MGT (PA)
Also Called: Professional Fleet Management
6405 Brch Hll Gna Pg 20 (45140)
PHONE................................513 677-6000
Michael Setzer, *Partner*
Thomas P Hock, *Partner*
Tom Hock, *Vice Pres*
EMP: 30
SQ FT: 950
SALES (est): 2MM **Privately Held**
WEB: www.ptmltd.com
SIC: 8741 7539 Management services; automotive repair shops

(G-13023)
RAPID PLUMBING INC
1407 State Route 28 (45140-8777)
PHONE................................513 575-1509
Walter D Minton, *President*
Ronald Minton, *Corp Secy*
EMP: 65
SQ FT: 4,500
SALES (est): 5.6MM **Privately Held**
WEB: www.rapidplumbing.net
SIC: 1711 Plumbing contractors

(G-13024)
RECREATIONAL GOLF INC
Also Called: Eastgate Advntres Golf G-Karts
203 Glen Lake Rd (45140-2603)
PHONE................................513 677-0347
Timothy C Jones, *President*
Mary Ellen Hofmann, *Corp Secy*
J Thomas Jones, *Vice Pres*
EMP: 25
SQ FT: 5,400
SALES (est): 506.9K **Privately Held**
SIC: 7999 Miniature golf course operation; go-cart raceway operation & rentals

(G-13025)
RVET OPERATING LLC
Also Called: Recruitmilitary
422 W Loveland Ave (45140-2322)
PHONE................................513 683-5020
Tim Best, *CEO*
Larry Slagel, *COO*
Robert Arndt, *Vice Pres*
Jennifer Hines, *Vice Pres*
Rick Jones, *Vice Pres*
EMP: 43
SALES (est): 924.6K
SALES (corp-wide): 13MM **Privately Held**
SIC: 7361 7389 Executive placement; advertising, promotional & trade show services; subscription fulfillment services: magazine, newspaper, etc.
PA: Bradley-Morris Holdings, Llc
　　1825 Barrett Lakes Blvd N
　　Kennesaw GA 30144
　　678 819-4171

(G-13026)
SEM VILLA INC
Also Called: SEM VILLA RETIREMENT COMMUNITY
6409 Small House Cir (45140-7524)
PHONE................................513 831-3262
Julie Foley, *Director*
Rosanna Stephenson, *Food Svc Dir*
EMP: 25
SQ FT: 400,000
SALES: 1.7MM **Privately Held**
SIC: 8361 Home for the aged

(G-13027)
SHAWCOR PIPE PROTECTION LLC
Also Called: Dsg Canusa
173 Commerce Dr (45140-7727)
P.O. Box 498830, Cincinnati (45249-8830)
PHONE................................513 683-7800
Jim Huntebrinker, *Branch Mgr*
EMP: 25
SALES (corp-wide): 1.6B **Privately Held**
WEB: www.bredero-shaw.com
SIC: 5084 Industrial machinery & equipment
HQ: Shawcor Pipe Protection Llc
　　3838 N Sam Houston Pkwy E # 300
　　Houston TX 77032

(G-13028)
SHAWNEESPRING HLTH CRE CNTR RL
390 Wards Corner Rd (45140-6969)
PHONE................................513 943-4000
Barry Bortz, *Principal*
EMP: 288
SALES (est): 171.1K
SALES (corp-wide): 74.2MM **Privately Held**
SIC: 8011 Offices & clinics of medical doctors
HQ: Shawneespring Health Care Center
　　10111 Simonson Rd
　　Harrison OH 45030
　　513 367-7780

(G-13029)
SMITH & ENGLISH II INC
12191 State Route 22 3 (45140-9355)
P.O. Box 750968, Dayton (45475-0968)
PHONE................................513 697-9300
John R Gierl, *Principal*
EMP: 45
SALES (est): 2.8MM **Privately Held**
SIC: 8748 8742 Business consulting; business consultant

(G-13030)
SOTTILE & BARILE LLC
394 Wards Corner Rd # 180 (45140-8339)
PHONE................................513 345-0592
Tony Sottile, *President*
EMP: 30
SALES: 3MM **Privately Held**
SIC: 8111 Legal services

(G-13031)
TALEMED LLC
6279 Tri Ridge Blvd # 110 (45140-8320)
PHONE................................513 774-7300
Randy Baker, *General Mgr*

▲ = Import ▼=Export
◆ =Import/Export

Libby Tracy,
EMP: 260
SALES (est): 12.5MM **Privately Held**
SIC: 7361 Nurses' registry

(G-13032)
WASHING SYSTEMS LLC (HQ)
167 Commerce Dr (45140-7727)
PHONE..................800 272-1974
John Walroth, *CEO*
Jonathan C Dill, *CFO*
▼ **EMP:** 110
SALES (est): 90MM
SALES (corp-wide): 13.4B **Privately Held**
WEB: www.washingsystems.com
SIC: 5169 2841 Detergents; industrial
chemicals; soap & other detergents
PA: Kao Corporation
1-14-10, Nihombashikayabacho
Chuo-Ku TKY 103-0
336 607-111

(G-13033)
**WEST SHELL GALE
SCHNETZER**
748 Wards Corner Rd (45140-8740)
PHONE..................513 683-3833
Gale Schnetzer, *Partner*
EMP: 50 EST: 1999
SALES (est): 1.2MM **Privately Held**
SIC: 6531 Real estate brokers & agents

(G-13034)
**WESTERN & SOUTHERN LF
INSUR CO**
6281 Tri Ridge Blvd # 310 (45140-8345)
PHONE..................513 891-0777
Robert Dennison, *Investment Ofcr*
Lawrence Sowders, *Manager*
EMP: 30
SQ FT: 6,473 **Privately Held**
SIC: 6411 Life insurance agents
HQ: The Western & Southern Life Insur-
ance Company
400 Broadway St
Cincinnati OH 45202
513 629-1800

(G-13035)
WILMARED INC
Also Called: Kinker Eveleigh Insurance
6279 Tri Ridge Blvd (45140-8396)
PHONE..................513 891-6615
Sam Tuten, *President*
George Seurkamp, *Vice Pres*
Vicky Tuten, *Treasurer*
EMP: 32
SQ FT: 4,100
SALES (est): 5.5MM **Privately Held**
WEB: www.ekinker.com
SIC: 6411 Insurance Agent/Broker

Lowell
Washington County

(G-13036)
BURKHART EXCAVATING INC
9950 State Route 60 (45744-7577)
PHONE..................740 896-3312
EMP: 35
SALES (est): 1.3MM **Privately Held**
SIC: 1794 Excavation Contractor

(G-13037)
BURKHART TRUCKING INC
Also Called: Burkhart Trucking & Excavating
9950 State Route 60 (45744-7577)
PHONE..................740 896-2244
William H Burkhart III, *President*
Bradley S Mason, *Treasurer*
EMP: 30
SQ FT: 3,200
SALES: 2.5MM **Privately Held**
SIC: 4212 1521 Dump truck haulage; coal
haulage, local; single-family housing con-
struction

(G-13038)
**MARIETTA TRANSFER
COMPANY**
Also Called: Mills Transfer
11569 State Route 60 (45744)
PHONE..................740 896-3565

Gene Davis, *President*
Dennis Davis, *Vice Pres*
EMP: 40
SALES (est): 1.1MM **Privately Held**
SIC: 4789 Transportation services

Lowellville
Mahoning County

(G-13039)
**BROWNING-FERRIS INDS OF
OHIO**
Site L08
8100 S State Line Rd (44436-9596)
PHONE..................330 536-8013
Mike Heher, *Manager*
EMP: 60
SALES (corp-wide): 10B **Publicly Held**
SIC: 4953 Sanitary landfill operation
HQ: Browning-Ferris Industries Of Ohio Inc
3870 Hendricks Rd
Youngstown OH 44515
330 793-7676

(G-13040)
ENERTECH ELECTRICAL INC
101 Yngstown Lwllville Rd (44436-1010)
PHONE..................330 536-2131
Gregory T Haren, *CEO*
John Donofrio Jr, *President*
John A Wilaj, *Vice Pres*
James Burgy, *Purch Mgr*
Ernie Yacovone, *Engineer*
▲ **EMP:** 30
SQ FT: 8,000
SALES (est): 6.7MM **Privately Held**
WEB: www.enertechelectrical.com
SIC: 1731 General electrical contractor

(G-13041)
M & M WINE CELLAR INC
Also Called: L'U Vabella
259 Bedford Rd (44436-9547)
PHONE..................330 536-6450
Frank Sergi, *President*
EMP: 30
SALES: 2MM **Privately Held**
SIC: 5499 5149 5182 Juices, fruit or veg-
etable; juices; wine

(G-13042)
REPUBLIC SERVICES INC
8100 S State Line Rd (44436-9596)
PHONE..................330 536-8013
Pete Stear, *Opers Mgr*
Mike Heher, *Branch Mgr*
EMP: 34
SALES (corp-wide): 10B **Publicly Held**
SIC: 4953 Refuse collection & disposal
services
PA: Republic Services, Inc.
18500 N Allied Way # 100
Phoenix AZ 85054
480 627-2700

(G-13043)
S E T INC
235 E Water St Ste C (44436-1273)
PHONE..................330 536-6724
Douglas Susany, *President*
Greg Susany, *Project Mgr*
EMP: 50
SQ FT: 3,500
SALES: 17MM **Privately Held**
WEB: www.setinc.com
SIC: 1794 Excavation work

(G-13044)
VIMAS PAINTING COMPANY INC
4328 Mccartney Rd (44436-9567)
P.O. Box 601, Campbell (44405-0601)
PHONE..................330 536-2222
Bessie Xipolitas, *President*
EMP: 40
SQ FT: 2,000
SALES: 5.3MM **Privately Held**
SIC: 1721 Industrial painting; bridge paint-
ing

Lucasville
Scioto County

(G-13045)
**CAMELOT REALTY
INVESTMENTS**
10689 Us 23 (45648)
P.O. Box 1312 (45648-1312)
PHONE..................740 357-5291
Stephen Todd Crabtree,
EMP: 30 EST: 2010
SALES: 1.3MM **Privately Held**
SIC: 6799 Investors

(G-13046)
**CONSULATE MANAGEMENT CO
LLC**
Also Called: Edgewood Manor Lucasville II
10098 Big Bear Creek Rd (45648-9168)
PHONE..................740 259-2351
Mike Bubinsky, *Manager*
EMP: 100
SALES (corp-wide): 580.2MM **Privately
Held**
WEB: www.tandemhealthcare.com
SIC: 8059 8051 Nursing home, except
skilled & intermediate care facility; skilled
nursing care facilities
PA: Consulate Management Company, Llc
800 Concourse Pkwy S
Maitland FL 32751
407 571-1550

(G-13047)
**CONSULATE MANAGEMENT CO
LLC**
10098 Big Bear Creek Rd (45648-9168)
PHONE..................740 259-5536
Carla Naegele,
EMP: 80
SALES (est): 1.3MM **Privately Held**
SIC: 8099 Health & allied services

(G-13048)
**EDGEWOOD MANOR OF
LUCASVILLE**
Also Called: Convalescent Center Lucasville
10098 Big Bear Creek Rd (45648-9168)
PHONE..................740 259-5536
Tom Barr, *Administration*
EMP: 120
SALES (est): 3.3MM **Privately Held**
SIC: 8051 Skilled nursing care facilities

(G-13049)
**FRIENDS OF GOOD SHEPHERD
MANOR**
374 Good Manor Rd (45648-9606)
PHONE..................740 289-2861
Normand Tremblay, *Director*
Helen Dovenbarger, *Associate Dir*
EMP: 92
SQ FT: 30,593
SALES: 1MM **Privately Held**
SIC: 8361 8052 Home for the mentally re-
tarded; intermediate care facilities

(G-13050)
**HEARTLAND HOSPICE
SERVICES LLC**
Also Called: Heartland HM Hlth Care Hospice
205 North St (45648)
P.O. Box 400 (45648-0400)
PHONE..................740 259-0281
Christina Williams, *Branch Mgr*
EMP: 53
SALES (corp-wide): 2.4B **Publicly Held**
SIC: 8082 Home health care services
HQ: Heartland Hospice Services, Llc
333 N Summit St
Toledo OH 43604

(G-13051)
HIGHWAY PATROL
7611 Us Highway 23 (45648-8419)
PHONE..................740 354-2888
John Kisik, *Principal*
EMP: 30
SALES (est): 129.9K **Privately Held**
SIC: 7381 Protective services, guard

(G-13052)
PORK CHAMP LLC
1136 Coldicott Hill Rd (45648-9595)
PHONE..................740 493-2164
Bryan Mc Coy, *Manager*
EMP: 58
SALES (corp-wide): 3.1MM **Privately
Held**
SIC: 0219 0291 General livestock; live-
stock farm, general
PA: Pork Champ Llc
5170 Blazer Pkwy
Dublin OH 43017
419 253-0637

(G-13053)
**SCIOTO COUNTY REGION WTR
DST 1**
Also Called: WATER 1
326 Robert Lucas Rd (45648-9204)
P.O. Box 310 (45648-0310)
PHONE..................740 259-2301
Johnathan King, *General Mgr*
Kathie Edwards, *Treasurer*
Kathie Martin, *Financial Exec*
James Estep, *Technology*
EMP: 29 EST: 1968
SALES: 4.5MM **Privately Held**
WEB: www.water1.org
SIC: 4941 Water supply

Luckey
Wood County

(G-13054)
HIRZEL FARMS INC
20790 Bradner Rd (43443-9727)
PHONE..................419 837-2710
Lou Kozma, *President*
Bridget Burgess, *General Mgr*
EMP: 25
SALES (est): 801.1K **Privately Held**
SIC: 0191 General farms, primarily crop

Lynchburg
Highland County

(G-13055)
SKW MANAGEMENT LLC
3841 Panhandle Rd (45142-9449)
PHONE..................937 382-7938
Samuel K Wilkin, *Mng Member*
EMP: 42 EST: 2009
SQ FT: 1,200
SALES: 1MM **Privately Held**
SIC: 6513 Apartment building operators

Lyons
Fulton County

(G-13056)
B W GRINDING CO
Also Called: Bw Supply Co.
15048 County Road 10 3 (43533-9713)
P.O. Box 307 (43533-0307)
PHONE..................419 923-1376
Martin Welch, *President*
EMP: 35
SQ FT: 30,000
SALES (est): 13.2MM **Privately Held**
WEB: www.bwsupplyco.com
SIC: 5085 3324 Industrial tools; commer-
cial investment castings, ferrous

Macedonia
Summit County

(G-13057)
**ABC PHONES NORTH
CAROLINA INC**
Also Called: A Wireless
8266 Golden Link Blvd (44067-2076)
PHONE..................330 752-0009
EMP: 26

SALES (corp-wide): 149.9MM **Privately Held**
SIC: **4812** Cellular telephone services
PA: Abc Phones Of North Carolina, Inc.
　8510 Colonnade Center Dr
　Raleigh NC 27615
　252 317-0388

(G-13058)
AGS CUSTOM GRAPHICS INC
Also Called: A G S Ohio
8107 Bavaria Rd (44056)
PHONE................................330 963-7770
John Green, *President*
Laura Williams, *Project Mgr*
Stephan Kolakowski, *Production*
Todd Henkel, *Accounts Mgr*
Bozena French, *Cust Mgr*
EMP: 74
SQ FT: 70,000
SALES (est): 20.6MM
SALES (corp-wide): 6.8B **Publicly Held**
WEB: www.automatedgraphic.com
SIC: **2752** 2721 7375 2791 Commercial printing, offset; periodicals; information retrieval services; typesetting; bookbinding & related work; commercial printing
PA: R. R. Donnelley & Sons Company
　35 W Wacker Dr Ste 3650
　Chicago IL 60601
　312 326-8000

(G-13059)
AVATAR MANAGEMENT SERVICES (PA)
Also Called: Avatar Solutions
8157 Bavaria Dr E (44056-2252)
PHONE................................330 963-3900
Mark G Gardner, *CEO*
Linda M Gardner, *President*
EMP: 25
SQ FT: 13,000
SALES (est): 3.5MM **Privately Held**
WEB: www.avatarms.com
SIC: **8742** Business consultant

(G-13060)
AWE HOSPITALITY GROUP LLC
9652 N Bedford Rd (44056-1008)
PHONE................................330 888-8836
Anthony Budroe, *President*
Rochelle Budroe, *Admin Sec*
EMP: 120 EST: 2011
SALES (est): 2.4MM **Privately Held**
SIC: **7011** Hotels & motels

(G-13061)
BAKER VEHICLE SYSTEMS INC
9035 Freeway Dr (44056-1508)
PHONE................................330 467-2250
Harland R Baker, *President*
A C Baker, *Principal*
Harland E Baker, *Principal*
Virginia M Baker, *Principal*
Richard A Baker, *Vice Pres*
EMP: 36 EST: 1940
SQ FT: 38,000
SALES (est): 16.2MM **Privately Held**
WEB: www.bakervehicle.com
SIC: **5012** 7359 Automobiles & other motor vehicles; equipment rental & leasing

(G-13062)
BENNETT SUPPLY OF OHIO LLC
8170 Roll And Hold Pkwy (44056-2146)
PHONE................................800 292-5577
David Bennett III,
Andrew C Bennett,
▼ EMP: 25
SALES: 19.6MM
SALES (corp-wide): 43.8MM **Privately Held**
SIC: **5031** Building materials, exterior
PA: Bennett Supply Co.
　300 Business Center Dr
　Cheswick PA 15024
　724 274-1700

(G-13063)
BURNS INDUSTRIAL EQUIPMENT INC
8155 Roll And Hold Pkwy (44056-2146)
PHONE................................330 425-2476

Chris Burns, *President*
EMP: 25
SALES (corp-wide): 62MM **Privately Held**
SIC: **5084** Materials handling machinery
PA: Burns Industrial Equipment, Inc.
　230 Thorn Hill Rd
　Warrendale PA 15086
　412 856-9253

(G-13064)
CAPITAL SENIOR LIVING CORP
9633 Valley View Rd Ofc C (44056-3017)
PHONE................................330 748-4204
Devan Owens, *Exec Dir*
EMP: 191
SALES (corp-wide): 460MM **Publicly Held**
SIC: **8082** Home health care services
PA: Capital Senior Living Corp
　14160 Dallas Pkwy Ste 300
　Dallas TX 75254
　972 770-5600

(G-13065)
CINEMARK USA INC
Also Called: Cinemark 15
8161 Macedonia Commons Bi (44056-1848)
PHONE................................330 908-1005
Carrie Walker, *Manager*
EMP: 25 **Publicly Held**
SIC: **7832** Motion picture theaters, except drive-in
HQ: Cinemark Usa, Inc.
　3900 Dallas Pkwy Ste 500
　Plano TX 75093
　972 665-1000

(G-13066)
CONSOLIDATED RAIL CORPORATION
401 Ledge Rd (44056-1020)
PHONE................................440 786-3014
Greg Drakulic, *Branch Mgr*
EMP: 60
SALES (corp-wide): 323.3MM **Privately Held**
SIC: **7699** Railroad car customizing
HQ: Consolidated Rail Corporation
　1717 Arch St Ste 1310
　Philadelphia PA 19103
　800 456-7509

(G-13067)
DAVEY TREE EXPERT COMPANY
837 Highland Rd E (44056-2113)
PHONE................................330 908-0833
Kent Winterhalter, *Branch Mgr*
EMP: 40
SALES (corp-wide): 1B **Privately Held**
SIC: **0783** Planting, pruning & trimming services
PA: The Davey Tree Expert Company
　1500 N Mantua St
　Kent OH 44240
　330 673-9511

(G-13068)
DUN RITE HOME IMPROVEMENT INC
8601 Freeway Dr (44056-1535)
PHONE................................330 650-5322
Jim Carson, *President*
EMP: 30
SQ FT: 5,400
SALES (est): 5.2MM **Privately Held**
WEB: www.calldunrite.com
SIC: **4959** 1761 5211 1521 Snowplowing; roofing contractor; door & window products; single-family home remodeling, additions & repairs

(G-13069)
FUN N STUFF AMUSEMENTS INC
661 Highland Rd E (44056-2109)
PHONE................................330 467-0821
Raymond Atwell, *President*
Bob Switalski, *General Mgr*
Victoria Noland, *Admin Sec*
▲ EMP: 66
SQ FT: 20,000

SALES (est): 2.2MM **Privately Held**
WEB: www.fun-n-stuff.com
SIC: **7996** Theme park, amusement

(G-13070)
GENERAL CRANE RENTAL LLC
9680 Freeway Dr (44056-1035)
PHONE................................330 908-0001
Dan Manos, *President*
EMP: 35
SQ FT: 10,000
SALES (est): 7.9MM **Privately Held**
WEB: www.generalcranerental.com
SIC: **7353** Cranes & aerial lift equipment, rental or leasing

(G-13071)
GIRL SCOUTS LAKE ERIE COUNCIL
1 Girl Scout Way (44056-2156)
PHONE................................330 864-9933
Cheryl Goggans, *CEO*
EMP: 46 EST: 1918
SQ FT: 15,000
SALES (est): 2.6MM **Privately Held**
WEB: www.gslec.org
SIC: **8641** Girl Scout organization

(G-13072)
GIRL SCOUTS NORTH EAST OHIO (PA)
1 Girl Scout Way (44056-2156)
PHONE................................330 864-9933
Jane Christyson, *CEO*
Brittany Zaehringer, *COO*
John Graves, *CFO*
Megan Millisor, *Manager*
Douglas Shaulis, *Manager*
EMP: 93
SQ FT: 35,000
SALES: 11.5MM **Privately Held**
SIC: **8641** Girl Scout organization

(G-13073)
HANDL-IT INC (PA)
360 Highland Rd E 2 (44056-2139)
PHONE................................330 468-0734
John S Peters, *Ch of Bd*
Jerry Peters, *President*
Don Barry, *CFO*
EMP: 125
SQ FT: 66,500
SALES (est): 9.6MM **Privately Held**
WEB: www.handlit.net
SIC: **4225** General warehousing

(G-13074)
HOWARD HANNA SMYTHE CRAMER
907 E Aurora Rd (44056-1905)
PHONE................................330 468-6833
Karen Griffith, *Manager*
EMP: 30
SALES (corp-wide): 73.7MM **Privately Held**
WEB: www.smythecramer.com
SIC: **6531** Real estate brokers & agents
HQ: Howard Hanna Smythe Cramer
　6000 Parkland Blvd
　Cleveland OH 44124
　216 447-4477

(G-13075)
INTER DISTR SVCS OF CLEVE
8055 Highland Pointe Pkwy (44056-2147)
PHONE................................330 468-4949
Jack A Russo, *President*
Jeffrey Fine, *Vice Pres*
Richard Kuzma, *CFO*
EMP: 27
SQ FT: 250,000
SALES (est): 2.6MM **Privately Held**
SIC: **4225** General warehousing & storage

(G-13076)
JAEKLE GROUP INC
1410 Highland Rd E (44056-2386)
PHONE................................330 405-9353
Greeg Jaekle, *President*
David Weldon, *Engineer*
Karen Spivak, *Office Admin*
Todd Mohr, *Administration*
EMP: 25

SALES (est): 3.3MM **Privately Held**
SIC: **7379** Computer related consulting services

(G-13077)
KAMAN CORPORATION
7900 Empire Pkwy (44056-2144)
PHONE................................330 468-1811
Andy Dalzell, *Principal*
Jerry Frank, *Accounts Mgr*
Jeff Schofield, *Sales Staff*
EMP: 42
SALES (corp-wide): 1.8B **Publicly Held**
WEB: www.bwrogers.com
SIC: **5085** Industrial supplies
PA: Kaman Corporation
　1332 Blue Hills Ave
　Bloomfield CT 06002
　860 243-7100

(G-13078)
NEWTOWN NINE INC (PA)
Also Called: Ohio Materials Handling
8155 Roll And Hold Pkwy (44056-2146)
PHONE................................440 781-0623
James P Orenga, *President*
Antoinette Orenga, *Admin Sec*
▲ EMP: 57
SQ FT: 38,000
SALES (est): 40MM **Privately Held**
WEB: www.ohiomaterialshandling.com
SIC: **5084** Lift trucks & parts; materials handling machinery

(G-13079)
OHIO STATE HOME SERVICES INC (PA)
Also Called: Ohio State Waterproofing
365 Highland Rd E (44056-2103)
PHONE................................330 467-1055
Nick Di Cello, *President*
Randy Hushour, *Purch Mgr*
Judith Garvin, *VP Finance*
Gay Schrom, *Human Res Dir*
EMP: 170
SQ FT: 15,000
SALES (est): 32.5MM **Privately Held**
WEB: www.ohiostatewaterproofing.com
SIC: **1799** Waterproofing

(G-13080)
PROGRESSIVE MACEDONIA LLC
Also Called: AVENUE AT MACEDONIA, THE
9730 Valley View Rd (44056-2040)
PHONE................................330 908-1260
Lisa Carter, *Director*
Robyn Doerr, *Administration*
EMP: 50
SQ FT: 79,000
SALES (est): 779.7K **Privately Held**
SIC: **8051** Skilled nursing care facilities

(G-13081)
REGENCY ROOFING COMPANIES INC (PA)
Also Called: Shakemasters
576 Highland Rd E Ste A (44056-2134)
PHONE................................330 468-1021
John J Zivich, *President*
EMP: 36 EST: 1974
SQ FT: 8,000
SALES (est): 4.2MM **Privately Held**
WEB: www.shakemaster.com
SIC: **1761** 1799 Roofing contractor; siding contractor; coating, caulking & weather, water & fireproofing

(G-13082)
SPECIALTY LUBRICANTS CORP
Also Called: SLC Custom Packaging
8300 Corporate Park Dr (44056-2300)
PHONE................................330 425-2567
Robin Bugenske, *CEO*
Sherry Bugenske, *President*
Paul Jones, *Purch Mgr*
Kahy Urner, *Human Res Mgr*
Kathy Turner, *Manager*
◆ EMP: 42
SQ FT: 64,000
SALES (est): 8.2MM **Privately Held**
WEB: www.slipkote.com
SIC: **7389** 5172 Packaging & labeling services; lubricating oils & greases

▲ = Import ▼=Export
◆ =Import/Export

(G-13083)
SYSTEMS PACK INC
649 Highland Rd E (44056-2109)
PHONE..................................330 467-5729
Ray Attwell, *President*
Laurene Neval, *CFO*
Sean Freeman, *Consultant*
Jeff Vranic, *Consultant*
EMP: 30 EST: 1977
SQ FT: 62,131
SALES: 8MM **Privately Held**
WEB: www.systemspackinc.com
SIC: 5199 7389 5113 2653 Packaging
materials; packaging & labeling services;
shipping supplies; corrugated & solid fiber
boxes

(G-13084)
THOMAS TRANSPORT
DELIVERY INC
9055 Freeway Dr Unit 1 (44056-1573)
PHONE..................................330 908-3100
Jeff Thomas, *President*
Glenn Berry, *Principal*
Frank Mandato, *Principal*
Bob Seaman, *Principal*
Sean Williams, *Vice Pres*
EMP: 40
SALES (est): 12.5MM **Privately Held**
WEB: www.thomastransportdelivery.com
SIC: 4212 Delivery service, vehicular

(G-13085)
TPC WIRE & CABLE CORP (HQ)
Also Called: Hoffman Products
9600 Valley View Rd (44056-2059)
PHONE..................................800 521-7935
Jeff Crane, *President*
Joseph Daprile, *Vice Pres*
Victor March, *CFO*
Paul M Barlak, *Asst Treas*
Henry Hathaway, *Regl Sales Mgr*
▲ EMP: 94
SALES (est): 62MM
SALES (corp-wide): 1.9B **Privately Held**
SIC: 5063 Electronic wire & cable
PA: Audax Group, L.P.
101 Huntington Ave # 2450
Boston MA 02199
617 859-1500

(G-13086)
TRADESMEN INTERNATIONAL
LLC (PA)
9760 Shepard Rd (44056-1124)
PHONE..................................440 349-3432
Joseph O Wesley, *President*
George Brophy, *President*
Joe Yeager, *President*
Ryan Allen, *General Mgr*
Christopher Bohn, *General Mgr*
EMP: 25
SQ FT: 3,000
SALES (est): 175.8MM **Privately Held**
WEB: www.tradesmen-intl.com
SIC: 7361 Labor contractors (employment
agency)

(G-13087)
TRADESMEN SERVICES LLC
Also Called: Tradesmen Services, Inc.
9760 Shepard Rd (44056-1124)
PHONE..................................440 349-3432
Joe Wesley, *President*
Elaine Kapusta, *CFO*
Patrick Flynn, *General Counsel*
EMP: 80
SALES: 950K **Privately Held**
WEB: www.tradesmen-intl.com
SIC: 7361 Employment agencies
PA: Tradesmen International, Llc
9760 Shepard Rd
Macedonia OH 44056

(G-13088)
VMI GROUP INC
8854 Valley View Rd (44056-2316)
PHONE..................................330 405-4146
Neille Vitale, *President*
Nick Bardall, *Project Mgr*
EMP: 90
SQ FT: 800
SALES: 1.8MM **Privately Held**
SIC: 1791 Precast concrete structural
framing or panels, placing of

(G-13089)
WESTERN RSRVE GIRL SCOUT
CNCIL
1 Girl Scout Way (44056-2156)
PHONE..................................330 864-9933
Fax: 330 864-5720
EMP: 30
SQ FT: 27,000
SALES: 11.7MM **Privately Held**
SIC: 8641 Girl Scout Council

(G-13090)
WW GRAINGER INC
Also Called: Grainger 165
8211 Bavaria Rd (44056)
PHONE..................................330 425-8387
Bob Holzer, *Branch Mgr*
EMP: 250
SALES (corp-wide): 11.2B **Publicly Held**
WEB: www.grainger.com
SIC: 4225 5085 Whol Industrial Supplies
Whol Electrical Equipment
PA: W.W. Grainger, Inc.
100 Grainger Pkwy
Lake Forest IL 60045
847 535-1000

(G-13091)
YOUNG MENS CHRISTIAN
ASSOC
Also Called: Longwood Family YMCA
8761 Shepard Rd (44056-1990)
PHONE..................................330 467-8366
John Herman, *Director*
EMP: 30
SALES (corp-wide): 16.8MM **Privately
Held**
WEB: www.campynoah.com
SIC: 8641 7991 8351 7032 Youth organi-
zations; physical fitness facilities; child
day care services; youth camps; individ-
ual & family services
PA: The Young Men's Christian Association
Of Akron Ohio
50 S Mn St Ste Ll100
Akron OH 44308
330 376-1335

Madison
Lake County

(G-13092)
AMERICAN EAGLE HLTH CARE
SVCS
Also Called: Cardinal Wds Skilled Nursing
6831 Chapel Rd (44057-2255)
PHONE..................................440 428-5103
Joyce Humphrey, *President*
EMP: 120
SQ FT: 2,237
SALES (est): 10.2MM **Privately Held**
SIC: 8051 Skilled nursing care facilities

(G-13093)
BRIGHTER HORIZONS
RESIDENTIAL
1899 Hubbard Rd (44057-2103)
PHONE..................................440 417-1751
Kelly Richmond, *President*
EMP: 50
SALES (est): 2.1MM **Privately Held**
WEB: www.brighterhorizonsinc.com
SIC: 8361 Home for the physically handi-
capped

(G-13094)
DAVITA INC
6830 N Ridge Rd (44057-2637)
PHONE..................................440 251-6237
EMP: 30 **Publicly Held**
SIC: 8092 Kidney dialysis centers
PA: Davita Inc.
2000 16th St
Denver CO 80202

(G-13095)
EASTWOOD RESIDENTIAL
LIVING
6261 Chapel Rd (44057-2160)
PHONE..................................440 417-0608
Louanne Busch, *Manager*
EMP: 36

SALES (est): 246.6K
SALES (corp-wide): 1.8MM **Privately
Held**
SIC: 8361 Home for the mentally handi-
capped
PA: Eastwood Residential Living Inc
6381 N Ridge Rd
Madison OH

(G-13096)
EASTWOOD RESIDENTIAL
LIVING
Also Called: Searidge
6412 N Ridge Rd (44057-2550)
PHONE..................................440 428-1588
Jim Victor, *Manager*
EMP: 40
SQ FT: 2,025
SALES (corp-wide): 1.8MM **Privately
Held**
SIC: 8361 Home for the mentally retarded
PA: Eastwood Residential Living Inc
6381 N Ridge Rd
Madison OH

(G-13097)
HOWARD HANNA SMYTHE
CRAMER
Also Called: Smythe-Cramer Co Madison
2757 Hubbard Rd (44057-2931)
PHONE..................................440 428-1818
Robin Tilbery, *Manager*
Alice Balsley, *Manager*
Janice Warren, *Real Est Agnt*
EMP: 28
SALES (corp-wide): 72.1MM **Privately
Held**
WEB: www.smythecramer.com
SIC: 6531 Real estate brokers & agents
HQ: Howard Hanna Smythe Cramer
6000 Parkland Blvd
Cleveland OH 44124
216 447-4477

(G-13098)
J P JENKS INC
4493 S Madison Rd (44057-9422)
P.O. Box 370 (44057-0370)
PHONE..................................440 428-4500
Ray Kennedy, *President*
EMP: 40 EST: 1972
SQ FT: 20,000
SALES (est): 4.9MM
SALES (corp-wide): 132.6MM **Privately
Held**
WEB: www.rwsidleyinc.com
SIC: 4213 4212 Contract haulers; local
trucking, without storage
PA: R. W. Sidley Incorporated
436 Casement Ave
Painesville OH 44077
440 352-9343

(G-13099)
LAKE COUNTY YMCA
Also Called: East End YMCA Pre School
730 N Lake St (44057-3153)
PHONE..................................440 428-5125
Susan Davis, *Finance Asst*
Dick Bennett, *Senior Mgr*
Michele Kuester, *Director*
EMP: 70
SALES (corp-wide): 8.9MM **Privately
Held**
SIC: 8641 7991 8351 7032 Youth organi-
zations; physical fitness facilities; child
day care services; youth camps; individ-
ual & family services
PA: Lake County Ymca
933 Mentor Ave Fl 2
Painesville OH 44077
440 352-3303

(G-13100)
LAKE METROPARKS
Also Called: Erie Shores Golf Club
7298 Lake Rd (44057-1512)
PHONE..................................440 428-3164
John Miller, *Manager*
EMP: 25
SALES (est): 473.5K
SALES (corp-wide): 20.9MM **Privately
Held**
WEB: www.lakemetroparks.com
SIC: 7999 Recreation services

PA: Lake Metroparks
11211 Spear Rd
Painesville OH 44077
440 639-7275

(G-13101)
LCN HOLDINGS INC
Also Called: Lake County Nursery
5052 S Ridge Rd (44057-9709)
P.O. Box 122, Perry (44081-0122)
PHONE..................................440 259-5571
Jeff Hyrne, *President*
Robert Pettorin, *VP Prdtn*
Joe Zampini, *VP Sales*
EMP: 34
SQ FT: 15,000
SALES (est): 4.1MM **Privately Held**
WEB: www.lakecountynursery.com
SIC: 5193 Flowers & nursery stock

(G-13102)
MADISON CARE INC
Also Called: FRANKLIN RIDGE CARE FA-
CILITY
7600 S Ridge Rd (44057-9746)
PHONE..................................440 428-1492
Susan Knowlson, *Director*
EMP: 100 EST: 1966
SQ FT: 69,000
SALES: 8MM
SALES (corp-wide): 85.7MM **Privately
Held**
SIC: 8051 Extended care facility
PA: Carington Health Systems
8200 Beckett Park Dr
Hamilton OH 45011
513 682-2700

(G-13103)
MADISON LOCAL SCHOOL
DISTRICT
Also Called: Memorial Complex
92 E Main St (44057-3224)
PHONE..................................440 428-5111
Maureen Fedor, *Principal*
EMP: 25
SALES (corp-wide): 32.2MM **Privately
Held**
WEB: www.madisonlocalschooldistrict.com
SIC: 8351 Preschool center
PA: Madison Local School District
1956 Red Bird Rd
Madison OH 44057
440 428-2166

(G-13104)
MADISON MEDICAL CAMPUS
Also Called: Lake Hospital Systems
6270 N Ridge Rd (44057-2567)
PHONE..................................440 428-6800
Rick Kondas, *Director*
EMP: 40
SALES (est): 1.6MM **Privately Held**
WEB: www.lakehospitalsystems.com
SIC: 8062 General medical & surgical hos-
pitals

(G-13105)
NORTH COAST PERENNIALS
INC
3754 Dayton Rd (44057-9782)
PHONE..................................440 428-1277
Mark Freshour, *Owner*
EMP: 35
SALES (est): 2.5MM **Privately Held**
WEB: www.northcoastperennials.com
SIC: 5193 Nursery stock

(G-13106)
NORTH RIDGE VETERINARY
HOSP
6336 N Ridge Rd (44057-2548)
PHONE..................................440 428-5166
Rw Pierce Dvm, *Owner*
EMP: 30
SQ FT: 11,000
SALES (est): 1.3MM **Privately Held**
SIC: 0742 Animal hospital services, pets &
other animal specialties

G
E
O
G
R
A
P
H
I
C

(G-13107)
PHOENIX RESIDENTIAL CTRS INC (PA)
1954 Hubbard Rd Ste 1 (44057-2154)
P.O. Box 40 (44057-0040)
PHONE..................................440 428-9082
Gary Toth, *President*
EMP: 26
SQ FT: 4,875
SALES (est): 3.2MM **Privately Held**
WEB: www.phoenixresidential.com
SIC: 8361 Home for the mentally handicapped

(G-13108)
RIDGE MANOR NUSERIES INC
Also Called: Willow Ridge Nursery
7925 N Ridge Rd (44057-3026)
PHONE..................................440 466-5781
Angelo Petitti, *President*
Frank Santore, *Sales Mgr*
Joe Dawson, *Marketing Staff*
EMP: 130
SQ FT: 200,000
SALES (est): 4.4MM
SALES (corp-wide): 18.7MM **Privately Held**
WEB: www.ridgemanor.com
SIC: 0181 Foliage, growing of; nursery stock, growing of
PA: Petitti Enterprises, Inc.
25018 Broadway Ave
Cleveland OH 44146
440 439-8636

(G-13109)
STEWART LODGE INC
7774 Warner Rd (44057-9547)
P.O. Box 520 (44057-0520)
PHONE..................................440 417-1898
John Dalsky, *Administration*
EMP: 84
SQ FT: 7,500
SALES (est): 2.7MM **Privately Held**
WEB: www.stewartlodge.com
SIC: 8059 Home for the mentally retarded, exc. skilled or intermediate

(G-13110)
WIRTZBERGER ENTERPRISES CORP
136 W Main St (44057-3183)
PHONE..................................440 428-1901
Michael Wirtzberger, *President*
Megan Herrick, *Corp Secy*
EMP: 25
SALES (est): 2.6MM **Privately Held**
WEB: www.wirtzberger.com
SIC: 1522 Residential construction

Magnolia
Stark County

(G-13111)
EAGLE INDUSTRIAL PAINTING LLC
3215 Magnolia Rd Nw (44643-9527)
PHONE..................................330 866-5965
Steve Zoumberakis, *Mng Member*
EMP: 30 **EST:** 2013
SQ FT: 217,800
SALES: 6MM **Privately Held**
SIC: 1721 Industrial painting; bridge painting

Maineville
Warren County

(G-13112)
AMS CONSTRUCTION INC
Also Called: Estephenson Brenda & John
7431 Windsor Park Dr (45039-9193)
PHONE..................................513 398-6689
John K Stephenson, *Branch Mgr*
EMP: 150
SALES (est): 4.1MM **Privately Held**
SIC: 1731 Electrical work
PA: Ams Construction, Inc.
10670 Loveland Madeira Rd
Loveland OH 45140

(G-13113)
CHARLES H HAMILTON CO
5875 S State Route 48 (45039-9798)
P.O. Box 99 (45039-0099)
PHONE..................................513 683-2442
Charles H Hamilton Jr, *President*
EMP: 85 **EST:** 1964
SQ FT: 8,000
SALES (est): 13.9MM **Privately Held**
WEB: www.charleshhamiltonco.com
SIC: 1794 1623 1771 Excavation & grading, building construction; water, sewer & utility lines; curb construction

(G-13114)
DAMASCUS STAFFING LLC
2263 W Us 22 And 3 (45039-9477)
PHONE..................................513 954-8941
Todd Wurzbacher, *Principal*
EMP: 60
SALES (est): 613.1K **Privately Held**
SIC: 7361 Employment agencies

(G-13115)
E F BAVIS & ASSOCIATES INC
201 Grandin Rd (45039-9762)
PHONE..................................513 677-0500
Edward F Bavis, *CEO*
William P Sieber, *President*
Mike Brown, *VP Mfg*
Susan Overbeck, *Treasurer*
Barbara Calhoun, *Human Resources*
EMP: 35 **EST:** 1970
SQ FT: 4,000
SALES (est): 13.2MM **Privately Held**
SIC: 5084 Conveyor systems

(G-13116)
MIKE WARD LANDSCAPING INC
Also Called: Eastgate Sod
424 E Us Highway 22 And 3 (45039-9650)
PHONE..................................513 683-6436
Kenneth Michael Ward, *President*
Nancy Giles, *Human Res Mgr*
Patty Simonton, *Administration*
EMP: 30
SQ FT: 15,441
SALES (est): 4.6MM **Privately Held**
WEB: www.eastgatesod.com
SIC: 0181 0782 Sod farms; lawn services; lawn care services; spraying services, lawn; turf installation services, except artificial

(G-13117)
PRIME HOME CARE LLC (PA)
2775 W Us Hwy 22 3 Ste 1 (45039)
PHONE..................................513 340-4183
Okshana Aminov,
Oksana Aminov,
EMP: 50 **EST:** 2009
SALES: 7.7MM **Privately Held**
SIC: 8082 Visiting nurse service

(G-13118)
SENSATION RESEARCH
1159 Chaucer Pl (45039-9134)
PHONE..................................513 602-1611
Cynthia Ward, *Owner*
EMP: 30 **EST:** 2012
SALES: 650K **Privately Held**
SIC: 8734 8731 Testing laboratories; commercial physical research

(G-13119)
THORNTON LANDSCAPE INC
424 E Us Highway 22 And 3 (45039-9650)
PHONE..................................513 683-8100
Richard Doesburg, *CEO*
Andrew Doesburg, *President*
Larry Henry, *Architect*
EMP: 35 **EST:** 1961
SQ FT: 12,000
SALES (est): 2.5MM **Privately Held**
WEB: www.thorntonlandscape.com
SIC: 0782 0781 Landscape contractors; landscape counseling & planning

(G-13120)
Z SNOW REMOVAL INC
8177 S State Route 48 (45039-9631)
PHONE..................................513 683-7719
Frank Ziebell, *Mng Member*
EMP: 45

SALES: 2.4MM **Privately Held**
WEB: www.oneworldholdings.net
SIC: 4959 Snowplowing

Malta
Morgan County

(G-13121)
EZ GROUT CORPORATION INC
Also Called: Ezg Manufacturing
1833 N Riverview Rd (43758-9303)
PHONE..................................740 962-2024
Damian Lang, *Owner*
Steve Wheeler, *Marketing Staff*
EMP: 40 **EST:** 2007
SALES (est): 13MM **Privately Held**
SIC: 5082 3499 3549 Masonry equipment & supplies; chests, fire or burglary resistive: metal; wiredrawing & fabricating machinery & equipment, ex. die

Malvern
Carroll County

(G-13122)
DR MICHAEL J HULIT
107 N Reed Ave (44644)
P.O. Box 937 (44644-0937)
PHONE..................................330 863-7173
Michael Hulit, *Owner*
EMP: 25
SALES (est): 852.3K **Privately Held**
SIC: 1522 8021 Residential construction; offices & clinics of dentists

(G-13123)
GREEN LINES TRANSPORTATION INC (PA)
7089 Alliance Rd Nw (44644-9428)
P.O. Box 377 (44644-0377)
PHONE..................................330 863-2111
Roger A Bettis, *President*
Kevin White, *General Mgr*
Michael Ragan, *Business Mgr*
Brad Yoder, *Vice Pres*
Jeff Cox, *Manager*
EMP: 50
SQ FT: 17,000
SALES (est): 13.6MM **Privately Held**
WEB: www.greenlines.net
SIC: 4213 Trucking, except local

(G-13124)
HOPPES CONSTRUCTION LLC
4036 Coral Rd Nw (44644-9468)
P.O. Box 604 (44644-0604)
PHONE..................................580 310-0090
Lynn Hoppe, *Branch Mgr*
EMP: 30 **Privately Held**
SIC: 1521 Single-family housing construction
PA: Hoppe"s Construction, Llc
12580 County Road 1538
Ada OK 74820

(G-13125)
LAKE MHAWK PRPERTY OWNERS ASSN
1 N Mohawk Dr (44644-9556)
PHONE..................................330 863-0000
Jack Buetner, *President*
Scott Noble, *General Mgr*
Robert Greene, *Director*
EMP: 36
SQ FT: 7,000
SALES: 1MM **Privately Held**
WEB: www.lake-mohawk.org
SIC: 8641 Homeowners' association

(G-13126)
ROGER BETTIS TRUCKING INC
7089 Alliance Rd Nw (44644-9428)
P.O. Box 396 (44644-0396)
PHONE..................................330 863-2111
Roger Bettis, *President*
Walt Downing, *Vice Pres*
EMP: 112
SQ FT: 14,000
SALES: 12MM **Privately Held**
SIC: 7513 Truck leasing, without drivers

Manchester
Adams County

(G-13127)
DAYTON POWER AND LIGHT COMPANY
Also Called: DPL
745 Us Highway 52 Unit 1 (45144-8450)
PHONE..................................937 549-2641
Troy Willia, *Safety Mgr*
John Knepfle, *Engineer*
James Saelens, *Engineer*
Melissa Hendrickson, *Financial Analy*
Ron Rodrique, *Branch Mgr*
EMP: 400
SQ FT: 1,040
SALES (corp-wide): 10.7B **Publicly Held**
WEB: www.waytogo.com
SIC: 4911 ; generation, electric power
HQ: The Dayton Power And Light Company
1065 Woodman Dr
Dayton OH 45432
937 331-4063

(G-13128)
DAYTON POWER AND LIGHT COMPANY
14869 Us 52 (45144-9332)
PHONE..................................937 549-2641
Dave Orme, *Plant Mgr*
Mike High, *Technology*
Lionel Smith, *Maintence Staff*
EMP: 60
SALES (corp-wide): 10.7B **Publicly Held**
WEB: www.waytogo.com
SIC: 4931 4932 4911 Electric & other services combined; gas & other services combined;
HQ: The Dayton Power And Light Company
1065 Woodman Dr
Dayton OH 45432
937 331-4063

(G-13129)
SPECIAL TOUCH HOMECARE LLC
207 Pike St (45144-1218)
PHONE..................................937 549-1843
Vickie Vivens, *Mng Member*
Conny Leonard,
EMP: 32
SALES (est): 461.3K **Privately Held**
SIC: 8082 Home health care services

Mansfield
Richland County

(G-13130)
3RD STREET COMMUNITY CLINIC
Also Called: 3RD STREET FAMILY HEALTH SERVI
600 W 3rd St (44906-2633)
PHONE..................................419 522-6191
Robert A Bowers, *CEO*
Gerad Pollick, *President*
Susan Cates, *Lic Prac Nurse*
EMP: 57 **EST:** 1994
SALES: 14.9MM **Privately Held**
SIC: 8011 Primary care medical clinic

(G-13131)
A TOUCH OF GRACE INC
787 Lexington Ave Ste 303 (44907-1998)
PHONE..................................567 560-2350
EMP: 62
SALES (corp-wide): 2.1MM **Privately Held**
SIC: 8082 Home health care services
PA: A Touch Of Grace, Inc.
809 Coshocton Ave Ste B
Mount Vernon OH 43050
740 397-7971

(G-13132)
ABF FREIGHT SYSTEM INC
25 S Mulberry St (44902-1907)
PHONE..................................419 525-0118
Rick Speckert, *Branch Mgr*
EMP: 200

SALES (corp-wide): 3B **Publicly Held**
SIC: 4731 Transportation agents & brokers
HQ: Abf Freight System, Inc.
3801 Old Greenwood Rd
Fort Smith AR 72903
479 785-8700

(G-13133)
ALLEN EST MANGEMENT LTD
132 Distl Ave (44902-2125)
PHONE..............................419 526-6505
Rod Shag, *President*
Melody Shag, *Vice Pres*
EMP: 30
SALES (est): 1.2MM **Privately Held**
WEB: www.allencabinetry.com
SIC: 6531 Real estate brokers & agents

(G-13134)
**ALLIED RESTAURANT SVC
OHIO INC (PA)**
187 Illinois Ave S (44905-2825)
PHONE..............................419 589-4759
Robert A Baxter, *President*
Tim Lawhorn, *Manager*
EMP: 26
SQ FT: 9,000
SALES (est): 5.8MM **Privately Held**
SIC: 1711 Heating & air conditioning con-
tractors

(G-13135)
**AMERICAN HLTH NTWRK &
FMLY PRC**
Also Called: Mansfield Family Practice
248 Blymyer Ave (44903-2306)
PHONE..............................419 524-2212
Raymond J Gardner, *Principal*
Terry Weston, *Principal*
EMP: 30
SALES (est): 1.3MM **Privately Held**
SIC: 8011 Physicians' office, including spe-
cialists; general & family practice, physi-
cian/surgeon

(G-13136)
**AMERICAN NATIONAL RED
CROSS**
Also Called: American Red Cross
39 Park St N (44902-1711)
PHONE..............................419 524-0311
EMP: 39
SALES (corp-wide): 2.5B **Privately Held**
SIC: 8322 Individual/Family Services
PA: The American National Red Cross
430 17th St Nw
Washington DC 20006
202 737-8300

(G-13137)
ASHLAND RAILWAY INC
803 N Main St (44902-4205)
PHONE..............................419 525-2822
Mike Mosley, *General Mgr*
Steve Nielsen, *Director*
EMP: 43
SALES (corp-wide): 10.6MM **Privately
Held**
SIC: 4011 4013 Railroads, line-haul oper-
ating; switching & terminal services
PA: The Ashland Railway Inc
6055d Kellers Church Rd
Pipersville PA 18947
215 795-8082

(G-13138)
**BAKERS CLLSION REPR
SPECIALIST**
595 5th Ave (44905-1946)
PHONE..............................419 524-1350
Toll Free:..............................866   -
Larry Baker, *President*
Delee Powell, *Owner*
EMP: 30
SQ FT: 18,500
SALES (est): 4.4MM **Privately Held**
WEB: www.bakerscollision.com
SIC: 7532 Body shop, automotive

(G-13139)
BBT FLEET SERVICES LLC
549 Russell Rd (44903-1928)
P.O. Box 542, Galion (44833-0542)
PHONE..............................419 462-7722
John Schmidt,

EMP: 38
SQ FT: 24,000
SALES: 2MM **Privately Held**
SIC: 7539 Trailer repair

(G-13140)
**BENJAMIN STEEL COMPANY
INC**
15 Industrial Pkwy (44903-8800)
PHONE..............................419 522-5500
Timothy Sinclair, *Branch Mgr*
EMP: 36
SALES (corp-wide): 86.5MM **Privately
Held**
WEB: www.benjaminsteel.com
SIC: 5051 Steel
PA: Benjamin Steel Company, Inc.
777 Benjamin Dr
Springfield OH 45502
937 322-8600

(G-13141)
**BIO-MDCAL APPLCATIONS
OHIO INC**
Also Called: FMC Dalysis Svcs Richland Cnty
680 Bally Row (44906-2969)
PHONE..............................419 774-0180
Jim Barsanti, *Manager*
EMP: 25
SALES (corp-wide): 18.9B **Privately Held**
WEB: www.fresenius.org
SIC: 8092 Kidney dialysis centers
HQ: Bio-Medical Applications Of Ohio, Inc.
920 Winter St
Waltham MA 02451

(G-13142)
BLACK RIVER GROUP INC (PA)
Also Called: Black River Display Group
140 Park Ave E (44902-1830)
P.O. Box 876 (44901-0876)
PHONE..............................419 524-6699
Terry Neff, *President*
Kurt Myers, *Prdtn Mgr*
Steve Winters, *Safety Mgr*
Chris Baldasare, *Accounting Mgr*
Chaz Schroeder, *Accounts Exec*
EMP: 65
SQ FT: 74,000
SALES: 120MM **Privately Held**
WEB: www.ds-creative.com
SIC: 7311 2752 2791 2789 Advertising
agencies; commercial printing, litho-
graphic; typesetting; bookbinding & re-
lated work

(G-13143)
**BLEVINS METAL FABRICATION
INC**
Also Called: Blevins Fabrication
288 Illinois Ave S (44905-2827)
PHONE..............................419 522-6082
Lloyd T Blevins, *President*
Sharon Thomas, *Buyer*
EMP: 25 EST: 1997
SQ FT: 13,000
SALES (est): 4.7MM **Privately Held**
SIC: 7692 3446 3444 3443 Welding re-
pair; architectural metalwork; sheet metal-
work; fabricated plate work (boiler shop);
fabricated structural metal

(G-13144)
BRAMARJAC INC
Also Called: Pebble Creek Golf Club
4300 Algire Rd (44904-9554)
PHONE..............................419 884-3434
George J Pidgeon, *President*
Marjorie L Pidgeon, *Corp Secy*
Bradley J Pidgeon, *Vice Pres*
EMP: 33
SQ FT: 5,000
SALES (est): 1MM **Privately Held**
WEB: www.pebblecreekgolfclub.com
SIC: 7992 5813 5941 7999 Public golf
courses; cocktail lounge; golf goods &
equipment; golf driving range

(G-13145)
BREITINGER COMPANY
595 Oakenwaldt St (44905-1900)
PHONE..............................419 526-4255
Milo Breitinger, *President*
Breitinger Kim, *CFO*
Kim Breitinger, *Manager*

Nikki Williams, *Admin Asst*
EMP: 120 EST: 1954
SQ FT: 106,000
SALES (est): 35.9MM **Privately Held**
WEB: www.breitingercompany.com
SIC: 3441 3469 7692 3444 Fabricated
structural metal; metal stampings; welding
repair; sheet metalwork; fabricated plate
work (boiler shop)

(G-13146)
**BROOKDALE SENIOR LIVING
INC**
Also Called: Sterling House of Mansfield
1841 Middle Bellville Rd (44904-1798)
PHONE..............................419 756-5599
Lana Mishey, *Branch Mgr*
Meredith Pasco, *Director*
Kim Wilson, *Hlthcr Dir*
EMP: 35
SALES (corp-wide): 4.5B **Publicly Held**
SIC: 8059 Rest home, with health care
PA: Brookdale Senior Living
111 Westwood Pl Ste 400
Brentwood TN 37027
615 221-2250

(G-13147)
**BROOKDALE SNIOR LVING
CMMNTIES**
Also Called: Sterling House of Mansfield
1841 Middle Bellville Rd (44904-1798)
PHONE..............................419 756-5599
Karel Freiwar, *Director*
EMP: 30
SALES (corp-wide): 4.5B **Publicly Held**
WEB: www.assisted.com
SIC: 8059 Rest home, with health care
HQ: Brookdale Senior Living Communities,
Inc.
6737 W Wa St Ste 2300
Milwaukee WI 53214
414 918-5000

(G-13148)
CASTO HEALTH CARE
Also Called: Lexington Court Care Center
20 N Mill St (44904-1251)
PHONE..............................419 884-6400
William Casto, *Owner*
Randy Casto, *Webmaster*
EMP: 60 EST: 2001
SALES (est): 1.3MM **Privately Held**
WEB: www.castohealthcare.com
SIC: 8051 8322 Convalescent home with
continuous nursing care; individual & fam-
ily services

(G-13149)
CENTAURUS FINANCIAL INC
58 W 3rd St Ste B (44902-1251)
PHONE..............................419 756-9747
Edward Klesack, *Principal*
EMP: 89 **Privately Held**
SIC: 6282 Investment advisory service
PA: Centaurus Financial, Inc.
2300 E Katella Ave # 200
Anaheim CA 92806

(G-13150)
**CENTER FOR INDIVIDUAL AND
FMLY (PA)**
Also Called: REHABILITATION SERVICES
OF NOR
741 Scholl Rd (44907-1571)
PHONE..............................419 522-4357
Veronica L Groff, *President*
Nancy Dean, *Marketing Staff*
Bethanie Vranekovic, *Manager*
EMP: 250
SQ FT: 30,000
SALES: 12.6MM **Privately Held**
WEB: www.cifcenter.org
SIC: 8093 8322 Mental health clinic, out-
patient; individual & family services

(G-13151)
**CHILDRENS CMPRHENSIVE
SVCS INC**
1451 Lucas Rd (44903-8682)
P.O. Box 2226 (44905-0226)
PHONE..............................419 589-5511
Steven Covington, *Branch Mgr*
EMP: 100

SALES (corp-wide): 10.7B **Publicly Held**
WEB: www.keystoneyouth.com
SIC: 8322 8361 Individual & family serv-
ices; residential care
HQ: Children's Comprehensive Services,
Inc.
3401 West End Ave Ste 400
Nashville TN 37203
615 250-0000

(G-13152)
COUNTY OF RICHLAND
Also Called: Rain Tree, The
721 Scholl Rd (44907-1571)
PHONE..............................419 774-4300
Lisa Gulian, *Director*
EMP: 100 **Privately Held**
WEB: www.mrcpl.org
SIC: 8361 Home for the mentally retarded
PA: County Of Richland
50 Park Ave E Ste 3
Mansfield OH 44902
419 774-5501

(G-13153)
COUNTY OF RICHLAND
Also Called: Richland County Prosectors Off
38 Park St S Ste B (44902-1717)
PHONE..............................419 774-5676
Mark Cains, *IT/INT Sup*
Martin Jones, *Director*
James Mayer Jr, *Administration*
EMP: 30 **Privately Held**
WEB: www.mrcpl.org
SIC: 8651 9111 9222 Political organiza-
tions; county supervisors' & executives'
offices
PA: County Of Richland
50 Park Ave E Ste 3
Mansfield OH 44902
419 774-5501

(G-13154)
COUNTY OF RICHLAND
Also Called: Dayspring Residential Care
3220 Olivesburg Rd (44903-8243)
PHONE..............................419 774-5894
Michelle Swank, *Director*
EMP: 40 **Privately Held**
WEB: www.mrcpl.org
SIC: 8322 Old age assistance
PA: County Of Richland
50 Park Ave E Ste 3
Mansfield OH 44902
419 774-5501

(G-13155)
COUNTY OF RICHLAND
Also Called: Children Services
731 Scholl Rd (44907-1571)
PHONE..............................419 774-4100
Randy Parker, *Manager*
EMP: 133 **Privately Held**
WEB: www.mrcpl.org
SIC: 8361 9111 8322 Children's home;
county supervisors' & executives' offices;
individual & family services
PA: County Of Richland
50 Park Ave E Ste 3
Mansfield OH 44902
419 774-5501

(G-13156)
COUNTY OF RICHLAND
Also Called: Dept of Human Services
171 Park Ave E (44902-1829)
PHONE..............................419 774-5400
Doug Theaker, *Director*
EMP: 105 **Privately Held**
WEB: www.mrcpl.org
SIC: 8322 9111 Social service center;
county supervisors' & executives' offices
PA: County Of Richland
50 Park Ave E Ste 3
Mansfield OH 44902
419 774-5501

(G-13157)
COUNTY OF RICHLAND
411 S Diamond St (44902-7812)
PHONE..............................419 774-5578
Ron Sopon, *Principal*
EMP: 65 **Privately Held**
WEB: www.mrcpl.org
SIC: 8361 Juvenile correctional facilities

PA: County Of Richland
50 Park Ave E Ste 3
Mansfield OH 44902
419 774-5501

(G-13158)
COUNTY OF RICHLAND
Also Called: Richland County Engineers
77 N Mulberry St (44902-1208)
PHONE....................................419 774-5591
Tom Beck, *Engineer*
Thomas Beck,
EMP: 50 **Privately Held**
WEB: www.mrcpl.org
SIC: 8711 9111 Engineering services;
county supervisors' & executives' offices
PA: County Of Richland
50 Park Ave E Ste 3
Mansfield OH 44902
419 774-5501

(G-13159)
COUNTY OF RICHLAND
Also Called: New Hope Center
314 Cleveland Ave (44902-8623)
PHONE....................................419 774-4200
Elizabeth Prather, *Principal*
Dawn Trosper, *HR Admin*
EMP: 350 **Privately Held**
WEB: www.mrcpl.org
SIC: 8059 9111 Home for the mentally re-
tarded, exc. skilled or intermediate;
county supervisors' & executives' offices
PA: County Of Richland
50 Park Ave E Ste 3
Mansfield OH 44902
419 774-5501

(G-13160)
CRITICAL LIFE INC
35 Logan Rd (44907-2810)
PHONE....................................419 525-0502
Jason Dotson, *President*
Carrie Dotson, *Corp Secy*
EMP: 30
SALES (est): 896.6K **Privately Held**
WEB: www.criticallife.com
SIC: 4119 Local passenger transportation

(G-13161)
CRYSTAL CARE CENTERS INC
458 Vanderbilt Rd Unit 1 (44904-8649)
P.O. Box 3167 (44904-0167)
PHONE....................................419 747-2666
Jerry Smith, *Administration*
EMP: 45 **Privately Held**
SIC: 8051 8052 Convalescent home with
continuous nursing care; intermediate
care facilities
PA: Crystal Care Centers Inc
1159 Wyandotte Ave
Mansfield OH 44906

(G-13162)
**CRYSTAL CARE CENTERS INC
(PA)**
Also Called: Crystal Care of Mansfield
1159 Wyandotte Ave (44906-1940)
PHONE....................................419 747-2666
Jerry Smith, *President*
Lorie Blanton, *Hlthcr Dir*
Anthony Wheaton, *Administration*
EMP: 90
SALES (est): 7.6MM **Privately Held**
SIC: 8051 8059 Convalescent home with
continuous nursing care; rest home, with
health care

(G-13163)
**CUMBERLAND MUTL FIRE
INSUR CO**
380 N Main St Ste 101 (44902-7307)
PHONE....................................419 525-4443
Nathan Jungeberg, *Technology*
Tracy Richards, *Prgrmr*
Blair Sturts, *Director*
EMP: 42
SALES (corp-wide): 99MM **Privately
Held**
SIC: 6411 Insurance agents
PA: Cumberland Mutual Fire Insurance
Company (Inc)
633 Shiloh Pike
Bridgeton NJ 08302
856 451-4050

(G-13164)
**D & S CRTIVE CMMUNICATIONS
INC**
Also Called: Black River Display
195 E 4th St (44902-1519)
PHONE....................................419 524-4312
EMP: 40
SALES (corp-wide): 120MM **Privately
Held**
SIC: 5023 5039 Wholesale Building Mate-
rials
PA: Black River Group, Inc.
140 Park Ave E
Mansfield OH 44902
419 524-6699

(G-13165)
DAYTON FREIGHT LINES INC
103 Cairns Rd (44903-8992)
PHONE....................................419 589-0350
Justin Sharky, *Branch Mgr*
EMP: 197
SALES (corp-wide): 971MM **Privately
Held**
SIC: 4789 Pipeline terminal facilities, inde-
pendently operated
PA: Dayton Freight Lines, Inc.
6450 Poe Ave Ste 311
Dayton OH 45414
937 264-4060

(G-13166)
**DEARMAN MOVING & STORAGE
CO**
961 N Main St (44903-8113)
P.O. Box 1992 (44901-1992)
PHONE....................................419 524-3456
Jeffrey L Campbell, *President*
Ruthann Campbell, *Vice Pres*
Tim Campbell, *Opers Staff*
Chris Campbell, *Sales Executive*
EMP: 40
SQ FT: 45,000
SALES (est): 4.6MM **Privately Held**
SIC: 4212 Moving services

(G-13167)
**DIRECTIONS CREDIT UNION
INC**
777 N Main St (44902-4203)
PHONE....................................419 524-7113
Pam Nottingham, *Branch Mgr*
EMP: 40
SALES (corp-wide): 34.8MM **Privately
Held**
SIC: 6062 6163 State credit unions, not
federally chartered; loan brokers
PA: Directions Credit Union, Inc.
5121 Whiteford Rd
Sylvania OH 43560
419 720-4769

(G-13168)
**DISABLED AMERICAN
VETERANS**
34 Park Ave W (44902-1603)
PHONE....................................419 526-0203
Hayne K Holstine, *Principal*
EMP: 400
SALES (corp-wide): 137MM **Privately
Held**
SIC: 8641 Veterans' organization
PA: Disabled American Veterans
3725 Alexandria Pike
Cold Spring KY 41076
859 441-7300

(G-13169)
DISCOVERY SCHOOL
855 Millsboro Rd (44903-1997)
PHONE....................................419 756-8880
Amy Oswalt, *Principal*
Shirley Heck, *Principal*
John Miller, *Principal*
Beth Parsons, *Teacher*
Maggie Bolin, *Assistant*
EMP: 25
SALES: 1.2MM **Privately Held**
WEB: www.discovery-school.net
SIC: 8211 8351 Private elementary
school; preschool center

(G-13170)
DTE INC
110 Baird Pkwy (44903-7909)
PHONE....................................419 522-3428
Rob Nelson, *CEO*
Dean Russell, *President*
Burke Melching, *Vice Pres*
EMP: 30
SQ FT: 45,000
SALES (est): 3.8MM **Privately Held**
WEB: www.dteinc.com
SIC: 7629 3661 Telephone set repair; tele-
phone & telegraph apparatus

(G-13171)
EDGE PLASTICS INC
Also Called: Jobs On Site
449 Newman St (44902-1123)
PHONE....................................419 522-6696
Sandy Cornett, *QC Mgr*
Diana White, *Manager*
EMP: 50
SALES (corp-wide): 32.8MM **Privately
Held**
SIC: 7363 Help supply services
PA: Edge Plastics, Inc.
449 Newman St
Mansfield OH 44902
419 522-6696

(G-13172)
**ELITE EXCAVATING COMPANY
INC**
Also Called: Elite Excavating Ohio Company
4500 Snodgrass Rd (44903-8065)
P.O. Box 290, Ontario (44862-0290)
PHONE....................................419 683-4200
Micheal Scott Fulmer, *President*
Patricia Fulmer, *Vice Pres*
EMP: 28
SQ FT: 8,000
SALES (est): 5MM **Privately Held**
SIC: 1794 Excavation work

(G-13173)
ESTES EXPRESS LINES INC
792 5th Ave (44905-1421)
PHONE....................................419 522-2641
Patricia Estes, *Branch Mgr*
EMP: 59
SALES (corp-wide): 2.7B **Privately Held**
SIC: 4213 Contract haulers
PA: Estes Express Lines, Inc.
3901 W Broad St
Richmond VA 23230
804 353-1900

(G-13174)
**FEDERAL EXPRESS
CORPORATION**
Also Called: Fedex
65 Paragon Pkwy (44903-8074)
PHONE....................................800 463-3339
EMP: 34
SALES (corp-wide): 65.4B **Publicly Held**
WEB: www.fedex.com
SIC: 4513 Package delivery, private air
HQ: Federal Express Corporation
3610 Hacks Cross Rd
Memphis TN 38125
901 369-3600

(G-13175)
FEDEX FREIGHT CORPORATION
160 Industrial Pkwy (44903-8999)
PHONE....................................800 390-0159
Chris Leonard, *Manager*
EMP: 32
SALES (corp-wide): 65.4B **Publicly Held**
SIC: 4213 Less-than-truckload (LTL) trans-
port
HQ: Fedex Freight Corporation
1715 Aaron Brenner Dr
Memphis TN 38120

(G-13176)
FIRST ASSEMBLY CHILD CARE
1000 Mcpherson St (44903-7145)
PHONE....................................419 529-6501
Kim McCoy, *Director*
Kim Glavic, *Deputy Dir*
EMP: 30

SALES (est): 1.1MM **Privately Held**
WEB: www.mansfieldfirstassembly.org
SIC: 8351 8661 Child day care services;
religious organizations

(G-13177)
**FIRST CHOICE MED STAFF OF
OHIO**
90 W 2nd St (44902-1917)
PHONE....................................419 521-2700
Charles Slone, *Branch Mgr*
EMP: 67
SALES (corp-wide): 4.6MM **Privately
Held**
SIC: 7361 Employment agencies
PA: First Choice Medical Staffing Of Ohio,
Inc.
1457 W 117th St
Cleveland OH 44107
216 521-2222

(G-13178)
**FRANS CHILD CARE-
MANSFIELD**
Also Called: YMCA
750 Scholl Rd (44907-1570)
PHONE....................................419 775-2500
Michael Kenyon, *CEO*
Mike Kenyon, *President*
Kerrick Franklin, *Director*
Megan Wolford, *Director*
EMP: 150
SQ FT: 120,000
SALES (est): 3MM **Privately Held**
SIC: 8641 7991 8351 8322 Youth organi-
zations; physical fitness facilities; child
day care services; individual & family
services

(G-13179)
**GORDON FLESCH COMPANY
INC**
2756 Lexington Ave (44904-1429)
PHONE....................................419 884-2031
Larry Layne, *Branch Mgr*
EMP: 25
SALES (corp-wide): 16.5MM **Privately
Held**
SIC: 5044 5045 5065 7359 Photocopy
machines; word processing equipment;
facsimile equipment; office machine
rental, except computers
PA: Gordon Flesch Company, Inc.
2675 Research Park Dr
Fitchburg WI 53711
608 271-2100

(G-13180)
**GRASAN EQUIPMENT
COMPANY INC**
440 S Illinois Ave (44907-1809)
PHONE....................................419 526-4440
Marian L Eilenfeld, *President*
Ed Eilenfeld, *Vice Pres*
Edward Eilenfeld Jr, *Vice Pres*
Chuck Ferguson, *Engineer*
Aaron Niswander, *Engineer*
▼ EMP: 65 EST: 1970
SQ FT: 62,000
SALES (est): 20.2MM **Privately Held**
WEB: www.grasan.com
SIC: 4953 3532 3559 3535 Recycling,
waste materials; crushers, stationary;
rock crushing machinery, stationary;
screeners, stationary; recycling machin-
ery; conveyors & conveying equipment;
construction machinery

(G-13181)
**HEALING HRTS CUNSELING
CTR INC**
680 Park Ave W (44906-3706)
PHONE....................................419 528-5993
Maja-Lisa Anderson, *President*
EMP: 35
SALES (est): 155.2K **Privately Held**
SIC: 8322 Individual & family services

(G-13182)
HEART OF OH CNCL BSA (PA)
3 N Main St Ste 303 (44902-1716)
PHONE....................................419 522-8300
Matthew Smith, *President*
Barry Norris, *Exec Dir*
EMP: 35

SALES: 1.6MM **Privately Held**
SIC: **8641** Boy Scout organization

(G-13183)
HORIZON MECHANICAL AND ELEC
Also Called: Buckeye Horizon
323 N Trimble Rd (44906-2539)
PHONE...................................419 529-2738
Mark Albert, *President*
Mark McClure, *Sales Staff*
Linda Albert, *Admin Sec*
EMP: 30
SALES (est): 4.8MM **Privately Held**
SIC: **1711** 1731 5999 Heating & air conditioning contractors; electrical work; plumbing & heating supplies

(G-13184)
IGH II INC
Also Called: Trugreen Chemlawn
110 Industrial Dr (44904-1339)
PHONE...................................419 874-3575
Terry Korczyk, *President*
EMP: 33 EST: 1987
SQ FT: 11,900
SALES (est): 2.9MM **Privately Held**
SIC: **0782** Lawn care services; landscape contractors

(G-13185)
IHEARTCOMMUNICATIONS INC
Also Called: Wman
1400 Radio Ln (44906-2525)
PHONE...................................419 529-2211
Diana Coon, *General Mgr*
EMP: 35 **Publicly Held**
SIC: **4832** Radio broadcasting stations, music format
HQ: Iheartcommunications, Inc.
20880 Stone Oak Pkwy
San Antonio TX 78258
210 822-2828

(G-13186)
INFO TRAK INCORPORATED
Also Called: Info Trak &
165 Marion Ave (44903-2223)
PHONE...................................419 747-9296
David W Satterfield, *President*
Ed Grove, *Director*
EMP: 40 EST: 1999
SQ FT: 1,700
SALES (est): 800K **Privately Held**
WEB: www.infotrakincorporated.com
SIC: **7381** Private investigator

(G-13187)
INFOCISION MANAGEMENT CORP
1404 Park Ave E (44905)
PHONE...................................419 529-8685
Jill Adamescu, *Branch Mgr*
EMP: 99
SALES (corp-wide): 242.3MM **Privately Held**
WEB: www.infocision.com
SIC: **7389** Telemarketing services
PA: Infocision Management Corporation
325 Springside Dr
Akron OH 44333
330 668-1411

(G-13188)
J & B EQUIPMENT & SUPPLY INC
Also Called: J & B Classical Glass & Mirror
2750 Lexington Ave (44904-1429)
P.O. Box 3028 (44904-0028)
PHONE...................................419 884-1155
Michael Chambers, *President*
Kim Miller, *Admin Sec*
EMP: 60
SQ FT: 10,000
SALES (est): 9.1MM **Privately Held**
WEB: www.jbacoustical.com
SIC: **5032** 5211 1793 1751 Drywall materials; lumber & other building materials; glass & glazing work; carpentry work

(G-13189)
J-TRAC INC
Also Called: Dearman Moving and Storage
961 N Main St (44903-8113)
P.O. Box 1992 (44901-1992)
PHONE...................................419 524-3456
Tim Cambell, *President*
Chris Cambell, *Vice Pres*
Chris Campbell, *Sales Staff*
EMP: 50
SALES (est): 3.3MM **Privately Held**
SIC: **4225** 4214 4213 4212 General warehousing; local trucking with storage; trucking, except local; local trucking, without storage

(G-13190)
JAMES RAY LOZIER
Also Called: TSA Inspections
84 Foxcroft Rd (44904-9705)
PHONE...................................419 884-2656
James R Lozier, *Owner*
Jim Luzier, *Owner*
EMP: 27
SALES (est): 450K **Privately Held**
SIC: **7389** Inspection & testing services

(G-13191)
JONES POTATO CHIP CO (PA)
823 Bowman St (44903-4107)
PHONE...................................419 529-9424
Robert Jones, *President*
Charles K Hellinger, *Principal*
Frederick W Jones, *Principal*
Darryl Jones, *Vice Pres*
Bob Martin, *Sales Mgr*
EMP: 46 EST: 1940
SQ FT: 50,000
SALES (est): 8.8MM **Privately Held**
WEB: www.joneschips.com
SIC: **2096** 5145 Potato chips & other potato-based snacks; potato chips

(G-13192)
KADEMENOS WISEHART HINES (PA)
6 W 3rd St Ste 200 (44902-1200)
PHONE...................................419 524-6011
Troy Wisehart, *President*
Victor P Kademenos, *Vice Pres*
EMP: 40
SALES (est): 4.5MM **Privately Held**
WEB: www.ckhlaw.com
SIC: **8111** General practice law office

(G-13193)
KEY OFFICE SERVICES
1999 Leppo Rd (44903-9076)
PHONE...................................419 747-9749
Brenda Upchuch, *Owner*
EMP: 29
SALES (est): 1.4MM **Privately Held**
WEB: www.keyofficeservices.com
SIC: **8748** Business consulting

(G-13194)
KINGWOOD CENTER
900 Park Ave W (44906)
PHONE...................................419 522-0211
Charles Gleabes, *Director*
Charles Gleaves, *Director*
EMP: 30
SALES (est): 1MM **Privately Held**
WEB: www.kingwoodcenter.org
SIC: **8412** Museum

(G-13195)
KOORSEN FIRE & SECURITY INC
100 Swarn Pkwy (44903-6515)
PHONE...................................419 526-2212
Randy Koorsen, *President*
EMP: 43
SALES (corp-wide): 244.8MM **Privately Held**
SIC: **7382** Protective devices, security
PA: Koorsen Fire & Security, Inc.
2719 N Arlington Ave
Indianapolis IN 46218
317 542-1800

(G-13196)
L A HAIR FORCE
1509 Lexington Ave (44907-2631)
PHONE...................................419 756-3101

Vicki Wittmer, *Owner*
EMP: 35
SALES (est): 416.9K **Privately Held**
SIC: **7231** Hairdressers

(G-13197)
LABORATORY CORPORATION AMERICA
418 E Broad St (44907)
PHONE...................................440 328-3275
Kathy Bruns, *Branch Mgr*
EMP: 40 **Publicly Held**
WEB: www.labcorp.com
SIC: **8071** Medical laboratories
HQ: Laboratory Corporation Of America
358 S Main St Ste 458
Burlington NC 27215
336 229-1127

(G-13198)
LEVERING MANAGEMENT INC
Also Called: Winchester Terrace
70 Winchester Rd (44907-2042)
PHONE...................................419 756-4747
L Bruce Levering, *President*
Alice Cree, *Administration*
EMP: 88
SALES (corp-wide): 27.7MM **Privately Held**
SIC: **8051** Convalescent home with continuous nursing care
PA: Levering Management, Inc.
201 N Main St
Mount Vernon OH 43050
740 397-3897

(G-13199)
LEXINGTON COURT CARE CENTER
Also Called: Burns International Staffing
250 Delaware Ave (44904-1215)
PHONE...................................419 884-2000
Toni Marone, *Administration*
EMP: 98
SALES (est): 3.3MM **Privately Held**
SIC: **8052** 8051 Intermediate care facilities; skilled nursing care facilities

(G-13200)
LYNNHAVEN XII LLC
Also Called: Woodlawn Nursing Home
535 Lexington Ave (44907-1502)
PHONE...................................419 756-7111
Richard Stewart, *Manager*
EMP: 125
SALES (corp-wide): 7.8MM **Privately Held**
SIC: **8051** Convalescent home with continuous nursing care
PA: Lynnhaven Xii, Llc
206 Southgate Dr
Boone NC 28607
828 265-0080

(G-13201)
MADISON LOCAL SCHOOL DISTRICT (PA)
1379 Grace St (44905-2742)
PHONE...................................419 589-2600
Jeff Meyers, *President*
Lee Kaple, *Superintendent*
Robin Klenk, *Purchasing*
Sandy Davis, *Asst Treas*
Mike Yost, *Training Spec*
EMP: 450
SALES (est): 26MM **Privately Held**
WEB: www.madison-lake.k12.oh.us
SIC: **8211** 8351 Public elementary & secondary schools; public junior high school; public senior high school; school board; child day care services

(G-13202)
MAJOR METALS COMPANY
844 Kochheiser Rd (44904-8637)
PHONE...................................419 886-4600
Jeffrey C Mason, *President*
Wayne Riffe, *Vice Pres*
Jason Dials, *Sales Mgr*
EMP: 30
SQ FT: 60,000

SALES (est): 13.7MM **Privately Held**
WEB: www.majormetalscompany.com
SIC: **3312** 5051 3317 Plate, sheet & strip, except coated products; iron or steel flat products; steel pipe & tubes

(G-13203)
MANFIELD LIVING CENTER LTD
Also Called: Twinoaks Living and Lrng Ctr
73 Madison Rd (44905-2830)
P.O. Box 1218 (44901-1218)
PHONE...................................419 512-1711
Tracy Robertson, *Manager*
Anthony Wheaton, *Exec Dir*
EMP: 30
SALES (est): 1.2MM **Privately Held**
SIC: **8361** Home for the mentally retarded

(G-13204)
MANSFIELD AMBULANCE INC
369 Marion Ave (44903-2064)
P.O. Box 2687 (44906-0687)
PHONE...................................419 525-3311
Tom Durbin, *President*
Margaret Neill, *Treasurer*
EMP: 40
SQ FT: 5,000
SALES (est): 1.9MM **Privately Held**
WEB: www.mansfieldambulance.com
SIC: **4119** Ambulance service

(G-13205)
MANSFIELD CITY BUILDING MAINT
30 N Diamond St (44902-1702)
PHONE...................................419 755-9698
Todd Dilley, *COO*
EMP: 38
SALES (est): 1.3MM **Privately Held**
SIC: **5087** Cleaning & maintenance equipment & supplies

(G-13206)
MANSFIELD HOTEL PARTNERSHIP
Also Called: Knights Inn
555 N Trimble Rd (44906-2101)
PHONE...................................419 529-2100
Sandy Keiser, *Manager*
EMP: 26
SALES (corp-wide): 2.5MM **Privately Held**
SIC: **7011** Hotels & motels
PA: Mansfield Hotel Partnership
500 N Trimble Rd
Mansfield OH 44906
419 529-1000

(G-13207)
MANSFIELD HOTEL PARTNERSHIP (PA)
Also Called: Quality Inn
500 N Trimble Rd (44906-2102)
PHONE...................................419 529-1000
Dr When Fu Chin, *Partner*
Ronald Fewster, *Partner*
Patrick Mc Allister, *Partner*
Sherry McNabb, *General Mgr*
Sandy Kiser, *Manager*
EMP: 60
SQ FT: 44,000
SALES (est): 2.5MM **Privately Held**
SIC: **7011** 7991 Hotel, franchised; physical fitness facilities

(G-13208)
MANSFIELD MEMORIAL HOMES
Also Called: Robert Sturges Memorial Homes
55 Wood St (44903-2251)
P.O. Box 966 (44901-0966)
PHONE...................................419 774-5100
Miles Parsons, *Principal*
Raymond L Loughman, *Exec Dir*
EMP: 125
SALES (est): 327.7K **Privately Held**
SIC: **6513** Apartment building operators

(G-13209)
MANSFIELD MEMORIAL HOMES LLC (PA)
Also Called: GERIATRICS CENTER OF MANSFIELD
50 Blymyer Ave (44903-2343)
P.O. Box 966 (44901-0966)
PHONE...................................419 774-5100

GEOGRAPHIC

Dan Miller,
Raymond Loughman,
EMP: 135 **EST:** 1953
SALES: 6.4MM **Privately Held**
WEB: www.mansfieldmh.com
SIC: 8051 8052 Convalescent home with continuous nursing care; intermediate care facilities

(G-13210)
MANSFIELD OPCO LLC
Also Called: Arbors At Mifflin
1600 Crider Rd (44903-9268)
PHONE..............................502 429-8062
Robert Norcross, *CEO*
EMP: 99
SQ FT: 60,000
SALES (est): 2.2MM **Privately Held**
SIC: 8051 Skilled nursing care facilities

(G-13211)
MANSFIELD TRUCK SLS & SVC INC
85 Longview Ave E (44903-4205)
P.O. Box 1516 (44901-1516)
PHONE..............................419 522-9811
Fred Bollon, *President*
Rod Rafael, *VP Opers*
EMP: 50
SALES (est): 5.3MM
SALES (corp-wide): 13MM **Privately Held**
SIC: 5012 5511 7538 Trucks, commercial; trucks, tractors & trailers: new & used; general truck repair
PA: Truck Sales & Service, Inc.
3429 Brightwood Rd
Midvale OH
740 922-3412

(G-13212)
MCELVAIN GROUP HOME
634 Mcbride Rd (44905-2962)
PHONE..............................419 589-6697
Kathy McElvain, *Partner*
Donald McElvain, *Partner*
EMP: 30
SALES (est): 816.3K **Privately Held**
SIC: 8361 Home for the mentally handicapped

(G-13213)
MECHANICS BANK (PA)
2 S Main St (44902-2931)
PHONE..............................419 524-0831
Mark Masters, *President*
Deborah Adams, *Senior VP*
Jason Painley, *CFO*
EMP: 35
SQ FT: 5,000
SALES: 21.4MM **Privately Held**
SIC: 6022 State commercial banks

(G-13214)
MEDCENTRAL HEALTH SYSTEM
Also Called: Med Central HM Hlth & Hospice
335 Glessner Ave (44903-2269)
PHONE..............................419 526-8442
Marte Alsleben, *Owner*
EMP: 30
SALES (corp-wide): 4B **Privately Held**
SIC: 8062 8082 8093 General medical & surgical hospitals; home health care services; specialty outpatient clinics
HQ: Medcentral Health System
335 Glessner Ave
Mansfield OH 44903
419 526-8000

(G-13215)
MEDCENTRAL HEALTH SYSTEM (HQ)
Also Called: Ohiohealth Mansfield Hospital
335 Glessner Ave (44903-2269)
PHONE..............................419 526-8000
Beth Hildreth, *Vice Pres*
Khanh Thai, *Med Doctor*
EMP: 53
SQ FT: 300,000
SALES: 269MM
SALES (corp-wide): 4B **Privately Held**
SIC: 8062 General medical & surgical hospitals

PA: Ohiohealth Corporation
180 E Broad St
Columbus OH 43215
614 788-8860

(G-13216)
MEDCENTRAL HEALTH SYSTEM
770 Balgreen Dr Ste 105 (44906-4106)
PHONE..............................419 526-8970
James Meyer, *Branch Mgr*
EMP: 80
SALES (corp-wide): 4B **Privately Held**
SIC: 8062 General medical & surgical hospitals
HQ: Medcentral Health System
335 Glessner Ave
Mansfield OH 44903
419 526-8000

(G-13217)
MEDCENTRAL HEALTH SYSTEM
Also Called: Med Cntral Hlth Sys Child Care
160 S Linden Rd (44906-3028)
PHONE..............................419 526-8043
Patricia Harding, *Director*
EMP: 26
SALES (corp-wide): 4B **Privately Held**
SIC: 8062 8351 General medical & surgical hospitals; child day care services
HQ: Medcentral Health System
335 Glessner Ave
Mansfield OH 44903
419 526-8000

(G-13218)
MEDIC RESPONSE SERVICE INC (PA)
98 S Diamond St (44902-7564)
PHONE..............................419 522-1998
Thomas F Wappner, *President*
William C Wappner, *Vice Pres*
EMP: 45
SQ FT: 1,600
SALES (est): 982.1K **Privately Held**
SIC: 4119 Ambulance service

(G-13219)
METAL CONVERSIONS LTD (PA)
849 Crawford Ave N (44905-1205)
P.O. Box 787 (44901-0787)
PHONE..............................419 525-0011
Steve Senser, *CEO*
Rob Care, *President*
Carl Roark, *Exec VP*
Jay Levant, *Vice Pres*
Andy Senser, *Vice Pres*
▲ **EMP:** 25
SQ FT: 16,000
SALES (est): 24.5MM **Privately Held**
SIC: 5051 Aluminum bars, rods, ingots, sheets, pipes, plates, etc.

(G-13220)
MICKIS CREATIVE OPTIONS INC
1841 S Main St (44907-2828)
PHONE..............................419 526-4254
Michele Stambaugh, *Principal*
EMP: 50
SALES (est): 1MM **Privately Held**
SIC: 8331 Job training & vocational rehabilitation services

(G-13221)
MID-OHIO HEART CLINIC INC
335 Glessner Ave (44903-2269)
PHONE..............................419 524-8151
William Polinsky MD, *President*
Michael Amalfitano MD, *Vice Pres*
Gregory Vigesaa MD, *Vice Pres*
Mary Alton, *Med Doctor*
EMP: 40
SALES (est): 4.5MM **Privately Held**
SIC: 8062 General medical & surgical hospitals

(G-13222)
MID-OHIO PIPELINE COMPANY INC
Also Called: Mid-Ohio Pipeline Services
4244 State Route 546 (44904-9327)
PHONE..............................419 884-3772
Chuck Austin, *President*
Gene F Yates, *Principal*
Thomas Lorenz, *Vice Pres*
EMP: 40 **EST:** 1970

SALES (est): 16.7MM **Privately Held**
SIC: 1623 Oil & gas pipeline construction; pipeline construction

(G-13223)
MILLIRON RECYCLING INC
Also Called: Milliron Iron & Metal
2384 Springmill Rd (44903-8712)
PHONE..............................419 747-6522
Brant Milliron, *President*
EMP: 60
SALES (est): 14.3MM **Privately Held**
SIC: 4953 Recycling, waste materials

(G-13224)
MIP INTERENT ENTERPRISES LLC
Also Called: Boxdrop Mansfield Mattress
720c 5th Ave (44905-1421)
PHONE..............................614 917-8705
Baron Johnson,
EMP: 35
SQ FT: 900
SALES (est): 2.9MM **Privately Held**
SIC: 2759 7336 Commercial printing; commercial art & graphic design

(G-13225)
MT BUSINESS TECHNOLOGIES INC (DH)
1150 National Pkwy (44906-1911)
PHONE..............................419 529-6100
Chuck Rounds, *President*
William Forrester, *Area Mgr*
Tammy Runion, *Marketing Mgr*
Adrienne Krizan, *Manager*
Debra Barker, *Sr Associate*
EMP: 130 **EST:** 1930
SQ FT: 64,000
SALES: 60MM
SALES (corp-wide): 9.8B **Publicly Held**
WEB: www.mtbustech.com
SIC: 5044 7378 7379 Copying equipment; computer peripheral equipment repair & maintenance; computer related consulting services

(G-13226)
NATIONAL WEATHER SERVICE
2101 Harrington Mem Rd (44903-8052)
PHONE..............................419 522-1375
EMP: 33 **Publicly Held**
SIC: 8999 9611 Weather forecasting; administration of general economic programs;
HQ: National Weather Service
1325 E West Hwy
Silver Spring MD 20910

(G-13227)
OAK GROVE MANOR INC
1670 Crider Rd (44903-9268)
PHONE..............................419 589-6222
Marlene Pachl, *Human Res Mgr*
Glenna Holley, *Manager*
Med Velasco, *Administration*
Linda Lamson, *Administration*
Chris Plantz, *Maintence Staff*
EMP: 114
SALES (est): 4.4MM **Privately Held**
SIC: 8051 Skilled nursing care facilities

(G-13228)
OHIO CANCER SPECIALISTS (PA)
1125 Aspira Ct (44906-4125)
PHONE..............................419 756-2122
Donald L Dewald, *Partner*
Saurabh Das, *Partner*
Shahzad Khan, *Partner*
EMP: 30
SQ FT: 6,000
SALES (est): 1.9MM **Privately Held**
WEB: www.ohcancer.com
SIC: 8011 Hematologist; internal medicine; physician/surgeon; oncologist

(G-13229)
OHIO EYE ASSOCIATES INC
Also Called: Marquardt, Richard F Od
466 S Trimble Rd (44906-3416)
PHONE..............................800 423-0694
John L Marquardt, *President*
Leonard D Quick, *Vice Pres*
Lori Conard, *Med Doctor*

EMP: 51
SQ FT: 32,000
SALES (est): 8.6MM **Privately Held**
WEB: www.ohioeyeassociates.com
SIC: 8011 Ophthalmologist

(G-13230)
PASSPRT ACCEPT FCLTY MANSFLD P
200 N Diamond St (44901-1240)
PHONE..............................419 755-4621
Robert Pelasky, *Post Master*
EMP: 145
SALES (est): 2.3MM **Privately Held**
SIC: 7389 Notary publics

(G-13231)
R G SMITH COMPANY
Also Called: Smith, R G of Mansfield
166 W 6th St (44902-1096)
P.O. Box 1057 (44901-1057)
PHONE..............................419 524-4778
Rick Reece, *Branch Mgr*
Mike Black, *Manager*
EMP: 25
SALES (corp-wide): 24MM **Privately Held**
SIC: 1541 Industrial buildings, new construction
PA: R. G. Smith Company
1249 Dueber Ave Sw
Canton OH 44706
330 456-3415

(G-13232)
RAMA TIKA DEVELOPERS LLC
719 Earick Rd (44903-8622)
PHONE..............................419 806-6446
Vaibhav Patel, *President*
EMP: 30
SQ FT: 85,000
SALES: 2MM **Privately Held**
SIC: 6552 8741 Subdividers & developers; hotel or motel management

(G-13233)
REBMAN TRUCK SERVICE INC
1004 Vanderbilt Rd (44904-8608)
PHONE..............................419 589-8161
James B Redman Jr, *President*
Denise Redman, *President*
EMP: 25
SALES (est): 2.6MM **Privately Held**
SIC: 7538 General truck repair

(G-13234)
RESEARCH & INVESTIGATION ASSOC
Also Called: Sonitrol Security Systems
186 Sturges Ave (44903-2313)
PHONE..............................419 526-1299
C Ray Gregory, *President*
Steve Miller, *Exec VP*
Chuck Gregory, *VP Opers*
Carol A Gregory, *Treasurer*
Thomas Cole, *Admin Sec*
EMP: 26
SQ FT: 3,500
SALES: 1.4MM **Privately Held**
SIC: 5999 5063 1731 7382 Alarm signal systems; electric alarms & signaling equipment; alarm systems; burglar alarm systems; fire detection & burglar alarm systems specialization; burglar alarm maintenance & monitoring

(G-13235)
RICHLAND COUNTY CHILD SUPPORT
161 Park Ave E (44902-1829)
PHONE..............................419 774-5700
Robert Sparks, *Director*
Dawn Bolinger, *Admin Sec*
EMP: 42
SALES (est): 459.7K **Privately Held**
SIC: 8322 Child guidance agency

(G-13236)
RICHLAND MALL SHOPPING CTR
2209 Lexington Ave (44907)
PHONE..............................419 529-4003
Richard E Jacobs, *Partner*
Barry Brown, *Info Tech Mgr*
EMP: 25

▲ = Import ▼=Export
◆ =Import/Export

SQ FT: 500,000
SALES (est): 1.6MM **Privately Held**
SIC: 8741 6552 6531 Management services; subdividers & developers; real estate agents & managers

(G-13237)
RICHLAND NEWHOPE INDUSTRIES (PA)
150 E 4th St (44902-1520)
P.O. Box 916 (44901-0916)
PHONE....................................419 774-4400
Peggy Hamblin, *Vice Pres*
Greg Young, *Prdtn Mgr*
Elizabeth Prather, *Exec Dir*
EMP: 250
SQ FT: 63,000
SALES: 6.4MM **Privately Held**
SIC: 0782 2448 7349 8331 Lawn & garden services; wood pallets & skids; building maintenance services; job training & vocational rehabilitation services; packaging & labeling services

(G-13238)
RICHLAND NEWHOPE INDUSTRIES
314 Cleveland Ave (44902-8623)
PHONE....................................419 774-4200
Anthony Persky, *HR Admin*
Jim Moore, *Marketing Mgr*
Jackie Fry, *Consultant*
Scott Anderson, *Information Mgr*
Jan Arnold, *Exec Dir*
EMP: 45
SALES (corp-wide): 6.4MM **Privately Held**
SIC: 8331 Job training & vocational rehabilitation services
PA: Richland Newhope Industries, Inc
150 E 4th St
Mansfield OH 44902
419 774-4400

(G-13239)
RICHLAND NEWHOPE INDUSTRIES
985 W Longview Ave (44906-2133)
PHONE....................................419 774-4496
Marsha Madden, *Principal*
EMP: 100
SALES (corp-wide): 6.4MM **Privately Held**
SIC: 8331 Job training & vocational rehabilitation services
PA: Richland Newhope Industries, Inc
150 E 4th St
Mansfield OH 44902
419 774-4400

(G-13240)
RICHLAND TRUST COMPANY (HQ)
3 N Main St Ste 1 (44902-1740)
P.O. Box 355 (44901-0355)
PHONE....................................419 525-8700
Timothy J Lehman, *President*
Jerrold Coon, *Corp Secy*
Ray Piar, *Vice Pres*
EMP: 84
SALES (est): 5.1MM
SALES (corp-wide): 411.9MM **Publicly Held**
WEB: www.richlandbank.com
SIC: 6022 8721 State trust companies accepting deposits, commercial; accounting, auditing & bookkeeping
PA: Park National Corporation
50 N 3rd St
Newark OH 43055
740 349-8451

(G-13241)
SC MADISON BUS GARAGE
Also Called: Madison Local School
600 Esley Ln (44905-2718)
PHONE....................................419 589-3373
Rodger Harramam, *Superintendent*
Mike Yost, *Training Spec*
EMP: 54
SALES (est): 1.5MM **Privately Held**
SIC: 4151 School buses

(G-13242)
SHAFFER POMEROY LTD
909 S Main St (44907-2037)
P.O. Box 3598 (44907-0598)
PHONE....................................419 756-7302
Keith A Amstutz,
EMP: 27
SALES: 250K **Privately Held**
SIC: 8711 Consulting engineer

(G-13243)
SKYBOX PACKAGING LLC
Also Called: Mr Box
1275 Pollock Pkwy (44905-1374)
P.O. Box 1567 (44901-1567)
PHONE....................................419 525-7209
Marc Miller, *President*
Jan Piko, *Regl Sales Mgr*
EMP: 73
SALES (est): 15.7MM
SALES (corp-wide): 882.3MM **Privately Held**
SIC: 3086 5199 Packaging & shipping materials, foamed plastic; packaging materials
PA: Atlantic Packaging Products Ltd
111 Progress Ave
Scarborough ON M1P 2
416 298-8101

(G-13244)
SOUTHERN TITLE OF OHIO LTD (PA)
58 W 3rd St Ste D (44902-1251)
P.O. Box 937 (44901-0937)
PHONE....................................419 525-4600
Mark Wilkinson, *President*
EMP: 27
SALES (est): 10.3MM **Privately Held**
WEB: www.southerntitleofohio.com
SIC: 6361 Title insurance

(G-13245)
SPECTRUM MGT HOLDG CO LLC
1280 Park Ave W (44906-2814)
PHONE....................................419 775-9292
EMP: 83
SALES (corp-wide): 43.6B **Publicly Held**
SIC: 4841 Cable television services
HQ: Spectrum Management Holding Company, Llc
400 Atlantic St
Stamford CT 06901
203 905-7801

(G-13246)
SPRING MEADOW EXTENDED CARE CE
105 S Main St (44902-7901)
PHONE....................................419 866-6124
Donald D Graber, *Branch Mgr*
EMP: 65
SALES (corp-wide): 1.4MM **Privately Held**
SIC: 8052 Intermediate care facilities
PA: Spring Meadow Extended Care Center Facility, Inc.
1125 Clarion Ave
Holland OH 43528
419 866-6124

(G-13247)
SURGICENTER OF MANSFIELD
1030 Cricket Ln (44906-4104)
PHONE....................................419 774-9410
Edroy McMillam, *Chairman*
EMP: 40
SALES (est): 2.1MM **Privately Held**
WEB: www.surgictr.com
SIC: 8093 Specialty outpatient clinics

(G-13248)
SYSTEMS JAY LLC NANOGATE (HQ)
150 Longview Ave E (44903-4206)
PHONE....................................419 524-3778
Ralf Zastrau, *CEO*
Michael Jung, *COO*
Daniel Seibert, *CFO*
EMP: 930 EST: 2016

SALES (est): 10.5MM
SALES (corp-wide): 219.6MM **Privately Held**
SIC: 1799 Coating of concrete structures with plastic
PA: Nanogate Se
Zum Schacht 3
Quierschied 66287
682 595-910

(G-13249)
SYSTEMS JAY LLC NANOGATE
Also Called: Kronis Coatings
1575 W Longview Ave (44906-1806)
PHONE....................................419 747-6639
Dick Ward, *Branch Mgr*
EMP: 45
SALES (corp-wide): 219.6MM **Privately Held**
WEB: www.jayindinc.com
SIC: 5198 Paints
HQ: Jay Nanogate Systems Llc
150 Longview Ave E
Mansfield OH 44903
419 524-3778

(G-13250)
TARA FLAHERTY
Also Called: Cuttin' It Close
1872 White Pine Dr (44904-1715)
PHONE....................................419 565-1334
Tara Flaherty, *Owner*
EMP: 27
SALES: 200K **Privately Held**
WEB: www.cuttinitclose.com
SIC: 7231 Beauty shops

(G-13251)
THE MANSFIELD STRL & ERCT CO (PA)
Also Called: Mansfield Fabricated Products
429 Park Ave E (44905-2844)
P.O. Box 427 (44901-0427)
PHONE....................................419 522-5911
Richard Gash, *President*
Barbara Gash, *Corp Secy*
EMP: 25 EST: 1924
SQ FT: 60,000
SALES (est): 6.3MM **Privately Held**
SIC: 3441 5051 Fabricated structural metal; metals service centers & offices

(G-13252)
THE MAPLE CITY ICE COMPANY
Also Called: Mansfield Distributing Co Div
1245 W Longview Ave (44906-1907)
PHONE....................................419 747-4777
Mary Berry, *Owner*
Michael J Berry, *Branch Mgr*
EMP: 25
SQ FT: 16,463
SALES (corp-wide): 26.9MM **Privately Held**
SIC: 4225 General warehousing
PA: Maple City Ice Company, The (Inc)
371 Cleveland Rd
Norwalk OH 44857
419 668-2531

(G-13253)
THINK-ABILITY LLC
1256 Warner Ave (44905-2619)
PHONE....................................419 589-2238
Michael Mazak,
EMP: 28
SALES (est): 826.2K **Privately Held**
SIC: 8082 Home health care services

(G-13254)
TMS INTERNATIONAL LLC
1344 Bowman St (44903-4009)
PHONE....................................419 747-5500
EMP: 40 **Privately Held**
SIC: 5093 Scrap And Waste Materials

(G-13255)
TRIUMPH HOSPITAL MANSFIELD
335 Glessner Ave (44903-2269)
PHONE....................................419 526-0777
Russell Test, *Principal*
EMP: 32
SALES (est): 3.1MM **Privately Held**
SIC: 8062 General medical & surgical hospitals

(G-13256)
TRUGREEN LIMITED PARTNERSHIP
Also Called: Tru Green-Chemlawn
110 Industrial Dr (44904-1339)
P.O. Box 3088 (44904-0088)
PHONE....................................419 884-3636
Jim Morris, *Manager*
EMP: 25
SALES (corp-wide): 3.4B **Privately Held**
SIC: 0782 Lawn care services
HQ: Trugreen Limited Partnership
1790 Kirby Pkwy
Memphis TN 38138
901 251-4128

(G-13257)
TUTTLE LANDSCAPING & GRDN CTR
1295 S Trimble Rd (44907-2699)
PHONE....................................419 756-7555
Charles A Tuttle, *President*
Tod Tuttle, *Vice Pres*
EMP: 25
SQ FT: 30,000
SALES: 750K **Privately Held**
SIC: 0782 5261 Landscape contractors; lawnmowers & tractors; garden supplies & tools; nursery stock, seeds & bulbs

(G-13258)
TWIN OAKS CARE CENTER INC
73 Madison Rd (44905-2830)
P.O. Box 1218 (44901-1218)
PHONE....................................419 524-1205
Michael Daffin, *President*
James Boyd III, *Vice Pres*
EMP: 25
SALES (est): 1.1MM **Privately Held**
SIC: 8051 8069 Skilled nursing care facilities; specialty hospitals, except psychiatric

(G-13259)
UNITED PARCEL SERVICE INC OH
Also Called: UPS
875 W Longview Ave (44906-2131)
PHONE....................................419 747-3080
Victor Jones, *Business Mgr*
Chuck Kastor, *Manager*
EMP: 112
SALES (corp-wide): 71.8B **Publicly Held**
WEB: www.upsscs.com
SIC: 4215 Package delivery, vehicular
HQ: United Parcel Service, Inc. (Oh)
55 Glenlake Pkwy
Atlanta GA 30328
404 828-6000

(G-13260)
VISITING NRSE ASSN OF CLVELAND
Also Called: Vna of Mid Ohio
40 W 4th St (44902-1206)
P.O. Box 1742 (44901-1742)
PHONE....................................419 522-4969
Cortney Swihart, *Exec Dir*
Dana Traxler, *Exec Dir*
EMP: 25
SALES (est): 2MM **Privately Held**
SIC: 8082 Visiting nurse service

(G-13261)
VOLUNTERS OF AMER GREATER OHIO
921 N Main St (44903-8113)
PHONE....................................419 524-5013
Lyle Draper, *Branch Mgr*
EMP: 30
SALES (corp-wide): 10.7MM **Privately Held**
WEB: www.voa.org
SIC: 8322 Individual & family services
PA: Volunteers Of America Ohio & Indiana
1776 E Broad St Frnt
Columbus OH 43203
614 253-6100

(G-13262)
WEDGEWOOD ESTATES
Also Called: Casto Health Care
600 S Trimble Rd (44906-3420)
PHONE....................................419 756-7400

William Casto, *Owner*
Lori Casto, *Sales Executive*
Gloria Saunders, *Nursing Dir*
Helen Sprowl, *Hlthcr Dir*
EMP: 30 **EST:** 1997
SALES (est): 1.8MM **Privately Held**
WEB: www.wedgewoodestates.com
SIC: 8059 8052 Convalescent home; in-
termediate care facilities

(G-13263)
WOMENS CARE INC
500 S Trimble Rd (44906-4103)
PHONE...........................419 756-6000
Thomas H Croghan, *President*
Edroy L Mc Millan, *Vice Pres*
Hunter Wilson, *Vice Pres*
Guy Capaldo, *Med Doctor*
Virginia Brown, *Director*
EMP: 77
SQ FT: 8,500
SALES (est): 5.8MM **Privately Held**
WEB: www.wcareinc.com
SIC: 8011 Gynecologist; obstetrician

Mantua
Portage County

(G-13264)
AWL TRANSPORT INC
4626 State Route 82 (44255-9654)
PHONE...........................330 899-3444
Jerry W Carlton, *President*
Linda Carlton, *General Mgr*
EMP: 34
SALES (est): 11.2MM **Privately Held**
SIC: 4213 Contract haulers

(G-13265)
COLUMBIAN CORPORATION MANTUA
Also Called: KNIGHTS OF COLUMBUS #3766
11845 State Route 44 (44255-9647)
P.O. Box 52 (44255-0052)
PHONE...........................330 274-2576
Bob Hartman, *President*
Mark Kasubick, *President*
EMP: 30
SALES: 52.9K **Privately Held**
SIC: 6512 Nonresidential building opera-
tors

(G-13266)
COMPASS PACKAGING LLC
10585 Main St (44255-9600)
P.O. Box 739, Parkman (44080-0739)
PHONE...........................330 274-2001
Phil Rath, *President*
Rory Groce, *Sales Staff*
▲ **EMP:** 41
SQ FT: 24,000
SALES (est): 21.8MM **Privately Held**
WEB: www.compasspackaging.com
SIC: 5199 Packaging materials

(G-13267)
HATTIE LARLHAM CENTER FOR (PA)
9772 Diagonal Rd (44255-9160)
PHONE...........................330 274-2272
Dennis Allen, *CEO*
Darryl E Mast, *COO*
Michelle Anderson, *Vice Pres*
Dotty Grexa, *Vice Pres*
Sandy Neal, *Vice Pres*
EMP: 246
SQ FT: 120,000
SALES: 19.8MM **Privately Held**
SIC: 8361 8322 8052 Home for the men-
tally retarded; individual & family services;
intermediate care facilities

(G-13268)
HATTIE LARLHAM CENTER FOR
9772 Diagonal Rd (44255-9160)
PHONE...........................330 274-2272
Dennis Allen, *CEO*
EMP: 83
SALES (corp-wide): 19.8MM **Privately Held**
SIC: 8361 Home for the mentally retarded

PA: Hattie Larlham Center For Children
With Disabilities
9772 Diagonal Rd
Mantua OH 44255
330 274-2272

(G-13269)
HATTIE LARLHAM COMMUNITY SVCS
Also Called: DOGGY DAY CARE
9772 Diagonal Rd (44255-9160)
PHONE...........................330 274-2272
Kayla Ferroni, *Manager*
Dennis Allen, *Exec Dir*
EMP: 50
SALES: 12.4MM
SALES (corp-wide): 5.2MM **Privately Held**
SIC: 8322 Association for the handicapped
PA: Hattie Larlham Community Living
7996 Darrow Rd
Twinsburg OH 44087
330 274-2272

(G-13270)
HATTIE LARLHAM COMMUNITY SVCS
9772 Diagonal Rd (44255-9160)
PHONE...........................330 274-2272
Jim Felter, *Controller*
EMP: 40
SALES: 13.5MM **Privately Held**
SIC: 8082 Home health care services

(G-13271)
LAKESIDE SAND & GRAVEL INC
3498 Frost Rd (44255-9136)
PHONE...........................330 274-2569
Larry Kotkowski, *President*
Ronald Kotkowski, *Corp Secy*
EMP: 25
SQ FT: 4,200
SALES: 1.6MM **Privately Held**
SIC: 1442 Construction sand mining;
gravel mining

(G-13272)
LARLHAM CARE HATTIE GROUP
9772 Diagonal Rd (44255-9128)
PHONE...........................330 274-2272
Dennis Allen, *CEO*
Elizabeth Jones, *Manager*
EMP: 53
SALES: 3.7MM **Privately Held**
SIC: 8099 Medical services organization

(G-13273)
MANTALINE CORPORATION
Also Called: Transportation Group
4754 E High St (44255-9201)
PHONE...........................330 274-2264
Bryan Fink, *Manager*
Bryan N Fink, *Manager*
EMP: 75
SALES (corp-wide): 35.2MM **Privately Held**
WEB: www.mantaline.com
SIC: 5169 3061 Synthetic rubber; me-
chanical rubber goods
PA: Mantaline Corporation
4754 E High St
Mantua OH 44255
330 274-2264

(G-13274)
OTTO FALKENBERG EXCAVATING
9350 Coit Rd (44255-9139)
PHONE...........................330 626-4215
Otto Falkenberg, *President*
Marilyn Falkenberg, *Vice Pres*
Carol Helmling, *Admin Sec*
EMP: 30
SALES (est): 2MM **Privately Held**
SIC: 1794 Excavation & grading, building
construction

(G-13275)
PIPER PLUMBING INC
2480 Bartlett Rd (44255-9417)
PHONE...........................330 274-0160
Irene Terry, *President*
David Terry, *Vice Pres*
John Terry, *Treasurer*
EMP: 25

SALES (est): 2.4MM **Privately Held**
WEB: www.terryproperties.com
SIC: 1711 Plumbing contractors

(G-13276)
STAMM CONTRACTING CO INC
4566 Orchard St (44255-9701)
P.O. Box 450 (44255-0450)
PHONE...........................330 274-8230
Hal Stamm, *President*
Elva Novotny, *Corp Secy*
Quinn Novotny, *Exec VP*
Jason Hielman, *Purch Agent*
Matt Tucek, *Sales Executive*
EMP: 40 **EST:** 1913
SQ FT: 1,500
SALES (est): 5.9MM **Privately Held**
WEB: www.stammcontracting.com
SIC: 3273 1541 1542 5211 Ready-mixed
concrete; industrial buildings & ware-
houses; commercial & office building con-
tractors; lumber & other building
materials; brick, stone & related material;
concrete work

(G-13277)
TRIPLE LADYS AGENCY INC (PA)
Also Called: T L Express
4626 State Route 82 (44255-9654)
PHONE...........................330 274-1100
Gloria G Vechery, *President*
Heather L Carlton, *Vice Pres*
Linda A Carlton, *Admin Sec*
EMP: 25
SQ FT: 10,000
SALES (est): 22MM **Privately Held**
SIC: 4213 4212 4225 Trucking, except
local; local trucking, without storage; gen-
eral warehousing

(G-13278)
VISUAL ART GRAPHIC SERVICES
5244 Goodell Rd (44255-9746)
PHONE...........................330 274-2775
George South, *President*
EMP: 30
SQ FT: 35,000
SALES (est): 3MM **Privately Held**
WEB: www.evisualarts.com
SIC: 2752 7336 Commercial printing, litho-
graphic; commercial art & graphic design

Maple Heights
Cuyahoga County

(G-13279)
AARONS INC
5420 Northfield Rd (44137-3113)
PHONE...........................216 587-2745
William Wagner, *Office Mgr*
EMP: 25
SALES (corp-wide): 3.8B **Publicly Held**
WEB: www.aaronrents.com
SIC: 7359 Furniture rental; home appli-
ance, furniture & entertainment rental
services
PA: Aaron's, Inc.
400 Galleria Pkwy Se # 300
Atlanta GA 30339
678 402-3000

(G-13280)
AGMET LLC
5463 Dunham Rd (44137-3644)
PHONE...........................216 662-6939
Dave Crose, *Office Mgr*
EMP: 35
SALES (corp-wide): 21.8MM **Privately Held**
WEB: www.agmetmetals.com
SIC: 5093 Ferrous metal scrap & waste
PA: Agmet Llc
7800 Medusa Rd
Cleveland OH 44146
440 439-7400

(G-13281)
AREA TEMPS INC
15689 Broadway Ave (44137-1121)
PHONE...........................216 518-2000
Tom Shea, *Manager*

EMP: 2305
SALES (corp-wide): 87.8MM **Privately Held**
WEB: www.areatemps.com
SIC: 7363 Temporary help service
PA: Area Temps, Inc.
4511 Rockside Rd Ste 190
Independence OH 44131
216 781-5350

(G-13282)
BRUDER INC
16900 Rockside Rd (44137-4333)
PHONE...........................216 791-9800
Robert Bruder, *President*
Michael Bruder, *Vice Pres*
▼ **EMP:** 27
SQ FT: 2,000
SALES (est): 5.9MM **Privately Held**
WEB: www.bruderinc.com
SIC: 5211 5032 Brick; tile, ceramic; roof-
ing material; aggregate

(G-13283)
CLIFTON STEEL COMPANY (PA)
16500 Rockside Rd (44137-4324)
PHONE...........................216 662-6111
Herbert C Neides, *President*
Howard Feldenkris, *Vice Pres*
Bruce Goodman, *Vice Pres*
Pamela Neides, *Human Res Mgr*
▲ **EMP:** 95
SQ FT: 160,000
SALES (est): 62.8MM **Privately Held**
WEB: www.cliftonsteel.com
SIC: 5051 3441 3443 3398 Steel; struc-
tural shapes, iron or steel; fabricated
structural metal; metal parts; metal heat
treating

(G-13284)
CUYAHOGA VENDING CO INC (PA)
Also Called: Cuyahoga Group, The
14250 Industrial Ave S # 104 (44137-3260)
PHONE...........................216 663-1457
James N Variglotti, *President*
David Karley, *Corp Secy*
Carla M Variglotti, *Vice Pres*
David W Heckel, *CFO*
EMP: 320
SQ FT: 20,000
SALES (est): 50.8MM **Privately Held**
SIC: 7359 Vending machine rental

(G-13285)
DAYNAS HOMECARE LLC
14616 Tabor Ave (44137-3859)
PHONE...........................216 323-0323
Dayna M Rasberry,
EMP: 30
SALES: 400K **Privately Held**
SIC: 8082 Home health care services

(G-13286)
EASTSIDE MULTI CARE INC
Also Called: Sunrise Pointe
19900 Clare Ave (44137-1806)
PHONE...........................216 662-3343
Motti Schonfeld, *President*
EMP: 135 **EST:** 2003
SALES (est): 7.5MM **Privately Held**
SIC: 8051 Convalescent home with contin-
uous nursing care

(G-13287)
HOME DEPOT USA INC
Also Called: Home Depot, The
21000 Libby Rd (44137-2931)
PHONE...........................216 581-6611
Randy Behm, *Manager*
EMP: 200
SALES (corp-wide): 108.2B **Publicly Held**
WEB: www.homerentalsdepot.com
SIC: 5211 7359 Home centers; tool rental
HQ: Home Depot U.S.A., Inc.
2455 Paces Ferry Ave
Atlanta GA 30339

(G-13288)
IN TERMINAL SERVICES CORP
5300 Greenhurst Ext (44137-1139)
PHONE...........................216 518-8407
Bill Donahue, *Branch Mgr*
EMP: 50

SALES (corp-wide): 14.7MM **Privately Held**
SIC: 7389 Crane & aerial lift service
PA: In Terminal Services Corporation
3111 167th St
Hazel Crest IL 60429
708 225-2400

(G-13289)
MAMMANA CUSTOM WOODWORKING INC
14400 Industrial Ave N (44137-3249)
PHONE......................216 581-9059
Max Mammana, *President*
EMP: 25
SQ FT: 18,000
SALES: 980K **Privately Held**
SIC: 1751 Cabinet & finish carpentry

(G-13290)
NORFOLK SOUTHERN CORPORATION
5300 Greenhurst Ext (44137-1139)
PHONE......................216 518-8407
Bill Donaghue, *Manager*
EMP: 32
SALES (corp-wide): 11.4B **Publicly Held**
WEB: www.nscorp.com
SIC: 4011 Railroads, line-haul operating
PA: Norfolk Southern Corporation
3 Commercial Pl Ste 1a
Norfolk VA 23510
757 629-2680

(G-13291)
PECK DISTRIBUTORS INC
Also Called: Peck Food Service
17000 Rockside Rd (44137-4345)
PHONE......................216 587-6814
Stephen Peck Jr, *President*
Kenneth Peck, *Vice Pres*
Scott Peck, *Treasurer*
David Peck, *Admin Sec*
▲ EMP: 35
SQ FT: 50,000
SALES (est): 24MM **Privately Held**
WEB: www.peckfoodservice.com
SIC: 5113 5149 5142 Industrial & personal service paper; canned goods: fruit, vegetables, seafood, meats, etc.; packaged frozen goods

(G-13292)
R L LIPTON DISTRIBUTING CO
5900 Pennsylvania Ave (44137-4302)
PHONE......................216 475-4150
Steve Eisenberg, *President*
W Terry Patrick, *Vice Pres*
W Bud Biggin, *Treasurer*
C Jack Amstutz, *Shareholder*
▲ EMP: 75
SQ FT: 70,000
SALES (est): 36.9MM **Privately Held**
SIC: 5181 5182 5149 Beer & other fermented malt liquors; wine; groceries & related products

(G-13293)
ROBERT A KAUFMANN INC
Also Called: Building Blocks Child Care Ctr
5210 Northfield Rd (44137-2466)
PHONE......................216 663-1150
Robert A Kaufmann, *President*
Mary Kaufmann, *Vice Pres*
EMP: 35
SQ FT: 3,000
SALES: 750K **Privately Held**
SIC: 8351 Child day care services

(G-13294)
SABER HEALTHCARE GROUP LLC
Also Called: Sunrise Pointe
19900 Clare Ave (44137-1806)
PHONE......................216 662-3343
Angela Hammons, *Administration*
EMP: 36
SALES (corp-wide): 157.7MM **Privately Held**
SIC: 8051 Skilled nursing care facilities
PA: Saber Healthcare Group, L.L.C.
26691 Richmond Rd Frnt
Bedford OH 44146
216 292-5706

(G-13295)
SHERWOOD FOOD DISTRIBUTORS LLC
Also Called: Sherwood Fd Dstrs Clveland Div
16625 Granite Rd (44137-4301)
PHONE......................216 662-8000
Doug Pierce, *Credit Mgr*
Jim Bell, *Mktg Dir*
John Politowski, *Marketing Staff*
Jake Lipson, *Manager*
Jaque Mathews, *Manager*
EMP: 88
SALES (corp-wide): 302.4MM **Privately Held**
SIC: 5147 5144 5146 Meats, fresh; poultry: live, dressed or frozen (unpackaged); fish, frozen, unpackaged
HQ: Sherwood Food Distributors, L.L.C.
12499 Evergreen Ave
Detroit MI 48228
313 659-7300

(G-13296)
SHERWOOD FOOD DISTRIBUTORS LLC
16625 Granite Rd (44137-4301)
PHONE......................216 662-6794
Bobby Lipson, *Exec VP*
Doug Pierce, *Credit Mgr*
Jim Bell, *Mktg Dir*
John Politowski, *Marketing Staff*
Mark Matheny, *Info Tech Dir*
EMP: 325
SQ FT: 350,000
SALES (corp-wide): 302.4MM **Privately Held**
WEB: www.sherwoodfoods.com
SIC: 5147 5146 5149 5141 Meats, fresh; fish & seafoods; specialty food items; groceries, general line; packaged frozen goods; meat, frozen; packaged
HQ: Sherwood Food Distributors, L.L.C.
12499 Evergreen Ave
Detroit MI 48228
313 659-7300

(G-13297)
ST LAWRENCE HOLDINGS LLC
16500 Rockside Rd (44137-4324)
PHONE......................330 562-9000
Herbert Neides, *President*
Jonh Zanin, *Controller*
Eileen Radcliffe, *Accounts Mgr*
EMP: 34
SALES: 8MM **Privately Held**
SIC: 5051 3443 3441 Steel; iron & steel (ferrous) products; fabricated plate work (boiler shop); fabricated structural metal

(G-13298)
STAR BEAUTY PLUS LLC (PA)
20900 Libby Rd (44137-2929)
PHONE......................216 662-9750
John Kim,
EMP: 40 EST: 1973
SQ FT: 13,000
SALES (est): 2.1MM **Privately Held**
SIC: 7231 Beauty Shop

(G-13299)
SUNRISE HEALTHCARE GROUP LLC
Also Called: SUNRISE POINTE CARE AND REHABILITATION CENTER
19900 Clare Ave (44137-1806)
PHONE......................216 662-3343
George S Repchick, *President*
William I Weisberg, *Vice Pres*
Sarah Depompei, *Assistant*
EMP: 193
SALES: 6.1MM
SALES (corp-wide): 157.7MM **Privately Held**
SIC: 8051 Convalescent home with continuous nursing care
PA: Saber Healthcare Group, L.L.C.
26691 Richmond Rd Frnt
Bedford OH 44146
216 292-5706

(G-13300)
SUNTWIST CORP
Also Called: Post-Up Stand
5461 Dunham Rd (44137-3644)
PHONE......................800 935-3534

Ram Tamir, *President*
Alon Weimer, *Vice Pres*
Tina Schulte, *Cust Mgr*
Fawn Patrick, *Marketing Staff*
▲ EMP: 76
SQ FT: 2,600
SALES (est): 3.9MM **Privately Held**
SIC: 7336 Graphic arts & related design

Marblehead
Ottawa County

(G-13301)
KELLEYS ISLE FERRY BOAT LINES
510 W Main St (43440-2250)
PHONE......................419 798-9763
Paula Moody, *Manager*
EMP: 25 **Privately Held**
WEB: www.kelleysislandferry.com
SIC: 4482 Ferries
PA: The Kelley's Island Ferry Boat Lines Inc
3203 Harvard Ave
Newburgh Heights OH 44105

Marengo
Morrow County

(G-13302)
DEARTH MANAGEMENT COMPANY
Also Called: Bennington Glen Nursing Home
825 State Route 61 (43334-9215)
P.O. Box 10 (43334-0010)
PHONE......................419 253-0144
Toll Free:......................888 -
Connie Deel, *Director*
Renee Forester, *Director*
Corey McFarland, *Director*
Tiffany Potter, *Nursing Dir*
Jim Deel, *Administration*
EMP: 110
SALES (corp-wide): 12.3MM **Privately Held**
WEB: www.schoenbrunnhealthcare.com
SIC: 8051 8052 Skilled nursing care facilities; intermediate care facilities
PA: Dearth Management Company
134 Northwoods Blvd Ste C
Columbus OH 43235
614 847-1070

(G-13303)
FISHBURN TANK TRUCK SERVICE
5012 State Route 229 (43334-9634)
P.O. Box 278 (43334-0278)
PHONE......................419 253-6031
Jack Fishburn, *Owner*
EMP: 60
SALES (est): 2.1MM **Privately Held**
SIC: 1389 Haulage, oil field

(G-13304)
RINGLER FEEDLOTS LLC
461 State Route 61 (43334-9415)
P.O. Box 249, Delaware (43015-0249)
PHONE......................419 253-5300
David Ringler, *President*
EMP: 25 EST: 2007
SALES (est): 1MM **Privately Held**
SIC: 4731 Brokers, shipping

(G-13305)
RINGLER INC
461 State Route 61 (43334-9415)
PHONE......................419 253-5300
Alexander Ringler, *President*
Alexander N Ringler, *President*
EMP: 25
SALES (est): 194.8K **Privately Held**
SIC: 0191 General farms, primarily crop

Maria Stein
Mercer County

(G-13306)
BROOKSIDE HOLDINGS LLC (PA)
Also Called: Brookside Trucking
8022 State Route 119 (45860-8708)
P.O. Box 68 (45860-0068)
PHONE......................419 925-4457
Ricky Uppenkamp,
Steve Cook,
John D Richards,
EMP: 43
SQ FT: 9,800
SALES (est): 3.8MM **Privately Held**
SIC: 4212 4213 Local trucking, without storage; trucking, except local

(G-13307)
HOMAN INC
6915 Olding Rd (45860-9735)
PHONE......................419 925-4349
Roger R Homan, *President*
Karen Boeke, *Office Mgr*
▲ EMP: 25
SQ FT: 13,700
SALES (est): 10.2MM **Privately Held**
WEB: www.homaninc.com
SIC: 1542 5999 Commercial & office building, new construction; farm machinery

(G-13308)
MOELLER TRUCKING INC
8100 Industrial Dr (45860-9544)
PHONE......................419 925-4799
Gary Moeller, *President*
Brenda Hamberg, *Terminal Mgr*
Art Moeller Jr, *Treasurer*
Terry Moeller, *Admin Sec*
EMP: 90
SQ FT: 3,500
SALES (est): 23MM **Privately Held**
SIC: 4213 4212 Contract haulers; local trucking, without storage

Marietta
Washington County

(G-13309)
AMEDISYS INC
Also Called: Home Health Agency
210 N 7th St (45750-2244)
PHONE......................740 373-8549
Pamela Parr, *Exec Dir*
EMP: 40 **Publicly Held**
WEB: www.amedisys.com
SIC: 8082 8051 8049 8361 Home health care services; skilled nursing care facilities; physical therapist; occupational therapist; speech therapist; rehabilitation center, residential: health care incidental
PA: Amedisys, Inc.
3854 American Way Ste A
Baton Rouge LA 70816

(G-13310)
AMERICAN PRODUCERS SUP CO INC (PA)
119 2nd St (45750-3102)
P.O. Box 1050 (45750-6050)
PHONE......................740 373-5050
Christopher L Brunton, *President*
Rick Blizzard, *Vice Pres*
Joseph Wesel, *Vice Pres*
Polly Stephens, *Purchasing*
Mark Magers, *Treasurer*
▲ EMP: 54 EST: 1963
SQ FT: 50,000
SALES (est): 37.2MM **Privately Held**
SIC: 5082 5085 Contractors' materials; abrasives

(G-13311)
AMERICAN STAR PAINTING CO LLC
Also Called: American Star Pntg & Coatings
201 Mitchells Ln (45750-6868)
PHONE......................740 373-5634
Toll Free:......................888 -

Garold Greenlees, *Mng Member*
Floyd G Dotson,
EMP: 25
SALES: 1.7MM **Privately Held**
SIC: 1721 1799 1752 Commercial paint-
ing; industrial painting; coating, caulking &
weather, water & fireproofing; access
flooring system installation

(G-13312)
ANTERO RESOURCES
CORPORATION
2335 State Route 821 (45750-5362)
PHONE......................................740 760-1000
EMP: 60 **Publicly Held**
SIC: 1382 Oil & gas exploration services
PA: Antero Resources Corporation
1615 Wynkoop St
Denver CO 80202

(G-13313)
APPALACHIAN DEVELOPMENT
CORP (PA)
1400 Pike St (45750-5196)
P.O. Box 520, Reno (45773-0520)
PHONE......................................740 374-9436
Heber Piatt, *President*
Gary Starner, *Vice Pres*
Joe Matthews, *Treasurer*
Misty Casto, *Admin Sec*
EMP: 82
SQ FT: 4,000
SALES: 232.3K **Privately Held**
SIC: 6163 Loan brokers

(G-13314)
B & L AGENCY LLC
1001 Pike St Ste 4 (45750-3516)
PHONE......................................740 373-8272
Brenda Frazier, *Principal*
EMP: 41
SALES (est): 1.2MM **Privately Held**
SIC: 8082 Home health care services

(G-13315)
BD OIL GATHERING CORP
649 Mitchells Ln (45750-6865)
PHONE......................................740 374-9355
Floyd Deer Sr, *President*
Keith Young, *Opers Mgr*
Floyd A Deer Jr, *Director*
Gordon J Deer, *Director*
Sarah Bober, *Admin Sec*
EMP: 29
SALES (est): 7MM **Privately Held**
WEB: www.bdoil.com
SIC: 5172 Crude oil

(G-13316)
BROOKDALE SENIOR LIVING
INC
150 Browns Rd (45750-9085)
PHONE......................................740 373-9600
Melanie Werdel, *Branch Mgr*
EMP: 42
SALES (corp-wide): 4.5B **Publicly Held**
SIC: 8052 Personal care facility
PA: Brookdale Senior Living
111 Westwood Pl Ste 400
Brentwood TN 37027
615 221-2250

(G-13317)
BUCKEYE HILLS-HCK VLY REG
DEV (HQ)
Also Called: Area Agency On Aging
1400 Pike St (45750-5196)
P.O. Box 520, Reno (45773-0520)
PHONE......................................740 373-0087
Misty Casto, *CEO*
Bret Allphin, *Director*
Denise Keyes, *Director*
Dawn Weber, *Director*
EMP: 59
SALES (est): 4.8MM
SALES (corp-wide): 232.3K **Privately**
Held
WEB: www.buckeyehills.org
SIC: 8748 Urban planning & consulting
services
PA: Appalachian Development Corporation
1400 Pike St
Marietta OH 45750
740 374-9436

(G-13318)
CERTIFIED PRESSURE TESTING
LLC (PA)
2019 State Route 821 (45750-5317)
PHONE......................................740 374-2071
Jason Corser, *Principal*
Max Rubin, *CFO*
Tanya Tinker, *Manager*
EMP: 41
SALES: 19MM **Privately Held**
SIC: 8734 Product testing laboratories

(G-13319)
COMMUNITY ACTION PROGRAM
CORP (PA)
218 Putnam St (45750-3014)
P.O. Box 144 (45750-0144)
PHONE......................................740 373-3745
David E Brightbill, *Exec Dir*
Cathy Rees, *Assistant*
EMP: 340 EST: 1967
SQ FT: 9,700
SALES (est): 9.9MM **Privately Held**
WEB: www.wmcap.org
SIC: 8399 Community action agency

(G-13320)
COMMUNITY ACTION PROGRAM
CORP
Also Called: Norwood School
205 Phillips St (45750-3427)
PHONE......................................740 373-6016
Rosie Foreman, *Director*
EMP: 30
SALES (est): 241.4K
SALES (corp-wide): 9.9MM **Privately**
Held
WEB: www.wmcap.org
SIC: 8399 8322 Community action
agency; individual & family services
PA: Community Action Program Corp
218 Putnam St
Marietta OH 45750
740 373-3745

(G-13321)
COUNTY OF WASHINGTON
Also Called: Washington Cnty Engineers Off
103 Westview Ave (45750-9403)
PHONE......................................740 376-7430
Roger Wright, *Engineer*
EMP: 37 **Privately Held**
WEB: www.washingtongov.org
SIC: 8711 Engineering services
PA: County Of Washington
205 Putnam St
Marietta OH 45750
740 373-6623

(G-13322)
COUNTY OF WASHINGTON
Also Called: Washington County Home
County House Ln (45750)
PHONE......................................740 373-2028
Ted Williams, *Administration*
EMP: 42 **Privately Held**
WEB: www.washingtongov.org
SIC: 8082 Home health care services
PA: County Of Washington
205 Putnam St
Marietta OH 45750
740 373-6623

(G-13323)
COUNTY OF WASHINGTON
Also Called: Department Jobs and Fmly Svcs
1115 Gilman Ave (45750-9428)
PHONE......................................740 373-5513
Thomas Ballengee, *Director*
EMP: 55 **Privately Held**
SIC: 8322 Social service center
PA: County Of Washington
205 Putnam St
Marietta OH 45750
740 373-6623

(G-13324)
DAVIS PICKERING & COMPANY
INC
Also Called: American Procomm
165 Enterprise Dr (45750-8051)
PHONE......................................740 373-5896
Jeffrey A Williamson, *CEO*
Dustin W Flinn, *President*
Kelly A Fisher, *Vice Pres*

Daniel M Fliehman, *Vice Pres*
EMP: 100
SQ FT: 6,000
SALES (est): 32.4MM **Privately Held**
SIC: 1731 General electrical contractor

(G-13325)
DAVITA INC
Also Called: Da Vita
1019 Pike St (45750-3500)
PHONE......................................740 376-2622
Scott Wagstaff, *Branch Mgr*
EMP: 31 **Publicly Held**
SIC: 8092 Kidney dialysis centers
PA: Davita Inc.
2000 16th St
Denver CO 80202

(G-13326)
E T B LTD
Also Called: John Deere Authorized Dealer
15 Acme St (45750-3305)
PHONE......................................740 373-6686
Chris Walters, *Branch Mgr*
Danny Neville, *Executive*
EMP: 30 **Privately Held**
SIC: 7359 5082 Stores & yards equipment
rental; construction & mining machinery
PA: E T B Ltd
500 Hall St
Bridgeport OH 43912

(G-13327)
EUREKA MIDSTREAM LLC
27710 State Route 7 (45750-5147)
PHONE......................................740 868-1325
Chris Akers, *CEO*
EMP: 40
SALES (est): 425.5K
SALES (corp-wide): 2.3B **Privately Held**
SIC: 4922 Pipelines, natural gas
HQ: Eureka Midstream Holdings, Llc
1111 La St Ste 4520
Houston TX 77002
732 203-4544

(G-13328)
FAMILY FORD LINCOLN INC
Also Called: Family Lincoln
909 Pike St (45750-5100)
P.O. Box 588 (45750-0588)
PHONE......................................740 373-9127
Carl Nourse, *President*
Sam Savage, *Sales Staff*
EMP: 60
SALES (est): 15.7MM **Privately Held**
SIC: 5511 7538 7514 7532 Automobiles,
new & used; general automotive repair
shops; hearse or limousine rental, without
drivers; top & body repair & paint shops

(G-13329)
FIRST SETTLEMENT
ORTHOPAEDICS (PA)
Also Called: Nayak, Naresh K MD
611 2nd St Ste A (45750-2167)
PHONE......................................740 373-8756
Gregory Krivchenia II, *President*
Naresh K Nayak, *Vice Pres*
Gary W Miller, *Treasurer*
John Henry, *Shareholder*
Jesse R Ada, *Admin Sec*
EMP: 32
SQ FT: 17,500
SALES (est): 5.8MM **Privately Held**
SIC: 8011 8049 Sports medicine special-
ist, physician; physical therapist

(G-13330)
GLENWOOD COMMUNITY INC
Also Called: Pines At Glenwood
200 Timberline Dr Apt 206 (45750-9372)
PHONE......................................740 376-9555
Margarine Shonard, *Exec Dir*
Caroline Beidler, *Executive*
EMP: 45
SALES (est): 3.7MM **Privately Held**
SIC: 8361 Home for the aged

(G-13331)
GOODWILL INDS CENTL OHIO
INC
1303 Colegate Dr (45750-1358)
PHONE......................................740 373-1304
F Pierpoint, *Branch Mgr*
EMP: 83

SALES (corp-wide): 48.1MM **Privately**
Held
SIC: 8331 Vocational rehabilitation agency
PA: Goodwill Industries Of Central Ohio,
Inc.
1331 Edgehill Rd
Columbus OH 43212
614 294-5181

(G-13332)
GREENLEAF LANDSCAPES INC
414 Muskingum Dr (45750-9306)
PHONE......................................740 373-1639
Albert J Lang, *President*
Pam McKitrick, *Regional Mgr*
Jeanne Lang, *Vice Pres*
Mike Ennemoser, *Manager*
Nick Mehl, *Manager*
EMP: 63
SQ FT: 3,500
SALES: 5.6MM **Privately Held**
WEB: www.greenleaflandscapes.com
SIC: 0782 5261 Landscape contractors;
nurseries & garden centers

(G-13333)
HARRISON CONSTRUCTION INC
Also Called: Harrison Contruction
1408 Colegate Dr (45750-1330)
PHONE......................................740 373-7000
Daniel Harrison, *President*
Gillian Harrison, *Treasurer*
Christie Fulmer, *Office Mgr*
EMP: 27
SQ FT: 7,100
SALES (est): 3.6MM **Privately Held**
SIC: 1521 5722 General remodeling, sin-
gle-family houses; kitchens, complete
(sinks, cabinets, etc.)

(G-13334)
HAVAR INC
416 3rd St (45750-2101)
P.O. Box 1107 (45750-6107)
PHONE......................................740 373-7175
Debbie Schmeiding, *Director*
EMP: 35
SALES (corp-wide): 3.6MM **Privately**
Held
WEB: www.havar.com
SIC: 8051 Extended care facility
PA: Havar Inc
396 Richland Ave
Athens OH 45701
740 594-3533

(G-13335)
HEALTH CARE RTREMENT
CORP AMER
Also Called: Heartland of Marietta
5001 State Route 60 (45750-5343)
PHONE......................................740 373-8920
Linda Daily, *Manager*
EMP: 100
SALES (corp-wide): 2.4B **Publicly Held**
WEB: www.hrc-manorcare.com
SIC: 8051 Convalescent home with contin-
uous nursing care
HQ: Health Care And Retirement Corpora-
tion Of America
333 N Summit St Ste 103
Toledo OH 43604
419 252-5500

(G-13336)
IEH AUTO PARTS LLC
Also Called: Auto Plus
123 Tennis Center Dr (45750-9765)
PHONE......................................740 373-8327
Scott Reynolds, *Branch Mgr*
EMP: 27
SALES (corp-wide): 11.7B **Publicly Held**
SIC: 5013 Automotive supplies & parts
HQ: Ieh Auto Parts Llc
1155 Roberts Blvd Nw # 175
Kennesaw GA 30144
770 701-5000

(G-13337)
IEH AUTO PARTS LLC
121 Tennis Center Dr (45750-9765)
PHONE......................................740 373-8151
EMP: 26
SALES (corp-wide): 11.7B **Publicly Held**
SIC: 5013 Automotive supplies & parts

2019 Harris Ohio
Services Directory

▲ = Import ▼=Export
◆ =Import/Export

HQ: Ieh Auto Parts Llc
1155 Roberts Blvd Nw # 175
Kennesaw GA 30144
770 701-5000

(G-13338)
INN AT MARIETTA LTD
150 Browns Rd Ofc (45750-9086)
PHONE....................................740 373-9600
Charlotte Forsyth, *Partner*
Deb Patrick, *Administration*
EMP: 80
SALES (est): 3MM **Privately Held**
SIC: 7011 8052 Inns; intermediate care facilities

(G-13339)
INTERIM HEALTHCARE SE OHIO INC
1017 Pike St (45750-3522)
PHONE....................................740 373-3800
Diane Hunter, *CEO*
Bradford C Hunter, *CFO*
EMP: 80
SQ FT: 2,100
SALES: 2.5MM **Privately Held**
SIC: 8082 Home health care services

(G-13340)
JANI-SOURCE LLC
478 Bramblewood Hts Rd (45750-8501)
PHONE....................................740 374-6298
Toll Free:....................................877 -
Ronald Burnworth, *Opers Mgr*
Bryan Waller, *Mng Member*
Judy Waller, *Mng Member*
EMP: 50
SQ FT: 2,400
SALES (est): 1.2MM **Privately Held**
WEB: www.janisource.com
SIC: 7349 5999 Janitorial service, contract basis; cleaning equipment & supplies

(G-13341)
JPMORGAN CHASE BANK NAT ASSN
125 Putnam St (45750-2936)
PHONE....................................740 374-2263
Dawn Wilson, *Manager*
EMP: 26
SALES (corp-wide): 131.4B **Publicly Held**
WEB: www.chase.com
SIC: 6021 National commercial banks
HQ: Jpmorgan Chase Bank, National Association
1111 Polaris Pkwy
Columbus OH 43240
614 436-3055

(G-13342)
KEMRON ENVIRONMENTAL SVCS INC
2343 State Route 821 (45750-5464)
PHONE....................................740 373-4071
David Vandenberg, *Branch Mgr*
EMP: 90
SALES (corp-wide): 35MM **Privately Held**
WEB: www.kemron.com
SIC: 8711 8748 8731 8734 Consulting engineer; environmental consultant; commercial physical research; testing laboratories
PA: Kemron Environmental Services, Inc.
1359-A Ellsworth
Atlanta GA 30318
404 601-6930

(G-13343)
KOROSEAL INTERIOR PRODUCTS LLC
700 Bf Goodrich Rd (45750-7849)
PHONE....................................855 753-5474
EMP: 40
SALES (corp-wide): 121MM **Privately Held**
SIC: 1541 Warehouse construction
PA: Koroseal Interior Products, Llc
3875 Embassy Pkwy Ste 110
Fairlawn OH 44333
330 668-7600

(G-13344)
LONGYEAR COMPANY
1010 Greene St (45750-2409)
PHONE....................................740 373-2190
EMP: 35 **Privately Held**
SIC: 1481 Test boring for nonmetallic minerals
HQ: Longyear Company
2455 S 3600 W
West Valley City UT 84119

(G-13345)
LOWES HOME CENTERS LLC
842 Pike St (45750-3503)
PHONE....................................740 374-2151
Paul REA, *Branch Mgr*
EMP: 150
SALES (corp-wide): 68.6B **Publicly Held**
SIC: 5211 5031 5722 5064 Home centers; building materials, exterior; building materials, interior; household appliance stores; electrical appliances, television & radio
HQ: Lowe's Home Centers, Llc
1605 Curtis Bridge Rd
Wilkesboro NC 28697
336 658-4000

(G-13346)
MARCH INVESTORS LTD
Also Called: Hampton Inn
508 Pike St (45750-3332)
PHONE....................................740 373-5353
David M Archer,
EMP: 25
SALES (est): 1.4MM **Privately Held**
SIC: 7011 Hotels

(G-13347)
MARIETTA AQUATIC CENTER
233 Pennsylvania Ave (45750-1663)
PHONE....................................740 373-2445
Peter Ianniciello, *Principal*
EMP: 30 **EST:** 2007
SALES (est): 233.2K **Privately Held**
SIC: 7999 Swimming pool, non-membership

(G-13348)
MARIETTA BANTAM BASEBALL LEAG
103 Chalet Ln (45750-9370)
PHONE....................................740 350-9844
Lisa Weekley, *Principal*
EMP: 31 **EST:** 2010
SALES: 30K **Privately Held**
SIC: 7997 Membership sports & recreation clubs

(G-13349)
MARIETTA CENTER FOR HEALTH &
Also Called: Marietta Nursing and Rehab Ctr
117 Bartlett St (45750-2683)
PHONE....................................740 373-1867
Randy Wright, *Director*
EMP: 150
SALES (est): 2.2MM
SALES (corp-wide): 6B **Privately Held**
WEB: www.kindredhealthcare.com
SIC: 8093 8051 Rehabilitation center, outpatient treatment; skilled nursing care facilities
HQ: Kindred Healthcare, Llc
680 S 4th St
Louisville KY 40202
502 596-7300

(G-13350)
MARIETTA COLLEGE
Also Called: Phisical Plant
213 4th St (45750-3004)
PHONE....................................740 376-4790
Fred Smith, *Manager*
EMP: 50
SALES (est): 970.5K
SALES (corp-wide): 36.2MM **Privately Held**
WEB: www.marietta.edu
SIC: 8221 4832 4813 College, except junior; educational; long distance telephone communications

PA: Marietta College
215 5th St Dept 32
Marietta OH 45750
740 376-4643

(G-13351)
MARIETTA COUNTRY CLUB INC
705 Pike St (45750-3502)
PHONE....................................740 373-7722
David Mitchem, *President*
EMP: 35 **EST:** 1932
SQ FT: 4,000
SALES: 779.6K **Privately Held**
WEB: www.mariettacountryclub.com
SIC: 7997 Country club, membership

(G-13352)
MARIETTA GYNECOLOGIC ASSOC
410 2nd St (45750-2115)
PHONE....................................740 374-3622
Warren L Cooper MD, *President*
Curtis D White MD, *Corp Secy*
Todd Myers MD, *Vice Pres*
EMP: 55
SQ FT: 13,000
SALES (est): 4.9MM **Privately Held**
WEB: www.gynassociates.com
SIC: 8011 Gynecologists

(G-13353)
MARIETTA INDUSTRIAL ENTPS INC (PA)
Also Called: Mie
17943 State Route 7 (45750-8239)
PHONE....................................740 373-2252
W Scott Elliott, *President*
Burt Elliott, *Vice Pres*
Grant Elliott, *Admin Sec*
EMP: 51 **EST:** 1955
SQ FT: 450,000
SALES (est): 11.1MM **Privately Held**
WEB: www.miecorp.com
SIC: 4491 4214 Marine cargo handling; local trucking with storage

(G-13354)
MARIETTA MEMORIAL HOSPITAL (PA)
Also Called: Memorial Health System
401 Matthew St (45750-1699)
PHONE....................................740 374-1400
Tom Tucker, *Ch of Bd*
J Stott Cantley, *President*
Inge Chenoweth, *General Mgr*
Orive E Fischer, *Vice Pres*
Lynne Miller, *Senior Buyer*
EMP: 1100
SQ FT: 100,000
SALES (est): 400.4MM **Privately Held**
SIC: 8062 8069 General medical & surgical hospitals; alcoholism rehabilitation hospital

(G-13355)
MARIETTA MEMORIAL HOSPITAL
Also Called: Home Nursing Service & Hospice
210 N 7th St Ste 300 (45750-2244)
PHONE....................................740 373-8549
Pam Parr, *Director*
EMP: 40
SALES (corp-wide): 400.4MM **Privately Held**
SIC: 8062 8082 General medical & surgical hospitals; visiting nurse service
PA: Marietta Memorial Hospital Inc
401 Matthew St
Marietta OH 45750
740 374-1400

(G-13356)
MARIETTA SILOS LLC
2417 Waterford Rd (45750-7828)
PHONE....................................740 373-2822
Dennis Blauser, *CEO*
Jordan Pomrenke, *Vice Pres*
EMP: 50
SQ FT: 50,000
SALES (est): 9.3MM **Privately Held**
WEB: www.mariettasilos.com
SIC: 1542 Silo construction, agricultural

(G-13357)
MC ALARNEY POOL SPAS AND BILLD
Also Called: McAlarney Pols Spas Billd More
908 Pike St (45750-3505)
PHONE....................................740 373-6698
Cheryl McAlarney, *President*
Wayne Mc Alarney, *Exec VP*
EMP: 25 **EST:** 1975
SQ FT: 6,500
SALES: 1.2MM **Privately Held**
WEB: www.mcalarney.com
SIC: 5091 3949 Swimming pools, equipment & supplies; spa equipment & supplies; billiard equipment & supplies; sporting & athletic goods

(G-13358)
MERCHANTS 5 STAR LTD
18192 State Route 7 (45750-8237)
P.O. Box 541 (45750-0541)
PHONE....................................740 373-0313
Jeffrey A Starner, *President*
Ellen Miller, *Treasurer*
Terry Lipps, *Admin Sec*
EMP: 100
SQ FT: 4,000
SALES (est): 6.5MM **Privately Held**
SIC: 4213 Trucking, except local

(G-13359)
MID OHIO VLY BULK TRNSPT INC
16380 State Route 7 (45750-8246)
P.O. Box 734 (45750-0734)
PHONE....................................740 373-2481
Mayeeta Merrill, *President*
Charles Merrill, *Corp Secy*
EMP: 30
SALES (est): 6.7MM
SALES (corp-wide): 8.6MM **Privately Held**
SIC: 4731 Freight transportation arrangement
PA: Mid-Ohio Valley Lime, Inc.
State Rt 7 S
Marietta OH 45750
740 373-1006

(G-13360)
MID-OHIO VALLEY LIME INC (PA)
State Rt 7 S (45750)
P.O. Box 734 (45750-0734)
PHONE....................................740 373-1006
Mayetta Merrill, *President*
Charles Merrill, *Corp Secy*
Orville Merrill, *Vice Pres*
EMP: 32 **EST:** 1973
SQ FT: 10,000
SALES (est): 8.6MM **Privately Held**
WEB: www.midohiovalleylime.com
SIC: 5032 Lime, except agricultural

(G-13361)
MORRISON INC
Also Called: Honeywell Authorized Dealer
410 Colegate Dr (45750-9549)
PHONE....................................740 373-5869
Kenneth Morrison, *President*
David M Haas, *Vice Pres*
Chase Hughes, *Project Mgr*
Ben Banks, *Manager*
Shawn Godfrey, *Manager*
EMP: 35 **EST:** 1955
SQ FT: 6,000
SALES (est): 5.7MM **Privately Held**
WEB: www.morrisonhvac.com
SIC: 1711 5722 Refrigeration contractor; warm air heating & air conditioning contractor; ventilation & duct work contractor; electric household appliances

(G-13362)
MOTEL INVESTMENTS MARIETTA INC
Also Called: Quality Inn
700 Pike St (45750-3501)
PHONE....................................740 374-8190
Thomas Dowdy, *President*
Jane Dowdy, *Vice Pres*
Jason Dowdy, *Vice Pres*
Byron Dowdy, *Treasurer*
EMP: 32

SALES (est): 1.6MM **Privately Held**
SIC: 7011 Motels

(G-13363)
NORTHPOINT SENIOR SERVICES LLC
Also Called: Arbors At Marietta
400 N 7th St (45750-2024)
PHONE.................................740 373-3597
Jill Jonas, *Manager*
Kenneth Leopold, *Director*
EMP: 117
SALES (corp-wide): 41.5MM **Privately Held**
WEB: www.extendicarehealth.com
SIC: 8051 8052 Convalescent home with continuous nursing care; intermediate care facilities
PA: Senior Northpoint Services Llc
7400 New Lagrange 100
Louisville KY 40222
502 429-8062

(G-13364)
OHIO STATE UNIVERSITY
Also Called: Ohio State University EXT
202 Davis Ave (45750-1415)
PHONE.................................740 376-7431
Eric Barrett, *Ch of Bd*
EMP: 66
SALES (corp-wide): 5.8B **Privately Held**
SIC: 8732 8221 Educational research; university
PA: The Ohio State University
Student Acade Servi Bldg
Columbus OH 43210
614 292-6446

(G-13365)
ONEILL SENIOR CENTER INC (PA)
333 4th St (45750-2002)
PHONE.................................740 373-3914
Connie Huntsman, *Psychologist*
Terry Zdrale, *Director*
Lisa Turner, *Asst Director*
EMP: 27
SALES: 1.3MM **Privately Held**
WEB: www.oneillcenter.com
SIC: 8322 Adult day care center; senior citizens' center or association

(G-13366)
PAWNEE MAINTENANCE INC
101 Rathbone Rd (45750-1437)
P.O. Box 269 (45750-0269)
PHONE.................................740 373-6861
Ted R Szabo, *President*
EMP: 60
SQ FT: 3,000
SALES (est): 4.5MM **Privately Held**
WEB: www.pawnee.com
SIC: 1541 3272 Industrial buildings & warehouses; concrete products

(G-13367)
PEOPLES BANCORP INC (PA)
138 Putnam St (45750-2923)
P.O. Box 738 (45750-0738)
PHONE.................................740 373-3155
David L Mead, *Ch of Bd*
Charles W Sulerzyski, *President*
Douglas V Wyatt, *Exec VP*
John C Rogers, *CFO*
Robyn A Stevens, *Ch Credit Ofcr*
EMP: 37
SALES: 208MM **Publicly Held**
WEB: www.peoplesbancorp.com
SIC: 6021 National commercial banks

(G-13368)
PEOPLES BANK (HQ)
138 Putnam St (45750-2923)
P.O. Box 738 (45750-0738)
PHONE.................................740 373-3155
Chuck Sulerziski, *President*
Charles W Sulerzyski, *President*
Mike De Jager, *Director*
EMP: 116 **EST:** 1914
SALES: 121.1MM
SALES (corp-wide): 208MM **Publicly Held**
SIC: 6022 State commercial banks

PA: Peoples Bancorp Inc.
138 Putnam St
Marietta OH 45750
740 373-3155

(G-13369)
PHYSICIANS CARE OF MARIETTA (PA)
Also Called: Physicians Care of Marrita
800 Pike St Ste 2 (45750-3507)
PHONE.................................740 373-2519
Lloyd Dennis, *President*
John Riggs MD, *Treasurer*
Edward Kappal, *Admin Sec*
EMP: 75
SALES (est): 3.8MM **Privately Held**
SIC: 8011 Offices & clinics of medical doctors

(G-13370)
PIONEER PIPE INC
Also Called: Pioneer Group
2021 Hanna Rd (45750-8255)
PHONE.................................740 376-2400
David M Archer, *President*
Matthew Hilverding, *Corp Secy*
Arlene M Archer, *Vice Pres*
Karl Robinson, *Vice Pres*
Larry Silvus, *Transptn Dir*
▲ **EMP:** 600
SQ FT: 24,800
SALES (est): 163.7MM **Privately Held**
WEB: www.pioneerpipeinc.com
SIC: 3498 1711 3443 3441 Pipe sections fabricated from purchased pipe; pipe fittings, fabricated from purchased pipe; plumbing contractors; warm air heating & air conditioning contractor; mechanical contractor; fabricated plate work (boiler shop); fabricated structural metal; blast furnaces & steel mills

(G-13371)
PITNEY BOWES INC
111 Marshall Rd (45750-1160)
PHONE.................................740 374-5535
Marcia Pawloski, *Branch Mgr*
EMP: 60
SALES (corp-wide): 3.5B **Publicly Held**
SIC: 3579 7359 Postage meters; business machine & electronic equipment rental services
PA: Pitney Bowes Inc.
3001 Summer St Ste 3
Stamford CT 06905
203 356-5000

(G-13372)
POWER SYSTEM ENGINEERING INC
Also Called: Pse
2349a State Route 821 (45750-5362)
PHONE.................................740 568-9220
Douglas R Joens, *President*
Bruce Lane, *Branch Mgr*
EMP: 29
SALES (corp-wide): 9.8MM **Privately Held**
SIC: 8711 Consulting engineer
PA: Power System Engineering, Inc.
1532 W Broadway
Monona WI 53713
608 268-3528

(G-13373)
PROMANCO INC
27823 State Route 7 (45750-9060)
PHONE.................................740 374-2120
Rudolph Lehman, *President*
EMP: 25 **EST:** 1988
SQ FT: 3,000
SALES (est): 3.2MM **Privately Held**
WEB: www.promanco.com
SIC: 1761 7349 Roofing contractor; building maintenance services

(G-13374)
R & J TRUCKING INC
14530 Sr 7 (45750)
PHONE.................................740 374-3050
Dennis Coe, *Technology*
Jeff Caltrider, *Maintence Staff*
EMP: 100 **Privately Held**
WEB: www.rjtrucking.com
SIC: 4212 4213 Dump truck haulage; heavy hauling

HQ: R & J Trucking, Inc.
8063 Southern Blvd
Youngstown OH 44512
800 262-9365

(G-13375)
REHABLTTION CTR AT MRIETTA MEM
Also Called: Rehabltltion Ctr At Mrtta Mmori
401 Matthew St (45750-1635)
PHONE.................................740 374-1407
Carol McAuley, *Director*
EMP: 65
SALES (est): 1.7MM **Privately Held**
SIC: 8093 8361 Rehabilitation center, outpatient treatment; residential care

(G-13376)
REO NETWORK INC
Also Called: Century 21
203 Pike St (45750-3320)
PHONE.................................740 374-8900
Lea Ioanou, *President*
EMP: 25
SALES (est): 1.4MM **Privately Held**
WEB: www.reonetwork.com
SIC: 6531 Real estate agent, residential

(G-13377)
RICHARDSON PRINTING CORP (PA)
Also Called: Zip Center, The-Division
201 Acme St (45750-3404)
P.O. Box 663 (45750-0663)
PHONE.................................740 373-5362
Dennis E Valentine, *President*
Robert Richardson Jr, *Shareholder*
Charles E Schwab, *Admin Sec*
▲ **EMP:** 65
SQ FT: 100,000
SALES (est): 4.4MM **Privately Held**
WEB: www.rpcprint.com
SIC: 7389 2752 Business Services Lithographic Commercial Printing

(G-13378)
SCHWENDEMAN AGENCY INC (PA)
Also Called: Schwendeman Sigafoos Agcy
109 Putnam St (45750-2924)
PHONE.................................740 373-6793
Mark Schewendeman, *President*
Larry Schewendeman, *Vice Pres*
Michael Schwendeman, *Vice Pres*
EMP: 30 **EST:** 1938
SQ FT: 5,000
SALES (est): 9.8MM **Privately Held**
WEB: www.schwendeman.com
SIC: 6411 Insurance agents

(G-13379)
SELBY GENERAL HOSPITAL
1338 Colegate Dr (45750-1369)
PHONE.................................740 568-2037
Steve Smith, *Branch Mgr*
EMP: 139
SALES (corp-wide): 43.7MM **Privately Held**
SIC: 8049 Physical therapist
PA: Selby General Hospital
1106 Colegate Dr
Marietta OH 45750
740 568-2000

(G-13380)
SELBY GENERAL HOSPITAL (PA)
1106 Colegate Dr (45750-1323)
PHONE.................................740 568-2000
Thomas Tucker, *Ch of Bd*
Steve Smith, *President*
Scott Cantley, *President*
Eric Young, *CFO*
EMP: 250
SQ FT: 65,000
SALES: 43.7MM **Privately Held**
WEB: www.selbygeneralhospital.com
SIC: 8062 Hospital, affiliated with AMA residency

(G-13381)
SHIV HOTELS LLC
700 Pike St (45750-3501)
PHONE.................................740 374-8190
Mahesh Nichani,

EMP: 30
SALES: 3MM **Privately Held**
SIC: 7011 Hotels

(G-13382)
SMITH BROTHERS ERECTION INC
101 Industry Rd (45750-9355)
PHONE.................................740 373-3575
Robert A Gribben Jr, *President*
Robert A Gribben III, *Director*
EMP: 45 **EST:** 2011
SALES: 1.2MM **Privately Held**
SIC: 1791 3449 Structural steel erection; bars, concrete reinforcing: fabricated steel

(G-13383)
SPAGNAS
301 Gilman Ave (45750)
PHONE.................................740 376-9245
Kevin Whitby, *Owner*
EMP: 25
SALES (est): 495.7K **Privately Held**
SIC: 5812 7299 Italian restaurant; banquet hall facilities

(G-13384)
STRATAGRAPH NE INC
116 Ellsworth Ave (45750-8607)
P.O. Box 59, Reno (45773-0059)
PHONE.................................740 373-3091
Walt Teer, *President*
EMP: 32
SQ FT: 2,400
SALES: 700K **Privately Held**
SIC: 1389 1381 Oil field services; drilling oil & gas wells

(G-13385)
THOMAS L MILLER
Also Called: Miller Engineering
111 Strecker HI (45750-1657)
PHONE.................................740 374-3041
Thomas L Miller, *Owner*
EMP: 77
SALES (est): 3MM **Privately Held**
SIC: 8711 Consulting engineer

(G-13386)
THOMSONS LANDSCAPING
26130 State Route 7 (45750-5113)
PHONE.................................740 374-9353
Russell Thomson, *Mng Member*
EMP: 25 **EST:** 1979
SQ FT: 2,500
SALES (est): 283.7K **Privately Held**
SIC: 0782 5261 Landscape contractors; lawn & garden supplies

(G-13387)
TRIAD ENERGY CORPORATION
125 Putnam St (45750-2936)
PHONE.................................740 374-2940
Kean Weaver, *President*
James R Bryden, *Vice Pres*
Brent Powell, *Safety Mgr*
Kim Arnold, *Human Res Mgr*
EMP: 26
SALES (est): 3.3MM **Privately Held**
SIC: 2992 1382 Lubricating oils & greases; oil & gas exploration services

(G-13388)
TRIAD OIL & GAS ENGINEERING
27724 State Route 7 (45750-5147)
PHONE.................................740 374-2940
Kean Weaver, *President*
EMP: 100
SQ FT: 7,800
SALES (est): 4.1MM **Privately Held**
SIC: 8742 Industry specialist consultants

(G-13389)
TRIAD PLL
27724 State Route 7 (45750-5147)
PHONE.................................740 374-2940
James R Briden, *Partner*
EMP: 35
SALES (est): 763.3K **Privately Held**
SIC: 6531 Real estate leasing & rentals

(G-13390)
TWIN COMM INC
Also Called: Telepage Communication Systems
2349 State Route 821 (45750-5362)
P.O. Box 487, Grove City (43123-0487)
PHONE..................................740 774-4701
Bruce Lane, *President*
EMP: 31
SQ FT: 6,000
SALES (est): 2.3MM **Privately Held**
WEB: www.telepagepaging.com
SIC: 4812 7389 5999 Radio pager (beeper) communication services; telephone answering service; telephone equipment & systems

(G-13391)
UBS FINANCIAL SERVICES INC
324 3rd St (45750-2901)
PHONE..................................740 336-7823
EMP: 43
SALES (corp-wide): 29.4B **Privately Held**
SIC: 7389 Financial services
HQ: Ubs Financial Services Inc.
1285 Ave Of The Americas
New York NY 10019
212 713-2000

(G-13392)
UNITED CHURCH HOMES INC
Also Called: Harmer Place
401 Harmar St (45750-2732)
PHONE..................................740 376-5600
Kenneth Daniel, *CEO*
James Henry, *Ch of Bd*
Susan K Boulton, *Administration*
EMP: 72
SALES (est): 7.7MM **Privately Held**
SIC: 8361 8051 Home for the aged; skilled nursing care facilities

(G-13393)
UNITED PARCEL SERVICE INC OH
Also Called: UPS
105 Industry Rd (45750-9355)
PHONE..................................740 373-0772
EMP: 158
SALES (corp-wide): 71.8B **Publicly Held**
SIC: 4215 Package delivery, vehicular
HQ: United Parcel Service, Inc. (Oh)
55 Glenlake Pkwy
Atlanta GA 30328
404 828-6000

(G-13394)
VADAKIN INC
110 Industry Rd (45750-9355)
P.O. Box 565 (45750-0565)
PHONE..................................740 373-7518
Sara Hooper, *President*
Mark Whiteley, *Vice Pres*
Greg Grose, *Manager*
EMP: 50
SQ FT: 16,000
SALES (est): 2.7MM **Privately Held**
WEB: www.vadakininc.com
SIC: 7349 Cleaning service, industrial or commercial

(G-13395)
VALLEY HOSPITALITY INC
Also Called: Holiday Inn
701 Pike St (45750-3502)
PHONE..................................740 374-9660
Andy Benson, *President*
Rita H Stephan, *Admin Sec*
EMP: 40
SQ FT: 50,000
SALES (est): 1.6MM **Privately Held**
SIC: 7011 5812 5813 7299 Hotels; family restaurants; bars & lounges; banquet hall facilities

(G-13396)
VETERANS HEALTH ADMINISTRATION
Also Called: Marietta Community Based
418 Colegate Dr (45750-9549)
PHONE..................................740 568-0412
Dianna Dowler, *Manager*
EMP: 264 **Publicly Held**
WEB: www.veterans-ru.org
SIC: 8011 9451 Clinic, operated by physicians; psychiatric clinic;
HQ: Veterans Health Administration
810 Vermont Ave Nw
Washington DC 20420

(G-13397)
VIKING FABRICATORS INC
2021 Hanna Rd (45750-8255)
PHONE..................................740 374-5246
David M Archer, *President*
James S Huggins, *Principal*
Matthew Hilverding, *Corp Secy*
Arlene M Archer, *Vice Pres*
EMP: 25
SQ FT: 20,000
SALES (est): 5.1MM **Privately Held**
SIC: 3441 7692 3446 3443 Fabricated structural metal; welding repair; architectural metalwork; fabricated plate work (boiler shop)

(G-13398)
WARREN BROS & SONS INC (PA)
Also Called: Warrens IGA
108b S 7th St (45750-3338)
PHONE..................................740 373-1430
Kin Brewer, *President*
Lisa G Brewer, *Admin Sec*
EMP: 75
SALES (est): 4.4MM **Privately Held**
SIC: 8721 Accounting, auditing & bookkeeping

(G-13399)
WARREN TWNSHP VLNTR FIRE DEPT
17305 State Route 550 (45750-8315)
PHONE..................................740 373-2424
Jeff Knowlton, *Principal*
Mark Wile, *Manager*
EMP: 30
SALES (est): 1.8MM **Privately Held**
SIC: 8621 Professional membership organizations

(G-13400)
WASCO INC (PA)
340 Muskingum Dr (45750-1435)
PHONE..................................740 373-3418
Joseph Faires, *CEO*
Tara Meeks, *Manager*
EMP: 31
SQ FT: 22,000
SALES (est): 3.3MM **Privately Held**
SIC: 8331 Sheltered workshop; job training services

(G-13401)
WESTFALL TOWING LLC
1200 Pike St (45750-5102)
PHONE..................................740 371-5185
Steve Griffith, *Manager*
EMP: 29
SALES (est): 173.1K **Privately Held**
SIC: 7549 Towing services

(G-13402)
YOUNG MENS CHRISTIAN ASSN
Also Called: MARIETTA FAMILY YMCA
300 N 7th St (45750-2243)
PHONE..................................740 373-2250
Roger Pitasky, *President*
Robert Ferguson, *Vice Pres*
Dennis Cooke, *Treasurer*
Suzy Zumwalde, *Exec Dir*
Al Miller, *Director*
EMP: 65
SQ FT: 35,000
SALES: 917.9K **Privately Held**
WEB: www.mariettaymca.org
SIC: 8641 8351 Recreation association; child day care services

(G-13403)
ZIDE SPORT SHOP OF OHIO INC (PA)
Also Called: Zide Screen Printing
253 2nd St (45750-2918)
PHONE..................................740 373-6446
Rodney Zide, *President*
Anita Zide, *Treasurer*
John Zide, *Shareholder*
EMP: 60

SQ FT: 19,000
SALES (est): 7.4MM **Privately Held**
SIC: 5941 5091 Bicycle & bicycle parts; golf goods & equipment; skiing equipment; sporting & recreation goods

Marion
Marion County

(G-13404)
AQUA TECH ENVMTL LABS INC (PA)
Also Called: Atel
1776 Marion Waldo Rd (43302-7428)
PHONE..................................740 389-5991
Paul Crerar, *President*
Rhonda Morris, *Manager*
EMP: 29
SQ FT: 5,000
SALES (est): 4.7MM **Privately Held**
WEB: www.atel2.com
SIC: 8734 Hazardous waste testing; soil analysis; water testing laboratory

(G-13405)
BIO-MDICAL APPLICATIONS RI INC
Also Called: Fresenius Medical Care
1730 Marion Waldo Rd (43302-7428)
PHONE..................................740 389-4111
EMP: 25
SALES (corp-wide): 18.9B **Privately Held**
SIC: 8092 8011 Kidney dialysis centers; offices & clinics of medical doctors
HQ: Bio-Medical Applications Of Rhode Island, Inc.
920 Winter St Ste A
Waltham MA 02451
781 699-9000

(G-13406)
BOISE CASCADE COMPANY
3007 Harding Hwy E (43302-2575)
PHONE..................................740 382-6766
Jeff Wiska, *Branch Mgr*
EMP: 26
SALES (corp-wide): 5B **Publicly Held**
SIC: 5031 Building materials, exterior; building materials, interior; composite board products, woodboard; lumber: rough, dressed & finished
PA: Boise Cascade Company
1111 W Jefferson St # 300
Boise ID 83702
208 384-6161

(G-13407)
BRIDGES TO INDEPENDENCE INC
117 N Greenwood St Ste 2 (43302-3129)
PHONE..................................740 375-5533
Chris Ritchie, *Manager*
EMP: 25
SALES (corp-wide): 3.4MM **Privately Held**
WEB: www.bridgestoindependence.com
SIC: 8051 Mental retardation hospital
PA: Bridges To Independence Inc
61 W William St
Delaware OH 43015
740 362-1996

(G-13408)
BURNS & SCALO ROOFING CO INC
2181 Innovation Dr # 101 (43302-8254)
PHONE..................................740 383-4639
Jack Scalo, *Owner*
EMP: 30
SALES (corp-wide): 33.1MM **Privately Held**
SIC: 1761 Roofing contractor
PA: Burns & Scalo Roofing Company, Inc.
22 Rutgers Rd Ste 200
Pittsburgh PA 15205
412 928-3060

(G-13409)
CARLSON HOTELS LTD PARTNERSHIP
Also Called: Marion Country Inn & Suites
2091 Marion Mt Gilead Rd (43302-8990)
PHONE..................................740 386-5451
Yantrini Patel, *Branch Mgr*
EMP: 60
SALES (corp-wide): 4B **Privately Held**
SIC: 7011 Hotels & motels
HQ: Carlson Hotels Limited Partnership
Carlson Parkway 701 Twr St Carlson Parkw
Minneapolis MN 55459
763 212-1000

(G-13410)
CENTER STREET CMNTY CLINIC INC
136 W Center St (43302-3704)
PHONE..................................740 751-6380
Cliff Edwards, *CEO*
EMP: 36
SALES: 3.8MM **Privately Held**
SIC: 8059 Personal care home, with health care

(G-13411)
CIRCLE T LOGISTICS INC
617 W Center St Ste 26 (43302-3569)
P.O. Box 357 (43301-0357)
PHONE..................................740 262-5096
Mark Lyon, *President*
EMP: 45
SQ FT: 11,000
SALES (est): 5.5MM **Privately Held**
SIC: 4213 Trucking, except local

(G-13412)
CITY OF MARION
Also Called: Sanitation & Garage Services
981 W Center St (43302-3463)
PHONE..................................740 382-1479
Bob Moats, *Manager*
EMP: 70 **Privately Held**
WEB: www.marionohio.org
SIC: 4212 8111 9111 Garbage collection & transport, no disposal; general practice attorney, lawyer; mayors' offices
PA: City Of Marion
233 W Center St
Marion OH 43302
740 387-2020

(G-13413)
COUNTY OF MARION
Also Called: Child Support Services
620 Leader St (43302-2230)
PHONE..................................740 387-6688
Roxanne Somerlot, *Director*
EMP: 40 **Privately Held**
WEB: www.co.marion.oh.us
SIC: 8322 9111 Public welfare center; county supervisors' & executives' offices
PA: County Of Marion
222 W Center St Ste A1031
Marion OH 43302
740 223-4030

(G-13414)
COUNTY OF MARION
Also Called: East Lawn Manor
1422 Mount Vernon Ave (43302-5629)
PHONE..................................740 389-4624
Barbara Balsley, *Administration*
EMP: 100
SQ FT: 500,000 **Privately Held**
WEB: www.co.marion.oh.us
SIC: 8051 Skilled nursing care facilities
PA: County Of Marion
222 W Center St Ste A1031
Marion OH 43302
740 223-4030

(G-13415)
COUNTY OF MARION
Also Called: Wadell Village Children Svcs
1680 Marion Waldo Rd (43302-7426)
PHONE..................................740 389-2317
Jacqueline Ringer, *Director*
EMP: 40 **Privately Held**
WEB: www.co.marion.oh.us
SIC: 8322 9111 Child related social services; county supervisors' & executives' offices

PA: County Of Marion
222 W Center St Ste A1031
Marion OH 43302
740 223-4030

(G-13416)
COUNTY OF MARION
Also Called: Board of Mrdd
2387 Harding Hwy E (43302-8529)
PHONE..............................740 387-1035
Cheryl Plaster, *Supervisor*
EMP: 95 **Privately Held**
WEB: www.co.marion.oh.us
SIC: 9111 8331 County supervisors' & executives' offices; job training & vocational rehabilitation services
PA: County Of Marion
222 W Center St Ste A1031
Marion OH 43302
740 223-4030

(G-13417)
COUNTY OF MARION
Also Called: Department of Transportation
1775 Mrn Williamsprt Rd E (43302-8512)
PHONE..............................740 382-0624
Bruce Mays, *Manager*
EMP: 30 **Privately Held**
WEB: www.co.marion.oh.us
SIC: 8742 Maintenance management consultant; food & beverage consultant
PA: County Of Marion
222 W Center St Ste A1031
Marion OH 43302
740 223-4030

(G-13418)
DEARTH MANAGEMENT COMPANY
Also Called: Morning View Care Center
677 Marion Cardington Rd (43302-7317)
P.O. Box 656 (43301-0656)
PHONE..............................740 389-1214
Fax: 740 389-2074
EMP: 25
SALES (corp-wide): 12.3MM **Privately Held**
SIC: 8052 8051 Intermediate Care Facility Skilled Nursing Care Facility
PA: Dearth Management Company
134 Northwoods Blvd Ste C
Columbus OH 43235
614 847-1070

(G-13419)
EPWORTH PRESCHOOL AND DAYCARE
Also Called: Epworth United Methodist Ch
249 E Center St (43302-3814)
PHONE..............................740 387-1062
Heder Mawler, *Director*
Robin Rick, *Director*
EMP: 40
SALES (est): 763.1K **Privately Held**
SIC: 8661 8351 Miscellaneous denomination church; child day care services

(G-13420)
EPWORTH UNITED METHODIST CH
249 E Center St (43302-3873)
PHONE..............................740 387-1062
Jim Hering Jr, *Minister*
Max L Williams, *Pastor*
Page Gustin, *Director*
Robin Rick, *Director*
Marlene La Shat, *Assoc Pastor*
EMP: 86
SALES (est): 2MM **Privately Held**
SIC: 8661 8351 Methodist Church; group day care center; preschool center

(G-13421)
FREDERICK C SMITH CLINIC INC (PA)
Also Called: Marion Area Health Center
1040 Delaware Ave (43302-6416)
PHONE..............................740 383-7000
Dalsukh Madia, *President*
Michael P Coyne, *Principal*
Ronald J Waldheger, *Principal*
J C Garvin MD, *Vice Pres*
EMP: 400
SQ FT: 100,000

SALES (est): 38MM **Privately Held**
WEB: www.marionareahealth.com
SIC: 8011 Physicians' office, including specialists; general & family practice, physician/surgeon

(G-13422)
GRAHAM INVESTMENT CO (PA)
Also Called: Casod Industrial Properties
3007 Harding Hwy E # 203 (43302-2575)
PHONE..............................740 382-0902
Ted Graham, *President*
Brian Grillot, *Supervisor*
EMP: 100 EST: 1969
SALES (est): 6.1MM **Privately Held**
WEB: www.micwarehouse.com
SIC: 6512 4225 Commercial & industrial building operation; general warehousing & storage

(G-13423)
HEALTH & HM CARE CONCEPTS INC
Also Called: Health & Homecare Concepts
353 S State St (43302-5019)
PHONE..............................740 383-4968
Thomas Veith, *President*
EMP: 45
SALES: 1.2MM **Privately Held**
SIC: 8082 Home health care services

(G-13424)
HEART OF OH CNCL BSA
1310 Mount Vernon Ave (43302-5627)
PHONE..............................740 389-4615
Sheryl Krassow, *Manager*
EMP: 26
SALES (corp-wide): 1.6MM **Privately Held**
SIC: 8641 Boy Scout organization
PA: Heart Of Ohio Council Inc., Boy Scouts Of America
3 N Main St Ste 303
Mansfield OH 44902
419 522-8300

(G-13425)
HOLBROOK & MANTER (PA)
181 E Center St (43302-3813)
P.O. Box 437 (43301-0437)
PHONE..............................740 387-8620
Brad Idge, *Partner*
Thomas Kalb, *Partner*
Linda Fargo, *CPA*
Bradley Ridge, *CPA*
EMP: 30
SQ FT: 6,270
SALES (est): 4.1MM **Privately Held**
SIC: 8721 Certified public accountant

(G-13426)
JPMORGAN CHASE BANK NAT ASSN
165 W Center St (43302-3742)
PHONE..............................740 382-7362
Tracie Wilson, *Branch Mgr*
EMP: 34
SALES (corp-wide): 131.4B **Publicly Held**
SIC: 6029 Commercial banks
HQ: Jpmorgan Chase Bank, National Association
1111 Polaris Pkwy
Columbus OH 43240
614 436-3055

(G-13427)
KINGSTON HEALTHCARE COMPANY
Also Called: Kingston Residence of Marion
464 James Way Ofc (43302-7817)
PHONE..............................740 389-2311
Linda Pfaff, *Office Mgr*
Carrie Hutchman, *Branch Mgr*
Dave Steer, *Supervisor*
EMP: 80
SQ FT: 47,452
SALES (corp-wide): 95.5MM **Privately Held**
WEB: www.kingstonhealthcare.com
SIC: 8361 Home for the aged
PA: Kingston Healthcare Company
1 Seagate Ste 1960
Toledo OH 43604
419 247-2880

(G-13428)
KNIGHTS OF COLUMBUS
1242 E Center St (43302-4406)
PHONE..............................740 382-3671
Gray Hubbard, *President*
EMP: 60
SALES (corp-wide): 2.3B **Privately Held**
WEB: www.kofc.org
SIC: 8641 Fraternal associations
PA: Knights Of Columbus
1 Columbus Plz Ste 1700
New Haven CT 06510
203 752-4000

(G-13429)
LEVERING MANAGEMENT INC
Also Called: Marion Manor Nursing Home
195 Executive Dr (43302-6343)
PHONE..............................740 387-9545
William Dunn, *Administration*
EMP: 90
SALES (corp-wide): 27.7MM **Privately Held**
SIC: 8741 8051 Management services; skilled nursing care facilities
PA: Levering Management, Inc.
201 N Main St
Mount Vernon OH 43050
740 397-3897

(G-13430)
LOWES HOME CENTERS LLC
1840 Marion Mt Gilead Rd (43302-5826)
PHONE..............................740 389-9737
Rhonda Walker, *Manager*
EMP: 150
SALES (corp-wide): 68.6B **Publicly Held**
SIC: 5211 5031 5722 5064 Home centers; building materials, exterior; building materials, interior; household appliance stores; electrical appliances, television & radio
HQ: Lowe's Home Centers, Llc
1605 Curtis Bridge Rd
Wilkesboro NC 28697
336 658-4000

(G-13431)
MAPLEWOOD NURSING CENTER INC
409 Bellefontaine Ave (43302-4811)
PHONE..............................740 383-2126
Paul A Granger, *President*
EMP: 50
SQ FT: 15,000
SALES (est): 1.8MM **Privately Held**
SIC: 8051 Convalescent home with continuous nursing care

(G-13432)
MARCA INDUSTRIES INC
2387 Harding Hwy E (43302-8531)
PHONE..............................740 387-1035
Liz Owens, *Director*
EMP: 39 EST: 1967
SQ FT: 50,000
SALES: 658.2K **Privately Held**
SIC: 8331 Sheltered workshop

(G-13433)
MARCY INDUSTRIES COMPANY LLC
1836 Likens Rd (43302-8652)
PHONE..............................740 943-2343
Dan Shew, *CEO*
EMP: 34 EST: 2009
SALES (est): 6.8MM **Privately Held**
SIC: 5084 Whol Industrial Equipment

(G-13434)
MARION AREA COUNSELING CTR (PA)
320 Executive Dr (43302-6373)
PHONE..............................740 387-5210
Beverly Young, *Director*
EMP: 109
SQ FT: 2,500
SALES: 5MM **Privately Held**
WEB: www.maccsite.com
SIC: 8322 8093 General counseling services; specialty outpatient clinics

(G-13435)
MARION CNTY BD DEV DSABILITIES
Also Called: Marion County Board of Mr Dd
2387 Harding Hwy E (43302-8529)
PHONE..............................740 387-1035
Lee Wedemeyer, *Superintendent*
Ken Padgett, *Manager*
Julie Cummins, *Director*
Victoria Dutton, *Admin Asst*
EMP: 95 EST: 2001
SALES (est): 3.6MM **Privately Held**
SIC: 8331 Community service employment training program

(G-13436)
MARION COUNTRY CLUB COMPANY
Also Called: Marion Country Club, The
2415 Crissinger Rd (43302-8231)
PHONE..............................740 387-0974
Bill Maybury, *General Mgr*
EMP: 25
SQ FT: 30,000
SALES (est): 940K **Privately Held**
SIC: 7997 5812 Country club, membership; golf club, membership; swimming club, membership; tennis club, membership; eating places

(G-13437)
MARION FAMILY YMCA
645 Barks Rd E (43302-6517)
PHONE..............................740 725-9622
Bob Houston, *President*
EMP: 60
SALES (est): 2.4MM **Privately Held**
WEB: www.marionymca.com
SIC: 8322 8641 Youth center; youth organizations

(G-13438)
MARION GEN SOCIAL WORK DEPT
Also Called: Marion General Hospital
1000 Mckinley Park Dr (43302-6399)
PHONE..............................740 383-8788
EMP: 25
SALES (est): 409.5K **Privately Held**
SIC: 8062 General Hospital

(G-13439)
MARION GENERAL HOSP HM HLTH
278 Barks Rd W (43302-7367)
PHONE..............................740 383-8770
Cindy Schifer, *Principal*
EMP: 31
SALES (est): 657.6K **Privately Held**
SIC: 8062 General medical & surgical hospitals

(G-13440)
MARION GENERAL HOSPITAL INC (HQ)
1000 Mckinley Park Dr (43302-6397)
PHONE..............................740 383-8400
John Sanders, *President*
Tim Watson, *Human Res Dir*
Andrea Benson, *Manager*
Christina Richards, *Manager*
Sheila Stewart, *Manager*
EMP: 58 EST: 1955
SQ FT: 247,000
SALES: 186.9MM
SALES (corp-wide): 4B **Privately Held**
WEB: www.mariongeneral.com
SIC: 8062 Hospital, AMA approved residency
PA: Ohiohealth Corporation
180 E Broad St
Columbus OH 43215
614 788-8860

(G-13441)
MARION GOODWILL INDUSTRIES (PA)
340 W Fairground St (43302-1728)
PHONE..............................740 387-7023
Bob Jordan, *Exec Dir*
EMP: 25 EST: 1977
SQ FT: 17,500

SALES: 16.6MM **Privately Held**
SIC: 5932 8331 Furniture, secondhand; sheltered workshop

(G-13442)
MARION HEAD START CENTER
2387 Harding Hwy E (43302-8529)
PHONE..............................740 382-6858
Andrew Devany, *CFO*
Jennifer Ishida, *Director*
EMP: 27
SALES (est): 300.9K **Privately Held**
SIC: 8351 Head start center, except in conjunction with school

(G-13443)
MARION MANOR
195 Executive Dr (43302-6343)
PHONE..............................740 387-9545
L Bruce Levering, *President*
William L Dunn, *Treasurer*
EMP: 75
SQ FT: 30,000
SALES (est): 2.6MM **Privately Held**
SIC: 8059 8051 Nursing home, except skilled & intermediate care facility; convalescent home; skilled nursing care facilities

(G-13444)
MATHEWS DODGE CHRYSLER JEEP
1866 Marion Waldo Rd (43302-7430)
PHONE..............................740 389-2341
Thurman Matthews, *President*
EMP: 30
SALES: 14MM **Privately Held**
SIC: 5511 7538 7515 Automobiles, new & used; general automotive repair shops; passenger car leasing

(G-13445)
MATHEWS KENNEDY FORD L-M INC (PA)
Also Called: Mathews Auto Group
1155 Delaware Ave (43302-6417)
PHONE..............................740 387-3673
Thurman R Mathews, *President*
Jean Mitchell, *Corp Secy*
Thomas Mathews,
EMP: 100
SQ FT: 35,000
SALES (est): 41.9MM **Privately Held**
WEB: www.mathewsautogroup.com
SIC: 5511 7538 7532 7515 Automobiles, new & used; general automotive repair shops; top & body repair & paint shops; passenger car leasing

(G-13446)
MC DANIEL MOTOR CO (INC)
1111 Mount Vernon Ave (43302-5699)
PHONE..............................740 389-2355
Michael Mc Daniel, *President*
James P Waddell, *Exec VP*
Matt Reynolds, *Info Tech Dir*
Becky Franco, *Executive*
Mark Vicars, *Executive*
EMP: 44
SQ FT: 60,000
SALES (est): 13.3MM **Privately Held**
WEB: www.mcdanieltoyota.com
SIC: 5511 7515 Automobiles, new & used; passenger car leasing

(G-13447)
MCCOY LANDSCAPE SERVICES INC
2391 Likens Rd (43302-8541)
PHONE..............................740 375-2730
Matt McCoy, *President*
Mark McCoy, *Vice Pres*
EMP: 35
SALES (est): 1.5MM **Privately Held**
WEB: www.mccoylandscape.com
SIC: 0782 5999 Landscape contractors; Christmas lights & decorations

(G-13448)
NATIONAL SERVICE INFORMATION
145 Baker St (43302-4111)
P.O. Box 6293 (43301-6293)
PHONE..............................740 387-6806
Cozy Lee Dixon, *President*

Kim Dixon, *Admin Sec*
EMP: 25
SQ FT: 6,700
SALES (est): 1.8MM **Privately Held**
WEB: www.nsii.net
SIC: 7338 8111 8999 Court reporting service; legal services; information bureau

(G-13449)
NEW HORIZONS SURGERY CENTER
1167 Independence Ave (43302-6360)
PHONE..............................740 375-5854
Brian Hempstead, *CEO*
EMP: 26
SALES (est): 3.2MM **Privately Held**
SIC: 8011 General & family practice, physician/surgeon

(G-13450)
OHIO HRTLAND CMNTY ACTION COMM (PA)
372 E Center St (43302-4126)
PHONE..............................740 387-1039
James Lavelle, *CFO*
Andrew J Devany, *Exec Dir*
Bonita Howard, *Director*
Betty Owens, *Admin Sec*
EMP: 45
SALES: 10.4MM **Privately Held**
SIC: 8399 Community action agency

(G-13451)
OHIO-AMERICAN WATER CO INC (HQ)
Also Called: Marion District
365 E Center St (43302-4155)
PHONE..............................740 382-3993
John E Eckart, *President*
T Wilkes Coleman, *Vice Pres*
Dwayne D Cole, *VP Opers*
Christine J Doron, *Treasurer*
Stephen B Givens, *Admin Sec*
EMP: 45
SQ FT: 8,500
SALES (est): 25.1MM
SALES (corp-wide): 3.4B **Publicly Held**
SIC: 4941 Water supply
PA: American Water Works Company, Inc.
1 Water St
Camden NJ 08102
856 955-4001

(G-13452)
ORDER OF SYMPOSIARCHS AMERICA
704 Vernon Heights Blvd (43302-5380)
PHONE..............................740 387-9713
James Greetham, *Treasurer*
EMP: 30
SALES (est): 940K **Privately Held**
SIC: 8641 Civic associations

(G-13453)
QUALITY MASONRY COMPANY INC
Also Called: Quality Maintenance Company
1001 S Prospect St # 101 (43302-6289)
PHONE..............................740 387-6720
William Bowers, *President*
Bret Bowers, *Vice Pres*
Justin Bowers, *Administration*
EMP: 30 EST: 1973
SQ FT: 2,000
SALES: 4.9MM **Privately Held**
WEB: www.qualitymasonryco.com
SIC: 1741 Masonry & other stonework

(G-13454)
REAL ESTATE SHOWCASE
731 E Center St (43302-4346)
PHONE..............................740 389-2000
Rick R Roe, *CEO*
EMP: 30
SALES (est): 1.7MM **Privately Held**
SIC: 6531 Real estate brokers & agents

(G-13455)
RESIDENTIAL HM ASSN OF MARION (PA)
Also Called: Rham
205 W Center St Ste 100 (43302-3700)
PHONE..............................740 387-9999

Shirley Russell, *Director*
EMP: 106
SALES: 3.1MM **Privately Held**
SIC: 8742 8361 6531 Management consulting services; home for the mentally retarded; real estate agents & managers

(G-13456)
RIVER ROCK REHABILITATION
990 S Prospect St Ste 4 (43302-6283)
PHONE..............................740 382-4035
William Reinbolt, *CEO*
Timothy Burkam, *COO*
EMP: 50
SALES (est): 2.1MM **Privately Held**
SIC: 8049 Physical therapist

(G-13457)
RK FAMILY INC
233 America Blvd (43302-7805)
PHONE..............................740 389-2674
Tim Lodes, *Principal*
EMP: 288
SALES (corp-wide): 1.5B **Privately Held**
SIC: 5099 Firearms & ammunition, except sporting
PA: Rk Family, Inc.
4216 Dewitt Ave
Mattoon IL 61938
217 235-7102

(G-13458)
SACK N SAVE INC
Also Called: King Saver
725 Richmond Ave (43302-1935)
PHONE..............................740 382-2464
David Fass, *Manager*
EMP: 30 **Privately Held**
SIC: 5411 6099 Grocery stores, chain; money order issuance
HQ: Sack 'n Save, Inc.
317 W Main Cross St
Findlay OH 45840
419 422-8090

(G-13459)
SIKA CORPORATION
1682 Mrn Williamsprt Rd E (43302-8694)
PHONE..............................740 387-9224
Todd Petrie, *VP Opers*
Ray Gear, *Purch Mgr*
Doug White, *Branch Mgr*
EMP: 62
SALES (corp-wide): 6.3B **Privately Held**
WEB: www.sikacorp.com
SIC: 2899 5169 3566 Concrete curing & hardening compounds; concrete additives; speed changers, drives & gears
HQ: Sika Corporation
201 Polito Ave
Lyndhurst NJ 07071
201 933-8800

(G-13460)
STOFCHECK AMBULANCE INC
Also Called: Stofcheck Ambulance Service
314 W Center St (43302-3614)
PHONE..............................740 383-2787
EMP: 200
SALES (est): 3.1MM **Privately Held**
SIC: 4119 Ambulance Service

(G-13461)
SUNBRDGE MARION HLTH CARE CORP
Also Called: Partners of Marion Care
524 James Way (43302-7801)
PHONE..............................740 389-6306
Shannon Kellogg, *Manager*
EMP: 90 **Publicly Held**
SIC: 8051 8093 Skilled nursing care facilities; rehabilitation center, outpatient treatment
HQ: Sunbridge Marion Health Care Llc
101 Sun Ave Ne
Albuquerque NM 87109
505 821-3355

(G-13462)
SUPERMEDIA LLC
Also Called: Verizon
19 E Central Ave Fl 1 Flr 1 (43302)
PHONE..............................740 369-2391
Jeff Germann, *Manager*
EMP: 80

SALES (corp-wide): 1.8B **Privately Held**
WEB: www.verizon.superpages.com
SIC: 4812 Cellular telephone services
HQ: Supermedia Llc
2200 W Airfield Dr
Dfw Airport TX 75261
972 453-7000

(G-13463)
TED GRAHAM
Also Called: G P Properties
3007 Harding Hwy E (43302-2575)
PHONE..............................740 223-3509
Ted Graham, *Owner*
EMP: 50
SQ FT: 1,300
SALES (est): 1.8MM **Privately Held**
WEB: www.tedgraham.com
SIC: 6512 Commercial & industrial building operation

(G-13464)
TONKA BAY DIALYSIS LLC
Also Called: Heart of Marion Dialysis
1221 Delaware Ave (43302-6419)
PHONE..............................740 375-0849
James K Hilger,
EMP: 26
SALES (est): 224.3K **Publicly Held**
SIC: 8092 Kidney dialysis centers
PA: Davita Inc.
2000 16th St
Denver CO 80202

(G-13465)
TRAFZER EXCAVATING INC
1560 Likens Rd (43302-8652)
PHONE..............................740 383-2616
James E Trafzer, *President*
EMP: 30
SQ FT: 6,000
SALES (est): 2.3MM **Privately Held**
SIC: 1794 Excavation & grading, building construction

(G-13466)
TURBO PARTS LLC
1676 Cascade Dr (43302-8509)
PHONE..............................740 223-1695
Tony Mitola, *Branch Mgr*
EMP: 30 **Privately Held**
SIC: 5013 Automotive supplies & parts
PA: Turbo Parts, Llc
767 Pierce Rd Ste 2
Clifton Park NY 12065

(G-13467)
UNION BANK COMPANY
111 S Main St (43302-3701)
PHONE..............................740 387-2265
EMP: 34
SALES (corp-wide): 24.3MM **Publicly Held**
SIC: 6022 State Commercial Bank
HQ: The Union Bank Company
100 S High St
Columbus Grove OH 45830
419 659-2141

(G-13468)
UNION TANK CAR COMPANY
939 Holland Rd W (43302-9406)
P.O. Box 1125 (43301-1125)
PHONE..............................419 864-7216
Mike Nestor, *Manager*
EMP: 119
SALES (corp-wide): 225.3B **Publicly Held**
WEB: www.utlx.com
SIC: 5099 Safety equipment & supplies
HQ: Union Tank Car Company
175 W Jackson Blvd # 2100
Chicago IL 60604
312 431-3111

(G-13469)
UNITE CHURC RESID OF OXFOR MIS (HQ)
Also Called: CHAPEL HILL COMMUNITY
170 E Center St (43302-3815)
P.O. Box 1806 (43301-1806)
PHONE..............................740 382-4885
Dorothy Eckert, *President*
John R Dickson, *Corp Secy*
Paul Kiewit, *Vice Pres*
EMP: 25

SQ FT: 20,000
SALES: 243.4K
SALES (corp-wide): 78.1MM **Privately Held**
SIC: 6513 Apartment building operators
PA: United Church Homes Inc
170 E Center St
Marion OH 43302
740 382-4885

(G-13470)
UNITED CHURCH HOMES
170 E Center St (43302-3815)
P.O. Box 1806 (43301-1806)
PHONE...........................740 382-4885
Kenneth Daniel, *President*
Brian Allen, *President*
John R Dickson, *Corp Secy*
Edwin R Allen Jr, *Vice Pres*
Laverne Joseph, *Vice Pres*
EMP: 60
SQ FT: 20,000
SALES: 325K
SALES (corp-wide): 78.1MM **Privately Held**
WEB: www.altenheimcommunity.org
SIC: 6513 Apartment building operators; nursing home, except skilled & intermediate care facility
PA: United Church Homes Inc
170 E Center St
Marion OH 43302
740 382-4885

(G-13471)
UNITED CHURCH HOMES INC (PA)
Also Called: Chapel Hill Community
170 E Center St (43302-3815)
P.O. Box 1806 (43301-1806)
PHONE...........................740 382-4885
Rev Kenneth Daniel, *CEO*
Brian S Allen, *President*
Edwin Allen, *Vice Pres*
Vincent Dent, *Vice Pres*
Timothy Hackett, *Vice Pres*
EMP: 60 EST: 1920
SQ FT: 20,000
SALES: 78.1MM **Privately Held**
WEB: www.altenheimcommunity.org
SIC: 8051 Skilled nursing care facilities

(G-13472)
UNITED PARCEL SERVICE INC OH
Also Called: UPS
1476 Likens Rd (43302-8788)
PHONE...........................614 383-4580
EMP: 158
SALES (corp-wide): 71.8B **Publicly Held**
SIC: 4215 Parcel delivery, vehicular
HQ: United Parcel Service, Inc. (Oh)
55 Glenlake Pkwy
Atlanta GA 30328
404 828-6000

(G-13473)
WHIRLPOOL CORPORATION
1300 Marion Agosta Rd (43302-9577)
PHONE...........................740 383-7122
Brian Gahr, *President*
Stan Kenneth, *Vice Pres*
David Strzalka, *Mfg Dir*
Barbara Klee, *Safety Dir*
Burl Davis, *Safety Mgr*
EMP: 250
SALES (corp-wide): 21B **Publicly Held**
WEB: www.whirlpoolcorp.com
SIC: 3633 5064 3632 Laundry dryers, household or coin-operated; washing machines; household refrigerators & freezers
PA: Whirlpool Corporation
2000 N M 63
Benton Harbor MI 49022
269 923-5000

Marshallville
Wayne County

(G-13474)
MARSHALLVILLE PACKING CO INC
50 E Market St (44645-9468)
P.O. Box 276 (44645-0276)
PHONE...........................330 855-2871
Frank T Tucker, *President*
Jeannette Tucker, *Corp Secy*
EMP: 29 EST: 1960
SQ FT: 35,000
SALES (est): 1.9MM **Privately Held**
SIC: 5421 5147 2013 2011 Meat markets, including freezer provisioniers; meats, fresh; sausages & other prepared meats; meat packing plants

(G-13475)
STOLL FARMS INC
15040 Fox Lake Rd (44645-9784)
PHONE...........................330 682-5786
Edward Stoll, *President*
Bonnie Stoll, *Admin Sec*
EMP: 35 EST: 1937
SALES: 2MM **Privately Held**
SIC: 0241 Dairy farms

Martins Ferry
Belmont County

(G-13476)
BELMONT METRO HSING AUTH (PA)
Also Called: Belmont Metro Hsing Auth A
100 S 3rd St (43935-1457)
PHONE...........................740 633-5085
Bruce Kinsel, *Owner*
EMP: 26
SQ FT: 63,000
SALES: 4.9MM **Privately Held**
SIC: 6513 Apartment building operators

(G-13477)
N F MANSUETTO & SONS INC
Also Called: Mansuetto Roofing Company
116 Wood St (43935-1710)
PHONE...........................740 633-7320
Matthew Mansuetto, *President*
Francis M Mansuetto, *Corp Secy*
Eugene Ochap, *Vice Pres*
EMP: 30
SQ FT: 10,000
SALES (est): 6.2MM **Privately Held**
SIC: 1761 Roofing contractor; sheet metalwork

(G-13478)
STONEY HOLLOW TIRE INC
1st & Hanover Sts (43935)
P.O. Box 310 (43935-0310)
PHONE...........................740 635-5200
John Seckman, *President*
Earl Buono, *Treasurer*
▲ **EMP:** 70
SQ FT: 80,000
SALES (est): 44.3MM **Privately Held**
WEB: www.stoneyhollowtire.com
SIC: 5014 Automobile tires & tubes; truck tires & tubes; tire & tube repair materials

(G-13479)
UNIFIED BANK (HQ)
Also Called: CITIZENS BANK
201 S 4th St (43935-1311)
P.O. Box 10 (43935-0010)
PHONE...........................740 633-0445
James W Everson, *Ch of Bd*
Scott Everson, *President*
Elmer Leeper, *Senior VP*
Michael A Lloyd, *Senior VP*
James Lodes, *Senior VP*
EMP: 40
SQ FT: 20,000
SALES: 21MM
SALES (corp-wide): 24.9MM **Publicly Held**
WEB: www.unitedbancorp.net
SIC: 6022 State commercial banks

PA: United Bancorp, Inc.
201 S 4th St
Martins Ferry OH 43935
740 633-0445

(G-13480)
UNITED STEELWORKERS
Also Called: Uswa
705 Main St (43935-1715)
PHONE...........................740 633-0899
Ken Apfenleiger, *President*
Carmen De Stefano, *VP Finance*
EMP: 32
SALES (corp-wide): 4.9MM **Privately Held**
WEB: www.uswa.org
SIC: 8631 Labor union
PA: United Steelworkers
60 Blvd Of The Allies # 902
Pittsburgh PA 15222
412 562-2400

(G-13481)
WHEELING HOSPITAL INC
Also Called: Valley Gstrnterology Endoscopy
90 N 4th St (43935-1648)
PHONE...........................740 633-4765
Ronald Violi, *CEO*
EMP: 35
SALES (corp-wide): 395.3MM **Privately Held**
SIC: 8011 Physical medicine, physician/surgeon
PA: Wheeling Hospital, Inc.
1 Medical Park
Wheeling WV 26003
304 243-3000

Marysville
Union County

(G-13482)
ACE RENTAL PLACE
Also Called: Ace Hardware
1299 W 5th St (43040-9291)
PHONE...........................937 642-2891
Dan Fitzgerald, *Owner*
Jim Fitzgerald, *Co-Owner*
EMP: 75
SALES (est): 5.6MM **Privately Held**
SIC: 7359 5251 Stores & yards equipment rental; hardware

(G-13483)
AREA ENERGY & ELECTRIC INC
19255 Smokey Rd (43040-9141)
PHONE...........................937 642-0386
Joe Lachey, *Manager*
EMP: 40
SALES (corp-wide): 58.8MM **Privately Held**
SIC: 1731 General electrical contractor
PA: Area Energy & Electric, Inc.
2001 Commerce Dr
Sidney OH 45365
937 498-4784

(G-13484)
BASINGER LFE ENHNCMNT SPRT SVC (PA)
Also Called: Bless
941 E 5th St (43040-1703)
PHONE...........................614 557-5461
Robert Basinger, *Mng Member*
EMP: 100
SALES (est): 5.4MM **Privately Held**
SIC: 8361 Residential care for the handicapped

(G-13485)
BROOKDALE SENIOR LIVING INC
1565 London Ave Frnt (43040-6808)
PHONE...........................937 738-7342
Angela Maxwell, *Director*
EMP: 86
SALES (corp-wide): 4.5B **Publicly Held**
SIC: 8361 Residential care
PA: Brookdale Senior Living
111 Westwood Pl Ste 400
Brentwood TN 37027
615 221-2250

(G-13486)
BY-LINE TRANSIT INC
17075 White Stone Rd (43040-9479)
PHONE...........................937 642-2500
Deborah Bywater, *President*
Ronald P Bywater, *Vice Pres*
EMP: 49
SQ FT: 1,600
SALES: 5MM **Privately Held**
SIC: 4213 Contract haulers; refrigerated products transport

(G-13487)
CARRIAGE CRT MRYSVLLE LTD PRTN
717 S Walnut St (43040-1639)
PHONE...........................937 642-2202
Rita Orahood, *Exec Dir*
EMP: 30
SALES (est): 1.3MM **Privately Held**
SIC: 8361 8052 Home for the aged; intermediate care facilities

(G-13488)
CASSENS TRANSPORT COMPANY
24777 Honda Pkwy (43040-9189)
PHONE...........................937 644-8886
Don Trainer, *Manager*
EMP: 125
SQ FT: 14,400
SALES (corp-wide): 217.5MM **Privately Held**
SIC: 4213 Automobiles, transport & delivery
HQ: Cassens Transport Company
145 N Kansas St
Edwardsville IL 62025
618 656-3006

(G-13489)
CELLCO PARTNERSHIP
Also Called: Verizon Wireless
1095 Delaware Ave (43040-9401)
PHONE...........................937 578-0022
Patricia Fisher, *Branch Mgr*
EMP: 71
SALES (corp-wide): 130.8B **Publicly Held**
SIC: 4812 Cellular telephone services
HQ: Cellco Partnership
1 Verizon Way
Basking Ridge NJ 07920

(G-13490)
COUNTY OF UNION
Also Called: Environmental Engineering Dept
128 S Main St Ste 203 (43040-1653)
PHONE...........................937 645-3018
Steve Stolte, *Principal*
EMP: 45 **Privately Held**
SIC: 8711 9111 Engineering services; county supervisors' & executives' offices
PA: County Of Union
227 E 5th St
Marysville OH 43040
937 642-6279

(G-13491)
COUNTY OF UNION
Also Called: Union Cnty Board of Devlpmt
1280 Charles Ln (43040-9797)
PHONE...........................937 645-6733
Jerry L Burger, *Superintendent*
EMP: 80 **Privately Held**
SIC: 9431 8322 ; social services for the handicapped
PA: County Of Union
227 E 5th St
Marysville OH 43040
937 642-6279

(G-13492)
COUNTY OF UNION
Also Called: Engineer's Office
128 S Main St Ste 203 (43040-1653)
PHONE...........................937 645-4145
Amy Hamilton, *CFO*
EMP: 78 **Privately Held**
SIC: 1623 Water, sewer & utility lines
PA: County Of Union
227 E 5th St
Marysville OH 43040
937 642-6279

▲ = Import ▼=Export
◆ =Import/Export

(G-13493)
CSX TRANSPORTATION INC
19835 Johnson Rd (43040-9252)
PHONE.................................937 642-2221
Dave Schmidt, *Branch Mgr*
EMP: 39
SALES (corp-wide): 12.2B **Publicly Held**
SIC: 4011 Railroads, line-haul operating
HQ: Csx Transportation, Inc.
500 Water St
Jacksonville FL 32202
904 359-3100

(G-13494)
DARBY CREEK GOLF COURSE INC
19300 Orchard Rd (43040-9044)
PHONE.................................937 349-7491
Scott Hanhart, *President*
Tony Benincasa, *Vice Pres*
Ralph M La Porte, *Vice Pres*
David Hanhart, *Shareholder*
Mark Stariniery, *Shareholder*
EMP: 25
SALES (est): 1.5MM **Privately Held**
WEB: www.darbycreekgolf.com
SIC: 7992 7999 5941 Public golf courses; golf driving range; golf goods & equipment

(G-13495)
FIVE COUNTY JOINT JUVENILE DET
Also Called: Central Ohio Youth Center
18100 State Route 4 (43040-8550)
PHONE.................................937 642-1015
Vicky Jordon, *Superintendent*
Travis Stillion, *Principal*
EMP: 40
SALES (est): 1.5MM **Privately Held**
SIC: 8361 Juvenile correctional facilities

(G-13496)
FRANKES UNLIMITED INC
825 Collins Ave (43040-1330)
PHONE.................................937 642-0706
Bill Franke, *President*
Christopher Franke, *Vice Pres*
Kevine Franke, *Vice Pres*
Michelle R Franke, *Admin Sec*
EMP: 30 EST: 1998
SALES: 3MM **Privately Held**
SIC: 7389 Field warehousing

(G-13497)
FRANKES WOOD PRODUCTS LLC
825 Collins Ave (43040-1330)
PHONE.................................937 642-0706
William Franke, *President*
Christopher S Franke, *Shareholder*
Kevin Franke, *Shareholder*
Michelle R Franke, *Shareholder*
EMP: 33
SQ FT: 93,800
SALES (est): 6.5MM **Privately Held**
SIC: 2448 2449 2493 3061 Cargo containers, wood; shipping cases & drums, wood; wirebound & plywood; fiberboard, other vegetable pulp; mechanical rubber goods; rubber scrap; marketing consulting services

(G-13498)
GABLES AT GREEN PASTURES
390 Gables Dr (43040-9582)
PHONE.................................937 642-3893
Lorie Whittington, *Director*
EMP: 112
SALES: 9.3MM **Privately Held**
WEB: www.gablesatgreenpastures.com
SIC: 8051 Convalescent home with continuous nursing care

(G-13499)
GEETA HOSPITALITY INC
Also Called: Hampton Inn
16610 Square Dr (43040-8558)
PHONE.................................937 642-3777
Amar Pandey, *President*
EMP: 25
SALES (est): 1.4MM **Privately Held**
SIC: 7011 7991 Hotels; physical fitness facilities

(G-13500)
GENRIC INC
433 Allenby Dr (43040-9355)
PHONE.................................937 553-9250
Philip C Drake, *CEO*
EMP: 337
SALES (corp-wide): 20MM **Privately Held**
SIC: 1731 7381 7382 Safety & security specialization; security guard service; security systems services; protective devices, security
PA: Genric Inc.
7380 W Sand Lake Rd # 500
Orlando FL 32819
407 476-2060

(G-13501)
HAWTHORNE HYDROPONICS LLC
Also Called: Hawthorne Hydroponics/Botanic
14111 Scottslawn Rd (43040-7800)
PHONE.................................480 777-2000
Chris Hagedorn,
Ross Haley,
▲ EMP: 100 EST: 1987
SALES (est): 1.3MM
SALES (corp-wide): 2.6B **Publicly Held**
SIC: 5083 2879 Hydroponic equipment & supplies; lawn & garden machinery & equipment; agricultural chemicals
HQ: The Hawthorne Garden Company
800 Port Washington Blvd
Port Washington NY 11050
516 883-6550

(G-13502)
HEALTH PARTNERS HEALTH CLINIC
19900 State Route 739 (43040-9256)
PHONE.................................937 645-8488
Tammy Allen, *Owner*
Darlene Luke, *Med Doctor*
Robert Shadel, *Medical Dir*
Michael Dick, *Executive*
▲ EMP: 25 EST: 2000
SALES (est): 1.3MM **Privately Held**
SIC: 8093 Mental health clinic, outpatient

(G-13503)
HONDA FEDERAL CREDIT UNION
24000 Honda Pkwy (43040-9251)
PHONE.................................937 642-6000
Joe Mattera, *Branch Mgr*
EMP: 40
SALES (corp-wide): 28.2MM **Privately Held**
SIC: 6061 Federal credit unions
PA: Honda Federal Credit Union
19701 Hamilton Ave # 130
Torrance CA 90502
310 217-0509

(G-13504)
HONDA NORTH AMERICA INC
24000 Honda Pkwy (43040-9251)
PHONE.................................937 642-5000
Takuji Yamada, *President*
Erik Berkman, *President*
Tomoni Kosaka, *President*
Richyard Schostek, *President*
Chitoshi Yokata, *President*
▼ EMP: 50 EST: 2014
SQ FT: 30,000
SALES (est): 58.6MM
SALES (corp-wide): 144.1B **Privately Held**
SIC: 5012 Automobiles
PA: Honda Motor Co., Ltd.
2-1-1, Minamiaoyama
Minato-Ku TKY 107-0
334 231-111

(G-13505)
HONDA OF AMERICA MFG INC
Also Called: Honda Support Office
19900 State Route 739 (43040-9256)
PHONE.................................937 644-0724
EMP: 200

SALES (corp-wide): 144.1B **Privately Held**
SIC: 3714 3711 3465 8742 Motor vehicle parts & accessories; motor vehicles & car bodies; automotive stampings; training & development consultant
HQ: Honda Of America Mfg., Inc.
24000 Honda Pkwy
Marysville OH 43040
937 642-5000

(G-13506)
HONDA TRADING AMERICA CORP
19900 State Route 739 (43040-9256)
PHONE.................................937 644-8004
Greg Norval, *Branch Mgr*
EMP: 140
SALES (corp-wide): 144.1B **Privately Held**
WEB: www.htaoh.honda.com
SIC: 5013 Automotive supplies & parts
HQ: Honda Trading America Corp
19210 Van Ness Ave
Torrance CA 90501
310 787-5000

(G-13507)
HOYER POURED WALLS INC
18205 Poling Rd (43040-9149)
PHONE.................................937 642-6148
Jerry Hoyer, *President*
John Dawson, *Vice Pres*
EMP: 25
SQ FT: 3,200
SALES (est): 2.6MM **Privately Held**
WEB: www.hoyerpouredwalls.com
SIC: 1771 Foundation & footing contractor

(G-13508)
J A GUY INC
Also Called: Mechanical Contractors
13116 Weaver Rd (43040-9057)
PHONE.................................937 642-3415
Barbara Guy Guess, *President*
Roger L Guess, *Vice Pres*
EMP: 30
SQ FT: 4,000
SALES: 2MM **Privately Held**
WEB: www.gregguy.com
SIC: 1711 1761 Warm air heating & air conditioning contractor; sheet metalwork

(G-13509)
KARE MEDICAL TRNSPT SVCS LLP
1002 Columbus Ave (43040-8563)
P.O. Box 110 (43040-0110)
PHONE.................................937 578-0263
Jason Keeran,
EMP: 30
SQ FT: 2,400
SALES (est): 1.2MM **Privately Held**
SIC: 4119 Ambulance service

(G-13510)
LINKS
200 Gallery Dr (43040-8347)
PHONE.................................937 644-9988
Scott Brown, *Manager*
EMP: 30
SALES (est): 1.2MM **Privately Held**
SIC: 6513 Apartment building operators

(G-13511)
LOWES HOME CENTERS LLC
15775 Us Highway 36 (43040-9484)
PHONE.................................937 578-4440
EMP: 158
SALES (corp-wide): 68.6B **Publicly Held**
SIC: 5211 5031 5722 5064 Home centers; building materials, exterior; building materials, interior; household appliance stores; electrical appliances, television & radio
HQ: Lowe's Home Centers, Llc
1605 Curtis Bridge Rd
Wilkesboro NC 28697
336 658-4000

(G-13512)
MAHONEY DIALYSIS LLC
Also Called: Meadowhawk Dialysis
491 Colemans Xing (43040-7068)
PHONE.................................937 642-0676
James K Hilger,

EMP: 30
SALES (est): 238.3K **Publicly Held**
SIC: 8092 Kidney dialysis centers
PA: Davita Inc.
2000 16th St
Denver CO 80202

(G-13513)
MARYHAVEN INC
715 S Plum St (43040-1631)
PHONE.................................937 644-9192
Paul Coleman, *Branch Mgr*
EMP: 35
SALES (est): 747.6K
SALES (corp-wide): 21.9MM **Privately Held**
SIC: 8093 Substance abuse clinics (outpatient)
PA: Maryhaven, Inc
1791 Alum Creek Dr
Columbus OH 43207
614 449-1530

(G-13514)
MARYSVILLE FOOD PANTRY
333 Ash St (43040-1543)
PHONE.................................937 644-3248
Gary Simpson, *Director*
EMP: 25
SALES (est): 87.4K **Privately Held**
SIC: 8699 Charitable organization

(G-13515)
MARYSVILLE STEEL INC
323 E 8th St (43040)
P.O. Box 383 (43040-0383)
PHONE.................................937 642-5971
Steven J Clayman, *CEO*
EMP: 31
SQ FT: 50,000
SALES (est): 10.6MM **Privately Held**
SIC: 3441 1791 5039 Fabricated structural metal; structural steel erection; joists

(G-13516)
MARYSVLLE OHIO SRGICAL CTR LLC (PA)
122 Professional Pkwy (43040-8053)
PHONE.................................937 642-6622
Daniel J Saale,
Jim Christie,
EMP: 69
SALES (est): 34.7MM **Privately Held**
SIC: 8062 General medical & surgical hospitals

(G-13517)
MARYSVLLE OHIO SRGICAL CTR LLC
17853 State Route 31 (43040-8520)
PHONE.................................937 578-4200
R Mark Stover, *Branch Mgr*
EMP: 637
SALES (corp-wide): 34.7MM **Privately Held**
SIC: 8011 Orthopedic physician
PA: Marysville Ohio Surgical Center, L.L.C.
122 Professional Pkwy
Marysville OH 43040
937 642-6622

(G-13518)
MEMORIAL HOSPITAL UNION COUNTY
660 London Ave (43040-1515)
PHONE.................................937 644-1001
Chip Hubbs, *Branch Mgr*
EMP: 200
SALES (corp-wide): 125.1MM **Privately Held**
SIC: 8062 General medical & surgical hospitals
PA: Memorial Hospital Of Union County
500 London Ave
Marysville OH 43040
937 644-6115

(G-13519)
MEMORIAL HOSPITAL UNION COUNTY (PA)
500 London Ave (43040-1594)
PHONE.................................937 644-6115
Olas A Hubbs, *CEO*
Dennis Stone, *Chairman*
James Taylor, *Pastor*

Mareva Page, *Assistant VP*
Victor Trianfo, *Vice Pres*
EMP: 600
SQ FT: 132,000
SALES: 125.1MM **Privately Held**
WEB: www.memorialhosp.org
SIC: 8062 Hospital, affiliated with AMA residency

(G-13520)
NISSIN INTL TRNSPT USA INC
16940 Square Dr (43040-9616)
PHONE.................................937 644-2644
EMP: 75
SALES (corp-wide): 2B **Privately Held**
WEB: www.nitusa.com
SIC: 4731 Freight forwarding
HQ: Nissin International Transport U.S.A.,
　　Inc.
　　1540 W 190th St
　　Torrance CA 90501
　　310 222-8500

(G-13521)
OHIO MEDICAL TRNSP INC
Also Called: Medical Flight 2
22758 Wilbur Rd (43040-9120)
PHONE.................................937 747-3540
Rod Crane, *Manager*
EMP: 25
SALES (est): 511.6K **Privately Held**
WEB: www.medflight.com
SIC: 4119 Ambulance service
PA: Ohio Medical Transportation, Inc.
　　2827 W Dblin Granville Rd
　　Columbus OH 43235

(G-13522)
PICKLESIMER TRUCKING INC
360 Palm Dr (43040-5534)
PHONE.................................937 642-1091
Charles Picklesimer, *President*
Patsy Picklesimer, *Corp Secy*
EMP: 25
SQ FT: 2,500
SALES (est): 1.7MM **Privately Held**
SIC: 4214 Local Trucking-With Storage

(G-13523)
PRECISION COATINGS SYSTEMS
948 Columbus Ave (43040-9501)
PHONE.................................937 642-4727
Fred Myers Jr, *President*
Mark Myers, *Vice Pres*
Sherry Myers, *Vice Pres*
Wendy Myers, *Vice Pres*
EMP: 30
SQ FT: 26,000
SALES: 2.4MM **Privately Held**
WEB: www.precisioncoatingsystems.com
SIC: 3479 7532 7549 7514 Painting of metal products; paint shop, automotive; collision shops, automotive; towing services; rent-a-car service

(G-13524)
R & D NESTLE CENTER INC (HQ)
Also Called: Nestle Product Technology Ctr
809 Collins Ave (43040-1308)
PHONE.................................937 642-7015
Mark Schneider, *CEO*
Gillian Anantharaman, *Vice Pres*
Kenneth G Boehm, *Vice Pres*
▲ **EMP:** 230
SALES (est): 30.1MM
SALES (corp-wide): 90.8B **Privately Held**
WEB: www.rdoh.nestle.com
SIC: 8731 Food research
PA: Nestle S.A.
　　Avenue Nestle 55
　　Vevey VD 1800
　　219 242-111

(G-13525)
RMI INTERNATIONAL INC
Also Called: Rodbat Security Services
24500 Honda Pwky (43040)
PHONE.................................937 642-5032
Marco Norman, *Manager*
EMP: 60
SALES (corp-wide): 25.5MM **Privately Held**
WEB: www.rmiintl.com
SIC: 7381 Guard services; protective services, guard

PA: Rmi International Inc
　　8125 Somerset Blvd
　　Paramount CA 90723
　　562 806-9098

(G-13526)
RYAN LOGISTICS INC
711 Clymer Rd (43040-9502)
PHONE.................................937 642-4158
Tracy Yoesting, *President*
Tammy Yelton, *Human Resources*
EMP: 80
SQ FT: 1,680
SALES (est): 27.2MM **Privately Held**
WEB: www.ryanlogistics.com
SIC: 4731 Freight forwarding

(G-13527)
SCIOTO SERVICES LLC (HQ)
405 S Oak St (43040-1735)
PHONE.................................937 644-0888
Thomas C Kruse, *CEO*
Mike Jones, *Regional Mgr*
Donnie Jones, *Area Mgr*
Beth Hazel, *Business Mgr*
Mark Fisher, *Project Mgr*
EMP: 42
SALES (est): 18MM
SALES (corp-wide): 302.2MM **Privately Held**
WEB: www.sciotocorp.com
SIC: 7349 1711 5085 Janitorial service, contract basis; mechanical contractor; industrial supplies
PA: Marsden Holding, L.L.C.
　　2124 University Ave W
　　Saint Paul MN 55114
　　651 641-1717

(G-13528)
SCOTTS COMPANY LLC (HQ)
Also Called: Scotts Miracle-Gro Products
14111 Scottslawn Rd (43040-7801)
P.O. Box 418 (43040-0418)
PHONE.................................937 644-0011
James Hagedorn, *CEO*
Ann Aquillo, *Vice Pres*
James Iovino, *Vice Pres*
Craig Izzo, *Vice Pres*
Jim King, *Vice Pres*
◆ **EMP:** 427
SALES (est): 1.6B
SALES (corp-wide): 2.6B **Publicly Held**
WEB: www.scottscompany.com
SIC: 2873 2874 2879 0782 Fertilizers: natural (organic), except compost; phosphates; fungicides, herbicides; insecticides, agricultural or household; lawn services; mulch, wood & bark; lawn & garden equipment; lawnmowers, residential: hand or power
PA: The Scotts Miracle-Gro Company
　　14111 Scottslawn Rd
　　Marysville OH 43040
　　937 644-0011

(G-13529)
SCOTTS MIRACLE-GRO COMPANY (PA)
14111 Scottslawn Rd (43040-7801)
PHONE.................................937 644-0011
James Hagedorn, *Ch of Bd*
Michael C Lukemire, *President*
Melanie Spare, *Business Mgr*
Tim Veasman, *Business Mgr*
Denise S Stump, *Exec VP*
▲ **EMP:** 277
SALES: 2.6B **Publicly Held**
WEB: www.scotts.com
SIC: 3542 0782 7342 2879 Machine tools, metal forming type; lawn & garden services; pest control services; insecticides & pesticides

(G-13530)
STRAIGHT 72 INC
Also Called: MAI Manufacturing
20078 State Route 4 (43040-9723)
PHONE.................................740 943-5730
Chris Vogelsang, *President*
Linda Wolf, *Vice Pres*
Mike Thomas, *QC Mgr*
Thomas J Muselin, *Hum Res Coord*
EMP: 60

SALES (est): 7.6MM **Privately Held**
SIC: 8711 3544 Acoustical engineering; special dies, tools, jigs & fixtures

(G-13531)
SUMITOMO ELC WIRG SYSTEMS INC
14800 Industrial Pkwy (43040-7507)
PHONE.................................937 642-7579
Federico Menendez, *QC Mgr*
EMP: 33
SALES (corp-wide): 28.9B **Privately Held**
SIC: 3714 5063 3694 Automotive wiring harness sets; wire & cable; engine electrical equipment
HQ: Sumitomo Electric Wiring Systems, Inc.
　　1018 Ashley St
　　Bowling Green KY 42102
　　270 782-7397

(G-13532)
SUMITOMO ELC WIRG SYSTEMS INC
Also Called: Honda Research Center
16960 Square Dr (43040-9616)
PHONE.................................937 642-7579
Mike Mirkovich, *Engineer*
Feng Xue, *Engineer*
Koji Morisada, *Branch Mgr*
Chad Boggs, *Manager*
EMP: 50
SALES (corp-wide): 28.9B **Privately Held**
WEB: www.sewsus.com
SIC: 8711 Engineering services
HQ: Sumitomo Electric Wiring Systems, Inc.
　　1018 Ashley St
　　Bowling Green KY 42102
　　270 782-7397

(G-13533)
THOMAS R TRUITT OD
Also Called: Truitt Thos R & Truitt Susan M
1001 W 5th St (43040-8666)
PHONE.................................937 644-8637
Thomas R Truitt, *President*
Tom R Truitt,
EMP: 25
SALES (est): 1.3MM **Privately Held**
SIC: 8042 Specialized optometrists

(G-13534)
U-CO INDUSTRIES INC
16900 Square Dr Ste 110 (43040-8948)
PHONE.................................937 644-3021
Teresa O'Connell, *Administration*
EMP: 71
SQ FT: 6,500
SALES: 1.2MM **Privately Held**
SIC: 8331 Sheltered workshop

(G-13535)
UNION RURAL ELECTRIC COOP INC (PA)
15461 Us Highway 36 (43040-9405)
P.O. Box 393 (43040-0393)
PHONE.................................937 642-1826
Roger Yoder, *President*
Anthony Smith, *President*
Michael Aquillo, *Vice Pres*
Ron Rockenbaugh, *Engineer*
Mike Rose, *Controller*
EMP: 39 **EST:** 1926
SQ FT: 4,000
SALES (est): 36.9MM **Privately Held**
WEB: www.ure.com
SIC: 4911 8611 Distribution, electric power; business associations

---
Mason
Warren County

(G-13536)
AERO FULFILLMENT SERVICES CORP (PA)
3900 Aero Dr (45040-8840)
PHONE.................................800 225-7145
Jon T Gimpel, *Ch of Bd*
Brenda Conaway, *VP Finance*
EMP: 100
SQ FT: 125,000

SALES: 23MM **Privately Held**
WEB: www.aerofulfillment.com
SIC: 4225 7374 7331 2759 General warehousing; data processing service; mailing service; commercial printing

(G-13537)
AFIDENCE INC
5412 Curseview Dr Ste 122 (45040)
PHONE.................................513 234-5822
Bryan Hogan, *President*
Barbara Hogan, *Vice Pres*
Lana Maric, *Marketing Staff*
Andy Hickey, *Manager*
Jim Hanna, *Consultant*
EMP: 28 **EST:** 2009
SALES (est): 3.9MM **Privately Held**
SIC: 7373 Computer integrated systems design

(G-13538)
ALTRIA GROUP DISTRIBUTION CO
4680 Parkway Dr Ste 450 (45040-7979)
PHONE.................................804 274-2000
Craig A Johnson, *President*
EMP: 104
SALES (corp-wide): 25.3B **Publicly Held**
SIC: 5159 Tobacco distributors & products
HQ: Altria Group Distribution Company
　　6601 W Broad St
　　Richmond VA 23230

(G-13539)
AMERICAN BUS PERSONNEL SVCS (PA)
7547 Central Parke Blvd (45040-6811)
PHONE.................................513 770-3300
Jim Wilson, *President*
Piotr Machon, *Regl Sales Mgr*
Kevin Mulholland, *Software Dev*
EMP: 50
SQ FT: 3,000
SALES (est): 3.5MM **Privately Held**
SIC: 7361 Executive placement

(G-13540)
ANDRE CORPORATION
4600 N Masn Montgomery Rd (45040-9176)
PHONE.................................574 293-0207
David Andre, *President*
EMP: 50
SQ FT: 50,000
SALES (est): 15.6MM **Privately Held**
WEB: www.andrecorp.com
SIC: 3452 3469 5085 Washers, metal; stamping metal for the trade; fasteners, industrial: nuts, bolts, screws, etc.

(G-13541)
ANTHEM MIDWEST INC
4361 Irwin Simpson Rd (45040-9479)
PHONE.................................614 433-8350
Larry Glasscock, *President*
Barry Martin, *Director*
EMP: 550
SALES (est): 67.4MM **Privately Held**
SIC: 6411 Insurance agents, brokers & service

(G-13542)
ARTIS SENIOR LIVING
6200 Snider Rd (45040-2640)
PHONE.................................513 229-7450
Jerry Craft, *Manager*
Diane Kloenne, *Exec Dir*
Diane Klaoenne, *Director*
EMP: 40
SALES (est): 791.9K **Privately Held**
SIC: 8322 Old age assistance

(G-13543)
ATOS IT SOLUTIONS AND SVCS INC
4705 Duke Dr (45040-7645)
PHONE.................................513 336-1000
Mike Mullins, *Project Mgr*
Brandy Wilhite, *Manager*
Rick Bostater, *Manager*
EMP: 451
SALES (corp-wide): 166.6MM **Privately Held**
SIC: 7379 Computer related maintenance services

HQ: Atos It Solutions And Services Inc.
2500 Westchester Ave Fl 3
Purchase NY 10577
914 881-3000

(G-13544)
BAYER & BECKER INC
Also Called: Becker & Becker
6900 Tylersville Rd Ste A (45040-1593)
PHONE..............................513 492-7297
Bob Garlock, *Manager*
EMP: 25
SALES (corp-wide): 5MM **Privately Held**
SIC: 8713 Surveying services
PA: Bayer & Becker, Inc.
6900 Tylersville Rd Ste A
Mason OH 45040
513 492-7401

(G-13545)
BAYER & BECKER INC (PA)
6900 Tylersville Rd Ste A (45040-1593)
PHONE..............................513 492-7401
Keith Becker, *President*
John Del Verne, *Vice Pres*
Greg Koch, *Project Mgr*
Tony Tuttle, *Project Mgr*
Mork Lachniet, *Engineer*
EMP: 36
SQ FT: 2,000
SALES: 5MM **Privately Held**
SIC: 8713 8711 Surveying services; civil engineering

(G-13546)
BROOKDALE SENIOR LIVING INC
5535 Irwin Simpson Rd (45040-8107)
PHONE..............................513 229-3155
EMP: 69
SALES (corp-wide): 4.5B **Publicly Held**
SIC: 8361 Residential care
PA: Brookdale Senior Living
111 Westwood Pl Ste 400
Brentwood TN 37027
615 221-2250

(G-13547)
BROOKSIDE EXTENDED CARE CENTER
780 Snider Rd (45040-1391)
P.O. Box 246 (45040-0246)
PHONE..............................513 398-1020
Mike Levenson, *CEO*
Rich Johnson, *President*
Becky Meister, *Vice Pres*
EMP: 215
SQ FT: 37,000
SALES: 7.6MM **Privately Held**
SIC: 8059 Home for the mentally retarded, exc. skilled or intermediate

(G-13548)
CARING HEARTS HOME HEALTH CARE (PA)
6677 Summer Field Dr (45040-7332)
PHONE..............................513 339-1237
Gloria Hayes, *President*
Tyrone Spears, *Vice Pres*
Ronnell Spears, *CFO*
EMP: 275
SALES (est): 5.3MM **Privately Held**
WEB: www.caringhearts.cc
SIC: 8082 Home health care services

(G-13549)
CARROLL PROPERTIES
5589 Kings Mills Rd (45040-2539)
P.O. Box 425, Kings Mills (45034-0425)
PHONE..............................513 398-8075
Rick Ziegeilmeyer, *General Mgr*
EMP: 30
SALES (corp-wide): 10.4MM **Privately Held**
WEB: www.carroll-properties.com
SIC: 7011 7991 Hotels & motels; physical fitness facilities
PA: Carroll Properties
12734 Kenwood Ln Ste 35
Fort Myers FL 33907
239 278-5900

(G-13550)
CARTER MANUFACTURING CO INC
4220 State Route 42 (45040-1931)
PHONE..............................513 398-7303
Chris Carter, *President*
EMP: 26
SALES (est): 885.7K **Privately Held**
WEB: www.cartermanufacturing.com
SIC: 3544 7692 3541 Dies & die holders for metal cutting, forming, die casting; jigs & fixtures; welding repair; machine tools, metal cutting type

(G-13551)
CDD LLC
6800 Cintas Blvd (45040-9151)
PHONE..............................905 829-2794
Ron L Sency, *Business Dir*
EMP: 500
SALES (est): 9.1MM **Privately Held**
SIC: 7389 Document & office record destruction

(G-13552)
CENGAGE LEARNING INC
South-Western
5191 Natorp Blvd Lowr (45040-7599)
PHONE..............................513 229-1000
Jennifer Castillo, *Publisher*
Kristen Meere, *Editor*
Rich EBY, *Vice Pres*
Richard Jensen, *Vice Pres*
Brian Kernan, *Vice Pres*
EMP: 500 **Privately Held**
WEB: www.thomsonlearning.com
SIC: 7371 Custom computer programming services
PA: Cengage Learning, Inc.
20 Channel Ctr St
Boston MA 02210

(G-13553)
CHARD SNYDER & ASSOCIATES LLC
Also Called: Chard Synder
6867 Cintas Blvd (45040)
PHONE..............................513 459-9997
Joyce Snyder, *President*
Kenneth Chard, *Exec VP*
John Gutzwiller, *Vice Pres*
Joe Rizzo, *Vice Pres*
Barb Yearout, *Vice Pres*
EMP: 165
SQ FT: 24,600
SALES (est): 14.4MM
SALES (corp-wide): 1.2B **Privately Held**
SIC: 8721 Payroll accounting service
PA: Ascensus, Inc.
200 Dryden Rd E Ste 1000
Dresher PA 19025
215 648-8000

(G-13554)
CHILDRENS HOSPITAL MEDICAL CTR
Also Called: Children's Outpatient North
9560 Children Dr (45040-9362)
PHONE..............................513 636-6800
Char Mason, *Branch Mgr*
Rebecca Brown, *Med Doctor*
Curtis Sheldon, *Med Doctor*
Murray Dock, *Fmly & Gen Dent*
EMP: 40
SALES (corp-wide): 1.6B **Privately Held**
WEB: www.cincinnatichildrens.org
SIC: 8733 8093 8011 8069 Medical research; specialty outpatient clinics; offices & clinics of medical doctors; children's hospital
PA: Children's Hospital Medical Center
3333 Burnet Ave
Cincinnati OH 45229
513 636-4200

(G-13555)
CINCOM SYSTEMS INC
4605 Duke Dr (45040-9410)
PHONE..............................513 459-1470
Thomas M Nies, *Branch Mgr*
EMP: 200
SALES (corp-wide): 109.6MM **Privately Held**
SIC: 7372 Business oriented computer software

PA: Cincom Systems, Inc.
55 Merchant St Ste 100
Cincinnati OH 45246
513 612-2300

(G-13556)
CINTAS CORPORATION NO 1 (HQ)
6800 Cintas Blvd (45040-9151)
PHONE..............................513 459-1200
Richard T Farmer, *Ch of Bd*
Robert Kohlhepp, *Vice Ch Bd*
Karen L Carnahan, *Vice Pres*
Michael Thompson, *Vice Pres*
William C Gale, *CFO*
◆ EMP: 1500
SQ FT: 75,000
SALES (est): 340.5MM
SALES (corp-wide): 6.4B **Publicly Held**
SIC: 7213 5136 5137 7549 Uniform supply; uniforms, men's & boys'; uniforms, women's & children's; automotive maintenance services
PA: Cintas Corporation
6800 Cintas Blvd
Cincinnati OH 45262
513 459-1200

(G-13557)
CINTAS CORPORATION NO 2
5800 Cintas Blvd (45040)
P.O. Box 636525, Cincinnati (45263-6525)
PHONE..............................513 459-1200
EMP: 1000
SALES (corp-wide): 6.4B **Publicly Held**
SIC: 5084 Safety equipment
HQ: Cintas Corporation No. 2
6800 Cintas Blvd
Mason OH 45040

(G-13558)
CINTAS CORPORATION NO 2 (HQ)
Also Called: Cintas First Aid & Safety
6800 Cintas Blvd (45040-9151)
P.O. Box 625737, Cincinnati (45262-5737)
PHONE..............................513 459-1200
Scott D Farmer, *CEO*
Thomas E Frooman, *Exec VP*
Robert J Kohlhepp, *Exec VP*
Mike L Thompson, *Treasurer*
▲ EMP: 2000
SALES (est): 3.4B
SALES (corp-wide): 6.4B **Publicly Held**
SIC: 5084 Safety equipment
PA: Cintas Corporation
6800 Cintas Blvd
Cincinnati OH 45262
513 459-1200

(G-13559)
CINTAS CORPORATION NO 2
6800 Cintas Blvd (45040-9151)
PHONE..............................513 459-1200
Judith Benatar, *Manager*
EMP: 99
SALES (corp-wide): 6.4B **Publicly Held**
SIC: 5047 Medical & hospital equipment
HQ: Cintas Corporation No. 2
6800 Cintas Blvd
Mason OH 45040

(G-13560)
CINTAS DOCUMENT MANAGEMENT LLC (HQ)
6800 Cintas Blvd (45040-9151)
PHONE..............................800 914-1960
Scott D Farmer, *CEO*
EMP: 36
SALES (est): 4.1MM
SALES (corp-wide): 6.4B **Publicly Held**
SIC: 7299 Personal document & information services
PA: Cintas Corporation
6800 Cintas Blvd
Cincinnati OH 45262
513 459-1200

(G-13561)
CINTAS-RUS LP (HQ)
6800 Cintas Blvd (45040-9151)
P.O. Box 625737, Cincinnati (45262-5737)
PHONE..............................513 459-1200
Scott D Farmer, *CEO*
EMP: 27

SALES (est): 39.2MM
SALES (corp-wide): 6.4B **Publicly Held**
SIC: 7218 Industrial uniform supply
PA: Cintas Corporation
6800 Cintas Blvd
Cincinnati OH 45262
513 459-1200

(G-13562)
CLEANER CARPET & JANTR INC
6516 Bluebird Ct (45040-9725)
PHONE..............................513 469-2070
Lary McGuffey, *President*
Brenda McGuffey, *Admin Sec*
EMP: 50
SQ FT: 2,000
SALES (est): 1.4MM **Privately Held**
WEB: www.ccjinc.com
SIC: 7349 Janitorial service, contract basis

(G-13563)
CLEVELAND CONSTRUCTION INC
5390 Curseview Dr Ste 200 (45040)
PHONE..............................440 255-8000
Jon D Small, *President*
Gary J Todd, *Controller*
David Kurilko, *Systems Mgr*
EMP: 30
SALES (corp-wide): 400.6MM **Privately Held**
SIC: 1542 1721 1742 1521 Commercial & office building contractors; commercial wallcovering contractor; plastering, drywall & insulation; single-family housing construction
PA: Cleveland Construction, Inc.
8620 Tyler Blvd
Mentor OH 44060
440 255-8000

(G-13564)
CLOPAY CORPORATION (HQ)
8585 Duke Blvd (45040-3100)
PHONE..............................800 282-2260
Gary Abyad, *President*
Eugene Colleran, *Senior VP*
Ellen Shoemaker, *Senior VP*
John Green, *Vice Pres*
Kevin Preston, *Opers Mgr*
▲ EMP: 231
SQ FT: 130,587
SALES (est): 981.8MM
SALES (corp-wide): 1.5B **Publicly Held**
WEB: www.clopay.com
SIC: 3081 3442 2431 1796 Plastic film & sheet; garage doors, overhead: metal; garage doors, overhead: wood; doors, wood; power generating equipment installation
PA: Griffon Corporation
712 5th Ave Fl 18
New York NY 10019
212 957-5000

(G-13565)
COMMUNITY CONCEPTS INC (PA)
Also Called: Community Concepts & Options
6699 Tri Way Dr (45040-2604)
PHONE..............................513 398-8181
Betty Davis, *President*
Deana M Davis, *Vice Pres*
Marc C Davis, *Vice Pres*
Wayne E Davis, *VP Opers*
Brad Davis, *Treasurer*
EMP: 110
SALES (est): 8.8MM **Privately Held**
WEB: www.communityconcepts.com
SIC: 8059 8082 Home for the mentally retarded, exc. skilled or intermediate; home health care services

(G-13566)
COMPLETE SERVICES INC (PA)
Also Called: Countrtops Cabinetry By Design
6345 Castle Dr (45040-9415)
PHONE..............................513 770-5575
Chris Holtz, *President*
EMP: 30
SQ FT: 5,200
SALES (est): 6.1MM **Privately Held**
SIC: 1799 Kitchen & bathroom remodeling

(G-13567)
CONNECT CALL GLOBAL LLC
7560 Central Parke Blvd (45040-6816)
P.O. Box 632 (45040-0632)
PHONE..................................513 348-1800
Chris Lutts, *President*
EMP: 29 **EST:** 2010
SQ FT: 47,000
SALES (est): 2.8MM **Privately Held**
SIC: 4813 Data telephone communications

(G-13568)
COUNTY ANIMAL HOSPITAL
1185 Reading Rd (45040-9154)
PHONE..................................513 398-8000
Gary Smith Dvm, *Owner*
Mary Wuest, *Office Mgr*
EMP: 30
SALES (est): 1MM **Privately Held**
SIC: 0742 Animal hospital services, pets &
   other animal specialties

(G-13569)
**CRAIG AND FRANCES LINDNER
CENT**
Also Called: LINDER CENTER OF HOPE
4075 Old Western Row Rd (45040-3104)
PHONE..................................513 536-4673
Paul E Keck Jr, *CEO*
Fred Bishop, *Principal*
Brian A Owens, *COO*
Lynn M Oswald, *Exec VP*
Jan Marhefka, *QA Dir*
EMP: 200 **EST:** 2006
SALES: 29.2MM **Privately Held**
SIC: 8093 Mental health clinic, outpatient

(G-13570)
**CREATIVE CHILDRENS WORLD
LLC (PA)**
7818 S Masn Montgomery Rd
(45040-9316)
PHONE..................................513 336-7799
Shawna McCastro, *Mng Member*
EMP: 28
SALES (est): 1.1MM **Privately Held**
SIC: 8351 Child Day Care Services

(G-13571)
**CREME DE LA CREME
COLORADO INC**
5324 Natorp Blvd (45040-7912)
PHONE..................................513 459-4300
Gale Sarant, *Branch Mgr*
EMP: 32
SALES (corp-wide): 16.7MM **Privately
Held**
SIC: 8351 Child day care services
PA: Creme De La Creme (Colorado), Inc.
   8400 E Prentice Ave # 1320
   Greenwood Village CO 80111
   303 662-9150

(G-13572)
**DASSAULT SYSTEMES SIMULIA
CORP**
Also Called: Central Region
5181 Natorp Blvd Ste 205 (45040-7987)
PHONE..................................513 275-1430
Curt Schrader, *Manager*
EMP: 33
SALES (corp-wide): 1.8B **Privately Held**
SIC: 7371 Computer software develop-
   ment
HQ: Dassault Systemes Simulia Corp.
   1301 Atwood Ave Ste 101w
   Johnston RI 02919
   401 531-5000

(G-13573)
DIGITAL MANAGEMENT INC
4660 Duke Dr Ste 100 (45040-8464)
PHONE..................................240 223-4800
EMP: 76
SALES (corp-wide): 350.2MM **Privately
Held**
SIC: 7379 Computer related maintenance
   services
PA: Digital Management, Llc
   6550 Rock Spring Dr Fl 7
   Bethesda MD 20817
   240 223-4800

(G-13574)
DIRECT EXPEDITING LLC
5311 Bentley Oak Dr (45040-8780)
P.O. Box 317 (45040-0317)
PHONE..................................513 459-0100
Mike Beegle,
EMP: 35
SQ FT: 10,000
SALES: 2MM **Privately Held**
SIC: 4119 Local rental transportation

(G-13575)
DRURY HOTELS COMPANY LLC
Also Called: Drury Inn Stes Cincinnati Masn
9956 Escort Dr (45040-9444)
P.O. Box 910, Cape Girardeau MO (63702-
0910)
PHONE..................................513 336-0108
Randol Hiett, *Principal*
Charles Drury, *Principal*
EMP: 50
SALES (est): 322.3K **Privately Held**
SIC: 7011 Hotels

(G-13576)
DUKE REALTY CORPORATION
Also Called: Duke Realty Investors
5181 Natorp Blvd Ste 600 (45040-5910)
PHONE..................................513 651-3900
Bob Fessler, *Manager*
EMP: 60
SALES (corp-wide): 947.8MM **Privately
Held**
WEB: www.dukeit.com
SIC: 6552 6531 Land subdividers & devel-
   opers, commercial; real estate agents &
   managers
PA: Duke Realty Corporation
   600 E 96th St Ste 100
   Indianapolis IN 46240
   317 808-6000

(G-13577)
ENGISYSTEMS INC
7588 Central Parke Blvd (45040-6857)
PHONE..................................513 229-8860
Gregory W Pierce, *President*
EMP: 100
SALES: 9MM **Privately Held**
SIC: 8711 Consulting engineer

(G-13578)
EVOKES LLC
8118 Corp Way Ste 212 (45040)
PHONE..................................513 947-8433
Daniel Lincoln, *President*
Tony Leslie, *Office Mgr*
EMP: 50 **EST:** 2015
SQ FT: 900
SALES (est): 2.4MM **Privately Held**
SIC: 3822 8011 Building services monitor-
   ing controls, automatic; surgeon

(G-13579)
FOOD CONCEPTS INTL INC
5010 Deerfield Blvd (45040-2504)
PHONE..................................513 336-7449
EMP: 84
SALES (corp-wide): 139.5MM **Privately
Held**
SIC: 5812 7929 Mexican restaurant; en-
   tertainment service
PA: Food Concepts International, Inc.
   4401 82nd St
   Lubbock TX 79424
   806 785-8686

(G-13580)
FORD MOTOR COMPANY
4680 Parkway Dr Ste 420 (45040-8117)
PHONE..................................513 573-1101
Greg Wedding, *President*
Melodee Parker, *Business Mgr*
Jim Splendore, *Manager*
EMP: 30
SALES (corp-wide): 160.3B **Publicly
Held**
WEB: www.ford.com
SIC: 6159 Automobile finance leasing
PA: Ford Motor Company
   1 American Rd
   Dearborn MI 48126
   313 322-3000

(G-13581)
**FORTE INDUS EQP SYSTEMS
INC**
Also Called: Forte Industries
6037 Commerce Ct (45040-8819)
PHONE..................................513 398-2800
Eugene A Forte, *President*
Doug Stamper, *Controller*
Eric Clark, *CIO*
Phyllis Forte, *Admin Sec*
EMP: 32
SQ FT: 16,000
SALES (est): 24.1MM
SALES (corp-wide): 36.3B **Privately Held**
WEB: www.forte-industries.com
SIC: 5084 8711 3537 Materials handling
   machinery; consulting engineer; industrial
   trucks & tractors
HQ: Swisslog Holding Ag
   Webereiweg 3
   Buchs AG 5033
   628 379-537

(G-13582)
G&K SERVICES LLC (HQ)
6800 Cintas Blvd (45040-9151)
PHONE..................................952 912-5500
Scott D Farmer, *CEO*
Kevin A Fancey, *President*
Thomas E Frooma, *Senior VP*
J Michael Hansen, *CFO*
◆ **EMP:** 300 **EST:** 1902
SALES (est): 880.2MM
SALES (corp-wide): 6.4B **Publicly Held**
WEB: www.gkservices.com
SIC: 7218 7213 7219 Industrial uniform
   supply; laundered mat & rug supply;
   treated equipment supply: mats, rugs,
   mops, cloths, etc.; work clothing supply;
   apron supply; towel supply; uniform sup-
   ply; garment making, alteration & repair
PA: Cintas Corporation
   6800 Cintas Blvd
   Cincinnati OH 45262
   513 459-1200

(G-13583)
GATESAIR INC (HQ)
5300 Kings Island Dr (45040-2353)
PHONE..................................513 459-3400
Bruce Swail, *CEO*
John Howell, *Principal*
Bryant Burke, *Vice Pres*
Joe Mack, *Vice Pres*
Joseph Mack, *Vice Pres*
▲ **EMP:** 150
SQ FT: 30,000
SALES (est): 16.5MM
SALES (corp-wide): 4B **Privately Held**
SIC: 1731 3663 7371 Communications
   specialization; radio & TV communica-
   tions equipment; computer software de-
   velopment & applications
PA: The Gores Group Llc
   9800 Wilshire Blvd
   Beverly Hills CA 90212
   310 209-3010

(G-13584)
GENERAL ELECTRIC COMPANY
4800 Parkway Dr Ste 100 (45040-9012)
PHONE..................................513 583-3626
Melvin Grimes, *Engineer*
Joe Ferrell, *Manager*
Sharon Wang, *Manager*
EMP: 150
SALES (corp-wide): 121.6B **Publicly
Held**
SIC: 8748 Business consulting
PA: General Electric Company
   41 Farnsworth St
   Boston MA 02210
   617 443-3000

(G-13585)
GENERAL MILLS INC
5181 Natorp Blvd Ste 540 (45040-2183)
PHONE..................................513 770-0558
Peter Baruk, *Branch Mgr*
EMP: 55
SALES (corp-wide): 15.7B **Publicly Held**
WEB: www.generalmills.com
SIC: 5141 2041 Food brokers; flour mixes
PA: General Mills, Inc.
   1 General Mills Blvd
   Minneapolis MN 55426
   763 764-7600

(G-13586)
**GENERAL REVENUE
CORPORATION (HQ)**
Also Called: G R C
4660 Duke Dr Ste 300 (45040-8466)
PHONE..................................513 469-1472
John Kane, *CEO*
Brian Hill, *President*
Michael Amstadt, *Managing Dir*
Justen Gay, *Vice Pres*
Eric Kiss, *Treasurer*
EMP: 480 **EST:** 1981
SQ FT: 100,000
SALES (est): 23.6MM
SALES (corp-wide): 4.9B **Publicly Held**
WEB: www.generalrevenue.com
SIC: 7322 6141 Collection agency, except
   real estate; personal credit institutions
PA: Navient Corporation
   123 S Justison St Ste 300
   Wilmington DE 19801
   302 283-8000

(G-13587)
GENSUITE LLC
4680 Parkway Dr Ste 400 (45040-8108)
PHONE..................................513 774-1000
Anshu Jha, *Opers Staff*
Christopher Barth, *Sales Staff*
R Mukund, *Mng Member*
Natasha Porter,
▲ **EMP:** 95
SQ FT: 16,000
SALES (est): 18.9MM **Privately Held**
SIC: 7371 Computer software systems
   analysis & design, custom

(G-13588)
**GLOBAL CNSLD HOLDINGS INC
(PA)**
3965 Marble Ridge Ln (45040-2892)
PHONE..................................513 703-0965
Mark Cohen, *President*
EMP: 52
SQ FT: 6,000
SALES (est): 3.4MM **Privately Held**
SIC: 8742 6719 Materials mgmt. (purchas-
   ing, handling, inventory) consultant; per-
   sonal holding companies, except banks

(G-13589)
**GREATER CINCINNATI CREDIT
UN**
7948 S Masn Montgomery Rd
(45040-8249)
PHONE..................................513 559-1234
Ben Sawyer, *Branch Mgr*
EMP: 27
SALES (corp-wide): 5.1MM **Privately
Held**
SIC: 6062 State credit unions, not federally
   chartered
PA: Greater Cincinnati Credit Union
   7221 Montgomery Rd Ste 1
   Cincinnati OH 45236
   513 559-1234

(G-13590)
GRIZZLY GOLF CENTER INC
Also Called: Golf Center At Kings Island
6042 Fairway Dr (45040-2006)
PHONE..................................513 398-5200
Peter Ryan, *General Mgr*
EMP: 300
SQ FT: 5,000
SALES (est): 6.5MM **Publicly Held**
WEB: www.thegolfcenter.com
SIC: 7992 5812 5941 0782 Public golf
   courses; eating places; golf goods &
   equipment; landscape contractors
HQ: Great American Insurance Company
   301 E 4th St Fl 8
   Cincinnati OH 45202
   513 369-5000

(G-13591)
HAAG-STREIT USA INC
5500 Courseview Dr (45040-2366)
PHONE..................................513 336-7255
Ernest Cavin, *CEO*

▲ = Import ▼=Export
◆ =Import/Export

EMP: 25
SALES (corp-wide): 1.2B Privately Held
SIC: 5047 Surgical equipment & supplies
HQ: Haag-Streit Usa Inc
3535 Kings Mills Rd
Mason OH 45040

(G-13592)
HAAG-STREIT USA INC (DH)
3535 Kings Mills Rd (45040-2303)
PHONE..................................513 336-7255
Ernest Cavin, CEO
Dominik Beck, President
Jeff Journey, Vice Pres
Steve Juenger, Vice Pres
Anthony Lanza, Engineer
EMP: 110
SQ FT: 22,988
SALES (est): 34.3MM
SALES (corp-wide): 1.2B Privately Held
SIC: 5047 5048 Surgical equipment &
supplies; ophthalmic goods

(G-13593)
HERITAGE CLUB
6690 Heritage Club Dr (45040-4649)
PHONE..................................513 459-7711
Lewis Rosenbloom, General Mgr
Chin Lin, Controller
Michelle Tegge, Director
Juan Campbell, Food Svc Dir
Jeffrey Brown, Executive
EMP: 100
SQ FT: 11,600
SALES: 2.5MM Privately Held
WEB: www.heritageclub.com
SIC: 7997 Golf club, membership

(G-13594)
HI-FIVE DEVELOPMENT SVCS INC
202 W Main St Ste C (45040-1882)
PHONE..................................513 336-9280
Mark Davis, President
Brian Zilch, President
Fred Hostetler, Superintendent
Stephen Daniels, Vice Pres
Larry Hatfield, Vice Pres
EMP: 27
SQ FT: 1,200
SALES (est): 4.8MM Privately Held
WEB: www.hifive1.com
SIC: 1542 Design & erection, combined:
non-residential

(G-13595)
HI-TEK MANUFACTURING INC
Also Called: System EDM of Ohio
6050 Hi Tek Ct (45040-2602)
PHONE..................................513 459-1094
Cletis Jackson, President
Scott Stang, Plant Mgr
George Carrington, QC Mgr
Michael Beech, Engineer
Craig Enderle, Engineer
▲ EMP: 180
SQ FT: 71,000
SALES (est): 69MM Privately Held
WEB: www.hitekmfg.com
SIC: 3599 7692 3724 3714 Machine
shop, jobbing & repair; welding repair; air-
craft engines & engine parts; motor vehi-
cle parts & accessories; special dies,
tools, jigs & fixtures

(G-13596)
ICR INC
Also Called: Icr Engineering
4770 Duke Dr Ste 370 (45040-8460)
PHONE..................................513 900-7007
Robert Dunn, President
EMP: 77
SALES (est): 1.3MM Privately Held
SIC: 8711 7371 Engineering services;
software programming applications

(G-13597)
ILLUMINATION RESEARCH INC
5947 Drfield Blvd Ste 203 (45040)
PHONE..................................513 774-9531
Jeff Bass, Principal
Kristin Bush, Vice Pres
Alice McConnell, Project Dir
Kelly Legault, Marketing Staff
Chris Breheim, Director
EMP: 25

SALES (est): 2.9MM Privately Held
SIC: 8732 8731 Business economic service; commercial physical research

(G-13598)
INTELLIGRATED SYSTEMS INC (HQ)
7901 Innovation Way (45040-9498)
PHONE..................................866 936-7300
Chris Cole, CEO
Jim McCarthy, President
Ed Puisis, CFO
▲ EMP: 800 EST: 1996
SQ FT: 390,000
SALES: 800MM
SALES (corp-wide): 41.8B Publicly Held
SIC: 3535 5084 7371 Conveyors & con-
veying equipment; industrial machinery &
equipment; computer software develop-
ment
PA: Honeywell International Inc.
115 Tabor Rd
Morris Plains NJ 07950
973 455-2000

(G-13599)
INTELLIGRATED SYSTEMS LLC
7901 Innovation Way (45040-9498)
PHONE..................................513 701-7300
Chris Cole, CEO
Jim McCarthy, President
Jim McKnight, Senior VP
Bryan Jones, Vice Pres
Ed Puisis, CFO
EMP: 2300
SQ FT: 260,000
SALES (est): 228.8MM
SALES (corp-wide): 41.8B Publicly Held
SIC: 3535 5084 7371 Conveyors & con-
veying equipment; materials handling ma-
chinery; computer software development
HQ: Intelligrated Systems, Inc.
7901 Innovation Way
Mason OH 45040
866 936-7300

(G-13600)
INTELLIGRATED SYSTEMS OHIO LLC (DH)
7901 Innovation Way (45040-9498)
PHONE..................................513 701-7300
Jim McCarthy, President
Stephen Ackerman, Exec VP
Stephen Causey, Vice Pres
◆ EMP: 600 EST: 2010
SQ FT: 332,000
SALES (est): 287.7MM
SALES (corp-wide): 41.8B Publicly Held
WEB: www.fxilogistex.com
SIC: 3535 5084 3537 Conveyors & con-
veying equipment; industrial machinery &
equipment; palletizers & depalletizers
HQ: Intelligrated Systems, Inc.
7901 Innovation Way
Mason OH 45040
866 936-7300

(G-13601)
INTERSTATE CONTRACTORS LLC
Also Called: Ic Roofing
762 Reading Rd G (45040-1362)
PHONE..................................513 372-5393
Young Chon Jung,
Jiah Jung,
EMP: 40
SALES (est): 2.8MM Privately Held
SIC: 8611 3444 Business associations;
metal roofing & roof drainage equipment

(G-13602)
J AND J ENVIRONMENTAL INC
Also Called: Tele-Vac Environmental
7611 Easy St (45040-9424)
PHONE..................................513 398-4521
Larry McCauley, President
Andy Andrews, Project Mgr
Pete Kellum, Project Mgr
Joe McCauley, Project Mgr
Jim Winchester, Treasurer
EMP: 28
SQ FT: 6,000
SALES (est): 4.9MM Privately Held
WEB: www.tele-vac.com
SIC: 7699 Sewer cleaning & rodding

(G-13603)
JEWISH HOME OF CINCINNATI
Also Called: CEDAR VILLAGE
5467 Cedar Village Dr (45040-8693)
PHONE..................................513 754-3100
Dan Fagan, CEO
Sally Korkin, Development
Connie Biederman, Director
EMP: 275 EST: 1883
SQ FT: 257,000
SALES: 21.9MM Privately Held
SIC: 8049 8051 Physical therapist; skilled
nursing care facilities

(G-13604)
KIDS R KIDS 1 OHIO INC
7439 S Masn Montgomery Rd
(45040-7828)
PHONE..................................513 398-9944
Doris Moore, Director
EMP: 36
SALES (est): 659.8K Privately Held
SIC: 8351 Child day care services

(G-13605)
KINANE INC
Also Called: Manor Hse Bnquet Cnference
Ctr
7440 S Masn Montgomery Rd
(45040-9762)
PHONE..................................513 459-0177
William Kinane, President
EMP: 60
SQ FT: 36,989
SALES (est): 4.5MM Privately Held
WEB: www.manorhouseohio.com
SIC: 7299 5812 Banquet hall facilities;
eating places

(G-13606)
KINDRED HEALTHCARE INC
411 Western Row Rd (45040-1438)
PHONE..................................513 336-0178
E Richard Crabtree, Branch Mgr
EMP: 37
SALES (corp-wide): 6B Privately Held
SIC: 8099 Blood related health services
HQ: Kindred Healthcare, Llc
680 S 4th St
Louisville KY 40202
502 596-7300

(G-13607)
KRIEGER ENTERPRISES INC
Also Called: Goddard School of Landon, The
3613 Scialville Foster Rd (45040-9335)
PHONE..................................513 573-9132
Karen Krieger, President
EMP: 25
SALES (est): 1.1MM Privately Held
SIC: 8351 Preschool center

(G-13608)
L-3 CMMNCATIONS NOVA ENGRG INC
4393 Digital Way (45040-7604)
P.O. Box 16850, Salt Lake City UT (84116-0850)
PHONE..................................877 282-1168
Mark Fischer, President
EMP: 150
SQ FT: 80,000
SALES (est): 8.7MM
SALES (corp-wide): 10.2B Publicly Held
WEB: www.l-3com.com
SIC: 8711 3663 Electrical or electronic en-
gineering; carrier equipment, radio com-
munications
PA: L3 Technologies, Inc.
600 3rd Ave Fl 34
New York NY 10016
212 697-1111

(G-13609)
LEEF BROS INC
Also Called: Leef Services
6800 Cintas Blvd (45040-9151)
PHONE..................................952 912-5500
Dan French, Principal
EMP: 170

SALES (est): 2.9MM
SALES (corp-wide): 6.4B Publicly Held
WEB: www.gkservices.com
SIC: 7218 Industrial uniform supply; wiping
towel supply; treated equipment supply:
mats, rugs, mops, cloths, etc.; laundered
mat & rug supply
HQ: G&K Services, Llc
6800 Cintas Blvd
Mason OH 45040
952 912-5500

(G-13610)
LIBERTY BIBLE ACADEMY ASSN
4900 Old Irwin Simpson Rd (45040-9751)
PHONE..................................513 754-1234
Dana Honerlaw, Principal
Ona Truesdale, Finance Mgr
Teresa Rynearson, Teacher
Julie Weber, Instructor
EMP: 33
SQ FT: 13,000
SALES: 1.8MM Privately Held
WEB: www.libertybibleacademy.org
SIC: 8351 Preschool center

(G-13611)
LIFE TIME FITNESS INC
Also Called: Lifetime
8310 Wilkens Blvd (45040-7364)
PHONE..................................513 234-0660
Schuana Lynn Doyle, Principal
EMP: 132
SALES (corp-wide): 773.5MM Privately Held
SIC: 7991 Athletic club & gymnasiums,
membership
HQ: Life Time, Inc.
2902 Corporate Pl
Chanhassen MN 55317

(G-13612)
LOWES HOME CENTERS LLC
9380 S Masn Montgomery Rd
(45040-7665)
PHONE..................................513 336-9741
Kathleen Barefield, Branch Mgr
EMP: 150
SALES (corp-wide): 68.6B Publicly Held
SIC: 5211 5031 5722 5064 Home centers; building materials, exterior; building
materials, interior; household appliance
stores; electrical appliances, television &
radio
HQ: Lowe's Home Centers, Llc
1605 Curtis Bridge Rd
Wilkesboro NC 28697
336 658-4000

(G-13613)
MACYS CR & CUSTOMER SVCS INC (DH)
9111 Duke Blvd (45040-8999)
PHONE..................................513 398-5221
Michael Gatio, President
David Faulk, Exec VP
Cynthia Walker, Vice Pres
Karen Foos, VP Human Res
Linda Harding, Payroll Mgr
EMP: 1200
SALES (est): 111.4MM
SALES (corp-wide): 25.7B Publicly Held
SIC: 7389 7322 6141 Credit card service;
adjustment & collection services; personal
credit institutions

(G-13614)
MARKETING INDUS SOLUTIONS CORP (HQ)
3965 Marble Ridge Ln (45040-2892)
PHONE..................................513 703-0965
Mark Cohen, President
EMP: 25
SALES (est): 6.8MM Privately Held
SIC: 8742 Materials mgmt. (purchasing,
handling, inventory) consultant

(G-13615)
MASON FAMILY RESORTS LLC
Also Called: Great Wolf Lodge
2501 Great Wolf Dr (45040-8085)
PHONE..................................513 339-0141
Patrick Alvaraz,
Jim Calder,
John Emery,
Alex Lombardo,

EMP: 450
SALES (est): 19.6MM
SALES (corp-wide): 2.7B Privately Held
SIC: 5812 7011 7299 Eating Place Hotel/Motel Operation Misc Personal Services
HQ: Great Wolf Resorts Holdings, Inc.
1255 Fourier Dr Ste 201
Madison WI 53717
608 662-4700

(G-13616)
MASON HEALTH CARE CENTER
5640 Cox Smith Rd (45040-2210)
PHONE...................513 398-2881
Shelley Owens, *Executive*
EMP: 90
SALES (est): 2.3MM Privately Held
SIC: 8051 8361 Convalescent home with continuous nursing care; home for the aged

(G-13617)
MCV HEALTH CARE FACILITIES
411 Western Row Rd (45040-1438)
PHONE...................513 398-1486
Donald Sams, *President*
Roger H Schwartz, *CFO*
EMP: 130
SQ FT: 79,000
SALES: 9.1MM Privately Held
SIC: 8051 8059 8052 Extended care facility; rest home, with health care; intermediate care facilities

(G-13618)
MERCY HEALTH
Also Called: Mercy Health - Deerfield
5232 Scialville Foster Rd (45040-9302)
PHONE...................513 339-0800
Brenda Meece, *Branch Mgr*
EMP: 33
SALES (corp-wide): 4.7B Privately Held
SIC: 8011 Offices & clinics of medical doctors
PA: Mercy Health
1701 Mercy Health Pl
Cincinnati OH 45237
513 639-2800

(G-13619)
MICROSOFT CORPORATION
4605 Duke Dr Ste 800 (45040-7627)
PHONE...................513 339-2800
Tom Taylor, *Partner*
Jack Lapan, *Branch Mgr*
EMP: 54
SALES (corp-wide): 110.3B Publicly Held
WEB: www.microsoft.com
SIC: 7372 Application computer software
PA: Microsoft Corporation
1 Microsoft Way
Redmond WA 98052
425 882-8080

(G-13620)
MILLENNIUM LEATHER LLC
Also Called: Andrew Philips Collection
4680 Parkway Dr Ste 200 (45040-8173)
PHONE...................201 541-7121
Fred Jagodzinski, *Manager*
Philip Kahan,
Donna L Kahan,
▲ **EMP: 35**
SQ FT: 20,000
SALES (est): 5.4MM Privately Held
WEB: www.millenniumleatherllc.com
SIC: 5199 Leather, leather goods & furs

(G-13621)
MVD COMMUNICATIONS LLC (PA)
Also Called: Mvd Connect
5188 Cox Smith Rd (45040-9005)
PHONE...................513 683-4711
Jeff Black, *Mng Member*
Thad Edmonds,
EMP: 65
SQ FT: 16,000
SALES (est): 27.6MM Privately Held
WEB: www.mvdcommunications.com
SIC: 4813 Data telephone communications

(G-13622)
NEXTRX LLC
Also Called: Wellpoint Health Networks
8990 Duke Blvd (45040-8943)
PHONE...................317 532-6000
Michael H Neumark,
EMP: 694 EST: 2000
SALES (est): 169.8MM
SALES (corp-wide): 141.6B Publicly Held
SIC: 6324 5961 Group hospitalization plans; health maintenance organization (HMO), insurance only; pharmaceuticals, mail order
HQ: Express Scripts, Inc.
1 Express Way
Saint Louis MO 63121
314 996-0900

(G-13623)
NORTHEAST CINCINNATI HOTEL LLC
9664 S Masn Montgomery Rd (45040-9397)
PHONE...................513 459-9800
Michael Hogan, *General Mgr*
Paul Pisegna, *Manager*
Christopher Stone, *Assistant*
▲ **EMP: 250 EST: 1995**
SQ FT: 197,115
SALES (est): 11.9MM Privately Held
SIC: 6513 7011 5813 5812 Residential hotel operation; hotels & motels; bar (drinking places); American restaurant

(G-13624)
P J & R J CONNECTION INC
Also Called: Goddard School, The
754 Reading Rd (45040-1362)
PHONE...................513 398-2777
Ron Herman, *President*
Paula Herman, *Vice Pres*
Amy Van Verth, *Director*
EMP: 28
SALES (est): 1.1MM Privately Held
SIC: 8351 Preschool center; group day care center

(G-13625)
PANASONIC CORP NORTH AMERICA
6402 Thornberry Ct (45040-7846)
PHONE...................513 770-9294
Michael Wilson, *Branch Mgr*
EMP: 53
SALES (corp-wide): 74.9B Privately Held
SIC: 5064 Electrical appliances, television & radio
HQ: Panasonic Corporation Of North America
2 Riverfront Plz Ste 200
Newark NJ 07102
201 348-7000

(G-13626)
PETSMART INC
8175 Arbor Square Dr (45040-5003)
PHONE...................513 336-0365
Rodney Cramer, *Branch Mgr*
EMP: 28
SALES (corp-wide): 12.1B Privately Held
WEB: www.petsmart.com
SIC: 5999 0752 Pets & pet supplies; training services, pet & animal specialties (not horses)
HQ: Petsmart, Inc.
19601 N 27th Ave
Phoenix AZ 85027
623 580-6100

(G-13627)
PIONEER CLDDING GLZING SYSTEMS (PA)
4074 Bethany Rd (45040-9047)
PHONE...................513 583-5925
Mike Robinson, *General Mgr*
Tom Heinold, *Principal*
Thomas Koogle, *Project Mgr*
Tim Moan, *Project Mgr*
Paul Robinson, *Project Mgr*
▲ **EMP: 90 EST: 1999**
SQ FT: 215,000
SALES (est): 56.9MM Privately Held
WEB: www.pioneerglazing.com
SIC: 1793 Glass & glazing work

(G-13628)
PRIMARY CR NTWRK PRMR HLTH PRT
4859 Nixon Park Dr Ste A (45040-8106)
PHONE...................513 492-5940
EMP: 47
SALES (corp-wide): 33.7MM Privately Held
SIC: 8011 General & family practice, physician/surgeon
PA: Primary Care Network Of Premier Health Partners
110 N Main St Ste 350
Dayton OH 45402
937 226-7085

(G-13629)
PRIMARY CR NTWRK PRMR HLTH PRT
7450 S Masn Montgomery Rd (45040-7802)
PHONE...................513 204-5785
EMP: 31
SALES (corp-wide): 33.7MM Privately Held
SIC: 8099 Childbirth preparation clinic
PA: Primary Care Network Of Premier Health Partners
110 N Main St Ste 350
Dayton OH 45402
937 226-7085

(G-13630)
PURE CONCEPT SALON INC
Also Called: Pure Concept Ecosalon & Spa
5625 Deerfield Cir (45040)
PHONE...................513 770-2120
Renee Hydrich, *Branch Mgr*
EMP: 47 Privately Held
WEB: www.pureconceptsalon.com
SIC: 7231 Cosmetology & personal hygiene salons; manicurist, pedicurist
PA: Pure Concept Salon, Inc.
8740 Montgomery Rd Ste 7
Cincinnati OH 45236

(G-13631)
QUOTIENT TECHNOLOGY INC
5191 Natorp Blvd Ste 420 (45040-7599)
PHONE...................513 229-8659
Leslie Brown, *Mktg Dir*
EMP: 50 Publicly Held
SIC: 7389 8742 8743 Advertising, promotional & trade show services; marketing consulting services; promotion service
PA: Quotient Technology Inc.
400 Logue Ave
Mountain View CA 94043

(G-13632)
RE MIDDLETON CNSTR LLC
503 W Main St (45040-1625)
PHONE...................513 398-9255
Robert Middelton,
EMP: 25
SALES (est): 2.6MM Privately Held
SIC: 1521 Single-family housing construction

(G-13633)
REGAL CINEMAS CORPORATION
5500 Deerfield Blvd (45040-2514)
PHONE...................513 770-0713
EMP: 30 Privately Held
SIC: 7832 Motion picture theaters, except drive-in
HQ: Regal Cinemas Corporation
101 E Blount Ave Ste 100
Knoxville TN 37920
865 922-1123

(G-13634)
REMTEC AUTOMATION LLC
6049 Hi Tek Ct (45040-2603)
PHONE...................877 759-8151
Keith Rosnell, *President*
EMP: 25
SALES (est): 220.9K
SALES (corp-wide): 12.9MM Privately Held
SIC: 8742 Automation & robotics consultant

PA: The C M Paula Company
6049 Hi Tek Ct
Mason OH 45040
513 759-7473

(G-13635)
REMTEC ENGINEERING
Also Called: Mbs Acquisition
6049 Hi Tek Ct (45040-2603)
PHONE...................513 860-4299
Keith Rosnell, *CEO*
EMP: 45
SQ FT: 25,000
SALES (est): 8.2MM Privately Held
WEB: www.remtecautomation.com
SIC: 3569 5084 Assembly machines, nonmetalworking; robots, assembly line: industrial & commercial; robots, industrial

(G-13636)
SEAPINE SOFTWARE INC (HQ)
6960 Cintas Blvd (45040-8922)
PHONE...................513 754-1655
Richard Riccetti, *President*
Richard Clyde, *President*
Kelly Riccetti, *Exec VP*
Judy Test, *CFO*
Matthew Disher, *CIO*
EMP: 50
SQ FT: 36,000
SALES (est): 12.5MM Privately Held
WEB: www.seapine.net
SIC: 7371 7372 Custom computer programming services; operating systems computer software

(G-13637)
SECURITY NAT AUTO ACCPTNCE LLC
6951 Cintas Blvd (45040-8923)
PHONE...................513 459-8118
Grant Skeens, *CEO*
Adam Catino, *CFO*
Adam Contino, *CFO*
Suzanne Rozniak, *Sales Staff*
Brian Denny, *Analyst*
EMP: 162
SQ FT: 24,000
SALES (est): 126MM Privately Held
SIC: 6141 6159 Personal credit institutions; automobile finance leasing

(G-13638)
SELECT HOTELS GROUP LLC
Also Called: Hyatt Pl Cincinnati-Northeast
5070 Natorp Blvd (45040-8263)
PHONE...................513 754-0003
Chris Larmour, *Branch Mgr*
EMP: 35
SALES (corp-wide): 4.4B Publicly Held
WEB: www.amerisuites.com
SIC: 7011 8741 6519 Hotels; hotel or motel management; real property lessors
HQ: Select Hotels Group, L.L.C.
71 S Wacker Dr
Chicago IL 60606
312 750-1234

(G-13639)
SHIVER SECURITY SYSTEMS INC
Also Called: Sonitrol of South West Ohio
6404 Thornberry Ct # 410 (45040-3502)
PHONE...................513 719-4000
Chip Shizer Sr, *Owner*
Dwayne Tackett, *Opers Mgr*
Monica Claxton, *Manager*
Greg Shockley, *Manager*
Randy Perkins, *Commercial*
EMP: 40
SALES (corp-wide): 6.1MM Privately Held
WEB: www.sonitrolsw.com
SIC: 1731 Fire detection & burglar alarm systems specialization
PA: Shiver Security Systems, Inc.
15 Pinnacle Point Dr
Miamisburg OH
937 228-7301

(G-13640)
SIBCY CLINE INC
Also Called: Sibcy Cline Realtors
7395 Mason Montgomery Rd (45040-7827)
PHONE...................513 677-1830
Madeline Hoge, *General Mgr*

EMP: 70
SALES (corp-wide): 2.1B **Privately Held**
WEB: www.sibcycline.com
SIC: 6531 Real estate agent, residential
PA: Sibcy Cline, Inc.
8044 Montgomery Rd # 300
Cincinnati OH 45236
513 984-4100

(G-13641)
STRESS ENGINEERING SVCS INC
7030 Stress Engrg Way (45040-7386)
PHONE...................................513 336-6701
Christopher Matice, *Principal*
Matt Berrey, *Engineer*
Kate Harvey, *Branch Mgr*
Matt Heidecker, *Associate*
EMP: 60
SALES (corp-wide): 110.8MM **Privately Held**
WEB: www.stress.com
SIC: 8711 Consulting engineer
PA: Stress Engineering Services, Inc.
13800 Westfair East Dr
Houston TX 77041
281 955-2900

(G-13642)
SUMMIT FUNDING GROUP INC (PA)
4680 Parkway Dr Ste 300 (45040-7979)
PHONE...................................513 489-1222
Richard Ross, *President*
Carlton Zwilling, *Senior VP*
Graham W R Strong, *Finance Mgr*
Scott Tenley, *Manager*
Louis Beck, *Shareholder*
EMP: 78
SQ FT: 19,395
SALES: 20.1MM **Privately Held**
WEB: www.summit-funding.com
SIC: 6159 Equipment & vehicle finance leasing companies

(G-13643)
SYNERGY HEALTH NORTH AMER INC
7086 Industrial Row Dr (45040-1363)
PHONE...................................513 398-6406
Mike Vell, *Manager*
EMP: 75
SALES (corp-wide): 2.6B **Privately Held**
SIC: 3841 7213 Surgical & medical instruments; linen supply
HQ: Synergy Health North America, Inc.
3903 Northdale Blvd 100e
Tampa FL 33624
813 891-9550

(G-13644)
TEC ENGINEERING INC (PA)
7288 Central Parke Blvd (45040-6776)
PHONE...................................513 771-8828
Rihab Saleh, *CEO*
Ali Saleh, *President*
Ed Williams, *Vice Pres*
Bryan Bender, *Project Mgr*
Robert Fluharty, *Project Mgr*
EMP: 35
SQ FT: 4,000
SALES: 1.5MM **Privately Held**
WEB: www.teceng.com
SIC: 8711 Professional engineer

(G-13645)
TELEDYNE INSTRUMENTS INC
Also Called: Teledyne Tekmar
4736 Scialville Foster Rd (45040-8265)
PHONE...................................513 229-7000
Martin Motz, *Engineer*
Cindy Leichty, *Human Res Dir*
Tammy Rellar, *Manager*
EMP: 25
SALES (corp-wide): 2.9B **Publicly Held**
SIC: 5049 3826 3829 3821 Laboratory equipment, except medical or dental; analytical instruments; environmental testing equipment; measuring & controlling devices; laboratory apparatus & furniture
HQ: Teledyne Instruments, Inc.
1049 Camino Dos Rios
Thousand Oaks CA 91360
805 373-4545

(G-13646)
TELEDYNE TEKMAR COMPANY (HQ)
Also Called: Tekmar-Dohrmann
4736 Scialville Foster Rd (45040-8265)
PHONE...................................513 229-7000
Robert Mehrabian, *Ch of Bd*
Ron Uchtman, *Opers Mgr*
Cindy Cancel, *Purchasing*
Stephen Proffitt, *Research*
Heather Beale, *Engineer*
EMP: 25
SQ FT: 40,000
SALES (est): 34.2MM
SALES (corp-wide): 2.9B **Publicly Held**
WEB: www.teledynetekmar.com
SIC: 5049 3826 3829 3821 Laboratory equipment, except medical or dental; analytical instruments; environmental testing equipment; measuring & controlling devices; laboratory apparatus & furniture
PA: Teledyne Technologies Inc
1049 Camino Dos Rios
Thousand Oaks CA 91360
805 373-4545

(G-13647)
TOP GUN SALES PERFORMANCE INC
5155 Financial Way Ste 1 (45040-2557)
PHONE...................................513 770-0870
J Steven Osborne, *CEO*
Barry Gorsun, *President*
Nancy Terselic, *Partner*
David Kessinger, *Vice Pres*
Michael Wlotzko, *Vice Pres*
EMP: 30
SALES (est): 5.9MM **Privately Held**
SIC: 7379 Computer related maintenance services

(G-13648)
TOUCHSTONE MDSE GROUP LLC (HQ)
7200 Industrial Row Dr (45040-1386)
PHONE...................................513 741-0400
Derek Block, *President*
Bill Bok, *President*
Andrew Backen, *Senior VP*
Chris Berger, *Senior VP*
Sydney Guttman, *Accounts Mgr*
▲ **EMP:** 64
SQ FT: 12,000
SALES (est): 20.8MM **Privately Held**
SIC: 7311 Advertising agencies

(G-13649)
TRIHEALTH HF LLC
7423 S Mason Mntgomery (45040-7828)
PHONE...................................513 398-3445
Brian Hoffman, *Mng Member*
EMP: 27 **EST:** 2012
SALES (est): 73K **Privately Held**
SIC: 8099 Health & allied services

(G-13650)
TRITON SERVICES INC
8162 Duke Blvd (45040-8111)
PHONE...................................513 679-6800
Majid H Samarghandi, *CEO*
Michael E Defrank, *Principal*
Scott Royer, *Project Mgr*
Larry Milillo, *CFO*
Donna Roesch, *Accountant*
EMP: 125
SALES (est): 37.9MM **Privately Held**
WEB: www.tritonservicesinc.com
SIC: 1711 Mechanical contractor

(G-13651)
TRUECHOICEPACK CORP
5155 Financial Way Ste 6 (45040-0055)
PHONE...................................937 630-3832
Heena Rathore, *President*
Christopher Che, *Chairman*
Rakesh Rathore, *COO*
EMP: 44
SALES (est): 2.4MM
SALES (corp-wide): 9.6MM **Privately Held**
SIC: 3089 3086 8748 7389 Blister or bubble formed packaging, plastic; packaging & shipping materials, foamed plastic; business consulting; field warehousing

PA: Che International Group, Llc
9435 Waterstone Blvd # 140
Cincinnati OH 45249
513 444-2072

(G-13652)
UC HEALTH LLC
Also Called: Uc Health Primary Care Mason
9313 S Mason Montgomery R (45040-8009)
PHONE...................................513 584-6999
Daniel Kessler, *Med Doctor*
Garvin Nickell, *Internal Med*
Emily Krans, *Nurse Practr*
EMP: 47 **Privately Held**
SIC: 8011 Internal medicine, physician/surgeon
PA: Uc Health, Llc.
3200 Burnet Ave
Cincinnati OH 45229

(G-13653)
VAN DYK MORTGAGE CORPORATION
4680 Parkway Dr Ste 100 (45040-8296)
PHONE...................................513 429-2122
Todd Bitter, *Principal*
EMP: 31
SALES (corp-wide): 90.5MM **Privately Held**
SIC: 6211 Mortgages, buying & selling
PA: Van Dyk Mortgage Corporation
2449 Camelot Ct Se
Grand Rapids MI 49546
616 940-3000

(G-13654)
VET PATH SERVICES INC
Also Called: Vps, Inc.
6450 Castle Dr (45040-9412)
PHONE...................................513 469-0777
Christopher Johnson, *President*
Philip Long, *Vice Pres*
EMP: 35
SQ FT: 13,000
SALES (est): 2.2MM **Privately Held**
WEB: www.vetpathservicesinc.com
SIC: 8071 Pathological laboratory

(G-13655)
WALL2WALL SOCCER LLC
846 Reading Rd (45040-1886)
PHONE...................................513 573-9898
Donte Rainone, *Mng Member*
EMP: 40
SALES (est): 975.8K **Privately Held**
WEB: www.wall2wallsoccer.com
SIC: 7941 Soccer club

Massillon
Stark County

(G-13656)
3-D SERVICE LTD (PA)
Also Called: Magnetech
800 Nave Rd Se (44646-9476)
PHONE...................................330 830-3500
Bernie Dewees, *President*
Tracy Tucker, *Human Res Mgr*
▲ **EMP:** 120
SQ FT: 85,000
SALES (est): 6.4MM **Privately Held**
WEB: www.3-dservice.com
SIC: 7694 7699 Electric motor repair; industrial equipment services

(G-13657)
A A HAMMERSMITH INSURANCE INC (PA)
210 Erie St N (44646-8400)
P.O. Box 591 (44648-0591)
PHONE...................................330 832-7411
Herold Weatherbee, *CEO*
Robert McAfee, *President*
Phillip Fox, *Vice Pres*
Richard Snyder, *Vice Pres*
Frank Sauser, *Admin Sec*
EMP: 27
SQ FT: 6,000
SALES (est): 8.7MM **Privately Held**
WEB: www.aahammersmith.com
SIC: 6411 Insurance agents

(G-13658)
A P & P DEV & CNSTR CO (PA)
2851 Lincoln Way E (44646-3769)
PHONE...................................330 833-8886
Nichkolas Maragas, *President*
EMP: 70
SQ FT: 2,000
SALES (est): 13.5MM **Privately Held**
SIC: 1542 6513 Commercial & office building, new construction; apartment building operators

(G-13659)
AAUW ACTION FUND INC
8400 Milmont St Nw (44646-1761)
PHONE...................................330 833-0520
Jacqueline Woods, *Exec Dir*
EMP: 25
SALES (corp-wide): 226.2K **Privately Held**
SIC: 8621 Education & teacher association
PA: Aauw Action Fund, Inc.
1310 L St Nw Ste 1000
Washington DC 20005
202 785-7700

(G-13660)
ADVANCED INDUSTRIAL ROOFG INC
1330 Erie St S (44646-7906)
PHONE...................................330 837-1999
Fred Horner, *President*
Jeff Rupert, *Vice Pres*
EMP: 75
SQ FT: 12,140
SALES (est): 14.4MM **Privately Held**
WEB: www.airoofing.com
SIC: 1761 Roofing contractor

(G-13661)
AMERICOLD LOGISTICS LLC
2140 17th St Sw (44647-7525)
PHONE...................................330 834-1742
Duane Wilson, *Facilities Mgr*
Ron Lair, *Branch Mgr*
Cheri Fabianich, *Director*
EMP: 90
SALES (corp-wide): 1.6B **Privately Held**
WEB: www.americoldlogistics.com
SIC: 4222 Warehousing, cold storage or refrigerated
HQ: Americold Logistics, Llc
10 Glenlake Pkwy Ste 324
Atlanta GA 30328
678 441-1400

(G-13662)
AMVETS POST NO 6 INC
8417 Audubon St Nw (44646-7811)
PHONE...................................330 833-5935
Orran Cahoun, *President*
EMP: 40
SALES: 4.5K **Privately Held**
SIC: 8641 Veterans' organization

(G-13663)
AQUA OHIO INC
Water Treatment Plant
870 3rd St Nw (44647-4206)
PHONE...................................330 832-5764
James Purtz, *Principal*
EMP: 25
SALES (corp-wide): 838MM **Publicly Held**
SIC: 4941 Water supply
HQ: Aqua Ohio, Inc.
6650 South Ave
Youngstown OH 44512
330 726-8151

(G-13664)
AULTCOMP INC
2458 Lincoln Way E (44646-5085)
P.O. Box 4817 (44648-4817)
PHONE...................................330 830-4919
Edward J Roth, *President*
EMP: 25
SQ FT: 4,200
SALES (est): 1.2MM **Privately Held**
WEB: www.aultcomp.com
SIC: 8741 Administrative management

(G-13665)
BRINKS INCORPORATED
300 Nova Dr Se (44646-8899)
PHONE......................330 832-6130
Scott Nichols, *Branch Mgr*
EMP: 27
SALES (corp-wide): 3.4B **Publicly Held**
WEB: www.brinksinc.com
SIC: 7381 Armored car services
HQ: Brink's, Incorporated
1801 Bayberry Ct Ste 400
Richmond VA 23226
804 289-9600

(G-13666)
BUTTERFIELD CO INC
Also Called: Finishing Touch Cleaning Svcs
401 26th St Nw (44647-5124)
PHONE......................330 832-1282
David M Butterfield, *President*
David Butterfield, *President*
Edwina Bowen, *Administration*
EMP: 75
SALES (est): 956.3K **Privately Held**
SIC: 7349 Cleaning service, industrial or commercial

(G-13667)
C-N-D INDUSTRIES INC
Also Called: Cnd Machine
359 State Ave Nw (44647-4269)
PHONE......................330 478-8811
Clyde Shetler, *President*
Don Rossbach, *CFO*
EMP: 42
SQ FT: 28,000
SALES (est): 8.6MM **Privately Held**
WEB: www.cndinc.com
SIC: 3441 3599 7692 3444 Fabricated structural metal; machine shop, jobbing & repair; welding repair; sheet metalwork

(G-13668)
CASE FARMS LLC
Also Called: Massillon Feed Mill
4001 Millennium Blvd Se (44646-9606)
PHONE......................330 832-0030
Thomas R Shelton, *Branch Mgr*
Josh Carney, *Manager*
EMP: 62 **Privately Held**
SIC: 0723 Feed milling custom services
PA: Case Farms, L.L.C.
385 Pilch Rd
Troutman NC 28166

(G-13669)
CHILDS INVESTMENT CO
Also Called: Hospitality House
205 Rohr Ave Nw (44646-3671)
PHONE......................330 837-2100
Steven Childs, *CEO*
EMP: 50
SQ FT: 20,000
SALES (est): 3.2MM **Privately Held**
SIC: 8052 8051 Intermediate care facilities; skilled nursing care facilities

(G-13670)
CHRISTIAN RIVERTREE SCHOOL
Also Called: Rivertreechristian.com
7373 Portage St Nw (44646-9315)
PHONE......................330 494-1860
Pamela Clevenger, *Director*
Cindy Hernandez, *Director*
EMP: 46
SALES (est): 1MM **Privately Held**
WEB: www.rivertreechristian.com
SIC: 8351 Preschool center

(G-13671)
CITY OF MASSILLON
Also Called: Waste Water Treatment Plant
100 Dig Indian Dr Sw (44646)
PHONE......................330 833-3304
Joseph R Ulrich, *Manager*
EMP: 29 **Privately Held**
SIC: 4941 Water supply
PA: City Of Massillon
1 James Duncan Plz Ste 7
Massillon OH 44646
330 830-1734

(G-13672)
CLOVERLEAF COLD STORAGE CO
950 Cloverleaf St Se (44646-9647)
PHONE......................330 833-9870
Al Harwick, *Manager*
EMP: 50
SALES (corp-wide): 76.3MM **Privately Held**
WEB: www.cloverleafco.com
SIC: 4222 Warehousing, cold storage or refrigerated
PA: Cloverleaf Cold Storage Co., Llc
401 Douglas St Ste 406
Sioux City IA 51101
712 279-8000

(G-13673)
CONSULATE MANAGEMENT CO LLC
Also Called: Legends Care Center
2311 Nave Rd Sw (44646)
PHONE......................330 837-1001
Tara Price, *Manager*
EMP: 100
SALES (corp-wide): 580.2MM **Privately Held**
WEB: www.tandemhealthcare.com
SIC: 8051 Skilled nursing care facilities
PA: Consulate Management Company, Llc
800 Concourse Pkwy S
Maitland FL 32751
407 571-1550

(G-13674)
COUNTY OF STARK
Also Called: Park Dist Maintenance
798 Genoa Ave Nw (44646)
PHONE......................330 477-3609
Robert Font, *Director*
EMP: 48 **Privately Held**
WEB: www.starkadas.org
SIC: 7699 9111 Miscellaneous automotive repair services; county supervisors' & executives' offices
PA: County Of Stark
110 Central Plz S Ste 240
Canton OH 44702
330 451-7371

(G-13675)
DOCTORS HOSP PHYSCN SVCS LLC
Also Called: Affinity Family Physicians
830 Amherst Rd Ne Ste 201 (44646-8518)
PHONE......................330 834-4725
Ron Bierman, *CEO*
EMP: 40
SALES (est): 12.5MM
SALES (corp-wide): 1.8B **Publicly Held**
SIC: 8011 General & family practice, physician/surgeon
PA: Quorum Health Corporation
1573 Mallory Ln Ste 100
Brentwood TN 37027
615 221-1400

(G-13676)
DUSK TO DAWN PROTECTIVE SVCS
3554 Lincoln Way E 3 (44646-8607)
PHONE......................330 837-9992
Ralph Ury, *Owner*
EMP: 25
SALES (est): 300K **Privately Held**
SIC: 7381 Security guard service

(G-13677)
EMSCO INC (HQ)
1000 Nave Rd Se (44646-9478)
P.O. Box 607 (44648-0607)
PHONE......................330 830-7125
James J Dyer, *President*
Greg Guggisberg, *Area Mgr*
Tom McWilliams, *Project Mgr*
Jim Dyer, *Purchasing*
Susan Hunter, *Engineer*
▲ EMP: 31
SQ FT: 55,000
SALES (est): 16.6MM
SALES (corp-wide): 924.5MM **Privately Held**
WEB: www.emsco.com
SIC: 7699 Industrial machinery & equipment repair

PA: Rowan Technologies, Inc.
10 Indel Ave
Rancocas NJ 08073
609 267-9000

(G-13678)
EMSCO INC
Emsco North Division
1000 Nave Rd Se (44646-9478)
PHONE......................330 833-5600
Paul D Wolanski, *Division Mgr*
EMP: 25
SALES (corp-wide): 924.5MM **Privately Held**
SIC: 7699 Industrial machinery & equipment repair
HQ: Emsco, Inc.
1000 Nave Rd Se
Massillon OH 44646
330 830-7125

(G-13679)
F W ARNOLD AGENCY CO INC
Also Called: Hammer Smith Agency
210 Erie St N (44646-8450)
PHONE......................330 832-1556
John L Muhlbach Jr, *President*
Charles Clark, *Vice Pres*
Faye Hedrick, *Treasurer*
Virginia Sorg, *Admin Sec*
EMP: 30 EST: 1876
SALES (est): 2.8MM **Privately Held**
WEB: www.fwarnold.com
SIC: 6411 Insurance agents

(G-13680)
FAIRPORT ENTERPRISES INC
Also Called: LAURELS OF MASSILLON, THE
2000 Sherman Cir Ne (44646-5219)
PHONE......................330 830-9988
Thomas F Franke, *Ch of Bd*
Dennis Sherman, *President*
Lynette Mock Sherman, *Asst Treas*
Diane McKeen, *Office Mgr*
Lori Miller, *Social Dir*
EMP: 150
SALES: 13MM **Privately Held**
SIC: 8051 Convalescent home with continuous nursing care
PA: Laurel Health Care Company Of North Worthington
8181 Worthington Rd
Westerville OH 43082

(G-13681)
FARRIS PRODUCE INC
2421 Lincoln Way Nw (44647-5111)
PHONE......................330 837-4607
Wanda Farris, *President*
Stephen Farris, *Treasurer*
EMP: 25
SQ FT: 9,996
SALES: 4.4MM **Privately Held**
WEB: www.farrisproduce.com
SIC: 5148 Fruits, fresh; vegetables

(G-13682)
FLORLINE GROUP INC
Also Called: Florline Midwest
800 Vista Ave Se (44646-7948)
PHONE......................330 830-3380
Christopher Reynolds, *President*
Peter W Reynolds, *Principal*
Shane Reynolds, *Vice Pres*
EMP: 25
SQ FT: 11,700
SALES (est): 5.7MM **Privately Held**
SIC: 1752 5162 Floor laying & floor work; resins

(G-13683)
FORT DIALYSIS LLC
Also Called: Massillon Community Dialysis
2112 Lincoln Way E (44646-7034)
PHONE......................330 837-7730
James K Hilger,
EMP: 35
SALES (est): 395K **Publicly Held**
SIC: 8092 Kidney dialysis centers
PA: Davita Inc.
2000 16th St
Denver CO 80202

(G-13684)
FRESENIUS USA INC
2474 Lincoln Way E (44646-5085)
PHONE......................330 837-2575
Mark Fawcett, *Branch Mgr*
EMP: 40
SALES (corp-wide): 18.9B **Privately Held**
SIC: 8092 Kidney dialysis centers
HQ: Fresenius Usa, Inc.
4040 Nelson Ave
Concord CA 94520
925 288-4218

(G-13685)
FRESH MARK INC (PA)
Also Called: Superior's Brand Meats
1888 Southway St Se (44646)
P.O. Box 571 (44648-0571)
PHONE......................330 834-3669
Neil Genshaft, *CEO*
David Cochenour, *President*
Tim Cranor, *President*
Richard Foster, *General Mgr*
Bob Goode, *Superintendent*
◆ EMP: 500 EST: 1932
SQ FT: 80,000
SALES: 1.3B **Privately Held**
WEB: www.freshmark.com
SIC: 2013 5147 2011 Prepared beef products from purchased beef; prepared pork products from purchased pork; sausages & related products, from purchased meat; meats & meat products; meat packing plants

(G-13686)
FRESH MARK INC
950 Cloverleaf St Se (44646-9647)
PHONE......................330 833-9870
Mike Portilla, *Branch Mgr*
EMP: 254
SALES (corp-wide): 1.3B **Privately Held**
SIC: 4222 Warehousing, cold storage or refrigerated
PA: Fresh Mark, Inc.
1888 Southway St Se
Massillon OH 44646
330 834-3669

(G-13687)
FRESH MARK INC
Also Called: Fresh Mark Sugardale
1888 Southway St Sw (44646-9429)
P.O. Box 571 (44648-0571)
PHONE......................330 832-7491
Tim Craner, *President*
Ryan Cucerzan, *Production*
Sherry Chidester, *Senior Engr*
Diane Doyle, *Accountant*
Mark Slaughter, *Director*
EMP: 350
SALES (corp-wide): 1.3B **Privately Held**
WEB: www.freshmark.com
SIC: 5147 2013 Meats & meat products; sausages & other prepared meats
PA: Fresh Mark, Inc.
1888 Southway St Se
Massillon OH 44646
330 834-3669

(G-13688)
GENCO OF LEBANON INC
Also Called: Genco Marketing Place
4300 Sterilite St Se (44646-7452)
PHONE......................330 837-0561
Marc Wittenberg, *Manager*
EMP: 2520
SALES (corp-wide): 262.7MM **Privately Held**
SIC: 1541 Industrial Building Construction
PA: Genco Of Lebanon, Inc.
700 Cranberry Woods Dr
Cranberry Township PA 16066
412 820-3747

(G-13689)
GREENLEAF AUTO RECYCLERS LLC
12192 Lincoln Way Nw (44647-9601)
PHONE......................330 832-6001
Jerr Banta, *Principal*
EMP: 31
SALES (corp-wide): 11.8B **Publicly Held**
SIC: 5013 Automotive supplies & parts

HQ: Greenleaf Auto Recyclers, Llc
904 S Intrstate 45 Svc Rd
Hutchins TX

(G-13690)
GREENLEAF OHIO LLC
Also Called: Grand Central Auto Recycling
12192 Lincoln Way Nw (44647-9601)
PHONE.................................330 832-6001
Eric Bagwell, *General Mgr*
EMP: 35
SQ FT: 5,000
SALES (est): 1.5MM **Privately Held**
SIC: 5015 5531 Automotive parts & supplies, used; automotive parts

(G-13691)
H & W CONTRACTORS INC
1722 1st St Ne (44646-4068)
P.O. Box 876 (44648-0876)
PHONE.................................330 833-0982
Fax: 330 833-5575
EMP: 26 EST: 1970
SQ FT: 7,000
SALES (est): 3.1MM **Privately Held**
SIC: 1623 Water/Sewer/Utility Construction

(G-13692)
HANOVER HOUSE INC
435 Avis Ave Nw (44646-3599)
PHONE.................................330 837-1741
Debbie Rorher, *Human Res Dir*
Hollis Garfield,
Albert Wiggins,
EMP: 160
SALES (est): 3.6MM **Privately Held**
SIC: 8051 Convalescent home with continuous nursing care

(G-13693)
HEALTH PLAN OF OHIO INC
Also Called: Massillon Cmnty Hosp Hlth Plan
100 Lillian Gish Blvd Sw # 301
(44647-6587)
PHONE.................................330 837-6880
William Epling, *President*
EMP: 160
SALES (est): 47.8MM
SALES (corp-wide): 434.2MM **Privately Held**
SIC: 6324 Health maintenance organization (HMO), insurance only
PA: Health Plan Of West Va Inc
1110 Main St
Wheeling WV 26003
740 695-3585

(G-13694)
HEALTH SERVICES INC
Also Called: Complete Home Care
2520 Wales Ave Nw Ste 120 (44646-2398)
PHONE.................................330 837-7678
Mervin Strine, *Ch of Bd*
James Budiscak, *President*
Richard Leffler, *Treasurer*
EMP: 30
SQ FT: 5,500
SALES (est): 460.4K
SALES (corp-wide): 11MM **Privately Held**
WEB: www.thehealthgroup.com
SIC: 8049 5999 Physical therapist; hospital equipment & supplies
PA: The Health Group
5425 High Mill Ave Nw
Massillon OH
330 833-3174

(G-13695)
HEARTLAND BHAVIORAL HEALTHCARE
3000 Erie St S (44646-7976)
PHONE.................................330 833-3135
Helen Stevens, *CEO*
EMP: 320
SALES (est): 22MM **Privately Held**
SIC: 8063 Psychiatric hospitals

(G-13696)
HYDRO-DYNE INC
225 Wetmore Ave Se (44646-6788)
P.O. Box 318 (44648-0318)
PHONE.................................330 832-5076
Rose Ann Dare, *President*
Lynn Neel, *Vice Pres*
Jean Holiday, *Manager*
Sherri McMillen, *Manager*

Ken Yeaman, *Manager*
▲ EMP: 30
SQ FT: 130,000
SALES (est): 8.2MM **Privately Held**
WEB: www.hydrodyneinc.com
SIC: 3585 8711 Evaporative condensers, heat transfer equipment; engineering services

(G-13697)
IDENTITEK SYSTEMS INC
Also Called: Adams Signs
1100 Industrial Ave Sw (44647-7608)
P.O. Box 347 (44648-0347)
PHONE.................................330 832-9844
Joseph Pugliese, *President*
Paul Boyer, *VP Sales*
EMP: 53
SQ FT: 70,000
SALES (est): 8MM **Privately Held**
WEB: www.adamsigns.com
SIC: 1799 3993 Sign installation & maintenance; signs & advertising specialties; electric signs

(G-13698)
IES INFRSTRCTURE SOLUTIONS LLC (HQ)
800 Nave Rd Se (44646-9476)
PHONE.................................330 830-3500
Michael Rice, *President*
EMP: 30
SALES (est): 81.2MM **Publicly Held**
SIC: 1731 Electrical work

(G-13699)
INN AT UNIV VLG MGT CO LLC
2650 Ohio State Dr Se (44646-9656)
PHONE.................................330 837-3000
Denise Beck, *Principal*
EMP: 34
SALES (est): 1.7MM **Privately Held**
SIC: 8052 Personal care facility

(G-13700)
J B M CLEANING & SUPPLY CO
Also Called: Jbm Cleaning
3106 Sheila St Nw (44646-3075)
P.O. Box 23 (44648-0023)
PHONE.................................330 837-8805
Patrick Leslie, *President*
Deborah Leslie, *Vice Pres*
EMP: 25
SALES (est): 500K **Privately Held**
WEB: www.jbmcleans.com
SIC: 7349 5999 Janitorial service, contract basis; concrete products, pre-cast

(G-13701)
JEFFREY CARR CONSTRUCTION INC
4164 Erie Ave Sw (44646-9668)
P.O. Box 1051 (44648-1051)
PHONE.................................330 879-5210
Jeffrey Carr, *President*
Jeff Carr, *Principal*
Terry Carr, *Admin Sec*
EMP: 50
SQ FT: 3,500
SALES (est): 15.9MM **Privately Held**
WEB: www.jcarrconstruction.com
SIC: 1542 Commercial & office buildings, renovation & repair

(G-13702)
KENMORE CONSTRUCTION CO INC
Also Called: American Sand & Gravel Div
9500 Forty Corners Rd Nw (44647-9309)
PHONE.................................330 832-8888
Chris Scala, *Manager*
EMP: 48
SALES (corp-wide): 93MM **Privately Held**
WEB: www.kenmorecompanies.com
SIC: 1611 1442 General contractor, highway & street construction; construction sand & gravel
PA: Kenmore Construction Co., Inc.
700 Home Ave
Akron OH 44310
330 762-8936

(G-13703)
LAND OLAKES INC
8485 Navarre Rd Sw (44646-8814)
PHONE.................................330 879-2158
Gary Hauenstin, *Manager*
EMP: 41
SALES (corp-wide): 10.4B **Privately Held**
WEB: www.landolakes.com
SIC: 2048 5191 2047 Livestock feeds; animal feeds; dog & cat food
PA: Land O'lakes, Inc.
4001 Lexington Ave N
Arden Hills MN 55126
651 375-2222

(G-13704)
LOWES HOME CENTERS LLC
101 Massillon Marketplace (44646-2015)
PHONE.................................330 832-1901
Ron Vyof, *Branch Mgr*
Joseph Bruck, *Manager*
Charles Housden, *Manager*
Margrethe Vagell, *Director*
EMP: 150
SALES (corp-wide): 68.6B **Publicly Held**
SIC: 5211 5031 5722 5064 Home centers; building materials, exterior; building materials, interior; household appliance stores; electrical appliances, television & radio
HQ: Lowe's Home Centers, Llc
1605 Curtis Bridge Rd
Wilkesboro NC 28697
336 658-4000

(G-13705)
LYDEN OIL COMPANY
3249 Wales Ave Nw (44646-1841)
PHONE.................................330 832-7800
Bren Lyden, *President*
EMP: 60
SALES (est): 11.9MM **Privately Held**
WEB: www.lydenoilcompany.com
SIC: 5172 Petroleum products

(G-13706)
MACKIN BOOK COMPANY
9326 Paulding St Nw (44646-9361)
PHONE.................................330 854-0099
Paula Crawford, *President*
EMP: 49
SALES (corp-wide): 210.4MM **Privately Held**
SIC: 5192 Books
PA: Mackin Book Company
3505 County Road 42 W
Burnsville MN 55306
952 895-9540

(G-13707)
MAGNETECH INDUSTRIAL SVCS INC (DH)
800 Nave Rd Se (44646-9476)
PHONE.................................330 830-3500
Michael P Moore, *President*
William Wisnieweski, *Vice Pres*
Stephen Rampa, *Controller*
Bob Codrea, *Sales Staff*
Pat Schottenheimer, *Sales Staff*
▲ EMP: 80
SALES (est): 36.8MM **Publicly Held**
SIC: 7629 Electrical equipment repair services
HQ: Ies Subsidiary Holdings, Inc
5433 Westheimer Rd # 500
Houston TX 77056
713 860-1500

(G-13708)
MAGNETECH INDUSTRIAL SVCS INC
800 Nave Rd Se (44646-9476)
PHONE.................................330 830-3500
Mike Rice, *Branch Mgr*
EMP: 120 **Publicly Held**
SIC: 7694 7699 Electric motor repair; industrial equipment services
HQ: Magnetech Industrial Services, Inc.
800 Nave Rd Se
Massillon OH 44646
330 830-3500

(G-13709)
MASSILLON AUTOMOBILE CLUB
Also Called: AAA Massillon Automobile Club
1972 Wales Rd Ne Ste 1 (44646-4197)
PHONE.................................330 833-1084
Jeff Bushman, *Director*
EMP: 26
SQ FT: 11,912
SALES (est): 40K **Privately Held**
SIC: 8699 Automobile owners' association

(G-13710)
MASSILLON CABLE TV INC (PA)
814 Cable Ct Nw (44647-4284)
P.O. Box 1000 (44648-1000)
PHONE.................................330 833-4134
Robert B Gessner, *President*
Robert Gessner, *General Mgr*
H Chas Hess, *Principal*
Jacob F Hess, *Principal*
M P L Kirchhofer, *Principal*
EMP: 75
SQ FT: 10,000
SALES (est): 26.5MM **Privately Held**
WEB: www.massilloncabletv.com
SIC: 4841 8748 4813 Cable television services; telecommunications consultant;

(G-13711)
MASSILLON CITY SCHOOL BUS GAR
1 George Red Bird Dr Se (44646-7176)
PHONE.................................330 830-1849
Ken McCune, *Director*
EMP: 30
SALES (est): 601.5K **Privately Held**
SIC: 4151 School buses

(G-13712)
MASSILLON HEALTH SYSTEM LLC
400 Austin Ave Nw (44646-3554)
PHONE.................................330 837-7200
Michael Richfeld,
EMP: 1451
SQ FT: 230,000
SALES (est): 456.2MM
SALES (corp-wide): 1.8B **Publicly Held**
SIC: 8062 General Hospital
PA: Quorum Health Corporation
1573 Mallory Ln Ste 100
Brentwood TN 37027
615 221-1400

(G-13713)
MATRIX SYS AUTO FINISHES LLC
600 Nova Dr Se (44646-8884)
PHONE.................................248 668-8135
W Kent Gardner, *President*
Sean Hook, *Director*
EMP: 100
SQ FT: 26,000
SALES (est): 37MM
SALES (corp-wide): 116.6MM **Privately Held**
WEB: www.matrixsystem.com
SIC: 5198 2851 Paints; paints & allied products
PA: Quest Specialty Chemicals, Inc.
225 Sven Farms Dr Ste 204
Charleston SC 29492
800 966-7580

(G-13714)
MEADOW WIND HLTH CARE CTR INC
300 23rd St Ne (44646-4996)
PHONE.................................330 833-2026
Robert Buchanan, *President*
Anne Marie King, *Personnel*
John Faust, *Director*
Jamie Hunt, *Administration*
EMP: 130
SQ FT: 32,000
SALES (est): 7.5MM **Privately Held**
SIC: 8051 Convalescent home with continuous nursing care

(G-13715)
MERCY PROFESSIONAL CARE
2859 Aaronwood Ave Ne (44646-2390)
PHONE.................................330 832-2280

EMP: 39
SALES (corp-wide): 5.2MM Privately Held
SIC: 8011 Offices & clinics of medical doctors
PA: Mercy Professional Care
1320 Mercy Dr Nw
Canton OH 44708
330 489-1435

(G-13716)
MIDWEST HEALTH SERVICES INC
107 Tommy Henrich Dr Nw (44647-5402)
PHONE................................330 828-0779
Joseph Knetzer, *President*
Kristine Knetzer, *Hlthcr Dir*
EMP: 125 EST: 1998
SALES (est): 6.9MM Privately Held
WEB: www.midwesths.com
SIC: 8361 Halfway group home, persons with social or personal problems

(G-13717)
NFM/WELDING ENGINEERS INC
1339 Duncan St Sw (44647-7843)
PHONE................................330 837-3868
Tim Boron, *Vice Pres*
Bob Kirkland, *Purch Agent*
Phil Roberson, *Manager*
EMP: 50
SALES (corp-wide): 43.2MM Privately Held
WEB: www.nfmwe.com
SIC: 5084 Plastic products machinery
PA: Nfm/Welding Engineers, Inc.
577 Oberlin Ave Sw
Massillon OH 44647
330 837-3868

(G-13718)
OHIO DRILLING COMPANY (PA)
2405 Bostic Blvd Sw (44647-7686)
PHONE................................330 832-1521
Jeff Brest, *President*
EMP: 25 EST: 1907
SQ FT: 23,000
SALES (est): 3.8MM Privately Held
SIC: 1781 Water well servicing

(G-13719)
PEOPLES CARTAGE INC
8045 Navarre Rd Sw (44648)
PHONE................................330 833-8571
Joseph Chevreau, *Principal*
EMP: 35 Privately Held
SIC: 4225 General warehousing
HQ: People's Cartage, Inc.
2207 Kimball Rd Se
Canton OH 44707
330 453-3709

(G-13720)
POLYMER PACKAGING INC (PA)
Also Called: Polymer Protective Packaging
8333 Navarre Rd Se (44646-9652)
PHONE................................330 832-2000
Larry L Lanham, *CEO*
Ronald Reagan, *President*
William D Lanham, *Exec VP*
Chris Thomazin, *Vice Pres*
Jeffrey S Davis, *CFO*
▲ **EMP: 65**
SQ FT: 36,000
SALES (est): 58.1MM Privately Held
WEB: www.polymerpkg.com
SIC: 5113 5162 2621 2821 Paper & products, wrapping or coarse; plastics products; wrapping & packaging papers; plastics materials & resins

(G-13721)
PROGRSSIVE OLDSMOBILE CADILLAC
Also Called: Progressive Dodge
7966 Hills & Dales Rd Ne (44646-5241)
PHONE................................330 833-8585
Toll Free:................................877 -
Dan Sanders, *President*
Carol Coates, *Treasurer*
EMP: 48
SQ FT: 20,000

SALES (est): 14.5MM Privately Held
WEB: www.progressivedodge.com
SIC: 5511 7538 5521 Automobiles, new & used; general automotive repair shops; used car dealers

(G-13722)
REPUBLIC SERVICES INC
2800 Erie St S (44646-7915)
PHONE................................330 830-9050
Ronald Setterlin, *Principal*
Pete Gutwin, *Branch Mgr*
Pete Gutwein, *Manager*
EMP: 34
SQ FT: 11,000
SALES (corp-wide): 10B Publicly Held
WEB: www.republicservices.com
SIC: 4953 Refuse collection & disposal services
PA: Republic Services, Inc.
18500 N Allied Way # 100
Phoenix AZ 85054
480 627-2700

(G-13723)
REPUBLIC SERVICES INC
2800 Erie St S (44646-7915)
PHONE................................800 247-3644
Ronald Setterlin, *Branch Mgr*
EMP: 34
SALES (corp-wide): 10B Publicly Held
WEB: www.republicservices.com
SIC: 4953 Refuse collection & disposal services
PA: Republic Services, Inc.
18500 N Allied Way # 100
Phoenix AZ 85054
480 627-2700

(G-13724)
ROBERT J MATTHEWS COMPANY (PA)
Also Called: P B S Animal Health
2780 Richville Dr Se (44646-8396)
PHONE................................330 834-3000
Della L Matthews, *Ch of Bd*
John K Cox, *Principal*
Robert J Matthews, *Principal*
J Stephen Matthews, *Vice Pres*
John D Matthews, *Vice Pres*
▲ **EMP: 60**
SQ FT: 40,000
SALES (est): 63MM Privately Held
WEB: www.horsehealthusa.com
SIC: 5122 Pharmaceuticals

(G-13725)
ROSE LN HLTH RHABILITATION INC
Also Called: Rose Lane Health Center
5425 High Mill Ave Nw (44646-9005)
PHONE................................330 833-3174
Karren Talbot, *CEO*
Dennis Potts, *President*
EMP: 240
SQ FT: 34,000
SALES (est): 9.1MM
SALES (corp-wide): 11MM Privately Held
WEB: www.roselane.org
SIC: 8051 Extended care facility
PA: The Health Group
5425 High Mill Ave Nw
Massillon OH
330 833-3174

(G-13726)
ROUND ROOM LLC
Also Called: Unknown
3 Massillon Mrktplc Dr Sw (44646-2014)
PHONE................................330 880-0660
EMP: 44 Privately Held
SIC: 4813 Local & long distance telephone communications
PA: Round Room, Llc
525 Congressional Blvd
Carmel IN 46032

(G-13727)
SEIFERT & GROUP INC
2323 Nave Rd Se (44646-8822)
PHONE................................330 833-2700
Tim Seifert, *President*
Michael Lee, *Vice Pres*
EMP: 89
SQ FT: 9,000

SALES (est): 4.5MM Privately Held
WEB: www.seifertgroup.com
SIC: 8748 8711 7375 7371 Business consulting; engineering services; information retrieval services; custom computer programming services; employment agencies

(G-13728)
SEIFERT TECHNOLOGIES INC (PA)
2323 Nave Rd Se (44646-8822)
PHONE................................330 833-2700
Timothy Seifert, *President*
Matthew D Ashton, *Vice Pres*
Richard T Kettler, *Vice Pres*
EMP: 65
SQ FT: 8,900
SALES (est): 12.7MM Privately Held
WEB: www.seifert.com
SIC: 7389 Drafting service, except temporary help; design services

(G-13729)
SHADY HOLLOW CNTRY CLB CO INC
4865 Wales Ave Nw (44646-9396)
PHONE................................330 832-1581
Keith Baklarc, *Manager*
EMP: 100
SALES (est): 5.4MM Privately Held
SIC: 7997 7992 7991 5941 Country club, membership; public golf courses; physical fitness facilities; sporting goods & bicycle shops; eating places

(G-13730)
SHEARERS FOODS LLC (PA)
Also Called: Shearer's Snacks
100 Lincoln Way E (44646-6634)
PHONE................................330 834-4030
C J Fraleigh, *CEO*
Christopher Fraleigh, *CEO*
Montgomery Pooley, *Exec VP*
Dennis Herod, *Prdtn Mgr*
Derrick Johnson, *Prdtn Mgr*
◆ **EMP: 700 EST: 1980**
SQ FT: 200,000
SALES (est): 590.9MM Privately Held
SIC: 2096 5145 Potato chips & similar snacks; snack foods

(G-13731)
STANDARDS TESTING LABS INC (PA)
1845 Harsh Ave Se (44646-7123)
P.O. Box 758 (44648-0758)
PHONE................................330 833-8548
Anthony E Efremoff, *President*
Darryl Fuller, *President*
Tim Dietz, *General Mgr*
Jason Sumney, *General Mgr*
Tim Flood, *Chief Engr*
▲ **EMP: 60 EST: 1972**
SQ FT: 84,000
SALES (est): 14.9MM Privately Held
WEB: www.stllabs.com
SIC: 3829 8734 8071 Testing equipment: abrasion, shearing strength, etc.; product testing laboratory, safety or performance; automobile proving & testing ground; medical laboratories

(G-13732)
STARK MEDICAL SPECIALTIES INC (PA)
323 Marion Ave Nw Ste 200 (44646-3639)
PHONE................................330 837-1111
Seth Brown, *President*
Dr John Uslick, *Corp Secy*
Dr Wayne Gross, *Vice Pres*
Dr George Seese, *Vice Pres*
EMP: 34 EST: 1970
SQ FT: 8,400
SALES (est): 4.6MM Privately Held
SIC: 8011 Physicians' office, including specialists

(G-13733)
TWELVE INC (PA)
Also Called: TWELVE OF OHIO, THE
619 Tremont Ave Sw (44647-6468)
P.O. Box 376 (44648-0376)
PHONE................................330 837-3555
Mark Huemme, *President*

Charles J Bendetta, *Vice Pres*
Linda Sirpilla, *Hum Res Coord*
John D Stoia, *Exec Dir*
Danelle Bryant, *Director*
EMP: 50 EST: 2002
SQ FT: 7,000
SALES: 2MM Privately Held
WEB: www.the12inc.org
SIC: 8361 8322 Boys' Towns; individual & family services

(G-13734)
WESTARK FAMILY SERVICES INC
42 1st St Ne (44646-8406)
PHONE................................330 832-5043
Nancy Maier, *Exec Dir*
EMP: 35
SALES: 888.9K Privately Held
WEB: www.westarkfamilyservices.com
SIC: 8322 Family counseling services

(G-13735)
WHISLER PLUMBING & HEATING INC
2521 Lincoln Way E (44646-5099)
PHONE................................330 833-2875
Jack Sponseller, *President*
Sharon Kannel, *Corp Secy*
Cindy Chapman, *Controller*
EMP: 40 EST: 1930
SQ FT: 2,500
SALES (est): 8.2MM Privately Held
SIC: 1711 Plumbing contractors; warm air heating & air conditioning contractor

(G-13736)
Y M C A CENTRAL STARK COUNTY
Also Called: Jackson Community YMCA
7389 Caritas Cir Nw (44646-9118)
PHONE................................330 830-6275
Jean Campbell, *Branch Mgr*
EMP: 27
SALES (corp-wide): 16.5MM Privately Held
SIC: 8641 7991 8351 7032 Youth organizations; physical fitness facilities; child day care services; youth camps; individual & family services
PA: Y M C A Of Central Stark County
1201 30th St Nw Ste 200a
Canton OH 44709
330 491-9622

(G-13737)
YMCA OF MASSILLON (PA)
Also Called: YMCA OF WESTERN STARK COUNTY
131 Tremont Ave Se (44646-6637)
PHONE................................330 837-5116
Jim Stamford, *Director*
EMP: 30
SQ FT: 16,342
SALES: 2.2MM Privately Held
WEB: www.massillonymca.org
SIC: 8641 Civic associations; youth organizations

(G-13738)
YUND INC
Also Called: Yund Car Care Center
205 1st St Nw (44647-5437)
PHONE................................330 837-9358
Robert K Yund, *President*
Douglad Drushal, *Treasurer*
EMP: 28
SQ FT: 6,764
SALES (est): 1.1MM Privately Held
SIC: 7542 7549 5411 Washing & polishing, automotive; lubrication service, automotive; grocery stores

(G-13739)
ZIEGLER TIRE AND SUPPLY CO (PA)
4150 Millennium Blvd Se (44646-7449)
PHONE................................330 353-1499
William C Ziegler, *President*
John Ziegler Jr, *Vice Pres*
Curtis A Hanner, *Director*
Hommer A Ray, *Director*
Oliver Ziegler, *Director*
EMP: 35 EST: 1919
SQ FT: 112,000

SALES (est): 80.9MM Privately Held
WEB: www.zieglertire.com
SIC: 5531 5014 Automotive tires; truck equipment & parts; truck tires & tubes

Masury
Trumbull County

(G-13740)
GONDA LAWN CARE LLC
7822 2nd St (44438-1435)
PHONE..................................330 701-7232
Steven Gonda, Principal
EMP: 50
SALES (est): 696.8K Privately Held
SIC: 0782 Lawn care services

(G-13741)
P I & I MOTOR EXPRESS INC (PA)
908 Broadway St (44438-1356)
P.O. Box 685, Sharon PA (16146-0685)
PHONE..................................330 448-4035
Joseph Kerola, President
William Kerola, Exec VP
Ray Tedesco, Opers Staff
James JW, Manager
EMP: 128
SQ FT: 76,000
SALES (est): 36.4MM Privately Held
WEB: www.piimx.com
SIC: 8741 4213 4212 Management services; trucking, except local; local trucking, without storage

(G-13742)
PENN-OHIO ELECTRICAL COMPANY
Also Called: Penn Ohio Electrical Contrs
1370 Sharon Hogue Rd (44438-8710)
PHONE..................................330 448-1234
Chris O'Brien, President
John P O'Brien, Vice Pres
Daniel O'Brien, Treasurer
Kirt J O'Brien, Admin Sec
EMP: 30
SQ FT: 5,000
SALES (est): 8.9MM Privately Held
SIC: 1731 General electrical contractor

(G-13743)
UPS GROUND FREIGHT INC
7945 3rd St (44438-1336)
PHONE..................................330 448-0440
Ike Henry, Manager
EMP: 42
SALES (corp-wide): 71.8B Publicly Held
WEB: www.overnite.com
SIC: 4213 Trucking, except local
HQ: Ups Ground Freight, Inc.
 1000 Semmes Ave
 Richmond VA 23224
 866 372-5619

Maumee
Lucas County

(G-13744)
A THOMAS DALAGIANNIS MD
1360 Arrowhead Dr (43537-1728)
PHONE..................................419 887-7000
Thomas Dalagiannis, Partner
Lawrence Baibak, Partner
Jeff Kesler, Partner
EMP: 25 EST: 2001
SALES (est): 350.9K Privately Held
SIC: 8011 Plastic surgeon

(G-13745)
ABOUTGOLF LIMITED (PA)
352 Tomahawk Dr (43537-1612)
PHONE..................................419 482-9095
William Bales, CEO
Bill Bales, Principal
Bill Branum, Technical Mgr
Pat Moore, Regl Sales Mgr
▲ EMP: 55
SQ FT: 20,000

SALES (est): 4.3MM Privately Held
WEB: www.aboutgolf.com
SIC: 7992 Public golf courses

(G-13746)
ACCESSRN INC
1540 S Hlland Sylvania Rd (43537)
PHONE..................................419 698-1988
Joseph Pettee, President
Mary Pettee, President
EMP: 99
SQ FT: 1,500
SALES (est): 8.3MM Privately Held
SIC: 8748 Business consulting

(G-13747)
AKTION ASSOCIATES INCORPORATED
1687 Woodlands Dr (43537-4018)
PHONE..................................419 893-7001
Scott E Irwin, President
EMP: 50
SALES (corp-wide): 69.7MM Privately Held
SIC: 8731 7371 Computer (hardware) development; computer software development & applications
PA: Aktion Associates, Incorporated
 1687 Woodlands Dr
 Maumee OH 43537
 419 893-7001

(G-13748)
AMERICAN FRAME CORPORATION (PA)
400 Tomahawk Dr (43537-1695)
PHONE..................................419 893-5595
Ronald J Mickel, President
Michael Cromly, Vice Pres
Larry Haddad, Vice Pres
Ronald Mickel, Research
Dana Dunbar, Treasurer
▲ EMP: 44
SQ FT: 33,000
SALES (est): 5.6MM Privately Held
WEB: www.americanframe.com
SIC: 7699 5961 5023 3444 Picture framing, custom; mail order house; home furnishings; sheet metalwork

(G-13749)
AMERICAN FRAME CORPORATION
1684 Woodlands Dr Ste 400 (43537-4099)
PHONE..................................419 893-5595
EMP: 31
SALES (corp-wide): 5.6MM Privately Held
SIC: 7699 Picture framing, custom
PA: American Frame Corporation
 400 Tomahawk Dr
 Maumee OH 43537
 419 893-5595

(G-13750)
AMERICAN HEALTH GROUP INC
570 Longbow Dr (43537-1724)
PHONE..................................419 891-1212
Warren Eckles MD, President
EMP: 70
SQ FT: 15,000
SALES: 10MM Privately Held
SIC: 8742 8748 Hospital & health services consultant; business consulting

(G-13751)
ANATRACE PRODUCTS LLC (HQ)
434 W Dussel Dr (43537-1624)
PHONE..................................419 740-6600
Ben Travis, President
Connie Cupilary, General Mgr
Ken Kreh, VP Opers
Mike Drury, CFO
Judy McCormick, Manager
EMP: 34
SALES (est): 7.3MM Privately Held
SIC: 5169 3585 Detergents & soaps, except specialty cleaning; refrigeration & heating equipment

(G-13752)
ANDERSONS INC
Also Called: Retail Distribution Center
1380 Ford St (43537-1733)
P.O. Box 119 (43537-0119)
PHONE..................................419 891-6479
Mike Anderson, Manager
EMP: 120
SALES (corp-wide): 3B Publicly Held
WEB: www.andersonsinc.com
SIC: 4225 General warehousing
PA: The Andersons Inc
 1947 Briarfield Blvd
 Maumee OH 43537
 419 893-5050

(G-13753)
ANDERSONS INC
Also Called: Anderson's Rail Car Service
421 Illinois Ave (43537-1705)
P.O. Box 119 (43537-0119)
PHONE..................................419 891-6634
Gary Beale, Manager
EMP: 38
SALES (corp-wide): 3B Publicly Held
SIC: 4789 Railroad maintenance & repair services
PA: The Andersons Inc
 1947 Briarfield Blvd
 Maumee OH 43537
 419 893-5050

(G-13754)
ANDERSONS INC (PA)
1947 Briarfield Blvd (43537-1690)
P.O. Box 119 (43537-0119)
PHONE..................................419 893-5050
Daniel T Anderson, President
Patrick E Bowe, President
Michael S Irmen, President
Corbett Jorgenson, President
Rasesh H Shah, President
EMP: 150
SQ FT: 245,000
SALES: 3B Publicly Held
WEB: www.andersonsinc.com
SIC: 0723 5191 2874 4789 Crop preparation services for market; cash grain crops market preparation services; farm supplies; fertilizers & agricultural chemicals; seeds & bulbs; phosphatic fertilizers; plant foods, mixed: from plants making phosphatic fertilizer; railroad car repair; rental of railroad cars; grains

(G-13755)
ANDERSONS INC
533 Illinois Ave (43537-1707)
PHONE..................................419 893-5050
Herm Kurrelmeier, Branch Mgr
EMP: 120
SALES (corp-wide): 3B Publicly Held
WEB: www.andersonsinc.com
SIC: 4225 General warehousing
PA: The Andersons Inc
 1947 Briarfield Blvd
 Maumee OH 43537
 419 893-5050

(G-13756)
ANDERSONS AGRICULTURE GROUP LP (HQ)
Also Called: Anderson's Farm
1947 Briarfield Blvd (43537-1690)
P.O. Box 119 (43537-0119)
PHONE..................................419 893-5050
Hal Reed, Partner
Naran Burchinow, Vice Pres
Chris Schwind, Branch Mgr
Jacqueline Woods, Bd of Directors
◆ EMP: 45
SALES (est): 54.1MM
SALES (corp-wide): 3B Publicly Held
SIC: 5191 Fertilizer & fertilizer materials
PA: The Andersons Inc
 1947 Briarfield Blvd
 Maumee OH 43537
 419 893-5050

(G-13757)
ANDY FRAIN SERVICES INC
1715 Indian Wood Cir # 200 (43537-4055)
PHONE..................................419 897-7909
Maryann Cook, Branch Mgr
EMP: 500

SALES (corp-wide): 244.6MM Privately Held
SIC: 7381 Security guard service
PA: Andy Frain Services, Inc.
 761 Shoreline Dr
 Aurora IL 60504
 630 820-3820

(G-13758)
APRIA HEALTHCARE LLC
Also Called: Young Medical
4062 Technology Dr (43537-9263)
PHONE..................................419 471-1919
Shawn Cowell, Branch Mgr
EMP: 54
SQ FT: 22,000 Privately Held
SIC: 5047 7352 Hospital equipment & furniture; medical equipment rental
HQ: Apria Healthcare Llc
 26220 Enterprise Ct
 Lake Forest CA 92630
 949 639-2000

(G-13759)
AUXILIARY ST LUKES HOSPITAL
Also Called: St Lukes Gift Shop
5901 Monclova Rd (43537-1841)
PHONE..................................419 893-5911
Iris Weirich, President
Irene Wolff, Manager
Cheresa Hadsell, Director
EMP: 50
SQ FT: 500
SALES (est): 2.1MM Privately Held
SIC: 5947 8699 Gift shop; charitable organization

(G-13760)
BARNES GROUP INC
Associated Spring Raymond
370 W Dussel Dr Ste A (43537-1604)
PHONE..................................419 891-9292
Peter Korczynski, Opers Mgr
Tracy Allison, Controller
EMP: 33
SALES (corp-wide): 1.5B Publicly Held
WEB: www.barnesgroupinc.com
SIC: 5072 3495 Hardware; wire springs
PA: Barnes Group Inc.
 123 Main St
 Bristol CT 06010
 860 583-7070

(G-13761)
BAUER LAWN MAINTENANCE INC
6341 Monclova Rd (43537-9760)
P.O. Box 8732 (43537-8732)
PHONE..................................419 893-5296
Craig Bauer, President
Lori Bauer, Admin Sec
Jodie Napolski,
EMP: 50
SQ FT: 2,000
SALES (est): 4MM Privately Held
WEB: www.bauerlawn.com
SIC: 0782 4959 Lawn care services; landscape contractors; snowplowing

(G-13762)
BENNETT ENTERPRISES INC
Also Called: Hampton Inn
1409 Reynolds Rd (43537-1625)
PHONE..................................419 893-1004
Ken Brandt, Manager
EMP: 30
SQ FT: 3,613
SALES (corp-wide): 66.6MM Privately Held
WEB: www.bennett-enterprises.com
SIC: 7011 Hotels & motels
PA: Bennett Enterprises, Inc.
 27476 Holiday Ln
 Perrysburg OH 43551
 419 874-1933

(G-13763)
BPF ENTERPRISES LTD
Also Called: Cold Fire Decor
1901 Middlesbrough Ct # 2 (43537-2202)
PHONE..................................419 855-2545
Brian Furlong,
EMP: 100
SALES (est): 3.1MM Privately Held
SIC: 7389 ;

(G-13764)
BPREX CLOSURES LLC
Also Called: Research & Development
1695 Indian Cir Ste 116 (43537)
PHONE................................812 424-2904
Michael Wenerd, *Plt & Fclts Mgr*
EMP: 100 **Publicly Held**
SIC: 5199 Packaging materials
HQ: Bprex Closures, Llc
101 Oakley St
Evansville IN 47710
812 424-2904

(G-13765)
BRANDYWINE MASTER ASSN
7705 Pilgrims Lndg (43537-9571)
PHONE................................419 866-0135
Charles Zsarnay, *Treasurer*
EMP: 56
SALES (est): 588.5K **Privately Held**
SIC: 8641 Condominium association

(G-13766)
BRIDGEPOINT RISK MGT LLC
1440 Arrowhead Dr (43537-4016)
PHONE................................419 794-1075
Greg Jones, *Branch Mgr*
EMP: 34
SALES (corp-wide): 9.6MM **Privately Held**
SIC: 8741 Management services
PA: Bridgepoint Risk Management Llc
5 Greenwich Office Park
Greenwich CT 06831
203 274-8010

(G-13767)
BRONDES ALL MAKES AUTO LEASING
1511 Reynolds Rd (43537-1601)
PHONE................................419 887-1511
Phillip Brondes Jr, *President*
EMP: 86
SALES (corp-wide): 4.2MM **Privately Held**
SIC: 7515 Passenger car leasing
PA: Ford Brondes
5545 Secor Rd
Toledo OH 43623
419 473-1411

(G-13768)
CELLCO PARTNERSHIP
Also Called: Verizon
1378 Conant St (43537-1610)
PHONE................................419 897-9133
David Johnson, *Branch Mgr*
EMP: 71
SALES (corp-wide): 130.8B **Publicly Held**
SIC: 4812 5999 Cellular telephone services; telephone equipment & systems
HQ: Cellco Partnership
1 Verizon Way
Basking Ridge NJ 07920

(G-13769)
CENTAUR MAIL INC
Also Called: Centaur Associates
4064 Technology Dr Ste A (43537-9739)
PHONE................................419 887-5857
Michael J Walters, *President*
Dennise Kamcza, *Exec VP*
Lisa Willford, *Vice Pres*
EMP: 50
SQ FT: 10,500
SALES (est): 5.9MM **Privately Held**
WEB: www.centaur-associates.com
SIC: 4215 Parcel delivery, vehicular

(G-13770)
CHECKER NOTIONS COMPANY INC (PA)
Also Called: Checker Distributors
400 W Dussel Dr Ste B (43537-1636)
PHONE................................419 893-3636
J Robert Krieger III, *President*
Bradley Krieger, *Vice Pres*
Jim Steedman, *Opers Mgr*
Kevin Phillips, *Warehouse Mgr*
Amy Hoard, *Receiver*
▲ **EMP:** 89
SQ FT: 120,000

SALES (est): 82MM **Privately Held**
WEB: www.checkerdist.com
SIC: 5131 5199 5949 5162 Sewing supplies & notions; art goods & supplies; quilting materials & supplies; plastics basic shapes

(G-13771)
COLGAN-DAVIS INC
1682 Lance Pointe Rd (43537-1600)
PHONE................................419 893-6116
Patrick Davis, *President*
Marlene Davis, *Corp Secy*
EMP: 25
SQ FT: 9,600
SALES: 4.9MM **Privately Held**
SIC: 1731 General electrical contractor

(G-13772)
COLONIAL COURIER SERVICE INC
409 Osage St (43537)
PHONE................................419 891-0922
Ken Miller, *Manager*
EMP: 29
SALES (corp-wide): 4.1MM **Privately Held**
WEB: www.forwardair.net
SIC: 4731 Truck transportation brokers
PA: Colonial Courier Service Inc
413 Osage St
Maumee OH 43537
419 891-0922

(G-13773)
COLONIAL COURIER SERVICE INC (PA)
413 Osage St (43537-1637)
PHONE................................419 891-0922
Judith J Miller, *President*
Robert E Miller, *Vice Pres*
EMP: 30
SQ FT: 35,000
SALES (est): 4.1MM **Privately Held**
SIC: 4731 Freight forwarding

(G-13774)
COLT ENTERPRISES INC
Also Called: Right At Home
133 E John St (43537-3341)
PHONE................................567 336-6062
John Baldwin, *Owner*
Connie Fox, *Assistant*
EMP: 30
SALES (est): 667.1K **Privately Held**
SIC: 8082 Visiting nurse service

(G-13775)
CONSULATE HEALTHCARE INC (PA)
Also Called: PARKSIDE MANOR
3231 Manley Rd (43537-9680)
PHONE................................419 865-1248
Lynn Buchlee, *President*
Jeff Orloski, *Exec Dir*
EMP: 50
SALES: 5.6MM **Privately Held**
SIC: 8051 8052 Skilled nursing care facilities; intermediate care facilities

(G-13776)
CONSULATE MANAGEMENT CO LLC
Also Called: Swan Point Care Center
3600 Butz Rd (43537-9691)
PHONE................................419 867-7926
Patrick Airson, *Administration*
EMP: 80
SALES (corp-wide): 580.2MM **Privately Held**
WEB: www.tandemhealthcare.com
SIC: 8051 Skilled nursing care facilities
PA: Consulate Management Company, Llc
800 Concourse Pkwy S
Maitland FL 32751
407 571-1550

(G-13777)
CRAIG TRANSPORTATION CO
819 Kingsbury St Ste 102 (43537-1861)
P.O. Box 1010, Perrysburg (43552-1010)
PHONE................................419 874-7981
Lance C Craig, *Principal*
Johnathan Craig, *COO*
Mike Craig, *Vice Pres*

Phil Jacks, *Vice Pres*
Chris Simmons, *Vice Pres*
EMP: 40 **EST:** 1929
SQ FT: 14,000
SALES (est): 22.6MM **Privately Held**
WEB: www.craigtransport.com
SIC: 4731 4213 Freight transportation arrangement; trucking, except local

(G-13778)
CROGHAN BANCSHARES INC
6465 Wheatstone Ct (43537-8610)
PHONE................................419 794-9399
Kirby Holman, *Branch Mgr*
EMP: 90 **Publicly Held**
SIC: 6029 6021 Commercial banks; national commercial banks
PA: Croghan Bancshares, Inc.
323 Croghan St
Fremont OH 43420

(G-13779)
DANBERRY CO
3555 Briarfield Blvd (43537-9383)
PHONE................................419 866-8888
Heather Lapoint, *Buyer*
Dan McQuillen, *Branch Mgr*
EMP: 60
SALES (corp-wide): 24MM **Privately Held**
SIC: 6531 Real estate agent, residential
PA: The Danberry Co
3242 Executive Pkwy # 203
Toledo OH 43606
419 534-6592

(G-13780)
DARI PIZZA ENTERPRISES II INC
1683 Woodlands Dr Ste A (43537-4052)
PHONE................................419 534-3000
Suzan Dari, *President*
Omar Dari, *Principal*
EMP: 150
SALES (est): 4.8MM **Privately Held**
SIC: 5812 8742 6531 Lunchrooms & cafeterias; new business start-up consultant; real estate agents & managers

(G-13781)
DEFINITIONS OF DESIGN INC
467 W Dussel Dr (43537-4210)
PHONE................................419 891-0188
EMP: 35
SALES (est): 863.2K **Privately Held**
SIC: 7231 Beauty Shop

(G-13782)
EATON-AEROQUIP LLC
1660 Indian Wood Cir (43537-4004)
PHONE................................419 891-7775
Howard Selland, *President*
EMP: 90 **Privately Held**
SIC: 8711 3594 3593 3561 Professional engineer; fluid power pumps & motors; fluid power cylinders & actuators; pumps & pumping equipment; fluid power valves & hose fittings; rubber & plastics hose & beltings
HQ: Eaton Aeroquip Llc
1000 Eaton Blvd
Cleveland OH 44122
216 523-5000

(G-13783)
ED SCHMIDT CHEVROLET INC
1425 Reynolds Rd (43537-1625)
P.O. Box 1180 (43537-8180)
PHONE................................419 897-8600
Robert E Schmidt, *President*
Charles R Schmidt, *Vice Pres*
John Schmidt, *Vice Pres*
William C Wagoner, *Treasurer*
Lynn Schmidt, *Admin Sec*
EMP: 60
SQ FT: 83,000
SALES (est): 11.7MM **Privately Held**
SIC: 5511 7515 Automobiles, new & used; passenger car leasing

(G-13784)
ELIZABETH SCOTT INC
Also Called: Elizabeth Scott Mem Care Ctr
2720 Albon Rd (43537-9752)
PHONE................................419 865-3002
Paul Bucher, *President*
Debra Bucher, *Vice Pres*

Deb Bucher, *Human Res Dir*
Patrick McSurley, *Director*
Kristin Kohring, *Nursing Dir*
EMP: 116
SQ FT: 73,000
SALES (est): 6.2MM **Privately Held**
SIC: 8059 Nursing home, except skilled & intermediate care facility

(G-13785)
ENTELCO CORPORATION (PA)
6528 Weatherfield Ct (43537-9468)
PHONE................................419 872-4620
Stephen Stranahan, *President*
EMP: 63
SQ FT: 3,000
SALES: 89.4K **Privately Held**
WEB: www.en-tel.com
SIC: 6719 Investment holding companies, except banks

(G-13786)
EPILEPSY CNTR OF NRTHWSTRN OH
1701 Holland Rd (43537-1699)
PHONE................................419 867-5950
Betty Hartman, *Marketing Staff*
Roy J Cherry, *Exec Dir*
Chad Bringman, *Director*
EMP: 56 **EST:** 1977
SALES: 3.4MM **Privately Held**
SIC: 8399 Fund raising organization, non-fee basis

(G-13787)
ERIE SHORES CREDIT UNION INC (PA)
1688 Woodlands Dr (43537-4069)
P.O. Box 9037 (43537-9037)
PHONE................................419 897-8110
Ralph Kubacki, *CEO*
Jim Troknya, *Ch of Bd*
EMP: 31
SQ FT: 8,536
SALES (est): 5.2MM **Privately Held**
SIC: 6062 State credit unions, not federally chartered

(G-13788)
FALLEN TIMBERS FMLY PHYSICIANS
Also Called: Bertka, Vicki M MD
5705 Monclova Rd (43537-1875)
PHONE................................419 893-3321
John Croci, *Business Mgr*
Vicki Bertka, *Corp Secy*
Donna Woodson, *Vice Pres*
Marcie Williams, *Manager*
Daniel R Sullivan, *Manager*
EMP: 55
SALES (est): 4.6MM **Privately Held**
WEB: www.ftfp.net
SIC: 8011 General & family practice, physician/surgeon

(G-13789)
FASTER INC
6560 Weatherfield Ct (43537-9468)
PHONE................................419 868-8197
Stijn Vriends, *President*
Francesco Arosio, *President*
Ted Frost, *Vice Pres*
Tammy Montgomery, *Vice Pres*
Nate Walton, *Regl Sales Mgr*
▲ **EMP:** 32
SQ FT: 16,000
SALES: 31MM
SALES (corp-wide): 352.2K **Privately Held**
WEB: www.fasterinc.com
SIC: 5085 Industrial fittings
HQ: Faster Srl
Via Ariosto 7
Rivolta D'adda CR 26027
036 337-7211

(G-13790)
FED EX ROB CARPENTER
4348 Beck Dr (43537-1804)
PHONE................................419 260-1889
EMP: 26
SALES: 1MM **Privately Held**
SIC: 4215 Courier Service

(G-13791)
FELLER FINCH & ASSOCIATES INC (PA)
1683 Woodlands Dr Ste A (43537-4052)
PHONE...................................419 893-3680
Donald L Feller, *President*
Chris Crisenbery, *Vice Pres*
Gregory N Feller, *Vice Pres*
EMP: 40
SQ FT: 5,000
SALES (est): 3.3MM **Privately Held**
WEB: www.fellerfinch.com
SIC: 8713 8711 Surveying services; civil engineering

(G-13792)
FITNESS INTERNATIONAL LLC
1361 Conant St (43537-1609)
PHONE...................................419 482-7740
Joe Walker, *Branch Mgr*
EMP: 34
SALES (corp-wide): 173.1MM **Privately Held**
SIC: 7991 Physical fitness facilities
PA: Fitness International, Llc
3161 Michelson Dr Ste 600
Irvine CA 92612
949 255-7200

(G-13793)
FOCUS HEALTHCARE OF OHIO LLC
1725 Timber Line Rd (43537-4015)
PHONE...................................419 891-9333
Carey Plummer,
EMP: 50
SALES (est): 2.5MM
SALES (corp-wide): 3.7MM **Privately Held**
WEB: www.focushc.com
SIC: 8063 Psychiatric hospitals
PA: Focus Healthcare Of Tennessee, Llc
7429 Shallowford Rd
Chattanooga TN 37421
423 308-2560

(G-13794)
FRITO-LAY NORTH AMERICA INC
6501 Monclova Rd (43537-9657)
PHONE...................................419 893-8171
Don Stupica, *Manager*
EMP: 80
SQ FT: 11,250
SALES (corp-wide): 64.6B **Publicly Held**
WEB: www.fritolay.com
SIC: 8741 5149 Management services; groceries & related products
HQ: Frito-Lay North America, Inc.
7701 Legacy Dr
Plano TX 75024

(G-13795)
GENTIVA HEALTH SERVICES INC
1745 Indian Wood Cir # 200 (43537-4042)
PHONE...................................419 887-6700
Rey Cilinsky, *Branch Mgr*
EMP: 100
SALES (corp-wide): 6B **Privately Held**
SIC: 8059 Personal care home, with health care
HQ: Gentiva Health Services, Inc.
3350 Riverwood Pkwy Se # 1
Atlanta GA 30339
770 951-6450

(G-13796)
GILMORE JASION MAHLER LTD (PA)
1715 Indian Wood Cir # 100 (43537-4055)
PHONE...................................419 794-2000
Kevin M Gilmore, *Managing Prtnr*
Adele Jasion, *Partner*
Andrew Mahler, *Partner*
Adele Jaison, *CPA*
EMP: 75
SALES: 10MM **Privately Held**
WEB: www.gjmltd.com
SIC: 8721 Certified public accountant

(G-13797)
GLASS CITY FEDERAL CREDIT UN (PA)
1340 Arrowhead Dr (43537-1741)
PHONE...................................419 887-1000
Mark Slates, *President*
David Kramb, *Exec VP*
Laura St John, *Manager*
EMP: 25
SQ FT: 22,190
SALES: 7.5MM **Privately Held**
WEB: www.glasscityfcu.com
SIC: 6061 Federal credit unions

(G-13798)
HANSON PRODUCTIONS INC
1695 Indian Wood Cir # 200 (43537-4082)
PHONE...................................419 327-6100
Steven Hanson, *President*
Jennifer Samson, *Treasurer*
John Ette Schweiss, *Manager*
EMP: 40
SQ FT: 8,000
SALES (est): 3.7MM **Privately Held**
WEB: www.hansoninc.com
SIC: 7922 Television program, including commercial producers

(G-13799)
HELM AND ASSOCIATES INC
501 W Sophia St Unit 8 (43537-1884)
PHONE...................................419 893-1480
Keith Helminski, *President*
Jerry Helminski, *Vice Pres*
Maria Iwinski, *Shareholder*
John Schrein, *Admin Sec*
EMP: 25
SQ FT: 6,900
SALES (est): 3.7MM **Privately Held**
WEB: www.helmandassociates.com
SIC: 1711 1731 1541 Warm air heating & air conditioning contractor; refrigeration contractor; plumbing contractors; electrical work; industrial buildings & warehouses

(G-13800)
HERITAGE HEALTH CARE SERVICES (PA)
1745 Indian Wood Cir # 252 (43537-4168)
PHONE...................................419 867-2002
Rich Adams, *President*
Marian Stillwell, *Opers Staff*
Liz Taylor, *Human Res Dir*
Emily Dickman, *Director*
EMP: 150
SQ FT: 2,500
SALES (est): 9.8MM **Privately Held**
SIC: 8082 Home health care services

(G-13801)
HIGH POINT ANIMAL HOSPITAL
6020 Manley Rd (43537-1531)
PHONE...................................419 865-3611
Thomas Mowery, *President*
EMP: 25
SALES (est): 1.8MM **Privately Held**
WEB: www.highpointanimalhospital.com
SIC: 0742 Animal hospital services, pets & other animal specialties

(G-13802)
IMAGE BY J & K LLC
1575 Henthorne Dr (43537-1372)
PHONE...................................888 667-6929
James Land IV, *Mng Member*
EMP: 400
SQ FT: 10,000
SALES (est): 51.6MM **Privately Held**
SIC: 3589 7217 7349 7342 Floor washing & polishing machines, commercial; carpet & upholstery cleaning; building & office cleaning services; service station cleaning & degreasing; air duct cleaning; rest room cleaning service

(G-13803)
INOVATIVE FACILITY SVCS LLC
1573 Henthorne Dr (43537-1372)
P.O. Box 1048, Holland (43528-1048)
PHONE...................................419 861-1710
Brett Harlett,
Richard Werderman,
EMP: 400

SALES (est): 6.1MM
SALES (corp-wide): 547.1MM **Privately Held**
WEB: www.kbs-clean.com
SIC: 7349 Janitorial service, contract basis
PA: Kellermyer Bergensons Services, Llc
1575 Henthorne Dr
Maumee OH 43537
419 867-4300

(G-13804)
INTERNATIONAL UNION UNITED AU
Also Called: Region 2b
1691 Woodlands Dr (43537-4018)
PHONE...................................419 893-4677
Lloyd Mahaffey, *Director*
EMP: 25
SALES (corp-wide): 237.6MM **Privately Held**
SIC: 8631 Labor union
PA: International Union, United Automobile, Aerospace And Agricultural Implement Workers Of Am
8000 E Jefferson Ave
Detroit MI 48214
313 926-5000

(G-13805)
JDI GROUP INC
360 W Dussel Dr (43537-1631)
PHONE...................................419 725-7161
Timothy Fry, *President*
Matthew Davis, *Principal*
Roxanne Manger, *Engineer*
Troy Woods, *Design Engr*
Lorin Hahn, *Sr Project Mgr*
EMP: 78
SQ FT: 27,000
SALES (est): 15MM **Privately Held**
WEB: www.cmdtechnologies.net
SIC: 8712 8711 Architectural engineering; engineering services

(G-13806)
JOHNSON CNTRLS SEC SLTIONS LLC
1722 Indian Wood Cir F (43537-4044)
PHONE...................................419 243-8400
Steve Carlson, *General Mgr*
EMP: 35 **Privately Held**
WEB: www.adt.com
SIC: 7382 Burglar alarm maintenance & monitoring; fire alarm maintenance & monitoring
HQ: Johnson Controls Security Solutions Llc
6600 Congress Ave
Boca Raton FL 33487
561 264-2071

(G-13807)
KELLERMYER BERGENSONS SVCS LLC (PA)
1575 Henthorne Dr (43537-1372)
PHONE...................................419 867-4300
Mark Minasian, *CEO*
Bob Thompson, *President*
Clay Davis, *Regional Mgr*
Maritza Morris, *Regional Mgr*
Marc Schwiesow, *Regional Mgr*
EMP: 60
SQ FT: 40,000
SALES (est): 547.1MM **Privately Held**
WEB: www.kbs-clean.com
SIC: 7349 Janitorial service, contract basis

(G-13808)
KUHLMAN CORPORATION (PA)
Also Called: Kuhlman Construction Products
1845 Indian Wood Cir (43537-4072)
P.O. Box 714, Toledo (43697-0714)
PHONE...................................419 897-6000
Timothy L Goligoski, *President*
Kenneth Kuhlman, *Vice Pres*
Terry Schaefer, *CFO*
Tim Casey, *Sales Mgr*
▲ EMP: 150 EST: 1901
SQ FT: 18,000
SALES (est): 50.1MM **Privately Held**
WEB: www.kuhlman-corp.com
SIC: 4226 5032 3273 Special warehousing & storage; brick, stone & related material; brick, except refractory; building blocks; sewer pipe, clay; ready-mixed concrete

(G-13809)
LIFE CONNECTION OF OHIO
3661 Brrfeld Blvd Ste 105 (43537)
PHONE...................................419 893-4891
Douglas Heiney, *President*
John Emmerich, *CFO*
Kara Steele, *Pub Rel Dir*
EMP: 35
SQ FT: 52,000
SALES: 8.7MM **Privately Held**
WEB: www.lifeconnectionofohio.org
SIC: 8099 Organ bank

(G-13810)
LMT ENTERPRISES MAUMEE INC
1772 Indian Wood Cir (43537-4006)
PHONE...................................419 891-7325
Mark E Thees, *President*
EMP: 45
SQ FT: 24,000
SALES (est): 3.5MM **Privately Held**
WEB: www.eventmakers.com
SIC: 6512 5812 Commercial & industrial building operation; caterers

(G-13811)
LOTT INDUSTRIES INCORPORATED
1645 Holland Rd (43537-1622)
PHONE...................................419 891-5215
Robert Stebbins, *Manager*
EMP: 371
SALES (corp-wide): 4.8MM **Privately Held**
WEB: www.lottindustries.com
SIC: 8331 Sheltered workshop
PA: Lott Industries Incorporated
3350 Hill Ave
Toledo OH 43607
419 534-4980

(G-13812)
MANNIK & SMITH GROUP INC (PA)
Also Called: M S G
1800 Indian Wood Cir (43537-4086)
PHONE...................................419 891-2222
C Michael Smith, *President*
Rich Bertz, *Principal*
John Browning, *Principal*
Brian Geer, *Principal*
Mark Smoley, *Principal*
EMP: 205 EST: 1955
SQ FT: 36,500
SALES: 34.3MM **Privately Held**
WEB: www.manniksmithgroup.com
SIC: 8711 8748 Consulting engineer; civil engineering; business consulting

(G-13813)
MARBLE RESTORATION INC
Also Called: Decorative Flooring Services
6539 Weatherfield Ct (43537-9018)
PHONE...................................419 865-9000
Dan Grant, *President*
Gary J Haskins, *Treasurer*
Michael McAuley, *Admin Sec*
▲ EMP: 75
SQ FT: 12,000
SALES (est): 5.9MM **Privately Held**
WEB: www.dfs-flooring.com
SIC: 5713 1752 Carpets; carpet laying

(G-13814)
MARITZ TRAVEL COMPANY
1740 Indian Wood Cir (43537-4174)
PHONE...................................660 626-1501
Janet Drummond, *Branch Mgr*
EMP: 312
SALES (corp-wide): 1.2B **Privately Held**
SIC: 4724 Travel Agency
HQ: Maritz Global Events Inc.
1395 N Highway Dr
Fenton MO 63026
636 827-4000

(G-13815)
MARITZCX RESEARCH LLC
1740 Indian Wood Cir (43537-4174)
PHONE...................................419 725-4000
Mary Gomoll, *Branch Mgr*
Shawn Stclair, *Director*
Babs Marshall, *Executive Asst*
EMP: 443

SALES (corp-wide): 1.2B **Privately Held**
SIC: 8732 Market analysis or research
HQ: Maritzcx Research Llc
1355 N Highway Dr
Fenton MO 63026
636 827-4000

(G-13816)
**MATRIX TECHNOLOGIES INC
(PA)**
1760 Indian Wood Cir (43537-4070)
PHONE.................................419 897-7200
David L Bishop, *President*
David J Blaida, *Vice Pres*
Donald J Krompak, *Treasurer*
EMP: 100
SQ FT: 39,000
SALES (est): 47.9MM **Privately Held**
WEB: www.matrixti.com
SIC: 8711 Engineering services

(G-13817)
**MAUMEE LODGE NO 1850
BNVLT**
Also Called: ELKS OF THE UNITED STATES
OF A
137 W Wayne St (43537-2150)
PHONE.................................419 893-7272
Charles E Scott, *Principal*
Tom Biggs, *Principal*
Harry Crooks, *Principal*
EMP: 25
SQ FT: 18,000
SALES: 601.2K **Privately Held**
SIC: 8641 Fraternal associations; bars &
restaurants, members only

(G-13818)
**MAUMEE LODGING
ENTERPRISES**
Also Called: Knights Inn
1520 S Hlland Sylvania Rd (43537)
PHONE.................................419 865-1380
Bobby Patel, *Principal*
EMP: 75
SQ FT: 51,552
SALES (est): 1.4MM **Privately Held**
SIC: 7011 Hotels & motels

(G-13819)
MAUMEE OB GYN ASSOC
660 Beaver Creek Cir # 200 (43537-1746)
PHONE.................................419 891-6201
Christine McMahon, *Manager*
EMP: 47
SALES (est): 2.2MM **Privately Held**
WEB: www.promedical.com
SIC: 8011 Gynecologist; general & family
practice, physician/surgeon

(G-13820)
**MCNAUGHTON-MCKAY ELC
OHIO INC**
355 Tomahawk Dr Unit 1 (43537-1757)
PHONE.................................419 891-0262
Timothy J Krucki, *Branch Mgr*
EMP: 45
SQ FT: 38,000
SALES (corp-wide): 822.5MM **Privately
Held**
WEB: www.mc.mc.com
SIC: 5063 Electrical supplies
HQ: Mcnaughton-Mckay Electric Company
Of Ohio, Inc.
2255 Citygate Dr
Columbus OH 43219
614 476-2800

(G-13821)
**MEYER HILL LYNCH
CORPORATION**
1771 Indian Wood Cir (43537-4009)
PHONE.................................419 897-9797
D Stuart Lovee, *President*
D Stuart Love, *President*
Robert Shick, *Vice Pres*
Chad King, *Project Mgr*
Jason Foster, *Engineer*
▼ **EMP:** 40
SQ FT: 20,000
SALES (est): 30.9MM **Privately Held**
WEB: www.mhl.com
SIC: 5045 Computer peripheral equipment

(G-13822)
MOSLEY PFUNDT & GLICK INC
6455 Wheatstone Ct (43537-9403)
PHONE.................................419 861-1120
Larry Mosley, *President*
Gary Pfundt, *Vice Pres*
Garth Tebay, *Mng Member*
Jane Glick, *Admin Sec*
EMP: 25
SQ FT: 4,974
SALES (est): 1.9MM **Privately Held**
WEB: www.tebaymosley.com
SIC: 8721 Certified public accountant

(G-13823)
NATIONAL AMUSEMENTS INC
Also Called: Showcase Cinemas
2300 Village Dr W # 1700 (43537-7550)
PHONE.................................419 215-3095
Elena Allen, *Manager*
EMP: 80
SALES (corp-wide): 14.5B **Publicly Held**
WEB: www.nationalamusements.com
SIC: 7832 Motion picture theaters, except
drive-in
PA: National Amusements, Inc.
846 University Ave
Norwood MA 02062
781 461-1600

(G-13824)
**NORTHWEST OHIO CHAPTER
CFMA**
145 Chesterfield Ln (43537-2209)
PHONE.................................419 891-1040
Georgia L Martin, *Principal*
EMP: 49
SALES: 42.4K **Privately Held**
SIC: 6022 State commercial banks

(G-13825)
NURSING RESOURCES CORP
3600 Brrfeld Blvd Ste 100 (43537)
PHONE.................................419 333-3000
David Venzke, *President*
Ann Worden, *Vice Pres*
EMP: 200
SALES (est): 7.8MM **Privately Held**
WEB: www.nursingresources.com
SIC: 8059 8082 7363 Personal care
home, with health care; home health care
services; help supply services

(G-13826)
**OHIOCARE AMBULATORY
SURGERY**
Also Called: Surgi Care Ambulatory
5959 Monclova Rd (43537-1888)
PHONE.................................419 897-5501
Dawn Lane, *Administration*
Frank L Bartell,
Gerald Cichocki,
EMP: 30
SQ FT: 16,000
SALES (est): 3.6MM **Privately Held**
SIC: 8011 Ambulatory surgical center; sur-
geon

(G-13827)
**OMICRON INVESTMENT
COMPANY LLC**
145 Chesterfield Ln (43537-2209)
PHONE.................................419 891-1040
William Vaughan,
Edwin Bergsmark,
Richard Bosleman,
William J Horst,
James Kline,
EMP: 51
SQ FT: 16,000
SALES (est): 1.3MM **Privately Held**
SIC: 8721 Certified public accountant

(G-13828)
**OPHTHALMOLOGY
ASSOCIATES OF**
Also Called: Eye Institute of Northwestern
3509 Briarfield Blvd (43537-9383)
PHONE.................................419 865-3866
Carol R Kollarits MD, *President*
John Bay, *Corp Secy*
Frank Kollarits, *Vice Pres*
EMP: 35
SQ FT: 8,500

SALES (est): 3.3MM **Privately Held**
SIC: 8011 Ophthalmologist

(G-13829)
ORC INTERNATIONAL INC
1900 Indian Wood Cir # 200 (43537-4039)
PHONE.................................419 893-0029
Terry Reilly, *Vice Pres*
Jeri Piehl, *Mktg Dir*
Debi Jankowski, *Manager*
EMP: 30 **Privately Held**
WEB: www.opinionresearch.com
SIC: 8732 Survey service: marketing, loca-
tion, etc.; market analysis or research
HQ: Orc International, Inc
902 Carnegie Ctr Ste 220
Princeton NJ 08540
609 452-5400

(G-13830)
PARAMOUNT CARE INC (DH)
Also Called: Paramount Health Care
1901 Indian Wood Cir (43537-4002)
P.O. Box 928, Toledo (43697-0928)
PHONE.................................419 887-2500
John C Randolph, *President*
Jeff Martin, *Vice Pres*
Mark Moser, *Vice Pres*
Rochelle Barmash, *Finance Mgr*
Timothy Dehoff, *Financial Analy*
EMP: 365
SQ FT: 59,900
SALES (est): 37.8MM
SALES (corp-wide): 2.1B **Privately Held**
WEB: www.paramounthealthcare.com
SIC: 6321 Accident insurance carriers;
health insurance carriers
HQ: Promedica Insurance Corp
1901 Indian Wood Cir
Maumee OH 43537
419 887-2500

(G-13831)
**PARK MANAGEMENT
SPECIALIST (PA)**
216 W Wayne St (43537-2125)
PHONE.................................419 893-4879
Dean S Skillman, *President*
EMP: 60 **EST:** 1979
SQ FT: 3,500
SALES (est): 3.8MM **Privately Held**
SIC: 6515 Mobile home site operators

(G-13832)
**PARKER STEEL
INTERNATIONAL INC (PA)**
Also Called: Parker Steel Company
1625 Indian Wood Cir (43537-4003)
P.O. Box 1508 (43537-8508)
PHONE.................................419 473-2481
Paul D Goldner, *Ch of Bd*
Jerry Hidalgo, *President*
Vicki Kretz, *VP Finance*
▲ **EMP:** 37
SQ FT: 6,500
SALES (est): 17MM **Privately Held**
WEB: www.metricmetal.com
SIC: 5051 Steel; aluminum bars, rods, in-
gots, sheets, pipes, plates, etc.; miscella-
neous nonferrous products

(G-13833)
PONTOON SOLUTIONS INC
1695 Indian Wood Cir # 200 (43537-4082)
PHONE.................................855 881-1533
EMP: 75
SALES (corp-wide): 27.9B **Privately Held**
SIC: 7363 Temporary help service
HQ: Pontoon Solutions, Inc.
1301 Riverplace Blvd # 1000
Jacksonville FL 32207
855 881-1533

(G-13834)
PROMEDICA
1695 Indian Wood Cir # 100 (43537-4083)
PHONE.................................419 291-3450
Benjamin Vickers, *Systems Dir*
EMP: 86
SALES (est): 17.5MM **Privately Held**
SIC: 8011 Clinic, operated by physicians

(G-13835)
**PROMEDICA HEALTH SYSTEMS
INC**
Also Called: Promedidcal Heath Syytem
660 Beaver Creek Cir # 200 (43537-1745)
PHONE.................................419 891-6201
EMP: 30
SALES (corp-wide): 2.1B **Privately Held**
SIC: 8011 Offices & clinics of medical doc-
tors
PA: Promedica Health Systems, Inc.
100 Madison Ave
Toledo OH 43604
567 585-7454

(G-13836)
**PRUDENTIAL INSUR CO OF
AMER**
1705 Indian Wood Cir # 115 (43537-4074)
PHONE.................................419 893-6227
Ronald Fleming, *Manager*
EMP: 50
SALES (corp-wide): 62.9B **Publicly Held**
SIC: 6411 Insurance agents, brokers &
service
HQ: The Prudential Insurance Company Of
America
751 Broad St
Newark NJ 07102
973 802-6000

(G-13837)
PSYCHIATRIC SOLUTIONS INC
1725 Timber Line Rd (43537-4015)
PHONE.................................419 891-9333
Elicia Bunch, *Manager*
EMP: 137
SALES (corp-wide): 10.7B **Publicly Held**
WEB: www.intermountainhospital.com
SIC: 8011 Psychiatric clinic
HQ: Psychiatric Solutions, Inc.
6640 Carothers Pkwy # 500
Franklin TN 37067
615 312-5700

(G-13838)
**PULMONARY CRTCAL CARE
SPCALIST**
1661 Holland Rd Ste 200 (43537-1659)
PHONE.................................419 843-7800
Hany Khalil MD Fccp, *President*
EMP: 30 **EST:** 1997
SQ FT: 3,700
SALES (est): 3.8MM **Privately Held**
WEB: www.pccsionline.com
SIC: 8011 Pulmonary specialist, physi-
cian/surgeon

(G-13839)
**QUEST QUALITY SERVICES
LLC**
8036 Joshua Ln (43537-9293)
PHONE.................................419 704-7407
Joe Braker, *CFO*
Stephen Bowen,
EMP: 100
SQ FT: 5,000
SALES (est): 1.3MM **Privately Held**
WEB: www.questtinc.com
SIC: 7549 Automotive maintenance serv-
ices

(G-13840)
**RANDSTAD PROFESSIONALS
US LLC**
Also Called: Mergis Group, The
1745 Indian Wood Cir # 150 (43537-4042)
PHONE.................................419 893-2400
Scott Gearig, *Principal*
EMP: 39
SALES (corp-wide): 27.2B **Privately Held**
SIC: 7363 Temporary help service
HQ: Randstad Professionals Us, Llc
150 Presidential Way Fl 4
Woburn MA 01801

(G-13841)
RANDY L FORK INC
Also Called: Honda East
1230 Conant St (43537-1608)
PHONE.................................419 891-1230
Sheryl Fork, *Owner*
Sheryl A Fork, *Vice Pres*
EMP: 36

SQ FT: 25,000
SALES (est): 6.3MM **Privately Held**
WEB: www.hondaeasttoledo.com
SIC: 7699 5571 Motorcycle repair service;
all-terrain vehicles

(G-13842)
RECYCLING SERVICES INC (PA)
Also Called: Allshred Services
3940 Technology Dr (43537-9264)
PHONE....................................419 381-7762
Willie Geiser, *President*
Jarret Silagyi, *Opers Staff*
Mallory Guerrero, *Human Res Mgr*
Jeffrey Green, *Sales Staff*
Staci Bailey, *Mktg Dir*
EMP: 40
SQ FT: 47,000
SALES (est): 9.5MM **Privately Held**
WEB: www.allshredservices.com
SIC: 7389 Document & office record de-
struction

(G-13843)
**RESIDENTIAL MANAGEMENT
SYSTEMS**
1446 Reynolds Rd Ste 100 (43537-1634)
PHONE....................................419 255-6060
Monica Schmidt, *Director*
EMP: 70
SALES (corp-wide): 4.5MM **Privately
Held**
SIC: 8361 Residential care for the handi-
capped
PA: Residential Management Systems, Inc
402 E Wilson Bridge Rd
Worthington OH 43085
614 880-6014

(G-13844)
RESOLUTE BANK
3425 Brrfeld Blvd Ste 100 (43537)
PHONE....................................419 868-1750
Kevin Rahe, *CEO*
Gary Hoyer, *Vice Pres*
G Mark Loreto, *Vice Pres*
Susan Martin, *Vice Pres*
Sarah Young, *Opers Mgr*
EMP: 70
SALES (est): 17.4MM **Privately Held**
SIC: 6036 Savings institutions, not feder-
ally chartered

(G-13845)
RICHARD J NELSON MD
Also Called: Toledo Ear Nose and Throat
6005 Monclova Rd Ste 320 (43537-1862)
PHONE....................................419 578-7555
Richard J Nelson, *Principal*
EMP: 50
SALES (est): 1.7MM **Privately Held**
SIC: 8011 Ears, nose & throat specialist:
physician/surgeon

(G-13846)
RITTER & ASSOCIATES INC
Also Called: Alta360 Research
1690 Woodlands Dr Ste 103 (43537-4165)
PHONE....................................419 535-5757
Stanley G Hart, *President*
Martin Petersen, *Accounts Mgr*
Jennifer Niswander, *Manager*
Kim Spradlin,
EMP: 50
SQ FT: 5,000
SALES (est): 6MM **Privately Held**
SIC: 8732 Market analysis or research
PA: Brand Equity Builders Inc
31 Bailey Ave Ste 1
Ridgefield CT 06877

(G-13847)
ROBERT E KOSE
1661 Holland Rd Ste 200 (43537-1659)
PHONE....................................419 843-7800
Robert E Kose, *Principal*
EMP: 30 EST: 2010
SALES (est): 464.4K **Privately Held**
SIC: 8011 Internal medicine, physician/sur-
geon

(G-13848)
SAR BIREN
Also Called: Baymont Inn & Suites
6425 Kit Ln (43537-8655)
PHONE....................................419 865-0407

Biren Sar, *Owner*
EMP: 29
SALES: 1,000K **Privately Held**
SIC: 7011 Inns

(G-13849)
**SAVAGE AND ASSOCIATES INC
(PA)**
655 Beaver Creek Cir (43537)
PHONE....................................419 475-8665
Ralph E Toland III, *President*
Phil Johnson, *Owner*
Mark Smigelski, *Owner*
Russell Karban, *Vice Pres*
Nick Camp, *CFO*
EMP: 130 EST: 1960
SALES: 73.9K **Privately Held**
WEB: www.savagefinancial.com
SIC: 6411 Life insurance agents; pension
& retirement plan consultants

(G-13850)
SEYMOUR & ASSOCIATES
1760 Manley Rd (43537-9400)
PHONE....................................419 517-7079
Dale Seymour, *Owner*
EMP: 35
SQ FT: 16,000
SALES (est): 4.9MM **Privately Held**
SIC: 6411 Insurance agents & brokers

(G-13851)
SHADOW VALLEY TENNIS CLUB
1661 S Hlland Sylvania Rd (43537)
PHONE....................................419 865-1141
Jim Davis, *Partner*
John Murmer, *Partner*
Carol Weiner, *Partner*
EMP: 25
SALES (est): 870K **Privately Held**
SIC: 7997 Tennis club, membership

(G-13852)
SOCCER CENTRE INC
1620 Market Place Dr # 1 (43537-4318)
PHONE....................................419 893-5419
Dave Hafner, *President*
Brant Smith, *Asst Mgr*
EMP: 25
SQ FT: 50,000
SALES (est): 1MM **Privately Held**
WEB: www.maumeesoccercentre.com
SIC: 7997 Soccer club, except professional
& semi-professional

(G-13853)
**SOCCER CENTRE OWNERS
LTD**
1620 Market Place Dr (43537-4318)
PHONE....................................419 893-5425
Brant Smith, *President*
EMP: 30 EST: 2012
SQ FT: 300,000
SALES (est): 970.8K **Privately Held**
SIC: 3949 7999 Pads: football, basketball,
soccer, lacrosse, etc.; indoor court clubs

(G-13854)
SORDYL & ASSOCIATES INC
2962 W Course Rd (43537-9624)
PHONE....................................419 866-6811
Michael Sordyl, *President*
EMP: 25
SALES (est): 1MM **Privately Held**
SIC: 7371 8748 Custom computer pro-
gramming services; business consulting

(G-13855)
ST LUKES HOSPITAL (PA)
Also Called: PROMEDICA
5901 Monclova Rd (43537-1899)
PHONE....................................419 893-5911
Frank J Bartell III, *President*
Stephen Bazeley, *Vice Pres*
April Snelling, *Opers Staff*
Joseph J Zigray, *CFO*
Sharon Dachenhaus, *Human Resources*
EMP: 62 EST: 1906
SQ FT: 324,324
SALES (est): 177.4MM **Privately Held**
SIC: 8062 5912 Hospital, affiliated with
AMA residency; drug stores

(G-13856)
**SUN FEDERAL CREDIT UNION
(PA)**
1625 Holland Rd (43537-1622)
PHONE..............................800 786-0945
Gary C Moritz, *President*
Marcia Bourdo, *Vice Pres*
Mark Deyoung, *Vice Pres*
Francesca Vogel, *Vice Pres*
Don Kruger, *VP Opers*
EMP: 40
SQ FT: 21,000
SALES: 17.6MM **Privately Held**
SIC: 6061 Federal credit unions

(G-13857)
SUNSHINE COMMUNITIES (PA)
Also Called: Sunshine Inc. Northwest Ohio
7223 Maumee Western Rd (43537-9755)
PHONE....................................419 865-0251
Tyson Stuckey, *Treasurer*
Nicole Beauch, *Manager*
Elizabeth J Holland, *Exec Dir*
Steffanie Brumett, *Director*
Susan Dorrington, *Director*
EMP: 280
SQ FT: 150,000
SALES: 185K **Privately Held**
WEB: www.sunshineincnwo.org
SIC: 8361 8052 8322 Home for the men-
tally retarded; intermediate care facilities;
individual & family services

(G-13858)
**SWAN PNTE FCLTY
OPERATIONS LLC**
Also Called: Addison Hts Hlth Rhblttion Ctr
3600 Butz Rd (43537-9691)
PHONE....................................419 867-7926
Joe Conte,
Carla Naegele,
EMP: 97 EST: 1994
SALES: 950K **Privately Held**
SIC: 8051 Skilled nursing care facilities

(G-13859)
**SYLVANIA FRANCISCAN
HEALTH (HQ)**
1715 Indian Wood Cir # 200 (43537-4055)
PHONE....................................419 882-8373
James Pope, *President*
William Waters, *Treasurer*
EMP: 47
SALES: 1.5MM **Privately Held**
WEB: www.fscsylvania.org
SIC: 8062 8741 General Hospital Man-
agement Services

(G-13860)
SYSTEMS ALTERNATIVES INTL
1705 Indian Wood Cir # 100 (43537-4097)
PHONE....................................419 891-1100
John W Underwood, *President*
Paul Trestan, *Vice Pres*
David A Youngman, *Vice Pres*
Brian Gribble, *CFO*
James B Haxton, *Admin Sec*
EMP: 28
SQ FT: 13,000
SALES (est): 4.3MM **Privately Held**
WEB: www.sysalt.com
SIC: 7371 7378 Computer software sys-
tems analysis & design, custom; computer
maintenance & repair

(G-13861)
TERMINIX INTL CO LTD PARTNR
6541 Weatherfield Ct (43537-9018)
PHONE....................................419 868-8290
Clint Geog, *Manager*
EMP: 29
SALES (corp-wide): 1.9B **Publicly Held**
SIC: 7342 Pest control services
HQ: The Terminix International Company
Limited Partnership
150 Peabody Pl
Memphis TN 38103
901 766-1400

(G-13862)
**TOLEDO MEDICAL EQUIPMENT
CO (PA)**
Also Called: Young Medical Services
4060 Technology Dr (43537-9263)
PHONE....................................419 866-7120

Timothy D Pontius, *President*
Kathy Mikolajczak, *Vice Pres*
EMP: 48
SQ FT: 20,000
SALES (est): 3.2MM **Privately Held**
SIC: 7352 5999 Medical equipment rental;
medical apparatus & supplies

(G-13863)
TRIAD RESIDENTIAL (PA)
1605 Holland Rd Ste A4 (43537-1630)
PHONE....................................419 482-0711
Podd Frick, *Partner*
EMP: 28
SALES (est): 2.2MM **Privately Held**
WEB: www.triad-residential.com
SIC: 8052 Home for the mentally retarded,
with health care

(G-13864)
**UNITED COLLECTION BUREAU
INC**
1345 Ford St (43537-1732)
PHONE....................................419 866-6227
Ka W Tsui, *Branch Mgr*
EMP: 49
SALES (corp-wide): 66.5MM **Privately
Held**
WEB: www.ucbinc.com
SIC: 7322 Collection agency, except real
estate
PA: United Collection Bureau, Inc.
5620 Southwyck Blvd
Toledo OH 43614
419 866-6227

(G-13865)
**UNITED PARCEL SERVICE INC
OH**
Also Called: UPS
1550 Holland Rd (43537-1657)
PHONE....................................419 891-6776
Karen Park, *Manager*
EMP: 4500
SALES (corp-wide): 71.8B **Publicly Held**
WEB: www.upsscs.com
SIC: 4215 Package delivery, vehicular; par-
cel delivery, vehicular
HQ: United Parcel Service, Inc. (Oh)
55 Glenlake Pkwy
Atlanta GA 30328
404 828-6000

(G-13866)
**UNITED SEATING & MOBILITY
LLC**
Also Called: Numotion
412 W Dussel Dr (43537-1686)
PHONE....................................567 302-4000
Shirley Frye, *Branch Mgr*
EMP: 36
SALES (corp-wide): 3.1B **Privately Held**
SIC: 5047 Medical equipment & supplies
HQ: United Seating & Mobility Llc
975 Hornet Dr
Hazelwood MO 63042
800 500-9150

(G-13867)
**WARNOCK TANNER & ASSOC
INC**
Also Called: Wta Consulting
959 Illinois Ave Ste C (43537-1744)
PHONE....................................419 897-6999
Roger Warnock, *President*
Ken Lynch, *Exec VP*
Richard Rusgo, *CFO*
Brie Warnock, *Marketing Mgr*
Brie Hobbs, *Marketing Staff*
EMP: 26
SQ FT: 3,000
SALES (est): 4.2MM **Privately Held**
SIC: 7379 7373 Computer related consult-
ing services; value-added resellers; com-
puter systems

(G-13868)
WHITEHURST COMPANY (PA)
6325 Garden Rd (43537-1271)
P.O. Box 351869, Toledo (43635-1869)
PHONE....................................419 865-0799
Herb Fultz, *President*
James Mc Innis, *Vice Pres*
EMP: 43

SALES: 500K **Privately Held**
WEB: www.thewhitehurstcompany.com
SIC: 6531 6513 Property Management &
Apartment Operator

(G-13869)
WILLIAM VAUGHAN COMPANY
Also Called: Northwest Ohio Practice
145 Chesterfield Ln (43537-2209)
PHONE......................................419 891-1040
William J Horst, *President*
Gregory J Arndt, *Vice Pres*
Michelle M Clement, *Vice Pres*
Aaron D Swiggum, *Vice Pres*
Jack C Hagmeyer, *Treasurer*
EMP: 63
SQ FT: 1,600
SALES (est): 7MM **Privately Held**
WEB: www.wvco.com
SIC: 8721 Certified public accountant

(G-13870)
YOUNG MENS CHRISTIAN ASSOCIAT
716 Askin St (43537-3602)
PHONE......................................419 794-7304
EMP: 103
SALES (corp-wide): 29.1MM **Privately Held**
SIC: 8641 Youth organizations
PA: The Young Men's Christian Association Of Greater Toledo
1500 N Superior St Fl 2
Toledo OH 43604
419 729-8135

(G-13871)
YOUNG MENS CHRISTIAN ASSOCIAT
2100 S Hlland Sylvania Rd (43537)
PHONE......................................419 866-9622
Vicki Coleman, *Manager*
Jill Morris, *Director*
EMP: 55
SALES (corp-wide): 29.1MM **Privately Held**
WEB: www.ymcastorercamps.org
SIC: 8641 7991 8351 7032 Youth organizations; physical fitness facilities; child day care services; youth camps; individual & family services
PA: The Young Men's Christian Association Of Greater Toledo
1500 N Superior St Fl 2
Toledo OH 43604
419 729-8135

Mayfield Heights
Cuyahoga County

(G-13872)
DATATRAK INTERNATIONAL INC
5900 Landerbrook Dr # 170 (44124-4085)
PHONE......................................440 443-0082
Alex Tabatabai, *Ch of Bd*
James R Ward, *President*
Varnesh Sritharan, *Vice Pres*
Shyla Jones, *Project Mgr*
Osman Muhammad, *Project Mgr*
EMP: 47
SQ FT: 4,300
SALES: 7.4MM **Privately Held**
WEB: www.datatrak.net
SIC: 7374 7372 Data processing & preparation; prepackaged software

(G-13873)
DTV INC
Also Called: Danny Veghs Home Entertainment
6505 Mayfield Rd (44124-3216)
PHONE......................................216 226-5465
Kathy Vegh, *CEO*
Frank Plutt, *Controller*
EMP: 35
SQ FT: 26,000

SALES (est): 9.6MM **Privately Held**
WEB: www.dannyveghs.com
SIC: 5046 7699 5962 5091 Vending machines, coin-operated; billiard table repair; vending machine repair; merchandising machine operators; billiard equipment & supplies; furniture stores; hobby, toy & game shops

(G-13874)
ELK & ELK CO LPA (PA)
6105 Parkland Blvd # 200 (44124-4258)
PHONE......................................800 355-6446
David J Elk, *Partner*
Arthur M Elk, *Partner*
Marilyn Elk, *CFO*
Brandon Roth, *Human Resources*
Ken Perdue, *Mktg Dir*
EMP: 70
SALES (est): 9.6MM **Privately Held**
SIC: 8111 General practice attorney, lawyer

(G-13875)
KIDDIE PARTY COMPANY LLC
1690 Lander Rd (44124-3301)
PHONE......................................440 273-7680
Tanisha Jamison, *Principal*
EMP: 25 EST: 2014
SALES (est): 448.5K **Privately Held**
SIC: 7299 Party planning service

(G-13876)
LITIGATION MANAGEMENT INC
6000 Parkland Blvd # 100 (44124-6120)
PHONE......................................440 484-2000
Elizabeth Juliano, *President*
Jerrod Vastag, *Partner*
Karen Brooks, *Opers Staff*
Melima Craddock, *Opers Staff*
Deborah Prokay, *Opers Staff*
EMP: 452
SQ FT: 2,000
SALES (est): 48.5MM **Privately Held**
WEB: www.medicineforthedefense.com
SIC: 8111 Legal aid service

(G-13877)
M W RECYCLING LLC (DH)
5875 Landerbrook Dr # 200 (44124-6511)
PHONE......................................440 753-5400
David Spector, *Mng Member*
EMP: 30
SALES (est): 19.1MM
SALES (corp-wide): 11.7B **Publicly Held**
SIC: 4953 Recycling, waste materials
HQ: Psc Metals, Llc
5875 Landerbrook Dr # 200
Mayfield Heights OH 44124
440 753-5400

(G-13878)
ONX ENTRPRISE SOLUTIONS US INC
5910 Landerbrook Dr 2 (44124-6508)
PHONE......................................440 569-2300
Mike Cox, *CEO*
Brian Nogar, *COO*
Chris Hamlin, *Project Mgr*
Kathleen Giblin, *Opers Mgr*
Casey Kerrick, *Opers Mgr*
EMP: 55
SALES (est): 809.7K
SALES (corp-wide): 1.3B **Publicly Held**
SIC: 7373 Systems software development services
HQ: Onx Holdings Llc
221 E 4th St
Cincinnati OH 45202
866 587-2287

(G-13879)
PARK PLACE TECHNOLOGIES LLC
Also Called: AMI
5910 Landerbrook Dr # 300 (44124-6500)
PHONE......................................610 544-0571
EMP: 390 **Privately Held**
SIC: 7378 Computer maintenance & repair
PA: Park Place Technologies, Llc
5910 Landerbrook Dr # 300
Mayfield Heights OH 44124

(G-13880)
PARK PLACE TECHNOLOGIES LLC (PA)
5910 Landerbrook Dr # 300 (44124-6500)
PHONE......................................877 778-8707
Ed Kenty, *CEO*
Tony Susi, *President*
Chris Adams, *COO*
Mike Knightly, *Exec VP*
Hal Malstrom, *Exec VP*
EMP: 161
SQ FT: 41,000
SALES (est): 143.9MM **Privately Held**
WEB: www.parkplaceintl.com
SIC: 7378 Computer maintenance & repair

(G-13881)
SEAL MAYFIELD LLC
Also Called: Staybridge Suites
6103 Landerhaven Dr (44124-4189)
PHONE......................................440 684-4100
Sheenal Patel,
EMP: 25
SALES (est): 136.5K **Privately Held**
SIC: 7011 Resort hotel, franchised

(G-13882)
TMW SYSTEMS INC (HQ)
6085 Parkland Blvd (44124-4184)
PHONE......................................216 831-6606
David Wangler, *President*
Rod Strata, *COO*
David Mook, *Exec VP*
Jeffrey Ritter, *Exec VP*
Scott Vanselous, *Exec VP*
EMP: 125
SQ FT: 32,500
SALES (est): 79.8MM
SALES (corp-wide): 3.1B **Publicly Held**
WEB: www.bulktrucker.com
SIC: 7372 Business oriented computer software
PA: Trimble Inc.
935 Stewart Dr
Sunnyvale CA 94085
408 481-8000

(G-13883)
TRUE NORTH ENERGY LLC
Also Called: Truenorth Energy
6411 Mayfield Rd (44124-3214)
PHONE......................................440 442-0060
EMP: 29
SALES (corp-wide): 265.4MM **Privately Held**
SIC: 5541 1382 Filling stations, gasoline; oil & gas exploration services
PA: True North Energy, Llc
10346 Brecksville Rd
Brecksville OH 44141
877 245-9336

Mayfield Village
Cuyahoga County

(G-13884)
CENTER SCHOOL ASSOCIATION
6625 Wilson Mills Rd (44143-3406)
PHONE......................................440 995-7400
EMP: 58
SALES: 26.8K **Privately Held**
SIC: 8621 Professional membership organizations

(G-13885)
FIRST REALTY PROPERTY MGT LTD
6690 Beta Dr Ste 220 (44143-2359)
PHONE......................................440 720-0100
Joseph T Aveni,
Marie Abazio,
William Pender,
EMP: 40
SALES (est): 4.3MM **Privately Held**
SIC: 6531 Real estate managers

(G-13886)
PROGRESSIVE CASUALTY INSUR CO (DH)
Also Called: PROGRESSIVE INSURANCE
6300 Wilson Mills Rd (44143-2109)
PHONE......................................440 461-5000

Susan Patricia Griffith, *CEO*
Jim Mauck, *COO*
Rick Dansko, *Opers Mgr*
Scott Feucht, *Facilities Mgr*
Jeff Bales, *Production*
▼ EMP: 3300
SALES: 7.4B
SALES (corp-wide): 31.9B **Publicly Held**
WEB: www.progressinsurance.com
SIC: 6351 6411 6321 6331 Surety insurance; credit & other financial responsibility insurance; insurance agents, brokers & service; insurance claim adjusters, not employed by insurance company; insurance agents & brokers; insurance agents; accident & health insurance; accident insurance carriers; fire, marine & casualty insurance & carriers

(G-13887)
SKODA MNTTI CRTIF PUB ACCNTNTS (HQ)
6685 Beta Dr (44143-2320)
PHONE......................................440 449-6800
Gregory Skoda, *CEO*
Michael Minotti, *President*
Mary Dolson, *Partner*
Tim Donovan, *Partner*
Dawn Gainer, *Managing Dir*
EMP: 62
SALES (est): 14.1MM
SALES (corp-wide): 18.6MM **Privately Held**
SIC: 8721 Certified public accountant
PA: Skoda Minotti Holdings Llc
6685 Beta Dr
Cleveland OH 44143
440 449-6800

(G-13888)
WIRELESS ENVIRONMENT LLC
Also Called: Mr. Beams
600 Beta Dr Ste 100 (44143-2355)
PHONE......................................216 455-0192
David Levine, *President*
Mike Recker, *CTO*
▲ EMP: 25
SQ FT: 1,000
SALES (est): 2.6MM **Publicly Held**
SIC: 1731 Lighting contractor
HQ: Ring Llc
1523 26th St
Santa Monica CA 90404
800 656-1918

Mc Arthur
Vinton County

(G-13889)
APPALACHIA WOOD INC (PA)
Also Called: McArthur Lumber and Post
31310 State Route 93 (45651-8924)
PHONE......................................740 596-2551
Fax: 740 596-2555
EMP: 30 EST: 1951
SQ FT: 150,000
SALES: 3.6MM **Privately Held**
SIC: 2491 2421 5031 2411 Wood Preserving Sawmill/Planing Mill Whol Lumber/Plywd/Millwk Logging

(G-13890)
HOPEWELL HEALTH CENTERS INC
31891 State Route 93 (45651-9006)
P.O. Box 308 (45651-0308)
PHONE......................................740 596-5249
Dawn Murray Do, *Principal*
EMP: 25
SALES (corp-wide): 33.1MM **Privately Held**
SIC: 8099 8011 Medical services organization; general & family practice, physician/surgeon
PA: Hopewell Health Centers, Inc.
1049 Western Ave
Chillicothe OH 45601
740 773-1006

(G-13891)
TWIN MAPLES NURSING HOME
31054 State Route 93 (45651-8925)
PHONE......................................740 596-5955

▲ = Import ▼ =Export
◆ =Import/Export

Virginia Ratliff, *President*
Fred Ratliff, *Corp Secy*
Crystal Ratliff, *Vice Pres*
EMP: 45 **EST:** 1974
SALES: 260.4MM **Privately Held**
SIC: 8051 8052 Convalescent home with continuous nursing care; intermediate care facilities

(G-13892)
VINTON COUNTY NAT BNK MCARTHUR (HQ)
Also Called: VINTON CO NATIONAL BANK
112 W Main St (45651-1214)
P.O. Box 460 (45651-0460)
PHONE................................740 596-2525
Stephen Hunter, *President*
Ron Collins, *President*
Mark Erslan, *Exec VP*
Audra Johnson, *Exec VP*
Jane Nickels, *Senior VP*
EMP: 43
SQ FT: 13,239
SALES: 40.5MM **Privately Held**
WEB: www.vintoncountybank.com
SIC: 6022 6162 State trust companies accepting deposits, commercial; mortgage bankers & correspondents
PA: Community Bancshares Inc
112 W Main St
Mc Arthur OH 45651
740 596-4561

Mc Clure
Henry County

(G-13893)
POGGEMEYER DESIGN GROUP INC
Also Called: Industrial Fluid Management
2926 Us Highway 6 (43534-9730)
PHONE................................419 748-7438
Richard Bennett, *President*
EMP: 25
SALES (corp-wide): 36.2MM **Privately Held**
WEB: www.poggemeyer.com
SIC: 8713 8711 9511 Surveying services; consulting engineer; waste management agencies
PA: Poggemeyer Design Group, Inc.
1168 N Main St
Bowling Green OH 43402
419 244-8074

Mc Comb
Hancock County

(G-13894)
GRUBB CONSTRUCTION INC
896 State Route 613 (45858-9303)
P.O. Box 728 (45858-0728)
PHONE................................419 293-2316
Norman Grubb, *President*
Nancy Grubb, *Corp Secy*
EMP: 30
SQ FT: 4,800
SALES (est): 3.1MM **Privately Held**
SIC: 1796 Machinery installation

Mc Connelsville
Morgan County

(G-13895)
RIVERSIDE CARE CENTER LLC
856 Riverside Dr S (43756)
PHONE................................740 962-5303
Brian Colleran, *President*
EMP: 62
SALES: 380.8MM **Privately Held**
WEB: www.riverside-care.net
SIC: 8051 Skilled nursing care facilities

Mc Dermott
Scioto County

(G-13896)
VOIERS ENTERPRISES INC
Also Called: Rest Haven Nursing Home
2274 Mc Dermott Pond Crk (45652)
PHONE................................740 259-2838
Deborah Akers, *CEO*
Sarah E Voiers, *President*
Steven Akers, *Principal*
Anna Clarke, *Treasurer*
EMP: 35
SALES (est): 2.1MM **Privately Held**
SIC: 8052 Personal care facility

Mc Donald
Trumbull County

(G-13897)
PREDATOR TRUCKING COMPANY (PA)
3181 Trumbull Ave (44437-1313)
P.O. Box 315 (44437-0315)
PHONE................................330 530-0712
Charles Haselow, *CEO*
Russell Golden, *President*
Gary Golden, *Owner*
James Golden, *Admin Sec*
EMP: 33
SQ FT: 1,000
SALES (est): 6.1MM **Privately Held**
SIC: 7513 Truck rental & leasing, no drivers

Mc Guffey
Hardin County

(G-13898)
ROHRS FARMS
810 Courtright St (45859)
P.O. Box 300 (45859-0300)
PHONE................................419 757-0110
John Rohrs, *General Mgr*
Jason Rohrs, *Principal*
EMP: 30
SALES (est): 8.1MM **Privately Held**
SIC: 0191 General farms, primarily crop

McConnelsville
Morgan County

(G-13899)
CARESERVE INC
Also Called: Genesis Health & Rehab
4114 N State Route 376 Nw (43756-9145)
PHONE................................740 962-3761
David Davis, *Director*
EMP: 145
SALES (corp-wide): 462MM **Privately Held**
SIC: 8051 Skilled nursing care facilities
HQ: Careserve
2991 Maple Ave
Zanesville OH 43701
740 454-4000

(G-13900)
FINLEY FIRE EQUIPMENT CO (PA)
5255 N State Route 60 Nw (43756-9630)
PHONE................................740 962-4328
John W Finley, *President*
George Owens, *Sales Mgr*
Kevin Hardwick, *Regl Sales Mgr*
Chris Antle, *Sales Staff*
Dennis Creamer, *Sales Staff*
EMP: 26
SQ FT: 34,000
SALES: 38.5MM **Privately Held**
WEB: www.finleyfire.com
SIC: 5087 Firefighting equipment

(G-13901)
MARY HMMOND ADULT ACTVTIES CTR
Also Called: Mary Hammond Center
900 S Riverside Dr Ne (43756-9102)
PHONE................................740 962-4200
Tom Neff, *President*
Diana Cline, *Business Mgr*
Bill Baker, *Vice Pres*
Scott Roberts, *Manager*
Wally Olszcewski, *Admin Sec*
EMP: 78
SQ FT: 20,000
SALES (est): 229.6K **Privately Held**
SIC: 8331 Work experience center

(G-13902)
MIBA BEARINGS US LLC
5037 N State Route 60 Nw (43756-9218)
PHONE................................740 962-4242
F Peter Mitterbauer, *Ch of Bd*
Heidi Suhoski, *Safety Mgr*
Broc Spears, *Production*
Shawn Gormley, *QA Dir*
Dave Ciacci, *Research*
▲ **EMP:** 300
SQ FT: 182,000
SALES (est): 143.9MM
SALES (corp-wide): 1B **Privately Held**
SIC: 5085 Bearings
PA: Mitterbauer Beteiligungs - Aktiengesellschaft
Dr. Mitterbauer-StraBe 3
Laakirchen 4663
761 325-41

(G-13903)
MORGAN COUNTY PUBLIC TRANSIT
37 S 5th St (43756-1203)
PHONE................................740 962-1322
Michael Reed, *Principal*
John Sampson, *Manager*
Shannon Well, *Commissioner*
Adam Shiver, *Commissioner*
Tim Zanhorn, *Commissioner*
EMP: 25
SALES: 600K **Privately Held**
SIC: 4119 Ambulance service

(G-13904)
OHIO MEDICAL TRNSP INC
975 E Airport Rd Ne (43756-9323)
PHONE................................740 962-2055
EMP: 53 **Privately Held**
SIC: 4119 Ambulance service
PA: Ohio Medical Transportation, Inc.
2827 W Dblin Granville Rd
Columbus OH 43235

Mechanicstown
Carroll County

(G-13905)
KINGS WELDING AND FABG INC
5259 Bane Rd Ne (44651-9020)
PHONE................................330 738-3592
Glen Richard King Sr, *President*
Diane Garrett, *Corp Secy*
Pat Sica, *Exec Dir*
EMP: 45
SQ FT: 9,500
SALES (est): 6.1MM **Privately Held**
SIC: 3599 7692 3498 3441 Machine shop, jobbing & repair; welding repair; fabricated pipe & fittings; fabricated structural metal

Medina
Medina County

(G-13906)
ADVOCATE PROPERTY SERVIC
620 E Smith Rd (44256-2692)
PHONE................................330 952-1313
Amanda Klein, *Principal*
Tresa Koein,
Tresa Klein,
EMP: 30 **EST:** 2010

SALES (est): 1MM **Privately Held**
SIC: 1522 Residential construction

(G-13907)
AHF OHIO INC
Also Called: Samaritan Care Center & Villa
806 E Washinton St (44256)
PHONE................................330 725-4123
Brad Willmore, *Administration*
EMP: 64
SALES (corp-wide): 22.6MM **Privately Held**
SIC: 8051 8361 Skilled nursing care facilities; residential care
PA: Ahf Ohio, Inc.
5920 Venture Dr Ste 100
Dublin OH 43017
614 760-7352

(G-13908)
ALICE TRAINING INSTITUTE LLC
2508 Medina Rd (44256-8144)
PHONE................................330 661-0106
Greg Crane, *President*
Christopher Schneider, *Principal*
Bob Kraft, *Vice Pres*
Matt Blotevogel, *Sales Staff*
Brett Joyce, *Program Mgr*
EMP: 80
SQ FT: 4,000
SALES (est): 5.5MM **Privately Held**
SIC: 8748 Safety training service

(G-13909)
ALTERNATIVE PATHS INC
246 Northland Dr Ste 200a (44256-3440)
PHONE................................330 725-9195
Jackie Owen, *Chairman*
Deborah Beckstett, *Exec Dir*
Tina Armeni, *Administration*
EMP: 30
SQ FT: 5,000
SALES: 3.2MM **Privately Held**
SIC: 8093 8322 Mental health clinic, outpatient; individual & family services

(G-13910)
AMF BOWLING CENTERS INC
201 Harding St (44256-1636)
PHONE................................330 725-4548
Ryan Sibert, *Manager*
EMP: 30
SALES (corp-wide): 323MM **Privately Held**
WEB: www.kidsports.org
SIC: 7933 Ten pin center
HQ: Amf Bowling Centers, Inc.
7313 Bell Creek Rd
Mechanicsville VA 23111

(G-13911)
AT&T CORP
1088 N Court St (44256-1586)
PHONE................................330 723-1717
Chad Dash, *Branch Mgr*
EMP: 96
SALES (corp-wide): 170.7B **Publicly Held**
SIC: 4812 Cellular telephone services
HQ: At&T Corp.
1 At&T Way
Bedminster NJ 07921
800 403-3302

(G-13912)
BATTERED WOMENS SHELTER
120 W Washington St 3e1 (44256-2260)
PHONE................................330 723-3900
Kathy Henninger, *Manager*
EMP: 49
SALES (corp-wide): 5MM **Privately Held**
SIC: 8322 Emergency shelters
PA: Battered Women's Shelter
974 E Market St
Akron OH 44305
330 374-0740

(G-13913)
BRIDGESHOME HEALTH CARE
Also Called: ROBERTSON BEREAVEMENT CENTER
5075 Windfall Rd (44256-8613)
PHONE................................330 764-1000
Kathy Segatta, *Finance*
Chris Baker, *Director*
Catherine Rohr, *Relations*

EMP: 30
SALES: 1.7MM
SALES (corp-wide): 89.8MM **Privately Held**
SIC: 8062 8082 General medical & surgical hospitals; home health care services
HQ: Hospice Of Medina County
5075 Windfall Rd
Medina OH 44256

(G-13914)
BROOKDALE SENIOR LIVING INC
49 Leisure Ln A (44256-1285)
PHONE..................................330 723-5825
EMP: 58
SALES (corp-wide): 4.5B **Publicly Held**
SIC: 8361 Residential care
PA: Brookdale Senior Living
111 Westwood Pl Ste 400
Brentwood TN 37027
615 221-2250

(G-13915)
CATHOLIC CHARITIES CORPORATION
4210 N Jefferson St (44256-5639)
PHONE..................................330 723-9615
Timothy Putka, *Director*
EMP: 397 **Privately Held**
SIC: 8322 Social service center
PA: Catholic Charities Corporation
7911 Detroit Ave
Cleveland OH 44102

(G-13916)
CELLCO PARTNERSHIP
2736 Medina Rd (44256-9660)
PHONE..................................330 722-6622
EMP: 31
SALES (corp-wide): 130.8B **Publicly Held**
SIC: 5065 4812 Telephone & telegraphic equipment; cellular telephone services
HQ: Cellco Partnership
1 Verizon Way
Basking Ridge NJ 07920

(G-13917)
CHICK MASTER INCUBATOR COMPANY (PA)
945 Lafayette Rd (44256-3510)
P.O. Box 704 (44258-0704)
PHONE..................................330 722-5591
Robert Holzer, *CEO*
Larry Stevens, *General Mgr*
Chad Daniels, *Vice Pres*
Alan Shandler, *Vice Pres*
Lou Sharp, *Vice Pres*
◆ EMP: 118
SQ FT: 100,000
SALES (est): 26.5MM **Privately Held**
WEB: www.chickmaster.com
SIC: 3523 1711 Incubators & brooders, farm; plumbing, heating, air-conditioning contractors

(G-13918)
CHILDTIME CHILDCARE INC
3550 Octagon Dr (44256-6836)
PHONE..................................330 723-8697
Chris Burkholder, *Owner*
EMP: 30
SALES (corp-wide): 340.2MM **Privately Held**
WEB: www.learninggroup.com
SIC: 8351 Preschool center
HQ: Childtime Childcare, Inc.
21333 Haggerty Rd Ste 300
Novi MI 48375
248 697-9000

(G-13919)
CHU MANAGEMENT CO INC (PA)
2875 Medina Rd (44256-9672)
PHONE..................................330 725-4571
Ding-Shu Chu, *President*
EMP: 40
SQ FT: 45,000
SALES: 1.7MM **Privately Held**
SIC: 8741 Manages Motel Operations

(G-13920)
CLARK BRANDS LLC
427 N Court St (44256-1869)
PHONE..................................330 723-9886
Al Carmen, *Principal*
EMP: 3098
SALES (corp-wide): 303.3MM **Privately Held**
SIC: 6794 Franchises, selling or licensing
PA: Clark Brands Llc
4200 Commerce Ct Ste 350
Lisle IL 60532
630 355-8918

(G-13921)
COMMUNITY LEGAL AID SERVICES
120 W Washington St 2c (44256-2271)
PHONE..................................330 725-1231
Sara Strattan, *Director*
EMP: 35
SALES (est): 1.5MM
SALES (corp-wide): 5.7MM **Privately Held**
SIC: 8111 Legal aid service
PA: Community Legal Aid Services, Inc
50 S Main St Ste 800
Akron OH 44308
330 535-4191

(G-13922)
CONSUMER SUPPORT SERVICES INC
2575 Medina Rd Ste A (44256-6606)
PHONE..................................330 764-4785
Barbie Knoll, *Manager*
EMP: 60
SALES (corp-wide): 26.7MM **Privately Held**
SIC: 8059 8322 Personal care home, with health care; individual & family services
PA: Consumer Support Services Inc
2040 Cherry Valley Rd # 1
Newark OH 43055
740 788-8257

(G-13923)
CONTROLS INC
5204 Portside Dr (44256-5966)
P.O. Box 368, Sharon Center (44274-0368)
PHONE..................................330 239-4345
Robert Cowen, *President*
Scott Izzo, *Vice Pres*
David Steinberg, *Engineer*
EMP: 25
SALES: 1.8MM **Privately Held**
WEB: www.controlsinc.com
SIC: 3625 7389 1731 Control equipment, electric; industrial controls: push button, selector switches, pilot; design services; electronic controls installation

(G-13924)
CORRPRO COMPANIES INC (DH)
1055 W Smith Rd (44256-2444)
PHONE..................................330 723-5082
David H Kroon, *President*
Jennifer Chrosniak, *General Mgr*
Jesse Corona, *Superintendent*
Sam Jeffery, *Area Mgr*
Dorwin Hawn, *Exec VP*
▼ EMP: 50
SQ FT: 8,000
SALES (est): 198.7MM
SALES (corp-wide): 1.3B **Publicly Held**
WEB: www.corrpro.com
SIC: 3699 8711 Electrical equipment & supplies; engineering services
HQ: Insituform Technologies, Llc
17988 Edison Ave
Chesterfield MO 63005
636 530-8000

(G-13925)
COUNTY OF MEDINA
Also Called: Medina County Home
6144 Wedgewood Rd (44256-7860)
PHONE..................................330 723-9553
Lynn Remington, *Manager*
Joyce Giles, *Manager*
EMP: 27
SQ FT: 33,504 **Privately Held**
WEB: www.mcbmrdd.org

SIC: 8361 9111 Rest home, with health care incidental; county supervisors' & executives' offices
PA: County Of Medina
144 N Brdwy St Rm 201
Medina OH 44256
330 722-9208

(G-13926)
COUNTY OF MEDINA
Also Called: Medina County Health Dept
4800 Ledgewood Dr (44256-7666)
PHONE..................................330 995-5243
David McElhatten, *General Mgr*
Daniel J Raub, *Commissioner*
Jeannie Bunch, *Supervisor*
Vickie O'Neill, *Clerk*
EMP: 70 **Privately Held**
WEB: www.mcbmrdd.org
SIC: 8399 9111 Health systems agency; county supervisors' & executives' offices
PA: County Of Medina
144 N Brdwy St Rm 201
Medina OH 44256
330 722-9208

(G-13927)
COUNTY OF MEDINA
Medina County Transportation
114 Bradway St (44256)
PHONE..................................330 723-9670
Michael Salamon, *Director*
EMP: 25
SQ FT: 1,080 **Privately Held**
WEB: www.mcbmrdd.org
SIC: 4731 9111 Freight transportation arrangement; county supervisors' & executives' offices
PA: County Of Medina
144 N Brdwy St Rm 201
Medina OH 44256
330 722-9208

(G-13928)
CUSTOM-PAK INC
Also Called: Custompak
885 W Smith Rd (44256-2424)
PHONE..................................330 725-0800
Ronald P Camaglia, *President*
Frederick Camaglia, *Vice Pres*
Renee Cranet, *Manager*
EMP: 65
SQ FT: 55,000
SALES (est): 3.9MM
SALES (corp-wide): 28.6MM **Privately Held**
WEB: www.custompakproducts.com
SIC: 7389 Packaging & labeling services
PA: Industrial Chemical Corp.
885 W Smith Rd
Medina OH 44256
330 725-0800

(G-13929)
DAIRY FARMERS AMERICA INC
1035 Medina Rd Ste 300 (44256-5398)
PHONE..................................330 670-7800
Glenn Wallace, *Chief*
EMP: 30
SALES (corp-wide): 14.6B **Privately Held**
WEB: www.dfamilk.com
SIC: 2022 2026 2021 0211 Cheese, natural & processed; fluid milk; creamery butter; beef cattle feedlots
PA: Dairy Farmers Of America, Inc.
1405 N 98th St
Kansas City KS 66111
816 801-6455

(G-13930)
DIPROINDUCA (USA) LIMITED LLC
Also Called: Diproinduca USA
2528 Medina Rd (44256-8144)
PHONE..................................330 722-4442
Efrain Riera, *President*
Mark Heuschkel, *Vice Pres*
Gerardo Ferreira, *Treasurer*
▼ EMP: 100
SQ FT: 4,300
SALES (est): 30.9MM **Privately Held**
SIC: 5093 8999 4959 Metal scrap & waste materials; earth science services; environmental cleanup services

(G-13931)
DISCOUNT DRUG MART INC (PA)
211 Commerce Dr (44256-1331)
PHONE..................................330 725-2340
Donald Boodjeh, *CEO*
Parviz Boodjeh, *Ch of Bd*
John Gains, *President*
Dough Boodjeh, *COO*
Matt Troup, *Store Mgr*
▲ EMP: 250
SQ FT: 500,000
SALES (est): 679.4MM **Privately Held**
WEB: www.discount-drugmart.com
SIC: 5912 5331 5411 5451 Drug stores; variety stores; grocery stores; dairy products stores; pharmaceuticals; home health care services

(G-13932)
DIVERSFIED EMPLYEE SLTIONS INC
3745 Medina Rd (44256-9510)
PHONE..................................330 764-4125
Thomas L Skeen, *Principal*
EMP: 500
SALES (est): 25.3MM **Privately Held**
WEB: www.des4you.com
SIC: 7361 Employment agencies

(G-13933)
DO IT BEST CORP
444 Independence Dr (44256-2407)
PHONE..................................330 725-3859
Rick Becker, *Site Mgr*
Mike Patalita, *Manager*
EMP: 150
SALES (corp-wide): 2.9B **Privately Held**
WEB: www.doitbestcorp.com
SIC: 5072 5211 5251 Builders' hardware; lumber & other building materials; hardware
PA: Do It Best Corp.
6502 Nelson Rd
Fort Wayne IN 46803
260 748-5300

(G-13934)
ENHANCED HOMECARE MEDINA INC
3745 Medina Rd Ste E (44256-9510)
PHONE..................................330 952-2331
Edward Swinarski, *Principal*
EMP: 50
SALES (est): 469.2K **Privately Held**
SIC: 8082 Home health care services

(G-13935)
ENVIROTEST SYSTEMS CORP
770 S Progress Dr (44256-1368)
PHONE..................................330 963-4464
EMP: 34
SQ FT: 7,400 **Privately Held**
WEB: www.il.etest.com
SIC: 7549 Emissions testing without repairs, automotive
HQ: Envirotest Systems Corp.
7 Kripes Rd
East Granby CT 06026

(G-13936)
FECHKO EXCAVATING INC
865 W Liberty St Ste 120 (44256-1332)
PHONE..................................330 722-2890
John Fechko, *President*
Matt Honigman, *Vice Pres*
Matthew Honigman, *Vice Pres*
Austin Steinbrenner, *Controller*
Dean Fechko, *Admin Sec*
EMP: 70
SQ FT: 4,000
SALES (est): 13.2MM **Privately Held**
WEB: www.fechko.com
SIC: 1794 Excavation & grading, building construction

(G-13937)
FECHKO EXCAVATING LLC
865 W Liberty St Ste 120 (44256-1332)
PHONE..................................330 722-2890
Austin Steinbrenner,
John Fechko,
EMP: 82
SALES (est): 5.3MM **Privately Held**
SIC: 1794 Excavation work

(G-13938)
FIORILLI CONSTRUCTION CO INC
1247 Medina Rd (44256-8135)
PHONE..............................216 696-5845
Carmen Fiorilli, *President*
Jeff Troxell, *Opers Staff*
Melissa Fiorilli, *Marketing Mgr*
EMP: 30
SALES (est): 13.2MM **Privately Held**
WEB: www.fio-con.com
SIC: 1542 Commercial & office building, new construction

(G-13939)
FNB CORPORATION
3613 Medina Rd (44256-8181)
PHONE..............................330 721-7484
Marguerite Krahe, *Manager*
EMP: 146
SALES (corp-wide): 1.4B **Publicly Held**
SIC: 6021 National commercial banks
PA: F.N.B. Corporation
1 N Shore Ctr 12 Fdral St
Pittsburgh PA 15212
800 555-5455

(G-13940)
FREE ENTERPRISES INCORPORATED
241 S State Rd (44256-2430)
P.O. Box 1199 (44258-1199)
PHONE..............................330 722-2031
James H Patneau Sr, *President*
Brian Fisher, *Business Mgr*
Annette M Patneau, *Vice Pres*
Cheley Emmert, *Manager*
EMP: 84
SQ FT: 14,590
SALES (est): 32.7MM **Privately Held**
SIC: 5172 5541 Gasoline; gasoline service stations

(G-13941)
GENE TOLLIVER CORP
Also Called: All American Heating AC
6222 Norwalk Rd (44256-9454)
PHONE..............................440 324-7727
Eugene Tolliver, *President*
Keith Tolliver, *Vice Pres*
EMP: 100
SQ FT: 4,300
SALES (est): 6.4MM **Privately Held**
SIC: 1711 Heating Air Conditioning & Refrigeration Contractor

(G-13942)
GENES REFRIGERATION HTG & AC
6222 Norwalk Rd (44256-9454)
PHONE..............................330 723-4104
Ralph E Tolliver, *President*
Gene Tolliver, *President*
Keith Tolliver, *President*
Emily M Berberich, *Principal*
Carolyn S Byrd, *Principal*
EMP: 43
SQ FT: 8,600
SALES (est): 8.7MM **Privately Held**
SIC: 1711 Warm air heating & air conditioning contractor; refrigeration contractor

(G-13943)
GERSPACHER COMPANIES
Also Called: Forest Meadow Villas
574 Leisure Ln (44256-1657)
PHONE..............................330 725-1596
Melvin Gerspacher, *President*
David Gerspacher, *Principal*
Diane Gerspacher, *Admin Sec*
EMP: 47
SQ FT: 22,000
SALES: 1.4MM **Privately Held**
WEB: www.camelotplace.net
SIC: 8361 Residential care

(G-13944)
GOLDEN LIVING LLC
Also Called: Beverly
555 Springbrook Dr (44256-3651)
PHONE..............................330 725-3393
Pam Haman, *Manager*
EMP: 100

SALES (corp-wide): 7.4MM **Privately Held**
SIC: 8059 8051 Convalescent home; skilled nursing care facilities
PA: Golden Living Llc
5220 Tennyson Pkwy # 400
Plano TX 75024
972 372-6300

(G-13945)
GRANGER TOWNSHIP
Also Called: Granger Township Fire & Rescue
3737 Ridge Rd (44256-7919)
PHONE..............................330 239-2111
John Hadam, *Chief*
EMP: 30 **Privately Held**
WEB: www.grangertwp.org
SIC: 9111 8699 City & town managers' offices; charitable organization
PA: Granger Township
3717 Ridge Rd
Medina OH 44256
330 239-3611

(G-13946)
H M T DERMATOLOGY INC
Also Called: Trillium Creek Dermatology
5783 Wooster Pike (44256-8816)
PHONE..............................330 725-0569
EMP: 30
SQ FT: 10,000
SALES (est): 3.5MM **Privately Held**
SIC: 8011 Medical Doctor's Office

(G-13947)
HASTINGS HOME HEALTH CTR INC
211 Commerce Dr (44256-1331)
PHONE..............................216 898-3300
David Ondrish, *Branch Mgr*
EMP: 34
SALES (corp-wide): 8.1MM **Privately Held**
SIC: 8082 Home health care services
PA: Hastings Home Health Center, Inc.
15210 Industrial Pkwy
Cleveland OH 44135
216 898-3300

(G-13948)
HERITAGE PTO
Also Called: Heritage Elemtary School
833 Guilford Blvd (44256-3028)
PHONE..............................330 636-4400
Tharen Houck, *Principal*
Carol Starrick, *Principal*
EMP: 40
SALES (est): 588.3K **Privately Held**
SIC: 8641 Parent-teachers' association

(G-13949)
HINCKLEY ROOFING INC
3587 Ridge Rd (44256-7917)
P.O. Box 458, Hinckley (44233-0458)
PHONE..............................330 722-7663
Ed Walkuski, *President*
Pam Walkuski, *Treasurer*
Steve Walkuski Jr, *Admin Sec*
EMP: 25
SQ FT: 2,000
SALES (est): 2.7MM **Privately Held**
SIC: 1761 Roofing contractor

(G-13950)
HMT DERMATOLOGY ASSOCIATES INC (PA)
Also Called: Trillium Creek Drmtlogy Srgery
5783 Wooster Pike (44256-8816)
PHONE..............................330 725-0569
Helen M Torok, *President*
EMP: 32 EST: 1979
SALES (est): 4.4MM **Privately Held**
SIC: 8011 Dermatologist

(G-13951)
HOSPICE OF THE WESTERN RESERVE
5075 Windfall Rd (44256-8613)
PHONE..............................330 800-2240
William E Finn, *CEO*
EMP: 57

SALES (corp-wide): 89.8MM **Privately Held**
SIC: 8082 8069 Home health care services; specialty hospitals, except psychiatric
PA: Hospice Of The Western Reserve, Inc
17876 Saint Clair Ave
Cleveland OH 44110
216 383-2222

(G-13952)
HOWARD HANNA SMYTHE CRAMER
3565 Medina Rd (44256-8182)
PHONE..............................330 725-4137
Karen Thompson, *Manager*
EMP: 53
SALES (corp-wide): 73.7MM **Privately Held**
WEB: www.smythecramer.com
SIC: 6531 6311 6141 6361 Real estate brokers & agents; life insurance; consumer finance companies; title insurance
HQ: Howard Hanna Smythe Cramer
6000 Parkland Blvd
Cleveland OH 44124
216 447-4477

(G-13953)
INDUSTRIAL CHEMICAL CORP (PA)
Also Called: Custom Pak
885 W Smith Rd (44256-2424)
PHONE..............................330 725-0800
Ron Camaglia, *President*
Frederick Camaglia, *CFO*
▲ EMP: 50
SQ FT: 55,000
SALES (est): 28.6MM **Privately Held**
SIC: 5169 7389 Chemicals, industrial & heavy; caustic soda; packaging & labeling services

(G-13954)
INN AT MEDINA LIMITED LLC
Also Called: Inn At Medina The
100 High Point Dr Ofc (44256-4363)
PHONE..............................330 723-0110
Dan Ihrig,
EMP: 70 EST: 2000
SQ FT: 60,000
SALES (est): 2.4MM **Privately Held**
SIC: 8322 Individual & family services

(G-13955)
INTEGRES GLOBAL LOGISTICS INC (DH)
Also Called: Integres Fast Forward Shipping
84 Medina Rd (44256-9616)
PHONE..............................866 347-2101
R Louis Schneeberger, *President*
EMP: 79
SQ FT: 20,954
SALES (est): 6.1MM
SALES (corp-wide): 3B **Publicly Held**
WEB: www.integres.com
SIC: 4213 Trucking, except local

(G-13956)
INTERACTIVE ENGINEERING CORP
884 Medina Rd (44256-9615)
PHONE..............................330 239-6888
Ming Zhang, *President*
Andy Dan, *Purchasing*
EMP: 25
SQ FT: 200,000
SALES (est): 3.3MM **Privately Held**
SIC: 8748 3672 Systems analysis & engineering consulting services; printed circuit boards

(G-13957)
INTERVENTION FOR PEACE INC
Also Called: Peace Foundation
689 W Liberty St Ste 7 (44256-2268)
PHONE..............................330 725-1298
Pattie Henighan, *Human Resources*
Rick Davidson, *Manager*
David Clardy, *Executive*
EMP: 55
SALES (est): 1.6MM **Privately Held**
WEB: www.interventionforpeace.com
SIC: 8082 Visiting nurse service

(G-13958)
JACOR LLC
1011 Lake Rd (44256-2450)
PHONE..............................330 441-4182
Chester Sipsock, *CFO*
Jeremy Carter,
Robert Zufra,
EMP: 600
SQ FT: 4,100
SALES (est): 18.2MM **Privately Held**
WEB: www.gojacor.com
SIC: 7361 Executive placement

(G-13959)
JAMES B OSWALD COMPANY
Also Called: Hoffman Group The
5000 Foote Rd (44256-5396)
PHONE..............................330 723-3637
Jaclyn Caniglia, *Client Mgr*
Robin Hammond, *Manager*
Michael Casey, *Executive*
EMP: 40
SALES (corp-wide): 165.6MM **Privately Held**
SIC: 6411 6331 6321 Insurance agents; fire, marine & casualty insurance; accident & health insurance
PA: The James B Oswald Company
1100 Superior Ave E # 1500
Cleveland OH 44114
216 367-8787

(G-13960)
JARRELLS MOVING & TRANSPORT CO
1155 Industrial Pkwy (44256-2492)
PHONE..............................330 952-1240
Robert S Zufra, *Branch Mgr*
EMP: 50
SALES (corp-wide): 10.6MM **Privately Held**
SIC: 4789 Pipeline terminal facilities, independently operated
PA: Jarrells Moving & Transport Co., Inc
5076 Park Ave W
Seville OH 44273
330 764-4333

(G-13961)
JPMORGAN CHASE BANK NAT ASSN
3626 Medina Rd (44256-8100)
PHONE..............................330 722-6626
Dave Cleckner, *Branch Mgr*
EMP: 26
SALES (corp-wide): 131.4B **Publicly Held**
WEB: www.chase.com
SIC: 6029 Commercial banks
HQ: Jpmorgan Chase Bank, National Association
1111 Polaris Pkwy
Columbus OH 43240
614 436-3055

(G-13962)
JUSTICE & CO INC
Also Called: Architectural Justice
2462 Pearl Rd (44256-9015)
PHONE..............................330 225-6000
James Justice, *President*
Annette Rieth, *Office Mgr*
▲ EMP: 25
SQ FT: 10,000
SALES (est): 5.3MM **Privately Held**
SIC: 5713 5032 Floor tile; granite building stone

(G-13963)
K & M CONSTRUCTION COMPANY
230 E Smith Rd (44256-2623)
PHONE..............................330 723-3681
Jerry A Schwab, *President*
David Schwab, *Vice Pres*
Mary Lynn Hites, *Treasurer*
Donna L Schwab, *Admin Sec*
EMP: 128
SQ FT: 2,000
SALES (est): 6MM
SALES (corp-wide): 29.7B **Privately Held**
SIC: 1611 1771 Resurfacing contractor; driveway, parking lot & blacktop contractors

HQ: Medina Supply Company
   230 E Smith Rd
   Medina OH 44256
   330 723-3681

(G-13964)
KAISER FOUNDATION HOSPITALS
Also Called: Medina Medical Offices
3443 Medina Rd (44256-5360)
PHONE............................800 524-7377
Marvin Baker, *Branch Mgr*
EMP: 593
SALES (corp-wide): 93B **Privately Held**
SIC: 8011 Offices & clinics of medical doctors
HQ: Kaiser Foundation Hospitals Inc
   1 Kaiser Plz
   Oakland CA 94612
   510 271-6611

(G-13965)
KENMAR LAWN & GRDN CARE CO LLC
Also Called: Kenmar Landscaping Company
3665 Ridge Rd (44256-7918)
P.O. Box 281 (44258-0281)
PHONE............................330 239-2924
Kenneth Bell, *Owner*
EMP: 48
SALES (est): 5.8MM **Privately Held**
SIC: 5083 Landscaping equipment

(G-13966)
KRAKOWSKI TRUCKING INC
1100 W Smith Rd (44256-3500)
PHONE............................330 722-7935
Barbara Krakowski, *President*
Lawrence C Krakowski, *President*
William Disbrow, *Vice Pres*
EMP: 39
SQ FT: 2,146
SALES (est): 4.5MM **Privately Held**
WEB: www.ktitrucking.com
SIC: 4731 Domestic freight forwarding

(G-13967)
KTIB INC
1100 W Smith Rd (44256-2443)
PHONE............................330 722-7935
Barbara J Krakowski, *President*
William R Disbrow, *Vice Pres*
EMP: 30
SALES (est): 2.8MM **Privately Held**
SIC: 4212 Local trucking, without storage

(G-13968)
MARKS CLEANING SERVICE INC
325 S Elmwood Ave (44256-2322)
PHONE............................330 725-5702
Eric Palmer, *President*
Mark Skoda, *President*
Bonnie Skoda, *Vice Pres*
Mike Hansen, *Opers Mgr*
Michael Gallucci, *Manager*
EMP: 37
SALES (est): 2MM **Privately Held**
WEB: www.markscleaning.com
SIC: 7217 7349 Carpet & upholstery cleaning on customer premises; janitorial service, contract basis

(G-13969)
MARVIN W MIELKE INC
Also Called: Mw Mielke
1040 Industrial Pkwy (44256-2449)
PHONE............................330 725-8845
David A Mielke, *President*
Terry Mielke, *Vice Pres*
Mary Jane Mielke, *Treasurer*
Amamda Prior, *Manager*
EMP: 100
SQ FT: 20,000
SALES: 25MM **Privately Held**
WEB: www.mwmielke.com
SIC: 1711 Plumbing contractors; sprinkler contractors; warm air heating & air conditioning contractor

(G-13970)
MEDINA ADVANTAGE INC
Also Called: Kids Country
3550 Octagon Dr (44256-6836)
PHONE............................330 723-8697
Christine Burkholder, *President*
Rick Burkholder, *Principal*

EMP: 30
SALES (est): 779.4K **Privately Held**
SIC: 8351 Group day care center

(G-13971)
MEDINA CNTY JVNILE DTNTION CTR
655 Independence Dr (44256-3547)
PHONE............................330 764-8408
Ronald Stollar, *Superintendent*
Reva Keaton, *Manager*
EMP: 33
SALES (est): 1.6MM **Privately Held**
SIC: 8361 Juvenile correctional home

(G-13972)
MEDINA COUNTY SANITARY
791 W Smith Rd (44256-2422)
P.O. Box 542 (44258-0542)
PHONE............................330 273-3610
Jim Troike, *Manager*
EMP: 37
SALES (est): 6MM **Privately Held**
SIC: 8711 Sanitary engineers

(G-13973)
MEDINA CREATIVE ACCESSIBILITY
232 N Court St (44256-1925)
PHONE............................330 591-4434
Diane De-Pasquale-Hagerty, *CEO*
Dianne De-Pasquale-Hagerty, *Principal*
EMP: 80
SALES: 3MM **Privately Held**
SIC: 8322 Association for the handicapped

(G-13974)
MEDINA GLASS BLOCK INC
Also Called: GBA Architectural Pdts Svcs
1213 Medina Rd Ste A (44256-5408)
PHONE............................330 239-0239
Jeffery W Boesch, *President*
Stephen J Boesch, *Vice Pres*
▲ EMP: 25
SQ FT: 38,000
SALES (est): 9MM **Privately Held**
WEB: www.medinaglassblock.com
SIC: 1793 5039 5231 Glass & glazing work; glass construction materials; glass

(G-13975)
MEDINA HOSPITAL
Life Support Team
1000 E Washington St (44256-2167)
PHONE............................330 723-3117
Ken Milligan, *Branch Mgr*
EMP: 30
SALES (corp-wide): 101.8MM **Privately Held**
SIC: 8062 General medical & surgical hospitals
PA: Medina Hospital
   1000 E Washington St
   Medina OH 44256
   330 725-1000

(G-13976)
MEDINA MANAGEMENT COMPANY LLC
Also Called: Medina Automall
3205 Medina Rd (44256-9631)
PHONE............................330 723-3291
Jim Brown, *Principal*
EMP: 70
SQ FT: 30,526
SALES (est): 1.3MM **Privately Held**
SIC: 5012 Automobiles

(G-13977)
MEDINA MEADOWS
550 Miner Dr (44256-1472)
PHONE............................330 725-1550
Sharona Grunspan, *President*
Sam Krichevsky, *Vice Pres*
EMP: 85
SQ FT: 28,000
SALES (est): 3.8MM **Privately Held**
SIC: 8051 Convalescent home with continuous nursing care

(G-13978)
MEDINA MEDICAL INVESTORS LTD
Also Called: Life Care Center of Medina
2400 Columbia Rd (44256-9414)
PHONE............................330 483-3131
Jim Everley, *Managing Dir*
Forrest I Preston, *General Ptnr*
Rob Berger, *Human Res Dir*
EMP: 180
SQ FT: 70,000
SALES: 8.5MM **Privately Held**
SIC: 8051 8059 Convalescent home with continuous nursing care; rest home, with health care

(G-13979)
MICHAEL T LEE DVM
Also Called: Animal Medical Center Medina
1060 S Court St (44256-2885)
PHONE............................330 722-5076
Michael T Lee Dvm, *Owner*
Kim Davey,
William Feeman,
EMP: 30 EST: 1980
SQ FT: 1,500
SALES (est): 1.4MM **Privately Held**
WEB:
www.animalmedicalcentreofmedina.com
SIC: 0742 Animal hospital services, pets & other animal specialties; veterinarian, animal specialties

(G-13980)
NEW BIRCH MANOR I ASSOC LLC
Also Called: Birch Manor Apartments I
23875 Miner Dr (44256)
PHONE............................330 723-3404
ABC Management, *Principal*
Larry Looney, *Mng Member*
EMP: 99
SALES: 1,000K **Privately Held**
SIC: 6513 Apartment building operators

(G-13981)
NORHTEAST OHIO MUSEUM
6807 Boneta Rd (44256-9771)
PHONE............................330 336-7657
Wayne H Lavin, *Owner*
EMP: 27
SALES (est): 366.7K **Privately Held**
SIC: 8412 Museum

(G-13982)
NORTH GATEWAY TIRE CO INC
4001 Pearl Rd (44256-9000)
PHONE............................330 725-8473
Robert H Dunlap, *CEO*
Darrell Hill, *President*
G E Mc Kittrick, *Corp Secy*
EMP: 41
SQ FT: 40,000
SALES (est): 1.9MM
SALES (corp-wide): 110MM **Privately Held**
WEB: www.northgatewaytire.com
SIC: 5531 5014 Automotive tires; automobile tires & tubes
PA: Dunlap & Kyle Company, Inc.
   280 Eureka St
   Batesville MS 38606
   662 563-7601

(G-13983)
NURTURY
250 N Spring Grove St (44256-1921)
PHONE............................330 723-1800
Mary Kubasta, *President*
Kent Kubasta, *Vice Pres*
EMP: 30
SQ FT: 7,500
SALES (est): 959K **Privately Held**
WEB: www.thenurturyschool.com
SIC: 8351 Nursery school; preschool center

(G-13984)
OHIO CAMP CHERITH INC
3854 Remsen Rd (44256-7656)
PHONE............................330 725-4202
Judy Kirsch, *President*
Gary Waldinger, *Vice Pres*
Sharon Lort, *Admin Sec*
EMP: 25

SALES: 57K **Privately Held**
SIC: 7032 Boys' camp; girls' camp; summer camp, except day & sports instructional

(G-13985)
PANTHER II TRANSPORTATION INC (DH)
84 Medina Rd (44256-9616)
PHONE............................800 685-0657
R Louis Schneeberger, *CEO*
Edward Wadel, *COO*
David Buss, *Vice Pres*
Allen Motter, *Vice Pres*
David Sosnowski, *Vice Pres*
EMP: 185
SQ FT: 33,000
SALES (est): 72.9MM
SALES (corp-wide): 3B **Publicly Held**
WEB: www.panther2.com
SIC: 4213 4212 4522 Trucking, except local; local trucking, without storage; air transportation, nonscheduled
HQ: Panther Premium Logistics, Inc.
   84 Medina Rd
   Medina OH 44256
   800 685-0657

(G-13986)
PANTHER PREMIUM LOGISTICS INC (HQ)
84 Medina Rd (44256-9616)
PHONE............................800 685-0657
R Louis Schneeberger, *President*
Edward Wadel, *COO*
David Buss, *Vice Pres*
Frank Ilacqua, *Vice Pres*
Bob Businger, *CFO*
EMP: 300
SQ FT: 50,000
SALES (est): 159.4MM
SALES (corp-wide): 3B **Publicly Held**
WEB: www.pantherii.com
SIC: 4213 4212 Trucking, except local; local trucking, without storage
PA: Arcbest Corporation
   8401 Mcclure Dr
   Fort Smith AR 72916
   479 785-6000

(G-13987)
PLASTIPAK PACKAGING INC
850 W Smith Rd (44256-2425)
PHONE............................330 725-0205
Frank Kovacek, *Maint Spvr*
Robert Jedreski, *Manager*
Larry Booth, *Manager*
EMP: 200
SQ FT: 60,000
SALES (corp-wide): 1.3B **Privately Held**
WEB: www.plastipak.com
SIC: 5199 Packaging materials
HQ: Plastipak Packaging, Inc.
   41605 Ann Arbor Rd E
   Plymouth MI 48170
   734 455-3600

(G-13988)
PRIME POLYMERS INC
Also Called: Engineered Polymer Systems
2600 Medina Rd (44256-8145)
P.O. Box 351, Sharon Center (44274-0351)
PHONE............................330 662-4200
Ronnie Rotli, *President*
EMP: 25
SQ FT: 80,000
SALES (est): 4.4MM **Privately Held**
WEB: www.primepolymers.com
SIC: 1771 1752 1799 1611 Concrete repair; floor laying & floor work; coating, caulking & weather, water & fireproofing; resurfacing contractor

(G-13989)
PROFESSIONAL RESTORATION SVC
Also Called: Serv Pro of Barberton/Norton
1170 Industrial Pkwy (44256-2486)
P.O. Box 22, Barberton (44203-0022)
PHONE............................330 825-1803
Michal Fosdick, *President*
EMP: 42 EST: 1996
SQ FT: 36,500

SALES (est): 1.7MM **Privately Held**
WEB: www.spbarberton.com
SIC: 7349 Building component cleaning service

(G-13990)
PSYCHOLOGY CONSULTANTS INC
3591 Reserve Commons Dr # 301 (44256-5334)
PHONE...................................330 764-7916
Thomas McArthy, *President*
Thomas I McArthy, *CFO*
Beth Plumley, *Administration*
EMP: 40
SALES (est): 1.5MM **Privately Held**
SIC: 8999 Psychological consultant

(G-13991)
PULTE HOMES INC
387 Medina Rd Ste 1700 (44256-9679)
PHONE...................................330 239-1587
Paul Spenthoff, *Vice Pres*
EMP: 30
SALES (est): 1.4MM **Privately Held**
SIC: 1522 Residential construction

(G-13992)
REA & ASSOCIATES INC
694 E Washington St (44256-2125)
PHONE...................................330 722-8222
Ted Klimczak, *CPA*
Vicki Cooper, *Sales Mgr*
Dan Watson, *Branch Mgr*
Janis Mack, *Office Admin*
EMP: 27
SQ FT: 6,400
SALES (corp-wide): 32.3MM **Privately Held**
WEB: www.reacpa.com
SIC: 8721 Certified public accountant
PA: Rea & Associates, Inc.
419 W High Ave
New Philadelphia OH 44663
330 339-6651

(G-13993)
REC CENTER
Also Called: Medina Community Recrtl Ctr
855 Weymouth Rd (44256-2039)
PHONE...................................330 721-6900
Darlene Donkin, *Manager*
Mike Wright, *Director*
EMP: 40 EST: 2011
SALES (est): 57K **Privately Held**
SIC: 7999 Recreation center

(G-13994)
REDEFINE ENTERPRISES LLC
Also Called: Rise Fitness
3839 Pearl Rd (44256-9001)
PHONE...................................330 952-2024
Andrew Hamlin, *Mng Member*
EMP: 28 EST: 2016
SQ FT: 12,500
SALES (est): 43.2K **Privately Held**
SIC: 7991 Physical fitness facilities

(G-13995)
REFLECTIONS HAIR STUDIO INC
3605 Medina Rd (44256-8181)
PHONE...................................330 725-5782
Lori Daso, *President*
EMP: 32
SQ FT: 3,000
SALES: 320K **Privately Held**
SIC: 7231 Hairdressers

(G-13996)
REGAL CINEMAS INC
Also Called: Huntington Street 16
200 W Reagan Pkwy (44256-1567)
PHONE...................................330 723-4416
Raymond Flato, *Manager*
EMP: 35 **Privately Held**
WEB: www.regalcinemas.com
SIC: 7832 Motion Picture Theaters
HQ: Regal Cinemas, Inc.
101 E Blount Ave Ste 100
Knoxville TN 37920
865 922-1123

(G-13997)
S&V INDUSTRIES INC (PA)
5054 Paramount Dr (44256-5363)
PHONE...................................330 666-1986

Senthil Sundarapandian, *CEO*
Senthil Kumar Sundarapandian, *CEO*
Mahesh Douglas, *President*
Joan Owens, *Vice Pres*
▲ EMP: 40
SQ FT: 1,618
SALES (est): 50MM **Privately Held**
WEB: www.svindustries.com
SIC: 5049 3089 3312 Engineers' equipment & supplies; casting of plastic; forgings, iron & steel

(G-13998)
SAMARITAN CARE CENTER & VILLA
806 E Washington St (44256-2194)
PHONE...................................330 725-4123
Bob Banasik, *President*
Amy Donaldson, *Administration*
Kirk Hartline, *Administration*
EMP: 100
SALES (est): 4.7MM
SALES (corp-wide): 9.1MM **Privately Held**
WEB: www.omnilife.net
SIC: 8059 8051 8052 Nursing home, except skilled & intermediate care facility; skilled nursing care facilities; intermediate care facilities
PA: Omnilife Health Care Systems, Inc.
50 W 5th Ave
Columbus OH 43201
614 299-3100

(G-13999)
SANDRIDGE FOOD CORPORATION
Also Called: Sandridge Gourmet Salads
133 Commerce Dr (44256-1333)
PHONE...................................330 725-8883
Barry Pioski, *Manager*
EMP: 225
SALES (corp-wide): 114.5MM **Privately Held**
WEB: www.sandridge.com
SIC: 2099 5141 Salads, fresh or refrigerated; groceries, general line
PA: Sandridge Food Corporation
133 Commerce Dr
Medina OH 44256
330 725-2348

(G-14000)
SENIOR CARE INC
Also Called: Elmcroft of Medina
1046 N Jefferson St (44256-1102)
PHONE...................................330 721-2000
Greg Kaminfki, *Branch Mgr*
EMP: 66 **Privately Held**
SIC: 8052 Intermediate care facilities
PA: Senior Care, Inc.
700 N Hurstbourne Pkwy # 200
Louisville KY 40222

(G-14001)
SIMMONS BROTHERS CORPORATION
780 W Smith Rd Ste A (44256-3513)
PHONE...................................330 722-1415
Donald Simmons, *CEO*
William Simmons, *President*
Stephen Hummel, *Vice Pres*
David Simmons, *Vice Pres*
EMP: 32 EST: 1959
SQ FT: 14,336
SALES (est): 6.4MM **Privately Held**
SIC: 1541 Industrial buildings, new construction

(G-14002)
SISLER HEATING & COOLING INC
249 S State Rd (44256-2430)
P.O. Box 308 (44258-0308)
PHONE...................................330 722-7101
Dennis Sisler, *President*
Christy Meadows, *Admin Sec*
EMP: 32
SQ FT: 7,500
SALES (est): 4MM **Privately Held**
SIC: 1711 1794 Ventilation & duct work contractor; warm air heating & air conditioning contractor; excavation work

(G-14003)
SOCIETY HANDICAPPED CITZ MEDIN
5810 Deerview Ln (44256-8003)
PHONE...................................330 722-1710
EMP: 88
SALES (corp-wide): 8MM **Privately Held**
SIC: 1521 New construction, single-family houses
PA: Society For Handicapped Citizens Of Medina County
4283 Paradise Rd
Seville OH 44273
330 722-1900

(G-14004)
SOUTH STAR CORP
Also Called: Number 1 Landscaping
3775 Ridge Rd (44256-7919)
PHONE...................................330 239-5466
Tom Csanyi, *President*
EMP: 30 EST: 1987
SQ FT: 2,226
SALES (est): 3.2MM **Privately Held**
WEB: www.southstarcorp.com
SIC: 0782 Landscape contractors

(G-14005)
STEINGASS MECHANICAL CONTG
754 S Progress Dr (44256-1368)
PHONE...................................330 725-6090
William Steingass, *Principal*
Linda Steingass, *Corp Secy*
Chad Barco, *Project Mgr*
Mike Steingass, *Purch Mgr*
Richard Mann, *Manager*
EMP: 30
SQ FT: 12,000
SALES (est): 7.4MM **Privately Held**
WEB: www.steingassmechanical.com
SIC: 1711 1794 Plumbing contractors; warm air heating & air conditioning contractor; fire sprinkler system installation; excavation & grading, building construction

(G-14006)
SUMMA HEALTH CENTER LK MEDINA
3780 Medina Rd Ste 220 (44256-9312)
PHONE...................................330 952-0014
Victoria J Meshekow, *Principal*
EMP: 39 EST: 2010
SALES (est): 4.1MM **Privately Held**
SIC: 8062 General medical & surgical hospitals

(G-14007)
SUMMIT MANAGEMENT SERVICES INC
201 Northland Dr Ofc (44256-1528)
PHONE...................................330 723-0864
EMP: 42
SALES (corp-wide): 6MM **Privately Held**
SIC: 6513 Apartment building operators
PA: Summit Management Services, Inc.
730 W Market St
Akron OH 44303
330 762-4011

(G-14008)
SUPER TAN
1110 N Court St (44256-1578)
PHONE...................................330 722-2799
Jodie James, *Owner*
EMP: 50
SALES (est): 343.8K **Privately Held**
SIC: 7299 Tanning salon

(G-14009)
TEKNOBILITY LLC
3013 Gary Kyle Ct (44256-6854)
PHONE...................................216 255-9433
Carmen Melillo, *President*
Carmen D Melillo, *Principal*
EMP: 45
SALES (est): 2.6MM **Privately Held**
SIC: 7373 Computer systems analysis & design

(G-14010)
TELCOM CONSTRUCTION SVCS INC
5067 Paramount Dr (44256-5364)
PHONE...................................330 239-6900
Joe Anello, *President*
EMP: 85 EST: 1998
SQ FT: 5,000
SALES (est): 12.4MM **Privately Held**
WEB: www.telcomcs.com
SIC: 4899 Communication signal enhancement network system

(G-14011)
TELINX SOLUTIONS LLC
961 Mallet Hill Ct (44256-3098)
PHONE...................................330 819-0657
Lola Cargill,
EMP: 25
SALES (est): 825.9K **Privately Held**
SIC: 7389 Telemarketing services; telephone solicitation service; fund raising organizations; subscription fulfillment services: magazine, newspaper, etc.

(G-14012)
VERMEER SALES & SERVICE INC (PA)
2389 Medina Rd (44256-9666)
PHONE...................................330 723-8383
Frank Sklarski, *President*
Cathie Sklarski, *Corp Secy*
Gary Snook, *Manager*
EMP: 39
SQ FT: 6,500
SALES (est): 26.5MM **Privately Held**
SIC: 5082 7699 Contractors' materials; construction equipment repair

(G-14013)
VEXOR TECHNOLOGY INC (PA)
955 W Smith Rd (44256-2446)
PHONE...................................330 721-9773
Joseph E Waters, *President*
Steven M Berry, *President*
F Phillip Stapf, *Principal*
Fred Stapf, *Vice Pres*
Brian Surane, *Vice Pres*
▲ EMP: 37
SQ FT: 60,800
SALES (est): 17.5MM **Privately Held**
WEB: www.vexortechnology.com
SIC: 4953 4212 Recycling, waste materials; local trucking, without storage

(G-14014)
WESTERN RSRVE MSONIC CMNTY INC
4931 Nettleton Rd # 4318 (44256-5353)
PHONE...................................330 721-3000
Jay Dettorre, *Exec Dir*
EMP: 150
SALES (est): 8.7MM **Privately Held**
SIC: 8059 8052 8051 Rest home, with health care; intermediate care facilities; skilled nursing care facilities
PA: Browning Mesonic Community Inc
8883 Browning Dr
Waterville OH 43566
419 878-4055

(G-14015)
WOLCOTT GROUP
1684 Medina Rd Ste 204 (44256-9316)
PHONE...................................330 666-5900
Daniel P Butcher, *Principal*
EMP: 31
SALES (est): 2.8MM **Privately Held**
SIC: 7379 Computer related consulting services

Mentor
Lake County

(G-14016)
ALLIANCE HOSPITALITY INC
Also Called: Comfort Inn
7701 Reynolds Rd (44060-5320)
PHONE...................................440 951-7333
Jessica Gilbride, *Manager*
EMP: 30

SALES (corp-wide): 11.2MM **Privately Held**
SIC: 7011 7999 Hotels & motels; swimming pool, non-membership; tennis courts, outdoor/indoor: non-membership
PA: Alliance Hospitality, Inc.
600 Enterprise Dr
Lewis Center OH 43035
614 846-6600

(G-14017)
ALTERCARE OF MENTOR CENTER
9901 Johnnycake Ridge Rd (44060-6739)
PHONE 440 953-4421
Gerald Schroer, *President*
EMP: 150
SALES (est): 1.5MM **Privately Held**
SIC: 8051 Convalescent home with continuous nursing care

(G-14018)
ANGELS IN WAITING HOME CARE
8336 Tyler Blvd (44060-4221)
PHONE 440 946-0349
Terri Jochum, *Branch Mgr*
EMP: 32
SALES (corp-wide): 1.1MM **Privately Held**
SIC: 8082 Home health care services
PA: Angels In Waiting Home Care
38052 Euclid Ave Ste 280
Willoughby OH 44094
440 946-0347

(G-14019)
AQUA OHIO INC
8644 Station St (44060-4316)
PHONE 440 255-3984
Lou Kreider, *Manager*
EMP: 25
SALES (corp-wide): 838MM **Publicly Held**
SIC: 4941 Water supply
HQ: Aqua Ohio, Inc.
6650 South Ave
Youngstown OH 44512
330 726-8151

(G-14020)
AVERY DENNISON CORPORATION
Also Called: Avery Dennison Materials Group
8080 Norton Pkwy (44060-5990)
PHONE 440 534-6000
Mike Kuhno, *Engineer*
Tim Merkel, *Accounts Exec*
Fabiana Wu, *Mktg Dir*
Rachel Berger, *Marketing Staff*
David Collins, *Manager*
EMP: 115
SALES (corp-wide): 7.1B **Publicly Held**
WEB: www.avery.com
SIC: 5199 7389 Packaging materials; packaging & labeling services
PA: Avery Dennison Corporation
207 N Goode Ave Ste 500
Glendale CA 91203
626 304-2000

(G-14021)
BEACON HEALTH
9220 Mentor Ave (44060-6412)
PHONE 440 354-9924
Spencer Kline, *CEO*
EMP: 150
SQ FT: 14,000
SALES: 6MM **Privately Held**
WEB: www.neighboring.org
SIC: 8093 Mental health clinic, outpatient

(G-14022)
BLACKBROOK COUNTRY CLUB INC
8900 Lake Shore Blvd (44060-1524)
PHONE 440 951-0010
Mary Lou Colbow, *President*
Karen Hillock, *Vice Pres*
EMP: 35
SQ FT: 3,500
SALES (est): 874.9K **Privately Held**
SIC: 7992 Public golf courses

(G-14023)
BURRIER SERVICE COMPANY INC
Also Called: Hvac
8669 Twinbrook Rd (44060-4340)
P.O. Box 661 (44061-0661)
PHONE 440 946-6019
Cary Burrier, *President*
Kevin Barry, *Vice Pres*
EMP: 30
SQ FT: 6,400
SALES (est): 5MM **Privately Held**
WEB: www.have.com
SIC: 1711 Warm air heating & air conditioning contractor; refrigeration contractor

(G-14024)
BUYERS PRODUCTS COMPANY (PA)
9049 Tyler Blvd (44060-4800)
PHONE 440 974-8888
Mark Saltzman, *President*
Dave Durst, *General Mgr*
Brian Smith, *COO*
Jeff Mueller, *Vice Pres*
Brian Lanican, *Mfg Dir*
▲ **EMP:** 160 **EST:** 1947
SQ FT: 172,000
SALES (est): 149MM **Privately Held**
WEB: www.buyersproducts.com
SIC: 5013 3714 Truck parts & accessories; motor vehicle parts & accessories

(G-14025)
CARDINALCOMMERCE CORPORATION
Also Called: C C
8100 Tyler Blvd Ste 100 (44060-4887)
PHONE 877 352-8444
Michael A Keresman III, *CEO*
Chandra Balasubramanian, *Exec VP*
Francis M Sherwin, *Exec VP*
Erik Enright, *Vice Pres*
Eric Goodman, *Vice Pres*
EMP: 60
SALES (est): 10.2MM **Privately Held**
SIC: 7361 Employment agencies

(G-14026)
CCI SUPPLY INC
8620 Tyler Blvd (44060-4300)
PHONE 440 953-0045
Tim Small, *President*
Ed Marko, *Vice Pres*
Jon Small, *Vice Pres*
Mark T Small, *Vice Pres*
Mark Small, *CFO*
EMP: 187
SQ FT: 22,000
SALES (est): 14.6MM **Privately Held**
SIC: 5032 5033 5211 Brick, stone & related material; insulation materials; lumber & other building materials; insulation material, building

(G-14027)
CELLCO PARTNERSHIP
Also Called: Verizon
7685 Mentor Ave (44060-5540)
PHONE 440 953-1155
Terry Tindel, *Branch Mgr*
EMP: 25
SALES (corp-wide): 130.8B **Publicly Held**
SIC: 4812 5999 Cellular telephone services; mobile telephones & equipment
HQ: Cellco Partnership
1 Verizon Way
Basking Ridge NJ 07920

(G-14028)
CHARTER HOTEL GROUP LTD PARTNR (PA)
Also Called: Courtyard By Marriott
5966 Heisley Rd (44060-1886)
PHONE 216 772-4538
Patricia Treaster, *Principal*
EMP: 35
SQ FT: 2,500
SALES (est): 1.6MM **Privately Held**
SIC: 7011 5812 Hotels; eating places

(G-14029)
CHEMSULTANTS INTERNATIONAL INC (PA)
9079 Tyler Blvd (44060-1868)
P.O. Box 1118 (44061-1118)
PHONE 440 974-3080
Judith Muny, *Corp Secy*
Keith Muny, *Vice Pres*
Mark Van Ness, *Prdtn Mgr*
Jennifer Muny, *Director*
Bonnie Cole-King, *Director*
EMP: 25
SQ FT: 10,000
SALES (est): 5.4MM **Privately Held**
SIC: 3821 8734 8742 Laboratory apparatus & furniture; product testing laboratory, safety or performance; industry specialist consultants

(G-14030)
CLASSIC INTERNATIONAL INC (PA)
Also Called: Classic Lexus
8470 Tyler Blvd (44060-4230)
P.O. Box 300 (44061-0300)
PHONE 440 975-1222
James Brown, *President*
Larry Villines, *CFO*
Barry Rice, *Sales Associate*
Vicky Prokop, *Admin Sec*
EMP: 62
SQ FT: 18,000
SALES (est): 24.1MM **Privately Held**
WEB: www.classiclexus.com
SIC: 5511 7538 Automobiles, new & used; general automotive repair shops

(G-14031)
CLEVELAND CONSTRUCTION INC (PA)
Also Called: CCI
8620 Tyler Blvd (44060-4348)
PHONE 440 255-8000
Jon Small, *President*
James Ferro, *General Mgr*
Scott Kershaw, *Superintendent*
Nick Small, *Superintendent*
Meghan Bracken, *Vice Pres*
▲ **EMP:** 50
SQ FT: 42,500
SALES (est): 400.6MM **Privately Held**
SIC: 1542 1742 1752 Commercial & office building contractors; commercial & office building, new construction; commercial & office buildings, renovation & repair; specialized public building contractors; plastering, plain or ornamental; drywall; insulation, buildings; acoustical & ceiling work; floor laying & floor work

(G-14032)
CLS FACILITIES MGT SVCS INC
Also Called: Cls Facilities Management Svcs
8061 Tyler Blvd (44060-4809)
PHONE 440 602-4600
Robert A Waldrip, *President*
Bill Brodnick, *CFO*
Penny Broski, *Accounts Mgr*
Jason Simons, *Administration*
EMP: 37
SQ FT: 10,000
SALES (est): 15.8MM **Privately Held**
WEB: www.clsfacilityservices.com
SIC: 5063 1731 Lighting fixtures, commercial & industrial; lighting contractor

(G-14033)
COMMUNITY DIALYSIS CTR MENTOR
8900 Tyler Blvd (44060-2185)
PHONE 440 255-5999
Diane Wish, *CEO*
EMP: 40
SQ FT: 8,000
SALES (est): 992.8K **Privately Held**
SIC: 8092 Kidney dialysis centers

(G-14034)
CONTRACT MARKETING INC
Also Called: Sales Building Systems
9325 Progress Pkwy (44060-1855)
PHONE 440 639-9100
Patricia White, *CEO*
Timothy Mc Carthy, *President*
Terry Goins, *Exec VP*

Cindy Venable, *Finance Other*
Alice Mc Carthy, *Admin Sec*
EMP: 60
SQ FT: 20,000
SALES (est): 4.3MM **Privately Held**
WEB: www.sbsteam.com
SIC: 8742 Marketing consulting services

(G-14035)
CONVENIENT FOOD MART INC (HQ)
6078 Pinecone Dr (44060-1865)
PHONE 800 860-4844
John Call, *President*
EMP: 30
SQ FT: 12,000
SALES (est): 11MM **Privately Held**
SIC: 5411 5541 6794 Convenience stores, chain; filling stations, gasoline; franchises, selling or licensing

(G-14036)
COUNTY OF LAKE
Also Called: Deepwood Center
8121 Deepwood Blvd (44060-7703)
PHONE 440 350-5100
Elfriede Roman, *Superintendent*
Susan March, *Finance Dir*
EMP: 650 **Privately Held**
WEB: www.lakecountyohio.gov
SIC: 8331 Job training & vocational rehabilitation services
PA: County Of Lake
8 N State St Ste 215
Painesville OH 44077
440 350-2500

(G-14037)
CROSSROADS LAKE COUNTY ADOLE (PA)
8445 Munson Rd (44060-2410)
PHONE 440 255-1700
Noel Walker, *Principal*
Kenneth Iwashita, *Principal*
Tim Vicars, *Finance Mgr*
Dan Porter, *Director*
EMP: 118
SALES: 7.5MM **Privately Held**
WEB: www.crossroads-lake.org
SIC: 8093 8322 8011 Mental health clinic, outpatient; individual & family services; offices & clinics of medical doctors

(G-14038)
CT CONSULTANTS INC (PA)
8150 Sterling Ct (44060-5698)
PHONE 440 951-9000
David Wiles, *President*
Wes Hall, *Vice Pres*
Dustin Doherty, *Project Mgr*
Don Shvegzda, *Engineer*
Jim Shumate, *Project Engr*
EMP: 128
SQ FT: 24,000
SALES (est): 40MM **Privately Held**
WEB: www.ctconsultants.com
SIC: 8713 8711 8712 Surveying services; civil engineering; structural engineering; electrical or electronic engineering; mechanical engineering; architectural services

(G-14039)
DCR SYSTEMS LLC (PA)
Also Called: Classic Accident Repair Center
8697 Tyler Blvd (44060-4346)
PHONE 440 205-9900
Mandy Wynn, *Manager*
Michael J Giarrizzo Jr,
Kevin Nugent, *Master*
EMP: 40
SALES (est): 4.5MM **Privately Held**
WEB: www.dcrsystems.net
SIC: 7538 General automotive repair shops

(G-14040)
DEEPWOOD INDUSTRIES INC
8121 Deepwood Blvd (44060-7703)
PHONE 440 350-5231
Brett Bevis, *President*
Laura Harig, *Treasurer*
EMP: 181

SALES: 815.4K **Privately Held**
WEB: www.deepwoodindustries.com
SIC: **8322** 8331 7331 Settlement house;
job training & vocational rehabilitation
services; direct mail advertising services

(G-14041)
DELTH CORPORATION
Also Called: Rainbow Connection Day Care
6312 Center St Ste C (44060-2449)
PHONE......................................440 255-7655
Delrene Showman, *President*
EMP: 35
SALES (est): 990.9K **Privately Held**
SIC: **8351** Preschool center; group day
care center

(G-14042)
EAST MENTOR RECREATION INC
Also Called: Scores Fun Center
65 Normandy Dr (44060)
PHONE......................................440 354-2000
George Eisenhart Jr, *President*
Jody Hainrock, *Admin Sec*
EMP: 30
SALES (est): 1.4MM **Privately Held**
SIC: **7933** Ten pin center

(G-14043)
ELECTRO-ANALYTICAL INC
Also Called: E A Group
7118 Industrial Park Blvd (44060-5314)
PHONE......................................440 951-3514
Patrick G Herbert, *President*
Timothy S Bowen, *Vice Pres*
Jeffrey A Herbert, *Vice Pres*
EMP: 33
SQ FT: 7,700
SALES: 4MM **Privately Held**
WEB: www.eagroup-ohio.com
SIC: **8734** Testing laboratories

(G-14044)
EUCLID FISH COMPANY
7839 Enterprise Dr (44060-5386)
P.O. Box 180 (44061-0180)
PHONE......................................440 951-6448
Charles L Young, *Ch of Bd*
John Young, *President*
Marilyn G Young, *Corp Secy*
EMP: 66
SQ FT: 18,000
SALES (est): 38.8MM **Privately Held**
WEB: www.euclidfish.com
SIC: **5141** 5142 5143 5144 Food bro-
kers; packaged frozen goods; frozen fish,
meat & poultry; fish, frozen: packaged;
meat, frozen: packaged; dairy products,
except dried or canned; poultry & poultry
products; meat & fish markets; fish &
seafood markets; fruit & vegetable mar-
kets

(G-14045)
EVERSTAFF LLC
7448 Mentor Ave (44060-5406)
PHONE......................................440 992-0238
Danny Spitz, *Branch Mgr*
EMP: 33 **Privately Held**
SIC: **7363** Temporary help service
PA: Everstaff, Llc
6150 Oak Tree Blvd # 175
Independence OH 44131

(G-14046)
FAITHFUL COMPANIONS INC
8500 Station St Ste 111 (44060-4963)
PHONE......................................440 255-4357
Diana K Ross, *President*
Kenneth B Ross, *Exec VP*
EMP: 25
SQ FT: 700
SALES: 158K **Privately Held**
WEB: www.faithfulcompanions.com
SIC: **8082** Home health care services

(G-14047)
FEDEX FREIGHT CORPORATION
7685 Saint Clair Ave (44060-5235)
PHONE......................................877 661-8956
Ken Cary, *Manager*
Ken Radford, *Manager*
EMP: 28

(G-14048)
FREEDOM STEEL INC
8200 Tyler Blvd Ste G (44060-4250)
P.O. Box 391377, Solon (44139-8377)
PHONE......................................440 266-6800
Timothy Jacobs, *President*
EMP: 25
SQ FT: 200,000
SALES (est): 18.7MM **Privately Held**
WEB: www.freedomsteel.net
SIC: **5051** Steel

(G-14049)
FREEWAY LANES BOWL GROUP LLC
7300 Palisades Pkwy (44060-5302)
PHONE......................................440 946-5131
Dave Patz,
EMP: 25
SQ FT: 50,000
SALES (est): 634.3K **Privately Held**
SIC: **7933** 5812 Ten pin center; snack bar

(G-14050)
GENERAL ELECTRIC COMPANY
8696 Applewood Ct (44060-2212)
PHONE......................................440 255-0930
EMP: 119
SALES (corp-wide): 123.6B **Publicly Held**
SIC: **6153** Short-Term Business Credit In-
stitution
PA: General Electric Company
41 Farnsworth St
Boston MA 02210
617 443-3000

(G-14051)
GILES MARATHON INC
8648 Tyler Blvd (44060-4348)
PHONE......................................440 974-8815
James Gils, *President*
Eric Giles, *Vice Pres*
Judy Giles, *Admin Sec*
EMP: 25
SQ FT: 3,500
SALES (est): 3.4MM **Privately Held**
SIC: **5541** 7538 Filling stations, gasoline;
general automotive repair shops

(G-14052)
GORDON FOOD SERVICE INC
Also Called: G F S Marketplace
7220 Mentor Ave (44060-7522)
PHONE......................................440 953-1785
Jay Sheldon, *Manager*
Veronica Cekada, *Manager*
EMP: 30
SALES (corp-wide): 13B **Privately Held**
WEB: www.gfs.com
SIC: **5141** Groceries, general line
PA: Gordon Food Service, Inc.
1300 Gezon Pkwy Sw
Wyoming MI 49509
888 437-3663

(G-14053)
GOVERNORS POINTE LLC
8506 Hendricks Rd Ofc (44060-8642)
PHONE......................................440 205-1570
Christopher C Randall,
EMP: 40
SALES (est): 1.3MM **Privately Held**
WEB: www.randallresidence.com
SIC: **8059** Personal care home, with health
care

(G-14054)
GRACE HOSPICE LLC
7314 Industrial Park Blvd (44060-5318)
PHONE......................................216 288-7413
Mark Mitchell, *Branch Mgr*
EMP: 102 **Privately Held**
SIC: **8052** Personal care facility
PA: Grace Hospice, Llc
500 Kirts Blvd Ste 250
Troy MI 48084

(G-14055)
GREAT LAKES HOME HLTH SVCS INC
5966 Heisley Rd Ste 100 (44060-5849)
PHONE......................................888 260-9835
William L Deary III, *CEO*
EMP: 50 **Privately Held**
SIC: **8082** Home health care services
PA: Great Lakes Home Health Services,
Inc.
900 Cooper St
Jackson MI 49202

(G-14056)
GREAT LAKES POWER PRODUCTS INC (PA)
Also Called: John Deere Authorized Dealer
7455 Tyler Blvd (44060-8389)
PHONE......................................440 951-5111
Harry Allen Jr, *CEO*
Harry L Allen Jr, *Ch of Bd*
Richard J Pennza, *President*
David Bell, *Vice Pres*
Sam Profio, *Vice Pres*
▲ EMP: 60
SQ FT: 55,000
SALES (est): 31.9MM **Privately Held**
WEB: www.glpowerlift.com
SIC: **5085** 5084 3566 Power transmission
equipment & apparatus; materials han-
dling machinery; speed changers (power
transmission equipment), except auto

(G-14057)
GREINER DENTAL ASSOCIATION
7553 Center St (44060-6001)
PHONE......................................440 255-2600
Steve Greiner, *Owner*
Victoria Cvitkovic, *Office Mgr*
EMP: 30
SALES (est): 1.8MM **Privately Held**
SIC: **8021** Dentists' office

(G-14058)
HABCO TOOL AND DEV CO INC
7725 Metric Dr (44060-4863)
PHONE......................................440 946-5546
Steven Sanders, *President*
Ron Giannetti, *Exec VP*
James Patchin, *Plant Mgr*
Kathy Fulmer, *Purchasing*
EMP: 46 EST: 1955
SQ FT: 24,000
SALES: 3MM **Privately Held**
WEB: www.habcotool.com
SIC: **3599** 7692 Machine shop, jobbing &
repair; welding repair

(G-14059)
HEALTH CARE RTREMENT CORP AMER
Also Called: Heartland of Mentor
8200 Mentor Hills Dr (44060-7861)
PHONE......................................440 946-1912
Elizabeth Schupp, *Manager*
EMP: 200
SALES (corp-wide): 2.4B **Publicly Held**
WEB: www.hrc-manorcare.com
SIC: **8051** Skilled nursing care facilities
HQ: Health Care And Retirement Corpora-
tion Of America
333 N Summit St Ste 103
Toledo OH 43604
419 252-5500

(G-14060)
HERITAGE BEVERAGE COMPANY LLC
7333 Corporate Blvd (44060-4857)
PHONE......................................440 255-5550
Scott Siegel,
▲ EMP: 85
SQ FT: 15,000
SALES (est): 6.9MM **Privately Held**
SIC: **5181** Beer & other fermented malt
liquors

(G-14061)
HOME DEPOT USA INC
Also Called: Home Depot, The
9615 Diamond Centre Dr (44060-1879)
PHONE......................................440 357-0428
Gregory L Loney, *Store Mgr*

EMP: 150
SALES (corp-wide): 108.2B **Publicly Held**
WEB: www.homerentalsdepot.com
SIC: **5211** 7359 Home centers; tool rental
HQ: Home Depot U.S.A., Inc.
2455 Paces Ferry Ave
Atlanta GA 30339

(G-14062)
HZW ENVIRONMENTAL CONS LLC (PA)
6105 Heisley Rd (44060-1837)
PHONE......................................800 804-8484
Phillip Shrout, *Ch of Bd*
Seline Griffith, *Bookkeeper*
Matthew D Knecht,
EMP: 27
SQ FT: 4,400
SALES: 7MM **Privately Held**
WEB: www.hzwenv.com
SIC: **8748** Environmental consultant

(G-14063)
INFINITE SHARES LLC
9401 Mentor Ave 167 (44060-4519)
PHONE......................................216 317-1601
EMP: 25
SALES (est): 925.8K **Privately Held**
SIC: **8741** Management Services

(G-14064)
ISOMEDIX OPERATIONS INC (DH)
5960 Heisley Rd (44060-1834)
PHONE......................................440 354-2600
Walter Rosebrough, *CEO*
Michael J Tokich, *Vice Pres*
Karen L Burton, *Treasurer*
Becky Aldhizer, *Manager*
EMP: 148
SQ FT: 5,000
SALES (est): 92.5MM
SALES (corp-wide): 2.6B **Privately Held**
SIC: **8734** Industrial sterilization service
HQ: Steris Corporation
5960 Heisley Rd
Mentor OH 44060
440 354-2600

(G-14065)
JIM BROWN CHEVROLET INC (PA)
6877 Center St (44060-4233)
P.O. Box 300 (44061-0300)
PHONE......................................440 255-5511
James Brown, *President*
Jeff Fortuna, *Corp Secy*
Frank Lakava, *Vice Pres*
EMP: 175
SQ FT: 47,000
SALES (est): 69.7MM **Privately Held**
WEB: www.classic.com
SIC: **5511** 7515 Automobiles, new & used;
passenger car leasing

(G-14066)
JIM BROWN CHEVROLET INC
Also Called: Classic Autobody
8490 Tyler Blvd (44060-4230)
P.O. Box 300 (44061-0300)
PHONE......................................440 255-5511
Dennis Macko, *Manager*
EMP: 35
SALES (corp-wide): 69.7MM **Privately Held**
WEB: www.classic.com
SIC: **7538** 7532 General automotive repair
shops; paint shop, automotive
PA: Jim Brown Chevrolet Inc
6877 Center St
Mentor OH 44060
440 255-5511

(G-14067)
JJO CONSTRUCTION INC
9045 Osborne Dr (44060-4326)
P.O. Box 713 (44061-0713)
PHONE......................................440 255-1515
Joseph J Orel, *President*
Lisa Howell, *Manager*
EMP: 25
SQ FT: 7,500

SALES: 22.7MM **Privately Held**
WEB: www.jjoconstruction.com
SIC: **1542** Commercial & office building, new construction; commercial & office buildings, renovation & repair

(G-14068)
JTO CLUB CORP
Also Called: Mentor Hsley Rcquet Fitnes CLB
6011 Heisley Rd (44060-1867)
PHONE..................................440 352-1900
Maureen Osborne, *CEO*
Jerome Osborne, *President*
EMP: 60
SQ FT: 70,000
SALES (est): 1.3MM
SALES (corp-wide): 19.7MM **Privately Held**
WEB: www.mentorheisleyfitness.com
SIC: **7991** Physical fitness facilities
PA: T O J Inc
6011 Heisley Rd
Mentor OH 44060
440 352-1900

(G-14069)
KAISER FOUNDATION HOSPITALS
Also Called: Mentor Medical Offices
7695 Mentor Ave (44060-5540)
PHONE..................................800 524-7377
EMP: 593
SALES (corp-wide): 93B **Privately Held**
SIC: **8011** Offices & clinics of medical doctors
HQ: Kaiser Foundation Hospitals Inc
1 Kaiser Plz
Oakland CA 94612
510 271-6611

(G-14070)
LABORATORY CORPORATION AMERICA
8300 Tyler Blvd (44060-4217)
PHONE..................................440 205-8299
Kolita Benedict, *Manager*
EMP: 25 **Publicly Held**
WEB: www.labcorp.com
SIC: **8071** Medical laboratories
HQ: Laboratory Corporation Of America
358 S Main St Ste 458
Burlington NC 27215
336 229-1127

(G-14071)
LAKE COUNTY COUNCIL ON AGING (PA)
8520 East Ave (44060-4302)
PHONE..................................440 205-8111
Joseph R Tomsick, *CEO*
Patricia McAteer, *Human Res Dir*
Brian Rice, *Human Res Dir*
Edgar Barnett Jr, *Exec Dir*
Lyle D Shull, *Exec Dir*
EMP: 45
SALES (est): 2.4MM **Privately Held**
WEB: www.lccoa.org
SIC: **8322** Senior citizens' center or association

(G-14072)
LAKE COUNTY FAMILY PRACTICE
Also Called: 7 Physcian Fmly Practice Group
9500 Mentor Ave Ste 100 (44060-8702)
PHONE..................................440 352-4880
Mark Komar, *President*
Eileen Sraj, *Administration*
EMP: 35
SQ FT: 37,000
SALES (est): 3.2MM **Privately Held**
WEB: www.lcfp.net
SIC: **8011** General & family practice, physician/surgeon

(G-14073)
LAKE COUNTY LOCAL HAZMAT
8505 Garfield Rd (44060-5961)
P.O. Box 480 (44061-0480)
PHONE..................................440 350-5499
Thomas Talcott, *Chief*
Larry Greene, *Manager*
EMP: 25

SALES (est): 550.1K **Privately Held**
SIC: **8631** Labor unions & similar labor organizations

(G-14074)
LAKE URGENT & FAMILY MED CTR (PA)
Also Called: Lake Urgent Care Centers
8655 Market St (44060-4170)
PHONE..................................440 255-6400
Joseph Saboca, *Director*
EMP: 40
SALES (est): 801.4K **Privately Held**
SIC: **8011** Freestanding emergency medical center; general & family practice, physician/surgeon

(G-14075)
LAND DESIGN CONSULTANTS
9025 Osborne Dr (44060-4326)
PHONE..................................440 255-8463
James R Pegoraro, *President*
Frank J Chorba, *Corp Secy*
EMP: 30
SQ FT: 5,000
SALES (est): 2.8MM **Privately Held**
WEB: www.ldcinc.net
SIC: **8711** **8713** Civil engineering; surveying services

(G-14076)
LAWNFIELD PROPERTIES LLC
Also Called: Best Wstn Lawnfield Inn Suites
8434 Mentor Ave (44060-5817)
PHONE..................................440 974-3572
Rob Kneen,
EMP: 25
SQ FT: 1,375
SALES (est): 1.8MM **Privately Held**
WEB: www.lawnfield.com
SIC: **7011** Hotels & motels

(G-14077)
LIFESERVICES DEVELOPMENT CORP
Also Called: Salidawoods
7685 Lake Shore Blvd (44060-3359)
PHONE..................................440 257-3866
Karen Harrell, *General Mgr*
EMP: 47 **Privately Held**
WEB: www.lifeservicesnetwork.com
SIC: **8399** **8052** Community development groups; intermediate care facilities
PA: Lifeservices Management Corporation
1625 Lowell Ave
Erie PA 16505

(G-14078)
LOWES HOME CENTERS LLC
9600 Mentor Ave (44060-4529)
PHONE..................................440 392-0027
Brian Braunstien, *Manager*
EMP: 150
SALES (corp-wide): 68.6B **Publicly Held**
SIC: **5211** **5031** **5722** **5064** Lumber & other building materials; building materials, exterior; building materials, interior; household appliance stores; electrical appliances, television & radio
HQ: Lowe's Home Centers, Llc
1605 Curtis Bridge Rd
Wilkesboro NC 28697
336 658-4000

(G-14079)
MC SIGN LLC (PA)
Also Called: Mc Group
8959 Tyler Blvd (44060-2184)
PHONE..................................440 209-6200
Ken Stinson, *Plant Mgr*
Dana Bellinger, *Project Mgr*
Kevin Kelley, *Prdtn Mgr*
Jennifer Hunt, *Sr Project Mgr*
Erin Buehler, *Program Mgr*
EMP: 185 EST: 1995
SALES (est): 63MM **Privately Held**
WEB: www.mcsign.com
SIC: **1731** Voice, data & video wiring contractor

(G-14080)
MENTOR EXEMPTED VLG SCHL DST
Also Called: Mentor School Service Trnsp
7060 Hopkins Rd (44060-4487)
PHONE..................................440 974-5260
Karen Gerardi, *Director*
EMP: 150
SALES (corp-wide): 103.9MM **Privately Held**
WEB: www.mboe.org
SIC: **4151** School buses
PA: Mentor Exempted Village School District
6451 Center St
Mentor OH 44060
440 255-4444

(G-14081)
MENTOR LAGOONS YACHT CLUB INC
8365 Harbor Dr (44060-1413)
P.O. Box 574 (44061-0574)
PHONE..................................440 205-3625
Cliff Gabriel, *CEO*
Jim Capp,
EMP: 60
SQ FT: 4,000
SALES: 54.3K **Privately Held**
SIC: **7997** Yacht club, membership

(G-14082)
MENTOR LUMBER AND SUPPLY CO (PA)
Also Called: Mentor Wholesale Lumber
7180 Center St (44060-4979)
P.O. Box 599 (44061-0599)
PHONE..................................440 255-8814
Jerome T Osborne, *Ch of Bd*
Reed H Martin, *President*
Robert Sanderson, *Senior VP*
Mack Stewart, *Vice Pres*
Barbie Rita, *CFO*
EMP: 120
SQ FT: 100,000
SALES (est): 41.9MM **Privately Held**
SIC: **5031** **5211** Lumber: rough, dressed & finished; lumber & other building materials

(G-14083)
MENTOR SURGERY CENTER LTD
9485 Mentor Ave Ste 1 (44060-8711)
PHONE..................................440 205-5725
Carol Gragg, *Manager*
David Wier, *Administration*
EMP: 50
SALES (est): 6.8MM **Privately Held**
SIC: **8011** Ambulatory surgical center

(G-14084)
MENTOR WAY NURSING & REHAB CEN
8881 Schaeffer St (44060-5035)
PHONE..................................440 255-9309
Fax: 440 205-9120
EMP: 150
SQ FT: 54,000
SALES (est): 11.4MM **Privately Held**
SIC: **8051** Skilled Nursing Care Facility

(G-14085)
MICHAELS INC
Also Called: Lamalfa Party Center
5783 Heisley Rd (44060-1883)
PHONE..................................440 357-0384
Michael Lamalfa Sr, *President*
Martin Lamalfa, *Vice Pres*
EMP: 77
SQ FT: 36,000
SALES (est): 3.3MM **Privately Held**
WEB: www.lamalfa.com
SIC: **7299** Banquet hall facilities

(G-14086)
MILL ROSE LABORATORIES INC
7310 Corp Blvd (44060)
PHONE..................................440 974-6730
Paul M Miller, *President*
Stephen W Kovalcheck Jr, *CFO*
Lawrence W Miller, *Admin Sec*
▲ EMP: 40 EST: 1977
SQ FT: 59,000

SALES (est): 6.3MM
SALES (corp-wide): 32.4MM **Privately Held**
WEB: www.millrose.com
SIC: **3991** **5047** Brooms & brushes; medical equipment & supplies
PA: The Mill-Rose Company
7995 Tyler Blvd
Mentor OH 44060
440 255-9171

(G-14087)
MILL-ROSE COMPANY (PA)
7995 Tyler Blvd (44060-4896)
PHONE..................................440 255-9171
Paul M Miller, *President*
Lawrence W Miller, *Vice Pres*
Diane Miller, *Admin Sec*
▲ EMP: 160
SQ FT: 61,000
SALES (est): 32.4MM **Privately Held**
WEB: www.millrose.com
SIC: **3841** **5085** **3991** **3624** Surgical instruments & apparatus; industrial supplies; brushes, industrial; brushes, household or industrial; carbon & graphite products; abrasive products

(G-14088)
MJ AUTO PARTS INC (PA)
Also Called: NAPA Auto Parts
7900 Tyler Blvd (44060-4806)
PHONE..................................440 205-6272
Lindy M Adelstein, *CEO*
James Starke, *President*
Jill Grinstead, *Vice Pres*
Susan Starke, *Treasurer*
◆ EMP: 30 EST: 1957
SQ FT: 12,000
SALES (est): 7.9MM **Privately Held**
SIC: **5531** **5013** Automobile & truck equipment & parts; automotive supplies & parts

(G-14089)
MONODE MARKING PRODUCTS INC (PA)
Also Called: Waldorf Marking Devices Div
9200 Tyler Blvd (44060-1882)
PHONE..................................440 975-8802
Tom Mackey, *President*
EMP: 65
SQ FT: 15,000
SALES (est): 12.3MM **Privately Held**
SIC: **3542** **5084** Marking machines; printing trades machinery, equipment & supplies

(G-14090)
MOVING SOLUTIONS INC
Also Called: Great Lakes Record Center
8001 Moving Way (44060-4898)
PHONE..................................440 946-9300
William Tyers, *President*
Lynne Mazeika, *Vice Pres*
Verne McCelland, *Admin Sec*
EMP: 60 EST: 1976
SQ FT: 100,000
SALES (est): 8MM **Privately Held**
WEB: www.yourmovingsolutions.com
SIC: **4214** **4731** Furniture moving & storage, local; household goods moving & storage, local; freight transportation arrangement

(G-14091)
MWD LOGISTICS INC
7236 Justin Way (44060-4881)
PHONE..................................440 266-2500
Rob Dibble, *Principal*
EMP: 52
SALES (corp-wide): 28.6MM **Privately Held**
SIC: **4212** Local trucking, without storage
PA: Mwd Logistics Inc
222 Tappan Dr N
Ontario OH 44906
419 522-3510

(G-14092)
OHIO RENAL CARE GROUP LLC
Also Called: Ohio Renal Care Grp Mentor Dia
8840 Tyler Blvd (44060-4361)
PHONE..................................440 974-3459
Mary Garber,
Ron Kuerbitz,
EMP: 53 EST: 2013

SALES (est): 518K **Privately Held**
SIC: 8092 Kidney dialysis centers

(G-14093)
OMNI CART SERVICES INC
Also Called: Ohio Carts
7370 Production Dr (44060-4859)
P.O. Box 366 (44061-0366)
PHONE......................................440 205-8363
Keith Woolf, *President*
William Jacobson, *Corp Secy*
Jennifer Chuha, *Human Resources*
Joel Levin, *Shareholder*
EMP: 35
SQ FT: 10,000
SALES (est): 7.9MM **Privately Held**
WEB: www.ocserv.com
SIC: 7699 Shopping cart repair

(G-14094)
OSBORNE CO
7954 Reynolds Rd (44060-5334)
P.O. Box 658 (44061-0658)
PHONE......................................440 942-7000
Jerome T Osborne, *President*
Gerald J Smith, *Admin Sec*
EMP: 60
SQ FT: 4,500
SALES (est): 2.2MM **Privately Held**
SIC: 1794 Excavation work

(G-14095)
PATHWAYS INC (PA)
7350 Palisades Pkwy (44060-5302)
PHONE......................................440 918-1000
James Limoli, *CEO*
Debbie Lambdin, *Principal*
Michelle Douglass, *Teacher*
EMP: 65
SALES: 229.9K **Privately Held**
WEB: www.pathwaysinc.com
SIC: 8322 Individual & family services; probation office

(G-14096)
PETSMART INC
9122 Mentor Ave (44060-6404)
PHONE......................................440 974-1100
Andrea Carlton, *Manager*
EMP: 30
SALES (corp-wide): 12.1B **Privately Held**
WEB: www.petsmart.com
SIC: 5999 0752 Pet food; animal specialty services
HQ: Petsmart, Inc.
19601 N 27th Ave
Phoenix AZ 85027
623 580-6100

(G-14097)
PLATFORM CEMENT INC
Also Called: Platform Contracting
7503 Tyler Blvd (44060-5403)
PHONE......................................440 602-9750
Jason Klar, *President*
Elizabeth Bechkowiak, *Principal*
Jeremy Kler, *Project Mgr*
Sally Murphy, *Admin Sec*
EMP: 35
SQ FT: 1,000
SALES (est): 5.7MM **Privately Held**
SIC: 1771 Concrete work

(G-14098)
PRUDENTIAL SELECT PROPERTIES (PA)
Also Called: Century 21
7395 Center St (44060-5801)
PHONE......................................440 255-1111
Frank Kaim, *President*
Jane Kaim, *Admin Sec*
EMP: 65
SQ FT: 6,000
SALES (est): 6.4MM **Privately Held**
WEB: www.pruselectprop.com
SIC: 6531 Real estate agent, residential

(G-14099)
PRUDENTIAL WELSH REALTY
7400 Center St (44060-5848)
PHONE......................................440 974-3100
Don Welsh, *Owner*
EMP: 25
SALES (est): 690.4K **Privately Held**
SIC: 6531 Rl Este Agntresidntl

(G-14100)
RAYMOND A GREINER DDS INC
Also Called: Greiner Dental & Associates
7553 Center St (44060-6001)
PHONE......................................440 951-6688
James N Greiner DDS, *Vice Pres*
Steven H Greiner DDS, *Vice Pres*
Marcia Tupa DDS, *Manager*
EMP: 32 EST: 1954
SQ FT: 4,000
SALES (est): 1.5MM **Privately Held**
SIC: 8021 Dentists' office

(G-14101)
RE/MAX REAL ESTATE EXPERTS
8444 Mentor Ave (44060-5817)
PHONE......................................440 255-6505
Cheryl Maggard, *Partner*
Liz Bauer, *Partner*
Mary Margaret Dacar, *Partner*
Karen Schultz, *Partner*
Kathy Thomas, *Partner*
EMP: 28
SALES (est): 1.3MM **Privately Held**
WEB: www.ohiorealestate4you.com
SIC: 6531 Real estate agent, residential

(G-14102)
REGISTERED CONTRACTORS INC
8425 Station St (44060-4924)
PHONE......................................440 205-0873
Edward A Krevas, *CEO*
Livio Stipcic, *President*
EMP: 40
SQ FT: 7,000
SALES (est): 5.3MM **Privately Held**
WEB: www.registeredcontractors.com
SIC: 1542 1541 1521 Commercial & office building contractors; industrial buildings & warehouses; single-family housing construction

(G-14103)
RELIABLE RNNERS CURIER SVC INC
8624 Station St (44060-4316)
PHONE......................................440 578-1011
Marc P Coben, *President*
EMP: 40
SQ FT: 2,800
SALES (est): 5.6MM **Privately Held**
WEB: www.rrunners.com
SIC: 4225 General warehousing & storage

(G-14104)
RICHCREEK BAILEY REHABILITATIO
Also Called: New Hope Vocational Services
7600 Tyler Blvd (44060-4853)
PHONE......................................440 527-8610
James Richcreek, *President*
James E Richcreek, *President*
Douglas M Bailey, *Principal*
Sherry L Richcreek, *Director*
EMP: 40
SALES (est): 42.5K **Privately Held**
SIC: 8331 Vocational rehabilitation agency

(G-14105)
RUNYON & SONS ROOFING INC
8745 Munson Rd (44060-4323)
PHONE......................................440 974-6810
Clyde Runyon Jr, *President*
Tom Runyon, *Vice Pres*
Jean Kovach, *Financial Exec*
Todd Runyon, *Sales Mgr*
EMP: 60
SALES (est): 6.4MM **Privately Held**
SIC: 1522 1542 1521 Multi-family dwelling construction; commercial & office building contractors; single-family home remodeling, additions & repairs

(G-14106)
SCHROER PROPERTIES INC
Also Called: Altercare of Mentor
9901 Johnnycake Ridge Rd (44060-6739)
PHONE......................................440 357-7900
Berry Lieberman, *Manager*
EMP: 115 **Privately Held**
SIC: 8051 Skilled nursing care facilities

PA: Schroer Properties, Inc
339 E Maple St
North Canton OH 44720

(G-14107)
SEACRIST LANDSCAPING AND CNSTR
9442 Mercantile Dr (44060-1889)
PHONE......................................440 946-2731
Charles Seacrist, *Owner*
Dale Stefancic, *Manager*
EMP: 25
SALES (est): 868.5K **Privately Held**
SIC: 0781 0782 Landscape architects; landscape contractors

(G-14108)
SHARP EDGE LLC
8855 Twinbrook Rd (44060-4334)
P.O. Box 1178 (44061-1178)
PHONE......................................440 255-5917
Peter Davenport, *Officer*
Robert Kennedy,
EMP: 25
SALES (est): 1.5MM **Privately Held**
SIC: 0782 Lawn care services

(G-14109)
SHIMA LIMOUSINE SERVICES INC
7555 Tyler Blvd Ste 12 (44060-4866)
PHONE......................................440 918-6400
George Shima, *President*
Michele Carothers, *Vice Pres*
Barbara Shima, *Shareholder*
EMP: 34
SALES (est): 1.9MM **Privately Held**
WEB: www.shimalimo.com
SIC: 4119 Limousine rental, with driver

(G-14110)
SOCIETY FOR REHABILITATION
Also Called: Society Rehabilitation
9290 Lake Shore Blvd (44060-1664)
PHONE......................................440 209-0135
Christopher Webb, *Director*
Elizabeth Ann Dietrich, *Director*
Mary Wilson, *Admin Sec*
EMP: 28
SQ FT: 12,000
SALES: 100.3K **Privately Held**
WEB: www.societyhelps.org
SIC: 8093 8049 Rehabilitation center, outpatient treatment; physical therapist; occupational therapist; speech therapist; audiologist

(G-14111)
SOURCEONE HEALTHCARE TECH INC (HQ)
Also Called: Mxr Sourceone
8020 Tyler Blvd (44060-4825)
PHONE......................................440 701-1200
Leo Zuckerman, *CEO*
Larry Lawson, *President*
Frank Krashoc, *General Mgr*
Bob Albright, *Regional Mgr*
Butch Davis, *Regional Mgr*
EMP: 147
SQ FT: 42,000
SALES (est): 63.9MM
SALES (corp-wide): 108MM **Privately Held**
SIC: 5047 Medical laboratory equipment
PA: Merry X-Ray Chemical Corporation
4909 Murphy Canyon Rd # 120
San Diego CA 92123
858 565-4472

(G-14112)
STODDARD IMPORTED CARS INC
Also Called: Audi Willoughby
8599 Market St (44060-4124)
PHONE......................................440 951-1040
Jerry Severin, *President*
Karl Colbary, *Business Mgr*
Lisa Mullin, *Business Mgr*
Frank Steffen, *Sales Mgr*
Mark Taylor, *Director*
▲ EMP: 51 EST: 1957
SQ FT: 22,000

SALES (est): 20.4MM **Privately Held**
WEB: www.stoddard.com
SIC: 5511 5013 Automobiles, new & used; automotive supplies & parts

(G-14113)
SUMMERVILLE SENIOR LIVING INC
Also Called: Summerville At Mentor
5700 Emerald Ct (44060-1870)
PHONE......................................440 354-5499
Russell Ragland, *President*
EMP: 60
SALES (corp-wide): 4.5B **Publicly Held**
SIC: 8361 Residential care
HQ: Summerville Senior Living, Inc.
3131 Elliott Ave Ste 500
Seattle WA 98121
206 298-2909

(G-14114)
T O J INC (PA)
6011 Heisley Rd (44060-1867)
PHONE......................................440 352-1900
Maureen Osborne, *President*
Jerry Osborne III, *President*
Loraine Mauk, *General Mgr*
Leong Tan, *Vice Pres*
Christine Baglione, *Safety Mgr*
EMP: 38
SQ FT: 32,000
SALES (est): 19.7MM **Privately Held**
WEB: www.jtoinc.com
SIC: 1542 1522 6552 4959 Commercial & office building, new construction; condominium construction; land subdividers & developers, commercial; snowplowing; health club

(G-14115)
TRICOUNTY AMBULANCE SERVICE
7000 Spinach Dr (44060-4958)
PHONE......................................440 951-4600
Kevin Farrell, *President*
John F Farrell, *Vice Pres*
Barb Baughman, *Opers Staff*
Beth Farrell, *Admin Sec*
EMP: 55
SQ FT: 8,000
SALES (est): 2.3MM **Privately Held**
SIC: 4119 Ambulance service

(G-14116)
TRUGREEN LIMITED PARTNERSHIP
Also Called: Tru Green-Chemlawn
7460 Clover Ave (44060-5212)
PHONE......................................440 290-3340
Jos Byers, *Service Mgr*
George Strata, *Manager*
EMP: 30
SQ FT: 20,000
SALES (corp-wide): 3.4B **Privately Held**
SIC: 0782 Lawn care services; spraying services, lawn
HQ: Trugreen Limited Partnership
1790 Kirby Pkwy
Memphis TN 38138
901 251-4128

(G-14117)
TYLINTER INC (HQ)
8570 Tyler Blvd (44060-4232)
PHONE......................................800 321-6188
Larry Polk, *President*
Judy Osgood, *Vice Pres*
◆ EMP: 65
SQ FT: 65,000
SALES (est): 19.3MM
SALES (corp-wide): 579.2MM **Privately Held**
WEB: www.wstyler.com
SIC: 5051 Metal wires, ties, cables & screening
PA: Haver & Boecker Ohg
Carl-Haver-Platz 3
Oelde 59302
252 230-0

(G-14118)
UNITED STATES ENDOSCOPY (DH)
Also Called: US Endoscopy
5976 Heisley Rd (44060-1873)
PHONE......................440 639-4494
Tony Siracusa, *CEO*
Ben Kingery, *General Mgr*
Heath Downs, *Regional Mgr*
Kenneith Turley, *Regional Mgr*
Bob Bradley, *Safety Dir*
▲ EMP: 153
SQ FT: 30,000
SALES (est): 110.8MM
SALES (corp-wide): 2.6B Privately Held
WEB: www.usendoscopy.com
SIC: 5047 Medical equipment & supplies
HQ: Steris Corporation
5960 Heisley Rd
Mentor OH 44060
440 354-2600

(G-14119)
UNIVERSITY HOSPITALS CLEVELAND
Also Called: Lake Univ Ireland Cancer Ctr
9485 Mentor Ave Ste 102 (44060-8722)
PHONE......................440 205-5755
Joel Saltzman, *Med Doctor*
Lois Teston, *Med Doctor*
Steven Waggoner, *Med Doctor*
Jeffrey Hardacre, *Surgeon*
Staton Gerson MD, *Director*
EMP: 45
SQ FT: 1,269
SALES (corp-wide): 580MM Privately Held
SIC: 8062 8011 General medical & surgical hospitals; oncologist
HQ: University Hospitals Of Cleveland
11100 Euclid Ave
Cleveland OH 44106
216 844-1000

(G-14120)
UNIVERSITY MEDNET
9000 Mentor Ave Ste 101 (44060-4496)
PHONE......................440 255-0800
Evelyn Havrillo, *Manager*
EMP: 200
SALES (corp-wide): 10.4MM Privately Held
SIC: 8011 8093 Clinic, operated by physicians; specialty outpatient clinics
PA: University Mednet
18599 Lake Shore Blvd
Euclid OH 44119
216 383-0100

(G-14121)
VECMAR CORPORATION
Also Called: Vecmar Computer Solutions
7595 Jenther Dr (44060-4872)
PHONE......................440 953-1119
Greg Pluscusky, *President*
Brian Dipasquale, *Vice Pres*
Philip R Pagon II, *Vice Pres*
Nick Zitnik, *Treasurer*
James Matonis, *Admin Sec*
▲ EMP: 30
SQ FT: 25,000
SALES (est): 10.8MM Privately Held
WEB: www.vecmar.com
SIC: 5045 Computers

(G-14122)
VINIFERA IMPORTS LTD
7551 Plaza Blvd (44060-5206)
PHONE......................440 942-9463
Matt Geisler, *Branch Mgr*
EMP: 36
SALES (corp-wide): 19MM Privately Held
SIC: 5099 Firearms & ammunition, except sporting
PA: Vinifera Imports, Ltd.
205 13th Ave
Ronkonkoma NY 11779
631 467-5907

(G-14123)
VIP ELECTRIC COMPANY
8358 Mentor Ave (44060-5748)
PHONE......................440 255-0180
Ellie Vayo, *President*

Kevin Vayo, *Vice Pres*
Erin Vayo, *Shareholder*
Rochelle Vayo, *Shareholder*
EMP: 30 EST: 1997
SQ FT: 2,000
SALES (est): 4.3MM Privately Held
WEB: www.vipelectric.com
SIC: 1731 General electrical contractor

(G-14124)
VOLK OPTICAL INC
7893 Enterprise Dr (44060-5309)
PHONE......................440 942-6161
Jyoti Gupta, *President*
Terry Cooper, *Regional Mgr*
Gary Webel, *Vice Pres*
Ezequiel Lukin, *Regl Sales Mgr*
Diane Drodouski, *Executive*
▲ EMP: 70 EST: 1974
SQ FT: 18,000
SALES (est): 12.5MM
SALES (corp-wide): 1.5B Privately Held
SIC: 8011 3851 3827 Offices & clinics of medical doctors; lenses, ophthalmic; optical instruments & lenses
HQ: Halma Holdings Inc.
11500 Northlake Dr # 306
Cincinnati OH 45249
513 772-5501

(G-14125)
WMK LLC
Also Called: Mobilityworks
7588 Tyler Blvd (44060-4871)
PHONE......................440 951-4335
EMP: 35
SALES (corp-wide): 404.9MM Privately Held
SIC: 7532 5999 1799 Van conversion; technical aids for the handicapped; home/office interiors finishing, furnishing & remodeling
PA: Wmk, Llc
4199 Kinross Lakes Pkwy # 300
Richfield OH 44286
234 312-2000

(G-14126)
WORK SOLUTIONS GROUP LLC
8324 Tyler Blvd (44060-4221)
PHONE......................440 205-8297
Terry Jochum,
EMP: 30
SALES (est): 472.9K Privately Held
SIC: 7361 Placement agencies

(G-14127)
WPMI INC
9325 Progress Pkwy (44060-1855)
PHONE......................440 392-2171
Stephanie Molnar, *CEO*
Lori Ware, *CFO*
Lori Wares, *Controller*
Chris Slomka, *Natl Sales Mgr*
Michael Reich, *Manager*
EMP: 30 EST: 2003
SALES (est): 4.8MM Privately Held
WEB: www.riversidecompany.com
SIC: 8742 Management consulting services

Mentor On The Lake
Lake County

(G-14128)
ABC PHONES NORTH CAROLINA INC
Also Called: A Wireless
5965 Andrews Rd Ste B (44060-8533)
PHONE......................440 290-4262
EMP: 26
SALES (corp-wide): 149.9MM Privately Held
SIC: 4812 Cellular telephone services
PA: Abc Phones Of North Carolina, Inc.
8510 Colonnade Center Dr
Raleigh NC 27615
252 317-0388

(G-14129)
MAIN SEQUENCE TECHNOLOGY INC (PA)
5370 Pinehill Dr (44060-1434)
PHONE......................440 946-5214
Martin Snyder, *President*
Jarrid Usmani, *Senior Engr*
Gretchen Kubicek, *CFO*
Patsy Lombardo, *Controller*
Bill Kubicek, *VP Sales*
EMP: 30
SALES (est): 6.9MM Privately Held
WEB: www.kubicek.net
SIC: 7371 Computer software development

Mesopotamia
Trumbull County

(G-14130)
HOPEWELL (PA)
Also Called: Hopewell Therapeutic Farm
9637 State Route 534 (44439)
P.O. Box 193 (44439-0193)
PHONE......................440 693-4074
William Hamilton, *Principal*
Richard Karges, *Director*
EMP: 29
SQ FT: 3,600
SALES (est): 4.5MM Privately Held
SIC: 8361 Home for the mentally handicapped

Metamora
Fulton County

(G-14131)
AMBOY CONTRACTORS LLC
424 E Main St (43540-9753)
P.O. Box H (43540-0207)
PHONE......................419 644-2111
Paul Hill, *Controller*
Michael S Anderzack,
Mike Anderzack,
James R Pitzen,
EMP: 80
SALES (est): 5.3MM Privately Held
WEB: www.wecandigit.com
SIC: 1623 Underground utilities contractor

(G-14132)
ANDERZACK-PITZEN CNSTR INC
424 E Main St (43540-9753)
P.O. Box H (43540-0207)
PHONE......................419 553-7015
Mike Anderzack, *President*
James R Pitzen, *Vice Pres*
Nathan Marlatt, *Project Mgr*
Nick Loeffler, *Purchasing*
Robert Booth, *Manager*
EMP: 50
SQ FT: 6,000
SALES (est): 20MM Privately Held
SIC: 1623 1794 Underground utilities contractor; excavation work

(G-14133)
TSCS INC
Also Called: Tristate Concrete
14293 State Route 64 (43540-9710)
PHONE......................419 644-3921
John Simon, *President*
Susan Simon, *Treasurer*
EMP: 25
SALES: 1.6MM Privately Held
SIC: 1771 Concrete work

Miamisburg
Montgomery County

(G-14134)
21ST CENTURY SOLUTIONS LTD
Also Called: Gokeyless
955 Mound Rd (45342-3263)
PHONE......................877 439-5377

Brandon Atchley, *Managing Prtnr*
Rob Faulconer, *Accounts Exec*
Jason Karrick, *Accounts Exec*
Steven Laskos, *Accounts Exec*
Hey White, *Accounts Exec*
EMP: 34 EST: 2003
SQ FT: 30,000
SALES: 20MM Privately Held
SIC: 5065 Electronic parts & equipment

(G-14135)
7NT ENTERPRISES LLC (PA)
3090 S Tech Blvd (45342-4860)
PHONE......................614 961-2026
Pratap Rajadhyaksha,
Travis Burr,
EMP: 45
SALES (est): 2.2MM Privately Held
SIC: 8711 8713 Engineering services; surveying services

(G-14136)
A-1 SPRINKLER COMPANY INC
2383 Northpointe Dr (45342-2989)
PHONE......................937 859-6198
Bill Hausmann, *CEO*
EMP: 68
SQ FT: 15,000
SALES (est): 9.6MM Privately Held
WEB: www.spkr.com
SIC: 3569 5087 Firefighting apparatus & related equipment; firefighting equipment

(G-14137)
ADVANCED SERVICE TECH LLC
Also Called: AST
885 Mound Rd (45342-2591)
PHONE......................937 435-4376
Jerry L Abner, *CEO*
Deorah Dobransky, *Vice Pres*
Brad McMartin, *Vice Pres*
Scott Abbott, *Technical Staff*
Michael Keck, *Technical Staff*
EMP: 29
SALES (est): 4MM Privately Held
WEB: www.astservice.com
SIC: 1731 7373 8243 Computer installation; computer integrated systems design; office computer automation systems integration; operator training, computer; repair training, computer; software training, computer

(G-14138)
ALDRICH CHEMICAL
Also Called: Sigma-Aldrich
3858 Benner Rd (45342-4304)
PHONE......................937 859-1808
Bob Becker, *Engineer*
John Shay, *Engineer*
Diane Szydell, *Manager*
Breet Eshbaugh, *Supervisor*
Michael Ferdelman, *Supervisor*
EMP: 70
SQ FT: 30,000
SALES (corp-wide): 16.9B Privately Held
SIC: 2819 5084 2899 2869 Isotopes, radioactive; chemical process equipment; chemical preparations; industrial organic chemicals
HQ: Aldrich Chemical
3050 Spruce St
Saint Louis MO 63103
314 771-5765

(G-14139)
ALIEN TECHNOLOGY LLC
3001 W Tech Blvd (45342-0824)
PHONE......................408 782-3900
Damon Bramble, *General Mgr*
EMP: 103 Privately Held
SIC: 7371 Computer software development
PA: Alien Technology, Llc
845 Embedded Way
San Jose CA 95138

(G-14140)
AMERICAN CUTTING EDGE INC
4475 Infirmary Rd (45342-1233)
PHONE......................937 866-5986
▲ EMP: 122
SQ FT: 4,000

▲ = Import ▼=Export
◆ =Import/Export

SALES (est): 5.6MM
SALES (corp-wide): 41.4MM **Privately Held**
SIC: 5122 Whol Commercial Cutting Blades
PA: Cb Manufacturing & Sales Co., Inc.
4455 Infirmary Rd
Miamisburg OH 45342
937 866-5986

(G-14141)
APRIA HEALTHCARE LLC
2029 Lyons Rd (45342-5453)
PHONE..................................937 291-2842
Susan Reffner-Bettinger, *Manager*
EMP: 30 **Privately Held**
WEB: www.apria.com
SIC: 8082 Visiting nurse service
HQ: Apria Healthcare Llc
26220 Enterprise Ct
Lake Forest CA 92630
949 639-2000

(G-14142)
ASHFORD TRS LESSEE LLC
Also Called: Doubletree Hotel
300 Prestige Pl (45342-5300)
PHONE..................................937 436-2400
Jennifer Brown, *Manager*
EMP: 48
SALES (corp-wide): 44.6MM **Privately Held**
SIC: 7011 Hotels
PA: Ashford Trs Lessee Llc
14185 Dallas Pkwy # 1100
Dallas TX 75254
972 490-9600

(G-14143)
AUTO-OWNERS INSURANCE COMPANY
1 Prestige Pl Ste 280 (45342-6146)
PHONE..................................937 432-6740
Mitchel Warner, *Manager*
EMP: 58
SALES (corp-wide): 2.4B **Privately Held**
WEB: www.autoownersinsurancecompany.com
SIC: 6411 Insurance agents
PA: Auto-Owners Insurance Company
6101 Anacapri Blvd
Lansing MI 48917
517 323-1200

(G-14144)
BELCAN SVCS GROUP LTD PARTNR
Also Called: Belcan Techservices
3494 Technical Dr (45342)
PHONE..................................937 859-8880
Gus Delucia, *Manager*
EMP: 60
SALES (corp-wide): 813.3MM **Privately Held**
SIC: 7363 Engineering help service; temporary help service
HQ: Belcan Services Group Limited Partnership
10200 Anderson Way
Blue Ash OH 45242
513 891-0972

(G-14145)
BLATCHFORD INC
Also Called: Endolite
1031 Byers Rd (45342-5487)
PHONE..................................937 291-3636
Steven Blatchford, *CEO*
Chris Nolan, *General Mgr*
Chris Feighner, *Mfg Mgr*
Jon Hawke, *Controller*
Tanya Shell, *Controller*
▲ **EMP:** 60
SQ FT: 22,000
SALES (est): 14.7MM **Privately Held**
SIC: 5047 5999 Artificial limbs; orthopedic equipment & supplies; orthopedic & prosthesis applications

(G-14146)
BRADY WARE & SCHOENFELD INC (PA)
Also Called: Brady Ware & Company
3601 Rigby Rd Ste 400 (45342-5039)
PHONE..................................937 223-5247

James Keiser, *CEO*
Brian Carr, *President*
Samuel Agresti, *Vice Pres*
Mary Beth Blake, *Vice Pres*
Gary Brown, *Vice Pres*
EMP: 60
SQ FT: 16,000
SALES (est): 15.6MM **Privately Held**
SIC: 8721 Certified public accountant

(G-14147)
C B MFG & SLS CO INC (PA)
4455 Infirmary Rd (45342-1299)
PHONE..................................937 866-5986
Charles S Biehn Jr, *CEO*
Richard Porter, *President*
Donald M Cain, *Vice Pres*
Roger Adams, *Plant Mgr*
Amanda Morris, *Production*
▲ **EMP:** 67
SQ FT: 90,000
SALES (est): 35.8MM **Privately Held**
WEB: www.cbmfg.us
SIC: 5085 3423 Knives, industrial; knives, agricultural or industrial

(G-14148)
CANON SOLUTIONS AMERICA INC
1 Prestige Pl (45342-3794)
PHONE..................................937 260-4495
Todd Kostkan, *Branch Mgr*
EMP: 75
SALES (corp-wide): 35.1B **Privately Held**
SIC: 5044 5045 Copying equipment; computer software
HQ: Canon Solutions America, Inc.
1 Canon Park
Melville NY 11747
631 330-5000

(G-14149)
CEC ENTERTAINMENT INC
Also Called: Chuck E. Cheese's
30 Prestige Pl (45342-5338)
PHONE..................................937 439-1108
Ralph Kick, *Branch Mgr*
EMP: 52
SQ FT: 10,200
SALES (corp-wide): 886.7MM **Privately Held**
WEB: www.chuckecheese.com
SIC: 5812 7299 Pizzeria, chain; party planning service
HQ: Cec Entertainment, Inc.
1707 Market Pl Ste 200
Irving TX 75063
972 258-8507

(G-14150)
CESO INC (PA)
3601 Rigby Rd Ste 310 (45342-5040)
PHONE..................................937 435-8584
David Oakes, *President*
James I Weprin, *Principal*
EMP: 51
SQ FT: 30,000
SALES (est): 16.2MM **Privately Held**
SIC: 8711 3674 8712 Civil engineering; light emitting diodes; architectural services

(G-14151)
CHANGE HLTH PRAC MGT SOLNS GRP
3131 Newmark Dr Ste 100 (45342-5400)
PHONE..................................937 291-7850
Glenn Goodpaster, *Branch Mgr*
EMP: 25
SALES (corp-wide): 208.3B **Publicly Held**
WEB: www.hserve.com
SIC: 7376 8742 8721 Computer facilities management; hospital & health services consultant; billing & bookkeeping service
HQ: Change Healthcare Practice Management Solutions Group, Inc.
7 Parkway Ctr Ste 400
Pittsburgh PA 15220

(G-14152)
CITY OF MIAMISBURG
Also Called: Miamisburg Pk Recreation Dept
10 N 1st St (45342-2300)
PHONE..................................937 866-4532
Kelsey Whipp, *Director*

EMP: 25 **Privately Held**
WEB: www.pipestonegolf.com
SIC: 7999 Recreation center
PA: City Of Miamisburg
10 N 1st St
Miamisburg OH 45342
937 866-3303

(G-14153)
CITY OF MIAMISBURG
Also Called: Pipestone Golf Course
4344 Benner Rd (45342-4314)
PHONE..................................937 866-4653
Kyle Kuhnle, *General Mgr*
Tom Saathoff, *Principal*
Emily Gilvin, *Manager*
EMP: 45
SQ FT: 1,464 **Privately Held**
WEB: www.pipestonegolf.com
SIC: 7992 Public golf courses
PA: City Of Miamisburg
10 N 1st St
Miamisburg OH 45342
937 866-3303

(G-14154)
CONNOR GROUP A RE INV FIRM LLC
10510 Springboro Pike (45342-4956)
PHONE..................................937 434-3095
Robert Holzapfel, *CFO*
Lawrence Connor, *Mng Member*
Connie Hart,
EMP: 475 **EST:** 1996
SALES (est): 11.9MM **Privately Held**
SIC: 6531 Real estate agents & managers

(G-14155)
CORNERSTONE RESEARCH GROUP INC
Also Called: C R G
510 Earl Blvd (45342-6411)
PHONE..................................937 320-1877
Patrick J Hood, *President*
Jeffrey Bennett, *Vice Pres*
Chrysa Theodore, *Vice Pres*
Deb Knapke, *CFO*
Carol Caldwell, *Manager*
EMP: 112
SQ FT: 20,979
SALES (est): 21.4MM **Privately Held**
WEB: www.crgrp.net
SIC: 8733 Scientific research agency

(G-14156)
COURTYARD BY MARRIOTT
100 Prestige Pl (45342-5340)
PHONE..................................937 433-3131
Bob Tate, *General Mgr*
Garry Kirkland, *Asst Mgr*
EMP: 80
SALES (est): 1.6MM **Privately Held**
SIC: 7011 Hotels & motels

(G-14157)
CRANE 1 SERVICES INC (PA)
1027 Byers Rd (45342-5487)
PHONE..................................937 704-9900
Steven Kutz, *Division Mgr*
William Smith, *Division Mgr*
Herbert E Horn, *Vice Pres*
Stephen Marsee, *Treasurer*
Deanna Nesbit, *Human Res Dir*
EMP: 40
SQ FT: 13,500
SALES: 47MM **Privately Held**
SIC: 7389 Crane & aerial lift service

(G-14158)
CSH GROUP
10100 Innovation Dr # 400 (45342-4966)
PHONE..................................937 226-0070
Herbert L Lemaster, *Partner*
Keri Grubbs, *Project Mgr*
Scott Deters, *Manager*
Brittany A Lawrence, *Manager*
Christine Vaughan, *Manager*
EMP: 25
SALES (corp-wide): 37.2MM **Privately Held**
WEB: www.cshco.com
SIC: 8721 Certified public accountant
PA: Clark, Schaefer, Hackett & Co.
1 E 4th St Ste 1200
Cincinnati OH 45202
513 241-3111

(G-14159)
DANIS BUILDING CONSTRUCTION CO (PA)
3233 Newmark Dr (45342-5422)
PHONE..................................937 228-1225
John Danis, *President*
Thomas P Hammelrath, *President*
Gordon Steadman, *President*
John Graf, *Superintendent*
Tom Kremer, *Superintendent*
EMP: 475
SQ FT: 29,000
SALES (est): 158.5MM **Privately Held**
SIC: 1542 1541 Commercial & office building, new construction; hospital construction; industrial buildings & warehouses

(G-14160)
DANIS COMPANIES
3233 Newmark Dr (45342-5422)
PHONE..................................937 228-1225
Thomas J Danis, *Ch of Bd*
Glenn P Schimpf, *Vice Ch Bd*
Richard C Russell, *President*
Nick Eden, *General Mgr*
Bret Anderson, *Superintendent*
EMP: 500
SQ FT: 42,784
SALES (est): 30MM **Privately Held**
SIC: 1629 Industrial plant construction; waste water & sewage treatment plant construction

(G-14161)
DANIS INDUSTRIAL CNSTR CO
3233 Newmark Dr (45342-5422)
PHONE..................................937 228-1225
John Danis, *CEO*
Jim Perkins, *Superintendent*
Steve Brown, *Project Mgr*
Greg Christensen, *Project Mgr*
Jim Lupidi, *Project Engr*
EMP: 75
SALES (est): 7.8MM **Privately Held**
SIC: 1522 Residential construction
PA: Danis Building Construction Company
3233 Newmark Dr
Miamisburg OH 45342

(G-14162)
DAVIS H ELLIOT CNSTR CO INC
1 S Gebhart Church Rd (45342-3646)
PHONE..................................937 847-8025
Eliot Davis, *Branch Mgr*
EMP: 160
SALES (corp-wide): 192.3MM **Privately Held**
SIC: 1731 General electrical contractor
HQ: Davis H. Elliot Construction Company , Inc.
673 Blue Sky Pkwy
Lexington KY 40509
859 263-5148

(G-14163)
DAYTON POWER AND LIGHT COMPANY
1 S Gebhart Church Rd (45342-3646)
PHONE..................................937 331-3032
Madonna Nessle, *Principal*
EMP: 25
SALES (corp-wide): 10.7B **Publicly Held**
WEB: www.waytogo.com
SIC: 4911 4932 4931 Generation, electric power; gas & other services combined; electric & other services combined
HQ: The Dayton Power And Light Company
1065 Woodman Dr
Dayton OH 45432
937 331-4063

(G-14164)
DEDICATED NURSING ASSOC INC
228 Byers Rd Ste 103 (45342-3675)
PHONE..................................937 886-4559
EMP: 66 **Privately Held**
SIC: 7361 Nurses' registry
PA: Dedicated Nursing Associates, Inc.
6536 State Route 22
Delmont PA 15626

(G-14165)
DEL MONDE INC
2485 Belvo Rd (45342-3909)
PHONE................................859 371-7780
Alan Mc Williams, *Manager*
EMP: 45
SALES (corp-wide): 17.2MM **Privately Held**
WEB: www.delmonde.com
SIC: 1711 Heating & air conditioning contractors
PA: Del Monde, Inc.
10107 Toebben Dr Ste 100
Independence KY 41051
937 847-8711

(G-14166)
DIGITAL CONTROLS CORPORATION (PA)
444 Alexandersville Rd (45342-3658)
PHONE................................513 746-8118
EMP: 52 EST: 1969
SQ FT: 24,000
SALES (est): 9.1MM **Privately Held**
SIC: 7379 7372 5045 8742 Computer Related Svcs Prepackaged Software Svc Whol Computer/Peripheral Mgmt Consulting Svcs

(G-14167)
DOUBLETREE GUEST SUITES DAYTON
300 Prestige Pl (45342-5300)
PHONE................................937 436-2400
Jennifer Brown, *General Mgr*
Kelly Brown, *Controller*
EMP: 60
SALES (est): 1.7MM **Privately Held**
SIC: 7011 Hotel, franchised

(G-14168)
ESKO-GRAPHICS INC (HQ)
Also Called: Eskoartwork
8535 Gander Creek Dr (45342-5436)
PHONE................................937 454-1721
Kurt Demeuleneere, *CEO*
Jill Gehrhardt, *President*
Mark Quinlan, *President*
Tony Wiley, *President*
Ellen Schipper, *General Mgr*
▲ EMP: 70
SQ FT: 27,000
SALES (est): 133.7MM
SALES (corp-wide): 19.8B **Publicly Held**
SIC: 5084 7372 Printing trades machinery, equipment & supplies; prepackaged software
PA: Danaher Corporation
2200 Penn Ave Nw Ste 800w
Washington DC 20037
202 828-0850

(G-14169)
EUBEL BRADY SUTTMAN ASSET MGT
Also Called: Ebs Asset Management
10100 Innovation Dr # 410 (45342-4965)
PHONE................................937 291-1223
Robert J Suttman, *President*
Mark E Brady, *COO*
David K Ray, *COO*
William Hazel, *Vice Pres*
Ken Leist, *Opers Staff*
EMP: 50
SQ FT: 12,000
SALES (est): 11.1MM **Privately Held**
WEB: www.ebs-asset.com
SIC: 6282 Investment advisory service

(G-14170)
FEDERAL EXPRESS CORPORATION
Also Called: Fedex
2578 Corporate Pl (45342-3656)
PHONE................................800 463-3339
Sam Salano, *General Mgr*
EMP: 100
SALES (corp-wide): 65.4B **Publicly Held**
WEB: www.federalexpress.com
SIC: 4513 4215 Air courier services; courier services, except by air
HQ: Federal Express Corporation
3610 Hacks Cross Rd
Memphis TN 38125
901 369-3600

(G-14171)
FINASTRA USA CORPORATION
8555 Gander Creek Dr (45342-5436)
PHONE................................937 435-2335
Connie Bruce, *Manager*
EMP: 49
SALES (corp-wide): 5.2B **Privately Held**
WEB: www.harlandfinancialsolutions.com
SIC: 7372 7389 Prepackaged software; personal service agents, brokers & bureaus
HQ: Finastra Usa Corporation
1320 Sw Broadway Ste 100
Portland OR 97201
407 804-6600

(G-14172)
FRONTIER SECURITY LLC
1041 Byers Rd (45342-5487)
PHONE................................937 247-2824
Holly Tsourides, *CEO*
Kelly Cain, *CFO*
EMP: 30
SQ FT: 20,000
SALES (est): 1.6MM **Privately Held**
SIC: 1731 Access control systems specialization

(G-14173)
GAYSTON CORPORATION
Also Called: Mulch Masters of Ohio
721 Richard St (45342-1840)
P.O. Box 523 (45343-0523)
PHONE................................937 743-6050
Adam Stone, *CEO*
Andrew Sheldrick, *COO*
Keith Bowers, *Engineer*
Paul Stone, *Engineer*
Ed Wach, *Engineer*
◆ EMP: 125 EST: 1951
SQ FT: 280,000
SALES (est): 44.5MM **Privately Held**
WEB: www.gayston.com
SIC: 1794 2819 3443 2499 Excavation & grading, building construction; aluminum compounds; cylinders, pressure: metal plate; mulch, wood & bark; military insignia

(G-14174)
GREENE MEMORIAL HOSP SVCS INC
Also Called: KETTERING HEALTH NETWORK
1 Prestige Pl Ste 910 (45342-6105)
PHONE................................937 352-2000
EMP: 48
SALES: 51.7MM
SALES (corp-wide): 1.7B **Privately Held**
SIC: 8062 Hospital, affiliated with AMA residency
PA: Kettering Adventist Healthcare
3535 Southern Blvd
Dayton OH 45429
937 298-4331

(G-14175)
HCL OF DAYTON INC
4000 Mmsbrg Ctrvle Rd 4 Ste (45342)
PHONE................................937 384-8300
Phillip B Douglas, *CEO*
EMP: 106
SALES (est): 2.2MM
SALES (corp-wide): 347.9MM **Privately Held**
SIC: 8062 General medical & surgical hospitals
HQ: Lifecare Holdings, Llc
5340 Legacy Dr Ste 150
Plano TX 75024
469 241-2100

(G-14176)
HEALTH CARE RTREMENT CORP AMER
Also Called: Heartland of Oak Ridge
450 Oak Ridge Blvd (45342-3673)
PHONE................................937 866-8885
Lee M Elliott, *Manager*
EMP: 130
SQ FT: 57,139
SALES (corp-wide): 2.4B **Publicly Held**
WEB: www.hrc-manorcare.com
SIC: 8051 Convalescent home with continuous nursing care

HQ: Health Care And Retirement Corporation Of America
333 N Summit St Ste 103
Toledo OH 43604
419 252-5500

(G-14177)
INVOTEC ENGINEERING INC (PA)
10909 Industry Ln (45342-0818)
PHONE................................937 886-3232
John C Hanna, *President*
Thomas Hahn, *Principal*
Mark Goode, *Safety Mgr*
Karen Brunke, *Engrg Dir*
Zachary Berger, *Engineer*
EMP: 60
SQ FT: 63,000
SALES (est): 21.4MM **Privately Held**
WEB: www.invotec.com
SIC: 8711 3599 Machine tool design; custom machinery

(G-14178)
KETTCOR INC
Also Called: Collaborative Pharmacy Svcs
4301 Lyons Rd (45342-6446)
PHONE................................937 458-4949
Russ Weatherall, *Vice Pres*
EMP: 303
SALES (est): 10.5MM
SALES (corp-wide): 1.7B **Privately Held**
WEB: www.gvh-svh.org
SIC: 8741 Nursing & personal care facility management
PA: Kettering Adventist Healthcare
3535 Southern Blvd
Dayton OH 45429
937 298-4331

(G-14179)
KETTERING ADVENTIST HEALTHCARE
Also Called: Kettering Health Network
1 Prestige Pl (45342-3794)
PHONE................................937 762-1361
EMP: 86
SALES (corp-wide): 1.7B **Privately Held**
SIC: 8062 General medical & surgical hospitals
PA: Kettering Adventist Healthcare
3535 Southern Blvd
Dayton OH 45429
937 298-4331

(G-14180)
KETTERING ADVENTIST HEALTHCARE
Also Called: Kettering Health Network Khn
2110 Leiter Rd (45342-3598)
PHONE................................937 395-8816
Joe Mendenhall, *President*
Howard D Drenth, *Branch Mgr*
EMP: 92
SALES (corp-wide): 1.7B **Privately Held**
SIC: 8062 General medical & surgical hospitals
PA: Kettering Adventist Healthcare
3535 Southern Blvd
Dayton OH 45429
937 298-4331

(G-14181)
KETTERING MEDICAL CENTER
Also Called: Sycamore Medical Center
4000 Mmsburg Cntrville Rd (45342)
PHONE................................937 866-0551
Clifton D Patten, *CFO*
EMP: 350
SQ FT: 110,000
SALES (corp-wide): 1.7B **Privately Held**
WEB: www.kmcfoundation.org
SIC: 8062 General medical & surgical hospitals
HQ: Kettering Medical Center
3535 Southern Blvd
Kettering OH 45429
937 298-4331

(G-14182)
KETTERING MEDICAL CENTER
Also Called: Sycamore Glen Retirement Cmnty
317 Sycamore Glen Dr Ofc (45342-5705)
PHONE................................937 866-2984

Gary Van Nostrand, *Director*
EMP: 60
SALES (corp-wide): 1.7B **Privately Held**
WEB: www.kmcfoundation.org
SIC: 6513 6531 Retirement hotel operation; real estate managers
HQ: Kettering Medical Center
3535 Southern Blvd
Kettering OH 45429
937 298-4331

(G-14183)
KINGSTON HEALTHCARE COMPANY
Also Called: Kingston of Miamisburg
1120 Dunaway St (45342-3839)
PHONE................................937 866-9089
George Rumman, *President*
Crissy Carpenter, *Human Res Mgr*
EMP: 115
SALES (corp-wide): 95.5MM **Privately Held**
SIC: 8051 Skilled nursing care facilities
PA: Kingston Healthcare Company
1 Seagate Ste 1960
Toledo OH 43604
419 247-2880

(G-14184)
LABORATORY CORPORATION AMERICA
415 Byers Rd Ste 100 (45342-3684)
PHONE................................937 866-8188
Rhonda Ellis, *Branch Mgr*
EMP: 25 **Publicly Held**
WEB: www.labcorp.com
SIC: 8071 Testing laboratories
HQ: Laboratory Corporation Of America
358 S Main St Ste 458
Burlington NC 27215
336 229-1127

(G-14185)
LEXISNEXIS GROUP (DH)
9443 Springboro Pike (45342-5490)
PHONE................................937 865-6800
Kurt Sanford, *CEO*
Doug Kaplan, *CEO*
▲ EMP: 148
SALES (est): 456.7MM
SALES (corp-wide): 9.7B **Privately Held**
SIC: 7375 2741 Data base information retrieval; miscellaneous publishing
HQ: Relx Inc.
230 Park Ave Ste 700
New York NY 10169
212 309-8100

(G-14186)
MANAGED TECHNOLOGY SVCS LLC
3366 S Tech Blvd (45342-0823)
PHONE................................937 247-8915
Jesse Alexander, *Mng Member*
Chris Petrini Poli,
EMP: 55
SALES: 39MM **Privately Held**
SIC: 8742 7371 Management consulting services; software programming applications

(G-14187)
MENARD INC
8480 Springboro Pike (45342-4407)
PHONE................................937 630-3550
Dennis Dixon, *Branch Mgr*
EMP: 118
SALES (corp-wide): 12.5B **Privately Held**
SIC: 5211 1521 Home centers; single-family home remodeling, additions & repairs
PA: Menard, Inc.
5101 Menard Dr
Eau Claire WI 54703
715 876-5911

(G-14188)
MERCHANT DATA SERVICE INC
2275 E Central Ave (45342-3628)
PHONE................................937 847-6585
Gerald Phipps, *President*
John Agmpfling, *Vice Pres*
Jerry Coleman, *Info Tech Mgr*
EMP: 120
SQ FT: 1,800

▲ = Import ▼=Export
◆ =Import/Export

SALES (est): 6.4MM **Privately Held**
WEB: www.merchantdata.com
SIC: **7389** 7374 Inventory Computing Service And Scan Auditing

(G-14189)
MERRILL LYNCH PIERCE FENNER
10100 Innovation Dr # 300 (45342-4966)
PHONE..................................937 847-4000
Michael Maroni, *Manager*
Mike Maroni, *Manager*
Scott Saad, *Advisor*
EMP: 50
SALES (corp-wide): 110.5B **Publicly Held**
WEB: www.merlyn.com
SIC: **6211** 8742 6282 6221 Security brokers & dealers; management consulting services; investment advice; commodity contracts brokers, dealers
HQ: Merrill Lynch, Pierce, Fenner & Smith Incorporated
111 8th Ave
New York NY 10011
800 637-7455

(G-14190)
METAL SHREDDERS INC
5101 Farmersville W (45342)
P.O. Box 244, Dayton (45449)
PHONE..................................937 866-0777
Ken Cohen, *President*
Wilbur Cohen, *Chairman*
EMP: 30
SQ FT: 8,000
SALES (est): 3.5MM **Privately Held**
WEB: www.metalshredders.com
SIC: **7389** 3341 Metal slitting & shearing; secondary nonferrous metals

(G-14191)
MIAMISBURG CITY SCHOOL DST
Also Called: Miamisburg Transportation Dept
200 N 12th St (45342-2548)
PHONE..................................937 866-1283
Dan Girvin, *Branch Mgr*
EMP: 60
SALES (corp-wide): 69MM **Privately Held**
WEB: www.miamisburg.k12.oh.us
SIC: **4151** School buses
PA: Miamisburg City School District
540 Park Ave
Miamisburg OH 45342
937 866-3381

(G-14192)
MIAMISBURG FAMILY PRACTICE
Also Called: Riddle, Kevin L MD
415 Byers Rd Ste 300 (45342-3684)
PHONE..................................937 866-2494
Dr David Page, *Owner*
Dr Mark Schmidt, *Officer*
EMP: 50
SALES (est): 3.4MM **Privately Held**
SIC: **8011** General & family practice, physician/surgeon

(G-14193)
MIDWEST FASTENERS INC
450 Richard St (45342-1863)
PHONE..................................937 866-0463
Thomas Hartmann, *President*
Brian Waterhouse, *Vice Pres*
George Bratz, *Engineer*
Nate Conley, *CFO*
Bill Smith, *Cust Mgr*
◆ EMP: 85
SQ FT: 46,000
SALES (est): 15MM **Privately Held**
WEB: www.midwestfasteners.com
SIC: **5085** Fasteners, industrial: nuts, bolts, screws, etc.

(G-14194)
MOODYS OF DAYTON INC (PA)
4359 Infirmary Rd (45342-1231)
PHONE..................................614 443-3898
John Wagner, *President*
Dave Upp, *Superintendent*
Douglas Wagner, *Vice Pres*
Leigh S Schierholt, *Bookkeeper*
Chris Towe, *Sales Staff*
EMP: 29

SQ FT: 12,500
SALES: 3.7MM **Privately Held**
WEB: www.moodysofdayton.com
SIC: **1781** Water well drilling

(G-14195)
MORRO DIALYSIS LLC
Also Called: Miamisburg Dialysis
290 Alexandersville Rd (45342-3611)
PHONE..................................937 865-0633
James K Hilger, *Mgr*
EMP: 31
SALES (est): 358.8K **Publicly Held**
SIC: **8092** Kidney dialysis centers
PA: Davita Inc.
2000 16th St
Denver CO 80202

(G-14196)
NATIONAL CITY MORTGAGE INC (HQ)
3232 Newmark Dr (45342-5433)
PHONE..................................937 910-1200
Leo E Knight Jr, *Ch of Bd*
Rick A Smalldon, *President*
Jack Case, *Exec VP*
Gregory A Davis, *Exec VP*
Todd A Householder, *Exec VP*
EMP: 1600 EST: 1955
SQ FT: 500,000
SALES (est): 401.2MM
SALES (corp-wide): 19.9B **Publicly Held**
WEB: www.nationalcitymortgage.com
SIC: **6162** Mortgage bankers & correspondents
PA: The Pnc Financial Services Group Inc
300 5th Ave
Pittsburgh PA 15222
412 762-2000

(G-14197)
NEW LFCARE HSPITALS DAYTON LLC
4000 Mmsburg Cntrville Rd (45342)
PHONE..................................937 384-8300
Phillip B Douglas, *Ch of Bd*
EMP: 352
SALES (est): 17.5MM
SALES (corp-wide): 347.9MM **Privately Held**
SIC: **8062** General Hospital
HQ: Lifecare Holdings, Llc
5340 Legacy Dr Ste 150
Plano TX 75024
469 241-2100

(G-14198)
NURSES CARE INC (PA)
9009 Springboro Pike (45342-4418)
PHONE..................................513 424-1141
Sheila Rush, *CEO*
Karen Hansen, *Director*
EMP: 100
SALES: 3.9MM **Privately Held**
WEB: www.nursescareinc.com
SIC: **8082** Home health care services

(G-14199)
OBERER DEVELOPMENT CO (PA)
Also Called: Oberer Companies
3445 Newmark Dr (45342-5426)
PHONE..................................937 910-0851
Bruce Brun, *Division Mgr*
George R Oberer Sr, *Chairman*
Robert McCann, *COO*
Chris Conley, *Vice Pres*
Ruth Slone, *Controller*
EMP: 40
SALES (est): 39MM **Privately Held**
SIC: **6552** 1521 1522 1542 Land subdividers & developers, commercial; single-family housing construction; residential construction; nonresidential construction; apartment building operators

(G-14200)
OBERER RESIDENTIAL CNSTR
Also Called: Gold Key Homes
3475 Newmark Dr (45342-5426)
PHONE..................................937 278-0851
George Oberer Jr, *President*
Bob McCann, *COO*
Walt Hibner, *Vice Pres*
Kerry Duncan, *Opers Mgr*

Elizabeth McDonough, *Controller*
EMP: 150
SALES (est): 11.5MM **Privately Held**
SIC: **1521** 6531 1522 New construction, single-family houses; real estate agents & managers; residential construction

(G-14201)
ONEIL & ASSOCIATES INC (PA)
495 Byers Rd (45342-3798)
PHONE..................................937 865-0800
Bob Heilman, *President*
Ralph E Heyman, *Principal*
Gerald D Rapp, *Principal*
Howard N Thiele Jr, *Principal*
John Staten, *Chairman*
EMP: 300 EST: 1947
SQ FT: 75,000
SALES (est): 33.9MM **Privately Held**
WEB: www.oneil.com
SIC: **2741** 8999 7336 Technical manuals: publishing only, not printed on site; technical manual preparation; commercial art & illustration

(G-14202)
PARK HOTELS & RESORTS INC
300 Prestige Pl (45342-5300)
PHONE..................................937 436-2400
Jennifer Brown, *Manager*
EMP: 50
SALES (corp-wide): 2.7B **Publicly Held**
WEB: www.esirvine.com
SIC: **7011** Hotels & motels
PA: Park Hotels & Resorts Inc.
1775 Tysons Blvd Fl 7
Tysons VA 22102
571 302-5757

(G-14203)
PATENTED ACQUISITION CORP (PA)
Also Called: Think Patented
2490 Cross Pointe Dr (45342-3584)
PHONE..................................937 353-2299
Ken McNerney, *President*
EMP: 101
SALES (est): 58.5MM **Privately Held**
WEB: www.thinkpatented.com
SIC: **7389** 7331 Printers' services: folding, collating; mailing service

(G-14204)
PCM SALES INC
3020 S Tech Blvd (45342-4860)
PHONE..................................937 885-6444
David Wright, *Manager*
EMP: 55
SALES (corp-wide): 2.1B **Publicly Held**
WEB: www.sarcom.com
SIC: **5045** Computers, peripherals & software
HQ: Pcm Sales, Inc.
1940 E Mariposa Ave
El Segundo CA 90245
310 354-5600

(G-14205)
PHYSICIAN HOSPITAL ALLIANCE
10050 Innovation Dr # 240 (45342-4935)
PHONE..................................937 558-3456
Troy Tyner, *President*
Sheila Harris, *Network Mgr*
Kathleen Beer, *Technology*
EMP: 25
SALES (est): 5.6MM
SALES (corp-wide): 1.7B **Privately Held**
SIC: **8062** General medical & surgical hospitals
PA: Kettering Adventist Healthcare
3535 Southern Blvd
Dayton OH 45429
937 298-4331

(G-14206)
PNC BANK-ATM
Also Called: Lexis Nexis
9333 Springboro Pike (45342-4424)
PHONE..................................937 865-6800
Doug Kaplan, *Exec VP*
Chris Koogler, *Manager*
James Kerins, *Consultant*
Christopher Bendel, *Info Tech Dir*
EMP: 35 EST: 2015

SALES (est): 21.2MM **Privately Held**
SIC: **6099** Automated teller machine (ATM) network

(G-14207)
PNC MORTGAGE COMPANY (DH)
3232 Newmark Dr Bldg 2 (45342-5433)
PHONE..................................412 762-2000
Robert Crowl, *Principal*
John Zlotow, *Loan Officer*
David V Derau, *Manager*
EMP: 56
SALES (est): 15.8MM
SALES (corp-wide): 19.9B **Publicly Held**
SIC: **6162** Mortgage Banker/Correspondent
HQ: Pnc Bank, National Association
222 Delaware Ave
Wilmington DE 19801
877 762-2000

(G-14208)
PULMONARY & MEDICINE DAYTON (PA)
4000 Miamisburg Centervil (45342-3908)
PHONE..................................937 439-3600
Ivo C Seni MD, *President*
Felipe Rubio, *Principal*
Hemant Shah, *Principal*
EMP: 32
SALES (est): 4.2MM **Privately Held**
SIC: **8011** Pulmonary specialist, physician/surgeon

(G-14209)
RELX INC
Lexis-Nexis Group
9443 Springboro Pike (45342-4425)
P.O. Box 933, Dayton (45401-0933)
PHONE..................................937 865-6800
Fax: 937 847-3090
EMP: 300
SALES (corp-wide): 9B **Privately Held**
SIC: **7375** Information Retrieval Services, Nsk
HQ: Relx Inc.
230 Park Ave
New York NY 10169
212 309-8100

(G-14210)
RELX INC
Also Called: Lexis Nexis
9443 Springboro Pike (45342-4425)
PHONE..................................937 865-6800
Michael Weber, *Branch Mgr*
EMP: 49
SALES (corp-wide): 9.7B **Privately Held**
WEB: www.lexis-nexis.com
SIC: **2721** 2731 7389 7999 Trade journals: publishing only, not printed on site; books: publishing only; trade show arrangement; exposition operation
HQ: Relx Inc.
230 Park Ave Ste 700
New York NY 10169
212 309-8100

(G-14211)
REQ/JQH HOLDINGS INC
Also Called: Homewood Suites
3100 Contemporary Ln (45342-5399)
PHONE..................................937 432-0000
Mark Landon, *General Mgr*
EMP: 100
SALES (corp-wide): 84.3MM **Privately Held**
WEB: www.whihotels.com
SIC: **7011** Hotels & motels
PA: Req/Jqh Holdings, Inc.
4243 Hunt Rd Ste 2
Blue Ash OH 45242
513 891-1066

(G-14212)
RETALIX INC
2490 Technical Dr (45342-6136)
PHONE..................................937 384-2277
Barry Shake, *CEO*
Barry Shaked, *President*
Karen Weaver, *Treasurer*
EMP: 155
SQ FT: 72,000

SALES (est): 9.8MM
SALES (corp-wide): 6.4B **Publicly Held**
SIC: 5734 7372 Software, business &
non-game; prepackaged software
HQ: Ncr Global Ltd
9 Dafna
Raanana 43662
747 756-677

(G-14213)
RETALIX USA INC
2490 Technical Dr (45342-6136)
PHONE............................937 384-2277
Tom Mandich, *Branch Mgr*
EMP: 110
SALES (corp-wide): 6.4B **Publicly Held**
WEB: www.retalixusa.com
SIC: 7371 Computer software develop-
ment
HQ: Retalix Usa, Inc.
6100 Tennyson Pkwy # 150
Plano TX 75024
469 241-8400

(G-14214)
**RIVER VALLEY CREDIT UNION
INC (PA)**
505 Earl Blvd (45342-6411)
PHONE............................937 859-1970
John Bowen, *CEO*
Rebecca Siciarz, *President*
Robert Delong, *Vice Pres*
Suzanne M Roush, *Vice Pres*
James Roberson Jr, *CFO*
EMP: 33
SQ FT: 10,000
SALES: 11MM **Privately Held**
SIC: 6061 State Chartered Credit Union

(G-14215)
RIVERAIN TECHNOLOGIES LLC
3020 S Tech Blvd (45342-4860)
PHONE............................937 425-6811
Steve Worrell, *CEO*
San Finkelstein, *President*
Jason Knapp, *Research*
Kelley Meade, *Sales Staff*
Kelley Wright, *Marketing Staff*
EMP: 30
SALES (est): 6.5MM **Privately Held**
WEB: www.riverainmedical.com
SIC: 5047 X-ray machines & tubes

(G-14216)
SCHUSTER CARDIOLOGY
Also Called: Saini, Hari MD
4000 Miamisburg Ctr Ste (45342)
PHONE............................937 866-0637
Benjamin Schuster MD, *Principal*
EMP: 50
SALES (est): 3.1MM **Privately Held**
SIC: 8011 Cardiologist & cardio-vascular
specialist

(G-14217)
SENIOR CARE INC
8630 Washington Church Rd (45342-3795)
PHONE............................937 291-3211
EMP: 25 **Privately Held**
SIC: 8361 8059 8051 Home for the aged;
convalescent home; skilled nursing care
facilities
PA: Senior Care, Inc.
700 N Hurstbourne Pkwy # 200
Louisville KY 40222

(G-14218)
SENTAGE CORPORATION
Also Called: Dental Services Group
1037 Byers Rd (45342-5487)
PHONE............................937 865-5900
Kirby Pickle, *CEO*
Allen Matthews, *Branch Mgr*
EMP: 35
SALES (corp-wide): 81MM **Privately
Held**
WEB: www.dentalservices.net
SIC: 8072 Artificial teeth production
PA: Sentage Corporation
146 2nd St N Ste 202
Saint Petersburg FL 33701
727 502-2069

(G-14219)
SGI MATRIX LLC (PA)
1041 Byers Rd (45342-5487)
PHONE............................937 438-9033
James Young, *President*
Jeffrey S Young, *Vice Pres*
John Schomburg, *CFO*
Jeff Stout, *VP Sales*
Bruce Rogoff,
EMP: 68 **EST:** 1977
SQ FT: 12,000
SALES (est): 30.5MM **Privately Held**
WEB: www.matrixsys.com
SIC: 8711 7373 3873 Engineering serv-
ices; computer integrated systems de-
sign; watches, clocks, watchcases & parts

(G-14220)
**SHAWNTECH
COMMUNICATIONS INC (PA)**
Also Called: SCI
8521 Gander Creek Dr (45342-5436)
PHONE............................937 898-4900
Lance Fancher, *President*
Amelia Fancher, *Treasurer*
Winifred Labomme, *Admin Sec*
EMP: 46
SALES (est): 17.3MM **Privately Held**
WEB: www.shawntech.com
SIC: 5065 5999 1731 Mobile telephone
equipment; telephone equipment; paging
& signaling equipment; communication
equipment; telephone equipment & sys-
tems; mobile telephones & equipment;
electrical work

(G-14221)
SIMPLEX TIME RECORDER LLC
8899 Gander Creek Dr (45342-5432)
PHONE............................937 291-0355
Krissy McCrudden, *Branch Mgr*
EMP: 53 **Privately Held**
SIC: 1731 Fire detection & burglar alarm
systems specialization
HQ: Simplex Time Recorder Llc
50 Technology Dr
Westminster MA 01441

(G-14222)
SKYLINE CM PORTFOLIO LLC
Also Called: Courtyard Dayton Mall
100 Prestige Pl (45342-5340)
PHONE............................937 433-3131
Mona Rigdon, *Principal*
Vadim Shub, *Principal*
EMP: 30
SALES (est): 481.3K **Privately Held**
SIC: 7011 Hotels & motels

(G-14223)
SOGETI USA LLC (DH)
10100 Innovation Dr # 200 (45342-4966)
PHONE............................937 291-8100
Rajnish Nath, *CEO*
Mike Pleiman, *Exec VP*
Cynthia Gibson, *Vice Pres*
Steve Hughes, *Vice Pres*
Prabhjeet Singh, *Vice Pres*
EMP: 150
SQ FT: 18,332
SALES (est): 292.3MM
SALES (corp-wide): 355MM **Privately
Held**
WEB: www.sogeti-usa.com
SIC: 7379
HQ: Capgemini North America, Inc.
79 5th Ave Frnt 3
New York NY 10003
212 314-8000

(G-14224)
SOURCELINK OHIO LLC
3303 W Tech Blvd (45342-0817)
PHONE............................937 885-8000
Don Landrum, *CEO*
Jim Wisnionski, *President*
Mike Dolan, *COO*
Scott Wolford, *Production*
Gordon Anderson, *CFO*
EMP: 120
SQ FT: 140,000

SALES (est): 29.9MM
SALES (corp-wide): 86.9MM **Privately
Held**
SIC: 7331 7374 2752 Direct mail advertis-
ing services; data processing service;
commercial printing, lithographic
PA: Sourcelink Acquisition, Llc
500 Park Blvd Ste 1425
Itasca IL 60143
866 947-6872

(G-14225)
SOUTH TOWN PAINTING INC
320 E Linden Ave (45342-2828)
PHONE............................937 847-1600
Ronald L Elmore, *President*
James David Elmore, *Vice Pres*
EMP: 40
SQ FT: 2,000
SALES (est): 3.4MM **Privately Held**
SIC: 1721 Commercial painting; residential
painting

(G-14226)
STEINER EOPTICS INC (PA)
Also Called: Sensor Technology Systems
3475 Newmark Dr (45342-5426)
PHONE............................937 426-2341
Alan Page, *General Mgr*
Doris Byerly Anderson, *Office Mgr*
EMP: 80
SQ FT: 50,000
SALES (est): 13.9MM **Privately Held**
SIC: 8731 3851 Electronic research; oph-
thalmic goods

(G-14227)
**TECH PRODUCTS
CORPORATION (DH)**
2215 Lyons Rd (45342-4465)
PHONE............................937 438-1100
Dan Rork, *President*
Hugh E Wall Jr, *Principal*
Peirce Wood, *Principal*
A M Zimmerman, *Principal*
Bryan Strayer, *Prdtn Mgr*
EMP: 29
SQ FT: 25,000
SALES (est): 5.4MM
SALES (corp-wide): 2.6MM **Privately
Held**
WEB: www.tpcdayton.com
SIC: 3625 5084 3829 3651 Noise control
equipment; noise control equipment;
measuring & controlling devices; house-
hold audio & video equipment
HQ: Fabreeka International Holdings, Inc.
1023 Turnpike St
Stoughton MA 02072
781 341-3655

(G-14228)
**TERADATA OPERATIONS INC
(HQ)**
10000 Innovation Dr (45342-4927)
PHONE............................937 242-4030
Victor Lund, *President*
John Emanuel, *President*
John Huffman, *Partner*
Paul Majchrzak, *Partner*
Oliver Ratzesberger, *COO*
EMP: 100
SALES (est): 396.9MM **Publicly Held**
SIC: 3571 7379 Electronic computers;
computer related consulting services

(G-14229)
**THINKPATH ENGINEERING
SVCS LLC (PA)**
9080 Springboro Pike # 300 (45342-4669)
PHONE............................937 291-8374
Robert Trick, *President*
Jeff Grawe, *Engineer*
Kelly Hankinson, *CFO*
Antoinette Quinless, *Controller*
Steve Bishop, *Accounts Mgr*
EMP: 33
SQ FT: 6,330
SALES (est): 8.8MM **Privately Held**
SIC: 7373 7361 8999 8711 Computer-
aided engineering (CAE) systems service;
executive placement; technical writing;
mechanical engineering

(G-14230)
THOMPSON HINE LLP
10050 Innovation Dr # 400 (45342-4934)
P.O. Box 8801, Dayton (45401-8801)
PHONE............................937 443-6859
Robert Curry, *General Ptnr*
Jessica Sachs, *Branch Mgr*
Paige Connelly, *Associate*
Diane K Klopsch, *Associate*
Jason Tutrone, *Associate*
EMP: 123
SALES (corp-wide): 176.3MM **Privately
Held**
SIC: 8111 General practice attorney,
lawyer
PA: Thompson Hine Llp
127 Public Sq
Cleveland OH 44114
216 566-5500

(G-14231)
**THYSSENKRUPP MATERIALS
NA INC**
Copper & Brass Sales
10100 Innovation Dr # 210 (45342-4966)
PHONE............................937 898-7400
Scot Marlin, *Vice Pres*
Paul Fairhurst, *Credit Staff*
Julie Mays, *Corp Comm Staff*
Sherry Whitaker, *Info Tech Mgr*
EMP: 25
SALES (corp-wide): 39.8B **Privately Held**
SIC: 5051 Metals service centers & offices
HQ: Thyssenkrupp Materials Na, Inc.
22355 W 11 Mile Rd
Southfield MI 48033
248 233-5600

(G-14232)
UBS FINANCIAL SERVICES INC
3601 Rigby Rd Ste 500 (45342-5039)
PHONE............................937 223-3141
Greg Mayeux, *Vice Pres*
Mark Pent, *Manager*
EMP: 35
SALES (corp-wide): 29.4B **Privately Held**
SIC: 6211 Security brokers & dealers
HQ: Ubs Financial Services Inc.
1285 Ave Of The Americas
New York NY 10019
212 713-2000

(G-14233)
**ULLIMAN SCHUTTE CNSTR LLC
(PA)**
Also Called: U S C
9111 Springboro Pike (45342-4420)
PHONE............................937 247-0375
Andy Van Scoy, *Project Mgr*
Herbert T Schutte,
Matthew S Ulliman,
EMP: 300 **EST:** 1998
SQ FT: 4,000
SALES: 1.9MM **Privately Held**
WEB: www.ullimanschutte.com
SIC: 1629 Waste water & sewage treat-
ment plant construction

(G-14234)
**VEOLIA ES TCHNCAL SLUTIONS
LLC**
4301 Infirmary Rd (45342-1231)
PHONE............................937 859-6101
Bob Luzanski, *Manager*
EMP: 55
SALES (corp-wide): 600.9MM **Privately
Held**
WEB: www.onyxes.com
SIC: 4953 Recycling, waste materials
HQ: Onyx Environmental Services Llc
700 E Bttrfeld Rd Ste 201
Lombard IL 60148
630 218-1500

(G-14235)
WALGREEN CO
Also Called: Walgreens
1260 E Central Ave (45342-3546)
PHONE............................937 859-3879
Steve Smith, *Manager*
EMP: 40

SALES (corp-wide): 131.5B **Publicly Held**
WEB: www.walgreens.com
SIC: 5912 7384 Drug stores; photofinishing laboratory
HQ: Walgreen Co.
200 Wilmot Rd
Deerfield IL 60015
847 315-2500

(G-14236)
WALKER AUTO GROUP INC
Also Called: Walker Mitsubishi
8457 Springboro Pike (45342-4403)
PHONE.................................937 433-4950
Jeff Walker, *President*
John Walker III, *President*
Kevin Newton, *General Mgr*
John V H Walker Jr, *Chairman*
Beverly Walker, *Corp Secy*
EMP: 90 EST: 1950
SQ FT: 65,000
SALES (est): 37.4MM **Privately Held**
WEB: www.jackwalker.com
SIC: 5511 7538 7532 5531 Automobiles, new & used; general automotive repair shops; top & body repair & paint shops; automotive & home supply stores; used car dealers

(G-14237)
WESTERN & SOUTHERN LF INSUR CO
2 Prestige Pl Ste 310 (45342-6142)
PHONE.................................937 435-1964
Mark J Cook, *Manager*
EMP: 30 **Privately Held**
SIC: 6311 Life insurance
HQ: The Western & Southern Life Insurance Company
400 Broadway St
Cincinnati OH 45202
513 629-1800

(G-14238)
WESTERN TRADEWINDS INC (PA)
521 Byers Rd (45342-7302)
P.O. Box 750608, Dayton (45475-0608)
PHONE.................................937 859-4300
Harry Bossey, *President*
Kevin Mooney, *Admin Sec*
◆ EMP: 30
SQ FT: 10,000
SALES (est): 5.3MM **Privately Held**
WEB: www.westerntradewinds.com
SIC: 5084 5065 5083 5013 Industrial machinery & equipment; electronic parts & equipment; farm & garden machinery; motor vehicle supplies & new parts

(G-14239)
WINSUPPLY INC
9300 Byers Rd (45342-4352)
PHONE.................................937 865-0796
Jeff Porter, *Manager*
Brock Smith, *Assistant*
EMP: 30
SALES (corp-wide): 4.9B **Privately Held**
SIC: 5074 Plumbing fittings & supplies
PA: Winsupply Inc.
3110 Kettering Blvd
Moraine OH 45439
937 294-5331

Miamitown
Hamilton County

(G-14240)
BRENNAN ELECTRIC LLC
6859 Cemetary Dr (45041)
P.O. Box 266 (45041-0266)
PHONE.................................513 353-2229
Timothy Brennan,
Debra Brennan,
EMP: 25 EST: 1971
SQ FT: 3,000
SALES (est): 2.4MM **Privately Held**
SIC: 1731 General electrical contractor

(G-14241)
GATEWAY CONCRETE FORMING SVCS
5938 Hamilton Cleves Rd (45041)
P.O. Box 130 (45041-0130)
PHONE.................................513 353-2000
Robert Bilz, *President*
Tim Hughey, *President*
Brandon Erfman, *Vice Pres*
Jean C Hughey, *Treasurer*
J Robert Hughey, *Shareholder*
EMP: 75
SQ FT: 3,000
SALES (est): 8MM **Privately Held**
WEB: www.gatewaybuildingproducts.com
SIC: 1771 3449 3496 3429 Foundation & footing contractor; bars, concrete reinforcing: fabricated steel; miscellaneous fabricated wire products; manufactured hardware (general)

(G-14242)
MERCHANDISE INC
Also Called: MI
5929 State Rte 128 (45041)
P.O. Box 10 (45041-0010)
PHONE.................................513 353-2200
Donald W Karches, *President*
Elizabeth Ann Karches, *Vice Pres*
Beth Schwarb, *Human Res Mgr*
Greg Christopfel, *Sales Executive*
Brian Longbottom, *Department Mgr*
▼ EMP: 70
SQ FT: 50,000
SALES (est): 42.6MM **Privately Held**
WEB: www.merchandise.com
SIC: 5085 5099 5122 5199 Industrial supplies; video & audio equipment; compact discs; tapes & cassettes, prerecorded; video cassettes, accessories & supplies; drugs, proprietaries & sundries; cosmetics; medicine cabinet sundries; general merchandise, non-durable

(G-14243)
SOUTHERN OHIO DOOR CONTRLS INC (PA)
8080 Furlong Dr (45041)
P.O. Box 331 (45041-0331)
PHONE.................................513 353-4793
Pete Nicolaou, *President*
Ronald Merkt, *Principal*
Chris Nicolaou, *Vice Pres*
Holly Nicolaou, *Admin Sec*
EMP: 33
SQ FT: 3,000
SALES: 4MM **Privately Held**
SIC: 5031 7699 Doors & windows; door & window repair

Miamiville
Clermont County

(G-14244)
AIM MRO HOLDINGS INC (PA)
Also Called: T&B Manufacturing
375 Center St 175 (45147)
PHONE.................................513 831-2938
Barry F Bucher, *Chairman*
Scott Bucher, *Vice Pres*
Scott Wandtke, *Vice Pres*
Tom Goila, *CFO*
◆ EMP: 60
SQ FT: 20,000
SALES (est): 36.2MM **Privately Held**
WEB: www.aimmro.com
SIC: 5088 Aircraft engines & engine parts

(G-14245)
D&M CARTER LLC
106 Glendale Milford Rd (45147)
P.O. Box 20 (45147-0020)
PHONE.................................513 831-8843
David Carter, *Mng Member*
Mark Carter,
EMP: 30
SALES (est): 924.5K **Privately Held**
SIC: 1611 Grading; highway & street paving contractor

Middle Point
Van Wert County

(G-14246)
COUNTY OF VAN WERT
Also Called: Lincolnway Home
17872 Lincoln Hwy (45863-9700)
PHONE.................................419 968-2141
Dan Qurik, *Manager*
EMP: 40 **Privately Held**
SIC: 8051 Skilled nursing care facilities
PA: County Of Van Wert
121 E Main St Rm 200
Van Wert OH 45891
419 238-7020

(G-14247)
OGLETHORPE MIDDLEPOINT LLC
Also Called: Ridgeview Hospital
17872 Lincoln Hwy (45863-9700)
PHONE.................................419 968-2950
Jamie Coyle, *Accountant*
Barbara Liuzzi, *Manager*
Scott Price, *Officer*
Randy La Fond,
Mike Ringwald, *Maintence Staff*
EMP: 33
SALES: 12.7MM **Privately Held**
SIC: 8063 Psychiatric hospitals

Middleburg Heights
Cuyahoga County

(G-14248)
BREWER-GARRETT CO (PA)
6800 Eastland Rd (44130-2402)
PHONE.................................440 243-3535
Lou Joseph, *President*
Michelle Brody, *Executive Asst*
EMP: 145 EST: 1959
SQ FT: 31,500
SALES (est): 41.5MM **Privately Held**
WEB: www.brewer-garrett.com
SIC: 1711 4961 8711 Mechanical contractor; steam & air-conditioning supply; engineering services

(G-14249)
CHEMSTEEL CONSTRUCTION COMPANY (PA)
7850 Freeway Cir Ste 110 (44130-6317)
PHONE.................................440 234-3930
Ernest Grochalski, *President*
Vicki Anderson, *Chairman*
David Morse, *Project Mgr*
Tony Deluca, *VP Human Res*
EMP: 25
SQ FT: 5,000
SALES: 10.5MM **Privately Held**
WEB: www.chemsteel.com
SIC: 1541 1711 1799 Industrial buildings & warehouses; mechanical contractor; coating of metal structures at construction site

(G-14250)
COMPASS HEALTH BRANDS CORP (PA)
Also Called: Roscoe Medical
6753 Engle Rd Ste A (44130-7935)
PHONE.................................800 947-1728
Paul Guth, *President*
Henry Lin, *COO*
Tony West, *Vice Pres*
Jim Hileman, *CFO*
Ryan Moore, *VP Sales*
◆ EMP: 110
SQ FT: 20,000
SALES (est): 131.2MM **Privately Held**
SIC: 5047 Medical equipment & supplies

(G-14251)
CONTINING HLTHCARE SLTIONS INC (PA)
7261 Engle Rd Ste 200 (44130-3479)
PHONE.................................216 772-1105
T Scott Sprenger, *President*
Chris Mallett, *Vice Pres*
Adam Dube, *Info Tech Dir*
EMP: 37
SALES (est): 7.9MM **Privately Held**
SIC: 8059 8361 Personal care home, with health care; rehabilitation center, residential: health care incidental

(G-14252)
FIDELITONE INC
17851 Englewood Dr Ste I (44130-3489)
PHONE.................................440 260-6523
EMP: 36
SALES (corp-wide): 225.9MM **Privately Held**
SIC: 4789 Pipeline terminal facilities, independently operated
PA: Fidelitone, Inc.
1260 Karl Ct
Wauconda IL 60084
847 487-3300

(G-14253)
HAMPTON INN & SUITE INC
7074 Engle Rd (44130-3423)
PHONE.................................440 234-0206
Mark Csepll, *Manager*
Mark Cseplo, *Manager*
EMP: 50
SALES (est): 1.8MM **Privately Held**
SIC: 7011 Hotels

(G-14254)
MARSDEN HOLDING LLC
6751 Engle Rd Ste H (44130-7900)
PHONE.................................440 973-7774
Linda Simek, *Branch Mgr*
EMP: 54
SALES (corp-wide): 302.2MM **Privately Held**
SIC: 8999 Artists & artists' studios
PA: Marsden Holding, L.L.C.
2124 University Ave W
Saint Paul MN 55114
651 641-1717

(G-14255)
OH-16 CLVLND ARPRT S PRPRTY SU
Also Called: Courtyard Cleveland Airport S
7345 Engle Rd (44130-3430)
PHONE.................................440 243-8785
Gregory Moundas, *Vice Pres*
EMP: 33 EST: 2014
SALES (est): 193.8K **Privately Held**
SIC: 7011 Hotels

(G-14256)
QUADAX INC (PA)
7500 Old Oak Blvd (44130-3343)
PHONE.................................440 777-6300
Thomas Hockman, *Ch of Bd*
R Ralph Daugstrup, *President*
John Leskiw, *President*
Anthony Petras, *COO*
Denise Ferguson, *Pastor*
EMP: 108
SQ FT: 2,000
SALES (est): 38.1MM **Privately Held**
WEB: www.quadax.net
SIC: 8721 Billing & bookkeeping service

(G-14257)
RICHS TOWING & SERVICE INC (PA)
20531 1st Ave (44130-2437)
PHONE.................................440 234-3435
Michael Tomasko, *President*
Scott Kellerhall, *COO*
Sandy Saponari, *Vice Pres*
EMP: 50
SQ FT: 5,000
SALES (est): 7.3MM **Privately Held**
SIC: 7549 Towing service, automotive; road service, automotive

(G-14258)
RIVALS SPORTS GRILLE LLC
6710 Smith Rd (44130-2656)
PHONE.................................216 267-0005
John Simmons,
EMP: 48
SQ FT: 4,368
SALES: 1.9MM **Privately Held**
SIC: 5812 7372 Grills (eating places); application computer software

GEOGRAPHIC

(G-14259)
SOUTHWEST GENERAL MED GROUP
18697 Bagley Rd (44130-3417)
PHONE....................................440 816-8000
Willliam Young, *CEO*
Susan L Ferrante, *Principal*
Walter Funk, *Vice Pres*
EMP: 2000
SALES (est): 25.1MM **Privately Held**
SIC: 8062 General medical & surgical hospitals

(G-14260)
TAZMANIAN FREIGHT FWDG INC (PA)
Also Called: Tazmanian Freight Systems
6640 Engle Rd Ste A (44130-7949)
P.O. Box 811090, Cleveland (44181-1090)
PHONE....................................216 265-7881
Robert Rossbach, *CEO*
Jerry Metzo, *General Mgr*
David Huesers, *District Mgr*
Brad Barton, *Opers Mgr*
Wayne Nutt, *Opers Staff*
EMP: 40
SALES (est): 67.9MM **Privately Held**
WEB: www.tazmanian.com
SIC: 4731 Freight forwarding

(G-14261)
THE INTERLAKE STEAMSHIP CO
7300 Engle Rd (44130-3429)
PHONE....................................440 260-6900
Paul R Tregurtha, *Vice Ch Bd*
Mark W Barker, *President*
James R Barker, *Chairman*
Robert F Dorn, *Senior VP*
Kimberly Noe, *Buyer*
EMP: 25
SQ FT: 18,456
SALES: 127MM
SALES (corp-wide): 127MM **Privately Held**
WEB: www.interlake-steamship.com
SIC: 4432 Freight transportation on the Great Lakes
PA: Interlake Holding Company
1 Landmark Sq Ste 710
Stamford CT 06901
203 977-8900

(G-14262)
TWIN MED LLC
Also Called: All-Med Medical Supply
6950 Engle Rd (44130-3445)
PHONE....................................440 973-4555
EMP: 34
SALES (corp-wide): 197.5MM **Privately Held**
SIC: 5047 Medical equipment & supplies
PA: Twin Med, Llc
11333 Greenstone Ave
Santa Fe Springs CA 90670
323 582-9900

(G-14263)
UNITED PARCEL SERVICE INC
Also Called: UPS
6940 Engle Rd Ste C (44130-3435)
PHONE....................................440 243-3344
Kevin Snow, *Purch Agent*
George Smith, *Manager*
EMP: 40
SALES (corp-wide): 71.8B **Publicly Held**
WEB: www.ups.com
SIC: 7389 Mailbox rental & related service
PA: United Parcel Service, Inc.
55 Glenlake Pkwy
Atlanta GA 30328
404 828-6000

(G-14264)
VERANTIS CORPORATION (HQ)
7251 Engle Rd Ste 300 (44130-3400)
PHONE....................................440 243-0700
William Jackson, *Senior VP*
▼ EMP: 30
SALES (est): 17.8MM **Privately Held**
SIC: 3564 5075 Air purification equipment; blowers & fans; air pollution control equipment & supplies

PA: Tanglewood Investments Inc.
5051 Westheimer Rd # 300
Houston TX 77056
713 629-5525

(G-14265)
WADSWORTH SERVICE INC
7851 Freeway Cir (44130-6308)
PHONE....................................419 861-8181
Nancy Steiger, *Administration*
EMP: 45
SALES (corp-wide): 10.6MM **Privately Held**
SIC: 1711 Refrigeration contractor
PA: Wadsworth Service, Inc.
1500 Michael Owens Way
Perrysburg OH 43551
216 391-7263

(G-14266)
WORLD EX SHIPG TRNSP FWDG SVCS (PA)
Also Called: Westainer Lines
17851 Jefferson Park Rd (44130-3461)
PHONE....................................440 826-5055
Brian Buckholz, *President*
John Morgan, *Vice Pres*
Jeff Ryer, *Treasurer*
EMP: 30
SQ FT: 2,800
SALES (est): 4MM **Privately Held**
WEB: www.westforwarding.com
SIC: 4731 Freight forwarding

(G-14267)
ZIN TECHNOLOGIES INC (PA)
6745 Engle Rd Ste 105 (44130-7993)
PHONE....................................440 625-2200
Daryl Z Laisure, *President*
Chris Sheehan, *Area Mgr*
Carlos Grodsinsky, *COO*
Brian Finley, *Vice Pres*
Debra Lyden, *QC Mgr*
EMP: 225
SQ FT: 60,000
SALES: 30MM **Privately Held**
SIC: 8731 8711 7379 Engineering laboratory, except testing; consulting engineer; computer related consulting services

---

Middlefield
Geauga County

(G-14268)
AIRGAS INC
14943 Madison Rd (44062-8403)
PHONE....................................440 632-1758
Woodrow Burton, *President*
EMP: 264
SALES (corp-wide): 125.9MM **Privately Held**
SIC: 5169 Industrial gases
HQ: Airgas, Inc.
259 N Radnor Chester Rd # 100
Radnor PA 19087
610 687-5253

(G-14269)
BRIAR HL HLTH CARE RSDENCE INC
Also Called: Briar Hill Hlth Care Residence
15950 Pierce St (44062-9577)
P.O. Box 277 (44062-0277)
PHONE....................................440 632-5241
George Ohman, *President*
Charles Ohman, *Vice Pres*
Donald Gray, *Treasurer*
Anderson Ohman, *Manager*
Judy Knepper, *Supervisor*
EMP: 95 EST: 1962
SQ FT: 10,000
SALES (est): 8.1MM **Privately Held**
SIC: 8051 Convalescent home with continuous nursing care

(G-14270)
HANS ROTHENBUHLER & SON INC
15815 Nauvoo Rd (44062-8501)
PHONE....................................440 632-6000
John Rothenbuhler, *President*
Joyce Filla, *General Mgr*
Gary Schoenwald, *Marketing Staff*

▲ EMP: 40
SALES (est): 12.3MM **Privately Held**
SIC: 2022 5451 5143 2023 Natural cheese; dairy products stores; dairy products, except dried or canned; dry, condensed, evaporated dairy products

(G-14271)
KRAFTMAID TRUCKING INC (PA)
16052 Industrial Pkwy (44062-9382)
P.O. Box 1055 (44062-1055)
PHONE....................................440 632-2531
Tom Chieffe, *President*
EMP: 100
SQ FT: 12,000
SALES (est): 16.7MM **Privately Held**
SIC: 4813 2517 Telephone communication, except radio; wood television & radio cabinets

(G-14272)
LAKE HOSPITAL SYSTEM INC
15050 S Springdale Ave (44062-9211)
PHONE....................................440 632-3024
Dave Ebel, *Branch Mgr*
EMP: 1100
SALES (corp-wide): 356.8MM **Privately Held**
SIC: 8062 8011 General Hospital Medical Doctor's Office
PA: Lake Hospital System, Inc.
7590 Auburn Rd
Painesville OH 44077
440 375-8100

(G-14273)
NORSTAR ALUMINUM MOLDS INC
Also Called: Starwood
15986 Valplast St (44062-9399)
PHONE....................................440 632-0853
Erik Adams, *Engineer*
Brian Gresch, *Branch Mgr*
EMP: 60
SALES (corp-wide): 8MM **Privately Held**
SIC: 7011 3444 Hotels & motels; sheet metalwork
PA: Norstar Aluminum Molds, Inc.
W66n622 Madison Ave
Cedarburg WI 53012
262 375-5600

(G-14274)
NORTH COAST SALES
15200 Madison Rd 101c (44062-8305)
P.O. Box 157 (44062-0157)
PHONE....................................440 632-0793
Bonnie Vaughan, *Owner*
James Vaughan III, *Owner*
EMP: 50
SALES (est): 1.3MM **Privately Held**
SIC: 7349 Janitorial service, contract basis

(G-14275)
RAVENWOOD MENTAL HEALTH CENTER
16030 E High St (44062-9474)
P.O. Box 246 (44062-0246)
PHONE....................................440 632-5355
Patrick Cantlin, *Controller*
Dave Boyle, *Branch Mgr*
EMP: 50
SALES (corp-wide): 7.5MM **Privately Held**
SIC: 8093 Mental health clinic, outpatient
PA: Ravenwood Mental Health Center, Inc.
12557 Ravenwood Dr
Chardon OH 44024
440 285-3568

(G-14276)
SANTAS HIDE AWAY HOLLOW INC
15400 Bundysburg Rd (44062-8437)
PHONE....................................440 632-5000
William Dietdrle, *Exec Dir*
EMP: 47
SALES: 214K **Privately Held**
SIC: 8351 Child day care services

(G-14277)
THE MIDDLEFIELD BANKING CO (HQ)
15985 E High St (44062-7229)
P.O. Box 35 (44062-0035)
PHONE....................................440 632-1666
Carolyn J Turk, *Ch of Bd*
Tom Caldwell, *President*
Charles O Moore, *President*
Michael L Allen, *Exec VP*
John D Lane, *Exec VP*
EMP: 25 EST: 1901
SQ FT: 2,500
SALES: 48.4MM
SALES (corp-wide): 54MM **Publicly Held**
WEB: www.middlefieldbank.com
SIC: 6022 State commercial banks
PA: Middlefield Banc Corp.
15985 E High St
Middlefield OH 44062
440 632-1666

(G-14278)
VALLEY TITLE & ESCROW AGENCY
15985 E High St Ste 203 (44062-7229)
P.O. Box 1269 (44062-1269)
PHONE....................................440 632-9833
Tom Hedrick, *CFO*
EMP: 30
SALES (est): 616.6K **Privately Held**
SIC: 6541 Title & trust companies

(G-14279)
WHITFORD WOODS CO INC
16192 Bundysburg Rd (44062-8444)
P.O. Box 290, Burton (44021-0290)
PHONE....................................440 693-4344
Bill Papenbrock, *President*
EMP: 35
SALES (est): 876.8K **Privately Held**
SIC: 6512 Commercial & industrial building operation

Middleport
Meigs County

(G-14280)
BEDFORD TOWNSHIP
Also Called: Meigs Cnty Dept Jobs Fmly Svcs
175 Race St (45760-1078)
P.O. Box 191 (45760-0191)
PHONE....................................740 992-2117
Michael Swisher, *Manager*
EMP: 50 **Privately Held**
WEB: www.meigsdjfs.net
SIC: 8322 9111 Social service center; county supervisors' & executives' offices
PA: County Of Meigs
100 E 2nd St Rm 201
Pomeroy OH 45769
740 992-5290

(G-14281)
MEIGS CENTER LTD
Also Called: Overbrook Center
333 Page St (45760-1391)
PHONE....................................740 992-6472
Charla Brown, *Partner*
David Snyder, *Administration*
EMP: 150
SQ FT: 36,000
SALES (est): 7.8MM **Privately Held**
SIC: 8051 8052 8093 Extended care facility; personal care facility; rehabilitation center, outpatient treatment

(G-14282)
MEIGS LOCAL SCHOOL DISTRICT
Also Called: Rutland Bus Garage
36895 State Route 124 (45760-9717)
PHONE....................................740 742-2990
Paul McElroy, *Manager*
EMP: 41
SALES (corp-wide): 16MM **Privately Held**
SIC: 4173 Bus terminal & service facilities
PA: Meigs Local School District
41765 Pomeroy Pike
Pomeroy OH 45769
740 992-5650

(G-14283)
SONS OF UN VTRANS OF CIVIL WAR
600 Grant St (45760-1214)
PHONE.................................740 992-6144
James Oiler, *Chief*
James Mourning, *Treasurer*
EMP: 60
SALES (est): 1.7MM **Privately Held**
SIC: 8699 Personal interest organization

Middletown
Butler County

(G-14284)
1440 CORPORATION INC
Also Called: Coldwell Banker
1440 S Breiel Blvd (45044-6702)
PHONE.................................513 424-2421
Michael Combs, *President*
Ron Davis, *Vice Pres*
EMP: 34
SALES: 1.5MM **Privately Held**
WEB: www.coldwellbankeroyer.com
SIC: 6531 Real estate agent, residential

(G-14285)
ABILITIES FIRST FOUNDATION INC (PA)
4710 Timber Trail Dr (45044-5399)
PHONE.................................513 423-9496
J Thomas Wheeler, *President*
Elaine Garver, *Vice Pres*
Ray Debrosse, *VP Finance*
Christine Alderman, *Human Res Dir*
Christine Kratzer, *Human Res Dir*
EMP: 86
SQ FT: 31,200
SALES: 5MM **Privately Held**
WEB: www.abilitiesfirst.org
SIC: 8211 8361 8049 8351 School for the retarded; home for the mentally handicapped; physical therapist; child day care services; job training & vocational rehabilitation services; employment agencies

(G-14286)
ADS MANUFACTURING OHIO LLC
1701 Reinartz Blvd (45042-2127)
PHONE.................................513 217-4502
Mark Booker, *Mng Member*
EMP: 70
SALES (est): 1.7MM **Privately Held**
SIC: 7389 Design services

(G-14287)
AK STEEL CORPORATION
1801 Crawford St (45044-4583)
PHONE.................................513 425-6541
MO Reed, *General Mgr*
Stephen W Gilby, *Managing Dir*
Dennis M Bench, *Principal*
R Jesseman, *Principal*
Lawrence Zizzo, *Vice Pres*
EMP: 148 **Publicly Held**
SIC: 8732 Commercial nonphysical research
HQ: Ak Steel Corporation
9227 Centre Pointe Dr
West Chester OH 45069
513 425-4200

(G-14288)
AMIX INC
Also Called: Pleasant Hill Golf Club
6487 Hankins Rd (45044-9712)
PHONE.................................513 539-7220
Dennis Meyer, *President*
Curtis L Meyer, *Corp Secy*
Lynn Meyer, *Vice Pres*
EMP: 25
SALES: 850K **Privately Held**
SIC: 7992 Public golf courses

(G-14289)
ATRIUM MEDICAL CENTER
Also Called: Sports Medicine and Spine Ctr
105 Mcknight Dr (45044)
PHONE.................................513 420-5013
Ron Hoehn, *Director*
EMP: 30

SALES (corp-wide): 17.2K **Privately Held**
SIC: 8062 8049 General medical & surgical hospitals; physical therapist
HQ: Atrium Medical Center
1 Medical Center Dr
Middletown OH 45005
513 424-2111

(G-14290)
BECK DIALYSIS LLC
Also Called: Atrium Dialysis
4421 Roosevelt Blvd Ste D (45044-9024)
PHONE.................................513 422-6879
James K Hilger,
EMP: 44
SALES (est): 655.3K **Publicly Held**
SIC: 8092 Kidney dialysis centers
PA: Davita Inc.
2000 16th St
Denver CO 80202

(G-14291)
BELCAN LLC
Also Called: Belcan Staffing Solutions
4490 Marie Dr (45044-6248)
PHONE.................................513 217-4562
Kimberly Roberts, *Branch Mgr*
EMP: 749
SALES (corp-wide): 813.3MM **Privately Held**
SIC: 7363 Engineering help service
PA: Belcan, Llc
10200 Anderson Way
Blue Ash OH 45242
513 891-0972

(G-14292)
BENCHMARK MASONRY CONTRACTORS
2924 Cincinnati Dayton Rd (45044-9313)
P.O. Box 976, Miamisburg (45343-0976)
PHONE.................................937 228-1225
Stephen R Hester, *President*
EMP: 80
SALES: 7K **Privately Held**
WEB: www.benchmarkmasonry.com
SIC: 1741 Masonry & other stonework

(G-14293)
BERNS GRNHSE & GRDN CTR INC (PA)
Also Called: Berns Garden Center
825 Greentree Rd (45044-8919)
PHONE.................................513 423-5306
Albert Berns, *Ch of Bd*
Cherie Berns, *President*
Greg Berns, *Vice Pres*
Jeff Berns, *Vice Pres*
Vickie Berns, *Vice Pres*
EMP: 25
SALES (est): 9.1MM **Privately Held**
SIC: 5261 0782 5191 Garden supplies & tools; nurseries; landscape contractors; garden supplies

(G-14294)
BROWNS RUN COUNTRY CLUB
6855 Sloebig Rd (45042-9448)
PHONE.................................513 423-6291
David Baril, *General Mgr*
Todd Dodge, *Superintendent*
Gerg Martin, *Treasurer*
Jennifer Fuller, *Admin Sec*
EMP: 52
SALES: 784.9K **Privately Held**
WEB: www.brownsruncc.com
SIC: 7997 Country club, membership

(G-14295)
CHURCH OF GOD RETIREMENT CMNTY
Also Called: Willow Knoll Nursing Center
4400 Vannest Ave (45042-2770)
PHONE.................................513 422-5600
West Johnson, *COO*
Sara Marshall, *Manager*
Dee Allen, *Director*
Pamela Van Nest, *Administration*
Diane Kloenne, *Administration*
EMP: 130
SQ FT: 28,000
SALES (est): 4.5MM **Privately Held**
SIC: 8051 8052 8361 Convalescent home with continuous nursing care; intermediate care facilities; residential care

(G-14296)
COHEN ELECTRONICS INC
Also Called: Cohen Middletown
3110 S Verity Pkwy (45044-7443)
PHONE.................................513 425-6911
Amy E Brown, *Principal*
Tammy Walling, *Asst Mgr*
David Dellostritto, *Director*
EMP: 99
SALES (est): 4.3MM
SALES (corp-wide): 78MM **Privately Held**
SIC: 5093 Ferrous metal scrap & waste
PA: Cohen Brothers, Inc.
1520 14th Ave
Middletown OH 45044
513 422-3696

(G-14297)
COMPREHENSIVE COUNSELING SVC
1659 S Breiel Blvd Ste A (45044-6705)
PHONE.................................513 424-0921
Charles Eastlick, *Exec Dir*
Henry Dorsman, *Director*
Deanna Proctor, *Director*
EMP: 45
SALES (est): 1.3MM **Privately Held**
WEB: www.comprehensivecounselingservice.com
SIC: 8093 Mental health clinic, outpatient

(G-14298)
CSX TRANSPORTATION INC
1003 Forrer St (45044-7516)
PHONE.................................513 422-2031
Pat Henry, *Branch Mgr*
Jerry Hughes, *Manager*
EMP: 25
SALES (corp-wide): 12.2B **Publicly Held**
WEB: www.csxt.com
SIC: 4011 Railroads, line-haul operating
HQ: Csx Transportation, Inc.
500 Water St
Jacksonville FL 32202
904 359-3100

(G-14299)
ELLIOTT AUTO BATH INC
901 Elliott Dr (45044-6213)
PHONE.................................513 422-3700
Patrice Drury, *President*
EMP: 26
SQ FT: 5,200
SALES (est): 110K **Privately Held**
SIC: 7542 Carwash, automatic; washing & polishing, automotive

(G-14300)
GARDEN MANOR EXTENDED CARE CEN
6898 Hmlton Middletown Rd (45044-7851)
PHONE.................................513 420-5972
Sam Boymel, *President*
Rachel Boymel, *Treasurer*
Peggy Frazier, *Manager*
EMP: 250
SQ FT: 10,000
SALES: 14.8MM **Privately Held**
SIC: 8051 8361 Convalescent home with continuous nursing care; residential care

(G-14301)
HART INDUSTRIES INC (PA)
Also Called: Hart Industrial Products Div
931 Jeanette St (45044-5701)
PHONE.................................513 541-4278
Herman E Hart, *CEO*
Roger Hart, *President*
Christopher Hart, *Treasurer*
▲ EMP: 34 EST: 1966
SQ FT: 47,000
SALES (est): 34.8MM **Privately Held**
WEB: www.hose.com
SIC: 5085 Hose, belting & packing; rubber goods, mechanical

(G-14302)
HOSPICE OF MIDDLETOWN
3909 Central Ave (45044-5006)
PHONE.................................513 424-2273
Rose Fromer, *Manager*
Amy Lindon, *Manager*
EMP: 35

SALES: 2.6MM **Privately Held**
SIC: 8069 Specialty hospitals, except psychiatric

(G-14303)
INTERSCOPE MANUFACTURING INC
2901 Carmody Blvd (45042-1761)
PHONE.................................513 423-8866
John Michael Brill, *CEO*
◆ EMP: 50
SQ FT: 175,000
SALES (est): 6.6MM **Privately Held**
WEB: www.interscopemfg.com
SIC: 3599 7389 Custom machinery; repossession service

(G-14304)
J P TRANSPORTATION COMPANY
2518 Oxford State Rd (45044-8909)
PHONE.................................513 424-6978
Kenneth Henderson, *President*
Donald Henderson, *Vice Pres*
EMP: 45
SQ FT: 3,200
SALES (est): 4.9MM **Privately Held**
SIC: 4213 4212 Contract haulers; local trucking, without storage

(G-14305)
LOWES HOME CENTERS LLC
3125 Towne Blvd (45044-6299)
PHONE.................................513 727-3900
Josh Crumrine, *Manager*
EMP: 150
SALES (corp-wide): 68.6B **Publicly Held**
SIC: 5211 5031 5722 5064 Home centers; building materials, exterior; building materials, interior; household appliance stores; electrical appliances, television & radio
HQ: Lowe's Home Centers, Llc
1605 Curtis Bridge Rd
Wilkesboro NC 28697
336 658-4000

(G-14306)
MARTIN GREG EXCAVATING INC
1501 S University Blvd (45044-5967)
PHONE.................................513 727-9300
Gregory L Martin, *President*
Rebecca Martin, *Corp Secy*
Herbert Martin, *Vice Pres*
EMP: 36
SQ FT: 27,500
SALES (est): 5.3MM **Privately Held**
SIC: 1794 Excavation & grading, building construction

(G-14307)
MECCO INC
2100 S Main St (45044-7345)
PHONE.................................513 422-3651
David T Morgan, *President*
Charles E Morgan, *Vice Pres*
Ron Price, *Vice Pres*
Stephen Rains, *Treasurer*
Brenda Burns, *Admin Sec*
EMP: 45 EST: 1956
SQ FT: 2,000
SALES (est): 4.3MM **Privately Held**
WEB: www.meccoconcrete.com
SIC: 3273 1442 Ready-mixed concrete; construction sand mining; gravel mining

(G-14308)
MIAMI UNIVERSITY
Also Called: Miami University-Middletown
4200 E University Blvd (45042)
PHONE.................................513 727-3200
Kelly Cowan, *Exec Dir*
EMP: 350
SALES (corp-wide): 551.7MM **Privately Held**
WEB: www.muohio.edu
SIC: 8221 8742 8331 University; training & development consultant; job training services
PA: Miami University
501 E High St
Oxford OH 45056
513 529-1809

(G-14309)
MIDDLETOWN CITY DIVISON FIRE
2300 Roosevelt Blvd (45044-4741)
PHONE..................................513 425-7996
Paul Lolli, *General Mgr*
John Sauter, *Chief*
EMP: 84
SALES (est): 1.4MM **Privately Held**
SIC: 0851 Fire fighting services, forest

(G-14310)
MIDDLETOWN SCHOOL VHCL SVC CTR
2951 Cincinnati Dayton Rd (45044-9313)
PHONE..................................513 420-4568
Thelma Hacker, *Principal*
Michael Hammond, *Manager*
EMP: 70 EST: 2002
SALES (est): 1.4MM **Privately Held**
SIC: 4151 School buses

(G-14311)
MIDDLTOWN AREA SENIOR CITIZENS
3907 Central Ave (45044-5006)
PHONE..................................513 423-1734
Ralph Conner, *President*
Alesia Childress, *President*
Basil Fleming, *President*
Alicia Chambers, *Exec Dir*
Ann Munafo, *Exec Dir*
EMP: 54
SQ FT: 22,000
SALES: 2.2MM **Privately Held**
WEB: www.middletownohioseniors.org
SIC: 8322 Senior citizens' center or association

(G-14312)
MIDDLTOWN CRDVSCULAR ASSOC INC
103 Mcknight Dr Ste A (45044-4891)
PHONE..................................513 217-6400
Thomas D Anthony, *President*
EMP: 38
SALES (est): 6.5MM **Privately Held**
SIC: 8011 Cardiologist & cardio-vascular specialist

(G-14313)
MIDUSA CREDIT UNION (PA)
1201 Crawford St (45044-4575)
PHONE..................................513 420-8640
Chris Johnson, *President*
Kelly Nugent, *Vice Pres*
EMP: 71
SQ FT: 6,000
SALES (est): 5.5MM **Privately Held**
WEB: www.midfirstcu.org
SIC: 6062 State credit unions

(G-14314)
MOOSE INTERNATIONAL INC
Also Called: Moose Fmly Ctr 501 Middletown
3009 S Main St (45044-7418)
PHONE..................................513 422-6776
Jerry Gabbard, *Administration*
EMP: 47
SALES (corp-wide): 48.4MM **Privately Held**
WEB: www.thalist.com
SIC: 8641 Civic associations
PA: Moose International, Incorporated
155 S International Dr
Mooseheart IL 60539
630 859-2000

(G-14315)
NU WAVES LTD
Also Called: Nuwaves Engineering
132 Edison Dr (45044-3269)
PHONE..................................513 360-0800
Jeffrey Wells, *President*
Jaclyn Thomas, *President*
Timothy Wurth, *Vice Pres*
Thoeun Huon, *Director*
Ryan Canning, *Business Dir*
EMP: 64 EST: 2003
SQ FT: 30,200
SALES (est): 15.3MM **Privately Held**
WEB: www.nuwaves-ltd.com
SIC: 8711 Electrical or electronic engineering

(G-14316)
OHIO TRANSPORT CORPORATION (PA)
5593 Hmlton Middletown Rd (45044-9703)
PHONE..................................513 539-0576
William C Hill, *President*
Chad Hill, *Corp Secy*
EMP: 25
SQ FT: 3,000
SALES: 3MM **Privately Held**
SIC: 4212 Local trucking, without storage

(G-14317)
OREILLY AUTOMOTIVE INC
1835 Central Ave (45044-4468)
PHONE..................................513 783-1343
EMP: 29 **Publicly Held**
SIC: 7538 General automotive repair shops
PA: O'reilly Automotive, Inc.
233 S Patterson Ave
Springfield MO 65802

(G-14318)
ORTHOPDIC SPT MDICINE CONS INC
275 N Breiel Blvd (45042-3807)
PHONE..................................513 777-7714
Jerry B Magone MD, *President*
Ray E Kiefhaber, *Principal*
M S True MD, *Med Doctor*
EMP: 30 EST: 1968
SQ FT: 12,000
SALES (est): 5.6MM **Privately Held**
WEB: www.ortho-sportsmed.com
SIC: 8011 Orthopedic Surgeon

(G-14319)
PAC WORLDWIDE CORPORATION
Also Called: Pac Manufacturing
3131 Cincinnati Dayton Rd (45044-8965)
PHONE..................................800 610-9367
EMP: 77 **Privately Held**
SIC: 5112 2677 Whol Stationery/Office Supplies Mfg Envelopes
HQ: Pac Worldwide Corporation
15435 Ne 92nd St
Redmond WA 98052
425 202-4000

(G-14320)
PHOENIX CORPORATION
Also Called: Phoenix Metals
1211 Hook Dr (45042-1713)
PHONE..................................513 727-4763
Mike Gara, *Principal*
EMP: 36
SALES (corp-wide): 11.5B **Publicly Held**
SIC: 5051 Steel
HQ: Phoenix Corporation
4685 Buford Hwy
Peachtree Corners GA 30071
770 447-4211

(G-14321)
PRECISION STRIP INC
4400 Oxford State Rd (45044-8914)
PHONE..................................513 423-4166
Darren Wolf, *Branch Mgr*
EMP: 85
SALES (corp-wide): 11.5B **Publicly Held**
WEB: www.precision-strip.com
SIC: 4225 General warehousing & storage
HQ: Precision Strip Inc.
86 S Ohio St
Minster OH 45865
419 628-2343

(G-14322)
PREMIER RSTRTION MECH SVCS LLC
2890 S Main St (45044-2800)
P.O. Box 8286, Franklin (45005-8286)
PHONE..................................513 420-1600
Jennifer Brown, *Principal*
EMP: 28
SALES (est): 5.5MM **Privately Held**
SIC: 1711 Mechanical contractor

(G-14323)
PREMIER SYSTEM INTEGRATORS INC
2660 Towne Blvd (45044-8986)
PHONE..................................513 217-7294
EMP: 73 **Privately Held**
SIC: 4813
PA: Premier System Integrators, Inc.
140 Weakley Ln
Smyrna TN 37167

(G-14324)
RITTENHOUSE
3000 Mcgee Ave (45044-4991)
PHONE..................................513 423-2322
Lisa Rice, *Exec Dir*
EMP: 37
SQ FT: 4,800
SALES: 746.4K **Privately Held**
WEB: www.mcknightterrace.com
SIC: 8059 Personal care home, with health care

(G-14325)
RMB ENTERPRISES INC
2742 Oxford State Rd (45044-8911)
PHONE..................................513 539-3431
Bill Bowling, *President*
Joe Brown, *General Mgr*
Mike Brooks, *Managing Dir*
Don Bowling, *Vice Pres*
EMP: 100
SALES (est): 7.6MM **Privately Held**
SIC: 4214 Local trucking with storage

(G-14326)
ROBINSON HTG AIR-CONDITIONING
1208 2nd Ave (45044-4210)
PHONE..................................513 422-6812
Stuart Robinson, *President*
Zereda Robinson, *Vice Pres*
Zereda Vega, *Technology*
EMP: 27
SQ FT: 4,000
SALES (est): 4.7MM **Privately Held**
WEB: www.robinsonheating.com
SIC: 1711 1731 Warm air heating & air conditioning contractor; electrical work

(G-14327)
SAWYER REALTORS
1505 S Breiel Blvd (45044-6703)
PHONE..................................513 423-6521
John Sawyer, *Owner*
EMP: 27
SALES (est): 1.1MM **Privately Held**
WEB: www.sawyerrealtors.com
SIC: 6552 6531 Subdividers & developers; real estate agents & managers

(G-14328)
SEMMA ENTERPRISES INC
Also Called: Hawthorn Glenn Nursing Center
5414 Hankins Rd (45044-9782)
PHONE..................................513 863-7775
Paul Depalma, *President*
Brain Gibbony, *Vice Pres*
Jo N Moon, *Director*
Ron Campbell, *Food Svc Dir*
Melissa Ruchel, *Hlthcr Dir*
EMP: 150
SALES (est): 2.8MM **Privately Held**
WEB: www.hawthornglennc.com
SIC: 8051 Skilled nursing care facilities

(G-14329)
SOUTHWEST OHIO AMBLATRY SRGERY
295 N Breiel Blvd (45042-3807)
PHONE..................................513 425-0930
Eugene D Herrmann, *President*
Jerry Magone, *Vice Pres*
Gary Cobb, *Treasurer*
Jeffrey Nicolai, *Administration*
EMP: 38
SQ FT: 11,500
SALES (est): 4.7MM **Privately Held**
WEB: www.magone.com
SIC: 8011 Ambulatory surgical center

(G-14330)
SSI FABRICATED INC
2860 Cincinnati Dayton Rd (45044-8902)
PHONE..................................513 217-3535

Richard Hall, *President*
Joel K Elkin, *Principal*
Mark Franks, *Vice Pres*
Jon Cooke, *Project Mgr*
Russ Weiandt, *Sales Staff*
EMP: 33
SQ FT: 6,000
SALES (est): 7.5MM **Privately Held**
WEB: www.steamsystems.com
SIC: 7699 5074 Industrial equipment services; heating equipment (hydronic)

(G-14331)
STANDARD LABORATORIES INC
2601 S Verity Pkwy (45044-7482)
PHONE..................................513 422-1088
Joy Wright, *Branch Mgr*
EMP: 28
SALES (corp-wide): 61.4MM **Privately Held**
SIC: 8734 Product testing laboratories
PA: Standard Laboratories, Inc.
147 11th Ave Ste 100
South Charleston WV 25303
304 744-6800

(G-14332)
STEVE S TOWING AND RECOVERY
6475 Trenton Franklin Rd (45042-1749)
PHONE..................................513 422-0254
Steve Gebhradt, *Principal*
EMP: 50
SALES (est): 1.1MM **Privately Held**
SIC: 7549 Towing service, automotive; towing services

(G-14333)
SUNCOKE ENERGY NC
Also Called: Mto Suncoke
3353 Yankee Rd (45044-8927)
PHONE..................................513 727-5571
Frederick Fritz A Henderson, *CEO*
Brian Bokovoy, *Safety Mgr*
David O'Brien, *Manager*
EMP: 40
SALES (est): 5.4MM **Privately Held**
SIC: 1241 Coal mining services

(G-14334)
SUPER SHINE INC
1549 S Breiel Blvd Ste A (45044-6861)
P.O. Box 146 (45042-0146)
PHONE..................................513 423-8999
Marsha Giltrow, *President*
EMP: 35
SALES: 500K **Privately Held**
SIC: 7349 7363 Janitorial service, contract basis; domestic help service

(G-14335)
TERMINIX INTL CO LTD PARTNR
4455 Salman Rd (45044)
PHONE..................................513 539-7846
Don Dunn, *Branch Mgr*
EMP: 29
SALES (corp-wide): 1.9B **Publicly Held**
SIC: 7342 7389 Pest control services; termite control; air pollution measuring service
HQ: The Terminix International Company Limited Partnership
150 Peabody Pl
Memphis TN 38103
901 766-1400

(G-14336)
TERMINIX INTL COML XENIA
4455 Salzman Rd (45044-9709)
PHONE..................................513 539-7846
Kathy Fitzgerald, *Principal*
EMP: 48 EST: 2010
SALES (est): 1.1MM **Privately Held**
SIC: 7342 Pest control in structures; pest control services

(G-14337)
TOMSON STEEL COMPANY
1400 Made Industrial Dr (45044-8936)
P.O. Box 940 (45044-0940)
PHONE..................................513 420-8600
Stephen Lutz, *President*
Larry L Knapp, *Principal*
Thomas Lutz, *Vice Pres*
Kelly Malone, *Sales Staff*

▲ = Import ▼=Export
◆ =Import/Export

Jim Strok, *Sales Staff*
EMP: 25
SQ FT: 94,000
SALES (est): 22.6MM **Privately Held**
WEB: www.tomsonsteel.com
SIC: 5051 3291 Steel; abrasive metal &
steel products

(G-14338)
TOPMIND/PLANEX
CONSTRUCTION
831 Elliott Dr (45044-6211)
PHONE...................248 719-0474
EMP: 35
SALES: 950K **Privately Held**
SIC: 1522 Residential Construction Contractor

(G-14339)
WELLS FARGO BANK
NATIONAL ASSN
1076 Summitt Dr (45042-3400)
PHONE...................513 424-6640
Lou Christy, *Branch Mgr*
EMP: 84
SALES (corp-wide): 101B **Publicly Held**
SIC: 6021 National commercial banks
HQ: Wells Fargo Bank, National Association
101 N Phillips Ave
Sioux Falls SD 57104
605 575-6900

(G-14340)
WMVH LLC
Also Called: Weatherwax
4616 Manchester Rd (45042-3818)
PHONE...................513 425-7886
Jim T Kraft, *Mng Member*
EMP: 60
SALES (est): 376.5K **Privately Held**
SIC: 7992 Public golf courses

Middletown
Warren County

(G-14341)
ACCESS COUNSELING
SERVICES LLC
4464 S Dixie Hwy (45005-5464)
PHONE...................513 649-8008
Deanna L Proctor,
Debra Cotter,
Judith Freeland,
Lynn Harris,
EMP: 101
SALES (est): 2.6MM **Privately Held**
SIC: 8322 General counseling services

(G-14342)
ATRIUM HEALTH SYSTEM (HQ)
1 Medical Center Dr (45005-2584)
PHONE...................937 499-5606
Mike Uhl, *President*
EMP: 1502
SALES (est): 211.1MM
SALES (corp-wide): 17.2K **Privately Held**
SIC: 8082 Home health care services
PA: Premier Health Partners
110 N Main St Ste 450
Dayton OH 45402
937 499-9596

(G-14343)
BARRETT PAVING MATERIALS
INC
3751 Commerce Dr (45005-5234)
PHONE...................513 271-6200
Janice Misch, *Human Res Mgr*
Gerald Bushelman, *Manager*
EMP: 200
SALES (corp-wide): 83.5MM **Privately Held**
WEB: www.barrettpaving.com
SIC: 5032 2951 1771 1611 Asphalt mixture; asphalt paving mixtures & blocks; driveway, parking lot & blacktop contractors; surfacing & paving; construction sand & gravel

HQ: Barrett Paving Materials Inc.
3 Becker Farm Rd Ste 307
Roseland NJ 07068
973 533-1001

(G-14344)
CBL & ASSOCIATES PRPTS INC
Also Called: Towne Mall
3461 Towne Blvd Unit 200 (45005-5533)
PHONE...................513 424-8517
Kelly Askine, *Manager*
EMP: 30 **Publicly Held**
WEB: www.yorkgalleriamall.com
SIC: 6512 Shopping center, property operation only
PA: Cbl & Associates Properties, Inc.
2030 Hamilton Place Blvd
Chattanooga TN 37421

(G-14345)
CELLCO PARTNERSHIP
Also Called: Verizon Wireless
3663 Towne Blvd (45005-5516)
PHONE...................513 422-3437
EMP: 76
SALES (corp-wide): 130.8B **Publicly Held**
SIC: 4812 Cellular telephone services
HQ: Cellco Partnership
1 Verizon Way
Basking Ridge NJ 07920

(G-14346)
ERMC II LP
Also Called: Towne Mall
3461 Towne Blvd Unit 250 (45005-5555)
PHONE...................513 424-8517
Emerson Russell, *Manager*
EMP: 30 **Privately Held**
WEB: www.ermc2.com
SIC: 7349 Lighting maintenance service
PA: Ermc Ii, L.P.
1 Park Pl 6148
Chattanooga TN 37421

(G-14347)
FACILITY SVC MAINT SYSTEMS
INC
Also Called: Facility Svcs & Maint Systems
3641 Commerce Dr (45005-5215)
P.O. Box 941 (45044-0941)
PHONE...................513 422-7060
Justin L Paulk, *President*
EMP: 58
SQ FT: 2,200
SALES (est): 500K **Privately Held**
SIC: 7349 Janitorial service, contract basis

(G-14348)
GREAT MIAMI VALLEY YMCA
5750 Innovation Dr (45005-5172)
PHONE...................513 217-5501
Donna Keith, *Director*
EMP: 85
SALES (corp-wide): 13MM **Privately Held**
SIC: 8641 Youth organizations
PA: Great Miami Valley Ymca
105 N 2nd St
Hamilton OH 45011
513 887-0001

(G-14349)
HIGHTOWERS PETROLEUM
COMPANY
3577 Commerce Dr (45005-5232)
PHONE...................513 423-4272
Steve Hightower Sr, *CEO*
Yudell Hightower, *Vice Pres*
Gary Visher, *CFO*
EMP: 50
SQ FT: 4,400
SALES: 308MM **Privately Held**
WEB: www.hightowerspetroleum.com
SIC: 5172 Diesel fuel; gasoline

(G-14350)
I-75 PIERSON AUTOMOTIVE INC
Also Called: Guyler Automotive
3456 S Dixie Hwy (45005-5718)
PHONE...................513 424-1881
Brenda Pierson, *President*
J Michael Guyler, *President*
EMP: 40
SQ FT: 30,000

SALES (est): 13MM **Privately Held**
SIC: 5511 7538 7532 Automobiles, new & used; trucks, tractors & trailers: new & used; general automotive repair shops; top & body repair & paint shops

(G-14351)
MIDUSA CREDIT UNION
3600 Towne Blvd Ste A (45005-5543)
PHONE...................513 420-8640
Christopher Johnson, *CEO*
EMP: 30
SQ FT: 56,744
SALES (est): 2.4MM
SALES (corp-wide): 5.5MM **Privately Held**
WEB: www.midfirstcu.org
SIC: 6062 State credit unions
PA: Midusa Credit Union
1201 Crawford St
Middleton OH 45044
513 420-8640

(G-14352)
OTTERBEIN SNIOR LFSTYLE
CHICES
105 Atrium Dr (45005-5166)
PHONE...................513 260-7690
EMP: 146
SALES (corp-wide): 58.4MM **Privately Held**
SIC: 8361 8059 8051 Home for the aged; nursing home, except skilled & intermediate care facility; skilled nursing care facilities
PA: Senior Otterbein Lifestyle Choices
585 N State Route 741
Lebanon OH 45036
513 933-5400

(G-14353)
PAYCHEX INC
3420 Atrium Blvd Ste 200 (45005-5186)
PHONE...................513 727-9182
Marcia Paulick, *President*
EMP: 37
SALES (corp-wide): 3.3B **Publicly Held**
SIC: 8721 Payroll accounting service
PA: Paychex, Inc.
911 Panorama Trl S
Rochester NY 14625
585 385-6666

(G-14354)
PRIMARY CR NTWRK PRMR
HLTH PRT
Also Called: Anne Camm, Psy.d., Company
1 Medical Center Dr (45005-2584)
PHONE...................513 420-5233
Christopher Danis, *CEO*
EMP: 32
SALES (corp-wide): 33.7MM **Privately Held**
SIC: 8011 General & family practice, physician/surgeon
PA: Primary Care Network Of Premier Health Partners
110 N Main St Ste 350
Dayton OH 45402
937 226-7085

(G-14355)
SPRINGHILLS LLC
Also Called: Spring Hills At Middletown
3851 Towne Blvd (45005-5595)
PHONE...................513 424-9999
Charlene Himes, *Manager*
Christina Jones, *Nurse*
EMP: 61
SALES (est): 1.8MM **Privately Held**
SIC: 8051 Skilled nursing care facilities
PA: Springhills Llc
515 Plainfield Ave
Edison NJ 08817

(G-14356)
UCC CHILDRENS CENTER
Also Called: Y M C A
5750 Innovation Dr (45005-5172)
PHONE...................513 217-5501
Donna Keith, *Director*
EMP: 35

SALES: 400K **Privately Held**
SIC: 8641 7991 8351 7032 Youth organizations; physical fitness facilities; child day care services; youth camps; individual & family services

---

Midvale
Tuscarawas County

(G-14357)
AMKO SERVICE COMPANY (DH)
Also Called: Dover Cryogenics
3211 Brightwood Rd (44653)
P.O. Box 280 (44653-0280)
PHONE...................330 364-8857
Darren Nippard, *President*
Duane R Yant, *Principal*
▲ **EMP:** 50
SALES (est): 6.2MM **Privately Held**
SIC: 7699 3443 7629 Tank repair & cleaning services; cryogenic tanks, for liquids & gases; electrical repair shops
HQ: Praxair, Inc.
10 Riverview Dr
Danbury CT 06810
203 837-2000

(G-14358)
HYDRAULIC SPECIALISTS INC
5655 Gundy Dr (44653)
PHONE...................740 922-3343
Dale Burkholder, *President*
Laraine Burkholder, *Corp Secy*
EMP: 25
SQ FT: 15,000
SALES (est): 3.7MM **Privately Held**
SIC: 3443 7699 3593 Industrial vessels, tanks & containers; hydraulic equipment repair; fluid power cylinders & actuators

---

Milan
Erie County

(G-14359)
BELLEVUE FOUR CNTY EMS N
CENTL
Also Called: Ems Service
12513 Us Highway 250 N (44846-9546)
PHONE...................419 483-3322
Don Ballah, *Director*
Donald Ballah, *Director*
EMP: 150
SALES (est): 1.9MM **Privately Held**
WEB: www.emsservice.com
SIC: 4119 Ambulance service

(G-14360)
COUNTY OF ERIE
Erie County Dept Envmtl Svcs
10102 Hoover Rd (44846-9711)
PHONE...................419 433-0617
Jack R Meyers, *Director*
EMP: 59 **Privately Held**
WEB: www.gem.org
SIC: 4953 9111 Sanitary landfill operation; county supervisors' & executives' offices
PA: County Of Erie
2900 Columbus Ave
Sandusky OH 44870
419 627-7682

(G-14361)
FREUDENBERG-NOK GENERAL
PARTNR
Transtec
11617 State Re 13 (44846)
P.O. Box 556 (44846-0556)
PHONE...................419 499-2502
David B Gardner, *President*
EMP: 300
SALES (corp-wide): 11B **Privately Held**
WEB: www.freudenberg-nok.com
SIC: 7389 5013 Packaging & labeling services; automotive supplies & parts
HQ: Freudenberg-Nok General Partnership
47774 W Anchor Ct
Plymouth MI 48170
734 451-0020

(G-14362)
MILAN SKILLED NURSING LLC
185 S Main St (44846-9765)
PHONE..................216 727-3996
Scott Sprenger, COO
Mark Sprenger, Vice Pres
Brian Haylor, CFO
Jeff Bunner, Exec Dir
Christopher Mallett, Exec Dir
EMP: 70
SALES (est): 808.1K Privately Held
SIC: 8049 Nurses & other medical assistants

(G-14363)
NORWALK AREA HEALTH SERVICES
Also Called: North Central Ems
12513 State Route 250 (44846-9546)
PHONE..................419 499-2515
Lisa Wildman, Exec Dir
Donald Ballah, Director
EMP: 150
SALES (corp-wide): 1.5MM Privately Held
SIC: 4119 Ambulance service
HQ: Norwalk Area Health Services
272 Benedict Ave
Norwalk OH 44857

(G-14364)
OLDE TOWNE WINDOWS INC
Also Called: Old Towne Windows & Doors
9501 Us Highway 250 N # 1 (44846-9377)
PHONE..................419 626-9613
Charles Hemker, Vice Pres
Lisa Hemker, Treasurer
Joyce Swint, Admin Sec
EMP: 40
SQ FT: 28,000
SALES (est): 6.2MM Privately Held
WEB: www.oldetownewindows.com
SIC: 5211 5031 5039 1761 Door & window products; windows; glass construction materials; siding contractor; patio & deck construction & repair

(G-14365)
PACKAGING & PADS R US LLC (PA)
12406 Us Highway 250 N C (44846-9382)
PHONE..................419 499-2905
Harry Perdue Jr, President
Lisa Brownell, Corp Secy
EMP: 30
SQ FT: 40,000
SALES (est): 6.6MM Privately Held
SIC: 5199 Packaging materials

(G-14366)
PRECISION PAVING INC
3414 State Route 113 E (44846-9426)
PHONE..................419 499-7283
Mike Kegarise, President
Matt Kluding, Corp Secy
Jeff Crecelius, Vice Pres
Missy Seidel, Comms Dir
EMP: 33
SQ FT: 10,000
SALES (est): 5.4MM Privately Held
WEB: www.precisionpaving.com
SIC: 1611 Surfacing & paving

(G-14367)
SCHLESSMAN SEED CO (PA)
11513 Us Highway 250 N (44846-9708)
PHONE..................419 499-2572
Daryl Deering, Ch of Bd
Vicki Zorn, Plant Mgr
Dave Herzer, Treasurer
Mark Skaggs, Controller
David Schlessman, Finance Mgr
EMP: 25
SQ FT: 100,000
SALES (est): 23.5MM Privately Held
WEB: www.schlessman-seed.com
SIC: 5191 2075 0723 0116 Seeds: field, garden & flower; soybean oil mills; crop preparation services for market; soybeans; corn; wheat

(G-14368)
XPO LOGISTICS FREIGHT INC
12518 State Route 250 (44846-9540)
PHONE..................419 499-8888

Jeffrey Mount, Manager
EMP: 50
SALES (corp-wide): 15.3B Publicly Held
WEB: www.con-way.com
SIC: 4213 Contract haulers
HQ: Xpo Logistics Freight, Inc..
2211 Old Earhart Rd # 100
Ann Arbor MI 48105
800 755-2728

Milford
Clermont County

(G-14369)
ALBRECHT INC (PA)
Also Called: Albrecht & Company
1040 Techne Center Dr (45150-2731)
PHONE..................513 576-9900
Vera Muzzillo, CEO
Brian Smith, President
Carl Albrecht, General Mgr
Pam Paeltz, Regional Mgr
Tom Rizzi, Senior VP
▲ EMP: 40
SQ FT: 6,500
SALES (est): 15.4MM Privately Held
WEB: www.albrechtcompany.com
SIC: 7311 Advertising agencies

(G-14370)
AMBULATORY MEDICAL CARE INC (PA)
Also Called: Doctor's Urgent Care Offices
935 State Route 28 (45150-1957)
PHONE..................513 831-8555
Paul J Amrhein, President
Dean Judkins, President
Paul Amrhein, Exec VP
EMP: 35
SQ FT: 6,000
SALES (est): 18.5MM Privately Held
WEB: www.amcareinc.com
SIC: 8011 Clinic, operated by physicians; medical centers

(G-14371)
AMERICAN NURSING CARE INC (DH)
1700 Edison Dr Ste 300 (45150-2729)
PHONE..................513 576-0262
Thomas J Karpinski, President
Mary Molnar, Opers Staff
Joanell Phillips, Opers Staff
James Graham, Technical Mgr
Jerry McKinney, CFO
EMP: 65 EST: 1976
SALES (est): 102.1MM Privately Held
WEB: www.americannursingcare.com
SIC: 8051 Convalescent home with continuous nursing care

(G-14372)
AW FARRELL SON INC
745 Us Route 50 (45150-9510)
PHONE..................513 334-0715
Craig Miller, General Mgr
EMP: 45
SALES (est): 1.8MM Privately Held
SIC: 1761 Roofing contractor

(G-14373)
AZTEC PLUMBING INC
Also Called: Aztec Plumbg
5989 Meijer Dr Ste 8 (45150-1544)
P.O. Box 121 (45150-0121)
PHONE..................513 732-3320
Gerald Blanchard, President
Catherine Blanchard, Treasurer
EMP: 30
SQ FT: 1,026
SALES (est): 2.5MM Privately Held
SIC: 1711 Plumbing contractors

(G-14374)
BURKE INC
Also Called: Burke Milford
25 Whitney Dr Ste 110 (45150-8400)
PHONE..................513 576-5700
Ron Tatham, Branch Mgr
EMP: 100
SALES (corp-wide): 55MM Privately Held
SIC: 8732 Market analysis or research

PA: Burke, Inc.
500 W 7th St
Cincinnati OH 45203
513 241-5663

(G-14375)
BZAK LANDSCAPING INC (PA)
Also Called: Bzak Ldscpg & Maintainance
931 Round Bottom Rd (45150-9520)
PHONE..................513 831-0907
Michael G Bieszczak, President
Awilda Lachtrop, Accounts Mgr
Mona Shaw, Manager
Joe Waters, Manager
Vicky Davis, Admin Asst
EMP: 30
SALES (est): 9.3MM Privately Held
SIC: 0781 0782 1521 5261 Landscape planning services; lawn care services; patio & deck construction & repair; nurseries & garden centers; farm & garden machinery

(G-14376)
CHI HEALTH AT HOME
1700 Edison Dr Ste 300 (45150-2729)
PHONE..................513 576-0262
EMP: 66
SALES (est): 462K Privately Held
SIC: 8082 Home health care services
HQ: Chi Health At Home
1700 Edison Dr Ste 300
Milford OH 45150

(G-14377)
CHI HEALTH AT HOME (DH)
1700 Edison Dr Ste 300 (45150-2729)
PHONE..................513 576-0262
Dan Dietz, President
L T Wilburn Jr, President
Rich Smith, Principal
EMP: 50
SALES (est): 103.6MM Privately Held
SIC: 7363 8093 Medical help service; specialty outpatient clinics
HQ: Bethesda, Inc.
619 Oak St 7n
Cincinnati OH 45206
513 569-6400

(G-14378)
CINCINNATI NATURE CENTER (PA)
4949 Tealtown Rd (45150-9737)
PHONE..................513 831-1711
Laura Schmid, Manager
William Hopple, Exec Dir
EMP: 45
SQ FT: 20,000
SALES: 7.7MM Privately Held
SIC: 8412 Arts or science center

(G-14379)
CINTAS CORPORATION NO 2
27 Whitney Dr (45150-9784)
PHONE..................513 965-0800
Scott Wolfe, Manager
EMP: 180
SALES (corp-wide): 6.4B Publicly Held
WEB: www.cintas-corp.com
SIC: 7218 7213 Industrial uniform supply; uniform supply
HQ: Cintas Corporation No. 2
6800 Cintas Blvd
Mason OH 45040

(G-14380)
CIVIL & ENVIRONMENTAL CONS INC
5899 Montclair Blvd (45150-3067)
PHONE..................513 985-0226
John Imbus, Principal
Amanda Clark, Admin Asst
EMP: 30
SALES (corp-wide): 134.8MM Privately Held
SIC: 0781 8711 Landscape architects; civil engineering
PA: Civil & Environmental Consultants, Inc.
333 Baldwin Rd Ste 1
Pittsburgh PA 15205
412 429-2324

(G-14381)
CLERMONT CARE INC
Also Called: Clearmont Nursing Convalecent
934 State Route 28 (45150-1912)
PHONE..................513 831-1770
Roger King, President
EMP: 190 EST: 1966
SQ FT: 50,000
SALES (est): 6.7MM Privately Held
SIC: 8051 Convalescent home with continuous nursing care

(G-14382)
COVINGTON CAR WASH INC
5942 Creekview Dr (45150-1518)
PHONE..................513 831-6164
Maureen Hein, President
Richard Hein, Vice Pres
EMP: 25
SALES (est): 330.5K Privately Held
SIC: 7542 Carwashes

(G-14383)
DAVEY TREE EXPERT COMPANY
Also Called: Davey Tree & Lawn Care
6065 Br Hill Guinea Pike (45150-2219)
PHONE..................513 575-1733
Rick Hannah, Manager
EMP: 40
SQ FT: 1,376
SALES (corp-wide): 1B Privately Held
SIC: 0783 Ornamental shrub & tree services
PA: The Davey Tree Expert Company
1500 N Mantua St
Kent OH 44240
330 673-9511

(G-14384)
DELANEYS TAX ACCUNTING SVC LTD
1157b State Route 131 (45150-2717)
PHONE..................513 248-2829
John Doughty, Owner
EMP: 30
SALES (est): 601.5K Privately Held
SIC: 7291 Tax return preparation services

(G-14385)
DNV GL HEALTHCARE USA INC
400 Techne Center Dr # 100 (45150-2792)
PHONE..................281 396-1610
Yehuda Dror, Branch Mgr
EMP: 44
SALES (corp-wide): 2.3B Privately Held
SIC: 8621 Medical field-related associations; professional standards review board
HQ: Dnv Gl Healthcare Usa, Inc.
1400 Ravello Rd
Katy TX 77449
281 396-1703

(G-14386)
DOWNING DISPLAYS INC (PA)
550 Techne Center Dr (45150-2763)
PHONE..................513 248-9800
Michael J Scherer, President
Catherine H Downing, Principal
Wesley Jacobs, Vice Pres
Peter O Toole, Vice Pres
Ed Moore, VP Opers
▲ EMP: 65
SQ FT: 110,000
SALES (est): 13.2MM Privately Held
WEB: www.downingdisplays.com
SIC: 7319 Display advertising service

(G-14387)
EPSILON
Also Called: Colloquy
1000 Summit Dr Unit 200 (45150-2724)
PHONE..................513 248-2882
Brian Kennedy, CEO
Julia Smith, President
Joan Deno, Business Mgr
Jim Kuschill, Senior VP
Patrick Lapointe, Senior VP
EMP: 190 EST: 1981
SQ FT: 38,000
SALES (est): 15.6MM Publicly Held
WEB: www.colloquy.com
SIC: 7371 Custom computer programming services

PA: Alliance Data Systems Corporation
7500 Dallas Pkwy Ste 700
Plano TX 75024

(G-14388)
FORWITH LOGISTICS LLC
6129 Guinea Pike (45150-2221)
PHONE..................................513 386-8310
Kevin Forwith, *Mng Member*
EMP: 40
SALES (est): 856K Privately Held
SIC: 8743 Public relations services

(G-14389)
FRESENIUS MED CARE
MILFORD LLC
Also Called: Fresenius Kidney Care Milford
5890 Meadow Creek Dr (45150-3087)
PHONE..................................513 248-1690
Mary Garber,
William Valle,
EMP: 30 EST: 2016
SALES (est): 326.1K Privately Held
SIC: 8092 Kidney dialysis centers

(G-14390)
FRONTLINE NATIONAL LLC
502 Techne Center Dr G (45150-8780)
PHONE..................................513 528-7823
Katherine Latham, *President*
Robert Latham,
Erika Latham, *Receptionist*
EMP: 90
SALES (est): 4.5MM Privately Held
WEB: www.frontlinenational.com
SIC: 7363 Medical help service

(G-14391)
GB LIQUIDATING COMPANY INC
22 Whitney Dr (45150-9783)
PHONE..................................513 248-7600
Cory Sherman, *Editor*
Leon Lovette, *Regional Mgr*
Kathy Kluska, *Human Res Dir*
Joe Leahy, *Marketing Staff*
Robert Sherman Jr,
EMP: 50
SALES (est): 4.5MM Privately Held
WEB: www.gordonbernard.com
SIC: 7371 2759 2741 2752 Custom computer programming services; commercial printing; miscellaneous publishing; calendar & card printing, lithographic

(G-14392)
GEM INTERIORS INC
769 Us Route 50 (45150-9510)
PHONE..................................513 831-6535
Greg E Massie, *President*
Greg Massie, *Manager*
EMP: 40
SQ FT: 8,000
SALES (est): 6.6MM Privately Held
SIC: 1542 Custom builders, non-residential

(G-14393)
GORDON BERNARD COMPANY
LLC
22 Whitney Dr (45150-9781)
PHONE..................................513 248-7600
Robert Sherman Jr, *President*
Cory Sherman, *Editor*
Leon Lovette, *Regional Mgr*
Kathy Kluska, *Human Res Dir*
Karyl Menchen, *Regl Sales Mgr*
EMP: 45
SQ FT: 25,000
SALES (est): 5.6MM Privately Held
SIC: 5199 2752 2741 Calendars; commercial printing, lithographic; miscellaneous publishing

(G-14394)
HENRY P THOMPSON COMPANY
(PA)
101 Main St Ste 300 (45150-1183)
PHONE..................................513 248-3200
William S Cantwell, *President*
Gary R Lubin, *Vice Pres*
Michael S Macy, *Vice Pres*
Joyce Widmeyer, *VP Opers*
EMP: 25
SQ FT: 16,000

SALES (est): 10.9MM Privately Held
WEB: www.hptthompson.com
SIC: 5084 7699 Pumps & pumping equipment; industrial equipment services

(G-14395)
HOMETOWN URGENT CARE
1068 State Route 28 Ste C (45150-2095)
PHONE..................................513 831-5900
EMP: 99
SALES (corp-wide): 73.2MM Privately Held
SIC: 8049 8011 Occupational therapist; medical centers
PA: Hometown Urgent Care
2400 Corp Exchange Dr # 102
Columbus OH 43231
614 505-7633

(G-14396)
ICON ENVIRONMENTAL GROUP
LLC
Also Called: Icon Property Rescue
24 Whitney Dr Ste D (45150-9521)
PHONE..................................513 426-6767
Larry Hensley, *President*
Paula Hensley, *Vice Pres*
Gina Lambrinides, *Manager*
EMP: 45
SALES (est): 5.7MM Privately Held
SIC: 8748 1521 1542 7217 Environmental consultant; repairing fire damage, single-family houses; commercial & office buildings, renovation & repair; carpet & upholstery cleaning; renovation, remodeling & repairs: industrial buildings

(G-14397)
INTERNATIONAL
TECHNEGROUP INC (PA)
5303 Dupont Cir (45150-2734)
PHONE..................................513 576-3900
Thomas A Gregory, *CEO*
Tom Gregory, *Exec VP*
Rendell Hughes, *Manager*
EMP: 100
SQ FT: 28,000
SALES (est): 22.3MM Privately Held
WEB: www.iti-oh.com.
SIC: 7371 Computer software development

(G-14398)
JARVIS MECHANICAL CONSTRS
INC (PA)
803 Us Route 50 (45150-9513)
PHONE..................................513 831-0055
Jeffery Jarvis, *President*
Brenda Holtzman, *Admin Sec*
EMP: 30
SQ FT: 13,500
SALES (est): 7.6MM Privately Held
WEB: www.jmc-afm.com
SIC: 1711 Mechanical contractor

(G-14399)
JPMORGAN CHASE BANK NAT
ASSN
967 Lila Ave (45150-1617)
PHONE..................................513 985-5350
Beth Hauke, *Manager*
EMP: 26
SALES (corp-wide): 131.4B Publicly Held
WEB: www.chase.com
SIC: 6021 National commercial banks
HQ: Jpmorgan Chase Bank, National Association
1111 Polaris Pkwy
Columbus OH 43240
614 436-3055

(G-14400)
LIBERTY INSULATION CO INC
5782 Deerfield Rd (45150-2657)
PHONE..................................513 621-0108
Russ Smith, *Manager*
EMP: 25
SALES (corp-wide): 4.7MM Privately Held
SIC: 4225 General warehousing
PA: Liberty Insulation Co Inc
2903 Kant Pl
Beavercreek OH 45431
513 621-0108

(G-14401)
LITTLE MIAMI HOME CARE INC
5371 S Milford Rd Apt 16 (45150-9502)
PHONE..................................513 248-8988
Susan Flynn, *President*
EMP: 40
SALES (est): 1.2MM Privately Held
SIC: 8082 Home health care services

(G-14402)
LOWES HOME CENTERS LLC
5694 Romar Dr (45150-8505)
PHONE..................................513 965-3280
EMP: 150
SALES (corp-wide): 68.6B Publicly Held
SIC: 5211 5031 5722 5064 Home centers; building materials, exterior; building materials, interior; household appliance stores; electrical appliances; television & radio
HQ: Lowe's Home Centers, Llc
1605 Curtis Bridge Rd
Wilkesboro NC 28697
336 658-4000

(G-14403)
LYKINS COMPANIES INC (PA)
Also Called: Lykins Energy Solutions
5163 Wlfpn Plsnt Hl Rd (45150-9632)
P.O. Box 643875, Cincinnati (45264-3875)
PHONE..................................513 831-8820
Jeff Lykins, *CEO*
Diana Brown, *Division Mgr*
Steve Krebs, *Division Mgr*
Billy Penn, *Plant Mgr*
Jacob Webster, *Safety Mgr*
EMP: 40
SQ FT: 10,000
SALES (est): 212.5MM Privately Held
SIC: 4213 5172 5411 Trucking, except local; gasoline; diesel fuel; fuel oil; convenience stores, chain

(G-14404)
LYKINS OIL COMPANY (HQ)
5163 Wlfpn Plsnt Hl Rd (45150-9632)
PHONE..................................513 831-8820
D Jeff Lykins, *President*
Ronald Lykins, *Vice Pres*
Robert J Manning, *CFO*
Joyce Mueller, *Sales Staff*
Mary U Gray, *Chief Mktg Ofcr*
EMP: 30
SQ FT: 12,000
SALES (est): 192.2MM
SALES (corp-wide): 212.5MM Privately Held
SIC: 5172 5983 Gasoline; diesel fuel; fuel oil; lubricating oils & greases; fuel oil dealers
PA: Lykins Companies, Inc.
5163 Wlfpn Plsnt Hl Rd
Milford OH 45150
513 831-8820

(G-14405)
LYKINS TRANSPORTATION INC
5163 Wlfpn Plsnt Hl Rd (45150-9632)
PHONE..................................513 831-8820
Donald F Lykins, *CEO*
Jeff Lykins, *President*
Ron Lykins, *Vice Pres*
Robert J Manning, *CFO*
Donald Lykins, *Manager*
EMP: 60 EST: 1996
SQ FT: 10,000
SALES (est): 12MM
SALES (corp-wide): 212.5MM Privately Held
WEB: www.lykinstransportation.com
SIC: 4213 Liquid petroleum transport, non-local
PA: Lykins Companies, Inc.
5163 Wlfpn Plsnt Hl Rd
Milford OH 45150
513 831-8820

(G-14406)
MADISON TREE CARE &
LDSCPG INC
636 Round Bottom Rd (45150-9568)
PHONE..................................513 576-6391
Frederick J Butcher, *President*
Dora Mae Butcher, *Exec VP*
Richard L E Butcher, *Vice Pres*
John Butcher, *Treasurer*

Brad Findley, *Technology*
EMP: 48
SALES (est): 4.5MM Privately Held
WEB: www.mtcandl.com
SIC: 0783 Ornamental shrub & tree services

(G-14407)
MAX DIXONS EXPRESSWAY
PARK
Also Called: Expressway Pk Softball Complex
689 Us Route 50 (45150-9102)
P.O. Box 402 (45150-0402)
PHONE..................................513 831-2273
Bob Owens, *President*
Betty Dixon, *Vice Pres*
EMP: 25
SQ FT: 2,400
SALES (est): 848.2K Privately Held
WEB: www.expresswaypark.com
SIC: 7999 Recreational Park

(G-14408)
MERCY HEALTH
201 Old Bank Rd Ste 103 (45150-2443)
PHONE..................................513 248-0100
EMP: 27
SALES (corp-wide): 4.7B Privately Held
SIC: 8011 Internal medicine, physician/surgeon
PA: Mercy Health
1701 Mercy Health Pl
Cincinnati OH 45237
513 639-2800

(G-14409)
MIAMI RIFLE PISTOL CLUB
P.O. Box 235 (45150-0235)
PHONE..................................513 732-9943
Ken Leyor, *Owner*
EMP: 100
SALES: 246.8K Privately Held
WEB: www.miamirifle-pistol.org
SIC: 7997 Membership sports & recreation clubs

(G-14410)
MIKE CASTRUCCI FORD
1020 State Route 28 (45150-2002)
PHONE..................................513 831-7010
Mike Castrucci, *Owner*
EMP: 150
SQ FT: 1,152
SALES (est): 37.2MM Privately Held
SIC: 5511 7538 7532 5521 Automobiles, new & used; general automotive repair shops; top & body repair & paint shops; used car dealers

(G-14411)
MILFORD COML CLG SVCS INC
701 Us Highway 50 Ste A (45150-9580)
P.O. Box 183 (45150-0183)
PHONE..................................513 575-5678
Tim Rhea, *President*
EMP: 30 EST: 2007
SALES (est): 1.1MM Privately Held
SIC: 7349 Cleaning service, industrial or commercial; janitorial service, contract basis

(G-14412)
MRP INC
Also Called: Medical Radiation Physics
5632 Sugar Camp Rd (45150-9673)
PHONE..................................513 965-9700
John Freshcorn, *President*
EMP: 30
SQ FT: 6,200
SALES: 7.8MM Privately Held
WEB: www.mrpinc.com
SIC: 8011 Radiologist

(G-14413)
NATIONAL AMUSEMENTS INC
Also Called: Nam Showcase Cinemas Milford
500 Rivers Edge (45150-1490)
PHONE..................................513 699-1500
James Warman, *Manager*
EMP: 41
SALES (corp-wide): 14.5B Publicly Held
WEB: www.nationalamusements.com
SIC: 7832 Motion picture theaters, except drive-in

PA: National Amusements, Inc.
846 University Ave
Norwood MA 02062
781 461-1600

(G-14414)
NORTHPOINT SENIOR SERVICES LLC
Also Called: Arbors At Milfor, The
5900 Meadow Creek Dr (45150-5641)
PHONE................................513 248-1655
Mark Johnston, *Administration*
EMP: 100
SALES (corp-wide): 41.5MM **Privately Held**
WEB: www.extendicarehealth.com
SIC: 8051 8052 Convalescent home with continuous nursing care; intermediate care facilities
PA: Senior Northpoint Services Llc
7400 New Lagrange 100
Louisville KY 40222
502 429-8062

(G-14415)
OPTION CARE ENTERPRISES INC
50 W Techne Center Dr J (45150-9798)
PHONE................................513 576-8400
Julie Koenig, *Manager*
EMP: 143
SALES (corp-wide): 1.4B **Privately Held**
SIC: 8082 Home health care services
HQ: Option Care Enterprises, Inc.
3000 Lakeside Dr Ste 300n
Bannockburn IL 60015

(G-14416)
OPTION CARE INFUSION SVCS INC
25 Whitney Dr Ste 114 (45150-8400)
PHONE................................513 576-8400
Ron Ferguson, *Manager*
EMP: 100
SALES (corp-wide): 1.4B **Privately Held**
SIC: 8082 Home health care services
HQ: Option Care Infusion Services, Inc.
3000 Lakeside Dr Ste 300n
Bannockburn IL 60015
312 940-2500

(G-14417)
PAGER PLUS ONE INC
927 Old State Rt 28 Ste G (45150)
PHONE................................513 748-3788
Roger Saddler, *President*
Logan A Saddler, *Vice Pres*
EMP: 240
SQ FT: 1,200
SALES: 356K **Privately Held**
SIC: 5065 Paging & signaling equipment

(G-14418)
PARKER MARKETING RESEARCH LLC
5405 Dupont Cir Ste B (45150-2798)
PHONE................................513 248-8100
Mike Brintzenhoff, *President*
Jim Whalen, *Exec VP*
Robert Goodwin, *Senior VP*
Greg Tetzloff, *CFO*
EMP: 26
SALES (est): 2.7MM **Privately Held**
WEB: www.parkerresearch.com
SIC: 8732 Market analysis or research

(G-14419)
PARKER-HANNIFIN CORPORATION
Also Called: Electromechanical North Amer
50 W Techne Center Dr H (45150-8403)
PHONE................................513 831-2340
Kenneth Sweet, *Branch Mgr*
EMP: 75
SALES (corp-wide): 14.3B **Publicly Held**
WEB: www.parker.com
SIC: 3577 7371 3575 3571 Computer peripheral equipment; computer software development; computer terminals; electronic computers
PA: Parker-Hannifin Corporation
6035 Parkland Blvd
Cleveland OH 44124
216 896-3000

(G-14420)
PAT HENRY GROUP LLC (PA)
Also Called: Phg Retail Services
6046 Bridgehaven Dr (45150-5623)
PHONE................................216 447-0831
Judith Hominy,
EMP: 25
SQ FT: 1,000
SALES (est): 4MM **Privately Held**
WEB: www.pathenry.com
SIC: 8742 Marketing consulting services

(G-14421)
PATRIOT INDUS CONTG SVCS LLC
200 Olympic Dr (45150-9522)
PHONE................................513 248-8222
Mike Wilkerson, *Principal*
Pat Booth, *Manager*
EMP: 30
SALES (est): 4.8MM **Privately Held**
WEB: www.patrioticsi.com
SIC: 7699 Repair Services

(G-14422)
PETSMART INC
245 Rivers Edge (45150-2592)
PHONE................................513 248-4954
Tim Irwin, *Branch Mgr*
EMP: 28
SALES (corp-wide): 12.1B **Privately Held**
WEB: www.petsmart.com
SIC: 5999 0752 Pet supplies; training services, pet & animal specialties (not horses)
HQ: Petsmart, Inc.
19601 N 27th Ave
Phoenix AZ 85027
623 580-6100

(G-14423)
PINNACLE PAVING & SEALING INC
787 Round Bottom Rd (45150-9509)
PHONE................................513 474-4900
Alan Vahumensky, *President*
Will Knight, *Vice Pres*
Lindsey Igo, *Manager*
EMP: 40
SALES: 7MM **Privately Held**
SIC: 1611 Surfacing & paving

(G-14424)
PIVOTEK LLC
910 Lila Ave Rear (45150-1631)
PHONE................................513 372-6205
Kent Hodson, *President*
Jerry Welte, *Project Mgr*
Doug Conradt, *Manager*
Heather Turpin, *Admin Sec*
Laura Poe, *Admin Asst*
◆ EMP: 35
SALES (est): 8.6MM **Privately Held**
SIC: 1542 1522 Commercial & office building contractors; residential construction

(G-14425)
PLUS REALTY CINCINNATI INC
Also Called: Remax Results Plus
1160 State Route 28 (45150-2155)
PHONE................................513 575-4500
Richard J Hoffman, *President*
Thomas Hoffman, *Vice Pres*
EMP: 25
SALES (est): 1.6MM **Privately Held**
SIC: 6531 1531 Selling agent, real estate; speculative builder, single-family houses

(G-14426)
PREMIER CLEANING SERVICES INC
Also Called: Cleaning Authority
5866 Wlfpen Plasant Hl Rd (45150)
PHONE................................513 831-2492
Michael A Randall, *President*
EMP: 32
SQ FT: 1,200
SALES (est): 2MM **Privately Held**
SIC: 7699 Cleaning services

(G-14427)
PROFESSIONAL LAMINATE MLLWK INC
Also Called: Pro-Lam
1003 Tech Dr (45150-9780)
PHONE................................513 891-7858
Shannon P Bitzer, *CEO*
Scott W Bitzer, *Vice Pres*
Jason O'Brien, *VP Opers*
Nikki Young, *Office Mgr*
Andrea Riddle,
▲ EMP: 42
SQ FT: 22,000
SALES (est): 18.8MM **Privately Held**
WEB: www.prolamonline.com
SIC: 5031 5712 Kitchen cabinets; customized furniture & cabinets

(G-14428)
ROCKWELL AUTOMATION OHIO INC (HQ)
1700 Edison Dr (45150-2729)
PHONE................................513 576-6151
Ralph Delisio, *General Mgr*
EMP: 75
SALES (est): 8.6MM **Publicly Held**
WEB: www.entek.com
SIC: 7373 7379 Systems software development services; computer systems analysis & design; computer related consulting services

(G-14429)
SCANNER APPLICATIONS LLC
Also Called: Scanner Applications, Inc.
400 Milford Pkwy (45150-9104)
PHONE................................513 248-5588
Robert W Gibson, *CEO*
Jay Griffiths, *General Mgr*
Jeffrey Gibson, *Vice Pres*
Jack Linberg, *Vice Pres*
John Turnau, *Vice Pres*
EMP: 48
SALES (est): 3.5MM **Privately Held**
WEB: www.scanapps.com
SIC: 8732 Business analysis
HQ: Inmar, Inc.
635 Vine St
Winston Salem NC 27101
800 765-1277

(G-14430)
SCHUMACHER & CO INC
920 Lila Ave (45150-1641)
PHONE................................859 655-9000
Steve Contois, *CEO*
Roy Young, *QC Mgr*
EMP: 33
SQ FT: 22,000
SALES (est): 1.6MM
SALES (corp-wide): 29.5MM **Privately Held**
WEB: www.schumacherco.com
SIC: 1752 Wood floor installation & refinishing
PA: CI Investments, Inc.
1050 Skillman Dr
Cincinnati OH 45215
513 771-2345

(G-14431)
SIEMENS PRODUCT LIFE MGMT SFTW
2000 Eastman Dr (45150-2712)
PHONE................................513 576-2400
Tony Asfusso, *President*
Tom Eberle, *General Mgr*
John Hembree, *Technology*
James Heywood, *Software Engr*
Eric Henggeler, *Graphic Designe*
EMP: 70
SALES (corp-wide): 95B **Privately Held**
WEB: www.ugs.com
SIC: 7371 Computer software development
HQ: Siemens Product Lifecycle Management Software Inc.
5800 Granite Pkwy Ste 600
Plano TX 75024
972 987-3000

(G-14432)
SILER EXCAVATION SERVICES
6025 Catherine Dr (45150-2203)
PHONE................................513 400-8628

Mike Siler,
EMP: 40 EST: 2007
SALES (est): 1.1MM **Privately Held**
SIC: 1794 1389 Excavation work; construction, repair & dismantling services

(G-14433)
SMITHPEARLMAN & CO
100 Techne Center Dr # 200 (45150-2780)
PHONE................................513 248-9210
Donald J Burkhardt, *President*
Judy Radloff, *Business Mgr*
Al Pearlman, *Corp Secy*
Kim Lorenzo, *Accountant*
Sheryl Sheshull, *Accountant*
EMP: 30
SALES (est): 3.1MM **Privately Held**
WEB: www.burkhardtcpa.com
SIC: 8721 Certified public accountant

(G-14434)
SMYTH AUTOMOTIVE INC
Also Called: Smyth Automotive Parts Plus
1900 State Route 131 (45150-2647)
PHONE................................513 575-2000
Joe Smyth, *Branch Mgr*
EMP: 33
SALES (corp-wide): 122.3MM **Privately Held**
WEB: www.smythautomotive.com
SIC: 5013 Automotive supplies & parts
PA: Smyth Automotive, Inc.
4275 Mt Carmel Tobasco Rd
Cincinnati OH 45244
513 528-2800

(G-14435)
TATA AMERICA INTL CORP
Also Called: Tata Consultancy Services
1000 Summit Dr Unit 1 (45150-2724)
PHONE................................513 677-6500
Sumanta Roy, *Regional Mgr*
Vikas Gupta, *Manager*
Brian Purvis, *Manager*
Alex Kellerman, *Software Dev*
EMP: 300
SALES (corp-wide): 81.3MM **Privately Held**
SIC: 7372 7373 7371 Prepackaged software; computer integrated systems design; custom computer programming services
HQ: Tata America International Corporation
101 Park Ave Rm 2603
New York NY 10178
212 557-8038

(G-14436)
TERRACE PARK COUNTRY CLUB INC
5341 S Milford Rd (45150-9744)
PHONE................................513 965-4061
Al Washvill, *General Mgr*
Matt Duwel, *Assistant*
EMP: 75
SQ FT: 17,000
SALES: 2.9MM **Privately Held**
SIC: 7997 Country club, membership

(G-14437)
TOTAL QUALITY LOGISTICS LLC
Also Called: Tql
1701 Edison Dr (45150-2728)
PHONE................................513 831-2600
Ken Oaks, *CEO*
EMP: 40
SALES (corp-wide): 2.9B **Privately Held**
SIC: 4731 Truck transportation brokers
HQ: Total Quality Logistics, Llc
4289 Ivy Pointe Blvd
Cincinnati OH 45245

(G-14438)
TOTAL QUALITY LOGISTICS LLC
1701 Edison Dr (45150-2728)
PHONE................................513 831-2600
Kenneth G Oaks, *CEO*
EMP: 150
SALES (corp-wide): 2.9B **Privately Held**
SIC: 4731 Truck transportation brokers
HQ: Total Quality Logistics, Llc
4289 Ivy Pointe Blvd
Cincinnati OH 45245

(G-14439)
TRIPACK LLC
401 Milford Pkwy Ste C (45150-9119)
PHONE.....................................513 248-1255
Tom S Linz, *Mng Member*
Nick Linz,
▲ EMP: 40
SQ FT: 6,000
SALES (est): 8MM Privately Held
WEB: www.tripack.net
SIC: 5084 7389 Packaging machinery &
equipment; labeling bottles, cans, car-
tons, etc.

(G-14440)
**UNITED MERCANTILE
CORPORATION**
575 Chamber Dr (45150-1498)
PHONE.....................................513 831-1300
Paul Spires, *Owner*
EMP: 30
SALES (est): 5MM Privately Held
SIC: 6794 Franchises, selling or licensing

(G-14441)
VALLEY ROOFING LLC
5293 Tech Valley Dr (45150-9762)
PHONE.....................................513 831-9444
Erich Manteuffel, *Owner*
Hans Philippo, *Mng Member*
Eric Manteuffel,
EMP: 40
SQ FT: 11,600
SALES (est): 1.9MM Privately Held
SIC: 1761 Roofing contractor

(G-14442)
VASCONCELLOS INC
400 Techne Center Dr # 406 (45150-2792)
PHONE.....................................513 576-1250
Timothy Vasconcellos, *Owner*
EMP: 50 EST: 2008
SALES (est): 710.9K Privately Held
SIC: 8322 Senior citizens' center or associ-
ation

(G-14443)
WESCOM SOLUTIONS INC
Also Called: Pointclickcare
300 Techne Center Dr A (45150-2795)
PHONE.....................................513 831-1207
Darcy Strong, *Manager*
Greg Roberts, *Manager*
EMP: 45
SALES (corp-wide): 77.3MM Privately
Held
SIC: 7373 Computer integrated systems
design
HQ: Pointclickcare Technologies Inc
5570 Explorer Dr
Mississauga ON L4W 0
905 858-8885

Milford Center
Union County

(G-14444)
**CHAMPAIGN PREMIUM GRN
GROWERS**
Also Called: Integrated AG Services
24320 Woodstock Rd (43045-8004)
P.O. Box 138 (43045-0138)
PHONE.....................................937 826-3003
David Scheiderer, *Principal*
Susan Follrod, *Principal*
EMP: 38
SALES (est): 1.4MM Privately Held
SIC: 8731 Agricultural research

(G-14445)
FORUM MANUFACTURING INC
77 Brown St (43045-8900)
PHONE.....................................937 349-8685
Nancy Kovacs, *President*
Jim J Kraus, *Principal*
Gerald Shannon, *Principal*
Mike Butcher, *Project Mgr*
▲ EMP: 25
SQ FT: 19,000
SALES (est): 4.2MM Privately Held
SIC: 1751 Cabinet building & installation;
cabinet & finish carpentry

Millbury
Wood County

(G-14446)
**BEST AIRE COMPRESSOR
SERVICE (DH)**
3648 Rockland Cir (43447-9804)
PHONE.....................................419 726-0055
Tracy D Paglary, *Principal*
EMP: 100
SQ FT: 37,100
SALES (est): 40.3MM
SALES (corp-wide): 2.6B Publicly Held
WEB: www.amsba.com
SIC: 5251 7699 5075 Pumps & pumping
equipment; compressor repair; compres-
sors, air conditioning

(G-14447)
DELVENTHAL COMPANY
3796 Rockland Cir (43447-9651)
PHONE.....................................419 244-5570
Steve Delventhal, *President*
Sharon Delventhal, *Corp Secy*
Tom Koepfler, *Project Mgr*
Todd Delventhal, *VP Sls/Mktg*
James Hahn, *CFO*
EMP: 30
SQ FT: 12,000
SALES: 10MM Privately Held
WEB: www.thedelventhalco.com
SIC: 1541 1542 Industrial buildings, new
construction; commercial & office building
contractors

(G-14448)
FORMLABS OHIO INC
Also Called: Spectra Photopolymers Inc.
27800 Lemoyne Rd Ste J (43447-9683)
PHONE.....................................419 837-9783
Alex Mejiritski, *President*
EMP: 28
SALES (est): 1.5MM Privately Held
SIC: 2899 5169 Chemical preparations;
chemicals & allied products

(G-14449)
**GETGO TRANSPORTATION CO
LLC**
28500 Lemoyne Rd (43447-9431)
PHONE.....................................419 666-6850
Anthony W Tomase,
EMP: 39
SQ FT: 14,000
SALES (est): 6MM Privately Held
SIC: 4214 4225 Local trucking with stor-
age; general warehousing

(G-14450)
MISTRAS GROUP INC
3094 Moline Martin Rd (43447-9691)
PHONE.....................................419 836-5904
Mike Hoy, *District Mgr*
EMP: 58 Publicly Held
SIC: 8734 Testing laboratories
PA: Mistras Group, Inc.
195 Clarksville Rd Ste 2
Princeton Junction NJ 08550

(G-14451)
STONEY LODGE INC
Also Called: Super 8 Motel
3491 Latcha Rd (43447-9786)
P.O. Box 701004, Plymouth MI (48170-
0957)
PHONE.....................................419 837-6409
William Nofar, *President*
EMP: 85
SALES (est): 3.9MM Privately Held
SIC: 7011 Hotels & motels

Millersburg
Holmes County

(G-14452)
77 COACH SUPPLY LTD
7426 County Road 77 (44654-9279)
PHONE.....................................330 674-1454
Atlee Kaufman,
EMP: 26

SALES (est): 3MM Privately Held
SIC: 5099 2499 Wood & wood by-products; decorative wood & woodwork

(G-14453)
A & R BUILDERS LTD
6914 County Road 672 (44654-8350)
PHONE.....................................330 893-2111
Alan Yoder, *Partner*
Erma Yoder, *Partner*
EMP: 25
SALES (est): 2.6MM Privately Held
SIC: 1521 New construction, single-family
houses; general remodeling, single-family
houses

(G-14454)
ALONOVUS CORP
7368 County Road 623 (44654-9256)
P.O. Box 358 (44654-0358)
PHONE.....................................330 674-2300
Michael Mast, *Principal*
David Mast, *Principal*
John Mast, *Principal*
Andy Vernon, *Manager*
Jim Marshall, *Author*
EMP: 56
SALES (est): 7.2MM Privately Held
SIC: 8742 2741 7371 Marketing consult-
ing services; miscellaneous publishing;
computer software development & appli-
cations

(G-14455)
ALTERCARE OF MILLERSBURG
105 Majora Ln (44654-8955)
PHONE.....................................330 674-4444
Diana Jackson, *Administration*
EMP: 80
SALES (est): 1.2MM Privately Held
SIC: 8051 Convalescent home with contin-
uous nursing care

(G-14456)
ASAP HOMECARE INC
31 N Mad Anthony St (44654-1169)
PHONE.....................................330 674-3306
EMP: 58
SALES (corp-wide): 6.9MM Privately
Held
SIC: 8082 Home health care services
PA: Asap Homecare Inc
1 Park Centre Dr Ste 107
Wadsworth OH 44281
330 334-7027

(G-14457)
B & L TRANSPORT INC (PA)
3149 State Route 39 (44654-8805)
P.O. Box 172, Walnut Creek (44687-0172)
PHONE.....................................866 848-2888
Ben Mast, *President*
Jon Mast, *Vice Pres*
EMP: 28
SQ FT: 4,500
SALES (est): 4MM Privately Held
SIC: 4212 Local trucking, without storage

(G-14458)
BERLIN CONSTRUCTION LTD
4740 Township Road 356 (44654-8719)
PHONE.....................................330 893-2003
Gideon Yoder, *Partner*
Jacob A Hershberger, *Partner*
EMP: 25
SALES (est): 6MM Privately Held
SIC: 1542 1521 Commercial & office build-
ing contractors; general remodeling, sin-
gle-family houses

(G-14459)
BERLIN TRANSPORTAION LLC
7576 State Route 241 (44654-8822)
PHONE.....................................330 674-3395
Thomas Wengerd,
Ken Wengard,
Marlin Wengerd,
EMP: 30
SQ FT: 6,000
SALES (est): 5.6MM Privately Held
WEB: www.berlintransportation.com
SIC: 4213 Contract haulers

(G-14460)
BIRD ENTERPRISES LLC
Also Called: Millersburg Hotel
35 W Jackson St (44654-1321)
P.O. Box 127 (44654-0127)
PHONE.....................................330 674-1457
Bill Robinson, *Manager*
EMP: 25
SQ FT: 20,000
SALES (corp-wide): 1.4MM Privately
Held
SIC: 7011 5812 7929 5813 Inns; restau-
rant, family: independent; entertainers &
entertainment groups; drinking places
PA: Bird Enterprises Llc
31 N Mad Anthony St
Millersburg OH 44654
330 674-2339

(G-14461)
**BLACK DIAMOND GOLF
COURSE**
7500 Township Road 103 (44654-8516)
PHONE.....................................330 674-6110
Walter Eppley, *President*
Jeffrey Eppley, *Vice Pres*
Debra Eppley, *Treasurer*
EMP: 25
SQ FT: 1,950
SALES (est): 696.4K Privately Held
WEB: www.blackdiamondgolfcourse.com
SIC: 7992 Public golf courses

(G-14462)
**CARTER-JONES COMPANIES
INC**
6139 State Route 39 (44654-8845)
PHONE.....................................330 674-0047
Steve Miller, *Branch Mgr*
EMP: 105
SALES (corp-wide): 1.4B Privately Held
SIC: 5031 Millwork
PA: Carter-Jones Companies, Inc.
601 Tallmadge Rd
Kent OH 44240
330 673-6100

(G-14463)
**CARTER-JONES LUMBER
COMPANY**
6139 State Route 39 (44654-8845)
PHONE.....................................330 674-9060
EMP: 104
SALES (corp-wide): 1.4B Privately Held
SIC: 5031 5211 2439 2434 Lumber, ply-
wood & millwork; lumber & other building
materials; structural wood members;
wood kitchen cabinets; millwork; hard-
wood dimension & flooring mills
HQ: The Carter-Jones Lumber Company
601 Tallmadge Rd
Kent OH 44240
330 673-6100

(G-14464)
CASTLE NURSING HOMES INC
Also Called: Sycamore Run Nursing
6180 State Route 83 (44654-9463)
PHONE.....................................330 674-0015
Kirk Hartline, *Branch Mgr*
EMP: 200
SALES (corp-wide): 256.1K Privately
Held
SIC: 8051 Skilled nursing care facilities
HQ: Castle Nursing Homes, Inc.
6967 Deer Trail Ave Ne
Canton OH 44721
440 793-2245

(G-14465)
CHRISTIAN AID MINISTRIES (PA)
Also Called: GOOD SAMARITAN, THE
4464 State Route 39 (44654-9677)
P.O. Box 360, Berlin (44610-0360)
PHONE.....................................330 893-2428
David N Troyer, *President*
Paul Weaver, *Principal*
Roman Mullet, *Finance Dir*
Karen Zook, *Manager*
Wendell Sommers, *Webmaster*
◆ EMP: 50
SQ FT: 8,160
SALES: 130.1MM Privately Held
SIC: 5999 8322 Religious goods; disaster
service

(G-14466)
**COMMERCIAL SVGS BANK
MILLERSBU (HQ)**
91 N Clay St (44654-1117)
PHONE..............................330 674-9015
Eddie Steiner, *CEO*
Molly Mohr, *President*
Brett A Gallion, *COO*
Paula Meiler, *Senior VP*
EMP: 28
SALES: 30.7MM
SALES (corp-wide): 34.4MM **Publicly
Held**
SIC: 6022 State commercial banks
PA: Csb Bancorp, Inc.
91 N Clay St
Millersburg OH 44654
330 674-9015

(G-14467)
COUNTY OF HOLMES
Also Called: Holmes County Fire Department
8478 State Route 39 (44654-9766)
P.O. Box 7 (44654-0007)
PHONE..............................330 674-1926
Scott Boulder, *Chief*
EMP: 27 **Privately Held**
WEB: www.district1fire.com
SIC: 9224 8322 ; emergency social serv-
ices
PA: County Of Holmes
2 Court St Ste 14
Millersburg OH 44654
330 674-1896

(G-14468)
COUNTY OF HOLMES
Also Called: Holmes County Health Dept
85 N Grant St B (44654-1166)
PHONE..............................330 674-5035
Dr Maurice Mullet, *Director*
EMP: 25 **Privately Held**
WEB: www.district1fire.com
SIC: 9431 7361 ; nurses' registry
PA: County Of Holmes
2 Court St Ste 14
Millersburg OH 44654
330 674-1896

(G-14469)
COUNTY OF HOLMES
Also Called: Engineer's Office
7191 State Route 39 (44654-9204)
P.O. Box 29 (44654-0029)
PHONE..............................330 674-5076
Chris Young, *Principal*
EMP: 33 **Privately Held**
WEB: www.district1fire.com
SIC: 1611 Highway & street maintenance
PA: County Of Holmes
2 Court St Ste 14
Millersburg OH 44654
330 674-1896

(G-14470)
COUNTY OF HOLMES
Also Called: Highway Department
75 E Clinton St (44654-1283)
PHONE..............................330 674-5916
Robert Kasner, *Manager*
EMP: 38 **Privately Held**
WEB: www.district1fire.com
SIC: 7521 9111 Parking garage; county
supervisors' & executives' offices
PA: County Of Holmes
2 Court St Ste 14
Millersburg OH 44654
330 674-1896

(G-14471)
COUNTY OF HOLMES
Also Called: Joel Pomerene Memorial Hosp
981 Wooster Rd (44654-1536)
PHONE..............................330 674-1015
Phillip W Smith, *CEO*
EMP: 213 **Privately Held**
WEB: www.district1fire.com
SIC: 8062 9111 General medical & surgi-
cal hospitals; county supervisors' & exec-
utives' offices
PA: County Of Holmes
2 Court St Ste 14
Millersburg OH 44654
330 674-1896

(G-14472)
COUNTY OF HOLMES
Also Called: Child Support Enforcement Agcy
85 N Grant St (44654-1166)
P.O. Box 72 (44654-0072)
PHONE..............................330 674-1111
Dan Jackson, *Director*
EMP: 42 **Privately Held**
WEB: www.district1fire.com
SIC: 8322 9111 8331 Individual & family
services; county supervisors' & execu-
tives' offices; job training services
PA: County Of Holmes
2 Court St Ste 14
Millersburg OH 44654
330 674-1896

(G-14473)
CSB BANCORP INC (PA)
91 N Clay St (44654-1117)
P.O. Box 232 (44654-0232)
PHONE..............................330 674-9015
Robert K Baker, *Ch of Bd*
Eddie L Steiner, *President*
Eric Gerber, *President*
Christopher Delatore, *Vice Pres*
Eric Strouse, *Vice Pres*
EMP: 40
SALES: 34.4MM **Publicly Held**
WEB: www.csb1.com
SIC: 6022 State commercial banks

(G-14474)
GRAPHIC PUBLICATIONS INC
Also Called: Bargain Hunter
7368 County Road 623 (44654-9256)
P.O. Box 358 (44654-0358)
PHONE..............................330 674-2300
Michael Mast, *President*
Frances Mast, *Corp Secy*
▲ **EMP:** 45
SQ FT: 12,000
SALES (est): 5.9MM **Privately Held**
WEB: www.gpubs.com
SIC: 2721 7336 Periodicals: publishing
only; graphic arts & related design

(G-14475)
**HOLMES LUMBER & BLDG CTR
INC**
Also Called: Holmes Lumber & Supply
6139 Hc 39 (44654)
PHONE..............................330 674-9060
Paul Miller, *President*
D Tim Yoder, *Credit Mgr*
EMP: 150 **EST:** 1952
SQ FT: 16,000
SALES (est): 971.4K **Privately Held**
WEB: www.holmeslumber.com
SIC: 5031 5211 2439 2434 Lumber, ply-
wood & millwork; lumber & other building
materials; structural wood members;
wood kitchen cabinets; millwork; hard-
wood dimension & flooring mills

(G-14476)
**HOLMES SIDING
CONTRACTORS**
6767 County Road 624 (44654-8840)
PHONE..............................330 674-2867
Edward Yoder, *Partner*
Daniel Mast, *Partner*
EMP: 75
SQ FT: 100,000
SALES (est): 7.1MM **Privately Held**
SIC: 1761 Siding contractor

(G-14477)
**HOLMES-WAYNE ELECTRIC
COOP**
6060 State Route 83 (44654-9172)
P.O. Box 112 (44654-0112)
PHONE..............................330 674-1055
Glenn Miller, *President*
EMP: 42
SQ FT: 25,000
SALES (est): 17.1MM **Privately Held**
WEB: www.hwecoop.com
SIC: 4911 Distribution, electric power

(G-14478)
**HONEY RUN RETREATS LLC
(PA)**
Also Called: Inn At Honey Run
6920 County Road 203 (44654)
PHONE..............................330 674-0011
Jason Nies,
EMP: 35
SALES: 2.9MM **Privately Held**
SIC: 7011 Hotels; bed & breakfast inn

(G-14479)
HUNTINGTON INSURANCE INC
212 N Washington St (44654-1123)
PHONE..............................330 674-2931
Ronald D Scherer, *Branch Mgr*
EMP: 37
SALES (corp-wide): 5.2B **Publicly Held**
SIC: 6411 Insurance agents
HQ: Huntington Insurance, Inc.
519 Madison Ave
Toledo OH 43604
419 720-7900

(G-14480)
**JOEL POMERENE MEMORIAL
HOSP (PA)**
Also Called: Pomerene Hospital
981 Wooster Rd (44654-1536)
PHONE..............................330 674-1015
P W Smith Jr, *CEO*
Constance Poulton, *Human Resources*
EMP: 270 **EST:** 1937
SQ FT: 45,000
SALES: 31.9MM **Privately Held**
SIC: 8062 General medical & surgical hos-
pitals

(G-14481)
LIEBEN WOOSTER LP
6834 County Road 672 # 102
(44654-8349)
PHONE..............................330 390-5722
Robert Schlabach, *Partner*
EMP: 25 **EST:** 2016
SALES (est): 150.1K **Privately Held**
SIC: 7011 Hotel, franchised

(G-14482)
MAST TRUCKING INC
6471 County Road 625 (44654-8833)
PHONE..............................330 674-8913
Willis Mast, *President*
Elsie Mast, *Vice Pres*
Kevin Mast, *Vice Pres*
Nikolas Marty, *Opers Mgr*
Ross Donnellan, *Parts Mgr*
EMP: 100
SALES (est): 28MM **Privately Held**
SIC: 4213 Contract haulers; refrigerated
products transport

(G-14483)
**MILLERSBURG TIRE SERVICE
INC**
7375 State Route 39 (44654-8319)
PHONE..............................330 674-1085
Brad Schmuker, *President*
▲ **EMP:** 30
SQ FT: 7,000
SALES (est): 12.1MM **Privately Held**
WEB: www.millersburgtireservice.com
SIC: 5014 5531 Automobile tires & tubes;
truck tires & tubes; motorcycle tires &
tubes; tires, used; automotive tires

(G-14484)
MULTI PRODUCTS COMPANY
7188 State Route 39 (44654-9204)
P.O. Box 1597, Gainesville TX (76241-
1597)
PHONE..............................330 674-5981
Jeff Berlin, *CEO*
William T Baker, *President*
Bud Doty, *Corp Secy*
Greg Guthrie, *Vice Pres*
▲ **EMP:** 42
SQ FT: 30,000
SALES (est): 12.5MM **Privately Held**
SIC: 3533 5084 Oil field machinery &
equipment; industrial machinery & equip-
ment

(G-14485)
N SAFE SOUND SECURITY INC
5555 County Road 203 (44654-8242)
PHONE..............................888 317-7233
Ryan Torrence, *President*
Jerry Anderson, *Director*
EMP: 40
SALES (est): 1.5MM **Privately Held**
SIC: 7389 Music & broadcasting services

(G-14486)
**PINECRAFT LAND HOLDINGS
LLC**
6834 County Road 672 # 102
(44654-8349)
PHONE..............................330 390-5722
David Schlabach, *Managing Prtnr*
Robert Schlabach, *Managing Prtnr*
EMP: 25
SALES (est): 136.5K **Privately Held**
SIC: 7011 Hotels & motels

(G-14487)
PIONEER TRAILS INC
7572 State Route 241 (44654-8822)
PHONE..............................330 674-1234
David Swartzentruber, *President*
EMP: 35
SQ FT: 16,000
SALES (est): 2.6MM **Privately Held**
WEB: www.pioneertrailsbus.com
SIC: 4142 Bus charter service, except local

(G-14488)
**PRECISION GEOPHYSICAL INC
(PA)**
2695 State Route 83 (44654-9455)
PHONE..............................330 674-2198
Steven Mc Crossin, *President*
EMP: 32
SALES (est): 4.8MM **Privately Held**
WEB: www.precisiongeophysical.com
SIC: 1382 Oil & gas exploration services

(G-14489)
REA & ASSOCIATES INC
212 N Washington St # 100 (44654-1122)
PHONE..............................330 674-6055
Chris Roush, *Branch Mgr*
Dustin Raber, *Senior Mgr*
EMP: 25
SALES (corp-wide): 32.3MM **Privately
Held**
WEB: www.reacpa.com
SIC: 8721 Certified public accountant
PA: Rea & Associates, Inc.
419 W High Ave
New Philadelphia OH 44663
330 339-6651

(G-14490)
ROY J MILLER
6739 State Route 241 (44654-9467)
PHONE..............................330 674-2405
Roy J Miller,
EMP: 36
SALES (est): 1.2MM **Privately Held**
SIC: 7389

(G-14491)
S AND R LEASING
9705 Township Rd (44654)
PHONE..............................330 276-3061
Donna Shreiner, *President*
David Shreiner, *Vice Pres*
Patrick Roche, *Treasurer*
EMP: 30
SALES (est): 1.2MM **Privately Held**
SIC: 7359 Equipment rental & leasing

(G-14492)
SAFE-N-SOUND SECURITY INC
5555 County Road 203 (44654-8242)
PHONE..............................330 491-1148
Ryan Torrence, *President*
Robert Hearn, *Opers Mgr*
EMP: 60
SALES (est): 6.3MM **Privately Held**
WEB: www.rusafensound.com
SIC: 7382 Security systems services

(G-14493)
SKYVIEW BAPTIST RANCH INC
7241 Township Road 319 (44654-8708)
PHONE..............................330 674-7511

▲ = Import ▼=Export
◆ =Import/Export

William E Roloff, *Director*
Sarah Kidner, *Admin Sec*
EMP: 46
SALES (est): 935.5K **Privately Held**
SIC: 8322 7032 0752 Multi-service center; summer camp, except day & sports instructional; animal specialty services

(G-14494)
T & L TRANSPORT INC
4395 County Road 58 (44654-9634)
P.O. Box 441 (44654-0441)
PHONE...................330 674-0655
Thomas Klein, *President*
Theresa Loder, *Treasurer*
Larry Loder, *Admin Sec*
EMP: 38
SALES (est): 5.2MM **Privately Held**
SIC: 4213 Refrigerated products transport

(G-14495)
TGS INTERNATIONAL INC
4464 State Route 39 (44654-9677)
P.O. Box 355, Berlin (44610-0355)
PHONE...................330 893-4828
Paul Weaver, *Vice Pres*
Roman Mullet, *Treasurer*
David Troyer, *Exec Dir*
EMP: 50
SALES (est): 2.6MM
SALES (corp-wide): 130.1MM **Privately Held**
SIC: 4731 2731 Freight forwarding; book publishing
PA: Christian Aid Ministries
4464 State Route 39
Millersburg OH 44654
330 893-2428

(G-14496)
THREE M ASSOCIATES
7488 State Route 241 (44654-8383)
PHONE...................330 674-9646
Dean Mullet, *Partner*
Dennis Mullet, *Partner*
Jacob Mullet, *Partner*
Duane Miller, *Data Proc Staff*
EMP: 70 EST: 1974
SQ FT: 1,716
SALES (est): 2.7MM **Privately Held**
WEB: www.mulletcabinet.com
SIC: 6512 Nonresidential building operators

(G-14497)
TROYER CHEESE INC
6597 County Road 625 (44654-9071)
PHONE...................330 893-2479
James A Troyer, *President*
Aaron Yoder, *Purch Mgr*
Steve Yoder, *Buyer*
Rob Ervin, *Controller*
Lori Durkin, *Financial Analy*
EMP: 45
SQ FT: 59,500
SALES (est): 20.5MM
SALES (corp-wide): 806.3MM **Privately Held**
WEB: www.troyercheese.com
SIC: 5147 2032 5143 5149 Meats, cured or smoked; ethnic foods: canned, jarred, etc.; cheese; specialty food items
PA: Lipari Foods Operating Company Llc
26661 Bunert Rd
Warren MI 48089
586 447-3500

(G-14498)
VILLAGE MOTORS INC
Also Called: Village Chrysler-Dodge
784 Wooster Rd (44654-1031)
PHONE...................330 674-2055
Thomas Green, *President*
Cory Allison, *Business Mgr*
Marc Miller, *Treasurer*
Deke Miller, *Sales Mgr*
Mike Emick, *Sales Associate*
EMP: 67
SQ FT: 11,200
SALES (est): 25.3MM **Privately Held**
WEB: www.villagemotorsinc.com
SIC: 5511 5521 5012 Automobiles, new & used; used car dealers; automobiles & other motor vehicles

(G-14499)
WASTE PARCHMENT INC
4510 Township Road 307 (44654-9656)
PHONE...................330 674-6868
Robert Smith, *President*
Elaine Smith, *Admin Sec*
EMP: 30
SQ FT: 80,000
SALES (est): 1MM **Privately Held**
SIC: 4953 2611 Recycling, waste materials; pulp mills

(G-14500)
WB SERVICES INC
6834 County Road 672 # 102 (44654-8349)
PHONE...................330 390-5722
Robert Schlabach, *President*
EMP: 72
SALES (est): 1.5MM **Privately Held**
SIC: 1522 Hotel/motel & multi-family home construction

Millersport
Fairfield County

(G-14501)
ASPLUNDH TREE EXPERT LLC
12488 Lancaster St # 94 (43046-8072)
PHONE...................740 467-1028
Debbie Tooper, *Manager*
EMP: 150
SALES (corp-wide): 4.5B **Privately Held**
WEB: www.asplundh.com
SIC: 0783 Tree trimming services for public utility lines
PA: Asplundh Tree Expert, Llc
708 Blair Mill Rd
Willow Grove PA 19090
215 784-4200

(G-14502)
CEDAR CREEK VTERINARY SVCS INC
12575 Lancaster St Ne (43046-8065)
PHONE...................740 467-2949
Steven Debruin, *President*
Edgar Biggie, *Vice Pres*
EMP: 25 EST: 2001
SQ FT: 3,502
SALES (est): 1.2MM **Privately Held**
SIC: 0742 Veterinarian, animal specialties

(G-14503)
PRE-FORE INC
Also Called: Professional Rfrgn & AC
410 Blacklick Rd (43046)
P.O. Box 518 (43046-0518)
PHONE...................740 467-2206
Gary Kendrick, *President*
Keith Schooley, *Vice Pres*
John Callow Sr, *Treasurer*
Tyler Evans, *Manager*
EMP: 35
SALES (est): 6.5MM **Privately Held**
WEB: www.pre-fore.com
SIC: 1711 Warm air heating & air conditioning contractor; refrigeration contractor

Millersville
Sandusky County

(G-14504)
CARMEUSE LIME INC
Also Called: Carmeuse Lime & Stone
3964 County Road 41 (43435-9619)
PHONE...................419 638-2511
Tim Haubert, *Purchasing*
Mike Klenda, *Branch Mgr*
EMP: 37 **Privately Held**
SIC: 1422 Crushed & broken limestone
HQ: Carmeuse Lime, Inc.
11 Stanwix St Fl 21
Pittsburgh PA 15222
412 995-5500

Millfield
Athens County

(G-14505)
FAST TRAXX PROMOTIONS LLC
17575 Jacksonville Rd (45761-9006)
PHONE...................740 767-3740
Shawna Bickley,
Norman Bickley,
EMP: 50
SALES (est): 590.6K **Privately Held**
WEB: www.fasttraxxracing.com
SIC: 7948 8743 Automotive race track operation; promotion service

Mineral City
Tuscarawas County

(G-14506)
M & L LEASING CO
8999 Bay Dr Ne (44656-9015)
PHONE...................330 343-8910
Michael Morris, *Partner*
Lionel Meister, *Partner*
EMP: 41
SQ FT: 80,000
SALES (est): 1.3MM **Privately Held**
SIC: 6512 7359 Commercial & industrial building operation; equipment rental & leasing

(G-14507)
MUSKINGUM WTRSHED CNSRVNCY DST
Also Called: Atwood Lake Park
4956 Shop Rd Ne (44656-8851)
PHONE...................330 343-6780
J Anthony Luther, *Superintendent*
EMP: 30
SALES (corp-wide): 93.5MM **Privately Held**
WEB: www.muskingumfoundation.org
SIC: 7996 7033 Amusement parks; trailer parks & campsites
PA: Muskingum Watershed Conservancy District
1319 3rd St Nw
New Philadelphia OH 44663
330 343-6647

Mineral Ridge
Trumbull County

(G-14508)
ADOLPH JOHNSON & SON CO
3497 Union St (44440-9009)
P.O. Box 1583, Youngstown (44501-1583)
PHONE...................330 544-8900
Paul Johnson, *President*
Warner Lawson, *Chairman*
James Johnson, *Vice Pres*
EMP: 25 EST: 1910
SQ FT: 4,300
SALES (est): 5.3MM **Privately Held**
WEB: www.adolphjohnson.com
SIC: 1542 1541 Commercial & office building, new construction; institutional building construction; industrial buildings & warehouses

(G-14509)
GLENN VIEW MANOR INC
3379 Main St Star Rt 46 (44440)
PHONE...................330 652-9901
Edward C Hood, *President*
Judy Grimes, *Admin Sec*
Joseph Ketchaver, *Administration*
EMP: 207 EST: 1964
SQ FT: 23,500
SALES (est): 4.9MM **Privately Held**
SIC: 8051 Skilled nursing care facilities

(G-14510)
L B FOSTER COMPANY
Also Called: Relay Rail Div.
1193 Salt Springs Rd (44440-9318)
PHONE...................330 652-1461
Scott Calahoun, *Manager*

EMP: 25
SQ FT: 3,000
SALES (corp-wide): 626.9MM **Publicly Held**
WEB: www.lbfoster.com
SIC: 1799 3743 Coating of metal structures at construction site; railroad equipment
PA: L. B. Foster Company
415 Holiday Dr Ste 1
Pittsburgh PA 15220
412 928-3400

(G-14511)
REINNOVATIONS CONTRACTING INC
3711 Main St (44440-9791)
PHONE...................330 505-9035
Jeffrey S McElhaney, *President*
George Wrataric, *Vice Pres*
EMP: 40
SALES (est): 3.8MM **Privately Held**
SIC: 1541 Renovation, remodeling & repairs: industrial buildings

(G-14512)
ROOD TRUCKING COMPANY INC (PA)
3505 Union St (44440-9007)
PHONE...................330 652-3519
George H Rood, *President*
Diane E Rood, *Vice Pres*
EMP: 121 EST: 1965
SQ FT: 10,000
SALES (est): 16.3MM **Privately Held**
WEB: www.roodtrucking.com
SIC: 4212 4213 Mail carriers, contract; trucking, except local

(G-14513)
TERRE FORME ENTERPRISES INC
Also Called: Clearview Lantern Suites
3000 Austintown Warren Rd (44440-9758)
PHONE...................330 847-6800
Stephen Sandberg, *President*
Betty Crews, *Vice Pres*
Kevin Sandberg, *Vice Pres*
Ellisa Sandberg-Roden, *Treasurer*
Kayla Wagner, *Office Mgr*
EMP: 32
SQ FT: 35,868
SALES (est): 1.7MM **Privately Held**
SIC: 8361 Home for the aged

(G-14514)
THE MAHONING VALLEY SANI DST
1181 Ohltown Mcdonald Rd (44440-9322)
P.O. Box 4119, Youngstown (44515-0119)
PHONE...................330 799-6315
Jack Vaughn, *President*
Thomas Holloway, *Chief Engr*
Alan Tatalovich, *Treasurer*
EMP: 53
SALES (est): 16.7MM **Privately Held**
SIC: 4941 Water supply

Minerva
Stark County

(G-14515)
AMERIDIAL INC
102 N Market St (44657-1614)
PHONE...................330 868-2000
Shannon Phillips, *Manager*
EMP: 60
SALES (corp-wide): 40MM **Privately Held**
SIC: 7389 Telemarketing services
HQ: Ameridial, Inc.
4535 Strausser St Nw
North Canton OH 44720
330 497-4888

(G-14516)
C C & S AMBULANCE SERVICE INC
Also Called: Bartley Ambulance
207 W Lincolnway (44657-1414)
P.O. Box 374 (44657-0374)
PHONE...................330 868-4114

Catherine Viola, *President*
David Viola, *Treasurer*
EMP: 50
SALES (est): 1.4MM **Privately Held**
SIC: 4119 Ambulance service

(G-14517)
CONSUMERS BANCORP INC
614 E Lincolnway (44657-2009)
P.O. Box 256 (44657-0256)
PHONE....................................330 868-7701
Laurie L McClellan, *Ch of Bd*
Ralph J Lober II, *President*
John P Furey, *Chairman*
Derek G Williams, *Senior VP*
Veronica Berresfrod, *Assistant VP*
EMP: 128
SALES: 20.9MM **Privately Held**
SIC: 6021 National commercial banks

(G-14518)
CONSUMERS NATIONAL BANK
(PA)
614 E Lincolnway (44657-2096)
PHONE....................................330 868-7701
Ralf Lober, *President*
Michele Catlett, *Assistant VP*
Sarah Chronister, *Assistant VP*
Theresa J Linder, *Assistant VP*
Debbie Miller, *Assistant VP*
EMP: 45
SQ FT: 6,000
SALES: 19.4MM **Privately Held**
WEB: www.consumersbank.com
SIC: 6021 National commercial banks

(G-14519)
FAMILY MEDICINE CENTER
MINERVA
Also Called: Minerva Medical Center
200 Carolyn Ct (44657-8758)
PHONE....................................330 868-4184
Joseph Khalil, *President*
EMP: 30
SQ FT: 6,000
SALES (est): 1.4MM **Privately Held**
SIC: 8011 General & family practice, physician/surgeon

(G-14520)
IMPERIAL ALUM - MINERVA LLC
217 Roosevelt St (44657-1541)
PHONE....................................330 868-7765
Mike Chenoweth, *Vice Pres*
David Riddell, *Vice Pres*
Gary Grim, *Plant Supt*
Shaun McLaughlin, *Manager*
David Kozin,
EMP: 55
SALES (est): 12.7MM **Privately Held**
SIC: 3334 5093 Slabs (primary), aluminum; scrap & waste materials

(G-14521)
MINERVA ELDER CARE INC
Also Called: Minerva Elderly Care
1035 E Lincolnway (44657-1297)
PHONE....................................330 868-4147
Edward Martell Sr, *President*
Pat Moschgat, *Director*
Tracy Randall, *Director*
Renee Forester, *Administration*
Martha Martell, *Admin Sec*
EMP: 35 EST: 1971
SQ FT: 12,000
SALES (est): 1.4MM **Privately Held**
SIC: 8051 Extended care facility

(G-14522)
MINERVA WELDING AND FABG
INC
22133 Us Route 30 (44657-9401)
P.O. Box 369 (44657-0369)
PHONE....................................330 868-7731
James A Gram, *President*
Stephen J Gram, *Treasurer*
Mike Gasper, *Manager*
Daniel E Gram, *Admin Sec*
Margie Wilson, *Admin Asst*
EMP: 40 EST: 1949
SQ FT: 10,000

SALES (est): 18.7MM **Privately Held**
WEB: www.minweld.com
SIC: 5084 3599 Industrial machinery & equipment; machine shop, jobbing & repair

(G-14523)
RTW INC (DH)
15245 Lincoln St Se (44657-8559)
PHONE....................................952 893-0403
Jeffrey B Murphy, *President*
Keith D Krueger, *COO*
Thomas J Byers, *Exec VP*
David M Dietz, *Vice Pres*
Keith Krueger, *Vice Pres*
EMP: 78
SQ FT: 31,930
SALES (est): 73.9MM
SALES (corp-wide): 1.5B **Publicly Held**
WEB: www.rtwi.com
SIC: 6331 Assessment associations: fire, marine & casualty insurance; workers' compensation insurance
HQ: Rockhill Holding Company
    700 W 47th St Ste 350
    Kansas City MO 64112
    816 412-2800

(G-14524)
SANDY CREEK JOINT FIRE DST
505 E Lincolnway (44657-2007)
PHONE....................................330 868-5193
Rudy Evanich, *Owner*
David Detchon, *Owner*
James Kiko, *Owner*
Richard McClellan, *Owner*
Laurie Peach, *Owner*
EMP: 45
SALES (est): 810.5K **Privately Held**
SIC: 8049 Paramedic

(G-14525)
ST LUKE LUTHERAN
COMMUNITY
4301 Woodale Ave Se (44657-8570)
PHONE....................................330 868-5600
Vicki Nicholson, *Principal*
EMP: 25
SALES (corp-wide): 15.5MM **Privately Held**
SIC: 8361 Home for the aged
PA: St. Luke Lutheran Community
    220 Applegrove St Ne
    Canton OH
    330 499-8341

Minford
Scioto County

(G-14526)
MINFORD RETIREMENT CENTER
LLC
9641 State Route 335 (45653-8904)
P.O. Box 276 (45653-0276)
PHONE....................................740 820-2821
Henry Collins,
Jeaneta Collins,
EMP: 42
SALES (est): 1.5MM **Privately Held**
SIC: 8059 Rest home, with health care

Mingo Junction
Jefferson County

(G-14527)
BELLAS CO
Also Called: Iron City Distributing
2670 Commercial Ave (43938-1613)
P.O. Box 2399, Steubenville (43953-0399)
PHONE....................................740 598-4171
Michael C Bellas, *Ch of Bd*
Robert M Chapman, *President*
Charles D Burrier Sr, *Principal*
Diane Bellas Terzis, *Corp Secy*
Albert Bellas, *Vice Pres*
▲ EMP: 50
SQ FT: 38,000

SALES (est): 9.8MM
SALES (corp-wide): 15.1MM **Privately Held**
WEB: www.ironcitydist.com
SIC: 5181 5182 5149 Beer & other fermented malt liquors; wine; soft drinks
PA: The K M C Corporation
    2670 Commercial Ave
    Mingo Junction OH 43938
    740 598-4171

(G-14528)
JSW STEEL USA OHIO INC
1500 Commercial St (43938-1096)
PHONE....................................740 535-8172
Cynthia L Woolheater, *President*
EMP: 120 EST: 2016
SALES (est): 1.4MM **Privately Held**
SIC: 5051 Metals service centers & offices
PA: Jsw Steel Limited
    Jsw Centre, Bandra Kurla Complex
    Mumbai MH 40005

(G-14529)
START-BLACK SERVICESJV
LLC
797 Cool Spring Rd (43938-1611)
PHONE....................................740 598-4891
Frank Hoagland,
EMP: 65
SALES (est): 540.8K **Privately Held**
SIC: 7381 Guard services

(G-14530)
SUNRISE TELEVISION CORP
Also Called: Wtov TV 9
9 Red Donely Plz (43938)
P.O. Box 9999, Steubenville (43952-6799)
PHONE....................................740 282-9999
EMP: 70
SALES (corp-wide): 674.9MM **Publicly Held**
SIC: 7622 4833 Radio/Television Repair Television Station
HQ: Sunrise Television Corp.
    1 W Exchange St Ste 5a
    Providence RI

Minster
Auglaize County

(G-14531)
ALBERT FREYTAG INC
306 Executive Dr (45865)
P.O. Box 5 (45865-0005)
PHONE....................................419 628-2018
William Freytag, *President*
Joseph Freytag, *Vice Pres*
EMP: 25
SQ FT: 1,200
SALES (est): 6.7MM **Privately Held**
SIC: 3441 1741 Fabricated structural metal; masonry & other stonework

(G-14532)
EMMYS BRIDAL INC
336 N Main St (45865-9561)
PHONE....................................419 628-7555
Lori Rindler, *President*
Anne Puthoff, *Vice Pres*
EMP: 25
SALES: 600K **Privately Held**
WEB: www.emmysbridal.com
SIC: 5621 7299 Bridal shops; clothing rental services

(G-14533)
GARMANN/MILLER & ASSOC
INC
Also Called: Garmann Miller Architects
38 S Lincoln Dr (45865-1220)
P.O. Box 71 (45865-0071)
PHONE....................................419 628-4240
Bruce Miller, *President*
Brad Garmann, *Vice Pres*
Matthew Kremer, *Engineer*
Kevin Rinderle, *Engineer*
Josh Miller, *Info Tech Dir*
EMP: 38
SQ FT: 2,800

SALES: 900K **Privately Held**
WEB: www.garmannmiller.com
SIC: 8712 8711 0781 Architectural engineering; engineering services; mechanical engineering; heating & ventilation engineering; electrical or electronic engineering; landscape architects

(G-14534)
GRAHAM PACKAGING
HOLDINGS CO
255 Southgate (45865-9552)
P.O. Box 123 (45865-0123)
PHONE....................................419 628-1070
Robert Andreas, *Branch Mgr*
EMP: 45
SALES (corp-wide): 1MM **Privately Held**
SIC: 5199 Packaging materials
HQ: Graham Packaging Holdings Co
    700 Indian Springs Dr # 100
    Lancaster PA 17601
    717 849-8500

(G-14535)
H A DORSTEN INC
146 N Main St (45865-1120)
P.O. Box 156 (45865-0156)
PHONE....................................419 628-2327
Ronald A Dorsten, *President*
Gregory Stricker, *Superintendent*
Ken Bertke, *Principal*
Frank P Connaughton, *Principal*
H A Dersten, *Principal*
EMP: 50 EST: 1953
SQ FT: 2,500
SALES: 11MM **Privately Held**
WEB: www.hadorsteninc.com
SIC: 1541 1542 Industrial buildings, new construction; commercial & office building, new construction

(G-14536)
HOSKINS INTERNATIONAL LLC
Also Called: Hoskins Intl SEC Invstigations
5116 State Route 119 (45865-9404)
PHONE....................................419 628-6015
James Hoskins,
James Joyce,
EMP: 26
SQ FT: 10,000
SALES: 2MM **Privately Held**
WEB: www.hoskinsinternational.com
SIC: 8748 1731 Energy conservation consultant; energy management controls

(G-14537)
KNIGHTS OF COLUMBUS
40 N Main St (45865-1119)
P.O. Box 48 (45865-0048)
PHONE....................................419 628-2089
Kurt Hilgefort, *President*
EMP: 37
SALES (corp-wide): 2.3B **Privately Held**
WEB: www.kofc.org
SIC: 8641 Fraternal associations
PA: Knights Of Columbus
    1 Columbus Plz Ste 1700
    New Haven CT 06510
    203 752-4000

(G-14538)
MINSTER BANK (PA)
95 W 4th St (45865-1060)
P.O. Box 90 (45865-0090)
PHONE....................................419 628-2351
Mark Henschen, *CEO*
Dale Luebke, *Exec VP*
Phyllis Rose, *Senior VP*
Daniel Heitmeyer, *Vice Pres*
Kenneth Wuebker, *CFO*
EMP: 42
SQ FT: 33,000
SALES: 17.9MM **Privately Held**
WEB: www.minsterbank.com
SIC: 6022 State trust companies accepting deposits, commercial

(G-14539)
PARK ARROWHEAD GOLF CLUB
INC
2211 Dirksen Rd (45865-9348)
P.O. Box 73 (45865-0073)
PHONE....................................419 628-2444
Mike Griner, *President*
Bruce Bernhole, *Treasurer*
Tom Griner, *Admin Sec*

EMP: 30
SALES (est): 1MM **Privately Held**
SIC: 7992 5941 Public golf courses; golf goods & equipment

(G-14540)
PRECISION STRIP INC (HQ)
86 S Ohio St (45865-1246)
P.O. Box 104 (45865-0104)
PHONE.............................419 628-2343
Thomas A Compton, *Ch of Bd*
Joe Wolf, *President*
▲ **EMP:** 200 **EST:** 1977
SQ FT: 300,000
SALES (est): 193.8MM
SALES (corp-wide): 11.5B **Publicly Held**
WEB: www.precision-strip.com
SIC: 4225 General warehousing & storage
PA: Reliance Steel & Aluminum Co.
    350 S Grand Ave Ste 5100
    Los Angeles CA 90071
    213 687-7700

Mogadore
Portage County

(G-14541)
ASW GLOBAL LLC (PA)
3375 Gilchrist Rd (44260-1253)
PHONE.............................330 733-6291
Andre Thornton, *CEO*
Carolyn Pizzuto, *Senior VP*
Laurie Quinn, *Human Res Mgr*
Pam Harris, *Manager*
Valerie Holloway, *Supervisor*
EMP: 70
SQ FT: 1,500,000
SALES (est): 84.5MM **Privately Held**
WEB: www.aswservices.com
SIC: 4225 General warehousing

(G-14542)
ASW GLOBAL LLC
Also Called: Asw Supply Chain Service
3325 Gilchrist Rd (44260-1253)
PHONE.............................330 798-5184
Nick Mihiylov, *Branch Mgr*
EMP: 100
SALES (corp-wide): 84.5MM **Privately Held**
WEB: www.aswservices.com
SIC: 4225 General warehousing
PA: Asw Global, Llc
    3375 Gilchrist Rd
    Mogadore OH 44260
    330 733-6291

(G-14543)
BICO AKRON INC
Also Called: Bico Steel Service Centers
3100 Gilchrist Rd (44260-1246)
PHONE.............................330 794-1716
Michael A Ensminger, *President*
▲ **EMP:** 65
SQ FT: 90,000
SALES (est): 28.5MM **Privately Held**
SIC: 5051 3443 Steel; fabricated plate work (boiler shop)

(G-14544)
BURGER IRON COMPANY
Also Called: Bico
3100 Gilchrist Rd (44260-1218)
P.O. Box 2219, Akron (44309-2219)
PHONE.............................330 794-1716
Thomas Fiocca, *President*
Richard Kearns, *Treasurer*
C Smith, *Admin Sec*
EMP: 190 **EST:** 1896
SALES (est): 70.2MM **Privately Held**
SIC: 5051 Steel

(G-14545)
CORNWELL QUALITY TOOLS COMPANY
200 N Cleveland Ave (44260-1205)
PHONE.............................330 628-2627
Bill Nobley, *Branch Mgr*
Dianna Stump, *Executive*
EMP: 75
SQ FT: 3,000

SALES (corp-wide): 173.8MM **Privately Held**
WEB: www.cornwelltools.com
SIC: 3423 5085 Hand & edge tools; industrial supplies
PA: The Cornwell Quality Tools Company
    667 Seville Rd
    Wadsworth OH 44281
    330 336-3506

(G-14546)
DAVEY TREE EXPERT COMPANY
1437 State Route 43 Ste A (44260-9670)
PHONE.............................330 628-1499
EMP: 25
SALES (corp-wide): 1B **Privately Held**
SIC: 0783 Ornamental shrub & tree services
PA: The Davey Tree Expert Company
    1500 N Mantua St
    Kent OH 44240
    330 673-9511

(G-14547)
DENNIS C MCCLUSKEY MD & ASSOC
754 S Cleveland Ave # 300 (44260-2210)
PHONE.............................330 628-2686
Dennis Mc Cluskey MD, *President*
Brian Cain, *Shareholder*
EMP: 42
SQ FT: 10,600
SALES (est): 1.8MM **Privately Held**
SIC: 8011 General & family practice, physician/surgeon

(G-14548)
EMPIRE ONE LLC
1532 State Route 43 (44260-8820)
PHONE.............................330 628-9310
Brian Taylor, *Principal*
EMP: 40
SALES (est): 1.7MM **Privately Held**
SIC: 7389 Water softener service

(G-14549)
H M MILLER CONSTRUCTION CO
1225 Waterloo Rd (44260-9598)
P.O. Box 131 (44260-0131)
PHONE.............................330 628-4811
John Smith, *President*
Mike Smith, *Treasurer*
Patrick Smith, *Admin Sec*
EMP: 55 **EST:** 1972
SQ FT: 20,000
SALES (est): 12.5MM **Privately Held**
SIC: 1623 7353 Sewer line construction; water main construction; heavy construction equipment rental

(G-14550)
HENRYS KING TOURING COMPANY
1369 Burbridge Dr (44260-1601)
PHONE.............................330 628-1886
Timothy Walsh, *Principal*
EMP: 35 **EST:** 2010
SALES (est): 46.4K **Privately Held**
SIC: 7929 Entertainers & entertainment groups

(G-14551)
HMS CONSTRUCTION & RENTAL CO
1225 Waterloo Rd (44260-9598)
P.O. Box 131 (44260-0131)
PHONE.............................330 628-4811
John Smith, *President*
EMP: 60
SQ FT: 1,200
SALES (est): 2.3MM **Privately Held**
SIC: 1521 New construction, single-family houses

(G-14552)
KIDS AHEAD INC
726 S Cleveland Ave (44260-2205)
PHONE.............................330 628-7404
Julie Begue, *Owner*
EMP: 35
SALES (est): 627.4K **Privately Held**
SIC: 8351 Group day care center

(G-14553)
OMEGA LABORATORIES INC
400 N Cleveland Ave (44260-1209)
PHONE.............................330 628-5748
John C Vitullo, *CEO*
Bill Corl, *CEO*
Jay Davis, *President*
EMP: 61 **EST:** 2000
SQ FT: 44,709
SALES (est): 12.6MM **Privately Held**
WEB: www.omegalabs.net
SIC: 8734 Testing laboratories

(G-14554)
PARRISH TIRE COMPANY OF AKRON
Also Called: Parrish McIntyre Tire
3833 Mogadore Indus Pkwy (44260-1216)
PHONE.............................330 628-6800
Logan Jackson, *President*
Mike Everhart, *Corp Secy*
Mike McIntyre, *Vice Pres*
EMP: 36
SQ FT: 8,800
SALES (est): 3.9MM **Privately Held**
SIC: 7538 General automotive repair shops

(G-14555)
R & R SANITATION INC
1447 Martin Rd (44260-1562)
PHONE.............................330 325-2311
EMP: 30
SALES (est): 2.3MM **Privately Held**
SIC: 4212 4953 Refuse System Local Trucking Operator

(G-14556)
TAYLOR CONSTRUCTION COMPANY
1532 State Route 43 (44260-8820)
PHONE.............................330 628-9310
Brian Taylor, *Principal*
Rick Taylor, *Principal*
EMP: 30
SALES (est): 2.9MM **Privately Held**
SIC: 1794 Excavation & grading, building construction

(G-14557)
TAYLOR TELECOMMUNICATIONS INC
3470 Gilchrist Rd (44260-1215)
PHONE.............................330 628-5501
Sherry Taylor, *President*
Chris Taylor, *Vice Pres*
Joe Taylor, *Treasurer*
Tam Taylor, *Admin Sec*
EMP: 95 **EST:** 1981
SQ FT: 4,000
SALES (est): 14.8MM **Privately Held**
SIC: 1731 Fiber optic cable installation

(G-14558)
THOMAS L STOVER INC
754 S Cleveland Ave # 300 (44260-2210)
PHONE.............................330 665-8060
Thomas L Stover, *President*
EMP: 30
SALES (est): 1.5MM **Privately Held**
SIC: 8011 Offices & clinics of medical doctors

Monclova
Lucas County

(G-14559)
SPARTAN CONSTRUCTION CO INC
2021 Mescher Dr (43542-9740)
PHONE.............................419 389-1854
Peter Vandenberg, *President*
Peter J Vandenberg, *President*
EMP: 35
SALES (est): 3.6MM **Privately Held**
SIC: 1741 1531 Masonry & other stonework;

Monroe
Butler County

(G-14560)
ASSEMBLY CENTER
913 Lebanon St (45050-1448)
PHONE.............................800 582-1099
Lenny Wyatt, *President*
EMP: 45
SALES (est): 1.1MM **Privately Held**
SIC: 6512 7299 Auditorium & hall operation; banquet hall facilities

(G-14561)
BAKER CONCRETE CNSTR INC (PA)
900 N Garver Rd (45050-1277)
PHONE.............................513 539-4000
Daniel L Baker, *President*
Jon Chastain, *General Mgr*
Wes Bradds, *Superintendent*
Gary L Benson, *Vice Pres*
Steven A Lydy, *Vice Pres*
◆ **EMP:** 700
SQ FT: 27,000
SALES (est): 771.2MM **Privately Held**
WEB: www.bakerconcrete.com
SIC: 1771 1611 Concrete work; concrete construction: roads, highways, sidewalks, etc.

(G-14562)
BAKER EQUIPMENT AND MTLS LTD
990 N Main St (45050)
P.O. Box 526 (45050-0526)
PHONE.............................513 422-6697
Robin Wells, *Transportation*
Cynthia S Baker, *Mng Member*
EMP: 30
SALES (est): 7MM
SALES (corp-wide): 771.2MM **Privately Held**
SIC: 7359 Equipment rental & leasing
PA: Baker Concrete Construction, Inc.
    900 N Garver Rd
    Monroe OH 45050
    513 539-4000

(G-14563)
BENEDICT ENTERPRISES INC (PA)
750 Lakeview Rd (45050-1707)
P.O. Box 370 (45050-0370)
PHONE.............................513 539-9216
Arnold Benedict, *President*
Elizabeth Benedict, *Exec VP*
Lisa Benedict, *Treasurer*
Lisa Staples, *Admin Sec*
Pam Wendt, *Administration*
EMP: 28
SQ FT: 20,528
SALES (est): 4.3MM **Privately Held**
WEB: www.bei-benedict.com
SIC: 7513 7519 5511 7538 Truck rental, without drivers; truck leasing, without drivers; trailer rental; trucks, tractors & trailers: new & used; general truck repair

(G-14564)
CONTINENTAL TRANSPORT INC
Also Called: CTI
997 Platte River Blvd (45050)
P.O. Box 100, Springboro (45066-0100)
PHONE.............................513 360-2960
James R Office, *President*
Steven L Messer, *Principal*
Allison Eder, *Vice Pres*
EMP: 50
SALES (est): 5.4MM **Privately Held**
SIC: 4212 Local trucking, without storage

(G-14565)
DICKERSON DISTRIBUTING COMPANY
150 Lawton Ave (45050-1212)
PHONE.............................513 539-8483
John Dickerson Jr, *Ch of Bd*
Michael Dickerson, *President*
▲ **EMP:** 60
SQ FT: 32,000

SALES (est): 24.1MM **Privately Held**
WEB: www.dickersondist.com
SIC: 5181 Beer & other fermented malt liquors

(G-14566)
DOMINGUEZ INC
1000 Reed Dr (45050-1724)
P.O. Box 693, Springboro (45066-0693)
PHONE.................................513 425-9955
Frank Dominguez, *President*
Francisco Dominguez, *Corp Secy*
Luz M Dominguez, *Treasurer*
EMP: 30
SALES (est): 3.9MM **Privately Held**
WEB: www.dominguezinc.net
SIC: 1752 Carpet laying; ceramic floor tile installation; wood floor installation & refinishing

(G-14567)
FORMWORK SERVICES LLC
900 N Garver Rd (45050-1241)
PHONE.................................513 539-4000
Daniel Baker, *President*
EMP: 50
SALES (est): 2.8MM **Privately Held**
SIC: 1771 Concrete work

(G-14568)
FOUR SEASONS ENVIRONMENTAL INC (PA)
43 New Garver Rd (45050-1281)
PHONE.................................513 539-2978
Daniel Tarkington, *CEO*
Timothy McDonald, *Business Mgr*
Dave Fryman, *Project Mgr*
Ron Wyrtzen, *Director*
EMP: 350
SQ FT: 9,500
SALES (est): 51.5MM **Privately Held**
WEB: www.fseinc.net
SIC: 8744 Facilities support services

(G-14569)
HCG INC
Also Called: Zack Pack
203 N Garver Rd (45050-1235)
P.O. Box 549, Springboro (45066-0549)
PHONE.................................513 539-9269
Mark Knue, *President*
Kenneth May, *Treasurer*
James R Office, *Admin Sec*
EMP: 40
SQ FT: 108,000
SALES (est): 4MM **Privately Held**
SIC: 4783 Packing goods for shipping

(G-14570)
J T EXPRESS INC
1200 N Main St (45050)
P.O. Box 439 (45050-0439)
PHONE.................................513 727-8185
Timothy Foister, *President*
Tim Foister, *President*
Jimmie Foister, *Principal*
EMP: 27
SQ FT: 30,000
SALES (est): 4.7MM **Privately Held**
SIC: 4213 4212 Trucking, except local; local trucking, without storage

(G-14571)
KAISER LOGISTICS LLC
201 Lawton Ave (45050-1213)
PHONE.................................937 534-0213
Dewey Weeda, *President*
EMP: 65
SALES (est): 5.6MM
SALES (corp-wide): 17.6B **Publicly Held**
SIC: 8741 Business management
PA: Performance Food Group Company
12500 West Creek Pkwy
Richmond VA 23238
804 484-7700

(G-14572)
KASTLE ELECTRIC COMPANY
Also Called: Kastle Technologies
100 Cart Path Dr (45050-1494)
PHONE.................................513 360-2901
EMP: 40
SALES (corp-wide): 22.7MM **Privately Held**
SIC: 1731 General Electrical Contractor

PA: Kastle Electric Company
4501 Kettering Blvd
Moraine OH 45439
937 254-2681

(G-14573)
KASTLE TECHNOLOGIES CO LLC (HQ)
100 Cart Path Dr (45050-1494)
PHONE.................................513 360-2901
Dennis Quebe, *CEO*
Lyman Smith, *President*
Gregory Ross, *COO*
William Page, *CFO*
EMP: 25
SQ FT: 20,000
SALES (est): 4.7MM
SALES (corp-wide): 66.4MM **Privately Held**
SIC: 1731 General electrical contractor
PA: Quebe Holdings, Inc.
1985 Founders Dr
Dayton OH 45420
937 222-2290

(G-14574)
LITHKO CONTRACTING LLC
900 N Garver Rd (45050-1241)
PHONE.................................513 863-5100
Westin Jensen, *Project Mgr*
Zach Proctor, *Project Mgr*
Garret Hossfeld, *Project Engr*
Curtis A Michael, *Manager*
EMP: 58
SALES (corp-wide): 177.7MM **Privately Held**
SIC: 1771 Foundation & footing contractor
PA: Lithko Contracting, Llc
2958 Crescentville Rd
West Chester OH 45069
513 564-2000

(G-14575)
LITHKO RESTORATION TECH LLC (PA)
990 N Main St (45050)
P.O. Box 569 (45050-0569)
PHONE.................................513 863-5500
Jim Dean, *Project Mgr*
Patrick Walsh, *Project Mgr*
Mike Pellegrini, *CFO*
Erik Henry, *Accounts Mgr*
Henry Frondorf, *Manager*
EMP: 80
SALES (est): 23.1MM **Privately Held**
SIC: 1771 Concrete repair

(G-14576)
MCGRAW/KOKOSING INC
101 Clark Blvd (45044-3216)
PHONE.................................614 212-5700
Daniel B Walker, *President*
Chris A Bergs, *Vice Pres*
Tim Freed, *CFO*
EMP: 500
SQ FT: 232,000
SALES (est): 133.4MM
SALES (corp-wide): 632.8MM **Privately Held**
WEB: www.mcgrawkokosing.com
SIC: 1541 Renovation, remodeling & repairs: industrial buildings
PA: Kokosing Inc.
6235 Wstrville Rd Ste 200
Westerville OH 43081
614 212-5700

(G-14577)
MONROE MECHANICAL INCORPORATED
Also Called: Monroe Heating and AC
150 Breaden Dr B (45050-1427)
PHONE.................................513 539-7555
William M Housh III, *President*
EMP: 35
SQ FT: 24,000
SALES (est): 7.5MM **Privately Held**
SIC: 1711 5075 Mechanical contractor; plumbing contractors; warm air heating & air conditioning

(G-14578)
OHIO PIZZA PRODUCTS INC (DH)
Also Called: Performnce Fodservice - Presto
201 Lawton Ave (45050-1213)
P.O. Box 549 (45050-0549)
PHONE.................................937 294-6969
Vito P Weeda, *Ch of Bd*
Jeff Schrand, *President*
Phil Weeda Sr, *Chairman*
Dewey Weeda, *Vice Pres*
Dale Lipa, *CFO*
EMP: 80
SQ FT: 80,000
SALES (est): 147MM
SALES (corp-wide): 17.6B **Publicly Held**
WEB: www.prestofoods.com
SIC: 5149 Pizza supplies; specialty food items; baking supplies
HQ: Institution Food House, Inc.
543 12th Street Dr Nw
Hickory NC 28601
800 800-0434

(G-14579)
OHIO PRESBT RETIREMENT SVCS
Also Called: Ohio Presbt Retirement Vlg
225 Britton Ln (45050-1154)
PHONE.................................513 539-7391
Stan Kappers, *Branch Mgr*
EMP: 250 **Privately Held**
WEB: www.nwo.oprs.org
SIC: 8361 8052 8051 Rest home, with health care incidental; intermediate care facilities; skilled nursing care facilities
PA: Ohio Living
1001 Kingsmill Pkwy
Columbus OH 43229

(G-14580)
PETERMANN
505 Yankee Rd (45050-1069)
PHONE.................................513 539-0324
Peter Settle, *Owner*
EMP: 25
SALES (est): 660K **Privately Held**
SIC: 4151 School buses

(G-14581)
RICHTER LANDSCAPING
240 Senate Dr (45050-1715)
PHONE.................................513 539-0300
Richard Richter, *Owner*
EMP: 30
SQ FT: 19,280
SALES (est): 1.7MM **Privately Held**
SIC: 0782 Landscape contractors

(G-14582)
SENIOR INDEPENDENCE ADULT
25 Indiana Ave (45050-1146)
PHONE.................................513 681-8174
Joan Punchfleming, *Manager*
EMP: 50
SALES (corp-wide): 2.7MM **Privately Held**
SIC: 8322 Adult day care center
PA: Senior Independence Adult Day Services
717 Neil Ave
Columbus OH 43215
614 224-5344

(G-14583)
SENIOR INDEPENDENCE ADULT
27 Indiana Ave (45050-1146)
PHONE.................................513 539-2697
Joan Punch-Fleming, *Manager*
EMP: 50
SALES (corp-wide): 2.7MM **Privately Held**
SIC: 8322 8082 Adult day care center; refugee service; home health care services
PA: Senior Independence Adult Day Services
717 Neil Ave
Columbus OH 43215
614 224-5344

(G-14584)
TEREX UTILITIES INC
Also Called: Cincinnati Division
920 Deneen Ave (45050-1210)
PHONE.................................513 539-9770
Rick Girffis, *Branch Mgr*
EMP: 53
SALES (corp-wide): 5.1B **Publicly Held**
WEB: www.craneamerica.com
SIC: 3531 7629 3536 Cranes; electrical repair shops; hoists, cranes & monorails
HQ: Terex Utilities, Inc.
12805 Sw 77th Pl
Tigard OR 97223
503 620-0611

(G-14585)
UNIVERSAL TRANSPORTATION SYSTE
220 Senate Dr (45050-1715)
PHONE.................................513 539-9491
Lori Vogft, *Branch Mgr*
EMP: 35
SALES (corp-wide): 18.3MM **Privately Held**
WEB: www.utswct.com
SIC: 4789 4111 Cargo loading & unloading services; local & suburban transit
PA: Universal Transportation Systems Llc
5284 Winton Rd
Fairfield OH 45014
513 829-1287

(G-14586)
VALICOR ENVIRONMENTAL SVCS LLC (HQ)
1045 Reed Dr Ste A (45050-1717)
PHONE.................................513 733-4666
James Devlin, *CEO*
Dave Brown, *COO*
Bill Hinton, *Officer*
▲ **EMP:** 70 **EST:** 1982
SQ FT: 16,000
SALES (est): 39.7MM
SALES (corp-wide): 1.8B **Privately Held**
WEB: www.unitedwastewater.com
SIC: 5039 Septic tanks
PA: Wind Point Partners, L.P.
676 N Michigan Ave # 3700
Chicago IL 60611
312 255-4800

(G-14587)
WORTHINGTON INDUSTRIES INC
Worthington Steel
350 Lawton Ave (45050-1216)
PHONE.................................513 539-9291
Dave Kleimeyer, *General Mgr*
David Kleimeyer, *Sales/Mktg Mgr*
EMP: 165
SQ FT: 120,000
SALES (corp-wide): 3.5B **Publicly Held**
WEB: www.worthingtonindustries.com
SIC: 3325 5051 3471 3441 Steel foundries; metals service centers & offices; plating & polishing; fabricated structural metal; blast furnaces & steel mills
PA: Worthington Industries, Inc.
200 W Old Wlson Bridge Rd
Worthington OH 43085
614 438-3210

Monroeville
Huron County

(G-14588)
HOMAN TRANSPORTATION INC
22 Fort Monroe Pkwy (44847-9411)
PHONE.................................419 465-2626
Andrew Homan, *President*
Angela Homan, *Admin Sec*
EMP: 80
SALES (est): 14.9MM **Privately Held**
SIC: 4213 Heavy hauling

(G-14589)
JHI GROUP INC (PA)
Also Called: Janotta & Herner
309 Monroe St (44847-9406)
PHONE.................................419 465-4611
James Shelley, *Ch of Bd*
James Limbird, *President*

Patti Anderson, *Vice Pres*
Steve Durbin, *Vice Pres*
Seth Herrnstein, *Vice Pres*
EMP: 165
SALES (est): 70.6MM **Privately Held**
WEB: www.janottaherner.com
SIC: 1542 Commercial & office building, new construction

(G-14590)
SHEARER FARM INC
Also Called: John Deere Authorized Dealer
13 Fort Monroe Pkwy (44847-9411)
PHONE..................................419 465-4622
Ivan Maibach, *Branch Mgr*
EMP: 35
SALES (corp-wide): 59.5MM **Privately Held**
SIC: 5046 5082 Commercial equipment; construction & mining machinery
PA: Shearer Farm Inc.
7762 Cleveland Rd
Wooster OH 44691
330 345-9023

(G-14591)
TUSING BUILDERS LTD
2596 Us Route 20 E (44847)
PHONE..................................419 465-3100
Jason Tusing, *Partner*
Todd Limpert, *Superintendent*
Greg Reynolds, *Project Mgr*
Jason Cleland, *Opers Mgr*
Colleen Shupe, *Controller*
EMP: 28
SALES (est): 6.7MM **Privately Held**
WEB: www.tusingbuilders.com
SIC: 1542 1521 Commercial & office building, new construction; single-family housing construction

(G-14592)
UNDERGROUND UTILITIES INC
416 Monroe St (44847-9789)
P.O. Box 428 (44847-0428)
PHONE..................................419 465-2587
John A Bores, *CEO*
Joseph Hossler, *Vice Pres*
Michael Prinatt, *Vice Pres*
Greg Schafer, *Vice Pres*
Mike Prenatt, *Project Mgr*
EMP: 96 **EST:** 1978
SQ FT: 12,000
SALES: 37MM **Privately Held**
SIC: 1623 Underground utilities contractor; sewer line construction

Montgomery
Hamilton County

(G-14593)
CITY OF MONTGOMERY (PA)
Also Called: CITY HALL
10101 Montgomery Rd (45242-5323)
PHONE..................................513 891-2424
Gerri Harbison, *Mayor*
EMP: 60 **Privately Held**
WEB: www.montgomeryoh.net
SIC: 9111 8611 ; business associations

(G-14594)
COLLIER NURSING SERVICE INC
9844 Zig Zag Rd (45242-6311)
PHONE..................................513 791-4357
Bette M Collier, *President*
EMP: 250
SALES (est): 8.2MM **Privately Held**
WEB: www.colliernursingservices.com
SIC: 7361 Nurses' registry

(G-14595)
INFORMATION BUILDERS INC
1 Financial Way Ste 307 (45242-5800)
PHONE..................................513 891-2338
Rick Rohde, *Manager*
EMP: 30
SALES (corp-wide): 262.6MM **Privately Held**
WEB: www.informationbuilders.com
SIC: 5734 7377 Computer software & accessories; computer rental & leasing

PA: Information Builders, Inc.
2 Penn Plz Fl 28
New York NY 10121
212 736-4433

(G-14596)
MONTGOMERY SWIM & TENNIS CLUB
9941 Orchard Club Dr (45242-4466)
PHONE..................................513 793-6433
Fax: 513 793-6433
EMP: 29
SQ FT: 1,963
SALES (est): 565.1K **Privately Held**
SIC: 7997 Membership Sport/Recreation Club

(G-14597)
O N EQUITY SALES COMPANY
Also Called: Onesco
1 Financial Way Ste 100 (45242-5800)
P.O. Box 371, Cincinnati (45201-0371)
PHONE..................................513 794-6794
Barbara Turner, *President*
Donna Clapp, *Vice Pres*
EMP: 600 **EST:** 1968
SALES (est): 46.1MM
SALES (corp-wide): 2.2MM **Privately Held**
WEB: www.hummelagency.com
SIC: 6211 Security brokers & dealers
HQ: Ohio National Financial Services, Inc.
1 Financial Way Ste 100
Montgomery OH 45242
513 794-6100

(G-14598)
OHIO NAT MUTL HOLDINGS INC (PA)
1 Financial Way Ste 100 (45242-5800)
PHONE..................................513 794-6100
Gary Huffman, *Ch of Bd*
Ronald Dolan, *Senior VP*
Michael S Haberkamp, *Vice Pres*
Roylene Broadwell, *Treasurer*
Matt Beerman, *Manager*
EMP: 750
SALES: 2.2MM **Privately Held**
SIC: 6311 Mutual association life insurance

(G-14599)
OHIO NATIONAL FINCL SVCS INC (HQ)
1 Financial Way Ste 100 (45242-5800)
P.O. Box 237, Cincinnati (45201-0237)
PHONE..................................513 794-6100
Gary T Huffman, *President*
Paul Boehm, *President*
Christopher A Carlson, *President*
Howard Clark, *President*
Arthur J Roberts, *President*
EMP: 700
SALES (est): 356.5MM
SALES (corp-wide): 2.2MM **Privately Held**
SIC: 6311 Mutual association life insurance
PA: Ohio National Mutual Holdings, Inc.
1 Financial Way Ste 100
Montgomery OH 45242
513 794-6100

(G-14600)
OHIO NATIONAL LIFE ASSURANCE
1 Financial Way Ste 100 (45242-5800)
P.O. Box 237, Cincinnati (45201-0237)
PHONE..................................513 794-6100
David B Omaley, *CEO*
Gates Smith, *Exec VP*
EMP: 716 **EST:** 1979
SALES (est): 88.1MM
SALES (corp-wide): 2.2MM **Privately Held**
WEB: www.ohionatl.com
SIC: 6411 Insurance agents
HQ: The Ohio National Life Insurance Company
1 Financial Way Ste 100
Montgomery OH 45242

(G-14601)
OHIO NATIONAL LIFE INSUR CO (DH)
Also Called: Ohio Casualty Insurance
1 Financial Way Ste 100 (45242-5800)
P.O. Box 237, Cincinnati (45201-0237)
PHONE..................................513 794-6100
David B Omaley, *CEO*
Ronald Heibert, *Vice Pres*
Ray Spears, *Vice Pres*
Michael Vogel, *Vice Pres*
Danny Leach, *Manager*
EMP: 80
SALES (est): 307MM
SALES (corp-wide): 2.2MM **Privately Held**
WEB: www.nslac.com
SIC: 6331 Fire, marine & casualty insurance
HQ: Ohio National Financial Services, Inc.
1 Financial Way Ste 100
Montgomery OH 45242
513 794-6100

(G-14602)
ORTHOPEDIC DIAGNSTC TRTMNT CTR
10547 Montgomery Rd 400a (45242-4418)
PHONE..................................513 791-6611
Thomas Carothers, *Branch Mgr*
Andrew S Islam, *Surgeon*
EMP: 26
SALES (corp-wide): 3MM **Privately Held**
SIC: 8011 Orthopedic physician
PA: Orthopedic Diagnostic & Treatment Center Inc
4600 Smith Rd Ste B
Cincinnati OH 45212
513 221-4848

(G-14603)
TRIHEALTH INC
Also Called: Trihealth Fitnes Hlth Pavilion
6200 Pfeiffer Rd Ste 330 (45242-5864)
PHONE..................................513 985-0900
Stacie Pabst, *General Mgr*
Deb Riggs, *Branch Mgr*
Marie Palladino, *Manager*
Kristie Ryan, *Supervisor*
Michael Moyer, *Director*
EMP: 134 **Privately Held**
WEB: www.trihealth.com
SIC: 8741 8011 Hospital management; offices & clinics of medical doctors
HQ: Trihealth, Inc.
619 Oak St
Cincinnati OH 45206
513 569-6111

(G-14604)
TRIHEALTH OS LLC
Also Called: Trihealth Orthpd & Spine Inst
10547 Montgomery Rd 400a (45242-4418)
PHONE..................................513 791-6611
Valerie Hall, *Manager*
EMP: 60 **Privately Held**
SIC: 8069 Orthopedic hospital
HQ: Trihealth Os, Llc
8311 Montgomery Rd
Cincinnati OH 45236
513 985-3700

Montpelier
Williams County

(G-14605)
B & H INDUSTRIES INC
14020 Us Highway 20a (43543-9270)
PHONE..................................419 485-8373
Ron Dean, *CEO*
Cindy Dennis, *VP Opers*
EMP: 28 **EST:** 1977
SQ FT: 4,000
SALES (est): 2.6MM
SALES (corp-wide): 12MM **Privately Held**
WEB: www.bryansystems.com
SIC: 4213 4212 Trucking, except local; local trucking, without storage
PA: Best Way Motor Lines, Inc.
14020 Us Highway 20a
Montpelier OH 43543
419 485-8373

(G-14606)
BEST WAY MOTOR LINES INC (PA)
Also Called: Bryan Systems
14020 Us Highway 20a (43543-9270)
PHONE..................................419 485-8373
Ronald W Dean, *Ch of Bd*
Larry H Dean, *President*
Cindy Dennis, *Vice Pres*
EMP: 115
SQ FT: 24,000
SALES (est): 12MM **Privately Held**
WEB: www.bryansystems.com
SIC: 4212 7513 4213 Local trucking, without storage; dump truck haulage; truck leasing, without drivers; contract haulers

(G-14607)
BOB MOR INC
Also Called: Quality Inn
13508 State Route 15 (43543-9737)
PHONE..................................419 485-5555
John P Kidston, *President*
Hal R Hendricks, *Vice Pres*
EMP: 130
SQ FT: 150,000
SALES (est): 4.4MM **Privately Held**
SIC: 7011 5812 Hotels & motels; eating places

(G-14608)
BRIDGEWATER DAIRY LLC
14587 County Road 8 50 (43543-9337)
PHONE..................................419 485-8157
Betty Deters, *Controller*
Leon D Weaver,
Tim Den Dulk,
Chris Weaver,
EMP: 35 **EST:** 1998
SALES (est): 7.7MM **Privately Held**
SIC: 0241 Milk production

(G-14609)
BRYAN TRUCK LINE INC
Also Called: Bryan Systems
14020 Us Hwy 20 Ste A (43543)
PHONE..................................419 485-8373
Ronald W Dean, *Ch of Bd*
Larry H Dean, *President*
Cindy Dennis, *Vice Pres*
Buck Muhlford, *CFO*
EMP: 100
SQ FT: 16,000
SALES (est): 12.4MM
SALES (corp-wide): 12MM **Privately Held**
WEB: www.bryansystems.com
SIC: 4212 4213 Local trucking, without storage; trucking, except local
PA: Best Way Motor Lines, Inc.
14020 Us Highway 20a
Montpelier OH 43543
419 485-8373

(G-14610)
COMMUNICARE HEALTH SVCS INC
Also Called: Evergreen Healthcare Center
924 Charlies Way (43543-1904)
PHONE..................................419 485-8307
Clarence Bell, *Director*
Fara Nickle, *Director*
Dee F Shoup, *Hlthcr Dir*
Terry Schollmeier, *Administration*
Robert Brailey, *Administration*
EMP: 70
SALES (corp-wide): 125.8MM **Privately Held**
WEB: www.atriumlivingcenters.com
SIC: 8051 Skilled nursing care facilities
PA: Communicare Health Services, Inc.
4700 Ashwood Dr Ste 200
Blue Ash OH 45241
513 530-1654

(G-14611)
COMMUNITY HSPTALS WLLNESS CTRS
Also Called: Montpelier Hospital
909 E Snyder Ave (43543-1251)
PHONE..................................419 485-3154
Phil Ennen, *CEO*
Matthew Stuckey, *Phys Thrpy Dir*
George T Magill, *Emerg Med Spec*
EMP: 76

SALES (corp-wide): 77.2MM **Privately Held**
SIC: 8062 General medical & surgical hospitals
PA: Community Hospitals And Wellness Centers
433 W High St
Bryan OH 43506
419 636-1131

(G-14612)
COUNTY OF WILLIAMS
Also Called: Williams County Health Dept
310 Lincoln Ave Ste A (43543-1274)
P.O. Box 146 (43543-0146)
PHONE...............................419 485-3141
James Watkins, *Director*
EMP: 25 **Privately Held**
SIC: 9431 8082 ; home health care services
PA: County Of Williams
1 Courthouse Sq Ste L
Bryan OH 43506
419 636-2059

(G-14613)
DECORATIVE PAINT INCORPORATED
700 Randolph St (43543-1464)
PHONE...............................419 485-0632
John Simon, *President*
Greg Dirrim, *Vice Pres*
Mike Avina, *Opers Mgr*
Mandy Hanna, *Materials Mgr*
Sandy Hough, *Personnel Assit*
EMP: 83
SALES: 1.2MM **Privately Held**
WEB: www.dpii.biz
SIC: 7532 Paint shop, automotive

(G-14614)
MONTPELIER AUTO AUCTION OHIO
14125 County Road M50 (43543-9233)
P.O. Box 47 (43543-0047)
PHONE...............................419 485-1691
Bob Hebergsen, *President*
EMP: 150
SALES (est): 12.9MM **Privately Held**
SIC: 5012 5521 Automobile auction; automobiles, used cars only

(G-14615)
MONTPELIER EXEMPTED VLG SCHL (PA)
1015 E Brown Rd (43543-2026)
P.O. Box 193 (43543-0193)
PHONE...............................419 485-3676
Jamison Grime, *Superintendent*
Carla Rice, *Purch Dir*
Lisa Fackler, *Asst Treas*
Connie Shoup, *Nurse*
EMP: 55
SALES: 14.3MM **Privately Held**
WEB: www.montpelier.k12.oh.us
SIC: 8211 7371 Public elementary & secondary schools; computer software development & applications

(G-14616)
MONTPELIER SENIOR CENTER
325 N Jonesville St (43543-1009)
PHONE...............................419 485-3218
Jewel Head, *Director*
EMP: 40
SALES: 71.6K **Privately Held**
SIC: 8399 Community development groups

(G-14617)
NORFOLK SOUTHERN CORPORATION
701 Linden St (43543-1886)
PHONE...............................419 485-3510
S E Smith, *Manager*
EMP: 25
SALES (corp-wide): 11.4B **Publicly Held**
WEB: www.nscorp.com
SIC: 4011 Railroads, line-haul operating
PA: Norfolk Southern Corporation
3 Commercial Pl Ste 1a
Norfolk VA 23510
757 629-2680

(G-14618)
STATE BANK AND TRUST COMPANY
1201 E Main St (43543-1247)
PHONE...............................419 485-5521
Al Fiser, *Branch Mgr*
EMP: 49
SALES (corp-wide): 56.1MM **Publicly Held**
SIC: 6022 6021 State trust companies accepting deposits, commercial; national commercial banks
HQ: The State Bank And Trust Company
401 Clinton St
Defiance OH 43512
419 783-8950

Moraine
Montgomery County

(G-14619)
AIRGAS INC
2400 Sandridge Dr (45439-1849)
PHONE...............................937 222-8312
EMP: 70
SALES (corp-wide): 125.9MM **Privately Held**
SIC: 5169 5084 Compressed gas; welding machinery & equipment
HQ: Airgas, Inc.
259 N Radnor Chester Rd # 100
Radnor PA 19087
610 687-5253

(G-14620)
ANDERSON SEC & FIRE SYSTEMS
Also Called: Anderson Security & Fire Systs
4600 S Dixie Dr (45439-2114)
PHONE...............................937 294-1478
Gaye Anderson, *President*
Sue Henry, *Vice Pres*
EMP: 50
SALES (est): 552.4K
SALES (corp-wide): 5.2MM **Privately Held**
WEB: www.anderson-security.com
SIC: 7381 Security guard service
PA: Anderson Security Inc
4600 S Dixie Dr
Moraine OH 45439
937 294-1478

(G-14621)
ANDERSON SECURITY INC (PA)
4600 S Dixie Dr (45439-2114)
PHONE...............................937 294-1478
Robert A Anderson, *President*
Gaye N Anderson, *President*
Gaye Anderson, *CFO*
EMP: 80
SQ FT: 6,500
SALES (est): 5.2MM **Privately Held**
WEB: www.anderson-security.com
SIC: 7381 7382 Security guard service; security systems services

(G-14622)
ANGEL HEARTS HOME HEALTH INC
2213 Arbor Blvd (45439-1521)
P.O. Box 49383, Dayton (45449-0383)
PHONE...............................937 263-6194
Jeniffer Jones, *President*
EMP: 200
SALES (est): 7.1MM **Privately Held**
SIC: 8059 Personal care home, with health care

(G-14623)
APRIL ENTERPRISES INC
Also Called: Walnut Creek Nursing Facility
5070 Lamme Rd (45439-3266)
PHONE...............................937 293-7703
Heather Isaacs, *Project Mgr*
Diane Gumbert, *CFO*
CAM Swift, *Financial Exec*
Yusef Thomas, *Human Res Dir*
Stephanie Miller, *Nursing Dir*
EMP: 319
SALES (est): 12.6MM **Privately Held**
WEB: www.wcreekoh.com
SIC: 8051 Skilled nursing care facilities

(G-14624)
BDS PACKAGING INC
3155 Elbee Rd Ste 201 (45439-2046)
PHONE...............................937 643-0530
Wendell T Bryant, *President*
Jeff Sloneker, *Vice Pres*
EMP: 58
SQ FT: 78,264
SALES (est): 11.6MM **Privately Held**
WEB: www.bdspackaging.com
SIC: 2653 3993 7389 Boxes, corrugated: made from purchased materials; displays & cutouts, window & lobby; packaging & labeling services

(G-14625)
BERRY NETWORK LLC (DH)
3100 Kettering Blvd (45439-1924)
P.O. Box 8818, Dayton (45401-8818)
PHONE...............................800 366-1264
Joni Arison, *President*
Michelle Hutchinson, *Vice Pres*
Frank McNauly, *Vice Pres*
Tom Smith, *Vice Pres*
Michele Hutchinson, *VP Opers*
EMP: 196
SQ FT: 55,000
SALES (est): 21.5K
SALES (corp-wide): 1.8B **Privately Held**
WEB: www.berrynetwork.com
SIC: 7319 Distribution of advertising material or sample services
HQ: Yp Holdings Llc
2247 Northlake Pkwy Fl 10
Tucker GA 30084
866 570-8863

(G-14626)
BLACK STONE CINCINNATI LLC
Also Called: Assisted Care By Black Stone
3044 Kettering Blvd (45439-1922)
PHONE...............................937 424-1370
David Tramontana, *Branch Mgr*
Kim Sposito, *Director*
EMP: 87
SALES (corp-wide): 13.8MM **Privately Held**
SIC: 8082 Home health care services
PA: Black Stone Of Cincinnati, Llc
4700 E Galbraith Rd Fl 3
Cincinnati OH 45236
513 924-1370

(G-14627)
BOBCAT OF DAYTON INC (PA)
2850 E River Rd Unit 1 (45439-1582)
PHONE...............................937 293-3176
Ruston Pettit, *President*
Byron Pettit, *Vice Pres*
Jack Fain, *Manager*
EMP: 30
SQ FT: 19,200
SALES (est): 10.2MM **Privately Held**
SIC: 5084 7359 Materials handling machinery; industrial truck rental

(G-14628)
BUCKEYE POWER SALES CO INC
Also Called: Lawn & Garden Equipment
5238 Cobblegate Blvd (45439-5114)
PHONE...............................937 346-8322
Jim Watson, *Branch Mgr*
EMP: 29
SALES (corp-wide): 70.1MM **Privately Held**
SIC: 5063 Generators
PA: Buckeye Power Sales Co., Inc.
6850 Commerce Court Dr
Blacklick OH 43004
513 755-2323

(G-14629)
BWI CHASSIS DYNAMICS NA INC
2582 E River Rd (45439-1514)
PHONE...............................937 455-5230
Jeff Zhao, *Branch Mgr*
EMP: 50
SALES (corp-wide): 7.3MM **Privately Held**
SIC: 8734 Testing laboratories

HQ: Bwi Chassis Dynamics (Na), Inc.
12501 Grand River Rd
Brighton MI 48116
937 455-5308

(G-14630)
BWI NORTH AMERICA INC
Also Called: Bwi Group NA
2582 E River Rd (45439-1514)
PHONE...............................937 212-2892
Greg Bowman, *Manager*
EMP: 50
SALES (corp-wide): 7.3MM **Privately Held**
WEB: www.delphiauto.com
SIC: 8734 Product testing laboratories
HQ: Bwi North America Inc.
3100 Res Blvd Ste 240
Kettering OH 45420

(G-14631)
CARAUSTAR INDUSTRIES INC
2601 E River Rd (45439-1533)
PHONE...............................937 298-9969
Bill Theado, *Manager*
EMP: 40
SALES (corp-wide): 3.8B **Publicly Held**
WEB: www.newarkpaperboardproducts.com
SIC: 4953 Recycling, waste materials
HQ: Caraustar Industries, Inc.
5000 Austell Powder Sprin
Austell GA 30106
770 948-3101

(G-14632)
CARDINAL HEALTH 414 LLC
2217 Arbor Blvd (45439-1521)
PHONE...............................937 438-1888
Gary Hoogland, *Sales/Mktg Mgr*
EMP: 30
SALES (corp-wide): 136.8B **Publicly Held**
WEB: www.syncor.com
SIC: 5122 Pharmaceuticals
HQ: Cardinal Health 414, Llc
7000 Cardinal Pl
Dublin OH 43017
614 757-5000

(G-14633)
COMMAND ROOFING CO
2485 Arbor Blvd (45439-1776)
PHONE...............................937 298-1155
Donald L Phlipot, *President*
Rob Hodge, *General Mgr*
Michael R Davis, *Vice Pres*
EMP: 110
SQ FT: 50,000
SALES: 12MM **Privately Held**
WEB: www.commandroofing.com
SIC: 1761 1751 Roofing contractor; carpentry work

(G-14634)
COMMSYS INC
3055 Kettering Blvd # 415 (45439-1900)
PHONE...............................937 220-4990
Robert S Turner, *President*
Linda Mullins, *Financial Analy*
Paul Webb, *Software Dev*
EMP: 26
SQ FT: 4,000
SALES (est): 3.9MM **Privately Held**
WEB: www.commsys.net
SIC: 7373 7371 Systems integration services; computer software systems analysis & design, custom

(G-14635)
COMMUNICATION SVC FOR DEAF INC
Also Called: Communication Svcs For Deaf
2448 W Dorothy Ln (45439-1828)
PHONE...............................937 299-0917
Mike Lamontagne, *Manager*
EMP: 200
SALES (corp-wide): 31.5MM **Privately Held**
WEB: www.relaysd.com
SIC: 4899 Data communication services
PA: Communication Service For The Deaf, Inc.
2028 E B White 240-5250
Austin TX 78741
844 222-0002

(G-14636)
COMPUNET CLINICAL LABS LLC (HQ)
Also Called: Compunet Clinical Labs
2308 Sandridge Dr (45439-1856)
PHONE................................937 296-0844
James Pancoast, *President*
Teresa Williams, *COO*
John Manier, *CFO*
EMP: 250
SALES (est): 47.4MM
SALES (corp-wide): 17.2K **Privately Held**
SIC: 8071 Medical laboratories
PA: Premier Health Partners
110 N Main St Ste 450
Dayton OH 45402
937 499-9596

(G-14637)
COUNTY OF MONTGOMERY
Also Called: Montgomery County N Incertr
2550 Sandridge Dr (45439-1851)
PHONE................................937 781-3046
Fax: 937 454-8133
EMP: 40
SQ FT: 672 **Privately Held**
SIC: 4953 Incinerator Operation
PA: County Of Montgomery
451 W 3rd St Fl 4
Dayton OH 45422
937 225-4000

(G-14638)
CUSHMAN & WAKEFIELD INC
Also Called: Cassidy Turley
3033 Kettering Blvd # 111 (45439-1948)
PHONE................................937 222-7884
Mark Burkhart, *President*
EMP: 48
SALES (corp-wide): 1.2MM **Privately Held**
SIC: 6531 Real estate agent, commercial
HQ: Cushman & Wakefield, Inc.
225 W Wacker Dr Ste 3000
Chicago IL 60606
312 424-8000

(G-14639)
DAVIS PAUL RESTORATION DAYTON
Also Called: Paul Davis Restoration
1960 W Dorothy Ln Ste 207 (45439-1818)
PHONE................................937 436-3411
Mark Adley, *Partner*
Scott Siens, *Project Mgr*
Mark Bradley,
EMP: 27
SQ FT: 2,400
SALES (est): 3.1MM **Privately Held**
SIC: 1521 Repairing fire damage, single-family houses

(G-14640)
DAY-MET CREDIT UNION INC (PA)
3199 S Dixie Dr (45439-2207)
P.O. Box 13087, Dayton (45413-0087)
PHONE................................937 236-2562
Walt Helman, *CEO*
Jerry Scalf, *Ch of Bd*
Tom Keyes, *Business Mgr*
Kevin Van Bibber, *Vice Pres*
Tammy Bretzfelder, *Loan Officer*
EMP: 26
SQ FT: 15,000
SALES: 4.6MM **Privately Held**
WEB: www.daymetcu.com
SIC: 6061 Federal credit unions

(G-14641)
DAY-MONT BHVORAL HLTH CARE INC (PA)
Also Called: Day-Mont Behavioral Hlth Care
2710 Dryden Rd (45439-1614)
PHONE................................937 222-8111
Gayle Johnson, *President*
Akil Sharif, *Vice Pres*
Marva Busby, *Exec Sec*
EMP: 100
SQ FT: 33,000
SALES: 5MM **Privately Held**
WEB: www.daymont.org
SIC: 8093 Specialty Outpatient Clinic

(G-14642)
DAYTON DOG TRAINING CLUB INC
3040 E River Rd Ste 5 (45439-1436)
PHONE................................937 293-5219
Cathy Hahn, *Director*
EMP: 30
SALES (est): 367.7K **Privately Held**
WEB: www.daytondogtraining.com
SIC: 0752 Training services, pet & animal specialties (not horses)

(G-14643)
DAYTON HEIDELBERG DISTRG CO (PA)
Also Called: Heidelberg Distributing Div
3601 Dryden Rd (45439-1411)
PHONE................................937 222-8692
Albert W Vontz III, *CEO*
Vail Miller, *Ch of Bd*
Steve Lowrey, *President*
Brian Gross, *General Mgr*
Bob Bilius, *Vice Pres*
▲ EMP: 200
SQ FT: 165,000
SALES (est): 369.4MM **Privately Held**
SIC: 5181 Beer & other fermented malt liquors

(G-14644)
DAYTON HEIDELBERG DISTRG CO
3601 Dryden Rd (45439-1411)
PHONE................................937 220-6450
EMP: 60
SALES (corp-wide): 369.4MM **Privately Held**
SIC: 5199 Advertising specialties
PA: Dayton Heidelberg Distributing Co.
3601 Dryden Rd
Moraine OH 45439
937 222-8692

(G-14645)
DAYTON HEIDELBERG DISTRG CO
Service Distributing Div
3601 Dryden Rd (45439-1411)
PHONE................................937 220-6450
Steven Lowery, *President*
EMP: 127
SALES (corp-wide): 369.4MM **Privately Held**
SIC: 5181 5182 5149 5921 Beer & other fermented malt liquors; wine; groceries & related products; beer (packaged)
PA: Dayton Heidelberg Distributing Co.
3601 Dryden Rd
Moraine OH 45439
937 222-8692

(G-14646)
DAYTON MARSHALL TIRE SALES CO
3091 S Dixie Dr (45439-2205)
PHONE................................937 293-8330
John Marshall, *President*
Charles L Marshall II, *Corp Secy*
Tony Fiori, *Manager*
Steve Whitehead, *Manager*
EMP: 26 EST: 1972
SQ FT: 24,000
SALES (est): 4.1MM **Privately Held**
SIC: 5531 5014 Automotive tires; automobile tires & tubes

(G-14647)
DAYTON POWER AND LIGHT COMPANY
1900 Dryden Rd (45439-1762)
P.O. Box 1247, Dayton (45401-1247)
PHONE................................937 331-4123
Charles F Hatfield, *Principal*
Nancy Clark, *Business Anlyst*
Ted Brewer, *Security Mgr*
Bruce Taylor, *Manager*
Georgene Dawson, *Manager*
EMP: 60
SALES (corp-wide): 10.7B **Publicly Held**
WEB: www.waytogo.com
SIC: 4931 4932 4923 4911 Electric & other services combined; gas & other services combined; gas transmission & distribution; electric services
HQ: The Dayton Power And Light Company
1065 Woodman Dr
Dayton OH 45432
937 331-4063

(G-14648)
DONNELLON MC CARTHY INC
2580 Lance Dr (45409-1512)
PHONE................................937 299-3564
Rob Lee, *Manager*
EMP: 35
SALES (corp-wide): 34.3MM **Privately Held**
WEB: www.dmdayton.com
SIC: 5044 Photocopy machines
PA: Donnellon Mc Carthy, Inc.
10855 Medallion Dr
Cincinnati OH 45241
513 769-7800

(G-14649)
DONNELLON MC CARTHY INC
2580 Lance Dr (45409-1512)
PHONE................................937 299-0200
Jim Donnellon, *General Mgr*
EMP: 50
SALES (corp-wide): 34.3MM **Privately Held**
WEB: www.dmdayton.com
SIC: 5999 5065 Photocopy machines; facsimile equipment
PA: Donnellon Mc Carthy, Inc.
10855 Medallion Dr
Cincinnati OH 45241
513 769-7800

(G-14650)
E S GALLON & ASSOCIATES
Also Called: Gallon, E S Associates
2621 Dryden Rd Ste 105 (45439-1646)
PHONE................................937 586-3100
Joseph Ebenger, *President*
David Saphire, *Treasurer*
Rebecca A Schott, *Administration*
Joann Brenner, *Admin Sec*
Pearlie Brewer,
EMP: 40 EST: 1953
SALES (est): 3.6MM **Privately Held**
WEB: www.esgallon.com
SIC: 8111 General practice law office; general practice attorney, lawyer

(G-14651)
ECG SCANNING & MEDICAL SVCS (DH)
3055 Kettering Blvd 219b (45439-1900)
PHONE................................888 346-5837
John Nasuti, *President*
Joseph Maclean, *COO*
Amanda Hayes, *Controller*
Denise Van Tongeren-Nicolai, *Officer*
EMP: 25
SQ FT: 7,500
SALES (est): 3.3MM
SALES (corp-wide): 399.4MM **Publicly Held**
WEB: www.ecgscanning.com
SIC: 8071 Testing laboratories
HQ: Cardionet, Llc
1000 Cedar Hollow Rd
Malvern PA 19355
610 729-7000

(G-14652)
ELASTIZELL SYSTEMS INC
2475 Arbor Blvd (45439-1754)
PHONE................................937 298-1313
Donald L Phlipot, *President*
Jeannine E Phlipot, *Treasurer*
Tom Buettmann, *Sales Mgr*
EMP: 50 EST: 1972
SQ FT: 6,000
SALES (est): 5.9MM **Privately Held**
SIC: 1771 Concrete work

(G-14653)
ENTING WATER CONDITIONING INC (PA)
Also Called: Superior Water Conditioning Co
3211 Dryden Rd Frnt Frnt (45439-1400)
PHONE................................937 294-5100
Mel Entingh, *CEO*
Dan Entingh, *President*
Amber Entingh, *Purchasing*
Karen Entingh, *Treasurer*
Doris Entingh, *Admin Sec*
▲ EMP: 31 EST: 1965
SQ FT: 43,440
SALES (est): 3.2MM **Privately Held**
WEB: www.enting.com
SIC: 3589 5999 5074 Water filters & softeners, household type; water purification equipment, household type; water treatment equipment, industrial; water purification equipment; water purification equipment; water softeners

(G-14654)
EVERYBODYS INC
Also Called: Everybodys Workplace Solutions
3050 Springboro Pike (45439-1812)
PHONE................................937 293-1010
Bill Kasch, *President*
Scot Freeman, *COO*
Thomas Shafer, *Vice Pres*
Bill Grace, *VP Bus Dvlpt*
EMP: 50
SQ FT: 80,000
SALES (est): 13.4MM **Privately Held**
WEB: www.everybodysinc.com
SIC: 5021 7641 5023 Office furniture; furniture repair & maintenance; carpets

(G-14655)
FAMILY SERVICE ASSOCIATION
Also Called: FAMILY SERVICES AND COMMUNITY
2211 Arbor Blvd (45439-1521)
PHONE................................937 222-9481
Bonnie Parrish, *Exec Dir*
EMP: 50 EST: 1896
SQ FT: 7,700
SALES: 1.5MM **Privately Held**
SIC: 8322 Social service center

(G-14656)
FEDERATED LOGISTICS
Also Called: Eletto Transfer
2260 Arbor Blvd (45439-1522)
PHONE................................937 294-3074
Mark Powell, *Opers Staff*
EMP: 25
SALES (est): 1.9MM **Privately Held**
SIC: 5021 Furniture

(G-14657)
FIDELITY HEALTH CARE
3170 Kettering Blvd (45439-1924)
PHONE................................937 208-6400
Paula Thompson, *President*
Renee Mock, *CFO*
EMP: 450
SQ FT: 30,000
SALES: 41.8MM
SALES (corp-wide): 968.3MM **Privately Held**
WEB: www.fidelityhealthcare.com
SIC: 8082 Home health care services
PA: Med America Health Systems Corporation
1 Wyoming St
Dayton OH 45409
937 223-6192

(G-14658)
FIELDSTONE LIMITED PARTNERSHIP (PA)
Also Called: Fox Run Apartments
4000 Miller Valentine Ct (45439)
PHONE................................937 293-0900
Dan Keller, *Principal*
Steve Ireland, *Vice Pres*
Kevin Kerr, *Project Mgr*
EMP: 200
SALES (est): 4.7MM **Privately Held**
SIC: 6513 Apartment building operators

(G-14659)
FLAGEL HUBER FLAGEL & CO (PA)
3400 S Dixie Dr (45439-2304)
PHONE................................937 299-3400
James R Harkwall, *Partner*
Linda Hadley, *General Mgr*
Randal Kuvin, *Mng Member*
Kevin Hagstrom, *Manager*
Erin Kliesch, *Manager*
EMP: 50
SQ FT: 13,200
SALES (est): 5.6MM **Privately Held**
WEB: www.fhf-cpa.com
SIC: 8721 Certified public accountant

(G-14660)
GARDA CL TECHNICAL SVCS INC
2690 Lance Dr (45409-1527)
PHONE...............................937 294-4099
Steve Fosnot, *Branch Mgr*
EMP: 34 Privately Held
SIC: 7381 3578 4513 Armored car services; coin counters; air courier services
HQ: Garda Cl Technical Services, Inc.
　700 S Federal Hwy Ste 300
　Boca Raton FL 33432

(G-14661)
GLEN ARBORS LTD PARTNERSHIP
4000 Miller Valentine Ct (45439)
PHONE...............................937 293-0900
Miller-Valentine Apts Etc, *Partner*
Edward Blake, *Manager*
EMP: 100 EST: 1997
SALES (est): 5.1MM Privately Held
SIC: 6512 Nonresidential building operators

(G-14662)
GLOBE FOOD EQUIPMENT COMPANY
2153 Dryden Rd (45439-1739)
PHONE...............................937 299-5493
Hilton Garner, *President*
Tom Randall, *Mfg Staff*
Michelle Throop, *Accountant*
Justin Fox, *Manager*
Stephanie Gray, *Technology*
▲ EMP: 39
SALES: 50MM
SALES (corp-wide): 2.7B Publicly Held
WEB: www.globeslicers.com
SIC: 5046 Restaurant equipment & supplies
PA: The Middleby Corporation
　1400 Toastmaster Dr
　Elgin IL 60120
　847 741-3300

(G-14663)
GLT INC
2691 Lance Dr (45409-1515)
PHONE...............................937 395-0508
Brad Labensky, *Branch Mgr*
EMP: 25
SALES (est): 891.8K
SALES (corp-wide): 11.3MM Privately Held
WEB: www.gltonline.com
SIC: 1796 Machinery installation
PA: Glt, Inc.
　3341 Successful Way
　Dayton OH 45414
　937 237-0055

(G-14664)
GRACE HOSPICE LLC
3033 Kettering Blvd # 220 (45439-1948)
PHONE...............................937 293-1381
Janice Urke, *Administration*
EMP: 115 Privately Held
SIC: 8052 Personal care facility
PA: Grace Hospice, Llc
　500 Kirts Blvd Ste 250
　Troy MI 48084

(G-14665)
GROUNDSYSTEMS INC
2929 Northlawn Ave (45439-1647)
PHONE...............................937 903-5325
Rachel Rorie, *Vice Pres*
Mike Graves, *Accounts Mgr*
Steve Barhorst, *Branch Mgr*
EMP: 30
SALES (corp-wide): 22.3MM Privately Held
SIC: 0782 Landscape contractors
PA: Groundsystems, Inc.
　11315 Williamson Rd
　Blue Ash OH 45241
　800 570-0213

(G-14666)
KASTLE ELECTRIC CO LLC
4501 Kettering Blvd (45439-2137)
PHONE...............................937 254-2681
Dennis Quebe, *CEO*
K Andrew Stuhlmiller, *President*

Gregory Ross, *COO*
William Page, *CFO*
EMP: 53
SQ FT: 20,000
SALES (est): 1.8MM
SALES (corp-wide): 66.4MM Privately Held
SIC: 1731 General electrical contractor
PA: Quebe Holdings, Inc.
　1985 Founders Dr
　Dayton OH 45420
　937 222-2290

(G-14667)
KASTLE ELECTRIC COMPANY
4501 Kettering Blvd (45439-2137)
P.O. Box 1451, Dayton (45401-1451)
PHONE...............................937 254-2681
K Andrew Stuhlmiller, *CEO*
Gregory P Brush, *President*
William S Page, *CFO*
Andy Stuhlmiller, *Admin Mgr*
EMP: 120 EST: 1925
SALES (est): 2.4MM Privately Held
WEB: www.kastle-elec.com
SIC: 1731 General electrical contractor

(G-14668)
KETTERING ADVENTIST HEALTHCARE
Also Called: Kettering Hospital Youth Svcs
5350 Lamme Rd (45439-3215)
PHONE...............................937 534-4651
Dorawbaugh David, *Manager*
EMP: 61
SALES (corp-wide): 1.7B Privately Held
SIC: 8062 General medical & surgical hospitals
PA: Kettering Adventist Healthcare
　3535 Southern Blvd
　Dayton OH 45429
　937 298-4331

(G-14669)
KIDS IN NEED FOUNDATION
3055 Kettering Blvd # 119 (45439-1900)
PHONE...............................937 296-1230
David Smith, *CEO*
Becky Shaw, *Accounting Dir*
Gina Palmer, *Program Dir*
Cheri Eck, *Executive Asst*
EMP: 25
SQ FT: 1,370
SALES: 121.9MM Privately Held
SIC: 8699 Charitable organization

(G-14670)
L M BERRY AND COMPANY (PA)
3170 Kettering Blvd (45439-1924)
PHONE...............................937 296-2121
Daniel J Graham, *President*
Greg Prince, *Opers Staff*
Joleen Neeley, *Manager*
Sonya Crocker, *Training Dir*
EMP: 650
SQ FT: 141,000
SALES (est): 69.2MM Privately Held
WEB: www.lmberry.com
SIC: 7311 2741 Advertising agencies; miscellaneous publishing

(G-14671)
MANDALAY INC
Also Called: Mandalay Banquet Center
2700 E River Rd (45439-1536)
PHONE...............................937 294-6600
Donald L Phillips, *Ch of Bd*
Cay Phillips, *President*
EMP: 42
SQ FT: 72,000
SALES (est): 2.1MM Privately Held
WEB: www.mandalaycatering.com
SIC: 7299 Banquet hall facilities

(G-14672)
MCGOHAN/BRABENDER AGENCY INC (PA)
Also Called: McGohan Brabender
3931 S Dixie Dr (45439-2313)
PHONE...............................937 293-1600
Scott McGohan, *CEO*
Patrick L McGohan, *CEO*
Tim Brabender, *President*
Lisa Block, *Vice Pres*
Bud Hauser, *VP Opers*
EMP: 73

SQ FT: 1,400
SALES (est): 34.2MM Privately Held
WEB: www.mcgohanbrabender.com
SIC: 6411 Insurance agents

(G-14673)
MDU RESOURCES GROUP INC
Also Called: Capital Electric
3150 Encrete Ln (45439-1902)
PHONE...............................937 424-2550
Steve Taulbee, *Branch Mgr*
EMP: 25
SALES (corp-wide): 4.5B Publicly Held
SIC: 1731 General electrical contractor
PA: Mdu Resources Group, Inc.
　1200 W Century Ave
　Bismarck ND 58503
　701 530-1000

(G-14674)
MED-TRANS INC
3510 Encrete Ln (45439-1951)
PHONE...............................937 293-9771
Jim Shiverdecker, *Manager*
EMP: 32
SALES (corp-wide): 18.6MM Privately Held
WEB: www.med-trans.com
SIC: 4119 Ambulance service
PA: Med-Trans, Inc
　714 W Columbia St
　Springfield OH 45504
　937 325-4926

(G-14675)
MEDICAL ACCOUNT SERVICES INC
3131 S Dixie Dr Ste 535 (45439-2223)
PHONE...............................937 297-6072
David Ackley, *CEO*
EMP: 30
SQ FT: 8,200
SALES (est): 1.5MM
SALES (corp-wide): 69.6MM Privately Held
WEB: www.medacct.com
SIC: 8721 8742 Billing & bookkeeping service; management consulting services
PA: Advantedge Healthcare Solutions, Inc.
　30 Technology Dr Ste 1n
　Warren NJ 07059
　908 279-8111

(G-14676)
MEDVET ASSOCIATES INC
2714 Springboro W (45439-1710)
PHONE...............................937 293-2714
EMP: 348 Privately Held
SIC: 0742 Veterinarian, animal specialties
PA: Medvet Associates, Inc
　300 E Wilson Bridge Rd # 100
　Worthington OH 43085

(G-14677)
MIAMI INDUSTRIAL TRUCKS INC (PA)
2830 E River Rd (45439-1500)
PHONE...............................937 293-4194
Mark Jones, *CEO*
Bill Miller, *Editor*
George Malacos, *Chairman*
Matt Malacos, *Vice Pres*
Jim Shriner, *Opers Mgr*
EMP: 75
SQ FT: 43,000
SALES (est): 51.9MM Privately Held
WEB: www.mitlift.com
SIC: 5084 7359 7699 Materials handling machinery; equipment rental & leasing; industrial equipment services; industrial truck repair

(G-14678)
MILLER CONSOLIDATED INDUSTRIES (PA)
2221 Arbor Blvd (45439-1521)
PHONE...............................937 294-2681
Larry Cartwright, *Vice Pres*
Tom Miller, *CFO*
Ben Eisbart, *Human Res Dir*
Kelly Henderson, *Director*
EMP: 106
SQ FT: 55,000

SALES (est): 19.3MM Privately Held
WEB: www.millerconsolidated.com
SIC: 5051 3398 Steel; metal heat treating

(G-14679)
MILLER-VALENTINE PARTNERS
4000 Miller Valentine Ct (45439-1465)
PHONE...............................937 293-0900
EMP: 200
SALES (est): 6.1MM Privately Held
SIC: 6512 Operator Of Commercial & Industrial Bldgs

(G-14680)
MIRACLECORP PRODUCTS (PA)
2425 W Dorothy Ln (45439-1827)
PHONE...............................937 293-9994
William M Sherk Jr, *President*
Patricia Weimer, *CFO*
Debbie Wietzel, *Sales Mgr*
Ron Castonguay, *Sales Staff*
Susie Lovy, *Mktg Dir*
◆ EMP: 55
SQ FT: 11,500
SALES: 21MM Privately Held
WEB: www.miraclecorp.com
SIC: 3999 0752 5999 Pet supplies; animal specialty services; pet supplies

(G-14681)
MOONLIGHT SECURITY INC
2710 Dryden Rd (45439-1614)
PHONE...............................937 252-1600
John Pawelski, *President*
EMP: 85
SQ FT: 13,000
SALES (est): 2.1MM Privately Held
SIC: 7381 Security guard service

(G-14682)
MV RESIDENTIAL DEVELOPMENT LLC
4000 Miller Valentine Ct (45439)
PHONE...............................937 293-0900
Pat George, *Superintendent*
Michael B Green, *Mng Member*
David R Liette, *Manager*
EMP: 25
SALES (est): 1.6MM Privately Held
SIC: 6552 Subdividers & developers

(G-14683)
NEXSTAR BROADCASTING INC
Also Called: Wdtn
4595 S Dixie Dr (45439-2111)
PHONE...............................937 293-2101
Jackie Lainhart, *Human Res Dir*
EMP: 80
SALES (corp-wide): 2.7B Publicly Held
WEB: www.wluk.com
SIC: 4833 Television broadcasting stations
HQ: Nexstar Broadcasting, Inc.
　545 E John Carpenter Fwy # 700
　Irving TX 75062
　972 373-8800

(G-14684)
NOLAND COMPANY (HQ)
Also Called: Greenville Noland
3110 Kettering Blvd (45439-1924)
PHONE...............................937 396-7980
Arjay Hoggard, *President*
James H Adcox, *COO*
Jack W Johnston, *Vice Pres*
Monte L Salsman, *Vice Pres*
Jeremy Streno, *Opers Mgr*
◆ EMP: 224 EST: 1915
SALES (est): 248.7MM
SALES (corp-wide): 4.9B Privately Held
WEB: www.noland.com
SIC: 5074 5075 5063 5085 Plumbing & hydronic heating supplies; air conditioning equipment, except room units; electrical supplies; industrial supplies
PA: Winsupply Inc.
　3110 Kettering Blvd
　Moraine OH 45439
　937 294-5331

(G-14685)
NORFOLK SOUTHERN CORPORATION
3101 Springboro Pike (45439-1970)
PHONE...............................937 297-5420
Mike Fender, *Manager*
EMP: 43

▲ = Import ▼=Export
◆ =Import/Export

SALES (corp-wide): 11.4B **Publicly Held**
WEB: www.nscorp.com
SIC: 4011 Railroads, line-haul operating
PA: Norfolk Southern Corporation
   3 Commercial Pl Ste 1a
   Norfolk VA 23510
   757 629-2680

(G-14686)
P C VPA
3033 Kettering Blvd # 100 (45439-1948)
PHONE..................................937 293-2133
EMP: 34 **Privately Held**
SIC: 8011 Geriatric specialist,
   physician/surgeon
PA: P C Vpa
   500 Kirts Blvd Ste 200
   Troy MI 48084

(G-14687)
PRIME TIME PARTY RENTAL INC
5225 Springboro Pike (45439-2970)
PHONE..................................937 296-9262
Bart A Nye, *President*
Dave Sercu, *General Mgr*
Frances McDonagh, *Opers Staff*
Christina Pearson, *Controller*
Christine Welsh, *Controller*
EMP: 33
SQ FT: 17,000
SALES (est): 5.7MM **Privately Held**
WEB: www.primetimepartyrental.com
SIC: 7359 Party supplies rental services

(G-14688)
PROVIDENCE HEALTH PARTNERS LLC
2912 Springboro W Ste 201 (45439-1674)
PHONE..................................937 297-8999
Susan Becker, *COO*
Cheryl Burns, *Project Mgr*
Mike Gross, *Director*
EMP: 50
SALES (est): 2.7MM **Privately Held**
SIC: 8741 Business management; financial
   management for business; administrative
   management

(G-14689)
PROVIDENCE MEDICAL GROUP INC
2912 Springboro W Ste 201 (45439-1674)
PHONE..................................937 297-8999
Susan Becker, *COO*
Brenden Wynn, *Opers Mgr*
Kim Hilton, *Purchasing*
Debbie Shockley, *Research*
Leslie Garrett, *Nurse*
EMP: 99
SALES (est): 11.3MM **Privately Held**
SIC: 8741 Administrative management

(G-14690)
QUALITY STEELS CORP (HQ)
2221 Arbor Blvd (45439-1521)
PHONE..................................937 294-4133
Thomas Miller, *President*
Alice L Miller, *Corp Secy*
EMP: 30
SQ FT: 42,000
SALES (est): 12MM
SALES (corp-wide): 19.3MM **Privately Held**
WEB: www.qualitysteels.com
SIC: 5051 Steel
PA: Miller Consolidated Industries Inc
   2221 Arbor Blvd
   Moraine OH 45439
   937 294-2681

(G-14691)
R G SELLERS COMPANY (PA)
Also Called: R G Seller Co
3185 Elbee Rd (45439-1919)
PHONE..................................937 299-1545
Doug Sellers, *CEO*
Barbara Sellers, *Corp Secy*
Tom Sellers, *Vice Pres*
EMP: 37
SQ FT: 10,500
SALES (est): 8.2MM **Privately Held**
SIC: 5141 Food brokers

(G-14692)
RANAC COMPUTER CORPORATION
3460 S Dixie Dr (45439-2304)
PHONE..................................317 844-0141
Keith A Pitzele, *President*
EMP: 26
SQ FT: 5,200
SALES (est): 2.2MM **Privately Held**
WEB: www.ranac.com
SIC: 7373 Turnkey vendors, computer sys-
   tems; value-added resellers, computer
   systems

(G-14693)
RSM US LLP
2000 W Dorothy Ln (45439-1820)
PHONE..................................937 298-0201
Charlie Foley, *Managing Prtnr*
EMP: 105
SALES (corp-wide): 2.1B **Privately Held**
SIC: 8721 Certified public accountant
PA: Rsm Us Llp
   1 S Wacker Dr Ste 800
   Chicago IL 60606
   312 384-6000

(G-14694)
SANDYS AUTO & TRUCK SVC INC
3053 Springboro W (45439-1811)
PHONE..................................937 461-4980
Ted Durig, *President*
Doug Thomas, *Vice Pres*
Ryan Templin, *Sales Staff*
EMP: 60
SQ FT: 14,000
SALES (est): 4.4MM **Privately Held**
WEB: www.sandystowing.com
SIC: 7549 Towing service, automotive

(G-14695)
SANDYS TOWING (PA)
3053 Springboro W (45439-1811)
PHONE..................................937 461-4980
Ted Durig, *President*
EMP: 28
SALES (est): 4.5MM **Privately Held**
SIC: 7549 Towing service, automotive; tow-
   ing services

(G-14696)
SERCO INC
2210 Arbor Blvd Ste 200 (45439-1506)
PHONE..................................937 331-4180
James Shaddox, *Branch Mgr*
Kathy Reeves, *Admin Asst*
EMP: 50
SALES (corp-wide): 3.9B **Privately Held**
WEB: www.serco.com
SIC: 8744 Facilities support services
HQ: Serco Inc.
   12930 Worldgate Dr # 600
   Herndon VA 20170

(G-14697)
SNYDER CONCRETE PRODUCTS INC (PA)
Also Called: Snyder Brick and Block
2301 W Dorothy Ln (45439-1825)
PHONE..................................937 885-5176
Lee E Snyder, *CEO*
Mark Snyder, *Vice Pres*
Julie Flory, *Treasurer*
Todd Hopf, *Controller*
Joe Rohrer, *Sales Mgr*
▲ EMP: 25
SQ FT: 50,000
SALES (est): 12.6MM **Privately Held**
WEB: www.snyderonline.com
SIC: 5032 3271 3272 Brick, except re-
   fractory; concrete & cinder building prod-
   ucts; blocks, concrete or cinder: standard;
   concrete products

(G-14698)
SOUTH COMMUNITY INC (PA)
3095 Kettering Blvd Ste 1 (45439-1983)
PHONE..................................937 293-8300
Carol Smerz, *President*
Marianne Saunders, *Mktg Dir*
Jeni Sand, *Marketing Mgr*
Maria Mathias, *Med Doctor*
Carol Gaeke, *Manager*
EMP: 205

SQ FT: 40,883
SALES: 19.1MM **Privately Held**
SIC: 8093 Mental health clinic, outpatient

(G-14699)
SOUTHTOWN HEATING & COOLING
3024 Springboro W (45439-1716)
PHONE..................................937 320-9900
Joe Trame, *President*
Terri Trame, *Vice Pres*
EMP: 26
SQ FT: 3,000
SALES (est): 4.8MM **Privately Held**
WEB: www.southtownheatingcooling.com
SIC: 1711 1731 7349 5999 Warm air
   heating & air conditioning contractor;
   electrical work; air duct cleaning; plumb-
   ing & heating supplies; fireplaces & wood
   burning stoves; oil & gas pipeline con-
   struction

(G-14700)
SUNRISE TELEVISION CORP
Also Called: Wdtn
4595 S Dixie Dr (45439-2111)
P.O. Box 741, Dayton (45401-0741)
PHONE..................................937 293-2101
EMP: 105
SALES (corp-wide): 674.9MM **Publicly Held**
SIC: 4833 Television Station
HQ: Sunrise Television Corp.
   1 W Exchange St Ste 5a
   Providence RI

(G-14701)
TANNER HEATING & AC INC
2238 E River Rd (45439-1520)
PHONE..................................937 299-2500
Robert F Tanner, *President*
David M Tanner, *Vice Pres*
Thomas Tanner, *Vice Pres*
EMP: 45
SQ FT: 17,500
SALES (est): 7.2MM **Privately Held**
WEB: www.tannerhtg-ac.com
SIC: 1711 Warm air heating & air condi-
   tioning contractor; ventilation & duct work
   contractor

(G-14702)
TESTAMERICA LABORATORIES INC
2017 Springboro W (45439-1665)
PHONE..................................937 294-6856
Debra Lowe, *Systems Mgr*
EMP: 75
SALES (corp-wide): 983.9MM **Privately Held**
WEB: www.stl-inc.com
SIC: 8734 Testing laboratories
HQ: Testamerica Laboratories, Inc.
   4101 Shuffel St Nw # 100
   North Canton OH 44720
   800 456-9396

(G-14703)
TYLER TECHNOLOGIES INC
Cole Layer Trumble Company Div
4100 Miller Valentine Ct (45439)
PHONE..................................937 276-5261
Kim Frisby, *Vice Pres*
Scott Scarborough, *Corp Comm Staff*
Bruce Nagel, *Branch Mgr*
Margie Belles, *Supervisor*
Mary Sue Livensperger, *Director*
EMP: 200
SALES (corp-wide): 935.2MM **Publicly Held**
WEB: www.tylertechnologies.com
SIC: 7389 Auction, appraisal & exchange
   services
PA: Tyler Technologies, Inc.
   5101 Tennyson Pkwy
   Plano TX 75024
   972 713-3700

(G-14704)
VAN MAYBERRYS & STORAGE INC
1850 Cardington Rd (45409-1503)
PHONE..................................937 298-8800
William Mayberry Jr, *President*
James Roberts, *General Mgr*

Victoria Voehringer, *Corp Secy*
Tom Maguire, *Opers Mgr*
EMP: 35
SQ FT: 35,000
SALES (est): 5.2MM **Privately Held**
SIC: 4213 4214 Household goods trans-
   port; local trucking with storage

(G-14705)
WAGNER INDUSTRIAL ELECTRIC INC (HQ)
Also Called: Wagner Smith Company
3178 Encrete Ln (45439-1902)
P.O. Box 55, Dayton (45401-0055)
PHONE..................................937 298-7481
James A Fortkamp, *President*
Thomas Cope, *Vice Pres*
Mark Blankenship, *Project Mgr*
Shawn Stamps, *Foreman/Supr*
Darrell Shryer, *Info Tech Mgr*
EMP: 25
SALES (est): 13.4MM
SALES (corp-wide): 4.5B **Publicly Held**
WEB: www.wagnersmith.com
SIC: 1731 Electrical Contractor
PA: Mdu Resources Group, Inc.
   1200 W Century Ave
   Bismarck ND 58503
   701 530-1000

(G-14706)
WAKONI DIALYSIS LLC
Also Called: Dayton South Dialysis
4700 Springboro Pike A (45439-1964)
PHONE..................................937 294-7188
Lisa Smiley, *Administration*
EMP: 31
SALES (est): 268.4K **Publicly Held**
SIC: 8092 Kidney dialysis centers
PA: Davita Inc.
   2000 16th St
   Denver CO 80202

(G-14707)
WINSUPPLY INC (PA)
Also Called: Wss- Dayton
3110 Kettering Blvd (45439-1924)
P.O. Box 1127, Dayton (45401-1127)
PHONE..................................937 294-5331
Roland Gordon, *President*
James Reese, *General Mgr*
Richard W Schwartz, *Chairman*
Bill Summers, *Area Mgr*
Jack Osenbaugh, *COO*
EMP: 100
SQ FT: 20,000
SALES (est): 4.9B **Privately Held**
SIC: 1542 5085 5074 Commercial & of-
   fice building contractors; industrial sup-
   plies; plumbing fittings & supplies

(G-14708)
YECK BROTHERS COMPANY
2222 Arbor Blvd (45439-1522)
P.O. Box 225, Dayton (45401-0225)
PHONE..................................937 294-4000
Bob Yeck, *President*
Janet Archer, *Accounts Mgr*
Mary Taylor, *Accounts Mgr*
Linda Brawley, *Manager*
Bev Roof, *Manager*
EMP: 35
SQ FT: 35,000
SALES: 3.4MM **Privately Held**
WEB: www.yeck.com
SIC: 1731 7331 Access control systems
   specialization; mailing service

(G-14709)
YOWELL TRANSPORTATION SVC INC
1840 Cardington Rd (45409-1503)
PHONE..................................937 294-5933
Victor Yowell, *President*
Neil T Yowell III, *Principal*
Joe Ford, *Vice Pres*
EMP: 75
SQ FT: 22,000
SALES (est): 13.1MM **Privately Held**
SIC: 4213 4214 Contract haulers; local
   trucking with storage

Moreland Hills
Cuyahoga County

(G-14710)
GALT ENTERPRISES INC
34555 Chagrin Blvd # 100 (44022-1068)
P.O. Box 22189, Cleveland (44122-0189)
PHONE....................................216 464-6744
Lee M Hoffman, *President*
Sherry Kahn, *Accountant*
Pam Sanford, *Accounts Mgr*
Mesut Kose, *IT/INT Sup*
Julianne M Seders, *Officer*
EMP: 50 **EST:** 1977
SQ FT: 5,000
SALES: 6.1MM **Privately Held**
WEB: www.galtenterprises.com
SIC: 6411 Insurance agents

Morral
Marion County

(G-14711)
FETTER AND SON LLC
Also Called: Fetter and Son Farms
2421 Mrral Krkptrick Rd W (43337-9314)
P.O. Box 38 (43337-0038)
PHONE....................................740 465-2961
Steven Fetter,
EMP: 39
SQ FT: 5,000
SALES: 5.3MM **Privately Held**
SIC: 4213 Contract haulers

(G-14712)
FETTER SON FARMS LTD LBLTY CO
2421 Mrral Krkptrick Rd W (43337-9314)
P.O. Box 38 (43337-0038)
PHONE....................................740 465-2961
Steven K Fetter, *Principal*
T Jane Fetter, *Principal*
Steven Fetter, *Mng Member*
EMP: 35
SALES (est): 3.1MM **Privately Held**
SIC: 4213 Contract haulers

(G-14713)
MORRAL COMPANIES LLC (HQ)
132 Postle Ave (43337-7505)
P.O. Box 26 (43337-0026)
PHONE....................................740 465-3251
Daryl Gates, *CEO*
Sandy Wampler, *Senior VP*
John Hartshorn, *QC Mgr*
Joe Cunningham, *CFO*
Brian Braumiller, *Sales Staff*
EMP: 46
SQ FT: 15,000
SALES: 25.4MM **Privately Held**
WEB: www.morralcompanies.com
SIC: 4783 5191 Packing & crating; fertilizer & fertilizer materials

Morrow
Warren County

(G-14714)
BEL-WOOD COUNTRY CLUB INC
5873 Ludlum Rd (45152-8364)
P.O. Box 195 (45152-0195)
PHONE....................................513 899-3361
Michelle Rooney, *General Mgr*
EMP: 60
SQ FT: 12,052
SALES (est): 3.4MM **Privately Held**
SIC: 7997 5812 Country club, membership; eating places

(G-14715)
BROWNING-FERRIS INDUSTRIES INC
Also Called: Site L10
2420 Mason Morrow Millgro (45152-9605)
PHONE....................................513 899-2942
Rob Dolder, *Manager*

EMP: 38
SQ FT: 5,896
SALES (corp-wide): 10B **Publicly Held**
WEB: www.alliedwaste.com
SIC: 4953 Sanitary landfill operation
HQ: Browning-Ferris Industries, Llc
　　18500 N Allied Way # 100
　　Phoenix AZ 85054
　　480 627-2700

(G-14716)
CONGREGATE LIVING OF AMERICA (PA)
463 E Pike St (45152-1221)
PHONE....................................513 899-2801
Oscar Jarnicki, *President*
Cynthia Jarnicki, *Treasurer*
EMP: 60
SALES (est): 4MM **Privately Held**
SIC: 8051 8052 Skilled nursing care facilities; intermediate care facilities

(G-14717)
VALLEY MACHINE TOOL CO INC
9773 Morrow Cozaddale Rd (45152-8589)
PHONE....................................513 899-2737
Larry R Wilson, *President*
Douglas Wilson, *Corp Secy*
Ralph Wilson, *Vice Pres*
EMP: 40
SQ FT: 11,000
SALES (est): 6.5MM **Privately Held**
SIC: 3599 7692 Machine shop, jobbing & repair; welding repair

(G-14718)
WORKSHOPS OF DAVID T SMITH
3600 Shawhan Rd (45152-9555)
PHONE....................................513 932-2472
David Smith, *Owner*
Julie Smith, *General Mgr*
Lora Smith, *Corp Secy*
EMP: 50
SALES (est): 10MM **Privately Held**
WEB: www.davidtsmith.com
SIC: 5021 5712 5023 5719 Furniture; furniture stores; pottery; pottery

(G-14719)
YOCKEY GROUP INC
6344 E Us Hwy 22 And 3 (45152-9417)
PHONE....................................513 899-2188
Jim Yockey, *President*
EMP: 45 **EST:** 1997
SALES (est): 4.5MM **Privately Held**
SIC: 7359 Equipment rental & leasing

Moscow
Clermont County

(G-14720)
DYNEGY ZIMMER LLC
1781 Us Rte 52 (45153)
PHONE....................................713 767-0483
EMP: 29
SALES (corp-wide): 9.1B **Publicly Held**
SIC: 4911 Electric services
HQ: Dynegy Zimmer, Llc
　　6555 Sierra Dr
　　Irving TX 75039
　　214 812-4600

(G-14721)
VISTRA ENERGY CORP
Also Called: William H Zimmer Power Station
1781 Us 52 (45153-9617)
PHONE....................................513 467-5289
Carl Cassell, *Opers Mgr*
Paul King, *Branch Mgr*
EMP: 250
SALES (corp-wide): 9.1B **Publicly Held**
SIC: 4911 Electric services
PA: Vistra Energy Corp.
　　6555 Sierra Dr
　　Irving TX 75039
　　214 812-4600

Mount Cory
Hancock County

(G-14722)
S&D FARMS INC (PA)
Also Called: Granary Gift & Furniture Barn
13466 Township Road 53 (45868-9634)
PHONE....................................419 859-3785
Steven E Schafer, *President*
Dianne S Schafer, *Corp Secy*
Andrew Schafer, *Vice Pres*
EMP: 25
SALES (est): 1.6MM **Privately Held**
WEB: www.ggbarn.com
SIC: 0191 5712 5947 General farms, primarily crop; furniture stores; gift, novelty & souvenir shop

Mount Eaton
Wayne County

(G-14723)
QUALITY BLOCK & SUPPLY INC (DH)
Rr 250 (44659)
PHONE....................................330 364-4411
Jerry A Schwab, *President*
David Schwab, *Vice Pres*
Donna Schwab, *Admin Sec*
EMP: 27
SQ FT: 4,000
SALES (est): 2.2MM
SALES (corp-wide): 29.7B **Privately Held**
SIC: 3271 3273 5032 Blocks, concrete or cinder: standard; ready-mixed concrete; concrete & cinder block
HQ: Schwab Industries, Inc.
　　2301 Progress St
　　Dover OH 44622
　　330 364-4411

Mount Gilead
Morrow County

(G-14724)
ANGELS HOME CARE LLC
4440 State Route 61 (43338-9781)
PHONE....................................419 947-9373
Mary Eckard, *Mng Member*
EMP: 38
SALES: 900K **Privately Held**
SIC: 8082 Oxygen tent service

(G-14725)
CONSOLIDATED ELECTRIC COOP INC
5255 State Route 95 (43338-9763)
P.O. Box 111 (43338-0111)
PHONE....................................419 947-3055
Richard Carter, *Ch of Bd*
Brian Newton, *President*
Nancy Salyer, *Vice Pres*
Jaimey Burden, *Opers Staff*
Wes Reinhardt, *CFO*
EMP: 55 **EST:** 1936
SQ FT: 18,000
SALES: 47.9MM **Privately Held**
WEB: www.conelec.com
SIC: 4911 8611 Distribution, electric power; business associations

(G-14726)
COUNTY OF MORROW
Also Called: Morrow Co Ed Service Center
27 W High St (43338-1251)
PHONE....................................419 946-2618
Thomas Ash, *Manager*
EMP: 38 **Privately Held**
WEB: www.morrowcountyhealth.org
SIC: 8741 Administrative management
PA: County Of Morrow
　　80 N Walnut St
　　Mount Gilead OH 43338
　　419 947-7535

(G-14727)
JPMORGAN CHASE BANK NAT ASSN
16 N Main St (43338-1344)
PHONE....................................419 946-3015
Allen Cooper, *Manager*
EMP: 50
SALES (corp-wide): 131.4B **Publicly Held**
WEB: www.chase.com
SIC: 6021 National commercial banks
HQ: Jpmorgan Chase Bank, National Association
　　1111 Polaris Pkwy
　　Columbus OH 43240
　　614 436-3055

(G-14728)
MORROW COUNTY CHILD CARE CTR
406 Bank St (43338-1300)
PHONE....................................419 946-5007
Terry Grieble, *President*
Lori Walters, *Director*
EMP: 60
SALES (est): 401.2K **Privately Held**
SIC: 8351 Group day care center

(G-14729)
MORROW COUNTY COUNCIL ON DRUGS
Also Called: McCad
950 Meadow Dr (43338-1389)
PHONE....................................419 947-4055
Eric Preuss, *Director*
EMP: 26
SALES (est): 950K **Privately Held**
SIC: 8069 Alcoholism rehabilitation hospital

(G-14730)
MORROW COUNTY FIRE FIGHTER
Also Called: Morrow County Emergency Squad
140 S Main St (43338-1408)
PHONE....................................419 946-7976
Jeff Sparks, *Controller*
EMP: 100
SALES (est): 2.3MM **Privately Held**
SIC: 4119 Ambulance service

(G-14731)
MORROW COUNTY HOSPITAL
Also Called: Morrow County Hospital MCH At
651 W Marion Rd (43338-1096)
PHONE....................................419 949-3085
Christopher Truax, *President*
EMP: 300
SALES (corp-wide): 28.9MM **Privately Held**
SIC: 8062 General medical & surgical hospitals
PA: Morrow County Hospital
　　651 W Marion Rd
　　Mount Gilead OH 43338
　　419 946-5015

(G-14732)
MORROW COUNTY HOSPITAL (PA)
Also Called: Morrow County Hospital HM Hlth
651 W Marion Rd (43338-1096)
PHONE....................................419 946-5015
Christopher Traux, *CEO*
EMP: 320
SQ FT: 89,702
SALES: 28.9MM **Privately Held**
WEB: www.morrowcountyhospital.com
SIC: 8062 General medical & surgical hospitals

(G-14733)
PAM JOHNSONIDENT
Also Called: McDonald's
535 W Marion Rd (43338-1025)
PHONE....................................419 946-4551
Pam Johnson, *President*
EMP: 60 **EST:** 1994
SALES (est): 1.2MM **Privately Held**
SIC: 5812 7221 Fast-food restaurant, chain; photographic studios, portrait

▲ = Import ▼=Export
◆ =Import/Export

(G-14734)
PUBLIC SAFETY OHIO DEPARTMENT
3980 County Road 172 (43338-7511)
PHONE..............................419 768-3955
C McGinty, *Branch Mgr*
EMP: 25 **Privately Held**
SIC: 7381 Protective services, guard
HQ: Ohio Department Of Public Safety
1970 W Broad St Fl 5
Columbus OH 43223

(G-14735)
WHETSTONE INDUSTRIES INC
Also Called: WHETSTONE SCHOOL
440 Douglas St (43338-1019)
PHONE..............................419 947-9222
Dr Richard A Kohler, *Principal*
David Keefer, *Finance Mgr*
Barb Gentille Green, *Director*
Anne Stock, *Director*
Kim Taber, *Director*
EMP: 30 **EST:** 1975
SALES: 110.3K **Privately Held**
WEB: www.whetstoneserves.org
SIC: 8211 8322 School for the retarded;
social services for the handicapped

(G-14736)
WOODSIDE VILLAGE CARE CENTER
841 W Marion Rd (43338-1094)
PHONE..............................419 947-2015
William Casto, *Partner*
Gary Casto, *Partner*
William R Casto, *Partner*
EMP: 95
SQ FT: 28,000
SALES (est): 3.8MM **Privately Held**
SIC: 8052 8051 Intermediate care facili-
ties; skilled nursing care facilities

Mount Hope
Holmes County

(G-14737)
MT HOPE AUCTION INC (PA)
Also Called: Farmers Produce Auction
8076 State Rte 241 (44660)
P.O. Box 82 (44660-0082)
PHONE..............................330 674-6188
Steven Mullett, *President*
Jim Mullet, *Manager*
EMP: 30
SALES (est): 14.5MM **Privately Held**
WEB: www.mthopeauction.com
SIC: 5154 7389 Auctioning livestock; auc-
tioneers, fee basis

(G-14738)
OVERHEAD DOOR CORPORATION
1 Door Dr (44660)
P.O. Box 67 (44660-0067)
PHONE..............................330 674-7015
EMP: 97
SALES (corp-wide): 3.6B **Privately Held**
SIC: 1751 Garage door, installation or
erection
HQ: Overhead Door Corporation
2501 S State Hwy 121 Ste
Lewisville TX 75067
469 549-7100

Mount Orab
Brown County

(G-14739)
CHILD FOCUS INC
710 N High St (45154-8349)
PHONE..............................937 444-1613
Jim Carter, *President*
EMP: 55
SALES (corp-wide): 17MM **Privately
Held**
WEB: www.child-focus.org
SIC: 8322 8351 Child related social serv-
ices; child day care services

PA: Child Focus, Inc.
4629 Aicholtz Rd Ste 2
Cincinnati OH 45244
513 752-1555

(G-14740)
EVERYDAY HOMECARE
711 S High St (45154-8947)
PHONE..............................937 444-1672
Vicky Cirley, *Owner*
EMP: 35
SALES (est): 930K **Privately Held**
SIC: 8082 Home health care services

(G-14741)
HOSPICE OF HOPE INC
215 Hughes Blvd (45154-8356)
PHONE..............................937 444-4900
Kavin Cartmell, *Branch Mgr*
EMP: 78 **Privately Held**
SIC: 8052 Personal care facility
PA: Hospice Of Hope, Inc.
909 Kenton Station Dr B
Maysville KY 41056

(G-14742)
MERCY HEALTH
Also Called: Mercy Health - Mt Orab Med Ctr
154 Health Partners Cir (45154-8611)
PHONE..............................513 981-4700
EMP: 53
SALES (corp-wide): 4.7B **Privately Held**
SIC: 8062 General medical & surgical hos-
pitals
PA: Mercy Health
1701 Mercy Health Pl
Cincinnati OH 45237
513 639-2800

(G-14743)
MT ORAB FIRE DEPARTMENT INC
Also Called: Mount Orab Ems
113 Spice St (45154-8932)
P.O. Box 454 (45154-0454)
PHONE..............................937 444-3945
Lisa Reeves, *Chief*
EMP: 27 **Privately Held**
WEB: www.mtorabfire.com
SIC: 4119 Ambulance service
PA: Mt Orab Fire Department Inc
105 Spice St
Mount Orab OH 45154
937 446-2379

Mount Saint Joseph
Hamilton County

(G-14744)
SISTERS OF CHARITY OF CINC (HQ)
5900 Delhi Rd (45051-1500)
PHONE..............................513 347-5200
Sister Bjoan Cook, *President*
Tim Molier, *CFO*
EMP: 82
SQ FT: 60,000
SALES (est): 60.2MM **Privately Held**
SIC: 8051 8661 Skilled nursing care facili-
ties; non-church religious organizations

Mount Sterling
Madison County

(G-14745)
KEIHIN THERMAL TECH AMER INC
10500 Oday Harrison Rd (43143-9474)
PHONE..............................740 869-3000
Tatsuhiko Arai, *President*
Scott Amortimer, *Vice Pres*
◆ **EMP:** 475
SALES (est): 133.1MM
SALES (corp-wide): 3.3B **Privately Held**
SIC: 5013 3714 Automotive engines & en-
gine parts; motor vehicle engines & parts
PA: Keihin Corporation
1-26-2, Nishishinjuku
Shinjuku-Ku TKY 160-0
333 453-411

(G-14746)
OHIO DEPT NATURAL RESOURCES
Also Called: Deer Creek State Park
20635 State Park Road 20 (43143-9541)
PHONE..............................740 869-3124
Mark Hoffhines, *Manager*
EMP: 50 **Privately Held**
WEB: www.ohiostateparks.com
SIC: 7999 9512 Beach & water sports
equipment rental & services;
HQ: Ohio Department Of Natural Re-
sources
2045 Morse Rd Bldg D-3
Columbus OH 43229

(G-14747)
STERLING JOINT AMBULANCE DST
24 S London St (43143-1133)
P.O. Box 51 (43143-0051)
PHONE..............................740 869-3006
Chief John McCalland, *Principal*
John McCalland, *Chief*
EMP: 40
SALES (est): 955.7K **Privately Held**
SIC: 4119 Ambulance service

Mount Vernon
Knox County

(G-14748)
A TOUCH OF GRACE INC (PA)
809 Coshocton Ave Ste B (43050-1900)
PHONE..............................740 397-7971
Carolyn Crow, *President*
Donna J Steele, *President*
Tammy Guillory, *Pharmacy Dir*
EMP: 100
SALES (est): 2.1MM **Privately Held**
SIC: 8082 Visiting nurse service

(G-14749)
BELCAN LLC
Also Called: Belcan Engineering Services
105 N Sandusky St (43050-2447)
PHONE..............................740 393-8888
EMP: 749
SALES (corp-wide): 813.3MM **Privately
Held**
SIC: 7363 Engineering help service
PA: Belcan, Llc
10200 Anderson Way
Blue Ash OH 45242
513 891-0972

(G-14750)
BRENNEMAN LUMBER CO
51 Parrott St (43050-4570)
P.O. Box 951 (43050-0951)
PHONE..............................740 397-0573
Charles Brenneman, *President*
Douglas J Brenneman Jr, *CFO*
▼ **EMP:** 36 **EST:** 1932
SQ FT: 20,000
SALES (est): 12.1MM **Privately Held**
WEB: www.brennemanlumber.com
SIC: 5031 Lumber: rough, dressed & fin-
ished

(G-14751)
C E S CREDIT UNION INC (PA)
1215 Yauger Rd (43050-9233)
P.O. Box 631 (43050-0631)
PHONE..............................740 397-1136
James Depue, *President*
Tracy Morgan, *Vice Pres*
Kelly Schermerhorn, *Vice Pres*
Colleen Kelly, *Manager*
EMP: 45
SQ FT: 7,800
SALES: 4MM **Privately Held**
WEB: www.cescu.com
SIC: 6061 Federal credit unions

(G-14752)
CELLCO PARTNERSHIP
Also Called: Verizon
1002 Coshocton Ave 3 (43050-1550)
PHONE..............................740 397-6609
John Tipton, *Branch Mgr*
EMP: 25

SALES (corp-wide): 130.8B **Publicly
Held**
SIC: 4812 5999 5731 Cellular telephone
services; mobile telephones & equipment;
radio, television & electronic stores
HQ: Cellco Partnership
1 Verizon Way
Basking Ridge NJ 07920

(G-14753)
CENTRAL OHIO CUSTOM CONTG LLC
10541 New Delaware Rd (43050-9144)
PHONE..............................614 579-4971
Kelly Kelley, *Principal*
EMP: 25
SALES: 300K **Privately Held**
SIC: 1799 Special trade contractors

(G-14754)
COLUMBIA GAS TRANSMISSION LLC
Columbia Energy
8484 Columbus Rd (43050)
PHONE..............................740 397-8242
R E Davidson, *Branch Mgr*
EMP: 41
SALES (corp-wide): 10.5B **Privately Held**
SIC: 4922 Pipelines, natural gas
HQ: Columbia Gas Transmission, Llc
200 Cizzic Ctr Dr
Columbus OH 43216
614 460-6000

(G-14755)
CONCEPTS IN COMMUNITY LIVING (PA)
700 Wooster Rd (43050-1488)
PHONE..............................740 393-0055
Karen Hendley, *President*
EMP: 25
SQ FT: 6,800
SALES (est): 2MM **Privately Held**
SIC: 8361 Home for the mentally retarded

(G-14756)
COUNTRY CLUB CENTER II LTD
Also Called: Country Club Retirement Cam-
pus
1350 Yauger Rd (43050-9233)
PHONE..............................740 397-2350
John Holland, *Partner*
Tonia Ressing, *Partner*
EMP: 150
SQ FT: 50,000
SALES (est): 6.1MM **Privately Held**
SIC: 8051 8052 Convalescent home with
continuous nursing care; intermediate
care facilities

(G-14757)
COUNTRY COURT LTD
Also Called: DELAWARE COURT
1076 Coshocton Ave (43050-1474)
PHONE..............................740 397-4125
L Bruce Levering, *Partner*
EMP: 136
SQ FT: 30,000
SALES: 6.8MM
SALES (corp-wide): 27.7MM **Privately
Held**
SIC: 8051 Convalescent home with contin-
uous nursing care
PA: Levering Management, Inc.
201 N Main St
Mount Vernon OH 43050
740 397-3897

(G-14758)
COUNTY OF KNOX
Also Called: Knox County Health Department
11660 Upper Gilchrist Rd (43050-9084)
PHONE..............................740 392-2200
Stacey Robinson, *Finance*
Dennis Murray, *Manager*
EMP: 49 **Privately Held**
WEB: www.knoxhealth.com
SIC: 9431 8082 ; home health care serv-
ices
PA: Knox County
117 E High St Rm 161
Mount Vernon OH 43050
740 393-6703

(G-14759)
COYNE GRAPHIC FINISHING INC
1301 Newark Rd (43050-4730)
PHONE...................................740 397-6232
Kevin Coyne, *President*
Robert Coyne, *Chairman*
Alice Ann Coyne, *Corp Secy*
EMP: 28 EST: 1926
SQ FT: 57,000
SALES: 3MM **Privately Held**
WEB: www.coynefinishing.com
SIC: 7336 Graphic arts & related design

(G-14760)
CREATIVE FOUNDATIONS INC
127 S Main St (43050-3323)
PHONE...................................614 832-2121
EMP: 27
SALES (corp-wide): 8MM **Privately Held**
SIC: 8051 Mental retardation hospital
PA: Creative Foundations, Inc.
57 N Sandusky St
Delaware OH 43015
740 362-5102

(G-14761)
DAILY SERVICES LLC
12 E Gambier St (43050-3316)
PHONE...................................740 326-6130
Ryan Mason, *Branch Mgr*
EMP: 199
SALES (corp-wide): 22.3MM **Privately Held**
SIC: 8999 Artists & artists' studios
PA: Daily Services Llc
1110 Morse Rd Ste B1
Columbus OH 43229
614 431-5100

(G-14762)
DECOSKY MOTOR HOLDINGS INC
Also Called: Decosky GM Center
510 Harcourt Rd 550 (43050-3920)
P.O. Box 351 (43050-0351)
PHONE...................................740 397-9122
John Decosky, *President*
EMP: 35 EST: 1956
SALES (est): 21.4MM **Privately Held**
SIC: 5511 7538 Automobiles, new & used; general automotive repair shops

(G-14763)
DIVERSIFIED PRODUCTS & SVCS
1250 Vernonview Dr (43050-1447)
PHONE...................................740 393-6202
Louis Ohara, *Director*
EMP: 118
SALES (est): 6.6MM **Privately Held**
SIC: 5199 2541 2511 Packaging materials; wood partitions & fixtures; wood household furniture

(G-14764)
EMMETT DAN HOUSE LTD PARTNR
Also Called: Amerihost Mt. Vernon
150 Howard St (43050-3596)
PHONE...................................740 392-6886
Tom Metcalf, *Managing Prtnr*
Colleen Mc Peek, *Manager*
EMP: 30
SQ FT: 50,000
SALES (est): 538.7K **Privately Held**
SIC: 7011 6512 5812 Bed & breakfast inn; nonresidential building operators; eating places

(G-14765)
EUROLINK INC
106 W Ohio Ave (43050-2442)
PHONE...................................740 392-1549
Mark Hauberg, *President*
Elaine Hauberg, *Treasurer*
▲ EMP: 30
SALES (est): 955.4K **Privately Held**
SIC: 5084 Machine tools & accessories

(G-14766)
FIRST-KNOX NATIONAL BANK (HQ)
Also Called: First-Knox National Division
1 S Main St (43050-3223)
PHONE...................................740 399-5500
Gordon E Yance, *President*
David L Trautman, *Chairman*
EMP: 140
SQ FT: 58,000
SALES (est): 7.4MM
SALES (corp-wide): 411.9MM **Publicly Held**
WEB: www.farmersandsavings.com
SIC: 6021 8721 National trust companies with deposits, commercial; accounting, auditing & bookkeeping
PA: Park National Corporation
50 N 3rd St
Newark OH 43055
740 349-8451

(G-14767)
HOME INSTEAD SENIOR CARE
Also Called: Senior Help Solutions
400 W High St (43050-2325)
PHONE...................................740 393-2500
Richard L Shoemaker, *President*
EMP: 32
SALES: 500K **Privately Held**
SIC: 8082 Home health care services

(G-14768)
HOSPICE OF KNOX COUNTY
17700 Coshocton Rd (43050-9218)
PHONE...................................740 397-5188
Kim Giffin, *Finance*
Austin Swallow, *Director*
April Hall, *Admin Sec*
Rachel Winegardner,
EMP: 36
SQ FT: 2,300
SALES: 6.9K **Privately Held**
WEB: www.hospiceofknox.org
SIC: 8082 8322 Home health care services; individual & family services

(G-14769)
INN AT HILLENVALE LTD
1615 Yauger Rd Ste B26 (43050-8342)
PHONE...................................740 392-8245
Chris Wolfard, *Director*
EMP: 67
SALES (est): 1.6MM **Privately Held**
SIC: 8059 Rest home, with health care

(G-14770)
KNOX AREA TRANSIT
Also Called: Knox Area Transit Kat
25 Columbus Rd (43050-4050)
PHONE...................................740 392-7433
Martin McAvoy, *Administration*
EMP: 42
SALES (est): 2MM **Privately Held**
SIC: 4121 Taxicabs

(G-14771)
KNOX AUTO LLC
Also Called: Chevrolet Buick GMC Mt Vernon
510 Harcourt Rd (43050-3920)
PHONE...................................330 701-5266
Stephen Shane,
EMP: 35
SALES: 100MM **Privately Held**
SIC: 5511 5013 7538 Automobiles, new & used; trailer parts & accessories; general automotive repair shops

(G-14772)
KNOX COMMUNITY HOSP FOUNDATION
1330 Coshocton Ave (43050-1440)
PHONE...................................740 393-9814
Jeff Scott, *President*
Jessica Beeman, *Human Res Mgr*
Carole Wagner, *Marketing Staff*
Chris White, *Marketing Staff*
David McCann, *Med Doctor*
EMP: 40
SALES: 10.6MM **Privately Held**
SIC: 8062 General medical & surgical hospitals

(G-14773)
KNOX COMMUNITY HOSPITAL
1330 Coshocton Ave (43050-1495)
PHONE...................................740 393-9000
Bruce White, *CEO*
Sheila Cochran, *CEO*
Michael Ambrosiani, *CFO*
Tom Beekman, *Accountant*
Darcy Bussard, *Accountant*
EMP: 628
SQ FT: 160,000
SALES: 149.6MM **Privately Held**
SIC: 8062 General medical & surgical hospitals

(G-14774)
KNOX COUNTY ENGINEER
422 Columbus Rd (43050-4499)
PHONE...................................740 397-1590
Jim Henry, *Principal*
EMP: 37
SALES (est): 9MM **Privately Held**
SIC: 8711 Engineering services

(G-14775)
KNOX COUNTY HEAD START INC (PA)
11700 Upper Gilchrist Rd B (43050-9232)
P.O. Box 1225 (43050-8225)
PHONE...................................740 397-1344
Margaret Tazewell, *Exec Dir*
EMP: 33
SQ FT: 4,000
SALES: 4.6MM **Privately Held**
SIC: 8351 Head start center, except in conjunction with school

(G-14776)
KNOX NEW HOPE INDUSTRIES INC
1375 Newark Rd (43050-4779)
PHONE...................................740 397-4601
Bill Bryant, *Transptn Dir*
Melissa Oxenford, *Manager*
Clare Bartlett, *Director*
EMP: 150
SQ FT: 30,000
SALES: 1.9MM **Privately Held**
SIC: 8331 Sheltered workshop

(G-14777)
LABELLE HMHEALTH CARE SVCS LLC
314 S Main St Ste B (43050-3333)
PHONE...................................740 392-1405
Eva Ingram, *Manager*
EMP: 85
SALES (corp-wide): 2.4MM **Privately Held**
SIC: 8082 Home health care services
PA: Labelle Homehealth Care Services Llc
1653 Brice Rd
Reynoldsburg OH 43068
614 367-0881

(G-14778)
LEVERING MANAGEMENT INC (PA)
Also Called: Marion Manor
201 N Main St (43050-2400)
PHONE...................................740 397-3897
William B Levering, *President*
EMP: 500
SQ FT: 2,000
SALES (est): 27.7MM **Privately Held**
SIC: 8051 Convalescent home with continuous nursing care

(G-14779)
LOWES HOME CENTERS LLC
1010 Coshocton Ave (43050-1411)
PHONE...................................740 393-5350
Ken Kaiser, *Manager*
EMP: 150
SALES (corp-wide): 68.6B **Publicly Held**
SIC: 5211 5031 5722 5064 Home centers; building materials, exterior; building materials, interior; household appliance stores; electrical appliances, television & radio
HQ: Lowe's Home Centers, Llc
1605 Curtis Bridge Rd
Wilkesboro NC 28697
336 658-4000

(G-14780)
MAUSER USA LLC
219 Commerce Dr (43050-4645)
PHONE...................................740 397-1762
Stefania Maschio, *Director*
EMP: 34
SALES (corp-wide): 1.1B **Privately Held**
WEB: www.mausergroup.com
SIC: 5093 Scrap & waste materials
HQ: Mauser Usa, Llc
35 Cotters Ln Ste C
East Brunswick NJ 08816
732 353-7100

(G-14781)
MAUSER USA LLC
219 Commerce Dr (43050-4645)
PHONE...................................740 397-1762
Robert Tiburzi, *Plant Mgr*
Chuck Sesco, *Manager*
EMP: 35
SALES (corp-wide): 1.1B **Privately Held**
WEB: www.mausergroup.com
SIC: 5085 Packing, industrial
HQ: Mauser Usa, Llc
35 Cotters Ln Ste C
East Brunswick NJ 08816
732 353-7100

(G-14782)
MOUNDBUILDERS GUIDANCE CTR INC
8402 Blackjack Rd (43050-9193)
PHONE...................................740 397-0442
Francis Deutschle, *Director*
EMP: 40
SALES (corp-wide): 9.3MM **Privately Held**
SIC: 8093 Mental health clinic, outpatient
PA: Behavorial Healthcare Partners Of Central Ohio, Inc.
65 Messimer Dr
Newark OH 43055
740 522-8477

(G-14783)
MOUNT VERNON NH LLC
Also Called: Mount Vrnon Hlth Rhbltn Ctr
1135 Gambier Rd (43050-3839)
PHONE...................................740 392-1099
Mordecai Rosenberg, *President*
Ronald Swartz, *CFO*
Lisa Schwartz, *Admin Sec*
EMP: 49 EST: 2015
SALES (est): 344.4K **Privately Held**
SIC: 8051 Skilled nursing care facilities

(G-14784)
OAK HEALTH CARE INVESTORS
Also Called: Laurels of Mt Vernon
13 Avalon Rd (43050-1403)
PHONE...................................740 397-3200
Dennis Sherman, *CEO*
Bev Campbell, *Human Res Dir*
Deb Amore, *Director*
EMP: 60 **Privately Held**
WEB: www.laurelhealth.com
SIC: 8051 8052 Convalescent home with continuous nursing care; intermediate care facilities
HQ: Oak Health Care Investors Of Mt Vernon, Inc
8181 Worthington Rd
Westerville OH 43082

(G-14785)
OHIO EASTERN STAR HOME
1451 Gambier Rd Ofc (43050-9299)
PHONE...................................740 397-1706
Linda Lamson, *Exec Dir*
Melanie Bolender, *Director*
Mark A Buddie, *Director*
Marci Thomas, *Director*
Laura Paalvast, *Executive*
EMP: 150
SQ FT: 60,000
SALES: 7.8MM **Privately Held**
WEB: www.oeshome.org
SIC: 8052 6513 8051 Intermediate care facilities; apartment building operators; skilled nursing care facilities

(G-14786)
REVLOCAL INC
895 Harcourt Rd Ste C (43050-4325)
P.O. Box 511 (43050-0511)
PHONE..........................740 392-9246
Cameron Gephart, *Business Mgr*
Sheryl Lanham, *Business Mgr*
David Robinson, *Business Mgr*
Aj Shull, *Business Mgr*
Kelly W Wick, *Business Mgr*
EMP: 82
SALES (est): 15.9MM **Privately Held**
SIC: 8742 Marketing consulting services

(G-14787)
RICHARD WOLFE TRUCKING INC
7299 Newark Rd (43050-9552)
PHONE..........................740 392-2445
Richard J Wolfe, *President*
EMP: 41
SALES (est): 9.9MM **Privately Held**
SIC: 4213 Heavy hauling

(G-14788)
S AND S GILARDI INC
Also Called: Lannings Foods
1033 Newark Rd (43050-4640)
PHONE..........................740 397-2751
Sam Gilardi, *President*
Brenda Giraldi, *Vice Pres*
Steve Gilardi, *Treasurer*
Cindy Smith, *Sales Executive*
Susan Combs, *Office Mgr*
EMP: 90
SQ FT: 20,000
SALES (est): 27.1MM **Privately Held**
WEB: www.lannings.com
SIC: 5147 5421 5451 5143 Meats, fresh; meat markets, including freezer provisioners; dairy products stores; dairy products, except dried or canned

(G-14789)
SANOH AMERICA INC
7905 Industrial Park Dr (43050-2776)
PHONE..........................740 392-9200
Eric Carroll, *Principal*
EMP: 220
SALES (corp-wide): 1.3B **Privately Held**
WEB: www.sanoh-america.com
SIC: 7539 3714 Automotive repair shops; motor vehicle parts & accessories
HQ: Sanoh America, Inc.
1849 Industrial Dr
Findlay OH 45840
419 425-2600

(G-14790)
SIEMENS ENERGY INC
105 N Sandusky St (43050-2447)
PHONE..........................740 393-8897
EMP: 252
SALES (corp-wide): 95B **Privately Held**
SIC: 1629 1731 3511 Power plant construction; energy management controls; turbines & turbine generator sets
HQ: Siemens Energy, Inc.
4400 N Alafaya Trl
Orlando FL 32826
407 736-2000

(G-14791)
W M V O 1300 AM
Also Called: Branch Clear Chan San Antonio
17421 Coshocton Rd (43050-9256)
PHONE..........................740 397-1000
Curtis Newland, *General Mgr*
Adam Klein, *General Mgr*
Shar Shingler, *Manager*
EMP: 25
SALES (est): 754.8K **Privately Held**
SIC: 4832 Radio broadcasting stations

(G-14792)
WHISPERING HILLS CARE CENTER
416 Wooster Rd (43050-1216)
PHONE..........................740 392-3982
Jessica Link, *Exec Dir*
EMP: 30
SALES (est): 1.2MM **Privately Held**
SIC: 8059 Convalescent home

(G-14793)
WQIO 93Q REQUEST
17421 Coshocton Rd (43050-9256)
PHONE..........................740 392-9370
Tom Klein, *CEO*
Jim Lorenzen, *President*
EMP: 50
SALES (est): 613.3K **Privately Held**
SIC: 4832 Radio broadcasting stations

(G-14794)
YOUNG MENS CHRISTIAN MT VERNON
Also Called: YMCA
103 N Main St (43050-2407)
PHONE..........................740 392-9622
Cameo Quick, *Finance Dir*
Wayne Uhrig, *Director*
EMP: 60
SQ FT: 53,000
SALES: 1.1MM **Privately Held**
SIC: 8641 7991 8351 7032 Youth organizations; physical fitness facilities; child day care services; youth camps; individual & family services

(G-14795)
YOUNG MNS CHRSTN ASSN GRTER NY
Also Called: Young Mens Christian Assn
103 N Main St (43050-2407)
PHONE..........................740 392-9622
Wayne Uhrig, *Exec Dir*
EMP: 55
SALES (corp-wide): 187.7MM **Privately Held**
SIC: 8641 7991 8351 7032 Youth organizations; physical fitness facilities; child day care services; youth camps; individual & family services
PA: Young Men's Christian Association Of Greater New York
5 W 63rd St Fl 6
New York NY 10023
212 630-9600

Mount Victory
Hardin County

(G-14796)
OHIO FRESH EGGS LLC
20449 County Road 245 (43340-9710)
P.O. Box 118 (43340-0118)
PHONE..........................937 354-2233
Brian Kinter, *Manager*
EMP: 30
SALES (est): 1.5MM
SALES (corp-wide): 25.9MM **Privately Held**
SIC: 5144 2015 0252 Eggs; poultry slaughtering & processing; chicken eggs
PA: Ohio Fresh Eggs, Llc
11212 Croton Rd
Croton OH 43013
740 893-7200

Munroe Falls
Summit County

(G-14797)
KYOCERA SGS PRECISION TOOLS (PA)
55 S Main St (44262-1635)
P.O. Box 187 (44262-0187)
PHONE..........................330 688-6667
Thomas Haag, *President*
Chris Sparks, *Engineer*
Aaron Holb, *Treasurer*
Raymond Gibson, *Chief Mktg Ofcr*
▲ EMP: 50
SQ FT: 45,000
SALES: 78.5MM **Privately Held**
WEB: www.sgstool.com
SIC: 3545 5084 Cutting tools for machine tools; industrial machinery & equipment

(G-14798)
MULBERRY GARDEN A L S
395 S Main St Apt 210 (44262-1671)
PHONE..........................330 630-3980

Maryann Ervin, *Administration*
EMP: 40
SALES (est): 1.3MM **Privately Held**
SIC: 6513 8361 Retirement hotel operation; residential care

(G-14799)
THOMPSON ELECTRIC INC
49 Northmoreland Ave (44262-1717)
PHONE..........................330 686-2300
Larry Thompson, *President*
Brian Lawrence, *Division Mgr*
Scott Manby, *Division Mgr*
Robert Mileski, *Division Mgr*
Bill Anderson, *Vice Pres*
EMP: 250
SQ FT: 33,000
SALES: 85.1MM **Privately Held**
SIC: 1731 General electrical contractor

Napoleon
Henry County

(G-14800)
CLOVERLEAF COLD STORAGE CO
1165 Independence Dr (43545-9718)
PHONE..........................419 599-5015
Tony Castle, *Branch Mgr*
EMP: 150
SALES (corp-wide): 76.3MM **Privately Held**
WEB: www.cloverleafco.com
SIC: 4225 4222 General warehousing; refrigerated warehousing & storage
PA: Cloverleaf Cold Storage Co., Llc
401 Douglas St Ste 406
Sioux City IA 51101
712 279-8000

(G-14801)
CLOVERLEAF TRANSPORT CO
1165 Independence Dr (43545-9718)
PHONE..........................419 599-5015
Dale Lilleholm, *General Mgr*
EMP: 50
SALES (corp-wide): 3.8MM **Privately Held**
SIC: 4119 Local passenger transportation
PA: Cloverleaf Transport Co
2800 Cloverleaf Ct
Sioux City IA 51111
712 279-8044

(G-14802)
COMUNIBANC CORP (PA)
122 E Washington St (43545-1646)
P.O. Box 72 (43545-0072)
PHONE..........................419 599-1065
William Wendt, *Principal*
EMP: 56 **Privately Held**
SIC: 6712 Bank holding companies

(G-14803)
COUNTY OF HENRY
Country View Haven
R858 County Road 15 (43545-7968)
PHONE..........................419 592-8075
Fax: 419 592-6620
EMP: 30 **Privately Held**
SIC: 8059 Nursing/Personal Care
PA: County Of Henry
1823 Oakwood Ave
Napoleon OH 43545
419 592-1956

(G-14804)
FILLING MEMORIAL HOME OF MERCY (PA)
N160 State Route 108 (43545-9278)
PHONE..........................419 592-6451
Paul E Oehrtman, *Principal*
Nancy Wiechers, *Human Res Dir*
Marty Daniel, *Manager*
Paul Oehrtman, *Administration*
EMP: 350
SQ FT: 53,000
SALES: 12.6MM **Privately Held**
WEB: www.fillinghome.org
SIC: 8052 Home for the mentally retarded, with health care

(G-14805)
FIRST CALL FOR HELP INC
600 Freedom Dr (43545-9038)
PHONE..........................419 599-1660
Joe Dildine, *CEO*
Lynda Sheets, *CFO*
EMP: 50
SQ FT: 10,000
SALES: 1.1MM **Privately Held**
WEB: www.fcfhnwo.org
SIC: 8093 Biofeedback center

(G-14806)
GERMAN MUTUAL INSURANCE CO
1000 Westmoreland Ave (43545-1257)
P.O. Box 191 (43545-0191)
PHONE..........................419 599-3993
Philip Menzel, *President*
EMP: 42
SALES (est): 7.5MM **Privately Held**
WEB: www.heartland-ins.com
SIC: 6411 Insurance agents

(G-14807)
GOLDEN LIVING LLC
Also Called: Beverly
240 Northcrest Dr (43545-7737)
PHONE..........................419 599-4070
Larry Cathcart, *Exec Dir*
EMP: 97
SALES (corp-wide): 7.4MM **Privately Held**
SIC: 8059 8051 Convalescent home; skilled nursing care facilities
PA: Golden Living Llc
5220 Tennyson Pkwy # 400
Plano TX 75024
972 372-6300

(G-14808)
HENRY COUNTY BANK (HQ)
122 E Washington St (43545-1646)
P.O. Box 72 (43545-0072)
PHONE..........................419 599-1065
William L Wendt, *President*
Anthony B Grieser, *Exec VP*
Kevin Yarnell, *Senior VP*
Sharon S Mack, *Vice Pres*
J Kevin Yarnell, *Vice Pres*
EMP: 50
SALES: 10.3MM **Privately Held**
WEB: www.thehenrycountybank.com
SIC: 6022 6163 State commercial banks; loan brokers

(G-14809)
HENRY COUNTY HOSPITAL INC
1600 E Riverview Ave Frnt (43545-9399)
PHONE..........................419 592-4015
Kim Bordenkircher, *CEO*
Tanna Ellert, *Manager*
Jeff Pompos, *Manager*
Ryan Thomas, *Systems Dir*
Michael Miller, *Administration*
EMP: 308
SQ FT: 100,000
SALES: 28MM **Privately Held**
SIC: 8062 General medical & surgical hospitals

(G-14810)
LEADERS FAMILY FARMS
0064 County Rd 16 (43545)
PHONE..........................419 599-1570
EMP: 30
SALES (est): 346.3K **Privately Held**
SIC: 7999 Amusement/Recreation Services

(G-14811)
MEL LANZER CO
2266 Scott St (43545-1064)
PHONE..........................419 592-2801
Charlotte Zgela, *President*
Cheryl Huffman, *Vice Pres*
Matthew Lanzer, *Vice Pres*
Dan Follett, *Treasurer*
Margaret Lanzer, *Admin Sec*
EMP: 33 EST: 1950
SQ FT: 5,000
SALES: 16.4MM **Privately Held**
WEB: www.mellanzer.com
SIC: 1541 1542 Industrial buildings, new construction; commercial & office building contractors; religious building construction

---

(G-14812)
MWA ENTERPRISES LTD
900 American Rd (43545-6498)
PHONE..................................419 599-3835
Michael Adams, *Principal*
Cheryl Khun, *Executive*
EMP: 28
SALES (est): 721.1K **Privately Held**
SIC: 6519 Landholding office

(G-14813)
NAPOLEON MACHINE LLC
476 E Riverview Ave (43545-1855)
PHONE..................................419 591-7010
Dave Rakay, *Project Mgr*
Anita Febrey, *Controller*
Kyle Rickner, *Marketing Staff*
Kevin Febrey,
EMP: 35
SALES: 2MM **Privately Held**
SIC: 3599 1721 Crankshafts & camshafts,
machining; electrical discharge machining
(EDM); commercial painting; exterior
commercial painting contractor; industrial
painting

(G-14814)
NAPOLEON WASH-N-FILL INC (PA)
485 N Perry St (43545-1706)
PHONE..................................419 592-0851
Mike Synder, *President*
Leo D Snyder Jr, *President*
Chauncey I Moore, *Corp Secy*
Michael Snyder, *Vice Pres*
EMP: 90 EST: 1969
SQ FT: 3,000
SALES (est): 859K **Privately Held**
SIC: 7542 5541 Carwashes; filling sta-
tions, gasoline

(G-14815)
NCOP LLC
Also Called: Orcha of North Livin & Rehab C
240 Northcrest Dr (43545-7737)
PHONE..................................419 599-4070
Andrew Fishman, *CEO*
Jeniffer Rohrs, *Exec Dir*
EMP: 99
SALES (est): 1.5MM **Privately Held**
SIC: 8051 Skilled nursing care facilities

(G-14816)
ROYAL ARCH MASONS OF OHIO
Also Called: Haly Chapter 136
109 E School St (43545-9217)
PHONE..................................419 762-5565
Dallas Andrew, *Admin Sec*
EMP: 30 EST: 1999
SALES (est): 337.6K **Privately Held**
SIC: 8699 Charitable organization

(G-14817)
SAFETY GROOVING & GRINDING LP
13226 County Road R (43545-5966)
P.O. Box 675, Abingdon MD (21009-0675)
PHONE..................................419 592-8666
Rex Parker, *Partner*
Tom Parker, *Partner*
Russell C Swank III, *General Ptnr*
EMP: 40
SALES (est): 3.1MM
SALES (corp-wide): 30MM **Privately Held**
WEB: www.swankco.com
SIC: 1799 Diamond drilling & sawing
PA: Swank Construction Company, Llc
632 Hunt Valley Cir
New Kensington PA 15068
724 727-3497

(G-14818)
TREP LTD
Also Called: Petrolube
900 American Rd (43545-6498)
PHONE..................................419 717-5624
Wayne Hitchcock, *General Mgr*
EMP: 30
SALES (est): 1.7MM **Privately Held**
SIC: 1711 5541 Mechanical contractor;

Nashport
Muskingum County

(G-14819)
HANBY FARMS INC
10790 Newark Rd (43830-9066)
P.O. Box 97 (43830-0097)
PHONE..................................740 763-3554
Ralph F Hanby, *President*
David R Hanby, *President*
Doug Hanby, *CFO*
Carol Hanby, *Admin Sec*
EMP: 34
SQ FT: 10,000
SALES (est): 7.8MM **Privately Held**
SIC: 2048 5153 5191 Livestock feeds;
corn; soybeans; fertilizer & fertilizer mate-
rials

(G-14820)
NEWARK DRYWALL INC
Also Called: A1 Drywall Supply
18122 Nashport Rd (43830-9629)
PHONE..................................740 763-3572
Rick Frenton, *President*
Jeffrey Frenton, *Principal*
Michael Frenton, *Principal*
EMP: 45 EST: 1977
SALES (est): 3MM **Privately Held**
SIC: 1742 Drywall

(G-14821)
OHIO OIL GATHERING CORPORATION (DH)
9320 Blackrun Rd (43830-9434)
P.O. Box 430, Frazeysburg (43822-0430)
PHONE..................................740 828-2892
Michael A Mayers, *President*
Michael McKee, *Vice Pres*
Robert Bumpus, *Asst Sec*
EMP: 25
SQ FT: 1,000
SALES (est): 4.9MM
SALES (corp-wide): 7.7B **Publicly Held**
WEB: www.ohiooil.com
SIC: 4213 4612 4212 Liquid petroleum
transport, non-local; crude petroleum
pipelines; local trucking, without storage
HQ: Clearfield Energy Inc
5 Radnor Corp Ctr Ste 400
Radnor PA 19087
610 293-0410

Navarre
Stark County

(G-14822)
CARMEN STEERING COMMITTEE
8074 Goodrich Rd Sw (44662-9436)
PHONE..................................330 756-2066
Edward V Smith Jr, *Principal*
EMP: 32
SALES (est): 470.8K **Privately Held**
SIC: 8699 Personal interest organization

(G-14823)
MDS FOODS INC (PA)
4676 Erie Ave Sw Ste A (44662-9658)
PHONE..................................330 879-9780
James Straughn, *President*
Pete Effinger, *Exec VP*
Misty D Lewis, *Vice Pres*
Lisa Straughn, *Vice Pres*
Scott Ward, *Maint Spvr*
EMP: 50
SQ FT: 40,000
SALES (est): 31.7MM **Privately Held**
WEB: www.mdsfoods.com
SIC: 5141 Groceries, general line

(G-14824)
PSC METALS INC
780 Warmington St Sw (44662-8120)
PHONE..................................330 879-5001
EMP: 4118 EST: 2015
SALES: 60.9K
SALES (corp-wide): 11.7B **Publicly Held**
SIC: 5093 Waste rags

HQ: Icahn Enterprises Holdings L.P.
767 5th Ave Fl 17
New York NY 10153
212 702-4300

(G-14825)
ROBERT G OWEN TRUCKING INC (PA)
9260 Erie Ave Sw (44662-9448)
P.O. Box 187 (44662-0187)
PHONE..................................330 756-1013
Steven Owen, *President*
Christopher Owen, *Vice Pres*
Patricia Owen, *Admin Sec*
EMP: 35
SQ FT: 8,000
SALES (est): 4.3MM **Privately Held**
SIC: 4213 Contract haulers

(G-14826)
YMCA OF MASSILLON
1226 Market St Ne (44662-8576)
PHONE..................................330 879-0800
Jim Stanford, *Manager*
EMP: 25
SALES (corp-wide): 2.2MM **Privately Held**
SIC: 8641 7991 8351 7032 Youth organi-
zations; physical fitness facilities; child
day care services; youth camps; individ-
ual & family services
PA: Ymca Of Massillon
131 Tremont Ave Se
Massillon OH 44646
330 837-5116

Negley
Columbiana County

(G-14827)
A M & O TOWING INC
11341 State Route 170 (44441-9713)
PHONE..................................330 385-0639
Mary Price, *President*
EMP: 40
SALES (est): 2.9MM **Privately Held**
SIC: 4492 Towing & tugboat service

Nelsonville
Athens County

(G-14828)
CORRECTONS COMM STHASTERN OHIO
16677 Riverside Dr (45764-9528)
PHONE..................................740 753-4060
Jeremy Tolson, *Chairman*
EMP: 60
SALES (est): 3.6MM **Privately Held**
WEB: www.seorj.com
SIC: 8744 Jails, privately operated

(G-14829)
DOCTORS HOSPITAL CLEVELAND INC
Also Called: Ohio Health
11 John Lloyd Evns Mem Dr (45764-2523)
PHONE..................................740 753-7300
Steve Swart, *President*
Lemar Wyse, *President*
Lewis New Berry, *CFO*
EMP: 185
SQ FT: 15,000
SALES (est): 21.6MM **Privately Held**
SIC: 8051 8062 Skilled nursing care facili-
ties; general medical & surgical hospitals

(G-14830)
ED MAP INC
296 S Harper St Ste 1 (45764-1600)
PHONE..................................740 753-3439
Michael Mark, *CEO*
Kerry Stoessel Pigman, *President*
Andrew J Herd, *Vice Pres*
Kelby Kostival, *Vice Pres*
Greg Smith, *CFO*
EMP: 83
SQ FT: 7,000

SALES (est): 74.8MM **Privately Held**
WEB: www.edmap.biz
SIC: 5192 Whol Books/Newspapers

(G-14831)
FIRST NAT BNK OF NELSONVILLE (PA)
11 Public Sq (45764-1132)
P.O. Box 149 (45764-0149)
PHONE..................................740 753-1941
Steven Cox, *President*
Mary Jane Lax, *Exec VP*
Eric Courtney, *Vice Pres*
Suzie Witmann, *Treasurer*
EMP: 32
SALES: 3.1MM **Privately Held**
WEB: www.fnbnelsonville.com
SIC: 6021 National commercial banks

(G-14832)
GEORGIA-BOOT INC
Also Called: Durango Boot
39 E Canal St (45764-1247)
PHONE..................................740 753-1951
Gerald M Cohn, *CEO*
Thomas R Morrison, *President*
EMP: 100
SALES (est): 17.7MM **Privately Held**
WEB: www.durangoboot.com
SIC: 5139 3144 3143 3021 Shoes;
women's footwear, except athletic; men's
footwear, except athletic; rubber & plas-
tics footwear

(G-14833)
HOCKING VLY CMNTY RSDNTIAL CTR
111 W 29 Dr (45764)
PHONE..................................740 753-4400
Elaine Downs, *Manager*
Tamara Bauman, *Director*
EMP: 26
SALES (est): 1.2MM **Privately Held**
SIC: 8361 Residential care

(G-14834)
LEHIGH OUTFITTERS LLC (HQ)
Also Called: Slipgrips
39 E Canal St (45764-1247)
PHONE..................................740 753-1951
Joseph J Sebes, *President*
Richard Simms, *Mng Member*
Joe Hanning, *Director*
◆ EMP: 200
SQ FT: 24,000
SALES (est): 130MM
SALES (corp-wide): 252.6MM **Publicly Held**
SIC: 5661 5139 Men's shoes; women's
shoes; shoes
PA: Rocky Brands, Inc.
39 E Canal St
Nelsonville OH 45764
740 753-1951

(G-14835)
PINE HILLS CONTINUING CARE CTR
1950 Mount Saint Marys Dr # 2 (45764-1280)
PHONE..................................740 753-1931
Lorina Harkless, *Director*
Steven Fwartz, *Administration*
EMP: 50
SALES (est): 542.7K **Privately Held**
SIC: 8062 General medical & surgical hos-
pitals

(G-14836)
S & B ENTERPRISES LLC
Also Called: Sanborn Vending
668 Poplar St (45764-1420)
PHONE..................................740 753-2646
Bill Wend,
EMP: 28 EST: 1940
SQ FT: 5,000
SALES (est): 413.8K **Privately Held**
SIC: 7993 5962 Amusement machine
rental, coin-operated; merchandising ma-
chine operators

(G-14837)
SECHKAR COMPANY
4831 2nd St (45764-9568)
PHONE..................................740 385-8900

▲ = Import ▼ =Export
◆ =Import/Export

Dan Sechkar, *Owner*
EMP: 42
SALES (est): 1.2MM **Privately Held**
SIC: 8322 Social services for the handicapped

Nevada
Wyandot County

(G-14838)
PHILLIP MC GUIRE
Also Called: H & R Block
1585 County Highway 62 (44849-9798)
PHONE.................................740 482-2701
Phillip Mc Guire, *Owner*
Charlene McGuire, *Co-Owner*
EMP: 50
SALES (est): 750.1K **Privately Held**
SIC: 7291 Tax return preparation services

New Albany
Franklin County

(G-14839)
**ABERCROMBIE & FITCH
TRADING CO (DH)**
6301 Fitch Path (43054-9269)
PHONE.................................614 283-6500
Fran Horowitz, *CEO*
Seth Johnson, *COO*
Wesley S McDonald, *CFO*
Jason Antonelli, *Analyst*
▼ **EMP:** 41 **EST:** 2000
SALES (est): 368.2MM
SALES (corp-wide): 3.5B **Publicly Held**
SIC: 5136 5137 5641 5621 Men's &
boys' clothing; women's & children's
clothing; children's & infants' wear stores;
women's clothing stores; men's & boys'
clothing stores

(G-14840)
ACCEL INC
9000 Smiths Mill Rd (43054-6647)
PHONE.................................614 656-1100
Tara Abraham, *CEO*
David Abraham, *President*
▲ **EMP:** 200
SQ FT: 305,000
SALES (est): 30.1MM **Privately Held**
SIC: 7389 Packaging & labeling services

(G-14841)
**AETNA HEALTH CALIFORNIA
INC**
7400 W Campus Rd Ste 100 (43054-8723)
PHONE.................................614 933-6000
Barb Hard, *Branch Mgr*
EMP: 50
SALES (corp-wide): 194.5B **Publicly
Held**
SIC: 6324 Health maintenance organization (HMO), insurance only
HQ: Aetna Health Of California, Inc.
515 S Flower St
Los Angeles CA 90071
925 543-9223

(G-14842)
ALLSTARS TRAVEL GROUP INC
Also Called: Troilo & Associates
7775 Walton Pkwy Ste 100 (43054-8202)
PHONE.................................614 901-4100
Torsten Krings, *President*
Tammy Troilo, *Vice Pres*
Joe Szablewski, *CFO*
Jeannie Thorne, *Human Res Dir*
Georgianna Huffman, *Manager*
EMP: 120
SALES (est): 30.6MM **Privately Held**
WEB: www.ts24.com
SIC: 4724 Tourist agency arranging transport, lodging & car rental

(G-14843)
BEST PLUMBING LIMITED
5791 Zarley St Ste A (43054-7091)
PHONE.................................614 855-1919
Jim Mullins,
Joe Electric,

EMP: 50 **EST:** 1995
SQ FT: 3,000
SALES (est): 6.1MM **Privately Held**
SIC: 1711 Plumbing contractors

(G-14844)
**BRIGHTVIEW LANDSCAPES
LLC**
Also Called: Brickman Facility Services
6530 W Campus Oval # 300 (43054-8726)
PHONE.................................614 741-8233
Scott Brickman, *CEO*
EMP: 56
SALES (corp-wide): 2.8B **Publicly Held**
SIC: 0781 0782 Landscape services; landscape contractors
HQ: Brightview Landscapes, Llc
401 Plymouth Rd Ste 500
Plymouth Meeting PA 19462
484 567-7204

(G-14845)
BRODHEAD VILLAGE LTD (PA)
Also Called: Wallick Company, The
160 W Main St (43054-1188)
PHONE.................................614 863-4640
Layne Hurst, *President*
Thomas A Feusse, *Partner*
Jerry Bowen, *General Mgr*
Paul Koehler, *Senior VP*
John Leonard, *Senior VP*
EMP: 60
SQ FT: 13,000
SALES (est): 5.6MM **Privately Held**
SIC: 6513 Apartment building operators

(G-14846)
**CAMPBELL FAMILY CHILDCARE
INC**
Also Called: Goddard School of New Albany
5351 New Albany Rd W (43054-8853)
PHONE.................................614 855-4780
Jeffrey Campbell, *Director*
Coleen Barber, *Director*
EMP: 26
SALES (est): 1MM **Privately Held**
SIC: 8351 Preschool center

(G-14847)
CAPITAL CITY ELECTRIC LLC
9798 Karmar Ct Ste B (43054-8210)
PHONE.................................614 933-8700
Danita Kessler, *Principal*
Blaze Bishop, *Project Engr*
Eric Baker, *Accounts Mgr*
Scott Barber, *Manager*
EMP: 45
SQ FT: 4,500
SALES (est): 8.3MM **Privately Held**
WEB: www.capcityelectric.com
SIC: 1731 General electrical contractor

(G-14848)
CAROL SCUDERE
Also Called: Domestic Connection
6912 Keesee Cir (43054-8876)
PHONE.................................614 839-4357
Carol Scudere, *Owner*
EMP: 28
SALES (est): 1.4MM **Privately Held**
WEB: www.pdspdi.com
SIC: 8742 8351 7363 7349 Industry specialist consultants; child day care services; domestic help service; maid
services, contract or fee basis; babysitting
bureau

(G-14849)
CASAGRANDE MASONRY INC
13530 Morse Rd Sw (43054-7792)
P.O. Box 1540, Pataskala (43062-1540)
PHONE.................................740 964-0781
Anthony A Casagrande, *President*
EMP: 50
SALES (est): 5MM **Privately Held**
SIC: 1741 Stone masonry

(G-14850)
**COLUMBUS CTR FOR HUMN
SVCS INC**
6227 Harlem Rd (43054-9707)
PHONE.................................614 245-8180
Rebecca Sharp, *CEO*
EMP: 37

SALES (corp-wide): 7.7MM **Privately
Held**
SIC: 8059 Home for the mentally retarded,
exc. skilled or intermediate
PA: Columbus Center For Human Services,
Inc.
540 Industrial Mile Rd
Columbus OH 43228
614 641-2904

(G-14851)
**DFS CORPORATE SERVICES
LLC**
Also Called: Discover Financial Services
6500 New Albany Rd E (43054-8730)
PHONE.................................614 283-2499
Don Probst, *Manager*
EMP: 30
SALES (corp-wide): 12.8B **Publicly Held**
WEB: www.discovercard.com
SIC: 6141 Consumer finance companies
HQ: Dfs Corporate Services Llc
2500 Lake Cook Rd 2
Riverwoods IL 60015
224 405-0900

(G-14852)
EVANS MECHWART HAM (PA)
Also Called: E M H & T
5500 New Albany Rd # 100 (43054-8704)
PHONE.................................614 775-4500
Nelson Kohman, *President*
Craig A Bohnin, *Vice Pres*
Gregory Comfort, *Vice Pres*
Jeffrey A Mill, *Vice Pres*
Douglas E Rome, *Vice Pres*
EMP: 285 **EST:** 1925
SQ FT: 13,200
SALES (est): 57.5MM **Privately Held**
WEB: www.emht.com
SIC: 8713 8711 Surveying services; consulting engineer

(G-14853)
EXHIBITPRO INC
8900 Smiths Mill Rd (43054-1281)
P.O. Box 537 (43054-0537)
PHONE.................................614 885-9541
Lori Miller, *CEO*
Lori J Miller, *CEO*
Edward Miller, *President*
Greg Lindsey, *Vice Pres*
Tammy Lawrence, *Office Mgr*
EMP: 30
SQ FT: 15,000
SALES (est): 4.8MM **Privately Held**
WEB: www.exhibitpro.net
SIC: 7336 7389 Commercial art & graphic
design; trade show arrangement

(G-14854)
**FRANKLIN CMPT SVCS GROUP
INC**
6650 Walnut St (43054-9138)
PHONE.................................614 431-3327
Mike Castrodale, *President*
Gail Gmelko, *Admin Sec*
EMP: 45
SALES (est): 1.7MM **Privately Held**
WEB: www.fcsg.com
SIC: 7379 Computer related consulting
services;

(G-14855)
GOLF CLUB CO
4522 Kitzmiller Rd (43054-9565)
P.O. Box 369 (43054-0369)
PHONE.................................614 855-7326
Grant Marrow, *Ch of Bd*
George McElroy, *Ch of Bd*
C T Rice, *President*
EMP: 35
SQ FT: 5,000
SALES (est): 3.2MM **Privately Held**
WEB: www.thegolfclub.com
SIC: 7997 Golf club, membership

(G-14856)
**HIGHLAND VILLAGE LTD
PARTNR**
Also Called: Wallick Co.
160 W Main St (43054-1188)
PHONE.................................614 863-4640
Kevin Allmandinger, *Partner*
EMP: 60

SALES (est): 2MM **Privately Held**
SIC: 6512 6513 Nonresidential building
operators; apartment building operators

(G-14857)
JEANNE B MCCOY COMM (PA)
Also Called: McCoy Center For The Arts
100 E Dublin Granville Rd (43054-8500)
P.O. Box 508 (43054-0508)
PHONE.................................614 245-4701
Jerry O Allen, *Managing Dir*
EMP: 30
SALES (est): 759.9K **Privately Held**
SIC: 8699 Art council

(G-14858)
**JOINT IMPLANT SURGEONS
INC**
Also Called: Ortholink Physicians
7727 Smiths Mill Rd 200 (43054)
PHONE.................................614 221-6331
Adolph V Lombardi Jr, *President*
Thomas H Mallory MD, *President*
Keith Berend, *Med Doctor*
Rebecca Dunaway, *Director*
EMP: 35
SQ FT: 2,500
SALES (est): 6.6MM **Privately Held**
WEB: www.jointimplantsurgeons.com
SIC: 8011 Orthopedic physician

(G-14859)
**MISSION ESSNTIAL
PERSONNEL LLC (PA)**
6525 W Campus Oval # 101 (43054-8830)
PHONE.................................614 416-2345
Al Pisani, *President*
Jeff Boushell, *Vice Pres*
Steve Frith, *Vice Pres*
Mark Halbig, *Vice Pres*
Jerry Blickenstaff, *Buyer*
EMP: 150
SQ FT: 8,000
SALES (est): 56MM **Privately Held**
WEB: www.aegismep.com
SIC: 7389 8748 Translation services;
safety training service

(G-14860)
MOUNT CARMEL HEALTH
55 N High St Ste A (43054-7098)
PHONE.................................614 855-4878
Diane Beggs, *Branch Mgr*
Steven Boysel, *Family Practiti*
EMP: 25
SALES (corp-wide): 18.3B **Privately Held**
SIC: 8062 General medical & surgical hospitals
HQ: Mount Carmel Health
793 W State St
Columbus OH 43222
614 234-5000

(G-14861)
**MOUNT CARMEL HEALTH
SYSTEM**
7333 Smiths Mill Rd (43054-9291)
PHONE.................................614 775-6600
Dick Denbeau, *CEO*
Dawn Buck, *Manager*
Verna Solove, *Manager*
Mark Reno, *Anesthesiology*
Michael Morris, *Surgeon*
EMP: 36
SALES (corp-wide): 18.3B **Privately Held**
SIC: 8062 General medical & surgical hospitals
HQ: Mount Carmel Health System
6150 E Broad St
Columbus OH 43213
614 234-6000

(G-14862)
**NEW ALBANY ATHC BOOSTER
CLB**
7600 Fodor Rd (43054-8738)
PHONE.................................614 413-8325
Tim Cline, *President*
EMP: 50
SALES (est): 834.2K **Privately Held**
SIC: 7997 Membership sports & recreation
clubs

GEOGRAPHIC

(G-14863)
NEW ALBANY CLEANING SERVICES
108 N High St Ste B (43054-8993)
P.O. Box 452 (43054-0452)
PHONE..................................614 855-9990
Greg Stanley, *President*
Jennifer Stanley, *Vice Pres*
EMP: 30
SALES (est): 1.4MM **Privately Held**
SIC: 7217 7349 Carpet & upholstery cleaning; cleaning service, industrial or commercial

(G-14864)
NEW ALBANY COUNTRY CLUB COMM A
1 Club Ln (43054-9377)
PHONE..................................614 939-8500
Leslie Wexner, *President*
Ted B Hipsher, *Principal*
Kate Williams, *Marketing Staff*
Bob Wesselman, *Manager*
Paul Valido, *Director*
EMP: 150
SQ FT: 55,000
SALES (est): 14.6MM **Privately Held**
WEB: www.nacc.com
SIC: 7997 Country club, membership

(G-14865)
NEW ALBANY LINKS DEV CO LTD
7100 New Albany Links Dr (43054-8194)
PHONE..................................614 939-5914
T Bruce Oldendick, *President*
Thomas Bruce Oldendick, *President*
Glenn Hay, *Superintendent*
Jessica Mahr, *Assistant*
EMP: 70
SQ FT: 1,932
SALES (est): 2.1MM **Privately Held**
SIC: 7997 Golf club, membership

(G-14866)
NEW ALBANY PLAIN LOC SC TRANSP
55 N High St Ste A (43054-7098)
PHONE..................................614 855-2033
Philip Vice, *Transportation*
Carol Mulbay, *Manager*
EMP: 35
SQ FT: 1,516
SALES: 1.5MM **Privately Held**
SIC: 4151 School buses

(G-14867)
NEW ALBANY SURGERY CENTER LLC
5040 Forest Dr Ste 100 (43054-9187)
PHONE..................................614 775-1616
Jacqueline A Primeau, *Principal*
Cindyrd Williams, *Technology*
EMP: 175
SQ FT: 95,000
SALES (est): 25.5MM
SALES (corp-wide): 18.3B **Privately Held**
SIC: 8062 General medical & surgical hospitals
HQ: Mount Carmel Health
793 W State St
Columbus OH 43222
614 234-5000

(G-14868)
QWAIDE ENTERPRISES LLC
Also Called: Gng Music Instruction
6044 Phar Lap Dr (43054-8106)
PHONE..................................614 209-0551
Gregory N Gould, *Owner*
EMP: 30 EST: 2008
SALES (est): 488.7K **Privately Held**
SIC: 8748 Business consulting

(G-14869)
RE/MAX CONSULTANT GROUP
6650 Walnut St (43054-9138)
PHONE..................................614 855-2822
Mara Ackermann, *CEO*
EMP: 70
SQ FT: 10,000
SALES: 300MM **Privately Held**
SIC: 6531 Real estate agent, residential

(G-14870)
READY SET GROW
5200 New Albany Rd (43054-8836)
PHONE..................................614 855-5100
Steve Lefkovitz, *Owner*
Michelle Rosser, *Co-Owner*
EMP: 30
SALES (est): 677.9K **Privately Held**
SIC: 8351 Preschool center

(G-14871)
RED ROOF INNS INC (HQ)
7815 Walton Pkwy (43054-8233)
PHONE..................................614 744-2600
Andrew Alexander, *CEO*
Joe Merz, *Vice Pres*
Brendan P Foley, *CFO*
Marina Macdonald, *Chief Mktg Ofcr*
EMP: 525
SALES (est): 430.6MM **Privately Held**
WEB: www.redroof.com
SIC: 7011 Hotels & motels

(G-14872)
ROSSMAN
Also Called: P C B
7795 Walton Pkwy Ste 360 (43054-8247)
P.O. Box 2051 (43054-2051)
PHONE..................................614 523-4150
Brad Rossman, *Principal*
Kevin Rossman, *Financial Exec*
EMP: 30 EST: 2010
SALES (est): 4.7MM **Privately Held**
SIC: 7322 Collection agency, except real estate

(G-14873)
RYDER LAST MILE INC (HQ)
Also Called: Mxd Group
7795 Walton Pkwy (43054-0001)
PHONE..................................866 711-3129
Terry Solvedt, *CEO*
Marie Graul, *CFO*
Julie Longbrake, *Manager*
Kathy Mohler, *Supervisor*
Josh Noblitt, *Director*
EMP: 70 EST: 1974
SALES (est): 344.6MM
SALES (corp-wide): 8.4B **Publicly Held**
SIC: 4213 7389 Trucking, except local; financial services
PA: Ryder System, Inc.
11690 Nw 105th St
Medley FL 33178
305 500-3726

(G-14874)
SHREMSHOCK ARCHITECTS INC (PA)
Also Called: S A I
7400 W Campus Rd Ste 150 (43054-8739)
PHONE..................................614 545-4550
Gerald Shremshock, *President*
EMP: 100
SQ FT: 18,000
SALES (est): 4.4MM **Privately Held**
WEB: www.shremshock.com
SIC: 8712 Architectural services

(G-14875)
STATE FARM MUTL AUTO INSUR CO
Also Called: State Farm Insurance
5400 New Albany Rd (43054-8861)
PHONE..................................614 775-2001
Jason McCrory, *Principal*
EMP: 750
SALES (corp-wide): 39.5B **Privately Held**
WEB: www.statefarm.com
SIC: 6411 6321 6311 Insurance agents & brokers; accident & health insurance; life insurance
PA: State Farm Mutual Automobile Insurance Company
1 State Farm Plz
Bloomington IL 61710
309 766-2311

(G-14876)
WALLICK CONSTRUCTION LLC
160 W Main St Ste 200 (43054-1189)
PHONE..................................614 863-4640
Bill Lepper, *President*
John Leonard, *Mng Member*
EMP: 40

SQ FT: 32,000
SALES (est): 1.1MM **Privately Held**
SIC: 1542 Commercial & office building, new construction

(G-14877)
WALLICK ENTERPRISES INC
Also Called: Wallick Companies Cnstr Prpts
160 W Main St (43054-1188)
PHONE..................................614 863-4640
Sanford Goldston, *Ch of Bd*
Bob Dayne, *President*
EMP: 60
SQ FT: 13,000
SALES (est): 3.7MM **Privately Held**
SIC: 6552 Subdividers & developers

(G-14878)
WALLICK PROPERTIES MIDWEST LLC (PA)
160 W Main St Ste 200 (43054-1189)
PHONE..................................419 381-7477
Howard Wallick, *Mng Member*
Tom Feusse,
Dave Hendy,
Troi Rambo,
Julie Wallick,
EMP: 650 EST: 1966
SQ FT: 32,000
SALES (est): 38.8MM **Privately Held**
WEB: www.wallickcos.com
SIC: 6531 Real estate managers

New Bavaria
Henry County

(G-14879)
FARMERS ELEV GRN & SPLY ASSOC (PA)
16917 County Road B (43548-9723)
PHONE..................................419 653-4132
Lynn Fitzwater, *President*
Dave Keeterle, *Vice Pres*
Tim Hockman, *Treasurer*
EMP: 28
SQ FT: 3,000
SALES: 55.7MM **Privately Held**
SIC: 5153 5191 Grain elevators; farm supplies

New Boston
Scioto County

(G-14880)
HERITAGE PROFESSIONAL SERVICES
Also Called: Heritage Square New Boston
3304 Rhodes Ave (45662-4914)
PHONE..................................740 456-8245
Gilbert E Lawson, *President*
Irene Leadingham, *Admin Sec*
EMP: 25
SALES (est): 1.4MM **Privately Held**
WEB: www.heritagesquareonline.com
SIC: 8052 Personal care facility

(G-14881)
NEW BOSTON AERIE 2271 FOE
Also Called: New Boston Eagles
3200 Rhodes Ave (45662-4912)
PHONE..................................740 456-0171
Oral Gulley, *President*
Jeff Gulley, *Vice Pres*
William David Jones, *Treasurer*
Scott Shope, *Admin Sec*
Don Cox,
EMP: 33
SALES (est): 477.1K **Privately Held**
SIC: 8641 Fraternal associations

(G-14882)
SCIOTO COUNTY OHIO
Also Called: Scioto County Child Services
3940 Gallia St (45662-4925)
PHONE..................................740 456-4164
Lisa Wiltshire, *Director*
EMP: 31 **Privately Held**
WEB:
www.sciotocountychildrenservices.com

SIC: 8322 9111 Children's aid society; county supervisors' & executives' offices
PA: Scioto County Ohio
602 7th St Rm 1
Portsmouth OH 45662
740 355-8313

(G-14883)
SOUTH CENTRAL OHIO EDUCTL CTR
522 Glenwood Ave (45662-5505)
PHONE..................................740 456-0517
Darren Jenkins, *Superintendent*
Andrew Riehl, *Treasurer*
Tom Hoggard, *Finance Other*
EMP: 109
SALES (est): 3.8MM **Privately Held**
SIC: 8299 8748 Arts & crafts schools; testing services

(G-14884)
SUPERIOR KRAFT HOMES LLC
3404 Rhodes Ave (45662-4916)
PHONE..................................740 947-7710
EMP: 61
SALES (est): 3.8MM **Privately Held**
SIC: 1522 Residential Construction

New Bremen
Auglaize County

(G-14885)
BROOKSIDE LABORATORIES INC
200 White Mountain Dr (45869-8603)
PHONE..................................419 977-2766
Thomas Menke, *Ch of Bd*
Mark Flock, *President*
Allen Metzger, *CFO*
Kari Long, *Director*
EMP: 34
SQ FT: 25,000
SALES (est): 4.2MM **Privately Held**
WEB: www.blinc.com
SIC: 8734 Soil analysis

(G-14886)
COUNTY OF AUGLAIZE
Also Called: Auglaize County Board of Mr/Dd
20 E 1st St (45869-1165)
PHONE..................................419 629-2419
Alvin Willis, *Superintendent*
EMP: 70 **Privately Held**
WEB: www.augmrdd.org
SIC: 8361 9111 Home for the mentally handicapped; county supervisors' & executives' offices
PA: County Of Auglaize
209 S Blackhoof St # 201
Wapakoneta OH 45895
419 739-6710

(G-14887)
CROWN EQUIPMENT CORPORATION (PA)
Also Called: Crown Lift Trucks
44 S Washington St (45869-1288)
P.O. Box 97 (45869-0097)
PHONE..................................419 629-2311
James F Dicke II, *Ch of Bd*
James F Dicke III, *President*
David J Besser, *Senior VP*
James R Mozer, *Senior VP*
Timothy S Quellhorst, *Senior VP*
◆ **EMP:** 4528
SQ FT: 25,000
SALES: 3.1B **Privately Held**
WEB: www.crown.com
SIC: 5084 Lift trucks & parts

(G-14888)
CROWN EQUIPMENT CORPORATION
40 S Washington St (45869-1247)
PHONE..................................419 629-2311
EMP: 65
SALES (corp-wide): 1.3B **Privately Held**
SIC: 5084 3537 Whol Industrial Equipment Mfg Industrial Trucks/Tractors

PA: Crown Equipment Corporation
44 S Washington St
New Bremen OH 45869
419 629-2311

New Carlisle
Clark County

(G-14889)
CHAMBER COMMERCE NEW CARLISLE
131 S Main St (45344-1952)
PHONE......................937 845-3911
Linda Campbell, *President*
EMP: 47
SALES (est): 619.7K **Privately Held**
SIC: 8611 Chamber of Commerce

(G-14890)
ELM VALLEY FISHING CLUB INC
5118 S Dayton Brandt Rd (45344-9611)
PHONE......................937 845-0584
Jack Weaver, *Principal*
EMP: 100
SQ FT: 2,646
SALES (est): 1MM **Privately Held**
SIC: 7997 Hunting club, membership

(G-14891)
INTEGRITY INFORMATION TECH INC
Also Called: Integrity It
2742 N Dayton Lakeview Rd (45344-8503)
PHONE......................937 846-1769
Mark Debreceni, *President*
Sara E Debreceni, *Owner*
John Simkins, *Principal*
EMP: 25
SALES: 3.3MM **Privately Held**
WEB: www.integrity-it.com
SIC: 7379

(G-14892)
KAFFENBARGER TRUCK EQP CO (PA)
10100 Ballentine Pike (45344-9534)
PHONE......................937 845-3804
Larry Kaffenbarger, *President*
Edward W Dunn, *Principal*
Everett L Kaffenbarger, *Principal*
◆ EMP: 110
SQ FT: 30,000
SALES (est): 38.4MM **Privately Held**
WEB: www.kaffenbarger.com
SIC: 3713 5013 Truck bodies (motor vehicles); truck parts & accessories

(G-14893)
LOUDERBACK FMLY INVSTMENTS INC
Also Called: Professional Property Maint
3545 S Dayton Lakeview Rd (45344-2345)
P.O. Box 24383, Dayton (45424-0383)
PHONE......................937 845-1762
Kevin Louderback, *President*
Don Louderback, *Executive*
EMP: 35
SQ FT: 6,000
SALES (est): 1.3MM **Privately Held**
SIC: 7349 0781 Building maintenance, except repairs; landscape services

(G-14894)
MIGRANT HEAD START
476 N Dayton Lakeview Rd (45344-2109)
PHONE......................937 846-0699
George Hardy, *Owner*
EMP: 45 EST: 2007
SALES (est): 62K **Privately Held**
SIC: 8351 Head start center, except in conjunction with school

(G-14895)
NEW CARLISLE SPT & FITNES CTR
524 N Dayton Lakeview Rd (45344-2111)
PHONE......................937 846-1000
Vijaya Devatha, *Owner*
EMP: 35

SALES (est): 787.8K **Privately Held**
SIC: 8099 7991 Nutrition services; health club

(G-14896)
ROOFING BY INSULATION INC
1727 Dalton Dr (45344-2309)
PHONE......................937 315-5024
Dave Dick, *President*
EMP: 27 EST: 2008
SALES: 1.2MM **Privately Held**
SIC: 1761 1742 Roofing contractor; insulation, buildings

(G-14897)
SCARFFS NURSERY INC
411 N Dayton Lakeview Rd (45344-2149)
PHONE......................937 845-3130
Peter Scarff, *President*
William N Scarff Sr, *Chairman*
EMP: 125
SQ FT: 8,000
SALES: 6MM **Privately Held**
WEB: www.scarffs.com
SIC: 0181 5992 0781 5261 Nursery stock, growing of; flowers, fresh; plants, potted; landscape architects; nurseries & garden centers; flowers & florists' supplies

(G-14898)
STUDEBAKER NURSERIES INC
Also Called: Studebaker Wholesale Nurseries
11140 Milton Carlisle Rd (45344-9298)
PHONE......................800 845-0584
William Studebaker, *President*
Dan W Studebaker, *Vice Pres*
EMP: 80
SQ FT: 2,500
SALES (est): 8.5MM **Privately Held**
WEB: www.studebakernurseries.com
SIC: 0181 Nursery stock, growing of

(G-14899)
WENCO INC
1807 Dalton Dr (45344-2305)
PHONE......................937 849-6002
Fax: 937 845-9221
EMP: 125
SQ FT: 12,000
SALES (est): 35.1MM **Privately Held**
SIC: 1542 1541 Nonresidential Construction Industrial Building Construction

New Concord
Muskingum County

(G-14900)
GUERNSY-MUSKINGUM ELC COOP INC (PA)
Also Called: Guernsey-Muskingum Elc Coop
17 S Liberty St (43762-1230)
PHONE......................740 826-7661
Shirley Stutz, *President*
Brian Hill, *President*
John Enos, *Corp Secy*
EMP: 44
SQ FT: 15,000
SALES: 34.4MM **Privately Held**
WEB: www.gmenergy.com
SIC: 4911 Distribution, electric power

(G-14901)
MUSKINGUM VLY SYMPHONIC WINDS
163 Stormont St (43762-1118)
PHONE......................740 826-8095
David Turrill, *CEO*
Kathy Brown, *Principal*
EMP: 25
SALES (est): 300.6K **Privately Held**
SIC: 7929 Entertainers & entertainment groups

(G-14902)
NEW CONCORD HEALTH CENTER
1280 Friendship Dr (43762-1024)
PHONE......................740 826-4135
Mark Richards, *Manager*
EMP: 137

SALES (est): 5MM **Privately Held**
WEB: www.zandex.com
SIC: 8059 Nursing/Personal Care

(G-14903)
SOUTHEASTERN OHIO SYMPHONY ORC
163 Stormont St (43762-1118)
P.O. Box 42 (43762-0042)
PHONE......................740 826-8197
Chris Stotler, *President*
Erin France, *Vice Pres*
EMP: 50
SALES: 53.4K **Privately Held**
SIC: 7929 Symphony orchestras

(G-14904)
TK GAS SERVICES INC
2303 John Glenn Hwy (43762-9310)
PHONE......................740 826-0303
Ted Korte, *President*
Jill Pattison, *Corp Secy*
EMP: 50
SQ FT: 4,000
SALES (est): 6.6MM **Privately Held**
SIC: 1389 Oil field services

(G-14905)
ZANDEX INC
Also Called: Beckett House
1280 Friendship Dr (43762-1024)
PHONE......................740 872-0809
Mark Richards, *Manager*
EMP: 120
SALES (corp-wide): 34MM **Privately Held**
SIC: 8052 8051 Intermediate care facilities; skilled nursing care facilities
PA: Zandex, Inc.
1122 Taylor St
Zanesville OH 43701
740 454-1400

(G-14906)
ZANDEX HEALTH CARE CORPORATION
Also Called: Beckett House At New Concord
1280 Friendship Dr (43762-1024)
PHONE......................740 454-1400
Margarett Richard, *Manager*
EMP: 140
SALES (corp-wide): 34MM **Privately Held**
SIC: 8052 8051 8361 Intermediate care facilities; skilled nursing care facilities; residential care
HQ: Zandex Health Care Corporation
1122 Taylor St
Zanesville OH 43701

New Franklin
Summit County

(G-14907)
CLINTON ALUMINUM DIST INC (PA)
6270 Van Buren Rd (44216-9743)
PHONE......................330 882-6743
Robert Krieger, *President*
Tom Dagenback, *Vice Pres*
Gregory Ertle, *Vice Pres*
Mark Jodon, *Manager*
▲ EMP: 113 EST: 2010
SQ FT: 165,000
SALES (est): 74.7MM **Privately Held**
SIC: 5051 Steel

(G-14908)
CONCEPT FREIGHT SERVICE INC
4386 Point Comfort Dr (44319-4076)
PHONE......................330 784-1134
Thomas L Cook, *President*
Jeffrey L Cook, *Vice Pres*
Allen Klever, *Vice Pres*
Jody Hamilton, *Treasurer*
Jan Good, *Manager*
EMP: 40
SQ FT: 9,600
SALES (est): 6.1MM **Privately Held**
WEB: www.conceptfreightinc.com
SIC: 4213 Trucking, except local

(G-14909)
EAST OHIO GAS COMPANY
Also Called: Dominion Energy Ohio
6500 Hampsher Rd (44216-8905)
PHONE......................330 266-2169
Greg Theril, *Manager*
EMP: 296
SALES (corp-wide): 13.3B **Publicly Held**
SIC: 4924 Natural gas distribution
HQ: The East Ohio Gas Company
1201 E 55th St
Cleveland OH 44103
800 362-7557

(G-14910)
JPMORGAN CHASE BANK NAT ASSN
5638 Manchester Rd (44319-4213)
PHONE......................330 972-1735
Connie Nagy, *Principal*
EMP: 26
SALES (corp-wide): 131.4B **Publicly Held**
SIC: 6021 National commercial banks
HQ: Jpmorgan Chase Bank, National Association
1111 Polaris Pkwy
Columbus OH 43240
614 436-3055

(G-14911)
OCCASIONS PARTY CENTRE
6800 Manchester Rd (44216-9491)
PHONE......................330 882-5113
Lisa Masey, *Owner*
EMP: 50
SQ FT: 30,471
SALES (est): 1.1MM **Privately Held**
WEB: www.occasionspartycentre.com
SIC: 7299 Banquet hall facilities

(G-14912)
SPRING HILLS GOLF CLUB
6571 Clvland Massillon Rd (44216-9342)
PHONE......................330 825-2439
Gary Kendron, *General Mgr*
EMP: 25
SALES (est): 900K **Privately Held**
SIC: 7992 Public golf courses

(G-14913)
ST LUKE LUTHERAN COMMUNITY
615 Latham Ln (44319-4338)
PHONE......................330 644-3914
John L Spieler, *President*
Ron Derry, *CFO*
EMP: 60
SQ FT: 4,000
SALES (est): 2.9MM **Privately Held**
SIC: 8052 Personal care facility

(G-14914)
ST LUKE LUTHERAN COMMUNITY
615 Latham Ln (44319-4338)
PHONE......................330 644-3914
Rev L W Lautenschlager, *Branch Mgr*
EMP: 80
SQ FT: 19,346
SALES (corp-wide): 15.5MM **Privately Held**
WEB: www.stlukelutherancommunity.org
SIC: 8052 Personal care facility
PA: St. Luke Lutheran Community
220 Applegrove St Ne
Canton OH
330 499-8341

(G-14915)
SUMMIT CLAIM SERVICES LLC
5511 Manchester Rd Ste C (44319-4282)
PHONE......................330 706-9898
Ron Costa,
EMP: 100 EST: 2008
SALES (est): 10.2MM **Privately Held**
SIC: 6411 7389 Insurance claim adjusters, not employed by insurance company; auction, appraisal & exchange services

New Haven
Huron County

(G-14916)
NEW HAVEN ESTATES INC (PA)
2744 E State Highway 224 (44850)
PHONE..419 933-2181
Thomas M Saas, *President*
David F Roberts, *Vice Pres*
Sheila Urie, *Vice Pres*
Ann W Von Saas, *Admin Sec*
EMP: 28
SQ FT: 38,000
SALES (est): 8.2MM **Privately Held**
WEB: www.newhavensupply.com
SIC: 5063 5085 5074 Electrical apparatus & equipment; industrial supplies; plumbing & hydronic heating supplies

New Knoxville
Auglaize County

(G-14917)
HOGE LUMBER COMPANY (PA)
Also Called: Hoge Brush
701 S Main St State (45871)
PHONE..419 753-2263
John H Hoge, *President*
Jack R Hoge, *Exec VP*
Clark T Froning, *Vice Pres*
Bruce L Hoge, *Vice Pres*
Bruce Eschmeyer, *Sales Mgr*
▲ EMP: 35
SQ FT: 400,000
SALES (est): 6.4MM **Privately Held**
WEB: www.hoge.com
SIC: 3448 1521 2521 Prefabricated metal buildings; new construction, single-family houses; cabinets, office: wood

New Lexington
Perry County

(G-14918)
COUNTY OF PERRY
445 W Broadway St Ste C (43764-1097)
PHONE..740 342-0416
Robin Demattia, *Branch Mgr*
EMP: 31 **Privately Held**
SIC: 9199 8051 7997 ; mental retardation hospital; country club, membership
PA: County Of Perry
121 W Brown St D
New Lexington OH 43764
740 342-2045

(G-14919)
COUNTY OF PERRY
Also Called: Perry County Engineer
2645 Old Somerset Rd (43764-9547)
PHONE..740 342-2191
Kenton C Cannon, *Director*
EMP: 35 **Privately Held**
SIC: 8711 Engineering services
PA: County Of Perry
121 W Brown St D
New Lexington OH 43764
740 342-2045

(G-14920)
LORI HOLDING CO (PA)
Also Called: Siemer Distributing
1400 Commerce Dr (43764-9500)
PHONE..740 342-3230
Joseph A Siemer III, *President*
EMP: 30
SALES (est): 10.8MM **Privately Held**
SIC: 5147 5143 5199 5142 Meats, fresh; cheese; ice, manufactured or natural; packaged frozen goods; manufactured ice

(G-14921)
MOUNT ALOYSIUS CORP
5375 Tile Plant Rd Se (43764-9801)
P.O. Box 598 (43764-0598)
PHONE..740 342-3343
William Shimp, *Ch of Bd*
Jean Ann Arbaugh, *President*

George Fisher, *Vice Pres*
EMP: 135 EST: 1969
SALES: 8.3MM **Privately Held**
SIC: 8361 8052 Home for the mentally retarded; intermediate care facilities

(G-14922)
NEW LEXINGTON CITY OF
Also Called: New Lexington Mncpl Water Plnt
215 S Main St (43764-1370)
PHONE..740 342-1633
Mark Cooper, *Superintendent*
EMP: 50
SALES (est): 7.4MM **Privately Held**
SIC: 4952 4941 Sewerage systems; water supply

(G-14923)
NEWLEX CLASSIC RIDERS INC
810 N Main St (43764-1042)
P.O. Box 27 (43764-0027)
PHONE..740 342-3885
Randy Altier, *President*
Ted Johnson, *Vice Pres*
EMP: 55
SALES (est): 824.5K **Privately Held**
WEB: www.newlexclassicriders.com
SIC: 7997 Membership sports & recreation clubs

(G-14924)
OXFORD MINING COMPANY INC
Also Called: Tunnell Hill Reclamation
2500 Township Rd 205 (43764)
PHONE..740 342-7666
Jeff Williams, *Superintendent*
EMP: 58
SALES (corp-wide): 1.3B **Privately Held**
SIC: 1221 Strip mining, bituminous
HQ: Oxford Mining Company, Inc.
544 Chestnut St
Coshocton OH 43812
740 622-6302

(G-14925)
PEOPLES NAT BNK OF NEW LXNGTON (PA)
110 N Main St (43764-1261)
P.O. Box 111 (43764-0111)
PHONE..740 342-5111
G Courtney Haning, *CEO*
Tony L Davis, *President*
Brenda Wright, *Exec VP*
EMP: 40
SALES: 5.5MM **Privately Held**
WEB: www.peoplesnational.com
SIC: 6021 National trust companies with deposits, commercial

(G-14926)
PERCO INC
2235 State Route 13 Ne (43764-9707)
PHONE..740 342-5156
Melissa Howell, *Principal*
Ron Spung, *Principal*
Janet Taylor, *Office Mgr*
Vikki Waymire, *Admin Sec*
EMP: 85
SQ FT: 14,000
SALES (est): 849.1K **Privately Held**
SIC: 8331 Vocational rehabilitation agency

(G-14927)
RESIDENTIAL INC
226 S Main St (43764-1369)
P.O. Box 101 (43764-0101)
PHONE..740 342-4158
Gretchen Brown, *Manager*
Linda Stonebrook, *Director*
EMP: 50
SQ FT: 1,000
SALES: 1.8MM **Privately Held**
SIC: 8361 Home for the mentally retarded

(G-14928)
SIEMER DISTRIBUTING COMPANY
1400 Commerce Dr (43764-9500)
PHONE..740 342-3230
Joseph A Siemer III, *President*
Veronica Rodgers, *Director*
Dolores Siemer, *Admin Sec*
EMP: 30
SQ FT: 3,000

SALES (est): 2.7MM
SALES (corp-wide): 10.8MM **Privately Held**
WEB: www.siemerdistributingcompany.com
SIC: 5147 5143 5199 Meats, fresh; cheese; ice, manufactured or natural
PA: Lori Holding Co.
1400 Commerce Dr
New Lexington OH 43764
740 342-3230

(G-14929)
SUNBRIDGE HEALTHCARE LLC
Also Called: New Lxngton Care Rhblttion Ctr
920 S Main St (43764-1552)
P.O. Box 507 (43764-0507)
PHONE..740 342-5161
Tammy Corp, *Facilities Dir*
Andy Iekies, *Manager*
EMP: 112 **Publicly Held**
WEB: www.innoventurehealthcare.com
SIC: 8052 8051 Intermediate care facilities; skilled nursing care facilities
HQ: Sunbridge Healthcare, Llc
101 Sun Ave Ne
Albuquerque NM 87109
505 821-3355

New London
Huron County

(G-14930)
204 W MAIN STREET OPER CO LLC
Also Called: Rehab Nursing Ctr At Firelands
204 W Main St (44851-1070)
PHONE..419 929-1563
Dena Mc Killips, *Nursing Dir*
Amy Donaldson, *Administration*
EMP: 85
SALES (est): 2.7MM **Privately Held**
WEB: www.hazelstreet.com
SIC: 8051 Skilled nursing care facilities

(G-14931)
CLARE-MAR CAMP INC
Also Called: Clare-Mar Lakes Rv Sales
47571 New Lndon Eastrn Rd (44851)
P.O. Box 229, Wellington (44090-0229)
PHONE..440 647-3318
Donald B Sears, *President*
Barbara J Sears, *Treasurer*
Brenda Sears, *Admin Sec*
Nicole Sosa,
EMP: 27
SALES (est): 1.3MM **Privately Held**
SIC: 7033 5561 Campgrounds; recreational vehicle dealers

(G-14932)
FIRELANDS AMBULANCE SERVICE
25 James St (44851-1211)
PHONE..419 929-1487
Paul Lortcher, *President*
Jeffrey Vanderpool,
EMP: 35 EST: 1978
SQ FT: 500
SALES: 200K **Privately Held**
SIC: 4119 Ambulance service

(G-14933)
NEW LONDON AREA HISTORICAL SOC
210 E Main St (44851-1154)
PHONE..419 929-3674
Thomas Neel, *President*
Martha Sturges, *Vice Pres*
Vaughn Neel, *Treasurer*
Jean Myers, *Admin Sec*
EMP: 81 EST: 1985
SALES: 11.5K **Privately Held**
SIC: 8412 Historical society

(G-14934)
PACE INTERNATIONAL UNION
100 New London Ave (44851-1186)
PHONE..419 929-1335
David Harlan, *Treasurer*
EMP: 45

SALES (corp-wide): 26.9MM **Privately Held**
SIC: 8631 Labor unions & similar labor organizations
PA: Pace International Union
5 Gateway Ctr
Pittsburgh PA 15222
412 562-2400

(G-14935)
PRIMETALS TECHNOLOGIES USA LLC
81 E Washburn St (44851-1247)
PHONE..419 929-1554
John Bailey, *Manager*
EMP: 50
SALES (corp-wide): 38.5B **Privately Held**
WEB: www.srt-ar.com
SIC: 7699 5084 Industrial equipment services; industrial machinery & equipment
HQ: Primetals Technologies Usa Llc
5895 Windward Pkwy Fl 2
Alpharetta GA 30005
770 740-3800

(G-14936)
U-HAUL NEIGHBORHOOD DEALER -CE
1005 Us Highway 250 S (44851-9110)
PHONE..419 929-3724
EMP: 25 EST: 2010
SALES (est): 336.5K **Privately Held**
SIC: 7519 7513 5099 4212 Utility Trailer Rental Truck Rental/Leasing Whol Durable Goods Local Trucking Operator

New Madison
Darke County

(G-14937)
LUDY GREENHOUSE MFG CORP (PA)
122 Railroad St (45346-5016)
P.O. Box 141 (45346-0141)
PHONE..800 255-5839
Stephan A Scantland, *President*
Deborah Scantland, *Vice Pres*
EMP: 62 EST: 1957
SQ FT: 2,500
SALES (est): 18.3MM **Privately Held**
SIC: 1542 3448 Greenhouse construction; greenhouses: prefabricated metal

(G-14938)
TRI VILLAGE RESCUE SERVICE
Also Called: Tri Village Joint Ambulance
320 N Main St (45346-9794)
P.O. Box 247 (45346-0247)
PHONE..937 996-3155
Eric Burns, *CEO*
Jerry Burns, *Principal*
EMP: 30
SALES (est): 300.9K **Privately Held**
SIC: 4119 Ambulance service

New Middletown
Mahoning County

(G-14939)
VENEZIA TRANSPORT SERVICE INC
Also Called: Venezia Hauling
6017 E Calla Rd (44442-9725)
P.O. Box 26, Bessemer PA (16112-0026)
PHONE..330 542-9735
Ted Habuda, *Manager*
EMP: 30
SALES (est): 1.5MM **Privately Held**
WEB: www.veneziainc.com
SIC: 4213 Contract haulers
PA: Venezia Transport Service, Inc.
86 Airport Rd
Pottstown PA 19464

GEOGRAPHIC

New Paris
Preble County

(G-14940)
BLUE BEACON USA LP II
Also Called: Blue Beacon Truck Wash
9787 Us Route 40 W (45347-1521)
PHONE.................................937 437-5533
Jody Cochrain, *Manager*
EMP: 35
SALES (corp-wide): 99MM **Privately Held**
WEB: www.bluebeacon.com
SIC: 7542 Truck wash
PA: Blue Beacon U.S.A., L.P. Ii
500 Graves Blvd
Salina KS 67401
785 825-2221

(G-14941)
CREATIVE LEARNING WORKSHOP
146 N Washington St (45347-1152)
PHONE.................................937 437-0146
Vincent E Fisher, *Manager*
EMP: 25
SALES (corp-wide): 7.2MM **Privately Held**
SIC: 8331 Vocational rehabilitation agency
PA: The Creative Learning Workshop
2460 Elm Rd Ne Ste 500
Warren OH 44483
330 393-5929

(G-14942)
FOUNDATIONS
Also Called: Cedar Springs
7739 Us Route 40 (45347-9048)
PHONE.................................937 437-2311
Tracey Ross, *Administration*
EMP: 75
SALES (est): 1.5MM **Privately Held**
SIC: 8052 Home for the mentally retarded, with health care

(G-14943)
HERITAGE PARK REHABILITA
Also Called: Cedar Springs Care Center
7739 Us Route 40 (45347-9048)
PHONE.................................937 437-2311
Suw Watts, *Manager*
EMP: 30
SALES (corp-wide): 230.6MM **Privately Held**
WEB: www.eldercareofwv.com
SIC: 8051 8052 Extended care facility; intermediate care facilities
HQ: Heritage Park Rehabilitation And Healthcare Center, Llc
5565 Bankers Ave
Baton Rouge LA 70808

(G-14944)
NORTHWEST FIRE AMBULANCE
135 N Washington St (45347-1151)
P.O. Box 66 (45347-0066)
PHONE.................................937 437-8354
Paul Cones, *Chief*
Brad Simpson, *Asst Chief*
EMP: 27
SALES (est): 607.9K **Privately Held**
SIC: 4119 Ambulance service

New Philadelphia
Tuscarawas County

(G-14945)
ALLSTATE TRK SLS OF ESTRN OH
Also Called: Alstate-Peterbilt-Trucks
327 Stonecreek Rd Nw (44663-6902)
PHONE.................................330 339-5555
Jesse Smitley, *Manager*
EMP: 33
SALES (corp-wide): 6.4MM **Privately Held**
SIC: 5511 5531 7538 Automobiles, new & used; automobile & truck equipment & parts; general truck repair

PA: Allstate Truck Sales Of Eastern Ohio, Llc
10700 Lyndale Ave S
Minneapolis MN 55420
952 703-3444

(G-14946)
AMERIDIAL INC
521 W High Ave (44663-2053)
PHONE.................................330 339-7222
Cathy McGee, *Branch Mgr*
EMP: 65
SALES (corp-wide): 40MM **Privately Held**
SIC: 7389 Telemarketing services
HQ: Ameridial, Inc.
4535 Strausser St Nw
North Canton OH 44720
330 497-4888

(G-14947)
BULK CARRIER TRNSP EQP CO
2743 Brightwood Rd Se (44663-6773)
PHONE.................................330 339-3333
Richard S Hartrick, *President*
Marcia Hartrick, *Vice Pres*
EMP: 26
SALES (est): 4.4MM **Privately Held**
WEB: www.bcte.com
SIC: 5012 2519 Trailers for trucks, new & used; household furniture, except wood or metal: upholstered

(G-14948)
CELLCO PARTNERSHIP
Also Called: Verizon Wireless
507 Mill Ave Se (44663-3864)
PHONE.................................330 308-0549
EMP: 57
SALES (corp-wide): 130.8B **Publicly Held**
SIC: 4812 Cellular telephone services
HQ: Cellco Partnership
1 Verizon Way
Basking Ridge NJ 07920

(G-14949)
CHILDRENS HOSP MED CTR AKRON
1045 W High Ave (44663-2071)
PHONE.................................330 308-5432
Susan Karitides, *Branch Mgr*
John Fargo, *Director*
EMP: 732
SALES (corp-wide): 747.4MM **Privately Held**
SIC: 8069 8062 Children's hospital; general medical & surgical hospitals
PA: Childrens Hospital Medical Center Of Akron
1 Perkins Sq
Akron OH 44308
330 543-1000

(G-14950)
CITY OF NEW PHILADELPHIA
Also Called: New Philadelphia General Svcs
1234 Commercial Ave Se (44663-2355)
PHONE.................................330 339-2121
Fred Neff, *Superintendent*
EMP: 35
SQ FT: 2,301 **Privately Held**
WEB: www.newphilaoh.com
SIC: 9111 7521 Mayors' offices; automobile storage garage
PA: City Of New Philadelphia
150 E High Ave Ste 15
New Philadelphia OH 44663
330 364-4491

(G-14951)
COPLEY OHIO NEWSPAPERS INC
Also Called: Times Reporter/Midwest Offset
629 Wabash Ave Nw (44663-4145)
P.O. Box 667 (44663-0667)
PHONE.................................330 364-5577
Kevin Kampman, *Publisher*
EMP: 245
SALES (corp-wide): 1.5B **Publicly Held**
WEB: www.timesreporter.com
SIC: 2711 2752 7313 2791 Commercial printing & newspaper publishing combined; commercial printing, offset; newspaper advertising representative; typesetting; bookbinding & related work

HQ: Copley Ohio Newspapers Inc
500 Market Ave S
Canton OH 44702
585 598-0030

(G-14952)
CORNERSTONE SUPPORT SERVICES (PA)
Also Called: Southeast
344 W High Ave (44663-2152)
PHONE.................................330 339-7850
Beth Powell, *Exec Dir*
Sandra Stevenson, *Director*
Carrie Baker, *Director*
Joe Wilson, *Director*
EMP: 75
SQ FT: 2,856
SALES (est): 2MM **Privately Held**
SIC: 8093 Mental health clinic, outpatient

(G-14953)
CORPORATION FOR OH APPALACHIAN
1260 Monroe St Nw Ste 39s (44663-4147)
PHONE.................................330 364-8882
Sherri Guthrie, *Branch Mgr*
EMP: 29
SALES (corp-wide): 25.3MM **Privately Held**
SIC: 8351 Head start center, except in conjunction with school
PA: Corporation For Ohio Appalachian Development
1 Pinchot Pl
Athens OH 45701
740 594-8499

(G-14954)
COUNTY OF TUSCARAWAS
Also Called: Child Support
154 2nd St Ne (44663-2854)
PHONE.................................330 343-0099
Linda Warner, *Director*
EMP: 45
SQ FT: 8,868 **Privately Held**
WEB: www.neohiotravel.com
SIC: 8322 9111 Child related social services; county supervisors' & executives' offices
PA: County Of Tuscarawas
125 E High Ave
New Philadelphia OH 44663
330 364-8811

(G-14955)
COUNTY OF TUSCARAWAS
Also Called: Tuscarawas Cnty Job Fmly Svcs
389 16th St Sw (44663-6401)
PHONE.................................330 339-7791
Lynn Angellzzi, *Manager*
EMP: 80 **Privately Held**
WEB: www.neohiotravel.com
SIC: 8322 9199 Probation office; adoption services; child related social services;
PA: County Of Tuscarawas
125 E High Ave
New Philadelphia OH 44663
330 364-8811

(G-14956)
DEARTH MANAGEMENT COMPANY
Also Called: Moring View Care Center
2594 E High Ave (44663-6737)
PHONE.................................330 339-3595
Denise La Creta, *Persnl Dir*
Loraine Lady, *Director*
EMP: 150
SALES (corp-wide): 12.3MM **Privately Held**
WEB: www.schoenbrunnhealthcare.com
SIC: 8052 8051 Personal care facility; skilled nursing care facilities
PA: Dearth Management Company
134 Northwoods Blvd Ste C
Columbus OH 43235
614 847-1070

(G-14957)
DISABLED AMERICAN VETERANS
824 Hardesty Ave Nw (44663-1132)
PHONE.................................330 364-1204
George Phillips, *President*
EMP: 330

SALES (corp-wide): 137MM **Privately Held**
SIC: 8641 Veterans' organization
PA: Disabled American Veterans
3725 Alexandria Pike
Cold Spring KY 41076
859 441-7300

(G-14958)
ENERGY POWER SERVICES INC
3251 Brightwood Rd Se (44663-7410)
PHONE.................................330 343-2312
Allen M Milarcik, *President*
EMP: 30
SALES (est): 254.8K **Privately Held**
SIC: 4212 Local trucking, without storage

(G-14959)
FENTON BROS ELECTRIC CO
Also Called: Fenton's Festival of Lights
235 Ray Ave Ne (44663-2813)
P.O. Box 996 (44663-0996)
PHONE.................................330 343-0093
Tom Fenton, *President*
Dennis Fenton, *Vice Pres*
Brian Fenton, *Treasurer*
Jim Hines, *Sales Staff*
Nancy Glenn, *Office Mgr*
EMP: 30 EST: 1947
SQ FT: 37,000
SALES (est): 23.4MM **Privately Held**
WEB: www.fentonbros.com
SIC: 5063 7694 Electrical supplies; electric motor repair

(G-14960)
HARBOR HOUSE INC
349 E High Ave (44663-2535)
P.O. Box 435 (44663-0435)
PHONE.................................740 498-7213
Starlene Lewis, *Exec Dir*
EMP: 25
SALES: 540K **Privately Held**
SIC: 8322 Emergency shelters

(G-14961)
HARCATUS TRI-COUNTY COMMUNITY (PA)
Also Called: Harcacus Tri-County Cmty Actn
225 Fair Ave Ne (44663-2837)
PHONE.................................740 922-0933
Rebecca Burkhart, *Nutritionist*
Alison Kerns, *Exec Dir*
Charles E Lorenz, *Exec Dir*
Charles Lorenz II, *Exec Dir*
Nancy Reed, *Exec Dir*
EMP: 46
SQ FT: 1,500
SALES: 7.5MM **Privately Held**
SIC: 8322 Social service center; referral service for personal & social problems; emergency social services; meal delivery program

(G-14962)
HARCATUS TRI-COUNTY COMMUNITY
504 Bowers Ave Nw (44663-4107)
PHONE.................................330 602-5442
EMP: 76
SALES (corp-wide): 7.5MM **Privately Held**
SIC: 8351 Head start center, except in conjunction with school
PA: Harcatus Tri-County Community Action Organization
225 Fair Ave Ne
New Philadelphia OH 44663
740 922-0933

(G-14963)
HARIBOL HARIBOL INC (PA)
Also Called: Holiday Inn
145 Bluebell Dr Sw (44663-9660)
PHONE.................................330 339-7731
Naresh Patel, *President*
EMP: 30
SALES (est): 1.2MM **Privately Held**
SIC: 7011 7299 Hotels; banquet hall facilities

(G-14964)
HICKS ROOFING INC
Also Called: Hicks Industrial Roofing
2162 Pleasant Vly Rd Ne (44663-8079)
PHONE..................................330 364-7737
Michael Hicks, *President*
Beth Hicks, *Vice Pres*
Bob Pryse, *Technical Mgr*
EMP: 40
SQ FT: 14,600
SALES (est): 5.7MM **Privately Held**
WEB: www.hicksroofing.com
SIC: 1761 Roofing contractor

(G-14965)
HOSPICE TUSCARAWAS COUNTY INC (PA)
Also Called: COMMUNITY HOSPICE
716 Commercial Ave Sw (44663-9367)
PHONE..................................330 343-7605
Norman Mast, *President*
Mike Griesen, *Vice Pres*
Nicholas Reynolds, *CFO*
Anissa Fuller, *Director*
Bonnie James, *Director*
EMP: 150
SQ FT: 22,500
SALES (est): 18.9MM **Privately Held**
WEB: www.hospiceoftusc.org
SIC: 8059 Nursing home, except skilled & intermediate care facility

(G-14966)
HYDRAULIC PARTS STORE INC
145 1st Dr Ne (44663-2857)
P.O. Box 808 (44663-0808)
PHONE..................................330 364-6667
Robert M Henning Sr, *President*
EMP: 30
SQ FT: 25,000
SALES (est): 14.6MM **Privately Held**
SIC: 5084 3594 3593 3492 Hydraulic systems equipment & supplies; fluid power pumps & motors; fluid power cylinders & actuators; fluid power valves & hose fittings

(G-14967)
J & D MINING INC
3497 University Dr Ne (44663-6711)
PHONE..................................330 339-4935
John R Demuth, *President*
James R Demuth, *Vice Pres*
EMP: 38
SQ FT: 1,000
SALES (est): 4.3MM **Privately Held**
SIC: 1221 Bituminous coal surface mining

(G-14968)
JPMORGAN CHASE BANK NAT ASSN
Also Called: Chase Bank and Atm
141 E High Ave (44663-2539)
PHONE..................................330 364-7242
Patricia Hile, *Principal*
EMP: 26
SALES (corp-wide): 131.4B **Publicly Held**
SIC: 6029 Commercial banks
HQ: Jpmorgan Chase Bank, National Association
    1111 Polaris Pkwy
    Columbus OH 43240
    614 436-3055

(G-14969)
KRUGLIAK WILKINS GRIFIYHD &
158 N Broadway St (44663-2628)
PHONE..................................330 364-3472
Terry Moore, *Branch Mgr*
Krugliak Wilkins, *Exec Dir*
Kelly Osborne, *Director*
Nathan Vaughan, *Executive*
John Schomer,
EMP: 36
SALES (corp-wide): 11.2MM **Privately Held**
SIC: 8111 General practice attorney, lawyer
PA: Krugliak, Wilkins, Griffiths And Dougherty Co Lpa
    4775 Munson St Nw
    Canton OH 44718
    330 497-0700

(G-14970)
LANDSCPING RCLMTION SPCIALISTS
3497 University Dr Ne (44663-6711)
PHONE..................................330 339-4900
John R Demuth, *President*
EMP: 50
SQ FT: 3,000
SALES (est): 2.9MM **Privately Held**
SIC: 1629 Land clearing contractor

(G-14971)
LOWES HOME CENTERS LLC
495 Mill Rd (44663)
PHONE..................................330 339-1936
Ken Kaiser, *Branch Mgr*
EMP: 50
SALES (corp-wide): 68.6B **Publicly Held**
SIC: 5211 5031 5722 5064 Home centers; building materials, exterior; building materials, interior; household appliance stores; electrical appliances, television & radio
HQ: Lowe's Home Centers, Llc
    1605 Curtis Bridge Rd
    Wilkesboro NC 28697
    336 658-4000

(G-14972)
MARATHON MFG & SUP CO
5165 Main St Ne (44663-8802)
P.O. Box 701 (44663-0701)
PHONE..................................330 343-2656
Emory Brumit, *President*
Peggy Brumit, *Treasurer*
EMP: 60 EST: 1969
SALES (est): 5.5MM **Privately Held**
SIC: 5199 3953 Advertising specialties; screens, textile printing

(G-14973)
MARK LUIKART INC
715 Cookson Ave Se (44663-6800)
PHONE..................................330 339-9141
Mark Luikart, *President*
EMP: 50
SQ FT: 6,400
SALES (est): 1.1MM **Privately Held**
WEB: www.marksplace.net
SIC: 7231 7299 5999 Hair care products; massage parlor; manicurist, pedicurist

(G-14974)
MUSKINGUM WTRSHED CNSRVNCY DST (PA)
1319 3rd St Nw (44663-1305)
P.O. Box 349 (44663-0349)
PHONE..................................330 343-6647
Boris Slogar, *Chief Engr*
James Cugliari, *Treasurer*
Matt Ott, *Technology*
John M Hoopingarner, *Exec Dir*
John Hoopingarner, *Exec Dir*
EMP: 350
SQ FT: 9,000
SALES (est): 93.5MM **Privately Held**
WEB: www.muskingumfoundation.org
SIC: 4941 Water supply

(G-14975)
N P MOTEL SYSTEM INC
Also Called: Holiday Inn
145 Bluebell Dr Sw (44663-9660)
PHONE..................................330 339-7731
Naresh Patel, *Principal*
EMP: 30
SALES (est): 733.9K **Privately Held**
WEB: www.radhe.net
SIC: 7011 Hotels & motels

(G-14976)
PERSONAL & FMLY COUNSELING SVC
1433 5th St Nw (44663-1223)
PHONE..................................330 343-8171
Nalini Morris, *Manager*
Pamela Trimmer, *Director*
Marilyn Henry, *Representative*
EMP: 38
SALES (est): 1.9MM **Privately Held**
SIC: 8322 Social service center

(G-14977)
REA & ASSOCIATES INC (PA)
419 W High Ave (44663-3621)
P.O. Box 1020 (44663-5120)
PHONE..................................330 339-6651
Leman G Beall, *President*
Jeremiah Senften, *Principal*
Debi Gellenbeck, *Corp Secy*
Tara Lengler, *Opers Staff*
Don McIntosh, *CFO*
EMP: 58
SQ FT: 680
SALES (est): 32.3MM **Privately Held**
WEB: www.reacpa.com
SIC: 8721 Certified public accountant

(G-14978)
REA & ASSOCIATES INC
122 4th St Nw (44663-1938)
P.O. Box 1020 (44663-5120)
PHONE..................................440 266-0077
Kent Beachy, *CPA*
Greg R Goodie, *CPA*
Jeff Tucker, *Branch Mgr*
EMP: 55
SALES (corp-wide): 32.3MM **Privately Held**
WEB: www.reacpa.com
SIC: 8721 Certified public accountant
PA: Rea & Associates, Inc.
    419 W High Ave
    New Philadelphia OH 44663
    330 339-6651

(G-14979)
S S T ENTERPRISES INC
Also Called: Marathon Manufacturing
5165 Main St Ne (44663-8802)
P.O. Box 701 (44663-0701)
PHONE..................................330 343-2656
Emery B Brumit, *President*
Peggy Brumit, *Corp Secy*
▲ EMP: 85
SALES (est): 6.4MM **Privately Held**
SIC: 5199 Advertising specialties

(G-14980)
SCHOENBRUNN HEALTHCARE
2594 E High Ave (44663-6737)
PHONE..................................330 339-3595
Shaul Flank, *Owner*
EMP: 100 EST: 2008
SALES: 6.4MM
SALES (corp-wide): 64.7MM **Privately Held**
SIC: 8059 8051 8011 Nursing home, except skilled & intermediate care facility; skilled nursing care facilities; clinic, operated by physicians
PA: Progressive Quality Care Inc
    5553 Broadview Rd
    Parma OH 44134
    216 661-6800

(G-14981)
SOUTH BROADWAY
Also Called: Amberwood Manor
245 S Broadway St 251 (44663-3842)
PHONE..................................330 339-2151
George S Repchick, *President*
William I Weisberg, *Vice Pres*
Debbie Kolat, *Director*
Kayla Arth, *Social Dir*
Yvette Schupbach, *Hlthcr Dir*
EMP: 54
SALES (est): 1.6MM
SALES (corp-wide): 157.7MM **Privately Held**
SIC: 8051 Convalescent home with continuous nursing care
PA: Saber Healthcare Group, L.L.C.
    26691 Richmond Rd Frnt
    Bedford OH 44146
    216 292-5706

(G-14982)
STALEY TECHNOLOGIES INC (PA)
1035 Front Ave Sw (44663-2077)
PHONE..................................330 339-2898
Timothy Staley, *President*
Brad Kandel, *Technician*
EMP: 45
SQ FT: 3,000

SALES (est): 7.1MM **Privately Held**
SIC: 5731 7622 Radios, two-way, citizens' band, weather, short-wave, etc.; radio repair shop

(G-14983)
STARLIGHT ENTERPRISES INC
Also Called: S.E.I.
400 E High Ave (44663-2549)
P.O. Box 1054 (44663-5154)
PHONE..................................330 339-2020
Cassie Elvin, *Director*
Eleanor Scott, *Admin Sec*
EMP: 175
SQ FT: 27,300
SALES (est): 1.8MM **Privately Held**
WEB: www.starlightenterprises.com
SIC: 8331 7349 Sheltered workshop; janitorial service, contract basis

(G-14984)
TANK LEASING CORP
Also Called: Bulk Carriers and Tank Leasing
2743 Brightwood Rd Se (44663-6773)
PHONE..................................330 339-3333
Marcia Hartrick, *President*
Richard Hartrick, *Vice Pres*
EMP: 25
SQ FT: 1,800
SALES (est): 5.6MM **Privately Held**
SIC: 5084 Tanks, storage

(G-14985)
TUCSON INC
3497 University Dr Ne (44663-6711)
PHONE..................................330 339-4935
James R Demuth, *President*
Becky Sharp, *Admin Asst*
EMP: 41 EST: 2001
SQ FT: 2,250
SALES (est): 7.4MM **Privately Held**
WEB: www.tucson.com
SIC: 1611 General contractor, highway & street construction

(G-14986)
TUSCARAWAS COUNTY HELP ME GROW
1433 5th St Nw (44663-1223)
PHONE..................................330 339-3493
Marilyn Henry, *Exec Dir*
Lisa Crites, *Director*
EMP: 50
SALES (est): 427.7K **Privately Held**
WEB: www.pfcs1.org
SIC: 8322 General counseling services

(G-14987)
UNITED PARCEL SERVICE INC OH
Also Called: UPS
241 8th Street Ext Sw (44663-2027)
PHONE..................................330 339-6281
Matt Walker, *Manager*
Brian Brahler, *Manager*
EMP: 150
SALES (corp-wide): 71.8B **Publicly Held**
WEB: www.upsscs.com
SIC: 4215 4513 Parcel delivery, vehicular; air courier services
HQ: United Parcel Service, Inc. (Oh)
    55 Glenlake Pkwy
    Atlanta GA 30328
    404 828-6000

(G-14988)
W E QUICKSALL AND ASSOC INC (PA)
554 W High Ave (44663-2006)
P.O. Box 646 (44663-0646)
PHONE..................................330 339-6676
David R Quicksall, *CEO*
Donald R Quicksall, *President*
Nathan Quicksall, *Opers Mgr*
John Snyder, *Engineer*
Cliff Easlick, *Controller*
EMP: 25 EST: 1959
SQ FT: 10,400
SALES (est): 2.3MM **Privately Held**
WEB: www.wequicksall.com
SIC: 8711 Consulting engineer

(G-14989)
WOOD ELECTRIC INC
210 11th St Nw (44663-1510)
PHONE..................................330 339-7002
Larry Wood, *President*
Al Ledrich, *Project Mgr*
Buck Ickes, *Manager*
Lisa Wood, *Executive*
EMP: 85
SQ FT: 8,000
SALES (est): 11.6MM **Privately Held**
SIC: 1731 General electrical contractor

(G-14990)
YOUR HOME COURT ADVANTAGE LLC
1243 Monroe St Nw (44663-4139)
PHONE..................................330 364-6602
EMP: 30
SALES (corp-wide): 1.7MM **Privately Held**
SIC: 6531 Real estate agents & managers
PA: Your Home Court Advantage, Llc
7953 Pittsburg Ave Nw
North Canton OH 44720
330 587-5587

New Plymouth
Vinton County

(G-14991)
HUNTLEY TRUCKING CO
23525 Pumpkin Ridge Rd (45654-8964)
P.O. Box 6 (45654-0006)
PHONE..................................740 385-7615
Steven Huntley, *Vice Pres*
Kent Maxwell, *Vice Pres*
Lee Huntley, *Admin Sec*
EMP: 35 **EST:** 1957
SALES: 3MM **Privately Held**
SIC: 4212 4213 Lumber & timber trucking; dump truck haulage; trucking, except local

New Richmond
Clermont County

(G-14992)
DAVE & BARB ENTERPRISES INC
Also Called: Janitec Building Service
Address Unknonwn (45157)
P.O. Box 242 (45157-0242)
PHONE..................................513 553-0050
Barbara Henry, *President*
Dave Henry, *Vice Pres*
EMP: 53
SQ FT: 2,000
SALES: 700K **Privately Held**
SIC: 7349 Janitorial service, contract basis

(G-14993)
DOBBINS NURSING HOME INC
400 Main St (45157-1129)
P.O. Box 54923, Cincinnati (45254-0923)
PHONE..................................513 553-4139
Howard Meeker, *President*
Steven Meeker, *Vice Pres*
Patricia A Meeker, *Treasurer*
EMP: 125 **EST:** 1950
SALES (est): 3.2MM
SALES (corp-wide): 4.7MM **Privately Held**
SIC: 8059 Nursing home, except skilled & intermediate care facility
PA: Locust Ridge Nursing Home Inc
12745 Elm Corner Rd
Williamsburg OH 45176
937 444-2920

(G-14994)
DUKE ENERGY OHIO INC
Also Called: Beckjord Power Station
757 Us 52 (45157-9709)
PHONE..................................513 467-5000
Jim Cumbow, *Manager*
EMP: 195
SALES (corp-wide): 24.5B **Publicly Held**
SIC: 4911 Electric services

HQ: Duke Energy Ohio, Inc.
139 E 4th St
Cincinnati OH 45202
704 382-3853

(G-14995)
JKL CONSTRUCTION INC
620 Hamilton St (45157-1267)
PHONE..................................513 553-3333
Guy Montgomery, *President*
EMP: 25
SQ FT: 1,500
SALES (est): 2.4MM **Privately Held**
SIC: 1542 Commercial & office building, new construction; commercial & office buildings, renovation & repair

New Springfield
Mahoning County

(G-14996)
ED WILSON & SON TRUCKING INC
14766 Woodworth Rd (44443-9738)
P.O. Box 2208 (44443-2208)
PHONE..................................330 549-9287
Edward Wilson, *President*
Gloria Wilson, *Vice Pres*
EMP: 25
SALES (est): 3MM **Privately Held**
SIC: 4212 Local trucking, without storage

(G-14997)
RURITAN
Also Called: Raritan National
3814 Columbiana Rd (44443-9776)
PHONE..................................330 542-2308
Francis Gebhardt, *Director*
EMP: 40
SALES (est): 282.3K **Privately Held**
WEB: www.ruritan.com
SIC: 8699 Charitable organization

(G-14998)
SNYDERS ANTIQUE AUTO PARTS INC
12925 Woodworth Rd (44443-8722)
PHONE..................................330 549-5313
Donald Snyder III, *President*
Donald Snyder Jr, *Vice Pres*
▲ **EMP:** 30
SALES (est): 5.5MM **Privately Held**
WEB: www.snydersantiqueauto.com
SIC: 5531 5013 Automotive parts; automotive supplies & parts

New Vienna
Clinton County

(G-14999)
SNOW HILL COUNTRY CLUB INC
11093 State Route 73 (45159-9638)
PHONE..................................937 987-2491
Jennifer Hodge, *Superintendent*
Nick Brunotte, *Manager*
EMP: 25 **EST:** 1924
SALES (est): 748K **Privately Held**
SIC: 7997 Country club, membership

New Washington
Crawford County

(G-15000)
BUCYRUS COMMUNITY PHYSICIANS
120 W Main St (44854-9431)
PHONE..................................419 492-2200
Tom Klitzka, *Principal*
EMP: 58 **EST:** 2010
SALES (est): 1.4MM
SALES (corp-wide): 444.6K **Privately Held**
SIC: 8011 Physical medicine, physician/surgeon

PA: Avita Health System
269 Portland Way S
Galion OH 44833
419 468-4841

(G-15001)
CREST BENDING INC
108 John St (44854-9702)
P.O. Box 458 (44854-0458)
PHONE..................................419 492-2108
Robert E Studer, *President*
EMP: 45 **EST:** 1966
SQ FT: 50,000
SALES (est): 8.8MM **Privately Held**
WEB: www.crestbending.com
SIC: 3312 7692 3498 3317 Tubes, steel & iron; welding repair; fabricated pipe & fittings; steel pipe & tubes

(G-15002)
MERCY HEALTH
202 W Mansfield St (44854-9532)
P.O. Box 397 (44854-0397)
PHONE..................................419 492-1300
EMP: 27
SALES (corp-wide): 4.7B **Privately Held**
SIC: 8011 General & family practice, physician/surgeon
PA: Mercy Health
1701 Mercy Health Pl
Cincinnati OH 45237
513 639-2800

(G-15003)
STUDER-OBRINGER INC
525 S Kibler St (44854-9524)
P.O. Box 278 (44854-0278)
PHONE..................................419 492-2121
Kenneth Falter, *President*
John Cronau, *Exec VP*
Jim Alt, *Vice Pres*
Mike Obringer, *Manager*
Andy Studer, *Manager*
EMP: 40
SQ FT: 1,500
SALES (est): 8.8MM **Privately Held**
SIC: 1542 1541 Commercial & office building, new construction; industrial buildings & warehouses

New Waterford
Columbiana County

(G-15004)
DYNAMIC STRUCTURES INC (PA)
3790 State Route 7 Ste B (44445-9784)
PHONE..................................330 892-0164
Scott McCrea, *President*
Tom Beckham, *Controller*
John Simon, *Supervisor*
EMP: 25
SQ FT: 4,500
SALES (est): 7.2MM **Privately Held**
SIC: 1751 1542 1541 Framing contractor; lightweight steel framing (metal stud) installation; nonresidential construction; industrial buildings & warehouses

(G-15005)
MAJESTIC MANUFACTURING INC
4536 State Route 7 (44445-9785)
P.O. Box 128 (44445-0128)
PHONE..................................330 457-2447
Paul Kudler, *President*
Jeff Kudler, *Vice Pres*
Rick Steed, *Purch Agent*
Vincent Kudler, *Treasurer*
▲ **EMP:** 45
SQ FT: 68,000
SALES (est): 8MM **Privately Held**
WEB: www.majesticrides.com
SIC: 3599 5087 Carnival machines & equipment, amusement park; carnival & amusement park equipment

(G-15006)
NEW WATERFORD FIREMAN
3766 E Main St (44445)
PHONE..................................330 457-2363
Harry Wilson, *Principal*
Bryland Henderson, *Chief*

Chief Bryland Henderson, *Chief*
EMP: 28
SALES: 33K **Privately Held**
SIC: 8611 Trade associations

New Weston
Darke County

(G-15007)
ELDORA ENTERPRISES INC
Also Called: Eldora Speedway
13929 State Route 118 (45348-9726)
PHONE..................................937 338-3815
Earl H Baltes, *President*
Starr Smith Myer, *Corp Secy*
Bernice Baltes, *Vice Pres*
Jonathan Bateman, *Webmaster*
EMP: 48
SALES (est): 2.5MM **Privately Held**
WEB: www.eldoraspeedway.com
SIC: 7948 7911 Automotive race track operation; dance hall or ballroom operation

Newark
Licking County

(G-15008)
ALLTEL COMMUNICATIONS CORP (DH)
66 N 4th St (43055-5000)
P.O. Box 3005 (43058-3005)
PHONE..................................740 349-8551
Dennis Mervis, *President*
Richard Mc Clain, *Area Mgr*
Ken Blake, *Vice Pres*
Giulio Freda, *Treasurer*
EMP: 60
SQ FT: 38,716
SALES (est): 144.9MM
SALES (corp-wide): 170.7B **Publicly Held**
SIC: 4813 4812 Local telephone communications; long distance telephone communications; radio telephone communication
HQ: Alltel Corporation
1001 Technology Dr
Little Rock AR 72223
866 255-8357

(G-15009)
ALPHA NURSING HOMES INC
Also Called: Autumn Health Care
17 Forry St (43055-4004)
PHONE..................................740 345-9197
Bob Huffman, *Manager*
EMP: 60
SQ FT: 1,400
SALES (corp-wide): 3.1MM **Privately Held**
WEB: www.alphanursingservice.com
SIC: 8052 8051 Intermediate care facilities; skilled nursing care facilities
PA: Alpha Nursing Homes, Inc
419 E Main St
Lancaster OH

(G-15010)
AMERICAN NATIONAL RED CROSS
Also Called: American Red Cross
1272 W Main St Bldg 5s (43055-2053)
PHONE..................................740 344-2510
EMP: 39
SALES (corp-wide): 2.5B **Privately Held**
SIC: 8322 Emergency social services
PA: The American National Red Cross
430 17th St Nw
Washington DC 20006
202 737-8300

(G-15011)
ARLINGTON CARE CTR
Also Called: FRANKLIN RIDGE CARE FACILITY
98 S 30th St (43055-1940)
PHONE..................................740 344-0303
Edward L Byington Sr, *President*
Betsy Mc Pherson, *Hlthcr Dir*
EMP: 200 **EST:** 1962
SQ FT: 50,000

GEOGRAPHIC

SALES: 10.1MM
SALES (corp-wide): 85.7MM **Privately Held**
SIC: 8051 8052 Skilled nursing care facilities; intermediate care facilities
PA: Carington Health Systems
8200 Beckett Park Dr
Hamilton OH 45011
513 682-2700

(G-15012)
ARMSTRONG STEEL ERECTORS INC
50 S 4th St (43055-5436)
P.O. Box 577 (43058-0577)
PHONE.................................740 345-4503
Diane M Reed, *President*
Roy Mc Intosh, *Vice Pres*
Roy McIntosh, *Vice Pres*
EMP: 50 **EST:** 1954
SQ FT: 20,000
SALES (est): 9.9MM **Privately Held**
WEB: www.armstrongsteelerectors.com
SIC: 1622 Bridge construction; highway construction, elevated

(G-15013)
BEHAVORIAL HEALTHCARE (PA)
65 Messimer Dr (43055-1874)
PHONE.................................740 522-8477
Kathryn E Saylor, *CEO*
Tim Gano, *Chief*
Theresa Gehr, *Case Mgr*
Cheryl L Hohl, *Manager*
Becky Stalter, *Officer*
EMP: 175 **EST:** 1955
SQ FT: 15,000
SALES: 9.3MM **Privately Held**
SIC: 8093 Mental health clinic, outpatient

(G-15014)
BOEING COMPANY
801 Irving Wick Dr W (43056-1199)
PHONE.................................740 788-4000
Stephen Feller, *Partner*
Jeremy Addy, *Engineer*
Daryl Dickerson, *Engineer*
Tony Hensley, *Engineer*
Mike Michaelian, *Engineer*
EMP: 25
SALES (corp-wide): 101.1B **Publicly Held**
SIC: 7629 3812 Electrical repair shops; search & navigation equipment
PA: The Boeing Company
100 N Riverside Plz
Chicago IL 60606
312 544-2000

(G-15015)
BROOKDALE SNIOR LVING CMMNTIES
Also Called: Sterling House of Newark
331 Goosepond Rd (43055-3184)
PHONE.................................740 366-0005
Marge Shawger, *Manager*
EMP: 30
SALES (corp-wide): 4.5B **Publicly Held**
WEB: www.assisted.com
SIC: 8059 Rest home, with health care
HQ: Brookdale Senior Living Communities, Inc.
6737 W Wa St Ste 2300
Milwaukee WI 53214
414 918-5000

(G-15016)
BROTHERHOOD OF LOCOMOTIVE ENGI
Also Called: Brothrhood Lcomotive Engineers
745 Sherman Ave (43055-6928)
PHONE.................................740 345-0978
Dave Moorhead, *Chairman*
EMP: 26
SALES (corp-wide): 20.9MM **Privately Held**
SIC: 8631 Labor union
PA: Brotherhood Of Locomotive Engineers & Trainmen
7061 E Pleasant Valley Rd
Independence OH 44131
216 241-2630

(G-15017)
BROWN DISTRIBUTING INC
51 Swans Rd Ne (43055-8809)
PHONE.................................740 349-7999
Richard L Brown, *President*
▲ **EMP:** 51
SALES (est): 11.9MM **Privately Held**
SIC: 5181 Beer & other fermented malt liquors

(G-15018)
BUCKEYE LINEN SERVICE INC
76 Jefferson St (43055-4936)
P.O. Box 159 (43058-0159)
PHONE.................................740 345-4046
Donald Struminger, *President*
David Struminger, *Exec VP*
Nancy P Alley, *Vice Pres*
John Crockford, *Vice Pres*
EMP: 70
SQ FT: 20,000
SALES (est): 4.1MM
SALES (corp-wide): 22.3MM **Privately Held**
WEB: www.mohenis.com
SIC: 7213 Uniform supply
PA: Mohenis Services, Inc.
875 E Bank St
Petersburg VA 23803
800 879-3315

(G-15019)
BURDENS MACHINE & WELDING
94 S 5th St (43055-5302)
P.O. Box 177 (43058-0177)
PHONE.................................740 345-9246
Donald Burden Sr, *President*
Robert Burden, *Corp Secy*
Darrell Burden, *Vice Pres*
Donald Burden Jr, *Vice Pres*
EMP: 26
SQ FT: 4,400
SALES: 1.9MM **Privately Held**
SIC: 1799 3599 Welding on site; machine shop, jobbing & repair

(G-15020)
CAMPOLO MICHAEL MD
1930 Tamarack Rd (43055-2303)
PHONE.................................740 522-7600
Michael Campolo, *President*
EMP: 50
SALES (est): 821.5K **Privately Held**
SIC: 8011 General & family practice, physician/surgeon

(G-15021)
CELLCO PARTNERSHIP
Also Called: Verizon
668 Hebron Rd (43056-1348)
P.O. Box 2266 (43056-0266)
PHONE.................................740 522-6446
Maggie Hallett, *Branch Mgr*
EMP: 25
SALES (corp-wide): 130.8B **Publicly Held**
SIC: 4812 5999 Cellular telephone services; mobile telephones & equipment
HQ: Cellco Partnership
1 Verizon Way
Basking Ridge NJ 07920

(G-15022)
CHERRY VALLEY LODGE
Also Called: Cherry Valley Lodge and Coco
2299 Cherry Valley Rd Se (43055-9393)
P.O. Box 771207, Houston TX (77215-1207)
PHONE.................................740 788-1200
Steve Hsu, *President*
Larry Murphy, *General Mgr*
Sherry Sorrell, *Sales Staff*
Bernadette Vinning, *Sales Staff*
Linda Reynolds, *Supervisor*
EMP: 45
SALES (est): 3.8MM **Privately Held**
SIC: 7011 5812 5091 Hotels; restaurant, family: independent; water slides (recreation park)

(G-15023)
COMMERCIAL ELECTRONICS INC
1294 N 21st St (43055-3061)
PHONE.................................740 281-0180
Chris Cover, *President*
EMP: 25
SALES (est): 1.7MM **Privately Held**
SIC: 5065 5999 Communication equipment; mobile telephones & equipment

(G-15024)
CONSUMER SUPPORT SERVICES (PA)
2040 Cherry Valley Rd # 1 (43055-1197)
PHONE.................................740 788-8257
Daniel F Swickard, *President*
EMP: 500
SQ FT: 5,000
SALES (est): 26.7MM **Privately Held**
SIC: 8059 8322 8082 Home for the mentally retarded, exc. skilled or intermediate; individual & family services; home health care services

(G-15025)
CONSUMER SUPPORT SERVICES INC
640 Industrial Pkwy (43056-1528)
PHONE.................................740 522-5464
EMP: 91
SALES (corp-wide): 26.7MM **Privately Held**
SIC: 8322 Social service center
PA: Consumer Support Services Inc
2040 Cherry Valley Rd # 1
Newark OH 43055
740 788-8257

(G-15026)
CONSUMER SUPPORT SERVICES INC
100 James St (43055-3931)
PHONE.................................740 344-3600
Lisa Cline, *Branch Mgr*
EMP: 73
SALES (corp-wide): 26.7MM **Privately Held**
SIC: 8322 Adult day care center
PA: Consumer Support Services Inc
2040 Cherry Valley Rd # 1
Newark OH 43055
740 788-8257

(G-15027)
CORPORATE HEALTH BENEFITS
1915 Tamarack Rd (43055-1300)
PHONE.................................740 348-1401
Bob Kamps, *President*
EMP: 34
SALES: 371.6K **Privately Held**
SIC: 6411 Insurance agents, brokers & service
PA: Licking Memorial Health Systems
1320 W Main St
Newark OH 43055

(G-15028)
COUGHLIN CHEVROLET TOYOTA INC
Also Called: Coughlin Automotive
1850 N 21st St (43055-3186)
P.O. Box 749, Pataskala (43062-0749)
PHONE.................................740 366-1381
Al Coughlin, *President*
Al Coughlin Jr, *Corp Secy*
Bill Vina, *Vice Pres*
Max Forster, *CFO*
Mark Hixon, *Sales Mgr*
EMP: 90
SQ FT: 50,000
SALES (est): 26.5MM
SALES (corp-wide): 95.1MM **Privately Held**
WEB: www.coughlinford.com
SIC: 5511 7532 5531 5521 Automobiles, new & used; top & body repair & paint shops; automotive & home supply stores; used car dealers
PA: Coughlin Chevrolet, Inc.
9000 Broad St Sw
Pataskala OH 43062
740 964-9191

(G-15029)
COURTESY AMBULANCE INC
1890 W Main St (43055-1134)
PHONE.................................740 522-8588
Lois Griggs, *President*
Clair Griggs, *Chairman*
EMP: 37
SQ FT: 1,000
SALES (est): 1.7MM **Privately Held**
SIC: 4119 Ambulance service

(G-15030)
DAWES ARBORETUM
7770 Jacksontown Rd (43056-9380)
PHONE.................................740 323-2355
Richard Larson, *Manager*
Gregory Payton, *Manager*
Luke Messinger, *Exec Dir*
Shana Byrd, *Director*
Michael Ecker, *Director*
EMP: 38
SALES (est): 1.8MM **Privately Held**
WEB: www.dawesarb.org
SIC: 8422 5261 Arboretum; nurseries & garden centers

(G-15031)
ENERGY COOPERATIVE INC (HQ)
1500 Granville Rd (43055-1536)
P.O. Box 4970 (43058-4970)
PHONE.................................740 348-1206
Dave Potter, *President*
David L Hite, *Principal*
Charles Manning, *Principal*
Gary Glover, *Manager*
Wayne Higgins, *IT/INT Sup*
EMP: 26
SALES (est): 65.2MM **Privately Held**
SIC: 8611 5983 4924 4911 Public utility association; fuel oil dealers; natural gas distribution; electric services
PA: Licking Rural Electrification Inc
11339 Mount Vernon Rd
Utica OH 43080
740 892-2071

(G-15032)
ENVIRONMENTAL SPECIALISTS INC
55 Builders Dr (43055-1343)
PHONE.................................740 788-8134
Ken Walls, *Branch Mgr*
EMP: 44 **Privately Held**
SIC: 8744
PA: Environmental Specialists, Inc.
1000 Andrews Ave
Youngstown OH 44505

(G-15033)
FIRST FDRAL SAV LN ASSN NEWARK (PA)
2 N 2nd St (43055-5610)
P.O. Box 4460 (43058-4460)
PHONE.................................740 345-3494
Paul M Thompson, *President*
Sarah R Wallace, *Chairman*
Michael S Young, *Vice Pres*
Glen L Griebel, *Treasurer*
Glen Griebel, *Treasurer*
EMP: 50
SQ FT: 5,000
SALES: 8.4MM **Privately Held**
SIC: 6035 Federal savings & loan associations

(G-15034)
FLYING COLORS PUBLIC PRESCHOOL
119 Union St (43055-3937)
PHONE.................................740 349-1629
Davelyn Ross, *Director*
EMP: 50
SALES (est): 765.5K **Privately Held**
WEB: www.flyingcolorspreschool.com
SIC: 8351 8211 Preschool center; elementary & secondary schools

(G-15035)
GENERATION HEALTH & REHAB CNTR
Also Called: Flint Ridge Nursing & Rehab
1450 W Main St (43055-1825)
PHONE.................................740 344-9465

▲ = Import ▼=Export
◆ =Import/Export

Karen Moss, *CFO*
John R Huges,
EMP: 92
SALES (est): 7.9MM **Privately Held**
SIC: 8052 8051 Intermediate care facilities; skilled nursing care facilities

(G-15036)
GEORGE W ARENSBERG PHRM INC
Also Called: Arensberg Home Health
1272 W Main St (43055-2053)
PHONE..................................740 344-2195
Jeff Read, *Manager*
EMP: 50
SALES (corp-wide): 7.4MM **Privately Held**
SIC: 5912 8049 Drug stores; nutritionist
PA: The George W Arensberg Pharmacy Inc
176 Hudson Ave
Newark OH 43055
740 345-9761

(G-15037)
GOLF GALAXY GOLFWORKS INC
Also Called: Golfworks, The
4820 Jacksontown Rd (43056-9377)
P.O. Box 3008 (43058-3008)
PHONE..................................740 328-4193
Mark McCormick, *CEO*
Richard C Nordvoid, *Principal*
Mark Wilson, *Vice Pres*
Jerry Datz, *CFO*
▲ **EMP:** 150 **EST:** 1974
SQ FT: 80,000
SALES (est): 58.7MM
SALES (corp-wide): 8.4B **Publicly Held**
WEB: www.golfworks.com
SIC: 5091 2731 3949 5941 Golf equipment; books; publishing only; golf equipment; shafts, golf club; golf, tennis & ski shops
HQ: Golf Galaxy, Llc
345 Court St
Coraopolis PA 15108

(G-15038)
GOODIN ELECTRIC INC
605 Garfield Ave Ste A (43055-6889)
PHONE..................................740 522-3113
John A Goodin, *CEO*
Howard Goodin, *Vice Pres*
EMP: 25
SQ FT: 10,000
SALES (est): 3MM **Privately Held**
SIC: 1731 General electrical contractor

(G-15039)
GW BUSINESS SOLUTIONS LLC
65 S 5th St (43055-5404)
PHONE..................................740 645-9861
EMP: 148 **EST:** 2013
SQ FT: 9,000
SALES (est): 3.9MM **Privately Held**
SIC: 8331 5932 Job Training/Related Services Ret Used Merchandise

(G-15040)
HEATH NURSING CARE CENTER
717 S 30th St (43056-1294)
PHONE..................................740 522-1171
Robert Lehman, *President*
Luke Sutherland, *Administration*
EMP: 180
SALES (est): 10.5MM **Privately Held**
WEB: www.carington.com
SIC: 8051 8059 Skilled nursing care facilities; convalescent home

(G-15041)
HOPEWELL DENTAL CARE
572 Industrial Pkwy Ste B (43056-1638)
PHONE..................................740 522-5000
Orest Kowalsky, *President*
EMP: 25 **EST:** 1981
SALES (est): 2MM **Privately Held**
WEB: www.hopewelldentalcare.com
SIC: 8021 Dentists' office

(G-15042)
HOSPICE OF CENTRAL OHIO (PA)
Also Called: Palliative Care of Ohio
2269 Cherry Valley Rd Se (43055-9323)
PHONE..................................740 344-0311
Kerry Hamilton, *CEO*
Calvin Robinson, *Principal*
Jim Jung, *CFO*
Mariann Day, *Program Mgr*
Barbara Ford, *Manager*
EMP: 130
SALES: 18.9MM **Privately Held**
WEB: www.hospiceofcentralohio.org
SIC: 8069 Specialty hospitals, except psychiatric

(G-15043)
HOUSTON DICK PLBG & HTG INC
Also Called: Houston Plumbing & Heating
724 Montgomery Rd Ne (43055-9461)
PHONE..................................740 763-3961
Richard F Houston, *President*
Patricia Houston, *Vice Pres*
Beverly Dodson, *Treasurer*
Beth L Cramer, *Admin Sec*
EMP: 40
SQ FT: 8,000
SALES: 5MM **Privately Held**
WEB: www.houstonplumbingheating.com
SIC: 1711 Plumbing contractors; warm air heating & air conditioning contractor

(G-15044)
INTERIM HALTHCARE COLUMBUS INC
Also Called: Interim Services
900 Sharon Valley Rd (43055-2804)
PHONE..................................740 349-8700
Susan Hamann, *Branch Mgr*
EMP: 743
SALES (corp-wide): 19.8MM **Privately Held**
SIC: 8082 Home health care services
HQ: Interim Healthcare Of Columbus, Inc.
784 Morrison Rd
Gahanna OH 43230
614 888-3130

(G-15045)
JOBES HENDERSON & ASSOC INC
59 Grant St (43055-3939)
PHONE..................................740 344-5451
Jim Roberts, *President*
Joseph Rutherford, *COO*
Jeremy Van Ostran, *Senior VP*
EMP: 40
SQ FT: 9,000
SALES (est): 5.3MM
SALES (corp-wide): 35.9MM **Privately Held**
WEB: www.jobeshenderson.com
SIC: 8713 8711 Surveying services; engineering services
PA: Hull & Associates, Inc.
6397 Emerald Pkwy Ste 200
Dublin OH 43016
614 793-8777

(G-15046)
KRIBHA LLC
Also Called: Hampton Inn-Newark/Heath
1008 Hebron Rd (43056-1121)
PHONE..................................740 788-8991
Ashok Patel, *Mng Member*
Vimal Patel,
EMP: 25
SALES (est): 1.6MM **Privately Held**
SIC: 7011 Hotels

(G-15047)
LABORATORY CORPORATION AMERICA
95 S Terrace Ave (43055-1355)
PHONE..................................740 522-2034
Diane Noland, *Branch Mgr*
EMP: 25 **Publicly Held**
WEB: www.labcorp.com
SIC: 8071 Testing laboratories
HQ: Laboratory Corporation Of America
358 S Main St Ste 458
Burlington NC 27215
336 229-1127

(G-15048)
LAYTON INC (PA)
169 Dayton Rd Ne (43055-8879)
PHONE..................................740 349-7101
Gerard Layton, *President*
Steve Carson, *Corp Secy*
EMP: 36
SQ FT: 9,200
SALES (est): 7.6MM **Privately Held**
SIC: 1794 Excavation work

(G-15049)
LEADS INC (PA)
Also Called: LEADS COMMUNITY ACTION AGENCY
159 Wilson St (43055-4921)
PHONE..................................740 349-8606
Ken Kempton, *CEO*
EMP: 25
SQ FT: 8,180
SALES (est): 9.1MM **Privately Held**
WEB: www.leadscaa.org
SIC: 8399 8322 Community action agency; individual & family services

(G-15050)
LICCO INC
600 Industrial Pkwy (43056-1528)
P.O. Box 4008 (43058-4008)
PHONE..................................740 522-8345
Gary Smith, *Business Mgr*
Kyle Miller, *Director*
EMP: 250
SQ FT: 32,000
SALES: 1.6MM **Privately Held**
WEB: www.liccoinc.com
SIC: 8331 8322 Sheltered workshop; individual & family services

(G-15051)
LICKING CNTY ALCOHOLISM PRVNTN
Also Called: ALCOHOLISM & CHEMICAL DEPENDEN
62 E Stevens St (43055-5969)
PHONE..................................740 281-3639
Jim Takacs, *Exec Dir*
James Takacs, *Exec Dir*
EMP: 42
SALES (est): 1.4MM **Privately Held**
SIC: 8322 Alcoholism counseling, nontreatment

(G-15052)
LICKING COUNTY AGING PROGRAM
1058 E Main St (43055-6940)
PHONE..................................740 345-0821
Martine Fuller, *General Mgr*
Marti Hartz, *Exec Dir*
David Bibler, *Director*
Janis Clark, *Director*
Bonnie Morton, *Director*
EMP: 85
SQ FT: 11,930
SALES: 4.8MM **Privately Held**
WEB: www.lcap.org
SIC: 8322 8399 Meal delivery program; old age assistance; general counseling services; health systems agency

(G-15053)
LICKING COUNTY BOARD OF MRDD
Also Called: Community Employment Services
116 N 22nd St (43055-2755)
P.O. Box 4910 (43058-4910)
PHONE..................................740 349-6588
Nancy Neely, *Superintendent*
EMP: 200
SALES (est): 5.7MM **Privately Held**
WEB: www.lcbmrdd.org
SIC: 8322 Social services for the handicapped
PA: County Of Licking
20 S 2nd St
Newark OH 43055
740 670-5040

(G-15054)
LICKING COUNTY PLAYERS INC
131 W Main St (43055-5007)
PHONE..................................740 349-2287
Christina Barth, *President*

EMP: 25
SALES: 59.7K **Privately Held**
SIC: 7922 Community theater production

(G-15055)
LICKING KNOX LABOR COUNCIL
34 N 4th St (43055-5010)
PHONE..................................740 345-1765
Dave McFortsh, *President*
EMP: 65
SALES (est): 212.5K **Privately Held**
SIC: 8631 Labor union

(G-15056)
LICKING MEMORIAL HLTH SYSTEMS (PA)
1320 W Main St (43055-1822)
PHONE..................................220 564-4000
Robert Montagnese, *President*
Sallie Arnett, *Vice Pres*
Rob Montagnese, *CFO*
Kim D Fleming, *Treasurer*
Lanita Garnack, *Analyst*
EMP: 990
SALES: 209.7MM **Privately Held**
SIC: 8741 6411 Hospital management; insurance agents, brokers & service

(G-15057)
LICKING MEMORIAL HOSPITAL (HQ)
Also Called: LICKING MEMORIAL HEALTH SYSTEMS
1320 W Main St (43055-3699)
PHONE..................................740 348-4137
Robert A Montagnese, *President*
Rob Montagnese, *Exec VP*
Sallie Arnett, *Vice Pres*
Craig Cairns, *Vice Pres*
Veronica Link, *Vice Pres*
EMP: 53 **EST:** 1898
SQ FT: 394,784
SALES: 223.3MM **Privately Held**
SIC: 8062 General medical & surgical hospitals

(G-15058)
LICKING MUSKINGUM CMNTY CORREC
20 S 2nd St (43055-5602)
PHONE..................................740 349-6980
EMP: 35
SALES (est): 1.4MM **Privately Held**
SIC: 8744 Facilities Support Services

(G-15059)
LICKING RHABILITATION SVCS INC
11177 Lambs Ln (43055-9779)
PHONE..................................740 345-2837
Cathy Konkler, *President*
Jeff Konkler, *Vice Pres*
Connie Bess, *Opers Staff*
Paul Kaple, *Director*
EMP: 25
SALES (est): 1.8MM **Privately Held**
SIC: 8049 Physical therapist; speech therapist; occupational therapist

(G-15060)
LICKING VALLEY LIONS CLUB
Also Called: International Assn Lions Clubs
3187 Licking Valley Rd (43055-9107)
PHONE..................................740 763-3733
EMP: 121
SALES: 24.2K **Privately Held**
SIC: 8699 Membership Organization

(G-15061)
LICKING-KNOX GOODWILL INDS INC (PA)
65 S 5th St (43055-5404)
P.O. Box 828 (43058-0828)
PHONE..................................740 345-9861
Timothy J Young, *CEO*
Vicki M Osborn, *CFO*
Lynn Fawcett, *VP Finance*
Lisa Baker, *Comms Dir*
Mari Church, *Office Mgr*
EMP: 60
SQ FT: 17,000

SALES: 9.3MM **Privately Held**
SIC: **8331** 8741 5932 Community service employment training program; sheltered workshop; vocational training agency; management services; used merchandise stores

(G-15062)
LORY DIALYSIS LLC
Also Called: Premiere Kidney Center Newark
65 S Terrace Ave (43055-1355)
PHONE..............................740 522-2955
Jim Hilger, *Principal*
EMP: 26
SALES (est): 541.6K **Publicly Held**
SIC: **8092** Kidney dialysis centers
PA: Davita Inc.
2000 16th St
Denver CO 80202

(G-15063)
LOWES HOME CENTERS LLC
888 Hebron Rd (43056-1399)
PHONE..............................740 522-0003
Jason Altemose, *Store Mgr*
John Armstrong, *Manager*
EMP: 150
SALES (corp-wide): 68.6B **Publicly Held**
SIC: **5211** 5031 5722 5064 Home centers; building materials, exterior; building materials, interior; household appliance stores; electrical appliances, television & radio
HQ: Lowe's Home Centers, Llc
1605 Curtis Bridge Rd
Wilkesboro NC 28697
336 658-4000

(G-15064)
MAIN PLACE INC (PA)
112 S 3rd St (43055-5335)
PHONE..............................740 345-6246
Kathy Vanwy, *Bookkeeper*
Janice Miller, *Case Mgr*
Cary Loughman, *Exec Dir*
Joe Boley, *Director*
Rhonda Gibson, *Director*
EMP: 27 EST: 2008
SALES: 1.3MM **Privately Held**
SIC: **8093** Mental health clinic, outpatient

(G-15065)
MATESICH DISTRIBUTING CO
1190 E Main St (43055-8803)
PHONE..............................740 349-8686
John C Matesich III, *CEO*
James M Matesich, *Corp Secy*
Garrett Oliver, *Accounts Mgr*
▲ EMP: 91
SQ FT: 103,000
SALES (est): 39.1MM **Privately Held**
SIC: **5181** Beer & other fermented malt liquors

(G-15066)
MATHEWS FORD INC
500 Hebron Rd (43056-1435)
P.O. Box 4220 (43058-4220)
PHONE..............................740 522-2181
Thurman Mathews, *President*
EMP: 77
SALES (est): 28.6MM **Privately Held**
SIC: **5511** 7538 7532 7549 Automobiles, new & used; general automotive repair shops; top & body repair & paint shops; automotive maintenance services

(G-15067)
MC MAHON REALESTATE CO (PA)
Also Called: Coldwell Banker
591 Country Club Dr (43055-2102)
PHONE..............................740 344-2250
Joseph Mc Mahon, *Owner*
Brittany Freas, *Broker*
Billie Allen, *Consultant*
Michelle Embrey, *Agent*
Timothy Cocanour, *Asst Broker*
EMP: 40
SALES (est): 2.6MM **Privately Held**
SIC: **6531** Real estate agent, residential

(G-15068)
MEDICAL AND SURGICAL ASSOC
Also Called: MSA Family Medicine
1930 Tamarack Rd (43055-2303)
PHONE..............................740 522-7600
Michael Campolo, *President*
EMP: 50
SALES (est): 3.8MM **Privately Held**
SIC: **8031** Offices & clinics of osteopathic physicians

(G-15069)
MEDICAL BENEFITS MUTL LF INSUR (PA)
Also Called: Medben Companies
1975 Tamarack Rd (43055-1300)
P.O. Box 1009 (43058-1009)
PHONE..............................740 522-8425
C Arthur Morrow, *Ch of Bd*
Douglas Freeman, *President*
Kurt Harden, *Senior VP*
Mike Ketron, *Regl Sales Mgr*
Thomas Hoffman, *Admin Sec*
EMP: 175
SQ FT: 32,000
SALES: 16.4MM **Privately Held**
SIC: **6411** Insurance agents

(G-15070)
MEDICAL BNFITS ADMNSTRTORS INC
Also Called: MEDBEN COMPANIES
1975 Tamarack Rd (43055-1300)
P.O. Box 1009 (43058-1009)
PHONE..............................740 522-8425
C Arthur Morrow, *Ch of Bd*
Douglas Freeman, *President*
Charlie Krajacic, *Corp Secy*
Kurt Hardin, *Senior VP*
Caroline Fraker, *Vice Pres*
EMP: 70
SQ FT: 32,000
SALES: 9.9MM
SALES (corp-wide): 16.4MM **Privately Held**
SIC: **6321** Accident & health insurance
PA: Medical Benefits Mutual Life Insurance Co
1975 Tamarack Rd
Newark OH 43055
740 522-8425

(G-15071)
MIDWAY GARAGE INC
140 Everett Ave (43055-5702)
P.O. Box 750 (43058-0750)
PHONE..............................740 345-0699
J Wine Gardner, *President*
EMP: 40
SQ FT: 26,000
SALES (est): 1.6MM **Privately Held**
WEB: www.midwaytt.com
SIC: **7538** Truck engine repair, except industrial

(G-15072)
MILESTONE VENTURES LLC
1776 Tamarack Rd (43055-1359)
PHONE..............................317 908-2093
Dittmar Schaefer, *Branch Mgr*
EMP: 25 **Privately Held**
SIC: **5031** Veneer
PA: Milestone Ventures, Llc
2924 Hallie Ln
Granville OH 43023

(G-15073)
MODERN WELDING CO OHIO INC
1 Modern Way (43055-3921)
P.O. Box 4430 (43058-4430)
PHONE..............................740 344-9425
John W Jones, *President*
Doug Routher, *General Mgr*
Bob Weidner, *COO*
James M Ruth, *Exec VP*
Doug Rothert, *Vice Pres*
EMP: 30
SQ FT: 52,000

SALES (est): 7.4MM
SALES (corp-wide): 126.3MM **Privately Held**
WEB: www.modweldco.net
SIC: **3443** 5051 Tanks, lined: metal plate; metals service centers & offices
PA: Modern Welding Company, Inc.
2880 New Hartford Rd
Owensboro KY 42303
270 685-4400

(G-15074)
MONTESSORI COMMUNITY SCHOOL
621 Country Club Dr (43055-1601)
PHONE..............................740 344-9411
Helen M Moore, *President*
Elizabeth Wells, *Director*
EMP: 34
SALES (est): 1.1MM **Privately Held**
WEB: www.montessorinewark.com
SIC: **8351** 8211 Nursery school; preschool center; Montessori child development center; kindergarten

(G-15075)
MOUND BUILDERS GUIDANCE CENTER
65 Messimer Dr Unit 2 (43055-1879)
PHONE..............................740 522-2828
Francis Deutshle, *Exec Dir*
Laura Maxwell, *Director*
EMP: 99
SALES: 1MM **Privately Held**
SIC: **8322** Individual & family services

(G-15076)
MOUNDBUILDERS COUNTRY CLUB CO
125 N 33rd St (43055-2014)
PHONE..............................740 344-4500
Joseph Moore, *General Mgr*
Joe Renaud,
EMP: 55
SQ FT: 50,000
SALES: 2MM **Privately Held**
WEB: www.moundbuilderscc.com
SIC: **7997** 5812 7992 5941 Country club, membership; golf club, membership; swimming club, membership; tennis club, membership; restaurant, family: independent; public golf courses; sporting goods & bicycle shops

(G-15077)
MPW INDUSTRIAL SERVICES INC
150 S 29th St (43055-1964)
PHONE..............................740 345-2431
Jared Black, *Branch Mgr*
EMP: 30
SALES (corp-wide): 208.7MM **Privately Held**
SIC: **8734** Water testing laboratory
HQ: Mpw Industrial Services, Inc.
9711 Lancaster Rd
Hebron OH 43025
800 827-8790

(G-15078)
MY PLACE CHILD CARE
1335 E Main St (43055-8848)
P.O. Box 4218 (43058-4218)
PHONE..............................740 349-3505
EMP: 33
SALES: 1MM **Privately Held**
SIC: **8351** Child Day Care Services

(G-15079)
NATIONAL GAS & OIL CORPORATION (DH)
Also Called: Permian Oil & Gas Division
1500 Granville Rd (43055-1500)
P.O. Box 4970 (43058-4970)
PHONE..............................740 344-2102
William Sullivan Jr, *Ch of Bd*
Patrick J Mc Gonagle, *President*
Gordon M King, *Vice Pres*
Todd P Ware, *Vice Pres*
EMP: 36
SQ FT: 10,000

SALES: 37.1MM
SALES (corp-wide): 65.2MM **Privately Held**
WEB: www.theenergycoop.com
SIC: **4922** 4924 4932 4911 Natural gas transmission; natural gas distribution; gas & other services combined; electric services; industrial gases
HQ: National Gas & Oil Company Inc
1500 Granville Rd
Newark OH 43055
740 344-2102

(G-15080)
NATIONAL YOUTH ADVOCATE PROGRA
Also Called: Nyap - Newark
15 N 3rd St Fl 3 (43055-5550)
PHONE..............................740 349-7511
Ken Larimore, *Branch Mgr*
EMP: 33
SALES (corp-wide): 53.3MM **Privately Held**
SIC: **8322** Individual & family services; child related social services; adoption services; family service agency
PA: National Youth Advocate Program, Inc.
1801 Watermark Dr Ste 200
Columbus OH 43215
614 487-8758

(G-15081)
NEW WORLD ENERGY RESOURCES (PA)
1500 Granville Rd (43055-1536)
PHONE..............................740 344-4087
John Manczak, *CEO*
EMP: 488
SALES (est): 18.8MM **Privately Held**
SIC: **1382** Geological exploration, oil & gas field

(G-15082)
NEWARK CARE CENTER LLC
Also Called: Price Rd Hlth Rhbilitation Ctr
151 Price Rd (43055-3317)
PHONE..............................740 366-2321
Mordecai Rosenberg, *President*
Ronald Swartz, *CFO*
Lisa Schwartz, *Admin Sec*
EMP: 99
SALES (est): 522.2K **Privately Held**
SIC: **8051** Convalescent home with continuous nursing care

(G-15083)
NEWARK LEASING LLC
Also Called: Newark Care and Rehabilitation
75 Mcmillen Dr (43055-1808)
PHONE..............................740 344-0357
Eli Gunzberg, *CEO*
EMP: 175
SALES (est): 82.9K **Privately Held**
SIC: **8051** Skilled nursing care facilities

(G-15084)
NEWARK MANAGEMENT PARTNERS LLC
Also Called: Newark Metropolitan Hotel
50 N 2nd St (43055-5622)
PHONE..............................740 322-6455
Martin Schrader,
Jane Simmons,
EMP: 80
SALES (est): 3.1MM **Privately Held**
SIC: **7011** Hotel, franchised

(G-15085)
NEWARK NH LLC
Also Called: NEWARK HILLS HEALTH AND REHABI
17 Forry St (43055-4004)
PHONE..............................740 345-9197
Mordecai Rosenberg, *President*
Ronald Swartz, *CFO*
Lisa Schwartz, *Admin Sec*
EMP: 74 EST: 2015
SALES (est): 406.7K **Privately Held**
SIC: **8051** Skilled nursing care facilities

(G-15086)
NEWARK RESIDENT HOMES INC
15 W Saint Clair St Apt C (43055-5732)
PHONE..............................740 345-7231
Dave Cook, *Exec Dir*

EMP: 75
SALES: 1.3MM **Privately Held**
SIC: 8361 Residential care

(G-15087)
NEWARK SLEEP DIAGNOSTIC CENTER
1900 Tamarack Rd Ste 1908 (43055-2303)
PHONE.................................740 522-9499
Gautam Samadder, *President*
EMP: 50
SALES (est): 563.2K **Privately Held**
SIC: 8069 Specialty hospitals, except psychiatric

(G-15088)
NOAHS ARK CREATIVE CARE
1255 Nadine Dr (43056-9234)
PHONE.................................740 323-3664
Jennifer Cominsky, *Owner*
Brett Cominsky, *Co-Owner*
EMP: 35 EST: 1999
SALES (est): 759.2K **Privately Held**
SIC: 8351 Preschool center

(G-15089)
PARK NATIONAL BANK (HQ)
50 N 3rd St (43055-5548)
P.O. Box 3500 (43058-3500)
PHONE.................................740 349-8451
Ben Rosensweet, *President*
David Trautman, *President*
Dan Delawder, *Chairman*
Thomas J Button, *Senior VP*
Cheryl Snyder, *Senior VP*
EMP: 150
SALES: 355.3MM
SALES (corp-wide): 411.9MM **Publicly Held**
WEB: www.parknationalbank.com
SIC: 6021 National commercial banks
PA: Park National Corporation
  50 N 3rd St
  Newark OH 43055
  740 349-8451

(G-15090)
PARK NATIONAL BANK
21 S 1st St Ste Front (43055-5634)
P.O. Box 3500 (43058-3500)
PHONE.................................740 349-8451
David C Bowers, *Manager*
Herbert Jarrod, *Administration*
EMP: 133
SALES (corp-wide): 411.9MM **Publicly Held**
WEB: www.parknationalbank.com
SIC: 6021 National commercial banks
HQ: The Park National Bank
  50 N 3rd St
  Newark OH 43055
  740 349-8451

(G-15091)
PATHWAYS OF CENTRAL OHIO
1627 Bryn Mawr Dr (43055-1505)
PHONE.................................740 345-6166
Maureen Barnes, *CFO*
Kristin McCloud, *Exec Dir*
Bobby Persinger, *Director*
EMP: 28
SQ FT: 7,000
SALES: 1MM **Privately Held**
WEB: www.pathwayslc.org
SIC: 8322 Social service center; crisis center

(G-15092)
PNC BANK NATIONAL ASSOCIATION
Also Called: National City Bank
68 W Church St Fl 1 (43055-5050)
PHONE.................................740 349-8431
Tom Decker, *Branch Mgr*
EMP: 30
SALES (corp-wide): 19.9B **Publicly Held**
WEB: www.allegiantbank.com
SIC: 6021 National commercial banks
HQ: Pnc Bank, National Association
  222 Delaware Ave
  Wilmington DE 19801
  877 762-2000

(G-15093)
PRIDE -N- JOY PRESCHOOL INC
1319 W Main St (43055-1821)
PHONE.................................740 522-3338
Mark Nutter, *President*
Vonnie Nutter, *Vice Pres*
EMP: 25
SQ FT: 3,000
SALES (est): 1MM **Privately Held**
SIC: 8351 Preschool center

(G-15094)
R & R PIPELINE INC (PA)
155 Dayton Rd Ne (43055-8879)
P.O. Box 37 (43058-0037)
PHONE.................................740 345-3692
Rick Reed, *President*
Jeff Emery, *Vice Pres*
Debbie Staley, *Real Est Agnt*
EMP: 55
SQ FT: 7,400
SALES (est): 11.1MM **Privately Held**
WEB: www.rrpipelineinc.com
SIC: 1623 Pipeline construction

(G-15095)
REESE PYLE DRAKE & MEYER (PA)
36 N 2nd St (43055-5610)
P.O. Box 919 (43058-0919)
PHONE.................................740 345-3431
J Andrew Crawford, *Partner*
Ann Munro Kennedy, *Partner*
William Douglas Lowe, *Partner*
David W Wenger, *Partner*
Robert Drake, *Counsel*
EMP: 44 EST: 1904
SQ FT: 12,000
SALES (est): 6.5MM **Privately Held**
WEB: www.rpdm.com
SIC: 8111 General practice attorney, lawyer

(G-15096)
RICHARDSON GLASS SERVICE INC (PA)
Also Called: RICHARDSON GLASS SERVICE INC DBA LEE'S GLASS SERVICE
1165 Mount Vernon Rd (43055-3032)
PHONE.................................740 366-5090
Toll Free:..........................888 -
Mark W McPeek, *President*
Steve Davis, *Principal*
John P Johnson II, *Principal*
Laura McPeek, *Vice Pres*
Gary Watson, *Project Mgr*
EMP: 52
SQ FT: 21,480
SALES: 13.1MM **Privately Held**
WEB: www.richardsonglass.com
SIC: 1793 Glass & glazing work

(G-15097)
SECURITY NATIONAL BANK & TR CO (HQ)
50 N 3rd St (43055-5523)
P.O. Box 1726, Springfield (45501-1726)
PHONE.................................740 426-6384
William C Fralick, *President*
Daniel M O'Keefe, *Vice Pres*
J William Stapleton, *CFO*
EMP: 120 EST: 1903
SQ FT: 40,000
SALES (est): 7.8MM
SALES (corp-wide): 411.9MM **Publicly Held**
WEB: www.securitynationalbank.com
SIC: 6021 National trust companies with deposits, commercial
PA: Park National Corporation
  50 N 3rd St
  Newark OH 43055
  740 349-8451

(G-15098)
SOUTHGATE CORP
1499 W Main St (43055-1988)
P.O. Box 397 (43058-0397)
PHONE.................................740 522-2151
Robert O'Neill, *President*
Robert O Neill, *President*
Russ Boren, *Project Mgr*
Mark Schillig, *Sales Staff*
EMP: 26

SALES (est): 3.6MM **Privately Held**
SIC: 6552 Land subdividers & developers, commercial

(G-15099)
ST FRANCIS DE SALES CHURCH (PA)
40 Granville St (43055-5084)
PHONE.................................740 345-9874
David Sizemore, *Pastor*
William Hritsko, *Pastor*
Dean Mathewson, *Pastor*
Maggie Wright, *Director*
R Penhallurick, *Post Master*
EMP: 95
SALES: 1.6MM **Privately Held**
SIC: 8661 8211 8351 Catholic Church; kindergarten; Catholic elementary school; Catholic junior high school; preschool center

(G-15100)
STATE FARM GENERAL INSUR CO
Also Called: State Farm Insurance
1440 Granville Rd (43055-1538)
PHONE.................................740 364-5000
Lee Baumann, *Vice Pres*
EMP: 89
SALES (corp-wide): 39.5B **Privately Held**
SIC: 6411 Insurance agents & brokers
HQ: State Farm General Insurance Co Inc
  1 State Farm Plz
  Bloomington IL 61701
  309 766-2311

(G-15101)
STATE FARM MUTL AUTO INSUR CO
Also Called: State Farm Insurance
1440 Granville Rd (43055-1538)
PHONE.................................740 364-5000
Lee Baumann, *Vice Pres*
EMP: 2000
SALES (corp-wide): 39.5B **Privately Held**
WEB: www.statefarm.com
SIC: 6411 Insurance agents & brokers
PA: State Farm Mutual Automobile Insurance Company
  1 State Farm Plz
  Bloomington IL 61710
  309 766-2311

(G-15102)
SURGICENTER LTD
Also Called: Speacialty Care Vision
1651 W Main St (43055-1345)
PHONE.................................740 522-3937
Leroy Bloomberg, *Principal*
Shahin Shahinfar, *Director*
EMP: 35
SALES (est): 1MM **Privately Held**
SIC: 8011 Eyes, ears, nose & throat specialist: physician/surgeon

(G-15103)
THERATRUST
23 Forry St (43055-4057)
PHONE.................................740 345-7688
Steve Hitchens, *Owner*
EMP: 50
SALES (est): 1.4MM **Privately Held**
WEB: www.theratrust.net
SIC: 8093 Rehabilitation center, outpatient treatment

(G-15104)
TRUE CORE FEDERAL CREDIT UNION
215 Deo Dr (43055-3051)
PHONE.................................740 345-6608
Fred Longstreth, *President*
Shani Smith, *Exec VP*
Dorothy Ridenbaugh, *Vice Pres*
Beth Sheets, *Marketing Staff*
Jocelyn Gayheart, *Manager*
EMP: 45
SALES: 5.6MM **Privately Held**
WEB: www.fiberglas.org
SIC: 6061 Federal credit unions

(G-15105)
UNITED STEELWORKERS
Also Called: Uswa
2100 James Pkwy (43056-1031)
PHONE.................................740 928-0157
Gary Sities, *President*
EMP: 240
SALES (corp-wide): 4.9MM **Privately Held**
WEB: www.uswa.org
SIC: 8631 Labor union
PA: United Steelworkers
  60 Blvd Of The Allies # 902
  Pittsburgh PA 15222
  412 562-2400

(G-15106)
UNIVERSAL VENEER MILL CORP
1776 Tamarack Rd (43055-1384)
PHONE.................................740 522-1147
Klaus Krajewski, *President*
William Cooper, *CFO*
Michael Funk, *CFO*
Aundrea Antritt, *Controller*
Jacob Preston, *Sales Staff*
EMP: 180
SQ FT: 75,000
SALES (est): 9.7MM **Privately Held**
SIC: 6512 Commercial & industrial building operation

(G-15107)
WASHINGTON SQUARE APARTMENTS
340 Eastern Ave Ofc (43055-6580)
PHONE.................................740 349-8353
Charles W Nobel, *President*
Sandy Henderson, *Director*
EMP: 28
SALES (est): 1.7MM **Privately Held**
SIC: 6513 6531 Apartment hotel operation; real estate agents & managers

(G-15108)
WASTE MANAGEMENT OHIO INC
100 Ecology Row (43055-8894)
PHONE.................................740 345-1212
Tim Giardina, *Manager*
EMP: 100
SALES (corp-wide): 14.9B **Publicly Held**
WEB: www.wm.com
SIC: 4953 Refuse systems
HQ: Waste Management Of Ohio, Inc.
  1700 N Broad St
  Fairborn OH 45324

(G-15109)
WILSON SHANNON & SNOW INC
10 W Locust St (43055-5508)
PHONE.................................740 345-6611
Philip Z Shannon, *President*
Noble B Snow III, *Corp Secy*
William W Weidaw, *Vice Pres*
Jodie Wheeler, *CPA*
Donna Yeager, *Admin Asst*
EMP: 28
SQ FT: 4,500
SALES (est): 2.8MM **Privately Held**
WEB: www.wssinc.net
SIC: 8721 Certified public accountant

(G-15110)
WILSONS HILLVIEW FARM INC
Also Called: Wilson's Garden Center
10923 Lambs Ln (43055-8897)
PHONE.................................740 763-2873
Ned Wilson, *President*
Brian Wilson, *General Mgr*
Mitzie Wilson, *Corp Secy*
Harry Wilson, *Vice Pres*
EMP: 40
SQ FT: 80,000
SALES: 2MM **Privately Held**
WEB: www.great-gardeners.com
SIC: 0181 5992 Shrubberies grown under cover (e.g. greenhouse production); flowers: grown under cover (e.g. greenhouse production); florists

GEOGRAPHIC

(G-15111)
WOODLNDS SRVING CENTL OHIO INC
Also Called: Family Counseling Services
68 W Church St Ste 318 (43055-5050)
PHONE..............................740 349-7051
Ann Rudrauf, Branch Mgr
EMP: 30
SALES (corp-wide): 1.5MM Privately Held
WEB: www.thewoodland.org
SIC: 8322 Social service center
PA: The Woodlands Serving Central Ohio Inc
195 Union St Ste B1
Newark OH 43055
740 349-7066

(G-15112)
YEATER ALENE K MD
Also Called: Govana Hospital
15 Messimer Dr (43055-1841)
PHONE..............................740 348-4694
Alene Yeater, Owner
EMP: 40
SALES (est): 128.2K Privately Held
SIC: 8011 Offices & clinics of medical doctors

Newburgh Heights
Cuyahoga County

(G-15113)
ALL INDUSTRIAL GROUP INC (PA)
1555 1/2 Harvard Ave (44105-3064)
PHONE..............................216 441-2000
Donald W Martinez, President
Rick Martinez, Treasurer
EMP: 34
SQ FT: 20,000
SALES (est): 5.8MM Privately Held
SIC: 4213 Contract haulers

(G-15114)
HOWMET CORPORATION (DH)
Also Called: Alcoa Power & Propulsion
1616 Harvard Ave (44105-3040)
PHONE..............................757 825-7086
David L Squier, President
Marklin Lasker, Senior VP
James R Stanley, Senior VP
Roland A Paul, Vice Pres
B Dennis Albrechtsen, VP Mfg
◆ EMP: 30
SQ FT: 10,000
SALES (est): 1.8B
SALES (corp-wide): 14B Publicly Held
WEB: www.alcoa.com
SIC: 3324 3542 5051 3479 Commercial investment castings, ferrous; machine tools, metal forming type; ferroalloys; ingots; coating of metals & formed products
HQ: Howmet Holdings Corporation
1 Misco Dr
Whitehall MI 49461
231 894-5686

(G-15115)
HUNT PRODUCTS INC
3982 E 42nd St (44105-3165)
PHONE..............................440 667-2457
Jo Ann Hunt, President
Laura Hunt, Vice Pres
EMP: 35 EST: 1970
SQ FT: 30,000
SALES (est): 2.2MM Privately Held
SIC: 7389 3544 3053 2675 Packaging & labeling services; special dies, tools, jigs & fixtures; gaskets, packing & sealing devices; die-cut paper & board; packaging paper & plastics film, coated & laminated; automotive & apparel trimmings

(G-15116)
WESTERN RSERVE WTR SYSTEMS INC
4133 E 49th St (44105-3267)
PHONE..............................216 341-9797
Joe Hooley, CEO
Michael D Eiermann, President
Bob Skocdopole, Plant Mgr
Bob Skocodopole, Plant Mgr

Alan Lauvray, Prdtn Mgr
◆ EMP: 70
SQ FT: 10,000
SALES: 12.5MM Privately Held
WEB: www.westernreservewater.com
SIC: 7389 Water softener service

Newbury
Geauga County

(G-15117)
ADVANCED TENTING SOLUTIONS
10750 Music St (44065-9559)
PHONE..............................216 291-3300
Kim Goodrick, Partner
EMP: 30
SALES (est): 2MM Privately Held
SIC: 7359 Tent & tarpaulin rental

(G-15118)
ANDOVER FLOOR COVERING
9950 Belleflower Cir (44065-9159)
PHONE..............................440 293-5339
Diana Hammer, Owner
EMP: 29
SQ FT: 1,000
SALES (est): 2.1MM Privately Held
SIC: 5713 1752 Carpets; floor laying & floor work

(G-15119)
CREATIVE MOLD AND MACHINE INC
10385 Kinsman Rd (44065-9701)
P.O. Box 323 (44065-0323)
PHONE..............................440 338-5146
Ray Lyons, President
Greg Davis, Vice Pres
Mishal Dedeck, Vice Pres
EMP: 25
SQ FT: 39,000
SALES (est): 4.3MM Privately Held
SIC: 7692 3599 Welding repair; machine shop, jobbing & repair

(G-15120)
FAIRMONT NURSING HOME INC
Also Called: Holly Hill Nursing Home
10190 Fairmount Rd (44065-9531)
P.O. Box 337 (44065-0337)
PHONE..............................440 338-8220
George Ohman, President
Ron Durkee, Maint Spvr
Jamie Linstra, Office Mgr
Stephanie Piecuch, Director
Catherine Dahlem, Nursing Dir
EMP: 95
SQ FT: 28,000
SALES (est): 6.3MM Privately Held
SIC: 8052 8051 Intermediate care facilities; skilled nursing care facilities

(G-15121)
GEAUGA SAVINGS BANK (PA)
10800 Kinsman Rd (44065-8701)
PHONE..............................440 564-9441
James Kleinfelter, President
David Leaver, Vice Pres
Ron Webb, Vice Pres
Greg Yurco, Vice Pres
Donna Light, Manager
EMP: 31
SALES: 12.9MM Privately Held
WEB: www.geaugasavings.com
SIC: 6036 State savings banks, not federally chartered

(G-15122)
KUHNLE BROTHERS INC
Also Called: Kuhnle Bros Trucking
14905 Cross Creek Pkwy (44065-9788)
P.O. Box 375 (44065-0375)
PHONE..............................440 564-7168
Kim Taylor Kuhnle, CEO
Robert Russell, Treasurer
Thomas Kuhnle, Admin Sec
EMP: 150 EST: 1963
SQ FT: 20,000
SALES: 270MM Privately Held
SIC: 4213 4212 Trucking, except local; local trucking, without storage

(G-15123)
MULLETT COMPANY
14980 Cross Creek Pkwy (44065-9788)
P.O. Box 5000 (44065-0509)
PHONE..............................440 564-9000
Owen A Mullett, President
Steve Mullett, General Mgr
Daniel Gingerich, Vice Pres
Dave Gingerich, Project Mgr
David Mullett, Treasurer
EMP: 25
SQ FT: 6,800
SALES (est): 8MM Privately Held
WEB: www.mullettco.com
SIC: 1541 1542 Industrial buildings, new construction; renovation, remodeling & repairs: industrial buildings; commercial & office building, new construction; commercial & office buildings, renovation & repair

(G-15124)
PRECIOUS CARGO TRANSPORTATION
15050 Cross Creek Pkwy (44065-9726)
P.O. Box 23617, Chagrin Falls (44023-0617)
PHONE..............................440 564-8039
Richard Wervey, President
Shawn Schofield, Officer
John Wervey, Master
EMP: 30
SQ FT: 10,000
SALES: 500K Privately Held
SIC: 4141 4119 4131 Local bus charter service; limousine rental, with driver; intercity & rural bus transportation

(G-15125)
SCOT BURTON CONTRACTORS LLC
11330 Kinsman Rd (44065-9666)
PHONE..............................440 564-1011
David Paulitsch,
Scot Paulitsch,
EMP: 40
SQ FT: 6,000
SALES (est): 7.8MM Privately Held
SIC: 1611 Highway & street paving contractor

(G-15126)
TW RECREATIONAL SERVICES INC
Also Called: Punderson Manor Resort
11755 Kinsman Rd (44065-9691)
P.O. Box 224 (44065-0224)
PHONE..............................440 564-9144
James Adamson, President
John Muller, General Mgr
Kate Patterson, Financial Exec
EMP: 40
SALES (est): 1.3MM Privately Held
WEB: www.pundersonmanorresort.com
SIC: 7011 Tourist camps, cabins, cottages & courts

(G-15127)
VAN NESS STONE INC
10500 Kinsman Rd (44065-9803)
P.O. Box 1000 (44065-0199)
PHONE..............................440 564-1111
Fred Van Ness, President
Scott Bennett, Sales Staff
EMP: 28 EST: 1969
SQ FT: 9,120
SALES (est): 3MM Privately Held
WEB: www.vannesstone.com
SIC: 1741 Stone masonry

(G-15128)
WICKED WOODS GULF CLUB INC
Also Called: Wicked Woods Golf Club
14085 Ravenna Rd (44065-9511)
PHONE..............................440 564-7960
Edith Zimerman, President
Sam Zimerman, Vice Pres
EMP: 40
SALES (est): 909.3K Privately Held
SIC: 7992 Public Golf Courses

Newcomerstown
Tuscarawas County

(G-15129)
DAVID BARBER CIVIC CENTER
1066 E State St (43832-1550)
P.O. Box 29 (43832-0029)
PHONE..............................740 498-4383
Heather Wells, President
EMP: 25
SALES (est): 380.1K Privately Held
SIC: 7999 Bingo hall

(G-15130)
EAGLE HARDWOODS INC
6138 Stonecreek Rd (43832-9162)
P.O. Box 96, Stone Creek (43840-0096)
PHONE..............................330 339-8838
Ronald D Furbay, President
Loy E Wiggins Jr, Vice Pres
▼ EMP: 40
SQ FT: 1,344
SALES (est): 12.3MM Privately Held
SIC: 5031 Lumber: rough, dressed & finished

(G-15131)
EXPRESS PACKAGING OHIO INC (PA)
301 Enterprise Dr (43832-9240)
PHONE..............................740 498-4700
Pam Hartzler, CEO
Fred Hartzler, Owner
Donald Faulhaber, Principal
Janet Earley, Traffic Mgr
Jason Hartzler, Manager
EMP: 395
SQ FT: 240,000
SALES (est): 102.1MM Privately Held
SIC: 7389 Packaging & labeling services

(G-15132)
GEORGE DARR
Also Called: Darr Farms
21284 Township Road 257 (43832-9660)
PHONE..............................740 498-5400
George Darr, Owner
Beverly Darr, Co-Owner
EMP: 40
SALES (est): 4.3MM Privately Held
SIC: 0161 0175 0116 0115 Vegetables & melons; deciduous tree fruits; soybeans; corn

(G-15133)
NEWCOMERSTOWN DEVELOPMENT INC
Also Called: Riverside Mnor Nrsing Rhab Ctr
1100 E State Rd (43832-9446)
PHONE..............................740 498-5165
Dwayne Shepherd, Administration
EMP: 125
SQ FT: 40,000
SALES: 5.2MM Privately Held
SIC: 8051 Skilled nursing care facilities

(G-15134)
NEWCOMERSTOWN PROGRESS CORP
Also Called: Riverside Manor
1100 E State Rd (43832-9446)
PHONE..............................740 498-5165
Terry Overholser, President
Roger Bambeck, Corp Secy
Wayne Mortine, Vice Pres
Dwayne Shepherd, Administration
EMP: 130
SQ FT: 35,000
SALES: 3.4MM Privately Held
WEB: www.riversidemanor.com
SIC: 8051 8049 Convalescent home with continuous nursing care; physical therapist

---

Newton Falls
Trumbull County

(G-15135)
AMERICAN LEGION POST
2025 E River Rd (44444)
PHONE..................................330 872-5475
Tom Greathouse, *Principal*
EMP: 25
SALES: 196.2K **Privately Held**
SIC: 8611 Business associations

(G-15136)
CADLE COMPANY II INC
100 N Center St (44444-1380)
PHONE..................................330 872-0918
Daniel C Cadle, *President*
Ruth Cadle, *Principal*
EMP: 120
SQ FT: 5,000
SALES (est): 14MM **Privately Held**
SIC: 6211 Investment bankers

(G-15137)
HOOBERRY ASSOCIATES INC
Also Called: LAURIE ANN NURSING HOME
2200 Milton Blvd (44444-8746)
PHONE..................................330 872-1991
Doris Hooberry, *President*
Sharon Jones, *Admin Sec*
EMP: 60
SQ FT: 15,415
SALES: 3.6MM **Privately Held**
SIC: 8051 Convalescent home with continuous nursing care

(G-15138)
LAURIE ANN HOME HEALTH CARE
2200 Milton Blvd (44444-8746)
PHONE..................................330 872-7512
Katherine Kolesar, *Owner*
EMP: 38
SALES (est): 1MM **Privately Held**
SIC: 8082 Home Health Care Services

(G-15139)
LEES ROBY INC
Also Called: Roby Lees Restaurant & Catrg
425 Ridge Rd (44444-1246)
PHONE..................................330 872-0983
Robert J Lee, *President*
Carolyn Lee, *Admin Sec*
EMP: 30
SALES (est): 1.1MM **Privately Held**
WEB: www.robylees.com
SIC: 5812 7299 Restaurant, family: independent; banquet hall facilities

(G-15140)
LIBERTY ASHTABULA HOLDINGS
Also Called: Holiday Inn
4185 State Route 5 (44444-9566)
PHONE..................................330 872-6000
Ketki Shah, *President*
Raxit Shah, *Corp Secy*
EMP: 25 EST: 1998
SALES (est): 1.1MM **Privately Held**
WEB: www.libertyg.com
SIC: 7011 Hotels & motels

(G-15141)
THE CADLE COMPANY (PA)
100 N Center St (44444-1380)
PHONE..................................330 872-0918
Daniel Cadle, *President*
Ruth Cadle, *Admin Sec*
EMP: 136
SQ FT: 25,000
SALES (est): 38MM **Privately Held**
SIC: 6211 6282 Mortgages, buying & selling; investment advice

---

Niles
Trumbull County

(G-15142)
AARIS THERAPY GROUP INC
950 Youngstown Warren Rd A
(44446-4626)
PHONE..................................330 505-1606
Tiffany Hurlbut, *President*
EMP: 40
SALES (est): 117.1K **Privately Held**
SIC: 8093 Rehabilitation center, outpatient treatment

(G-15143)
ALTOBELLI REALESTATE (PA)
304 Vienna Ave (44446-2628)
PHONE..................................330 652-0200
Jerry Altobelli, *Owner*
EMP: 33
SALES (est): 1.6MM **Privately Held**
SIC: 6531 Real estate brokers & agents

(G-15144)
AMERICAN TITLE SERVICES INC
700 Youngstown Warren Rd (44446-3552)
PHONE..................................330 652-1609
Ralph Zuzolo Sr, *President*
Renee Zuzolo, *Vice Pres*
Ralph Zuzolo Jr, *Treasurer*
Christopher Zuzolo, *Admin Sec*
Ralph Susalow Sr,
EMP: 34 EST: 1975
SALES (est): 1.1MM **Privately Held**
WEB: www.americantitleservices.com
SIC: 6541 8111 6531 Title abstract offices; legal services; real estate agents & managers

(G-15145)
AT&T CORP
5412 Youngstown Warren Rd
(44446-4910)
PHONE..................................330 505-4200
EMP: 46
SALES (corp-wide): 170.7B **Publicly Held**
SIC: 5065 4812 Telephone & telegraphic equipment; cellular telephone services
HQ: At&t Corp.
1 At&T Way
Bedminster NJ 07921
800 403-3302

(G-15146)
AUTUMN HILLS CARE CENTER INC
2565 Niles Vienna Rd (44446-4400)
PHONE..................................330 652-2053
Michael J Coats, *President*
Dr Carl R Gillette, *Vice Pres*
EMP: 200
SQ FT: 37,000
SALES (est): 10MM **Privately Held**
WEB: www.autumnhills.com
SIC: 8051 Convalescent home with continuous nursing care

(G-15147)
BECDEL CONTROLS INCORPORATED
1869 Warren Ave (44446-1143)
PHONE..................................330 652-1386
Kerry Beck, *President*
John Schell III, *Vice Pres*
EMP: 32
SALES (est): 3.2MM **Privately Held**
SIC: 1731 General electrical contractor

(G-15148)
C R G HEALTH CARE SYSTEMS
Also Called: Manor, The
2567 Niles Vienna Rd Ofc (44446-5406)
PHONE..................................330 498-8107
Cynthia Woodford, *Director*
EMP: 35
SALES (est): 1.1MM **Privately Held**
WEB: www.manorautumnhills.com
SIC: 8082 8052 Home health care services; intermediate care facilities

(G-15149)
CAFARO CO
Also Called: Eastwood Mall Kids Club
5555 Youngstown Warren Rd
(44446-4804)
PHONE..................................330 652-6980
Ken Koler, *Manager*
EMP: 25
SALES (est): 591.7K **Privately Held**
SIC: 8641 Youth organizations

(G-15150)
CARARO CO INC
Also Called: Eastwood Mall
492 Eastwood Mall (44446)
PHONE..................................330 652-6980
William M Cafaro, *Ch of Bd*
Ken Kollar, *President*
Anthony M Cafaro, *Vice Pres*
Joseph Nohra, *Treasurer*
EMP: 42
SALES (est): 2.6MM **Privately Held**
SIC: 6512 Commercial & industrial building operation

(G-15151)
CLEVELAND CLINIC FOUNDATION
650 Youngstown Warren Rd (44446-4356)
PHONE..................................330 505-2280
Guiyun Wu, *Manager*
EMP: 85
SALES (corp-wide): 8.9B **Privately Held**
SIC: 6733 Trusts
PA: The Cleveland Clinic Foundation
9500 Euclid Ave
Cleveland OH 44195
216 636-8335

(G-15152)
COATES CAR CARE INC
59 Youngstown Warren Rd (44446-4592)
PHONE..................................330 652-4180
James M Coates Sr, *President*
Jamie Williams, *Corp Secy*
James M Coates Jr, *Vice Pres*
EMP: 35
SQ FT: 38,000
SALES (est): 2.7MM **Privately Held**
SIC: 7539 7542 7549 Automotive repair shops; carwash, self-service; lubrication service, automotive; automotive customizing services, non-factory basis

(G-15153)
CONSUMER SUPPORT SERVICES INC
1254 Yngstwn Wrrn Rd B (44446)
PHONE..................................330 652-8800
Patty Beckley, *Exec Dir*
EMP: 146
SALES (corp-wide): 26.7MM **Privately Held**
SIC: 8082 Home health care services
PA: Consumer Support Services Inc
2040 Cherry Valley Rd # 1
Newark OH 43055
740 788-8257

(G-15154)
FAIRHAVEN SHELTERED WORKSHOP
6000 Youngstown Warren Rd
(44446-4624)
PHONE..................................330 652-1116
Rocco Maiorca, *Branch Mgr*
EMP: 178
SALES (corp-wide): 4.5MM **Privately Held**
SIC: 8331 Sheltered workshop
PA: Fairhaven Sheltered Workshop
45 North Rd
Niles OH 44446
330 505-3644

(G-15155)
FAIRHAVEN SHELTERED WORKSHOP (PA)
45 North Rd (44446-1918)
PHONE..................................330 505-3644
Douglas Burkhardt, *Principal*
EMP: 205
SALES (est): 4.5MM **Privately Held**
SIC: 8331 Sheltered workshop

(G-15156)
FARMERS NATIONAL BANK
51 S Main St (44446-5011)
PHONE..................................330 544-7447
Frank Padenk, *President*
Desirae Monaco, *Branch Mgr*
Kerry Pizzulo, *Executive*
EMP: 67
SALES (corp-wide): 117.2MM **Publicly Held**
SIC: 6021 6022 National commercial banks; state commercial banks
HQ: Farmers National Bank
20 S Broad St
Canfield OH 44406
330 533-3341

(G-15157)
HOMES FOR KIDS OF OHIO INC
165 E Park Ave (44446-2352)
P.O. Box 683 (44446-0683)
PHONE..................................330 544-8005
Debra Wilson, *President*
EMP: 50
SALES: 4.3MM **Privately Held**
SIC: 8322 Children's aid society

(G-15158)
MARION PLAZA INC
Also Called: Eastwood Mall
5577 Youngstown Warren Rd
(44446-4803)
P.O. Box 2186, Youngstown (44504-0186)
PHONE..................................330 747-2661
Vincent Morgione, *CEO*
John Sinclair, *Accountant*
EMP: 60
SALES: 950K **Privately Held**
SIC: 6531 Real estate managers

(G-15159)
MIENCORP INC
706 Robbins Ave (44446-2416)
P.O. Box 8726, Warren (44484-0726)
PHONE..................................330 978-8511
Greg Mientkiewicz, *President*
EMP: 50
SALES: 6MM **Privately Held**
SIC: 1541 7389 Renovation, remodeling & repairs: industrial buildings; ; estimating service, construction

(G-15160)
MIKE COATES CNSTR CO INC
800 Summit Ave (44446-3695)
PHONE..................................330 652-0190
Michael J Coates Sr, *President*
Michael J Coates Jr, *Vice Pres*
Jim Huffman, *Project Mgr*
Joanne Coates, *Admin Sec*
EMP: 150
SQ FT: 15,000
SALES (est): 40.2MM **Privately Held**
SIC: 1542 1541 Institutional building construction; commercial & office building contractors; industrial buildings & warehouses

(G-15161)
NATIONAL VETERINARY ASSOC INC
1007 Youngstown Warren Rd
(44446-4620)
PHONE..................................330 652-0055
EMP: 51
SALES (corp-wide): 876MM **Privately Held**
SIC: 0742 Animal hospital services, pets & other animal specialties
PA: National Veterinary Associates, Inc.
29229 Canwood St Ste 100
Agoura Hills CA 91301
805 777-7722

(G-15162)
NILES HISTORICAL SOCIETY
503 Brown St (44446-1443)
P.O. Box 368 (44446-0368)
PHONE..................................330 544-2143
Jessie Scott, *President*
Fred Kubli, *President*
Ann Townley, *President*
EMP: 51
SQ FT: 3,909
SALES: 42.6K **Privately Held**
SIC: 8699 Historical club

(PA)=Parent Co (HQ)=Headquarters (DH)=Div Headquarters
✪ = New Business established in last 2 years

(G-15163)
**NILES IRON & METAL COMPANY
LLC (PA)**
Also Called: Niles Scrap Iron & Metal Co
700 S Main St (44446-1372)
P.O. Box 166 (44446-0166)
PHONE................................330 652-2262
Gary Clayman, *Mng Member*
Michael Clayman, *Mng Member*
EMP: 50
SQ FT: 2,000
SALES (est): 33.3MM **Privately Held**
SIC: 5093 Ferrous metal scrap & waste

(G-15164)
NILES RESIDENTIAL CARE LLC
Also Called: Manor At Autumn Hills
2567 Niles Vienna Rd (44446-5401)
PHONE................................216 727-3996
Brian Haylor, *Principal*
Jeff Bunner, *Principal*
Christopher Mallett, *Principal*
Benjamin Parsons, *Principal*
Mark Sprenger, *Principal*
EMP: 65 EST: 2016
SALES (est): 391.4K **Privately Held**
SIC: 8059 Nursing & personal care

(G-15165)
NRG POWER MIDWEST LP
Also Called: Niles Generating Station
1047 Belmont Ave (44446-1356)
PHONE................................330 505-4327
EMP: 54 **Publicly Held**
SIC: 4911 Electric Services
HQ: Nrg Power Midwest Lp
1000 Main St
Houston TX 77002

(G-15166)
**PALISDES BSBAL A CAL LTD
PRTNR**
Also Called: Mahoning Valley Scrappers
111 Eastwood Mall Blvd (44446-4841)
PHONE................................330 505-0000
Alan Levin, *Partner*
Clayton Sibilla, *Manager*
EMP: 175 EST: 1994
SALES (est): 197.6K **Privately Held**
WEB: www.palisadesbaseball.com
SIC: 7941 Baseball club, professional &
semi-professional

(G-15167)
PETSMART INC
5812 Youngstown Warren Rd
(44446-4706)
PHONE................................330 544-1499
Jim Moroco, *Manager*
EMP: 30
SALES (corp-wide): 12.1B **Privately Held**
WEB: www.petsmart.com
SIC: 5999 0752 Pet food; animal specialty
services
HQ: Petsmart, Inc.
19601 N 27th Ave
Phoenix AZ 85027
623 580-6100

(G-15168)
SEARS ROEBUCK AND CO
Also Called: Sears Auto Center
5555 Youngstown Warren Rd # 120
(44446-4899)
PHONE................................330 652-5128
EMP: 150
SALES (corp-wide): 16.7B **Publicly Held**
SIC: 7549 Automotive Services
HQ: Sears, Roebuck And Co.
3333 Beverly Rd
Hoffman Estates IL 60179
847 286-2500

(G-15169)
SELECT STEEL INC
1825 Hunter Ave (44446-1672)
PHONE................................330 652-1756
Jeffrey A Gotthardt, *President*
Glenn E Gotthardt, *Corp Secy*
Danielle Tenney, *Manager*
EMP: 40
SQ FT: 76,000
SALES (est): 20.8MM **Privately Held**
WEB: www.selectstl.com
SIC: 5051 Steel

(G-15170)
**SOUTHSIDE ENVMTL GROUP
LLC**
1806 Warren Ave (44446-1144)
P.O. Box 372 (44446-0372)
PHONE................................330 299-0027
Matthew J Schimley, *Principal*
EMP: 30
SALES (est): 3.8MM **Privately Held**
SIC: 8744 0781 ; landscape services

(G-15171)
TIMKEN COMPANY
1819 N Main St (44446-1251)
P.O. Box 477905, Broadview Heights
(44147-7905)
PHONE................................234 262-3000
Richard Hill, *Manager*
EMP: 100
SALES (corp-wide): 3.5B **Publicly Held**
SIC: 5085 Bearings
PA: The Timken Company
4500 Mount Pleasant St Nw
North Canton OH 44720
234 262-3000

(G-15172)
**TRAICHAL CONSTRUCTION
COMPANY (PA)**
Also Called: Warren Door
332 Plant St (44446-1895)
P.O. Box 70 (44446-0070)
PHONE................................800 255-3667
Edward Traichal, *President*
EMP: 30
SQ FT: 15,000
SALES (est): 7.8MM **Privately Held**
WEB: www.plantia.com
SIC: 3442 1751 5199 5031 Metal doors;
rolling doors for industrial buildings or
warehouses, metal; window & door instal-
lation & erection; advertising specialties;
doors & windows

(G-15173)
**W T C S A HEADSTART NILES
CTR**
Also Called: Casaro Headstart
309 N Rhodes Ave (44446-3821)
PHONE................................330 652-0338
James W Abicht, *President*
Jeanne Wall, *Director*
EMP: 40
SALES (est): 442.9K **Privately Held**
SIC: 8299 8399 Educational services; so-
cial services

(G-15174)
WEST CORPORATION
5185 Youngstown Warren Rd
(44446-4906)
PHONE................................330 574-0510
James Evans, *Branch Mgr*
EMP: 269
SALES (corp-wide): 2.2B **Privately Held**
SIC: 7389 Automobile recovery service
HQ: West Corporation
11808 Miracle Hills Dr
Omaha NE 68154

(G-15175)
**WESTERN RESERVE
MECHANICAL INC**
3041 S Main St (44446-1313)
PHONE................................330 652-3888
Linda Leger, *President*
Mark Leger, *President*
Larry Moore, *Vice Pres*
Mike Jewell, *Manager*
EMP: 50
SALES (est): 8.9MM **Privately Held**
WEB: www.wrmech.com
SIC: 1711 Mechanical contractor

North Baltimore
Wood County

(G-15176)
CSX TRANSPORTATION INC
17000 Deshler Rd (45872-8719)
PHONE................................419 257-1225
Jaime Reyes, *Business Anlyst*

Steven M Loewengart, *Branch Mgr*
EMP: 36
SALES (corp-wide): 12.2B **Publicly Held**
SIC: 4011 Railroads, line-haul operating
HQ: Csx Transportation, Inc.
500 Water St
Jacksonville FL 32202
904 359-3100

(G-15177)
**HANCOCK-WOOD ELECTRIC
COOP INC (PA)**
1399 Business Park Dr S (45872-8716)
P.O. Box 190 (45872-0190)
PHONE................................419 257-3241
George Walton, *President*
Ryan Marquette, *Info Tech Mgr*
EMP: 35 EST: 1938
SALES (est): 42.2MM **Privately Held**
WEB: www.hwelectric.com
SIC: 4911 Distribution, electric power

(G-15178)
HPJ INDUSTRIES INC (PA)
510 W Broadway St (45872-9521)
P.O. Box 860, Bowling Green (43402-0860)
PHONE................................419 278-1000
Chris Beck, *CEO*
Scott M Rothweiler, *President*
EMP: 90
SALES (est): 14.1MM **Privately Held**
SIC: 4953 Recycling, waste materials

(G-15179)
POLYONE CORPORATION
733 E Water St (45872-1434)
P.O. Box 247 (45872-0247)
PHONE................................440 930-1000
Pete Jacob, *Vice Pres*
EMP: 80 **Publicly Held**
WEB: www.polyone.com
SIC: 2821 5169 3087 Vinyl resins; syn-
thetic resins, rubber & plastic materials;
custom compound purchased resins
PA: Polyone Corporation
33587 Walker Rd
Avon Lake OH 44012

(G-15180)
USIC LOCATING SERVICES LLC
12769 Eagleville Rd B (45872-9656)
PHONE................................419 874-9988
Fax: 419 874-9988
EMP: 36 **Privately Held**
SIC: 1623 Water/Sewer/Utility Construction
HQ: Usic Locating Services, Llc
9045 River Rd Ste 300
Indianapolis IN 46240
317 575-7800

North Bend
Hamilton County

(G-15181)
ASTON OAKS GOLF CLUB
1 Aston Oaks Dr (45052-9621)
PHONE................................513 467-0070
Andrew Macke, *Vice Pres*
EMP: 40
SALES (est): 1.3MM **Privately Held**
WEB: www.astonoaks.com
SIC: 7992 Public golf courses

(G-15182)
**MARTIN MARIETTA MATERIALS
INC**
Martin Marietta Aggregates
10905 Us 50 (45052)
PHONE................................513 353-1400
Bernie Jelen, *Branch Mgr*
EMP: 55 **Publicly Held**
WEB: www.martinmarietta.com
SIC: 1422 Crushed & broken limestone
PA: Martin Marietta Materials Inc
2710 Wycliff Rd
Raleigh NC 27607

(G-15183)
VISTRA ENERGY CORP
Also Called: Miami Fort Power Station
11021 Brower Rd (45052-9755)
PHONE................................513 467-4900
Chris Osterbrink, *General Mgr*

Jeff Foglesong, *Technical Mgr*
John Gulasy, *Electrical Engi*
Tim Thiemann, *Manager*
EMP: 205
SALES (corp-wide): 9.1B **Publicly Held**
SIC: 4911
PA: Vistra Energy Corp.
6555 Sierra Dr
Irving TX 75039
214 812-4600

North Canton
Stark County

(G-15184)
**ADVANTAGE HOME HEALTH
SVCS INC**
7951 Pittsburg Ave Nw (44720-5669)
PHONE................................330 491-8161
Kun Woo Nam, *President*
Maria N Swisher, *Vice Pres*
EMP: 35
SALES: 7.9MM **Privately Held**
SIC: 8082 Home health care services

(G-15185)
**ADVANTAGE TANK LINES INC
(HQ)**
4366 Mount Pleasant St Nw (44720-5446)
PHONE................................330 491-0474
Dennis Nash, *President*
Bill Downey, *Exec VP*
Robert Schurer, *Exec VP*
Carl H Young, *CFO*
EMP: 35
SALES (est): 29.6MM
SALES (corp-wide): 2.4B **Privately Held**
WEB: www.advantagemgmtgroup.com
SIC: 4213 Trucking, except local
PA: The Kenan Advantage Group Inc
4366 Mount Pleasant St Nw
North Canton OH 44720
800 969-5419

(G-15186)
**AKRON-CANTON REGIONAL
AIRPORT**
Also Called: Akron Canton Airport
5400 Lauby Rd Ste 9 (44720-1598)
PHONE................................330 499-4059
Richard McQueen, *President*
Kristie Vanauken, *Senior VP*
Kevin Ripple, *Manager*
EMP: 48
SQ FT: 150,000
SALES (est): 9.3MM **Privately Held**
WEB: www.akroncantonairport.com
SIC: 4581 8721 Airport; accounting, audit-
ing & bookkeeping

(G-15187)
ALL ABOUT KIDS DAYCARE N
6199 Frank Ave Nw (44720-7207)
PHONE................................330 494-8700
Melvin Clark, *President*
Julie Lenox, *Principal*
EMP: 26
SALES (est): 479.8K **Privately Held**
SIC: 8351 Group day care center

(G-15188)
AMERIDIAL INC
4535 Strausser St Nw (44720-6979)
PHONE................................330 479-8044
James McGeorge, *Branch Mgr*
EMP: 70
SALES (corp-wide): 40MM **Privately
Held**
SIC: 7389 Telemarketing services
HQ: Ameridial, Inc.
4535 Strausser St Nw
North Canton OH 44720
330 497-4888

(G-15189)
AMERIDIAL INC (HQ)
4535 Strausser St Nw (44720-6979)
PHONE................................330 497-4888
Partho Choudhury, *President*
James McGeorge, *President*
Matt McGeorge, *Exec VP*
Richard Smalley, *CIO*
Brent Pellman, *Technology*

2019 Harris Ohio
Services Directory

▲ = Import ▼=Export
◆ =Import/Export

EMP: 429
SQ FT: 3,000
SALES (est): 40MM **Privately Held**
WEB: www.ameridial.com
SIC: 7389 Telemarketing services
PA: Fusion Bpo Services, Inc.
1147 E Lone Peak Ln
Draper UT 84020
866 581-0038

(G-15190)
ARTHUR MIDDLETON CAPITAL HOLDN (PA)
8000 Freedom Ave Nw (44720-6912)
PHONE....................................330 966-9000
Rodney L Napier, *Ch of Bd*
Lisa Loy, *Vice Pres*
Dean Petersen, *Vice Pres*
Roxanne Sims, *Human Res Mgr*
Eric Barker, *Mktg Dir*
EMP: 42
SALES (est): 56.9MM **Privately Held**
SIC: 8111 8721 8741 Legal services; accounting, auditing & bookkeeping; administrative management

(G-15191)
AWP INC (PA)
Also Called: Area Wide Protective
4244 Mount Pleasant St Nw # 100
(44720-5469)
PHONE....................................330 677-7401
William A Fink, *President*
John Sypek, *President*
Robert Metz, *Area Mgr*
Jack Peak, *Exec VP*
Don Weidig, *CFO*
EMP: 600
SQ FT: 5,500
SALES (est): 172.7MM **Privately Held**
SIC: 7381 Security guard service

(G-15192)
CAVENEY INC
Also Called: SERVPRO
7801 Cleveland Ave Nw (44720-5657)
PHONE....................................330 497-4600
John Caveney, *President*
Linda L Caveney, *Treasurer*
EMP: 85
SQ FT: 5,200
SALES (est): 3.1MM **Privately Held**
SIC: 7349 Building maintenance services

(G-15193)
CPI - CNSTR POLYMERS INC (PA)
7576 Freedom Ave Nw (44720-6902)
PHONE....................................330 861-5200
Dirk Benthien, *CEO*
Jack Demita, *COO*
▲ EMP: 27 EST: 1998
SQ FT: 35,000
SALES (est): 4.3MM **Privately Held**
WEB: www.cpifoam.com
SIC: 5084 Industrial machinery & equipment

(G-15194)
CPX CANTON AIRPORT LLC
Also Called: Embassy Stes Akrn-Canton Arprt
7883 Freedom Ave Nw (44720-6907)
PHONE....................................330 305-0500
Gordon Snyder, *President*
EMP: 110 EST: 2015
SQ FT: 129,291
SALES (est): 1MM **Privately Held**
SIC: 7011 Hotels

(G-15195)
CUTLER REAL ESTATE
203 Applegrove St Nw (44720-1613)
PHONE....................................330 499-9922
Richard Motts, *Branch Mgr*
EMP: 63 **Privately Held**
SIC: 6531 Real estate brokers & agents
PA: Cutler Real Estate
4618 Dressler Rd Nw
Canton OH 44718

(G-15196)
DESIGN RSTRTION RECONSTRUCTION
4305 Mount Pleasant St Nw # 103
(44720-5429)
PHONE....................................330 563-0010
Ray Santiago, *President*
Greg Campbell, *Vice Pres*
Mike Rankin, *Treasurer*
Don Schultz, *Shareholder*
EMP: 38
SQ FT: 9,000
SALES: 3MM **Privately Held**
WEB: www.designrestoration.net
SIC: 1799 Post-disaster renovations

(G-15197)
DOCUMENT CONCEPTS INC
Also Called: Office Furniture Solution
607 S Main St A (44720-3065)
PHONE....................................330 575-5685
Tim Barr, *President*
Terry A Moore, *Admin Sec*
EMP: 30
SQ FT: 15,000
SALES (est): 4.2MM **Privately Held**
WEB: www.document-concepts.com
SIC: 7389 Printers' services: folding, collating

(G-15198)
EMERGENCY MEDICAL TRANSPORT
Also Called: Emt Ambulance
7100 Whipple Ave Nw Ste A (44720-7167)
PHONE....................................330 484-4000
Kenneth J Joseph, *President*
Bill Soplata, *Technology*
EMP: 88
SQ FT: 5,000
SALES (est): 4.9MM **Privately Held**
WEB: www.emtambulance.com
SIC: 4119 8621 Ambulance service; professional membership organizations

(G-15199)
EMLAB P&K LLC (DH)
Also Called: Test America
4101 Shuffel St Nw # 200 (44720-6900)
PHONE....................................330 497-9396
Rachel Brydon Jannetta, *President*
Heather Collins Villemaire, *CFO*
Jenny L Stewart, *Admin Sec*
EMP: 69
SALES (est): 9.3MM
SALES (corp-wide): 983.9MM **Privately Held**
WEB: www.emlabpk.com
SIC: 8734 Testing laboratories
HQ: Testamerica Holdings, Inc.
4101 Shuffel St Nw
North Canton OH 44720
330 497-9396

(G-15200)
ENVIROSERVE INC (HQ)
7640 Whipple Ave Nw (44720-6924)
PHONE....................................330 966-0910
James Kozak, *President*
Kenneth Kozak, *Admin Sec*
EMP: 130
SQ FT: 7,200
SALES: 14.7MM
SALES (corp-wide): 1B **Privately Held**
WEB: www.sunproservices.com
SIC: 8748 1731 8744 Environmental consultant; electrical work;
PA: Savage Companies
901 W Legacy Center Way
Midvale UT 84047
801 944-6600

(G-15201)
EVANS CONSTRUCTION
4585 Aultman Ave Nw (44720)
PHONE....................................330 305-9355
Dean Evans, *Principal*
Craig Evans, *Principal*
Dave Evans, *Principal*
EMP: 40
SALES (est): 1.3MM **Privately Held**
SIC: 1521 Single-family housing construction

(G-15202)
EYE CENTERS OF OHIO INC
6407 Frank Ave Nw (44720-7263)
PHONE....................................330 966-1111
John Malik, *Manager*
EMP: 50
SALES (est): 3.2MM
SALES (corp-wide): 4.7MM **Privately Held**
WEB: www.eyecentersofohio.com
SIC: 8011 Ophthalmologist
PA: Eye Centers Of Ohio Inc
1330 Mercy Dr Nw Ste 310
Canton OH 44708
330 489-1441

(G-15203)
FISHER FOODS MARKETING INC (PA)
4855 Frank Ave Nw (44720-7425)
PHONE....................................330 497-3000
Jeffrey A Fisher, *President*
Jack B Fisher, *Vice Pres*
Debbie Grasse, *Buyer*
Melanie Veigel, *Accounting Mgr*
Lee Karelitz, *Asst Office Mgr*
EMP: 200 EST: 1930
SQ FT: 100,000
SALES (est): 110.8MM **Privately Held**
WEB: www.fisherfoods.com
SIC: 5411 8741 Supermarkets, independent; management services

(G-15204)
FORTIS NORTH CANTON LLC
6174 Promler St Nw (44720-7640)
PHONE....................................330 682-5984
Mike Jarrett,
EMP: 30
SALES (est): 227.9K **Privately Held**
SIC: 5812 7371 Fast food restaurants & stands; computer software development & applications

(G-15205)
FRED OLIVIERI CONSTRUCTION CO (PA)
6315 Promway Ave Nw (44720-7695)
PHONE....................................330 494-1007
Alfred A Olivieri, *CEO*
Dean L Olivieri, *President*
Edward French, *Vice Pres*
Virginia C Olivieri, *Vice Pres*
Aaron Fritz, *Project Mgr*
▲ EMP: 153
SQ FT: 12,600
SALES (est): 87.5MM **Privately Held**
WEB: www.fredolivieri.com
SIC: 1542 Commercial & office building, new construction

(G-15206)
GBS CORP (PA)
Also Called: GBS Printech Solutions
7233 Freedom Ave Nw (44720-7123)
P.O. Box 2340, Canton (44720-0340)
PHONE....................................330 494-5330
Eugene Calabria, *President*
Ryan Hamsher, *General Mgr*
Laurence Merriman, *Chairman*
Bob Campolito, *Opers Staff*
Michele Benson, *CFO*
▲ EMP: 150 EST: 1971
SQ FT: 115,000
SALES: 72.8MM **Privately Held**
WEB: www.gbscorp.com
SIC: 5045 5112 2675 2672 Computers, peripherals & software; business forms; folders, filing, die-cut: made from purchased materials; labels (unprinted), gummed: made from purchased materials; tape, pressure sensitive: made from purchased materials; manifold business forms; commercial printing

(G-15207)
GRAPHIC ENTERPRISES INC
3874 Highland Park Nw (44720-4538)
PHONE....................................800 553-6616
Brian Frank, *President*
Michael Brigner, *VP Opers*
Rick Plant, *Facilities Mgr*
Kim Allen, *Purchasing*
Yvonne Brown, *CFO*
▲ EMP: 54 EST: 2003

SQ FT: 10,000
SALES (est): 31.8MM
SALES (corp-wide): 270MM **Privately Held**
WEB: www.geiohio.com
SIC: 5044 Photocopy machines; copying equipment
PA: Visual Edge Technology, Inc.
3874 Highland Park Nw
Canton OH 44720
330 494-9694

(G-15208)
GRAPHIC ENTPS OFF SLUTIONS INC
3874 Highland Park Nw (44720-4538)
PHONE....................................800 553-6616
Austin Vanchieri, *CEO*
Brian Frank, *President*
Les Beyeler, *Vice Pres*
Yvonne Brown, *CFO*
Debra Pyles, *Human Resources*
EMP: 75
SALES (est): 17.9MM **Privately Held**
SIC: 5044 Copying equipment

(G-15209)
HABEGGER CORPORATION
7580 Whipple Ave Nw (44720-6922)
PHONE....................................330 499-4328
EMP: 31
SALES (corp-wide): 91.9MM **Privately Held**
SIC: 5074 Plumbing & hydronic heating supplies
PA: The Habegger Corporation
4995 Winton Rd
Cincinnati OH 45232
513 853-6644

(G-15210)
HAINES & COMPANY INC (PA)
Also Called: Criss Cross Directories
8050 Freedom Ave Nw A (44720-6985)
P.O. Box 2117 (44720-0117)
PHONE....................................330 494-9111
William K Haines Jr, *Ch of Bd*
Leonard W Haines, *Principal*
Harriett E Jones, *Principal*
Delores Ball, *Treasurer*
Elizabeth Lowe, *Accounts Exec*
▲ EMP: 130 EST: 1932
SQ FT: 20,000
SALES (est): 35MM **Privately Held**
WEB: www.haines.com
SIC: 2741 7331 2752 2759 Directories: publishing & printing; mailing list compilers; commercial printing, lithographic; commercial printing

(G-15211)
HOME SAVINGS BANK
600 S Main St (44720-3031)
PHONE....................................330 499-1900
Rick Hull, *Manager*
EMP: 77
SALES (corp-wide): 133.9MM **Publicly Held**
SIC: 6036 Savings & loan associations, not federally chartered
HQ: Home Savings Bank
275 W Federal St
Youngstown OH 44503
330 742-0500

(G-15212)
INDIAN NATION INC
1051 Skyline Cir Se (44709-1154)
PHONE....................................740 532-6143
EMP: 50
SALES (est): 2.6MM **Privately Held**
SIC: 1794 7353 Excavation Contractor Heavy Construction Equipment Rental

(G-15213)
J & C AMBULANCE SERVICES INC (PA)
Also Called: Life Care Medical Services
7100 Whipple Ave Nw Ste G (44720-7167)
PHONE....................................330 899-0022
James Caplinger, *President*
Rick Reed, *Executive*
EMP: 180 EST: 1999
SQ FT: 4,500
SALES: 10.9MM **Privately Held**
SIC: 4119 Ambulance service

(G-15214)
KAISER FOUNDATION HOSPITALS
Also Called: North Canton Medical Offices
4914 Portage Rd (44720)
PHONE.....................................800 524-7377
EMP: 593
SALES (corp-wide): 93B Privately Held
SIC: 8011 Offices & clinics of medical doctors
HQ: Kaiser Foundation Hospitals Inc
1 Kaiser Plz
Oakland CA 94612
510 271-6611

(G-15215)
KARCHER GROUP INC
5590 Lauby Rd Ste 8 (44720-1500)
PHONE.....................................330 493-6141
Geoff Karcher, President
EMP: 42
SALES (est): 4.6MM Privately Held
WEB: www.tkg.com
SIC: 7374 Computer graphics service

(G-15216)
KENAN ADVANTAGE GROUP INC (PA)
Also Called: Transport Service Co.
4366 Mount Pleasant St Nw (44720-5446)
PHONE.....................................800 969-5419
Bruce Blaise, President
Boyd Brown, General Mgr
Grant Mitchell, COO
Tom Baughman, Vice Pres
Mike Calnon, Vice Pres
EMP: 114
SQ FT: 86,500
SALES (est): 2.4B Privately Held
SIC: 4212 4213 Local trucking, without storage; petroleum haulage, local; liquid petroleum transport, non-local

(G-15217)
KIRK KEY INTERLOCK COMPANY LLC
9048 Meridian Cir Nw (44720-8387)
PHONE.....................................330 833-8223
Scott Life, President
Greg Wise, Production
Emily McDaniel, Marketing Staff
James G Owens, Mng Member
James R Fink,
▲ EMP: 47
SQ FT: 26,000
SALES (est): 12.4MM
SALES (corp-wide): 1.5B Privately Held
WEB: www.kirkkey.com
SIC: 3429 5063 Keys, locks & related hardware; electrical apparatus & equipment
PA: Halma Public Limited Company
Misbourne Court
Amersham BUCKS HP7 0
149 472-1111

(G-15218)
LEMMON & LEMMON INC
1201 S Main St Ste 200 (44720-4283)
PHONE.....................................330 497-8686
William J Lemmon, President
Stephen Lemmon, Vice Pres
EMP: 160
SQ FT: 9,600
SALES (est): 15.3MM Privately Held
WEB: www.lemmonandlemmon.com
SIC: 1521 1522 New construction, single-family houses; apartment building construction; condominium construction

(G-15219)
MEDICAL TRANSPORT SYSTEMS INC
Also Called: Stark Summit Ambulance
909 Las Olas Blvd Nw (44720-6130)
PHONE.....................................330 837-9818
Ronald Cordray, President
Karla McClaskey, Vice Pres
Jeffrey Finkelstein, Treasurer
Arthur Leb, Admin Sec
EMP: 100 EST: 1978
SALES (est): 2.7MM Privately Held
WEB: www.starksummit.com
SIC: 4119 Ambulance service

(G-15220)
MICROPLEX INC
7568 Whipple Ave Nw (44720-6922)
PHONE.....................................330 498-0600
Valerie Walters, President
John Walters, Vice Pres
Jo A Schwenning, Purch Agent
Susan Harst, Treasurer
Cheri Rowlands, Accounts Mgr
EMP: 30
SQ FT: 12,000
SALES (est): 6.2MM Privately Held
WEB: www.microplex.com
SIC: 3496 3679 5045 Cable, uninsulated wire: made from purchased wire; harness assemblies for electronic use: wire or cable; computer peripheral equipment

(G-15221)
MIDWEST COMMUNICATIONS INC
Also Called: Group Midwest
4721 Eagle St Nw (44720-7083)
PHONE.....................................800 229-4756
George K Dixon, CEO
Brian Stimer, President
Tom Lyon, Vice Pres
EMP: 92
SQ FT: 160,000
SALES (est): 10.2MM Privately Held
WEB: www.groupmidwest.com
SIC: 5065 Telephone equipment

(G-15222)
MIDWEST DIGITAL INC
4721 Eagle St Nw (44720-7083)
PHONE.....................................330 966-4744
Brian Stimer, President
EMP: 65
SALES (est): 19MM Privately Held
SIC: 5065 Communication equipment

(G-15223)
NEXTEL PARTNERS OPERATING CORP
Also Called: Sprint
6791 Strip Ave Nw (44720-7093)
PHONE.....................................330 305-1365
EMP: 30
SALES (corp-wide): 85.9B Publicly Held
WEB: www.nymobilellc.com
SIC: 4812 Cellular telephone services
HQ: Nextel Partners Operating Corp.
6200 Sprint Pkwy
Overland Park KS 66251
800 829-0965

(G-15224)
NORTHSTAR ASPHALT INC
7345 Sunset Strip Ave Nw (44720-7040)
P.O. Box 2646 (44720-0646)
PHONE.....................................330 497-0936
Howard J Wenger, President
EMP: 45
SQ FT: 10,000
SALES (est): 4.2MM Privately Held
SIC: 1771 1611 Blacktop (asphalt) work; highway & street construction

(G-15225)
ORCHARD PHRM SVCS LLC
Also Called: Envision Rx Options
7835 Freedom Ave Nw (44720-6907)
PHONE.....................................330 491-4200
Bruce Scott, President
John Baker Sr, Vice Pres
Eugene Samuels, Admin Sec
EMP: 112
SALES (est): 48.4MM
SALES (corp-wide): 21.5B Publicly Held
SIC: 5122 Pharmaceuticals
PA: Rite Aid Corporation
30 Hunter Ln
Camp Hill PA 17011
717 761-2633

(G-15226)
OREILLY AUTOMOTIVE INC
1233 N Main St (44720-1925)
PHONE.....................................330 494-0042
Phillip Oreilly, Branch Mgr
EMP: 59 Publicly Held
SIC: 5531 5013 Batteries, automotive & truck; automotive supplies & parts

PA: O'reilly Automotive, Inc.
233 S Patterson Ave
Springfield MO 65802

(G-15227)
PRIME PRODATA INC
800 N Main St (44720-2011)
PHONE.....................................330 497-2578
Susan Caghan, President
EMP: 30
SALES (est): 4.3MM Privately Held
SIC: 7379 Computer related consulting services

(G-15228)
PROVANTAGE LLC
7576 Freedom Ave Nw (44720-6902)
PHONE.....................................330 494-3781
Arno Zirngibl, CEO
Alison Carey, General Mgr
Scott Dibattista, COO
Carol Baker, Purch Mgr
Dan Gray, VP Human Res
▼ EMP: 60
SQ FT: 30,000
SALES (est): 225MM Privately Held
WEB: www.provantage.com
SIC: 5961 5719 5734 5045 Computer software, mail order; computers & peripheral equipment, mail order; housewares; computer software & accessories; computers, peripherals & software

(G-15229)
QUESTAR SOLUTIONS LLC
Also Called: Questar, Inc.
7948 Freedom Ave Nw (44720-6910)
PHONE.....................................330 966-2070
Kevin Gray, General Mgr
Mike Mountain, General Mgr
▼ EMP: 35
SQ FT: 20,000
SALES (est): 24.7MM
SALES (corp-wide): 1.1B Privately Held
WEB: www.questarusa.com
SIC: 5199 5084 Packaging materials; pollution control equipment, air (environmental); safety equipment
HQ: Industrial Container Services Llc
2600 Mtland Ctr Pkwy 20 # 200
Maitland FL 32751
407 930-4182

(G-15230)
REPUBLIC TELCOM WORLDWIDE LLC
8000 Freedom Ave Nw (44720-6912)
PHONE.....................................330 244-8285
Monica Wallace, Branch Mgr
EMP: 52 Privately Held
SIC: 7389 Telephone services
HQ: Republic Telcom Worldwide, Llc
3939 Everhard Rd Nw
Canton OH 44709

(G-15231)
SCHROER PROPERTIES INC (PA)
Also Called: Altercare of Navarre
339 E Maple St (44720-2593)
P.O. Box 2279 (44720-0279)
PHONE.....................................330 498-8200
Gerald F Schroer, President
Suzanne F Schroer, Treasurer
Casey Knox, Pharmacist
INA Lauer, Program Dir
Laurie Huntington, Assistant
EMP: 76
SQ FT: 30,000
SALES (est): 14.4MM Privately Held
SIC: 8082 Home health care services

(G-15232)
SCI DIRECT LLC
7800 Whipple Ave Nw (44720-6928)
PHONE.....................................330 494-5504
EMP: 570 EST: 1968
SQ FT: 170,000
SALES (est): 13.5MM Privately Held
SIC: 8742 Management Consulting Services

(G-15233)
SPECTRUM ORTHPEDICS INC CANTON (PA)
7442 Frank Ave Nw (44720-7022)
PHONE.....................................330 455-5367
Mark Shepard, President
Dr Robert Manns, Corp Secy
P W Welch, Vice Pres
EMP: 45
SQ FT: 6,000
SALES (est): 6.4MM Privately Held
WEB: www.spectrumortho.com
SIC: 8011 Orthopedic physician; surgeon

(G-15234)
STARK INDUSTRIAL LLC
5103 Stoneham Rd (44720-1540)
P.O. Box 3030 (44720-8030)
PHONE.....................................330 493-9773
Ray Wilkof,
Samuel Wilkof,
▼ EMP: 40
SQ FT: 25,000
SALES (est): 24.2MM Privately Held
WEB: www.starkindustrial.com
SIC: 5085 3545 Industrial supplies; machine tool accessories

(G-15235)
STOLLE MACHINERY COMPANY LLC
4337 Excel St (44720-6995)
PHONE.....................................330 453-2015
Jim McClung, Branch Mgr
EMP: 58
SALES (corp-wide): 262.3MM Privately Held
SIC: 5084 Industrial machinery & equipment
PA: Stolle Machinery Company, Llc
6949 S Potomac St
Centennial CO 80112
303 708-9044

(G-15236)
SURGERE INC
5399 Lauby Rd Ste 200 (44720-1554)
PHONE.....................................330 526-7971
William J Wappler, President
Michael Curran, Director
EMP: 26
SQ FT: 3,000
SALES (est): 4.1MM Privately Held
SIC: 8742 Business consultant

(G-15237)
TESTAMERICA LABORATORIES INC (DH)
4101 Shuffel St Nw # 100 (44720-6900)
PHONE.....................................800 456-9396
Rachel Brydon Jannetta, CEO
Heather Collins Villemaire, CFO
Jenny L Stewart, Admin Sec
EMP: 139
SALES (est): 475.6MM
SALES (corp-wide): 983.9MM Privately Held
WEB: www.stl-inc.com
SIC: 8734 Soil analysis; water testing laboratory
HQ: Testamerica Holdings, Inc.
4101 Shuffel St Nw
North Canton OH 44720
330 497-9396

(G-15238)
TIGER 2010 LLC (PA)
6929 Portage St Nw (44720-6535)
PHONE.....................................330 236-5100
Anthony T Ferrante,
Debra L Ferrante,
EMP: 31
SQ FT: 2,400
SALES (est): 1.4MM Privately Held
WEB: www.homesaroundohio.com
SIC: 6531 Real estate agent, residential

(G-15239)
TIMKEN CORPORATION (DH)
4500 Mount Pleasant St Nw (44720-5450)
PHONE.....................................330 471-3378
Richard G Kyle, CEO
Nancy Noeske, President
William R Burkhart, Exec VP
Christopher A Coughlin, Exec VP

Ronald J Myers, *Vice Pres*
◆ EMP: 50 EST: 1957
SALES (est): 240.6MM
SALES (corp-wide): 3.5B **Publicly Held**
WEB: www.timken.com
SIC: 5085 5051 Bearings; aluminum bars, rods, ingots, sheets, pipes, plates, etc.
HQ: Timken Us Llc
336 Mechanic St
Lebanon NH 03766
603 443-5217

(G-15240)
TRI-STATE AMBLNCE PRAMEDIC SVC
7100 Whipple Ave Nw Ste C (44720-7167)
PHONE..................................304 233-2331
Robert Ritner, *Director*
EMP: 30
SQ FT: 3,000
SALES (est): 860.3K **Privately Held**
SIC: 4119 Ambulance service

(G-15241)
TSG RESOURCES INC
339 E Maple St Ste 110 (44720-2593)
PHONE..................................330 498-8200
Dennis Conley, *CEO*
EMP: 3609
SALES (est): 5.6MM **Privately Held**
SIC: 8742 Business planning & organizing services

(G-15242)
ULTIMATE JETCHARTERS LLC
Also Called: Ultimate Air Shuttle
6061 W Airport Dr (44720-1447)
PHONE..................................330 497-3344
John Gordon, *CEO*
Jeff Moneypenny, *Vice Pres*
Dave Parsons, *Opers Staff*
Michael Degirolamo, *CFO*
EMP: 98
SQ FT: 30,000
SALES (est): 20.7MM
SALES (corp-wide): 23.5MM **Privately Held**
WEB: www.ultimatejetcharters.com
SIC: 4581 Airports, flying fields & services
PA: Onejet, Inc.
1100 Larkspur Landing Cir # 108
Larkspur CA
844 663-5381

(G-15243)
UNITED ARCHITECTURAL MTLS INC
7830 Cleveland Ave Nw (44720-5658)
PHONE..................................330 433-9220
Shelly Nesbitt, *President*
Robert W Eckinger, *Principal*
Greg Reed, *Plant Mgr*
Maria Liossis, *Controller*
Robin Cespedes, *Admin Asst*
EMP: 36
SALES (est): 9.5MM **Privately Held**
SIC: 8712 Architectural services

(G-15244)
WILLIAMS PARTNERS LP
7235 Whipple Ave Nw (44720-7137)
PHONE..................................330 966-3674
EMP: 245 **Publicly Held**
SIC: 1311 Natural gas production
PA: Williams Partners L.P.
1 Williams Ctr
Tulsa OK 74172

North Fairfield
Huron County

(G-15245)
DRW PACKING INC
Also Called: Doug Walcher Farms
866 State Route 162 E (44855-9687)
PHONE..................................419 744-2427
Kevin Holphouse, *President*
Ken Holphouse, *Vice Pres*
Kirk Holphouse, *Vice Pres*
Steve Holphouse, *Vice Pres*
Becky Phillips, *Admin Sec*
EMP: 100

SALES (est): 4.5MM **Privately Held**
SIC: 0161 0119 Vegetables & melons; pea & bean farms (legumes)

North Jackson
Mahoning County

(G-15246)
HILLTRUX TANK LINES INC
200 Rosemont Rd (44451-9631)
P.O. Box 696 (44451-0696)
PHONE..................................330 538-3700
Brad Hille, *President*
Marvin Carroll, *Safety Dir*
CJ Woodring, *Office Mgr*
Viola Foster, *Administration*
Lori Rupert, *Administration*
EMP: 50
SALES (est): 2.5MM **Privately Held**
SIC: 4213 Contract haulers

(G-15247)
JS PARIS EXCAVATING INC
12240 Commissioner Dr (44451-9641)
P.O. Box 219 (44451-0219)
PHONE..................................330 538-3048
James S Paris Jr, *President*
James S Paris Sr, *Corp Secy*
Jason A Paris, *Vice Pres*
Jason Paris, *Vice Pres*
Nicholas Rossi, *Manager*
EMP: 50
SQ FT: 80,000
SALES: 11.1MM **Privately Held**
SIC: 1794 1795 Excavation & grading; building construction; demolition, buildings & other structures

(G-15248)
LIBERTY STEEL PRODUCTS INC (PA)
11650 Mahoning Ave (44451-9688)
P.O. Box 175 (44451-0175)
PHONE..................................330 538-2236
Andrew J Weller Jr, *CEO*
James T Weller Sr, *Ch of Bd*
James M Grasso, *CFO*
Tom McCullough, *Sales Mgr*
Mike Kelly, *Sales Associate*
◆ EMP: 40
SQ FT: 110,000
SALES (est): 74MM **Privately Held**
SIC: 5051 Steel

(G-15249)
NILCO LLC
489 Rosemont Rd (44451-9717)
PHONE..................................330 538-3386
Scott Honthy, *Branch Mgr*
EMP: 30
SALES (corp-wide): 800MM **Privately Held**
SIC: 5031 Lumber: rough, dressed & finished; building materials, exterior
HQ: Nilco, Llc
1221 W Maple St Ste 100
Hartville OH 44632
888 248-5151

(G-15250)
OHIO UTILITIES PROTECTION SVC
12467 Mahoning Ave (44451-9617)
P.O. Box 729 (44451-0729)
PHONE..................................800 311-3692
Roger L Lipscomb Jr, *President*
Jami Novak, *Vice Pres*
Mary A Dornon, *Finance*
Tom Hackstedde, *Supervisor*
Lee Richards, *Exec Dir*
EMP: 51
SQ FT: 2,000
SALES: 6.6MM **Privately Held**
SIC: 8611 8748 1623 Public utility association; business consulting; underground utilities contractor

(G-15251)
PAM TRANSPORTATION SVCS INC
12274 Mahoning Ave (44451-9617)
PHONE..................................330 270-7900
Glenn J Schwartz, *Branch Mgr*

EMP: 478
SALES (corp-wide): 533.2MM **Publicly Held**
SIC: 4789 Pipeline terminal facilities, independently operated
PA: P.A.M. Transportation Services, Inc.
297 W Henri De Tonti
Tontitown AR 72770
479 361-9111

(G-15252)
PMC SYSTEMS LIMITED
12155 Commissioner Dr (44451-9640)
P.O. Box 486 (44451-0486)
PHONE..................................330 538-2268
John Frano, *President*
Randy G Yakubek, *President*
Paul Graff, *Vice Pres*
EMP: 30
SQ FT: 3,000
SALES (est): 5.7MM **Privately Held**
SIC: 3625 8711 Electric controls & control accessories, industrial; electrical or electronic engineering

(G-15253)
RAILWORKS TRACK SERVICES INC
1550 N Bailey Rd (44451-8601)
P.O. Box 555, Sewell NJ (08080-0555)
PHONE..................................330 538-2261
Roger K Boggess, *President*
Pablo Gonzalez, *Vice Pres*
Gene Cellini, *Treasurer*
Alexander Motamed, *Treasurer*
Mary Nemeth, *Office Mgr*
EMP: 300
SQ FT: 3,000
SALES: 28.7MM
SALES (corp-wide): 1.8B **Privately Held**
WEB: www.railworks.com
SIC: 1629 Railroad & railway roadbed construction
HQ: Railworks Corporation
5 Penn Plz
New York NY 10001
212 502-7900

(G-15254)
TRANSPORT CORP AMERICA INC
1951 N Bailey Rd (44451-9621)
PHONE..................................330 538-3328
Marjorie Plant, *Manager*
EMP: 31
SQ FT: 2,378
SALES (corp-wide): 3.7B **Privately Held**
WEB: www.transportamerica.com
SIC: 4213 Contract haulers
HQ: Transport Corporation Of America, Inc.
1715 Yankee Doodle Rd # 100
Eagan MN 55121
651 686-2500

(G-15255)
TRI COUNTY TOWER SERVICE
8900 Mahoning Ave (44451-9750)
PHONE..................................330 538-9874
Frank Kovach, *Partner*
Doug Henry, *Partner*
▼ EMP: 28
SALES (est): 4.3MM **Privately Held**
SIC: 1623 7389 Transmitting tower (telecommunication) construction;

(G-15256)
WASTE MANAGEMENT OHIO INC
12201 Council Dr (44451-9650)
P.O. Box 368 (44451-0368)
PHONE..................................866 797-9018
James Judge, *Principal*
EMP: 50
SALES (corp-wide): 14.9B **Publicly Held**
WEB: www.wm.com
SIC: 4953 Rubbish collection & disposal
HQ: Waste Management Of Ohio, Inc.
1700 N Broad St
Fairborn OH 45324

North Kingsville
Ashtabula County

(G-15257)
GREG FORD SWEET INC
Also Called: Greg Sweet Ford
4011 E Center St (44068)
P.O. Box 659 (44068-0659)
PHONE..................................440 593-7714
Gregory Sweet, *President*
Michael Kelly, *Finance Mgr*
Chris Ritchey, *Sales Mgr*
Loretta Tratar, *Cust Mgr*
EMP: 35
SQ FT: 25,000
SALES: 9MM **Privately Held**
SIC: 5511 7538 Automobiles, new & used; trucks, tractors & trailers: new & used; general automotive repair shops; general truck repair

North Lawrence
Stark County

(G-15258)
ELMS COUNTRY CLUB INC
1608 Manchester Ave Sw (44666-9432)
PHONE..................................330 833-2668
Mark Sweany, *President*
Lance Manion, *General Mgr*
EMP: 40
SALES (est): 1.2MM **Privately Held**
WEB: www.elmscc.com
SIC: 7997 5812 5813 Country club, membership; American restaurant; bar (drinking places)

(G-15259)
ELMS OF MASSILLON INC
Also Called: Elms Country Club
1608 Manchester Ave Sw (44666-9432)
P.O. Box 846, Massillon (44648-0846)
PHONE..................................330 833-2668
Johnny Lambada, *President*
EMP: 29
SALES: 39.3K **Privately Held**
SIC: 7997 Country club, membership

(G-15260)
US TUBULAR PRODUCTS INC
Also Called: Benmit Division
14852 Lincoln Way W (44666)
PHONE..................................330 832-1734
Jeffrey J Cunningham, *President*
Connye Cunningham, *Corp Secy*
Brian Cunningham, *Vice Pres*
EMP: 60 EST: 1973
SQ FT: 100,000
SALES (est): 9.2MM **Privately Held**
SIC: 8734 3498 Hydrostatic testing laboratory; tube fabricating (contract bending & shaping)

North Lima
Mahoning County

(G-15261)
ABF FREIGHT SYSTEM INC
11000 Market St (44452-9801)
PHONE..................................330 549-3800
James Rimstidt, *Opers Spvr*
Cliff Willoughby, *Manager*
EMP: 50
SALES (corp-wide): 3B **Publicly Held**
WEB: www.abfs.com
SIC: 4213 Contract haulers
HQ: Abf Freight System, Inc.
3801 Old Greenwood Rd
Fort Smith AR 72903
479 785-8700

(G-15262)
ARMSTRONG UTILITIES INC
Also Called: Armstrong Cable Services
9328 Woodworth Rd (44452-9712)
PHONE..................................330 758-6411
Dan McGahagan, *General Mgr*
Robert Meredith, *Opers Mgr*

GEOGRAPHIC

Paul Wachtel, *Manager*
EMP: 40 **Privately Held**
SIC: 4841 Cable & other pay television services
HQ: Armstrong Utilities, Inc.
1 Armstrong Pl
Butler PA 16001
724 283-0925

(G-15263)
ASSOCIATED PAPER STOCK INC (PA)
11510 South Ave (44452-9527)
P.O. Box 470 (44452-0470)
PHONE..............................330 549-5311
Thomas Yanko, *President*
Dan Betz, *Admin Sec*
EMP: 35
SQ FT: 10,000
SALES (est): 9.2MM **Privately Held**
WEB: www.associatedpaperstock.com
SIC: 5093 Waste paper

(G-15264)
ASSUMPTION VILLAGE
Also Called: Marian Living Center
9800 Market St (44452-9560)
PHONE..............................330 549-2434
Kathryn Barnhart, *Finance*
Mary Luke, *Administration*
EMP: 200 **EST:** 1974
SQ FT: 7,440
SALES: 14.1MM **Privately Held**
SIC: 8051 Skilled nursing care facilities

(G-15265)
B & T EXPRESS INC (PA)
400 Miley Rd (44452-8545)
P.O. Box 468 (44452-0468)
PHONE..............................330 549-0000
Breen O'Malley, *President*
Tom Cook, *Vice Pres*
Bill Rypcinski, *VP Opers*
John Redmon, *Office Mgr*
Mike Harter, *Manager*
EMP: 74
SQ FT: 25,000
SALES (est): 13.6MM **Privately Held**
WEB: www.btair.com
SIC: 4213 Heavy hauling

(G-15266)
B G TRUCKING & CONSTRUCTION
11330 Market St (44452-9720)
P.O. Box 308 (44452-0308)
PHONE..............................234 759-3440
Bernard Lewis, *President*
Alicia Lewis, *Corp Secy*
Geneva Lewis, *Vice Pres*
EMP: 50
SALES (est): 8.1MM **Privately Held**
SIC: 1771 5211 Blacktop (asphalt) work; concrete repair; masonry materials & supplies

(G-15267)
CAPRICE HEALTH CARE INC
Also Called: Caprice Health Care Center
9184 Market St (44452-9558)
PHONE..............................330 965-9200
Celeste Hawkins, *Office Mgr*
Jeniffer See, *Administration*
EMP: 150 **EST:** 1998
SALES (est): 9.4MM **Privately Held**
SIC: 8051 8093 8082 8052 Skilled nursing care facilities; specialty outpatient clinics; home health care services; intermediate care facilities

(G-15268)
DART TRUCKING COMPANY INC (PA)
11017 Market St (44452-9782)
P.O. Box 157 (44452-0157)
PHONE..............................330 549-0994
John Polli, *President*
James Pazzanita, *Vice Pres*
David Lynch, *CFO*
EMP: 25
SQ FT: 12,000
SALES (est): 1.8MM **Privately Held**
SIC: 4213 Trucking, except local

(G-15269)
GUARDIAN ELDER CARE LLC
Also Called: Rolling Acres Care Center
9625 Market St (44452-8564)
PHONE..............................330 549-0898
Laurie Ference, *Branch Mgr*
EMP: 120 **Privately Held**
SIC: 8051 Convalescent home with continuous nursing care
PA: Guardian Elder Care, Llc
8796 Route 219
Brockway PA 15824

(G-15270)
JOE DICKEY ELECTRIC INC
180 W South Range Rd (44452-9578)
P.O. Box 158 (44452-0158)
PHONE..............................330 549-3976
Joseph Dickey Jr, *CEO*
David A Dickey, *President*
Brian Crumbacher, *Superintendent*
Eric Carlson, *Vice Pres*
Joseph Dickey III, *Vice Pres*
EMP: 80
SALES (est): 20.4MM **Privately Held**
WEB: www.dickeyelectric.com
SIC: 1731 General electrical contractor

(G-15271)
LAKESIDE MANOR INC
Also Called: Glenellen
9661 Market St (44452-8564)
PHONE..............................330 549-2545
James E McMurray, *President*
Roger F Herrmann, *Vice Pres*
EMP: 31
SALES (est): 1.9MM **Privately Held**
SIC: 8361 8052 Home for the aged; rehabilitation center, residential; health care incidental; rest home, with health care incidental; self-help group home; intermediate care facilities

(G-15272)
MKM DISTRIBUTION SERVICES INC
100 Eastgate Dr (44452-8563)
PHONE..............................330 549-9670
EMP: 60
SALES (corp-wide): 50.5MM **Privately Held**
SIC: 4789 Transportation Services
PA: Mkm Distribution Services Inc
8256 Zionsville Rd
Indianapolis IN 46268
317 334-7900

(G-15273)
NORTH LIMA DAIRY QUEEN INC (PA)
10067 Market St (44452-8560)
P.O. Box 125 (44452-0125)
PHONE..............................330 549-3220
Dean Rapp, *Owner*
Rick Firestone, *Corp Secy*
Randy Rapp, *Vice Pres*
EMP: 38 **EST:** 1961
SQ FT: 24,713
SALES (est): 1.2MM **Privately Held**
SIC: 5812 7542 Ice cream stands or dairy bars; carwash, automatic

(G-15274)
R T VERNAL PAVING INC
11299 South Ave (44452-9731)
P.O. Box 519 (44452-0519)
PHONE..............................330 549-3189
Richard Vernal, *President*
Jo Anne Vernal, *Corp Secy*
EMP: 40
SALES (est): 1.4MM **Privately Held**
SIC: 1794 1611 Excavation & grading; building construction; highway & street paving contractor

(G-15275)
USF HOLLAND LLC
Also Called: USFreightways
10855 Market St (44452-9562)
PHONE..............................330 549-2917
Vince Secarro, *Manager*
EMP: 150

SALES (corp-wide): 5B **Publicly Held**
WEB: www.usfc.com
SIC: 4213 Less-than-truckload (LTL) transport
HQ: Usf Holland Llc
700 S Waverly Rd
Holland MI 49423
616 395-5000

North Olmsted
Cuyahoga County

(G-15276)
AFFILIATED FM INSURANCE CO
25050 Country Club Blvd # 400 (44070-5356)
PHONE..............................216 362-4820
Brian Nyquist, *Branch Mgr*
EMP: 26
SALES (corp-wide): 4.4B **Privately Held**
SIC: 6331 Fire, marine & casualty insurance
HQ: Affiliated Fm Insurance Company
270 Central Ave
Johnston RI 02919
401 275-3000

(G-15277)
AFFORDABLE CARS & FINANCE INC (PA)
Also Called: Halleen Kia
27932 Lorain Rd (44070-4024)
PHONE..............................440 777-2424
Carl Halleen, *President*
Eric Halleen, *Vice Pres*
Ronald Kula, *Admin Sec*
EMP: 30
SQ FT: 3,200
SALES (est): 8.4MM **Privately Held**
WEB: www.halleenkia.com
SIC: 5511 6141 Automobiles, new & used; financing: automobiles, furniture, etc., not a deposit bank

(G-15278)
CARGILL INCORPORATED
24950 Country Club Blvd # 450 (44070-5333)
PHONE..............................440 716-4664
Toni Payne, *Marketing Staff*
Dale Sehrenbach, *Manager*
EMP: 75
SALES (corp-wide): 114.7B **Privately Held**
WEB: www.cargill.com
SIC: 5169 Industrial salts & polishes
PA: Cargill, Incorporated
15407 Mcginty Rd W
Wayzata MN 55391
952 742-7575

(G-15279)
CELLCO PARTNERSHIP
Also Called: Verizon Wireless
24121 Lorain Rd (44070-2163)
PHONE..............................440 779-1313
Larry Shiever, *General Mgr*
EMP: 25
SALES (corp-wide): 130.8B **Publicly Held**
SIC: 7629 5065 5999 Telephone set repair; mobile telephone equipment; telephone & communication equipment
HQ: Cellco Partnership
1 Verizon Way
Basking Ridge NJ 07920

(G-15280)
CHAMPLAIN ENTERPRISES LLC (PA)
Also Called: Commutair
24950 Country Club Blvd # 300 (44070-5333)
PHONE..............................440 779-4588
John Sullivan, *Ch of Bd*
Joel Raymond, *Vice Pres*
EMP: 200
SQ FT: 41,000
SALES: 120MM **Privately Held**
WEB: www.commutair.com
SIC: 4512 Air passenger carrier, scheduled

(G-15281)
CHEMICAL BANK
25000 Country Club Blvd # 200 (44070-5344)
PHONE..............................440 779-0807
Timothy Atkinson, *Senior VP*
Kathy Shaw, *Vice Pres*
EMP: 36
SALES (corp-wide): 924.5MM **Publicly Held**
SIC: 6022 State commercial banks
HQ: Chemical Bank
333 E Main St
Midland MI 48640
989 631-9200

(G-15282)
CITY OF NORTH OLMSTED
Also Called: Olmsted Parks and Recreation
26000 Lorain Rd (44070-2738)
PHONE..............................440 734-8200
Ted Disaldo, *Commissioner*
EMP: 53 **Privately Held**
WEB: www.north-olmsted.com
SIC: 7999 Recreation center; swimming pool, non-membership; tennis club, non-membership; tennis courts, outdoor/indoor: non-membership
PA: City Of North Olmsted
5200 Dover Center Rd
North Olmsted OH 44070
440 716-4171

(G-15283)
CITY OF NORTH OLMSTED
Also Called: Springvale Golf Crse Ballroom
5873 Canterbury Rd (44070)
PHONE..............................440 777-0678
Marty Young, *Branch Mgr*
EMP: 50 **Privately Held**
WEB: www.north-olmsted.com
SIC: 7389 Convention & show services
PA: City Of North Olmsted
5200 Dover Center Rd
North Olmsted OH 44070
440 716-4171

(G-15284)
CONSTRUCTION BIDDINGCOM LLC
31269 Bradley Rd (44070-3875)
PHONE..............................440 716-4087
EMP: 50
SALES (est): 5.1MM **Privately Held**
SIC: 4813 Telephone Communications

(G-15285)
DAVID SCOTT SALON
107a Great Northern Mall (44070-3301)
PHONE..............................440 734-7595
David Petrella, *Partner*
Scott Stettin, *Partner*
EMP: 30
SALES (est): 841.7K **Privately Held**
SIC: 7231 Hairdressers

(G-15286)
ENT AND ALLERGY HEALTH SVCS (PA)
25761 Lorain Rd Fl 3 (44070-3369)
PHONE..............................440 779-1112
Jeffrey E Binder Do, *President*
Mark Mehle, *Vice Pres*
▲ **EMP:** 48
SQ FT: 5,000
SALES (est): 6.9MM **Privately Held**
WEB: www.enthealth.com
SIC: 8011 Allergist

(G-15287)
FACTORY MUTUAL INSURANCE CO
Also Called: FM Global
25050 Country Club Blvd # 400 (44070-5356)
PHONE..............................440 779-0651
Lisa Muckley, *Opers Staff*
Maralee Rodgers, *Human Resources*
Angela Edwards, *Admin Asst*
EMP: 120
SALES (corp-wide): 4.4B **Privately Held**
SIC: 6331 Property damage insurance

▲ = Import ▼=Export
◆ =Import/Export

PA: Factory Mutual Insurance Co
270 Central Ave
Johnston RI 02919
401 275-3000

(G-15288)
FORTNEY & WEYGANDT INC
31269 Bradley Rd (44070-3875)
PHONE..................................440 716-4000
Robert L Fortney, *President*
Greg Freeh, *Corp Secy*
Ruth Fortney, *Vice Pres*
EMP: 50
SQ FT: 21,000
SALES: 76MM **Privately Held**
WEB: www.fwprojects.com
SIC: 1541 1542 Industrial buildings, new
construction; commercial & office build-
ing, new construction
PA: R. L. Fortney Management, Inc.
31269 Bradley Rd
North Olmsted OH 44070
440 716-4000

(G-15289)
**FOUNDATIONS HLTH
SOLUTIONS INC**
Also Called: Provider Services
25000 Country Club Blvd (44070-5344)
PHONE..................................440 793-0200
Daniel Parker, *President*
EMP: 70
SALES (est): 14.1MM **Privately Held**
SIC: 8721 8361 8322 8052 Certified public accountant; accounting services, except auditing; rehabilitation center,
residential; health care incidental; home
for the mentally handicapped; old age assistance; intermediate care facilities; personal care facility; health maintenance
organization

(G-15290)
FRESENIUS USA INC
Also Called: Fresenius Medical Care
25050 Country Club Blvd # 250
(44070-5356)
PHONE..................................440 734-7474
Tim Martin, *Branch Mgr*
EMP: 40
SALES (corp-wide): 18.9B **Privately Held**
WEB: www.fresenius.org
SIC: 8092 Kidney dialysis centers
HQ: Fresenius Usa, Inc.
4040 Nelson Ave
Concord CA 94520
925 288-4218

(G-15291)
**GRAND HERITAGE HOTEL
PORTLAND**
Also Called: Hampton Inn Cleveland
25105 Country Club Blvd (44070-5312)
PHONE..................................440 734-4477
Meghan Carruthers, *General Mgr*
EMP: 45
SALES (est): 1.1MM
SALES (corp-wide): 6.1MM **Privately
Held**
SIC: 7011 Hotels
PA: Grand Heritage Hotel Portland
39 Bay Dr
Annapolis MD 21403
410 280-9800

(G-15292)
HIGH-TECH POOLS INC
31330 Industrial Pkwy (44070-4787)
PHONE..................................440 979-5070
Jeff Hammerschmidt, *President*
Frank Duale, *Project Mgr*
Terry Brennan, *Sales Mgr*
Tim Flury, *Admin Asst*
▲ EMP: 30
SQ FT: 7,800
SALES (est): 5.5MM **Privately Held**
WEB: www.hightechpools.com
SIC: 1799 Swimming pool construction

(G-15293)
**INTERNTONAL ALIANCE THEA
STAGE**
Also Called: Local 883
4689 Georgette Ave (44070-3735)
PHONE..................................440 734-4883

Diane M Burke, *Principal*
EMP: 30
SALES (est): 406.3K **Privately Held**
SIC: 7922 Theatrical producers & services

(G-15294)
JOHN ATWOOD INC
Also Called: Aquasonic Auto & Van Wash
28800 Lorain Rd (44070-4012)
PHONE..................................440 777-4147
John Atwood Jr, *President*
Jim Capone, *Vice Pres*
Cindy Shalala, *Vice Pres*
EMP: 50
SALES (est): 747.8K **Privately Held**
SIC: 7542 Washing & polishing, automo-
tive

(G-15295)
**LAKETEC COMMUNICATIONS
INC**
27881 Lorain Rd (44070-4023)
PHONE..................................440 892-2001
Joseph Little, *President*
Joe Little, *General Mgr*
Matt Burns, *Accounts Exec*
Louise Aigner, *Manager*
Matthew Jacobson, *Network Enginr*
EMP: 25
SQ FT: 10,000
SALES (est): 6.1MM **Privately Held**
WEB: www.laketec.net
SIC: 7379 Computer related maintenance
services

(G-15296)
MANOR CARE OF AMERICA INC
23225 Lorain Rd (44070-1624)
PHONE..................................440 779-6900
Dian Zawadzki, *Manager*
EMP: 200
SALES (corp-wide): 2.4B **Publicly Held**
WEB: www.trisunhealthcare.com
SIC: 8051 Convalescent home with contin-
uous nursing care
HQ: Manor Care Of America, Inc.
333 N Summit St Ste 103
Toledo OH 43604
419 252-5500

(G-15297)
**MARRIOTT INTERNATIONAL
INC**
Also Called: Courtyard By Marriott
24901 Country Club Blvd (44070-5308)
PHONE..................................440 716-9977
Erica Todhunter, *General Mgr*
EMP: 28
SALES (corp-wide): 20.7B **Publicly Held**
SIC: 7011 Hotels & motels
PA: Marriott International, Inc.
10400 Fernwood Rd
Bethesda MD 20817
301 380-3000

(G-15298)
**MORRIS CADILLAC BUICK GMC
(PA)**
26100 Lorain Rd (44070-2740)
PHONE..................................440 327-4181
Robert Morris III, *President*
Eshghy Dean, *Finance Mgr*
Dale Freeman, *Sales Mgr*
Mark Yonke, *Sales Staff*
EMP: 55
SQ FT: 20,000
SALES (est): 19.7MM **Privately Held**
SIC: 5511 7538 Automobiles, new & used;
pickups, new & used; general automotive
repair shops

(G-15299)
**MOTORISTS MUTUAL
INSURANCE CO**
28111 Lorain Rd (44070-4027)
PHONE..................................440 779-8900
Robert Hart, *Branch Mgr*
EMP: 30
SQ FT: 9,696
SALES (corp-wide): 352.1MM **Privately
Held**
SIC: 6331 6411 Fire, marine & casualty in-
surance: mutual; insurance agents

PA: Motorists Mutual Insurance Company
471 E Broad St Ste 200
Columbus OH 43215
614 225-8211

(G-15300)
NEW YORK COMMUNITY BANK
4800 Great Northern Blvd (44070-3444)
PHONE..................................440 734-7040
Chris Cinmisenick, *Manager*
EMP: 31 **Publicly Held**
WEB: www.amtrustinvest.com
SIC: 6035 Federal savings & loan associa-
tions
HQ: New York Community Bank
615 Merrick Ave
Westbury NY 11590
516 203-0010

(G-15301)
OLMSTED LANES INC
Also Called: Buckeye Lanes
24488 Lorain Rd (44070-2167)
PHONE..................................440 777-6363
Jim Carney Jr, *President*
EMP: 30
SQ FT: 60,000
SALES (est): 1.3MM **Privately Held**
SIC: 7933 Ten pin center

(G-15302)
**OLMSTED MANOR NURSING
HOME**
27500 Mill Rd (44070-3197)
PHONE..................................440 250-4080
Fax: 440 777-5796
EMP: 130 EST: 1967
SQ FT: 25,000
SALES (est): 4.2MM **Privately Held**
SIC: 8051 8052 Skilled & Intermediate
Nursing Care

(G-15303)
**OLMSTED MNOR RTRMENT
CMNTY LTD**
27420 Mill Rd (44070-3190)
PHONE..................................440 779-8886
John Coury, *Business Mgr*
Katherine Mossrbruger, *Administration*
EMP: 35
SQ FT: 17,690
SALES (est): 1.6MM **Privately Held**
SIC: 6513 8051 Retirement hotel opera-
tion; skilled nursing care facilities

(G-15304)
PALMER HOLLAND INC
25000 Country Club Blvd # 444
(44070-5331)
PHONE..................................440 686-2300
Bryn Irvine, *CEO*
C Bradley Steven, *President*
Katie Ritondaro, *Partner*
Bert D Bradley, *Principal*
Fred H Palmer III, *Principal*
▲ EMP: 95 EST: 1925
SALES (est): 126.3MM **Privately Held**
SIC: 5169 Industrial chemicals

(G-15305)
**PROFESSIONAL TRAVEL INC
(PA)**
25000 Country Club Blvd # 170
(44070-5338)
PHONE..................................440 734-8800
Bob Sturm, *CEO*
Rob Turk, *Exec VP*
Todd Stoneman, *Vice Pres*
Cheryl Viscomi, *Vice Pres*
Andrew Lazar, *Engineer*
EMP: 75
SQ FT: 6,000
SALES (est): 24.4MM **Privately Held**
WEB: www.protrav.com
SIC: 4724 Travel agencies

(G-15306)
PROLINE XPRESS INC
24371 Lorain Rd Ste 206 (44070-2108)
PHONE..................................440 777-8120
Charlene Penn, *President*
EMP: 25
SQ FT: 2,500
SALES (est): 3.8MM **Privately Held**
SIC: 4212 Local trucking, without storage

(G-15307)
**R L FORTNEY MANAGEMENT
INC (PA)**
Also Called: FORTNEY & WEYGANDT
31269 Bradley Rd (44070-3875)
PHONE..................................440 716-4000
Ruth Fortney, *President*
Jo Young, *Business Mgr*
Scott Zanick, *Project Mgr*
EMP: 101 EST: 1978
SALES: 76MM **Privately Held**
SIC: 1542 Commercial & office building,
new construction

(G-15308)
RADISSON HOTEL CLEVE
25070 Country Club Blvd (44070-5309)
PHONE..................................440 734-5060
Syed M Zaman, *Partner*
EMP: 38
SALES (est): 950K **Privately Held**
SIC: 7011 Hotels

(G-15309)
SCHIRMER CONSTRUCTION CO
31350 Industrial Pkwy (44070-4787)
PHONE..................................440 716-4900
Fred Schirmer, *CEO*
James A Yungman, *CEO*
Nick Iafigliola, *President*
Frederick Schirmer, *Exec VP*
John M Roche, *Vice Pres*
EMP: 45
SQ FT: 38,500
SALES (est): 15.1MM **Privately Held**
SIC: 1541 1542 Industrial buildings, new
construction; renovation, remodeling & re-
pairs: industrial buildings; commercial &
office building, new construction; com-
mercial & office buildings, renovation &
repair; institutional building construction

(G-15310)
SMART (PA)
Also Called: Smart - Transportation Div
24950 Country Club Blvd # 340
(44070-5342)
PHONE..................................216 228-9400
John Previsich, *President*
C F Lane, *Principal*
Charles Luna, *Principal*
Dan Johnson, *Treasurer*
Myles Oreilly, *Supervisor*
EMP: 120 EST: 1969
SQ FT: 50,000
SALES: 27.7MM **Privately Held**
SIC: 8631 6411 Labor union; insurance
agents, brokers & service

(G-15311)
SPRINT SPECTRUM LP
25363 Lorain Rd (44070-2061)
PHONE..................................440 686-2600
David Latto, *Manager*
EMP: 30
SALES (corp-wide): 85.9B **Publicly Held**
WEB: www.sprintpcs.com
SIC: 4813 Local & long distance telephone
communications
HQ: Sprint Spectrum L.P.
6800 Sprint Pkwy
Overland Park KS 66251

(G-15312)
SUNNYSIDE TOYOTA INC
27000 Lorain Rd (44070-3212)
PHONE..................................440 777-9911
Kirt Frye, *President*
Jordon Baker, *Finance Mgr*
Brian Harris, *Finance Mgr*
Matt Stolarski, *Sales Mgr*
Jeff Knopf, *Manager*
EMP: 100
SALES (est): 31.7MM **Privately Held**
SIC: 5511 7538 7532 7515 Automobiles,
new & used; general automotive repair
shops; top & body repair & paint shops;
passenger car leasing; automotive &
home supply stores; used car dealers

(G-15313)
SUNSET MEMORIAL PARK ASSN
6265 Columbia Rd (44070-4620)
P.O. Box 729 (44070-0729)
PHONE..................................440 777-0450
Bryn Baracskai, *President*

GEOGRAPHIC

Thomas Baracskai, *Vice Pres*
Edward Shubeck Jr, *Vice Pres*
EMP: 50
SQ FT: 3,000
SALES: 6.7MM **Privately Held**
SIC: 6553 Cemeteries, real estate opera-
tion; cemetery association; mausoleum
operation

(G-15314)
THIRD FEDERAL SAVINGS
26949 Lorain Rd (44070-3211)
PHONE..................................440 716-1865
Liz M Robinson, *Manager*
Diana Kincaid, *Manager*
EMP: 25
SALES (corp-wide): 894.9MM **Publicly
Held**
SIC: 6035 Federal savings & loan associa-
tions
HQ: Third Federal Savings And Loan Asso-
ciation Of Cleveland
7007 Broadway Ave
Cleveland OH 44105
800 844-7333

(G-15315)
UNITED STEELWORKERS
Also Called: Uswa
24371 Lorain Rd Ste 207 (44070-2108)
PHONE..................................440 979-1050
John Majorek, *Manager*
EMP: 44
SALES (corp-wide): 4.9MM **Privately
Held**
SIC: 8631 Labor union
PA: United Steelworkers
60 Blvd Of The Allies # 902
Pittsburgh PA 15222
412 562-2400

(G-15316)
WELLINGTON PLACE LLC
Also Called: O'Neil Healthcare - N Olmstead
4800 Clague Rd Apt 108 (44070-6209)
PHONE..................................440 734-9933
John O'Neill,
EMP: 65
SALES (est): 4MM **Privately Held**
WEB: www.wellingtonplace.net
SIC: 8052 Intermediate care facilities

(G-15317)
XPO CNW INC
5498 Dorothy Dr (44070-4263)
PHONE..................................440 716-8971
Daniel Conway, *Principal*
EMP: 155
SALES (corp-wide): 15.3B **Publicly Held**
WEB: www.cnf.com
SIC: 4213 Trucking, except local
HQ: Xpo Cnw, Inc.
2211 Old Earhart Rd
Ann Arbor MI 48105
734 757-1444

North Ridgeville
Lorain County

(G-15318)
0714 INC
32648 Center Ridge Rd (44039-2457)
PHONE..................................440 327-2123
Adrian Frederick, *President*
Willoughby Hills, *Broker*
Linda Blackstone, *Sales Staff*
EMP: 44
SQ FT: 2,229
SALES (est): 2.7MM **Privately Held**
SIC: 8742 6531 Real estate consultant;
construction project management consult-
ant; real estate agents & managers

(G-15319)
**ALL AMERICAN SPORTS CORP
(HQ)**
Also Called: Riddell All American Sport
7501 Performance Ln (44039-2765)
PHONE..................................440 366-8225
Don Gleisner, *President*
▲ **EMP:** 1000

SALES: 5MM **Privately Held**
SIC: 7699 Recreational sporting equipment
repair services

(G-15320)
ALTERCARE INC (PA)
Also Called: Northridge Health Center
35990 Westminister Ave (44039-1399)
PHONE..................................440 327-5285
Robert A Wickes, *President*
Teresa Brown, *Nursing Dir*
EMP: 45
SQ FT: 30,000
SALES (est): 10MM **Privately Held**
SIC: 8051 Skilled nursing care facilities

(G-15321)
**BANK ENGLAND MORTGAGE
CORP**
37723 Center Ridge Rd (44039-2817)
PHONE..................................440 327-5626
Ray Bolin, *Regional Mgr*
Raymond E Bolin, *Administration*
EMP: 67
SALES (corp-wide): 53.9MM **Privately
Held**
SIC: 6162 Mortgage bankers & correspon-
dents
PA: Bank Of England Mortgage Corporation
5 Statehouse Plz Ste 500
Little Rock AR 72201
501 687-2265

(G-15322)
BOWLERO CORP
Also Called: Brunswick Center Ridge Lanes
38931 Center Ridge Rd (44039-2753)
PHONE..................................440 327-1190
Matt Schneider, *Manager*
EMP: 32
SQ FT: 432
SALES (corp-wide): 323MM **Privately
Held**
SIC: 7933 Ten pin center
PA: Bowlero Corp.
222 W 44th St
New York NY 10036
212 777-2214

(G-15323)
CASTLE CARE
Also Called: Castle Care Landscaping
6043 Oakwood Cir (44039-2661)
PHONE..................................440 327-3700
John Krakowski, *Owner*
Lori Krakowski, *Manager*
EMP: 25
SALES: 500K **Privately Held**
SIC: 0782 Landscape contractors

(G-15324)
**CENTER RIDGE NURSING HOME
INC**
Also Called: Oneill Hlthcare - N Ridgeville
38600 Center Ridge Rd (44039-2837)
PHONE..................................440 808-5500
John T O'Neill, *President*
EMP: 200
SQ FT: 45,000
SALES (est): 5.4MM **Privately Held**
WEB: www.centerridgenursinghome.com
SIC: 8059 8052 8051 Nursing home, ex-
cept skilled & intermediate care facility; in-
termediate care facilities; skilled nursing
care facilities

(G-15325)
CHAPIN LOGISTICS INC
Also Called: Chapin Leasing
39111 Center Ridge Rd (44039-2744)
P.O. Box 1317, Elyria (44036-1317)
PHONE..................................440 327-1360
Timothy J Watson, *President*
EMP: 25
SALES (est): 3.1MM **Privately Held**
WEB: www.chapinlogistics.com
SIC: 4212 Local trucking, without storage

(G-15326)
CITY OF NORTH RIDGEVILLE
Also Called: Dept of Streets
35010 Bainbridge Rd (44039-4072)
PHONE..................................440 327-8326
Chris Rangus, *Branch Mgr*
EMP: 33 **Privately Held**
SIC: 1611 Highway & street maintenance

PA: City Of North Ridgeville
7307 Avon Belden Rd
North Ridgeville OH 44039
440 353-0819

(G-15327)
**CLEVELAND CLINIC
FOUNDATION**
Also Called: Cleveland Clinic Health System
35105 Center Ridge Rd (44039-3081)
PHONE..................................440 327-1050
EMP: 2554
SALES (corp-wide): 8.9B **Privately Held**
SIC: 8062 General medical & surgical hos-
pitals
PA: The Cleveland Clinic Foundation
9500 Euclid Ave
Cleveland OH 44195
216 636-8335

(G-15328)
**DAVITA HEALTHCARE
PARTNERS INC**
35143 Center Ridge Rd (44039-3089)
PHONE..................................440 353-0114
Gregory Beattie, *Branch Mgr*
EMP: 27 **Publicly Held**
SIC: 8092 Kidney dialysis centers
PA: Davita Inc.
2000 16th St
Denver CO 80202

(G-15329)
ESTES EXPRESS LINES INC
38495 Center Ridge Rd (44039-2833)
PHONE..................................440 327-3884
Ron Jordan, *Mktg Dir*
Tom Lamb, *Manager*
Maggie Hales, *Executive*
EMP: 75
SALES (corp-wide): 2.7B **Privately Held**
WEB: www.estes-express.com
SIC: 4213 Heavy hauling
PA: Estes Express Lines, Inc.
3901 W Broad St
Richmond VA 23230
804 353-1900

(G-15330)
FOREVERGREEN LAWN CARE
38601 Sugar Ridge Rd (44039-3526)
PHONE..................................440 327-8987
Michael J Babet, *President*
Pam Karkoff, *Manager*
Debbie M Babet,
EMP: 35
SALES: 1MM **Privately Held**
SIC: 0782 0783 Lawn care services; plant-
ing, pruning & trimming services

(G-15331)
JIMS ELECTRIC INC
39221 Center Ridge Rd (44039-2747)
PHONE..................................440 327-8800
James Tweardy, *President*
Kim Tweardy, *Corp Secy*
EMP: 40
SQ FT: 14,000
SALES (est): 5.2MM **Privately Held**
SIC: 1731 General electrical contractor

(G-15332)
KIDDIE KOLLEGE INC
33169 Center Ridge Rd (44039-2566)
PHONE..................................440 327-5435
Joanne Mollel, *Branch Mgr*
EMP: 25 **Privately Held**
SIC: 8351 Group day care center
PA: Kiddie Kollege Inc
660 Dover Center Rd Ste 2
Bay Village OH 44140

(G-15333)
LASER CRAFT INC
38900 Taylor Pkwy (44035-6259)
PHONE..................................440 327-4300
Greg Claycomb, *President*
William Flickinger, *Vice Pres*
Joe Schmitt, *Vice Pres*
Leonard J Sikora, *Vice Pres*
Mark Ralph, *Prdtn Mgr*
EMP: 25
SALES (est): 4MM **Privately Held**
WEB: www.lasercraftusa.com
SIC: 7389 Metal slitting & shearing

(G-15334)
LIFESTYLE LANDSCAPING INC
34613 Center Ridge Rd (44039-3157)
PHONE..................................440 353-0333
Donald Hoffman, *CEO*
David Hoffman, *President*
Karen Hoffman, *Corp Secy*
EMP: 25
SALES (est): 2.1MM **Privately Held**
WEB: www.lifestylelandscaping.com
SIC: 0781 Landscape planning services;
landscape services

(G-15335)
MERCY HEALTH
6115 Emerald St (44039-2047)
PHONE..................................440 327-7372
Douglas J Potoczak, *Family Practiti*
EMP: 27
SALES (corp-wide): 4.7B **Privately Held**
SIC: 8062 General medical & surgical hos-
pitals
PA: Mercy Health
1701 Mercy Health Pl
Cincinnati OH 45237
513 639-2800

(G-15336)
MERCY HEALTH
39263 Center Ridge Rd (44039-2759)
PHONE..................................440 366-5577
EMP: 32
SALES (corp-wide): 4.7B **Privately Held**
SIC: 8011 Primary care medical clinic; oc-
cupational & industrial specialist, physi-
cian/surgeon
PA: Mercy Health
1701 Mercy Health Pl
Cincinnati OH 45237
513 639-2800

(G-15337)
MILLS CREEK ASSOCIATION
5175 Mills Creek Ln (44039-2332)
P.O. Box 39084 (44039-0084)
PHONE..................................440 327-5336
Warren Blakely, *President*
Art Hubble, *Vice Pres*
Richard Bartels, *Treasurer*
Janice Kennard, *Admin Sec*
EMP: 28
SALES: 280K **Privately Held**
WEB: www.millscreek.org
SIC: 8641 Homeowners' association

(G-15338)
**NEUTRAL TELECOM
CORPORATION**
6472 Monroe Ln Ste 200 (44039-5306)
PHONE..................................440 377-4700
Beth Ellen Davis, *President*
EMP: 40
SQ FT: 40,000
SALES: 10MM **Privately Held**
SIC: 8748 Telecommunications consultant

(G-15339)
PETRO-COM CORP (PA)
32523 Lorain Rd (44039-3423)
PHONE..................................440 327-6900
Manny Sclimenti Jr, *President*
Sharon Sclimenti, *Vice Pres*
Teresa Curtis, *Opers Mgr*
EMP: 29
SQ FT: 10,000
SALES (est): 4MM **Privately Held**
WEB: www.petrocomcorp.com
SIC: 7699 Service station equipment repair

(G-15340)
RHENIUM ALLOYS INC (PA)
38683 Taylor Pkwy (44035-6200)
P.O. Box 245, Elyria (44036-0245)
PHONE..................................440 365-7388
Mike Prokop, *President*
Todd Leonhardt, *Vice Pres*
William McVicker, *Controller*
Tim Carlson, *Sales Executive*
Martin Buck, *CTO*
▲ **EMP:** 60 **EST:** 1994
SQ FT: 35,500

SALES (est): 14.2MM Privately Held
WEB: www.rhenium.com
SIC: 3313 3356 3498 3339 Electrometal-lurgical products; tungsten, basic shapes; fabricated pipe & fittings; primary nonfer-rous metals; chemical preparations; fer-roalloy ores, except vanadium

(G-15341)
RIDDELL INC
7501 Performance Ln (44039-2765)
PHONE...................................440 366-8225
Robert Kelly, *Manager*
EMP: 25 Privately Held
WEB: www.riddellsports.com
SIC: 5091 Athletic goods
HQ: Riddell, Inc.
1700 E Higgins Rd Ste 500
Des Plaines IL 60018
847 292-1472

(G-15342)
SAFARI CLUB INTERNATIONAL
Also Called: SCI Ohio
5084 Garrett Dr (44039-2014)
PHONE...................................440 247-8614
Jim Hayes, *President*
EMP: 40
SALES (est): 36.5K Privately Held
SIC: 7997 Membership sports & recreation clubs

(G-15343)
SCHILL LANDSCAPING AND LAWN CA (PA)
Also Called: Schill Grounds Management
5000 Mills Indus Pkwy (44039-1971)
PHONE...................................440 327-3030
Joseph H Schill, *President*
Gerald J Schill Jr, *Vice Pres*
James Schill, *Vice Pres*
EMP: 63
SQ FT: 10,000
SALES (est): 10.4MM Privately Held
WEB: www.schilllandscaping.com
SIC: 0781 0782 4959 Landscape archi-tects; lawn services; snowplowing

(G-15344)
UNITED STTES BOWL CONGRESS INC
38931 Center Ridge Rd (44039-2753)
PHONE...................................440 327-0102
EMP: 51
SALES (corp-wide): 32.9MM Privately Held
SIC: 7933 Ten pin center
PA: United States Bowling Congress, Inc.
621 Six Flags Dr
Arlington TX 76011
817 385-8200

North Royalton
Cuyahoga County

(G-15345)
AARON LANDSCAPE INC
Also Called: Accucut
14900 York Rd (44133-4526)
PHONE...................................440 838-8875
Aaron Zaremba, *President*
Tom Fritsch, *Manager*
EMP: 30 EST: 1993
SALES (est): 3.8MM Privately Held
WEB: www.aaronlandscaping.com
SIC: 0781 Landscape services

(G-15346)
ABC FIRE INC
10250 Royalton Rd (44133-4429)
PHONE...................................440 237-6677
Richard W Watson, *President*
Joe Watson, *Sales Mgr*
Dan Jindra, *Sales Associate*
Eric Cathcart, *Manager*
EMP: 25
SQ FT: 13,500

SALES (est): 10.2MM Privately Held
WEB: www.abcfireinc.net
SIC: 5099 1731 1711 8748 Safety equip-ment & supplies; fire detection & burglar alarm systems specialization; fire sprin-kler system installation; safety training service; fire alarm maintenance & moni-toring

(G-15347)
B & D AUTO & TOWING INC
14290 State Rd Ste 1 (44133-5129)
PHONE...................................440 237-3737
David Quinn, *President*
EMP: 30
SQ FT: 87,120
SALES (est): 179.6K Privately Held
SIC: 7549 Towing service, automotive

(G-15348)
BERARDIS FRESH ROAST INC
12029 Abbey Rd (44133-2637)
PHONE...................................440 582-4303
Patrick Leneghan, *CEO*
Brian Leneghan, *Vice Pres*
Sean Leneghan, *CFO*
EMP: 40
SQ FT: 17,000
SALES (est): 8.3MM Privately Held
WEB: www.berardiscoffee.com
SIC: 5149 Coffee, green or roasted; tea; cocoa

(G-15349)
CHILDRENS FOREVER HAVEN INC (PA)
Also Called: Haven Hill Home
10983 Abbey Rd (44133-2537)
PHONE...................................440 652-6749
Sharon Curlett, *Human Res Mgr*
Kelly Simmons, *Manager*
Halle Weber, *Director*
EMP: 47
SQ FT: 9,000
SALES: 96.1K Privately Held
SIC: 8052 Personal care facility

(G-15350)
CLASSROOM ANTICS INC
10143 Royalton Rd Ste G (44133-4468)
PHONE...................................800 595-3776
Marjorie Andrews, *Business Mgr*
Tara Foote, *Director*
Toby Foote, *Program Dir*
EMP: 30
SQ FT: 1,800
SALES (est): 587.7K Privately Held
SIC: 7032 Summer camp, except day & sports instructional

(G-15351)
D C TRANSPORTATION SERVICE
Also Called: Commercial Drivers
5740 Royalwood Rd Ste C (44133-3936)
PHONE...................................440 237-0900
Thomas Fink, *President*
Liz Krauth, *Accounting Mgr*
EMP: 190
SALES (est): 5.4MM Privately Held
SIC: 7363 Employee leasing service

(G-15352)
DAVE COMMERCIAL GROUND MGT
9956 Akins Rd (44133-4547)
PHONE...................................440 237-5394
Vito Montelbone, *Principal*
EMP: 28
SALES: 3.3MM Privately Held
SIC: 8741 Management services

(G-15353)
DIGIOIA/SUBURBAN EXCVTG LLC
11293 Royalton Rd (44133-4409)
PHONE...................................440 237-1978
Nick Di Gioia Jr,
Terry Monnolly,
EMP: 85 EST: 1976
SQ FT: 23,000
SALES (est): 20.5MM Privately Held
SIC: 1623 1794 Water main construction; sewer line construction; excavation work

---

(G-15354)
EMPIRE MASONRY COMPANY INC
Also Called: Empire Poured Walls
12359 Abbey Rd Ste B (44133-2642)
PHONE...................................440 230-2800
Bernard Nofel, *President*
Kathlene Nofel, *Manager*
EMP: 70
SQ FT: 2,000
SALES (est): 4MM Privately Held
SIC: 1741 Masonry & other stonework

(G-15355)
EPILOGUE INC
Also Called: Ltc Nursing
12333 Ridge Rd Ste E (44133-3700)
PHONE...................................440 582-5555
Richard Buesch, *President*
Andrea Wisniewski, *Nurse*
EMP: 56
SALES (est): 3.2MM Privately Held
SIC: 7361 Nurses' registry

(G-15356)
GRABER METAL WORKS INC
9664 Akins Rd Ste 1 (44133-4595)
PHONE...................................440 237-8422
Steve M Graber Sr, *President*
Michael R Horvath, *Vice Pres*
Katherine Graber, *Treasurer*
EMP: 30 EST: 1965
SQ FT: 25,000
SALES (est): 3MM Privately Held
WEB: www.grabermetal.com
SIC: 3599 5051 3446 3444 Machine shop, jobbing & repair; tubing, flexible metallic; metals service centers & offices; architectural metalwork; sheet metalwork; fabricated plate work (boiler shop); fabri-cated structural metal

(G-15357)
H & D STEEL SERVICE INC
Also Called: H & D Steel Service Center
9960 York Alpha Dr (44133-3588)
PHONE...................................440 237-3390
Raymond Gary Schreiber, *Ch of Bd*
Joseph Bubba, *President*
Joseph A Cachat, *Principal*
R M Jones, *Principal*
R G Schreiber, *Principal*
▲ EMP: 50
SQ FT: 125,000
SALES (est): 53.9MM Privately Held
WEB: www.hdsteel.com
SIC: 5051 3541 5085 Iron or steel flat products; sheets, metal; tubing, metal; bars, metal; home workshop machine tools, metalworking; industrial tools

(G-15358)
HANNA HOLDINGS INC
Also Called: Howard Hanna RE & Mrtg Svcs
9485 W Sprague Rd (44133-1210)
PHONE...................................440 971-5600
Stacy Nickels, *Branch Mgr*
EMP: 50
SALES (corp-wide): 73.7MM Privately Held
SIC: 6531 6111 Real estate brokers & agents; Federal Home Loan Mortgage Corporation
PA: Hanna Holdings, Inc.
1090 Freeport Rd Ste 1a
Pittsburgh PA 15238
412 967-9000

(G-15359)
HARMONY HOME CARE INC
12608 State Rd Ste 1a (44133-3281)
PHONE...................................440 877-1977
Christine Tharp, *President*
EMP: 50
SALES (est): 1.7MM Privately Held
SIC: 8361 Residential care

(G-15360)
HCR MANORCARE MED SVCS FLA LLC
Also Called: Arden Courts of Parma
9205 W Sprague Rd (44133-1286)
PHONE...................................440 887-1442
Stephanie Chambers, *Director*
EMP: 65

SALES (corp-wide): 2.4B Publicly Held
WEB: www.manorcare.com
SIC: 8322 8051 Old age assistance; skilled nursing care facilities
HQ: Hcr Manorcare Medical Services Of Florida, Llc
333 N Summit St Ste 100
Toledo OH 43604
419 252-5500

(G-15361)
HOWARD HANNA SMYTHE CRAMER
5730 Wallings Rd (44133-3015)
PHONE...................................440 237-8888
Joesephine Calabro, *Manager*
EMP: 30
SALES (corp-wide): 72.1MM Privately Held
SIC: 6531 Real estate brokers & agents
HQ: Howard Hanna Smythe Cramer
6000 Parkland Blvd
Cleveland OH 44124
216 447-4477

(G-15362)
MANOR CARE OF AMERICA INC
9055 W Sprague Rd (44133-1285)
PHONE...................................440 345-9300
Hans Larsen, *Branch Mgr*
EMP: 200
SALES (corp-wide): 2.4B Publicly Held
SIC: 8051 Convalescent home with contin-uous nursing care
HQ: Manor Care Of America, Inc.
333 N Summit St Ste 103
Toledo OH 43604
419 252-5500

(G-15363)
OAK BROOK GARDENS
Also Called: Oak Brook Garden Apartments
13911 Oakbrook Dr Apt 205 (44133-4641)
PHONE...................................440 237-3613
Harley Gross, *President*
Gary Gross, *Partner*
Morton J Gross, *Partner*
EMP: 90
SQ FT: 500
SALES (est): 3.6MM Privately Held
SIC: 6513 6531 Apartment building opera-tors; real estate agents & managers

(G-15364)
PREMIER ASPHALT PAVING CO INC
10519 Royalton Rd (44133-4401)
PHONE...................................440 237-6600
Ronald Fabricius Sr, *President*
Ronald Fabricius Jr, *Vice Pres*
Troy Fabricius, *Vice Pres*
EMP: 25
SQ FT: 7,000
SALES (est): 5.6MM Privately Held
WEB: www.premierasphaltpaving.com
SIC: 1611 1771 Highway & street paving contractor; blacktop (asphalt) work

(G-15365)
ROYAL REDEEMER LUTHERAN CHURCH
Also Called: Royal Rdeemer Lutheran Ch Schl
11680 Royalton Rd (44133-4461)
PHONE...................................440 237-7958
John Zahrte, *Pastor*
James Martin, *Pastor*
Gary Likowski, *Director*
EMP: 40
SQ FT: 69,342
SALES (est): 891K Privately Held
SIC: 8661 8351 8211 8322 Lutheran Church; preschool center; kindergarten; social service center

(G-15366)
ROYALTON SENIOR LIVING INC
Also Called: Royalton Woods
14277 State Rd (44133-5130)
PHONE...................................440 582-4111
Linda Arduini, *Director*
EMP: 44
SQ FT: 18,407
SALES: 2MM Privately Held
SIC: 8059 Rest home, with health care

GEOGRAPHIC

(G-15367)
SHEARER FARM INC
Also Called: John Deere Authorized Dealer
11204 Royalton Rd (44133-4417)
PHONE....................................440 237-4806
EMP: 35
SALES (corp-wide): 59.5MM Privately
Held
SIC: 5261 5084 5083 Lawnmowers &
tractors; industrial machinery & equip-
ment; tractors, agricultural
PA: Shearer Farm, Inc
7762 Cleveland Rd
Wooster OH 44691
330 345-9023

(G-15368)
SUBURBAN MAINT & CNSTR
INC
16330 York Rd Ste 2 (44133-5551)
P.O. Box 33009, Cleveland (44133-0009)
PHONE....................................440 237-7765
Brian Stucky, President
EMP: 35
SQ FT: 12,000
SALES (est): 3.8MM Privately Held
SIC: 1799 1771 Waterproofing; concrete
repair

(G-15369)
SUBURBAN MAINTENANCE &
CONTRS
16330 York Rd (44133-5551)
PHONE....................................440 237-7765
Donna Gallo, Principal
EMP: 25
SALES (est): 1.4MM Privately Held
SIC: 7349 Building maintenance services

(G-15370)
VERIZON SELECT SERVICES
INC
12300 Ridge Rd (44133-3745)
PHONE....................................908 559-2054
EMP: 30
SALES (corp-wide): 126B Publicly Held
SIC: 4822 Telephone Communications
HQ: Verizon Select Services Inc.
4255 Patriot Dr Ste 400
Grapevine TX 76051

Northfield
Summit County

(G-15371)
1ST CLASS HOME HEALTH
CARE SER
Also Called: 1st Class Wellness Healty Eats
10333 Nrthfeld Rd Unit 30 (44067)
P.O. Box 39254, Solon (44139-0254)
PHONE....................................216 678-0213
Tisha Maire, Mng Member
James Randolph,
EMP: 50
SALES: 1MM Privately Held
SIC: 8082 Home health care services

(G-15372)
ADESA-OHIO LLC
Also Called: Adesa Cleveland
210 E Twinsburg Rd (44067-2848)
PHONE....................................330 467-8280
Jim Hellet, Ch of Bd
Don Harris, COO
Frank Birkas, Opers Mgr
William Stackhouse, CFO
Karen Drebo, Human Res Mgr
EMP: 200
SQ FT: 150,000
SALES (est): 27MM Publicly Held
WEB: www.adesa.com
SIC: 5012 Automobile auction
HQ: Adesa Corporation, Llc
13085 Hamilton Crossing B
Carmel IN 46032

(G-15373)
BALANCED CARE
CORPORATION
Also Called: Outlook Pointe
997 W Aurora Rd (44067-1605)
PHONE....................................330 908-1166

Pete Szigeti, Principal
Toni Montgomery, Director
EMP: 50 Privately Held
SIC: 8741 8051 8621 Nursing & personal
care facility management; skilled nursing
care facilities; professional membership
organizations
PA: Balanced Care Corporation
5000 Ritter Rd Ste 202
Mechanicsburg PA 17055

(G-15374)
BAVAN & ASSOCIATES
Also Called: Bevan and Associates Lpa
10360 Northfield Rd (44067-1445)
PHONE....................................330 650-0088
Keith Bavan, President
Dale S Economus, Partner
Raymond M Powell
Charlene Gedeon, Legal Staff
EMP: 30
SQ FT: 7,000
SALES (est): 2.2MM Privately Held
WEB: www.bevanlaw.com
SIC: 8111 General practice attorney,
lawyer

(G-15375)
BRENTWOOD LIFE CARE
COMPANY
Also Called: Brentwood Health Care Center
907 W Aurora Rd (44067-1605)
PHONE....................................330 468-2273
Brent Classen, Owner
Autumn Richmond, Director
EMP: 135
SQ FT: 38,700
SALES (est): 8MM Privately Held
SIC: 8051 Convalescent home with contin-
uous nursing care

(G-15376)
CLEVELND CLNC HLTH SYSTM
EAST
Also Called: Sagamore Hills Medical Center
863 W Aurora Rd (44067-1603)
PHONE....................................330 468-0190
Jennifer Simmons, Branch Mgr
EMP: 40
SALES (corp-wide): 8.9B Privately Held
SIC: 8062 8093 General medical & surgi-
cal hospitals; specialty outpatient clinics
HQ: Cleveland Clinic Health System-East
Region
6803 Mayfield Rd Ste 500
Cleveland OH 44124
440 312-6010

(G-15377)
DENNIS & CAROL LIEDERBACH
8651 Wood Hollow Rd (44067-1852)
PHONE....................................256 582-6200
David Lienback, General Mgr
EMP: 35
SALES (est): 1.8MM Privately Held
SIC: 7389 Business services

(G-15378)
FARMERS GROUP INC
Also Called: Farmers Insurance
500 W Aurora Rd Ste 115 (44067-2166)
PHONE....................................330 467-6575
Jose Quiles, Branch Mgr
EMP: 25
SALES (corp-wide): 65.1B Privately Held
SIC: 6411 Insurance agents, brokers &
service
HQ: Farmers Group, Inc.
6301 Owensmouth Ave
Woodland Hills CA 91367
323 932-3200

(G-15379)
FERFOLIA FUNERAL HOMES
INC
356 W Aurora Rd (44067-2104)
PHONE....................................216 663-4222
Donald Berfolia, President
Donald L Berfolia, President
Alice Ferfolia, Treasurer
Theresa Ferfolia, Admin Sec
EMP: 36
SQ FT: 15,000

SALES (est): 3.7MM Privately Held
WEB: www.ferfolia.com
SIC: 7261 Funeral home

(G-15380)
INNOVATIVE LOGISTICS SVCS
INC
201 E Twinsburg Rd (44067-2847)
P.O. Box 560206, Macedonia (44056-0206)
PHONE....................................330 468-6422
Dale Hug, President
Cynthia Hug, Corp Secy
EMP: 55
SQ FT: 8,000
SALES (est): 8.8MM Privately Held
WEB: www.innlogistics.com
SIC: 4212 Local trucking, without storage

(G-15381)
JACKSON COMFORT SYSTEMS
INC
Also Called: Jackson Comfort Htg Coolg Sys
499 E Twinsburg Rd (44067-2851)
PHONE....................................330 468-3111
Paul Jackson, President
Mark Jackson, Vice Pres
Matt Rhodes, Vice Pres
Gary Jackson, Treasurer
Keith McCann, Sales Mgr
EMP: 30 EST: 1976
SQ FT: 13,000
SALES (est): 5.6MM Privately Held
WEB: www.jacksoncomfort.com
SIC: 1711 Hydronics heating contractor;
warm air heating & air conditioning con-
tractor; refrigeration contractor

(G-15382)
LOWES HOME CENTERS LLC
8224 Golden Link Blvd (44067-2067)
PHONE....................................330 908-2750
Al Rito, Office Mgr
Dave Rhodes, Manager
EMP: 150
SALES (corp-wide): 68.6B Publicly Held
SIC: 5211 5031 5722 5064 Home cen-
ters; building materials, exterior; building
materials, interior; household appliance
stores; electrical appliances, television &
radio
HQ: Lowe's Home Centers, Llc
1605 Curtis Bridge Rd
Wilkesboro NC 28697
336 658-4000

(G-15383)
MENTAL HEALTH AND ADDI
SERV
Also Called: Northcast Bhvral Halthcare Sys
1756 Sagamore Rd (44067-1086)
PHONE....................................330 467-7131
Douglas Kern, CEO
EMP: 300 Privately Held
SIC: 8063 9431 Psychiatric hospitals;
mental health agency administration, gov-
ernment;
HQ: Ohio Department Of Mental Health
And Addiction Services
30 E Broad St Fl 8
Columbus OH 43215

(G-15384)
NORTHFIELD PRESBT DAY
CARE CTR
7755 S Boyden Rd (44067-2452)
PHONE....................................330 467-4411
Ann Kujawski, Administration
EMP: 40
SALES (est): 826.9K Privately Held
SIC: 8351 Child day care services

(G-15385)
REVILLE TIRE CO (PA)
Also Called: Reville Wholesale Distributing
8044 Olde 8 Rd (44067-2830)
PHONE....................................330 468-1900
Robert J Reville, President
James S Bidlake, Principal
Michael Reville, Vice Pres
Raymond L Reville III, Vice Pres
Richard H Reville, Vice Pres
EMP: 65 EST: 1970
SQ FT: 30,000

SALES (est): 40.1MM Privately Held
WEB: www.revillewhs.com
SIC: 5014 Automobile tires & tubes

(G-15386)
SPITZER CHEVROLET INC
333 E Aurora Rd (44067-2022)
PHONE....................................330 467-4141
Alan Spitzer, Ch of Bd
Janet May, Treasurer
Gary Blanchard, Admin Sec
EMP: 70
SQ FT: 45,000
SALES (est): 21.3MM Privately Held
SIC: 5511 7539 7538 5521 Automobiles,
new & used; automotive repair shops;
general automotive repair shops; used
car dealers

(G-15387)
THOMAS E ANDERSON DDS INC
147 E Aurora Rd (44067-2084)
PHONE....................................330 467-6466
Thomas E Anderson, President
EMP: 25
SALES (est): 717.9K Privately Held
SIC: 8021 Dentists' office

Northwood
Wood County

(G-15388)
A E D INC
Also Called: Interstate Coml GL & Door
2845 Crane Way (43619-1098)
PHONE....................................419 661-9999
Daniel Erickson, President
Walter Erickson, Vice Pres
Pamela Erickson, Admin Sec
EMP: 33
SQ FT: 11,500
SALES (est): 7.2MM Privately Held
WEB: www.icgad.com
SIC: 1793 Glass & glazing work

(G-15389)
BLOCK COMMUNICATIONS INC
Also Called: Buckeye Broadband
2700 Oregon Rd (43619-1057)
PHONE....................................419 724-2539
Walter H Carstensen, President
EMP: 350
SALES (corp-wide): 921.6MM Privately
Held
SIC: 4841 4813 Cable television services;
local & long distance telephone communi-
cations
PA: Block Communications, Inc.
405 Madison Ave Ste 2100
Toledo OH 43604
419 724-6212

(G-15390)
BUCKEYE TELESYSTEM INC
(HQ)
2700 Oregon Rd (43619-1057)
P.O. Box 1116, Holland (43528-1116)
PHONE....................................419 724-9898
Thomas K Dawson, Vice Pres
Kirk Dombek, Vice Pres
John E Martin, Vice Pres
Harry Kuebler, Technical Mgr
Brian Mysko, Engineer
EMP: 153
SALES (est): 27.9MM
SALES (corp-wide): 921.6MM Privately
Held
WEB: www.blockcommunications.com
SIC: 4813
PA: Block Communications, Inc.
405 Madison Ave Ste 2100
Toledo OH 43604
419 724-6212

(G-15391)
CAMPBELL INC (PA)
Also Called: Total Solutions
2875 Crane Way (43619-1098)
PHONE....................................419 476-4444
K Keith Campbell, President
Robert A Eaton, Vice Pres
Dan Feasby, Engineer
Peter J Vavrinek, CFO

Todd Kocsis, *Sales Staff*
EMP: 47 **EST:** 1968
SQ FT: 14,650
SALES: 10.7MM **Privately Held**
WEB: www.campbellinc.com
SIC: 1711 Mechanical contractor

(G-15392)
EMI ENTERPRISES INC
Also Called: Envelope Mart
2639 Tracy Rd (43619-1006)
P.O. Box 307, Toledo (43697-0307)
PHONE.................................419 666-0012
Norman Shapiro, *President*
Gregory Shapiro, *Vice Pres*
Myron Shapiro, *Vice Pres*
Susan Hauff, *Manager*
Eric Zolciak, *Manager*
EMP: 45
SQ FT: 15,000
SALES (est): 13.5MM **Privately Held**
WEB: www.envelopemart.com
SIC: 5112 Envelopes

(G-15393)
FEDERAL EXPRESS CORPORATION
Also Called: Fedex
7600 Caple Blvd (43619-1091)
PHONE.......................800 463-3339
EMP: 109
SALES (corp-wide): 65.4B **Publicly Held**
WEB: www.federalexpress.com
SIC: 4513 Package delivery, private air
HQ: Federal Express Corporation
3610 Hacks Cross Rd
Memphis TN 38125
901 369-3600

(G-15394)
FEDEX FREIGHT CORPORATION
7779 Arbor Dr (43619-7506)
PHONE.......................800 728-8190
Scott Kolling, *Senior Mgr*
EMP: 150
SQ FT: 62,424
SALES (corp-wide): 65.4B **Publicly Held**
SIC: 4213 4731 Less-than-truckload (LTL) transport; freight transportation arrangement
HQ: Fedex Freight Corporation
1715 Aaron Brenner Dr
Memphis TN 38120

(G-15395)
HIRZEL CANNING COMPANY (PA)
Also Called: Dei Fratelli
411 Lemoyne Rd (43619-1699)
PHONE.................................419 693-0531
Karl A Hirzel Jr, *President*
Bill Hirzel, *Plant Mgr*
Rick Kopec, *Plant Mgr*
Emily Neuenschwander, *QA Dir*
Isaac Schroeder, *Plant Engr*
▲ **EMP:** 100 **EST:** 1923
SQ FT: 250,000
SALES (est): 29.6MM **Privately Held**
WEB: www.hirzel.com
SIC: 2033 8611 2034 Tomato products: packaged in cans, jars, etc.; tomato juice: packaged in cans, jars, etc.; tomato paste: packaged in cans, jars, etc.; tomato purees: packaged in cans, jars, etc.; business associations; dehydrated fruits, vegetables, soups

(G-15396)
INSTALLED BUILDING PDTS LLC
Also Called: Royalty Mooney & Moses
6412 Fairfield Dr Ste A (43619-7514)
PHONE.................................419 662-4524
Joe Loch, *Principal*
EMP: 40
SALES (est): 1.6MM **Privately Held**
SIC: 1742 5211 Insulation, buildings; insulation material, building; bathroom fixtures, equipment & supplies

(G-15397)
LAKEWOOD GREENHOUSE INC
909 Lemoyne Rd (43619-1817)
PHONE.................................419 691-3541
Walter F Krueger Jr, *President*
Mary M Krueger, *Corp Secy*
Mary Ann Franke, *Manager*

▲ **EMP:** 45
SQ FT: 20,000
SALES (est): 4.1MM **Privately Held**
SIC: 0181 Flowers: grown under cover (e.g. greenhouse production)

(G-15398)
MACOMB GROUP INC
Also Called: Macomb Group Toledo Division
2830 Crane Way (43619-1095)
PHONE.................................419 666-6899
Mark D Calzolano, *Vice Pres*
Dale Coffield, *Manager*
Randall Heck, *Information Mgr*
EMP: 30
SALES (corp-wide): 200MM **Privately Held**
SIC: 5085 Industrial supplies
PA: The Macomb Group Inc
6600 15 Mile Rd
Sterling Heights MI 48312
586 274-4100

(G-15399)
MOTOR CARRIER SERVICE INC
815 Lemoyne Rd (43619-1815)
PHONE.................................419 693-6207
Keith A Tuttle, *President*
Ronda Sherrer, *Purch Dir*
David Slesinski, *Controller*
John Vasko, *Director*
Kaydee Forgette, *Representative*
EMP: 110
SQ FT: 10,000
SALES (est): 31MM **Privately Held**
SIC: 4213 Contract haulers

(G-15400)
NATIONAL ASSN LTR CARRIERS
Also Called: N A L C
4437 Woodville Rd (43619-1859)
PHONE.................................419 693-8392
Robert T Newbold, *President*
EMP: 53
SALES (corp-wide): 1.4B **Privately Held**
WEB: www.nalc.org
SIC: 8631 Labor union
PA: National Association Of Letter Carriers
100 Indana Ave Nw Ste 709
Washington DC 20001
202 393-4695

(G-15401)
NORTH AMERCN SCIENCE ASSOC INC (PA)
Also Called: Namsa
6750 Wales Rd (43619-1012)
PHONE.................................419 666-9455
John J Gorski, *President*
Alan Alexander, *Exec VP*
Jane A Kervin, *Vice Pres*
Mike Brookman, *CFO*
John Amat, *Ch Credit Ofcr*
EMP: 250
SQ FT: 135,000
SALES (est): 121.4MM **Privately Held**
WEB: www.namsa.com
SIC: 8731 8734 Medical research, commercial; testing laboratories

(G-15402)
NORTH AMERCN SCIENCE ASSOC INC
Also Called: Namsa Sterilzation Products
2261 Tracy Rd (43619-1397)
PHONE.................................419 666-9455
Richard Wallin, *Branch Mgr*
EMP: 142
SALES (corp-wide): 121.4MM **Privately Held**
SIC: 8731 Medical research, commercial
PA: North American Science Associates, Inc.
6750 Wales Rd
Northwood OH 43619
419 666-9455

(G-15403)
NWO BEVERAGE INC
Also Called: N W O
6700 Wales Rd (43619-1012)
PHONE.................................419 725-2162
Pj Sullivan, *Vice Pres*
Joe Schetz, *Vice Pres*
Patrick J Sullivan, *Vice Pres*
Jeff Stewart, *Opers Mgr*

Brenda Johnson, *Office Mgr*
EMP: 48
SALES (est): 18.6MM **Privately Held**
SIC: 5181 Beer & other fermented malt liquors

(G-15404)
OH ST TRANS DIST 02 OUTPOST
200 Lemoyne Rd (43619-1630)
PHONE.................................419 693-8870
Herman Munn, *Manager*
EMP: 30
SALES (est): 920.5K **Privately Held**
SIC: 4789 Transportation services

(G-15405)
PRESCRIPTION SUPPLY INC
2233 Tracy Rd (43619-1302)
PHONE.................................419 661-6600
Thomas Schoen, *President*
Jacquelyn J Harbauer, *Corp Secy*
Candace Harbauer, *Vice Pres*
Julie A Lewandowski, *Controller*
Howard Serling, *Accounts Exec*
EMP: 75
SQ FT: 30,000
SALES (est): 67.9MM **Privately Held**
WEB: www.prescriptionsupply.com
SIC: 5122 Pharmaceuticals

(G-15406)
SATTLERPEARSON INC
Also Called: Wright Harvey House, The
3055 E Plaza Blvd (43619-2037)
PHONE.................................419 698-3822
Patricia Pearson, *President*
Jenny Bucher, *Mktg Dir*
Chris Mills, *Office Mgr*
Natalie Tousley, *Director*
Paula Cluckey, *Food Svc Dir*
EMP: 26
SALES: 800K **Privately Held**
WEB: www.wrightharvey.com
SIC: 8361 Geriatric residential care

(G-15407)
THYSSENKRUPP LOGISTICS INC (DH)
Also Called: Copper and Brass Sales Div
8001 Thyssenkrupp Pkwy (43619-2082)
PHONE.................................419 662-1800
Joachim Limberg, *Chairman*
James Baber, *Vice Pres*
Daniel Burroughs, *Technical Staff*
EMP: 62
SALES (est): 22.3MM
SALES (corp-wide): 39.8B **Privately Held**
SIC: 4213 Trucking, except local
HQ: Thyssenkrupp Materials Na, Inc.
22355 W 11 Mile Rd
Southfield MI 48033
248 233-5600

(G-15408)
THYSSENKRUPP ONLINEMETALS LLC
8001 Thyssenkrupp Pkwy (43619-2082)
PHONE.................................206 285-8603
Matt Miller, *Director*
EMP: 25
SALES (est): 760.1K
SALES (corp-wide): 39.8B **Privately Held**
SIC: 5051 Nonferrous metal sheets, bars, rods, etc.
HQ: Thyssenkrupp Onlinemetals, Llc
1138 W Ewing St
Seattle WA 98119

(G-15409)
TKX LOGISTICS
Also Called: Thyssen Krupp Logistics
8001 Thyssenkrupp Pkwy (43619-2082)
PHONE.................................419 662-1800
Joachim Limberg, *Chairman*
EMP: 35
SALES (est): 9.3MM **Privately Held**
SIC: 4213 Trucking, except local

(G-15410)
TL INDUSTRIES INC (PA)
2541 Tracy Rd (43619-1097)
PHONE.................................419 666-8144
Joseph Young, *Vice Pres*
Theodore Stetschulte, *Vice Pres*
Paul Rodgers, *Prdtn Mgr*
Keith Kogler, *Purch Agent*

EMP: 105
SQ FT: 36,000
SALES (est): 31.6MM **Privately Held**
SIC: 8711 3444 3623 3679 Electrical or electronic engineering; sheet metalwork; battery chargers, rectifying or nonrotating; loads, electronic

(G-15411)
TOWLIFT INC
2860 Crane Way (43619-1095)
PHONE.................................419 666-1333
Brent Cannon, *Manager*
EMP: 50
SALES (corp-wide): 106.6MM **Privately Held**
SIC: 5084 7353 7699 Materials handling machinery; heavy construction equipment rental; industrial equipment services
PA: Towlift, Inc.
1395 Valley Belt Rd
Brooklyn Heights OH 44131
216 749-6800

(G-15412)
TREU HOUSE OF MUNCH INC
8000 Arbor Dr (43619-7505)
PHONE.................................419 666-7770
Richard G Esser, *President*
Todd Esser, *Vice Pres*
Rick Niehaus, *Vice Pres*
James Layman, *Treasurer*
Greg Hipp, *Human Res Dir*
EMP: 100 **EST:** 1875
SQ FT: 120,000
SALES (est): 29.1MM **Privately Held**
WEB: www.treuhouse.com
SIC: 5181 Beer & other fermented malt liquors

(G-15413)
WASTE MANAGEMENT OHIO INC
Also Called: Waste Management Ohio NW
6525 Wales Rd (43619-1330)
PHONE.................................866 409-4671
John Stark, *Manager*
EMP: 65
SALES (corp-wide): 14.9B **Publicly Held**
SIC: 4953 Rubbish collection & disposal
HQ: Waste Management Of Ohio, Inc.
1700 N Broad St
Fairborn OH 45324

(G-15414)
WESCO DISTRIBUTION INC
6519 Fairfield Dr (43619-7507)
PHONE.................................419 666-1670
Chad Marrison, *Branch Mgr*
EMP: 28 **Publicly Held**
SIC: 5085 3699 Industrial supplies; electrical equipment & supplies
HQ: Wesco Distribution, Inc.
225 W Station Square Dr # 700
Pittsburgh PA 15219

(G-15415)
WOJOS HEATING & AC INC
5523 Woodville Rd (43619-2209)
PHONE.................................419 693-3220
Thomas Wojo Ciehowfki, *President*
Chuck Westenbarger, *Opers Mgr*
Robert Shamy, *Sales Mgr*
Leann St Johns, *Manager*
EMP: 25
SALES (est): 3.1MM **Privately Held**
SIC: 1711 Warm air heating & air conditioning contractor; heating & air conditioning contractors

(G-15416)
YANFENG US AUTOMOTIVE
Also Called: Johnson Contrls Authorized Dlr
7560 Arbor Dr (43619-7500)
PHONE.................................419 662-4905
Keith Wandell, *President*
EMP: 96
SALES (corp-wide): 55MM **Privately Held**
SIC: 2531 5075 Public building & related furniture; warm air heating & air conditioning

(PA)=Parent Co (HQ)=Headquarters (DH)=Div Headquarters
✿ = New Business established in last 2 years

2019 Harris Ohio
Services Directory

GEOGRAPHIC

HQ: Yanfeng Us Automotive Interior Systems I Llc
41935 W 12 Mile Rd
Novi MI 48377
248 319-7333

Norton
Summit County

(G-15417)
BARBERTON TREE SERVICE INC
3307 Clark Mill Rd (44203-1027)
PHONE..................................330 848-2344
Keith Luck, *President*
EMP: 50 **EST:** 1978
SQ FT: 5,000
SALES (est): 7MM **Privately Held**
WEB: www.barbertontree.com
SIC: 0783 Pruning services, ornamental tree; removal services, bush & tree; surgery services, ornamental tree

(G-15418)
COMPASS SYSTEMS & SALES LLC
5185 New Haven Cir (44203-4672)
PHONE..................................330 733-2111
Robert S Sherrod, *President*
Mark Rubin, *Vice Pres*
Brenda Pavlantos, *Treasurer*
Phil Hart, *Admin Sec*
▼ **EMP:** 56
SQ FT: 43,500
SALES (est): 14.6MM **Privately Held**
SIC: 3542 0724 Mechanical (pneumatic or hydraulic) metal forming machines; cotton ginning

(G-15419)
DRIVERS ON CALL LLC
1263 Norton Ave (44203-6528)
PHONE..................................330 867-5193
Andrew W McPherson, *President*
Michael Cyc, *CFO*
EMP: 129 **EST:** 2011
SQ FT: 2,200
SALES: 3MM **Privately Held**
SIC: 4212 Moving services

(G-15420)
NARAGON COMPANIES INC
2197 Wadsworth Rd (44203-5328)
PHONE..................................330 745-7700
Michael Naragon, *President*
Jeff Naragon, *Vice Pres*
EMP: 30
SQ FT: 1,780
SALES (est): 5.1MM **Privately Held**
SIC: 1711 5261 Irrigation sprinkler system installation; hydroponic equipment & supplies

(G-15421)
NELSEN CORPORATION (PA)
3250 Barber Rd (44203-1012)
P.O. Box 1028 (44203-9428)
PHONE..................................330 745-6000
Ronald E Nelsen, *CEO*
David Nelsen, *President*
Jeanette Nelsen, *Corp Secy*
Kim Bell, *Vice Pres*
◆ **EMP:** 50
SQ FT: 33,000
SALES (est): 34.1MM **Privately Held**
WEB: www.nelsencorp.com
SIC: 5084 Pumps & pumping equipment

(G-15422)
ROMASTER CORP
3013 Wadsworth Rd (44203-5310)
PHONE..................................330 825-1945
Valentin Roman, *President*
EMP: 65
SALES (est): 1.7MM **Privately Held**
SIC: 7349 Janitorial service, contract basis

(G-15423)
WILLIAMS CONCRETE CNSTR CO INC
2959 Barber Rd Ste 100 (44203-1005)
PHONE..................................330 745-6388
Nancy C Williams, *President*

EMP: 36
SQ FT: 4,000
SALES (est): 4.4MM **Privately Held**
SIC: 1771 Concrete pumping

Norwalk
Huron County

(G-15424)
ADVANCED CMPT CONNECTIONS LLC
Also Called: Wireless Connections
166 Milan Ave (44857-1146)
PHONE..................................419 668-4080
Michael Cowan, *President*
David Peterson, *Engineer*
Melinda Wiley, *Sales Dir*
John Staley, *Sales Engr*
Susan Sweeting, *Sales Staff*
EMP: 32
SQ FT: 28,000
SALES (est): 21MM **Privately Held**
WEB: www.acc-corp.net
SIC: 5045 4813 Computer peripheral equipment; computer software;

(G-15425)
BACKOFFICE ASSOCIATES LLC
16 Executive Dr Ste 200 (44857-2486)
PHONE..................................419 660-4600
Nick Woolaver, *Branch Mgr*
EMP: 65 **Privately Held**
SIC: 8742 Management consulting services
HQ: Backoffice Associates, Llc
75 Perseverance Way 201a
Hyannis MA 02601

(G-15426)
CITY OF NORWALK
Also Called: Street Deparment
42 Woodlawn Ave (44857-2257)
PHONE..................................419 663-6715
Richard Moore, *Superintendent*
EMP: 27
SQ FT: 1,224 **Privately Held**
SIC: 1611 9111 Highway & street paving contractor; mayors' offices
PA: City Of Norwalk
38 Whittlesey Ave
Norwalk OH 44857
419 663-6700

(G-15427)
CIVISTA BANK
16 Executive Dr (44857-2486)
P.O. Box 5016, Sandusky (44871-5016)
PHONE..................................419 744-3100
EMP: 35 **Publicly Held**
SIC: 6022 6021 State commercial banks; national commercial banks
HQ: Civista Bank
100 E Water St
Sandusky OH 44870
419 625-4121

(G-15428)
CLE TRANSPORTATION COMPANY
203 Republic St (44857-1157)
PHONE..................................567 805-4008
Igor Stankic, *President*
Daniela Stankic, *Vice Pres*
EMP: 62 **EST:** 2016
SALES (est): 8MM **Privately Held**
SIC: 4213 Trucking, except local

(G-15429)
CLI INCORPORATED
306 S Norwalk Rd W (44857-9529)
PHONE..................................419 668-8840
John Schwartz, *President*
EMP: 125 **EST:** 1976
SQ FT: 20,000
SALES (est): 2.2MM **Privately Held**
SIC: 8331 Sheltered workshop

(G-15430)
COUNSELING CENTER HURON COUNTY
Also Called: Fireland Hospital
292 Benedict Ave (44857-2374)
PHONE..................................419 663-3737

Bruce Kijowski, *Manager*
Renee Jerome, *Manager*
EMP: 31
SALES (est): 728.3K **Privately Held**
SIC: 8093 8322 Mental health clinic, outpatient; emergency social services

(G-15431)
COUNTY OF HURON
Also Called: Job and Family Services
185 Shady Lane Dr (44857-2397)
PHONE..................................419 668-8126
Jill Eversol Nolan, *Director*
EMP: 95
SQ FT: 25,000 **Privately Held**
WEB: www.huroncountyema.com
SIC: 8322 9111 7361 Public welfare center; children's aid society; county supervisors' & executives' offices; employment agencies
PA: County Of Huron
180 Milan Ave Ste 7
Norwalk OH 44857
419 668-3092

(G-15432)
COUNTY OF HURON
Also Called: Children Service Unit
185 Shady Lane Dr (44857-2397)
PHONE..................................419 663-5437
Judy Fegen, *Director*
EMP: 90 **Privately Held**
WEB: www.huroncountyema.com
SIC: 8322 9111 Child related social services; county supervisors' & executives' offices
PA: County Of Huron
180 Milan Ave Ste 7
Norwalk OH 44857
419 668-3092

(G-15433)
DURABLE CORPORATION
75 N Pleasant St (44857-1218)
P.O. Box 290 (44857-0290)
PHONE..................................800 537-1603
Jon M Anderson, *CEO*
Tom Secor, *President*
Marcia Norris, *Principal*
Cathy McGinn, *Human Res Mgr*
Kaci White, *Mktg Dir*
◆ **EMP:** 60
SQ FT: 3,000
SALES (est): 12.6MM **Privately Held**
WEB: www.durablecorp.com
SIC: 3069 2273 5013 Mats or matting, rubber; molded rubber products; rubber automotive products; mats & matting; bumpers

(G-15434)
ERIE HURON CAC HEADSTART INC
11 E League St (44857-1378)
PHONE..................................419 663-2623
Janice Alexander, *Director*
EMP: 25
SALES (est): 251.1K **Privately Held**
SIC: 8351 Child day care services

(G-15435)
FIRELANDS REGIONAL HEALTH SYS
Also Called: FireInds Cnsling Recovery Svcs
292 Benedict Ave (44857-2374)
PHONE..................................419 663-3737
Renee Gerome, *Manager*
EMP: 28
SALES (corp-wide): 280.7MM **Privately Held**
SIC: 8093 8322 Alcohol clinic, outpatient; emergency social services
PA: Firelands Regional Health System
1111 Hayes Ave
Sandusky OH 44870
419 557-7400

(G-15436)
FISHER-TITUS MEDICAL CENTER
368 Milan Ave Ste D (44857-3106)
PHONE..................................419 663-6464
Deborah Keith, *President*
EMP: 131

SALES (corp-wide): 138MM **Privately Held**
SIC: 8011 Medical centers
PA: Fisher-Titus Medical Center
272 Benedict Ave
Norwalk OH 44857
419 668-8101

(G-15437)
FISHER-TITUS MEDICAL CENTER
Also Called: Carriage House
175 Shady Lane Dr Off (44857-2387)
PHONE..................................419 668-4228
Terri William, *Administration*
EMP: 25
SALES (corp-wide): 138MM **Privately Held**
WEB: www.fisher-titus.com
SIC: 8052 Intermediate care facilities
PA: Fisher-Titus Medical Center
272 Benedict Ave
Norwalk OH 44857
419 668-8101

(G-15438)
FISHER-TITUS MEDICAL CENTER (PA)
272 Benedict Ave (44857-2374)
PHONE..................................419 668-8101
Robert Andrews, *Ch of Bd*
Virginia Poling, *Vice Ch Bd*
Patrick J Martin, *President*
Duane Woods, *Vice Pres*
John Payne, *Treasurer*
▲ **EMP:** 600
SQ FT: 83,000
SALES: 138MM **Privately Held**
WEB: www.fisher-titus.com
SIC: 8052 8062 Intermediate care facilities; general medical & surgical hospitals

(G-15439)
GAYMONT NURSING HOMES INC
Also Called: Gaymont Nursing Center
66 Norwood Ave (44857-2385)
PHONE..................................419 668-8258
William C Dotson, *President*
EMP: 95
SQ FT: 34,500
SALES (est): 6.6MM **Privately Held**
SIC: 8051 8052 Skilled Nursing Care Facility Intermediate Care Facility

(G-15440)
KAISER-WELLS INC
Also Called: Kaiser Wells Pharmacy
251 Benedict Ave (44857-2346)
PHONE..................................419 668-7651
John G Kaiser Jr, *President*
Donald A Baur, *Vice Pres*
Lisa R Nestor, *Vice Pres*
EMP: 30
SQ FT: 8,000
SALES (est): 5.9MM **Privately Held**
SIC: 5912 8082 Drug stores; home health care services

(G-15441)
LAKE ERIE CONSTRUCTION CO
25 S Norwalk Rd E (44857-9259)
P.O. Box 777 (44857-0777)
PHONE..................................419 668-3302
David P Bleile, *President*
Raymond Chapin, *Vice Pres*
Michael Bleile, *Treasurer*
Matt Chapin, *Supervisor*
Kenneth Bleile, *Admin Sec*
EMP: 200
SQ FT: 6,000
SALES (est): 31MM **Privately Held**
WEB: www.lec-co.com
SIC: 1611 Guardrail construction, highways; highway & street sign installation

(G-15442)
LAKE ERIE HOME REPAIR
257 Milan Ave (44857-1123)
PHONE..................................419 871-0687
John Jackson, *Principal*
Darell Williams, *Manager*
EMP: 25
SALES (est): 950K **Privately Held**
SIC: 1522 Residential construction

(G-15443)
MARK SCHAFFER EXCVTG TRCKG INC
1623 Old State Rd N (44857-9377)
PHONE..................................419 668-5990
Mark Schaffer, *President*
Mary Jo Moyer, *Vice Pres*
Cheri Perry, *Admin Sec*
Diane Schaffer, *Admin Sec*
EMP: 55
SQ FT: 100,000
SALES (est): 11.5MM **Privately Held**
SIC: 1794 1623 1795 Excavation & grading, building construction; water, sewer & utility lines; wrecking & demolition work

(G-15444)
MC FADDEN CONSTRUCTION INC
4426 Old State Rd N (44857-9139)
P.O. Box 463 (44857-0463)
PHONE..................................419 668-4165
Marvin Smith, *President*
Michael F McFadden, *Superintendent*
Neil E McFadden, *Principal*
EMP: 30
SALES (est): 1.3MM **Privately Held**
SIC: 1799 Exterior cleaning, including sandblasting

(G-15445)
NEWCOMER CONCRETE SERVICES INC (PA)
646 Townline Road 151 (44857-9255)
P.O. Box 672 (44857-0672)
PHONE..................................419 668-2789
Jeffery Newcomer, *CEO*
David Newcomer, *CFO*
Linda Newcomer Holmer, *Admin Sec*
EMP: 64
SQ FT: 13,000
SALES (est): 9.2MM **Privately Held**
WEB: www.newcomerconcrete.com
SIC: 1771 1794 Concrete pumping; excavation & grading, building construction

(G-15446)
NORTHERN OHIO RURAL WATER
2205 Us Highway 20 E (44857-9521)
P.O. Box 96, Collins (44826-0096)
PHONE..................................419 668-7213
Thomas Reese, *Director*
EMP: 35
SALES (est): 6.7MM **Privately Held**
SIC: 4941 Water supply

(G-15447)
NORWALK AREA HEALTH SERVICES (HQ)
272 Benedict Ave (44857-2374)
PHONE..................................419 668-8101
Patrick Martin, *President*
Paul Douglas, *VP Finance*
Jason Smith,
EMP: 150
SALES: 7.5MM
SALES (corp-wide): 1.5MM **Privately Held**
SIC: 4119 Ambulance service
PA: Norwalk Area Health Systems, Inc.
272 Benedict Ave
Norwalk OH 44857
419 668-8101

(G-15448)
NORWALK AREA HLTH SYSTEMS INC (PA)
272 Benedict Ave (44857-2374)
PHONE..................................419 668-8101
Patrick J Martin, *President*
EMP: 800
SQ FT: 200,000
SALES: 1.5MM **Privately Held**
WEB: www.ftmc.com
SIC: 8062 8051 General medical & surgical hospitals; skilled nursing care facilities

(G-15449)
NORWALK CLINIC INC
257 Benedict Ave Ste C1 (44857-2391)
PHONE..................................419 668-4851
James A Gottfried, *President*
EMP: 30 EST: 1962

SQ FT: 4,000
SALES (est): 2.1MM **Privately Held**
SIC: 8011 Clinic, operated by physicians

(G-15450)
NORWALK GOLF PROPERTIES INC
Also Called: Eagle Creek Golf Club
2406 New State Rd (44857-7100)
PHONE..................................419 668-8535
Robert Bleile, *President*
Marc Schaffer, *Vice Pres*
Gary Wilkins, *Treasurer*
Ken Bleile, *Admin Sec*
EMP: 30
SQ FT: 100
SALES (est): 1.4MM **Privately Held**
WEB: www.eaglecreekgolf.com
SIC: 7992 6514 Public golf courses; dwelling operators, except apartments

(G-15451)
PALAZZO BROTHERS ELECTRIC INC
2811 State Route 18 (44857-8829)
PHONE..................................419 668-1100
Joseph M Palazzo, *President*
Doug Stang, *Opers Mgr*
EMP: 32
SQ FT: 2,674
SALES (est): 7.4MM **Privately Held**
SIC: 1731 1799 General electrical contractor; sign installation & maintenance

(G-15452)
PAYNE NICKLES & CO CPA (PA)
Also Called: Furlong, Lawrence P CPA
257 Benedict Ave Ste D (44857-2715)
PHONE..................................419 668-2552
Carl McGookey, *President*
John Payne, *President*
Dave Brink, *Vice Pres*
Ennis Camp, *Vice Pres*
Allen Nickles, *Vice Pres*
EMP: 28
SALES (est): 4MM **Privately Held**
SIC: 8721 Certified public accountant

(G-15453)
R & L TRANSFER INC
Also Called: R & L Carriers
1403 State Route 18 (44857-9519)
PHONE..................................216 531-3324
Chris Viock, *Branch Mgr*
EMP: 225 **Privately Held**
WEB: www.robertsarena.com
SIC: 4213 4212 Trucking, except local; local trucking, without storage
HQ: R & L Transfer, Inc.
600 Gilliam Rd
Wilmington OH 45177
937 382-1494

(G-15454)
RENAISSANCE HOUSE INC
48 Executive Dr Ste 1 (44857-2492)
PHONE..................................419 663-1316
Joan Tommas, *Manager*
EMP: 35
SALES (corp-wide): 4MM **Privately Held**
WEB: www.renaissancehouseinc.com
SIC: 8361 Home for the mentally retarded
PA: Renaissance House Inc
103 N Washington St
Tiffin OH 44883
419 447-7901

(G-15455)
RON JOHNSON PLUMBING AND HTG
14805 Shawmill Rd (44857-9633)
PHONE..................................419 433-5365
Sandra S Johnson, *President*
Scott Johnson, *Corp Secy*
EMP: 25
SQ FT: 22,000
SALES (est): 3.1MM **Privately Held**
WEB: www.johnsonphe.com
SIC: 1711 Plumbing contractors; warm air heating & air conditioning contractor

(G-15456)
STEIN HOSPICE SERVICES INC
150 Milan Ave (44857-2620)
PHONE..................................419 663-3222

Annabelle Stewart, *Manager*
EMP: 89
SALES (corp-wide): 28.8MM **Privately Held**
SIC: 8069 8052 Chronic disease hospital; personal care facility
PA: Stein Hospice Services, Inc.
1200 Sycamore Line
Sandusky OH 44870
800 625-5269

(G-15457)
THE MAPLE CITY ICE COMPANY (PA)
371 Cleveland Rd (44857-9027)
PHONE..................................419 668-2531
Patricia Hipp, *President*
John Hipp, *Vice Pres*
Jeff Hipp, *Treasurer*
Joel Hipp, *Sales Executive*
Gerard Hipp, *Admin Sec*
EMP: 41
SQ FT: 57,000
SALES (est): 26.9MM **Privately Held**
SIC: 5181 Beer & other fermented malt liquors

(G-15458)
TWILIGHT GARDENS HEALTHCARE
Also Called: TWILIGHT GARDENS HOME
196 W Main St (44857-1915)
PHONE..................................419 668-2086
George S Repchick, *President*
William I Weisberg, *Vice Pres*
Sarah Depompei, *Assistant*
EMP: 40
SQ FT: 5,500
SALES: 5.2MM
SALES (corp-wide): 157.7MM **Privately Held**
SIC: 8051 8052 Skilled nursing care facilities; intermediate care facilities
PA: Saber Healthcare Group, L.L.C.
26691 Richmond Rd Frnt
Bedford OH 44146
216 292-5706

(G-15459)
WASINIAK CONSTRUCTION INC
2519 State Route 61 (44857-9181)
PHONE..................................419 668-8624
John Wasiniak, *President*
James Wasiniak, *Vice Pres*
Edward Will, *Vice Pres*
EMP: 60
SQ FT: 1,000
SALES (est): 6.8MM **Privately Held**
SIC: 1741 1771 Masonry & other stonework; concrete work

(G-15460)
ZEITER TRUCKING INC
Also Called: Zeiter Leasing
2590 State Route 18 (44857-8831)
PHONE..................................419 668-2229
Richard D Zeiter, *President*
Mark Zeiter, *Vice Pres*
Steven Zeiter, *Vice Pres*
Kim Zieter, *Admin Sec*
EMP: 45 EST: 1963
SALES: 6MM **Privately Held**
SIC: 4212 Dump truck haulage

Norwood
Hamilton County

(G-15461)
CUSHMAN & WAKEFIELD INC
Also Called: Cassidy Turley
4600 Montgomery Rd (45212-2697)
PHONE..................................513 631-1121
EMP: 44
SALES (corp-wide): 1.2MM **Privately Held**
SIC: 6531 Real estate agents & managers
HQ: Cushman & Wakefield, Inc.
225 W Wacker Dr Ste 3000
Chicago IL 60606
312 424-8000

(G-15462)
EMD MILLIPORE CORPORATION
2909 Highland Ave (45212-2411)
PHONE..................................513 631-0445
Michael Mulligan, *Vice Pres*
Daryl Hayslip, *Info Tech Dir*
Sandra Heyob, *Associate*
EMP: 150
SQ FT: 100,000
SALES (corp-wide): 16.9B **Privately Held**
WEB: www.emdchemicals.com
SIC: 8731 3295 2899 2842 Biotechnical research, commercial; minerals, ground or treated; chemical preparations; specialty cleaning, polishes & sanitation goods; biological products, except diagnostic
HQ: Emd Millipore Corporation
400 Summit Dr
Burlington MA 01803
781 533-6000

(G-15463)
TEXO INTERNATIONAL INC
2828 Highland Ave (45212-2410)
PHONE..................................513 731-6350
Robert W Fisher, *President*
Craig Berkhart, *Principal*
Michael A Fisher, *Exec VP*
Marc D Fisher, *Treasurer*
EMP: 80
SALES (est): 7.8MM **Privately Held**
SIC: 5169 Specialty cleaning & sanitation preparations

Novelty
Geauga County

(G-15464)
ASM INTERNATIONAL
9639 Kinsman Rd (44073-0002)
PHONE..................................440 338-5151
Thomas Dudley, *CEO*
William Mahoney, *Managing Dir*
Amy Nolan, *Editor*
Joanne Miller, *Prdtn Mgr*
Veronica Becker, *Controller*
▲ EMP: 80
SQ FT: 55,000
SALES: 8.3MM **Privately Held**
WEB: www.aeromat.com
SIC: 2731 2721 7389 7999 Books: publishing only; periodicals: publishing only; advertising, promotional & trade show services; promoters of shows & exhibitions; trade show arrangement; exhibition operation

(G-15465)
O C I CONSTRUCTION CO INC
8560 Pekin Rd (44072-9717)
PHONE..................................440 338-3166
Robert Wantz, *President*
Daniel Wantz, *Vice Pres*
EMP: 30
SQ FT: 3,000
SALES (est): 4.6MM **Privately Held**
SIC: 1623 Telephone & communication line construction

(G-15466)
PATTIE GROUP INC (PA)
Also Called: Pattie's Landscaping
15533 Chillicothe Rd (44072-9646)
PHONE..................................440 338-1288
Steve Pattie, *President*
Mike Kramer, *Project Dir*
Danielle Beausoleil, *Project Mgr*
Randy Collins, *Project Mgr*
William Pattie, *Treasurer*
EMP: 95
SQ FT: 2,000
SALES (est): 13.9MM **Privately Held**
WEB: www.pattiegroup.com
SIC: 0781 Landscape services

(G-15467)
WIEGANDS LAKE PARK INC
9390 Kinsman Rd (44072-9633)
PHONE..................................440 338-5795
William B Frantz, *President*
Wendy Wiegand, *Vice Pres*
EMP: 45

GEOGRAPHIC

SALES (est): 1MM **Privately Held**
WEB: www.wiegandslakepark.com
SIC: 7999 7389 Picnic ground operation; convention & show services

Oak Harbor
Ottawa County

(G-15468)
BENTON-CARROLL-SALEM
Also Called: Benton School Bus Garage
601 N Benton St (43449-1009)
PHONE..............................419 898-6214
Ginger Staymancho, *Principal*
EMP: 30
SALES (corp-wide): 15.9MM **Privately Held**
SIC: 4151 School buses
PA: Benton Carroll Salem Local School District
11685 W State Route 163
Oak Harbor OH 43449
419 898-6210

(G-15469)
COUNTY OF OTTAWA
275 N Toussaint South Rd (43449-9086)
PHONE..............................419 898-7433
Bill Lowe, *Director*
EMP: 37 **Privately Held**
WEB: www.ottawacocpcourt.com
SIC: 4119 9111 Local passenger transportation; county supervisors' & executives' offices
PA: County Of Ottawa
315 Madison St Ste 201
Port Clinton OH 43452
419 734-6700

(G-15470)
COUNTY OF OTTAWA
Also Called: Ottawa Cnty Sr Healthcare
8180 W State Route 163 (43449-8855)
PHONE..............................419 898-6459
Cara Densic, *Manager*
Lisa Barrett, *Director*
Lisa Dobbelare, *Nursing Dir*
John Ambrosecchia, *Administration*
Beth Greer, *Admin Asst*
EMP: 200
SQ FT: 20,000 **Privately Held**
WEB: www.ottawacocpcourt.com
SIC: 8051 9111 8111 Convalescent home with continuous nursing care; county supervisors' & executives' offices; general practice attorney, lawyer
PA: County Of Ottawa
315 Madison St Ste 201
Port Clinton OH 43452
419 734-6700

(G-15471)
COUNTY OF OTTAWA
Also Called: Ottawa County Dept Human Svcs
8444 W State Route 163 # 102 (43449-8884)
PHONE..............................419 898-2089
Jim Adkins, *Manager*
Juan Cortez, *Web Proj Mgr*
Doris James, *Director*
EMP: 50 **Privately Held**
WEB: www.ottawacocpcourt.com
SIC: 8322 9111 8111 Individual & family services; county supervisors' & executives' offices; general practice attorney, lawyer
PA: County Of Ottawa
315 Madison St Ste 201
Port Clinton OH 43452
419 734-6700

(G-15472)
FIRSTENERGY CORP
5501 N State Route 2 (43449-9752)
PHONE..............................419 321-7114
Anthony J Alexander, *President*
Angie Ayres, *General Mgr*
Alex Garza, *Opers Mgr*
Paul West, *Maint Spvr*
Steven Osting, *Engineer*
EMP: 37
SALES (est): 16MM **Privately Held**
SIC: 4911 Electric services

(G-15473)
JERSEY CENTRAL PWR & LIGHT CO
Also Called: Firstenergy
5501 N State Route 2 (43449-9752)
PHONE..............................419 321-7207
Howard Bergendahl, *Manager*
EMP: 35 **Publicly Held**
WEB: www.jersey-central-power-light.monmouth.n
SIC: 7629 Telecommunication equipment repair (except telephones)
HQ: Jersey Central Power & Light Company
76 S Main St
Akron OH 44308
800 736-3402

(G-15474)
MID COUNTY EMS
222 W Washington St (43449-1148)
P.O. Box 88 (43449-0088)
PHONE..............................419 898-9366
Marcia Eehlmer, *Chief*
EMP: 30
SALES (est): 608.9K **Privately Held**
SIC: 4119 Ambulance service

(G-15475)
OAK HARBOR LIONS CLUB
101 S Brookside Dr (43449-1276)
P.O. Box 144 (43449-0144)
PHONE..............................419 898-3828
EMP: 34
SALES: 17.1K **Privately Held**
SIC: 8611 Business Association

(G-15476)
OTTAWA COUNTY BOARD M R D D
Also Called: Services & Support ADM
235 N Toussaint St (43449)
PHONE..............................419 734-6650
Melinda Felusser, *Director*
EMP: 50
SQ FT: 5,000
SALES (est): 1.2MM **Privately Held**
SIC: 8322 Social services for the handicapped

(G-15477)
OTTAWA COUNTY TRANSIT BOARD
275 N Toussaint South Rd (43449-9086)
PHONE..............................419 898-7433
Laurie Cleaver, *Manager*
Bill Lowe, *Exec Dir*
EMP: 29
SALES: 950K **Privately Held**
SIC: 4173 Bus terminal & service facilities

(G-15478)
RIVERVIEW INDUSTRIES INC
8380 W State Route 163 (43449-8859)
PHONE..............................419 898-5250
Brenda Smith, *Director*
EMP: 180
SALES: 3.5MM **Privately Held**
SIC: 8331 Manpower training

(G-15479)
TOLEDO EDISON COMPANY
Also Called: Davis Beese Nuclear Power Stn
5501 N State Route 2 (43449-9752)
PHONE..............................419 321-8488
Jon Hook, *Engineer*
James J Powers, *Engineer*
Connie Moore, *Supervisor*
EMP: 50 **Publicly Held**
SIC: 4911 Generation, electric power
HQ: The Toledo Edison Company
76 S Main St Bsmt
Akron OH 44308
800 447-3333

Oak Hill
Jackson County

(G-15480)
H & H RETREADING INC
5400 State Route 93 (45656-9361)
P.O. Box 236 (45656-0236)
PHONE..............................740 682-7721
Noah Hickman, *President*
Joel Hickman Jr, *Corp Secy*
EMP: 74 EST: 1970
SQ FT: 2,000
SALES (est): 4.2MM **Privately Held**
SIC: 7534 Tire recapping

(G-15481)
LEGRAND SERVICES INC
Also Called: Fantastic Sams
230 W Hill St (45656-1012)
PHONE..............................740 682-6046
Don Legrand, *President*
EMP: 42
SALES (est): 655.3K **Privately Held**
SIC: 7231 Unisex hair salons

Oakwood
Montgomery County

(G-15482)
KUNESH EYE CENTER INC
Also Called: Oakwood Optical
2601 Far Hills Ave Ste 2 (45419-1634)
PHONE..............................937 298-1703
Kristine K Part MD, *President*
Kristine Kunesh-Part MD, *President*
Michael T Kunesh, *Vice Pres*
John Kunesh, *Admin Sec*
Lucy Helmers, *Administration*
EMP: 35
SALES (est): 5.1MM **Privately Held**
SIC: 8011 Ophthalmologist

Oakwood
Paulding County

(G-15483)
COOPER HATCHERY INC (PA)
Also Called: Cooper Farms
22348 Road 140 (45873)
PHONE..............................419 594-3325
James R Cooper, *President*
Gary A Cooper, *COO*
Emily Smith, *COO*
Neil Diller, *Vice Pres*
Janice Fiely, *CFO*
EMP: 225 EST: 1934
SQ FT: 47,000
SALES (est): 256.7MM **Privately Held**
WEB: www.cooperfarm.com
SIC: 0254 0253 2015 5153 Poultry hatcheries; turkey farm; turkey, processed; grains; prepared feeds

(G-15484)
STONECO INC
13762 Road 179 (45873-9012)
PHONE..............................419 393-2555
Rick Welch, *Superintendent*
EMP: 25
SALES (corp-wide): 29.7B **Privately Held**
WEB: www.stoneco.net
SIC: 1422 2951 Crushed & broken limestone; asphalt paving mixtures & blocks
HQ: Stoneco, Inc.
1700 Fostoria Ave Ste 200
Findlay OH 45840
419 422-8854

Oakwood Village
Cuyahoga County

(G-15485)
AIRGAS USA LLC
7600 Oak Leaf Rd (44146-5554)
PHONE..............................440 786-2864
John Mazzola, *Branch Mgr*
EMP: 100
SALES (corp-wide): 125.9MM **Privately Held**
WEB: www.us.linde-gas.com
SIC: 5169 Industrial gases
HQ: Airgas Usa, Llc
259 N Radnor Chester Rd # 100
Radnor PA 19087
610 687-5253

(G-15486)
BRIGHTVIEW LANDSCAPES LLC
25072 Broadway Ave (44146-6309)
PHONE..............................216 398-1289
Brad McBride, *Branch Mgr*
EMP: 38
SALES (corp-wide): 2.8B **Publicly Held**
SIC: 0781 Landscape services
HQ: Brightview Landscapes, Llc
401 Plymouth Rd Ste 500
Plymouth Meeting PA 19462
484 567-7204

(G-15487)
BUILDING INTEGRATED SVCS LLC
7777 First Pl (44146-6733)
PHONE..............................330 733-9191
Scott K Jordan,
EMP: 60
SALES (est): 1.4MM **Privately Held**
SIC: 1711 Plumbing, heating, air-conditioning contractors

(G-15488)
CRYSTAL CLEAR BLDG SVCS INC
26118 Broadway Ave Ste B (44146-6530)
PHONE..............................440 439-2288
Jim Lesko, *President*
Stephen M Lesko, *Principal*
EMP: 90 EST: 1997
SALES (est): 3.2MM **Privately Held**
SIC: 7349 Janitorial service, contract basis

(G-15489)
FLOWERLAND GARDEN CENTERS (PA)
Also Called: Petitti Garden Centers
25018 Broadway Ave (44146-6309)
PHONE..............................440 439-8636
Angelo Petitti, *President*
▲ EMP: 26
SALES (est): 30MM **Privately Held**
SIC: 5193 Flowers & florists' supplies

(G-15490)
MEDICAL SPECIALTIES DISTRS LLC
26350 Broadway Ave (44146-6517)
PHONE..............................440 232-0320
Carl Farago, *Branch Mgr*
EMP: 37
SALES (corp-wide): 208.3B **Publicly Held**
WEB: www.msdistributors.com
SIC: 7352 Medical equipment rental
HQ: Medical Specialties Distributors, Llc
800 Technology Center Dr # 3
Stoughton MA 02072
781 344-6000

(G-15491)
MID-CONTINENT CONSTRUCTION CO
7235 Free Ave Ste A (44146-5461)
PHONE..............................440 439-6100
Thomas McDonald, *CEO*
Darryl Wilkins, *CEO*
William Schmid, *Vice Pres*
Chad Jurisch, *Vice Pres*
Ray Krankowski, *Vice Pres*
EMP: 25
SQ FT: 8,000
SALES (est): 6.3MM **Privately Held**
SIC: 1542 1541 Commercial & office building, new construction; industrial buildings, new construction

(G-15492)
PERFORMANCE PAINTING LLC
7603 First Pl (44146-6703)
PHONE..................................440 735-3340
Keith Donaldson,
Tim Wilson,
EMP: 25
SALES (est): 1.2MM **Privately Held**
SIC: 1721 Painting & paper hanging

(G-15493)
ROCK HOUSE ENTRMT GROUP INC
7809 First Pl (44146-6707)
PHONE..................................440 232-7625
Matt Radicelli, *President*
▲ EMP: 120
SALES (est): 732K **Privately Held**
WEB: www.rockthehousedj.net
SIC: 7929 Disc jockey service; entertainment service

(G-15494)
SWIFT FILTERS INC (PA)
24040 Forbes Rd (44146-5650)
PHONE..................................440 735-0995
Edwin C Swift Jr, *President*
Charles C Swift, *Vice Pres*
Michelle Pacino, *Purchasing*
Cheryl Segulin, *Info Tech Mgr*
EMP: 38
SQ FT: 6,000
SALES (est): 6.9MM **Privately Held**
WEB: www.swiftfilters.com
SIC: 3569 5075 Filters; air filters

(G-15495)
THERMO FISHER SCIENTIFIC INC
Also Called: Remel Products
1 Thermo Fisher Way (44146-6536)
PHONE..................................800 871-8909
Debra Dicillo, *Manager*
EMP: 150
SALES (corp-wide): 24.3B **Publicly Held**
SIC: 5047 2835 3841 Diagnostic equipment, medical; in vitro & in vivo diagnostic substances; surgical & medical instruments
PA: Thermo Fisher Scientific Inc.
168 3rd Ave
Waltham MA 02451
781 622-1000

(G-15496)
VIEWRAY TECHNOLOGIES INC
2 Thermo Fisher Way (44146-6536)
PHONE..................................440 703-3210
Scott Drake, *President*
Chris A Raanes, *President*
Shar Matin, *COO*
Peter Sullivan, *Exec VP*
Robert Bea, *Senior VP*
▲ EMP: 70
SALES: 80.9MM **Privately Held**
SIC: 3845 5047 Electromedical equipment; therapy equipment

Oberlin
Lorain County

(G-15497)
AGRINOMIX LLC
300 Creekside Dr (44074-1272)
PHONE..................................440 774-2981
Joe Smith, *VP Mfg*
George Andulics, *Engineer*
Neil Mabrouk, *Engineer*
Mary Haber, *Human Res Mgr*
Mike Herring, *Sales Staff*
▲ EMP: 36
SQ FT: 74,800
SALES: 14MM **Privately Held**
WEB: www.agrinomix.com
SIC: 5083 5084 Planting machinery & equipment; materials handling machinery

(G-15498)
ALLIED WASTE INDUSTRIES LLC
Also Called: Site R24
43502 Oberlin Elyria Rd (44074-9591)
PHONE..................................440 774-3100
David Matthews, *General Mgr*
EMP: 30
SALES (corp-wide): 10B **Publicly Held**
SIC: 4953 Recycling, waste materials; sanitary landfill operation
HQ: Allied Waste Industries, Llc
18500 N Allied Way # 100
Phoenix AZ 85054
480 627-2700

(G-15499)
CITY OF OBERLIN (PA)
Also Called: OBERLIN MUNICIPAL LIGHT & POWE
85 S Main St (44074-1603)
PHONE..................................440 775-1531
Ron Rimbert, *President*
Eric Norenberg, *Principal*
Sharon Soucy, *Vice Pres*
Rob Disperdo, *Manager*
EMP: 47
SQ FT: 10,000 **Privately Held**
WEB: www.oberlinpd.com
SIC: 9111 8611 City & town managers' offices; ; business associations

(G-15500)
CUSTOM CLEANING SERVICE LLC
305 Artino St Unit A (44074-1277)
PHONE..................................440 774-1222
Stacy Fenderson,
EMP: 46
SALES (est): 936.1K **Privately Held**
SIC: 7349 Janitorial service, contract basis

(G-15501)
DOVIN DAIRY FARMS LLC
Also Called: Dovin Land Company
15967 State Route 58 (44074-9581)
PHONE..................................440 653-7000
Billie Jo Dovin, *Mng Member*
John M Dovin,
Lisa Gilbert,
EMP: 28
SALES (est): 5.3MM **Privately Held**
SIC: 0241 Milk production

(G-15502)
EXPRESS SEED COMPANY
51051 Us Highway 20 (44074-1253)
PHONE..................................440 774-2259
John Van Wingerden, *Owner*
Dawn Van Wingerden, *Admin Sec*
▲ EMP: 60 EST: 1982
SQ FT: 30,000
SALES (est): 11.9MM **Privately Held**
SIC: 5193 5191 Plants, potted; flower & field bulbs

(G-15503)
GREEN CIRCLE GROWERS INC (PA)
51051 Us Highway 20 (44074-9637)
PHONE..................................440 775-1411
John Van Wingerden, *President*
Dawn Van Wingerden, *Vice Pres*
Dan Reed, *Opers Mgr*
Bob Shepherd, *Purch Mgr*
Norman Daxter, *CFO*
◆ EMP: 125 EST: 1972
SQ FT: 2,500
SALES (est): 107.1MM **Privately Held**
WEB: www.greencirclehome.com
SIC: 0181 Flowers: grown under cover (e.g. greenhouse production); plants, potted: growing of

(G-15504)
GREEN CIRCLE GROWERS INC
15650 State Route 511 (44074-9699)
PHONE..................................440 775-1411
Van Wingerden John, *Branch Mgr*
Mark Sheldon, *Maintence Staff*
EMP: 475

SALES (corp-wide): 107.1MM **Privately Held**
SIC: 0181 Flowers: grown under cover (e.g. greenhouse production); plants, potted: growing of
PA: Green Circle Growers, Inc.
51051 Us Highway 20
Oberlin OH 44074
440 775-1411

(G-15505)
INDICO LLC (HQ)
528 E Lorain St (44074-1238)
PHONE..................................440 775-7777
Rene Yang, *Vice Pres*
Terry Schubert, *Purchasing*
Frank Sulen, *VP Finance*
Kathy Schwartzer, *Finance*
Dawn Glow, *Sales Staff*
EMP: 85
SQ FT: 162,000
SALES (est): 14.5MM
SALES (corp-wide): 30MM **Privately Held**
WEB: www.nacscorp.com
SIC: 5045 5192 Computer software; books
PA: National Association Of College Stores, Inc.
500 E Lorain St
Oberlin OH 44074
440 775-7777

(G-15506)
KENDAL AT OBERLIN
600 Kendal Dr (44074-1900)
PHONE..................................440 775-0094
Barbara Thomas, *CEO*
George Bent, *President*
Ryan Stalzkowski, *Opers Staff*
Rebecca Butler, *Human Resources*
Teresa Maynard, *Office Mgr*
EMP: 222
SALES: 22.5MM **Privately Held**
WEB: www.kao.kendal.org
SIC: 8051 8052 Skilled nursing care facilities; intermediate care facilities

(G-15507)
LOCKES GARDEN CENTER INC
461 E Lorain St (44074-1217)
PHONE..................................440 774-6981
Charles H Annable, *President*
EMP: 46
SQ FT: 5,000
SALES: 250K **Privately Held**
SIC: 0782 5261 Landscape contractors; nurseries

(G-15508)
MCCONNELL EXCAVATING LTD
15804 State Route 58 (44074-9580)
PHONE..................................440 774-4578
Eric McConnell, *General Ptnr*
EMP: 47
SALES (est): 13.7MM **Privately Held**
SIC: 1794 7389 Excavation & grading, building construction;

(G-15509)
MERCY HEALTH
319 W Lorain St (44074-1027)
PHONE..................................440 775-1881
EMP: 33
SALES (corp-wide): 4.7B **Privately Held**
SIC: 8011 Offices & clinics of medical doctors
PA: Mercy Health
1701 Mercy Health Pl
Cincinnati OH 45237
513 639-2800

(G-15510)
MERCY HEALTH
200 W Lorain St (44074-1026)
PHONE..................................440 775-1211
EMP: 37
SALES (corp-wide): 4.7B **Privately Held**
SIC: 4119 Ambulance service
PA: Mercy Health
1701 Mercy Health Pl
Cincinnati OH 45237
513 639-2800

(G-15511)
MERCY HEALTH
Also Called: Mercy Allen Hospital
200 W Lorain St (44074-1026)
PHONE..................................440 774-6800
EMP: 91
SALES (corp-wide): 4.7B **Privately Held**
SIC: 8062 General medical & surgical hospitals
PA: Mercy Health
1701 Mercy Health Pl
Cincinnati OH 45237
513 639-2800

(G-15512)
OBERLIN CLINIC INC
224 W Lorain St Ste P (44074-1042)
PHONE..................................440 774-7337
Toll Free:..................................866 -
Jim Schaum, *President*
Donna Moyers, *Admin Sec*
EMP: 150
SQ FT: 24,000
SALES (est): 5.4MM **Privately Held**
SIC: 8011 Clinic, operated by physicians

(G-15513)
OBERLIN COLLEGE
Also Called: Oberlin College Recreation Ctr
200 Woodland St (44074-1051)
PHONE..................................440 775-8519
Timothy Elgren, *Dean*
Betsy Bruce, *Manager*
EMP: 125
SALES (corp-wide): 185.5MM **Privately Held**
WEB: www.oberlin.edu
SIC: 8221 7997 7999 College, except junior; membership sports & recreation clubs; recreation center
PA: Oberlin College
173 W Lorain St
Oberlin OH 44074
440 775-8121

(G-15514)
OBERLIN COLLEGE
Also Called: Athletic Dept
200 Woodland St (44074-1051)
PHONE..................................440 775-8500
Clif Barnes, *Safety Dir*
Richard Wood, *Facilities Mgr*
Calvin Frye, *IT/INT Sup*
Victor Lananna, *Director*
Kirk Warren, *Technician*
EMP: 41
SALES (corp-wide): 185.5MM **Privately Held**
WEB: www.oberlin.edu
SIC: 8221 8699 University; athletic organizations
PA: Oberlin College
173 W Lorain St
Oberlin OH 44074
440 775-8121

(G-15515)
OBERLIN COLLEGE
Also Called: Oberlin Inn
10 E College St (44074-1613)
PHONE..................................440 935-1475
William Barlow, *Vice Pres*
Rex Angle, *Manager*
Pam Snyder, *Director*
EMP: 75
SALES (corp-wide): 185.5MM **Privately Held**
WEB: www.oberlin.edu
SIC: 5812 7011 American restaurant; hotels
PA: Oberlin College
173 W Lorain St
Oberlin OH 44074
440 775-8121

(G-15516)
OBERLIN EARLY CHILDHOOD CENTER
317 E College St (44074-1316)
PHONE..................................440 774-8193
Debbie Marvin, *Exec Dir*
Nancy Sabath, *Director*
EMP: 30
SQ FT: 16,000
SALES: 977.6K **Privately Held**
SIC: 8351 Group day care center

(G-15517)
PHYSICIANS IN FAMILY PRACTICE
319 W Lorain St (44074-1027)
PHONE...................................440 775-1881
John M Jonesco, *President*
Jane Jonesco, *Vice Pres*
EMP: 25
SQ FT: 1,800
SALES (est): 858.2K **Privately Held**
SIC: 8031 8011 Offices & clinics of osteopathic physicians; offices & clinics of medical doctors

(G-15518)
REPUBLIC SERVICES INC
Also Called: Lorain County Landfill
43502 Oberlin Elyria Rd (44074-9591)
PHONE...................................440 774-4060
EMP: 34
SALES (corp-wide): 10B **Publicly Held**
SIC: 4953 Refuse collection & disposal services
PA: Republic Services, Inc.
18500 N Allied Way # 100
Phoenix AZ 85054
480 627-2700

(G-15519)
RIDGE MURRAY PROD CTR OBERLIN
285 Artino St (44074-1207)
PHONE...................................440 774-7400
David Blevins, *Marketing Staff*
Edgar Barnett, *Director*
EMP: 39
SALES (est): 1.7MM **Privately Held**
SIC: 8051 8331 Mental retardation hospital; job training & vocational rehabilitation services

(G-15520)
SUPERS LANDSCAPING INC
48211 State Route 511 (44074-9205)
PHONE...................................440 775-0027
Greg Supers, *Exec VP*
EMP: 30
SQ FT: 10,000
SALES (est): 800K **Privately Held**
WEB: www.superslandscape.com
SIC: 0782 4959 5261 7699 Landscape contractors; lawn services; snowplowing; lawn & garden equipment; lawn mower repair shop

(G-15521)
WESSELL GENERATIONS INC
Also Called: Welcome Nursing Home
417 S Main St (44074-1749)
PHONE...................................440 775-1491
Jill Herron, *President*
Heidi Freas, *Vice Pres*
Connie Haswell, *Hlthcr Dir*
Kelly Wessell, *Admin Sec*
Meghan Wessell, *Asst Sec*
EMP: 140
SQ FT: 40,766
SALES (est): 8.4MM **Privately Held**
SIC: 8051 Convalescent home with continuous nursing care

Obetz
Franklin County

(G-15522)
AUCTION SERVICES INC
4700 Groveport Rd (43207-5217)
PHONE...................................614 497-2000
Alexis A Jacobs, *President*
Brett Vanmeter, *Principal*
Leslie Ivery, *Human Res Mgr*
Cicly Sellers, *Administration*
EMP: 700
SQ FT: 60,000
SALES: 64.7K **Privately Held**
SIC: 7389 Auctioneers, fee basis

(G-15523)
CAPITOL CITY TRAILERS INC
3960 Groveport Rd (43207-5127)
PHONE...................................614 491-2616
Buck Stewart, *President*
Scott Brown, *Vice Pres*
Tim Stewart, *Vice Pres*
Jeff Steen, *Sales Engr*
Rob Ryder, *Director*
EMP: 58
SQ FT: 20,000
SALES (est): 10.8MM **Privately Held**
WEB: www.capitolcitytrailers.net
SIC: 7539 3792 Trailer repair; travel trailers & campers

(G-15524)
CARDINAL HEALTH INC
2320 Mcgaw Rd (43207-4805)
PHONE...................................614 497-9552
Kelly Byrd, *Branch Mgr*
Joe Bowman, *Manager*
EMP: 74
SALES (corp-wide): 136.8B **Publicly Held**
SIC: 5122 5047 8741 Pharmaceuticals; biologicals & allied products; druggists' sundries; blood plasma; surgical equipment & supplies; hospital equipment & supplies; management services
PA: Cardinal Health, Inc.
7000 Cardinal Pl
Dublin OH 43017
614 757-5000

(G-15525)
COLUMBUS FAIR AUTO AUCTION INC
Also Called: Wednesday Auto Auction
4700 Groveport Rd (43207-5217)
P.O. Box 32490, Columbus (43232-0490)
PHONE...................................614 497-2000
Keith Whann, *CEO*
Jeff Baerga, *Vice Pres*
Chris Hayes, *Facilities Mgr*
Bill Stackhouse, *CFO*
Mary Wheeler, *CFO*
EMP: 1240
SQ FT: 60,000
SALES (est): 221.8MM **Privately Held**
SIC: 5012 5521 Automobile auction; used car dealers

(G-15526)
HUTTIG BUILDING PRODUCTS INC
Also Called: Huttig Sash & Door Co
2160 Mcgaw Rd (43207-4801)
PHONE...................................614 492-8248
Dave McCormack, *Branch Mgr*
Jamie Lashbrook, *Manager*
Jordan Post, *Manager*
EMP: 50
SQ FT: 100,000
SALES (corp-wide): 839.6MM **Publicly Held**
WEB: www.huttig.com
SIC: 5031 Door frames, all materials
PA: Huttig Building Products, Inc.
555 Maryville University
Saint Louis MO 63141
314 216-2600

(G-15527)
JACOBSON WAREHOUSE COMPANY INC
Also Called: Xpo Logistics
3880 Groveport Rd (43207-5125)
PHONE...................................614 314-1091
EMP: 142
SALES (corp-wide): 15.3B **Publicly Held**
SIC: 4226 Special warehousing & storage
HQ: Jacobson Warehouse Company, Inc.
3811 Dixon St
Des Moines IA 50313
515 263-0854

(G-15528)
PAR INTERNATIONAL INC
2160 Mcgaw Rd (43207-4801)
PHONE...................................614 529-1300
Eli Goldach, *President*
Dan Stergiou, *Exec VP*
Dan Goldach, *Vice Pres*
▼ EMP: 30
SQ FT: 300,000
SALES (est): 10MM **Privately Held**
WEB: www.parinternational.com
SIC: 5013 5199 Automotive supplies & parts; gifts & novelties

(G-15529)
S P RICHARDS COMPANY
2410 Mcgaw Rd (43207-4513)
PHONE...................................614 497-2270
Dennis Reid, *General Mgr*
EMP: 50
SALES (corp-wide): 18.7B **Publicly Held**
WEB: www.sprichards.com
SIC: 5112 5021 Office supplies; office furniture
HQ: S. P. Richards Company
6300 Highlands Pkwy Se
Smyrna GA 30082
770 434-4571

(G-15530)
SYNERGY HOTELS LLC
Also Called: Holiday Inn
4870 Old Rathmell Ct (43207-4580)
PHONE...................................614 492-9000
Mike Duncan, *General Mgr*
Stephen Berger, *Manager*
EMP: 30
SALES: 500K **Privately Held**
SIC: 7011 7991 Hotels; physical fitness facilities

(G-15531)
UNITED PARCEL SERVICE INC OH
Also Called: UPS
2450 Rathmell Rd (43207-4591)
P.O. Box 557, Holland (43528-0557)
PHONE...................................614 272-8500
Paul Stotridge, *Manager*
EMP: 158
SALES (corp-wide): 71.8B **Publicly Held**
SIC: 4215 Parcel delivery, vehicular
HQ: United Parcel Service, Inc. (Oh)
55 Glenlake Pkwy
Atlanta GA 30328
404 828-6000

Okeana
Butler County

(G-15532)
KISSEL ENTERTAINMENT LLC
Also Called: Kissel Rides & Shows
3748 State Line Rd (45053-9506)
P.O. Box 2340, Clanton AL (35046-2340)
PHONE...................................513 266-4505
Tammy Kissel, *Manager*
Russell Kissel,
EMP: 45
SALES: 950K **Privately Held**
SIC: 7999 Amusement/Recreation Services

Olmsted Falls
Cuyahoga County

(G-15533)
DOVER INVESTMENTS INC
7989 Columbia Rd (44138-2019)
P.O. Box 450739, Westlake (44145-0615)
PHONE...................................440 235-5511
EMP: 45 **Privately Held**
SIC: 5082 Ladders
PA: Dover Investments Inc
694 Dover Center Rd
Westlake OH 44145

(G-15534)
KIDS FIRST LEARNING CENTERS
26184 Bagley Rd (44138-1812)
PHONE...................................440 235-2500
Coleen Siss, *Exec Dir*
EMP: 60
SALES (est): 882.2K **Privately Held**
SIC: 8351 Preschool center

Olmsted Twp
Cuyahoga County

(G-15535)
E J LINKS CO THE INC
Also Called: Links At The Renaissance
26111 John Rd (44138-1223)
PHONE...................................440 235-0501
Fax: 440 235-5161
EMP: 40
SALES: 500K
SALES (corp-wide): 4.4MM **Privately Held**
SIC: 7992 Public Golf Course
HQ: The Eliza Jennings Home Inc
10603 Detroit Ave
Cleveland OH 44102
216 226-0282

(G-15536)
JENNINGS ELIZA SENIOR CARE (PA)
26376 John Rd Ofc C (44138-1283)
PHONE...................................216 226-5000
Deborah Hiller, *CEO*
Jim Rogerson, *COO*
EMP: 600
SALES: 3.8MM **Privately Held**
WEB: www.therapypartnersohio.com
SIC: 8051 Skilled nursing care facilities

(G-15537)
LENAU PARK
Also Called: Donauschwaben's Grmnamrcn Cltr
7370 Columbia Rd (44138-1502)
P.O. Box 38160, Olmsted Falls (44138-0160)
PHONE...................................440 235-2646
Frank Rimps, *President*
Anita Kalkhof, *Vice Pres*
Reinhard Keck, *Vice Pres*
Erika Knowles, *Admin Asst*
EMP: 40
SQ FT: 32,075
SALES: 562.2K **Privately Held**
SIC: 7997 8641 Country club, membership; civic social & fraternal associations

(G-15538)
LINK & RENEISSANCE INC
Also Called: Links Golf Course
26111 John Rd (44138-1223)
PHONE...................................440 235-0501
Jim Rogerson, *President*
John Garus, *General Mgr*
EMP: 30
SALES (est): 1.2MM **Privately Held**
WEB: www.linksgolfcourse.com
SIC: 7992 Public golf courses

(G-15539)
OLMSTED RESIDENCE CORPORATION
Also Called: RENAISSANCE, THE
26376 John Rd Ofc (44138-1283)
PHONE...................................440 235-7100
Deborah Hiller, *CEO*
EMP: 200
SQ FT: 256,000
SALES: 7.3MM **Privately Held**
WEB: www.therapypartnersohio.com
SIC: 8322 6531 Senior citizens' center or association; real estate managers
PA: Jennings, Eliza Senior Care Network
26376 John Rd Ofc C
Olmsted Twp OH 44138

(G-15540)
PTA OLMS FALLS INT SCH
Also Called: Olmstedfalls Intermediate Schl
27043 Bagley Rd (44138-1103)
PHONE...................................440 427-6500
Donald Svec, *Principal*
Don Svec, *Principal*
EMP: 70
SALES (est): 1MM **Privately Held**
SIC: 8641 Parent-teachers' association

(G-15541)
STRIKE ZONE INC
Also Called: Swings N Things Family Fun Pk
8501 Stearns Rd (44138-1738)
PHONE....................................440 235-4420
Tim Sorge, *President*
Steve Bonham, *General Mgr*
Helen Burko, *Financial Exec*
Brian Novak, *Manager*
EMP: 85 EST: 1982
SQ FT: 24,000
SALES (est): 1.1MM **Privately Held**
WEB: www.swings-n-things.com
SIC: 7999 7993 5812 Recreation serv-
ices; baseball batting cage; miniature golf
course operation; go-cart raceway opera-
tion & rentals; video game arcade; ice
cream stands or dairy bars

Ontario

Richland County

(G-15542)
ADENA CORPORATION
1310 W 4th St (44906-1828)
PHONE....................................419 529-4456
Randy A Payne, *President*
Dave Heyl, *Superintendent*
Dwight Farmer, *Vice Pres*
Brad Geissman, *Vice Pres*
Josh Darling, *Project Mgr*
EMP: 160
SQ FT: 7,000
SALES: 65MM **Privately Held**
WEB: www.adenacorporation.com
SIC: 1541 1542 Industrial buildings, new
construction; nonresidential construction

(G-15543)
**ADVANTAGE CREDIT UNION
INC (PA)**
700 Stumbo Rd (44906-1279)
P.O. Box 2674, Mansfield (44906-0674)
PHONE....................................419 529-5603
Wesley P Volz, *President*
EMP: 28
SALES: 1.1MM **Privately Held**
SIC: 6061 Federal credit unions

(G-15544)
**ALL AMERICAN TRNSP SVCS
LLC**
575 Beer Rd (44906-1214)
PHONE....................................419 589-7433
James Blevins, *Mng Member*
EMP: 35
SALES (est): 105.9K **Privately Held**
SIC: 4789 Cargo loading & unloading serv-
ices

(G-15545)
CENTRAL STAR
Also Called: Central Star Home Health Svcs
2003 W 4th St Ste 116 (44906-1865)
PHONE....................................419 756-9449
Steve Sternbock, *CEO*
Julie Charlton, *Administration*
EMP: 120
SALES (est): 1.7MM
SALES (corp-wide): 32.5MM **Privately
Held**
SIC: 8082 Home health care services
PA: Star Multi Care Services, Inc.
115 Broadhollow Rd # 275
Melville NY 11747
631 423-6689

(G-15546)
CINEMARK USA INC
2355 Walker Lake Rd (44903-6529)
PHONE....................................419 589-7300
Yolanda Hubbard, *Branch Mgr*
EMP: 34 **Publicly Held**
SIC: 7832 Motion picture theaters, except
drive-in
HQ: Cinemark Usa, Inc.
3900 Dallas Pkwy Ste 500
Plano TX 75093
972 665-1000

(G-15547)
**DIVERSICARE OF MANSFIELD
LLC**
Also Called: Ontario Commons
2124 Park Ave W (44906-3807)
PHONE....................................419 529-6447
EMP: 63 EST: 2014
SALES (est): 1.9MM
SALES (corp-wide): 563.4MM **Publicly
Held**
SIC: 8051 Skilled nursing care facilities
PA: Diversicare Healthcare Services, Inc.
1621 Galleria Blvd
Brentwood TN 37027
615 771-7575

(G-15548)
DTA INC
Also Called: Arnold's Landscaping
3128 Park Ave W (44906-1051)
PHONE....................................419 529-2920
Darrell Arnold, *President*
EMP: 30
SQ FT: 4,000
SALES (est): 6.8MM **Privately Held**
WEB: www.stone-creations.net
SIC: 5083 0782 Landscape contractors

(G-15549)
**EXECUTIVE MANAGEMENT
SERVICES**
1225 Home Rd N (44906-1407)
PHONE....................................419 529-8800
Lawrence Grin, *President*
EMP: 250
SALES (est): 4.3MM
SALES (corp-wide): 301.8MM **Privately
Held**
WEB: www.outsourcepartners.net
SIC: 7349 Janitorial service, contract basis
HQ: U.S. Security Holdings, Inc.
200 Mansell Ct E Ste 500
Roswell GA 30076
770 625-1400

(G-15550)
GORDON FOOD SERVICE INC
Also Called: G F S Marketplace
1310 N Lexngtn Sprngmill (44906-1127)
PHONE....................................419 747-1212
Jeff White, *Manager*
EMP: 25
SALES (corp-wide): 13B **Privately Held**
WEB: www.gfs.com
SIC: 5149 5142 Groceries & related prod-
ucts; packaged frozen goods
PA: Gordon Food Service, Inc.
1300 Gezon Pkwy Sw
Wyoming MI 49509
888 437-3663

(G-15551)
**GRAHAM CHEVROLET-
CADILLAC CO (PA)**
Also Called: Ford
1515 W 4th St (44906-1857)
P.O. Box 340, Zanesville (43702-0340)
PHONE....................................419 989-4012
James Graham, *President*
Ken Williams, *Vice Pres*
Clay Graham, *Treasurer*
Brian Graham, *Admin Sec*
EMP: 82
SQ FT: 44,000
SALES (est): 64.1MM **Privately Held**
WEB: www.grahamjeep.com
SIC: 5511 7515 7513 5521 Automobiles,
new & used; passenger car leasing; truck
rental & leasing, no drivers; used car
dealers; automobiles & other motor vehi-
cles

(G-15552)
HOME DEPOT USA INC
Also Called: Home Depot, The
2000 August Dr (44906-3350)
PHONE....................................419 529-0015
Rob Haner, *Manager*
EMP: 200
SALES (corp-wide): 108.2B **Publicly
Held**
WEB: www.homerentalsdepot.com
SIC: 5211 7359 Home centers; tool rental

HQ: Home Depot U.S.A., Inc.
2455 Paces Ferry Ave
Atlanta GA 30339

(G-15553)
**HOSPICE OF NORTH CENTRAL
OHIO**
2131 Park Ave W (44906-1226)
PHONE....................................419 524-9200
Anne Shelley, *CEO*
Jennifer Clark, *Director*
EMP: 34
SALES (est): 514.1K **Privately Held**
SIC: 8082 Home health care services

(G-15554)
**INTERCITY AMATEUR RDO CLB
INC**
Also Called: Iarc
120 Homewood Rd (44906-1324)
PHONE....................................419 989-3429
Derrick Martin, *Principal*
EMP: 40
SALES (est): 353K **Privately Held**
SIC: 8641 Civic social & fraternal associa-
tions

(G-15555)
INTERSTATE OPTICAL CO (DH)
680 Lindaire Ln E (44906-1760)
P.O. Box 308, Mansfield (44901-0308)
PHONE....................................419 529-6800
John Art, *President*
Robert Art, *Vice Pres*
Bud Stanton, *Vice Pres*
Greg Pugh, *Production*
Deborah L Art, *Treasurer*
▲ EMP: 61
SQ FT: 14,000
SALES (est): 34.5MM
SALES (corp-wide): 283.5MM **Privately
Held**
WEB: www.interstateoptical.com
SIC: 5048 Ophthalmic goods
HQ: Essilor Laboratories Of America Hold-
ing Co., Inc.
13555 N Stemmons Fwy
Dallas TX 75234
214 496-4141

(G-15556)
**JOHNNY APPLESEED
BROADCASTING**
Also Called: Wvno-FM
2900 Park Ave W (44906-1062)
PHONE....................................419 529-5900
Gunther S Meisse, *President*
EMP: 42
SQ FT: 17,000
SALES (est): 4.1MM **Privately Held**
WEB: www.wmfd.com
SIC: 4832 4833 Radio broadcasting sta-
tions; television broadcasting stations

(G-15557)
JOYCE BUICK INC
Also Called: Joyce Buick GMC of Mansfield
1400 Park Ave W (44906-2799)
PHONE....................................419 529-3211
William F Joyce, *President*
Brian M Joyce, *Vice Pres*
Chad Cooper, *Manager*
Heather Figley, *Executive*
EMP: 37
SQ FT: 32,000
SALES (est): 15.7MM **Privately Held**
WEB: www.saturnofmansfield.com
SIC: 5511 7532 Automobiles, new & used;
body shop, automotive

(G-15558)
LAKE ERIE ELECTRIC INC
Also Called: Charnan Div
539 Home Rd N (44906-2325)
P.O. Box 2539, Mansfield (44906-0539)
PHONE....................................419 529-4611
Keith Rowland, *General Mgr*
Larry Mooney, *Manager*
EMP: 25
SALES (corp-wide): 137.9MM **Privately
Held**
SIC: 1731 General electrical contractor

PA: Erie Lake Electric Inc
25730 1st St
Westlake OH 44145
440 835-5565

(G-15559)
LOWES HOME CENTERS LLC
940 N Lexington Spring Rd (44906-1119)
PHONE....................................419 747-1920
Dan Messord, *Manager*
EMP: 150
SALES (corp-wide): 68.6B **Publicly Held**
SIC: 5211 5031 5722 5064 Home cen-
ters; building materials, exterior; building
materials, interior; household appliance
stores; electrical appliances, television &
radio
HQ: Lowe's Home Centers, Llc
1605 Curtis Bridge Rd
Wilkesboro NC 28697
336 658-4000

(G-15560)
**MANSFIELD WHSNG & DIST INC
(HQ)**
Also Called: Mansfield Express
222 Tappan Dr N (44906-1333)
P.O. Box 2685, Mansfield (44906-0685)
PHONE....................................419 522-3510
Stuart Lichter, *Ch of Bd*
Brian Glowaski, *President*
Dawn Stevenson, *General Mgr*
Chris Swearingen, *Facilities Mgr*
Aaron Taylor, *Sales Mgr*
EMP: 130
SQ FT: 1,500,000
SALES (est): 11.4MM
SALES (corp-wide): 28.6MM **Privately
Held**
SIC: 4225 4213 General warehousing;
trucking, except local
PA: Mwd Logistics Inc
222 Tappan Dr N
Ontario OH 44906
419 522-3510

(G-15561)
MARCO PHOTO SERVICE INC
1655 Nussbaum Pkwy (44906-2300)
PHONE....................................419 529-9010
Rick Casey, *President*
Selena Baker, *COO*
Dave Elick, *COO*
Jay Allred, *Vice Pres*
Richard Casey, *Vice Pres*
EMP: 75 EST: 1965
SQ FT: 45,000
SALES (est): 10.1MM **Privately Held**
WEB: www.marcophotoservice.com
SIC: 7384 Photofinishing laboratory

(G-15562)
MEDCENTRAL HEALTH SYSTEM
Also Called: Medcentral Hlth Sys Spt Mdcine
1750 W 4th St Ste 1 (44906-1796)
PHONE....................................419 526-8900
Brian Brickner, *Director*
EMP: 25
SALES (corp-wide): 4B **Privately Held**
SIC: 8062 8011 General medical & surgi-
cal hospitals; occupational & industrial
specialist, physician/surgeon
HQ: Medcentral Health System
335 Glessner Ave
Mansfield OH 44903
419 526-8000

(G-15563)
MEDCENTRAL WORKABLE
1750 W 4th St Ste 5 (44906-1796)
PHONE....................................419 526-8444
Marcia Rice, *Manager*
EMP: 25
SALES (est): 698.6K **Privately Held**
SIC: 8071 Medical laboratories

(G-15564)
**MID OHIO EMPLOYMENT
SERVICES (PA)**
2282 Village Mall Dr # 2 (44906-1151)
PHONE....................................419 747-5466
Beth Delaney, *President*
Ashle Finley, *Area Mgr*
Ann Smith, *VP Opers*
Jan Horn, *Treasurer*
Amie Walker, *Branch Mgr*

EMP: 25
SALES (est): 2.2MM **Privately Held**
SIC: 7361 Employment agencies

(G-15565)
MID OHIO HOME HEALTH LTD
1332 W 4th St (44906-1828)
PHONE...................................419 529-3883
Kelly Purvis, *CEO*
EMP: 40
SALES (est): 1.6MM **Privately Held**
SIC: 8082 Home Health Care Services

(G-15566)
NORFOLK SOUTHERN CORPORATION
2586 Park Ave W (44906-1235)
PHONE...................................419 529-4574
Julius Chirumbolo, *Principal*
EMP: 43
SALES (corp-wide): 11.4B **Publicly Held**
SIC: 4011 Railroads, line-haul operating
PA: Norfolk Southern Corporation
   3 Commercial Pl Ste 1a
   Norfolk VA 23510
   757 629-2680

(G-15567)
OHIO DISTRICT 5 AREA
2131 Park Ave W (44906-1226)
PHONE...................................419 522-5612
Duana Patton, *CEO*
James Hairston, *COO*
EMP: 123
SALES: 40.7MM **Privately Held**
WEB: www.agingnorthcentralohio.org
SIC: 8322 Senior citizens' center or association

(G-15568)
ONTARIO LOCAL SCHOOL DISTRICT
Also Called: Transportation Department
3644 Pearl St (44906-1066)
PHONE...................................419 529-3814
Pat Duffner, *Director*
EMP: 33 **Privately Held**
SIC: 4151 School buses
PA: Ontario Local School District
   457 Shelby Ontario Rd
   Ontario OH 44906

(G-15569)
ONTARIO MECHANICAL LLC
2880 Park Ave W (44906-1026)
PHONE...................................419 529-2578
Dave Baker, *Vice Pres*
Kenneth Earhart, *Mng Member*
EMP: 30 **EST:** 2012
SALES (est): 6.8MM **Privately Held**
SIC: 3449 1761 1791 Custom roll formed products; sheet metalwork; structural steel erection

(G-15570)
P R MACHINE WORKS INC
1825 Nussbaum Pkwy (44906-2360)
PHONE...................................419 529-5748
Mark Romanchuk, *President*
Mark J Romanchuk, *President*
Jerry Schwall, *Vice Pres*
Mike Strench, *Purch Mgr*
Andrea Dill, *Human Res Mgr*
▲ **EMP:** 75
SQ FT: 14,100
SALES: 9.5MM **Privately Held**
WEB: www.prmachineworks.com
SIC: 3599 1531 Machine shop, jobbing & repair;

(G-15571)
SHEARER FARM INC
Also Called: John Deere Authorized Dealer
2715 W 4th St (44906-1212)
PHONE...................................419 529-6160
Ivan Maibach, *Manager*
EMP: 25
SALES (corp-wide): 59.5MM **Privately Held**
WEB: www.shearerequipment.com
SIC: 5083 5999 Farm implements; farm machinery
PA: Shearer Farm, Inc
   7762 Cleveland Rd
   Wooster OH 44691
   330 345-9023

(G-15572)
SHELLY AND SANDS INC
Mansfield Saphalt Paving
1300 W 4th St Rear (44906-1828)
P.O. Box 1321, Mansfield (44901-1321)
PHONE...................................419 529-8455
Tom Ellis, *Manager*
EMP: 75
SQ FT: 5,000
SALES (corp-wide): 276.3MM **Privately Held**
WEB: www.shellyandsands.com
SIC: 1611 Highway & street paving contractor
PA: Shelly And Sands, Inc.
   3570 S River Rd
   Zanesville OH 43701
   740 453-0721

(G-15573)
SLICK AUTOMATED SOLUTIONS INC
1825 Nussbaum Pkwy (44906-2360)
PHONE...................................567 247-1080
Zoi Romanchuk, *President*
Mark Romanchuk, *Vice Pres*
Jeff Blanchard, *Engineer*
Donald Metz, *Design Engr*
EMP: 26
SALES (est): 4.9MM **Privately Held**
SIC: 8711 Engineering services

(G-15574)
SOUTHERN CARE INC
41 Briggs Dr (44906-3805)
PHONE...................................419 774-0555
Michael Pardy, *Branch Mgr*
EMP: 50 **Privately Held**
SIC: 8082 Home health care services
PA: Southern Care, Inc
   1000 Urban Center Dr # 115
   Vestavia AL 35242

(G-15575)
SPITZER MOTOR CITY INC
Also Called: Spitzer Motors of Mansfield
1777 W 4th St (44906-1704)
PHONE...................................567 307-7119
EMP: 26
SALES (corp-wide): 9.3MM **Privately Held**
SIC: 7538 General Auto Repair
PA: Spitzer Motor City, Inc.
   13001 Brookpark Rd
   Cleveland OH 44142
   216 267-2100

(G-15576)
STARTEK INC
850 W 4th St (44906-2534)
PHONE...................................419 528-7801
Brenda Young, *Branch Mgr*
EMP: 137 **Publicly Held**
WEB: www.startek.com
SIC: 7389 Telemarketing services
HQ: Startek, Inc.
   8200 E Maplewood Ave # 100
   Greenwood Village CO 80111
   303 262-4500

(G-15577)
UNIVERSAL ENTERPRISES INC (PA)
Also Called: Universal Refrigeration Div
545 Beer Rd (44906-1214)
PHONE...................................419 529-3500
Ralph Ridenour, *President*
George Reece, *Owner*
Todd Kiger, *Vice Pres*
Rob Ridenour, *Vice Pres*
Mike Bugg, *Info Tech Dir*
EMP: 180 **EST:** 1952
SALES (est): 27.7MM **Privately Held**
WEB: www.universalrefrigeration.com
SIC: 1711 7374 Warm air heating & air conditioning contractor; computer graphics service

(G-15578)
WALLOWA DIALYSIS LLC
Also Called: Mid Ohio Dialysis
2148 W 4th St (44906-1200)
PHONE...................................419 747-4039
James K Hilger,
EMP: 30 **EST:** 2013

SALES (est): 324K **Publicly Held**
SIC: 8092 Kidney dialysis centers
PA: Davita Inc.
   2000 16th St
   Denver CO 80202

(G-15579)
WESTERN & SOUTHERN LF INSUR CO
Also Called: Western Southern Life Insur
1989 W 4th St (44906-1708)
PHONE...................................419 524-1800
Barry Danko, *Manager*
EMP: 40 **Privately Held**
SIC: 6411 Insurance agents, brokers & service
HQ: The Western & Southern Life Insurance Company
   400 Broadway St
   Cincinnati OH 45202
   513 629-1800

Oregon
Lucas County

(G-15580)
AA BOOS & SONS INC
2015 Pickle Rd (43616-3155)
PHONE...................................419 691-2329
Robert Boos, *CEO*
Robert D Boos, *CEO*
James Cousino, *President*
Bret Boos, *Vice Pres*
Cheryl Koeniger, *CFO*
EMP: 80 **EST:** 1948
SQ FT: 6,000
SALES: 42MM **Privately Held**
WEB: www.aaboos.com
SIC: 1541 1542 Industrial buildings, new construction; renovation, remodeling & repairs: industrial buildings; commercial & office building, new construction; commercial & office buildings, renovation & repair

(G-15581)
ABC APPLIANCE INC
3012 Navarre Ave (43616-3308)
PHONE...................................419 693-4414
J R Pruss, *Manager*
EMP: 30
SALES (corp-wide): 300.7MM **Privately Held**
WEB: www.abcwarehouse.com
SIC: 3639 5722 5731 5065 Major kitchen appliances, except refrigerators & stoves; vacuum cleaners; high fidelity stereo equipment; telephone equipment; photocopy machines
PA: Abc Appliance, Inc.
   1 W Silverdome Indus Park
   Pontiac MI 48342
   248 335-4222

(G-15582)
AECOM ENERGY & CNSTR INC
Also Called: Washington Group
4001 Cedar Point Rd (43616-1310)
P.O. Box 696, Toledo (43697-0696)
PHONE...................................419 698-6277
EMP: 125
SALES (corp-wide): 20.1B **Publicly Held**
WEB: www.wgint.com
SIC: 1542 2911 Nonresidential construction; petroleum refining
HQ: Aecom Energy & Construction, Inc.
   1999 Avenue Of The Stars
   Los Angeles CA 90067
   213 593-8100

(G-15583)
ASSOCTED CTRACT LASER SURGEONS
Also Called: Center For Prgressive Eye Care
2740 Navarre Ave (43616-3216)
PHONE...................................419 693-4444
William G Martin MD, *President*
Robert G Wiley MD, *Vice Pres*
EMP: 25
SQ FT: 4,500
SALES (est): 824.6K **Privately Held**
SIC: 8011 Ophthalmologist

(G-15584)
BUCKEYE PIPE LINE SERVICES CO
3321 York St (43616-1215)
P.O. Box 167567 (43616-7567)
PHONE...................................419 698-8770
Bob McDowel, *Manager*
EMP: 28
SALES (corp-wide): 4.1B **Publicly Held**
SIC: 4613 Refined petroleum pipelines
HQ: Buckeye Pipe Line Services Company
   5002 Buckeye Rd
   Emmaus PA 18049
   484 232-4000

(G-15585)
C & W TANK CLEANING COMPANY
50 N Lallendorf Rd (43616-1847)
PHONE...................................419 691-1995
James C Parker, *President*
Ben Patterson, *Safety Dir*
Brian Francis, *Opers Mgr*
Christy Schramm, *Human Res Mgr*
Steve Stamper, *Manager*
EMP: 65
SQ FT: 6,000
SALES (est): 9.3MM **Privately Held**
WEB: www.nk.com
SIC: 7699 Tank & boiler cleaning service

(G-15586)
CAPITAL CITY GROUP INC
4314 Corduroy Rd (43616-1820)
PHONE...................................419 931-6757
EMP: 44 **Privately Held**
SIC: 7353 Cranes & aerial lift equipment, rental or leasing
PA: Capital City Group, Inc.
   2299 Performance Way
   Columbus OH 43207

(G-15587)
CHARLES MERCY HLTH-ST HOSPITA (HQ)
2600 Navarre Ave (43616-3207)
PHONE...................................419 696-7200
Jeffrey Dempseyn, *CEO*
Jacalyn Liebowitz, *President*
F J Gallagher, *Principal*
Joseph W Rossler, *Principal*
Rolf H Scheidel, *Principal*
EMP: 75
SQ FT: 515,000
SALES: 133.5MM
SALES (corp-wide): 4.7B **Publicly Held**
SIC: 8062 General medical & surgical hospitals
PA: Mercy Health
   1701 Mercy Health Pl
   Cincinnati OH 45237
   513 639-2800

(G-15588)
CSX TRANSPORTATION INC
600 Millard Ave (43616)
PHONE...................................419 697-2323
Paul Lecomtte, *Manager*
EMP: 75
SALES (corp-wide): 12.2B **Publicly Held**
WEB: www.csxt.com
SIC: 4011 Railroads, line-haul operating
HQ: Csx Transportation, Inc.
   500 Water St
   Jacksonville FL 32202
   904 359-3100

(G-15589)
DAVITA INC
3310 Dustin Rd (43616-3302)
PHONE...................................419 697-2191
Anil Mehta, *Branch Mgr*
EMP: 35 **Publicly Held**
SIC: 8092 Kidney dialysis centers
PA: Davita Inc.
   2000 16th St
   Denver CO 80202

(G-15590)
DESOTO DIALYSIS LLC
Also Called: Lucas County Home Training
2702 Navarre Ave Ste 203 (43616-3224)
PHONE...................................419 691-1514
James K Hilger,
EMP: 35

▲ = Import ▼=Export
◆ =Import/Export

SALES (est): 507.3K **Publicly Held**
SIC: **8092** Kidney dialysis centers
PA: Davita Inc.
2000 16th St
Denver CO 80202

(G-15591)
DURE INVESTMENTS LLC
Also Called: Sleep Inn
1761 Meijers Cir (43616-4923)
PHONE....................................419 697-7800
Darrell Ducat,
Rudolph Eckert III,
EMP: 25
SQ FT: 42,478
SALES (est): 1MM **Privately Held**
SIC: **7011** Hotels & motels

(G-15592)
E S WAGNER COMPANY
Also Called: Esw
840 Patchen Rd (43616-3132)
PHONE....................................419 691-8651
Lewis John Wagner, *CEO*
Scott Boyle, *Superintendent*
Jim Pilewski, *Vice Pres*
John C Wagner, *Vice Pres*
Doug Spencer, *Project Mgr*
EMP: 60
SQ FT: 8,500
SALES (est): 30.7MM **Privately Held**
WEB: www.eswagner.com
SIC: **1794** 1622 1611 1623 Excavation &
grading, building construction; bridge con-
struction; concrete construction: roads,
highways, sidewalks, etc.; sewer line con-
struction; railroad & subway construction

(G-15593)
EASTERN MUMEE BAY ARTS COUNCIL
595 Sylvandale Ave (43616-2721)
PHONE....................................419 690-5718
Martin Danekind, *President*
Vernon Pattont, *Vice Pres*
Steve Sheskey, *Treasurer*
Claudia Winn, *Admin Sec*
EMP: 50
SALES (est): 274.3K **Privately Held**
WEB: www.maumeebay.org
SIC: **8699** Art council

(G-15594)
ENVIROSAFE SERVICES OF OHIO (DH)
876 Otter Creek Rd (43616-1243)
PHONE....................................419 698-3500
Doug Roberts, *President*
EMP: 48
SALES (est): 24.3MM **Privately Held**
WEB: www.envirosafeservices.com
SIC: **4953** Hazardous waste collection &
disposal
HQ: Tms International Corporation
12 Monongahela Ave
Glassport PA 15045
412 675-8251

(G-15595)
FRESENIUS USA INC
555 Blue Heron Dr (43616-1849)
PHONE....................................419 691-2475
Gary Heleman, *Manager*
EMP: 28
SQ FT: 58,000
SALES (corp-wide): 18.9B **Privately Held**
WEB: www.fresenius.org
SIC: **8092** Kidney dialysis centers
HQ: Fresenius Usa, Inc.
4040 Nelson Ave
Concord CA 94520
925 288-4218

(G-15596)
GREAT EASTERN THEATRE COMPANY
4500 Navarre Ave (43616-3520)
PHONE....................................419 691-9668
Kevin Christy, *Branch Mgr*
EMP: 73
SALES (corp-wide): 4.7MM **Privately Held**
SIC: **7832** Motion picture theaters, except
drive-in

PA: Great Eastern Theatre Company
3361 Executive Pkwy # 300
Toledo OH 43606
419 537-9682

(G-15597)
HCR MANORCARE MED SVCS FLA LLC
Also Called: Heartland of Oregon
3953 Navarre Ave (43616-3437)
PHONE....................................419 691-3088
Abby Taylor, *Manager*
EMP: 110
SQ FT: 30,158
SALES (corp-wide): 2.4B **Publicly Held**
WEB: www.manorcare.com
SIC: **8051** Skilled Nursing Care Facility
HQ: Hcr Manorcare Medical Services Of
Florida, Llc
333 N Summit St Ste 100
Toledo OH 43604
419 252-5500

(G-15598)
HOLIDAY INN
3154 Navarre Ave (43616-3310)
PHONE....................................419 691-8800
Saad Roumaya,
Frank Shallal,
EMP: 26
SQ FT: 5,694
SALES (est): 2MM **Privately Held**
SIC: **7011** Hotels & motels

(G-15599)
JEFFERS CRANE SERVICE INC (HQ)
5421 Navarre Ave (43616-3551)
P.O. Box 167789 (43616-7789)
PHONE....................................419 693-0421
Toll Free:..................................888 -
Michael C Liptak Jr, *President*
David E Bucher, *General Mgr*
Barb Tillison, *Vice Pres*
Lawrence Liptak, *Treasurer*
Mike Calevro, *Sales Staff*
EMP: 56
SQ FT: 20,000
SALES (est): 9.5MM
SALES (corp-wide): 93.3MM **Privately Held**
SIC: **7353** Cranes & aerial lift equipment,
rental or leasing
PA: All Erection' & Crane Rental Corp
4700 Acorn Dr Ste 100
Cleveland OH 44131
216 524-6550

(G-15600)
MERCY HEALTH - ST
Also Called: St Charles Child Dev Center
2600 Navarre Ave (43616-3207)
PHONE....................................419 696-7465
Bobbie Kehlmeier, *Exec Dir*
Christina Cassaubon, *Director*
Adnan A Al-Khaleefa, *Oncology*
EMP: 30
SALES (corp-wide): 4.7B **Privately Held**
SIC: **8062** 8322 General medical & surgi-
cal hospitals; child guidance agency
HQ: Mercy Health - St. Charles Hospital Llc
2600 Navarre Ave
Oregon OH 43616
419 696-7200

(G-15601)
NORTHTOWN SQUARE LTD PARTNR
Also Called: Comfort Inn
2930 Navarre Ave (43616-3373)
PHONE....................................419 691-8911
Darrell Ducat, *General Ptnr*
Karen Magnone, *Manager*
EMP: 30
SQ FT: 36,000
SALES (est): 1.6MM **Privately Held**
SIC: **7011** Hotels & motels

(G-15602)
OPTIVUE INC
Also Called: Ohio Vision of Toledo Inc Opt
2740 Navarre Ave (43616-3216)
PHONE....................................419 891-1391
Mary Martin, *President*
William Martin, *Principal*

Connie Richards, *COO*
EMP: 126
SALES (est): 14.3MM **Privately Held**
SIC: **8011** 8042 Ophthalmologist; special-
ized optometrists

(G-15603)
ORCHARD VILLA INC
2841 Munding Dr (43616-3290)
PHONE....................................419 697-4100
Bruce Daskal, *Owner*
Rey Nevarez, *Director*
Jill Schlievert, *Administration*
EMP: 200
SALES (est): 5.9MM **Privately Held**
SIC: **8059** 8052 8051 Nursing home, ex-
cept skilled & intermediate care facility; in-
termediate care facilities; skilled nursing
care facilities

(G-15604)
OREGON CLEAN ENERGY CENTER
816 N Lallendorf Rd (43616-1339)
PHONE....................................419 566-9466
Moe Collins, *Principal*
EMP: 25
SALES (est): 41.9K **Privately Held**
SIC: **7699** Cleaning services

(G-15605)
OREGON FORD INC
Also Called: Mathews Ford-Oregon
2811 Navarre Ave (43616-3397)
PHONE....................................419 698-4444
Timothy W Mathews, *President*
Lauren Jarzeboski, *Sales Staff*
Alan Robinson, *Sales Staff*
EMP: 110
SQ FT: 33,000
SALES (est): 46MM **Privately Held**
SIC: **5511** 7538 7532 7515 Automobiles,
new & used; trucks, tractors & trailers:
new & used; general automotive repair
shops; top & body repair & paint shops;
passenger car leasing

(G-15606)
OTTIVUE (PA)
Also Called: Optio-Vision By Kahn & Diehl
2740 Navarre Ave (43616-3216)
PHONE....................................419 693-4444
Connie Richards, *CEO*
EMP: 100
SALES (est): 1.8MM **Privately Held**
WEB: www.optivue.com
SIC: **8042** Specialized optometrists

(G-15607)
RBM ENVIRONMENTAL AND CNSTR
4526 Bayshore Rd (43616-1035)
PHONE....................................419 693-5840
Bob J Petty, *President*
Mike S Petty, *Vice Pres*
EMP: 40
SALES (est): 4.9MM **Privately Held**
SIC: **1794** 7699 7692 3498 Excavation
work; tank & boiler cleaning service; weld-
ing repair; fabricated pipe & fittings; fabri-
cated structural metal

(G-15608)
SISTERS OF LITTLE
Also Called: Scared Heart Nursing Home
930 S Wynn Rd (43616-3530)
PHONE....................................419 698-4331
Mother Contance, *Administration*
Martha Dunn, *Administration*
Cecilia Sartorius, *Administration*
EMP: 120
SALES (corp-wide): 8.6MM **Privately Held**
SIC: **8051** Skilled nursing care facilities
PA: Little Sisters Of The Poor, Baltimore,
Inc.
601 Maiden Choice Ln
Baltimore MD 21228
410 744-9367

(G-15609)
SISTERS OF MERCY AMER REG COMM
Also Called: Mercy Ctr For Hlth Promtn St
1001 Isaac Streets Dr (43616-3205)
PHONE....................................419 696-7203
Rick Gray, *Director*
EMP: 75
SALES (corp-wide): 19.1MM **Privately Held**
SIC: **8049** Nurses, registered & practical
PA: Sisters Of Mercy Of The Union In The
United States Of America
2335 Grandview Ave Fl 5
Cincinnati OH 45206
513 475-6700

(G-15610)
TESCO-TRANSPORTION EQP SLS
6401 Seaman Rd (43616-4223)
P.O. Box 167230 (43616-7230)
PHONE....................................419 836-2835
Noel E Graham Jr, *President*
EMP: 50 EST: 2007
SALES (est): 1.6MM **Privately Held**
SIC: **4142** 5012 Bus charter service, ex-
cept local; buses

(G-15611)
TOLEDO REFINING COMPANY LLC (DH)
1819 Woodville Rd (43616-3159)
PHONE....................................419 698-6600
Tom Nimbley, *CEO*
Michael D Gayda, *President*
Jeffrey Dill, *Senior VP*
Matthew C Lucey, *Senior VP*
Paul Davis, *Vice Pres*
EMP: 151
SALES (est): 178.3MM
SALES (corp-wide): 27.1B **Publicly Held**
SIC: **1629** Oil refinery construction

(G-15612)
TOLEDO SWISS SINGERS
3860 Starr Ave (43616-2438)
PHONE....................................419 693-4110
Charles Justus, *President*
Ernie Bollinger, *Principal*
John Murr, *Vice Pres*
EMP: 40
SALES (est): 301K **Privately Held**
SIC: **7929** Musicians

(G-15613)
TW RECREATIONAL SERVICES
Also Called: Maumee Bay Golf Course
1750 State Park Rd 2 (43616-5800)
PHONE....................................419 836-1466
Don Karns, *Principal*
EMP: 25
SQ FT: 1,800
SALES (est): 680.8K **Privately Held**
SIC: **7992** Public golf courses

(G-15614)
WALLEYE POWER LLC
4701 Bay Shore Rd (43616-1038)
PHONE....................................567 298-7400
Joanne Piasecki, *Treasurer*
Shawn Smith,
EMP: 62
SALES: 49MM **Privately Held**
SIC: **4911**

(G-15615)
YOUNG MENS CHRISTIAN ASSOCIAT
Also Called: Eastern Community YMCA
2960 Pickle Rd (43616-4051)
PHONE....................................419 691-3523
Tracy Adams, *Director*
EMP: 80
SALES (corp-wide): 29.1MM **Privately Held**
WEB: www.ymcastorercamps.org
SIC: **8641** 7991 8351 7032 Youth organi-
zations; physical fitness facilities; child
day care services; youth camps; individ-
ual & family services

GEOGRAPHIC

PA: Young Men's Christian Association Of
Greater Toledo
1500 N Superior St Fl 2
Toledo OH 43604
419 729-8135

Oregonia
Warren County

(G-15616)
DAYTON SOCIETY NATURAL HISTORY
Also Called: Fort Ancient State Memorial
6123 State Route 350 (45054-9708)
PHONE..................................513 932-4421
Jack Blosser, *Branch Mgr*
EMP: 43
SQ FT: 20,526
SALES (est): 604.2K
SALES (corp-wide): 4.2MM **Privately Held**
SIC: 8412 8699 Museum; historical club
PA: Dayton Society Of Natural History
2600 Deweese Pkwy
Dayton OH 45414
937 275-7431

(G-15617)
ROGER SHAWN HOUCK
Also Called: Prengers
7887 Wilmington Rd (45054-9448)
PHONE..................................513 933-0563
Roger S Houck, *Partner*
EMP: 45
SALES (est): 2.8MM **Privately Held**
SIC: 5083 Dairy machinery & equipment

(G-15618)
YOUNG MENS CHRISTIAN ASSOC
Also Called: Dayton YMCA Camp Kern
5291 State Route 350 (45054-9746)
PHONE..................................513 932-3756
C Addison, *Exec Dir*
EMP: 90
SALES (est): 1.6MM
SALES (corp-wide): 26.1MM **Privately Held**
WEB: www.daytonymca.org
SIC: 8641 7032 Youth organizations; summer camp, except day & sports instructional
PA: Young Men's Christian Association Of
Greater Dayton
118 W 1st St Ste 300
Dayton OH 45402
937 223-5201

Orient
Pickaway County

(G-15619)
EITEL TOWING SERVICE INC
Also Called: Eitels Amrcas Towing Trnsp Svc
7111 Stahl Rd (43146-9601)
PHONE..................................614 877-4139
Stacy L Wills, *President*
Denise Buyaky, *General Mgr*
Larry Cyrus, *Administration*
EMP: 30
SQ FT: 10,000
SALES (est): 3.9MM **Privately Held**
WEB: www.eitelstowing.com
SIC: 7549 Towing service, automotive

(G-15620)
KMJ LEASING LTD
Also Called: B & B Industries
7001 Harrisburg Pike (43146-9468)
PHONE..................................614 871-3883
Kenneth A Harwood,
Mary A Harwood,
EMP: 38 **EST:** 1971
SQ FT: 5,000
SALES (est): 6.6MM **Privately Held**
WEB: www.bandbindustriesinc.com
SIC: 4213 3799 Contract haulers; golf carts, powered

(G-15621)
SPLIT ROCK GOLF CLUB INC
10210 Scioto Darby Rd (43146-9016)
PHONE..................................614 877-9755
Glen B Gulick, *President*
Lucinda Gulick, *Corp Secy*
EMP: 30
SALES (est): 1MM **Privately Held**
SIC: 7992 Public golf courses

Orrville
Wayne County

(G-15622)
AMTRAC OF OHIO INC
Also Called: Amtrac Railroad Contrs Ohio
11842 Lincoln Way E (44667-9597)
PHONE..................................330 683-7206
Rickey J Geib, *President*
Lynn Lawson, *President*
Mary A Shank, *Corp Secy*
Brian L Lawson, *Vice Pres*
EMP: 55
SQ FT: 10,000
SALES (est): 8.4MM **Privately Held**
WEB: www.amtracohio.com
SIC: 1629 Railroad & railway roadbed construction

(G-15623)
ASPIRE ENERGY OF OHIO LLC (HQ)
300 Tracy Bridge Rd (44667-9384)
PHONE..................................330 682-7726
Tony Kovacevich, *President*
Ralph Knoll, *Vice Pres*
EMP: 39
SQ FT: 11,446
SALES (est): 17.7MM
SALES (corp-wide): 717.4MM **Publicly Held**
WEB: www.gatherco.com
SIC: 4923 Gas transmission & distribution
PA: Chesapeake Utilities Corporation
909 Silver Lake Blvd
Dover DE 19904
302 734-6799

(G-15624)
AULTMAN HEALTH FOUNDATION
832 S Main St (44667-2208)
PHONE..................................330 682-3010
Jessica Immel, *Office Mgr*
EMP: 2381
SALES (corp-wide): 1.1MM **Privately Held**
SIC: 8062 General medical & surgical hospitals
PA: Aultman Health Foundation
2600 6th St Sw
Canton OH 44710
330 452-9911

(G-15625)
BEN D IMHOFF INC
Also Called: Imhoff Construction
315 E Market St (44667-1805)
PHONE..................................330 683-4498
Scott Imhoff, *President*
Lisle Liston, *Vice Pres*
Tom Miller, *Shareholder*
EMP: 40
SQ FT: 9,000
SALES (est): 10.9MM **Privately Held**
WEB: www.imhoffinc.com
SIC: 1542 1541 Institutional building construction; commercial & office building, new construction; commercial & office buildings, renovation & repair; industrial buildings, new construction; renovation, remodeling & repairs: industrial buildings

(G-15626)
BRENN FIELD NURSING CENTER
1980 Lynn Dr (44667-2337)
PHONE..................................330 683-4075
Jeanne Stepfield, *President*
Sandy Brockman, *Corp Secy*
Tom Brockman, *Vice Pres*
EMP: 116
SQ FT: 30,000

SALES (est): 5.3MM **Privately Held**
WEB: www.brenn-field.com
SIC: 8051 8322 Convalescent home with continuous nursing care; individual & family services

(G-15627)
CONSUMERS GAS COOPERATIVE
298 Tracy Bridge Rd (44667-9383)
PHONE..................................330 682-4144
Anthony Kovakevich, *President*
EMP: 45
SALES (est): 2.1MM **Privately Held**
SIC: 4922 Natural gas transmission

(G-15628)
DUNLAP FAMILY PHYSICIANS INC (PA)
830 S Main St Ste Rear (44667-2218)
PHONE..................................330 684-2015
Larry Sander, *President*
Andrew Naumoff, *Family Practiti*
EMP: 34
SALES (est): 4.5MM **Privately Held**
SIC: 8011 General & family practice, physician/surgeon

(G-15629)
DUTCH CNTRY APPLE DMPLINGS INC
229 W Market St (44667-1848)
P.O. Box 603 (44667-0603)
PHONE..................................330 683-0646
Andrew Hamsher, *President*
Creg Rohr, *General Mgr*
EMP: 70
SQ FT: 12,000
SALES (est): 5.3MM **Privately Held**
SIC: 5149 Whol Groceries

(G-15630)
FAMILY PRACTICE CENTER INC
830 S Main St Ste Rear (44667-9598)
PHONE..................................330 682-3075
Oliver Eshenaur Do, *President*
Dr Charles D Milligan, *Corp Secy*
Dr Douglas R Brown, *Vice Pres*
EMP: 31
SQ FT: 10,300
SALES (est): 2.2MM **Privately Held**
SIC: 8031 Offices & clinics of osteopathic physicians

(G-15631)
FARMERS NATIONAL BANK
112 W Market St (44667-1847)
PHONE..................................330 682-1010
EMP: 122
SALES (corp-wide): 117.2MM **Publicly Held**
SIC: 6021 National commercial banks
HQ: Farmers National Bank
20 S Broad St
Canfield OH 44406
330 533-3341

(G-15632)
FARMERS NATIONAL BANK
1444 N Main St (44667-9169)
P.O. Box 57 (44667-0057)
PHONE..................................330 682-1030
Jim Griffith, *Manager*
EMP: 54
SALES (corp-wide): 117.2MM **Publicly Held**
WEB: www.fnborrville.com
SIC: 6021 National commercial banks
HQ: Farmers National Bank
20 S Broad St
Canfield OH 44406
330 533-3341

(G-15633)
GENERAL BUILDING MAINTENANCE
500 Jefferson Ave (44667-1811)
PHONE..................................330 682-2238
James M Corbett, *President*
Lavinia Corbett, *Vice Pres*
EMP: 80
SQ FT: 140
SALES (est): 2.4MM **Privately Held**
SIC: 7349 Janitorial service, contract basis

(G-15634)
HOFSTETTER ORRAN INC (PA)
12024 Lincoln Way E (44667-9639)
P.O. Box 237 (44667-0237)
PHONE..................................330 683-8070
John N Hofstetter, *Ch of Bd*
Kathy Hofstetter, *Treasurer*
EMP: 25
SQ FT: 15,000
SALES (est): 2.8MM **Privately Held**
SIC: 4213 4212 4491 4225 Trucking, except local; local trucking, without storage; loading vessels; unloading vessels; general warehousing & storage

(G-15635)
HUMMEL GROUP INC
461 Wadsworth Rd (44667-9215)
P.O. Box 3 (44667-0003)
PHONE..................................330 683-1050
Tony Rohrer, *Branch Mgr*
EMP: 30
SALES (corp-wide): 21.4MM **Privately Held**
SIC: 6411 Insurance agents
PA: Hummel Group, Inc.
4585 State Rt 39
Berlin OH
330 893-2600

(G-15636)
JARRETT LOGISTICS SYSTEMS INC
1347 N Main St (44667-9761)
PHONE..................................330 682-0099
Michael Jarrett, *President*
William McCabe, *Adv Board Mem*
Matt Angell, *Vice Pres*
Ellen Wood, *Hum Res Coord*
Duke Price, *Sales Staff*
EMP: 150
SQ FT: 73,000
SALES (est): 100MM **Privately Held**
WEB: www.jarrettlogistics.com
SIC: 8742 4731 Transportation consultant; freight transportation arrangement

(G-15637)
ORRVILLA INC
333 E Sassafras St (44667-2250)
PHONE..................................330 683-4455
Morris Stutcman, *Chairman*
George Bixler, *Director*
EMP: 25
SALES: 1.3MM **Privately Held**
WEB: www.orrvilla.com
SIC: 6513 Retirement hotel operation

(G-15638)
ORRVILLA RETIREMENT COMMUNITY
Also Called: Manor 1
333 E Sassafras St (44667-2250)
PHONE..................................330 683-4455
George Bixler, *Director*
EMP: 35
SALES (est): 1.2MM **Privately Held**
SIC: 8361 Home for the aged

(G-15639)
ORRVILLE BOYS AND GIRLS CLUB
820 N Ella St (44667-1155)
P.O. Box 17 (44667-0017)
PHONE..................................330 683-4888
Kevin Platz, *Exec Dir*
EMP: 32
SALES (est): 1.6MM **Privately Held**
WEB: www.oabgc.org
SIC: 8641 Youth organizations

(G-15640)
ORRVILLE HOSPITAL FOUNDATION
Also Called: Aultman Orrville Hospital
832 S Main St (44667-2208)
PHONE..................................330 684-4700
Marchelle Suppan, *CEO*
Kim Gossard, *Human Resources*
EMP: 240
SQ FT: 90,000
SALES: 25.2MM **Privately Held**
SIC: 8062 General medical & surgical hospitals

(G-15641)
ORRVILLE TRUCKING &
GRADING CO (PA)
475 Orr St (44667-9764)
P.O. Box 220 (44667-0220)
PHONE..................................330 682-4010
Auvil Richmond, *President*
John H Wilson, *Treasurer*
EMP: 50
SQ FT: 15,000
SALES (est): 7.4MM **Privately Held**
SIC: 3273 3272 5031 Ready-mixed concrete; concrete products; building materials, exterior; building materials, interior

(G-15642)
ORVILLE PET SPA & RESORT
1669 N Main St (44667-9171)
PHONE..................................330 683-3335
Anne Kollier, *Office Mgr*
Anne Weiser, *Manager*
EMP: 25
SALES (est): 473.1K **Privately Held**
SIC: 0752 Boarding services, kennels

(G-15643)
PACKSHIP USA INC (PA)
1347 N Main St (44667-9761)
PHONE..................................330 682-7225
W Michael Jarrett, *President*
Diane Jarrett, *Vice Pres*
EMP: 56
SQ FT: 15,000
SALES (est): 7.3MM **Privately Held**
WEB: www.packshipusa.com
SIC: 7389 4783 4731 Packaging & labeling services; packing & crating; freight transportation arrangement

(G-15644)
PINES GOLF CLUB
1319 N Millborne Rd (44667-9500)
P.O. Box 308 (44667-0308)
PHONE..................................330 684-1414
Glen Miller, *Partner*
Ron Contini, *Partner*
Gary Ertle, *Partner*
Glenn Miller, *Partner*
Howard Wenger, *Partner*
EMP: 25
SALES (est): 1.3MM **Privately Held**
SIC: 7992 5812 7299 5941 Public golf courses; eating places; banquet hall facilities; sporting goods & bicycle shops

(G-15645)
REGENCY PARK
230 S Crown Hill Rd (44667-1328)
PHONE..................................330 682-2273
Robert Kline, *President*
Harvey Rickert Sr, *President*
Harvey Rickert Jr, *Vice Pres*
EMP: 80 **EST:** 1996
SALES (est): 1.1MM **Privately Held**
SIC: 8059 Nursing home, except skilled & intermediate care facility

(G-15646)
REGENCY PARK NURSING &
REHAB
230 S Crown Hill Rd (44667-1328)
PHONE..................................330 682-2273
Robert Klein, *President*
Alan Jaffa, *Treasurer*
EMP: 55
SALES (est): 2.1MM **Privately Held**
SIC: 8059 Nursing home, except skilled & intermediate care facility

(G-15647)
SIDLE TRANSIT SERVICE INC
5454 N Crown Hill Rd (44667-9134)
PHONE..................................330 683-2807
Dennis I Sidle, *President*
Duane B Sidle, *Corp Secy*
EMP: 35 **EST:** 1954
SALES (est): 3.3MM **Privately Held**
SIC: 4212 Liquid haulage, local

(G-15648)
SMITHFOODS ORRVILLE INC
1381 Dairy Ln (44667-2503)
PHONE..................................330 683-8710
Jerry Cosentino, *Purch Mgr*
John Owens, *Manager*

EMP: 99
SALES (corp-wide): 202.1MM **Privately Held**
SIC: 5143 Dairy products, except dried or canned
HQ: Smithfoods Orrville Inc.
1381 Dairy Ln
Orrville OH 44667
330 683-8710

(G-15649)
WILL-BURT COMPANY (PA)
169 S Main St (44667-1801)
P.O. Box 900 (44667-0900)
PHONE..................................330 682-7015
Jeffrey Evans, *President*
Phil Tryon, *General Mgr*
John Glenn, *Regional Mgr*
Thomas Howard, *Business Mgr*
Travis Powell, *Business Mgr*
▲ **EMP:** 275 **EST:** 1918
SQ FT: 170,000
SALES (est): 63.8MM **Privately Held**
WEB: www.willburt.com
SIC: 3599 5039 3443 3449 Machine shop, jobbing & repair; prefabricated structures; fabricated plate work (boiler shop); miscellaneous metalwork; lighting equipment; sheet metalwork

(G-15650)
WILL-BURT COMPANY
312 Collins Blvd (44667-9727)
P.O. Box 900 (44667-0900)
PHONE..................................330 682-7015
Andrew Wasson, *Engineer*
Jeffrey O Evans, *Manager*
EMP: 37
SALES (corp-wide): 63.8MM **Privately Held**
WEB: www.willburt.com
SIC: 3443 3449 3599 5039 Fabricated plate work (boiler shop); miscellaneous metalwork; machine shop, jobbing & repair; prefabricated structures
PA: The Will-Burt Company
169 S Main St
Orrville OH 44667
330 682-7015

Orwell
Ashtabula County

(G-15651)
COUNTRY NEIGHBOR
PROGRAM INC (PA)
39 S Maple St (44076-9501)
P.O. Box 212 (44076-0212)
PHONE..................................440 437-6311
Lester Marrison, *President*
Kasey Obrien, *President*
Barbara Klingensmith, *Exec Dir*
William Enstrom, *Bd of Directors*
Carl Plickert, *Admin Sec*
EMP: 40
SQ FT: 8,000
SALES (est): 1.8MM **Privately Held**
WEB: www.countryneighbor.org
SIC: 8322 Referral service for personal & social problems

Osgood
Darke County

(G-15652)
DYNAMIC WELD CORPORATION
242 N St (45351)
P.O. Box 127 (45351-0127)
PHONE..................................419 582-2900
Harry Heitkamp, *President*
Sue Heitkamp, *Finance Mgr*
EMP: 44
SQ FT: 35,000
SALES (est): 11.8MM **Privately Held**
WEB: www.dynamicweld.com
SIC: 3444 7692 Sheet metalwork; welding repair

(G-15653)
OSGOOD STATE BANK (INC)
(PA)
275 W Main St (45351)
P.O. Box 69 (45351-0069)
PHONE..................................419 582-2681
Jon Alexander, *Chairman*
Mandy Ranly, *Branch Mgr*
Tony Kaiser, *Officer*
Katey Wibbenmeyer, *Officer*
EMP: 40 **EST:** 1915
SQ FT: 4,500
SALES: 9.6MM **Privately Held**
SIC: 6022 6163 State trust companies accepting deposits, commercial; loan brokers

Ostrander
Delaware County

(G-15654)
MILL CREEK GOLF COURSE
CORP
Also Called: Mill Creek Golf Club
7259 Penn Rd (43061-9430)
PHONE..................................740 666-7711
Jeanne Bash, *President*
Janice E Curtis, *Treasurer*
Nancy Plant, *Admin Sec*
EMP: 35 **EST:** 1972
SQ FT: 1,700
SALES: 1MM **Privately Held**
WEB: www.millcreekgolfclub.com
SIC: 7992 7997 Public golf courses; golf club, membership

(G-15655)
SHELLY MATERIALS INC
8328 Watkins Rd (43061-9311)
PHONE..................................740 666-5841
Keith Siler, *Vice Pres*
EMP: 25
SALES (corp-wide): 29.7B **Privately Held**
SIC: 2951 1611 3274 1422 Asphalt & asphaltic paving mixtures (not from refineries); surfacing & paving; lime; crushed & broken limestone
HQ: Shelly Materials, Inc.
80 Park Dr
Thornville OH 43076
740 246-6315

(G-15656)
T & B ELECTRIC LTD
7464 Watkins Rd (43061-9309)
PHONE..................................740 881-5696
Lynn Vara,
Thomas Beshara,
EMP: 40
SQ FT: 3,600
SALES (est): 4.7MM **Privately Held**
SIC: 1731 General electrical contractor

Ottawa
Putnam County

(G-15657)
BROOKHILL CENTER
INDUSTRIES
7989 State Route 108 (45875-9678)
PHONE..................................419 876-3932
Bill Unterbink, *President*
EMP: 115
SQ FT: 16,000
SALES: 1.8MM **Privately Held**
SIC: 8331 2448 Sheltered workshop; wood pallets & skids

(G-15658)
CROYS MOWING LLC
440 N Maple St (45875-1331)
PHONE..................................419 523-5884
Lyle Croy, *Accounts Mgr*
Donald Croy,
EMP: 25
SALES (est): 1.5MM **Privately Held**
SIC: 0782 Mowing services, lawn

(G-15659)
HOVEST CONSTRUCTION
4997 Old State Route 224 (45875-9763)
PHONE..................................419 456-3426
Ed Hovest Jr, *President*
Charles Hovest, *Corp Secy*
EMP: 30
SALES (est): 1.8MM **Privately Held**
WEB: www.hovestconstruction.com
SIC: 1741 1791 1771 Masonry & other stonework; structural steel erection; concrete work

(G-15660)
NELSON MANUFACTURING
COMPANY
6448 State Route 224 (45875-9789)
PHONE..................................419 523-5321
Anthony Niese, *President*
Chad Stall, *Vice Pres*
Patricia Taylor, *Treasurer*
Amy Niece, *Admin Sec*
▼ **EMP:** 80 **EST:** 1947
SQ FT: 46,000
SALES: 17.6MM **Privately Held**
WEB: www.nelsontrailer.com
SIC: 3715 7539 Semitrailers for truck tractors; trailer repair

(G-15661)
NIESE TRANSPORT INC
Also Called: Niese Leasing
418 N Agner St (45875-1537)
P.O. Box 226 (45875-0226)
PHONE..................................419 523-4400
Jerry Niese, *President*
Kevin Niese, *Vice Pres*
Sam Langhals, *Manager*
EMP: 30
SALES (est): 1.7MM **Privately Held**
SIC: 4789 Transportation services

(G-15662)
ORTHODONTIC ASSOCIATION
1020 N Perry St (45875-1158)
PHONE..................................419 523-4014
Thomas Ahman, *Mng Member*
EMP: 50
SALES (est): 366.5K **Privately Held**
SIC: 8021 Orthodontist

(G-15663)
PANDORA MANUFACTURING
LLC (PA)
157 W Main St (45875-1721)
PHONE..................................419 384-3241
Dave Roper, *Mng Member*
Patrick Parks,
EMP: 51
SQ FT: 113,000
SALES (est): 6.7MM **Privately Held**
WEB: www.pandoramfg.com
SIC: 7389 Packaging & labeling services

(G-15664)
PIKE RUN GOLF CLUB INC
10807 Road H (45875-9655)
PHONE..................................419 538-7000
Charles Miller, *President*
Steve Radcliff, *General Mgr*
Kenneth Pester, *Vice Pres*
James Hattery, *Treasurer*
Robert Buckland, *Admin Sec*
EMP: 27
SQ FT: 4,100
SALES: 704.4K **Privately Held**
SIC: 7997 5813 5812 Golf club, membership; cocktail lounge; eating places

(G-15665)
PUTNAM CNTY HOMECARE &
HOSPICE
575 Ottawa (45875)
P.O. Box 312 (45875-0312)
PHONE..................................419 523-4449
Jodie Lammers, *Principal*
Pamela Sager, *Exec Dir*
EMP: 63
SALES: 1.4MM **Privately Held**
SIC: 8082 Home health care services

GEOGRAPHIC

(G-15666)
R K INDUSTRIES INC
725 N Locust St (45875-1466)
P.O. Box 306 (45875-0306)
PHONE....................................419 523-5001
Ann Woodyard, *President*
Joe Maag, *Vice Pres*
Barry Woodyard, *Manager*
Kimberly French, *Admin Sec*
▲ **EMP:** 85
SQ FT: 45,000
SALES (est): 8.8MM **Privately Held**
WEB: www.rkindustries.org
SIC: 7692 3465 Automotive welding; automotive stampings

(G-15667)
YOUNG MENS CHRISTIAN ASSOC
Also Called: Putnam County Y M C A
101 Putnam Pkwy (45875-8657)
PHONE....................................419 523-5233
Lynn Watchnan, *Manager*
EMP: 84
SALES (corp-wide): 16.8MM **Privately Held**
WEB: www.campynoah.com
SIC: 8641 8351 Recreation association; child day care services
PA: The Young Men's Christian Association Of Akron Ohio
50 S Mn St Ste LI100
Akron OH 44308
330 376-1335

Ottawa Hills
Lucas County

(G-15668)
OTTAWA HILLS MEMORIAL PARK
4210 W Central Ave Ste 1 (43606-2270)
PHONE....................................419 539-0218
Jay M Brammer, *President*
EMP: 35
SQ FT: 1,350
SALES (est): 1.5MM **Privately Held**
SIC: 6553 Cemeteries, real estate operation; mausoleum operation

(G-15669)
SUNSET RTRMENT COMMUNITIES INC (PA)
4040 Indian Rd (43606-2266)
PHONE....................................419 724-1200
Vicky Bartlett, *CEO*
Cynthia Williams, *Trustee*
Christine Gladieux, *CFO*
Joseph Zigray, *Treasurer*
Tiffany Dowling, *Human Res Dir*
EMP: 100 **EST:** 1873
SALES: 17.4MM **Privately Held**
SIC: 6513 8361 Retirement hotel operation; home for the aged

Ottoville
Putnam County

(G-15670)
MILLER CONTRACTING GROUP INC
17359 S Rt E 66 (45876)
P.O. Box 162 (45876-0162)
PHONE....................................419 453-3825
Alan J Miller, *President*
Patrick Miller, *Vice Pres*
EMP: 44
SALES (est): 12.9MM **Privately Held**
WEB: www.millercontractinggroup.com
SIC: 1542 1521 Commercial & office building, new construction; single-family housing construction

Owensville
Clermont County

(G-15671)
DEVELOPMENTAL DISABILITIES
Also Called: Thomas A Wildey School
204 State Rte Hwy 50ben (45160)
P.O. Box 8 (45160-0008)
PHONE....................................513 732-7015
Jay Williams, *Principal*
EMP: 100
SALES (corp-wide): 2.7MM **Privately Held**
WEB: www.ccmrdd.org
SIC: 8322 Individual & family services
PA: Clermont County Board Of Developmental Disabilities
2040 Us Highway 50
Batavia OH 45103
513 732-7000

Oxford
Butler County

(G-15672)
ALEXANDER HOUSE INC
Also Called: Governor's Room
118 Hilltop Rd (45056-1521)
PHONE....................................513 523-4569
Steve Friede, *President*
EMP: 25
SALES (est): 599.9K **Privately Held**
SIC: 7011 Bed & breakfast inn

(G-15673)
BETA THETA PI FRATERNITY (PA)
5134 Bonham Rd (45056-1429)
P.O. Box 6277 (45056-6067)
PHONE....................................513 523-7591
Clark V Carbioo, *Finance*
Jeff Runtel, *Admin Sec*
Stephen B Becker, *Admin Sec*
EMP: 30
SQ FT: 18,000
SALES: 6.3MM **Privately Held**
SIC: 8641 University club

(G-15674)
BUTLER RURAL ELECTRIC COOP
3888 Stillwell Beckett Rd (45056-9115)
PHONE....................................513 867-4400
Thomas Mc Quiston, *President*
Michael Sims, *General Mgr*
Michael L Sims, *Principal*
Mary Beth Dorrel, *Corp Secy*
Kim Gebhart, *Vice Pres*
EMP: 38
SQ FT: 27,000
SALES: 32.1MM **Privately Held**
WEB: www.butlerrural.coop
SIC: 4911 Distribution, electric power

(G-15675)
CAPITOL VARSITY SPORTS INC
6723 Ringwood Rd (45056-9709)
P.O. Box 669 (45056-0669)
PHONE....................................513 523-4126
Bob Fawley, *President*
Scott Trostel, *Marketing Staff*
EMP: 30
SQ FT: 22,000
SALES (est): 5.2MM **Privately Held**
WEB: www.capitolvarsitysports.com
SIC: 5941 7699 Specialty sport supplies; team sports equipment; football equipment; baseball equipment; recreational sporting equipment repair services

(G-15676)
CASH FLOW SOLUTIONS INC
5166 College Corner Pike (45056-1004)
PHONE....................................513 524-2320
Kasey Princell, *President*
EMP: 51
SQ FT: 6,000
SALES (est): 20.2MM **Privately Held**
SIC: 8748 Business consulting

(G-15677)
FIRST MIAMI STUDENT CREDIT UN
117 Shriver Ctr (45056)
PHONE....................................513 529-1251
Randi M Thomas, *Chairman*
EMP: 50
SALES: 28.9K **Privately Held**
SIC: 6061 Federal Credit Union

(G-15678)
INDIAN RIDGE GOLF CLUB L L C
2600 Oxford Millville Rd (45056-9415)
PHONE....................................513 524-4653
Jim Robefon,
Tim Derickson,
Dale Leirman,
Jim Rohr,
EMP: 40
SALES (est): 1.9MM **Privately Held**
WEB: www.theindianridgegolfclub.com
SIC: 7992 Public golf courses

(G-15679)
MAPLE KNOLL COMMUNITIES INC
6727 Contreras Rd (45056-8769)
PHONE....................................513 524-7990
Lina Mares, *Exec Dir*
EMP: 30
SALES (est): 566.9K
SALES (corp-wide): 43.4MM **Privately Held**
SIC: 8051 8361 Convalescent home with continuous nursing care; residential care
PA: Knoll Maple Communities Inc
11100 Springfield Pike
Cincinnati OH 45246
513 782-2400

(G-15680)
MCCULLOUGH-HYDE MEM HOSP INC (PA)
110 N Poplar St (45056-1204)
PHONE....................................513 523-2111
Bryan D Hehemann, *President*
Richard Norman, *Chairman*
Alan D Oak, *Corp Secy*
Chris Lauer, *CFO*
Sherry Callahan, *Manager*
EMP: 500
SQ FT: 115,000
SALES: 55.4MM **Privately Held**
SIC: 8062 General medical & surgical hospitals

(G-15681)
MIAMI UNIVERSITY
Also Called: Marcum Conference Center
Fisher Dr (45056)
PHONE....................................513 529-6911
Cornch Waite, *Manager*
EMP: 75
SALES (corp-wide): 551.7MM **Privately Held**
WEB: www.muohio.edu
SIC: 8221 7389 University; convention & show services
PA: Miami University
501 E High St
Oxford OH 45056
513 529-1809

(G-15682)
MIAMI UNIVERSITY
First Miami University Student
701 E Spring St Ste 117 (45056-2801)
PHONE....................................513 529-1251
Willard Hopkins, *Manager*
EMP: 50
SALES (corp-wide): 551.7MM **Privately Held**
WEB: www.muohio.edu
SIC: 6061 8221 Federal credit unions; university
PA: Miami University
501 E High St
Oxford OH 45056
513 529-1809

(G-15683)
MIAMI UNIVERSITY
Also Called: Office of Divisional Support
725 E Chestnut St (45056-3450)
PHONE....................................513 529-1230

Jane Whitehead, *Vice Pres*
Coleman Barnes, *Director*
Jennifer Clark, *Director*
Jay Fridy, *Director*
Jill Gaby, *Director*
EMP: 80
SQ FT: 2,001
SALES (corp-wide): 551.7MM **Privately Held**
WEB: www.muohio.edu
SIC: 7389 8221 Fund raising organizations; university
PA: Miami University
501 E High St
Oxford OH 45056
513 529-1809

(G-15684)
MILLER BROTHERS CNSTR DEM LLC
3685 Oxford Millville Rd (45056-9038)
PHONE....................................513 257-1082
Frederick Click,
Mitch Stevenson,
Steve Stevenson II,
EMP: 35
SQ FT: 2,000
SALES (est): 1.9MM **Privately Held**
SIC: 1795 Demolition, buildings & other structures

(G-15685)
MINI UNIVERSITY INC
401 Western College Dr (45056-1902)
PHONE....................................513 275-5184
Ruth Williamson, *Director*
EMP: 69
SALES (corp-wide): 1MM **Privately Held**
SIC: 8351 Child day care services
PA: Mini University Inc
115 Harbert Dr Ste A
Beavercreek OH 45440
937 426-1414

(G-15686)
OXFORD COUNTRY CLUB INC
6200 Contreras Rd (45056-9736)
P.O. Box 229 (45056-0229)
PHONE....................................513 524-0801
Reed Maltbie, *President*
Jeff McDonald, *Vice Pres*
Jack Cotter, *Treasurer*
Jj Slager, *Admin Sec*
EMP: 28
SALES (est): 1.4MM **Privately Held**
SIC: 7997 Country club, membership; golf club, membership; swimming club, membership; tennis club, membership

(G-15687)
OXFORD HOSPITALITY GROUP INC
Also Called: Comfort Inn
5056 College Corner Pike (45056-1103)
PHONE....................................513 524-0114
Dennis Day, *President*
EMP: 25
SALES (est): 914.2K **Privately Held**
SIC: 7011 Hotels & motels

(G-15688)
RDI CORPORATION
110 S Locust St Ste A (45056-1751)
PHONE....................................513 524-3320
George Trebbi, *President*
EMP: 100
SALES (corp-wide): 80.7MM **Privately Held**
SIC: 7389 Telemarketing services
PA: The Rdi Corporation
4350 Glendale Milford Rd # 250
Blue Ash OH 45242
513 984-5927

(G-15689)
RED BRICK PROPERTY MGT LLC
21 N Poplar St (45056-1254)
PHONE....................................513 524-9340
Matt Rodro, *President*
EMP: 50
SQ FT: 1,938
SALES (est): 3.4MM **Privately Held**
WEB: www.redbrickproperty.com
SIC: 6531 Real estate managers

▲ = Import ▼=Export
◆ =Import/Export

(G-15690)
TIME WARNER CABLE INC
114 S Locust St (45056-1717)
PHONE................................513 523-6333
Danny Schiffer, *Manager*
EMP: 83
SALES (corp-wide): 43.6B **Publicly Held**
SIC: 4841 Cable television services
HQ: Spectrum Management Holding Company, Llc
400 Atlantic St
Stamford CT 06901
203 905-7801

Painesville
Lake County

(G-15691)
ABLE CONTRACTING GROUP INC (PA)
Also Called: Able Fence & Guard Rail Co
11117 Caddie Ln (44077-8939)
PHONE................................440 951-0880
Donna Richards, *President*
Douglas J Richards, *COO*
Marianne Richards, *Treasurer*
EMP: 25 EST: 1971
SQ FT: 12,500
SALES (est): 3.3MM **Privately Held**
WEB: www.ablefence.com
SIC: 1611 0782 5211 Highway & street maintenance; guardrail construction, highways; highway & street sign installation; highway lawn & garden maintenance services; fencing

(G-15692)
AEROCONTROLEX GROUP INC (DH)
313 Gillett St (44077-2918)
PHONE................................440 352-6182
Raymond Laubenthal, *President*
Mario Jurcevic, *Engineer*
Robert George, *Treasurer*
Michael Carney, *Sales Dir*
Bob Miller, *IT/INT Sup*
EMP: 99
SQ FT: 55,000
SALES (est): 18.7MM
SALES (corp-wide): 3.8B **Publicly Held**
WEB: www.aerocontrolex.com
SIC: 3492 5084 3594 Valves, hydraulic, aircraft; industrial machinery & equipment; fluid power pumps & motors

(G-15693)
ANESTHESIA ASSOCIATES INC
7757 Auburn Rd Ste 15 (44077-9604)
PHONE................................440 350-0832
James Donohue, *President*
EMP: 30
SQ FT: 1,000
SALES (est): 3.3MM **Privately Held**
SIC: 8011 Anesthesiologist

(G-15694)
AROUND CLOCK HOME CARE
7757 Auburn Rd Ste 6 (44077-9604)
PHONE................................440 350-2547
Carmen Ettinger, *Director*
EMP: 75
SALES: 898.9K **Privately Held**
WEB: www.lcghd.org
SIC: 8049 8082 Nurses, registered & practical; home health care services

(G-15695)
BENEVOLENT/PROTECTV ORDER ELKS
Also Called: Elks Lodge 549
723 Liberty St (44077-3623)
PHONE................................440 357-6943
Dave Larsen, *Principal*
EMP: 27 EST: 1972
SALES: 310.3K **Privately Held**
SIC: 8641 Civic associations; fraternal associations

(G-15696)
BURGESS & NIPLE INC
100 W Erie St (44077-3203)
PHONE................................440 354-9700

Charles J Zibbel, *Manager*
EMP: 75
SALES (corp-wide): 122.1MM **Privately Held**
WEB: www.burgessniple.com
SIC: 8711 8712 Consulting engineer; architectural services
PA: Burgess & Niple, Inc.
5085 Reed Rd
Columbus OH 43220
502 254-2344

(G-15697)
C & M EXPRESS LOGISTICS INC
342 Blackbrook Rd (44077-1217)
PHONE................................440 350-0802
Michael Pettrey, *President*
EMP: 25
SQ FT: 6,000
SALES: 7MM **Privately Held**
SIC: 4731 Freight forwarding

(G-15698)
CINTAS CORPORATION NO 2
800 Renaissance Pkwy (44077-1287)
PHONE................................440 352-4003
Richard Farmer, *Branch Mgr*
EMP: 98
SALES (corp-wide): 6.4B **Publicly Held**
WEB: www.cintas-corp.com
SIC: 7213 Uniform supply
HQ: Cintas Corporation No 2
6800 Cintas Blvd
Mason OH 45040

(G-15699)
CITY OF PAINESVILLE
Also Called: Painesville Municipal Electric
325 Richmond St (44077-3262)
P.O. Box 601 (44077-0601)
PHONE................................440 392-5954
Thomas A Green, *Superintendent*
EMP: 43 **Privately Held**
WEB: www.pmcourt.com
SIC: 4911 ; distribution, electric power; transmission, electric power
PA: City Of Painesville
7 Richmond St
Painesville OH 44077
440 352-9301

(G-15700)
CITY OF PAINESVILLE
Also Called: Utilities Dept
7 Richmond St (44077-3222)
P.O. Box 601 (44077-0601)
PHONE................................440 392-5795
Timothy Petric, *Director*
EMP: 294 **Privately Held**
WEB: www.pmcourt.com
SIC: 4939 Combination utilities
PA: City Of Painesville
7 Richmond St
Painesville OH 44077
440 352-9301

(G-15701)
CLASSIC BUICK OLDS CADILLAC
Also Called: Classic Oldsmobile
1700 Mentor Ave (44077-1438)
PHONE................................440 639-4500
Ralph W Wilson, *President*
EMP: 75
SQ FT: 35,000
SALES (est): 22.8MM **Privately Held**
WEB: www.classicoldsmobile.com
SIC: 5511 7515 Automobiles, new & used; passenger car leasing

(G-15702)
CLEVELAND ELC ILLUMINATING CO
7755 Auburn Rd (44077-9177)
PHONE................................440 953-7650
Tom McGonnell, *Manager*
EMP: 70 **Publicly Held**
SIC: 4911 Distribution, electric power
HQ: The Cleveland Electric Illuminating Company
76 S Main St
Akron OH 44308
800 589-3101

(G-15703)
COMFORT KEEPERS
368 Blackbrook Rd (44077-1285)
P.O. Box 1000 (44077-8280)
PHONE................................440 721-0100
Dale Gassor, *Owner*
EMP: 45
SALES (est): 782.9K **Privately Held**
SIC: 8082 Visiting nurse service

(G-15704)
CONCORD BIOSCIENCES LLC
10845 Wellness Way (44077-9041)
PHONE................................440 357-3200
Clifford W Croley, *CEO*
Michael W Martell, *Exec VP*
Mike O'Neill, *Research*
William Janz, *Engineer*
Art Cooper, *Manager*
EMP: 94
SQ FT: 260,000
SALES (est): 12.5MM
SALES (corp-wide): 43.6MM **Privately Held**
WEB: www.ricerca.com
SIC: 8731 Medical research, commercial
PA: Frontage Laboratories, Inc.
700 Pennsylvania Dr
Exton PA 19341
610 232-0100

(G-15705)
CONSULTNTS IN GASTROENTEROLOGY
7530 Fredle Dr (44077-9406)
PHONE................................440 386-2250
Davivd Gottesman, *President*
Fred Kessler, *Principal*
Peter Yang, *Principal*
Don Brinberg, *Vice Pres*
Miriam Vishny, *Admin Sec*
EMP: 30
SALES (est): 1.8MM **Privately Held**
SIC: 8011 Gastronomist

(G-15706)
CROSSROADS LAKE COUNTY ADOLE
Also Called: Cross Roads Head Start
1083 Mentor Ave (44077-1829)
PHONE................................440 358-7370
Susan Walsh, *Manager*
EMP: 25
SALES (corp-wide): 7.5MM **Privately Held**
WEB: www.crossroads-lake.org
SIC: 8351 Head start center, except in conjunction with school
PA: Crossroads Lake County Adolescent Counseling Service
8445 Munson Rd
Mentor OH 44060
440 255-1700

(G-15707)
D B BENTLEY INC
Also Called: Bentley Excavating
2649 Narrows Rd (44077-4908)
PHONE................................440 352-8495
Mike Bentley, *President*
Dennis R Bentley, *Vice Pres*
Dennis B Bentley, *Treasurer*
Joshua Vance, *Advisor*
EMP: 25 EST: 1976
SALES: 5MM **Privately Held**
WEB: www.bentleyexc.com
SIC: 1611 1794 General contractor, highway & street construction; excavation work

(G-15708)
DE NORA TECH LLC (DH)
7590 Discovery Ln (44077-9190)
PHONE................................440 710-5300
Paolo Dellacha, *CEO*
Charlotte Valencic, *General Mgr*
Frank J McGorty, *COO*
Tony Friedrich, *Plant Mgr*
Donna Shipman, *Buyer*
◆ EMP: 80 EST: 1982
SQ FT: 20,000

SALES (est): 40.9MM **Privately Held**
WEB: www.eltechsystems.com
SIC: 3624 3589 7359 Electrodes, thermal & electrolytic uses: carbon, graphite; sewage & water treatment equipment; equipment rental & leasing
HQ: Industrie De Nora Spa
Via Leonardo Bistolfi 35
Milano MI 20134
022 129-1

(G-15709)
DIZER CORP (PA)
1912 Mentor Ave (44077-1325)
PHONE................................440 368-0200
Jagdish Medarametla, *President*
Mohammed Ghouse, *Engineer*
Gopi Krishna, *Consultant*
Ranjith Patel, *Technology*
Srikkanth Reddy, *IT/INT Sup*
EMP: 27
SQ FT: 2,300
SALES (est): 7.9MM **Privately Held**
WEB: www.dizercorp.com
SIC: 7371 8711 Computer software development; engineering services

(G-15710)
DOLBEY SYSTEMS INC (PA)
7280 Auburn Rd (44077-9724)
PHONE................................440 392-9900
Kris Wilson, *President*
Matt Turner, *Regional Mgr*
Chris Casto, *Vice Pres*
Patricia Dempsey, *Sales Mgr*
EMP: 37
SQ FT: 26,000
SALES (est): 7.2MM **Privately Held**
SIC: 5045 Computer software

(G-15711)
DWORKEN & BERNSTEIN CO LPA
60 S Park Pl Fl 2 (44077-3417)
PHONE................................440 352-3391
Toll Free:................................877 -
Howard Rebb, *Manager*
Ann Bollas, *Admin Asst*
William Crosby, *Administration*
Kim Rawley, *Receptionist*
Patrick Brickman, *Associate*
EMP: 40
SALES (corp-wide): 5.7MM **Privately Held**
WEB: www.dworken-bernstein.com
SIC: 8111 General practice attorney, lawyer
PA: Dworken & Bernstein Co Lpa
1468 W 9th St Ste 135
Cleveland OH 44113
216 861-4211

(G-15712)
EMILY MANAGEMENT INC
Also Called: Quality Plus
10280 Pinecrest Rd (44077-9795)
PHONE................................440 354-6713
Elizabeth Bauer, *President*
Debbie Jasic, *Manager*
EMP: 60
SALES (est): 1.4MM **Privately Held**
SIC: 7363 Temporary help service

(G-15713)
ENVIROTEST SYSTEMS CORP
Also Called: Ohio E Check
1755 N Ridge Rd (44077-4811)
PHONE................................330 963-4464
Mike Hensley, *Manager*
EMP: 25 **Privately Held**
SIC: 7549 Emissions testing without repairs, automotive
HQ: Envirotest Systems Corp.
7 Kripes Rd
East Granby CT 06026

(G-15714)
FIRST FRANCIS COMPANY INC (HQ)
Also Called: Federal Hose Manufacturing
25 Florence Ave (44077-1103)
PHONE................................440 352-8927
Ron George, *President*
Dave Lally, *Vice Pres*
Debbie Middleton, *Vice Pres*
John Lally, *Controller*

EMP: 28 **EST:** 1997
SALES (est): 6.8MM
SALES (corp-wide): 66.3MM **Publicly Held**
WEB: www.federalhose.com
SIC: 5085 3599 3444 3429 Hose, belting & packing; hose, flexible metallic; sheet metalwork; manufactured hardware (general)
PA: Hickok Incorporated
10514 Dupont Ave
Cleveland OH 44108
216 541-8060

(G-15715)
HOMESTEAD II HEALTHCARE GROUP
60 Wood St (44077-3396)
PHONE.................................440 352-0788
George S Repchick, *President*
William I Weisberg, *Vice Pres*
Sarah Depompei, *Assistant*
EMP: 321 **EST:** 2012
SALES: 3.8MM
SALES (corp-wide): 157.7MM **Privately Held**
SIC: 8051 Skilled nursing care facilities
PA: Saber Healthcare Group, L.L.C.
26691 Richmond Rd Frnt
Bedford OH 44146
216 292-5706

(G-15716)
JERSEY CENTRAL PWR & LIGHT CO
Also Called: Firstenergy
7755 Auburn Rd (44077-9177)
PHONE.................................440 953-7651
Heintz Limer, *Manager*
EMP: 100 **Publicly Held**
WEB: www.jersey-central-power-light.monmouth.n
SIC: 4911 Electric services
HQ: Jersey Central Power & Light Company
76 S Main St
Akron OH 44308
800 736-3402

(G-15717)
JPMORGAN CHASE BANK NAT ASSN
30 S Park Pl Ste 100 (44077-3467)
PHONE.................................440 352-5969
Janet Cummings, *Manager*
EMP: 500
SALES (corp-wide): 131.4B **Publicly Held**
WEB: www.chase.com
SIC: 6021 Natl Commercial Banks
HQ: Jpmorgan Chase Bank, National Association
1111 Polaris Pkwy
Columbus OH 43240
614 436-3055

(G-15718)
LAKE COUNTY YMCA (PA)
933 Mentor Ave Fl 2 (44077-2519)
PHONE.................................440 352-3303
Richard Bennett, *CEO*
Janet Storer, *Business Mgr*
Bob Diak, *COO*
Erin Pinkston, *Vice Pres*
Lori Franceschini, *Human Resources*
EMP: 150
SQ FT: 80,000
SALES: 8.9MM **Privately Held**
SIC: 8641 7991 8351 7032 Youth organizations; physical fitness facilities; child day care services; youth camps; individual & family services

(G-15719)
LAKE HOSPITAL SYSTEM INC (PA)
Also Called: Tripoint Medical Center
7590 Auburn Rd (44077-9176)
PHONE.................................440 375-8100
Cynthia Moore-Hardy, *President*
Richard Cicero, *Senior VP*
Michael E Kittoe, *Senior VP*
Jim Mortach, *Opers Mgr*
Earl Inks, *Senior Buyer*
EMP: 1200

SQ FT: 150,000
SALES: 356.8MM **Privately Held**
WEB: www.lakehospitalsystem.com
SIC: 8062 Hospital, affiliated with AMA residency

(G-15720)
LAKE METROPARKS (PA)
11211 Spear Rd (44077-8902)
P.O. Box 1140, Columbus (43216-1140)
PHONE.................................440 639-7275
Jean Hacker, *General Mgr*
Skip Dugan, *Opers Staff*
Christopher Brassell, *CFO*
Sharon Sharpnack, *Marketing Mgr*
Sharon Jenkins, *Marketing Staff*
EMP: 350
SQ FT: 25,000
SALES (est): 20.9MM **Privately Held**
WEB: www.lakemetroparks.com
SIC: 7999 Recreation services

(G-15721)
LAKETRAN
555 Lakeshore Blvd (44077-1121)
P.O. Box 158, Grand River (44045-0158)
PHONE.................................440 350-1000
Ray Jurkowski, *CEO*
Andrew Alpenweg, *General Mgr*
EMP: 210
SQ FT: 150,000
SALES: 2.2MM **Privately Held**
WEB: www.laketran.com
SIC: 4111 Subway operation

(G-15722)
LEROY TWP FIRE DEPT
13028 Leroy Center Rd (44077-9317)
PHONE.................................440 254-4124
Franklin Huffman, *Chief*
EMP: 30 **Privately Held**
SIC: 9224 8099 Fire department, volunteer; medical rescue squad

(G-15723)
MADISON ROUTE 20 LLC
Also Called: Little Mountain Country Club
7667 Hermitage Rd (44077-9770)
PHONE.................................440 358-7888
Richard M Osbourne Sr,
Steven A Calabrese,
EMP: 50
SALES: 2MM **Privately Held**
SIC: 7997 7992 5941 5813 Golf club, membership; public golf courses; sporting goods & bicycle shops; drinking places; eating places

(G-15724)
MC NEAL INDUSTRIES INC
835 Richmond Rd (44077-1123)
PHONE.................................440 721-0400
Randall McNeil, *President*
Randall J Mc Neil, *President*
Justine McNeal, *Vice Pres*
EMP: 30
SALES (est): 5.6MM **Privately Held**
SIC: 5085 Seals, industrial

(G-15725)
MCCALLISTERS LANDSCAPING & SUP
2519 N Ridge Rd (44077-4801)
PHONE.................................440 259-3348
James McCallister, *President*
Carla McCallister, *Vice Pres*
EMP: 29
SALES (est): 963.7K **Privately Held**
SIC: 0782 5261 Landscape contractors; lawn & garden supplies

(G-15726)
MCNEIL INDUSTRIES INC
835 Richmond Rd Ste 2 (44077-1123)
PHONE.................................440 951-7756
Randall J McNeil, *President*
Jordan Owens, *Exec VP*
Robert Madden, *Vice Pres*
Sandy Warner, *Receptionist*
▲ **EMP:** 30
SQ FT: 18,000
SALES (est): 8.4MM **Privately Held**
WEB: www.mcneilindustries.com
SIC: 3366 5085 Bushings & bearings; seals, industrial

(G-15727)
MELZERS FUEL SERVICE INC
755 E Erie St (44077-4403)
P.O. Box 1400 (44077-7325)
PHONE.................................800 367-0203
Richard G Melzer II, *President*
Andrew J Melzer I, *Vice Pres*
Adelle Melzer, *Admin Sec*
EMP: 25
SQ FT: 1,300
SALES: 5.5MM **Privately Held**
WEB: www.melzersfuel.com
SIC: 5172 Petroleum products

(G-15728)
MULTI-CARE INC
Also Called: Homestead II
60 Wood St (44077-3332)
PHONE.................................440 352-0788
Morton J Weisburg, *Manager*
P K K Yakkundi, *Director*
EMP: 100
SALES (corp-wide): 6.1MM **Privately Held**
WEB: www.nursehome.com
SIC: 8051 Skilled nursing care facilities
PA: Multi-Care, Inc
26691 Richmond Rd Frnt
Bedford OH 44146
216 292-5706

(G-15729)
NVR INC
408 Greenfield Ln (44077-6149)
PHONE.................................440 639-0525
EMP: 33 **Publicly Held**
SIC: 1521 New construction, single-family houses
PA: Nvr, Inc.
11700 Plaza America Dr # 500
Reston VA 20190

(G-15730)
OLON RICERCA BIOSCIENCE LLC
7528 Auburn Rd (44077-9176)
PHONE.................................440 357-3300
Paolo Tubertini, *CEO*
Nicole Daugherty, *Admin Asst*
EMP: 99 **EST:** 2017
SALES (est): 87.2K **Privately Held**
SIC: 8731 Commercial physical research
HQ: Olon Spa
Strada Provinciale Rivoltana 6/7
Rodano MI 20090
029 523-1

(G-15731)
OMEGA SEA LLC
1000 Bacon Rd (44077-4637)
PHONE.................................440 639-2372
Martin Crews, *Vice Pres*
Jim Randall, *Vice Pres*
Dan Crews, *Manager*
Dennis Crews,
◆ **EMP:** 40 **EST:** 2010
SALES (est): 8.8MM **Privately Held**
SIC: 5146 Fish & seafoods

(G-15732)
PAINESVILLE DENTAL GROUP INC (PA)
128 Mentor Ave (44077-3232)
PHONE.................................440 354-2183
Donald Brekholder, *President*
EMP: 30
SALES (est): 2.6MM **Privately Held**
WEB: www.painesville.com
SIC: 8021 Dentists' office; orthodontist

(G-15733)
PERSONACARE OF OHIO INC
Also Called: Kindred Transitional Care and
70 Normandy Dr (44077-1616)
PHONE.................................440 357-1311
Vesta Jones, *Administration*
EMP: 150
SALES (corp-wide): 6B **Privately Held**
SIC: 8052 Intermediate care facilities
HQ: Personacare Of Ohio Inc
1801 Macy Dr
Roswell GA 30076

(G-15734)
QUAIL HOLLOW MANAGEMENT INC
Also Called: Quail Hollow Resort Cntry CLB
11295 Quail Hollow Dr (44077-9036)
PHONE.................................440 639-4000
Eric Affeldt, *President*
EMP: 80
SQ FT: 17,000
SALES (est): 2.7MM
SALES (corp-wide): 477MM **Privately Held**
SIC: 7997 5812 7992 7011 Golf club, membership; eating places; public golf courses; hotels & motels; sporting goods & bicycle shops; drinking places
HQ: Clubcorp Usa, Inc.
3030 Lyndon B Johnson Fwy
Dallas TX 75234
972 243-6191

(G-15735)
R W SIDLEY INCORPORATED (PA)
436 Casement Ave (44077-3817)
P.O. Box 150 (44077-0150)
PHONE.................................440 352-9343
Robert C Sidley, *Ch of Bd*
Robert J Buescher, *President*
Brad Busher, *General Mgr*
Iola Black, *Principal*
R H Bostick, *Principal*
▲ **EMP:** 30
SQ FT: 10,000
SALES (est): 132.6MM **Privately Held**
WEB: www.rwsidleyinc.com
SIC: 1771 3299 Concrete work; blocks & brick, sand lime

(G-15736)
R W SIDLEY INCORPORATED
Mining & Materials Division
436 Casement Ave (44077-3817)
P.O. Box 150 (44077-0150)
PHONE.................................440 352-9343
Bob Buescher, *President*
EMP: 30
SALES (corp-wide): 132.6MM **Privately Held**
WEB: www.rwsidleyinc.com
SIC: 1422 Cement rock, crushed & broken-quarrying
PA: R. W. Sidley Incorporated
436 Casement Ave
Painesville OH 44077
440 352-9343

(G-15737)
REAL LIVING TITLE AGENCY LTD
7470b Auburn Rd (44077-9703)
PHONE.................................440 974-7810
EMP: 35
SALES (corp-wide): 24.2MM **Privately Held**
SIC: 6531 Real Estate Agent/Manager
PA: Real Living Title Agency Ltd
77 E Nationwide Blvd
Columbus OH 43215
614 459-7400

(G-15738)
RIDERS 1812 INN
792 Mentor Ave (44077-2516)
PHONE.................................440 354-0922
Elaine Crane, *Owner*
Gary Herman, *Co-Owner*
EMP: 25
SALES (est): 453.4K **Privately Held**
SIC: 5812 7011 Eating places; bed & breakfast inn

(G-15739)
SABER HEALTHCARE GROUP LLC
60 Wood St (44077-3332)
PHONE.................................440 352-0788
EMP: 107
SALES (corp-wide): 157.7MM **Privately Held**
SIC: 8099 Childbirth preparation clinic
PA: Saber Healthcare Group, L.L.C.
26691 Richmond Rd Frnt
Bedford OH 44146
216 292-5706

(G-15740)
SINES INC
1744 N Ridge Rd (44077-4812)
PHONE....................................440 352-6572
Suanne Sines, *President*
Raymond Sines, *Treasurer*
Pam Schlaugh, *Shareholder*
EMP: 30
SQ FT: 1,800
SALES (est): 16.7MM **Privately Held**
WEB: www.sines.com
SIC: 5172 5541 5531 Fuel oil; filling stations, gasoline; automotive tires

(G-15741)
STAFAST PRODUCTS INC (PA)
Also Called: Stafast West
505 Lakeshore Blvd (44077-1197)
PHONE....................................440 357-5546
Donald S Selle, *President*
Elmer T Elbrecht, *Principal*
John G Roberts, *Principal*
Joan Selle, *Corp Secy*
Kirk Hedger, *Opers Mgr*
▲ **EMP:** 40
SQ FT: 20,600
SALES (est): 27.3MM **Privately Held**
WEB: www.stafast.com
SIC: 5085 3452 Fasteners, industrial: nuts, bolts, screws, etc.; bolts, nuts, rivets & washers

(G-15742)
STERILTEK INC (PA)
11910 Briarwyck Woods Dr (44077-9392)
PHONE....................................615 627-0241
William O'Riordian, *CEO*
William Aamonth, *Vice Pres*
Jon Backholm, *VP Finance*
EMP: 35
SQ FT: 15,000
SALES (est): 4.5MM **Privately Held**
WEB: www.steriltek.com
SIC: 7389 Product sterilization service

(G-15743)
TRANSCRIPTIONGEAR INC
Also Called: Transcriptiongear.com
7280 Auburn Rd (44077-9724)
PHONE....................................888 834-2392
Kris Wilson, *President*
Jerry Dolbey, *Corp Secy*
EMP: 45
SALES: 6MM **Privately Held**
SIC: 5045 Computer software

(G-15744)
TRIPOINT MEDICAL CENTER
Also Called: Lake Health
7590 Auburn Rd (44077-9176)
PHONE....................................440 375-8100
John Mirch, *Business Mgr*
Leslie Manzo, *Vice Pres*
Lisa Freibergmackey, *Opers Staff*
Kathy Lautanen, *Opers Staff*
Adam Sornberger, *Opers Staff*
EMP: 825
SQ FT: 300,000
SALES: 324.4MM **Privately Held**
SIC: 8062 General medical & surgical hospitals

(G-15745)
UNITED REST HOMES INC
Also Called: Ivy House Care Center
308 S State St (44077-3532)
PHONE....................................440 354-2131
Marie Swaim, *President*
EMP: 30
SALES (est): 1.2MM **Privately Held**
SIC: 8059 Personal care home, with health care

(G-15746)
UNITED STEELWORKERS
Also Called: Uswa
50 Branch Ave (44077-3819)
PHONE....................................440 354-2328
John Gombos, *Branch Mgr*
EMP: 50
SALES (corp-wide): 4.9MM **Privately Held**
WEB: www.uswa.org
SIC: 8631 Labor union

PA: United Steelworkers
60 Bolevard Of The Allies
Pittsburgh PA 15222
412 562-2400

(G-15747)
WEINSTEIN DONALD JAY PHD
Also Called: Weinstein and Associates
54 S State St (44077-3445)
PHONE....................................216 831-1040
Donald Weinstein, *President*
EMP: 25
SALES (corp-wide): 1.4MM **Privately Held**
WEB: www.djweinstein.com
SIC: 8049 Clinical psychologist
PA: Weinstein, Donald Jay Phd, Inc
25700 Science Park Dr # 200
Beachwood OH 44122
216 831-1040

(G-15748)
WILLIAM R MORSE
Also Called: Morse Van Line
83 S State St (44077-3405)
PHONE....................................440 352-2600
William R Morse, *Owner*
EMP: 25
SALES (est): 3.2MM **Privately Held**
SIC: 4731 4213 4214 Freight transportation arrangement; trucking, except local; local trucking with storage

(G-15749)
YARDMASTER INC (PA)
1447 N Ridge Rd (44077-4494)
PHONE....................................440 357-8400
Kurt Kluznik, *CEO*
Jerry Kunco, *General Mgr*
Ed Gallagher, *COO*
Rick Colwell, *Vice Pres*
Cyndi Paskell, *Controller*
EMP: 100
SQ FT: 6,000
SALES: 15MM **Privately Held**
WEB: www.yardmaster.com
SIC: 0782 Landscape contractors; lawn care services; garden maintenance services

---

Pandora
Putnam County

(G-15750)
DRC HOLDINGS INC
Also Called: Shirleys Gourmet Popcorn Co
17623 Road 4 (45877-8714)
P.O. Box 131, Bluffton (45817-0131)
PHONE....................................419 230-0188
J Peter Suter, *President*
Kimberly Suter, *Vice Pres*
EMP: 40
SALES: 850K **Privately Held**
SIC: 5441 7832 Popcorn, including caramel corn; motion picture theaters, except drive-in

(G-15751)
FIRST NATIONAL BANK OF PANDORA (DH)
102 E Main St (45877-8706)
P.O. Box 329 (45877-0329)
PHONE....................................419 384-3221
Todd Monson, *President*
Shari Schwab, *Assoc VP*
Alison Hovest, *Opers-Prdtn-Mfg*
Jim Downhower, *CFO*
Jennifer Vastano, *Mktg Dir*
EMP: 28
SQ FT: 10,000
SALES: 7.6MM
SALES (corp-wide): 6.6MM **Privately Held**
WEB: www.e-fnb.com
SIC: 6021 National commercial banks
HQ: Pandora Bancshares, Incorporated
102 E Main St
Pandora OH 45877
419 384-3221

(G-15752)
HILTY CHILD CARE CENTER
304 Hilty Dr (45877-9476)
P.O. Box 359 (45877-0359)
PHONE....................................419 384-3220
Heather Sanchez, *Director*
EMP: 50
SALES (est): 226.9K **Privately Held**
SIC: 8351 Group day care center

(G-15753)
HILTY MEMORIAL HOME INC
304 Hilty Dr (45877-9476)
P.O. Box 359 (45877-0359)
PHONE....................................419 384-3218
Laura Both, *CEO*
Jason Cox, *Exec Dir*
Kristen Niekamp, *Director*
Cathy Lucas, *Nursing Dir*
Marsha Stechschulte, *Records Dir*
EMP: 157
SQ FT: 25,707
SALES: 5.8MM **Privately Held**
SIC: 8051 8322 8049 Convalescent home with continuous nursing care; old age assistance; physical therapist; speech therapist

(G-15754)
PANDORA BANCSHARES INC (HQ)
102 E Main St (45877-8706)
P.O. Box 329 (45877-0329)
PHONE....................................419 384-3221
Todd A Mason, *President*
James Downhower, *CFO*
EMP: 34
SQ FT: 15,000
SALES (est): 7.6MM
SALES (corp-wide): 6.6MM **Privately Held**
SIC: 6021 National commercial banks
PA: Pandora Banchares Inc
102 E Main St
Pandora OH 45877
419 384-3221

(G-15755)
SUTER PRODUCE INC
12200 Pandora Rd (45877-9501)
PHONE....................................419 384-3665
Jerry Suter, *President*
EMP: 80 **EST:** 1977
SALES (est): 4.4MM **Privately Held**
SIC: 0191 0171 0161 General farms, primarily crop; strawberry farm; corn farm, sweet

---

Paris
Stark County

(G-15756)
D L BELKNAP TRUCKING INC
3526 Baird Ave Se (44669-9732)
PHONE....................................330 868-7766
Denver Belknap, *President*
Norma Belknap, *Treasurer*
EMP: 84 **EST:** 1972
SQ FT: 30,000
SALES (est): 9.5MM **Privately Held**
SIC: 4213 Contract haulers

(G-15757)
STALLION OILFIELD CNSTR LLC
3361 Baird Ave Se (44669-9769)
PHONE....................................330 868-2083
Chrysta Dansby, *Branch Mgr*
EMP: 27 **Privately Held**
SIC: 1389 Oil field services
PA: Stallion Oilfield Construction, Llc
950 Corbindale Rd Ste 400
Houston TX 77024

Parma
Cuyahoga County

(G-15758)
3G OPERATING COMPANY LLC
Also Called: Wickliffe Country Place
12380 Plaza Dr (44130-1043)
PHONE....................................440 944-9400
Bruce Daskal,
EMP: 330 **EST:** 2007
SALES (est): 4.2MM **Privately Held**
SIC: 8051 Convalescent home with continuous nursing care

(G-15759)
ADVANCED GRAPHITE MACHINING US
12300 Snow Rd (44130-1001)
PHONE....................................216 658-6521
Baker Kearney, *CEO*
Hunter Kearney, *Sales Staff*
Keith Kearney,
EMP: 25
SQ FT: 430,702
SALES: 12MM **Privately Held**
SIC: 5051 Metals service centers & offices

(G-15760)
AMERICAN NATIONAL RED CROSS
5585 Pearl Rd (44129-2544)
PHONE....................................216 303-5476
EMP: 39
SALES (corp-wide): 2.5B **Privately Held**
SIC: 8322 Individual & family services
PA: The American National Red Cross
430 17th St Nw
Washington DC 20006
202 737-8300

(G-15761)
BROADVIEW NURSING HOME INC
Also Called: Broadview Multi-Care Center
5520 Broadview Rd (44134-1699)
PHONE....................................216 661-5084
Harold Shachter, *President*
Mike Flank, *Vice Pres*
Erna Laufer, *Admin Sec*
EMP: 250
SQ FT: 68,000
SALES (est): 12.5MM **Privately Held**
WEB: www.broadviewmulticare.com
SIC: 8051 Extended care facility

(G-15762)
COMPREHENSIVE LOGISTICS CO INC
5520 Chevrolet Blvd (44130-1419)
PHONE....................................330 233-0805
Eric Williams, *Branch Mgr*
EMP: 25 **Privately Held**
SIC: 4225 General warehousing & storage
PA: Comprehensive Logistics, Co., Inc.
4944 Belmont Ave Ste 202
Youngstown OH 44505

(G-15763)
COX COMMUNICATIONS INC
12221 Plaza Dr (44130-1059)
PHONE....................................216 712-4500
Todd Smith, *Director*
EMP: 86
SALES (corp-wide): 32.5B **Privately Held**
SIC: 4841 Cable television services
HQ: Cox Communications, Inc.
6205 B Pchtree Dunwody Ne
Atlanta GA 30328

(G-15764)
COX OHIO TELCOM LLC
Also Called: Cox Business
12221 Plaza Dr (44130-1059)
PHONE....................................216 535-3500
Tom Hamilton, *Principal*
EMP: 76
SALES (corp-wide): 32.5B **Privately Held**
SIC: 4813 Telephone communication, except radio
HQ: Cox Ohio Telcom, L.L.C.
1400 Lake Hearn Dr Ne
Brookhaven GA 30319

(G-15765)
DEDICATED NURSING ASSOC INC
1339a Rockside Rd (44134-2776)
PHONE................................877 547-9144
EMP: 41 **Privately Held**
SIC: 7361 7363 8051 Nurses' registry; medical help service; skilled nursing care facilities
PA: Dedicated Nursing Associates, Inc.
　　6536 State Route 22
　　Delmont PA 15626

(G-15766)
ELECTRA SOUND INC (PA)
Also Called: Electrasound TV & Appl Svc
5260 Commerce Pkwy W (44130-1271)
PHONE................................216 433-9600
Robert C Masa Jr, *CEO*
Charles C Masa, *President*
Patricia Masa, *Vice Pres*
Rodger Miller, *Asst Controller*
Nancy Reschke, *VP Mktg*
EMP: 70
SQ FT: 28,000
SALES (est): 31MM **Privately Held**
WEB: www.electrasound.com
SIC: 3694 7622 5065 5731 Automotive electrical equipment; television repair shop; radio repair shop; video repair; sound equipment, electronic; sound equipment, automotive

(G-15767)
GES GRAPHITE INC (PA)
Also Called: G E S
12300 Snow Rd (44130-1001)
PHONE................................216 658-6660
Keith Kearney, *CEO*
Baker Kearney, *President*
Hunter Kearney, *Treasurer*
◆ EMP: 45
SQ FT: 100,000
SALES (est): 14.1MM **Privately Held**
WEB: www.geselectrodes.com
SIC: 5085 Industrial supplies

(G-15768)
METROPOLITAN POOL SERVICE CO
Also Called: Metropolitan Pools
3427 Brookpark Rd (44134-1298)
PHONE................................216 741-9451
Robert Matney, *CEO*
Todd Whitlock, *President*
Erin Norton, *Manager*
Matt Spring, *Director*
EMP: 50 **EST**: 1961
SQ FT: 6,000
SALES (est): 5.1MM **Privately Held**
WEB: www.metropools.com
SIC: 1799 5999 5091 7389 Swimming pool construction; swimming pool chemicals, equipment & supplies; swimming pools, equipment & supplies; swimming pool & hot tub service & maintenance; lifeguard service

(G-15769)
NATIONWIDE HEALTH MGT LLC
5700 Chevrolet Blvd (44130-1412)
PHONE................................440 888-8888
Chanthou Phay,
EMP: 75
SALES (est): 195.5K **Privately Held**
SIC: 8082 Home health care services

(G-15770)
OWNERS MANAGEMENT COMPANY
5555 Powers Blvd (44129-5462)
PHONE................................440 439-3800
Paul T Wilms, *Controller*
EMP: 40
SALES (est): 807.8K **Privately Held**
SIC: 6513 6531 Apartment building operators; real estate agents & managers

(G-15771)
PARMA COMMUNITY GENERAL HOSP (PA)
7007 Powers Blvd (44129-5437)
P.O. Box 73270n, Cleveland (44193-0001)
PHONE................................440 743-3000
Patricia A Ruflin, *President*

Robert Jacobson, *Ch Radiology*
Terrance Deis, *Vice Pres*
Elizabeth Myers, *Materials Dir*
Pamela Yusz, *Opers Staff*
EMP: 1667
SQ FT: 415,000
SALES: 179.1MM **Privately Held**
SIC: 8062 General medical & surgical hospitals

(G-15772)
PARMA COMMUNITY GENERAL HOSP
7007 Powers Blvd (44129-5437)
PHONE................................440 743-4280
M Furgeson, *Exec Dir*
EMP: 293
SALES (corp-wide): 179.1MM **Privately Held**
SIC: 8699 Charitable organization
PA: Parma Community General Hospital
　　7007 Powers Blvd
　　Parma OH 44129
　　440 743-3000

(G-15773)
PROGRESSIVE QUALITY CARE INC (PA)
5553 Broadview Rd (44134-1604)
PHONE................................216 661-6800
Mike Flank, *President*
Evan Hamilton, *Director*
EMP: 30
SQ FT: 500,000
SALES (est): 64.7MM **Privately Held**
SIC: 7389 Personal service agents, brokers & bureaus

(G-15774)
RYCON CONSTRUCTION INC
7661 W Ridgewood Dr (44129-5537)
PHONE................................440 481-3770
EMP: 64
SALES (corp-wide): 244MM **Privately Held**
SIC: 1521 Single-family housing construction
PA: Rycon Construction, Inc.
　　2501 Smallman St Ste 100
　　Pittsburgh PA 15222
　　412 392-2525

(G-15775)
SEBESTA INC
2802 Tuxedo Ave (44134-1329)
PHONE................................216 351-7621
Mark Banas, *Principal*
EMP: 25
SALES (corp-wide): 418MM **Publicly Held**
SIC: 8711 Consulting engineer
HQ: Sebesta, Inc.
　　1450 Energy Park Dr # 300
　　Saint Paul MN 55108

(G-15776)
SHEET METAL WORKERS LOCAL NO (PA)
12515 Corporate Dr (44130-9322)
PHONE................................216 267-1645
Reggie Hohenberter, *President*
Wayne Fletcher, *Corp Secy*
EMP: 30
SALES: 624K **Privately Held**
SIC: 6371 Union welfare, benefit & health funds

(G-15777)
ST AUGUSTINE MANOR
Also Called: Holy Family Home and Hospice
6707 State Rd (44134-4517)
PHONE................................440 888-7722
Peggy Rossi, *Mktg Dir*
Kristin Graham, *Director*
Michael Debs, *Director*
EMP: 330
SALES (corp-wide): 34.1MM **Privately Held**
SIC: 8082 Home health care services
PA: St Augustine Manor
　　7801 Detroit Ave
　　Cleveland OH
　　216 634-7400

(G-15778)
TRADESOURCE INC
5504 State Rd (44134-2250)
PHONE................................216 801-4944
EMP: 101 **Privately Held**
SIC: 7361 Employment agencies
PA: Tradesource, Inc.
　　205 Hallene Rd Unit 211
　　Warwick RI 02886

(G-15779)
UNIVERSITY HOSPITALS
Also Called: University Hospitals Parma
7007 Powers Blvd (44129-5437)
PHONE................................440 743-3000
Kathi O'Connor, *Vice Pres*
Suzanne Hoover, *Purch Dir*
Meghan Ramic, *QA Dir*
Mila Davidovic, *Podiatrist*
Valerie Hennessy, *Director*
EMP: 2000
SALES (corp-wide): 580MM **Privately Held**
SIC: 8062 8011 8741 General medical & surgical hospitals; offices & clinics of medical doctors; hospital management; nursing & personal care facility management
PA: University Hospitals Health System, Inc.
　　3605 Warrensville Ctr Rd
　　Shaker Heights OH 44122
　　216 767-8900

(G-15780)
XPO LOGISTICS FREIGHT INC
12901 Snow Rd (44130-1004)
PHONE................................216 433-1000
Gene Carson, *Branch Mgr*
EMP: 140
SALES (corp-wide): 15.3B **Publicly Held**
WEB: www.con-way.com
SIC: 4213 4212 Contract haulers; local trucking, without storage
HQ: Xpo Logistics Freight, Inc.
　　2211 Old Earhart Rd # 100
　　Ann Arbor MI 48105
　　800 755-2728

(G-15781)
Y & E ENTERTAINMENT GROUP LLC
Also Called: Make Believe
8303 Day Dr (44129-5610)
PHONE................................440 385-5500
Yuri Abramovich, *Mng Member*
Elena Abramovich,
EMP: 47
SQ FT: 23,000
SALES (est): 366.3K **Privately Held**
SIC: 7996 Amusement parks

Pataskala
Licking County

(G-15782)
ALLEN REFRACTORIES COMPANY
131 Shackelford Rd (43062-9106)
PHONE................................740 927-8000
James A Shackelford, *President*
Margaret O'Connor Shackelford, *Exec VP*
James Gibson, *Vice Pres*
EMP: 245
SQ FT: 32,000
SALES (est): 39.2MM **Privately Held**
WEB: www.allenrefractories.com
SIC: 1741 5085 Refractory or acid brick masonry; refractory material

(G-15783)
CONTRACT LUMBER INC (PA)
3245 Hazelton Etna Rd Sw (43062-8532)
PHONE................................740 964-3147
Richard Hiegel, *President*
Harold T Bieser, *Chairman*
James Holloway, *CFO*
EMP: 150
SQ FT: 35,000
SALES (est): 76.6MM **Privately Held**
SIC: 1761 5211 1751 Roofing contractor; siding contractor; lumber & other building materials; framing contractor

(G-15784)
COUGHLIN CHEVROLET INC (PA)
Also Called: Coughlin Automotive Group
9000 Broad St Sw (43062-7879)
P.O. Box 1480 (43062-1480)
PHONE................................740 964-9191
Al Coughlin, *President*
Dan Turner, *General Mgr*
Frederick J Simon, *Principal*
Michael Coughlin, *Vice Pres*
Brian Griffie, *Parts Mgr*
EMP: 100
SALES (est): 95.1MM **Privately Held**
WEB: www.coughlinford.com
SIC: 5511 5012 7538 7532 Automobiles, new & used; pickups, new & used; automobiles & other motor vehicles; general automotive repair shops; top & body repair & paint shops; automotive & home supply stores

(G-15785)
DYNAMIC CONSTRUCTION INC
172 Coors Blvd (43062-7313)
PHONE................................740 927-8898
Mark S Gray, *President*
Ron Nichols, *Vice Pres*
Chris Bell, *Project Mgr*
Adam Messerall, *Project Mgr*
Lisa Wynd, *Admin Sec*
EMP: 60
SQ FT: 1,200
SALES (est): 14.1MM **Privately Held**
SIC: 1623 Transmitting tower (telecommunication) construction

(G-15786)
NURSING CARE MGT AMER INC
Also Called: Pataskala Oaks Care Center
144 E Broad St (43062-7536)
PHONE................................740 927-9888
Butch Wright, *Maintenance Dir*
Teresa Roberts, *Manager*
Jennifer May, *Director*
Anita Butler, *Nursing Dir*
EMP: 100
SALES (corp-wide): 25.9MM **Privately Held**
WEB: www.nursinghomeinfo.org
SIC: 8741 8051 8059 Nursing & personal care facility management; skilled nursing care facilities; nursing home, except skilled & intermediate care facility
PA: Nursing Care Management Of America, Inc.
　　7265 Kenwood Rd Ste 300
　　Cincinnati OH 45236
　　513 793-8804

(G-15787)
SALO INC
350 S Main St B (43062-9626)
PHONE................................740 964-2904
EMP: 2784
SALES (corp-wide): 19.8MM **Privately Held**
SIC: 8082 Home health care services
PA: Salo, Inc.
　　960 Checkrein Ave Ste A
　　Columbus OH 43229
　　614 436-9404

(G-15788)
THAYER PWR COMM LINE CNSTR LLC (PA)
Also Called: Thayer Power & Comm Line
12345 Worthington Rd Nw (43062)
PHONE................................740 927-0021
Timothy Luden, *Mng Member*
EMP: 42
SQ FT: 16,000
SALES (est): 60.5MM **Privately Held**
SIC: 1623 Communication line & transmission tower construction

Patriot
Gallia County

(G-15789)
BUCKEYE RURAL ELC COOP INC
4848 State Route 325 (45658-8960)
P.O. Box 200, Rio Grande (45674-0200)
PHONE....................................740 379-2025
David Lester, *Ch of Bd*
Tonda Meadows, *Exec VP*
Tedd Mollohon, *Vice Pres*
Maggie M Rucker, *CFO*
EMP: 45 EST: 1938
SALES: 38.2MM **Privately Held**
WEB: www.aceinter.net
SIC: 4911 Distribution, electric power

Paulding
Paulding County

(G-15790)
ALEX PRODUCTS INC
810 W Gasser Rd (45879-8770)
PHONE....................................419 399-4500
Dave Dondeylon, *Manager*
EMP: 110
SALES (corp-wide): 110.3MM **Privately Held**
WEB: www.alexproducts.com
SIC: 3499 5013 3714 Automobile seat frames, metal; automotive supplies & parts; motor vehicle parts & accessories
PA: Alex Products, Inc.
19911 County Rd T
Ridgeville Corners OH 43555
419 267-5240

(G-15791)
COMMUNITY HLTH PRFSSIONALS INC
Also Called: Paulding Area Visiting Nurses
250 Dooley Dr Ste A (45879-8846)
PHONE....................................419 399-4708
Peggy Carnhan, *Manager*
EMP: 33
SALES (corp-wide): 13.1MM **Privately Held**
SIC: 8082 Visiting nurse service
PA: Community Health Professionals, Inc.
1159 Westwood Dr
Van Wert OH 45891
419 238-9223

(G-15792)
COUNTY OF CUYAHOGA
112 N Williams St (45879-1281)
PHONE....................................419 399-8260
Anna Campbell, *Branch Mgr*
EMP: 650 **Privately Held**
SIC: 8322 Probation office
PA: County Of Cuyahoga
1215 W 3rd St
Cleveland OH 44113
216 443-7022

(G-15793)
COUNTY OF PAULDING
Also Called: Westwood Bhvioural Hlth Centre
501 Mc Donald Pike (45879-9239)
PHONE....................................419 399-3636
Tom Stricker, *Director*
EMP: 30 **Privately Held**
WEB: www.pauldingcountycourt.com
SIC: 9431 8322 8063 Mental health agency administration, government; family counseling services; hospital for the mentally ill
PA: County Of Paulding
115 N Williams St
Paulding OH 45879
419 399-8280

(G-15794)
HERBERT E ORR COMPANY
335 W Wall St (45879-1163)
P.O. Box 209 (45879-0209)
PHONE....................................419 399-4866
Greg Johnson, *President*
Bruce Whitman, *Supervisor*

Ken Metzger, *Admin Sec*
EMP: 125
SQ FT: 48,000
SALES (est): 46.1MM **Privately Held**
WEB: www.heorr.com
SIC: 5013 3479 Wheels, motor vehicle; painting of metal products

(G-15795)
P C WORKSHOP INC
900 W Caroline St (45879-1381)
P.O. Box 390 (45879-0390)
PHONE....................................419 399-4805
Megan Sierra, *CEO*
Brenda Miller, *Director*
EMP: 100
SALES: 1.2MM **Privately Held**
WEB: www.pcworkshop.com
SIC: 7389 3711 Document & office record destruction; automobile assembly, including specialty automobiles

(G-15796)
PAULDING COUNTY HOSPITAL
1035 W Wayne St (45879-9235)
PHONE....................................419 399-4080
Gary Adkins, *CEO*
Randy Ruge, *CEO*
Michael Winans, *Ch of Bd*
Ron Etzler, *Corp Secy*
Tom Litzenberg, *Vice Pres*
EMP: 213
SQ FT: 36,000
SALES: 22.3MM **Privately Held**
WEB: www.pauldingcountyhospital.com
SIC: 8062 Hospital, affiliated with AMA residency

(G-15797)
PAULDING EXEMPTED VLG SCHL DST (PA)
405 N Water St (45879-1251)
PHONE....................................419 594-3309
Greg Reinhart, *President*
John Baysinger, *Superintendent*
Nancy Ruhe, *Psychologist*
Patricia Carlisle, *Med Doctor*
Joann Adams, *Comp Spec*
EMP: 230
SALES: 19.8MM **Privately Held**
SIC: 8351 8211 Preschool center; elementary & secondary schools

(G-15798)
PAULDING-PUTNAM ELECTRIC COOP (PA)
Also Called: PAULDING PUTNAM ELECTRIC COOPE
401 Mc Donald Pike (45879-9270)
PHONE....................................419 399-5015
George Carter, *President*
Renee Boss, *Human Resources*
Erika Willitzer, *Marketing Staff*
Derek George, *Technician*
Mary Arend,
EMP: 30 EST: 1935
SALES: 40.2MM **Privately Held**
SIC: 4911 Distribution, electric power

(G-15799)
SHAFER CONFESSION
411 E Jackson St (45879-1229)
PHONE....................................419 399-4662
Terry J Shafer, *Principal*
EMP: 45
SALES (est): 546.2K **Privately Held**
SIC: 8399 Social services

Pedro
Lawrence County

(G-15800)
NECCO CENTER
115 Private Road 977 (45659-8608)
PHONE....................................740 534-1386
Dr J Kulkari, *President*
EMP: 65
SALES (est): 3MM **Privately Held**
SIC: 8361 Children's home

Peebles
Adams County

(G-15801)
GENERAL ELECTRIC COMPANY
1200 Jaybird Rd (45660-9550)
PHONE....................................937 587-2631
Kevin Hunter, *Opers Staff*
Terry Craig, *Senior Engr*
Dean Schultz, *Manager*
Dane Clark, *Manager*
EMP: 200
SALES (corp-wide): 121.6B **Publicly Held**
SIC: 8734 Testing laboratories
PA: General Electric Company
41 Farnsworth St
Boston MA 02210
617 443-3000

(G-15802)
HANSON AGGREGATES EAST LLC
Plum Run Stone Division
848 Plum Run Rd (45660-9706)
PHONE....................................937 587-2671
Terry Lauderback, *Manager*
Terry Louderback, *Manager*
EMP: 50
SALES (corp-wide): 20.6B **Privately Held**
SIC: 1422 3274 3273 Crushed & broken limestone; lime; ready-mixed concrete
HQ: Hanson Aggregates East Llc
3131 Rdu Center Dr
Morrisville NC 27560
919 380-2500

(G-15803)
J MCCOY LUMBER CO LTD (PA)
6 N Main St (45660-1243)
P.O. Box 306 (45660-0306)
PHONE....................................937 587-3423
Jack McCoy, *Owner*
EMP: 40
SQ FT: 2,400
SALES (est): 4.4MM **Privately Held**
SIC: 5031 2426 2431 Lumber: rough, dressed & finished; dimension, hardwood; moldings, wood: unfinished & prefinished

Pemberville
Wood County

(G-15804)
HIRZEL TRANSFER CO
115 Columbus St (43450-7029)
P.O. Box A (43450-0428)
PHONE....................................419 287-3288
Joseph Hirzel, *President*
William Hirzel, *Treasurer*
Karl Hirzel Jr, *Admin Sec*
EMP: 35
SALES: 500K
SALES (corp-wide): 29.6MM **Privately Held**
WEB: www.hirzel.com
SIC: 4212 Truck rental with drivers
PA: Hirzel Canning Company
411 Lemoyne Rd
Northwood OH 43619
419 693-0531

(G-15805)
NORTH BRANCH NURSERY INC
3359 Kesson Rd (43450-9204)
P.O. Box 353 (43450-0353)
PHONE....................................419 287-4679
Thomas Oberhouse, *President*
Lynnette Oberhouse, *Vice Pres*
Kelsey Gahler, *Production*
Craig Baldauf, *Human Res Dir*
Sara Schleicher, *Sales Staff*
EMP: 50
SQ FT: 3,200
SALES (est): 3.5MM **Privately Held**
WEB: www.northbranchnursery.com
SIC: 0782 5261 5193 1521 Landscape contractors; nurseries & garden centers; flowers & florists' supplies; patio & deck construction & repair; flowers: grown under cover (e.g. greenhouse production)

(G-15806)
OTTERBEIN PORTAGE VALLEY INC
Also Called: Otterbein Portage Vly Rtrmnt
20311 Pemberville Rd Ofc (43450-9411)
PHONE....................................888 749-4950
Toll Free:....................................888 -
Thomas Keith, *Director*
EMP: 150
SQ FT: 96,000
SALES: 5.1MM
SALES (corp-wide): 58.4MM **Privately Held**
SIC: 8051 8052 6513 Skilled nursing care facilities; intermediate care facilities; apartment building operators
PA: Senior Otterbein Lifestyle Choices
585 N State Route 741
Lebanon OH 45036
513 933-5400

(G-15807)
SOCIETY PLASTICS ENGINEERS INC
15520 S River Rd (43450-9303)
PHONE....................................419 287-4898
Jamie Prybylski, *Treasurer*
EMP: 150
SALES (corp-wide): 3.6MM **Privately Held**
WEB: www.4spe.org
SIC: 8621 8711 Engineering association; engineering services
PA: Society Of Plastics Engineers, Incorporated
6 Berkshire Blvd Ste 306
Bethel CT 06801
203 740-5422

Peninsula
Summit County

(G-15808)
A & C WELDING INC
80 Cuyahoga Fls Indus Pkwy (44264-9568)
PHONE....................................330 762-4777
Carl Lamancusa, *President*
Michael Lamancusa, *Vice Pres*
Timothy Gorbach, *Treasurer*
EMP: 25
SALES (est): 5.9MM **Privately Held**
SIC: 3444 7692 Sheet metalwork; welding repair

(G-15809)
BELFOR USA GROUP INC
79 Cuyahoga Fls Indus Par (44264-9567)
PHONE....................................330 916-6468
Brandon Carr, *Manager*
EMP: 25
SALES (corp-wide): 1.5B **Privately Held**
SIC: 1521 1541 1542 Repairing fire damage, single-family houses; renovation, remodeling & repairs: industrial buildings; commercial & office buildings, renovation & repair
HQ: Belfor Usa Group Inc.
185 Oakland Ave Ste 150
Birmingham MI 48009

(G-15810)
BRANDYWINE COUNTRY CLUB INC
Also Called: Brandywine Golf Course
5555 Akron Peninsula Rd (44264-9528)
PHONE....................................330 657-2525
Brett Yesberger, *President*
Scott Yesberger, *President*
EMP: 25 EST: 1963
SQ FT: 1,500
SALES (est): 1MM **Privately Held**
SIC: 7992 5812 Public golf courses; eating places

(G-15811)
CONSERV FOR CYHG VLLY NAT PRK
Also Called: CVNPA
1403 W Hines Hill Rd (44264-9646)
PHONE....................................330 657-2909
Deb Yandala, *CEO*
Barb Greene, *Principal*

Mary K Holmes, *Principal*
Sandy Kuban, *Finance Dir*
Emily Heninger, *Comms Mgr*
EMP: 55
SALES: 8.6MM **Privately Held**
WEB: www.cvnpa.org
SIC: 8699 Charitable organization

(G-15812)
ROADRUNNER TRNSP SYSTEMS INC
89 Cuyhoga Fls Indus Pkwy (44264-9567)
PHONE.............................330 920-4101
Dan Arnold, *President*
EMP: 29
SALES (corp-wide): 2.2B **Publicly Held**
SIC: 4731 Freight forwarding
PA: Roadrunner Transportation Systems, Inc.
      1431 Opus Pl Ste 530
      Downers Grove IL 60515
      414 615-1500

(G-15813)
SUNCREST GARDENS INC
5157 Akron Cleveland Rd (44264-9515)
PHONE.............................330 650-4969
Richard Haury, *President*
Barb Heffelman, *Financial Exec*
Rob Cowie, *Sales Executive*
Kolin Atkinson, *Director*
EMP: 125 **EST:** 1976
SQ FT: 1,000
SALES (est): 17.8MM **Privately Held**
WEB: www.suncrestgardens.com
SIC: 0781 0782 Landscape services; lawn & garden services

(G-15814)
WAYSIDE FARMS INC
Also Called: Wayside Farms Nursing
4557 Quick Rd (44264-9708)
PHONE.............................330 666-7716
Rebecca K Pool, *President*
Dr Loren Pool, *Vice Pres*
EMP: 95
SQ FT: 14,000
SALES: 6.6MM **Privately Held**
WEB: www.waysidefarms.com
SIC: 8051 Skilled nursing care facilities

(G-15815)
WHOLECYCLE INC
Also Called: State 8 Motorcycle & Atv
100 Cyhoga Fls Indus Pkwy (44264-9569)
PHONE.............................330 929-8123
R Kirk Compton, *President*
Brett H Huff, *Business Mgr*
Gar Compton, *Corp Secy*
Paul Compton, *Vice Pres*
Chris Geiger, *Sales Mgr*
◆ **EMP:** 40
SQ FT: 25,000
SALES (est): 12.9MM **Privately Held**
SIC: 5012 5571 3799 Motorcycles; motorcycles; all terrain vehicles (ATV)

(G-15816)
WINKING LIZARD INC
1615 Main St (44264-9754)
PHONE.............................330 467-1002
Carla Wauscoe, *Manager*
EMP: 75
SALES (corp-wide): 103.7MM **Privately Held**
SIC: 7299 5812 Banquet hall facilities; caterers
PA: Winking Lizard, Inc.
      25380 Miles Rd
      Bedford OH 44146
      216 831-0022

Pepper Pike
Cuyahoga County

(G-15817)
FRANK SANTO LLC
Also Called: Santo Salon & Spa
31100 Pinetree Rd (44124-5963)
PHONE.............................216 831-9374
Frank Santo Schiciano,
EMP: 29

SALES: 1.4MM **Privately Held**
SIC: 7231 Hairdressers

(G-15818)
HOWARD HANNA SMYTHE CRAMER
Also Called: Howard Hanna Real Estate Svcs
3550 Lander Rd Ste 300 (44124-5727)
PHONE.............................216 831-9310
Barbara Reynolds, *Manager*
EMP: 100
SALES (corp-wide): 73.7MM **Privately Held**
SIC: 6531 Real estate brokers & agents
HQ: Howard Hanna Smythe Cramer
      6000 Parkland Blvd
      Cleveland OH 44124
      216 447-4477

(G-15819)
JEWISH DAY SCHL ASSOC GRTR CLV (PA)
Also Called: SCHECHTER, GROSS DAY SCHOOL
27601 Fairmount Blvd (44124-4614)
PHONE.............................216 763-1400
Rabbi Jim Rogozen, *Headmaster*
Randy Boroff, *Headmaster*
Jim Walker, *Facilities Mgr*
Rachel Gonsenhauser, *Hlthcr Dir*
Susan Foley, *Teacher*
EMP: 60
SQ FT: 59,000
SALES: 4.3MM **Privately Held**
WEB: www.grossschechter.org
SIC: 8211 8351 Private elementary & secondary schools; group day care center

---

Perry
Lake County

(G-15820)
C M BROWN NURSERIES INC
4906 Middle Ridge Rd (44081-8700)
PHONE.............................440 259-5403
Shane S Brown, *President*
Mary Jane Brown, *Corp Secy*
EMP: 30
SALES (est): 2.7MM **Privately Held**
WEB: www.cmbrown.com
SIC: 5193 Nursery stock

(G-15821)
CAR PARTS WAREHOUSE INC
3382 N Ridge Rd (44081-9530)
PHONE.............................440 259-2991
Tony Difiore, *President*
EMP: 40
SALES (corp-wide): 96.9MM **Privately Held**
SIC: 5013 Automotive supplies & parts
PA: Car Parts Warehouse, Inc.
      5200 W 130th St
      Brookpark OH 44142
      216 281-4500

(G-15822)
COTTAGE GARDENS INC
4992 Middle Ridge Rd (44081-8700)
PHONE.............................440 259-2900
Thomas Varcak, *Branch Mgr*
EMP: 90
SQ FT: 3,640
SALES (corp-wide): 61.2MM **Privately Held**
WEB: www.cottagegardensinc.com
SIC: 0181 5193 Nursery stock, growing of; flowers & florists' supplies
PA: The Cottage Gardens Inc
      2611 S Waverly Hwy
      Lansing MI 48911
      517 882-5728

(G-15823)
JPMORGAN CHASE BANK NAT ASSN
2772 N Ridge Rd (44081-9553)
PHONE.............................440 352-5491
Charles Fay, *Principal*
EMP: 26
SALES (corp-wide): 131.4B **Publicly Held**
SIC: 6021 National commercial banks

HQ: Jpmorgan Chase Bank, National Association
      1111 Polaris Pkwy
      Columbus OH 43240
      614 436-3055

(G-15824)
LAKE COUNTY YMCA
Also Called: Outdoor Family Center
4540 River Rd (44081-8613)
PHONE.............................440 259-2724
Dave Saifman, *Marketing Staff*
Steve Gause, *Property Mgr*
Dale Nissley, *Exec Dir*
Richard Bennett, *Director*
Sue Dietrich, *Director*
EMP: 40
SALES (corp-wide): 8.9MM **Privately Held**
SIC: 8641 7991 8351 7032 Youth organizations; physical fitness facilities; child day care services; youth camps; individual & family services
PA: Lake County Ymca
      933 Mentor Ave Fl 2
      Painesville OH 44077
      440 352-3303

(G-15825)
MAC KENZIE NURSERY SUPPLY INC
3891 Shepard Rd (44081-9633)
P.O. Box 322 (44081-0322)
PHONE.............................440 259-3517
Douglas Mackenzie, *President*
Wilson J Burr, *Treasurer*
▲ **EMP:** 35 **EST:** 1977
SQ FT: 5,000
SALES (est): 3.4MM **Privately Held**
WEB: www.mackenzie-nsy-supply.com
SIC: 5193 5191 Flowers & nursery stock; greenhouse equipment & supplies

(G-15826)
MID-WEST MATERIALS INC
3687 Shepard Rd (44081-9694)
P.O. Box 345 (44081-0345)
PHONE.............................440 259-5200
Noreen Goldstein, *President*
Brian D Robbins, *Principal*
Mark Chabot, *Plant Mgr*
Lynn Clark, *Purch Mgr*
David Goldstein, *Inv Control Mgr*
EMP: 49
SQ FT: 220,000
SALES: 58.7MM **Privately Held**
WEB: www.mid-westmaterials.com
SIC: 5051 Steel

(G-15827)
PERRY TRANSPORTATION DEPT
3829 Main St (44081-8502)
PHONE.............................440 259-3005
Michael Sawyers, *Superintendent*
EMP: 35
SALES (est): 1.2MM **Privately Held**
SIC: 4151 School buses

(G-15828)
SOUTH SHORE CONTROLS INC
4485 N Ridge Rd (44081-9760)
PHONE.............................440 259-2500
Rick Stark, *President*
George Strekal, *Vice Pres*
EMP: 45
SQ FT: 22,000
SALES: 7MM **Privately Held**
WEB: www.southshorecontrols.com
SIC: 3549 5084 Metalworking machinery; instruments & control equipment

(G-15829)
WILLOWBEND NURSERIES LLC
4654 Davis Rd (44081-9667)
PHONE.............................440 259-3121
Brent Cherkala, *CFO*
Angelo Petitti,
Peggy Norris,
▲ **EMP:** 150
SALES (est): 14.1MM **Privately Held**
SIC: 0181 Nursery stock, growing of; shrubberies grown in field nurseries

---

(G-15830)
XZAMCORP
4119 Logans Way (44081-8654)
PHONE.............................330 629-2218
Craig Zamary, *Principal*
EMP: 25 **EST:** 1998
SALES (est): 1.5MM **Privately Held**
WEB: www.xzamcorp.com
SIC: 8742 General management consultant

Perrysburg
Wood County

(G-15831)
A RENEWED MIND
Also Called: CITY OF COMPASSION
885 Commerce Dr Ste D (43551-5268)
PHONE.............................419 214-0606
Matthew Rizzo, *CEO*
Cheri Gorajewski, *CFO*
Martha Campbell, *Psychologist*
Steve Kaighin, *Administration*
EMP: 90
SALES: 14.8MM **Privately Held**
SIC: 8322 Rehabilitation services

(G-15832)
ABC DETROIT/TOLEDO AUTO AUCTN
9797 Fremont Pike 3 (43551-4221)
PHONE.............................419 872-0872
Michael Hockett, *President*
EMP: 50
SQ FT: 9,600
SALES (est): 6.5MM
SALES (corp-wide): 72.6MM **Privately Held**
SIC: 5012 Automobile auction
PA: Auction Broadcasting Company Llc
      1919 S Post Rd
      Indianapolis IN 46239
      317 862-7325

(G-15833)
AUCTION BROADCASTING CO LLC
Also Called: ABC Detroit/Toledo
9797 Fremont Pike (43551-4221)
PHONE.............................419 872-0872
Mary Haller, *Branch Mgr*
EMP: 140
SALES (corp-wide): 72.6MM **Privately Held**
SIC: 5012 Automobile auction
PA: Auction Broadcasting Company Llc
      1919 S Post Rd
      Indianapolis IN 46239
      317 862-7325

(G-15834)
AUTOMATION & CONTROL TECH LTD
28210 Cedar Park Blvd (43551-4865)
PHONE.............................419 661-6400
Dan Pfouts, *General Mgr*
Kathy Dominiak, *Purch Mgr*
Chris Farrar, *Sales Mgr*
Mike Losure, *Sales Mgr*
Jason Miller, *Accounts Mgr*
▲ **EMP:** 27
SQ FT: 8,500
SALES (est): 5.7MM **Privately Held**
SIC: 7629 Electronic equipment repair

(G-15835)
BAYES INC
7414 Ponderosa Rd (43551-4857)
PHONE.............................419 661-3933
Christopher Bayes, *President*
Joan E Bayes, *CFO*
EMP: 25
SQ FT: 13,800
SALES (est): 5.9MM **Privately Held**
WEB: www.bayesinc.com
SIC: 1711 Mechanical contractor

(G-15836)
BEHAVRAL CNNCTIONS WD CNTY INC
27072 Carronade Dr Ste A (43551-5363)
PHONE.............................419 872-2419

Mark Haskin, *Director*
EMP: 26
SALES (corp-wide): 4.8MM **Privately Held**
SIC: **8093** 8322 Alcohol clinic, outpatient; individual & family services
PA: Behavioral Connections Of Wood County, Inc.
280 S Main St
Bowling Green OH 43402
419 352-5387

(G-15837)
BELMONT COUNTRY CLUB
29601 Bates Rd (43551-3899)
PHONE..................................419 666-1472
Bill Ammann, *President*
Gary Kovach, *General Mgr*
EMP: 75
SALES: 1.2MM **Privately Held**
SIC: **7997** Country club, membership; golf club, membership

(G-15838)
BENNETT ENTERPRISES INC
Also Called: Holiday Inn
10630 Fremont Pike (43551-3354)
P.O. Box 268 (43552-0268)
PHONE..................................419 874-3111
Carol Sattler, *Manager*
EMP: 350
SALES (corp-wide): 66.6MM **Privately Held**
WEB: www.bennett-enterprises.com
SIC: **7011** 5812 5947 7991 Hotels; restaurant, family: chain; gift shop; physical fitness facilities
PA: Bennett Enterprises, Inc.
27476 Holiday Ln
Perrysburg OH 43551
419 874-1933

(G-15839)
BIO-MDCAL APPLCATIONS OHIO INC
Also Called: Fresenius Med Care Perrysburg
701 Commerce Dr (43551-5271)
PHONE..................................419 874-3447
Jacque Cady, *Principal*
EMP: 31
SALES (corp-wide): 18.9B **Privately Held**
SIC: **8092** Kidney dialysis centers
HQ: Bio-Medical Applications Of Ohio, Inc.
920 Winter St
Waltham MA 02451

(G-15840)
BOTTOMLINE INK CORPORATION
7829 Ponderosa Rd (43551-4854)
PHONE..................................419 897-8000
Mike Davison, *President*
Nicholas J Cron, *Principal*
Darla Lay, *Accounts Mgr*
Emily Schwab, *Accounts Mgr*
Dave Tulk, *Info Tech Mgr*
▲ EMP: 29
SQ FT: 58,000
SALES (est): 6.8MM **Privately Held**
WEB: www.bottomlineink.com
SIC: **2759** 5199 Advertising literature: printing; advertising specialties

(G-15841)
BRAND TECHNOLOGIES INC
Also Called: Bluefin Media
2262 Levis Commons Blvd (43551-7142)
PHONE..................................419 873-6600
EMP: 50
SALES (est): 2.3MM **Privately Held**
SIC: **4899** Communication Services

(G-15842)
BROWN & BROWN OF OHIO LLC
360 3 Meadows Dr (43551-3197)
P.O. Box 428 (43552-0428)
PHONE..................................419 874-1974
James K Mc Whinnie, *CEO*
Daniel E Dumbauld, *COO*
Jack N Conley, *Vice Pres*
James Bailey, *Sales Staff*
Angela Krueger, *Department Mgr*
EMP: 102
SQ FT: 20,000

SALES (est): 609.1K
SALES (corp-wide): 2B **Publicly Held**
SIC: **6411** Insurance agents, brokers & service
PA: Brown & Brown, Inc.
220 S Ridgewood Ave # 180
Daytona Beach FL 32114
386 252-9601

(G-15843)
BUCKINGHAM MANAGEMENT LLC
1000 Hollister Ln (43551-6950)
PHONE..................................844 361-5559
EMP: 137 **Privately Held**
SIC: **6513** Apartment building operators
PA: Buckingham Management, L.L.C.
941 N Meridian St
Indianapolis IN 46204

(G-15844)
BURKETT AND SONS INC
Also Called: Burkett Restaurant Equipment
28740 Glenwood Rd (43551-3014)
P.O. Box 984, Toledo (43697-0984)
PHONE..................................419 242-7377
Jameel Burkett, *President*
Rachel Miller, *Principal*
Jackie Brown, *Human Res Mgr*
Jon Stambaugh, *Representative*
▼ EMP: 50
SQ FT: 95,000
SALES (est): 44.3MM **Privately Held**
SIC: **5046** Restaurant equipment & supplies

(G-15845)
CAPITAL SENIOR LIVING CORP
7100 S Wilkinson Way (43551-2590)
PHONE..................................419 874-2564
EMP: 110
SALES (est): 460MM **Publicly Held**
SIC: **6513** Retirement hotel operation
PA: Capital Senior Living Corp
14160 Dallas Pkwy Ste 300
Dallas TX 75254
972 770-5600

(G-15846)
CARGOTEC SERVICES USA INC
12233 Williams Rd (43551-6802)
PHONE..................................419 482-6000
Lennart Brelin, *President*
James Anasticio, *Senior VP*
Greg Betz, *Purch Mgr*
Trevor Lockyer, *Purch Agent*
Conor Trainor, *Engineer*
EMP: 62
SALES (est): 3.1MM
SALES (corp-wide): 3.8B **Privately Held**
WEB: www.cargotecservices.com
SIC: **8741** Management services
PA: Cargotec Oyj
Porkkalankatu 5
Helsinki 00180
207 774-000

(G-15847)
CAVINS TRUCKING & GARAGE LLC (PA)
100 J St C (43551-4418)
PHONE..................................419 661-9947
Rocky Cavins, *Mng Member*
Belinda Cavin, *
EMP: 30
SALES: 1.2MM **Privately Held**
SIC: **4213** Contract haulers

(G-15848)
CITY OF PERRYSBURG
Also Called: Bureau of Sanitation
11980 Route Roached Rd (43551)
PHONE..................................419 872-8020
Jon Eckeo, *Manager*
EMP: 30
SQ FT: 1,664 **Privately Held**
WEB: www.perrysburgcourt.com
SIC: **4953** 9111 Refuse systems; mayors' offices
PA: City Of Perrysburg
201 W Indiana Ave
Perrysburg OH 43551
419 873-6225

(G-15849)
COMMERCIAL COMFORT SYSTEMS INC
26610 Eckel Rd Ste 3a (43551-1254)
P.O. Box 8792, Maumee (43537-8792)
PHONE..................................419 481-4444
Francis Lanciaux, *President*
Laurel Lanzio, *Treasurer*
EMP: 34
SQ FT: 25,300
SALES (est): 6.5MM **Privately Held**
WEB: www.commercialcomfort.com
SIC: **1711** Warm air heating & air conditioning contractor

(G-15850)
CORRIGAN MOVING SYSTEMS-ANN AR
12377 Williams Rd (43551-1981)
PHONE..................................419 874-2900
William Axel, *General Mgr*
EMP: 25
SALES (corp-wide): 13.2MM **Privately Held**
SIC: **4213** 4214 4212 Household goods transport; household goods moving & storage, local; moving services
HQ: Corrigan Moving Systems-Ann Arbor, Inc.
23923 Research Dr
Farmington Hills MI 48335
248 471-4000

(G-15851)
CRAWFORD GROUP INC
12611 Eckel Junction Rd (43551-1304)
PHONE..................................419 873-7360
Andy Bouza, *Branch Mgr*
EMP: 54
SALES (corp-wide): 4.9B **Privately Held**
SIC: **7514** Rent-a-car service
PA: The Crawford Group Inc
600 Corporate Park Dr
Saint Louis MO 63105
314 512-5000

(G-15852)
CRITICAL BUSINESS ANALYSIS INC
Also Called: CBA
133 W 2nd St Ste 1 (43551-1479)
PHONE..................................419 874-0800
John Gordon, *CEO*
Donald Monteleone, *President*
Bob Ferris, *Vice Pres*
Paul Deraedt, *Mktg Dir*
Vickie Laskey, *Sr Consultant*
EMP: 48
SQ FT: 5,000
SALES: 3.1MM **Privately Held**
WEB: www.cbainc.com
SIC: **8243** 7371 8742 8741 Software training, computer; custom computer programming services; construction project management consultant; business consultant; financial management for business; construction management

(G-15853)
CUTTING EDGE COUNTERTOPS INC
1300 Flagship Dr (43551-1375)
PHONE..................................419 873-9500
Brad Burns, *President*
Jon Cousino, *Principal*
Rob Loughridge, *Principal*
Jeff Erickson, *COO*
Brian Burns, *Vice Pres*
▼ EMP: 32
SQ FT: 24,000
SALES (est): 6.1MM **Privately Held**
WEB: www.cectops.com
SIC: **3281** 1743 Granite, cut & shaped; marble installation, interior

(G-15854)
DAYTON FREIGHT LINES INC
28240 Oregon Rd (43551-4739)
PHONE..................................419 661-8600
Bill Nieset, *Manager*
EMP: 50
SALES (corp-wide): 971MM **Privately Held**
SIC: **4213** Trucking, except local

PA: Dayton Freight Lines, Inc.
6450 Poe Ave Ste 311
Dayton OH 45414
937 264-4060

(G-15855)
DAYTON HEIDELBERG DISTRG CO
Also Called: Burman Wine
912 3rd St (43551-4356)
PHONE..................................419 666-9783
Tom McHugh, *Manager*
EMP: 150
SALES (corp-wide): 369.4MM **Privately Held**
SIC: **4225** 5182 5181 General warehousing & storage; wine & distilled beverages; beer & ale
PA: Dayton Heidelberg Distributing Co.
3601 Dryden Rd
Moraine OH 45439
937 222-8692

(G-15856)
DAYTON HEIDELBERG DISTRG CO
912 3rd St (43551-4356)
PHONE..................................419 666-9783
Matthew Clark, *Technical Mgr*
Tom McHugh, *Manager*
EMP: 90
SALES (corp-wide): 369.4MM **Privately Held**
SIC: **5181** Beer & other fermented malt liquors
PA: Dayton Heidelberg Distributing Co.
3601 Dryden Rd
Moraine OH 45439
937 222-8692

(G-15857)
DCO LLC (HQ)
900 E Boundary St Ste 8a (43551-2406)
PHONE..................................419 931-9086
Michael L Debacker, *Mng Member*
Bricy Stringham, *
◆ EMP: 277 EST: 1904
SALES (est): 3.1MM
SALES (corp-wide): 35.6MM **Privately Held**
WEB: www.dana.com
SIC: **3751** 8741 Motor scooters & parts; financial management for business
PA: Enstar Holdings (Us) Llc
150 2nd Ave N Fl 3
Saint Petersburg FL 33701
727 217-2900

(G-15858)
DEACONIS ASSOCATION INC
Also Called: Deaconis Association
27062 Oakmead Dr (43551-2657)
PHONE..................................419 874-9008
Felicia Evans, *Director*
Marlene Burke, *Administration*
EMP: 75
SALES (est): 722K **Privately Held**
SIC: **8621** Professional membership organizations

(G-15859)
DILLIN ENGINEERED SYSTEMS CORP
8030 Broadstone Rd (43551-4856)
PHONE..................................419 666-6789
David A Smith, *President*
Mike Brickner, *Project Mgr*
Kathy McCormick, *Finance*
Chris Mc Ilroy, *Manager*
Marty Shaffer, *Data Proc Dir*
EMP: 50
SQ FT: 40,000
SALES (est): 10.9MM **Privately Held**
SIC: **8711** 3535 Mechanical engineering; conveyors & conveying equipment

(G-15860)
DOLD HOMES INC (PA)
26610 Eckel Rd (43551-1247)
PHONE..................................419 874-2535
William H Dold, *President*
Mary Lou Dold, *Admin Sec*
EMP: 45 EST: 1976
SQ FT: 16,000

SALES (est): 14MM **Privately Held**
WEB: www.doldhomes.com
SIC: **1521** 1531 New construction, single-family houses; speculative builder, single-family houses

(G-15861)
E H SCHMIDT EXECUTIVE
26785 Dixie Hwy (43551-1714)
P.O. Box 111 (43552-0111)
PHONE..........................419 874-4331
Thomas G Schmidt, *President*
Edward H Schmidt, *Vice Pres*
EMP: 100
SALES (est): 3.3MM **Privately Held**
SIC: **7513** 7515 Truck rental & leasing, no drivers; passenger car leasing

(G-15862)
ECKEL LOGISTICS INC
14617 Deerwood Ct (43551-6224)
PHONE..........................419 349-3118
Paul Eckel, *President*
EMP: 25 EST: 2017
SALES (est): 993.7K **Privately Held**
SIC: **4731** Freight forwarding

(G-15863)
ED SCHMIDT AUTO INC
26875 Dixie Hwy (43551-1716)
PHONE..........................419 874-4331
Thomas G Schmidt, *President*
Adam Stockburger, *Business Mgr*
Matt Urbaniak, *Business Mgr*
Nick Ort, *Sales Mgr*
Kevin Cook, *Sales Staff*
EMP: 250
SQ FT: 55,000
SALES (est): 71.8MM **Privately Held**
SIC: **5511** 5521 5012 7538 Automobiles, new & used; pickups, new & used; vans, new & used; used car dealers; automobiles & other motor vehicles; general automotive repair shops; top & body repair & paint shops; automotive & home supply stores

(G-15864)
ENVIRCARE LAWN LANDSCACAPE LLC
24112 Lime City Rd (43551-9043)
PHONE..........................419 874-6779
Jeffrey D Eberly, *President*
EMP: 30
SALES (est): 2.7MM **Privately Held**
WEB: www.envirocarelawn.com
SIC: **0782** Lawn care services

(G-15865)
FIRST 2 MARKET PRODUCTS LLC
25671 Fort Meigs Rd Ste A (43551-1191)
PHONE..........................419 874-5444
Danny Sackett,
▲ EMP: 32
SQ FT: 20,000
SALES (est): 2.6MM **Privately Held**
SIC: **5199** Packaging materials

(G-15866)
FLUX A SALON BY HAZELTON
131 W Indiana Ave (43551-1578)
PHONE..........................419 841-5100
Greg Hazelton, *Owner*
EMP: 35
SALES (est): 188.8K **Privately Held**
WEB: www.fluxasalon.com
SIC: **7231** Beauty shops

(G-15867)
FRAM GROUP OPERATIONS LLC
Also Called: Honeywell
28399 Cedar Park Blvd (43551-4864)
P.O. Box 981729, El Paso TX (79998-1729)
PHONE..........................419 661-6700
Jerry Bolser, *Principal*
Jim Lamb, *Vice Pres*
Daniel Groszkiewicz, *VP Opers*
Cyndi Holt, *Sales Staff*
Lee Bennett, *Branch Mgr*
EMP: 100 **Privately Held**
WEB: www.honeywell.com

SIC: **3714** 3694 8734 8731 Motor vehicle engines & parts; filters: oil, fuel & air, motor vehicle; spark plugs for internal combustion engines; testing laboratories; commercial physical research
HQ: Fram Group Operations Llc
      1900 W Field Ct 4w-516
      Lake Forest IL 60045

(G-15868)
GENOX TRANSPORTATION INC
25750 Oregon Rd (43551-9778)
PHONE..........................419 837-2023
Kevin Matthews, *President*
Lisa Mathews, *CFO*
EMP: 50 EST: 2013
SALES (est): 138.6K **Privately Held**
SIC: **4789** Transportation services

(G-15869)
GLOW INDUSTRIES INC (PA)
12962 Eckel Junction Rd (43551-1309)
PHONE..........................419 872-4772
David P Glowacki, *President*
Jason Glowacki, *Vice Pres*
◆ EMP: 30
SQ FT: 40,000
SALES (est): 22.7MM **Privately Held**
SIC: **5199** 5331 Variety store merchandise; variety stores

(G-15870)
HCF OF PERRYSBURG INC
Also Called: Manor At Perrysburg, The
250 Manor Dr (43551-3118)
PHONE..........................419 874-0306
Kenneth Zeilinski, *Manager*
EMP: 99
SALES (est): 993.1K
SALES (corp-wide): 154.8MM **Privately Held**
SIC: **8051** Skilled nursing care facilities
PA: Hcf Management, Inc.
      1100 Shawnee Rd
      Lima OH 45805
      419 999-2010

(G-15871)
HEALTH CARE RTREMENT CORP AMER
10540 Fremont Pike (43551-3356)
PHONE..........................419 874-3578
Sara Louk, *Branch Mgr*
EMP: 113
SALES (corp-wide): 2.4B **Publicly Held**
WEB: www.hrc-manorcare.com
SIC: **8051** Skilled nursing care facilities
HQ: Health Care And Retirement Corporation Of America
      333 N Summit St Ste 103
      Toledo OH 43604
      419 252-5500

(G-15872)
HEARTLAND HOSPICE SERVICES LLC
Also Called: Heartland HM Hlth Care Hospice
28555 Starbright Blvd E (43551-5662)
PHONE..........................419 531-0440
Amy Marino, *Manager*
EMP: 56
SALES (corp-wide): 2.4B **Publicly Held**
SIC: **8082** Home health care services
HQ: Heartland Hospice Services, Llc
      333 N Summit St
      Toledo OH 43604

(G-15873)
HERB THYME FARMS INC
8600 S Wilkinson Way G (43551-2598)
PHONE..........................866 386-0854
Howard Roeder, *President*
EMP: 500 EST: 2000
SALES (est): 12MM **Privately Held**
SIC: **0191** General farms, primarily crop

(G-15874)
HIAB USA INC (HQ)
12233 Williams Rd (43551-6802)
PHONE..........................419 482-6000
Roland Sunden, *President*
Lennart Brelin, *President*
John Pielli, *Regional Mgr*
Joakim Andersson, *Vice Pres*
Conor Magee, *Vice Pres*
◆ EMP: 70 EST: 1962

SQ FT: 56,000
SALES (est): 89.5MM
SALES (corp-wide): 3.8B **Privately Held**
SIC: **5084** 3536 Cranes, industrial; hoists; cranes, industrial plant; hoists
PA: Cargotec Oyj
      Porkkalankatu 5
      Helsinki 00180
      207 774-000

(G-15875)
HOSPICE OF NORTHWEST OHIO (PA)
30000 E River Rd (43551-3429)
PHONE..........................419 661-4001
Angie Baltzell, *Manager*
Tracy Schinharl, *Info Tech Dir*
Judy Seibenick, *Exec Dir*
Judy Lang, *Exec Dir*
Sue Miller, *Director*
EMP: 300
SQ FT: 48,000
SALES: 28.7MM **Privately Held**
SIC: **8052** Personal care facility

(G-15876)
HOSTER HOTELS LLC
Also Called: Home2 Suites, The
5995 Levis Commons Blvd (43551-7112)
PHONE..........................419 931-8900
Robert Volker, *Mng Member*
EMP: 30
SALES (est): 137.8K **Privately Held**
SIC: **7011** Hotels

(G-15877)
IMCO CARBIDE TOOL INC
Also Called: Toledo Cutting Tools
28170 Cedar Park Blvd (43551-4872)
PHONE..........................419 661-6313
Perry L Osburn, *Ch of Bd*
Matthew S Osburn, *Vice Pres*
Julie Whitlow, *Admin Sec*
EMP: 90
SQ FT: 25,000
SALES (est): 38.5MM **Privately Held**
WEB: www.imcousa.com
SIC: **5084** 3545 Machine tools & accessories; tools & accessories for machine tools

(G-15878)
INDEPENDENT EVALUATORS INC
27457 Holiday Ln Ste B (43551-5364)
PHONE..........................419 872-5650
Charles Burke, *President*
Dawn N Schmidt, *Administration*
EMP: 100
SALES (est): 6MM **Privately Held**
WEB: www.independentevaluators.com
SIC: **8742** Compensation & benefits planning consultant

(G-15879)
INGRAM ENTRMT HOLDINGS INC
668 1st St (43551-4480)
PHONE..........................419 662-3132
EMP: 41
SALES (corp-wide): 400MM **Privately Held**
SIC: **7929** Entertainers & entertainment groups
PA: Ingram Entertainment Holdings Inc.
      2 Ingram Blvd
      La Vergne TN 37089
      615 287-4000

(G-15880)
INVESTEK MANAGEMENT SVCS F/C
1090 W South Boundary St # 100 (43551-5234)
PHONE..........................419 873-1236
John Aubry, *Owner*
Anne Weilgopolski, *Manager*
EMP: 26 EST: 2011
SALES (est): 2.7MM **Privately Held**
SIC: **8741** Management services

(G-15881)
INVESTEK REALTY LLC
1090 W South Boundary St # 100 (43551-5285)
PHONE..........................419 873-1236
John Anbury,
EMP: 25 EST: 2001
SALES (est): 2.1MM **Privately Held**
SIC: **6531** Real estate managers

(G-15882)
JERL MACHINE INC
11140 Avenue Rd (43551-2825)
PHONE..........................419 873-0270
Robert L Brossia, *CEO*
Carol Coe, *President*
Eileen Brossia, *Vice Pres*
David Kessler, *Foreman/Supr*
Rodney Burris, *CFO*
EMP: 61
SQ FT: 76,000
SALES (est): 10.6MM **Privately Held**
WEB: www.jerl.com
SIC: **7692** 3599 Welding repair; machine shop, jobbing & repair

(G-15883)
JON R DVORAK MD
Also Called: Weeber-Morse, Carmen MD
1090 W South Boundary St # 5 (43551-5234)
PHONE..........................419 872-7700
Jon R Dvorak MD, *Med Doctor*
Morse C Weeber, *Med Doctor*
EMP: 25
SALES (est): 884.9K **Privately Held**
SIC: **8011** Pediatrician; general & family practice, physician/surgeon

(G-15884)
K WEST GROUP LLC
8305 Fremont Pike (43551-9427)
PHONE..........................972 722-3874
Martha Kwest, *Principal*
EMP: 116
SALES (corp-wide): 36.4MM **Privately Held**
SIC: **1611** General contractor, highway & street construction
PA: K. West Group, Llc
      8305 Fremont Pike
      Perrysburg OH 43551
      419 874-4284

(G-15885)
KENS FLOWER SHOP INC
140 W South Boundary St (43551-1754)
PHONE..........................419 841-9590
Art Balk, *Manager*
EMP: 28
SQ FT: 3,000
SALES (corp-wide): 12.1MM **Privately Held**
WEB: www.kensflowers.com
SIC: **5992** 5193 Flowers, fresh; flowers, fresh
PA: Ken's Flower Shop, Inc
      140 W South Boundary St
      Perrysburg OH 43551
      419 874-1333

(G-15886)
KIEMLE-HANKINS COMPANY (PA)
94 H St (43551-4497)
P.O. Box 507, Toledo (43697-0507)
PHONE..........................419 661-2430
Tim Martindale, *President*
Kevin Napierala, *Division Mgr*
Stephen Martindale, *Chairman*
Robert Schuck, *Purchasing*
Jeffrey Lee, *CFO*
EMP: 50
SQ FT: 50,000
SALES: 20MM **Privately Held**
WEB: www.kiemlehankins.com
SIC: **7694** 7629 3699 Electric motor repair; electrical equipment repair services; electrical equipment & supplies

(G-15887)
KINGSTON RSDNCE PERRYSBURG LLC
333 E Boundary St (43551-2861)
PHONE..........................419 872-6200

▲ = Import ▼=Export
◆ =Import/Export

Cheryl Hartman, *Exec Dir*
Karen Burnard, *Exec Dir*
William Nichols, *Director*
Diana Oreck, *Director*
EMP: 53
SALES (est): 3.9MM
SALES (corp-wide): 95.5MM **Privately Held**
WEB: www.kingstonhealthcare.com
SIC: 8361 8051 Home for the aged; skilled nursing care facilities
PA: Kingston Healthcare Company
1 Seagate Ste 1960
Toledo OH 43604
419 247-2880

(G-15888)
LAND ART INC (PA)
7728 Ponderosa Rd (43551-4851)
P.O. Box 879 (43552-0879)
PHONE.....................419 666-5296
Martin W Strassner Jr, *President*
EMP: 30 **EST:** 1974
SQ FT: 12,000
SALES (est): 3MM **Privately Held**
SIC: 0783 0782 Spraying services, ornamental tree; fertilizing services, lawn

(G-15889)
LEVIS COMMONS HOTEL LLC
Also Called: Hilton Garden Inn Perrysburg
6165 Levis Commons Blvd (43551-7269)
PHONE.....................419 873-3573
Izzet Sueri, *Manager*
EMP: 98
SALES (est): 5.8MM
SALES (corp-wide): 7.4MM **Privately Held**
WEB: www.ghghotels.net
SIC: 7011 Hotel, franchised
PA: Gateway Hospitality Group Inc
8921 Canyon Falls Blvd # 140
Twinsburg OH 44087
330 405-9800

(G-15890)
LOWER GREAT LAKES KENWORTH INC
Also Called: Whiteford Kenworth
12650 Eckel Junction Rd (43551-1303)
P.O. Box 387 (43552-0387)
PHONE.....................419 874-3511
Roger Euler, *Manager*
EMP: 33
SQ FT: 10,000
SALES (corp-wide): 84.6MM **Privately Held**
WEB: www.lglk.com
SIC: 5012 7538 5013 Trucks, commercial; general automotive repair shops; motor vehicle supplies & new parts
PA: Lower Great Lakes Kenworth, Inc.
4625 W Western Ave
South Bend IN 46619
574 234-9007

(G-15891)
LOWES HOME CENTERS LLC
10295 Fremont Pike (43551-3334)
PHONE.....................419 874-6758
Darcy Mueller, *Branch Mgr*
EMP: 150
SALES (corp-wide): 68.6B **Publicly Held**
SIC: 5211 5031 5722 5064 Home centers; building materials, exterior; building materials, interior; household appliance stores; electrical appliances, television & radio
HQ: Lowe's Home Centers, Llc
1605 Curtis Bridge Rd
Wilkesboro NC 28697
336 658-4000

(G-15892)
MAUMEE PLUMBING & HTG SUP INC (PA)
Also Called: Waterhouse Bath and Kit Studio
12860 Eckel Junction Rd (43551-1307)
P.O. Box 309 (43552-0309)
PHONE.....................419 874-7991
Douglas Williams, *President*
Greg Williams, *Vice Pres*
Tony Cannon, *Purch Agent*
Frank Mata, *Purch Agent*
Keith Weidner, *Purchasing*
EMP: 25

SQ FT: 48,000
SALES (est): 13.4MM **Privately Held**
WEB: www.maumeesupply.com
SIC: 5074 Plumbing fittings & supplies

(G-15893)
MERRILL LYNCH PIERCE FENNER
3292 Levis Commons Blvd (43551-7144)
PHONE.....................419 891-2091
Alan Lynch, *Branch Mgr*
EMP: 27
SALES (corp-wide): 110.5B **Publicly Held**
WEB: www.ml.com
SIC: 6211 Stock brokers & dealers
HQ: Merrill Lynch, Pierce, Fenner & Smith Incorporated
111 8th Ave
New York NY 10011
800 637-7455

(G-15894)
MIDWEST CHURCH CNSTR LTD
634 Eckel Rd Ste A (43551-6031)
PHONE.....................419 874-0838
Ken Miller,
EMP: 28 **EST:** 1998
SALES (est): 4.9MM **Privately Held**
WEB: www.midwestchurch.com
SIC: 1542 Religious building construction

(G-15895)
MIDWEST ENVIRONMENTAL INC
28757 Glenwood Rd (43551-3015)
PHONE.....................419 382-9200
Dale Bruhl, *President*
EMP: 30 **EST:** 2014
SALES (est): 2.5MM **Privately Held**
SIC: 8744

(G-15896)
OHIO & MICHIGAN PAPER COMPANY
350 4th St (43551-4338)
P.O. Box 621, Toledo (43697-0621)
PHONE.....................419 666-1500
Alan Leininger, *President*
Robert Steve Fronk, *Corp Secy*
Phillip Christensen, *Vice Pres*
Laura Malosh, *Marketing Staff*
EMP: 25 **EST:** 1868
SQ FT: 75,000
SALES (est): 17.4MM **Privately Held**
SIC: 5111 5112 5113 Printing paper; stationery; paper & products, wrapping or coarse

(G-15897)
OHIO MACHINERY CO
Also Called: Caterpillar Authorized Dealer
25970 Dixie Hwy (43551-1701)
PHONE.....................419 874-7975
Randy McCabe, *Manager*
EMP: 101
SQ FT: 19,000
SALES (corp-wide): 222.7MM **Privately Held**
WEB: www.enginesnow.com
SIC: 5082 7359 General construction machinery & equipment; equipment rental & leasing
PA: Ohio Machinery Co.
3993 E Royalton Rd
Broadview Heights OH 44147
440 526-6200

(G-15898)
OHIOANS HOME HEALTH CARE INC
28315 Kensington Ln (43551-4164)
PHONE.....................419 843-4422
Josh Adams, *President*
Matt Anderson, *Business Mgr*
Christa Firsdon, *Human Res Dir*
Don Kristufek, *Mktg Coord*
Samantha Fain, *Office Admin*
EMP: 95
SQ FT: 3,500
SALES (est): 4.1MM **Privately Held**
SIC: 8082 Visiting nurse service

(G-15899)
PEAK TRANSPORTATION INC
26624 Glenwood Rd (43551-4846)
P.O. Box 150 (43552-0150)
PHONE.....................419 874-5201
Milton F Knight, *President*
Debbie Knight, *Admin Sec*
EMP: 66
SQ FT: 20,000
SALES (est): 3.5MM **Privately Held**
SIC: 4212 4213 Local trucking, without storage; trucking, except local

(G-15900)
PENSKE TRUCK LEASING CO LP
12222 Williams Rd (43551-6803)
PHONE.....................419 873-8611
Mike Pritchard, *Manager*
EMP: 40
SALES (corp-wide): 2.6B **Privately Held**
WEB: www.pensketruckleasing.com
SIC: 7513 Truck leasing, without drivers
PA: Penske Truck Leasing Co., L.P.
2675 Morgantown Rd
Reading PA 19607
610 775-6000

(G-15901)
PERRY PRO TECH INC
1270 Flagship Dr (43551-1381)
PHONE.....................419 475-9030
Courtney King, *Accounts Mgr*
John Rees, *Manager*
EMP: 30
SALES (corp-wide): 59.6MM **Privately Held**
SIC: 5044 Office equipment
PA: Perry Pro Tech, Inc.
545 W Market St Lowr Lowr
Lima OH 45801
419 228-1360

(G-15902)
PERRYSBURG BOARD OF EDUCATION
Also Called: Perrysburg Bus Garage
25715 Fort Meigs Rd (43551-1138)
PHONE.....................419 874-3127
Michael Cline, *Manager*
EMP: 30
SALES (corp-wide): 17.1MM **Privately Held**
SIC: 4151 School buses
PA: Perrysburg Board Of Education Inc
140 E Indiana Ave
Perrysburg OH 43551
419 874-9131

(G-15903)
PERRYSBURG PEDIATRICS
1601 Brigham Dr Ste 200 (43551-7117)
PHONE.....................419 872-7700
Kenneth Turk, *Principal*
EMP: 25 **EST:** 2001
SALES (est): 1MM **Privately Held**
SIC: 8011 General & family practice, physician/surgeon

(G-15904)
PERRYSBURG RSDNTIAL SEAL CTING
26651 Eckel Rd (43551-1209)
P.O. Box 170 (43552-0170)
PHONE.....................419 872-7325
Richard Jambor, *Owner*
EMP: 30
SALES (est): 1.6MM **Privately Held**
SIC: 1611 Surfacing & paving

(G-15905)
PRECISION STRIP INC
7401 Ponderosa Rd (43551-4858)
PHONE.....................419 661-1100
Greg Bergman, *Manager*
EMP: 70
SALES (corp-wide): 11.5B **Publicly Held**
WEB: www.precision-strip.com
SIC: 4225 General warehousing & storage
HQ: Precision Strip Inc.
86 S Ohio St
Minster OH 45865
419 628-2343

(G-15906)
PROHEALTH PARTNERS INC
12661 Eckel Junction Rd (43551)
PHONE.....................419 491-7150
Rich Adam, *President*
EMP: 50
SALES (est): 1.8MM **Privately Held**
SIC: 8049 Physical therapist

(G-15907)
PRUETER ENTERPRISES LTD
Also Called: Great Lakes Medical Staffing
25660 Dixie Hwy Ste 2 (43551-2167)
PHONE.....................419 872-5343
E Kyle Prueter, *President*
Ann M Prueter, *Vice Pres*
EMP: 212
SQ FT: 2,400
SALES (est): 5.8MM **Privately Held**
SIC: 7363 Employee leasing service

(G-15908)
PUPS PARADISE
12615 Roachton Rd (43551-1349)
PHONE.....................419 873-6115
Ron Deleeuw, *Owner*
EMP: 25
SALES (est): 214.7K **Privately Held**
SIC: 0752 Boarding services, kennels; grooming services, pet & animal specialties

(G-15909)
QUINCY AMUSEMENTS INC
2005 Hollenbeck Dr (43551-7137)
PHONE.....................419 874-2154
Elena Allen, *Principal*
EMP: 50
SALES (est): 397.5K **Privately Held**
SIC: 7832 Motion picture theaters, except drive-in

(G-15910)
R & J TRUCKING INC
3423 Genoa Rd (43551-9703)
PHONE.....................419 837-9937
Mike Schnider, *Manager*
EMP: 30 **Privately Held**
WEB: www.rjtrucking.com
SIC: 4212 Dump truck haulage
HQ: R & J Trucking, Inc.
8063 Southern Blvd
Youngstown OH 44512
800 262-9365

(G-15911)
R & L CARRIERS INC
134 W South Boundary St (43551-1763)
PHONE.....................419 874-5976
EMP: 27 **Privately Held**
SIC: 4213 Contract haulers
PA: R & L Carriers, Inc.
600 Gilliam Rd
Wilmington OH 45177

(G-15912)
RENHILL STFFING SRVCES-AMERICA (HQ)
28315 Kensington Ln Ste B (43551-4164)
PHONE.....................419 254-2800
Joseph T Braden, *President*
EMP: 25
SQ FT: 6,000
SALES (est): 3.7MM
SALES (corp-wide): 7.5MM **Privately Held**
SIC: 7363 Temporary help service
PA: Renhill Group Inc
28315 Kensington Ln Ste B
Perrysburg OH 43551
419 254-2800

(G-15913)
RIVER ROAD FAMILY PHYSICIANS
1601 Brigham Dr Ste 250 (43551-7115)
PHONE.....................419 872-7745
Jason Evans, *Owner*
EMP: 15
SALES (est): 940K **Privately Held**
SIC: 8011 General & family practice, physician/surgeon

G E O G R A P H I C

(G-15914)
ROBEX LLC
8600 S Wilkinson Way A (43551-2598)
PHONE..................................419 270-0770
Jon Parker, *CEO*
EMP: 55
SALES: 10MM **Privately Held**
SIC: 8742 Automation & robotics consultant

(G-15915)
RRP PACKAGING
327 5th St (43551-4919)
PHONE..................................419 666-6119
Jeff Freiburger, *Principal*
Robert Hinkle, *Vice Pres*
EMP: 50 EST: 2008
SALES (est): 3.4MM **Privately Held**
SIC: 5199 Packaging materials

(G-15916)
RYDER TRUCK RENTAL INC
1380 4th St (43551-4365)
PHONE..................................419 666-9833
Jon Rodgers, *Site Mgr*
Henry Alexander, *Manager*
Brad Lehman, *Manager*
EMP: 50
SALES (corp-wide): 8.4B **Publicly Held**
SIC: 7513 Truck rental, without drivers
HQ: Ryder Truck Rental, Inc.
　11690 Nw 105th St
　Medley FL 33178
　305 500-3726

(G-15917)
SALON HAZELTON
131 W Indiana Ave (43551-1578)
PHONE..................................419 874-9404
Greg Hazelton, *Owner*
EMP: 26
SQ FT: 1,420
SALES (est): 836.1K **Privately Held**
WEB: www.salonhazelton.com
SIC: 7231 5999 Cosmetologist; hair care products

(G-15918)
SARO TRUCK DISPATCH INC
26180 Glenwood Rd (43551-4822)
PHONE..................................419 873-1358
Sandra Ankney, *President*
Jeff Mc Coy, *Vice Pres*
EMP: 42
SALES (est): 5.2MM **Privately Held**
SIC: 4213 Heavy hauling

(G-15919)
SCHMIDT DAILY RENTAL INC
Also Called: Ed Schmidt Chevrolet
26875 Dixie Hwy (43551-1716)
PHONE..................................419 874-4331
Thomas Schmidt, *President*
EMP: 61
SALES: 44.6MM **Privately Held**
SIC: 7514 Passenger car rental

(G-15920)
SHAMAS LTD
102 W Indiana Ave (43551-1577)
PHONE..................................419 872-9908
Rhonda Broadway, *Partner*
Tony Shamas, *Partner*
EMP: 40
SALES (est): 1.2MM **Privately Held**
WEB: www.shamas.com
SIC: 7231 Hairdressers

(G-15921)
SIGMA TECHNOLOGIES LTD
27096 Oakmead Dr (43551-2657)
PHONE..................................419 874-9262
Jay Carpenter, *Opers Mgr*
Matthew Zalaiskalns, *Engineer*
Philip Mathieu, *Accountant*
Brandon Lerette, *Manager*
John Hamilton, *Technical Staff*
EMP: 45
SALES (est): 8.8MM **Privately Held**
WEB: www.teamsigma.com
SIC: 8711 Consulting engineer

(G-15922)
SOTO SALON & SPA
580 Craig Dr Ste 6 (43551-1776)
PHONE..................................419 872-5555

Denise Soto, *Owner*
EMP: 28
SALES (est): 870K **Privately Held**
WEB: www.salonsoto.com
SIC: 7231 Cosmetologist

(G-15923)
SOUTHERN GRAPHIC SYSTEMS INC
9648 Grassy Creek Dr (43551-3544)
PHONE..................................419 662-9873
Christine Wood, *Manager*
EMP: 415
SALES (corp-wide): 272.7MM **Privately Held**
SIC: 7389 Personal service agents, brokers & bureaus
HQ: Southern Graphic Systems, Llc
　626 W Main St Ste 500
　Louisville KY 40202
　502 637-5443

(G-15924)
SPIEKER COMPANY
8350 Fremont Pike (43551-9427)
PHONE..................................419 872-7000
Norman T White, *President*
Marty Almester, *Superintendent*
Dennis Hoodlebrink, *Superintendent*
Frank McDonald, *Superintendent*
Matt Berg, *Vice Pres*
EMP: 50
SQ FT: 22,000
SALES (est): 22.2MM **Privately Held**
WEB: www.spiekercompany.com
SIC: 1542 1541 1611 Commercial & office building, new construction; industrial buildings, new construction; general contractor, highway & street construction

(G-15925)
STATE FARM MUTL AUTO INSUR CO
Also Called: State Farm Insurance
13001 Roachton Rd (43551-1357)
PHONE..................................419 873-0100
Keith Kirkpatrick, *Branch Mgr*
Patrici Kirkpatrick, *Agent*
Barry Hoozen, *Real Est Agnt*
EMP: 89
SALES (corp-wide): 39.5B **Privately Held**
SIC: 6411 Insurance agents & brokers
PA: State Farm Mutual Automobile Insurance Company
　1 State Farm Plz
　Bloomington IL 61710
　309 766-2311

(G-15926)
TMT INC
Also Called: Tmt Logistics
655 D St (43551-4908)
P.O. Box 408 (43552-0408)
PHONE..................................419 592-1041
Tony Marks, *President*
EMP: 250
SALES (est): 9.6MM **Privately Held**
SIC: 4789 3999 Railroad maintenance & repair services; dock equipment & supplies, industrial

(G-15927)
TRT MANAGEMENT CORPORATION (PA)
Also Called: Kenakore Solutions
487 J St (43551-4303)
PHONE..................................419 661-1233
Bruce Gonring, *CEO*
Chris Huver, *President*
Denise Keeran, *Administration*
EMP: 35 EST: 2015
SQ FT: 128,000
SALES: 1.1MM **Privately Held**
SIC: 4225 General warehousing

(G-15928)
UNITED PARCEL SERVICE INC OH
Also Called: UPS
12171 Eckel Rd (43551-1241)
PHONE..................................419 872-0211
Marv N Thress, *Manager*
EMP: 115

SALES (corp-wide): 71.8B **Publicly Held**
WEB: www.upsscs.com
SIC: 4215 7538 Parcel delivery, vehicular; general automotive repair shops; general truck repair
HQ: United Parcel Service, Inc. (Oh)
　55 Glenlake Pkwy
　Atlanta GA 30328
　404 828-6000

(G-15929)
UNITED RENTALS NORTH AMER INC
620 Eckel Rd (43551-1202)
P.O. Box 240 (43552-0240)
PHONE..................................800 877-3687
April Mitchell, *Sales Staff*
Mike Lowell, *Branch Mgr*
EMP: 25
SALES (corp-wide): 8B **Publicly Held**
WEB: www.ur.com
SIC: 7353 7359 Cranes & aerial lift equipment, rental or leasing; equipment rental & leasing
HQ: United Rentals (North America), Inc.
　100 Frederick St 700
　Stamford CT 06902
　203 622-3131

(G-15930)
US UTILITY ELECTRICAL SVCS
3592 Genoa Rd (43551-9702)
PHONE..................................419 837-9753
Gerald Heminger, *President*
Kathryn Chlebowski, *Vice Pres*
EMP: 40
SQ FT: 2,400
SALES (est): 1.7MM **Privately Held**
SIC: 1731 General electrical contractor

(G-15931)
VAN TASSEL CONSTRUCTION CORP
25591 Fort Meigs Rd Ste A (43551-1394)
P.O. Box 698, Sylvania (43560-0698)
PHONE..................................419 873-0188
Fax: 419 873-0190
EMP: 30
SQ FT: 20,000
SALES (est): 2.8MM **Privately Held**
SIC: 1541 1542 General Construction Commercial

(G-15932)
W W WILLIAMS COMPANY LLC
3325 Libbey Rd (43551-9740)
P.O. Box 427, Lemoyne (43441-0427)
PHONE..................................419 837-5067
Alan Gatlin, *President*
John M Stephenson, *Branch Mgr*
Led McIntyre, *Manager*
EMP: 25
SALES (corp-wide): 4.8B **Privately Held**
WEB: www.williamsdistribution.com
SIC: 7538 5013 5084 5063 Diesel engine repair: automotive; automotive supplies & parts; industrial machinery & equipment; electrical apparatus & equipment
HQ: The W W Williams Company Llc
　5025 Bradenton Ave # 130
　Dublin OH 43017
　614 228-5000

(G-15933)
W W WILLIAMS COMPANY LLC
3325 Libbey Rd (43551-9740)
PHONE..................................419 837-5067
W Williams, *Branch Mgr*
EMP: 67
SALES (corp-wide): 4.8B **Privately Held**
SIC: 5013 Truck parts & accessories
HQ: The W W Williams Company Llc
　5025 Bradenton Ave # 130
　Dublin OH 43017
　614 228-5000

(G-15934)
WADSWORTH-SLAWSON INC
Also Called: Wadsworth Solutions Northeast
1500 Michael Owens Way (43551-2975)
PHONE..................................216 391-7263
Brit R Wadsworth, *CEO*
Thomas H McClave, *President*
Britt Wadsworth, *General Mgr*
Gary L McClave, *Vice Pres*
David Sommer, *Vice Pres*

EMP: 32
SALES (est): 18.3MM **Privately Held**
SIC: 5075 Warm air heating & air conditioning

(G-15935)
WESTHAVEN SERVICES CO LLC
Also Called: Omnicare of Northwest Ohio
7643 Ponderosa Rd (43551-4862)
P.O. Box 1030 (43552-1030)
PHONE..................................419 661-2200
Sue Neuber, *Exec VP*
EMP: 300
SALES (est): 57.8MM
SALES (corp-wide): 194.5B **Publicly Held**
SIC: 5122 Pharmaceuticals
HQ: Neighborcare Pharmacy Services, Inc.
　201 E 4th St Ste 900
　Cincinnati OH 45202

(G-15936)
WHELCO INDUSTRIAL LTD
28210 Cedar Park Blvd (43551-4865)
PHONE..................................419 873-6134
Mike Farar, *Branch Mgr*
EMP: 36
SALES (corp-wide): 5.1MM **Privately Held**
WEB: www.whelco.com
SIC: 7694 Electric motor repair
PA: Whelco Industrial, Ltd
　28210 Cedar Park Blvd
　Perrysburg OH 43551
　419 385-4627

(G-15937)
XPO LOGISTICS FREIGHT INC
28291 Glenwood Rd (43551-4809)
PHONE..................................419 666-3022
Robert Bull, *Manager*
EMP: 60
SALES (corp-wide): 15.3B **Publicly Held**
WEB: www.con-way.com
SIC: 4213 Contract haulers
HQ: Xpo Logistics Freight, Inc.
　2211 Old Earhart Rd # 100
　Ann Arbor MI 48105
　800 755-2728

(G-15938)
YOUNG MENS CHRISTIAN ASSOCIAT
Also Called: YMCA of Greater Toledo
13415 Eckel Junction Rd (43551-1320)
PHONE..................................419 251-9622
Joe Hillrich, *Principal*
Glen King, *Vice Pres*
EMP: 240
SALES (corp-wide): 29.1MM **Privately Held**
SIC: 8641 Youth organizations
PA: Young Men's Christian Association Of Greater Toledo
　1500 N Superior St Fl 2
　Toledo OH 43604
　419 729-8135

┌─────────────────────────────┐
│　　　　**Perrysville**　　　　│
│　　　*Ashland County*　　　│
└─────────────────────────────┘

(G-15939)
AYERS FARMS INC
820 State Route 39 (44864-9539)
PHONE..................................419 938-7707
Carl Ayers, *President*
Steve Ayers, *Vice Pres*
EMP: 25
SALES: 500K **Privately Held**
SIC: 0211 0119 0241 Beef cattle feedlots; bean (dry field & seed) farm; milk production

(G-15940)
COWEN TRUCK LINE INC
2697 State Route 39 (44864-9535)
P.O. Box 480 (44864-0480)
PHONE..................................419 938-3401
Tim Cowen, *President*
Marianne Cowell, *COO*
Wayne Heller, *Business Dir*
EMP: 85

SQ FT: 20,000
SALES (est): 17MM **Privately Held**
WEB: www.cowentruckline.com
SIC: 4213 4212 Contract haulers; local trucking, without storage

(G-15941)
MANSFIELD PLUMBING PDTS LLC (HQ)
150 E 1st St (44864-9421)
P.O. Box 620 (44864-0620)
PHONE...............................419 938-5211
Jim Morando, *President*
◆ EMP: 600
SQ FT: 700,000
SALES (est): 177.7MM **Privately Held**
SIC: 3261 3463 3088 3431 Vitreous plumbing fixtures; plumbing fixture forgings, nonferrous; plastics plumbing fixtures; bathtubs: enameled iron, cast iron or pressed metal; shower stalls, metal; plumbing fixture fittings & trim; plumbing fittings & supplies

(G-15942)
NATURAL RESOURCES OHIO DEPT
Also Called: Mohican State Park Lodge & Con
1098 Ashlnd Cnty Rd 300 (44864)
PHONE...............................419 938-5411
Laura Weirick, *Manager*
EMP: 100 **Privately Held**
WEB: www.ohiostateparks.com
SIC: 7011 9512 5813 5812 Hotels; land, mineral & wildlife conservation; ; drinking places; eating places
HQ: Ohio Department Of Natural Resources
2045 Morse Rd Bldg D-3
Columbus OH 43229

Petersburg
Mahoning County

(G-15943)
DAVE SUGAR EXCAVATING LLC
11640 S State Line Rd (44454-9705)
P.O. Box 459, New Middletown (44442-0459)
PHONE...............................330 542-1100
Dave Sugar,
EMP: 35
SALES (est): 2.7MM **Privately Held**
SIC: 1794 1795 1623 Excavation work; wrecking & demolition work; water. sewer & utility lines

---

Pettisville
Fulton County

(G-15944)
PHEASANTS FOREVER INC
Also Called: Chapter 492
173 Main St (43553)
PHONE...............................567 454-6319
Kenneth Frey, *President*
EMP: 38
SALES (corp-wide): 67.8MM **Privately Held**
SIC: 8699 Animal humane society
PA: Pheasants Forever, Inc.
1783 Buerkle Cir
Saint Paul MN 55110
651 773-2000

Pickerington
Fairfield County

(G-15945)
AMERICAN MOTORCYCLE ASSN (PA)
Also Called: AMERICAN MOTORCYCLIST ASSOCIAT
13515 Yarmouth Dr (43147-8273)
PHONE...............................614 856-1900
Robert M Dingman, *President*
Joel Moor, *COO*

Darcel Higgins, *CFO*
Carolyn Stewart, *Human Res Dir*
Kaitlyn Sesco, *Marketing Staff*
EMP: 85 EST: 1952
SQ FT: 30,000
SALES: 12.6MM **Privately Held**
WEB: www.americanmotorcyclist.com
SIC: 8699 Automobile owners' association

(G-15946)
ANOTHER CHANCE INC
9866 Haverford Pl (43147-9544)
PHONE...............................614 868-3541
Robert Scott, *President*
EMP: 33
SALES (est): 26.1K **Privately Held**
WEB: www.anotherchance.com
SIC: 7389 Personal service agents, brokers & bureaus

(G-15947)
ANTIOCH CNNCTION CANTON MI LLC
799 Windmiller Dr (43147-8199)
PHONE...............................614 531-9285
Gary Smelser, *Mng Member*
EMP: 50 EST: 2013
SQ FT: 86,000
SALES (est): 184.4K **Privately Held**
SIC: 8059 Nursing home, except skilled & intermediate care facility

(G-15948)
ANTIOCH SALEM FIELDS FREDERICK
799 Windmiller Dr (43147-8199)
PHONE...............................614 531-9285
Gary Smelser, *Mng Member*
EMP: 50
SQ FT: 90,000
SALES (est): 181.9K **Privately Held**
SIC: 8059 Nursing home, except skilled & intermediate care facility

(G-15949)
BUCKEYE COMMERCIAL CLEANING
12936 Stonecreek Dr Ste F (43147-8846)
PHONE...............................614 866-4700
David Myers, *President*
EMP: 42
SALES (est): 1.2MM **Privately Held**
SIC: 7349 Janitorial service, contract basis

(G-15950)
BUREAU WORKERS COMPENSATION
Also Called: Safety and Hygiene
13430 Yarmouth Dr (43147-8310)
PHONE...............................614 466-5109
Mark Garver, *Superintendent*
EMP: 45
SALES (est): 2.3MM **Privately Held**
SIC: 7382 Security systems services

(G-15951)
CITY OF PICKERINGTON
Also Called: Municipal Golf Course
1145 Clubhouse Ln (43147-8715)
PHONE...............................614 645-8474
Scott Jones, *Manager*
EMP: 50 **Privately Held**
SIC: 7992 Public golf courses
PA: City Of Pickerington
100 Lockville Rd
Pickerington OH 43147
614 833-2289

(G-15952)
COLDWELL BANKER KING THOMPSON
176 Clint Dr (43147-7994)
PHONE...............................614 759-0808
Kevin Strait, *Owner*
Consuela Floyd, *Sales Associate*
Vanessav Simmons, *Consultant*
Margaret Fenters, *Real Est Agnt*
Darlene Kuzmic, *Real Est Agnt*
EMP: 60
SALES (est): 2.2MM **Privately Held**
SIC: 6531 Real estate agent, residential

(G-15953)
COLONIAL HEATING & COOLING CO
Also Called: Honeywell Authorized Dealer
671 Windmiller Dr (43147-8192)
PHONE...............................614 837-6100
Robert L Posey Jr, *President*
Rob Elkins, *Vice Pres*
Lora Posey, *Treasurer*
EMP: 50
SQ FT: 12,000
SALES (est): 7.6MM **Privately Held**
WEB: www.colonialheating.com
SIC: 1711 Warm air heating & air conditioning contractor

(G-15954)
COMO INC
8670 Hill Rd S (43147-8536)
PHONE...............................614 830-2666
Robert Hart, *President*
EMP: 28
SQ FT: 1,970
SALES (est): 1.3MM **Privately Held**
SIC: 0782 Landscape contractors

(G-15955)
COOKIE CUTTERS HAIRCUTTERS
1726 Hill Rd N (43147-8880)
PHONE...............................614 522-0220
Alison Celento, *Owner*
EMP: 30
SALES (est): 233.3K **Privately Held**
SIC: 7231 Unisex hair salons

(G-15956)
DONLEY CONCRETE CUTTING
151 W Borland St (43147-1206)
PHONE...............................614 834-0300
David Donley, *Branch Mgr*
EMP: 60
SALES (corp-wide): 5.9MM **Privately Held**
SIC: 1771 Concrete work
PA: Donley Concrete Cutting
1441 Gest St
Cincinnati OH 45203
513 421-1950

(G-15957)
HER INC
1450 Tussing Rd (43147-9499)
PHONE...............................614 864-7400
Michael Kocher, *Partner*
Ed Caldwell, *Manager*
EMP: 100
SALES (corp-wide): 14.3MM **Privately Held**
WEB: www.eassent.com
SIC: 6531 Real estate agent, residential
PA: Her, Inc
4261 Morse Rd
Columbus OH 43230
614 221-7400

(G-15958)
HOME ECHO CLUB INC
Also Called: Echo Manor Extended Care Ctr
10270 Blacklick Rd (43147-9225)
PHONE...............................614 864-1718
William T Johnson, *President*
Gary Brand, *Administration*
EMP: 107
SQ FT: 66,000
SALES (est): 5MM **Privately Held**
SIC: 8052 8051 Intermediate care facilities; skilled nursing care facilities

(G-15959)
HUNTINGTON HLLS RECREATION CLB
6600 Springbrook Dr (43147-9142)
P.O. Box 75 (43147-0075)
PHONE...............................614 837-0293
Jon Hanna, *President*
EMP: 30
SALES: 114.3K **Privately Held**
SIC: 7999 Swimming pool, non-membership

(G-15960)
JPMORGAN CHASE BANK NAT ASSN
7915 Refugee Rd (43147-9428)
PHONE...............................614 834-3120
Sheila Williamslee, *Branch Mgr*
EMP: 26
SALES (corp-wide): 131.4B **Publicly Held**
WEB: www.chase.com
SIC: 6029 Commercial banks
HQ: Jpmorgan Chase Bank, National Association
1111 Polaris Pkwy
Columbus OH 43240
614 436-3055

(G-15961)
KINDRED NURSING CENTERS E LLC
Also Called: Kindred Transitional Care
1300 Hill Rd N (43147-8986)
PHONE...............................314 631-3000
Brian Newman, *Branch Mgr*
EMP: 121
SALES (corp-wide): 6B **Privately Held**
WEB: www.salemhaven.com
SIC: 8051 Convalescent home with continuous nursing care
HQ: Kindred Nursing Centers East, L.L.C.
680 S 4th St
Louisville KY 40202
502 596-7300

(G-15962)
LBS INTERNATIONAL INC
Also Called: Friendly Care Agency
12920 Sheffield Dr (43147-7706)
PHONE...............................614 866-3688
Sam I Lantsman, *President*
Larisa B Lantsman, *Exec VP*
EMP: 100 EST: 1994
SALES: 1MM **Privately Held**
SIC: 8082 Visiting nurse service

(G-15963)
MARCUS THEATRES CORPORATION
Also Called: Pickerington Marcus Cinemas
1776 Hill Rd N (43147-8880)
PHONE...............................614 759-6500
Alan Zetting, *Manager*
EMP: 41
SALES (corp-wide): 707.1MM **Publicly Held**
SIC: 7832 Motion picture theaters, except drive-in
HQ: Marcus Theatres Corporation
100 E Wisconsin Ave
Milwaukee WI 53202
414 905-1500

(G-15964)
NATIONWIDE CHILDRENS HOSPITAL
1310 Hill Rd N (43147-7814)
PHONE...............................614 864-9216
EMP: 830
SALES (corp-wide): 2.3B **Privately Held**
SIC: 8069 Children's hospital
PA: Nationwide Children's Hospital
700 Childrens Dr
Columbus OH 43205
614 722-2000

(G-15965)
PROVENITFINANCE LLC
195 Fox Glen Dr W (43147-8097)
PHONE...............................888 958-1060
Craig Hollenbeck, *Partner*
William Miller, *Mng Member*
EMP: 25
SALES: 5MM **Privately Held**
SIC: 8742 Business consultant

(G-15966)
R G BARRY CORPORATION (HQ)
13405 Yarmouth Rd Nw (43147)
PHONE...............................614 864-6400
Bob Mullaney, *President*
Jerry Hemphill, *President*
Garry Bincoski, *COO*
Yvonne E Kalucis, *Senior VP*
Thomas J Z Konecki, *Senior VP*
▲ EMP: 86 EST: 1947

SQ FT: 55,000
SALES (est): 114MM
SALES (corp-wide): 94.2MM **Privately Held**
WEB: www.rgbarry.com
SIC: **5136** 5137 5139 Men's & boys' furnishings; handbags; slippers, house
PA: Mrgb Hold Co.
　382 Greenwich Ave Apt 1
　Greenwich CT 06830
　203 987-3500

(G-15967)
RAINBOW STATION DAY CARE INC (PA)
226 Durand St (43147-7941)
PHONE..................................614 759-8667
Bonnie Gibbs, *President*
EMP: 36
SQ FT: 7,000
SALES: 2.5MM **Privately Held**
WEB: www.rainbowstation.com
SIC: **8351** Group day care center

(G-15968)
SPORTS MEDICINE GRANT INC
417 Hill Rd N Ste 401 (43147-1310)
PHONE..................................614 461-8199
Raymond J Tesner, *Principal*
EMP: 26
SALES (corp-wide): 6.5MM **Privately Held**
SIC: **8099** Childbirth preparation clinic
PA: Sports Medicine Grant Inc
　323 E Town St Ste 100
　Columbus OH 43215
　614 461-8174

(G-15969)
VOLUNTEER ENERGY SERVICES INC (PA)
790 Windmiller Dr Ste A (43147-6879)
PHONE..................................614 856-3128
Richard Curnutte Sr, *President*
Jim Raver, *Business Mgr*
Marc Runck, *CFO*
Jordan Zornes, *Accountant*
Rick Pyles, *Sales Mgr*
EMP: 50
SQ FT: 8,000
SALES (est): 21.8MM **Privately Held**
WEB: www.volunteerenergy.com
SIC: **4911** Electric services

┌─────────────────────┐
│ **Piketon**   │
│ *Pike County*   │
└─────────────────────┘

(G-15970)
ACORD RK LUMBER COMPANY
125 W 4th St (45661-9650)
PHONE..................................740 289-3761
Randy Acord, *Owner*
EMP: 29
SALES (est): 2.1MM **Privately Held**
SIC: **5031** Lumber: rough, dressed & finished

(G-15971)
ATOMIC CREDIT UNION INC (PA)
711 Beaver Creek Rd (45661-9140)
PHONE..................................740 289-5060
Thomas Griffith, *President*
Lindsey Barnhouse, *Technology*
EMP: 25
SALES: 12.1MM **Privately Held**
WEB: www.2mycu.com
SIC: **6062** State credit unions, not federally chartered

(G-15972)
CDM SMITH INC
3930 Us Rte 23 S (45661)
PHONE..................................740 897-2937
EMP: 50
SALES (corp-wide): 1.2B **Privately Held**
SIC: **8711** Engineering Services
PA: Smith Cdm Inc
　75 State St Ste 701
　Boston MA 02109
　617 452-6000

(G-15973)
COMMUNITY ACTION COMM PIKE CNT (PA)
941 Market St (45661-9757)
P.O. Box 799 (45661-0799)
PHONE..................................740 289-2371
Rebecca Adkins, *CFO*
Barb Crabtree, *Marketing Staff*
Gary Roberts, *Exec Dir*
Ray Roberts, *Exec Dir*
Cindy Balzer, *Director*
EMP: 115
SQ FT: 21,360
SALES (est): 22.1MM **Privately Held**
SIC: **8322** Family service agency

(G-15974)
DKM CONSTRUCTION INC
W Perimeter Rd (45661)
PHONE..................................740 289-3006
Dennis Martin, *President*
Debbie Martin, *Corp Secy*
William Martin, *Vice Pres*
EMP: 35
SQ FT: 2,400
SALES: 10.6MM **Privately Held**
SIC: **1541** 1542 Industrial buildings & warehouses; commercial & office building, new construction

(G-15975)
FLUOR-BWXT PORTSMOUTH LLC
3930 Us Route 23 S (45661)
P.O. Box 548 (45661-0548)
PHONE..................................866 706-6992
Tracy Heidelberg, *CFO*
Mark Ashby, *Mng Member*
EMP: 1200
SALES (est): 158.5MM
SALES (corp-wide): 19.1B **Publicly Held**
SIC: **1795** Wrecking & demolition work
PA: Fluor Corporation
　6700 Las Colinas Blvd
　Irving TX 75039
　469 398-7000

(G-15976)
H C F INC
Also Called: Pleasant Hl Otptent Thrapy Ctr
7143 Us Rte 23 (45661)
PHONE..................................740 289-2528
Jim Unverferth, *President*
EMP: 220
SALES (est): 3MM **Privately Held**
SIC: **8059** Nursing home, except skilled & intermediate care facility

(G-15977)
HCF MANAGEMENT INC
7143 Us Highway 23 (45661-9527)
PHONE..................................740 289-2394
Abby Walls, *Human Res Dir*
Amy Clemons, *Administration*
EMP: 170
SALES (corp-wide): 154.8MM **Privately Held**
SIC: **8051** 8322 Skilled nursing care facilities; rehabilitation services
PA: Hcf Management, Inc.
　1100 Shawnee Rd
　Lima OH 45805
　419 999-2010

(G-15978)
INNOVTIVE SLTONS UNLIMITED LLC (PA)
1862 Shyville Rd (45661-9749)
PHONE..................................740 289-3282
Steve Barbarits, *General Mgr*
Josh Oudeh, *Opers Staff*
Ed Jordan, *Engineer*
Jennifer Barbarits, *Mng Member*
Frank Barbarits,
EMP: 41
SQ FT: 3,000
SALES (est): 16MM **Privately Held**
WEB: www.insolves.com
SIC: **8711** 7363 Consulting engineer; employee leasing service

(G-15979)
INNOVTIVE SLTONS UNLIMITED LLC
1862 Shyville Rd (45661-9749)
PHONE..................................740 289-3282
Richard Warner, *Business Mgr*
EMP: 100
SQ FT: 5,000 **Privately Held**
WEB: www.insolves.com
SIC: **8711** 7363 Engineering services; help supply services
PA: Innovative Solutions Unlimited, Llc
　1862 Shyville Rd
　Piketon OH 45661

(G-15980)
OHIO DEPARTMENT OF EDUCATION
Also Called: South Central Ohio Cmpt Assn
175 Beaver Creek Rd (45661-9114)
P.O. Box 577 (45661-0577)
PHONE..................................740 289-2908
Dennis Decamp, *Superintendent*
Shawn Clemmons, *Exec Dir*
Christopher Long, *Technician*
EMP: 40 **Privately Held**
WEB: www.osd.oh.gov
SIC: **8741** 9411 Management services;
HQ: Department Of Education Ohio
　25 S Front St
　Columbus OH 43215

(G-15981)
OHIO VALLEY ELECTRIC CORP (HQ)
Also Called: AEP
3932 Us Rte 23 (45661)
P.O. Box 468 (45661-0468)
PHONE..................................740 289-7200
Nicholas Akins, *President*
Thomas Denney, *Principal*
Freeman T Eagleson, *Principal*
Clarence Laylin, *Principal*
John Brodt, *Corp Secy*
EMP: 93
SQ FT: 100,000
SALES: 457MM
SALES (corp-wide): 16.2B **Publicly Held**
SIC: **4911** Generation, electric power; transmission, electric power; distribution, electric power
PA: American Electric Power Company, Inc.
　1 Riverside Plz Fl 1 # 1
　Columbus OH 43215
　614 716-1000

(G-15982)
OHIO VALLEY ELECTRIC CORP
Also Called: Power Scheduling Group
3932 Us Rt 23 (45661)
P.O. Box 468 (45661-0468)
PHONE..................................740 289-7225
David Jones, *Branch Mgr*
EMP: 83
SALES (corp-wide): 16.2B **Publicly Held**
SIC: **4911**
HQ: Ohio Valley Electric Corporation
　3932 Us Rte 23
　Piketon OH 45661
　740 289-7200

(G-15983)
PACE INTERNATIONAL UNION
Also Called: Local 5-689
2288 Wakefield Mound Rd (45661-9660)
P.O. Box 467 (45661-0467)
PHONE..................................740 289-2368
Daniel Mintor, *President*
EMP: 33
SALES (corp-wide): 26.9MM **Privately Held**
SIC: **8631** Labor unions & similar labor organizations
PA: Pace International Union
　5 Gateway Ctr
　Pittsburgh PA 15222
　412 562-2400

(G-15984)
PAVILION AT PIKETON FOR NURSIN
Also Called: Pavilion At Piketon, The
7143 Us Highway 23 (45661-9527)
PHONE..................................740 289-2394
Rafael A Moerman,

EMP: 99
SALES (est): 1.1MM **Privately Held**
SIC: **8399** Advocacy group

(G-15985)
PIKE COUNTY HEAD START INC
941 Market St (45661-9757)
P.O. Box 799 (45661-0799)
PHONE..................................740 289-2371
Chris Ervin, *CTO*
Raymond Roberts, *Exec Dir*
Barb Tackett, *Director*
Cindy Balzer, *Director*
Keith Pitts, *Deputy Dir*
EMP: 60
SALES (est): 958.6K **Privately Held**
SIC: **8351** Head start center, except in conjunction with school

(G-15986)
PIKETON NURSING CENTER INC
300 Overlook Dr (45661-9760)
PHONE..................................740 289-4074
James Renacci, *President*
EMP: 65
SALES (est): 2.8MM
SALES (corp-wide): 580.2MM **Privately Held**
WEB: www.tandemhealthcare.com
SIC: **8051** Convalescent home with continuous nursing care
PA: Consulate Management Company, Llc
　800 Concourse Pkwy S
　Maitland FL 32751
　407 571-1550

(G-15987)
PLEASANT HILL LEASING LLC
Also Called: Pleasant Hill Manor
7143 Us Rte 23 S (45661)
PHONE..................................740 289-2394
Eli Gunzburg,
Jody Kupchak, *Executive Asst*
EMP: 130 EST: 2016
SALES (est): 147.7K **Privately Held**
SIC: **8051** Mental retardation hospital

(G-15988)
RITCHIES FOOD DISTRIBUTORS INC
527 S West St (45661-8042)
PHONE..................................740 443-6303
James P Ritchie, *President*
Nancy Ritchie, *Corp Secy*
Joyce Lightle, *Vice Pres*
Twyla Suter, *Vice Pres*
Steve Spencer, *Buyer*
EMP: 31
SALES (est): 14MM **Privately Held**
SIC: **5146** 5147 5142 5149 Seafoods; meats, fresh; packaged frozen goods; canned goods: fruit, vegetables, seafood, meats, etc.

(G-15989)
UNITED STATES ENRICHMENT CORP
Also Called: Usec
3930 Us Highway 23 Anx (45661-9113)
P.O. Box 628 (45661-0628)
PHONE..................................740 897-2331
Ralph Donnelly, *Branch Mgr*
EMP: 1200
SALES (corp-wide): 193MM **Publicly Held**
WEB: www.portslab.com
SIC: **8742** Public utilities consultant
HQ: United States Enrichment Corporation
　6901 Rockledge Dr Ste 800
　Bethesda MD 20817
　301 564-3200

(G-15990)
UNITED STATES ENRICHMENT CORP
3930 Us Rte 23 S (45661)
PHONE..................................740 897-2457
Ray Jordan, *Manager*
EMP: 1160
SALES (corp-wide): 193MM **Publicly Held**
WEB: www.portslab.com
SIC: **8742** 8351 Public utilities consultant; child day care services

HQ: United States Enrichment Corporation
6901 Rockledge Dr Ste 800
Bethesda MD 20817
301 564-3200

(G-15991)
URANIUM DISPOSITION SVCS LLC
3930 Us Highway 23 Anx (45661-9113)
PHONE..................................740 289-3620
Paul Kreitz, *Branch Mgr*
EMP: 156
SALES (corp-wide): 33.7MM **Privately Held**
SIC: 1629 Waste disposal plant construction
PA: Uranium Disposition Services, Llc
1020 Monarch St Ste 100
Lexington KY 40513
859 296-0023

(G-15992)
WASTREN - ENERGX MISSION
Also Called: Wems
1571 Shyville Rd (45661-9201)
P.O. Box 307 (45661-0307)
PHONE..................................740 897-3724
Steven Moore, *CEO*
Glenn Henderson, *COO*
Jim Gardner, *Vice Pres*
Keith Tucker, *Vice Pres*
Eric Anderson, *Med Doctor*
EMP: 170
SALES (est): 23.2MM **Privately Held**
SIC: 8744 Facilities support services
PA: Wastren Advantage, Inc.
1571 Shyville Rd
Piketon OH 45661

(G-15993)
WASTREN ADVANTAGE INC (PA)
1571 Shyville Rd (45661-9201)
PHONE..................................970 254-1277
Steve Moore, *President*
Charlie Anderson, *General Mgr*
Glenn Henderson, *COO*
Jim Gardner, *Exec VP*
Keith Tucker, *Vice Pres*
EMP: 30
SALES (est): 105MM **Privately Held**
SIC: 4959 8744 8711 Sanitary services; facilities support services; engineering services

---

Piqua
Miami County

(G-15994)
A M LEONARD INC
Also Called: Gardeners Edge
241 Fox Dr (45356-9265)
P.O. Box 816 (45356-0816)
PHONE..................................937 773-2694
Betty L Ziegler, *President*
Chris Campbell, *Train & Dev Mgr*
Angela Lewis, *Human Resources*
Nicole Allenbaugh, *Accounts Mgr*
Teresa Bailey, *Accounts Mgr*
◆ EMP: 90 EST: 1885
SQ FT: 120,000
SALES (est): 43.4MM **Privately Held**
WEB: www.amleo.com
SIC: 5072 5191 Garden tools, hand; farm supplies; garden supplies

(G-15995)
AARONS INC
1305 E Ash St (45356-4108)
PHONE..................................937 778-3577
Matthew Bradley, *Branch Mgr*
EMP: 25
SALES (corp-wide): 3.8B **Publicly Held**
WEB: www.aaronrents.com
SIC: 7359 Furniture rental; home appliance, furniture & entertainment rental services
PA: Aaron's, Inc.
400 Galleria Pkwy Se # 300
Atlanta GA 30339
678 402-3000

(G-15996)
B D TRANSPORTATION INC
9590 Looney Rd (45356-2584)
PHONE..................................937 773-9280
John Douglas, *President*
Teresa Douglas, *Vice Pres*
Phil Douglas, *Manager*
EMP: 30
SQ FT: 1,000
SALES (est): 7.1MM **Privately Held**
WEB: www.bdtransport.com
SIC: 4213 4212 Contract haulers; local trucking, without storage

(G-15997)
BLACK STONE CINCINNATI LLC
Also Called: Home Care By Black Stone
106 W Ash St Ste 504 (45356-2343)
PHONE..................................937 773-8573
Regina Carroll, *Branch Mgr*
EMP: 27
SALES (corp-wide): 13.8MM **Privately Held**
SIC: 8099 Blood related health services
PA: Black Stone Of Cincinnati, Llc
4700 E Galbraith Rd Fl 3
Cincinnati OH 45236
513 924-1370

(G-15998)
BROOKDALE SNIOR LVING CMMNTIES
Also Called: Sterling House of Piqua
1744 W High St Ofc (45356-8333)
PHONE..................................937 773-0500
Ida Hecht, *General Mgr*
EMP: 25
SALES (corp-wide): 4.5B **Publicly Held**
WEB: www.assisted.com
SIC: 8059 Rest home, with health care
HQ: Brookdale Senior Living Communities, Inc.
6737 W Wa St Ste 2300
Milwaukee WI 53214
414 918-5000

(G-15999)
BUCKEYE STATE MUTUAL INSUR CO (PA)
Also Called: Buckeye Insurance Group
1 Heritage Pl (45356-4148)
PHONE..................................937 778-5000
R Douglas Haines, *President*
Rob Bornhorst, *CFO*
EMP: 70
SQ FT: 17,000
SALES (est): 27.9MM **Privately Held**
SIC: 6331 Fire, marine & casualty insurance & carriers

(G-16000)
COILPLUS INC
Also Called: Coilplus Berwick
100 Steelway Dr (45356-7530)
PHONE..................................937 778-8884
Terry Harold, *Manager*
EMP: 51
SALES (corp-wide): 71B **Privately Held**
SIC: 5051 Steel
HQ: Coilplus, Inc.
6250 N River Rd Ste 6050
Rosemont IL 60018
847 384-3000

(G-16001)
COUNCIL ON RUR SVC PRGRAMS INC (PA)
201 Robert M Davis Pkwy B (45356-8342)
PHONE..................................937 778-5220
Daniel Schwanitz, *Exec Dir*
EMP: 40
SALES: 15.7MM **Privately Held**
WEB: www.corsp.org
SIC: 8399 Community action agency

(G-16002)
COUNCIL ON RUR SVC PRGRAMS INC
Also Called: Beary Land
285 Robert M Davis Pkwy (45356-8342)
PHONE..................................937 773-0773
Shirley Hathaway, *Director*
EMP: 40

SALES (corp-wide): 15.7MM **Privately Held**
WEB: www.corsp.org
SIC: 8399 8351 8322 Community action agency; child day care services; individual & family services
PA: Council On Rural Service Programs, Inc.
201 Robert M Davis Pkwy B
Piqua OH 45356
937 778-5220

(G-16003)
CRANE PUMPS & SYSTEMS INC
Also Called: Pacific Valve
420 3rd St (45356-3918)
PHONE..................................937 773-2442
Allan Oak, *Branch Mgr*
EMP: 280
SALES (corp-wide): 3.3B **Publicly Held**
SIC: 5085 3494 Valves & fittings; valves & pipe fittings
HQ: Crane Pumps & Systems, Inc.
420 3rd St
Piqua OH 45356
937 773-2442

(G-16004)
FIRST ACCEPTANCE CORPORATION
987 E Ash St (45356-4133)
PHONE..................................937 778-8888
Shela Schipper, *Principal*
EMP: 27
SALES (corp-wide): 347.5MM **Publicly Held**
SIC: 6411 Insurance agents, brokers & service
PA: First Acceptance Corporation
3813 Green Hills Vlg Dr
Nashville TN 37215
615 844-2800

(G-16005)
GARBRY RIDGE ASSISTED LIVING
1567 Garbry Rd (45356-8238)
PHONE..................................937 778-9385
Debbie Adkins, *Exec Dir*
Rhonda McConnaughey, *Director*
Pam Miller, *Director*
Marianne Emmert, *Food Svc Dir*
EMP: 35
SQ FT: 2,234
SALES (est): 1.2MM **Privately Held**
WEB: www.garbryridge.com
SIC: 8052 Intermediate care facilities

(G-16006)
HARTZELL HARDWOODS INC (PA)
1025 S Roosevelt Ave (45356-3713)
P.O. Box 919 (45356-0919)
PHONE..................................937 773-7054
Jeffery Bannister, *CEO*
James Robert Hartzell, *Ch of Bd*
Kelly Hostetter, *President*
Jane Osborn, *Admin Sec*
▼ EMP: 90
SQ FT: 275,000
SALES (est): 30.1MM **Privately Held**
WEB: www.hartzellhardwoods.com
SIC: 5031 2421 2426 Lumber: rough, dressed & finished; sawmills & planing mills, general; hardwood dimension & flooring mills

(G-16007)
HARTZELL INDUSTRIES INC (PA)
1025 S Roosevelt Ave (45356-3713)
P.O. Box 919 (45356-0919)
PHONE..................................937 773-6295
Jeff Bannister, *CEO*
James Robert Hartzell, *Ch of Bd*
Michael Bardo, *President*
Chris Oliss, *CFO*
Randi Pearson, *Treasurer*
EMP: 73 EST: 1964
SQ FT: 20,000
SALES (est): 12.5MM **Privately Held**
WEB: www.hartzellfan.com
SIC: 2435 6719 Veneer stock, hardwood; personal holding companies, except banks

(G-16008)
HCF OF PIQUA INC
Also Called: Piqua Manor
1840 W High St (45356-9399)
PHONE..................................937 773-0040
James Unberferth, *President*
Jodell Karns, *Technology*
Ashley Moore, *Executive*
EMP: 99
SQ FT: 41,920
SALES (est): 3.5MM
SALES (corp-wide): 154.8MM **Privately Held**
SIC: 8051 Convalescent home with continuous nursing care
PA: Hcf Management, Inc.
1100 Shawnee Rd
Lima OH 45805
419 999-2010

(G-16009)
HEALTH CARE RTREMENT CORP AMER
Also Called: Heartland of Piqua
275 Kienle Dr (45356-4119)
PHONE..................................937 773-9346
Stacie Atherton, *Branch Mgr*
EMP: 92
SQ FT: 27,568
SALES (corp-wide): 2.4B **Publicly Held**
WEB: www.hrc-manorcare.com
SIC: 8051 Convalescent home with continuous nursing care
HQ: Health Care And Retirement Corporation Of America
333 N Summit St Ste 103
Toledo OH 43604
419 252-5500

(G-16010)
HOME AND FARM INSURANCE CO
Also Called: Buckeye Insurance
1 Heritage Pl (45356-4148)
PHONE..................................937 778-5000
Doug Haynes, *President*
Lisa Wesner, *Human Resources*
Elizabeth Platzer, *Manager*
EMP: 60
SQ FT: 500
SALES (est): 11.1MM
SALES (corp-wide): 27.9MM **Privately Held**
WEB: www.buckeye-ins.com
SIC: 6411 6331 Insurance agents; fire, marine & casualty insurance
PA: The Buckeye State Mutual Insurance Company
1 Heritage Pl
Piqua OH 45356
937 778-5000

(G-16011)
INDUSTRY PRODUCTS CO (PA)
500 W Statler Rd (45356-8281)
PHONE..................................937 778-0585
Linda Cleveland, *President*
Bob Axe, *VP Opers*
Tom Craft, *Mfg Dir*
Tyler Furrow, *Project Mgr*
Joel Roy, *Project Mgr*
▲ EMP: 366 EST: 1966`
SQ FT: 335,000
SALES: 76MM **Privately Held**
WEB: www.industryproductsco.com
SIC: 7692 3053 3714 3544 Automotive welding; gaskets, all materials; motor vehicle parts & accessories; motor vehicle body components & frame; special dies, tools, jigs & fixtures; unsupported plastics film & sheet

(G-16012)
M&C HOTEL INTERESTS INC
Also Called: Comfort Inn
987 E Ash St Ste 171 (45356-4198)
PHONE..................................937 778-8100
Larry Chester, *Manager*
EMP: 30 **Privately Held**
WEB: www.richfield.com
SIC: 7011 Hotels & motels
HQ: M&C Hotel Interests, Inc.
6560 Greenwood Plaza Blvd # 300
Greenwood Village CO 80111

(G-16013)
MIAMI CO YMCA CHILD CARE
325 W Ash St (45356-2203)
PHONE................................937 778-5241
James McMaken, *Exec Dir*
EMP: 30
SALES (est): 105.2K **Privately Held**
SIC: 8641 Youth organizations

(G-16014)
MIAMI VALLEY STEEL SERVICE INC
201 Fox Dr (45356-9265)
PHONE................................937 773-7127
Louis Moran, *CEO*
Guy House, *Vice Pres*
Lou Moran, *Vice Pres*
Chip Lamoreaux, *Plant Mgr*
Brian Layne, *Maint Mgr*
▼ EMP: 140
SQ FT: 320,000
SALES (est): 149.7MM **Privately Held**
SIC: 5051 Steel

(G-16015)
MURRAY WLLS WNDELN RBNSON CPAS (PA)
Also Called: Murray Wells Wendeln & Robinsn
326 N Wayne St (45356-2230)
P.O. Box 613 (45356-0613)
PHONE................................937 773-6373
Tony Wendeln, *CEO*
Samuel Robinson, *President*
Karen Benanzer, *Bd of Directors*
Molli Baker, *Associate*
EMP: 26
SQ FT: 5,000
SALES (est): 2.7MM **Privately Held**
SIC: 8721 Certified public accountant

(G-16016)
PIONEER RURAL ELECTRIC COOP (PA)
344 W Us Route 36 (45356-9255)
PHONE................................800 762-0997
Ronald Salyer, *President*
EMP: 62 EST: 1936
SQ FT: 32,000
SALES: 72.1MM **Privately Held**
WEB: www.pioneerec.com
SIC: 4911 Distribution, electric power

(G-16017)
PIQUA COUNTRY CLUB HOLDING CO
Also Called: PIQUA COUNTRY CLUB POOL
9812 Country Club Rd (45356-9594)
PHONE................................937 773-7744
Don Goettpmoeller, *Treasurer*
Don Grieshop, *Treasurer*
EMP: 40
SQ FT: 9,000
SALES: 1.4MM **Privately Held**
SIC: 7997 5812 7911 Country club, membership; golf club, membership; swimming club, membership; eating places; dance hall or ballroom operation

(G-16018)
PIQUA INDUSTRIAL CUT & SEW
727 E Ash St (45356-2411)
P.O. Box 1657 (45356-4657)
PHONE................................937 773-7397
Yvonne Mc Greevy, *President*
EMP: 35
SQ FT: 4,800
SALES: 750K **Privately Held**
SIC: 7389 Sewing contractor

(G-16019)
PIQUA MATERIALS INC
Also Called: Piqua Mineral Division
1750 W Statler Rd (45356-9264)
PHONE................................937 773-4824
Brent Phillips, *Safety Mgr*
John Harris, *Branch Mgr*
EMP: 30
SQ FT: 16,808
SALES (corp-wide): 10.1MM **Privately Held**
SIC: 1422 3274 Limestones, ground; lime

PA: Piqua Materials Inc
11641 Mosteller Rd Ste 1
Cincinnati OH 45241
513 771-0820

(G-16020)
PIQUA STEEL CO
Also Called: PSC Crane & Rigging
4243 W Us Route 36 (45356-9334)
PHONE................................937 773-3632
James R Sever, *President*
Earl F Sever III, *Chairman*
Randy Sever, *Exec VP*
Jill Larger, *Purchasing*
Nancy J Sever, *Treasurer*
EMP: 75
SQ FT: 30,000
SALES: 31.9MM **Privately Held**
WEB: www.piquasteel.com
SIC: 4225 7353 1796 7359 General warehousing; cranes & aerial lift equipment, rental or leasing; machine moving & rigging; equipment rental & leasing

(G-16021)
PIQUA TRANSFER & STORAGE CO
9782 Looney Rd (45356-2587)
P.O. Box 823 (45356-0823)
PHONE................................937 773-3743
John D Laughman, *President*
Damita Hoblit, *Corp Secy*
H L Lane, *Vice Pres*
John Basye, *Safety Mgr*
Steve Nash, *Accounting Mgr*
EMP: 86 EST: 1904
SQ FT: 24,000
SALES (est): 11.8MM **Privately Held**
SIC: 4213 4214 Contract haulers; local trucking with storage

(G-16022)
PIQUA VILLAGE REHAB LLC
1345 Covington Ave (45356-2813)
PHONE................................937 773-9537
Tom Lusk, *Principal*
Dametri Coleman, *Principal*
EMP: 25
SALES (est): 197.9K **Privately Held**
SIC: 8093 Rehabilitation center, outpatient treatment

(G-16023)
PLASTIC RECYCLING TECH INC (PA)
Also Called: Prt
9054 N County Road 25a (45356-7522)
PHONE................................937 615-9286
Matthew Kreigel, *President*
Stephen Larger, *Vice Pres*
Brian E Voisard, *Plant Mgr*
Mark Miller, *CFO*
Stacy Jent, *Admin Sec*
EMP: 30
SALES (est): 45.2MM **Privately Held**
SIC: 4953 Recycling, waste materials

(G-16024)
PRO CARE JANITOR SUPPLY
317 N Main St (45356-2315)
P.O. Box 1748 (45356-4748)
PHONE................................937 778-2275
Mark Miller, *Owner*
Connie Miller, *Manager*
EMP: 50
SQ FT: 1,800
SALES (est): 1.1MM **Privately Held**
SIC: 7349 Janitorial service, contract basis

(G-16025)
R C HEMM GLASS SHOPS INC (PA)
514 S Main St (45356-3942)
PHONE................................937 773-5591
Jeff Hemm, *President*
Michelle Baker, *Project Mgr*
Casey Brooks, *Project Mgr*
Josh Hesse, *Project Mgr*
Trent Karn, *Project Mgr*
EMP: 32 EST: 1948
SQ FT: 20,000
SALES (est): 10.4MM **Privately Held**
WEB: www.hemmglass.com
SIC: 1793 5231 Glass & glazing work; glass

(G-16026)
R K HYDRO-VAC INC (PA)
322 Wyndham Way (45356-9267)
P.O. Box 915 (45356-0915)
PHONE................................937 773-8600
Rusty D Kimmel, *Principal*
Randy Kimmel, *Vice Pres*
Don Borchers, *VP Opers*
Chris Apple, *Manager*
Kerry Murphy, *Manager*
EMP: 50
SALES (est): 10.9MM **Privately Held**
SIC: 7349 Cleaning service, industrial or commercial

(G-16027)
S & H RISNER INC
Also Called: Hr Associates Personnel Svc
314 N Wayne St (45356-2230)
PHONE................................937 778-8563
Heather Risner, *CEO*
EMP: 63
SALES (est): 3.2MM **Privately Held**
SIC: 7361 Executive placement

(G-16028)
SCOTT STEEL LLC
125 Clark Ave (45356-3807)
PHONE................................937 552-9670
John Scott, *Mng Member*
Aaron Scott, *Manager*
Joan Hager, *Receptionist*
EMP: 30
SALES (est): 3.6MM **Privately Held**
SIC: 5051 Steel

(G-16029)
SPECTRUM MGT HOLDG CO LLC
Time Warner
614 N Main St (45356-2347)
PHONE................................937 306-6082
Charlotte Small,
EMP: 83
SQ FT: 3,608
SALES (corp-wide): 43.6B **Publicly Held**
SIC: 4841 Cable television services
HQ: Spectrum Management Holding Company, Llc
400 Atlantic St
Stamford CT 06901
203 905-7801

(G-16030)
SUNRISE COOPERATIVE INC
215 Looney Rd (45356-4147)
P.O. Box 870, Fremont (43420-0870)
PHONE................................937 575-6780
EMP: 450
SALES (corp-wide): 62MM **Privately Held**
SIC: 5153 5191 Grains; farm supplies
PA: Sunrise Cooperative, Inc.
2025 W State St Ste A
Fremont OH 43420
419 332-6468

(G-16031)
TK HOLDINGS INC
Also Called: T K Holdings
1401 Innovation Pkwy (45356-7524)
PHONE................................937 778-9713
Monica Bauthn, *Manager*
EMP: 25
SALES (corp-wide): 4B **Privately Held**
SIC: 2399 5013 Seat belts, automobile & aircraft; motor vehicle supplies & new parts
HQ: Tk Holdings Inc.
4611 Wiseman Blvd
San Antonio TX 78251
210 509-0762

(G-16032)
UNITED PARCEL SERVICE INC OH
Also Called: UPS
8460 Industry Park Dr (45356-8538)
PHONE................................937 773-4762
Paul Francis, *Branch Mgr*
EMP: 110
SALES (corp-wide): 71.8B **Publicly Held**
WEB: www.upsscs.com
SIC: 4215 Parcel delivery, vehicular

HQ: United Parcel Service, Inc. (Oh)
55 Glenlake Pkwy
Atlanta GA 30328
404 828-6000

(G-16033)
UNITY NATIONAL BANK (HQ)
Also Called: Third Savings
215 N Wayne St (45356-2227)
P.O. Box 913 (45356-0913)
PHONE................................937 773-0752
Scott Rasor, *President*
Scott Gabriel, *President*
EMP: 42
SQ FT: 6,000
SALES (est): 2MM
SALES (corp-wide): 411.9MM **Publicly Held**
WEB: www.unitynationalbk.com
SIC: 6021 National commercial banks
PA: Park National Corporation
50 N 3rd St
Newark OH 43055
740 349-8451

(G-16034)
UPPER VALLEY FAMILY CARE
200 Kienle Dr (45356-4120)
PHONE................................937 339-5355
James S Burkhardt Do, *Principal*
Beth Burroughs, *Project Mgr*
Joni Walker, *Admin Asst*
EMP: 45 EST: 2001
SALES (est): 1.2MM **Privately Held**
WEB: www.uvfc.com
SIC: 8011 General & family practice, physician/surgeon

(G-16035)
UPPER VALLEY FINANCIAL INC
1262 E Ash St (45356-4160)
P.O. Box 1214 (45356-1214)
PHONE................................937 381-0054
Bill Young, *Principal*
EMP: 40
SALES (est): 1.8MM **Privately Held**
SIC: 8742 Financial consultant

(G-16036)
USI CABLE CORP
102 Fox Dr (45356-9269)
P.O. Box 820 (45356-0820)
PHONE................................937 606-2636
Carol Gaston, *President*
John Gaston, *Manager*
EMP: 30
SALES (est): 2.3MM **Privately Held**
SIC: 4841 Cable television services

(G-16037)
VALLEY REGIONAL SURGERY CENTER
Also Called: Sydney ASC
283 Looney Rd (45356-4147)
P.O. Box 914 (45356-0914)
PHONE................................877 858-5029
Randall Welsh, *Partner*
Robert McDevitt, *Partner*
Anita Couchot, *Executive*
EMP: 25
SQ FT: 6,700
SALES (est): 4.1MM **Privately Held**
SIC: 8011 Ambulatory surgical center; surgeon

(G-16038)
WEST OHIO CONFERENCE OF
Also Called: Drop In Babysitting Service
415 W Greene St (45356-2113)
PHONE................................937 773-5313
Debbie Fraser, *Manager*
EMP: 30
SALES (corp-wide): 5.6MM **Privately Held**
WEB: www.cliftonumc.com
SIC: 8661 8351 Methodist Church; child day care services
PA: The West Ohio Conference Of United Methodist Church
32 Wesley Blvd
Worthington OH 43085
614 844-6200

(G-16039)
WESTERN & SOUTHERN LF INSUR CO
1255 E Ash St Ste 2 (45356-4141)
PHONE.........................937 773-5303
Terry Bosworth, *District Mgr*
EMP: 30 **Privately Held**
SIC: 6411 Life insurance agents
HQ: The Western & Southern Life Insurance Company
400 Broadway St
Cincinnati OH 45202
513 629-1800

Plain City
Madison County

(G-16040)
A-1 ADVANCED PLUMBING INC
8299 Memorial Dr (43064-8623)
PHONE.........................614 873-0548
Wesley Zimmer, *President*
Eearl Sagraves, *Exec VP*
EMP: 30
SQ FT: 4,500
SALES (est): 3.7MM **Privately Held**
SIC: 1711 Plumbing contractors

(G-16041)
A2Z FIELD SERVICES LLC
7450 Industrial Pkwy # 105 (43064-8789)
P.O. Box 3215, Dublin (43016-0100)
PHONE.........................614 873-0211
William McMullen III, *CEO*
Amie Sparks, *Senior VP*
Jennifer Sells, *Manager*
EMP: 130
SQ FT: 6,000
SALES: 23.5MM **Privately Held**
SIC: 7389 Building inspection service

(G-16042)
ABBRUZZESE BROTHERS INC (PA)
7775 Smith Calhoun Rd (43064-9192)
P.O. Box 215, Hilliard (43026-0215)
PHONE.........................614 873-1550
Jim Abbruzzese, *President*
John Abbruzzese, *Vice Pres*
Brian Roudabush, *Production*
Joe Abbruzzese, *CFO*
EMP: 31
SQ FT: 7,200
SALES (est): 4MM **Privately Held**
WEB: www.abbzinc.com
SIC: 0782 Lawn care services; landscape contractors

(G-16043)
AMERICAN COATINGS CORPORATION
Also Called: Americoat
7510 Montgomery Rd (43064-8611)
PHONE.........................614 335-1000
Philip Freedman, *President*
Dan Wiginton, *Sales Mgr*
EMP: 30
SALES (est): 3.7MM **Privately Held**
WEB: www.americoat.net
SIC: 1771 Driveway contractor

(G-16044)
ARCHITECTURAL SYSTEMS INC
Also Called: A S I
8633 Memorial Dr (43064-8608)
PHONE.........................614 873-2057
David Phillips, *President*
EMP: 55
SQ FT: 6,000
SALES (est): 9.2MM **Privately Held**
SIC: 1761 Roofing contractor

(G-16045)
BENCHMARK LANDSCAPE CNSTR INC
9600 Industrial Pkwy (43064-9426)
PHONE.........................614 873-8080
Roy Ed Veley, *President*
Mark Chamberlain, *Vice Pres*
Matt Hecht, *Mng Member*
Doug Heindel, *Mng Member*

Devon Stanley, *Mng Member*
EMP: 38
SQ FT: 1,900
SALES (est): 3.8MM **Privately Held**
WEB: www.benchmarkohio.com
SIC: 0782 Landscape contractors

(G-16046)
BINDERY & SPC PRESSWORKS INC
351 W Bigelow Ave (43064-1152)
PHONE.........................614 873-4623
Dick Izzard, *President*
Betty Izzard, *Vice Pres*
Doug Izzard, *Vice Pres*
Mark Izzard, *Vice Pres*
Tami Roberts, *Admin Sec*
EMP: 74
SQ FT: 42,000
SALES (est): 18.1MM **Privately Held**
SIC: 2791 2759 2752 2789 Typesetting; commercial printing; commercial printing, offset; bookbinding & related work; mailing service

(G-16047)
BULK TRANSIT CORPORATION (PA)
7177 Indl Pkwy (43064)
PHONE.........................614 873-4632
Ronald De Wolf, *President*
Paul F Beery, *Principal*
Amanda Schramm, *Supervisor*
Gloria De Wolf, *Admin Sec*
Jessie Ferguson, *Receptionist*
EMP: 40
SQ FT: 5,000
SALES (est): 26.7MM **Privately Held**
WEB: www.bulktransit.com
SIC: 4213 Contract haulers

(G-16048)
CSI COMPLETE INC
8080 Corporate Blvd (43064-9220)
PHONE.........................800 343-0641
Doug Webb, *CEO*
Daniel Adkins, *Info Tech Mgr*
EMP: 50
SALES (est): 841.2K **Privately Held**
SIC: 7374 Data processing service
PA: Douglas Webb & Associates, Inc.
8080 Corporate Blvd
Plain City OH 43064

(G-16049)
DKMP CONSULTING INC
8000 Corporate Blvd (43064-9220)
PHONE.........................614 733-0979
Mark Patel, *President*
Matthew S Patel, *President*
EMP: 105
SQ FT: 33,000
SALES: 18MM **Privately Held**
WEB: www.pkcontrols.com
SIC: 8711 Engineering services
HQ: Ohio Transmission Corporation
1900 Jetway Blvd
Columbus OH 43219
614 342-6247

(G-16050)
DUTCHMAN HOSPITALITY GROUP INC
Also Called: Der Dutchman's Restaurant
445 S Jefferson Ave (43064-1166)
PHONE.........................614 873-3414
Dan Yoder, *Branch Mgr*
Victor Meleshchua, *Manager*
EMP: 200
SALES (corp-wide): 46.4MM **Privately Held**
SIC: 5812 5947 5149 Italian restaurant; gift shop; bakery products
PA: Dutchman Hospitality Group, Inc.
4985 State Rte 515
Walnut Creek OH 44687
330 893-2926

(G-16051)
EMSI INC (PA)
8220 Industrial Pkwy (43064-9371)
P.O. Box 175, Dublin (43017-0175)
PHONE.........................614 876-9988
Mark Wehinger, *President*
Gregory C Farell, *Principal*

Brandon Gepper, *Project Mgr*
Tom Kiefer, *CFO*
Mark Gamble, *Manager*
EMP: 40
SALES (est): 10.1MM **Privately Held**
SIC: 0782 Landscape contractors

(G-16052)
EVOLUTION AG LLC
Also Called: Kubota Authorized Dealer
13275 Us Highway 42 N (43064-8748)
PHONE.........................740 363-1341
James R Henkel, *Ch of Bd*
Thomas M Hill, *President*
Nick Crist, *Parts Mgr*
David P Shipley, *Treasurer*
Judy Curry, *Accounting Mgr*
EMP: 36
SALES: 24.5MM **Privately Held**
SIC: 5083 Farm implements; agricultural machinery & equipment

(G-16053)
FAIRFIELD HOMES INC
Also Called: Madison Square Apartments
445 Fairfield Dr Ofc (43064-1274)
PHONE.........................614 873-3533
Leonard F Gorsuch, *Branch Mgr*
EMP: 200
SALES (corp-wide): 20.4MM **Privately Held**
WEB: www.gorsuch-homes.com
SIC: 6513 1522 6531 1542 Apartment building operators; residential construction; real estate agents & managers; non-residential construction; nonresidential building operators
PA: Fairfield Homes Inc.
603 W Wheeling St
Lancaster OH 43130
740 653-3583

(G-16054)
HERITAGE EQUIPMENT COMPANY
9000 Heritage Dr (43064-8744)
PHONE.........................614 873-3941
Louis Cascelli, *CEO*
Eric J Zwirner, *President*
Eric Ferry, *Transportation*
Don Behna, *Financial Exec*
John Licklider, *Sales Staff*
▲ **EMP:** 30 **EST:** 1982
SQ FT: 10,000
SALES (est): 18.6MM **Privately Held**
WEB: www.heritage-equipment.com
SIC: 5084 Dairy products manufacturing machinery; food product manufacturing machinery

(G-16055)
INTEGRITY GYMNSTICS CHRLEADING
8185 Business Way (43064-9216)
PHONE.........................614 733-0818
Les Hood, *Mng Member*
John Brooks, *Manager*
Randy Cline, *Manager*
Bill Wilson, *Manager*
EMP: 34
SALES (est): 1MM **Privately Held**
SIC: 7999 Gymnastic instruction, non-membership

(G-16056)
K AMALIA ENTERPRISES INC
Also Called: Mjr Sales
8025 Corporate Blvd (43064-9208)
PHONE.........................614 733-3800
Jeff Bradshaw, *President*
Mark Laufersweiler, *Vice Pres*
Michael Cacchio, *CFO*
▲ **EMP:** 90
SQ FT: 53,000
SALES (est): 8MM **Privately Held**
WEB: www.kamalia.com
SIC: 5699 5136 Designers, apparel; men's & boys' clothing

(G-16057)
LITHKO CONTRACTING LLC
8065 Corporate Blvd (43064-9208)
PHONE.........................614 733-0300
Randy Doss, *Manager*
EMP: 125

SALES (corp-wide): 177.7MM **Privately Held**
SIC: 1771 Foundation & footing contractor
PA: Lithko Contracting, Llc
2958 Crescentville Rd
West Chester OH 45069
513 564-2000

(G-16058)
MADE FROM SCRATCH INC (PA)
Also Called: Celebrations
7500 Montgomery Rd (43064-8611)
PHONE.........................614 873-3344
Larry G Clark, *President*
EMP: 31
SQ FT: 12,000
SALES (est): 3.9MM **Privately Held**
WEB: www.made-from-scratch.com
SIC: 7359 5812 5149 5992 Party supplies rental services; caterers; bakery products; florists

(G-16059)
MAZA INC
7635 Commerce Pl (43064-9223)
PHONE.........................614 760-0003
Chris Watson, *President*
▲ **EMP:** 50
SQ FT: 15,400
SALES (est): 7.6MM
SALES (corp-wide): 68.6B **Publicly Held**
WEB: www.mgworks.com
SIC: 5211 5999 5032 Masonry materials & supplies; monuments & tombstones; marble building stone
PA: Lowe's Companies, Inc.
1000 Lowes Blvd
Mooresville NC 28117
704 758-1000

(G-16060)
MEDIA SOURCE INC (PA)
7858 Industrial Pkwy (43064-9468)
PHONE.........................614 873-7635
Steve Zales, *CEO*
Victor F Ganzi, *Ch of Bd*
Randall J Asmo, *President*
Tracey Fenton, *Vice Pres*
Gerry Nemeth, *Opers Staff*
EMP: 60
SQ FT: 4,800
SALES (est): 31.6MM **Privately Held**
WEB: www.juniorlibraryguild.com
SIC: 5192 Books

(G-16061)
MJ DESIGN ASSOCIATES INC
Also Called: Landscape Dsgn-Bld-Maintenance
8463 Estates Ct (43064-8015)
PHONE.........................614 873-7333
Joel John, *President*
Molly John, *Vice Pres*
EMP: 25
SALES (est): 3.1MM **Privately Held**
WEB: www.mjdesignassociates.com
SIC: 0781 Landscape architects

(G-16062)
NO CAGES HARLEY-DAVIDSON
7610 Commerce Pl (43064-9222)
PHONE.........................614 764-2453
Lynn Loomis, *Partner*
EMP: 25
SALES (est): 178.8K **Privately Held**
SIC: 7699 Motorcycle repair service

(G-16063)
PAINTING COMPANY
6969 Industrial Pkwy (43064-8799)
PHONE.........................614 873-1334
David Asman, *Vice Pres*
Terry Asman, *Vice Pres*
Jeffery D Sammons, *Incorporator*
EMP: 105
SALES: 10MM **Privately Held**
WEB: www.thepaintingcompany.com
SIC: 1721 Commercial painting; industrial painting; wallcovering contractors

(G-16064)
SCHEIDERER TRANSPORT INC
8520 State Route 161 E (43064-9101)
PHONE.........................614 873-5103
Roger C Scheiderer, *President*
EMP: 55

SQ FT: 10,000
SALES: 6.5MM **Privately Held**
SIC: 4213 Contract haulers

(G-16065)
SHALOM MINISTRIES INTL INC
Also Called: Discovering The Jewish Jesus
9018 Heritage Dr (43064-9493)
P.O. Box 777, Blissfield MI (49228-0077)
PHONE................................614 504-6052
Kirt A Schneider, *President*
Cynthia Schneider, *Human Resources*
EMP: 35
SALES: 7MM **Privately Held**
SIC: 7812 Motion picture & video production

(G-16066)
SHARRON GROUP INC (PA)
Also Called: Buckeye Western Star
7605 Commerce Pl (43064-9223)
PHONE................................614 873-5856
Thomas A Ewers, *President*
George Ritter, *Parts Mgr*
Gil Sears, *Controller*
Cody Martindale, *Sales Staff*
Linda Ewers, *Manager*
EMP: 25
SALES (est): 9.6MM **Privately Held**
WEB: www.buckeyewesternstar.com
SIC: 5012 7699 Commercial vehicles; industrial truck repair

(G-16067)
STALEY INC
8040 Corporate Blvd (43064-9220)
PHONE................................614 552-2333
Fax: 614 552-2349
EMP: 30
SALES (corp-wide): 84.2MM **Privately Held**
SIC: 1731 Installation & Cabling Of Lan Systems
PA: Staley, Inc.
8101 Fourche Rd
Little Rock AR 72209
501 565-3006

(G-16068)
STOVER EXCAVATING INC
7500 Industrial Pkwy (43064-9005)
PHONE................................614 873-5865
Anthony Stover, *President*
Pat Kalinkiewicz, *Project Mgr*
Chad Turner, *Project Mgr*
Vickie Watson, *Office Mgr*
Karen Swartz,
EMP: 28 EST: 2006
SALES (est): 4MM **Privately Held**
SIC: 1794 Excavation & grading, building construction

(G-16069)
TOMITA USA INC (HQ)
7801 Corp Blvd Unit G (43064)
PHONE................................614 873-6509
Kaoru Tomita, *President*
Masahiko Yatsuyanagi, *Corp Secy*
Perry Lambert, *Accounts Mgr*
▲ EMP: 50
SQ FT: 6,000
SALES: 16MM **Privately Held**
SALES (corp-wide): 223.9MM **Privately Held**
SIC: 5084 Pneumatic tools & equipment
PA: Tomita Co., Ltd.
1-18-16, Omorinaka
Ota-Ku TKY 143-0
337 651-219

(G-16070)
TRADESMEN GROUP INC
8465 Rausch Dr (43064-8064)
PHONE................................614 799-0889
Melissa West, *President*
Karen Suvak, *Controller*
EMP: 40
SQ FT: 12,000
SALES: 11.2MM **Privately Held**
WEB: www.tradesmengroup.com
SIC: 1541 Renovation, remodeling & repairs; industrial buildings

(G-16071)
VELOCYS INC
7950 Corporate Blvd (43064-9230)
PHONE................................614 733-3300
David Pummell, *CEO*
Jeff McDaniel, *General Mgr*
Dr Paul F Schubert, *COO*
Brian Blackstone, *Research*
Anthony Detrick, *Research*
EMP: 60
SQ FT: 26,800
SALES (est): 10.3MM
SALES (corp-wide): 1MM **Privately Held**
WEB: www.velocys.com
SIC: 8731 3559 Commercial physical research; environmental research; electronic research; medical research, commercial; sewing machines & hat & zipper making machinery; refinery, chemical processing & similar machinery
PA: Velocys Plc
173 Curie Avenue
Didcot OXON OX11
123 583-8621

Pleasant City
Guernsey County

(G-16072)
TIMOTHY SINFIELD
54962 Marietta Rd (43772-9601)
PHONE................................740 685-3684
Timothy Sinfield, *Director*
EMP: 47
SALES (est): 1MM **Privately Held**
SIC: 1389 Oil & gas field services

Pleasant Plain
Warren County

(G-16073)
ENDEAVOR CONSTRUCTION LTD
6801 Long Spurling Rd (45162-9742)
PHONE................................513 469-1900
David Beiersdorfer, *President*
Valerie Webster, *Vice Pres*
EMP: 50
SQ FT: 3,000
SALES (est): 5.3MM **Privately Held**
SIC: 1522 1521 Residential construction; single-family housing construction

(G-16074)
MID-WESTERN CHILDRENS HOME
Also Called: VILLAGE CHRISTIAN SCHOOLS
4585 Long Spurling Rd (45162-9790)
P.O. Box 48 (45162-0048)
PHONE................................513 877-2141
James Frampton, *President*
Cotton Blakely, *Vice Pres*
Ron Hartman, *Treasurer*
Barry Boverie, *Administration*
EMP: 38
SQ FT: 68,283
SALES: 2.4MM **Privately Held**
WEB: www.village-christian.com
SIC: 8361 Children's home

(G-16075)
MILLER INDUSTRIAL SVC TEAM INC
8485 State Route 132 (45162-9226)
P.O. Box 188, Morrow (45152-0188)
PHONE................................513 877-2708
Debbie Miller, *President*
Jim Miller, *Opers Mgr*
EMP: 100
SQ FT: 11,590
SALES: 52.6MM **Privately Held**
SIC: 1542 Commercial & office building, new construction; commercial & office buildings, renovation & repair

---

Plymouth
Huron County

(G-16076)
BESTWAY TRANSPORT CO (PA)
2040 Sandusky St (44865-9412)
PHONE................................419 687-2000
Rich M Myers, *President*
Beverly Tuttle, *Corp Secy*
EMP: 38
SQ FT: 5,300
SALES: 5.5MM **Privately Held**
WEB: www.bestwaytransport.com
SIC: 4213 Trucking, except local

(G-16077)
JOHN F STAMBAUGH & CO
5063 Bevier Rd (44865)
PHONE................................419 687-6833
Charles F Hanline, *President*
EMP: 35
SQ FT: 1,332
SALES (est): 3.5MM **Privately Held**
SIC: 0161 0134 Onion farm; Irish potatoes

Point Pleasant
Clermont County

(G-16078)
CENTRAL REPAIR SERVICE INC
1606 Locust St (45153-9784)
PHONE................................513 943-0500
Garrett Sloane, *President*
EMP: 25 EST: 1997
SALES (est): 1.2MM **Privately Held**
WEB: www.centralrepairservice.com
SIC: 5963 7629 Appliance sales, house-to-house; clothing sales, house-to-house; electrical household appliance repair

---

Poland
Mahoning County

(G-16079)
ACME COMPANY
9495 Harvard Blvd (44514-3369)
PHONE................................330 758-2313
Carmine Zarlenga Jr, *President*
Adam Lonardo, *Opers Mgr*
John M Newman, *Incorporator*
EMP: 60 EST: 1934
SQ FT: 10,000
SALES (est): 13.3MM **Privately Held**
SIC: 5032 3423 1422 3295 Sand, construction; hand & edge tools; crushed & broken limestone; minerals, ground or treated

(G-16080)
ALPHA SECURITY LLC
87 W Mckinley Way Ste 1 (44514-1975)
PHONE................................330 406-2181
Steven Liller,
EMP: 100
SALES: 1MM **Privately Held**
SIC: 7381 Security guard service; guard services

(G-16081)
C-Z TRUCKING CO
Also Called: C-Z Trckng Co
9495 Harvard Blvd (44514-3369)
PHONE................................330 758-2313
Dan Zarlingo, *President*
Carmine Zarlingo Jr, *Treasurer*
Martha Zarlingo, *Admin Sec*
EMP: 65
SQ FT: 1,000
SALES: 3MM **Privately Held**
SIC: 4212 Local trucking, without storage

(G-16082)
CHEMICAL BANK
2 S Main St (44514-1914)
PHONE................................330 314-1395
EMP: 36

SALES (corp-wide): 924.5MM **Publicly Held**
SIC: 6035 Federal savings & loan associations
HQ: Chemical Bank
333 E Main St
Midland MI 48640
989 631-9200

(G-16083)
COLDWELL BANKER FIRST PLACE RE
1275 Boardman Poland Rd # 1 (44514-3911)
PHONE................................330 726-8161
Eric Caspray, *Principal*
EMP: 100
SALES (est): 4.1MM **Privately Held**
SIC: 6531 Real estate agent, residential

(G-16084)
HAMPTON WOODS NURSING CTR INC
Also Called: WOODLANDS AT HAMPTON
1525 E Western Reserve Rd (44514-3254)
PHONE................................330 707-1400
Kathy Prasad, *Principal*
EMP: 34
SALES: 6.1MM **Privately Held**
SIC: 8051 8059 Convalescent home with continuous nursing care; nursing & personal care

(G-16085)
HANNA HOLDINGS INC
100 W Mckinley Way (44514-1954)
PHONE................................330 707-1000
Ann Delacroix, *Manager*
EMP: 70
SALES (corp-wide): 73.7MM **Privately Held**
WEB: www.howardhanna.com
SIC: 6531 Real estate brokers & agents
PA: Hanna Holdings, Inc.
1090 Freeport Rd Ste 1a
Pittsburgh PA 15238
412 967-9000

(G-16086)
LAKE CLUB
1140 Paulin Rd (44514-3239)
PHONE................................330 549-3996
Ed Muransky, *Owner*
Joe Larocca, *COO*
Samantha Villella,
Erin Hirschbeck, *Receptionist*
Debbie Kish, *Receptionist*
EMP: 200
SALES (est): 1.1MM **Privately Held**
SIC: 7997 Golf club, membership; country club, membership

(G-16087)
RESERVE RUN GOLF CLUB LLC
Also Called: Quarry Pines
625 E Western Reserve Rd (44514-3356)
P.O. Box 14189 (44514-7189)
PHONE................................330 758-1017
Scott Macdonald, *Partner*
EMP: 80
SALES (est): 816.1K **Privately Held**
WEB: www.reserverungolf.com
SIC: 7992 Public golf courses

(G-16088)
SHANE SECURITY SERVICES INC
7217 Pennsylvania Ave (44514-1652)
P.O. Box 5366 (44514-0366)
PHONE................................330 757-4001
Conrad Childers, *President*
Geraldine Childers, *President*
EMP: 75 EST: 1976
SALES (est): 1.1MM **Privately Held**
SIC: 7381 6211 Protective services, guard; detective services; security brokers & dealers

(G-16089)
SHEPHERD OF THE VALLEY LUTHERA
Also Called: Shepards Meadows
301 W Western Reserve Rd (44514-3527)
PHONE................................330 726-7110
Kelly Stansloski, *Director*

EMP: 45
SALES (corp-wide): 33MM Privately
Held
WEB: www.shepherdofthevalley.com
SIC: 6513 Retirement hotel operation
PA: Shepherd Of The Valley Lutheran Retirement Services, Inc.
5525 Silica Rd
Youngstown OH 44515
330 530-4038

(G-16090)
SUNRISE SENIOR LIVING LLC
Also Called: Sunrise of Poland
335 W Mckinley Way (44514-1681)
PHONE.............................330 707-1313
Nicole Lagata, *Branch Mgr*
EMP: 50
SALES (corp-wide): 4.7B Publicly Held
WEB: www.sunrise.com
SIC: 8051 Skilled nursing care facilities
HQ: Sunrise Senior Living, Llc
7902 Westpark Dr
Mc Lean VA 22102

(G-16091)
TRUGREEN-CHEM LAWN
8529 South Ave (44514-3699)
P.O. Box 5070 (44514-0070)
PHONE.............................330 533-2839
Dave Slott, *President*
EMP: 60
SALES (est): 1.6MM Privately Held
SIC: 0782 Lawn care services

Polk
Ashland County

(G-16092)
FALLING STAR FARM LTD
Also Called: Dairy Farm
626 State Route 89 (44866-9712)
PHONE.............................419 945-2651
Karen Meyer, *Owner*
Dewey Meyer, *Principal*
Duane Schrier, *Human Res Mgr*
Holly Fullmer,
EMP: 25
SALES (est): 2.9MM Privately Held
WEB: www.meyerhatchery.com
SIC: 0241 Dairy farms

Pomeroy
Meigs County

(G-16093)
BEDFORD TOWNSHIP
Also Called: Meigs County Emrgncy Med Svcs
Mulburry Heights Stn 11 (45769)
P.O. Box 748 (45769-0748)
PHONE.............................740 992-6617
Patsy Warner, *Director*
EMP: 35
SQ FT: 2,000 Privately Held
WEB: www.meigsdjfs.net
SIC: 4119 Ambulance service
PA: Bedford Township
100 E 2nd St Rm 201
Pomeroy OH 45769
740 992-5290

(G-16094)
FARMERS BANK & SAVINGS CO INC (PA)
211 W 2nd St (45769-1037)
PHONE.............................740 992-0088
Paul Reed, *President*
Mark Groves, *COO*
Edna Weber, *Assistant VP*
Donna Schmoll, *Vice Pres*
Woody Stein, *Vice Pres*
EMP: 45
SALES: 14.7MM Privately Held
WEB: www.fbsc.com
SIC: 6021 National commercial banks

(G-16095)
MEIGS COUNTY COUNCIL ON AGING
112 E Memorial Dr Fl 1 (45769-9569)
P.O. Box 722 (45769-0722)
PHONE.............................740 992-2161
Beth Shaver, *Exec Dir*
EMP: 50
SALES: 1MM Privately Held
WEB: www.meigsseniors.com
SIC: 8322 Old age assistance

(G-16096)
PDK CONSTRUCTION INC
34070 Crew Rd (45769-9715)
P.O. Box 683 (45769-0683)
PHONE.............................740 992-6451
Phillip R Harrison, *President*
Donald Roush, *Vice Pres*
EMP: 45
SQ FT: 4,080
SALES (est): 7.8MM Privately Held
SIC: 1611 Guardrail construction, highways; highway & street sign installation

(G-16097)
SYRACUSE WATER DEPT
2581 3rd St (45769)
P.O. Box 323, Syracuse (45779-0323)
PHONE.............................740 992-7777
Gordon Winerenner, *President*
Allen Gran, *Bd of Directors*
Dencil Hudson, *Bd of Directors*
EMP: 26
SALES (est): 955.5K Privately Held
SIC: 4941 Water supply

(G-16098)
TAYLORS STAFFING LLC
37817 State Route 124 (45769-9302)
PHONE.............................740 446-3305
Frances Taylor, *Owner*
EMP: 83
SALES: 100K Privately Held
SIC: 7361 7363 Nurses' registry; help supply services

Port Clinton
Ottawa County

(G-16099)
ANIMAL MGT SVCS OHIO INC
Also Called: African Safari Wildlife Park
267 S Lightner Rd (43452-3851)
PHONE.............................248 398-6533
Jon Mikosz, *Principal*
EMP: 35 Privately Held
WEB:
www.animalmanagementservices.com
SIC: 8422 Zoological garden, noncommercial
PA: Animal Management Services Of Ohio Inc.
25600 Woodward Ave Ste 11
Royal Oak MI 48067

(G-16100)
BROWN CONTRACTING & DEV LLC
318 Madison St (43452-1921)
PHONE.............................419 341-3939
William A Brown, *Principal*
EMP: 27
SALES (est): 2.1MM Privately Held
SIC: 1799 Special trade contractors

(G-16101)
CATAWBA-CLEVELAND DEV CORP (PA)
Also Called: Catawba Island Marina
4235 E Beachclub Rd (43452-3009)
PHONE.............................419 797-4424
James V Stouffer, *CEO*
EMP: 99
SQ FT: 4,500
SALES (est): 8.1MM Privately Held
WEB: www.cicclub.com
SIC: 7997 4493 6519 Country club, membership; marinas; real property lessors

(G-16102)
COMMODORE PRRY INNS SUITES LLC
255 W Lakeshore Dr (43452-9477)
PHONE.............................419 732-2645
Edward R Fitzgerald,
EMP: 80
SALES (est): 2.2MM Privately Held
SIC: 7011 5812 Hotels; eating places

(G-16103)
COMMODORE RESORTS INC
Also Called: Commodore Motel
255 W Lakeshore Dr (43452-9477)
PHONE.............................419 285-3101
Edward Fitzgerald, *President*
EMP: 30 EST: 1967
SALES (est): 1.3MM Privately Held
WEB: www.commodoreresorts.com
SIC: 7011 Motels

(G-16104)
COVENANT CARE OHIO INC
Also Called: Edgewood Manor Nursing Center
1330 Fulton St (43452-9297)
PHONE.............................419 898-5506
Denise Day, *Branch Mgr*
EMP: 94 Privately Held
WEB: www.villageorgetown.com
SIC: 8051 Convalescent home with continuous nursing care
HQ: Covenant Care Ohio, Inc.
27071 Aliso Creek Rd # 100
Aliso Viejo CA 92656
949 349-1200

(G-16105)
D & G FOCHT CONSTRUCTION CO
2040 E State Rd (43452-2525)
P.O. Box 446 (43452-0446)
PHONE.............................419 732-2412
Douglas Focht, *President*
Joy Taylor, *General Mgr*
Jeanette Focht, *Corp Secy*
EMP: 35 EST: 1975
SQ FT: 5,000
SALES (est): 6.8MM Privately Held
WEB: www.fochtconstruction.com
SIC: 1541 1542 Industrial buildings, new construction; commercial & office building, new construction; institutional building construction

(G-16106)
DUBLIN COML PROPERTY SVCS INC
127 Madison St (43452-1103)
PHONE.............................419 732-6732
James E McKinney, *President*
Judith McKinney, *Vice Pres*
Gregory A Staib, *Vice Pres*
Jim McKinney, *Manager*
EMP: 25
SQ FT: 3,000
SALES (est): 1MM Privately Held
WEB: www.dublincps.com
SIC: 7349 Janitorial service, contract basis

(G-16107)
GOOFY GOLF II INC
Also Called: Monsoon Lagoon Water Park
1530 S Danbury Rd (43452-3920)
PHONE.............................419 732-6671
John Heilman, *President*
Patricia Heilman, *Corp Secy*
EMP: 65
SQ FT: 5,000
SALES (est): 1.5MM Privately Held
WEB: www.monsoonlagoonwaterpark.com
SIC: 7999 Miniature golf course operation

(G-16108)
GUNDLACH SHEET METAL WORKS INC
Also Called: Shilling AC Heating & Plumbing
2439 E Gill Rd (43452)
PHONE.............................419 734-7351
Roger Gundlach, *President*
EMP: 40

SALES (est): 1.6MM
SALES (corp-wide): 18.7MM Privately
Held
WEB: www.gundlach-hvac.com
SIC: 1711 Warm air heating & air conditioning contractor
PA: Gundlach Sheet Metal Works, Inc.
910 Columbus Ave
Sandusky OH 44870
419 626-4525

(G-16109)
H B MAGRUDER MEMORIAL HOSPITAL
611 Fulton St (43452-2008)
PHONE.............................419 734-4539
EMP: 365
SALES (corp-wide): 55.1MM Privately
Held
SIC: 8062 General medical & surgical hospitals
PA: H B Magruder Memorial Hospital
615 Fulton St
Port Clinton OH 43452
419 734-3131

(G-16110)
ISLAND HOUSE INC
Also Called: Island House Inn
102 Madison St (43452-1104)
PHONE.............................419 734-0100
Dave Walerie, *President*
EMP: 40 EST: 1990
SALES (est): 1.4MM Privately Held
SIC: 5812 7011 5813 Restaurant, family: chain; cafe; hotels; tavern (drinking places)

(G-16111)
KUEHNE + NAGEL INC
Erie Industrial Park # 2 (43452-9412)
PHONE.............................419 635-4051
Jeffrey Crosby, *Manager*
EMP: 50
SALES (corp-wide): 20.9B Privately Held
WEB: www.kuehnenagel.com
SIC: 4225 General warehousing & storage
HQ: Kuehne + Nagel Inc.
10 Exchange Pl Fl 19
Jersey City NJ 07302
201 413-5500

(G-16112)
LODGING INDUSTRY INC
Also Called: Quality Inn
1723 E Perry St (43452-1425)
PHONE.............................419 732-2929
Jacqueline Seibold, *General Mgr*
EMP: 31
SALES (corp-wide): 1.5MM Privately
Held
SIC: 7011 Hotels & motels
PA: Lodging Industry Inc
910 Lorain Blvd Ste N
Elyria OH
440 323-9820

(G-16113)
MJS SNOW & LANDSCAPE LLC
6660 W Fritchie Rd (43452-8408)
PHONE.............................419 656-6724
Matthew Holcomb,
EMP: 71
SALES: 12MM Privately Held
SIC: 0781 Landscape services

(G-16114)
PORT CLNTON BPO ELKS LDGE 1718
231 Buckeye Blvd (43452-1421)
PHONE.............................419 734-1900
Heath Krupp, *President*
Luis Catania, *General Mgr*
EMP: 25
SALES: 228K Privately Held
SIC: 8641 Civic associations

(G-16115)
REPUBLIC SERVICES INC
530 N Camp Rd (43452-9599)
PHONE.............................419 635-2367
John Logsdon, *Branch Mgr*
EMP: 34
SALES (corp-wide): 10B Publicly Held
SIC: 4953 Refuse collection & disposal services

PA: Republic Services, Inc.
18500 N Allied Way # 100
Phoenix AZ 85054
480 627-2700

(G-16116)
RJ RUNGE COMPANY INC
3539 Ne Catawba Rd (43452-9609)
P.O. Box 977 (43452-0977)
PHONE..................................419 740-5781
Richard J Runge, *CEO*
Amy Runge, *President*
EMP: 30
SQ FT: 3,000
SALES (est): 4.8MM **Privately Held**
WEB: www.rjrunge.com
SIC: 8741 1731 8748 Construction management; electrical work; business consulting

(G-16117)
SHIP SHAPE MARINE INC
410 W Perry St (43452-1048)
P.O. Box 387 (43452-0387)
PHONE..................................419 734-1554
Kevin Leneghan, *President*
Michelle Miller, *Corp Secy*
Brian Holly, *Vice Pres*
Jenna Sandvick, *Manager*
EMP: 25
SALES (est): 2.2MM **Privately Held**
SIC: 4499 4226 Boat cleaning; special warehousing & storage

(G-16118)
SPECTRUM MGT HOLDG CO LLC
Also Called: Time Warner
2853 East Harbor Rd Ste A (43452-2679)
PHONE..................................419 386-0040
Kathryn Warner, *Branch Mgr*
EMP: 83
SALES (corp-wide): 43.6B **Publicly Held**
SIC: 4841 Cable television services
HQ: Spectrum Management Holding Company, Llc
400 Atlantic St
Stamford CT 06901
203 905-7801

(G-16119)
TACK-ANEW INC
Also Called: Brands' Marina
451 W Lakeshore Dr (43452-9478)
PHONE..................................419 734-4212
Dalton Brand, *President*
Darrell A Brand, *President*
EMP: 26
SQ FT: 15,000
SALES: 2MM **Privately Held**
WEB: www.brandsmarina.com
SIC: 4493 3731 Boat yards, storage & incidental repair; shipbuilding & repairing

(G-16120)
ZINK CALLS
30 Park Dr (43452-2075)
PHONE..................................419 732-6171
Dawn Zink, *Principal*
▲ **EMP:** 32
SALES (est): 1.3MM **Privately Held**
SIC: 7929 Entertainment service

Port Washington
Tuscarawas County

(G-16121)
BATES METAL PRODUCTS INC
403 E Mn St (43837)
P.O. Box 68 (43837-0068)
PHONE..................................740 498-8371
James A Bates, *President*
Betty Bates, *Corp Secy*
Terry L Bates, *Vice Pres*
EMP: 60 **EST:** 1956
SQ FT: 106,500
SALES (est): 15.4MM **Privately Held**
WEB: www.batesmetal.com
SIC: 4783 2542 3993 3469 Packing & crating; racks, merchandise display or storage: except wood; signs & advertising specialties; metal stampings; automotive & apparel trimmings

Portage
Wood County

(G-16122)
COUNTY OF WOOD
Also Called: Portage Group Werner Home
351 W Main St (43451-9802)
PHONE..................................419 686-6951
Cathy Miller, *Manager*
EMP: 350 **Privately Held**
WEB: www.woodmrdd.org
SIC: 8059 8052 Home for the mentally retarded, exc. skilled or intermediate; intermediate care facilities
PA: County Of Wood
1 Courthouse Sq
Bowling Green OH 43402
419 354-9100

Portsmouth
Scioto County

(G-16123)
AAA SOUTH CENTRAL OHIO INC
1414 12th St (45662-4206)
PHONE..................................740 354-5614
Robert L Morton, *President*
Micheal Morgan, *President*
Brenda Thacker, *Manager*
Gerald Baker, *Director*
EMP: 40 **EST:** 1917
SALES (est): 771.1K **Privately Held**
SIC: 8699 Automobile owners' association

(G-16124)
ADVANTAGE HOME HEALTH CARE
1656 Coles Blvd (45662-2632)
PHONE..................................800 636-2330
Kathy Pierrion, *President*
EMP: 80
SALES (est): 1.5MM **Privately Held**
SIC: 8082 Visiting nurse service

(G-16125)
BIG SANDY FURNITURE INC
Also Called: Big Sandy Furniture Store 5
730 10th St (45662-4033)
PHONE..................................740 354-3193
Tyler Conley, *Branch Mgr*
EMP: 30 **Privately Held**
WEB: www.bigsandyfurniture.com
SIC: 4225 5722 5712 General warehousing & storage; gas household appliances; furniture stores
HQ: Big Sandy Furniture, Inc.
8375 Gallia Pike
Franklin Furnace OH 45629
740 574-2113

(G-16126)
BOONE COLEMAN CONSTRUCTION INC
32 State Route 239 (45663-8929)
PHONE..................................740 858-6661
Timothy Coleman, *President*
EMP: 35
SQ FT: 500
SALES (est): 5.4MM **Privately Held**
SIC: 1623 Water, sewer & utility lines

(G-16127)
CANTER INNS INC (HQ)
Also Called: Ramada Inn
711 2nd St (45662-4001)
PHONE..................................740 354-7711
Jeff Albrecht, *President*
Gary Albrecht, *Corp Secy*
EMP: 26
SQ FT: 38,000
SALES (est): 1.3MM **Privately Held**
WEB: www.ramadaportsmouth.com
SIC: 7011 Hotels & motels
PA: Albrecht's Ohio Inns, Inc.
711 2nd St Ste 35
Portsmouth OH 45662
740 354-7711

(G-16128)
CITY OF PORTSMOUTH
Also Called: Portsmouth Health Department
605 Washington St (45662-3919)
PHONE..................................740 353-5153
Don Walden, *Manager*
Celeste Tucker, *Officer*
EMP: 37 **Privately Held**
WEB: www.pmcourt.org
SIC: 8399 Health systems agency; health & welfare council
PA: City Of Portsmouth
728 2nd St Rm 1
Portsmouth OH 45662
740 354-8807

(G-16129)
CITY OF PORTSMOUTH
Also Called: Public Service Dept
55 Mary Ann St (45662-4647)
PHONE..................................740 353-5419
Bill Beaumont, *Director*
Teresa Harmon, *Clerk*
EMP: 34 **Privately Held**
WEB: www.pmcourt.org
SIC: 1611 9111 Highway & street maintenance; mayors' offices
PA: City Of Portsmouth
728 2nd St Rm 1
Portsmouth OH 45662
740 354-8807

(G-16130)
CITY OF PORTSMOUTH
Also Called: City Garage
55 Mary Ann St (45662-4647)
PHONE..................................740 353-3459
Christopher Murphy, *Manager*
EMP: 40 **Privately Held**
WEB: www.pmcourt.org
SIC: 7521 Parking garage
PA: City Of Portsmouth
728 2nd St Rm 1
Portsmouth OH 45662
740 354-8807

(G-16131)
COMMUNITY ACTION COMM PIKE CNT
Also Called: Valley View Health Center
621 Broadway St (45662-4788)
PHONE..................................740 961-4011
Cheryl Tackett, *Asst Director*
EMP: 50
SALES (corp-wide): 22.1MM **Privately Held**
SIC: 8322 Family service agency
PA: The Community Action Committee Of Pike County
941 Market St
Piketon OH 45661
740 289-2371

(G-16132)
COMMUNITY ACTION ORGANIZATION (PA)
433 3rd St (45662-3811)
P.O. Box 1525 (45662-1525)
PHONE..................................740 354-7541
Carolyn Powell, *Comptroller*
Tami Wellman, *Manager*
Steve Sturgill, *Exec Dir*
Katie Andrews, *Bd of Directors*
EMP: 200
SQ FT: 6,000
SALES: 14.8MM **Privately Held**
SIC: 8322 8331 Social service center; community service employment training program

(G-16133)
COMPASS COMMUNITY HEALTH
1634 11th St (45662-4526)
PHONE..................................740 355-7102
Ed Hughes, *CEO*
Lora Gampp, *CFO*
EMP: 40 **EST:** 2012
SALES: 2.3MM **Privately Held**
SIC: 8011 8093 Offices & clinics of medical doctors; mental health clinic, outpatient

(G-16134)
CRYSTAL CARE CENTER PORTSMOUTH
1319 Spring St (45662-2675)
P.O. Box 439 (45662-0439)
PHONE..................................740 354-6619
Kim Nye, *Administration*
EMP: 30
SQ FT: 7,900
SALES (est): 950K **Privately Held**
WEB: www.crystalcarecenters.com
SIC: 8051 Convalescent home with continuous nursing care

(G-16135)
DESCO FEDERAL CREDIT UNION (PA)
401 Chillicothe St (45662-4013)
P.O. Box 1546 (45662-1546)
PHONE..................................740 354-7791
Richard Powell, *President*
Chris Hamilton, *Assistant VP*
Lou Bennett, *Vice Pres*
Joyce Myers, *Vice Pres*
Teresa Noel, *Mfg Spvr*
EMP: 85 **EST:** 1963
SQ FT: 10,000
SALES: 9.9MM **Privately Held**
SIC: 6061 Federal credit unions

(G-16136)
DIALYSIS CLINIC INC
1207 17th St (45662-3573)
PHONE..................................740 351-0596
Andrew Mazon, *Manager*
EMP: 25
SALES (corp-wide): 760.1MM **Privately Held**
WEB: www.dciinc.org
SIC: 8092 Kidney dialysis centers
PA: Dialysis Clinic, Inc.
1633 Church St Ste 500
Nashville TN 37203
615 327-3061

(G-16137)
EARL TWINAM
550 Field Rd (45662-8919)
PHONE..................................740 820-2654
Earl Twinam, *General Mgr*
EMP: 25
SALES (est): 1.5MM **Privately Held**
SIC: 8711 Engineering services

(G-16138)
GENESIS RESPIRATORY SVCS INC (PA)
Also Called: Genesis Oxygen & Home Med Eqp
4132 Gallia St (45662-5511)
PHONE..................................740 354-4363
Rosalie Kay Williams, *President*
James Blair, *Vice Pres*
Steve Mefford, *Safety Mgr*
E B Lowman, *Shareholder*
EMP: 105 **EST:** 1977
SQ FT: 8,000
SALES (est): 14MM **Privately Held**
SIC: 5999 8093 Medical apparatus & supplies; respiratory therapy clinic

(G-16139)
GEORGE P PETTIT MD INC
Also Called: Dr Darren Adams Dr Grge Pettit
1729 27th St Bldg G (45662-2638)
PHONE..................................740 354-1434
George P Pettit MD, *President*
EMP: 40
SALES (est): 4.1MM **Privately Held**
SIC: 8011 Gynecologist; obstetrician; physicians' office, including specialists

(G-16140)
GLENNCO SYSTEMS INC
928 16th St (45662-2901)
PHONE..................................740 353-4328
Dan Glenn, *President*
Sue Glenn, *Vice Pres*
EMP: 25
SQ FT: 2,000
SALES: 2.5MM **Privately Held**
SIC: 1711 Plumbing contractors

▲ = Import ▼ =Export
◆ =Import/Export

(G-16141)
GRACIE PLUM INVESTMENTS INC
609 2nd St Unit 2 (45662-3974)
PHONE.............................740 355-9029
Francesca G Hartop, CEO
Aaron Prose, Vice Pres
Nancy Prose, Controller
▼ EMP: 27
SQ FT: 3,150
SALES: 4.3MM Privately Held
WEB: www.yostengineering.com
SIC: 7372 7374 7371 Application computer software; data processing & preparation; custom computer programming services

(G-16142)
HCR MANORCARE MED SVCS FLA LLC
35 Bierly Rd Ste 2 (45662-8503)
PHONE.............................419 252-5500
Criag Thurston, CEO
EMP: 105
SALES (corp-wide): 2.4B Publicly Held
SIC: 8051 Convalescent home with continuous nursing care
HQ: Hcr Manorcare Medical Services Of Florida, Llc
333 N Summit St Ste 100
Toledo OH 43604
419 252-5500

(G-16143)
HEALTH CARE RTREMENT CORP AMER
Also Called: Heartland of Portsmouth
20 Easter Dr (45662-8659)
PHONE.............................740 354-4505
Lois Clay, Administration
EMP: 126
SALES (corp-wide): 2.4B Publicly Held
WEB: www.hrc-manorcare.com
SIC: 8051 Skilled nursing care facilities
HQ: Health Care And Retirement Corporation Of America
333 N Summit St Ste 103
Toledo OH 43604
419 252-5500

(G-16144)
HEARTLAND HOSPICE SERVICES LLC
35 Bierly Rd Ste 2 (45662-8503)
PHONE.............................740 351-0575
EMP: 100
SALES (corp-wide): 3.8B Publicly Held
SIC: 8082 Home Health Care Service
HQ: Heartland Hospice Services, Llc
333 N Summit St
Toledo OH 43604

(G-16145)
HEMPSTEAD MANOR
727 8th St (45662-4020)
PHONE.............................740 354-8150
Linda Purek, President
EMP: 130
SQ FT: 80,000
SALES (est): 4.6MM Privately Held
SIC: 8051 8052 Convalescent home with continuous nursing care; intermediate care facilities

(G-16146)
HILL VIEW RETIREMENT CENTER
1610 28th St (45662-2641)
PHONE.............................740 354-3135
John Prose, President
Mike Hodge, Purch Agent
Kane Bazler, Human Res Dir
Kevin Blume, Manager
Tom Decamp, Info Tech Mgr
EMP: 174
SQ FT: 14,500
SALES: 14.2MM Privately Held
WEB: www.hillviewretirement.org
SIC: 8051 Skilled nursing care facilities

(G-16147)
HORIZON HOUSE APARTMENTS LLC
700 2nd St (45662-4064)
PHONE.............................740 354-6393
Michelle Hert,
EMP: 55
SALES: 320K Privately Held
SIC: 6513 Apartment building operators

(G-16148)
HOSPICE OF SOUTHERN OHIO
Also Called: Somc Hospice
2201 25th St (45662-3259)
PHONE.............................740 356-2567
Teresa Ruby, Director
EMP: 80
SALES (est): 3.6MM Privately Held
SIC: 8062 General medical & surgical hospitals

(G-16149)
INFRA-METALS CO
1 Sturgill Way (45662-5179)
PHONE.............................740 353-1350
Oak Williams, Branch Mgr
EMP: 25
SALES (corp-wide): 11.5B Publicly Held
SIC: 5051 Steel
HQ: Infra-Metals Co.
580 Middletown Blvd D100
Langhorne PA 19047
215 741-1000

(G-16150)
INTERIM HEALTHCARE (PA)
4130 Gallia St (45662-5511)
PHONE.............................740 354-5550
Donna Southworth, President
Rosie Williams, Vice Pres
EMP: 82
SALES (est): 3.8MM Privately Held
SIC: 8082 Home health care services

(G-16151)
J&H RNFRCING STRL ERECTORS INC
Also Called: J & H Erectors
55 River Ave (45662-4712)
P.O. Box 60 (45662-0060)
PHONE.............................740 355-0141
Donald Hadsell, President
Lisa Hadsell, Corp Secy
Wanda Fannin, Clerk
EMP: 150
SQ FT: 30,000
SALES (est): 33.3MM Privately Held
WEB: www.jherectors.com
SIC: 1542 1791 Commercial & office building contractors; iron work, structural

(G-16152)
KENTUCKY HEART INSTITUTE INC
2001 Scioto Trl Ste 200 (45662-2845)
PHONE.............................740 353-8100
Debbie Bell, Principal
EMP: 41
SALES (corp-wide): 92.7K Privately Held
SIC: 8011 Offices & clinics of medical doctors
PA: Kentucky Heart Institute, Inc
613 23rd St
Ashland KY 41101
606 329-1997

(G-16153)
LUTE SUPPLY INC (PA)
3920 Us Highway 23 (45662-6468)
P.O. Box 721 (45662-0721)
PHONE.............................740 353-1447
Christopher H Lute, President
Dave Fleming, Vice Pres
Brian Hancock, Vice Pres
Phil Markins, Purchasing
Jason C Lute, Treasurer
EMP: 25 EST: 1952
SALES (est): 78.5MM Privately Held
WEB: www.lutesupply.com
SIC: 5074 5075 5031 5087 Plumbing fittings & supplies; air conditioning & ventilation equipment & supplies; warm air heating equipment & supplies; kitchen cabinets; service establishment equipment; tools

(G-16154)
MECHANICAL CONSTRUCTION CO
Also Called: McCo
2302 8th St (45662-4798)
PHONE.............................740 353-5668
Darrell Stapleton, President
Jackie Enz, Corp Secy
W Michael Stapleton, Vice Pres
Tony Dingus, Project Mgr
Brian Enz, Office Admin
EMP: 50 EST: 1957
SQ FT: 10,000
SALES (est): 10.7MM Privately Held
SIC: 1711 1761 Plumbing contractors; warm air heating & air conditioning contractor; sheet metalwork

(G-16155)
NORFOLK SOUTHERN CORPORATION
2435 8th St (45662-4781)
PHONE.............................740 353-4529
Dianne Ravizee, Manager
EMP: 54
SALES (corp-wide): 11.4B Publicly Held
WEB: www.nscorp.com
SIC: 4011 Railroads, line-haul operating
PA: Norfolk Southern Corporation
3 Commercial Pl Ste 1a
Norfolk VA 23510
757 629-2680

(G-16156)
PAINTERS LOCAL UNION 555
2101 7th St (45662-4726)
PHONE.............................740 353-1431
Joe Crytser, Manager
EMP: 65 EST: 1932
SQ FT: 2,800
SALES (est): 1.2MM Privately Held
SIC: 8631 Trade union

(G-16157)
PEOPLES BANK
503 Chillicothe St (45662-4015)
PHONE.............................740 354-3177
EMP: 52
SALES (corp-wide): 208MM Publicly Held
SIC: 6035 Federal savings & loan associations
HQ: Peoples Bank
138 Putnam St
Marietta OH 45750
740 373-3155

(G-16158)
PORTSMOUTH AMBULANCE
2796 Gallia St (45662-4807)
PHONE.............................740 289-2932
Sherri Fannin, Owner
EMP: 180
SALES (est): 2.3MM Privately Held
SIC: 4119 Ambulance service

(G-16159)
PORTSMOUTH HOSPITAL CORP
Also Called: KING'S DAUGHTERS' MEDICAL CENT
1901 Argonne Rd (45662-2827)
P.O. Box 151, Ashland KY (41105-0151)
PHONE.............................740 991-4000
David Jones, Chairman
Charlie Borders, Finance Dir
Dan Cassidy, Director
Fred Jackson, Director
Alex Krivchenia MD, Director
EMP: 2082
SALES: 24.4MM
SALES (corp-wide): 485.1MM Privately Held
SIC: 8011 Medical centers
HQ: Ashland Hospital Corporation
2201 Lexington Ave
Ashland KY 41101
606 408-4000

(G-16160)
PORTSMOUTH LODGE 154 B P O E (PA)
Also Called: Elks
544 4th St (45662-3838)
P.O. Box 871 (45662-0871)
PHONE.............................740 353-1013
Clark Thompson, Director
Gary Plant, Director
EMP: 50
SALES (est): 1.1MM Privately Held
SIC: 8641 Fraternal associations

(G-16161)
PORTSMOUTH METRO HOUSING AUTH (PA)
Also Called: Section 8 Housing Assistance
410 Court St (45662-3949)
PHONE.............................740 354-4547
Teresa Everett, Finance
Stephanie Sands, Manager
Peggy Rice, Director
Helen Adams, Director
EMP: 45
SALES (est): 3.7MM Privately Held
WEB: www.pmha.us
SIC: 8322 Individual & family services

(G-16162)
PORTSMUTH EMRGNCY AMBLANCE SVC
2796 Gallia St (45662-4807)
PHONE.............................740 354-3122
Michael L Adkins, President
Trina Adkins, Vice Pres
Rachael Estep, Treasurer
Michael R Adkins, Admin Sec
EMP: 500
SQ FT: 11,000
SALES (est): 9.4MM Privately Held
SIC: 4119 Ambulance service

(G-16163)
REHABCARE GROUP MGT SVCS INC
Also Called: Somc Speech and Hearing Svcs
1202 18th St (45662-2922)
PHONE.............................740 356-6160
Kevin Staimpert, Director
EMP: 68
SALES (corp-wide): 6B Privately Held
WEB: www.rehabcare.com
SIC: 8093 Rehabilitation center, outpatient treatment
HQ: Rehabcare Group Mgt Svcs Inc
680 S 4th St
Louisville KY 40202
502 596-7300

(G-16164)
REYNOLDS & CO INC
Also Called: Reynolds & Company Cpa's
839 Gallia St (45662-4137)
P.O. Box 1364 (45662-1364)
PHONE.............................740 353-1040
Greg Brown, Principal
Ronald F Champan, Treasurer
Amanda Caldwell, Accountant
Debra Coburn, Accountant
Melania Cox, Accountant
EMP: 35 EST: 1967
SQ FT: 6,000
SALES (est): 2.5MM Privately Held
WEB: www.reynolds-cpa.com
SIC: 8721 Certified public accountant

(G-16165)
ROYCE LEASING CO LLC
Also Called: Bridgeport Healthcare Center
2125 Royce St (45662-4714)
PHONE.............................740 354-1240
EMP: 99
SALES (est): 3.3MM
SALES (corp-wide): 114.3MM Privately Held
SIC: 8051 Skilled nursing care facilities
HQ: Health Care Facility Management, Llc
4700 Ashwood Dr Ste 200
Blue Ash OH 45241

(G-16166)
SCIOTO COUNTY C A O HEADSTART
Also Called: Highland Ctr Early Head Start
1511 Hutchins St (45662-3615)
P.O. Box 1525 (45662-1525)
PHONE.............................740 354-3333
Robert Walton, Exec Dir
Mary Parker, Director
EMP: 33

G
E
O
G
R
A
P
H
I
C

SALES (est): 950K **Privately Held**
SIC: 8351 Head start center, except in conjunction with school

(G-16167)
**SCIOTO COUNTY COUNSELING
CTR (PA)**
Also Called: COUNSELING CENTER, THE
1634 11th St (45662-4526)
PHONE..................................740 354-6685
Michael Ralstin, *Opers Staff*
Melanie Colmer, *CFO*
Ed Hughes, *Exec Dir*
Rick Calvin, *Director*
Penny Moore, *Director*
EMP: 59
SALES: 11.9MM **Privately Held**
SIC: 8322 Alcoholism counseling, nontreatment; drug abuse counselor, nontreatment; family counseling services

(G-16168)
**SCIOTO RESIDENTIAL
SERVICES**
2333 Vinton Ave (45662-3741)
PHONE..................................740 353-0288
Lisa Francis, *Principal*
EMP: 27
SALES (corp-wide): 4.8MM **Privately
Held**
SIC: 8361 Home for the mentally retarded
PA: Scioto Residential Services, Inc
9 Plaza Dr
Portsmouth OH 45662
740 354-7958

(G-16169)
SHAWNEE ANIMAL CLINIC INC
101 Bierly Rd (45662-8805)
PHONE..................................740 353-5758
Gail Counts Dvm, *President*
EMP: 25
SALES (est): 2.4MM **Privately Held**
SIC: 0742 Animal hospital services, pets & other animal specialties

(G-16170)
SOMC FOUNDATION INC
1805 27th St (45662-2686)
PHONE..................................740 356-5000
Stewart Yes, *President*
EMP: 60
SALES (est): 1.2K **Privately Held**
SIC: 8011 Physicians' office, including specialists

(G-16171)
**SOUTHERN OHIO MEDICAL
CENTER (PA)**
Also Called: SCIOTO MEMORIAL HOSPITAL
CAMPU
1805 27th St (45662-2640)
PHONE..................................740 354-5000
Robert E Dever, *Ch of Bd*
Randal M Arnett, *President*
Claudia Burchett, *Vice Pres*
Myrna Wamsley, *Buyer*
Kendall Stewart MD, *Director*
▲ EMP: 200 EST: 1954
SALES: 394.6MM **Privately Held**
SIC: 8062 General medical & surgical hospitals

(G-16172)
**SOUTHERN OHIO MEDICAL
CENTER**
Also Called: Somc Urgent Care Ctr Prtsmouth
1248 Kinneys Ln (45662-2927)
PHONE..................................740 356-5000
Addam King, *Manager*
Greg Gilliland, *Director*
EMP: 30
SALES (corp-wide): 394.6MM **Privately
Held**
SIC: 8062 General medical & surgical hospitals
PA: Southern Ohio Medical Center
1805 27th St
Portsmouth OH 45662
740 354-5000

(G-16173)
**SOUTHERN OHIO MEDICAL
CENTER**
Also Called: Somc
1805 27th St (45662-2640)
PHONE..................................740 354-5000
Emily Van Loon, *CFO*
Elizabeth Blevins, *Director*
EMP: 2000
SALES (corp-wide): 394.6MM **Privately
Held**
SIC: 8062 General medical & surgical hospitals
PA: Southern Ohio Medical Center
1805 27th St
Portsmouth OH 45662
740 354-5000

(G-16174)
STAR INC
2625 Gallia St (45662-4805)
PHONE..................................740 354-1517
John Kantz, *President*
John Burke, *Vice Pres*
Nancy Bays, *Manager*
Kelly Hunter, *Director*
EMP: 150
SQ FT: 32,000
SALES: 2.1MM **Privately Held**
SIC: 8331 7349 Job training services; vocational rehabilitation agency; building maintenance services

(G-16175)
**UNITED PARCEL SERVICE INC
OH**
Also Called: UPS
21 Gingersnap Rd (45662-8825)
PHONE..................................740 962-7971
EMP: 316
SALES (corp-wide): 71.8B **Publicly Held**
SIC: 7389 Personal service agents, brokers & bureaus
HQ: United Parcel Service, Inc. (Oh)
55 Glenlake Pkwy
Atlanta GA 30328
404 828-6000

(G-16176)
**UNITED SCOTO SENIOR
ACTIVITIES (PA)**
Also Called: SENIOR CITIZENS CENTER
117 Market St 119 (45662)
P.O. Box 597 (45662-0597)
PHONE..................................740 354-6672
Chester Neff, *President*
Laurna Garlinger, *Principal*
Renee Ellis, *Director*
EMP: 32
SALES: 688.4K **Privately Held**
SIC: 8322 8111 7349 5812 Senior citizens' center or association; legal services; building maintenance services; eating places; local passenger transportation; local & suburban transit

(G-16177)
**UNITY I HOME HEALTHCARE
LLC**
221 Market St (45662-3831)
PHONE..................................740 351-0500
Trish Larkin,
EMP: 30
SQ FT: 1,926
SALES (est): 1.5MM **Privately Held**
SIC: 8082 Home health care services

(G-16178)
**US BANK NATIONAL
ASSOCIATION**
Also Called: US Bank
602 Chillicothe St Frnt (45662-4095)
P.O. Box 1151 (45662-1151)
PHONE..................................740 353-4151
James Barrett, *Manager*
EMP: 25
SALES (corp-wide): 25.7B **Publicly Held**
WEB: www.firstar.com
SIC: 6021 National commercial banks
HQ: U.S. Bank National Association
425 Walnut St Fl 14
Cincinnati OH 45202
513 632-4234

(G-16179)
USSA INC
Also Called: Golden Buckeye Program
117 119 Market St (45662)
P.O. Box 597 (45662-0597)
PHONE..................................740 354-6672
Lorna Garlinger, *Principal*
Renee Ellis, *Exec Dir*
EMP: 34
SALES (est): 1.3MM **Privately Held**
SIC: 8322 8082 7299 Social service center; home health care services; personal appearance services

(G-16180)
**VALLEY WHOLESALE FOODS
INC (PA)**
Also Called: V F
415 Market St (45662-3834)
P.O. Box 1281 (45662-1281)
PHONE..................................740 354-5216
Ernest J Vastine Sr, *President*
Jay Vastine, *Principal*
Jim Vastine, *Principal*
Zack Vastine, *Principal*
Kristi Vastine-Mckenzie, *Principal*
EMP: 35
SQ FT: 40,000
SALES (est): 17.1MM **Privately Held**
SIC: 5141 Food brokers

(G-16181)
**WESTERN & SOUTHERN LF
INSUR CO**
35 Bierly Rd Ste 1 (45662-8503)
PHONE..................................740 354-2848
David Carle, *Manager*
Dave Carle, *Manager*
EMP: 32 **Privately Held**
SIC: 6411 Life insurance agents
HQ: The Western & Southern Life Insurance Company
400 Broadway St
Cincinnati OH 45202
513 629-1800

(G-16182)
**ZEBU COMPLIANCE SOLUTIONS
LLC**
609 2nd St Unit 2 (45662-3974)
PHONE..................................740 355-9029
Francesca Hartop, *President*
EMP: 25
SALES (est): 371.6K
SALES (corp-wide): 7.3MM **Privately
Held**
SIC: 7389 Financial services
PA: United Claim Solutions Llc
23048 N 15th Ave
Phoenix AZ 85027
602 863-1651

Powell
Delaware County

(G-16183)
ADVOCATE RADIOLOGY BIL
10567 Swmill Pkwy Ste 100 (43065)
PHONE..................................614 210-1885
Kirk Reinitz, *President*
Samuel J Merandi, *Principal*
Mike Nicholas, *Opers Staff*
Ashley Petiya, *Human Res Mgr*
Ashley Lavin, *Marketing Mgr*
EMP: 169
SALES (est): 20.7MM **Privately Held**
SIC: 8011 Radiologist

(G-16184)
ARMADA LTD
23 Clairedan Dr (43065-8064)
PHONE..................................614 505-7256
Thomas Foos, *President*
Jeff Podracky, *Admin Sec*
Tim McVey, *Sr Associate*
EMP: 70
SALES (est): 6.1MM **Privately Held**
WEB: www.armadausa.com
SIC: 8742 Management consulting services

(G-16185)
AT&T CORP
10654 Brettridge Dr (43065-7860)
PHONE..................................614 271-8911
EMP: 105
SALES (corp-wide): 170.7B **Publicly
Held**
SIC: 4813 Telephone communication, except radio
HQ: At&T Corp.
1 At&T Way
Bedminster NJ 07921
800 403-3302

(G-16186)
**BOENNING & SCATTERGOOD
INC**
9922 Brewster Ln (43065-7571)
PHONE..................................614 336-8851
Cortney Hart, *Manager*
EMP: 43
SALES (corp-wide): 63.5MM **Privately
Held**
SIC: 8742 Management Consulting Services
PA: Boenning & Scattergood Inc.
200 Barr Harbor Dr # 300
Conshohocken PA 19428
610 832-1212

(G-16187)
**BROADVIEW MORTGAGE
COMPANY (PA)**
3982 Powell Rd Ste 230 (43065-7662)
PHONE..................................614 854-7000
Steve Schenck, *President*
Steven K Hartzler, *Chairman*
John C Rosenberger, *Admin Sec*
EMP: 58
SQ FT: 10,000
SALES (est): 6.5MM **Privately Held**
WEB: www.aemc.cc
SIC: 6162 Mortgage bankers

(G-16188)
CLICK4CARE INC
50 S Liberty St Ste 200 (43065-4006)
PHONE..................................614 431-3700
Rob Gillette, *CEO*
EMP: 65
SQ FT: 10,000
SALES (est): 5.7MM
SALES (corp-wide): 32MM **Privately
Held**
WEB: www.click4care.com
SIC: 7371 Computer software systems analysis & design, custom
PA: Healthedge Software, Inc.
30 Corporate Dr Ste 150
Burlington MA 01803
781 285-1300

(G-16189)
COCHRAN ELECTRIC INC
Also Called: Cochran W R Industrial Elc
90 Grace Dr (43065-9331)
PHONE..................................614 847-0035
Donna E Cochran, *President*
Carol Cameron, *COO*
William R Cochran, *Vice Pres*
Dan Walker, *Project Mgr*
EMP: 25
SQ FT: 10,000
SALES (est): 3.7MM **Privately Held**
SIC: 1731 General electrical contractor

(G-16190)
**COLUMBUS ZOOLOGICAL PARK
ASSN (PA)**
Also Called: Columbus Zoo and Aquarium
4850 Powell Rd (43065-7288)
P.O. Box 400 (43065-0400)
PHONE..................................614 645-3400
Tom Stalf, *President*
John Gannon, *Senior VP*
Lewis Greene, *Senior VP*
Terri Kepes, *Senior VP*
Greg Bell, *CFO*
EMP: 200
SQ FT: 25,000
SALES: 85MM **Privately Held**
WEB: www.czda.org
SIC: 8422 5947 7992 Zoological garden, noncommercial; gift shop; public golf courses

(G-16191)
COMPREHENSIVE MED DATA MGT LLC
Also Called: Cmdm
9980 Brewster Ln Ste 100 (43065-7278)
PHONE..................................614 717-9840
Dan Crocker, *Owner*
Kirk Reinitz, *Principal*
Susan Bolton, *Controller*
EMP: 65
SQ FT: 22,000
SALES (est): 2.4MM **Privately Held**
WEB: www.cmdm.com
SIC: 8721 Billing & bookkeeping service

(G-16192)
CONTINENTAL GL SLS & INV GROUP
Also Called: Continental Group
315 Ashmoore Ct (43065-7486)
P.O. Box 1764 (43065-1764)
PHONE..................................614 679-1201
Sean Snyder, *Partner*
Chris Snyder, *Partner*
Mark McClain, *Vice Pres*
▲ EMP: 400
SQ FT: 100,000
SALES (est): 33.7MM **Privately Held**
SIC: 3441 7011 3211 Fabricated structural metal; hotels; structural glass

(G-16193)
CTV MEDIA INC (PA)
1490 Manning Pkwy (43065-9171)
PHONE..................................614 848-5800
Kathryn C Dixon, *President*
Scott Mangini, *Vice Pres*
Abigail Levi, *Buyer*
Emil Stackpoole, *Buyer*
Laura Huber, *Research*
EMP: 30 EST: 1980
SQ FT: 20,000
SALES (est): 8.8MM **Privately Held**
WEB: www.ctvmedia.com
SIC: 7313 7319 Electronic media advertising representatives; media buying service

(G-16194)
FIRST COMMONWEALTH BANK
10149 Brewster Ln (43065-7571)
PHONE..................................614 336-2280
Fred Fowler, *Branch Mgr*
EMP: 27
SALES (corp-wide): 380.8MM **Publicly Held**
SIC: 6021 National commercial banks
HQ: First Commonwealth Bank
601 Philadelphia St
Indiana PA 15701
724 349-7220

(G-16195)
GANZHORN SUITES INC
10272 Sawmill Pkwy (43065-9189)
PHONE..................................614 356-9810
Eleanor Alvarez, *President*
EMP: 65 EST: 2015
SALES (est): 1.8MM **Privately Held**
SIC: 8322 Old age assistance

(G-16196)
GS OHIO INC
Also Called: Maple Lee Greenhouse
8573 Owenfield Dr (43065-9835)
PHONE..................................614 885-5350
George S Davis, *Ch of Bd*
Charles Davis, *President*
Steven Davis, *Vice Pres*
Leza Cutforth, *Treasurer*
Sherrie Robinson, *Admin Sec*
EMP: 90
SQ FT: 17,000
SALES (est): 3MM **Privately Held**
SIC: 5992 5947 5193 5261 Flowers, fresh; gift shop; flowers, fresh; florists' supplies; nurseries & garden centers

(G-16197)
IMPROVEDGE LLC
9878 Brewster Ln 210 (43065-7980)
PHONE..................................614 793-1738
Karen H Majidzadeh,
EMP: 25

SALES (est): 1.4MM **Privately Held**
WEB: www.improvedge.com
SIC: 8748 7389 Business consulting;

(G-16198)
JBENTLEY STUDIO & SPA LLC
8882 Moreland St (43065-6678)
PHONE..................................614 790-8828
John Paton,
Kelsey Mason, *Graphic Designe*
EMP: 55
SQ FT: 7,500
SALES (est): 1.2MM **Privately Held**
SIC: 7231 7991 Unisex hair salons; spas

(G-16199)
JPMORGAN CHASE BANK NAT ASSN
4066 Powell Rd (43065-7898)
PHONE..................................614 248-3315
Elaine Borling, *Branch Mgr*
EMP: 26
SALES (corp-wide): 131.4B **Publicly Held**
WEB: www.chasebank.com
SIC: 6029 Commercial banks
HQ: Jpmorgan Chase Bank, National Association
1111 Polaris Pkwy
Columbus OH 43240
614 436-3055

(G-16200)
KAISER CONSULTING LLC
818 Riverbend Ave (43065-7067)
PHONE..................................614 378-5361
Lori Kaiser, *Mng Member*
EMP: 50
SALES (est): 1.8MM **Privately Held**
SIC: 8721 8742 Accounting, auditing & bookkeeping; financial consultant

(G-16201)
KF EXPRESS LLC
10440 Delwood Pl (43065-7896)
PHONE..................................614 258-8858
Kevin Flaherty, *President*
Chris Henneforth, *Mng Member*
EMP: 35
SQ FT: 6,500
SALES (est): 6MM **Privately Held**
SIC: 4212 4213 Local trucking, without storage; trucking, except local

(G-16202)
KINSALE GOLF & FITNES CLB LLC
3737 Village Club Dr (43065-8196)
PHONE..................................740 881-6500
Donald Kenny, *Mng Member*
EMP: 189
SQ FT: 1,537
SALES (est): 12.1MM **Privately Held**
WEB: www.golfkinsale.com
SIC: 7992 7991 Public golf courses; health club

(G-16203)
MKC ASSOCIATES INC
90 Hidden Ravines Dr (43065-8736)
PHONE..................................740 657-3202
Patrick Carroll, *Branch Mgr*
EMP: 31
SALES (corp-wide): 6MM **Privately Held**
WEB: www.mkcinc.com
SIC: 8712 8711 Architectural engineering; engineering services
PA: Mkc Associates, Inc.
40 W 4th St
Mansfield OH
419 525-1102

(G-16204)
NEW PATH INTERNATIONAL LLC
1476 Manning Pkwy Ste A (43065-7295)
PHONE..................................614 410-3974
Damon Canfield, *Mng Member*
Neil Macivor,
▲ EMP: 50
SQ FT: 13,000

SALES (est): 8.1MM **Privately Held**
WEB: www.npi.com
SIC: 3639 7389 8711 Major kitchen appliances, except refrigerators & stoves; design, commercial & industrial; engineering services

(G-16205)
PRIMROSE SCHOOL AT GOLF VLG
8771 Moreland St (43065-7177)
PHONE..................................740 881-5830
CAM Struck, *Owner*
EMP: 30
SALES (est): 774.1K **Privately Held**
SIC: 8351 Preschool center

(G-16206)
RICHARD ALLEN GROUP LLC (PA)
391 Glenside Ln (43065-9484)
PHONE..................................614 623-2654
Roy Johnson,
EMP: 100
SALES: 22MM **Privately Held**
SIC: 7389 6282 ; futures advisory service

(G-16207)
ROLLS REALTY
6706 Harriott Rd (43065-8408)
PHONE..................................614 792-5662
Christopher Gregory, *President*
EMP: 35
SALES (est): 1.9MM **Privately Held**
SIC: 6531 Real estate agent, residential; real estate brokers & agents

(G-16208)
SCIOTO RESERVE INC (PA)
Also Called: Scioto Reserve Golf & Athc CLB
7383 Scioto Pkwy (43065-7956)
PHONE..................................740 881-9082
Joe Bush, *General Mgr*
Regan Koivesto, *Principal*
Jeff Olson, *Principal*
Andy Montgomery, *Opers Staff*
Ann Marie Brockman, *Director*
EMP: 81 EST: 1990
SALES (est): 7.3MM **Privately Held**
WEB: www.sciotoreserve.com
SIC: 7992 7997 7991 Public golf courses; membership sports & recreation clubs; physical fitness facilities

(G-16209)
SCIOTO RESERVE INC
Also Called: Scioto Reserve Country Club
3982 Powell Rd Ste 332 (43065-7662)
PHONE..................................740 881-6500
EMP: 79
SALES (corp-wide): 7.3MM **Privately Held**
SIC: 7992 Public golf courses
PA: Scioto Reserve, Inc.
7383 Scioto Pkwy
Powell OH 43065
740 881-9082

(G-16210)
SEARCH 2 CLOSE COLUMBUS LTD (PA)
10254 Sawmill Pkwy (43065-9189)
PHONE..................................614 389-5353
Kevin Alexander,
Brooke Munekata,
EMP: 25
SQ FT: 6,000
SALES (est): 2.2MM **Privately Held**
WEB: www.search2close.com
SIC: 6541 Title abstract offices

(G-16211)
SMOKY ROW CHILDRENS CENTER
8615 Smoky Row Rd (43065-9201)
PHONE..................................614 766-2122
Judy Chosy, *Owner*
EMP: 30
SALES (est): 978.8K **Privately Held**
SIC: 8351 Preschool center

(G-16212)
W R SHEPHERD INC (PA)
390 W Olentangy St (43065-8716)
PHONE..................................614 889-2896

William R Shepherd, *President*
Sharon Shepherd, *Corp Secy*
Brad Shepperd, *Vice Pres*
EMP: 50
SQ FT: 4,000
SALES (est): 2.3MM **Privately Held**
SIC: 1752 Floor laying & floor work

(G-16213)
WEDGEWOOD GOLF & COUNTRY CLUB
9600 Wedgewood Blvd (43065-8788)
PHONE..................................614 793-9600
James Simonton, *President*
Matt Neff, *Superintendent*
Pat Dugan, *Vice Pres*
Steve Jackson, *Vice Pres*
Lee Slone, *Facilities Mgr*
EMP: 140
SQ FT: 43,500
SALES (est): 7.4MM **Privately Held**
SIC: 7997 Country club, membership

Powhatan Point
Belmont County

(G-16214)
COAL SERVICES INC
Also Called: Coal Services Group
155 Highway 7 S (43942-1033)
PHONE..................................740 795-5220
Don Gentry, *President*
Michael O McKown, *Principal*
Robert Moore, *Principal*
Bonnie Froehlich, *Manager*
EMP: 90
SALES (est): 12MM
SALES (corp-wide): 4.8B **Publicly Held**
WEB: www.coalservices.com
SIC: 8741 8711 1231 1222 Management services; engineering services; anthracite mining; bituminous coal-underground mining; bituminous coal & lignite-surface mining; coal mining services
HQ: The American Coal Company
9085 Highway 34 N
Galatia IL 62935
618 268-6311

Proctorville
Lawrence County

(G-16215)
A&L HOME CARE & TRAINING CTR
6101 County Road 107 (45669-5022)
P.O. Box 1010 (45669-1010)
PHONE..................................740 886-7623
Dawnetta Abbett, *Owner*
EMP: 160
SALES (est): 2.2MM **Privately Held**
SIC: 8361 Residential care

(G-16216)
FORTHS FOODS INC
Also Called: Proctorville Food Fair
7604 County Road 107 (45669-8173)
PHONE..................................740 886-9769
Don Plybon, *Manager*
EMP: 48
SALES (corp-wide): 99.8MM **Privately Held**
WEB: www.foodfairmarkets.com
SIC: 5141 5411 Groceries, general line; grocery stores
PA: Forth's Foods, Inc.
3090 Woodville Dr
Huntington WV 25701
304 525-3293

(G-16217)
HOLZER CLINIC LLC
Also Called: Holzer Clinic Lawrence County
98 State St (45669-8163)
P.O. Box 646 (45669-0646)
PHONE..................................740 886-9403
Nathan Miller, *Manager*
EMP: 26

SALES (corp-wide): 323.8MM **Privately Held**
WEB: www.holzerclinic.com
SIC: 8011 8049 General & family practice, physician/surgeon; physical therapist
HQ: Holzer Clinic Llc
    90 Jackson Pike
    Gallipolis OH 45631
    740 446-5411

(G-16218)
KINDER KARE DAY NURSERY
627 County Road 411 (45669-9407)
PHONE..................................740 886-6905
Aimee Sites, *Director*
Amiee Sites, *Director*
EMP: 25
SALES (est): 393K **Privately Held**
SIC: 8351 Group day care center

(G-16219)
SUPERIOR MARINE WAYS INC
5852 County Rd 1 Suoth Pt (45669)
P.O. Box 519 (45669-0519)
PHONE..................................740 894-6224
Dale Manns, *Manager*
EMP: 120
SALES (corp-wide): 16.3MM **Privately Held**
WEB: www.superiormarine.on.ca
SIC: 3731 7699 Barges, building & repairing; boat repair
PA: Superior Marine Ways, Inc.
    5852 County Road 1
    South Point OH 45680
    740 894-6224

(G-16220)
THERMAL SOLUTIONS INC
9329 County Road 107 (45669-8732)
P.O. Box 661 (45669-0661)
PHONE..................................740 886-2861
John Stevens, *President*
Tommy Crank, *Project Mgr*
John Browning, *CFO*
EMP: 100
SQ FT: 1,200
SALES (est): 14.6MM **Privately Held**
SIC: 1742 1799 Insulation, buildings; fireproofing buildings

Prospect
Marion County

(G-16221)
CUMMINS BUILDING MAINT INC
5202 Marion Waldo Rd (43342-9758)
P.O. Box 350, Waldo (43356-0350)
PHONE..................................740 726-9800
Ronald H Cummins, *CEO*
Myra Cummins, *CFO*
Missy Haas, *Accounts Mgr*
EMP: 70
SALES (est): 1.5MM **Privately Held**
WEB: www.cumminsmaint.com
SIC: 7349 1721 Janitorial service, contract basis; painting & paper hanging

(G-16222)
CUMMINS FACILITY SERVICES LLC
5202 Marion Waldo Rd (43342-9758)
P.O. Box 350, Waldo (43356-0350)
PHONE..................................740 726-9800
Missy Haas, *VP Admin*
Jill Frey, *Mng Member*
Vernon Barry, *Supervisor*
Dawn Murr, *Supervisor*
Chris Osborne, *Officer*
EMP: 350
SALES (est): 6.4MM **Privately Held**
SIC: 7349 Cleaning service, industrial or commercial

(G-16223)
FLEMING CONSTRUCTION CO
Also Called: Scioto Sand & Gravel
5298 Marion Marysville Rd (43342-9342)
P.O. Box 31, Marion (43301-0031)
PHONE..................................740 494-2177
Gerald E Fleming, *President*
Sonya Fleming, *Vice Pres*
EMP: 35

SQ FT: 2,400
SALES (est): 6.7MM **Privately Held**
SIC: 1542 1541 1623 1442 Commercial & office building, new construction; industrial buildings, new construction; sewer line construction; gravel mining; excavation & grading, building construction

Put In Bay
Ottawa County

(G-16224)
CAPITAL CITY INDUS SYSTEMS LLC
1494 Langram Rd (43456-6721)
PHONE..................................614 519-5047
Dennis Bryant, *President*
EMP: 25
SALES (est): 697.2K **Privately Held**
SIC: 8748 Business consulting

(G-16225)
ISLAND BIKE RENTAL INC
2071 Langram Rd (43456)
PHONE..................................419 285-2016
Charles Duggan, *President*
Mike Steidl, *Manager*
EMP: 25
SALES (est): 1MM **Privately Held**
WEB: www.islandbikerental.com
SIC: 7999 Bicycle rental

(G-16226)
ISLAND SERVICE COMPANY
Also Called: Middle Bass Ferry Company, The
341 Bayview Ave (43456-5503)
P.O. Box 360 (43456-0360)
PHONE..................................419 285-3695
Marvin Booker, *CEO*
Pat Thwaite, *Treasurer*
EMP: 130
SQ FT: 250,000
SALES (est): 4.8MM **Privately Held**
WEB: www.the-boardwalk.com
SIC: 5812 5541 7997 4493 Eating places; marine service station; boating club, membership; marinas; cocktail lounge; management services

(G-16227)
MILLER BOAT LINE INC (PA)
Also Called: ISLAND VIEW GIFTS
535 Bayview Ave (43456-6524)
PHONE..................................419 285-2421
William C Market, *President*
Mary Ann Market, *Vice Pres*
Scott E Market, *VP Opers*
Julene Marie Market, *Treasurer*
EMP: 57
SQ FT: 1,800
SALES (est): 10.1MM **Privately Held**
WEB: www.millerferry.com
SIC: 4482 5947 Ferries; gift, novelty & souvenir shop

(G-16228)
PUT IN BAY TRANSPORTATION
2009 Langram Rd (43456-6734)
P.O. Box 190 (43456-0190)
PHONE..................................419 285-4855
Charles Duggan, *President*
Dianne Duggan, *Principal*
EMP: 25
SALES (est): 1MM **Privately Held**
WEB: www.put-in-bay-trans.com
SIC: 4142 Bus charter service, except local

Racine
Meigs County

(G-16229)
J D DRILLING CO
107 S 3rd St (45771-9552)
P.O. Box 369 (45771-0369)
PHONE..................................740 949-2512
James E Diddle, *President*
EMP: 25
SQ FT: 6,000
SALES (est): 3.8MM **Privately Held**
SIC: 1381 Drilling oil & gas wells

Randolph
Portage County

(G-16230)
EAST MANUFACTURING CORPORATION (PA)
1871 State Rte 44 (44265)
P.O. Box 277 (44265-0277)
PHONE..................................330 325-9921
Howard D Booher, *CEO*
David De Poincy, *President*
Mark T Tate, *Corp Secy*
Robert J Bruce, *Vice Pres*
Charlie Wells, *Vice Pres*
▼ EMP: 267
SQ FT: 350,000
SALES (est): 68.3MM **Privately Held**
WEB: www.eastmfg.com
SIC: 3715 5013 7539 Trailer bodies; truck parts & accessories; automotive repair shops

(G-16231)
JPMORGAN CHASE BANK NAT ASSN
4000 Waterloo Rd (44265)
P.O. Box 186 (44265-0186)
PHONE..................................330 325-7855
Peggy Tyrakowski, *Manager*
EMP: 26
SALES (corp-wide): 131.4B **Publicly Held**
WEB: www.chase.com
SIC: 6029 Commercial banks
HQ: Jpmorgan Chase Bank, National Association
    1111 Polaris Pkwy
    Columbus OH 43240
    614 436-3055

Ravenna
Portage County

(G-16232)
AMANDAS PLAYROOM INC (PA)
Also Called: Amanda's Garden
6709 Cleveland Rd (44266-1847)
PHONE..................................330 296-3934
Linda McClellan, *President*
Robbie McClellan, *Admin Sec*
EMP: 26
SQ FT: 6,000
SALES: 549K **Privately Held**
SIC: 8351 Preschool center

(G-16233)
BUCKEYE RSDNTIAL SOLUTIONS LLC
320 E Main St Ste 301 (44266-3102)
PHONE..................................330 235-9183
Chad Konkle, *CEO*
Matthew Ferrell, *CFO*
Paul Lynn, *Officer*
EMP: 75 EST: 2012
SQ FT: 12,000
SALES (est): 215K **Privately Held**
SIC: 8082 Home health care services

(G-16234)
CARDIOLOGY SPECIALISTS INC
6847 N Chestnut St # 100 (44266-3929)
PHONE..................................330 297-6110
A R Tsai MD, *President*
Leslie Tobias, *Vice Pres*
EMP: 32
SALES (est): 1.1MM **Privately Held**
SIC: 8011 Cardiologist & cardio-vascular specialist

(G-16235)
CHEMICAL BANK
999 E Main St (44266-3325)
PHONE..................................330 298-0510
Lisa Lee, *Manager*
EMP: 70

SALES (corp-wide): 924.5MM **Publicly Held**
WEB: www.dlkbank.com
SIC: 6035 Federal savings & loan associations; federal savings banks
HQ: Chemical Bank
    333 E Main St
    Midland MI 48640
    989 631-9200

(G-16236)
COLEMAN PROFESSIONAL SVCS INC
3920 Lovers Ln (44266-4200)
PHONE..................................330 296-8313
Nelson Burns, *CEO*
EMP: 70
SALES (est): 1.1MM
SALES (corp-wide): 51.3MM **Privately Held**
SIC: 8093 8049 Mental health clinic, outpatient; clinical psychologist
PA: Coleman Professional Services, Inc.
    5982 Rhodes Rd
    Kent OH 44240
    330 673-1347

(G-16237)
COMPETITIVE INTERIORS INC
625 Enterprise Pkwy (44266-8058)
PHONE..................................330 297-1281
Paul Cunningham, *President*
Nancy Cunningham, *Vice Pres*
Erik Cunningham, *Project Mgr*
Mike Ricketson, *Warehouse Mgr*
Don Denbow, *Foreman/Supr*
EMP: 120
SQ FT: 5,104
SALES (est): 13.1MM **Privately Held**
WEB: www.competitiveinteriors.com
SIC: 1751 1742 Carpentry work; drywall

(G-16238)
COUNTY OF PORTAGE
Also Called: Portage County Engineer Office
5000 Newton Falls Rd (44266-9602)
PHONE..................................330 296-6411
Don Van Metre, *Superintendent*
Tom Medzie, *Purch Mgr*
Stan Carlisle, *Sales Staff*
Michael Marozzi, *Manager*
Mary Smith, *Director*
EMP: 65 **Privately Held**
WEB: www.portageprosecutor.com
SIC: 8711 1611 0782 Engineering services; highway & street construction; lawn & garden services
PA: County Of Portage
    449 S Meridian St Fl 7
    Ravenna OH 44266
    330 297-3561

(G-16239)
COUNTY OF PORTAGE
Sanitary Engineer
449 S Meridian St Fl 3 (44266-2914)
P.O. Box 1217 (44266-1217)
PHONE..................................330 297-3670
John Vence, *Design Engr*
Harold G Huff, *Director*
John Evans, *Technician*
EMP: 40 **Privately Held**
WEB: www.portageprosecutor.com
SIC: 4953 Refuse systems
PA: County Of Portage
    449 S Meridian St Fl 7
    Ravenna OH 44266
    330 297-3561

(G-16240)
COUNTY OF PORTAGE
Prosecuting Attorney's Office
466 S Chestnut St (44266-3006)
PHONE..................................330 297-3850
Victor Valuchi, *Principal*
Jennifer E Redman,
Sean Scahill,
EMP: 40 **Privately Held**
WEB: www.portageprosecutor.com
SIC: 9222 8111 Public prosecutors' offices; legal services
PA: County Of Portage
    449 S Meridian St Fl 7
    Ravenna OH 44266
    330 297-3561

(G-16241)
CUTLER REAL ESTATE
525 N Scranton St (44266-1429)
PHONE...................................330 733-7575
EMP: 60
SALES (corp-wide): 5.3MM Privately
Held
SIC: 6531 Real estate agent, residential
PA: Cutler Real Estate
2800 W Market St
Fairlawn OH 44333
330 836-9141

(G-16242)
ECLIPSE BLIND SYSTEMS INC
7154 State Route 88 (44266-9189)
PHONE...................................330 296-0112
James W Watson, President
Dennis Miller, Purchasing
EMP: 165
SQ FT: 110,000
SALES (est): 15.2MM Privately Held
SIC: 3089 7371 Extruded finished plastic
products; custom computer programming
services
HQ: Turnils (Uk) Limited
10 Fountain Crescent Inchinnan Busi-
ness Park
Renfrew PA4 9
141 812-3322

(G-16243)
**FAMILY CMNTY SVCS PORTAGE
CNTY**
Also Called: FAMILIES THAT WORK
705 Oakwood St (44266-2191)
PHONE...................................330 297-0078
Greg Musci, Finance Dir
Mark Srisone, Exec Dir
Mark Frisone, Exec Dir
Tom Albanese, Associate Dir
EMP: 110
SQ FT: 800
SALES: 8.1MM Privately Held
SIC: 8322 Individual & family services

(G-16244)
GOLDEN LIVING LLC
Also Called: Beverly
565 Bryn Mawr St (44266-9696)
PHONE...................................330 297-5781
Debbie Shrieve, Director
EMP: 150
SALES (corp-wide): 7.4MM Privately
Held
SIC: 8059 8052 8051 Convalescent
home; intermediate care facilities; skilled
nursing care facilities
PA: Golden Living Llc
5220 Tennyson Pkwy # 400
Plano TX 75024
972 372-6300

(G-16245)
HAASZ AUTOMALL LLC
4886 State Route 59 (44266-8838)
PHONE...................................330 296-2866
Kevin Haasz, President
Heather Mayle, Business Mgr
Mary Scott, Finance Mgr
Justin Bracken, Sales Mgr
Christine Cosma, Sales Mgr
EMP: 38
SALES (est): 5.6MM Privately Held
SIC: 5531 7539 Automotive parts; auto-
motive repair shops

(G-16246)
**HUMMEL CONSTRUCTION
COMPANY**
127 E Main St (44266-3103)
PHONE...................................330 274-8584
Eric W Hummel, President
Marty Snode, Vice Pres
Ronald Ayers, Controller
EMP: 40 EST: 1971
SQ FT: 5,000
SALES (est): 10.2MM Privately Held
WEB: www.hummelconstruction.com
SIC: 1542 Commercial & office building,
new construction

(G-16247)
**INDEPENDENCE FOUNDATION
INC**
161 E Main St (44266-3129)
PHONE...................................330 296-2851
Anna Barrett, Exec Dir
EMP: 134
SALES: 254.5K
SALES (corp-wide): 4.3MM Privately
Held
SIC: 8641 Civic social & fraternal associa-
tions
PA: Independence Of Portage County Inc
161 E Main St
Ravenna OH 44266
330 296-2851

(G-16248)
**KENMORE RESEARCH
COMPANY**
935 N Freedom St (44266-2496)
PHONE...................................330 297-1407
Gave Moorehouse, Branch Mgr
EMP: 100
SALES (corp-wide): 940.1MM Privately
Held
SIC: 8731 8734 Commercial physical re-
search; testing laboratories
HQ: Kenmore Research Company
29500 Solon Rd
Cleveland OH 44139
440 248-4600

(G-16249)
**LONGMEADOW CARE CENTER
INC**
565 Bryn Mawr St (44266-9696)
PHONE...................................330 297-5781
Dave Cruser, Principal
EMP: 120
SALES (est): 5.5MM Privately Held
SIC: 8052 Intermediate care facilities

(G-16250)
**NEIGHBORHOOD
DEVELOPMENT SVCS**
Also Called: Nds
120 E Main St (44266-3104)
PHONE...................................330 296-2003
William Hale, CEO
David Vauthan, President
Michael Bogo, President
Stacy Brown, President
EMP: 30
SQ FT: 1,500
SALES: 5.7MM Privately Held
SIC: 8399 8742 8641 Community devel-
opment groups; financial consultant; civic
social & fraternal associations

(G-16251)
**NON EMERGENCY AMBULANCE
SVC**
4830 Harding Ave (44266-8813)
PHONE...................................330 296-4541
Robert Turley, President
EMP: 25
SALES (est): 787.2K Privately Held
SIC: 4119 Ambulance service

(G-16252)
PARIS CLEANERS INC
Also Called: Paris Healthcare Linen
650 Enterprise Pkwy (44266-8054)
PHONE...................................330 296-3300
Lisa Long, Human Res Dir
Sean Flanders, Branch Mgr
Janet Bland, Supervisor
EMP: 150
SALES (corp-wide): 67.2MM Privately
Held
WEB: www.parisco.com
SIC: 7213 Uniform supply
PA: Paris Cleaners, Inc.
67 Hoover Ave
Du Bois PA 15801
814 375-9700

(G-16253)
**PORTAGE BANCSHARES INC
(PA)**
Also Called: Portage Community Bank
1311 E Main St (44266-3329)
PHONE...................................330 296-8090

Richard Coe, President
Connie Bennett, President
Jill Conard, President
Kevin Lewis, Officer
EMP: 85
SQ FT: 10,000 Privately Held
WEB: www.pcbbank.com
SIC: 6712 Bank holding companies

(G-16254)
**PORTAGE COMMUNITY BANK
INC (HQ)**
1311 E Main St (44266-3329)
PHONE...................................330 296-8090
Donald Herman, CEO
Richard Coe, President
John Forberg, COO
Deb Bish, Vice Pres
Tom Cargo, Vice Pres
EMP: 55
SALES: 13.9MM Privately Held
WEB: www.portagecommunitybank.com
SIC: 6022 State commercial banks
PA: Portage Bancshares Inc
1311 E Main St
Ravenna OH 44266
330 296-8090

(G-16255)
PORTAGE COUNTY BOARD
Also Called: Happy Day School
2500 Brady Lake Rd (44266-1610)
PHONE...................................330 678-2400
Gail McAlister, Principal
EMP: 80
SALES (corp-wide): 21.5MM Privately
Held
SIC: 8322 Social services for the handi-
capped
PA: Portage County Board Of Developmen-
tal Disabilities
2606 Brady Lake Rd
Ravenna OH 44266
330 297-6209

(G-16256)
PORTAGE COUNTY BOARD (PA)
2606 Brady Lake Rd (44266-1604)
PHONE...................................330 297-6209
Patrick Macke, Superintendent
Dennis Coble, Principal
Tim Torch, HR Admin
Diane Cotton, Executive
EMP: 34
SALES: 21.5MM Privately Held
SIC: 8361 Home for the mentally handi-
capped; residential care for the handi-
capped

(G-16257)
PORTAGE INDUSTRIES INC
7008 State Route 88 (44266-9134)
PHONE...................................330 296-3996
Philip Miller, President
Jaime Nichols, Manager
EMP: 200
SQ FT: 48,000
SALES: 1.7MM Privately Held
WEB: www.portageind.org
SIC: 8331 Sheltered workshop

(G-16258)
PORTAGE PEDIATRICS
6847 N Chestnut St # 200 (44266-3929)
PHONE...................................330 297-8824
Cheryl Kemerer, Principal
EMP: 40
SALES (est): 1.2MM Privately Held
SIC: 8011 Pediatrician

(G-16259)
PORTAGE PRIVATE INDUSTRY
Also Called: PORTAGE LEARNING CEN-
TERS
145 N Chestnut St Lowr (44266-4008)
PHONE...................................330 297-7795
James Tinnin, Chairman
Suzanne Livinggood, Exec Dir
Karen Johnson, Director
Rebecca Gorczyca, Admin Sec
EMP: 70
SALES: 3.3MM Privately Held
SIC: 8351 8331 Head start center, except
in conjunction with school; job training
services

(G-16260)
**RAVENNA ASSEMBLY OF GOD
INC**
6401 State Route 14 (44266-9692)
PHONE...................................330 297-1493
Gary Beck, Pastor
EMP: 39
SQ FT: 25,000
SALES: 800K Privately Held
WEB: www.ravennaag.com
SIC: 8661 8211 8351 Pentecostal
Church; elementary & secondary schools;
child day care services

(G-16261)
REHAB CENTER
Also Called: Rehabcenter
6847 N Chestnut St (44266-3929)
P.O. Box 1204 (44266-1204)
PHONE...................................330 297-2770
Stephen Colecchi, CEO
David Baldwin, Principal
Richard E Clough, COO
Linda Breedlove, Vice Pres
EMP: 28
SALES (est): 735.4K Privately Held
WEB: www.rmh2.org
SIC: 8049 8093 Physical therapist; reha-
bilitation center, outpatient treatment

(G-16262)
**ROBINSON HEALTH SYSTEM
INC**
Also Called: Robinson Surgery Center
6847 N Chestnut St (44266-3929)
PHONE...................................330 678-4100
Janis Barnes, Director
EMP: 25
SALES (corp-wide): 580MM Privately
Held
SIC: 8062 8093 General medical & surgi-
cal hospitals; specialty outpatient clinics
HQ: Robinson Health System, Inc.
6847 N Chestnut St
Ravenna OH 44266
330 297-0811

(G-16263)
**ROBINSON HEALTH SYSTEM
INC (HQ)**
Also Called: University Hosp Prtage Med Ctr
6847 N Chestnut St (44266-3929)
P.O. Box 1204 (44266-1204)
PHONE...................................330 297-0811
Stephen Colecchi, President
Bradley Raum, President
Linda Breedlove, Vice Pres
Neil Everett, Vice Pres
Mandy Moneypenny, Manager
EMP: 1200
SQ FT: 307,000
SALES (est): 222.5MM
SALES (corp-wide): 580MM Privately
Held
SIC: 8062 8011 General medical & surgi-
cal hospitals; offices & clinics of medical
doctors
PA: University Hospitals Health System,
Inc.
3605 Warrensville Ctr Rd
Shaker Heights OH 44122
216 767-8900

(G-16264)
**ROBINSON VISITN NRS
ASOC/HOSPC**
6847 N Chestnut St (44266-3929)
PHONE...................................330 297-8899
Bill Kahl, Exec Dir
EMP: 50
SALES (est): 1.1MM Privately Held
SIC: 8082 Visiting nurse service

(G-16265)
ROOTSTOWN TOWNSHIP
4268 Sandy Lake Rd (44266-9324)
PHONE...................................330 296-8240
Bonnie Howe, Trustee
Diane Dillon, Trustee
Bret Howe, Trustee
EMP: 40
SALES (est): 2.5MM Privately Held
WEB: www.rootstowntwp.com
SIC: 6512 Auditorium & hall operation

GEOGRAPHIC

(G-16266)
SIRNA & SONS INC (PA)
Also Called: Sirna's Market & Deli
7176 State Route 88 (44266-9189)
PHONE...................................330 298-2222
Joseph Sirna, *CEO*
Tom Sirna, *President*
Serena Wagner, *Corp Secy*
Vince Sirna, *Vice Pres*
Troy Bennington, *Opers Mgr*
EMP: 150 **EST:** 1979
SQ FT: 20,000
SALES (est): 133.5MM **Privately Held**
WEB: www.sirnaandsonsproduce.com
SIC: 5148 Fruits, fresh; vegetables, fresh

(G-16267)
SIX C FABRICATION INC
5245 S Prospect St (44266-9032)
PHONE...................................330 296-5594
EMP: 60
SQ FT: 400,000
SALES (est): 2.3MM **Privately Held**
SIC: 1799 1623 5039 Trade Contractor
Water/Sewer/Utility Construction Whol
Construction Materials

(G-16268)
SMITHERS RAPRA INC
Also Called: Compliance Testing
1150 N Freedom St (44266-2457)
PHONE...................................330 297-1495
Tom Cerjak, *General Mgr*
EMP: 25
SQ FT: 30,000
SALES (corp-wide): 63.6MM **Privately Held**
WEB: www.smithersconsulting.com
SIC: 8734 Product testing laboratories
HQ: Smithers Rapra Inc.
425 W Market St
Akron OH 44303
330 762-7441

(G-16269)
TSK ASSISTED LIVING SERVICES
Also Called: Visiting Angels
240 W Riddle Ave (44266-2949)
PHONE...................................330 297-2000
Steven W Kastenhuber, *President*
EMP: 35
SALES (est): 1.1MM **Privately Held**
SIC: 8082 Home health care services

(G-16270)
W POL CONTRACTING INC
4188 Ohio 14 (44266)
PHONE...................................330 325-7177
Wade Pol, *President*
Christine Pol, *Treasurer*
EMP: 26
SQ FT: 6,640
SALES: 6.5MM **Privately Held**
SIC: 1629 Oil refinery construction

(G-16271)
WOODLANDS HEALTHCARE GROUP LLC
Also Called: WoodInds Hlth Rhbilitation Ctr
6831 N Chestnut St (44266-3929)
PHONE...................................330 297-4564
EMP: 40
SALES (corp-wide): 944.2K **Privately Held**
WEB: www.portageprosecutor.com
SIC: 8051 Skilled nursing care facilities
PA: Woodlands Healthcare Group, Llc
6831 N Chestnut St
Ravenna OH 44266
330 297-4564

Rayland
Jefferson County

(G-16272)
HEAVENLY HOME HEALTH
1800 Old State Route 7 (43943-7962)
PHONE...................................740 859-4735
Colin Goff, *Owner*
Karen Dowell, *Co-Owner*
EMP: 30

SALES: 350K **Privately Held**
SIC: 8082 Home health care services

(G-16273)
SHELLY AND SANDS INC
Also Called: Tri-State Asphalt Co
1731 Old State Route 7 (43943-7962)
P.O. Box 66 (43943-0066)
PHONE...................................740 859-2104
Mark Haverty, *General Mgr*
EMP: 60
SALES (corp-wide): 276.3MM **Privately Held**
WEB: www.shellyandsands.com
SIC: 2951 1542 Asphalt paving mixtures & blocks; nonresidential construction
PA: Shelly And Sands, Inc.
3570 S River Rd
Zanesville OH 43701
740 453-0721

(G-16274)
VALLEY HOSPICE INC (PA)
10686 State Route 150 (43943-7847)
PHONE...................................740 859-5041
Karen Nicols, *President*
EMP: 30
SALES: 14.2MM **Privately Held**
WEB: www.valleyhospice.com
SIC: 8051 Skilled nursing care facilities

Raymond
Union County

(G-16275)
HONDA R&D AMERICAS INC
Also Called: Honda Marysville Location
21001 State Route 739 (43067-9705)
PHONE...................................937 644-0439
Noboru Hashimoto, *Branch Mgr*
EMP: 25
SALES (corp-wide): 144.1B **Privately Held**
WEB: www.hra.com
SIC: 8732 Market analysis or research
HQ: Honda R&D Americas, Inc.
1900 Harpers Way
Torrance CA 90501
310 781-5500

Reno
Washington County

(G-16276)
BUCKEYE HILLS-HCK VLY REG DEV
Also Called: Area Agency On Aging
P.O. Box 368 (45773-0368)
PHONE...................................740 373-6400
Maryann Sims, *Human Res Mgr*
Pat Palmer, *Branch Mgr*
EMP: 27
SALES (corp-wide): 232.3K **Privately Held**
WEB: www.buckeyehills.org
SIC: 8082 Home health care services
HQ: Buckeye Hills Hocking Valley Regional
Development District
1400 Pike St
Marietta OH 45750
740 373-0087

(G-16277)
MONDO POLYMER TECHNOLOGIES INC
27620 State Rte 7 (45773)
P.O. Box 250 (45773-0250)
PHONE...................................740 376-9396
Mark Mondo, *President*
Maggie Ellis, *General Mgr*
Judy Mondo, *Vice Pres*
Rick Hockenberry, *Opers Mgr*
Marc Mondo, *QC Mgr*
EMP: 40
SQ FT: 3,200
SALES (est): 15.2MM **Privately Held**
WEB: www.mondopolymer.com
SIC: 4953 2822 Recycling, waste materials; synthetic rubber

Reynoldsburg
Franklin County

(G-16278)
ABACUS CORPORATION
1676 Brice Rd (43068-2704)
PHONE...................................614 367-7000
April Calausi, *Branch Mgr*
EMP: 445
SALES (corp-wide): 234.6MM **Privately Held**
SIC: 7361 Executive placement
PA: Abacus Corporation
610 Gusryan St
Baltimore MD 21224
410 633-1900

(G-16279)
ACCURATE ELECTRIC CNSTR INC
6901 Americana Pkwy (43068-4116)
PHONE...................................614 863-1844
Robert S Beal, *President*
Ralph Stout, *Vice Pres*
Dan Nussbaum, *Project Mgr*
Kevin Ledy, *Human Res Dir*
Joe Schmidt, *Manager*
EMP: 160
SQ FT: 10,000
SALES (est): 31.6MM **Privately Held**
WEB: www.aecohio.com
SIC: 1731 General electrical contractor

(G-16280)
ALLIANCE DATA SYSTEMS CORP
6939 Americana Pkwy (43068-4171)
PHONE...................................614 729-5800
Peg Hansel, *Manager*
Matthew Lazzaro, *Manager*
Angela Risacher, *Manager*
Kelly Kroskie, *Director*
EMP: 160 **Publicly Held**
WEB: www.alliancedatasystems.com
SIC: 7389 Credit card service
PA: Alliance Data Systems Corporation
7500 Dallas Pkwy Ste 700
Plano TX 75024

(G-16281)
AMERICAN CRANE INC
Also Called: American Crane & Lift Trck Svc
7791 Taylor Rd Sw Ste A (43068-9632)
PHONE...................................614 496-2268
Richard W Palmer Jr, *President*
Scott Hughes, *Vice Pres*
Steve Cole, *Marketing Staff*
Bryan McAfee, *Manager*
EMP: 34
SQ FT: 25,000
SALES (est): 4.9MM **Privately Held**
WEB: www.americancraneinc.com
SIC: 7389 7353 5082 Crane & aerial lift service; cranes & aerial lift equipment, rental or leasing; cranes, construction

(G-16282)
AMERICAN JERSEY CATTLE ASSN (PA)
6486 E Main St (43068-2349)
PHONE...................................614 861-3636
Neal Smith, *CEO*
Vickie White, *Treasurer*
EMP: 35
SQ FT: 9,000
SALES: 3.8MM **Privately Held**
WEB: www.infojersey.com
SIC: 8611 Trade associations

(G-16283)
AMERICAN KENDA RBR INDUS LTD (HQ)
Also Called: Kenda USA
7095 Americana Pkwy (43068-4118)
PHONE...................................866 536-3287
CHI-Jen Yang, *President*
Charles Rechter, *Purchasing*
Jeff Pizzola, *CFO*
Ching-Huey Yang, *Treasurer*
Robin Kamal, *Controller*
▲ **EMP:** 45
SQ FT: 100,000

SALES (est): 27.2MM
SALES (corp-wide): 1B **Privately Held**
SIC: 5014 Tires & tubes
PA: Kenda Rubber Ind. Co., Ltd.
146, Chung Shan Rd., Sec. 1,
Yuanlin Chen CHA 51064
483 451-71

(G-16284)
ARMOR PAVING & SEALING
6900 Americana Pkwy (43068-4115)
PHONE...................................614 751-6900
Donald S Trasin, *President*
EMP: 25
SALES (est): 3.9MM **Privately Held**
WEB: www.armorpavingandsealing.com
SIC: 1611 Highway & street paving contractor; surfacing & paving

(G-16285)
BILLING CONNECTION INC
6422 E Main St Ste 202 (43068-2302)
PHONE...................................740 964-0043
Willis Wolf, *President*
EMP: 26
SALES (est): 2.1MM **Privately Held**
SIC: 8721 Billing & bookkeeping service

(G-16286)
BREATHING AIR SYSTEMS INC
8855 E Broad St (43068-9602)
PHONE...................................614 864-1235
Mark Schuster, *President*
Lou Howard, *Treasurer*
EMP: 32
SALES (est): 5.4MM **Privately Held**
SIC: 5084 Compressors, except air conditioning

(G-16287)
BUSINESS ADMNSTRATORS CONS INC (PA)
6331 E Livingston Ave (43068-2756)
P.O. Box 107 (43068-0107)
PHONE...................................614 863-8780
Richard Raup, *President*
EMP: 47
SQ FT: 4,600
SALES: 6.3MM **Privately Held**
WEB: www.bactpa.com
SIC: 6411 Insurance information & consulting services

(G-16288)
CENTIMARK CORPORATION
7077 Americana Pkwy (43068-4118)
PHONE...................................614 536-1960
Steve Caudill, *Branch Mgr*
EMP: 45
SALES (corp-wide): 625.8MM **Privately Held**
SIC: 1761 Roofing contractor
PA: Centimark Corporation
12 Grandview Cir
Canonsburg PA 15317
724 514-8700

(G-16289)
CENTRAL CREDIT CORP
2040 Brice Rd Ste 200 (43068-3460)
PHONE...................................614 856-5840
Rhett Ricart, *President*
Paul F Ricart Jr, *Shareholder*
EMP: 55
SALES (est): 9.3MM **Privately Held**
WEB: www.centralcreditcorp.com
SIC: 6141 Automobile loans, including insurance

(G-16290)
CENTRAL OHIO PRIMARY CARE
6488 E Main St Ste C (43068-7310)
PHONE...................................614 552-2300
EMP: 60 **Privately Held**
SIC: 8011 General & family practice, physician/surgeon
PA: Central Ohio Primary Care Physicians, Inc.
570 Polaris Pkwy Ste 250
Westerville OH 43082

(G-16291)
CHARDON LABORATORIES INC
7300 Tussing Rd (43068-4111)
PHONE...................................614 860-1000
Robert S Butt, *CEO*

▲ = Import ▼=Export
◆ =Import/Export

Chris Mace, *Engineer*
Mark Davenport, *CFO*
Cynthia King, *Human Res Mgr*
Mike Chaffee, *Sales Engr*
EMP: 50
SQ FT: 10,000
SALES: 7.5MM **Privately Held**
WEB: www.chardonlabs.com
SIC: 7389 Water softener service

(G-16292)
COLUMBUS DIESEL SUPPLY CO INC
3100 Delta Marine Dr (43068-3992)
PHONE..................................614 445-8391
Brad Fry, *General Mgr*
Susan Boone, *Office Mgr*
EMP: 25
SALES (corp-wide): 13.6MM **Privately Held**
WEB: www.columbusdieselsupply.com
SIC: 7538 5013 Diesel engine repair: automotive; automotive supplies & parts; automotive supplies
PA: Columbus Diesel Supply Co Inc
    4710 Allmond Ave
    Louisville KY 40209
    502 361-1181

(G-16293)
COLUMBUS FRKLN CNTY PK
Also Called: Blacklick Wods Mtro Golf Crses
7309 E Livingston Ave (43068-3019)
P.O. Box 3 (43068-0003)
PHONE..................................614 861-3193
Chuck Doran, *Manager*
EMP: 28
SALES (corp-wide): 18.3MM **Privately Held**
WEB: www.metroparks.net
SIC: 7992 Public golf courses
PA: Columbus & Franklin County Metropolitan Park District
    1069 W Main St Unit B
    Westerville OH 43081
    614 891-0700

(G-16294)
CONTRACT FREIGHTERS INC
945 Mahle Dr (43068-6797)
PHONE..................................614 577-0447
EMP: 563
SALES (corp-wide): 3.7B **Privately Held**
SIC: 4213 Trucking, except local
HQ: Contract Freighters, Inc.
    4701 E 32nd St
    Joplin MO 64804
    417 623-5229

(G-16295)
DA VINCI GROUP INC
7815 Pembrook Dr (43068-3129)
PHONE..................................614 419-2393
Jeff Porter, *President*
◆ **EMP:** 30
SALES (est): 2.2MM **Privately Held**
SIC: 1542 Commercial & office building contractors

(G-16296)
DATACOMM TECH
Also Called: Techdisposal
6606 Tussing Rd Ste B (43068-4174)
PHONE..................................614 755-5100
Sepehr Rajaie, *President*
EMP: 40
SQ FT: 60,000
SALES (est): 3.5MM **Privately Held**
WEB: www.techdisposal.com
SIC: 7379 Computer related consulting services

(G-16297)
DENTAL SERVICS OF OHIO DANIEL
6323 Tussing Rd (43068-3984)
P.O. Box 11568, Overland Park KS (66207-4268)
PHONE..................................614 863-2222
EMP: 99
SQ FT: 1,500
SALES (est): 1.8MM **Privately Held**
SIC: 8021 Dentist's Office

(G-16298)
DIEWALD & POPE INC
245 Connell Ct (43068-4307)
PHONE..................................614 861-6160
Joseph Pope, *President*
Jesse Pope, *Treasurer*
EMP: 25 **EST:** 1974
SQ FT: 3,000
SALES (est): 1.4MM **Privately Held**
SIC: 1711 Plumbing contractors; heating & air conditioning contractors

(G-16299)
DIMENSIONAL METALS INC (PA)
Also Called: D M I
58 Klema Dr N (43068-9691)
PHONE..................................740 927-3633
Stephen C Wissman, *CEO*
Phillip Gastaldo, *President*
Steven Gastaldo, *Vice Pres*
Shawn Walters, *Prdtn Mgr*
Brian Peck, *Purchasing*
EMP: 52
SQ FT: 34,000
SALES (est): 12.7MM **Privately Held**
WEB: www.dmimetals.com
SIC: 1761 3444 3531 Sheet metalwork; sheet metalwork; roofing equipment

(G-16300)
DREIER & MALLER INC (PA)
6508 Taylor Rd Sw (43068-9633)
PHONE..................................614 575-0065
Stewart Dreier, *President*
Bruce Stevenson, *Business Mgr*
Steve Maller, *Corp Secy*
Amanda Madrigrano, *Admin Asst*
EMP: 28
SALES (est): 3.6MM **Privately Held**
WEB: www.dreierandmaller.com
SIC: 7389 7699 5084 Pipeline & power line inspection service; sewer cleaning & rodding; measuring & testing equipment, electrical

(G-16301)
DUCKWORTH ENTERPRISES LLC
Also Called: Scwashtan
2020 Brice Rd Ste 210 (43068-3457)
PHONE..................................614 575-2900
Thomas M Duckworth, *Mng Member*
EMP: 25 **EST:** 2001
SALES (est): 1.5MM **Privately Held**
SIC: 7218 Industrial launderers

(G-16302)
ECHO 24 INC (PA)
167 Cypress St Sw Ste A (43068-9692)
PHONE..................................740 964-7081
Anthony J Gunter, *President*
Lisa L Gunter, *CPA*
Debbie Spicer, *Office Mgr*
EMP: 40
SQ FT: 2,000
SALES: 6MM **Privately Held**
SIC: 4813 Telephone communication, except radio

(G-16303)
ENTERPRISE HOLDINGS INC (PA)
6501 Tussing Rd (43068-3990)
PHONE..................................614 866-1480
EMP: 53
SALES (corp-wide): 4.9B **Privately Held**
SIC: 7514 Rent-a-car service
HQ: Enterprise Holdings, Inc.
    600 Corporate Park Dr
    Saint Louis MO 63105
    314 512-5000

(G-16304)
FIRST HOSPITALITY COMPANY LLC
Also Called: Fairfield Inn
2826 Taylor Road Ext (43068-9555)
PHONE..................................614 864-4555
Amar Pandey, *Partner*
EMP: 50
SALES (est): 2.8MM **Privately Held**
SIC: 7011 Hotels & motels

(G-16305)
GLOBAL TRANSPORTATION SERVICES
7139 Americana Pkwy (43068-4120)
PHONE..................................614 409-0770
EMP: 29
SALES (corp-wide): 853.4MM **Privately Held**
SIC: 4731 Freight forwarding; customhouse brokers
HQ: Global Transportation Services, Inc
    18209 80th Ave S Ste A
    Kent WA 98032
    425 207-1500

(G-16306)
GOLIATH CONTRACTING LTD
405 Waggoner Rd (43068-9729)
PHONE..................................614 568-7878
Steve Hatton, *President*
EMP: 25
SQ FT: 2,500
SALES: 4MM **Privately Held**
SIC: 1751 1542 Store fixture installation; commercial & office building contractors

(G-16307)
GPAX LTD
555 Lancaster Ave (43068-1128)
PHONE..................................614 501-7622
Gary James, *Partner*
EMP: 50
SALES (est): 4.1MM
SALES (corp-wide): 59.5MM **Privately Held**
WEB: www.gpax.com
SIC: 5199 Packaging materials
PA: Dynalab, Inc.
    555 Lancaster Ave
    Reynoldsburg OH 43068
    614 866-9999

(G-16308)
GREEN KING COMPANY INC
9562 Taylor Rd Sw (43068-3228)
PHONE..................................614 861-4132
Adam T High, *President*
Erik High, *Vice Pres*
EMP: 30
SQ FT: 4,000
SALES (est): 2.2MM **Privately Held**
SIC: 0782 Landscape contractors

(G-16309)
HOME DEPOT USA INC
Also Called: Home Depot, The
2480 Brice Rd (43068-5431)
PHONE..................................614 577-1601
Mark Smith, *Manager*
EMP: 160
SALES (corp-wide): 108.2B **Publicly Held**
WEB: www.homerentalsdepot.com
SIC: 5211 7359 Home centers; tool rental
HQ: Home Depot U.S.A., Inc.
    2455 Paces Ferry Ave
    Atlanta GA 30339

(G-16310)
J & D HOME IMPROVEMENT INC (PA)
Also Called: J & D Basement Sytems
13659 E Main St (43068)
PHONE..................................740 927-0722
Tom Johnston, *President*
Ronald Greenbaum, *Vice Pres*
EMP: 65
SQ FT: 13,000
SALES (est): 13MM **Privately Held**
WEB: www.crawlspacemaintenance.com
SIC: 1799 1771 1521 1741 Waterproofing; foundation & footing contractor; general remodeling, single-family houses; foundation building; plumbing contractors

(G-16311)
JPMORGAN CHASE BANK NAT ASSN
8445 E Main St (43068-4707)
PHONE..................................614 759-8955
Carissa Davis, *Branch Mgr*
EMP: 34

SALES (corp-wide): 131.4B **Publicly Held**
SIC: 6029 6022 6021 Commercial banks; state commercial banks; national commercial banks
HQ: Jpmorgan Chase Bank, National Association
    1111 Polaris Pkwy
    Columbus OH 43240
    614 436-3055

(G-16312)
JPMORGAN CHASE BANK NAT ASSN
2025 Brice Rd (43068-3447)
P.O. Box 1651 (43068-6651)
PHONE..................................614 248-2410
E C Carter, *Principal*
EMP: 26
SALES (corp-wide): 131.4B **Publicly Held**
SIC: 6021 National commercial banks
HQ: Jpmorgan Chase Bank, National Association
    1111 Polaris Pkwy
    Columbus OH 43240
    614 436-3055

(G-16313)
KARST & SONS INC
6496 Taylor Rd Sw (43068-9633)
PHONE..................................614 501-9530
John G Karst, *President*
EMP: 45
SALES (est): 1.1MM **Privately Held**
SIC: 1741 Masonry & other stonework

(G-16314)
KINDERCARE LEARNING CTRS LLC
Also Called: Reynoldsburg Kindercare
6601 Bartlett Rd (43068-2382)
PHONE..................................614 866-4446
Debi Standiford, *Branch Mgr*
EMP: 25
SALES (corp-wide): 1.2B **Privately Held**
WEB: www.kindercare.com
SIC: 8351 Group day care center
HQ: Kindercare Learning Centers, Llc
    650 Ne Holladay St # 1400
    Portland OR 97232
    503 872-1300

(G-16315)
KRISTI BRITTON
Also Called: Comtron Professional Cons
6400 E Main St Ste 203 (43068-2348)
PHONE..................................614 868-7612
Kristi Britton, *Owner*
EMP: 30 **EST:** 1978
SQ FT: 1,000
SALES (est): 1.3MM **Privately Held**
SIC: 7379 Computer related consulting services

(G-16316)
LIFE CENTER ADULT DAY CARE
Also Called: LIFE CENTER AT WESLEY RIDGE
2225 State Route 256 (43068)
PHONE..................................614 866-7212
Crystal Busher, *Manager*
Elizabeth Vogt, *Director*
EMP: 30
SALES: 238.1K **Privately Held**
SIC: 8322 8351 Adult day care center; child day care services

(G-16317)
LOWES HOME CENTERS LLC
8231 E Broad St (43068-9732)
PHONE..................................614 769-9940
Jeff Fetters, *Branch Mgr*
Becky Boudreaux, *Admin Asst*
EMP: 150
SALES (corp-wide): 68.6B **Publicly Held**
SIC: 5211 5031 5722 5064 Home centers; building materials, exterior; building materials, interior; household appliance stores; electrical appliances, television & radio
HQ: Lowe's Home Centers, Llc
    1605 Curtis Bridge Rd
    Wilkesboro NC 28697
    336 658-4000

(G-16318)
LQ MANAGEMENT LLC
Also Called: La Quinta Inn
2447 Brice Rd (43068-3455)
PHONE..................................614 866-6456
Ed Sosa, *General Mgr*
EMP: 30
SQ FT: 27,145
SALES (corp-wide): 1.8B **Publicly Held**
WEB: www.neubayern.net
SIC: 7011 Hotels
HQ: Lq Management L.L.C.
909 Hidden Rdg Ste 600
Irving TX 75038
214 492-6600

(G-16319)
MAST INDUSTRIES INC
Also Called: Mast Global Fashions
8655 E Broad St (43068-9715)
PHONE..................................614 856-6000
Richard Paul, *President*
EMP: 52
SALES (corp-wide): 13.2B **Publicly Held**
SIC: 5137 5136 Women's & children's
clothing; men's & boys' clothing
HQ: Mast Industries, Inc.
2 Limited Pkwy
Columbus OH 43230
614 415-7000

(G-16320)
METROPOLITIAN FAMILY CARE INC
Also Called: Metropolitan Family Care
7094 E Main St (43068-2010)
PHONE..................................614 237-1067
Andrew J Pultz MD, *President*
Diana Max, *Manager*
EMP: 25
SALES (est): 2.9MM **Privately Held**
SIC: 8011 General & family practice, physician/surgeon

(G-16321)
NATIONAL ALL-JERSEY INC (PA)
6486 E Main St (43068-2349)
PHONE..................................614 861-3636
Neal Smith, *CEO*
Vickie J White, *Treasurer*
EMP: 25 EST: 1957
SQ FT: 1,350
SALES: 967.5K **Privately Held**
WEB: www.usjersey.com
SIC: 8611 Trade associations

(G-16322)
OAKWOOD MANAGEMENT COMPANY (PA)
6950 Americana Pkwy Ste A (43068-4126)
PHONE..................................614 866-8702
John D Wymer, *President*
Rose Gore, *Regional Mgr*
Donald W Kelley, *Vice Pres*
Dana L Moore, *Vice Pres*
Patrick J Kelley, *Treasurer*
EMP: 45
SQ FT: 10,000
SALES: 4.3MM **Privately Held**
WEB: www.oakwoodmgmt.com
SIC: 6531 Real estate managers

(G-16323)
OHIO FEDERATION OF SOIL AND WA
Also Called: OFSWCD
8995 E Main St (43068-3342)
PHONE..................................614 784-1900
Melinda Bankey, *CEO*
Kris Swartz, *President*
Jack Hazelbaker, *Corp Secy*
Harold Neuenschwander, *Vice Pres*
Bob Short, *Vice Pres*
EMP: 40
SALES: 1MM **Privately Held**
SIC: 8699 Charitable organization

(G-16324)
PXP OHIO
6800 Tussing Rd (43068-7044)
PHONE..................................614 575-4242
Greg Scott, *Owner*
Linda Scott, *Co-Owner*
Dan Robinson, *COO*
Kyle Paugh, *Sales Staff*

Mark July, *Sr Project Mgr*
EMP: 31
SQ FT: 15,688
SALES (est): 2.9MM **Privately Held**
SIC: 7389 Printing broker

(G-16325)
REM-OHIO INC
Also Called: REM Ohio Waivered Services
6402 E Main St Ste 103 (43068-2356)
PHONE..................................614 367-1370
Theresa Setser, *Director*
EMP: 80
SALES (est): 2MM
SALES (corp-wide): 2.8MM **Privately Held**
WEB: www.remohio.com
SIC: 8361 Home for the mentally retarded
PA: Rem-Ohio, Inc
6921 York Ave S
Minneapolis MN 55435
952 925-5067

(G-16326)
REYNOLDSBURG CITY SCHOOLS
Also Called: School Bus Garage
7932 E Main St (43068-1239)
PHONE..................................614 501-1041
Mike Rosenberger, *Director*
EMP: 45
SQ FT: 8,640
SALES (corp-wide): 93.4MM **Privately Held**
SIC: 4173 Maintenance facilities, buses
PA: Reynoldsburg City Schools
7244 E Main St
Reynoldsburg OH 43068
614 501-1020

(G-16327)
REYNOLDSBURG SWIM CLUB INC
7215 E Main St (43068-2000)
PHONE..................................614 866-3211
Fax: 614 866-5270
EMP: 30
SQ FT: 4,000
SALES (est): 901.4K **Privately Held**
SIC: 7997 Membership Sport/Recreation Club

(G-16328)
RGIS LLC
6488 E Main St Ste B (43068-7310)
PHONE..................................248 651-2511
Art Alexander, *Manager*
EMP: 65
SALES (corp-wide): 6.8B **Publicly Held**
WEB: www.rgisinv.com
SIC: 7389 7374 Inventory computing service; data processing & preparation
HQ: Rgis, Llc
2000 Taylor Rd
Auburn Hills MI 48326
248 651-2511

(G-16329)
RIVERSIDE COMMONS LTD PARTNR
6880 Tussing Rd (43068-4101)
PHONE..................................614 863-4640
Sandsord Goldston, *CEO*
Sandy Goldston, *Chairman*
EMP: 60
SQ FT: 17,000
SALES (est): 2.8MM **Privately Held**
SIC: 6513 Apartment building operators

(G-16330)
ROSE TRANSPORT INC
6747 Taylor Rd Sw (43068-9674)
PHONE..................................614 864-4004
John W Spencer, *President*
Ralph Spencer, *Vice Pres*
EMP: 25
SQ FT: 14,000
SALES (est): 3.5MM
SALES (corp-wide): 49.3MM **Privately Held**
WEB: www.mulchmfg.com
SIC: 4212 Local trucking, without storage

PA: Mulch Manufacturing, Inc.
6747 Taylor Rd Sw
Reynoldsburg OH 43068
614 864-4004

(G-16331)
SATCOM SERVICE LLC
7052 Americana Pkwy (43068-4117)
PHONE..................................614 863-6470
Steve Farber, *President*
Ken Farber, *CFO*
Patty Jackson, *Manager*
EMP: 60
SQ FT: 50,000
SALES (est): 1.8MM **Privately Held**
SIC: 4841 Direct broadcast satellite services (DBS)

(G-16332)
TENDER NURSING CARE
7668 Slate Ridge Blvd (43068-8160)
PHONE..................................614 856-3508
Maria Thacker, *Principal*
EMP: 25
SALES (est): 1.3MM **Privately Held**
SIC: 8051 Skilled nursing care facilities

(G-16333)
TM WALLICK RSDNTL PRPTS I LTD
6880 Tussing Rd (43068-4101)
PHONE..................................614 863-4640
Park Lawrence,
EMP: 83
SALES: 950K **Privately Held**
SIC: 6513 Apartment building operators

(G-16334)
TS TECH AMERICAS INC (HQ)
8458 E Broad St (43068-9749)
PHONE..................................614 575-4100
Minoru Maeda, *President*
Jason J MA, *Exec VP*
Hiroshi Suzuki, *Exec VP*
Takayuki Taniuchi, *Exec VP*
Katharine Pezzatta, *Buyer*
▲ EMP: 350 EST: 2013
SALES (est): 988.6MM
SALES (corp-wide): 4.5B **Privately Held**
SIC: 5099 Child restraint seats, automotive
PA: Ts Tech Co., Ltd.
3-7-27, Sakaecho
Asaka STM 351-0
484 621-121

(G-16335)
UNIVERSAL GREEN ENERGY SOLUTIO
2086 Belltree Dr (43068-3505)
PHONE..................................844 723-7768
Kerry E Fletcher, *President*
EMP: 25
SQ FT: 1,700
SALES (est): 851.8K **Privately Held**
SIC: 4939 7382 Combination utilities; security systems services

(G-16336)
VALMER LAND TITLE AGENCY (PA)
2227 State Route 256 B (43068-9326)
PHONE..................................614 860-0005
Valerie Lambert, *President*
Monica Merriman, *Vice Pres*
Monica Merryman, *Vice Pres*
Chris Borgan, *Sales Mgr*
EMP: 25
SALES (est): 20MM **Privately Held**
SIC: 6361 Real estate title insurance

(G-16337)
WESLEY RIDGE INC
Also Called: METHODIST ELDER CARE SERVICES
2225 Taylor Park Dr (43068-8053)
PHONE..................................614 759-0023
Robert L Rouse, *CEO*
Dinah Cason, *Exec Dir*
Wesley Ridge, *Exec Dir*
Mary Lemaster, *Director*
Maureen Keebaugh, *Associate*
EMP: 126 EST: 1996

SALES: 6MM **Privately Held**
WEB: www.wesleyridge.com
SIC: 8059 8052 Personal care home, with health care; intermediate care facilities

(G-16338)
WHITE BARN CANDLE CO
7 Limited Pkwy E (43068-5300)
PHONE..................................614 856-6000
Diane Neal, *CEO*
EMP: 1000
SALES (est): 126.1MM
SALES (corp-wide): 13.2B **Publicly Held**
WEB: www.limited.com
SIC: 5199 Candles
PA: L Brands, Inc.
3 Limited Pkwy
Columbus OH 43230
614 415-7000

(G-16339)
WHITESTONE GROUP INC
6422 E Main St Ste 101 (43068-2342)
PHONE..................................614 501-7007
John Clark, *President*
Pam Gentile, *President*
R Gene Hart, *Vice Pres*
Bill Smith, *CFO*
EMP: 300
SQ FT: 2,500
SALES (est): 24MM **Privately Held**
SIC: 7381 Guard services

(G-16340)
WOODWARD EXCAVATING CO
7340 Tussing Rd (43068-4111)
PHONE..................................614 866-4384
John Woodward, *President*
Clay Woodward, *Corp Secy*
Brad Woodward, *Vice Pres*
EMP: 25
SQ FT: 7,200
SALES: 1.9MM **Privately Held**
SIC: 1623 Underground utilities contractor; sewer line construction; water main construction

(G-16341)
XTREME CONTRACTING LTD
7600 Asden Ct (43068-9757)
PHONE..................................614 568-7030
Steven Hatton, *President*
EMP: 25
SQ FT: 2,500
SALES: 4MM **Privately Held**
SIC: 5211 1542 Bathroom fixtures, equipment & supplies; commercial & office building contractors

```
Richfield
Summit County
```

(G-16342)
AETNA LIFE INSURANCE COMPANY
4059 Kinros Lake Pkwy # 300
(44286-9253)
PHONE..................................330 659-8000
Scott Ushkowitz, *Branch Mgr*
EMP: 50
SALES (corp-wide): 194.5B **Publicly Held**
SIC: 6324 Health maintenance organization (HMO), insurance only
HQ: Aetna Life Insurance Company Inc
151 Farmington Ave
Hartford CT 06156
860 273-0123

(G-16343)
ALL AERIALS LLC
4945 Brecksville Rd (44286-9244)
PHONE..................................330 659-9600
Kimberly Kasparek, *Manager*
Susi Motz,
▼ EMP: 25
SALES (est): 5.9MM **Privately Held**
WEB: www.allaerials.com
SIC: 7353 Cranes & aerial lift equipment, rental or leasing

(G-16344)
AMERICAN ENVMTL GROUP LTD
3600 Brecksville Rd # 100 (44286-9668)
PHONE..................................330 659-5930
Carl Apicella, *President*
Peter Augustin, *Opers Mgr*
Ernest Vallorz, *CFO*
Mike Maurer,
▲ EMP: 450
SALES (est): 70.4MM
SALES (corp-wide): 2.9B **Publicly Held**
WEB: www.aegl.net
SIC: 8748 Environmental consultant
PA: Tetra Tech, Inc.
  3475 E Foothill Blvd
  Pasadena CA 91107
  626 351-4664

(G-16345)
AMERICAN HIGHWAYS INSUR AGCY
3250 Interstate Dr (44286-9000)
PHONE..................................330 659-8900
Alan Spachman, *Principal*
EMP: 104
SALES (est): 10.1MM **Publicly Held**
WEB: www.nationalinterstate.com
SIC: 6411 Insurance agents
HQ: National Interstate Corporation
  3250 Interstate Dr
  Richfield OH 44286
  330 659-8900

(G-16346)
AMERICAN ROADWAY LOGISTICS INC
3920 Congress Pkwy (44286-9745)
PHONE..................................330 659-2003
Heidi Claxton, *President*
Chad Moag, *Division Mgr*
Gary Tytko, *Division Mgr*
Rick Sutton, *Superintendent*
Jonathon Claxton, *Vice Pres*
EMP: 30
SALES (est): 5.9MM **Privately Held**
SIC: 7359 Work zone traffic equipment
  (flags, cones, barrels, etc.)

(G-16347)
BRECKSVILLE LEASING CO LLC
Also Called: Pine Valley Care Center
4360 Brecksville Rd (44286-9457)
PHONE..................................330 659-6166
Christina Grezlik, *Human Res Mgr*
Stephen Rosedale,
EMP: 140
SALES (est): 5.7MM **Privately Held**
SIC: 8051 Convalescent home with continuous nursing care

(G-16348)
CARRARA COMPANIES INC
3774 Congress Pkwy (44286-9041)
PHONE..................................330 659-2800
Toll Free:..............................888 -
Justin Sucato, *President*
Julie Sucato, *Corp Secy*
EMP: 58 EST: 1996
SQ FT: 16,000
SALES: 10.4MM **Privately Held**
WEB: www.steamaticneo.com
SIC: 7349 6331 Cleaning service, industrial or commercial; property damage insurance

(G-16349)
CHARLES SCHWAB & CO INC
4150 Kinross Lakes Pkwy (44286-9369)
P.O. Box 5050 (44286-5050)
PHONE..................................330 908-4478
Rick Haseltine, *General Mgr*
Mary Coss, *Client Mgr*
Staci Probst, *Client Mgr*
Marianne Thompson, *Client Mgr*
Nancy Morris, *Property Mgr*
EMP: 50
SALES (corp-wide): 10.9B **Publicly Held**
WEB: www.schwab.com
SIC: 6211 Brokers, security
HQ: Charles Schwab & Co., Inc.
  211 Main St Fl 17
  San Francisco CA 94105
  415 636-7000

(G-16350)
CISCO SYSTEMS INC
4125 Highlander Pkwy (44286-9085)
PHONE..................................330 523-2000
Mark Fahmi, *Engineer*
Greg Edwards, *Corp Comm Staff*
Michael Wyss, *Branch Mgr*
Tim Esker, *Manager*
Kate Hagan, *Manager*
EMP: 239
SALES (corp-wide): 48B **Publicly Held**
WEB: www.cisco.com
SIC: 7373 Local area network (LAN) systems integrator
PA: Cisco Systems, Inc.
  170 W Tasman Dr
  San Jose CA 95134
  408 526-4000

(G-16351)
COLUMBUS EQUIPMENT COMPANY
3942 Brecksville Rd (44286-9627)
PHONE..................................330 659-6681
Jeff Thornburg, *Branch Mgr*
Jeff Badner, *Asst Mgr*
EMP: 30
SQ FT: 20,000
SALES (corp-wide): 84.2MM **Privately Held**
WEB: www.colsequipment.com
SIC: 5082 General construction machinery & equipment
PA: The Columbus Equipment Company
  2323 Performance Way
  Columbus OH 43207
  614 437-0352

(G-16352)
DAWSON COMPANIES
3900 Kinross Lakes Pkwy (44286-9381)
PHONE..................................440 333-9000
Chuck Putnam, *Division Mgr*
Rob Odney, *Principal*
Rick Cote, *Exec VP*
Darren Faye, *Exec VP*
Bob Grevey, *Exec VP*
EMP: 79
SALES (est): 57.3MM **Privately Held**
SIC: 6321 Health insurance carriers

(G-16353)
DENTAL CERAMICS INC
3404 Brecksville Rd (44286-9662)
PHONE..................................330 523-5240
John Lavicka, *President*
Jan Bittner, *Office Mgr*
EMP: 37
SALES (est): 4.3MM **Privately Held**
WEB: www.dentalceramics.net
SIC: 8072 3843 Crown & bridge production; dental equipment & supplies

(G-16354)
EMPACO EQUIPMENT CORPORATION (PA)
Also Called: Emil Pawuk & Associates
2958 Brecksville Rd (44286-9747)
P.O. Box 535 (44286-0535)
PHONE..................................330 659-9393
Emil M Pawuk Sr, *President*
L R Gaiduk, *Principal*
C B Wheeler, *Principal*
Emil M Pawuk Jr, *Vice Pres*
Paul Backo, *Project Mgr*
EMP: 40
SQ FT: 11,280
SALES (est): 11.6MM **Privately Held**
WEB: www.empacoequipment.com
SIC: 1799 Service station equipment installation & maintenance

(G-16355)
EXPLORER RV INSURANCE AGCY INC
Also Called: GMAC Insurance
3250 Interstate Dr (44286-9000)
P.O. Box 568 (44286-0568)
PHONE..................................330 659-8900
Alan R Spachman, *Principal*
EMP: 125
SALES (est): 10.6MM **Publicly Held**
WEB: www.explorerrv.com
SIC: 6411 Insurance agents

HQ: National Interstate Corporation
  3250 Interstate Dr
  Richfield OH 44286
  330 659-8900

(G-16356)
FEDEX GROUND PACKAGE SYS INC
3245 Henry Rd (44286-9701)
PHONE..................................800 463-3339
Chad Fogle, *Manager*
EMP: 34
SALES (corp-wide): 65.4B **Publicly Held**
WEB: www.fedex.com
SIC: 4513 Letter delivery, private air; parcel delivery, private air
HQ: Fedex Ground Package System, Inc.
  1000 Fed Ex Dr
  Coraopolis PA 15108
  800 463-3339

(G-16357)
FEDEX GROUND PACKAGE SYS INC
3201 Columbia Rd (44286-9622)
PHONE..................................800 463-3339
EMP: 200
SALES (corp-wide): 65.4B **Publicly Held**
SIC: 4215 Package delivery, vehicular; parcel delivery, vehicular
HQ: Fedex Ground Package System, Inc.
  1000 Fed Ex Dr
  Coraopolis PA 15108
  800 463-3339

(G-16358)
FRONTIER TANK CENTER INC
3800 Congress Pkwy (44286-9745)
P.O. Box 460 (44286-0460)
PHONE..................................330 659-3888
James S Hollabaugh, *President*
Mary Hollabaugh, *Admin Sec*
EMP: 25
SQ FT: 25,000
SALES (est): 3.2MM **Privately Held**
WEB: www.frontiertrailer.com
SIC: 7699 5013 3714 Tank repair; trailer parts & accessories; motor vehicle body components & frame

(G-16359)
GROUP MANAGEMENT SERVICES INC (PA)
3750 Timberlake Dr (44286-9187)
PHONE..................................330 659-0100
Mike Kahoe, *President*
Mark Watkins, *Vice Pres*
Mike Johnson, *CFO*
Jennifer Shuster, *Hum Res Coord*
Jenna Berkemeyer, *Accounts Mgr*
EMP: 30
SQ FT: 47,000
SALES (est): 12MM **Privately Held**
WEB: www.groupmgmt.com
SIC: 8742 Compensation & benefits planning consultant; human resource consulting services

(G-16360)
I-TRAN INC
Also Called: Low Country Metal
4100 Congress Pkwy W (44286-9732)
PHONE..................................330 659-0801
◆ EMP: 25 EST: 2007
SALES (est): 1.2MM **Privately Held**
SIC: 4953 Refuse System

(G-16361)
IRG REALTY ADVISORS LLC (PA)
4020 Kinross Lakes Pkwy (44286-9084)
PHONE..................................330 659-4060
Tracy C Green, *President*
Sam Maj, *Project Mgr*
Frank Kelley, *Opers Mgr*
Lou Palumbo, *Opers Mgr*
Joseph Staeuble, *Opers Mgr*
EMP: 30
SQ FT: 1,200
SALES (est): 44.6MM **Privately Held**
WEB: www.ohiorealtyadvisors.com
SIC: 6531 Real estate managers

(G-16362)
MAS INC (PA)
2718 Brecksville Rd (44286-9735)
P.O. Box 526 (44286-0526)
PHONE..................................330 659-3333
C Edwin Howard, *Ch of Bd*
Brian T Parsell, *President*
Ken E Weegar, *Exec VP*
◆ EMP: 41
SQ FT: 80,000
SALES (est): 34.2MM **Privately Held**
WEB: www.masdist.com
SIC: 5092 5064 Video games; electrical entertainment equipment

(G-16363)
NATIONAL INTERSTATE CORP (HQ)
3250 Interstate Dr (44286-9000)
PHONE..................................330 659-8900
Anthony J Mercurio, *President*
Arthur J Gonzales, *Senior VP*
Terry E Phillips, *Senior VP*
Chris Mikolay, *Assistant VP*
Michelle Wiltgen, *Assistant VP*
EMP: 69
SQ FT: 143,000
SALES: 625.7MM **Publicly Held**
WEB: www.nationalinterstate.com
SIC: 6331 6411 Fire, marine & casualty insurance; property & casualty insurance agent

(G-16364)
NATIONAL INTERSTATE INSUR CO (DH)
3250 Interstate Dr (44286-9000)
PHONE..................................330 659-8900
David W Michelson, *President*
Alan R Spachman, *Chairman*
George Skuggen, *Senior VP*
Arthur M Kraus, *Treasurer*
Jay Baer, *Accountant*
EMP: 200
SQ FT: 22,000
SALES (est): 269.8MM **Publicly Held**
SIC: 6331 Fire, marine & casualty insurance
HQ: National Interstate Corporation
  3250 Interstate Dr
  Richfield OH 44286
  330 659-8900

(G-16365)
NEWARK CORPORATION
Newark Electronics Div
4180 Highlander Pkwy (44286-9352)
PHONE..................................330 523-4457
Vicky Villicana, *General Mgr*
Michelle Evans, *Manager*
EMP: 300
SALES (corp-wide): 19B **Publicly Held**
WEB: www.newarkinone.com
SIC: 5065 Electronic parts
HQ: Newark Corporation
  300 S Riverside Plz # 2200
  Chicago IL 60606
  773 784-5100

(G-16366)
NEWARK ELECTRONICS CORPORATION
4180 Highlander Pkwy (44286-9352)
PHONE..................................330 523-4912
Tim Smith, *Branch Mgr*
EMP: 150
SALES (corp-wide): 19B **Publicly Held**
SIC: 5065 5063 Electronic parts; electrical apparatus & equipment
HQ: Newark Electronics Corporation
  300 S Riverside Plz
  Chicago IL 60606
  773 784-5100

(G-16367)
OECONNECTION LLC (PA)
4205 Highlander Pkwy (44286-9077)
PHONE..................................888 776-5792
Chuck Rotuno, *CEO*
Ron Coill, *COO*
Ike Herman, *COO*
Philip Firrell, *Exec VP*
Paul Johnson, *Exec VP*
EMP: 95

SALES (est): 60.6MM **Privately Held**
WEB: www.oeconnection.com
SIC: 7371 Computer software systems analysis & design, custom

(G-16368)
OHIO ASSN PUB SCHL EMPLOYEES
3380 Brecksville Rd # 101 (44286-9801)
PHONE..................330 659-7335
Marc Beallor, *Manager*
EMP: 55
SALES (corp-wide): 9.9MM **Privately Held**
SIC: 8631 Labor union
PA: Ohio Association Of Public School Employees
6805 Oak Creek Dr Ste 1
Columbus OH 43229
614 890-4770

(G-16369)
OHIO TPK & INFRASTRUCTURE COMM
Also Called: Boston Maintenance Bldg
3245 Boston Mills Rd (44286-9455)
PHONE..................440 234-2081
Lynn Parker, *Manager*
EMP: 25
SQ FT: 24,800 **Privately Held**
WEB: www.ohioturnpike.net
SIC: 1611 0782 9621 Highway & street maintenance; highway lawn & garden maintenance services; regulation, administration of transportation;
HQ: Ohio Turnpike And Infrastructure Commission
682 Prospect St
Berea OH 44017
440 234-2081

(G-16370)
OLDER WISER LIFE SERVICES LLC
4028 Broadview Rd Ste 1 (44286-9231)
PHONE..................330 659-2111
Cheryl M Bass,
EMP: 30 EST: 2014
SALES (est): 95.3K **Privately Held**
SIC: 8322 Senior citizens' center or association

(G-16371)
QUALITY PLANT PRODUCTIONS INC
4586 Newton Rd (44286-9609)
PHONE..................440 526-8711
EMP: 30
SQ FT: 1,600
SALES (est): 1.3MM **Privately Held**
WEB: www.qualityplantinc.com
SIC: 0181 0175 Shrubberies grown in field nurseries; deciduous tree fruits

(G-16372)
QUILALEA CORPORATION
3861 Sawbridge Dr (44286-9679)
PHONE..................330 487-0777
Mark Sinreich, *President*
EMP: 40
SALES (est): 6.9MM **Privately Held**
WEB: www.avid-tech.com
SIC: 8711 5045 Consulting engineer; computer software

(G-16373)
RECEIVABLE MGT SVCS CORP
4836 Brecksville Rd (44286-9177)
PHONE..................330 659-1000
Dan Leo Montenaro, *Branch Mgr*
EMP: 65 **Privately Held**
SIC: 7322 Collection agency, except real estate
HQ: The Receivable Management Services Corporation
240 Emery St
Bethlehem PA 18015
484 242-4000

(G-16374)
REGIONAL EXPRESS INC
4615 W Streetsboro Rd (44286-9227)
PHONE..................516 458-3514
Salvatore Caiazzo Jr, *President*
EMP: 54

SALES: 2.5MM **Privately Held**
SIC: 4731 Freight transportation arrangement

(G-16375)
RICHFIELD BANQUET & CONFER
Also Called: Quality Inn
4742 Brecksville Rd (44286-9619)
PHONE..................330 659-6151
Sandip Tharkar,
EMP: 43
SALES (est): 2.6MM **Privately Held**
SIC: 7011 Hotels & motels

(G-16376)
RICOH USA INC
Also Called: American Business Machines
4125 Highlander Pkwy # 175 (44286-8903)
PHONE..................330 523-3900
Rex Swartz, *Branch Mgr*
EMP: 80
SALES (corp-wide): 19.3B **Privately Held**
WEB: www.ikon.com
SIC: 5044 Photocopy machines
HQ: Ricoh Usa, Inc.
70 Valley Stream Pkwy
Malvern PA 19355
610 296-8000

(G-16377)
SAIA MOTOR FREIGHT LINE LLC
2920 Brecksville Rd Ste B (44286-9265)
PHONE..................330 659-4277
M Pawuk, *Branch Mgr*
EMP: 31
SALES (corp-wide): 1.6B **Publicly Held**
WEB: www.saia.com
SIC: 4213 Contract haulers
HQ: Saia Motor Freight Line, Llc
11465 Johns Creek Pkwy # 400
Duluth GA 30097
770 232-5067

(G-16378)
SCHNEIDER ELECTRIC USA INC
Also Called: Schneider Electric Svcs
3623 Brecksville Rd Ste A (44286-9264)
PHONE..................440 526-9070
Bill McHenry, *Manager*
EMP: 25
SALES (corp-wide): 355.8K **Privately Held**
WEB: www.squared.com
SIC: 5063 Electrical supplies
HQ: Schneider Electric Usa, Inc.
201 Wshington St Ste 2700
Boston MA 02108
978 975-9600

(G-16379)
SHREE SHANKAR LLC
Also Called: La Quinta Inn
3971 Evergreen Ln (44286-9593)
PHONE..................440 734-4477
Palak Patel,
EMP: 25
SALES (est): 196.5K **Privately Held**
SIC: 7011 Hotels & motels

(G-16380)
THORSON BAKER & ASSOC INC (PA)
3030 W Streetsboro Rd (44286-9632)
PHONE..................330 659-6688
Michael Thorson, *President*
Gordon Baker, *Vice Pres*
Jayson Tarantino, *Engineer*
Karen Sherwood, *Finance*
EMP: 121
SQ FT: 48,000
SALES (est): 17.1MM **Privately Held**
WEB: www.thorsonbaker.com
SIC: 8711 Professional engineer; consulting engineer

(G-16381)
TRANSITWORKS LLC (HQ)
4199 Kinross Lakes Pkwy (44286-9010)
PHONE..................330 861-1118
Ken Richards, *Business Mgr*
Rick Cook, *Purchasing*
Roger Vartanian, *Sales Staff*
Debbie Beiter, *Manager*

John Bollinger, *Manager*
▲ EMP: 99
SALES (est): 5.9MM
SALES (corp-wide): 404.9MM **Privately Held**
WEB: www.mobilityworks.net
SIC: 7532 5511 Customizing services, non-factory basis; automobiles, new & used
PA: Wmk, Llc
4199 Kinross Lakes Pkwy # 300
Richfield OH 44286
234 312-2000

(G-16382)
UPS GROUND FREIGHT INC
3495 Brecksville Rd (44286-9663)
PHONE..................330 659-6693
Jerry Ruediger, *Manager*
Ken Brown, *Manager*
EMP: 200
SQ FT: 3,500
SALES (corp-wide): 71.8B **Publicly Held**
WEB: www.overnite.com
SIC: 4213 4212 Contract haulers; local trucking, without storage
HQ: Ups Ground Freight, Inc.
1000 Semmes Ave
Richmond VA 23224
866 372-5619

(G-16383)
WARD TRUCKING LLC
2800 Brecksville Rd (44286-9740)
PHONE..................330 659-6658
Robert Kane, *Manager*
EMP: 50
SALES (corp-wide): 168.8MM **Privately Held**
SIC: 4213 Contract haulers
PA: Ward Trucking, Llc
1436 Ward Trucking Dr
Altoona PA 16602
814 944-0803

(G-16384)
WMK INC
Also Called: MOBILITY WORKS FOUNDATION, THE
4199 Kinross Lakes Pkwy (44286-9010)
PHONE..................630 782-1900
William M Koeblitz, *Principal*
EMP: 29
SALES: 377.1K **Privately Held**
SIC: 4789 Cargo loading & unloading services

(G-16385)
YRC INC
Also Called: Yellow Transportation
5250 Brecksville Rd (44286-9461)
PHONE..................330 659-4151
Joel Campbell, *Manager*
EMP: 52
SQ FT: 800
SALES (corp-wide): 5B **Publicly Held**
WEB: www.roadway.com
SIC: 4213 4212 Contract haulers; local trucking, without storage
HQ: Yrc Inc.
10990 Roe Ave
Overland Park KS 66211
913 696-6100

Richmond
Jefferson County

(G-16386)
OHI-RAIL CORP (PA)
992 State Route 43 (43944-6958)
P.O. Box 728, Steubenville (43952-5728)
PHONE..................740 765-5083
Teresa C Schiappa, *President*
Richard Delatore, *Vice Pres*
EMP: 30 EST: 1982
SQ FT: 2,000
SALES (est): 3.2MM **Privately Held**
WEB: www.ohirail.com
SIC: 4011 Railroads, line-haul operating

(G-16387)
SIGN AMERICA INCORPORATED
3887 State Route 43 (43944-7912)
P.O. Box 396 (43944-0396)
PHONE..................740 765-5555
Judith A Hilty, *President*
Bob Hilty, *Vice Pres*
Scott Hilty Jr, *Vice Pres*
John D Bray, *Executive*
John Bray, *Admin Sec*
EMP: 40
SQ FT: 6,000
SALES (est): 9.6MM **Privately Held**
WEB: www.signamericainc.com
SIC: 5046 3993 Signs, electrical; neon signs; signs & advertising specialties

Richmond Heights
Cuyahoga County

(G-16388)
CAPITAL SENIOR LIVING CORP
261 Richmond Rd (44143-4422)
PHONE..................216 289-9800
EMP: 110
SALES (corp-wide): 460MM **Publicly Held**
SIC: 6513 Retirement hotel operation
PA: Capital Senior Living Corp
14160 Dallas Pkwy Ste 300
Dallas TX 75254
972 770-5600

(G-16389)
FLIGHT OPTIONS INC (PA)
26180 Curtiss Wright Pkwy (44143-1453)
PHONE..................216 261-3880
Michael J Silvestro, *CEO*
Darnell H Martens, *President*
Robert Pinkas, *President*
David H Davies, *Principal*
Kenneth Ricci, *Chairman*
EMP: 500
SQ FT: 30,000
SALES (est): 61.7MM **Privately Held**
SIC: 7359 Aircraft rental

(G-16390)
FLIGHT OPTIONS INTL INC (HQ)
355 Richmond Rd (44143-4405)
PHONE..................216 261-3500
Ed Mc Donald, *President*
EMP: 33
SQ FT: 15,000
SALES (est): 14.4MM
SALES (corp-wide): 61.7MM **Privately Held**
SIC: 7359 Aircraft rental
PA: Flight Options, Inc.
26180 Curtiss Wright Pkwy
Richmond Heights OH 44143
216 261-3880

(G-16391)
INTEX SUPPLY COMPANY
26301 Curtiss Wright Pkwy (44143-4413)
PHONE..................216 535-4300
Ken Vuylsteke, *President*
Jack Levine, *Vice Pres*
Tom Friedl, *CFO*
Dan Soukup, *Controller*
Patrick Fitz Maurice, *Finance Dir*
▼ EMP: 50
SQ FT: 12,500
SALES (est): 10.5MM **Privately Held**
SIC: 5093 Waste rags; waste paper

(G-16392)
PK MANAGEMENT LLC (PA)
26301 Curtiss Wright Pkwy (44143-4413)
PHONE..................216 472-1870
Amy Nutter, *Area Mgr*
Yvette Rouff, *Vice Pres*
Cheryl London, *Opers Staff*
Teresita Jones, *Controller*
Elizabeth Reink, *Accountant*
EMP: 106
SALES: 52.1MM **Privately Held**
SIC: 8741 Management services

(G-16393)
REGAL CINEMAS CORPORATION
631 Richmond Rd (44143-2915)
PHONE.............................440 720-0500
EMP: 30 **Privately Held**
SIC: 7832 Motion picture theaters, except drive-in
HQ: Regal Cinemas Corporation
101 E Blount Ave Ste 100
Knoxville TN 37920
865 922-1123

(G-16394)
RICHMOND MEDICAL CENTER (PA)
27100 Chardon Rd (44143-1116)
PHONE.............................440 585-6500
Laurie Delgado, *President*
Jason Klein, *Med Doctor*
Sami E Moufawad, *Manager*
Naushad Banani, *Podiatrist*
Amy A Barko, *Podiatrist*
EMP: 400 EST: 1996
SALES (est): 17.1MM **Privately Held**
SIC: 8062 8011 General medical & surgical hospitals; medical centers

(G-16395)
TRANZONIC COMPANIES (PA)
Also Called: Ccp Industries
26301 Curtiss Wright Pkwy # 200 (44143-1454)
PHONE.............................216 535-4300
Thomas Friedl, *CEO*
Melissa Sims, *Partner*
Rudy Garcia, *District Mgr*
Tim Kline, *Area Mgr*
Paul Lee, *Area Mgr*
◆ EMP: 150
SALES (est): 295.9MM **Privately Held**
SIC: 2842 2273 5087 2676 Sanitation preparations, disinfectants & deodorants; mats & matting; cleaning & maintenance equipment & supplies; napkins, sanitary: made from purchased paper

(G-16396)
YOUTH MNTRNG & AT RSK INTRVNTN
2092 Washington Dr (44143-1357)
PHONE.............................216 324-2451
Willie L Gary, *Exec Dir*
EMP: 50
SALES: 75K **Privately Held**
SIC: 8322 Individual & family services

Richwood
Union County

(G-16397)
RICHWOOD BANKING COMPANY (HQ)
28 N Franklin St (43344-1027)
PHONE.............................740 943-2317
Nancy K Hoffman, *President*
Chad Hoffman, *Vice Pres*
EMP: 27
SALES: 21.6MM **Privately Held**
WEB: www.richwoodbank.com
SIC: 6022 State trust companies accepting deposits, commercial

Ridgeville Corners
Henry County

(G-16398)
RIDGEVILLE COMMUNITY CHOIR
633 First St (43555)
PHONE.............................419 267-3820
Pat Basselman, *Treasurer*
Steven Basselman, *Director*
EMP: 40 EST: 2010
SALES (est): 303.2K **Privately Held**
SIC: 8699 Charitable organization

Rio Grande
Gallia County

(G-16399)
AREA AGENCY ON AGING DST 7 INC (PA)
160 Dorsey Dr (45674-7517)
P.O. Box 500 (45674-0500)
PHONE.............................800 582-7277
Becky Simon, *General Mgr*
Kristy Bowman, *Human Resources*
Vicky Abdella, *Pub Rel Dir*
Jenni Dovyak-Lewis, *Comms Mgr*
Sherri McCollum, *Office Mgr*
EMP: 130
SALES: 61MM **Privately Held**
SIC: 8322 Senior citizens' center or association

Ripley
Brown County

(G-16400)
LEGACY INDUSTRIAL SERVICES LLC
9272 Scoffield Rd (45167-9627)
PHONE.............................606 584-8953
Phillip Truesdell,
EMP: 25
SALES (est): 759.7K **Privately Held**
SIC: 1791 7389 Structural steel erection;

(G-16401)
OHIO VALLEY MANOR INC
5280 Us Highway 62 And 68 (45167-8650)
PHONE.............................937 392-4318
Dave Seesholtz, *President*
Evelyn Seesholtz, *President*
George Balz, *Vice Pres*
Gary Seesholtz, *Treasurer*
Dale G Wilson, *Admin Sec*
EMP: 230
SQ FT: 72,000
SALES: 11.7MM **Privately Held**
SIC: 8059 8052 8051 Convalescent home; intermediate care facilities; skilled nursing care facilities

(G-16402)
OVM INVESTMENT GROUP LLC
5280 Us Hwy 62 & 88 (45167)
PHONE.............................937 392-0145
Steven Boymel, *President*
Allan Acheson, *CFO*
EMP: 220
SQ FT: 150,000
SALES (est): 574.2K **Privately Held**
SIC: 8051 Skilled nursing care facilities

Rittman
Wayne County

(G-16403)
APOSTOLIC CHRISTIAN HOME INC
10680 Steiner Rd (44270-9518)
PHONE.............................330 927-1010
Ellen Gasser, *Manager*
Megan Brownlee, *Director*
Eugene Petrilla, *Director*
Susan Miller, *Social Dir*
Lashayna McCourt, *Food Svc Dir*
EMP: 90
SQ FT: 23,000
SALES: 5.6MM **Privately Held**
SIC: 8059 8052 8051 Nursing home, except skilled & intermediate care facility; intermediate care facilities; skilled nursing care facilities

(G-16404)
BAUMAN ORCHARDS INC
161 Rittman Ave (44270-1253)
PHONE.............................330 925-6861
Marion E Bauman, *President*
William Bauman, *Corp Secy*
Doug Bauman, *Vice Pres*

EMP: 43
SQ FT: 13,500
SALES (est): 3.3MM **Privately Held**
WEB: www.baumanorchards.com
SIC: 0175 Peach orchard

(G-16405)
EMBASSY AUTUMNWOOD MGT LLC
275 E Sunset Dr (44270-1165)
PHONE.............................330 927-2060
Darla Handler, *COO*
Jill Hoffman, *Finance Dir*
EMP: 99
SALES (est): 356.7K **Privately Held**
SIC: 8051 Skilled nursing care facilities

(G-16406)
LARIA CHEVROLET-BUICK INC
112 E Ohio Ave (44270-1537)
PHONE.............................330 925-2015
Toll Free:.............................866 -
John W Laria, *President*
EMP: 40 EST: 1934
SALES (est): 17.3MM **Privately Held**
WEB: www.lariachevybuick.com
SIC: 5511 5521 5012 Automobiles, new & used; used car dealers; automobiles & other motor vehicles

(G-16407)
MORTON SALT INC
151 Industrial Ave (44270-1593)
PHONE.............................330 925-3015
Mark Wallace, *Branch Mgr*
EMP: 150
SALES (corp-wide): 4.6B **Privately Held**
WEB: www.mortonintl.com
SIC: 5149 2899 Salt, edible; chemical preparations
HQ: Morton Salt, Inc.
444 W Lake St Ste 3000
Chicago IL 60606

(G-16408)
RITTMAN CITY OF INC
Also Called: Ems Station
25 N State St (44270-1584)
PHONE.............................330 925-2065
Larry Boggs, *Manager*
EMP: 35 **Privately Held**
SIC: 4119 Ambulance service
PA: Rittman, City Of Inc
30 N Main St
Rittman OH 44270
330 925-2045

(G-16409)
RITTMAN INC
Also Called: Mull Iron
10 Mull Dr (44270-9777)
PHONE.............................330 927-6855
Chester Mull Jr, *President*
Robert A O'Neil, *Principal*
Richard J Wendelken, *Principal*
Beth Mull, *Corp Secy*
William Mull, *Vice Pres*
EMP: 60
SQ FT: 34,000
SALES (est): 14.7MM **Privately Held**
SIC: 3441 1791 Fabricated structural metal; structural steel erection

(G-16410)
U SAVE AUTO RENTAL
Also Called: U-Save Auto Rental
112 E Ohio Ave (44270-1537)
PHONE.............................330 925-2015
John Laria, *Owner*
EMP: 50
SALES (est): 1.1MM **Privately Held**
SIC: 7514 Rent-a-car service

Rock Creek
Ashtabula County

(G-16411)
GLENBEIGH (PA)
Also Called: Rock Creek Medical Center
2863 State Route 45 N (44084-0298)
P.O. Box 298 (44084-0298)
PHONE.............................440 563-3400
Pat Weston-Hall, *CEO*

Joseph Vendel, *Chairman*
Tessa Kingus, *COO*
Joanna Calabris, *Supervisor*
Kim Hochschild, *Info Tech Mgr*
EMP: 48
SALES (est): 5.9MM **Privately Held**
SIC: 8069 Drug addiction rehabilitation hospital

(G-16412)
GLENBEIGH HEALTH SOURCES INC (PA)
2863 State Route 45 N (44084-9352)
P.O. Box 298 (44084-0298)
PHONE.............................440 951-7000
Patricia Weston-Hall, *CEO*
Tom Dailey, *Director*
Barbara Rodney, *Nurse*
EMP: 180
SALES: 28.2MM **Privately Held**
SIC: 8069 Drug addiction rehabilitation hospital

Rockbridge
Hocking County

(G-16413)
GLENLAUREL INC
Also Called: Glenlurel-A Scottish Cntry Inn
14940 Mount Olive Rd (43149-9736)
PHONE.............................740 385-4070
Greg Leonard, *President*
Rick Brown, *Opers Mgr*
EMP: 25
SQ FT: 20,000
SALES (est): 1MM **Privately Held**
WEB: www.glenlaurelinn.com
SIC: 5812 7011 Eating places; inns

Rockford
Mercer County

(G-16414)
ECO GLOBAL CORP
10803 Erastus Durbin Rd (45882-9654)
PHONE.............................419 363-2681
Lloyd Linton, *Principal*
EMP: 37
SALES (est): 827.5K **Privately Held**
SIC: 4953 Recycling, waste materials

(G-16415)
GLM TRANSPORT INC (PA)
12806 State Route 118 (45882-9354)
PHONE.............................419 363-2041
Daniel Ruhe, *President*
Tyson Bailey, *Vice Pres*
Ty Conrad, *Vice Pres*
Edward Ruhe, *Vice Pres*
Samantha Wiswell, *Marketing Staff*
EMP: 30
SALES (est): 11.4MM **Privately Held**
SIC: 4212 4213 Local trucking, without storage; trucking, except local

(G-16416)
HEALTHCARE MANAGEMENT CONS
Also Called: Colonial Nursing Home
201 Buckeye St (45882-9266)
PHONE.............................419 363-2193
Paul Bergener, *President*
EMP: 32 EST: 1949
SQ FT: 3,500
SALES (est): 1.9MM **Privately Held**
WEB: www.colonialnursingcenter.com
SIC: 8741 8052 Nursing & personal care facility management; intermediate care facilities

(G-16417)
TIRE WASTE TRANSPORT INC
10803 Erastus Durbin Rd (45882-9654)
PHONE.............................419 363-2681
Lloyd Linton, *CEO*
EMP: 320
SQ FT: 13,000
SALES (est): 19.4MM **Privately Held**
SIC: 5014 Tires & tubes

(G-16418)
TSM LOGISTICS LLC
4567 Old Town Run Rd (45882-9331)
PHONE................................419 234-6074
Steve Marks, *Branch Mgr*
EMP: 45
SALES (est): 1.6MM
SALES (corp-wide): 600K **Privately Held**
SIC: 4212 Local trucking, without storage
PA: Tsm Logistics, Llc
2421 S Nappanee St
Elkhart IN 46517
419 363-2041

Rocky Ridge
Ottawa County

(G-16419)
BLATT TRUCKING CO INC (PA)
1205 Main St (43458)
P.O. Box 100 (43458-0100)
PHONE................................419 898-0002
Russell Blatt, *President*
EMP: 40
SALES (est): 4.8MM **Privately Held**
SIC: 4213 4212 Contract haulers; local
trucking, without storage

Rocky River
Cuyahoga County

(G-16420)
A W S INC
Also Called: S A W - Rocky River Adult Trai
20120 Detroit Rd (44116-2421)
PHONE................................440 333-1791
Katherine L Johnson, *Branch Mgr*
EMP: 200
SALES (corp-wide): 7.8MM **Privately Held**
SIC: 8331 7331 Vocational training
agency; direct mail advertising services
PA: A W S Inc
1275 Lakeside Ave E
Cleveland OH 44114
216 861-0250

(G-16421)
ACE HARDWARE CORPORATION
20200 Detroit Rd (44116-2422)
PHONE................................440 333-4223
EMP: 139
SALES (corp-wide): 5.3B **Privately Held**
SIC: 5251 5072 Hardware; hardware
PA: Ace Hardware Corporation
2200 Kensington Ct
Oak Brook IL 60523
866 681-1836

(G-16422)
AMERICAN MULTI-CINEMA INC
Also Called: AMC
21653 Center Ridge Rd (44116-3917)
PHONE................................440 331-2826
Eric Supple, *Manager*
EMP: 30
SALES (corp-wide): 7.3MM **Publicly Held**
WEB: www.arrowheadtownecenter.com
SIC: 7832 Motion picture theaters, except
drive-in
HQ: American Multi-Cinema, Inc.
1 Amc Way
Leawood KS 66211
913 213-2000

(G-16423)
AUTOMOTIVE EVENTS INC (PA)
19111 Detroit Rd Ste 306 (44116-1740)
PHONE................................440 356-1383
John Thorne, *President*
Iain Dobson, *President*
Charles E Wern Jr, *Principal*
EMP: 25
SQ FT: 3,000
SALES (est): 6.6MM **Privately Held**
WEB: www.automotive-events.com
SIC: 8743 8742 Sales promotion; training
& development consultant

(G-16424)
BOUNDLESS FLIGHT INC (PA)
20226 Detroit Rd (44116-2422)
P.O. Box 360109, Strongsville (44136-0002)
PHONE................................440 610-3683
Gary Baney, *CEO*
Joanna Orloff, *Principal*
EMP: 25
SALES (est): 3.5MM **Privately Held**
WEB: www.boundlessflight.com
SIC: 7371 Computer software writers, free-
lance

(G-16425)
CAPITAL SENIOR LIVING (PA)
Also Called: Harbor Court
22900 Center Ridge Rd (44116-3000)
PHONE................................440 356-5444
Xen Zapis, *Partner*
EMP: 50
SQ FT: 19,064
SALES (est): 4.3MM **Privately Held**
WEB: www.theharbourcourt.com
SIC: 8059 6531 Rest home, with health
care; real estate agents & managers

(G-16426)
CHILD & ELDER CARE INSIGHTS
18500 Lake Rd Ste 200 (44116-1746)
PHONE................................440 356-2900
Elisabeth Bryenton, *CEO*
EMP: 27
SQ FT: 2,500
SALES (est): 692.5K **Privately Held**
WEB: www.carereports.com
SIC: 7299 Information services, consumer

(G-16427)
CLEVELAND PHLHRMONIC ORCHESTRA
1158 Bates Rd (44116-2173)
PHONE................................216 556-1800
Lisa Wilson, *Exec Dir*
EMP: 90
SALES (est): 48.2K **Privately Held**
SIC: 7929 Orchestras or bands

(G-16428)
CONVIVO NETWORK LLC
22564 Sunnyhill Dr (44116-3727)
PHONE................................216 631-9000
Roland Straubs, *Mng Member*
EMP: 50
SALES: 500K **Privately Held**
SIC: 7389 Decoration service for special
events

(G-16429)
COWEN AND COMPANY LLC
20006 Detroit Rd Ste 100 (44116-2406)
PHONE................................440 331-3531
Allen Gerard, *Branch Mgr*
Ethan Johnson, *Technology*
EMP: 50 **Publicly Held**
SIC: 6211 Securities flotation companies
HQ: Cowen And Company, Llc
599 Lexington Ave Fl 19
New York NY 10022
646 562-1000

(G-16430)
DAVITA INC
19133 Hilliard Blvd (44116-2907)
PHONE................................216 712-4700
EMP: 27 **Publicly Held**
SIC: 8092 Kidney dialysis centers
PA: Davita Inc.
2000 16th St
Denver CO 80202

(G-16431)
EARNEST MACHINE PRODUCTS CO (PA)
1250 Linda St Ste 301 (44116-1854)
PHONE................................440 895-8400
Kirk P Zehnder, *President*
Paul Zehnder, *Principal*
Victor Zehnder, *Principal*
John P Zehnder, *Co-President*
Timothy D Weber, *Vice Pres*
▲ EMP: 50 EST: 1951
SQ FT: 68,000

SALES (est): 36.2MM **Privately Held**
SIC: 5085 Fasteners, industrial: nuts, bolts,
screws, etc.

(G-16432)
EXCHANGEBASE LLC
18500 Lake Rd (44116-1744)
P.O. Box 16790 (44116-0790)
PHONE................................440 331-3600
Alex Kowalski,
EMP: 25
SALES (est): 6MM **Privately Held**
SIC: 6792 Oil royalty traders

(G-16433)
FITWORKS HOLDING LLC
20001 Center Ridge Rd (44116-3659)
PHONE................................440 333-4141
Max Stillwagon, *Manager*
EMP: 40 **Privately Held**
SIC: 7991 7997 Health club; membership
sports & recreation clubs
PA: Fitworks Holding, Llc
849 Brainard Rd
Cleveland OH 44143

(G-16434)
GOLDWOOD PRIMARY SCHOOL PTA
Also Called: Goldwood Pta
21600 Center Ridge Rd (44116-3918)
PHONE................................440 356-6720
Chris Albano, *President*
EMP: 37
SALES: 51.4K **Privately Held**
SIC: 8641 Parent-teachers' association

(G-16435)
HERITAGE HOME HEALTH CARE
20800 Center Ridge Rd # 401
(44116-4312)
PHONE................................440 333-1925
Ray Cancelliere, *Director*
EMP: 40
SALES (est): 762.7K **Privately Held**
WEB: www.heritagehomehealthcare.com
SIC: 8082 Home health care services

(G-16436)
HOWARD HANNA SMYTHE CRAMER
19204 Detroit Rd (44116-1706)
PHONE................................440 333-6500
William Brink, *Manager*
Aileen Fitzgerald, *Agent*
EMP: 45
SQ FT: 576
SALES (corp-wide): 73.7MM **Privately Held**
WEB: www.smythecramer.com
SIC: 6531 Real estate agent, residential
HQ: Howard Hanna Smythe Cramer
6000 Parkland Blvd
Cleveland OH 44124
216 447-4477

(G-16437)
JAG HEALTHCARE INC
220 Buckingham Rd (44116-1623)
PHONE................................440 385-4370
James Griffiths, *President*
Richard Gebhard, *Vice Pres*
Miriam Walters, *Vice Pres*
Micheal McBride, *Opers Staff*
David Cooley, *CFO*
EMP: 650
SALES (est): 14MM **Privately Held**
SIC: 8082 Home health care services

(G-16438)
JP RECOVERY SERVICES INC
Also Called: Patient Financial Services
20220 Center Ridge Rd # 200
(44116-3501)
PHONE................................440 331-2200
John Beirne, *President*
John Murray, *Vice Pres*
EMP: 90
SQ FT: 23,500
SALES (est): 9.9MM **Privately Held**
WEB: www.jprecovery.com
SIC: 7322 Collection agency, except real
estate

(G-16439)
KAISER FOUNDATION HOSPITALS
Also Called: Rocky River Medical Offices
20575 Ctr Ridgerd Ste 500 (44116)
PHONE................................216 524-7377
EMP: 593
SALES (corp-wide): 19.1B **Privately Held**
SIC: 8011 Medical Doctor's Office
PA: Kaiser Foundation Hospitals Inc
1 Kaiser Plz Ste 2600
Oakland CA 94612
510 271-5800

(G-16440)
LOWES HOME CENTERS LLC
20639 Center Ridge Rd (44116-3449)
PHONE................................440 331-1027
Lorie Thomas, *Branch Mgr*
Justin Bain, *Manager*
EMP: 150
SALES (corp-wide): 68.6B **Publicly Held**
SIC: 5211 5031 5722 5064 Home cen-
ters; building materials, exterior; building
materials, interior; household appliance
stores; electrical appliances, television &
radio
HQ: Lowe's Home Centers, Llc
1605 Curtis Bridge Rd
Wilkesboro NC 28697
336 658-4000

(G-16441)
MSAB PARK CREEK LLC
Also Called: Park Creek Center
20375 Center Ridge Rd # 204
(44116-3561)
PHONE................................440 842-5100
David A Farkas, *Mng Member*
Valerie Farkas,
EMP: 38
SALES (est): 1.3MM **Privately Held**
WEB: www.parkcreekretirement.com
SIC: 8059 Personal care home, with health
care

(G-16442)
NL OF KY INC
Also Called: Neace Lukens
1340 Depot St Ste 300 (44116-1741)
PHONE................................216 643-7100
Skip Vogelsberger, *Manager*
EMP: 30 **Privately Held**
SIC: 6411 Insurance agents & brokers
HQ: Nl Of Ky, Inc.
2305 River Rd
Louisville KY 40206

(G-16443)
NORMANDY MANOR OF ROCKY RIVER
22709 Lake Rd (44116-1021)
PHONE................................440 333-5401
David Orlean, *Partner*
Debra Sue Orlean, *Partner*
Susan Orlean, *Partner*
Stephanie Johnson, *Purch Agent*
David Rodgers, *Controller*
EMP: 150 EST: 1988
SALES (est): 15.1MM **Privately Held**
WEB: www.normandyretirement.com
SIC: 8051 Convalescent home with contin-
uous nursing care

(G-16444)
PRODUCER GROUP LLC (PA)
Also Called: Todd Organization, The
19111 Detroit Rd Ste 304 (44116-1740)
PHONE................................440 871-7700
Scott Holton, *COO*
William Holton, *Vice Pres*
Tammy Jasiek, *Broker*
Gene Forsythe, *Consultant*
Graham Gerlach, *Consultant*
EMP: 26
SQ FT: 25,000
SALES (est): 4.6MM **Privately Held**
SIC: 6411 8742 Pension & retirement plan
consultants; franchising consultant

(G-16445)
RUFFING MONTESSORI SCHOOL
1285 Orchard Park Dr (44116-2045)
PHONE................................440 333-2250

▲ = Import ▼=Export
◆ =Import/Export

John McNamara, *Director*
Lori Coticchia, *Administration*
EMP: 26
SQ FT: 34,727
SALES: 3.3MM **Privately Held**
WEB: www.ruffingmontessori.org
SIC: 8211 8351 Private elementary & secondary schools; Montessori child development center

(G-16446)
SUNRISE SENIOR LIVING INC
Also Called: Sunrise of Rocky River
21600 Detroit Rd (44116-2218)
PHONE...................................440 895-2383
Natalie Antosh, *Manager*
EMP: 58
SALES (corp-wide): 4.7B **Publicly Held**
WEB: www.sunrise.com
SIC: 8051 8361 Skilled nursing care facilities; home for the aged
HQ: Sunrise Senior Living, Llc
7902 Westpark Dr
Mc Lean VA 22102

(G-16447)
VER-A-FAST CORP
20545 Center Ridge Rd # 300
(44116-3423)
PHONE...................................440 331-0250
Robert Bensman, *President*
Steve Lucek, *President*
Michelle Steer, *Prdtn Mgr*
Cathleen Soprano, *CFO*
Beth Lusk, *Contractor*
EMP: 45
SQ FT: 13,000
SALES (est): 5.7MM **Privately Held**
WEB: www.verafast.com
SIC: 8743 Public relations & publicity

(G-16448)
WESTWOOD COUNTRY CLUB COMPANY
22625 Detroit Rd (44116-2024)
P.O. Box 16459 (44116-0459)
PHONE...................................440 331-3016
Richard McClure, *President*
Thomas M Cawley, *Vice Pres*
Robert J Koepke, *Treasurer*
Jamie Kearney, *Controller*
Raymond Strah, *Asst Mgr*
EMP: 75
SQ FT: 53,000
SALES: 6.2MM **Privately Held**
WEB: www.westwoodcountryclub.org
SIC: 7997 Country club, membership

(G-16449)
WOMENS WELSH CLUBS OF AMERICA
Also Called: Welsh Home For The Aged
22199 Center Ridge Rd (44116-3925)
PHONE...................................440 331-0420
Chasity Smith, *Bookkeeper*
Sarah Cook, *Administration*
EMP: 100
SQ FT: 31,206
SALES: 8.8MM **Privately Held**
SIC: 8361 8051 Home for the aged; rest home, with health care incidental; convalescent home with continuous nursing care

Rootstown
Portage County

(G-16450)
JET RUBBER COMPANY
4457 Tallmadge Rd (44272-9610)
PHONE...................................330 325-1821
Franklin R Brubaker, *Principal*
Karen Crooks, *Corp Secy*
Ken Beachy, *Sales Mgr*
EMP: 43 EST: 1954
SQ FT: 20,000

SALES (est): 8.5MM **Privately Held**
WEB: www.jetrubber.com
SIC: 3069 3053 3533 5085 Molded rubber products; gaskets, packing & sealing devices; gaskets & sealing devices; gas field machinery & equipment; oil field machinery & equipment; rubber goods, mechanical

(G-16451)
LEEDA SERVICES INC
4123 Tallmadge Rd (44272-9657)
PHONE...................................330 325-1560
EMP: 118
SALES (corp-wide): 4.8MM **Privately Held**
SIC: 8322 Social service center
PA: Leeda Services Inc
1441 Parkman Rd Nw
Warren OH 44485
330 392-6006

(G-16452)
MILLER TRANSFER AND RIGGING CO (HQ)
3833 State Route 183 (44272-9799)
P.O. Box 453 (44272-0453)
PHONE...................................330 325-2521
Mitchell J Unger, *President*
Norman Hartline, *President*
Mike Raus, *Regional Mgr*
Kenneth H Rusinoff, *Corp Secy*
David Cochran, *Vice Pres*
EMP: 50
SQ FT: 10,000
SALES (est): 61.4MM
SALES (corp-wide): 64.6MM **Privately Held**
WEB: www.millertransfer.com
SIC: 4213 Heavy machinery transport
PA: United Transport Industries, Inc
1310 N King St
Wilmington DE 19801
330 325-2521

Roseville
Muskingum County

(G-16453)
ACCCO INC
451 Gordon St (43777-1110)
P.O. Box 35 (43777-0035)
PHONE...................................740 697-2005
Peter Petratsaf, *President*
Rick Emmert, *Vice Pres*
▲ EMP: 50
SQ FT: 50,000
SALES (est): 11.7MM **Privately Held**
WEB: www.accco-inc.com
SIC: 5032 Ceramic wall & floor tile

(G-16454)
CLAY BURLEY PRODUCTS CO (PA)
455 Gordon St (43777-1110)
P.O. Box 35 (43777-0035)
PHONE...................................740 452-3633
Peter Petratsas, *President*
Emmett Abella, *Traffic Mgr*
Bobbi Bennett, *Sales Executive*
▲ EMP: 50
SQ FT: 180,000
SALES (est): 8.3MM **Privately Held**
WEB: www.burleyclay.com
SIC: 3269 5032 Stoneware pottery products; art & ornamental ware, pottery; ceramic wall & floor tile

(G-16455)
RMX FREIGHT SYSTEMS INC (PA)
Also Called: R M X
4550 Roseville Rd (43777-9720)
P.O. Box 185, White Cottage (43791-0185)
PHONE...................................740 849-2374
Jeff Moore, *President*
Derek Dunn, *Traffic Dir*
EMP: 25
SQ FT: 10,000
SALES (est): 6MM **Privately Held**
SIC: 4212 Local trucking, without storage

Ross
Butler County

(G-16456)
GUENTHER & SONS INC
2578 Long St (45061)
P.O. Box 28 (45061-0028)
PHONE...................................513 738-1448
James Guenther, *President*
Steve Guenther, *Vice Pres*
Gary Guenther, *Treasurer*
Glenn Guenther, *Admin Sec*
EMP: 42
SQ FT: 6,280
SALES: 1.5MM **Privately Held**
SIC: 4213 Contract haulers

Rossburg
Darke County

(G-16457)
CAL-MAINE FOODS INC
3078 Washington Rd (45362-9500)
PHONE...................................937 337-9576
Leonard Kropp, *General Mgr*
EMP: 43
SALES (corp-wide): 1.5B **Publicly Held**
WEB: www.calmainefoods.com
SIC: 0252 2015 Chicken eggs; poultry slaughtering & processing
PA: Cal-Maine Foods, Inc.
3320 W Woodrow Wilson Ave
Jackson MS 39209
601 948-6813

(G-16458)
COOPER FRMS SPRING MADOW FARMS
13243 Cochran Rd (45362-9753)
PHONE...................................419 375-4119
Marvin Lefeld, *CFO*
EMP: 35
SALES (est): 1.7MM **Privately Held**
SIC: 5144 Eggs

Rossford
Wood County

(G-16459)
ALLIEDBARTON SECURITY SVCS LLC
Also Called: Allied Barton Security Svcs
1001 Dixie Hwy Ste F (43460-1389)
PHONE...................................419 874-9005
Timothy Dotson, *Manager*
EMP: 50
SALES (corp-wide): 3.2B **Privately Held**
WEB: www.alliedsecurity.com
SIC: 7381 Security guard service
HQ: Alliedbarton Security Services Llc
8 Tower Bridge 161 Wshgtn
Conshohocken PA 19428
610 239-1100

(G-16460)
COURTYARD BY MARRIOTT ROSSFORD
9789 Clark Dr (43460-1700)
PHONE...................................419 872-5636
Arne Sorenson's, *President*
Carrie Brettschneider, *Manager*
Andrew Groom, *Info Tech Mgr*
Jan Widdel, *Info Tech Mgr*
EMP: 25
SALES: 1.1MM **Privately Held**
SIC: 7011 Hotels & motels

(G-16461)
INDUSTRIAL POWER SYSTEMS INC
Also Called: I P S
146 Dixie Hwy (43460-1215)
PHONE...................................419 531-3121
Kevin Gray, *President*
John Gray, *Vice Pres*
Jeremiah Johnson, *Vice Pres*
Brian Baumgartner, *Project Mgr*

Tim Grosteffon, *Project Mgr*
EMP: 250
SQ FT: 20,000
SALES: 67.2MM **Privately Held**
WEB: www.indpowsys.com
SIC: 1711 1796 1731 Mechanical contractor; machinery installation; electrical work

(G-16462)
INTERSTATE LANES OF OHIO LTD
819 Lime City Rd (43460-1613)
PHONE...................................419 666-2695
Nicholas Veronica, *Partner*
Barbara Golbinec, *Partner*
Howard Teifke, *Partner*
Sue Penske, *Manager*
Sue Pinski, *Webmaster*
EMP: 28 EST: 1981
SQ FT: 30,000
SALES (est): 1MM **Privately Held**
WEB: www.interstatelanes.com
SIC: 7933 5813 Ten pin center; cocktail lounge

(G-16463)
OBR COOLING TOWERS INC
9665 S Compass Dr (43460-1740)
PHONE...................................419 243-3443
Peter Poll, *President*
John Hall, *Exec VP*
Philip Poll, *Treasurer*
Debra Haas, *Admin Sec*
EMP: 45
SQ FT: 6,000
SALES (est): 7.7MM **Privately Held**
WEB: www.obrcoolingtowers.com
SIC: 7699 3444 Industrial equipment services; cooling towers, sheet metal

(G-16464)
ROSSFORD HOSPITALITY GROUP INC
Also Called: Hampton Inn
9753 Clark Dr (43460-1700)
PHONE...................................419 874-2345
Thomas Shoemaker, *Owner*
EMP: 25
SALES: 950K **Privately Held**
SIC: 7011 Hotels & motels

Rushville
Fairfield County

(G-16465)
RICHLAND TOWNSHIP FIRE DEPT
3150 Market St (43150-9750)
PHONE...................................740 536-7313
Kenneth Rookard, *Chief*
Scott Baker, *Chief*
EMP: 35 **Privately Held**
SIC: 9224 8999 Fire department, volunteer; search & rescue service

Russia
Shelby County

(G-16466)
FRANCIS-SCHULZE CO
3880 Rangeline Rd (45363-9711)
P.O. Box 245 (45363-0245)
PHONE...................................937 295-3941
Ralph Schulze, *President*
Rita Schulze, *Treasurer*
EMP: 45 EST: 1943
SQ FT: 50,000
SALES (est): 7.8MM **Privately Held**
WEB: www.francisschulze.com
SIC: 3442 5031 Metal doors; building materials, exterior

Sabina
Clinton County

(G-16467)
EARLEY & ROSS LTD
Also Called: Autumn Years Nursing Center
580 E Washington St (45169-1253)
PHONE.....................................740 634-3301
Tim Ross, *Partner*
EMP: 62
SALES (est): 4.7MM **Privately Held**
SIC: 8052 Intermediate care facilities

Saint Clairsville
Belmont County

(G-16468)
ALTERNATIVE RESIDENCES TWO (PA)
Also Called: WILEY AVENUE GROUP HOME
67051 Executive Dr (43950-8473)
PHONE.....................................740 526-0514
Shirley M Johnson, *Chairman*
Lavelle Lloyd, *Corp Secy*
EMP: 150
SALES: 899.1K **Privately Held**
SIC: 8361 8052 Home for the mentally
handicapped; home for the mentally re-
tarded; intermediate care facilities

(G-16469)
AMBULATORY CARE SOLUTIONS LLC
103 Plaza Dr Ste A (43950-7729)
PHONE.....................................740 695-3721
EMP: 108
SALES (corp-wide): 3.3MM **Privately Held**
SIC: 8093 Mental health clinic, outpatient
PA: Ambulatory Care Solutions, Llc
5080 Spectrum Dr 1200w
Addison TX 75001
502 580-2007

(G-16470)
BELCO WORKS INC
340 Fox Shannon Pl (43950)
PHONE.....................................740 695-0500
Kim Cain, *Opers Staff*
Debbie Alexander, *HR Admin*
Sherri Marlin, *Manager*
Anne Haning, *Director*
EMP: 350 EST: 1966
SQ FT: 5,000
SALES: 3.2MM **Privately Held**
WEB: www.belcoworks.com
SIC: 8331 3993 3931 2448 Sheltered
workshop; signs & advertising specialties;
musical instruments; wood pallets & skids

(G-16471)
BELLMONT COUNTY
Also Called: Sargus Juvenille Center
210 Fox Shannon Pl (43950)
PHONE.....................................740 695-9750
Beth Oprisch, *Exec Dir*
EMP: 32
SALES (est): 1MM **Privately Held**
SIC: 8361 Juvenile correctional facilities

(G-16472)
BELMONT COUNTY HOME
Also Called: Park Health Center
100 Pine Ave (43950-9738)
PHONE.....................................740 695-4925
Gordy Longshaw, *Commissioner*
Chuck Probst, *Commissioner*
Mark Thomas, *Commissioner*
Mike Maistros, *Director*
EMP: 100
SALES (est): 2.7MM **Privately Held**
SIC: 8051 Skilled nursing care facilities
PA: Belmont County Of Ohio
101 W Main St
Saint Clairsville OH 43950
740 695-2121

(G-16473)
BELMONT COUNTY OF OHIO
Also Called: Belmont County Sani Sewer Dst
67711 Oak View Rd (43950-7719)
P.O. Box 457 (43950-0457)
PHONE.....................................740 695-3144
Mark Esposito, *Director*
EMP: 40 **Privately Held**
WEB: www.belmontsheriff.com
SIC: 4941 4952 Water supply; sewerage
systems
PA: Belmont County Of Ohio
101 W Main St
Saint Clairsville OH 43950
740 695-2121

(G-16474)
BELMONT COUNTY OF OHIO
Also Called: Belmont County Children Svcs
101 N Market St Ste A (43950-1270)
PHONE.....................................740 695-3813
Jeff Felton, *Partner*
EMP: 29 **Privately Held**
WEB: www.belmontsheriff.com
SIC: 8322 Public welfare center
PA: Belmont County Of Ohio
101 W Main St
Saint Clairsville OH 43950
740 695-2121

(G-16475)
BELMONT COUNTY OF OHIO
68421 Hammond Rd (43950-8783)
PHONE.....................................740 695-0460
Jamie Bauman, *Principal*
EMP: 100 **Privately Held**
SIC: 8211 8322 Public special education
school; individual & family services
PA: Belmont County Of Ohio
101 W Main St
Saint Clairsville OH 43950
740 695-2121

(G-16476)
BELMONT COUNTY OF OHIO
Also Called: Belmont County Engineering
101 W Maint St (43950)
PHONE.....................................740 695-1580
Dave Sloan, *Superintendent*
EMP: 50 **Privately Held**
WEB: www.belmontsheriff.com
SIC: 1611 Highway & street maintenance
PA: Belmont County Of Ohio
101 W Main St
Saint Clairsville OH 43950
740 695-2121

(G-16477)
BELMONT HILLS COUNTRY CLUB
47080 National Rd (43950-8711)
PHONE.....................................740 695-2181
Thomas Dowler, *President*
EMP: 75
SQ FT: 30,000
SALES: 1.4MM **Privately Held**
SIC: 7997 Country club, membership

(G-16478)
BELMONT SAVINGS BANK
215 W Main St (43950-1141)
P.O. Box 71 (43950-0071)
PHONE.....................................740 695-0140
Nick Rocchio, *Manager*
EMP: 30
SALES (corp-wide): 14.3MM **Privately Held**
SIC: 6036 State savings banks, not feder-
ally chartered
PA: Belmont Savings Bank
3301 Guernsey St
Bellaire OH 43906
740 676-1165

(G-16479)
BHC FOX RUN HOSPITAL INC
Also Called: Fox Run Cntr For Chldrn & Adol
67670 Traco Dr (43950-9375)
PHONE.....................................740 695-2131
Karen Maxwell, *CEO*
William Hale, *Senior VP*
Joe Smith, *CFO*
EMP: 146
SQ FT: 8,200
SALES (est): 11MM **Privately Held**
WEB: www.foxrunhospital.com
SIC: 8063 8093 Psychiatric hospitals;
mental health clinic, outpatient

(G-16480)
BORDAS & BORDAS PLLC
106 E Main St (43950-1526)
PHONE.....................................740 695-8141
Michelle Marinacci, *Executive*
Jay Stoneking, *Executive*
Linda Bordas,
Scott Blass,
James Bordas Jr,
EMP: 26
SALES (est): 1.1MM
SALES (corp-wide): 8.3MM **Privately Held**
SIC: 8111 General practice attorney,
lawyer
PA: Bordas & Bordas Pllc
1358 National Rd
Wheeling WV 26003
304 242-8410

(G-16481)
BRYAN ELECTRIC INC
46139 National Rd (43950-8715)
PHONE.....................................740 695-9834
Joseph Dallison, *President*
EMP: 30
SQ FT: 12,000
SALES (est): 3.3MM **Privately Held**
SIC: 1731 General electrical contractor

(G-16482)
CELLCO PARTNERSHIP
Also Called: Verizon Wireless
50641 Valley Plaza Dr (43950-1750)
PHONE.....................................740 695-3600
EMP: 71
SALES (corp-wide): 130.8B **Publicly Held**
SIC: 4812 Cellular telephone services
HQ: Cellco Partnership
1 Verizon Way
Basking Ridge NJ 07920

(G-16483)
COMMUNITY ACTION COMSN BELMONT (PA)
Also Called: Community Action Comm Blmont C
153 1/2 W Main St (43950-1224)
PHONE.....................................740 695-0293
Gary Obloy, *Exec Dir*
Shirley Mallory, *Admin Director*
EMP: 30
SQ FT: 3,600
SALES: 4.1MM **Privately Held**
WEB: www.cacbelmont.org
SIC: 8322 8351 1742 Social service cen-
ter; referral service for personal & social
problems; head start center, except in
conjunction with school; insulation, build-
ings

(G-16484)
COMMUNITY MENTAL HEALTH SVC (PA)
Also Called: Community Mental Health Svcs
68353 Bannock Rd (43950-9736)
PHONE.....................................740 695-9344
Jack Stephens, *Treasurer*
Mary Denoble, *Exec Dir*
Katherine Whinnery, *Admin Sec*
EMP: 61 EST: 1970
SQ FT: 6,000
SALES (est): 3.5MM **Privately Held**
WEB: www.cmhs.net
SIC: 8011 8093 Clinic, operated by physi-
cians; specialty outpatient clinics

(G-16485)
CRESTVIEW HEALTH CARE CENTER
Also Called: Crestview Nursing Home
68637 Bannock Rd (43950-9736)
PHONE.....................................740 695-2500
Thomas D Nordquist, *President*
EMP: 100

SALES (est): 2.7MM **Privately Held**
SIC: 8361 8092 8051 Rehabilitation center, residential: health care incidental; kidney dialysis centers; skilled nursing care
facilities

(G-16486)
DAYS INN
52601 Holiday Dr (43950-9313)
PHONE.....................................740 695-0100
Rajendra Patel, *President*
Debbie Britton, *General Mgr*
EMP: 28
SQ FT: 5,000
SALES (est): 1.7MM **Privately Held**
SIC: 7011 Hotels & motels

(G-16487)
GULFPORT ENERGY CORPORATION
67185 Executive Dr (43950-8494)
PHONE.....................................740 251-0407
William Sowards, *Facilities Mgr*
Jen Masters, *Engineer*
Cindy Gray, *Branch Mgr*
EMP: 41
SALES (corp-wide): 1.3B **Publicly Held**
SIC: 1311 Crude petroleum production
PA: Gulfport Energy Corporation
3001 Quail Springs Pkwy
Oklahoma City OK 73134
405 252-4600

(G-16488)
HARRISON COUNTY COAL COMPANY (PA)
46226 National Rd (43950-8742)
PHONE.....................................740 338-3100
Jason D Witt, *Manager*
EMP: 38
SALES (est): 22MM **Privately Held**
SIC: 1241 Coal mining services

(G-16489)
HUNTINGTON NATIONAL BANK
154 W Main St (43950-1225)
P.O. Box 249 (43950-0249)
PHONE.....................................740 695-3323
Susan Neal, *Site Mgr*
Carol Debonis, *Branch Mgr*
EMP: 50
SALES (corp-wide): 5.2B **Publicly Held**
WEB: www.huntingtonnationalbank.com
SIC: 6029 6022 Commercial banks; state
commercial banks
HQ: The Huntington National Bank
17 S High St Fl 1
Columbus OH 43215
614 480-4293

(G-16490)
LAMAR ADVERTISING COMPANY
52610 Holiday Dr (43950-9313)
PHONE.....................................740 699-0000
Shane Walters, *Manager*
EMP: 48 **Publicly Held**
WEB: www.lamar.com
SIC: 7312 Billboard advertising
PA: Lamar Advertising Company
5321 Corporate Blvd
Baton Rouge LA 70808

(G-16491)
LANCIA NURSING HOME INC
Also Called: Belmont Manor Nursing Home
51999 Guirino Dr (43950-8314)
PHONE.....................................740 695-4404
Karen Layman, *Manager*
EMP: 50
SALES (corp-wide): 8MM **Privately Held**
SIC: 8051 Convalescent home with contin-
uous nursing care
PA: Lancia Nursing Home Inc
1852 Sinclair Ave
Steubenville OH 43953
740 264-7101

(G-16492)
LM CONSTRCTION TRRY LVRINI INC
67682 Clark Rd (43950-9257)
P.O. Box 339 (43950-0339)
PHONE.....................................740 695-9604
Terry Lavorini, *President*

▲ = Import ▼=Export
◆ =Import/Export

Lisa Lavorini, *Vice Pres*
Mickey Mickler, *Admin Sec*
EMP: 50
SQ FT: 10,000
SALES (est): 13.3MM **Privately Held**
SIC: 1542 1742 1541 Commercial & office building, new construction; commercial & office buildings, renovation & repair; plastering, plain or ornamental; industrial buildings & warehouses

(G-16493)
LOWES HOME CENTERS LLC
50421 Valley Plaza Dr (43950-1749)
PHONE..................................740 699-3000
Cary Johnson, *Manager*
EMP: 150
SALES (corp-wide): 68.6B **Publicly Held**
SIC: 5211 5031 5722 5064 Home centers; building materials, exterior; building materials, interior; household appliance stores; electrical appliances, television & radio
HQ: Lowe's Home Centers, Llc
1605 Curtis Bridge Rd
Wilkesboro NC 28697
336 658-4000

(G-16494)
MARIETTA COAL CO (PA)
67705 Friends Church Rd (43950-9500)
PHONE..................................740 695-2197
Paul Gill, *President*
George Nicolozakes, *Chairman*
John Nicolozakes, *Vice Pres*
EMP: 50 **EST:** 1946
SQ FT: 4,300
SALES (est): 8.2MM **Privately Held**
WEB: www.mcatee.biz
SIC: 1221 Surface mining, bituminous

(G-16495)
MCKEEN SECURITY INC
69100 Bayberry Dr Ste 200 (43950-9194)
P.O. Box 740 (43950-0740)
PHONE..................................740 699-1301
David McKeen, *President*
Ranelle Klan, *Technology*
EMP: 100
SALES (est): 1.8MM **Privately Held**
SIC: 7381 Security guard service

(G-16496)
MURRAY AMERICAN ENERGY INC
46226 National Rd (43950-8742)
PHONE..................................740 338-3100
Robert E Murray, *President*
Robert D Moore, *Vice Pres*
Michael D Loiacono, *Treasurer*
Jason D Witt, *Admin Sec*
EMP: 2667 **EST:** 2013
SALES (est): 443.4K
SALES (corp-wide): 4.8B **Publicly Held**
SIC: 1221 Bituminous coal surface mining
PA: Murray Energy Corporation
46226 National Rd
Saint Clairsville OH 43950
740 338-3100

(G-16497)
OHIO POWER COMPANY
47687 National Rd (43950-8714)
P.O. Box 99 (43950-0099)
PHONE..................................740 695-7800
Phil Lewis, *Manager*
EMP: 100
SALES (corp-wide): 16.2B **Publicly Held**
SIC: 4911 Electric services
HQ: Ohio Power Company
1 Riverside Plz
Columbus OH 43215
614 716-1000

(G-16498)
OHIO VALLEY COAL COMPANY (DH)
46226 National Rd (43950-8742)
PHONE..................................740 926-1351
Robert E Murray, *CEO*
Ryan M Murray, *President*
John R Forrelli, *Senior VP*
Michael O McKown, *Senior VP*
Robert D Moore, *Vice Pres*
EMP: 395
SQ FT: 40,380

SALES (est): 218.7MM
SALES (corp-wide): 4.8B **Publicly Held**
SIC: 1221 Bituminous coal & lignite-surface mining
HQ: Ohio Valley Resources, Inc.
29325 Chagrin Blvd # 300
Beachwood OH 44122
216 765-1240

(G-16499)
OHIO VALLEY RESOURCES INC
Also Called: Ohio Valley Coal
46226 National Rd (43950-8742)
PHONE..................................740 795-5220
Robert E Murray, *CEO*
McKown Michael, *Vice Pres*
Andrew Wentz, *Purchasing*
Bo Putsock, *Accounting Dir*
Colt McVey, *Manager*
EMP: 30
SALES (corp-wide): 4.8B **Publicly Held**
SIC: 1241 Coal mining services
HQ: Ohio Valley Resources, Inc.
29325 Chagrin Blvd # 300
Beachwood OH 44122
216 765-1240

(G-16500)
OHIO VALLEY TRANSLOADING CO
46226 National Rd (43950-8742)
PHONE..................................740 795-4967
Robert Murray, *CEO*
EMP: 2566
SALES (est): 57.6MM
SALES (corp-wide): 4.8B **Publicly Held**
SIC: 1241 Bituminous coal mining services, contract basis
HQ: Ohio Valley Resources, Inc.
29325 Chagrin Blvd # 300
Beachwood OH 44122
216 765-1240

(G-16501)
PARAMOUNT SUPPORT SERVICE
252 W Main St Ste H (43950-1065)
P.O. Box 543 (43950-0543)
PHONE..................................740 526-0540
Brent Kovalski, *President*
Jay Van Horn, *Supervisor*
Cheryl Howells, *Representative*
EMP: 86
SALES (est): 1.5MM **Privately Held**
SIC: 8082 Home health care services

(G-16502)
PSYCHIATRIC SOLUTIONS INC
67670 Traco Dr (43950-9375)
PHONE..................................740 695-2131
Karen Maxwell, *CEO*
EMP: 137
SALES (corp-wide): 10.7B **Publicly Held**
WEB: www.intermountainhospital.com
SIC: 8011 Psychiatric clinic
HQ: Psychiatric Solutions, Inc.
6640 Carothers Pkwy # 500
Franklin TN 37067
615 312-5700

(G-16503)
RED ROOF INNS INC
68301 Red Roof Ln (43950-1706)
PHONE..................................740 695-4057
Chris Bolt, *Manager*
EMP: 30 **Privately Held**
WEB: www.redroof.com
SIC: 7011 Hotels & motels
HQ: Red Roof Inns, Inc.
7815 Walton Pkwy
New Albany OH 43054
614 744-2600

(G-16504)
RES-CARE INC
66387 Airport Rd (43950-9421)
PHONE..................................740 526-0285
Tonya Bartyzel, *Branch Mgr*
EMP: 48
SALES (corp-wide): 23.7B **Privately Held**
SIC: 8361 Residential care
HQ: Res-Care, Inc.
805 N Whittington Pkwy
Louisville KY 40222
502 394-2100

(G-16505)
SOMNUS CORPORATION
Also Called: Hampton Inn
51130 National Rd (43950-9118)
PHONE..................................740 695-3961
Edward Hitchman, *President*
Christopher Chesebrough, *General Mgr*
EMP: 35
SALES (est): 2.1MM **Privately Held**
SIC: 7011 Hotels & motels

(G-16506)
ST CLAIR 60 MINUTE CLRS INC (PA)
Also Called: Glo-Tone Cleaners
116 N Sugar St (43950-1303)
PHONE..................................740 695-3100
Paul G Yochum, *President*
Phyllis June Yochum, *Principal*
Peter Yochum, *Vice Pres*
EMP: 35 **EST:** 1959
SQ FT: 9,000
SALES: 2MM **Privately Held**
SIC: 7216 7215 Drycleaning collecting & distributing agency; curtain cleaning & repair; laundry, coin-operated

(G-16507)
TRI COUNTY HELP CENTER INC (PA)
104 1/2 N Marietta St (43950-1255)
P.O. Box 494 (43950-0494)
PHONE..................................740 695-5441
Karen Scott, *Exec Dir*
EMP: 43
SQ FT: 2,021
SALES: 1.3MM **Privately Held**
SIC: 8322 Emergency shelters; alcoholism counseling, nontreatment; drug abuse counselor, nontreatment

(G-16508)
UNITED PARCEL SERVICE INC OH
Also Called: UPS
44191 Lafferty Rd (43950-9743)
PHONE..................................740 968-3508
James Stickradt, *Manager*
EMP: 50
SALES (corp-wide): 71.8B **Publicly Held**
WEB: www.upsscs.com
SIC: 4215 Parcel delivery, vehicular
HQ: United Parcel Service, Inc. (Oh)
55 Glenlake Pkwy
Atlanta GA 30328
404 828-6000

(G-16509)
VETERANS HEALTH ADMINISTRATION
Also Called: St Clairsville V A Primary
103 Plaza Dr Ste A (43950-7729)
PHONE..................................740 695-9321
Misty Reynolds, *Manager*
EMP: 264 **Publicly Held**
WEB: www.veterans-ru.org
SIC: 8011 9451 Clinic, operated by physicians; psychiatric clinic;
HQ: Veterans Health Administration
810 Vermont Ave Nw
Washington DC 20420

(G-16510)
WESTERN KY COAL RESOURCES LLC
46226 National Rd (43950-8742)
PHONE..................................740 338-3100
Robert E Murray, *President*
EMP: 400
SALES (est): 3.7MM
SALES (corp-wide): 4.8B **Publicly Held**
SIC: 1222 Bituminous coal-underground mining
HQ: Murray Kentucky Energy, Inc.
46226 National Rd
Saint Clairsville OH 43950
740 338-3100

(G-16511)
WHEELING HOSPITAL INC
107 Plaza Dr Ste D (43950-8735)
PHONE..................................740 695-2090
EMP: 35

SALES (corp-wide): 395.3MM **Privately Held**
SIC: 8011 General & family practice, physician/surgeon
PA: Wheeling Hospital, Inc.
1 Medical Park
Wheeling WV 26003
304 243-3000

(G-16512)
ZANDEX INC
Also Called: Beacon House, The
100 Reservoir Rd Ofc 2 (43950-1033)
PHONE..................................740 695-3281
Cathy Kocher, *Manager*
EMP: 34
SALES (corp-wide): 34MM **Privately Held**
SIC: 8052 Intermediate care facilities
PA: Zandex, Inc.
1122 Taylor St
Zanesville OH 43701
740 454-1400

(G-16513)
ZANDEX INC
Also Called: Forest Hill Care Center
100 Reservoir Rd Ofc 1 (43950-1063)
PHONE..................................740 695-7233
Heather Borkoski, *Administration*
EMP: 150
SALES (corp-wide): 34MM **Privately Held**
SIC: 8052 8051 Intermediate care facilities; skilled nursing care facilities
PA: Zandex, Inc.
1122 Taylor St
Zanesville OH 43701
740 454-1400

(G-16514)
ZANDEX HEALTH CARE CORPORATION
Also Called: Forest Hill Retirement Cmnty
100 Reservoir Rd (43950-1064)
PHONE..................................740 695-7233
Heather Borkoski, *Manager*
Eileen Kanzic, *Nursing Dir*
EMP: 150
SQ FT: 1,920
SALES (corp-wide): 34MM **Privately Held**
SIC: 8052 8051 8059 Personal care facility; skilled nursing care facilities; nursing home, except skilled & intermediate care facility
HQ: Zandex Health Care Corporation
1122 Taylor St
Zanesville OH 43701

Saint Henry
Mercer County

(G-16515)
BRUNS BUILDING & DEV CORP INC
Also Called: Ohio and Indiana Roofing Co
1429 Cranberry Rd (45883-9749)
PHONE..................................419 925-4095
Robert E Bruns, *CEO*
Mike Bruns, *President*
Dave Bruns, *Exec VP*
Dan Bruns, *Vice Pres*
Steve Elston, *Project Mgr*
▲ **EMP:** 86
SQ FT: 10,000
SALES (est): 27.4MM **Privately Held**
WEB: www.brunsbuilding.com
SIC: 1761 Roofing contractor

(G-16516)
LCS INC
411 Stachler Dr (45883-9581)
P.O. Box 414 (45883-0414)
PHONE..................................419 678-8600
Dan Lennartz, *President*
Theresa Lennartz, *Corp Secy*
EMP: 35 **EST:** 2001
SQ FT: 4,000
SALES: 2.8MM **Privately Held**
SIC: 1541 Industrial buildings & warehouses

(G-16517)
STACHLER CONCRETE INC
431 Stachler Dr (45883-9581)
PHONE..................................419 678-3867
Andy Stockwood, *President*
Janice Ridler, *Office Mgr*
EMP: 28
SQ FT: 1,200
SALES: 4MM **Privately Held**
SIC: 1799 Erection & dismantling of forms
for poured concrete

Saint Louisville
Licking County

(G-16518)
HOUSE OF NEW HOPE
8135 Mount Vernon Rd (43071-9670)
PHONE..................................740 345-5437
Edward Sharp, *President*
Shirley Sharp, *Vice Pres*
Jeffrey Greene PHD, *Exec Dir*
Glenn McCleese, *Director*
EMP: 35
SQ FT: 18,000
SALES: 4MM **Privately Held**
SIC: 8361 Residential care

(G-16519)
LAW EXCAVATING INC
9128 Mount Vernon Rd (43071-9637)
PHONE..................................740 745-3420
Tom Law, *President*
Veronica Edwards, *Corp Secy*
Nick Edwards, *Vice Pres*
EMP: 45
SQ FT: 120
SALES (est): 3.6MM **Privately Held**
SIC: 1794 Excavation work

Saint Marys
Auglaize County

(G-16520)
CAPABILITIES INC (PA)
124 S Front St (45885-2301)
PHONE..................................419 394-0003
Karen Blumhorst, *CEO*
William Blumhorst, *CFO*
Katie Blumhorst, *Human Resources*
Belinda Bockrath, *Manager*
Lisa Bowling, *Consultant*
EMP: 45
SQ FT: 2,720
SALES (est): 3.2MM **Privately Held**
SIC: 8331 Sheltered workshop; vocational
rehabilitation agency

(G-16521)
**COMMUNICARE HEALTH SVCS
INC**
Also Called: Saint Marys Living Center
1209 Indiana Ave (45885-1310)
PHONE..................................419 394-7611
Jane Fiely, *Director*
EMP: 75
SALES (corp-wide): 125.8MM **Privately
Held**
WEB: www.atriumlivingcenters.com
SIC: 6531 8052 8051 Real estate agents
& managers; intermediate care facilities;
skilled nursing care facilities
PA: Communicare Health Services, Inc.
4700 Ashwood Dr Ste 200
Blue Ash OH 45241
513 530-1654

(G-16522)
CONAG INC
Also Called: Con-AG
16672 County Road 66a (45885-9212)
PHONE..................................419 394-8870
Robert Hirschfeld, *President*
John Hirschfeld, *President*
Lee Kuck, *Corp Secy*
Johnathan Hirschfeld, *Vice Pres*
EMP: 35
SALES (est): 3.5MM **Privately Held**
WEB: www.conag.com
SIC: 1422 Limestones, ground

(G-16523)
**JOINT TOWNSHIP DST MEM
HOSP**
Also Called: Grand Lake Primary Care
1040 Hager St (45885-2421)
PHONE..................................419 394-9959
Jeffrey W Vossler, *Vice Pres*
EMP: 64
SALES (corp-wide): 76.8MM **Privately
Held**
SIC: 8062 General medical & surgical hos-
pitals
PA: Joint Township District Memorial Hospi-
tal
200 Saint Clair Ave
Saint Marys OH 45885
419 394-3335

(G-16524)
**JOINT TOWNSHIP DST MEM
HOSP (PA)**
Also Called: GRAND LAKE HEALTH SYS-
TEM
200 Saint Clair Ave (45885-2494)
PHONE..................................419 394-3335
Kevin W Harlan, *CEO*
Jeff Vossler, *Treasurer*
Jill Dickman, *Admin Sec*
Kelsey Eickholt, *Personnel Assit*
EMP: 400
SQ FT: 170,000
SALES: 76.8MM **Privately Held**
WEB: www.jtdmh.org
SIC: 8062 8051 General medical & surgi-
cal hospitals; skilled nursing care facilities

(G-16525)
**JOINT TOWNSHIP HOME
HEALTH**
1122 E Spring St (45885-2402)
PHONE..................................419 394-3335
Linda Haines, *Principal*
EMP: 35
SALES (est): 426.5K
SALES (corp-wide): 76.8MM **Privately
Held**
WEB: www.jtdmh.org
SIC: 8082 Home health care services
PA: Joint Township District Memorial Hospi-
tal
200 Saint Clair Ave
Saint Marys OH 45885
419 394-3335

(G-16526)
**JPMORGAN CHASE BANK NAT
ASSN**
125 W Spring St (45885-2313)
PHONE..................................419 394-2358
Larry Gautschi, *Principal*
EMP: 26
SALES (corp-wide): 131.4B **Publicly
Held**
SIC: 6021 National commercial banks
HQ: Jpmorgan Chase Bank, National Asso-
ciation
1111 Polaris Pkwy
Columbus OH 43240
614 436-3055

(G-16527)
JTD HEALTH SYSTEMS INC
Also Called: Speech Center
200 Saint Clair Ave (45885-2400)
PHONE..................................419 394-3335
Jeff Vossler, *Treasurer*
Kevin W Harlan, *Administration*
Jill Dickman, *Admin Sec*
EMP: 600
SQ FT: 150,000
SALES: 90MM **Privately Held**
SIC: 8741 Hospital management

(G-16528)
**NATURAL RESOURCES OHIO
DEPT**
Division of Parks
834 Edgewater Dr (45885-1132)
PHONE..................................419 394-3611
Brian Miller, *Manager*
EMP: 30 **Privately Held**
WEB: www.ohiostateparks.com
SIC: 7033 9512 Trailer parks & campsites;

HQ: Ohio Department Of Natural Resources
2045 Morse Rd Bldg D-3
Columbus OH 43229

(G-16529)
OMNISOURCE LLC
04575 County Road 33a (45885-9655)
PHONE..................................419 394-3351
Mlike Starkey, *Branch Mgr*
EMP: 25 **Publicly Held**
WEB: www.omnisource.com
SIC: 5093 Ferrous metal scrap & waste
HQ: Omnisource, Llc
7575 W Jefferson Blvd
Fort Wayne IN 46804
260 422-5541

(G-16530)
**OTTERBEIN SNIOR LFSTYLE
CHICES**
Also Called: Otterbein St Marys Retrmnt
11230 State Route 364 (45885-9534)
PHONE..................................419 394-2366
Ed Bray, *Trustee*
Fred Wiswell, *Manager*
Teresa Wenning,
EMP: 120
SALES (corp-wide): 58.4MM **Privately
Held**
SIC: 8322 8361 8051 Geriatric social
service; residential care; skilled nursing
care facilities
PA: Senior Otterbein Lifestyle Choices
585 N State Route 741
Lebanon OH 45036
513 933-5400

(G-16531)
PET FOOD HOLDINGS INC
1601 Mckinley Rd (45885-1864)
PHONE..................................419 394-3374
Jim Wiegmann, *President*
EMP: 93
SALES (corp-wide): 114.7B **Privately
Held**
SIC: 6719 Investment holding companies,
except banks
PA: Cargill, Incorporated
15407 Mcginty Rd W
Wayzata MN 55391
952 742-7575

(G-16532)
**ST MARYS CITY BOARD
EDUCATION**
Also Called: Saint Marys Cy Schools-Bus Gar
1445 Celina Rd (45885-1210)
PHONE..................................419 394-1116
Kurt Kuffner, *Manager*
EMP: 25
SALES (corp-wide): 1.5MM **Privately
Held**
WEB: www.smriders.net
SIC: 8211 7699 Public elementary & sec-
ondary schools; miscellaneous automo-
tive repair services
PA: St Marys City Board Of Education
2250 State Route 66
Saint Marys OH 45885
419 394-4312

(G-16533)
**ST MARYS CITY BOARD
EDUCATION**
Also Called: East Elementary School
650 Armstrong St (45885-1840)
PHONE..................................419 394-2616
Susan Sherman, *Principal*
EMP: 60
SALES (corp-wide): 1.5MM **Privately
Held**
WEB: www.smriders.net
SIC: 8211 8351 Public elementary & sec-
ondary schools; child day care services
PA: St Marys City Board Of Education
2250 State Route 66
Saint Marys OH 45885
419 394-4312

Saint Paris
Champaign County

(G-16534)
**THE FIRST CENTRAL NATIONAL
BNK (PA)**
103 S Springfield St (43072-7704)
P.O. Box 730 (43072-0730)
PHONE..................................937 663-4186
Jeff McCulla, *President*
Curtis Blake, *Vice Pres*
EMP: 25 EST: 1880
SALES: 3.5MM **Privately Held**
WEB: www.firststparis.com
SIC: 6021 National commercial banks

Salem
Columbiana County

(G-16535)
AT&T CORP
1098 E State St Ste A (44460-2212)
PHONE..................................330 337-3505
EMP: 69
SALES (corp-wide): 146.8B **Publicly
Held**
SIC: 4813 Telephone Communications
HQ: At&T Corp.
1 At&T Way
Bedminster NJ 07921
800 403-3302

(G-16536)
BENTLEY LEASING CO LLC
Also Called: Salem West Healthcare Center
2511 Bentley Dr (44460-2503)
PHONE..................................330 337-9503
Charles Stoltz, *CEO*
Steve Rosedale, *COO*
Isaac Rosedale, *CFO*
EMP: 3830
SALES (est): 2.7MM **Privately Held**
SIC: 8051 Skilled nursing care facilities

(G-16537)
BFI WASTE SERVICES LLC
1717 Pennsylvania Ave (44460-2781)
PHONE..................................800 437-1123
John Carlson, *Branch Mgr*
EMP: 48
SALES (corp-wide): 10B **Publicly Held**
SIC: 4212 4953 Garbage collection &
transport, no disposal; refuse collection &
disposal services
HQ: Bfi Waste Services, Llc
18500 N Allied Way # 100
Phoenix AZ 85054
480 627-2700

(G-16538)
**BLOSSOM NURSING & REHAB
CENTER**
Also Called: Blossom Nrsing Rhblitation Ctr
109 Blossom Ln (44460-4284)
PHONE..................................330 337-3033
David Keast, *Director*
Joseph Pilla, *Director*
EMP: 110
SALES (est): 5MM **Privately Held**
SIC: 8071 8051 Medical laboratories;
skilled nursing care facilities

(G-16539)
BOC WATER HYDRAULICS INC
12024 Salem Warren Rd (44460-7649)
P.O. Box 1028 (44460-8028)
PHONE..................................330 332-4444
Todd Olson, *President*
Donald Olson, *Vice Pres*
EMP: 44
SQ FT: 14,000
SALES: 8.2MM **Privately Held**
SIC: 7699 Hydraulic equipment repair

(G-16540)
COUNTRY SAW AND KNIFE INC
1375 W State St (44460-1952)
P.O. Box 887 (44460-0887)
PHONE..................................330 332-1611
Stanley Glista, *President*

Daniel Glista, *Vice Pres*
Anthony Glista, *Treasurer*
Richard Mercer, *Admin Sec*
▲ **EMP:** 40
SQ FT: 4,800
SALES (est): 4.3MM **Privately Held**
WEB: www.countrysaw.com
SIC: 7699 5072 Knife, saw & tool sharpening & repair; saw blades

(G-16541)
CTM INTEGRATION INCORPORATED
1318 Quaker Cir (44460-1051)
P.O. Box 589 (44460-0589)
PHONE..............................330 332-1800
Thomas C Rumsey, *President*
Dan Mc Laughlin, *Exec VP*
Dan McLaughlin, *Exec VP*
Kevin Marshall, *Plant Mgr*
Mike Kennedy, *Engineer*
EMP: 36
SQ FT: 30,000
SALES (est): 10.9MM **Privately Held**
WEB: www.ctmint.com
SIC: 3565 5084 3549 Packaging machinery; industrial machinery & equipment; metalworking machinery

(G-16542)
DONNELL FORD-LINCOLN
152 Continental Dr (44460-2506)
P.O. Box 765 (44460-0765)
PHONE..............................330 332-0031
Tim Loudon, *CEO*
Hank Loudon Jr, *President*
Tom Poponak, *General Mgr*
Bruce Mansfield, *Manager*
EMP: 40
SALES (est): 8.6MM **Privately Held**
WEB: www.loudonford.com
SIC: 5511 5521 7538 7532 Automobiles, new & used; used car dealers; general automotive repair shops; top & body repair & paint shops

(G-16543)
FAMILY PRACTICE CTR SALEM INC
2370 Southeast Blvd (44460-3498)
PHONE..............................330 332-9961
Richard Banning, *President*
Richard Fawcett, *Med Doctor*
EMP: 25
SALES (est): 2.7MM **Privately Held**
SIC: 8011 General & family practice, physician/surgeon

(G-16544)
FRENCOR INC
Also Called: Visiting Angels
409 E 2nd St Ste 6 (44460-2862)
P.O. Box 67 (44460-0067)
PHONE..............................330 332-1203
Mark Frenger, *President*
Susan Frenger, *Vice Pres*
EMP: 60
SALES (est): 1.6MM **Privately Held**
SIC: 8082 Home health care services

(G-16545)
GORDON BROTHERS INC (PA)
Also Called: Gordon Bros Water
776 N Ellsworth Ave (44460-1600)
P.O. Box 358 (44460-0358)
PHONE..............................800 331-7611
Bruce Gordon, *Ch of Bd*
Ned Jones, *President*
EMP: 39
SQ FT: 4,500
SALES: 4.7MM **Privately Held**
WEB: www.gordonbros.com
SIC: 7359 5999 5078 5074 Equipment rental & leasing; water purification equipment; refrigeration equipment & supplies; plumbing & hydronic heating supplies

(G-16546)
HICKEY METAL FABRICATION ROOFG
873 Georgetown Rd (44460-9710)
PHONE..............................330 337-9329
Bob Hickey, *President*
Robert R Hickey, *Principal*
Leo Hickey, *Vice Pres*

Nick Peters, *Vice Pres*
Robert Peters, *Vice Pres*
▲ **EMP:** 30
SALES: 6.9MM **Privately Held**
WEB: www.hickeymetal.com
SIC: 1761 Sheet metalwork

(G-16547)
HOME CARE ADVANTAGE
718 E 3rd St Ste C (44460-2915)
PHONE..............................330 337-4663
Carolyn Crookston, *Principal*
Cynthia Kenst, *Principal*
EMP: 60
SALES (est): 1.4MM **Privately Held**
SIC: 8082 Visiting nurse service

(G-16548)
HUNTINGTON INSURANCE INC
193 S Lincoln Ave (44460-3101)
PHONE..............................330 337-9933
David B Hazen, *Branch Mgr*
EMP: 37
SALES (corp-wide): 5.2B **Publicly Held**
WEB: www.skyinsure.com
SIC: 6411 Insurance agents, brokers & service
HQ: Huntington Insurance, Inc.
      519 Madison Ave
      Toledo OH 43604
      419 720-7900

(G-16549)
INTEGRATED PRJ RESOURCES LLC
600 E 2nd St (44460-2916)
PHONE..............................330 272-0998
Tina Hertzel, *Mng Member*
John Hertzel,
EMP: 28
SQ FT: 2,500
SALES: 3MM **Privately Held**
WEB: www.iprglobal.net
SIC: 8742 Management consulting services

(G-16550)
L B BRUNK & SONS INC
Also Called: Brunk's Stoves
10460 Salem Warren Rd (44460-9666)
PHONE..............................330 332-0359
Lawrence B Brunk, *President*
Joseph Brunk, *Treasurer*
EMP: 35
SQ FT: 2,000
SALES (est): 7.1MM **Privately Held**
WEB: www.brunks.com
SIC: 5074 5561 Fireplaces, prefabricated; stoves, wood burning; recreational vehicle dealers

(G-16551)
LAKE FRONT II INC
Also Called: Salem Hills Golf and Cntry CLB
12688 Salem Warren Rd (44460-9668)
PHONE..............................330 337-8033
Clement L Ross, *President*
EMP: 30
SQ FT: 12,000
SALES (est): 1.2MM **Privately Held**
SIC: 7997 Country club, membership

(G-16552)
MAC MANUFACTURING INC
1453 Allen Rd (44460-1004)
PHONE..............................330 829-1680
Cora McDonald, *Branch Mgr*
EMP: 104
SALES (est): 36.2MM **Privately Held**
SIC: 3715 5012 Truck trailers; trailers for trucks, new & used; truck bodies
PA: Mac Manufacturing, Inc.
      14599 Commerce St Ne
      Alliance OH 44601

(G-16553)
MOBILE MEALS OF SALEM INC
1995 E State St (44460-2423)
PHONE..............................330 332-2160
Jeff Goll, *President*
Barb Plummer, *Vice Pres*
Laura Todd, *Treasurer*
Marilyn McBride, *Admin Sec*
EMP: 45
SALES (est): 720.2K **Privately Held**
SIC: 8322 Meal delivery program

(G-16554)
POLLOCK RESEARCH & DESIGN INC
Simmers Crane Design & Svc Co
1134 Salem Pkwy (44460-1063)
PHONE..............................330 332-3300
Randy L Stull, *Manager*
EMP: 45
SALES (corp-wide): 73.1MM **Privately Held**
SIC: 8711 7389 7353 3537 Civil engineering; mechanical engineering; structural engineering; crane & aerial lift service; heavy construction equipment rental; industrial trucks & tractors
PA: Pollock Research & Design, Inc.
      11 Vanguard Dr
      Reading PA 19606
      610 582-7203

(G-16555)
QUALITY FABRICATED METALS INC
14000 W Middletown Rd (44460-9184)
PHONE..............................330 332-7008
Danny Beegle, *President*
EMP: 25
SQ FT: 42,000
SALES (est): 4.7MM **Privately Held**
WEB: www.gtd-qfm.com
SIC: 3469 1799 Metal stampings; welding on site

(G-16556)
R K CAMPF CORP
Also Called: R-K-Campf Transport
465 Newgarden Ave (44460-3042)
PHONE..............................330 332-7089
Rob Campf, *President*
Karrin Campf, *Vice Pres*
EMP: 50
SALES (est): 4.3MM **Privately Held**
WEB: www.rkcampf.com
SIC: 4213 4214 Contract haulers; local trucking with storage

(G-16557)
RENT-A-CENTER INC
2870 E State St Ste 500 (44460-9335)
PHONE..............................330 337-1107
Anthony Dieudenil, *Manager*
Robert Hensley, *Manager*
EMP: 56
SALES (corp-wide): 2.6B **Publicly Held**
WEB: www.rentacenter.com
SIC: 7359 Appliance rental; furniture rental; home entertainment equipment rental; television rental
PA: Rent-A-Center, Inc.
      5501 Headquarters Dr
      Plano TX 75024
      972 801-1100

(G-16558)
SALEM AREA VSITING NURSE ASSOC
718 E 3rd St Ste A (44460-2915)
PHONE..............................330 332-9986
Susan K Yoder, *Exec Dir*
EMP: 50
SQ FT: 9,000
SALES: 1.8MM **Privately Held**
WEB: www.salemohiovna.com
SIC: 8082 Visiting nurse service

(G-16559)
SALEM COMMUNITY CENTER INC
1098 N Ellsworth Ave (44460-1536)
PHONE..............................330 332-5885
George Morris, *Systems Dir*
Heather Young, *Exec Dir*
Mark Equizi, *Exec Dir*
Caroline Stone, *Exec Dir*
Cory Wonner, *Director*
EMP: 75
SALES: 2.4MM **Privately Held**
SIC: 8322 Community center

(G-16560)
SALEM COMMUNITY HOSPITAL (PA)
Also Called: SALEM HOME MEDICAL
1995 E State St (44460-2400)
PHONE..............................330 332-1551
Anita Hackstedde MD, *CEO*
Mike Giangardella, *Vice Pres*
Michael Giangardella, *CFO*
Joan Creel, *Director*
Chris Dunn, *Social Dir*
EMP: 988
SQ FT: 300,000
SALES: 105.5MM **Privately Held**
WEB: www.salemhosp.com
SIC: 8062 8051 General medical & surgical hospitals; skilled nursing care facilities

(G-16561)
SALEM HEALTHCARE MGT LLC
1985 E Pershing St (44460-3411)
PHONE..............................330 332-1588
Alan Schwartz, *Mng Member*
EMP: 40
SALES (est): 4MM **Privately Held**
SIC: 8741 Nursing & personal care facility management

(G-16562)
SALEM HISTORICAL SOC MUSEUM
208 S Broadway Ave (44460-3004)
PHONE..............................330 337-6733
David Stratton, *Director*
EMP: 25
SALES: 1.7MM **Privately Held**
SIC: 8412 Museum

(G-16563)
SALEM INTERNAL MEDICINE ASSOC
564 E 2nd St (44460-2914)
PHONE..............................330 332-5232
Fax: 330 332-4771
EMP: 32
SQ FT: 2,400
SALES (est): 1.8MM **Privately Held**
SIC: 8011 Medical Doctor's Office

(G-16564)
TFI TRANSPORTATION INC
10370 W South Range Rd (44460-9621)
P.O. Box 310 (44460-0310)
PHONE..............................330 332-4655
Verona Lippiatt, *President*
Sam Lippiatt, *Vice Pres*
Bill Sinclair, *Vice Pres*
Sue Sinclair, *Treasurer*
Mary McLaughlin, *Admin Sec*
EMP: 35
SALES (est): 3.4MM **Privately Held**
SIC: 4213 Heavy machinery transport; building materials transport

(G-16565)
VENTRA SALEM LLC
383 Mullins St (44460-3016)
PHONE..............................330 337-3240
Sid Ravelli, *Manager*
EMP: 25
SALES (corp-wide): 3.4B **Privately Held**
SIC: 4225 General warehousing & storage
HQ: Ventra Salem, Llc
      800 Pennsylvania Ave
      Salem OH 44460

(G-16566)
VENTRA SALEM LLC (HQ)
800 Pennsylvania Ave (44460-2783)
PHONE..............................330 337-8002
Tammy Anderson, *Human Res Mgr*
Shahid Khan,
▲ **EMP:** 750
SQ FT: 400,000
SALES (est): 221.8MM
SALES (corp-wide): 3.4B **Privately Held**
WEB: www.flex-n-gate.com
SIC: 5013 Automotive supplies & parts
PA: Flex-N-Gate Llc
      1306 E University Ave
      Urbana IL 61802
      217 384-6600

(G-16567)
WITMERS INC
39821 Salem Unity Rd (44460-9696)
P.O. Box 368, Columbiana (44408-0368)
PHONE.........................330 427-2147
Ralph Witmer, *CEO*
Nelson Witmer, *President*
Grace Styer, *Corp Secy*
EMP: 30
SQ FT: 20,000
SALES (est): 5.9MM **Privately Held**
SIC: 5999 1542 7699 Farm equipment &
  supplies; agricultural building contractors;
  farm machinery repair

Salesville
Guernsey County

(G-16568)
**SOUTHEASTERN
REHABILITATION**
62222 Frankfort Rd (43778-9638)
PHONE.........................740 679-2111
Renee Nelson, *Owner*
Sheri Vandyne, *Admin Sec*
EMP: 35
SALES (est): 635.8K **Privately Held**
SIC: 8322 Rehabilitation services

(G-16569)
WAMPUM HARDWARE CO
60711 Dynamite Rd (43778-9756)
PHONE.........................740 685-2585
Bob Wright, *Manager*
EMP: 45
SALES (corp-wide): 36.1MM **Privately
Held**
WEB: www.wampumhardware.com
SIC: 5169 Explosives
PA: Wampum Hardware Co.
  636 Paden Rd
  New Galilee PA 16141
  724 336-4501

Salineville
Columbiana County

(G-16570)
**CIRCLE J HOME HEALTH CARE
(PA)**
412 State Route 164 (43945-7701)
PHONE.........................330 482-0877
Betty Johnson, *President*
EMP: 67
SALES (est): 1.5MM **Privately Held**
SIC: 8082 Home health care services

(G-16571)
M3 MIDSTREAM LLC
Also Called: Salineville Office
10 E Main St (43945-1134)
PHONE.........................330 679-5580
EMP: 28
SALES (corp-wide): 54.9MM **Privately
Held**
SIC: 1311 Natural gas production
PA: M3 Midstream Llc
  600 Travis St Ste 5600
  Houston TX 77002
  713 783-3000

Sandusky
Erie County

(G-16572)
ABILITY WORKS INC
Also Called: MRDD
3920 Columbus Ave (44870-5791)
PHONE.........................419 626-1048
Lisa Moore, *General Mgr*
Laura Lagodney, *COO*
Allison Young, *Director*
EMP: 125
SALES: 2.1MM **Privately Held**
WEB: www.doublejind.com
SIC: 8331 8322 7389 Sheltered work-
  shop; individual & family services;

(G-16573)
AKIL INCORPORATED
Also Called: Akil Industrial Cleaning
2525 W Monroe St (44870-1902)
PHONE.........................419 625-0857
Fax: 419 627-8182
EMP: 40
SQ FT: 33,000
SALES (est): 1.4MM **Privately Held**
SIC: 7699 1622 1611 Repair Services
  Bridge/Tunnel Cnstn Highway/Street
  Cnstn

(G-16574)
**ALL PHASE POWER AND LTG
INC**
Also Called: INSIGHT TECHNICAL SERV-
ICES
2122 Campbell St (44870-4816)
P.O. Box 2515 (44871-2515)
PHONE.........................419 624-9640
William Tunnell, *President*
Frank Kath, *President*
Jude Poggiali, *Vice Pres*
Janice Tunnell, *Vice Pres*
EMP: 35
SQ FT: 6,400
SALES (est): 9.1MM **Privately Held**
WEB: www.4-insight.com
SIC: 1731 General electrical contractor;
  switchgear & related devices installation

(G-16575)
AMERICAS BEST VALUE INN
Also Called: Ramada Inn
5608 Milan Rd (44870-5879)
PHONE.........................419 626-9890
EMP: 35
SALES (est): 618.8K **Privately Held**
SIC: 7011 6512 5812 Hotel/Motel Opera-
  tion Nonresidential Building Operator Eat-
  ing Place

(G-16576)
AUGUST CORSO SONS INC
Also Called: Corso's Flower & Garden Center
3404 Milan Rd (44870-5678)
P.O. Box 1575 (44871-1575)
PHONE.........................419 626-0765
August J Corso, *CEO*
Chad Corso, *President*
John Corso, *Vice Pres*
▲ **EMP:** 120
SQ FT: 8,000
SALES: 43.4MM **Privately Held**
WEB: www.corsos.com
SIC: 5193 5261 Flowers & nursery stock;
  nurseries & garden centers

(G-16577)
**BAYSHORE COUNSELING SVC
INC (PA)**
1634 Sycamore Line (44870-4132)
PHONE.........................419 626-9156
Tim Naughton, *Exec Dir*
EMP: 40
SQ FT: 3,700
SALES: 1.5MM **Privately Held**
SIC: 8093 Mental health clinic, outpatient

(G-16578)
BROOK PLUM COUNTRY CLUB
3712 Galloway Rd (44870-6021)
PHONE.........................419 625-5394
Dan Moncher, *President*
Craig Wood, *Vice Pres*
EMP: 100
SQ FT: 33,469
SALES: 2MM **Privately Held**
WEB: www.pbcc.net
SIC: 7997 Country club, membership

(G-16579)
CAFARO PEACHCREEK CO LTD
Also Called: Clarion Hotel
1119 Sandusky Mall Blvd (44870)
PHONE.........................419 625-6280
Mary Sartor, *Manager*
EMP: 60
SALES (corp-wide): 4.1MM **Privately
Held**
WEB: www.millcreekmall.net
SIC: 7011 Hotels & motels

PA: Cafaro Peachcreek Co Ltd
  5577 Youngstown Warren Rd
  Niles OH 44446
  330 747-2661

(G-16580)
CANTON S-GROUP LTD
4000 Columbus Ave (44870-7325)
PHONE.........................419 625-7003
John Stock, *Partner*
Becky Stock, *Partner*
Tim Wade, *Partner*
EMP: 400
SALES (est): 11.5MM **Privately Held**
SIC: 7389 Personal service agents, bro-
  kers & bureaus

(G-16581)
CARE & SHARE OF ERIE COUNT
241 Jackson St (44870-2608)
PHONE.........................419 624-1411
L M More, *Exec Dir*
Linda Miller More, *Exec Dir*
EMP: 100
SALES: 149.8K **Privately Held**
SIC: 8322 Senior citizens' center or associ-
  ation

(G-16582)
CEDAR FAIR LP (PA)
1 Cedar Point Dr (44870-5259)
PHONE.........................419 626-0830
Richard A Zimmerman, *President*
Tim V Fisher, *COO*
Lee A Alexakos, *Vice Pres*
Carrie Boldman, *Vice Pres*
Leslie Bradshaw, *Vice Pres*
▲ **EMP:** 600
SALES: 1.3B **Publicly Held**
WEB: www.cedarfair.com
SIC: 7996 Theme park, amusement

(G-16583)
CEDAR POINT PARK LLC
Also Called: Castaway Bay
2001 Cleveland Rd (44870-4403)
PHONE.........................419 627-2500
Tyler Adams, *Sales Executive*
Robert Gigliotti, *Manager*
EMP: 100
SALES (corp-wide): 1.3B **Publicly Held**
WEB: www.cedarfair.com
SIC: 7996 7011 Theme park, amusement;
  resort hotel
HQ: Cedar Point Park Llc
  1 Cedar Point Dr
  Sandusky OH 44870
  419 626-0830

(G-16584)
CITY OF SANDUSKY
Engineering Department
222 Meigs St (44870-2835)
PHONE.........................419 627-5829
Kathryn McKillips, *Director*
EMP: 61 **Privately Held**
SIC: 8711 Engineering services
PA: City Of Sandusky
  222 Meigs St
  Sandusky OH 44870
  419 627-5844

(G-16585)
CITY OF SANDUSKY
Also Called: Sewer Department
304 Harrison St (44870)
PHONE.........................419 627-5907
Jeff Meinert, *Manager*
EMP: 30 **Privately Held**
SIC: 4952 9111 Sewerage systems; may-
  ors' offices
PA: City Of Sandusky
  222 Meigs St
  Sandusky OH 44870
  419 627-5844

(G-16586)
CIVISTA BANK (HQ)
100 E Water St (44870-2524)
P.O. Box 5016 (44871-5016)
PHONE.........................419 625-4121
James O Miller, *CEO*
David A Voight, *Ch of Bd*
John O Bacon, *President*
Douglas Greulich, *Senior VP*
Charles C Riesterer, *Senior VP*

EMP: 100 **EST:** 1898
SQ FT: 23,000
SALES: 74.9MM **Publicly Held**
WEB: www.citizensbankco.com
SIC: 6022 State trust companies accepting
  deposits, commercial

(G-16587)
**CLEVELAND CLINIC
FOUNDATION**
Also Called: North Coast Cancer Campus
417 Quarry Lakes Dr (44870-8635)
PHONE.........................419 609-2812
EMP: 72
SALES (corp-wide): 8.9B **Privately Held**
SIC: 8062 8011 8741 General medical &
  surgical hospitals; medical centers; man-
  agement services
PA: The Cleveland Clinic Foundation
  9500 Euclid Ave
  Cleveland OH 44195
  216 636-8335

(G-16588)
COACHS SPORTS CORNER INC
1130 Cleveland Rd (44870-4036)
PHONE.........................419 609-3737
James E Fischer, *President*
Greg Fischer, *Vice Pres*
Emily J Fischer, *Treasurer*
EMP: 32
SQ FT: 7,250
SALES (est): 3.6MM **Privately Held**
WEB: www.csc1st.com
SIC: 5091 5941 Sporting & recreation
  goods; sporting goods & bicycle shops

(G-16589)
**COMMODORE DENIG POST NO
83**
3615 Hayes Ave (44870-5324)
P.O. Box 2101 (44871-2101)
PHONE.........................419 625-3274
Jim Caldwell, *Commissioner*
EMP: 40
SALES: 307.1K **Privately Held**
SIC: 8641 Veterans' organization

(G-16590)
COMMONS OF PROVIDENCE
Also Called: Providence Care Centers
5000 Providence Dr Ste 1 (44870-1415)
PHONE.........................419 624-1171
Rick Ryan, *CEO*
Angel Wadsworth, *Director*
Rick Didomenici, *Administration*
EMP: 75
SALES: 4.9MM **Privately Held**
SIC: 8361 6513 8052 Group foster home;
  apartment building operators; intermedi-
  ate care facilities

(G-16591)
**COMMUNITY ACTION
COMMISSION (PA)**
908 Seavers Way (44870-4659)
P.O. Box 2500 (44871-2500)
PHONE.........................419 626-6540
Emma Moore, *Treasurer*
Janice W Warner, *Exec Dir*
Pervis D Brown, *Admin Sec*
EMP: 40
SQ FT: 10,934
SALES: 4.4MM **Privately Held**
WEB: www.ehcac.com
SIC: 8399 Community action agency

(G-16592)
CONCORD HEALTH CARE INC
Also Called: Briarfield of Sandusky
620 W Strub Rd (44870-5779)
PHONE.........................419 626-5373
Dianne McFarlyn, *Administration*
EMP: 50
SALES (est): 740.8K **Privately Held**
SIC: 8051 Skilled nursing care facilities
PA: Concord Health Care Inc
  202 Churchill Hubbard Rd
  Youngstown OH 44505

(G-16593)
CONSTRUCTION EQP & SUP LTD
3015 Old Railroad Rd (44870-9636)
P.O. Box 436 (44871-0436)
PHONE.............................419 625-7192
Lisa Wagner, *President*
Walt Foreman, *Sales Staff*
Kurt Martin, *Sales Staff*
EMP: 26
SQ FT: 30,000
SALES: 10.6MM **Privately Held**
SIC: 7353 Heavy construction equipment rental

(G-16594)
COOPER/T SMITH CORPORATION
2705 W Monroe St (44870-1831)
P.O. Box 2647 (44871-2647)
PHONE.............................419 626-0801
Ron House, *Manager*
EMP: 37
SALES (corp-wide): 525.8MM **Privately Held**
SIC: 4491 Docks, piers & terminals
PA: Smith Cooper/T Corporation
   118 N Royal St Ste 1000
   Mobile AL 36602
   251 431-6100

(G-16595)
COUNTY OF ERIE
Also Called: Child Support Enforcement Agcy
221 W Parish St (44870-4877)
PHONE.............................419 626-6781
Judith K Englehart, *Director*
EMP: 125 **Privately Held**
WEB: www.gem.org
SIC: 8322 9111 Probation office; county supervisors' & executives' offices
PA: County Of Erie
   2900 Columbus Ave
   Sandusky OH 44870
   419 627-7682

(G-16596)
COUNTY OF ERIE
Also Called: Erie County Hwy Dept
2700 Columbus Ave (44870-5551)
PHONE.............................419 627-7710
John Farschman, *Principal*
EMP: 33 **Privately Held**
WEB: www.gem.org
SIC: 8711 9111 Engineering services; county supervisors' & executives' offices
PA: County Of Erie
   2900 Columbus Ave
   Sandusky OH 44870
   419 627-7682

(G-16597)
ECONO LODGE
1904 Cleveland Rd (44870-4307)
PHONE.............................419 627-8000
George Spadaro, *President*
EMP: 70
SALES (est): 1.4MM **Privately Held**
SIC: 7011 Motels

(G-16598)
ERIE BLACKTOP INC
4507 Tiffin Ave (44870-9646)
P.O. Box 2308 (44871-2308)
PHONE.............................419 625-7374
Dean Wikel, *President*
Chris Schaeffer, *Vice Pres*
Dan White, *QC Dir*
James Kromer, *CFO*
Mario Barone, *Manager*
EMP: 30
SQ FT: 560
SALES (est): 6.3MM
SALES (corp-wide): 45.6MM **Privately Held**
WEB: www.erieblacktop.com
SIC: 1611 Highway & street paving contractor
PA: Erie Materials, Inc.
   4507 Tiffin Ave
   Sandusky OH 44870
   419 625-7374

(G-16599)
ERIE CONSTRUCTION GROUP INC
4507 Tiffin Ave (44870-9646)
P.O. Box 2308 (44871-2308)
PHONE.............................419 625-7374
Dean Wikel, *President*
Chris Schaffer, *Vice Pres*
Chris Walters, *Treasurer*
EMP: 50
SALES: 1.4MM
SALES (corp-wide): 45.6MM **Privately Held**
WEB: www.eriematerials.com
SIC: 1611 General contractor, highway & street construction
PA: Erie Materials, Inc.
   4507 Tiffin Ave
   Sandusky OH 44870
   419 625-7374

(G-16600)
ERIE COUNTY CABLEVISION INC
Also Called: Cable System, The
409 E Market St (44870-2814)
PHONE.............................419 627-0800
David Huey, *President*
Patrick L Deville, *Vice Pres*
EMP: 33
SQ FT: 8,600
SALES (est): 4MM
SALES (corp-wide): 921.6MM **Privately Held**
WEB: www.blockcommunications.com
SIC: 4841 Cable television services
PA: Block Communications, Inc.
   405 Madison Ave Ste 2100
   Toledo OH 43604
   419 724-6212

(G-16601)
ERIE RESIDENTIAL LIVING INC
Also Called: Erie Residential Living Home I
706 E Park St (44870-3301)
PHONE.............................419 625-0060
Donna Frost, *Exec Dir*
EMP: 30 **EST:** 1976
SALES: 918.4K **Privately Held**
SIC: 8361 Home for the mentally handicapped

(G-16602)
ERIE TRUCKING INC
4507 Tiffin Ave (44870-9646)
P.O. Box 2308 (44871-2308)
PHONE.............................419 625-7374
Dean Wikel, *President*
Chris Walters, *Corp Secy*
Chris Schaeffer, *Vice Pres*
Ned Wikel, *Manager*
EMP: 30 **EST:** 1927
SQ FT: 1,000
SALES (est): 3.3MM
SALES (corp-wide): 45.6MM **Privately Held**
WEB: www.eriematerials.com
SIC: 4213 Contract haulers
PA: Erie Materials, Inc.
   4507 Tiffin Ave
   Sandusky OH 44870
   419 625-7374

(G-16603)
FEICK CONTRACTORS INC
224 E Water St (44870-2545)
PHONE.............................419 625-3241
John A Feick, *President*
Carl M Feick, *Vice Pres*
EMP: 30
SQ FT: 4,000
SALES: 783.7K **Privately Held**
SIC: 1542 Commercial & office building, new construction

(G-16604)
FIRELANDS REGIONAL HEALTH SYS (PA)
Also Called: FIRELANDS REGIONAL MEDICAL CEN
1111 Hayes Ave (44870-3323)
PHONE.............................419 557-7400
Martin E Tursky, *CEO*
Daniel Moncher, *CFO*
Shelly De Lamattere, *Director*

EMP: 1300
SQ FT: 320,000
SALES: 280.7MM **Privately Held**
SIC: 8062 General medical & surgical hospitals

(G-16605)
FIRELANDS REGIONAL HEALTH SYS
Also Called: Out Patient
1101 Decatur St (44870-3364)
PHONE.............................419 626-7400
Patty Martin, *Director*
EMP: 150
SALES (corp-wide): 280.7MM **Privately Held**
SIC: 6324 Hospital & medical service plans
PA: Firelands Regional Health System
   1111 Hayes Ave
   Sandusky OH 44870
   419 557-7400

(G-16606)
FIRELANDS SECURITY SERVICES
1210 Sycamore Line (44870-4029)
P.O. Box 2587 (44871-2587)
PHONE.............................419 627-0562
Brian Dietrich, *President*
EMP: 30
SQ FT: 400
SALES (est): 601.6K **Privately Held**
WEB: www.firelandssecurityservices.com
SIC: 7381 4215 Security guard service; private investigator; lie detection service; courier services, except by air

(G-16607)
FIRST AMERICAN TITLE INSUR CO
143 E Water St (44870-2525)
PHONE.............................419 625-8505
EMP: 25 **Publicly Held**
SIC: 6361 Title Insurance Carrier
HQ: First American Title Insurance Company
   1 First American Way
   Santa Ana CA 92707
   800 854-3643

(G-16608)
FIRST CHOICE MEDICAL STAFFING
1164 Cleveland Rd (44870-4036)
PHONE.............................419 626-9740
Charles Slone, *President*
EMP: 38
SALES (corp-wide): 4.6MM **Privately Held**
WEB: www.rxprn.com
SIC: 8742 Hospital & health services consultant
PA: First Choice Medical Staffing Of Ohio, Inc.
   1457 W 117th St
   Cleveland OH 44107
   216 521-2222

(G-16609)
FRESCH ELECTRIC INC
1414 Milan Rd (44870-4194)
PHONE.............................419 626-2535
Dan Fresch, *President*
Albert J Fresch, *President*
Daniel J Fresch, *Treasurer*
EMP: 25
SQ FT: 5,000
SALES (est): 3MM **Privately Held**
WEB: www.sanduskyohio.com
SIC: 1731 General electrical contractor

(G-16610)
GILBERT HEATING & AC
Also Called: Gilbert Heating AC & Plumb
2121 Cleveland Rd Ste A (44870-4493)
PHONE.............................419 625-8875
Thomas Runkle, *President*
EMP: 30
SQ FT: 8,500
SALES: 2MM **Privately Held**
SIC: 1711 Warm air heating & air conditioning contractor; plumbing contractors

(G-16611)
GOODWILL INDUSTRIES OF ERIE (PA)
Also Called: Goodw Indus of Erie, Huron, Ot
419 W Market St (44870-2411)
PHONE.............................419 625-4744
Eric Kochendoerfer, *CEO*
Robert Talcott, *President*
Jason Stout, *VP Finance*
Steven Timmerman, *Marketing Mgr*
Bambi Link, *Manager*
EMP: 50
SQ FT: 30,000
SALES: 8.9MM **Privately Held**
SIC: 8322 5932 Individual & family services; clothing, secondhand

(G-16612)
GOOFY GOLF INC
3020 Milan Rd (44870-5676)
PHONE.............................419 625-1308
Roger Andrews, *President*
Diane Andrews, *Principal*
Dianne Andrews, *Vice Pres*
EMP: 38
SALES (est): 1.1MM **Privately Held**
SIC: 7999 5599 Recreation center; go-carts

(G-16613)
GREAT BEAR LODGE SANDUSKY LLC
Also Called: Great Wolf Lodge
4600 Milan Rd (44870-5840)
PHONE.............................419 609-6000
John Emery, *CEO*
Jim Calder, *CFO*
Alex Lombardo, *Treasurer*
Elan Blutinger, *Director*
Randy Churchey, *Director*
EMP: 300 **EST:** 2000
SALES (est): 4MM **Privately Held**
SIC: 7011 Resort hotel

(G-16614)
GUNDLACH SHEET METAL WORKS INC (PA)
Also Called: Honeywell Authorized Dealer
910 Columbus Ave (44870-3594)
PHONE.............................419 626-4525
Roger M Gundlach, *President*
Terry W Gundlach, *Chairman*
Terry Kette, *Vice Pres*
Andrew Gundluch, *Admin Sec*
EMP: 76
SQ FT: 17,000
SALES (est): 18.7MM **Privately Held**
WEB: www.gundlach-hvac.com
SIC: 1711 3444 Warm air heating & air conditioning contractor; refrigeration contractor; sheet metalwork

(G-16615)
HEAP HOME ENERGY ASSISTANCE
908 Seavers Way (44870-4659)
PHONE.............................419 626-6540
Janice Alexander, *Exec Dir*
EMP: 85
SALES (est): 685.7K **Privately Held**
SIC: 8322 Individual & family services

(G-16616)
HOME DEPOT USA INC
Also Called: Home Depot, The
715 Crossings Rd (44870-8903)
PHONE.............................419 626-6493
James Mieden, *Manager*
EMP: 120
SALES (corp-wide): 108.2B **Publicly Held**
WEB: www.homerentalsdepot.com
SIC: 5211 7359 Home centers; tool rental
HQ: Home Depot U.S.A., Inc.
   2455 Paces Ferry Ave
   Atlanta GA 30339

(G-16617)
HOTY ENTERPRISES INC (PA)
5003 Milan Rd (44870-5845)
PHONE.............................419 609-7000
John M Hoty, *President*
Todd Hart, *Vice Pres*
Angelo Hoty, *Vice Pres*
Zack Hoty, *Vice Pres*

GEOGRAPHIC

Kula Hoty Lynch, *Admin Sec*
EMP: 28
SQ FT: 6,000
SALES (est): 4MM **Privately Held**
WEB: www.hoty.com
SIC: 6512 Commercial & industrial building operation

(G-16618)
IHEARTCOMMUNICATIONS INC
Also Called: Wmjk FM
1640 Cleveland Rd (44870-4357)
PHONE..................................419 625-1010
Adam Klein, *Manager*
EMP: 30 **Publicly Held**
SIC: 4832 Radio broadcasting stations
HQ: Iheartcommunications, Inc.
20880 Stone Oak Pkwy
San Antonio TX 78258
210 822-2828

(G-16619)
JERSEY CENTRAL PWR & LIGHT CO
Also Called: Firstenergy
2508 W Perkins Ave (44870-1917)
PHONE..................................419 366-2915
Jim Gill, *Manager*
EMP: 60 **Publicly Held**
WEB: www.jersey-central-power-light.monmouth.n
SIC: 4911 Electric services
HQ: Jersey Central Power & Light Company
76 S Main St
Akron OH 44308
800 736-3402

(G-16620)
K & K INTERIORS INC
2230 Superior St (44870-1843)
PHONE..................................419 627-0039
Kyle Camp, *President*
Mark Wall, *Vice Pres*
◆ **EMP:** 53 **EST:** 1996
SQ FT: 125,000
SALES (est): 22.5MM **Privately Held**
WEB: www.kkinteriors.com
SIC: 5092 Arts & crafts equipment & supplies

(G-16621)
KIDDLE KORRAL
Also Called: Kiddie Korral
315 W Follett St (44870-4881)
PHONE..................................419 626-9082
Diedre Bartemes, *Exec Dir*
EMP: 45
SALES (est): 789.3K **Privately Held**
SIC: 8351 Preschool center

(G-16622)
KOCH ALUMINUM MFG INC
1615 E Perkins Ave (44870-5199)
PHONE..................................419 625-5956
Randall G Koch, *President*
EMP: 30 **EST:** 1952
SQ FT: 25,000
SALES (est): 9.5MM **Privately Held**
WEB: www.kochdoorsandwindows.com
SIC: 5031 5211 Building materials, exterior; building materials, interior; doors, wood or metal, except storm

(G-16623)
LMN DEVELOPMENT LLC (PA)
Also Called: Kalahari Resort
7000 Kalahari Dr (44870-8628)
PHONE..................................419 433-7200
Todd Nelson, *President*
Brian Shanle, *General Mgr*
Mary Bonte-Stath, *CFO*
Kari Johnson, *Finance*
Richard McCadden, *Sales Mgr*
EMP: 95
SALES (est): 67.3MM **Privately Held**
SIC: 7011 7996 5091 Resort hotel; amusement parks; water slides (recreation park)

(G-16624)
LODGING INDUSTRY INC
Also Called: Super 8 Motel
7704 Milan Rd (44870-8356)
PHONE..................................440 323-7488
Michael Ruta, *Owner*

EMP: 31
SALES (corp-wide): 1.5MM **Privately Held**
SIC: 7011 5813 Hotels & motels; drinking places
PA: Lodging Industry Inc
910 Lorain Blvd Ste N
Elyria OH
440 323-9820

(G-16625)
LOWES HOME CENTERS LLC
5500 Milan Rd Ste 304 (44870-7805)
PHONE..................................419 624-6000
Fred Schlick, *Branch Mgr*
EMP: 150
SALES (corp-wide): 68.6B **Publicly Held**
SIC: 5211 5031 5722 5064 Home centers; building materials, exterior; building materials, interior; household appliance stores; electrical appliances, television & radio
HQ: Lowe's Home Centers, Llc
1605 Curtis Bridge Rd
Wilkesboro NC 28697
336 658-4000

(G-16626)
MAGNUM MANAGEMENT CORPORATION
1 Cedar Point Dr (44870-5259)
PHONE..................................419 627-2334
Richard L Kinzel, *CEO*
Nathaniel Whitt, *Area Mgr*
Craig J Freeman, *Vice Pres*
Duffield E Milkie, *Vice Pres*
Alan L Schwartz, *Vice Pres*
▲ **EMP:** 800
SQ FT: 6,000
SALES (est): 87.4MM
SALES (corp-wide): 1.3B **Publicly Held**
WEB: www.cedarpointresorts.com
SIC: 4785 6552 7996 Toll bridge operation; subdividers & developers; amusement parks
PA: Cedar Fair, L.P.
1 Cedar Point Dr
Sandusky OH 44870
419 626-0830

(G-16627)
MURRAY & MURRAY CO LPA (PA)
111 E Shoreline Dr Ste 2 (44870-2579)
PHONE..................................419 624-3000
John Murray, *President*
Charles Murray, *President*
Dennis E Murray Sr, *President*
Dennis E Murray Jr, *President*
James Murray, *President*
EMP: 36
SQ FT: 33,000
SALES (est): 5.3MM **Privately Held**
WEB: www.murrayandmurray.com
SIC: 8111 General practice attorney, lawyer

(G-16628)
MV TRANSPORTATION INC
1230 N Depot St (44870-3165)
PHONE..................................419 627-0740
Peter Carey, *Branch Mgr*
EMP: 76
SALES (corp-wide): 1.4B **Privately Held**
SIC: 4111 Local & suburban transit
PA: Mv Transportation, Inc.
2711 N Haskell Ave
Dallas TX 75204
214 265-3400

(G-16629)
NORTH COAST PROF CO LLC
Also Called: Firelands Physicians Group
1031 Pierce St (44870-4669)
PHONE..................................419 557-5541
Martin Tursky, *CEO*
EMP: 191
SALES (est): 19.4MM **Privately Held**
SIC: 8011 Primary care medical clinic

(G-16630)
NORTHERN OHIO MED SPCLISTS LLC
Also Called: Bayshore Obgyn
2500 W Strub Rd Ste 210 (44870-5390)
PHONE..................................419 625-2841
William D Bruner, *Manager*
EMP: 29
SALES (corp-wide): 38.7MM **Privately Held**
WEB: www.nomsdrs.com
SIC: 8011 Gynecologist
PA: Northern Ohio Medical Specialists Llc
3004 Hayes Ave
Sandusky OH 44870
419 626-6161

(G-16631)
O E MEYER CO (PA)
3303 Tiffin Ave (44870-9752)
P.O. Box 479 (44871-0479)
PHONE..................................419 625-1256
Rodney S Belden, *CEO*
David Belden, *President*
Craig A Wood, *President*
Eric Wood, *President*
Jim Frederick, *Division Mgr*
▲ **EMP:** 155
SQ FT: 46,000
SALES (est): 92.8MM **Privately Held**
WEB: www.oemeyer.com
SIC: 5084 5047 Welding machinery & equipment; medical & hospital equipment

(G-16632)
PNC BANK NATIONAL ASSOCIATION
Also Called: National City Bank
129 W Perkins Ave (44870-4802)
PHONE..................................419 621-2930
Josephine Angelo, *Vice Pres*
Robert Johns, *Branch Mgr*
EMP: 25
SALES (corp-wide): 19.9B **Publicly Held**
WEB: www.allegiantbank.com
SIC: 6021 National commercial banks
HQ: Pnc Bank, National Association
222 Delaware Ave
Wilmington DE 19801
877 762-2000

(G-16633)
PROVIDENCE CARE CENTER
2025 Hayes Ave (44870-4739)
PHONE..................................419 627-2273
Amy Fox, *Opers Mgr*
Shirl Felder, *Social Dir*
Donna Novak, *Executive*
Denice Day, *Administration*
Stacy Lemco, *Administration*
EMP: 160
SALES: 12.9MM **Privately Held**
WEB: www.providencecenters.org
SIC: 8062 Hospital, affiliated with AMA residency

(G-16634)
RENAISSANCE HOUSE INC
158 E Market St Ste 805 (44870-2556)
PHONE..................................419 626-1110
Robert Weinhardt, *Director*
EMP: 55
SALES (corp-wide): 4MM **Privately Held**
WEB: www.renaissancehouseinc.com
SIC: 8741 8052 Hospital management; nursing & personal care facility management; intermediate care facilities
PA: Renaissance House Inc
103 N Washington St
Tiffin OH 44883
419 447-7901

(G-16635)
REPUBLIC SERVICES INC
4005 Tiffin Ave (44870-9689)
PHONE..................................419 626-2454
Neil Carlson, *Branch Mgr*
EMP: 34
SALES (corp-wide): 10B **Publicly Held**
SIC: 4953 Refuse collection & disposal services
PA: Republic Services, Inc.
18500 N Allied Way # 100
Phoenix AZ 85054
480 627-2700

(G-16636)
REXEL USA INC
Also Called: Brohl & Appell
140 Lane St (44870-3560)
PHONE..................................419 625-6761
Mary Ebert, *Regional Mgr*
Loren Gosser, *Sales Mgr*
EMP: 29
SALES (corp-wide): 2.2MM **Privately Held**
SIC: 5063 5074 Electrical supplies; plumbing & hydronic heating supplies
HQ: Rexel Usa, Inc.
14951 Dallas Pkwy
Dallas TX 75254

(G-16637)
SANDUSKY AREA YMCA FOUNDATION
Also Called: Sandusky YMCA
224 E Water St 2 (44870-2526)
PHONE..................................419 621-9622
Donald Yontz, *President*
William Parker, *Vice Pres*
John Bacon, *Treasurer*
Paul Mc Callister, *Exec Dir*
Bjorn Wiberg, *Director*
EMP: 29 **EST:** 1960
SALES: 882K **Privately Held**
SIC: 8641 8351 Youth organizations; child day care services

(G-16638)
SANDUSKY HARBOR MARINA INC
Also Called: Sandusky Harbour Marina
1 Huron St (44870-1805)
PHONE..................................419 627-1201
Jerry Parsons, *Manager*
EMP: 37
SALES: 4MM **Privately Held**
WEB: www.sanduskyharbor.com
SIC: 4493 Boat yards, storage & incidental repair

(G-16639)
SANDUSKY NEWSPAPERS INC (PA)
Also Called: Sandusky Newspaper Group
314 W Market St (44870-2410)
PHONE..................................419 625-5500
Dudley A White Jr, *Ch of Bd*
David A Rau, *President*
Kathy Lilje, *Editor*
Aimee Miller, *Vice Pres*
Susan E White, *Admin Sec*
EMP: 140
SQ FT: 45,000
SALES (est): 98.3MM **Privately Held**
WEB: www.sanduskyregister.com
SIC: 4832 2711 2752 Radio broadcasting stations; newspapers; commercial printing, lithographic

(G-16640)
SANDUSKY REGISTER
314 W Market St (44870-2410)
P.O. Box 5071 (44871-5071)
PHONE..................................419 625-5500
Tim Kelly, *President*
Dudley White, *Principal*
Rachel Jagel, *Sales Staff*
Teri Gerber, *Manager*
Kelli Braun, *Graphic Designe*
EMP: 26
SALES (est): 2.8MM **Privately Held**
SIC: 7313 5994 Newspaper advertising representative; newsstand

(G-16641)
SANDUSKY YACHT CLUB INC
529 E Water St (44870-2875)
PHONE..................................419 625-6567
Mike Thuemmler, *General Mgr*
David Dunn, *General Mgr*
Penny Williams, *Manager*
EMP: 80 **EST:** 1894
SQ FT: 25,000
SALES: 1.8MM **Privately Held**
WEB: www.sanduskyyachtclub.com
SIC: 7997 Boating club, membership; yacht club, membership

▲ = Import ▼ =Export
◆ =Import/Export

(G-16642)
SMILE BRANDS INC
Also Called: Bright Dental
1313 W Bogart Rd Ste D (44870-5704)
PHONE..............................419 627-1255
Jeana Janik, *Branch Mgr*
EMP: 30
SALES (corp-wide): 565MM **Privately
Held**
WEB: www.monarchdental.com
SIC: 8021 Dental clinic
HQ: Smile Brands Inc.
100 Spectrum Center Dr # 1
Irvine CA 92618
714 668-1300

(G-16643)
**SORTINO MANAGEMENT & DEV
CO**
Also Called: Greentree Inn
1935 Cleveland Rd (44870-4308)
PHONE..............................419 626-6761
Fax: 419 624-1204
EMP: 50
SQ FT: 80,000
SALES (corp-wide): 7.3MM **Privately
Held**
SIC: 7011 5812 7933 Hotel/Motel Opera-
tion Eating Place Bowling Center
PA: Sortino Management & Development
Co
1210 Sycamore Line
Sandusky OH 44870
419 625-0362

(G-16644)
**ST STEPHEN UNITED CHURCH
CHRST**
905 E Perkins Ave (44870-5067)
PHONE..............................419 624-1814
Robert C Patton, *Pastor*
Kenneth L Heintzelman, *Pastor*
EMP: 30
SALES (est): 916.9K **Privately Held**
SIC: 8661 8351 Church of Christ; child
day care services

(G-16645)
STEIN HOSPICE SERVICES INC
1200 Sycamore Line (44870-4029)
P.O. Box Camore Lin (44870)
PHONE..............................419 447-0475
Carl Stein, *Branch Mgr*
EMP: 89
SALES (corp-wide): 28.8MM **Privately
Held**
SIC: 8069 Specialty hospitals, except psy-
chiatric
PA: Stein Hospice Services, Inc.
1200 Sycamore Line
Sandusky OH 44870
800 625-5269

(G-16646)
STEIN HOSPICE SERVICES INC
126 Columbus Ave (44870-2502)
PHONE..............................419 502-0019
Gail Shatzer, *Branch Mgr*
EMP: 71
SALES (corp-wide): 28.8MM **Privately
Held**
SIC: 8069 Specialty hospitals, except psy-
chiatric
PA: Stein Hospice Services, Inc.
1200 Sycamore Line
Sandusky OH 44870
800 625-5269·

(G-16647)
**STEIN HOSPICE SERVICES INC
(PA)**
1200 Sycamore Line (44870-4029)
PHONE..............................800 625-5269
Jan Bucholz, *CEO*
Larry Robinson, *Associate Dir*
Dorene Frost, *Lic Prac Nurse*
▲ **EMP:** 370
SALES (est): 28.8MM **Privately Held**
WEB: www.steinhospice.com
SIC: 8069 Chronic disease hospital

(G-16648)
**STERLING HEIGHTS GSA PRPTS
LTD**
5003 Milan Rd (44870-5845)
PHONE..............................419 609-7000
John M Hoty,
EMP: 37
SALES: 175K **Privately Held**
SIC: 6531 Real estate agents & managers

(G-16649)
**TRADESMEN INTERNATIONAL
LLC**
2419 E Perkins Ave (44870-7998)
PHONE..............................419 502-9140
EMP: 153 **Privately Held**
SIC: 7361 Labor contractors (employment
agency)
PA: Tradesmen International, Llc
9760 Shepard Rd
Macedonia OH 44056

(G-16650)
UBS FINANCIAL SERVICES INC
111 E Shoreline Dr Ste 3 (44870-2579)
PHONE..............................419 624-6800
Tim Vansimaeys, *Branch Mgr*
James N Samson, *Branch Mgr*
EMP: 43
SALES (corp-wide): 29.4B **Privately Held**
SIC: 7389 Financial services
HQ: Ubs Financial Services Inc.
1285 Ave Of The Americas
New York NY 10019
212 713-2000

(G-16651)
UNITED CHURCH HOMES INC
Also Called: Parkview Health Care
3800 Boardwalk Blvd (44870-7044)
PHONE..............................419 621-1900
Ken Keller, *Administration*
EMP: 150
SALES (corp-wide): 78.1MM **Privately
Held**
WEB: www.altenheimcommunity.org
SIC: 8051 Skilled nursing care facilities
PA: United Church Homes Inc
170 E Center St
Marion OH 43302
740 382-4885

(G-16652)
**UNITED STATES DEPT
AGRICULTURE**
2900 Columbus Ave (44870-5574)
PHONE..............................419 626-8439
Valarie Grahl, *Branch Mgr*
EMP: 81 **Publicly Held**
WEB: www.usda.gov
SIC: 9641 5191 Agriculture fair board,
government; farm supplies
HQ: United States Department Of Agricul-
ture
1400 Independence Ave Sw
Washington DC 20250
202 720-3631

(G-16653)
**US TSUBAKI POWER TRANSM
LLC**
Also Called: Engineering Chain Div
1010 Edgewater Ave (44870-1601)
PHONE..............................419 626-4560
Myron Timmer, *Vice Pres*
Steve Funni, *Mfg Staff*
Chuck Kaman, *Design Engr Mgr*
Vic Hostetter, *Engineer*
Dave Piasecki, *Engineer*
EMP: 180
SALES (corp-wide): 2B **Privately Held**
SIC: 5049 3568 3714 3462 Engineers'
equipment & supplies; chain, power trans-
mission; motor vehicle parts & acces-
sories; iron & steel forgings
HQ: U.S. Tsubaki Power Transmission Llc
301 E Marquardt Dr
Wheeling IL 60090
847 459-9500

(G-16654)
**VACATIONLAND FEDERAL
CREDIT UN**
2911 Hayes Ave (44870-7206)
PHONE..............................440 967-5155
Kevin Ralofsky, *CEO*
Mary Jackson, *Officer*
Derek Callin, *Tech/Comp Coord*
EMP: 25
SALES (corp-wide): 8MM **Privately Held**
SIC: 6061 Federal credit unions
PA: Vacationland Federal Credit Union
2409 E Perkins Ave
Sandusky OH 44870
419 625-9025

(G-16655)
WAGNER QUARRIES COMPANY
Also Called: Hanson Aggregates
4203 Milan Rd (44870-5880)
PHONE..............................419 625-8141
Norman Jacobs, *Plant Mgr*
Chris Kinner, *Plant Mgr*
Bill Hoelzer, *Sales Staff*
Chuck Cashan, *Manager*
Andrew Harper, *Manager*
EMP: 48
SQ FT: 2,400
SALES (est): 4.5MM **Privately Held**
SIC: 1422 Limestones, ground

(G-16656)
WOLFF BROS SUPPLY INC
2800 W Strub Rd (44870-5368)
PHONE..............................330 400-5990
Bill Rutherford, *Marketing Staff*
Pete Doyle, *Manager*
Jeff Pycraft, *Asst Mgr*
EMP: 32
SALES (corp-wide): 114.4MM **Privately
Held**
WEB: www.wolffbros.com
SIC: 5074 Plumbing & hydronic heating
supplies
PA: Wolff Bros. Supply, Inc
6078 Wolff Rd
Medina OH 44256
330 725-3451

(G-16657)
YMCA OF SANDUSKY OHIO INC
Also Called: International MGT Counsel
2101 W Perkins Ave (44870-2057)
PHONE..............................419 621-9622
Jared Williams, *Exec Dir*
Steve Snyder, *Exec Dir*
EMP: 45
SALES (est): 1MM **Privately Held**
SIC: 8641 Youth organizations; recreation
association

Sardinia
Brown County

(G-16658)
**CORNERSTONE CONCRETE
CNSTR INC**
12577 Us Highway 62 (45171)
PHONE..............................937 442-2805
Harold Dorsey, *President*
Vicky Dorsey, *Office Mgr*
EMP: 25
SQ FT: 6,500
SALES (est): 3.6MM **Privately Held**
SIC: 1771 Concrete work

(G-16659)
G & D ALTERNATIVE LIVING INC
Also Called: Pinewood Home
121 Charles St (45171-9338)
P.O. Box 341 (45171-0341)
PHONE..............................937 446-2803
Gordon L Fitzpatrick, *President*
Keith Crothers, *Director*
Diana Fitzpatrick, *Administration*
EMP: 35
SQ FT: 6,400
SALES (est): 1.2MM **Privately Held**
SIC: 8361 Home for the mentally handi-
capped

(G-16660)
SARDINIA LIFE SQUAD
159 Winchester St (45171-9326)
P.O. Box 380 (45171-0380)
PHONE..............................937 446-2178
EMP: 29 **EST:** 1975
SALES: 127.4K **Privately Held**
SIC: 4119 Local Passenger Transportation

Sardis
Monroe County

(G-16661)
**SLAY TRANSPORTATION CO
INC**
Rr 7 Box 34684 (43946)
PHONE..............................740 865-2910
Gary Slay, *President*
EMP: 110
SALES (corp-wide): 142.9MM **Privately
Held**
SIC: 4213 4231 4212 Trucking, except
local; trucking terminal facilities; local
trucking, without storage
HQ: Slay Transportation Co., Inc.
1441 Hampton Ave
Saint Louis MO 63139
800 852-7529

Scio
Harrison County

(G-16662)
BHF INCORPORATED
Also Called: Bhfi
147 E College St (43988-8732)
PHONE..............................740 945-6410
James W Anderson III, *CEO*
EMP: 35
SALES (est): 1.3MM **Privately Held**
SIC: 8711 Engineering services

(G-16663)
M3 MIDSTREAM LLC
Also Called: Harrison Hub
37950 Crimm Rd (43988)
PHONE..............................740 945-1170
EMP: 57
SALES (corp-wide): 54.9MM **Privately
Held**
SIC: 1311 Crude petroleum & natural gas
PA: M3 Midstream Llc
600 Travis St Ste 5600
Houston TX 77002
713 783-3000

(G-16664)
TAPPAN LAKE MARINA INC
Also Called: Tappan Marina
33315 Cadiz Dennison Rd (43988-9724)
PHONE..............................740 269-2031
Dick Henry, *President*
Sandra Henry, *Partner*
Cathrine Cramblett, *Vice Pres*
EMP: 36
SALES (est): 49.8K **Privately Held**
SIC: 5812 4493 Ethnic food restaurants;
marinas

Seaman
Adams County

(G-16665)
**ADAMS COUNTY REGIONAL
MED CTR**
230 Medical Center Dr (45679-8002)
PHONE..............................937 386-3001
Bill May, *CEO*
Heather Shoemaker, *Human Res Dir*
Becky Hawkins, *Mktg Dir*
Radah Brown, *Manager*
Tami Graham, *Manager*
EMP: 250
SQ FT: 94,600
SALES: 26.6MM **Privately Held**
SIC: 8062 General medical & surgical hos-
pitals

Sebring
Mahoning County

(G-16666)
COPELAND OAKS
715 S Johnson Rd (44672-1709)
PHONE..................................330 938-1050
David Mannigan, *Administration*
EMP: 344
SALES (corp-wide): 14.7MM **Privately Held**
SIC: 6513 Retirement hotel operation
PA: Copeland Oaks
800 S 15th St
Sebring OH 44672
330 938-6126

(G-16667)
COPELAND OAKS (PA)
800 S 15th St (44672-2099)
PHONE..................................330 938-6126
Phillip Braisted, *CEO*
Dave Mannion, *CFO*
EMP: 48
SQ FT: 383,672
SALES: 14.7MM **Privately Held**
WEB: www.copelandoaks.com
SIC: 6513 Retirement hotel operation

(G-16668)
CRANDALL MEDICAL CENTER INC
800 S 15th St Apt 7318 (44672-2085)
PHONE..................................330 938-6126
Linda Thomas, *QC Dir*
Jennifer Gier, *Human Res Dir*
Jeanie Ramser, *Human Res Dir*
Don Piccianno, *Pub Rel Dir*
Debbie Reho, *Pub Rel Dir*
EMP: 200
SQ FT: 77,300
SALES: 15.2MM **Privately Held**
SIC: 8051 Convalescent home with continuous nursing care

(G-16669)
FAMOUS ENTERPRISES INC
350 Courtney Rd (44672-1337)
PHONE..................................330 938-6350
Tanja Kozul, *Branch Mgr*
EMP: 29 **Privately Held**
WEB: www.jfgood.com
SIC: 5074 Plumbing fittings & supplies
PA: Famous Enterprises, Inc.
2620 Ridgewood Rd Ste 200
Akron OH 44313

Senecaville
Guernsey County

(G-16670)
MUSKINGUM WTRSHED CNSRVNCY DST
Also Called: Seneca Lake Park
22172 Park Rd (43780-9613)
PHONE..................................740 685-6013
Gary Perrish, *Superintendent*
EMP: 40
SALES (est): 806.4K
SALES (corp-wide): 93.5MM **Privately Held**
WEB: www.muskingumfoundation.org
SIC: 7996 Amusement parks
PA: Muskingum Watershed Conservancy District
1319 3rd St Nw
New Philadelphia OH 44663
330 343-6647

Seven Hills
Cuyahoga County

(G-16671)
ALEX N SILL COMPANY (PA)
6000 Lombardo Ctr Ste 600 (44131-6911)
PHONE..................................216 524-9999
Michael Perlmuter, *President*
Dean Harclerode, *Vice Pres*
Michael Hickle, *Vice Pres*
Preston Hoopes, *Vice Pres*
Jeffrey O'Connor, *Vice Pres*
EMP: 35 **EST:** 1928
SQ FT: 7,500
SALES (est): 13.9MM **Privately Held**
WEB: www.sill.com
SIC: 6411 Policyholders' consulting service

(G-16672)
BLUE CHIP CONSULTING GROUP LLC
6000 Lombardo Ctr Ste 650 (44131-6916)
PHONE..................................216 503-6001
James Filicko, *Mng Member*
Jim Peelman,
EMP: 28
SQ FT: 14,000
SALES (est): 3.7MM **Privately Held**
SIC: 7379 ; computer related consulting services

(G-16673)
CITY OF SEVEN HILLS
7777 Summitview Dr (44131-4441)
PHONE..................................216 524-6262
Jennifer Burger, *Chief*
Sonja Herwick, *Finance*
EMP: 116 **Privately Held**
SIC: 7999 Recreation center
PA: City Of Seven Hills
7325 Summitview Dr
Seven Hills OH 44131
216 524-4421

(G-16674)
EQUITY CONSULTANTS LLC
5800 Lombardo Ctr Ste 202 (44131-2588)
PHONE..................................330 659-7600
Goran Marich,
Ryko Marich,
EMP: 60
SQ FT: 10,000
SALES (est): 3.7MM **Privately Held**
WEB: www.equityconsultants.org
SIC: 6163 Mortgage brokers arranging for loans, using money of others

(G-16675)
EXPERIS FINANCE US LLC
6000 Lombardo Ctr Ste 400 (44131-6926)
PHONE..................................216 621-0200
Edward Primisoch, *Director*
EMP: 35 **Publicly Held**
SIC: 8721 Accounting, auditing & bookkeeping
HQ: Experis Finance Us, Llc
100 W Manpower Pl
Milwaukee WI 53212

(G-16676)
JPMORGAN CHASE BANK NAT ASSN
7703 Broadview Rd (44131-5724)
PHONE..................................216 524-0600
Jim Henderson, *Manager*
EMP: 26
SQ FT: 2,631
SALES (corp-wide): 131.4B **Publicly Held**
WEB: www.chase.com
SIC: 6029 Commercial banks
HQ: Jpmorgan Chase Bank, National Association
1111 Polaris Pkwy
Columbus OH 43240
614 436-3055

(G-16677)
NELSON
Also Called: Ka Architecture
6000 Lombardo Ctr Ste 500 (44131-6910)
PHONE..................................216 781-9144
James B Heller, *President*
Thomas M Milanich, *COO*
Alan W Siliko, *CFO*
EMP: 108 **EST:** 1960
SQ FT: 30,000
SALES (est): 16MM **Privately Held**
WEB: www.kainc.com
SIC: 8712 Architectural services

(G-16678)
OHIO EDUCATIONAL CREDIT UNION (PA)
4141 Rockside Rd Ste 400 (44131-2537)
P.O. Box 93079, Cleveland (44101-5079)
PHONE..................................216 621-6296
Jerome R Valco, *CEO*
Richard Gore, *President*
Art Boehm, *CFO*
Bob Becker, *Officer*
Tony H Smith Sr, *Admin Sec*
EMP: 38 **EST:** 1933
SQ FT: 27,000
SALES: 7.7MM **Privately Held**
WEB: www.ohioedcu.com
SIC: 6061 Federal credit unions

(G-16679)
OHIO KEPRO INC
5700 Lombardo Ctr Ste 100 (44131-2542)
PHONE..................................216 447-9604
Joe Dougher, *CEO*
Donald Harrop, *Ch of Bd*
Linda Greel, *Office Mgr*
Keisha Chavers, *Webmaster*
Liz Simpson, *Admin Asst*
EMP: 48
SQ FT: 12,000
SALES (est): 2.8MM
SALES (corp-wide): 78.2MM **Privately Held**
WEB: www.ohiokepro.com
SIC: 8099 Medical services organization
PA: Keystone Peer Review Organization, Inc.
777 E Park Dr
Harrisburg PA 17111
717 564-8288

(G-16680)
SCA ACQUISITIONS INC (HQ)
4141 Rockside Rd Ste 210 (44131-2537)
PHONE..................................216 777-2750
Christopher M Valerian, *CEO*
John D Landefeld, *CFO*
EMP: 702
SALES (corp-wide): 172.4MM **Privately Held**
SIC: 6719 Investment holding companies, except banks
PA: Sweep America Intermediate Holdings, Llc
4141 Rockside Rd Ste 210
Seven Hills OH 44131
216 777-2750

(G-16681)
SEVEN HILLS FIREMAN ASSN
7195 Broadview Rd (44131-4210)
PHONE..................................216 524-3321
Charles Osta, *President*
EMP: 35
SALES (est): 634.8K **Privately Held**
SIC: 8641 6331 Civic social & fraternal associations; workers' compensation insurance

Seville
Medina County

(G-16682)
BENCHMARK CRAFTSMAN INC
Also Called: Benchmark Craftsmen
4700 Greenwich Rd (44273-8848)
PHONE..................................330 975-4214
Nathan Sublett, *President*
EMP: 30
SALES (est): 4.1MM **Privately Held**
WEB: www.benchmarkcraftsmen.com
SIC: 7389 3993 Exhibit construction by industrial contractors; displays & cutouts, window & lobby

(G-16683)
BLEACHTECH LLC
320 Ryan Rd (44273-9109)
PHONE..................................216 921-1980
Joseph Traylinek, *Maintenance Dir*
William Schaad, *Plant Mgr*
Richard Immerman, *Mng Member*
Bill Shadd, *Manager*
Benjamin Calkins,
EMP: 25
SALES (est): 2MM **Privately Held**
SIC: 7349 5169 2819 Chemical cleaning services; chemicals & allied products; bleaching powder, lime bleaching compounds

(G-16684)
ELITE TRANSPORTATION SVCS LLC
Also Called: Elite Logistics Worldwide
4940 Enterprise Pkwy (44273-8929)
PHONE..................................330 769-5830
Maggie Petrush, *Administration*
EMP: 30
SALES (est): 3.7MM
SALES (corp-wide): 3B **Publicly Held**
WEB: www.elitepdx.com
SIC: 4731 Foreign freight forwarding; freight forwarding
HQ: Panther Ii Transportation, Inc.
84 Medina Rd
Medina OH 44256

(G-16685)
ENCORE HEALTHCARE LLC
Also Called: Meadowview Care Center
83 High St (44273-9308)
PHONE..................................330 769-2015
Fax: 330 769-3790
EMP: 120
SALES (corp-wide): 24MM **Privately Held**
SIC: 8059 8051 Nursing/Personal Care Skilled Nursing Care Facility
PA: Encore Healthcare, Llc
7150 Columbia Gateway Dr A
Columbia MD 21046
443 539-2350

(G-16686)
JARRELLS MOVING & TRANSPORT CO (PA)
Also Called: J M T Freight Specialists
5076 Park Ave W (44273-8916)
PHONE..................................330 764-4333
Robert S Zufra, *CEO*
David J Jarrell, *Exec VP*
Randy J Jarrell, *Exec VP*
Chester A Sipsock, *CFO*
EMP: 70 **EST:** 1997
SQ FT: 8,200
SALES (est): 10.6MM **Privately Held**
WEB: www.gojmt.com
SIC: 4213 Trucking, except local

(G-16687)
PROFESSIONAL SALES ASSOCIATES
5045 Park Ave W Ste 1b (44273-8963)
PHONE..................................330 299-7343
James McGonigal, *President*
EMP: 34
SALES (est): 4.8MM **Privately Held**
WEB: www.profsales.com
SIC: 5047 Dental equipment & supplies

(G-16688)
RAWIGA COUNTRY CLUB INC
10353 Rawiga Rd (44273-9700)
PHONE..................................330 336-2220
Jeanne Pritchard, *Principal*
EMP: 75
SQ FT: 19,000
SALES: 1.2MM **Privately Held**
SIC: 7992 Public golf courses

(G-16689)
SOCIETY HANDICAPPED CITZ MEDIN (PA)
4283 Paradise Rd (44273-9353)
PHONE..................................330 722-1900
Roger Ware, *Maintenance Dir*
Deborah Haumesser, *Opers Staff*
Michael Beh, *Finance*
Janine Dalton, *Director*
Shelly Wharton, *Director*
EMP: 35
SQ FT: 4,800
SALES: 8MM **Privately Held**
WEB: www.shc-medina.org
SIC: 8361 8052 Home for the mentally handicapped; home for the physically handicapped; intermediate care facilities

(G-16690)
SOCIEY FOR HANDICAPPED CITIZEN
Also Called: Camp Paradise
4283 Paradise Rd (44273-9353)
PHONE...................................330 725-7041
Janine Dalton, *Exec Dir*
EMP: 180
SALES (est): 1.5MM **Privately Held**
SIC: 8361 8052 Home for the mentally handicapped; intermediate care facilities

(G-16691)
SON-RISE HOTELS INC
Also Called: Comfort Inn
4949 Park Ave W (44273-9313)
PHONE...................................330 769-4949
Fateme Shaikary, *President*
Abbas Shaikary MD, *Vice Pres*
EMP: 28
SALES (est): 1.1MM **Privately Held**
SIC: 7011 Hotels & motels

(G-16692)
STELLAR SRKG ACQUISITION LLC
Also Called: Stellar Automotive Group
4935 Enterprise Pkwy (44273-8930)
PHONE...................................330 769-8484
Justin Archer,
▲ **EMP:** 33
SQ FT: 40,000
SALES (est): 12.7MM **Privately Held**
WEB: www.stellargroup.com
SIC: 5013 Automotive supplies & parts

(G-16693)
WORLD TRCK TOWING RECOVERY INC
4970 Park Ave W (44273-9376)
PHONE...................................330 723-1116
Mike Schoen, *Principal*
EMP: 29
SALES (est): 6.4MM **Privately Held**
SIC: 7549 4789 5521 Towing services; cargo loading & unloading services; trucks, tractors & trailers: used

Shadyside
Belmont County

(G-16694)
DJD EXPRESS INC
56461 Ferry Landing Rd (43947-9705)
P.O. Box 124, Powhatan Point (43942-0124)
PHONE...................................740 676-7464
Nancy Lucas, *Office Mgr*
EMP: 55
SALES (est): 136.9K **Privately Held**
SIC: 8742 Management consulting services

(G-16695)
H L C TRUCKING INC
57245 Ferry Landing Rd (43947-9701)
P.O. Box 127, Powhatan Point (43942-0127)
PHONE...................................740 676-6181
Dennis Hendershot, *President*
Roger Lewis, *Business Mgr*
Dennis Winkler, *Vice Pres*
Donald Hendershot, *Treasurer*
Robin Burkhart, *Human Res Dir*
EMP: 62
SALES (est): 7.2MM **Privately Held**
WEB: www.hlctrucking.com
SIC: 4212 Local trucking, without storage

(G-16696)
LYNDCO INC
56805 Ferry Landing Rd 8a (43947-8769)
PHONE...................................740 671-9098
Lynda Hendershot, *President*
EMP: 50
SQ FT: 10,000
SALES (est): 6.8MM **Privately Held**
SIC: 1611 Surfacing & paving

(G-16697)
OHIO EDISON COMPANY
Also Called: Burger Plant
57246 Ferry Landing Rd (43947-9701)
P.O. Box 8 (43947-0008)
PHONE...................................740 671-2900
Peter Robinson, *Manager*
EMP: 140 **Publicly Held**
SIC: 4911 4939 Generation, electric power; combination utilities
HQ: Ohio Edison Company
76 S Main St Bsmt
Akron OH 44308
800 736-3402

(G-16698)
VIRGINIA OHIO-WEST EXCVTG CO
Also Called: Owv Exc
56461 Ferry Landing Rd (43947-9705)
P.O. Box 128, Powhatan Point (43942-0128)
PHONE...................................740 676-7464
Dennis Hendershot, *CEO*
Roger Lewis, *President*
Brian Hendershot, *Vice Pres*
Matt Cavanaugh, *Project Mgr*
Shawn Starr, *Project Mgr*
EMP: 120
SQ FT: 2,800
SALES: 37MM **Privately Held**
WEB: www.owvexcavating.com
SIC: 1611 General contractor, highway & street construction

(G-16699)
WHEELING HOSPITAL INC
Also Called: Shadyside Health Center
4000 Central Ave (43947-1209)
PHONE...................................740 671-0850
Ronald L Violi, *CEO*
EMP: 53
SALES (corp-wide): 395.3MM **Privately Held**
SIC: 8099 Childbirth preparation clinic
PA: Wheeling Hospital, Inc.
1 Medical Park
Wheeling WV 26003
304 243-3000

(G-16700)
ZANDEX INC
Also Called: Shadyside Care Center
60583 State Route 7 (43947-9704)
PHONE...................................740 676-8381
Joni Fox, *Manager*
EMP: 125
SALES (corp-wide): 34MM **Privately Held**
SIC: 8051 Convalescent home with continuous nursing care
PA: Zandex, Inc.
1122 Taylor St
Zanesville OH 43701
740 454-1400

Shaker Heights
Cuyahoga County

(G-16701)
1ST ALL FILE RECOVERY USA
Also Called: Data Recovery
3570 Warrensville Ctr Rd (44122-5288)
PHONE...................................800 399-7150
Dmitry Belkin, *CEO*
EMP: 40
SALES (est): 2.8MM **Privately Held**
WEB: www.dataretrieval.com
SIC: 7374 Data processing service

(G-16702)
ABA INSURANCE SERVICES INC
3401 Tuttle Rd Ste 300 (44122-6393)
PHONE...................................800 274-5222
John N Wells, *CEO*
Alena Dreskin, *Opers-Prdtn-Mfg*
Amber Williams, *Opers-Prdtn-Mfg*
Luba Sudnitsyn, *Software Dev*
Joshua Holden, *Executive*
EMP: 56
SALES: 17MM **Publicly Held**
SIC: 6411 Insurance agents

PA: American Financial Group, Inc.
301 E 4th St Fl 8
Cincinnati OH 45202

(G-16703)
BELLEFAIRE JEWISH CHLD BUR (PA)
22001 Fairmount Blvd (44118-4819)
PHONE...................................216 932-2800
Betty Schieferstein, *Human Res Dir*
Vincent Wisser, *Psychologist*
Karen McHenry, *Program Mgr*
Karin Hess, *Manager*
Sheila Reynolds, *Manager*
EMP: 400
SQ FT: 102,000
SALES: 50.6MM **Privately Held**
WEB: www.bellefairejcb.org
SIC: 8361 8322 Home for the emotionally disturbed; individual & family services

(G-16704)
CELLULAR TECHNOLOGY LIMITED
Also Called: Ctl Analyzers
20521 Chagrin Blvd # 200 (44122-5350)
PHONE...................................216 791-5084
Paul V Lehmann,
EMP: 40
SQ FT: 30,000
SALES (est): 6MM **Privately Held**
SIC: 8071 3821 Medical laboratories; clinical laboratory instruments, except medical & dental

(G-16705)
CENTERS FOR DIALYSIS CARE INC (PA)
18720 Chagrin Blvd (44122-4855)
PHONE...................................216 295-7000
Cheryl Winterich, *Vice Pres*
Alan Zarach, *Technical Mgr*
David Oppenland, *CFO*
Melissa Lesiak, *Accountant*
Sylvia Young, *Human Res Mgr*
EMP: 125
SQ FT: 25,000
SALES: 38.4MM **Privately Held**
SIC: 8011 8092 Clinic, operated by physicians; kidney dialysis centers

(G-16706)
COMMUNITY DIALYSIS CENTER
18720 Chagrin Blvd (44122-4855)
PHONE...................................216 295-7000
Linda Floyd, *Manager*
EMP: 332 **Privately Held**
SIC: 8092 Kidney dialysis centers
PA: Community Dialysis Center
18720 Chagrin Blvd
Shaker Heights OH 44122

(G-16707)
DURABLE SLATE CO
3530 Warrensville Ctr Rd (44122-5278)
PHONE...................................216 751-0151
Cleveland Slate, *Branch Mgr*
EMP: 30
SALES (corp-wide): 21.5MM **Privately Held**
SIC: 1761 Gutter & downspout contractor; roofing contractor
PA: The Durable Slate Co
3933 Groves Rd
Columbus OH 43232
614 299-5522

(G-16708)
EQUITY ENGINEERING GROUP INC (PA)
20600 Chagrin Blvd # 1200 (44122-5342)
PHONE...................................216 283-9519
David A Osage, *President*
Joel Andreani, *Treasurer*
Joseph Simari, *Admin Sec*
EMP: 60
SQ FT: 27,000
SALES (est): 17.9MM **Privately Held**
WEB: www.equityeng.com
SIC: 8711 Engineering services

(G-16709)
HANNA PERKINS SCHOOL
Also Called: HANNA PERKIN CENTER
19910 Malvern Rd (44122-2823)
PHONE...................................216 991-4472
Karen Baer, *CEO*
Zach France, *Treasurer*
Barbara Streeter, *Director*
Beth Watson, *Director*
Burt Griffin, *Bd of Directors*
EMP: 25 **EST:** 1952
SQ FT: 33,000
SALES: 1.1MM **Privately Held**
SIC: 8351 8211 Preschool center; kindergarten

(G-16710)
MFF SOMERSET LLC
Also Called: SHAKER GARDENS NURSING & REHAB
3550 Northfield Rd (44122-5253)
PHONE...................................216 752-5600
Michael F Flanagan,
EMP: 29
SALES: 4MM **Privately Held**
SIC: 8051 Skilled nursing care facilities

(G-16711)
MYCITY TRANSPORATATION CO
16781 Shgrin Blvd Ste 283 (44120)
PHONE...................................216 591-1900
James R Crosby, *CEO*
EMP: 45
SQ FT: 4,500
SALES: 2.5MM **Privately Held**
SIC: 4119 Local passenger transportation

(G-16712)
SHAKER HEIGHTS COUNTRY CLUB CO
3300 Courtland Blvd (44122-2810)
PHONE...................................216 991-3324
Phil Boova, *CEO*
Gerald Breen, *President*
D H Tilden, *Principal*
Allen Waddle, *Vice Pres*
Michael Abdalian, *Treasurer*
EMP: 225
SQ FT: 62,000
SALES (est): 4.8MM **Privately Held**
WEB: www.shakerheightscc.org
SIC: 7997 Country club, membership

(G-16713)
SOFTWARE SUPPORT GROUP INC
Also Called: Ssg
22211 Westchester Rd (44122-2968)
PHONE...................................216 566-0555
David Rosenblatt, *Ch of Bd*
Drew Sellers, *President*
EMP: 62
SQ FT: 4,000
SALES (est): 3.6MM **Privately Held**
WEB: www.ssgcom.com
SIC: 8748 Business consulting

(G-16714)
SPECIALIZED ALTERNATIVES FOR F
Also Called: Safy of Cleveland
20600 Chagrin Blvd # 320 (44122-5334)
PHONE...................................216 295-7239
Dru Whitaker, *Principal*
EMP: 156
SALES (corp-wide): 19.7MM **Privately Held**
SIC: 8322 Child related social services
PA: Specialized Alternatives For Families And Youth Of Ohio, Inc.
10100 Elida Rd
Delphos OH 45833
419 695-8010

(G-16715)
SUBURBAN PEDIATRICS INC (PA)
Also Called: University Prmry Care Physcans
20220 Farnsleigh Rd (44122-3643)
PHONE...................................440 498-0065
Andrew Hertz MD, *President*
Janet Benish, *Med Doctor*
Elizabeth Carpenter, *Pediatrics*
EMP: 27

SALES (est): 2.7MM **Privately Held**
WEB: www.suburbanpediatrics.com
SIC: **8062** General medical & surgical hospitals

(G-16716)
SUPERIOR STREET PARTNERS LLC
19010 Shaker Blvd (44122-2544)
PHONE..................216 862-0058
Jon Herbst, *President*
EMP: 100
SALES (est): 4.5MM **Privately Held**
SIC: **6799** Investors

(G-16717)
UNIVERSITY HOSPITALS (PA)
3605 Warrensville Ctr Rd (44122-5203)
PHONE..................216 767-8900
Thomas S Zenty, *CEO*
Janet L Miller, *Senior VP*
Elizabeth Novak, *Vice Pres*
Michael Szubski, *CFO*
Bradley Bond, *Treasurer*
▲ EMP: 950
SALES: 580MM **Privately Held**
SIC: **8062** 8011 8741 General medical & surgical hospitals; offices & clinics of medical doctors; hospital management; nursing & personal care facility management

(G-16718)
UNIVERSITY HOSPITALS CLEVELAND
3605 Warrensville Ctr Rd (44122-5203)
PHONE..................216 844-3323
Ryan Hooper, *Counsel*
Harlin Adelman, *Vice Pres*
David Gillum, *Finance Mgr*
Tierney Kimmerle, *Mktg Coord*
Janet Miller, *Branch Mgr*
EMP: 607
SALES (corp-wide): 580MM **Privately Held**
SIC: **8062** General medical & surgical hospitals
HQ: University Hospitals Of Cleveland
11100 Euclid Ave
Cleveland OH 44106
216 844-1000

(G-16719)
VIGILANT GLOBAL TRADE SVCS LLC (PA)
3140 Courtland Blvd # 3400 (44122-2808)
PHONE..................260 417-1825
David Moore, *President*
Derek Abramovitch,
EMP: 25
SALES: 2.2MM **Privately Held**
SIC: **8611** 7389 Trade associations;

(G-16720)
WINGSPAN CARE GROUP (PA)
22001 Fairmount Blvd (44118-4819)
PHONE..................216 932-2800
Adam G Jacobs PHD, *President*
Jeanne Williamson, *Accountant*
Kelli Michaud, *Human Res Dir*
Leigh Johnson, *Manager*
Raymond Fink, *Info Tech Dir*
EMP: 41
SALES: 8MM **Privately Held**
SIC: **8621** Medical field-related associations

Shandon
Butler County

(G-16721)
R & B CONTRACTORS LLC
Also Called: Robert McConnell
3730 Schloss Ln (45063)
PHONE..................513 738-0954
Robert R McConnell, *Owner*
EMP: 35
SALES (est): 3.2MM **Privately Held**
SIC: **1761** Roofing contractor

Sharon Center
Medina County

(G-16722)
HOLLAND MANAGEMENT INC (PA)
1383 Sharon Copley Rd (44274)
PHONE..................330 239-4474
John E Holland Jr, *President*
Teresa Holland, *Admin Sec*
EMP: 300
SALES (est): 18.1MM **Privately Held**
SIC: **6513** 6512 Apartment building operators; nonresidential building operators

(G-16723)
HOLLAND PROFESSIONAL GROUP
Also Called: Holand Management
1343 Sharon Copley (44274)
PHONE..................330 239-4474
John E Holland Jr, *President*
John Houghton, *Architect*
EMP: 65 EST: 1972
SQ FT: 2,000
SALES (est): 4.1MM **Privately Held**
SIC: **8712** Architectural services

(G-16724)
RUHLIN COMPANY (PA)
6931 Ridge Rd (44274)
PHONE..................330 239-2800
James L Ruhlin, *President*
George Seanor, *General Mgr*
Michael Deiwert, *Vice Pres*
Scott McCarthy, *Vice Pres*
Charles Schreckenberger, *Vice Pres*
EMP: 151 EST: 1915
SQ FT: 16,500
SALES (est): 109.6MM **Privately Held**
WEB: www.ruhlin.com
SIC: **1542** 1541 1622 1611 Commercial & office building, new construction; industrial buildings, new construction; bridge construction; general contractor, highway & street construction

(G-16725)
SHARON TWNSHIP FRFIGHTERS ASSN
1274 Sharon Copley Rd (44274)
P.O. Box 310 (44274-0310)
PHONE..................330 239-4992
Michael George, *President*
Valerie Mravepc, *Admin Sec*
Bill Spalin,
EMP: 35
SALES: 35.6K **Privately Held**
SIC: **8399** Fund raising organization, non-fee basis

(G-16726)
SOUTHEAST SECURITY CORPORATION
1385 Wolf Creek Trl (44274)
P.O. Box 326 (44274-0326)
PHONE..................330 239-4600
Matt Lentine, *President*
David Brown, *General Mgr*
Thomas Cutlip, *Project Mgr*
Mike Kelly, *Project Mgr*
Jim Laube, *Project Mgr*
EMP: 40
SQ FT: 8,000
SALES (est): 9.2MM **Privately Held**
WEB: www.southeastsecurity.com
SIC: **1731** Fire detection & burglar alarm systems specialization

(G-16727)
VELOTTA COMPANY
6740 Ridge Rd (44274)
P.O. Box 267 (44274-0267)
PHONE..................330 239-1211
Robert P Velotta, *President*
Carolann V Stercula, *Vice Pres*
Michael Velotta, *Vice Pres*
Thomas F Velotta, *Vice Pres*
EMP: 50
SQ FT: 4,500

SALES (est): 11.7MM **Privately Held**
WEB: www.velottacompany.com
SIC: **1611** 1622 General contractor, highway & street construction; bridge construction; highway construction, elevated

---

Sharonville
Hamilton County

(G-16728)
DCP HOLDING COMPANY
Also Called: DENTAL CARE PLUS GROUP (DCPG)
100 Crowne Point Pl (45241-5427)
PHONE..................513 554-1100
Stephen T Schuler, *Ch of Bd*
Anthony A Cook, *President*
Jodi M Fronczek, *COO*
Robert C Hodgkins Jr, *CFO*
EMP: 77
SALES: 112.5MM **Privately Held**
SIC: **6324** Dental insurance

(G-16729)
INNOMARK COMMUNICATIONS LLC
12080 Mosteller Rd (45241-5510)
PHONE..................937 425-6152
Gary P Boens,
EMP: 30
SALES (corp-wide): 82.8MM **Privately Held**
SIC: **7319** Display advertising service
PA: Innomark Communications Llc
420 Distribution Cir
Fairfield OH 45014
888 466-6627

(G-16730)
RICOH USA INC
400 E Business Way # 125 (45241-2223)
PHONE..................513 984-9898
Charles Dews, *Branch Mgr*
Michael Pantano, *Executive*
EMP: 70
SALES (corp-wide): 19.3B **Privately Held**
WEB: www.ikon.com
SIC: **5044** 5065 7359 5112 Photocopy machines; copying equipment; facsimile equipment; office machine rental, except computers; photocopying supplies; photocopying & duplicating services; machinery & equipment finance leasing
HQ: Ricoh Usa, Inc.
70 Valley Stream Pkwy
Malvern PA 19355
610 296-8000

Sheffield Village
Lorain County

(G-16731)
ABC PHONES NORTH CAROLINA INC
Also Called: Verizon
5255 Detroit Rd (44054-2902)
PHONE..................440 328-4331
Barney Stinson, *Branch Mgr*
EMP: 46
SALES (corp-wide): 149.9MM **Privately Held**
SIC: **4812** Cellular telephone services
PA: Abc Phones Of North Carolina, Inc.
8510 Colonnade Center Dr
Raleigh NC 27615
252 317-0388

(G-16732)
ADVANCED DESIGN INDUSTRIES INC
Also Called: ADI
4686 French Creek Rd (44054-2716)
PHONE..................440 277-4141
Jerome Winiasz, *President*
R G Brooks Jr, *Principal*
Edward J Winiasz, *Principal*
Thomas Winiasz, *Corp Secy*
▲ EMP: 25
SQ FT: 27,000

SALES (est): 7.3MM **Privately Held**
SIC: **3569** 3599 8711 Robots, assembly line: industrial & commercial; machine shop, jobbing & repair; designing: ship, boat, machine & product

(G-16733)
BRENTWOOD GOLF CLUB INC
4456 Abbe Rd (44054-2910)
PHONE..................440 322-9254
Walter Jalowiec Jr, *President*
John Jalowiec, *General Mgr*
Henry Jalowiec, *Principal*
EMP: 30
SQ FT: 5,000
SALES (est): 1.2MM **Privately Held**
WEB: www.golfwillow.com
SIC: **7992** Public golf courses

(G-16734)
GREEN IMPRESSIONS LLC
842 Abbe Rd (44054-2302)
PHONE..................440 240-8508
Joseph Schill, *President*
James P Louth, *Vice Pres*
Jim Louth, *Vice Pres*
Terri Healey, *Administration*
EMP: 45
SALES: 3.6MM **Privately Held**
SIC: **0781** 7349 4959 0782 Landscape services; building maintenance services; snowplowing; lawn & garden services

(G-16735)
J E DAVIS CORPORATION
5187 Smith Ct Ste 100 (44054-2470)
PHONE..................440 377-4700
Doug Davis, *President*
EMP: 37
SQ FT: 2,500
SALES (est): 4.9MM **Privately Held**
SIC: **4813** Telephone communications broker

(G-16736)
JACK COOPER TRANSPORT CO INC
5211 Oster Rd (44054-1568)
PHONE..................440 949-2044
Larry Suscha, *Branch Mgr*
EMP: 131
SALES (corp-wide): 667.8MM **Privately Held**
SIC: **4213** Automobiles, transport & delivery
HQ: Jack Cooper Transport Company, Inc.
1100 Walnut St Ste 2400
Kansas City MO 64106
816 983-4000

(G-16737)
JOSEPH A GIRGIS MD INC (PA)
Also Called: Superior Medical Care
5334 Meadow Lane Ct (44035-1469)
PHONE..................440 930-6095
Joseph A Girgis, *President*
EMP: 39
SALES (est): 6.1MM **Privately Held**
SIC: **8011** 5912 Medical centers; drug stores

(G-16738)
LUXURY HEATING CO
Also Called: L & H Wholesale & Supply
5327 Ford Rd (44035-1349)
PHONE..................440 366-0971
William Samek, *President*
Paul Samek, *COO*
Michael Samek, *Vice Pres*
Jodie Reynolds, *Office Mgr*
Barry Racz, *Manager*
EMP: 65 EST: 1947
SALES: 7MM **Privately Held**
SIC: **1711** 5075 Warm air heating & air conditioning contractor; warm air heating & air conditioning

(G-16739)
MERCY HEALTH
5054 Waterford Dr (44035-1497)
PHONE..................440 934-8344
EMP: 37
SALES (corp-wide): 4.7B **Privately Held**
SIC: **8011** Offices & clinics of medical doctors

PA: Mercy Health
1701 Mercy Health Pl
Cincinnati OH 45237
513 639-2800

(G-16740)
MONTROSE SHEFFIELD LLC
5033 Detroit Rd (44054-2810)
PHONE...............................440 934-6699
Doug Beasley, *Parts Mgr*
Michael Thompson, *Mng Member*
Christopher Mills,
Joseph M Stefanini,
Mary Lou Taylor,
EMP: 36
SALES (est): 2.4MM **Privately Held**
SIC: 7539 5511 Automotive repair shops;
automobiles, new & used

(G-16741)
NICHOLAS CARNEY-MC INC
Also Called: Carney McNicholas
2931 Abbe Rd (44054-2424)
PHONE...............................440 243-8560
Tim Carney, *Manager*
EMP: 30
SALES (est): 2.2MM
SALES (corp-wide): 2.2MM **Privately
Held**
WEB: www.cmcn.com
SIC: 4212 Local Trucking Operator
PA: Nicholas Carney-Mc Inc
100 Victoria Rd
Youngstown OH 44515
330 792-5460

(G-16742)
**WESTSHORE PRMRY CARE
ASSOC INC**
5323 Meadow Lane Ct (44035-1469)
PHONE...............................440 934-0276
Ellen Egan, *Branch Mgr*
EMP: 95
SALES (corp-wide): 8.3MM **Privately
Held**
SIC: 8011 General & family practice, physi-
cian/surgeon
PA: Westshore Primary Care Associates,
Inc.
26908 Detroit Rd Ste 201
Westlake OH 44145
440 808-1283

Shelby
Richland County

(G-16743)
**CENTRAL OHIO ASSOCIATES
LTD**
Central Oh Ind 18 (44875)
P.O. Box 646 (44875-0646)
PHONE...............................419 342-2045
Stephen Rosen, *Partner*
Uehuda Mendelson, *Partner*
Benjamin Rosen, *Partner*
EMP: 33
SQ FT: 2,500,000
SALES (est): 3.2MM **Privately Held**
SIC: 6512 Nonresidential building opera-
tors

(G-16744)
CORNELL COMPANIES INC
Also Called: Abraxas Foundation of Ohio
2775 State Route 39 (44875-9466)
PHONE...............................419 747-3322
Bruce Tessena, *Director*
Erich Dumbeck, *Administration*
EMP: 110
SALES (corp-wide): 2.3B **Privately Held**
WEB: www.cornellcorrections.com
SIC: 8069 8361 Substance abuse hospi-
tals; residential care
HQ: Cornell Companies, Inc.
621 Nw 53rd St Ste 700
Boca Raton FL 33487

(G-16745)
DECOATING INC
3955 Industrial Pkwy (44875-9259)
P.O. Box 5100 (44875-5100)
PHONE...............................419 347-9191
Dave Wagner, *President*

David Wagner, *President*
Pearl Biller, *Finance Mgr*
EMP: 25
SQ FT: 10,000
SALES: 750K **Privately Held**
WEB: www.decoating.com
SIC: 1799 Paint & wallpaper stripping

(G-16746)
**GLEN SURPLUS SALES INC
(PA)**
14 E Smiley Ave (44875-1080)
PHONE...............................419 347-1212
Glen H Arms, *President*
Bobby Arms, *Vice Pres*
James Arms, *Vice Pres*
Jennifer Arms, *Vice Pres*
EMP: 25 EST: 1978
SQ FT: 109,000
SALES (est): 3MM **Privately Held**
SIC: 5399 5199 Surplus & salvage goods;
variety store merchandise

(G-16747)
MEDCENTRAL HEALTH SYSTEM
199 W Main St (44875-1490)
PHONE...............................419 342-5015
Ronald Distl, *Director*
EMP: 200
SALES (corp-wide): 4B **Privately Held**
SIC: 8062 8049 General medical & surgi-
cal hospitals; physical therapist
HQ: Medcentral Health System
335 Glessner Ave
Mansfield OH 44903
419 526-8000

(G-16748)
MWD LOGISTICS INC
Also Called: Mansfield Warehouse & Distrg
151 S Martin Dr (44875-1750)
PHONE...............................419 342-6253
Stuart Lichter, *Chairman*
EMP: 34
SALES (corp-wide): 28.6MM **Privately
Held**
WEB: www.mwdlogistics.com
SIC: 4225 General warehousing
PA: Mwd Logistics Inc
222 Tappan Dr N
Ontario OH 44906
419 522-3510

(G-16749)
**PHILLIPS MFG AND TOWER CO
(PA)**
Also Called: Shelby Welded Tube Div
5578 State Route 61 N (44875-9564)
P.O. Box 125 (44875-0125)
PHONE...............................419 347-1720
Angela Phillip, *CEO*
Theresa Wallace, *CFO*
Lori Metheney, *Administration*
EMP: 85
SQ FT: 90,000
SALES (est): 29.7MM **Privately Held**
WEB: www.shelbytube.com
SIC: 3312 3498 3317 7692 Tubes, steel
& iron; fabricated pipe & fittings; steel
pipe & tubes; welding repair

(G-16750)
R & J TRUCKING INC
147 Curtis Dr (44875-9501)
PHONE...............................330 758-0841
EMP: 56 **Privately Held**
SIC: 4212 Dump truck haulage
HQ: R & J Trucking, Inc.
8063 Southern Blvd
Youngstown OH 44512
800 262-9365

(G-16751)
**YOUNG MENS CHRISTN ASSN
SHELBY**
Also Called: Y M C A
111 W Smiley Ave (44875-2112)
PHONE...............................419 347-1312
Jeff Ream, *President*
Joyce Douglas, *Business Mgr*
Kevin Herring, *Treasurer*
Rich Haight, *Exec Dir*
Kim Stover, *Director*
EMP: 60

SALES: 439.2K **Privately Held**
SIC: 8641 7997 7991 Youth organizations; membership sports & recreation
clubs; physical fitness facilities

Sherrodsville
Carroll County

(G-16752)
ATWOOD YACHT CLUB INC
2637 Lodge Rd Sw (44675-9719)
P.O. Box 165 (44675-0165)
PHONE...............................330 735-2135
Joseph Montero, *Principal*
Norma Campbell, *Manager*
Phil Eberhart,
EMP: 25
SQ FT: 7,719
SALES: 395.9K **Privately Held**
WEB: www.atwoodyc.com
SIC: 7997 Yacht club, membership

Shreve
Wayne County

(G-16753)
CRW INC
3716 S Elyria Rd (44676-9529)
PHONE...............................330 264-3785
Chris Wood, *President*
Charles R Wood, *Vice Pres*
EMP: 52
SQ FT: 9,800
SALES (est): 9.5MM **Privately Held**
SIC: 4213 Contract haulers

(G-16754)
**QUALITY CLEANING SYSTEMS
LLC**
7945 Shreve Rd (44676-9565)
PHONE...............................330 567-2050
Steven Pogue,
EMP: 47
SALES (est): 846.9K **Privately Held**
SIC: 7349 Janitorial service, contract basis

Sidney
Shelby County

(G-16755)
1157 DESIGN CONCEPTS LLC
210 S Lester Ave (45365-7057)
PHONE...............................937 497-1157
Evelyn Flock, *President*
EMP: 25
SALES (est): 3.7MM **Privately Held**
SIC: 7699 Customizing services

(G-16756)
**AAA SHELBY COUNTY MOTOR
CLUB**
Also Called: World Wide Travel Service
920 Wapakoneta Ave (45365-1471)
PHONE...............................937 492-3167
Debra Barga, *CEO*
Keith Putman, *President*
EMP: 25 EST: 1922
SQ FT: 10,400
SALES (est): 4MM **Privately Held**
WEB: www.shelbycounty.aaa.com
SIC: 4724 Travel agencies

(G-16757)
AG TRUCKING INC
798 S Vandemark Rd (45365-8139)
PHONE...............................937 497-7770
Katie Stamp, *Manager*
EMP: 28
SALES (corp-wide): 34MM **Privately
Held**
WEB: www.ag-trucking.com
SIC: 4213 4212 Contract haulers; local
trucking, without storage
PA: Ag Trucking Inc
2430 Lincolnway E
Goshen IN 46526
574 642-3351

(G-16758)
AMOS MEDIA COMPANY (PA)
Also Called: Coin World
911 S Vandemark Rd (45365-8974)
P.O. Box 4129 (45365-4129)
PHONE...............................937 498-2111
John O Amos, *Ch of Bd*
Bruce Boyd, *President*
William Gibbs, *Editor*
Phyllis Stegemoller, *Sales Associate*
Victoria Hardy, *Marketing Staff*
▲ EMP: 200 EST: 1876
SQ FT: 90,000
SALES (est): 36.4MM **Privately Held**
SIC: 2721 2711 2796 7389 Magazines:
publishing only, not printed on site; news-
papers, publishing & printing; platemaking
services; appraisers, except real estate;
miscellaneous publishing

(G-16759)
**AREA ENERGY & ELECTRIC INC
(PA)**
Also Called: Honeywell Authorized Dealer
2001 Commerce Dr (45365-9393)
PHONE...............................937 498-4784
Kenneth Schlater, *Principal*
Joe Lachey, *Vice Pres*
EMP: 219
SQ FT: 20,000
SALES (est): 58.8MM **Privately Held**
SIC: 1731 1711 General electrical contrac-
tor; heating & air conditioning contractors

(G-16760)
BAUMFOLDER CORPORATION
1660 Campbell Rd (45365-2480)
PHONE...............................937 492-1281
Janice Benanzer, *President*
Jason Muldoon, *President*
Ruth Souder, *Buyer*
Lee Trisler, *Engineer*
Mark Stonerock, *Project Engr*
▲ EMP: 45 EST: 1917
SQ FT: 125,000
SALES: 10MM
SALES (corp-wide): 3B **Privately Held**
WEB: www.baumfolder.com
SIC: 3579 7389 3554 Binding machines,
plastic & adhesive; packaging & labeling
services; folding machines, paper
HQ: Heidelberg Americas Inc
1000 Gutenberg Dr Nw
Kennesaw GA 30144

(G-16761)
BELL HENSLEY INC
Also Called: AMS
804 W Parkwood St (45365-3626)
PHONE...............................937 498-1718
EMP: 35
SALES (est): 3.2MM **Privately Held**
SIC: 1541 Constructor Of Machine Equip-
ment

(G-16762)
**BELTING COMPANY OF
CINCINNATI**
Also Called: Cbt Company
301 Stolle Ave (45365-7807)
PHONE...............................937 498-2104
James E Stahl Jr, *President*
EMP: 28
SALES (corp-wide): 207.7MM **Privately
Held**
SIC: 5063 Electrical apparatus & equip-
ment
PA: The Belting Company Of Cincinnati
5500 Ridge Ave
Cincinnati OH 45213
513 621-9050

(G-16763)
BULK TRANSIT CORPORATION
1377 Riverside Dr (45365-9197)
PHONE...............................937 497-9573
Scott Woods, *Manager*
EMP: 30
SALES (corp-wide): 26.7MM **Privately
Held**
WEB: www.bulktransit.com
SIC: 4213 Contract haulers

GEOGRAPHIC

PA: Bulk Transit Corporation
7177 Indl Pkwy
Plain City OH 43064
614 873-4632

(G-16764)
CHOICE ONE ENGINEERING CORP
440 E Hoewisher Rd (45365-8450)
PHONE....................................937 497-0200
Anthony Schroeder, *Owner*
Steven E Bowersox, *Owner*
Thomas Coverstone, *Owner*
Jeffery M Kunk, *Owner*
Sharon Maurice, *Owner*
EMP: 25
SALES (est): 3.6MM **Privately Held**
WEB: www.choiceoneengineering.com
SIC: 8711 8713 Consulting engineer; surveying services

(G-16765)
CHS MIAMI VALLEY INC
Also Called: Sidney Care Center
510 Buckeye Ave (45365-1214)
PHONE....................................330 204-1040
Edward L Byington, *President*
EMP: 50 **EST:** 2002
SALES: 3.4MM **Privately Held**
SIC: 8051 Convalescent home with continuous nursing care

(G-16766)
CLEAN ALL SERVICES INC
324 Adams St Bldg 1 (45365-2328)
P.O. Box 4127 (45365-4127)
PHONE....................................937 498-4146
Steve Shuchat, *President*
Gary Shuchat, *Chairman*
Sarah Wesbecher, *Human Res Mgr*
Tracy Burgan, *Manager*
Rebecca Fair, *Manager*
EMP: 203
SQ FT: 6,000
SALES (est): 7.3MM **Privately Held**
SIC: 7349 Janitorial service, contract basis

(G-16767)
CONTINENTAL EXPRESS INC
10450 State Route 47 W (45365-9009)
PHONE....................................937 497-2100
Russell L Gottemoeller, *President*
Rene Gottemoeller, *Vice Pres*
Daniel Subler, *Opers Mgr*
Mark Goubeaux, *Persnl Dir*
Becky Schmiesing, *Office Mgr*
EMP: 350
SQ FT: 31,000
SALES: 96.3MM **Privately Held**
SIC: 4213 4212 Refrigerated products transport; local trucking, without storage

(G-16768)
COPELAND ACCESS + INC
1675 Campbell Rd (45365-2479)
P.O. Box 669 (45365-0669)
PHONE....................................937 498-3802
Clinton Clay, *Principal*
Jan Burns, *Assistant VP*
Judy Peterson, *Human Res Mgr*
◆ **EMP:** 28
SALES (est): 23MM
SALES (corp-wide): 17.4B **Publicly Held**
WEB: www.copeland-corp.com
SIC: 5075 Warm air heating & air conditioning
HQ: Emerson Climate Technologies, Inc.
1675 Campbell Rd
Sidney OH 45365
937 498-3011

(G-16769)
COUNCIL ON RUR SVC PRGRAMS INC
Also Called: Shelby County Child Care
1502 N Main Ave (45365-1761)
PHONE....................................937 492-8787
Brenda Lillicrap, *Manager*
EMP: 34
SALES (corp-wide): 15.7MM **Privately Held**
WEB: www.corsp.org
SIC: 8399 8351 Community action agency; head start center, except in conjunction with school

PA: Council On Rural Service Programs, Inc.
201 Robert M Davis Pkwy B
Piqua OH 45356
937 778-5220

(G-16770)
COUNTY OF SHELBY
Also Called: Shelby County Highway Dept
500 Gearhart Rd (45365-9404)
PHONE....................................937 498-7244
Robert Geuy, *Manager*
EMP: 32
SQ FT: 3,200 **Privately Held**
WEB: www.shelbycountyauditors.com
SIC: 1611 Highway & street construction
PA: County Of Shelby
129 E Court St
Sidney OH 45365
937 498-7226

(G-16771)
COUNTY OF SHELBY
Also Called: Fair Haven Shelby County Home
2901 Fair Rd (45365-9534)
PHONE....................................937 492-6900
Melissa Malone, *Site Mgr*
Judy McCorkle, *Human Res Dir*
Miguel Topolov, *Director*
Anita Miller, *Administration*
EMP: 150 **Privately Held**
WEB: www.shelbycountyauditors.com
SIC: 8059 8052 8051 Nursing home, except skilled & intermediate care facility; intermediate care facilities; skilled nursing care facilities
PA: County Of Shelby
129 E Court St
Sidney OH 45365
937 498-7226

(G-16772)
COVER CROP SHOP LLC
Also Called: Center Seeds
739 S Vandemark Rd (45365-8959)
PHONE....................................937 417-3972
Eric L Belcher, *Mng Member*
Jane Ford, *Manager*
EMP: 78
SALES (corp-wide): 5.3MM **Privately Held**
SIC: 5191 Seeds: field, garden & flower
PA: Cover Crop Shop, Llc
40 W 4th St
Minster OH 45865
937 417-3972

(G-16773)
DICKMAN SUPPLY INC (PA)
1991 St Marys Ave (45365)
P.O. Box 569 (45365-0569)
PHONE....................................937 492-6166
Tim Geise, *President*
Timothy Geise, *President*
Marla Geise, *Corp Secy*
Chris Geise, *Vice Pres*
Jason Borchers, *Purchasing*
EMP: 110
SQ FT: 28,000
SALES (est): 114MM **Privately Held**
WEB: www.electro-controls.com
SIC: 5063 5084 Electrical apparatus & equipment; drilling bits; paper, sawmill & woodworking machinery

(G-16774)
DICKMAN SUPPLY INC
Also Called: Electro Controls
1991 St Mary Ave (45365)
P.O. Box 569 (45365-0569)
PHONE....................................937 492-6166
Chris Geise, *Manager*
EMP: 50
SALES (est): 6.9MM
SALES (corp-wide): 114MM **Privately Held**
WEB: www.electro-controls.com
SIC: 5063 Electrical supplies
PA: Dickman Supply, Inc.
1991 St Marys Ave
Sidney OH 45365
937 492-6166

(G-16775)
EAGLE BRIDGE CO
800 S Vandemark Rd (45365-8139)
P.O. Box 59 (45365-0059)
PHONE....................................937 492-5654
Richard Franz, *President*
Thomas Frantz, *Vice Pres*
EMP: 80
SALES (est): 17.2MM **Privately Held**
WEB: www.eaglebridge.net
SIC: 1622 Bridge construction

(G-16776)
FAULKNER GRMHSEN KEISTER SHENK (PA)
100 S Main Ave (45365-2771)
PHONE....................................937 492-1271
Ralph F Keister, *Partner*
Ralph Keister, *Partner*
James R Shenk, *Partner*
EMP: 28
SALES (est): 3.5MM **Privately Held**
WEB: www.fgks-law.com
SIC: 8111 General practice law office

(G-16777)
FERGUSON CONSTRUCTION COMPANY (PA)
400 Canal St (45365-2312)
P.O. Box 726 (45365-0726)
PHONE....................................937 498-2243
Martin Given, *President*
Jason Stiver, *Vice Pres*
John Brown, *Safety Dir*
Ted Lyons, *Project Mgr*
Keith Overmyer, *Project Mgr*
EMP: 150
SQ FT: 40,000
SALES (est): 106.3MM **Privately Held**
WEB: www.ferguson-construction.com
SIC: 1541 1542 Industrial Building Construction Nonresidential Construction

(G-16778)
FOOT & ANKLE CARE CENTER
1000 Michigan St (45365-2404)
PHONE....................................937 492-1211
Eric Polanski DPM, *President*
EMP: 30
SALES (est): 425.4K **Privately Held**
SIC: 8043 Offices & clinics of podiatrists

(G-16779)
FREISTHLER PAVING INC
2323 Campbell Rd (45365-9529)
PHONE....................................937 498-4802
Michael J Freisthler, *President*
Janet Freisthler, *Corp Secy*
Chad Moos, *Exec VP*
EMP: 48
SQ FT: 14,000
SALES (est): 3MM **Privately Held**
SIC: 1771 Blacktop (asphalt) work

(G-16780)
FRESHWAY FOODS INC (PA)
Also Called: Fresh and Limited
601 Stolle Ave (45365-8895)
PHONE....................................937 498-4664
Frank Gilardi Jr, *Ch of Bd*
Phil Gilardi, *President*
Devon Beer, *CFO*
EMP: 147
SQ FT: 90,000
SALES: 109MM **Privately Held**
SIC: 5148 2099 Vegetables, fresh; food preparations

(G-16781)
FRESHWAY FOODS INC
601 Stolle Ave (45365-8895)
PHONE....................................937 498-4664
Devon Beer, *Branch Mgr*
EMP: 241
SALES (corp-wide): 109MM **Privately Held**
SIC: 4731 Transportation agents & brokers
PA: Freshway Foods, Inc.
601 Stolle Ave
Sidney OH 45365
937 498-4664

(G-16782)
HEIDELBERG USA INC
Also Called: Baum USA
1660 Campbell Rd (45365-2480)
PHONE....................................937 492-1281
Micheal Gravel, *Branch Mgr*
EMP: 30
SALES (corp-wide): 3B **Privately Held**
SIC: 5084 Printing trades machinery, equipment & supplies
HQ: Heidelberg Usa, Inc.
1000 Gutenberg Dr Nw
Kennesaw GA 30144
770 419-6500

(G-16783)
KIRK NATIONALEASE CO (PA)
3885 Michigan St (45365-8623)
P.O. Box 4369 (45365-4369)
PHONE....................................937 498-1151
Jeff Phlitot, *President*
James R Harvey, *Vice Pres*
Deb Hovestreybt, *Vice Pres*
Tom Menker, *CFO*
EMP: 40 **EST:** 1920
SQ FT: 20,000
SALES (est): 44.6MM **Privately Held**
WEB: www.knl.cc
SIC: 7513 7538 Truck leasing, without drivers; truck rental, without drivers; truck engine repair, except industrial

(G-16784)
LOCHARD INC
Also Called: Do It Best
903 Wapakoneta Ave (45365-1409)
PHONE....................................937 492-8811
Michael Lochard, *President*
Donald W Lochard, *Vice Pres*
Tim Kleptz, *VP Opers*
Doug Grewe, *Plant Mgr*
Chris Hutson, *Accountant*
EMP: 58 **EST:** 1945
SQ FT: 44,500
SALES: 7MM **Privately Held**
WEB: www.lochard-inc.com
SIC: 1711 5251 Mechanical contractor; hardware

(G-16785)
LOWES HOME CENTERS LLC
2700 W Michigan St (45365-9007)
PHONE....................................937 498-8400
Mike Herrera, *Manager*
EMP: 150
SALES (corp-wide): 68.6B **Publicly Held**
SIC: 5211 5031 5722 5064 Home centers; building materials, exterior; building materials, interior; household appliance stores; electrical appliances, television & radio
HQ: Lowe's Home Centers, Llc
1605 Curtis Bridge Rd
Wilkesboro NC 28697
336 658-4000

(G-16786)
MCCRATE DELAET & CO
Also Called: McCrate Delaet & Co Cpa's
100 S Main Ave Ste 203 (45365-2771)
P.O. Box 339 (45365-0339)
PHONE....................................937 492-3161
Fax: 937 492-8050
EMP: 25
SALES (est): 2.2MM **Privately Held**
SIC: 8721 Accounting/Auditing/Bookkeeping

(G-16787)
NK PARTS INDUSTRIES INC
Also Called: Nkp West
2640 Campbell Rd (45365-8836)
PHONE....................................937 493-4651
Tammy Eilerman, *Manager*
EMP: 30
SALES (corp-wide): 1.7B **Privately Held**
SIC: 5013 5015 Motor vehicle supplies & new parts; motor vehicle parts, used
HQ: Nk Parts Industries, Inc.
777 S Kuther Rd
Sidney OH 45365
937 498-4651

(G-16788)
OCCUPATIONAL HEALTH SERVICES
Also Called: Wilson Mem Hosp Occptnal Clnic
915 Michigan St (45365-2401)
PHONE..................................937 492-7296
Cindy Bay, *Manager*
EMP: 25
SALES (est): 541.4K **Privately Held**
SIC: 8011 8748 8049 Internal medicine; physician/surgeon; business consulting; offices of health practitioner

(G-16789)
OHIO PRESBT RETIREMENT SVCS
Also Called: Dorothy Love Retirement Cmnty
3003 Cisco Rd (45365-9343)
PHONE..................................937 498-2391
Anne Roller, *Principal*
Lou Ann Presser, *Marketing Staff*
EMP: 300 **Privately Held**
WEB: www.nwo.oprs.org
SIC: 8059 8051 8052 Rest home, with health care; skilled nursing care facilities; intermediate care facilities
PA: Ohio Living
1001 Kingsmill Pkwy
Columbus OH 43229

(G-16790)
OHIO VALLEY INTEGRATION SVCS
2005 Commerce Dr (45365-9393)
PHONE..................................937 492-0008
John M Garmhausen, *President*
EMP: 35
SALES (est): 3.9MM
SALES (corp-wide): 58.8MM **Privately Held**
WEB: www.ohiovalleyintegration.com
SIC: 7382 Burglar alarm maintenance & monitoring
PA: Area Energy & Electric, Inc.
2001 Commerce Dr
Sidney OH 45365
937 498-4784

(G-16791)
PEOPLES FEDERAL SAV & LN ASSN (HQ)
101 E Court St (45365-3021)
P.O. Box 727 (45365-0727)
PHONE..................................937 492-6129
Douglas Stewart, *President*
Debra Geuy, *CFO*
EMP: 31
SALES: 4.4MM
SALES (corp-wide): 4.3MM **Publicly Held**
SIC: 6035 Federal savings & loan associations
PA: Peoples-Sidney Financial Corporation
101 E Court St
Sidney OH 45365
937 492-6129

(G-16792)
PEOPLES-SIDNEY FINANCIAL CORP (PA)
101 E Court St (45365-3021)
P.O. Box 727 (45365-0727)
PHONE..................................937 492-6129
Douglas Stewart, *President*
Debra Geuy, *CFO*
EMP: 32 EST: 1997
SALES (est): 4.3MM **Publicly Held**
SIC: 6035 Federal savings & loan associations

(G-16793)
PERFECTION BAKERIES INC
1900 Progress Way (45365-8961)
PHONE..................................937 492-2220
Kelly Henry, *Branch Mgr*
EMP: 57
SALES (corp-wide): 515.3MM **Privately Held**
SIC: 5149 Bakery products
PA: Perfection Bakeries, Inc.
350 Pearl St
Fort Wayne IN 46802
260 424-8245

(G-16794)
PRIMARY EYECARE ASSOCIATES (PA)
1086 Fairington Dr (45365-8913)
PHONE..................................937 492-2351
Jeffery Ahrns, *CEO*
Jeffrey R Ahrns,
EMP: 25
SALES (est): 2.9MM **Privately Held**
WEB: www.primaryeyecare.org
SIC: 8042 8011 Offices & clinics of optometrists; offices & clinics of medical doctors

(G-16795)
REGAL PLUMBING & HEATING CO
9303 State Route 29 W (45365)
PHONE..................................937 492-2894
Gary Thoma, *President*
Phil Wyen, *Shareholder*
Sandy Bruns, *Admin Sec*
EMP: 45
SQ FT: 21,000
SALES (est): 11.5MM **Privately Held**
WEB: www.regalplbg-htg.com
SIC: 1711 Mechanical contractor

(G-16796)
REPUBLIC SERVICES INC
1600 Riverside Dr (45365-9156)
PHONE..................................937 492-3470
EMP: 34
SALES (corp-wide): 8.1B **Publicly Held**
SIC: 4953 Refuse System
PA: Republic Services, Inc.
18500 N Allied Way # 100
Phoenix AZ 85054
480 627-2700

(G-16797)
SHELBY COUNTY MEM HOSP ASSN (PA)
Also Called: Wilson Health
915 Michigan St (45365-2401)
PHONE..................................937 498-2311
Mark Dooley, *President*
Cindy Cable, *President*
Craig Lannoye, *COO*
Linda Maurer, *Vice Pres*
Greg Freistuhler, *Opers Staff*
EMP: 679
SQ FT: 116,000
SALES: 112.5MM **Privately Held**
SIC: 8062 General medical & surgical hospitals

(G-16798)
SHELBY COUNTY MEM HOSP ASSN
Also Called: The Pavilion
705 Fulton St (45365-3203)
PHONE..................................937 492-9591
Marianne Wildermuth, *Executive*
EMP: 80
SALES (corp-wide): 112.5MM **Privately Held**
SIC: 8051 8062 Skilled nursing care facilities; general medical & surgical hospitals
PA: Shelby County Memorial Hospital Association
915 Michigan St
Sidney OH 45365
937 498-2311

(G-16799)
SIDNEY ELECTRIC COMPANY (PA)
840 S Vandemark Rd (45365-8139)
PHONE..................................419 222-1109
John S Frantz, *President*
Mike Ellett, *Vice Pres*
EMP: 59
SQ FT: 20,000
SALES (est): 15.2MM **Privately Held**
SIC: 1731 General electrical contractor

(G-16800)
SIDNEY-SHELBY COUNTY YMCA (PA)
300 E Parkwood St (45365-1642)
PHONE..................................937 492-9134
Ed Thomas, *CEO*
Dennis Ruble, *Exec Dir*

Michele Dotson, *Director*
EMP: 35
SALES: 126.2K **Privately Held**
WEB: www.sidney-ymca.org
SIC: 8641 8661 8322 Youth organizations; religious organizations; individual & family services

(G-16801)
SLAGLE MECHANICAL CONTRACTORS
877 W Russell Rd (45365-8633)
P.O. Box 823 (45365-0823)
PHONE..................................937 492-4151
Jerry Kingseed, *President*
Gary Smith, *Vice Pres*
Bob Snarr, *Vice Pres*
Rick Williams, *Project Mgr*
John Short, *Purchasing*
EMP: 45
SQ FT: 32,000
SALES (est): 13.6MM **Privately Held**
WEB: www.slaglemech.com
SIC: 1711 1761 Plumbing contractors; warm air heating & air conditioning contractor; ventilation & duct work contractor; mechanical contractor; sheet metalwork

(G-16802)
TIME WARNER CABLE INC
1602 Wapakoneta Ave (45365-1434)
PHONE..................................937 492-4145
Jerry Degrazia, *Branch Mgr*
EMP: 83
SALES (corp-wide): 43.6B **Publicly Held**
SIC: 4841 Cable television services
HQ: Spectrum Management Holding Company, Llc
400 Atlantic St
Stamford CT 06901
203 905-7801

(G-16803)
US BANK NATIONAL ASSOCIATION
Also Called: US Bank
115 E Court St (45365-3021)
PHONE..................................937 498-1131
Jamie Wurstner, *Vice Pres*
Perrica Short, *Branch Mgr*
EMP: 43
SALES (corp-wide): 25.7B **Publicly Held**
WEB: www.firstar.com
SIC: 6021 National commercial banks
HQ: U.S. Bank National Association
425 Walnut St Fl 14
Cincinnati OH 45202
513 632-4234

(G-16804)
VICTORY MACHINE AND FAB
920 S Vandemark Rd (45365-8140)
PHONE..................................937 693-3171
Hannah Wilcox, *Principal*
EMP: 28
SALES (est): 3MM **Privately Held**
SIC: 7699 Industrial machinery & equipment repair

(G-16805)
WAPPOO WOOD PRODUCTS INC
Also Called: Interntnal Pckg Pallets Crates
12877 Kirkwood Rd (45365-8102)
PHONE..................................937 492-1166
Thomas G Baker, *Ch of Bd*
T Adam Baker, *President*
Gary O'Connor, *Principal*
Matthew Baker, *Office Mgr*
EMP: 40
SQ FT: 21,800
SALES (est): 19.1MM **Privately Held**
WEB: www.wappoowood.com
SIC: 5031 2435 2436 2421 Lumber: rough, dressed & finished; hardwood veneer & plywood; softwood veneer & plywood; sawmills & planing mills, general; hardwood dimension & flooring mills

(G-16806)
XPO LOGISTICS FREIGHT INC
2021 Campbell Rd (45365-2474)
PHONE..................................937 492-3899
Jeff Farrell, *Manager*
EMP: 30

SALES (corp-wide): 15.3B **Publicly Held**
WEB: www.con-way.com
SIC: 4213 Contract haulers
HQ: Xpo Logistics Freight, Inc.
2211 Old Earhart Rd # 100
Ann Arbor MI 48105
800 755-2728

Silver Lake
Summit County

(G-16807)
F B AND S MASONRY INC
Also Called: Brown, Frank R & Sons
3021 Harriet Rd (44224-3811)
PHONE..................................330 608-3442
Thomas Earl Brown, *President*
Paula Brown, *Vice Pres*
EMP: 30
SQ FT: 3,000
SALES (est): 2.5MM **Privately Held**
SIC: 1741 Masonry & other stonework

(G-16808)
S P S & ASSOCIATES INC
2926 Ivanhoe Rd (44224-3012)
PHONE..................................330 283-4267
Sterling Paul Shand, *President*
▲ EMP: 30
SALES (est): 2MM **Privately Held**
WEB: www.spsassociates.com
SIC: 1741 Stone masonry

(G-16809)
SILVER LAKE COUNTRY CLUB
1325 Graham Rd (44224-2999)
PHONE..................................330 688-6066
Bob Dedman Jr, *Ch of Bd*
Mike Stevens, *General Mgr*
Doug Koepnick, *Chairman*
EMP: 65 EST: 1957
SQ FT: 15,000
SALES (est): 2.7MM **Privately Held**
WEB: www.teemonline.com
SIC: 7997 7992 5941 5812 Country club, membership; public golf courses; sporting goods & bicycle shops; eating places

(G-16810)
SILVER LAKE MANAGEMENT CORP
Also Called: Sliver Lake Country Club
1325 Graham Rd (44224-2940)
PHONE..................................330 688-6066
Doug Koepnick, *General Mgr*
EMP: 120
SQ FT: 15,000
SALES (est): 2MM
SALES (corp-wide): 477MM **Privately Held**
WEB: www.remington-gc.com
SIC: 7997 Country club, membership
HQ: Clubcorp Usa, Inc.
3030 Lyndon B Johnson Fwy
Dallas TX 75234
972 243-6191

Smithville
Wayne County

(G-16811)
METRO HEALTH SYSTEM
6022 N Honeytown Rd (44677-9563)
PHONE..................................330 669-2249
Alexia Harris, *Education*
EMP: 69
SALES (est): 1.5MM **Privately Held**
SIC: 8099 8031 8011 Health & allied services; offices & clinics of osteopathic physicians; offices & clinics of medical doctors

---

Solon
Cuyahoga County

(G-16812)
1 EDI SOURCE INC
31875 Solon Rd (44139-3553)
P.O. Box 391466 (44139-8466)
PHONE.....................................440 519-7800
John Onysko, *CEO*
David Lowman, *President*
Sime Suminguit, *Partner*
Bill Brinkman, *CFO*
Correen Brown, *Finance*
EMP: 105
SQ FT: 30,000
SALES (est): 18.6MM **Privately Held**
WEB: www.1edisource.com
SIC: 7379 7371 Computer related consulting services; software programming applications

(G-16813)
ABSOLUTE CLEANING SERVICES
5349 Harper Rd (44139-1517)
PHONE.....................................440 542-1742
Mikheil Kavtaradze, *President*
EMP: 89
SALES: 1,000K **Privately Held**
SIC: 7349 Janitorial service, contract basis

(G-16814)
ACLARA TECHNOLOGIES LLC
30400 Solon Rd (44139-3416)
PHONE.....................................440 528-7200
Randy Clark, *Prdtn Mgr*
Rich Goetter, *Purch Agent*
Timothy Figura, *Engineer*
Hari Moorthy, *Engineer*
Mark Fredebaugh, *Train & Dev Mgr*
EMP: 120
SALES (corp-wide): 4.4B **Publicly Held**
SIC: 3824 3825 3829 7371 Mechanical & electromechanical counters & devices; instruments to measure electricity; measuring & controlling devices; custom computer programming services; computer integrated systems design
HQ: Aclara Technologies Llc
77 West Port Plz Ste 500
Saint Louis MO 63146
314 895-6400

(G-16815)
ACOSTA INC
30600 Aurora Rd Ste 100 (44139-2761)
PHONE.....................................440 498-7370
Tim McShane, *Branch Mgr*
EMP: 61
SALES (corp-wide): 6B **Privately Held**
WEB: www.acosta.com
SIC: 5141 Food brokers
PA: Acosta Inc.
6600 Corporate Ctr Pkwy
Jacksonville FL 32216
904 332-7986

(G-16816)
AGILYSYS INC
Also Called: Solon Branch
6521 Davis Indus Pkwy (44139-3549)
PHONE.....................................440 519-6262
Frank Petsock, *Manager*
EMP: 30
SALES (corp-wide): 127.3MM **Publicly Held**
SIC: 5065 5045 Electronic parts & equipment; computers, peripherals & software
PA: Agilysys, Inc.
1000 Windward Concourse # 250
Alpharetta GA 30005
770 810-7800

(G-16817)
AHERN RENTALS INC
29001 Solon Rd Ste 17 (44139-3468)
PHONE.....................................440 498-0869
Scott Mellenger, *Principal*
EMP: 38
SALES (corp-wide): 470.5MM **Privately Held**
SIC: 7359 Equipment rental & leasing

PA: Ahern Rentals, Inc.
1401 Mineral Ave
Las Vegas NV 89106
702 362-0623

(G-16818)
AIR VENTURI LTD
5135 Naiman Pkwy (44139-1003)
PHONE.....................................216 292-2570
Joshua Unger, *CEO*
Valentin Gamerman, *President*
EMP: 54
SQ FT: 70,000
SALES (est): 5MM **Privately Held**
SIC: 5091 Sporting & recreation goods
PA: Pyramyd Air Ltd.
5135 Naiman Pkwy
Solon OH 44139

(G-16819)
ALL PRO CLEANING SERVICES INC
29500 Aurora Rd Ste 14 (44139-7214)
P.O. Box 391711, Cleveland (44139-8711)
PHONE.....................................440 519-0055
Steven Altman, *President*
S Altman, *Technology*
EMP: 75
SQ FT: 2,000
SALES (est): 1.9MM **Privately Held**
SIC: 7349 Janitorial service, contract basis

(G-16820)
AMG MARKETING RESOURCES INC
Also Called: AMG Advertising & PR
30670 Bnbridge Rd Ste 200 (44139)
PHONE.....................................216 621-1835
Anthony Fatica, *President*
Marilyn Clark, *Corp Secy*
Kip Botirius, *Vice Pres*
Annette Fatica, *Vice Pres*
Crystal Madrilejos, *Vice Pres*
EMP: 25
SQ FT: 7,500
SALES: 1.2MM **Privately Held**
WEB: www.amgadvertising.com
SIC: 7311 Advertising consultant

(G-16821)
ARCO HEATING & AC CO (PA)
5325 Naiman Pkwy Ste J (44139-1019)
PHONE.....................................216 663-3211
Brian Friedman, *President*
EMP: 50
SQ FT: 50,000
SALES (est): 5.2MM **Privately Held**
WEB: www.arcohvac.com
SIC: 1711 Warm air heating & air conditioning contractor

(G-16822)
ARROW ELECTRONICS INC
Power & Signal Group
5440 Naiman Pkwy (44139-1010)
PHONE.....................................800 722-5273
EMP: 87
SALES (corp-wide): 29.6B **Publicly Held**
WEB: www.arrow.com
SIC: 5065 Electronic parts
PA: Arrow Electronics, Inc.
9201 E Dry Creek Rd
Centennial CO 80112
303 824-4000

(G-16823)
ARROW ELECTRONICS INC
6675 Parkland Blvd (44139-4345)
PHONE.....................................440 498-6400
Amer Pelasko, *Manager*
EMP: 53
SALES (corp-wide): 29.6B **Publicly Held**
SIC: 5065 Electronic parts
PA: Arrow Electronics, Inc.
9201 E Dry Creek Rd
Centennial CO 80112
303 824-4000

(G-16824)
ATS GROUP LLC
5845 Harper Rd (44139-1832)
P.O. Box 391202 (44139-8202)
PHONE.....................................216 744-5757
Maryna Svilovich, *President*
EMP: 176

SALES (est): 2.4MM **Privately Held**
SIC: 7349 Building maintenance services

(G-16825)
AURORA WHOLESALERS LLC (PA)
Also Called: Mazel Company, The
31000 Aurora Rd (44139-2769)
PHONE.....................................440 248-5200
Carrie Messer, *Traffic Mgr*
James Standring, *Foreman/Supr*
Linda Taylor, *Asst Controller*
Richard Goroff, *Marketing Mgr*
Debbie Love, *Marketing Mgr*
◆ EMP: 74
SQ FT: 1,000,000
SALES: 53.2MM **Privately Held**
WEB: www.mazelcompany.com
SIC: 5199 General merchandise, non-durable

(G-16826)
B D G WRAP-TITE INC
6200 Cochran Rd (44139-3308)
PHONE.....................................440 349-5400
Suresh Bafna, *CEO*
Sunil Daga, *President*
◆ EMP: 80
SQ FT: 89,000
SALES (est): 11MM **Privately Held**
WEB: www.jainco.com
SIC: 3069 5199 Film, rubber; leather goods, except footwear, gloves, luggage, belting

(G-16827)
BELCAN LLC
Also Called: Specialty Equipment Engrg Div
32125 Solon Rd Ste 150 (44139-3557)
PHONE.....................................513 891-0972
Robert Brehm, *Project Mgr*
Angela Noyes, *Project Mgr*
Robert McCoy, *Opers Mgr*
Kieron Powell, *Opers Mgr*
Neil Davis, *Engineer*
EMP: 85
SALES (corp-wide): 813.3MM **Privately Held**
SIC: 7363 Engineering help service
PA: Belcan, Llc
10200 Anderson Way
Blue Ash OH 45242
513 891-0972

(G-16828)
BREEZY POINT LTD PARTNERSHIP (PA)
Also Called: Heritage Development
30575 Bnbridge Rd Ste 100 (44139)
PHONE.....................................440 247-3363
James A Schoff,
John Mc Gill,
Bert Wolstein,
Scott Wolstein,
EMP: 130
SQ FT: 6,000
SALES (est): 11.8MM **Privately Held**
SIC: 6552 7997 Land subdividers & developers, residential; golf club, membership

(G-16829)
BRENNAN INDUSTRIES INC
30205 Solon Rd (44139-3411)
PHONE.....................................440 248-7088
David Carr, *President*
EMP: 30
SALES (corp-wide): 40.1MM **Privately Held**
WEB: www.brennaninc.com
SIC: 5085 Valves, pistons & fittings
PA: Brennan Industries, Inc.
6701 Cochran Rd
Cleveland OH 44139
440 248-1880

(G-16830)
BROWNING-FERRIS INDUSTRIES LLC
Also Called: Republic Services
30300 Pettibone Rd (44139-5414)
PHONE.....................................440 786-9390
Dave Matthews, *Branch Mgr*
EMP: 38

SALES (corp-wide): 10B **Publicly Held**
SIC: 4953 Refuse collection & disposal services
HQ: Browning-Ferris Industries, Llc
18500 N Allied Way # 100
Phoenix AZ 85054
480 627-2700

(G-16831)
CARNEGIE COMPANIES INC
6190 Cochran Rd Ste A (44139-3323)
PHONE.....................................440 232-2300
Paul Pesses, *President*
Peter Meisel, *Exec VP*
Mary Egan, *Property Mgr*
Michele Alcorn, *Manager*
Frank Leitaa, *Associate*
EMP: 50
SQ FT: 20,000
SALES (est): 4.8MM **Privately Held**
WEB: www.carnegiecos.com
SIC: 6531 Real estate agent, commercial; real estate agent, residential

(G-16832)
CARTEMP USA INC (PA)
29100 Aurora Rd (44139-1855)
PHONE.....................................440 715-1000
Ed Hammer, *Partner*
Snappy Funding Corp, *General Ptnr*
EMP: 250
SALES (est): 4.2MM **Privately Held**
SIC: 7514 Rent-a-car service

(G-16833)
CASTLE HEATING & AIR INC
30355 Solon Indus Pkwy (44139-4325)
PHONE.....................................216 696-3940
Mark Boucher, *President*
EMP: 25
SQ FT: 14,000
SALES (est): 4.4MM **Privately Held**
WEB: www.castlehvac.net
SIC: 1711 Warm air heating & air conditioning contractor

(G-16834)
CELLCO PARTNERSHIP
Also Called: Verizon Wireless
6440 Som Center Rd Ste C (44139-6806)
PHONE.....................................440 542-9631
Antonio Martin, *Manager*
EMP: 71
SALES (corp-wide): 130.8B **Publicly Held**
SIC: 4812 Cellular telephone services
HQ: Cellco Partnership
1 Verizon Way
Basking Ridge NJ 07920

(G-16835)
CINCINNATI EQUITABLE INSUR CO
Also Called: Equitable Life Assurance
5910 Harper Rd Ste 100 (44139-1886)
PHONE.....................................440 349-2210
Ken Uveges, *President*
John Lohrman, *Sales Mgr*
Gary Uveges, *Admin Sec*
EMP: 27 **Privately Held**
WEB: www.1826.com
SIC: 6411 Insurance agents, brokers & service
HQ: Cincinnati Equitable Insurance Company
525 Vine St Ste 1925
Cincinnati OH 45202
513 621-1826

(G-16836)
CITY OF SOLON
Also Called: Solon Fire Department
34025 Bainbridge Rd (44139-3002)
PHONE.....................................440 248-6939
William Shaw, *Chief*
EMP: 50 **Privately Held**
SIC: 7389 Fire protection service other than forestry or public
PA: City Of Solon
34200 Bainbridge Rd
Solon OH 44139
440 248-1155

▲ = Import ▼=Export
◆ =Import/Export

(G-16837)
CORE-MARK OHIO
30300 Emerald Valley Pkwy (44139-4394)
PHONE..............................650 589-9445
Tom Perkins, *CEO*
EMP: 150 **EST:** 2014
SQ FT: 179,000
SALES (est): 100.6MM **Privately Held**
SIC: 5194 Cigarettes

(G-16838)
CORPORATE PLANS INC
Also Called: CPI-Hr
6830 Cochran Rd (44139-3966)
PHONE..............................440 542-7800
James Hopkins, *CEO*
Brian Meharry, *President*
Mike Grinnell, *Vice Pres*
Kirsten Tudman, *Vice Pres*
Tom Wirbel, *Vice Pres*
EMP: 35
SQ FT: 3,000
SALES (est): 3.9MM **Privately Held**
WEB: www.cpihr.com
SIC: 8742 6411 Compensation & benefits
planning consultant; insurance agents,
brokers & service

(G-16839)
**COSMAX USA INC COSMAX USA
CORP**
30701 Carter St (44139-3515)
PHONE..............................440 600-5738
Howard Lim, *Principal*
Kent Puthoff, *Purch Mgr*
Barbara Hach, *QC Mgr*
Leroy Lee, *Sales Dir*
Angelina Lee, *Sales Staff*
▲ **EMP:** 50
SALES (est): 46.4MM
SALES (corp-wide): 50MM **Privately
Held**
SIC: 5122 Cosmetics
PA: Cosmax Bti, Inc.
Rm F-801 Pangyo Innovalley
Seongnam 13486
823 178-9330

(G-16840)
CREATIVE PLAYROOM
Also Called: Solon Creative Playroom Center
32750 Solon Rd Ste 3 (44139-2865)
PHONE..............................440 248-3100
Joan Wenk, *Owner*
EMP: 35
SALES (corp-wide): 999K **Privately Held**
SIC: 8351 Montessori child development
center
PA: Creative Playroom
16574 Broadway Ave
Cleveland OH 44137
216 475-6464

(G-16841)
**CREATIVE PLAYROOMS INC
(PA)**
32750 Solon Rd Ste 3 (44139-2865)
PHONE..............................440 349-9111
Joan P Wenk, *President*
EMP: 25
SQ FT: 5,440
SALES (est): 3.7MM **Privately Held**
SIC: 8351 Child day care services

(G-16842)
**CUSTOM PRODUCTS
CORPORATION (PA)**
7100 Cochran Rd (44139-4306)
PHONE..............................440 528-7100
Timothy Stepanek, *President*
John Stepanek, *Vice Pres*
William Stepanek Jr, *Vice Pres*
Ashley Cross, *Buyer*
Pam Gall, *Purchasing*
▲ **EMP:** 78 **EST:** 1974
SQ FT: 82,000
SALES (est): 14.6MM **Privately Held**
WEB: www.customproducts.net
SIC: 7389 5131 5199 2761 Packaging &
labeling services; labels; packaging mate-
rials; manifold business forms; commer-
cial printing; packaging paper & plastics
film, coated & laminated

(G-16843)
**EFFICIENT COLLABORATIVE
RETAIL (PA)**
Also Called: Ecrm
27070 Miles Rd Ste A (44139-1162)
PHONE..............................440 498-0500
Greg Farrar, *CEO*
Brian Nelson, *CFO*
EMP: 56
SQ FT: 6,000
SALES (est): 34.2MM **Privately Held**
WEB: www.ecrm-epps.com
SIC: 8742 Marketing consulting services

(G-16844)
**EMERGENCY RESPONSE &
TRNNG**
Also Called: Erts
6001 Cochran Rd (44139-3310)
P.O. Box 72333, Cleveland (44192-0002)
PHONE..............................440 349-2700
Clay Richter, *President*
Ed Ballash, *Vice Pres*
Jon Wright, *Vice Pres*
Nate Walden, *VP Opers*
Matt Andrle, *Project Mgr*
EMP: 50
SALES (est): 1.9MM
SALES (corp-wide): 450.6MM **Privately
Held**
WEB: www.ertsonline.com
SIC: 8748 Environmental consultant
PA: Hepaco, Llc
2711 Burch Dr
Charlotte NC 28269
704 598-9787

(G-16845)
**ENTERPRISE CONSTRUCTION
INC**
30505 Bnbridge Rd Ste 200 (44139)
PHONE..............................440 349-3443
David Jezek, *President*
EMP: 25
SALES (est): 3.3MM **Privately Held**
SIC: 1521 1542 New construction, single-
family houses; commercial & office build-
ing, new construction

(G-16846)
ENVIROCHEMICAL INC
29325 Aurora Rd (44139-1848)
PHONE..............................440 287-2200
Brian Fox, *President*
A Richard Valore, *Principal*
Jacqueline Knack, *COO*
Keith Karakul, *Vice Pres*
Kristen McKenna, *Purchasing*
EMP: 35
SALES (est): 9MM **Privately Held**
WEB: www.envirochemical.net
SIC: 5087 Janitors' supplies

(G-16847)
F I L US INC (HQ)
Also Called: Baldwin International
30403 Bruce Indus Pkwy (44139-3941)
PHONE..............................440 248-9500
Edward Webber, *CEO*
G W Goertz, *President*
Edward Weber, *COO*
J D Sherwood, *Vice Pres*
▲ **EMP:** 25
SQ FT: 44,500
SALES (est): 6.8MM
SALES (corp-wide): 2.5B **Privately Held**
WEB: www.filus.com
SIC: 5051 Steel
PA: Russel Metals Inc
6600 Financial Dr
Mississauga ON L5N 7
905 819-7777

(G-16848)
FAK GROUP INC
Also Called: Raf Automation
6750 Arnold Miller Pkwy (44139-4363)
PHONE..............................440 498-8465
Thomas J Koly, *President*
Willard E Frissell, *Corp Secy*
EMP: 28 **EST:** 1953
SQ FT: 22,000

SALES (est): 6.8MM
SALES (corp-wide): 136.8MM **Privately
Held**
WEB: www.raffluidpower.com
SIC: 7629 Electrical equipment repair serv-
ices
PA: Electro-Matic Ventures, Inc.
23409 Industrial Park Ct
Farmington Hills MI 48335
248 478-1182

(G-16849)
FINDAWAY WORLD LLC
31999 Aurora Rd (44139-2853)
PHONE..............................440 893-0808
Mitch Kroll, *CEO*
▲ **EMP:** 100
SALES (est): 15.4MM **Privately Held**
WEB: www.playawaydigital.com
SIC: 5999 8331 3669 5192 Audio-visual
equipment & supplies; job training & vo-
cational rehabilitation services; visual
communication systems; periodicals

(G-16850)
**GARDINER SERVICE COMPANY
LLC (PA)**
31200 Bainbridge Rd Ste 1 (44139-2298)
P.O. Box 39280 (44139-0280)
PHONE..............................440 248-3400
Robert M Case, *CEO*
William H Gardiner, *Ch of Bd*
Todd Barnhart, *President*
Michael R Reder, *Treasurer*
Donald Sabetta, *Accounts Mgr*
EMP: 132
SQ FT: 32,000
SALES: 64.2MM **Privately Held**
WEB: www.gardinertrane.com
SIC: 5075 1711 7623 Air conditioning &
ventilation equipment & supplies; plumb-
ing, heating, air-conditioning contractors;
refrigeration service & repair; air condi-
tioning repair

(G-16851)
GLAVIN INDUSTRIES INC
Also Called: Glavin Specialty Co
6835 Cochran Rd Ste A (44139-3927)
P.O. Box 391316 (44139-8316)
PHONE..............................440 349-0049
Julia S Glavin, *CEO*
David H Glavin, *President*
EMP: 25
SQ FT: 23,000
SALES (est): 15.6MM **Privately Held**
SIC: 5084 3993 2759 Industrial machin-
ery & equipment; signs & advertising spe-
cialties; screen printing

(G-16852)
**GLAZERS DISTRIBUTORS OHIO
INC**
7800 Cochran Rd (44139-4342)
PHONE..............................440 542-7000
EMP: 25
SALES (corp-wide): 7.2B **Privately Held**
SIC: 5181 5182 Beer & ale; wine & dis-
tilled beverages
HQ: Southern Glazer's Distributors Of Ohio,
Llc
4800 Poth Rd
Columbus OH 43213

(G-16853)
**GORBETT ENTERPRISES OF
SOLON (PA)**
Also Called: Great Lakes Cold Storage
6531 Cochran Rd (44139-3959)
PHONE..............................440 248-3950
Patrick J Gorbett, *President*
John Grill, *Controller*
EMP: 30
SQ FT: 240,000
SALES (est): 13.1MM **Privately Held**
SIC: 4222 Warehousing, cold storage or
refrigerated

(G-16854)
**GREAT LAKES TEXTILES INC
(PA)**
Also Called: Glt Products
6810 Cochran Rd (44139-3908)
PHONE..............................440 914-1122
Steven Wake, *President*

Joel Hammer, *Vice Pres*
Jeff Robinson, *Vice Pres*
Patrick Burch, *Plant Mgr*
Marinko Milos, *CFO*
◆ **EMP:** 47
SQ FT: 117,000
SALES (est): 15.8MM **Privately Held**
WEB: www.gltproducts.com
SIC: 2821 5033 5131 5085 Polyvinyli-
dene chloride resins; insulation materials;
tape, textile; industrial supplies

(G-16855)
GRL ENGINEERS INC (PA)
30725 Aurora Rd (44139-2735)
PHONE..............................216 831-6131
Patrick Hannigan, *President*
Mohamad Hussein, *Vice Pres*
George Piscsalko, *Vice Pres*
Mark Rawlings, *Site Mgr*
Karen Webster, *Site Mgr*
EMP: 30 **EST:** 1976
SALES (est): 5.4MM **Privately Held**
SIC: 8734 Testing laboratories

(G-16856)
HAB INC
Also Called: Hab Computer Services
28925 Fountain Pkwy (44139-4356)
PHONE..............................608 785-7650
Michael Juran, *President*
EMP: 25
SALES (est): 2.4MM
SALES (corp-wide): 151.1MM **Privately
Held**
WEB: www.habinc.com
SIC: 7371 7372 Computer software devel-
opment & applications; prepackaged soft-
ware
PA: Mri Software Llc
28925 Fountain Pkwy
Solon OH 44139
800 321-8770

(G-16857)
**HD SUPPLY FACILITIES MAINT
LTD**
30311 Emerald Valley Pkwy (44139-4339)
PHONE..............................440 542-9188
Steve Yaney, *Manager*
EMP: 40 **Publicly Held**
SIC: 5087 5072 5085 Cleaning & mainte-
nance equipment & supplies; hardware;
industrial supplies
HQ: Hd Supply Facilities Maintenance, Ltd.
3100 Cumberland Blvd Se # 1700
Atlanta GA 30339
770 852-9000

(G-16858)
**HOWARD HANNA SMYTHE
CRAMER**
6240 Som Center Rd # 100 (44139-2950)
PHONE..............................440 248-3000
EMP: 50
SALES (corp-wide): 73.7MM **Privately
Held**
SIC: 6531 Real estate brokers & agents
HQ: Howard Hanna Smythe Cramer
6000 Parkland Blvd
Cleveland OH 44124
216 447-4477

(G-16859)
**HUNTER DEFENSE TECH INC
(PA)**
Also Called: Hdt Engineered Technologies
30500 Aurora Rd Ste 100 (44139-2776)
PHONE..............................216 438-6111
Sean Bond, *President*
Frederick Strader, *President*
Robin Carney, *Exec VP*
Greg Miller, *Senior VP*
Bob Demarchi, *Vice Pres*
▲ **EMP:** 50
SQ FT: 26,000
SALES (est): 261.5MM **Privately Held**
SIC: 3433 3569 3822 8331 Room & wall
heaters, including radiators; filters; auto
controls regulating residntl & coml envi-
ronmt & applncs; sheltered workshop; en-
gineering services; assembly machines,
including robotic

(G-16860)
IMPERIAL HEATING AND COOLG INC (PA)
30685 Solon Industrial Pk (44139-4388)
PHONE..................................440 498-1788
Todd Rickard Ozanich, *President*
Bob Campus, *Technology*
Gary O'Neil, *Technology*
EMP: 54
SQ FT: 19,000
SALES (est): 12.8MM **Privately Held**
WEB: www.imperialhvac.com
SIC: **1711** Warm air heating & air conditioning contractor

(G-16861)
INTERDESIGN INC
Also Called: Swiss Tech Products
30725 Solon Indus Pkwy (44139-4380)
P.O. Box 39606 (44139-0606)
PHONE..................................440 248-0136
Chris Quinn, *CEO*
Robert Immerman, *President*
Robert Woolnough, *Vice Pres*
◆ EMP: 280 EST: 1974
SQ FT: 178,096
SALES (est): 178MM **Privately Held**
WEB: www.interdesignusa.com
SIC: **5023** Home furnishings

(G-16862)
IRON MOUNTAIN INFO MGT LLC
5101 Naiman Pkwy Ste B (44139-1018)
PHONE..................................440 248-0999
Travis Glasper, *Manager*
EMP: 101
SALES (corp-wide): 4.2B **Publicly Held**
SIC: **4226 8742** Document & office records storage; management consulting services
HQ: Iron Mountain Information Management, Llc
　　1 Federal St
　　Boston MA 02110
　　800 899-4766

(G-16863)
JAINCO INTERNATIONAL INC
Also Called: Jaincotech
30405 Solon Rd Ste 9 (44139-3477)
PHONE..................................440 519-0100
Suresh Bafna, *CEO*
Jasvinder Mandair, *President*
Vijay Sharma, *CFO*
▲ EMP: 250
SQ FT: 30,000
SALES (est): 20.4MM **Privately Held**
SIC: **5032** Granite building stone

(G-16864)
KEITHLEY INSTRUMENTS LLC (DH)
28775 Aurora Rd (44139-1891)
PHONE..................................440 248-0400
Joseph P Keithley, *President*
Linda C Rae, *COO*
Philip R Etsler, *Vice Pres*
Mark A Hoersten, *Vice Pres*
Mark Hoersten, *Vice Pres*
▲ EMP: 118 EST: 1946
SQ FT: 125,000
SALES (est): 94.9MM
SALES (corp-wide): 6.4B **Publicly Held**
SIC: **3823 7371 3825** Computer interface equipment for industrial process control; computer software development; test equipment for electronic & electric measurement
HQ: Tektronix, Inc.
　　14150 Sw Karl Braun Dr
　　Beaverton OR 97005
　　800 833-9200

(G-16865)
KINDERCARE LEARNING CTRS LLC
Also Called: Kindercare Child Care Network
6140 Kruse Dr (44139-2374)
PHONE..................................440 248-5437
Julie Felder, *Manager*
EMP: 25
SALES (corp-wide): 1.2B **Privately Held**
WEB: www.kindercare.com
SIC: **8351** Group day care center

HQ: Kindercare Learning Centers, Llc
　　650 Ne Holladay St # 1400
　　Portland OR 97232
　　503 872-1300

(G-16866)
LP INSURANCE SERVICES LLC
Also Called: Loan Protector Insurance Svcs
6000 Cochran Rd (44139-3318)
PHONE..................................877 369-5121
Dennis Swit, *CEO*
EMP: 200
SQ FT: 21,000
SALES (est): 3.2MM **Privately Held**
SIC: **6411** Insurance agents & brokers

(G-16867)
LUTHERAN MEDICAL CENTER (HQ)
Also Called: Lutheran Hospital
33001 Solon Rd Ste 112 (44139-2864)
PHONE..................................216 696-4300
David Pesre MD, *CEO*
Christopher Winters, *CFO*
J Bradley Burns, *Diag Radio*
EMP: 320
SQ FT: 350,000
SALES: 111MM
SALES (corp-wide): 8.9B **Privately Held**
SIC: **8062 8011 8069** General medical & surgical hospitals; offices & clinics of medical doctors; specialty hospitals, except psychiatric
PA: The Cleveland Clinic Foundation
　　9500 Euclid Ave
　　Cleveland OH 44195
　　216 636-8335

(G-16868)
M & A DISTRIBUTING CO INC (PA)
Also Called: M & A Distribution
31031 Diamond Pkwy (44139-5463)
PHONE..................................440 703-4580
John M Antonucci, *President*
EMP: 37 EST: 1981
SQ FT: 12,000
SALES (est): 53.7MM **Privately Held**
SIC: **5182 5181** Wine & distilled beverages; beer & other fermented malt liquors

(G-16869)
MAJESTIC TOOL AND MACHINE INC
30700 Carter St Ste C (44139-3585)
PHONE..................................440 248-5058
Walter Krueger, *President*
Kurt Krueger, *Vice Pres*
Todd Krueger, *Vice Pres*
EMP: 32
SQ FT: 30,000
SALES: 2.5MM **Privately Held**
SIC: **3599 7692 3544** Machine shop, jobbing & repair; welding repair; special dies, tools, jigs & fixtures

(G-16870)
MANTUA MANUFACTURING CO (PA)
Also Called: Mantua Bed Frames
31050 Diamond Pkwy (44139-5478)
PHONE..................................800 333-8333
David Jaffe, *CEO*
Charles Bastien, *Vice Pres*
Dirk Smith, *Vice Pres*
Jeff Wick, *Vice Pres*
Frank Barkley, *Plant Mgr*
◆ EMP: 120 EST: 1952
SQ FT: 67,500
SALES (est): 109.4MM **Privately Held**
WEB: www.bedframes.com
SIC: **5021 2514** Bedsprings; frames for box springs or bedsprings: metal

(G-16871)
MARRIOTT
31225 Bainbridge Rd Ste A (44139-2293)
PHONE..................................440 542-2375
Amy Oblinger, *Owner*
Charles Kirkland, *Human Res Dir*
EMP: 30
SALES (est): 1.6MM **Privately Held**
SIC: **7011** Hotels & motels

(G-16872)
MILES FARMERS MARKET INC
28560 Miles Rd (44139-1184)
PHONE..................................440 248-5222
Frank Cangemi, *President*
Joe Degaetano, *Vice Pres*
Joseph Degaetano, *Vice Pres*
Dave Rondini, *Vice Pres*
Debbie Slak, *Office Mgr*
EMP: 150
SQ FT: 50,000
SALES (est): 14.9MM **Privately Held**
WEB: www.milesfarmersmarket.com
SIC: **5431 5148** Fruit stands or markets; vegetable stands or markets; fruits, fresh; vegetables, fresh

(G-16873)
MP BIOMEDICALS LLC
29525 Fountain Pkwy (44139-4351)
PHONE..................................440 337-1200
Dragon Kraojovic, *Branch Mgr*
Viktor Kuzmanov, *Manager*
Randy Mayner, *Manager*
Akshaya Manai, *Executive*
EMP: 130
SALES (corp-wide): 379MM **Privately Held**
WEB: www.mpbio.com
SIC: **8731 2869 2834 8071** Biological research; enzymes; pharmaceutical preparations; medical laboratories; medical research
HQ: Mp Biomedicals, Llc
　　3 Hutton Centre Dr # 100
　　Santa Ana CA 92707
　　949 833-2500

(G-16874)
MRI SOFTWARE LLC (PA)
28925 Fountain Pkwy (44139-4356)
PHONE..................................800 321-8770
Patrick Ghilani, *CEO*
Ben Berk, *Partner*
Nick Constantino, *Vice Pres*
Oren Rosen, *Vice Pres*
Helene Slosarik, *Vice Pres*
EMP: 145
SQ FT: 44,000
SALES (est): 151.1MM **Privately Held**
WEB: www.mrisoftware.com
SIC: **7374 7371 6531** Data processing & preparation; computer software development; real estate agents & managers; real estate managers

(G-16875)
MUSTARD SEED HEALTH FD MKT INC
6025 Kruse Dr Ste 100 (44139-2378)
PHONE..................................440 519-3663
Margaret Kanfer-Nabors, *Ch of Bd*
Bill Goodwin, *Financial Exec*
EMP: 35
SALES (corp-wide): 59.5MM **Privately Held**
WEB: www.mustardseedmarket.com
SIC: **5499 7299 5812 2051** Gourmet food stores; banquet hall facilities; caterers; bread, cake & related products
PA: Mustard Seed Health Food Market, Inc.
　　3885 Medina Rd
　　Akron OH 44333
　　330 666-7333

(G-16876)
NATIONAL ENTP SYSTEMS INC (PA)
Also Called: Nes
29125 Solon Rd (44139-3442)
PHONE..................................440 542-1360
Ernest Pollak, *President*
Ellen Pollak, *Vice Pres*
EMP: 102 EST: 1987
SQ FT: 48,000
SALES (est): 29MM **Privately Held**
WEB: www.nes1.com
SIC: **7322** Collection agency, except real estate

(G-16877)
NETSMART TECHNOLOGIES INC
Also Called: Trend Consulting Services
30775 Bnbridge Rd Ste 200 (44139)
PHONE..................................440 942-4040
Michael Valentine, *CEO*
Kim Schnebelin, *Prgrmr*
EMP: 39
SALES (corp-wide): 219.5MM **Privately Held**
SIC: **7379 7372** Computer related consulting services; business oriented computer software
HQ: Netsmart Technologies, Inc.
　　4950 College Blvd
　　Overland Park KS 66211

(G-16878)
NOBLE-DAVIS CONSULTING INC
6190 Cochran Rd Ste D (44139-3323)
PHONE..................................440 519-0850
Pamela Noble, *President*
Jan L Davis, *Vice Pres*
EMP: 25
SQ FT: 7,200
SALES (est): 4.5MM **Privately Held**
WEB: www.noblepension.com
SIC: **6411** Pension & retirement plan consultants

(G-16879)
NOCO COMPANY
30339 Diamond Pkwy # 102 (44139-5473)
PHONE..................................216 464-8131
William K Nook, *President*
Luke Case, *Vice Pres*
Rick Stanfield, *Engineer*
Jeffrey Weiner, *VP Sales*
Lindsey Walters, *Accounts Mgr*
◆ EMP: 500 EST: 1914
SQ FT: 100,000
SALES (est): 32.2MM **Privately Held**
WEB: www.noco-usa.com
SIC: **3694 3714 3315 2899** Battery cable wiring sets for internal combustion engines; booster (jump-start) cables, automotive; filters: oil, fuel & air, motor vehicle; steel wire & related products; chemical preparations; wire & cable; power tools & accessories

(G-16880)
P K WADSWORTH HEATING & COOLG
34280 Solon Rd Frnt (44139-2668)
PHONE..................................440 248-4821
Paul K Wadsworth Jr, *President*
Tyler Wadsworth, *Design Engr*
EMP: 45
SQ FT: 6,000
SALES (est): 8.9MM **Privately Held**
WEB: www.pkwadsworth.com
SIC: **1711** Warm air heating & air conditioning contractor

(G-16881)
PAUL MOSS LLC
Also Called: Moss Affiliate Marketing
5895 Harper Rd (44139-1832)
PHONE..................................216 765-1580
Pamela Kleinman, *Opers Staff*
Paul Moss,
EMP: 35 EST: 2009
SALES (est): 3.5MM **Privately Held**
SIC: **6411** Insurance information & consulting services

(G-16882)
PERMATEX INC
6875 Parkland Blvd (44139-4377)
PHONE..................................440 914-3100
Doug Weaver, *Branch Mgr*
EMP: 25
SALES (corp-wide): 71MM **Privately Held**
SIC: **5085** Abrasives & adhesives
PA: Permatex, Inc.
　　10 Columbus Blvd Ste 1
　　Hartford CT 06106
　　860 543-7500

(G-16883)
PICASSO FOR NAIL LLC
35494 Spatterdock Ln (44139-5094)
PHONE..........................440 308-4470
Deborah Washington,
EMP: 30
SALES (est): 122.6K **Privately Held**
SIC: 7231 Manicurist, pedicurist

(G-16884)
**PIPELINE PACKAGING
CORPORATION (HQ)**
30310 Emerald Valley Pkwy (44139-4394)
PHONE..........................440 349-3200
Christopher I Page, *Ch of Bd*
Christopher Nelson, *President*
Daniel Herbert, *CFO*
▲ EMP: 30
SQ FT: 85,000
SALES (est): 114.3MM
SALES (corp-wide): 131.9MM **Privately
Held**
SIC: 5099 Containers: glass, metal or plastic
PA: Cleveland Steel Container Corporation
30310 Emerald Valley Pkwy
Solon OH 44139
440 349-8000

(G-16885)
PRIORITY DISPATCH INC
5385 Naiman Pkwy (44139-1007)
PHONE..........................216 332-9852
Dan Walter, *Branch Mgr*
EMP: 25
SALES (corp-wide): 14.7MM **Privately
Held**
SIC: 4212 4215 Delivery service, vehicular; courier services, except by air
PA: Priority Dispatch, Inc.
4665 Malsbary Rd
Blue Ash OH 45242
513 791-3900

(G-16886)
PTMJ ENTERPRISES
32000 Aurora Rd (44139-2875)
P.O. Box 391437 (44139-8437)
PHONE..........................440 543-8000
Peter Joyce, *President*
Joe Miller, *Opers Staff*
◆ EMP: 180
SALES (est): 34.4MM **Privately Held**
WEB: www.signum-inc.com
SIC: 2541 1799 Display fixtures, wood;
closet organizers, installation & design

(G-16887)
PYRAMYD AIR LTD (PA)
5135 Naiman Pkwy (44139-1003)
PHONE..........................216 896-0893
Val Gamerman, *Partner*
Joshua Ungier, *General Ptnr*
Tom Chandler, *Business Mgr*
Jack Antalek, *Purch Mgr*
Robin Karlozi, *Human Res Dir*
▲ EMP: 40
SQ FT: 22,500
SALES (est): 9.7MM **Privately Held**
WEB: www.pyramydair.com
SIC: 5941 5092 Firearms; toys

(G-16888)
R & D NESTLE CENTER INC
5750 Harper Rd (44139-1831)
PHONE..........................440 349-5757
EMP: 53
SALES (corp-wide): 90.8B **Privately Held**
SIC: 8731 Food research
HQ: R & D Nestle Center Inc
809 Collins Ave
Marysville OH 43040
937 642-7015

(G-16889)
**R L MORRISSEY & ASSOC INC
(PA)**
Also Called: American Ring & Tool Co
30450 Bruce Indus Pkwy (44139-3940)
P.O. Box 75510, Cleveland (44101-4200)
PHONE..........................440 498-3730
James N Morrissey, *President*
William F Chinnock, *Principal*
Robert H Morrissey, *Corp Secy*
Jack Morrissey, *Vice Pres*

▲ EMP: 40
SQ FT: 28,000
SALES (est): 23.4MM **Privately Held**
SIC: 5085 5051 5013 Fasteners, industrial: nuts, bolts, screws, etc.; stampings,
metal; automotive supplies & parts

(G-16890)
REIMER LAW CO
30455 Solon Rd Ste 1 (44139-3415)
PHONE..........................440 600-5500
Dennis Reimer, *President*
Jill Cohn, *Human Res Dir*
Jeannie Mocny, *Manager*
Nicole Caprara, *Director*
Michele Stockdale, *Director*
EMP: 150
SALES (est): 7.1MM **Privately Held**
WEB: www.reimerlaw.com
SIC: 8111 General practice attorney,
lawyer

(G-16891)
RELAM INC
Also Called: Railway Equipment Lsg & Maint
7695 Bond St (44139-5350)
PHONE..........................440 232-3354
Carl Eberhardt, *President*
Linda Ertel, *Corp Secy*
David Horth, *Shareholder*
EMP: 35
SQ FT: 4,800
SALES (est): 10.4MM **Privately Held**
SIC: 7353 Heavy construction equipment
rental

(G-16892)
REXEL USA INC
2699 Solon Sales 30310 (44139)
PHONE..........................440 248-3800
Orman Malkes, *Accounts Mgr*
Dave Gerding, *Branch Mgr*
Dave Longo, *Manager*
EMP: 70
SQ FT: 5,000
SALES (corp-wide): 2.2MM **Privately
Held**
WEB: www.rexelusa.com
SIC: 5063 Electrical supplies
HQ: Rexel Usa, Inc.
14951 Dallas Pkwy
Dallas TX 75254

(G-16893)
**ROTO-ROOTER SERVICES
COMPANY**
5375 Naiman Pkwy (44139-1007)
PHONE..........................216 429-1928
Rick Beechy, *Manager*
EMP: 40
SALES (corp-wide): 1.7B **Publicly Held**
SIC: 7699 Sewer cleaning & rodding
HQ: Roto-Rooter Services Company
255 E 5th St Ste 2500
Cincinnati OH 45202
513 762-6690

(G-16894)
RSR PARTNERS LLC
Also Called: Regency Technologies LLC
6111 Cochran Rd (44139-3305)
PHONE..........................440 248-3991
Jim Levine, *CEO*
Chris Pinchot, *Facilities Mgr*
Scott Artrip, *Sales Staff*
EMP: 284
SALES (corp-wide): 90.9MM **Privately
Held**
SIC: 4953 Recycling, waste materials
PA: Rsr Partners Llc
1831 Highland Rd
Twinsburg OH 44087
440 519-1768

(G-16895)
SCHWEBEL BAKING COMPANY
Also Called: Schwebel Baking Co-Solon Bky
6250 Camp Industrial Rd (44139-2750)
PHONE..........................440 248-1500
Grant West, *Manager*
EMP: 150

SALES (corp-wide): 170MM **Privately
Held**
WEB: www.schwebels.com
SIC: 5461 5149 2051 Bread; groceries &
related products; bread, cake & related
products
PA: Schwebel Baking Company
965 E Midlothian Blvd
Youngstown OH 44502
330 783-2860

(G-16896)
**SERVICELINK FIELD SERVICES
LLC**
30825 Aurora Rd Ste 140 (44139-2733)
PHONE..........................440 424-0058
Robert J Caruso, *President*
Brian Davis, *Assistant VP*
EMP: 1257
SALES (est): 28.1MM
SALES (corp-wide): 1.1B **Publicly Held**
SIC: 7389 Inspection & testing services
HQ: Black Knight Infoserv, Llc
601 Riverside Ave
Jacksonville FL 32204

(G-16897)
SIGNUM LLC
32000 Aurora Rd Ste C (44139-2849)
PHONE..........................440 248-2233
Todd McCuaig,
EMP: 100
SALES: 12MM **Privately Held**
SIC: 7319 Sample distribution

(G-16898)
SNF WADSWORTH LLC
Also Called: Golden Leaf
5625 Emerald Ridge Pkwy (44139-1860)
PHONE..........................330 336-3472
Melissa Nelson, *Mng Member*
EMP: 80
SALES (est): 672.3K **Privately Held**
SIC: 8051 Skilled nursing care facilities

(G-16899)
**SOLON LODGING ASSOCIATES
LLC**
Also Called: Springhill Suites
30100 Aurora Rd (44139-2730)
PHONE..........................440 248-9600
Pamela Keeven, *General Mgr*
Ron Kindall,
EMP: 26
SALES (est): 2.3MM
SALES (corp-wide): 20.7B **Publicly Held**
WEB: www.buffalolodging.com
SIC: 7011 Hotels & motels
PA: Marriott International, Inc.
10400 Fernwood Rd
Bethesda MD 20817
301 380-3000

(G-16900)
**SOLON PNTE AT EMRALD
RIDGE LLC**
5625 Emerald Ridge Pkwy (44139-1860)
PHONE..........................440 498-3000
Mark P McGrievy,
EMP: 36
SALES: 7.5MM **Privately Held**
SIC: 8051 Convalescent home with continuous nursing care

(G-16901)
**SOURCE DIAGNOSTICS LLC
(PA)**
5275 Naiman Pkwy Ste E (44139-1033)
PHONE..........................440 542-9481
Keith Marchand, *Mng Member*
David Burns,
EMP: 95
SALES (est): 1.8MM **Privately Held**
WEB: www.sourcediagnostics.com
SIC: 8082 Home health care services

(G-16902)
STRATFORD COMMONS INC
7000 Cochran Rd (44139-4304)
PHONE..........................440 914-0900
Maureen Moffatte, *President*
Prentice Lipsey, *Administration*
EMP: 179

SALES (est): 8MM **Privately Held**
WEB: www.stratfordcommons.com
SIC: 8059 8052 Nursing home, except
skilled & intermediate care facility; intermediate care facilities

(G-16903)
**SUPERIOR BEVERAGE
COMPANY INC**
31031 Diamond Pkwy (44139-5463)
PHONE..........................440 703-4580
John R Antonucci, *President*
John Fleming, *Vice Pres*
David Robinson, *Vice Pres*
EMP: 70
SQ FT: 42,000
SALES (est): 20.2MM **Privately Held**
SIC: 5181 5182 Beer & other fermented
malt liquors; wine

(G-16904)
**SUPERIOR BEVERAGE GROUP
LTD (PA)**
31031 Diamond Pkwy (44139-5463)
PHONE..........................440 703-4580
Mike Caffrey, *Partner*
John W Fleming, *Partner*
Mike Marchese, *Division Mgr*
Tom Hennes, *Area Mgr*
Gregg Shellhorn, *Vice Pres*
▲ EMP: 101
SALES (est): 98.5MM **Privately Held**
SIC: 5149 5499 Beverages, except coffee
& tea; beverage stores

(G-16905)
SWAGELOK COMPANY
31400 Aurora Rd (44139-2764)
PHONE..........................440 349-5934
Bill Ponikvar, *Electrical Engi*
Nick Lubar, *Manager*
EMP: 100
SALES (corp-wide): 940.1MM **Privately
Held**
WEB: www.swagelok.com
SIC: 5051 3593 3498 3494 Tubing,
metal; fluid power cylinders & actuators;
fabricated pipe & fittings; valves & pipe fittings; fabricated plate work (boiler shop)
PA: Swagelok Company
29500 Solon Rd
Solon OH 44139
440 248-4600

(G-16906)
SWAGELOK COMPANY
32550 Old South Miles Rd (44139-2829)
PHONE..........................440 542-1250
Bruce Schneider, *Branch Mgr*
Joe Mossbarger, *Manager*
EMP: 35
SALES (corp-wide): 940.1MM **Privately
Held**
SIC: 5085 Valves & fittings
PA: Swagelok Company
29500 Solon Rd
Solon OH 44139
440 248-4600

(G-16907)
**SYLVANIA LIGHTING SVCS
CORP**
35405 Spatterdock Ln (44139-6500)
PHONE..........................440 742-8208
EMP: 25
SALES (corp-wide): 4.7B **Privately Held**
SIC: 7349 Lighting maintenance service
HQ: Sylvania Lighting Services Corp.
200 Ballardvale St
Wilmington MA 01887
978 570-3000

(G-16908)
**TAMERAN GRAPHIC SYSTEMS
INC**
30300 Solon Ind Pkwy F (44139-4382)
PHONE..........................440 349-7100
Mark A Wise, *CEO*
Karl Kuckelheim, *Purch Dir*
▲ EMP: 50 EST: 2000
SQ FT: 40,000
SALES (est): 6.3MM **Privately Held**
WEB: www.tameran.com
SIC: 5044 Office equipment

(G-16909)
TTI FLOOR CARE NORTH AMER INC (DH)
Also Called: Royal Appliance Manufacturing
7005 Cochran Rd (44139-4303)
PHONE..................................440 996-2000
Chris Gurreri, *President*
Mike Ferris, *President*
Nora Covarrubias, *Buyer*
Doug Rukavina, *Engineer*
Steven Kegg, *Senior Engr*
▲ EMP: 350
SQ FT: 450,000
SALES (est): 224.7MM
SALES (corp-wide): 6B **Privately Held**
SIC: 5072 3825 Power tools & accessories; power measuring equipment, electrical
HQ: Royal Appliance Mfg. Co.
     7005 Cochran Rd
     Cleveland OH 44139
     440 996-2000

(G-16910)
ULYSSES CAREMARK HOLDING CORP
29100 Aurora Rd (44139-1855)
PHONE..................................440 542-4214
Kenneth Kramer, *VP Opers*
Wendy Brantley, *Branch Mgr*
EMP: 158
SALES (corp-wide): 374.8MM **Privately Held**
SIC: 6311 Life insurance
PA: Ulysses Caremark Holding Corp
     44 S Broadway Fl 12f
     White Plains NY 10601
     914 934-5200

(G-16911)
VAN DYNE-CROTTY CO
Also Called: Spirit Services
30400 Bruce Indus Pkwy (44139-3929)
PHONE..................................440 248-6935
Jeff Brewer, *Manager*
EMP: 47
SQ FT: 41,454
SALES (corp-wide): 35.9MM **Privately Held**
WEB: www.getspirit.com
SIC: 7218 7213 Industrial uniform supply; linen supply
PA: Van Dyne-Crotty Co.
     2150 Fairwood Ave
     Columbus OH 43207
     614 684-0048

(G-16912)
VINCENT LTG SYSTEMS CO INC (PA)
6161 Cochran Rd Ste D (44139-3324)
PHONE..................................216 475-7600
Paul Vincent, *CEO*
Bill Groener, *President*
Patrick Spicuzza, *COO*
Christopher Shick, *Vice Pres*
Walter Weber, *Vice Pres*
EMP: 29
SALES (est): 17.4MM **Privately Held**
SIC: 5063 7359 5999 Lighting fixtures; equipment rental & leasing; theatrical equipment & supplies

(G-16913)
WASTE MANAGEMENT OHIO INC
6705 Richmond Rd (44139-2130)
PHONE..................................440 201-1235
Alan Bosiacki, *Accounts Mgr*
Paul Pispomo, *Manager*
EMP: 100
SALES (corp-wide): 14.9B **Publicly Held**
WEB: www.wm.com
SIC: 4953 4212 Refuse systems; local trucking, without storage
HQ: Waste Management Of Ohio, Inc.
     1700 N Broad St
     Fairborn OH 45324

(G-16914)
WESTON INC
32000 Aurora Rd (44139-2875)
PHONE..................................440 349-9001
Edward Asher, *Branch Mgr*
EMP: 26

SALES (corp-wide): 26.1MM **Privately Held**
SIC: 6531 6519 Real estate managers; real property lessors
PA: Weston Inc
     4760 Richmond Rd Ste 200
     Cleveland OH 44128
     440 349-9000

(G-16915)
WEYMOUTH VALLEY INC
Also Called: Signature Solon Golf Course
39000 Signature Dr (44139-5266)
PHONE..................................440 498-8888
Gary Cramer, *CEO*
Bonnie Napora, *Director*
Lauren Baker,
EMP: 31
SQ FT: 5,734
SALES (est): 2MM **Privately Held**
WEB: www.pgmi.net
SIC: 7997 5813 5812 Country club, membership; drinking places; eating places

(G-16916)
WINNCOM TECHNOLOGIES CORP
28900 Ftn Pkwy Unit B (44139)
PHONE..................................440 498-9510
Gregory Raskin, *President*
Adriana Chavarro, *Regional Mgr*
Vyacheslav Kz, *Business Mgr*
Igor Dovgun, *Project Mgr*
Diane Burns, *Purch Mgr*
◆ EMP: 47
SQ FT: 16,000
SALES (est): 55.2MM **Privately Held**
WEB: www.winncom.com
SIC: 5065 Communication equipment; radio & television equipment & parts; radio parts & accessories
HQ: Winncom Technologies Holding Limited
     15 Herbert Street
     Dublin

(G-16917)
WORKSPEED MANAGEMENT LLC
28925 Fountain Pkwy (44139-4356)
PHONE..................................917 369-9025
EMP: 25
SALES (est): 1.8MM **Privately Held**
SIC: 7372 Prepackaged Software Services

Somerset
Perry County

(G-16918)
SOMERSET NH LLC
Also Called: SOMERSET HEALTH AND REHABILITA
411 S Columbus St (43783-9415)
PHONE..................................740 743-2924
Mordecai Rosenberg, *President*
Ronald Swartz, *CFO*
Dawn Wozniak, *Exec Dir*
Lisa Schwartz, *Admin Sec*
EMP: 79
SALES (est): 422.2K **Privately Held**
SIC: 8051 Skilled nursing care facilities

Somerville
Butler County

(G-16919)
TRI TECH SERVICE SYSTEMS INC
9501 Pleasant Valley Rd (45064-9329)
PHONE..................................937 787-4664
Justin Paulk, *President*
EMP: 200
SALES (est): 2.2MM **Privately Held**
WEB: www.tritechservicesystems.com
SIC: 7349 Cleaning service, industrial or commercial

(G-16920)
WOODLAND COUNTRY MANOR INC
4166 Somerville Rd (45064-9707)
PHONE..................................513 523-4449
Ealeta Dingeldine, *President*
Lori Auer, *Administration*
EMP: 35
SQ FT: 1,401
SALES (est): 5.2MM **Privately Held**
SIC: 8051 Convalescent home with continuous nursing care

South Amherst
Lorain County

(G-16921)
ECHOING HILLS VILLAGE INC
Also Called: Echoing Lake/Renourd Home
235 W Main St (44001-2925)
PHONE..................................440 986-3085
Pat McCraken, *Manager*
EMP: 56
SQ FT: 3,682
SALES (corp-wide): 27MM **Privately Held**
WEB: www.echoinghillsvillage.org
SIC: 7032 8059 Sporting & recreational camps; home for the mentally retarded, exc. skilled or intermediate
PA: Echoing Hills Village, Inc.
     36272 County Road 79
     Warsaw OH 43844
     740 327-2311

(G-16922)
REM-OHIO INC
214 W Main St (44001-2926)
PHONE..................................440 986-3337
Carla Parker, *Director*
EMP: 25
SALES (corp-wide): 2.8MM **Privately Held**
WEB: www.remohio.com
SIC: 8399 Community development groups
PA: Rem-Ohio, Inc
     6921 York Ave S
     Minneapolis MN 55435
     952 925-5067

South Charleston
Clark County

(G-16923)
BW ENTERPRISES INC
Also Called: National Golf Links
276 Clubhouse Dr (45368-8767)
PHONE..................................937 568-9660
Robert W Whitmer, *President*
Patsy L Whitmer, *Admin Sec*
EMP: 28
SQ FT: 5,000
SALES (est): 500K **Privately Held**
SIC: 7992 Public golf courses

(G-16924)
GARICK LLC
Also Called: Paygro
11000 Huntington Rd B (45368-8800)
PHONE..................................937 462-8350
EMP: 30
SALES (corp-wide): 58.2MM **Privately Held**
WEB: www.garick.com
SIC: 5261 5031 Lawn & garden supplies; lumber, plywood & millwork
PA: Garick, Llc
     13600 Broadway Ave Ste 1
     Cleveland OH 44125
     216 581-0100

(G-16925)
SUNRISE COOPERATIVE INC
149 N Chillicothe St (45368-9744)
P.O. Box R (45368-0818)
PHONE..................................937 462-8341
Michael Taylor, *Manager*
EMP: 26

SALES (corp-wide): 56.3MM **Privately Held**
SIC: 5191 Feed
PA: Sunrise Cooperative, Inc.
     2025 W State St Ste A
     Fremont OH 43420
     419 332-6468

South Lebanon
Warren County

(G-16926)
LOWES HOME CENTERS LLC
575 Corwin Nixon Blvd (45065-1199)
PHONE..................................513 445-1000
Bill Goodlick, *Branch Mgr*
EMP: 158
SALES (corp-wide): 68.6B **Publicly Held**
SIC: 5211 5031 5722 5064 Home centers; building materials, exterior; building materials, interior; household appliance stores; electrical appliances, television & radio
HQ: Lowe's Home Centers, Llc
     1605 Curtis Bridge Rd
     Wilkesboro NC 28697
     336 658-4000

(G-16927)
NVR INC
5153 Riverview Dr (45065-8782)
PHONE..................................513 494-0167
Ryan McCarthy, *Branch Mgr*
EMP: 33 **Publicly Held**
SIC: 1521 New construction, single-family houses
PA: Nvr, Inc.
     11700 Plaza America Dr # 500
     Reston VA 20190

South Point
Lawrence County

(G-16928)
ARMSTRONG UTILITIES INC
9651 County Road 1 (45680-8447)
PHONE..................................740 894-3886
Gordon Waters, *General Mgr*
D Johnson, *Manager*
EMP: 30 **Privately Held**
SIC: 4899 4813 Television antenna construction & rental
HQ: Armstrong Utilities, Inc.
     1 Armstrong Pl
     Butler PA 16001
     724 283-0925

(G-16929)
CHATHAM STEEL CORPORATION
235 Commerce Dr (45680-8465)
PHONE..................................740 377-9310
EMP: 25
SALES (corp-wide): 8.4B **Publicly Held**
SIC: 5051 Metal Service Center
HQ: Chatham Steel Corporation
     501 W Boundary St
     Savannah GA 31401
     912 233-4182

(G-16930)
DBI SERVICES LLC
2393 County Road 1 (45680-8462)
PHONE..................................410 590-4181
Paul D Deangelo, *President*
EMP: 30 **Privately Held**
SIC: 0783 Ornamental shrub & tree services
PA: Dbi Services, Llc
     100 N Conahan Dr
     Hazleton PA 18201

(G-16931)
DICKSON INDUSTRIAL PARK INC
Also Called: General Refrigeration
719 County Road 1 (45680-8881)
P.O. Box 617 (45680-0617)
PHONE..................................740 377-9162
John M Smith, *President*

▲ = Import ▼=Export
◆ =Import/Export

Mike E Clagg, *Vice Pres*
EMP: 25
SALES (est): 4.5MM **Privately Held**
WEB: www.refrigind.com
SIC: 1711 7623 Refrigeration contractor;
refrigeration repair service

(G-16932)
DOLIN SUPPLY CO
702 Solida Rd (45680-8953)
PHONE..................................304 529-4171
Mark Sparks,
EMP: 45
SQ FT: 83,000
SALES (est): 6MM **Publicly Held**
WEB: www.mscdirect.com
SIC: 5085 7353 7694 3496 Industrial
supplies; heavy construction equipment
rental; armature rewinding shops; miscel-
laneous fabricated wire products
PA: Msc Industrial Direct Co., Inc.
75 Maxess Rd
Melville NY 11747

(G-16933)
EARLY CONSTRUCTION CO
Also Called: Early Construction Company
307 County Road 120 S (45680-7807)
P.O. Box 551, Huntington WV (25710-
0551)
PHONE..................................740 894-5150
Jack W Tolliver, *President*
EMP: 25 EST: 1982
SQ FT: 6,000
SALES (est): 5.9MM **Privately Held**
WEB: www.earlycc.com
SIC: 1799 8711 1542 Construction site
cleanup; engineering services; commer-
cial & office building contractors

(G-16934)
GRAND VIEW INN INC
Also Called: Grandview Inn
154 County Road 450 (45680-8853)
PHONE..................................740 377-4388
Victor Hardan, *President*
EMP: 61
SALES (est): 2.8MM **Privately Held**
SIC: 7011 Hotels

(G-16935)
H & W HOLDINGS LLC
Also Called: Trucking and Logistics
341 County Road 120 S (45680-7807)
P.O. Box 679 (45680-0679)
PHONE..................................800 826-3560
Mike Herman, *Owner*
EMP: 50 **Privately Held**
WEB: www.hwtruck.com
SIC: 4212 Local trucking, without storage
HQ: H & W Holdings, Llc
829 Graves St
Kernersville NC 27284
336 992-0288

(G-16936)
**HEALTH CARE RTREMENT
CORP AMER**
Also Called: Heartland of Riverview
7743 County Road 1 (45680-7822)
PHONE..................................740 894-3287
Lois Clay, *Branch Mgr*
EMP: 100
SALES (corp-wide): 2.4B **Publicly Held**
WEB: www.hrc-manorcare.com
SIC: 8051 Convalescent home with contin-
uous nursing care
HQ: Health Care And Retirement Corpora-
tion Of America
333 N Summit St
Toledo OH 43604
419 252-5500

(G-16937)
**HEARTLND-RIVERVIEW S PT OH
LLC**
Also Called: HEARTLAND OF RIVERVIEW
#4148
7743 County Road 1 (45680-7822)
P.O. Box 10086 (45680)
PHONE..................................740 894-3287
Mark Stewart, *Administration*
EMP: 110

SALES: 9.7MM
SALES (corp-wide): 2.4B **Publicly Held**
SIC: 8051 8093 Convalescent home with
continuous nursing care; rehabilitation
center, outpatient treatment
HQ: Manor Care, Inc.
333 N Summit St Ste 103
Toledo OH 43604

(G-16938)
**LAWRENCE CNTY BD DEV
DSBLITIES**
Also Called: Lawrence Cnty Early Chldhd Ctr
1749 County Road 1 (45680-8850)
PHONE..................................740 377-2356
Sue Canderhoof, *Director*
EMP: 50 **Privately Held**
SIC: 8322 8351 Child related social serv-
ices; child day care services
PA: Lawrence County Board Of Dev Dis-
abilities
604 Carlton Davidson Ln
Coal Grove OH 45638
740 532-7401

(G-16939)
LOWES HOME CENTERS LLC
294 County Road 120 S (45680)
PHONE..................................740 894-7120
Edgel Castle, *Manager*
EMP: 190
SALES (corp-wide): 68.6B **Publicly Held**
SIC: 5211 5031 5722 5064 Home cen-
ters; building materials, exterior; building
materials, interior; household appliance
stores; electrical appliances, television &
radio
HQ: Lowe's Home Centers, Llc
1605 Curtis Bridge Rd
Wilkesboro NC 28697
336 658-4000

(G-16940)
MCGINNIS INC (HQ)
502 2nd St E (45680-9446)
P.O. Box 534 (45680-0534)
PHONE..................................740 377-4391
Bruce D McGinnis, *CEO*
Rickey Lee Griffith, *President*
Bill Jessie, *Corp Secy*
D Dwaine Stephens, *Vice Pres*
EMP: 193 EST: 1971
SQ FT: 5,000
SALES (est): 43.9MM
SALES (corp-wide): 152.4MM **Privately
Held**
WEB: www.mcginnisinc.com
SIC: 4491 3731 Marine cargo handling;
barges, building & repairing
PA: Mcnational, Inc.
502 2nd St E
South Point OH 45680
740 377-4391

(G-16941)
MCNATIONAL INC (PA)
502 2nd St E (45680-9446)
P.O. Box 534 (45680-0534)
PHONE..................................740 377-4391
Bruce D McGinnis, *CEO*
Rick Griffith, *President*
C Barry Gipson, *Principal*
Aaron Canfield, *Technology*
C Clayton Johnson, *Admin Sec*
EMP: 26
SQ FT: 5,000
SALES (est): 152.4MM **Privately Held**
SIC: 3731 7699 4491 Barges, building &
repairing; cargo vessels, building & re-
pairing; aircraft & heavy equipment repair
services; marine cargo handling

(G-16942)
MERCIERS INCORPORATED
Also Called: Mercier's Tree Experts
2393 County Road 1 (45680-8462)
PHONE..................................410 590-4181
Craig Mercier, *President*
EMP: 110
SQ FT: 2,500
SALES (est): 15MM **Privately Held**
WEB: www.merciers.com
SIC: 0783 Ornamental shrub & tree serv-
ices

(G-16943)
MIKE ENYART & SONS INC
Also Called: Mesi
77 Private Drive 615 (45680-1259)
P.O. Box 9 (45680-0009)
PHONE..................................740 523-0235
Michael Enyart, *President*
Tommy Enyart, *Vice Pres*
EMP: 85
SALES (est): 16.9MM **Privately Held**
SIC: 1623 1794 Sewer line construction;
excavation work

(G-16944)
**QUALITY CARE NURSING SVCS
LLC**
Also Called: Ultimate Health Care
501 Washington St Ste 13 (45680-9606)
PHONE..................................740 377-9095
Douglas Freeman, *CEO*
James Carver, *Vice Pres*
EMP: 200
SQ FT: 5,500
SALES (est): 6.4MM **Privately Held**
WEB: www.qcnservices.com
SIC: 8082 8051 Home health care serv-
ices; skilled nursing care facilities

(G-16945)
**RIVERS BEND HEALTH CARE
LLC**
335 Township Road 1026 (45680-7842)
P.O. Box 947 (45680-0947)
PHONE..................................740 894-3476
Ronald Lyons,
EMP: 100
SQ FT: 27,341
SALES: 5MM **Privately Held**
SIC: 8051 8052 Convalescent home with
continuous nursing care; intermediate
care facilities

(G-16946)
**TRIBUTE CONTRACTING &
CONS LLC**
2125 County Road 1 (45680-5001)
PHONE..................................740 451-1010
Todd Harrah, *Manager*
Tom Enyart,
EMP: 26
SALES (est): 147.7K **Privately Held**
SIC: 8748 1623 Business consulting;
water, sewer & utility lines; water & sewer
line construction; manhole construction;
pumping station construction

(G-16947)
XPO LOGISTICS FREIGHT INC
96 Private Drive 339 (45680-8919)
PHONE..................................740 894-3859
Andrew Sikes, *Manager*
EMP: 27
SALES (corp-wide): 15.3B **Publicly Held**
WEB: www.con-way.com
SIC: 4213 Contract haulers
HQ: Xpo Logistics Freight, Inc.
2211 Old Earhart Rd # 100
Ann Arbor MI 48105
800 755-2728

South Vienna
Clark County

(G-16948)
**OHIO ENTERTAINMENT
SECURITY**
3749 Mahar Rd (45369-9728)
PHONE..................................937 325-7216
Gregory Powell, *President*
Wilford Potter, *Vice Pres*
Carter Feltner, *Treasurer*
EMP: 99
SALES (est): 1.2MM **Privately Held**
WEB: www.ohioentertainmentsecurity.com
SIC: 7381 Security guard service

(G-16949)
VIENNA ENTERPRISES INC
Also Called: Sharonview Nursing Home
125 E National Rd (45369-9742)
P.O. Box 339 (45369-0339)
PHONE..................................937 568-4524

Helen Diener, *CEO*
Donald H Diener, *President*
Pierre Sweeney, *Administration*
EMP: 40
SQ FT: 5,000
SALES (est): 1.2MM **Privately Held**
SIC: 8059 8051 8052 Convalescent
home; nursing home, except skilled & in-
termediate care facility; skilled nursing
care facilities; intermediate care facilities

South Webster
Scioto County

(G-16950)
ALLARD EXCAVATION LLC
8336 Bennett Schl Hse Rd (45682-9029)
PHONE..................................740 778-2242
Margaret Allard, *Mng Member*
Mark Allard,
EMP: 68
SALES (est): 3.3MM **Privately Held**
SIC: 1794 Excavation work

South Zanesville
Muskingum County

(G-16951)
**FIRST AMERICAN TITLE INSUR
CO**
961 Linden Ave (43701-3049)
PHONE..................................740 450-0006
Wendy Mallett, *Branch Mgr*
EMP: 25 **Publicly Held**
WEB: www.firstam.com
SIC: 6361 Real estate title insurance
HQ: First American Title Insurance Com-
pany
1 First American Way
Santa Ana CA 92707
800 854-3643

Southington
Trumbull County

(G-16952)
AMERICAN LEGION POST
4200 Herner Cnty Line Rd (44470-9562)
PHONE..................................330 393-9858
Norman Doyen, *Principal*
EMP: 70
SALES (est): 349.7K **Privately Held**
SIC: 8641 Veterans' organization

Spencer
Medina County

(G-16953)
ENVIROTEST SYSTEMS CORP
408 E Main St (44275-9564)
PHONE..................................330 963-4464
EMP: 34
SQ FT: 5,601 **Privately Held**
WEB: www.il.etest.com
SIC: 7549 Emissions testing without re-
pairs, automotive
HQ: Envirotest Systems Corp.
7 Kripes Rd
East Granby CT 06026

(G-16954)
FARMERS SAVINGS BANK (PA)
111 W Main St (44275-9565)
P.O. Box 38 (44275-0038)
PHONE..................................330 648-2441
Thomas W Lee, *CEO*
John W Donley, *Vice Pres*
Sandra Davis, *Branch Mgr*
Janice Clark, *Technology*
Jackie Simmons, *Officer*
EMP: 29
SQ FT: 13,802
SALES: 9.7MM **Privately Held**
SIC: 6029 Commercial banks

GEOGRAPHIC

Spencerville
Allen County

(G-16955)
CHARLES RIVER LABORATORIES INC
Also Called: Pre-Clinical Services
640 N Elizabeth St (45887-1064)
PHONE...................................419 647-4196
Malcolm Blair PHD, *Manager*
EMP: 135
SALES (corp-wide): 2.2B **Publicly Held**
WEB: www.criver.com
SIC: 8731 Biotechnical research, commercial
HQ: Charles River Laboratories, Inc.
   251 Ballardvale St
   Wilmington MA 01887
   781 222-6000

(G-16956)
HCF OF ROSELAWN INC
420 E 4th St (45887-1210)
PHONE...................................419 647-4115
David Walsh, *Vice Pres*
Ronald Ringwald, *Director*
Kelly Miller, *Education*
EMP: 146
SALES (est): 177.8K
SALES (corp-wide): 154.8MM **Privately Held**
SIC: 8051 8322 8093 Convalescent home with continuous nursing care; rehabilitation services; rehabilitation center, outpatient treatment
PA: Hcf Management, Inc.
   1100 Shawnee Rd
   Lima OH 45805
   419 999-2010

Spring Valley
Greene County

(G-16957)
CENTURY 21 ELITE PERFORMANCE
2905 River Edge Cir (45370-9797)
PHONE...................................937 438-8221
Thomas Fitzgibbons, *President*
Sandy Yount, *Admin Sec*
EMP: 25
SQ FT: 2,160
SALES (est): 1.5MM **Privately Held**
WEB: www.century21ep.com
SIC: 6531 Real estate agent, residential

(G-16958)
DAYS OF DISCOVERY
3195 Clear Springs Rd (45370-7731)
PHONE...................................937 862-4465
Janine Speck, *Owner*
EMP: 45
SALES (est): 434.6K **Privately Held**
SIC: 8351 Child day care services

(G-16959)
TIM MUNDY
Also Called: My Lawn Ldscp & Irrigation Co
3159 State Route 42 (45370-9736)
P.O. Box 249 (45370-0249)
PHONE...................................937 862-8686
Tim Mundy, *Owner*
Ed Blair, *Finance Mgr*
EMP: 25
SALES (est): 1.4MM **Privately Held**
SIC: 0781 0782 7389 Landscape services; lawn & garden services;

Springboro
Warren County

(G-16960)
ADVANCED ENGRG SOLUTIONS INC
Also Called: Aesi
250 Advanced Dr (45066-1802)
PHONE...................................937 743-6900

Khang Do, *President*
Thomas J Harrington, *Principal*
Pat Croskey, *Program Mgr*
Jim Haws, *Manager*
EMP: 70
SQ FT: 44,000
SALES (est): 12.9MM **Privately Held**
SIC: 8711 3544 Consulting engineer; special dies, tools, jigs & fixtures

(G-16961)
ALFONS HAAR INC
150 Advanced Dr (45066-1800)
PHONE...................................937 560-2031
Thomas Haar, *President*
Betty Vankerkoerle, *Purchasing*
Bernd Haar, *Treasurer*
Bryan Johnson, *Marketing Staff*
▲ EMP: 31
SQ FT: 5,000
SALES (est): 8MM
SALES (corp-wide): 53.1MM **Privately Held**
WEB: www.alfonshaar.com
SIC: 5084 3599 8711 Packaging machinery & equipment; custom machinery; engineering services
PA: Alfons Haar Maschinenbau Gmbh & Co. Kg
   Fangdieckstr. 67
   Hamburg 22547
   408 339-10

(G-16962)
AST ENVIRONMENTAL INC
70 Commercial Way (45066-3080)
PHONE...................................937 743-0002
Robert Welsh, *President*
Duane Guilfoil, *Vice Pres*
William Guilfoil, *Vice Pres*
William Shackelford, *Administration*
EMP: 27
SQ FT: 6,000
SALES (est): 7.7MM **Privately Held**
WEB: www.astenvironmental.com
SIC: 4959 Environmental cleanup services

(G-16963)
BRIGHT BEGINNINGS
60 E North St (45066-1367)
PHONE...................................937 748-2612
Susan Stalcup, *President*
Suzanne Allen, *Pastor*
Kim Crosen, *Director*
Kim Criosen, *Director*
EMP: 35
SALES (est): 300K **Privately Held**
SIC: 8351 Preschool center

(G-16964)
BROTHERS TRADING CO INC (PA)
Also Called: Victory Wholesale Grocery
400 Victory Ln (45066-3046)
P.O. Box 216 (45066-0216)
PHONE...................................937 746-1010
David Kantor, *President*
Richard Kantor, *Vice Pres*
Scott Mattis, *Vice Pres*
◆ EMP: 150
SQ FT: 25,000
SALES (est): 295.8MM **Privately Held**
SIC: 5141 5122 5149 Groceries, general line; drugs, proprietaries & sundries; groceries & related products

(G-16965)
CHILDVINE INC
Also Called: Kids 'r' Kids 3 OH
790 N Main St (45066-8944)
PHONE...................................937 748-1260
Edward Doczy, *President*
Bonnie Doczy, *Vice Pres*
EMP: 45
SQ FT: 15,000
SALES (est): 1.8MM **Privately Held**
SIC: 8351 Preschool center

(G-16966)
COLDWELL BNKR HRITG RLTORS LLC
535 N Main St (45066-9555)
PHONE...................................937 748-5500
Karen Powell, *Manager*
EMP: 29

SALES (corp-wide): 6.5MM **Privately Held**
SIC: 6531 Real estate agent, residential
PA: Coldwell Banker Heritage Realtors Llc
   2000 Hewitt Ave
   Dayton OH 45440
   937 434-7600

(G-16967)
GRAPHIC SYSTEMS SERVICES INC
Also Called: G S S
400 S Pioneer Blvd (45066-3001)
PHONE...................................937 746-0708
Daniel L Green, *President*
James Copeland, *Corp Secy*
John Sillies, *Exec VP*
John Fillies, *Opers Staff*
Kim Sweet, *Purch Agent*
EMP: 41
SQ FT: 100,000
SALES (est): 6.6MM **Privately Held**
WEB: www.gsspress.com
SIC: 7699 3555 Industrial equipment services; printing presses

(G-16968)
HARDY DIAGNOSTICS
Also Called: Quickslide
429 S Pioneer Blvd (45066-3002)
PHONE...................................937 550-2768
Shelly Austin, *Manager*
EMP: 75
SALES (corp-wide): 45MM **Privately Held**
SIC: 5047 Medical equipment & supplies
PA: Hardy Diagnostics
   1430 W Mccoy Ln
   Santa Maria CA 93455
   805 346-2766

(G-16969)
HEATHERWOODE GOLF COURSE
88 Heatherwoode Blvd (45066-1577)
PHONE...................................937 748-3222
Steve Marino, *General Mgr*
EMP: 131
SALES (est): 1.8MM **Privately Held**
SIC: 7992 7299 Public golf courses; banquet hall facilities

(G-16970)
HILLSPRING HEALTH CARE CENTER
Also Called: CARESPRING
325 E Central Ave (45066)
PHONE...................................937 748-1100
Barry Dortz, *CEO*
Greg Weaver, *Branch Mgr*
EMP: 40 EST: 1997
SQ FT: 55,611
SALES: 13.3MM
SALES (corp-wide): 97.1MM **Privately Held**
SIC: 8051 Convalescent home with continuous nursing care
PA: Carespring Health Care Management, Llc
   390 Wards Corner Rd
   Loveland OH 45140
   513 943-4000

(G-16971)
KELCHNER INC (DH)
50 Advanced Dr (45066-1805)
PHONE...................................937 704-9890
Todd Kelchner, *CEO*
Troy Norvell, *President*
Kelly Dawson, *Superintendent*
Jeff Kelchner, *Vice Pres*
Jeremy White, *Project Mgr*
EMP: 134 EST: 1948
SQ FT: 8,600
SALES: 93MM
SALES (corp-wide): 5.3B **Privately Held**
SIC: 1794 1389 Excavation work; mud service, oil field drilling; bailing wells
HQ: Wood Group Uk Limited
   15 Justice Mill Lane
   Aberdeen AB11
   122 437-3772

(G-16972)
KIDS R KIDS SCHOOLS QULTY LRNG
790 N Main St (45066-8944)
PHONE...................................937 748-1260
Edward Doczy, *Principal*
EMP: 32 EST: 2007
SALES (est): 688.2K **Privately Held**
SIC: 8351 Preschool center

(G-16973)
M J J B LTD
Also Called: Day Academy
505 N Main St (45066-9555)
PHONE...................................937 748-4414
Jill S Brown, *President*
Shayna Donley, *Director*
EMP: 28
SQ FT: 20,374
SALES (est): 652.6K **Privately Held**
SIC: 8351 Group day care center

(G-16974)
MIAMI-LUKEN INC (PA)
Also Called: Paramount Confection Co
265 S Pioneer Blvd (45066-3307)
PHONE...................................937 743-7775
Tony Rattini, *CEO*
Joseph Mastandrea, *Ch of Bd*
Anthony V Rattini, *Principal*
William Knerr III, *Admin Sec*
EMP: 64
SQ FT: 60,000
SALES (est): 214.6MM **Privately Held**
WEB: www.miamiluken.com
SIC: 5122 Drugs, proprietaries & sundries

(G-16975)
MIDWEST SEAFOOD INC (PA)
475 Victory Ln (45066-3047)
PHONE...................................937 746-8856
William Easton, *President*
Joseph Perry, *Vice Pres*
EMP: 70
SQ FT: 10,000
SALES (est): 12.2MM **Privately Held**
SIC: 5146 Fish, fresh; fish, frozen, unpackaged

(G-16976)
MONRO INC
Also Called: Monro Muffler Brake
4 Remick Blvd (45066-9168)
PHONE...................................937 999-3202
EMP: 61
SALES (corp-wide): 1.1B **Publicly Held**
SIC: 7533 Muffler shop, sale or repair & installation
PA: Monro, Inc.
   200 Holleder Pkwy
   Rochester NY 14615
   585 647-6400

(G-16977)
MOUND TECHNOLOGIES INC
25 Mound Park Dr (45066-2402)
PHONE...................................937 748-2937
Thomas Miller, *President*
John Barger, *Vice Pres*
Luke Brongersma, *Project Mgr*
Troy Stevens, *Project Mgr*
Teresa Profitt, *Purch Mgr*
EMP: 45
SQ FT: 40,000
SALES: 20.9MM
SALES (corp-wide): 38.1MM **Privately Held**
WEB: www.moundtechnologies.com
SIC: 3441 1791 3446 Building components, structural steel; structural steel erection; gates, ornamental metal; grillwork, ornamental metal
PA: Heartland, Inc.
   1005 N 19th St
   Middlesboro KY 40965
   606 248-7323

(G-16978)
NATIONS ROOF OF OHIO LLC
Also Called: Affiliate of Nations Roof
275 S Pioneer Blvd (45066-1180)
PHONE...................................937 439-4160
Chuck Painter, *President*
Andrew Strauser, *Vice Pres*
EMP: 50

SALES: 87.4MM **Privately Held**
SIC: **1761** Roofing contractor; siding contractor

(G-16979)
PDI COMMUNICATION SYSTEMS INC (PA)
Also Called: P D I
40 Greenwood Ln (45066-3033)
PHONE.................................937 743-6010
Lou Vilardo, *Owner*
Kent Carver, *COO*
Cindy Doxrud, *Admin Sec*
▲ EMP: 60 EST: 1976
SQ FT: 78,000
SALES (est): 23.8MM **Privately Held**
WEB: www.pdiarm.com
SIC: **5047** Medical equipment & supplies

(G-16980)
PEOPLES BANK
95 Edgebrooke Dr (45066-1036)
P.O. Box 338 (45066-0338)
PHONE.................................937 748-0067
Steven Harding, *Manager*
EMP: 30
SALES (corp-wide): 208MM **Publicly Held**
SIC: **6021** National commercial banks
HQ: Peoples Bank
138 Putnam St
Marietta OH 45750
740 373-3155

(G-16981)
PHOENIX GROUP HOLDING CO
4 Sycamore Creek Dr Ste A (45066-2311)
PHONE.................................937 704-9850
George Coates, *CEO*
Robert D Gray, *CFO*
Robert Gray, *CFO*
Renee Bremer, *Administration*
EMP: 140
SQ FT: 1,200
SALES (est): 10.2MM **Privately Held**
WEB: www.phoenixgrouphc.com
SIC: **8711** Consulting engineer; machine tool design

(G-16982)
PIONEER AUTOMOTIVE TECH INC (DH)
100 S Pioneer Blvd (45066-1177)
PHONE.................................937 746-2293
Steven Moerner, *President*
Tina Groves, *Production*
Mike Honda, *Treasurer*
▲ EMP: 175
SQ FT: 155,000
SALES (est): 81.1MM
SALES (corp-wide): 3.4B **Privately Held**
SIC: **5013 3714 3651** Motor vehicle supplies & new parts; motor vehicle parts & accessories; household audio & video equipment
HQ: Pioneer North America, Inc.
2050 W 190th St Ste 100
Torrance CA 90504
310 952-2000

(G-16983)
RIGHT AT HOME
Also Called: Health Right
15 Dinsley Pl (45066-7422)
PHONE.................................937 291-2244
EMP: 60
SALES (est): 1.2MM **Privately Held**
SIC: **8082** Home Health Care Services

(G-16984)
SPRINGBORO SERVICE CENTER
Also Called: City Springsboro Public Works
220 E Mill St (45066-1430)
PHONE.................................937 748-0020
Barry Conway, *Director*
EMP: 30
SALES (est): 2.4MM **Privately Held**
SIC: **1611** Highway & street maintenance

(G-16985)
SYCAMORE CREEK COUNTRY CLUB
8300 Country Club Ln (45066-8436)
PHONE.................................937 748-0791

David Gagner, *President*
Bradley Pollak, *COO*
EMP: 120 EST: 1959
SALES: 2.8MM **Privately Held**
SIC: **7997** Country club, membership

(G-16986)
TRUGREEN LIMITED PARTNERSHIP
Also Called: Tru Green-Chemlawn
760 Pleasant Valley Dr (45066-1157)
PHONE.................................937 557-0060
Edmund Mackey, *Branch Mgr*
EMP: 50
SALES (corp-wide): 3.4B **Privately Held**
SIC: **0782** Lawn care services
HQ: Trugreen Limited Partnership
1790 Kirby Pkwy
Memphis TN 38138
901 251-4128

(G-16987)
WATKINS MECHANICAL INC (PA)
Also Called: Watkins Mechanical Services
10 Parker Dr (45066-1334)
PHONE.................................937 748-0220
David Watkins, *President*
Lisa Watkins, *General Mgr*
Jason Redmon, *Manager*
Elliot Watkins, *Technology*
EMP: 25
SALES (est): 4.1MM **Privately Held**
WEB: www.watkinsheating.com
SIC: **1711** Warm air heating & air conditioning contractor; heating & air conditioning contractors

(G-16988)
WILLOW AND CANE LLC
Also Called: Willow & Cane
1110 Lakemont Dr (45066-8185)
PHONE.................................609 280-1150
Christopher Meyer,
EMP: 25
SALES (est): 2.2MM **Privately Held**
SIC: **5091** Sporting & recreation goods

(G-16989)
WOODHULL LLC (PA)
125 Commercial Way (45066-3079)
PHONE.................................937 294-5311
Susan S Woodhull, *Owner*
Lance A Gildner,
EMP: 33
SQ FT: 6,500
SALES (est): 9.2MM **Privately Held**
WEB: www.woodhullusa.com
SIC: **5999 7699** Photocopy machines; photocopy machine repair

(G-16990)
YOUNG MENS CHRISTIAN ASSOC
Also Called: Coffman Branch
88 Remick Blvd (45066-9168)
PHONE.................................937 223-5201
Dale Brunner, *Director*
EMP: 120
SQ FT: 2,512
SALES (corp-wide): 26.1MM **Privately Held**
WEB: www.daytonymca.org
SIC: **8641 8351 7997 7991** Youth organizations; child day care services; membership sports & recreation clubs; physical fitness facilities; individual & family services
PA: Young Men's Christian Association Of Greater Dayton
118 W 1st St Ste 300
Dayton OH 45402
937 223-5201

Springfield
Clark County

(G-16991)
56 PLUS MANAGEMENT LLC
Also Called: First Diversity MGT Group
560 E High St (45505-1010)
PHONE.................................937 323-4114
Miguel Ten, *President*

Bruce Smith, *Exec VP*
EMP: 50
SALES (est): 2.1MM **Privately Held**
SIC: **7361** Placement agencies

(G-16992)
AETNA BUILDING MAINTENANCE INC
525 N Yellow Springs St (45504-2462)
P.O. Box 1985 (45501-1985)
PHONE.................................937 324-5711
Julian Greenland, *Principal*
EMP: 96
SALES (corp-wide): 29.6MM **Privately Held**
SIC: **7349** Window cleaning; janitorial service, contract basis
HQ: Aetna Building Maintenance, Inc.
646 Parsons Ave
Columbus OH 43206
614 476-1818

(G-16993)
AMERICAN NATIONAL RED CROSS
1830 N Limestone St Ste 1 (45503-2677)
PHONE.................................937 399-3872
Jon Low, *Director*
EMP: 78
SALES (corp-wide): 2.5B **Privately Held**
SIC: **8699 8621** Charitable organization; medical field-related associations
PA: The American National Red Cross
430 17th St Nw
Washington DC 20006
202 737-8300

(G-16994)
AMERICAN NATIONAL RED CROSS
1830 N Limestone St Ste 1 (45503-2677)
PHONE.................................937 631-9315
EMP: 29
SALES (corp-wide): 2.5B **Privately Held**
SIC: **8322** Individual & family services
PA: The American National Red Cross
430 17th St Nw
Washington DC 20006
202 737-8300

(G-16995)
AMERICAN SECURITY INSURANCE CO
1 Assurant Way (45505-4717)
PHONE.................................937 327-7700
Michael Lawson, *Principal*
EMP: 32
SALES (corp-wide): 8B **Publicly Held**
WEB: www.assurantsolutions.com
SIC: **6311** Life insurance
HQ: American Security Insurance Company
260 Interstate N Cir Se
Atlanta GA 30339
770 763-1000

(G-16996)
ARCHDIOCESE OF CINCINNATI
Also Called: Second Harvest Food Bank
701 E Columbia St (45503-4404)
PHONE.................................937 323-6507
Bill Leaver, *Manager*
EMP: 25
SALES (corp-wide): 229.4MM **Privately Held**
WEB: www.catholiccincinnati.org
SIC: **8322** Individual & family services
PA: Archdiocese Of Cincinnati
100 E 8th St Fl 8
Cincinnati OH 45202
513 421-3131

(G-16997)
ARCTECH FABRICATING INC (PA)
1317 Lagonda Ave (45503-4001)
P.O. Box 1447 (45501-1447)
PHONE.................................937 525-9353
Leonard McConnaghey, *CEO*
James C Roberts II, *President*
Len McConnaughey, *Vice Pres*
Tim Bussen, *Sales Mgr*
Joe Wood, *Manager*
EMP: 29
SQ FT: 13,200

SALES (est): 5MM **Privately Held**
WEB: www.arctechfabricating.com
SIC: **7692 3441** Welding repair; fabricated structural metal

(G-16998)
BENJAMIN STEEL COMPANY INC
777 Benjamin Dr (45502-8846)
PHONE.................................937 233-1212
Vincent Demana, *Owner*
Shawn Taylor, *Branch Mgr*
EMP: 40
SQ FT: 36,000
SALES (corp-wide): 86.5MM **Privately Held**
WEB: www.benjaminsteel.com
SIC: **5051 3498 3334 3317** Steel; tube fabricating (contract bending & shaping); primary aluminum; steel pipe & tubes; cold finishing of steel shapes; blast furnaces & steel mills
PA: Benjamin Steel Company, Inc.
777 Benjamin Dr
Springfield OH 45502
937 322-8600

(G-16999)
BOARD OF DIR OF WITTENBE
134 W Ward St (45504-2118)
PHONE.................................937 327-6231
Chuck Dominick, *Vice Pres*
Ken Irwin, *Librarian*
EMP: 49
SQ FT: 3,636
SALES (corp-wide): 70.2MM **Privately Held**
SIC: **7389** Fund raising organizations
PA: The Board Of Directors Of Wittenberg College
200 W Ward St
Springfield OH 45504
937 327-6231

(G-17000)
BOARD OF DIR OF WITTENBE
Also Called: Wittenberg University
225 N Fountain Ave (45504-2534)
P.O. Box 720 (45501-0720)
PHONE.................................937 327-6310
Mary Jo Darr, *Branch Mgr*
EMP: 26
SALES (corp-wide): 70.2MM **Privately Held**
WEB: www.wittenberg.edu
SIC: **8221 6163** University; loan brokers
PA: The Board Of Directors Of Wittenberg College
200 W Ward St
Springfield OH 45504
937 327-6231

(G-17001)
BOB EVANS TRANSPORTATION
6088 Green Field Dr (45502-7979)
PHONE.................................937 322-4447
EMP: 5012 EST: 2013
SALES (est): 1.1MM **Publicly Held**
SIC: **4789** Transportation services
HQ: Bob Evans Farms, Inc.
8111 Smiths Mill Rd
New Albany OH 43054
614 491-2225

(G-17002)
BROOKDALE LVING CMMUNITIES INC
Also Called: Cardinal Retirement Village
2981 Vester Ave (45503-1565)
PHONE.................................937 399-1216
Katherine Hitchcock, *Manager*
EMP: 36
SALES (corp-wide): 4.5B **Publicly Held**
WEB: www.parkplace-spokane.com
SIC: **8059** Rest home, with health care
HQ: Brookdale Living Communities, Inc.
515 N State St Ste 1750
Chicago IL 60654

(G-17003)
CANUS HOSPITALITY LLC
383 E Leffel Ln (45505-4746)
PHONE.................................937 323-8631
Andy Mullick, *Manager*
Jeremy L Trahan,
EMP: 40

SQ FT: 200
SALES: 1.6MM **Privately Held**
SIC: 7011 Hotels

(G-17004)
CARDIOLOGIST OF CLARK & CHAMP
1911 E High St (45505-1227)
PHONE....................................937 323-1404
Bonnie Davis, *Manager*
EMP: 26
SALES (est): 1.9MM **Privately Held**
WEB: www.cambridgewhoswho.com
SIC: 8011 Internal medicine practitioners

(G-17005)
CATHOLIC CHARITIES OF SOUTHWST
701 E Columbia St (45503-4404)
PHONE....................................937 325-8715
Kathleen Donnellan, *Exec Dir*
EMP: 99
SALES: 10.2MM **Privately Held**
SIC: 8322 Social service center

(G-17006)
CENTRAL FIRE PROTECTION CO INC
583 Selma Rd (45505-2071)
P.O. Box 1448 (45501-1448)
PHONE....................................937 322-0713
Gary Adkins, *President*
Helen Gifford, *Vice Pres*
Karla Brown, *Plant Mgr*
Jack Kaney, *Project Mgr*
Helen D Gifford, *Manager*
EMP: 34
SALES: 700MM **Privately Held**
SIC: 1799 Coating, caulking & weather, water & fireproofing

(G-17007)
CHI OMEGA SORORITY
2 Ferncliff Pl (45504-2512)
PHONE....................................937 325-9323
Louise Smockey, *President*
EMP: 50
SALES (est): 411.8K **Privately Held**
SIC: 7041 Sorority residential house

(G-17008)
CLARK SCHAEFER HACKETT & CO
14 E Main St Ste 500 (45502-1364)
PHONE....................................937 399-2000
John McKinnon, *Principal*
Nichole King, *Accountant*
Suzanne Klein, *Technology*
EMP: 40
SALES (corp-wide): 37.2MM **Privately Held**
WEB: www.cshco.com
SIC: 8721 Certified public accountant
PA: Clark, Schaefer, Hackett & Co.
   1 E 4th St Ste 1200
   Cincinnati OH 45202
   513 241-3111

(G-17009)
CLARK COUNTY BOARD OF DEVELOPM (PA)
Also Called: Town & Country School
2527 Kenton St (45505-3352)
PHONE....................................937 328-2675
Jennifer Rousculp-Miller, *Superintendent*
Ravi Shankar, *Comptroller*
Robert Bender, *Director*
EMP: 28
SQ FT: 15,000
SALES: 32MM **Privately Held**
SIC: 8322 Rehabilitation services

(G-17010)
CLARK COUNTY BOARD OF DEVELOPM
Also Called: Clark County Mrdd Trnsp
50 W Leffel Ln (45506-3520)
PHONE....................................937 328-5240
Elmer M Beard, *Director*
EMP: 53
SQ FT: 1,270
SALES (corp-wide): 32MM **Privately Held**
SIC: 4119 Local passenger transportation

PA: Clark County Board Of Developmental Disabilities
   2527 Kenton St
   Springfield OH 45505
   937 328-2675

(G-17011)
CLARK COUNTY BOARD OF DEVELOPM
110 W Leffel Ln (45506-3522)
PHONE....................................937 328-5200
Mary Brandstetter, *Director*
EMP: 236
SALES (corp-wide): 32MM **Privately Held**
SIC: 8361 Home for the mentally retarded
PA: Clark County Board Of Developmental Disabilities
   2527 Kenton St
   Springfield OH 45505
   937 328-2675

(G-17012)
CLARK COUNTY COMBINED HLTH DST (PA)
529 E Home Rd (45503-2710)
PHONE....................................937 390-5600
Charles A Patterson, *Commissioner*
EMP: 77
SALES (est): 5.5MM **Privately Held**
SIC: 8621 Health association

(G-17013)
CLARK MEMORIAL HOME ASSN
106 Kewbury Rd (45504-1199)
PHONE....................................937 399-4262
Sylvia Rosenlieb, *Director*
EMP: 27
SALES: 745.4K **Privately Held**
SIC: 8361 Home for the aged

(G-17014)
CLARK SHAWNEE SCHL TRANSPRTN
725 E Leffel Ln (45505-4753)
PHONE....................................937 328-5382
Debbie Finkes, *Superintendent*
Wayne Leis, *Principal*
EMP: 30
SALES: 830K **Privately Held**
SIC: 4151 School buses

(G-17015)
CLEANERS EXTRAORDINAIRE INC
128 Eagle City Rd (45502-9502)
PHONE....................................937 324-8488
Jeff Clouse, *Manager*
EMP: 70
SALES: 2MM **Privately Held**
SIC: 8322 Helping hand service (Big Brother, etc.)

(G-17016)
COILPLUS INC
Coilplus Ohio
4801 Gateway Blvd (45502-8866)
PHONE....................................937 322-4455
James Ralston, *Division Pres*
Kim Noble, *Purchasing*
Dave Lecocq, *Manager*
Toby Schofield, *Manager*
EMP: 42
SALES (corp-wide): 71B **Privately Held**
WEB: www.coilplusohio.com
SIC: 5051 Steel
HQ: Coilplus, Inc.
   6250 N River Rd Ste 6050
   Rosemont IL 60018
   847 384-3000

(G-17017)
COMFORT KEEPERS INC
101 N Fountain Ave (45502-1118)
PHONE....................................937 322-6288
Cris Clum, *President*
EMP: 50
SALES (corp-wide): 133.3MM **Privately Held**
WEB: www.comfortkeepers.com
SIC: 8082 Visiting nurse service
HQ: Comfort Keepers, Inc.
   6640 Poe Ave Ste 200
   Dayton OH 45414
   937 832-2454

(G-17018)
COMMUNICARE HEALTH SVCS INC
Also Called: Homestead Healthcare Center
2615 Derr Rd (45503-2445)
PHONE....................................937 399-9217
Maryanne Strauk, *Administration*
EMP: 137
SALES (corp-wide): 125.8MM **Privately Held**
WEB: www.atriumlivingcenters.com
SIC: 8051 Convalescent home with continuous nursing care
PA: Communicare Health Services, Inc.
   4700 Ashwood Dr Ste 200
   Blue Ash OH 45241
   513 530-1654

(G-17019)
COMMUNITY MERCY HLTH PARTNERS (DH)
Also Called: MERCY HEALTH FOUNDATION, SPRIN
100 Medical Center Dr (45504-2687)
PHONE....................................937 523-6670
Paul Hiltz, *CEO*
Gary A Hagens, *COO*
Sherry Nelson, *Vice Pres*
Marianne Potina, *Vice Pres*
John Dempsey, *CFO*
EMP: 33
SALES: 316MM
SALES (corp-wide): 4.7B **Privately Held**
SIC: 8062 General medical & surgical hospitals

(G-17020)
COMPUNET CLINICAL LABS LLC
2100 Emmanuel Way Ste C (45502-7218)
PHONE....................................937 342-0015
Melissa Williams, *Branch Mgr*
EMP: 61
SALES (corp-wide): 17.2K **Privately Held**
SIC: 8071 Medical laboratories
HQ: Compunet Clinical Laboratories, Llc
   2308 Sandridge Dr
   Moraine OH 45439
   937 296-0844

(G-17021)
CORROTEC INC
1125 W North St (45504-2713)
PHONE....................................937 325-3585
David A Stratton, *CEO*
Aristides G Gianakopoulos, *President*
Walter A Wildman, *Principal*
John C Stratton, *Vice Pres*
EMP: 35 **EST:** 1981
SQ FT: 28,500
SALES (est): 9.2MM **Privately Held**
WEB: www.corrotec.com
SIC: 3559 7699 3479 3625 Electroplating machinery & equipment; tank repair; coating of metals with plastic or resins; electric controls & control accessories, industrial

(G-17022)
COUNTY OF CLARK
Also Called: Environmental Health Dept
529 E Home Rd (45503-2710)
PHONE....................................937 390-5600
Charles Patterson, *Commissioner*
EMP: 75 **Privately Held**
WEB: www.ccpl.lib.oh.us
SIC: 8099 Health screening service
PA: County Of Clark
   50 E Columbia St Fl 5
   Springfield OH 45502
   937 521-2005

(G-17023)
COUNTY OF CLARK
Also Called: Clark County Human Services
1345 Lagonda Ave (45503-4001)
PHONE....................................937 327-1700
Robert Suver, *Branch Mgr*
EMP: 250 **Privately Held**
WEB: www.ccpl.lib.oh.us
SIC: 8322 Public welfare center
PA: County Of Clark
   50 E Columbia St Fl 5
   Springfield OH 45502
   937 521-2005

(G-17024)
COUNTY OF CLARK
Clark County Job & Family Svc
1346 Lagonda Ave (45503-4041)
PHONE....................................937 327-1700
Robert B Suver, *Branch Mgr*
EMP: 290 **Privately Held**
WEB: www.ccpl.lib.oh.us
SIC: 8322 Child related social services
PA: County Of Clark
   50 E Columbia St Fl 5
   Springfield OH 45502
   937 521-2005

(G-17025)
COUNTY OF CLARK
Also Called: Child Support
1345 Lagonda Ave (45503-4001)
PHONE....................................937 327-1700
Nancy Zimmerman, *Manager*
EMP: 300 **Privately Held**
WEB: www.ccpl.lib.oh.us
SIC: 8322 Child related social services
PA: County Of Clark
   50 E Columbia St Fl 5
   Springfield OH 45502
   937 521-2005

(G-17026)
COVENANT CARE OHIO INC
Also Called: Villa Springfield
701 Villa Rd (45503-1330)
PHONE....................................937 399-5551
Tammy Nall, *Human Res Dir*
Rhonda Nissley, *Branch Mgr*
EMP: 90 **Privately Held**
WEB: www.villagegeorgetown.com
SIC: 8051 Skilled nursing care facilities
HQ: Covenant Care Ohio, Inc.
   27071 Aliso Creek Rd # 100
   Aliso Viejo CA 92656
   949 349-1200

(G-17027)
CREFIII WARAMAUG
Also Called: Courtyard Springfield Downtown
100 S Fountain Ave (45502-1208)
PHONE....................................937 322-3600
Becky Krieger, *General Mgr*
Jose Batista, *General Mgr*
Craig Nussbaum, *Vice Pres*
EMP: 60
SALES (est): 992.9K **Privately Held**
SIC: 5812 7011 American restaurant; resort hotel

(G-17028)
D C MINNICK CONTRACTING LTD (PA)
Also Called: D.C.minnick Heating and AC
328 Ravenwood Dr (45504-3367)
PHONE....................................937 322-1012
David Minnick, *CEO*
Mike L Cole, *Shareholder*
Darlene R Minnick, *Shareholder*
EMP: 37
SQ FT: 10,800
SALES: 5.3MM **Privately Held**
SIC: 1731 1711 General electrical contractor; plumbing contractors

(G-17029)
DAVIS 5 STAR HOLDINGS LLC (PA)
14 E Main St Ste 300 (45502-1358)
PHONE....................................954 470-8456
Derek Davis Sr, *CEO*
Terrel Carlson, *COO*
EMP: 25
SQ FT: 12,500
SALES: 50MM **Privately Held**
SIC: 8742 Marketing consulting services

(G-17030)
DOLE FRESH VEGETABLES INC
600 Benjamin Dr (45502-8860)
PHONE....................................937 525-4300
Elena Jordan, *Opers Mgr*
Melissa Cooley, *Plant Engr*
Michael Locke, *Controller*
Cathleen Entler, *Human Res Mgr*
Lenny Pelifian, *Branch Mgr*
EMP: 190

SALES (corp-wide): 11.5B **Privately Held**
SIC: 5148 2099 Fruits, fresh; food preparations
HQ: Dole Fresh Vegetables, Inc.
2959 Salinas Hwy
Monterey CA 93940
831 422-8871

(G-17031)
EAGLEWOOD CARE CENTER
2000 Villa Rd (45503-1761)
PHONE..............................937 399-7195
Babur Khaan, *Administration*
EMP: 160
SQ FT: 29,000
SALES (est): 7.7MM **Privately Held**
SIC: 8051 6513 Convalescent home with continuous nursing care; apartment building operators

(G-17032)
EBY-BROWN COMPANY LLC
1982 Commerce Cir (45504-2012)
PHONE..............................937 324-1036
Rich Haen, *Sales Dir*
Tom Oktavec, *Marketing Staff*
Jeff Bundy, *Info Tech Mgr*
EMP: 225 **Privately Held**
WEB: www.eby-brown.com
SIC: 5194 5145 5141 5122 Whol Tobacco Products Whol Confectionery Whol General Groceries
PA: Eby-Brown Company, Llc
1415 W Diehl Rd Ste 300
Naperville IL 60563

(G-17033)
ELDERLY UNITED OF SPRINGFIELD (PA)
Also Called: UNITED SENIOR SERVICES
125 W Main St (45502-1296)
PHONE..............................937 323-4948
Lisa McDonough, *Cust Mgr*
Maureen Fagans, *Exec Dir*
Joyce Ware, *Asst Director*
Randy Yontz, *Asst Director*
EMP: 99
SQ FT: 24,000
SALES: 4.8MM **Privately Held**
WEB: www.elderlyunited.org
SIC: 8322 Senior citizens' center or association

(G-17034)
ENCOMPASS HEALTH CORPORATION
Also Called: HealthSouth
2685 E High St (45505-1412)
PHONE..............................205 970-4869
Melissa Halley, *Administration*
EMP: 28
SALES (corp-wide): 4.2B **Publicly Held**
WEB: www.healthsouth.com
SIC: 8062 General medical & surgical hospitals
PA: Encompass Health Corporation
9001 Liberty Pkwy
Birmingham AL 35242
205 967-7116

(G-17035)
F H BONN
Also Called: F H Bonn Company
4300 Gateway Blvd (45502-8819)
P.O. Box 12388, Fort Pierce FL (34979-2388)
PHONE..............................937 323-7024
Neal Bonn, *Owner*
EMP: 45
SALES (est): 1.4MM **Privately Held**
SIC: 6512 Commercial & industrial building operation

(G-17036)
FAMILY PRACTICE & ASSOCIATES
2701 Moorefield Rd (45502-8207)
PHONE..............................937 399-6650
Sally Abbott MD, *Partner*
Richard Gordon MD, *Partner*
EMP: 25
SALES (est): 2.2MM **Privately Held**
SIC: 8011 General & family practice, physician/surgeon

(G-17037)
FDC ENTERPRISES INC
5470 Ballentine Pike (45502-9011)
P.O. Box 189, New Albany (43054-0189)
PHONE..............................614 774-9182
Fred D Circle, *President*
Tom Schwartz, *Marketing Mgr*
Liz Hammond, *Manager*
Mike Retterer, *Manager*
EMP: 26
SQ FT: 2,000
SALES (est): 2.3MM **Privately Held**
WEB: www.fdcenterprises.com
SIC: 0783 Removal services, bush & tree

(G-17038)
FIRST DIVERSITY STAFFING GROUP
560 E High St (45505-1010)
PHONE..............................937 323-4114
George Ten, *President*
Ten Geroge, *President*
Bruce Smith, *Business Mgr*
Robin Williams, *Human Res Mgr*
Tony Abriola, *Sales Staff*
EMP: 500 EST: 2008
SQ FT: 6,000
SALES (est): 27.2MM **Privately Held**
SIC: 7361 Executive placement

(G-17039)
FIRST OHIO HOME FINANCE INC
1021 N Limestone St (45503-3613)
PHONE..............................937 322-3396
Anthony Coplen, *President*
EMP: 25
SALES (est): 1.6MM **Privately Held**
SIC: 6162 Mortgage bankers & correspondents

(G-17040)
FRATERNAL ORDER OF EAGLES
Also Called: Champion Aerie 397
1802 Selma Rd (45505-4242)
PHONE..............................937 323-0671
Matt Garst, *President*
Robert Miller, *President*
Charlie Heinz, *Trustee*
Louim WER, *Treasurer*
Margie Wheeler, *Office Mgr*
EMP: 40
SALES (est): 499.7K **Privately Held**
SIC: 8641 Fraternal associations

(G-17041)
GAMMA PHI BETA SORORITY ALPHA
628 Woodlawn Ave (45504-2124)
PHONE..............................937 324-3436
Alexa Berklin, *President*
EMP: 72
SQ FT: 5,048
SALES: 58.2K **Privately Held**
SIC: 8641 University club

(G-17042)
GOOD SHEPARD VILLAGE LLC
422 N Burnett Rd (45503-4821)
PHONE..............................937 322-1911
Curtis Springer,
EMP: 70
SALES (est): 4.4MM **Privately Held**
SIC: 8051 Convalescent home with continuous nursing care

(G-17043)
GRANDVIEW HT LTD PARTNR OHIO
Also Called: Holiday Inn
383 E Leffel Ln (45505-4746)
PHONE..............................937 766-5519
Fax: 937 323-5389
EMP: 73
SALES (corp-wide): 8.7MM **Privately Held**
SIC: 7011 5812 7299 7991 Hotel/Motel Operation Eating Place Misc Personal Service Physical Fitness Faclty Drinking Place
PA: Grandview Hotel Limited Partnership Of Ohio
740 Centre View Blvd
Crestview Hills KY

(G-17044)
HEALTH CARE RTREMENT CORP AMER
Also Called: Heartland of Springfield
2615 Derr Rd (45503-2445)
PHONE..............................937 390-0005
Kelly Meckstroch, *Branch Mgr*
EMP: 110
SALES (corp-wide): 2.4B **Publicly Held**
WEB: www.hrc-manorcare.com
SIC: 8051 Convalescent home with continuous nursing care
HQ: Health Care And Retirement Corporation Of America
333 N Summit St Ste 103
Toledo OH 43604
419 252-5500

(G-17045)
HOMETOWN URGENT CARE
1200 Vester Ave (45503-1304)
PHONE..............................937 342-9520
Toni Rogers, *Branch Mgr*
EMP: 197
SALES (corp-wide): 73.2MM **Privately Held**
SIC: 8062 8049 8011 General medical & surgical hospitals; occupational therapist; medical centers
PA: Hometown Urgent Care
2400 Corp Exchange Dr # 102
Columbus OH 43231
614 505-7633

(G-17046)
HOMETOWN URGENT CARE
1301 W 1st St (45504-1920)
PHONE..............................937 322-6222
EMP: 148
SALES (corp-wide): 73.2MM **Privately Held**
SIC: 8011 Medical centers
PA: Hometown Urgent Care
2400 Corp Exchange Dr # 102
Columbus OH 43231
614 505-7633

(G-17047)
HORNER INDUSTRIAL SERVICES INC
Also Called: Scherer Industrial Group
5330 Prosperity Dr (45502-9074)
PHONE..............................937 390-6667
Michael Harper, *Director*
EMP: 25
SALES (corp-wide): 46.7MM **Privately Held**
SIC: 5063 7694 Motors, electric; electric motor repair
PA: Horner Industrial Services, Inc.
1521 E Washington St
Indianapolis IN 46201
317 639-4261

(G-17048)
HOSPICE OF MIAMI VALLEY LLC
1948 N Limestone St (45503-2648)
PHONE..............................937 521-1444
EMP: 26
SALES (corp-wide): 16MM **Privately Held**
SIC: 8082 8069 Home health care services; specialty hospitals, except psychiatric
PA: Hospice Of The Miami Valley, L.L.C.
46 N Detroit St Ste B
Xenia OH 45385
937 458-6028

(G-17049)
HUSTEAD EMERGENCY MEDICAL SVC
6215 Springfield Xenia Rd (45502-8142)
PHONE..............................937 324-3031
Heather Kaufman, *Opers Staff*
EMP: 25
SALES (est): 630.3K **Privately Held**
SIC: 4119 Ambulance service

(G-17050)
IMPERIAL EXPRESS INC
202 N Limestone St # 300 (45503-4246)
P.O. Box 1607 (45501-1607)
PHONE..............................937 399-9400
Charles Crabill, *President*

Dale Briggs, *Vice Pres*
James Valentine, *Admin Sec*
EMP: 44
SQ FT: 4,000
SALES: 6MM **Privately Held**
SIC: 4212 Local trucking, without storage

(G-17051)
INDEPENDENT LIVING OF OHIO
530 S Burnett Rd (45505-2720)
PHONE..............................937 323-8400
Deborah Ackley, *President*
EMP: 45
SQ FT: 4,500
SALES (est): 1.1MM **Privately Held**
SIC: 8082 Home health care services

(G-17052)
INSIDE OUT (PA)
Also Called: INSIDE OUT CHILD CARE
501 S Wittenberg Ave (45506-2101)
PHONE..............................937 525-7880
William R Stout, *President*
EMP: 75
SQ FT: 60,000
SALES: 215.5K **Privately Held**
SIC: 8322 Social service center

(G-17053)
INSURANCE CLAIMS MGT INC
14 E Main St Fl 4 (45502-1359)
PHONE..............................937 328-4300
Dan Wilson, *CEO*
EMP: 130
SALES (corp-wide): 87.7MM **Privately Held**
SIC: 6411 Insurance claim adjusters, not employed by insurance company
HQ: Insurance Claims Management Inc.
404 S Barstow St
Eau Claire WI 54701

(G-17054)
INTEGRATED YOUTH SERVICES INC
1055 E High St (45505-1157)
PHONE..............................937 427-3837
Dave Nuscher, *CEO*
Dave Nusher, *CEO*
EMP: 45
SALES: 2MM **Privately Held**
SIC: 8093 Mental health clinic, outpatient

(G-17055)
INTERNATIONAL TRUCK & ENG CORP
6125 Urbana Rd (45502-9279)
PHONE..............................937 390-4045
John R Horne, *CEO*
Mr Daniel Ustian, *Ch of Bd*
Bob Baker, *Principal*
Robert A Boardman, *Senior VP*
Robert C Lannert, *CFO*
EMP: 1500 EST: 1999
SALES (est): 71.9MM **Privately Held**
SIC: 4212 Local trucking, without storage

(G-17056)
JERSEY CENTRAL PWR & LIGHT CO
Also Called: Firstenergy
420 York St (45505-2143)
PHONE..............................937 327-1218
Tom Clark, *Manager*
EMP: 80 **Publicly Held**
WEB: www.jersey-central-power-light.monmouth.n
SIC: 4911 Generation, electric power
HQ: Jersey Central Power & Light Company
76 S Main St
Akron OH 44308
800 736-3402

(G-17057)
JKL DEVELOPMENT COMPANY (PA)
Also Called: Splish Splash Auto Bath
2101 E Home Rd (45503-2516)
PHONE..............................937 390-0358
Jack Sayers, *President*
EMP: 30
SALES (est): 2.2MM **Privately Held**
SIC: 7542 Carwash, automatic

(G-17058)
K - O - I WAREHOUSE INC
622 W Main St (45504-2637)
PHONE.............................937 323-5585
Bob Curry, *Branch Mgr*
EMP: 25
SALES (corp-wide): 834.8MM **Privately Held**
WEB: www.koiwarehouse.com
SIC: 5013 5531 Automotive supplies & parts; automotive parts
HQ: K - O - I Warehouse, Inc.
    2701 Spring Grove Ave
    Cincinnati OH 45225
    513 357-2400

(G-17059)
KAPP CONSTRUCTION INC
329 Mount Vernon Ave (45503-4143)
P.O. Box 629 (45501-0629)
PHONE.............................937 324-0134
Randy Kapp, *President*
EMP: 45
SALES (est): 15.3MM **Privately Held**
WEB: www.kappconstruction.com
SIC: 1542 1541 Commercial & office building, new construction; commercial & office buildings, renovation & repair; industrial buildings & warehouses; renovation, remodeling & repairs: industrial buildings

(G-17060)
LATEEF ELMIN MHAMMAD INV GROUP
Also Called: Imam WD Mohammed Comm Devt
524 W Liberty St (45506-2024)
PHONE.............................937 450-3388
Jihad Muhammad, *CEO*
Robert Rhinehardt, *Principal*
Olenthia Rhinehart, *Vice Pres*
Yahya R El Amin, *CFO*
Lori El Amin, *Treasurer*
EMP: 56
SALES: 950K **Privately Held**
SIC: 8748 Business consulting

(G-17061)
LINEAGE LOGISTICS LLC
1985 Airpark Dr (45502-7976)
PHONE.............................937 328-3349
EMP: 40
SALES (corp-wide): 1.1B **Privately Held**
SIC: 8741 Administrative management
HQ: Lineage Logistics, Llc
    46500 Humboldt Dr
    Novi MI 48377
    248 863-4400

(G-17062)
LINKS AT WINDY KNOLL LLC
Also Called: Windy Knoll Golf Club
500 Roscommon Dr (45503-7133)
PHONE.............................937 631-3744
Dan D'Arrigo, *Mng Member*
EMP: 65
SQ FT: 4,900
SALES (est): 2MM **Privately Held**
SIC: 7992 5941 Public golf courses; golf goods & equipment

(G-17063)
LOBBY SHOPPES INC (PA)
Also Called: Lobby Shoppes Inc-Springfield
200 N Murray St (45503-4297)
P.O. Box 1200 (45501-1200)
PHONE.............................937 324-0002
Michael H Chakeres, *President*
Tony Taylor, *Sales Associate*
EMP: 200
SQ FT: 15,000
SALES (est): 4.2MM **Privately Held**
SIC: 5812 5145 Concessionaire; confectionery

(G-17064)
LOCUST HILLS GOLF INC
Also Called: Locust Hills Golf Course
5575 N River Rd (45502-6324)
PHONE.............................937 265-5152
John Lee Kitchen, *President*
Carol Kitchen, *Principal*
Joann Kitchen, *Principal*
Richard Lee Kitchen, *Vice Pres*
EMP: 45

SQ FT: 5,232
SALES: 1MM **Privately Held**
WEB: www.locusthillsgc.com
SIC: 7992 Public golf courses

(G-17065)
LOWES HOME CENTERS LLC
1601 N Bechtle Ave (45504-1576)
PHONE.............................937 327-6000
Mark Sprague, *Manager*
EMP: 120
SALES (corp-wide): 68.6B **Publicly Held**
SIC: 5211 5031 5722 5064 Home centers; building materials, exterior; building materials, interior; household appliance stores; electrical appliances, television & radio
HQ: Lowe's Home Centers, Llc
    1605 Curtis Bridge Rd
    Wilkesboro NC 28697
    336 658-4000

(G-17066)
MAINES COLLISION REPR & BDY SP
Also Called: Maines Towing & Recovery Svc
1717 E Pleasant St (45505-3313)
P.O. Box 1045 (45501-1045)
PHONE.............................937 322-4618
Fred E Maine, *President*
John Hawke Jr, *Senior VP*
Scott Hennigan, *Vice Pres*
Stacy Pavalatos, *Treasurer*
Mike Catanzaro, *Admin Sec*
EMP: 60
SQ FT: 20,000
SALES (est): 6.8MM **Privately Held**
WEB: www.mainescr.com
SIC: 7532 7549 4213 7538 Body shop, automotive; towing service, automotive; trucking, except local; heavy machinery transport; truck engine repair, except industrial

(G-17067)
MASONIC HEALTHCARE INC
3 Masonic Dr (45504-3658)
PHONE.............................937 525-3001
Marion Leeman, *President*
Nancy Archabold, *Principal*
Greg Holm, *COO*
Jerry Guess, *Vice Pres*
David Stacy, *CFO*
EMP: 500 EST: 1995
SALES (est): 7.4MM **Privately Held**
WEB: www.masonichealthcare.com
SIC: 8051 Convalescent home with continuous nursing care

(G-17068)
MCKINLEY HALL INC
2624 Lexington Ave (45505-2620)
PHONE.............................937 328-5300
Wendy Doolittle, *CEO*
EMP: 50
SQ FT: 31,770
SALES: 4.4MM **Privately Held**
SIC: 8069 8093 8051 Alcoholism rehabilitation hospital; drug addiction rehabilitation hospital; specialty outpatient clinics; skilled nursing care facilities

(G-17069)
MED-TRANS INC (PA)
714 W Columbia St (45504-2734)
P.O. Box 1048 (45501-1048)
PHONE.............................937 325-4926
William George, *Ch of Bd*
Luanne George, *President*
Susan Crutchfield, *Partner*
Diana Taylor, *Partner*
Edward G Bailey, *Vice Pres*
EMP: 100
SQ FT: 7,600
SALES (est): 18.6MM **Privately Held**
WEB: www.med-trans.com
SIC: 4119 Ambulance service

(G-17070)
MENTAL HEALTH SERVICE
474 N Yellow Springs St (45504-2463)
PHONE.............................937 399-9500
Curt Gillespie, *CEO*
Jo Marenberg, *Human Res Dir*
James Perry, *CIO*
James Gibfried, *Director*

EMP: 28 EST: 2014
SALES (est): 2.2MM **Privately Held**
SIC: 8052 Home for the mentally retarded, with health care

(G-17071)
MENTAL HLTH SERV FOR CL & MAD
1086 Mound St (45505-1298)
PHONE.............................937 390-7980
Jim Wade, *Manager*
EMP: 50
SALES (corp-wide): 12.5MM **Privately Held**
WEB: www.mhscc.com
SIC: 8063 8322 Hospital for the mentally ill; social worker
PA: Mental Health Services For Clark And Madison Counties, Inc.
    474 N Yellow Springs St
    Springfield OH 45504
    937 399-9500

(G-17072)
MENTAL HLTH SERV FOR CL & MAD (PA)
474 N Yellow Springs St (45504-2463)
PHONE.............................937 399-9500
Jeff Hughes, *Vice Ch Bd*
James P Perry PHD, *President*
Jeff Darding, *Vice Pres*
Mary B Taylor, *CFO*
Phoebe Peczkowski, *Human Res Dir*
EMP: 219 EST: 1969
SQ FT: 30,000
SALES: 12.5MM **Privately Held**
WEB: www.mhscc.com
SIC: 8063 Hospital for the mentally ill

(G-17073)
MERCY HEALTH
160 Tuttle Rd (45503-5234)
PHONE.............................937 323-4585
EMP: 27
SALES (corp-wide): 4.7B **Privately Held**
SIC: 8099 Childbirth preparation clinic
PA: Mercy Health
    1701 Mercy Health Pl
    Cincinnati OH 45237
    513 639-2800

(G-17074)
MERCY HEALTH
211 Northparke Dr Ste 101 (45503-1117)
PHONE.............................937 390-1700
EMP: 54
SALES (corp-wide): 4.7B **Privately Held**
SIC: 8062 General medical & surgical hospitals
PA: Mercy Health
    1701 Mercy Health Pl
    Cincinnati OH 45237
    513 639-2800

(G-17075)
MERCY HEALTH
100 W Mccreight Ave # 400 (45504-1885)
P.O. Box 1380 (45501-1380)
PHONE.............................937 390-9665
EMP: 109
SALES (corp-wide): 4.7B **Privately Held**
SIC: 8052 Personal care facility
PA: Mercy Health
    1701 Mercy Health Pl
    Cincinnati OH 45237
    513 639-2800

(G-17076)
MERCY HEALTH
Also Called: Commun Mer OCC Healh & Medici
2501 E High St (45505-1410)
PHONE.............................937 328-8700
EMP: 53
SALES (corp-wide): 4.7B **Privately Held**
SIC: 8062 General medical & surgical hospitals
PA: Mercy Health
    1701 Mercy Health Pl
    Cincinnati OH 45237
    513 639-2800

(G-17077)
MERCY HEALTH
2600 N Limestone St (45503-1114)
PHONE.............................937 390-5075

EMP: 27
SALES (corp-wide): 4.7B **Privately Held**
SIC: 8049 Physical therapist
PA: Mercy Health
    1701 Mercy Health Pl
    Cincinnati OH 45237
    513 639-2800

(G-17078)
MERCY HEALTH - SPRINGFIELD C
148 W North St (45504-2547)
PHONE.............................937 323-5001
Paul Hiltz, *CEO*
EMP: 35 EST: 2011
SALES (est): 2.5MM
SALES (corp-wide): 4.7B **Privately Held**
SIC: 8011 Oncologist
HQ: Community Mercy Health Partners
    100 Medical Center Dr
    Springfield OH 45504

(G-17079)
MERCY HEALTH FOUNDATION
100 W Mccreight Ave # 200 (45504-1885)
PHONE.............................937 523-6670
Kristy Kohl McCready, *President*
Amy Aman, *Executive Asst*
EMP: 434
SALES (est): 7.5MM
SALES (corp-wide): 4.7B **Privately Held**
SIC: 6732 Charitable trust management
HQ: Community Mercy Health Partners
    100 Medical Center Dr
    Springfield OH 45504

(G-17080)
MERCY MEDICAL CENTER
1343 N Fountain Blvd (45504-1499)
P.O. Box 688 (45501-0688)
PHONE.............................937 390-5000
Andrew McCulloch, *President*
Freddy Katai, *Ch Radiology*
EMP: 868 EST: 1949
SQ FT: 25,160
SALES (est): 44.1MM **Privately Held**
SIC: 8062 General medical & surgical hospitals

(G-17081)
MERRILL LYNCH PIERCE FENNER
1155 Scanlon Ln (45503-6666)
PHONE.............................614 225-3197
EMP: 27
SALES (corp-wide): 110.5B **Publicly Held**
SIC: 6211 Security brokers & dealers
HQ: Merrill Lynch, Pierce, Fenner & Smith Incorporated
    111 8th Ave
    New York NY 10011
    800 637-7455

(G-17082)
METALS USA CRBN FLAT RLLED INC
5750 Lower Valley Pike (45502-9101)
PHONE.............................937 882-6354
Jeff Taugh, *Manager*
EMP: 54
SALES (corp-wide): 11.5B **Publicly Held**
SIC: 5051 3312 Steel; blast furnaces & steel mills
HQ: Metals Usa Carbon Flat Rolled, Inc.
    1070 W Liberty St
    Wooster OH 44691
    330 264-8416

(G-17083)
MIAMI VLY CHILD DEV CTRS INC
Also Called: Clark County Office
1450 S Yellow Springs St (45506-2545)
PHONE.............................937 325-2559
Diane Johnson, *Manager*
EMP: 106
SALES (corp-wide): 32MM **Privately Held**
WEB: www.mvcdc.org
SIC: 8351 Preschool center
PA: Miami Valley Child Development Centers, Inc.
    215 Horace St
    Dayton OH 45402
    937 226-5664

▲ = Import ▼=Export
◆ =Import/Export

(G-17084)
MID-OHIO HARLEY-DAVIDSON INC
2100 Quality Ln (45505-3623)
PHONE..................................937 322-3590
Roland Ude, *President*
Melody Ude, *Corp Secy*
Brian Cubbage, *Vice Pres*
EMP: 25
SQ FT: 19,000
SALES (est): 6.1MM **Privately Held**
WEB: www.midohiohd.com
SIC: 5571 7699 Motorcycles; motorcycle parts & accessories; motorcycle repair service

(G-17085)
MIDWEST REINFORCING CONTRS
1839 N Fountain Blvd (45504-1406)
P.O. Box 2060 (45501-2060)
PHONE..................................937 390-8998
Katherine A Heinzen, *President*
Scott Heinzen, *Vice Pres*
EMP: 25
SALES: 1.1MM **Privately Held**
SIC: 1791 Concrete reinforcement, placing of

(G-17086)
MILLERS TEXTILE SERVICES INC
540 E Columbia St (45503-4200)
PHONE..................................614 262-1206
Jim Bode, *Branch Mgr*
John Engle, *Manager*
EMP: 25
SALES (corp-wide): 15MM **Privately Held**
WEB: www.millerstextile.com
SIC: 7213 Uniform supply
PA: Miller's Textile Services, Inc.
520 Commerce Rd
Wapakoneta OH
419 738-3551

(G-17087)
NAVISTAR INTL TRNSP CORP
5975 Urbana Rd (45502-9537)
PHONE..................................937 390-4242
Tom Tullis, *President*
Donna Wenzel, *Purch Agent*
Brad Shroyer, *Engineer*
Thomas Tebeje, *Engineer*
Randy Johnson, *Controller*
EMP: 200
SALES (est): 13.6MM **Privately Held**
SIC: 7538 General truck repair

(G-17088)
NEW NGHBORS RSDENTIAL SVCS INC
4230 E National Rd (45505-1759)
PHONE..................................937 717-5731
Brenda McAlexander, *CEO*
EMP: 35
SALES: 1.2MM **Privately Held**
SIC: 8361 Home for the mentally handicapped

(G-17089)
NIGHTINGALE MONTESSORI INC
Also Called: Nightingale Montessori School
1106 E High St (45505-1122)
PHONE..................................937 324-0336
Maria Taylor, *President*
Sheila Brown, *Corp Secy*
Cole Taylor, *Technology*
Guyia Wilson, *Director*
Nancy Schwab, *Administration*
EMP: 34
SALES: 1.1MM **Privately Held**
SIC: 8211 8351 Private elementary & secondary schools; private elementary school; Montessori child development center

(G-17090)
NORTHWEST COLUMBUS UROLOGY
Also Called: Springfield Urology
1164 E Home Rd Ste J (45503-2726)
PHONE..................................937 342-9260

Tina Stuart, *Office Mgr*
Eric Espinosa, *Med Doctor*
EMP: 25 **Privately Held**
SIC: 8011 Urologist
PA: Northwest Columbus Urology
551 W Central Ave Ste 102
Delaware OH 43015

(G-17091)
OESTERLEN-SERVICES FOR YOUTH
Also Called: SOCIAL MINISTRY ORGANIZATION
1918 Mechanicsburg Rd (45503-3147)
PHONE..................................937 399-6101
Lucy Yu, *Accountant*
Kathryn Murphy, *Finance*
Mark Derr, *Marketing Staff*
Emily Blanford, *Manager*
Amy Selvage, *Manager*
EMP: 150
SQ FT: 10,204
SALES: 6.1MM **Privately Held**
WEB: www.oesterlen.org
SIC: 8211 8661 8361 Private special education school; community church; residential care

(G-17092)
OHIO MASONIC RETIREMENT VLG
4 Masonic Dr (45504-3695)
PHONE..................................937 525-1743
John Nofsinger, *President*
EMP: 65
SALES (est): 913.7K **Privately Held**
SIC: 8641 Civic associations

(G-17093)
OHIO VALLEY MEDICAL CENTER LLC
100 E Main St (45502-1308)
PHONE..................................937 521-3900
James Cromwell, *Ch of Bd*
Steve Eisentrager, *President*
Ajay Mangal, *Principal*
Ronny Shumaker, *COO*
Dean Stoughton, *Plant Mgr*
EMP: 70
SALES (est): 30.9MM **Privately Held**
SIC: 8062 General medical & surgical hospitals

(G-17094)
PARK NATIONAL BANK
40 S Limestone St (45502-1222)
PHONE..................................937 324-6800
H Egger, *Principal*
EMP: 30
SALES (corp-wide): 411.9MM **Publicly Held**
SIC: 6021 National commercial banks
HQ: The Park National Bank
50 N 3rd St
Newark OH 43055
740 349-8451

(G-17095)
PEDIATRIC ASSOC OF SPRINGFIELD
1640 N Limestone St (45503-2652)
PHONE..................................937 328-2320
Raymond Cooper MD, *President*
EMP: 58
SALES (est): 5.4MM **Privately Held**
SIC: 8011 Pediatrician

(G-17096)
PENTAFLEX INC
4981 Gateway Blvd (45502-8867)
PHONE..................................937 325-5551
Dave Arndt, *President*
Bob Jones, *Vice Pres*
Julie McGregor, *Treasurer*
Mark McClain, *Controller*
Melissa McCrillis, *Human Res Dir*
◆ **EMP:** 110
SQ FT: 146,000
SALES (est): 28.2MM **Privately Held**
WEB: www.pentaflex.com
SIC: 3469 7692 Stamping metal for the trade; welding repair

(G-17097)
PEPSI-COLA METRO BTLG CO INC
233 Dayton Ave (45506-1205)
PHONE..................................937 328-6750
Phyllis Beach, *Regional Mgr*
EMP: 99
SALES (corp-wide): 64.6B **Publicly Held**
WEB: www.joy-of-cola.com
SIC: 5149 Soft drinks
HQ: Pepsi-Cola Metropolitan Bottling Company, Inc.
1111 Westchester Ave
White Plains NY 10604
914 767-6000

(G-17098)
PHYSICIANS SURGEONS FOR WOMEN
1821 E High St (45505-1225)
PHONE..................................937 323-7340
David R Billing MD, *Partner*
Lisa M Delong MD, *Partner*
EMP: 25 **EST:** 1975
SQ FT: 6,000
SALES (est): 2.8MM **Privately Held**
WEB: www.cpso.on.ca
SIC: 8011 Gynecologist; obstetrician

(G-17099)
R&M MATERIALS HANDLING INC
Also Called: R & M
4501 Gateway Blvd (45502-8863)
PHONE..................................937 328-5100
Jim Vandegrift, *President*
Steve Mayes, *Treasurer*
Guy Shumaker, *VP Finance*
Angel Becerra, *Regl Sales Mgr*
Damian Mulcahy, *Regl Sales Mgr*
▼ **EMP:** 41
SQ FT: 110,000
SALES (est): 18.3MM
SALES (corp-wide): 3.7B **Privately Held**
WEB: www.rmhoist.com
SIC: 5084 Materials handling machinery; hoists
HQ: Kci Holding Usa Inc.
4401 Gateway Blvd
Springfield OH 45502

(G-17100)
REAL ESTATE II INC
1140 E Home Rd (45503-2726)
PHONE..................................937 390-3119
Sue Smedley, *President*
Charlene McAllister, *Manager*
EMP: 26 **EST:** 1979
SQ FT: 2,000
SALES: 21MM **Privately Held**
SIC: 6531 Real estate agent, residential

(G-17101)
RICHWOOD BANKING COMPANY
2454 N Limestone St (45503-1110)
PHONE..................................937 390-0470
EMP: 30 **Privately Held**
SIC: 6035 Federal savings & loan associations
HQ: The Richwood Banking Company
28 N Franklin St
Richwood OH 43344
740 943-2317

(G-17102)
ROBINSON INSULATION CO INC
Also Called: Ohio Gypsum Supply
4715 Urbana Rd (45502-9503)
PHONE..................................937 323-9599
Garth S Robinson, *President*
Ryan J Robinson, *Vice Pres*
Jennifer Robinson, *Treasurer*
EMP: 35 **EST:** 1975
SQ FT: 8,000
SALES (est): 4.9MM **Privately Held**
SIC: 1742 5032 Insulation, buildings; drywall materials

(G-17103)
ROCKING HORSE CHLD HLTH CTR (PA)
651 S Limestone St (45505-1965)
PHONE..................................937 328-7266

James Duffy, *Partner*
Shonda Wallace, *Finance*
Stacy Lee, *Office Mgr*
Sue Carter, *Nurse*
Chelsey Lupher, *Nurse*
EMP: 28
SALES: 13.9MM **Privately Held**
WEB: www.rockinghorsecenter.org
SIC: 8011 8322 Pediatrician; individual & family services

(G-17104)
ROEDIGER REALTY INC
331 Mount Vernon Ave (45503-4143)
PHONE..................................937 322-0352
James Roediger, *President*
EMP: 30
SALES (est): 1.5MM **Privately Held**
WEB: www.roedigerrealty.com
SIC: 6531 Real estate agent, residential

(G-17105)
ROLLINS MOVING AND STORAGE INC
1050 Wheel St (45503-3545)
PHONE..................................937 525-4013
Clyde Depuy, *Branch Mgr*
EMP: 30
SALES (corp-wide): 21.4MM **Privately Held**
WEB: www.rollins3pl.com
SIC: 4214 4213 Household goods moving & storage, local; household goods transport
PA: Rollins Moving And Storage, Inc.
1900 E Leffel Ln
Springfield OH 45505
937 325-2484

(G-17106)
ROSE CITY MANUFACTURING INC
900 W Leffel Ln (45506-3538)
P.O. Box 1103 (45501-1103)
PHONE..................................937 325-5561
Daniel McGregor, *President*
Hugh Barnett, *Principal*
Dane A Belden, *Principal*
▲ **EMP:** 60
SQ FT: 44,000
SALES (est): 9.1MM **Privately Held**
WEB: www.rosecitymfg.com
SIC: 7692 Automotive welding

(G-17107)
SAGAR SATYAVOLU MD
1911 E High St (45505-1227)
PHONE..................................937 323-1404
Sagar Satyavolu, *Principal*
EMP: 40 **EST:** 2001
SALES (est): 476.4K **Privately Held**
SIC: 8011 Cardiologist & cardio-vascular specialist

(G-17108)
SAWMILL ROAD MANAGEMENT CO LLC (PA)
1990 Kingsgate Rd Ste A (45502-8225)
PHONE..................................937 342-9071
Judy Ross, *Mng Member*
EMP: 30
SALES (est): 1.9MM **Privately Held**
SIC: 6531 2421 Buying agent, real estate; sawmills & planing mills, general

(G-17109)
SDX HOME CARE OPERATIONS LLC
Also Called: Comfort Keepers
101 N Fountain Ave (45502-1118)
PHONE..................................937 322-6288
Kristina Butler, *President*
EMP: 99
SALES (est): 2.4MM **Privately Held**
SIC: 8082 Home health care services

(G-17110)
SECURITY NATIONAL BANK & TR CO
40 S Limestone St (45502-1222)
PHONE..................................937 324-6800
William Fralick, *President*
EMP: 210

SALES (corp-wide): 411.9MM **Publicly Held**
WEB: www.securitynationalbank.com
SIC: 6021 6141 National trust companies with deposits, commercial; consumer finance companies
HQ: The Security National Bank And Trust Co
50 N 3rd St
Newark OH 43055
740 426-6384

(G-17111)
SELF RELIANCE INC
3674 E National Rd Ste 3 (45505-1545)
PHONE...............................937 525-0809
William Smith, *President*
Jay Crawford, *Vice Pres*
EMP: 32
SALES (est): 1.6MM **Privately Held**
SIC: 8322 Social services for the handicapped

(G-17112)
SERVICE EXPERTS HTG & AC LLC
2600 S Limestone St (45505-4940)
PHONE...............................937 426-3444
Mark Weaver, *General Mgr*
EMP: 30
SALES (corp-wide): 985.7MM **Privately Held**
SIC: 1711 Heating & air conditioning contractors
HQ: Service Experts Heating & Air Conditioning Llc
3820 American Dr Ste 200
Plano TX 75075
972 535-3800

(G-17113)
SOUTHBROOK HEALTH CARE CTR INC
Also Called: Southbrook Care Center
2299 S Yellow Springs St (45506-3368)
PHONE...............................937 322-3436
Harold Sosna, *President*
Nikki Lee, *Director*
EMP: 110
SALES: 4.4MM **Privately Held**
SIC: 8051 Skilled nursing care facilities

(G-17114)
SPECTRUM MGT HOLDG CO LLC
Also Called: Time Warner
75 W Main St (45502-1309)
PHONE...............................937 552-5760
Cindy Ohagan, *Vice Pres*
EMP: 83
SALES (corp-wide): 43.6B **Publicly Held**
SIC: 4841 Cable television services; subscription television services
HQ: Spectrum Management Holding Company, Llc
400 Atlantic St
Stamford CT 06901
203 905-7801

(G-17115)
SPRINGFLED RGNAL OTPATIENT CTR
2610 N Limestone St (45503-1114)
PHONE...............................937 390-8310
Cindy Morgan, *Director*
EMP: 30 EST: 2009
SALES (est): 580.3K **Privately Held**
SIC: 8093 Specialty outpatient clinics

(G-17116)
SPRINGFIELD UNFRM-LINEN SUP INC
Also Called: Miller's Textiles
141 N Murray St (45503-4321)
PHONE...............................937 323-5544
Robert Hager, *President*
Jim Romaker, *Corp Secy*
EMP: 68
SQ FT: 12,000

SALES (est): 896.6K
SALES (corp-wide): 15MM **Privately Held**
WEB: www.millerstextile.com
SIC: 7213 7219 7218 7217 Linen supply; laundry, except power & coin-operated; industrial launderers; carpet & upholstery cleaning
PA: Miller's Textile Services, Inc.
520 Commerce Rd
Wapakoneta OH
419 738-3551

(G-17117)
SPRINGFIELD BUSINESS EQP CO (PA)
3783 W National Rd (45504-3516)
PHONE...............................937 322-3828
J D Lindeman, *President*
Lisa Lindeman, *Corp Secy*
Jeff Austin, *Vice Pres*
Shonda Lindeman, *Vice Pres*
EMP: 31 EST: 1970
SALES (est): 18.4MM **Privately Held**
SIC: 5044 5021 Office equipment; office furniture

(G-17118)
SPRINGFIELD COUNTRY CLUB CO
2315 Signal Hill Rd (45504-1042)
P.O. Box 1642 (45501-1642)
PHONE...............................937 399-4215
Craig Taylor, *General Mgr*
Valerie McKinley, *Controller*
EMP: 50 EST: 1896
SQ FT: 28,000
SALES: 1.8MM **Privately Held**
SIC: 7997 5812 5813 5941 Country club, membership; golf club, membership; swimming club, membership; tennis club, membership; eating places; bar (drinking places); sporting goods & bicycle shops

(G-17119)
SPRINGFIELD FAMILY Y M C A
300 S Limestone St (45505-1071)
PHONE...............................937 323-3781
Paul Hanus, *Director*
EMP: 85 EST: 1854
SQ FT: 47,125
SALES: 1.5MM **Privately Held**
SIC: 8641 7991 8351 7032 Youth organizations; physical fitness facilities; child day care services; youth camps; individual & family services

(G-17120)
SUE SMEDLEY
417 Wildwood Dr (45504-1052)
PHONE...............................937 399-5155
Sue Smedley, *Partner*
EMP: 50
SALES (est): 1.6MM **Privately Held**
SIC: 6531 Real estate agent, residential

(G-17121)
SUN VALLEY INFOSYS LLC
1750 N Fountain Blvd (45504-1466)
PHONE...............................937 267-6435
Jude Stanley, *Mng Member*
Jessie Behl,
Marshall Behl,
WEI Cao,
EMP: 52
SQ FT: 2,000
SALES (est): 3.3MM **Privately Held**
SIC: 8742 Management consulting services

(G-17122)
SUNRISE COOPERATIVE INC
821 N Belmont Ave (45503-3515)
PHONE...............................937 323-7536
Tom Waddle, *Manager*
EMP: 25
SALES (corp-wide): 62MM **Privately Held**
SIC: 5191 Farm supplies
PA: Sunrise Cooperative, Inc.
2025 W State St Ste A
Fremont OH 43420
419 332-6468

(G-17123)
TAC INDUSTRIES INC (PA)
Also Called: TAC Enterprises
2160 Old Selma Rd (45505-4600)
PHONE...............................937 328-5200
Mary Brandstetter, *CEO*
Michael Ahern, *CFO*
Kevin Spriggs, *Manager*
Karol See, *Info Tech Mgr*
EMP: 340
SQ FT: 52,800
SALES (est): 5.2MM **Privately Held**
WEB: www.tacind.com
SIC: 8741 2399 8331 Management services; nets, launderers & dyers; work experience center

(G-17124)
TAC INDUSTRIES INC
Also Called: Town & Country Adult Services
2160 Old Selma Rd (45505-4600)
PHONE...............................937 328-5200
W K Hoke, *Branch Mgr*
EMP: 218
SALES (corp-wide): 5.2MM **Privately Held**
WEB: www.tacind.com
SIC: 8331 Job training & vocational rehabilitation services
PA: Tac Industries, Inc.
2160 Old Selma Rd
Springfield OH 45505
937 328-5200

(G-17125)
TEREX UTILITIES INC
4401 Gateway Blvd (45502-9339)
PHONE...............................937 293-6526
EMP: 104
SALES (corp-wide): 5.1B **Publicly Held**
SIC: 7699 Aircraft & heavy equipment repair services
HQ: Terex Utilities, Inc.
12805 Sw 77th Pl
Tigard OR 97223
503 620-0611

(G-17126)
TIER ONE DISTRIBUTION LLC
Also Called: Tri State Forest Products
2105 Sheridan Ave (45505-2419)
PHONE...............................937 323-6325
Tom Berghouse, *Mng Member*
EMP: 60
SALES (est): 7MM **Privately Held**
SIC: 4731 Freight forwarding

(G-17127)
TRI-STATE FOREST PRODUCTS INC (PA)
2105 Sheridan Ave (45505-2419)
PHONE...............................937 323-6325
Tom Latham, *CEO*
Becky Siderits, *COO*
Rob Latham, *Vice Pres*
Aaron Kreinbrink, *Foreman/Supr*
Tom Berghouse, *CFO*
▲ EMP: 44
SQ FT: 68,000
SALES (est): 75.9MM **Privately Held**
WEB: www.tsfpi.com
SIC: 5031 Lumber: rough, dressed & finished

(G-17128)
TRIEC ELECTRICAL SERVICES INC
1630 Progress Rd (45505-4467)
PHONE...............................937 323-3721
Scott Yeazell, *President*
Michael Cain, *Vice Pres*
Mike Cain, *Vice Pres*
EMP: 35
SQ FT: 10,500
SALES: 6.7MM **Privately Held**
WEB: www.triec.com
SIC: 1731 General electrical contractor

(G-17129)
U S XPRESS INC
825 W Leffel Ln (45506-3535)
PHONE...............................937 328-4100
Richard Schaefer, *Branch Mgr*
EMP: 50 **Publicly Held**
SIC: 4213 Contract haulers

HQ: U. S. Xpress, Inc.
4080 Jenkins Rd
Chattanooga TN 37421
866 266-7270

(G-17130)
VICTORY LANES INC
1906 Commerce Cir (45504-2012)
PHONE...............................937 323-8684
Jim Zabakos, *President*
Ann Klein, *President*
Pearl Romanoff, *President*
Charles Kerney, *Treasurer*
EMP: 35
SQ FT: 40,000
SALES (est): 783.4K **Privately Held**
SIC: 7933 5813 Ten pin center; cocktail lounge

(G-17131)
WALLACE & TURNER INSURANCE INC
30 Warder St Ste 200 (45504-2581)
P.O. Box 209 (45501-0209)
PHONE...............................937 324-8492
Gerald Simonton, *President*
Michael Trempe, *Partner*
Patrick Field, *Principal*
David McLaughlin, *Principal*
Michelle Sweeney, *Agent*
EMP: 25
SQ FT: 6,500
SALES (est): 3.9MM **Privately Held**
WEB: www.wtins.com
SIC: 6411 Insurance agents

(G-17132)
WALLICK CONSTRUCTION CO
Also Called: Eaglewood Villa
3001 Middle Urbana Rd (45502-9284)
PHONE...............................937 399-7009
Kay Dotson, *Systems Mgr*
EMP: 27
SALES (corp-wide): 64.6MM **Privately Held**
WEB: www.eaglewoodvillage.com
SIC: 6513 8361 Retirement hotel operation; residential care
PA: Wallick Construction Co.
6880 Tussing Rd
Reynoldsburg OH 43068
614 863-4640

(G-17133)
WALMART INC
2100 N Bechtle Ave (45504-1575)
PHONE...............................937 399-0370
Heather Price, *Manager*
EMP: 200
SALES (corp-wide): 514.4B **Publicly Held**
WEB: www.walmartstores.com
SIC: 5311 5411 7231 Department stores, discount; supermarkets, hypermarket; manicurist, pedicurist
PA: Walmart Inc.
702 Sw 8th St
Bentonville AR 72716
479 273-4000

(G-17134)
WERNER ENTERPRISES INC
4395 Laybourne Rd (45505-3619)
PHONE...............................937 325-5403
Donovan Knight, *Manager*
EMP: 70
SALES (corp-wide): 2.4B **Publicly Held**
WEB: www.werner.com
SIC: 4213 Contract haulers
PA: Werner Enterprises, Inc
14507 Frontier Rd
Omaha NE 68138
402 895-6640

(G-17135)
WESTERN & SOUTHERN LF INSUR CO
30 Warder St Ste 130 (45504-2579)
PHONE...............................937 399-7696
EMP: 26 **Privately Held**
SIC: 6411 Life Insurance Agency
HQ: The Western & Southern Life Insurance Company
400 Broadway St
Cincinnati OH 45202
513 629-1800

(G-17136)
WESTFIELD STEEL INC
Also Called: Remington Steel
1120 S Burnett Rd (45505-3408)
PHONE......................................937 322-2414
Fritz Prine, *President*
Harry Osborne, *Vice Pres*
Debbie Funderburg, *Treasurer*
Myra Starr, *Human Res Mgr*
Frank Bair, *Branch Mgr*
EMP: 60
SALES (est): 11.5MM
SALES (corp-wide): 140.5MM **Privately Held**
SIC: 5051 3714 Steel; clutches, motor vehicle
PA: Westfield Steel Inc
530 W State Road 32
Westfield IN 46074
317 896-5587

(G-17137)
WOODROW MANUFACTURING CO
4300 River Rd (45502-7517)
P.O. Box 1567 (45501-1567)
PHONE......................................937 399-9333
John K Woodrow, *President*
Patrick T McAtee, *Treasurer*
EMP: 40
SQ FT: 26,000
SALES (est): 5MM **Privately Held**
WEB: www.woodrowcorp.com
SIC: 7336 3479 2752 2396 Silk screen design; etching on metals; commercial printing, lithographic; automotive & apparel trimmings

(G-17138)
WOODRUFF ENTERPRISES INC
4951 Gateway Blvd (45502-8867)
PHONE......................................937 399-9300
Todd Woodruff, *President*
Jeff Stoner, *Project Leader*
EMP: 43
SALES (est): 8.2MM **Privately Held**
WEB: www.woodruffenterprises.net
SIC: 4222 4789 Refrigerated warehousing & storage; pipeline terminal facilities, independently operated

---

Steubenville
Jefferson County

(G-17139)
ACUITY HEALTHCARE LP
Acuityhealthcare,
380 Summit Ave Fl 3 (43952-2667)
PHONE......................................740 283-7499
Judy Weaver, *CEO*
Edward Cooper, *Branch Mgr*
Tracey Cutri, *Case Mgmt Dir*
EMP: 88
SALES (corp-wide): 54.5MM **Privately Held**
SIC: 8741 8742 Hospital management; hospital & health services consultant
PA: Acuity Healthcare, Lp
10200 Mallard Creek Rd # 300
Charlotte NC 28262
877 228-4893

(G-17140)
BARRINGTON DIALYSIS LLC
Also Called: STEUBENVILLE HOME TRAINING
1799 Sinclair Ave Ste 2 (43953-3373)
P.O. Box 2037, Tacoma WA (98401-2037)
PHONE......................................740 346-2740
Bob Badal, *Principal*
EMP: 44
SALES: 1.6MM **Publicly Held**
SIC: 8092 Kidney dialysis centers
PA: Davita Inc.
2000 16th St
Denver CO 80202

(G-17141)
BLUEFOOT INDUSTRIAL LLC
Also Called: Bluefoot Energy Services
224 N 3rd St (43952-2121)
PHONE......................................740 314-5299
Clyde Larsen,

Peter Urie,
EMP: 25
SQ FT: 7,000
SALES (est): 4MM **Privately Held**
SIC: 7353 2899 7359 1623 Heavy construction equipment rental; fluxes: brazing, soldering, galvanizing & welding; industrial truck rental; oil & gas pipeline construction; crude petroleum pipelines

(G-17142)
CAPITAL HEALTH HOMECARE
201 Luray Dr 2a (43953-3973)
P.O. Box 2615, Wintersville (43953-0615)
PHONE......................................740 264-8815
Shari Jo Watkins, *Administration*
EMP: 30
SALES (est): 1.1MM **Privately Held**
SIC: 8082 Home health care services

(G-17143)
CARMIKE CINEMAS INC
100 Mall Dr Unit C20 (43952-3093)
PHONE......................................740 264-1680
Ross Paino, *Manager*
EMP: 28
SALES (corp-wide): 7.3MM **Publicly Held**
WEB: www.carmike.com
SIC: 7832 Exhibitors, itinerant: motion picture
HQ: Carmike Cinemas, Llc
11500 Ash St
Leawood KS 66211
913 213-2000

(G-17144)
CARRIAGE HOUSE ASSISTED LIVING
63102 Saint Charles Dr (43952)
PHONE......................................740 264-7667
Robert Huff, *President*
Megan Green, *Manager*
EMP: 45
SALES (est): 977.1K **Privately Held**
SIC: 8361 Residential care

(G-17145)
CARRIAGE INN OF STEUBENVILLE
3102 Saint Charles Dr (43952-3556)
PHONE......................................740 264-7161
Brad Conto, *Administration*
EMP: 130
SALES (corp-wide): 8.9MM **Privately Held**
SIC: 8051 Skilled nursing care facilities
PA: Carriage Inn Of Steubenville, Inc
5020 Philadelphia Dr C
Dayton OH 45415
740 264-7161

(G-17146)
CATHERINES CARE CENTER INC
717 N 6th Ave (43952-1832)
PHONE......................................740 282-3605
Steve Bolger, *Administration*
EMP: 65
SALES (est): 1.7MM **Privately Held**
SIC: 8051 Convalescent home with continuous nursing care

(G-17147)
CHARITY HOSPICE INC
500 Luray Dr (43953-3972)
P.O. Box 2483, Wintersville (43953-0483)
PHONE......................................740 264-2280
Cathy Marie Cich, *Owner*
Connie Robb, *Accountant*
Tiffany Hartzell, *Relations*
EMP: 25
SALES: 1.1MM **Privately Held**
SIC: 8069 Specialty hospitals, except psychiatric

(G-17148)
COLUMBIA GAS OF OHIO INC
300 Luray Dr (43953-3901)
P.O. Box 2160 (43953-0160)
PHONE......................................740 264-5577
Clair M Colburn Jr, *Branch Mgr*
EMP: 46
SALES (corp-wide): 5.1B **Publicly Held**
WEB: www.meterrepairshop.com
SIC: 4924 Natural gas distribution

HQ: Columbia Gas Of Ohio, Inc.
290 W Nationwide Blvd # 114
Columbus OH 43215
614 460-6000

(G-17149)
COMCAST CBLE CMMUNICATIONS LLC
100 Welday Ave Ste A (43953-3779)
PHONE......................................503 372-9144
Heather Cipriani, *Branch Mgr*
EMP: 101
SALES (corp-wide): 94.5B **Publicly Held**
SIC: 4841 Cable television services
HQ: Comcast Cable Communications, Llc
1701 John F Kennedy Blvd
Philadelphia PA 19103

(G-17150)
COMMUNICARE HEALTH SVCS INC
Also Called: Dixon Health Care Center
135 Reichart Ave (43953-4050)
PHONE......................................740 264-1155
James Burke, *Office Mgr*
EMP: 100
SALES (corp-wide): 125.8MM **Privately Held**
WEB: www.atriumlivingcenters.com
SIC: 8051 Skilled nursing care facilities
PA: Communicare Health Services, Inc.
4700 Ashwood Dr Ste 200
Blue Ash OH 45241
513 530-1654

(G-17151)
DIALYSIS CLINIC INC
4227 Mall Dr (43952-3011)
PHONE......................................740 264-6687
Ruth Ann Blackburn, *Manager*
EMP: 25
SALES (corp-wide): 760.1MM **Privately Held**
WEB: www.dciinc.org
SIC: 8092 Kidney dialysis centers
PA: Dialysis Clinic, Inc.
1633 Church St Ste 500
Nashville TN 37203
615 327-3061

(G-17152)
DLC TRANSPORT INC
320 N 5th St (43952-2016)
PHONE......................................740 282-1763
Donna Colalella, *President*
EMP: 40
SQ FT: 43,000
SALES: 2.3MM **Privately Held**
SIC: 4213 Contract haulers

(G-17153)
FAYETTE PARTS SERVICE INC
1512 Sunset Blvd (43952-1303)
PHONE......................................740 282-4547
EMP: 138
SALES (corp-wide): 58MM **Privately Held**
SIC: 5013 Automotive supplies & parts
PA: Fayette Parts Service, Inc.
325 E Main St
Uniontown PA
724 785-2506

(G-17154)
FEDEX GROUND PACKAGE SYS INC
103 Anart St (43953-7262)
PHONE......................................412 859-2653
EMP: 152
SALES (corp-wide): 47.4B **Publicly Held**
SIC: 4212 Local Trucking Operator
HQ: Fedex Ground Package System, Inc.
1000 Fed Ex Dr
Coraopolis PA 15108
412 269-1000

(G-17155)
GOODMAN PROPERTIES INC
Also Called: Fort Steuben Mall
100 Mall Dr Ofc Ofc (43952-3012)
PHONE......................................740 264-7781
Michael Glenn, *Manager*
EMP: 25

SALES (corp-wide): 12.1MM **Privately Held**
WEB: www.ftsteubenmall.com
SIC: 6552 6512 Land subdividers & developers, commercial; shopping center, property operation only
PA: Goodman Properties, Inc.
777 S Flagler Dr Ste 136
West Palm Beach FL 33401
561 833-3777

(G-17156)
GPC CONTRACTING COMPANY
500 E Church St Ste 3 (43953-3701)
P.O. Box 4372 (43952-8372)
PHONE......................................740 264-6060
Gary E Speece Sr, *President*
EMP: 30 EST: 2009
SALES (est): 339K **Privately Held**
SIC: 1721 Industrial painting

(G-17157)
GRAE-CON CONSTRUCTION INC (PA)
Also Called: Grae-Con Contructions
880 Kingsdale Rd (43952-4361)
P.O. Box 1778 (43952-7778)
PHONE......................................740 282-6830
Robert A Gribben Jr, *President*
Shirley Gribben, *Corp Secy*
Robert A Gribben III, *Vice Pres*
John A Humpe III, *Vice Pres*
Jeremy Benton, *Buyer*
EMP: 80
SQ FT: 23,000
SALES (est): 39.1MM **Privately Held**
WEB: www.graecon.com
SIC: 1542 Commercial & office building, new construction; commercial & office buildings, renovation & repair

(G-17158)
JEFFERSON BEHAVIORAL HLTH SYS (PA)
1 Ross Park Blvd Ste 201 (43952-2671)
PHONE......................................740 264-7751
Anthony Sheposh, *CEO*
EMP: 115 **EST:** 1988
SQ FT: 60,000
SALES: 4.2MM **Privately Held**
WEB: www.jbhsorg.com
SIC: 8621 Health association

(G-17159)
JEFFERSON CNTY CMMNTY ACTION (PA)
114 N 4th St (43952-2132)
PHONE......................................740 282-0971
Barbara West, *Exec Dir*
EMP: 160
SALES: 4MM **Privately Held**
WEB: www.co.jefferson.wa.us
SIC: 8399 9111 Community action agency; county supervisors' & executives' offices

(G-17160)
JEFFERSON INVSTGTORS SCURITIES
1439 Sunset Blvd (43952-1521)
PHONE......................................740 283-3681
Robert J D'Anniballe, *President*
Robert Herceg, *Manager*
EMP: 60
SALES (est): 1.1MM **Privately Held**
WEB: www.danniballe.com
SIC: 7381 Private investigator; security guard service

(G-17161)
LABELLE NEWS AGENCY INC
814 University Blvd (43952-1794)
PHONE......................................740 282-9731
Thomas Pentes, *President*
Arthur D'Anniballe, *Treasurer*
Andy Pentes, *Admin Sec*
EMP: 25
SQ FT: 17,200
SALES (est): 4.4MM **Privately Held**
WEB: www.labellenews.com
SIC: 5199 Anatomical specimens & research material

(G-17162)
LANCIA NURSING HOME INC (PA)
Also Called: Lancia Villa Royal
1852 Sinclair Ave (43953-3328)
PHONE..................................740 264-7101
Joseph Lancia, *President*
Linda Lancia, *Vice Pres*
EMP: 40
SQ FT: 5,000
SALES: 3.8MM **Privately Held**
SIC: 8051 Skilled nursing care facilities

(G-17163)
LAUREL HEALTH CARE COMPANY
Also Called: Laurels of Steubenville, The
500 Stanton Blvd (43952-3706)
PHONE..................................740 264-5042
Steve Welhorsky, *Branch Mgr*
Paul Desarro, *Director*
Jamie Maley, *Food Svc Dir*
EMP: 100 **Privately Held**
SIC: 8051 Skilled nursing care facilities
HQ: Laurel Health Care Company
8181 Worthington Rd Uppr
Westerville OH 43082

(G-17164)
LOWES HOME CENTERS LLC
4115 Mall Dr (43952-3007)
PHONE..................................740 266-3500
Kevin Santon, *General Mgr*
EMP: 180
SALES (corp-wide): 68.6B **Publicly Held**
SIC: 5211 5031 5722 5064 Home centers; building materials, exterior; building materials, interior; household appliance stores; electrical appliances, television & radio
HQ: Lowe's Home Centers, Llc
1605 Curtis Bridge Rd
Wilkesboro NC 28697
336 658-4000

(G-17165)
MEDI HOME HEALTH AGENCY INC (HQ)
Also Called: Medi-Home Care
105 Main St (43953-3733)
PHONE..................................740 266-3977
Ronnie L Young, *President*
James Hardman, *Vice Pres*
John Keim, *CFO*
Mary Craver, *Director*
Ciji Johnson, *Admin Asst*
EMP: 50
SALES (est): 6.3MM
SALES (corp-wide): 180.5MM **Privately Held**
SIC: 8082 7361 5169 Home health care services; nurses' registry; oxygen
PA: Medical Services Of America, Inc.
171 Monroe Ln
Lexington SC 29072
803 957-0500

(G-17166)
MEDICAL GROUP ASSOCIATES INC
114 Brady Cir E (43952-1478)
PHONE..................................740 283-4773
Stephen G Kuruc, *President*
EMP: 29
SQ FT: 16,400
SALES (est): 1.5MM **Privately Held**
SIC: 8011 Physicians' office, including specialists; gastronomist; hematologist; oncologist

(G-17167)
MOUGIANIS INDUSTRIES INC
Also Called: Alexander Great Distributing
1626 Cadiz Rd (43953-7630)
P.O. Box 2100 (43953-0100)
PHONE..................................740 264-6372
Anthony N Mougianis, *President*
EMP: 60
SQ FT: 8,000
SALES (est): 2.6MM **Privately Held**
SIC: 7349 5087 Janitorial service, contract basis; cleaning & maintenance equipment & supplies

(G-17168)
NATIONAL COLLOID COMPANY
906 Adams St (43952-2709)
P.O. Box 309 (43952-5309)
PHONE..................................740 282-1171
Michael Barber Jr, *President*
▲ EMP: 25 EST: 1938
SQ FT: 45,000
SALES (est): 11.9MM **Privately Held**
WEB: www.natcoll.com
SIC: 2869 5169 2899 2842 Industrial organic chemicals; caustic soda; calcium chloride; chemical preparations; specialty cleaning, polishes & sanitation goods; industrial inorganic chemicals; alkalies & chlorine

(G-17169)
PHILIP ICUSS JR
Also Called: Legal Hair and Day Spa
2311 Sunset Blvd (43952-2433)
PHONE..................................740 264-4647
Philip Icuss Jr, *Partner*
EMP: 40
SQ FT: 6,000
SALES (est): 841.3K **Privately Held**
SIC: 7231 Hairdressers

(G-17170)
STATE PARK MOTORS INC
766 Canton Rd (43953-4108)
P.O. Box 2328 (43953-0328)
PHONE..................................740 264-3113
Sam Davis, *President*
Willard L Davis, *Vice Pres*
Norman Davis, *Treasurer*
EMP: 25
SALES (est): 6MM **Privately Held**
WEB: www.stateparkmotors.com
SIC: 5012 Vans, commercial; automotive brokers

(G-17171)
STEUBENVILLE COUNTRY CLB MANOR
575 Lovers Ln (43953-3311)
PHONE..................................740 266-6118
James Bolger, *President*
Rena Bolger, *Vice Pres*
Denise Boyle, *Treasurer*
Becky Aceto, *Director*
Stephen Bolger, *Admin Sec*
EMP: 70
SALES (est): 2.9MM **Privately Held**
WEB: www.bolgerhealthcare.com
SIC: 8059 Nursing home, except skilled & intermediate care facility

(G-17172)
STEUBENVILLE COUNTRY CLUB INC
413 Lovers Ln (43953-3309)
PHONE..................................740 264-0521
Robert Chapman, *President*
Anthony Sheposh, *Vice Pres*
EMP: 75
SQ FT: 5,000
SALES: 2MM **Privately Held**
WEB: www.steubenvillecountryclub.com
SIC: 7997 Country club, membership

(G-17173)
STEUBENVILLE TRUCK CENTER INC
620 South St (43952-2802)
P.O. Box 1741 (43952-7741)
PHONE..................................740 282-2711
Larry A Remp, *President*
Mary Stead, *Corp Secy*
Marney Remp, *Vice Pres*
EMP: 25
SQ FT: 7,500
SALES (est): 5.7MM **Privately Held**
WEB: www.ohiovolvo.com
SIC: 7538 5511 7692 Truck engine repair, except industrial; trucks, tractors & trailers: new & used; welding repair

(G-17174)
TIDEWATER RIVER RAIL OPER LLC
440 S 3rd St (43952-2903)
PHONE..................................817 659-0091
Scott Prince, *CEO*
Scott Spence, *COO*

Rob Crawley, *CFO*
EMP: 90
SALES: 5MM **Privately Held**
SIC: 4491 4013 Marine terminals; railroad terminals

(G-17175)
TRANSMERICA SVCS TECHNICAL SUP
Also Called: Hanna Chevrolet Cadillac
4404 Scioto Dr (43953-3320)
P.O. Box 38 (43952-5038)
PHONE..................................740 282-3695
Makram A Hanna, *President*
Doreen M Deleonardis, *Principal*
D A Frazee, *Principal*
Peter S Olivito, *Principal*
Mary Hanna, *Corp Secy*
EMP: 28
SQ FT: 15,000
SALES (est): 5.5MM **Privately Held**
SIC: 5511 4212 Automobiles, new & used; local trucking, without storage

(G-17176)
TRINITY HEALTH SYSTEM
Also Called: Radiology Department
380 Summit Ave (43952-2667)
PHONE..................................740 283-7848
Fred Bowers, *President*
EMP: 219 **Privately Held**
SIC: 8741 Hospital management; nursing & personal care facility management
HQ: Trinity Health System
380 Summit Ave
Steubenville OH 43952

(G-17177)
TRINITY HEALTH SYSTEM
Also Called: Trinity Health West
4000 Johnson Rd Fl 1 (43952-2300)
PHONE..................................740 264-8000
Fred Brower, *President*
Nutan Shah, *Anesthesiology*
EMP: 625 **Privately Held**
SIC: 8741 8062 Hospital management; general medical & surgical hospitals
HQ: Trinity Health System
380 Summit Ave
Steubenville OH 43952

(G-17178)
TRINITY HEALTH SYSTEM
Also Called: Medical Records
4000 Johnson Rd Fl 1 (43952-2300)
PHONE..................................740 264-8101
Kim Dudich, *Manager*
EMP: 30 **Privately Held**
SIC: 8741 8062 Hospital management; general medical & surgical hospitals
HQ: Trinity Health System
380 Summit Ave
Steubenville OH 43952

(G-17179)
TRINITY HEALTH SYSTEM (DH)
Also Called: Trinity Medical Center East
380 Summit Ave (43952-2667)
PHONE..................................740 283-7000
Fred Brower, *CEO*
Elizabeth Allen, *CFO*
Janet Gratzmiller, *Admin Sec*
Erin Mulrooney, *Recruiter*
EMP: 300
SQ FT: 1,004,854
SALES: 256MM **Privately Held**
SIC: 8062 8011 General medical & surgical hospitals; hospital, AMA approved residency; offices & clinics of medical doctors
HQ: Sylvania Franciscan Health
1715 Indian Wood Cir # 200
Maumee OH 43537
419 882-8373

(G-17180)
TRINITY HOSPITAL HOLDING CO (DH)
Also Called: Trinity Medical Center East
380 Summit Ave (43952-2667)
PHONE..................................740 264-8000
Clyde Metzger MD, *Ch of Bd*
Fred B Bower, *President*
Albert Pavlik, *Admin Sec*
EMP: 600

SALES: 231.4MM **Privately Held**
SIC: 8062 8741 General medical & surgical hospitals; management services

(G-17181)
TRINITY WEST
4000 Johnson Rd Fl 1 (43952-2300)
PHONE..................................740 264-8000
Fred B Brower, *President*
EMP: 1640
SQ FT: 600,000
SALES (est): 69.8MM **Privately Held**
SIC: 8062 General medical & surgical hospitals
HQ: Trinity Hospital Holding Company
380 Summit Ave
Steubenville OH 43952
740 264-8000

(G-17182)
TRUEBLUE INC
Also Called: Labor Ready
2125 Sunset Blvd (43952-2469)
PHONE..................................740 282-1079
Jason Callihan, *Manager*
EMP: 26
SALES (corp-wide): 2.5B **Publicly Held**
WEB: www.laborready.com
SIC: 7363 Temporary help service
PA: Trueblue, Inc.
1015 A St
Tacoma WA 98402
253 383-9101

Stockport
Morgan County

(G-17183)
STOCKPORT MILL COUNTRY INN INC
Also Called: Restaurant On The Dam
1995 Broadway St (43787-9120)
PHONE..................................740 559-2822
Toll Free:..................................877 -
Laura Smith, *President*
Randy Smith, *Vice Pres*
EMP: 40
SALES (est): 1.2MM **Privately Held**
SIC: 7011 5812 7999 4931 Inns; American restaurant; beach & water sports equipment rental & services; electric & other services combined

---

Stony Ridge
Wood County

(G-17184)
JTI TRANSPORTATION INC
5601 Cherry St (43463)
P.O. Box 187 (43463-0187)
PHONE..................................419 661-9360
Jim Jacobs, *Principal*
EMP: 40
SALES (est): 621.6K **Privately Held**
SIC: 4789 Transportation services

(G-17185)
NOLLENBERGER TRUCK CENTER (PA)
5320 Fremont Pike (43463)
PHONE..................................419 837-5996
Virginia M Nollenberger, *President*
George Mitchell, *Vice Pres*
Krystal Shubarga, *Admin Sec*
EMP: 41
SQ FT: 10,000
SALES (est): 6.3MM **Privately Held**
WEB: www.inttrucks.com
SIC: 5012 5511 Trucks, commercial; new & used car dealers

Stoutsville
Fairfield County

(G-17186)
CLEARCREEK CONSTRUCTION
11050 16th Rd Sw (43154-9592)
PHONE..................................740 420-3568

John E Hite, *Owner*
Melisa Hite, *Co-Owner*
EMP: 25
SQ FT: 7,000
SALES (est): 3.3MM **Privately Held**
SIC: 1711 Mechanical contractor

Stow
Summit County

(G-17187)
ACRT INC (PA)
4500 Courthouse Blvd # 150 (44224-6837)
PHONE..............................800 622-2562
Michael Weidner, *CEO*
Todd Jones, *Vice Pres*
Cliff Benedict, *Opers Mgr*
David Burke, *Opers Mgr*
Derrick Caringi, *Opers Mgr*
EMP: 35
SALES: 68MM **Privately Held**
WEB: www.acrtinc.com
SIC: 8748 Environmental consultant

(G-17188)
ACRT SERVICES INC
4500 Courthouse Blvd # 150 (44224-6837)
PHONE..............................330 945-7500
Michael Weidner, *President*
Linda Zaremski, *Accountant*
EMP: 1100
SALES: 80MM **Privately Held**
SIC: 8748 Business consulting

(G-17189)
AKRON METROPOLITAN HSING AUTH
500 Hardman Dr (44224-4883)
PHONE..............................330 920-1652
EMP: 149 **Privately Held**
SIC: 9531 8211 7299 6513 Housing authority, non-operating: government; kindergarten; apartment locating service; apartment building operators
PA: Akron Metropolitan Housing Authority
100 W Cedar St Ste 100 # 100
Akron OH 44307
330 762-9631

(G-17190)
ALL AROUND CHILDREN MONTESSORI
Also Called: Stow Montessori Center
4117 Bridgewater Pkwy (44224-6191)
PHONE..............................330 928-1444
Joan Wenk, *Owner*
Ashley Peterson, *Director*
EMP: 25
SALES (est): 450K **Privately Held**
WEB: www.creativeplayrooms.com
SIC: 8351 Montessori child development center

(G-17191)
AUDIO-TECHNICA US INC (HQ)
1221 Commerce Dr (44224-1760)
PHONE..............................330 686-2600
K Matsushita, *Ch of Bd*
Philip Cajka, *President*
Marc Lee Shannon, *Vice Pres*
Richard Sprunlgle, *Vice Pres*
▲ **EMP:** 77
SQ FT: 70,000
SALES (est): 71.2MM
SALES (corp-wide): 290.5MM **Privately Held**
WEB: www.atus.com
SIC: 5065 5731 Sound equipment, electronic; consumer electronic equipment
PA: Audio-Technica Corporation
2-46-1, Nishinaruse
Machida TKY 194-0
427 399-111

(G-17192)
BERMEX INC
4500 Courthouse Blvd # 150 (44224-6837)
PHONE..............................330 945-7500
Todd Jones, *President*
David Mack, *Manager*
EMP: 271

SALES: 12.3MM
SALES (corp-wide): 68MM **Privately Held**
SIC: 7389 Meter readers, remote
PA: Acrt, Inc.
4500 Courthouse Blvd # 150
Stow OH 44224
800 622-2562

(G-17193)
BRIARWOOD LTD
Also Called: Briarwood Healthcare Center
3700 Englewood Dr (44224-3223)
PHONE..............................330 688-1828
John Trimble, *Partner*
Dana Dixon, *Human Res Mgr*
Bryan Baker, *Director*
Melissa Frankish, *Social Dir*
EMP: 100
SQ FT: 37,000
SALES (est): 6.2MM **Privately Held**
SIC: 8059 8051 Rest home, with health care; convalescent home with continuous nursing care

(G-17194)
CENTIMARK CORPORATION
Also Called: Questmark
4665 Allen Rd Ste C (44224-1055)
PHONE..............................330 920-3560
EMP: 120
SALES (corp-wide): 540.7MM **Privately Held**
SIC: 1761 1752 Roofing/Siding Contractor
Floor Laying Contractor
PA: Centimark Corporation
12 Grandview Cir
Canonsburg PA 15317
724 743-7777

(G-17195)
CHEMIMAGE FILTER TECH LLC
1100 Campus Dr Ste 500 (44224-1767)
PHONE..............................330 686-2829
George Ventouris, *Principal*
EMP: 47
SALES (corp-wide): 4.6MM **Privately Held**
SIC: 8731 Commercial physical research
PA: Chemimage Filter Technologies, Llc
7301 Penn Ave
Pittsburgh PA 15208
412 241-7335

(G-17196)
CUSTOM MOVERS SERVICES INC
Also Called: CMS
3290 Kent Rd (44224-4512)
PHONE..............................330 564-0507
Dean Barker, *President*
EMP: 30
SALES (est): 2.8MM **Privately Held**
WEB: www.custommoversservices.com
SIC: 4212 Moving services

(G-17197)
CUTLER AND ASSOCIATES INC
3653 Darrow Rd Ste 1 (44224-4012)
PHONE..............................330 688-2100
June Harvey, *Manager*
EMP: 35
SALES (corp-wide): 8.4MM **Privately Held**
WEB: www.cutlerhomes.com
SIC: 6531 Real estate agents & managers
PA: Cutler And Associates, Inc
4618 Dressler Rd Nw
Canton OH 44718
330 493-9323

(G-17198)
CUTLER REAL ESTATE
3653 Darrow Rd (44224-4012)
PHONE..............................330 688-2100
Shirley Chimento, *Manager*
EMP: 35 **Privately Held**
SIC: 6531 Real estate brokers & agents
PA: Cutler Real Estate
4618 Dressler Rd Nw
Canton OH 44718

(G-17199)
DAVEY TREE EXPERT COMPANY
Also Called: Davey Tree & Lawn Care
4576 Allen Rd (44224-1036)
PHONE..............................330 928-4911
Scott Heim, *Manager*
EMP: 25
SALES (corp-wide): 1B **Privately Held**
SIC: 0782 0783 Lawn services; ornamental shrub & tree services
PA: The Davey Tree Expert Company
1500 N Mantua St
Kent OH 44240
330 673-9511

(G-17200)
ELECTRONIC PRINTING PDTS INC
Also Called: Laser Label Technologies
4560 Darrow Rd (44224-1888)
PHONE..............................330 689-3930
James Peruzzi, *President*
Jerry S Krempa, *President*
Sheri H Edison, *Vice Pres*
Ted F Unton, *Treasurer*
James W Ransom, *Director*
EMP: 32
SQ FT: 30,000
SALES: 12MM
SALES (corp-wide): 2.3B **Privately Held**
WEB: www.lltproducts.com
SIC: 5131 5112 Labels; laserjet supplies
HQ: Morgan Adhesives Company, Llc
4560 Darrow Rd
Stow OH 44224
330 688-1111

(G-17201)
EMERITUS CORPORATION
Also Called: Emeritus At Stow
5511 Fishcreek Rd (44224-1435)
PHONE..............................330 342-0934
Kelli Phillips, *Branch Mgr*
EMP: 44
SALES (corp-wide): 4.5B **Publicly Held**
SIC: 8052 Personal care facility
HQ: Emeritus Corporation
3131 Elliott Ave Ste 500
Milwaukee WI 53214

(G-17202)
ENVIROSCIENCE INC (PA)
5070 Stow Rd (44224-1530)
PHONE..............................330 688-0111
Daniel G Dunstan, *CEO*
Martin A Hilovsky, *President*
James Krejsa, *Vice Pres*
Gregory F Zimmerman, *Vice Pres*
Brian Burkhardt, *Director*
EMP: 110
SQ FT: 24,000
SALES (est): 23.2MM **Privately Held**
WEB: www.enviroscienceinc.com
SIC: 8734 8748 Water testing laboratory; business consulting

(G-17203)
EVANT (PA)
1221 Commerce Dr (44224-1744)
PHONE..............................330 920-1517
Renee Richardson, *Human Res Dir*
Peter Spadafino, *Sales Executive*
Gene Woodling, *Manager*
Sherry D Gedeon, *Exec Dir*
Karen Deem, *Associate*
EMP: 36
SALES: 4.3MM **Privately Held**
WEB: www.evant.com
SIC: 8361 Home for the mentally handicapped

(G-17204)
FISH CREEK PLAZA LTD
Also Called: Lawrence Saltis Plaza
3000 Graham Rd Unit Ofc (44224-3623)
PHONE..............................330 688-0450
Walter Grund, *Partner*
Jennifer Hardee, *Principal*
Leeann Morein, *Principal*
EMP: 99
SALES (est): 3.4MM **Privately Held**
SIC: 6513 Apartment building operators

(G-17205)
FITWORKS HOLDING LLC
4301 Kent Rd Ste 26 (44224-4364)
PHONE..............................330 688-2329
Chuck Ortiz, *Manager*
EMP: 32 **Privately Held**
SIC: 7991 Health club
PA: Fitworks Holding, Llc
849 Brainard Rd
Cleveland OH 44143

(G-17206)
FOX DEN FAIRWAYS INC
Also Called: Fox Den Golf Course
2770 Call Rd (44224-1510)
PHONE..............................330 678-6792
Herb Rake, *President*
Dennis Whalen, *President*
Jay Drennan, *Vice Pres*
Tom Mc Kinney, *Manager*
Mark Paxton, *Asst Mgr*
EMP: 46
SQ FT: 3,500
SALES (est): 1.2MM **Privately Held**
WEB: www.foxdengolf.com
SIC: 7992 5812 5941 Public golf courses; eating places; golf goods & equipment

(G-17207)
FUTURE ADVANTAGE INC
Also Called: Kids Country
4923 Hudson Dr (44224-1726)
PHONE..............................330 686-7707
Chris Burkholder, *President*
EMP: 35
SALES (est): 666.6K **Privately Held**
WEB: www.futureadvantage.com
SIC: 8351 Group day care center

(G-17208)
GENEVA CHERVENIC REALTY INC
3589 Darrow Rd (44224-4000)
PHONE..............................330 686-8400
David Chervenic, *President*
EMP: 65
SQ FT: 2,500
SALES (est): 4.9MM **Privately Held**
WEB: www.chervenicrealty.com
SIC: 6531 Real estate agent, residential

(G-17209)
HOBBY LOBBY STORES INC
4332 Kent Rd Ste 3 (44224-4394)
PHONE..............................330 686-1508
EMP: 30
SALES (corp-wide): 4.5B **Privately Held**
SIC: 5945 5023 Arts & crafts supplies; frames & framing, picture & mirror
PA: Hobby Lobby Stores, Inc.
7707 Sw 44th St
Oklahoma City OK 73179
405 745-1100

(G-17210)
HOPE HOMES INC
2044 Bryn Mawr Dr (44224-2616)
PHONE..............................330 688-4935
Dayna Worthy, *Branch Mgr*
EMP: 35
SALES (corp-wide): 2MM **Privately Held**
SIC: 8082 Home health care services
PA: Hope Homes, Inc
2300 Call Rd
Stow OH 44224
330 686-5342

(G-17211)
HOTEL STOW LP
Also Called: Courtyard By Marriott
4047 Bridgewater Pkwy (44224-6306)
PHONE..............................330 945-9722
Jason Jackson, *General Mgr*
EMP: 25
SALES (est): 1.3MM **Privately Held**
SIC: 7011 Hotels & motels

(G-17212)
HOWARD HANNA SMYTHE CRAMER
3925 Darrow Rd Ste 101 (44224-2600)
PHONE..............................330 686-1166
Julie Domenick, *Manager*
EMP: 50

GEOGRAPHIC

SALES (corp-wide): 73.7MM **Privately Held**
WEB: www.smythecramer.com
SIC: 6531 Real estate brokers & agents
HQ: Howard Hanna Smythe Cramer
　6000 Parkland Blvd
　Cleveland OH 44124
　216 447-4477

(G-17213)
INSTANTWHIP FOODS INC
4870 Hudson Dr (44224-1708)
PHONE..............................330 688-8825
Dave Owen, *Manager*
EMP: 35
SQ FT: 16,905
SALES (corp-wide): 47.5MM **Privately Held**
WEB: www.instantwhip.com
SIC: 5143 5142 Dairy products, except dried or canned; packaged frozen goods
PA: Instantwhip Foods, Inc.
　2200 Cardigan Ave
　Columbus OH 43215
　614 488-2536

(G-17214)
INSTANTWHIP-AKRON INC
4870 Hudson Dr (44224-1708)
PHONE..............................614 488-2536
Fred Smith, *President*
G Frederick Smith, *President*
Kevin Sheaffer, *General Mgr*
Thomas Michaelides, *Treasurer*
Michael Bennett, *Manager*
EMP: 40
SALES (est): 14.3MM **Privately Held**
SIC: 5143 Milk & cream, fluid

(G-17215)
KELLER WILLIAMS RLTY M WALKER
3589 Darrow Rd (44224-4008)
PHONE..............................330 571-2020
Latonya Keths, *Principal*
Jana Chervenic, *Real Est Agnt*
Barbara Simkoff, *Real Est Agnt*
EMP: 45 EST: 2011
SALES (est): 1.4MM **Privately Held**
SIC: 6531 Real estate agent, residential

(G-17216)
LABORATORY CORPORATION AMERICA
4482 Darrow Rd (44224-1885)
PHONE..............................330 686-0194
Advancecom Technolog, *Branch Mgr*
EMP: 25 **Publicly Held**
WEB: www.labcorp.com
SIC: 8071 Testing laboratories
HQ: Laboratory Corporation Of America
　358 S Main St Ste 458
　Burlington NC 27215
　336 229-1127

(G-17217)
LAW OFFICES OF JOHN D CLUNK C
4500 Courthouse Blvd # 400 (44224-6839)
PHONE..............................330 436-0300
John D Clunk, *Owner*
EMP: 55 EST: 1999
SALES (est): 6.6MM **Privately Held**
WEB: www.johndclunk.com
SIC: 8111 Bankruptcy law

(G-17218)
LOWES HOME CENTERS LLC
3570 Hudson Dr (44224-2907)
PHONE..............................330 920-9280
EMP: 150
SQ FT: 134,995
SALES (corp-wide): 68.6B **Publicly Held**
SIC: 5211 5031 5722 5064 Home centers; building materials, exterior; building materials, interior; household appliance stores; electrical appliances, television & radio
HQ: Lowe's Home Centers, Llc
　1605 Curtis Bridge Rd
　Wilkesboro NC 28697
　336 658-4000

(G-17219)
MATCO TOOLS CORPORATION (HQ)
Also Called: Nmtc, Inc.
4403 Allen Rd (44224-1096)
P.O. Box 1429 (44224-0429)
PHONE..............................330 929-4949
Timothy J Gilmore, *President*
Rich McKenna, *Regional Mgr*
Mike McCaleb, *District Mgr*
Brian Rose, *District Mgr*
Kelly Smith, *District Mgr*
▲ EMP: 400
SALES (est): 150.6MM
SALES (corp-wide): 6.4B **Publicly Held**
WEB: www.matcotools.com
SIC: 5251 5072 3469 3423 Hardware; hardware; metal stampings; hand & edge tools; tools & equipment, automotive
PA: Fortive Corporation
　6920 Seaway Blvd
　Everett WA 98203
　425 446-5000

(G-17220)
MOISTURE GUARD CORPORATION
4370 Allen Rd (44224-1032)
PHONE..............................330 928-7200
Matthew Kuhn, *President*
Nancy J Kuhn, *Vice Pres*
Rick Hein, *Project Mgr*
EMP: 30
SQ FT: 3,000
SALES (est): 3.5MM **Privately Held**
WEB: www.moisture-guard.com
SIC: 1761 Roofing contractor

(G-17221)
OMEGA TITLE AGENCY LLC
4500 Courthouse Blvd # 100 (44224-6835)
PHONE..............................330 436-0600
Kimberly Clunk,
EMP: 53
SALES (est): 14.7MM **Privately Held**
SIC: 6361 Title insurance

(G-17222)
OSMANS PIES INC
3678 Elm Rd (44224-3954)
PHONE..............................330 607-9083
Ethel Osman, *President*
Terry Osman, *Vice Pres*
Cheryl Osman Crowe, *Admin Sec*
EMP: 30
SQ FT: 3,500
SALES (est): 600K **Privately Held**
SIC: 5461 5149 2052 2051 Bakeries; bakery products; cookies & crackers; bread, cake & related products

(G-17223)
P3 INFRASTRUCTURE INC
3105 Preakness Dr (44224-6243)
PHONE..............................330 686-1129
Puneet Singh, *Principal*
EMP: 1811
SALES (est): 38.4MM **Privately Held**
SIC: 7389

(G-17224)
PRECISION ENDOSCOPY AMER INC (PA)
4575 Hudson Dr (44224-1725)
PHONE..............................410 527-9598
John Thormann, *CEO*
Christian Mills, *President*
Ted Honeywell, *Vice Pres*
EMP: 30
SQ FT: 13,000
SALES (est): 2MM **Privately Held**
SIC: 7699 Medical equipment repair, non-electric

(G-17225)
PRUSA INC
Also Called: Lawnmark
1049 Mccauley Rd (44224-1009)
PHONE..............................330 688-8500
John Prusa, *President*
EMP: 43
SALES (est): 6.5MM **Privately Held**
SIC: 0782 Lawn care services

(G-17226)
QUALITY CLEANERS OF OHIO INC
3773 Darrow Rd (44224-4035)
PHONE..............................330 688-5616
James Croyle, *President*
EMP: 40
SQ FT: 8,300
SALES (est): 1MM **Privately Held**
SIC: 7216 7219 Drycleaning plants, except rugs; garment alteration & repair shop

(G-17227)
ROCE GROUP LLC
Also Called: Fairfield Inn
4170 Steels Pointe (44224-6808)
PHONE..............................330 969-2627
Bharat Patel, *Manager*
Arvind Patel,
Kishore Patel,
Leena Patel,
EMP: 30 EST: 2015
SQ FT: 49,043
SALES (est): 268.6K **Privately Held**
SIC: 7011 Hotels & motels

(G-17228)
RON MARHOFER COLLISION CENTER
1585 Commerce Dr (44224-1711)
PHONE..............................330 686-2262
Ron Marhofer, *CEO*
EMP: 30
SALES (est): 966.9K **Privately Held**
SIC: 7532 Body shop, automotive

(G-17229)
SERVICE KING HOLDINGS LLC
Also Called: Service King Cllision Repr Ctr
26 E Steels Corners Rd (44224-4918)
PHONE..............................330 926-0100
EMP: 50
SALES (corp-wide): 347.9MM **Privately Held**
SIC: 7532 Antique & classic automobile restoration
PA: Service King Holdings, Llc
　2375 N Glenville Dr
　Richardson TX 75082
　972 960-7595

(G-17230)
SHOTSTOP BALLISTICS LLC
4319 Lorwood Dr Ste 102 (44224-2734)
P.O. Box 1393 (44224-0393)
PHONE..............................330 686-0020
Pepa Iliev, *Vice Pres*
Vall Iliev,
EMP: 26
SALES (est): 330.8K **Privately Held**
SIC: 8742 8748 8711 7389 Management engineering; systems engineering consultant, ex. computer or professional; mechanical engineering;

(G-17231)
STOW DENTAL GROUP INC
Also Called: Schlosser, David W DDS
3506 Darrow Rd (44224-4098)
PHONE..............................330 688-6456
David Wiedie DDS, *President*
Dr Mark Iati, *Vice Pres*
Dr Eric Schikowski, *Vice Pres*
Dr David Scholsser, *Treasurer*
Dr Kenneth Sladky, *Admin Sec*
EMP: 39
SQ FT: 3,500
SALES (est): 3.7MM **Privately Held**
SIC: 8021 Dental clinic

(G-17232)
STOW OPCO LLC
Also Called: Arbors At Stow
2910 Lermitage Pl (44224-5219)
PHONE..............................502 429-8062
Robert Norcross, *CEO*
Tracey Cugini, *Hlthcr Dir*
Lisa Chester, *Executive*
Kimberly Joye, *Administration*
EMP: 99
SQ FT: 60,000
SALES (est): 1.7MM **Privately Held**
SIC: 8051 Skilled nursing care facilities

(G-17233)
STRUKTOL COMPANY AMERICA LLC (HQ)
201 E Steels Corners Rd (44224-4921)
P.O. Box 1649 (44224-0649)
PHONE..............................330 928-5188
Gilbret Hamrick, *President*
Rita Robinette, *Business Mgr*
Michael Bergfield, *Mfg Mgr*
Mike Irby, *Purchasing*
Peter Blohm, *VP Finance*
◆ EMP: 105 EST: 1977
SQ FT: 60,000
SALES (est): 88.8MM
SALES (corp-wide): 173.5MM **Privately Held**
WEB: www.struktol.com
SIC: 5169 Chemicals & allied products
PA: Schill + Seilacher "struktol" Gmbh
　Moorfleeter Str. 28
　Hamburg 22113
　407 336-20

(G-17234)
SUMMA HEALTH
Also Called: Lab Care
3869 Darrow Rd Ste 208 (44224-2677)
PHONE..............................330 688-4531
Carla Davenport, *Branch Mgr*
EMP: 45
SALES (corp-wide): 1B **Privately Held**
WEB: www.barbhosp.com
SIC: 8062 8071 General medical & surgical hospitals; medical laboratories
PA: Summa Health
　525 E Market St
　Akron OH 44304
　330 375-3000

(G-17235)
TERSIGNI CARGILL ENTPS LLC
Also Called: Amber Gardens
4315 Hudson Dr (44224-2216)
PHONE..............................330 351-0942
Michael J Tercini,
Kurt Cargill,
EMP: 35
SQ FT: 8,000
SALES: 1.7MM **Privately Held**
WEB: www.ambergardens.com
SIC: 5261 0782 Lawn & garden supplies; lawn services

(G-17236)
TRAXIUM LLC
Also Called: Printing Concepts
4246 Hudson Dr (44224-2251)
PHONE..............................330 572-8200
George Schmutz, *President*
EMP: 49
SQ FT: 45,000
SALES (est): 7.3MM **Privately Held**
WEB: www.printingconcepts.com
SIC: 2759 2752 7331 2789 Letterpress printing; commercial printing, offset; direct mail advertising services; bookbinding & related work

(G-17237)
TWIN PINES RETREAT CARE CENTER
456 Seasons Rd (44224-1020)
PHONE..............................330 688-5553
Scott Phillips, *President*
EMP: 47
SQ FT: 13,500
SALES (est): 1.8MM **Privately Held**
WEB: www.twinpinesretreatcarecenter.cc
SIC: 8052 Intermediate care facilities

(G-17238)
VIZMEG LANDSCAPE INC
778 Mccauley Rd Unit 100 (44224-1067)
PHONE..............................330 686-0901
George Vizmeg, *Principal*
EMP: 25
SALES (est): 4.3MM **Privately Held**
WEB: www.vizmeglandscape.com
SIC: 0782 Landscape contractors

▲ = Import ▼=Export
◆ =Import/Export

(G-17239)
WHEATON & SPRAGUE ENGINEERING (PA)
Also Called: Wheaton Sprague Bldg Envelope
1151 Campus Dr Ste 100 (44224-1762)
PHONE................................330 923-5560
John L Wheaton, *President*
Richard Sprague, *Vice Pres*
EMP: 28
SQ FT: 3,000
SALES: 2.1MM **Privately Held**
WEB: www.wheatonsprague.com
SIC: 8711 Professional engineer

Strasburg
Tuscarawas County

(G-17240)
TUSCO IMAA CHAPTER NO 602
Also Called: Tusco RC Club
6607 Cherry Run Rd Nw (44680-9026)
PHONE................................330 878-7369
David Dessecker, *President*
Darlinda Scwartz, *Treasurer*
EMP: 27 **EST:** 1997
SALES (est): 311.2K **Privately Held**
SIC: 8641 Social club, membership

(G-17241)
VILLAGE OF STRASBURG
Village Clerk
358 5th St Sw (44680-1254)
PHONE................................330 878-7115
Ron Lambert, *Administration*
EMP: 29
SQ FT: 592 **Privately Held**
SIC: 8111 Administrative & government law
PA: Village Of Strasburg
358 5th St Sw
Strasburg OH 44680
330 878-7115

Stratton
Jefferson County

(G-17242)
JERSEY CENTRAL PWR & LIGHT CO
Also Called: Firstenergy
29503 State Route 7 (43961)
PHONE................................740 537-6308
EMP: 200 **Publicly Held**
SIC: 4911 Electric services
HQ: Jersey Central Power & Light Company
76 S Main St
Akron OH 44308
800 736-3402

Streetsboro
Portage County

(G-17243)
A DUIE PYLE INC
10225 Philipp Pkwy (44241-4040)
PHONE................................330 342-7750
Rich Gadus, *Branch Mgr*
EMP: 63
SALES (corp-wide): 481MM **Privately Held**
SIC: 4225 7519 General warehousing; trailer rental
PA: A. Duie Pyle Inc.
650 Westtown Rd
West Chester PA 19382
610 696-5800

(G-17244)
AERO-MARK INC
10423 Danner Dr (44241-5071)
PHONE................................330 995-0100
Mike Krenn, *President*
Curt Huffman, *Vice Pres*
EMP: 40
SQ FT: 3,600

SALES (est): 5.3MM **Privately Held**
SIC: 1721 Pavement marking contractor

(G-17245)
AGRATRONIX LLC
10375 State Route 43 (44241-4992)
PHONE................................330 562-2222
James Falbo, *Vice Pres*
Randy Beck, *Purch Mgr*
Dawn Decker, *Human Res Mgr*
Andrew Laflame, *VP Sales*
Gerald Stephens, *Mng Member*
▲ **EMP:** 30
SALES (est): 10.2MM **Privately Held**
WEB: www.agratronix.com
SIC: 5039 3699 3446 Wire fence, gates & accessories; electric fence chargers; fences, gates, posts & flagpoles

(G-17246)
ARTS AND EXHIBITIONS INTL LLC
10145 Philipp Pkwy D (44241-4706)
PHONE................................330 995-9300
EMP: 75
SQ FT: 1,000
SALES (est): 1.4MM **Privately Held**
SIC: 8412 Museum/Art Gallery

(G-17247)
BLADE-TECH INDUSTRIES INC
10125 Wellman Rd (44241-1614)
PHONE................................877 331-5793
Bryce Wegner, *Ch of Bd*
Tom Crawford, *COO*
Paul Hodgson, *Treasurer*
Steve Avila, *Shareholder*
Tim Wegner, *Shareholder*
▲ **EMP:** 80
SQ FT: 10,500
SALES (est): 43.9MM **Privately Held**
WEB: www.blade-tech.com
SIC: 5162 Plastics materials & basic shapes

(G-17248)
CELLCO PARTNERSHIP
Also Called: Verizon Wireless
9315 State Route 14 (44241-3800)
PHONE................................330 626-0524
EMP: 71
SALES (corp-wide): 130.8B **Publicly Held**
SIC: 4812 Cellular telephone services
HQ: Cellco Partnership
1 Verizon Way
Basking Ridge NJ 07920

(G-17249)
CER HOTELS LLC
Also Called: TownePlace Suites By Marriott
795 Mondial Pkwy (44241-4574)
PHONE................................330 422-1855
Maninder S Chhabra, *Mng Member*
EMP: 50
SALES (est): 158.8K **Privately Held**
SIC: 7011 Hotel, franchised

(G-17250)
CITY OF STREETSBORO
Also Called: Service Dept
2094 State Route 303 (44241-1707)
PHONE................................330 626-2856
Bill Miller, *Director*
EMP: 25
SQ FT: 2,312 **Privately Held**
WEB: www.cityofstreetsboro.com
SIC: 1611 Highway & street maintenance
PA: City Of Streetsboro
9184 State Route 43
Streetsboro OH 44241
330 626-4942

(G-17251)
CORPORATE IMAGEWORKS LLC
10375 State Route 43 (44241-4992)
PHONE................................216 292-8800
Stafford Worley,
Gerald Stephens,
▲ **EMP:** 30
SALES (est): 3.6MM **Privately Held**
WEB: www.corporateimageworks.com
SIC: 5199 Advertising specialties

(G-17252)
GARDENS WESTERN RESERVE INC (PA)
9975 Greentree Pkwy (44241-4328)
PHONE................................330 342-9100
Richard Piekarski, *Owner*
EMP: 75
SALES (est): 4.4MM **Privately Held**
WEB: www.gardensofwesternreserve.com
SIC: 8059 8322 Rest home, with health care; adult day care center

(G-17253)
GEIS CONSTRUCTION INC
Also Called: Geis Companies
10020 Aurora Hudson Rd (44241-1621)
PHONE................................330 528-3500
Jeff Martin, *President*
Jim Flauraud, *Superintendent*
Daniel McKee, *Superintendent*
Gregory Seifert, *Vice Pres*
Jesse Powers, *Project Mgr*
EMP: 56
SQ FT: 10,000
SALES (est): 54.4MM **Privately Held**
SIC: 1541 Industrial buildings, new construction

(G-17254)
GORELL ENTERPRISES INC (PA)
Also Called: Gorell Windows & Doors
10250 Philipp Pkwy (44241-4765)
PHONE................................724 465-1800
Wayne C Gorell, *Ch of Bd*
Brian Zimmerman, *President*
Michael A Rempel, *Vice Pres*
Arnold S Levitt, *CFO*
EMP: 370
SQ FT: 240,000
SALES (est): 34.5MM **Privately Held**
WEB: www.gorell.com
SIC: 3089 5031 Plastic hardware & building products; doors & windows

(G-17255)
HAMPTON INNS LLC
800 Mondial Pkwy (44241-4540)
PHONE................................330 422-0500
Rose Mills, *Branch Mgr*
EMP: 29
SALES (corp-wide): 2.7B **Publicly Held**
WEB: www.premierhotels.us
SIC: 7011 Hotels & motels
HQ: Hampton Inns, Llc
755 Crossover Ln
Memphis TN 38117
901 374-5000

(G-17256)
HIGHLAND SOM DEVELOPMENT (PA)
Also Called: Geis Company
10020 Aurora Hudson Rd (44241-1621)
PHONE................................330 528-3500
Erwin Geis, *Partner*
EMP: 32
SALES (est): 20.1MM **Privately Held**
WEB: www.geis-companies.com
SIC: 6552 Land subdividers & developers, commercial

(G-17257)
IS ACQUISITION INC (HQ)
Also Called: Integrity Stainless
3000 Crane Centre Dr (44241-5035)
PHONE................................440 287-0150
Andy Markowitz, *Vice Pres*
▲ **EMP:** 45
SALES (est): 50.6MM
SALES (corp-wide): 1.3B **Publicly Held**
WEB: www.integritystainless.com
SIC: 5051 Steel
PA: Olympic Steel, Inc.
22901 Millcreek Blvd # 650
Cleveland OH 44122
216 292-3800

(G-17258)
JOSEPH INDUSTRIES INC
Also Called: BUCKEYE FASTENERS COMPANY
10039 Aurora Hudson Rd (44241-1600)
PHONE................................330 528-0091
Patrick Finnegan, *President*

Linda Kerekes, *Corp Secy*
Wendy Lovejoy, *Purch Mgr*
Audrey Jackson, *Controller*
Courtney Mahan, *Asst Controller*
▲ **EMP:** 52
SQ FT: 76,260
SALES: 10.9MM
SALES (corp-wide): 42.3MM **Privately Held**
WEB: www.joseph.com
SIC: 3714 5084 3713 3566 Motor vehicle parts & accessories; lift trucks & parts; truck & bus bodies; speed changers, drives & gears
PA: Fastener Industries, Inc.
1 Berea Cmns Ste 209
Berea OH 44017
440 243-0034

(G-17259)
LOWES HOME CENTERS LLC
1210 State Route 303 (44241-4591)
PHONE................................330 626-2980
Tim Mercer, *Branch Mgr*
EMP: 150
SALES (corp-wide): 68.6B **Publicly Held**
SIC: 5211 5031 5722 5064 Home centers; building materials, exterior; building materials, interior; household appliance stores; electrical appliances, television & radio
HQ: Lowe's Home Centers, Llc
1605 Curtis Bridge Rd
Wilkesboro NC 28697
336 658-4000

(G-17260)
MEANDER HSPTALITY GROUP II LLC
Also Called: Hampton Inn
800 Mondial Pkwy (44241-4540)
PHONE................................330 422-0500
Celine Kovas,
Bill Kovas,
EMP: 25
SQ FT: 1,232
SALES (est): 1.6MM **Privately Held**
SIC: 7011 Hotels & motels

(G-17261)
MED CENTER ONE STREETSBORO
9318 State Route 14 (44241-5224)
PHONE................................330 626-3455
Jack Mondo, *Administration*
EMP: 50
SALES (est): 1.7MM **Privately Held**
SIC: 8011 Ambulatory surgical center

(G-17262)
MONDELEZ GLOBAL LLC
Also Called: Nabisco
545 Mondial Pkwy (44241-4510)
P.O. Box 340, Meadow Lands PA (15347-0340)
PHONE................................330 626-6500
Doug Evans, *Branch Mgr*
EMP: 60 **Publicly Held**
SIC: 5149 Crackers, cookies & bakery products
HQ: Mondelez Global Llc
3 N Pkwy Ste 300
Deerfield IL 60015
847 943-4000

(G-17263)
OLYMPIC STEEL INC
Also Called: Integrity Stainless
3000 Crane Centre Dr (44241-5035)
PHONE................................440 287-0150
Andy Markowitz, *Division Pres*
EMP: 35
SALES (corp-wide): 1.3B **Publicly Held**
SIC: 5051 Steel
PA: Olympic Steel, Inc.
22901 Millcreek Blvd # 650
Cleveland OH 44122
216 292-3800

(G-17264)
ONEX CONSTRUCTION INC
1430 Miller Pkwy (44241-4640)
PHONE................................330 995-9015
Ken Finnerty, *President*
Aaron Smigelski, *Controller*
Paul Marshal, *Shareholder*

▲ EMP: 40 EST: 1996
SQ FT: 20,000
SALES: 20MM Privately Held
WEB: www.onexconstruction.com
SIC: 1741 Refractory or acid brick masonry

(G-17265)
PENSKE LOGISTICS LLC
9777 Mopar Dr (44241-5220)
PHONE....................................330 626-7623
EMP: 59
SALES (corp-wide): 2.6B Privately Held
WEB: www.penskelogistics.com
SIC: 4213 Trucking, except local
HQ: Penske Logistics Llc
2675 Morgantown Rd
Reading PA 19607
610 775-6000

(G-17266)
PORTAGE FAMILY MEDICINE
9480 Rosemont Dr (44241-4569)
PHONE....................................330 626-5566
Philip Kennedy MD, President
EMP: 25
SALES (est): 2.1MM Privately Held
SIC: 8011 General & family practice, physician/surgeon

(G-17267)
R & H SERVICE INC
Also Called: Americas Best Value Inn
9420 State Route 14 (44241-5226)
PHONE....................................330 626-2888
Rajni S Patel, President
Hema R Patel, Manager
EMP: 25
SALES (est): 1MM Privately Held
WEB: www.rhservice.com
SIC: 7011 Inns

(G-17268)
ROBINSON MEMORIAL HOSPITAL
Also Called: Robinson Hlth Affl Med Ctr One
9424 State Route 14 (44241-5226)
PHONE....................................330 626-3455
Marcy Burch, Principal
EMP: 30
SALES (corp-wide): 580MM Privately Held
SIC: 8062 8011 General medical & surgical hospitals; primary care medical clinic
HQ: Robinson Health System, Inc.
6847 N Chestnut St
Ravenna OH 44266
330 297-0811

(G-17269)
SINGER STEEL COMPANY
1 Singer Dr (44241)
P.O. Box 2279 (44241-0279)
PHONE....................................330 562-7200
Bruce Alexander, President
Eric Shaw, Vice Pres
EMP: 50
SQ FT: 100,000
SALES (est): 9.1MM Privately Held
WEB: www.singersteel.com
SIC: 5051 Metals service centers & offices

(G-17270)
SOJOURN LODGING INC
Also Called: TownePlace Suites By Marriott
795 Mondial Pkwy (44241-4574)
PHONE....................................330 422-1855
Christine Zebris, Manager
EMP: 25
SALES (corp-wide): 5MM Privately Held
SIC: 7011 Hotel, franchised
PA: Sojourn Lodging, Inc.
265 Kings Grant Rd # 106
Virginia Beach VA 23452
757 463-1907

(G-17271)
SOUTHERN GLAZERS WINE AND SP
Also Called: 55 Degrees
9450 Rosemont Dr (44241-4563)
PHONE....................................330 422-9463
Diane Dubin, Manager
EMP: 67
SALES (corp-wide): 7.2B Privately Held
SIC: 5182 5181 Wine; beer & ale

HQ: Southern Glazer's Wine And Spirits Of Texas, Llc
2001 Diplomat Dr
Farmers Branch TX 75234
972 277-2000

(G-17272)
STREETSBORO BOARD EDUCATION
Also Called: Streetsboro Bus Garage
1901 Annalane Dr (44241-1730)
PHONE....................................330 626-4909
Sharon Deyoung, Director
Lori Thomson, Teacher
Megan Holtz, Education
EMP: 30
SALES (corp-wide): 25.8MM Privately Held
WEB: www.rock889.com
SIC: 4151 School buses
PA: Streetsboro Board Of Education
9000 Kirby Ln
Streetsboro OH 44241
330 626-4900

(G-17273)
STREETSBORO OPCO LLC
Also Called: Arbors At Streetsboro
1645 Maplewood Dr (44241-5662)
PHONE....................................502 429-8062
Robert Norcross, CEO
Yvette Kline, Manager
EMP: 99
SALES (est): 2.3MM Privately Held
SIC: 8051 Skilled nursing care facilities

(G-17274)
TECHNOLOGY HOUSE LTD (PA)
Also Called: North Cape Manufacturing
10036 Aurora Hudson Rd (44241-1640)
PHONE....................................440 248-3025
Chip Gear,
Pamela Gear,
EMP: 46
SQ FT: 14,000
SALES (est): 18.8MM Privately Held
SIC: 8711 3544 3369 Industrial engineers; machine tool design; mechanical engineering; special dies, tools, jigs & fixtures; nonferrous foundries

(G-17275)
UNITED TECHNICAL SUPPORT SVCS
10325 State Route 43 F (44241-4945)
PHONE....................................330 562-3330
James Cecil, CEO
Larry Cornell, Admin Sec
EMP: 75
SQ FT: 5,000
SALES (est): 14.9MM Privately Held
SIC: 7373 Local area network (LAN) systems integrator

(G-17276)
UNITY HEALTH NETWORK LLC
9150 Market Square Dr (44241-4571)
PHONE....................................330 626-0549
Terry Kingery, Branch Mgr
EMP: 34
SALES (corp-wide): 14.5MM Privately Held
SIC: 8043 8011 5999 Offices & clinics of podiatrists; orthopedic physician; orthopedic & prosthesis applications
PA: Unity Health Network, Llc
3033 State Rd
Cuyahoga Falls OH 44223
330 923-5899

(G-17277)
WESTERN RESERVE RACQUET CLUB
11013 Aurora Hudson Rd (44241-1630)
PHONE....................................330 653-3103
Terry Travies, General Mgr
EMP: 30
SQ FT: 80,000
SALES (est): 1.2MM Privately Held
WEB: www.wrrfc.com
SIC: 7997 Racquetball club, membership

Strongsville
Cuyahoga County

(G-17278)
A-ROO COMPANY LLC (HQ)
22360 Royalton Rd (44149-3826)
P.O. Box 360050 (44136-0001)
PHONE....................................440 238-8850
Bill Harshbarger, Plant Mgr
Ronda Orick, Purch Agent
Phil Basak, Mktg Dir
Nick Schalk, Marketing Staff
Kevin Shuman, Manager
▲ EMP: 55
SQ FT: 50,000
SALES (est): 25.5MM Privately Held
SIC: 5199 Packaging materials
PA: Professional Packaging Company Inc
22360 Royalton Rd
Strongsville OH 44149
440 238-8850

(G-17279)
ACCESS CATALOG COMPANY LLC
21848 Commerce Pkwy # 100 (44149-5559)
PHONE....................................440 572-5377
Jim Vangieson, Manager
EMP: 33
SALES (corp-wide): 206.3MM Privately Held
WEB: www.courtesyproducts.com
SIC: 5065 5046 Electronic parts & equipment; coffee brewing equipment & supplies
HQ: Access Catalog Company, L.L.C.
10880 Linpage Pl
Saint Louis MO 63132
314 301-3300

(G-17280)
ACUATIVE CORPORATION
8237 Dow Cir (44136-1761)
PHONE....................................440 202-4500
Joseph Jean, Engineer
Brian Mandell, Sales Staff
Bob Cain, Branch Mgr
Dennis Diller, Manager
Susan Bauck, Director
EMP: 60
SALES (corp-wide): 95.8MM Privately Held
SIC: 5065 Telephone & telegraphic equipment
PA: Acuative Corporation
695 Rte 46 W Ste 305
Fairfield NJ 07004
862 926-5600

(G-17281)
ADT SECURITY
13022 Pearl Rd (44136-3442)
PHONE....................................440 397-5751
EMP: 57 Privately Held
SIC: 9229 9224 9221 7382 Public order & safety; fire protection; police protection; security systems services

(G-17282)
AKA WIRELESS INC
Also Called: Verizon Wireless Authorized Ret
14150 Pearl Rd (44136-8708)
PHONE....................................440 572-5777
Brandon Parham, Branch Mgr
EMP: 26 Privately Held
SIC: 4812 Cellular telephone services
HQ: Aka Wireless, Inc.
7505 S Louise Ave
Sioux Falls SD 57108
605 275-3733

(G-17283)
ALL FOILS INC
16100 Imperial Pkwy (44149-0600)
PHONE....................................440 572-3645
Kevin C Foos, President
Robert F Gesing, Treasurer
Karen Mittman, Controller
Honie Latak, Sales Mgr
Honie Dalton, Sales Staff
◆ EMP: 75
SQ FT: 140,000

SALES (est): 46.4MM Privately Held
WEB: www.allfoils.com
SIC: 5051 Metals service centers & offices

(G-17284)
ALTENHEIM FOUNDATION INC
18627 Shurmer Rd (44136-6150)
PHONE....................................440 238-3361
Greg McDaniels, President
EMP: 49
SALES: 234.6K Privately Held
WEB: www.altenheim.com
SIC: 8051 Convalescent home with continuous nursing care

(G-17285)
APPLIED MINT SUPS SLUTIONS LLC (HQ)
14790 Foltz Pkwy (44149-4723)
PHONE....................................216 456-3600
Robert Onorato, Vice Pres
Greg Edwards, Purch Mgr
Michael Murray, Finance
EMP: 50
SQ FT: 102,850
SALES (est): 79MM
SALES (corp-wide): 3B Publicly Held
SIC: 5085 Industrial supplies
PA: Applied Industrial Technologies, Inc.
1 Applied Plz
Cleveland OH 44115
216 426-4000

(G-17286)
ARCHWAY MARKETING SERVICES INC
20770 Westwood Dr (44149-3907)
P.O. Box 360450, Cleveland (44136-0041)
PHONE....................................440 572-0725
Lawrence Zimmering, CEO
Laura Lapohn, Technology
EMP: 200 Privately Held
SIC: 8742 Marketing consulting services
HQ: Archway Marketing Services, Inc.
19850 S Diamond Lake Rd
Rogers MN 55374

(G-17287)
AT&T MOBILITY LLC
17970 Royalton Rd (44136-5149)
PHONE....................................440 846-3232
Anita Carile, Branch Mgr
EMP: 26
SALES (corp-wide): 170.7B Publicly Held
SIC: 4812 Cellular telephone services
HQ: At&T Mobility Llc
1025 Lenox Park Blvd Ne
Brookhaven GA 30319
800 331-0500

(G-17288)
BRIGHTON-BEST INTL INC
21855 Commerce Pkwy (44149-5560)
PHONE....................................440 238-1350
Steve Andrasik, Regional Mgr
EMP: 40
SALES (corp-wide): 375.1MM Privately Held
SIC: 5072 Screws
HQ: Brighton-Best International, Inc.
5855 Obispo Ave
Long Beach CA 90805
562 808-8000

(G-17289)
CELLCO PARTNERSHIP
Also Called: Verizon
17290 Royalton Rd (44136-4400)
PHONE....................................440 846-8881
Scott Goodrich, Manager
EMP: 25
SALES (corp-wide): 130.8B Publicly Held
SIC: 4812 5999 Cellular telephone services; mobile telephones & equipment
HQ: Cellco Partnership
1 Verizon Way
Basking Ridge NJ 07920

(G-17290)
CLERAC LLC (DH)
Also Called: National Car Rental
8249 Mohawk Dr (44136-1795)
PHONE....................................440 345-3999
Scott Vaccaro, Vice Pres

Chryssa Alexis, *Manager*
Todd Delong, *Supervisor*
Kashmini Morgan, *Info Tech Mgr*
Aimee Sully, *Executive Asst*
EMP: 50
SQ FT: 11,894
SALES (est): 24.3MM
SALES (corp-wide): 4.9B **Privately Held**
SIC: 7515 7514 Passenger car leasing;
rent-a-car service
HQ: Enterprise Holdings, Inc.
600 Corporate Park Dr
Saint Louis MO 63105
314 512-5000

(G-17291)
CLEVELAND JSM INC
Also Called: Tenk Machine
11792 Alameda Dr (44149-3011)
PHONE.....................440 876-3050
Dave Holm, *General Mgr*
Ray Knapp, *Principal*
Paul Skidmore, *Plant Mgr*
Brad Shrock, *Manager*
EMP: 65 **EST:** 1942
SALES (est): 393.5K **Privately Held**
SIC: 3599 7699 7692 Custom machinery;
industrial machinery & equipment repair;
welding repair

(G-17292)
CLEVELAND METROPARKS
9485 Eastland Rd (44149-1418)
PHONE.....................216 739-6040
Steve Dice, *Manager*
EMP: 450
SALES (corp-wide): 57.3MM **Privately
Held**
WEB: www.clemetparks.com
SIC: 7999 Recreation services
PA: Cleveland Metroparks
4101 Fulton Pkwy
Cleveland OH 44144
216 635-3200

(G-17293)
CLEVELAND METROPARKS
Also Called: Chalet
16200 Valley Pkwy (44149)
PHONE.....................440 572-9990
Rob Muntz, *Manager*
EMP: 30
SALES (corp-wide): 57.3MM **Privately
Held**
WEB: www.clemetparks.com
SIC: 7999 Recreation services; astrologer
PA: Cleveland Metroparks
4101 Fulton Pkwy
Cleveland OH 44144
216 635-3200

(G-17294)
CREATIVE PLAYROOMS INC
16000 Foltz Pkwy (44149-5502)
PHONE.....................440 572-9365
Lisa Roff, *Director*
EMP: 30
SQ FT: 16,532
SALES (corp-wide): 3.7MM **Privately
Held**
SIC: 8351 Child day care services
PA: Creative Playrooms, Inc.
32750 Solon Rd Ste 3
Solon OH 44139
440 349-9111

(G-17295)
**CUYAHOGA LANDMARK INC
(PA)**
21079 Westwood Dr (44149-2901)
P.O. Box 361189 (44136-0020)
PHONE.....................440 238-3900
Gary Smith, *President*
EMP: 40 **EST:** 1934
SQ FT: 25,640
SALES (est): 19.9MM **Privately Held**
WEB: www.cfgh.hbocvan.com
SIC: 5172 5541 5983 Gasoline; fuel oil;
filling stations, gasoline; fuel oil dealers

(G-17296)
DANIELS BOARDING KENNELS
21782 Royalton Rd (44149-3816)
PHONE.....................440 238-7179
James Strachen, *Partner*
Denes Pal, *Partner*

Rosalie Strachen, *Partner*
EMP: 25 **EST:** 2001
SQ FT: 6,100
SALES (est): 576.3K **Privately Held**
WEB: www.drdenespal.com
SIC: 0742 Veterinarian, animal specialties

(G-17297)
DARICE INC (DH)
Also Called: Pat Catan's Craft Centers
13000 Darice Pkwy 82 (44149-3800)
PHONE.....................440 238-9150
Michael Catanzarite, *President*
◆ **EMP:** 150
SQ FT: 100,000
SALES (est): 193.9MM
SALES (corp-wide): 5.2B **Publicly Held**
SIC: 5945 5193 5999 Arts & crafts sup-
plies; flowers & florists' supplies; picture
frames, ready made
HQ: Michaels Stores, Inc.
8000 Bent Branch Dr
Irving TX 75063
972 409-1300

(G-17298)
**DWA MRKTING PRMTIONAL
PDTS LLC**
Also Called: Art Wall
17000 Foltz Pkwy (44149-5522)
PHONE.....................216 476-0635
David Aheimer, *CEO*
David Khieu, *President*
Brian Peabody, *Manager*
EMP: 32
SALES (est): 2MM **Privately Held**
SIC: 5023 5091 5141 5092 Decorative
home furnishings & supplies; sporting &
recreation goods; groceries, general line;
toys & hobby goods & supplies; gifts &
novelties

(G-17299)
EDRICH SUPPLY CO
22700 Royalton Rd (44149-3838)
PHONE.....................440 238-9440
Richard A Puzzitiello, *President*
EMP: 50
SQ FT: 1,500
SALES (est): 3.3MM **Privately Held**
SIC: 1521 5031 General remodeling, sin-
gle-family houses; lumber, plywood & mill-
work

(G-17300)
EMSCO (PA)
Also Called: Emsco Distributors
22350 Royalton Rd (44149-3826)
P.O. Box 360660 (44136-0011)
PHONE.....................440 238-2100
Mark Stoyanoff, *President*
Richard Laneve, *Vice Pres*
Richard Foltz, *Controller*
Nancy Kane, *Admin Sec*
EMP: 28
SQ FT: 100,000
SALES (est): 41MM **Privately Held**
WEB: www.emscocorp.com
SIC: 5091 Swimming pools, equipment &
supplies

(G-17301)
ENABLING PARTNERS LLC
13862 Basswood Cir (44136-2693)
PHONE.....................440 878-9418
John Ice, *Principal*
EMP: 25
SQ FT: 10,000
SALES (est): 767K **Privately Held**
WEB: www.enablingpartners.com
SIC: 8742 Business consultant; productiv-
ity improvement consultant

(G-17302)
EUTHENICS INC (PA)
8235 Mohawk Dr (44136-1795)
PHONE.....................440 260-1555
Ron Bender, *President*
Richard S Wasosky, *Vice Pres*
Ronald Bender, *Sales Executive*
Vince Bobkovich, *Manager*
Dan Bender, *Comp Tech*
EMP: 33
SQ FT: 8,000

SALES (est): 4MM **Privately Held**
WEB: www.euthenics-inc.com
SIC: 8711 Civil engineering

(G-17303)
FALLING LEASING CO LLC
Also Called: Falling Water Healthcare Ctr
18840 Falling Water Rd (44136-4200)
PHONE.....................440 238-1100
Stephen L Rosedale, *Chairman*
Charles R Stoltz, *Exec VP*
Ronald S Wilheim, *Exec VP*
Mark Morley, *Director*
David Trimble,
EMP: 202
SQ FT: 60,000
SALES: 1.5MM **Privately Held**
SIC: 8051 Convalescent home with contin-
uous nursing care

(G-17304}
FAY INDUSTRIES INC
17200 Foltz Pkwy (44149-5526)
P.O. Box 360947, Cleveland (44136-0016)
PHONE.....................440 572-5030
Richard Schnaterbeck, *President*
Jack Notarianni, *Vice Pres*
▲ **EMP:** 59 **EST:** 1974
SQ FT: 60,000
SALES (est): 46.2MM **Publicly Held**
SIC: 5051 Steel
PA: Ryerson Holding Corporation
227 W Monroe St Fl 27
Chicago IL 60606

(G-17305)
FOUNDATION SOFTWARE INC
17999 Foltz Pkwy (44149-5565)
PHONE.....................330 220-8383
Fred Ode, *CEO*
Thomas Ross, *Project Mgr*
Jason Stypick, *Project Mgr*
Denise Prescott, *Controller*
Mike Ode, *Sales Mgr*
EMP: 92
SQ FT: 16,000
SALES (est): 15.6MM **Privately Held**
SIC: 7372 7371 Prepackaged software;
software programming applications; cus-
tom computer programming services

(G-17306)
**GOING HOME MEDICAL
HOLDING CO**
15830 Foltz Pkwy (44149-4745)
PHONE.....................305 340-1034
Ryan Hawley, *President*
EMP: 25 **EST:** 2016 **Privately Held**
SIC: 6719 Holding companies

(G-17307)
**GOODWILL IDSTRS GRTR
CLVLND L**
16160 Pearl Rd (44136-6036)
PHONE.....................440 783-1168
EMP: 32
SALES (corp-wide): 27.6MM **Privately
Held**
SIC: 8331 Job training & vocational reha-
bilitation services
PA: Goodwill Industries Of Greater Cleve-
land And East Central Ohio, Inc.
408 9th St Sw
Canton OH 44707
330 454-9461

(G-17308)
HEALTHCARE CIRCLE INC
18149 Williamsburg Oval (44136-7091)
PHONE.....................440 331-7347
Tammy Haseley, *President*
EMP: 75
SALES (est): 1MM **Privately Held**
SIC: 8082 Home health care services

(G-17309)
HEWLETTCO INC
Also Called: Goddard School
13590 Falling Water Rd (44136-4319)
PHONE.....................440 238-4600
Robyn T Hewlett, *President*
Craig Bach, *Principal*
Tracy Swanson, *Principal*
L Dale Todd, *Vice Pres*
Maragaret Todd, *Admin Sec*
EMP: 25

SQ FT: 10,000
SALES (est): 963.7K **Privately Held**
SIC: 8351 Preschool center

(G-17310)
HIRTS GREENHOUSE INC
Also Called: Hirts Greenhouse and Flowers
14407 Pearl Rd (44136-8797)
PHONE.....................440 238-8200
Claire Hirt, *President*
EMP: 35
SQ FT: 20,000
SALES (est): 1.8MM **Privately Held**
SIC: 0181 5992 Nursery stock, growing of;
flowers, fresh

(G-17311)
HOME DEPOT USA INC
Also Called: Home Depot, The
8199 Pearl Rd (44136-1633)
PHONE.....................440 826-9092
Ron Salizar, *Manager*
EMP: 150
SALES (corp-wide): 108.2B **Publicly
Held**
WEB: www.homerentalsdepot.com
SIC: 5211 7359 Home centers; tool rental
HQ: Home Depot U.S.A., Inc.
2455 Paces Ferry Ave
Atlanta GA 30339

(G-17312)
HUGHES CORPORATION (PA)
Also Called: Weschler Instruments
16900 Foltz Pkwy (44149-5520)
PHONE.....................440 238-2550
David E Hughes, *President*
Esther Carpenter, *Principal*
Michael F Dorman, *Exec VP*
Douglas Hughes, *Vice Pres*
Ryan Hughes, *Vice Pres*
EMP: 30
SQ FT: 11,500
SALES (est): 32.4MM **Privately Held**
WEB: www.weschler.com
SIC: 5063 3825 Electrical apparatus &
equipment; instruments to measure elec-
tricity

(G-17313)
HUGHES CORPORATION
Also Called: Mac Group, The
16900 Foltz Pkwy (44149-5520)
PHONE.....................440 238-2550
David Hughes, *CEO*
EMP: 25
SALES (corp-wide): 32.4MM **Privately
Held**
WEB: www.weschler.com
SIC: 5065 Electronic parts & equipment
PA: Hughes Corporation
16900 Foltz Pkwy
Strongsville OH 44149
440 238-2550

(G-17314)
ICE LAND USA LTD
15381 Royalton Rd (44136-5440)
PHONE.....................440 268-2800
William Neiheiser, *President*
Katie Nieheiser, *Vice Pres*
EMP: 80
SQ FT: 97,000
SALES (est): 3.3MM **Privately Held**
SIC: 7999 5812 Ice skating rink operation;
eating places

(G-17315)
ILEAD LLC
Also Called: Ilead Marketing
20376 Kelsey Ln (44149-0965)
PHONE.....................440 846-2346
Scott Flanagan,
EMP: 30
SALES (est): 2.6MM **Privately Held**
SIC: 8742 Marketing consulting services

(G-17316)
INTRALOT INC
13500 Darice Pkwy Ste C (44149-3840)
PHONE.....................440 268-2900
EMP: 25 **Privately Held**
SIC: 7379

HQ: Intralot, Inc.
11360 Technology Cir
Duluth GA 30097
678 473-7200

(G-17318)
JOHNSON CONTROLS
17295 Foltz Pkwy Ste G (44149-5568)
PHONE..................440 268-1160
Anthony Warner, *Branch Mgr*
Pierre St Arnaud, *Manager*
Sean Cromwell, *Technology*
EMP: 112 **Privately Held**
WEB: www.simplexgrinnell.com
SIC: 1711 Fire sprinkler system installation
HQ: Johnson Controls Fire Protection Lp
6600 Congress Ave
Boca Raton FL 33487
561 988-7200

(G-17319)
KAISER FOUNDATION HOSPITALS
Also Called: Strongsville Medical Offices
17406 Royalton Rd (44136-5151)
PHONE..................216 524-7377
EMP: 593
SALES (corp-wide): 93B **Privately Held**
SIC: 8011 Medical centers
HQ: Kaiser Foundation Hospitals Inc
1 Kaiser Plz
Oakland CA 94612
510 271-6611

(G-17320)
KEMPER COMPANY
Also Called: Kemper House of Strongsville
10890 Prospect Rd (44149-2256)
PHONE..................440 846-1100
John Kemper, *Branch Mgr*
Kathy Busch, *Nursing Mgr*
EMP: 85
SALES (corp-wide): 24.5MM **Privately Held**
SIC: 8748 Business consulting
PA: The Kemper Company
10307 Detroit Ave # 101
Cleveland OH 44102
216 472-4200

(G-17321)
KENNEDY GROUP ENTERPRISES INC
13370 Prospect Rd 2c (44149-3854)
PHONE..................440 879-0078
Ronald J Kennedy, *Owner*
Jennifer George, *Cust Mgr*
Carol Miranda, *Manager*
Craig D Kennedy, *Admin Sec*
EMP: 30
SQ FT: 3,500
SALES (est): 2.2MM **Privately Held**
SIC: 8721 8742 8748 Billing & bookkeeping service; management information systems consultant; business consulting

(G-17321)
LAMRITE WEST INC (HQ)
Also Called: Darice
13000 Darice Pkwy (44149-3800)
PHONE..................440 238-9150
Michael Catanzarite, *President*
David Catanzarite, *Vice Pres*
Joe Rudolph, *CFO*
▲ **EMP:** 200
SQ FT: 125,000
SALES (est): 65.6MM
SALES (corp-wide): 5.2B **Publicly Held**
WEB: www.darice.com
SIC: 5999 5199 5092 Artists' supplies & materials; artificial flowers; art goods & supplies; toys & hobby goods & supplies
PA: The Michaels Companies Inc
8000 Bent Branch Dr
Irving TX 75063
972 409-1300

(G-17322)
LAMRITE WEST INC
Also Called: A C Supply
17647 Foltz Pkwy (44149-5535)
PHONE..................440 572-9946
Rocco Catan, *Manager*
EMP: 25

SALES (corp-wide): 5.2B **Publicly Held**
WEB: www.darice.com
SIC: 5199 Art goods & supplies
HQ: Lamrite West, Inc.
13000 Darice Pkwy
Strongsville OH 44149
440 238-9150

(G-17323)
LAMRITE WEST INC
Also Called: Pat Catan's
14225 Pearl Rd (44136-8711)
PHONE..................440 268-0634
Greg Alberty, *Manager*
EMP: 43
SQ FT: 77,530
SALES (corp-wide): 5.2B **Publicly Held**
WEB: www.darice.com
SIC: 5092 Arts & crafts equipment & supplies
HQ: Lamrite West, Inc.
13000 Darice Pkwy
Strongsville OH 44149
440 238-9150

(G-17324)
LOWES HOME CENTERS LLC
9149 Pearl Rd (44136-1414)
PHONE..................440 239-2630
Bob Kaine, *Sales Staff*
John Lerch, *Manager*
EMP: 150
SALES (corp-wide): 68.6B **Publicly Held**
SIC: 5211 5031 5722 5064 Home centers; building materials, exterior; building materials, interior; household appliance stores; electrical appliances, television & radio
HQ: Lowe's Home Centers, Llc
1605 Curtis Bridge Rd
Wilkesboro NC 28697
336 658-4000

(G-17325)
MAINTENANCE UNLIMITED INC
12351 Prospect Rd (44149-2995)
PHONE..................440 238-1162
Joseph Friscone, *President*
EMP: 50
SQ FT: 10,000
SALES (est): 6.6MM **Privately Held**
WEB: www.maintenanceunlimited.com
SIC: 1623 1541 1629 1794 Sewer line construction; oil & gas pipeline construction; renovation, remodeling & repairs: industrial buildings; trenching contractor; excavation & grading, building construction

(G-17326)
MANCAN INC
13500 Pearl Rd Ste 109 (44136-3428)
PHONE..................440 884-9675
EMP: 1336
SALES (corp-wide): 124MM **Privately Held**
SIC: 8742 7361 Industrial & labor consulting services; employment agencies
PA: Mancan, Inc.
48 1st St Nw
Massillon OH 44647
330 832-4595

(G-17327)
MANHATTAN ASSOCIATES INC
10153 S Bexley Cir (44136-2565)
PHONE..................440 878-0771
Raymond Bernard, *Branch Mgr*
EMP: 90 **Publicly Held**
SIC: 7371 Software programming applications
PA: Manhattan Associates, Inc.
2300 Windy Ridge Pkwy Se 1000n
Atlanta GA 30339

(G-17328)
MARIA GARDENS LLC (PA)
20465 Royalton Rd (44149-4967)
P.O. Box 360256, Cleveland (44136-0005)
PHONE..................440 238-7637
David Stopper, *President*
Dave Stopper Sr, *Principal*
Rosemary Stopper, *Vice Pres*
EMP: 45
SQ FT: 85,000

SALES (est): 3.5MM **Privately Held**
SIC: 0181 5193 5992 Flowers: grown under cover (e.g. greenhouse production); plants, potted; plants, potted

(G-17329)
MASSAGE ENVY
Also Called: Dhr
6 Southpark Ctr (44136-9334)
PHONE..................440 878-0500
Kim Lau, *Sales Mgr*
Sarah Zarife, *Manager*
EMP: 25 **EST:** 2008
SALES (est): 305.9K **Privately Held**
SIC: 7299 Massage parlor

(G-17330)
MEDICAL MUTUAL OF OHIO
15885 W Sprague Rd (44136-1772)
PHONE..................440 878-4800
Jan Santoli, *Vice Pres*
Brian Berman, *Engineer*
Robert Klubert, *VP Sales*
Michael Nugent, *Info Tech Mgr*
Tom Stepec, *Executive*
EMP: 85
SALES (corp-wide): 1.2B **Privately Held**
SIC: 6411 Insurance agents
PA: Medical Mutual Of Ohio
2060 E 9th St Frnt Ste
Cleveland OH 44115
216 687-7000

(G-17331)
MEDICAL MUTUAL SERVICES LLC (HQ)
Also Called: Antares Management Solutions
17800 Royalton Rd (44136-5149)
PHONE..................440 878-4800
Ed Twardzik, *Technology*
Edward J Hartzell,
Ken Sidon,
EMP: 250
SQ FT: 15,000
SALES (est): 34.5MM
SALES (corp-wide): 1.2B **Privately Held**
WEB: www.antaressolutions.com
SIC: 7374 7375 Data processing & preparation; information retrieval services
PA: Medical Mutual Of Ohio
2060 E 9th St Frnt Ste
Cleveland OH 44115
216 687-7000

(G-17332)
MEDINA WORLD CARS INC
11800 Pearl Rd (44136-3329)
PHONE..................330 725-4901
Paul Hrnchar, *President*
Steve Karg, *Vice Pres*
EMP: 40
SQ FT: 16,000
SALES (est): 2.5MM **Privately Held**
WEB: www.4worldcars.com
SIC: 7532 5511 7538 7515 Body shop, automotive; automobiles, new & used; general automotive repair shops; passenger car leasing; automotive & home supply stores

(G-17333)
MERRICK CHEVROLET CO
15303 Royalton Rd (44136-5440)
PHONE..................440 878-6700
Robert Serpentini Jr, *President*
Paul Serpentini, *Corp Secy*
Mary Jo Root, *Human Res Mgr*
EMP: 80
SQ FT: 18,000
SALES (est): 20.3MM **Privately Held**
SIC: 5511 7515 Automobiles, new & used; pickups, new & used; trucks, tractors & trailers: new & used; passenger car leasing

(G-17334)
MOHAWK RE-BAR SERVICES INC
15110 Foltz Pkwy Ste 106 (44149-4765)
P.O. Box 8468, Canton (44711-8468)
PHONE..................440 268-0780
EMP: 30
SQ FT: 1,500
SALES (est): 2.1MM **Privately Held**
SIC: 1791 Reinforcing Steel Contractor

(G-17335)
MUELLER ART COVER & BINDING CO
12005 Alameda Dr (44149-3016)
P.O. Box 360829 (44136-0014)
PHONE..................440 238-3303
Toll Free:..................888 -
Edmond Mueller, *President*
Bob Mueller, *COO*
Daniel Mack, *Vice Pres*
Robert Mueller, *Manager*
EMP: 45
SQ FT: 38,000
SALES (est): 5.9MM **Privately Held**
WEB: www.muellerartcover.com
SIC: 2782 7336 Looseleaf binders & devices; graphic arts & related design; silk screen design

(G-17336)
NATIONAL AUTO EXPERTS LLC
8370 Dow Cir Ste 100 (44136-1797)
PHONE..................440 274-5114
Kelly Price, *Principal*
Ryan Nelson, *Vice Pres*
David Neuenschwander, *Vice Pres*
EMP: 39
SALES (est): 7.3MM **Privately Held**
SIC: 7538 General automotive repair shops

(G-17337)
OPTIONS FOR FAMILY & YOUTH
11351 Pearl Rd Ste 103 (44136-3331)
PHONE..................216 267-7070
Michael Rush, *President*
EMP: 40
SALES: 1.6MM **Privately Held**
SIC: 8322 Adoption services

(G-17338)
PARK GROUP CO OF AMERICA INC
22700 Royalton Rd (44149-3838)
PHONE..................440 238-9440
Richard Puzzitello Jr, *President*
Chris Bender, *Senior VP*
EMP: 50
SQ FT: 1,000
SALES (est): 3.5MM **Privately Held**
SIC: 1521 New construction, single-family houses

(G-17339)
PPG ARCHITECTURAL FINISHES INC
Glidden Professional Paint Ctr
16651 W Sprague Rd (44136-1757)
PHONE..................440 826-5100
Patricia Starrett, *Manager*
EMP: 300
SALES (corp-wide): 15.3B **Publicly Held**
WEB: www.gliddenpaint.com
SIC: 8731 Commercial research laboratory
HQ: Ppg Architectural Finishes, Inc.
1 Ppg Pl
Pittsburgh PA 15272
412 434-3131

(G-17340)
RADEBAUGH-FETZER COMPANY
Also Called: Gill Podiatry Supply Co
22400 Ascoa Ct (44149-4766)
PHONE..................440 878-4700
Eric Boggs, *President*
Laurie Appenzeller, *General Mgr*
Dave Adriano, *Purch Dir*
Brian Murphy, *Sales Staff*
Jim Rief, *Sales Staff*
EMP: 30
SQ FT: 42,000
SALES (est): 13.1MM **Privately Held**
WEB: www.gillpodiatry.com
SIC: 5047 Physician equipment & supplies; surgical equipment & supplies; orthopedic equipment & supplies; hospital equipment & supplies

(G-17341)
ROBERT E MCGRATH INC
Also Called: Olympia Candies
11606 Pearl Rd (44136-3320)
PHONE..................440 572-7747
Robert McGrath, *President*

▲ = Import ▼=Export
◆ =Import/Export

Celia McGrath, *Vice Pres*
EMP: 25
SQ FT: 15,000
SALES: 750K **Privately Held**
WEB: www.olympiacandy.com
SIC: 5145 5441 2096 2066 Candy; candy; potato chips & similar snacks; chocolate & cocoa products; ice cream & frozen desserts

(G-17342)
SEVEN SECURED INC
15830 Foltz Pkwy (44149-4745)
PHONE...................................281 362-2887
Peter Martin, *President*
EMP: 25
SALES (est): 344.7K **Privately Held**
SIC: 7381 Detective & armored car services

(G-17343)
SGL CARBON TECHNIC LLC
21945 Drake Rd (44149-6608)
PHONE...................................440 572-3600
Ken Manning, *President*
Libby Knowles, *General Mgr*
Libby Knowle, *Plant Mgr*
Jake Desso, *Project Mgr*
Alex Olszewski, *Purch Mgr*
▼ EMP: 36
SQ FT: 46,004
SALES: 16.5MM
SALES (corp-wide): 1.2B **Privately Held**
SIC: 5084 Heat exchange equipment, industrial
PA: Sgl Carbon Se
    Sohnleinstr. 8
    Wiesbaden 65201
    611 602-90

(G-17344)
SHORELINE EXPRESS INC
20137 Progress Dr (44149-3215)
P.O. Box 360341 (44136-0006)
PHONE...................................440 878-3750
Don Sparks, *Principal*
EMP: 27
SALES (est): 4.5MM **Privately Held**
SIC: 4213 Trucking, except local

(G-17345)
SHORELINE TRANSPORTATION INC
Also Called: Shoreline Company
20137 Progress Dr (44149-3215)
PHONE...................................440 878-2000
Janeen Mazzeo-Sparks, *President*
Donald Sparks, *Vice Pres*
EMP: 240
SQ FT: 35,000
SALES (est): 26.4MM **Privately Held**
WEB: www.shorelinetransportation.com
SIC: 4212 4213 4731 Local trucking, without storage; trucking, except local; transportation agents & brokers

(G-17346)
SHURMER PLACE AT ALTENHEIM
18821 Shurmer Rd (44136-6100)
PHONE...................................440 238-9001
Paul Pasota, *Exec Dir*
Paul Pasotam, *Exec Dir*
EMP: 50 EST: 2000
SALES (est): 2.2MM **Privately Held**
SIC: 8361 Residential care

(G-17347)
SOUTHWEST GENERAL HEALTH CTR
18181 Pearl Rd Ste B104 (44136-6950)
PHONE...................................440 816-4900
Barb Stec, *Manager*
Deborah Traine, *Manager*
Donna SRP, *Gastroenterlgy*
EMP: 110
SALES (corp-wide): 363.2MM **Privately Held**
SIC: 8062 8011 General medical & surgical hospitals; medical centers
PA: Southwest General Health Center
    18697 Bagley Rd
    Cleveland OH 44130
    440 816-8000

(G-17348)
STRONGSVILLE LODGING ASSOC 1
Also Called: Holiday Inn
15471 Royalton Rd (44136-5441)
PHONE...................................440 238-8800
Robert Cole, *Partner*
Robert Flanders, *Partner*
Strongsville Lodging Associate, *Partner*
EMP: 175
SQ FT: 65,414
SALES (est): 8.3MM **Privately Held**
SIC: 7011 Hotels & motels

(G-17349)
STRONGVILLE RECREATION COMPLEX
18688 Royalton Rd (44136-5127)
PHONE...................................440 580-3230
Colleen Grady, *Branch Mgr*
Frank Pientka, *Executive*
Ronald Stolz, *Executive*
EMP: 203
SALES (corp-wide): 5MM **Privately Held**
SIC: 7996 Theme park, amusement
PA: Strongville Recreation Complex
    18100 Royalton Rd
    Cleveland OH 44136
    440 878-6000

(G-17350)
SUMITOMO DEMAG PLSTC MACHINERY
11792 Alameda Dr (44149-3011)
PHONE...................................440 876-8960
John Martich, *Vice Pres*
David Jersak, *Engineer*
Shari Fortune, *Asst Controller*
Karen Freeman, *Credit Mgr*
Beth Belay, *Accounts Mgr*
EMP: 25
SALES (corp-wide): 7.4B **Privately Held**
SIC: 5084 Plastic products machinery
HQ: Sumitomo (Shi) Demag Plastics Machinery North America, Inc.
    1266 Oakbrook Dr
    Norcross GA 30093

(G-17351)
TELETRONIC SERVICES INC (PA)
Also Called: Teletronics Communications
22550 Ascoa Ct (44149-4700)
PHONE...................................216 778-6500
Gale Kenney, *CEO*
Thomas Ursem, *President*
Gary Reffert, *Vice Pres*
EMP: 33
SQ FT: 12,000
SALES (est): 17.3MM **Privately Held**
SIC: 5065 Telephone equipment

(G-17352)
TERSHER CORPORATION
Also Called: Shamrock Moving & Storage Co
17000 Foltz Pkwy (44149-5522)
PHONE...................................440 439-8383
Sharon Mc Gee, *President*
Robert Struck, *Vice Pres*
EMP: 100 EST: 1977
SQ FT: 40,000
SALES (est): 6.8MM **Privately Held**
SIC: 4213 4731 4214 Household goods transport; agents, shipping; household goods moving & storage, local

(G-17353)
UNION HOME MORTGAGE CORP (PA)
Also Called: Vloan
8241 Dow Cir (44136-1761)
PHONE...................................440 234-4300
Bill Cosgrove, *CEO*
C William Cosgrove, *President*
Rob Lane, *Partner*
Karen Moreno, *Partner*
Denise Young, *Partner*
EMP: 35
SQ FT: 15,000
SALES (est): 28.7MM **Privately Held**
WEB: www.unmco.com
SIC: 6162 Mortgage bankers

(G-17354)
UNITED AMERICAN INSURANCE CO
10749 Pearl Rd Ste D (44136-3347)
PHONE...................................440 265-9200
Karen E Dolan, *Branch Mgr*
EMP: 25
SALES (corp-wide): 4.3B **Publicly Held**
WEB: www.unitedamerican.com
SIC: 6411 6311 Life insurance agents; insurance agents; life insurance carriers
HQ: United American Insurance Company
    3700 S Stonebridge Dr
    Mckinney TX 75070
    800 331-2512

(G-17355)
UNITED PARCEL SERVICE INC
Also Called: UPS
13500 Pearl Rd Ste 139 (44136-3428)
PHONE...................................440 846-6000
Mark Munoz, *Owner*
EMP: 38
SALES (corp-wide): 71.8B **Publicly Held**
SIC: 4215 Package delivery, vehicular
PA: United Parcel Service, Inc.
    55 Glenlake Pkwy
    Atlanta GA 30328
    404 828-6000

(G-17356)
UNIVAR USA INC
21600 Drake Rd (44149-6615)
PHONE...................................440 238-8550
Jennifer Lechner, *Buyer*
Al Bernhardt, *Manager*
EMP: 80
SALES (corp-wide): 8.6B **Publicly Held**
SIC: 5169 Industrial chemicals
HQ: Univar Usa Inc.
    3075 Highland Pkwy # 200
    Downers Grove IL 60515
    331 777-6000

(G-17357)
VAN MILLS LINES INC
14675 Foltz Pkwy (44149-4720)
PHONE...................................440 846-0200
Donald Mills II, *President*
Michael McGill, *Vice Pres*
Robert Mills, *Vice Pres*
Robert Simmon, *CFO*
EMP: 110
SQ FT: 160,000
SALES (est): 17.3MM **Privately Held**
SIC: 4213 4214 4212 Household goods transport

(G-17358)
WALLOVER ENTERPRISES INC (DH)
21845 Drake Rd (44149-6610)
PHONE...................................440 238-9250
George M Marquis, *President*
William C Cutri, *Vice Pres*
EMP: 30
SQ FT: 28,000
SALES (est): 25.1MM **Privately Held**
SIC: 2992 8734 Oils & greases, blending & compounding; re-refining lubricating oils & greases; product testing laboratories
HQ: Houghton International Inc.
    945 Madison Ave
    Norristown PA 19403
    888 459-9844

(G-17359)
WEST SIDE DTSCHER FRUEN VEREIN
Also Called: Altenheim
18627 Shurmer Rd (44136-6150)
PHONE...................................440 238-3361
Paul Psota, *CEO*
Karina Gross, *Manager*
EMP: 300
SALES: 14.8MM **Privately Held**
SIC: 8051 Skilled nursing care facilities

Struthers
Mahoning County

(G-17360)
CASEY EQUIPMENT CORPORATION
15 Union St Bldg 1 (44471-2901)
PHONE...................................330 750-1005
Angela Williams, *Mktg Dir*
James Rugh, *Branch Mgr*
Paul Ulam, *Manager*
Donna Orbin, *Officer*
EMP: 40
SALES (corp-wide): 9.9MM **Privately Held**
WEB: www.caseyusa.com
SIC: 5084 Industrial machinery & equipment
PA: Casey Equipment Corporation
    275 Kappa Dr
    Pittsburgh PA 15238
    412 963-1111

(G-17361)
CLEMENTE-MC KAY AMBULANCE INC (PA)
700 5th St Ste 1 (44471-1772)
PHONE...................................330 755-1401
EMP: 50
SQ FT: 10,200
SALES (est): 4MM **Privately Held**
SIC: 4119 Transportation Services

(G-17362)
CRED-KAP INC
Also Called: Maple Crest Nrsing HM For Aged
400 Sexton St (44471-1141)
P.O. Box 5185, Poland (44514-0185)
PHONE...................................330 755-1466
Christopher Daprile, *President*
Lisa Daprile, *Vice Pres*
EMP: 55 EST: 1960
SALES (est): 4.2MM **Privately Held**
SIC: 8052 Personal care facility

(G-17363)
DAVIDSON BECKER INC
11 Spring St (44471-1745)
PHONE...................................330 755-2111
Kelly Becker, *President*
Daniel Becker, *President*
Margaret L Becker, *Vice Pres*
EMP: 25
SALES (est): 1.5MM **Privately Held**
SIC: 7261 Funeral home

(G-17364)
GOLD CROSS LIMOUSINE SERVICE
26 Sexton St (44471-1773)
PHONE...................................330 757-3053
Grant Williams, *Manager*
EMP: 50
SALES (est): 1.3MM **Privately Held**
WEB: www.goldcrosslimo.com
SIC: 4119 Limousine rental, with driver

(G-17365)
JS BOVA EXCAVATING LLC
235 State St (44471-1958)
P.O. Box 296 (44471-0296)
PHONE...................................234 254-4040
Louis J Bova, *Mng Member*
Sherri Bova,
EMP: 36
SQ FT: 2,100
SALES: 8.5MM **Privately Held**
SIC: 1794 1623 Excavation work; underground utilities contractor

(G-17366)
L B INDUSTRIES INC
Also Called: Lally Pipe & Tube
534 Lowellville Rd (44471-2077)
P.O. Box 69 (44471-0069)
PHONE...................................330 750-1002
Josh Ball, *Asst Controller*
James Mocker, *Branch Mgr*
EMP: 36

SALES (corp-wide): 110MM **Privately Held**
WEB: www.lallypipe.com
SIC: 5051 7692 Pipe & tubing, steel; steel; welding repair
PA: L B Industries, Inc.
　8770 Railroad Dr
　Taylor Mill KY 41015
　859 431-8300

(G-17367)
RUDZIK EXCAVATING INC
401 Lowellville Rd (44471-2076)
P.O. Box 206 (44471-0206)
PHONE............................330 755-1540
Jeffrey A Rudzik, *Owner*
Bonnie L Rudzik, *Corp Secy*
EMP: 45 EST: 1998
SQ FT: 3,000
SALES (est): 9.7MM **Privately Held**
WEB: www.rudzikexcavating.com
SIC: 1794 1799 Excavation & grading, building construction; building site preparation

(G-17368)
TINY TOTS DAY NURSERY
310 Argonne St (44471-1671)
PHONE............................330 755-6473
D Fontez, *Owner*
EMP: 28
SALES (est): 569.1K **Privately Held**
WEB: www.tinytotsdaynursery.com
SIC: 8351 Nursery school

Stryker
Williams County

(G-17369)
CORRECTION COMMISSION NW OHIO
3151 County Road 2425 (43557-9418)
PHONE............................419 428-3800
Denny Stantz, *Maint Spvr*
Jim Dennis, *Exec Dir*
EMP: 187
SQ FT: 189,000
SALES (est): 15MM **Privately Held**
WEB: www.ccnoregionaljail.org
SIC: 8744 Correctional facility

(G-17370)
QUADCO REHABILITATION CTR INC (PA)
Also Called: Northwest Products
427 N Defiance St (43557-9472)
PHONE............................419 682-1011
Terry Fruth, *CFO*
Bruce Abell, *Exec Dir*
EMP: 287
SQ FT: 24,000
SALES: 247.7K **Privately Held**
SIC: 8331 2448 2441 Vocational rehabilitation agency; wood pallets & skids; nailed wood boxes & shook

(G-17371)
R & S LINES INC
102 Ellis St (43557-9333)
P.O. Box 410 (43557-0410)
PHONE............................419 682-7807
Robert Liechty, *President*
Sharon Liechty, *Vice Pres*
EMP: 25
SQ FT: 12,000
SALES (est): 3.1MM **Privately Held**
SIC: 4213 Trucking, except local

(G-17372)
WOOLACE ELECTRIC CORP
1978 County Road 22a (43557-9778)
PHONE............................419 428-3161
William D Woolace, *President*
Eric Woolace, *Vice Pres*
John Schlatter, *Safety Dir*
Catherine Salisbury, *Engineer*
Benjamin Woolace, *Treasurer*
EMP: 35
SQ FT: 2,600
SALES (est): 6.1MM **Privately Held**
SIC: 1731 General electrical contractor

Sugar Grove
Fairfield County

(G-17373)
COLUMBIA GULF TRANSMISSION LLC
Also Called: Columbia Energy
6175 Old Logan Rd (43155-9795)
PHONE............................740 746-9105
Larry Brown, *Branch Mgr*
EMP: 30
SALES (corp-wide): 10.5B **Privately Held**
WEB: www.columbiagastrans.com
HQ: Columbia Gulf Transmission, Llc
　5151 San Felipe St # 2500
　Houston TX 77056
　713 386-3701

(G-17374)
HIDE-A-WAY HILLS CLUB
29042 Hide Away Hills Rd (43155-9607)
PHONE............................740 746-9589
Rogers Childers, *President*
John Vanderbuilt, *Treasurer*
EMP: 30
SQ FT: 2,000
SALES (est): 1.8MM **Privately Held**
WEB: www.hide-a-wayhillsclub.com
SIC: 8641 7011 Social club, membership; resort hotel

(G-17375)
POWERS EQUIPMENT
7265 Sugar Grove Rd (43155-9785)
P.O. Box 43 (43155-0043)
PHONE............................740 746-8220
Mark Powers, *Owner*
EMP: 32
SQ FT: 2,189
SALES (est): 1.6MM **Privately Held**
SIC: 4212 Local trucking, without storage

Sugarcreek
Tuscarawas County

(G-17376)
ANDREAS FURNITURE COMPANY
580 Belden Pkwy Ne (44681-7695)
PHONE............................330 852-2494
Stephanie Saulnier, *Mktg Coord*
Tim Sisler, *Branch Mgr*
EMP: 46
SALES (corp-wide): 15.4MM **Privately Held**
WEB: www.andreasfurniture.com
SIC: 4226 Household goods & furniture storage
PA: Andreas Furniture Company
　114 Dover Rd Ne
　Sugarcreek OH 44681
　330 852-2494

(G-17377)
DRASC ENTERPRISES INC
Also Called: Gordon Milk Transport
9060 Bollman Rd Sw (44681-8008)
P.O. Box 707 (44681-0707)
PHONE............................330 852-3254
Rodney Gordon, *President*
EMP: 50 EST: 2001
SQ FT: 1,600
SALES (est): 5.7MM **Privately Held**
SIC: 4212 4213 Liquid haulage, local; trucking, except local

(G-17378)
DUTCH CREEK FOODS INC
1411 Old Route 39 Ne (44681-7400)
PHONE............................330 852-2631
Mike Palmer, *President*
Lynn Dessecker, *Opers Mgr*
Doug Myers, *Sales Associate*
Shawn Houze, *Manager*
EMP: 27
SQ FT: 25,000

SALES (est): 13.9MM
SALES (corp-wide): 46.4MM **Privately Held**
WEB: www.dutchcreekfoods.com
SIC: 5147 Meats, fresh
PA: Dutchman Hospitality Group, Inc.
　4985 State Rte 515
　Walnut Creek OH 44687
　330 893-2926

(G-17379)
PROVIA HOLDINGS INC (PA)
Also Called: Provia - Heritage Stone
2150 State Route 39 (44681-9201)
PHONE............................330 852-4711
Brian Miller, *President*
Bill Mullet, *Principal*
Willis Schlabach, *Principal*
Phil Wengerd, *Vice Pres*
Mike Yoder, *Plant Mgr*
EMP: 180 EST: 1972
SQ FT: 280,000
SALES: 140.5MM **Privately Held**
WEB: www.precisionentry.com
SIC: 3442 5031 Metal doors; door frames, all materials

(G-17380)
RUBIN ERB
Also Called: Sugar Valley Meats
2149 Dutch Valley Dr Nw (44681-7922)
PHONE............................330 852-4423
Rubin Erb, *Owner*
EMP: 25
SALES (est): 1.2MM **Privately Held**
SIC: 5421 0751 Meat markets, including freezer provisioners; slaughtering: custom livestock services

(G-17381)
YODER DRILLING AND GEOTHERMAL
997 State Route 93 Nw (44681-7728)
PHONE............................330 852-4342
Daniel Yoder, *President*
Timothy Yoder, *Vice Pres*
Elaine Beech, *Admin Sec*
EMP: 34
SALES (est): 7.4MM **Privately Held**
WEB: www.yodergeothermal.com
SIC: 5082 Wellpoints (drilling equipment); bailey bridges; blades for graders, scrapers, dozers & snow plows

Sunbury
Delaware County

(G-17382)
AMERICAN SHOWA INC
677 W Cherry St (43074-9803)
PHONE............................740 965-4040
Greg Cockerel, *Branch Mgr*
Brenda Cox, *Planning*
EMP: 30
SALES (corp-wide): 2.7B **Privately Held**
SIC: 8731 Commercial research laboratory
HQ: American Showa, Inc.
　707 W Cherry St
　Sunbury OH 43074
　740 965-1133

(G-17383)
BLACKSTAR DRYWALL INC
9821 E State Route 37 (43074-9635)
P.O. Box 550, Westerville (43086-0550)
PHONE............................614 242-4242
Jim Williams, *President*
Bobby Porter Jr, *Vice Pres*
EMP: 25
SQ FT: 1,100
SALES (est): 1.8MM **Privately Held**
SIC: 1742 Drywall

(G-17384)
BST & G JOINT FIRE DISTRICT
350 W Cherry St (43074-7508)
PHONE............................740 965-3841
Jeff Wilson, *Chief*
EMP: 32
SALES (est): 2MM **Privately Held**
SIC: 7389 Fire protection service other than forestry or public

(G-17385)
CHAMPIONSHIP MANAGEMENT CO
Also Called: North Star Golf Club
1150 Wilson Rd (43074-9633)
PHONE............................740 524-4653
Robert Weiler, *President*
Bill Gallant, *General Mgr*
EMP: 75
SALES: 3MM **Privately Held**
SIC: 7992 Public golf courses

(G-17386)
DBP ENTERPRISES LLC
Also Called: Holiday Inn
7301 E State Route 37 (43074-9210)
PHONE............................740 513-2399
Daxa Patel, *Mng Member*
EMP: 30
SALES (est): 1.6MM **Privately Held**
SIC: 7011 Hotels & motels

(G-17387)
FACEMYER BACKHOE AND DOZER SVC
Also Called: FM Earth
72 Holmes St (43074)
P.O. Box 304 (43074-0304)
PHONE............................740 965-1137
Cameron L Facemyer, *President*
Joyce Facemyer, *Office Mgr*
EMP: 25
SQ FT: 1,312
SALES (est): 2.9MM **Privately Held**
SIC: 1794 Excavation & grading, building construction

(G-17388)
FIRE GUARD LLC
35 E Granville St (43074-9130)
P.O. Box 730, Centerburg (43011-0730)
PHONE............................740 625-5181
Nick McGovern, *President*
EMP: 50
SALES (est): 3.2MM **Privately Held**
SIC: 1711 Fire sprinkler system installation

(G-17389)
J & J ENTPS WESTERVILLE INC
Also Called: Arrow Industrial Supply
660 Kintner Pkwy (43074-8038)
PHONE............................614 898-5997
Colleen Jordan, *President*
Kurt Campagna, *Vice Pres*
Jeffery Jordan, *Vice Pres*
Zena Trout, *CFO*
Curt Campagna, *VP Sales*
EMP: 8,000
SQ FT: 8,000
SALES: 3MM **Privately Held**
WEB: www.arrowindustrialsupply.com
SIC: 5085 Fasteners, industrial: nuts, bolts, screws, etc.

(G-17390)
MINE EQUIPMENT SERVICES LLC (PA)
Also Called: Mes
3958 State Route 3 (43074-9660)
P.O. Box 120 (43074-0120)
PHONE............................740 936-5427
Christopher Wagner,
Tony Schiavi,
EMP: 25 EST: 2012
SQ FT: 10,000
SALES (est): 3.4MM **Privately Held**
SIC: 5084 3535 7699 Industrial machinery & equipment; belt conveyor systems, general industrial use; construction equipment repair; pumps & pumping equipment repair; industrial equipment services; industrial machinery & equipment repair

(G-17391)
MORNING VIEW DELAWARE INC
Also Called: Country View of Sunbury
14961 N Old 3c Rd (43074-9716)
PHONE............................740 965-3984
Brian Colleran, *President*
Daniel Parker, *Vice Pres*
John Krystowski, *Treasurer*
Sandy Muir, *Manager*
Ryan Kray, *Admin Sec*
EMP: 150

▲ = Import ▼=Export
◆ =Import/Export

SALES (est): 380K **Privately Held**
SIC: 8059 Nursing home, except skilled & intermediate care facility

(G-17392)
NOAHS ARK LEARNING CENTER
100 Tippett Ct Ste 103 (43074-8572)
PHONE.....................................740 965-1668
Kim Low, *Owner*
Jeff Low, *Co-Owner*
EMP: 25
SALES (est): 801.5K **Privately Held**
SIC: 8351 Preschool center

(G-17393)
OHASHI TECHNICA USA INC (HQ)
111 Burrer Dr (43074-9323)
PHONE.....................................740 965-5115
Hikaru Tateiwa, *President*
Mamoru Shibasaki, *Principal*
Masaki Takafuji, *Sales Staff*
Anthony White, *Manager*
▲ EMP: 50
SQ FT: 110,000
SALES: 90MM
SALES (corp-wide): 365.8MM **Privately Held**
SIC: 5013 5072 3452 Automotive supplies & parts; automotive supplies; hardware; bolts, nuts, rivets & washers
PA: Ohashi Technica Inc.
4-3-13, Toranomon
Minato-Ku TKY 105-0
354 044-411

(G-17394)
RESTAURANT SPECIALTIES INC
Also Called: RSI Construction
801 W Cherry St Ste 200 (43074-8598)
PHONE.....................................614 885-9707
Paul Tanzillo, *President*
Gregory Hunt, *Vice Pres*
EMP: 32
SQ FT: 4,000
SALES: 31.5MM **Privately Held**
WEB: www.rsibuilds4u.com
SIC: 1542 Restaurant construction; commercial & office buildings, renovation & repair

Swanton
Fulton County

(G-17395)
CESSNA AIRCRAFT COMPANY
Also Called: Cessna Toledo Citation Svc Ctr
11591 W Airport Service R (43558-9618)
PHONE.....................................419 866-6761
EMP: 82
SQ FT: 42,358
SALES (corp-wide): 12.1B **Publicly Held**
SIC: 4581 Airport/Airport Services
HQ: The Cessna Aircraft Company
1 Cessna Blvd
Wichita KS 67215
316 517-6000

(G-17396)
EAGLE INDUSTRIAL TRUCK MFG LLC
Also Called: Eagle Tugs
1 Air Cargo Pkwy E (43558-9490)
PHONE.....................................734 442-1000
Mark Iddon, *President*
Connie Sroufe, *Mktg Dir*
John Morgan,
Jace Morgan,
◆ EMP: 30 EST: 2000
SQ FT: 70,000
SALES (est): 17.5MM
SALES (corp-wide): 10B **Privately Held**
WEB: www.eaglegse.com
SIC: 5085 3537 Industrial supplies; industrial trucks & tractors
HQ: Tronair, Inc.
1 Air Cargo Pkwy E
Swanton OH 43558
419 866-6301

(G-17397)
FOUNDATION STEEL LLC
12525 Airport Hwy (43558-9613)
P.O. Box 210 (43558-0210)
PHONE.....................................419 402-4241
Charlotte A Dymarkowski, *President*
Jim Starr, *Manager*
EMP: 90
SALES (est): 12.8MM **Privately Held**
SIC: 1791 1622 Iron work, structural; bridge, tunnel & elevated highway

(G-17398)
GENICON INC
12150 Monclova Rd (43558-8706)
PHONE.....................................419 491-4478
Jason Byrd, *President*
EMP: 45
SQ FT: 1,500
SALES (est): 1.7MM **Privately Held**
SIC: 7549 5511 Towing service, automotive; new & used car dealers

(G-17399)
HARBORSIDE HEALTHCARE CORP
Also Called: Swanton Vly Care Rhbltttion Ctr
401 W Airport Hwy (43558-1447)
PHONE.....................................419 825-1111
Steven Dood, *Branch Mgr*
Darlene Bellman, *Social Dir*
EMP: 125 **Publicly Held**
SIC: 8051 Skilled nursing care facilities
HQ: Harborside Healthcare Corporation
5100 Sun Ave Ne
Albuquerque NM 87109

(G-17400)
JAMES C SASS ATTY
226 N Main St (43558-1034)
PHONE.....................................419 843-3545
James Sass, *Principal*
EMP: 29
SALES (est): 1.3MM **Privately Held**
SIC: 8111 General practice attorney, lawyer

(G-17401)
MAPLEVIEW FARMS INC (PA)
2425 S Fulton Lucas Rd (43558-9658)
PHONE.....................................419 826-3671
William J Schmidt, *President*
Allen J Schmidt, *Vice Pres*
Allen Schmidt, *Vice Pres*
Joseph L Schmidt, *Vice Pres*
Lawrence H Schmidt, *Treasurer*
EMP: 35
SQ FT: 33,100
SALES: 3.7MM **Privately Held**
WEB: www.mapleviewfarm.com
SIC: 6519 7359 Farm land leasing; equipment rental & leasing

(G-17402)
NATIONAL FLIGHT SERVICES INC (HQ)
10971 E Airport Svc Rd (43558)
PHONE.....................................419 865-2311
Tom Wiles, *President*
Larry Lowry, *Vice Pres*
Larry Mates, *Opers Mgr*
Bev Sanders, *Human Res Mgr*
John Crummey, *Admin Sec*
EMP: 75
SQ FT: 49,000
SALES (est): 18.2MM **Privately Held**
WEB: www.nationalflight.com
SIC: 4581 Aircraft servicing & repairing

(G-17403)
OHIO TPK & INFRASTRUCTURE COMM
Also Called: Swanton Maintenance Building
8891 County Road 1 (43558-8678)
PHONE.....................................419 826-4831
EMP: 38 **Privately Held**
SIC: 1611 0782 9621 Highway/Street Construction Lawn/Garden Services
HQ: Ohio Turnpike And Infrastructure Commission
682 Prospect St
Berea OH 44017
440 234-2081

(G-17404)
SCHENKER INC
2 Air Cargo Pkwy E (43558-9312)
PHONE.....................................419 491-1055
EMP: 30
SALES (corp-wide): 23.3MM **Privately Held**
WEB: www.schenkerlogisticsusa.com
SIC: 7349 Cleaning service, industrial or commercial
HQ: Schenker, Inc.
1305 Executive Blvd # 200
Chesapeake VA 23320
757 821-3400

(G-17405)
SCHENKER INC
1 Air Cargo Pkwy E (43558-9490)
PHONE.....................................419 866-6390
EMP: 28 **Privately Held**
SIC: 4731 Freight Transportation Arrangement
HQ: Schenker, Inc.
41 Pinelawn Rd 110
Melville NY 23320
757 821-3400

(G-17406)
SCHMIDT BROS INC
420 N Hallett Ave (43558)
PHONE.....................................419 826-3671
Lawrence Schmidt, *President*
Robert J Schmidt, *President*
Allen J Schmidt, *Vice Pres*
William J Schmidt, *Vice Pres*
Michael P Schmidt, *Treasurer*
▲ EMP: 30
SQ FT: 610,000
SALES (est): 3.1MM
SALES (corp-wide): 3.7MM **Privately Held**
WEB: www.schmidtbrosinc.com
SIC: 0181 5193 Bedding plants, growing of; flowers & florists' supplies
PA: Mapleview Farms, Inc
2425 S Fulton Lucas Rd
Swanton OH 43558
419 826-3671

(G-17407)
SWANTON HLTH CARE RTREMENT CTR
214 S Munson Rd (43558-1210)
PHONE.....................................419 825-1145
Lisa Mitchell, *President*
Scott Mitchell, *Vice Pres*
EMP: 90
SQ FT: 19,000
SALES: 5MM **Privately Held**
WEB: www.swantonhealthcare.com
SIC: 8051 8052 Convalescent home with continuous nursing care; intermediate care facilities

(G-17408)
TOLEDO-LUCAS COUNTY PORT AUTH
Also Called: Toledo Express Airport
11013 Airport Hwy Ste 11 (43558-9403)
PHONE.....................................419 865-2351
Paul L Toht Jr, *Director*
EMP: 25
SALES (corp-wide): 15MM **Privately Held**
SIC: 4581 Airport
PA: Toledo-Lucas County Port Authority
1 Maritime Plz Ste 701
Toledo OH 43604
419 243-8251

(G-17409)
VALLEYWOOD GOLF CLUB INC
13501 Airport Hwy (43558)
PHONE.....................................419 826-3991
Ron Dickson, *President*
Louie Carson, *Treasurer*
Neil Toeppe, *Admin Sec*
EMP: 45
SQ FT: 6,500
SALES (est): 1.8MM **Privately Held**
SIC: 7992 Public golf courses

Sycamore
Wyandot County

(G-17410)
CREATIVE PLASTIC CONCEPTS LLC (HQ)
206 S Griffith St (44882-9694)
PHONE.....................................419 927-9588
Nick Reinhart, *President*
▲ EMP: 56
SALES (est): 21MM
SALES (corp-wide): 35.2MM **Privately Held**
SIC: 2499 5085 Clothes dryers (clothes horses), wood; bins & containers, storage
PA: Jansan Acquisition, Llc
11840 Westline Industrial
Saint Louis MO 63146
314 656-4321

Sylvania
Lucas County

(G-17411)
ABILITY CTR OF GREATER TOLEDO (PA)
5605 Monroe St (43560-2702)
PHONE.....................................419 517-7123
Susan Golden, *Ch of Bd*
Timothy Harrington, *President*
Richard Gunden, *President*
Richard R Brown, *Treasurer*
James L Fischer, *Admin Sec*
EMP: 43
SQ FT: 13,000
SALES: 3.8MM **Privately Held**
WEB: www.abilitycenter.org
SIC: 8361 Residential care for the handicapped

(G-17412)
BOBBART INDUSTRIES INC
Also Called: American Custom Industries
5035 Alexis Rd Ste 1 (43560-1637)
PHONE.....................................419 350-5477
Bart Lea, *President*
Laura Lea, *Corp Secy*
EMP: 25
SQ FT: 45,000
SALES: 1.7MM **Privately Held**
WEB: www.acivette.com
SIC: 3711 3082 7532 3714 Motor vehicles & car bodies; unsupported plastics profile shapes; top & body repair & paint shops; motor vehicle parts & accessories; plastics plumbing fixtures

(G-17413)
BUCKEYE LAUNDERER AND CLRS LLC
4930 N Holland Sylvania (43560-2178)
PHONE.....................................419 592-2941
Patrick Jackson, *Mng Member*
EMP: 85
SALES (est): 3.9MM **Privately Held**
SIC: 7211 Power laundries, family & commercial

(G-17414)
CENTENNIAL TERRACE & QUARRY
5773 Centennial Rd (43560-9846)
PHONE.....................................419 885-7106
Ken Katafias, *Director*
EMP: 30
SALES (est): 521K **Privately Held**
SIC: 7999 Swimming pool, non-membership

(G-17415)
CITY OF SYLVANIA
Also Called: Tam-O-Shanter Sports Complex
7060 Sylvania Ave (43560-3680)
PHONE.....................................419 885-1167
Tom Cline, *Manager*
EMP: 25
SQ FT: 3,775 **Privately Held**
WEB: www.cityofsylvania.com
SIC: 7999 7997 Ice skating rink operation; membership sports & recreation clubs

PA: City Of Sylvania
6730 Monroe St Ste 201
Sylvania OH 43560
419 885-8930

(G-17416)
CREATIVE MARKETING ENTERPRISES
6711 Monroe St Ste 4c (43560-1968)
PHONE..................................419 867-4444
Lynn P Brown, *President*
Martha L Brown, *Corp Secy*
B Joyce Clevenger, *Exec VP*
EMP: 80
SQ FT: 11,000
SALES (est): 3.3MM **Privately Held**
WEB: www.cmeinet.com
SIC: 8732 Market analysis or research

(G-17417)
DAVE WHITE CHEVROLET INC
Also Called: White Cars
5880 Monroe St (43560-2200)
PHONE..................................419 885-4444
Hugh David White, *CEO*
Hugh David White Jr, *President*
James F White Jr, *Vice Pres*
Steven R Justinger, *CFO*
EMP: 110
SQ FT: 30,000
SALES (est): 41.9MM **Privately Held**
SIC: 5511 5521 7538 7532 Automobiles, new & used; used car dealers; general automotive repair shops; top & body repair & paint shops; passenger car leasing

(G-17418)
DI SALLE REAL ESTATE CO
4904 Holland Sylvania Rd (43560-2119)
PHONE..................................419 885-4475
Thomas Dull, *Manager*
EMP: 25
SALES (corp-wide): 6.1MM **Privately Held**
SIC: 6531 Real estate brokers & agents
PA: Di Salle Real Estate Co
1909 River Rd
Maumee OH 43537
419 893-0751

(G-17419)
DIRECTIONS CREDIT UNION INC (PA)
5121 Whiteford Rd (43560-2987)
PHONE..................................419 720-4769
Barry Shaner, *President*
Diane Harris, *President*
Katherine Martin, *President*
Patricia Decesare, *Business Mgr*
Frederick Comes, *Vice Pres*
EMP: 57
SQ FT: 15,000
SALES: 34.8MM **Privately Held**
SIC: 6062 State credit unions, not federally chartered

(G-17420)
DRESCH TOLSON DENTAL LABS
8730 Resource Park Dr (43560-8939)
PHONE..................................419 842-6730
Joseph Gerace, *Owner*
EMP: 90
SALES (est): 2MM **Privately Held**
SIC: 8072 3843 Crown & bridge production; dental equipment & supplies

(G-17421)
EBONY CONSTRUCTION CO
3510 Centennial Rd (43560-9739)
PHONE..................................419 841-3455
Amy Hall, *President*
Michael Bass, *Vice Pres*
Tim Wiegand, *Manager*
EMP: 35
SQ FT: 2,200
SALES (est): 6.7MM **Privately Held**
WEB: www.ebonyco.com
SIC: 1611 5082 Highway & street paving contractor; construction & mining machinery

(G-17422)
ENDOSCOPY CENTER
5700 Monroe St Unit 102 (43560-2779)
PHONE..................................419 843-7993
Kevin K Koffel MD, *President*
EMP: 25
SQ FT: 4,800
SALES (est): 1.2MM **Privately Held**
SIC: 8011 Ambulatory surgical center; gastronomist

(G-17423)
ENTERPRISE SYSTEMS SFTWR LLC
Also Called: Esd
3351 Silica Rd (43560-9726)
PHONE..................................419 841-3179
Joseph M Torti, *President*
Sonya Sparks, *Controller*
Michelle Becorest, *Human Res Dir*
Jospeh M Torti, *Mng Member*
Stephen Muigai, *Consultant*
EMP: 76
SQ FT: 2,500
SALES (est): 7.2MM **Privately Held**
WEB: www.bootycallsystems.com
SIC: 7379 Computer related consulting services

(G-17424)
EXPEDITUS TRANSPORT LLC
6600 Sylvania Ave Ste 220 (43560-3935)
PHONE..................................419 464-9450
Adam Scuralli,
EMP: 38 **EST:** 2012
SALES (est): 22.1MM **Privately Held**
SIC: 4212 Truck rental with drivers

(G-17425)
FLOWER HOSPITAL
Also Called: Lake Park At Flower Hospital
5100 Harroun Rd (43560-2110)
PHONE..................................419 824-1000
Mark Mullahy, *Manager*
EMP: 350
SALES (corp-wide): 2.1B **Privately Held**
WEB: www.flowerhospital.com
SIC: 8051 8052 Extended care facility; intermediate care facilities
HQ: Flower Hospital
5200 Harroun Rd
Sylvania OH 43560
419 824-1444

(G-17426)
FLOWER HOSPITAL (HQ)
5200 Harroun Rd (43560-2196)
PHONE..................................419 824-1444
Kevin Webb, *President*
Scott Fought, *Finance Dir*
Sonya Garcia, *Manager*
Paul Beauch, *Director*
Cathy Shirley, *Director*
EMP: 889 **EST:** 1910
SALES: 229.1MM
SALES (corp-wide): 2.1B **Privately Held**
WEB: www.flowerhospital.com
SIC: 8062 General medical & surgical hospitals
PA: Promedica Health Systems, Inc.
100 Madison Ave
Toledo OH 43604
567 585-7454

(G-17427)
GRENADA STAMPING ASSEMBLY INC (HQ)
3810 Herr Rd (43560-8925)
PHONE..................................419 842-3600
Jeffrey Snavely, *Principal*
EMP: 32
SALES (est): 25.7MM
SALES (corp-wide): 100MM **Privately Held**
SIC: 8999 Art related services
PA: Ice Industries, Inc.
3810 Herr Rd
Sylvania OH 43560
419 842-3612

(G-17428)
GUARDIAN ANGLS HOME HLTH SVCS
Also Called: Guardian Angels Senior HM Svc
8553 Sylvania Metamora Rd (43560-9629)
PHONE..................................419 517-7797
Sharee Youssef, *President*
Randy Duvall, *General Mgr*
EMP: 70
SQ FT: 2,000
SALES (est): 116.6K **Privately Held**
SIC: 8082 Home health care services

(G-17429)
HARBORSIDE SYLVANIA LLC
Also Called: Sylvania Center
5757 Whiteford Rd (43560-1632)
PHONE..................................419 882-1875
Stephen Guillard, *Ch of Bd*
EMP: 70
SQ FT: 5,000
SALES (est): 2.7MM **Publicly Held**
WEB: www.harborsideuniversity.com
SIC: 8052 8051 Intermediate care facilities; skilled nursing care facilities
HQ: Genesis Healthcare Corporation
101 E State St
Kennett Square PA 19348
610 444-6350

(G-17430)
HICKMAN CANCER CENTER
5200 Harroun Rd (43560-2168)
PHONE..................................419 824-1952
Kevin Webb, *Principal*
EMP: 80
SALES (est): 1.1MM **Privately Held**
SIC: 8011 Internal medicine, physician/surgeon; oncologist

(G-17431)
HUNT CLUB LLC
5600 Alexis Rd (43560-2342)
PHONE..................................419 885-4647
Flecia Sobzaka, *Property Mgr*
Joe Goodell,
Gary Van Cleef,
EMP: 25
SALES (est): 1.3MM **Privately Held**
WEB: www.huntclub.com
SIC: 6531 Real estate agents & managers

(G-17432)
JDRM ENGINEERING INC
5604 Main St Ste 200 (43560-1950)
PHONE..................................419 824-2400
Steve Morris, *President*
Roger Debelly, *Senior Partner*
Dave Desjardins, *Senior Partner*
Daniel Rosenberger, *Corp Secy*
Darren T Keil, *Vice Pres*
EMP: 44
SQ FT: 8,500
SALES (est): 7.3MM **Privately Held**
WEB: www.jdrm.com
SIC: 8711 Mechanical engineering; designing: ship, boat, machine & product

(G-17433)
JEFF CREQUE FARMS INC
Also Called: Creque's Greenhouse
9700 Sylvania Ave (43560-9662)
PHONE..................................419 829-2941
Jeffery L Creque, *President*
Eileen Creque, *Treasurer*
EMP: 44
SALES: 800K **Privately Held**
SIC: 0181 0191 Flowers: grown under cover (e.g. greenhouse production); general farms, primarily crop

(G-17434)
JEWISH CMNTY CTR OF TOLEDO
Also Called: Jcc
6465 Sylvania Ave (43560-3916)
PHONE..................................419 885-4485
Debbie Frison, *Manager*
Eric Goldstein, *Exec Dir*
EMP: 60
SQ FT: 50,000
SALES: 68.5K **Privately Held**
SIC: 8322 Community center

(G-17435)
KINGSTON HEALTHCARE COMPANY
4125 King Rd (43560-4445)
PHONE..................................419 824-4200
Don Ferguson, *Branch Mgr*
EMP: 83
SALES (corp-wide): 95.5MM **Privately Held**
SIC: 8361 8052 Residential care; intermediate care facilities
PA: Kingston Healthcare Company
1 Seagate Ste 1960
Toledo OH 43604
419 247-2880

(G-17436)
LEISURE SPORTS INC
Also Called: Cottonwd Crk At Spytn-Dyvl
9501 Central Ave (43560-9787)
PHONE..................................419 829-2891
Gary Shaneck, *President*
Susan Shaneck, *Vice Pres*
EMP: 30
SQ FT: 3,600
SALES (est): 1.8MM **Privately Held**
SIC: 7997 Golf club, membership

(G-17437)
MARK FELDSTEIN & ASSOC INC
6703 Monroe St (43560-1962)
PHONE..................................419 867-9500
Mark S Feldstein, *President*
Annette Donnelly, *Sales Mgr*
Emily Clouser, *Accounts Mgr*
Howard Feldstein, *Mktg Dir*
◆ **EMP:** 25
SQ FT: 30,000
SALES (est): 7.6MM **Privately Held**
WEB: www.mfagifts.com
SIC: 5199 5065 Gifts & novelties; electronic parts & equipment

(G-17438)
NORTHERN OHIO INVESTMENT CO
Also Called: Noic
6444 Monroe St Ste 6 (43560-1455)
P.O. Box 787 (43560-0787)
PHONE..................................419 885-8300
Ralph D Vinciguerra, *President*
April Soss, *Senior VP*
Pauline Schnell, *Assistant VP*
Kaylene Schaar, *Vice Pres*
Marty Vihn, *Vice Pres*
EMP: 53 **EST:** 1926
SQ FT: 5,000
SALES (est): 14.1MM **Privately Held**
WEB: www.noic.com
SIC: 6162 Mortgage bankers

(G-17439)
NORTHWEST OHIO ORTHOPEDICS
6444 Monroe St Ste 1 (43560-1455)
PHONE..................................419 885-2553
Robert Hartwig, *President*
Jackie Oehlers, *General Mgr*
EMP: 30 **EST:** 1948
SALES (est): 1.6MM **Privately Held**
WEB: www.nwo-ortho.com
SIC: 8011 Orthopedic physician

(G-17440)
OHIO CON SAWING & DRLG INC (PA)
8534 Central Ave (43560-9748)
PHONE..................................419 841-1330
James R Aston, *President*
Jamison Gee, *Division Mgr*
Thomas A Lenix, *Vice Pres*
CJ Harrison, *Office Mgr*
Amie Hempy, *Admin Asst*
EMP: 29
SALES (est): 14.7MM **Privately Held**
WEB: www.gp-radar.com
SIC: 1771 Concrete repair

(G-17441)
OVERCASHIER AND HORST HTG & AC
3745 Centennial Rd (43560-9734)
PHONE..................................419 841-3333
Duane Horst, *President*

EMP: 45
SQ FT: 9,000
SALES (est): 7.1MM **Privately Held**
WEB: www.ohcomfort.com
SIC: 1711 Warm air heating & air conditioning contractor

(G-17442)
PROFESSNAL GLFERS ASSN OF AMER
5201 Corey Rd (43560-2202)
PHONE...............................419 882-3197
Jason Stuller, *Principal*
EMP: 36 EST: 2010
SALES (est): 217.7K
SALES (corp-wide): 7.5MM **Privately Held**
SIC: 8699 Athletic organizations
PA: Jason Stuller Pro Shop, Llc
5201 Corey Rd
Sylvania OH 43560
419 882-3197

(G-17443)
PROME CONTI CARE SERV CORPO
Also Called: PROMEDICA HOME HEALTH CARE
5855 Monroe St Ste 200 (43560-2270)
PHONE...............................419 885-1715
Randy Oostra, *CEO*
Elizabeth O Williams, *Manager*
Cynthia J Tuttle, *Nurse Practr*
EMP: 520
SALES: 50.6MM
SALES (corp-wide): 2.1B **Privately Held**
SIC: 8082 Home health care services
PA: Promedica Health Systems, Inc.
100 Madison Ave
Toledo OH 43604
567 585-7454

(G-17444)
PROMEDICA PHYSCN CNTINUUM SVCS
Also Called: Promedica Physician Group
5855 Monroe St Fl 1 (43560-2270)
PHONE...............................419 824-7200
Lee Hammerling MD, *President*
Jackie Giles, *Mktg Dir*
EMP: 101
SALES (est): 39.4MM
SALES (corp-wide): 2.1B **Privately Held**
SIC: 8741 7361 8721 Management services; employment agencies; accounting, auditing & bookkeeping
PA: Promedica Health Systems, Inc.
100 Madison Ave
Toledo OH 43604
567 585-7454

(G-17445)
REGENCY HOSPITAL TOLEDO LLC
5220 Alexis Rd (43560-2504)
PHONE...............................419 318-5700
Laura Van Liere, *Facilities Mgr*
Rod Laughlin, *Mng Member*
Jason Bickley, *Director*
Brett Johnson, *Officer*
Jeff Boyd,
EMP: 30
SALES: 17.2MM
SALES (corp-wide): 3.7B **Publicly Held**
SIC: 8062 Hospital, medical school affiliated with nursing & residency
HQ: Select Medical Corporation
4714 Gettysburg Rd
Mechanicsburg PA 17055
717 972-1100

(G-17446)
REVERSE CENTER CLINIC
Also Called: Toledo Ctr For Eting Disorders
5465 Main St (43560-2155)
PHONE...............................419 885-8800
David M Garner, *Owner*
EMP: 30
SALES (est): 523K **Privately Held**
WEB: www.eatingdisorders-toledo.com
SIC: 8049 Clinical psychologist

(G-17447)
REVES SALON & SPA
5633 Main St (43560-1929)
PHONE...............................419 885-1140
Carmen Gauer-Wigma, *Owner*
EMP: 50
SQ FT: 1,200
SALES (est): 1.2MM **Privately Held**
SIC: 7231 Manicurist, pedicurist

(G-17448)
ROOT INC (PA)
Also Called: Root Map Module
5470 Main St Ste 100 (43560-2164)
PHONE...............................419 874-0077
Jim Haudan, *CEO*
Kurt Cumming, *Managing Dir*
Ed Francis, *Managing Dir*
Heather Lee, *Managing Dir*
Carl Wagner, *Managing Dir*
EMP: 58
SQ FT: 17,000
SALES (est): 22.7MM **Privately Held**
WEB: www.rootlearning.com
SIC: 8742 8748 Business consultant; test development & evaluation service

(G-17449)
ROSARY CARE CENTER
6832 Convent Blvd (43560-4805)
PHONE...............................419 824-3600
Cheryl King, *Administration*
EMP: 80
SALES: 4.6MM **Privately Held**
WEB: www.rosarycare.org
SIC: 8051 Skilled nursing care facilities

(G-17450)
S A STORER AND SONS COMPANY
3135 Centennial Rd (43560-9689)
PHONE...............................419 843-3133
Jeffery R Storer, *President*
Robert W Dixon, *Vice Pres*
Amy Trumbull, *Office Mgr*
EMP: 60
SALES (est): 4.2MM **Privately Held**
SIC: 1741 Masonry & other stonework

(G-17451)
SMILE DEVELOPMENT INC
Also Called: Syvania Pediatric Dental Care
5860 Alexis Rd Ste 1 (43560-2347)
PHONE...............................419 882-7187
Rodney W Owen, *President*
Joe Inman, *Vice Pres*
EMP: 30
SQ FT: 14,376
SALES (est): 2.4MM **Privately Held**
SIC: 8021 Orthodontist; dental clinic

(G-17452)
SMITH TRUCKING INC
3775 Centennial Rd (43560-9734)
P.O. Box 9, Blissfield MI (49228-0009)
PHONE...............................419 841-8676
Henry Smith, *President*
EMP: 35
SALES (est): 3.4MM **Privately Held**
SIC: 4213 Trucking, except local

(G-17453)
STANSLEY MINERAL RESOURCES INC (PA)
3793 Silica Rd B (43560-9814)
PHONE...............................419 843-2813
Rick Stansley, *CEO*
Richard Stansley Jr, *Corp Secy*
Jeff Stansley, *COO*
Mandy Billau, *Manager*
EMP: 35
SQ FT: 10,000
SALES (est): 15MM **Privately Held**
SIC: 1442 Gravel mining

(G-17454)
SYLVANIA COMMUNITY SVCS CTR
4747 N Hlland Sylvania Rd (43560)
PHONE...............................419 885-2451
Claire A Proctor, *Exec Dir*
EMP: 35

SALES: 1.8MM **Privately Held**
WEB: www.scsonline.org
SIC: 8322 8351 Child related social services; child day care services

(G-17455)
SYLVANIA COUNTRY CLUB
5201 Corey Rd (43560-2202)
PHONE...............................419 392-0530
Shawne Lnd, *President*
EMP: 60 EST: 1916
SALES: 2.1MM **Privately Held**
SIC: 7997 Country club, membership

(G-17456)
SYLVANIA VETERINARY HOSPITAL (PA)
4801 N Hlland Sylvania Rd (43560)
PHONE...............................419 885-4421
Robert B Esplin, *President*
Carol Esplin, *Vice Pres*
EMP: 43 EST: 1974
SQ FT: 2,250
SALES (est): 3.6MM **Privately Held**
WEB: www.sylvaniavet.com
SIC: 0742 Animal hospital services, pets & other animal specialties

(G-17457)
SYLVESTER MATERIALS CO
7901 Sylvania Ave (43560-9732)
PHONE...............................419 841-3874
Charles Stansley, *President*
Richard B Stansley Jr, *Corp Secy*
Frank Mihalik, *Vice Pres*
EMP: 120
SQ FT: 10,000
SALES (est): 6.7MM **Privately Held**
SIC: 4212 5032 Local trucking, without storage; sand, construction

(G-17458)
TOLEDO DISTRICT NURSES ASSN
Also Called: VISITING NURSES ASSOCIATION
5520 Monroe St (43560-2538)
PHONE...............................419 255-0983
Judy E Rogers, *Director*
Andy J Hoehn, *Officer*
EMP: 170 EST: 1901
SQ FT: 16,700
SALES: 1.2MM **Privately Held**
SIC: 8049 8082 Nurses, registered & practical; home health care services

(G-17459)
TOLEDO HOSPITAL
Caring Services
5520 Monroe St (43560-2538)
PHONE...............................419 291-2273
Debbie Turner, *Finance*
Laura Bachmann, *Pharmacist*
Carrol Scholtz, *Director*
EMP: 250
SALES (corp-wide): 2.1B **Privately Held**
SIC: 8361 8082 Rehabilitation center, residential: health care incidental; home health care services
HQ: The Toledo Hospital
2142 N Cove Blvd
Toledo OH 43606
419 291-4000

(G-17460)
TOLEDO MEMORIAL PK & MAUSOLEUM
6382 Monroe St (43560-1428)
PHONE...............................419 882-7151
Jeffrey Clegg, *President*
EMP: 25
SQ FT: 7,000
SALES: 4.3MM **Privately Held**
WEB: www.toledomemorialpark.com
SIC: 6553 0782 Cemetery association; mausoleum operation; lawn & garden services

(G-17461)
UBS FINANCIAL SERVICES INC
5757 Monroe St (43560-2739)
PHONE...............................419 318-5525
James Porea, *Branch Mgr*
Timothy Van Simaeys, *Manager*
Karyn Keilholz, *Advisor*

EMP: 60
SALES (corp-wide): 29.4B **Privately Held**
SIC: 6211 Stock brokers & dealers
HQ: Ubs Financial Services Inc.
1285 Ave Of The Americas
New York NY 10019
212 713-2000

(G-17462)
VIN DEVERS (PA)
5570 Monroe St (43560-2560)
PHONE...............................888 847-9535
Jason Perry, *Principal*
Erin McCarthy, *Business Mgr*
Justin Schmehl, *Foreman/Supr*
Clark Blackford, *Parts Mgr*
Linda Cymbola, *Controller*
EMP: 110
SQ FT: 40,000
SALES (est): 47.8MM **Privately Held**
WEB: www.vindevers.com
SIC: 5511 5521 7538 7515 Automobiles, new & used; used car dealers; general automotive repair shops; passenger car leasing; truck rental & leasing, no drivers; local trucking, without storage

(G-17463)
WEBER OBRIEN LTD
Also Called: Webert & Co
5580 Monroe St Ste 210 (43560-2561)
PHONE...............................419 885-8338
James F Weber, *Owner*
R David O'Brien, *Partner*
Steven Weber, *Partner*
Steve M Weber, *Principal*
Jim Weber, *CPA*
EMP: 45
SALES (est): 4.3MM **Privately Held**
WEB: www.weberobrien.com
SIC: 8721 8742 8748 Certified public accountant; accounting services, except auditing; financial consultant; business consulting

(G-17464)
WHITE FAMILY COLLISION CENTER
5328 Alexis Rd (43560-2432)
P.O. Box 196 (43560-0196)
PHONE...............................419 885-8885
David White Sr, *Owner*
Dave White Jr, *General Mgr*
EMP: 26
SALES (est): 987.2K **Privately Held**
SIC: 7532 Body shop, automotive

Symmes Twp
Hamilton County

(G-17465)
BEST PAYMENT SOLUTIONS INC (HQ)
8500 Governors Hill Dr (45249-1384)
PHONE...............................630 321-0117
Jared Warner, *President*
EMP: 35
SALES (est): 2.6MM
SALES (corp-wide): 3.9B **Publicly Held**
WEB: www.best-payment.com
SIC: 7389 Credit card service
PA: Worldpay, Inc.
8500 Governors Hill Dr
Symmes Twp OH 45249
513 900-5250

(G-17466)
NPC GROUP INC
8500 Governors Hill Dr (45249-1384)
PHONE...............................312 627-6000
Charles D Drucker, *CEO*
EMP: 2493 EST: 2013
SALES (est): 30.6MM
SALES (corp-wide): 3.9B **Publicly Held**
SIC: 7389 Credit card service
PA: Worldpay, Inc.
8500 Governors Hill Dr
Symmes Twp OH 45249
513 900-5250

(G-17467)
WORLDPAY INC (PA)
8500 Governors Hill Dr (45249-1384)
PHONE...............................513 900-5250
Jeffrey Stiefler, *Ch of Bd*
Charles D Drucker, *President*
Royal Cole, *President*
Robert Demeuse, *President*
Matthew Taylor, *President*
EMP: 133
SALES: 3.9B **Publicly Held**
SIC: 7389 Credit card service

(G-17468)
WORLDPAY LLC (DH)
Also Called: Vantiv, LLC
8500 Governors Hill Dr (45249-1384)
PHONE...............................877 713-5964
Charles Drucker, *President*
George A Schafer Jr, *President*
Kayla Venter, *Partner*
Sarah Owen, *General Mgr*
Tj Casey, *Vice Pres*
EMP: 350
SALES (est): 802MM
SALES (corp-wide): 3.9B **Publicly Held**
SIC: 7374 Data processing service
HQ: Worldpay Holding, Llc
8500 Governors Hill Dr
Symmes Twp OH 45249
513 358-6192

Syracuse
Meigs County

(G-17469)
MEIGS INDUSTRIES INC
Also Called: CARLETON SCHOOL
1310 Carleton St (45779)
P.O. Box 307 (45779-0307)
PHONE...............................740 992-6681
Kay Davis, *Director*
EMP: 40
SALES: 533.1K **Privately Held**
SIC: 8331 Sheltered workshop

Tallmadge
Summit County

(G-17470)
BUSINESS DATA SYSTEMS INC
1267 Southeast Ave Ste 5 (44278-3148)
PHONE...............................330 633-1221
James Coffelt, *President*
EMP: 34
SQ FT: 2,500
SALES: 4.5MM **Privately Held**
WEB: www.businessdatasystems.net
SIC: 5045 5046 5044 Terminals, computer; computer software; commercial cooking & food service equipment; cash registers

(G-17471)
CHILDRENS HOSP MED CTR AKRON
Also Called: Family Child Learning Center
143 Northwest Ave Bldg A (44278-1806)
PHONE...............................330 633-2055
Marilyn Espesherwindt, *Director*
EMP: 27
SALES (corp-wide): 747.4MM **Privately Held**
WEB: www.cincinnatichildrens.org
SIC: 8733 8322 Medical research; child related social services
PA: Childrens Hospital Medical Center Of Akron
1 Perkins Sq
Akron OH 44308
330 543-1000

(G-17472)
COMMUNICARE HEALTH SVCS INC
Also Called: Colony Healthcare Center, The
563 Colony Park Dr (44278-2859)
PHONE...............................330 630-9780
Dawn Koma, *Principal*
EMP: 92

SALES (corp-wide): 125.8MM **Privately Held**
SIC: 6531 8051 Real estate agents & managers; skilled nursing care facilities
PA: Communicare Health Services, Inc.
4700 Ashwood Dr Ste 200
Blue Ash OH 45241
513 530-1654

(G-17473)
COUNTY OF SUMMIT
Also Called: Developmental Disabilities Bd
89 E Howe Rd (44278-1003)
PHONE...............................330 634-8193
Gary Peters, *Project Mgr*
Laurie Williams, *Hum Res Coord*
Tricia Perduk, *Comms Mgr*
Thomas Armstrong, *Manager*
Cheryl Funk, *Manager*
EMP: 600 **Privately Held**
WEB: www.cpcourt.summitoh.net
SIC: 9431 8322 ; individual & family services
PA: County Of Summit
650 Dan St
Akron OH 44310
330 643-2500

(G-17474)
DERMAMED COATINGS COMPANY LLC
381 Geneva Ave (44278-2732)
PHONE...............................330 634-9449
Phil Brady, *Mng Member*
Steve Collins,
Brian Leek,
▲ EMP: 40
SQ FT: 10,000
SALES (est): 10.9MM **Privately Held**
WEB: www.dermamed.net
SIC: 5047 Medical & hospital equipment

(G-17475)
HANGER PROSTHETICS & (HQ)
33 North Ave Ste 101 (44278-1900)
PHONE...............................330 633-9807
Vinit K Asar, *CEO*
Samuel M Liang, *President*
Anurag W Kedia, *Family Practiti*
EMP: 34
SALES (est): 25.4MM
SALES (corp-wide): 1B **Publicly Held**
SIC: 5999 8741 Orthopedic & prosthesis applications; management services
PA: Hanger, Inc.
10910 Domain Dr Ste 300
Austin TX 78758
512 777-3800

(G-17476)
HEATHER KNOLL RETIREMENT VLG
Also Called: Heather Knoll Nursing Center
1134 North Ave (44278-1065)
PHONE...............................330 688-8600
Lisa Slomovitz, *President*
EMP: 160
SALES: 9.4MM **Privately Held**
SIC: 8051 Convalescent home with continuous nursing care

(G-17477)
HEAVEN BOUND ASCENSIONS
Also Called: Fun Makers
66 N Village View Rd (44278-2040)
PHONE...............................330 633-3288
Dennis Wellser, *President*
EMP: 30
SALES: 400K **Privately Held**
WEB: www.fun-makers.com
SIC: 5945 7999 Toys & games; tennis services & professionals

(G-17478)
J D WILLIAMSON CNSTR CO INC
441 Geneva Ave (44278-2704)
P.O. Box 113 (44278-0113)
PHONE...............................330 633-1258
Joel D Williamson, *President*
John Englehart, *Vice Pres*
Veronica Williamson, *Vice Pres*
EMP: 99
SQ FT: 3,000

SALES (est): 19.6MM **Privately Held**
SIC: 1542 Commercial & office building, new construction

(G-17479)
J RUSSELL CONSTRUCTION
180 Southwest Ave (44278-2231)
PHONE...............................330 633-6462
James Russell Wilson, *Owner*
EMP: 45
SQ FT: 4,500
SALES (est): 4.7MM **Privately Held**
SIC: 1521 General remodeling, single-family houses

(G-17480)
LEPPO INC (PA)
Also Called: LEPPO EQUIPMENT
176 West Ave (44278-2145)
P.O. Box 154 (44278-0154)
PHONE...............................330 633-3999
Dale Leppo, *CEO*
Glenn Leppo, *President*
John Dovala, *Parts Mgr*
Brian Ulman, *Parts Mgr*
Joanne Sweeney, *Treasurer*
EMP: 128 EST: 1945
SQ FT: 44,000
SALES: 70.6MM **Privately Held**
WEB: www.leppos.com
SIC: 5082 7353 7629 General construction machinery & equipment; heavy construction equipment rental; business machine repair, electric

(G-17481)
LIVING ASSISTANCE SERVICES
Also Called: Visiting Angels
22 Northwest Ave (44278-1808)
PHONE...............................330 733-1532
Jodi Wood, *President*
EMP: 65
SALES (est): 2.3MM **Privately Held**
SIC: 8082 Home health care services

(G-17482)
NORTHEAST FAMILY HEALTH CARE
Also Called: Dorman, Regina MD
65 Community Rd Ste C (44278-2358)
PHONE...............................330 630-2332
Mark Meyers Do, *President*
EMP: 35
SQ FT: 3,500
SALES (est): 2.3MM **Privately Held**
SIC: 8011 Physicians' office, including specialists

(G-17483)
NOVUS CLINIC
518 West Ave (44278-2117)
PHONE...............................330 630-9699
Donald C Stephens MD, *Principal*
EMP: 29
SALES (est): 2.3MM **Privately Held**
WEB: www.novusclinic.com
SIC: 8099 Health & allied services

(G-17484)
PIONEER PHYSICIANS NETWORKING
Also Called: North East Family Healthcare
65 Community Rd Ste C (44278-2358)
PHONE...............................330 633-6601
Kathy Ray, *Site Mgr*
EMP: 30 **Privately Held**
WEB: www.pioneerphysicians.com
SIC: 8721 8011 Billing & bookkeeping service; physicians' office, including specialists
PA: Pioneer Physicians Networking, Inc
3515 Massillon Rd Ste 150
Uniontown OH 44685

(G-17485)
RAINBOW RESIDENTIALS LLC
193 East Ave Ste 103 (44278-2341)
PHONE...............................330 819-4202
Angela Parnell-Jackson, *Principal*
EMP: 41 EST: 2008
SALES (est): 1.2MM **Privately Held**
SIC: 8082 Home health care services

(G-17486)
S D MYERS INC
180 South Ave (44278-2864)
PHONE...............................330 630-7000
Scott Myers, *Ch of Bd*
Dale Bissonette, *President*
Allan Ross, *Vice Pres*
David Myers, *Admin Sec*
EMP: 230
SQ FT: 220,000
SALES (est): 36.3MM **Privately Held**
SIC: 8734 7629 Testing laboratories; electrical equipment repair services; electrical equipment repair, high voltage

(G-17487)
SD MYERS LLC
180 South Ave (44278-2864)
PHONE...............................330 630-7000
Scott Myers, *CEO*
Dale Bissonette, *President*
Ed Muckley, *Finance*
Beth Raies, *Admin Sec*
Sindi Harrison,
EMP: 200
SQ FT: 200,000
SALES: 30MM **Privately Held**
SIC: 8734 Testing laboratories

(G-17488)
SPEELMAN ELECTRIC INC
358 Commerce St (44278-2139)
PHONE...............................330 633-1410
Richard Speelman, *President*
Christeen Parsons, *CFO*
EMP: 80
SQ FT: 7,000
SALES (est): 43.5MM **Privately Held**
WEB: www.speelmanelectric.com
SIC: 3825 1731 Test equipment for electronic & electric measurement; general electrical contractor

(G-17489)
SUMMA HEALTH
Also Called: Summa Physicians
182 East Ave (44278-2311)
PHONE...............................330 630-9726
Jeffrey Bachtel, *Branch Mgr*
EMP: 25
SALES (corp-wide): 1B **Privately Held**
SIC: 8062 General medical & surgical hospitals
PA: Summa Health
525 E Market St
Akron OH 44304
330 375-3000

(G-17490)
SUMMIT FACILITY OPERATIONS LLC
Also Called: Summit Villa Care Center
330 Southwest Ave (44278-2235)
PHONE...............................330 633-0555
James Renacci, *President*
C Douglas Warner, *Vice Pres*
Ann J Warner, *Treasurer*
Christy Yoho, *Director*
Janice Collins, *Administration*
EMP: 94
SALES (est): 3.7MM
SALES (corp-wide): 580.2MM **Privately Held**
WEB: www.tandemhealthcare.com
SIC: 8051 8052 Skilled nursing care facilities; intermediate care facilities
PA: Consulate Management Company, Llc
800 Concourse Pkwy S
Maitland FL 32751
407 571-1550

(G-17491)
SYSTEM OPTICS CSMT SRGCAL ARTS
518 West Ave (44278-2117)
PHONE...............................330 630-9699
Todd L Beyer Do, *President*
EMP: 50
SQ FT: 11,378
SALES (est): 4.2MM **Privately Held**
WEB: www.glassline.com
SIC: 8011 Ophthalmologist

▲ = Import ▼=Export
◆ =Import/Export

(G-17492)
SYSTEM OPTICS LASER VISION CTR
518 West Ave (44278-2117)
PHONE...............................330 630-2451
Scott Weekly, *Administration*
EMP: 52
SALES (est): 3.4MM **Privately Held**
SIC: 8011 Eyes, ears, nose & throat specialist: physician/surgeon

(G-17493)
TALLMADGE BOARD OF EDUCATION
Also Called: Tallmadge Schools Bus Garage
89 W Overdale Dr (44278-1935)
PHONE...............................330 633-2215
Bev Alestock, *Branch Mgr*
EMP: 45
SALES (corp-wide): 10.8MM **Privately Held**
SIC: 7538 General automotive repair shops
PA: Tallmadge Board Of Education
486 East Ave
Tallmadge OH 44278
330 633-3291

(G-17494)
TALLMADGE COLLISION CENTER (PA)
195 Northeast Ave (44278-1450)
P.O. Box 458 (44278-0458)
PHONE...............................330 630-2188
Kenneth Dixon, *CEO*
Robert Black III, *President*
EMP: 33
SQ FT: 11,000
SALES (est): 4MM **Privately Held**
WEB: www.tallmadgecollision.com
SIC: 7532 Collision shops, automotive

(G-17495)
TWO HAPPY FROGS INCORPORATED
165 Northeast Ave (44278-1450)
P.O. Box 516 (44278-0516)
PHONE...............................330 633-1666
Bobbie Tilton, *President*
David Pape, *Vice Pres*
EMP: 35 EST: 1980
SQ FT: 32,000
SALES (est): 8.7MM **Privately Held**
SIC: 5199 Rubber, crude

(G-17496)
UNITED DENTAL LABORATORIES (PA)
261 South Ave (44278-2819)
P.O. Box 428 (44278-0428)
PHONE...............................330 253-1810
Richard Delapa Jr, *President*
EMP: 35
SQ FT: 15,000
SALES (est): 5.3MM **Privately Held**
WEB: www.uniteddentallab.com
SIC: 8072 3843 Denture production; dental equipment & supplies

(G-17497)
UNITY HEALTH NETWORK LLC
116 East Ave (44278-2300)
PHONE...............................330 633-7782
Robert A Kent, *Administration*
EMP: 47
SALES (corp-wide): 14.5MM **Privately Held**
SIC: 8099 Blood related health services
PA: Unity Health Network, Llc
3033 State Rd
Cuyahoga Falls OH 44223
330 923-5899

(G-17498)
WARDJET LLC
180 South Ave (44278-2813)
PHONE...............................330 677-9100
Rich Ward, *President*
Kelly Eastman, *Materials Mgr*
Benjie Massara, *Purch Agent*
Leah Runyon, *Buyer*
Jon Deamicis, *Engineer*
◆ EMP: 91
SQ FT: 12,000

SALES (est): 15.2MM
SALES (corp-wide): 25.5MM **Privately Held**
WEB: www.wardjet.com
SIC: 5084 Industrial machinery & equipment
PA: Axyz International Inc
5330 South Service Rd
Burlington ON L7L 5
905 634-4940

(G-17499)
WARREN GUILLARD BRICKLAYERS
Also Called: Warren Guillard Brick Layers
107 Potomac Ave (44278-2754)
PHONE...............................330 633-3855
Warren Guillard, *President*
Gene Guillard, *Treasurer*
EMP: 45
SQ FT: 2,000
SALES: 4MM **Privately Held**
SIC: 1741 Masonry & other stonework

Terrace Park
Hamilton County

(G-17500)
ST THOMAS EPISCOPAL CHURCH
Also Called: St Thomas Nursery School
100 Miami Ave (45174-1175)
PHONE...............................513 831-6908
Becky Peharry, *Director*
EMP: 25 **Privately Held**
WEB: www.stthomasepiscopal.org
SIC: 8351 Child day care services
PA: St Thomas Episcopal Church
100 Miami Ave
Terrace Park OH 45174

(G-17501)
WILKRIS COMPANY
411 Terrace Pl (45174-1164)
P.O. Box 230 (45174-0230)
PHONE...............................513 271-9344
William J Van EE, *President*
Bonnie Van EE, *Corp Secy*
Bill Vanee, *Senior Engr*
Bonnie V EE, *Treasurer*
Russ Darrow, *Sales Staff*
EMP: 50
SALES (est): 2.6MM **Privately Held**
SIC: 8711 5084 Engineering services; industrial machinery & equipment

---

The Plains
Athens County

(G-17502)
ATHENS COUNTY EMRGNCY MED SVCS
36 N Plains Rd Ste 2 (45780-2003)
PHONE...............................740 797-9560
Rick Ballebes, *Director*
EMP: 54
SALES (est): 514K **Privately Held**
SIC: 4119 Ambulance service

(G-17503)
LINDLEY INN
Also Called: Athens Health Partners
9000 Hocking Hills Dr (45780-1209)
PHONE...............................740 797-9701
Roger Benson, *President*
EMP: 50
SALES (est): 2.3MM **Privately Held**
WEB: www.lindley.cc
SIC: 8361 Geriatric residential care

Thornville
Perry County

(G-17504)
BOWMAN ORGANIC FARMS LTD
Also Called: Bowman Agricultural RES Ctr
8100 Blackbird Ln (43076-9625)
P.O. Box 29 (43076-0029)
PHONE...............................740 246-3936
EMP: 47
SALES (est): 1.3MM **Privately Held**
SIC: 5148 Whol Fruits/Vegetables

(G-17505)
ENGLEFIELD INC
Also Called: BP
10636 Jacksontown Rd (43076-8865)
PHONE...............................740 323-2077
EMP: 73
SALES (corp-wide): 615.5MM **Privately Held**
SIC: 7231 Unisex hair salons
PA: Englefield, Inc.
447 James Pkwy
Heath OH 43056
740 928-8215

(G-17506)
SHELLY MATERIALS INC (DH)
Also Called: Shelly Company, The
80 Park Dr (43076-9397)
P.O. Box 266 (43076-0266)
PHONE...............................740 246-6315
John Power, *President*
Ted Lemon, *Vice Pres*
Doug Radabaugh, *Treasurer*
EMP: 100 EST: 1938
SALES (est): 809.6MM
SALES (corp-wide): 29.7B **Privately Held**
SIC: 1422 1442 2951 4492 Crushed & broken limestone; construction sand & gravel; concrete, asphaltic (not from refineries); tugboat service
HQ: Shelly Company
80 Park Dr
Thornville OH 43076
740 246-6315

(G-17507)
THORNVILLE NH LLC
Also Called: THORNVILLE HEALTH AND REHABILI
14100 Zion Rd (43076-9408)
PHONE...............................740 246-5253
Mordecai Rosenberg, *President*
Ronald Swartz, *CFO*
Dawn Wozniak, *Exec Sec*
EMP: 73
SALES (est): 488.2K **Privately Held**
SIC: 8051 Skilled nursing care facilities

Thurman
Gallia County

(G-17508)
DOT SMITH LLC
3607 Garners Ford Rd (45685-9301)
PHONE...............................740 245-5105
David Martin, *General Mgr*
John Smith, *Principal*
EMP: 25 EST: 2013
SALES: 692.5K **Privately Held**
SIC: 4212 Local trucking, without storage

Tiffin
Seneca County

(G-17509)
ATLAS INDUSTRIES INC
401 Wall St (44883-1369)
PHONE...............................419 637-2117
Donald Rickard, *Manager*
EMP: 302

SALES (corp-wide): 133.9MM **Privately Held**
WEB: www.atlasindustries.com
SIC: 3599 5013 3714 Crankshafts & camshafts, machining; automotive supplies & parts; motor vehicle parts & accessories
PA: Atlas Industries, Inc.
1750 E State St
Fremont OH 43420
419 355-1000

(G-17510)
BALLREICH BROS INC
Also Called: Ballreichs Potato Chips Snacks
186 Ohio Ave (44883-1746)
PHONE...............................419 447-1814
Brian Reis, *President*
Joseph Weininger, *Controller*
Linda Reis, *Financial Exec*
Haley Thomas, *Sales Dir*
Regina Miller, *Manager*
EMP: 105
SQ FT: 48,000
SALES (est): 10.2MM **Privately Held**
WEB: www.ballreich.com
SIC: 2096 2099 4226 Potato chips & other potato-based snacks; food preparations; special warehousing & storage

(G-17511)
CAMDEN FLS RCPTION CNFRNCE CTR
Also Called: Carmella's Italian Restaurant
2460 S State Route 231 (44883-9314)
P.O. Box 221 (44883-0221)
PHONE...............................419 448-7699
Dominic Fabrizio, *Partner*
EMP: 30
SALES (est): 630.6K **Privately Held**
SIC: 7299 Banquet hall facilities

(G-17512)
CONCORDNCE HLTHCARE SLTONS LLC (PA)
Also Called: Seneca Medical
85 Shaffer Park Dr (44883-9290)
PHONE...............................419 455-2153
Roger Benz, *Co-President*
Tom Harris, *Co-President*
Jaysen Stevenson, *COO*
Todd Howell, *CFO*
EMP: 90
SALES (est): 790.7MM **Privately Held**
SIC: 5047 Medical & hospital equipment

(G-17513)
COUNTY OF SENECA
Also Called: Seneca County Highway Dept
3210 S State Route 100 (44883-8869)
PHONE...............................419 447-3863
Joe Rumschlag, *Manager*
EMP: 25 **Privately Held**
WEB: www.senecapros.org
SIC: 1611 Highway & street maintenance
PA: County Of Seneca
111 Madison St
Tiffin OH 44883
419 447-4550

(G-17514)
COUNTY OF SENECA
Also Called: Seneca County Human Services
3362 S Township Rd (44883)
PHONE...............................419 447-5011
Kathy Oliver, *Manager*
EMP: 90 **Privately Held**
WEB: www.senecapros.org
SIC: 6371 Welfare pensions
PA: County Of Seneca
111 Madison St
Tiffin OH 44883
419 447-4550

(G-17515)
CUSTOM MACHINE INC
3315 W Township Road 158 (44883-9453)
PHONE...............................419 986-5122
David Hammer, *President*
Jeffery Hammer, *Vice Pres*
Phyllis Hammer, *Treasurer*
EMP: 30
SQ FT: 19,200

SALES: 2.9MM **Privately Held**
WEB: www.custom-machine-inc.com
SIC: 3544 3599 7692 Special dies &
tools; machine shop, jobbing & repair;
welding repair

(G-17516)
ELMWOOD CENTER INC
Also Called: Elmwood At Shawhan
54 S Washington St (44883-2377)
PHONE.....................................419 447-6885
Teresa Jones, *Manager*
EMP: 60
SALES (corp-wide): 9.2MM **Privately
Held**
WEB: www.elmwoodassistedliving.com
SIC: 8052 Home for the mentally retarded,
with health care
PA: Elmwood Center Inc
441 N Broadway St
Green Springs OH 44836
419 639-2581

(G-17517)
FAMILY LRNG CTR AT SENTINEL
797 E Township Road 201 (44883-8861)
PHONE.....................................419 448-5079
Heather Justen, *Director*
EMP: 50
SALES (est): 639.4K **Privately Held**
SIC: 8351 Preschool center

(G-17518)
**FIRELANDS REGIONAL HEALTH
SYS**
Also Called: Firelands Counseling Recovery
76 Ashwood Dr (44883-1908)
PHONE.....................................419 448-9440
Robin Reeves, *Manager*
EMP: 50
SALES (corp-wide): 280.7MM **Privately
Held**
SIC: 8361 Home for the mentally handi-
capped
PA: Firelands Regional Health System
1111 Hayes Ave
Sandusky OH 44870
419 557-7400

(G-17519)
**FRIEDMAN VLG RETIREMENT
CMNTY**
Also Called: Heart & HM Assistant Friedman
175 Saint Francis Ave (44883-3457)
PHONE.....................................419 443-1540
Kim Henry, *Vice Pres*
EMP: 25
SALES (est): 301.2K **Privately Held**
SIC: 8361 Residential care

(G-17520)
**INSTITUTIONAL CARE
PHARMACY (PA)**
1815 W County Road 54 (44883-7723)
PHONE.....................................419 447-6216
James W Unverferth, *President*
Todd Hendrickson, *Pharmacist*
Chad Orr, *Pharmacist*
Kari Wedge, *Pharmacist*
Sue Hawkins, *Info Tech Mgr*
EMP: 95 EST: 1985
SQ FT: 22,000
SALES (est): 53.8MM **Privately Held**
WEB: www.icp.com
SIC: 5122 5047 5912 Patent medicines;
medical & hospital equipment; drug stores
& proprietary stores

(G-17521)
LOWES HOME CENTERS LLC
1025 W Market St (44883-2541)
PHONE.....................................419 447-4101
Jean Lowe, *Branch Mgr*
EMP: 158
SALES (corp-wide): 68.6B **Publicly Held**
SIC: 5211 5031 5722 5064 Home cen-
ters; building materials, exterior; building
materials, interior; household appliance
stores; electrical appliances, television &
radio
HQ: Lowe's Home Centers, Llc
1605 Curtis Bridge Rd
Wilkesboro NC 28697
336 658-4000

(G-17522)
M G Q INC
Also Called: Maple Grove Companies
1525 W County Road 42 (44883-8457)
P.O. Box 130, Old Fort (44861-0130)
PHONE.....................................419 992-4236
Lynn Radabaugh, *President*
Tim Bell, *President*
Bruce Chubb, *Principal*
Jeff Murphy, *Principal*
Bob Chesebro, *Corp Secy*
EMP: 45
SALES (est): 3.5MM **Privately Held**
WEB: www.mgq.com
SIC: 4214 1481 Local trucking with stor-
age; mine & quarry services, nonmetallic
minerals

(G-17523)
MCPAUL CORP
Also Called: Quality Inn
981 S Morgan St (44883-2535)
PHONE.....................................419 447-6313
George Paul, *President*
Charlie Mc Carthy, *Principal*
EMP: 25
SQ FT: 30,000
SALES (est): 1MM **Privately Held**
WEB: www.mcpaul.com
SIC: 7011 5812 5813 Hotels; eating
places; cocktail lounge

(G-17524)
**MERCY HEALTH - TIFFIN HOSP
LLC (HQ)**
45 St Lawrence Dr (44883-8310)
PHONE.....................................419 455-7000
Lynn Detterman, *President*
EMP: 102
SQ FT: 241,000
SALES: 75.2MM
SALES (corp-wide): 4.7B **Privately Held**
SIC: 8062 General medical & surgical hos-
pitals
PA: Mercy Health
1701 Mercy Health Pl
Cincinnati OH 45237
513 639-2800

(G-17525)
MOHAWK GOLF CLUB
4399 S State Route 231 (44883-9308)
P.O. Box 506 (44883-0506)
PHONE.....................................419 447-5876
Robert Durbin, *President*
Robert Sankey, *Vice Pres*
EMP: 33
SALES: 461.4K **Privately Held**
SIC: 7997 5812 5813 Golf club, member-
ship; eating places; bar (drinking places)

(G-17526)
**MOLYET CROP PRODUCTION
INC**
546 E County Road 51 (44883-9609)
PHONE.....................................419 992-4288
Bernard Molyet, *President*
Gregory Molyet, *Partner*
Jeffery Molyet, *Partner*
Michael Molyet, *Partner*
Ruth Molyet, *Partner*
EMP: 40
SALES (est): 2.3MM **Privately Held**
SIC: 0111 0115 0116 0161 Wheat; corn;
soybeans; vegetables & melons

(G-17527)
NYE F A & SONS ENTERPRISES
7443 N Township Road 70 (44883-9454)
P.O. Box 398, Bettsville (44815-0398)
PHONE.....................................419 986-5400
Gary Nye, *President*
Franklin Nye, *Vice Pres*
EMP: 26
SALES (est): 1.9MM **Privately Held**
SIC: 4789 Cargo loading & unloading serv-
ices

(G-17528)
OHIO DEPARTMENT OF HEALTH
Also Called: Tiffin Developmental Center
600 N River Rd (44883-1173)
PHONE.....................................419 447-1450
Peggy S Bockey, *Manager*
EMP: 400 **Privately Held**

WEB: www.jchealth.com
SIC: 8361 9431 Home for the mentally
handicapped;
HQ: Department Of Health Ohio
246 N High St
Columbus OH 43215

(G-17529)
OHIO POWER COMPANY
2622 S State Route 100 (44883-8972)
PHONE.....................................419 443-4634
Carl McCue, *Branch Mgr*
EMP: 30
SALES (corp-wide): 16.2B **Publicly Held**
SIC: 1731 Electrical work
HQ: Ohio Power Company
1 Riverside Plz
Columbus OH 43215
614 716-1000

(G-17530)
OLD FORT BANKING COMPANY
Also Called: Invest
33 E Market St (44883-2829)
P.O. Box 627 (44883-0627)
PHONE.....................................419 447-4790
Scott Kromer, *Assistant VP*
Sandy Rau, *Manager*
EMP: 59
SALES (corp-wide): 20.2MM **Privately
Held**
WEB: www.oldfortbank.com
SIC: 6022 State trust companies accepting
deposits, commercial
HQ: The Old Fort Banking Company
8034 Main St
Old Fort OH 44861
419 447-6150

(G-17531)
ORIANA HOUSE INC
3055 S State Route 100 (44883-8868)
PHONE.....................................419 447-1444
Jason Varney, *Branch Mgr*
EMP: 212
SALES (corp-wide): 51.1MM **Privately
Held**
SIC: 7322 Collection agency, except real
estate
PA: Oriana House, Inc.
885 E Buchtel Ave
Akron OH 44305
330 535-8116

(G-17532)
PIASANS MILL INC
255 Riverside Dr (44883-1609)
PHONE.....................................419 448-0100
Scott Lyons, *President*
EMP: 35
SALES: 950K **Privately Held**
SIC: 8742 Management consulting serv-
ices

(G-17533)
QUICK TAB II INC (PA)
241 Heritage Dr (44883-9504)
P.O. Box 723 (44883-0723)
PHONE.....................................419 448-6622
Chuck Daughenbaugn, *CEO*
Mike Daughenbaugh, *Vice Pres*
Marty Ward, *Traffic Mgr*
Charles Eingle, *CFO*
Melissa Chester, *Human Res Mgr*
▼ EMP: 64
SQ FT: 30,000
SALES (est): 12.1MM **Privately Held**
WEB: www.qt2.com
SIC: 2752 5112 2791 2789 Business
forms, lithographed; stationery & office
supplies; typesetting; bookbinding & re-
lated work

(G-17534)
RK FAMILY INC
2300 W Market St (44883-8877)
PHONE.....................................419 443-1663
Tim F Lode, *Principal*
EMP: 128
SALES (corp-wide): 1.5B **Privately Held**
SIC: 0191 General farms, primarily crop
PA: Rk Family, Inc.
4216 Dewitt Ave
Mattoon IL 61938
217 235-7102

(G-17535)
SALVATION ARMY
505 E Market St (44883-1767)
P.O. Box 341 (44883-0341)
PHONE.....................................419 447-2252
George Polariek, *Branch Mgr*
EMP: 91
SQ FT: 86,946
SALES (corp-wide): 4.3B **Privately Held**
WEB: www.salvationarmy.org
SIC: 5932 8741 8641 Used merchandise
stores; management services; civic social
& fraternal associations
HQ: The Salvation Army
440 W Nyack Rd Ofc
West Nyack NY 10994
845 620-7200

(G-17536)
SENECA COUNTY EMS
126 Hopewell Ave (44883-2636)
PHONE.....................................419 447-0266
Dan Stahl, *Manager*
Ken Majors,
EMP: 140
SALES: 300K **Privately Held**
SIC: 8099 Health & allied services

(G-17537)
**SENECA COUNTY FIREMENS
ASSN**
1070 S County Road 17 (44883-9408)
PHONE.....................................419 447-7909
Dennis Wilkinson, *Corp Secy*
EMP: 99
SALES (est): 834.1K **Privately Held**
SIC: 8641 Civic social & fraternal associa-
tions

(G-17538)
SENECA DIALYSIS LLC
Also Called: Seneca County Dialysis
10 St Lawrence Dr (44883-8310)
PHONE.....................................419 443-1051
Bob Badal, *Principal*
EMP: 53
SALES (est): 1.6MM **Publicly Held**
WEB: www.davita.com
SIC: 8092 Kidney dialysis centers
PA: Davita Inc.
2000 16th St
Denver CO 80202

(G-17539)
SENECA MEDICAL LLC (HQ)
85 Shaffer Park Dr (44883-9290)
P.O. Box 399 (44883-0399)
PHONE.....................................419 447-0236
Roger Benz, *CEO*
Buddy Wert, *President*
Todd Howell, *CFO*
Dave Myers, *Ch Credit Ofcr*
Michelle Clouse, *Marketing Staff*
▲ EMP: 235
SALES (est): 447.2MM
SALES (corp-wide): 790.7MM **Privately
Held**
WEB: www.senecamedical.com
SIC: 5047 Medical equipment & supplies;
surgical equipment & supplies
PA: Concordance Healthcare Solutions Llc
85 Shaffer Park Dr
Tiffin OH 44883
419 455-2153

(G-17540)
**SENECA-CRAWFORD AREA
TRNSP (PA)**
Also Called: S C A T
3446 S Township Road 151 (44883-9499)
P.O. Box 922 (44883-0922)
PHONE.....................................419 937-2428
Mary Habig, *CEO*
EMP: 35
SALES: 1.4MM **Privately Held**
SIC: 4119 Vanpool operation

(G-17541)
TECTA AMERICA CORP
Also Called: JB Roofing
1480 S County Road 594 (44883-2677)
PHONE.....................................419 447-1716
EMP: 60

SALES (corp-wide): 12.9MM **Privately Held**
SIC: 1761 Roofing contractor
HQ: Tecta America Corp.
9450 Bryn Mawr Ave
Rosemont IL 60018
847 581-3888

(G-17542)
TIFFIN CMNTY YMCA RCRATION CTR (PA)
180 Summit St (44883-3168)
PHONE.................................419 447-8711
Kathy Jentgen, *President*
Paul Fortney, *Opers Staff*
Stacie Routzahn, *Finance*
Jillian Shaferly, *Director*
EMP: 80
SQ FT: 70,000
SALES: 1.9MM **Privately Held**
SIC: 7997 8641 Membership sports & recreation clubs; community membership club

(G-17543)
TIFFIN LOADER CRANE COMPANY
4151 W State Route 18 (44883-8997)
PHONE.................................419 448-8156
Mark Woody, *President*
Ed Gerken, *General Mgr*
Luke Kelly, *General Mgr*
Anthony J Reser, *Admin Sec*
EMP: 55
SQ FT: 60,000
SALES (est): 20.6MM
SALES (corp-wide): 242.1K **Privately Held**
SIC: 5084 Cranes, industrial; materials handling machinery
HQ: Palfinger Ag
Lamprechtshausener BundesstraBe 8
Bergheim 5101
662 228-10

(G-17544)
TIFFIN PAPER COMPANY (PA)
Also Called: TPC Food Service
265 6th Ave (44883-1083)
P.O. Box 129 (44883-0129)
PHONE.................................419 447-2121
Thomas M Maiberger, *President*
Tony Paulus, *Vice Pres*
Angie Kimmet, *Purchasing*
Scott Maiberger, *Accountant*
Stephen Musil, *Hum Res Coord*
EMP: 45
SQ FT: 40,000
SALES (est): 38.9MM **Privately Held**
WEB: www.tpcfoodservice.com
SIC: 5113 5149 5145 Paper & products, wrapping or coarse; groceries & related products; confectionery

(G-17545)
TRINITY HEALTH CORPORATION
485 W Market St (44883)
PHONE.................................419 448-3124
Dave McBicker, *Director*
EMP: 30
SALES (corp-wide): 18.3B **Privately Held**
WEB: www.trinity-health.com
SIC: 8742 Management consulting services
PA: Trinity Health Corporation
20555 Victor Pkwy
Livonia MI 48152
734 343-1000

(G-17546)
VOLUNTERS AMER CARE FACILITIES
Also Called: Volunteer of Amer Autemwood CA
670 E State Route 18 (44883-1856)
PHONE.................................419 447-7151
Sally Turner, *Branch Mgr*
EMP: 130
SALES (corp-wide): 66.7MM **Privately Held**
SIC: 8051 Convalescent home with continuous nursing care
PA: Volunteers Of America Care Facilities
7530 Market Place Dr
Eden Prairie MN 55344
952 941-0305

(G-17547)
WORK CONNECTIONS INTL LLC
525 Wall St Ste A (44883-1370)
PHONE.................................419 448-4655
Ryan Shultz, *Principal*
EMP: 25
SALES (est): 3.5MM **Privately Held**
SIC: 8731 Natural resource research

Tipp City
Miami County

(G-17548)
AFFORD-A-CAR INC
8973 State 201 (45371)
PHONE.................................937 235-2700
Don Gilliam, *President*
EMP: 25
SALES (est): 2MM **Privately Held**
SIC: 5521 7514 Automobiles, used cars only; trucks, tractors & trailers: used; passenger car rental

(G-17549)
ANNAS CHILD CARE LRNG CTR INC (PA)
Also Called: Early Beginnings
4949 S County Road 25a (45371-2946)
PHONE.................................937 667-1903
Drew Shock, *President*
Jacquelyn Shock, *Admin Sec*
EMP: 85
SALES (est): 2.7MM **Privately Held**
SIC: 8351 Group day care center

(G-17550)
CALVARY CONTRACTING INC
4125 Gibson Dr (45371-9064)
PHONE.................................937 754-0300
John C Moon, *President*
Denise Moon, *Vice Pres*
Cliff Dech, *Project Mgr*
Sterling Williams, *Project Mgr*
Kim Rector, *Controller*
EMP: 27
SQ FT: 3,600
SALES (est): 7.9MM **Privately Held**
WEB: www.calvarycontracting.com
SIC: 1542 Commercial & office building, new construction; commercial & office buildings, renovation & repair

(G-17551)
CHARLES C SMITH DDS INC
Also Called: Saleh, Hady DMD
110 S Tippecanoe Dr Ste A (45371-3109)
PHONE.................................937 667-2417
Charles C Smith DDS, *President*
EMP: 30
SQ FT: 10,176
SALES (est): 1.4MM **Privately Held**
SIC: 8021 Dentists' office

(G-17552)
CHILD & ADOLESCENT SPECIALITY
1483 W Main St (45371-2803)
PHONE.................................937 667-7711
Kevin Horvath MD, *President*
EMP: 30
SALES (est): 4MM **Privately Held**
SIC: 8011 Pediatrician

(G-17553)
COMMUNITY SERVICES INC
3 E Main St (45371-1925)
P.O. Box 242 (45371-0242)
PHONE.................................937 667-8631
Kathy Taylor, *Director*
EMP: 100
SALES: 375.2K **Privately Held**
WEB: www.tmcomservices.org
SIC: 8322 7032 Community center; sporting & recreational camps

(G-17554)
D&M SALES & SOLUTIONS LLC
9465 S State Route 202 # 1 (45371-8301)
PHONE.................................937 667-8713
Dale Landes, *President*
EMP: 30

(G-17555)
DAIHEN INC (HQ)
Also Called: Advanced Welding Division
1400 Blauser Dr (45371-2471)
PHONE.................................937 667-0800
Masanobu Uchida, *President*
Mike Monnin, *General Mgr*
Todd Griffieth, *Opers Mgr*
Larry Barley, *Engineer*
Jeffrey Preston, *Engineer*
▲ EMP: 38 EST: 1979
SQ FT: 45,000
SALES: 26.3MM
SALES (corp-wide): 1.4B **Privately Held**
SIC: 5084 Welding machinery & equipment
PA: Daihen Corporation
2-1-11, Tagawa, Yodogawa-Ku
Osaka OSK 532-0
663 011-212

(G-17556)
ENVIRONMENT CTRL OF MIAMI CNTY
7939 S County Road 25a A (45371-9107)
P.O. Box 877 (45371-0877)
PHONE.................................937 669-9900
Ted Pauling, *President*
Sheryl Pauling, *Corp Secy*
William Schneider, *Shareholder*
EMP: 65
SQ FT: 3,000
SALES (est): 2.4MM **Privately Held**
SIC: 7349 Janitorial service, contract basis

(G-17557)
HIGH POWER INC
15 Industry Park Ct (45371-3060)
P.O. Box 533 (45371-0533)
PHONE.................................937 667-1772
Brent Black, *President*
EMP: 25
SQ FT: 10,000
SALES (est): 742.4K **Privately Held**
SIC: 7349 Building maintenance services

(G-17558)
HIGH-TEC INDUSTRIAL SERVICES
15 Industry Park Ct (45371-3060)
P.O. Box 533 (45371-0533)
PHONE.................................937 667-1772
Brent Black, *President*
William E Oldham, *President*
Christopher Taylor, *Vice Pres*
Chris Taylor, *Manager*
EMP: 139
SQ FT: 18,000
SALES (est): 25.3MM **Privately Held**
WEB: www.hightecindustrial.com
SIC: 3589 7349 Commercial cooking & foodwarming equipment; building & office cleaning services

(G-17559)
HOMESTEAD GOLF COURSE INC
5327 Worley Rd (45371-9681)
PHONE.................................937 698-4876
David Knife, *President*
Ester Knife, *Corp Secy*
Karen Knife, *Vice Pres*
EMP: 39
SQ FT: 5,000
SALES (est): 1.4MM **Privately Held**
WEB: www.homesteadgolfcourse.com
SIC: 7992 Public golf courses

(G-17560)
HOSS II INC
Also Called: Voss Honda
155 S Garber Dr (45371-1147)
PHONE.................................937 669-4300
John Voss, *President*
John E Voss, *President*
EMP: 40
SALES (est): 12.2MM **Privately Held**
WEB: www.vosshonda.com
SIC: 5511 7539 Automobiles, new & used; automotive repair shops

(G-17561)
JASON WILSON
5575 Ross Rd (45371-9710)
PHONE.................................937 604-8209
Jason Wilson, *Mng Member*
Mark Nelson,
EMP: 27
SALES: 1.5MM **Privately Held**
SIC: 3663 7389 3229 Radio & TV communications equipment; ; fiber optics strands

(G-17562)
MILLER PIPELINE LLC
11990 Peters Pike (45371-9669)
PHONE.................................937 506-8837
Jim Wilson, *Manager*
EMP: 400
SALES (corp-wide): 10.5B **Publicly Held**
WEB: www.millerpipeline.com
SIC: 1623 Pipeline construction
HQ: Miller Pipeline, Llc
8850 Crawfordsville Rd
Indianapolis IN 46234
317 293-0278

(G-17563)
OHIO WINDOW CLEANING INC
Also Called: Kentucky Window Cleaning
4582 Us Route 40 (45371-9025)
P.O. Box 24026, Dayton (45424-0026)
PHONE.................................937 877-0832
Toll Free:.................................888 -
H Bernard Wilson, *President*
Brad Wilson, *General Mgr*
Brian Brabson, *Area Mgr*
Lisa Joiner, *Office Mgr*
Zach Wilson, *Manager*
EMP: 54
SALES (est): 1.9MM **Privately Held**
SIC: 7349 Window cleaning

(G-17564)
POLYMERSHAPES LLC
1480 Blauser Dr (45371-2471)
PHONE.................................937 877-1903
Patrick Welsh, *Opers Mgr*
Nick Roach, *Cust Svc Mgr*
EMP: 30
SALES (corp-wide): 179.8MM **Privately Held**
WEB: www.sabic-ip.com
SIC: 5162 Plastics materials & basic shapes
PA: Polymershapes Llc
10130 Perimeter Pkwy # 500
Charlotte NC 28216
866 333-0651

(G-17565)
PRECISION STRIP INC
315 Park Ave (45371-1887)
PHONE.................................937 667-6255
Jerry Huber, *Manager*
EMP: 52
SQ FT: 3,080
SALES (corp-wide): 11.5B **Publicly Held**
WEB: www.precision-strip.com
SIC: 4225 3312 General warehousing & storage; blast furnaces & steel mills
HQ: Precision Strip Inc.
86 S Ohio St
Minster OH 45865
419 628-2343

(G-17566)
SAFTEK INDUSTRIAL SERVICE INC
Also Called: High TEC Industrial Services
15 Industry Park Ct (45371-3060)
P.O. Box 533 (45371-0533)
PHONE.................................937 667-1772
Brent Black, *President*
EMP: 25
SALES (est): 690K **Privately Held**
SIC: 7349 Janitorial service, contract basis

(G-17567)
TIME WARNER CABLE INC
1440 Commerce Park Dr (45371-2845)
PHONE.................................937 667-8302
Lois Kerns, *Principal*
EMP: 83
SQ FT: 693
SALES (corp-wide): 43.6B **Publicly Held**
SIC: 4841 Cable television services

HQ: Spectrum Management Holding Company, Llc
400 Atlantic St
Stamford CT 06901
203 905-7801

(G-17568)
TIPP CITY VETERINARY HOSP INC
4900 S County Road 25a (45371-2912)
PHONE..................................937 667-8489
James Mathias, *President*
Ben Spinks, *Treasurer*
Jennie Accuntius, *Department Mgr*
Jim Mathias, *Director*
EMP: 61
SALES (est): 2.2MM Privately Held
WEB: www.tippvet.com
SIC: 0742 Animal hospital services, pets & other animal specialties; veterinarian, animal specialties

(G-17569)
TIPP-MONROE COMMUNITY SVCS INC
3 E Main St (45371-1925)
P.O. Box 242 (45371-0242)
PHONE..................................937 667-8631
Denise Gross, *President*
Deb Jackson, *Treasurer*
EMP: 49
SALES (est): 491.8K Privately Held
SIC: 8399 Community development groups; community action agency

(G-17570)
TOOL TESTING LAB INC
11601 N Dixie Dr (45371-9108)
PHONE..................................937 898-5696
Ted Bowden, *President*
EMP: 35
SALES (est): 5.8MM Privately Held
SIC: 8734 5251 Product certification, safety or performance; tools
PA: Tool Testing Lab, Inc.
11601 N Dixie Dr
Tipp City OH 45371

(G-17571)
TOOL TESTING LAB INC (PA)
11601 N Dixie Dr (45371-9108)
PHONE..................................937 898-5696
Ted Bowden, *President*
Patricia Bowden, *Treasurer*
Terri Howard, *Manager*
Robb Thomas, *Manager*
EMP: 57
SQ FT: 1,000
SALES (est): 7.7MM Privately Held
WEB: www.ttlcal.com
SIC: 8734 Product testing laboratory, safety or performance

(G-17572)
UVMC NURSING CARE INC
Also Called: Springmeade
4375 S County Road 25a (45371-2956)
PHONE..................................937 667-7500
Tom Nick, *Administration*
EMP: 150
SALES (corp-wide): 20.3MM Privately Held
WEB: www.koesterpavilion.com
SIC: 8361 8051 Home for the aged; skilled nursing care facilities
PA: Uvmc Nursing Care, Inc.
3130 N County Road 25a
Troy OH 45373
937 440-4000

```
┌─────────────────────┐
│       Toledo        │
│    Lucas County     │
└─────────────────────┘
```

(G-17573)
21ST CENTURY HEALTH SPA INC (PA)
343 New Towne Square Dr (43612-4626)
PHONE..................................419 476-5585
Ronald R Hemelgarn, *Owner*
EMP: 50
SQ FT: 10,000
SALES (est): 2.9MM Privately Held
SIC: 5091 Fitness equipment & supplies

(G-17574)
A & K RAILROAD MATERIALS INC
2750 Hill Ave (43607-2926)
PHONE..................................419 537-9470
Joe Shinsky, *Manager*
EMP: 25
SQ FT: 10,868
SALES (corp-wide): 150.1MM Privately Held
WEB: www.akrailroad.com
SIC: 5088 Railroad equipment & supplies
PA: A & K Railroad Materials, Inc.
1505 S Redwood Rd
Salt Lake City UT 84104
801 974-5484

(G-17575)
A AND S VENTURES INC
Also Called: Winter Drive In Theater
4311 Garden Estates Dr (43623-3414)
PHONE..................................419 376-3934
Anthony J Arite, *President*
EMP: 35 Privately Held
SIC: 6719 Personal holding companies, except banks

(G-17576)
A R E A TITLE AGENCY INC (PA)
5450 Monroe St Ste 2 (43623-2879)
PHONE..................................419 242-5485
Michael D Repass, *President*
EMP: 25
SALES (est): 4.9MM Privately Held
WEB: www.areatitle.com
SIC: 6541 6361 Title & trust companies; title insurance

(G-17577)
AAA CLUB ALLIANCE INC (PA)
Also Called: AAA Mid-Atlantic
3201 Meijer Dr (43617)
PHONE..................................419 843-1200
Karl Halbedl, *President*
Patty Hicks, *Opers Staff*
Ann Martin, *Agent*
EMP: 83
SQ FT: 24,000
SALES (est): 16.2MM Privately Held
SIC: 8699 Automobile owners' association

(G-17578)
AAA STANDARD SERVICES INC
4117 South Ave (43615-6231)
PHONE..................................419 535-0274
Steven Johnson, *President*
Dale Johnson Sr, *Principal*
Dee Dee Thorsby, *Manager*
EMP: 60
SQ FT: 24,500
SALES: 4MM Privately Held
WEB: www.aaastandardservices.com
SIC: 7349 1521 Janitorial service, contract basis; window cleaning; repairing fire damage, single-family houses

(G-17579)
ABBOTT TOOL INC
Also Called: ATI
405 Dura Ave (43612-2619)
PHONE..................................419 476-6742
Karle Stange, *President*
Kevin Webb, *General Mgr*
Arthur Stange, *Vice Pres*
Leonard Livecchi, *Vice Pres*
EMP: 27
SQ FT: 12,000
SALES (est): 5.5MM Privately Held
SIC: 3469 7692 Machine parts, stamped or pressed metal; welding repair

(G-17580)
ABCO CONTRACTING LLC
947 Belmont Ave (43607-4244)
PHONE..................................419 973-4772
Floyd W Abercrombie Jr,
EMP: 37
SQ FT: 100
SALES: 200K Privately Held
SIC: 1522 1542 4214 6531 Apartment building construction; commercial & office building contractors; local trucking with storage; real estate agents & managers

(G-17581)
ACCURATE NURSE STAFFING
4165 Monroe St (43606-2009)
PHONE..................................419 475-2424
Donna Martin, *Principal*
EMP: 50
SALES (est): 525.6K Privately Held
SIC: 8049 Nurses, registered & practical

(G-17582)
ADECCO USA INC
336 N Superior St 200 (43604-1422)
PHONE..................................419 720-0111
Ken Davis, *Branch Mgr*
EMP: 30
SALES (corp-wide): 27.9B Privately Held
WEB: www.usadecco.com
SIC: 7363 Temporary help service
HQ: Adecco Usa, Inc.
10151 Deerwood Park Blvd
Jacksonville FL 32256
940 360-2000

(G-17583)
ADVOCTES FOR BSIC LGAL EQALITY (PA)
Also Called: ABLE
525 Jefferson Ave (43604-1094)
PHONE..................................419 255-0814
Will Shryock, *Info Tech Mgr*
Susan Frantz, *Web Dvlpr*
Joe Tafelski, *Exec Dir*
Joseph Tafelski, *Director*
Denise Saxon, *Director*
EMP: 50
SALES: 7.7MM Privately Held
SIC: 8111 Legal aid service

(G-17584)
AL PEAKE & SONS INC
4949 Stickney Ave (43612-3716)
PHONE..................................419 243-9284
Philip Peake, *President*
Jeff Goldsmith, *Opers Mgr*
Jack Gilkerson, *Warehouse Mgr*
Joe Deeb, *Sales Mgr*
Ann Beck, *Sales Staff*
EMP: 30
SQ FT: 57,408
SALES (est): 18.3MM Privately Held
WEB: www.alpeake.com
SIC: 5148 Fruits, fresh

(G-17585)
ALBRING VENDING COMPANY
702 Galena St (43611)
PHONE..................................419 726-8059
Bob Albring, *President*
EMP: 30
SQ FT: 2,000
SALES (corp-wide): 2.9MM Privately Held
SIC: 4225 General warehousing
PA: Albring Vending Company
13570 Wayne Rd
Livonia MI 48150
419 726-8059

(G-17586)
ALRO STEEL CORPORATION
3003 Airport Hwy (43609-1405)
P.O. Box 964 (43697-0964)
PHONE..................................419 720-5300
Adam Cristek, *Manager*
EMP: 40
SALES (corp-wide): 1.9B Privately Held
WEB: www.alro.com
SIC: 5051 5085 5162 3444 Steel; aluminum bars, rods, ingots, sheets, pipes, plates, etc.; nonferrous metal sheets, bars, rods, etc.; industrial supplies; plastics materials; sheet metalwork
PA: Alro Steel Corporation
3100 E High St
Jackson MI 49203
517 787-5500

(G-17587)
AMERICAN BROADBAND TELECOM CO
1 Seagate Ste 600 (43604-4512)
PHONE..................................419 824-5800
Jeff Ansted, *President*
EMP: 36
SQ FT: 5,500

SALES (est): 6MM Privately Held
SIC: 8748 Telecommunications consultant

(G-17588)
AMERICAN GOLF CORPORATION
Also Called: Detwiler Park Golf Course
4001 N Summit St (43611-3067)
PHONE..................................419 726-9353
Lynne Murnan, *Manager*
EMP: 28 Publicly Held
SIC: 7997 Country club, membership
HQ: American Golf Corporation
909 N Pacific Coast Hwy
El Segundo CA 90245
310 664-4000

(G-17589)
AMERICAN GOLF CORPORATION
Also Called: Collins Park Golf Course
3915 Heatherdowns Blvd (43614-3268)
PHONE..................................419 693-1991
Jim Linenkugl, *Manager*
EMP: 46 Publicly Held
SIC: 7997 7992 Membership Sport/Recreation Club Public Golf Course
HQ: American Golf Corporation
909 N Pacific Coast Hwy
El Segundo CA 90245
310 664-4000

(G-17590)
AMERICAN INTERIORS INC (PA)
302 S Byrne Rd Bldg 100 (43615-6208)
PHONE..................................419 324-0365
Steve Essig, *President*
Rick Essig, *Vice Pres*
Chris Froling, *Accounts Exec*
Abby Krause, *Director*
◆ EMP: 50
SQ FT: 140,000
SALES (est): 54.1MM Privately Held
SIC: 5021 Office furniture

(G-17591)
AMERICAN MARITIME OFFICERS
1 Maritime Plz Fl 2 (43604-1885)
PHONE..................................419 255-3940
Fax: 419 255-2350
EMP: 25
SALES (est): 1.4MM Privately Held
SIC: 6512 Nonresidential Building Operator

(G-17592)
AMERICAN NATIONAL RED CROSS
1111 Research Dr (43614-2798)
PHONE..................................419 382-2707
Arkia Blackman, *Materials Mgr*
Mary Rietzke, *Manager*
EMP: 170
SALES (corp-wide): 2.5B Privately Held
WEB: www.redcross.org
SIC: 8322 Social service center; disaster service
PA: The American National Red Cross
430 17th St Nw
Washington DC 20006
202 737-8300

(G-17593)
AMERICAN POSTS LLC
810 Chicago St (43611-3609)
PHONE..................................419 720-0652
David Feniger, *Mng Member*
Andrew Spoering, *Supervisor*
EMP: 30
SALES (est): 7.8MM Privately Held
WEB: www.americanposts.com
SIC: 3312 5051 Rods, iron & steel: made in steel mills; steel

(G-17594)
ANN ARBOR RAILROAD INC
4058 Chrysler Dr (43608-4100)
P.O. Box 5128 (43611-0128)
PHONE..................................419 726-4181
Fax: 419 726-2250
EMP: 30
SALES (corp-wide): 8.5MM Privately Held
SIC: 4011 Railroad Company

HQ: Ann Arbor Railroad Inc
121 S Walnut St
Howell MI
517 548-3930

(G-17595)
ANSPACH MEEKS ELLENBERGER LLP (PA)
300 Madison Ave Ste 1600 (43604-2633)
PHONE..................................419 447-6181
Tami Lang, *President*
Deanna Whitley, *President*
Robert M Anspach, *Partner*
Richard F Ellenberg, *Partner*
Mark D Meeks, *Partner*
EMP: 36
SQ FT: 9,000
SALES (est): 9.1MM **Privately Held**
SIC: 8111 General practice attorney, lawyer; general practice law office

(G-17596)
ANTONIO SOFO SON IMPORTING CO (PA)
Also Called: Sofo Importing Company
253 Waggoner Blvd (43612-1952)
PHONE..................................419 476-4211
Antonio J Sofo, *CEO*
Mike Sofo, *President*
Paul Peer, *Principal*
Joseph J Sofo Jr, *Principal*
Wilma Jean Sofo, *Principal*
▲ EMP: 206 EST: 1940
SQ FT: 180,000
SALES (est): 63.6MM **Privately Held**
WEB: www.sofofoods.com
SIC: 5499 5149 Gourmet food stores; specialty food items

(G-17597)
APS MEDICAL BILLING
Also Called: A P S Medical Billing
5620 Southwyck Blvd (43614-1501)
PHONE..................................419 866-1804
Nancy Condon, *President*
Harold S Rickard, *Principal*
Margaret Rickard, *Treasurer*
Judy Udell, *Admin Sec*
EMP: 65
SALES (est): 7.9MM
SALES (corp-wide): 66.5MM **Privately Held**
WEB: www.apsmedicalbilling.com
SIC: 8721 Billing & bookkeeping service
PA: United Collection Bureau, Inc.
5620 Southwyck Blvd
Toledo OH 43614
419 866-6227

(G-17598)
ARCADIS US INC
1 Seagate Ste 700 (43604-4508)
PHONE..................................419 473-1121
Bob Casaletta, *Branch Mgr*
EMP: 87
SALES (corp-wide): 2.8B **Privately Held**
WEB: www.arcadis-us.com
SIC: 8748 Environmental consultant
HQ: Arcadis U.S., Inc.
630 Plaza Dr Ste 200
Highlands Ranch CO 80129
720 344-3500

(G-17599)
AREA OFFICE ON AGING OF NWSTRN
2155 Arlington Ave (43609-1997)
PHONE..................................419 382-0624
Jayne Wagner, *Project Mgr*
Billie Johnson, *Exec Dir*
John Bleau, *Director*
EMP: 96
SALES: 33.3MM **Privately Held**
WEB: www.areaofficeonaging.com
SIC: 8322 8082 Senior citizens' center or association; home health care services

(G-17600)
ARNOLDS HOME IMPROVEMENT LLC
1770 Premainsville (43613)
PHONE..................................734 847-9600
Jason Arnold, *Owner*
EMP: 30

SALES (corp-wide): 1.9MM **Privately Held**
SIC: 1542 1521 Commercial & office buildings, renovation & repair; general remodeling, single-family houses
PA: Arnold's Home Improvement Llc
1770 Tremainsville Rd
Toledo OH 43613
419 354-7663

(G-17601)
ASSET PROTECTION CORPORATION
5211 Renwyck Dr (43615-5923)
PHONE..................................419 531-3400
Kim Klewer, *President*
William Mishka, *COO*
Bill Mishka, *Senior VP*
Roy Chase, *CFO*
Gary Lemle, *Consultant*
EMP: 25
SALES (est): 5.3MM **Privately Held**
WEB: www.assetprotection.net
SIC: 5063 5065 7382 Alarm systems; fire alarm systems; closed circuit television; security systems services

(G-17602)
ASSOCIATED IMAGING CORPORATION
Also Called: M R I Center
3830 Woodley Rd Ste A (43606-1176)
PHONE..................................419 517-0500
Tom Thompson, *President*
Marty Connors, *Treasurer*
Diane Moreno, *Manager*
EMP: 30
SQ FT: 5,000
SALES: 11.2K **Privately Held**
SIC: 8071 X-ray laboratory, including dental

(G-17603)
AUTO WAREHOUSING CO INC
4405 Chrysler Dr (43608-4050)
PHONE..................................419 727-1534
Carlos Sanchez, *General Mgr*
Jose Lopez, *Manager*
EMP: 33
SALES (corp-wide): 194.2MM **Privately Held**
SIC: 4226 Automobile dead storage
PA: Auto Warehousing Co.
2810 Marshall Ave Ste B
Tacoma WA 98421
253 719-1700

(G-17604)
BAGEL PLACE INC (PA)
Also Called: Barry Bagel's Place
3715 King Rd (43617-1417)
PHONE..................................419 885-1000
Mark Greenblatt, *President*
Judie A Greenblatt, *Vice Pres*
EMP: 50
SQ FT: 10,000
SALES (est): 30.2MM **Privately Held**
SIC: 5461 5411 5812 5149 Bagels; delicatessens; caterers; bakery products

(G-17605)
BARRINGTON TOLEDO LLC
Also Called: W N W O
300 S Byrne Rd (43615-6217)
PHONE..................................419 535-0024
Chris Popf, *General Mgr*
Victoria Scott, *Business Mgr*
EMP: 50
SALES (est): 1.7MM
SALES (corp-wide): 143.8MM **Privately Held**
WEB: www.barringtontv.com
SIC: 4833 Television broadcasting stations
HQ: Barrington Broadcasting Group Llc
1270 Ave Of The Amer Fl 9
New York NY 10020
847 884-1877

(G-17606)
BAY PARK COMMUNITY HOSPITAL (HQ)
Also Called: Promedica
100 Madison Ave (43604-1516)
PHONE..................................567 585-9600
Randy Oostra, *President*

Doug Bush, *President*
Dawn Buskey, *President*
Michael Browning, *CFO*
Melanie Rittenour, *Human Res Mgr*
EMP: 86 EST: 1986
SQ FT: 270,000
SALES: 76.3MM
SALES (corp-wide): 2.1B **Privately Held**
SIC: 8062 General medical & surgical hospitals
PA: Promedica Health Systems, Inc.
100 Madison Ave
Toledo OH 43604
567 585-7454

(G-17607)
BAYVIEW RETIREES GOLF COURSE
3900 N Summit St (43611-3042)
PHONE..................................419 726-8081
Harold Rodgers, *Director*
EMP: 70
SALES (est): 2.1MM **Privately Held**
SIC: 7992 Public golf courses

(G-17608)
BEACON OF LIGHT LTD
Also Called: Beacon of Light Health Agency
242 S Reynolds Rd Ste A (43615-6164)
PHONE..................................419 531-9060
Shirley Foster, *Mng Member*
Calandra Strong,
EMP: 35 EST: 2007
SQ FT: 4,500
SALES (est): 2.3MM **Privately Held**
SIC: 8051 8742 Convalescent home with continuous nursing care; hospital & health services consultant

(G-17609)
BEAUTY BAR LLC
2919 W Central Ave (43606-3027)
PHONE..................................419 537-5400
David Czehut, *Manager*
Sara Stallino,
EMP: 40
SQ FT: 5,170
SALES (est): 969.4K **Privately Held**
SIC: 7231 Cosmetology & personal hygiene salons

(G-17610)
BELLE TIRE DISTRIBUTORS INC
5253 Secor Rd (43623-2401)
PHONE..................................419 473-1393
James Stevenson, *Manager*
EMP: 50
SALES (corp-wide): 489.4MM **Privately Held**
WEB: www.belletire.com
SIC: 5014 Automobile tires & tubes
PA: Belle Tire Distributors, Inc.
1000 Enterprise Dr
Allen Park MI 48101
888 462-3553

(G-17611)
BENCHMARK TECHNOLOGIES CORP
3161 N Republic Blvd (43615-1507)
PHONE..................................419 843-6691
Gary A Cooper, *Ch of Bd*
Rand Palmer, *Manager*
EMP: 30
SQ FT: 17,000
SALES: 3.4MM **Privately Held**
WEB: www.benchmark-usa.com
SIC: 8741 8748 7699 8742 Test development & evaluation service; caliper, gauge & other machinists' instrument repair; management consulting services; business management

(G-17612)
BERNER TRUCKING
4310 Lagrange St (43612-1413)
P.O. Box 660, Dover (44622-0660)
PHONE..................................419 476-0207
Jim Kniesly, *President*
Kathy Brinkerhoff, *Human Resources*
Tim Tritt, *Manager*
Ben Goehring, *Maintence Staff*
EMP: 25

SALES (est): 1.6MM **Privately Held**
SIC: 4212 Dump truck haulage

(G-17613)
BINKELMAN CORPORATION (PA)
2601 Hill Ave (43607-2922)
PHONE..................................419 537-9333
Dan Kazmierczak, *President*
Brad Fitzgerald, *General Mgr*
Dave Grana, *Vice Pres*
Clay Grieffendorf, *Vice Pres*
Brian Elsner, *Accounts Mgr*
EMP: 33
SQ FT: 30,000
SALES (est): 36.2MM **Privately Held**
SIC: 5085 Power transmission equipment & apparatus; bearings; hose, belting & packing

(G-17614)
BIOMAT USA INC
3217 Dorr St Ste B (43607-2716)
PHONE..................................419 531-3332
Nate Ringenberg, *Manager*
EMP: 38
SALES (corp-wide): 741MM **Privately Held**
SIC: 8099 Blood bank
HQ: Biomat Usa, Inc.
2410 Lillyvale Ave
Los Angeles CA 90032
323 225-2221

(G-17615)
BIONIX SAFETY TECHNOLOGIES LTD (HQ)
5154 Enterprise Blvd (43612-3807)
PHONE..................................419 727-0552
Andrew Milligan, *President*
Dr James Huttner, *Vice Pres*
EMP: 49
SALES (est): 7.7MM
SALES (corp-wide): 12.1MM **Privately Held**
WEB: www.nst-usa.com
SIC: 3825 3826 3829 Test equipment for electronic & electric measurement; analytical instruments; gas testing apparatus; industrial machinery & equipment; measuring & controlling devices
PA: Bionix Development Corporation
315 Matzinger Rd
Toledo OH 43612
419 727-8421

(G-17616)
BOHL CRANE INC (PA)
534 W Laskey Rd (43612-3207)
PHONE..................................419 476-7525
Douglas E Bohl, *President*
Steven C Bohl, *Vice Pres*
Jonathon Balduf, *Project Mgr*
Bernice Lampley, *Project Mgr*
Thomas Velker, *Project Engr*
EMP: 75
SQ FT: 16,400
SALES: 16.1MM **Privately Held**
WEB: www.bohlcrane.com
SIC: 5084 Materials handling machinery

(G-17617)
BOHL EQUIPMENT COMPANY (PA)
534 W Laskey Rd (43612-3299)
PHONE..................................419 476-7525
Robert D Bohl, *President*
Steven Bohl, *Vice Pres*
Dave Klopping, *Project Mgr*
Ron Demars, *Parts Mgr*
Douglas E Bohl, *Treasurer*
▲ EMP: 75
SQ FT: 11,300
SALES (est): 22.4MM **Privately Held**
WEB: www.bohlco.com
SIC: 5084 Materials handling machinery

(G-17618)
BOLLIN & SONS INC
Also Called: Bollin Label Systems
6001 Brent Dr (43611-1090)
PHONE..................................419 693-6573
Mark D Bollin, *President*
Chris Younkman, *Vice Pres*
EMP: 40

SQ FT: 21,000
SALES (est): 23.2MM **Privately Held**
WEB: www.bollin.com
SIC: 5084 7389 2851 2759 Packaging machinery & equipment; design services; paints & allied products; commercial printing; packaging paper & plastics film, coated & laminated; adhesive papers, labels or tapes: from purchased material

(G-17619)
BOLT EXPRESS LLC (PA)
Also Called: Strike Logistics
7255 Crossleigh Ct # 108 (43617-1556)
P.O. Box 759 (43697-0759)
PHONE...................................419 729-6698
Guy Sanderson, *CEO*
Chuck King, *COO*
EMP: 98
SQ FT: 5,000
SALES: 80MM **Privately Held**
WEB: www.bolt-express.com
SIC: 4731 Transportation agents & brokers

(G-17620)
BOSTWICK-BRAUN COMPANY (PA)
7349 Crossleigh Ct (43617-3108)
PHONE...................................419 259-3600
Chris Beach, *Principal*
▲ EMP: 55 EST: 1855
SQ FT: 23,000
SALES (est): 146.5MM **Privately Held**
SIC: 5072 5084 5063 5083 Builders' hardware; industrial machinery & equipment; electrical apparatus & equipment; lawn & garden machinery & equipment; home furnishings

(G-17621)
BOWSER-MORNER INC
Also Called: Bowser Morner and Associates
1419 Miami St (43605-3314)
P.O. Box 838 (43697-0838)
PHONE...................................419 691-4800
Dick Hoppenjans, *Manager*
EMP: 50
SALES (corp-wide): 19MM **Privately Held**
WEB: www.bowser-morner.com
SIC: 8734 Metallurgical testing laboratory
PA: Bowser-Morner, Inc.
　　4518 Taylorsville Rd
　　Dayton OH 45424
　　937 236-8805

(G-17622)
BOYS & GIRLS CLUB OF TOLEDO (PA)
Also Called: Boys Club Camp Association
2250 N Detroit Ave (43606-4690)
PHONE...................................419 241-4258
Dave Wehrmeister, *Exec Dir*
EMP: 32 EST: 1892
SQ FT: 35,000
SALES: 37.6K **Privately Held**
WEB: www.bgctoledo.org
SIC: 8641 Boy Scout organization; youth organizations

(G-17623)
BRAND ENERGY & INFRASTRUCTURE
Also Called: Empire Refractory Services
2961 South Ave (43609-1327)
PHONE...................................419 324-1305
David Varanese, *Branch Mgr*
EMP: 30
SALES (corp-wide): 3B **Privately Held**
SIC: 5085 Industrial supplies
PA: Brand Industrial Services, Inc.
　　1325 Cobb Intl Dr Nw A1
　　Kennesaw GA 30152
　　678 285-1400

(G-17624)
BRENT INDUSTRIES INC
2922 South Ave (43609-1328)
PHONE...................................419 382-8693
Royse Willie, *Branch Mgr*
EMP: 30
SQ FT: 42,000

SALES (corp-wide): 9.1MM **Privately Held**
WEB: www.brentind.com
SIC: 7218 Safety glove supply
PA: Brent Industries, Inc.
　　10501 Highway 5
　　Brent AL 35034
　　205 926-4801

(G-17625)
BRINKS INCORPORATED
1265 Matzinger Rd (43612-3853)
PHONE...................................419 729-5389
John Stepek, *Manager*
EMP: 45
SALES (corp-wide): 3.4B **Publicly Held**
WEB: www.brinksinc.com
SIC: 7381 Armored car services
HQ: Brink's, Incorporated
　　1801 Bayberry Ct Ste 400
　　Richmond VA 23226
　　804 289-9600

(G-17626)
BROADBAND EXPRESS LLC
1915 Nebraska Ave (43607-3800)
PHONE...................................419 536-9127
Mike Common, *District Mgr*
EMP: 52
SALES (corp-wide): 3.1B **Publicly Held**
WEB: www.broadbandexpress.net
SIC: 1731 1623 Cable television installation; communication line & transmission tower construction
HQ: Broadband Express, Llc
　　374 Westdale Ave Ste B
　　Westerville OH 43082
　　614 823-6464

(G-17627)
BRONDES FORD (PA)
Also Called: Brondes Ford Toledo
5545 Secor Rd (43623-1998)
PHONE...................................419 473-1411
Phillip Brondes Sr, *President*
Drew Conkle, *General Mgr*
John Stedcke, *General Mgr*
Diana Tymiak, *Sales Staff*
Tony Tepper, *Technology*
▼ EMP: 100
SALES (est): 4.2MM **Privately Held**
WEB: www.brondesford.com
SIC: 7515 7538 7532 5511 Passenger car leasing; general automotive repair shops; top & body repair & paint shops; automobiles, new & used

(G-17628)
BROOKESIDE AMBULANCE SERVICES
Also Called: Rumpf Ambulance
640 Phillips Ave (43612-1370)
PHONE...................................419 476-7442
Donald Kish, *President*
Deborah Kish, *Admin Sec*
EMP: 38
SQ FT: 3,800
SALES: 1.4MM **Privately Held**
WEB: www.rumpfambulance.com
SIC: 4119 Ambulance service

(G-17629)
BROWN MOTOR SALES CO (PA)
Also Called: Brown Motors
5625 W Central Ave (43615-1505)
PHONE...................................419 531-0151
Rob Brown Jr, *President*
Robert W Brown Jr, *Exec VP*
EMP: 39
SQ FT: 46,000
SALES (est): 38.7MM **Privately Held**
WEB: www.brownpontiac.com
SIC: 7538 7532 7515 5531 General automotive repair shops; top & body repair & paint shops; passenger car leasing; automotive & home supply stores; used car dealers

(G-17630)
BRUCE KLINGER
Also Called: Northwestern Mutual Inv Svcs
3950 Sunforest Ct Ste 200 (43623-4522)
PHONE...................................419 473-2270
Bruce Klinger, *Owner*
Nathan Danziger, *Agent*
Brian Kurtz, *Representative*

EMP: 40
SALES (est): 9.4MM **Privately Held**
SIC: 6411 Insurance agents

(G-17631)
BUCKEYE CABLE SYSTEMS INC
4212 South Ave (43615-6234)
PHONE...................................419 724-2539
Ron Durham, *President*
EMP: 30 EST: 1998
SALES (est): 1.5MM **Privately Held**
SIC: 1799 1731 Cable splicing service; electrical work

(G-17632)
BURBANK INC
Also Called: Seagate Roofg & Waterproofing
623 Burbank Dr (43607-3234)
PHONE...................................419 698-3434
Thomas K Elder, *President*
EMP: 40
SQ FT: 10,000
SALES (est): 5.1MM **Privately Held**
WEB: www.seagateroofing.com
SIC: 1761 1799 1751 Roofing contractor; siding contractor; waterproofing; window & door (prefabricated) installation

(G-17633)
C & B BUCK BROS ASP MAINT LLC
2742 Victory Ave (43607-3272)
P.O. Box 735, Holland (43528-0735)
PHONE...................................419 536-7325
Ched Buck,
Brad Buck,
EMP: 25
SQ FT: 2,560
SALES (est): 1.1MM **Privately Held**
SIC: 0782 1629 4959 5032 Landscape contractors; tennis court construction; snowplowing; building stone

(G-17634)
CANAAN COMPANIES INC
328 21st St (43604-5037)
PHONE...................................419 842-8373
James House, *President*
EMP: 42
SQ FT: 12,000
SALES: 5.4MM **Privately Held**
SIC: 1542 1799 1741 1541 Nonresidential construction; commercial & office buildings, renovation & repair; coating, caulking & weather, water & fireproofing; masonry & other stonework; industrial buildings, new construction

(G-17635)
CAPITAL TIRE INC (PA)
Also Called: Wholesale Tire Division
1001 Cherry St (43608-2995)
PHONE...................................419 241-5111
Thomas B Geiger, *Ch of Bd*
Thomas B Geiger Jr, *President*
Joe Ballachino, *General Mgr*
Brian Haas, *Senior VP*
Carl J EBY, *Vice Pres*
▲ EMP: 40 EST: 1920
SQ FT: 100,000
SALES (est): 95.9MM **Privately Held**
WEB: www.capitaltire.com
SIC: 5014 Automobile tires & tubes; truck tires & tubes

(G-17636)
CAPITAL TIRE INC
Also Called: Wholesale Tire Division
2220 S Reynolds Rd (43614-1413)
PHONE...................................419 865-7151
EMP: 32
SALES (corp-wide): 95.9MM **Privately Held**
SIC: 5014 Automobile tires & tubes
PA: Capital Tire, Inc.
　　1001 Cherry St
　　Toledo OH 43608
　　419 241-5111

(G-17637)
CARLISLE FLUID TECH INC
Also Called: Devilbiss Auto Refinishing
320 Phillips Ave (43612-1467)
PHONE...................................419 825-5186
Hans Horstik, *Branch Mgr*
EMP: 25

SALES (corp-wide): 4.4B **Publicly Held**
SIC: 5198 Paints, varnishes & supplies
HQ: Carlisle Fluid Technologies, Inc.
　　16430 N Scottsdale Rd
　　Scottsdale AZ 85254
　　480 781-5250

(G-17638)
CAROL BURTON MANAGEMENT LLC
Also Called: Econo Lodge
1800 Miami St (43605-3318)
PHONE...................................419 666-5120
Denny Jirjis, *Manager*
EMP: 35
SALES (corp-wide): 7.6MM **Privately Held**
SIC: 7011 Hotels
PA: Burton Carol Management
　　4832 Richmond Rd Ste 200
　　Cleveland OH 44128
　　216 464-5130

(G-17639)
CASSENS TRANSPORT COMPANY
633 Matzinger Rd (43612-2630)
PHONE...................................419 727-0520
Gregory Foster, *General Mgr*
Greg Foster, *Site Mgr*
EMP: 130
SQ FT: 28,432
SALES (corp-wide): 217.5MM **Privately Held**
SIC: 4213 Automobiles, transport & delivery
HQ: Cassens Transport Company
　　145 N Kansas St
　　Edwardsville IL 62025
　　618 656-3006

(G-17640)
CELLCO PARTNERSHIP
Also Called: Verizon Wireless
1260 S Reynolds Rd (43615-6962)
PHONE...................................419 381-1726
EMP: 74
SALES (corp-wide): 130.8B **Publicly Held**
SIC: 4812 Cellular telephone services
HQ: Cellco Partnership
　　1 Verizon Way
　　Basking Ridge NJ 07920

(G-17641)
CELLCO PARTNERSHIP
Also Called: Verizon
6710 W Central Ave Ste 20 (43617-1149)
PHONE...................................419 843-2995
Dave Johnson, *Manager*
EMP: 35
SALES (corp-wide): 130.8B **Publicly Held**
SIC: 4812 5999 Cellular telephone services; telephone & communication equipment
HQ: Cellco Partnership
　　1 Verizon Way
　　Basking Ridge NJ 07920

(G-17642)
CENTER FOR SPINAL DISORDERS
3000 Arlington Ave (43614-2595)
PHONE...................................419 383-4878
Beth Fields, *Principal*
EMP: 35
SALES (est): 1.5MM **Privately Held**
WEB: www.centerforspinaldisorders.com
SIC: 8062 General medical & surgical hospitals

(G-17643)
CENTRAL COCA-COLA BTLG CO INC
3970 Catawba St (43612-1404)
PHONE...................................419 476-6622
Paul Kenny, *Manager*
EMP: 110

SALES (corp-wide): 35.4B **Publicly Held**
WEB: www.colasic.net
SIC: 2086 2087 5149 Carbonated beverages, nonalcoholic: bottled & canned; soft drinks: packaged in cans, bottles, etc.; fruit drinks (less than 100% juice): packaged in cans, etc.; syrups, drink; concentrates, drink; groceries & related products
HQ: Central Coca-Cola Bottling Company, Inc.
555 Taxter Rd Ste 550
Elmsford NY 10523
914 789-1100

(G-17644)
CENTRAL TRAVEL & TICKET INC (PA)
Also Called: Central 'travel
4540 Heatherdowns Blvd # 2 (43614-3155)
PHONE...............................419 897-2070
Janie Miller, *CEO*
Jani Miller, *President*
Richard Westmeyer, *President*
John Miller, *Treasurer*
Christianne Lehman, *Consultant*
EMP: 25
SQ FT: 4,700
SALES: 15MM **Privately Held**
WEB: www.centraltravel.com
SIC: 4724 Tourist agency arranging transport, lodging & car rental

(G-17645)
CENTURY EQUIPMENT INC (PA)
5959 Angola Rd (43615-6332)
P.O. Box 352889 (43635-2889)
PHONE...............................419 865-7400
Robert E O'Brien, *Ch of Bd*
Martin O'Brien, *President*
Rick Puffenberger, *CFO*
EMP: 35 EST: 1950
SQ FT: 42,000
SALES (est): 41.7MM **Privately Held**
WEB: www.centuryequip.com
SIC: 5083 5088 Mowers, power; lawn machinery & equipment; garden machinery & equipment; irrigation equipment; golf carts

(G-17646)
CHAMBERS LEASING SYSTEMS CORP (PA)
3100 N Summit St (43611-3250)
P.O. Box 5337 (43611-0337)
PHONE...............................419 726-9747
James Chambers, *President*
Edman Lee, *Vice Pres*
EMP: 31
SQ FT: 6,200
SALES: 9MM **Privately Held**
SIC: 4213 Trucking, except local

(G-17647)
CHAMPION SPARK PLUG COMPANY (HQ)
900 Upton Ave (43607)
PHONE...............................419 535-2567
Richard Keller, *President*
William Whipple, *Plant Mgr*
F J Raeske, *Engineer*
Gerald Johnston, *Technician*
▲ EMP: 55 EST: 1907
SQ FT: 15,000
SALES (est): 7.1MM
SALES (corp-wide): 11.7B **Publicly Held**
SIC: 8731 Commercial physical research
PA: Tenneco Inc.
500 N Field Dr
Lake Forest IL 60045
847 482-5000

(G-17648)
CHARIOTT FOODS INC
6163 Valley Park Dr (43623-2555)
PHONE...............................419 243-1101
Michael Okdie, *President*
Shirley Okdie, *Technology*
EMP: 34
SQ FT: 40,000
SALES (est): 8MM **Privately Held**
SIC: 5148 Fruits, fresh; vegetables, fresh

(G-17649)
CHELMSFORD APARTMENTS LTD
Also Called: Glendale, The
5020 Ryan Rd (43614-2065)
PHONE...............................419 389-0800
Dr Thomas Sollas, *Managing Prtnr*
Pete Olina, *Maintenance Dir*
Ellen Matteson, *Facilities Dir*
Jodi Kimball, *Director*
Keith Stroder, *Nursing Dir*
EMP: 25
SQ FT: 33,000
SALES (est): 2.1MM **Privately Held**
WEB: www.chelmsfordapartments.com
SIC: 6513 8052 Apartment building operators; intermediate care facilities

(G-17650)
CHERRY ST MISSION MINISTRIES (PA)
105 17th St (43604-6785)
PHONE...............................419 242-5141
Cuauhtemoc Valdiviez, *CEO*
Dan Rogers, *President*
Kathleen Clink, *Finance Mgr*
Nikki Morey, *Comms Mgr*
Dawn Bongratz, *Manager*
EMP: 43 EST: 1947
SQ FT: 120,000
SALES: 6.5MM **Privately Held**
WEB: www.cherrystreetmission.org
SIC: 8361 Rehabilitation center, residential: health care incidental

(G-17651)
CHI LIVING COMMUNITIES
Also Called: St Clare Commons
5942 Renaissance Pl Ste A (43623-4716)
PHONE...............................567 455-0414
Alisa Iffland, *Vice Pres*
Bonnie Szabo, *Admin Asst*
EMP: 86 EST: 2012
SALES (est): 10.7MM **Privately Held**
SIC: 8051 Skilled nursing care facilities

(G-17652)
CHRISTEN & SONS COMPANY (PA)
Also Called: Christen Detroit
714 George St (43608-2914)
P.O. Box 547 (43697-0547)
PHONE...............................419 243-4161
Frederick R Christen, *President*
Tim Davis, *Superintendent*
Bill Kaiser, *CFO*
Marlene Christen, *Treasurer*
EMP: 50
SQ FT: 60,000
SALES (est): 7.6MM **Privately Held**
SIC: 1761 Roofing, siding & sheet metal work

(G-17653)
CITIGROUP GLOBAL MARKETS INC
Also Called: Smith Barney
7124 W Central Ave (43617-1117)
PHONE...............................419 842-5383
Jeffrey Botruba, *Manager*
EMP: 50
SALES (corp-wide): 72.8B **Publicly Held**
WEB: www.salomonsmithbarney.com
SIC: 6211 Security brokers & dealers
HQ: Citigroup Global Markets Inc.
388 Greenwich St Fl 18
New York NY 10013
212 816-6000

(G-17654)
CITY OF TOLEDO
Also Called: Utilities Department
420 Madison Ave Ste 100 (43604-1219)
PHONE...............................419 245-1800
Robert C Stevenson, *Principal*
Abby Arnold, *Administration*
EMP: 90 **Privately Held**
WEB: www.ci.toledo.oh.us
SIC: 4941 9111 4952 4924 Water supply; mayors' offices; sewerage systems; natural gas distribution; electric services
PA: City Of Toledo
1 Government Ctr Ste 2050
Toledo OH 43604
419 245-1050

(G-17655)
CITY OF TOLEDO
Also Called: Municipal Government
1 Government Ctr Ste 2200 (43604-2295)
PHONE...............................419 245-1001
Sullivan Nicholls, *General Mgr*
Wade Kapszukiewicz, *Mayor*
Jesse Torrence, *Exec Dir*
EMP: 2800 **Privately Held**
WEB: www.ci.toledo.oh.us
SIC: 8611 9111 Business associations; mayors' offices
PA: City Of Toledo
1 Government Ctr Ste 2050
Toledo OH 43604
419 245-1050

(G-17656)
CITY OF TOLEDO
Also Called: Toledo City Parks
2201 Ottawa Dr (43606-4338)
PHONE...............................419 936-2875
Tom Crothers, *Branch Mgr*
Lisa Ward, *Commissioner*
EMP: 30 **Privately Held**
WEB: www.ci.toledo.oh.us
SIC: 8999 9221 Natural resource preservation service; police protection
PA: City Of Toledo
1 Government Ctr Ste 2050
Toledo OH 43604
419 245-1050

(G-17657)
CITY OF TOLEDO
Also Called: Sewer & Drainage Services
4032 Creekside Ave (43612-1478)
PHONE...............................419 936-2924
Kelly O'Brien, *Manager*
EMP: 129
SQ FT: 102,840 **Privately Held**
WEB: www.ci.toledo.oh.us
SIC: 4952 9111 4959 Sewerage systems; mayors' offices; sanitary services
PA: City Of Toledo
1 Government Ctr Ste 2050
Toledo OH 43604
419 245-1050

(G-17658)
CITY OF TOLEDO
Also Called: Dept of Neighborhoods
1 Government Ctr Ste 1800 (43604-2275)
PHONE...............................419 245-1400
Tom Carouthers, *Branch Mgr*
EMP: 70 **Privately Held**
WEB: www.ci.toledo.oh.us
SIC: 9531 8742 Housing programs, planning & development: government; business associations
PA: City Of Toledo
1 Government Ctr Ste 2050
Toledo OH 43604
419 245-1050

(G-17659)
CITY OF TOLEDO
Also Called: Fleet Operations
555 N Expressway Dr (43608-1512)
PHONE...............................419 936-2507
Ken Naeidert, *Manager*
EMP: 80 **Privately Held**
WEB: www.ci.toledo.oh.us
SIC: 7538 General truck repair
PA: City Of Toledo
1 Government Ctr Ste 2050
Toledo OH 43604
419 245-1050

(G-17660)
CITY OF TOLEDO
600 Jefferson Ave Ste 300 (43604-1012)
PHONE...............................419 936-2275
Warian E Henry, *Commissioner*
EMP: 60 **Privately Held**
WEB: www.ci.toledo.oh.us
SIC: 8711 Engineering services
PA: City Of Toledo
1 Government Ctr Ste 2050
Toledo OH 43604
419 245-1050

(G-17661)
CIVIL & ENVIRONMENTAL CONS INC
4841 Monroe St Ste 103 (43623-4390)
PHONE...............................419 724-5281
Nicholas Berkholz, *Manager*
EMP: 30
SALES (corp-wide): 134.8MM **Privately Held**
SIC: 8999 Scientific consulting
PA: Civil & Environmental Consultants, Inc.
333 Baldwin Rd Ste 1
Pittsburgh PA 15205
412 429-2324

(G-17662)
CLARK SCHAEFER HACKETT & CO
3166 N Republic Blvd (43615-1507)
PHONE...............................419 243-0218
Clayton Holt, *Principal*
John R Moster, *Principal*
EMP: 100
SALES (corp-wide): 37.2MM **Privately Held**
WEB: www.cshco.com
SIC: 8721 Certified public accountant
PA: Clark, Schaefer, Hackett & Co.
1 E 4th St Ste 1200
Cincinnati OH 45202
513 241-3111

(G-17663)
CLEAN CARE INC
511 Phillips Ave (43612-1328)
PHONE...............................419 725-2100
Jon Steingass, *President*
Joel Groober, *Vice Pres*
Tim Steingass, *Cust Mgr*
Joel Groover, *Director*
EMP: 150
SQ FT: 6,500
SALES (est): 3.9MM **Privately Held**
SIC: 7349 Janitorial service, contract basis

(G-17664)
CLEAR VISION ENGINEERING LLC
Also Called: Palmer Associates
4401 Jackman Rd (43612-1529)
PHONE...............................419 478-7151
Tariq Alkhairy, *CEO*
EMP: 30
SQ FT: 12,000
SALES: 5MM **Privately Held**
WEB: www.palmerassoc.com
SIC: 8711 8742 Consulting engineer; mechanical engineering; electrical or electronic engineering; designing: ship, boat, machine & product; automation & robotics consultant

(G-17665)
CLIFTONLARSONALLEN LLP
1 Seagate Ste 2650 (43604-1522)
PHONE...............................419 244-3711
Donna Dawson, *Branch Mgr*
Todd Deindoerfer, *Mng Member*
EMP: 25
SALES (corp-wide): 755.1MM **Privately Held**
WEB: www.cliftoncpa.com
SIC: 8721 Certified public accountant
PA: Cliftonlarsonallen Llp
220 S 6th St Ste 300
Minneapolis MN 55402
612 376-4500

(G-17666)
COACT ASSOCIATES LTD
2748 Centennial Rd (43617-1829)
PHONE...............................866 646-4400
Mark Frasco, *President*
EMP: 30
SQ FT: 10,000
SALES: 2.5MM **Privately Held**
SIC: 8748 Environmental consultant

(G-17667)
COLLABORATIVE INC
1 Seagate Park Level 118 (43604)
PHONE...............................419 242-7405
Paul Hollenbeck, *Chairman*
Dan J Tabor, *Corp Secy*
Michael Dinardo, *Vice Pres*

Paul Meneilly, *Project Mgr*
Rich Pace, *Project Mgr*
EMP: 50 **EST:** 1973
SQ FT: 12,000
SALES (est): 8.8MM **Privately Held**
WEB: www.thecollaborativeinc.com
SIC: 8712 0781 7389 5021 Architectural
engineering; landscape architects; interior
designer; office & public building furniture;
office equipment

(G-17668)
COLUMBIA GAS OF OHIO INC
2901 E Manhattan Blvd (43611-1713)
PHONE....................419 539-6046
Jack Klein, *Branch Mgr*
EMP: 100
SQ FT: 80,340
SALES (corp-wide): 5.1B **Publicly Held**
WEB: www.meterrepairshop.com
SIC: 4924 Natural gas distribution
HQ: Columbia Gas Of Ohio, Inc.
290 W Nationwide Blvd # 114
Columbus OH 43215
614 460-6000

(G-17669)
COMMERCE PAPER COMPANY
302 S Byrne Rd Bldg 200 (43615-6208)
P.O. Box 140395 (43614-0395)
PHONE....................419 241-9101
Craig D Roberts, *President*
Jeffrey M Roberts, *Vice Pres*
Chas L Smith Et Al, *Incorporator*
George E Kirk, *Incorporator*
Morgan Levi, *Incorporator*
EMP: 45
SQ FT: 100,000
SALES (est): 26.8MM **Privately Held**
WEB: www.commercepaper.com
SIC: 5113 Industrial & personal service
paper

(G-17670)
COMMUNI CARE INC
Also Called: Advanced Health Care Center
955 Garden Lake Pkwy (43614-2777)
PHONE....................419 382-2200
Linda Hudson, *Purch Mgr*
Ramzieh Shousher, *Exec Dir*
EMP: 50
SALES (est): 72.1K **Privately Held**
SIC: 8051 Convalescent home with contin-
uous nursing care

(G-17671)
COMMUNICA INC (PA)
31 N Erie St (43604-6942)
PHONE....................419 244-7766
Jeff Kimble, *CEO*
Debra Monagan, *President*
John Edwards, *Principal*
Tom Kopp, *Business Mgr*
Susan Doktor, *Vice Pres*
EMP: 26
SQ FT: 8,500
SALES (est): 6.5MM **Privately Held**
WEB: www.communica-usa.com
SIC: 8742 Marketing consulting services

(G-17672)
COMMUNITY ISP INC
3035 Moffat Rd (43615-1836)
PHONE....................419 867-6060
Jeffrey Klingshirn, *CEO*
Dustin Wade, *President*
EMP: 35
SQ FT: 42,000
SALES (est): 6.2MM **Privately Held**
WEB: www.cisp.com
SIC: 4813 7375 ; information retrieval
services

(G-17673)
COMPASS CORP FOR RECOVERY SVCS
Also Called: Sasi
2005 Ashland Ave (43620-1163)
PHONE....................419 241-8827
Robert Stokes, *President*
Ross Chaban, *Vice Pres*
Jim Schultz, *Vice Pres*
EMP: 100
SALES: 3.7MM **Privately Held**
SIC: 8069 Drug addiction rehabilitation
hospital

(G-17674)
COMPREHENSIVE ADDICTION SVC SY
Also Called: Compass
2005 Ashland Ave (43620-1703)
PHONE....................419 241-8827
Ross Chaban, *Exec Dir*
EMP: 63
SQ FT: 68,000
SALES (est): 2.7MM **Privately Held**
WEB: www.ccrscompass.org
SIC: 8361 8093 Rehabilitation center, resi-
dential: health care incidental; specialty
outpatient clinics

(G-17675)
CONCEPT REHAB INC (PA)
7150 Granite Cir Ste 200 (43617-3114)
PHONE....................419 843-6002
Joan E Bayer, *CEO*
Kim Saylor, *President*
Martha Shaker, *President*
Marianne Hassen, *Senior VP*
EMP: 71
SQ FT: 3,000
SALES (est): 29.5MM **Privately Held**
WEB: www.conceptrehab.com
SIC: 8093 Rehabilitation center, outpatient
treatment

(G-17676)
CONCORD CARE CENTER OF TOLEDO
Also Called: Briarfield At Glanzman Road
3121 Glanzman Rd (43614-3802)
PHONE....................419 385-6616
Debra A Ifft, *CEO*
Fran Johnson, *Nursing Dir*
Maria Laubenthal, *Food Svc Dir*
Nick Mancini, *Records Dir*
Gail Fischer, *Administration*
EMP: 90
SALES (est): 4.2MM **Privately Held**
SIC: 8051 Skilled nursing care facilities

(G-17677)
CONSULTANTS LABORATORY MEDICI
2130 W Central Ave # 300 (43606-3819)
PHONE....................419 535-9629
F Michael Walsh, *Principal*
EMP: 38
SALES (est): 255K **Privately Held**
SIC: 8071 Pathological laboratory
HQ: Aurora Diagnostics, Llc
11025 Rca Center Dr # 300
Palm Beach Gardens FL 33410

(G-17678)
CONTAINER GRAPHICS CORP
305 Ryder Rd (43607-3105)
PHONE....................419 531-5133
Bill Beaker, *Branch Mgr*
EMP: 100
SQ FT: 24,200
SALES (corp-wide): 3MM **Privately Held**
WEB: www.containergraphics.com
SIC: 7336 3545 3944 Graphic arts & re-
lated design; cutting tools for machine
tools; dice & dice cups
PA: Container Graphics Corp.
114 Ednbrgh S Dr Ste 104
Cary NC 27511
919 481-4200

(G-17679)
COOPER-SMITH ADVERTISING LLC
3500 Granite Cir (43617-1172)
PHONE....................419 470-5900
James D Cooper, *CEO*
Brad Rieger, *COO*
Michele Hall, *Senior VP*
Michael Jacob, *Vice Pres*
Karen Hudock, *Buyer*
EMP: 40
SQ FT: 11,000
SALES (est): 9.8MM **Privately Held**
WEB: www.cooper-smith.com
SIC: 7311 Advertising consultant

(G-17680)
COUNTY OF LUCAS
Also Called: Child Support Enforcement Agcy
701 Adams St (43604-6623)
PHONE....................419 213-3000
Mary Carol Torsok, *Director*
EMP: 170 **Privately Held**
WEB: www.lucascountyoh.gov
SIC: 8322 9111 Individual & family serv-
ices; county supervisors' & executives' of-
fices
PA: County Of Lucas
1 Government Ctr Ste 600
Toledo OH 43604
419 213-4406

(G-17681)
COUNTY OF LUCAS
Also Called: Lucas County Prosecution
700 Adams St Ste 150 (43604-5661)
PHONE....................419 213-4700
Gene Atkins, *Branch Mgr*
EMP: 114 **Privately Held**
WEB: www.lucascountyoh.gov
SIC: 8111 9111 Specialized law offices, at-
torneys; county supervisors' & executives'
offices
PA: County Of Lucas
1 Government Ctr Ste 600
Toledo OH 43604
419 213-4406

(G-17682)
COUNTY OF LUCAS
Also Called: Job and Family Services Dept
3210 Monroe St (43606-7738)
P.O. Box 10007 (43699-0007)
PHONE....................419 213-8999
Issacc Palmer, *Director*
EMP: 400 **Privately Held**
WEB: www.lucascountyoh.gov
SIC: 8322 9111 Individual & family serv-
ices; county supervisors' & executives' of-
fices
PA: County Of Lucas
1 Government Ctr Ste 600
Toledo OH 43604
419 213-4406

(G-17683)
COUNTY OF LUCAS
Also Called: Lucas County Regional Hlth Dst
635 N Erie St (43604-5317)
PHONE....................419 213-4018
Joanne Melamed, *General Mgr*
David L Grossman, *Med Doctor*
Ross Buckingham, *Director*
Dennis Cole, *Director*
Peter Ujvagi, *Administration*
EMP: 120 **Privately Held**
WEB: www.lucascountyoh.gov
SIC: 8011 Health maintenance organiza-
tion
PA: County Of Lucas
1 Government Ctr Ste 600
Toledo OH 43604
419 213-4406

(G-17684)
COUNTY OF LUCAS
Also Called: Board Lucas Cnty Commission-
ers
1 Government Ctr Ste 800 (43604-2259)
PHONE....................419 213-4500
Dan Hiskey, *Manager*
Dave Sigler, *Executive*
Michael Beazley, *Administration*
EMP: 45 **Privately Held**
WEB: www.lucascountyoh.gov
SIC: 9121 8721 ; accounting, auditing &
bookkeeping
PA: County Of Lucas
1 Government Ctr Ste 600
Toledo OH 43604
419 213-4406

(G-17685)
COUNTY OF LUCAS
1154 Larc Ln (43614-2768)
PHONE....................419 385-6021
John Trunk, *Manager*
EMP: 52 **Privately Held**
SIC: 9411 8051 ; skilled nursing care fa-
cilities

PA: County Of Lucas
1 Government Ctr Ste 600
Toledo OH 43604
419 213-4406

(G-17686)
COUSINS WASTE CONTROL LLC (PA)
1701 E Matzinger Rd (43612-3841)
PHONE....................419 726-1500
Brian Recatto, *Mng Member*
EMP: 64
SQ FT: 4,000
SALES (est): 3.3MM **Privately Held**
SIC: 4212 4959 Hazardous waste trans-
port; oil spill cleanup

(G-17687)
COVENANT CARE OHIO INC
Also Called: Fairview Skilled Nursing & Reh
4420 South Ave (43615-6417)
PHONE....................419 531-4201
Jim Framsted, *Manager*
EMP: 90 **Privately Held**
WEB: www.villagegeorgetown.com
SIC: 8051 Skilled nursing care facilities
HQ: Covenant Care Ohio, Inc.
27071 Aliso Creek Rd # 100
Aliso Viejo CA 92656
949 349-1200

(G-17688)
CRIMINAL JSTICE CRDNTING CNCIL
1 Government Ctr Ste 1720 (43604-2230)
PHONE....................567 200-6850
Holly Mathews, *Exec Dir*
EMP: 42
SALES (est): 6.5MM **Privately Held**
WEB: www.lucascountyoh.gov
SIC: 8111 Legal services

(G-17689)
CROWNE PLAZA TOLEDO
444 N Summit St (43604-1514)
PHONE....................419 241-1411
EMP: 80
SALES: 5MM **Privately Held**
SIC: 7011 Hotel/Motel Operation

(G-17690)
CUMULUS MEDIA INC
Also Called: Wxkr
3225 Arlington Ave (43614-2427)
PHONE....................419 725-5700
Andy Stuart, *Manager*
Rick Sharp, *Manager*
EMP: 60
SALES (corp-wide): 1.1B **Publicly Held**
WEB: www.cumulusmedia.com
SIC: 4832 Radio broadcasting stations
PA: Cm Wind Down Topco Inc.
3280 Peachtree Rd Ne Ne2300
Atlanta GA 30305
404 949-0700

(G-17691)
CUMULUS MEDIA INC
Also Called: K 100 Radio Station
3225 Arlington Ave (43614-2427)
PHONE....................419 240-1000
John Dickie, *President*
EMP: 93
SALES (corp-wide): 1.1B **Publicly Held**
WEB: www.cumulusmedia.com
SIC: 4832 Radio broadcasting stations
PA: Cm Wind Down Topco Inc.
3280 Peachtree Rd Ne Ne2300
Atlanta GA 30305
404 949-0700

(G-17692)
DAVID LEE GROSSMAN MD
Also Called: Alexis Medical Center
1000 Regency Ct Ste 102 (43623-3074)
PHONE....................419 843-8150
David Lee Grossman-Md, *Principal*
Susan Kirkbride, *Manager*
Helena Howe, *Info Tech Mgr*
Morgan Rethman,
Andrea Rutan,
EMP: 32
SALES (est): 1.1MM **Privately Held**
SIC: 8011 Internal medicine, physician/sur-
geon

(G-17693)
DAYTON HCRI PLACE DENVER
4500 Dorr St (43615-4040)
PHONE...............................419 247-2800
Mary Ellen Pisanelli, *Principal*
Kevin Kirn, *Vice Pres*
Shawn French, *Engineer*
Amy Berg, *Manager*
Diane Brown, *Manager*
EMP: 27
SALES (est): 2.7MM **Privately Held**
SIC: 6512 Nonresidential building operators

(G-17694)
DAYTON-DIXIE MUFFLERS INC (PA)
Also Called: Midas Muffler
1101 Monroe St (43604-5811)
PHONE...............................419 243-7281
Calvin Katz, *President*
Arthur Katz, *Treasurer*
EMP: 25
SALES (est): 1.9MM **Privately Held**
SIC: 7533 Muffler shop, sale or repair & installation

(G-17695)
DEALER SUPPLY AND EQP LTD
1549 Campbell St (43607-4321)
PHONE...............................419 724-8473
Thomas W Heintschel, *President*
EMP: 30
SALES (est): 666.3K **Privately Held**
SIC: 7549 Automotive maintenance services

(G-17696)
DECAHEALTH INC
7071 W Central Ave Ste C (43617-2700)
PHONE...............................866 908-3514
Michael S McGowan, *President*
William James, *President*
Chad Graham, *CFO*
Lisa Seel, *Business Dir*
April Martin, *Admin Asst*
EMP: 80
SALES: 4.8MM **Privately Held**
SIC: 8082 Home health care services

(G-17697)
DENNIS TOP SOIL & LANDSCAPING
Also Called: Gardenland
6340 Dorr St (43615-4310)
P.O. Box 10, Blissfield MI (49228-0010)
PHONE...............................419 865-5656
Robert T Dennis, *President*
EMP: 40 EST: 1960
SQ FT: 7,270
SALES (est): 2.4MM **Privately Held**
SIC: 0782 5261 5193 Landscape contractors; nursery stock, seeds & bulbs; garden supplies & tools; nursery stock

(G-17698)
DENVER WHOLESALE FLORISTS CO
Also Called: D W F
14 N Erie St (43604-6940)
PHONE...............................419 241-7241
John Smith, *Branch Mgr*
EMP: 25
SALES (corp-wide): 100.1MM **Privately Held**
WEB: www.dwfwholesale.com
SIC: 5193 Flowers, fresh; florists' supplies; plants, potted
PA: Denver Wholesale Florists Company
4800 Dahlia St Ste A
Denver CO 80216
303 399-0970

(G-17699)
DEVELPMNTAL DSBLTIES OHIO DEPT
Also Called: Northwest Ohio Dvlopmental Ctr
1101 S Detroit Ave (43614-2704)
PHONE...............................419 385-0231
Dan Housepian, *Manager*
EMP: 340 **Privately Held**
SIC: 8361 9431 Home for the mentally retarded;

HQ: Ohio Department Of Developmental Disabilities
30 E Broad St Fl 13
Columbus OH 43215

(G-17700)
DHL SUPPLY CHAIN (USA)
1717 E Matzinger Rd (43612-3841)
PHONE...............................419 727-4318
Rory Hammerstrom, *General Mgr*
David Williams, *General Mgr*
Eugene Hartman, *Opers Mgr*
John Shadler, *Safety Mgr*
Don Bolles, *Branch Mgr*
EMP: 30
SALES (corp-wide): 70.4B **Privately Held**
WEB: www.exel-logistics.com
SIC: 4225 8741 4214 General warehousing; management services; local trucking with storage
HQ: Exel Inc.
570 Polaris Pkwy
Westerville OH 43082
614 865-8500

(G-17701)
DIMECH SERVICES INC
5505 Enterprise Blvd (43612-3858)
PHONE...............................419 727-0111
Janice Sheahan, *President*
James E Sheahan, *President*
Josh Quinlivan, *Vice Pres*
Ronald Sheahan, *Vice Pres*
Roger Sheahan, *Treasurer*
EMP: 30
SQ FT: 12,700
SALES: 10.1MM **Privately Held**
WEB: www.dimech.com
SIC: 1711 Mechanical contractor

(G-17702)
DIOCESE OF TOLEDO
Also Called: Catholic Club
1601 Jefferson Ave (43604-5724)
PHONE...............................419 243-7255
Hope Bland, *Director*
EMP: 47
SALES (corp-wide): 90.2MM **Privately Held**
SIC: 8351 Child day care services
PA: Roman Catholic Diocese Of Toledo
1933 Spielbusch Ave
Toledo OH 43604
419 244-6711

(G-17703)
DMC TECHNOLOGY GROUP
Also Called: DMC Consulting
7657 Kings Pointe Rd (43617-1514)
PHONE...............................419 535-2900
J Patrick Sheehan, *President*
Jenny Becker, *Accounting Mgr*
EMP: 30
SQ FT: 13,000
SALES (est): 7.8MM **Privately Held**
SIC: 7379 7371 5045 7378 Computer related consulting services; custom computer programming services; computers, peripherals & software; computer maintenance & repair

(G-17704)
DSC LOGISTICS LLC
1260 W Laskey Rd (43612-2909)
PHONE...............................847 390-6800
Dean Whitacre, *Manager*
EMP: 59
SALES (corp-wide): 355MM **Privately Held**
SIC: 4225 General warehousing & storage
PA: Dsc Logistics, Llc
1750 S Wolf Rd
Des Plaines IL 60018
847 390-6800

(G-17705)
DUMOUCHELLE ART GALLERIES
409 Jefferson Ave (43604)
PHONE...............................419 255-7606
Lawrence Dumouchelle, *Principal*
EMP: 30
SALES (est): 225.2K **Privately Held**
SIC: 8412 Art gallery

(G-17706)
DUNBAR MECHANICAL INC (PA)
2806 N Reynolds Rd (43615-2034)
P.O. Box 352350 (43635-2350)
PHONE...............................734 856-6601
Stephen E Dunbar, *President*
Jean Elkins, *General Mgr*
Bill Bailey, *Superintendent*
Dale R Dunbar, *Principal*
Delbert R Dunbar, *Principal*
EMP: 65 EST: 1956
SQ FT: 115,000
SALES (est): 48.6MM **Privately Held**
WEB: www.dunbarmechanical.com
SIC: 1711 Mechanical contractor

(G-17707)
E N T TOLEDO INC
2865 N Reynolds Rd # 260 (43615-2070)
PHONE...............................419 578-7555
Peter Vander Meer, *President*
EMP: 45 EST: 2001
SALES (est): 922.3K **Privately Held**
WEB: www.toledoent.com
SIC: 8011 Ears, nose & throat specialist: physician/surgeon

(G-17708)
EAST TOLEDO FAMILY CENTER (PA)
1020 Varland Ave (43605-3299)
PHONE...............................419 691-1429
Kim Partin, *Director*
EMP: 75
SQ FT: 23,755
SALES: 2.2MM **Privately Held**
SIC: 8322 Community center

(G-17709)
EASTMAN & SMITH LTD
1 Seagate Ste 2400 (43604-1576)
P.O. Box 10032 (43699-0032)
PHONE...............................419 241-6000
Laura Pinardo, *President*
Mark C Abramson, *Partner*
Richard E Antonini, *Partner*
Kenneth C Baker, *Partner*
Morton Bobowick, *Partner*
EMP: 150 EST: 1844
SQ FT: 48,000
SALES: 7.8K **Privately Held**
WEB: www.eastmansmith.com
SIC: 8111 General practice attorney, lawyer

(G-17710)
ELECTRO PRIME GROUP LLC (PA)
4510 Lint Ave Ste B (43612-2658)
PHONE...............................419 476-0100
Brett Grachek, *Vice Pres*
Jim Vellequette, *Plant Mgr*
Don Lublin, *QC Mgr*
Brent Leist, *Accounting Mgr*
John L Lauffer, *Mng Member*
▲ EMP: 70
SQ FT: 20,100
SALES (est): 20MM **Privately Held**
WEB: www.electroprime.com
SIC: 3471 5169 Plating & polishing; anti-corrosion products

(G-17711)
ELLIS RICHARD CB REICHLE KLEIN
Also Called: CB Richard Ellis
1 Seagate Fl 26 (43604-1527)
PHONE...............................419 861-1100
Daniel M Klein, *President*
Harlan E Reichle, *Vice Pres*
Chelsie Donley, *Manager*
EMP: 35
SQ FT: 6,000
SALES (est): 3.6MM **Privately Held**
SIC: 6531 Real estate agent, commercial

(G-17712)
EMERGENCY MEDICAL GROUP INC
5620 Southwyck Blvd 2 (43614-1501)
PHONE...............................419 866-6009
EMP: 50
SALES (est): 2.6MM **Privately Held**
SIC: 8011 Medical Doctor's Office

(G-17713)
EMPLOYBRIDGE HOLDING COMPANY
4400 Heatherdowns Blvd 5c (43614-3147)
PHONE...............................419 874-7125
EMP: 163
SALES (corp-wide): 577.1MM **Privately Held**
SIC: 7361 Employment agencies
PA: Employbridge Holding Company
1040 Crown Pointe Pkwy # 1040
Atlanta GA 30338
770 671-1900

(G-17714)
EMPOWERED FOR EXCELLENCE
3170 W Central Ave Ste B (43606-2945)
PHONE...............................567 316-7253
Jonathan James, *CEO*
EMP: 25
SALES (est): 612.3K **Privately Held**
SIC: 8093 Mental health clinic, outpatient

(G-17715)
ENDEVIS LLC (PA)
7643 Kings Pointe Rd # 100 (43617-1514)
PHONE...............................419 482-4848
Mark Melfi, *Mng Member*
Michael Fecko,
Mick Fecko,
Ron Walters,
EMP: 25
SQ FT: 3,500
SALES: 12MM **Privately Held**
WEB: www.staffingmaster.com
SIC: 7361 Executive placement

(G-17716)
ERIE CONSTRUCTION MID-WEST INC (PA)
4271 Monroe St (43606-1968)
P.O. Box 2698 (43606-0698)
PHONE...............................419 472-4200
Patrick J Trompeter, *CEO*
Philip C Davis, *Principal*
Adam Reed, *Mktg Dir*
Timothy Sink, *Info Tech Mgr*
Katie Vancs, *Executive Asst*
EMP: 45
SQ FT: 14,000
SALES (est): 50.6MM **Privately Held**
SIC: 1751 1761 Window & door (prefabricated) installation; siding contractor

(G-17717)
ERNST & YOUNG LLP
Also Called: Ey
1 Seagate Ste 2510 (43604-1591)
PHONE...............................419 244-8000
Thomas F Eagan, *Principal*
Randy M Kummer, *Principal*
Christine L Mabrey, *Manager*
EMP: 150
SALES (corp-wide): 4.3B **Privately Held**
WEB: www.ey.com
SIC: 8721 Certified public accountant
PA: Ernst & Young Llp
5 Times Sq Fl Conlv1
New York NY 10036
212 773-3000

(G-17718)
ESTES EXPRESS LINES INC
Also Called: Estes Express Lines 92
5330 Angola Rd Ste B (43615-6379)
PHONE...............................419 531-1500
Bruce Roberts, *Manager*
EMP: 50
SALES (corp-wide): 2.7B **Privately Held**
WEB: www.estes-express.com
SIC: 4213 Less-than-truckload (LTL) transport
PA: Estes Express Lines, Inc.
3901 W Broad St
Richmond VA 23230
804 353-1900

(G-17719)
EXPRESSO CAR WASH SYSTEMS INC
5440 W Central Ave (43615-1502)
PHONE...............................419 536-7540
Scott Beck, *President*
EMP: 60

SALES (corp-wide): 2.5MM **Privately Held**
WEB: www.expressocarwash.com
SIC: 7542 Washing & polishing, automotive
PA: Expresso Car Wash Systems Inc
  201 Illinois Ave
  Maumee OH 43537
  419 893-1406

(G-17720)
EXPRESSO CAR WASH SYSTEMS INC
Also Called: Expresso Car Wash 5
1750 S Reynolds Rd (43614-1404)
PHONE..................................419 866-7099
Jason Ikenburg, *Branch Mgr*
EMP: 35
SALES (corp-wide): 2.5MM **Privately Held**
WEB: www.expressocarwash.com
SIC: 7542 Carwash, automatic
PA: Expresso Car Wash Systems Inc
  201 Illinois Ave
  Maumee OH 43537
  419 893-1406

(G-17721)
EXTREME DETAIL CLG CNSTR SVCS
1724 Barrows St (43613-4618)
P.O. Box 140743 (43614-0743)
PHONE..................................419 392-3243
Julie Lake, *Partner*
Melissa Leeper, *Partner*
EMP: 34
SALES: 950K **Privately Held**
SIC: 1799 7349 Construction site cleanup; janitorial service, contract basis

(G-17722)
EYE INST OF NORTHWESTERN OH IN
5555 Airport Hwy (43615-7380)
PHONE..................................419 865-3866
Carol R Kollarits MD, *President*
Frank Kollarits, *Vice Pres*
EMP: 25
SQ FT: 9,000
SALES (est): 1MM **Privately Held**
SIC: 8011 Medical centers; ophthalmologist

(G-17723)
FAMILY & CHILD ABUSE (PA)
2460 Cherry St (43608-2667)
PHONE..................................419 244-3053
Christie Jenkins, *CEO*
Darla McCarty, *Office Mgr*
Christie Jenkins, *Manager*
Lynn Wilkins, *Manager*
EMP: 30
SQ FT: 3,000
SALES: 1.4MM **Privately Held**
SIC: 8322 Child related social services

(G-17724)
FAMILY HEALTH PLAN INC
2200 Jefferson Ave Fl 6 (43604-7102)
PHONE..................................419 241-6501
Tom Beaty, *President*
Lauri Oakes, *Vice Pres*
Randy Hoffman, *CFO*
Dr Mark Tucker, *Medical Dir*
Warren K D, *Pediatrics*
EMP: 170
SQ FT: 20,000
SALES: 108MM
SALES (corp-wide): 4.7B **Privately Held**
WEB: www.fhpl.net
SIC: 6324 8011 Health maintenance organization (HMO), insurance only; offices & clinics of medical doctors
PA: Mercy Health
  1701 Mercy Health Pl
  Cincinnati OH 45237
  513 639-2800

(G-17725)
FAMILY SERVICE OF NW OHIO (PA)
701 Jefferson Ave Ste 301 (43604-6957)
P.O. Box 1010 (43697-1010)
PHONE..................................419 321-6455
Tim Yenrick, *President*

Linda Condit, *Vice Pres*
EMP: 93
SQ FT: 12,000
SALES: 6.4MM **Privately Held**
SIC: 8322 8082 Social service center; home health care services

(G-17726)
FAMOUS ENTERPRISES INC
Also Called: Johnson Contrls Authorized Dlr
220 Matzinger Rd (43612-2625)
PHONE..................................419 478-0343
Therese Stambaugh, *Manager*
EMP: 30
SQ FT: 59,155 **Privately Held**
WEB: www.jfgood.com
SIC: 5211 5075 Lumber & other building materials; warm air heating & air conditioning
PA: Famous Enterprises, Inc.
  2620 Ridgewood Rd Ste 200
  Akron OH 44313

(G-17727)
FAURECIA EMISSIONS CONTROL SYS (DH)
543 Matzinger Rd (43612-2638)
P.O. Box 64010 (43612-0010)
PHONE..................................812 341-2000
David Degraaf, *President*
Christophe Schmidt,
Mark Stidham,
▲ EMP: 130
SQ FT: 40,000
SALES (est): 1.5B
SALES (corp-wide): 342.9MM **Privately Held**
WEB: www.franklin.faurecia.com
SIC: 3714 5013 Mufflers (exhaust), motor vehicle; motor vehicle supplies & new parts

(G-17728)
FCA US LLC
Also Called: Toledo Assembly Complex
4400 Chrysler Dr (43608-4000)
PHONE..................................419 727-2800
Robert Seabolt, *Principal*
EMP: 32
SALES (corp-wide): 130.8B **Privately Held**
SIC: 7538 General automotive repair shops
HQ: Fca Us Llc
  1000 Chrysler Dr
  Auburn Hills MI 48326

(G-17729)
FCA US LLC
Also Called: Trucking Division
5925 Hagman Rd (43612-3919)
PHONE..................................419 729-5959
Fred Prenal, *Branch Mgr*
EMP: 100
SALES (corp-wide): 130.8B **Privately Held**
SIC: 4731 Freight transportation arrangement
HQ: Fca Us Llc
  1000 Chrysler Dr
  Auburn Hills MI 48326

(G-17730)
FEDEX FREIGHT CORPORATION
5657 Enterprise Blvd (43612-3816)
PHONE..................................419 729-1755
EMP: 50
SQ FT: 7,000
SALES (corp-wide): 47.4B **Publicly Held**
SIC: 4213 Trucking Operator-Nonlocal
HQ: Fedex Freight Corporation
  1715 Aaron Brenner Dr
  Memphis TN 38120
  901 434-3100

(G-17731)
FEDEX GROUND PACKAGE SYS INC
650 S Reynolds Rd (43615-6345)
PHONE..................................800 463-3339
EMP: 400
SALES (corp-wide): 65.4B **Publicly Held**
SIC: 4212 4215 Delivery service, vehicular; courier services, except by air

HQ: Fedex Ground Package System, Inc.
  1000 Fed Ex Dr
  Coraopolis PA 15108
  800 463-3339

(G-17732)
FEED LUCAS COUNTY CHILDREN INC
Also Called: FLCC MEALS
1501 Monroe St Ste 27 (43604-5760)
P.O. Box 9363 (43697-9363)
PHONE..................................419 260-1556
Tony Siebeneck, *Director*
EMP: 52
SQ FT: 3,852
SALES: 973.8K **Privately Held**
WEB: www.feedlucaschildren.org
SIC: 8322 Children's aid society

(G-17733)
FIFTH THIRD BANK
606 Madison Ave Fl 8 (43604-1120)
PHONE..................................419 259-7820
John Schinharl, *Senior VP*
Bob McLair, *Sales/Mktg Mgr*
EMP: 25
SQ FT: 750
SALES (corp-wide): 7.9B **Publicly Held**
WEB: www.53rd.com
SIC: 6022 State trust companies accepting deposits, commercial
HQ: The Fifth Third Bank
  38 Fountain Square Plz
  Cincinnati OH 45202
  513 579-5203

(G-17734)
FIFTH THIRD BANK OF NW OHIO
1 Seagate Ste 2200 (43604-1525)
P.O. Box 1868 (43603-1868)
PHONE..................................419 259-7820
Robert Laclair, *President*
Kelly Davidson, *Office Mgr*
Fulton Wick, *Manager*
EMP: 300
SALES (est): 131.9MM
SALES (corp-wide): 7.9B **Publicly Held**
WEB: www.53.com
SIC: 6022 State commercial banks
PA: Fifth Third Bancorp
  38 Fountain Square Plz
  Cincinnati OH 45202
  800 972-3030

(G-17735)
FINANCE SYSTEM OF TOLEDO INC (PA)
2821 N Holland Sylvania R (43615-1871)
P.O. Box 351297 (43635-1297)
PHONE..................................419 578-4300
Randall Parker, *President*
Amy Pfeiffer, *Manager*
EMP: 25
SQ FT: 5,000
SALES (est): 2.2MM **Privately Held**
SIC: 7322 Collection agency, except real estate

(G-17736)
FINANCIAL DESIGN GROUP INC (PA)
3230 Central Park W # 100 (43617-1019)
PHONE..................................419 843-4737
Michael Clements, *President*
James Strasser, *President*
Jason Strasser, *Principal*
Kay Preston, *Marketing Staff*
Mary Bertke, *Manager*
EMP: 25 EST: 1994
SALES (est): 4.5MM **Privately Held**
WEB: www.fdgonline.com
SIC: 6411 8742 Insurance agents, brokers & service; management consulting services

(G-17737)
FINDLEY INC (PA)
1 Seagate Ste 2050 (43604-1558)
PHONE..................................419 255-1360
John M Weber, *President*
Kyle Pifher, *Vice Pres*
Robert J Rogers, *Vice Pres*
Marc Stockwell, *Vice Pres*
Lisa Kay, *Marketing Mgr*
EMP: 75

SQ FT: 15,000
SALES (est): 18.2MM **Privately Held**
WEB: www.findleydavies.com
SIC: 8742 Compensation & benefits planning consultant; human resource consulting services

(G-17738)
FIRST APOSTOLIC CHURCH
Also Called: Apostolic Christian Academy
5701 W Sylvania Ave (43623-3308)
PHONE..................................419 885-4888
Brandon Buford, *Principal*
Gary Grzcinski, *Principal*
Ryan Jordan, *Principal*
Gary Trzcinski, *Principal*
J Mark Jordan, *Pastor*
EMP: 40
SQ FT: 47,957
SALES: 31.7K **Privately Held**
WEB: www.factoledo.com
SIC: 8661 8211 8351 Apostolic Church; private elementary & secondary schools; child day care services

(G-17739)
FIRST CHOICE MEDICAL STAFFING
5445 Sthwyck Blvd Ste 208 (43614)
PHONE..................................419 861-2722
Christopher Sterben, *Branch Mgr*
EMP: 57
SALES (corp-wide): 4.6MM **Privately Held**
SIC: 8082 Home health care services
PA: First Choice Medical Staffing Of Ohio, Inc.
  1457 W 117th St
  Cleveland OH 44107
  216 521-2202

(G-17740)
FIRST LOUISVILLE ARDEN LLC (DH)
333 N Summit St (43604-1531)
PHONE..................................419 252-5500
Paul A Ormond, *CEO*
EMP: 40
SALES (est): 2.4MM
SALES (corp-wide): 2.4B **Publicly Held**
SIC: 8051 Skilled nursing care facilities
HQ: Manor Care Of America, Inc.
  333 N Summit St Ste 103
  Toledo OH 43604
  419 252-5500

(G-17741)
FIRST STUDENT INC
419 N Westwood Ave (43607-3347)
PHONE..................................419 382-9915
Inez Evans, *Manager*
EMP: 45
SALES (corp-wide): 8.9B **Privately Held**
WEB: www.leag.com
SIC: 4151 School buses
HQ: First Student, Inc.
  600 Vine St Ste 1400
  Cincinnati OH 45202

(G-17742)
FLEETPRIDE WEST INC
200 Indiana Ave (43604-8220)
PHONE..................................419 243-3161
Joe Gears, *Branch Mgr*
EMP: 30 **Publicly Held**
SIC: 7539 Automotive repair shops
HQ: Fleetpride West, Inc.
  600 E Las Coli Blvd Ste
  Irving TX 75014
  469 249-7500

(G-17743)
FLEX REALTY
Also Called: Flex Property Management
5763 Talmadge Rd Ste C2 (43623-1555)
PHONE..................................419 841-6208
Jim Moody, *Partner*
EMP: 30
SALES (est): 2.7MM **Privately Held**
WEB: www.flexrealty.com
SIC: 6531 Real estate agent, residential

(G-17744)
FLORALANDSCAPE INC
130 Elmdale Rd (43607-2914)
PHONE..................................419 536-7640

Douglas J Bettinger, *CEO*
EMP: 65
SQ FT: 6,480
SALES (est): 3.2MM **Privately Held**
WEB: www.floralandscape.com
SIC: 0782 0781 Lawn care services; landscape planning services

(G-17745)
FLOYD P BUCHER & SON INC
5743 Larkhall Dr (43614-1136)
PHONE....................................419 867-8792
Dan Bucher, *President*
Roger Bucher, *Corp Secy*
Verl Frazier, *Exec VP*
EMP: 50 **EST:** 1947
SQ FT: 10,000
SALES (est): 8.8MM **Privately Held**
WEB: www.floydpbucherandsoninc.com
SIC: 1541 1542 Industrial buildings, new construction; commercial & office building, new construction

(G-17746)
FRANCISCAN CARE CTR SYLVANIA
4111 N Hlland Sylvania Rd (43623)
PHONE....................................419 882-2087
Shawn T Litton, *CEO*
EMP: 130
SQ FT: 25,712
SALES: 9.4MM **Privately Held**
WEB: www.fccsylvania.org
SIC: 8051 Skilled nursing care facilities
HQ: Sylvania Franciscan Health
1715 Indian Wood Cir # 200
Maumee OH 43537
419 882-8373

(G-17747)
FRED CHRISTEN & SONS COMPANY (PA)
714 George St (43608-2914)
P.O. Box 547 (43697-0547)
PHONE....................................419 243-4161
Fredrick R Christen, *President*
Marlene P Christen, *Corp Secy*
Marlene Christen, *Treasurer*
Michael Schreiber, *Director*
EMP: 60 **EST:** 1929
SQ FT: 32,000
SALES (est): 21MM **Privately Held**
WEB: www.fredchristenandsons.com
SIC: 1761 Roofing contractor; sheet metalwork

(G-17748)
FREIGHT RITE INC (PA)
4352 W Sylvania Ave Ste M (43623-3441)
P.O. Box 6964 (43612-0964)
PHONE....................................419 478-7400
Todd Sanderson, *General Mgr*
Matthew J Paden, *Principal*
Gary Jackson, *Principal*
EMP: 25
SALES (est): 11.3MM **Privately Held**
SIC: 4731 Freight forwarding

(G-17749)
FULLER & HENRY LTD (PA)
1 Seagate Ste 1700 (43604-1504)
P.O. Box 2633 (43606-0633)
PHONE....................................419 247-2500
Stephen J Stanford, *Partner*
David R Bainbridge, *Partner*
Michael E Born, *Partner*
Alan C Boyd, *Partner*
Martin D Carrigan, *Partner*
EMP: 50
SQ FT: 15,000
SALES (est): 5MM **Privately Held**
SIC: 8111 Attorneys

(G-17750)
FURNEY GROUP HOME
4656 Glendale Ave (43614-1965)
PHONE....................................419 389-0152
Carlina Moore, *Director*
EMP: 35
SALES (est): 289.1K **Privately Held**
SIC: 8361 8052 Residential care; intermediate care facilities

(G-17751)
G G MARCK & ASSOCIATES INC (PA)
300 Phillips Ave (43612-1470)
PHONE....................................419 478-0900
Gary Marck, *President*
Christopher Miller, *CFO*
Joe Marck, *Natl Sales Mgr*
Amy Bee, *Cust Mgr*
Cary Kingsley, *Sales Staff*
▲ **EMP:** 44
SQ FT: 300,000
SALES: 30MM **Privately Held**
WEB: www.marckassoc.com
SIC: 5023 Kitchenware

(G-17752)
GA BUSINESS PURCHASER LLC
Also Called: Guardian Alarm
3222 W Central Ave (43606-2929)
PHONE....................................419 255-8400
Dennis Simmons, *Sales Mgr*
Cris Zielinski, *Branch Mgr*
EMP: 60
SALES (est): 4.5MM
SALES (corp-wide): 86.7MM **Privately Held**
SIC: 1731 5063 7382 Fire detection & burglar alarm systems specialization; burglar alarm systems; security systems services
PA: Ga Business Purchaser Llc
20800 Southfield Rd
Southfield MI 48075
248 423-1000

(G-17753)
GALLON TAKACS BOISSONEAULT & S (PA)
3516 Granite Cir (43617-1172)
P.O. Box 352018 (43635-2018)
PHONE....................................419 843-2001
Jack E Gallon, *President*
Stephanie Keith, *President*
William E Takacs, *Vice Pres*
Jeffrey Julius, *Treasurer*
EMP: 100
SQ FT: 30,728
SALES (est): 15.8MM **Privately Held**
WEB: www.gallonlaw.com
SIC: 8111 General practice attorney, lawyer

(G-17754)
GARDA CL GREAT LAKES INC
Also Called: Metropolitan Armored Car
3635 Marine Rd (43609-1019)
PHONE....................................419 385-2411
Michael Odunn, *Manager*
EMP: 25
SQ FT: 500 **Privately Held**
WEB: www.gocashlink.com
SIC: 7381 Armored car services
HQ: Garda Cl Technical Services, Inc.
700 S Federal Hwy Ste 300
Boca Raton FL 33432

(G-17755)
GARDEN II LEASING CO LLC
Also Called: Advanced Specialty Hosp Toledo
1015 Garden Lake Pkwy (43614-2779)
PHONE....................................419 381-0037
Robert Desotelle, *CEO*
Lauren Avigdor, *Human Res Dir*
Gail Bechtel, *Hlthcr Dir*
EMP: 100
SALES (est): 12.4MM
SALES (corp-wide): 125.8MM **Privately Held**
SIC: 8062 General medical & surgical hospitals
PA: Communicare Health Services, Inc.
4700 Ashwood Dr Ste 200
Blue Ash OH 45241
513 530-1654

(G-17756)
GARDNER CEMENT CONTRACTORS
821 Warehouse Rd (43615-6472)
PHONE....................................419 389-0768
Robert W Gardner, *President*
Lynn A Gardner, *Corp Secy*
Mark Hogrefe, *Manager*
EMP: 75

SQ FT: 6,200
SALES (est): 6.4MM **Privately Held**
SIC: 1771 Concrete work

(G-17757)
GEDDIS PAVING & EXCAVATING INC
1019 Wamba Ave (43607-3256)
PHONE....................................419 536-8501
Robert J Geddis Jr, *President*
Steve Oliver, *Vice Pres*
Stella Ellerbrock, *Safety Dir*
Benjamin Geddis, *Treasurer*
Kimberly Geddis, *Admin Sec*
EMP: 26 **EST:** 1949
SQ FT: 4,200
SALES (est): 4.9MM **Privately Held**
WEB: www.geddispaving.com
SIC: 1794 1771 Excavation work; blacktop (asphalt) work

(G-17758)
GEMINI PROPERTIES
Also Called: West Park Place
3501 Executive Pkwy Ofc (43606-1369)
PHONE....................................419 531-9211
Kristen Pickle, *Director*
EMP: 50
SALES (corp-wide): 6.8MM **Privately Held**
WEB: www.geminiproperties.com
SIC: 6513 Retirement hotel operation
PA: Gemini Properties
1516 S Boston Ave Ste 301
Tulsa OK 74119
918 592-4400

(G-17759)
GEO GRADEL CO
3135 Front St (43605-1009)
P.O. Box 8337 (43605-0337)
PHONE....................................419 691-7123
John F Gradel, *President*
Frederick T Sander, *Vice Pres*
Alan Raven, *Treasurer*
Frank Justen, *Admin Sec*
EMP: 65 **EST:** 1903
SQ FT: 12,200
SALES (est): 22.4MM **Privately Held**
SIC: 1794 Excavation & grading, building construction

(G-17760)
GEORGE P BALLAS BUICK GMC TRCK (PA)
Also Called: Budget Rent-A-Car
5715 W Central Ave (43615-1401)
P.O. Box 352470 (43635-2470)
PHONE....................................419 535-1000
George P Ballas, *President*
Robert Fowler, *Vice Pres*
Richard Farrar, *Admin Sec*
EMP: 58 **EST:** 1968
SQ FT: 55,000
SALES (est): 13MM **Privately Held**
SIC: 5511 7514 7532 5521 Automobiles, new & used; rent-a-car service; top & body repair & paint shops; used car dealers; automobiles & other motor vehicles

(G-17761)
GIAMMARCO PROPERTIES LLC
5252 Monroe St (43623-3140)
PHONE....................................419 885-4844
Pasquale Giammarco, *President*
EMP: 30
SALES (est): 1.6MM **Privately Held**
SIC: 6531 Real estate agent, commercial

(G-17762)
GIANT INDUSTRIES INC
900 N Westwood Ave (43607-3261)
PHONE....................................419 531-4600
Raymond Simon, *CEO*
Edward Simon, *President*
Wolfgang Drescher, *Admin Sec*
▲ **EMP:** 40
SQ FT: 83,000
SALES (est): 8.6MM **Publicly Held**
WEB: www.giantpumps.com
SIC: 3581 3589 5084 3594 Automatic vending machines; car washing machinery; pumps & pumping equipment; fluid power pumps & motors; pumps & pumping equipment; sanitary paper products

PA: Marathon Petroleum Corporation
539 S Main St
Findlay OH 45840

(G-17763)
GIRL SCOUTS OF WESTERN OHIO
Also Called: Girl Scuts Wstn Ohio Tledo Div
2244 Collingwood Blvd (43620-1147)
PHONE....................................567 225-3557
EMP: 44
SALES (corp-wide): 13.7MM **Privately Held**
SIC: 8641 Girl Scout organization
PA: Girl Scouts Of Western Ohio
4930 Cornell Rd
Blue Ash OH 45242
513 489-1025

(G-17764)
GIRL SCUTS WSTN OHIO TLEDO DIV (PA)
2244 Collingwood Blvd (43620-1147)
PHONE....................................419 243-8216
Fax: 419 245-5357
EMP: 38 **EST:** 1917
SQ FT: 22,000
SALES (est): 1.2MM **Privately Held**
SIC: 8641 Civic/Social Association

(G-17765)
GLOBE TRUCKING INC
5261 Stickney Ave (43612-3722)
PHONE....................................419 727-8307
David L Drago, *President*
EMP: 56
SQ FT: 9,000
SALES (est): 7.6MM **Privately Held**
WEB: www.globetrucking.com
SIC: 4213 Contract haulers

(G-17766)
GOODREMONTS
1017 W Sylvania Ave (43612-1701)
P.O. Box 1728, Mansfield (44901-1728)
PHONE....................................419 476-1492
EMP: 28
SQ FT: 17,000
SALES (est): 3.1MM **Privately Held**
SIC: 5044 Whol Office Equipment

(G-17767)
GOODWILL INDS NW OHIO INC (PA)
1120 Madison Ave (43604-7538)
P.O. Box 336 (43697-0336)
PHONE....................................419 255-0070
Robert Huber, *President*
Bob Huber, *Vice Pres*
Amy Wachob, *Vice Pres*
Sarah Semer, *Opers Mgr*
Raymond W Byers, *CFO*
EMP: 100
SQ FT: 66,000
SALES: 19.2MM **Privately Held**
WEB: www.goodwillnwohio.com
SIC: 5932 8331 Clothing, secondhand; shoes, secondhand; home furnishings, secondhand; vocational rehabilitation agency; sheltered workshop

(G-17768)
GRAY TELEVISION GROUP INC
Also Called: Wtvg-TV
4247 Dorr St (43607-2134)
PHONE....................................419 531-1313
Peter Veto, *Vice Pres*
Mark Sexton, *Sales Mgr*
Mark Stroud, *Technology*
EMP: 54
SALES (corp-wide): 1B **Publicly Held**
SIC: 4833 Television translator station
HQ: Gray Television Group, Inc.
4370 Peachtree Rd Ne # 500
Brookhaven GA 30319
404 266-8333

(G-17769)
GREAT LAKES HOME HLTH SVCS INC
3425 Executive Pkwy # 206 (43606-1334)
PHONE....................................888 260-9835
Adam D Nielsen, *President*
EMP: 50 **Privately Held**
SIC: 8082 Home health care services

PA: Great Lakes Home Health Services, Inc.
900 Cooper St
Jackson MI 49202

(G-17770)
GREAT LAKES MKTG ASSOC INC
3361 Executive Pkwy # 201 (43606-1337)
PHONE....................................419 534-4700
Lori Dixon, *President*
Ed Schweickert, *Director*
EMP: 35
SQ FT: 5,151
SALES (est): 3.8MM **Privately Held**
WEB: www.greatlakesmarketing.com
SIC: 8732 Market analysis or research

(G-17771)
GREENFIELD HEALTH SYSTEMS CORP (PA)
Also Called: Dialysis Partners of NW Ohio
3401 Glendale Ave Ste 110 (43614-2490)
PHONE....................................419 389-9681
Deanna Shaffer, *President*
Eva Costilla, *Admin Sec*
EMP: 48
SQ FT: 10,000
SALES (est): 4.2MM **Privately Held**
SIC: 8092 Kidney dialysis centers

(G-17772)
GROGANS TOWNE CHRYSLER INC (PA)
6100 Telegraph Rd (43612-4575)
PHONE....................................419 476-0761
Mark Floyd, *President*
Marc Ray, *Partner*
Dennis Amrhein, *General Mgr*
Denny Amrhiem, *Vice Pres*
Ed J Lishewski, *Treasurer*
▼ **EMP:** 100
SQ FT: 50,000
SALES (est): 38.7MM **Privately Held**
SIC: 5511 7515 7513 7538 Automobiles, new & used; passenger car leasing; truck leasing, without drivers; general automotive repair shops; top & body repair & paint shops; used car dealers

(G-17773)
GROSS ELECTRIC INC (PA)
2807 N Reynolds Rd (43615-2080)
P.O. Box 352377 (43635-2377)
PHONE....................................419 537-1818
Richard J Gross, *Ch of Bd*
Laurie Gross, *President*
Joseph Gross, *Vice Pres*
Jessica Inwood, *Store Mgr*
H C Reinhard, *Treasurer*
EMP: 35 **EST:** 1910
SQ FT: 36,000
SALES (est): 40.8MM **Privately Held**
WEB: www.grosselectric.com
SIC: 5063 5719 Electrical supplies; lighting fixtures; lighting fixtures

(G-17774)
GRUNWELL-CASHERO CO
5212 Tractor Rd (43612-3440)
PHONE....................................419 476-2426
Anthony Serra, *Branch Mgr*
EMP: 25
SQ FT: 3,880
SALES (corp-wide): 18MM **Privately Held**
WEB: www.grunwell-cashero.com
SIC: 1541 Renovation, remodeling & repairs: industrial buildings
PA: Grunwell-Cashero Co.
1041 Major St
Detroit MI 48217
313 843-8440

(G-17775)
GW SUTHERLAND MD
2865 N Reynolds Rd # 160 (43615-2068)
PHONE....................................419 578-7200
Gw Sutherland, *Principal*
EMP: 25 **EST:** 2001
SALES (est): 378.1K **Privately Held**
SIC: 8011 Offices & clinics of medical doctors

(G-17776)
H C R CORP
Also Called: Heartland Holly Glen Care Ctr
4293 Monroe St (43606-1943)
PHONE....................................419 472-0076
Becky Abbey, *President*
Robert G Mason, *President*
La Donna Mason, *Corp Secy*
EMP: 80
SALES (est): 2.1MM **Privately Held**
SIC: 8059 Nursing home, except skilled & intermediate care facility

(G-17777)
HANDY HUBBY
2010 N Reynolds Rd (43615-3512)
PHONE....................................419 754-1150
John Bothe, *Owner*
EMP: 25
SQ FT: 958
SALES (est): 1.4MM **Privately Held**
WEB: www.handyhubbyhomeimprovement.com
SIC: 1521 General remodeling, single-family houses

(G-17778)
HANSEN-MUELLER CO
1800 N Water St (43611)
P.O. Box 50497 (43605-0497)
PHONE....................................419 729-5535
Mike Burget, *Manager*
EMP: 26
SALES (corp-wide): 85.6MM **Privately Held**
WEB: www.hmgrain.com
SIC: 5153 2041 Grains; flour & other grain mill products
PA: Hansen-Mueller Co.
12231 Emmet St Ste 1
Omaha NE 68164
402 491-3385

(G-17779)
HARBOR (PA)
6629 W Central Ave Ste 1 (43617-1098)
P.O. Box 8970 (43623-0970)
PHONE....................................419 479-3233
Dale Shreve, *CEO*
Donna Corsoe, *Med Doctor*
Dave Timmerman, *Director*
EMP: 90 **EST:** 1941
SQ FT: 22,400
SALES: 40.2MM **Privately Held**
WEB: www.harbor.org
SIC: 8093 Mental health clinic, outpatient

(G-17780)
HARBOR
123 22nd St Ste 1 (43604-2706)
PHONE....................................419 241-6191
Dale Shreve, *Branch Mgr*
EMP: 100
SALES (corp-wide): 40.2MM **Privately Held**
WEB: www.harbor.org
SIC: 8093 8361 Mental health clinic, outpatient; rehabilitation center, residential; health care incidental
PA: Harbor
6629 W Central Ave Ste 1
Toledo OH 43617
419 479-3233

(G-17781)
HARBOR
Also Called: Mayfair School
5331 Bennett Rd (43612-3403)
PHONE....................................800 444-3353
Rachel Holland, *Manager*
EMP: 40
SALES (corp-wide): 40.2MM **Privately Held**
WEB: www.harbor.org
SIC: 8093 8052 Mental health clinic, outpatient; home for the mentally retarded, with health care
PA: Harbor
6629 W Central Ave Ste 1
Toledo OH 43617
419 479-3233

(G-17782)
HARBORSIDE POINTE PLACE LLC
Also Called: Point Place
6101 N Summit St (43611-1242)
PHONE....................................419 727-7870
George V Hager Jr, *Principal*
Mark Grieselding, *Principal*
Tom Durbin, *Administration*
EMP: 101
SALES (est): 1,000K **Privately Held**
SIC: 8051 Skilled nursing care facilities

(G-17783)
HART ASSOCIATES INC
811 Madison Ave (43604-5684)
PHONE....................................419 893-9600
Michael K Hart, *President*
Marc Paulenich, *Senior VP*
Mike Bell, *Vice Pres*
James Calhoun, *Vice Pres*
Susan Degens, *Vice Pres*
EMP: 55
SQ FT: 13,000
SALES (est): 13.3MM **Privately Held**
WEB: www.hartinc.com
SIC: 7311 Advertising consultant

(G-17784)
HARVEST FACILITY HOLDINGS LP
Also Called: Alexis Gardens
4560 W Alexis Rd Apt 9 (43623-1082)
PHONE....................................419 472-7115
Bob Allen, *Manager*
EMP: 25 **Privately Held**
WEB: www.holidaytouch.com
SIC: 6513 Retirement hotel operation
HQ: Harvest Facility Holdings Lp
5885 Meadows Rd Ste 500
Lake Oswego OR 97035
503 370-7070

(G-17785)
HCR MANOR CARE SVC FLA III INC (DH)
Also Called: Heartland Hospice Services
333 N Summit St (43604-1531)
PHONE....................................419 252-5500
Michael John Reed, *President*
EMP: 34
SALES (est): 4MM
SALES (corp-wide): 2.4B **Publicly Held**
SIC: 8051 Skilled nursing care facilities

(G-17786)
HCR MANORCARE MED SVCS FLA LLC
Also Called: Heartland Care Partners 3555
3450 W Central Ave # 230 (43606-1416)
P.O. Box 10086 (43699-0086)
PHONE....................................419 531-2127
Barry A Lazarus, *Branch Mgr*
EMP: 105
SALES (corp-wide): 2.4B **Publicly Held**
SIC: 8051 Convalescent home with continuous nursing care
HQ: Hcr Manorcare Medical Services Of Florida, Llc
333 N Summit St Ste 100
Toledo OH 43604
419 252-5500

(G-17787)
HCR MANORCARE MED SVCS FLA LLC (DH)
Also Called: Manor Care
333 N Summit St Ste 100 (43604-2617)
P.O. Box 10086 (43699-0086)
PHONE....................................419 252-5500
Paul Ormond, *Ch of Bd*
Keith Weikel, *COO*
R Jeffrey Bixler, *Vice Pres*
Steve Cavannough, *CFO*
Douglas G Haag, *Treasurer*
EMP: 200
SQ FT: 210,000
SALES (est): 94.6MM
SALES (corp-wide): 2.4B **Publicly Held**
WEB: www.manorcare.com
SIC: 8051 Convalescent home with continuous nursing care

HQ: Manor Care Of America, Inc.
333 N Summit St Ste 103
Toledo OH 43604
419 252-5500

(G-17788)
HEALTH CARE RETIREMENT CORP
333 N Summit St Ste 100 (43604-2615)
P.O. Box 10086 (43699-0086)
PHONE....................................419 252-5500
Paul A Ormond, *President*
Michael Keith Weikel, *Vice Pres*
Spencer Molen, *Treasurer*
Jeff Bixler, *Admin Sec*
EMP: 500
SQ FT: 10,000
SALES (est): 14.1MM
SALES (corp-wide): 2.4B **Publicly Held**
WEB: www.hrc-manorcare.com
SIC: 8051 Skilled nursing care facilities
HQ: Health Care And Retirement Corporation Of America
333 N Summit St Ste 103
Toledo OH 43604
419 252-5500

(G-17789)
HEALTH CARE RTREMENT CORP AMER (DH)
333 N Summit St Ste 103 (43604-2617)
P.O. Box 10086 (43699-0086)
PHONE....................................419 252-5500
Paul A Ormond, *Ch of Bd*
Stephen Guillard, *Senior VP*
Spence C Moler, *Vice Pres*
Richard Parr, *Vice Pres*
Steven Cavanaugh, *CFO*
EMP: 243
SALES (est): 45.2MM
SALES (corp-wide): 2.4B **Publicly Held**
WEB: www.hrc-manorcare.com
SIC: 8051 Convalescent home with continuous nursing care

(G-17790)
HEALTH CARE RTREMENT CORP AMER
Also Called: Heartland - Holly Glen
4293 Monroe St (43606-1943)
PHONE....................................419 474-6021
Kelly Lindeman, *Administration*
EMP: 100
SALES (corp-wide): 2.4B **Publicly Held**
WEB: www.hrc-manorcare.com
SIC: 8051 Skilled nursing care facilities
HQ: Health Care And Retirement Corporation Of America
333 N Summit St Ste 103
Toledo OH 43604
419 252-5500

(G-17791)
HEALTHCARE FACILITY MGT LLC
Also Called: Advanced Healtcare Center
955 Garden Lake Pkwy (43614-2777)
PHONE....................................419 382-2200
Elaine Hetherwick, *Manager*
EMP: 90
SALES (corp-wide): 125.8MM **Privately Held**
WEB: www.communicarehealth.com
SIC: 8051 Skilled nursing care facilities
PA: Communicare Health Services, Inc.
4700 Ashwood Dr Ste 200
Blue Ash OH 45241
513 530-1654

(G-17792)
HEARTLAND EMPLOYMENT SVCS LLC
333 N Summit St Ste 103 (43604-2617)
PHONE....................................419 252-5500
Bruce M Helberg, *Principal*
EMP: 715
SALES (est): 83.9K
SALES (corp-wide): 2.4B **Publicly Held**
SIC: 7363 Medical help service
HQ: Manor Care, Inc.
333 N Summit St Ste 103
Toledo OH 43604

(G-17793)
HEARTLAND FORT MYERS FL LLC (DH)
333 N Summit St (43604-1531)
PHONE.................................419 252-5500
Michael G Meyer, *Treasurer*
EMP: 37
SALES (est): 2.9MM
SALES (corp-wide): 2.4B **Publicly Held**
SIC: 8051 Skilled nursing care facilities

(G-17794)
HEARTLAND HEALTHCARE SVCS LLC (PA)
4755 South Ave (43615-6422)
PHONE.................................419 535-8435
Jeffrey Cremean, *CFO*
Dorothy Kuhl, *CFO*
EMP: 200
SQ FT: 72,000
SALES: 204.4MM **Privately Held**
WEB: www.hhstol.org
SIC: 5122 Pharmaceuticals

(G-17795)
HEARTLAND HOME CARE LLC (DH)
333 N Summit St Ste 100 (43604-2617)
PHONE.................................419 252-5500
EMP: 53
SALES (est): 5.3MM
SALES (corp-wide): 2.4B **Publicly Held**
SIC: 8059 Personal care home, with health care
HQ: Heartland Rehabilitation Services, Inc.
3425 Executive Pkwy # 128
Toledo OH 43606
419 537-0764

(G-17796)
HEARTLAND RHBLITATION SVCS INC (DH)
3425 Executive Pkwy # 128 (43606-1326)
PHONE.................................419 537-0764
Pat Smith, *Principal*
EMP: 75
SALES (est): 15.1MM
SALES (corp-wide): 2.4B **Publicly Held**
WEB: www.hrs-contracts.com
SIC: 8093 Rehabilitation center, outpatient treatment

(G-17797)
HECKS DIRECT MAIL & PRTG SVC (PA)
417 Main St (43605-2057)
PHONE.................................419 697-3505
Edward Heck, *CEO*
▲ EMP: 40 EST: 1943
SQ FT: 30,000
SALES (est): 4.4MM **Privately Held**
WEB: www.hecksprinting.com
SIC: 7331 2752 2791 2789 Addressing service; commercial printing, offset; typesetting; bookbinding & related work; commercial printing

(G-17798)
HECKS DIRECT MAIL & PRTG SVC
Also Called: Heck's Diamond Printing
202 W Florence Ave (43605-3304)
P.O. Box 8266 (43605-0266)
PHONE.................................419 661-6028
Cosino Trina, *Vice Pres*
EMP: 25
SALES (corp-wide): 4.4MM **Privately Held**
WEB: www.hecksprinting.com
SIC: 2752 7331 5192 Offset & photolithographic printing; direct mail advertising services; books, periodicals & newspapers
PA: Heck's Direct Mail & Printing Service Inc
417 Main St
Toledo OH 43605
419 697-3505

(G-17799)
HEIDTMAN STEEL PRODUCTS
2401 Front St (43605-1199)
PHONE.................................419 691-4646
EMP: 800

SALES (est): 53.4MM **Privately Held**
SIC: 5051 Metals Service Center

(G-17800)
HEIDTMAN STEEL PRODUCTS INC
Also Called: Heidtman Toledo Blank
135 N Flearing Blvd (43609)
PHONE.................................419 385-0636
John C Bates, *CEO*
EMP: 87
SALES (corp-wide): 296.3MM **Privately Held**
SIC: 5051 Steel
HQ: Heidtman Steel Products, Inc.
2401 Front St
Toledo OH 43605
419 691-4646

(G-17801)
HENRY GURTZWEILER INC
921 Galena St (43611-3717)
PHONE.................................419 729-3955
William H Myers, *President*
Greg Myers, *Vice Pres*
Robert Thomason, *CFO*
EMP: 75 EST: 1946
SQ FT: 15,000
SALES (est): 13.7MM **Privately Held**
WEB: www.henrygurtzweiler.com
SIC: 1791 Precast concrete structural framing or panels, placing of

(G-17802)
HERITAGE ENVMTL SVCS LLC
Also Called: Crystal Clean Parts Washer Svc
5451 Enterprise Blvd (43612-3812)
PHONE.................................419 729-1321
Adam Hoy, *Manager*
EMP: 50
SALES (corp-wide): 225.3MM **Privately Held**
WEB: www.heritage-enviro.com
SIC: 8748 Environmental consultant
HQ: Heritage Environmental Services, Llc
7901 W Morris St
Indianapolis IN 46231
317 243-0811

(G-17803)
HGCC OF ALLENTOWN INC
333 N Summit St (43604-1531)
PHONE.................................419 252-5500
Paul A Ormond, *Principal*
EMP: 96
SALES (est): 439.9K
SALES (corp-wide): 2.4B **Publicly Held**
SIC: 8051 Skilled nursing care facilities
HQ: Health Care And Retirement Corporation Of America
333 N Summit St Ste 103
Toledo OH 43604
419 252-5500

(G-17804)
HOLLYWOOD CASINO TOLEDO
1968 Miami St (43605-3359)
PHONE.................................419 661-5200
Chris Wilson, *Principal*
EMP: 61
SALES (est): 5.3MM **Privately Held**
SIC: 7011 Casino hotel

(G-17805)
HOME DEPOT USA INC
Also Called: Home Depot, The
1035 W Alexis Rd (43612-4201)
PHONE.................................419 476-4573
Darcy Miller, *Manager*
EMP: 200
SQ FT: 9,900
SALES (corp-wide): 108.2B **Publicly Held**
WEB: www.homerentalsdepot.com
SIC: 5211 7359 Home centers; tool rental
HQ: Home Depot U.S.A., Inc.
2455 Paces Ferry Ave
Atlanta GA 30339

(G-17806)
HOME DEPOT USA INC
Also Called: Home Depot, The
3200 Secor Rd (43606-1515)
PHONE.................................419 537-1920
Don Mandabille, *Manager*
EMP: 140

SALES (corp-wide): 108.2B **Publicly Held**
WEB: www.homerentalsdepot.com
SIC: 5211 7359 Home centers; tool rental
HQ: Home Depot U.S.A., Inc.
2455 Paces Ferry Ave
Atlanta GA 30339

(G-17807)
HOOVER & WELLS INC
Also Called: REZ STONE
2011 Seaman St (43605-1908)
PHONE.................................419 691-9220
Margaret Hoover, *Ch of Bd*
Barbara Corsini, *President*
John Corsini, *Vice Pres*
James Mc Collum, *Vice Pres*
Nichole Simon, *Vice Pres*
EMP: 120
SQ FT: 23,448
SALES: 37.3MM **Privately Held**
WEB: www.hooverwells.com
SIC: 1752 2891 2851 Wood floor installation & refinishing; adhesives & sealants; paints & allied products

(G-17808)
HORIZONS EMPLOYMENT SVCS LLC
Also Called: Apple A Day Healthcare Svcs
2024 W Terrace View St (43607-1063)
PHONE.................................419 254-9644
Jerome A Parker, *Mng Member*
EMP: 300
SQ FT: 1,300
SALES: 3.5MM **Privately Held**
SIC: 7361 Employment agencies

(G-17809)
HOUSEHOLD CENTRALIZED SVC INC
2052 W Sylvania Ave (43613-4527)
PHONE.................................419 474-5754
David Tobian, *President*
Richard Chase, *Vice Pres*
Tamara Tobian, *Admin Sec*
EMP: 26
SQ FT: 10,000
SALES (est): 2.8MM **Privately Held**
WEB:
www.householdcentralizedservice.com
SIC: 7629 7622 Electrical household appliance repair; television repair shop; stereophonic equipment repair; video repair; radio repair shop

(G-17810)
HS EXPRESS LLC
6003 Benore Rd (43612-3905)
PHONE.................................419 729-2400
Houston Vaughn, *CEO*
Larry Hall, *President*
EMP: 85
SQ FT: 3,000
SALES (est): 1.6MM
SALES (corp-wide): 219MM **Privately Held**
SIC: 4213 Trucking, except local
PA: Ps Logistics, Llc
1810 Avenue C
Birmingham AL 35218
205 788-4000

(G-17811)
HUB CITY TERMINALS INC
811 Madison Ave Ste 601 (43604-5684)
PHONE.................................419 217-5200
EMP: 47
SALES (corp-wide): 3.6B **Publicly Held**
WEB: www.hubgroup.com
SIC: 4731 Freight transportation arrangement
HQ: Hub City Terminals, Inc.
2000 Clearwater Dr
Oak Brook IL 60523
630 271-3600

(G-17812)
HULL & ASSOCIATES INC
219 S Erie St (43604-8607)
PHONE.................................419 385-2018
John Hull, *President*
EMP: 40

SALES (corp-wide): 108.2B **Publicly Held**
WEB: www.hullinc.com
SIC: 8711 Consulting engineer
PA: Hull & Associates, Inc.
6397 Emerald Pkwy Ste 200
Dublin OH 43016
614 793-8777

(G-17813)
HUNTINGTON INSURANCE INC (DH)
519 Madison Ave (43604-1206)
PHONE.................................419 720-7900
Paul Baldwin, *President*
Mary Beth Sullivan, *President*
Robert C Hawker Cpcu Arm, *Senior VP*
Ronald L Murray, *Senior VP*
Stu Peterson, *Vice Pres*
EMP: 150 EST: 1898
SALES (est): 93.9MM
SALES (corp-wide): 5.2B **Publicly Held**
WEB: www.skyinsure.com
SIC: 6411 Insurance agents
HQ: The Huntington National Bank
17 S High St Fl 1
Columbus OH 43215
614 480-4293

(G-17814)
HYLANT ADMINISTRATIVE SERVICES (PA)
811 Madison Ave Fl 11 (43604-5626)
P.O. Box 2083 (43603-2083)
PHONE.................................419 255-1020
Joe Seay, *President*
Michael Ugljesa, *President*
Dennis Michel, *Vice Pres*
Bill Petro, *Vice Pres*
Becky Stewart, *Vice Pres*
EMP: 35 EST: 1994
SALES (est): 3.3MM **Privately Held**
WEB: www.ohioplan.com
SIC: 6411 Insurance agents

(G-17815)
HYLANT GROUP INC (PA)
811 Madison Ave Fl 11 (43604-5626)
P.O. Box 1687 (43603-1687)
PHONE.................................419 255-1020
Michael Hylant, *CEO*
Patrick Hylant, *Ch of Bd*
Todd Belden, *President*
William F Buckley, *President*
John W Chaney, *President*
EMP: 180
SQ FT: 80,000
SALES: 129.8MM **Privately Held**
WEB: www.hylant.com
SIC: 6411 Insurance agents

(G-17816)
IET INC
3539 Glendale Ave Ste C (43614-3457)
PHONE.................................419 385-1233
Timothy C Stansfield, *President*
Ronda Massey, *Vice Pres*
Dan Holman, *Engineer*
Bhanu Jayanthi, *Engineer*
Philip Leinbach, *Engineer*
EMP: 40
SQ FT: 14,000
SALES (est): 6.3MM **Privately Held**
WEB: www.ieteng.com
SIC: 8711 Consulting engineer

(G-17817)
ILLINOIS CENTRAL RAILROAD CO
4820 Schwartz Rd (43611-1726)
PHONE.................................419 726-6028
EMP: 50
SALES (corp-wide): 10.2B **Privately Held**
SIC: 4011 Interurban railways
HQ: Illinois Central Railroad Company
17641 Ashland Ave
Homewood IL 60430
708 332-3500

(G-17818)
IMPACT PRODUCTS LLC (DH)
2840 Centennial Rd (43617-1898)
PHONE.................................419 841-2891
Terry Neal, *CEO*
Jeff Beery, *CFO*

▲ **EMP:** 155 **EST:** 2001
SQ FT: 155,000
SALES: 35MM
SALES (corp-wide): 18.7B **Publicly Held**
WEB: www.impact-products.com
SIC: 5084 5087 2392 3089 Safety equipment; janitors' supplies; mops, floor & dust; buckets, plastic; tissue dispensers, plastic
HQ: S. P. Richards Company
   6300 Highlands Pkwy Se
   Smyrna GA 30082
   770 434-4571

(G-17819)
IN HOME HEALTH LLC
Also Called: Heartland HM Hlth Care Hospice
3450 W Central Ave # 132 (43606-1416)
PHONE..............................419 531-0440
Fax: 419 531-0437
EMP: 50
SALES (corp-wide): 3.8B **Publicly Held**
SIC: 8082 Home Health Care Services
HQ: In Home Health, Llc
   333 N Summit St
   Toledo OH 43604
   419 252-5500

(G-17820)
INFINITE SEC SOLUTIONS LLC
663 Gawil Ave (43609-1115)
PHONE..............................419 720-5678
Lawrence Leizerman, *Principal*
EMP: 25
SALES (est) 341.2K **Privately Held**
SIC: 7381 Detective & armored car services

(G-17821)
INNOVATIVE CONTROLS CORP
1354 E Broadway St (43605-3667)
PHONE..............................419 691-6684
Louis M Soltis, *President*
Anson F Schultz, *Vice Pres*
Mark Benton, *Engineer*
Bryan Hanthorn, *Engineer*
Walter King, *Info Tech Mgr*
EMP: 63
SQ FT: 20,000
SALES (est): 14.1MM **Privately Held**
WEB: www.innovativecontrolscorp.com
SIC: 3613 3535 3711 3823 Control panels, electric; conveyors & conveying equipment; engineering services; industrial instrmnts msrmnt display/control process variable; relays & industrial controls; food products machinery

(G-17822)
INNOVATIVE DIALYSIS
Also Called: U.S. Rnal Care NW Ohio Dialysis
3829 Woodley Rd Ste 12 (43606-1173)
PHONE..............................419 473-9900
Shannon C Weills, *CEO*
Stephen Pirri, *President*
EMP: 25 **Privately Held**
SIC: 8092 Kidney dialysis centers

(G-17823)
INTEGRITY WALL & CEILING INC
5242 Angola Rd Ste 180 (43615-6336)
PHONE..............................419 381-1855
Mario Dominguez, *President*
EMP: 30
SQ FT: 7,200
SALES (est): 2.8MM **Privately Held**
WEB: www.iwctoledo.com
SIC: 1742 Drywall

(G-17824)
INTERTEC CORPORATION
3400 Executive Pkwy (43606-1396)
PHONE..............................419 537-9711
George B Seifried, *President*
Scott A Slater, *Vice Pres*
Darrel G Howard, *Admin Sec*
Darrel Howard, *Admin Sec*
◆ **EMP:** 300 **EST:** 1978
SQ FT: 1,000
SALES (est): 855.3K **Privately Held**
WEB: www.mspro.com
SIC: 3559 1796 3523 Glass making machinery: blowing, molding, forming, etc.; machinery installation; farm machinery & equipment

(G-17825)
INVERNESS CLUB
4601 Dorr St Ste 1 (43615-4038)
PHONE..............................419 578-9000
E C Benington, *President*
EMP: 63
SALES: 6.4MM **Privately Held**
SIC: 7997 Country club, membership; golf club, membership

(G-17826)
J & B LEASING INC OF OHIO
435 Dura Ave (43612-2619)
PHONE..............................419 269-1440
James M Bashore, *President*
EMP: 40
SQ FT: 6,240
SALES (est): 5.4MM **Privately Held**
SIC: 4213 Refrigerated products transport

(G-17827)
J & S INDUSTRIAL MCH PDTS INC
123 Oakdale Ave (43605-3322)
PHONE..............................419 691-1380
Nancy Colyer, *Principal*
Elton E Bowland, *Principal*
George Bowland, *Principal*
John Sehr, *Principal*
Donald R Colyer, *Vice Pres*
EMP: 70 **EST:** 1946
SQ FT: 32,000
SALES (est): 9.2MM **Privately Held**
WEB: www.jsindustrialmachine.com
SIC: 3559 7692 Glass making machinery: blowing, molding, forming, etc.; welding repair

(G-17828)
J SCHOEN ENTERPRISES INC (PA)
Also Called: Cleaner & Dryer Restoration
5056 Angola Rd (43615-6415)
PHONE..............................419 536-0970
Jon Schoen, *President*
Ying Xu, *Bookkeeper*
EMP: 26
SQ FT: 5,000
SALES (est): 4.2MM **Privately Held**
SIC: 7389 Fire protection service other than forestry or public

(G-17829)
JB MANAGEMENT INC
6540 W Central Ave Ste A (43617-1095)
PHONE..............................419 841-2596
William Beck, *President*
Joe Janicki, *Vice Pres*
EMP: 90
SALES (est): 400K **Privately Held**
SIC: 7363 Employee leasing service

(G-17830)
JENNITE CO
4694 W Bancroft St (43615-3946)
PHONE..............................419 531-1791
Robert Wheeler Jr, *President*
Thomas Wheeler, *Corp Secy*
Tom Wheeler, *Vice Pres*
EMP: 40
SQ FT: 2,800
SALES (est): 5.3MM **Privately Held**
WEB: www.jennite.com
SIC: 1771 Blacktop (asphalt) work

(G-17831)
JOB1USA INC (HQ)
701 Jefferson Ave Ste 202 (43604-6957)
P.O. Box 1480 (43603-1480)
PHONE..............................419 255-5005
Bruce F Rumpf, *President*
Chris Hammye, *Area Mgr*
Ray Kasparian, *Area Mgr*
Charles Reedy, *Area Mgr*
Sue Daniels, *Vice Pres*
EMP: 91
SQ FT: 35,000

SALES (est): 30.1MM
SALES (corp-wide): 31.1MM **Privately Held**
WEB: www.joboneusa.com
SIC: 7381 7363 7361 Security guard service; protective services, guard; temporary help service; medical help service; employment agencies; executive placement
PA: The Rumpf Corporation
   701 Jefferson Ave Ste 201
   Toledo OH 43604
   419 255-5005

(G-17832)
JONES & HENRY ENGINEERS LTD (PA)
3103 Executive Pkwy # 300 (43606-1372)
PHONE..............................419 473-9611
Bradley F Lowery, *President*
Fraur Morsches, *Principal*
Tim Warren, *Project Mgr*
Gary Bauer, *Engineer*
Troy Brehmer, *Engineer*
EMP: 50 **EST:** 1926
SALES: 10MM **Privately Held**
WEB: www.jheng.com
SIC: 8711 Consulting engineer

(G-17833)
JOSINA LOTT FOUNDATION
Also Called: Josina Lott Residential Home
120 S Holland Sylvania Rd (43615-5622)
P.O. Box 352049 (43635-2049)
PHONE..............................419 866-9013
Carol Parcell, *Info Tech Dir*
Michael Malone, *Director*
Beth Baumert, *Director*
Patty Schlosser, *Associate Dir*
EMP: 50
SQ FT: 23,600
SALES (est): 104.1K **Privately Held**
WEB: www.josinalott.org
SIC: 8361 Home for the mentally handicapped

(G-17834)
K-LIMITED CARRIER LTD (PA)
131 Matzinger Rd (43612-2623)
PHONE..............................419 269-0002
Dean Kaplan, *CEO*
Kim Kaplan, *President*
John Spurling, *Vice Pres*
Dennis Perna, *CFO*
Thurston Kristi, *Human Resources*
EMP: 110
SQ FT: 8,200
SALES: 23MM **Privately Held**
WEB: www.k-ltd.com
SIC: 4213 Contract haulers

(G-17835)
KA BERGQUIST INC (PA)
1100 King Rd (43617-2002)
P.O. Box 351330 (43635-1330)
PHONE..............................419 865-419€
Robert Barry, *President*
Hilda C Bergquist, *Principal*
Karl Bergquist, *Principal*
Charles E Ide Jr, *Principal*
Larry Hinkley, *Chairman*
▼ **EMP:** 30
SQ FT: 30,000
SALES (est): 43MM **Privately Held**
WEB: www.bergquistinc.com
SIC: 5084 1711 Propane conversion equipment; plumbing, heating, air-conditioning contractors

(G-17836)
KACE LOGISTICS LLC
1515 Matzinger Rd (43612-3828)
PHONE..............................419 273-3388
EMP: 55
SALES (est): 2.2MM **Privately Held**
SIC: 4212 Local Trucking Operator

(G-17837)
KATHLEEN K KAROL MD
2865 N Reynolds Rd # 170 (43615-2076)
PHONE..............................419 878-7992
Richard Torchia, *President*
EMP: 60 **EST:** 2001
SALES (est): 820.4K **Privately Held**
SIC: 8011 Ophthalmologist

(G-17838)
KELLI WOODS MANAGEMENT INC
Also Called: Advance Cleaning Contractors
4708 Angola Rd (43615-6409)
PHONE..............................419 478-1200
Robert F Swan, *President*
Josh Carmody, *General Mgr*
Thomas Woods, *Vice Pres*
Janice Porter, *Admin Sec*
EMP: 140
SQ FT: 7,000
SALES (est): 3.8MM **Privately Held**
SIC: 7349 Janitorial service, contract basis

(G-17839)
KEYSTONE FOODS LLC
M & M Restaurant Supply Div
4763 High Oaks Blvd (43623-1087)
PHONE..............................419 843-3009
Ronald Enser, *Manager*
EMP: 120
SQ FT: 80,000 **Privately Held**
WEB: www.keystonefoods.com
SIC: 5141 5113 Food brokers; industrial & personal service paper
HQ: Keystone Foods Llc
   905 Airport Rd Ste 400
   West Chester PA 19380
   610 667-6700

(G-17840)
KINGSTON HEALTHCARE COMPANY (PA)
Also Called: Kingston Residence
1 Seagate Ste 1960 (43604-1592)
PHONE..............................419 247-2880
M George Rumman, *President*
Beth Connors, *Regional Mgr*
Kent Libbe, *Vice Pres*
Joyce Hartford, *QC Dir*
Larry A Nirschl, *Treasurer*
EMP: 50
SQ FT: 3,000
SALES (est): 95.5MM **Privately Held**
WEB: www.kingstonhealthcare.com
SIC: 8059 8741 Nursing home, except skilled & intermediate care facility; personal care home, with health care; nursing & personal care facility management

(G-17841)
KNIGHT CROCKETT MILLER INS
Also Called: K C M Consulting
22 N Erie St Ste A (43604-2723)
PHONE..............................419 254-2400
Boyd Bonner, *CEO*
Kenneth Knight, *Ch of Bd*
Diane Hipp, *COO*
Diane Roe, *Vice Pres*
Tracy Barber, *Personnel*
EMP: 25
SQ FT: 2,000
SALES (est): 7.3MM **Privately Held**
WEB: www.knightinsurance.com
SIC: 6411 Insurance agents

(G-17842)
KNS FINANCIAL INC
2034 Austin Bluffs Ct (43615-3098)
PHONE..............................800 215-1136
Marquis Kimble, *CEO*
EMP: 25
SALES (est): 371.6K **Privately Held**
SIC: 7389 Investment advice

(G-17843)
KONICA MINOLTA BUSINESS SOLUTI
3131 Executive Pkwy # 101 (43606-1367)
PHONE..............................419 536-7720
Pat Brighton, *Branch Mgr*
EMP: 32
SALES (corp-wide): 9.6B **Privately Held**
WEB: www.konicabt.com
SIC: 5044 Photocopy machines
HQ: Konica Minolta Business Solutions U.S.A., Inc.
   100 Williams Dr
   Ramsey NJ 07446
   201 825-4000

(G-17844)
KWIK PARKING
709 Madison Ave Ste 205 (43604-6624)
PHONE..................................419 246-0454
George Jones, *President*
Jim Kiniep, *Vice Pres*
EMP: 50
SQ FT: 1,110
SALES (est): 1.5MM **Privately Held**
WEB: www.kwikparking.com
SIC: 7521 6531 Parking garage; real estate agents & managers

(G-17845)
L A KING TRUCKING INC
434 Matzinger Rd (43612-2628)
PHONE..................................419 727-9398
Russell King, *CEO*
EMP: 50
SALES (est): 3.2MM **Privately Held**
SIC: 4213 Trucking, except local

(G-17846)
**L VAN & ASSOCIATES
CORPORATION**
4151 Emmajean Rd (43607-1073)
PHONE..................................419 208-9145
Tori Costen, *Principal*
EMP: 25
SALES (est): 371.6K **Privately Held**
SIC: 7389

(G-17847)
LAIBE ELECTRIC CO
Also Called: Laibe Electric/Technology
404 N Byrne Rd (43607-2609)
PHONE..................................419 724-8200
Jim Deaton, *President*
Joe Perkins, *General Mgr*
Lauren Dzierwa, *Corp Secy*
Joseph P Deaton, *Vice Pres*
Mike Deaton, *Project Mgr*
EMP: 85 **EST:** 1930
SQ FT: 7,200
SALES (est): 19.8MM **Privately Held**
WEB: www.laibe.com
SIC: 1731 General electrical contractor

(G-17848)
LAKEFRONT LINES INC
Also Called: Lakefront Trailways
3152 Hill Ave (43607-2933)
PHONE..................................419 537-0677
Mike Schmul, *Manager*
Kate Henke, *Manager*
EMP: 50
SQ FT: 8,944
SALES (corp-wide): 4.5B **Privately Held**
WEB: www.lakefrontlines.com
SIC: 4119 4142 Limousine rental, with driver; bus charter service, except local
HQ: Lakefront Lines, Inc.
　　13315 Brookpark Rd
　　Brookpark OH 44142
　　216 267-8810

(G-17849)
LATHROP COMPANY INC (DH)
28 N Saint Clair St (43604-1001)
PHONE..................................419 893-7000
Steven M Johnson, *President*
Joseph R Kovaleski, *Vice Pres*
Douglas F Martin, *Vice Pres*
Consie Taylor, *Purch Agent*
Mark T Kusner, *Treasurer*
EMP: 50
SQ FT: 20,000
SALES (est): 26.9MM
SALES (corp-wide): 579.6MM **Privately Held**
SIC: 1542 8741 1541 Commercial & office building, new construction; construction management; industrial buildings & warehouses
HQ: Turner Construction Company Inc
　　375 Hudson St Fl 6
　　New York NY 10014
　　212 229-6000

(G-17850)
**LEADER NURING &
REHABILITATION (DH)**
Also Called: Hcr Manor Care
333 N Summit St (43604-1531)
P.O. Box 10086 (43699-0086)
PHONE..................................419 252-5718
Paul A Ormond, *President*
Steven Guillard, *COO*
Steve Cavanaugh, *CFO*
Jeremy Barr, *Software Dev*
Charles Brown, *Telecom Exec*
EMP: 150
SALES (est): 19.1MM
SALES (corp-wide): 2.4B **Publicly Held**
SIC: 8051 Skilled nursing care facilities
HQ: Hcr Manorcare Medical Services Of Florida, Llc
　　333 N Summit St Ste 100
　　Toledo OH 43604
　　419 252-5500

(G-17851)
LEGAL AID WESTERN OHIO INC
Also Called: Lawo
525 Jefferson Ave 400 (43604-1094)
PHONE..................................419 724-0030
Kevin Mulder, *Director*
Janet Boswell, *Director*
Meg Bowers, *Legal Staff*
Patrick Maloney, *Legal Staff*
EMP: 60
SALES (est): 5.6MM **Privately Held**
SIC: 8111 Legal aid service

(G-17852)
LEXAMED
705 Front St (43605-2107)
PHONE..................................419 693-5307
James Kulla, *Senior VP*
Kelly Farhbach, *Project Mgr*
Jeff Leverenz, *Manager*
James Latham, *Consultant*
Robin Wilson, *Supervisor*
EMP: 40
SALES (est): 6.8MM **Privately Held**
SIC: 8734 Testing laboratories

(G-17853)
LIBBEY INC
Also Called: Cordelia Martin Hlth Ctr
1250 Western Ave (43609-2208)
PHONE..................................419 671-6000
Joy Gregory, *Branch Mgr*
EMP: 1468 **Publicly Held**
SIC: 8011 Offices & clinics of medical doctors
PA: Libbey Inc.
　　300 Madison Ave
　　Toledo OH 43604

(G-17854)
LIFESTAR AMBULANCE INC
1402 Lagrange St (43608-2928)
PHONE..................................419 245-6210
William Sutton, *President*
EMP: 200
SALES (est): 5MM **Privately Held**
SIC: 4119 Ambulance service

(G-17855)
LIGHTING MAINT HARMON SIGN
7844 W Central Ave (43617-1530)
PHONE..................................419 841-6658
Dan Kasper, *President*
EMP: 60
SALES (est): 1.9MM **Privately Held**
SIC: 1799 Sign installation & maintenance

(G-17856)
LOGISTICS INC
6010 Skyview Dr (43612-4715)
PHONE..................................419 478-1514
Aaron Alberts, *Branch Mgr*
EMP: 50
SALES (corp-wide): 13.7MM **Privately Held**
WEB: www.metrorush.com
SIC: 7389 Courier or messenger service
PA: Logistics Inc.
　　21450 Trolley Indus Dr
　　Taylor MI 48180
　　734 641-1600

(G-17857)
LOGOS LOGISTICS INC ✪
5657 Enterprise Blvd (43612-3816)
PHONE..................................734 304-1777
Jonguk Kim, *President*
EMP: 26 **EST:** 2018
SALES (est): 618.7K **Privately Held**
SIC: 4213 Trucking, except local

(G-17858)
**LOTT INDUSTRIES
INCORPORATED**
5500 Telegraph Rd (43612-3631)
PHONE..................................419 476-2516
John Roberts, *Manager*
EMP: 400
SALES (est): 1.1MM
SALES (corp-wide): 4.8MM **Privately Held**
WEB: www.lottindustries.com
SIC: 8331 Sheltered Workshop
PA: Lott Industries Incorporated
　　3350 Hill Ave
　　Toledo OH 43607
　　419 534-4980

(G-17859)
**LOTT INDUSTRIES
INCORPORATED (PA)**
3350 Hill Ave (43607-2937)
PHONE..................................419 534-4980
Jeff Holland, *CEO*
EMP: 1001
SALES (est): 4.8MM **Privately Held**
WEB: www.lottindustries.com
SIC: 8331 8741 Job Training/Related Services Management Services

(G-17860)
**LOTT INDUSTRIES
INCORPORATED**
3350 Hill Ave (43607-2937)
PHONE..................................419 534-4980
Laura Odiari, *Manager*
EMP: 480
SALES (corp-wide): 4.8MM **Privately Held**
WEB: www.lottindustries.com
SIC: 8331 Job Training/Related Services
PA: Lott Industries Incorporated
　　3350 Hill Ave
　　Toledo OH 43607
　　419 534-4980

(G-17861)
**LOUIEVILLE TITLE AGNCY FOR
NRT**
626 Madison Ave Ste 100 (43604-1106)
PHONE..................................419 248-4611
John Martin, *President*
Vicky Feze, *Vice Pres*
William Harlet, *Vice Pres*
James Lenzey, *Vice Pres*
William Wise, *Vice Pres*
EMP: 65
SALES (est): 4.3MM **Privately Held**
SIC: 6411 Insurance agents

(G-17862)
**LOUISVLLE TITLE AGCY FOR
NW OH (PA)**
626 Madison Ave Ste 100 (43604-1106)
PHONE..................................419 248-4611
John W Martin, *President*
Deb Tussing, *Prdtn Mgr*
Kelsey Cardell, *Sales Staff*
Dennis O'Shea, *Sales Staff*
Esther Johnson, *Marketing Staff*
EMP: 91 **EST:** 1948
SQ FT: 20,000
SALES (est): 25.6MM **Privately Held**
WEB: www.louisvilletitle.com
SIC: 6361 Title insurance

(G-17863)
**LOVING FAMILY HOME CARE
INC**
2600 N Reynolds Rd 101a (43615-2067)
PHONE..................................888 469-2178
Solarix Fireheart, *CEO*
EMP: 60
SQ FT: 1,400
SALES (est): 1.3MM **Privately Held**
SIC: 8082 Visiting nurse service

(G-17864)
LOWES HOME CENTERS LLC
5501 Airport Hwy (43615-7303)
PHONE..................................419 389-9464
Salam Hawry, *Branch Mgr*
EMP: 150
SALES (corp-wide): 68.6B **Publicly Held**
SIC: 5211 5031 5722 5064 Home centers; building materials, exterior; building materials, interior; household appliance stores; electrical appliances, television & radio
HQ: Lowe's Home Centers, Llc
　　1605 Curtis Bridge Rd
　　Wilkesboro NC 28697
　　336 658-4000

(G-17865)
LOWES HOME CENTERS LLC
7000 W Central Ave (43617-1115)
PHONE..................................419 843-9758
Jim Weirick, *Manager*
EMP: 150
SALES (corp-wide): 68.6B **Publicly Held**
SIC: 5211 5031 5722 5064 Home centers; building materials, exterior; building materials, interior; household appliance stores; electrical appliances, television & radio
HQ: Lowe's Home Centers, Llc
　　1605 Curtis Bridge Rd
　　Wilkesboro NC 28697
　　336 658-4000

(G-17866)
LOWES HOME CENTERS LLC
1136 W Alexis Rd (43612-4204)
PHONE..................................419 470-2491
John Swisher, *Department Mgr*
Randy Kitts, *Manager*
EMP: 150
SALES (corp-wide): 68.6B **Publicly Held**
SIC: 5211 5031 5722 5064 Home centers; building materials, exterior; building materials, interior; household appliance stores; electrical appliances, television & radio
HQ: Lowe's Home Centers, Llc
　　1605 Curtis Bridge Rd
　　Wilkesboro NC 28697
　　336 658-4000

(G-17867)
LUCAS COUNTY ASPHALT INC
Also Called: Buckeye Asphalt Paving Co
7540 Hollow Creek Dr (43617-1652)
P.O. Box 353094 (43635-3094)
PHONE..................................419 476-0705
EMP: 25
SQ FT: 4,800
SALES (est): 1.7MM **Privately Held**
SIC: 1771 2951 Asphalt Paving Contractor & Mfg Asphalt Paving Mixtures

(G-17868)
**LUCAS COUNTY BOARD OF
DEVELOPM**
1154 Larc Ln (43614-2768)
PHONE..................................419 380-4000
Deb Yenrick, *Superintendent*
EMP: 100 **EST:** 2010
SALES (est): 3MM **Privately Held**
SIC: 8322 Individual & family services

(G-17869)
**LUCAS METROPOLITAN HSING
AUTH**
Also Called: Parkwood Apartments
435 Nebraska Ave (43604-8539)
PHONE..................................419 259-9457
Lawrence Gaster, *Branch Mgr*
EMP: 100 **Privately Held**
SIC: 7241 Barber shops
PA: Lucas Metropolitan Housing Authority
　　435 Nebraska Ave
　　Toledo OH 43604
　　419 259-9400

(G-17870)
LUTHERAN HOME
131 N Wheeling St Ofc (43605-1545)
PHONE..................................419 724-1414
Thomas Keith, *President*
David Roberts, *Director*
Tina Sherer, *Director*

Julie Kurtz, *Admin Asst*
Fancy Moreland, *Assistant*
EMP: 70 **EST:** 1997
SQ FT: 2,979
SALES: 8.6MM **Privately Held**
SIC: 8361 Halfway group home, persons with social or personal problems

(G-17871)
LUTHERAN HOMES SOCIETY INC
2411 Seaman St (43605-1519)
PHONE..................................419 724-1525
James Dumke, *Branch Mgr*
Amanda Schroeder, *Exec Dir*
EMP: 28
SALES (est): 1.4MM
SALES (corp-wide): 51.9MM **Privately Held**
SIC: 8361 Residential care
PA: Lutheran Homes Society, Inc.
2021 N Mccord Rd
Toledo OH 43615
419 861-4990

(G-17872)
LUTHERAN HOUSING SERVICES INC
2021 N Mccord Rd Ste B (43615-3030)
PHONE..................................419 861-4990
David Roberts, *Director*
EMP: 30
SALES (est): 377.4K **Privately Held**
SIC: 8741 Management services

(G-17873)
LUTHERAN MEMORIAL HOME INC
2021 N Mccord Rd (43615-3030)
PHONE..................................419 502-5700
Jason Bennett, *Exec Dir*
Jennifer Flounders, *Executive*
EMP: 80 **EST:** 1974
SQ FT: 44,000
SALES (est): 3.9MM **Privately Held**
SIC: 8052 8059 Personal care facility; rest home, with health care

(G-17874)
LYDEN COMPANY
Also Called: True North Trucking
310 S Reynolds Rd Ste A (43615-5972)
PHONE..................................419 868-6800
Geoffrey W Lyden III, *CEO*
Mark Lyden, *President*
Kathy Gorski, *Manager*
EMP: 32
SQ FT: 14,000
SALES (est): 8.4MM **Privately Held**
SIC: 4213 Contract haulers

(G-17875)
LYMAN W LIGGINS URBAN AFFAIRS
Also Called: Nutrition Program
2155 Arlington Ave (43609-1903)
PHONE..................................419 385-2532
Lisa Hughley, *Director*
EMP: 100
SALES (est): 1.3MM **Privately Held**
SIC: 8322 Senior citizens' center or association

(G-17876)
M&M HEATING & COOLING INC
Also Called: M & M Heating & Cooling
1515 Washington St (43604-5705)
PHONE..................................419 243-3005
Mark Janowiecki, *President*
Mike Janowiecki, *Corp Secy*
EMP: 61
SQ FT: 18,000
SALES (est): 10.2MM **Privately Held**
WEB: www.m-mhvac.com
SIC: 1711 Warm air heating & air conditioning contractor

(G-17877)
MACMILLAN SOBANSKI & TODD LLC (PA)
1 Maritime Plz Fl 5 (43604-1879)
PHONE..................................419 255-5900
Thomas Brainard, *Counsel*
Rhonda Russell, *Manager*
Chad Imbrogno, *IT/INT Sup*

Richard Mac Millan,
Chad Robinson, *Admin Asst*
EMP: 38
SQ FT: 8,000
SALES (est): 5.8MM **Privately Held**
WEB: www.mstfirm.com
SIC: 8111 Patent, trademark & copyright law

(G-17878)
MADISON AVENUE MKTG GROUP INC
1600 Madison Ave (43604-5464)
PHONE..................................419 473-9000
Gerald R Brown Jr, *President*
EMP: 25
SQ FT: 7,000
SALES (est): 2.8MM **Privately Held**
WEB: www.businessvoice.com
SIC: 7313 8999 7311 7812 Electronic media advertising representatives; advertising copy writing; advertising agencies; advertising consultant; video production; music video production; marketing consulting services

(G-17879)
MAIL IT CORP
380 S Erie St (43604-4634)
P.O. Box 768 (43697-0768)
PHONE..................................419 249-4848
Karen Smith, *President*
Marion Howard, *Vice Pres*
Ken Yohn, *Prdtn Mgr*
H Russell Troyan, *Treasurer*
Michelle Beard, *Manager*
EMP: 50
SALES (est): 6.8MM **Privately Held**
WEB: www.mailitcorp.com
SIC: 7331 Mailing service

(G-17880)
MANOR CARE INC (HQ)
333 N Summit St Ste 103 (43604-2617)
P.O. Box 10086 (43699-0086)
PHONE..................................419 252-5500
Paul A Ormond, *President*
Stephen L Guillard, *COO*
Lynn M Hood, *Vice Pres*
Spencer C Moler, *Vice Pres*
David B Parker, *Vice Pres*
EMP: 66
SALES (est): 2.2B
SALES (corp-wide): 2.4B **Publicly Held**
WEB: www.hcr-manorcare.com
SIC: 8051 8082 8062 Extended care facility; home health care services; general medical & surgical hospitals
PA: The Carlyle Group L P
1001 Pennsylvania Ave Nw 220s
Washington DC 20004
202 729-5626

(G-17881)
MANOR CARE NURSING CENTER (DH)
333 N Summit St Ste 100 (43604-2617)
PHONE..................................419 252-5500
Mark H Boss, *Principal*
EMP: 26
SALES (est): 3.2MM
SALES (corp-wide): 2.4B **Publicly Held**
SIC: 8051 Skilled nursing care facilities

(G-17882)
MANOR CARE OF BOYNTON BEACH (DH)
333 N Summit St Ste 103 (43604-2617)
PHONE..................................419 252-5500
Paul A Ormond, *Chairman*
Steve Cavanaugh, *CFO*
EMP: 200
SALES (est): 10.2MM
SALES (corp-wide): 2.4B **Publicly Held**
WEB: www.manorcare.com
SIC: 8051 Skilled nursing care facilities
HQ: Hcr Manorcare Medical Services Of Florida, Llc
333 N Summit St Ste 100
Toledo OH 43604
419 252-5500

(G-17883)
MANOR CARE OF KANSAS INC (DH)
333 N Summit St Ste 100 (43604-2617)
PHONE..................................419 252-5500
Deb Houke, *Administration*
EMP: 100
SQ FT: 43,000
SALES (est): 11.5MM
SALES (corp-wide): 2.4B **Publicly Held**
SIC: 8051 8093 Skilled nursing care facilities; rehabilitation center, outpatient treatment
HQ: Hcr Manorcare Medical Services Of Florida, Llc
333 N Summit St Ste 100
Toledo OH 43604
419 252-5500

(G-17884)
MANOR CARE OF NORTH OLMSTED
333 N Summit St Ste 100 (43604-2617)
P.O. Box 10086 (43699-0086)
PHONE..................................419 252-5500
Paul Ormond, *President*
Stewart Bainum Jr, *President*
Donald C Tomasso, *President*
James A Maccutcheon, *Vice Pres*
EMP: 385
SQ FT: 47,000
SALES (est): 3.4MM
SALES (corp-wide): 2.4B **Publicly Held**
WEB: www.manorcare.com
SIC: 8051 Skilled nursing care facilities
HQ: Hcr Manorcare Medical Services Of Florida, Llc
333 N Summit St Ste 100
Toledo OH 43604
419 252-5500

(G-17885)
MANOR CARE OF PLANTATION INC
333 N Summit St Ste 100 (43604-2617)
PHONE..................................419 252-5500
Stewart Bainum Jr, *Ch of Bd*
Stewart Bainum Sr, *Vice Ch Bd*
Nadja Papillon, *President*
Gilda Anderson, *President*
EMP: 120
SQ FT: 48,670
SALES (est): 1.1MM
SALES (corp-wide): 2.4B **Publicly Held**
WEB: www.manorcare.com
SIC: 8051 Skilled nursing care facilities
HQ: Hcr Manorcare Medical Services Of Florida, Llc
333 N Summit St Ste 100
Toledo OH 43604
419 252-5500

(G-17886)
MANOR CARE OF YORK NORTH INC
Also Called: Manor Care-North
333 N Summit St Ste 100 (43604-2617)
PHONE..................................419 252-5500
Criag Thurston, *President*
Marion Bittner, *Principal*
James H Rempe, *Vice Pres*
Kim Rocheleau, *Administration*
EMP: 160
SQ FT: 47,000
SALES (est): 1.9MM
SALES (corp-wide): 2.4B **Publicly Held**
WEB: www.manorcare.com
SIC: 8051 Skilled nursing care facilities
HQ: Hcr Manorcare Medical Services Of Florida, Llc
333 N Summit St Ste 100
Toledo OH 43604
419 252-5500

(G-17887)
MANOR CARE WILMINGTON INC (DH)
333 N Summit St Ste 100 (43604-2617)
PHONE..................................419 252-5500
Stewart Bainum Jr, *Ch of Bd*
EMP: 42
SALES (est): 2.7MM
SALES (corp-wide): 2.4B **Publicly Held**
SIC: 8051 Skilled nursing care facilities

HQ: Hcr Manorcare Medical Services Of Florida, Llc
333 N Summit St Ste 100
Toledo OH 43604
419 252-5500

(G-17888)
MANOR CARE YORK (SOUTH) INC
333 N Summit St Ste 100 (43604-2617)
PHONE..................................419 252-5500
Paul A Ormond, *CEO*
EMP: 200
SALES (est): 2.2MM
SALES (corp-wide): 2.4B **Publicly Held**
WEB: www.manorcare.com
SIC: 8051 Skilled nursing care facilities
HQ: Hcr Manorcare Medical Services Of Florida, Llc
333 N Summit St Ste 100
Toledo OH 43604
419 252-5500

(G-17889)
MANOR CR-MPRIAL RCHMOND VA LLC (DH)
333 N Summit St (43604-1531)
PHONE..................................419 252-5000
Hcr IV Healthcare, *Mng Member*
EMP: 53
SALES (est): 11.2MM
SALES (corp-wide): 2.1B **Privately Held**
SIC: 8051 Skilled nursing care facilities
HQ: Hcr Manorcare, Inc.
333 N Summit St
Toledo OH 43604
419 252-5743

(G-17890)
MANORCARE HEALTH SERVICES LLC (DH)
333 N Summit St Ste 100 (43604-2617)
PHONE..................................419 252-5500
Barry A Lazarus, *Principal*
EMP: 42
SALES (est): 4.4MM
SALES (corp-wide): 2.4B **Publicly Held**
SIC: 8051 Skilled nursing care facilities

(G-17891)
MANORCARE HEALTH SVCS VA INC (DH)
333 N Summit St Ste 100 (43604-2617)
P.O. Box 10086 (43699-0086)
PHONE..................................419 252-5500
Paul Ormond, *CEO*
Steve Cavanaugh, *CFO*
EMP: 61
SALES (est): 5MM
SALES (corp-wide): 2.4B **Publicly Held**
SIC: 8051 Skilled nursing care facilities
HQ: Hcr Manorcare Medical Services Of Florida, Llc
333 N Summit St Ste 100
Toledo OH 43604
419 252-5500

(G-17892)
MANORCARE OF KINGSTON COURT
333 N Summit St Ste 100 (43604-2617)
PHONE..................................419 252-5500
Deb Slemmons, *Administration*
Deb Slemons, *Administration*
EMP: 135
SQ FT: 35,570
SALES (est): 1.3MM
SALES (corp-wide): 2.4B **Publicly Held**
WEB: www.manorcare.com
SIC: 8051 Skilled nursing care facilities
HQ: Hcr Manorcare Medical Services Of Florida, Llc
333 N Summit St Ste 100
Toledo OH 43604
419 252-5500

(G-17893)
MANORCARE OF WILLOUGHBY INC
333 N Summit St Ste 100 (43604-2617)
P.O. Box 10086 (43699-0086)
PHONE..................................419 252-5500
Paul Ormond, *President*
Keith Weikel, *COO*
Jeff Meyers, *CFO*

EMP: 183
SALES (est): 2.4MM
SALES (corp-wide): 2.4B **Publicly Held**
WEB: www.manorcare.com
SIC: 8051 8052 Skilled nursing care facilities; intermediate care facilities
HQ: Hcr Manorcare Medical Services Of Florida, Llc
333 N Summit St Ste 100
Toledo OH 43604
419 252-5500

(G-17894)
MARCOS INC
Also Called: Marco's Pizza
5252 Monroe St (43623-3140)
PHONE...........................419 885-4844
Pasquale Giammarco, *President*
Anne Giammarco, *Vice Pres*
Rick Stanbridge, *Vice Pres*
Brieanne Sanders, *Opers Staff*
Wendy Stephens, *Sales Staff*
EMP: 250
SQ FT: 1,000
SALES (est): 5.9MM **Privately Held**
SIC: 5812 6794 Pizzeria, chain; franchises, selling or licensing

(G-17895)
MARRIK DISH COMPANY LLC
Also Called: Suite Solutions Technologies
4102 Monroe St (43606-2060)
P.O. Box 2891 (43606-0891)
PHONE...........................419 475-6538
Mark Ralston,
EMP: 25
SALES (est): 3MM **Privately Held**
SIC: 4841 Cable television services

(G-17896)
MARSHALL & MELHORN LLC
4 Seagate Ste 800 (43604-1599)
PHONE...........................419 249-7100
Kassi Billick, *President*
Justice G Johnson Jr, *Partner*
Marshall A Bennett Jr, *Partner*
Jennifer J Dawson, *Partner*
Lori W Decker, *Partner*
EMP: 90
SQ FT: 21,270
SALES (est): 12.7MM **Privately Held**
WEB: www.bennettlex.com
SIC: 8111 General practice law office; patent solicitor

(G-17897)
MARTIN + WD APPRISAL GROUP LTD
43 S Saint Clair St (43604-8735)
PHONE...........................419 241-4998
Kenneth Wood, *President*
EMP: 30
SQ FT: 3,000
SALES (est): 3.1MM **Privately Held**
WEB: www.martinwoodappraisal.com
SIC: 6531 Appraiser, real estate

(G-17898)
MARTIN TRNSP SYSTEMS INC
320 Matzinger Rd (43612-2627)
PHONE...........................419 726-1348
June Brown, *Branch Mgr*
EMP: 85
SALES (est): 3.1MM
SALES (corp-wide): 91.1MM **Privately Held**
SIC: 4212 4213 Local trucking, without storage; trucking, except local
PA: Martin Transportation Systems Inc.
7300 Clyde Park Ave Sw
Byron Center MI 49315
616 455-8850

(G-17899)
MCNERNEY & SON INC
1 Maritime Plz Fl 7 (43604-1853)
PHONE...........................419 666-0200
John H Mc Nerney, *President*
Allan L Kessler, *Principal*
F A Messerschmidt, *Principal*
N James McNerney, *Treasurer*
Terri Cochran, *Office Mgr*
EMP: 25 EST: 1900
SQ FT: 4,000

SALES (est): 6.5MM **Privately Held**
WEB: www.mcnerneyson.com
SIC: 1542 5021 1541 Commercial & office building, new construction; furniture; industrial buildings, new construction; warehouse construction

(G-17900)
MEDCORP INC (PA)
745 Medcorp Dr (43608-1376)
PHONE...........................419 727-7000
Fred Isch, *President*
EMP: 92
SQ FT: 5,000
SALES (est): 10.9MM **Privately Held**
SIC: 8082 4119 Home Health Care Services Local Passenger Transportation

(G-17901)
MEDICAL COLLEGE OF OHIO
Also Called: University Toledo Physicians
3355 Glendale Ave Fl 3 (43614-2426)
PHONE...........................419 383-7100
Gerard L Otten,
EMP: 38
SALES (est): 7.1MM **Privately Held**
SIC: 8011 Physical medicine, physician/surgeon

(G-17902)
MEDICAL MUTUAL OF OHIO
3737 W Sylvania Ave (43623-4482)
P.O. Box 943 (43697-0943)
PHONE...........................419 473-7100
Joel Mercer, *Principal*
Dave Dearth, *Director*
Dwain Bradshaw,
EMP: 500
SALES (corp-wide): 1.2B **Privately Held**
SIC: 6324 Hospital & medical service plans
PA: Medical Mutual Of Ohio
2060 E 9th St Frnt Ste
Cleveland OH 44115
216 687-7000

(G-17903)
MENARD INC
1415 E Alexis Rd (43612-3978)
PHONE...........................419 726-4029
John Menard, *Branch Mgr*
EMP: 25
SALES (corp-wide): 12.5B **Privately Held**
SIC: 5072 Hardware
PA: Menard, Inc.
5101 Menard Dr
Eau Claire WI 54703
715 876-5911

(G-17904)
MENTAL HEALTH AND ADDI SERV
Also Called: Northcoast Behavior Healthcare
930 S Detroit Ave (43614-2701)
PHONE...........................419 381-1881
Joe Reichert, *President*
EMP: 250 **Privately Held**
SIC: 8063 9431 Psychiatric hospitals; mental health agency administration, government;
HQ: Ohio Department Of Mental Health And Addiction Services
30 E Broad St Fl 8
Columbus OH 43215

(G-17905)
MERCY HEALTH
2213 Cherry St (43608-2603)
PHONE...........................419 251-2659
Susan Woolner, *Partner*
Deb Stiemann, *Vice Pres*
EMP: 87
SALES (corp-wide): 4.7B **Privately Held**
SIC: 8011 Offices & clinics of medical doctors
PA: Mercy Health
1701 Mercy Health Pl
Cincinnati OH 45237
513 639-2800

(G-17906)
MERCY HEALTH
3930 Sunforest Ct Ste 100 (43623-4441)
PHONE...........................419 407-3990
EMP: 43
SALES (corp-wide): 4.7B **Privately Held**
SIC: 7299 Personal appearance services

PA: Mercy Health
1701 Mercy Health Pl
Cincinnati OH 45237
513 639-2800

(G-17907)
MERCY HEALTH
3425 Executive Pkwy 200nw (43606-1326)
PHONE...........................419 475-4666
EMP: 43
SALES (corp-wide): 4.7B **Privately Held**
SIC: 8011 Offices & clinics of medical doctors
PA: Mercy Health
1701 Mercy Health Pl
Cincinnati OH 45237
513 639-2800

(G-17908)
MERCY HEALTH SYS - NTHRN REG (HQ)
2200 Jefferson Ave (43604-7101)
PHONE...........................419 251-1359
Steven Mickus, *President*
Christine Browning, *President*
Kathleen A Osborne, *President*
Samantha Platzke, *CFO*
EMP: 500
SQ FT: 4,000
SALES (est): 226.9MM
SALES (corp-wide): 4.7B **Privately Held**
SIC: 8062 General medical & surgical hospitals
PA: Mercy Health
1701 Mercy Health Pl
Cincinnati OH 45237
513 639-2800

(G-17909)
MERCY HLTH ST VINCENT MED LLC (PA)
Also Called: St. Vincent Hospit
2213 Cherry St (43608-2603)
PHONE...........................419 251-3232
Beverly J McBride, *Ch of Bd*
Tim Koder, *President*
Steven Mickus, *President*
Robert A Sullivan, *Treasurer*
Joan Rutherford, *Finance Dir*
EMP: 3600 EST: 1875
SQ FT: 634,165
SALES: 478.7MM **Privately Held**
SIC: 8062 General medical & surgical hospitals

(G-17910)
MERCY HLTH ST VINCENT MED LLC
Also Called: Mercy Clinic
2200 Jefferson Ave (43604-7101)
PHONE...........................419 251-0580
Steven L Mickus, *Principal*
EMP: 812
SALES (corp-wide): 478.7MM **Privately Held**
SIC: 8011 Clinic, operated by physicians
PA: Mercy Health St Vincent Med Llc
2213 Cherry St
Toledo OH 43608
419 251-3232

(G-17911)
MERIT HOUSE LLC
4645 Lewis Ave (43612-2336)
PHONE...........................419 478-5131
John Stone, *President*
Paula Pineda, *Director*
Kim Vandeneynde, *Nursing Dir*
EMP: 150
SALES (est): 3MM **Privately Held**
SIC: 8051 Skilled nursing care facilities

(G-17912)
MICHAELS GOURMET CATERING
Also Called: Michael's Cafe & Bakery
101 Main St Ste 7 (43605-2076)
PHONE...........................419 698-2988
Michael F Armstrong, *Partner*
Michael Armstrong, *President*
Laura Armstrong, *Vice Pres*
Cathy Ireland, *Admin Sec*
EMP: 30

SALES (est): 1.2MM **Privately Held**
WEB: www.michaelsoftoledo.com
SIC: 5812 5149 Caterers; cafe; bakery products

(G-17913)
MIDAS AUTO SYSTEMS EXPERTS (PA)
Also Called: Midas Muffler
1101 Monroe St (43604-5811)
PHONE...........................419 243-7281
Randolph Katz, *Principal*
Ted Behnken, *Vice Pres*
Randy Lindhurst, *VP Opers*
Ian Katz, *General Counsel*
EMP: 47
SALES (est): 36.1MM **Privately Held**
SIC: 7533 Muffler shop, sale or repair & installation

(G-17914)
MIDWEST INDUSTRIAL SUPPLY INC
1929 E Manhattan Blvd (43608-1534)
PHONE...........................800 321-0699
EMP: 26
SALES (corp-wide): 67MM **Privately Held**
SIC: 1799 5169 Coating, caulking & weather, water & fireproofing; specialty cleaning & sanitation preparations
PA: Midwest Industrial Supply, Inc.,
1101 3rd St Se
Canton OH 44707
330 456-3121

(G-17915)
MIDWEST MOSAIC INC
Also Called: Mw Mosaic
2268 Robinwood Ave (43620-1019)
PHONE...........................419 377-3894
Malcolm Campbell, *Owner*
EMP: 50
SALES: 2.5MM **Privately Held**
SIC: 1743 Mosaic work; tile installation, ceramic

(G-17916)
MIDWEST OPTOELECTRONICS LLC
2801 W Bancroft St 230 (43606-3328)
PHONE...........................419 724-0565
Stanley Rubini,
EMP: 200
SALES (est): 6.7MM **Privately Held**
SIC: 8731 Environmental research

(G-17917)
MIDWEST TRMNLS TLEDO INTL INC
Also Called: Facility 1
3518 Saint Lawrence Dr (43605-1079)
PHONE...........................419 897-6868
Jason Tipton, *COO*
Brad Hendricks, *Manager*
EMP: 35
SALES (corp-wide): 19MM **Privately Held**
SIC: 4225 4491 General warehousing; stevedoring
HQ: Midwest Terminals Of Toledo, International, Inc.
383 W Dussel Dr
Maumee OH 43537
419 897-6868

(G-17918)
MIDWEST TRMNLS TLEDO INTL INC
3518 Saint Lawrence Dr (43605-1079)
PHONE...........................419 698-8171
Lori Vonseggern, *Controller*
Doug Struvle, *Branch Mgr*
EMP: 50
SALES (corp-wide): 19MM **Privately Held**
SIC: 4789 4225 Cargo loading & unloading services; general warehousing & storage
HQ: Midwest Terminals Of Toledo, International, Inc.
383 W Dussel Dr
Maumee OH 43537
419 897-6868

(G-17919)
MIZAR MOTORS INC (HQ)
Also Called: Great Lakes Western Star
6003 Benore Rd (43612-3905)
PHONE....................................419 729-2400
Rudy Vogel, *President*
Linda K Shinkle, *Principal*
John C Bates, *Chairman*
Simon Les, *Chairman*
Mark Ridenour, *Corp Secy*
EMP: 60
SQ FT: 60,000
SALES (est): 8.7MM
SALES (corp-wide): 296.3MM **Privately
Held**
WEB: www.freightlineroftoledo.com
SIC: 4213 7538 5511 Heavy hauling;
　truck engine repair, except industrial;
　trucks, tractors & trailers: new & used
PA: Centaur, Inc.
　　2401 Front St
　　Toledo OH 43605
　　419 469-8000

(G-17920)
MJ-6 LLC
2621 Liverpool Ct (43617-2327)
PHONE....................................419 517-7725
Juana Barrow, *General Mgr*
Matt Barrow, *General Mgr*
Matthew Barrow,
EMP: 25
SALES (est): 6.1MM **Privately Held**
SIC: 7361 Labor contractors (employment
　agency)

(G-17921)
MOBILE CARDIAC IMAGING LLC
2409 Cherry St Ste 100 (43608-2670)
PHONE....................................419 251-3711
Amir Kabour,
Thomas Welch,
EMP: 25
SALES (est): 601.6K **Privately Held**
SIC: 8011 Cardiologist & cardio-vascular
　specialist

(G-17922)
**MODERN BUILDERS SUPPLY
INC (PA)**
Also Called: Polaris Technologies
3500 Phillips Ave (43608-1070)
P.O. Box 80025 (43608-0025)
PHONE....................................419 241-3961
Kevin Leggett, *CEO*
Larry Leggett, *Ch of Bd*
Eric Leggett, *Vice Pres*
Jack Marstellar, *Vice Pres*
Tony Puntel, *Vice Pres*
EMP: 200
SQ FT: 40,000
SALES (est): 347.7MM **Privately Held**
WEB: www.polaristechnologies.com
SIC: 3089 5032 3446 3442 Windows,
　plastic; doors, folding: plastic or plastic
　coated fabric; brick, stone & related mate-
　rial; architectural metalwork; metal doors,
　sash & trim

(G-17923)
**MOORE TRANSPORT OF TULSA
LLC**
4015 Stickney Ave (43612-2687)
PHONE....................................419 726-4499
George Wofford, *Branch Mgr*
EMP: 88
SALES (corp-wide): 34.7MM **Privately
Held**
SIC: 4213 Trucking, except local
PA: Moore Transport Of Tulsa, Llc
　　700 E Park Blvd Ste 104
　　Plano TX 75074
　　972 907-3688

(G-17924)
MORGAN SERVICES INC
34 10th St (43604-6912)
PHONE....................................419 243-2214
Pat Wheeler, *Branch Mgr*
EMP: 50
SALES (corp-wide): 38.6MM **Privately
Held**
WEB: www.morganservices.com
SIC: 7213 7218 Linen supply; industrial
　launderers

PA: Morgan Services, Inc.
　　323 N Michigan Ave
　　Chicago IL 60601
　　312 346-3181

(G-17925)
MRC GLOBAL (US) INC
3110 Frenchmens Rd (43607-2917)
P.O. Box 352918 (43635-2918)
PHONE....................................419 324-0039
Larry Whitney, *Principal*
Wendy Wilkins, *Manager*
EMP: 25 **Publicly Held**
SIC: 5085 Valves & fittings
HQ: Mrc Global (Us) Inc.
　　1301 Mckinney St Ste 2300
　　Houston TX 77010
　　877 294-7574

(G-17926)
MSSTAFF LLC
5950 Airport Hwy Ste 12 (43615-7362)
PHONE....................................419 868-8536
Kim Grabill, *Manager*
EMP: 200
SALES (corp-wide): 816.4MM **Publicly
Held**
SIC: 7363 8049 Medical help service;
　nurses & other medical assistants
HQ: Msstaff, Llc
　　901 Nw 51st St Ste 110
　　Boca Raton FL 33431

(G-17927)
MY FIRST DAYS DAYCARE LLC
580 N Byrne Rd (43607-2611)
PHONE....................................419 466-3354
Kashaundra Besteda, *Director*
EMP: 25 EST: 2011
SALES (est): 278.2K **Privately Held**
SIC: 8351 Child day care services

(G-17928)
NATIONAL BLANKING LLC
135 N Fearing Blvd (43607-3604)
PHONE....................................419 385-0636
Matt McCaffrey,
EMP: 25
SALES (est): 3MM **Privately Held**
SIC: 1761 Sheet metalwork

(G-17929)
NATIONAL EXCHANGE CLUB
3050 W Central Ave (43606-1700)
P.O. Box 1034, Fremont (43420-8034)
PHONE....................................419 535-3232
Tracey Edwards, *Exec VP*
Kristie Lindau, *Comms Dir*
EMP: 25 EST: 1918
SALES: 1.8MM **Privately Held**
SIC: 7997 Membership sports & recreation
　clubs

(G-17930)
**NATIONAL EXCHANGE CLUB
FOUNDAT**
Also Called: National Service Club
3050 W Central Ave (43606-1757)
PHONE....................................419 535-3232
Chris Rice, *Exec VP*
Russ Finney, *Vice Pres*
Elizabeth Grantham, *Vice Pres*
Tom Karnes, *Vice Pres*
EMP: 25 EST: 1911
SQ FT: 22,500
SALES: 476.6K **Privately Held**
SIC: 8322 Child related social services

(G-17931)
**NATIONAL HERITG ACADEMIES
INC**
Also Called: Bennett Venture Academy
5130 Bennett Rd (43612-3422)
PHONE....................................419 269-2247
Xavier Owens, *Branch Mgr*
EMP: 54 **Privately Held**
SIC: 8741 Management services
PA: National Heritage Academies, Inc.
　　3850 Broadmoor Se # 201
　　Grand Rapids MI 49512

(G-17932)
**NATIONAL HERITG ACADEMIES
INC**
Also Called: Winterfield Venture Academy
305 Wenz Rd (43615-6244)
PHONE....................................419 531-3285
Nate Preston, *Branch Mgr*
EMP: 54 **Privately Held**
SIC: 8741 Management services
PA: National Heritage Academies, Inc.
　　3850 Broadmoor Ave Se # 201
　　Grand Rapids MI 49512

(G-17933)
**NATIONAL RAILROAD PASS
CORP**
Also Called: Amtrak
415 Emerald Ave (43604-8817)
PHONE....................................419 246-0159
Ted Craig, *Manager*
EMP: 50 **Publicly Held**
WEB: www.amtrak.com
SIC: 9621 4013 ; switching & terminal
　services
HQ: National Railroad Passenger Corpora-
　tion
　　1 Massachusetts Ave Nw
　　Washington DC 20001
　　202 906-3000

(G-17934)
NATURAL FOODS INC (PA)
Also Called: Bulkfoods.com
3040 Hill Ave (43607-2983)
PHONE....................................419 537-1713
Frank Dietrich, *President*
Richard A Cohen, *Principal*
Rita Jester, *Treasurer*
Rosalie Dezandt, *Admin Sec*
▼ EMP: 31 EST: 1938
SQ FT: 424,845
SALES (est): 13.6MM **Privately Held**
WEB: www.bulkfoods.com
SIC: 5149 Health foods; natural & organic
　foods

(G-17935)
**NEIGHBORHOOD HEALTH ASSO
(PA)**
Also Called: Toledo Family Health Center
313 Jefferson Ave (43604-1004)
PHONE....................................419 720-7883
Doni Miller, *CEO*
Miranda Hoffman, *CFO*
Larry Leyland, *CFO*
John Uche, *Director*
John Shousher, *Bd of Directors*
EMP: 70
SQ FT: 9,000
SALES: 6.3MM **Privately Held**
SIC: 8093 Specialty outpatient clinics

(G-17936)
**NEIGHBORHOOD HSG SERVS
TOLEDO**
Also Called: NHS WEATHERIZATION PRO-
GRAM
704 2nd St (43605-2113)
P.O. Box 8125 (43605-0125)
PHONE....................................419 691-2900
William E Farnsel, *Exec Dir*
William Farnsel, *Exec Dir*
Michael Sachs, *Deputy Dir*
EMP: 36
SQ FT: 2,500
SALES: 4.2MM **Privately Held**
WEB: www.nhstoledo.org
SIC: 8399 Neighborhood development
　group

(G-17937)
**NEIGHBORHOOD PROPERTIES
INC**
2753 W Central Ave (43606-3439)
PHONE....................................419 473-2604
John Hoover, *President*
Lori Tyler, *Manager*
EMP: 50
SALES: 8.3MM **Privately Held**
WEB: www.neighborhoodproperties.org
SIC: 6513 6531 Retirement hotel opera-
　tion; real estate agents & managers

(G-17938)
**NEUROSURGICAL NETWORK
INC**
3909 Woodley Rd Ste 600 (43606-1179)
P.O. Box 824 (43697-0824)
PHONE....................................419 251-1155
Edmont P Lawrence, *President*
Scott Dull, *Principal*
Sean Logan, *Principal*
Leo J P Clark, *Vice Pres*
Michael Healey, *Treasurer*
EMP: 43
SQ FT: 10,000
SALES (est): 3.8MM **Privately Held**
WEB: www.neurosurgical-network.com
SIC: 8011 Surgeon; neurologist

(G-17939)
NEW TECHNOLOGY STEEL LLC
135 N Fearing Blvd (43607-3604)
PHONE....................................419 385-0636
EMP: 100
SQ FT: 63,404
SALES (corp-wide): 15.3MM **Privately
Held**
SIC: 5051 Steel Service Center
PA: New Technology Steel, Llc
　　2401 Front St
　　Toledo OH 43605
　　419 385-0636

(G-17940)
**NEW TECHNOLOGY STEEL LLC
(PA)**
2401 Front St (43605-1145)
PHONE....................................419 385-0636
▲ EMP: 42
SQ FT: 153,000
SALES (est): 15.3MM **Privately Held**
SIC: 5051 Metals Service Center

(G-17941)
**NEXTEL PARTNERS OPERATING
CORP**
Also Called: Sprint
5350 Airport Hwy Ste 110 (43615-6813)
PHONE....................................419 380-2000
Jeff Bradish, *Branch Mgr*
EMP: 30
SALES (corp-wide): 85.9B **Publicly Held**
WEB: www.nymobilellc.com
SIC: 4812 Cellular telephone services
HQ: Nextel Partners Operating Corp.
　　6200 Sprint Pkwy
　　Overland Park KS 66251
　　800 829-0965

(G-17942)
NHS - TOTCO INC
704 2nd St (43605-2113)
PHONE....................................419 691-2900
William Farnsel, *Exec Dir*
EMP: 40
SQ FT: 10,000
SALES (est): 1.9MM **Privately Held**
SIC: 1521 Single-family housing construc-
　tion

(G-17943)
**NONEMAN REAL ESTATE
COMPANY**
3519 Secor Rd (43606-1504)
PHONE....................................419 531-4020
Dennis J Noneman, *President*
EMP: 30
SQ FT: 3,200
SALES (est): 2.8MM **Privately Held**
WEB: www.noneman.com
SIC: 6531 Real estate brokers & agents

(G-17944)
NORDMANN ROOFING CO INC
1722 Starr Ave (43605-2461)
PHONE....................................419 691-5737
Robert Mac Kinnon, *President*
Neil A Mac Kinnon Jr, *Chairman*
Robert R Carns, *Vice Pres*
Steven N Saum, *Admin Sec*
EMP: 40 EST: 1931
SQ FT: 10,000
SALES (est): 11.1MM **Privately Held**
WEB: www.nordmannroofing.com
SIC: 1542 1761 Nonresidential construc-
　tion; roofing contractor; sheet metalwork

(G-17945)
NORFOLK SOUTHERN CORPORATION
2101 Hill Ave (43607-3621)
PHONE...............................419 381-5505
EMP: 44
SALES (corp-wide): 11.4B Publicly Held
SIC: 4011 Railroads, line-haul operating
PA: Norfolk Southern Corporation
3 Commercial Pl Ste 1a
Norfolk VA 23510
757 629-2680

(G-17946)
NORFOLK SOUTHERN CORPORATION
341 Emerald Ave (43604-3815)
PHONE...............................419 254-1562
Doug Williams, Manager
EMP: 75
SALES (corp-wide): 11.4B Publicly Held
WEB: www.nscorp.com
SIC: 4011 Railroads, line-haul operating
PA: Norfolk Southern Corporation
3 Commercial Pl Ste 1a
Norfolk VA 23510
757 629-2680

(G-17947)
NORON INC
Also Called: Honeywell Authorized Dealer
5465 Enterprise Blvd (43612-3812)
PHONE...............................419 726-2677
Kevin Boeke, President
EMP: 35
SQ FT: 15,000
SALES (est): 5.5MM Privately Held
WEB: www.noroninc.com
SIC: 1711 Warm air heating & air conditioning contractor

(G-17948)
NORTHWEST FIRESTOP INC
328 21st St (43604-5037)
PHONE...............................419 517-4777
James House, President
EMP: 25
SQ FT: 8,000
SALES (est): 3.9MM Privately Held
SIC: 1799 Fireproofing buildings

(G-17949)
NORTHWEST OHIO CARDIOLOGY CONS (PA)
2121 Hughes Dr Ste 850 (43606-5135)
PHONE...............................419 842-3000
Everett M Bush MD, President
James Bingle, Vice Pres
Daryl Moreau, Admin Sec
EMP: 70
SQ FT: 5,000
SALES (est): 6MM Privately Held
SIC: 8011 Cardiologist & cardio-vascular specialist

(G-17950)
NORTHWEST OHIO URGENT CARE INC
1421 S Reynolds Rd (43615-7413)
PHONE...............................419 720-7363
EMP: 50
SALES (corp-wide): 4.2MM Privately Held
SIC: 8011 Medical Doctor's Office
PA: Northwest Ohio Urgent Care, Inc.
1015 Conant St
Maumee OH 43537
419 891-0525

(G-17951)
NORTHWEST TTL AGY OF OH MI IN (PA)
328 N Erie St (43604-6601)
PHONE...............................419 241-8195
Fax: 419 241-9302
EMP: 55
SALES (est): 6.2MM Privately Held
SIC: 6361 8111 Title Insurance Carrier Legal Services Office

(G-17952)
NUCENTURY TEXTILE SERVICES LLC (PA)
1 Southard Ave (43604-5215)
P.O. Box 20130 (43610-0130)
PHONE...............................419 241-2267
Jim Pacitti, Owner
Mike Gigandet, Sales Mgr
EMP: 91
SQ FT: 1,000
SALES (est): 5.4MM Privately Held
SIC: 7213 Linen supply

(G-17953)
NURSING CARE MGT AMER INC
Also Called: Foundation Park Care Center
1621 S Byrne Rd (43614-3456)
PHONE...............................419 385-3958
Eric Valuckas, Administration
EMP: 150
SALES (corp-wide): 25.9MM Privately Held
WEB: www.nursinghomeinfo.org
SIC: 8051 Skilled nursing care facilities
PA: Nursing Care Management Of America, Inc.
7265 Kenwood Rd Ste 300
Cincinnati OH 45236
513 793-8804

(G-17954)
NWO GASTROENTEROLOGY ASSOC INC
4841 Monroe St Ste 110 (43623-4390)
PHONE...............................419 471-1317
Peter Reilly, President
EMP: 30
SALES (est): 1MM Privately Held
SIC: 8011 Gastronomist

(G-17955)
NZR RETAIL OF TOLEDO INC
4820 Monroe St (43623-4310)
PHONE...............................419 724-0005
Nick Hasan, CEO
Yazeed Qaimari, Principal
EMP: 85
SQ FT: 2,000,000
SALES (est): 110MM Privately Held
SIC: 5172 Gasoline

(G-17956)
OAKLEAF TOLEDO LTD PARTNERSHIP
Also Called: Oakleaf Village
4220 N Hllnd Sylvnia Ofc (43623)
PHONE...............................419 885-3934
Sanford Goldston, General Ptnr
Deborah Kelsik, Mktg Dir
David Moyer, Manager
EMP: 50
SQ FT: 106,000
SALES (est): 3.3MM Privately Held
SIC: 8361 6513 Home for the aged; retirement hotel operation

(G-17957)
OEM PARTS OUTLET
1815 W Sylvania Ave (43613-4637)
PHONE...............................419 472-2237
Julie O'Donnell, Owner
EMP: 25
SALES (est): 1MM Privately Held
WEB: www.oempartsoutlet.com
SIC: 5075 Warm air heating equipment & supplies

(G-17958)
OHIO SKATE INC (PA)
5735 Opportunity Dr (43612-2902)
PHONE...............................419 476-2808
Joseph Yambor, President
EMP: 50
SQ FT: 24,000
SALES: 120K Privately Held
WEB: www.ohioskate.com
SIC: 7999 5941 Roller skating rink operation; skating rink operation services; skating equipment

(G-17959)
OLD DOMINION FREIGHT LINE INC
5950 Stickney Ave (43612-3946)
PHONE...............................419 726-4032

Robert Bolin, Branch Mgr
EMP: 48
SALES (corp-wide): 4B Publicly Held
WEB: www.odfl.com
SIC: 4213 Less-than-truckload (LTL) transport
PA: Old Dominion Freight Line Inc
500 Old Dominion Way
Thomasville NC 27360
336 889-5000

(G-17960)
OLIVER HOUSE REST COMPLEX
27 Broadway St Ste A (43604-8701)
PHONE...............................419 243-1302
Patricia Appold, President
James Appold, Vice Pres
EMP: 70
SQ FT: 70,000
SALES (est): 5MM Privately Held
SIC: 1522 1542 6513 6512 Remodeling, multi-family dwellings; commercial & office buildings, renovation & repair; apartment building operators; commercial & industrial building operation

(G-17961)
OMNISOURCE LLC
2453 Hill Ave (43607-3610)
PHONE...............................419 537-1631
Jon Kinsman, Branch Mgr
EMP: 68 Publicly Held
WEB: www.omnisource.com
SIC: 5093 Ferrous metal scrap & waste
HQ: Omnisource, Llc
7575 W Jefferson Blvd
Fort Wayne IN 46804
260 422-5541

(G-17962)
OMNISOURCE LLC
5130 N Detroit Ave (43612-3515)
PHONE...............................419 537-9400
Art Cheloff, Branch Mgr
EMP: 218 Publicly Held
WEB: www.omnisource.com
SIC: 5093 Ferrous metal scrap & waste
HQ: Omnisource, Llc
7575 W Jefferson Blvd
Fort Wayne IN 46804
260 422-5541

(G-17963)
ONE MAIN FINANCIAL SERVICES
Also Called: Springleaf Financial Svc.
2232 Centennial Rd (43617-1870)
PHONE...............................419 841-0785
Gerald Oslakodic, Branch Mgr
EMP: 226
SALES (corp-wide): 2.3B Privately Held
SIC: 7389 6021 Finishing services; national commercial banks
PA: Springleaf Financial Holdings, Llc
601 Nw 2nd St
Evansville IN 47708
800 961-5577

(G-17964)
ONLINE MEGA SELLERS CORP (PA)
Also Called: Distinct Advantage Cabinetry
4236 W Alexis Rd (43623-1255)
PHONE...............................888 384-6468
Timothy Baker, President
Craig Poupard, Vice Pres
EMP: 53
SQ FT: 250,000
SALES: 7.2MM Privately Held
SIC: 2434 7371 7373 Wood kitchen cabinets; computer software systems analysis & design, custom; computer software development; systems software development services

(G-17965)
ORAL & MAXILLOFACIAL SURGEONS (PA)
1850 Eastgate Rd Ste A (43614-3024)
PHONE...............................419 385-5743
Patrick McCabe, President
Howard I Feig DDS, President
EMP: 50
SQ FT: 3,354

SALES (est): 3.4MM Privately Held
WEB: www.oralmaxsurgeons.com
SIC: 8021 8093 Dental surgeon; specialty outpatient clinics

(G-17966)
ORAL & MAXILLOFACIAL SURGEONS
4646 Nantuckett Dr Ste A (43623-3194)
PHONE...............................419 471-0300
Connie Smith, Manager
Sandy Kerschbaum, Admin Asst
EMP: 32
SALES (est): 4.7MM
SALES (corp-wide): 3.4MM Privately Held
SIC: 8021 Dental surgeon
PA: Oral & Maxillofacial Surgeons Inc
1850 Eastgate Rd Ste A
Toledo OH 43614
419 385-5743

(G-17967)
OVERHEAD INC (PA)
Also Called: Overhead Door Co of Toledo
340 New Towne Square Dr (43612-4606)
PHONE...............................419 476-7811
Lee J Huss, President
Michael Huss, President
Moody Telb, General Mgr
Diane Huss, Vice Pres
Mike Huss, Sales Executive
EMP: 40
SQ FT: 27,000
SALES (est): 12.4MM Privately Held
WEB: www.overheadinc.com
SIC: 1751 5211 5719 Garage door, installation or erection; garage doors, sale & installation; windows, storm: wood or metal; fireplaces & wood burning stoves

(G-17968)
OWENS CORNING SALES LLC (HQ)
1 Owens Corning Pkwy (43659-0001)
PHONE...............................419 248-8000
Michael H Thaman, Ch of Bd
Rhonda L Brooks, President
Carl B Hedlund, President
George E Kiemle, President
William E Lebaron, President
◆ EMP: 1000 EST: 2006
SQ FT: 400,000
SALES (est): 3B Publicly Held
WEB: www.owenscorning.com
SIC: 3296 2952 3229 3089 Fiberglass insulation; insulation: rock wool, slag & silica minerals; acoustical board & tile; mineral wool; roofing mats, mineral wool; asphalt felts & coatings; glass fibers, textile; yarn, fiberglass; windows, plastic; roofing, siding & sheet metal work

(G-17969)
P & W PAINTING CONTRACTORS INC
3031 Front St (43605-1007)
PHONE...............................419 698-2209
Paul Branstutter, President
Virginia Branstutter, Corp Secy
EMP: 50
SQ FT: 2,500
SALES (est): 5.1MM Privately Held
SIC: 1721 Industrial painting

(G-17970)
PARK INN
101 N Summit St (43604-1033)
PHONE...............................419 241-3000
Michael Sapara, Principal
EMP: 30 EST: 2008
SALES (est): 2.6MM Privately Held
SIC: 7011 Hotels & motels

(G-17971)
PARKCLIFFE DEVELOPMENT
4226 Parkcliff Ln (43615-7113)
PHONE...............................419 381-9447
Wayne Bucher, Partner
Tom Butler, Partner
Natalie Tousley, Director
Charlene Sutton, Program Dir
EMP: 65

SALES (est): 3.4MM **Privately Held**
WEB: www.parkcliffe.com
SIC: 8051 8361 Skilled nursing care facilities; residential care

(G-17972)
PARKVIEW MANOR INC
Also Called: Liberty West Nursing Center
2051 Collingwood Blvd (43620-1649)
PHONE..............................419 243-5191
Amanda Gibson, *Manager*
EMP: 170
SALES (corp-wide): 3.1MM **Privately Held**
SIC: 8051 Convalescent home with continuous nursing care
PA: Parkview Manor Inc
425 Lauricella Ct
Englewood OH 45322
937 296-1550

(G-17973)
PATHOLOGY LABORATORIES INC (DH)
Also Called: Pathlabs
1946 N 13th St Ste 301 (43604-7264)
PHONE..............................419 255-4600
Marian C McVicker, *President*
Donna Sandwisch, *Human Res Mgr*
Shelley Hughes, *Accounts Exec*
Marian McVicker, *Supervisor*
Daniel Hanson, *Pathologist*
EMP: 160
SQ FT: 18,000
SALES (est): 15.9MM **Privately Held**
SIC: 8071 Pathological laboratory

(G-17974)
PATHWAY INC
505 Hamilton St (43604-8520)
PHONE..............................419 242-7304
Cheryl Grice, *CEO*
Virginia Mayfield, *Opers Staff*
Robert Jordan, *CFO*
INA Jones, *Case Mgr*
Cheryl Toska, *Director*
EMP: 30
SQ FT: 13,000
SALES: 6MM **Privately Held**
WEB: www.eopa.org
SIC: 8322 7361 Social service center; employment agencies

(G-17975)
PENETRATING R GROUND (PA)
Also Called: Gprs
5217 Monroe St (43623-4601)
PHONE..............................419 843-9804
Matt Aston, *President*
Chad Fischer, *VP Opers*
Michael Brown, *Project Mgr*
Joshua Gonzales, *Project Mgr*
Chase Johnson, *Project Mgr*
EMP: 25
SALES (est): 44.7MM **Privately Held**
SIC: 8713 Surveying services

(G-17976)
PHILIO INC
Also Called: NEW CONCEPTS
5301 Reynolds Rd (43615)
P.O. Box 20068 (43610-0068)
PHONE..............................419 531-5544
Janice Edwards, *Exec Dir*
EMP: 35 EST: 2012
SALES: 2.9MM **Privately Held**
SIC: 8093 Substance abuse clinics (outpatient); mental health clinic, outpatient

(G-17977)
PINEWOOD PLACE APARTMENTS
1210 Collingwood Blvd (43604-8112)
PHONE..............................419 243-1413
Leean Morein, *Partner*
EMP: 3900
SALES (est): 43.4MM **Privately Held**
SIC: 6513 Apartment building operators

(G-17978)
PITT-OHIO EXPRESS LLC
5200 Stickney Ave (43612-3723)
PHONE..............................419 726-6523
Shelley Hart, *Opers Mgr*
Dean Miller, *Opers Mgr*
Jim Brywczynski,

EMP: 109
SALES (corp-wide): 457MM **Privately Held**
SIC: 4213 Contract haulers
PA: Pitt-Ohio Express, Llc
15 27th St
Pittsburgh PA 15222
412 232-3015

(G-17979)
PITT-OHIO EXPRESS LLC
5200 Stickney Ave (43612-3723)
PHONE..............................419 729-8173
Robert Divel, *Manager*
EMP: 80
SALES (corp-wide): 457MM **Privately Held**
SIC: 4213 Trucking, except local
PA: Pitt-Ohio Express, Llc
15 27th St
Pittsburgh PA 15222
412 232-3015

(G-17980)
PLANNED PARENTHOOD NW OHIO INC
1301 Jefferson Ave (43604-5850)
PHONE..............................419 255-1115
Scott Hamner, *Treasurer*
Johnetta McCollough, *Exec Dir*
EMP: 33
SQ FT: 11,600
SALES: 1.7MM **Privately Held**
WEB: www.ppnwo.org
SIC: 8093 Family planning clinic

(G-17981)
PNC BANK NATIONAL ASSOCIATION
Also Called: National City Bank
405 Madison Ave Ste 4 (43604-1263)
P.O. Box 1688 (43603-1688)
PHONE..............................419 259-5466
Scot Masell, *Branch Mgr*
EMP: 350
SALES (corp-wide): 19.9B **Publicly Held**
WEB: www.allegiantbank.com
SIC: 6021 National commercial banks
HQ: Pnc Bank, National Association
222 Delaware Ave
Wilmington DE 19801
877 762-2000

(G-17982)
PORT LAWRENCE TITLE AND TR CO (DH)
4 Seagate Ste 101 (43604-1173)
PHONE..............................419 244-4605
Marggretta Laskey, *President*
Victor Crouch, *Vice Pres*
Steve Sczesny, *Vice Pres*
Gerald Stewart, *Vice Pres*
Pat Lammon, *Director*
EMP: 40
SQ FT: 16,200
SALES (est): 29.6MM **Publicly Held**
SIC: 6361 6531 Real estate title insurance; guarantee of titles; real estate agents & managers
HQ: First American Title Insurance Company
1 First American Way
Santa Ana CA 92707
800 854-3643

(G-17983)
POTTER TECHNOLOGIES LLC
843 Warehouse Rd (43615-6472)
PHONE..............................419 380-8404
Michael Teadt,
Jeffrey Potter,
EMP: 83 EST: 2010
SALES (est): 6.8MM **Privately Held**
SIC: 8731 Commercial physical research

(G-17984)
PRECISION STEEL SERVICES INC (PA)
31 E Sylvania Ave (43612-1474)
PHONE..............................419 476-5702
David L Kelley, *President*
Greg Forrester, *Vice Pres*
Ramin Kalaty, *Vice Pres*
Kathy Zolciak, *Vice Pres*
Jordan Demchyna, *Opers Mgr*

EMP: 60 EST: 1975
SQ FT: 35,000
SALES (est): 62.4MM **Privately Held**
WEB: www.precision-steel.com
SIC: 5051 3441 3444 Steel; fabricated structural metal; sheet metalwork

(G-17985)
PREMIUM TRNSP LOGISTICS LLC (PA)
5445 Sthwyck Blvd Ste 210 (43614)
PHONE..............................419 861-3430
Chris Koehring, *Vice Pres*
David L Swartz,
EMP: 80
SALES (est): 13.5MM **Privately Held**
SIC: 4213 Trucking, except local

(G-17986)
PRESIDIO INFRASTRUCTURE
20 N Saint Clair St (43604-1074)
PHONE..............................419 241-8303
Kirsten Smith, *Branch Mgr*
EMP: 51
SALES (corp-wide): 1.1B **Publicly Held**
SIC: 7373 Office computer automation systems integration
HQ: Presidio Infrastructure Solutions Llc
6355 E Paris Ave Se
Caledonia MI 49316
616 871-1500

(G-17987)
PRICEWATERHOUSECOOPERS LLP
406 Washington St Ste 200 (43604-1046)
PHONE..............................419 254-2500
Pam Schlosser, *Branch Mgr*
Brandon Gabel, *Director*
Molly McCartney, *Admin Sec*
EMP: 40
SQ FT: 2,500
SALES (corp-wide): 7.8B **Privately Held**
WEB: www.pwcglobal.com
SIC: 8721 Certified public accountant
PA: Pricewaterhousecoopers Llp
300 Madison Ave Fl 24
New York NY 10017
646 471-4000

(G-17988)
PRIME HOME CARE LLC
3454 Oak Alley Ct Ste 304 (43606-1365)
PHONE..............................419 535-1414
Nataliya Romanova, *Branch Mgr*
EMP: 31
SALES (corp-wide): 1.6MM **Privately Held**
SIC: 8059 8082 Personal care home, with health care; home health care services
PA: Prime Home Care Llc
2775 W Us Hwy 22 3 Ste 1
Maineville OH 45039
513 340-4183

(G-17989)
PROFESSIONAL ELECTRIC PDTS CO
Also Called: Pepco
501 Phillips Ave (43612-1328)
P.O. Box 12020 (43612-0020)
PHONE..............................419 269-3790
Glen McNeil, *Opers Mgr*
Jim Deraedt, *Branch Mgr*
EMP: 30
SQ FT: 24,394
SALES (corp-wide): 90.8MM **Privately Held**
WEB: www.pepconet.com
SIC: 5063 Motors, electric
PA: Professional Electric Products Co Inc
33210 Lakeland Blvd
Eastlake OH 44095
440 946-3790

(G-17990)
PROGRSSIVE SWEEPING CONTRS INC (PA)
5202 Enterprise Blvd (43612-3809)
PHONE..............................419 464-0130
Michael R Lucht, *President*
Karen S Lucht, *Corp Secy*
Gregg Blair, *Opers Staff*
Brandi Linder, *Admin Asst*
EMP: 25

SQ FT: 4,800
SALES (est): 20.2MM **Privately Held**
SIC: 4959 Sweeping service: road, airport, parking lot, etc.

(G-17991)
PROMEDICA GI PHYSICIANS LLC
Also Called: Digestive Health Gastrologist
3439 Granite Cir (43617)
PHONE..............................419 843-7996
Anita Eurner, *Office Mgr*
EMP: 30 EST: 2010
SALES (est): 722.7K **Privately Held**
SIC: 8011 Gastronomist

(G-17992)
PROMEDICA GNT-URINARY SURGEONS (PA)
2100 W Central Ave (43606-3800)
PHONE..............................419 531-8558
Gregor K Emmert MD, *President*
Mayer Waynestein MD, *Vice Pres*
Tapper Richard I, *Treasurer*
Daniel S Murtagh MD, *Admin Sec*
EMP: 33
SQ FT: 7,000
SALES (est): 4.4MM **Privately Held**
WEB: www.parkwaysc.org
SIC: 8011 Urologist

(G-17993)
PROMEDICA HEALTH SYSTEMS INC (PA)
100 Madison Ave (43604-1516)
PHONE..............................567 585-7454
Alan W Brass, *CEO*
Gary Akenberger, *Vice Pres*
Tom Borer, *Vice Pres*
Jered Wilson, *Vice Pres*
Stella Wohlgamuth, *Auditor*
EMP: 4500
SALES (est): 2.1B **Privately Held**
SIC: 8062 6324 8351 8741 General medical & surgical hospitals; health maintenance organization (HMO), insurance only; child day care services; management services

(G-17994)
PTI QLITY CNTNMENT SLTIONS LLC
5655 Opportunity Dr Ste 4 (43612-2934)
PHONE..............................313 304-8677
Rodney Yates, *Director*
EMP: 54
SALES (corp-wide): 36.3MM **Privately Held**
SIC: 4785 Inspection services connected with transportation
PA: Pti Quality Containment Solutions Llc
18615 Sherwood St
Detroit MI 48234
313 365-3999

(G-17995)
PUBLIC BROADCASTING FOUND NW (PA)
Also Called: Wgte-Tv-Fm
1270 S Detroit Ave (43614-2794)
PHONE..............................419 380-4600
Marlon P Kiser, *President*
EMP: 70 EST: 1953
SQ FT: 45,000
SALES: 4MM **Privately Held**
WEB: www.wgte.pbs.org
SIC: 4833 4832 Television broadcasting stations; radio broadcasting stations

(G-17996)
R I D INC
Also Called: Mahajan Tita & Katra
2222 Cherry St Ste 1400 (43608-2669)
PHONE..............................419 251-4790
James Tita, *President*
EMP: 25
SALES (est): 1.7MM **Privately Held**
SIC: 8011 8031 Pulmonary specialist, physician/surgeon; offices & clinics of osteopathic physicians

(G-17997)
REGENCY PARK EYE ASSOCIATES (PA)
Also Called: Associated Eye Care
1000 Regency Ct Ste 100 (43623-3074)
PHONE..............................419 882-0588
Richard H Koop MD, *President*
Kathryn Koop, *Treasurer*
Elaine Leonard, *Manager*
EMP: 45 EST: 1970
SALES (est): 5.1MM **Privately Held**
SIC: 8011 Ophthalmologist

(G-17998)
REGENT ELECTRIC INC
5235 Tractor Rd (43612-3439)
PHONE..............................419 476-8333
Kevin Mc Carthy, *President*
Chas Slates, *Principal*
Gail Taylor, *Principal*
James Tice, *Principal*
Brian Mc Carthy, *Vice Pres*
EMP: 75
SQ FT: 10,000
SALES (est): 10.2MM **Privately Held**
SIC: 1731 General electrical contractor

(G-17999)
REHABILITATION AQUATICS
Also Called: Central Pk W Rhabilitation Ctr
3130 Central Park W Ste A (43617-1088)
PHONE..............................419 843-2500
Fax: 419 843-8288
EMP: 25
SQ FT: 10,000
SALES (est): 1.4MM **Privately Held**
SIC: 8049 Health Practitioner's Office

(G-18000)
REHMANN LLC
7124 W Central Ave (43617-1117)
PHONE..............................419 865-8118
John Hills, *Branch Mgr*
EMP: 60
SALES (corp-wide): 103.9MM **Privately Held**
SIC: 8721 Certified public accountant
PA: Rehmann, Llc
1500 W Big Beaver Rd
Macomb MI 48044
866 799-9580

(G-18001)
REMINGER CO LPA
405 Madison Ave Ste 2300 (43604-1212)
PHONE..............................419 254-1311
Laurie Avery, *Partner*
EMP: 71
SALES (corp-wide): 52.2MM **Privately Held**
SIC: 8111 Specialized law offices, attorneys
PA: Reminger Co., L.P.A.
101 W Prospect Ave # 1400
Cleveland OH 44115
216 687-1311

(G-18002)
RENT-A-CENTER INC
3418 Glendale Ave (43614-2428)
PHONE..............................419 382-8585
Rodney Rodriguez, *Branch Mgr*
EMP: 64
SALES (corp-wide): 2.6B **Publicly Held**
WEB: www.rentacenter.com
SIC: 7359 Appliance rental; furniture rental; home entertainment equipment rental; television rental
PA: Rent-A-Center, Inc.
5501 Headquarters Dr
Plano TX 75024
972 801-1100

(G-18003)
REPUBLIC SERVICES INC
6196 Hagman Rd (43612-3922)
PHONE..............................419 726-9465
EMP: 34
SALES (corp-wide): 10B **Publicly Held**
SIC: 4953 Rubbish collection & disposal
PA: Republic Services, Inc.
18500 N Allied Way # 100
Phoenix AZ 85054
480 627-2700

(G-18004)
RESCUE INCORPORATED
Also Called: Rescue Mental HLTh&addctn Svcs
3350 Collingwood Blvd # 2 (43610-1173)
PHONE..............................419 255-9585
John Debruyne, *CEO*
Linda Condit, *CFO*
Kul Gupta, *Director*
Jan Eppard, *Nursing Dir*
Winona Robinson, *Lic Prac Nurse*
EMP: 125
SQ FT: 13,500
SALES: 7MM **Privately Held**
WEB: www.rescuemhs.com
SIC: 8063 8361 8093 Hospital for the mentally ill; residential care; specialty outpatient clinics

(G-18005)
REUBEN CO (PA)
24 S Huron St (43604-8706)
PHONE..............................419 241-3400
George S Wade Sr, *Ch of Bd*
Penny Celestino, *Finance*
EMP: 42
SQ FT: 1,000
SALES (est): 2.7MM **Privately Held**
SIC: 6531 Real estate managers; real estate agent, commercial; real estate agent, residential

(G-18006)
REYNOLDS ROAD SURGICAL CTR LLC
Also Called: WILDWOOD SURGICAL CENTER
2865 N Reynolds Rd # 190 (43615-2076)
PHONE..............................419 578-7500
Casey Johnson, *Business Mgr*
EMP: 53
SALES: 6.9MM **Privately Held**
WEB: www.wildwoodsurgical.com
SIC: 8011 Plastic surgeon

(G-18007)
RICHARD HEALTH SYSTEMS LLC
5237 Renwyck Dr Ste A (43615-5963)
PHONE..............................419 534-2371
Takang N Abunaw,
Takang Abunaw, *Administration*
EMP: 200
SALES: 24.6K **Privately Held**
WEB: www.richardhealthsystems.com
SIC: 8082 Visiting nurse service

(G-18008)
RIVERSIDE MARINE INDS INC
Also Called: H Hansen Industries
2824 N Summit St (43611-3425)
PHONE..............................419 729-1621
Tony La Mantia, *President*
Jerry Norton, *Corp Secy*
Larry Ansler, *Vice Pres*
EMP: 60
SQ FT: 30,000
SALES (est): 10.6MM **Privately Held**
SIC: 7699 Nautical repair services

(G-18009)
RMF NOOTER INC
915 Matzinger Rd (43612-3820)
PHONE..............................419 727-1970
Jimmy Nelson, *President*
Mike Pollans, *Vice Pres*
Roger Sheidler, *Vice Pres*
Ron Blubaugh, *Project Mgr*
George Childress, *Project Mgr*
EMP: 100
SALES (est): 21MM
SALES (corp-wide): 678.7MM **Privately Held**
WEB: www.nooter.com
SIC: 7699 1711 1731 Boiler & heating repair services; mechanical contractor; electrical work
HQ: Nooter Construction Company
1500 S 2nd St
Saint Louis MO 63104
314 621-6000

(G-18010)
ROBERT F LINDSAY CO (PA)
4268 Rose Garden Dr (43623-3457)
PHONE..............................419 476-6221
Thomas Lindsay, *President*
Marge Czarnecki, *Vice Pres*
Timothy O'Leary, *Vice Pres*
Ann Veasey, *Vice Pres*
Margaret M Lindsay, *Admin Sec*
EMP: 60
SQ FT: 2,500
SALES (est): 2.5MM **Privately Held**
WEB: www.rflindsay.com
SIC: 6531 Real estate brokers & agents

(G-18011)
ROBERT STOUGH VENTURES CORP
Also Called: Whitewater Car & Van Wash Co
5409 Monroe St (43623-2817)
PHONE..............................419 882-4073
Robert A Stough, *President*
EMP: 50
SQ FT: 3,400
SALES (est): 1MM **Privately Held**
SIC: 7542 Carwash, automatic

(G-18012)
ROEMER LAND INVESTMENT CO
3912 Sunforest Ct Ste A (43623-4486)
PHONE..............................419 475-5151
Wellington F Roemer I, *President*
Wayne Shawaker, *Vice Pres*
EMP: 45 EST: 1942
SQ FT: 9,500
SALES (est): 2.3MM **Privately Held**
SIC: 6512 Commercial & industrial building operation

(G-18013)
ROMANOFF ELECTRIC CO LLC
5570 Enterprise Blvd (43612-3860)
PHONE..............................937 640-7925
Dennis Quebe, *CEO*
EMP: 396 EST: 1927
SALES (est): 23MM
SALES (corp-wide): 66.4MM **Privately Held**
WEB: www.romanoffelectric.com
SIC: 1731 General electrical contractor
PA: Quebe Holdings, Inc.
1985 Founders Dr
Dayton OH 45420
937 222-2290

(G-18014)
RUMPF CORPORATION (PA)
Also Called: Job1usa
701 Jefferson Ave Ste 201 (43604-6957)
P.O. Box 1480 (43603-1480)
PHONE..............................419 255-5005
Bruce F Rumpf, *CEO*
Elizabeth B Rumpf, *Admin Sec*
EMP: 40
SQ FT: 35,000
SALES (est): 31.1MM **Privately Held**
SIC: 7361 7363 7381 Employment agencies; temporary help service; employee leasing service; security guard service; protective services, guard

(G-18015)
RUSK INDUSTRIES INC
Also Called: Everdry Waterproofing Toledo
2930 Centennial Rd (43617-1833)
PHONE..............................419 841-6055
Kenneth Rusk, *President*
Jerry Jacobiak, *QC Mgr*
Gil Ramirez, *Sales Dir*
Dawn Curtis, *Admin Sec*
EMP: 60
SQ FT: 9,000
SALES (est): 7.4MM **Privately Held**
WEB: www.everdrytoledo.com
SIC: 1799 Waterproofing

(G-18016)
SABCO INDUSTRIES INC
5242 Angola Rd Ste 150 (43615-6334)
PHONE..............................419 531-5347
Robert Sulier, *President*
John Pershing, *Vice Pres*
CB M Ash, *Treasurer*
▲ EMP: 28 EST: 1961

SALES (est): 3.6MM **Privately Held**
WEB: www.kegs.com
SIC: 7699 5085 3993 3412 Tank repair & cleaning services; barrels, new or reconditioned; signs & advertising specialties; metal barrels, drums & pails

(G-18017)
SAIA MOTOR FREIGHT LINE LLC
1919 E Manhattan Blvd (43608-1534)
PHONE..............................419 726-9761
Jim Bryan, *Branch Mgr*
EMP: 31
SALES (corp-wide): 1.6B **Publicly Held**
WEB: www.saia.com
SIC: 4213 Contract haulers
HQ: Saia Motor Freight Line, Llc
11465 Johns Creek Pkwy # 400
Duluth GA 30097
770 232-5067

(G-18018)
SAMUEL SON & CO (USA) INC
Samuel Automotive N.a
1500 Coining Dr (43612-2905)
PHONE..............................419 470-7070
David A Oliva, *General Mgr*
John Mrkonjic, *Vice Pres*
Alf Keddy, *Opers Mgr*
Bernie H Schroeter, *Controller*
Tammy Schulte, *Sales Mgr*
EMP: 75
SALES (corp-wide): 1.8B **Privately Held**
SIC: 5051 Steel
HQ: Samuel, Son & Co. (Usa) Inc.
1401 Davey Rd Ste 300
Woodridge IL 60517
630 783-8900

(G-18019)
SAR ENTERPRISES LLC
Also Called: Home Instead Senior Care
2631 W Central Ave (43606-3548)
PHONE..............................419 472-8181
Scott Rozanski,
Lisa Rozanski,
EMP: 80 EST: 2000
SALES (est): 2.5MM **Privately Held**
SIC: 8082 Home health care services

(G-18020)
SATURN OF TOLEDO INC
6141 W Central Ave (43615-1805)
PHONE..............................419 841-9070
Frank Kisler, *President*
EMP: 28
SALES (est): 5.2MM **Privately Held**
SIC: 5511 7515 Automobiles, new & used; passenger car leasing

(G-18021)
SCHROEDER COMPANY (PA)
4668 Talmadge Rd (43623-3007)
PHONE..............................419 473-3139
Edward J Schroeder Jr, *President*
◆ EMP: 40
SQ FT: 1,500
SALES (est): 5.3MM **Privately Held**
SIC: 1522 6531 Apartment building construction; real estate managers

(G-18022)
SCOTTS TOWING CO
Also Called: Scotts Commercial Truck Svcs
5930 Benore Rd (43612-3955)
PHONE..............................419 729-7888
Ronald L Scott, *President*
Mark Scott, *Corp Secy*
Dona Scott, *Vice Pres*
EMP: 25
SQ FT: 5,000
SALES (est): 3.4MM **Privately Held**
WEB: www.scott-truck.com
SIC: 7549 7538 5078 Towing services; truck engine repair, except industrial; refrigeration units, motor vehicles

(G-18023)
SEAWAY SPONGE & CHAMOIS CO (PA)
Also Called: Seaway Building Services
458 2nd St (43605-2006)
P.O. Box 8037 (43605-0037)
PHONE..............................419 691-4694
Terry Vandervlucht, *President*

EMP: 45
SALES (est): 750K **Privately Held**
SIC: 7349 5087 Janitorial service, contract basis; janitors' supplies

(G-18024)
SENIOR CARE MANAGEMENT INC
3501 Executive Pkwy # 219 (43606-1321)
PHONE..................................419 578-7000
Kathy Brentlinger, *Principal*
EMP: 73
SALES (est): 1.5MM **Privately Held**
WEB: www.seniorcaremanagement.com
SIC: 8082 Home health care services

(G-18025)
SENTINEL FLUID CONTROLS LLC (DH)
5702 Opportunity Dr (43612-2903)
PHONE..................................419 478-9086
Larry Peterson, *Mng Member*
Terry Moore,
EMP: 50
SALES (est): 36.1MM
SALES (corp-wide): 3B **Publicly Held**
WEB: www.sentinelfluidcontrols.com
SIC: 5084 Food industry machinery; hydraulic systems equipment & supplies

(G-18026)
SERVICE CORPS RETIRED EXECS
Also Called: S C O R E
2200 Jefferson Ave Fl 1 (43604-7101)
PHONE..................................419 259-7598
Larry King, *Chairman*
EMP: 30
SALES (corp-wide): 13.1MM **Privately Held**
WEB: www.score199.mv.com
SIC: 8611 Business associations
PA: Service Corps Of Retired Executives Association
1175 Herndon Pkwy Ste 900
Herndon VA 20170
703 487-3612

(G-18027)
SFC GRAPHICS INC
110 E Woodruff Ave (43604-5226)
PHONE..................................419 255-1283
Tom Clark, *CEO*
Gary Crider, *Principal*
Scott Flom, *Vice Pres*
Steve Macy, *Controller*
Kevin Marsh, *Info Tech Mgr*
EMP: 45
SALES (est): 7.4MM **Privately Held**
SIC: 7336 Commercial art & graphic design

(G-18028)
SFN GROUP INC
Also Called: Spherion Outsourcing Group
1212 E Alexis Rd (43612-3974)
PHONE..................................419 727-4104
Peter Rogowski, *Manager*
EMP: 33
SALES (corp-wide): 27.2B **Privately Held**
SIC: 7363 Temporary help service
HQ: Sfn Group, Inc.
2050 Spectrum Blvd
Fort Lauderdale FL 33309
954 308-7600

(G-18029)
SHADOW VALLEY TENNIS & FITNESS
1661 N Hlland Sylvania Rd (43615)
PHONE..................................419 861-3986
Carol Weiner, *President*
Jim Davis, *Vice Pres*
EMP: 25
SQ FT: 85,768
SALES (est): 370.7K **Privately Held**
SIC: 7997 Tennis club, membership

(G-18030)
SHINDLER NEFF HOLMES SCHLAG
300 Madison Ave Ste 1200 (43604-1567)
PHONE..................................419 243-6281
Daniel A Worline, *Partner*
Charles K Boxell, *Partner*

Paul S Goldberg, *Partner*
Martin J Holmes, *Partner*
Mark E Lupe, *Partner*
EMP: 45
SALES (est): 5.1MM **Privately Held**
WEB: www.snhslaw.com
SIC: 8111 General practice attorney, lawyer

(G-18031)
SHORT FREIGHT LINES INC
6180 Benore Rd (43612-4801)
PHONE..................................419 729-1691
Dee Palmerton, *Manager*
EMP: 40
SALES (corp-wide): 9.5MM **Privately Held**
SIC: 4213 4231 Trucking, except local; trucking terminal facilities
PA: Short Freight Lines, Inc.
459 S River Rd
Bay City MI
989 893-3505

(G-18032)
SHRADER TIRE & OIL INC (PA)
2045 W Sylvania Ave # 51 (43613-4588)
PHONE..................................419 472-2128
James W Shrader Jr, *Ch of Bd*
Joseph W Schrader, *President*
Zach Park, *Business Mgr*
Mark Meyer, *Corp Secy*
Jim McCabe, *Vice Pres*
▲ **EMP:** 35 **EST:** 1948
SQ FT: 33,000
SALES: 69.9MM **Privately Held**
WEB: www.shradertireandoil.com
SIC: 5014 5172 5013 Tires & tubes; petroleum products; lubricating oils & greases; motor vehicle supplies & new parts

(G-18033)
SHUMAKER LOOP & KENDRICK LLP (PA)
1000 Jackson St (43604-5573)
PHONE..................................419 241-9000
David F Waterman, *Managing Prtnr*
Kenneth Crooks, *COO*
Paul Favorite, *COO*
Susan Kowlaski, *CFO*
Wendy Zimmerman, *Human Res Dir*
EMP: 210
SQ FT: 110,000
SALES: 115MM **Privately Held**
SIC: 8111 General practice law office

(G-18034)
SIGNATURE ASSOCIATES INC
Also Called: Signature Assoc-A Cushman
4 Seagate Ste 608 (43604-2612)
PHONE..................................419 244-7505
EMP: 25
SALES (est): 18.5MM **Privately Held**
SIC: 8742 6531 6552 Mgmt Consulting Svcs Real Estate Agent/Mgr Subdivider/Developer
PA: Signature Associates, Inc.
1 Towne Sq Ste 1200
Southfield MI 48076
248 948-9000

(G-18035)
SISTERS OF NOTRE D
Also Called: Maria Child Care
3912 Sunforest Ct Ste B (43623-4486)
PHONE..................................419 471-0170
Carrie Craun, *Administration*
EMP: 25
SALES (corp-wide): 8.4MM **Privately Held**
WEB: www.stjamesvalley.org
SIC: 8351 Child day care services
PA: Sisters Of Notre Dame Of Toledo Ohio, The (Inc)
3837 Secor Rd
Toledo OH 43623
419 474-5485

(G-18036)
SLEEP NETWORK INC (PA)
3450 W Central Ave # 346 (43606-1418)
PHONE..................................419 535-9282
Terry Shiffer, *President*
Joseph I Shaffer, *President*

Bob Drager, *Vice Pres*
Terry Shaffer, *Admin Sec*
EMP: 100
SQ FT: 3,000
SALES (est): 9MM **Privately Held**
WEB: www.sleepnetwork.com
SIC: 8741 Management services

(G-18037)
SLIDDY ENT LLC
Also Called: Sliddy Entertainment
417 Bronson Ave (43608-1938)
PHONE..................................419 376-1797
Charles Lee, *Principal*
Michelle Lee, *Principal*
Troy Reed, *Principal*
EMP: 50
SALES (est): 157.2K **Privately Held**
SIC: 7929 Entertainers & entertainment groups

(G-18038)
SMB CONSTRUCTION CO INC (PA)
5120 Jackman Rd (43613-2923)
PHONE..................................419 269-1473
Jim Mossing, *President*
Rob Keel, *Vice Pres*
Jeff Mossing, *Vice Pres*
EMP: 47
SQ FT: 33,000
SALES (est): 7.4MM **Privately Held**
WEB: www.smbconstruction.com
SIC: 1521 6513 1542 Repairing fire damage, single-family houses; apartment building operators; commercial & office buildings, renovation & repair

(G-18039)
SOLOMON LEI & ASSOCIATES INC
Also Called: Solomon, Lei & Associates
947 Belmont Ave (43607-4244)
PHONE..................................419 246-6931
Floyd Abercrombie, *CEO*
EMP: 27
SALES (est): 477.7K **Privately Held**
SIC: 7389

(G-18040)
SPA FITNESS CENTERS INC (PA)
Also Called: Utah Spas
343 New Towne Square Dr (43612-4626)
PHONE..................................419 476-6018
Robert Rice, *President*
Kenneth Melby, *Vice Pres*
EMP: 50
SQ FT: 1,200
SALES (est): 4.6MM **Privately Held**
SIC: 7991 Spas

(G-18041)
SPENGLER NATHANSON PLL
4 Seagate Ste 400 (43604-2622)
PHONE..................................419 241-2201
Richard Wolff, *Managing Prtnr*
B Gary Mc Bride, *Managing Prtnr*
James C Anderson, *Partner*
Michael W Bragg, *Partner*
Byron S Choka, *Partner*
EMP: 55
SQ FT: 26,000
SALES (est): 7.5MM **Privately Held**
SIC: 8111 General practice attorney, lawyer

(G-18042)
SPORTS CARE REHABILITATION
2865 N Reynolds Rd # 110 (43615-2069)
PHONE..................................419 578-7530
Mike Heifferon, *Director*
EMP: 40
SALES (est): 1.1MM **Privately Held**
WEB: www.sportscarept.com
SIC: 8011 Sports medicine specialist, physician

(G-18043)
SPRINT COMMUNICATIONS CO LP
1708 W Alexis Rd (43613-2349)
PHONE..................................419 725-2444
EMP: 39

SALES (corp-wide): 85.9B **Publicly Held**
SIC: 4813 Local & long distance telephone communications
HQ: Sprint Communications Company L.P.
6391 Sprint Pkwy
Overland Park KS 66251
800 829-0965

(G-18044)
SPRYANCE INC
3101 Executive Pkwy # 600 (43606-5301)
PHONE..................................678 808-0600
EMP: 34
SALES (est): 639K
SALES (corp-wide): 1.9B **Publicly Held**
SIC: 8099 Health And Allied Services, Nec, Nsk
HQ: Transcend Services, Inc.
1 Glenlake Pkwy Ste 800
Atlanta GA 30328
800 205-7047

(G-18045)
ST ANNE MERCY HOSPITAL
3404 W Sylvania Ave (43623-4480)
PHONE..................................419 407-2663
Richard Evans, *CEO*
Mahjabeen M Islam MD, *Principal*
Agha Shahid MD, *Principal*
EMP: 39
SALES (est): 113.2MM **Privately Held**
SIC: 8062 General medical & surgical hospitals

(G-18046)
ST PAULS COMMUNITY CENTER
230 13th St (43604-5443)
P.O. Box 9564 (43697-9564)
PHONE..................................419 255-5520
Ruth Arden, *Exec Dir*
EMP: 51
SQ FT: 9,464
SALES: 2.2MM **Privately Held**
SIC: 8322 Community center; temporary relief service; emergency shelters

(G-18047)
STEPHEN R SADDEMI MD
Also Called: Medical College of Ohio
2865 N Reynolds Rd # 160 (43615-2076)
PHONE..................................419 578-7200
Stephen R Saddemi, *Owner*
EMP: 25
SALES (est): 359.4K **Privately Held**
SIC: 8049 Offices of health practitioner

(G-18048)
STERICYCLE INC
1301 E Alexis Rd (43612-3977)
PHONE..................................419 729-1934
John Ertle, *Manager*
EMP: 36
SALES (corp-wide): 3.4B **Publicly Held**
WEB: www.stericycle.com
SIC: 4953 Medical waste disposal
PA: Stericycle, Inc.
28161 N Keith Dr
Lake Forest IL 60045
847 367-5910

(G-18049)
STORK STUDIOS INC
Also Called: Sylvania Ultrasound Institute
3830 Woodley Rd Ste A (43606-1176)
PHONE..................................419 841-7766
Rose Gozdowski, *President*
EMP: 27
SALES (est): 1.9MM **Privately Held**
SIC: 8071 Ultrasound laboratory

(G-18050)
STRANAHAN THEATRE TRUST
Also Called: Stranahan Theatre & Great Hall
4645 Heatherdowns Blvd # 2 (43614-3192)
PHONE..................................419 381-8851
Ward Whiting, *Manager*
EMP: 55
SQ FT: 50,000
SALES: 2.2MM **Privately Held**
WEB: www.stranahantheater.com
SIC: 6512 7922 6519 5812 Auditorium & hall operation; theatrical producers & services; real property lessors; eating places

GEOGRAPHIC

(G-18051)
STS RESTAURANT MANAGEMENT INC
Also Called: STS Management
420 Madison Ave Ste 103 (43604-1209)
PHONE....................................419 246-0730
David Ball, *President*
EMP: 65
SQ FT: 144,000
SALES (est): 5.5MM **Privately Held**
SIC: 6531 Real estate managers

(G-18052)
SUN FEDERAL CREDIT UNION
3341 Executive Pkwy (43606-1316)
PHONE....................................419 537-0200
Rick Cherry, *President*
EMP: 100
SQ FT: 5,000
SALES (est): 10MM **Privately Held**
SIC: 6062 6061 State credit unions, not federally chartered; federal credit unions

(G-18053)
SUNFOREST OB GYN ASSOCIATES
Also Called: Promedica Physician
3740 W Sylvania Ave # 103 (43623-4461)
PHONE....................................419 473-6622
Mary Kerr, *Manager*
Jane Szumigala, *Nursing Dir*
EMP: 26
SQ FT: 9,200
SALES (est): 5.2MM **Privately Held**
SIC: 8011 Gynecologist

(G-18054)
SUNRISE TELEVISION CORP
Also Called: W U P W
4 Seagate Ste 101 (43604-1520)
PHONE....................................419 244-2197
Fax: 419 244-8842
EMP: 50
SALES (corp-wide): 674.9MM **Publicly Held**
SIC: 4832 4833 Tv Station
HQ: Sunrise Television Corp.
1 W Exchange St Ste 5a
Providence RI

(G-18055)
SUNSET HOUSE INC
Also Called: WOODLANDS AT SUNSET HOUSE
4020 Indian Rd (43606-2292)
PHONE....................................419 536-4645
Vickie Bartlett, *CEO*
Peggy Kramer, *Human Res Dir*
Gayle Young, *Marketing Staff*
Carol Jones, *Manager*
Judy Bishop-Pierce, *Director*
EMP: 170 EST: 1873
SQ FT: 1,800
SALES (est): 4.3MM **Privately Held**
SIC: 8361 8052 Home for the aged; intermediate care facilities

(G-18056)
SUPERIOR PACKAGING TOLEDO LLC
2970 Airport Hwy (43609-1404)
PHONE....................................419 380-3335
Steve Kovar, *President*
Jennifer Moore, *Vice Pres*
EMP: 40 EST: 2007
SALES (est): 5MM **Privately Held**
SIC: 5199 Packaging materials

(G-18057)
SUPREME COURT UNITED STATES
Also Called: US Probation
1946 N 13th St Ste 292 (43604-7264)
PHONE....................................419 213-5800
Eric Corns, *Branch Mgr*
EMP: 27 **Publicly Held**
WEB: www.ao.uscourts.gov
SIC: 8322 9211 Probation office; courts;
HQ: Supreme Court, United States
1 1st St Ne
Washington DC 20543
202 479-3000

(G-18058)
TAMARON GOLF LLC
Also Called: Tamaron Country Club
2162 W Alexis Rd (43613-2216)
PHONE....................................419 474-5067
Tony Fuhrman, *President*
Anthony A Fuhrman,
EMP: 58
SALES (est): 2.8MM **Privately Held**
SIC: 7992 Public golf courses

(G-18059)
TASC NEW TOWN LLC
701 Jefferson Ave Ste 101 (43604-6956)
PHONE....................................419 242-9955
Johnetta McCollough, *Exec Dir*
EMP: 30
SALES (est): 184.1K **Privately Held**
SIC: 8322 Individual & family services
PA: Tasc Of Northwest Ohio, Inc.
701 Jefferson Ave Ste 101
Toledo OH 43604

(G-18060)
TASC OF NORTHWEST OHIO INC (PA)
Also Called: LUCAS COUNTY TASC
701 Jefferson Ave Ste 101 (43604-6956)
PHONE....................................419 242-9955
Larry Leyland, *Manager*
Johnetta McCollough, *Exec Dir*
EMP: 30
SALES: 2.1MM **Privately Held**
SIC: 8322 Social service center

(G-18061)
TEGNA INC
Also Called: Wtol
730 N Summit St (43604-1808)
PHONE....................................419 248-1111
EMP: 120
SALES (corp-wide): 2.2B **Publicly Held**
SIC: 4833 Television broadcasting stations
PA: Tegna Inc.
8350 Broad St Ste 2000
Tysons VA 22102
703 873-6600

(G-18062)
TELEPHONE & CMPT CONTRS INC
5560 308th St (43611-2354)
PHONE....................................419 726-8142
Patricia Futrell, *President*
Dennis M Futrell, *Vice Pres*
EMP: 25
SQ FT: 15,000
SALES: 2.3MM **Privately Held**
WEB: www.tccontractor.com
SIC: 1731 Communications specialization

(G-18063)
TEMBEC BTLSR INC
2112 Sylvan Ave (43606-4767)
P.O. Box 2570 (43606-0570)
PHONE....................................419 244-5856
James M Lopez, *President*
Lawrence Rowley, *General Mgr*
Dan Wozniak, *Admin Sec*
▲ EMP: 32
SQ FT: 84,000
SALES (est): 8.8MM **Privately Held**
WEB: www.btlresins.com
SIC: 2821 5169 Plastics materials & resins; industrial chemicals
HQ: Tembec Inc
4 Place Ville-Marie Bureau 100
Montreal QC H3B 2
514 871-0137

(G-18064)
THOS A LUPICA
608 Madison Ave Ste 1000 (43604-1169)
PHONE....................................419 252-6298
Thomas Lupica, *Owner*
EMP: 70
SALES (est): 1.8MM **Privately Held**
SIC: 8111 General practice attorney, lawyer

(G-18065)
THREAD INFORMATION DESIGN INC
Also Called: Thread Marketing Group
4635 W Alexis Rd (43623-1005)
PHONE....................................419 887-6801
Judy McFarland, *CEO*
Mark Luetke, *President*
Joe Sharp, *Principal*
EMP: 35
SQ FT: 11,000
SALES (est): 5.6MM **Privately Held**
WEB: www.threadgroup.com
SIC: 7311 Advertising agencies

(G-18066)
TJ METZGERS INC
207 Arco Dr (43607-2906)
PHONE....................................419 861-8611
Thomas H Metzger, *CEO*
Jackie Klempner, *Accounts Mgr*
Mary Schuck, *Accounts Mgr*
Aaron Meyer, *Manager*
EMP: 100
SQ FT: 63,146
SALES (est): 26.7MM **Privately Held**
WEB: www.metzgers.com
SIC: 2752 2759 2789 2791 Commercial printing, offset; commercial printing; bookbinding & related work; photocomposition, for the printing trade; color separation, photographic & movie film

(G-18067)
TK HOMECARE LLC
Also Called: Visiting Angels
7110 W Central Ave Ste A (43617-3118)
PHONE....................................419 517-7000
Tamera Riggs, *President*
EMP: 132
SALES (est): 700.4K **Privately Held**
SIC: 8082 Home health care services

(G-18068)
TKY ASSOCIATES LLC
Also Called: Comfort Keepers
2451 N Reynolds Rd (43615-2840)
PHONE....................................419 535-7777
Julie Kuney, *General Mgr*
Todd A Kuney, *Mng Member*
Todd Kuney, *Manager*
EMP: 85 EST: 2011
SQ FT: 1,600
SALES (est): 4.1MM **Privately Held**
SIC: 8082 8049 Visiting nurse service; nurses & other medical assistants

(G-18069)
TLC EYECARE
3000 Regency Ct Ste 100 (43623-3081)
PHONE....................................419 882-2020
Sue Demott, *President*
EMP: 30 EST: 2001
SALES (est): 730.3K **Privately Held**
SIC: 8011 Ophthalmologist

(G-18070)
TLEVAY INC
Also Called: Foundation Pk Alzheimers Care
1621 S Byrne Rd (43614-3456)
PHONE....................................419 385-3958
James L Farley, *Principal*
Michael J Scharfenberger, *Principal*
EMP: 140
SALES (est): 2.4MM
SALES (corp-wide): 26.1MM **Privately Held**
SIC: 8051 Skilled nursing care facilities
PA: Nursing Care Management Of America, Inc.
7265 Kenwood Rd Ste 300
Cincinnati OH 45236
513 793-8804

(G-18071)
TODD ALSPAUGH & ASSOCIATES
415 E State Line Rd (43612-4795)
PHONE....................................419 476-8126
Todd Alspaugh, *President*
Curt Asplaugh, *Vice Pres*
EMP: 45
SQ FT: 4,000
SALES (est): 4.5MM **Privately Held**
SIC: 1629 1794 1623 Land preparation construction; excavation work; sewer line construction

(G-18072)
TOLCO CORPORATION
1920 Linwood Ave (43604-5293)
PHONE....................................419 241-1113
George L Notarianni, *President*
James Reising, *Regional Mgr*
Tricia Thomas, *Design Engr*
Carole Rayle, *Credit Staff*
Robin Chlebowski, *Sales Staff*
▲ EMP: 75
SQ FT: 30,000
SALES (est): 32.6MM **Privately Held**
WEB: www.tolco.com
SIC: 5085 3563 3586 3561 Bottler supplies; spraying outfits: metals, paints & chemicals (compressor); vacuum pumps, except laboratory; measuring & dispensing pumps; pumps & pumping equipment; specialty cleaning, polishes & sanitation goods

(G-18073)
TOLEDO AREA INSULATOR WKRS JAC
Also Called: Heat and Frost Insulators Jatc
4535 Hill Ave (43615-5301)
PHONE....................................419 531-5911
Lynette Jones, *Principal*
EMP: 85
SALES (est): 4.2MM **Privately Held**
SIC: 1799 Special trade contractors

(G-18074)
TOLEDO AREA RGIONAL TRNST AUTH (PA)
Also Called: Tarta
1127 W Central Ave (43610-1062)
P.O. Box 792 (43697-0792)
PHONE....................................419 243-7433
James K Gee, *General Mgr*
EMP: 73 EST: 1971
SQ FT: 8,000
SALES (est): 22.5MM **Privately Held**
WEB: www.tarta.com
SIC: 4111 Bus line operations

(G-18075)
TOLEDO BUILDING SERVICES CO
2121 Adams St (43604-5088)
P.O. Box 2223 (43603-2223)
PHONE....................................419 241-3101
Joel B Friedman, *Ch of Bd*
Lawrence M Friedman, *President*
Ward Whiting, *Vice Pres*
Judith Friedman, *Admin Sec*
EMP: 940
SQ FT: 20,000
SALES (est): 17.4MM **Privately Held**
WEB: www.toledobuildingservices.com
SIC: 7349 Cleaning service, industrial or commercial

(G-18076)
TOLEDO CARDIOLOGY CONS INC (PA)
2409 Cherry St Ste 100 (43608-2670)
PHONE....................................419 251-6183
Thomas G Welch MD, *President*
Ameer Kabour MD, *Vice Pres*
Tracy Bates, *Office Mgr*
EMP: 56
SQ FT: 8,000
SALES (est): 7.2MM **Privately Held**
SIC: 8011 Cardiologist & cardio-vascular specialist

(G-18077)
TOLEDO CARDIOLOGY INC
Also Called: Nahhas, Ahed T MD
4235 Secor Rd (43623-4231)
PHONE....................................419 479-5690
Richard A Fell, *President*
EMP: 25
SALES (est): 1.2MM **Privately Held**
SIC: 8011 Cardiologist & cardio-vascular specialist

(G-18078)
TOLEDO CLINIC INC (PA)
4235 Secor Rd (43623-4299)
PHONE...................................419 473-3561
Ian S Elliot, *President*
E L Doermann, *Principal*
Edward G Seybold, *Principal*
Peggy Barton, *Business Mgr*
Timothy Husted, *Corp Secy*
▲ EMP: 500
SQ FT: 14,600
SALES (est): 118.9MM Privately Held
SIC: 8011 Physicians' office, including specialists

(G-18079)
TOLEDO CLINIC INC
1414 S Byrne Rd (43614-2363)
PHONE...................................419 381-9977
Jessica Makowski, *Branch Mgr*
EMP: 78
SALES (corp-wide): 118.9MM Privately Held
SIC: 8043 Offices & clinics of podiatrists
PA: Toledo Clinic, Inc.
4235 Secor Rd
Toledo OH 43623
419 473-3561

(G-18080)
TOLEDO CLINIC INC
3909 Woodley Rd Ste 800 (43606-1180)
PHONE...................................419 841-1600
Cherri Brothers, *Branch Mgr*
Peter Klein, *Surgeon*
EMP: 117
SALES (corp-wide): 118.9MM Privately Held
SIC: 8011 Offices & clinics of medical doctors
PA: Toledo Clinic, Inc.
4235 Secor Rd
Toledo OH 43623
419 473-3561

(G-18081)
TOLEDO CLUB
235 14th St (43604-5475)
PHONE...................................419 243-2200
Ronald Paerson, *President*
EMP: 78 EST: 1889
SQ FT: 20,000
SALES: 5MM Privately Held
SIC: 7997 8641 Country club, membership; social club, membership

(G-18082)
TOLEDO CY PUB UTLITY WTR DISTR
Also Called: City of Toledo Div Wtr Dist
401 S Erie St (43604-4611)
PHONE...................................419 936-2506
Sherman Mosser, *Commissioner*
EMP: 155
SALES (est): 5.7MM Privately Held
SIC: 4941 Water supply

(G-18083)
TOLEDO FAMILY HEALTH CENTER
Also Called: Mildred Byer Clnic For Hmeless
313 Jefferson Ave (43604-1004)
PHONE...................................419 241-1554
Doni Miller, *Exec Dir*
EMP: 52
SQ FT: 2,100
SALES: 4.9MM Privately Held
WEB: www.nhainc.org
SIC: 8011 Clinic, operated by physicians

(G-18084)
TOLEDO GLASS LLC (PA)
Also Called: Toledo Mirror & Glass
103 Avondale Ave (43604-8207)
PHONE...................................419 241-3151
James P Nicholson, *Mng Member*
EMP: 32 EST: 1918
SQ FT: 40,000
SALES (est): 5.7MM Privately Held
SIC: 1793 Glass & glazing work

(G-18085)
TOLEDO HOSPITAL
Also Called: Family Medicine Residency
2051 W Central Ave (43606-3948)
PHONE...................................419 291-2051
Luoito Edje, *Principal*
EMP: 40
SALES (corp-wide): 2.1B Privately Held
SIC: 8011 General & family practice, physician/surgeon
HQ: The Toledo Hospital
2142 N Cove Blvd
Toledo OH 43606
419 291-4000

(G-18086)
TOLEDO HOSPITAL (HQ)
Also Called: PROMEDICA TOLEDO HOSPITAL
2142 N Cove Blvd (43606-3896)
PHONE...................................419 291-4000
Alan Brass, *CEO*
Barbara Steele, *President*
Kevin Webb, *President*
Heather Baumgartner, *Purchasing*
Lani Brighton, *Research*
EMP: 4900 EST: 1876
SALES (corp-wide): 854.4MM
SALES (corp-wide): 2.1B Privately Held
SIC: 8011 8062 Medical centers; hospital, professional nursing school with AMA residency
PA: Promedica Health Systems, Inc.
100 Madison Ave
Toledo OH 43604
567 585-7454

(G-18087)
TOLEDO HOSPITAL
Also Called: Promedica
2150 W Central Ave Ste A (43606-3859)
PHONE...................................419 291-8701
Kathy Jaworski, *Manager*
EMP: 100
SALES (corp-wide): 2.1B Privately Held
SIC: 8062 General medical & surgical hospitals
HQ: The Toledo Hospital
2142 N Cove Blvd
Toledo OH 43606
419 291-4000

(G-18088)
TOLEDO JEWELERS SUPPLY CO
245 23rd St (43604-6519)
PHONE...................................419 241-4181
David Perlmutter, *President*
Steven Perlmutter, *Vice Pres*
James Kersten, *Controller*
EMP: 27
SQ FT: 19,000
SALES (est): 5.8MM
SALES (corp-wide): 13MM Privately Held
SIC: 5094 Watches & parts; jewelry
PA: Peoples Jewelry Company Inc
245 23rd St
Toledo OH
419 241-4181

(G-18089)
TOLEDO LEGAL AID SOCIETY
520 Madison Ave Ste 640 (43604-1307)
PHONE...................................419 720-3048
Robert Comes, *Exec Dir*
EMP: 28 EST: 1950
SQ FT: 5,800
SALES: 1.5MM Privately Held
SIC: 8111 Legal aid service

(G-18090)
TOLEDO METRO AREA CNCL GVRNMNT
300 M Luther King Jr Dr (43604)
P.O. Box 9508 (43697-9508)
PHONE...................................419 241-9155
Anthony L Reams, *President*
William Best, *Info Tech Mgr*
Jennifer Allen, *Exec Sec*
EMP: 27
SQ FT: 12,200
SALES: 792.6K Privately Held
WEB: www.tmacog.org
SIC: 8748 City planning

(G-18091)
TOLEDO MUD HENS BASBAL CLB INC
406 Washington St Fl 5 (43604-1046)
PHONE...................................419 725-4367
Michael Miller, *Owner*
Joe Napoli, *General Mgr*
Charles Bracken, *Corp Secy*
Greg Setola, *Opers Staff*
Nathan Steinmetz, *Marketing Staff*
EMP: 85
SALES (est): 8.5MM Privately Held
WEB: www.mudhens.com
SIC: 7941 Baseball club, professional & semi-professional

(G-18092)
TOLEDO MUSEUM OF ART
2445 Monroe St (43620-1500)
P.O. Box 1013 (43697-1013)
PHONE...................................419 255-8000
Brian Kennedy, *President*
Carol Bintz, *COO*
Mary K Siefke, *CFO*
Lynn Miller, *Human Res Dir*
Scott Boberg, *Manager*
▲ EMP: 225
SQ FT: 200,000
SALES: 23MM Privately Held
WEB: www.toledomuseum.org
SIC: 8412 Museum

(G-18093)
TOLEDO OPCO LLC
Also Called: ARBORS AT SYLVANIA
7120 Port Sylvania Dr (43617-1158)
PHONE...................................502 429-8062
Robert Norcross, *CEO*
EMP: 99
SQ FT: 60,000
SALES: 5.1MM Privately Held
SIC: 8051 Skilled nursing care facilities

(G-18094)
TOLEDO OPTICAL LABORATORY INC
1201 Jefferson Ave (43604-5836)
P.O. Box 2028 (43603-2028)
PHONE...................................419 248-3384
Irland Tashima, *President*
Jeffrey Seymenski, *Vice Pres*
Mary Johnson, *Manager*
Julie Shook, *Manager*
Jeff Szymanski, *Manager*
EMP: 52
SQ FT: 10,000
SALES (est): 8.1MM Privately Held
SIC: 3851 5048 Eyeglasses, lenses & frames; lenses, ophthalmic; frames, ophthalmic

(G-18095)
TOLEDO PUBLIC SCHOOLS
Also Called: Toledo Maintance Center
130 S Hawley St (43609-2318)
PHONE...................................419 243-6422
Gary Sautter, *Director*
EMP: 62
SALES (corp-wide): 454.8MM Privately Held
WEB: www.tps.org
SIC: 7349 School custodian, contract basis
PA: Toledo Public Schools
1609 N Summit St
Toledo OH 43604
419 729-8200

(G-18096)
TOLEDO SCIENCE CENTER
Also Called: IMAGINATION STATION
1 Discovery Way (43604-1579)
PHONE...................................419 244-2674
Chip Hambro, *COO*
Daniel Frick, *CFO*
Leslie Roth, *Hum Res Coord*
Lori Hauser, *Exec Dir*
Amy Hering, *Director*
EMP: 50
SQ FT: 100,000
SALES: 4.2MM Privately Held
SIC: 8412 Museum

(G-18097)
TOLEDO SHREDDING LLC
275 Millard Ave Bldg 3 (43605-1071)
PHONE...................................419 698-1153
Mike Valentine, *General Mgr*
Mel Rukin,
◆ EMP: 30
SQ FT: 11,360
SALES (est): 4.7MM Privately Held
SIC: 7389 Scrap steel cutting
PA: Protrade Steel Company, Ltd.
5700 Darrow Rd Ste 114
Hudson OH 44236

(G-18098)
TOLEDO SIGN COMPANY INC (PA)
2021 Adams St (43604-5431)
PHONE...................................419 244-4444
Brad Heil, *President*
Brian Heil Jr, *Vice Pres*
Daniel Fink, *Engineer*
Myra Gueli, *Sales Staff*
Wendy Jones, *Manager*
EMP: 25
SQ FT: 34,000
SALES (est): 3MM Privately Held
SIC: 7389 Sign painting & lettering shop

(G-18099)
TOLEDO SPORTS CENTER INC
1516 Starr Ave (43605-2472)
PHONE...................................419 693-0687
Andy Vasko, *President*
Bruce E Davis, *President*
James E Walter, *Vice Pres*
Thomas A Davis, *Treasurer*
Ivadelle Davis, *Admin Sec*
EMP: 25
SQ FT: 34,500
SALES (est): 829.8K Privately Held
WEB: www.toledokaraoke.com
SIC: 7933 Bowling centers

(G-18100)
TOLEDO TELEVISION INVESTORS LP
Also Called: Wnwo-TV
300 S Byrne Rd (43615-6217)
PHONE...................................419 535-0024
Brett Cornwell, *President*
John B Nizamis, *General Mgr*
Ralph E Becker, *Chairman*
EMP: 56
SQ FT: 12,000
SALES (est): 3.2MM Privately Held
SIC: 4833 Television broadcasting stations

(G-18101)
TOLEDO ZOO
2700 Broadway St (43609-3100)
PHONE...................................419 385-5721
Lorie Wittler, *Director*
Jeff Sailer, *Director*
EMP: 33
SALES (est): 3.4MM Privately Held
SIC: 8422 Animal & reptile exhibit

(G-18102)
TOLEDO ZOOLOGICAL SOCIETY (PA)
2 Hippo Way (43609-4100)
P.O. Box 140130 (43614-0130)
PHONE...................................419 385-4040
Lamont Thurston, *President*
Anne Baker, *Director*
Laura Elvey, *Administration*
EMP: 450
SALES (est): 34.3MM Privately Held
WEB: www.toledozoo.org
SIC: 8422 Zoological garden, noncommercial

(G-18103)
TOLEDO-LUCAS COUNTY PORT AUTH (PA)
Also Called: Seaport Division
1 Maritime Plz Ste 701 (43604-1853)
PHONE...................................419 243-8251
Paul L Toth Jr, *CEO*
Matthew A Sapara, *COO*
Anthony Schumaker, *Project Engr*
Thomas J Winston, *CFO*
Michele Lashuay, *Manager*
EMP: 25

SQ FT: 6,000
SALES (est): 12MM Privately Held
SIC: 4491 Marine cargo handling

(G-18104)
TOLSON ENTERPRISES INC
Also Called: Tolson Investment Property
6591 W Central Ave # 100 (43617-1097)
PHONE..................................419 843-6465
Harvey Tolson, *President*
Stephanie Lucio, *Bookkeeper*
Karen Renard, *Bookkeeper*
Hazel Taulbee, *Bookkeeper*
Galina Kagan, *Finance*
EMP: 26
SALES (est): 1.6MM Privately Held
SIC: 6531 Real estate managers

(G-18105)
**TONY PACKOS TOLEDO LLC
(PA)**
Also Called: Tony Packo's Food Company
1902 Front St (43605-1226)
PHONE..................................419 691-6054
Tony Packo, *CEO*
Emily Bennett, *Owner*
Brian Smith, *General Mgr*
Anthony Packo III, *Vice Pres*
Scott Radel, *Vice Pres*
EMP: 60
SQ FT: 7,500
SALES (est): 7.7MM Privately Held
WEB: www.tonypacko.com
SIC: 5812 5149 Carry-out only (except
pizza) restaurant; pickles, preserves, jel-
lies & jams

(G-18106)
TOWLIFT INC
Also Called: Forklift of Toledo
140 N Byrne Rd (43607-2603)
PHONE..................................419 531-6110
James Schuller, *Branch Mgr*
EMP: 33
SQ FT: 14,408
**SALES (corp-wide): 106.6MM Privately
Held**
SIC: 5084 Materials handling machinery
PA: Towlift, Inc.
1395 Valley Belt Rd
Brooklyn Heights OH 44131
216 749-6800

(G-18107)
**TRANSCO RAILWAY PRODUCTS
INC**
4800 Schwartz Rd (43611-1726)
P.O. Box 5009 (43611-0009)
PHONE..................................419 726-3383
Jim Smith, *QA Dir*
Antwan Smith, *Branch Mgr*
EMP: 30
**SALES (corp-wide): 96.7MM Privately
Held**
SIC: 3537 7699 Industrial trucks & trac-
tors; railroad car customizing
HQ: Transco Railway Products Inc.
200 N La Salle St # 1550
Chicago IL 60601
312 427-2818

(G-18108)
TRANSTAR ELECTRIC INC
767 Warehouse Rd Ste B (43615-6491)
PHONE..................................419 385-7573
Daniel L Bollin, *President*
Scott Bollin, *COO*
Jerry Buchhop, *Vice Pres*
Bob Turpening, *Project Mgr*
Becky Bollin, *CFO*
EMP: 60
SQ FT: 7,000
SALES (est): 15.3MM Privately Held
SIC: 1731 General electrical contractor

(G-18109)
TRI-STATE ALUMINIUM INC (HQ)
1663 Tracy St (43605-3463)
PHONE..................................419 666-0100
Marc A Schupan, *President*
EMP: 25
SQ FT: 28,000

SALES (est): 10.6MM
**SALES (corp-wide): 94.1MM Privately
Held**
WEB: www.tristate-aluminum.com
SIC: 5051 Aluminum bars, rods, ingots,
sheets, pipes, plates, etc.; steel
PA: Schupan & Sons, Inc.
2619 Miller Rd
Kalamazoo MI 49001
269 382-0000

(G-18110)
TSL LTD (PA)
5217 Monroe St Ste A1 (43623-4604)
P.O. Box 23100 (43623-0100)
PHONE..................................419 843-3200
Donald J Finnegan, *President*
Anne Marlow, *Admin Sec*
EMP: 2500
SQ FT: 3,600
SALES (est): 39.5MM Privately Held
WEB: www.tsl1.com
SIC: 7363 Truck driver services

(G-18111)
TTL ASSOCIATES INC (PA)
1915 N 12th St (43604-5305)
PHONE..................................419 241-4556
Thomas R Uhler, *President*
Charles Chambers, *VP Admin*
Jeffrey Elliot, *Vice Pres*
Timothy Pedro, *Vice Pres*
Curtis Roupe, *Vice Pres*
EMP: 110
SQ FT: 40,000
SALES: 13MM Privately Held
WEB: www.ttlassoc.com
SIC: 8711 8748 8741 Consulting engi-
neer; environmental consultant; construc-
tion management

(G-18112)
TUFFY ASSOCIATES CORP (PA)
Also Called: Tuffy Auto Service Centers
7150 Granite Cir Ste 100 (43617-3114)
PHONE..................................419 865-6900
Adina Harel, *Ch of Bd*
Yoav Navon, *Vice Ch Bd*
Roger Hill, *President*
Albert Nissim, *Vice Pres*
Karen Velliquette, *CFO*
EMP: 50
SQ FT: 5,000
SALES (est): 99.4MM Privately Held
WEB: www.tuffy.com
SIC: 6794 7533 7539 Franchises, selling
or licensing; muffler shop, sale or repair &
installation; brake repair, automotive

(G-18113)
TWO MEN & TRUCK INC
Also Called: Two Men and A Truck
2800 Tremainsville Rd A (43613-3583)
P.O. Box 258, Van Buren (45889-0258)
PHONE..................................419 882-1002
Duane Sell, *President*
Luann Wendeo, *Financial Exec*
EMP: 28
SQ FT: 7,000
SALES (est): 2.2MM Privately Held
SIC: 4212 Moving services

(G-18114)
**U HAUL CO OF
NORTHWESTERN OHIO (DH)**
Also Called: U-Haul
50 W Alexis Rd (43612-3692)
PHONE..................................419 478-1101
Lonnie Enderle, *President*
Ali Gillentine, *President*
Pamela D Davis, *Corp Secy*
Christopher Johnson, *Vice Pres*
EMP: 40
SQ FT: 14,000
SALES (est): 5.2MM
SALES (corp-wide): 3.6B Publicly Held
SIC: 7513 7519 7359 Truck rental & leas-
ing, no drivers; trailer rental; equipment
rental & leasing
HQ: U-Haul International, Inc.
2727 N Central Ave
Phoenix AZ 85004
602 263-6011

(G-18115)
**UNISON BEHAVIORAL HEALTH
GROUP**
Also Called: East Center
1425 Starr Ave (43605-2456)
P.O. Box 10015 (43699-0015)
PHONE..................................419 693-0631
Larry Hamme MD, *Director*
EMP: 200
**SALES (corp-wide): 20.7MM Privately
Held**
WEB: www.unisonbhg.org
SIC: 8093 Mental health clinic, outpatient
PA: Unison Behavioral Health Group, Inc.
1425 Starr Ave
Toledo OH 43605
419 214-4673

(G-18116)
**UNISON BHVIORAL HLTH
GROUP INC (PA)**
1425 Starr Ave (43605-2456)
P.O. Box 10015 (43699-0015)
PHONE..................................419 214-4673
Jeff De Lay, *President*
Melissa Studer, *Chairman*
Linda Torbet, *Chairman*
Stacey Bock, *CFO*
Lee Vivod, *Treasurer*
EMP: 75 **EST:** 1972
SQ FT: 17,100
SALES: 20.7MM Privately Held
WEB: www.unisonbhg.org
SIC: 8093 Mental health clinic, outpatient

(G-18117)
**UNITED COLLECTION BUREAU
INC (PA)**
Also Called: Ucb
5620 Southwyck Blvd (43614-1501)
PHONE..................................419 866-6227
Harold Sam Rickard, *Ch of Bd*
Moira Lechtenberg, *President*
Harold S Rickard III, *President*
Sanju Sharma, *President*
Michael R Karosas, *COO*
EMP: 165
SQ FT: 3,500
SALES (est): 66.5MM Privately Held
WEB: www.ucbinc.com
SIC: 7322 Collection agency, except real
estate

(G-18118)
**UNITED INSURANCE COMPANY
AMER**
1650 N Reynolds Rd (43615-3600)
PHONE..................................419 531-4289
Anthony Powell, *Branch Mgr*
EMP: 27
SQ FT: 2,550
SALES (corp-wide): 3.7B Publicly Held
WEB: www.unitedinsure.com
SIC: 6411 Insurance agents
HQ: United Insurance Company Of America
12115 Lackland Rd
Saint Louis MO 63146
314 819-4300

(G-18119)
**UNITED PARCEL SERVICE INC
OH**
Also Called: UPS
1212 E Alexis Rd (43612-3974)
PHONE..................................419 891-6841
Dave Bardram, *Site Mgr*
EMP: 70
SALES (corp-wide): 71.8B Publicly Held
WEB: www.upsscs.com
SIC: 4215 Package delivery, vehicular
HQ: United Parcel Service, Inc. (Oh)
55 Glenlake Pkwy
Atlanta GA 30328
404 828-6000

(G-18120)
UNITED ROAD SERVICES INC
Also Called: Mpg Transport
27400 Luckey Rd (43605)
PHONE..................................419 837-2703
Joseph Mell, *General Mgr*
EMP: 56

**SALES (corp-wide): 331MM Privately
Held**
WEB: www.unitedroad.com
SIC: 4213 Automobiles, transport & deliv-
ery
PA: United Road Services, Inc.
10701 Middlebelt Rd
Romulus MI 48174
734 946-3232

(G-18121)
**UNITED STTES BOWL
CONGRESS INC**
5062 Dorr St (43615-3852)
PHONE..................................419 531-4058
Robert Huss Jr, *Branch Mgr*
EMP: 51
**SALES (corp-wide): 32.9MM Privately
Held**
SIC: 8699 Athletic organizations
PA: United States Bowling Congress, Inc.
621 Six Flags Dr
Arlington TX 76011
817 385-8200

(G-18122)
**UNITED WAY OF GREATER
TOLEDO (PA)**
424 Jackson St (43604-1495)
PHONE..................................419 254-4742
Bill Kitson, *CEO*
Kathleen Doty, *COO*
Karen Mathison, *COO*
Jane Moore, *Vice Pres*
Kim Sidwell, *Vice Pres*
EMP: 60 **EST:** 1918
SQ FT: 25,000
SALES: 11.5MM Privately Held
WEB: www.namitoledo.com
SIC: 8322 Individual & family services

(G-18123)
**UNIVERSAL MARKETING
GROUP LLC**
5454 Airport Hwy (43615-7302)
PHONE..................................419 720-9696
Steven Horst, *Managing Prtnr*
Jason Birch, *CFO*
EMP: 99
SALES (est): 2.7MM Privately Held
SIC: 8742 5963 Marketing consulting
services; direct sales, telemarketing

(G-18124)
**UNIVERSITY OF TLEDO
FOUNDATION**
2801 W Bancroft St 1002 (43606-3398)
PHONE..................................419 530-7730
Brenda Lee, *President*
Derek Groves, *COO*
Lawrence Burns, *Vice Pres*
EMP: 40
SQ FT: 2,336
SALES: 37.7MM Privately Held
SIC: 8399 Community development groups

(G-18125)
UNIVERSITY OF TOLEDO
Also Called: Hsc Dept of Psychiatry
3120 Glendale Ave Ste 79 (43614)
PHONE..................................419 534-3770
Dr Marijo Tamburriono, *Principal*
EMP: 60
**SALES (corp-wide): 728.1MM Privately
Held**
WEB: www.utoledo.edu
SIC: 8011 8221 Psychiatrist; university
PA: The University Of Toledo
2801 W Bancroft St
Toledo OH 43606
419 530-4636

(G-18126)
UNIVERSITY OF TOLEDO
Also Called: University Toledo Medical Ctr
4430 N Hllnd Sylvnia Rd (43623)
PHONE..................................419 383-3556
Samir Fahed, *Manager*
EMP: 33
**SALES (corp-wide): 728.1MM Privately
Held**
WEB: www.utoledo.edu
SIC: 8011 8221 Offices & clinics of med-
ical doctors; university

(PA)=Parent Co (HQ)=Headquarters (DH)=Div Headquarters   2019 Harris Ohio
✪ = New Business established in last 2 years   Services Directory

731

PA: The University Of Toledo
2801 W Bancroft St
Toledo OH 43606
419 530-4636

(G-18127)
UNIVERSITY OF TOLEDO
Also Called: University of Toledo Med Ctr
3000 Arlington Ave (43614-2598)
PHONE..............................419 383-4000
Joan Stasa, *Sales Staff*
Keith Lewis, *Supervisor*
Theresa Gallup, *Anesthesiology*
Robert Booth Jr, *Pathologist*
Robert Mrak, *Pathologist*
EMP: 3200
SALES (corp-wide): 728.1MM **Privately Held**
SIC: 8062 8221 Hospital, affiliated with AMA residency; college, except junior
PA: The University Of Toledo
2801 W Bancroft St
Toledo OH 43606
419 530-4636

(G-18128)
UNIVERSITY OF TOLEDO
Also Called: Health Science Campus
3000 Arlington Ave (43614-2598)
PHONE..............................419 383-5322
Jeffrey Gold, *President*
EMP: 33
SALES (corp-wide): 728.1MM **Privately Held**
WEB: www.utoledo.edu
SIC: 8011 8221 Radiologist; university
PA: The University Of Toledo
2801 W Bancroft St
Toledo OH 43606
419 530-4636

(G-18129)
UNIVERSITY OF TOLEDO
Health Science Campus
3000 Arlington Ave (43614-2598)
PHONE..............................419 383-3759
Dr Lloyd Jacobs, *Principal*
EMP: 3579
SALES (corp-wide): 728.1MM **Privately Held**
WEB: www.utoledo.edu
SIC: 8062 8221 Hospital, affiliated with AMA residency; college, except junior
PA: The University Of Toledo
2801 W Bancroft St
Toledo OH 43606
419 530-4636

(G-18130)
UNIVERSITY OF TOLEDO
Also Called: Health Science Campus
3000 Arlington Ave (43614-2598)
PHONE..............................419 383-4229
Lloyd Jacobs, *President*
EMP: 322
SALES (corp-wide): 728.1MM **Privately Held**
WEB: www.utoledo.edu
SIC: 8221 8062 University; hospital, medical school affiliation
PA: The University Of Toledo
2801 W Bancroft St
Toledo OH 43606
419 530-4636

(G-18131)
URSULINE CONVENT SACRED HEART
Also Called: Ursuline Center
4035 Indian Rd (43606-2226)
PHONE..............................419 531-8990
Kathleen Voyles, *Administration*
EMP: 47
SALES (corp-wide): 2.5MM **Privately Held**
SIC: 8361 8661 Rest home, with health care incidental; convent
PA: The Ursuline Convent Of The Sacred Heart
4045 Indian Rd
Toledo OH
419 536-9587

(G-18132)
USI INC
1120 Madison Ave (43604-7538)
PHONE..............................419 243-1191
Benjamin Brown, *Vice Pres*
EMP: 90 **Privately Held**
SIC: 6411 Insurance agents
PA: Usi, Inc.
200 Summit Lake Dr # 350
Valhalla NY 10595

(G-18133)
V M SYSTEMS INC
3125 Hill Ave (43607-2987)
PHONE..............................419 535-1044
Craig Gabel, *President*
Ronald H Gabel, *President*
Trent Bloomfield, *Vice Pres*
Kevin Phillips, *Project Mgr*
Ron Snyder, *Facilities Mgr*
EMP: 100
SQ FT: 24,000
SALES (est): 26MM **Privately Held**
WEB: www.vmsystemsinc.com
SIC: 1711 3444 Warm air heating & air conditioning contractor; ventilation & duct work contractor; sheet metalwork

(G-18134)
VAN STEVENS LINES INC
64 N Fearing Blvd (43607-3601)
PHONE..............................419 729-8871
Rich Evasius, *Manager*
EMP: 25
SALES (corp-wide): 72.7MM **Privately Held**
WEB: www.stevensworldwide.com
SIC: 4213 4214 Household goods transport; local trucking with storage
HQ: Van Stevens Lines Inc
527 W Morley Dr
Saginaw MI 48601
989 755-3000

(G-18135)
VANCE PROPERTY MANAGEMENT LLC
4200 South Ave (43615-6254)
P.O. Box 365, Maumee (43537-0365)
PHONE..............................419 467-9548
Winston Vance, *Branch Mgr*
EMP: 56
SALES (est): 1.2MM **Privately Held**
SIC: 0781 4214 Landscape services; household goods moving & storage, local
PA: Vance Property Management Llc
4200 South Ave
Toledo OH 43615

(G-18136)
VANCE PROPERTY MANAGEMENT LLC (PA)
4200 South Ave (43615-6254)
P.O. Box 365, Maumee (43537-0365)
PHONE..............................419 887-1878
Winston Vance, *Mng Member*
James W Nightingale,
EMP: 67
SQ FT: 7,500
SALES: 1.4MM **Privately Held**
SIC: 8741 Management services

(G-18137)
VERITIV OPERATING COMPANY
Also Called: International Paper
1320 Locust St (43608-2938)
P.O. Box 567 (43697-0567)
PHONE..............................419 243-6100
Bruce E Lang, *Branch Mgr*
EMP: 49
SALES (corp-wide): 8.7B **Publicly Held**
WEB: www.internationalpaper.com
SIC: 5111 5943 Printing & writing paper; office forms & supplies
HQ: Veritiv Operating Company
1000 Abernathy Rd
Atlanta GA 30328
770 391-8200

(G-18138)
VETERANS HEALTH ADMINISTRATION
Also Called: Toledo V A Outpatient Clinic
3333 Glendale Ave (43614-2426)
PHONE..............................419 259-2000

Jennifer Sherman, *Manager*
EMP: 70 **Publicly Held**
WEB: www.veterans-ru.org
SIC: 8011 9451 Clinic, operated by physicians; psychiatric clinic;
HQ: Veterans Health Administration
810 Vermont Ave Nw
Washington DC 20420

(G-18139)
VISION ASSOCIATES INC (PA)
Also Called: Ofori, Jason MD
2865 N Reynolds Rd # 170 (43615-2076)
PHONE..............................419 578-7598
Rodney McCarthy, *Principal*
J G Rosenthal MD, *Bd of Directors*
EMP: 51
SALES (est): 5.6MM **Privately Held**
SIC: 8042 Offices & clinics of optometrists

(G-18140)
VOLUNTEERS OF AMERICA NW OHIO
701 Jefferson Ave Ste 203 (43604-6957)
PHONE..............................419 248-3733
Sue Reamsnyder, *President*
EMP: 50
SALES (est): 2.5MM **Privately Held**
WEB: www.voa.org
SIC: 8699 8322 Personal interest organization; individual & family services

(G-18141)
W DAVID MAUPIN INC
Also Called: Royal Building Cleaning Svcs
3564 Marine Rd (43609-1018)
P.O. Box 903 (43697-0903)
PHONE..............................419 389-0458
W David Maupin, *President*
EMP: 28
SQ FT: 13,000
SALES: 330K **Privately Held**
SIC: 7349 Building cleaning service

(G-18142)
W S O S COMMUNITY A
1500 N Superior St # 303 (43604-2157)
PHONE..............................419 729-8035
Cheryl Denny, *Planning*
EMP: 45
SALES (corp-wide): 33MM **Privately Held**
SIC: 8351 Head start center, except in conjunction with school
PA: W. S. O. S. Community Action Commission, Inc.
127 S Front St
Fremont OH 43420
419 333-6068

(G-18143)
W W W M
3225 Arlington Ave (43614-2427)
PHONE..............................419 240-1055
Loulew Dickey, *President*
Paul Smith, *Principal*
EMP: 37
SALES (est): 1.7MM **Privately Held**
SIC: 5064 Radios

(G-18144)
WABE MAQUAW HOLDINGS INC
17 Corey Creek Rd (43623-1183)
PHONE..............................419 243-1191
Dennis G Johnson, *President*
Paul Johnson, *Principal*
Jim Stengle, *Senior VP*
Kevin Brennan, *Vice Pres*
Ben Brown, *Vice Pres*
EMP: 90
SQ FT: 20,000
SALES (est): 3MM **Privately Held**
WEB: www.brooksinsurance.com
SIC: 6411 Insurance agents

(G-18145)
WALMAN OPTICAL COMPANY
1201 Jefferson Ave (43604-5836)
PHONE..............................419 248-3384
EMP: 93
SALES (corp-wide): 404.2MM **Privately Held**
SIC: 5048 Optometric equipment & supplies

PA: The Walman Optical Company
801 12th Ave N Ste 1
Minneapolis MN 55411
612 520-6000

(G-18146)
WASHINGTON LOCAL SCHOOLS
Also Called: Bus Garage & Maintenance Dept
5201 Douglas Rd (43613-2640)
PHONE..............................419 473-8356
John Bettis, *Manager*
EMP: 75
SALES (corp-wide): 93.4MM **Privately Held**
SIC: 4173 4151 Maintenance facilities for motor vehicle passenger transport; school buses
PA: Washington Local Schools
3505 W Lincolnshr Blvd Of Ofc
Toledo OH 43606
419 473-8224

(G-18147)
WATERFORD BANK NATIONAL ASSN (HQ)
3900 N Mccord Rd (43617-1049)
PHONE..............................419 720-3900
Mike White, *President*
Rod Frey, *Vice Pres*
Jeremy Zeisloft, *Vice Pres*
Debra Beyer, *CFO*
EMP: 63
SALES: 30.6MM **Privately Held**
SIC: 6021 National commercial banks

(G-18148)
WELCH PACKAGING GROUP INC
1240 Matzinger Rd (43612-3849)
PHONE..............................419 726-3491
Robert Dorst, *Principal*
EMP: 250
SALES (corp-wide): 546.3MM **Privately Held**
SIC: 5199 Packaging materials
PA: Welch Packaging Group, Inc.
1020 Herman St
Elkhart IN 46516
574 295-2460

(G-18149)
WELLES BOWEN REALTY INC
2460 N Reynolds Rd (43615-2884)
PHONE..............................419 535-0011
David Browning, *President*
Kevin Smith, *Vice Pres*
Linda McDougle, *Office Mgr*
Melissa Sargent, *Office Mgr*
Elaine Schlagheck, *Director*
EMP: 65
SALES (est): 5.1MM **Privately Held**
WEB: www.wellesbowen.com
SIC: 6531 6163 Real estate agent, residential; mortgage brokers arranging for loans, using money of others

(G-18150)
WELLS FARGO CLEARING SVCS LLC
Also Called: Wells Fargo Advisors
3450 W Central Ave # 130 (43606-1416)
PHONE..............................419 356-3272
Linda Zachel, *Vice Pres*
Gerald L Sliemers, *Manager*
EMP: 26
SQ FT: 750
SALES (corp-wide): 101B **Publicly Held**
SIC: 6211 Stock brokers & dealers
HQ: Wells Fargo Clearing Services, Llc
1 N Jefferson Ave Fl 7
Saint Louis MO 63103
314 955-3000

(G-18151)
WELLS FARGO CLEARING SVCS LLC
Also Called: Wells Fargo Advisors
7335 Crossleigh Ct # 100 (43617-3124)
PHONE..............................419 720-9700
EMP: 33
SALES (corp-wide): 101B **Publicly Held**
SIC: 6211 Stock brokers & dealers

HQ: Wells Fargo Clearing Services, Llc
1 N Jefferson Ave Fl 7
Saint Louis MO 63103
314 955-3000

(G-18152)
WELLTOWER INC (PA)
4500 Dorr St (43615-4040)
PHONE..................419 247-2800
Thomas J Derosa, CEO
Jeffrey H Donahue, Ch of Bd
Tim McHugh, President
Lisa Schmaltz, President
Cheryl O'Connor, Counsel
▲ EMP: 392
SALES: 4.7B Publicly Held
WEB: www.hcreit.com
SIC: 6513 Apartment building operators

(G-18153)
WEST PARK FAMILY PHYSICIAN
Also Called: West Park Health Partners
3425 Executive Pkwy # 100 (43606-1326)
PHONE..................419 472-1124
Mark D Hillard, Partner
EMP: 30
SALES (est): 1.2MM Privately Held
SIC: 8011 Offices & clinics of medical doctors

(G-18154)
WEST SIDE MONTESSORI
7115 W Bancroft St (43615-3010)
PHONE..................419 866-1931
Lynn Fisher, President
Dawn Westley, Director
EMP: 85 EST: 1975
SQ FT: 22,700
SALES: 6MM Privately Held
WEB: www.wsmctoledo.org
SIC: 8211 8351 Private elementary school; Montessori child development center

(G-18155)
WESTGATE LIMITED PARTNERSHIP
Also Called: Ramada Hotel & Conference Ctr
457 S Reynolds Rd (43615-5953)
PHONE..................419 535-7070
Ken Maclaren, Partner
Ken McLaren, Partner
Stephen Swigart, Partner
EMP: 150
SQ FT: 216,000
SALES (est): 7.5MM Privately Held
WEB: www.clariontoledo.com
SIC: 7011 6513 5813 Hotels; residential hotel operation; drinking places

(G-18156)
WHITEFORD GREENHOUSE
4554 Whiteford Rd (43623-2759)
PHONE..................419 882-4110
Roger F Barrow, Owner
EMP: 50
SQ FT: 58,000
SALES (est): 2.7MM Privately Held
SIC: 0181 Bedding plants, growing of; flowers: grown under cover (e.g. greenhouse production)

(G-18157)
WILEY HOMES INC
4011 Angola Rd (43615-6509)
P.O. Box 351688 (43635-1688)
PHONE..................419 535-3988
Stephanie C Wiley, President
EMP: 80
SALES (est): 1.9MM Privately Held
SIC: 8361 Home for the mentally retarded

(G-18158)
WILLIAMS HOMES LLC
1841 Eastgate Rd (43614-3034)
PHONE..................419 472-1005
Brian Williams, Mng Member
EMP: 25
SALES (est): 356.8K Privately Held
SIC: 6531 Real estate brokers & agents

(G-18159)
WILLIS DAY MANAGEMENT INC (PA)
4100 Bennett Rd Ste 1 (43612-1970)
P.O. Box 676 (43697-0676)
PHONE..................419 476-8000
Jeffrey K Day, President
Stephen Day, Vice Pres
Willis Day IV, Admin Sec
EMP: 25
SQ FT: 60,000
SALES (est): 1.8MM Privately Held
SIC: 6512 5084 4214 4225 Commercial & industrial building operation; materials handling machinery; local trucking with storage; general warehousing

(G-18160)
WOLVES CLUB INC
5930 Dalton Rd (43612-4210)
PHONE..................419 476-4418
Joe Brescol, CEO
EMP: 42
SQ FT: 960
SALES (est): 1.4MM Privately Held
SIC: 8641 Civic social & fraternal associations

(G-18161)
WORLD TABLEWARE INC (DH)
300 Madison Ave Fl 4 (43604-1567)
P.O. Box 10060 (43699-0060)
PHONE..................419 325-2608
John Myer, CEO
▲ EMP: 100
SALES (est): 39.6MM Publicly Held
SIC: 5023 Kitchenware
HQ: Libbey Glass Inc.
300 Madison Ave Fl 4
Toledo OH 43604
419 325-2100

(G-18162)
WRWK 1065
Also Called: 94 5 Xkr Rdo Stn Bus & Sls Off
3225 Arlington Ave (43614-2427)
PHONE..................419 725-5700
Andy Stuart, Manager
EMP: 50
SALES (est): 555.4K Privately Held
SIC: 4832 Radio broadcasting stations

(G-18163)
WUPW LLC
730 N Summit St (43604-1808)
PHONE..................419 244-3600
Traci Grimm, Accountant
EMP: 50
SALES (est): 1.2MM Privately Held
SIC: 4833 Television broadcasting stations

(G-18164)
WURTEC INCORPORATED (PA)
6200 Brent Dr (43611-1081)
PHONE..................419 726-1066
Steven P Wurth, President
Rob Wurth, President
Jane A Wurth, Corp Secy
Jeff Wagenhauser, Mfg Mgr
◆ EMP: 62
SQ FT: 43,000
SALES (est): 24.5MM Privately Held
SIC: 5065 5084 Telephone & telegraphic equipment; elevators

(G-18165)
XEROX CORPORATION
600 Jefferson Ave Ste 200 (43604-1012)
PHONE..................419 418-6500
Jeffrey Wenger, Owner
EMP: 50
SALES (corp-wide): 9.8B Publicly Held
WEB: www.xerox.com
SIC: 7699 Photocopy machine repair
PA: Xerox Corporation
201 Merritt 7
Norwalk CT 06851
203 968-3000

(G-18166)
YARK AUTOMOTIVE GROUP INC (PA)
Also Called: Yark Subaru
6019 W Central Ave (43615-1803)
PHONE..................419 841-7771

Douglas Kearns, CEO
John W Yark, President
Dj Yark, Vice Pres
Max Forster, CFO
David Duncan, Finance Mgr
EMP: 550
SQ FT: 40,000
SALES (est): 71.8MM Privately Held
WEB: www.yarkbmw.net
SIC: 5511 7515 7521 Automobiles, new & used; passenger car leasing; indoor parking services

(G-18167)
YOUNG MENS CHRISTIAN ASSOC (PA)
Also Called: YMCA of Greater Toledo
1500 N Superior St Fl 2 (43604-2149)
PHONE..................419 729-8135
Todd Tibbits, President
Casey Holck, COO
Stephanie Dames, Vice Pres
Wilma Dimanna, Vice Pres
Brian Keel, CFO
EMP: 50 EST: 1865
SQ FT: 2,500
SALES (est): 29.1MM Privately Held
WEB: www.ymcastorercamps.org
SIC: 8641 7991 8351 7032 Youth organizations; physical fitness facilities; child day care services; youth camps; individual & family services

(G-18168)
YOUNG MENS CHRISTIAN ASSOCIAT
2110 Tremainsville Rd (43613-3409)
PHONE..................419 475-3496
Jason Trame, Exec Dir
EMP: 240
SALES (corp-wide): 29.1MM Privately Held
SIC: 8641 Youth organizations
PA: The Young Men's Christian Association Of Greater Toledo
1500 N Superior St Fl 2
Toledo OH 43604
419 729-8135

(G-18169)
YOUNG MENS CHRISTIAN ASSOCIAT
1500 N Superior St Fl 2 (43604-2149)
PHONE..................419 474-3995
Regina Carter, Principal
EMP: 45
SALES (corp-wide): 29.1MM Privately Held
WEB: www.ymcastorercamps.org
SIC: 8641 7991 8351 7032 Youth organizations; physical fitness facilities; child day care services; youth camps; individual & family services
PA: Young Men's Christian Association Of Greater Toledo
1500 N Superior St Fl 2
Toledo OH 43604
419 729-8135

(G-18170)
YOUNG MENS CHRISTIAN ASSOCIAT
Also Called: Y M C A
2020 Tremainsville Rd (43613)
PHONE..................419 475-3496
Fax: 419 475-8837
EMP: 120
SALES (corp-wide): 29.4MM Privately Held
SIC: 8641 7991 8351 7032 Civic/Social Association Physical Fitness Faclty Child Day Care Services Sport/Recreation Camp Individual/Family Svcs
PA: Young Men's Christian Association Of Greater Toledo
1500 N Superior St Fl 2
Toledo OH 43604
419 729-8135

(G-18171)
YOUNG SERVICES INC (PA)
Also Called: Toddler's School
806 Starr Ave (43605-2362)
PHONE..................419 704-2009
Michael Tersigni, President

EMP: 25
SALES (est): 6.1MM Privately Held
SIC: 8351 8211 Group day care center; elementary & secondary schools

(G-18172)
YOUNG WOMENS CHRISTIAN
1018 Jefferson Ave (43604-5941)
PHONE..................419 241-3235
Taryn Payne, Principal
Shelly Ulrich, Principal
Lisa McDuffie, Exec Dir
Winda Birt, Director
Jan Bruggeman, Director
EMP: 70 EST: 1891
SQ FT: 82,470
SALES: 3.8MM Privately Held
SIC: 8351 7032 8322 Child day care services; youth camps; emergency shelters

(G-18173)
YOUNG WOMNS CHRSTN ASSC LIMA
Also Called: YWCA
1018 Jefferson Ave (43604-5941)
PHONE..................419 241-3230
Carol Simons, President
Marianne Carreno, Office Mgr
Renee Wells, Office Mgr
Ali Hufane, Case Mgr
Debra Monroe, Program Mgr
EMP: 45
SQ FT: 5,156
SALES: 4.5MM Privately Held
SIC: 8641 Youth organizations

(G-18174)
YRC INC
Also Called: Roadway Express
4431 South Ave (43615-6416)
PHONE..................419 729-0631
John McAbier, General Mgr
John Mc Aber, Manager
EMP: 300
SALES (corp-wide): 5B Publicly Held
WEB: www.roadway.com
SIC: 4213 4212 Contract haulers; local trucking, without storage
HQ: Yrc Inc.
10990 Roe Ave
Overland Park KS 66211
913 696-6100

(G-18175)
ZEPF CENTER
905 Nebraska Ave (43607-4222)
PHONE..................419 255-4050
Jennifer Moses, CEO
EMP: 40
SALES (corp-wide): 37.8MM Privately Held
SIC: 8093 Mental health clinic, outpatient
PA: Zepf Center
6605 W Central Ave # 100
Toledo OH 43617
419 841-7701

(G-18176)
ZEPF CENTER (PA)
6605 W Central Ave # 100 (43617-1000)
PHONE..................419 841-7701
Adam Nutt, CFO
Nancy Paige, Office Mgr
Marilyn Ryder, Office Mgr
Krystal Hughes, Case Mgr
Beth Ayer, Manager
EMP: 70
SQ FT: 25,000
SALES: 37.8MM Privately Held
WEB: www.zepfcom.com
SIC: 8093 Mental health clinic, outpatient

(G-18177)
ZEPF CENTER
Network
6605 W Central Ave # 100 (43617-1000)
PHONE..................419 213-5627
Jennifer Moses, Branch Mgr
EMP: 30
SALES (corp-wide): 37.8MM Privately Held
WEB: www.zepfcom.com
SIC: 8093 8331 Mental health clinic, outpatient; job training & vocational rehabilitation services

PA: Zepf Center
6605 W Central Ave # 100
Toledo OH 43617
419 841-7701

(G-18178)
ZEPF CENTER
525 Hamilton St Ste 101a (43604-8547)
PHONE..................................419 255-4050
Frank Ayers, *Principal*
EMP: 30
SALES (corp-wide): 37.8MM **Privately Held**
WEB: www.zepfcom.com
SIC: 8093 8011 Mental health clinic, outpatient; clinic, operated by physicians
PA: Zepf Center
6605 W Central Ave # 100
Toledo OH 43617
419 841-7701

(G-18179)
ZEPF CENTER
Network
1301 Monroe St (43604-5815)
PHONE..................................419 213-5627
Jennifer Moses, *Branch Mgr*
EMP: 30
SALES (corp-wide): 37.8MM **Privately Held**
WEB: www.zepfcom.com
SIC: 8093 Mental health clinic, outpatient
PA: Zepf Center
6605 W Central Ave # 100
Toledo OH 43617
419 841-7701

(G-18180)
ZEPF HOUSING CORP ONE INC
Also Called: Ottawa House
5310 Hill Ave (43615-5805)
PHONE..................................419 531-0019
Kendell Alexander, *Exec Dir*
EMP: 125
SALES: 86.2K
SALES (corp-wide): 37.8MM **Privately Held**
WEB: www.zepfcom.com
SIC: 6513 Apartment building operators
PA: Zepf Center
6605 W Central Ave # 100
Toledo OH 43617
419 841-7701

Toronto
Jefferson County

(G-18181)
BUCKEYE MECHANICAL CONTG INC
2325 Township Road 370 (43964-7992)
PHONE..................................740 282-0089
Robert Hickle, *President*
Dennis Hickle, *Vice Pres*
Aimee Glenn, *Treasurer*
Earla Hickle, *Treasurer*
Melody Larkins, *Admin Sec*
EMP: 46
SALES (est): 5.6MM **Privately Held**
SIC: 1711 7389 Mechanical contractor;

(G-18182)
CARL MILLS
1005 Franklin St (43964-1153)
PHONE..................................740 282-2382
Carl Mills, *Owner*
EMP: 100 **EST:** 1991
SALES (est): 891.1K **Privately Held**
SIC: 8082 Home health care services

(G-18183)
CATTRELL COMPANIES INC
906 Franklin St (43964-1152)
P.O. Box 367 (43964-0367)
PHONE..................................740 537-2481
Christine Hargrave, *President*
George R Cattrell, *Corp Secy*
Thomas L Wilson, *Vice Pres*
Brad Burkhead, *Project Mgr*
Tom Schiffer, *Project Mgr*
EMP: 52 **EST:** 1939
SQ FT: 4,000

SALES: 16MM **Privately Held**
WEB: www.cattrell.com
SIC: 1711 1731 1542 Mechanical contractor; general electrical contractor; commercial & office building contractors

(G-18184)
EXPRESS ENERGY SVCS OPER LP
1515 Franklin St (43964-1029)
PHONE..................................740 337-4530
EMP: 42
SALES (corp-wide): 825.2MM **Privately Held**
SIC: 1389 Oil field services
PA: Express Energy Services Operating, Lp
9800 Richmond Ave Ste 500
Houston TX 77042
713 625-7400

(G-18185)
SHADCO INC
Also Called: Trans World Alloys
100 Titanium Way (43964-1990)
PHONE..................................310 217-8777
Marc Donegan, *CEO*
Liz Fritzinger, *Treasurer*
▲ **EMP:** 26
SQ FT: 5,400
SALES (est): 7MM
SALES (corp-wide): 225.3B **Publicly Held**
SIC: 5051 Nonferrous metal sheets, bars, rods, etc.; aluminum bars, rods, ingots, sheets, pipes, plates, etc.; iron & steel (ferrous) products
HQ: Precision Castparts Corp.
4650 Sw Mcdam Ave Ste 300
Portland OR 97239
503 946-4800

(G-18186)
TORONTO EMERGENCY MEDICAL SVC
Also Called: Tems
201 S 4th St (43964-1369)
P.O. Box 307 (43964-0307)
PHONE..................................740 537-3891
John Olesky, *President*
EMP: 27
SALES (est): 578.2K **Privately Held**
SIC: 4119 Ambulance service

Trenton
Butler County

(G-18187)
CAL CRIM INC
Also Called: Business Consultants Limited
384 Deer Run Dr (45067-1653)
PHONE..................................513 563-5500
Claude Hinds, *Ch of Bd*
Gregg E Hollenbaugh, *President*
Nancy S Baker, *Treasurer*
Randall K Hollenbaugh, *Treasurer*
Terri S Hollenbaugh, *Admin Sec*
EMP: 130 **EST:** 1913
SQ FT: 2,250
SALES (est): 2.9MM **Privately Held**
WEB: www.calcrim.net
SIC: 7381 Protective services, guard; security guard service; private investigator

(G-18188)
LESAINT LOGISTICS LLC
5564 Alan B Shepherd St (45067-9401)
PHONE..................................513 988-0101
Delbert Murphy, *Manager*
Kevin Rhymer, *Manager*
EMP: 80
SALES (corp-wide): 95.7MM **Privately Held**
WEB: www.intrupa.com
SIC: 4731 4225 8742 Freight transportation arrangement; general warehousing & storage; materials mgmt. (purchasing, handling, inventory) consultant
PA: Lesaint Logistics, Llc
868 W Crossroads Pkwy
Romeoville IL 60446
630 243-5950

(G-18189)
NOAHS ARK CHILD DEV CTR
3259 Wayne Madison Rd (45067-9532)
P.O. Box 138 (45067-0138)
PHONE..................................513 988-0921
Rebecca Ncey, *Director*
Jeff Marshall, *Administration*
EMP: 34
SALES (est): 892.1K **Privately Held**
SIC: 8351 Child day care services

(G-18190)
PROCESS PUMP & SEAL INC
2993 Woodsdale Rd (45067-9754)
PHONE..................................513 988-7000
Daniel Quenneville, *Principal*
Martin Onkst, *Vice Pres*
EMP: 28
SQ FT: 12,000
SALES: 10MM **Privately Held**
WEB: www.processpumpandseal.com
SIC: 5085 5084 Packing, industrial; seals, industrial; pumps & pumping equipment

Trotwood
Montgomery County

(G-18191)
BIO-MDCAL APPLCATIONS OHIO INC
Also Called: Fresenius Med Care Dayton W
4100 Salem Ave (45416)
PHONE..................................937 279-3120
Ron Kuerbitz, *CEO*
Mary Garber, *Manager*
EMP: 30
SALES (est): 880K **Privately Held**
SIC: 8092 Kidney dialysis centers

(G-18192)
CARRIAGE INN OF TROTWOOD INC
Also Called: SHILOH SPRINGS CARE CENTER
3500 Shiloh Springs Rd (45426-2260)
PHONE..................................937 854-1180
Ken Bernsen, *President*
EMP: 104
SQ FT: 6,500
SALES: 6.4MM **Privately Held**
SIC: 8051 Convalescent home with continuous nursing care

(G-18193)
E T FINANCIAL SERVICE INC
Also Called: Jackson Hewitt Tax Service
4550 Salem Ave (45416-1700)
PHONE..................................937 716-1726
Emmanuel Umoren, *President*
Theo Adegdoruwa, *Vice Pres*
EMP: 40
SQ FT: 1,800
SALES (est): 871.4K **Privately Held**
SIC: 7291 8721 7389 Tax return preparation services; billing & bookkeeping service; financial services

Troy
Miami County

(G-18194)
ARC ABRASIVES INC
Also Called: A R C
2131 Corporate Dr (45373-1067)
P.O. Box 10 (45373-0010)
PHONE..................................800 888-4885
Anthony H Stayman, *CEO*
Anthony Stayman, *President*
▲ **EMP:** 76 **EST:** 1960
SALES (est): 67.1MM **Privately Held**
WEB: www.arcabrasives.com
SIC: 5085 3291 2296 Abrasives; abrasive products; tire cord & fabrics

(G-18195)
ARETT SALES CORP
1261 Brukner Dr (45373-3843)
PHONE..................................937 552-2005
David McCarthy, *Branch Mgr*
EMP: 65

SALES (corp-wide): 127.4MM **Privately Held**
WEB: www.arett.com
SIC: 4225 General warehousing
PA: Arett Sales Corporation
9285 Commerce Hwy
Pennsauken NJ 08110
856 751-1224

(G-18196)
BIGELOW CORPORATION (PA)
Also Called: Troy Bowl
1530 Mckaig Ave (45373-2641)
PHONE..................................937 339-3315
Rex Bigelow, *President*
Jan Bigelow, *Treasurer*
EMP: 30
SQ FT: 7,500
SALES (est): 1.2MM **Privately Held**
SIC: 7933 5941 Ten pin center; sporting goods & bicycle shops

(G-18197)
BRACKETT BUILDERS INC (PA)
185 Marybill Dr S (45373-1074)
PHONE..................................937 339-7505
Eric Stahl, *President*
Ed Langenkamp, *Superintendent*
Andy Middendorf, *Superintendent*
Thomas Hoying, *Vice Pres*
Vern Hoying, *Vice Pres*
EMP: 27
SQ FT: 9,200
SALES: 42.2MM **Privately Held**
WEB: www.brackettbuilders.com
SIC: 1542 Commercial & office buildings, renovation & repair; commercial & office building, new construction; hospital construction; institutional building construction

(G-18198)
CITY OF TROY
Also Called: Troy City Water Distribution
1400 Experiment Farm Rd (45373-8788)
PHONE..................................937 335-1914
Rosaleen Rayman, *Branch Mgr*
Larry Lewis, *Manager*
EMP: 40
SQ FT: 23,760 **Privately Held**
WEB: www.troyohio.gov
SIC: 4941 Water supply
PA: City Of Troy
100 S Market St Ste 1
Troy OH 45373
937 335-2224

(G-18199)
COUNTY OF MIAMI
Also Called: Miami Co Highway Dept
2100 N County Road 25a (45373-1333)
PHONE..................................937 335-1314
Jeff Vore, *Foreman/Supr*
Jerry Jackson, *Manager*
Sandy Curtis, *Admin Sec*
EMP: 30 **Privately Held**
WEB: www.co.miami.oh.us
SIC: 8744 Base maintenance (providing personnel on continuing basis)
PA: County Of Miami
201 W Main St
Troy OH 45373
937 440-5900

(G-18200)
DUNGAN & LEFEVRE CO LPA (PA)
210 W Main St (45373-3240)
PHONE..................................937 339-0511
William J Mc Graw III, *President*
Alan M Kappers,
Karen Breeze, *Legal Staff*
James D Brookshire, *Associate*
EMP: 30
SQ FT: 4,200
SALES (est): 3.9MM **Privately Held**
WEB: www.dungan-lefevre.com
SIC: 8111 General practice attorney, lawyer

(G-18201)
EVER GREEN LAWN CARE INC
Also Called: Ever-Green Turf & Landscape
625 Olympic Dr (45373-2305)
PHONE..................................937 335-6418
Joseph Duncan, *President*

Gina Duncan, *Corp Secy*
Kirk Persinger, *Vice Pres*
Patty Johnston, *Office Mgr*
Mark Eickhoff, *Manager*
EMP: 30 **EST:** 1970
SQ FT: 6,000
SALES (est): 1.9MM **Privately Held**
SIC: 0782 0781 Lawn care services; land-scape services

(G-18202)
FTECH R&D NORTH AMERICA INC (HQ)
1191 Horizon West Ct (45373-7560)
PHONE..................................937 339-2777
Bing Liu, *COO*
EMP: 56
SQ FT: 50,000
SALES (est): 8.4MM
SALES (corp-wide): 2.1B **Privately Held**
SIC: 8731 3714 Commercial physical re-search; motor vehicle parts & accessories
PA: F-Tech Inc.
19, Showanuma, Shobucho
Kuki STM 346-0
480 855-211

(G-18203)
GENESIS HEALTHCARE
Also Called: TROY CENTER
2 Crescent Dr (45373-2714)
PHONE..................................937 875-4604
EMP: 1161 **EST:** 2014
SALES: 11MM **Publicly Held**
SIC: 8351 Child day care services
HQ: Toledo Harborside Limited Partnership
101 Sun Ave Ne
Albuquerque NM 87109

(G-18204)
GREENTECH CORPORATION
Also Called: Greentech Lawn and Irrigation
1405 S County Road 25a (45373-4243)
P.O. Box 679 (45373-0679)
PHONE..................................937 339-4758
Larry Smith, *President*
EMP: 35
SQ FT: 2,400
SALES (est): 4.2MM **Privately Held**
SIC: 0782 Lawn care services; lawn serv-ices

(G-18205)
HARBORSIDE TROY LLC
Also Called: Troy Center
512 Crescent Dr (45373-2718)
PHONE..................................937 335-7161
Rick Edwards, *Treasurer*
EMP: 99
SALES (est): 294.8K **Privately Held**
SIC: 8051 Skilled nursing care facilities

(G-18206)
HOBART BROS STICK ELECTRODE
101 Trade Sq E (45373-2476)
PHONE..................................937 332-5375
Steve Knostman, *Owner*
EMP: 109
SALES (est): 3.2MM **Privately Held**
SIC: 7692 Welding repair

(G-18207)
HOSPICE OF MIAMI COUNTY INC
550 Summit Ave Ste 101 (45373-3047)
P.O. Box 502 (45373-0502)
PHONE..................................937 335-5191
Susan Hemm, *Marketing Staff*
Nancy Magel, *Exec Dir*
EMP: 50
SALES: 9.8MM **Privately Held**
WEB: www.homc.org
SIC: 8082 Home health care services

(G-18208)
ITW FOOD EQUIPMENT GROUP LLC (HQ)
Also Called: Hobart
701 S Ridge Ave (45374-0001)
PHONE..................................937 332-2396
Tom Szafranski, *President*
Chris O Herlihy, *Exec VP*
Jennifer Monnin, *Vice Pres*
Jeff CPM, *Manager*

Trudy Tolbert, *Manager*
◆ **EMP:** 1100
SALES (est): 528.4MM
SALES (corp-wide): 14.7B **Publicly Held**
SIC: 5046 3556 Restaurant equipment & supplies; food products machinery
PA: Illinois Tool Works Inc.
155 Harlem Ave
Glenview IL 60025
847 724-7500

(G-18209)
KEY II SECURITY INC
110 W Main St (45373-3214)
P.O. Box 434, Tipp City (45371-0434)
PHONE..................................937 339-8530
Jack D Cheaddle, *President*
EMP: 50
SALES (est): 955K **Privately Held**
SIC: 7381 Detective agency

(G-18210)
LEOS LA PIAZZA INC
Also Called: La Piazza Pasta & Grill
2 N Market St (45373-3216)
PHONE..................................937 339-5553
Leo Anticoli, *President*
Peggy Anticoli, *Vice Pres*
Mike Anticoli, *Treasurer*
EMP: 40
SQ FT: 3,000
SALES (est): 1.5MM **Privately Held**
SIC: 5812 7299 Italian restaurant; banquet hall facilities

(G-18211)
LOWES HOME CENTERS LLC
2000 W Main St (45373-1019)
PHONE..................................937 339-2544
Mike Haehl, *Store Mgr*
Jerry Breger, *Manager*
EMP: 155
SALES (corp-wide): 68.6B **Publicly Held**
SIC: 5211 5031 5722 5064 Home cen-ters; building materials, exterior; building materials, interior; household appliance stores; electrical appliances, television & radio
HQ: Lowe's Home Centers, Llc
1605 Curtis Bridge Rd
Wilkesboro NC 28697
336 658-4000

(G-18212)
MIAMI CNTY CMNTY ACTION CUNCIL
Also Called: MIAMI COUNTY JOB TRAINING PART
1695 Troy Sidney Rd (45373-9794)
PHONE..................................937 335-7921
Jack Baird, *Director*
EMP: 35 **EST:** 1966
SQ FT: 11,000
SALES: 688.9K **Privately Held**
SIC: 8399 6513 Community action agency; apartment building operators

(G-18213)
MIAMI COUNTY CHILDRENS SVCS BD
510 W Water St Ste 210 (45373-2982)
PHONE..................................937 335-4103
June Cannon, *Exec Dir*
EMP: 32
SALES (est): 599.9K **Privately Held**
SIC: 8322 Child related social services; substance abuse counseling

(G-18214)
MIAMI COUNTY PARK DISTRICT
2645 E State Route 41 (45373-9692)
PHONE..................................937 335-6273
Jerry Eldred, *Director*
EMP: 40
SALES (est): 1.4MM **Privately Held**
WEB: www.miamicountyparks.com
SIC: 8999 8641 Natural resource preser-vation service; civic social & fraternal as-sociations

(G-18215)
MIGHTY MAC INVESTMENTS INC (PA)
1494 Lytle Rd (45373-9401)
P.O. Box 39 (45373-0039)
PHONE..................................937 335-2928
Jeffrey W Earhart, *President*
Matt Welch, *Business Mgr*
Dan Mader, *Vice Pres*
Jason Reynolds, *Vice Pres*
Tim Anderson, *Opers Staff*
EMP: 40
SQ FT: 21,000
SALES (est): 72.3MM **Privately Held**
WEB: www.earhartpetroleum.com
SIC: 5172 5541 5983 Fuel oil; lubricating oils & greases; gasoline; filling stations, gasoline; fuel oil dealers

(G-18216)
MILCON CONCRETE INC
1360 S County Road 25a 25 A (45373)
PHONE..................................937 339-6274
Mark Miller, *President*
EMP: 25
SALES (est): 4MM **Privately Held**
WEB: www.millmark-inc.com
SIC: 1771 Concrete work
PA: Millmark Construction, Inc
1360 S County Rd 25a
Troy OH

(G-18217)
NATIONWIDE TRUCK BROKERS INC
3355 S County Road 25a (45373-9384)
PHONE..................................937 335-9229
Mike Wilcox, *Branch Mgr*
EMP: 25
SALES (corp-wide): 44.8MM **Privately Held**
SIC: 4213 Contract haulers
PA: Nationwide Truck Brokers, Inc.
4203 R B Chaffee Mem Dr
Wyoming MI 49548
616 878-5554

(G-18218)
OHIO & INDIANA ROOFING
17 S Market St (45373-3217)
PHONE..................................937 339-8768
Michael Bruns, *Principal*
EMP: 25
SALES (est): 109K **Privately Held**
SIC: 1761 Roof repair

(G-18219)
OHIO INNS INC
Also Called: Residence Inn By Marriott
87 Troy Town Dr (45373-2327)
PHONE..................................937 440-9303
Frank Crisofia, *President*
Julie Isely, *VP Sales*
EMP: 30
SALES (est): 1.4MM **Privately Held**
WEB: www.ohioinns.com
SIC: 7011 Hotels & motels

(G-18220)
OHIO MACHINERY CO
Also Called: Caterpillar
1281 Brukner Dr (45373-3843)
PHONE..................................937 335-7660
Toll Free:......................................888
John Fiedler, *Sales Staff*
Tj Perkins, *Marketing Staff*
Greg Hallaway, *Manager*
EMP: 57
SALES (corp-wide): 222.7MM **Privately Held**
WEB: www.enginesnow.com
SIC: 5082 General construction machinery & equipment
PA: Ohio Machinery Co.
3993 E Royalton Rd
Broadview Heights OH 44147
440 526-6200

(G-18221)
PANASONIC CORP NORTH AMERICA
America Matsushita Electronic
1400 W Market St (45373-3889)
PHONE..................................201 392-6872
Seiji Kasamatsu, *President*

Adam Yamamoto, *QC Dir*
EMP: 25
SALES (corp-wide): 74.9B **Privately Held**
WEB: www.panasonic.com
SIC: 5064 Electrical appliances, television & radio
HQ: Panasonic Corporation Of North Amer-ica
2 Riverfront Plz Ste 200
Newark NJ 07102
201 348-7000

(G-18222)
PUBLIC SAFETY OHIO DEPARTMENT
Also Called: Testing and Inspection Fcilty
1275 Experiment Farm Rd (45373-1065)
PHONE..................................937 335-6209
EMP: 32 **Privately Held**
SIC: 9221 8011 5399 State highway pa-trol; physicians' office, including special-ists; surplus & salvage goods
HQ: Ohio Department Of Public Safety
1970 W Broad St Fl 5
Columbus OH 43223

(G-18223)
R P L CORPORATION
Also Called: Motel 6
1375 W Market St (45373-3858)
PHONE..................................937 335-0021
William A Roll MD, *President*
Juan M Palomar MD, *Treasurer*
Frank Scott, *Admin Sec*
EMP: 105
SQ FT: 200,000
SALES (est): 2.1MM **Privately Held**
SIC: 7011 5812 5813 Motels; family restaurants; cocktail lounge

(G-18224)
R T INDUSTRIES INC (PA)
Also Called: CHAMPION INDUSTRIES DIV
110 Foss Way (45373-1430)
PHONE..................................937 335-5784
Ann Hinkle, *Superintendent*
Karen Mayer, *Superintendent*
EMP: 146
SQ FT: 18,000
SALES: 4.3MM **Privately Held**
SIC: 3579 8331 7349 2789 Paper cut-ters, trimmers & punches; sheltered work-shop; janitorial service, contract basis; bookbinding & related work; home for the mentally handicapped

(G-18225)
R T INDUSTRIES INC
Also Called: Riverside of Miami County
1625 Troy Sidney Rd (45373-9794)
PHONE..................................937 339-8313
Brian Green, *Superintendent*
Karen Mayer, *Branch Mgr*
EMP: 140
SALES (corp-wide): 4.3MM **Privately Held**
SIC: 8331 9111 Sheltered workshop; county supervisors' & executives' offices
PA: R T Industries Inc
110 Foss Way
Troy OH 45373
937 335-5784

(G-18226)
REM-OHIO INC
721 Lincoln Ave (45373-3176)
PHONE..................................937 335-8267
EMP: 40
SALES (corp-wide): 2.8MM **Privately Held**
SIC: 8361 Home for the mentally retarded
PA: Rem-Ohio, Inc
6921 York Ave S
Minneapolis MN 55435
952 925-5067

(G-18227)
REMEDI SENIORCARE OF OHIO LLC (HQ)
962 S Dorset Rd (45373-4705)
PHONE..................................800 232-4239
Rene Deller, *General Mgr*
John Jay Meyer,
EMP: 41
SQ FT: 20,000

SALES (est): 143.4MM **Privately Held**
SIC: 5122 Pharmaceuticals

(G-18228)
S P S INC
Also Called: Hampton Inn
45 Troy Town Dr (45373-2327)
PHONE.................................937 339-7801
Thomas J Schippel, *President*
Sheila Patel, *Manager*
Raman Patel, *Admin Sec*
EMP: 30
SALES (est): 2.1MM **Privately Held**
SIC: 7011 7991 5813 Hotels; physical fitness facilities; drinking places

(G-18229)
ST PATRICK CHURCH INC (PA)
Also Called: St Patrick School
409 E Main St (45373-3431)
PHONE.................................937 335-2833
Thomas Brunner, *Pastor*
EMP: 26
SALES (est): 1MM **Privately Held**
WEB: www.stpattroy.org
SIC: 8661 8211 8351 Catholic Church; Catholic elementary school; preschool center

(G-18230)
TIME WARNER CABLE INC
1450 Experiment Farm Rd (45373-8788)
PHONE.................................937 483-5152
Danny Schiffer, *Branch Mgr*
EMP: 50
SQ FT: 12,900
SALES (corp-wide): 43.6B **Publicly Held**
SIC: 4841 Cable television services
HQ: Spectrum Management Holding Company, Llc
400 Atlantic St
Stamford CT 06901
203 905-7801

(G-18231)
TONI & MARIE BADER
831 E Main St (45373-3420)
PHONE.................................937 339-3621
Toni O Bader, *Agent*
EMP: 30
SALES (est): 1MM **Privately Held**
SIC: 8742 Real estate consultant

(G-18232)
TRANSFREIGHT INC
3355 S County Road 25a B (45373-9384)
PHONE.................................937 332-0366
Darrell Dewberry, *Manager*
EMP: 32
SALES (corp-wide): 2.6B **Privately Held**
SIC: 4731 Freight forwarding
HQ: Penske Logistics Canada Ltd
3065 King St E
Kitchener ON N2A 1
519 650-0123

(G-18233)
TROY CHRISTIAN SCHOOL
1586 Mckaig Rd (45373-2670)
PHONE.................................937 339-5692
Gary Wilber, *Superintendent*
EMP: 60
SQ FT: 32,000
SALES: 6.8MM **Privately Held**
SIC: 8211 8351 Catholic combined elementary & secondary school; kindergarten; private elementary school; child day care services

(G-18234)
TROY COUNTRY CLUB INC
1830 Peters Rd (45373-3868)
P.O. Box 459 (45373-0459)
PHONE.................................937 335-5691
Philip Zwierzchowski, *Manager*
Phil Zwierzchowski, *Manager*
EMP: 50
SQ FT: 5,000
SALES: 1MM **Privately Held**
WEB: www.troycountryclub.com
SIC: 7997 Country club, membership

(G-18235)
UNITED RETAIL LOGISTICS SVCS
1501 Experiment Farm Rd (45373-9466)
PHONE.................................937 332-1500
Rafael Benaria, *President*
Kent Frauenberger, *Vice Pres*
EMP: 160
SQ FT: 4,000
SALES (est): 8.1MM **Privately Held**
WEB: www.unitedretail.com
SIC: 4225 General warehousing & storage

(G-18236)
US BANK NATIONAL ASSOCIATION
Also Called: US Bank
910 W Main St (45373-2846)
PHONE.................................937 335-8351
Thomas Atkinson, *Branch Mgr*
EMP: 40
SALES (corp-wide): 25.7B **Publicly Held**
WEB: www.firstar.com
SIC: 6021 National commercial banks
HQ: U.S. Bank National Association
425 Walnut St Fl 14
Cincinnati OH 45202
513 632-4234

(G-18237)
UVMC MANAGEMENT CORPORATION (HQ)
3130 N County Road 25a (45373-1309)
PHONE.................................937 440-4000
Michael Maiberger, *President*
EMP: 66
SQ FT: 169,000
SALES (est): 25.6MM
SALES (corp-wide): 17.2K **Privately Held**
SIC: 8051 8062 Skilled nursing care facilities; general medical & surgical hospitals
PA: Premier Health Partners
110 N Main St Ste 450
Dayton OH 45402
937 499-9596

(G-18238)
UVMC NURSING CARE INC
Also Called: Koester Pavilion Nursing Home
3232 N County Road 25a (45373-1338)
PHONE.................................937 440-7663
Jessica Suba, *Corp Comm Staff*
Pat Meyer, *Manager*
Joseph Hughes, *Director*
Amy Kentner, *Administration*
EMP: 200
SQ FT: 57,216
SALES (corp-wide): 20.3MM **Privately Held**
WEB: www.koesterpavilion.com
SIC: 8051 Skilled nursing care facilities
PA: Uvmc Nursing Care, Inc.
3130 N County Road 25a
Troy OH 45373
937 440-4000

(G-18239)
VULCAN FEG
750 Lincoln Ave (45373-3137)
PHONE.................................937 332-2763
EMP: 80
SQ FT: 1,250,000
SALES (est): 5.3MM **Privately Held**
SIC: 5046 Commercial cooking & food service equipment

(G-18240)
ZEBO PRODUCTIONS
1875 Barnhart Rd (45373-9589)
PHONE.................................937 339-0397
Mike Fischer, *President*
EMP: 55
SALES (est): 310.8K **Privately Held**
SIC: 7822 Motion picture & tape distribution

Twinsburg
Summit County

(G-18241)
ADVANTAGE WAYPOINT LLC
9458 Ravenna Rd (44087-2104)
PHONE.................................248 919-3144
Marylou Wethington, *Admin Mgr*
EMP: 28
SALES (corp-wide): 200MM **Privately Held**
SIC: 5141 Food brokers
PA: Advantage Waypoint Llc
13521 Prestige Pl
Tampa FL 33635
813 358-5900

(G-18242)
AIR SUPPLY CO (PA)
Also Called: Allied Separation
2300 E Enterprise Pkwy (44087-2349)
PHONE.................................704 732-8034
Michael E Williams, *President*
Pam Caskey, *Sales Staff*
Lori Williams, *Executive*
◆ **EMP:** 31
SALES (est): 8.6MM **Privately Held**
WEB: www.airsupplycompany.com
SIC: 5085 Filters, industrial

(G-18243)
AMERICAN ROCK MECHANICS INC
9241 Ravenna Rd Ste 6 (44087-2451)
PHONE.................................330 963-0550
EMP: 27
SQ FT: 5,500
SALES: 3MM **Privately Held**
SIC: 8711 Engineering Services

(G-18244)
ANDERSEN & ASSOCIATES INC
1960 Summit Commerce Park (44087-2372)
PHONE.................................330 425-8500
Tom Forrester, *Vice Pres*
EMP: 50
SALES (est): 4.1MM
SALES (corp-wide): 86.6MM **Privately Held**
SIC: 5084 Materials handling machinery
PA: Andersen & Associates, Inc.
30575 Anderson Ct
Wixom MI 48393
248 960-6800

(G-18245)
APPLE GATE OPERATING CO INC
Also Called: Hilton Garden Inn Twinsburg
8971 Wilcox Dr (44087-1945)
PHONE.................................330 405-4488
Robert Voelker, *President*
EMP: 40
SALES (est): 2.7MM **Privately Held**
SIC: 7011 Hotels & motels

(G-18246)
ASSURAMED INC (HQ)
1810 Summit Commerce Park (44087-2300)
PHONE.................................330 963-6998
Michael B Petras Jr, *CEO*
Kurt Packer, *COO*
Andy Hinkle, *Vice Pres*
Chris Lindroth, *Vice Pres*
Mark Wells, *Vice Pres*
EMP: 39
SALES (est): 76.4MM
SALES (corp-wide): 136.8B **Publicly Held**
SIC: 5047 Medical & hospital equipment
PA: Cardinal Health, Inc.
7000 Cardinal Pl
Dublin OH 43017
614 757-5000

(G-18247)
ATLAS STEEL PRODUCTS CO (PA)
Also Called: AB Tube Company
7990 Bavaria Rd (44087-2252)
PHONE.................................330 425-1600
John Adams, *President*
Fred Barrera, *COO*
Claude Bianchi, *Opers Mgr*
Mike Lozar, *Traffic Mgr*
Victoria Widmor, *Finance Mgr*
◆ **EMP:** 80 **EST:** 1957
SQ FT: 120,000
SALES (est): 58.5MM **Privately Held**
WEB: www.atlassteel.com
SIC: 5051 Sheets, metal; steel

(G-18248)
AVID TECHNOLOGIES INC
2112 Case Pkwy Ste 1 (44087-2378)
P.O. Box 468 (44087-0468)
PHONE.................................330 487-0770
David Shen, *CEO*
Arnie Grever, *President*
Joseph R Daprile, *Vice Pres*
Paul M Barlak, *Treasurer*
EMP: 45 **EST:** 2014
SQ FT: 12,000
SALES: 10.4MM
SALES (corp-wide): 19B **Publicly Held**
SIC: 8711 5045 Consulting engineer; computer software
HQ: Premier Farnell Corp.
4180 Highlander Pkwy
Richfield OH 44286
216 525-4300

(G-18249)
BASEMENT SYSTEMS OHIO INC
8295 Darrow Rd (44087-2307)
PHONE.................................330 423-4430
Michael Rusk, *President*
Joseph Rusk, *Vice Pres*
EMP: 105
SQ FT: 65,000
SALES (est): 7.6MM **Privately Held**
WEB: www.basementsystemsohio.com
SIC: 1799 Waterproofing

(G-18250)
BEACON SALES ACQUISITION INC
Also Called: North Coast Coml Roofg Systems
2440 Edison Blvd (44087-2340)
PHONE.................................330 425-3359
Sam Flora, *Opers Mgr*
Britt Cherry, *Engineer*
Michael Leanza, *Credit Mgr*
April Stewart, *Credit Staff*
Steve Keyes, *Sales Mgr*
EMP: 200
SALES (corp-wide): 4.3B **Publicly Held**
SIC: 5033 Roofing, asphalt & sheet metal
HQ: Beacon Sales Acquisition, Inc.
50 Webster Ave
Somerville MA 02143
877 645-7663

(G-18251)
CEM-BASE INC
Also Called: Trimor
8530 N Boyle Pkwy (44087-2267)
PHONE.................................330 963-3101
John R Morris III, *President*
Steve Taylor, *Vice Pres*
Jeremy Neff, *Project Mgr*
EMP: 25
SALES (est): 2.9MM **Privately Held**
SIC: 1771 Concrete work

(G-18252)
CHILDRENS HOSP MED CTR AKRON
8054 Darrow Rd (44087-2381)
PHONE.................................330 425-3344
Jeanne Fenton, *Branch Mgr*
Jane Messemer, *Med Doctor*
EMP: 732
SALES (corp-wide): 747.4MM **Privately Held**
SIC: 8062 General medical & surgical hospitals

PA: Childrens Hospital Medical Center Of Akron
1 Perkins Sq
Akron OH 44308
330 543-1000

(G-18253)
CLEVELAND ELECTRIC LABS CO (PA)
Also Called: Cleveland Electric Labs
1776 Enterprise Pkwy (44087-2246)
PHONE...................................800 447-2207
Jack Allan Lieske, *President*
C M Lemmon, *Principal*
Val Jean Lieske, *Vice Pres*
Rebecca Lieske, *Admin Sec*
EMP: 50
SQ FT: 30,000
SALES (est): 10.5MM **Privately Held**
WEB: www.clevelandelectriclabs.com
SIC: 3823 7699 Thermocouples, industrial process type; professional instrument repair services; industrial machinery & equipment repair

(G-18254)
CLEVELAND PUMP REPR & SVCS LLC
Also Called: C P R
1761 Highland Rd (44087-2220)
PHONE...................................330 963-3100
James Durkin, *General Mgr*
Tony Dailey,
EMP: 25
SQ FT: 23,000
SALES (est): 6.3MM **Privately Held**
WEB: www.clevelandpumprepair.com
SIC: 7699 Industrial machinery & equipment repair; pumps & pumping equipment repair

(G-18255)
CME ACQUISITIONS LLC
Also Called: Cleveland Metal Exchange
1900 Case Pkwy S (44087-2358)
PHONE...................................216 464-4480
Jeff Haas, *President*
Paul Kytta, *Traffic Mgr*
Ron Glazer, *CFO*
Debbie Albee, *Sales Staff*
Tom Consolo, *Sales Staff*
▲ EMP: 35
SALES: 3MM **Privately Held**
WEB: www.clevelandmetal.com
SIC: 5051 Steel

(G-18256)
CONTRACTORS STEEL COMPANY
8383 Boyle Pkwy (44087-2236)
PHONE...................................330 425-3050
Mitch Kubasek, *Manager*
EMP: 49
SQ FT: 58,000
SALES (corp-wide): 250.1MM **Privately Held**
WEB: www.contractorssteel.com
SIC: 5051 3498 3312 Steel; plates, metal; sheets, metal; strip, metal; fabricated pipe & fittings; blast furnaces & steel mills
HQ: Contractors Steel Company
36555 Amrhein Rd
Livonia MI 48150
734 464-4000

(G-18257)
COWAN SYSTEMS LLC
1882 Highland Rd (44087-2223)
PHONE...................................330 963-8483
Dave Feder, *Branch Mgr*
EMP: 48 **Privately Held**
SIC: 4213 Automobiles, transport & delivery
PA: Cowan Systems, Llc
4555 Hollins Ferry Rd
Baltimore MD 21227

(G-18258)
DMD MANAGEMENT INC
Also Called: Legacy Place
2463 Sussex Blvd (44087-2442)
PHONE...................................330 405-6040
Amy Kraynak, *Branch Mgr*
EMP: 45
SQ FT: 41,918 **Privately Held**

SIC: 8051 Convalescent home with continuous nursing care
PA: Dmd Management, Inc.
12380 Plaza Dr
Cleveland OH 44130

(G-18259)
EARLE M JORGENSEN COMPANY
Also Called: EMJ Cleveland
2060 Enterprise Pkwy (44087-2210)
PHONE...................................330 425-1500
Joanna Janic, *Human Res Mgr*
Ed King, *Branch Mgr*
Ruben Borunda, *Manager*
Jim Garcia, *Manager*
EMP: 100
SQ FT: 75,000
SALES (corp-wide): 11.5B **Publicly Held**
WEB: www.emjmetals.com
SIC: 5051 Pipe & tubing, steel; bars, metal
HQ: Earle M. Jorgensen Company
10650 Alameda St
Lynwood CA 90262
323 567-1122

(G-18260)
ENVIRONMENT CTRL BEACHWOOD INC
1897 E Aurora Rd (44087-1917)
PHONE...................................330 405-6201
James Hennessy, *President*
EMP: 70
SQ FT: 4,000
SALES (est): 1.8MM **Privately Held**
SIC: 7349 Cleaning service, industrial or commercial

(G-18261)
ENVIROTEST SYSTEMS CORP
2180 Pinnacle Pkwy (44087-2379)
PHONE...................................330 963-4464
Steve Peterson, *Manager*
EMP: 25 **Privately Held**
SIC: 7549 Emissions testing without repairs, automotive
HQ: Envirotest Systems Corp.
7 Kripes Rd
East Granby CT 06026

(G-18262)
ENVIROTEST SYSTEMS CORP
2180 Pinnacle Pkwy (44087-2379)
PHONE...................................330 963-4464
Steve Peterson, *Branch Mgr*
EMP: 34 **Privately Held**
WEB: www.il.etest.com
SIC: 7549 Emissions testing without repairs, automotive
HQ: Envirotest Systems Corp.
7 Kripes Rd
East Granby CT 06026

(G-18263)
ENVISION PHRM SVCS LLC
Also Called: Envision Rx Options
2181 E Aurora Rd Ste 201 (44087-1974)
PHONE...................................330 405-8080
Ben Bulkley, *CEO*
EMP: 320
SALES (est): 83.6MM
SALES (corp-wide): 21.5B **Publicly Held**
WEB: www.envisionrx.com
SIC: 6411 Insurance claim processing, except medical
PA: Rite Aid Corporation
30 Hunter Ln
Camp Hill PA 17011
717 761-2633

(G-18264)
ESSENDANT CO
2100 Highland Rd (44087-2229)
PHONE...................................330 425-4001
Dan Wolfe, *Exec VP*
Dave Martin, *Manager*
EMP: 126
SALES (corp-wide): 5B **Privately Held**
WEB: www.ussco.com
SIC: 5112 5044 Office supplies; office equipment
HQ: Essendant Co.
1 Parkway North Blvd # 100
Deerfield IL 60015
847 627-7000

(G-18265)
FACIL NORTH AMERICA INC (HQ)
Also Called: Streetsboro Operations
2242 Pinnacle Pkwy # 100 (44087-5301)
PHONE...................................330 487-2500
Rene Achten, *CEO*
Daniel Michiels, *CFO*
◆ EMP: 210
SQ FT: 150,000
SALES (est): 142.6MM
SALES (corp-wide): 5.9MM **Privately Held**
WEB: www.flexalloy.com
SIC: 5072 3452 5085 Nuts (hardware); bolts; screws; nuts, metal; fasteners, industrial: nuts, bolts, screws, etc.
PA: Facil Corporate
Geleenlaan 20
Genk 3600
894 104-50

(G-18266)
FILING SCALE COMPANY INC
1500 Enterprise Pkwy (44087-2240)
PHONE...................................330 425-3092
Kenneth J Filing Sr, *CEO*
Kenneth J Filing Jr, *President*
Linda Filing, *Vice Pres*
Rosemarie Filing, *Admin Sec*
EMP: 35
SQ FT: 12,000
SALES (est): 7.8MM **Privately Held**
WEB: www.filing-lts.com
SIC: 5046 7359 7699 Scales, except laboratory; equipment rental & leasing; scale repair service

(G-18267)
FNB CORPORATION
10071 Darrow Rd (44087-1564)
PHONE...................................330 425-1818
Jamie Williams, *Branch Mgr*
EMP: 97
SALES (corp-wide): 1.4B **Publicly Held**
SIC: 7389 6162 6029 6021 Financial services; mortgage bankers & correspondents; commercial banks; national commercial banks
PA: F.N.B. Corporation
1 N Shore Ctr 12 Fdral St
Pittsburgh PA 15212
800 555-5455

(G-18268)
FOREST CITY ERECTORS INC
Also Called: CLEVELAND CRANE RENTAL
8200 Boyle Pkwy Ste 1 (44087-2248)
PHONE...................................330 425-2345
Denise M Beers, *President*
James Mirgliotta, *Vice Pres*
EMP: 100
SQ FT: 6,000
SALES (est): 25.6MM **Privately Held**
WEB: www.forestcityerectors.com
SIC: 1791 Iron work, structural

(G-18269)
FRENCH COMPANY LLC
Also Called: Facility Connect
8289 Darrow Rd (44087-2307)
PHONE...................................330 963-4344
Scott Dahl, *CEO*
John Durkey, *President*
Christine Callahan, *Vice Pres*
David Mechenbier, *CFO*
Tony D'Ambrosio, *Accountant*
EMP: 75
SALES: 7.4MM
SALES (corp-wide): 1.8MM **Privately Held**
WEB: www.thefrenchcompany.com
SIC: 7699 8741 Cleaning services; management services
HQ: Technibilt, Ltd.
700 Technibilt Dr
Newton NC 28658
828 464-7388

(G-18270)
FUCHS LUBRICANTS CO
Also Called: Fuchs Franklin Div
8036 Bavaria Rd (44087-2262)
PHONE...................................330 963-0400
Kipp Kofsky, *Branch Mgr*
EMP: 25

SALES (corp-wide): 2.9B **Privately Held**
WEB: www.fuchs.com
SIC: 4225 2992 2899 2851 General warehousing & storage; lubricating oils & greases; chemical preparations; paints & allied products; specialty cleaning, polishes & sanitation goods
HQ: Fuchs Lubricants Co.
17050 Lathrop Ave
Harvey IL 60426
708 333-8901

(G-18271)
GATEWAY HOSPITALITY GROUP INC (PA)
8921 Canyon Falls Blvd # 140 (44087-3900)
PHONE...................................330 405-9800
Bob F Voelker, *CEO*
Rhonda Staples, *General Mgr*
Ron Hutcheson, *CFO*
Mayra Santiago, *Accounting Mgr*
Diana Smrz, *Admin Sec*
EMP: 110
SQ FT: 2,000
SALES (est): 7.4MM **Privately Held**
WEB: www.ghghotels.net
SIC: 7011 Hotels

(G-18272)
GED HOLDINGS INC
9280 Dutton Dr (44087-1967)
PHONE...................................330 963-5401
William Weaver, *President*
Dave Lewis, *Research*
EMP: 141 EST: 2000
SALES (est): 16.5MM **Privately Held**
SIC: 3559 3549 5084 Glass making machinery; blowing, molding, forming, etc.; cutting & slitting machinery; industrial machinery & equipment

(G-18273)
GENERAL ELECTRIC INTL INC
8941 Dutton Dr (44087-1939)
PHONE...................................330 963-2066
Jeffrey Pack, *Manager*
EMP: 30
SALES (corp-wide): 121.6B **Publicly Held**
SIC: 5084 3561 Compressors, except air conditioning; pumps, oil well & field
HQ: General Electric International, Inc.
191 Rosa Parks St
Cincinnati OH 45202
617 443-3000

(G-18274)
GIESECKE & DEVRIENT AMER INC
Also Called: G & D Twinsburg
2020 Enterprise Pkwy (44087-2210)
PHONE...................................330 425-1515
Tina Atwell, *VP Admin*
Randy Gurganus, *Vice Pres*
Dale Ridel, *Plant Mgr*
Ray Daines, *Purch Mgr*
Tina Coleman, *Purch Agent*
EMP: 120
SALES (corp-wide): 308.9K **Privately Held**
SIC: 2672 5044 Coated & laminated paper; office equipment
HQ: Giesecke+Devrient Currency Technology America, Inc.
45925 Horseshoe Dr # 100
Dulles VA 20166
703 480-2000

(G-18275)
GODDARD SCHOOL OF TWINSBURG
2608 Glenwood Dr (44087-2835)
PHONE...................................330 487-0394
Jim Lindley, *Director*
EMP: 30
SALES (est): 424.3K **Privately Held**
SIC: 8351 Preschool center

(G-18276)
GREAT LAKES FASTENERS INC
1962 Case Pkwy (44087-4327)
PHONE...................................330 425-4488
Kevin Weidinger, *President*
Tim Umberger, *Vice Pres*

Jeff McConnell, *Buyer*
Matt Macomber, *Sales Engr*
Rob Myers, *Program Mgr*
▲ EMP: 25
SQ FT: 20,000
SALES: 2.9MM **Privately Held**
SIC: 5085 Fasteners, industrial: nuts, bolts, screws, etc.

(G-18277)
HAHS FACTORY OUTLET
1993 Case Pkwy (44087-4328)
PHONE.....................330 405-4227
Gerry Haas, *Owner*
EMP: 50
SALES (est): 3.5MM **Privately Held**
SIC: 1081 Test boring, metal mining

(G-18278)
HEALTHSPAN INTEGRATED CARE
Also Called: Kaiser Foundation Health Plan
8920 Canyon Falls Blvd (44087-1990)
PHONE.....................330 486-2800
Patricia Kennedy Scott, *Manager*
EMP: 29
SALES (corp-wide): 4.7B **Privately Held**
SIC: 6324 Hospital & medical service plans
HQ: Healthspan Integrated Care
　　1001 Lakeside Ave E # 1200
　　Cleveland OH 44114
　　216 621-5600

(G-18279)
HITACHI HLTHCARE AMERICAS CORP
Also Called: Hitachi Medical Systems Amer
1959 Summit Commerce Park
(44087-2371)
PHONE.....................330 425-1313
Donald Broomfield, *President*
Vickie Campbell, *Regional Mgr*
Tony Giblin, *Regional Mgr*
Josh Nice, *Area Mgr*
William Bishop, *Vice Pres*
▲ EMP: 370
SQ FT: 54,000
SALES: 194.8MM
SALES (corp-wide): 87.9B **Privately Held**
WEB: www.hitachimed.com
SIC: 5047 Diagnostic equipment, medical; medical equipment & supplies
HQ: Hitachi Healthcare Manufacturing, Ltd.
　　2-1, Shintoyofuta
　　Kashiwa CHI 277-0
　　471 314-336

(G-18280)
HOLLAND ROOFING INC
9221 Ravenna Rd (44087-2472)
PHONE.....................330 963-0237
Joe Arway, *Branch Mgr*
EMP: 44
SALES (corp-wide): 47.8MM **Privately Held**
SIC: 1761 Roofing contractor
PA: Holland Roofing, Inc.
　　7450 Industrial Rd
　　Florence KY 41042
　　859 525-0887

(G-18281)
ICM DISTRIBUTING COMPANY INC
Also Called: Inventory Controlled Mdsg
1755 Entp Pkwy Ste 200 (44087)
PHONE.....................234 212-3030
Harry Singer, *President*
Phillip B Singer, *Vice Pres*
Dan Cohen, *Senior Buyer*
Gary Hawvermale, *Controller*
Bernard Harrigan, *Cust Mgr*
▼ EMP: 35
SQ FT: 80,000
SALES (est): 27.1MM
SALES (corp-wide): 31.2MM **Privately Held**
SIC: 5122 5049 5199 5092 Hair preparations; cosmetics; school supplies; general merchandise, non-durable; toys
PA: Sandusco, Inc.
　　1755 Entp Pkwy Ste 200
　　Twinsburg OH 44087
　　440 357-5964

(G-18282)
INTEGRTED PRCISION SYSTEMS INC
9321 Ravenna Rd Ste C (44087-2461)
PHONE.....................330 963-0064
James Butkovic, *President*
Greg Ponchak, *Vice Pres*
Tyler Jewel, *Marketing Staff*
Valerie Fink, *Office Admin*
Ronald Karpus, *Technician*
EMP: 25
SQ FT: 4,000
SALES (est): 4.8MM **Privately Held**
WEB: www.ipsid.com
SIC: 7382 Security systems services

(G-18283)
J T EATON & CO INC
1393 Highland Rd (44087-2213)
PHONE.....................330 425-7801
Stanley Baker, *Chairman*
Bart Baker, *Exec VP*
Benjamin Baker, *Exec VP*
Jack A Polenick, *CFO*
Paul Millet, *Admin Sec*
◆ EMP: 30 EST: 1932
SQ FT: 45,000
SALES (est): 5.1MM **Privately Held**
WEB: www.jteaton.com
SIC: 7342 Pest control services

(G-18284)
JADE INVESTMENTS
2300 E Aurora Rd (44087-1928)
P.O. Box 1090 (44087-9090)
PHONE.....................330 425-3141
William Lieberman, *Partner*
Russell Garron, *Partner*
Gary Bauman, *Ltd Ptnr*
EMP: 50
SALES (est): 2.1MM **Privately Held**
WEB: www.jadeinvestments.com
SIC: 6512 Commercial & industrial building operation

(G-18285)
JADE-STERLING STEEL CO INC (PA)
2300 E Aurora Rd (44087-1987)
P.O. Box 1090 (44087-9090)
PHONE.....................330 425-3141
Howard Fertel, *CEO*
Scott Herman, *President*
Lisa Krolikowski, *General Mgr*
Bill Lieberman, *Chairman*
Dean Musarra, *Vice Pres*
▲ EMP: 45 EST: 1965
SQ FT: 375,000
SALES (est): 54.4MM **Privately Held**
WEB: www.jadesterling.com
SIC: 5051 Steel

(G-18286)
K & M INTERNATIONAL INC (PA)
Also Called: Wild Republic
1955 Midway Dr Ste A (44087-1961)
PHONE.....................330 425-2550
Gopala B Pillai, *CEO*
Vishnu Chandran, *President*
Kamala Pillai, *Vice Pres*
Dan Davies, *CFO*
Daniel Davis, *CFO*
▲ EMP: 65
SQ FT: 100,000
SALES: 38MM **Privately Held**
WEB: www.kmtoys.com
SIC: 5092 5199 Toys; gifts & novelties; bags, baskets & cases; art goods

(G-18287)
KAISER FOUNDATION HOSPITALS
Also Called: Twinsburg Medical Offices
8920 Canyon Falls Blvd (44087-1990)
PHONE.....................330 486-2800
EMP: 593
SALES (corp-wide): 93B **Privately Held**
SIC: 8011 Medical centers
HQ: Kaiser Foundation Hospitals Inc
　　1 Kaiser Plz
　　Oakland CA 94612
　　510 271-6611

(G-18288)
KIMBLE COMPANIES INC
8500 Chamberlin Rd (44087-2096)
PHONE.....................330 963-5493
Peter Gutwein, *Branch Mgr*
EMP: 67 **Privately Held**
SIC: 4953 Refuse collection & disposal services
PA: Kimble Recycling & Disposal, Inc.
　　3596 State Route 39 Nw
　　Dover OH 44622

(G-18289)
KINDERCARE EDUCATION LLC
Also Called: Childrens World Learning Ctr
2572 Glenwood Dr (44087-2698)
PHONE.....................330 405-5556
Jill Gay, *Director*
EMP: 27
SALES (corp-wide): 1.2B **Privately Held**
WEB: www.knowledgelearning.com
SIC: 8351 Group day care center
PA: Kindercare Education Llc
　　650 Ne Holladay St # 1400
　　Portland OR 97232
　　503 872-1300

(G-18290)
LAUDAN PROPERTIES LLC
2204 E Enterprise Pkwy (44087-2356)
PHONE.....................234 212-3225
Kevin Weidinger, *President*
Erin King, *Supervisor*
Lisa Murphy, *Supervisor*
Tim Umberger, *Director*
EMP: 29 EST: 2008
SQ FT: 3,000
SALES: 15.5MM **Privately Held**
SIC: 6512 Nonresidential building operators

(G-18291)
LEIDOS INC
8866 Commons Blvd Ste 201
(44087-2177)
PHONE.....................330 405-9810
Jeffrey Dick, *Manager*
EMP: 30
SALES (corp-wide): 10.1B **Publicly Held**
WEB: www.saic.com
SIC: 8731 Commercial physical research
HQ: Leidos, Inc.
　　11951 Freedom Dr Ste 500
　　Reston VA 20190
　　571 526-6000

(G-18292)
LEIDOS ENGINEERING LLC
8866 Commons Blvd Ste 201
(44087-2177)
PHONE.....................330 405-9810
Robin Giles, *HR Admin*
Steven Visocky, *Branch Mgr*
EMP: 54
SALES (corp-wide): 10.1B **Publicly Held**
SIC: 8731 Commercial physical research
HQ: Leidos Engineering, Llc
　　11951 Freedom Dr
　　Reston VA 20190
　　571 526-6000

(G-18293)
LIGHTING SERVICES INC
9001 Dutton Dr (44087-1930)
PHONE.....................330 405-4879
Kim Allerman, *President*
Darcy Gilbert, *General Mgr*
Kurt Allerman, *Vice Pres*
EMP: 33
SQ FT: 5,000
SALES: 6.3MM **Privately Held**
SIC: 5063 Lighting fixtures

(G-18294)
LOU RITENOUR DECORATORS INC
Also Called: Ritenour Industrial
2066 Case Pkwy S (44087-2360)
PHONE.....................330 425-3232
Michael Ritenour, *President*
Tracey Smartt, *Project Mgr*
Karen Ritenour, *Treasurer*
Aldo Sainato, *Manager*
EMP: 100
SQ FT: 8,000
SALES (est): 10.8MM **Privately Held**
SIC: 1721 Interior commercial painting contractor; wallcovering contractors

(G-18295)
MARSAM METALFAB INC
1870 Enterprise Pkwy (44087-2206)
PHONE.....................330 405-1520
Mark Brownfield, *President*
EMP: 25
SQ FT: 30,000
SALES (est): 3.9MM **Privately Held**
SIC: 1799 3441 7692 3444 Welding on site; fabricated structural metal; welding repair; sheet metalwork

(G-18296)
MAVAL INDUSTRIES LLC
Also Called: Maval Manufacturing
1555 Enterprise Pkwy (44087-2239)
PHONE.....................330 405-1600
John Dougherty, *President*
Dale Lumby, *Vice Pres*
Steve Summerville, *Plant Mgr*
Ralph Wolanin, *QC Mgr*
Dan Denavich, *Engineer*
▲ EMP: 203
SQ FT: 88,000
SALES: 30MM
SALES (corp-wide): 10.5B **Publicly Held**
WEB: www.mavalgear.com
SIC: 3714 8711 Power steering equipment, motor vehicle; consulting engineer
HQ: Borgwarner Pds (Indiana) Inc.
　　13975 Borg Warner Dr
　　Noblesville IN 46060
　　800 372-3555

(G-18297)
MEDIA COLLECTIONS INC
Also Called: Joseph, Mann & Creed
8948 Canyon Falls Blvd # 200
(44087-1900)
P.O. Box 22253, Beachwood (44122-0253)
PHONE.....................216 831-5626
Perry Creed, *President*
Bill Mann, *Admin Sec*
EMP: 63
SQ FT: 10,000
SALES (est): 7.5MM **Privately Held**
WEB: www.jmcbiz.com
SIC: 7322 Collection agency, except real estate

(G-18298)
MERC ACQUISITIONS INC
Also Called: Electric Sweeper Service Co
1933 Highland Rd (44087-2224)
PHONE.....................216 925-5918
Robert Merckle, *President*
Gale Merckle, *Vice Pres*
▲ EMP: 28 EST: 1924
SQ FT: 27,000
SALES (est): 22.7MM **Privately Held**
SIC: 5064 Appliance parts, household; vacuum cleaners, household

(G-18299)
MIRKA USA INC
2375 Edison Blvd (44087-2376)
PHONE.....................330 963-6421
Mark Kush, *President*
Tracy Burns, *Sales Staff*
Julie Schilling, *Marketing Mgr*
Nathan Swanson, *Marketing Staff*
Jed Fiske, *Manager*
▲ EMP: 80
SQ FT: 24,000
SALES (est): 32.9MM
SALES (corp-wide): 548.2MM **Privately Held**
WEB: www.mirkausa.com
SIC: 5085 Abrasives
HQ: Mirka Oy
　　Pensalantie 210
　　Jepua 66850
　　207 602-111

(G-18300)
NATIONAL TRNSP SOLUTIONS INC
1831 Highland Rd (44087-2222)
PHONE.....................330 405-2660
Larry Musarra, *President*
Ron Glazer, *CFO*
EMP: 55

SQ FT: 140,000
SALES: 14MM **Privately Held**
SIC: 4213 4212 Trucking, except local; local trucking, without storage

(G-18301)
NEXEO SOLUTIONS LLC
Also Called: Ashland Distribution
1842 Enterprise Pkwy (44087-2289)
PHONE..................................330 405-0461
David Newhart, *Branch Mgr*
EMP: 27
SALES (corp-wide): 8.6B **Publicly Held**
WEB: www.ashland.com
SIC: 5169 Industrial chemicals
HQ: Nexeo Solutions, Llc
3 Waterway Square Pl # 1000
The Woodlands TX 77380

(G-18302)
PEPPERL + FUCHS INC (DH)
1600 Enterprise Pkwy (44087-2245)
PHONE..................................330 425-3555
Wolfgang Mueller, *President*
Kishore K Kumble, *General Mgr*
Jessica Mercurio, *General Mgr*
Michael Fuchs, *Managing Dir*
Seitz Juergen, *Managing Dir*
▲ EMP: 130
SQ FT: 55,050
SALES (est): 100.4MM
SALES (corp-wide): 744.1MM **Privately Held**
WEB: www.pepperlfuchs.com
SIC: 5065 3625 3822 3674 Electronic parts & equipment; relays & industrial controls; auto controls regulating residntl & coml environmt & applncs; semiconductors & related devices
HQ: Pepperl + Fuchs Enterprises, Inc.
1600 Enterprise Pkwy
Twinsburg OH 44087
330 425-3555

(G-18303)
PEPPERL + FUCHS AMERICAS INC
1600 Enterprise Pkwy (44087-2245)
PHONE..................................330 425-3555
Alexander Gress, *President*
EMP: 80
SALES (est): 1.4MM
SALES (corp-wide): 744.1MM **Privately Held**
SIC: 5065 Electronic parts
HQ: Pepperl + Fuchs Enterprises, Inc.
1600 Enterprise Pkwy
Twinsburg OH 44087
330 425-3555

(G-18304)
PEPSI-COLA METRO BTLG CO INC
1999 Enterprise Pkwy (44087-2253)
PHONE..................................330 963-0426
Joshua Robison, *Prdtn Mgr*
Richard Michaud, *Production*
Michael Gatto, *Sales Staff*
Charlie Powers, *Manager*
Frank O'Neill, *Manager*
EMP: 500
SALES (corp-wide): 64.6B **Publicly Held**
WEB: www.joy-of-cola.com
SIC: 2086 5149 Bottled & canned soft drinks; groceries & related products
HQ: Pepsi-Cola Metropolitan Bottling Company, Inc.
1111 Westchester Ave
White Plains NY 10604
914 767-6000

(G-18305)
PHARMERICA LONG-TERM CARE INC
Also Called: Ltc Pharmacy
1750 Highland Rd Ste F (44087-2275)
PHONE..................................330 425-4450
Rob Koch, *Branch Mgr*
EMP: 25 **Privately Held**
WEB: www.pharmerica.com
SIC: 7352 Invalid supplies rental
HQ: Pharmerica Long-Term Care, Llc
3625 Queen Palm Dr
Tampa FL 33619
877 975-2273

(G-18306)
PRECISION FUNDING CORP
2132 Case Pkwy Ste A (44087-2383)
PHONE..................................330 405-1313
Dominic Di Franco, *President*
EMP: 32
SQ FT: 12,800
SALES: 2.5MM **Privately Held**
SIC: 6162 6163 Mortgage bankers & correspondents; loan brokers

(G-18307)
PRESTIGE INTERIORS INC
2239 E Enterprise Pkwy (44087-2347)
PHONE..................................330 425-1690
David Maag, *President*
EMP: 35
SQ FT: 2,500
SALES: 2.5MM **Privately Held**
WEB: www.prestigeinteriorsinc.com
SIC: 1542 Commercial & office building, new construction; commercial & office buildings, renovation & repair

(G-18308)
PSI ASSOCIATES INC
2112 Case Pkwy Ste 10 (44087-2378)
P.O. Box 468 (44087-0468)
PHONE..................................330 425-8474
Steve Rosenberg, *President*
Dr Colleen Lorberl, *COO*
Cyndie Nicholl, *Manager*
Barbara Taylor-Ross, *Manager*
Karen Heichel, *Supervisor*
EMP: 300 EST: 1977
SQ FT: 1,500
SALES (est): 16.3MM **Privately Held**
SIC: 7361 8049 Employment agencies; clinical psychologist

(G-18309)
QSR PARENT CO
1700 Highland Rd (44087-2221)
PHONE..................................330 425-8472
Randy Ross, *CEO*
EMP: 914
SALES (corp-wide): 1.8B **Privately Held**
SIC: 6719 Investment holding companies, except banks
HQ: Q Holding Company
1700 Highland Rd
Twinsburg OH 44087
330 425-8472

(G-18310)
REGENCY WINDOWS CORPORATION
2288 E Aurora Rd (44087-1926)
P.O. Box 6743, Cleveland (44101-1743)
PHONE..................................330 963-4077
David Gordon, *CEO*
Kim Gaebelein, *Vice Pres*
Joe Tripi Jr, *Vice Pres*
Bruce Gorrell, *CFO*
EMP: 65
SQ FT: 17,000
SALES (est): 9.4MM **Privately Held**
WEB: www.regencywindow.com
SIC: 5211 5713 1761 1751 Siding; carpets; siding contractor; window & door (prefabricated) installation

(G-18311)
RESERVE FTL LLC
Also Called: Reserve Management Group
1831 Highland Rd (44087-2222)
PHONE..................................440 519-1768
Robert Evenhouse, *Branch Mgr*
EMP: 30 **Privately Held**
WEB: www.reservemarine.com
SIC: 4491 Marine terminals
PA: Reserve Ftl, Llc
11600 S Burley Ave
Chicago IL 60617

(G-18312)
RIGHTWAY INVESTMENTS LLC
1959 Edgewood Dr (44087-1637)
P.O. Box 27211, Cleveland (44127-0211)
PHONE..................................216 854-7697
Bernard Motley, *Mng Member*
EMP: 50
SALES: 950K **Privately Held**
SIC: 6799 Investment clubs

(G-18313)
ROGER ZATKOFF COMPANY
Also Called: Zatkoff Seals & Packings
2475 Edison Blvd (44087-2340)
PHONE..................................248 478-2400
Richard Dahm, *Sales Engr*
Brian Gilboy, *Manager*
EMP: 25
SALES (corp-wide): 126.3MM **Privately Held**
WEB: www.zatkoff.com
SIC: 5085 Seals, industrial
PA: Roger Zatkoff Company
23230 Industrial Park Dr
Farmington Hills MI 48335
248 478-2400

(G-18314)
RX OPTIONS LLC (HQ)
Also Called: Envision Pharmaceutical Svcs
2181 E Aurora Rd Ste 101 (44087-1962)
PHONE..................................330 405-8080
Barry Katz, *President*
William M Toomajian, *Principal*
Catherine Stroutman, *Vice Pres*
EMP: 75
SQ FT: 2,500
SALES (est): 31.5MM
SALES (corp-wide): 40.1MM **Privately Held**
SIC: 8742 Compensation & benefits planning consultant
PA: Envision Pharmaceutical Holdings Llc
2181 E Aurora Rd Ste 201
Twinsburg OH 44087
800 361-4542

(G-18315)
S & E ELECTRIC INC
1521 Highland Rd (44087-2254)
PHONE..................................330 425-7866
Fax: 330 425-2745
EMP: 30
SQ FT: 20,000
SALES: 4.1MM **Privately Held**
SIC: 1731 Electrical Contractors

(G-18316)
SAFRAN POWER USA LLC
8380 Darrow Rd (44087-2329)
PHONE..................................330 487-2000
Chris Plumb, *President*
Kirk Bailey, *Safety Mgr*
Terry McGlothlin, *Engineer*
Edward Tompkin, *Project Engr*
Moshe Hoyat, *Design Engr*
EMP: 140
SALES (est): 27.2MM
SALES (corp-wide): 833.4MM **Privately Held**
SIC: 8711 8741 Engineering services; business management
HQ: Safran Usa, Inc.
700 S Washington St # 320
Alexandria VA 22314
703 351-9898

(G-18317)
SAMUEL STEEL PICKLING COMPANY (PA)
1400 Enterprise Pkwy (44087-2242)
PHONE..................................330 963-3777
Rick Snyder, *COO*
William Vason, *Opers Mgr*
Sylvia Herrmann, *Accountant*
EMP: 70
SQ FT: 115,000
SALES: 15MM **Privately Held**
SIC: 7389 5051 3471 3398 Metal slitting & shearing; metals service centers & offices; plating & polishing; metal heat treating; blast furnaces & steel mills

(G-18318)
SAW SYSTEMS INC (PA)
1579 Enterprise Pkwy (44087-2239)
PHONE..................................330 963-2992
Natalie Brillhart, *President*
Jerry Brillhart, *Principal*
Lawrence C Gould, *Principal*
David A Berkey, *Vice Pres*
Mark Rotondo, *Vice Pres*
EMP: 26
SQ FT: 12,000

SALES (est): 5.4MM **Privately Held**
WEB: www.sawsystemsinc.com
SIC: 7699 Knife, saw & tool sharpening & repair

(G-18319)
SCHUSTER ELECTRONICS INC
Also Called: Schuster/Cleveland
2057d E Aurora Rd (44087-1921)
PHONE..................................330 425-8134
Anne Bailey, *Branch Mgr*
EMP: 26
SALES (corp-wide): 8.6MM **Privately Held**
WEB: www.schusterusa.com
SIC: 5065 5088 Electronic parts; transportation equipment & supplies
PA: Schuster Electronics, Inc.
11320 Grooms Rd
Blue Ash OH 45242
513 489-1400

(G-18320)
SHELLY COMPANY
8920 Canyon Falls Blvd # 3 (44087-1990)
PHONE..................................330 425-7861
Doug Rauh, *Branch Mgr*
EMP: 50
SALES (corp-wide): 29.7B **Privately Held**
SIC: 1611 Highway & street construction
HQ: Shelly Company
80 Park Dr
Thornville OH 43076
740 246-6315

(G-18321)
SODEXO INC
2333 Sandalwood Dr (44087-1383)
PHONE..................................330 425-0709
EMP: 39
SALES (corp-wide): 145.8MM **Privately Held**
SIC: 8742 Management Consulting Services
HQ: Sodexo, Inc.
9801 Washingtonian Blvd # 1
Gaithersburg MD 20878
301 987-4000

(G-18322)
SOLUPAY CONSULTING INC
1900 Entp Pkwy Ste A (44087)
PHONE..................................216 535-9016
Joe Musitano Jr, *Managing Prtnr*
Jayme Moss, *Managing Prtnr*
EMP: 97
SQ FT: 4,000
SALES: 4.5MM **Privately Held**
SIC: 7389 Credit card service

(G-18323)
SSP FITTINGS CORP (PA)
8250 Boyle Pkwy (44087-2200)
PHONE..................................330 425-4250
Jeffrey E King, *CEO*
F B Douglas, *Principal*
O F Douglas, *Principal*
H M Hunter, *Principal*
Jo Soukup, *CFO*
▲ EMP: 150 EST: 1926
SQ FT: 165,000
SALES (est): 63.2MM **Privately Held**
WEB: www.sspfittings.com
SIC: 3494 5085 3498 3492 Pipe fittings; industrial supplies; fabricated pipe & fittings; fluid power valves & hose fittings

(G-18324)
STEEL PLATE LLC
8333 Boyle Pkwy (44087-2236)
PHONE..................................888 894-8818
Joe Curry, *Vice Pres*
Kristy Konic, *Accounts Exec*
Parker Warnock, *Sales Staff*
Ron Stuart, *Manager*
EMP: 25 **Privately Held**
SIC: 5051 Steel
PA: Steel Plate, L.L.C.
140 S Holland Dr
Pendergrass GA 30567

(G-18325)
STONEMOR PARTNERS LP
Also Called: Crown Hill Cemetery
8592 Darrow Rd (44087-2128)
PHONE..................................330 425-8128

Tony Cusma, *Manager*
EMP: 26
SQ FT: 2,768
SALES (corp-wide): 316.1MM **Publicly Held**
WEB: www.stonemor.com
SIC: 6553 Cemeteries, real estate operation
PA: Stonemor Partners L.P.
　　3600 Horizon Blvd Ste 100
　　Trevose PA 19053
　　215 826-2800

(G-18326)
THE MAU-SHERWOOD SUPPLY CO (PA)
Also Called: M S
8400 Darrow Rd Ste 1 (44087-2375)
PHONE......................330 405-1200
JC Rexroth, *President*
Mg McAleenan, *Principal*
WD Turner, *Principal*
▼ **EMP:** 25
SQ FT: 11,000
SALES (est): 11.9MM **Privately Held**
WEB: www.mausherwood.com
SIC: 5085 5169 5072 Valves & fittings; chemicals & allied products; hardware

(G-18327)
TIMEWARE INC
9329 Ravenna Rd Ste D (44087-2457)
PHONE......................330 963-2700
Michael Farhat, *President*
Rebecca Farhat, *Vice Pres*
EMP: 30
SQ FT: 1,782
SALES (est): 1.8MM **Privately Held**
WEB: www.timeware.net
SIC: 7371 Computer software development

(G-18328)
TRI COUNTY CONCRETE INC (PA)
9423 Darrow Rd (44087-1415)
P.O. Box 665 (44087-0665)
PHONE......................330 425-4464
Tony Farenacci, *President*
Fred Farenacci, *Vice Pres*
EMP: 30
SQ FT: 62,000
SALES (est): 4.8MM **Privately Held**
SIC: 3273 3272 1442 Ready-mixed concrete; concrete products; construction sand & gravel

(G-18329)
TRI-MOR CORP
Also Called: Trimor
8530 N Boyle Pkwy (44087-2267)
PHONE......................330 963-3101
John R Morris III, *President*
Rich Desgee, *Principal*
James Vitale, *Vice Pres*
Frank Perry, *Project Mgr*
Neille Morris, *Credit Mgr*
EMP: 120
SALES (est): 21.2MM **Privately Held**
WEB: www.trimor.com
SIC: 1771 Blacktop (asphalt) work

(G-18330)
TURFSCAPE INC
8490 Tower Dr (44087-2000)
PHONE......................330 405-0741
George M Hohman Jr, *President*
Christopher White, *Opers Staff*
Marysue Hohman, *Treasurer*
Fred Krause, *Accounts Mgr*
Jodi Reimer, *Sales Staff*
EMP: 110
SALES (est): 11.9MM **Privately Held**
WEB: www.turfscapeohio.com
SIC: 0782 Landscape contractors

(G-18331)
TWIN HAVEN RECEPTION HALL
10439 Ravenna Rd (44087-1726)
PHONE......................330 425-1616
Robert Friedo, *Pastor*
EMP: 25
SALES (est): 404K **Privately Held**
SIC: 5812 7299 Caterers; banquet hall facilities

(G-18332)
U S A WATERPROOFING INC
1632 Enterprise Pkwy (44087-2282)
PHONE......................330 425-2440
Steven Rusk, *President*
Mark Nemeth, *General Mgr*
James Rusk, *Vice Pres*
Jim Rusk, *Human Res Dir*
EMP: 40
SQ FT: 8,000
SALES (est): 3.3MM **Privately Held**
SIC: 1799 Waterproofing

(G-18333)
UNIVAR USA INC
1686 Highland Rd (44087-2219)
PHONE......................330 425-4330
Nancy Reddy, *Marketing Staff*
Michael Sebenoler, *Branch Mgr*
EMP: 40
SALES (corp-wide): 8.6B **Publicly Held**
SIC: 5169 Industrial chemicals
HQ: Univar Usa Inc.
　　3075 Highland Pkwy # 200
　　Downers Grove IL 60515
　　331 777-6000

(G-18334)
US FOODS INC
8000 Bavaria Rd (44087-2262)
PHONE......................330 963-6789
Steve Preston, *Branch Mgr*
EMP: 250 **Publicly Held**
WEB: www.usfoodservice.com
SIC: 5141 5149 Food brokers; groceries & related products
HQ: Us Foods, Inc.
　　9399 W Higgins Rd Ste 500
　　Rosemont IL 60018

(G-18335)
VENTURE LIGHTING INTL INC (HQ)
2451 E Enterprise Pkwy (44087-2351)
PHONE......................800 451-2606
Wayne Vespoli, *President*
Sabu Krishnan, *Co-President*
Amy Patrick, *Vice Pres*
Anupama Krishnan, *Purchasing*
Rob Adams, *Sales Mgr*
◆ **EMP:** 68
SQ FT: 330,000
SALES (est): 51.1MM **Privately Held**
SIC: 5063 Lighting fixtures

(G-18336)
VERIZON WIRELESS
2000 Highland Rd (44087-2227)
PHONE......................330 963-1300
Jeffrey Gardner, *CFO*
James Andres, *Manager*
Craig Brown, *Analyst*
EMP: 25
SALES (est): 1.9MM
SALES (corp-wide): 6.5MM **Privately Held**
SIC: 4812 Cellular telephone services
PA: Verizon Wireless
　　15505 Sand Canyon Ave
　　Irvine CA 92618
　　949 286-7000

(G-18337)
WEBMD HEALTH CORP
2045 Midway Dr (44087-1933)
PHONE......................330 425-3241
Mike Mc Manus, *Branch Mgr*
EMP: 30
SALES (corp-wide): 705MM **Privately Held**
WEB: www.wellmed.com
SIC: 7375 Information retrieval services
HQ: Webmd Health Corp.
　　395 Hudson St Fl 3
　　New York NY 10014
　　212 624-3700

(G-18338)
YOUNG CHEMICAL CO LLC (HQ)
1755 Entp Pkwy Ste 400 (44087)
PHONE......................330 486-4210
Brian McCue, *President*
Mike Leighty, *CFO*
EMP: 32

SALES (est): 8MM
SALES (corp-wide): 31MM **Privately Held**
SIC: 5169 Industrial chemicals
PA: Paro Services Co.
　　1755 Entp Pkwy Ste 100
　　Twinsburg OH 44087
　　330 467-1300

Uhrichsville
Tuscarawas County

(G-18339)
BARBOUR PUBLISHING INC (PA)
Also Called: Heartsong Presents
1810 Barbour Dr Se (44683-1084)
P.O. Box 719 (44683-0719)
PHONE......................740 922-1321
Tim Martins, *CEO*
Mary Burns, *President*
George Kourkounakis, *Exec VP*
Kelly McIntosh, *Vice Pres*
David Applin, *Prdtn Mgr*
◆ **EMP:** 47
SQ FT: 74,000
SALES (est): 8.9MM **Privately Held**
WEB: www.barbourbooks.com
SIC: 5942 5192 Ret Books Whol Books/Newspapers

(G-18340)
EMBER COMPLETE CARE (PA)
1800 N Water Street Ext (44683-1044)
P.O. Box 369 (44683-0369)
PHONE......................740 922-6888
Lois Ann Grandison, *President*
Dennis Jock Grandison, *Vice Pres*
Cindy Peterson, *Executive*
EMP: 150
SALES (est): 5.7MM **Privately Held**
SIC: 8082 Visiting nurse service

(G-18341)
EMBER HOME CARE
730 N Water St (44683-1456)
PHONE......................740 922-6968
Dennis Grandison, *Owner*
Jock Grandison, *Owner*
EMP: 300
SALES (est): 5.2MM **Privately Held**
SIC: 8082 Home health care services

(G-18342)
IMCO RECYCLING OF OHIO LLC
7335 Newport Rd Se (44683-6368)
PHONE......................740 922-2373
Sean M Stack, *CEO*
Robert R Holian, *Vice Pres*
▲ **EMP:** 164
SALES (est): 20.3MM **Privately Held**
WEB: www.imcorecycling.com
SIC: 3341 4953 Aluminum smelting & refining (secondary); recycling, waste materials
HQ: Aleris Rolled Products, Inc.
　　25825 Science Park Dr # 400
　　Beachwood OH 44122
　　216 910-3400

(G-18343)
ROSEBUD MINING COMPANY
5600 Pleasant Vly Rd Se (44683-9502)
PHONE......................740 922-9122
Greg Blainer, *Branch Mgr*
EMP: 33
SALES (corp-wide): 605.3MM **Privately Held**
WEB: www.rosebudmining.com
SIC: 1222 1221 Bituminous coal-underground mining; strip mining, bituminous
PA: Rosebud Mining Company
　　301 Market St
　　Kittanning PA 16201
　　724 545-6222

(G-18344)
SUPERIOR CLAY CORP
6566 Superior Rd Se (44683-7487)
P.O. Box 352 (44683-0352)
PHONE......................740 922-4122
Elmer W McClave III, *President*
Joe Berni, *Corp Secy*

Tyler McClave, *Vice Pres*
Nan Giumenti, *Technology*
Dana Martini, *Technician*
◆ **EMP:** 75 **EST:** 1936
SQ FT: 190,000
SALES (est): 9.9MM **Privately Held**
WEB: www.superiorclay.com
SIC: 3259 8611 Sewer pipe or fittings, clay; flue lining, clay; wall coping, clay; stove lining, clay; business associations

(G-18345)
U S ARMY CORPS OF ENGINEERS
86801 Eslick Rd (44683-9614)
PHONE......................740 269-2681
Jerry Herman, *Branch Mgr*
EMP: 65 **Publicly Held**
SIC: 8711 Engineering services
HQ: U S Army Corps Of Engineers
　　441 G St Nw
　　Washington DC 20314
　　202 761-0001

(G-18346)
UHRICHSVILLE HEALTH CARE CTR
Also Called: Beacon Point Rehab
5166 Spanson Dr Se (44683-1346)
PHONE......................740 922-2208
Brian Colleran, *President*
EMP: 83 **EST:** 1981
SQ FT: 25,000
SALES: 4.6MM **Privately Held**
SIC: 8051 Convalescent home with continuous nursing care

(G-18347)
UNITED STTES BOWL CONGRESS INC
710 Gorley St (44683-1626)
PHONE......................740 922-3120
EMP: 51
SALES (corp-wide): 32.9MM **Privately Held**
SIC: 8699 Athletic organizations
PA: United States Bowling Congress, Inc.
　　621 Six Flags Dr
　　Arlington TX 76011
　　817 385-8200

(G-18348)
VISION EXPRESS INC
801 W 1st St (44683-2205)
PHONE......................740 922-8848
Todd Evans, *President*
Randy Jones, *Director*
EMP: 35
SQ FT: 10,000
SALES: 4MM **Privately Held**
SIC: 4212 4213 Local trucking, without storage; contract haulers

(G-18349)
XPO LOGISTICS FREIGHT INC
2401 N Water Street Ext (44683)
PHONE......................740 922-5614
Larry McCraken, *Branch Mgr*
EMP: 30
SALES (corp-wide): 15.3B **Publicly Held**
WEB: www.con-way.com
SIC: 4213 Trucking, except local
HQ: Xpo Logistics Freight, Inc.
　　2211 Old Earhart Rd # 100
　　Ann Arbor MI 48105
　　800 755-2728

Union
Montgomery County

(G-18350)
DILLARD ELECTRIC INC
106 Quinter Farm Rd (45322-9705)
PHONE......................937 836-5381
John Dillard, *President*
EMP: 30
SALES (est): 2.9MM **Privately Held**
WEB: www.dillardelectric.net
SIC: 1731 General electrical contractor

(G-18351)
PROCTER & GAMBLE DISTRG LLC
1800 Union Park Blvd (45377)
P.O. Box 2628, Burlington NC (27216-2628)
PHONE.................................937 387-5189
Robert Fix, *General Mgr*
EMP: 178
SALES (corp-wide): 66.8B **Publicly Held**
SIC: 5169 Detergents
HQ: Procter & Gamble Distributing Llc
1 Procter And Gamble Plz
Cincinnati OH 45202
513 983-1100

Union City
Darke County

(G-18352)
CAL-MAINE FOODS INC
1039 Zumbrum Rd (45390-8646)
PHONE.................................937 968-4874
Chuck Jenkins, *Branch Mgr*
EMP: 35
SALES (corp-wide): 1.5B **Publicly Held**
WEB: www.calmainefoods.com
SIC: 0252 2015 Chicken eggs; eggs, processed: frozen
PA: Cal-Maine Foods, Inc.
3320 W Woodrow Wilson Ave
Jackson MS 39209
601 948-6813

(G-18353)
CROTINGER NURSING HOME INC
Also Called: Center of Hope
907 E Central St (45390-1605)
PHONE.................................937 968-5284
Meta Sue Livingston, *President*
Jamie Livingston, *Vice Pres*
Eric Hiatt, *Treasurer*
Phil Crawford, *Administration*
EMP: 70
SQ FT: 16,000
SALES (est): 1.8MM **Privately Held**
WEB: www.centerofhope.com
SIC: 8051 Skilled nursing care facilities

(G-18354)
RL PAINTING AND MFG INC
Also Called: Livingston Painting
10001 Oh In State Line (45390-9050)
P.O. Box 145 (45377-0145)
PHONE.................................937 968-5526
Richard Livingston, *President*
EMP: 30
SALES (est): 2.7MM **Privately Held**
SIC: 1721 Exterior residential painting contractor; commercial painting; industrial painting

(G-18355)
U C M RESIDENTIAL SERVICES
400 Gade Ave (45390)
PHONE.................................937 643-3757
Robert Thompson, *Owner*
Cheryl Juhl, *Administration*
EMP: 70
SALES (est): 886.6K **Privately Held**
SIC: 8051 Skilled nursing care facilities

(G-18356)
UNION CHRISTEL MANOR INC
Also Called: Union City Crystal Manor
400 S Melvin Eley Ave (45390-8611)
PHONE.................................937 968-6265
Robert Thompson III, *President*
Cheryl Juhl, *Admin Sec*
EMP: 75
SALES (est): 2.5MM **Privately Held**
SIC: 8051 Mental retardation hospital

Uniontown
Stark County

(G-18357)
BIO-MDCAL APPLCATIONS OHIO INC
Also Called: Akron Canton Kidney Center
1575 Corp Woods Pkwy # 100 (44685-7842)
PHONE.................................330 896-6311
Jacqueline Powers, *Manager*
EMP: 30
SALES (corp-wide): 18.9B **Privately Held**
WEB: www.fresenius.org
SIC: 8092 Kidney dialysis centers
HQ: Bio-Medical Applications Of Ohio, Inc.
920 Winter St
Waltham MA 02451

(G-18358)
BONTRAGER EXCAVATING CO INC
11087 Cleveland Ave Nw (44685-8677)
PHONE.................................330 499-8775
Brian Bontrager, *President*
Helen Bontrager, *Corp Secy*
Eric Bontrager, *Vice Pres*
EMP: 27 EST: 1972
SALES (est): 4.5MM **Privately Held**
SIC: 1794 Excavation work

(G-18359)
CAHILL CORPORATION
3951 Creek Wood Ln (44685-7786)
PHONE.................................330 724-1224
Edwin A Huth Jr, *President*
Lori Martin, *Principal*
EMP: 25 EST: 1907
SQ FT: 5,000
SALES: 9.8MM **Privately Held**
WEB: www.cahillcorp.com
SIC: 1711 Mechanical contractor; process piping contractor

(G-18360)
CAMBRIA GREEN MANAGEMENT LLC
Also Called: Cambria Stes Akrn-Canton Arprt
1787 Thorn Dr (44685-9573)
PHONE.................................330 899-1263
Chris Bitikofer, *General Mgr*
Laura Groves, *Manager*
Karen Friedt, *Executive*
EMP: 34 EST: 2006
SALES (est): 1.1MM **Privately Held**
SIC: 7011 Hotels

(G-18361)
CBIZ INC
13680 Cleveland Ave Nw (44685-8098)
PHONE.................................330 644-2044
Michael Stickard, *Manager*
EMP: 77 **Publicly Held**
SIC: 8748 6411 Business consulting; pension & retirement plan consultants
PA: Cbiz, Inc.
6050 Oak Tree Blvd # 500
Cleveland OH 44131

(G-18362)
CBORD GROUP INC
3800 Tabs Dr (44685-9564)
PHONE.................................330 498-2702
Matthew Irwin, *Marketing Mgr*
John Stroia, *Branch Mgr*
Paul Mercina, *Director*
EMP: 200
SQ FT: 17,000
SALES (corp-wide): 5.1B **Publicly Held**
WEB: www.cbord.com
SIC: 7699 Automated teller machine (ATM) repair
HQ: The Cbord Group Inc
950 Danby Rd Ste 100c
Ithaca NY 14850
607 257-2410

(G-18363)
COMDOC INC (DH)
3458 Massillon Rd (44685-9503)
P.O. Box 908, Akron (44309-0908)
PHONE.................................330 896-2346

Riley Lochridge, *Ch of Bd*
Gordy Opitz, *President*
Larry Frank, *COO*
Tricia Taliani, *Site Mgr*
Steven T Owen, *CFO*
EMP: 125 EST: 1955
SQ FT: 60,000
SALES (est): 90MM
SALES (corp-wide): 9.8B **Publicly Held**
SIC: 7699 5044 7359 Photocopy machine repair; office equipment; business machine & electronic equipment rental services

(G-18364)
CORPORATE LADDER SEARCH
1549 Boettler Rd Ste D (44685-7766)
PHONE.................................330 776-4390
Kristen Babbin, *President*
Heidi Hopkins, *Vice Pres*
Kelsey Kloss, *Manager*
Ann Messina, *Manager*
Doreen Thorne, *Admin Asst*
EMP: 25 EST: 2013
SALES (est): 95.6K **Privately Held**
SIC: 8748 7361 Business consulting; employment agencies

(G-18365)
CROWN HEATING & COOLING INC
Also Called: Honeywell Authorized Dealer
11197 Cleveland Ave Nw (44685-9401)
P.O. Box 1030 (44685-1030)
PHONE.................................330 499-4988
Eugene Seifert, *President*
Arlene Seifert, *Vice Pres*
Nancy Maciag, *Purch Agent*
Tim Earnsberger, *Consultant*
EMP: 70
SQ FT: 43,054
SALES (est): 12.1MM **Privately Held**
SIC: 1711 Warm air heating & air conditioning contractor

(G-18366)
DENTAL SUPPORT SPECIALTIES LLC
Also Called: Dss
1790 Graybill Rd Ste 100 (44685-7993)
PHONE.................................330 639-1333
Mary Beth Bajornas, *Mng Member*
EMP: 35
SALES (est): 396.8K **Privately Held**
SIC: 8621 Dental association

(G-18367)
DIRECTION HOME AKRON CANTON AR (PA)
1550 Corporate Woods Pkwy (44685-8730)
PHONE.................................330 896-9172
Becky Newman, *President*
Gary Cook, *COO*
Christopher Fagerstrom, *Assistant VP*
Abigail Morgan, *Vice Pres*
Barbara Kallenbach, *CFO*
EMP: 135
SQ FT: 19,502
SALES: 52.8MM **Privately Held**
SIC: 8322 Senior citizens' center or association; geriatric social service

(G-18368)
DREES COMPANY
3906 Kenway Blvd (44685-6230)
PHONE.................................330 899-9554
Hailey Collier, *Manager*
EMP: 27
SALES (corp-wide): 722.6MM **Privately Held**
SIC: 1521 New construction, single-family houses
PA: The Drees Company
515 S Captal Of Texas Hwy
West Lake Hills TX 78746
859 578-4200

(G-18369)
FEDEX CUSTOM CRITICAL INC (HQ)
1475 Boettler Rd (44685-9584)
P.O. Box 5000, Green (44232-5000)
PHONE.................................800 463-3339
Virginia Albanese, *CEO*

Alan B Graf Jr, *Ch of Bd*
Michael Lombardi, *Facilities Mgr*
Steve Dezenzo, *Finance*
Micheal Abood, *Human Res Mgr*
EMP: 500
SQ FT: 103,000
SALES (est): 94MM
SALES (corp-wide): 65.4B **Publicly Held**
SIC: 4731 Freight transportation arrangement
PA: Fedex Corporation
942 Shady Grove Rd S
Memphis TN 38120
901 818-7500

(G-18370)
FEDEX TRUCKLOAD BROKERAGE INC
1475 Boettler Rd (44685-9584)
P.O. Box 5000, Green (44232-5000)
PHONE.................................800 463-3339
Virginia Albanese, *President*
EMP: 123
SALES (est): 34.5MM
SALES (corp-wide): 65.4B **Publicly Held**
WEB: www.FedEx.com
SIC: 4731 Freight transportation arrangement
HQ: Fedex Custom Critical, Inc.
1475 Boettler Rd
Uniontown OH 44685
800 463-3339

(G-18371)
FIRST UNION BANC CORP
1559 Corporate Woods Pkwy (44685-7872)
PHONE.................................330 896-1222
Beth Mosley, *President*
EMP: 31
SALES (est): 3.2MM **Privately Held**
SIC: 6162 Mortgage bankers

(G-18372)
GREENTOWN VOLUNTEER FIRE DEPT
10100 Cleveland Ave Nw (44685-9413)
PHONE.................................330 494-3002
Aaron Baker, *President*
Vincent Harris, *Chief*
Thomas Radomski-Bomba, *Vice Pres*
Nicholas Nicholson, *Treasurer*
Paul Weigand, *Admin Sec*
EMP: 38
SALES: 1.1MM **Privately Held**
SIC: 7389 Fire protection service other than forestry or public

(G-18373)
HANKOOK TIRE AMERICA CORP
Also Called: Hankook Tire Akron Office
3535 Forest Lake Dr (44685-8105)
PHONE.................................330 896-6199
Alex Hwang, *General Mgr*
Ray Labuda, *Vice Pres*
Raymond Labuda, *Manager*
Karla Jones, *Administration*
EMP: 40
SALES (corp-wide): 66.4MM **Privately Held**
WEB: www.hankook-atc.com
SIC: 5014 5013 Automobile tires & tubes; truck tires & tubes; automotive batteries; wheels, motor vehicle
HQ: Hankook Tire America Corporation
333 Commerce St Ste 600
Nashville TN 37201
615 432-0700

(G-18374)
HOWARD HANNA SMYTHE CRAMER
Also Called: Smythe Cramer Co
3700 Massillon Rd Ste 300 (44685-9558)
PHONE.................................330 896-3333
Bruce Heath, *Manager*
EMP: 40
SALES (corp-wide): 73.7MM **Privately Held**
WEB: www.smythecramer.com
SIC: 6531 Real estate brokers & agents
HQ: Howard Hanna Smythe Cramer
6000 Parkland Blvd
Cleveland OH 44124
216 447-4477

(G-18375)
KIDS COUNTRY
1801 Town Park Blvd (44685-7963)
PHONE....................330 899-0909
Christine Burkholder, *Owner*
Aimee Coia, *Asst Director*
EMP: 25
SALES (est): 636.2K **Privately Held**
SIC: 8351 Group day care center

(G-18376)
KIDS-PLAY INC
Also Called: Kids Play Green
1651 Boettler Rd (44685-7705)
PHONE....................330 896-2400
Stephanie Shriver, *Director*
EMP: 30
SQ FT: 15,500
SALES (corp-wide): 4.8MM **Privately Held**
SIC: 8351 Group day care center; pre-school center
PA: Kids-Play Inc
　　388 S Main St Ste 100
　　Akron OH 44311
　　330 253-2373

(G-18377)
LOUISVILLE CHILD CARE CENTER
Also Called: Marilyn Wagner
3477 Elmhurst Cir (44685-8143)
PHONE....................330 875-4303
Fax: 330 875-9144
EMP: 25
SQ FT: 4,980
SALES (est): 550K **Privately Held**
SIC: 8351 Child Day Care Services

(G-18378)
MAYFAIR COUNTRY CLUB INC
2229 Raber Rd (44685-8844)
PHONE....................330 699-2209
David Springer, *President*
Jeannie Springer, *Vice Pres*
EMP: 55
SQ FT: 15,582
SALES (est): 1.3MM **Privately Held**
WEB: www.mayfaircountryclub.com
SIC: 7992 Public golf courses

(G-18379)
MOTORISTS MUTUAL INSURANCE CO
3532 Massillon Rd (44685-7859)
P.O. Box 7647, Akron (44306-0697)
PHONE....................330 896-9311
Randy McKinney, *Branch Mgr*
EMP: 28
SALES (corp-wide): 352.1MM **Privately Held**
SIC: 6331 Fire, marine & casualty insurance
PA: Motorists Mutual Insurance Company
　　471 E Broad St Ste 200
　　Columbus OH 43215
　　614 225-8211

(G-18380)
NEW INNOVATIONS INC
3540 Forest Lake Dr (44685-8105)
PHONE....................330 899-9954
Stephen C Reed, *CEO*
Denise M Reed, *CFO*
Lee Neal, *Finance Asst*
Stephanie Husmann, *Web Dvlpr*
Jason Baxter, *Software Dev*
EMP: 31
SQ FT: 7,500
SALES (est): 3.8MM **Privately Held**
WEB: www.new-innov.com
SIC: 7371 Computer software development

(G-18381)
NEW NV CO LLC
3777 Boettler Oaks Dr (44685-7733)
PHONE....................330 896-7611
David Logsdon, *Mng Member*
Kim Hamrick,
EMP: 140
SALES (est): 5.4MM **Privately Held**
SIC: 1521 Single-family housing construction

(G-18382)
PHIL WAGLER CONSTRUCTION INC
Also Called: Wagler Homes
3710 Tabs Dr (44685)
PHONE....................330 899-0316
Philip E Wagler, *Ch of Bd*
Phil E Wagler, *President*
EMP: 40
SQ FT: 9,000
SALES (est): 3.4MM **Privately Held**
SIC: 1521 1531 New construction, single-family houses; speculative builder, single-family houses

(G-18383)
PRUDENTIAL INSUR CO OF AMER
3515 Massillon Rd Ste 200 (44685-6113)
PHONE....................330 896-7200
Ed Twele, *General Mgr*
EMP: 45
SALES (corp-wide): 62.9B **Publicly Held**
SIC: 6411 Insurance agents, brokers & service
HQ: The Prudential Insurance Company Of America
　　751 Broad St
　　Newark NJ 07102
　　973 802-6000

(G-18384)
RAINTREE COUNTRY CLUB INC
4350 Mayfair Rd (44685-8137)
PHONE....................330 699-3232
John Rainieri Sr, *President*
John Rainieri Jr, *Vice Pres*
Melinda Haynes, *Admin Sec*
EMP: 40
SQ FT: 10,000
SALES (est): 1.9MM **Privately Held**
WEB: www.raintreegc.com
SIC: 7997 Country club, membership

(G-18385)
SCHEESER BUCKLEY MAYFIELD LLC
1540 Corporate Woods Pkwy (44685-8730)
PHONE....................330 896-4664
Ron Radabaugh, *Project Engr*
James E Eckman P E,
EMP: 43
SALES: 2MM **Privately Held**
SIC: 8711 Consulting engineer

(G-18386)
SECURITAS ELECTRONIC SEC INC (DH)
3800 Tabs Dr (44685-9564)
PHONE....................855 331-0359
Santiago Galaz, *CEO*
Tony Byerly, *President*
Frederick W London, *Vice Pres*
Thomas C Cantlon, *Treasurer*
EMP: 103
SALES (est): 132MM
SALES (corp-wide): 10.9B **Privately Held**
SIC: 7382 Protective devices, security
HQ: Securitas Security Services Usa, Inc.
　　9 Campus Dr
　　Parsippany NJ 07054
　　973 267-5300

(G-18387)
SYNERGY CONSULTING GROUP INC
3700 Massillon Rd Ste 300 (44685-9558)
PHONE....................330 899-9301
Craig Mueller, *President*
EMP: 30
SALES (est): 3.1MM **Privately Held**
SIC: 8742 Human resource consulting services

(G-18388)
TOTAL LOOP INC
1790 Town Park Blvd Ste A (44685-7972)
PHONE....................888 614-5667
Vincenzo Rubino, *President*
EMP: 100 EST: 2012
SALES: 2.2MM **Privately Held**
SIC: 5045 Computer software

(G-18389)
VCA GREEN ANIMAL MEDICAL CTR
Also Called: VCA Green Animal Hospital
1620 Corporate Woods Cir (44685-7819)
PHONE....................330 896-4040
Terry White, *General Mgr*
EMP: 30
SALES (est): 598.8K **Privately Held**
SIC: 0742 Animal hospital services, pets & other animal specialties

(G-18390)
WH MIDWEST LLC (PA)
Also Called: Wayne Homes
3777 Boettler Oaks Dr (44685-7733)
PHONE....................330 896-7611
William A Post, *COO*
Steve Wessel, *Senior VP*
David E Logsdon, *Mng Member*
EMP: 120
SQ FT: 16,000
SALES (est): 23.3MM **Privately Held**
WEB: www.waynehomes.com
SIC: 1521 New construction, single-family houses

(G-18391)
XPO LOGISTICS FREIGHT INC
3733 Massillon Rd (44685-7730)
PHONE....................330 896-7300
Jeff Teague, *Manager*
EMP: 82
SALES (corp-wide): 15.3B **Publicly Held**
WEB: www.con-way.com
SIC: 4213 4231 4212 Contract haulers; trucking terminal facilities; local trucking, without storage
HQ: Xpo Logistics Freight, Inc.
　　2211 Old Earhart Rd # 100
　　Ann Arbor MI 48105
　　800 755-2728

(G-18392)
Y M C A CENTRAL STARK COUNTY
Also Called: YMCA
11928 King Church Ave Nw (44685-8220)
PHONE....................330 877-8933
Linda Phillips, *Branch Mgr*
EMP: 27
SALES (corp-wide): 16.5MM **Privately Held**
SIC: 8641 7991 8351 7032 Youth organizations; physical fitness facilities; child day care services; youth camps; individual & family services
PA: Y M C A Of Central Stark County
　　1201 30th St Nw Ste 200a
　　Canton OH 44709
　　330 491-9622

Upper Arlington
Franklin County

(G-18393)
ARLINGTON COURT NURSING (PA)
Also Called: Arlington Court Skilled
1605 Nw Prof Plz (43220-3866)
PHONE....................614 545-5502
Allan Vrable, *President*
Linda Vrable, *Vice Pres*
James Merrill, *CFO*
Brian Hennis, *Administration*
EMP: 126
SQ FT: 50,000
SALES (est): 5.7MM **Privately Held**
SIC: 8052 8051 Intermediate care facilities; extended care facility

(G-18394)
AUTO DES SYS INC
3518 Riverside Dr (43221-1735)
PHONE....................614 488-7984
Chris Yessios, *President*
David Kropp, *Vice Pres*
Alexandra Yessios, *Vice Pres*
Paul Helm, *Technical Staff*
Matthew Holewinski, *Technical Staff*
EMP: 30
SQ FT: 2,000

SALES (est): 3MM **Privately Held**
WEB: www.autodessys.com
SIC: 7371 7372 Computer software development; prepackaged software

(G-18395)
BARRINGTON ELEM SCHOOL PTO
1780 Barrington Rd (43221-3839)
PHONE....................614 487-5180
Jason Fine, *Principal*
Angie Ullum, *Principal*
EMP: 90
SALES: 176.1K **Privately Held**
SIC: 8641 Parent-teachers' association

(G-18396)
DELTA GAMMA FRATERNITY (PA)
Also Called: ANCHOR TRADER
3250 Riverside Dr (43221-1725)
P.O. Box 21397, Columbus (43221-0397)
PHONE....................614 481-8169
Betsy Fouss, *Exec Dir*
Heather Daverio, *Exec Dir*
EMP: 45
SQ FT: 22,000
SALES: 6.3MM **Privately Held**
SIC: 8641 Fraternal associations

(G-18397)
DELTA GAMMA FRATERNITY
3220 Riverside Dr Ste A2 (43221-1736)
PHONE....................614 487-5599
Nancy Brittle, *Principal*
EMP: 38
SALES (corp-wide): 6.3MM **Privately Held**
SIC: 8641 University club
PA: Delta Gamma Fraternity
　　3250 Riverside Dr
　　Upper Arlington OH 43221
　　614 481-8169

(G-18398)
HOME INSTEAD SENIOR CARE
3220 Riverside Dr Ste C4 (43221-1736)
PHONE....................614 432-8524
Nancy S Barrett-Paschke, *President*
Nancy Barrett Paschke, *Owner*
Ralph B Samson, *Treasurer*
EMP: 53
SQ FT: 1,200
SALES (est): 1.3MM **Privately Held**
SIC: 8082 Home health care services

(G-18399)
KAPPA HOUSE CORP OF DELTA
3220 Riverside Dr Ste A2 (43221-1736)
PHONE....................614 487-9461
Beth Koukol, *Director*
EMP: 39
SALES: 409.7K **Privately Held**
SIC: 8741 Management services

(G-18400)
KENEXIS CONSULTING CORPORATION
3366 Riverside Dr Ste 200 (43221-1734)
PHONE....................614 451-7031
Edward Marszal, *President*
Edward M Marszal, *President*
EMP: 25
SALES: 2.5MM **Privately Held**
SIC: 8711 Engineering services

(G-18401)
MANIFEST SOLUTIONS CORP
Also Called: Manifest Software
2035 Riverside Dr (43221-4012)
PHONE....................614 930-2800
Nancy Matijasich, *President*
Barb Muncie, *Office Admin*
James Balmert, *Consultant*
James Drayer, *Consultant*
Steve Russell, *Consultant*
EMP: 65
SALES (est): 7.3MM **Privately Held**
WEB: www.manifest-solutions.com
SIC: 7371 7373 Computer software systems analysis & design, custom; local area network (LAN) systems integrator

(G-18402)
SUNRISE SENIOR LIVING INC
Also Called: Sunrise On The Scioto
3500 Riverside Dr (43221-1753)
PHONE................................614 457-3500
Suzanne Johns, *Manager*
EMP: 70
SALES (corp-wide): 4.7B **Publicly Held**
WEB: www.sunrise.com
SIC: 8059 8051 Rest home, with health
care; skilled nursing care facilities
HQ: Sunrise Senior Living, Llc
7902 Westpark Dr
Mc Lean VA 22102

Upper Sandusky
Wyandot County

(G-18403)
ANGELINE INDUSTRIES INC
11028 County Highway 44 (43351-9056)
PHONE................................419 294-4488
Todd Dilley, *Director*
EMP: 45
SALES: 1MM **Privately Held**
WEB: www.angeline.com
SIC: 8331 Sheltered workshop

(G-18404)
COUNTY OF WYANDOT
Also Called: Wyandot County Home
7830 State Highway 199 (43351-9333)
PHONE................................419 294-1714
David Oucid, *Owner*
EMP: 92 **Privately Held**
WEB: www.co.wyandot.oh.us
SIC: 8059 Nursing home, except skilled &
intermediate care facility
PA: County Of Wyandot
109 S Sandusky Ave Rm.10
Upper Sandusky OH 43351
419 294-6436

(G-18405)
CUSTOM AGRI SYSTEMS INC
1289 N Warpole St (43351-9381)
PHONE................................419 209-0940
Rick Storch, *President*
EMP: 30
SALES (corp-wide): 57.1MM **Privately
Held**
SIC: 0723 Grain drying services
PA: Custom Agri Systems, Inc.
255 County Road R
Napoleon OH 43545
419 599-5180

(G-18406)
**FAIRBORN EQUIPMENT
COMPANY INC (PA)**
225 Tarhe Trl (43351-8700)
P.O. Box 123 (43351-0123)
PHONE................................419 209-0760
Mark Dillon, *President*
John H Elgin, *Principal*
Jeff Shreve, *Project Mgr*
Dan Kott, *Opers Mgr*
Bob Hare, *VP Sales*
EMP: 60 EST: 1991
SQ FT: 55,000
SALES (est): 51.6MM **Privately Held**
WEB: www.fairbornequipment.com
SIC: 5084 Materials handling machinery

(G-18407)
**FIRST CITIZENS NAT BNK INC
(PA)**
100 N Sandusky Ave (43351-1270)
P.O. Box 299 (43351-0299)
PHONE................................419 294-2351
Mark Johnson, *President*
Robert McClure, *Exec VP*
Brant Zucker, *Vice Pres*
Eli Smith, *Loan Officer*
Mona Fridley, *Cust Mgr*
EMP: 40
SALES: 10.1MM **Privately Held**
SIC: 6021 National commercial banks

(G-18408)
**JPMORGAN CHASE BANK NAT
ASSN**
335 N Sandusky Ave (43351-1139)
PHONE................................419 294-4944
Karen Kline, *Principal*
EMP: 26
SALES (corp-wide): 131.4B **Publicly
Held**
SIC: 6021 National commercial banks
HQ: Jpmorgan Chase Bank, National Asso-
ciation
1111 Polaris Pkwy
Columbus OH 43240
614 436-3055

(G-18409)
**KALMBACH PORK FINISHING
LLC**
7148 State Highway 199 (43351-9346)
PHONE................................419 294-3838
Paul M Kalmbach, *President*
EMP: 100
SALES (est): 15.3MM **Privately Held**
WEB: www.kalmbachfeeds.com
SIC: 5154 Hogs

(G-18410)
KIMMEL CLEANERS INC (PA)
225 N Sandusky Ave (43351-1233)
P.O. Box 98 (43351-0098)
PHONE................................419 294-1959
Kurt Kimmel, *President*
Debbie Amos, *Corp Secy*
Mark Kimmel, *Vice Pres*
Brian Kimmel, *Manager*
EMP: 58
SQ FT: 30,000
SALES (est): 3.4MM **Privately Held**
WEB: www.kimmelcleaners.com
SIC: 7216 7218 7213 Drycleaning plants,
except rugs; laundered mat & rug supply;
industrial uniform supply; towel supply

(G-18411)
**LUCAS FUNERAL HOMES INC
(PA)**
Also Called: Lucas-Batton Funeral Homes
476 S Sandusky Ave (43351-1597)
PHONE................................419 294-1985
Daniel P Lucas, *President*
EMP: 36
SQ FT: 3,000
SALES: 715K **Privately Held**
WEB: www.lucasfh.com
SIC: 7261 5999 Funeral home; alarm &
safety equipment stores

(G-18412)
SCHMIDT MACHINE COMPANY
Also Called: S M C
7013 State Highway 199 (43351-9347)
PHONE................................419 294-3814
Bill, *President*
Randy F Schmidt, *President*
Dorothy M Schmidt, *Principal*
Kevin Schmidt, *Vice Pres*
Darlene Mooney, *Treasurer*
EMP: 50 EST: 1935
SQ FT: 2,500
SALES: 17MM **Privately Held**
WEB: www.schmidtmachine.com
SIC: 3599 7692 5083 Machine shop, job-
bing & repair; welding repair; farm equip-
ment parts & supplies

(G-18413)
STS LOGISTICS INC
13863 County Highway 119 (43351-9413)
PHONE................................419 294-1498
Stephen T Smith, *President*
EMP: 25
SALES (est): 1.8MM **Privately Held**
SIC: 4231 Trucking terminal facilities

(G-18414)
UNITED CHURCH HOMES INC
Also Called: Fairhaven Community
850 Marseilles Ave (43351-1648)
PHONE................................419 294-4973
Daniel Miller, *Director*
EMP: 180

SALES (corp-wide): 78.1MM **Privately
Held**
WEB: www.altenheimcommunity.org
SIC: 8059 8661 8052 Personal care
home, with health care; religious organi-
zations; intermediate care facilities
PA: United Church Homes Inc
170 E Center St
Marion OH 43302
740 382-4885

(G-18415)
WYANDOT COUNTY AG SOC
Also Called: Wyandot County Fair
10171 State Highway 53 N (43351-9272)
P.O. Box 3 (43351-0003)
PHONE................................419 294-4320
Philip Kin, *President*
Nick Derr, *Vice Pres*
Bonnie Miller, *Admin Sec*
EMP: 25
SALES (est): 543.9K **Privately Held**
SIC: 7999 Agricultural fair

(G-18416)
**WYANDOT MEMORIAL
HOSPITAL**
885 N Sandusky Ave (43351-1098)
PHONE................................419 294-4991
Joseph D'Ettorre, *CEO*
J Craig Bowman, *Chairman*
Ty Shaull, *COO*
Abel Walton, *Opers Staff*
Keith Koehler, *Engineer*
EMP: 200 EST: 1950
SQ FT: 68,000
SALES: 43.4MM **Privately Held**
WEB: www.wyandotmemorial.com
SIC: 8062 General medical & surgical hos-
pitals

(G-18417)
**WYANDOT TRACTOR &
IMPLEMENT CO**
Also Called: John Deere Authorized Dealer
10264 County Highway 121 (43351-9798)
P.O. Box 147 (43351-0147)
PHONE................................419 294-2349
Bruce Kuenzli, *President*
Martha Mosser, *Corp Secy*
EMP: 28
SQ FT: 10,000
SALES (est): 4.8MM **Privately Held**
SIC: 5083 Agricultural machinery & equip-
ment

(G-18418)
XPO LOGISTICS FREIGHT INC
1850 E Wyandot Ave (43351-9652)
PHONE................................419 294-5728
Paul Masano, *Manager*
EMP: 25
SALES (corp-wide): 15.3B **Publicly Held**
WEB: www.con-way.com
SIC: 4213 Contract haulers
HQ: Xpo Logistics Freight, Inc.
2211 Old Earhart Rd # 100
Ann Arbor MI 48105
800 755-2728

Urbana
Champaign County

(G-18419)
**BEN EL CHILD DEVELOPMENT
CTR**
1150 Scioto St Ste 200 (43078-2291)
P.O. Box 755 (43078-0755)
PHONE................................937 465-0010
Douglas Stiner, *Director*
Douglas Steiner, *Director*
EMP: 30
SALES: 1MM **Privately Held**
SIC: 8322 General counseling services

(G-18420)
C T WIRELESS
Also Called: C T Communication
731 Scioto St (43078-2147)
PHONE................................937 653-2208
Michael Conrad, *President*
EMP: 56

SALES (est): 1.1MM **Privately Held**
SIC: 4813 4841 5999 ; cable & other pay
television services; telephone equipment
& systems

(G-18421)
**CARDIOLOGIST CLARK &
CHAMPAIGN**
900 E Court St (43078-1887)
PHONE................................937 653-8897
Akber Mohammed, *President*
EMP: 28
SALES (est): 506.6K **Privately Held**
SIC: 8011 Cardiologist & cardio-vascular
specialist

(G-18422)
**CHAMPAIGN CNTY BOARD OF
DD**
Also Called: Champaign County Board of
Mrdd
1250 E Us Highway 36 (43078-8002)
PHONE................................937 653-5217
Jeanne Bowman, *President*
Max Coates, *Vice Pres*
Bill Kremer, *Admin Sec*
EMP: 28
SALES (est): 1.4MM **Privately Held**
SIC: 8322 9431 Individual & family serv-
ices; child health program administration,
government
PA: County Of Champaign
1250 E State Rt 29 Ste 3
Urbana OH 43078
937 653-5217

(G-18423)
**CHAMPAIGN LANDMARK INC
(PA)**
304 Bloomfield Ave (43078-1206)
P.O. Box 828 (43078-0828)
PHONE................................937 652-2135
Dean Terrill, *Ch of Bd*
John T Dunbar, *President*
Doug Mueting, *Treasurer*
Brett Zimmerman, *Admin Sec*
EMP: 40 EST: 1923
SQ FT: 32,400
SALES (est): 23.9MM **Privately Held**
WEB: www.champaignlandmark.com
SIC: 5153 5191 5172 Grains; farm sup-
plies; fertilizer & fertilizer materials;
seeds: field, garden & flower; petroleum
products

(G-18424)
**CHAMPAIGN NATIONAL BANK
URBANA (HQ)**
601 Scioto St (43078-2134)
PHONE................................937 653-1100
Michael J Lamping, *President*
Roger Felch, *Vice Pres*
Steven A Glock, *Vice Pres*
Aaron Stephens, *Vice Pres*
Robert Gantzer, *CFO*
EMP: 36
SQ FT: 8,000
SALES: 18.1MM **Privately Held**
WEB: www.champaignbank.com
SIC: 6021 National commercial banks

(G-18425)
**CHAMPAIGN RESIDENTIAL
SVCS INC (PA)**
1150 Scioto St Ste 201 (43078-2292)
P.O. Box 29 (43078-0029)
PHONE................................937 653-1320
Than Johnson, *CEO*
Ed Corwin, *Chairman*
Scott Delong, *CFO*
Jeff McCulla, *Treasurer*
Steve Loffing, *Human Res Dir*
EMP: 70
SQ FT: 40,000
SALES: 40.1MM **Privately Held**
WEB: www.crsi-oh.com
SIC: 8361 Home for the mentally retarded

(G-18426)
**CHAMPAIGN TELEPHONE
COMPANY (PA)**
Also Called: CT Communications
126 Scioto St (43078-2199)
PHONE................................937 653-4000
Michael Conrad, *President*

Cynthia J Huffman, *Treasurer*
EMP: 25
SQ FT: 5,000
SALES (est): 13.4MM **Privately Held**
WEB: www.ctcn.net
SIC: 4813 Local telephone communications; long distance telephone communications

(G-18427)
CITIZENS NAT BNK URBANA OHIO (HQ)
1 Monument Sq (43078-9918)
PHONE..................................937 653-1200
James Wilson, *President*
Timothy Bunnell, *Vice Pres*
EMP: 45
SQ FT: 8,000
SALES (est): 1.7MM
SALES (corp-wide): 411.9MM **Publicly Held**
WEB: www.citnatbk.com
SIC: 6021 National commercial banks
PA: Park National Corporation
50 N 3rd St
Newark OH 43055
740 349-8451

(G-18428)
CMBB LLC
Also Called: Bundy Baking Solutions
417 E Water St (43078-2367)
P.O. Box 150 (43078-0150)
PHONE..................................937 652-2151
William McCoy, *Principal*
Elizabeth A Bundy, *Corp Secy*
Russell T Bundy, *Mng Member*
EMP: 170
SQ FT: 55,800
SALES (est): 4.8MM **Privately Held**
SIC: 5046 7699 Bakery equipment & supplies; baking pan glazing & cleaning

(G-18429)
COMMUNITY MERCY HLTH PARTNERS
Also Called: Mercy McAuley Center
906 Scioto St (43078-2226)
PHONE..................................937 653-5432
Robin Cornett, *Director*
EMP: 250
SALES (corp-wide): 4.7B **Privately Held**
SIC: 8741 8051 Hospital management; skilled nursing care facilities
HQ: Community Mercy Health Partners
100 Medical Center Dr
Springfield OH 45504

(G-18430)
COUNTY OF CHAMPAIGN
Also Called: Champaign County Engineer
428 Beech St (43078-1920)
P.O. Box 669 (43078-0669)
PHONE..................................937 653-4848
Stephen McCall, *Engineer*
EMP: 31 **Privately Held**
SIC: 8711 Consulting engineer
PA: County Of Champaign
1250 E State Rt 29 Ste 3
Urbana OH 43078
937 653-5217

(G-18431)
DINGLEDINE TRUCKING COMPANY
1000 Phoenix Dr (43078-9387)
PHONE..................................937 652-3454
Kim S Damewood, *President*
Betty Sherman, *Corp Secy*
Brad Damewood, *Vice Pres*
Gerald W Damewood, *Vice Pres*
EMP: 40 **EST:** 1918
SQ FT: 8,700
SALES (est): 7.9MM **Privately Held**
SIC: 4213 4212 Contract haulers; local trucking, without storage

(G-18432)
FARMERS EQUIPMENT INC (PA)
Also Called: Kubota Authorized Dealer
1749 E Us Highway 36 A (43078-9698)
PHONE..................................419 339-7000
Todd Channel, *General Mgr*
Clay Halterman, *Personnel*
Judy McClorey, *Accounts Mgr*

EMP: 42
SALES (est): 12MM **Privately Held**
WEB: www.farmersequipment.com
SIC: 5083 Farm implements; agricultural machinery & equipment

(G-18433)
FIRST TRANSIT INC
2200 S Us Highway 68 (43078-9470)
PHONE..................................937 652-4175
Pam Hoffner, *Branch Mgr*
EMP: 54
SALES (corp-wide): 8.9B **Privately Held**
SIC: 4111 Bus transportation
HQ: First Transit, Inc.
600 Vine St Ste 1400
Cincinnati OH 45202
513 241-2200

(G-18434)
FUTURA BANC CORP (PA)
Also Called: Champagne National Bank
601 Scioto St (43078-2134)
PHONE..................................937 653-1167
Michael J Lamping, *President*
Lee Jordan, *Vice Pres*
Robert Gantzer, *CFO*
Patricia Cromwell, *VP Human Res*
Judy Kizer, *Sales Staff*
EMP: 75
SQ FT: 8,000
SALES (est): 21.2MM **Privately Held**
SIC: 6021 National commercial banks

(G-18435)
GRACE BAPTIST CHURCH (PA)
Also Called: Grace Baptist Preschool
960 Childrens Home Rd (43078-9132)
PHONE..................................937 652-1133
George Riddell, *Pastor*
Joseph Fortna, *Pastor*
Steven Smith, *Pastor*
EMP: 25
SQ FT: 6,300
SALES (est): 955.2K **Privately Held**
SIC: 8661 8211 8351 Baptist Church; elementary & secondary schools; child day care services

(G-18436)
GRIMES AEROSPACE COMPANY
Also Called: Honeywell
550 State Route 55 (43078-9482)
PHONE..................................937 484-2001
Bruce Blagg, *Branch Mgr*
EMP: 300
SALES (corp-wide): 41.8B **Publicly Held**
SIC: 5088 7699 3812 3769 Aircraft & parts; aircraft & heavy equipment repair services; search & navigation equipment; guided missile & space vehicle parts & auxiliary equipment; vehicular lighting equipment
HQ: Grimes Aerospace Company
550 State Route 55
Urbana OH 43078
937 484-2000

(G-18437)
J & J SCHLAEGEL INC
1250 E Us Highway 36 (43078-8002)
PHONE..................................937 652-2045
Jerry Schlaegel, *President*
Jeff Schlaegel, *Vice Pres*
EMP: 25
SQ FT: 625
SALES (est): 5.1MM **Privately Held**
SIC: 1622 Bridge construction

(G-18438)
LAWNVIEW INDUSTRIES INC
1250 E Us Highway 36 (43078-8002)
P.O. Box 38147 (43078-8147)
PHONE..................................937 653-5217
Micheal Misler, *Director*
EMP: 175
SQ FT: 6,000
SALES: 423.2K **Privately Held**
SIC: 3999 3914 2392 2499 Plaques, picture, laminated; trophies; towels, fabric & nonwoven; made from purchased materials; surveyors' stakes, wood; packaging & labeling services; carwashes

(G-18439)
MC AULEY CENTER
906 Scioto St (43078-2299)
PHONE..................................937 653-5432
J Tollefson, *Exec Dir*
Jennifer Tollefson, *Exec Dir*
EMP: 125
SALES: 7.1MM **Privately Held**
SIC: 8051 Convalescent home with continuous nursing care

(G-18440)
MERCY HEALTH
1300 S Us Highway 68 (43078-8409)
PHONE..................................937 653-3445
EMP: 43
SALES (corp-wide): 4.7B **Privately Held**
SIC: 8062 General medical & surgical hospitals
PA: Mercy Health
1701 Mercy Health Pl
Cincinnati OH 45237
513 639-2800

(G-18441)
MESILLA DIALYSIS LLC
Also Called: Midwest Urbana Dialysis
1430 E Us Highway 36 (43078-9112)
PHONE..................................937 484-4600
Jeffrey Spiers, *Principal*
Dianne Baumgardner, *Administration*
EMP: 40
SALES (est): 550.9K **Publicly Held**
SIC: 8092 Kidney dialysis centers
PA: Davita Inc.
2000 16th St
Denver CO 80202

(G-18442)
OHIO HI POINT CAREER CENTER
412 N Main St (43078-1608)
PHONE..................................937 599-3010
Sharon Halter, *President*
EMP: 25
SALES (corp-wide): 16.9MM **Privately Held**
SIC: 8049 Physical therapist
PA: Ohio Hi Point Career Center
2280 State Route 540
Bellefontaine OH 43311
937 599-3010

(G-18443)
RICHARD H FREYHOF (PA)
Also Called: Champaign Realty
1071 S Main St (43078-2578)
P.O. Box 284 (43078-0284)
PHONE..................................937 653-5837
Richard H Freyhof, *Owner*
EMP: 26
SALES (est): 1MM **Privately Held**
SIC: 6531 Selling agent, real estate

(G-18444)
RUSSELL T BUNDY ASSOCIATES INC (PA)
Also Called: Pan-Glo of St Louis
417 E Water St Ste 1 (43078-2154)
P.O. Box 150 (43078-0150)
PHONE..................................937 652-2151
Eric Lang, *General Mgr*
Russell T Bundy, *Principal*
Elizabeth A Bundy, *Corp Secy*
Douglas H Geiser, *Vice Pres*
Scott Mouton, *VP Opers*
◆ **EMP:** 55
SQ FT: 55,800
SALES (est): 62MM **Privately Held**
SIC: 5046 7699 Bakery equipment & supplies; baking pan glazing & cleaning

(G-18445)
THE PEOPLES SAVINGS AND LN CO (PA)
10 Monument Sq (43078-2001)
PHONE..................................937 653-1600
L Richard Kadel, *Ch of Bd*
Brice L Kadel, *President*
Brian Nicol, *Senior VP*
Bill Evans, *Assistant VP*
Ellen Pond, *Assistant VP*
EMP: 25 **EST:** 1892

SALES: 4.8MM **Privately Held**
SIC: 6036 6163 Savings & loan associations, not federally chartered; loan brokers

(G-18446)
WHITES SERVICE CENTER INC
Also Called: White' S Ford
1246 N Main St (43078-5000)
P.O. Box 38129 (43078-8129)
PHONE..................................937 653-5279
Jeffrey White, *President*
James Donahue, *Vice Pres*
James White, *Treasurer*
Leah Timmons, *Finance Mgr*
Lance White, *Sales Staff*
EMP: 32 **EST:** 1948
SQ FT: 18,000
SALES (est): 13.9MM **Privately Held**
SIC: 5511 5013 5012 Automobiles, new & used; automotive supplies & parts; trucks, commercial

(G-18447)
YMCA
191 Community Dr (43078-6001)
PHONE..................................937 653-9622
Paul Waldsmith, *CEO*
Kathy Finney, *Director*
EMP: 100
SALES (est): 1.2MM **Privately Held**
SIC: 7999 8322 7991 Recreation center; individual & family services; physical fitness facilities

---

Urbancrest
Franklin County

(G-18448)
DECISIONONE CORPORATION
3425 Urbancrest Indus Dr (43123-1775)
PHONE..................................614 883-0228
Mike Barnett, *Business Mgr*
John Tennyson, *Business Mgr*
Liz Fravel, *Financial Exec*
Dave Perorazio, *Manager*
Kevin Leapley, *Manager*
EMP: 50
SALES (corp-wide): 49MM **Privately Held**
WEB: www.decisionone.com
SIC: 7378 7374 Computer & data processing equipment repair/maintenance; data processing service
HQ: Decisionone Corporation
640 Lee Rd Frnt
Wayne PA 19087
610 296-6000

(G-18449)
IRON MOUNTAIN INCORPORATED
3250 Urbancrest Indus Dr (43123-1768)
PHONE..................................614 801-0151
Roxann Mc Naughton, *Branch Mgr*
EMP: 51
SALES (corp-wide): 4.2B **Publicly Held**
SIC: 4226 Document & office records storage
PA: Iron Mountain Incorporated
1 Federal St Fl 7
Boston MA 02110
617 535-4766

(G-18450)
MCKESSON MEDICAL-SURGICAL INC
3500 Centerpoint Dr (43123-1495)
PHONE..................................614 539-2600
Steve Robenolt, *Vice Pres*
Bill Heiser, *Branch Mgr*
Josh Morton, *Supervisor*
EMP: 200
SALES (corp-wide): 208.3B **Publicly Held**
WEB: www.gmholdings.com
SIC: 5047 Medical equipment & supplies
HQ: Mckesson Medical-Surgical Inc.
9954 Mayland Dr Ste 4000
Richmond VA 23233
804 264-7500

(G-18451)
PALMER-DONAVIN MFG CO
3210 Centerpoint Dr (43123-1464)
PHONE.....................................614 277-2777
David Zimmerman, *Vice Pres*
EMP: 81
SALES (corp-wide): 242MM **Privately Held**
WEB: www.palmerdonavin.com
SIC: 5031 Building materials, exterior
PA: The Palmer-Donavin Manufacturing Company
3210 Centerpoint Dr
Columbus OH 43212
800 652-1234

(G-18452)
UNITED PARCEL SERVICE INC OH
Also Called: UPS
3500 Centerpoint Dr (43123-1495)
PHONE.....................................614 277-3300
EMP: 316
SALES (corp-wide): 71.8B **Publicly Held**
SIC: 7389 Mailbox rental & related service
HQ: United Parcel Service, Inc. (Oh)
55 Glenlake Pkwy
Atlanta GA 30328
404 828-6000

(G-18453)
YOUNG MENS CHRISTIAN ASSOC
Also Called: Southwest Community Center
3500 1st Ave (43123-1390)
PHONE.....................................614 539-1770
Linda Day-Mackessy, *Vice Pres*
Kim Jordan, *Branch Mgr*
Scott Debney, *Software Dev*
Nancy Brody, *Director*
Caroline Rankin, *Training Spec*
EMP: 30
SALES (corp-wide): 44.9MM **Privately Held**
WEB: www.ymca-columbus.com
SIC: 8641 7991 8351 7032 Youth organizations; physical fitness facilities; child day care services; youth camps; individual & family services
PA: Young Men's Christian Association Of Central Ohio
40 W Long St
Columbus OH 43215
614 389-4409

Utica
Licking County

(G-18454)
C E S CREDIT UNION INC
8 N Main St (43080-7706)
PHONE.....................................740 892-3323
Kathy Robinson, *Manager*
EMP: 25
SALES (corp-wide): 4MM **Privately Held**
SIC: 6062 State credit unions
PA: C E S Credit Union, Inc.
1215 Yauger Rd
Mount Vernon OH 43050
740 397-1136

(G-18455)
CROUSE IMPLEMENT
14149 North St (43080-9437)
PHONE.....................................740 892-2086
Richard Crouse, *Owner*
EMP: 25
SALES (est): 2.7MM **Privately Held**
SIC: 5083 Farm implements

(G-18456)
LICKING RURAL ELECTRIFICATION (PA)
11339 Mount Vernon Rd (43080-7703)
P.O. Box 455 (43080-0455)
PHONE.....................................740 892-2071
Charles Manning, *President*
Dave Mussard, *Chairman*
Arland K Rogers, *Corp Secy*
George Charles Manning, *COO*
Neil Buxton, *Vice Pres*
EMP: 58 EST: 1936
SQ FT: 20,000

SALES (est): 65.2MM **Privately Held**
SIC: 4911 Distribution, electric power

(G-18457)
LIVING CARE ALTRNTVES OF UTICA
Also Called: Utica Nursing Home
233 N Main St (43080-7705)
P.O. Box 518 (43080-0518)
PHONE.....................................740 892-3414
Thomas J Rosser, *President*
EMP: 50 EST: 1960
SQ FT: 7,500
SALES (est): 1.8MM **Privately Held**
SIC: 8052 Personal care facility

(G-18458)
UTICA VOLUNTEER EMRGNCY SQUAD
39 Spring St (43080-9010)
P.O. Box 147 (43080-0147)
PHONE.....................................740 892-2369
William Cronin, *Chief*
Rex Stevenson, *Vice Pres*
EMP: 25
SALES: 350.8K **Privately Held**
SIC: 4119 Ambulance service

Valley City
Medina County

(G-18459)
CHGC INC
Also Called: Cherokee Hills Golf Club
5740 Center Rd (44280-9746)
PHONE.....................................330 225-6122
Ed Haddad, *President*
Marcia Haddad, *Treasurer*
Mark Haddad, *Admin Sec*
EMP: 85
SQ FT: 20,000
SALES (est): 3.9MM **Privately Held**
WEB: www.cherokeehillsgolf.com
SIC: 7992 5812 Public golf courses; eating places

(G-18460)
DAVIS TREE FARM & NURSERY INC
6126 Neff Rd (44280-9530)
PHONE.....................................330 483-3324
Michael Davis, *President*
EMP: 40 EST: 1989
SALES (est): 1.2MM **Privately Held**
SIC: 5193 Nursery stock

(G-18461)
DUNLOP AND JOHNSTON INC
5498 Innovation Dr (44280-9352)
PHONE.....................................330 220-2700
William H Spencer, *CEO*
Randolph B Spencer, *President*
EMP: 30 EST: 1910
SQ FT: 15,000
SALES (est): 10.5MM **Privately Held**
WEB: www.dunlopandjohnston.com
SIC: 1542 1541 Commercial & office building, new construction; industrial buildings & warehouses

(G-18462)
EMH INC (PA)
Also Called: Engineered Material Handling
550 Crane Dr (44280-9361)
PHONE.....................................330 220-8600
Edis Hazne, *President*
Dave Comiono, *Vice Pres*
Barbara Held, *Purchasing*
Don Fenton, *Regl Sales Mgr*
◆ EMP: 40
SQ FT: 65,000
SALES (est): 10MM **Privately Held**
WEB: www.emh-inc.com
SIC: 3536 8711 3441 Cranes & monorail systems; hoists; fabricated structural metal

(G-18463)
INDEPENDENT STEEL COMPANY LLC
615 Liverpool Dr (44280-9717)
P.O. Box 472 (44280-0472)
PHONE.....................................330 225-7741
Mark Schwertner, *President*
Mark A Schwertner, *Vice Pres*
John F Krupinski, *Mng Member*
James P Bouchard,
Thomas Modrowski,
▲ EMP: 50 EST: 1957
SQ FT: 110,000
SALES (est): 25.4MM **Privately Held**
WEB: www.independentsteel.com
SIC: 5051 7389 3316 Steel; metal cutting services; cold finishing of steel shapes
PA: Esmark Steel Group, Llc
2500 Euclid Ave
Chicago Heights IL 60411

(G-18464)
LIFE CARE CENTERS AMERICA INC
Also Called: Life Care Centers of Medina
2400 Columbia Rd (44280)
PHONE.....................................330 483-3131
Steve Wolf, *Manager*
EMP: 200
SALES (corp-wide): 119.8MM **Privately Held**
SIC: 8051 8052 Skilled nursing care facilities; intermediate care facilities
PA: Life Care Centers Of America, Inc.
3570 Keith St Nw
Cleveland TN 37312
423 472-9585

(G-18465)
LIVERPOOL COIL PROCESSING INC
Also Called: Liverpool-Coil-Processing
880 Steel Dr (44280-9310)
PHONE.....................................330 558-2600
Ramzi Hermiz, *CEO*
James Fanello, *Vice Pres*
Robert Grissinger, *Treasurer*
David J Hessler, *Admin Sec*
EMP: 101
SQ FT: 223,000
SALES (est): 10MM **Publicly Held**
WEB: www.shiloh.com
SIC: 4225 General warehousing & storage
PA: Shiloh Industries, Inc.
880 Steel Dr
Valley City OH 44280

(G-18466)
LUK-AFTERMARKET SERVICE INC
Also Called: As Automotive Systems
5370 Wegman Dr (44280-9700)
PHONE.....................................330 273-4383
Gerald Hinderhan, *President*
◆ EMP: 65 EST: 1996
SQ FT: 100,000
SALES (est): 11.2MM
SALES (corp-wide): 68.1B **Privately Held**
WEB: www.lukclutch.com
SIC: 5013 Motor vehicle supplies & new parts
HQ: Iho Holding Gmbh & Co. Kg
Industriestr. 1-3
Herzogenaurach 91074
913 282-0

(G-18467)
MTD HOLDINGS INC (PA)
5965 Grafton Rd (44280-9329)
P.O. Box 368022, Cleveland (44136-9722)
PHONE.....................................330 225-2600
Curtis E Moll, *Ch of Bd*
Jason Belsito, *Opers Mgr*
Jeff Deuch, *Treasurer*
▼ EMP: 500
SALES (est): 2.4B **Privately Held**
SIC: 3524 3544 3469 6141 Lawn & garden equipment; lawnmowers, residential: hand or power; special dies & tools; metal stampings; financing: automobiles, furniture, etc., not a deposit bank

(G-18468)
RUSTY OAK NURSERY LTD
1547 Marks Rd (44280-9779)
P.O. Box 436 (44280-0436)
PHONE.....................................330 225-7704
Charlie Bailey, *Foreman/Supr*
Joe Vasel, *Sales Staff*
Chad Cekada, *Supervisor*
Mario Cekada,
Karen Cekada,
EMP: 30
SQ FT: 8,000
SALES (est): 2.4MM **Privately Held**
SIC: 5193 Nursery stock

(G-18469)
SHILOH MANUFACTURING LLC (HQ)
880 Steel Dr (44280-9736)
PHONE.....................................330 558-2693
Ramzi Hermiz, *CEO*
Thomas Dugan, *President*
EMP: 50
SALES (est): 57.1MM **Publicly Held**
SIC: 5013 Automotive supplies & parts

(G-18470)
THREE D METALS INC (PA)
5462 Innovation Dr (44280-9352)
PHONE.....................................330 220-0451
David Dickens Sr, *CEO*
David D Dickens Jr, *President*
Matt Hutchison, *General Mgr*
Jeffrey Cox, *Vice Pres*
Jeremy Storrow, *Plant Mgr*
▲ EMP: 72
SQ FT: 146,000
SALES (est): 62.4MM **Privately Held**
WEB: www.threedmetals.com
SIC: 5051 Strip, metal

Van Wert
Van Wert County

(G-18471)
ALEXANDER AND BEBOUT INC
10098 Lincoln Hwy (45891-9351)
PHONE.....................................419 238-9567
Thomas Alexander, *President*
T J Staude, *Vice Pres*
Charlie Salway, *Project Mgr*
Lori Dasher, *Treasurer*
Sylvia Alexander, *Admin Sec*
EMP: 62 EST: 1965
SQ FT: 9,500
SALES (est): 10.1MM **Privately Held**
WEB: www.alexanderbebout.com
SIC: 1521 Single-family housing construction

(G-18472)
ALL AMERICA INSURANCE COMPANY (HQ)
Also Called: CENTRAL INSURANCE COMPANIES
800 S Washington St (45891-2357)
PHONE.....................................419 238-1010
Francis W Purmort III, *President*
Jon A Rhoades, *Principal*
Karl Waite, *Principal*
Jeffrey L Hanson, *Vice Pres*
Michael Thompson, *Vice Pres*
EMP: 350
SQ FT: 200,000
SALES: 101.9MM
SALES (corp-wide): 535.3MM **Privately Held**
SIC: 6411 Insurance agents, brokers & service
PA: Central Mutual Insurance Company
800 S Washington St
Van Wert OH 45891
419 238-1010

(G-18473)
AYERS-STERRETT INC
222 N Market St (45891-1245)
PHONE.....................................419 238-5480
Stan Ayers Jr, *President*
Kim Ayers, *Corp Secy*
EMP: 25

SALES (est): 2.5MM **Privately Held**
WEB: www.ayers-sterrett.com
SIC: 1711 Mechanical contractor

(G-18474)
CENTRAL MUTUAL INSURANCE CO (PA)
Also Called: CENTRAL INSURANCE COMPANIES
800 S Washington St (45891-2357)
PHONE.............................419 238-1010
Francis W Purmort III, *Ch of Bd*
Jeff Hanson, *Vice Pres*
Thad Eikenbary, *Treasurer*
Edward Buhl, *Admin Sec*
EMP: 385
SQ FT: 200,000
SALES: 535.3MM **Privately Held**
WEB: www.central-insurance.com
SIC: 6331 Fire, marine & casualty insurance

(G-18475)
COMMUNITY HLTH PRFSSIONALS INC (PA)
Also Called: CELINA AREA VISITING NURSES AS
1159 Westwood Dr (45891-2464)
PHONE.............................419 238-9223
Brent Tow, *President*
EMP: 140
SQ FT: 13,500
SALES: 13.1MM **Privately Held**
SIC: 8082 7361 Visiting nurse service; nurses' registry

(G-18476)
COMPREHENSIVE HEALTH CARE INC
140 Fox Rd Ste 402 (45891-3406)
PHONE.............................419 238-7777
Paul Kalogerou, *President*
Judy Kalogerou, *Treasurer*
Byron Kalogerou, *Admin Sec*
EMP: 25
SALES (est): 1.1MM **Privately Held**
WEB: www.chc-mso.com
SIC: 8011 General & family practice, physician/surgeon

(G-18477)
ELMCO ENGINEERING OH INC
1171 Grill Rd (45891-9386)
P.O. Box 705 (45891-0705)
PHONE.............................419 238-1100
John Metzger, *President*
David Lilly, *Corp Secy*
Robert Beherns, *Vice Pres*
EMP: 25
SQ FT: 3,200
SALES (est): 5.3MM **Privately Held**
WEB: www.elmco-press.com
SIC: 7699 Industrial machinery & equipment repair; industrial tool grinding

(G-18478)
GKN FREIGHT SERVICES INC (DH)
700 Fox Rd (45891-2441)
PHONE.............................419 232-5623
Russell Davies, *Managing Dir*
Peter Cook, *Vice Pres*
Terry Brooks, *Opers Staff*
Andrew Buller, *Finance*
Scott Long, *Manager*
◆ EMP: 34
SALES (est): 22.6MM
SALES (corp-wide): 2.7B **Privately Held**
WEB: www.gknfreightservices.com
SIC: 4731 Freight forwarding
HQ: Gkn America Corp.
　　1180 Peachtree St Ne # 2450
　　Atlanta GA 30309
　　630 972-9300

(G-18479)
HCF OF VAN WERT INC
Also Called: Van Wert Manor
160 Fox Rd (45891-2440)
PHONE.............................419 999-2010
James Unberferth, *President*
Van Wert, *Human Resources*
Meghan Dicke, *Pub Rel Dir*
Lisa Kiel, *Technology*
Tina Hulbert, *Executive*

EMP: 95
SALES: 950K
SALES (corp-wide): 154.8MM **Privately Held**
SIC: 8051 Convalescent home with continuous nursing care
PA: Hcf Management, Inc.
　　1100 Shawnee Rd
　　Lima OH 45805
　　419 999-2010

(G-18480)
HOSPICE CARING WAY
1159 Westwood Dr (45891-2464)
PHONE.............................419 238-9223
Brent Tow, *President*
Linda Boggs, *Vice Pres*
EMP: 950
SALES: 950K **Privately Held**
SIC: 8082 Visiting nurse service

(G-18481)
JOHNSON ADAMS & PROTROUSKI
1178 Professional Dr (45891-2461)
PHONE.............................419 238-6251
Robert Adams MD, *Partner*
Terrence Johnson MD, *Partner*
EMP: 40
SALES (est): 2.1MM **Privately Held**
SIC: 8011 General & family practice, physician/surgeon

(G-18482)
LIFE STAR RESCUE INC
1171 Production Dr (45891-9390)
PHONE.............................419 238-2507
Jim Dondlinger, *President*
Dond Linger, *Principal*
Jim Snyder, *Principal*
Lyle Halstead, *Vice Pres*
EMP: 25
SQ FT: 50,000
SALES (est): 6.3MM
SALES (corp-wide): 1.6B **Privately Held**
WEB: www.holmanenterprises.com
SIC: 5521 5012 3713 Pickups & vans, used; ambulances; ambulance bodies
PA: Holman Enterprises Inc.
　　244 E Kings Hwy
　　Maple Shade NJ 08052
　　856 663-5200

(G-18483)
LINCOLNVIEW LOCAL SCHOOLS (PA)
15945 Middle Point Rd (45891-9769)
PHONE.............................419 968-2226
Troy Bowersock, *Treasurer*
Deb Stetler, *Librarian*
Greg Leeth, *Athletic Dir*
Doug Fries, *Administration*
EMP: 120 EST: 1960
SALES (est): 4.5MM **Privately Held**
SIC: 8211 8741 Public elementary school; public senior high school; management services

(G-18484)
MARSH FOUNDATION
1229 Lincoln Hwy (45891-1877)
P.O. Box 150 (45891-0150)
PHONE.............................419 238-1695
James E Price, *Treasurer*
Jeff Grothouse, *Exec Dir*
EMP: 50 EST: 1925
SALES: 6.7MM **Privately Held**
WEB: www.marshfoundation.org
SIC: 8211 8322 Boarding school; individual & family services

(G-18485)
OPTIMIST INTERNATIONAL
1008 Woodland Ave (45891-1433)
PHONE.............................419 238-5086
Jane Moss, *President*
EMP: 61
SALES: 93.8K **Privately Held**
WEB: www.optimistinternational.com
SIC: 8641 Social associations

(G-18486)
PLASTIC RECYCLING TECH INC
7600 Us Route 127 (45891-9363)
PHONE.............................419 238-9395
Matt Kreigel, *Branch Mgr*

EMP: 50
SALES (corp-wide): 45.2MM **Privately Held**
SIC: 4953 Recycling, waste materials
PA: Plastic Recycling Technology, Inc.
　　9054 N County Road 25a
　　Piqua OH 45356
　　937 615-9286

(G-18487)
PRIVATE DUTY SERVICES INC
1157 Westwood Dr (45891-2464)
PHONE.............................419 238-3714
Brent Tow, *President*
EMP: 200
SQ FT: 5,000
SALES: 2.6MM **Privately Held**
SIC: 8082 8322 Visiting nurse service; individual & family services

(G-18488)
SCHUMM RICHARD A PLBG & HTG
Also Called: Schumm Plumbing & Heating
9883 Liberty Union Rd (45891-9142)
PHONE.............................419 238-4994
Richard A Schumm, *President*
Phyllis A Schumm, *Corp Secy*
Erna W Schumm, *Vice Pres*
EMP: 28
SQ FT: 10,000
SALES (est): 3.2MM **Privately Held**
SIC: 1711 1794 Warm air heating & air conditioning contractor; excavation work

(G-18489)
STORE & HAUL INC
Also Called: Store & Haul Trucking
1165 Grill Rd (45891-9386)
PHONE.............................419 238-4284
Curt Rager, *President*
Jerry Rager, *Vice Pres*
EMP: 38
SQ FT: 13,000
SALES: 5.5MM **Privately Held**
SIC: 4213 Trucking, except local

(G-18490)
UNITED STEELWORKERS
Also Called: Uswa
351 Pleasant St Ste 1 (45891-1923)
PHONE.............................419 238-7980
Patrick Herman, *Manager*
EMP: 25
SALES (corp-wide): 4.9MM **Privately Held**
WEB: www.uswa.org
SIC: 8631 Labor union
PA: United Steelworkers
　　60 Bolevard Of The Allies
　　Pittsburgh PA 15222
　　412 562-2400

(G-18491)
VAN RUE INCORPORATED
Also Called: Vancrest Health Care Center
10357 Van Wert Decatur Rd (45891-8425)
PHONE.............................419 238-0715
Mark A White, *President*
Connie Elder, *Purch Mgr*
Michelle White, *Purch Agent*
Steve White, *Treasurer*
Tammy Gregory, *Human Res Dir*
EMP: 250
SQ FT: 90,000
SALES (est): 12.5MM **Privately Held**
SIC: 8051 Convalescent home with continuous nursing care

(G-18492)
VAN WERT COUNTY DAY CARE INC
Also Called: WEE CARE LEARNING CENTER
10485 Van Wert Decatur Rd (45891-9209)
P.O. Box 107 (45891-0107)
PHONE.............................419 238-9918
Faith Fadian, *Director*
EMP: 39
SALES: 847.8K **Privately Held**
SIC: 8351 Group day care center

(G-18493)
VAN WERT COUNTY ENGINEERS
1192 Grill Rd (45891-9389)
PHONE.............................419 238-0210
Kyle Wendel, *Engineer*
EMP: 35
SALES (est): 2.2MM **Privately Held**
SIC: 7549 Road service, automotive

(G-18494)
VAN WERT COUNTY HOSPITAL ASSN (PA)
1250 S Washington St (45891-2551)
PHONE.............................419 238-2390
Mark Minick, *President*
Angela Snyder, *Principal*
Jon Bagley, *Chairman*
Sheila Brokenshire, *Vice Pres*
Tiffany Unverferth, *Human Res Dir*
EMP: 69 EST: 1905
SQ FT: 80,000
SALES: 55.1MM **Privately Held**
SIC: 8062 General medical & surgical hospitals

(G-18495)
VAN WERT COUNTY HOSPITAL ASSN
140 Fox Rd Ste 201 (45891-2492)
PHONE.............................419 232-2077
Nick Spoonmore, *Branch Mgr*
EMP: 120
SALES (corp-wide): 55.1MM **Privately Held**
SIC: 8011 General & family practice, physician/surgeon
PA: The Van Wert County Hospital Association
　　1250 S Washington St
　　Van Wert OH 45891
　　419 238-2390

(G-18496)
VAN WERT MEDICAL SERVICES LTD
140 Fox Rd Ste 105 (45891-2490)
PHONE.............................419 238-7727
Mark Minick, *President*
EMP: 281
SALES (est): 2.2MM
SALES (corp-wide): 55.1MM **Privately Held**
SIC: 8062 General medical & surgical hospitals
PA: The Van Wert County Hospital Association
　　1250 S Washington St
　　Van Wert OH 45891
　　419 238-2390

(G-18497)
WESTWOOD BEHAVIORAL HEALTH CTR
1158 Westwood Dr (45891-2449)
P.O. Box 601 (45891-0601)
PHONE.............................419 238-3434
Thomas Stricker, *Exec Dir*
EMP: 25
SQ FT: 6,245
SALES: 3.5MM **Privately Held**
SIC: 8093 Mental health clinic, outpatient

(G-18498)
YOUNG MENS CHRISTIAN ASSN
Also Called: YMCA
241 W Main St (45891-1673)
PHONE.............................419 238-0443
Heather Tribolet, *Office Mgr*
Brad Perrot, *Director*
Kristin Lichtensteiger, *Director*
Kevin Morrison, *Director*
Clint Myers, *Director*
EMP: 32
SALES: 1.2MM **Privately Held**
SIC: 8641 7991 8351 7032 Youth organizations; physical fitness facilities; child day care services; youth camps; individual & family services

(G-18499)
YOUNG WOMENS CHRISTIAN
Also Called: YWCA
408 E Main St (45891-1809)
PHONE...................................419 238-6639
Jennifer Jackson, *Principal*
EMP: 30
SALES (corp-wide): 7.3MM **Privately Held**
SIC: 8641 7991 8351 7032 Youth organizations; physical fitness facilities; child day care services; youth camps; individual & family services
PA: The Young Women's Christian Association Of The City Of New York
52 Broadway
New York NY 10004
212 755-4500

Vandalia
Montgomery County

(G-18500)
A M COMMUNICATIONS LTD
4431 Old Springfield Rd (45377-9739)
PHONE...................................419 528-3051
Alan Miller, *Branch Mgr*
EMP: 81
SALES (corp-wide): 22.2MM **Privately Held**
PA: A M Communications, Ltd.
5707 State Route 309
Galion OH 44833
419 528-3051

(G-18501)
AMERICAN AIRLINES INC
Also Called: US Airways
10398 Freight Dr (45377-3304)
PHONE...................................937 454-7472
Dave Loving, *Branch Mgr*
EMP: 100
SALES (corp-wide): 44.5B **Publicly Held**
WEB: www.usair.com
SIC: 4512 Scheduled Air Transportation
HQ: American Airlines, Inc.
4333 Amon Carter Blvd
Fort Worth TX 76155
817 963-1234

(G-18502)
AMERICAN AIRLINES INC
3600 Terminal Rd Ste 1 (45377-1079)
PHONE...................................937 890-6668
Cyrus Spaulding, *General Mgr*
EMP: 40
SALES (corp-wide): 44.5B **Publicly Held**
WEB: www.aa.com
SIC: 4512 Air passenger carrier, scheduled
HQ: American Airlines, Inc.
4333 Amon Carter Blvd
Fort Worth TX 76155
817 963-1234

(G-18503)
AMERICAN WAY VAN AND STOR INC
Also Called: American Way Van & Storage
1001 S Brown School Rd (45377-9632)
P.O. Box 547 (45377-0547)
PHONE...................................937 898-7294
Robert G Vann, *President*
Diana Vann, *Vice Pres*
Adam Vann, *Opers Mgr*
Wanda Lacey, *Accountant*
Christine Cox, *Manager*
EMP: 30
SQ FT: 30,000
SALES: 4.4MM **Privately Held**
WEB: www.awvs.com
SIC: 4214 Local trucking with storage

(G-18504)
ASET CORPORATION (PA)
407 Corporate Center Dr (45377-1176)
P.O. Box 247 (45377-0247)
PHONE...................................937 890-8881
Teresa Lucas, *Vice Pres*
Charles Carroll, *Sales Executive*
EMP: 25

SALES (est): 3.8MM **Privately Held**
SIC: 8299 7381 Educational services; detective & armored car services; detective services

(G-18505)
AVIS ADMINISTRATION
3300 Valet Dr (45377-1000)
PHONE...................................937 898-2581
Robert Salerno, *President*
Dwayne Clark, *General Mgr*
Cindy Rose, *Manager*
Kris Skinner, *Manager*
EMP: 99
SALES (est): 2.4MM **Privately Held**
SIC: 7514 Rent-a-car service

(G-18506)
BALANCING COMPANY INC (PA)
898 Center Dr (45377-3130)
PHONE...................................937 898-9111
Donald K Belcher, *President*
Michael W Belcher, *President*
Jack Boeke, *Vice Pres*
Jack Pequignot, *Accountant*
Doug Kelchner, *Manager*
EMP: 31 EST: 1967
SQ FT: 53,000
SALES (est): 6.5MM **Privately Held**
WEB: www.balco.com
SIC: 3599 8734 3544 Machine shop, jobbing & repair; testing laboratories; special dies, tools, jigs & fixtures

(G-18507)
BASIC DRUGS INC
Also Called: Basic Vitamins
300 Corporate Center Dr (45377-1162)
P.O. Box 412 (45377-0412)
PHONE...................................937 898-4010
Doris Fischer Lamb, *Ch of Bd*
Nancy Green, *President*
Robert F Fischer Jr, *Corp Secy*
Sharon Erbaugh, *VP Opers*
John Fischer, *Manager*
EMP: 36
SQ FT: 12,200
SALES (est): 9.1MM **Privately Held**
WEB: www.basicvitamins.com
SIC: 5122 Vitamins & minerals

(G-18508)
BND RENTALS INC
Also Called: Vandalia Rental
950 Engle Rd (45377-9690)
P.O. Box 160 (45377-0160)
PHONE...................................937 898-5061
Randy Barney, *President*
Jack W Barney, *Principal*
Carl B Nickel, *Principal*
Kathy Barney, *Corp Secy*
EMP: 32
SQ FT: 25,000
SALES (est): 7MM **Privately Held**
WEB: www.vandaliarental.com
SIC: 7359 Tool rental

(G-18509)
BUDGET RENT A CAR SYSTEM INC
Also Called: Budget Rent-A-Car
3300 Valet Dr (45377-1072)
PHONE...................................937 898-1396
Dick Hagopian, *General Mgr*
EMP: 50
SALES (corp-wide): 9.1B **Publicly Held**
WEB: www.blackdogventures.com
SIC: 7515 7514 Passenger car leasing; passenger car rental
HQ: Budget Rent A Car System, Inc.
6 Sylvan Way Ste 1
Parsippany NJ 07054
973 496-3500

(G-18510)
BUILDERS FIRSTSOURCE INC
4173 Old Springfield Rd (45377-9574)
PHONE...................................937 898-1358
Denny Edwards, *Branch Mgr*
EMP: 30
SQ FT: 11,250
SALES (corp-wide): 7.7B **Publicly Held**
WEB: www.hopelumber.com
SIC: 5031 1751 Lumber, plywood & millwork; cabinet & finish carpentry

PA: Builders Firstsource, Inc.
2001 Bryan St Ste 1600
Dallas TX 75201
214 880-3500

(G-18511)
BUTLER ASPHALT CO LLC
7500 Johnson Station Rd (45377-9465)
PHONE...................................937 890-1141
Jamie Voisard, *Accountant*
David A Poynter,
EMP: 37
SQ FT: 3,000
SALES (est): 4.6MM
SALES (corp-wide): 84MM **Privately Held**
WEB: www.jrjnet.com
SIC: 1611 Highway & street paving contractor; surfacing & paving
PA: John R. Jurgensen Co.
11641 Mosteller Rd
Cincinnati OH 45241
513 771-0820

(G-18512)
CAREY ELECTRIC CO
3925 Vanco Ln (45377-9743)
PHONE...................................937 669-3399
Rick O'Cull, *President*
Anita Bernard, *Vice Pres*
Ryan O'Cull, *Project Mgr*
Doug Smith, *Manager*
EMP: 40
SQ FT: 3,500
SALES: 7.3MM **Privately Held**
WEB: www.careyelectric.com
SIC: 1731 General electrical contractor

(G-18513)
CHARTER VANS INC
Also Called: Charter Vans Tours
303 Corporate Center Dr # 100 (45377-1178)
P.O. Box 90035, Dayton (45490-0035)
PHONE...................................937 898-4043
Marianne Smith, *General Mgr*
Beverly J Mc Kiban, *Corp Secy*
Gregory Mc Kiban, *Vice Pres*
EMP: 33
SALES (est): 2MM **Privately Held**
WEB: www.chartervans.com
SIC: 4111 4141 Airport transportation; local bus charter service

(G-18514)
CIRCUITS & CABLES INC
Also Called: C & C Industries
815 S Brown School Rd (45377-9632)
PHONE...................................937 415-2070
Michael Seibert, *President*
Cindy Seibert, *Vice Pres*
Jerriann Doll, *Electrical Engi*
EMP: 40
SQ FT: 40,000
SALES (est): 11.3MM **Privately Held**
WEB: www.circuitsandcables.com
SIC: 8711 Consulting engineer

(G-18515)
CITY OF DAYTON
Also Called: Aviation, Department of
3600 Terminal Rd Ste 300 (45377-3313)
PHONE...................................937 454-8200
Michael Etter, *Chief*
Pam Hixon, *Business Mgr*
Gilbert Turner, *Opers Staff*
Jim Davis, *Finance Mgr*
Michael Brading, *Supervisor*
EMP: 135
SQ FT: 672 **Privately Held**
WEB: www.daytonconventioncenter.com
SIC: 4581 4512 Airport; air transportation, scheduled
PA: City Of Dayton
101 W 3rd St
Dayton OH 45402
937 333-3333

(G-18516)
CITY OF DAYTON
Also Called: Department of Aviation
3848 Wright Dr (45377-1004)
PHONE...................................937 454-8231
Joseph Homan, *Finance*
Sarah Spees, *Sales Executive*
Dan France, *Branch Mgr*

Mark Kowalski, *Supervisor*
EMP: 40 **Privately Held**
WEB: www.daytonconventioncenter.com
SIC: 4581 Airport
PA: City Of Dayton
101 W 3rd St
Dayton OH 45402
937 333-3333

(G-18517)
CITY OF VANDALIA
Also Called: Cassel Hills Golf Course
201 Clubhouse Way (45377-9693)
PHONE...................................937 890-1300
John Marchi, *Manager*
EMP: 35 **Privately Held**
WEB: www.vandaliaohio.net
SIC: 7992 7299 Public golf courses; banquet hall facilities
PA: City Of Vandalia
333 James Bohanan Dr # 3
Vandalia OH 45377
937 898-5891

(G-18518)
COLDWELL BNKR HRITG RLTORS LLC
356 N Dixie Dr Ste 1 (45377-2063)
PHONE...................................937 890-2200
Linda Gabbard, *Manager*
EMP: 39
SALES (corp-wide): 6.5MM **Privately Held**
WEB: www.coldwellbankerdayton.com
SIC: 6531 Real estate agent, residential
PA: Coldwell Banker Heritage Realtors Llc
2000 Hewitt Ave
Dayton OH 45440
937 434-7600

(G-18519)
DATWYLER SLING SLTIONS USA INC
Also Called: Columbia
875 Center Dr (45377-3129)
PHONE...................................937 387-2800
Mark Bueltel, *Accountant*
Denise Bagaieh, *Human Res Mgr*
Brian Bueltel, *Sales Staff*
◆ EMP: 67
SQ FT: 100,000
SALES (est): 22MM
SALES (corp-wide): 1.3B **Privately Held**
WEB: www.columbiaerd.com
SIC: 5085 3069 3061 Seals, industrial; gaskets; molded rubber products; mechanical rubber goods
HQ: Keystone Holdings, Inc.
875 Center Dr
Vandalia OH 45377

(G-18520)
DOOR FABRICATION SERVICES INC
3250 Old Springfield Rd # 1 (45377-9599)
PHONE...................................937 454-9207
Brian Hakers, *Manager*
▲ EMP: 45
SALES (est): 4.8MM
SALES (corp-wide): 2.1B **Publicly Held**
WEB: www.masonite.com
SIC: 5046 2431 Partitions; millwork
PA: Masonite International Corporation
201 N Franklin St Ste 300
Tampa FL 33602
800 895-2723

(G-18521)
FAR OAKS ORTHOPEDISTS INC
55 Elva Ct Ste 100 (45377-1875)
PHONE...................................937 298-0452
Dan Morris, *Manager*
EMP: 50
SALES (corp-wide): 6.5MM **Privately Held**
SIC: 8011 Offices & clinics of medical doctors
PA: Far Oaks Orthopedists, Inc.
6490 Centervl Bus Pkwy
Dayton OH 45459
937 433-5309

(G-18522)
FEDERAL EXPRESS CORPORATION
Also Called: Fedex
3605 Concorde Dr (45377-3310)
PHONE......................800 463-3339
EMP: 75
SALES (corp-wide): 65.4B **Publicly Held**
WEB: www.federalexpress.com
SIC: 4513 Letter delivery, private air; package delivery, private air; parcel delivery, private air
HQ: Federal Express Corporation
3610 Hacks Cross Rd
Memphis TN 38125
901 369-3600

(G-18523)
FEDERAL EXPRESS CORPORATION
Also Called: Fedex
10340 Freight Dr (45377-1033)
PHONE......................937 898-3474
EMP: 80
SALES (corp-wide): 47.4B **Publicly Held**
SIC: 4513 4215 Air Courier Services Courier Service
HQ: Federal Express Corporation
3610 Hacks Cross Rd
Memphis TN 38125
901 369-3600

(G-18524)
GE AVIATION SYSTEMS LLC
740 E National Rd (45377-3062)
PHONE......................937 898-5881
Victor Bonneau, *Branch Mgr*
EMP: 300
SALES (corp-wide): 121.6B **Publicly Held**
SIC: 8711 3643 3625 3624 Aviation &/or aeronautical engineering; current-carrying wiring devices; relays & industrial controls; carbon & graphite products; motors & generators
HQ: Ge Aviation Systems Llc
1 Neumann Way
Cincinnati OH 45215
937 898-9600

(G-18525)
HERAEUS PRECIOUS METALS NORTH
970 Industrial Park Dr (45377-3116)
PHONE......................937 264-1000
Jrgen Heraeus, *Chairman*
Alex Christofis, *Manager*
Santosh K Gupta,
Robert Housman,
Ram B Sharma,
▲ EMP: 31
SQ FT: 28,000
SALES (est): 8.8MM
SALES (corp-wide): 96.1K **Privately Held**
SIC: 2869 2819 8731 Industrial organic chemicals; chemicals, high purity: refined from technical grade; chemical laboratory, except testing
HQ: Heraeus Holding Gesellschaft Mit Beschrankter Haftung
Heraeusstr. 12-14
Hanau 63450
618 135-0

(G-18526)
HERTZ CORPORATION
James Cox Intrl Arpt (45377)
PHONE......................937 890-2721
Wm Noble, *Branch Mgr*
EMP: 30
SQ FT: 6,500
SALES (corp-wide): 8.8B **Publicly Held**
WEB: www.hertz.com
SIC: 7514 5521 Rent-a-car service; automobiles, used cars only
HQ: The Hertz Corporation
8501 Williams Rd
Estero FL 33928
239 301-7000

(G-18527)
HERTZ CORPORATION
3350 S Valet Cir (45377-1068)
PHONE......................937 898-5806
Grant Funk, *Site Mgr*

Jeff Waple, *Manager*
EMP: 80
SALES (corp-wide): 8.8B **Publicly Held**
WEB: www.hertz.com
SIC: 7514 Rent-a-car service
HQ: The Hertz Corporation
8501 Williams Rd
Estero FL 33928
239 301-7000

(G-18528)
HESTER MASONRY CO INC
10867 Engle Rd (45377-9439)
PHONE......................937 890-2283
EMP: 35
SQ FT: 8,400
SALES: 2MM **Privately Held**
SIC: 1741 Masonry/Stone Contractor

(G-18529)
HORIZON HOME HEALTH CARE
410 Corporate Center Dr (45377-1164)
PHONE......................937 264-3155
Nicole Hardin, *Owner*
EMP: 35
SALES (est): 2.6MM **Privately Held**
SIC: 8099 Blood related health services

(G-18530)
KOORSEN FIRE & SECURITY INC
3577 Concorde Dr (45377-3308)
PHONE......................937 324-9405
Lowell Fredrickson, *Principal*
EMP: 25
SALES (corp-wide): 244.8MM **Privately Held**
WEB: www.koorsen.com
SIC: 7389 7382 1731 5999 Fire extinguisher servicing; fire alarm maintenance & monitoring; fire detection & burglar alarm systems specialization; fire extinguishers
PA: Koorsen Fire & Security, Inc.
2719 N Arlington Ave
Indianapolis IN 46218
317 542-1800

(G-18531)
MIAMI VALLEY HOSPITAL
211 Kenbrook Dr (45377-2400)
PHONE......................937 208-7065
Bill Quilter, *Manager*
EMP: 814
SALES (corp-wide): 968.3MM **Privately Held**
SIC: 8062 General medical & surgical hospitals
HQ: Miami Valley Hospital
1 Wyoming St
Dayton OH 45409
937 208-8000

(G-18532)
NATIONAL RENTAL (US) INC
Also Called: National Rent A Car
3600 Terminal Rd (45377-3312)
PHONE......................937 890-0100
Kurt Zorss, *Manager*
EMP: 45
SALES (corp-wide): 4.9B **Privately Held**
WEB: www.specialtyrentals.com
SIC: 7514 Rent-a-car service
HQ: National Rental (Us) Llc
14002 E 21st St Ste 1500
Tulsa OK 74134

(G-18533)
NIMERS & WOODY II INC
7482 Webster St (45377)
PHONE......................937 898-2060
Clay Adams, *Project Mgr*
Roger Clinard, *QC Mgr*
Brad Nimer, *Manager*
Julie Lovett, *Info Tech Mgr*
EMP: 70
SALES (corp-wide): 51MM **Privately Held**
WEB: www.mac-cable.com
SIC: 5063 Wire & cable
PA: Nimers & Woody Ii, Inc.
1625 Fieldstone Way
Vandalia OH 45377
937 454-0722

(G-18534)
OHIO ASSN PUB TREASURERS
333 James Bohanan Dr (45377-2319)
PHONE......................937 415-2237
William Loy, *Mayor*
EMP: 135
SALES (est): 1.6MM **Privately Held**
WEB: www.airshowvandalia.com
SIC: 8611 Business associations

(G-18535)
PRIMARY CR NTWRK PRMR HLTH PRT
900 S Dixie Dr Ste 40 (45377-2656)
PHONE......................937 890-6644
EMP: 39
SALES (corp-wide): 33.7MM **Privately Held**
SIC: 8011 Physical medicine, physician/surgeon
PA: Primary Care Network Of Premier Health Partners
110 N Main St Ste 350
Dayton OH 45402
937 226-7085

(G-18536)
PSA AIRLINES INC
3634 Cargo Rd (45377-1008)
PHONE......................937 454-9338
Keith Houk, *President*
EMP: 77
SALES (corp-wide): 44.5B **Publicly Held**
SIC: 4512 Air passenger carrier, scheduled
HQ: Psa Airlines, Inc.
3400 Terminal Rd
Vandalia OH 45377
937 454-1116

(G-18537)
PSA AIRLINES INC (HQ)
Also Called: US Airways Express
3400 Terminal Rd (45377-1041)
PHONE......................937 454-1116
Keith D Houk, *President*
James Schear, *Vice Pres*
Timothy Keuscher, *VP Opers*
Aaron Workman, *Info Tech Dir*
EMP: 250
SQ FT: 18,600
SALES (est): 92.3K
SALES (corp-wide): 44.5B **Publicly Held**
SIC: 4512 Air passenger carrier, scheduled
PA: American Airlines Group Inc.
4333 Amon Carter Blvd
Fort Worth TX 76155
817 963-1234

(G-18538)
R B JERGENS CONTRACTORS INC
11418 N Dixie Dr (45377-9736)
PHONE......................937 669-9799
William Jergens, *President*
Randy Hubley, *Project Mgr*
Devon Muir, *Project Mgr*
Greg Meyer, *Opers Mgr*
John Duff, *Controller*
EMP: 99
SALES (est): 27.7MM **Privately Held**
SIC: 1611 General contractor, highway & street construction; highway & street paving contractor; concrete construction: roads, highways, sidewalks, etc.

(G-18539)
R D JERGENS CONTRACTORS INC (PA)
11418 N Dixie Dr (45377-9736)
P.O. Box 309 (45377-0309)
PHONE......................937 669-9799
William Jergens, *President*
Kevin Harshberger, *Vice Pres*
Dave Tennery, *Vice Pres*
Ruth Jergens, *Treasurer*
EMP: 100
SQ FT: 14,000
SALES (est): 29.4MM **Privately Held**
SIC: 1611 1623 Highway & street construction; underground utilities contractor

(G-18540)
REPUBLIC PARKING SYSTEM INC
3600 Terminal Rd (45377-3312)
PHONE......................937 415-0016
EMP: 46
SALES (corp-wide): 400MM **Privately Held**
SIC: 7521 Automobile Parking
PA: Republic Parking System, Inc.
633 Chestnut St Ste 2000
Chattanooga TN 37450
423 756-2771

(G-18541)
STEVENS AVIATION INC
3500 Hangar Dr (45377-1055)
P.O. Box 399 (45377-0399)
PHONE......................937 890-0189
Ron Tennyson, *Branch Mgr*
EMP: 60
SALES (corp-wide): 121.8MM **Privately Held**
WEB: www.stevensaviation.com
SIC: 4581 Airport terminal services
PA: Stevens Aviation, Inc.
600 Delaware St
Greenville SC 29605
864 678-6000

(G-18542)
SUPERIOR ABRASIVES LLC
1620 Fieldstone Way (45377-9357)
P.O. Box 13086, Dayton (45413-0086)
PHONE......................937 278-9123
Lynne Henson, *President*
Amber Collett, *Purch Agent*
Delma Overman, *Engineer*
Linda Newberry, *Human Res Mgr*
Christie Hinshaw, *Director*
▲ EMP: 32
SALES (est): 4.3MM **Privately Held**
SIC: 7389

(G-18543)
SUPREME COURT OF OHIO
Also Called: Vandalia Municipal Court
245 James Bohanan Dr (45377-2375)
P.O. Box 428 (45377-0428)
PHONE......................937 898-3996
Jerry Kaylor, *Principal*
EMP: 30
SQ FT: 5,461 **Privately Held**
WEB: www.judicialstudies.com
SIC: 9211 8111 State courts; ; legal services
HQ: The Supreme Court Of Ohio
65 S Front St Fl 1
Columbus OH 43215
614 387-9000

(G-18544)
TRIAD TECHNOLOGIES LLC (PA)
985 Falls Creek Dr (45377-9686)
PHONE......................937 832-2861
Doug Wissman, *CEO*
Tom Eyer, *CFO*
Todd Baumgartner, *Sales Mgr*
Mark Mosher, *Sales Staff*
Lew Daly, *Info Tech Dir*
EMP: 29
SALES: 43.6MM **Privately Held**
WEB: www.triadtechnologies.com
SIC: 5084 Hydraulic systems equipment & supplies

(G-18545)
TRUGREEN LIMITED PARTNERSHIP
Also Called: Tru Green-Chemlawn
800 Center Dr (45377-3130)
P.O. Box 578 (45377-0578)
PHONE......................937 410-4055
Joan Thorton, *Manager*
EMP: 75
SALES (corp-wide): 3.4B **Privately Held**
SIC: 0782 Lawn care services
HQ: Trugreen Limited Partnership
1790 Kirby Pkwy
Memphis TN 38138
901 251-4128

(G-18546)
UNITED AIRLINES INC
Also Called: Continental Airlines
3600 Terminal Rd Ste 213 (45377-1093)
PHONE..................................937 454-2009
Robert Hall, *Manager*
EMP: 35
SALES (corp-wide): 41.3B **Publicly Held**
WEB: www.continental.com
SIC: 4512 Air passenger carrier, scheduled
HQ: United Airlines, Inc.
   233 S Wacker Dr Ste 710
   Chicago IL 60606
   872 825-4000

(G-18547)
US EXPEDITING LOGISTICS LLC
4311 Old Springfield Rd (45377-9576)
PHONE..................................937 235-1014
Joel Timmons,
EMP: 32
SALES (est): 4.6MM **Privately Held**
SIC: 4731 Freight transportation arrangement

(G-18548)
US SECURITY ASSOCIATES INC
69 N Dixie Dr Ste F (45377-2060)
PHONE..................................937 454-9035
Greg Reynolds, *General Mgr*
Victor Lay, *Director*
EMP: 113
SALES (corp-wide): 13.5MM **Privately Held**
SIC: 7381 Security guard service
HQ: U.S. Security Associates, Inc.
   200 Mansell Ct E Fl 5
   Roswell GA 30076

(G-18549)
VANCARE INC
Also Called: Vandalia Park
208 N Cassel Rd (45377-2926)
PHONE..................................937 898-4202
Mark Schertzinger, *Administration*
EMP: 250 **EST:** 1996
SQ FT: 10,000
SALES (est): 5.4MM **Privately Held**
SIC: 8051 8052 Skilled nursing care facilities; intermediate care facilities

(G-18550)
WRIGHT BROTHERS AERO INC (PA)
3700 Mccauley Dr Ste C (45377-1069)
PHONE..................................937 890-8900
Kevin Keeley, *President*
Emerson R Keck, *Principal*
Gerald L Turner, *Principal*
Sharon S Keeley, *Chairman*
EMP: 57 **EST:** 1977
SQ FT: 47,000
SALES (est): 8.1MM **Privately Held**
WEB: www.wrightbrosaero.com
SIC: 4581 Airport terminal services

Vermilion
Erie County

(G-18551)
CABBAGE INC (PA)
4700 Liberty Ave Fl 2 (44089-3205)
P.O. Box 890 (44089-0890)
PHONE..................................440 899-9171
David Hille, *President*
EMP: 26
SQ FT: 3,800
SALES (est): 20MM **Privately Held**
WEB: www.cabbageinc.com
SIC: 5148 Vegetables, fresh

(G-18552)
ELDEN PROPERTIES LTD PARTNR
Also Called: Elden & Strauss
15008 Holiday Dr Ste A (44089-9291)
PHONE..................................440 967-0521
John A Elden Jr, *Partner*
Carol Elden, *Partner*
Dan Strauss, *Partner*
EMP: 30
SALES (est): 1.5MM **Privately Held**
SIC: 6531 Real estate agents & managers

(G-18553)
HULL BUILDERS SUPPLY INC
685 Main St (44089-1311)
P.O. Box 432 (44089-0432)
PHONE..................................440 967-3159
Steve Holovacs, *President*
EMP: 28
SALES: 1,000K **Privately Held**
SIC: 5032 3273 5211 Limestone; ready-mixed concrete; lumber & other building materials

(G-18554)
IRG OPERATING LLC
Also Called: Cleveland Quarries
850 W River Rd (44089-1530)
PHONE..................................440 963-4008
Jim Penkava, *Facilities Mgr*
Zach Carpenter, *Mng Member*
EMP: 36
SALES: 3.6MM **Privately Held**
SIC: 1411 Sandstone, dimension-quarrying

(G-18555)
KINGSTON HEALTHCARE COMPANY
Also Called: Kingston of Vermilion
4210 Telegraph Ln (44089-3748)
PHONE..................................440 967-1800
Heather Shirley, *Branch Mgr*
Rhonda Prusak, *Director*
EMP: 110
SALES (corp-wide): 95.5MM **Privately Held**
WEB: www.kingstonhealthcare.com
SIC: 8051 8059 Skilled nursing care facilities; home for the mentally retarded, exc. skilled or intermediate
PA: Kingston Healthcare Company
   1 Seagate Ste 1960
   Toledo OH 43604
   419 247-2880

(G-18556)
LINWOOD PARK COMPANY
4920 Liberty Ave (44089-1434)
PHONE..................................440 963-0481
Anne Peters, *President*
EMP: 30
SALES (est): 993.2K **Privately Held**
SIC: 7996 Theme park, amusement

(G-18557)
MERCY HEALTH
1607 State Route 50 Ste 6 (44089)
PHONE..................................440 967-8713
EMP: 33
SALES (corp-wide): 4.7B **Privately Held**
SIC: 8011 Offices & clinics of medical doctors
PA: Mercy Health
   1701 Mercy Health Pl
   Cincinnati OH 45237
   513 639-2800

(G-18558)
MILL MANOR NURSING HOME INC
983 Exchange St (44089-1256)
PHONE..................................440 967-6614
Ted Dush, *President*
Edie Dush, *Vice Pres*
Mary Ellen Smith, *Bookkeeper*
EMP: 39
SQ FT: 8,000
SALES (est): 1.8MM **Privately Held**
SIC: 8051 8052 Convalescent home with continuous nursing care; intermediate care facilities

(G-18559)
SIX SIGMA LOGISTICS INC
6745 Ciffside Dr (44089)
PHONE..................................440 666-6026
Ron O'Connell, *President*
EMP: 50
SALES (est): 641.1K **Privately Held**
SIC: 7389 Courier or messenger service

(G-18560)
STEP BY STEP EMPLYMENT TRINING
664 Exchange St (44089-1301)
P.O. Box 551 (44089-0551)
PHONE..................................440 967-9042

Susan Fischer, *President*
EMP: 35
SALES (est): 619.3K **Privately Held**
SIC: 8331 Job training services

(G-18561)
VERMILION BOARD OF EDUCATION
Also Called: Vermilion School Bus Garage
1065 Decatur St (44089-1167)
PHONE..................................440 204-1700
George Harizal, *Principal*
Linda Griffin, *Branch Mgr*
EMP: 50
SALES (corp-wide): 26.3MM **Privately Held**
SIC: 4151 School buses
PA: Vermilion Board Of Education
   1250 Sanford St Ste A
   Vermilion OH 44089
   440 204-1700

(G-18562)
VERMILION BOAT CLUB INC
5416 Liberty Ave (44089-1334)
PHONE..................................440 967-6634
Karen Mathews, *Principal*
Rj Hickey, *Commodore*
George Vegotis, *Rear Commodore*
Roger McCoy, *Treasurer*
Barry Masin, *Admin Sec*
EMP: 25
SQ FT: 9,200
SALES: 1.2MM **Privately Held**
WEB: www.vermilionboatclub.com
SIC: 7997 5812 4493 Boating club, membership; eating places; marinas

(G-18563)
VERMILION FAMILY YMCA
320 Aldrich Rd (44089-2286)
PHONE..................................440 967-4208
Jim Turton, *President*
Anne Stock, *Vice Pres*
Don Lebeau, *Treasurer*
W Robert Johnston II, *Director*
Jo Brown, *Admin Sec*
EMP: 40
SQ FT: 37,000
SALES: 678.4K **Privately Held**
SIC: 8351 8641 7991 7997 Child day care services; youth organizations; physical fitness facilities; membership sports & recreation clubs; individual & family services

(G-18564)
VERMILION FARM MARKET
2901 Liberty Ave (44089-2534)
PHONE..................................440 967-9666
Thomas Rottel, *President*
EMP: 43
SQ FT: 19,000
SALES (est): 2.6MM **Privately Held**
WEB: www.vermilionfarmmarket.com
SIC: 5431 5148 Fruit stands or markets; fresh fruits & vegetables

---

Versailles
Darke County

(G-18565)
A L SMITH TRUCKING INC
8984 Murphy Rd (45380-9752)
PHONE..................................937 526-3651
Dave Fullenkamp, *President*
Chad Kelch, *Manager*
EMP: 38 **EST:** 1956
SQ FT: 9,600
SALES (est): 7.2MM **Privately Held**
WEB: www.alsmithtrucking.com
SIC: 4213 4212 Contract haulers; local trucking, without storage

(G-18566)
BNSF LOGISTICS LLC
Also Called: T E S - East
611 Marker Rd (45380-9334)
P.O. Box 176 (45380-0176)
PHONE..................................937 526-3141
Sarah Davis, *Transportation*
Chuck Borchers, *Branch Mgr*
EMP: 40

SALES (corp-wide): 225.3B **Publicly Held**
WEB: www.bnsflogistics.com
SIC: 4731 Transportation agents & brokers
HQ: Bnsf Logistics, Llc
   2710 S 48th St
   Springdale AR 72762
   800 275-8521

(G-18567)
CLASSIC CARRIERS INC (PA)
151 Industrial Pkwy (45380-9756)
P.O. Box 295 (45380-0295)
PHONE..................................937 604-8118
Jim Subler, *President*
Jeffrey Grote, *Manager*
EMP: 50
SALES (est): 15.7MM **Privately Held**
WEB: www.classiccarrier.com
SIC: 4213 Contract haulers

(G-18568)
COUNTY OF DARKE
Also Called: Y M C A
10242 Versailles Se Rd (45380-9583)
PHONE..................................937 526-4488
Amy Wagner, *Director*
EMP: 40 **Privately Held**
WEB: www.darkecountyfair.com
SIC: 8641 8322 Youth organizations; individual & family services
PA: County Of Darke
   520 S Broadway St
   Greenville OH 45331
   937 547-7370

(G-18569)
COVENANT CARE OHIO INC
Also Called: Versailles Health Care Center
200 Marker Rd (45380-9494)
PHONE..................................937 526-5570
Martin Grilliot, *Human Res Dir*
Marilyn Barga, *Branch Mgr*
Amber Bey, *Branch Mgr*
Sara Becher, *Manager*
Tami Stover, *Info Tech Mgr*
EMP: 85 **Privately Held**
WEB: www.villageorgetown.com
SIC: 8051 8011 Convalescent home with continuous nursing care; offices & clinics of medical doctors
HQ: Covenant Care Ohio, Inc.
   27071 Aliso Creek Rd # 100
   Aliso Viejo CA 92656
   949 349-1200

(G-18570)
PHELAN INSURANCE AGENCY INC (PA)
863 E Main St (45380-1533)
P.O. Box 1 (45380-0001)
PHONE..................................800 843-3069
James B Phelan, *Ch of Bd*
Tim P Grow, *President*
Ron D Stauffer, *Vice Pres*
Mike Westgerdes, *Accounting Mgr*
Karen Knopp, *Empl Benefits*
EMP: 31
SQ FT: 10,000
SALES (est): 1MM **Privately Held**
WEB: www.phelanins.com
SIC: 6411 Insurance agents

(G-18571)
PREMIER HEALTH PARTNERS
Also Called: Still Water Family Care
471 Marker Rd (45380-9324)
PHONE..................................937 526-3235
Daniel Elshoff MD, *President*
EMP: 70
SALES (corp-wide): 17.2K **Privately Held**
SIC: 8011 General & family practice, physician/surgeon
PA: Premier Health Partners
   110 N Main St Ste 450
   Dayton OH 45402
   937 499-9596

(G-18572)
VILLAGE OF VERSAILLES
Also Called: Versailles Util Dept
177 N Center St (45380-1206)
P.O. Box 288 (45380-0288)
PHONE..................................937 526-4191
Randy Gump, *Director*
EMP: 30 **Privately Held**

SIC: 8611 Public utility association
PA: Village Of Versailles
177 N Center St
Versailles OH 45380
937 526-3294

(G-18573)
WEAVER BROS INC (PA)
Also Called: Tri County Eggs
895 E Main St (45380-1533)
P.O. Box 333 (45380-0333)
PHONE..................................937 526-3907
Timothy John Weaver, *President*
Audrey Weaver, *Principal*
Geo L Weaver, *Principal*
John D Weaver, *Principal*
Kreg Kohli, *Vice Pres*
▲ **EMP:** 60 **EST:** 1931
SQ FT: 20,000
SALES (est): 55MM **Privately Held**
SIC: 0252 5143 2015 Chicken eggs; dairy products, except dried or canned; cheese; butter; poultry slaughtering & processing

(G-18574)
WEAVER BROS INC
Also Called: Weaver Brothers Farm
10638 State Route 47 (45380-9743)
PHONE..................................937 526-4777
Phil Borchers, *General Mgr*
EMP: 25
SALES (corp-wide): 55MM **Privately Held**
SIC: 0252 Chicken eggs
PA: Weaver Bros., Inc.
895 E Main St
Versailles OH 45380
937 526-3907

Vickery
Sandusky County

(G-18575)
SR IMPROVEMENTS SERVICES LLC
1485 County Road 268 (43464-9701)
PHONE..................................567 207-6488
Ron Wilson, *General Ptnr*
Ronald E Wilson,
EMP: 40
SALES (est): 583.1K **Privately Held**
SIC: 7299 7349 Handyman service; building maintenance services

(G-18576)
WASTE MANAGEMENT OHIO INC
3956 State Route 412 (43464-9791)
PHONE..................................419 547-7791
Steve Lonneman, *Branch Mgr*
EMP: 28
SALES (corp-wide): 14.9B **Publicly Held**
WEB: www.wm.com
SIC: 4953 Hazardous waste collection & disposal
HQ: Waste Management Of Ohio, Inc.
1700 N Broad St
Fairborn OH 45324

Vienna
Trumbull County

(G-18577)
AVALON GOLF & COUNTRY CLUB
761 Youngstown Kingsvlle (44473-8615)
PHONE..................................330 539-5008
Christine Bell, *General Mgr*
EMP: 68 **EST:** 1922
SQ FT: 10,000
SALES (est): 1.5MM **Privately Held**
SIC: 7997 7992 Country club, membership; public golf courses

(G-18578)
COLE SELBY FUNERAL INC
3966 Warren Sharon Rd (44473-9524)
PHONE..................................330 856-4695
Bob Moses, *President*
EMP: 25

SALES (est): 562.5K **Privately Held**
SIC: 7261 Funeral home

(G-18579)
GLOWE-SMITH INDUSTRIAL INC
Also Called: G. S. I.
812 Youngstwn Kgsvl Rd Se (44473)
P.O. Box 625, Cortland (44410-0625)
PHONE..................................330 638-5088
EMP: 136
SQ FT: 2,600
SALES (est): 4.6MM **Privately Held**
SIC: 8711 8734 Engineering Consultants

(G-18580)
LATROBE SPCIALTY MTLS DIST INC (HQ)
1551 Vienna Pkwy (44473-8703)
PHONE..................................330 609-5137
Gregory A Pratt, *Ch of Bd*
Timothy R Armstrong, *Vice Pres*
Thomas F Cramsey, *Vice Pres*
James D Dee, *Vice Pres*
Matthew S Enoch, *Vice Pres*
◆ **EMP:** 80
SQ FT: 189,000
SALES (est): 69.2MM
SALES (corp-wide): 2.1B **Publicly Held**
SIC: 5051 3312 Steel; stainless steel
PA: Carpenter Technology Corporation
1735 Market St Fl 15
Philadelphia PA 19103
610 208-2000

(G-18581)
LITCO INTERNATIONAL INC (PA)
1 Litco Dr (44473-9600)
P.O. Box 150 (44473-0150)
PHONE..................................330 539-5433
Lionel F Trebilcock, *CEO*
Gary L Trebilcock, *President*
Gary Sharon, *Vice Pres*
Chameika Patterson, *Human Res Mgr*
Pete Snyder, *Human Res Mgr*
◆ **EMP:** 30
SQ FT: 13,000
SALES (est): 4MM **Privately Held**
WEB: www.litco.com
SIC: 2448 5031 Pallets, wood; particleboard

(G-18582)
MILLWOOD INC (PA)
3708 International Blvd (44473-9796)
PHONE..................................330 393-4400
Steven J Miller, *President*
Lionel W Trebilcock, *President*
Ronald C Ringness, *Exec VP*
Brad Arnold, *VP Opers*
Craig Gretter, *CFO*
▲ **EMP:** 30
SQ FT: 20,000
SALES (est): 418.5MM **Privately Held**
WEB: www.millwoodinc.com
SIC: 4225 4731 General warehousing & storage; freight transportation arrangement

(G-18583)
MILLWOOD NATURAL LLC
3708 International Blvd (44473-9796)
PHONE..................................330 393-4400
Lionel Trebilcock, *Partner*
EMP: 105
SALES (est): 11.6MM **Privately Held**
SIC: 3565 4731 Packaging machinery; freight transportation arrangement
PA: Millwood, Inc.
3708 International Blvd
Vienna OH 44473

(G-18584)
WINNER AVIATION CORPORATION
1453 Youngstown Kingsvill (44473-9788)
PHONE..................................330 856-5000
Rick Hale, *CEO*
Charles R Hale, *President*
Karen Hale, *Vice Pres*
Lee McCracken, *CFO*
Jeffrey A McCandless, *Treasurer*
EMP: 75
SQ FT: 5,000

SALES (est): 18.3MM **Privately Held**
WEB: www.winneraviation.com
SIC: 4581 5172 7359 Hangars & other aircraft storage facilities; aircraft fueling services; equipment rental & leasing

Vincent
Washington County

(G-18585)
DECKER DRILLING INC
11565 State Route 676 (45784-5636)
PHONE..................................740 749-3939
Dean Decker, *President*
Pat Decker, *Vice Pres*
EMP: 42
SALES (est): 6.6MM **Privately Held**
WEB: www.deandecker.com
SIC: 1381 Redrilling oil & gas wells

Vinton
Gallia County

(G-18586)
STEELIAL WLDG MET FBRCTION INC
Also Called: Steelial Cnstr Met Fabrication
70764 State Route 124 (45686-8545)
PHONE..................................740 669-5300
Larry Allen Hedrick Jr, *President*
Krista Lynnete Hedrick, *Admin Sec*
EMP: 32 **EST:** 1998
SQ FT: 40,000
SALES (est): 11MM **Privately Held**
WEB: www.steelial.com
SIC: 1623 3441 3444 Pipe laying construction; fabricated structural metal; sheet metalwork

Wadsworth
Medina County

(G-18587)
AKRON INN LIMITED PARTNERSHIP
Also Called: Ramada Inn
5 Park Centre Dr (44281-9431)
PHONE..................................330 336-7692
Shawn Leattherman, *Owner*
Kim Outritch, *Principal*
Rosemary Knepp, *Manager*
EMP: 25
SALES (est): 919.8K **Privately Held**
SIC: 7011 Hotels & motels

(G-18588)
ALTERCARE INC
Also Called: Altercare of Wadsworth
147 Garfield St (44281-1431)
PHONE..................................330 335-2555
Diana Jackson, *Manager*
Mitzi Speicher, *Manager*
Jodi Tarnasky, *Director*
EMP: 120
SALES (corp-wide): 7.7MM **Privately Held**
SIC: 8051 8052 Skilled nursing care facilities; intermediate care facilities
PA: Altercare, Inc.
35990 Westminister Ave
North Ridgeville OH 44039
440 327-5285

(G-18589)
AMERICAN HOSPITALITY GROUP INC (HQ)
Also Called: A H G
200 Smokerise Dr Ste 300 (44281-9499)
P.O. Box 438 (44282-0438)
PHONE..................................330 336-6684
Robert Leatherman Sr, *Ch of Bd*
Robert Leatherman Jr, *President*
Phyllis Leatherman, *Corp Secy*
Neil Winger, *Vice Pres*
Robin Winger, *Vice Pres*
EMP: 550 **EST:** 1972
SQ FT: 20,000

SALES (est): 60.2MM
SALES (corp-wide): 21.8MM **Privately Held**
SIC: 8741 Hotel or motel management
PA: Leatherman Nursing Centers Corporation
200 Smokerise Dr Ste 300
Wadsworth OH 44281
330 336-6684

(G-18590)
ASAP HOMECARE INC (PA)
1 Park Centre Dr Ste 107 (44281-9482)
PHONE..................................330 334-7027
Luke Harmon, *CEO*
Dayna Harmon, *Principal*
EMP: 35
SALES (est): 6.9MM **Privately Held**
WEB: www.asaphomecare.com
SIC: 8082 Home health care services

(G-18591)
BARBERTON HEALTHCARE GROUP LLC
Also Called: SABER SKILLED NURSING UNIT AT
540 Great Oaks Trl (44281-8799)
PHONE..................................330 615-3717
George S Repchick, *President*
William I Weisberg, *Vice Pres*
Sarah Depompei, *Assistant*
EMP: 45 **EST:** 2013
SALES: 2.4MM **Privately Held**
SIC: 8062 General medical & surgical hospitals

(G-18592)
CITY OF WADSWORTH
Also Called: Electrical Service Dept
120 Maple St (44281-1865)
PHONE..................................330 334-1581
Peter A Giacomo, *Superintendent*
EMP: 30 **Privately Held**
SIC: 7629 9111 Electrical repair shops; mayors' offices
PA: City Of Wadsworth
120 Maple St Uppr
Wadsworth OH 44281
330 335-1521

(G-18593)
COMMUNITY CAREGIVERS
230 Quadral Dr Ste D (44281-8375)
PHONE..................................330 725-9800
Michael T Nemeth, *Branch Mgr*
EMP: 36
SALES (corp-wide): 2.2MM **Privately Held**
SIC: 8082 Home health care services
PA: Community Caregivers
66 S Miller Rd Ste 200
Fairlawn OH 44333
330 836-8585

(G-18594)
CORNWELL QUALITY TOOLS COMPANY
Also Called: Distribution Service Company
635 Seville Rd (44281-1077)
PHONE..................................330 335-2933
Dal Ringler, *Manager*
EMP: 46
SALES (corp-wide): 173.8MM **Privately Held**
WEB: www.cornwelltools.com
SIC: 5013 5085 Tools & equipment, automotive; industrial supplies
PA: The Cornwell Quality Tools Company
667 Seville Rd
Wadsworth OH 44281
330 336-3506

(G-18595)
DAVITA INC
195 Wadsworth Rd (44281-9504)
PHONE..................................330 335-2300
Julie Zubek, *Branch Mgr*
EMP: 26 **Publicly Held**
SIC: 8092 Kidney dialysis centers
PA: Davita Inc.
2000 16th St
Denver CO 80202

(G-18596)
GOLDEN LIVING LLC
Also Called: Beverly
365 Johnson Rd (44281-8609)
PHONE...................330 335-1558
Rick Michell, *General Mgr*
EMP: 75
SQ FT: 28,324
SALES (corp-wide): 7.4MM **Privately Held**
SIC: 8059 8052 8051 Convalescent home; intermediate care facilities; skilled nursing care facilities
PA: Golden Living Llc
5220 Tennyson Pkwy # 400
Plano TX 75024
972 372-6300

(G-18597)
HEALTHSPAN INTEGRATED CARE
Also Called: Kaiser Foundation Health Plan
120 High St (44281-1855)
PHONE...................330 334-1549
Sue Cieslack, *Branch Mgr*
EMP: 29
SALES (corp-wide): 4.7B **Privately Held**
SIC: 6324 Hospital & medical service plans
HQ: Healthspan Integrated Care
1001 Lakeside Ave E # 1200
Cleveland OH 44114
216 621-5600

(G-18598)
HEART TO HEART HOME HEALTH
250 Smokerise Dr Apt 302 (44281-8263)
PHONE...................330 335-9999
Rosemary Knepp, *General Mgr*
Nancy Kirby, *Administration*
EMP: 40 EST: 1999
SALES (est): 1.2MM **Privately Held**
WEB: www.h2hhomehealth.com
SIC: 8082 8071 Home health care services; medical laboratories

(G-18599)
HOME INSTEAD SENIOR CARE
1 Park Centre Dr Ste 15 (44281-9452)
PHONE...................330 334-4664
Pam Myers, *President*
EMP: 100 EST: 1970
SALES (est): 2.5MM **Privately Held**
SIC: 8082 8322 Home health care services; individual & family services

(G-18600)
HUBBELL POWER SYSTEMS INC
Ohio Brass
8711 Wadsworth Rd (44281-8438)
PHONE...................330 335-2361
Patrick Clemente, *President*
Chris Davis, *Branch Mgr*
EMP: 75
SALES (corp-wide): 4.4B **Publicly Held**
SIC: 5063 Electrical apparatus & equipment
HQ: Hubbell Power Systems, Inc.
200 Center Point Cir # 200
Columbia SC 29210
803 216-2600

(G-18601)
JERSEY CENTRAL PWR & LIGHT CO
9681 Silvercreek Rd (44281-9008)
PHONE...................330 336-9884
Anthony Alexander, *Branch Mgr*
EMP: 67 **Publicly Held**
WEB: www.jersey-central-power-light.monmouth.n
SIC: 4911 Electric services
HQ: Jersey Central Power & Light Company
76 S Main St
Akron OH 44308
800 736-3402

(G-18602)
LEATHERMAN NURSING CTRS CORP (PA)
200 Smokerise Dr Ste 300 (44281-9499)
PHONE...................330 336-6684

Robert Leatherman, *President*
Phyllis Leatherman, *Corp Secy*
EMP: 550
SQ FT: 20,000
SALES (est): 21.8MM **Privately Held**
SIC: 8741 Management services

(G-18603)
LIBERTY RESIDENCE II
1054 Freedom Dr Apt 115 (44281-7900)
PHONE...................330 334-3262
Michelle Crinich, *Manager*
EMP: 38 EST: 2001
SALES (est): 1.3MM **Privately Held**
SIC: 8052 Intermediate care facilities

(G-18604)
LIFECARE HOSPICE
Also Called: Lifecare Pallivative Medicine
102 Main St (44281-1453)
PHONE...................330 336-6595
Greg Tesniarz, *Principal*
EMP: 90 **Privately Held**
SIC: 8322 Individual & family services
PA: Lifecare Hospice
1900 Akron Rd
Wooster OH 44691

(G-18605)
LOUIS PERRY & ASSOCIATES INC
165 Smokerise Dr (44281-8702)
PHONE...................330 334-1585
Louis B Perry, *President*
Thomas R Payne, *Senior VP*
James T Calderone, *Vice Pres*
James Calderone, *Vice Pres*
William Sage, *Project Mgr*
EMP: 135
SQ FT: 31,000
SALES: 11MM
SALES (corp-wide): 1.1B **Privately Held**
WEB: www.louisperry.com
SIC: 8711 8712 Consulting engineer; building construction consultant; architectural services
PA: Cdm Smith Inc
75 State St Ste 701
Boston MA 02109
617 452-6000

(G-18606)
LOWES HOME CENTERS LLC
1065 Wlliams Reserve Blvd (44281-9316)
PHONE...................330 335-1900
Dave Labuda, *Manager*
EMP: 150
SQ FT: 137,480
SALES (corp-wide): 68.6B **Publicly Held**
SIC: 5211 5031 5722 5064 Home centers; building materials, exterior; building materials, interior; household appliance stores; electrical appliances, television & radio
HQ: Lowe's Home Centers, Llc
1605 Curtis Bridge Rd
Wilkesboro NC 28697
336 658-4000

(G-18607)
MASTERS AGENCY INC
Also Called: American Benefits Management
1108 Ledgestone Dr (44281-8113)
PHONE...................330 805-5985
Paul Cantwell, *President*
EMP: 42
SQ FT: 10,000
SALES (est): 6.3MM **Privately Held**
WEB: www.americanbenefits.org
SIC: 6411 Insurance agents, brokers & service

(G-18608)
MEDINA COUNTY SHELTERED INDS
Also Called: WINDFALL INDUSTRIES
150 Quadral Dr Ste D (44281-8352)
PHONE...................330 334-4491
Amanda Fulton, *Controller*
Wendy Bassak, *Accountant*
Kathy Javorsky, *Manager*
Jim Brown, *Exec Dir*
EMP: 315
SQ FT: 40,000
SALES: 2.9MM **Privately Held**
SIC: 8331 Sheltered workshop

(G-18609)
NCS HEALTHCARE OF OHIO LLC
Also Called: Omnicare of Dover
1360 Reimer Rd (44281-8164)
PHONE...................330 364-5011
Jerry Marlowe, *Director*
EMP: 44
SALES (corp-wide): 194.5B **Publicly Held**
SIC: 5122 Pharmaceuticals
HQ: Ncs Healthcare Of Ohio, Llc
201 E 4th St Ste 900
Cincinnati OH 45202

(G-18610)
OHIO EDISON COMPANY
9681 Silvercreek Rd (44281-9008)
PHONE...................330 336-9880
Bruce J Busse, *Branch Mgr*
EMP: 120 **Publicly Held**
SIC: 4911 Electric services
HQ: Ohio Edison Company
76 S Main St Bsmt
Akron OH 44308
800 736-3402

(G-18611)
PEPSI-COLA METRO BTLG CO INC
904 Seville Rd (44281-8316)
PHONE...................330 336-3553
Scott Sutkaytis, *Regional Mgr*
Don Cooper, *Branch Mgr*
EMP: 50
SALES (corp-wide): 64.6B **Publicly Held**
WEB: www.joy-of-cola.com
SIC: 4225 5149 General warehousing & storage; soft drinks
HQ: Pepsi-Cola Metropolitan Bottling Company, Inc.
1111 Westchester Ave
White Plains NY 10604
914 767-6000

(G-18612)
PERRAM ELECTRIC INC
6882 Ridge Rd (44281-9706)
PHONE...................330 239-2661
Zoltan J Kovacs, *President*
Dale B Perram, *Chairman*
Dale Perram, *Chairman*
Dave Powell, *Vice Pres*
Lori A Stanley, *Vice Pres*
EMP: 40
SQ FT: 2,500
SALES: 14.3MM **Privately Held**
WEB: www.perramelectric.com
SIC: 1731 General electrical contractor

(G-18613)
PLASTICS R UNIQUE INC
330 Grandview Ave (44281-1161)
PHONE...................330 334-4820
Kenneth R Boersma, *President*
EMP: 30
SQ FT: 12,300
SALES (est): 5.2MM **Privately Held**
SIC: 3089 5162 Plastic containers, except foam; plastics materials

(G-18614)
RELIABLE POLYMER SERVICES LP
300 1st St (44281-2084)
PHONE...................800 321-0954
Michael Fagan, *President*
Jim Talarico, *CFO*
EMP: 39
SALES (est): 1.8MM **Privately Held**
SIC: 7389

(G-18615)
RETAIL RENOVATIONS INC (PA)
7530 State Rd (44281-9794)
PHONE...................330 334-4501
Gary Williams, *CEO*
Frank Northcutt, *President*
Rhonda Williams, *Treasurer*
Lisa Williams, *Admin Sec*
EMP: 29
SALES (est): 5.8MM **Privately Held**
WEB: www.retailrenovations.com
SIC: 1542 Commercial & office building, new construction

(G-18616)
SUMMA HEALTH SYSTEM
195 Wadsworth Rd (44281-9504)
PHONE...................330 334-1504
Becky Shields, *Business Mgr*
Mark Kovacik, *Research*
Beth McKee, *Administration*
Heidi Cahoon, *Administration*
EMP: 520
SALES (corp-wide): 1B **Privately Held**
SIC: 8062 General medical & surgical hospitals
PA: Summa Health
525 E Market St
Akron OH 44304
330 375-3000

(G-18617)
VERIZON COMMUNICATIONS INC
1114 Williams Reserve (44281-9318)
PHONE...................330 334-1268
Kevin Fruth, *Branch Mgr*
EMP: 107
SALES (corp-wide): 130.8B **Publicly Held**
SIC: 4813 4812 Local & long distance telephone communications; cellular telephone services
PA: Verizon Communications Inc.
1095 Ave Of The Americas
New York NY 10036
212 395-1000

(G-18618)
WADSWORTH GALAXY REST INC
201 Park Centre Dr (44281-7106)
PHONE...................330 334-3663
Robert Leatherman, *President*
Phyllis Leatherman, *Corp Secy*
Robert Leatherman Jr, *Vice Pres*
Neil Winger, *Vice Pres*
Robin Winger, *Vice Pres*
EMP: 80
SALES (est): 216.5K **Privately Held**
WEB: www.galaxyrestaurant.com
SIC: 8741 5812 Restaurant management; eating places

Wakeman
Huron County

(G-18619)
BETTCHER INDUSTRIES INC (PA)
6801 State Route 60 (44889-8509)
P.O. Box 336, Vermilion (44089-0336)
PHONE...................440 965-4422
Don Esch, *President*
Terry Blaine, *Regional Mgr*
Dallas Watson, *Regional Mgr*
Paul Pirozzola, *Vice Pres*
Tom Tomasula, *Vice Pres*
▲ **EMP:** 165 EST: 1944
SQ FT: 65,000
SALES (est): 28.8MM **Privately Held**
WEB: www.bettcher.com
SIC: 5084 Food product manufacturing machinery; counterbores

(G-18620)
CONCAST METAL PRODUCTS CO
14315 State Route 113 (44889-8320)
PHONE...................440 965-4455
Alfred D Barbour, *President*
John Dorsey, *COO*
Martin Little, *Exec VP*
Dean Mora, *Vice Pres*
Pete Zimmerman, *Opers Mgr*
▲ **EMP:** 80
SALES (est): 33.4MM
SALES (corp-wide): 38.5MM **Privately Held**
SIC: 5051 Metals service centers & offices
PA: A Cubed Corporation
131 Myoma Rd
Mars PA 16046
724 538-4000

(G-18621)
FISHER-TITUS MEDICAL CENTER
24 Hyde St (44889-9301)
PHONE.....................440 839-2226
EMP: 94
SALES (corp-wide): 138MM Privately Held
SIC: 8011 Physicians' office, including specialists
PA: Fisher-Titus Medical Center
272 Benedict Ave
Norwalk OH 44857
419 668-8101

Walbridge
Wood County

(G-18622)
GEM INDUSTRIAL INC (HQ)
6842 Commodore Dr (43465-9793)
P.O. Box 716, Toledo (43697-0716)
PHONE.....................419 666-6554
Hussien Shousher, President
Bill Rudolph, Chairman
Douglas R Heyman, Corp Secy
Daniel Stark, Project Mgr
Bryan Darling, Project Engr
EMP: 100
SQ FT: 33,000
SALES (est): 48.3MM
SALES (corp-wide): 567.7MM Privately Held
WEB: www.gemindustrial.com
SIC: 1711 1731 1796 Mechanical contractor; boiler maintenance contractor; general electrical contractor; machinery installation
PA: The Rudolph/Libbe Companies Inc
6494 Latcha Rd
Walbridge OH 43465
419 241-5000

(G-18623)
PROFESSIONAL TRANSPORTATION
Also Called: P T I
30801 Drouillard Rd (43465-1037)
PHONE.....................419 661-0576
Justin Purkey, Branch Mgr
EMP: 109 Privately Held
SIC: 4119 7363 Local passenger transportation; help supply services
PA: Professional Transportation Inc
3700 E Morgan Ave
Evansville IN 47715

(G-18624)
RUDOLPH LIBBE INC (HQ)
Also Called: RUDOLPH/LIBBE
6494 Latcha Rd (43465-9788)
PHONE.....................419 241-5000
Timothy Alter, President
Tammy Euler, Superintendent
Mark Murray, Superintendent
William Rudolph, Chairman
Bob Jacobs, District Mgr
EMP: 186
SQ FT: 50,000
SALES: 362.9MM
SALES (corp-wide): 567.7MM Privately Held
WEB: www.rlcos.com
SIC: 1541 1542 Industrial buildings, new construction; nonresidential construction
PA: The Rudolph/Libbe Companies Inc
6494 Latcha Rd
Walbridge OH 43465
419 241-5000

(G-18625)
RUDOLPH/LIBBE COMPANIES INC (PA)
6494 Latcha Rd (43465-9788)
PHONE.....................419 241-5000
Allan J Libbe, President
Frederick W Rudolph, President
Philip J Rudolph, President
Bill Rudolph, Chairman
Mike Rokicki, Project Mgr
EMP: 52
SQ FT: 40,000

SALES: 567.7MM Privately Held
SIC: 1541 1542 Industrial buildings & warehouses; commercial & office building contractors

(G-18626)
UNIVAR USA INC
30450 Tracy Rd (43465-9775)
PHONE.....................419 666-7880
Scott Post, Research
EMP: 44
SALES (corp-wide): 8.6B Publicly Held
SIC: 5169 Industrial chemicals
HQ: Univar Usa Inc.
3075 Highland Pkwy # 200
Downers Grove IL 60515
331 777-6000

(G-18627)
WESTERN STATES ENVELOPE CO
Also Called: Western States Envelope Label
6859 Commodore Dr (43465-9765)
PHONE.....................419 666-7480
Shelly Hinkle, Manager
EMP: 70
SALES (corp-wide): 203.2MM Privately Held
WEB: www.westernstatesenvelope.com
SIC: 5112 2677 Envelopes; envelopes
PA: Western States Envelope Company
4480 N 132nd St
Butler WI 53007
262 781-5540

(G-18628)
WOLFES ROOFING INC
6568 State Route 795 (43465-9760)
PHONE.....................419 666-6233
David A Wolfe, President
Daniel Wolfe, Project Engr
Becky Petrusky, Bookkeeper
Frank Wright, Manager
EMP: 40
SALES (est): 4.8MM Privately Held
SIC: 1761 Roofing contractor

Waldo
Marion County

(G-18629)
COLUMBUS DISTRIBUTING COMPANY
Delmar Distributing
6829 Waldo Delaware Rd (43356-9115)
PHONE.....................740 726-2211
Tom Wallsmith, Manager
EMP: 50
SALES (corp-wide): 96.7MM Privately Held
WEB: www.delmardistributing.com
SIC: 5181 Beer & other fermented malt liquors
PA: The Columbus Distributing Company
4949 Freeway Dr E
Columbus OH 43229
614 846-1000

(G-18630)
OHIGRO INC (PA)
6720 Gillette Rd (43356)
P.O. Box 196 (43356-0196)
PHONE.....................740 726-2429
Jerry Ward, President
Jerry A Ward, President
James H Ward, Vice Pres
David Fierbaugh, Plant Mgr
Jeffrey Schweinfurth, Plant Mgr
EMP: 36
SQ FT: 9,600
SALES: 12.9MM Privately Held
WEB: www.ohigro.com
SIC: 5191 5261 2875 0723 Fertilizer & fertilizer materials; fertilizer; fertilizers, mixing only; crop preparation services for market

Walnut Creek
Holmes County

(G-18631)
COBLENTZ DISTRIBUTING INC
Also Called: Walnut Creek Foods
2641 State R 39 39 R (44687)
P.O. Box 240 (44687-0240)
PHONE.....................330 852-2888
Dennis Schladach, Branch Mgr
EMP: 110
SALES (corp-wide): 162.2MM Privately Held
SIC: 5143 Cheese
PA: Coblentz Distributing, Inc.
3850 State Route 39
Millersburg OH 44654
800 543-6848

(G-18632)
WALNUT CREEK CHOCOLATE COMPANY
Also Called: Coblentz Chocolate Co
4917 State Rte 515 (44687)
PHONE.....................330 893-2995
Jason Coblentz, President
Amy Yoder, Mktg Dir
EMP: 25
SQ FT: 2,000
SALES (est): 4.6MM Privately Held
SIC: 2064 2066 5149 5441 Chocolate covered dates; fruit, chocolate covered (except dates); chocolate candy, solid; chocolate; candy

(G-18633)
WALNUT HILLS INC
4748 Olde Pump St (44687)
P.O. Box 127 (44687-0127)
PHONE.....................330 852-2457
Levi Troyer, CEO
David Miller, President
Lillis Troyer, Admin Sec
EMP: 150
SQ FT: 36,000
SALES (est): 5.7MM Privately Held
WEB: www.walnuthillsliving.com
SIC: 8052 8051 Intermediate care facilities; skilled nursing care facilities

Walnut Hills
Hamilton County

(G-18634)
GREATER CINCINNATI BEHAVIORAL (PA)
1501 Madison Rd (45206-1706)
PHONE.....................513 354-7000
Jeff O'Neil, CEO
Kathy Schellinger, Superintendent
David Meek, Business Mgr
Steve Goldsberry, Vice Pres
Roger Rosenberger, VP Opers
EMP: 220
SQ FT: 25,000
SALES: 29.7MM Privately Held
WEB: www.gcbhs.com
SIC: 8093 Mental health clinic, outpatient

(G-18635)
GREATER CINCINNATI BEHAVIORAL
1501 Madison Rd Fl 1 (45206-1706)
PHONE.....................513 755-2203
Jeff O'Neil, Branch Mgr
EMP: 98
SALES (corp-wide): 28.2MM Privately Held
WEB: www.gcbhs.com
SIC: 8322 Social service center
PA: Greater Cincinnati Behavioral Health Services
1501 Madison Rd
Walnut Hills OH 45206
513 354-7000

Walton Hills
Cuyahoga County

(G-18636)
GOODYEAR TIRE & RUBBER COMPANY
7230 Northfield Rd (44146-6157)
PHONE.....................440 735-9910
Chad Nelson, Branch Mgr
EMP: 25
SALES (corp-wide): 15.4B Publicly Held
WEB: www.wingfootct.com
SIC: 7534 Tire retreading & repair shops
PA: The Goodyear Tire & Rubber Company
200 E Innovation Way
Akron OH 44316
330 796-2121

(G-18637)
MASON STRUCTURAL STEEL INC
Also Called: Mason Steel
7500 Northfield Rd (44146-6187)
PHONE.....................440 439-1040
Leonard N Polster, CEO
Keith Polster, President
J Moldaver, Principal
Joseph Patchan, Principal
Sol W Wyman, Principal
EMP: 100 EST: 1958
SQ FT: 75,000
SALES (est): 30.1MM Privately Held
WEB: www.masonsteel.com
SIC: 3441 5031 5074 Fabricated structural metal; doors & windows; window frames, all materials; fireplaces, prefabricated

(G-18638)
SMITH & OBY COMPANY
7676 Northfield Rd (44146-5519)
PHONE.....................440 735-5333
Michael A Brandt, CEO
Ronald Vranich, President
Gary Y Klie, Chairman
Charles E Caye, Exec VP
Matthew P Kittelberger, Vice Pres
EMP: 80
SQ FT: 6,500
SALES (est): 21MM Privately Held
WEB: www.smithandoby.com
SIC: 1711 Warm air heating & air conditioning contractor; ventilation & duct work contractor; plumbing contractors

Wapakoneta
Auglaize County

(G-18639)
COM NET INC
13888 County Road 25a (45895-8316)
PHONE.....................419 739-3100
Tim Berelsman, CEO
David Frey, CFO
Randall Plaisier, CTO
EMP: 60
SALES: 15.3MM Privately Held
WEB: www.cniteam.com
SIC: 4813 7375 ; information retrieval services

(G-18640)
COUNTY OF AUGLAIZE
Auglaize Acres Nursing Home
13093 Infirmary Rd (45895-9325)
PHONE.....................419 738-3816
Kim Sudhoff, Business Mgr
Bob Coverstone, Manager
Kathy Kohler, Telecom Exec
EMP: 125 Privately Held
WEB: www.augmrdd.org
SIC: 8059 9121 Nursing home, except skilled & intermediate care facility; legislative bodies
PA: County Of Auglaize
209 S Blackhoof St # 201
Wapakoneta OH 45895
419 739-6710

(G-18641)
CY SCHWIETERMAN INC
10097 Kohler Rd (45895-8232)
PHONE...............................419 753-2566
Michael Schwieterman, *President*
EMP: 40
SALES (est): 1.4MM **Privately Held**
SIC: 1521 1522 Single-family housing
construction; residential construction

(G-18642)
FRATERNAL ORDER EAGLES INC
Also Called: Foe 691
25 E Auglaize St (45895-1503)
P.O. Box 1977 (45895-0977)
PHONE...............................419 738-2582
Jack Piercefield, *Manager*
EMP: 26
SALES (corp-wide): 5.7MM **Privately Held**
WEB: www.fraternalorderofeagles.tribe.net
SIC: 8641 Fraternal associations
PA: Fraternal Order Of Eagles, Bryan Aerie
2233 Of Bryan, Ohio
221 S Walnut St
Bryan OH 43506
419 636-7812

(G-18643)
FROST ROOFING INC
2 Broadway St (45895-2056)
PHONE...............................419 739-2701
Jj Smithey, *President*
Chad Dunlap, *Business Mgr*
Suellen Smith, *Admin Asst*
Marty Borchers, *Administration*
EMP: 65
SQ FT: 200,000
SALES (est): 8MM **Privately Held**
WEB: www.frost-roofing.com
SIC: 1761 Roofing contractor

(G-18644)
GARDENS AT WAPAKONETA
Also Called: Trans Healthcare
505 Walnut St (45895-1868)
PHONE...............................419 738-0725
Teresa Ireland, *Exec Dir*
Debbie McElroy, *Director*
EMP: 31
SALES (est): 1.4MM **Privately Held**
SIC: 8051 Convalescent home with continuous nursing care

(G-18645)
HCF OF WAPAKONETA INC
Also Called: Wapakoneta Manor
1010 Lincoln Hwy (45895-9347)
PHONE...............................419 738-3711
Elaine Steinke, *Personnel*
Josiah Meyer, *Manager*
Bill Sheipline, *Supervisor*
Amy Shilling, *Director*
EMP: 99
SALES (est): 2.6MM **Privately Held**
SIC: 8051 Convalescent home with continuous nursing care

(G-18646)
HELP ME GROW
214 S Wagner Ave (45895-1714)
PHONE...............................419 738-4773
Charlotte Axe, *Director*
EMP: 28
SALES (est): 331.4K **Privately Held**
SIC: 8322 Youth self-help agency

(G-18647)
JPMORGAN CHASE BANK NAT ASSN
801 Defiance St (45895-1020)
PHONE...............................419 739-3600
Rob Armentrout, *Branch Mgr*
Sandy Truesdale, *Branch Mgr*
EMP: 26
SALES (corp-wide): 131.4B **Publicly Held**
WEB: www.chase.com
SIC: 6021 National commercial banks
HQ: Jpmorgan Chase Bank, National Association
1111 Polaris Pkwy
Columbus OH 43240
614 436-3055

(G-18648)
LIMA MEMORIAL HOSPITAL LA
1251 Lincoln Hwy (45895-7356)
PHONE...............................419 738-5151
Joy Brown, *Branch Mgr*
EMP: 368
SALES (est): 270.4K
SALES (corp-wide): 189.6MM **Privately Held**
SIC: 8062 General medical & surgical hospitals
HQ: Lima Memorial Hospital
1001 Bellefontaine Ave
Lima OH 45804
419 228-3335

(G-18649)
LOWES HOME CENTERS LLC
1340 Bellefontaine St (45895-9776)
PHONE...............................419 739-1300
Rich Phillips, *Branch Mgr*
EMP: 158
SALES (corp-wide): 68.6B **Publicly Held**
SIC: 5211 5031 5722 5064 Lumber & other building materials; building materials, exterior; building materials, interior; household appliance stores; electrical appliances, television & radio
HQ: Lowe's Home Centers, Llc
1605 Curtis Bridge Rd
Wilkesboro NC 28697
336 658-4000

(G-18650)
MILLERS TEXTILE SERVICES INC
1002 Bellefontaine St (45895-9701)
P.O. Box 239 (45895-0239)
PHONE...............................419 738-3552
Bob Hager, *Branch Mgr*
EMP: 68
SALES (corp-wide): 15MM **Privately Held**
WEB: www.millerstextile.com
SIC: 7213 5113 Uniform supply; patterns, paper
PA: Miller's Textile Services, Inc.
520 Commerce Rd
Wapakoneta OH
419 738-3551

(G-18651)
OHIO DEPARTMENT TRANSPORTATION
Also Called: Hwy Garage
511 Converse Dr (45895)
PHONE...............................419 738-4214
Ted Hemleben, *Manager*
EMP: 25 **Privately Held**
SIC: 1611 9621 Highway & street maintenance;
HQ: Ohio Department Of Transportation
1980 W Broad St
Columbus OH 43223

(G-18652)
PETERSON CONSTRUCTION COMPANY
18817 State Route 501 (45895-9392)
P.O. Box 2058 (45895-0558)
PHONE...............................419 941-2233
Donald J Bergfeld, *President*
Douglas J Crusey, *Vice Pres*
Ty Bergfeld, *Project Mgr*
Matt Brackman, *Project Mgr*
Ty Salisbury, *Project Mgr*
EMP: 150
SQ FT: 5,000
SALES (est): 83.9MM **Privately Held**
SIC: 1542 1629 Commercial & office building, new construction; institutional building construction; school building construction; waste water & sewage treatment plant construction

(G-18653)
S & S MANAGEMENT INC
Also Called: Holiday Inn
1510 Saturn Dr (45895-9782)
PHONE...............................567 356-4151
Philip M Valentine, *President*
EMP: 30

SALES (corp-wide): 6.9MM **Privately Held**
SIC: 7011 5812 7999 Hotel, franchised; eating places; pool parlor
PA: S & S Management Inc
550 Folkerth Ave 100
Sidney OH 45365
937 498-9645

(G-18654)
SUPERIOR CREDIT UNION INC
202 Willipie St (45895-1919)
PHONE...............................419 738-4512
Phil Buell, *Branch Mgr*
Jayne Vaske, *Assistant*
EMP: 50
SALES (corp-wide): 36.5MM **Privately Held**
WEB: www.limasuperiorfederalcreditunion.com
SIC: 6061 Federal credit unions
PA: Superior Credit Union, Inc.
4230 Elida Rd
Lima OH 45807
419 223-9746

(G-18655)
TED RUCK CO INC
101 N Wood St (45895-1661)
P.O. Box 1327, Hilliard (43026-6327)
PHONE...............................419 738-2613
Todd Ruck, *President*
Mike Ruck, *General Mgr*
EMP: 50
SQ FT: 2,000
SALES (est): 3.1MM **Privately Held**
SIC: 4212 7538 Mail carriers, contract; general truck repair

(G-18656)
TRI COUNTY VISITNG NRS PRVT
803 Brewfield Dr (45895-9394)
PHONE...............................419 738-7430
Donna Grimm, *Owner*
EMP: 30
SALES (est): 505.5K **Privately Held**
WEB: www.comhealthpro.com
SIC: 8082 Visiting nurse service

(G-18657)
TSC COMMUNICATIONS INC
Also Called: Telephone Service Company
2 Willipie St (45895-1969)
P.O. Box 408 (45895-0408)
PHONE...............................419 739-2200
Lonnie D Pedersen, *President*
EMP: 49
SQ FT: 40,000
SALES: 20MM
SALES (corp-wide): 15.5MM **Privately Held**
WEB: www.brighthosting.net
SIC: 4813 4812 7375 ; paging services; information retrieval services
PA: Telephone Service Company
2 Willipie St
Wapakoneta OH 45895
419 739-2200

(G-18658)
TSC TELEVISION INC
2 Willipie St (45895-1969)
P.O. Box 408 (45895-0408)
PHONE...............................419 941-6001
Terrance Schwieterman, *CEO*
Lonnie Pederson, *President*
Clint Conover, *Vice Pres*
EMP: 56 **EST:** 1996
SALES (est): 2.3MM **Privately Held**
SIC: 4841 4813 Cable television services; telephone communication, except radio

(G-18659)
WAPAKONETA YMCA
1100 Defiance St (45895-1022)
PHONE...............................419 739-9622
Joshua Little, *CEO*
Lisa Atkins, *Director*
EMP: 55
SALES (est): 2.7MM **Privately Held**
WEB: www.wapakymca.org
SIC: 8641 8661 8699 Youth organizations; religious organizations; charitable organization

---

(G-18660)
AIR MANAGEMENT GROUP LLC
Also Called: Avalon Inn and Resort
1 American Way Ne 20 (44484-5531)
PHONE...............................330 856-1900
Merry H Pieper, *Principal*
John Kouvas, *Principal*
EMP: 75
SALES (est): 3.7MM **Privately Held**
SIC: 7011 Hotels

(G-18661)
AJAX TOCCO MAGNETHERMIC CORP (HQ)
1745 Overland Ave Ne (44483-2860)
PHONE...............................330 372-8511
Thomas Illencik, *President*
Chun Lee, *General Mgr*
Scott Tewell, *General Mgr*
Ron Akers, *Vice Pres*
Gerald Jackson, *Vice Pres*
◆ EMP: 200
SQ FT: 200,000
SALES (est): 18.8MM
SALES (corp-wide): 1.6B **Publicly Held**
WEB: www.ajaxtocco.com
SIC: 3567 7699 3612 Metal melting furnaces, industrial: electric; industrial machinery & equipment repair; electric furnace transformers
PA: Park-Ohio Holdings Corp.
6065 Parkland Blvd Ste 1
Cleveland OH 44124
440 947-2000

(G-18662)
AMERICAN FUTURE SYSTEMS INC
5000 E Market St (44484-2260)
PHONE...............................330 394-1555
Irene Plum, *Branch Mgr*
EMP: 27
SALES (corp-wide): 134.8MM **Privately Held**
SIC: 5112 Business forms
PA: American Future Systems, Inc.
370 Technology Dr
Malvern PA 19355
610 695-8600

(G-18663)
AMERICAN NATIONAL RED CROSS
Also Called: American Red Cross Med Educa
126 Valley Cir Ne (44484-1090)
PHONE...............................330 469-6403
EMP: 49
SALES (corp-wide): 2.5B **Privately Held**
SIC: 8099 Childbirth preparation clinic
PA: The American National Red Cross
430 17th St Nw
Washington DC 20006
202 737-8300

(G-18664)
AMERICAN WASTE MGT SVCS INC
Also Called: Awms
1 American Way Ne (44484-5531)
PHONE...............................330 856-8800
Kenneth McMahon, *President*
Mark Cawthorne, *Vice Pres*
Tim Coxson, *Treasurer*
John Zwahl, *Sales Mgr*
EMP: 25
SQ FT: 3,000
SALES (est): 6.3MM
SALES (corp-wide): 55.8MM **Publicly Held**
WEB: www.awmsi.com
SIC: 4212 Hazardous waste transport
PA: Avalon Holdings Corporation
1 American Way Ne
Warren OH 44484
330 856-8800

(G-18665)
ANDERSON AND DUBOSE INC (PA)
Also Called: Anderson-Dubose Co, The
5300 Tod Ave Sw (44481-9767)
PHONE.............................440 248-8800
Warren Anderson, *President*
EMP: 100
SQ FT: 55,000
SALES: 518.2MM **Privately Held**
WEB: www.anderson-dubose.com
SIC: 5142 5141 Packaged frozen goods;
groceries, general line

(G-18666)
APTIV SERVICES US LLC
Also Called: Warren Plant 11
1265 N River Rd Ne (44483-2352)
P.O. Box 431 (44486-0001)
PHONE.............................330 373-3568
Brenda Jamison, *Controller*
Stephanie Pennel, *Branch Mgr*
EMP: 31
SALES (corp-wide): 16.6B **Privately Held**
SIC: 7549 8712 Automotive maintenance
services; architectural services
HQ: Aptiv Services Us, Llc
5725 Innovation Dr
Troy MI 48098

(G-18667)
APTIV SERVICES US LLC
Also Called: Delphi
Larchmond North River Rd (44483)
PHONE.............................330 373-7666
Steve Duca, *Branch Mgr*
EMP: 350
SALES (corp-wide): 16.6B **Privately Held**
SIC: 8711 Engineering services
HQ: Aptiv Services Us, Llc
5725 Innovation Dr
Troy MI 48098

(G-18668)
ATLAS RECYCLING INC
1420 Burton St Se (44484-5129)
P.O. Box 2037 (44484-0037)
PHONE.............................800 837-1520
Martin L Wilhelm, *President*
Scott A Wilhelm, *Corp Secy*
EMP: 40
SQ FT: 6,200
SALES (est): 2.6MM
SALES (corp-wide): 110.5MM **Privately
Held**
WEB: www.atlasrecycling.com
SIC: 4953 Recycling, waste materials
PA: Metalico, Inc.
135 Dermody St
Cranford NJ 07016
908 497-9610

(G-18669)
ATTITUDES NEW INC
1543 Westview Dr Ne (44483-5254)
PHONE.............................330 856-1143
Deneen Genaro, *President*
EMP: 26
SQ FT: 3,567
SALES (est): 770K **Privately Held**
SIC: 7231 Manicurist, pedicurist

(G-18670)
AUTO WAREHOUSING CO INC
1950 Halloock Young (44481)
P.O. Box 757, North Jackson (44451-0757)
PHONE.............................330 824-5149
Jim Zdanczewski, *General Mgr*
EMP: 50
SALES (corp-wide): 194.2MM **Privately
Held**
SIC: 7549 Automotive maintenance serv-
ices
PA: Auto Warehousing Co.
2810 Marshall Ave Ste B
Tacoma WA 98421
253 719-1700

(G-18671)
AUTUMN INDUSTRIES INC (PA)
518 Perkins Jones Rd Ne (44483-1849)
PHONE.............................330 372-5002
Sandra N Clark, *President*
Michael T Carney, *Senior VP*
EMP: 47
SQ FT: 20,000

SALES: 11.5MM **Privately Held**
SIC: 4213 4212 Trucking Operator-Nonlocal Local Trucking Operator

(G-18672)
AVALON GOLF AND CNTRY CLB INC
1 American Way Ne (44484-5531)
PHONE.............................330 856-8898
Ronald E Klingle, *Principal*
EMP: 75
SALES (est): 2.5MM
SALES (corp-wide): 55.8MM **Publicly
Held**
SIC: 7997 Golf club, membership
PA: Avalon Holdings Corporation
1 American Way Ne
Warren OH 44484
330 856-8800

(G-18673)
AVALON HOLDINGS CORPORATION (PA)
1 American Way Ne (44484-5531)
PHONE.............................330 856-8800
Ronald E Klingle, *Ch of Bd*
Kenneth J McMahon, *President*
Bryan P Saksa, *CFO*
Clifford P Davis, *CTO*
Frances R Klingle, *Officer*
EMP: 51
SQ FT: 37,000
SALES: 55.8MM **Publicly Held**
WEB: www.avalonholdings.com
SIC: 4953 7999 7991 4724 Hazardous
waste collection & disposal; golf services
& professionals; golf, pitch-n-putt; physi-
cal fitness facilities; travel agencies

(G-18674)
AVALON INN SERVICES INC
9519 E Market St (44484-5599)
PHONE.............................330 856-1900
Thomas Keegan, *President*
John Kouvas, *Manager*
EMP: 154
SALES (est): 2.9MM **Privately Held**
WEB: www.avaloninn.com
SIC: 7011 5813 Hotel, franchised; cocktail
lounge

(G-18675)
AVALON LAKES GOLF INC (HQ)
Also Called: Avalon Lakes Pro Shop
1 American Way Ne (44484-5531)
PHONE.............................330 856-8898
Jeff Shaffer, *President*
EMP: 36
SALES (est): 5.4MM
SALES (corp-wide): 55.8MM **Publicly
Held**
WEB: www.avalonlakesgolf.com
SIC: 7992 Public golf courses
PA: Avalon Holdings Corporation
1 American Way Ne
Warren OH 44484
330 856-8800

(G-18676)
AVALON RESORT AND SPA LLC
9519 E Market St (44484-5511)
PHONE.............................330 856-1900
Bunny Bronson, *Credit Mgr*
Bryan Saksa,
EMP: 99
SQ FT: 50,000
SALES (est): 441.1K
SALES (corp-wide): 55.8MM **Publicly
Held**
SIC: 7011 Hotels & motels
PA: Avalon Holdings Corporation
1 American Way Ne
Warren OH 44484
330 856-8800

(G-18677)
AVI FOOD SYSTEMS INC (PA)
2590 Elm Rd Ne (44483-2997)
PHONE.............................330 372-6000
Anthony J Payiavlas, *CEO*
John Payiavlas, *Ch of Bd*
Patrice Kouvas, *President*
Bill Parker, *President*
Robert A Sunday, *President*
EMP: 120
SQ FT: 11,000

SALES (est): 609.6MM **Privately Held**
WEB: www.avifoodsystems.com
SIC: 5962 5812 8742 Merchandising machine operators; caterers; food & beverage consultant

(G-18678)
BARRISTERS OF OHIO LLC
223 Niles Cortland Rd Se # 1
(44484-5720)
PHONE.............................330 898-5600
Alfred R Corsi Jr, *Branch Mgr*
EMP: 25
SALES (corp-wide): 5MM **Privately Held**
SIC: 6361 Title insurance
PA: Barristers Of Ohio, Llc
6000 Parkland Blvd Fl 2
Cleveland OH 44124
216 986-7600

(G-18679)
BERK ENTERPRISES INC (PA)
Also Called: Berk Paper & Supply
1554 Thomas Rd Se (44484-5119)
P.O. Box 2187 (44484-0187)
PHONE.............................330 369-1192
Robert A Berk, *President*
Franks Valley, *CFO*
▲ **EMP:** 81 **EST:** 1976
SQ FT: 240,000
SALES (est): 77.9MM **Privately Held**
WEB: www.berkleysquare.net
SIC: 5113 Bags, paper & disposable plas-
tic

(G-18680)
BIG BLUE TRUCKING INC
518 Perkins Jones Rd Ne (44483-1849)
PHONE.............................330 372-1421
Sandra N Clark, *President*
EMP: 47
SALES (est): 7.7MM **Privately Held**
SIC: 4212 Local trucking, without storage

(G-18681)
BROTHERS AUTO TRANSPORT LLC
2188 Lyntz Townline Rd Sw (44481-8702)
PHONE.............................330 824-0082
Dan Carney, *CEO*
EMP: 50 **Privately Held**
SIC: 4789 Pipeline terminal facilities, inde-
pendently operated
PA: Brothers Auto Transport, Llc
593 Male Rd
Wind Gap PA 18091

(G-18682)
BROWNING-FERRIS INDUSTRIES LLC
1901 Pine Ave Se (44483-6541)
PHONE.............................330 393-0385
Paul Stacharczyk, *Manager*
EMP: 53
SALES (corp-wide): 10B **Publicly Held**
WEB: www.alliedwaste.com
SIC: 4953 4212 Medical waste disposal;
local trucking, without storage
HQ: Browning-Ferris Industries, Llc
18500 N Allied Way # 100
Phoenix AZ 85054
480 627-2700

(G-18683)
CHILDRENS REHABILITATION CTR
885 Howland Wilson Rd Ne (44484-2100)
PHONE.............................330 856-2107
Robert C Foster, *Director*
EMP: 38
SQ FT: 14,000
SALES: 1MM **Privately Held**
SIC: 8093 8351 Rehabilitation center, out-
patient treatment; child day care services

(G-18684)
CLEAN BREAK INC
300 Muirwood Dr Ne (44484-4110)
PHONE.............................330 638-5648
David Eppley, *President*
EMP: 35
SALES: 750K **Privately Held**
SIC: 7349 Janitorial service, contract basis

(G-18685)
COLE-VALLEY MOTOR CO (PA)
4111 Elm Rd Ne (44483)
P.O. Box 1500 (44482-1500)
PHONE.............................330 372-1665
David Cole, *Partner*
Tom Cole, *Partner*
EMP: 62
SQ FT: 25,000
SALES (est): 29.1MM **Privately Held**
WEB: www.colecars.com
SIC: 5511 5531 7538 Automobiles, new &
used; automotive parts; automotive ac-
cessories; general automotive repair
shops

(G-18686)
COMMUNITY BUS SERVICES INC
1976 Niles Rd Se (44484-5117)
PHONE.............................330 369-6060
Will Amero, *Manager*
EMP: 26
SALES (corp-wide): 8.2MM **Privately
Held**
WEB: www.com-bus.com
SIC: 4151 School buses
PA: Community Bus Services, Inc.
1415 Gibson St
Youngstown OH 44502
330 743-7726

(G-18687)
COMMUNITY DIALYSIS CENTER
Also Called: Cdc of Warren
1950 Niles Cortland Rd Ne # 12
(44484-1077)
PHONE.............................330 609-0370
Donna Guerra, *Controller*
Mike Brajer, *Manager*
EMP: 25 **Privately Held**
WEB: www.curvesohio.com
SIC: 8092 Kidney dialysis centers
PA: Community Dialysis Center
18720 Chagrin Blvd
Shaker Heights OH 44122

(G-18688)
COMMUNITY HEALTH SYSTEMS INC
Also Called: Valley Care Health System
1350 E Market St (44483-6608)
PHONE.............................330 841-9011
Cindy Burns, *Principal*
Justin Snyder, *Pharmacist*
Briana Esteban,
Briana Montano,
EMP: 85 **EST:** 2010
SALES (est): 6.6MM **Privately Held**
SIC: 8082 Home health care services

(G-18689)
COMMUNITY SKILLED HEALTH CARE
1320 Mahoning Ave Nw (44483-2002)
PHONE.............................330 373-1160
Tony Kulisc, *CIO*
Janet Williams, *Systems Dir*
Leslie Terry, *Director*
Robert Annaess, *Administration*
EMP: 200
SQ FT: 42,000
SALES: 8.8MM **Privately Held**
WEB: www.communityskilled.com
SIC: 8051 Convalescent home with contin-
uous nursing care

(G-18690)
COMMUNITY SOLUTIONS ASSN
320 High St Ne (44481-1222)
PHONE.............................330 394-9090
Amy Bugos, *Accounts Mgr*
Ken Lloyd, *Director*
EMP: 40 **EST:** 2000
SALES: 1.3MM **Privately Held**
WEB:
www.commissioners.co.trumbull.oh.us
SIC: 8093 8322 Mental health clinic, out-
patient; substance abuse clinics (outpa-
tient); individual & family services

(G-18691)
COUNTRYSIDE VETERINARY SERVICE
Also Called: R L Baugher, Dvm
4680 Mahoning Ave Nw (44483-1419)
PHONE..................................330 847-7337
R L Baugher, *Treasurer*
EMP: 30
SALES (corp-wide): 6.6MM Privately Held
SIC: 0742 Veterinarian, animal specialties; animal hospital services, pets & other animal specialties
PA: Countryside Veterinary Service
8004 State Route 5
Kinsman OH 44428
330 876-5555

(G-18692)
COUNTY OF TRUMBULL
Also Called: Trumbull County Engineers
650 N River Rd Nw (44483-2255)
PHONE..................................330 675-2640
John Latell, *Director*
EMP: 74 Privately Held
WEB: www.co.trumbull.oh.us
SIC: 1611 9111 Highway & street maintenance; county supervisors' & executives' offices
PA: County Of Trumbull
160 High St Nw
Warren OH 44481
330 675-2420

(G-18693)
COV-RO INC
3900 E Market St Ste 1 (44484-4708)
PHONE..................................330 856-3176
Albert Covelli, *President*
Michael Marando, *Admin Sec*
EMP: 40 EST: 1964
SQ FT: 16,000
SALES: 536K Privately Held
SIC: 7699 7623 5661 Restaurant equipment repair; air conditioning repair; refrigeration repair service; men's shoes; women's shoes

(G-18694)
COVELLI FAMILY LTD PARTNERSHIP (PA)
Also Called: Panera Bread
3900 E Market St (44484-4708)
PHONE..................................330 856-3176
Kevin Ricci, *Managing Prtnr*
EMP: 38
SALES (est): 28.2MM Privately Held
SIC: 5812 5461 6794 Cafe; bread; franchises, selling or licensing

(G-18695)
CRAWFORD & COMPANY
6752 Brookhollow Dr Sw (44481-8645)
PHONE..................................330 652-3296
EMP: 38
SALES (corp-wide): 1.1B Publicly Held
WEB: www.crawfordandcompany.com
SIC: 8741 Management services
PA: Crawford & Company
5335 Triangle Pkwy Ofc C
Peachtree Corners GA 30092
404 300-1000

(G-18696)
CREATIVE LEARNING WORKSHOP (PA)
2460 Elm Rd Ne Ste 500 (44483-2949)
PHONE..................................330 393-5929
Caren Painter,
EMP: 43
SALES (est): 7.2MM Privately Held
SIC: 8331 Vocational rehabilitation agency

(G-18697)
CUSTOM PKG & INSPECTING INC
5232 Tod Ave Sw Ste 3 (44481-9729)
PHONE..................................330 399-8961
Christopher Harrison, *President*
EMP: 40
SQ FT: 8,000
SALES (est): 1.6MM Privately Held
SIC: 7389 Packaging & labeling services

(G-18698)
DACAS NURSING SYSTEMS INC
Also Called: Forum At Homes
8747 Squires Ln Ne (44484-1649)
PHONE..................................330 884-2530
Walter J Pishkur, *President*
Michael Seelman, *Director*
EMP: 200
SALES: 19.1K Privately Held
SIC: 8082 Home health care services

(G-18699)
DASHER LAWLESS AUTOMATION LLC
310 Dana St Ne (44483-3850)
PHONE..................................855 755-7275
Alex Mendikyan, *VP Finance*
Christopher Alan,
EMP: 28
SALES (est): 12MM Privately Held
SIC: 7521 7389 3534 Automobile storage garage; design services; automobile elevators

(G-18700)
DAWN INCORPORATED
2861 Sferra Ave Nw (44483-2273)
PHONE..................................330 652-7711
Dawn Ochman, *President*
Niloufer Patel, *Director*
EMP: 25
SQ FT: 2,500
SALES: 8MM Privately Held
SIC: 1541 Industrial buildings & warehouses

(G-18701)
DIAMOND ROOFING SYSTEMS LLP
8031 E Market St Ste 6 (44484-2200)
PHONE..................................330 856-2500
Amanda Marsco, *Director*
EMP: 30 EST: 2013
SQ FT: 2,000
SALES: 5MM Privately Held
SIC: 1761 Roofing contractor

(G-18702)
DIANE SAUER CHEVROLET INC
700 Niles Rd Se (44483-5951)
PHONE..................................330 373-1600
Diane Sauer, *President*
EMP: 80
SALES (est): 25MM Privately Held
WEB: www.dianesauerchevy.com
SIC: 5511 7513 7359 Automobiles, new & used; truck leasing, without drivers; business machine & electronic equipment rental services

(G-18703)
DO CUT SALES & SERVICE INC
Also Called: Do-Cut True Value
3375 Youngstown Rd Se (44484-5299)
PHONE..................................330 533-9878
Dante Terzigni, *Manager*
EMP: 30
SQ FT: 17,000
SALES (corp-wide): 6.7MM Privately Held
WEB: www.docut.com
SIC: 5072 5191 5251 5261 Hardware; garden supplies; hardware; lawnmowers & tractors
PA: Do-Cut Sales And Service, Inc.
3375 Youngstown Rd Se
Warren OH 44484
330 369-2345

(G-18704)
E AND P WAREHOUSE SERVICES LTD
1666 Mcmyler St Nw (44485-2703)
PHONE..................................330 898-4800
George Halkias,
Anna Halkias,
EMP: 25
SQ FT: 35,000
SALES: 200K Privately Held
SIC: 4225 General warehousing

(G-18705)
EASTERN OHIO P-16
4314 Mahoning Ave Nw (44483-1931)
PHONE..................................330 675-7623

Anthony Paglia, *Principal*
Jennifer Good, *Research*
Sarah Braun, *Manager*
Stephanie L Shaw, *Exec Dir*
EMP: 50
SALES: 387.7K Privately Held
SIC: 6021 National commercial banks

(G-18706)
EATON GROUP GMAC REAL ESTATE
Also Called: GMAC Realestate
382 Niles Cortland Rd Ne (44484-1940)
PHONE..................................330 726-9999
Mary Lou Maloy, *President*
EMP: 31
SALES (est): 1.5MM Privately Held
WEB: www.janetswhite.com
SIC: 6531 Real estate brokers & agents

(G-18707)
ERIE ISLAND RESORT AND MARINA
150 E Market St Ste 300 (44481-1141)
PHONE..................................419 734-9117
John Gronvall,
EMP: 50
SALES (est): 3.5MM Privately Held
WEB: www.erieislandsresort.com
SIC: 4493 Marina Operation

(G-18708)
FAIRHAVEN SHELTERED WORKSHOP
455 Educational Hwy Nw (44483-1967)
PHONE..................................330 847-7275
Rick Mistovich, *Manager*
David Sekerak, *Manager*
EMP: 150
SALES (corp-wide): 4.5MM Privately Held
SIC: 8331 Sheltered workshop
PA: Fairhaven Sheltered Workshop
45 North Rd
Niles OH 44446
330 505-3644

(G-18709)
GILLETTE ASSOCIATES LP
3310 Elm Rd Ne (44483-2614)
PHONE..................................330 372-1960
Nadile Stein, *Partner*
Charles E Stein, *General Ptnr*
EMP: 90
SQ FT: 27,947
SALES (est): 4.1MM Privately Held
SIC: 8059 Nursing home, except skilled & intermediate care facility

(G-18710)
GILLETTE NURSING HOME INC
3310 Elm Rd Ne (44483-2662)
PHONE..................................330 372-1960
Charles E Stein, *President*
Janet L Stein, *Vice Pres*
EMP: 95
SQ FT: 42,000
SALES (est): 5.7MM Privately Held
SIC: 8052 8051 Intermediate care facilities; skilled nursing care facilities

(G-18711)
HAYS ENTERPRISES INC
Also Called: Carts of America
1901 Ellsworth Bailey Rd (44481-9283)
PHONE..................................330 392-2278
Doris Hays, *President*
Jay Hays, *Exec VP*
EMP: 25
SQ FT: 22,000
SALES: 1.9MM Privately Held
WEB: www.haysenterprises.com
SIC: 7699 5199 Shopping cart repair; general merchandise, non-durable

(G-18712)
HOMETOWN URGENT CARE
1997 Niles Cortland Rd Se (44484-3037)
PHONE..................................330 505-9400
Tammy Russell, *President*
EMP: 123
SALES (corp-wide): 73.2MM Privately Held
SIC: 8011 Medical centers

PA: Hometown Urgent Care
2400 Corp Exchange Dr # 102
Columbus OH 43231
614 505-7633

(G-18713)
HOPE CTR FOR CNCER CARE WARREN
1745 Niles Crtlnd Rd Ne (44484)
PHONE..................................330 856-8600
Bruce Giambattifta, *Principal*
Terry Piperata, *Administration*
EMP: 60
SALES (est): 253.5K Privately Held
SIC: 8011 8093 Oncologist; specialty outpatient clinics

(G-18714)
HOWLAND CORNERS TWN & CTRY VET
Also Called: Towne & Country Vet Clinic
8000 E Market St (44484-2228)
PHONE..................................330 856-1862
Rufus Sparks, *President*
Charles Moxley, *Vice Pres*
EMP: 30
SALES (est): 1.6MM Privately Held
SIC: 0742 0741 Veterinarian, animal specialties; animal hospital services, livestock

(G-18715)
INTERNATIONAL STEEL GROUP
2234 Main Street Ext Sw (44481-9602)
PHONE..................................330 841-2800
Rodney Mott, *President*
Jeff Foster, *General Mgr*
EMP: 135
SALES (est): 15.3MM
SALES (corp-wide): 9.1B Privately Held
WEB: www.internationalsteelgroup.com
SIC: 3312 1011 Blast furnaces & steel mills; iron ores
HQ: Arcelormittal Usa Llc
1 S Dearborn St Ste 1800
Chicago IL 60603
312 346-0300

(G-18716)
J V HANSEL INC
Also Called: Institutional Foods
6055 Louise Ct Nw (44481-9006)
PHONE..................................330 716-0806
John J Hansel, *President*
Connie Radich, *Admin Sec*
EMP: 26
SQ FT: 26,000
SALES (est): 5MM Privately Held
SIC: 5113 5411 5141 5451 Industrial & personal service paper; grocery stores; groceries, general line; dairy products stores; party favors

(G-18717)
JACK GIBSON CONSTRUCTION CO
2460 Parkman Rd Nw (44485-1757)
PHONE..................................330 394-5280
John C Gibson Jr, *CEO*
E James Breese, *President*
John C Gibson Sr, *Chairman*
Marilyn E Hughes, *Corp Secy*
Bill Butch, *Vice Pres*
EMP: 100
SQ FT: 27,000
SALES: 15.4MM Privately Held
WEB: www.jackgibsonconstruction.com
SIC: 1542 1629 8741 1541 School building construction; industrial plant construction; construction management; industrial buildings & warehouses

(G-18718)
JARO TRANSPORTATION SVCS INC (PA)
975 Post Rd Nw (44483-2083)
P.O. Box 1890 (44482-1890)
PHONE..................................330 393-5659
James S Ffy, *CEO*
Terry Fiorina, *Corp Secy*
Rick Pompeo, *Vice Pres*
EMP: 79
SQ FT: 5,000
SALES: 39.4MM Privately Held
WEB: www.jarotrans.com
SIC: 4213 Trucking, except local

(G-18719)
KIDZ BY RIVERSIDE INC
421 Main Ave Sw (44481-1015)
PHONE................................330 392-0700
Crystal Anderson, *Administration*
EMP: 26
SALES (est): 691.3K **Privately Held**
SIC: 8351 Group day care center

(G-18720)
KING COLLISION INC
2000 N River Rd Ne (44483-2530)
PHONE................................330 372-3242
Douglas Fenstermaker, *President*
EMP: 25
SALES (est): 1.6MM **Privately Held**
WEB: www.kingcollision.net
SIC: 7532 Body shop, automotive

(G-18721)
LANDMARK AMERICA INC (PA)
1268 N River Rd Ne Ste 1 (44483-2371)
P.O. Box 4302 (44482-4302)
PHONE................................330 372-6800
Rokki Rogan, *CEO*
Robert Delisio, *President*
EMP: 32
SALES (est): 2.3MM **Privately Held**
SIC: 7389 Financial services

(G-18722)
LEEDA SERVICES INC (PA)
1441 Parkman Rd Nw (44485-2156)
PHONE................................330 392-6006
Winifred Hosking, *President*
EMP: 30
SALES (est): 4.8MM **Privately Held**
SIC: 8052 Home for the mentally retarded,
with health care

(G-18723)
LEWIS PRICE REALTY CO
8031 E Market St (44484-2200)
PHONE................................330 856-1911
Dennis Lewis, *Partner*
Patricia Potts, *Partner*
Gordon Price, *Partner*
EMP: 25
SALES (est): 1.2MM **Privately Held**
WEB: www.noas.com
SIC: 6512 6531 Commercial & industrial
building operation; shopping center, prop-
erty operation only; real estate brokers &
agents

(G-18724)
LIBERTY STEEL INDUSTRIES INC
2207 Larchmont Ave Ne (44483-2834)
PHONE................................330 372-6363
James T Weller, *President*
Phil Lapmardo, *CFO*
EMP: 104 EST: 2015
SQ FT: 145,000
SALES (est): 74.1MM **Privately Held**
SIC: 5051 Steel

(G-18725)
LOWES HOME CENTERS LLC
940 Niles Cortland Rd Se (44484-2537)
PHONE................................330 609-8000
Jack Swedzo, *Manager*
EMP: 150
SQ FT: 1,315
SALES (corp-wide): 68.6B **Publicly Held**
SIC: 5211 5031 5722 5064 Home cen-
ters; building materials, exterior; building
materials, interior; household appliance
stores; electrical appliances, television &
radio
HQ: Lowe's Home Centers, Llc
1605 Curtis Bridge Rd
Wilkesboro NC 28697
336 658-4000

(G-18726)
MAIN LITE ELECTRIC CO INC
3000 Sferra Ave Nw (44483-2266)
P.O. Box 828 (44482-0828)
PHONE................................330 369-8333
Toni M Harnar, *President*
Colleen Beil, *Vice Pres*
Kevin D Beil, *CFO*
Tracy Raschilla, *Office Mgr*
John H Harnar, *Admin Sec*

(G-18727)
EMP: 43
SQ FT: 13,000
SALES: 8.1MM **Privately Held**
SIC: 1731 1623 General electrical con-
tractor; electric power line construction

(G-18727)
MASTERPIECE PAINTING COMPANY
546 Washington St Ne (44483-4933)
PHONE................................330 395-9900
John Handerhan, *CEO*
EMP: 25
SQ FT: 3,305
SALES (est): 1.6MM **Privately Held**
WEB:
www.masterpiecepaintingcompany.com
SIC: 1721 Interior commercial painting
contractor; exterior commercial painting
contractor; industrial painting

(G-18728)
MED STAR EMGNCY MDCL SRV (PA)
1600 Youngstown Rd Se (44484-4251)
P.O. Box 2156 (44484-0156)
PHONE................................330 394-6611
Joseph W Robinson, *President*
EMP: 35
SQ FT: 4,800
SALES (est): 1.5MM **Privately Held**
SIC: 4119 Ambulance service

(G-18729)
MERCY HEALTH
8600 E Market St Ste 5 (44484-2375)
PHONE................................330 841-4406
EMP: 38
SALES (corp-wide): 4.7B **Privately Held**
SIC: 8734 Testing laboratories
PA: Mercy Health
1701 Mercy Health Pl
Cincinnati OH 45237
513 639-2800

(G-18730)
MERCY HEALTH YOUNGSTOWN LLC
Also Called: St. Joseph Warren Hospital
667 Eastland Ave Se (44484-4503)
PHONE................................330 841-4000
Kathy Cook, *President*
EMP: 900
SALES (corp-wide): 4.7B **Privately Held**
SIC: 8062 Hospital, affiliated with AMA res-
idency
HQ: Mercy Health Youngstown Llc
1044 Belmont Ave
Youngstown OH 44504

(G-18731)
MOCHA HOUSE INC (PA)
467 High St Ne (44481-1226)
PHONE................................330 392-3020
George N Liakaris, *President*
Nick G Liakaris, *Vice Pres*
Bill M Axiotis, *Treasurer*
EMP: 35
SQ FT: 10,000
SALES (est): 1.1MM **Privately Held**
WEB: www.mochahouse.com
SIC: 5812 5461 7299 Coffee shop; deli-
catessen (eating places); bakeries; ban-
quet hall facilities

(G-18732)
MSSL CONSOLIDATED INC
8640 E Market St (44484-2346)
PHONE................................330 766-5510
Vc Sehgal, *Chairman*
Sukant Gupta, *Vice Pres*
Laksh V Sehgal, *Director*
EMP: 409
SALES: 202MM
SALES (corp-wide): 1.1B **Privately Held**
SIC: 6719 Investment holding companies,
except banks
PA: Motherson Sumi Systems Limited
Sector-127, Plot No.1, 11th Floor,
Noida UP 20130
120 667-9500

(G-18733)
NEOCAP/CBCF
Also Called: Northeast Ohio Community Alter
411 Pine Ave Se (44483-5706)
PHONE................................330 675-2669
Rachel Defazio, *Opers Mgr*
Natalie Carr, *Case Mgr*
Jeigh Maynard, *Case Mgr*
Shauna Nadzan, *Case Mgr*
Eric Anderson, *Manager*
EMP: 35 EST: 1998
SALES (est): 3.7MM **Privately Held**
SIC: 8744 Correctional facility

(G-18734)
NORTH WOOD REALTY
Also Called: Century 21
1985 Niles Cortland Rd Se (44484-3037)
PHONE................................330 856-3915
Marlin Palich, *Manager*
EMP: 40
SALES (corp-wide): 5.5MM **Privately Held**
WEB: www.mikeshomecenter.com
SIC: 6531 Real estate agent, residential
PA: North Wood Realty
1315 Boardman Poland Rd # 7
Youngstown OH 44514
330 423-0837

(G-18735)
NORTHEAST OHIO COMMUNIC
Also Called: Neocom
2910 Youngstown Rd Se (44484-5259)
PHONE................................330 399-2700
Eric Tobin, *CEO*
Linda Money, *President*
EMP: 60
SQ FT: 12,000
SALES (est): 2.5MM **Privately Held**
WEB: www.rooms-r-us.com
SIC: 8748 Communications consulting

(G-18736)
NORTHEAST OHIO DUKES
4289 N Park Ave (44483-1531)
PHONE................................330 360-0968
Raymond Kohn, *Principal*
EMP: 40 EST: 2010
SALES (est): 168.9K **Privately Held**
SIC: 7929 Entertainers & entertainment
groups

(G-18737)
PSY-CARE INC
8577 E Market St (44484-2390)
PHONE................................330 856-6663
Douglas Darnall, *CEO*
Terrence Heltzel, *Director*
Susan Mills,
Vanessa Brocco, *Social Worker*
EMP: 30
SALES (est): 1.9MM **Privately Held**
SIC: 8093 8011 Mental health clinic, out-
patient; psychiatric clinic

(G-18738)
REM ELECTRONICS SUPPLY CO INC (PA)
525 S Park Ave (44483-5731)
P.O. Box 831 (44482-0831)
PHONE................................330 373-1300
Robert E Miller Sr, *CEO*
Randall Miller, *President*
Richard Cowin, *Vice Pres*
EMP: 25
SQ FT: 30,000
SALES (est): 9.6MM **Privately Held**
SIC: 5065 Electronic parts

(G-18739)
SANESE SERVICES INC (PA)
2590 Elm Rd Ne (44483-2904)
P.O. Box 110 (44482-0110)
PHONE................................614 436-1234
Ralph Sanese, *President*
Doris Sanese, *Principal*
Victoria Steck, *Vice Pres*
William Z Esch, *CFO*
Steve Hoffman, *CFO*
EMP: 300
SQ FT: 100,000

SALES (est): 119.3MM **Privately Held**
WEB: www.sanese.com
SIC: 5962 5812 7389 Food vending machines; eating places; cafeteria; caterers;
coffee service

(G-18740)
SANFREY FREIGHT SERVICES INC
695 Summit St Nw Ste 1 (44485-2800)
P.O. Box 1770 (44482-1770)
PHONE................................330 372-1883
William Sanfrey, *President*
EMP: 25
SALES (corp-wide): 3.3MM **Privately Held**
SIC: 4212 4213 Local trucking, without
storage; contract haulers
PA: Sanfrey Freight Services Inc
1256 Elm Rd Ne
Warren OH 44483
330 372-1883

(G-18741)
SEVEN SEVENTEEN CREDIT UN INC (PA)
3181 Larchmont Ave Ne (44483-2498)
PHONE................................330 372-8100
Gary L Soukenik, *CEO*
Jerome J McGee, *CFO*
Karen De Salvo, *VP Mktg*
EMP: 250
SQ FT: 40,000
SALES: 40.1MM **Privately Held**
SIC: 6163 6062 Loan brokers; state credit
unions, not federally chartered

(G-18742)
SEVEN SEVENTEEN CREDIT UN INC
100 Brewster Dr Se (44484-2462)
PHONE................................330 372-8100
Andy Wollam, *Branch Mgr*
EMP: 25
SALES (corp-wide): 40.1MM **Privately Held**
SIC: 6163 6062 Loan brokers; state credit
unions, not federally chartered
PA: Seven Seventeen Credit Union, Inc.
3181 Larchmont Ave Ne
Warren OH 44483
330 372-8100

(G-18743)
SIGNATURE HEALTHCARE LLC
2473 North Rd Ne (44483-3054)
PHONE................................330 372-1977
Crys Blankenship, *Branch Mgr*
EMP: 92 **Privately Held**
SIC: 8099 Blood related health services
PA: Signature Healthcare, Llc
12201 Bluegrass Pkwy
Louisville KY 40299

(G-18744)
SIMS BUICK-G M C TRUCK INC
Also Called: Sims GMC Trucks
3100 Elm Rd Ne (44483-2698)
PHONE................................330 372-3500
William Sims, *President*
Kenneth Sims, *Corp Secy*
Ronald Edwards, *Director*
EMP: 54
SQ FT: 36,000
SALES (est): 20.3MM **Privately Held**
WEB: www.simsnissan.com
SIC: 5511 5012 Automobiles, new & used;
trucks, tractors & trailers: new & used; au-
tomobiles & other motor vehicles

(G-18745)
SPECTRUM MGT HOLDG CO LLC
Also Called: Time Warner
8600 E Market St Ste 4 (44484-2375)
PHONE................................330 856-2343
Dan Beblo, *Manager*
EMP: 83
SALES (corp-wide): 43.6B **Publicly Held**
SIC: 4841 Cable television services
HQ: Spectrum Management Holding Com-
pany, Llc
400 Atlantic St
Stamford CT 06901
203 905-7801

(G-18746)

STEEL VALLEY CONSTRUCTION CO

135 Pine Ave Se Ste 203 (44481-1249)
PHONE.................................330 392-8391
Lois Shockey, *President*
David Shay, *Vice Pres*
Victor Shockey, *Admin Sec*
EMP: 25
SQ FT: 1,800
SALES (est): 2.4MM **Privately Held**
WEB: www.steelvalley.org
SIC: 1521 1711 New construction, single-family houses; general remodeling, single-family houses; plumbing contractors

(G-18747)

STERICYCLE INC

1901 Pine Ave Se (44483-6541)
PHONE.................................330 393-0370
Steve Pantano, *Manager*
EMP: 75
SALES (corp-wide): 3.4B **Publicly Held**
WEB: www.stericycle.com
SIC: 4953 Medical waste disposal
PA: Stericycle, Inc.
28161 N Keith Dr
Lake Forest IL 60045
847 367-5910

(G-18748)

STEWARD TRUMBULL MEM HOSP INC

1350 E Market St (44483-6608)
P.O. Box 1269 (44482-1269)
PHONE.................................330 841-9011
Ronald Bierman, *President*
Shawn Dilmore, *COO*
Steven Snyder, *CFO*
Bettina Dohn, *Manager*
EMP: 1000 EST: 1984
SQ FT: 600,000
SALES: 130.5MM
SALES (corp-wide): 2.5B **Privately Held**
SIC: 8062 8049 General medical & surgical hospitals; physical therapist
HQ: Steward Health Care System Llc
1900 N Pearl St Ste 2400
Dallas TX 75201
469 341-8800

(G-18749)

SU-JON ENTERPRISES

2448 Weir Rd Ne (44483-2516)
P.O. Box 1190 (44482-1190)
PHONE.................................330 372-1100
John Bellando, *Co-Owner*
Billie Sue Bellando, *Co-Owner*
EMP: 28
SALES (est): 1.8MM **Privately Held**
SIC: 4212 Local trucking, without storage

(G-18750)

SURGERY CENTER HOWLAND LTD

1934 Niles Cortland Rd Ne (44484-1055)
PHONE.................................330 609-7874
Kathy Cook, *Administration*
EMP: 27
SALES (est): 1.3MM **Privately Held**
SIC: 8011 Ambulatory surgical center

(G-18751)

THOMAS STEEL STRIP CORPORATION

Also Called: Tata Steel Plating
2518 W Market St (44485)
PHONE.................................330 841-6429
William Boyd, *President*
Jonathan M Jarvis, *Vice Pres*
▲ EMP: 300
SALES (est): 211.3MM
SALES (corp-wide): 9.2B **Privately Held**
WEB: www.corusgroup.com
SIC: 5051 Steel
HQ: Tata Steel Europe Limited
30 Millbank
London SW1P
207 975-8382

(G-18752)

TRUE2FORM COLLISION REPAIR CTR (PA)

3924 Youngstown Rd Se (44484-2839)
PHONE.................................330 399-6659
Rex Dunn, *President*
Clark Plucinski, *Exec VP*
Rick Paukstitus, *Vice Pres*
John Sanders, *Vice Pres*
Gary Erculiani, *Site Mgr*
EMP: 29
SALES (est): 13.9MM **Privately Held**
WEB: www.true2form.com
SIC: 7532 Collision shops, automotive

(G-18753)

TRUMBALL CNTY FIRE CHIEFS ASSN

Also Called: Trumball Cnty Hzardous Mtl Bur
640 N River Rd Nw (44483-2255)
PHONE.................................330 675-6602
Fred Youngbluth, *President*
Rick Bauman, *Vice Pres*
EMP: 60
SALES (est): 2.3MM **Privately Held**
SIC: 8322 Emergency social services

(G-18754)

TRUMBULL CMNTY ACTION PROGRAM (PA)

1230 Palmyra Rd Sw (44485-3730)
PHONE.................................330 393-2507
Ms Mamie C Hunt, *Bd of Directors*
Henry Angelo, *Bd of Directors*
Phyllis Cayson, *Bd of Directors*
Dr Kraig Markland, *Bd of Directors*
B J Pollard, *Bd of Directors*
EMP: 48
SALES: 7.1MM **Privately Held**
SIC: 8331 Work experience center

(G-18755)

TRUMBULL COUNTY ENGINEERING (PA)

650 N River Rd Nw (44483-2255)
PHONE.................................330 675-2640
Randy Smith, *Principal*
Nicole Klingeman, *Foreman/Supr*
Heather Richard, *Admin Sec*
EMP: 60
SALES (est): 7.6MM **Privately Held**
SIC: 8711 Engineering services

(G-18756)

TRUMBULL COUNTY ONE STOP

280 N Park Ave (44481-1123)
PHONE.................................330 675-2000
William Turner, *Principal*
EMP: 99
SALES (est): 1.6MM **Privately Held**
SIC: 8322 Social service center

(G-18757)

TRUMBULL HOUSING DEV CORP

4076 Youngstown Rd Se # 101 (44483-3367)
PHONE.................................330 369-1533
Heidi Scanlon, *Manager*
Donald Emerson, *Director*
EMP: 75
SALES: 445.1K **Privately Held**
SIC: 8748 9531 Urban planning & consulting services; housing programs

(G-18758)

TRUMBULL INDUSTRIES INC

850 Bronze Rd Ne (44483-2759)
PHONE.................................330 393-6624
EMP: 34
SALES (corp-wide): 150.3MM **Privately Held**
SIC: 5074 Plumbing & hydronic heating supplies
PA: Trumbull Industries, Inc.
300 Dietz Rd Ne
Warren OH 44483
330 393-6624

(G-18759)

TRUMBULL MANUFACTURING INC

400 Dietz Rd Ne (44483-2749)
P.O. Box 30 (44482-0030)
PHONE.................................330 393-6624
Murray Miller, *President*
Ken Miller, *CFO*
Julian Lehman, *Treasurer*
Chick Haering, *VP Sales*
Curtis Straubhaar, *Sales Staff*
▲ EMP: 89
SQ FT: 16,000
SALES (est): 14.8MM **Privately Held**
SIC: 3432 3433 5074 Plumbing fixture fittings & trim; heating equipment, except electric; plumbing & hydronic heating supplies

(G-18760)

TRUMBULL MEM HOSP FOUNDATION

Also Called: Mahoning Vly Hmtology Oncology
1350 E Market St (44483-6608)
PHONE.................................330 841-9376
Charles Johns, *President*
Henry Sebold, *CFO*
EMP: 3000
SALES: 725.3K **Privately Held**
SIC: 8011 Hematologist

(G-18761)

TRUMBULL SPECIAL COURIER INC

346 Willard Ave Se (44483-6238)
PHONE.................................330 841-0074
EMP: 30
SALES (est): 1.4MM **Privately Held**
SIC: 7389 Courier Service

(G-18762)

TURN AROUND GROUP INC

Also Called: Sunrise Industries Harps Jantr
1512 Phoenix Rd Ne (44483-2855)
PHONE.................................330 372-0064
Jeff Swogger, *President*
EMP: 80
SALES: 1.6MM **Privately Held**
WEB: www.tagdn.com
SIC: 7349 Janitorial service, contract basis

(G-18763)

ULTIMATE BUILDING MAINTENANCE

3229 Youngstown Rd Se (44484-5265)
P.O. Box 4313 (44482-4313)
PHONE.................................330 369-9771
James Dobson, *CEO*
EMP: 100
SALES (est): 1.4MM **Privately Held**
WEB: www.ultimatemaintenance.com
SIC: 7349 Building maintenance services

(G-18764)

US SAFETYGEAR INC (PA)

5001 Enterprise Dr Nw (44481-8713)
P.O. Box 309, Leavittsburg (44430-0309)
PHONE.................................330 898-1344
Tarry A Alberini, *President*
John C Conley, *CFO*
Dave Sherock, *Sales Staff*
Adam Talanca, *Info Tech Mgr*
EMP: 40
SQ FT: 102,000
SALES (est): 21.9MM **Privately Held**
WEB: www.ohioglove.com
SIC: 5084 5199 Safety equipment; packaging materials

(G-18765)

VALLEY TITLE & ESCRO AGENCY

2833 Elm Rd Ne (44483-2603)
PHONE.................................330 392-6171
Gilbert L Rieger, *President*
EMP: 30
SALES (est): 1.2MM **Privately Held**
SIC: 6512 Nonresidential building operators

(G-18766)

VIBRA HEALTHCARE LLC

1350 E Market St (44483-6608)
PHONE.................................330 675-5555
EMP: 71
SALES (corp-wide): 325.2MM **Privately Held**
SIC: 8062 General medical & surgical hospitals
PA: Vibra Healthcare, Llc
4600 Lena Dr Ste 100
Mechanicsburg PA 17055
717 591-5700

(G-18767)

VWC LIQUIDATION COMPANY LLC

1701 Henn Pkwy Sw (44481-8656)
PHONE.................................330 372-6776
Jamie Mallery, *Project Mgr*
James E Collins Sr, *Mng Member*
Daniel J McCarthy,
EMP: 130
SQ FT: 50,000
SALES (est): 23.4MM **Privately Held**
WEB: www.vistawindowco.com
SIC: 1799 5031 Window treatment installation; lumber, plywood & millwork

(G-18768)

WARREN CITY BOARD EDUCATION

Also Called: Transportation Center
600 Roanoke Ave Sw (44483-6473)
PHONE.................................330 841-2265
Phyllis Linderman, *Principal*
EMP: 42
SALES (corp-wide): 88.8MM **Privately Held**
SIC: 4226 Special warehousing & storage
PA: Warren City Board Of Education
105 High St Ne
Warren OH 44481
330 841-2321

(G-18769)

WARREN DRMATOLOGY ALLERGIES PC

Also Called: Warren Dermatology and Allergy
735 Niles Cortland Rd Se (44484-2475)
PHONE.................................330 856-6365
Kristen Lynch, *President*
EMP: 25
SALES (est): 1.8MM **Privately Held**
SIC: 8011 Dermatologist

(G-18770)

WARREN HOUSING DEVELOPMENT

4076 Youngstown Rd Se # 101 (44484-3367)
PHONE.................................330 369-1533
Donald Emerson, *Director*
EMP: 80
SALES: 2.9MM **Privately Held**
SIC: 6552 Subdividers & developers

(G-18771)

WEE CARE DAYCARE

Also Called: Lads and Lasses
1145 Niles Cortland Rd Se (44484-2542)
PHONE.................................330 856-1313
Donna McGrach, *Owner*
Sheri Baily, *Director*
EMP: 25
SALES (est): 318.1K **Privately Held**
WEB: www.ladsandlasses.com
SIC: 8351 Preschool center

(G-18772)

WILLIAM ZAMARELLI REALTORS

Also Called: Zamarelli William Relators
8700 E Market St Ste 6 (44484-2340)
PHONE.................................330 856-2299
William Zamarelli, *President*
EMP: 31
SALES (est): 1.8MM **Privately Held**
WEB: www.williamzamarelli.com
SIC: 6531 Real estate agent, residential

(G-18773)
WJ SERVICE CO INC (PA)
Also Called: W J Alarm Service
2592 Elm Rd Ne (44483-2904)
PHONE....................................330 372-5040
James Paylavlas, President
Tony Paylavlas, Corp Secy
Nicholas Paylavlas, Vice Pres
EMP: 45
SQ FT: 29,704
SALES (est): 5MM Privately Held
WEB: www.osscompanies.com
SIC: 7349 7382 Janitorial service, contract
basis; security systems services

(G-18774)
**WSB REHABILITATION SVCS
INC**
4329 Mahoning Ave Nw B (44483-1974)
PHONE....................................330 847-7819
Kelly Jenkins, Branch Mgr
EMP: 540
SALES (corp-wide): 26.6MM Privately
Held
SIC: 8093 Rehabilitation center, outpatient
treatment
PA: Wsb Rehabilitation Services, Inc.
510 W Main St Ste B
Canfield OH 44406
330 533-1338

(G-18775)
XPO LOGISTICS FREIGHT INC
6700 Muth Rd Sw (44481-9276)
PHONE....................................330 824-2242
Farris Scott, Manager
EMP: 150
SALES (corp-wide): 15.3B Publicly Held
WEB: www.con-way.com
SIC: 4213 Contract haulers
HQ: Xpo Logistics Freight, Inc.
2211 Old Earhart Rd # 100
Ann Arbor MI 48105
800 755-2728

Warrensville Heights
Cuyahoga County

(G-18776)
**ARSLANIAN BROS CRPT RUG
CLG CO**
Also Called: Arslanian Brothers Company
19499 Miles Rd (44128-4109)
PHONE....................................216 271-6888
Ted Arslanian, President
Henry Arslanian, Vice Pres
Armen Arslanian, Admin Sec
EMP: 25
SQ FT: 6,000
SALES (est): 2.2MM Privately Held
WEB: www.arslanianblind.com
SIC: 7217 Carpet & furniture cleaning on
location

(G-18777)
DIVAL INC (PA)
Also Called: W.F. Hann & Sons
26401 Miles Rd (44128-5930)
PHONE....................................216 831-4200
Karen Johnson, President
Jeff Williams, Director
Fred Disanto, Shareholder
Carl Grassi, Shareholder
EMP: 60
SQ FT: 12,500
SALES (est): 11.9MM Privately Held
SIC: 1711 Plumbing contractors; warm air
heating & air conditioning contractor; re-
frigeration contractor

(G-18778)
GOLDFISH SWIM SCHOOL
4670 Richmond Rd Ste 100 (44128-6411)
PHONE....................................216 364-9090
Soneli Morris, General Mgr
Renee Camporeale, General Mgr
Jamie Fernandez, General Mgr
Andrew Joseph, General Mgr
Emily Ryan, General Mgr
EMP: 45
SALES (est): 1.1MM Privately Held
SIC: 7999 7299 Swimming instruction; fa-
cility rental & party planning services

(G-18779)
GRACE HOSPITAL
20000 Harvard Ave (44122-6805)
PHONE....................................216 687-1500
EMP: 55
SALES (corp-wide): 17.4MM Privately
Held
SIC: 8062 Hospital, affiliated with AMA res-
idency
PA: Grace Hospital
2307 W 14th St
Cleveland OH 44113
216 687-1500

(G-18780)
SISTERS OF LITTLE
Also Called: St Mary & Joseph Home
4291 Richmond Rd (44122-6103)
PHONE....................................216 464-1222
Anne Donnelly, President
EMP: 150
SALES (corp-wide): 8.6MM Privately
Held
SIC: 8051 8052 Skilled nursing care facili-
ties; intermediate care facilities
PA: Little Sisters Of The Poor, Baltimore,
Inc.
601 Maiden Choice Ln
Baltimore MD 21228
410 744-9367

(G-18781)
**SPECIAL METALS
CORPORATION (DH)**
4832 Richmond Rd Ste 100 (44128-5993)
PHONE....................................216 755-3030
Ken Buck, President
James M Hensler, Vice Pres
Joseph Snowden, Vice Pres
Chris Conner, Controller
Dave Janosko, Manager
◆ EMP: 461
SQ FT: 14,000
SALES (est): 612.4MM
SALES (corp-wide): 225.3B Publicly
Held
SIC: 5051 Metals service centers & offices
HQ: Precision Castparts Corp.
4650 Sw Mcdam Ave Ste 300
Portland OR 97239
503 946-4800

(G-18782)
TRICKERATION INC
Also Called: Donegal Bay
26055 Emery Rd Ste E (44128-6211)
PHONE....................................216 360-9966
Timothy Hewitt, President
Mike Volchko, Controller
EMP: 26
SQ FT: 40,000
SALES (est): 4.3MM
SALES (corp-wide): 1.6B Publicly Held
WEB: www.pkoh.com.cn
SIC: 5122 Drugs, proprietaries & sundries
HQ: Park-Ohio Industries, Inc.
6065 Parkland Blvd Ste 1
Cleveland OH 44124
440 947-2000

Warsaw
Coshocton County

(G-18783)
**ECHOING HILLS VILLAGE INC
(PA)**
Also Called: ECHOING RIDGE RESIDEN-
TIAL CENT
36272 County Road 79 (43844-9770)
PHONE....................................740 327-2311
Buddy Busch, CEO
Harry C Busch, President
Bill Bell, Maintenance Dir
Mikael Lundqvist, Director
Kassondra Reed, Director
EMP: 110
SQ FT: 2,500

SALES: 27MM Privately Held
WEB: www.echoinghillsvillage.org
SIC: 7032 8051 8361 8322 Sporting &
recreational camps; mental retardation
hospital; residential care; individual &
family services; real estate agents & managers

Washington Court Hou
Fayette County

(G-18784)
NB TRUCKING INC
Also Called: Nickle Bakery
1659 Rte 22 E (43160)
PHONE....................................740 335-9331
Nickle Bakery, Owner
EMP: 40
SALES (corp-wide): 205MM Privately
Held
SIC: 4212 Local trucking, without storage
HQ: Nb Trucking Inc
26 Main St N
Navarre OH 44662

Washington Township
Montgomery County

(G-18785)
L A FITNESS INTL LLC
45 W Alex Bell Rd (45459-3007)
PHONE....................................937 439-2795
EMP: 29
SALES (corp-wide): 117.3MM Privately
Held
SIC: 7991 Physical Fitness Facility
PA: L. A. Fitness International, Llc
3021 Michelson Dr
Irvine CA 92612
949 255-7200

Waterford
Washington County

(G-18786)
**LANG MASONRY
CONTRACTORS INC**
405 Watertown Rd (45786-5248)
PHONE....................................740 749-3512
Damian Lang, President
Doug Taylor, CFO
EMP: 70
SALES (est): 12.2MM Privately Held
WEB: www.langmasonry.com
SIC: 1741 Stone masonry

(G-18787)
**WATERTOWN STEEL COMPANY
LLC**
405 Watertown Rd (45786-5248)
PHONE....................................740 749-3512
Ken Funk,
Ed Ewing,
Damien Lang,
EMP: 25
SALES: 2.5MM Privately Held
SIC: 1542 Commercial & office building
contractors

Waterville
Lucas County

(G-18788)
**BROWNING MESONIC
COMMUNITY (PA)**
8883 Browning Dr (43566-9757)
PHONE....................................419 878-4055
Dave Subleski, Director
EMP: 35
SQ FT: 350,000
SALES (est): 8.7MM Privately Held
SIC: 8361 Home for the aged

(G-18789)
**HEALTH CARE RTREMENT
CORP AMER**
Also Called: Heartland of Waterville
8885 Browning Dr (43566-9701)
PHONE....................................419 878-8523
Vivian Kiraly, Administration
EMP: 160
SALES (corp-wide): 2.4B Publicly Held
WEB: www.hrc-manorcare.com
SIC: 8051 Convalescent home with contin-
uous nursing care
HQ: Health Care And Retirement Corpora-
tion Of America
333 N Summit St Ste 103
Toledo OH 43604
419 252-5500

(G-18790)
**PARKER-HANNIFIN
CORPORATION**
Also Called: Fluid Connector Group
1290 Wtrville Monclova Rd (43566-1066)
PHONE....................................419 878-7000
Tom Boyer, Branch Mgr
Steve Dezort, Manager
EMP: 55
SQ FT: 46,642
SALES (corp-wide): 14.3B Publicly Held
WEB: www.parker.com
SIC: 4225 General warehousing
PA: Parker-Hannifin Corporation
6035 Parkland Blvd
Cleveland OH 44124
216 896-3000

(G-18791)
PER DIEM NURSE STAFFING LLT
18 N 3rd St Lowr (43566-1532)
PHONE....................................419 878-8880
Brenda Michalski, Partner
Mary Everly, Supervisor
William Everly, IT/INT Sup
EMP: 40
SALES: 1MM Privately Held
SIC: 7361 Labor contractors (employment
agency)

(G-18792)
**SOMETHING SPECIAL LRNG
CTR INC (PA)**
8251 Wterville Swanton Rd (43566-9725)
PHONE....................................419 878-4190
Mary Wolfe, President
EMP: 28
SQ FT: 5,000
SALES (est): 2.9MM Privately Held
SIC: 8351 Group day care center; nursery
school

(G-18793)
ST LUKES HOSPITAL
Also Called: St Lukes Wtrvlle Physcl Thrapy
900 Wterville Monclova Rd (43566-1168)
PHONE....................................419 441-1002
Scott Giest, Branch Mgr
EMP: 1496
SALES (corp-wide): 177.4MM Privately
Held
SIC: 8049 8071 Physical therapist; med-
ical laboratories
PA: St. Luke's Hospital
5901 Monclova Rd
Maumee OH 43537
419 893-5911

(G-18794)
SURFACE COMBUSTION INC
1270 Wtrville Monclova Rd (43566-1066)
PHONE....................................419 878-8444
Jeff Valuck, Sales Dir
Dennis Wolke, Branch Mgr
EMP: 30
SALES (est): 2MM
SALES (corp-wide): 23.8MM Privately
Held
WEB: www.surfacecombustion.com
SIC: 4225 General warehousing
PA: Surface Combustion, Inc.
1700 Indian Wood Cir
Maumee OH 43537
419 891-7150

▲ = Import ▼=Export
◆ =Import/Export

(G-18795)
WATERVILLE CARE LLC
Also Called: ARBORS AT WATERVILLE
555 Anthony Wayne Trl (43566-1516)
PHONE...................................419 878-3901
Erin Montag, *Administration*
Elyse Aasen,
EMP: 90
SALES: 4.6MM **Privately Held**
SIC: 8051 Skilled nursing care facilities

Wauseon
Fulton County

(G-18796)
ALANO CLUB INC
Also Called: Fulton County Alano Club
222 S Brunell St (43567-1360)
P.O. Box 1 (43567-0001)
PHONE...................................419 335-6211
Kent Bacon, *President*
EMP: 65
SALES: 11.8K **Privately Held**
SIC: 7997 Membership sports & recreation clubs

(G-18797)
COUNTY OF FULTON
Fulton County Engineers
9120 County Road 14 (43567-9669)
PHONE...................................419 335-3816
Paul Bieber, *Foreman/Supr*
Frank T Onweller, *Director*
EMP: 25 **Privately Held**
WEB: www.fultoncountyoh.com
SIC: 8711 Engineering services
PA: County Of Fulton
152 S Fulton St Ste 270
Wauseon OH 43567
419 337-9214

(G-18798)
DAVES SAND & STONE INC
Also Called: Greiser Transportation
19230 County Road F (43567-9481)
PHONE...................................419 445-9256
David A Grieser, *President*
Jason Grieser, *Vice Pres*
Kathleen Grieser, *Admin Sec*
EMP: 35 EST: 1978
SQ FT: 18,000
SALES: 4MM **Privately Held**
SIC: 4212 4213 Dump truck haulage; trucking, except local

(G-18799)
DONS AUTOMOTIVE GROUP LLC
720 N Shoop Ave (43567-1838)
P.O. Box 208 (43567-0208)
PHONE...................................419 337-3010
Larry Roush, *Transptn Dir*
Nikki Henry, *Sales Mgr*
Don Hayati,
EMP: 35
SALES (est): 11.8MM **Privately Held**
SIC: 5511 5521 5012 Automobiles, new & used; used car dealers; automobiles & other motor vehicles

(G-18800)
FOUR COUNTY FAMILY CENTER
7320 State Route 108 A (43567-9244)
P.O. Box 1010, Toledo (43697-1010)
PHONE...................................800 693-6000
Kathy Short, *Director*
EMP: 30
SALES (est): 1.2MM **Privately Held**
SIC: 8322 Social worker

(G-18801)
FULTON COUNTY HEALTH CENTER
Also Called: Fulton Manor Nursing Home
725 S Shoop Ave (43567-1701)
PHONE...................................419 335-2017
Patricia Finn, *CEO*
EMP: 111
SALES (corp-wide): 83.7MM **Privately Held**
WEB: www.fulhealth.org
SIC: 8062 8051 General medical & surgical hospitals; skilled nursing care facilities

PA: Fulton County Health Center
725 S Shoop Ave
Wauseon OH 43567
419 335-2015

(G-18802)
FULTON COUNTY HEALTH CENTER
Also Called: Fulton Stress Unit
725 S Shoop Ave (43567-1701)
PHONE...................................419 337-8661
Fax: 419 330-2776
EMP: 50
SALES (est): 1.8MM **Privately Held**
SIC: 8093 Specialty Outpatient Clinic

(G-18803)
FULTON COUNTY HEALTH CENTER (PA)
725 S Shoop Ave (43567-1701)
PHONE...................................419 335-2015
Patti Finn, *CEO*
Carl Hill, *President*
Jenee Seibert, *Principal*
Mark Hagans, *Treasurer*
Niki Thourot, *Controller*
EMP: 652 EST: 1927
SQ FT: 164,276
SALES: 83.7MM **Privately Held**
WEB: www.fulhealth.org
SIC: 8062 General medical & surgical hospitals

(G-18804)
FULTON COUNTY HEALTH DEPT
606 S Shoop Ave (43567-1712)
PHONE...................................419 337-0915
Sandy Heising, *Principal*
Michael Oricko, *Commissioner*
Kim Cupp, *Director*
Cynthia Rose, *Director*
Luanne Stanley, *Director*
EMP: 40
SALES (est): 2.4MM **Privately Held**
SIC: 8093 Family planning clinic

(G-18805)
FULTON COUNTY SENIOR CENTER
240 Clinton St (43567-1109)
PHONE...................................419 337-9299
Sandra Griggs, *Director*
Sheri Rychener, *Director*
EMP: 50
SALES (est): 1.7MM **Privately Held**
SIC: 8322 Social service center

(G-18806)
HEALTH CARE RTREMENT CORP AMER
Also Called: Heartland of Wauseon
303 W Leggett St (43567-1341)
PHONE...................................419 337-3050
Bill McDaniel, *Administration*
EMP: 50
SALES (corp-wide): 2.4B **Publicly Held**
WEB: www.hrc-manorcare.com
SIC: 8051 Skilled nursing care facilities
HQ: Health Care And Retirement Corporation Of America
333 N Summit St Ste 103
Toledo OH 43604
419 252-5500

(G-18807)
MRS DENNIS POTATO FARM INC
15370 County Road K (43567-8891)
PHONE...................................419 335-2778
Suzanne Dennis, *President*
Timothy Dennis, *Corp Secy*
EMP: 30
SQ FT: 27,000
SALES (est): 16.9MM **Privately Held**
SIC: 5148 Potatoes, fresh

(G-18808)
NOFZIGER DOOR SALES INC (PA)
Also Called: Haas Doors
320 Sycamore St (43567-1100)
PHONE...................................419 337-9900
Edward L Nofziger, *President*
Carol Nofziger, *Corp Secy*
▼ EMP: 173
SQ FT: 200,000

SALES (est): 35.1MM **Privately Held**
WEB: www.haasdoor.com
SIC: 3442 1751 5211 Metal doors; garage doors, overhead: metal; garage door, installation or erection; doors, wood or metal, except storm

(G-18809)
QUALITY CLG SVC OF NW OHIO
861 N Fulton St (43567-1054)
P.O. Box 142 (43567-0142)
PHONE...................................419 335-9105
Michael Draper, *President*
Linda Draper, *Treasurer*
EMP: 60
SQ FT: 400
SALES (est): 1.9MM **Privately Held**
SIC: 7349 Building cleaning service; building maintenance, except repairs

(G-18810)
SARAS GARDEN
620 W Leggett St (43567-1348)
P.O. Box 150 (43567-0150)
PHONE...................................419 335-7272
Bill Frank, *President*
William Frank, *Principal*
Amy Murphy, *Principal*
Matthew Rychener, *Principal*
David Burkholder, *Vice Pres*
EMP: 66
SALES: 3.1MM **Privately Held**
SIC: 8011 Medical centers

(G-18811)
WAUSEON DIALYSIS LLC
721 S Shoop Ave (43567-1729)
PHONE...................................419 335-0695
James K Hilger,
EMP: 31
SALES (est): 395.5K **Publicly Held**
WEB: www.davita.com
SIC: 8092 Kidney dialysis centers
PA: Davita Inc.
2000 16th St
Denver CO 80202

(G-18812)
WAUSEON MACHINE & MFG INC (PA)
995 Enterprise Ave (43567-9333)
PHONE...................................419 337-0940
Russell P Dominique, *CEO*
Eric Patty, *President*
Douglas A Weddelman, *Principal*
Chad Desgrange, *Opers Mgr*
Jackie Dominique, *Purch Mgr*
▲ EMP: 75
SQ FT: 24,000
SALES (est): 18.4MM **Privately Held**
WEB: www.wauseonmachine.com
SIC: 3599 3441 3559 7629 Machine shop, jobbing & repair; fabricated structural metal; automotive related machinery; electrical repair shops; rolling mill machinery; special dies, tools, jigs & fixtures

Waverly
Pike County

(G-18813)
ALOMIE DIALYSIS LLC
Also Called: Pike County Dialysis
609 W Emmitt Ave (45690-1013)
PHONE...................................740 941-1688
James K Hilger,
EMP: 35 EST: 2014
SALES (est): 348.8K **Publicly Held**
SIC: 8092 Kidney dialysis centers
PA: Davita Inc.
2000 16th St
Denver CO 80202

(G-18814)
BRISTOL VILLAGE HOMES
660 E 5th St (45690-1551)
PHONE...................................740 947-2118
Tanya Kim Hahn, *President*
Angela McCatherine, *Office Mgr*
EMP: 26

SALES: 5MM
SALES (corp-wide): 38.2MM **Privately Held**
SIC: 8059 Nursing home, except skilled & intermediate care facility
PA: National Church Residences
2335 N Bank Dr
Columbus OH 43220
614 451-2151

(G-18815)
BUCKEYE COMMUNITY SERVICES INC
Also Called: Grandview Avenue Home
207 Remy Ct (45690-2000)
PHONE...................................740 941-1639
Jeff Adkins, *Director*
EMP: 193
SALES (corp-wide): 12.7MM **Privately Held**
SIC: 8059 Home for the mentally retarded, exc. skilled or intermediate
PA: Buckeye Community Services, Incorporated
220 Morton St
Jackson OH 45640
740 286-5039

(G-18816)
CLEARFIELD OHIO HOLDINGS INC
300 E 2nd St (45690-1323)
PHONE...................................740 947-5121
Brian Jonard, *Branch Mgr*
EMP: 67
SALES (corp-wide): 11.4MM **Privately Held**
SIC: 1389 Gas field services
PA: Clearfield Ohio Holdings Inc
Radnor Corp Ctr Bdg5 40
Radnor PA 19087
610 293-0410

(G-18817)
COMMUNITY ACTION COMM PIKE CNT
Also Called: Beaver Clinic
227 Valley View Dr (45690-9135)
PHONE...................................740 947-7726
Cheryl Tackett, *Asst Director*
Sarah Williams, *Dental Hygenist*
EMP: 36
SALES (corp-wide): 22.1MM **Privately Held**
SIC: 8011 Clinic, operated by physicians
PA: The Community Action Committee Of Pike County
941 Market St
Piketon OH 45661
740 289-2371

(G-18818)
FIRST NATIONAL BANK OF WAVERLY (PA)
107 N Market St (45690-1354)
P.O. Box 147 (45690-0147)
PHONE...................................740 947-2136
Robert E Foster, *President*
Dwight A Massie, *Vice Pres*
Mitch Shumate, *Vice Pres*
Peggy Smith, *Vice Pres*
Dwight Massie, *CFO*
EMP: 50 EST: 1901
SQ FT: 17,000
SALES: 6.2MM **Privately Held**
WEB: www.thefirstnational.com
SIC: 6021 National commercial banks

(G-18819)
PEOPLES BANCORP INC
951 W Emmitt Ave (45690-1098)
PHONE...................................740 947-4372
EMP: 40
SALES (corp-wide): 208MM **Publicly Held**
SIC: 6035 Savings institutions, federally chartered
PA: Peoples Bancorp Inc.
138 Putnam St
Marietta OH 45750
740 373-3155

(G-18820)
PIKE CNTY ADULT ACTIVITIES CTR
301 Clough St (45690-1112)
PHONE....................740 947-7503
Tracy Noble, *Exec Dir*
EMP: 25
SALES: 1.5MM **Privately Held**
SIC: 8399 Health systems agency

(G-18821)
PIKE CNTY RECOVERY COUNCIL INC (PA)
218 E North St (45690-1148)
PHONE....................740 835-8437
Pam Johnson, *Exec Dir*
EMP: 38
SALES: 3.1MM **Privately Held**
SIC: 8069 Drug addiction rehabilitation hospital

(G-18822)
PIKE COUNTY YMCA
400 Pride Dr (45690-8979)
PHONE....................740 947-8862
Tim Conley, *CEO*
John Pennington, *Exec Dir*
Arlie Adams, *Director*
Sharon Christopher, *Director*
Donna Dutcher, *Director*
EMP: 25
SALES: 747.7K **Privately Held**
WEB: www.pikecountyymca.org
SIC: 8641 7991 8351 7032 Youth organizations; physical fitness facilities; child day care services; youth camps; individual & family services

(G-18823)
RES-CARE INC
Also Called: RES Care
212 Saint Anns Ln (45690-1039)
PHONE....................740 941-1178
EMP: 47
SALES (corp-wide): 23.7B **Privately Held**
SIC: 8052 Home for the mentally retarded, with health care
HQ: Res-Care, Inc.
     805 N Whittington Pkwy
     Louisville KY 40222
     502 394-2100

(G-18824)
WAVERLY CARE CENTER INC
Also Called: National Ch Rsdnces Brstol Vlg
444 Cherry St Frnt (45690-1276)
PHONE....................740 947-2113
Tanya Kim Hahn, *CEO*
Vickie J Nickell, *Executive*
Kay J Smallwood, *Administration*
EMP: 33
SALES (est): 5.7MM
SALES (corp-wide): 38.2MM **Privately Held**
SIC: 8051 Skilled nursing care facilities
PA: National Church Residences
     2335 N Bank Dr
     Columbus OH 43220
     614 451-2151

Wayne
Wood County

(G-18825)
C & G TRANSPORTATION INC
11100 Wayne Rd (43466-9846)
PHONE....................419 288-2653
Gary Harrison, *President*
Cathy Harrison, *Vice Pres*
EMP: 50
SALES (est): 6.7MM **Privately Held**
SIC: 4212 Local trucking, without storage

(G-18826)
S & D APPLICATION LLC (PA)
158 Church St (43466-9783)
PHONE....................419 288-3660
Doug Miller,
EMP: 36 EST: 1997
SQ FT: 15,000
SALES (est): 7MM **Privately Held**
SIC: 0711 5191 Fertilizer application services; fertilizer & fertilizer materials

---

Waynesburg
Stark County

(G-18827)
ACE ASSEMBLY PACKAGING INC
133 N Mill St (44688-9124)
P.O. Box 55 (44688-0055)
PHONE....................330 866-9117
Dency S Cilona, *President*
EMP: 30
SALES (est): 2.4MM **Privately Held**
SIC: 7389 3999 Packaging & labeling services; manufacturing industries

(G-18828)
AMERICAN LANDFILL INC
Also Called: Waste Management
7916 Chapel St Se (44688-9700)
PHONE....................330 866-3265
A Maurice Myers, *Ch of Bd*
EMP: 25
SQ FT: 26,000
SALES (est): 3.7MM
SALES (corp-wide): 14.9B **Publicly Held**
WEB: www.americanlandfill.com
SIC: 4953 Sanitary landfill operation
HQ: Waste Management Holdings Inc
     1001 Fannin St Ste 4000
     Houston TX 77002
     713 512-6200

(G-18829)
QUAD AMBULANCE DISTRICT
6930 Minerva Rd Se (44688-9320)
P.O. Box 33 (44688-0033)
PHONE....................330 866-9847
Steven Van Meter, *Chief*
Steven Vanmeter, *Chief*
EMP: 30
SQ FT: 1,200
SALES: 686.7K **Privately Held**
SIC: 4119 Ambulance service

(G-18830)
TERRA STAR INC
111 N Main St (44688)
PHONE....................405 200-1336
Bradley Wittrock, *CEO*
Tommy Peck, *Foreman/Supr*
EMP: 29
SALES (corp-wide): 12.6MM **Privately Held**
SIC: 1389 Cementing oil & gas well casings
PA: Terra Star Inc
     1515 S 7th St Ste 300
     Kingfisher OK 73750
     405 200-1336

Waynesville
Warren County

(G-18831)
GRANDMAS GARDENS INC
8107 State Route 48 (45068-9232)
PHONE....................937 885-2973
Douglas B Rhinehart, *President*
Pat Rhinehart, *Corp Secy*
James B Rhinehart, *Vice Pres*
Donna Trent, *Purch Mgr*
Jerry Schelhorn, *Manager*
EMP: 40
SQ FT: 2,500
SALES: 6MM **Privately Held**
SIC: 5261 0782 Nursery stock, seeds & bulbs; landscape contractors

(G-18832)
HOME THE FRIENDS INC
Also Called: Friends Boarding Home
514 High St (45068-9784)
P.O. Box 677 (45068-0677)
PHONE....................513 897-6050
Sherry Lamb, *Manager*
Woodie Davis, *Director*
Wendy Waters, *Administration*
Wendy Waters-Connell, *Administration*
EMP: 105

SQ FT: 35,000
SALES: 6.7MM **Privately Held**
SIC: 8051 Skilled nursing care facilities

(G-18833)
INTERNATIONAL UNION UNITED AU
8137 Lytle Trails Rd (45068-9231)
PHONE....................513 897-4939
EMP: 100
SALES (corp-wide): 237.6MM **Privately Held**
SIC: 8631 Labor union
PA: International Union, United Automobile, Aerospace And Agricultural Implement Workers Of Am
     8000 E Jefferson Ave
     Detroit MI 48214
     313 926-5000

(G-18834)
MBI TREE SERVICE LLC
9447 Cold Springs Ln (45068-9019)
PHONE....................513 926-9857
Luis Paez, *Principal*
EMP: 29
SALES (est): 323.5K **Privately Held**
SIC: 0783 Planting, pruning & trimming services

(G-18835)
QUAKER HEIGHTS NURSING HM INC
Also Called: Quaker Heights Care Community
514 High St (45068-9784)
PHONE....................513 897-6050
Barry Robbins, *Vice Pres*
Wendy Waters Connell, *Exec Dir*
Amanda Yauger, *Administration*
EMP: 99
SALES (est): 3.8MM **Privately Held**
SIC: 8051 Convalescent home with continuous nursing care

(G-18836)
SYNTHETIC STUCCO CORPORATION
4571 Isaac Ct (45068-8113)
PHONE....................513 897-9227
Gary W Bentley, *President*
Pamela S Bentley, *Corp Secy*
EMP: 30
SALES (est): 1.6MM **Privately Held**
SIC: 1742 Plastering, plain or ornamental

(G-18837)
VERIZON BUS NETWRK SVCS INC
9073 Lytle Ferry Rd (45068-9494)
PHONE....................513 897-1501
David Estell, *Manager*
EMP: 25
SQ FT: 81,086
SALES (corp-wide): 130.8B **Publicly Held**
WEB: www.gtl.net
SIC: 4813 Telephone communication, except radio
HQ: Verizon Business Network Services Inc.
     1 Verizon Way
     Basking Ridge NJ 07920
     908 559-2000

Wellington
Lorain County

(G-18838)
COUNTY OF LORAIN
Also Called: South Lrrain Cnty Amblance Dst
179 E Herrick Ave (44090-1302)
PHONE....................440 647-5803
Pat Wilkinson, *Manager*
EMP: 25 **Privately Held**
WEB: www.lcmhb.org
SIC: 4119 Ambulance service
PA: County Of Lorain
     226 Middle Ave
     Elyria OH 44035
     440 329-5201

(G-18839)
EDWARD W DANIEL LLC
46950 State Route 18 S (44090-9791)
PHONE....................440 647-1960
Ken Wrona, *CFO*
Robert Oriti,
Stuart W Cordell,
EMP: 36 EST: 1922
SQ FT: 75,000
SALES (est): 5.8MM **Privately Held**
WEB: www.ewdaniel.com
SIC: 3429 5085 3494 3463 Manufactured hardware (general); industrial supplies; valves & pipe fittings; nonferrous forgings; iron & steel forgings; bolts, nuts, rivets & washers

(G-18840)
ELMS RETIREMENT VILLAGE INC
136 S Main St Rear (44090-3301)
P.O. Box 88126, Carol Stream IL (60188-0126)
PHONE....................440 647-2414
Anthony Sprenger, *President*
Michael Springer, *President*
Mark A Sprenger, *Exec VP*
Donel Sprenger, *Vice Pres*
Mark Sprenger, *Admin Sec*
EMP: 80
SQ FT: 21,000
SALES: 4.5MM **Privately Held**
WEB: www.smithvillewestern.com
SIC: 8052 8059 8051 Intermediate care facilities; convalescent home; skilled nursing care facilities
PA: Sprenger Enterprises, Inc.
     2198 Gladstone Ct
     Glendale Heights IL 60139

(G-18841)
GRACE CONSULTING INC (PA)
510 Dickson St Lowr (44090-1502)
P.O. Box 58 (44090-0058)
PHONE....................440 647-6672
Carl Vineyard, *CEO*
Scott Teague, *President*
Hal Stiles, *Vice Pres*
Darryl Christy, *Mktg Dir*
EMP: 25
SALES: 10MM **Privately Held**
WEB: www.graceconsultinginc.com
SIC: 8748 8734 Environmental consultant; pollution testing

(G-18842)
KRYSTOWSKI TRACTOR SALES INC
Also Called: Krystowski Ford Tractor Sales
47117 State Route 18 (44090-9264)
PHONE....................440 647-2015
Jill Sheparovich, *President*
Lawrence Krystowski, *Vice Pres*
Richard Krystowski, *Treasurer*
Ronald Krystowski, *Admin Sec*
EMP: 25 EST: 1945
SQ FT: 15,000
SALES: 6MM **Privately Held**
WEB: www.krystowskitractor.com
SIC: 5999 5083 Farm equipment & supplies; farm & garden machinery

(G-18843)
MODERN POURED WALLS INC
41807 State Route 18 (44090-9677)
P.O. Box 598, Lagrange (44050-0598)
PHONE....................440 647-6661
W S Smith, *President*
EMP: 100 EST: 1976
SQ FT: 2,500
SALES (est): 12.7MM **Privately Held**
SIC: 1771 1794 Foundation & footing contractor; excavation work

(G-18844)
MPW CONSTRUCTION SERVICES
41807 State Route 18 (44090-9677)
P.O. Box 598, Lagrange (44050-0598)
PHONE....................440 647-6661
Scott Smith, *President*
EMP: 50
SALES (est): 3.6MM **Privately Held**
SIC: 1771 Concrete work

(G-18845)
WEBER HEALTH CARE CENTER INC
214 E Herrick Ave (44090-1315)
P.O. Box 386 (44090-0386)
PHONE...................................440 647-2088
Adelbert Weber, *President*
EMP: 140 **EST:** 1957
SQ FT: 20,000
SALES (est): 4.1MM **Privately Held**
SIC: 8051 8052 Extended care facility; intermediate care facilities

(G-18846)
WELLINGTON IMPLEMENT CO INC (PA)
625 S Main St (44090-1368)
PHONE...................................440 647-3725
Bill Stannard, *President*
William Stannard, *President*
Robt Stannard, *Principal*
Walter Young, *Principal*
Patricia Young, *Corp Secy*
EMP: 35 **EST:** 1929
SQ FT: 24,000
SALES (est): 14.6MM **Privately Held**
WEB: www.ohiotractor.com
SIC: 5083 Farm & garden machinery

Wellston
Jackson County

(G-18847)
AMERICAN ELECTRIC POWER CO INC
3 W 13th St (45692-9505)
PHONE...................................740 384-7981
EMP: 37
SALES (corp-wide): 16.2B **Publicly Held**
SIC: 4911 Distribution, electric power
PA: American Electric Power Company, Inc.
1 Riverside Plz Fl 1 # 1
Columbus OH 43215
614 716-1000

(G-18848)
CITY OF WELLSTON
Also Called: Wellston Auditor's Office
203 E Broadway St (45692-1521)
PHONE...................................740 384-2428
Chris Dupree, *Auditor*
EMP: 60 **Privately Held**
SIC: 9111 8721 City & town managers' offices; auditing services
PA: City Of Wellston
203 E Broadway St
Wellston OH 45692
740 384-2720

(G-18849)
EDGEWOOD MANOR OF WELLSTON
Also Called: Consulate Healthcare
405 N Park Ave (45692)
PHONE...................................740 384-5611
Jeff Jellerson, *President*
EMP: 50
SALES (est): 2.4MM **Privately Held**
SIC: 8052 Intermediate care facilities

(G-18850)
J-VAC INDUSTRIES INC
202 S Pennsylvania Ave (45692-1797)
PHONE...................................740 384-2155
Frank Declemente, *President*
Richard Moore, *Director*
Ann Ogletree, *Director*
EMP: 74
SQ FT: 8,300
SALES (est): 28.4K **Privately Held**
SIC: 8331 3269 Sheltered workshop; art & ornamental ware, pottery

(G-18851)
JACKSON COUNTY HLTH FACILITIES
Also Called: Jenkins Memorial Health Fcilty
142 Jenkins Memorial Rd (45692-9561)
PHONE...................................740 384-0722
David Nichols, *CFO*
Theresa Womeldorf, *Administration*
EMP: 97

SALES: 5.1MM **Privately Held**
SIC: 8051 Skilled nursing care facilities

(G-18852)
JACKSON-VINTON CMNTY ACTION (PA)
Also Called: JACKSON VINTON COMMUNITY ACTIO
118 S New York Ave (45692-1540)
PHONE...................................740 384-3722
Michelle Green, *Manager*
Tammy Riegel, *Manager*
Jerry Hall, *Cnty Cmsnr*
Cheryl Thiessen, *Exec Dir*
John Peoples, *Director*
EMP: 30
SQ FT: 12,000
SALES: 4MM **Privately Held**
SIC: 8399 9111 Community action agency; county supervisors' & executives' offices

(G-18853)
MONTGOMERY TRUCKING COMPANY
103 E 13th St (45692-2305)
P.O. Box 21 (45692-0021)
PHONE...................................740 384-2138
Phillip Fain, *President*
Mary B Casteel, *Corp Secy*
Jeffrey Fain, *Purch Agent*
Carol Wallace, *Purch Agent*
Betsy Fain, *Human Res Mgr*
EMP: 50
SQ FT: 7,200
SALES (est): 5.5MM **Privately Held**
WEB: www.mgotrucking.com
SIC: 4212 4213 Light haulage & cartage, local; refrigerated products transport; household goods transport

(G-18854)
PEOPLES BANK
101 E A St (45692-1211)
PHONE...................................740 286-6773
Chuck Sulerzyski, *President*
EMP: 35
SALES (corp-wide): 208MM **Publicly Held**
SIC: 6022 State commercial banks
HQ: Peoples Bank
138 Putnam St
Marietta OH 45750
740 373-3155

West Alexandria
Preble County

(G-18855)
COUNTY OF PREBLE
1251 State Route 503 N (45381-9733)
PHONE...................................937 839-5845
EMP: 52 **Privately Held**
SIC: 6733 Trusts
PA: County Of Preble
101 E Main St
Eaton OH 45320
937 456-8143

West Carrollton
Montgomery County

(G-18856)
RECOVERY WORKS HEALING CTR LLC
100 Elmwood Park Dr (45449-5402)
PHONE...................................937 384-0580
EMP: 38
SALES (est): 297.2K **Privately Held**
SIC: 8069 Drug addiction rehabilitation hospital

(G-18857)
UNITED PARCEL SERVICE INC
Also Called: UPS
225 S Alex Rd (45449-1910)
PHONE...................................937 859-2314
Mick Tasso, *Branch Mgr*
EMP: 86
SALES (corp-wide): 71.8B **Publicly Held**
SIC: 4215 Package delivery, vehicular

PA: United Parcel Service, Inc.
55 Glenlake Pkwy
Atlanta GA 30328
404 828-6000

West Chester
Butler County

(G-18858)
ABF FREIGHT SYSTEM INC
6290 Allen Rd (45069-3854)
P.O. Box 1063 (45071-1063)
PHONE...................................513 779-7888
Jon Koopman, *Sales Mgr*
Matthew Godfrey, *Branch Mgr*
EMP: 50
SALES (corp-wide): 3B **Publicly Held**
WEB: www.abfs.com
SIC: 4213 Contract haulers
HQ: Abf Freight System, Inc.
3801 Old Greenwood Rd
Fort Smith AR 72903
479 785-8700

(G-18859)
ADVANTAGE RN LLC (PA)
Also Called: Advantage Local
9021 Meridian Way (45069-6539)
PHONE...................................866 301-4045
Dawn Rider-Carter, *Sales Dir*
Anne Donlin, *Client Mgr*
Charlotte Yenney, *Manager*
Rock Mann, *Consultant*
Brian Cherry, *Info Tech Mgr*
EMP: 100
SQ FT: 8,400
SALES (est): 42.3MM **Privately Held**
WEB: www.advantagern.com
SIC: 7361 Placement agencies

(G-18860)
ADVANTAGE TECHNOLOGY GROUP (PA)
7723 Tylers Place Blvd # 132 (45069-4684)
PHONE...................................513 563-3560
Douglas W Lantz, *President*
EMP: 26
SQ FT: 2,000
SALES (est): 1.8MM **Privately Held**
WEB: www.advtechgroup.com
SIC: 7371 7379 Computer software development & applications; computer related consulting services

(G-18861)
AERO FULFILLMENT SERVICES CORP
6023 Un Centre Blvd Steb (45069)
PHONE...................................513 874-4112
Jon T Gimpel, *Branch Mgr*
EMP: 75
SQ FT: 264,000
SALES (corp-wide): 23MM **Privately Held**
SIC: 4225 General warehousing
PA: Aero Fulfillment Services Corporation
3900 Aero Dr
Mason OH 45040
800 225-7145

(G-18862)
AFFILIATES IN ORAL & MAXLOFCL
7795 Discovery Dr Ste C (45069-2903)
PHONE...................................513 829-8080
Michelle Maupin, *Manager*
EMP: 30
SALES (est): 1MM
SALES (corp-wide): 3.5MM **Privately Held**
SIC: 8069 8021 8011 Specialty hospitals, except psychiatric; specialized dental practitioners; surgeon
PA: Affiliates In Oral & Maxilliofacial Surgery Inc
5188 Winton Rd
Fairfield OH 45014
513 829-8080

(G-18863)
ALL GONE TERMITE & PEST CTRL
9037 Sutton Pl (45011-9316)
PHONE...................................513 874-7500
Tony White, *President*
Sandy Nellon, *Office Mgr*
EMP: 32 **EST:** 1997
SALES (est): 2.8MM **Privately Held**
SIC: 7342 Pest control in structures; pest control services

(G-18864)
ALS SERVICES USA CORP
8961 Steeplechase Way (45069-5874)
PHONE...................................513 582-8277
Kenneth Parks, *Branch Mgr*
EMP: 59 **Privately Held**
SIC: 8734 Testing laboratories
HQ: Als Services Usa, Corp.
10450 Stncliff Rd Ste 210
Houston TX 77099
281 530-5656

(G-18865)
ALT & WITZIG ENGINEERING INC
6205 Schumacher Park Dr (45069-4806)
PHONE...................................513 777-9890
Mark Conroy, *Manager*
EMP: 30
SALES (corp-wide): 28.7MM **Privately Held**
WEB: www.altwitzig.com
SIC: 8711 Consulting engineer
PA: Alt & Witzig Engineering Inc
4105 W 99th St
Carmel IN 46032
317 875-7000

(G-18866)
AMERIMED INC
9961 Cincinnati Dayton Rd (45069-3823)
PHONE...................................513 942-3670
Dan Deitz, *CEO*
Dan Dietz, *CEO*
EMP: 25
SQ FT: 6,300
SALES (est): 3.4MM **Privately Held**
WEB: www.americannursingcare.com
SIC: 5999 7363 5047 Medical apparatus & supplies; help supply services; medical & hospital equipment
HQ: American Nursing Care, Inc.
1700 Edison Dr Ste 300
Milford OH 45150
513 576-0262

(G-18867)
AMICA MUTUAL INSURANCE COMPANY
9277 Centre Pointe Dr # 230 (45069-4844)
PHONE...................................866 942-6422
R Daily, *Branch Mgr*
EMP: 48
SALES (corp-wide): 2B **Privately Held**
WEB: www.amica.com
SIC: 6331 Fire, marine & casualty insurance: mutual
PA: Amica Mutual Insurance Company
100 Amica Way
Lincoln RI 02865
800 992-6422

(G-18868)
ANIXTER INC
4440 Muhlhauser Rd # 200 (45011-9767)
PHONE...................................513 881-4600
Dave Wallace, *Manager*
EMP: 30
SALES (corp-wide): 8.4B **Publicly Held**
SIC: 5063 Wire & cable
HQ: Anixter Inc.
2301 Patriot Blvd
Glenview IL 60026
800 323-8167

(G-18869)
ASD SPECIALTY HEALTHCARE LLC
Also Called: Besse Medical
9075 Centre Pointe Dr (45069-4890)
PHONE...................................513 682-3600
Susan Coldren, *Principal*
Mick Besse, *Branch Mgr*

GEOGRAPHIC

EMP: 98
SALES (corp-wide): 167.9B **Publicly Held**
SIC: 5047 Medical equipment & supplies
HQ: Asd Specialty Healthcare, Llc
    5025 Plano Pkwy
    Carrollton TX 75010
    469 365-8000

(G-18870)
AXIS INTERIOR SYSTEMS INC (PA)
8216 Prnceton Glendale Rd (45069-1675)
PHONE....................................513 642-0039
Michael Ansari, *CEO*
Mark Thuney, *Vice Pres*
Greg Weldon, *Project Engr*
Zeyu Zhao, *Project Engr*
▲ EMP: 28
SQ FT: 18,000
SALES: 16.5MM **Privately Held**
WEB: www.axisinteriorsystems.com
SIC: 1752 Access flooring system installation; asphalt tile installation; ceramic floor tile installation; resilient floor laying

(G-18871)
BAG-PACK INC
Also Called: Bagpack
9486 Sutton Pl (45011-9698)
PHONE....................................513 346-3900
Steven Dreyer, *President*
Ronald C Dreyer, *Vice Pres*
Ken Harney, *Production*
EMP: 30
SQ FT: 40,000
SALES (est): 6.4MM **Privately Held**
WEB: www.bag-pack.com
SIC: 5199 Packaging materials

(G-18872)
BAKEMARK USA LLC
Bakemark Cincinnati
9401 Le Saint Dr (45014-5447)
PHONE....................................513 870-0880
Doug Townsend, *Branch Mgr*
EMP: 100
SALES (corp-wide): 598.7MM **Privately Held**
SIC: 5149 5046 Baking supplies; commercial equipment
PA: Bakemark Usa Llc
    7351 Crider Ave
    Pico Rivera CA 90660
    562 949-1054

(G-18873)
BECKETT RIDGE COUNTRY CLUB
5595 Beckett Ridge Blvd # 2 (45069-1897)
PHONE....................................513 874-2710
Jeff Galkin, *Manager*
EMP: 65
SQ FT: 1,800
SALES (est): 6.3MM **Privately Held**
SIC: 5941 7992 Golf goods & equipment; public golf courses

(G-18874)
BECKETT SPRINGS LLC (PA)
Also Called: Beckett Springs Hospital
8614 Shepherd Farm Dr (45069-1128)
PHONE....................................513 942-9500
Stacey D Banks, *President*
Christy Flick, *Director*
Sarayah McKinney,
EMP: 28 EST: 2013
SALES: 9.9MM **Privately Held**
SIC: 8062 General medical & surgical hospitals

(G-18875)
BELCAN LLC
9100 Centre Pointe Dr (45069-4846)
PHONE....................................513 645-1509
Lance Kwasniewski, *Branch Mgr*
EMP: 749
SALES (corp-wide): 813.3MM **Privately Held**
SIC: 7363 Engineering help service
PA: Belcan, Llc
    10200 Anderson Way
    Blue Ash OH 45242
    513 891-0972

(G-18876)
BHATTI ENTERPRISES INC
8045 Vegas Cir (45069-9291)
PHONE....................................513 886-6000
Santokh S Bhatti, *President*
EMP: 50
SQ FT: 4,000
SALES (est): 2.7MM **Privately Held**
SIC: 8111 Corporate, partnership & business law

(G-18877)
BOBCAT ENTERPRISES INC (PA)
9605 Prnceton Glendale Rd (45011-8802)
P.O. Box 46345, Cincinnati (45246-0345)
PHONE....................................513 874-8945
Thomas L Trapp, *CEO*
Lois Trapp, *Admin Sec*
▲ EMP: 85
SQ FT: 15,000
SALES (est): 44.4MM **Privately Held**
SIC: 5082 7353 Contractors' materials; cranes, construction; heavy construction equipment rental; cranes & aerial lift equipment, rental or leasing

(G-18878)
BRANDS INSURANCE AGENCY INC
6449 Allen Rd Ste 1 (45069-3803)
P.O. Box 62267, Cincinnati (45262-0267)
PHONE....................................513 777-7775
Alfred T Brands, *President*
Mat Brands, *President*
Steven Murry, *COO*
Allison Brands, *Treasurer*
Marcus Wyatt, *Software Dev*
EMP: 30 EST: 1967
SQ FT: 4,400
SALES (est): 7.4MM **Privately Held**
SIC: 6411 Insurance agents

(G-18879)
BRANDSAFWAY SERVICES LLC
9536 Glades Dr (45011-9400)
PHONE....................................513 860-2626
Tim Debolt, *Branch Mgr*
EMP: 50
SALES (corp-wide): 3B **Privately Held**
WEB: www.safway.com
SIC: 5082 Scaffolding
HQ: Brandsafway Services Llc
    N19w24200 Riverwood Dr
    Waukesha WI 53188

(G-18880)
CAMEO SOLUTIONS INC
Also Called: Bcbd
9078 Union Centre Blvd # 200 (45069-4992)
PHONE....................................513 645-4220
Mark Handermann, *President*
Kish Jha, *President*
John Leonhardt, *President*
Benjamin R Stockton, *Chairman*
Greg Paulson, *Exec VP*
EMP: 40
SQ FT: 6,800
SALES: 8.2MM **Privately Held**
SIC: 7373 Value-added resellers, computer systems
PA: Cameo Global, Inc.
    4695 Chabot Dr Ste 101
    Pleasanton CA 94588

(G-18881)
CECO CONCRETE CNSTR DEL LLC
4535 Port Union Rd (45011-9766)
PHONE....................................513 874-6953
Ronald D Worth, *Sales & Mktg St*
Rick Cevasco, *Manager*
EMP: 100 **Privately Held**
WEB: www.cecoconcrete.com
SIC: 1799 1771 Erection & dismantling of forms for poured concrete; concrete work
HQ: Ceco Concrete Construction Delaware, L.L.C.
    10100 N Ambassador Dr
    Kansas City MO 64153

(G-18882)
CEDAR ELEC HOLDINGS CORP
5440 W Chester Rd (45069-2950)
PHONE....................................773 804-6288
Chris Cowger, *CEO*
Manuel Jaime, *Chief Engr*
Gail Babitt, *CFO*
Dave Smidebush, *Branch Mgr*
Jonas Forsberg, *Officer*
EMP: 70
SALES (corp-wide): 139.2MM **Privately Held**
SIC: 3812 5013 5015 Navigational systems & instruments; tools & equipment, automotive; automotive supplies, used
PA: Cedar Electronics Holdings Corp.
    6500 W Cortland St
    Chicago IL 60707
    630 862-7282

(G-18883)
CELLCO PARTNERSHIP
Also Called: Verizon Wireless
7606 Trailside Dr (45069-7588)
PHONE....................................513 755-1666
EMP: 76
SALES (corp-wide): 130.8B **Publicly Held**
SIC: 4812 Cellular telephone services
HQ: Cellco Partnership
    1 Verizon Way
    Basking Ridge NJ 07920

(G-18884)
CHESTER WEST DENTAL GROUP INC
5900 W Chester Rd Ste A (45069-2951)
PHONE....................................513 942-8181
Sanjeev Goel, *President*
Jayne McAfee, *Office Mgr*
Edward Maag, *Fmly & Gen Dent*
EMP: 50
SALES (est): 3.9MM **Privately Held**
SIC: 8021 Dentists' office

(G-18885)
CHESTER WEST MEDICAL CENTER
Also Called: West Chester Hospital
7700 University Dr (45069-2505)
PHONE....................................513 298-3000
Dana Lovell, *Obstetrician*
Edward Crane, *Director*
Amber Finkelstein, *Social Dir*
Lisa Davis, *Hlthcr Dir*
Tom Daskalakis, *Officer*
EMP: 1200
SALES (est): 37.6MM **Privately Held**
SIC: 8062 General medical & surgical hospitals
PA: Uc Health, Llc.
    3200 Burnet Ave
    Cincinnati OH 45229

(G-18886)
CHRIST HOSPITAL
7589 Tylers Place Blvd (45069-6308)
PHONE....................................513 755-4700
EMP: 146
SALES (corp-wide): 929.7MM **Privately Held**
SIC: 8062 General medical & surgical hospitals
PA: The Christ Hospital
    2139 Auburn Ave
    Cincinnati OH 45219
    513 585-2000

(G-18887)
CINCINNATI HYDRAULIC SVC INC
9431 Sutton Pl (45011-9705)
PHONE....................................513 874-0540
Tom Hook, *President*
EMP: 30
SQ FT: 20,000
SALES (est): 1.5MM **Privately Held**
WEB: www.cinhyd.com
SIC: 7699 Hydraulic equipment repair

(G-18888)
CINMAR LLC (DH)
Also Called: Frontgate Catalog
5566 W Chester Rd (45069-2914)
PHONE....................................513 603-1000

Paul Tarvin, *Managing Prtnr*
Andrew Daniel, *Vice Pres*
David Landis, *Vice Pres*
Jenn Reeves, *Vice Pres*
Bill Daly, *Store Mgr*
◆ EMP: 120
SQ FT: 131,000
SALES (est): 45.8MM **Publicly Held**
SIC: 5961 5023 5712 Catalog sales; rugs; bedding & bedsprings

(G-18889)
CIP INTERNATIONAL INC
Also Called: Commercial Interior Products
9575 Le Saint Dr (45014-5447)
PHONE....................................513 874-9925
Thomas Huff, *Ch of Bd*
Kathleen Huff, *President*
Mark Elmlinger, *Vice Pres*
Jay Voss, *CFO*
EMP: 83 EST: 1975
SQ FT: 140,000
SALES: 33MM **Privately Held**
WEB: www.cipinternational.net
SIC: 7389 2541 Interior designer; lettering & sign painting services; store fixtures, wood; cabinets, except refrigerated: show, display, etc.: wood

(G-18890)
CL ZIMMERMAN DELAWARE LLC
Also Called: G M Z
5115 Excello Ct (45069-3091)
PHONE....................................513 860-9300
Tom Wells, *President*
Marsha Hummel, *Sales Staff*
▲ EMP: 30
SQ FT: 70,000
SALES (est): 38.3MM
SALES (corp-wide): 355.8K **Privately Held**
SIC: 5169 Industrial chemicals
HQ: Azelis Americas, Llc
    262 Harbor Dr
    Stamford CT 06902
    203 274-8691

(G-18891)
CLARK THEDERS INSURANCE AGENCY
9938 Crescent Park Dr (45069-3895)
PHONE....................................513 779-2800
Richard R Theders, *CEO*
Jonathan Theders, *President*
Jason M Randolph, *CFO*
EMP: 28
SQ FT: 6,000
SALES (est): 6.2MM **Privately Held**
WEB: www.ctia.com
SIC: 6411 Insurance agents

(G-18892)
CLARKDIETRICH ENGINEERING SERV
9100 Centre Pointe Dr (45069-4846)
PHONE....................................513 870-1100
William Courtney, *CEO*
Greg Ralph, *Exec VP*
Keith Harr, *Admin Sec*
EMP: 58
SALES (est): 1.2MM
SALES (corp-wide): 20.2B **Privately Held**
SIC: 8711 Consulting engineer
HQ: Clarkwestern Dietrich Building Systems Llc
    9050 Centre Pointe Dr
    West Chester OH 45069

(G-18893)
CLARKE CONTRACTORS CORP
4475 Muhlhauser Rd (45011-9788)
PHONE....................................513 285-7844
Matt Clarke, *President*
Peter Chadwick, *Project Mgr*
Mike Mercer, *Project Mgr*
Tonya Holbrook, *Sales Staff*
EMP: 30
SQ FT: 4,000
SALES (est): 5.4MM **Privately Held**
WEB: www.clarkecontractors.com
SIC: 1521 Repairing fire damage, single-family houses

▲ = Import ▼=Export
◆ =Import/Export

(G-18894)
COLDWELL BANKER WEST SHELL
9106 W Chester Towne Ctr (45069-3102)
PHONE..................................513 829-4000
Lisa Morales, *Real Est Agnt*
Mary Schneider, *Real Est Agnt*
EMP: 46
SALES (corp-wide): 15.3MM **Privately Held**
SIC: 6531 Real estate agent, residential
PA: Coldwell Banker West Shell
9321 Montgomery Rd Ste C
Cincinnati OH 45242
513 794-9494

(G-18895)
COLDWELL BANKER WEST SHELL
7311 Tylers Corner Dr (45069-6344)
PHONE..................................513 777-7900
Gayle Tipp, *Vice Pres*
Becky Mannix, *Project Mgr*
Matthew Schneider, *Sales Staff*
Sue Hughes, *Sales Associate*
Robin Johnson, *Sales Associate*
EMP: 75
SALES (corp-wide): 15.3MM **Privately Held**
WEB: www.coldwellbankerwestshell.com
SIC: 6531 Real estate agent, residential
PA: Coldwell Banker West Shell
9321 Montgomery Rd Ste C
Cincinnati OH 45242
513 794-9494

(G-18896)
CONTAINERPORT GROUP INC
Also Called: CONTAINERPORT GROUP, INC.
2700 Crescentville Rd (45069-4828)
PHONE..................................513 771-0275
Ken Kraus, *Manager*
EMP: 40
SQ FT: 750
SALES (corp-wide): 274.1MM **Privately Held**
WEB: www.containerport.com
SIC: 4493 Boat yards, storage & incidental repair
HQ: Containerport Group, Inc.
1340 Depot St Fl 2
Cleveland OH 44116
440 333-1330

(G-18897)
CONTECH TRCKG & LOGISTICS LLC
9025 Centre Pointe Dr # 400 (45069-9700)
PHONE..................................513 645-7000
Steve Kerls, *Treasurer*
Rick Gaynorr, *Mng Member*
EMP: 74
SALES (est): 12.4MM **Privately Held**
SIC: 4731 Freight forwarding
HQ: Contech Engineered Solutions Llc
9025 Centre Pointe Dr # 400
West Chester OH 45069
513 645-7000

(G-18898)
CORNERSTONE BRANDS INC (DH)
5568 W Chester Rd (45069-2914)
P.O. Box 1308 (45071-1308)
PHONE..................................513 603-1000
Judy A Schmeling, *President*
Andrea Huff, *Superintendent*
Lisa Barnes, *Vice Pres*
Bryon Colby, *Vice Pres*
Andy Franzoni, *Vice Pres*
◆ EMP: 1000
SQ FT: 55,000
SALES (est): 1.4B **Publicly Held**
SIC: 5021 Furniture

(G-18899)
CORNERSTONE BRANDS GROUP INC
5568 W Chester Rd (45069-2914)
PHONE..................................513 603-1000
Judy A Schmeling, *President*
▼ EMP: 918
SQ FT: 1,000,000

SALES (est): 413.8K **Publicly Held**
SIC: 5961 8742 Catalog & mail-order houses; marketing consulting services
HQ: Cornerstone Brands, Inc.
5568 W Chester Rd
West Chester OH 45069
513 603-1000

(G-18900)
CORT BUSINESS SERVICES CORP
Also Called: Cort Furniture Rental
7400 Squire Ct (45069-2313)
PHONE..................................513 759-8181
Mark Robertson, *Manager*
EMP: 60
SQ FT: 30,000
SALES (corp-wide): 225.3B **Publicly Held**
SIC: 7359 5932 Furniture rental; furniture, secondhand
HQ: Cort Business Services Corporation
15000 Conference
Chantilly VA 20151
703 968-8500

(G-18901)
COURTYARD BY MARRIOTT
6250 Muhlhauser Rd (45069-4988)
PHONE..................................513 341-4140
John Sukola, *General Mgr*
EMP: 30
SALES (est): 1.7MM **Privately Held**
SIC: 7011 Hotels & motels

(G-18902)
COURTYARD LTD (PA)
7373 Kingsgate Way (45069-2453)
PHONE..................................513 777-5530
Carol Packett, *Manager*
EMP: 38 EST: 1975
SQ FT: 14,300
SALES (est): 939.3K **Privately Held**
WEB: www.courtyard.com
SIC: 7997 7991 Racquetball club, membership; physical fitness facilities

(G-18903)
COWAN SYSTEMS LLC
2751 Crescentville Rd (45069-3816)
PHONE..................................513 721-6444
EMP: 129 **Privately Held**
SIC: 4213 Trucking, except local
PA: Cowan Systems, Llc
4555 Hollins Ferry Rd
Baltimore MD 21227

(G-18904)
COX AUTOMOTIVE INC
4969 Muhlhauser Rd (45011-9789)
PHONE..................................513 874-9310
Ryan Edwards, *Manager*
EMP: 150
SALES (corp-wide): 32.5B **Privately Held**
WEB: www.manheim.com
SIC: 5012 Automobile auction
HQ: Cox Automotive, Inc.
6205-A Pchtree Dnwoody Rd
Atlanta GA 30328
404 843-5000

(G-18905)
CR BRANDS INC (DH)
8790 Beckett Rd (45069-2904)
PHONE..................................513 860-5039
Richard Owen, *CEO*
John Samoya, *CFO*
Joe Cilurzo, *Sales Dir*
Elli Frasier, *Director*
▼ EMP: 82
SQ FT: 5,000
SALES (est): 27.5MM **Publicly Held**
WEB: www.redoxbrands.com
SIC: 2841 5169 3999 Soap & other detergents; detergents & soaps, except specialty cleaning; atomizers, toiletry

(G-18906)
CRESCENT PARK CORPORATION (PA)
9817 Crescent Park Dr (45069-3867)
PHONE..................................513 759-7000
Chris Taylor, *CEO*
David E Taylor Sr, *Ch of Bd*
Tom Schwallie, *Exec VP*
David Combs, *CFO*

EMP: 160
SQ FT: 700,000
SALES (est): 53MM **Privately Held**
SIC: 4213 4222 4225 7389 General warehousing & storage; refrigerated warehousing & storage; packaging & labeling services; management services; packing & crating

(G-18907)
CUMMINS INC
5400 Rialto Rd (45069-3092)
PHONE..................................513 563-6670
Peter Zelinskas, *Marketing Staff*
Robert Fontilla, *Branch Mgr*
EMP: 40
SALES (corp-wide): 23.7B **Publicly Held**
WEB: www.cummins.com
SIC: 5084 Engines & parts, diesel
PA: Cummins Inc.
500 Jackson St
Columbus IN 47201
812 377-5000

(G-18908)
DATATECH DEPOT (EAST) INC
4750 Ashley Dr (45011-9704)
PHONE..................................513 860-5651
Tom Le, *President*
EMP: 35
SALES (est): 2MM
SALES (corp-wide): 4.1MM **Privately Held**
SIC: 7378 Computer & data processing equipment repair/maintenance; computer peripheral equipment repair & maintenance
PA: Datatech Depot, Inc.
249 E Emerson Ave Ste G
Orange CA 92865

(G-18909)
DEDICATED LOGISTICS INC
6019 Union Centre Blvd (45014-2290)
PHONE..................................513 275-1135
Ryan Usher, *Branch Mgr*
EMP: 99
SALES (corp-wide): 262.7MM **Privately Held**
SIC: 4213 4212 4225 Trucking, except local; local trucking, without storage; general warehousing & storage
HQ: Dedicated Logistics, Inc.
2900 Granada Ln N
Oakdale MN 55128

(G-18910)
DIALYSIS CLINIC INC
7650 University Dr (45069)
PHONE..................................513 777-0855
Roy Dansro, *Administration*
EMP: 25
SQ FT: 51,052
SALES (corp-wide): 760.1MM **Privately Held**
WEB: www.dciinc.org
SIC: 8092 Kidney dialysis centers
PA: Dialysis Clinic, Inc.
1633 Church St Ste 500
Nashville TN 37203
615 327-3061

(G-18911)
DILLON HOLDINGS LLC
Also Called: Visiting Angels Lvng Asst
8050 Beckett Center Dr # 103 (45069-5017)
PHONE..................................513 942-5600
Tabatha Dillon, *Marketing Staff*
Tom Dillon,
Debbie Dillon,
EMP: 105
SQ FT: 1,200
SALES (est): 2MM **Privately Held**
SIC: 8082 Home health care services

(G-18912)
DIMENSIONMARK LTD
2909 Crescentville Rd (45069-3883)
PHONE..................................513 305-3525
Todd Parnell, *Mng Member*
EMP: 25
SALES: 6.5MM **Privately Held**
SIC: 8741 Business management

(G-18913)
DIRECT OPTIONS INC
9565 Cncnnati Columbus Rd (45069-4242)
PHONE..................................513 779-4416
Jan S Moore, *President*
Paul Wiehe, *Vice Pres*
EMP: 28
SQ FT: 10,000
SALES: 7MM **Privately Held**
WEB: www.directoptions.com
SIC: 8742 Marketing consulting services

(G-18914)
DITTMAN-ADAMS COMPANY
4946 Rialto Rd (45069-2927)
PHONE..................................513 870-7530
Garry Adams, *President*
Ryan Smith, *Vice Pres*
Kathy Peterson, *Credit Mgr*
Marco Mikesell, *Accountant*
Sandra Hendrix, *Human Res Dir*
EMP: 43
SQ FT: 60,000
SALES (est): 22.8MM **Privately Held**
WEB: www.dittman-adams.com
SIC: 5194 Cigarettes; cigars; chewing tobacco; smoking tobacco

(G-18915)
DIXON BUILDERS & DEVELOPERS
8050 Beckett Center Dr # 213 (45069-5018)
PHONE..................................513 887-6400
Brian Byington, *President*
James M Dixon, *Founder*
Jeffrey L Nelson, *CFO*
Mark Schraffenberger, *Admin Sec*
EMP: 100
SQ FT: 4,000
SALES (est): 6.2MM **Privately Held**
WEB: www.dixonbuilders.com
SIC: 1521 1522 1531 New construction, single-family houses; condominium construction; operative builders

(G-18916)
DYNCORP
9266 Meridian Way (45069-6521)
PHONE..................................513 942-6500
EMP: 200
SALES (corp-wide): 16.3B **Privately Held**
SIC: 7373 Computer Systems Design
PA: Dyncorp Llc
1700 Old Meadow Rd
Mc Lean VA 22102
571 722-0210

(G-18917)
E-TECHNOLOGIES GROUP LLC (HQ)
Also Called: E Technologies Group
5530 Union Centre Dr (45069-4821)
PHONE..................................513 771-7271
Ralph Carter, *CEO*
Henry Stacey, *Project Mgr*
Chris Beard, *Engineer*
Scott Burngasser, *Engineer*
Nick Hasselbeck, *Engineer*
EMP: 71
SQ FT: 7,000
SALES (est): 38.8MM
SALES (corp-wide): 7.2MM **Privately Held**
WEB: www.etech-group.com
SIC: 8711 Consulting engineer
PA: E-Technologies Group, Inc.
5530 Union Centre Dr
West Chester OH 45069
513 771-7271

(G-18918)
ENSAFE INC
8187 Fox Knoll Dr (45069-2898)
PHONE..................................513 621-7233
Robert Goodman, *Branch Mgr*
EMP: 25
SALES (corp-wide): 63.1MM **Privately Held**
SIC: 8731 Commercial physical research
PA: Ensafe Inc.
5724 Summer Trees Dr
Memphis TN 38134
901 372-7962

(G-18919)
ENTERTRAINMENT INC
Also Called: Entertrainment Junction
7379 Squire Ct (45069-2314)
PHONE.................................513 898-8000
Donald Oeters, *President*
Sue Anne Allen, *Accounts Mgr*
EMP: 30
SALES (est): 1.9MM **Privately Held**
SIC: 7993 Amusement arcade

(G-18920)
ESTES EXPRESS LINES INC
6459 Allen Rd (45069-3848)
PHONE.................................513 779-9581
John Flynn, *Branch Mgr*
EMP: 70
SALES (corp-wide): 2.7B **Privately Held**
WEB: www.estes-express.com
SIC: 4213 Contract haulers
PA: Estes Express Lines, Inc.
3901 W Broad St
Richmond VA 23230
804 353-1900

(G-18921)
F B WRIGHT CO CINCINNATI (PA)
Also Called: FB Wright of Cincinnati
4689 Ashley Dr (45011-9706)
PHONE.................................513 874-9100
Jack Doerr, *CEO*
William Reno, *President*
Arthur Colburn, *President*
EMP: 27
SQ FT: 18,000
SALES (est): 15.9MM **Privately Held**
WEB: www.fbw-cincy.com
SIC: 5085 5162 Hose, belting & packing;
plastics products

(G-18922)
FASTEMS LLC
9850 Windisch Rd (45069-3806)
PHONE.................................513 779-4614
Pekka Lammasaari, *Project Mgr*
Michael Bell, *Opers Staff*
Jussi Hiukka, *Engineer*
Robert Humphreys, *VP Sales*
Bob Baldizzi, *Sales Staff*
EMP: 35
SALES (est): 5.4MM **Privately Held**
SIC: 7371 Computer software development

(G-18923)
FERGUSON ENTERPRISES INC
Also Called: Ferguson Integrated Services
2945 Crescentville Rd (45069-3883)
P.O. Box 2940, Newport News VA (23609-0940)
PHONE.................................513 771-6566
Mark Harp, *Cust Mgr*
Andy Norkey, *Branch Mgr*
Matthew Richey, *Manager*
EMP: 50
SALES (corp-wide): 20.7B **Privately Held**
WEB: www.ferguson.com
SIC: 5074 Plumbing & hydronic heating
supplies
HQ: Ferguson Enterprises, Inc.
12500 Jefferson Ave
Newport News VA 23602
757 874-7795

(G-18924)
FITNESS INTERNATIONAL LLC
Also Called: La Fitness West Chester
7730 Dudley Dr (45069-2400)
PHONE.................................513 298-0134
Caitlin Waters, *Branch Mgr*
EMP: 30
SALES (corp-wide): 173.1MM **Privately Held**
SIC: 7991 Physical fitness facilities
PA: Fitness International, Llc
3161 Michelson Dr Ste 600
Irvine CA 92612
949 255-7200

(G-18925)
FOCUS ON YOUTH INC
8904 Brookside Ave (45069-3139)
PHONE.................................513 644-1030
Penny Dugan, *Finance Mgr*
Penny Dougan, *Finance*

Christina Kappn, *Program Mgr*
Leah Weimer, *Supervisor*
Bryan Forney, *Exec Dir*
EMP: 30
SQ FT: 6,200
SALES: 3.1MM **Privately Held**
SIC: 8322 Youth center

(G-18926)
FREDRICS CORPORATION (PA)
7664 Voice Of America Ctr (45069-2794)
PHONE.................................513 874-2226
Frederic Holzberger, *President*
Gary J Trame, *CFO*
▲ EMP: 140
SQ FT: 35,000
SALES (est): 16.7MM **Privately Held**
WEB: www.puregiving.com
SIC: 5087 5122 Barber shop equipment &
supplies; drugs, proprietaries & sundries

(G-18927)
FRITO-LAY NORTH AMERICA INC
7781 Service Center Dr (45069-2440)
PHONE.................................513 759-1000
Dan Carley, *Manager*
EMP: 200
SALES (corp-wide): 64.6B **Publicly Held**
WEB: www.fritolay.com
SIC: 5145 Snack foods
HQ: Frito-Lay North America, Inc.
7701 Legacy Dr
Plano TX 75024

(G-18928)
FUSION INTERIOR SERVICES LTD (PA)
9823 Cincinnati Dayton Rd (45069-3825)
PHONE.................................513 759-4100
John Planes, *President*
Heath Carrier, *Vice Pres*
▲ EMP: 33
SALES (est): 1.6MM **Privately Held**
SIC: 7699 Office equipment & accessory
customizing

(G-18929)
G R B INC (PA)
Also Called: Triangle Label
6392 Gano Rd (45069-4869)
PHONE.................................800 628-9195
Roger Neiheisel, *President*
Allen Backscheider, *Vice Pres*
Dean Backscheider, *Vice Pres*
Joseph Hennekes, *Opers Dir*
Gary McDougle, *Opers Mgr*
▲ EMP: 75
SQ FT: 225,000
SALES (est): 84.8MM **Privately Held**
WEB: www.bgrinc.com
SIC: 5199 Packaging materials

(G-18930)
GE AVIATION SYSTEMS LLC
7831 Ashford Glen Ct (45069-1614)
PHONE.................................513 786-4555
EMP: 300
SALES (corp-wide): 121.6B **Publicly Held**
SIC: 4581 Airports, flying fields & services
HQ: Ge Aviation Systems Llc
1 Neumann Way
Cincinnati OH 45215
937 898-9600

(G-18931)
GENERAL MOTORS LLC
9287 Meridian Way (45069-6523)
PHONE.................................513 874-0535
Gene Lauer, *Plant Mgr*
EMP: 190 **Publicly Held**
SIC: 4225 5013 General warehousing &
storage; motor vehicle supplies & new
parts
HQ: General Motors Llc
300 Renaissance Ctr L1
Detroit MI 48243

(G-18932)
GENERAL MOTORS LLC
8752 Jacquemin Dr (45069-4859)
PHONE.................................513 603-6600
Lisa Veneziano, *Manager*
EMP: 185 **Publicly Held**

SIC: 5015 5013 4226 Motor vehicle parts,
used; motor vehicle supplies & new parts;
special warehousing & storage
HQ: General Motors Llc
300 Renaissance Ctr L1
Detroit MI 48243

(G-18933)
GLOBAL WORKPLACE SOLUTIONS LLC (PA)
Also Called: G W S
9823 Cincinnati Dayton Rd (45069-3825)
PHONE.................................513 759-6000
Tom Meyer, *President*
John Sabatalo, *President*
Kyle Skeldon, *President*
Jeff Ankenbauer, *Senior VP*
Brian H Bowers, *Vice Pres*
EMP: 31
SALES (est): 11.1MM **Privately Held**
SIC: 4213 Trucking, except local

(G-18934)
GRAPHEL CORPORATION
Also Called: Carbon Products
6115 Centre Park Dr (45069-3869)
P.O. Box 369 (45071-0369)
PHONE.................................513 779-6166
Cliff Kersker, *President*
Mark Grammer, *CFO*
EMP: 140 EST: 1965
SQ FT: 35,000
SALES (est): 64.2MM
SALES (corp-wide): 36MM **Privately Held**
WEB: www.graphel.com
SIC: 5052 3599 3624 Coal & other minerals & ores; machine shop, jobbing & repair; electrodes, thermal & electrolytic uses: carbon, graphite
PA: Graphite Metallizing Corp
1050 Nepperhan Ave
Yonkers NY 10703
914 968-8400

(G-18935)
GREAT TRADITIONS HOMES
7267 Hamilton Mason Rd (45069)
PHONE.................................513 759-7444
Tom Humes, *President*
EMP: 30
SALES (est): 1MM **Privately Held**
SIC: 1521 Single-family housing construction

(G-18936)
GROUNDSPRO LLC
9405 Sutton Pl (45011-9705)
PHONE.................................513 242-1700
Anthony Wilson, *Mng Member*
EMP: 130
SALES (est): 546.2K **Privately Held**
SIC: 0782 Highway lawn & garden maintenance services

(G-18937)
GUARDIAN PROTECTION SVCS INC
Also Called: Honeywell Authorized Dealer
9852 Windisch Rd (45069-3806)
PHONE.................................513 422-5319
Gerry Deehan, *Manager*
EMP: 60 **Privately Held**
WEB: www.guardianprotection.com
SIC: 7382 Burglar alarm maintenance &
monitoring
HQ: Guardian Protection Services, Inc.
174 Thorn Hill Rd
Warrendale PA 15086
412 788-2580

(G-18938)
GUARDIAN SAVINGS BANK (PA)
Also Called: FEDERAL SAVINGS BANK
6100 W Chester Rd (45069-2943)
PHONE.................................513 942-3535
Louis Beck, *Ch of Bd*
Richard L Burkhart, *President*
Paul Warner, *Senior VP*
Yvonne Rich, *Vice Pres*
Bill Voorhees, *Vice Pres*
EMP: 45
SQ FT: 4,000

SALES: 42.4MM **Privately Held**
WEB: www.guardiansavingsbank.com
SIC: 6163 6035 Loan brokers; federal savings banks

(G-18939)
GWS FF&E LLC
9823 Cincinnati Dayton Rd (45069-3825)
PHONE.................................513 759-6000
John Planes, *Principal*
EMP: 38
SALES (est): 3MM **Privately Held**
SIC: 7389 4214 Styling of fashions, apparel, furniture, textiles, etc.; furniture moving & storage, local
PA: Global Workplace Solutions Llc
9823 Cincinnati Dayton Rd
West Chester OH 45069

(G-18940)
HAIRY CACTUS SALON INC
Also Called: Salon Spa & Wellness Center
9437 Civic Centre Blvd B (45069-7118)
PHONE.................................513 771-9335
Sharon Hargis, *President*
Sandra Reader, *Corp Secy*
Sandy Reder, *Treasurer*
EMP: 43
SQ FT: 3,100
SALES (est): 837.3K **Privately Held**
SIC: 7231 Hairdressers

(G-18941)
HAMMACHER SCHLEMMER & CO INC
9180 La Saint Dr (45069)
PHONE.................................513 860-4570
Don Rogers, *Branch Mgr*
EMP: 200
SALES (est): 10MM
SALES (corp-wide): 71.8MM **Privately Held**
WEB: www.hammacher.com
SIC: 5199 General merchandise, nondurable
PA: Hammacher, Schlemmer & Co., Inc.
9307 N Milwaukee Ave
Niles IL 60714
847 581-8600

(G-18942)
HARMON INC
4290 Port Union Rd (45011-9713)
PHONE.................................513 645-1550
Roger Matthews, *Branch Mgr*
EMP: 41
SALES (corp-wide): 1.3B **Publicly Held**
WEB: www.harmoninc.com
SIC: 5039 Glass construction materials
HQ: Harmon, Inc.
7900 Xerxes Ave S # 1800
Bloomington MN 55431
952 944-5700

(G-18943)
HILLANDALE HEALTHCARE INC
8073 Tylersville Rd (45069-2589)
PHONE.................................513 813-5595
Greg Dixon, *President*
Don Dixon, *Vice Pres*
Steve Dixon, *Treasurer*
Rex Richardson, *Mktg Dir*
James E Dixon, *Exec Dir*
EMP: 80
SQ FT: 12,000
SALES (est): 3.9MM **Privately Held**
SIC: 8051 Skilled nursing care facilities

(G-18944)
HOME2 BY HILTON
7145 Liberty Centre Dr (45069-2585)
PHONE.................................513 422-3454
EMP: 30
SALES (est): 201.8K **Privately Held**
SIC: 7011 Hotel/Motel Operation

(G-18945)
HWZ CONTRACTING LLC
4730 Ashley Dr (45011-9704)
PHONE.................................513 671-3300
EMP: 51
SALES (est): 1.9MM
SALES (corp-wide): 24.8MM **Privately Held**
SIC: 1761 Roofing contractor

▲ = Import ▼=Export
◆ =Import/Export

PA: Bradcorp Ohio Ii, Llc
3195 Profit Dr
Fairfield OH 45014
513 671-3300

(G-18946)
INDUSTRIAL CONTROLS DISTRS LLC
9407 Meridian Way (45069-6525)
PHONE..................................513 733-5200
Danny Cordeiro, *Engineer*
John Kelly, *Engineer*
Michael McNaught, *Engineer*
Johnpaul Valentino, *Engineer*
Brian McBroom, *Accounts Mgr*
EMP: 32 **Privately Held**
WEB: www.industrialcontrolsonline.com
SIC: 5074 5075 Heating equipment (hydronic); air conditioning equipment, except room units
HQ: Industrial Controls Distributors, Llc
17 Christopher Way
Eatontown NJ 07724
732 918-9000

(G-18947)
INET INTERACTIVE LLC
9100 W Chester Towne Ctr (45069-3106)
PHONE..................................513 322-5600
Troy Augustine, *President*
John Skinner, *CFO*
Ahmad Permessur, *Manager*
EMP: 35
SALES (est): 3.4MM
SALES (corp-wide): 2.3B **Privately Held**
WEB: www.inetinteractive.com
SIC: 7371 4899 Computer software development; data communication services
HQ: Informa Media, Inc.
605 3rd Ave Fl 22
New York NY 10158
212 204-4200

(G-18948)
IRON MOUNTAIN INCORPORATED
9247 Meridian Way (45069-6523)
PHONE..................................513 874-3535
Debbie Davis, *Manager*
EMP: 51
SALES (corp-wide): 4.2B **Publicly Held**
SIC: 4226 Document & office records storage
PA: Iron Mountain Incorporated
1 Federal St Fl 7
Boston MA 02110
617 535-4766

(G-18949)
IRON MOUNTAIN INFO MGT LLC
9247 Meridian Way (45069-6523)
PHONE..................................513 297-1906
Don Garza, *Manager*
EMP: 38
SALES (corp-wide): 4.2B **Publicly Held**
SIC: 4226 Document & office records storage
HQ: Iron Mountain Information Management, Llc
1 Federal St
Boston MA 02110
800 899-4766

(G-18950)
J & B INTERESTS INC (PA)
Also Called: JB Steel
9430 Sutton Pl (45011-9698)
PHONE..................................513 874-1722
Terry Estes, *President*
Greg Wilson,
EMP: 70
SQ FT: 5,000
SALES (est): 6.1MM **Privately Held**
SIC: 1791 Concrete reinforcement, placing of

(G-18951)
J&B STEEL ERECTORS INC
Also Called: J&B Steel Contractors
9430 Sutton Pl (45011-9698)
PHONE..................................513 874-1722
Toya Estes, *President*
EMP: 107
SQ FT: 32,000

SALES: 15MM **Privately Held**
SIC: 1611 General contractor, highway & street construction

(G-18952)
JLS ENTERPRISES INC
Also Called: Jimmy's Limousine Service
7879 Cincinnati Dayton Rd (45069-2008)
PHONE..................................513 769-1888
Danielle Little, *President*
James W Barnes, *Vice Pres*
EMP: 30
SQ FT: 8,000
SALES (est): 1.1MM **Privately Held**
SIC: 4119 Limousine rental, with driver

(G-18953)
JOHNSON CONTROLS
9685 Cincinnati Dayton Rd (45069-3829)
PHONE..................................513 874-1227
Pat Markey, *Sales Mgr*
Tom Goyer, *Branch Mgr*
Dan Thieken, *Manager*
Bernie Weiss, *Manager*
Frederick Shivadecker, *Supervisor*
EMP: 60 **Privately Held**
WEB: www.simplexgrinnell.com
SIC: 1711 Fire sprinkler system installation
HQ: Johnson Controls Fire Protection Lp
6600 Congress Ave
Boca Raton FL 33487
561 988-7200

(G-18954)
JP FLOORING SYSTEMS INC
9097 Union Centre Blvd (45069-4861)
PHONE..................................513 346-4300
Phil Shrimper, *President*
Scott M Slovin, *Principal*
Kenneth Robert Thompson II, *Principal*
Linda B Woodrow, *Principal*
EMP: 50
SQ FT: 100,000
SALES (est): 26.7MM **Privately Held**
WEB: www.jpflooring.com
SIC: 5023 5713 Wood flooring; floor tile

(G-18955)
KEMBA CREDIT UNION INC (PA)
8763 Union Centre Blvd # 101 (45069-1207)
PHONE..................................513 762-5070
Stephen Behler, *President*
EMP: 75
SQ FT: 34,000
SALES: 26.8MM **Privately Held**
SIC: 6062 State credit unions

(G-18956)
KIDS R KIDS 2 OHIO
9077 Union Centre Blvd (45069-4861)
PHONE..................................513 860-3197
Emily Grabit, *General Mgr*
Debbie Even, *Administration*
EMP: 48
SALES (est): 244.5K **Privately Held**
SIC: 8351 Preschool center

(G-18957)
KLEINGERS GROUP INC (PA)
6305 Centre Park Dr (45069-3863)
PHONE..................................513 779-7851
Jim Kleingers Pe PS, *CEO*
Steve Korte Pe, *Vice Pres*
Jay S Aicp, *Director*
Dave Cox PS, *Director*
EMP: 55
SQ FT: 15,000
SALES (est): 14.7MM **Privately Held**
WEB: www.kleingers.com
SIC: 8711 8713 0781 Consulting engineer; surveying services; landscape architects

(G-18958)
LESAINT LOGISTICS INC
4487 Le Saint Ct (45014-2229)
PHONE..................................513 874-3900
Jeff Pennington, *President*
Steven Wormus, *Controller*
Scott Riddle, *Director*
Allison Gruendl, *Executive*
EMP: 232
SQ FT: 900,000

SALES (est): 33.9MM
SALES (corp-wide): 95.7MM **Privately Held**
WEB: www.lesaint.com
SIC: 4225 4212 General warehousing & storage; local trucking, without storage
PA: Lesaint Logistics, Llc
868 W Crossroads Pkwy
Romeoville IL 60446
630 243-5950

(G-18959)
LESAINT LOGISTICS LLC
4487 Le Saint Ct (45014-2229)
P.O. Box 960522, Cincinnati (45296-0001)
PHONE..................................513 874-3900
Dan Harmon, *Manager*
EMP: 50
SALES (corp-wide): 95.7MM **Privately Held**
WEB: www.lesaint.com
SIC: 4225 General warehousing
PA: Lesaint Logistics, Llc
868 W Crossroads Pkwy
Romeoville IL 60446
630 243-5950

(G-18960)
LEVEL 3 TELECOM LLC
Also Called: Time Warner Telecom
9490 Meridian Way (45069-6527)
PHONE..................................513 682-7806
Thomas Cloud, *Principal*
EMP: 29
SALES (corp-wide): 23.4B **Publicly Held**
SIC: 4813 Telephone communication, except radio
HQ: Level 3 Telecom, Llc
10475 Park Meadows Dr
Lone Tree CO 80124
303 566-1000

(G-18961)
LEVEL 3 TELECOM LLC
Also Called: Time Warner Telecom
9490 Meridian Way (45069-6527)
PHONE..................................513 682-7806
Thomas Cloud, *Branch Mgr*
EMP: 29
SALES (corp-wide): 23.4B **Publicly Held**
SIC: 4813 Telephone communication, except radio
HQ: Level 3 Telecom, Llc
10475 Park Meadows Dr
Lone Tree CO 80124
303 566-1000

(G-18962)
LEVEL 3 TELECOM LLC
Also Called: Time Warner Telecom
9490 Meridian Way (45069-6527)
PHONE..................................513 682-7806
Thomas Cloud, *Branch Mgr*
EMP: 29
SALES (corp-wide): 23.4B **Publicly Held**
SIC: 4813 Telephone communication, except radio
HQ: Level 3 Telecom, Llc
10475 Park Meadows Dr
Lone Tree CO 80124
303 566-1000

(G-18963)
LITHKO CONTRACTING LLC (PA)
2958 Crescentville Rd (45069-4827)
PHONE..................................513 564-2000
Robert Strobel, *President*
Perry Hausfeld, *Vice Pres*
Greg Jones, *Info Tech Dir*
Kevin Garman, *Director*
EMP: 150 EST: 1994
SQ FT: 10,000
SALES (est): 177.7MM **Privately Held**
SIC: 1771 Concrete work; foundation & footing contractor; flooring contractor; concrete repair

(G-18964)
LONG-STANTON MFG COMPANY
9388 Sutton Pl (45011-9702)
PHONE..................................513 874-8020
Daniel B Cunningham, *President*
Richard Hassinger, *General Mgr*
Tom Kachovec, *COO*
Tim Hershey, *CFO*

Lisa Wetterich, *Human Res Mgr*
▲ EMP: 50
SQ FT: 66,000
SALES (est): 11.7MM **Privately Held**
WEB: www.longstanton.com
SIC: 3444 7692 3469 3544 Sheet metalwork; welding repair; metal stampings; special dies, tools, jigs & fixtures; fabricated plate work (boiler shop)

(G-18965)
LONGWORTH ENTERPRISES INC
8050 Beckett Center Dr (45069-5017)
PHONE..................................513 738-4663
Marc Longworth II, *CEO*
EMP: 300 EST: 2009
SALES (est): 2.8MM **Privately Held**
SIC: 7299 Home improvement & renovation contractor agency

(G-18966)
LOWES HOME CENTERS LLC
7975 Tylersville Sq Rd (45069-4691)
PHONE..................................513 755-4300
EMP: 150
SALES (corp-wide): 68.6B **Publicly Held**
SIC: 5211 5031 5722 5064 Home centers; building materials, exterior; building materials, interior; household appliance stores; electrical appliances, television & radio
HQ: Lowe's Home Centers, Llc
1605 Curtis Bridge Rd
Wilkesboro NC 28697
336 658-4000

(G-18967)
MACYS CR & CUSTOMER SVCS INC
9249 Meridian Way (45069-6523)
PHONE..................................513 881-9950
Tom Schneider, *Manager*
EMP: 100
SALES (corp-wide): 25.7B **Publicly Held**
SIC: 7389 7331 Credit card service; mailing service
HQ: Macy's Credit And Customer Services, Inc.
9111 Duke Blvd
Mason OH 45040

(G-18968)
MAILENDER INC
9500 Glades Dr (45011-9400)
PHONE..................................513 942-5453
Ken Mailender, *CEO*
Andrew Abel, *President*
Chris Ward, *Vice Pres*
Jim Fleissner Jr, *Warehouse Mgr*
Chris Hardiman, *Purchasing*
▲ EMP: 62
SQ FT: 65,000
SALES (est): 42.5MM **Privately Held**
WEB: www.mailender.com
SIC: 5113 Paper & products, wrapping or coarse

(G-18969)
MARKETVISION RESEARCH INC
5426 W Chester Rd (45069-2950)
PHONE..................................513 603-6340
Kelly Farmer, *Research*
Dawn Hoskins, *Branch Mgr*
EMP: 40
SALES (corp-wide): 13.7MM **Privately Held**
WEB: www.copyvision.com
SIC: 8732 Market analysis or research
PA: Marketvision Research, Inc.
5151 Pfeiffer Rd Ste 300
Blue Ash OH 45242
513 791-3100

(G-18970)
MARTIN MARIETTA MATERIALS INC
Also Called: Martin Marietta Aggragate
9277 Centre Pointe Dr # 250 (45069-4844)
P.O. Box 30013, Raleigh NC (27622-0013)
PHONE..................................513 701-1140
Harry Charles, *Manager*
EMP: 40 **Publicly Held**
WEB: www.martinmarietta.com

G
E
O
G
R
A
P
H
I
C

SIC: 1423 1422 3295 3297 Crushed & broken granite; crushed & broken limestone; magnesite, crude: ground, calcined or dead-burned; nonclay refractories; construction sand & gravel
PA: Martin Marietta Materials Inc
2710 Wycliff Rd
Raleigh NC 27607

(G-18971)
MARTIN-BROWER COMPANY LLC
Also Called: Distribution Center
4260 Port Union Rd (45011-9768)
PHONE................................513 773-2301
Ryan Rozen, General Mgr
Jeanne Malone, Manager
EMP: 275 **Privately Held**
SIC: 2013 2015 5087 Frozen meats from purchased meat; poultry, processed: frozen; restaurant supplies
HQ: The Martin-Brower Company L L C
6250 N River Rd Ste 9000
Rosemont IL 60018
847 227-6500

(G-18972)
MIDWEST TRAILER SALES & SVC
Also Called: Mike's Truck & Trailer
3000 Crescentville Rd (45069-3887)
PHONE................................513 772-2818
Dan McCabe, President
EMP: 25
SALES (est): 1.4MM
SALES (corp-wide): 24.7MM **Privately Held**
WEB: www.eeienv.com
SIC: 7538 General truck repair
PA: Environmental Enterprises Inc
10163 Cncinnati Dayton Rd
Cincinnati OH 45241
513 772-2818

(G-18973)
MITCHELLS SALON & DAY SPA
7795 University Ct Ste A (45069)
PHONE................................513 793-0900
Karen Rueckert, Human Res Mgr
Sherry Williams, Branch Mgr
EMP: 195
SALES (corp-wide): 7.7MM **Privately Held**
SIC: 7231 Beauty shops
PA: Mitchell's Salon & Day Spa Inc
5901 E Galbraith Rd # 230
Cincinnati OH 45236
513 793-0900

(G-18974)
MITEL (DELAWARE) INC
Also Called: Inter Tel
9100 W Chester Towne Ctr (45069-3106)
PHONE................................513 733-8000
Dan Ziezerink, Branch Mgr
EMP: 25
SALES (corp-wide): 987.6MM **Privately Held**
WEB: www.inter-tel.com
SIC: 3661 5045 4813 5065 Telephone & telegraph apparatus; computer software; long distance telephone communications; telephone equipment; telephone & telephone equipment installation; equipment rental & leasing
HQ: Mitel (Delaware). Inc.
1146 N Alma School Rd
Mesa AZ 85201
480 449-8900

(G-18975)
MKJB INC
Also Called: Meadows Healthcare
4515 Guildford Dr (45069-8571)
PHONE................................513 851-8400
Karen Jamison, CEO
EMP: 130
SALES (corp-wide): 4.4MM **Privately Held**
WEB: www.mkjb.com
SIC: 8059 Nursing home, except skilled & intermediate care facility; skilled nursing care facilities

PA: Mkjb Inc
3536 Washington Ave
Cincinnati OH 45229
513 751-4900

(G-18976)
MOLLETT SEAMLESS GUTTER CO
Also Called: Cincinnati Gutter Supply
9345 Prnceton Glendale Rd (45011-9707)
PHONE................................513 825-0500
Radford Mollett, President
EMP: 25
SQ FT: 18,000
SALES (est): 1.7MM **Privately Held**
SIC: 1761 1629 Gutter & downspout contractor; trenching contractor

(G-18977)
MRC GLOBAL (US) INC
Also Called: M R C
9085 Le Saint Dr (45014-2242)
PHONE................................513 489-6922
Dawn Stepp, District Mgr
EMP: 25 **Publicly Held**
SIC: 5085 Valves & fittings
HQ: Mrc Global (Us) Inc.
1301 Mckinney St Ste 2300
Houston TX 77010
877 294-7574

(G-18978)
OHIO AUTOMOBILE CLUB
8210 Highland Pointe Dr (45069-4520)
PHONE................................513 870-0951
EMP: 36
SALES (corp-wide): 59.9MM **Privately Held**
SIC: 7997 Membership sports & recreation clubs
PA: The Ohio Automobile Club
90 E Wilson Bridge Rd # 1
Worthington OH 43085

(G-18979)
OLD DOMINION FREIGHT LINE INC
6431 Centre Park Dr (45069-4801)
PHONE................................513 771-1486
Brian Houser, Manager
EMP: 48
SALES (corp-wide): 4B **Publicly Held**
WEB: www.odfl.com
SIC: 4213 Less-than-truckload (LTL) transport
PA: Old Dominion Freight Line Inc
500 Old Dominion Way
Thomasville NC 27360
336 889-5000

(G-18980)
OMNI FIREPROOFING CO LLC
9305 Le Saint Dr (45014-5447)
PHONE................................513 870-9115
Thomas Hochhausler, Mng Member
Ken Brosnan,
Greg Shields,
EMP: 55
SQ FT: 15,000
SALES (est): 6.1MM **Privately Held**
WEB: www.omnifp.com
SIC: 1799 1742 Fireproofing buildings; acoustical & insulation work

(G-18981)
OVERHEAD DOOR CO-CINCINNATI
9345 Prnceton Glendale Rd (45011-9707)
P.O. Box 8187 (45069-8187)
PHONE................................513 346-4000
Fred S Klipsch, Vice Ch Bd
Terry Sarbinoff, President
Charlie Lanham, Treasurer
EMP: 145
SQ FT: 70,000
SALES (est): 17.1MM
SALES (corp-wide): 64.1MM **Privately Held**
SIC: 5211 1761 1751 1742 Garage doors, sale & installation; roofing, siding & sheet metal work; carpentry work; plastering, drywall & insulation

PA: Garage Door Systems, Llc
8811 Bash St
Indianapolis IN 46256
317 842-7444

(G-18982)
PLANES MOVING & STORAGE INC (PA)
Also Called: Planes Companies
9823 Cincinnati Dayton Rd (45069-3825)
PHONE................................513 759-6000
John J Planes, CEO
Greg Hallas, President
Darren S Montgomery, President
John Sabatalo, President
Vince Serraino, President
EMP: 217 **EST:** 1928
SQ FT: 250,000
SALES (est): 72.8MM **Privately Held**
SIC: 4214 4213 Household goods moving & storage, local; trucking, except local

(G-18983)
POPE & ASSOCIATES INC
Also Called: Pope Consulting
9277 Centre Pointe Dr # 150 (45069-4964)
PHONE................................513 671-1277
Patricia Pope, President
Lea Ann Hilboldt, Manager
EMP: 27
SQ FT: 1,650
SALES (est): 2.7MM **Privately Held**
WEB: www.popeandassociates.com
SIC: 8742 General management consultant; personnel management consultant

(G-18984)
PREMIERE SERVICE MORTGAGE CORP (PA)
6266 Centre Park Dr (45069-3865)
PHONE................................513 546-9895
Gerald Matyow, President
Graham Strong, Vice Pres
Steve Fried, Shareholder
Rob Uebel, Shareholder
EMP: 40
SALES (est): 5MM **Privately Held**
SIC: 6163 Mortgage brokers arranging for loans, using money of others

(G-18985)
PRESTIGE TECHNICAL SVCS INC (PA)
7908 Cincinnati Dayton Rd T (45069-3382)
PHONE................................513 779-6800
Joan Mears, President
EMP: 32
SQ FT: 2,700
SALES (est): 5.7MM **Privately Held**
WEB: www.prestigetechnical.com
SIC: 7363 Engineering help service

(G-18986)
PRIMETECH COMMUNICATIONS INC
4505 Muhlhauser Rd (45011-9788)
P.O. Box 531730, Cincinnati (45253-1730)
PHONE................................513 942-6000
Brad Shoemaker, President
Marcia Shoemaker, Vice Pres
EMP: 60
SQ FT: 17,000
SALES (est): 8.8MM **Privately Held**
SIC: 1731 Cable television installation; fiber optic cable installation

(G-18987)
PROSCAN IMAGING LLC
Also Called: First Scan Imaging
7307 Tylers Corner Dr (45069-6344)
PHONE................................513 759-7350
Stephen Pomeranz, CEO
Thom O'Donnell, Exec VP
Jenn Malone, Office Mgr
EMP: 31
SALES (corp-wide): 37.6MM **Privately Held**
SIC: 8011 Radiologist
PA: Proscan Imaging, Llc
5400 Kennedy Ave Ste 1
Cincinnati OH 45213
513 281-3400

(G-18988)
QUASONIX INC (PA)
6025 Schumacher Park Dr (45069-4812)
PHONE................................513 942-1287
Terrance Hill, President
Norman Eichenberger, Engineer
Tim O'Connell, Engineer
Sean Wilson, Engineer
Pamela S Hill, Treasurer
EMP: 28
SQ FT: 15,000
SALES: 15MM **Privately Held**
WEB: www.quasonix.com
SIC: 5065 3663 3812 3669 Communication equipment; airborne radio communications equipment; antennas, radar or communications; intercommunication systems, electric; physical research, noncommercial

(G-18989)
QUEEN CITY POLYMERS INC (PA)
6101 Schumacher Park Dr (45069-3818)
PHONE................................513 779-0990
James M Powers, President
James L Powers, Principal
EMP: 42
SQ FT: 33,000
SALES (est): 11.2MM **Privately Held**
WEB: www.qcpinc.net
SIC: 3089 5162 Injection molding of plastics; plastics products

(G-18990)
RAM CONSTRUCTION SERVICES OF
4710 Ashley Dr (45011-9704)
PHONE................................513 297-1857
Bob Mazur, President
Jeff Clapper, Superintendent
John Mazur, Vice Pres
Joe Fisher, Project Mgr
Dino Hubbard, Project Mgr
EMP: 60
SALES (est): 4.7MM
SALES (corp-wide): 106.8MM **Privately Held**
SIC: 1799 1541 1542 Waterproofing; renovation, remodeling & repairs: industrial buildings; commercial & office buildings, renovation and repair
PA: Ram Construction Services Of Michigan, Inc.
13800 Eckles Rd
Livonia MI 48150
734 464-3800

(G-18991)
REPS RESOURCE LLC
9120 Union Centre Blvd # 300 (45069-4896)
PHONE................................513 874-0500
Daryl Fultz, Principal
Bill Schoultheis, Senior Engr
Barbara Fisher, Accountant
Shelly Rubi, Manager
Dave Caddell, Senior Mgr
EMP: 30
SALES: 3MM **Privately Held**
WEB: www.reps-resource.com
SIC: 8711 Aviation &/or aeronautical engineering

(G-18992)
RES-CARE INC
7908 Cincinnati Dayton Rd (45069-6608)
PHONE................................513 858-4550
Angie Mick, Branch Mgr
EMP: 48
SALES (corp-wide): 23.7B **Privately Held**
SIC: 8082 Home health care services
HQ: Res-Care, Inc.
805 N Whittington Pkwy
Louisville KY 40222
502 394-2100

(G-18993)
RICKERIER AND ECKLER
9277 Centre Pointe Dr # 100 (45069-4844)
PHONE................................513 870-6565
Mark Engel, Partner
EMP: 25

SALES (est): 757.9K **Privately Held**
SIC: 8111 General practice attorney, lawyer

(G-18994)
RIVER CITY FURNITURE LLC (PA)
Also Called: Rcf Group
6454 Centre Park Dr (45069-4800)
PHONE....................513 612-7303
Carl Satterwhite,
Bryan Lindholz,
Scott Robertson,
EMP: 53
SQ FT: 7,500
SALES: 68.9MM **Privately Held**
WEB: www.r-c-f.com
SIC: 7389 5712 1752 0782 Interior design services; office furniture; resilient floor laying; mowing services, lawn; furniture moving, local: without storage; furniture moving & storage, local

(G-18995)
RIVERFRONT DIVERSIFIED INC
Also Called: Ever Dry of Cincinnati
9814 Harwood Ct (45014-7589)
PHONE....................513 874-7200
James Gielty, *President*
Dorothy Hay, *Financial Exec*
Connie Fahmy, *Manager*
EMP: 70
SQ FT: 12,000
SALES (est): 7.9MM **Privately Held**
SIC: 1799 Waterproofing

(G-18996)
RRR EXPRESS LLC
Also Called: Rrr Logistics
6432 Centre Park Dr (45069-4800)
PHONE....................800 723-3424
Steven D Hall, *Mng Member*
Lee Scheven,
EMP: 120
SQ FT: 31,000
SALES (est): 23MM **Privately Held**
WEB: www.rrrexpress.com
SIC: 4213 Trucking, except local

(G-18997)
SCHNEIDER ELECTRIC USA INC
9870 Crescent Park Dr (45069-3800)
PHONE....................513 755-5000
Regis Ganley, *Partner*
Alexander Gorski, *Partner*
Darren Meiser, *District Mgr*
CAM Slaughter, *District Mgr*
Todd Gilliam, *Business Mgr*
EMP: 75
SALES (corp-wide): 355.8K **Privately Held**
WEB: www.squared.com
SIC: 3613 3643 3612 3823 Mfg Electrical Distribution & Industrial Products Systems & Services
HQ: Schneider Electric Usa, Inc.
201 Wshington St Ste 2700
Boston MA 02108
978 975-9600

(G-18998)
SCHOLASTIC BOOK FAIRS INC
5459 W Chester Rd Ste C (45069-2915)
PHONE....................513 714-1000
Anthony Hopkins, *Manager*
EMP: 60
SALES (corp-wide): 1.6B **Publicly Held**
WEB: www.scholasticbookfairs.com
SIC: 5192 5199 Books; posters
HQ: Scholastic Book Fairs, Inc.
1080 Greenwood Blvd
Lake Mary FL 32746
407 829-7300

(G-18999)
SCHRUDDER PRFMCE GROUP LLC
7723 Tylers Place Blvd (45069-4684)
PHONE....................513 652-7675
Mitchell R Schrudder,
EMP: 50
SALES: 12MM **Privately Held**
WEB: www.schrudderperformance.com
SIC: 8742 Management consulting services

(G-19000)
SCOTT D PHILLIPS
9277 Centre Pointe Dr (45069-4844)
PHONE....................513 870-8200
Scott D Phillips, *Principal*
EMP: 30
SALES (est): 779.6K **Privately Held**
SIC: 8111 General practice attorney, lawyer

(G-19001)
SELECT STAFFING
Also Called: Remedy Intelligent Staffing
7682 Overglen Dr (45069-9214)
PHONE....................513 247-9772
Jason Guyler, *Manager*
EMP: 71
SALES (corp-wide): 577.1MM **Privately Held**
SIC: 7363 Temporary help service
HQ: Select Staffing
301 Mentor Dr 210
Santa Barbara CA 93111

(G-19002)
SENIOR LIFESTYLE CORPORATION
Also Called: West Chester, Barrington of
7222 Heritagespring Dr (45069-6589)
PHONE....................513 777-4457
Stephanie Weihrman, *Director*
EMP: 55
SALES (corp-wide): 320.8MM **Privately Held**
SIC: 8361 8059 8011 6513 Home for the aged; convalescent home; clinic, operated by physicians; retirement hotel operation
PA: Senior Lifestyle Corporation
303 E Wacker Dr Ste 2400
Chicago IL 60601
312 673-4333

(G-19003)
SHANCLIFF INVESTMENTS LTD
9463 Chardon Cir Apt 301 (45069-2999)
PHONE....................330 883-5560
EMP: 35
SALES (est): 1.7MM **Privately Held**
SIC: 6799 Investors

(G-19004)
SHETLER MOVING & STOR OF OHIO
Also Called: Shelter Moving & Storage
9917 Charter Park Dr (45069-3890)
PHONE....................513 755-0700
Thomas J Shelter Sr, *President*
Thomas J Shetler Jr, *President*
Robert O Shetler, *General Mgr*
EMP: 30
SQ FT: 25,000
SALES (est): 4.4MM **Privately Held**
SIC: 4213 4214 Household goods transport; furniture moving & storage, local

(G-19005)
SIBCY CLINE INC
Also Called: Sibcy Cline Realtors
7677 Voice Of Amer Ctr Dr (45069-2795)
PHONE....................513 777-8100
Patty Letzler, *Manager*
EMP: 90
SALES (corp-wide): 2.1B **Privately Held**
WEB: www.sibcycline.com
SIC: 6531 6162 Real estate agent, residential; mortgage bankers
PA: Sibcy Cline, Inc.
8044 Montgomery Rd # 300
Cincinnati OH 45236
513 984-4100

(G-19006)
SIGHT RESOURCE CORPORATION (PA)
8100 Beckett Center Dr (45069-5015)
PHONE....................513 942-4423
E Dean Butler, *Ch of Bd*
Carene S Kunkler, *President*
Duane Kimble, *Exec VP*
Sandra K Likes, *Vice Pres*
Donald L Radcliff, *CFO*
EMP: 60
SQ FT: 7,500

SALES (est): 20.5MM **Privately Held**
SIC: 8042 5048 Group & corporate practice optometrists; optometric equipment & supplies

(G-19007)
SIMPLEX TIME RECORDER LLC
8910 Beckett Rd (45069-7054)
PHONE....................800 746-7539
Daniel Thiecen, *Branch Mgr*
EMP: 30 **Privately Held**
WEB: www.comtec-alaska.com
SIC: 1731 Fire detection & burglar alarm systems specialization
HQ: Simplex Time Recorder Llc
50 Technology Dr
Westminster MA 01441

(G-19008)
SKATE TOWN U S A
8730 N Pavillion (45069-4894)
PHONE....................513 874-9855
Ken Roesel, *Managing Prtnr*
EMP: 30
SALES (est): 688.6K **Privately Held**
SIC: 7999 Roller skating rink operation

(G-19009)
SKIDMORE SALES & DISTRG CO INC (PA)
9889 Cincinnati Dayton Rd (45069-3825)
PHONE....................513 755-4200
Douglas S Skidmore, *CEO*
Jim McCarthy, *President*
Gerald Skidmore, *Chairman*
Mark Overbeck, *Vice Pres*
Steppi Frey, *CFO*
▲ **EMP:** 36 **EST:** 1963
SQ FT: 150,000
SALES (est): 164.9MM **Privately Held**
WEB: www.foodingr.com
SIC: 5149 5169 Groceries & related products; chemicals & allied products

(G-19010)
SMYTH AUTOMOTIVE INC
Also Called: Parts Plus
8868 Cincinnati Columbus (45069-3516)
PHONE....................513 777-6400
Bob Smyth, *Branch Mgr*
EMP: 33
SALES (corp-wide): 122.3MM **Privately Held**
WEB: www.smythautomotive.com
SIC: 5013 Automotive supplies & parts
PA: Smyth Automotive, Inc.
4275 Mt Carmel Tobasco Rd
Cincinnati OH 45244
513 528-2800

(G-19011)
SPRANDEL ENTERPRISES INC
Also Called: Quality Towing
6467 Gano Rd (45069-4830)
P.O. Box 1873 (45071-1873)
PHONE....................513 777-6622
Michael Sprandel, *President*
EMP: 25
SALES (est): 3.3MM **Privately Held**
SIC: 7549 Towing service, automotive; road service, automotive

(G-19012)
STAR ONE HOLDINGS INC
6875 Fountains Blvd Ste A (45069-5149)
PHONE....................513 779-9500
Tricia A Abel, *Vice Pres*
Sandy Sieve, *Vice Pres*
Mark Meinhardt, *Manager*
Elizabeth Lautner,
Mark Stehlin, *Real Est Agnt*
EMP: 35
SALES (corp-wide): 8.8MM **Privately Held**
WEB: www.nkybuilders.com
SIC: 6531 Real estate agent, residential; real estate brokers & agents
PA: Star One Holdings, Inc.
3895 Woodridge Blvd
Fairfield OH 45014
513 870-9100

(G-19013)
STERLING LAND TITLE AGENCY
7594 Cox Ln (45069-6519)
PHONE....................513 755-3700

Pam Felino, *President*
EMP: 25
SALES (est): 2.5MM **Privately Held**
SIC: 6361 Title insurance

(G-19014)
SUNESIS CONSTRUCTION COMPANY
2610 Crescentville Rd (45069-3819)
PHONE....................513 326-6000
Rick Jones, *President*
Jason Shaw, *General Mgr*
Albert C Eiselein Jr, *Principal*
Richard Jones, *Principal*
Steve Abernathy, *Vice Pres*
EMP: 125
SQ FT: 3,000
SALES: 40MM **Privately Held**
WEB: www.sunesisconstruction.com
SIC: 1623 1622 1611 Water, sewer & utility lines; bridge construction; general contractor, highway & street construction

(G-19015)
THYSSENKRUPP BILSTEIN AMER INC
4440 Muhlhauser Rd (45011-9767)
PHONE....................513 881-7600
Jimmy Brentle, *Manager*
EMP: 25
SALES (corp-wide): 39.8B **Privately Held**
SIC: 5013 3714 Automotive supplies & parts; motor vehicle parts & accessories
HQ: Thyssenkrupp Bilstein Of America, Inc.
8685 Bilstein Blvd
Hamilton OH 45015
513 881-7600

(G-19016)
TITAN TRANSFER INC
6432 Centre Park Dr (45069-4800)
PHONE....................513 458-4233
Greg Hall, *Branch Mgr*
EMP: 64
SALES (corp-wide): 59.2MM **Privately Held**
SIC: 4213 Contract haulers
PA: Titan Transfer, Inc.
1200 Stanley Blvd
Shelbyville TN 37160
931 684-0255

(G-19017)
TOTAL QUALITY LOGISTICS LLC
8488 Shepherd Farm Dr (45069-5933)
PHONE....................800 580-3101
Larry Shepherd, *Branch Mgr*
EMP: 50
SALES (corp-wide): 2.9B **Privately Held**
SIC: 4789 Cargo loading & unloading services
HQ: Total Quality Logistics, Llc
4289 Ivy Pointe Blvd
Cincinnati OH 45245

(G-19018)
TOYOTA INDUSTRIES N AMER INC
Also Called: Prolift Industrial Equipment
9890 Charter Park Dr (45069-4803)
PHONE....................513 779-7500
Keith Ingels, *Branch Mgr*
EMP: 50
SALES (corp-wide): 18.8B **Privately Held**
SIC: 5084 Materials handling machinery
HQ: Toyota Industries North America, Inc.
3030 Barker Dr
Columbus IN 47201
812 341-3810

(G-19019)
TRANSFORCE INC
8080 Beckett Center Dr # 202 (45069-5047)
PHONE....................513 860-4402
Julie Neff, *President*
EMP: 33 **Privately Held**
SIC: 7699 Industrial equipment services
PA: Transforce, Inc.
5520 Cherokee Ave Ste 200
Alexandria VA 22312

(G-19020)
UC HEALTH LLC
7700 University Ct # 1800 (45069-7202)
PHONE.....................................513 475-7458
Rhonada Brown, *Manager*
Bart Branam, *Surgeon*
Linda Jamison, *Director*
Sara Deem, *Radiology Dir*
EMP: 75 **Privately Held**
SIC: 8011 Radiologist
PA: Uc Health, Llc.
    3200 Burnet Ave
    Cincinnati OH 45229

(G-19021)
UC HEALTH LLC
Also Called: U C Health Dermatology
7690 Discovery Dr # 1700 (45069-6551)
PHONE.....................................513 475-7630
EMP: 197 **Privately Held**
SIC: 8748 Business consulting
PA: Uc Health, Llc.
    3200 Burnet Ave
    Cincinnati OH 45229

(G-19022)
UC HEALTH LLC
7700 University Ct (45069-7202)
PHONE.....................................513 475-8881
EMP: 75 **Privately Held**
SIC: 8011 Surgeon
PA: Uc Health, Llc.
    3200 Burnet Ave
    Cincinnati OH 45229

(G-19023)
UC HEALTH LLC
7798 Discovery Dr Ste F (45069-7747)
PHONE.....................................513 298-3000
EMP: 210 **Privately Held**
SIC: 8741 Hospital management
PA: Uc Health, Llc.
    3200 Burnet Ave
    Cincinnati OH 45229

(G-19024)
UC HEALTH LLC
7710 University Ct (45069)
PHONE.....................................513 475-7777
EMP: 28 **Privately Held**
WEB: www.precisionradiotherapy.com
SIC: 8011 Medical centers
PA: Uc Health, Llc.
    3200 Burnet Ave
    Cincinnati OH 45229

(G-19025)
UC HEALTH LLC
7798 Discovery Dr Ste E (45069-7747)
PHONE.....................................513 475-7500
EMP: 75 **Privately Held**
SIC: 8011 Medical centers
PA: Uc Health, Llc.
    3200 Burnet Ave
    Cincinnati OH 45229

(G-19026)
UNION CENTRE HOTEL LLC
Also Called: Marriott
6189 Muhlhauser Rd (45069-4842)
PHONE.....................................513 874-7335
Brian Perkins, *General Mgr*
EMP: 167
SALES (est): 5.7MM **Privately Held**
SIC: 7011 Hotels & motels

(G-19027)
**UNIVERSITY MOVING &
STORAGE CO**
Also Called: North American Van Lines
8735 Rite Track Way (45069-7361)
PHONE.....................................248 615-7000
Mark Bruns, *Manager*
Diana West, *Agent*
EMP: 35
SALES (corp-wide): 18.9MM **Privately
Held**
SIC: 4214 Household goods moving &
    storage, local
PA: University Moving & Storage Company
    23305 Commerce Dr
    Farmington Hills MI 48335
    248 615-7000

(G-19028)
VALLEN DISTRIBUTION INC
Also Called: Innosource
9407 Meridian Way (45069-6525)
PHONE.....................................513 942-9100
Brian Ramstetter, *Opers Staff*
Shannon Eads, *Buyer*
John Kramer, *Branch Mgr*
EMP: 60
SALES (corp-wide): 12.2MM **Privately
Held**
WEB: www.idgventures.com
SIC: 5085 Mill supplies
HQ: Vallen Distribution, Inc.
    2100 The Oaks Pkwy
    Belmont NC 28012

(G-19029)
VARO ENGINEERS INC
6039 Schumacher Park Dr (45069-4812)
PHONE.....................................513 729-9313
Tim Burnham, *CEO*
EMP: 60
SALES (corp-wide): 27.4MM **Privately
Held**
SIC: 8711 Consulting engineer
PA: Varo Engineers, Inc.
    2751 Tuller Pkwy
    Dublin OH 43017
    614 459-0424

(G-19030)
VENDORS SUPPLY INC
Also Called: Vendor Supply of Ohio
6448 Gano Rd (45069-4829)
P.O. Box 62883, Cincinnati (45262-0883)
PHONE.....................................513 755-2111
Ken Morgan, *Manager*
Sarah McGuire, *Receptionist*
EMP: 30
SALES (corp-wide): 47.2MM **Privately
Held**
SIC: 5141 Food brokers
PA: Vendors Supply, Inc.
    201 Saluda River Rd
    Columbia SC 29210
    803 772-6390

(G-19031)
VIGILANT DEFENSE
Also Called: Vigilant Technology Solutions
8366 Princeton Glendale (45069-5935)
PHONE.....................................513 309-0672
Chris Nyhuis, *Owner*
Katherine Nyhuis, *CFO*
EMP: 40 EST: 2009
SALES (est): 4.4MM **Privately Held**
SIC: 7382 Security systems services

(G-19032)
VIKING OFFICE PRODUCTS INC
4700 Muhlhauser Rd (45011-9796)
PHONE.....................................513 881-7200
Bruce Harris, *Branch Mgr*
EMP: 400
SALES (corp-wide): 11B **Publicly Held**
SIC: 5943 5044 Office forms & supplies;
    office equipment
HQ: Viking Office Products, Inc.
    3366 E Willow St
    Signal Hill CA 90755
    562 490-1000

(G-19033)
VITRAN EXPRESS INC
2789 Crescentville Rd (45069-3816)
PHONE.....................................513 771-4894
Mike Scott, *Manager*
EMP: 30
SALES (corp-wide): 109.4MM **Privately
Held**
SIC: 4213 Less-than-truckload (LTL) trans-
    port
PA: Vitran Express, Inc.
    12225 Stephens Rd
    Warren MI 48089
    317 803-4000

(G-19034)
**WARSTEINER IMPORTERS
AGENCY**
Also Called: Warsteiner USA
9359 Allen Rd (45069-3846)
PHONE.....................................513 942-9872
Geoffery Westapher, *President*
Kevin Berning, *Controller*

John Burke, *Regl Sales Mgr*
Ed Dellapiana, *Regl Sales Mgr*
Rob Emmer, *Regl Sales Mgr*
▲ EMP: 50
SQ FT: 10,000
SALES: 24.5MM **Privately Held**
WEB: www.warsteiner-usa.com
SIC: 5181 Beer & other fermented malt
    liquors
PA: Warsteiner International Kg
    Domring 4-10
    Warstein
    290 280-220

(G-19035)
WEST CHESTER CHRSTN CHLD
7951 Tylersville Rd (45069-2508)
PHONE.....................................513 777-6300
Kathleen Wiseman, *Director*
EMP: 25
SALES: 394.8K **Privately Held**
SIC: 8351 Group day care center

(G-19036)
**WETHERNGTON GOLF CNTRY
CLB INC (PA)**
7337 Country Club Ln (45069-1598)
PHONE.....................................513 755-2582
Michael Purich, *Principal*
Donna Kiessling, *Asst Controller*
Terri England, *Exec Dir*
Jason Rose, *Director*
Khalid Mafazy, *Executive*
EMP: 65
SALES: 1.3MM **Privately Held**
WEB: www.wetheringtongcc.com
SIC: 7997 Country club, membership

(G-19037)
**WINDWOOD SWIM & TENNIS
CLUB**
6649 N Windwood Dr (45069-4329)
P.O. Box 8037 (45069-8037)
PHONE.....................................513 777-2552
Barb Russell, *President*
Karen Gabriel, *Manager*
EMP: 25
SALES: 170.3K **Privately Held**
SIC: 7941 Sports clubs, managers & pro-
    moters

(G-19038)
WINELCO INC
6141 Centre Park Dr (45069-3869)
PHONE.....................................513 755-8050
Michael Ullman, *President*
Robert Gomez, *Opers Staff*
Mary Holsinger, *Manager*
EMP: 40
SQ FT: 17,000
SALES (est): 8.2MM **Privately Held**
WEB: www.winelco.com
SIC: 7699 5084 Industrial equipment serv-
    ices; industrial machinery & equipment

West Chester
Hamilton County

(G-19039)
A-T CONTROLS INC (PA)
9955 International Blvd (45246-4853)
PHONE.....................................513 530-5175
Brian Wright, *President*
Brad Mueller, *Principal*
Jeremy Pitzel, *Regional Mgr*
Pat Combs, *COO*
Ronald Ruehlmann, *Vice Pres*
▲ EMP: 32
SQ FT: 17,500
SALES (est): 19.9MM **Privately Held**
WEB: www.atcontrols.com
SIC: 5085 Valves & fittings; valves, pistons
    & fittings

(G-19040)
ACCURATE HEALTHCARE INC
4681 Interstate Dr (45246-1109)
PHONE.....................................513 208-6988
James Hobbs, *President*
EMP: 49 EST: 2016
SQ FT: 8,000

SALES (est): 165.7K **Privately Held**
SIC: 8059 Nursing home, except skilled &
    intermediate care facility

(G-19041)
**ATLAS MACHINE AND SUPPLY
INC**
4985 Provident Dr (45246-1020)
PHONE.....................................502 584-7262
Kurt Colwell, *Div Sub Head*
Sonny Welker, *Manager*
EMP: 32
SALES (corp-wide): 43.5MM **Privately
Held**
WEB: www.atlasmachine.com
SIC: 5084 3599 Compressors, except air
    conditioning; machine shop, jobbing & re-
    pair
PA: Atlas Machine And Supply, Inc.
    7000 Global Dr
    Louisville KY 40258
    502 584-7262

(G-19042)
BEIERSDORF INC
5232 E Provident Dr (45246-1040)
PHONE.....................................513 682-7300
Gayle Gao, *President*
Dan Heil, *Opers Mgr*
Aneesa Khan, *Human Res Dir*
Melanie Peck, *Human Res Mgr*
Jim Kenton, *Branch Mgr*
EMP: 168
SALES (corp-wide): 12.1B **Privately Held**
WEB: www.bdfusa.com
SIC: 2844 5122 3842 2841 Face creams
    or lotions; antiseptics; bandages & dress-
    ings; stockinette, surgical; soap: granu-
    lated, liquid, cake, flaked or chip; tape,
    pressure sensitive: made from purchased
    materials
HQ: Beiersdorf, Inc.
    45 Danbury Rd
    Wilton CT 06897
    203 563-5800

(G-19043)
BELFOR USA GROUP INC
4710 Interstate Dr Ste L (45246-1144)
PHONE.....................................513 860-3111
Beth Goodhart, *Manager*
EMP: 45
SALES (corp-wide): 1.5B **Privately Held**
SIC: 1799 7349 Post-disaster renovations;
    building maintenance services
HQ: Belfor Usa Group Inc.
    185 Oakland Ave Ste 150
    Birmingham MI 48009

(G-19044)
BENCO DENTAL SUPPLY CO
10014 International Blvd (45246-4839)
PHONE.....................................317 845-5356
David Brod, *Branch Mgr*
EMP: 96
SALES (corp-wide): 621.9MM **Privately
Held**
SIC: 5047 Dental equipment & supplies
PA: Benco Dental Supply Co.
    295 Centerpoint Blvd
    Pittston PA 18640
    570 602-7781

(G-19045)
BLUELINX CORPORATION
400 Circle Freeway Dr (45246-1214)
P.O. Box 46444, Cincinnati (45246-0444)
PHONE.....................................513 874-6770
Rick Carlson, *Branch Mgr*
EMP: 26
SQ FT: 100,000
SALES (corp-wide): 1.8B **Publicly Held**
WEB: www.bluelinx.com
SIC: 5031 Millwork
HQ: Bluelinx Corporation
    1950 Spectrum Cir Se # 300
    Marietta GA 30067
    770 953-7000

(G-19046)
BRIDGE LOGISTICS INC
5 Circle Freeway Dr (45246-1201)
PHONE.....................................513 874-7444
James Campbell, *CEO*
William P Lanham, *Vice Pres*
Joe Campbell, *Opers Mgr*

Tony Campbell, *Opers Staff*
Sharon Smith, *Accounts Mgr*
EMP: 30
SQ FT: 10,000
SALES: 15MM **Privately Held**
WEB: www.bridgelogisticsinc.com
SIC: 4214 Local trucking with storage

(G-19047)
BRIGHTVIEW LANDSCAPES LLC
10139 Transportation Way (45246-1317)
PHONE.................................513 874-6484
Mark McClanahan, *General Mgr*
EMP: 56
SALES (corp-wide): 2.8B **Publicly Held**
SIC: 0781 Landscape services
HQ: Brightview Landscapes, Llc
   401 Plymouth Rd Ste 500
   Plymouth Meeting PA 19462
   484 567-7204

(G-19048)
E S I INC (DH)
4696 Devitt Dr (45246-1104)
PHONE.................................513 454-3741
Tom Schrout, *President*
Cahrley Hartshorn, *Vice Pres*
Douglas Hurley, *Vice Pres*
Gary Laidman, *Vice Pres*
Paul Clark, *Project Mgr*
EMP: 100
SQ FT: 9,000
SALES (est): 35.7MM
SALES (corp-wide): 4.5B **Publicly Held**
WEB: www.esielectrical.com
SIC: 1731 General electrical contractor
HQ: Mdu Construction Services Group, Inc.
   1150 W Century Ave
   Bismarck ND 58503
   701 530-1000

(G-19049)
ESSENDANT CO
9775 International Blvd (45246-4855)
PHONE.................................513 942-1354
Glynn Magness, *Branch Mgr*
EMP: 96
SALES (corp-wide): 5B **Privately Held**
WEB: www.ussco.com
SIC: 5112 Office supplies
HQ: Essendant Co.
   1 Parkway North Blvd # 100
   Deerfield IL 60015
   847 627-7000

(G-19050)
ESSIG RESEARCH INC
497 Circle Freeway Dr # 236 (45246-1257)
PHONE.................................513 942-7100
Joseph P Daly, *President*
Mark Ridge, *Project Mgr*
Tiffany Spencer, *Engineer*
EMP: 28
SQ FT: 5,000
SALES (est): 4.7MM **Privately Held**
SIC: 8711 Consulting engineer

(G-19051)
EXPRESS TWING RECOVERY SVC INC
9772 Prnceton Glendale Rd (45246-1022)
PHONE.................................513 881-1900
Mark Groteke, *President*
EMP: 44
SQ FT: 3,000
SALES (est): 4.7MM **Privately Held**
WEB: www.expressautotransport.com
SIC: 4213 Automobiles, transport & delivery

(G-19052)
FEDEX GROUND PACKAGE SYS INC
9667 Inter Ocean Dr (45246-1029)
PHONE.................................513 942-4330
EMP: 100
SALES (corp-wide): 47.4B **Publicly Held**
SIC: 4213 4212 Trucking Delivery Services
HQ: Fedex Ground Package System, Inc.
   1000 Fed Ex Dr
   Coraopolis PA 15108
   412 269-1000

(G-19053)
FILTERFRESH COFFEE SERVICE INC
4890 Duff Dr Ste D (45246-1100)
PHONE.................................513 681-8911
Yasna Hood, *Manager*
EMP: 25 **Publicly Held**
SIC: 7389 Coffee service
HQ: Filterfresh Coffee Service Inc.
   1101 Market St Fl 7
   Philadelphia PA 19107

(G-19054)
FRITO-LAY NORTH AMERICA INC
4696 Devitt Dr (45246-1104)
PHONE.................................513 874-0112
Russell White, *Branch Mgr*
EMP: 61
SQ FT: 12,500
SALES (corp-wide): 64.6B **Publicly Held**
WEB: www.fritolay.com
SIC: 5145 Snack foods
HQ: Frito-Lay North America, Inc.
   7701 Legacy Dr
   Plano TX 75024

(G-19055)
FULFILLMENT TECHNOLOGIES LLC
Also Called: Filltek Fulfillment Services
5389 E Provident Dr (45246-1044)
PHONE.................................513 346-3100
Craig Kerl, *Opers Mgr*
Tony Mazzone, *Controller*
Kim Fielden, *Client Mgr*
David H Cook, *Mng Member*
Terry Cooper, *Supervisor*
▲ **EMP:** 150 **EST:** 2000
SQ FT: 304,000
SALES (est): 12.6MM **Privately Held**
WEB: www.filltek.com
SIC: 4225 4841 Warehousing, self-storage; multipoint distribution systems services (MDS)

(G-19056)
FULL RANGE REHAB LLC
4722 Interstate Dr Ste K (45246-1145)
PHONE.................................513 330-5995
Jerry Weiner, *Facilities Mgr*
Cory Alvarez, *Regl Sales Mgr*
Roland Seymor, *Sales Staff*
Brenda Witkowski, *Marketing Mgr*
Jay Weiner,
EMP: 27
SALES: 5.6MM **Privately Held**
SIC: 5047 Medical & hospital equipment

(G-19057)
GSF NORTH AMERICAN JANTR SVC
9850 Prnceton Glendale Rd (45246-1034)
PHONE.................................513 733-1451
Tim Rupard, *President*
EMP: 199
SALES (corp-wide): 86MM **Privately Held**
SIC: 7349 Janitorial service, contract basis
HQ: Gsf North American Janitorial Service Inc
   107 S Penn St Ste 300
   Indianapolis IN 46204
   317 262-1133

(G-19058)
HANSER MUSIC GROUP INC (PA)
9615 Inter Ocean Dr (45246-1029)
PHONE.................................859 817-7100
John F Hanser III, *President*
Timothy J Hanser, *Corp Secy*
Gary Hanser, *Vice Pres*
David F Rasfeld, *CFO*
Carlos Vargas, *Sales Mgr*
◆ **EMP:** 80 **EST:** 1924
SQ FT: 121,000
SALES (est): 21.7MM **Privately Held**
WEB: www.powerwerks.com
SIC: 5099 3931 Musical instruments; musical instruments

(G-19059)
HELPING HANDS HEALTH CARE INC
9692 Cncnnati Columbus Rd (45241-1071)
PHONE.................................513 755-4181
Chris Ellis, *CEO*
EMP: 160 **EST:** 1999
SALES: 6.1MM **Privately Held**
WEB: www.helpinghandshealthcare.com
SIC: 8082 Home health care services

(G-19060)
HILLMAN GROUP INC
Sealtight
9950 Prnceton Glendale Rd (45246-1116)
PHONE.................................513 874-5905
David Quehl, *Manager*
EMP: 35
SALES (corp-wide): 838.3MM **Privately Held**
WEB: www.sealtite.com
SIC: 7319 Aerial advertising services
HQ: The Hillman Group Inc
   10590 Hamilton Ave
   Cincinnati OH 45231
   513 851-4900

(G-19061)
INTELLIGENT INFORMATION INC
4838 Duff Dr Ste C (45246-1143)
PHONE.................................513 860-4233
George Wagenheim, *President*
Colleen Cavanaugh, *Opers Mgr*
EMP: 25
SALES (est): 1.5MM **Privately Held**
SIC: 7378 Computer maintenance & repair

(G-19062)
INTERNASH GLOBAL SVC GROUP LLC
4621 Interstate Dr (45246-1109)
PHONE.................................513 772-0430
Jennifer Campos, *Branch Mgr*
EMP: 55
SALES (corp-wide): 19.9MM **Privately Held**
SIC: 7629 Electrical equipment repair services
PA: Internash Global Services, Llc
   8219 Kempwood Dr
   Houston TX 77055
   713 722-0320

(G-19063)
LEIDOS TECHNICAL SERVICES INC
Also Called: Lockheed Martin
497 Circle Freeway Dr # 236 (45246-1257)
PHONE.................................513 672-8400
Fax: 513 674-5798
EMP: 60
SALES (corp-wide): 7B **Publicly Held**
SIC: 8731 Research & Development Of Space Launch Vehicles
HQ: Leidos Technical Services, Inc.
   700 N Frederick Ave
   Gaithersburg MD 20879
   301 240-7000

(G-19064)
LOUIS TRAUTH DAIRY LLC (HQ)
9991 Commerce Park Dr (45246-1331)
P.O. Box 721770, Newport KY (41072-1770)
PHONE.................................859 431-7553
Greg Engles, *CEO*
Rachael A Gonzalez, *Principal*
Steven J Kemps, *Principal*
Gary Sparks, *Senior VP*
Dan Smith, *Vice Pres*
EMP: 260 **EST:** 1920
SQ FT: 160,000
SALES (est): 39.2MM **Publicly Held**
WEB: www.trauthdairy.com
SIC: 5149 2033 2026 2024 Beverages, except coffee & tea; mineral or spring water bottling; tea; canned fruits & specialties; fluid milk; ice cream & frozen desserts; milk & cream, fluid

(G-19065)
MCCC SPORTSWEAR INC
9944 Prnceton Glendale Rd (45246-1116)
PHONE.................................513 583-9210
Marta Callahan, *President*
Sue Kollstedt, *Vice Pres*
Debbie Johnson, *Art Dir*
Pam Bedell,
▲ **EMP:** 30
SQ FT: 45,000
SALES: 8MM **Privately Held**
WEB: www.mccc-sportswear.com
SIC: 5137 2395 5136 Women's & children's clothing; embroidery & art needlework; men's & boys' clothing

(G-19066)
MH LOGISTICS CORP
Also Called: Mh Equipment
106 Circle Freeway Dr (45246-1204)
PHONE.................................513 681-2200
Steve Meinken, *Foreman/Supr*
Mark Hoerst, *Parts Mgr*
Scott Streicher, *Sales Staff*
Charles Blankenship, *Manager*
Tom Weiner, *Manager*
EMP: 55
SALES (corp-wide): 247.9MM **Privately Held**
WEB: www.mhlogistics.com
SIC: 5084 Materials handling machinery
PA: M.H. Logistics Corp.
   8901 N Industrial Rd
   Peoria IL 61615
   309 579-8020

(G-19067)
MID-AMERICA GUTTERS INC (PA)
862 E Crescentville Rd (45246-4843)
PHONE.................................513 671-4000
Lee J Brown, *President*
EMP: 48
SQ FT: 37,000
SALES (est): 3.6MM **Privately Held**
SIC: 1761 Gutter & downspout contractor

(G-19068)
MIDWEST MFG SOLUTIONS LLC
Also Called: Definity Partners
5474 Spellmire Dr (45246-4842)
P.O. Box 28, Pleasant Plain (45162-0028)
PHONE.................................513 381-7200
Ray Attiyah, *Administration*
Jay Kuhn,
EMP: 30
SALES (est): 3.5MM **Privately Held**
SIC: 8742 Manufacturing management consultant

(G-19069)
MILLIKEN MILLWORK INC
Also Called: Mmi Ii
400 Circle Freeway Dr (45246-1214)
PHONE.................................513 874-6771
Rick Carlson, *General Mgr*
Debbie Olding, *Human Res Dir*
EMP: 100 **Publicly Held**
WEB: www.millikenmillwork.com
SIC: 5031 Millwork; door frames, all materials; doors
HQ: Milliken Millwork, Inc.
   6361 Sterling Dr N
   Sterling Heights MI 48312
   586 264-0950

(G-19070)
MOTION INDUSTRIES INC
Apache
9965 Farr Ct (45246-1119)
PHONE.................................513 860-8400
Mark Benedetti, *Administration*
EMP: 66
SALES (corp-wide): 18.7B **Publicly Held**
SIC: 5085 Industrial supplies
HQ: Motion Industries, Inc.
   1605 Alton Rd
   Birmingham AL 35210
   205 956-1122

(G-19071)
ORS NASCO INC
9901 Princeton Glendale (45246-1115)
PHONE.................................918 781-5300
Greg Hawkins, *Branch Mgr*
EMP: 43
SALES (corp-wide): 5B **Privately Held**
SIC: 5085 1541 Fasteners & fastening equipment; industrial buildings & warehouses

HQ: Ors Nasco, Inc.
　　907 S Detroit Ave Ste 400
　　Tulsa OK 74120
　　918 781-5300

(G-19072)
PITNEY BOWES PRESORT SVCS INC
10085 International Blvd (45246-4845)
PHONE....................513 860-3607
David Overley, *President*
David Bush, *General Mgr*
EMP: 84
SALES (corp-wide): 3.5B **Publicly Held**
WEB: www.psigroupinc.com
SIC: 7389 Presorted mail service
HQ: Pitney Bowes Presort Services, Inc.
　　10110 I St
　　Omaha NE 68127

(G-19073)
PITT-OHIO EXPRESS LLC
5000 Duff Dr (45246-1309)
PHONE....................513 860-3424
Brent Acton, *Business Mgr*
Brant Actin, *Manager*
EMP: 100
SALES (corp-wide): 457MM **Privately Held**
SIC: 4213 4212 Contract haulers; local trucking, without storage
PA: Pitt-Ohio Express, Llc
　　15 27th St
　　Pittsburgh PA 15222
　　412 232-3015

(G-19074)
PUTMAN JANITORIAL SERVICE INC
4836 Duff Dr Ste D (45246-1194)
PHONE....................513 942-1900
James Putman, *President*
EMP: 36
SQ FT: 1,800
SALES (est): 1MM **Privately Held**
SIC: 7349 Building maintenance services

(G-19075)
READING ROCK RESIDENTIAL LLC
Also Called: Installed Products & Services
4677 Devitt Dr (45246-1103)
P.O. Box 46387, Cincinnati (45246-0387)
PHONE....................513 874-4770
Gordan Rich,
Richard Butcher,
Brian Campbell,
Kim Hammelrath,
Jesse Willoughby,
▼ EMP: 36
SALES (est): 6.4MM **Privately Held**
WEB: www.installps.com
SIC: 5074 1791 Fireplaces, prefabricated; structural steel erection

(G-19076)
RECKER AND BOERGER INC
Also Called: Recker & Boerger Appliances
10115 Transportation Way (45246-1317)
PHONE....................513 942-9663
Allen Boerger, *CEO*
Steven A Boerger, *President*
Jim Recker, *Vice Pres*
Eric Engelhardt, *Accounts Mgr*
Al Boerger, *Sales Associate*
▲ EMP: 100 EST: 1962
SALES (est): 19.9MM **Privately Held**
WEB: www.reckerandboerger.com
SIC: 5722 1711 Electric household appliances, major; warm air heating & air conditioning contractor

(G-19077)
ROYAL PAPER STOCK COMPANY INC
339 Circle Freeway Dr (45246-1207)
PHONE....................513 870-5780
Dan Price, *Manager*
EMP: 25
SALES (corp-wide): 16.4MM **Privately Held**
WEB: www.royalpaperstock.com
SIC: 4953 Recycling, waste materials

PA: Royal Paper Stock Company Inc
　　1300 Norton Rd
　　Columbus OH 43228
　　614 851-4714

(G-19078)
SALON ALEXANDRE INC
9755 Cncnnati Columbus Rd (45241-1074)
PHONE....................513 207-8406
Alexandre Zinovieve, *President*
EMP: 33
SALES (est): 406.2K **Privately Held**
SIC: 7231 Beauty shops

(G-19079)
SCHINDLER ELEVATOR CORPORATION
5426 Duff Dr (45246-1323)
PHONE....................513 341-2600
Brian Billings, *Superintendent*
Catherine Morgan, *Manager*
Sean Cain, *Network Mgr*
EMP: 40
SALES (corp-wide): 10.9B **Privately Held**
WEB: www.us.schindler.com
SIC: 7699 Elevators: inspection, service & repair
HQ: Schindler Elevator Corporation
　　20 Whippany Rd
　　Morristown NJ 07960
　　973 397-6500

(G-19080)
SEXTON INDUSTRIAL INC
366 Circle Freeway Dr (45246-1208)
PHONE....................513 530-5555
Abbe Sexton, *President*
Dan Towne, *Corp Secy*
Ron Sexton, *Vice Pres*
EMP: 150
SQ FT: 85,000
SALES (est): 39.2MM **Privately Held**
WEB: www.artisanmechanical.com
SIC: 1711 3443 Mechanical contractor; industrial vessels, tanks & containers

(G-19081)
SIMPLEX TIME RECORDER LLC
Also Called: Simplex Time Recorder 514
10182 International Blvd (45246-4846)
PHONE....................513 874-1227
Dan Thieken, *Branch Mgr*
EMP: 30 **Privately Held**
WEB: www.comtec-alaska.com
SIC: 5063 1731 Electrical apparatus & equipment; safety & security specialization
HQ: Simplex Time Recorder Llc
　　50 Technology Dr
　　Westminster MA 01441

(G-19082)
SLUSH PUPPIE
44 Carnegie Way (45246-1224)
PHONE....................513 771-0940
Will Radcliff, *Ch of Bd*
Dan Keating, *President*
Robert Schwartz, *Admin Sec*
EMP: 90
SQ FT: 40,000
SALES (est): 7.6MM **Privately Held**
WEB: www.slushpuppie.net
SIC: 2087 5078 Syrups, drink; cocktail mixes, nonalcoholic; soda fountain equipment, refrigerated

(G-19083)
STAR DIST & MANUFACTURRING LLC
Also Called: Star Manufacturing
9818 Prnceton Glendale Rd (45246-1017)
PHONE....................513 860-3573
Rick Hancock, *Mng Member*
EMP: 57
SQ FT: 60,000
SALES (est): 11.4MM **Privately Held**
SIC: 1731 7629 Electrical work; electrical repair shops

(G-19084)
STOROPACK INC (DH)
Also Called: Foam Pac Materials Company
4758 Devitt Dr (45246-1106)
PHONE....................513 874-0314
Hans Reichenecker, *Ch of Bd*
Daniel Wachter, *President*

Thomas G Eckel, *Vice Pres*
Joe Lagrasta, *Vice Pres*
Lester Whisnant, *Vice Pres*
▲ EMP: 50
SQ FT: 35,000
SALES: 110MM
SALES (corp-wide): 443.7MM **Privately Held**
WEB: www.storopack.com
SIC: 5199 3086 2671 Packaging materials; packaging & shipping materials, foamed plastic; packaging paper & plastics film, coated & laminated
HQ: Storopack Deutschland Gmbh + Co. Kg
　　Untere Rietstr. 30
　　Metzingen 72555
　　712 316-40

(G-19085)
SUPERIOR BULK LOGISTICS INC
Also Called: Superior Carriers
4963 Provident Dr (45246-1020)
PHONE....................513 874-3440
Robert P Foltz, *Manager*
EMP: 30
SALES (corp-wide): 595.7MM **Privately Held**
WEB: www.superiorbulklogistics.com
SIC: 4213 Contract haulers
PA: Superior Bulk Logistics, Inc.
　　711 Jorie Blvd Ste 101n
　　Oak Brook IL 60523
　　630 573-2555

(G-19086)
SUPERIOR ENVMTL SLTONS SES INC
Also Called: S E S
9976 Joseph James Dr (45246-1340)
PHONE....................513 874-6910
Peter Cowling, *Purchasing*
Chester Yeager, *Branch Mgr*
EMP: 259
SALES (corp-wide): 34.5MM **Privately Held**
SIC: 8999 Earth science services
PA: Superior Environmental Solutions Llc
　　9996 Joseph James Dr
　　West Chester OH 45246
　　513 874-8355

(G-19087)
SUPERIOR ENVMTL SOLUTIONS LLC (PA)
Also Called: S E S
9996 Joseph James Dr (45246-1340)
PHONE....................513 874-8355
Dean Wallace, *President*
Chester Yeager, *Vice Pres*
Michael Malone, *Safety Dir*
EMP: 126
SQ FT: 10,000
SALES: 34.5MM **Privately Held**
SIC: 4959 Environmental cleanup services

(G-19088)
T&T ENTERPRISES OF OHIO INC
5100 Duff Dr (45246-1311)
PHONE....................513 942-1141
Eric O Trautman Sr, *CEO*
EMP: 42
SQ FT: 8,500
SALES (est): 7.3MM **Privately Held**
SIC: 4212 Mail carriers, contract

(G-19089)
TAYLOR DISTRIBUTING COMPANY
9756 International Blvd (45246-4854)
PHONE....................513 771-1850
Rex Taylor, *President*
Drew Taylor, *Vice Pres*
James B Taylor, *Vice Pres*
John A Taylor, *Vice Pres*
▲ EMP: 80
SALES: 3.9MM **Privately Held**
WEB: www.taylorwarehouse.com
SIC: 4214 Local trucking with storage

(G-19090)
TAYLOR LOGISTICS INC (PA)
9756 International Blvd (45246-4854)
PHONE....................513 771-1850
Rex C Taylor, *President*
John A Taylor, *Principal*
Pam Gural, *Accountant*
EMP: 25
SQ FT: 192,000
SALES: 21.7MM **Privately Held**
WEB: www.taylor-logistics.net
SIC: 4731 Transportation agents & brokers

(G-19091)
TAYLOR WAREHOUSE CORPORATION
9756 International Blvd (45246-4854)
PHONE....................513 771-2956
Rex C Taylor, *President*
James B Taylor, *Vice Pres*
John A Taylor, *Vice Pres*
EMP: 25 EST: 1972
SALES: 1.8MM **Privately Held**
WEB: www.taylorwarehouse.com
SIC: 4225 General warehousing

(G-19092)
TRADEGLOBAL LLC
5389 E Provident Dr (45246-1044)
PHONE....................866 345-5835
Dave Cook, *CEO*
Dave Eckley, *President*
Russ Carter, *Vice Pres*
Tony Mazzone, *Vice Pres*
Chris Pacetti, *Vice Pres*
EMP: 52
SALES (est): 13.4MM
SALES (corp-wide): 948.8MM **Privately Held**
SIC: 7371 Custom computer programming services
PA: Singapore Post Limited
　　10 Eunos Road 8
　　Singapore 40860
　　684 120-00

(G-19093)
TRI-STATE TRAILER SALES INC
5230 Duff Dr (45246-1313)
PHONE....................412 747-7777
Naomi Carr, *Manager*
EMP: 25
SALES (corp-wide): 48MM **Privately Held**
WEB: www.tristatetrailer.com
SIC: 5012 Trucks, commercial
PA: Tri-State Trailer Sales, Inc.
　　3111 Grand Ave
　　Pittsburgh PA 15225
　　412 747-7777

(G-19094)
UNITED GROUP SERVICES INC (PA)
9740 Near Dr (45246-1013)
PHONE....................800 633-9690
Daniel Freese, *President*
Clarence Evenson, *Vice Pres*
Kevin Sell, *Vice Pres*
John Long, *Project Mgr*
Matt Mofield, *Project Mgr*
EMP: 200
SQ FT: 45,500
SALES: 50.4MM **Privately Held**
WEB: www.united-gs.com
SIC: 3498 1711 Fabricated pipe & fittings; process piping contractor; mechanical contractor

(G-19095)
UNIVAR USA INC
4600 Dues Dr (45246-1009)
PHONE....................513 714-5264
Charles Miller, *Accounts Mgr*
Gary Southern, *Branch Mgr*
EMP: 150
SQ FT: 129,100
SALES (corp-wide): 8.6B **Publicly Held**
SIC: 5169 2819 2869 2891 Industrial chemicals; industrial inorganic chemicals; industrial organic chemicals; chemical preparations; specialty cleaning, polishes & sanitation goods

HQ: Univar Usa Inc.
3075 Highland Pkwy # 200
Downers Grove IL 60515
331 777-6000

(G-19096)
US FOODS INC
5445 Spellmire Dr (45246-4842)
PHONE....................................614 539-7993
Ron Jordon, *Manager*
EMP: 3300 **Publicly Held**
WEB: www.usfoodservice.com
SIC: **5141** 5149 5148 5143 Food brokers; groceries & related products; fresh fruits & vegetables; dairy products, except dried or canned; packaged frozen goods
HQ: Us Foods, Inc.
9399 W Higgins Rd Ste 500
Rosemont IL 60018

(G-19097)
USF HOLLAND LLC
Also Called: USFreightways
10074 Prncton Glendale Rd (45246-1210)
PHONE....................................513 874-8960
Rick Cook, *Accounts Exec*
Dave Botos, *Branch Mgr*
EMP: 128
SALES (corp-wide): 5B **Publicly Held**
WEB: www.usfc.com
SIC: **4213** 4212 Less-than-truckload (LTL) transport; local trucking, without storage
HQ: Usf Holland Llc
700 S Waverly Rd
Holland MI 49423
616 395-5000

(G-19098)
W W WILLIAMS COMPANY LLC
4806 Interstate Dr (45246-1114)
PHONE....................................800 336-6651
EMP: 67
SALES (corp-wide): 4.8B **Privately Held**
SIC: **5084** Engines & parts, diesel
HQ: The W W Williams Company Llc
5025 Bradenton Ave # 130
Dublin OH 43017
614 228-5000

(G-19099)
WACHTER INC
10186 International Blvd (45246-4846)
PHONE....................................513 777-0701
Ken Hennings, *Branch Mgr*
EMP: 175
SALES (corp-wide): 232.7MM **Privately Held**
SIC: **1731** 1623 General electrical contractor; voice, data & video wiring contractor; cable laying construction
PA: Wachter, Inc.
16001 W 99th St
Lenexa KS 66219
913 541-2500

(G-19100)
XPO LOGISTICS FREIGHT INC
5289 Duff Dr (45246-1330)
PHONE....................................513 870-0044
Donald Gallam, *Manager*
EMP: 230
SALES (corp-wide): 15.3B **Publicly Held**
WEB: www.con-way.com
SIC: **4213** 4212 Contract haulers; local trucking, without storage
HQ: Xpo Logistics Freight, Inc.
2211 Old Earhart Rd # 100
Ann Arbor MI 48105
800 755-2728

(G-19101)
YRC INC
Also Called: Yellow Transportation
10074 Prncton Glendale Rd (45246-1210)
PHONE....................................513 874-9320
Bill Pierson, *Managing Dir*
Bryan Reifsnyder, *Vice Pres*
Tyrone Dixon, *Opers Mgr*
Bob Braun, *Materials Mgr*
David Rodis, *Accounts Mgr*
EMP: 200
SALES (corp-wide): 5B **Publicly Held**
WEB: www.roadway.com
SIC: **4213** Less-than-truckload (LTL) transport

HQ: Yrc Inc.
10990 Roe Ave
Overland Park KS 66211
913 696-6100

West Farmington
Trumbull County

(G-19102)
REYNOLDS INDUSTRIES INC
380 W Main St (44491-9712)
P.O. Box 6 (44491-0006)
PHONE....................................330 889-9466
Gregory A Reynolds, *President*
EMP: 25
SQ FT: 3,500
SALES (est): 2.6MM **Privately Held**
SIC: **3069** 4783 Rubber hardware; packing goods for shipping

West Jefferson
Madison County

(G-19103)
ARBORS WEST LLC
Also Called: ARBORS WEST SUBACUTE & REHABIL
375 W Main St (43162-1298)
PHONE....................................614 879-7661
Tina Smith, *Hlthcr Dir*
Alison Morris, *Administration*
EMP: 100
SQ FT: 50,000
SALES: 6.9MM **Privately Held**
SIC: **8059** 8051 Nursing home, except skilled & intermediate care facility; skilled nursing care facilities

(G-19104)
BATTELLE MEMORIAL INSTITUTE
Hc 142 (43162)
PHONE....................................614 424-5435
Greg Kastner, *Branch Mgr*
Mark Cloran, *Manager*
EMP: 299
SALES (corp-wide): 2.5B **Privately Held**
WEB: www.battelle.org
SIC: **8731** Commercial physical research
PA: Battelle Memorial Institute Inc
505 King Ave
Columbus OH 43201
614 424-6424

(G-19105)
BATTELLE MEMORIAL INSTITUTE
Also Called: Battelle W Jfferson Operations
1425 State Route 142 Ne (43162-9647)
PHONE....................................614 424-5435
Greg Enwen, *Manager*
Jim Estep, *Manager*
EMP: 230
SALES (corp-wide): 2.5B **Privately Held**
WEB: www.battelle.org
SIC: **8731** Commercial physical research; medical research, commercial; environmental research; electronic research
PA: Battelle Memorial Institute Inc
505 King Ave
Columbus OH 43201
614 424-6424

(G-19106)
DENNIS TODD PAINTING INC
6055 Us Highway 40 (43162-9789)
PHONE....................................614 879-7952
Dennis Todd, *President*
EMP: 30
SALES (est): 1.9MM **Privately Held**
SIC: **1721** Commercial painting; commercial wallcovering contractor

(G-19107)
FEDEX FREIGHT CORPORATION
10 Commerce Pkwy (43162-9419)
PHONE....................................800 344-6448
EMP: 80
SQ FT: 8,405

SALES (corp-wide): 65.4B **Publicly Held**
SIC: **4213** Trucking, except local
HQ: Fedex Freight Corporation
1715 Aaron Brenner Dr
Memphis TN 38120

(G-19108)
FISHER CAST STEEL PRODUCTS INC (PA)
6 W Town St (43162-1293)
P.O. Box 1368, Delaware (43015-8368)
PHONE....................................614 879-8325
John Harmeyer, *President*
Richard Metcalf, *Principal*
Max Robbins, *Principal*
Brad Dennis, *Vice Chairman*
Michelle Hansberry, *Prdtn Mgr*
▲ EMP: 45 EST: 1956
SQ FT: 800
SALES (est): 18.1MM **Privately Held**
WEB: www.fishercaststeel.com
SIC: **5051** Metals service centers & offices

(G-19109)
FORREST TRUCKING COMPANY
540 Taylor Blair Rd (43162-9718)
PHONE....................................614 879-8642
Ace Forrest, *Branch Mgr*
EMP: 38
SALES (corp-wide): 5.5MM **Privately Held**
SIC: **4212** Dump truck haulage
PA: Forrest Trucking Company
7 E 1st St
London OH 43140
614 879-7347

(G-19110)
M H EBY INC
4435 State Route 29 (43162-9544)
P.O. Box 137 (43162-0137)
PHONE....................................614 879-6901
Fax: 614 879-6904
EMP: 50 **Privately Held**
SIC: **5012** 3444 Whol Autos/Motor Vehicles Mfg Sheet Metalwork

(G-19111)
MADISON TREE & LANDSCAPE CO
3180 Glade Run Rd (43162-9530)
P.O. Box 71 (43162-0071)
PHONE....................................614 207-5422
David Spegal, *Owner*
EMP: 36 EST: 1986
SALES (est): 2.4MM **Privately Held**
SIC: **0781** Landscape services

(G-19112)
TARGET CORPORATION
1 Walker Way (43162-9406)
PHONE....................................614 801-6700
Gerri Commodore, *General Mgr*
EMP: 344
SALES (corp-wide): 75.3B **Publicly Held**
WEB: www.target.com
SIC: **4226** Special warehousing & storage
PA: Target Corporation
1000 Nicollet Mall
Minneapolis MN 55403
612 304-6073

(G-19113)
WEST JEFFERSON PLUMBING HTG
Also Called: West Jefferson Plbg Htg Coolin
174 E Main St (43162-1248)
PHONE....................................614 879-9606
Ivan Mast Jr, *President*
James Schrock, *Vice Pres*
Wayne Yoder, *Vice Pres*
EMP: 32
SQ FT: 8,800
SALES (est): 5MM **Privately Held**
SIC: **1711** Plumbing contractors; warm air heating & air conditioning contractor

West Lafayette
Coshocton County

(G-19114)
JONES METAL PRODUCTS COMPANY
Jones-Zylon Company
305 N Center St (43845-1001)
PHONE....................................740 545-6341
Todd Kohl, *Manager*
EMP: 40
SALES (est): 2.3MM
SALES (corp-wide): 9.5MM **Privately Held**
WEB: www.joneszylon.com
SIC: **5047** 3842 Hospital equipment & supplies; surgical appliances & supplies
PA: Jones Metal Products Company
200 N Center St
West Lafayette OH 43845
740 545-6381

(G-19115)
KINDRED HEALTHCARE OPER INC
Also Called: West Lafytt Rehabltion
620 E Main St (43845-1267)
PHONE....................................740 545-6355
Ira C Gross, *Principal*
Jackie Wolgamott, *Administration*
EMP: 68
SALES (corp-wide): 6B **Privately Held**
WEB: www.salemhaven.com
SIC: **8051** 8093 8052 Skilled nursing care facilities; rehabilitation center, outpatient treatment; intermediate care facilities
HQ: Kindred Healthcare Operating, Llc
680 S 4th St
Louisville KY 40202
502 596-7300

(G-19116)
RIVER GREENS GOLF COURSE INC
22749 State Route 751 (43845-9737)
PHONE....................................740 545-7817
Doug Davis, *President*
Lee Russell, *Corp Secy*
Lynn Russell, *Vice Pres*
EMP: 30
SQ FT: 3,000
SALES (est): 1.2MM **Privately Held**
WEB: www.rivergreens.com
SIC: **7992** Public golf courses

West Liberty
Logan County

(G-19117)
ADRIEL SCHOOL INC (PA)
414 N Detroit St (43357-9690)
P.O. Box 188 (43357-0188)
PHONE....................................937 465-0010
Michael Mullins, *CEO*
Amy Bennett, *Director*
Jacquie Linville, *Director*
Terri McGarry, *Director*
Jessica Smith, *Director*
EMP: 100 EST: 1896
SQ FT: 60,000
SALES: 7.2MM **Privately Held**
SIC: **8361** 8063 8211 Home for the emotionally disturbed; group foster home; hospital for the mentally ill; private special education school

(G-19118)
COMMUNITY HEALTH & WELLNESS PA
4879 Us Rt 68 S (43357)
PHONE....................................937 599-1411
Tara Wagner, *CEO*
EMP: 67
SALES: 5.5MM **Privately Held**
SIC: **8011** Primary care medical clinic

GEOGRAPHIC

(G-19119)
CONSOLIDATED CARE INC
1521 N Detroit St (43357)
P.O. Box 817 (43357-0817)
PHONE..................................937 465-8065
Randell Reminder, *President*
Sally J Willolby, *Vice Pres*
EMP: 50
SALES (est): 5.2MM **Privately Held**
WEB: www.lightofheartsvilla.org
SIC: 8322 Family counseling services

(G-19120)
CONSOLIDATED CARE INC (PA)
1521 N Detroit St (43357)
P.O. Box 817 (43357-0817)
PHONE..................................937 465-8065
Jennifer Dempster, *President*
EMP: 30
SQ FT: 3,000
SALES: 4.4MM **Privately Held**
WEB: www.ccibhp.com
SIC: 8322 8093 8049 8011 Family coun-
seling services; mental health clinic, out-
patient; psychiatric social worker;
psychiatrists & psychoanalysts

(G-19121)
OAKHILL MEDICAL ASSOCIATES
4879 Us Highway 68 S (43357-9525)
PHONE..................................937 599-1411
Roger Kauffman, *President*
Charles Kratz MD, *Principal*
Kenneth Miller MD, *Principal*
John Wenger Do, *Principal*
EMP: 35
SALES (est): 4.4MM **Privately Held**
SIC: 8011 General & family practice, physi-
cian/surgeon

(G-19122)
WEST LIBERTY CARE CENTER INC
Also Called: GREEN HILLS
6557 Us Highway 68 S (43357-9536)
PHONE..................................937 465-5065
Mike Ray, *President*
Stacie Cingle, *Human Res Dir*
Karen Oder, *Director*
Elizabeth Siegenthaler, *Director*
Jennifer Wren, *Director*
EMP: 170
SQ FT: 47,346
SALES: 10MM **Privately Held**
SIC: 8051 8052 8351 Skilled nursing care
facilities; intermediate care facilities; child
day care services

West Manchester
Preble County

(G-19123)
BIRCHWOOD GENETICS INC (PA)
465 Stephens Rd (45382-9716)
P.O. Box 137 (45382-0137)
PHONE..................................937 678-9313
Dave Flory, *President*
Philip Dorn, *General Mgr*
Pamela Flory, *Vice Pres*
Mindy Barden, *Opers Mgr*
Griff Tomlin, *Opers Mgr*
EMP: 30
SQ FT: 1,000
SALES: 12.6MM **Privately Held**
SIC: 0752 Animal breeding services

West Mansfield
Logan County

(G-19124)
HEARTLAND QUALITY EGG FARM
Also Called: Dufresh Farms
9800 County Road 26 (43358-9552)
PHONE..................................937 355-5103
Tim Weaver, *Owner*
▲ **EMP:** 40

SALES (est): 1.3MM **Privately Held**
SIC: 0252 Chicken eggs

(G-19125)
HERITAGE COOPERATIVE INC (PA)
11177 Township Road 133 (43358-9709)
P.O. Box 68 (43358-0068)
PHONE..................................419 294-2371
Eric N Parthemore, *CEO*
Ray Etgen, *Division Mgr*
Tim Rooney, *Division Mgr*
Don Hotelling, *Superintendent*
John T Dunbar, *COO*
EMP: 85
SQ FT: 7,000
SALES (est): 500.1MM **Privately Held**
SIC: 5153 5261 4925 4932 Grains; fertil-
izer; liquefied petroleum gas, distribution
through mains; gas & other services com-
bined

West Milton
Miami County

(G-19126)
BRUMBAUGH ENGRG SURVEYING LLC
1105 S Miami St Ste 1 (45383-1260)
PHONE..................................937 698-3000
John Brumbaugh, *Mng Member*
Barbara Brumbaugh,
Philip C Brumbaugh,
Steve Brumbaugh,
EMP: 35
SQ FT: 1,000
SALES: 1MM **Privately Held**
SIC: 8711 Civil engineering

(G-19127)
TOWE & ASSOCIATES INC
Also Called: Towe and Associates
415 S Miami St Ste 415 # 415
(45383-1558)
PHONE..................................937 275-0900
Carl Towe, *President*
Shawna Towe, *Info Tech Dir*
EMP: 26
SQ FT: 3,972
SALES (est): 2.2MM **Privately Held**
SIC: 8748 Business consulting

West Salem
Wayne County

(G-19128)
JOHNSON BROS RUBBER CO INC (PA)
42 W Buckeye St (44287-9747)
P.O. Box 812 (44287-0812)
PHONE..................................419 853-4122
Lawrence G Cooke, *President*
Eric Vail, *Vice Pres*
Michelle Green, *Materials Mgr*
Jill Lifer, *Train & Dev Mgr*
Tom Fisher, *Sales Mgr*
▲ **EMP:** 100 **EST:** 1947
SQ FT: 70,000
SALES (est): 54.4MM **Privately Held**
SIC: 5199 3061 Foams & rubber; mechan-
ical rubber goods

West Union
Adams County

(G-19129)
ADAMS CNTY /OHIO VLY SCHL DST
Also Called: West Union Elementary School
555 Lloyd Rd (45693-9654)
PHONE..................................937 544-2951
Rodney Wallace, *Superintendent*
EMP: 90
SALES (corp-wide): 59.5MM **Privately Held**
SIC: 8211 8351 Elementary/Secondary
School Child Day Care Services

PA: Adams County /Ohio Valley School District
141 Lloyd Rd
West Union OH 45693
937 544-5586

(G-19130)
ADAMS CNTY SNIOR CTZENS CUNCIL
10835 State Route 41 (45693-9671)
PHONE..................................937 544-7459
Mary Stout, *Exec Dir*
EMP: 30
SALES: 951.6K **Privately Held**
SIC: 8399 8322 Council for social agency;
geriatric social service

(G-19131)
ADAMS COUNTY MANOR
10856 State Route 41 (45693-9671)
PHONE..................................937 544-2205
John Houser, *President*
Ben Houser, *Vice Pres*
Ralph Houser, *Manager*
Stacey Dick, *Exec Dir*
Nicole Mc Caughey, *Administration*
EMP: 60
SQ FT: 6,700
SALES (est): 2.6MM **Privately Held**
SIC: 8052 8051 Personal care facility;
skilled nursing care facilities

(G-19132)
ADAMS RURAL ELECTRIC COOP INC
4800 State Route 125 (45693-9329)
P.O. Box 247 (45693-0247)
PHONE..................................937 544-2305
Gary Kennedy, *President*
Chris Koenig, *Manager*
Alice Baird,
EMP: 33 **EST:** 1940
SQ FT: 11,400
SALES: 16.6MM **Privately Held**
WEB: www.adamsrec.com
SIC: 4911 Distribution, electric power

(G-19133)
BRUSH CREEK MOTORSPORTS
720 E Main St (45693-1109)
PHONE..................................937 515-1353
Tom Partin, *Owner*
EMP: 30
SALES: 95K **Privately Held**
SIC: 7948 Motor vehicle racing & drivers

(G-19134)
CLAYTON RAILROAD CNSTR LLC
500 Lane Rd (45693-9440)
PHONE..................................937 549-2952
Jim McAdams, *President*
Jim McAdams Jr, *Superintendent*
Bob Staun, *Accountant*
EMP: 40
SQ FT: 1,000
SALES (est): 7.6MM **Privately Held**
SIC: 1622 Bridge construction

(G-19135)
COUNTY OF ADAMS
Also Called: Children Services
300 N Wilson Dr (45693-1157)
PHONE..................................937 544-5067
Jill Wright, *Director*
EMP: 30 **Privately Held**
SIC: 8322 Child related social services
PA: County Of Adams
11260 State Route 41
West Union OH 45693
937 544-3286

(G-19136)
EAGLE CREEK HLTHCARE GROUP INC
Also Called: EAGLE CREEK NURSING CEN-
TER
141 Spruce Ln (45693-8807)
PHONE..................................937 544-5531
George S Repchick, *President*
William I Weisberg, *Vice Pres*
Sarah Depompei, *Assistant*
EMP: 40
SQ FT: 15,551

SALES: 5.6MM
SALES (corp-wide): 157.7MM **Privately Held**
SIC: 8051 8052 Skilled nursing care facili-
ties; intermediate care facilities
PA: Saber Healthcare Group, L.L.C.
26691 Richmond Rd Frnt
Bedford OH 44146
216 292-5706

(G-19137)
OAKDALE ESTATES II INV LLC
310 Rice Dr (45693-9545)
PHONE..................................216 520-1250
Frank Sinito,
EMP: 99
SALES (est): 3.7MM **Privately Held**
SIC: 6799 Investors

(G-19138)
SABER HEALTHCARE GROUP LLC
141 Spruce Ln (45693-8807)
PHONE..................................937 779-4150
EMP: 193
SALES (corp-wide): 157.7MM **Privately Held**
SIC: 8051 Convalescent home with contin-
uous nursing care
PA: Saber Healthcare Group, L.L.C.
26691 Richmond Rd Frnt
Bedford OH 44146
216 292-5706

(G-19139)
VENTURE PRODUCTIONS INC
11516 State Route 41 (45693-9434)
PHONE..................................937 544-2823
Dan Mitchell, *CEO*
Liz Lafferty, *Director*
EMP: 60
SALES: 262K **Privately Held**
SIC: 8322 Social services for the handi-
capped

West Unity
Williams County

(G-19140)
CONVERSION TECH INTL INC
700 Oak St (43570-9457)
P.O. Box 707 (43570-0707)
PHONE..................................419 924-5566
Chester Cromwell, *President*
Jason Cromwell, *Principal*
▲ **EMP:** 33
SQ FT: 130,000
SALES (est): 8.9MM **Privately Held**
WEB: www.conversiontechnologies.com
SIC: 2891 7389 Adhesives; laminating
service

(G-19141)
THREE-D TRANSPORT INC
14237 Us Highway 127 (43570-9799)
PHONE..................................419 924-5368
Daniel Meyers, *President*
Debra Meyers, *Treasurer*
EMP: 40
SQ FT: 15,200
SALES (est): 8.3MM **Privately Held**
SIC: 4213 Trucking, except local

Westerville
Delaware County

(G-19142)
ABB INC
Also Called: ABB Industrial Systems
579 Executive Campus Dr (43082-9801)
PHONE..................................614 818-6300
Roger Billy, *Branch Mgr*
EMP: 160
SALES (corp-wide): 34.3B **Privately Held**
WEB: www.elsterelectricity.com
SIC: 5063 Power transmission equipment,
electric
HQ: Abb Inc.
305 Gregson Dr
Cary NC 27511

▲ = Import ▼=Export
◆ =Import/Export

(G-19143)
AHV DEVELOPMENT LLC
Also Called: Ahv Construction
592 Office Pkwy (43082-7985)
PHONE..................................614 890-1440
Greg Filbrun, *Mng Member*
EMP: 52
SQ FT: 4,000
SALES: 8MM **Privately Held**
SIC: 1522 Apartment building construction

(G-19144)
AMERICAN CERAMIC SOCIETY (PA)
Also Called: Pottery Making Illustrate
550 Polaris Pkwy Ste 510 (43082-7132)
PHONE..................................614 890-4700
Michael Johnson, *CFO*
Scott Steen, *Exec Dir*
EMP: 35
SQ FT: 10,126
SALES: 7.5MM **Privately Held**
WEB: www.ceramics.org
SIC: 8621 2721 Medical field-related associations; engineering association; scientific membership association; periodicals: publishing & printing

(G-19145)
ARCHER-MEEK-WEILER AGENCY INC
440 Polaris Pkwy Ste 400 (43082-7229)
PHONE..................................614 212-1009
Steven Weiler, *President*
Alan R Weiler, *Chairman*
Charles Schaeffer, *Vice Pres*
Shirley A Blades, *Admin Sec*
EMP: 37
SQ FT: 5,000
SALES (est): 4.4MM **Privately Held**
WEB: www.archer-meek.com
SIC: 6411 Insurance agents

(G-19146)
BAKERWELL INC
6295 Maxtown Rd Ste 300 (43082-8885)
P.O. Box 1678 (43086-1678)
PHONE..................................614 898-7590
Rex Baker, *President*
Jeff Baker, *Corp Secy*
EMP: 51 **EST:** 1981
SALES (est): 2.9MM **Privately Held**
WEB: www.bakerwell.com
SIC: 1382 Oil & gas exploration services

(G-19147)
BANC AMER PRCTICE SLUTIONS INC
600 N Cleveland Ave # 300 (43082-6920)
PHONE..................................614 794-8247
Roy Best, *Principal*
John Fiore, *Senior VP*
Charlee Rocha, *Senior VP*
EMP: 250
SQ FT: 115,000
SALES: 9.2MM
SALES (corp-wide): 110.5B **Publicly Held**
SIC: 8742 Banking & finance consultant
PA: Bank Of America Corporation
100 N Tryon St Ste 170
Charlotte NC 28202
704 386-5681

(G-19148)
BANK OF AMERICA
600 N Cleveland Ave # 300 (43082-6926)
PHONE..................................614 882-4319
Kay Griffith, *Principal*
Joseph Dinicola, *Senior VP*
Josh Contrucci, *Sales Staff*
EMP: 108
SALES (est): 73.9MM **Privately Held**
SIC: 6021 National commercial banks

(G-19149)
BROADBAND EXPRESS LLC
374 Westdale Ave Ste A (43082-6069)
PHONE..................................614 823-6464
John Kuhn,
EMP: 30
SQ FT: 36,000

SALES (est): 2.2MM
SALES (corp-wide): 538.2K **Privately Held**
SIC: 1731 Cable television installation
PA: Broadband Installation Services, Llc
374 Westdale Ave
Westerville OH 43082
614 823-6464

(G-19150)
CENTER FOR SRGCAL DRMTLOGY INC
428 County Line Rd W (43082-7294)
PHONE..................................614 847-4100
Ronald J Siegle, *President*
Peter C Seline, *Vice Pres*
Brian P Biernat, *Treasurer*
EMP: 60
SQ FT: 19,200
SALES (est): 6.7MM **Privately Held**
SIC: 8011 Dermatologist

(G-19151)
CENTRAL OHIO PRIMARY CARE
507 Executive Campus Dr # 160
(43082-9838)
PHONE..................................614 891-9505
Katrina Tansky, *Branch Mgr*
EMP: 37 **Privately Held**
SIC: 8011 Pediatrician
PA: Central Ohio Primary Care Physicians, Inc.
570 Polaris Pkwy Ste 250
Westerville OH 43082

(G-19152)
CENTRAL OHIO PRIMARY CARE (PA)
570 Polaris Pkwy Ste 250 (43082-7923)
PHONE..................................614 326-2672
J William Wulf, *CEO*
Jeffrey L Hunter Do, *President*
Michael Ashanin, *COO*
Lee Budin MD, *Vice Pres*
Paul Westfall, *Purchasing*
EMP: 60
SALES (est): 133MM **Privately Held**
WEB: www.copcp.com
SIC: 8011 Internal medicine, physician/surgeon

(G-19153)
CENTRAL OHIO SLEEP MEDICINE
Also Called: Central Ohio Pulmonary Disease
484 County Line Rd W # 130 (43082-7080)
PHONE..................................614 475-6700
Sherri Whalen, *Director*
EMP: 30
SALES (est): 647.6K **Privately Held**
SIC: 8049 Offices of health practitioner

(G-19154)
CSC INSURANCE AGENCY INC
Also Called: Pro Century
550 Polaris Pkwy Ste 300 (43082-7113)
P.O. Box 163340, Columbus (43216-3340)
PHONE..................................614 895-2000
Chrisopher J Timm, *CEO*
EMP: 100
SQ FT: 16,000
SALES: 12.9MM
SALES (corp-wide): 255K **Privately Held**
WEB: www.centurysurety.com
SIC: 6411 Insurance brokers
HQ: Century Surety Company
465 N Cleveland Ave
Westerville OH 43082
614 895-2000

(G-19155)
CSX TRANSPORTATION INC
426 Landings Loop E (43082-7421)
PHONE..................................614 898-3651
Kim Sherman, *Branch Mgr*
EMP: 42
SALES (corp-wide): 12.2B **Publicly Held**
SIC: 4011 Interurban railways
HQ: Csx Transportation, Inc.
500 Water St
Jacksonville FL 32202
904 359-3100

(G-19156)
D L RYAN COMPANIES LLC
Also Called: Ryan Partnership
440 Polaris Pkwy Ste 350 (43082-7262)
PHONE..................................614 436-6558
Peter Tarnapoll, *Principal*
EMP: 32 **Publicly Held**
SIC: 8743 8742 Sales promotion; marketing consulting services
HQ: D. L. Ryan Companies, Llc
10 Westport Rd Unit 10 # 10
Wilton CT 06897
203 210-3000

(G-19157)
DHL EXPRESS (USA) INC
570 Polaris Pkwy Ste 110 (43082-7902)
PHONE..................................614 865-8325
Nick Kaufman, *Branch Mgr*
EMP: 31
SALES (corp-wide): 70.4B **Privately Held**
SIC: 4513 Air courier services
HQ: Dhl Express (Usa), Inc.
1210 S Pine Island Rd
Plantation FL 33324
954 888-7000

(G-19158)
DHL SUPPLY CHAIN (USA)
Also Called: Sam's Distribution Center
570 Polaris Pkwy Ste 110 (43082-7902)
PHONE..................................614 895-1959
John Hummel, *Manager*
EMP: 55
SALES (corp-wide): 70.4B **Privately Held**
WEB: www.exel-logistics.com
SIC: 4225 General warehousing & storage
HQ: Exel Inc.
570 Polaris Pkwy
Westerville OH 43082
614 865-8500

(G-19159)
DONALD R KENNEY & COMPANY (PA)
Also Called: Triangle Commercial Properties
470 Olde Worthington Rd # 101
(43082-8986)
PHONE..................................614 540-2404
Donald R Kenney, *Owner*
Evan Fracasso, *Sales Staff*
Perry Smith, *Sales Staff*
Kathrine Kasas, *Property Mgr*
Aimee D'Amore, *Director*
EMP: 70 **EST:** 1968
SQ FT: 5,000
SALES (est): 8.3MM **Privately Held**
WEB: www.drkrealtors.com
SIC: 1522 Apartment building construction

(G-19160)
DOOR SHOP & SERVICE INC
7385 State Route 3 Ste 52 (43082-8654)
PHONE..................................614 423-8043
EMP: 35
SQ FT: 3,000
SALES: 2.5MM **Privately Held**
SIC: 1751 Carpentry Contractor

(G-19161)
EXEL HOLDINGS (USA) INC (DH)
570 Polaris Pkwy Ste 110 (43082-7902)
PHONE..................................614 865-8500
Scott Sureddin, *CEO*
Jose Fernando Nava, *CEO*
Jose Nava, *CEO*
Lynn Anderson, *Vice Pres*
Tim Sprosty, *Vice Pres*
EMP: 200
SALES (est): 7.5B
SALES (corp-wide): 70.4B **Privately Held**
SIC: 4226 4213 Special warehousing & storage; household goods transport
HQ: Exel Limited
Ocean House
Bracknell BERKS RG12
134 430-2000

(G-19162)
EXEL INC
Also Called: Genesis Logistics
570 Polaris Pkwy Ste 110 (43082-7902)
PHONE..................................614 865-8294
Brian Locasto, *Branch Mgr*
EMP: 30

SALES (corp-wide): 70.4B **Privately Held**
WEB: www.exel-logistics.com
SIC: 4225 General warehousing
HQ: Exel Inc.
570 Polaris Pkwy
Westerville OH 43082
614 865-8500

(G-19163)
EXEL INC (DH)
Also Called: Dhl
570 Polaris Pkwy (43082-7900)
P.O. Box 1590 (43086-1590)
PHONE..................................614 865-8500
Scott Sureddin, *CEO*
Scott Cubbler, *President*
Luis Eraa, *President*
Jim Gehr, *President*
Mark Kunar, *President*
◆ **EMP:** 500 **EST:** 1983
SALES (est): 7.5B
SALES (corp-wide): 70.4B **Privately Held**
WEB: www.exel-logistics.com
SIC: 4213 4225 4581 Trucking, except local; general warehousing; air freight handling at airports
HQ: Exel Holdings (Usa) Inc.
570 Polaris Pkwy Ste 110
Westerville OH 43082
614 865-8500

(G-19164)
FEAZEL ROOFING COMPANY
5855 Chandler Ct (43082-9050)
PHONE..................................614 898-7663
Leo Ruberto, *President*
Matt Mabe, *General Mgr*
Todd Feazel, *Vice Pres*
Nick Warmath, *Vice Pres*
Tony Satira, *Controller*
EMP: 46
SQ FT: 9,000
SALES: 30MM **Privately Held**
WEB: www.feazelroofingcompany.com
SIC: 1761 Roofing contractor; roofing & gutter work; siding contractor

(G-19165)
FERIDEAN COMMONS LLC
6885 Freeman Rd (43082-9113)
PHONE..................................614 898-7488
Fred H Powrie III, *Mng Member*
Judy Pyle, *Manager*
Gale Koehler, *Social Dir*
EMP: 40
SQ FT: 1,748
SALES (est): 2.4MM **Privately Held**
SIC: 8361 Home for the aged

(G-19166)
FERIDEAN GROUP INC
6885 Freeman Rd (43082-9113)
PHONE..................................614 898-7488
Frederick H Powrie, *President*
Ron Pyle, *Vice Pres*
EMP: 40
SALES (est): 1.2MM **Privately Held**
SIC: 6517 Railroad property lessors

(G-19167)
FUSION ALLIANCE LLC
440 Polaris Pkwy Ste 500 (43082-6083)
PHONE..................................614 852-8000
Vince Nelson, *Branch Mgr*
EMP: 40
SALES (corp-wide): 58.5MM **Privately Held**
SIC: 8742 Management information systems consultant
HQ: Fusion Alliance, Llc
301 Pennsylvania Pkwy 2
Carmel IN 46032
317 955-1300

(G-19168)
GRACE BRTHREN CH COLUMBUS OHIO (PA)
Also Called: Grace Polaris Church
8724 Olde Worthington Rd (43082-8840)
P.O. Box 1650 (43086-1650)
PHONE..................................614 888-7733
Tom Anglea, *Principal*
Michael L Yoder, *Pastor*
James S Kanzeg, *Finance Dir*
EMP: 107 **EST:** 1964

SALES: 8.2MM **Privately Held**
SIC: 8661 8351 Brethren Church; child day care services

(G-19169)
HARRIS MACKESSY & BRENNAN
Also Called: Hmb Information Sys Developers
570 Polaris Pkwy Ste 125 (43082-7924)
PHONE..................................614 221-6831
Thomas Harris, *President*
Tom Harris, *President*
Mark Buchy, *Vice Pres*
John Mackessy, *Admin Sec*
EMP: 150
SQ FT: 9,000
SALES (est): 36.4MM **Privately Held**
WEB: www.hmbnet.com
SIC: 8742 3577 Management consulting services; decoders, computer peripheral equipment

(G-19170)
HEALTH CARE PLUS (HQ)
470 Olde Worthington Rd # 200 (43082-9127)
PHONE..................................614 340-7587
Randall A Mason, *President*
EMP: 150
SALES (est): 2.3MM
SALES (corp-wide): 7.7MM **Privately Held**
WEB: www.mardencompanies.com
SIC: 8082 7361 8351 Home health care services; nurses' registry; child day care services
PA: Marden Rehabilitation Assoc
200 Putnam St Ste 800
Marietta OH 45750
740 373-9446

(G-19171)
HEITMEYER GROUP LLC
140 Commerce Park Dr C (43082-7811)
PHONE..................................614 573-5571
Norm Heitmeyer,
EMP: 300
SQ FT: 1,500
SALES (est): 12MM **Privately Held**
SIC: 7361 Employment agencies

(G-19172)
HER INC
Also Called: H E R
413 N State St (43082-8276)
PHONE..................................614 890-7400
Gloria Raul, *General Mgr*
EMP: 106
SALES (corp-wide): 14.3MM **Privately Held**
WEB: www.eassent.com
SIC: 6531 Real estate brokers & agents
PA: Her, Inc
4261 Morse Rd
Columbus OH 43230
614 221-7400

(G-19173)
HUMAN RESOURCES SERVICES
465 Buckstone Pl (43082-8281)
PHONE..................................740 587-3484
Keith Jenkins, *Principal*
EMP: 45
SALES (est): 1.3MM **Privately Held**
SIC: 7361 Employment agencies

(G-19174)
HUNTSEY CORPORATION
Also Called: Synergy Homecare
470 Olde Worthington Rd (43082-8985)
PHONE..................................614 568-5030
Barbara Hawley, *President*
EMP: 30 EST: 2008
SALES (est): 512.1K **Privately Held**
SIC: 8082 Home health care services

(G-19175)
INSPECTION GROUP INCORPORATED
440 Polaris Pkwy Ste 170 (43082-7987)
PHONE..................................614 891-3606
Saul Himelstein, *President*
Robert Gardier, *COO*
Clarence Buck, *Vice Pres*
Keith Lavrar, *Vice Pres*
Matt Lavrar, *Vice Pres*

EMP: 50
SQ FT: 2,500
SALES (est): 3.7MM **Privately Held**
WEB: www.theinspectiongroup.com
SIC: 7389 Building inspection service

(G-19176)
JULIAN & GRUBE INC
Also Called: Trimble & Julian
333 County Line Rd W A (43082-6908)
PHONE..................................614 846-1899
Steven Julian, *Ch of Bd*
Julian Sfeve, *President*
Mark Grube, *Partner*
EMP: 35
SQ FT: 4,000
SALES (est): 3.2MM **Privately Held**
WEB: www.tjginc.com
SIC: 8721 Certified public accountant

(G-19177)
KLEINGERS GROUP INC
350 Worthington Rd Ste B (43082-8327)
PHONE..................................614 882-4311
Steven R Korte, *Manager*
EMP: 85 **Privately Held**
WEB: www.kleingers.com
SIC: 8711 Civil engineering
PA: The Kleingers Group Inc
6305 Centre Park Dr
West Chester OH 45069

(G-19178)
LAKES GOLF & COUNTRY CLUB INC
6740 Worthington Rd (43082-9491)
PHONE..................................614 882-2582
Tod Ortlip, *President*
Jim Spragg, *COO*
Leigh Allen, *Trustee*
Jay Ortlip, *Trustee*
EMP: 50
SQ FT: 40,000
SALES: 7.1MM **Privately Held**
SIC: 7997 Country club, membership

(G-19179)
LAUREL DEVELOPMENT CORPORATION
8181 Worthington Rd (43082-8067)
PHONE..................................614 794-8800
Dennis Sherman, *President*
Thomas Franke, *Chairman*
Jack Alcott, *Vice Pres*
Kevin Belew, *Vice Pres*
James Franke, *Vice Pres*
EMP: 25
SALES (est): 1.9MM **Privately Held**
SIC: 6552 Land subdividers & developers, commercial
PA: Laurel Health Care Company Of North Worthington
8181 Worthington Rd
Westerville OH 43082

(G-19180)
LAUREL HEALTH CARE COMPANY (HQ)
8181 Worthington Rd Uppr (43082-8071)
PHONE..................................614 794-8800
Bradford Payne, *President*
Jack Alcott, *Vice Pres*
Carol Bailey, *Vice Pres*
Carol Hofbauer, *Vice Pres*
Barbara Lombardi, *Vice Pres*
EMP: 54
SALES (est): 92.7MM **Privately Held**
WEB: www.laurelsofnorworth.com
SIC: 8051 Skilled nursing care facilities

(G-19181)
LAUREL HLTH CARE BATTLE CREEK (HQ)
Also Called: Laurels of Bedford, The
8181 Worthington Rd (43082-8067)
PHONE..................................614 794-8800
Dennis Sherman, *President*
Thomas Franke, *Owner*
Jack Alcott, *Vice Pres*
Kevin Belew, *Vice Pres*
James Franke, *Vice Pres*
EMP: 40
SALES (est): 2.9MM **Privately Held**
WEB: www.laurelsofbedford.com
SIC: 8051 Skilled nursing care facilities

(G-19182)
LAUREL HLTH CARE OF MT PLASANT (HQ)
Also Called: Laurels of Mt Pleasant
8181 Worthington Rd # 2 (43082-8067)
PHONE..................................614 794-8800
Dennis Sherman, *President*
Thomas Franke, *Chairman*
Jack Alcott, *Vice Pres*
Kevin Belew, *Vice Pres*
James Franke, *Vice Pres*
EMP: 63 EST: 1962
SALES (est): 3.2MM **Privately Held**
WEB: www.laurelsofmtpleasant.com
SIC: 8051 Skilled nursing care facilities

(G-19183)
LIBERTY MUTUAL INSURANCE CO
440 Polaris Pkwy Ste 150 (43082-7261)
PHONE..................................614 855-6193
Graham Powers, *Branch Mgr*
EMP: 35
SALES (corp-wide): 38.3B **Privately Held**
WEB: www.libertymutual.com
SIC: 6321 6331 Accident insurance carriers; health insurance carriers; reinsurance carriers, accident & health; workers' compensation insurance
HQ: Liberty Mutual Insurance Company
175 Berkeley St
Boston MA 02116
617 357-9500

(G-19184)
MARK HUMRICHOUSER
Also Called: Jae Co 2
6295 Maxtown Rd Ste 100 (43082-8883)
PHONE..................................614 324-5231
Mark Humrichouser, *Owner*
EMP: 45
SALES: 5.2MM **Privately Held**
SIC: 5722 5087 Kitchens, complete (sinks, cabinets, etc.); service establishment equipment

(G-19185)
MEDALLION CLUB (PA)
5000 Club Dr (43082-9551)
PHONE..................................614 794-6999
Tateo Tanigawa, *President*
Chris Ramsay, *Sales Staff*
Pete Ulliman, *Director*
Ron Dyer,
EMP: 105
SQ FT: 57,000
SALES: 8.3MM **Privately Held**
WEB: www.medallionclub.com
SIC: 7997 7991 5941 5813 Country club, membership; physical fitness facilities; sporting goods & bicycle shops; drinking places; eating places

(G-19186)
MODERN MEDICAL INC
250 Progressive Way (43082-9615)
P.O. Box 549, Lewis Center (43035-0549)
PHONE..................................800 547-3330
Joseph G Favazzo, *President*
Raymond Black, *Vice Pres*
EMP: 130
SQ FT: 40,000
SALES (est): 14.8MM
SALES (corp-wide): 226.2B **Publicly Held**
SIC: 5999 5912 5047 Medical apparatus & supplies; drug stores & proprietary stores; medical & hospital equipment
HQ: Healthcare Solutions, Inc.
2736 Meadow Church Rd # 300
Duluth GA 30097

(G-19187)
NATIONAL AUTO CARE CORPORATION
440 Polaris Pkwy Ste 250 (43082-6082)
PHONE..................................800 548-1875
Christina Schrank, *President*
Paul Leary, *Exec VP*
Steven Juresich, *Senior VP*
EMP: 53
SQ FT: 15,000

SALES (est): 14.3MM
SALES (corp-wide): 47.7MM **Privately Held**
WEB: www.natlauto.com
SIC: 6411 Insurance agents
PA: Trivest Partners, L.P.
550 S Dixie Hwy Ste 300
Coral Gables FL 33146
305 858-2200

(G-19188)
NATIONWIDE CHILDRENS HOSPITAL
Also Called: Close To Home Health Care Ctr
433 N Cleveland Ave (43082-8095)
PHONE..................................614 355-8300
Larry Long, *Director*
Heather Moorehead, *Technician*
EMP: 50
SALES (corp-wide): 2.3B **Privately Held**
SIC: 8069 8082 Children's hospital; home health care services
PA: Nationwide Children's Hospital
700 Childrens Dr
Columbus OH 43205
614 722-2000

(G-19189)
NATIONWIDE MUTUAL INSURANCE CO
955 County Line Rd W (43082-7237)
PHONE..................................614 948-4153
EMP: 40
SALES (corp-wide): 15.9B **Privately Held**
SIC: 6411 Insurance Agent/Broker
PA: Nationwide Mutual Insurance Company
1 Nationwide Plz
Columbus OH 43215
614 249-7111

(G-19190)
NEUMERIC TECHNOLOGIES CORP
470 Olde Worthington Rd # 325 (43082-9380)
PHONE..................................248 204-0652
Sudheer Gaddam, *President*
Vijay Reddy, *Research*
Boilla Bhaskar, *Sales Staff*
Bharath Neumeric, *Marketing Mgr*
Sandeep Reddy, *Senior Mgr*
EMP: 98
SQ FT: 1,300
SALES (est): 6.7MM **Privately Held**
WEB: www.ntc-us.com
SIC: 7371 Computer software development

(G-19191)
NORTHEAST CONCRETE & CNSTR
7243 Saddlewood Dr (43082-9372)
PHONE..................................614 898-5728
Thomas R Gehrlich, *President*
Samuel E Gehrlich, *Vice Pres*
EMP: 85
SQ FT: 1,500
SALES: 12.5MM **Privately Held**
WEB: www.neconcreteconstruction.com
SIC: 1771 Concrete work

(G-19192)
OAK HEALTH CARE INVESTOR (DH)
8181 Worthington Rd (43082-8067)
PHONE..................................614 794-8800
Dennis Sherman, *President*
Tom Franke, *Principal*
EMP: 49
SALES (est): 3.4MM **Privately Held**
SIC: 6512 Nonresidential building operators

(G-19193)
OAK HEALTH CARE INVESTORS (HQ)
Also Called: Laurels of Defiance, The
8181 Worthington Rd (43082-8067)
PHONE..................................614 794-8800
Dennis Sherman, *President*
Thomas Franke, *Chairman*
Jack Alcott, *Vice Pres*
Kevin Belew, *Vice Pres*
James Franke, *Vice Pres*
EMP: 30

SALES (est): 2.1MM **Privately Held**
SIC: 8051 Skilled nursing care facilities

(G-19194)
OHIO BUILDERS RESOURCES LLC
Also Called: Ohio Resources
5901 Chandler Ct Ste D (43082-9149)
PHONE 614 865-0306
Richard Mely, *President*
Scott Hoff, *General Mgr*
Sally Mealey, *Corp Secy*
Liz Mealey, *Marketing Mgr*
EMP: 26
SALES (est): 2.5MM **Privately Held**
WEB: www.ohio-resources.com
SIC: 1521 1751 Single-family home remodeling, additions & repairs; carpentry work

(G-19195)
OHIO CIVIL SERVICE EMPLOYEES A
Also Called: O.C.S.E.a
390 Worthington Rd Ste A (43082-8329)
PHONE 614 865-4700
Ron Alexander, *President*
Kathleen M Stewart, *Corp Secy*
Eddie L Parks, *Vice Pres*
Buffy Andrews, *Opers Staff*
Bruce Thompson, *Treasurer*
EMP: 92
SQ FT: 40,000
SALES (est): 10.5MM **Privately Held**
WEB: www.ocsea.org
SIC: 8631 8611 Labor union; business associations

(G-19196)
OPTUMRX INC
250 Progressive Way (43082-9615)
PHONE 614 794-3300
EMP: 530
SALES (corp-wide): 226.2B **Publicly Held**
SIC: 6411 Medical insurance claim processing, contract or fee basis
HQ: Optumrx, Inc.
2300 Main St
Irvine CA 92614

(G-19197)
ORTON EDWARD JR CRMIC FNDATION
6991 S Old 3c Hwy (43082-9026)
P.O. Box 2760 (43086-2760)
PHONE 614 895-2663
Jonathan Hinton, *Ch of Bd*
J Gary Childress, *General Mgr*
Dr Stephen Freiman, *Trustee*
Dr John Morral, *Trustee*
Dr James Williams, *Trustee*
▼ **EMP:** 31
SQ FT: 34,260
SALES: 5MM **Privately Held**
WEB: www.ortonceramic.com
SIC: 3269 3826 3825 8748 Cones, pyrometric: earthenware; analytical instruments; instruments to measure electricity; testing services

(G-19198)
PERMEDION INC
350 Worthington Rd Ste H (43082-8327)
PHONE 614 895-9900
William Lucia, *President*
Thomas A Schultz, *Vice Pres*
EMP: 60
SQ FT: 25,000
SALES (est): 3.3MM
SALES (corp-wide): 598.2MM **Publicly Held**
WEB: www.hmsy.com
SIC: 8741 Hospital management
HQ: Health Management Systems Inc
5615 High Point Dr # 100
Irving TX 75038
214 453-3000

(G-19199)
POLARIS INNKEEPERS INC
Also Called: Fairfield Inn
9000 Worthington Rd (43082-8851)
PHONE 614 568-0770
Laura Focht, *Sales Executive*

Kezia Cromer, *Manager*
EMP: 25
SALES (est): 622.4K **Privately Held**
SIC: 7011 Hotels & motels

(G-19200)
POWELL ENTERPRISES INC
Also Called: Goddard School, The
8750 Olde Worthington Rd (43082-8853)
PHONE 614 882-0111
Steve Powell, *President*
Marykay Weite, *Director*
EMP: 25
SALES: 1MM **Privately Held**
SIC: 8351 Group day care center

(G-19201)
PRECISION BROADBND INSTALLATNS
7642 Red Bank Rd (43082-8210)
PHONE 614 523-2917
Frederick P Steininger, *CEO*
Chris Steininger, *President*
Dave Bay, *Technology*
EMP: 140
SALES (est): 23.4MM **Privately Held**
SIC: 1731 Cable television installation

(G-19202)
PREFERRED RE INVESTMENTS LLC
Also Called: Preferred Living
470 Olde Worthington Rd # 470 (43082-8985)
PHONE 614 901-2400
Michael J Kenney, *President*
Jennifer King, *COO*
Wayne S Chang, *CFO*
Mindy Greer, *Marketing Mgr*
Amy Long, *Manager*
EMP: 30
SALES (est): 5.9MM **Privately Held**
SIC: 6531 Real estate managers

(G-19203)
PRIMROSE SCHOOL AT POLARIS
561 Westar Blvd (43082-7806)
PHONE 614 899-2588
Ashley Clement, *Owner*
EMP: 30
SALES (est): 524.1K **Privately Held**
SIC: 8351 Preschool center

(G-19204)
PROGRESSIVE ENTPS HOLDINGS INC
250 Progressive Way (43082-9615)
PHONE 614 794-3300
Jamie Oliver, *Human Res Mgr*
Susan N Paris, *Sales Staff*
Alison Cowan, *CTO*
Howard Peppercorn, *Information Mgr*
EMP: 531
SALES (est): 17.7MM **Privately Held**
SIC: 8742 Compensation & benefits planning consultant

(G-19205)
QUICK SOLUTIONS INC
440 Polaris Pkwy Ste 500 (43082-6083)
PHONE 614 825-8000
Tom Campbell, *CEO*
Rick Mariotti, *President*
Adam Frumkin, *Mfg Staff*
Valerie Coomes, *Manager*
Paul Moore, *Manager*
EMP: 200
SQ FT: 22,000
SALES (est): 27.6MM
SALES (corp-wide): 58.5MM **Privately Held**
WEB: www.quicksolutions.net
SIC: 8742 Management consulting services
PA: Fusion Alliance Holdings, Inc.
301 Pennsylvania Pkwy
Indianapolis IN 46280
317 955-1300

(G-19206)
R & E JOINT VENTURE INC
6843 Regency Dr (43082-8480)
PHONE 614 891-9404
Richard Hames, *President*

EMP: 30
SALES (est): 1.5MM **Privately Held**
SIC: 7212 Pickup station, laundry & drycleaning

(G-19207)
REVOLUTION GROUP INC
600 N Cleveland Ave # 110 (43082-6921)
PHONE 614 212-1111
Richard Snide, *President*
Polly Clavijo, *Vice Pres*
Carlos Clavijo, *CFO*
Cindy Snide, *Mktg Dir*
Amit Joshi, *Manager*
EMP: 80
SALES (est): 7.6MM **Privately Held**
SIC: 7379 7372 4813 8741 Computer related consulting services; prepackaged software; ; ; management services

(G-19208)
RWC INC
6210 Frost Rd (43082-9027)
PHONE 614 890-0600
Wesley Osburn, *CEO*
EMP: 25
SALES (corp-wide): 8.8MM **Privately Held**
SIC: 5169 0782 Industrial chemicals; lawn & garden services
PA: Rwc, Inc.
248 Lockhouse Rd
Westfield MA 01085
614 890-0600

(G-19209)
SHAMROCK TOWING INC (PA)
6333 Frost Rd (43082-9027)
PHONE 614 882-3555
Charles N Duffey, *CEO*
Tim Duffey, *President*
Mike Nelson, *Corp Secy*
EMP: 30 **EST:** 1952
SALES (est): 4.1MM **Privately Held**
WEB: www.shamrocktowinginc.com
SIC: 7549 Towing service, automotive

(G-19210)
SOGETI USA LLC
579 Executive Campus Dr # 300 (43082-9801)
PHONE 614 847-4477
Thomas Wesseling, *Manager*
Mike Pasquale, *Consultant*
Kevin Cheesman, *Director*
EMP: 50
SALES (corp-wide): 355MM **Privately Held**
WEB: www.sogeti-usa.com
SIC: 7379 7373 ; computer integrated systems design
HQ: Sogeti Usa Llc
10100 Innovation Dr # 200
Miamisburg OH 45342
937 291-8100

(G-19211)
STATUS SOLUTIONS LLC
999 County Line Rd W A (43082-7237)
PHONE 866 846-7272
Michael Macleod, *Manager*
EMP: 37
SALES (corp-wide): 12.1MM **Privately Held**
SIC: 8748 Business consulting
PA: Status Solutions, Llc
1180 Seminole Trl Ste 440
Charlottesville VA 22901
434 296-1789

(G-19212)
SUDHI INFOMATICS INC
470 Olde Worthington Rd (43082-8985)
PHONE 614 882-7309
Sudheer Gaddam, *CEO*
Sandeep Reddy, *Sales Staff*
EMP: 32
SALES (est): 318.8K **Privately Held**
SIC: 7379 Computer related consulting services

(G-19213)
TALON TITLE AGENCY LLC (PA)
570 Polaris Pkwy Ste 140 (43082-7902)
PHONE 614 818-0500
William L Robinson Jr, *CEO*

Joseph J Barone, *President*
Byron Ross, *Opers Staff*
Myla Sabanalromero, *Human Res Mgr*
Michelle Ohler, *Manager*
EMP: 40 **EST:** 2012
SALES (est): 2.5MM **Privately Held**
SIC: 6541 Title & trust companies

(G-19214)
TRG MAINTENANCE LLC
514 N State St Ste B (43082-9073)
PHONE 614 891-4850
Kristy McGrath, *Principal*
EMP: 899
SALES (est): 13.2MM **Privately Held**
SIC: 7349 Building maintenance services
PA: Titan Restaurant Group, Llc
514 N State St Ste B
Westerville OH 43082

(G-19215)
VERTIV CORPORATION
610 Executive Campus Dr (43082-8870)
PHONE 614 841-6400
EMP: 250
SALES (corp-wide): 322.9MM **Privately Held**
SIC: 7378 Computer maintenance & repair
HQ: Vertiv Corporation
1050 Dearborn Dr
Columbus OH 43085
614 888-0246

(G-19216)
VILLAGE COMMUNITIES LLC
470 Olde Worthington Rd # 100 (43082-8986)
PHONE 614 540-2400
Tre Giller, *Principal*
Chris Fleet, *Principal*
Joe Thomas, *Vice Pres*
Steve Godek, *Project Mgr*
Janie Boykin, *CFO*
EMP: 113
SALES (est): 15MM **Privately Held**
SIC: 6531 Rental agent, real estate

Westerville
Franklin County

(G-19217)
AFFINION GROUP LLC
300 W Schrock Rd (43081-1189)
PHONE 614 895-1803
Peg Ayers, *Branch Mgr*
EMP: 800
SALES (corp-wide): 953.1MM **Privately Held**
SIC: 8699 Personal interest organization
HQ: Affinion Group, Llc
6 High Ridge Park Bldg A
Stamford CT 06905
203 956-1000

(G-19218)
ALADDINS ENTERPRISES INC
Also Called: Aladdin Limousines
3408 E Dblin Granville Rd (43081-9722)
PHONE 614 891-3440
Archie Synder, *President*
Janice Snyder, *Vice Pres*
EMP: 25
SQ FT: 1,000
SALES (est): 5.6MM **Privately Held**
SIC: 5511 4119 Automobiles, new & used; limousine rental, with driver

(G-19219)
ALLIANCE DATA SYSTEMS CORP
220 W Schrock Rd (43081-2873)
PHONE 614 729-5000
John Cowan, *Manager*
Michael Tasker, *Manager*
Bill Harbison, *Info Tech Mgr*
EMP: 263 **Publicly Held**
WEB: www.alliancedatasystems.com
SIC: 7389 Credit card service
PA: Alliance Data Systems Corporation
7500 Dallas Pkwy Ste 700
Plano TX 75024

(G-19220)
ANNEHURST VETERINARY HOSPITAL
25 Collegeview Rd (43081-1463)
PHONE...........................614 818-4221
Mark Harris, *Owner*
Adam Ballard, *Manager*
EMP: 30
SQ FT: 2,000
SALES (est): 1.7MM **Privately Held**
WEB: www.reprovet.com
SIC: 0742 0752 Animal hospital services, pets & other animal specialties; animal boarding services

(G-19221)
AQUA PENNSYLVANIA INC
5481 Buenos Aires Blvd (43081-4203)
PHONE...........................614 882-6586
EMP: 45
SALES (corp-wide): 838MM **Publicly Held**
SIC: 4941 Water supply
HQ: Aqua Pennsylvania, Inc.
　762 W Lancaster Ave
　Bryn Mawr PA 19010
　610 525-1400

(G-19222)
ASSOC DVLPMTLY DISABLED (PA)
Also Called: A D D
769 Brooksedge Blvd (43081-2821)
PHONE...........................614 486-4361
Robert L Archer, *CEO*
J Clifford Wilcox, *President*
Rebecca Baird, *Vice Pres*
John Poston, *Treasurer*
Gary Pocock, *Manager*
EMP: 38
SQ FT: 10,000
SALES: 17.2MM **Privately Held**
WEB: www.add1.com
SIC: 8361 8322 Home for the mentally handicapped; individual & family services

(G-19223)
ASSOCIATION FOR MIDDLE LVL EDU
4151 Executive Pkwy # 300 (43081-3867)
PHONE...........................614 895-4730
Jeff La Roux, *President*
Nancy Polinseo, *President*
Jeff Ward, *CFO*
William Waidelich, *Exec Dir*
EMP: 27
SALES: 2.4MM **Privately Held**
WEB: www.nmsa.org
SIC: 8621 Education & teacher association

(G-19224)
AT&T CORP
814 Green Crest Dr (43081-2839)
PHONE...........................614 223-5318
Don Hamilton, *Branch Mgr*
Michael Peoples, *Manager*
EMP: 69
SALES (corp-wide): 170.7B **Publicly Held**
SIC: 4813 Telephone communication, except radio
HQ: At&T Corp.
　1 At&T Way
　Bedminster NJ 07921
　800 403-3302

(G-19225)
AT&T DATACOMM LLC
814 Green Crest Dr (43081-2839)
PHONE...........................614 223-5799
Don Hamilton, *Branch Mgr*
EMP: 25
SALES (corp-wide): 170.7B **Publicly Held**
SIC: 4813 Data telephone communications
HQ: At&T Datacomm, Llc
　175 E Houston St Ste 100
　San Antonio TX 78205
　210 821-4105

(G-19226)
AUTOMATIC DATA PROCESSING INC
Also Called: ADP
713 Brooksedge Plaza Dr (43081-4913)
PHONE...........................614 895-7700
Dave Darbutt, *Branch Mgr*
EMP: 190
SALES (corp-wide): 13.3B **Publicly Held**
SIC: 7374 Data processing service
PA: Automatic Data Processing, Inc.
　1 Adp Blvd Ste 1 # 1
　Roseland NJ 07068
　973 974-5000

(G-19227)
BON APPETIT MANAGEMENT CO
100 W Home St (43081-1408)
PHONE...........................614 823-1880
Bill Taylor, *General Mgr*
EMP: 66
SALES (corp-wide): 29.6B **Privately Held**
WEB: www.cafebonappetit.com
SIC: 8741 Restaurant management
HQ: Bon Appetit Management Co.
　100 Hamilton Ave Ste 400
　Palo Alto CA 94301
　650 798-8000

(G-19228)
BROOKDALE SENIOR LIVING INC
690 Cooper Rd Apt 514 (43081-8756)
PHONE...........................614 794-2499
Nicky Caudill, *Principal*
EMP: 90
SALES (corp-wide): 4.5B **Publicly Held**
SIC: 8361 Residential care
PA: Brookdale Senior Living
　111 Westwood Pl Ste 400
　Brentwood TN 37027
　615 221-2250

(G-19229)
BUCKEYE HOME HEALTHCARE INC (PA)
635 Park Madow Rd Ste 110 (43081)
PHONE...........................614 776-3372
Kinzi Farah, *President*
EMP: 25
SALES (est): 1.8MM **Privately Held**
SIC: 8082 Home health care services

(G-19230)
CANNON GROUP INC
Also Called: Pdi Plastics
5037 Pine Creek Dr (43081-4849)
PHONE...........................614 890-0343
Frank T Cannon Jr, *President*
Terrence A Grady, *Principal*
Todd Wilson, *Exec VP*
Cindy Stapleton, *Treasurer*
Ronald A Taylor, *Controller*
▲ EMP: 25
SQ FT: 6,800
SALES (est): 12.6MM **Privately Held**
WEB: www.pdisaneck.com
SIC: 5113 5162 Bags, paper & disposable plastic; plastics resins

(G-19231)
CEIBA ENTERPRISES INCORPORATED
Also Called: Gracor Language Services
159 Baranof W (43081-6205)
PHONE...........................614 818-3220
Rosario Hubbard, *President*
Thomas Hubbard Jr, *Vice Pres*
EMP: 102 EST: 1994
SALES: 1.1MM **Privately Held**
WEB: www.gracor.com
SIC: 7389 Translation services

(G-19232)
CENTRAL BNFITS ADMNSTRTORS INC
5150 E Dublin Grnvlle 3 (43081-8701)
PHONE...........................614 797-5200
John B Reinhardt Jr, *Ch of Bd*
Ted M Georges, *Vice Pres*
Scott M Vandergriff, *Vice Pres*
Joseph H Hoffman, *CFO*
David P Tague, *Accounts Mgr*
EMP: 100
SALES (est): 15MM **Privately Held**
SIC: 6411 Medical insurance claim processing, contract or fee basis

(G-19233)
CENTRAL OHIO PRIMARY CARE
285 W Schrock Rd (43081-2874)
PHONE...........................614 818-9550
EMP: 66
SIC: 8049 8011 Acupuncturist; offices & clinics of medical doctors
PA: Central Ohio Primary Care Physicians, Inc.
　570 Polaris Pkwy Ste 250
　Westerville OH 43082

(G-19234)
CENTRAL OHIO PRIMARY CARE
Also Called: Columbus Infectious Disease
615 Cpland Mill Rd Ste 2d (43081)
PHONE...........................614 508-0110
EMP: 59 **Privately Held**
SIC: 8011 Medical Doctor's Office
PA: Central Ohio Primary Care Physicians, Inc.
　570 Polaris Pkwy Ste 250
　Westerville OH 43082

(G-19235)
CENTRAL OHIO PRIMARY CARE
Also Called: Northside Internal Medicine
555 W Schrock Rd Ste 110 (43081-8739)
PHONE...........................614 882-0708
EMP: 42 **Privately Held**
SIC: 8011 Internal medicine practitioners; physics consultant
PA: Central Ohio Primary Care Physicians, Inc.
　570 Polaris Pkwy Ste 250
　Westerville OH 43082

(G-19236)
CITY OF WESTERVILLE
Also Called: Public Services Department
350 Park Meadow Dr (43081-2894)
PHONE...........................614 901-6500
Frank Wiseman, *Branch Mgr*
Christian Lord, *Manager*
EMP: 45 **Privately Held**
SIC: 4941 9631 4971 4952 Water supply; public service commission, except transportation: government; irrigation systems; sewerage systems; highway & street construction
PA: City Of Westerville
　21 S State St
　Westerville OH 43081
　614 901-6406

(G-19237)
CITY OF WESTERVILLE
Also Called: Electric Division
139 E Broadway Ave (43081-1507)
PHONE...........................614 901-6700
Andy Boatwright, *General Mgr*
Chris Monacelli, *Manager*
EMP: 37 **Privately Held**
SIC: 4911 Electric services
PA: City Of Westerville
　21 S State St
　Westerville OH 43081
　614 901-6406

(G-19238)
COLS HEALTH & WELLNESS TESTING
5050 Pine Creek Dr Ste B (43081-4852)
PHONE...........................614 839-2781
Marty Luxeder, *Owner*
EMP: 35
SALES (est): 662.3K **Privately Held**
WEB: www.appsparamedical.com
SIC: 8099 8071 Health screening service; blood analysis laboratory

(G-19239)
COLUMBUS CLNY FOR ELDERLY CARE
Also Called: COLUMBUS COLONY ELDERLY CARE
1150 Colony Dr (43081-3624)
PHONE...........................614 891-5055
Richard Huebner, *President*
Howard Snyder, *Treasurer*
Kristyn Eck, *Director*

EMP: 180 EST: 1977
SQ FT: 50,000
SALES: 10.3MM **Privately Held**
SIC: 8051 Convalescent home with continuous nursing care

(G-19240)
COLUMBUS FRKLN CNTY PK
Also Called: Blendonwoods Metro Park
4265 E Dblin Granville Rd (43081-4478)
PHONE...........................614 895-6219
Dan Bissonette, *General Mgr*
EMP: 33
SALES (corp-wide): 18.3MM **Privately Held**
SIC: 7996 Amusement parks
PA: Columbus & Franklin County Metropolitan Park District
　1069 W Main St Unit B
　Westerville OH 43081
　614 891-0700

(G-19241)
COLUMBUS FRKLN CNTY PK (PA)
Also Called: Metro Parks
1069 W Main St Unit B (43081-1186)
PHONE...........................614 891-0700
Bruce Dudley, *Opers Staff*
Renee Telfer, *Human Res Dir*
Marshall Reese, *Park Mgr*
Matthew Thompson, *Park Mgr*
Danny Sorgini, *Manager*
EMP: 50 EST: 1945
SALES (est): 18.3MM **Privately Held**
WEB: www.metroparks.net
SIC: 7999 Recreation services

(G-19242)
COLUMBUS FRKLN CNTY PK
Also Called: District Office
1069 W Main St (43081-1181)
PHONE...........................614 891-0700
John Omeara, *Branch Mgr*
EMP: 25
SALES (corp-wide): 18.3MM **Privately Held**
WEB: www.metroparks.net
SIC: 7032 Sporting & recreational camps
PA: Columbus & Franklin County Metropolitan Park District
　1069 W Main St Unit B
　Westerville OH 43081
　614 891-0700

(G-19243)
COLUMBUS PRESCR PHRMS INC
975 Eastwind Dr Ste 155 (43081-3344)
PHONE...........................614 294-1600
Mark A Witchey, *President*
Nick T Kalogeras, *Vice Pres*
Jack A Witchey, *Vice Pres*
EMP: 113 EST: 1976
SQ FT: 15,000
SALES (est): 19.5MM **Privately Held**
SIC: 5047 5912 Surgical equipment & supplies; drug stores

(G-19244)
COMMUNICATIONS III INC (PA)
921 Eastwind Dr Ste 104 (43081-5316)
PHONE...........................614 901-7720
Scott Halliday, *President*
Hugh Cathey, *Chairman*
Peter Halliday, *Shareholder*
Steve Vogelmeier, *Admin Sec*
EMP: 27
SQ FT: 12,000
SALES (est): 7.5MM **Privately Held**
WEB: www.comiii.com
SIC: 5065 8748 Communication equipment; telecommunications consultant

(G-19245)
CONCORD
Also Called: CONCORD COUNSELING SERVICES
700 Brooksedge Blvd (43081-2820)
PHONE...........................614 882-9338
Mary Sommer, *Exec Dir*
Neil Edgar, *Director*
EMP: 50
SQ FT: 4,300

SALES: 5.9MM **Privately Held**
SIC: **8399** 8322 Health & welfare council; individual & family services

(G-19246)
CONTINUUM INC
Also Called: Automated Transaction MGT
142 Wetherby Ln (43081-4957)
PHONE...................................614 891-9200
Bud Phillips, *President*
EMP: 25
SALES (est): 2MM **Privately Held**
SIC: **7359** 5044 Electronic equipment rental, except computers; bank automatic teller machines

(G-19247)
CORNA KOKOSING CONSTRUCTION CO
6235 Westerville Rd (43081-4041)
PHONE...................................614 901-8844
Mark Corna, *President*
Jim Negron, *Exec VP*
Josh Corna, *Senior VP*
James Graves, *Treasurer*
▲ EMP: 200 EST: 1995
SQ FT: 23,000
SALES (est): 101MM **Privately Held**
WEB: www.corna.com
SIC: **1541** 1542 Industrial buildings & warehouses; nonresidential construction

(G-19248)
DELIASS ASSETS CORP
780 Brooksedge Plaza Dr (43081-4914)
P.O. Box 6143 (43086-6143)
PHONE...................................614 891-0101
EMP: 75
SALES (corp-wide): 136.6MM **Publicly Held**
SIC: **4813** Customer Communciation Service
HQ: Delias's Assets Corp
50 W 23rd St Rear 10
New York NY
212 807-9060

(G-19249)
DIVERSIFIED SYSTEMS INC
100 Dorchester Sq N # 103 (43081-7305)
PHONE...................................614 476-9939
Archie D Williamson Jr, *President*
Nathan Paige, *Managing Prtnr*
Mike Beard, *Exec VP*
Kristina Mallorca, *Manager*
Will Thomas, *Manager*
EMP: 35
SQ FT: 3,000
SALES: 12.9MM **Privately Held**
WEB: www.diversifiedsystems.com
SIC: **7379** 8742 7371 Data processing consultant; management consulting services; computer software systems analysis & design, custom

(G-19250)
DOME DIALYSIS LLC
Also Called: Park Side Dialysis
241 W Schrock Rd (43081-2874)
PHONE...................................614 882-1734
Jim Hilger, *Principal*
EMP: 39 EST: 2011
SALES: 548.5K **Publicly Held**
SIC: **8092** Kidney dialysis centers
PA: Davita Inc.
2000 16th St
Denver CO 80202

(G-19251)
EATON PLUMBING INC
Also Called: Plumbing Contractor
5600 E Walnut St (43081-8229)
PHONE...................................614 891-7005
John F Eaton, *President*
Max Eaton, *Vice Pres*
EMP: 36 EST: 1974
SQ FT: 3,200
SALES (est): 5.3MM **Privately Held**
WEB: www.eatonplumbing.com
SIC: **1711** Plumbing contractors

(G-19252)
ELECTRIC CONNECTION INC
5441 Westerville Rd (43081-8940)
PHONE...................................614 436-1121
Judson G Voorhees, *President*

Randy L Harmon, *Vice Pres*
Chad Moore, *Financial Exec*
EMP: 100
SQ FT: 7,000
SALES (est): 13MM **Privately Held**
SIC: **1731** General electrical contractor

(G-19253)
EXEL N AMERCN LOGISTICS INC (DH)
570 Players Pkwy (43081)
PHONE...................................800 272-1052
Randy Briggs, *President*
Hugh Evans, *Vice Pres*
EMP: 125
SQ FT: 100,000
SALES (est): 100.4MM
SALES (corp-wide): 70.4B **Privately Held**
SIC: **4731** Freight forwarding

(G-19254)
FAMILY PHYSICIAN ASSOCIATES
291 W Schrock Rd (43081-2895)
PHONE...................................614 901-2273
Jeffrey Hunter, *President*
John E Verhoff MD, *President*
Mary J Welker MD, *Vice Pres*
EMP: 41
SQ FT: 2,500
SALES (est): 761.7K **Privately Held**
SIC: **8011** General & family practice, physician/surgeon

(G-19255)
FEDEX OFFICE & PRINT SVCS INC
604 W Schrock Rd (43081-8996)
PHONE...................................614 898-0000
EMP: 40
SALES (corp-wide): 65.4B **Publicly Held**
WEB: www.kinkos.com
SIC: **7334** 2759 2396 Photocopying & duplicating services; commercial printing; automotive & apparel trimmings
HQ: Fedex Office And Print Services, Inc.
7900 Legacy Dr
Plano TX 75024
800 463-3339

(G-19256)
FIDELITY NATIONAL FINCL INC
4111 Executive Pkwy # 304 (43081-3869)
PHONE...................................614 865-1562
Mark Sinkhorn, *General Mgr*
EMP: 25
SALES (corp-wide): 7.5B **Publicly Held**
SIC: **6361** Real estate title insurance
PA: Fidelity National Financial, Inc.
601 Riverside Ave Fl 4
Jacksonville FL 32204
904 854-8100

(G-19257)
GANNETT FLEMING INC
Also Called: Gannet Fleming Engr & Archt
4151 Executive Pkwy # 350 (43081-3863)
PHONE...................................614 794-9424
Joseph Rikk, *Branch Mgr*
Raychelle Staron, *Regional*
EMP: 32
SALES (corp-wide): 423.5MM **Privately Held**
WEB: www.gfnet.com
SIC: **8711** Consulting engineer
HQ: Fleming Gannett Inc
207 Senate Ave
Camp Hill PA 17011
717 763-7211

(G-19258)
HALLEY CONSULTING GROUP LLC
1224 Oak Bluff Ct (43081-3222)
P.O. Box 118 (43086-0118)
PHONE...................................614 899-7325
Marc D Halley, *CEO*
Michael J Ferry, *President*
Jennifer Snider, *Vice Pres*
Karen Bridges, *CFO*
EMP: 25
SALES: 6MM **Privately Held**
SIC: **8748** 8742 Business consulting; management consulting services; marketing consulting services

(G-19259)
HARRINGTON HEALTH SERVICES INC (DH)
Also Called: Fiserv Health
780 Brooksedge Plaza Dr (43081-4914)
PHONE...................................614 212-7000
Jeff Mills, *President*
Terry Moore, *CFO*
EMP: 130 EST: 2000
SQ FT: 24,000
SALES (est): 116.5MM
SALES (corp-wide): 226.2B **Publicly Held**
WEB: www.harringtonbenefits.com
SIC: **6411** Insurance claim processing, except medical
HQ: Umr, Inc.
11 Scott St
Wausau WI 54403
800 826-9781

(G-19260)
HCR MANORCARE MED SVCS FLA LLC
Also Called: Manorcare Hlth Svcs Wsterville
140 Old County Line Rd (43081-1002)
PHONE...................................614 882-1511
Cara Aranette, *Director*
EMP: 160
SALES (corp-wide): 2.4B **Publicly Held**
WEB: www.manorcare.com
SIC: **8051** 8069 Convalescent home with continuous nursing care; specialty hospitals, except psychiatric
HQ: Hcr Manorcare Medical Services Of Florida, Llc
333 N Summit St Ste 100
Toledo OH 43604
419 252-5500

(G-19261)
HEALTH CARE RTREMENT CORP AMER
Also Called: Village At Wstrvlle Retiremnt
215 Huber Village Blvd (43081-3339)
PHONE...................................614 882-3782
Beverly Cabb, *Manager*
EMP: 75
SQ FT: 59,241
SALES (corp-wide): 2.4B **Publicly Held**
WEB: www.hrc-manorcare.com
SIC: **8051** Convalescent home with continuous nursing care
HQ: Health Care And Retirement Corporation Of America
333 N Summit St Ste 103
Toledo OH 43604
419 252-5500

(G-19262)
HEALTHSCOPE BENEFITS INC
5150 E Dublin Granvll 3 (43081-8701)
PHONE...................................614 797-5200
Dave Tague, *Branch Mgr*
Melvin Cox, *Director*
EMP: 38 **Privately Held**
WEB: www.healthscopebenefits.com
SIC: **8741** Hospital management; nursing & personal care facility management
PA: Healthscope Benefits, Inc.
27 Corporate Hill Dr
Little Rock AR 72205

(G-19263)
IBI GROUP ENGRG SVCS USA INC (HQ)
Also Called: M-E Companies, Inc.
635 Brooksedge Blvd (43081-2817)
PHONE...................................614 818-4900
Tim Foley, *CEO*
EMP: 65
SALES (est): 20MM
SALES (corp-wide): 283.1MM **Privately Held**
SIC: **6799** 8711 Real estate investors, except property operators; consulting engineer
PA: Ibi Group Inc
55 St Clair Ave W Suite 700
Toronto ON M4V 2
416 596-1930

(G-19264)
IFS FINANCIAL SERVICES INC (DH)
370 S Cleveland Ave (43081-8917)
PHONE...................................513 362-8000
Jill T McGruder, *President*
Mark E Caner, *President*
EMP: 35
SQ FT: 2,000
SALES (est): 23.9MM **Privately Held**
SIC: **6211** 6282 Security brokers & dealers; investment advice
HQ: The Western & Southern Life Insurance Company
400 Broadway St
Cincinnati OH 45202
513 629-1800

(G-19265)
IMMEDIATE HEALTH ASSOCIATES
Also Called: Wedgewood Urgent Care
575 Cpland Mill Rd Ste 1d (43081)
PHONE...................................614 794-0481
Frank Orth Do, *President*
Edward Boudreau Do, *Vice Pres*
Patricia Robitaille, *Vice Pres*
EMP: 30
SALES (est): 6.1MM **Privately Held**
WEB: www.ihainc.org
SIC: **8011** Freestanding emergency medical center

(G-19266)
JOHNSON CONTROLS INC
835 Green Crest Dr (43081-2838)
PHONE...................................614 895-6600
Stephen Carter, *Branch Mgr*
EMP: 72 **Privately Held**
SIC: **1711** Heating & air conditioning contractors
HQ: Johnson Controls, Inc.
5757 N Green Bay Ave
Milwaukee WI 53209
414 524-1200

(G-19267)
JPMORGAN CHASE BANK NAT ASSN
275 W Schrock Rd (43081-2874)
P.O. Box 711038, Columbus (43271-0001)
PHONE...................................614 248-5800
Jim Merriman, *Manager*
EMP: 65
SALES (corp-wide): 131.4B **Publicly Held**
WEB: www.chase.com
SIC: **6021** National commercial banks
HQ: Jpmorgan Chase Bank, National Association
1111 Polaris Pkwy
Columbus OH 43240
614 436-3055

(G-19268)
JPMORGAN CHASE BANK NAT ASSN
713 Brooksedge Plaza Dr (43081-4913)
PHONE...................................614 248-7505
Jeff Benton, *Branch Mgr*
EMP: 26
SALES (corp-wide): 131.4B **Publicly Held**
WEB: www.chase.com
SIC: **6021** National commercial banks
HQ: Jpmorgan Chase Bank, National Association
1111 Polaris Pkwy
Columbus OH 43240
614 436-3055

(G-19269)
JPMORGAN CHASE BANK NAT ASSN
800 Brooksedge Blvd (43081-2822)
PHONE...................................614 248-5800
Amy Gorski, *Vice Pres*
Randy Lightbpdy, *Manager*
EMP: 250
SALES (corp-wide): 131.4B **Publicly Held**
WEB: www.chase.com
SIC: **6021** National commercial banks

HQ: Jpmorgan Chase Bank, National Association
1111 Polaris Pkwy
Columbus OH 43240
614 436-3055

(G-19270)
KOKOSING CONSTRUCTION CO INC (HQ)
6235 Westerville Rd (43081-4041)
P.O. Box 226, Fredericktown (43019-0226)
PHONE.................................614 228-1029
W Barth Burgett, *CEO*
Marsha Rinehart, *Exec VP*
Daniel J Compston, *Senior VP*
Daniel Walker, *Senior VP*
Timothy Freed, *CFO*
▲ EMP: 200
SALES (est): 449.1MM
SALES (corp-wide): 632.8MM **Privately Held**
WEB: www.kokosing-inc.com
SIC: 1611 1622 1629 1542 General contractor, highway & street construction; highway & street paving contractor; bridge construction; waste water & sewage treatment plant construction; commercial & office building, new construction; industrial buildings, new construction; renovation, remodeling & repairs; industrial buildings; sewer line construction; water main construction
PA: Kokosing Inc.
6235 Wstrville Rd Ste 200
Westerville OH 43081
614 212-5700

(G-19271)
KOKOSING CONSTRUCTION CO INC
6235 Westerville Rd (43081-4041)
PHONE.................................614 228-1029
Mike Helbing, *Manager*
EMP: 25
SQ FT: 2,527
SALES (corp-wide): 632.8MM **Privately Held**
WEB: www.kokosing-inc.com
SIC: 1611 1622 General contractor, highway & street construction; bridge, tunnel & elevated highway
HQ: Kokosing Construction Company, Inc.
6235 Westerville Rd
Westerville OH 43081
614 228-1029

(G-19272)
KOKOSING INC (PA)
6235 Wstrville Rd Ste 200 (43081)
PHONE.................................614 212-5700
Dan Compston, *President*
William B Burgett, *Principal*
Tom Muraski, *Principal*
Dan Walker, *Principal*
Marsha Rianhart, *Admin Sec*
EMP: 100
SALES (est): 632.8MM **Privately Held**
SIC: 1611 General contractor, highway & street construction; highway & street paving contractor

(G-19273)
KOKOSING INDUSTRIAL INC (HQ)
6235 Westerville Rd (43081-4041)
PHONE.................................614 212-5700
W Brian Burgett, *CEO*
EMP: 400
SALES (est): 47.2MM
SALES (corp-wide): 632.8MM **Privately Held**
SIC: 1623 1629 Water, sewer & utility lines; dams, waterways, docks & other marine construction
PA: Kokosing Inc.
6235 Wstrville Rd Ste 200
Westerville OH 43081
614 212-5700

(G-19274)
KROGER CO
4111 Executive Pkwy # 100 (43081-3800)
PHONE.................................614 898-3200
Merritt Henderson, *Manager*
EMP: 300
SQ FT: 27,252

SALES (corp-wide): 121.1B **Publicly Held**
WEB: www.kroger.com
SIC: 5411 5122 Supermarkets, chain; pharmaceuticals
PA: The Kroger Co
1014 Vine St Ste 1000
Cincinnati OH 45202
513 762-4000

(G-19275)
LOS ALAMOS TECHNICAL ASSOC INC
Also Called: Lata
756 Park Meadow Rd (43081-2871)
PHONE.................................614 508-1200
Rob Pfendler, *Branch Mgr*
Dean Gehlhausen, *Technology*
EMP: 30
SALES (corp-wide): 40.1MM **Privately Held**
SIC: 8711 4959 Industrial engineers; environmental cleanup services
PA: Los Alamos Technical Associates, Inc.
6501 Americas Pkwy Ne # 200
Albuquerque NM 87110
505 884-3800

(G-19276)
LUTHERAN OUTDR MINISTRIES OH (PA)
863 Eastwind Dr (43081-3309)
PHONE.................................614 890-2267
Penny Christensen, *Exec Dir*
EMP: 38
SALES (est): 1.4MM **Privately Held**
WEB: www.lomocamps.org
SIC: 7032 Sporting & recreational camps

(G-19277)
M CONSULTANTS LLC
Also Called: M-Engineering
750 Brooksedge Blvd (43081-2820)
PHONE.................................614 839-4639
Katie Evans, *Engineer*
Matt Garee, *Electrical Engi*
Harry Jacobs, *Electrical Engi*
David Gonzalez,
Monique Davis, *Executive Asst*
EMP: 57
SALES (est): 6.8MM **Privately Held**
SIC: 8711 Consulting engineer

(G-19278)
M RETAIL ENGINEERING INC
750 Brooksedge Blvd (43081-2820)
PHONE.................................614 818-2323
Dan Gilmore, *President*
Dave Gonzollaz, *President*
David Gonzalez, *Vice Pres*
Ron Koons, *Vice Pres*
Shigeyoshi A Mori, *Vice Pres*
EMP: 45
SQ FT: 10,000
SALES (est): 2.8MM **Privately Held**
SIC: 8711 Consulting engineer

(G-19279)
MICRO INDUSTRIES CORPORATION (PA)
8399 Green Meadows Dr N (43081)
PHONE.................................740 548-7878
John Curran, *CEO*
Michael Curran, *President*
Amanda Curran, *Vice Pres*
William Jackson, *Vice Pres*
EMP: 67
SQ FT: 52,000
SALES (est): 11.9MM **Privately Held**
WEB: www.microindustries.com
SIC: 8711 3674 Engineering services; semiconductor circuit networks; microcircuits, integrated (semiconductor)

(G-19280)
MID-OHIO PDIATRICS ADOLESCENTS
595 Cpland Mill Rd Ste 2a (43081)
PHONE.................................614 899-0000
Richard Anthony Petrella, *President*
EMP: 31
SQ FT: 5,200
SALES (est): 4.8MM **Privately Held**
SIC: 8011 Pediatrician

(G-19281)
MODERN OFFICE METHODS INC
929 Eastwind Dr Ste 220 (43081-3362)
PHONE.................................614 891-3693
Dan Vail, *Vice Pres*
Dale Schwartzmiller, *Manager*
EMP: 40
SALES (corp-wide): 27.8MM **Privately Held**
WEB: www.momnet.com
SIC: 5999 7629 Business machines & equipment; business machine repair, electric
PA: Modern Office Methods, Inc.
4747 Lake Forest Dr # 200
Blue Ash OH 45242
513 791-0909

(G-19282)
MOUNT CARMEL CENTRAL OHIO
955 Eastwind Dr Ste B (43081-3376)
PHONE.................................614 268-9561
David Yashon MD, *President*
EMP: 52
SALES (est): 4.1MM **Privately Held**
SIC: 8011 Surgeon

(G-19283)
MOUNT CARMEL HEALTH
Also Called: Mount Carmel Home Care
501 W Schrock Rd Ste 350 (43081-7155)
PHONE.................................614 234-0100
Erin Denholm, *CEO*
Cindy Salvator, *Director*
EMP: 80
SALES (corp-wide): 18.3B **Privately Held**
SIC: 8062 General medical & surgical hospitals
HQ: Mount Carmel Health
793 W State St
Columbus OH 43222
614 234-5000

(G-19284)
NATIONAL GROUND WATER ASSN INC
Also Called: Ngwa
601 Dempsey Rd (43081-8978)
PHONE.................................614 898-7791
Kevin B McCray, *CEO*
Richard Thron, *President*
Jeffrey Williams, *Vice Pres*
Paul Humes, *CFO*
Mark Mohanna, *Sales Staff*
EMP: 34
SQ FT: 13,600
SALES: 5.4MM **Privately Held**
WEB: www.ngwa.org
SIC: 8611 Trade associations

(G-19285)
NEW RIVER ELECTRICAL CORP
6005 Westerville Rd (43081-4055)
PHONE.................................614 891-1142
Tom Wolden, *Manager*
EMP: 25
SALES (corp-wide): 293.1MM **Privately Held**
WEB: www.newriverelectrical.com
SIC: 1731 General electrical contractor
PA: New River Electrical Corporation
15 Cloverdale Pl
Cloverdale VA 24077
540 966-1650

(G-19286)
OFFICEMAX NORTH AMERICA INC
87 Huber Village Blvd (43081-3311)
PHONE.................................614 899-6186
Ron Pierce, *Manager*
EMP: 26
SALES (corp-wide): 11B **Publicly Held**
WEB: www.copymax.net
SIC: 7641 5943 Reupholstery & furniture repair; office forms & supplies
HQ: Officemax North America, Inc.
263 Shuman Blvd
Naperville IL 60563
630 717-0791

(G-19287)
OHIO LBRERS FRNGE BNEFT PRGRAM
800 Hillsdowne Rd (43081-3302)
PHONE.................................614 898-9006
Mathew Archer, *President*
Denise Sikes, *Benefits Mgr*
Matt Archer, *Admin Mgr*
Michael Ossing, *Technology*
EMP: 30
SALES: 8.2MM **Privately Held**
WEB: www.olfbp.com
SIC: 8631 Labor union

(G-19288)
OPTIMUM SYSTEM PRODUCTS INC (PA)
Also Called: Optimum Graphics
921 Eastwind Dr Ste 133 (43081-3363)
PHONE.................................614 885-4464
John Martin, *CEO*
Dorothy Martin, *President*
EMP: 40
SQ FT: 75,000
SALES (est): 10.5MM **Privately Held**
WEB: www.optimumsystem.com
SIC: 2752 5112 Business form & card printing, lithographic; business forms

(G-19289)
ORTHONEURO (PA)
Also Called: Ortho Neuro
70 S Cleveland Ave (43081-1397)
PHONE.................................614 890-6555
Francis O Donnell, *President*
Patti Jasin, *Purch Mgr*
Rachel Conwell, *Human Res Mgr*
Tina Carmos, *Hum Res Coord*
Ying Chen, *Med Doctor*
EMP: 30
SQ FT: 20,000
SALES (est): 21.2MM **Privately Held**
SIC: 8011 Orthopedic physician; neurologist; neurosurgeon

(G-19290)
OURDAY AT MESSIAH PRESCHOOL
51 N State St (43081-2123)
PHONE.................................614 882-4416
Charity Monroe, *Exec Dir*
EMP: 32 EST: 1979
SALES (est): 502.7K **Privately Held**
SIC: 8351 Preschool center

(G-19291)
PATROL URBAN SERVICES LLC
4563 E Walnut St (43081-9693)
PHONE.................................614 620-4672
Robert S Urban, *President*
EMP: 35
SALES: 1.3MM **Privately Held**
SIC: 7381 Security guard service; private investigator

(G-19292)
PERCEPTIONIST INC
178 W Schrock Rd Ste C (43081-2973)
PHONE.................................614 384-7500
Tiger Downey, *President*
Scott Mackenzie, *Shareholder*
EMP: 26
SQ FT: 3,000
SALES: 1.4MM **Privately Held**
SIC: 7389 Telephone answering service

(G-19293)
PORTER DRYWALL INC
297 Old County Line Rd (43081-1602)
P.O. Box 550 (43086-0550)
PHONE.................................614 890-2111
Robert E Porter, *President*
EMP: 100 EST: 1969
SQ FT: 10,000
SALES (est): 7.5MM **Privately Held**
WEB: www.porterdrywall.com
SIC: 1742 Drywall

(G-19294)
PRESCRIPTION HOPE INC
253 N State St Ste 250 (43081-1585)
P.O. Box 2700 (43086-2700)
PHONE.................................877 296-4673
Douglas K Pierce, *President*
Bryan Hildreth, *COO*

Sarah Hildreth, *Director*
EMP: 30 **EST:** 2006
SALES (est): 324.4K **Privately Held**
SIC: 8399 Advocacy group

(G-19295)
PTA OH CONG MCVAY ELEM PTA
270 S Hempstead Rd (43081-2714)
PHONE..............................614 797-7230
Amy Miller, *Principal*
EMP: 80
SALES (est): 832.4K **Privately Held**
SIC: 8641 Parent-teachers' association

(G-19296)
QUADAX INC
4151 Executive Pkwy # 360 (43081-3820)
PHONE..............................614 882-1200
Fax: 614 882-7133
EMP: 25
SALES (corp-wide): 26MM **Privately Held**
SIC: 8721 7374 Accounting, Auditing, And Bookkeeping
PA: Quadax, Inc.
7500 Old Oak Blvd
Middleburg Heights OH 44130
216 765-1144

(G-19297)
QUANDEL CONSTRUCTION GROUP INC
Also Called: Quandel Group Main Office
774 Park Meadow Rd (43081-2871)
PHONE..............................717 657-0909
Richard Krisch, *Project Mgr*
Roland Tokarski, *Manager*
EMP: 50
SALES (corp-wide): 161.1MM **Privately Held**
WEB: www.quandel-ohio.com
SIC: 1542 8741 Commercial & office building contractors; institutional building construction; construction management
HQ: The Quandel Construction Group Inc
3003 N Front St Ste 203
Harrisburg PA 17110
717 657-0909

(G-19298)
RAISIN RACK INC (PA)
Also Called: Raisin Rack Natural Food Mkt
2545 W Schrock Rd (43081-8956)
PHONE..............................614 882-5886
Toll Free:............................888 -
Donald L Caster, *President*
Matt Patchin, *Opers Mgr*
Bill Kerekes, *Buyer*
John Marulli, *VP Mktg*
Jan Sehlmeyer, *Manager*
EMP: 42
SQ FT: 6,500
SALES (est): 3.6MM **Privately Held**
WEB: www.wholesomelife.com
SIC: 5499 5122 Health foods; vitamins & minerals

(G-19299)
ROMANELLI & HUGHES BUILDING CO
Also Called: Romanelli & Hughes Contractors
148 W Schrock Rd (43081-4915)
PHONE..............................614 891-2042
David Hughes, *President*
Darrel R Miller, *Corp Secy*
Vincent Romanelli, *Vice Pres*
EMP: 42
SQ FT: 5,000
SALES (est): 7.4MM **Privately Held**
WEB: www.rh-homes.com
SIC: 1521 1542 New construction, single-family houses; commercial & office building, new construction

(G-19300)
ROUSH EQUIPMENT INC (PA)
Also Called: Roush Honda
100 W Schrock Rd (43081-2832)
PHONE..............................614 882-1535
Jeffrey A Brindley, *President*
Karen Matthews, *General Mgr*
Brian Kadlec, *Parts Mgr*
Kandy Lazarrus, *Purchasing*
Mark Vanbenschoten, *CFO*

EMP: 129
SQ FT: 16,000
SALES (est): 58.9MM **Privately Held**
WEB: www.roushhonda.com
SIC: 5511 7538 7532 7515 Automobiles, new & used; general automotive repair shops; top & body repair & paint shops; passenger car leasing; truck rental & leasing, no drivers; used car dealers

(G-19301)
THOMAS ROSSER
Also Called: Financial Perspective Company
855 S Sunbury Rd (43081-9553)
PHONE..............................614 890-2900
Thomas Rosser, *Owner*
EMP: 125
SQ FT: 1,000
SALES (est): 4.6MM **Privately Held**
SIC: 8741 8721 Management Services Accounting/Auditing/Bookkeeping

(G-19302)
THYSSENKRUPP ELEVATOR CORP
929 Eastwind Dr Ste 218 (43081-3362)
PHONE..............................614 895-8930
Glen Steel, *Commissioner*
EMP: 50
SALES (corp-wide): 39.8B **Privately Held**
WEB: www.tyssenkrupp.com
SIC: 1796 7699 5084 Elevator installation & conversion; elevators: inspection, service & repair; elevators
HQ: Thyssenkrupp Elevator Corporation
11605 Haynes Bridge Rd # 650
Alpharetta GA 30009
678 319-3240

(G-19303)
TURTLE GOLF MANAGEMENT LTD (HQ)
Also Called: Little Turtle Golf Club
5400 Little Turtle Way W (43081-7821)
PHONE..............................614 882-5920
Garth Walker,
Michael Hill,
EMP: 26
SQ FT: 23,000
SALES (est): 2.4MM **Privately Held**
SIC: 8742 7997 General management consultant; country club, membership

(G-19304)
UNITED STATES TROTTING ASSN (PA)
6130 S Sunbury Rd (43081-9309)
PHONE..............................614 224-2291
Michael Panner, *CEO*
Dan Leary, *Marketing Staff*
Sherry Antion-Mohr, *Info Tech Dir*
Tc Lane, *Director*
Kathy Burlingame,
EMP: 60
SQ FT: 20,000
SALES: 7.9MM **Privately Held**
WEB: www.ustrotting.com
SIC: 8611 Trade associations

(G-19305)
WESTERVILLE DERMATOLOGY INC
235 W Schrock Rd (43081-2874)
PHONE..............................614 895-0400
Kevin B Karikomi Do, *President*
Joyce Miller, *Manager*
EMP: 25
SQ FT: 1,882
SALES (est): 1.7MM **Privately Held**
WEB: www.westervilledermatology.com
SIC: 8011 Dermatologist

(G-19306)
WESTERVILLE-WORTHINGTON LEARNI
149 Charring Cross Dr S (43081-2860)
PHONE..............................614 891-4105
Debra Jennings, *Owner*
EMP: 30
SALES (est): 378.1K **Privately Held**
SIC: 8351 Child day care services

Westfield Center
Medina County

(G-19307)
AMERICAN SELECT INSURANCE CO
1 Park Cir (44251-9700)
P.O. Box 5001 (44251-5001)
PHONE..............................330 887-0101
Robert Kiraty, *Treasurer*
Wayne Hartzler, *Info Tech Mgr*
EMP: 1500 **EST:** 1850
SQ FT: 100,000
SALES (est): 234.4MM
SALES (corp-wide): 1.7B **Privately Held**
WEB: www.westfieldgrp.com
SIC: 6331 Fire, marine & casualty insurance
PA: Ohio Farmers Insurance Company
1 Park Cir
Westfield Center OH 44251
800 243-0210

(G-19308)
OHIO FARMERS INSURANCE COMPANY (PA)
Also Called: Westfield Group
1 Park Cir (44251-9700)
P.O. Box 5001 (44251-5001)
PHONE..............................800 243-0210
Edward J Largent III, *CEO*
Ed Largent, *President*
Connie Frey, *Division Mgr*
Alex Mosyjowski, *General Mgr*
Rick Poling, *General Mgr*
EMP: 1753
SQ FT: 200,000
SALES (est): 1.7B **Privately Held**
WEB: www.westfieldgrp.com
SIC: 6411 6331 Property & casualty insurance agent; fire, marine & casualty insurance

(G-19309)
WESTFIELD BANK FSB (HQ)
2 Park Cir (44251-9744)
P.O. Box 5002 (44251-5002)
PHONE..............................800 368-8930
Jon Park, *CEO*
Timothy E Phillips, *President*
Gary Clark, *COO*
Michael Toth, *Exec VP*
Kurt Kappa, *Vice Pres*
EMP: 40
SALES: 56.9MM **Privately Held**
SIC: 6029 Commercial banks

Westlake
Cuyahoga County

(G-19310)
ACHIEVEMENT CTRS FOR CHILDREN
24211 Center Ridge Rd (44145-4211)
PHONE..............................440 250-2520
Scott Peplin, *Manager*
EMP: 30
SALES (corp-wide): 10MM **Privately Held**
WEB: www.achievementcenters.org
SIC: 8322 Individual & family services
PA: Achievement Centers For Children
4255 Northfield Rd
Cleveland OH 44128
216 292-9700

(G-19311)
ADVANCED TRANSLATION/CNSLTNG
Also Called: Spanish Portugese Translation
3751 Willow Run (44145-5720)
PHONE..............................440 716-0820
Hugo R Urizar, *Owner*
EMP: 30
SALES (est): 1.4MM **Privately Held**
SIC: 7389 2791 Translation services; typesetting

(G-19312)
ALL METAL SALES INC
29260 Clemens Rd Ste 3 (44145-1020)
PHONE..............................440 617-1234
Thomas Klocker, *President*
Alison Klocker, *Vice Pres*
Steve Scalf, *Opers Mgr*
Ryan Fowler, *Engineer*
Jim Vandevelde, *Sales Staff*
▲ **EMP:** 26
SQ FT: 69,000
SALES (est): 20MM **Privately Held**
WEB: www.allmetalsalesinc.com
SIC: 5051 Ferrous metals; nonferrous metal sheets, bars, rods, etc.

(G-19313)
ALL PRO FREIGHT SYSTEMS INC (PA)
1006 Crocker Rd (44145-1031)
PHONE..............................440 934-2222
Chris Haas, *President*
Matt Demyan, *Vice Pres*
Ken Gruman, *Vice Pres*
Matt Seedhouse, *VP Opers*
James Pozone, *Opers Staff*
EMP: 80
SQ FT: 109,000
SALES (est): 30.9MM **Privately Held**
WEB: www.allprofreight.com
SIC: 4214 4225 4213 Local trucking with storage; general warehousing; trucking, except local; contract haulers

(G-19314)
ALLIED ENTERPRISES INC (PA)
26021 Center Ridge Rd (44145-4013)
PHONE..............................440 808-8760
Eric Pfaff, *President*
Mark Pfaff, *Vice Pres*
Dennis Williams, *Sales Staff*
▲ **EMP:** 25 **EST:** 1954
SALES (est): 6.9MM **Privately Held**
WEB: www.alliedenterprisesinc.com
SIC: 5065 Electronic parts

(G-19315)
ALTA PARTNERS LLC
902 Westpoint Pkwy # 320 (44145-1534)
PHONE..............................440 808-3654
Ann Hanzel, *Opers Staff*
Jennifer Peregord, *Finance Mgr*
Jennifer Dalton, *Senior Mgr*
Mike Michelakis, *Info Tech Dir*
Dan Kasinc,
EMP: 30
SALES (est): 3.3MM **Privately Held**
WEB: www.altapartnersllc.com
SIC: 8011 General & family practice, physician/surgeon

(G-19316)
ALUMINUM LINE PRODUCTS COMPANY (PA)
Also Called: Alpco
24460 Sperry Cir (44145-1591)
PHONE..............................440 835-8880
Edward Murray, *Principal*
Chris Harrington, *Vice Pres*
Richard Daniel, *CFO*
Wendy L Wilson-Kieding, *Treasurer*
▲ **EMP:** 100 **EST:** 1960
SQ FT: 100,000
SALES: 100MM **Privately Held**
WEB: www.aluminumline.com
SIC: 5051 3365 3999 Metals service centers & offices; aluminum foundries; barber & beauty shop equipment

(G-19317)
APPLIED MARKETING SERVICES (HQ)
Also Called: Medical & Home Health
28825 Ranney Pkwy (44145-1173)
PHONE..............................440 716-9962
David J Marquard II, *President*
Sandi Kinley, *Purch Agent*
C V Guggenviller, *CFO*
Cathy Marquard, *Controller*
Jane Binzer, *Sales Staff*
▲ **EMP:** 28
SQ FT: 20,000

GEOGRAPHIC

SALES (est): 5.8MM **Privately Held**
WEB: www.applied-inc.com
SIC: 3569 8742 Gas producers, generators & other gas related equipment; marketing consulting services; new products & services consultants
PA: Oxygo Hq Florida Llc
7380 W Sand Lake Rd # 500
Orlando FL 32819
440 716-9962

(G-19318)
ARDMORE POWER LOGISTICS LLC
Also Called: Ardmore Logistics
24610 Detroit Rd Ste 1200 (44145-2561)
PHONE..................................216 502-0640
David Cottenden, *Chairman*
Scott Dolan, *Opers Mgr*
Debbie Suhy, *Human Res Mgr*
Greg Giuliano, *Accounts Mgr*
Jason Gus, *Manager*
EMP: 29
SQ FT: 6,000
SALES (est): 7.9MM **Privately Held**
WEB: www.ardmorelogistics.com
SIC: 8742 4731 Transportation consultant; domestic freight forwarding

(G-19319)
ASSOCIATES IN DERMATOLOGY INC (PA)
26908 Detroit Rd Ste 103 (44145-2399)
PHONE..................................440 249-0274
Paul G Hazen, *President*
John Jay Stewart, *Assistant VP*
Conley W Engstrom, *Vice Pres*
Karen Turgeon, *Treasurer*
Paul Hazen, *Dermatology*
EMP: 32
SQ FT: 5,000
SALES (est): 4.8MM **Privately Held**
SIC: 8011 Dermatologist

(G-19320)
BAY FURNACE SHEET METAL CO
Also Called: Bay Heating & Air Conditioning
24530 Sperry Dr (44145-1578)
PHONE..................................440 871-3777
Lynn Robinson, *President*
Cori Robinson, *Treasurer*
Kori Robinson, *Treasurer*
Korie Szabo, *Financial Exec*
Paul Dooney, *Sales Executive*
EMP: 30
SQ FT: 4,800
SALES (est): 3.2MM **Privately Held**
WEB: www.bayfurnace.com
SIC: 1711 Warm air heating & air conditioning contractor

(G-19321)
BAY VILLAGE MONTESSORI INC
Also Called: MONTESSORI CHILDREN SCHOOL
28370 Bassett Rd (44145-3022)
PHONE..................................440 871-8773
Barbara Kincade, *President*
EMP: 30
SQ FT: 1,092
SALES: 1MM **Privately Held**
SIC: 8351 Montessori child development center

(G-19322)
BELLA CAPELLI INC
Also Called: Bella Capelli Salon
24350 Center Ridge Rd (44145-4212)
PHONE..................................440 899-1225
Sandra Borrelli, *President*
Serina Peck, *Vice Pres*
EMP: 30 EST: 1997
SALES (est): 1.3MM **Privately Held**
WEB: www.bellacapelli.com
SIC: 7231 Hairdressers

(G-19323)
BORCHERS AMERICAS INC (HQ)
Also Called: Om Group
811 Sharon Dr (44145-1522)
PHONE..................................440 899-2950
Joseph Scaminace, *CEO*
◆ EMP: 60

SQ FT: 30,000
SALES (est): 41.4MM
SALES (corp-wide): 1.4B **Privately Held**
SIC: 8731 2819 2899 2992 Commercial physical research; industrial inorganic chemicals; chemical preparations; lubricating oils & greases; industrial organic chemicals
PA: The Jordan Company L P
399 Park Ave Fl 30
New York NY 10022
212 572-0800

(G-19324)
BROOKDALE SENIOR LIVING INC
28550 Westlake Village Dr (44145-7608)
PHONE..................................440 892-4200
Jeanne Barnard, *Branch Mgr*
Dellana Kinkopf, *Pathologist*
EMP: 35
SALES (corp-wide): 4.5B **Publicly Held**
SIC: 8059 Nursing home, except skilled & intermediate care facility
PA: Brookdale Senior Living
111 Westwood Pl Ste 400
Brentwood TN 37027
615 221-2250

(G-19325)
BUDGET DUMPSTER LLC (PA)
Also Called: Budget Dumpster Rental
830 Canterbury Rd (44145-1419)
PHONE..................................866 284-6164
John Fenn,
Mark Campbell,
EMP: 31 EST: 2009
SALES (est): 4.6MM **Privately Held**
SIC: 7359 Equipment rental & leasing

(G-19326)
CAREER CNNCTIONS STAFFING SVCS
Also Called: Go 2 It Group
26260 Center Ridge Rd (44145-4016)
PHONE..................................440 471-8210
Beverly Sandvick, *Agent*
EMP: 50
SQ FT: 1,500
SALES (est): 5.6MM **Privately Held**
WEB: www.go2itgroup.com
SIC: 7361 Employment agencies

(G-19327)
CARNEGIE MANAGEMENT & DEV CORP
27500 Detroit Rd Ste 300 (44145-5913)
PHONE..................................440 892-6800
Rustom R Khouri, *CEO*
Steven M Edelman, *COO*
James McKinney, *Vice Pres*
Mary Khouri,
EMP: 30
SQ FT: 17,000
SALES (est): 4.9MM **Privately Held**
SIC: 6512 6552 Commercial & industrial building operation; subdividers & developers

(G-19328)
CD BLOCK K HOTEL LLC
Also Called: Hyatt Place
2020 Crocker Rd (44145-1963)
PHONE..................................440 871-3100
Todd Lentz, *General Mgr*
EMP: 34
SALES (est): 115.4K **Privately Held**
SIC: 7011 Hotels

(G-19329)
CERES ENTERPRISES LLC
Also Called: Hilton
835 Sharon Dr Ste 400 (44145-7704)
PHONE..................................440 617-9385
Kelli Peterson, *Purch Agent*
David Crisafi, *Mng Member*
Frank Crisafi, *Mng Member*
EMP: 55
SALES (est): 1.2MM **Privately Held**
SIC: 7011 Hotels & motels

(G-19330)
CHARLES SCHWAB CORPORATION
2211 Crocker Rd Ste 100 (44145-7603)
PHONE..................................440 617-2301
Karen Barrett, *Manager*
Roger Baranovic, *Manager*
Deborah Brock, *Manager*
EMP: 26
SALES (corp-wide): 10.9B **Publicly Held**
WEB: www.schwab.com
SIC: 6211 Brokers, security
PA: The Charles Schwab Corporation
211 Main St Fl 17
San Francisco CA 94105
415 667-7000

(G-19331)
CHILDRENS FOREVER HAVEN INC
Also Called: Center Ridge House
28700 Center Ridge Rd (44145-5213)
PHONE..................................440 250-9182
Lynne Urbanski, *Director*
Denise Mendiola, *Asst Admin*
EMP: 45
SALES (corp-wide): 96.1K **Privately Held**
SIC: 8052 Home for the mentally retarded, with health care
PA: Childrens Forever Haven Inc
10983 Abbey Rd
North Royalton OH 44133
440 652-6749

(G-19332)
CITY OF WESTLAKE
Also Called: Meadowood Golf Course
29800 Center Ridge Rd (44145-5121)
PHONE..................................440 835-6442
Bret Smith, *Manager*
EMP: 25 **Privately Held**
SIC: 7992 Public golf courses
PA: City Of Westlake
27700 Hilliard Blvd
Cleveland OH 44145
440 871-3300

(G-19333)
CLEVELAND AIRPORT HOSPITALITY
1100 Crocker Rd (44145-1033)
PHONE..................................440 871-6000
Steve Burroughs, *General Mgr*
Tom Hipman, *General Mgr*
EMP: 96
SALES (est): 15.4MM **Publicly Held**
SIC: 7011 5813 5812 Hotels; drinking places; eating places
PA: Wyndham Destinations, Inc.
6277 Sea Harbor Dr
Orlando FL 32821

(G-19334)
CLEVELAND WESTLAKE
29690 Detroit Rd (44145-1934)
PHONE..................................440 892-0333
Gia Polo, *General Mgr*
Tyler Wulf, *Manager*
EMP: 25
SALES (est): 780K **Privately Held**
SIC: 7011 Hotels

(G-19335)
COMCAST SPOTLIGHT
Also Called: Adelphia
27887 Clemens Rd Ste 3 (44145-1181)
PHONE..................................440 617-2280
Michelle Radio, *Manager*
EMP: 50
SALES (corp-wide): 94.5B **Publicly Held**
WEB: www.cablecomcast.com
SIC: 4841 Cable television services
HQ: Comcast Spotlight
55 W 46th St Fl 33
New York NY 10036
212 907-8641

(G-19336)
COMPREHENSIVE PEDIATRICS
2001 Crocker Rd Ste 600 (44145-6972)
PHONE..................................440 835-8270
Cynthia Strieter, *Partner*
Laura Kilbane, *Admin Sec*
EMP: 35

SALES (est): 3.5MM **Privately Held**
WEB: www.comprehensivepediatrics.com
SIC: 8011 Pediatrician

(G-19337)
CORPORATE UNITED INC
24651 Center Ridge Rd # 527 (44145-5674)
PHONE..................................440 895-0938
Gregg Mylett, *CEO*
Doug Blossey, *President*
Christopher Zirke, *President*
Mark Molnar, *CFO*
EMP: 27 EST: 1996
SALES (est): 5.1MM
SALES (corp-wide): 12.6MM **Privately Held**
WEB: www.corporateunited.com
SIC: 7389 Personal service agents, brokers & bureaus
PA: Omnia Partners, Inc.
840 Crescent Centre Dr
Franklin TN 37067
866 875-3299

(G-19338)
COURTYARD BY MARRIOTT
25050 Sperry Dr (44145-1535)
PHONE..................................440 871-3756
David Bragan, *General Mgr*
Al Schreiber, *Principal*
EMP: 31
SALES (est): 1MM **Privately Held**
SIC: 7011 Hotels & motels

(G-19339)
DCT TELECOM GROUP INC
27877 Clemens Rd (44145-1167)
PHONE..................................440 892-0300
Anthony S Romano, *CEO*
Anthony Rehak, *President*
Tony Romano Jr, *CFO*
EMP: 35 EST: 1993
SALES (est): 13MM **Privately Held**
WEB: www.4dct.com
SIC: 4813 ; local & long distance telephone communications; local telephone communications; long distance telephone communications

(G-19340)
FACTS MANAGEMENT COMPANY
Also Called: Private School Aid Service
28446 W Preston Pl (44145-6782)
PHONE..................................440 892-4272
David J Byrnes, *Branch Mgr*
EMP: 50
SALES (corp-wide): 1.7B **Publicly Held**
SIC: 7389 Financial services
HQ: Facts Management Company
121 S 13th St Ste 201
Lincoln NE 68508
402 466-1063

(G-19341)
FAIRVIEW HOSPITAL
850 Columbia Rd Ste 100 (44145-7213)
PHONE..................................440 871-1063
Mary K Kelly, *Manager*
EMP: 100
SALES (corp-wide): 8.9B **Privately Held**
SIC: 8062 General medical & surgical hospitals
HQ: Fairview Hospital
18101 Lorain Ave
Cleveland OH 44111
216 476-7000

(G-19342)
FAR WEST CENTER (PA)
29133 Health Campus Dr (44145-5256)
PHONE..................................440 835-6212
Kelly Dylag, *Director*
Eduardo D Vazquez, *Psychiatry*
EMP: 25
SQ FT: 10,000
SALES: 1.5MM **Privately Held**
WEB: www.farwestcenter.com
SIC: 8322 8399 Family counseling services; health systems agency

▲ = Import ▼=Export
◆ =Import/Export

(G-19343)
FASTENER CORP OF AMERICA INC
1133 Bassett Rd (44145-1193)
PHONE....................................440 835-5100
Rufus Lumbgao, *President*
Harvey Lumchek, *Principal*
Bob Douglas, *Sales Staff*
Sharon Eggert, *Office Admin*
EMP: 25
SQ FT: 12,000
SALES (est): 2.8MM **Privately Held**
WEB: www.fastenercorp.com
SIC: 5072 Miscellaneous fasteners

(G-19344)
GLOBAL TCHNICAL RECRUITERS INC (PA)
27887 Clemens Rd Ste 1 (44145-1181)
PHONE....................................216 251-9560
Patrick T Murphy, *CEO*
Robert J Murphy, *President*
Cory Pallutch, *Manager*
Laura Norman, *Director*
EMP: 36
SALES: 22MM **Privately Held**
SIC: 7361 Executive placement

(G-19345)
GLOBAL TCHNICAL RECRUITERS INC
27887 Clemens Rd Ste 1 (44145-1181)
PHONE....................................440 365-1670
Robert Murphy, *President*
EMP: 58
SALES (corp-wide): 22MM **Privately Held**
SIC: 7361 Executive placement
PA: Global Technical Recruiters Inc.
27887 Clemens Rd Ste 1
Westlake OH 44145
216 251-9560

(G-19346)
GROUND EFFECTS LLC
31000 Viking Pkwy (44145-1019)
PHONE....................................440 565-5925
Jim Scott, *President*
EMP: 50
SALES (corp-wide): 4.4B **Privately Held**
SIC: 7549 Automotive customizing services, non-factory basis
HQ: Ground Effects Llc
3302 Kent St
Flint MI 48503
810 250-5560

(G-19347)
HARBORSIDE CLVELAND LTD PARTNR
Also Called: West Bay Care Rhbilitation Ctr
27601 Westchester Pkwy (44145-1251)
PHONE....................................440 871-5900
Bob Kuhn, *Info Tech Mgr*
Nadine Kodysz, *Director*
EMP: 85 **Publicly Held**
SIC: 8051 Skilled nursing care facilities
HQ: Harborside Of Cleveland Limited Partnership
101 Sun Ave Ne
Albuquerque NM 87109
505 821-3355

(G-19348)
HCR MANORCARE MED SVCS FLA LLC
Also Called: Arden Crts Manorcare Hlth Svcs
28400 Center Ridge Rd (44145-3805)
PHONE....................................440 808-9275
Allison Marrow, *Manager*
EMP: 50
SQ FT: 24,400
SALES (corp-wide): 2.4B **Publicly Held**
WEB: www.manorcare.com
SIC: 8051 Convalescent home with continuous nursing care
HQ: Hcr Manorcare Medical Services Of Florida, Llc
333 N Summit St Ste 100
Toledo OH 43604
419 252-5500

(G-19349)
HEAD MERCANTILE CO INC
29065 Clemens Rd Ste 200 (44145-1179)
PHONE....................................440 847-2700
James Scharfeld, *President*
Steven Scharfeld, *Vice Pres*
EMP: 80 **EST:** 1975
SQ FT: 12,000
SALES (est): 722.3K **Privately Held**
SIC: 7322 Adjustment & collection services

(G-19350)
HMC GROUP INC
29065 Clemens Rd Ste 200 (44145-1179)
PHONE....................................440 847-2720
Leonard B Scharfeld, *President*
Lee Scharfeld, *Corp Secy*
James Scharfeld, *Exec VP*
Steven Scharfeld, *Exec VP*
EMP: 30
SQ FT: 4,100
SALES (est): 4.8MM **Privately Held**
WEB: www.hmcgrp.com
SIC: 7322 Collection agency, except real estate

(G-19351)
HOSPICE OF THE WESTERN RESERVE
30080 Hospice Way (44145-1077)
PHONE....................................440 414-7349
EMP: 32
SALES (corp-wide): 97.5MM **Privately Held**
SIC: 8059 Personal care home, with health care
PA: Hospice Of The Western Reserve, Inc
17876 Saint Clair Ave
Cleveland OH 44110
216 383-2222

(G-19352)
HOWLEY BREAD GROUP LTD (PA)
Also Called: Panera Bread
159 Crocker Park Blvd # 290 (44145-8131)
PHONE....................................440 808-1600
Lee Howley, *President*
Leslie Pakush, *Vice Pres*
Dennis Abbuhl, *CFO*
EMP: 92
SQ FT: 3,500
SALES (est): 28MM **Privately Held**
SIC: 5812 6794 Cafe; franchises, selling or licensing

(G-19353)
HS FINANCIAL GROUP LLC
25651 Detroit Rd Ste 203 (44145-2415)
P.O. Box 451193 (44145-0630)
PHONE....................................440 871-8484
Timothy M Sullivan, *Mng Member*
Ken Wojtach, *Manager*
Sheilah Steiner, *Info Tech Mgr*
Crystal Duplay, *Officer*
EMP: 50
SALES (est): 4.8MM **Privately Held**
SIC: 7322 Collection agency, except real estate

(G-19354)
HUB CITY TERMINALS INC
27476 Detroit Rd Ste 102 (44145-2394)
PHONE....................................440 779-2226
EMP: 51
SALES (corp-wide): 3.6B **Publicly Held**
SIC: 4731 Freight transportation arrangement
HQ: Hub City Terminals, Inc.
2000 Clearwater Dr
Oak Brook IL 60523
630 271-3600

(G-19355)
HYLAND SOFTWARE INC (HQ)
28500 Clemens Rd (44145-1145)
PHONE....................................440 788-5000
Bill Priemer, *CEO*
Christopher J Hyland, *Ch of Bd*
Tom Vongunden, *Editor*
Noreen Kilbane, *Senior VP*
Brenda Kirk, *Senior VP*
EMP: 1800
SQ FT: 150,000

SALES (est): 496.8MM
SALES (corp-wide): 492.6MM **Privately Held**
WEB: www.onbase.com
SIC: 7372 Application computer software
PA: Thoma Cressey Bravo, Inc.
300 N La Salle Dr # 4350
Chicago IL 60654
312 254-3300

(G-19356)
IEWC CORP
1991 Crocker Rd Ste 110 (44145-6970)
PHONE....................................440 835-5601
Jim Wojan, *Branch Mgr*
EMP: 25
SALES (corp-wide): 60.1MM **Privately Held**
WEB: www.iewc.com
SIC: 5063 Electronic wire & cable
HQ: Iewc Corp.
5001 S Towne Dr
New Berlin WI 53151
262 782-2255

(G-19357)
INFINITY HEALTH SERVICES INC (PA)
Also Called: American Home Health Services, 975 Crocker Rd A (44145-1030)
PHONE....................................440 614-0145
Norma Goodman, *President*
EMP: 68
SQ FT: 2,700
SALES (est): 2.5MM **Privately Held**
SIC: 8082 Home health care services

(G-19358)
IRISH ENVY LLC
Also Called: Massage Envy
30307 Detroit Rd (44145-1950)
PHONE....................................440 808-8000
Kevin Flynn, *Mng Member*
Brian Quinn,
EMP: 30
SQ FT: 2,500
SALES (est): 680.5K **Privately Held**
SIC: 7299 Massage parlor

(G-19359)
ITS TRAFFIC SYSTEMS INC
28915 Clemens Rd Ste 200 (44145-1177)
PHONE....................................440 892-4500
Randall Houlas, *President*
Robert Houlas, *Principal*
Lori Spencer, *Opers Staff*
EMP: 57
SQ FT: 10,000
SALES (est): 10.9MM **Privately Held**
WEB: www.itstraffic.com
SIC: 8748 Traffic consultant

(G-19360)
J P FARLEY CORPORATION (PA)
29055 Clemens Rd (44145-1135)
P.O. Box 458022 (44145-8022)
PHONE....................................440 250-4300
James P Farley, *President*
Patricia Hannigan, *Vice Pres*
Mike Farley, *CFO*
EMP: 50
SQ FT: 15,000
SALES (est): 30.7MM **Privately Held**
WEB: www.jpfarley.com
SIC: 6311 6321 6324 Life insurance; accident & health insurance; hospital & medical service plans

(G-19361)
JORDAN KYLI ENTERPRISES INC
Also Called: Jke
24650 Center Ridge Rd (44145-5637)
PHONE....................................216 256-3773
EMP: 25
SALES (est): 560K **Privately Held**
SIC: 7349 Janitorial Services And Cleaning Chemical Distribution

(G-19362)
JTEKT AUTO TENN MORRISTOWN
29570 Clemens Rd (44145-1007)
PHONE....................................440 835-1000
▲ **EMP:** 204

SALES (est): 128.3K
SALES (corp-wide): 13.5B **Privately Held**
SIC: 7538 General Auto Repair
HQ: Jtekt Automotive Tennessee-Morristown, Inc.
5932 Commerce Blvd
Morristown TN 37814
423 585-2544

(G-19363)
KING JAMES GROUP IV LTD
Also Called: Westwat Management
24700 Center Ridge Rd G50 (44145-5636)
PHONE....................................440 250-1851
Lewis Wallner Jr, *Owner*
Bob Lubick, *Partner*
Robert Miller, *Partner*
Lewis E Wallner Sr, *Partner*
EMP: 25
SALES (est): 1.7MM **Privately Held**
WEB: www.kingjameshomes.com
SIC: 6512 Commercial & industrial building operation

(G-19364)
KING JAMES PARK LTD
Also Called: King James Group
24700 Center Ridge Rd G50 (44145-5636)
PHONE....................................440 835-1100
Robert J Lubick, *Partner*
EMP: 50 **EST:** 1975
SQ FT: 5,000
SALES (est): 3.1MM **Privately Held**
WEB: www.kingjamesgroup.com
SIC: 6512 Commercial & industrial building operation

(G-19365)
KNOXBI COMPANY LLC
27500 Detroit Rd (44145-5915)
PHONE....................................440 892-6800
Robert Berryhill,
EMP: 55
SALES: 950K **Privately Held**
SIC: 6531 Real estate agent, commercial

(G-19366)
LAKE ERIE ELECTRIC INC (PA)
25730 1st St (44145-1432)
P.O. Box 450859 (44145-0619)
PHONE....................................440 835-5565
Peter J Corogin, *President*
Linda L Bottegal, *Principal*
Kenneth R Beck, *Senior VP*
Armando Francisco, *Vice Pres*
Steven Warnock, *Vice Pres*
EMP: 65 **EST:** 1952
SQ FT: 15,000
SALES (est): 137.9MM **Privately Held**
SIC: 1731 General electrical contractor

(G-19367)
LAKESIDE TITLE ESCROW AGCY INC
29550 Detroit Rd Ste 301 (44145-1994)
PHONE....................................216 503-5600
Dennis L Obrien, *President*
EMP: 45
SALES (est): 2.3MM **Privately Held**
SIC: 6541 Title & trust companies

(G-19368)
LE CHAPERON ROUGE COMPANY
27390 Center Ridge Rd (44145-3957)
PHONE....................................440 899-9477
Stella Moga, *Owner*
EMP: 25
SALES (corp-wide): 1.2MM **Privately Held**
SIC: 8351 Child day care services
PA: Le Chaperon Rouge Company
30121 Lorain Rd
North Olmsted OH
440 779-5671

(G-19369)
LIFE CARE CENTERS AMERICA INC
Also Called: Life Care Center of Cleveland
26520 Center Ridge Rd (44145-4033)
PHONE....................................440 871-3030
Laura Garsky, *Chf Purch Ofc*
Mary Ann Dubyoski, *Administration*
EMP: 160

SALES (corp-wide): 119.8MM **Privately Held**
WEB: www.lcca.com
SIC: 8051 Convalescent home with continuous nursing care
PA: Life Care Centers Of America, Inc.
3570 Keith St Nw
Cleveland TN 37312
423 472-9585

(G-19370)
LORAD LLC
Also Called: Diversified Fall Protection
24400 Sperry Dr (44145-1565)
PHONE....................216 265-2862
Jeff Schneid, *Mng Member*
Carla R Burton,
▲ **EMP:** 30
SALES (est): 2.4MM **Privately Held**
SIC: 1799 Home/office interiors finishing, furnishing & remodeling

(G-19371)
MATRIX POINTE SOFTWARE LLC
30400 Detroit Rd Ste 400 (44145-1855)
PHONE....................216 333-1263
Joseph Whang,
EMP: 25
SQ FT: 10,000
SALES (est): 1.9MM **Privately Held**
SIC: 7371 Computer software development

(G-19372)
MEDICAL ADMINISTRATORS INC
28301 Ranney Pkwy (44145-1161)
PHONE....................440 899-2229
Tom Spooner, *President*
Margaret Carnish, *VP Opers*
Sandy Tomaro, *Opers Mgr*
Edward Shine, *Manager*
Lisa Lachendro, *Exec Dir*
EMP: 30
SALES (est): 1.7MM **Privately Held**
WEB: www.medadmin.com
SIC: 7322 Adjustment & collection services

(G-19373)
METROHEALTH SYSTEM
Also Called: Metrohealth Premier Health Ctr
25200 Center Ridge Rd (44145-4141)
PHONE....................216 957-3200
EMP: 26
SALES (corp-wide): 859.8MM **Privately Held**
SIC: 8062 General Hospital
PA: The Metrohealth System
2500 Metrohealth Dr
Cleveland OH 44109
216 398-6000

(G-19374)
MIDWEST FITNESS LLC
25935 Detroit Rd Ste 336 (44145-2452)
PHONE....................216 965-5694
Roman Liscynesky, *VP Admin*
William Dane, *Mng Member*
Glenn Silvidi, *Mng Member*
EMP: 40
SALES: 1.5MM **Privately Held**
SIC: 7991 Physical fitness facilities

(G-19375)
MONRO INC
Also Called: Monro Muffler Brake
29778 Detroit Rd (44145-1937)
PHONE....................440 835-2393
EMP: 71
SALES (corp-wide): 1.1B **Publicly Held**
SIC: 5531 7533 7538 Automotive tires; muffler shop, sale or repair & installation; general automotive repair shops
PA: Monro, Inc.
200 Holleder Pkwy
Rochester NY 14615
585 647-6400

(G-19376)
MORGAN STANLEY
159 Crocker Park Blvd # 460 (44145-8132)
PHONE....................440 835-6750
Tim Adkins, *Manager*
EMP: 50
SALES (corp-wide): 40.1B **Publicly Held**
SIC: 6211 Security brokers & dealers

PA: Morgan Stanley
1585 Broadway
New York NY 10036
212 761-4000

(G-19377)
NATIONS LENDING CORPORATION
30700 Center Ridge Rd # 3 (44145-5197)
PHONE....................440 842-4817
EMP: 42
SALES (corp-wide): 28.2MM **Privately Held**
SIC: 6162 Mortgage bankers & correspondents
PA: Nations Lending Corporation
4 Summit Park Dr Ste 200
Independence OH 44131
440 842-4817

(G-19378)
NEFF GROUP DISTRIBUTORS INC
Also Called: Fluidtrols
909 Canterbury Rd Ste G (44145-7212)
PHONE....................440 835-7010
John J Neff, *CEO*
EMP: 30
SALES (corp-wide): 57.8MM **Privately Held**
SIC: 5084 Instruments & control equipment
PA: Neff Group Distributors, Inc.
7114 Innovation Blvd
Fort Wayne IN 46818
260 489-6007

(G-19379)
NICK MAYER LINCOLN-MERCURY INC
24400 Center Ridge Rd (44145-4213)
PHONE....................440 835-3700
Patricia Mayer, *President*
Greg Gromack, *General Mgr*
Chad Mayer, *General Mgr*
Jack Gannon, *Vice Pres*
Paul Prenatt, *Sales Staff*
EMP: 40
SALES (est): 17.6MM **Privately Held**
SIC: 5511 7538 7515 Automobiles, new & used; general automotive repair shops; passenger car leasing

(G-19380)
NORTH BAY CONSTRUCTION INC
Also Called: Pe
25800 1st St Ste 1 (44145-1481)
PHONE....................440 835-1898
James J Manns, *CEO*
Michael S Kovatch, *Vice Pres*
Michael Kovatch, *Vice Pres*
Thomas Rice, *Project Mgr*
Kevin Anthony, *Engineer*
EMP: 25
SQ FT: 12,000
SALES (est): 5.7MM **Privately Held**
SIC: 8744 1799 7389 1796 Facilities support services; hydraulic equipment, installation & service; design, commercial & industrial; installing building equipment; plumbing, heating, air-conditioning contractors; water, sewer & utility lines

(G-19381)
NORTH EAST MECHANICAL INC
Also Called: Westland Heating & AC
26200 1st St (44145-1460)
PHONE....................440 871-7525
Zachary Mitchell, *President*
Andy France, *Engineer*
Fran Banda, *Bookkeeper*
EMP: 50
SQ FT: 6,000
SALES (est): 6.6MM **Privately Held**
SIC: 1711 Refrigeration contractor; warm air heating & air conditioning contractor

(G-19382)
NORTH SHORE GSTRENTEROLOGY INC
Also Called: North Shore Gastroenterology &
850 Columbia Rd Ste 200 (44145-7215)
PHONE....................440 808-1212
Tabbaa Mousab MD, *President*
Mark Wiedt, *COO*

EMP: 80
SALES (est): 11.1MM **Privately Held**
SIC: 8011 Gastronomist

(G-19383)
NORTHERN TIER HOSPITALITY LLC
Also Called: Best Western Grnd Victoria Inn
1100 Crocker Rd (44145-1033)
PHONE....................570 888-7711
Satish Duggal,
EMP: 60
SALES (est): 3.1MM **Privately Held**
SIC: 7011 Hotels

(G-19384)
OBRIEN LAW FIRM COMPANY LPA
29550 Detroit Rd (44145-1994)
PHONE....................216 685-7500
Dennis O'Brien, *President*
EMP: 32
SALES (est): 1.7MM **Privately Held**
SIC: 8111 Specialized law offices, attorneys

(G-19385)
OH-16 CLEVELAND WESTLAKE
Also Called: TownePlace Suites
25052 Sperry Dr (44145-1535)
PHONE....................440 892-4275
Mona Rigdon,
Richard Horne,
EMP: 30
SALES (est): 679.7K **Privately Held**
SIC: 7011 Hotels & motels

(G-19386)
OHIO MEDICAL GROUP (PA)
29325 Health Campus Dr # 3 (44145-8201)
PHONE....................440 414-9400
Othma Shemisa MD, *President*
EMP: 50
SALES (est): 4.3MM **Privately Held**
SIC: 8011 Cardiologist & cardio-vascular specialist

(G-19387)
OLMSTED MANOR RETIREMENT PRPTS
26612 Center Ridge Rd (44145-4035)
PHONE....................440 250-4080
EMP: 26
SALES: 1.2MM **Privately Held**
SIC: 8059 Nursing/Personal Care

(G-19388)
ORTHOPEDIC ASSOCIATES INC
24723 Detroit Rd (44145-2526)
PHONE....................440 892-1440
Manuel Martinez, *Principal*
Michael M Lew, *Surgeon*
Drew Lisa, *Technology*
EMP: 40
SALES (est): 891.4K **Privately Held**
SIC: 8011 Orthopedic physician

(G-19389)
OSBORN MARKETING RESEARCH CORP
1818 Century Oaks Dr (44145-3654)
PHONE....................440 871-1047
Ronald Kornokovich, *President*
Frank Amelia, *Vice Pres*
EMP: 40
SQ FT: 5,000
SALES (est): 2.9MM **Privately Held**
SIC: 8732 Market analysis or research

(G-19390)
OUR HOUSE INC
27633 Bassett Rd (44145-3093)
PHONE....................440 835-2110
Marguerite Vanderwyst, *President*
EMP: 47
SQ FT: 44,000
SALES (est): 3.7MM **Privately Held**
SIC: 6514 Dwelling operators, except apartments

(G-19391)
PHARMED CORPORATION
Also Called: Pharmed Institutional Pharmacy
24340 Sperry Dr (44145-1565)
PHONE....................440 250-5400
Elias J Coury, *President*
Charles Freireich, *Principal*
Samuel Laderman, *Principal*
Nancy Thorne, *Principal*
Norman Fox, *Corp Secy*
EMP: 130 **EST:** 1971
SQ FT: 36,000
SALES (est): 44MM **Privately Held**
WEB: www.pharmedcorp.com
SIC: 5047 5122 Medical & hospital equipment; drugs & drug proprietaries; pharmaceuticals

(G-19392)
PINES MANUFACTURING INC (PA)
Also Called: Pines Technology
29100 Lakeland Blvd (44145)
PHONE....................440 835-5553
Donald Rebar, *Ch of Bd*
Ian Williamson, *President*
Dan Wilczynski, *Plant Mgr*
Tom Wright, *Manager*
Bob Nosky, *Real Est Agnt*
▲ **EMP:** 43
SQ FT: 48,000
SALES (est): 13.6MM **Privately Held**
WEB: www.pines-mfg.com
SIC: 5084 3542 3549 3547 Industrial machinery & equipment; bending machines; metalworking machinery; rolling mill machinery

(G-19393)
PREMIER PHYSICIANS CENTERS INC (PA)
24651 Center Ridge Rd # 350 (44145-5627)
PHONE....................440 895-5085
Mark Wiedt, *CEO*
Antonios Paras, *President*
Nl Dasari, *Vice Pres*
Isam Diab, *Treasurer*
Steve Hurd, *Human Res Dir*
EMP: 36
SQ FT: 7,000
SALES (est): 18.8MM **Privately Held**
SIC: 8011 General & family practice, physician/surgeon

(G-19394)
R AND J CORPORATION
Also Called: Haynes Manufacturing Company
24142 Detroit Rd (44145-1515)
PHONE....................440 871-6009
Beth Kloos, *President*
Timothy Kloos, *Vice Pres*
Sheri Bohning, *Purchasing*
Ric Thornton, *Project Engr*
Matt Rogan, *Sales Engr*
EMP: 42
SQ FT: 23,000
SALES (est): 15.8MM **Privately Held**
WEB: www.haynesmfg.com
SIC: 3556 5084 7389 3053 Food products machinery; food industry machinery; design, commercial & industrial; gaskets, packing & sealing devices; lubricating oils & greases

(G-19395)
R E WARNER & ASSOCIATES INC
25777 Detroit Rd Ste 200 (44145-2484)
PHONE....................440 835-9400
David W Sminchak, *President*
Anthony Murphy, *Engineer*
Mitchell Reynolds, *Engineer*
Farres Sarrouh, *Engineer*
Lydia Janis, *Mktg Coord*
EMP: 68
SQ FT: 23,473
SALES (est): 10.2MM **Privately Held**
SIC: 8713 8712 8711 Surveying services; architectural engineering; mechanical engineering

(G-19396)
RADIOMETER AMERICA INC
810 Sharon Dr (44145-1598)
PHONE.................................440 871-8900
Cheryl Borcher, *General Mgr*
Daniel Comas, *Vice Pres*
Robert Strenk, *Vice Pres*
Sheryl Rocher, *Finance Mgr*
Lindsey Anderson, *Regl Sales Mgr*
EMP: 100
SALES (corp-wide): 19.8B **Publicly Held**
SIC: 5047 Medical equipment & supplies
HQ: Radiometer America Inc.
250 S Kraemer Blvd Ms
Brea CA 92821
800 736-0600

(G-19397)
RAE-ANN HOLDINGS INC
Also Called: Rae Ann West Lake
28303 Detroit Rd (44145-2157)
PHONE.................................440 871-0500
Sue Griffith, *Manager*
Sue Williams, *Nursing Dir*
EMP: 80
SQ FT: 45,176
SALES (corp-wide): 36.6MM **Privately Held**
SIC: 8059 8052 8051 Nursing home, except skilled & intermediate care facility; intermediate care facilities; skilled nursing care facilities
PA: Rae-Ann Holdings, Inc.
27310 W Oviatt Rd
Bay Village OH 44140
440 835-3004

(G-19398)
RAE-ANN SUBURBAN INC
29505 Detroit Rd (44145-1932)
P.O. Box 40175, Bay Village (44140-0175)
PHONE.................................440 871-5181
John Griffiths, *President*
Robert Coveney, *Business Mgr*
EMP: 125
SALES (est): 2.2MM **Privately Held**
SIC: 8051 Skilled nursing care facilities

(G-19399)
REGAL CINEMAS INC
Also Called: Regal Entertainment Group
30147 Detroit Rd (44145-1946)
PHONE.................................440 871-4546
Frank Scott, *General Mgr*
EMP: 30 **Privately Held**
WEB: www.regalcinemas.com
SIC: 7832 Motion picture theaters, except drive-in
HQ: Regal Cinemas, Inc.
101 E Blount Ave Ste 100
Knoxville TN 37920
865 922-1123

(G-19400)
RETINA ASSOCIATE OF CLEVELAND
4350 Crocker Rd Ste 200 (44145-6329)
PHONE.................................216 221-2878
Warren Laurita, *Administration*
EMP: 35
SALES (corp-wide): 10.8MM **Privately Held**
SIC: 8011 Ophthalmologist
PA: Retina Associate Of Cleveland Inc
3401 Entp Pkwy Ste 300
Beachwood OH 44122
216 831-5700

(G-19401)
RMS OF OHIO INC
Also Called: RMS Management
24651 Center Ridge Rd Ste 300
(44145-5635)
PHONE.................................440 617-6605
EMP: 324
SALES (corp-wide): 11.8MM **Privately Held**
SIC: 8742 8741 Management consulting services; business management
PA: Rms Of Ohio, Inc
733 E Dublin Granville Rd # 100
Columbus OH 43229
614 844-6767

(G-19402)
ROMETRICS TOO HAIR NAIL GLLERY
26155 Detroit Rd (44145-2430)
PHONE.................................440 808-1391
Sherry Young, *Owner*
EMP: 25
SALES (est): 231.2K **Privately Held**
SIC: 7231 Beauty shops

(G-19403)
SCOTT FETZER COMPANY (DH)
Also Called: Kirby Vacuum Cleaner
28800 Clemens Rd (44145-1197)
PHONE.................................440 892-3000
Kenneth J Semelsberger, *Ch of Bd*
Bob McBride, *Principal*
Vince Nardy, *COO*
John Grepta, *Treasurer*
▲ EMP: 40
SQ FT: 80,000
SALES (est): 412.3MM
SALES (corp-wide): 225.3B **Publicly Held**
SIC: 7699 Industrial equipment services

(G-19404)
SEA-LAND CHEMICAL CO (PA)
821 Westpoint Pkwy (44145-1545)
PHONE.................................440 871-7887
Joseph Clayton, *President*
Jennifer Altstadt, *President*
Mark Christeon, *Exec VP*
Mark Getsay, *CFO*
◆ EMP: 54
SQ FT: 8,000
SALES (est): 118.5MM **Privately Held**
SIC: 5169 Industrial chemicals

(G-19405)
SHAMROCK COMPANIES INC (PA)
Also Called: Shamrock Acquisition Company
24090 Detroit Rd (44145-1513)
P.O. Box 450980 (44145-0623)
PHONE.................................440 899-9510
Tim Connor, *CEO*
Robert E Troop, *Ch of Bd*
Dave Fechter, *COO*
Gary A Lesjak, *CFO*
Jen Barnhart, *Sales Staff*
▲ EMP: 65
SQ FT: 42,500
SALES (est): 87.9MM **Privately Held**
WEB: www.shamrockcompanies.net
SIC: 5112 5199 7336 7389 Business forms; advertising specialties; art design services; brokers' services; commercial printing, gravure; pleating & stitching

(G-19406)
SIMPLIFIED LOGISTICS LLC
28915 Clemens Rd Ste 220 (44145-1177)
PHONE.................................440 250-8912
David Klugman, *CEO*
Doug Brownley, *President*
Robert H Maisch Jr, *President*
Samuel Avampato, *COO*
Sheila Taylor, *CFO*
EMP: 27
SALES (est): 9.9MM **Privately Held**
SIC: 7375 On-line data base information retrieval

(G-19407)
SPRING VALLEY GOLF & ATHC CLB
257 Crocker Park Blvd (44145-8142)
PHONE.................................440 365-1411
John Galligan, *President*
Wilfred Tremblay, *Treasurer*
Charles Bush, *Admin Sec*
EMP: 85
SQ FT: 5,000
SALES (est): 2.7MM **Privately Held**
SIC: 7997 Golf club, membership

(G-19408)
SPRINGCAR COMPANY LLC
27500 Detroit Rd Ste 300 (44145-5913)
PHONE.................................440 892-6800
Mary Cory,
EMP: 28
SALES (est): 736K **Privately Held**
SIC: 6531 Real estate agents & managers

(G-19409)
STANDARD RETIREMENT SVCS INC
24610 Detroit Rd Ste 2000 (44145-2543)
PHONE.................................440 808-2724
John J Griffith Jr, *President*
Don Daleffandro, *Manager*
EMP: 40
SALES (corp-wide): 34.1B **Privately Held**
SIC: 8741 6282 Administrative management; investment advisory service
HQ: Standard Retirement Services, Inc.
1100 Sw 6th Ave Ste 711
Portland OR 97204
412 249-3200

(G-19410)
SUNRISE SENIOR LIVING INC
Also Called: Brighton Gardens of Westlake
27819 Center Ridge Rd Ofc (44145-3920)
PHONE.................................440 808-0074
Michael Beard, *Principal*
EMP: 58
SALES (corp-wide): 4.7B **Publicly Held**
WEB: www.sunrise.com
SIC: 8051 Skilled nursing care facilities
HQ: Sunrise Senior Living, Llc
7902 Westpark Dr
Mc Lean VA 22102

(G-19411)
TA OPERATING LLC (HQ)
Also Called: Petro Stopping Center
24601 Center Ridge Rd # 200
(44145-5677)
PHONE.................................440 808-9100
Thomas O Brien, *CEO*
ARA Bagdasarian, *Exec VP*
Andrew J Rebholz, *Exec VP*
Barry Richards, *Exec VP*
Shery Hill, *Human Resources*
EMP: 300
SQ FT: 60,000
SALES (est): 4.1B **Publicly Held**
SIC: 5541 7538 5812 5411 Filling stations, gasoline; truck stops; general truck repair; eating places; fast food restaurants & stands; convenience stores; franchises, selling or licensing

(G-19412)
TECHNOLOGY RECOVERY GROUP LTD (PA)
Also Called: Trg Repair
31390 Viking Pkwy (44145-1063)
PHONE.................................440 250-9970
Sean Kennedy, *President*
Dan Zirkle, *Vice Pres*
Will McFadden, *Parts Mgr*
Thomas Benedict, *Manager*
EMP: 100
SQ FT: 20,000
SALES (est): 30.6MM **Privately Held**
SIC: 7379 Computer related consulting services

(G-19413)
TRAVELCENTERS AMERICA INC (HQ)
24601 Center Ridge Rd # 200
(44145-5634)
PHONE.................................440 808-9100
Timothy Doane, *Ch of Bd*
Edwin P Kuhn, *Chairman*
Michael J Lombardi, *Exec VP*
Andrew J Rebholz, *Exec VP*
Barry A Richards, *Exec VP*
EMP: 700
SQ FT: 60,000
SALES (est): 1.2B **Publicly Held**
WEB: www.tatravelcenters.com
SIC: 5541 7538 5812 5411 Filling stations, gasoline; truck stops; general truck repair; eating places; fast food restaurants & stands; convenience stores

(G-19414)
TRAVELCENTERS OF AMERICA LLC
Also Called: Quaker Steak and Lube
24601 Center Ridge Rd # 200
(44145-5634)
PHONE.................................724 981-9464
EMP: 420 **Publicly Held**

(G-19415)
TRAVELCENTERS OF AMERICA LLC (PA)
Also Called: Quaker Steak & Lube
24601 Center Ridge Rd # 200
(44145-5634)
P.O. Box 451100 (44145-0627)
PHONE.................................440 808-9100
Thomas M O'Brien, *President*
Jason Davis, *General Mgr*
Tim Hoekzema, *General Mgr*
Steve Krakowski, *General Mgr*
Robert Chadwick, *Regional Mgr*
EMP: 600
SALES: 6.2B **Publicly Held**
WEB: www.iowa80group.com
SIC: 5812 7538 5541 American restaurant; coffee shop; general truck repair; truck stops

(G-19416)
UBS FINANCIAL SERVICES INC
2055 Crocker Rd Ste 201 (44145-2197)
PHONE.................................440 414-2740
Dale Alexander, *Senior VP*
John Bellow, *Branch Mgr*
Brian Cahill, *Advisor*
EMP: 43
SALES (corp-wide): 29.4B **Privately Held**
SIC: 7389 6029 Financial services; commercial banks
HQ: Ubs Financial Services Inc.
1285 Ave Of The Americas
New York NY 10019
212 713-2000

(G-19417)
UHHS WESTLAKE MEDICAL CENTER
960 Clague Rd Ste 3201 (44145-1588)
PHONE.................................440 250-2070
Fred Barton, *Med Doctor*
Anna Kessler, *Administration*
EMP: 200
SALES (est): 4.3MM **Privately Held**
SIC: 8062 General medical & surgical hospitals

(G-19418)
UNIVERSITY HOSPITALS
960 Clague Rd Ste 2410 (44145-1587)
PHONE.................................440 250-2001
Charles Nock, *Branch Mgr*
Robert Anderson, *Med Doctor*
Joan Tamburro, *Med Doctor*
EMP: 270
SALES (corp-wide): 580MM **Privately Held**
SIC: 8062 8221 Hospital, medical school affiliation; university
PA: University Hospitals Health System, Inc.
3605 Warrensville Ctr Rd
Shaker Heights OH 44122
216 767-8900

(G-19419)
UNIVERSITY HOSPITALS ST JOHN
29000 Center Ridge Rd (44145-5219)
PHONE.................................440 835-8000
Cliff Coker, *President*
Donald Sheldon, *President*
Amy Wing, *Manager*
Greg Bloxdorf, *Emerg Med Spec*
Stephen Evans,
EMP: 1200
SALES: 157.8MM
SALES (corp-wide): 580MM **Privately Held**
SIC: 8062 General medical & surgical hospitals
PA: University Hospitals Health System, Inc.
3605 Warrensville Ctr Rd
Shaker Heights OH 44122
216 767-8900

GEOGRAPHIC

(G-19420)
VERIZON COMMUNICATIONS INC
30171 Detroit Rd (44145-1946)
PHONE....................................440 892-4504
EMP: 107
SALES (corp-wide): 130.8B **Publicly Held**
SIC: **4813** 4812 4841 Local & long distance telephone communications; local telephone communications; voice telephone communications; ; cellular telephone services; cable & other pay television services
PA: Verizon Communications Inc.
1095 Ave Of The Americas
New York NY 10036
212 395-1000

(G-19421)
WELLINGTON TECHNOLOGIES INC
802 Sharon Dr (44145-1539)
PHONE....................................440 238-4377
Joseph Jasko, President
Jim Bizjak, Vice Pres
Ed Griglak, Vice Pres
Brenda Miller, Accounting Mgr
EMP: 37
SQ FT: 13,000
SALES (est): 3.2MM **Privately Held**
WEB: www.wtimaintains.com
SIC: 7378 Computer maintenance & repair

(G-19422)
WELLS FARGO CLEARING SVCS LLC
Also Called: Wells Fargo Advisors
25 Main St Fl 2 (44145-6975)
PHONE....................................440 835-9250
Matthew Clemens, Consultant
Tim Atkins, Systems Staff
Randall Keller, Officer
EMP: 30
SQ FT: 3,500
SALES (corp-wide): 101B **Publicly Held**
WEB: www.wachoviasec.com
SIC: 6211 Stock brokers & dealers
HQ: Wells Fargo Clearing Services, Llc
1 N Jefferson Ave Fl 7
Saint Louis MO 63103
314 955-3000

(G-19423)
WEST-WAY MANAGEMENT COMPANY
24700 Center Ridge Rd G50 (44145-5636)
PHONE....................................440 250-1851
Lewis E Wallner Jr, President
Lewis E Wallner Sr, Vice Pres
Robert J Lubick, Treasurer
EMP: 26
SQ FT: 2,000
SALES (est): 1.5MM **Privately Held**
SIC: 6531 Real estate managers

(G-19424)
WESTLAKE MARRIOTT
30100 Clemens Rd (44145-1013)
PHONE....................................440 892-6887
Kristen Weaver, Manager
EMP: 30
SALES (est): 357.4K **Privately Held**
SIC: 7011 Motels

(G-19425)
WESTLAKE MNTSR SCHL & CHLD DV
Also Called: Creative Playrooms
26830 Detroit Rd (44145-2368)
PHONE....................................440 835-5858
Joan Wenk, President
EMP: 31
SQ FT: 12,000
SALES (est): 565.3K **Privately Held**
SIC: 8351 Montessori child development center

(G-19426)
YOUNG MNS CHRSTN ASSN CLVELAND
Also Called: Westshore Ymca/Westlake Chrn
1575 Columbia Rd (44145-2404)
PHONE....................................440 808-8150

Laurie Wise, Branch Mgr
EMP: 100
SALES (corp-wide): 29.2MM **Privately Held**
SIC: **8641** 8661 8322 7991 Youth organizations; religious organizations; individual & family services; physical fitness facilities
PA: Young Men's Christian Association Of Cleveland
1801 Superior Ave E # 130
Cleveland OH 44114
216 781-1337

Wheelersburg
Scioto County

(G-19427)
ACCURATE MECHANICAL INC
8732 Ohio River Rd (45694-1918)
PHONE....................................740 353-4328
Thomas White, President
EMP: 25
SALES (corp-wide): 26.3MM **Privately Held**
SIC: 1711 Warm air heating & air conditioning contractor
PA: Accurate Mechanical, Inc.
3001 River Rd
Chillicothe OH
740 775-5005

(G-19428)
BEST CARE NRSING RHBLTTION CTR
2159 Dogwood Ridge Rd (45694-9044)
PHONE....................................740 574-2558
Wanda Meade, Vice Pres
EMP: 150
SQ FT: 40,000
SALES (est): 4.6MM
SALES (corp-wide): 563.4MM **Publicly Held**
SIC: 8051 8093 Skilled nursing care facilities; specialty outpatient clinics
HQ: Diversicare Management Services Co.
277 Mallory Station Rd # 130
Franklin TN 37067

(G-19429)
CATSI INC
7991 Ohio River Rd (45694-1620)
P.O. Box 263 (45694-0263)
PHONE....................................800 922-0468
Chris Rennion, President
EMP: 40
SALES (est): 2MM **Privately Held**
SIC: 7389 Inspection & testing services

(G-19430)
COLLINS ASSOC TCHNCAL SVCS INC
7991 Ohio River Rd (45694-1620)
P.O. Box 263 (45694-0263)
PHONE....................................740 574-2320
James L Collins, President
Joe Klapp, Engineer
EMP: 125 EST: 1980
SQ FT: 8,000
SALES (est): 4.5MM **Privately Held**
WEB: www.catsi.com
SIC: 8741 Construction management

(G-19431)
COMMUNITY CHOICE HOME CARE
7318 Ohio River Rd (45694)
P.O. Box 148 (45694-0148)
PHONE....................................740 574-9900
L Cunningham, Director
EMP: 50 EST: 1996
SALES (est): 1.1MM **Privately Held**
SIC: 8082 Visiting nurse service

(G-19432)
CONCORD HLTH RHABILITATION CTR
1242 Crescent Dr (45694-9376)
PHONE....................................740 574-8441
Jennifer Chaffin, Director
EMP: 43 EST: 2010

SALES: 6.4MM **Privately Held**
SIC: **8082** 8059 8052 8051 Home health care services; nursing home, except skilled & intermediate care facility; personal care facility; skilled nursing care facilities

(G-19433)
DIVERSICARE LEASING CORP
2159 Dogwood Ridge Rd (45694-9044)
PHONE....................................615 771-7575
Brenda Wimsatt, Director
Lisa Tyler, Admin Sec
EMP: 99
SALES (est): 1.3MM **Privately Held**
SIC: 8051 Skilled nursing care facilities

(G-19434)
GIGGLES & WIGGLES INC (PA)
1207 Dogwood Ridge Rd (45694-9219)
PHONE....................................740 574-4536
Judie Hedrick, President
EMP: 32
SQ FT: 4,500
SALES (est): 894.4K **Privately Held**
SIC: 8351 Group day care center

(G-19435)
LOWES HOME CENTERS LLC
7915 Ohio River Rd (45694-1618)
PHONE....................................740 574-6200
Brian Clifford, Manager
EMP: 150
SALES (corp-wide): 68.6B **Publicly Held**
SIC: **5211** 5031 5722 5064 Home centers; building materials, exterior; building materials, interior; household appliance stores; electrical appliances, television & radio
HQ: Lowe's Home Centers, Llc
1605 Curtis Bridge Rd
Wilkesboro NC 28697
336 658-4000

(G-19436)
NORFOLK SOUTHERN CORPORATION
914 Hayport Rd (45694-7504)
PHONE....................................740 574-8491
Charles Waggoner, Branch Mgr
EMP: 41
SALES (corp-wide): 11.4B **Publicly Held**
WEB: www.nscorp.com
SIC: 4011 Railroads, line-haul operating
PA: Norfolk Southern Corporation
3 Commercial Pl Ste 1a
Norfolk VA 23510
757 629-2680

(G-19437)
PEOPLES BANCORP INC
7920 Ohio River Rd (45694-1675)
PHONE....................................740 574-9100
EMP: 60
SALES (corp-wide): 208MM **Publicly Held**
SIC: 6035 Federal savings & loan associations
PA: Peoples Bancorp Inc.
138 Putnam St
Marietta OH 45750
740 373-3155

(G-19438)
PROACTIVE OCCPATIONAL MEDICINE
Also Called: Proactive Occpational Medicine
1661 State Route 522 # 3 (45694-8120)
P.O. Box 64 (45694-0064)
PHONE....................................740 574-8728
Jeff Brown,
EMP: 30
SALES: 2MM **Privately Held**
SIC: 8082 Visiting nurse service

(G-19439)
PROACTIVE OCCPTNAL MDICINE INC
Also Called: Brown Medical Services
1661 State Route 522 (45694-8120)
PHONE....................................740 574-8728
Jeffrey A Brown, President
Wendi Collins, Executive
James Scott Smith,
EMP: 45

SQ FT: 5,000
SALES: 3.5MM **Privately Held**
SIC: 8099 Health screening service; hearing testing service

(G-19440)
SELECTIVE NETWORKING INC
Also Called: Alternative Nursing & HM Care
8407 Hayport Rd (45694-1832)
P.O. Box 338 (45694-0338)
PHONE....................................740 574-2682
Tammy Hitower, President
EMP: 75
SALES (est): 1.7MM **Privately Held**
SIC: 8082 Visiting nurse service

(G-19441)
TRI-AMERICA CONTRACTORS INC (PA)
1664 State Route 522 (45694-7828)
PHONE....................................740 574-0148
Teresa Smith, CEO
Scott Taylor, President
John Mauk, General Mgr
Gregory Stanley, General Mgr
Paul Montgomery, Superintendent
EMP: 37
SQ FT: 34,000
SALES: 12MM **Privately Held**
WEB: www.triaminc.com
SIC: **3498** 3441 1629 Fabricated pipe & fittings; fabricated structural metal; industrial plant construction

---

Whipple
Washington County

(G-19442)
NEXEO SOLUTIONS LLC
7577 State Route 821 (45788-5164)
PHONE....................................330 405-0461
David Bradley, Mng Member
EMP: 90
SALES (est): 5.5MM **Privately Held**
SIC: 5169 Industrial chemicals

Whitehouse
Lucas County

(G-19443)
ANTHONY WAYNE LOCAL SCHOOLS
Also Called: Anthony Wayne Trnsp Dept
6320 Industrial Pkwy (43571-9792)
P.O. Box 2487 (43571-0487)
PHONE....................................419 877-0451
Randy Hardy, Superintendent
EMP: 100
SQ FT: 5,580
SALES (corp-wide): 51.2MM **Privately Held**
SIC: **4151** 4111 School buses; local & suburban transit
PA: Anthony Wayne Local Schools
9565 Bucher Rd
Whitehouse OH 43571
419 877-0466

(G-19444)
BITTERSWEET INC (PA)
Also Called: BITTERSWEET FARMS
12660 Archbold Whthuse Rd (43571-9566)
PHONE....................................419 875-6986
Vicki Obee-Hilty, Exec Dir
EMP: 62
SQ FT: 20,000
SALES: 6.7MM **Privately Held**
WEB: www.bittersweetfarms.org
SIC: **8361** 2032 8052 Home for the mentally handicapped; canned specialties; intermediate care facilities

(G-19445)
BLUE CREEK HEALTHCARE LLC
11239 Waterville St (43571-9813)
PHONE....................................419 877-5338
Paul Bergsten,
EMP: 95
SALES (est): 265K **Privately Held**
SIC: 8051 Skilled nursing care facilities

▲ = Import ▼=Export
◆ =Import/Export

(G-19446)
DOTSON COMPANY
6848 Providence St (43571-9572)
P.O. Box 2429 (43571-0429)
PHONE..................................419 877-5176
Mark Dotson, *President*
Kurt Dotson, *Corp Secy*
Rodd Dotson, *Vice Pres*
EMP: 25
SQ FT: 2,700
SALES: 7.3MM **Privately Held**
WEB: www.dotsoncompany.com
SIC: 1541 1542 Industrial buildings, new construction; commercial & office building contractors

(G-19447)
FROG & TOAD INC
Also Called: Whitehouse Inn
10835 Waterville St (43571-9181)
P.O. Box 2506 (43571-0506)
PHONE..................................419 877-1180
John Fronk, *President*
Anthony Fronk, *Admin Sec*
EMP: 50
SALES (est): 1.3MM **Privately Held**
SIC: 7011 Inns

(G-19448)
GARCIA SURVEYORS INC (PA)
6655 Providence St (43571-9638)
P.O. Box 2628 (43571-0628)
PHONE..................................419 877-0400
Anthony Garcia, *President*
EMP: 25
SALES: 60K **Privately Held**
SIC: 8713 Surveying services

(G-19449)
KINDRED HEALTHCARE OPERATING
11239 Waterville St (43571-9813)
P.O. Box 2760 (43571-0760)
PHONE..................................419 877-5338
Deborah Townsend, *Manager*
EMP: 99
SALES (corp-wide): 6B **Privately Held**
WEB: www.salemhaven.com
SIC: 8052 8051 Intermediate care facilities; skilled nursing care facilities
HQ: Kindred Healthcare Operating, Llc
680 S 4th St
Louisville KY 40202
502 596-7300

(G-19450)
LEADERSHIP CIRCLE LLC
10918 Springbrook Ct (43571-9674)
PHONE..................................801 518-2980
William Adams, *CEO*
Betsy Leatherman, *President*
Nicolai Tillisch, *Partner*
Greg Piercy, *Opers Staff*
Nathan Delahunty, *CFO*
EMP: 30
SALES: 7.5MM **Privately Held**
SIC: 7379

(G-19451)
PROGRESSIVE FISHING ASSN
8050 Schadel Rd (43571-9538)
PHONE..................................419 877-9909
Mike Adcok, *President*
EMP: 80
SQ FT: 3,282
SALES: 30.8K **Privately Held**
SIC: 7997 Country club, membership

(G-19452)
WHITEHOUSE OPERATOR LLC
Also Called: Whitehouse Country Manor
11239 Waterville St (43571-9813)
PHONE..................................419 877-5338
Wendy Hartman,
EMP: 99
SQ FT: 27,015
SALES (est): 5.6MM **Privately Held**
SIC: 8361 Geriatric residential care

Wickliffe
Lake County

(G-19453)
A AAA H JACKS PLUMBING HTG CO
29930 Lakeland Blvd (44092-1744)
PHONE..................................440 946-1166
John Langer, *Principal*
EMP: 40
SALES (est): 3.2MM **Privately Held**
SIC: 1711 Plumbing contractors

(G-19454)
A1 MR LIMO INC
29555 Lakeland Blvd (44092-2221)
PHONE..................................440 943-5466
Lawrence Chrystal, *President*
Judy Chrystal, *Vice Pres*
Carmen Labbato, *Technology*
EMP: 35 **EST:** 1995
SALES: 1MM **Privately Held**
WEB: www.a1mrlimo.com
SIC: 4119 Limousine rental, with driver

(G-19455)
DINOS CATERING INC
30605 Ridge Rd (44092-1165)
PHONE..................................440 943-1010
Pat Tibaldi, *President*
Mark Tibaldi, *Vice Pres*
EMP: 50
SALES (est): 1.9MM **Privately Held**
WEB: www.dinoscatering.com
SIC: 7299 5812 Banquet hall facilities; eating places

(G-19456)
DMD MANAGEMENT INC
Also Called: Legacy Health Services
1919 Bishop Rd (44092-2518)
PHONE..................................440 944-9400
EMP: 236 **Privately Held**
SIC: 8741 Nursing & personal care facility management
PA: Dmd Management, Inc.
12380 Plaza Dr
Cleveland OH 44130

(G-19457)
EAST OHIO GAS COMPANY
Also Called: Dominion Energy Ohio
29555 Clayton Ave (44092-1924)
PHONE..................................216 736-6917
Mike Reed, *Manager*
EMP: 200
SALES (corp-wide): 13.3B **Publicly Held**
SIC: 4924 Natural gas distribution
HQ: The East Ohio Gas Company
1201 E 55th St
Cleveland OH 44103
800 362-7557

(G-19458)
FAIRWAYS
30630 Ridge Rd (44092-1166)
PHONE..................................440 943-2050
Michelle Gorman, *Exec Dir*
EMP: 56
SALES (est): 1.6MM **Privately Held**
WEB: www.fairwaysindoorgolf.com
SIC: 8361 Home for the aged

(G-19459)
FOTI CONSTRUCTION COMPANY LLP
1164 Lloyd Rd (44092-2314)
PHONE..................................440 347-0728
Fred Innamorato,
EMP: 50
SQ FT: 11,000
SALES (est): 2.4MM **Privately Held**
WEB: www.foticonstruction.com
SIC: 1741 1542 Masonry & other stonework; commercial & office building, new construction; commercial & office buildings, renovation & repair

(G-19460)
FOTI CONTRACTING LLC
1164 Lloyd Rd (44092-2314)
PHONE..................................330 656-3454

Fred Innamorato,
Edward P Wojnaroski,
EMP: 250
SALES (est): 27MM **Privately Held**
SIC: 1542 Nonresidential construction

(G-19461)
GREAT LAKES CRUSHING LTD
30831 Euclid Ave (44092-1042)
PHONE..................................440 944-5500
Mark M Belich, *General Ptnr*
EMP: 47 **EST:** 1996
SQ FT: 10,000
SALES (est): 23.9MM **Privately Held**
SIC: 1429 7359 1623 1629 Igneous rock, crushed & broken-quarrying; equipment rental & leasing; office machine rental, except computers; underground utilities contractor; land clearing contractor; grading

(G-19462)
GTM SERVICE INC (PA)
Also Called: Parts Pro Automotive Warehouse
1366 Rockefeller Rd (44092-1973)
PHONE..................................440 944-5099
Michael McPhee, *President*
Sue Naght, *Sales Mgr*
Jean Sweigert, *Manager*
EMP: 40 **EST:** 1981
SQ FT: 12,000
SALES (est): 85.5MM **Privately Held**
WEB: www.partsproautomotive.com
SIC: 5013 Truck parts & accessories

(G-19463)
HI TECMETAL GROUP INC
Also Called: Brite Brazing
28910 Lakeland Blvd (44092-2321)
PHONE..................................440 373-5101
Duane Heinrich, *Manager*
EMP: 40
SALES (corp-wide): 25.2MM **Privately Held**
SIC: 3398 7692 Metal heat treating; welding repair
PA: Hi Tecmetal Group Inc
1101 E 55th St
Cleveland OH 44103
216 881-8100

(G-19464)
HORIZON PERSONNEL RESOURCES (PA)
1516 Lincoln Rd (44092-2411)
PHONE..................................440 585-0031
Daniel L Schivitz, *President*
Stephen Majercik, *COO*
Walter Nelson, *Executive*
EMP: 150
SQ FT: 2,200
SALES (est): 5.6MM **Privately Held**
WEB: www.hprjobs.com
SIC: 7363 7361 Temporary help service; employment agencies

(G-19465)
INN AT WICKLIFFE LLC
Also Called: Ramada Inn
28600 Ridgehills Dr (44092-2788)
PHONE..................................440 585-0600
Ghanshyam Patel, *Mng Member*
Asmita Barot,
EMP: 34
SALES (est): 1.7MM **Privately Held**
SIC: 7011 Hotels & motels

(G-19466)
IWI INCORPORATED (PA)
1399 Rockefeller Rd (44092-1972)
PHONE..................................440 585-5900
Robert J Iacco Sr, *Ch of Bd*
Jeffery Iacco, *President*
Mark Merickel, *Opers Mgr*
Sherrie Janz, *Accounts Mgr*
Marty Slunski, *Sales Engr*
EMP: 30 **EST:** 1972
SQ FT: 9,875
SALES (est): 22.7MM **Privately Held**
WEB: www.yalepart.com
SIC: 5084 Materials handling machinery; pollution control equipment, air (environmental)

(G-19467)
LAKE DATA CENTER INC
800 Lloyd Rd (44092-2334)
PHONE..................................440 944-2020
Tony Saranita, *President*
EMP: 70 **EST:** 1980
SQ FT: 3,500
SALES (est): 3.4MM **Privately Held**
WEB: www.lakedata.com
SIC: 7374 Data entry service

(G-19468)
LAZAR BROTHERS INC
Also Called: Stanley Steemer
30030 Lakeland Blvd (44092-1745)
PHONE..................................440 585-9333
Terrance Lazar, *President*
Dennis E Lazar, *Corp Secy*
Donald Lazar, *Vice Pres*
EMP: 25
SQ FT: 8,100
SALES (est): 2.2MM **Privately Held**
SIC: 7217 Carpet & furniture cleaning on location; upholstery cleaning on customer premises

(G-19469)
MCSTEEN & ASSOCIATES INC
1415 E 286th St (44092-2506)
PHONE..................................440 585-9800
Debbie Feller, *President*
Tim Feller, *Vice Pres*
Bradley Forbes, *Project Mgr*
Bill Feller, *Sales Staff*
Trellis Grubbs, *Marketing Staff*
EMP: 40
SQ FT: 4,000
SALES (est): 3.6MM **Privately Held**
SIC: 8713 Surveying services

(G-19470)
MULLINAX EAST LLC
Also Called: Autonation Ford East
28825 Euclid Ave (44092-2528)
PHONE..................................440 296-3020
Charles E Mullinax, *President*
Rickey Limbers, *Manager*
EMP: 100
SQ FT: 34,000
SALES (est): 30.8MM
SALES (corp-wide): 21.4B **Publicly Held**
WEB: www.mullinaxfordeast.com
SIC: 5511 7538 7532 5521 Automobiles, new & used; general automotive repair shops; top & body repair & paint shops; used car dealers; automobiles & other motor vehicles
HQ: An Dealership Holding Corp.
200 Sw 1st Ave
Fort Lauderdale FL 33301
954 769-7000

(G-19471)
NORTHCOAST MOVING ENTERPRISING
Also Called: TWO MEN AND A TRUCK/CLEVELAND
1420 Lloyd Rd (44092-2320)
PHONE..................................440 943-3900
Lynn Meilander, *President*
EMP: 60
SQ FT: 27,000
SALES (est): 4.8MM **Privately Held**
SIC: 4212 Moving services

(G-19472)
OFEQ INSTITUTE INC
28772 Johnson Dr (44092-2652)
PHONE..................................440 943-1497
Abraham Shoshana, *Director*
EMP: 26
SALES: 135.6K **Privately Held**
SIC: 8733 Noncommercial research organizations

(G-19473)
PERFECT CUT-OFF INC
29201 Anderson Rd (44092-2337)
PHONE..................................440 943-0000
Michael V Picciano, *President*
Valerie Picciano, *Treasurer*
EMP: 35 **EST:** 1973
SALES (est): 5.2MM **Privately Held**
WEB: www.perfectcutoff.com
SIC: 7389 Metal cutting services

(G-19474)
PROTERRA INC (PA)
29103 Euclid Ave (44092-2467)
PHONE................................216 383-8449
Michael Zychowski, *President*
Jonathan Varcelli, *Vice Pres*
EMP: 25 EST: 2008
SQ FT: 8,000
SALES (est): 2.4MM **Privately Held**
SIC: 4214 5032 Local trucking with storage; stone, crushed or broken

(G-19475)
RIDGEHILLS HOTEL LTD PARTNR
Also Called: Holiday Inn
28600 Ridgehills Dr (44092-2788)
PHONE................................440 585-0600
Patti Martin, *Manager*
EMP: 60
SQ FT: 53,998
SALES (corp-wide): 1.7MM **Privately Held**
WEB: www.ridgehillshotel.com
SIC: 7011 5813 5812 Hotels & motels; drinking places; eating places
PA: Ridgehills Hotel Limited Partnership
1350 W 3rd St
Cleveland OH 44113
216 464-2860

(G-19476)
UNITED SKATES AMERICA INC
30325 Palisades Pkwy (44092-1567)
PHONE................................440 944-5300
Bruce Aster, *Manager*
EMP: 30
SALES (corp-wide): 9.6MM **Privately Held**
SIC: 7999 Roller skating rink operation
PA: United Skates Of America, Inc.
3362 Refugee Rd
Columbus OH 43232
614 802-2440

(G-19477)
WICKLIFFE ASSOCIATES PARTNR
Also Called: Wickliffe Lanes
30315 Euclid Ave (44092-1549)
PHONE................................440 585-3505
Gerald Appel, *Partner*
Frank King, *Partner*
Jeff Gierman, *Manager*
EMP: 40
SQ FT: 15,000
SALES (est): 2.1MM **Privately Held**
WEB: www.wickliffelanes.com
SIC: 6512 Commercial & industrial building operation

(G-19478)
WICKLIFFE COUNTRY PLACE LTD
1919 Bishop Rd (44092-2586)
PHONE................................440 944-9400
Mark Yantek, *Administration*
EMP: 150
SALES (est): 3.4MM
SALES (corp-wide): 11.3MM **Privately Held**
SIC: 8051 Skilled nursing care facilities
PA: Wickliffe Country Place Ltd
12380 Plaza Dr
Parma OH 44130
216 898-8399

Willard
Huron County

(G-19479)
CSX CORPORATION
2826 Liberty Rd (44890-9382)
PHONE................................419 933-5027
Bill Loar, *Manager*
EMP: 149
SALES (corp-wide): 12.2B **Publicly Held**
WEB: www.csx.com
SIC: 4011 Railroads, line-haul operating
PA: Csx Corporation
500 Water St Fl 15
Jacksonville FL 32202
904 359-3200

(G-19480)
FAMILY HEALTH PARTNERS INC
Also Called: Brown, Chris R & Vicki J
315 Crestwood Dr (44890-1652)
PHONE................................419 935-0196
Eric Prack, *President*
Chris Brown, *Med Doctor*
EMP: 28
SALES (est): 2.7MM **Privately Held**
WEB: www.family-health-partners.com
SIC: 8011 Offices & clinics of medical doctors

(G-19481)
HOLTHOUSE FARMS OF OHIO INC (PA)
Also Called: Holthouse Farms of Michigan
4373 State Route 103 S (44890-9219)
PHONE................................419 935-1041
Stanton Holthouse, *Principal*
Carol Holthouse, *Principal*
Connie Holthouse, *Principal*
Jordon Holthouse, *Principal*
Kirk Holthouse, *Sales Executive*
EMP: 125
SQ FT: 20,000
SALES (est): 14.3MM **Privately Held**
SIC: 0161 0191 Vegetables & melons; general farms, primarily crop

(G-19482)
K & P TRUCKING LLC
3862 State Route 103 S (44890-9042)
P.O. Box 179 (44890-0179)
PHONE................................419 935-8646
William Koerner,
J Harold Cashman,
Kent Knaus,
EMP: 60
SALES (est): 3.3MM **Privately Held**
SIC: 4213 Trucking, except local

(G-19483)
LIBERTY NURSING OF WILLARD
Also Called: Hillside Acres Nursing Home
370 E Howard St (44890-1656)
PHONE................................419 935-0148
Linda Blackurek, *President*
EMP: 70
SQ FT: 58,000
SALES (est): 2.5MM **Privately Held**
WEB: www.lbkhealthcare.com
SIC: 8051 8052 Skilled nursing care facilities; intermediate care facilities
PA: Lbk Health Care, Inc.
4336 W Franklin St Ste A
Bellbrook OH 45305

(G-19484)
MERCY HEALTH
218 S Myrtle Ave (44890-1408)
PHONE................................419 935-0187
EMP: 54
SALES (corp-wide): 4.7B **Privately Held**
SIC: 8011 Gynecologist
PA: Mercy Health
1701 Mercy Health Pl
Cincinnati OH 45237
513 639-2800

(G-19485)
PAM TRANSPORTATION SVCS INC
2501 Miller Rd (44890-9555)
P.O. Box 383 (44890-0383)
PHONE................................419 935-9501
Fred Blank, *Manager*
David R Grana, *Manager*
EMP: 60
SALES (corp-wide): 533.2MM **Publicly Held**
SIC: 4213 4231 Trucking, except local; trucking terminal facilities
PA: P.A.M. Transportation Services, Inc.
297 W Henri De Tonti
Tontitown AR 72770
479 361-9111

(G-19486)
PRISTINE SENIOR LIVING OF
Also Called: Pristine Senior Living and
370 E Howard St (44890-1656)
PHONE................................419 935-0148
Brian Femia, *Mng Member*
EMP: 60

SALES (est): 645.4K **Privately Held**
SIC: 8059 Nursing & personal care

(G-19487)
SHARPNACK CHVRLET BICK CDILLAC
1330 S Conwell Ave (44890-9148)
PHONE................................419 935-0194
Tom Sharpnack, *President*
Rhonda Holbrook, *Office Mgr*
EMP: 100
SALES: 10MM **Privately Held**
SIC: 5511 7532 Automobiles, new & used; collision shops, automotive

(G-19488)
SISTERS OF MRCY OF WLLARD OHIO (DH)
Also Called: Mercy Hospital of Willard
1100 Neal Zick Rd (44890-9287)
PHONE................................419 964-5000
Lynn Detterman, *President*
Ronald E Heinlen, *Principal*
EMP: 175
SQ FT: 70,000
SALES: 24.7MM
SALES (corp-wide): 4.7B **Privately Held**
SIC: 8062 General medical & surgical hospitals
HQ: Mercy Health Cincinnati Llc
1701 Mercy Health Pl
Cincinnati OH 45237
513 952-5000

(G-19489)
TRILOGY HEALTH SERVICES LLC
Also Called: Willows At Willard, The
1050 Neal Zick Rd (44890-9288)
PHONE................................419 935-6511
Randall Bufford, *CEO*
D Phillips, *Exec Dir*
Jeff Orlowski, *Hlthcr Dir*
EMP: 100
SQ FT: 28,442
SALES (corp-wide): 67.1MM **Privately Held**
SIC: 8051 8361 Skilled nursing care facilities; residential care
HQ: Trilogy Health Services, Llc
303 N Hurstbourne Pkwy # 200
Louisville KY 40222

Williamsburg
Clermont County

(G-19490)
CECOS INTERNATIONAL INC
Also Called: Site K62
5092 Aber Rd (45176-9532)
PHONE................................513 724-6114
Connie Dall, *Controller*
EMP: 28
SALES (corp-wide): 10B **Publicly Held**
SIC: 4953 Refuse collection & disposal services
HQ: Cecos International, Inc.
5600 Niagara Falls Blvd
Niagara Falls NY 14304
716 282-2676

(G-19491)
CLERCOM INC
Also Called: Diesel-Eagle
3710 State Route 133 (45176-9798)
PHONE................................513 724-6101
Marlyon E Abrams, *President*
Jessie Abrams, *Corp Secy*
▲ EMP: 100 EST: 1968
SQ FT: 104,000
SALES (est): 10MM **Privately Held**
SIC: 5065 5199 Communication equipment; citizens band radios; radio parts & accessories; general merchandise, nondurable

(G-19492)
CROSWELL OF WILLIAMSBURG LLC (PA)
Also Called: Croswell VIP Motor Couch Svc
975 W Main St (45176-1147)
PHONE................................513 724-2206

John W Croswell, *President*
Marion Croswell, *Corp Secy*
Robert S Croswell III, *Vice Pres*
Susan Mahan, *Vice Pres*
Ellen Gedling, *Director*
EMP: 25 EST: 1921
SQ FT: 21,000
SALES: 7MM **Privately Held**
WEB: www.croswell-bus.com
SIC: 4142 4141 Bus charter service, except local; local bus charter service

(G-19493)
DUALITE SALES & SERVICE INC (PA)
1 Dualite Ln (45176-1121)
PHONE................................513 724-7100
Gregory Schube, *CEO*
Kenneth Syberg, *Senior VP*
Greg Hoffer, *Vice Pres*
Paula Mueller, *Vice Pres*
Rob Shephard, *Vice Pres*
◆ EMP: 250
SQ FT: 214,500
SALES: 32MM **Privately Held**
SIC: 5099 Signs, except electric

(G-19494)
LOCUST RIDGE NURSING HOME INC (PA)
12745 Elm Corner Rd (45176-9621)
PHONE................................937 444-2920
Howard L Meeker, *President*
Ruth Osborn, *CFO*
Steven L Meeker, *Admin Sec*
EMP: 125
SQ FT: 20,000
SALES (est): 4.7MM **Privately Held**
SIC: 8051 Convalescent home with continuous nursing care

(G-19495)
PINE RIDGE PINE VLLG RESDNTL H
146 N 3rd St (45176-1322)
PHONE................................513 724-3460
Tracy Watson, *Manager*
Verna Wiedenbein, *Administration*
EMP: 28
SALES (est): 893.4K **Privately Held**
SIC: 8361 Residential care for the handicapped

(G-19496)
RESCARE OHIO INC (DH)
Also Called: Willimsburg Rsdntial Altrntves
348 W Main St (45176-1352)
PHONE................................513 724-1177
Dwight Finch, *Director*
Fred Duley, *Director*
Lynn Hibbard, *Director*
EMP: 50
SALES (est): 10.3MM
SALES (corp-wide): 23.7B **Privately Held**
SIC: 8361 8052 Self-help group home; intermediate care facilities
HQ: Res-Care, Inc.
805 N Whittington Pkwy
Louisville KY 40222
502 394-2100

(G-19497)
RESIDENTIAL CONCEPTS INC
117 Kermit Ave (45176-1511)
PHONE................................513 724-6067
Jim Sprags, *President*
EMP: 40
SALES (est): 699.3K **Privately Held**
SIC: 8052 Home for the mentally retarded, with health care

Williamsport
Pickaway County

(G-19498)
CONNECTIVITY SYSTEMS INC (PA)
Also Called: Csi International
8120 State Route 138 (43164-9767)
P.O. Box 417 (43164-0417)
PHONE................................740 420-5400
John A Rankin, *Ch of Bd*

John Byrnes, *President*
Katie Shaw, *Accounts Exec*
EMP: 30
SQ FT: 4,000
SALES (est): 3.2MM **Privately Held**
WEB: www.e-vse.com
SIC: 7371 Computer software development

(G-19499)
INTERNATIONAL ASSN LIONS
Also Called: New Holland Lions Club
24920 Locust Grove Rd (43164-9780)
PHONE..............................740 986-6502
Fay Washburn, *President*
Marty Mace, *Treasurer*
Charlotte Riley, *Admin Sec*
EMP: 29
SALES (est): 250.2K **Privately Held**
SIC: 8641 Civic associations

Williston
Ottawa County

(G-19500)
LUTHER HOME OF MERCY
Also Called: WILLISTON LUTHER HOME OF MERCY
5810 N Main St (43468)
P.O. Box 187 (43468-0187)
PHONE..............................419 836-3918
Rev Donald Wukotich, *Exec Dir*
Jean Witt, *Director*
EMP: 499
SQ FT: 150,000
SALES: 3.4MM **Privately Held**
SIC: 8052 Intermediate care facilities

Willoughby
Lake County

(G-19501)
A J GOULDER ELECTRIC CO
4307 Hamann Pkwy (44094-5625)
PHONE..............................440 942-4026
Keith Eldridge, *President*
Connie Eldridge, *Corp Secy*
Amy Gallo, *Vice Pres*
Bret Thomas, *Vice Pres*
EMP: 44
SQ FT: 4,500
SALES (est): 3.5MM **Privately Held**
SIC: 1731 General electrical contractor

(G-19502)
AEROCON PHOTOGRAMMETRIC SVCS (PA)
4515 Glenbrook Rd (44094-8215)
PHONE..............................440 946-6277
James Liberty, *Principal*
Judith Liberty, *Admin Sec*
EMP: 27
SQ FT: 10,000
SALES (est): 4.1MM **Privately Held**
WEB: www.aerocon.com
SIC: 7389 7335 Photogrammatic mapping; aerial photography, except mapmaking

(G-19503)
ALL LIFT SERVICE COMPANY INC
Also Called: All Industrial Engine Service
4607 Hamann Pkwy (44094-5631)
PHONE..............................440 585-1542
John L Gelsimino, *President*
John P Gelsimino, *Owner*
Holly Rolf, *Accounting Mgr*
Chris Collins, *Accounts Mgr*
Denise Germano, *Manager*
EMP: 47 **EST:** 1972
SQ FT: 38,000
SALES (est): 10.9MM **Privately Held**
WEB: www.alllift.com
SIC: 7699 5013 7359 5084 Industrial truck repair; truck parts & accessories; industrial truck rental; trucks, industrial

(G-19504)
ALPHA IMAGING LLC (PA)
4455 Glenbrook Rd (44094-8219)
PHONE..............................440 953-3800
Albert D Perrico, *President*
Pete Davis, *President*
Scott Macgregor, *Vice Pres*
Michael Perrico, *Vice Pres*
Svijetlana Celan, *Accountant*
EMP: 42
SQ FT: 7,500
SALES (est): 26MM **Privately Held**
WEB: www.alpha-imaging.com
SIC: 5047 7699 X-ray machines & tubes; X-ray equipment repair

(G-19505)
ANDREWS APARTMENTS LTD
4420 Sherwin Rd (44094-7994)
PHONE..............................440 946-3600
Douglas Price, *Principal*
EMP: 155 **EST:** 2008
SALES (est): 2MM
SALES (corp-wide): 27MM **Privately Held**
SIC: 6513 Apartment building operators
PA: The K&D Group Inc
4420 Sherwin Rd Ste 1
Willoughby OH 44094
440 946-3600

(G-19506)
ASCENDTECH INC
4772 E 355th St (44094-4632)
PHONE..............................216 458-1101
Igor Lapinskiy, *President*
Gary Lapinskiy, *General Mgr*
EMP: 35
SALES (est): 8.3MM **Privately Held**
SIC: 5045 7379 3571 7378 Computer peripheral equipment; computer related maintenance services; electronic computers; computer peripheral equipment repair & maintenance; electrical repair shops; scrap & waste materials

(G-19507)
AT&T CORP
34808 Euclid Ave (44094-4504)
PHONE..............................440 951-5309
EMP: 69
SALES (corp-wide): 170.7B **Publicly Held**
SIC: 4812 Cellular telephone services
HQ: At&T Corp.
1 At&T Way
Bedminster NJ 07921
800 403-3302

(G-19508)
BEVCORP LLC (PA)
4711 E 355th St (44094-4631)
PHONE..............................440 954-3500
John Schein, *Plant Supt*
Stephen Soukup, *Project Mgr*
Michael Connelly, *Mng Member*
Donald Albert,
Vicki Connelly,
▲ **EMP:** 65
SQ FT: 40,000
SALES (est): 39.5MM **Privately Held**
WEB: www.bevcorp.com
SIC: 5084 Industrial machinery & equipment

(G-19509)
CASCIA LLC
Also Called: Lake Cnty Captains Prof Basbal
Classic Pk 35300 Vine St Classic Park (44095)
PHONE..............................440 975-8085
Rita Murphy Carfagna,
Peter A Carfagna,
Ray Murphy,
EMP: 45
SALES (est): 2MM **Privately Held**
SIC: 7997 7941 Baseball club, except professional & semi-professional; baseball club, professional & semi-professional

(G-19510)
CITY OF WILLOUGHBY
Also Called: Willoughby City Garage
37400 N Industrial Pkwy (44094-6213)
PHONE..............................440 942-0215
Neil Pinckney, *Superintendent*

EMP: 35 **Privately Held**
WEB: www.willoughbyohio.com
SIC: 4173 Maintenance facilities for motor vehicle passenger transport
PA: City Of Willoughby
1 Public Sq
Willoughby OH 44094
440 953-4191

(G-19511)
CITY OF WILLOUGHBY
Road Department
1 Public Sq (44094-7827)
PHONE..............................440 953-4111
Sam Trost, *Manager*
EMP: 75 **Privately Held**
WEB: www.willoughbyohio.com
SIC: 1611 Highway & street maintenance
PA: City Of Willoughby
1 Public Sq
Willoughby OH 44094
440 953-4191

(G-19512)
CITY OF WILLOUGHBY
Service Dept
1 Public Sq (44094-7827)
PHONE..............................440 953-4111
David E Anderson, *Mayor*
EMP: 254 **Privately Held**
WEB: www.willoughbyohio.com
SIC: 6531 Cemetery management service
PA: City Of Willoughby
1 Public Sq
Willoughby OH 44094
440 953-4191

(G-19513)
CITY OF WILLOUGHBY
Also Called: Lost Nation Golf Course
38890 Hodgson Rd (44094-7572)
PHONE..............................440 953-4280
Mitch Allan, *Manager*
EMP: 30 **Privately Held**
WEB: www.willoughbyohio.com
SIC: 7992 Public golf courses
PA: City Of Willoughby
1 Public Sq
Willoughby OH 44094
440 953-4191

(G-19514)
CLEVELAND COIN MCH EXCH INC (HQ)
3860 Ben Hur Ave Unit 2 (44094-6377)
PHONE..............................847 842-6310
EMP: 60 **EST:** 1947
SQ FT: 40,000
SALES (est): 16.6MM **Privately Held**
SIC: 5087 5046 Whol Service Establishment Equipment Whol Commercial Equipment
PA: Family Entertainment Group Llc
1265 Hamilton Pkwy
Itasca IL 60143
847 842-6310

(G-19515)
COMMUNITY CHOICE FINANCIAL INC
34302 Euclid Ave Unit 7 (44094-3334)
PHONE..............................440 602-9922
Jim Frauenberg, *President*
EMP: 100 **Privately Held**
WEB: www.buckeyecheckcashing.com
SIC: 6099 Check cashing agencies
HQ: Buckeye Check Cashing, Inc.
6785 Bobcat Way Ste 200
Dublin OH 43016
614 798-5900

(G-19516)
COUNTY OF LAKE
Also Called: Lake Cnty Deptmntl Retrdtn/Dvl
2100 Joseph Lloyd Pkwy (44094-8032)
PHONE..............................440 269-2193
Gary Metelko, *Director*
EMP: 72 **Privately Held**
WEB: www.lakecountyohio.gov
SIC: 8322 8331 3441 Individual & family services; job training & vocational rehabilitation services; fabricated structural metal

PA: County Of Lake
8 N State St Ste 215
Painesville OH 44077
440 350-2500

(G-19517)
CUSTOM CLEANING AND MAINT
38046 2nd St (44094-6105)
PHONE..............................440 946-7028
Joe Lambardo, *President*
Sandra Sidley, *Vice Pres*
EMP: 30
SALES (est): 792.8K **Privately Held**
SIC: 7349 Janitorial service, contract basis

(G-19518)
DEPENDABLE CLEANING CONTRS
Also Called: Willo Maintenance
38230 Glenn Ave (44094-7808)
PHONE..............................440 953-9191
Wayne A Trubiano, *President*
EMP: 70
SQ FT: 2,500
SALES (est): 2MM **Privately Held**
WEB: www.unimar.com
SIC: 7349 Janitorial service, contract basis

(G-19519)
EAST END RO BURTON INC
Also Called: Riders Inn
792 Mentor Ave (44094)
PHONE..............................440 942-2742
Elaine R Crane, *President*
EMP: 25
SQ FT: 7,801
SALES (est): 910K **Privately Held**
SIC: 7011 Motels

(G-19520)
EMERITUS CORPORATION
Also Called: Brookdale Willoughby
35300 Kaiser Ct (44094-6633)
PHONE..............................440 269-8600
Laurie Bonarrigo, *Exec Dir*
EMP: 39
SALES (corp-wide): 4.5B **Publicly Held**
SIC: 8361 Residential care
HQ: Emeritus Corporation
3131 Elliott Ave Ste 500
Milwaukee WI 53214

(G-19521)
ERIESIDE MEDICAL GROUP
38429 Lake Shore Blvd (44094-7009)
PHONE..............................440 918-6270
Winston Ho, *Partner*
Harris Freedman, *Partner*
James Mandelick, *Partner*
EMP: 30
SALES (est): 2.9MM **Privately Held**
SIC: 8011 Internal medicine practitioners

(G-19522)
EXODUS INTEGRITY SERVICE
Also Called: Eis
37111 Euclid Ave Ste F (44094-5659)
PHONE..............................440 918-0140
Jim Ciricola, *President*
Pete Mc Millan, *Vice Pres*
EMP: 63
SQ FT: 2,200
SALES (est): 3.9MM **Privately Held**
WEB: www.exodusintegrity.com
SIC: 7371 7361 Custom computer programming services; employment agencies

(G-19523)
FEDEX OFFICE & PRINT SVCS INC
34800 Euclid Ave (44094-4504)
PHONE..............................440 946-6353
EMP: 34
SALES (corp-wide): 65.4B **Publicly Held**
WEB: www.fedex.com
SIC: 7334 Photocopying & duplicating services
HQ: Fedex Office And Print Services, Inc.
7900 Legacy Dr
Plano TX 75024
800 463-3339

GEOGRAPHIC

(G-19524)
FIVE STAR TRUCKING INC
4380 Glenbrook Rd (44094-8213)
PHONE.....................................440 953-9300
John J Gramc, *President*
Jeff Ratcliffe, *COO*
Ralph Godic, *Vice Pres*
John Gramc, *Vice Pres*
Joseph J Gramc, *Vice Pres*
EMP: 32
SQ FT: 19,000
SALES: 22.5MM Privately Held
WEB: www.fivestartrucking.com
SIC: 4213 4212 Contract haulers; local
trucking, without storage

(G-19525)
FLUID LINE PRODUCTS INC
38273 Western Pkwy (44094-7591)
P.O. Box 1000 (44096-1000)
PHONE.....................................440 946-9470
John Skalicki, *Ch of Bd*
John J Hetzer, *President*
Stella Ann Hetzer, *Corp Secy*
Zelko Skalicki, *Vice Pres*
Robert Skalicki, *Admin Asst*
EMP: 128
SQ FT: 62,000
SALES (est): 42.5MM Privately Held
WEB: www.fluidline.com
SIC: 5084 Hydraulic systems equipment &
supplies

(G-19526)
GLENRIDGE MACHINE CO
4610 Beidler Rd (44094-4603)
PHONE.....................................440 975-1055
Mark Negrelli Jr, *Ch of Bd*
Jerry Negrelli, *President*
Mark Negrelli III, *Vice Pres*
Michael Genzen, *Engineer*
Phil Zendarski, *Senior Engr*
▲ EMP: 33
SQ FT: 66,000
SALES (est): 7.8MM Privately Held
WEB: www.glenridgemachine.com
SIC: 3599 7692 Machine shop, jobbing &
repair; welding repair

(G-19527)
GOLDEN LIVING LLC
Also Called: Beverly
9679 Chillicothe Rd (44094-8503)
PHONE.....................................440 256-8100
Jim Homa, *Exec Dir*
EMP: 200
SALES (corp-wide): 7.4MM Privately
Held
SIC: 8059 Convalescent home
PA: Golden Living Llc
5220 Tennyson Pkwy # 400
Plano TX 75024
972 372-6300

(G-19528)
HI TECMETAL GROUP INC
HI Tech Aero
34800 Lakeland Blvd (44095-5224)
PHONE.....................................440 946-2280
Scott St Claire, *Branch Mgr*
EMP: 27
SQ FT: 17,433
SALES (corp-wide): 25.2MM Privately
Held
SIC: 7692 3398 Welding repair; brazing
(hardening) of metal
PA: Hi Tecmetal Group Inc
1101 E 55th St
Cleveland OH 44103
216 881-8100

(G-19529)
HOLDEN ARBORETUM
9500 Sperry Rd (44094-5172)
PHONE.....................................440 946-4400
Clem Hamilton, *President*
Dave Lowery, *Vice Pres*
Jim Ansberry, *Treasurer*
Peg Weir, *Manager*
Brian Schoch, *Officer*
EMP: 62
SQ FT: 80,000
SALES: 7.2MM Privately Held
WEB: www.holdenarb.org
SIC: 8422 Arboretum

(G-19530)
**HOWARD HANNA SMYTHE
CRAMER**
Also Called: Paul Paratto
34601 Ridge Rd Ste 3 (44094-3032)
PHONE.....................................440 516-4444
Nancy Tracz, *Sales/Mktg Mgr*
EMP: 27
SALES (corp-wide): 73.7MM Privately
Held
WEB: www.smythecramer.com
SIC: 6531 Real estate agent, residential
HQ: Howard Hanna Smythe Cramer
6000 Parkland Blvd
Cleveland OH 44124
216 447-4477

(G-19531)
K & D ENTERPRISES INC
4420 Sherwin Rd Ste 1 (44094-7995)
P.O. Box 219 (44096-0219)
PHONE.....................................440 946-3600
Karen Harrison, *President*
Doug Price, *Admin Sec*
EMP: 50
SALES (est): 2.3MM Privately Held
SIC: 6513 Apartment building operators

(G-19532)
K&D GROUP INC (PA)
4420 Sherwin Rd Ste 1 (44094-7995)
P.O. Box 219 (44096-0219)
PHONE.....................................440 946-3600
Douglas E Price III, *CEO*
Karen M Harrison, *President*
Steven Johnson, *Maintenance Dir*
Mauri-Lynn Feemster, *Controller*
EMP: 25
SQ FT: 33,000
SALES (est): 27MM Privately Held
SIC: 6513 Apartment building operators

(G-19533)
**KAISER FOUNDATION
HOSPITALS**
Also Called: Willoughby Medical Offices
5105 S O M Center Rd (44094)
PHONE.....................................216 524-7377
EMP: 454
SALES (corp-wide): 19.1B Privately Held
SIC: 6733 Trust Management
PA: Kaiser Foundation Hospitals Inc
1 Kaiser Plz Ste 2600
Oakland CA 94612
510 271-5800

(G-19534)
**KIRTLAND COUNTRY CLUB
COMPANY**
39438 Kirtland Rd (44094-9201)
PHONE.....................................440 942-4400
Brian Bollar, *President*
Mark T Petzinc, *General Mgr*
Roy Johnson, *Controller*
EMP: 100
SQ FT: 15,000
SALES: 5.6MM Privately Held
WEB: www.kirtlandcc.org
SIC: 7997 Country club, membership

(G-19535)
**KOTTLER METAL PRODUCTS
CO INC**
1595 Lost Nation Rd (44094-7329)
PHONE.....................................440 946-7473
Barry Feldman, *President*
Harold Feldman, *Vice Pres*
Mike Mangan, *Mfg Staff*
Ron McCloud, *Mfg Staff*
Pat Garrett, *Sales Mgr*
▲ EMP: 25
SALES: 7.4MM Privately Held
WEB: www.kottlermetal.com
SIC: 3498 3441 7692 3547 Pipe sections
fabricated from purchased pipe; tube fab-
ricating (contract bending & shaping); fab-
ricated structural metal; welding repair;
rolling mill machinery

(G-19536)
**KUCERA INTERNATIONAL INC
(PA)**
38133 Western Pkwy (44094-7589)
PHONE.....................................440 975-4230
John W Antalovich Sr, *Ch of Bd*
John W Antalovich Jr, *President*
Robert Weston, *Project Mgr*
Scott Antalovich, *Treasurer*
Denise O'Donnell, *Accounting Mgr*
EMP: 65 EST: 1948
SQ FT: 20,000
SALES: 7MM Privately Held
WEB: www.hendersonaerial.com
SIC: 7335 8713 7389 8711 Aerial photog-
raphy, except mapmaking; surveying
services; photogrammetric engineering;
photogrammatic mapping; mining engi-
neer

(G-19537)
**LABORATORY CORPORATION
AMERICA**
38429 Lake Shore Blvd (44094-7009)
PHONE.....................................440 951-6841
EMP: 25
SALES (corp-wide): 8.6B Publicly Held
SIC: 8071 Medical Laboratory
HQ: Laboratory Corporation Of America
358 S Main St Ste 458
Burlington NC 27215
336 229-1127

(G-19538)
LAKE COUNTY YMCA
Also Called: West End Branch
37100 Euclid Ave (44094-5612)
PHONE.....................................440 946-1160
Robert Hoffman, *Branch Mgr*
EMP: 150
SALES (corp-wide): 8.9MM Privately
Held
SIC: 8641 7991 8351 7032 Youth organi-
zations; physical fitness facilities; child
day care services; youth camps; individ-
ual & family services
PA: Lake County Ymca
933 Mentor Ave Fl 2
Painesville OH 44077
440 352-3303

(G-19539)
LAKE HOSPITAL SYSTEM INC
Also Called: Lake-West Hospital
36000 Euclid Ave (44094-4625)
PHONE.....................................440 953-9600
Cynthia Moore Hardy, *Principal*
Cynthia Hardy, *Principal*
EMP: 1000
SALES (corp-wide): 356.8MM Privately
Held
WEB: www.lakehospitalsystem.com
SIC: 8062 General medical & surgical hos-
pitals
PA: Lake Hospital System, Inc.
7590 Auburn Rd
Painesville OH 44077
440 375-8100

(G-19540)
LAKE METROPARKS
8668 Kirtland Chardon Rd (44094-8608)
PHONE.....................................440 256-1404
Ann Bugeda, *General Mgr*
Dan Burnett, *Manager*
EMP: 30
SALES (est): 437.8K
SALES (corp-wide): 20.9MM Privately
Held
WEB: www.lakemetroparks.com
SIC: 7999 Recreation services
PA: Lake Metroparks
11211 Spear Rd
Painesville OH 44077
440 639-7275

(G-19541)
LAKELAND FOUNDATION
7700 Clocktower Dr C2089 (44094-5198)
PHONE.....................................440 525-7094
Bob Cahen, *Exec Dir*
EMP: 48
SALES: 910.9K Privately Held
SIC: 8299 7371 Educational services;
computer software development & appli-
cations

(G-19542)
LANHAN CONTRACTORS INC
2220 Lost Nation Rd (44094-7535)
PHONE.....................................440 918-1099
William Lanhan, *Owner*
EMP: 30
SALES (est): 1MM Privately Held
SIC: 0781 Landscape architects

(G-19543)
LAURELWOOD HOSPITAL (PA)
Also Called: LAURELWOOD CENTER FOR
BEHAVIOU
35900 Euclid Ave (44094-4648)
PHONE.....................................440 953-3000
Richard Warden, *President*
EMP: 319
SQ FT: 160,000
SALES: 36.5MM Privately Held
WEB: www.laurelwoodhospital.com
SIC: 8063 8069 Psychiatric hospitals; sub-
stance abuse hospitals

(G-19544)
LEIKIN MOTOR COMPANIES INC
38750 Mentor Ave (44094-7929)
PHONE.....................................440 946-6900
Ronald Leikin, *President*
Brian Rapoport, *Business Mgr*
Mike Bonitati, *Manager*
Ron Leikin, *Manager*
Steve Ours, *Manager*
EMP: 62
SQ FT: 40,000
SALES (est): 22.7MM Privately Held
WEB: www.leikenvolvo.com
SIC: 5511 7532 7514 5531 Automobiles,
new & used; top & body repair & paint
shops; passenger car rental; automotive
& home supply stores; used car dealers

(G-19545)
LOST NATION SPORTS PARK
38630 Jet Center Pl (44094-8174)
PHONE.....................................440 602-4000
Mike Srsen, *CEO*
Michelle Almady, *Director*
Dave Boyza, *Director*
Danny Bartulovic, *Program Dir*
EMP: 30
SALES (est): 2MM Privately Held
WEB: www.lnsportspark.com
SIC: 7996 Amusement parks

(G-19546)
LOWES HOME CENTERS LLC
36300 Euclid Ave (44094-4415)
PHONE.....................................440 942-2759
Richard Brown, *Branch Mgr*
Aaron Ladson, *Manager*
EMP: 150
SALES (corp-wide): 68.6B Publicly Held
SIC: 5211 5031 5722 5064 Home cen-
ters; building materials, exterior; building
materials, interior; household appliance
stores; electrical appliances, television &
radio
HQ: Lowe's Home Centers, Llc
1605 Curtis Bridge Rd
Wilkesboro NC 28697
336 658-4000

(G-19547)
M J LANESE LANDSCAPING INC
37115 Code Ave (44094-6337)
PHONE.....................................440 942-3444
Matt Lanese, *Owner*
EMP: 30
SALES (est): 1.8MM Privately Held
SIC: 0782 Landscape contractors

(G-19548)
MANOR CARE OF AMERICA INC
37603 Euclid Ave (44094-5923)
PHONE.....................................440 951-5551
Erlinda Gonzalez, *Branch Mgr*
EMP: 110
SALES (corp-wide): 2.4B Publicly Held
WEB: www.trisunhealthcare.com
SIC: 8051 Convalescent home with contin-
uous nursing care
HQ: Manor Care Of America, Inc.
333 N Summit St Ste 103
Toledo OH 43604
419 252-5500

2019 Harris Ohio
Services Directory

▲ = Import ▼=Export
◆ =Import/Export

(G-19549)
MARKETING COMM RESOURCE INC
4800 E 345th St (44094-4607)
PHONE..................................440 484-3010
Dominic Tiunno, *CEO*
Frank Tiunno, *Exec VP*
EMP: 57
SALES (est): 6.9MM **Privately Held**
SIC: 4961 2759 Steam/Air-Conditioning Supply Commercial Printing

(G-19550)
MAROUS BROTHERS CNSTR INC
1702 Joseph Lloyd Pkwy (44094-8028)
PHONE..................................440 951-3904
Adelbert Marous, *President*
Doug Richardson, *General Mgr*
Kenneth Marous, *Corp Secy*
Scott Marous, *Vice Pres*
Daniel Crofoot, *Project Mgr*
EMP: 300
SQ FT: 22,000
SALES (est): 133MM **Privately Held**
WEB: www.marousbrothers.com
SIC: 1521 1751 New construction, single-family houses; carpentry work

(G-19551)
MOODY NAT CY WILLOUGHBY MT LLC
Also Called: Courtyard By Marriott
35103 Maplegrove Rd (44094-9698)
PHONE..................................440 530-1100
Dena Heinlein, *Manager*
EMP: 50
SALES: 950K **Privately Held**
SIC: 7011 Hotels

(G-19552)
MORRIS SCHNEIDER WITTSTADT LLC
35110 Euclid Ave Ste 2 (44094-4523)
PHONE..................................440 942-5168
Dean Talaganis, *Branch Mgr*
EMP: 28
SALES (corp-wide): 11.6MM **Privately Held**
SIC: 8111 Legal services
PA: Morris Schneider Wittstadt Llc
120 Interstate North Pkwy
Atlanta GA 30339
678 298-2100

(G-19553)
NATIONAL METAL TRADING LLC
3950 Ben Hur Ave (44094-6371)
PHONE..................................440 487-9771
Ron Vaughn,
Frank Demilta,
EMP: 35
SQ FT: 5,000
SALES (est): 5.2MM **Privately Held**
WEB: www.demiltairon.com
SIC: 5051 Iron or steel flat products

(G-19554)
NELSON & BOLD INC
Also Called: Bold, E Luke MD PH D
36060 Euclid Ave Ste 201 (44094-4661)
PHONE..................................440 975-1422
Scott Nelson, *President*
EMP: 30
SALES (est): 649K **Privately Held**
SIC: 8011 5999 Ears, nose & throat specialist: physician/surgeon; hearing aids

(G-19555)
NEUNDORFER INC
Also Called: Neundorfer Engineering Service
4590 Hamann Pkwy (44094-5691)
PHONE..................................440 942-8990
Michael Neundorfer, *CEO*
EMP: 42
SQ FT: 38,000
SALES (est): 8.4MM **Privately Held**
WEB: www.neundorfer.com
SIC: 8711 3564 Pollution control engineering; precipitators, electrostatic

(G-19556)
NORTHWEST COUNTRY PLACE INC
9223 Amber Wood Dr (44094-9350)
PHONE..................................440 488-2700
Thomas A Armagno, *Branch Mgr*
EMP: 52 **Privately Held**
SIC: 8742 Management consulting services
PA: Northwest Country Place Inc
9223 Amber Wood Dr
Willoughby OH 44094

(G-19557)
OHIO BROACH & MACHINE COMPANY
35264 Topps Indus Pkwy (44094-4684)
PHONE..................................440 946-1040
Charles P Van De Motter, *CEO*
Christopher C Van De Motter, *President*
Neil Van De Motter, *Vice Pres*
Richard Van De Motter, *Vice Pres*
James L Lutz, *Treasurer*
▼ EMP: 34 EST: 1956
SQ FT: 52,000
SALES (est): 6.2MM **Privately Held**
WEB: www.ohiobroach.com
SIC: 3541 7699 3545 3599 Broaching machines; knife, saw & tool sharpening & repair; machine tool accessories; machine shop, jobbing & repair

(G-19558)
OHIO LIVING
Also Called: Breckenridge Village
36855 Ridge Rd (44094-4128)
PHONE..................................440 942-4342
Jeannie Zuydhoek, *Branch Mgr*
Michael Baranauskus, *Director*
Eric Myers, *Director*
Amy Palermo, *Hlthcr Dir*
EMP: 400 **Privately Held**
WEB: www.nwo.oprs.org
SIC: 8361 Home for the aged
PA: Ohio Living
1001 Kingsmill Pkwy
Columbus OH 43229

(G-19559)
OHIO PAVING & CNSTR CO INC
38220 Willoughby Pkwy (44094-7583)
PHONE..................................440 975-8929
John Delillo, *President*
EMP: 35
SQ FT: 10,000
SALES (est): 5.6MM **Privately Held**
WEB: www.ohiopaving.com
SIC: 1611 Surfacing & paving

(G-19560)
PALMER EXPRESS INCORPORATED
Also Called: Willo Transportation
34799 Curtis Blvd Ste A (44095-4025)
PHONE..................................440 942-3333
Robert Palmer, *President*
EMP: 47
SQ FT: 500
SALES (est): 2.5MM **Privately Held**
SIC: 4151 4215 School buses; package delivery, vehicular

(G-19561)
PAULO PRODUCTS COMPANY
Also Called: American Brzing Div Paulo Pdts
4428 Hamann Pkwy (44094-5628)
PHONE..................................440 942-0153
Bob Muto, *Branch Mgr*
Jim Loveland, *Manager*
EMP: 38
SALES (corp-wide): 98.4MM **Privately Held**
WEB: www.paulo.com
SIC: 7692 1799 Brazing; coating of concrete structures with plastic
PA: Paulo Products Company
5711 W Park Ave
Saint Louis MO 63110
314 647-7500

(G-19562)
PLATINUM RE PROFESSIONALS LLC
10 Public Sq (44094-7843)
PHONE..................................440 942-2100

Steven Sears,
EMP: 42
SALES: 827K **Privately Held**
WEB: MyPlatinumRealEstate.com
SIC: 6531 Real estate agent, residential; real estate brokers & agents

(G-19563)
POWER-PACK CONVEYOR COMPANY
38363 Airport Pkwy (44094-7562)
PHONE..................................440 975-9955
Kevin Ensinger, *President*
James L Ensinger, *President*
Donnell Ensinger, *Exec VP*
Harry Cook, *VP Mfg*
Eric Ensinger, *CFO*
EMP: 25 EST: 1929
SQ FT: 48,000
SALES: 5.6MM **Privately Held**
WEB: www.power-packconveyor.com
SIC: 5084 3531 3535 Industrial machinery & equipment; road construction & maintenance machinery; unit handling conveying systems

(G-19564)
PSYCHIATRIC SOLUTIONS INC
35900 Euclid Ave (44094-4623)
PHONE..................................440 953-3000
Cynthia Danko, *Branch Mgr*
EMP: 137
SALES (corp-wide): 10.7B **Publicly Held**
SIC: 8011 8049 Psychiatric clinic; clinical psychologist
HQ: Psychiatric Solutions, Inc.
6640 Carothers Pkwy # 500
Franklin TN 37067
615 312-5700

(G-19565)
RED OAK CAMP
Also Called: Red Barn
9057 Kirtland Chardon Rd (44094-5156)
PHONE..................................440 256-0716
Leonard K Roskos, *Director*
EMP: 40
SALES: 464.4K **Privately Held**
SIC: 7032 Youth camps

(G-19566)
REGAL CINEMAS INC
Also Called: Willoughby Commons 16
36655 Euclid Ave (44094-4450)
PHONE..................................440 975-8820
EMP: 35 **Privately Held**
WEB: www.regalcinemas.com
SIC: 7832 Motion picture theaters, except drive-in
HQ: Regal Cinemas, Inc.
101 E Blount Ave Ste 100
Knoxville TN 37920
865 922-1123

(G-19567)
REMAX HOMESOURCE
3500 Kaiser Ct Ste 300 (44095)
PHONE..................................440 951-2500
Michael Sivo, *Partner*
Alan Benjamin, *Partner*
EMP: 40
SALES (est): 1.3MM **Privately Held**
SIC: 6531 Real estate agent, residential

(G-19568)
RENTECH SOLUTIONS INC
4934 Campbell Rd Ste C (44094-3332)
PHONE..................................216 398-1111
Daniel E Collins, *President*
EMP: 89
SQ FT: 4,000
SALES (est): 10.1MM **Privately Held**
SIC: 7359 Audio-visual equipment & supply rental

(G-19569)
RYNO 24 INC
Also Called: Eagle Protective Services
4429 Hamann Pkwy Frnt (44094-5627)
PHONE..................................440 946-7700
Stephen Tryon, *President*
Frank Budic, *Vice Pres*
William Tryon, *Vice Pres*
Richard Toma, *Transportation*
EMP: 47

SALES (est): 1.2MM **Privately Held**
WEB: www.eagle-protective.com
SIC: 7381 Security guard service

(G-19570)
SENIOR INDEPENDENCE ADULT
36855 Ridge Rd (44094-4128)
PHONE..................................440 954-8372
Tina Witt, *Branch Mgr*
EMP: 35
SALES (corp-wide): 2.7MM **Privately Held**
SIC: 8322 Adult day care center
PA: Senior Independence Adult Day Services
717 Neil Ave
Columbus OH 43215
614 224-5344

(G-19571)
SIGNATURE HEALTH INC
Also Called: NORTH COAST CENTER
38882 Mentor Ave (44094-7875)
PHONE..................................440 953-9999
Jonathan Lee, *Director*
EMP: 312
SALES (est): 35.4MM **Privately Held**
SIC: 8093 Mental health clinic, outpatient

(G-19572)
SIMA MARINE SALES INC (PA)
200 Forest Dr (44095-1504)
PHONE..................................440 269-3200
John Sima, *President*
Barbara Remley, *Corp Secy*
James C Sima, *Vice Pres*
Eleanor Sima, *Asst Sec*
EMP: 30
SQ FT: 15,000
SALES (est): 5.2MM **Privately Held**
SIC: 5551 4493 Motor boat dealers; marinas

(G-19573)
SNPJ RECREATION FARM
10946 Heath Rd (44094-5183)
PHONE..................................440 256-3423
Joseph Blotneck, *Admin Sec*
EMP: 25
SALES (est): 457.9K **Privately Held**
WEB: www.snpj.org
SIC: 7299 Banquet hall facilities

(G-19574)
STEWART TITLE COMPANY
4212 State Route 306 (44094-9248)
PHONE..................................440 520-7130
EMP: 25
SALES (corp-wide): 1.9B **Publicly Held**
SIC: 6361 Real estate title insurance
HQ: Stewart Title Company
1980 Post Oak Blvd Ste 80
Houston TX 77056
713 625-8100

(G-19575)
TECHNICAL ASSURANCE INC
38112 2nd St (44094-6107)
PHONE..................................440 953-3147
William Roess, *President*
James Solether, *Vice Pres*
David Bebout, *Project Mgr*
Christin Miller, *Manager*
Scott Krabill, *Technology*
EMP: 50
SQ FT: 6,500
SALES (est): 4.1MM **Privately Held**
WEB: www.technicalassurance.com
SIC: 7389 8711 8744 1541 Building inspection service; engineering services; facilities support services; industrial buildings & warehouses; architectural engineering; computer facilities management

(G-19576)
TOM SCHAEFER PLUMBING INC
4350 Glenbrook Rd (44094-8213)
P.O. Box 547 (44096-0547)
PHONE..................................440 602-7300
Thomas E Schaefer, *President*
EMP: 30
SALES (est): 1.3MM **Privately Held**
SIC: 1711 Plumbing, heating, air-conditioning contractors

GEOGRAPHIC

(G-19577)
TRAMZ HOTELS LLC
Also Called: Fairfield Inn
35110 Maplegrove Rd (44094-9692)
PHONE................................440 975-9922
Craig Roback, *Vice Pres*
EMP: 51
SQ FT: 2,400
SALES (corp-wide): 27.2MM **Privately Held**
SIC: 7011 Hotels & motels
PA: Tramz Hotels, Llc
    31 Mountain Blvd Bldg U
    Warren NJ 07059
    908 753-7400

(G-19578)
TWO M PRECISION CO INC
Also Called: United Hydraulics
1747 Joseph Lloyd Pkwy # 3 (44094-8067)
PHONE................................440 946-2120
Mate Brkic, *President*
Nate Brkic, *Vice Pres*
Frank Bortnick, *Purchasing*
Doris Brkic, *Treasurer*
EMP: 45
SQ FT: 35,000
SALES (est): 7.2MM **Privately Held**
WEB: www.twomprecision.com
SIC: 3599 3569 7692 Machine shop, job-
bing & repair; grinding castings for the
trade; filter elements, fluid, hydraulic line;
welding repair

(G-19579)
**UNIVERSITY PRMRY CARE
PRCTICES (HQ)**
Also Called: University Hosp Hlth Sys Shake
4212 State Route 306 # 304 (44094-9258)
PHONE................................440 946-7391
Michael Nochomitz, *President*
Phyllis Hall, *CFO*
Mary Ella Rohwer, *Controller*
EMP: 26
SALES (est): 855.7K
SALES (corp-wide): 580MM **Privately
Held**
SIC: 8011 Pediatrician
PA: University Hospitals Health System,
    Inc.
    3605 Warrensville Ctr Rd
    Shaker Heights OH 44122
    216 767-8900

(G-19580)
**US MOLDING MACHINERY CO
INC**
38294 Pelton Rd (44094-7765)
PHONE................................440 918-1701
Zac Cohen, *President*
Jerry Harper, *Vice Pres*
Robert Luck, *Vice Pres*
Bill Sprowls, *Vice Pres*
Roger Anderson, *Plant Engr*
EMP: 28
SQ FT: 12,500
SALES (est): 5.2MM **Privately Held**
WEB: www.usmolding.com
SIC: 3089 7699 Injection molding of plas-
tics; industrial equipment services

(G-19581)
VECTOR TECHNICAL INC
38033 Euclid Ave Ste T9 (44094-6162)
PHONE................................440 946-8800
Tim Bleich, *President*
EMP: 150
SQ FT: 2,000
SALES (est): 7.2MM **Privately Held**
WEB: www.vectortechnicalinc.com
SIC: 7361 Executive placement

(G-19582)
WILLO SECURITY INC (PA)
38230 Glenn Ave (44094-7808)
PHONE................................440 953-9191
Raymond D Disanto, *President*
EMP: 32
SQ FT: 1,200
SALES (est): 7.4MM **Privately Held**
SIC: 7381 Security guard service

(G-19583)
WILLOUGHBY LODGING LLC
Also Called: Courtyard By Marriott
35103 Maplegrove Rd Fl 3 (44094-9698)
PHONE................................440 530-1100
Ken Hiller, *Manager*
EMP: 25
SALES (corp-wide): 1.1MM **Privately
Held**
SIC: 7011 Hotels & motels
PA: Willoughby Lodging Llc
    5966 Heisley Rd
    Mentor OH 44060
    440 701-1000

(G-19584)
**WILLOUGHBY MONTESSORI
DAY SCHL**
5543 Som Center Rd (44094-4281)
PHONE................................440 942-5602
Kathy Li, *Director*
EMP: 30
SQ FT: 10,000
SALES (est): 890K **Privately Held**
SIC: 8351 Preschool center; group day
care center; Montessori child develop-
ment center

(G-19585)
WOODHILL SUPPLY INC (PA)
4665 Beidler Rd (44094-4645)
PHONE................................440 269-1100
Arnold Kaufman, *President*
Bruce Silverberg, *Purchasing*
Bruce Shaw, *Controller*
Ann Norris, *Credit Mgr*
Edward Carpenter, *Sales Mgr*
EMP: 47 EST: 1958
SQ FT: 150,000
SALES: 13MM **Privately Held**
WEB: www.woodhillsupply.com
SIC: 5074 Plumbing fittings & supplies

Willoughby Hills
Lake County

(G-19586)
ANIMAL HOSPITAL INC
2735 Som Center Rd (44094-9121)
PHONE................................440 946-2800
Deborah Dennis, *President*
Dr J S Murray, *President*
Kelli Kerwin, *Executive*
EMP: 25
SALES (est): 3.2MM **Privately Held**
WEB: www.animalhospitalinc.com
SIC: 0742 Veterinarian, animal specialties

(G-19587)
CITY OF WILLOUGHBY HILLS
Also Called: Fire Department
35455 Chardon Rd (44094-9195)
PHONE................................440 942-7207
Robert Disanto, *Chief*
EMP: 35 **Privately Held**
WEB: www.willoughbyhills.net
SIC: 9224 8322 ; hotline
PA: City Of Willoughby Hills
    35405 Chardon Rd
    Willoughby Hills OH 44094
    440 942-9111

(G-19588)
**HOSPICE OF THE WESTERN
RESERVE**
34900 Chardon Rd Ste 105 (44094-9161)
PHONE................................440 951-8692
Kathy Maltry, *Director*
EMP: 85
SALES (corp-wide): 97.5MM **Privately
Held**
SIC: 8051 Skilled nursing care facilities
PA: Hospice Of The Western Reserve, Inc
    17876 Saint Clair Ave
    Cleveland OH 44110
    216 383-2222

(G-19589)
**HOSPICE OF THE WESTERN
RESERVE**
34900 Chardon Rd Ste 105 (44094-9161)
PHONE................................440 357-5833

Cathy Maltry, *Principal*
EMP: 100
SALES (corp-wide): 97.5MM **Privately
Held**
SIC: 8059 Convalescent home
PA: Hospice Of The Western Reserve, Inc
    17876 Saint Clair Ave
    Cleveland OH 44110
    216 383-2222

(G-19590)
**KAVAL-LEVINE MANAGEMENT
CO**
34500 Chardon Rd Ste 5 (44094-8239)
PHONE................................440 944-5402
Marcie Levine, *President*
EMP: 25
SALES (est): 2.6MM **Privately Held**
SIC: 6531 Real estate managers

(G-19591)
MICRO PRODUCTS CO INC
26653 Curtiss Wright Pkwy (44092-2832)
PHONE................................440 943-0258
Arthur Anton, *President*
Reese Armstrong, *Safety Mgr*
Frank Roddy, *CFO*
Ernie Mansour, *Admin Sec*
EMP: 70 EST: 1981
SQ FT: 10,000
SALES (est): 3.7MM
SALES (corp-wide): 940.1MM **Privately
Held**
WEB: www.swagelok.com
SIC: 3471 7389 Plating & polishing; grind-
ing, precision: commercial or industrial
PA: Swagelok Company
    29500 Solon Rd
    Solon OH 44139
    440 248-4600

(G-19592)
**PRIMEHALTH WNS HLTH
SPECIALIST**
35040 Chardon Rd Ste 205 (44094-9004)
PHONE................................440 918-4630
Cynthia Moore-Heardy, *CEO*
EMP: 30
SALES (est): 1.7MM **Privately Held**
SIC: 8011 Obstetrician

(G-19593)
S & P SOLUTIONS INC
35000 Chardon Rd Ste 110 (44094-9018)
PHONE................................440 918-9111
Gary Bates, *President*
EMP: 130
SQ FT: 8,500
SALES (est): 11.4MM **Privately Held**
WEB: www.sps-solutions.com
SIC: 7379 5734 8243 5045 Data pro-
cessing consultant; computer software &
accessories; operator training, computer;
computers, peripherals & software

(G-19594)
SOUTH EAST CHEVROLET CO
2810 Bishop Rd (44092-2604)
PHONE................................440 585-9300
Patt Obrien, *President*
EMP: 42
SQ FT: 48,000
SALES (est): 7.7MM **Privately Held**
SIC: 5511 7515 7513 5012 Automobiles,
new & used; passenger car leasing; truck
rental & leasing, no drivers; automobiles
& other motor vehicles

Willow Wood
Lawrence County

(G-19595)
MANNON PIPELINE LLC
9160 State Route 378 (45696-9014)
PHONE................................740 643-1534
Darren Mannon,
EMP: 39 EST: 2010
SALES (est): 5.9MM **Privately Held**
SIC: 1623 Pipeline construction

Willowick
Lake County

(G-19596)
**BAUR LEO CENTURY 21
REALTY**
32801 Vine St Ste D (44095-3380)
PHONE................................440 585-2300
Tim Baur, *Owner*
EMP: 26
SALES: 1.4MM **Privately Held**
SIC: 6531 Real estate agent, residential

(G-19597)
DAWNCHEM INC
Also Called: Dawn Chemical
30510 Lakeland Blvd Frnt (44095-5239)
PHONE................................440 943-3332
Edward Rossi, *President*
Brian Benson, *Vice Pres*
Janine Thomas, *Opers Mgr*
Dave Vranic, *Purch Mgr*
Todd Readence, *Accounts Mgr*
EMP: 40
SQ FT: 40,000
SALES (est): 25.1MM **Privately Held**
WEB: www.dawnchem.com
SIC: 5169 5087 5113 Specialty cleaning
& sanitation preparations; cleaning &
maintenance equipment & supplies; in-
dustrial & personal service paper

(G-19598)
**EXCALIBUR AUTO BODY INC
(PA)**
Also Called: Excalibur Body & Frame
30520 Lakeland Blvd (44095-5202)
PHONE................................440 942-5550
Mitchell Rudolph, *Principal*
EMP: 32
SQ FT: 14,000
SALES (est): 4.4MM **Privately Held**
SIC: 7532 Body shop, automotive; paint
shop, automotive

Wilmington
Clinton County

(G-19599)
797 ELKS GOLF CLUB INC
2593 E Us Highway 22 3 (45177-8947)
P.O. Box 469 (45177-0469)
PHONE................................937 382-2666
John Wynn, *Superintendent*
Robert Holmes, *Treasurer*
EMP: 27
SQ FT: 1,152
SALES (est): 740.3K **Privately Held**
SIC: 7992 7997 7999 5941 Public golf
courses; golf club, membership; golf driv-
ing range; golf goods & equipment

(G-19600)
ABX AIR INC (HQ)
145 Hunter Dr (45177-9550)
PHONE................................937 382-5591
Joe Hete, *CEO*
John Starkovich, *President*
James E Bushman, *Principal*
James H Carey, *Principal*
Jeffrey A Dominick, *Principal*
EMP: 500
SQ FT: 37,000
SALES (est): 152.8MM **Publicly Held**
SIC: 4513 5088 4581 8299 Letter deliv-
ery, private air; package delivery, private
air; parcel delivery, private air; aircraft &
parts; aircraft servicing & repairing; flying
instruction

(G-19601)
ABX AIR INC
Abx Equipment and Facility Svc
145 Hunter Dr (45177-9550)
PHONE................................937 366-2282
Jim Osborne, *Branch Mgr*
EMP: 849 **Publicly Held**
SIC: 4513 Letter delivery, private air

2019 Harris Ohio
Services Directory

▲ = Import ▼=Export
◆ =Import/Export

HQ: Abx Air, Inc.
145 Hunter Dr
Wilmington OH 45177
937 382-5591

(G-19602)
ACCURATE MECHANICAL INC
363 E Main St (45177-2314)
PHONE..................................937 382-1436
Thomas White, *President*
EMP: 25
SALES (corp-wide): 26.3MM **Privately Held**
SIC: 1711 Warm air heating & air conditioning contractor
PA: Accurate Mechanical, Inc.
3001 River Rd
Chillicothe OH
740 775-5005

(G-19603)
AIR TRANSPORT SVCS GROUP INC (PA)
Also Called: Atsg
145 Hunter Dr (45177-9550)
P.O. Box 966 (45177-0966)
PHONE..................................937 382-5591
Randy D Rademacher, *Ch of Bd*
Joseph C Hete, *President*
Jack Greenwood, *General Mgr*
Richard F Corrado, *COO*
W Joseph Payne, *Senior VP*
EMP: 56
SQ FT: 310,000
SALES: 892.3MM **Publicly Held**
SIC: 4513 Air courier services

(G-19604)
AIRBORNE MAINT ENGRG SVCS INC
1111 Airport Rd (45177-8904)
PHONE..................................937 366-2559
James McIntosh, *Sales Staff*
Brady Price, *Branch Mgr*
EMP: 502 **Publicly Held**
SIC: 7699 5088 Aircraft & heavy equipment repair services; aircraft & parts
HQ: Airborne Maintenance And Engineering Services, Inc.
145 Hunter Dr
Wilmington OH 45177

(G-19605)
AIRBORNE MAINT ENGRG SVCS INC (HQ)
145 Hunter Dr (45177-9550)
PHONE..................................937 382-5591
Brady Templeton, *President*
Scott Glasser, *President*
Joseph Ryan, *COO*
Gary Stover, *Vice Pres*
Richard Ratliff, *Project Mgr*
EMP: 86
SALES (est): 89.2MM **Publicly Held**
SIC: 7699 5088 Aircraft & heavy equipment repair services; aircraft & parts

(G-19606)
AMES MATERIAL SERVICES INC
145 Hunter Dr (45177-9550)
P.O. Box 966 (45177-0966)
PHONE..................................937 382-5591
Joseph Hete, *President*
John Graver, *President*
EMP: 800
SALES (est): 73MM **Publicly Held**
WEB: www.abxair.com
SIC: 4513 Air courier services
PA: Air Transport Services Group, Inc.
145 Hunter Dr
Wilmington OH 45177

(G-19607)
CHAMPONS IN MAKING DAYCARE LLC
160 Park Dr (45177-2041)
PHONE..................................937 728-4886
Tamara Rollins, *Director*
Hope Wilson-Belle,
EMP: 28 EST: 2006
SALES (est): 397.1K **Privately Held**
SIC: 8351 Group day care center

(G-19608)
CITY OF WILMINGTON
Also Called: Wilmington City Cab Service
260 Charles St (45177-2883)
PHONE..................................937 382-7961
Jeanie Foster, *Branch Mgr*
EMP: 45 **Privately Held**
WEB: www.ci.wilmington.oh.us
SIC: 4111 9111 Airport transportation; mayors' offices
PA: City Of Wilmington
69 N South St
Wilmington OH 45177
937 382-1880

(G-19609)
CLINTON COUNTY BOARD OF DD
4425 State Route 730 (45177-8661)
PHONE..................................937 382-7519
Kyle Lewis, *Superintendent*
EMP: 27
SALES (est): 1MM **Privately Held**
SIC: 8322 8093 Referral service for personal & social problems; specialty outpatient clinics

(G-19610)
CLINTON COUNTY COMMUNITY ACTN (PA)
789 N Nelson Ave (45177-8348)
P.O. Box 32 (45177-0032)
PHONE..................................937 382-8365
Ray Camp, *Comptroller*
Doug Tucker, *Manager*
Dean Knapp, *Director*
Stella Cramer, *Director*
Susan Stai, *Director*
EMP: 82
SQ FT: 11,782
SALES: 4.6MM **Privately Held**
SIC: 8399 Community action agency

(G-19611)
CLINTON COUNTY COMMUNITY ACTN
Also Called: Clinton County Head Start
789 N Nelson Ave (45177-8348)
P.O. Box 32 (45177-0032)
PHONE..................................937 382-5624
Carole Erdman, *Director*
EMP: 32
SALES (corp-wide): 4.6MM **Privately Held**
SIC: 8399 8351 Community action agency; head start center, except in conjunction with school
PA: Clinton County Community Action Program, Inc
789 N Nelson Ave
Wilmington OH 45177
937 382-8365

(G-19612)
CLINTON COUNTY DEPT JOBS/FMLY
Also Called: Job & Family Svcs Clinton Cnty
1025 S South St Ste 200 (45177-2788)
PHONE..................................937 382-0963
Bart Barber, *Director*
EMP: 60
SALES (est): 17.1MM **Privately Held**
SIC: 6371 9441 Pension, health & welfare funds;

(G-19613)
CLINTON MEMORIAL HOSPITAL (PA)
610 W Mn St (45177)
P.O. Box 600 (45177-0600)
PHONE..................................937 382-6611
Mark Dooley, *President*
Bradley Mabry, *COO*
Bob Curtis, *Maint Spvr*
Ken Peters, *Buyer*
Sheila Rose, *Buyer*
EMP: 630
SQ FT: 200,000
SALES (est): 59.5MM **Privately Held**
WEB: www.cmhregional.com
SIC: 8062 General medical & surgical hospitals

(G-19614)
CLINTON MEMORIAL HOSPITAL
Also Called: Clinton Memorial Fmly Hlth Ctr
825 W Locust St (45177-2118)
PHONE..................................937 383-3402
Greg Taulbee, *Principal*
EMP: 41
SALES (corp-wide): 59.5MM **Privately Held**
WEB: www.cmhregional.com
SIC: 6733 8011 8093 Trusts; general & family practice, physician/surgeon; specialty outpatient clinics
PA: Clinton Memorial Hospital
610 W Mn St
Wilmington OH 45177
937 382-6611

(G-19615)
CLINTON MEMORIAL HOSPITAL
Also Called: Foster J Boyd MD Regnl Cncr CT
31 Farquhar Ave (45177-2188)
PHONE..................................937 283-2273
Becky Allen, *Branch Mgr*
EMP: 45
SALES (corp-wide): 59.5MM **Privately Held**
WEB: www.cmhregional.com
SIC: 8011 Medical centers
PA: Clinton Memorial Hospital
610 W Mn St
Wilmington OH 45177
937 382-6611

(G-19616)
COMMUNITY ACTION PROGRAM INC
789 N Nelson Ave (45177-8348)
P.O. Box 32 (45177-0032)
PHONE..................................937 382-0225
Dean Knapp, *Administration*
EMP: 85
SALES (est): 1.6MM **Privately Held**
SIC: 8399 Social Services

(G-19617)
COMMUNITY CARE HOSPICE
1669 Rombach Ave (45177-1965)
P.O. Box 123 (45177-0123)
PHONE..................................937 382-5400
Patricia Settlemyre, *Administration*
Michelle Huffman,
EMP: 43
SALES: 2.6MM **Privately Held**
SIC: 8069 Specialty hospitals, except psychiatric

(G-19618)
COMPTON METAL PRODUCTS INC
416 Steele Rd (45177-9332)
PHONE..................................937 382-2403
James Compton, *President*
EMP: 82
SQ FT: 2,000
SALES (est): 2.4MM **Privately Held**
SIC: 7699 3599 7692 Engine repair & replacement, non-automotive; machine shop, jobbing & repair; welding repair

(G-19619)
COUNTY OF CLINTON
Also Called: Clinton County Childrens Svcs
1025 S South St Ste 300 (45177-2788)
PHONE..................................937 382-2449
John Hosler, *Director*
EMP: 40 **Privately Held**
WEB: www.clincohd.com
SIC: 8322 Child related social services
PA: County Of Clinton
46 S South St Rm 213
Wilmington OH 45177
937 382-2103

(G-19620)
COUNTY OF CLINTON
Also Called: Clinton County Highway Dept
1326 Fife Ave (45177-2462)
PHONE..................................937 382-2078
Jeffrey Linkous, *Principal*
EMP: 40 **Privately Held**
WEB: www.clincohd.com
SIC: 1611 Highway & street maintenance

PA: County Of Clinton
46 S South St Rm 213
Wilmington OH 45177
937 382-2103

(G-19621)
DASH LOGISTICS INC
259 Olinger Cir (45177-2484)
PHONE..................................937 382-9110
Tim Williams, *President*
Tracy Zammert, *Office Mgr*
Steve Barton, *Admin Sec*
EMP: 30
SALES (est): 2.8MM **Privately Held**
SIC: 7389 Courier or messenger service

(G-19622)
EQUIPMENT MGT SVC & REPR INC
Also Called: Emsar
270 Davids Dr (45177-2491)
PHONE..................................937 383-1052
Renee Lapine, *President*
Rob Hedrick, *Business Mgr*
Shari Woods, *Opers Staff*
Stephanie Rogers, *Accounting Mgr*
Rebecca Bryant, *Human Res Mgr*
▲ EMP: 27
SQ FT: 10,000
SALES (est): 6.4MM
SALES (corp-wide): 32.2MM **Privately Held**
WEB: www.emsar.com
SIC: 7699 Medical equipment repair, non-electric
PA: Csa Service Solutions, Llc
9208 Waterford Ctr
Austin TX 78758
877 487-5360

(G-19623)
FERNO-WASHINGTON INC (PA)
70 Weil Way (45177-9300)
PHONE..................................877 733-0911
Elroy Bourgraf, *Ch of Bd*
Joseph Bourgraf, *President*
Sandy Frazier, *General Mgr*
Becky Jenkins, *General Mgr*
Bruce Whitaker, *Managing Dir*
◆ EMP: 149 EST: 1955
SQ FT: 212,000
SALES (est): 93.5MM **Privately Held**
SIC: 5047 Medical equipment & supplies

(G-19624)
G & J PEPSI-COLA BOTTLERS INC
3500 Progress Way (45177-8974)
PHONE..................................937 393-5744
Jim Malone, *Branch Mgr*
EMP: 25
SALES (corp-wide): 418.3MM **Privately Held**
WEB: www.gjpepsi.com
SIC: 4225 General warehousing
PA: G & J Pepsi-Cola Bottlers Inc
9435 Waterstone Blvd # 390
Cincinnati OH 45249
513 785-6060

(G-19625)
JET MINTENANCE CONSULTING CORP
1113 Airport Rd Ste Jmcc (45177-8904)
PHONE..................................937 205-2406
Joseph Merry, *President*
Stephen Huffman, *Manager*
EMP: 25 EST: 2013
SALES: 500K **Privately Held**
SIC: 7363 8249 Pilot service, aviation; aviation school

(G-19626)
LABORATORY CORPORATION AMERICA
630 W Main St (45177-2170)
PHONE..................................937 383-6964
Brian Ondulick, *Branch Mgr*
EMP: 25 **Publicly Held**
SIC: 8071 Testing laboratories
HQ: Laboratory Corporation Of America
358 S Main St Ste 458
Burlington NC 27215
336 229-1127

GEOGRAPHIC

(G-19627)
LGSTX SERVICES INC (HQ)
145 Hunter Dr (45177-9550)
PHONE.................................866 931-2337
Gary Stover, *President*
Nicholas Reed, *Opers Spvr*
Mark Pauley, *Purch Agent*
Todd Reed, *Bus Dvlpt Dir*
Jack Anderson, *Manager*
EMP: 31
SALES (est): 15MM **Publicly Held**
SIC: 4513 Air courier services

(G-19628)
LIBERTY CAPITAL INC (PA)
3435 Airborne Rd Ste B (45177-8951)
PHONE.................................937 382-1000
James R Powell, *President*
Tim Fiedler, *Manager*
Kent Powell, *Shareholder*
John H Powell, *Admin Sec*
Elaine Warren, *Admin Sec*
EMP: 71
SALES: 30.5MM **Privately Held**
SIC: 6035 Federal savings & loan associations

(G-19629)
LIBERTY SAVINGS BANK FSB (HQ)
2251 Rombach Ave (45177-1995)
P.O. Box 1000 (45177-1000)
PHONE.................................937 382-1000
James R Powell, *Ch of Bd*
John H Powell, *Vice Ch Bd*
Robert E Reed, *President*
Fred Blume, *Principal*
Bruce Clapp, *Vice Pres*
EMP: 113
SQ FT: 50,000
SALES: 28.1MM
SALES (corp-wide): 30.5MM **Privately Held**
WEB: www.liberty-direct.com
SIC: 6022 State commercial banks
PA: Liberty Capital, Inc.
　　3435 Airborne Rd Ste B
　　Wilmington OH 45177
　　937 382-1000

(G-19630)
LOWES HOME CENTERS LLC
1175 Rombach Ave (45177-1940)
PHONE.................................937 383-7000
Darryl Allen, *Branch Mgr*
EMP: 150
SALES (corp-wide): 68.6B **Publicly Held**
SIC: 5211 5031 5722 5064 Home centers; building materials, exterior; building materials, interior; household appliance stores; electrical appliances, television & radio
HQ: Lowe's Home Centers, Llc
　　1605 Curtis Bridge Rd
　　Wilkesboro NC 28697
　　336 658-4000

(G-19631)
LT LAND DEVELOPMENT LLC
94 N South St Ste A (45177-2097)
PHONE.................................937 382-0072
Ralph Larry Roberts, *Mng Member*
Terri Roberts,
EMP: 30
SALES (est): 1.4MM **Privately Held**
SIC: 6552 6531 Subdividers & developers; real estate leasing & rentals

(G-19632)
M C TRUCKING COMPANY LLC
Also Called: Melvin Stone
228 Melvin Rd (45177-8750)
P.O. Box 158, Sabina (45169-0158)
PHONE.................................937 584-2486
Dennis Garrison,
EMP: 40 EST: 1951
SQ FT: 2,000
SALES (est): 3.5MM **Privately Held**
SIC: 4212 Local trucking, without storage

(G-19633)
MARK E GROSINGER (PA)
Also Called: Montgomery Ear Nose/Throat CL
1150 W Locust St Ste 500 (45177-2062)
PHONE.................................937 382-2000
Mark E Grosinger, *Owner*

EMP: 25
SALES (est): 891.4K **Privately Held**
SIC: 8011 Ears, nose & throat specialist: physician/surgeon

(G-19634)
MB FINANCIAL INC
2251 Rombach Ave (45177-1995)
PHONE.................................937 283-2027
EMP: 86
SALES (corp-wide): 7.9B **Publicly Held**
SIC: 8742 6162 6029 Financial consultant; mortgage bankers & correspondents; commercial banks
HQ: Mb Financial, Inc.
　　800 W Madison St
　　Chicago IL 60607

(G-19635)
MENTAL HEALTH & RECOVERY CTR (PA)
Also Called: Crisis Counseling Center
953 S South St (45177-2921)
PHONE.................................937 383-3031
Phyllis Mitchell, *Director*
EMP: 25
SQ FT: 5,200
SALES: 5.3K **Privately Held**
WEB: www.mhrccc.org
SIC: 8093 8322 8069 Specialty Outpatient Fac Individual/Family Svcs Specialty Hospital

(G-19636)
NATIONAL WEATHER SERVICE
Also Called: Ohio River Forecast
1901 S State Route 134 (45177-9708)
PHONE.................................937 383-0031
Ken Haydu, *Manager*
EMP: 44 **Publicly Held**
SIC: 8999 9611 7389 Weather forecasting; administration of general economic programs; ; music & broadcasting services
HQ: National Weather Service
　　1325 E West Hwy
　　Silver Spring MD 20910

(G-19637)
PC CONNECTION INC
3336 Progress Way Bldg 11 (45177-8928)
PHONE.................................937 382-4800
Angie Hargett, *Controller*
Gretchen Myers, *Human Res Mgr*
John Moran, *Manager*
Jeffrey Curry, *Manager*
Ben Norman, *Technology*
EMP: 175
SALES (corp-wide): 2.7B **Publicly Held**
SIC: 4226 5045 Special warehousing & storage; computers, peripherals & software
PA: Pc Connection, Inc.
　　730 Milford Rd
　　Merrimack NH 03054
　　603 683-2000

(G-19638)
PC CONNECTION SALES CORP
2870 Old State 1 (45177)
PHONE.................................937 382-4800
John Moran, *Manager*
EMP: 125
SALES (corp-wide): 2.7B **Publicly Held**
SIC: 4225 5961 General warehousing & storage; computers & peripheral equipment, mail order
HQ: Pc Connection Sales Corp
　　730 Milford Rd
　　Merrimack NH 03054
　　603 423-2000

(G-19639)
PC CONNECTION SERVICES
Also Called: Distribution Center
2870 Old State Route 73 # 1 (45177-8997)
PHONE.................................937 382-4800
EMP: 148
SALES (est): 47.7MM **Privately Held**
SIC: 7379 Computer Related Services

(G-19640)
PEOPLES BANK
48 N South St (45177-2212)
PHONE.................................937 382-1441
John Limbert, *President*
EMP: 68

EMP: 200
SALES (corp-wide): 208MM **Publicly Held**
SIC: 6021 National commercial banks
HQ: Peoples Bank
　　138 Putnam St
　　Marietta OH 45750
　　740 373-3155

(G-19641)
PREMIER FEEDS LLC
238 Melvin Rd (45177-8750)
PHONE.................................937 584-2411
John Haynes, *Manager*
EMP: 25
SALES (corp-wide): 16.2MM **Privately Held**
SIC: 5191 Feed
HQ: Premier Feeds, Llc
　　292 N Howard St
　　Sabina OH 45169
　　937 584-2411

(G-19642)
R+L PRAMOUNT TRNSP SYSTEMS INC
Also Called: RI Global Services
600 Gilliam Rd (45177-9089)
P.O. Box 271 (45177-0271)
PHONE.................................937 382-1494
Michael Shroyer, *President*
Ralph L Roberts, *Vice Pres*
Robby L Roberts, *Vice Pres*
Tom Roberts, *Vice Pres*
EMP: 400
SALES (est): 28.6MM **Privately Held**
WEB: www.rlcarriers.com
SIC: 4213 Trucking, except local
PA: R & L Carriers, Inc.
　　600 Gilliam Rd
　　Wilmington OH 45177

(G-19643)
RCHP - WILMINGTON LLC (PA)
Also Called: Clinton Memorial Hospital
610 W Main St (45177-2125)
P.O. Box 600 (45177-0600)
PHONE.................................937 382-6611
Greg Nielsen, *CEO*
Marcy Hawley, *Chairman*
James Reynolds, *Chairman*
Mark Rembert, *Vice Chairman*
Eric Jost, *CFO*
EMP: 72
SALES: 78.4MM **Privately Held**
SIC: 8062 8361 General medical & surgical hospitals; rehabilitation center, residential: health care incidental

(G-19644)
RENAL LIFE LINK INC
Also Called: Willow Dialysis Cntr
1675 Alex Dr (45177-2446)
PHONE.................................937 383-3338
Angela Parkins, *Branch Mgr*
EMP: 25 **Publicly Held**
WEB: www.davita.com
SIC: 8092 Kidney dialysis centers
HQ: Renal Life Link, Inc.
　　2000 16th St
　　Denver CO 80202
　　253 280-9501

(G-19645)
RLR INVESTMENTS LLC
600 Gilliam Rd (45177-9089)
PHONE.................................937 382-1494
Mark Sherman, *Director*
James S Wachs,
EMP: 100
SALES (est): 17.3MM **Privately Held**
SIC: 4222 Warehousing, cold storage or refrigerated

(G-19646)
ROSE & DOBYNS AN OHIO PARTNR (PA)
97 N South St (45177-1644)
PHONE.................................937 382-2838
Gordon Rose, *Partner*
Michael Campbell, *Partner*
J Michael Dobyns, *Partner*
Richard Federle Jr, *Partner*
John Porter, *Partner*
EMP: 68

SALES (est): 3.8MM **Privately Held**
WEB: www.rosedobynslaw.com
SIC: 8111 General practice attorney, lawyer

(G-19647)
S & S MANAGEMENT INC
Also Called: Holiday Inn
155 Holiday Dr (45177-8763)
PHONE.................................937 382-5858
Bryan Powell, *General Mgr*
EMP: 25
SALES (corp-wide): 6.9MM **Privately Held**
SIC: 7011 Hotels
PA: S & S Management Inc
　　550 Folkerth Ave 100
　　Sidney OH 45365
　　937 498-9645

(G-19648)
SEWELL LEASING CORPORATION
Also Called: Sewell Motor Express
370 Davids Dr (45177-2424)
PHONE.................................937 382-3847
Janet Sewell, *CEO*
Jay Sewell, *President*
Leslie Williams, *Vice Pres*
▲ EMP: 70 EST: 1921
SQ FT: 90,000
SALES (est): 10.7MM **Privately Held**
WEB: www.sewellmotorexpress.com
SIC: 4213 4212 Contract haulers; local trucking, without storage

(G-19649)
STOKES FRUIT FARM
3182 Center Rd (45177-9490)
PHONE.................................937 382-4004
Dale Stokes, *Owner*
EMP: 40
SALES (est): 1.6MM **Privately Held**
SIC: 0171 0115 0111 Raspberry farm; corn; wheat

(G-19650)
SUNRISE COOPERATIVE INC
1425 Rombach Ave (45177-1946)
P.O. Box 512 (45177-0512)
PHONE.................................937 382-1633
Steve Haines, *Branch Mgr*
EMP: 28
SALES (corp-wide): 56.3MM **Privately Held**
SIC: 5191 Feed
PA: Sunrise Cooperative, Inc.
　　2025 W State St Ste A
　　Fremont OH 43420
　　419 332-6468

(G-19651)
TECHNICOLOR THOMSON GROUP
Also Called: Technicolor Entertainment Svcs
3418 Progress Way (45177-8952)
PHONE.................................937 383-6000
Tim Burke, *Manager*
EMP: 250
SALES (corp-wide): 62.9MM **Privately Held**
WEB: www.technicolor.com
SIC: 7819 7822 7829 5043 Video tape or disk reproduction; developing & printing of commercial motion picture film; motion picture & tape distribution; motion picture distribution services; photographic equipment & supplies
HQ: Technicolor Thomson Group, Inc
　　2233 N Ontario St Ste 300
　　Burbank CA 91504
　　818 260-3600

(G-19652)
UNITED PARCEL SERVICE INC OH
Also Called: UPS
2500 S Us Highway 68 (45177-8698)
PHONE.................................937 382-0658
Dave Bartko, *Manager*
Mark Moscinski, *Manager*
EMP: 158
SALES (corp-wide): 71.8B **Publicly Held**
WEB: www.martrac.com
SIC: 4215 Package delivery, vehicular

▲ = Import ▼=Export
◆ =Import/Export

HQ: United Parcel Service, Inc. (Oh)
55 Glenlake Pkwy
Atlanta GA 30328
404 828-6000

(G-19653)
WILMINGTON HALTHCARE GROUP INC
Also Called: Wilmington Nrsng & Rehab Cntr
75 Hale St (45177-2104)
PHONE...................................937 382-1621
George S Repchick, *President*
William I Weisberg, *Vice Pres*
Sarah Depompei, *Finance Asst*
EMP: 100
SQ FT: 15,000
SALES (est): 3.2MM **Privately Held**
SIC: 8051 Skilled nursing care facilities

(G-19654)
WILMINGTON IRON AND MET CO INC
2149 S Us Highway 68 (45177-8629)
PHONE...................................937 382-3867
Robert Raizk, *President*
Dennis Hayes, *Vice Pres*
EMP: 25
SQ FT: 2,500
SALES (est): 6.3MM **Privately Held**
SIC: 5093 Ferrous metal scrap & waste; nonferrous metals scrap

(G-19655)
WILMINGTON MEDICAL ASSOCIATES
1184 W Locust St (45177-2009)
PHONE...................................937 382-1616
Thomas Neville MD, *President*
Tracy Coomer, *Administration*
EMP: 65
SQ FT: 10,000
SALES (est): 5.8MM **Privately Held**
SIC: 8011 General & family practice, physician/surgeon; pediatrician

(G-19656)
WRIGHT EXECUTIVE HT LTD PARTNR
123 Gano Rd (45177-8848)
PHONE...................................937 283-3200
Gray Campbell, *Manager*
EMP: 128 **Privately Held**
WEB: www.hwdaytonfairborn.com
SIC: 7011 Hotels & motels
PA: Wright Executive Hotel Limited Partnership
2800 Presidential Dr
Beavercreek OH 45324

Wilmot
Stark County

(G-19657)
AMISH DOOR INC (PA)
Also Called: Amish Door Restaurant
1210 Winesburg St (44689)
P.O. Box 215 (44689-0215)
PHONE...................................330 359-5464
Milo Miller, *President*
Eric Gerber, *Vice Pres*
Yvonne Torrence, *Treasurer*
Katherine Miller, *Shareholder*
EMP: 294
SQ FT: 7,500
SALES (est): 17.4MM **Privately Held**
WEB: www.amishdoor.com
SIC: 5947 5812 7011 2051 Gift shop; restaurant, family: independent; hotels & motels; bread, cake & related products

Winchester
Adams County

(G-19658)
1ST STOP INC (PA)
Also Called: Cantrell's Motel
18856 State Route 136 (45697-9793)
P.O. Box 175 (45697-0175)
PHONE...................................937 695-0318
Robert Cantrell, *President*

Mike Gregory, *Info Tech Mgr*
Linda Cantrell, *Admin Sec*
EMP: 30
SQ FT: 12,000
SALES (est): 37.1MM **Privately Held**
SIC: 5411 7011 Convenience stores, independent; motels

(G-19659)
ADAMS & BROWN COUNTIES ECONOMI
Also Called: Adams Brown Wthrzation Program
19211 Main St (45697)
P.O. Box 188 (45697-0188)
PHONE...................................937 695-0316
Gary Tabor, *Admin Director*
EMP: 30
SALES (corp-wide): 10.4MM **Privately Held**
SIC: 8399 Community action agency
PA: Adams & Brown Counties Economic Opportunities, Inc.
406 W Plum St
Georgetown OH 45121
937 378-6041

(G-19660)
CANTRELL OIL COMPANY
Also Called: Winchester Wholesale
18856 State Route 136 (45697-9793)
P.O. Box 175 (45697-0175)
PHONE...................................937 695-8003
Robert Cantrell Jr, *President*
Linda Cantrell, *Admin Sec*
EMP: 46
SQ FT: 4,800
SALES (est): 29.7MM **Privately Held**
SIC: 5141 5169 Food brokers; essential oils

(G-19661)
FIRST STATE BANK (PA)
19230 State Route 136 (45697-9571)
PHONE...................................937 695-0331
Michael Pell, *President*
Chris Baxla, *COO*
Judd Johnson, *Vice Pres*
David Richey, *CFO*
Jo Hanson, *Human Res Mgr*
EMP: 30 EST: 1884
SQ FT: 9,363
SALES: 19.8MM **Privately Held**
WEB: www.fsbadamscounty.com
SIC: 6022 State commercial banks

(G-19662)
HANSON AGGREGATES EAST LLC
13526 Overstake Rd (45697-9644)
PHONE...................................937 442-6009
Bob Roades, *Plant Mgr*
Bobby Roades, *Branch Mgr*
EMP: 30
SALES (corp-wide): 20.6B **Privately Held**
SIC: 1422 Crushed & broken limestone
HQ: Hanson Aggregates East Llc
3131 Rdu Center Dr
Morrisville NC 27560
919 380-2500

Windham
Portage County

(G-19663)
RICK KUNTZ TRUCKING INC
9056 State Route 88 (44288-9726)
P.O. Box 775, Ravenna (44266-0775)
PHONE...................................330 296-9311
Rick Kuntz, *President*
Valarie Kuntz, *Corp Secy*
EMP: 35
SQ FT: 7,000
SALES (est): 4.9MM **Privately Held**
SIC: 4212 Local trucking, without storage

(G-19664)
TURNPIKE AND INFRASTRUCTURE CO
Also Called: Hiram Maintenance Bldg
9196 State Route 700 (44288-9744)
PHONE...................................330 527-2169
R Underwood, *Superintendent*

EMP: 80 **Privately Held**
WEB: www.ohioturnpike.net
SIC: 1611 0782 9621 Highway & street maintenance; highway lawn & garden maintenance services; regulation, administration of transportation;
HQ: Ohio Turnpike And Infrastructure Commission
682 Prospect St
Berea OH 44017
440 234-2081

Windsor
Ashtabula County

(G-19665)
LYNNHAVEN V LLC
Also Called: Grand Valley Country Manor
5165 State Route 322 (44099-9623)
PHONE...................................440 272-5600
Dr Kenneth Hubbard, *CEO*
Stanley Huffman, *President*
EMP: 125
SALES: 3.5MM **Privately Held**
SIC: 8051 8052 Skilled nursing care facilities; intermediate care facilities

Winesburg
Holmes County

(G-19666)
R W SAUDER INC
Also Called: Sauder's Quality Eggs
2648 Us Rt 62 (44690)
PHONE...................................330 359-5440
Wayne Troyer, *Manager*
EMP: 48
SALES (corp-wide): 180MM **Privately Held**
WEB: www.sauderseggs.com
SIC: 5144 Eggs
PA: R. W. Sauder Inc.
570 Furnace Hills Pike
Lititz PA 17543
717 626-2074

Wintersville
Jefferson County

(G-19667)
ADDUS HOMECARE CORPORATION
Also Called: Addus Home Care
1406 Cadiz Rd (43953-9058)
PHONE...................................866 684-0385
EMP: 674 **Publicly Held**
SIC: 8082 Home health care services
PA: Addus Homecare Corporation
6801 Gaylord Pkwy Ste 110
Frisco TX 75034

(G-19668)
BATES BROS AMUSEMENT CO
1506 Fernwood Rd (43953-7640)
PHONE...................................740 266-2950
Eric Bates, *President*
Dolores Bates, *President*
EMP: 75
SALES (est): 4.1MM **Privately Held**
WEB: www.batesbros.com
SIC: 7999 Amusement ride

(G-19669)
COMMUNICARE HEALTH SVCS INC
Also Called: Salem West Healthcare Center
135 Reichart Ave (43953-4050)
PHONE...................................877 366-5306
Toni Fuzo, *Manager*
EMP: 140
SQ FT: 33,805
SALES (corp-wide): 125.8MM **Privately Held**
WEB: www.atriumlivingcenters.com
SIC: 8051 Skilled nursing care facilities

PA: Communicare Health Services, Inc.
4700 Ashwood Dr Ste 200
Blue Ash OH 45241
513 530-1654

(G-19670)
FAYETTE PARTS SERVICE INC
618 Canton Rd (43953-4118)
PHONE...................................724 880-3616
Carl Dellapenna, *Branch Mgr*
EMP: 103
SALES (corp-wide): 58MM **Privately Held**
SIC: 7549 Automotive maintenance services
PA: Fayette Parts Service, Inc.
325 E Main St
Uniontown PA
724 785-2506

Woodsfield
Monroe County

(G-19671)
BOARD MENTAL RETARDATION DVLPM
Also Called: Monroe Achievement Center
47011 State Route 26 (43793-9330)
P.O. Box 623 (43793-0623)
PHONE...................................740 472-1712
Helen Ring, *Superintendent*
Duane Burton, *Principal*
EMP: 32
SALES (est): 1MM **Privately Held**
SIC: 8322 Social services for the handicapped

(G-19672)
CITIZENS NATIONAL BANK (PA)
143 S Main St (43793-1022)
P.O. Box 230 (43793-0230)
PHONE...................................740 472-1696
Stanley Heft, *Ch of Bd*
Carey Bott, *President*
Bruce Climber, *Vice Pres*
Lois Sivard, *Vice Pres*
EMP: 30
SQ FT: 3,500
SALES: 3.1MM **Privately Held**
SIC: 6021 National commercial banks

(G-19673)
COUNTY OF MONROE
Also Called: Monroe County Engineers Dept
47026 Moore Ridge Rd (43793-9050)
P.O. Box 555 (43793-0555)
PHONE...................................740 472-0760
Bruce Jones, *Superintendent*
Lonnie Tustin, *Principal*
EMP: 32 **Privately Held**
WEB: www.monroevets.net
SIC: 1611 Highway & street construction
PA: County Of Monroe
101 N Main St Rm 34
Woodsfield OH 43793
740 472-1341

(G-19674)
COUNTY OF MONROE
Also Called: Monroe County Care Center
47045 Moore Ridge Rd (43793-9484)
P.O. Box 352 (43793-0352)
PHONE...................................740 472-0144
Marilyn Stepp, *Manager*
Robin Groves, *Program Dir*
EMP: 78 **Privately Held**
WEB: www.monroevets.net
SIC: 8051 Skilled nursing care facilities
PA: County Of Monroe
101 N Main St Rm 34
Woodsfield OH 43793
740 472-1341

(G-19675)
MACO INC
Also Called: MONROE ADULT CRAFTS ORGANIZATI
47013 State Route 26 (43793-9330)
P.O. Box 564 (43793-0564)
PHONE...................................740 472-5445
Don Longwel, *Principal*
Daniel Lollathin, *Director*
Misty Dierkes, *Admin Sec*

EMP: 50
SALES: 128.6K **Privately Held**
WEB: www.maco.com
SIC: 8322 Individual & family services

(G-19676)
MONROE COUNTY ASSOCIATION FOR
47011 State Route 26 (43793-9330)
P.O. Box 623 (43793-0623)
PHONE.......................................740 472-1712
Helen Ring, *President*
EMP: 32
SALES (est): 597.4K **Privately Held**
SIC: 8621 Professional membership organizations

(G-19677)
MONROE FAMILY HEALTH CENTER
Also Called: Ohio Hills Health Service
37984 Airport Rd (43793-9247)
P.O. Box 658 (43793-0658)
PHONE.......................................740 472-0757
Donna Secrest, *Manager*
Theodore Koler, *Exec Dir*
EMP: 25
SALES (est): 1.8MM **Privately Held**
SIC: 8011 8071 Clinic, operated by physicians; medical laboratories

(G-19678)
SAFE AUTO INSURANCE COMPANY
47060 Black Walnut Pkwy (43793-9521)
PHONE.......................................740 472-1900
Jon P Diamond, *Branch Mgr*
EMP: 156
SALES (corp-wide): 678.8MM **Privately Held**
SIC: 6331 Automobile insurance
HQ: Safe Auto Insurance Company
4 Easton Oval
Columbus OH 43219

(G-19679)
WOODSFIELD OPCO LLC
Also Called: Arbors At Woodsfield
37930 Airport Rd (43793-9247)
PHONE.......................................502 429-8062
Robert Norcross, *Mng Member*
EMP: 99
SQ FT: 60,000
SALES (est): 1MM **Privately Held**
SIC: 8051 Skilled nursing care facilities

Woodstock
Champaign County

(G-19680)
SABER HEALTHCARE GROUP LLC
Also Called: Spring Meadows Care Center
1649 Park Rd (43084-9713)
PHONE.......................................937 826-3351
Heather Mudgett, *Administration*
EMP: 36
SALES (corp-wide): 157.7MM **Privately Held**
SIC: 8051 Skilled nursing care facilities
PA: Saber Healthcare Group, L.L.C.
26691 Richmond Rd Frnt
Bedford OH 44146
216 292-5706

(G-19681)
WOODSTOCK HEALTHCARE GROUP INC
Also Called: Spring Meadows Care Center
1649 Park Rd (43084-9713)
PHONE.......................................937 826-3351
George S Repchick, *President*
William I Weisberg, *Vice Pres*
Sarah Depompei, *Assistant*
EMP: 50
SQ FT: 20,000
SALES (est): 3MM **Privately Held**
WEB: www.chicagowilderness.org
SIC: 8051 Skilled nursing care facilities

Woodville
Sandusky County

(G-19682)
PREDATOR TRUCKING COMPANY
1121 State Route 105 (43469-9754)
PHONE.......................................419 849-2601
Steve Frasure, *General Mgr*
EMP: 25 **Privately Held**
SIC: 4213 Trucking, except local
PA: Predator Trucking Company
3181 Trumbull Ave
Mc Donald OH 44437

(G-19683)
ROUEN CHRYSLER PLYMOUTH DODGE
Also Called: Rouen Dodge
1091 Fremont Pike (43469-9606)
P.O. Box 1330, Maumee (43537-8330)
PHONE.......................................419 837-6228
Michael J Rouen, *President*
Kevin Carnicom, *Vice Pres*
Robert Graham, *Sales Associate*
Michael Rouen, *Manager*
EMP: 31
SQ FT: 20,000
SALES (est): 12.3MM **Privately Held**
SIC: 5511 7515 7513 5521 Automobiles, new & used; passenger car leasing; truck rental & leasing, no drivers; used car dealers

Wooster
Wayne County

(G-19684)
ALAN MANUFACTURING INC
3927 E Lincoln Way (44691-8997)
P.O. Box 24875, Cleveland (44124-0875)
PHONE.......................................330 262-1555
Richard Bluestone, *President*
Dean Weidner, *Manager*
▲ **EMP:** 36 **EST:** 1993
SQ FT: 110,000
SALES (est): 3.9MM **Privately Held**
SIC: 3444 3822 1711 1761 Sheet metalwork; auto controls regulating residntl & coml environmt & applncs; plumbing, heating, air-conditioning contractors; roofing, siding & sheet metal work

(G-19685)
ALBRIGHT WELDING SUPPLY CO INC (PA)
3132 E Lincoln Way (44691-3757)
P.O. Box 35 (44691-0035)
PHONE.......................................330 264-2021
James E Horst, *President*
Rebecca Horst, *Corp Secy*
Robert V Horst Jr, *Vice Pres*
Greg Patterson, *Manager*
EMP: 35 **EST:** 1928
SQ FT: 14,500
SALES (est): 11.8MM **Privately Held**
WEB: www.albrightwelding.com
SIC: 5084 5085 5999 Welding machinery & equipment; welding supplies; welding supplies

(G-19686)
ALICE NOBLE ICE ARENA
851 Oldman Rd (44691-9072)
PHONE.......................................330 345-8686
David Noble, *Principal*
EMP: 25
SQ FT: 1,296
SALES (est): 772.5K **Privately Held**
SIC: 7999 Ice skating rink operation

(G-19687)
ANAZAO COMMUNITY PARTNERS (PA)
2587 Back Orrville Rd (44691-9523)
PHONE.......................................330 264-9597
Kevin Bowen, *Finance Dir*
Ken Ward, *Exec Dir*
EMP: 27
SQ FT: 4,000

SALES: 2.4MM **Privately Held**
SIC: 8322 8093 Substance abuse counseling; child related social services; specialty outpatient clinics

(G-19688)
ASAP HOMECARE INC
133 Beall Ave (44691-3676)
PHONE.......................................330 263-4733
EMP: 103
SALES (corp-wide): 6.9MM **Privately Held**
SIC: 8082 Home health care services
PA: Asap Homecare Inc
1 Park Centre Dr Ste 107
Wadsworth OH 44281
330 334-7027

(G-19689)
BAUER CORPORATION (PA)
Also Called: Bauer Ladder
2540 Progress Dr (44691-7970)
PHONE.......................................800 321-4760
Mark McConnell, *President*
Richard Stoner, *General Mgr*
Ward McConnel, *Chairman*
John Vasichko, *Vice Pres*
Bruce Worstell, *Plant Mgr*
EMP: 30
SQ FT: 71,500
SALES (est): 17.1MM **Privately Held**
WEB: www.bauerladder.com
SIC: 5082 3499 3446 3441 Ladders; metal ladders; architectural metalwork; fabricated structural metal

(G-19690)
BEST WOOSTER INC
Also Called: Best Western Wooster Plaza
243 E Liberty St Ste 11 (44691-4366)
PHONE.......................................330 264-7750
Stephen Sun, *President*
EMP: 40
SQ FT: 97,000
SALES (est): 2.7MM **Privately Held**
SIC: 7011 Hotels

(G-19691)
BLACK TIE AFFAIR INC
Also Called: Greenbriar CONference& Pty Ctr
50 Riffel Rd (44691-8596)
PHONE.......................................330 345-8333
EMP: 50
SQ FT: 40,000
SALES (est): 1.6MM **Privately Held**
SIC: 5812 7299 Catering Service Facility Rental

(G-19692)
BLUESKY HEALTHCARE INC
Also Called: Smithville Western Commons
4110 E Smithville Wstn Rd (44691)
PHONE.......................................330 345-9050
Carrie Horst, *Branch Mgr*
EMP: 150
SALES (corp-wide): 13.2MM **Privately Held**
SIC: 8051 8052 Skilled nursing care facilities; intermediate care facilities
PA: Bluesky Healthcare Inc.
3885 Oberlin Ave
Lorain OH 44053
440 989-5200

(G-19693)
BOGNER CONSTRUCTION COMPANY
305 Mulberry St (44691-4735)
P.O. Box 887 (44691-0887)
PHONE.......................................330 262-6730
Theodore R Bogner, *President*
Robert E Bogner, *Vice Pres*
Adam Bogner, *Project Mgr*
Michael Bogner, *Project Mgr*
Bonnie Fink, *Manager*
EMP: 75 **EST:** 1979
SQ FT: 5,000
SALES (est): 23.8MM **Privately Held**
WEB: www.bognergroup.com
SIC: 1542 Commercial & office building, new construction

(G-19694)
BROOKDALE PLACE WOOSTER LLC
1615 Cleveland Rd (44691-2335)
PHONE.......................................330 262-1615
Ann Worley, *Manager*
EMP: 43 **EST:** 2009
SALES (est): 429.9K
SALES (corp-wide): 4.5B **Publicly Held**
SIC: 8322 Rehabilitation services
PA: Brookdale Senior Living
111 Westwood Pl Ste 400
Brentwood TN 37027
615 221-2250

(G-19695)
BROOKDALE SENIOR LIVING INC
1615 Cleveland Rd (44691-2335)
PHONE.......................................330 262-1615
Ann Worley, *Branch Mgr*
EMP: 27
SALES (corp-wide): 4.5B **Publicly Held**
SIC: 6513 Retirement hotel operation
PA: Brookdale Senior Living
111 Westwood Pl Ste 400
Brentwood TN 37027
615 221-2250

(G-19696)
CAMPBELL CONSTRUCTION INC (PA)
1159 Blachleyville Rd (44691-9750)
PHONE.......................................330 262-5186
John Campbell, *President*
Nancy J Campbell, *Principal*
Robert B Campbell, *Principal*
Mary Louise Campbell, *Corp Secy*
Richard Hauenstein, *Exec VP*
EMP: 68
SQ FT: 12,000
SALES (est): 18.2MM **Privately Held**
SIC: 1542 Commercial & office building, new construction

(G-19697)
CCJ ENTERPRISES INC
Also Called: Acres of Fun
3889 Friendsville Rd (44691-9601)
PHONE.......................................330 345-4386
Darlene Johns, *President*
Bob Johns, *Corp Secy*
EMP: 30
SQ FT: 15,750
SALES (est): 1.3MM **Privately Held**
SIC: 7996 Amusement parks

(G-19698)
CELLCO PARTNERSHIP
Also Called: Verizon
4164 Burbank Rd (44691-9077)
PHONE.......................................330 345-6465
Amy Schafer, *Manager*
EMP: 71
SALES (corp-wide): 130.8B **Publicly Held**
SIC: 4812 5999 Cellular telephone services; communication equipment
HQ: Cellco Partnership
1 Verizon Way
Basking Ridge NJ 07920

(G-19699)
CERTIFIED ANGUS BEEF LLC (HQ)
206 Riffel Rd (44691-8588)
PHONE.......................................330 345-2333
John Stika, *President*
Farias Ivette, *Minister*
Brent Eichar, *Senior VP*
Mark A McCully, *Assistant VP*
Tracey Erickson, *Vice Pres*
EMP: 90
SQ FT: 42,000
SALES (est): 15.4MM
SALES (corp-wide): 55.4MM **Privately Held**
SIC: 8611 Business associations
PA: American Angus Association Inc
3201 Frederick Ave
Saint Joseph MO 64506
816 383-5100

(G-19700)
CHRISTIAN CHLD HM OHIO INC
2685 Armstrong Rd (44691-9041)
P.O. Box 765 (44691-0765)
PHONE....................................330 345-7949
Steve Porter, *President*
Kevin R Hewitt, *Exec Dir*
Kevin Hewitt, *Director*
EMP: 100
SQ FT: 12,000
SALES: 8.3MM **Privately Held**
WEB: www.ccho.org
SIC: 8361 8093 8322 Children's home;
substance abuse clinics (outpatient); indi-
vidual & family services

(G-19701)
CHRISTIAN WOOSTER SCHOOL
4599 Burbank Rd Ste B (44691-9099)
PHONE....................................330 345-6436
Randy Claes, *Principal*
Karen Anderson, *Admin Sec*
Jerrand Claes, *Administration*
Joyce Atkins, *Teacher*
Lisa Falkenberg, *Teacher*
EMP: 43
SALES (est): 1.2MM **Privately Held**
WEB: www.woosterchristianschool.com
SIC: 8211 8351 Private elementary & sec-
ondary schools; preschool center

(G-19702)
CINEMARK USA INC
Also Called: Cinemark Movies 10
4108 Burbank Rd (44691-9077)
PHONE....................................330 345-2610
Nancy Keller, *Manager*
EMP: 27 **Publicly Held**
SIC: 7832 Motion picture theaters, except
drive-in
HQ: Cinemark Usa, Inc.
3900 Dallas Pkwy Ste 500
Plano TX 75093
972 665-1000

(G-19703)
CITY OF WOOSTER
1761 Beall Ave (44691-2342)
PHONE....................................330 263-8636
Alex Davis, *Manager*
EMP: 25 **Privately Held**
WEB: www.woosteroh.com
SIC: 8082 Home health care services
PA: City Of Wooster
538 N Market St
Wooster OH 44691
330 263-5200

(G-19704)
CITY OF WOOSTER
Also Called: Wooster Division Fire
510 N Market St (44691-3406)
PHONE....................................330 263-5266
Robert Eyler, *Chief*
EMP: 40 **Privately Held**
WEB: www.woosteroh.com
SIC: 7389 9111 Fire protection service
other than forestry or public; mayors' of-
fices
PA: City Of Wooster
538 N Market St
Wooster OH 44691
330 263-5200

(G-19705)
CITY OF WOOSTER
Also Called: Wooster Community Hospital
1761 Beall Ave (44691-2342)
PHONE....................................330 263-8100
William Sheron, *CEO*
Osama M D, *Med Doctor*
Stuart Workman, *Director*
Shannon Dye, *Admin Sec*
Cyril S Ofori, *Cardiovascular*
EMP: 854 **Privately Held**
WEB: www.woosteroh.com
SIC: 8062 5912 General medical & surgi-
cal hospitals; drug stores
PA: City Of Wooster
538 N Market St
Wooster OH 44691
330 263-5200

(G-19706)
CLASSIC IMPORTS INC (PA)
Also Called: Funky People
2018 Great Trails Dr (44691-3740)
PHONE....................................330 262-5277
Raj Arora, *President*
Ramesh Arora, *Vice Pres*
Sarvesh Arora, *Vice Pres*
Rachna Walia, *Vice Pres*
▲ **EMP:** 37
SQ FT: 45,000
SALES: 10MM **Privately Held**
SIC: 5137 Women's & children's clothing

(G-19707)
CLEVELAND CLINIC
FOUNDATION
Also Called: Womans Health Center
1739 Cleveland Rd (44691-2203)
PHONE....................................330 287-4930
Cathy Fischer, *Manager*
EMP: 30
SALES (corp-wide): 8.9B **Privately Held**
SIC: 8011 8062 Physicians' office, includ-
ing specialists; general medical & surgical
hospitals
PA: The Cleveland Clinic Foundation
9500 Euclid Ave
Cleveland OH 44195
216 636-8335

(G-19708)
CLEVELAND CLINIC
FOUNDATION
Also Called: Cleveland Clinic Wooster
1740 Cleveland Rd (44691-2204)
PHONE....................................330 287-4500
Jennifer Kirsop, *Research*
Duane Golden, *Engineer*
Crystal Hill, *Engineer*
Lauren Indorf, *Treasurer*
Ryan Bretz, *Accountant*
EMP: 85
SALES (corp-wide): 8.9B **Privately Held**
SIC: 6733 Trusts
PA: The Cleveland Clinic Foundation
9500 Euclid Ave
Cleveland OH 44195
216 636-8335

(G-19709)
CLEVELND CLNC HLTH SYSTM
EAST
Also Called: Cleveland Clinic Wooster
721 E Milltown Rd (44691-1331)
PHONE....................................330 287-4830
Wendy Simmons, *Principal*
Greg Barton, *Med Doctor*
Richard Guttmajr, *Med Doctor*
EMP: 30
SALES (corp-wide): 8.9B **Privately Held**
SIC: 8062 8093 General medical & surgi-
cal hospitals; specialty outpatient clinics
HQ: Cleveland Clinic Health System-East
Region
6803 Mayfield Rd Ste 500
Cleveland OH 44124
440 312-6010

(G-19710)
COMMUNITY ACTION-
WAYNE/MEDINA (PA)
905 Pittsburg Ave (44691-4296)
PHONE....................................330 264-8677
Donald Ackerman, *CFO*
EMP: 80
SQ FT: 1,700
SALES (est): 7.5MM **Privately Held**
WEB: www.cawm.org
SIC: 8322 Social service center

(G-19711)
COMPAK INC
1130 Riffel Rd (44691-8502)
PHONE....................................330 345-5666
Jerry Baker, *President*
EMP: 35
SALES (est): 2.5MM **Privately Held**
SIC: 4225 General warehousing & storage

(G-19712)
COUNSELING CTR WAYNE
HOLMES CT (PA)
2285 Benden Dr (44691-2568)
PHONE....................................330 264-9029
Susan Buchwalter, *CEO*
Karen Berry, *Vice Pres*
Dave Snyder, *Vice Pres*
Jacquelyn Kraps, *Psychologist*
Bob Howard, *Manager*
EMP: 150 **EST:** 1953
SALES: 8.1MM **Privately Held**
WEB: www.ccwhc.org
SIC: 8322 Individual & family services

(G-19713)
COUNTRY ACRES OF WAYNE
COUNTY
1240 Wildwood Dr (44691-1984)
PHONE....................................330 698-2031
Leota Hutchinson, *President*
EMP: 26
SALES (est): 320.6K **Privately Held**
SIC: 8059 Nursing home, except skilled &
intermediate care facility

(G-19714)
COUNTRY POINTE SKILLED
NURSING
3071 N Elyria Rd (44691-9379)
PHONE....................................330 264-7881
Rick Gebhard, *Administration*
EMP: 35 **EST:** 1999
SALES (est): 1.6MM **Privately Held**
SIC: 8051 Extended care facility

(G-19715)
COUNTY OF WAYNE
Also Called: Wayne County Care Center
876 S Geyers Chapel Rd (44691-3908)
PHONE....................................330 262-1786
Carol Van Pelt, *Administration*
EMP: 100 **Privately Held**
WEB: www.waynecsb.org
SIC: 8059 9111 Personal care home, with
health care; county supervisors' & execu-
tives' offices
PA: County Of Wayne
428 W Liberty St
Wooster OH 44691
330 287-5400

(G-19716)
COUNTY OF WAYNE
Also Called: Wayne Employment Training Ctr
356 W North St (44691-4822)
P.O. Box 76 (44691-0076)
PHONE....................................330 264-5060
Becky Wagner, *Director*
EMP: 31 **Privately Held**
SIC: 7361 Employment agencies
PA: County Of Wayne
428 W Liberty St
Wooster OH 44691
330 287-5400

(G-19717)
COUNTY OF WAYNE
Also Called: Wayne County Childrens Svcs
2534 Burbank Rd (44691-1675)
PHONE....................................330 345-5340
Thomas Roelant, *Director*
EMP: 62 **Privately Held**
SIC: 8361 9111 Children's home; county
supervisors' & executives' offices
PA: County Of Wayne
428 W Liberty St
Wooster OH 44691
330 287-5400

(G-19718)
COUNTY OF WAYNE
Also Called: Wayne County Child Support
428 W Liberty St Ste 11 (44691-4851)
PHONE....................................330 287-5600
Marjorie Butler, *Director*
EMP: 32 **Privately Held**
WEB: www.waynecsb.org
SIC: 8322 Child related social services
PA: County Of Wayne
428 W Liberty St
Wooster OH 44691
330 287-5400

(G-19719)
COUNTY OF WAYNE
Also Called: Wayne County Engineers
Wooster
3151 W Old Lincoln Way (44691-3262)
PHONE....................................330 287-5500
Roger K Terrell, *Branch Mgr*
EMP: 52 **Privately Held**
WEB: www.waynecsb.org
SIC: 8711 Heating & ventilation engineer-
ing
PA: County Of Wayne
428 W Liberty St
Wooster OH 44691
330 287-5400

(G-19720)
CRITCHFELD CRTCHFIELD
JOHNSTON (PA)
Also Called: Ccj
225 N Market St (44691-3511)
P.O. Box 599 (44691-0599)
PHONE....................................330 264-4444
Robert C Berry, *Partner*
J Douglas Drushal, *Partner*
Robert C Gorman, *Partner*
John C Johnston III, *Partner*
Daniel H Plumly, *Partner*
EMP: 88
SALES (est): 12MM **Privately Held**
SIC: 8111 General practice law office

(G-19721)
DANBURY WOODS OF
WOOSTER
939 Portage Rd (44691-2100)
PHONE....................................330 264-0355
Wesley Hess, *Director*
EMP: 45
SALES (est): 697.9K **Privately Held**
SIC: 8322 Old age assistance

(G-19722)
ENGINEERING ASSOCIATES INC
1935 Eagle Pass (44691-5316)
PHONE....................................330 345-6556
Kent Baker, *President*
Frederick A Seling, *Vice Pres*
Gary Daugherty, *Treasurer*
Ronny Portz, *Admin Sec*
EMP: 25 **EST:** 1957
SQ FT: 9,000
SALES (est): 3MM **Privately Held**
WEB: www.eaohio.com
SIC: 8711 Civil engineering

(G-19723)
GLENDORA HEALTH CARE
CENTER
1552 N Honeytown Rd (44691-9511)
PHONE....................................330 264-0912
Shaw Flank, *President*
Terry J Ferguson, *President*
Linda Ferguson, *Vice Pres*
EMP: 56
SQ FT: 11,000
SALES (est): 2.8MM **Privately Held**
WEB: www.glendoracarecenter.com
SIC: 8051 Convalescent home with contin-
uous nursing care

(G-19724)
GOLF COURSE MAINTENANCE
1599 Mechanicsburg Rd (44691-2766)
PHONE....................................330 262-9141
Joe Hatlla, *President*
Larry Barnett, *President*
Scott McLain, *Principal*
EMP: 76
SQ FT: 1,200
SALES (est): 697.6K **Privately Held**
SIC: 7997 Country club, membership

(G-19725)
GOODWILL INDUSTRIES (PA)
1034 Nold Ave (44691-3642)
P.O. Box 1188 (44691-7083)
PHONE....................................330 264-1300
Judy Delaney, *President*
James Carpenter, *Vice Pres*
EMP: 30
SQ FT: 21,000

SALES: 5.4MM **Privately Held**
WEB: www.woostergoodwill.org
SIC: 8331 5932 Sheltered workshop; used
  merchandise stores

(G-19726)
H & R BLOCK INC
2831 Cleveland Rd (44691-1737)
PHONE..............................330 345-1040
Sandy Easterlay, *Manager*
EMP: 25
SALES (corp-wide): 3.1B **Publicly Held**
WEB: www.hrblock.com
SIC: 7291 Tax return preparation services
PA: H&R Block, Inc.
  1 H&R Block Way
  Kansas City MO 64105
  816 854-3000

(G-19727)
HERMAN BAIR ENTERPRISE
Also Called: Ej Therapy
210 E Milltown Rd Ste A (44691-1200)
PHONE..............................330 262-4449
Eunice Herman, *President*
EMP: 27
SALES: 800K **Privately Held**
SIC: 8049 Nutrition specialist

(G-19728)
HOMETOWN URGENT CARE
4164 Burbank Rd (44691-9077)
PHONE..............................937 252-2000
EMP: 123
SALES (corp-wide): 73.2MM **Privately
Held**
SIC: 8049 8011 7291 Occupational thera-
  pist; medical centers; tax return prepara-
  tion services
PA: Hometown Urgent Care
  2400 Corp Exchange Dr # 102
  Columbus OH 43231
  614 505-7633

(G-19729)
**HORIZONS
TUSCARAWAS/CARROLL**
527 N Market St (44691-3495)
PHONE..............................330 262-4183
Jack Robinson, *Manager*
EMP: 35
SALES (corp-wide): 6.8MM **Privately
Held**
SIC: 8361 Home for the mentally handi-
  capped
PA: Horizons Of Tuscarawas/Carroll
  220 W 4th St
  Dover OH 44622
  330 874-1060

(G-19730)
**HORN NURSING AND REHAB
CENTER (HQ)**
Also Called: Horn Nursing Rehabilation Ctr
230 N Market St (44691-3512)
PHONE..............................330 262-2951
Fax: 330 264-1254
EMP: 70 EST: 1960
SQ FT: 5,000
SALES (est): 8.6MM **Privately Held**
SIC: 8051 8052 Skilled Nursing Care/In-
  termediate Nursing Facility

(G-19731)
**HOWARD HANNA SMYTHE
CRAMER**
177 W Milltown Rd Unit A (44691-7289)
PHONE..............................330 345-2244
Howard Hannah, *Principal*
EMP: 30
SALES (corp-wide): 72.1MM **Privately
Held**
SIC: 6531 Real estate brokers & agents
HQ: Howard Hanna Smythe Cramer
  6000 Parkland Blvd
  Cleveland OH 44124
  216 447-4477

(G-19732)
HUNTINGTON INSURANCE INC
121 N Market St Ste 600 (44691-4880)
PHONE..............................330 262-6611
Scott Schaffter, *President*
EMP: 37

SALES (corp-wide): 5.2B **Publicly Held**
WEB: www.skyinsure.com
SIC: 6411 Insurance agents
HQ: Huntington Insurance, Inc.
  519 Madison Ave
  Toledo OH 43604
  419 720-7900

(G-19733)
**JPMORGAN CHASE BANK NAT
ASSN**
601 Portage Rd (44691-2029)
PHONE..............................330 287-5101
Glenda Farver, *Principal*
Nicole McGregor, *Principal*
EMP: 26
SALES (corp-wide): 131.4B **Publicly
Held**
SIC: 6021 National commercial banks
HQ: Jpmorgan Chase Bank, National Asso-
  ciation
  1111 Polaris Pkwy
  Columbus OH 43240
  614 436-3055

(G-19734)
**JPMORGAN CHASE BANK NAT
ASSN**
601 Portage Rd (44691-2029)
PHONE..............................330 287-5101
Rob Carter, *Manager*
EMP: 26
SALES (corp-wide): 131.4B **Publicly
Held**
WEB: www.chase.com
SIC: 6021 National commercial banks
HQ: Jpmorgan Chase Bank, National Asso-
  ciation
  1111 Polaris Pkwy
  Columbus OH 43240
  614 436-3055

(G-19735)
K S BANDAG INC
737 Industrial Blvd (44691-8999)
PHONE..............................330 264-9237
John Kauffman, *President*
Earl Shaw, *Corp Secy*
Mark Hershberger, *Vice Pres*
EMP: 25
SQ FT: 15,500
SALES (est): 1.6MM **Privately Held**
SIC: 7534 Rebuilding & retreading tires

(G-19736)
KEIM CONCRETE LLC
4175 W Old Lincoln Way (44691-3241)
PHONE..............................330 264-5313
Jonas Keim,
EMP: 31 EST: 1974
SALES (est): 3.1MM **Privately Held**
SIC: 1771 Concrete work

(G-19737)
KEN MILLER SUPPLY INC
1537 Blachleyville Rd (44691-9752)
P.O. Box 1086 (44691-7081)
PHONE..............................330 264-9146
Kirk Miller, *CEO*
Lindy Chandler, *CEO*
◆ EMP: 70 EST: 1959
SQ FT: 5,000
SALES (est): 77.1MM **Privately Held**
SIC: 5084 Oil well machinery, equipment &
  supplies

(G-19738)
KENOIL INC
1537 Blachleyville Rd (44691-9752)
P.O. Box 1085 (44691-7081)
PHONE..............................330 262-1144
Steve Fleisher, *Vice Pres*
EMP: 50 EST: 1982
SALES (est): 2.7MM **Privately Held**
SIC: 1311 Crude petroleum & natural gas
  production

(G-19739)
**KOKOSING CONSTRUCTION
INC**
1516 Timken Rd (44691-9401)
PHONE..............................330 263-4168
Brian Burgett, *President*
▲ EMP: 2500
SQ FT: 20,000

SALES (est): 99.7MM **Privately Held**
SIC: 1611 Highway & street paving contractor

(G-19740)
LADDER MAN INC
1505 E Bowman St (44691-3128)
PHONE..............................614 784-1120
Jeff Monastra, *Vice Pres*
EMP: 25
SALES (est): 1.2MM **Privately Held**
SIC: 8748 Business consulting

(G-19741)
LIFECARE HOSPICE (PA)
Also Called: LIFECARE PALLIVATIVE MEDI-
CINE
1900 Akron Rd (44691-2518)
PHONE..............................330 264-4899
Kurt Holmes, *CEO*
Tim Pettorini, *Ch of Bd*
Debra Meadows, *Nurse*
EMP: 30
SQ FT: 8,006
SALES: 10.8MM **Privately Held**
WEB: www.wchospice.org
SIC: 8322 Individual & family services

(G-19742)
LOWES HOME CENTERS LLC
3788 Burbank Rd (44691-9076)
PHONE..............................330 287-2261
EMP: 150
SALES (corp-wide): 68.6B **Publicly Held**
SIC: 5211 5031 5722 5064 Home centers; building materials, exterior; building
  materials, interior; household appliance
  stores; electrical appliances, television &
  radio
HQ: Lowe's Home Centers, Llc
  1605 Curtis Bridge Rd
  Wilkesboro NC 28697
  336 658-4000

(G-19743)
MCCLINTOCK ELECTRIC INC
402 E Henry St (44691-4393)
PHONE..............................330 264-6380
Michael J McClintock, *President*
Steve Curtis, *Superintendent*
Ralph D McClintock, *Vice Pres*
Misty Shields, *Warehouse Mgr*
Kimberley Simmons, *Controller*
EMP: 35 EST: 1963
SQ FT: 2,400
SALES (est): 6.8MM **Privately Held**
WEB: www.mcclintockelectric.com
SIC: 1731 General electrical contractor;
  fiber optic cable installation; voice, data &
  video wiring contractor; fire detection &
  burglar alarm systems specialization

(G-19744)
**METALS USA FLAT RLLED CNTL
INC**
1070 W Liberty St (44691-3308)
PHONE..............................618 451-4700
Tom Calhoun, *General Mgr*
EMP: 35 EST: 1979
SALES (est): 22.7MM
SALES (corp-wide): 11.5B **Publicly Held**
WEB: www.metalsusa.com
SIC: 5051 Metals Service Center
HQ: Metals Usa, Inc.
  4901 Nw 17th Way Ste 405
  Fort Lauderdale FL 33309
  954 202-4000

(G-19745)
**MIDLAND COUNCIL
GOVERNMENTS**
Also Called: Tri-County Computer Svcs Assn
2125 Eagle Pass (44691-5320)
PHONE..............................330 264-6047
Stuart Workman, *Exec Dir*
EMP: 35
SQ FT: 10,000
SALES (est): 2.9MM **Privately Held**
SIC: 7374 8211 Data processing & prepa-
  ration; elementary & secondary schools

(G-19746)
MILITARY RESOURCES LLC
1036 Burbank Rd (44691)
PHONE..............................330 263-1040
EMP: 50

SALES (corp-wide): 3MM **Privately Held**
SIC: 3559 7389 Mfg Misc Industry Machinery Business Services
PA: Military Resources, Llc
  1834 Cleveland Rd Ste 301
  Wooster OH 44691
  330 309-9970

(G-19747)
MILITARY RESOURCES LLC (PA)
1834 Cleveland Rd Ste 301 (44691-2206)
PHONE..............................330 309-9970
William D Johnson, *CEO*
Arthur Summerville,
Roger Williams,
▼ EMP: 59
SQ FT: 3,000
SALES: 3MM **Privately Held**
WEB: www.militaryresources.com
SIC: 3559 7389 Business Services Mfg
  Misc Industry Machinery

(G-19748)
**MILLER SUPPLY OF WVA INC
(PA)**
1537 Blachleyville Rd (44691-9752)
P.O. Box 1086 (44691-7081)
PHONE..............................330 264-9146
Jack K Miller, *President*
Kenneth R Miller, *Corp Secy*
Max A Miller, *Vice Pres*
▲ EMP: 50
SALES (est): 30.7MM **Privately Held**
SIC: 5084 Oil well machinery, equipment &
  supplies

(G-19749)
**NEW PITTSBURGH FIRE &
RESCUE F**
3311 N Elyria Rd (44691-7645)
PHONE..............................330 264-1230
Ken Becker, *Chief*
EMP: 31
SALES (est): 386.3K **Privately Held**
SIC: 8641 Civic social & fraternal associa-
  tions

(G-19750)
NICK AMSTER INC (PA)
1700b Old Mansfield Rd (44691-7212)
PHONE..............................330 264-9667
Rich Patterson, *CEO*
EMP: 120
SQ FT: 18,000
SALES: 3.9MM **Privately Held**
WEB: www.nickamster.com
SIC: 8331 Sheltered workshop

(G-19751)
NICK AMSTER INC
326 N Hillcrest Dr Ste C (44691-3745)
PHONE..............................330 264-9667
Rich Patterson, *General Mgr*
EMP: 74
SALES (est): 435.7K
SALES (corp-wide): 3.9MM **Privately
Held**
WEB: www.nickamster.com
SIC: 8322 Social service center
PA: Nick Amster, Inc.
  1700b Old Mansfield Rd
  Wooster OH 44691
  330 264-9667

(G-19752)
**NOBLE TECHNOLOGIES CORP
(PA)**
Also Called: Nobletek
2020 Noble Dr (44691-5353)
PHONE..............................330 287-1530
Uday Vaidya, *CEO*
Kurt Jauert, *General Mgr*
John Stevens, *Vice Pres*
Michael Murzin, *Engineer*
Roy Zinsky, *Engineer*
EMP: 40
SALES: 8.8MM **Privately Held**
WEB: www.tgstech.com
SIC: 7371 Computer software develop-
  ment

(G-19753)
OHIO LIGHT OPERA
1189 Beall Ave (44691-2393)
PHONE..............................330 263-2345

Steven Daigle, *Director*
EMP: 100
SALES (est): 5.6MM **Privately Held**
SIC: 7832 7922 Motion picture theaters, except drive-in; theatrical producers & services

(G-19754)
OHIO STATE UNIVERSITY
Also Called: O A R D C
1680 Madison Ave (44691-4114)
PHONE..................................330 263-3700
Steven A Slack, *Director*
EMP: 550
SALES (corp-wide): 5.8B **Privately Held**
WEB: www.ohio-state.edu
SIC: 8731 8221 Agricultural research; university
PA: The Ohio State University
Student Acade Servi Bldg
Columbus OH 43210
614 292-6446

(G-19755)
OHIO STATE UNIVERSITY
Also Called: Ohio Agriculture RES & Dev Ctr
1680 Madison Ave (44691-4114)
PHONE..................................330 263-3701
Steven A Slack, *Director*
EMP: 400
SALES (corp-wide): 5.8B **Privately Held**
WEB: www.ohio-state.edu
SIC: 8733 8221 Physical research, non-commercial; university
PA: The Ohio State University
Student Acade Servi Bldg
Columbus OH 43210
614 292-6446

(G-19756)
ONEEIGHTY INC
Also Called: STEPS AT LIBERTY CENTER
104 Spink St (44691-3652)
PHONE..................................330 263-6021
Thomas Fenzl, *Ch of Bd*
Bobbi Bresson, *Info Tech Mgr*
Bobbi Douglas, *Exec Dir*
EMP: 75
SQ FT: 25,000
SALES: 5.4MM **Privately Held**
WEB: www.everywomanshouse.org
SIC: 8322 Family counseling services

(G-19757)
OUTREACH COMMUNITY LIVING SVCS
337 W North St (44691-4821)
PHONE..................................330 263-0862
Mary Lloyd, *Exec Dir*
EMP: 30
SQ FT: 4,500
SALES: 770.9K **Privately Held**
WEB: www.oclswooster.org
SIC: 8322 Social services for the handicapped

(G-19758)
PERSONAL TOUCH HM CARE IPA INC
543 Riffel Rd Ste F (44691-8591)
PHONE..................................330 263-1112
Norene Scheck, *Branch Mgr*
Ann Plecha, *Manager*
EMP: 1509
SALES (corp-wide): 363MM **Privately Held**
SIC: 8082 Home health care services
PA: Personal Touch Home Care Ipa, Inc.
1985 Marcus Ave Ste 202
New Hyde Park NY 11042
718 468-4747

(G-19759)
PLAZ-WAY INC
Also Called: Wayne Lanes
1983 E Lincoln Way (44691-3813)
PHONE..................................330 264-9025
Raymond Jeffries, *President*
Carol Jeffries, *Vice Pres*
EMP: 27 **EST:** 1956
SQ FT: 25,000
SALES (est): 1MM **Privately Held**
WEB: www.waynelanes.com
SIC: 7933 5812 5813 Ten pin center; snack bar; bars & lounges

(G-19760)
PSC METALS - WOOSTER LLC
972 Columbus Rd (44691-4600)
PHONE..................................330 264-8956
David N Spector,
EMP: 90
SQ FT: 43,200
SALES (est): 9.9MM
SALES (corp-wide): 11.7B **Publicly Held**
WEB: www.pscmetals.com
SIC: 5093 Ferrous metal scrap & waste; nonferrous metals scrap
HQ: Psc Metals, Llc
5875 Landerbrook Dr # 200
Mayfield Heights OH 44124
440 753-5400

(G-19761)
RK FAMILY INC
3541 E Lincoln Way (44691-3716)
PHONE..................................330 264-5475
Tom Waites, *Principal*
EMP: 351
SALES (corp-wide): 1.5B **Privately Held**
SIC: 5099 Firearms & ammunition, except sporting
PA: Rk Family, Inc.
4216 Dewitt Ave
Mattoon IL 61938
217 235-7102

(G-19762)
ROD LIGHTNING MUTUAL INSUR CO (PA)
1685 Cleveland Rd (44691-2335)
P.O. Box 36 (44691-0036)
PHONE..................................330 262-9060
F Emerson Logee, *Vice Ch Bd*
John P Murphy, *President*
Kevin Day, *Exec VP*
Jim Geopfert, *Assistant VP*
Robert George, *Vice Pres*
EMP: 265
SQ FT: 46,100
SALES: 77.1MM **Privately Held**
WEB: www.wrg-ins.com
SIC: 6411 Insurance agents, brokers & service

(G-19763)
RXP WIRELESS LLC
Also Called: Verizon Wireless
3417 Cleveland Rd (44691-1213)
PHONE..................................330 264-1500
Jared Bogner, *Branch Mgr*
EMP: 25
SALES (corp-wide): 20MM **Privately Held**
SIC: 4813 Telephone communication, except radio
HQ: Rxp Wireless, Llc
262 S 3rd St
Columbus OH 43215
614 397-2844

(G-19764)
SANTMYER OIL CO INC (PA)
3000 Old Airport Rd (44691-9520)
P.O. Box 146 (44691-0146)
PHONE..................................330 262-6501
Terry Santmyer, *Principal*
EMP: 55
SQ FT: 1,000
SALES (est): 93.8MM **Privately Held**
WEB: www.santmyeroil.com
SIC: 5172 5983 4212 5531 Fuel oil; gasoline; fuel oil dealers; petroleum haulage, local; automotive parts

(G-19765)
SCHMID MECHANICAL INC
207 N Hillcrest Dr (44691-3720)
PHONE..................................330 264-3633
Timothy Schmid, *President*
EMP: 45
SQ FT: 2,400
SALES (est): 7.2MM **Privately Held**
WEB: www.schmid-net.com
SIC: 1711 Plumbing contractors

(G-19766)
SCHMIDS SERVICE NOW INC
Also Called: Snyder's Service Now
258 S Columbus Ave (44691-4826)
PHONE..................................330 264-2040
Lee Painter, *Branch Mgr*

EMP: 42 **Privately Held**
SIC: 1711 5722 Warm air heating & air conditioning contractor; electric household appliances
PA: Schmid's Service Now, Inc
807 N Main St
Canton OH 44720

(G-19767)
SCOT INDUSTRIES INC
6578 Ashland Rd (44691-9233)
P.O. Box 1106 (44691-7081)
PHONE..................................330 262-7585
Mike Bannert, *Plant Mgr*
Cody Wesson, *Prdtn Mgr*
Tammy Myers, *Human Resources*
Robert G Gralinski, *Manager*
Keith Hodkinson, *Manager*
EMP: 40
SQ FT: 2,018
SALES (corp-wide): 155.5MM **Privately Held**
WEB: www.scotindustries.com
SIC: 5051 7389 3498 3471 Steel; pipe & tubing, steel; metal cutting services; fabricated pipe & fittings; plating & polishing
PA: Scot Industries, Inc.
3756 Fm 250 N
Lone Star TX 75668
903 639-2551

(G-19768)
SHEARER FARM INC (PA)
Also Called: John Deere Authorized Dealer
7762 Cleveland Rd (44691-7700)
PHONE..................................330 345-9023
Brian Giauque, *President*
Gerald Shearer, *Principal*
EMP: 45 **EST:** 1937
SQ FT: 9,400
SALES (est): 59.5MM **Privately Held**
WEB: www.shearerequipment.com
SIC: 3523 5082 Fertilizing machinery, farm; construction & mining machinery

(G-19769)
SHEER PROFESSIONALS INC
2912 Cleveland Rd (44691-1655)
PHONE..................................330 345-8666
Donna Beem, *Owner*
EMP: 32
SALES (est): 534.4K **Privately Held**
WEB: www.sheerprofessionals.com
SIC: 7231 Hairdressers

(G-19770)
STYX ACQUISITION LLC
3540 Burbank Rd (44691-8539)
PHONE..................................330 264-9900
Daniel Shanahan, *President*
EMP: 2091
SALES (corp-wide): 240MM **Privately Held**
SIC: 6799 Investors
PA: Styx Acquisition, Llc
1401 Old Mansfield Rd
Wooster OH 44691
330 264-4355

(G-19771)
SUNRISE SENIOR LIVING LLC
Also Called: Sunrise of Wooster
1615 Cleveland Rd (44691-2335)
PHONE..................................330 262-1615
Ann Worley, *Manager*
EMP: 48
SALES (corp-wide): 4.7B **Publicly Held**
WEB: www.sunrise.com
SIC: 8051 8361 Skilled nursing care facilities; residential care
HQ: Sunrise Senior Living, Llc
7902 Westpark Dr
Mc Lean VA 22102

(G-19772)
SURREAL ENTERTAINMENT LLC
2018 Great Trails Dr (44691-3740)
PHONE..................................330 262-5277
Sarvish Arora, *Mng Member*
▲ **EMP:** 27 **EST:** 2014
SALES (est): 100K **Privately Held**
SIC: 5162 Plastics products

(G-19773)
TRICOR INDUSTRIAL INC (PA)
Also Called: Tricor Metals
3225 W Old Lincoln Way (44691-3258)
P.O. Box 752 (44691-0752)
PHONE..................................330 264-3299
Nancy A Stitzlein, *CEO*
Michael D Stitzlein, *President*
◆ **EMP:** 77
SQ FT: 140,000
SALES: 50MM **Privately Held**
WEB: www.tricormetals.com
SIC: 5051 5169 3444 5085 Metals service centers & offices; chemicals & allied products; sheet metalwork; fasteners, industrial: nuts, bolts, screws, etc.

(G-19774)
TRICOR METALS
Also Called: Tricor Industrial
3225 W Old Lincoln Way (44691-3258)
P.O. Box 752 (44691-0752)
PHONE..................................330 264-3299
Mike Ftitzlein, *President*
EMP: 100
SALES (est): 33.5MM **Privately Held**
SIC: 5085 Industrial supplies

(G-19775)
UNITED PARCEL SERVICE INC OH
Also Called: UPS
3250 Old Airport Rd (44691-9580)
PHONE..................................440 826-3320
EMP: 158
SALES (corp-wide): 71.8B **Publicly Held**
SIC: 4215 Parcel delivery, vehicular
HQ: United Parcel Service, Inc. (Oh)
55 Glenlake Pkwy
Atlanta GA 30328
404 828-6000

(G-19776)
VILLAGE NETWORK (PA)
2000 Noble Dr (44691-5353)
P.O. Box 518, Smithville (44677-0518)
PHONE..................................330 264-0650
James T Miller, *CEO*
Richard W Rodman, *Exec VP*
Bel Klockenga, *CFO*
EMP: 216
SQ FT: 16,816
SALES: 41.3MM **Privately Held**
SIC: 8361 Boys' Towns

(G-19777)
WASTE MANAGEMENT OHIO INC
116 N Bauer Rd (44691-8624)
PHONE..................................800 910-2831
Bill Sigler, *Manager*
EMP: 43
SALES (corp-wide): 14.9B **Publicly Held**
WEB: www.wm.com
SIC: 4953 Waste materials, disposal at sea
HQ: Waste Management Of Ohio, Inc.
1700 N Broad St
Fairborn OH 45324

(G-19778)
WAYNE MUTUAL INSURANCE CO
3873 Cleveland Rd (44691-1297)
PHONE..................................330 345-8100
Ralph Gresser, *Ch of Bd*
Alvin C Ramseyer, *Vice Ch Bd*
Tod Carmony, *President*
R Michael Miller, *Vice Pres*
David Tschantz, *Vice Pres*
EMP: 38 **EST:** 1910
SQ FT: 5,600
SALES: 15MM **Privately Held**
WEB: www.waynemutual.com
SIC: 6331 Fire, marine & casualty insurance

(G-19779)
WAYNE SAVINGS BANCSHARES INC (PA)
151 N Market St (44691-4809)
PHONE..................................330 264-5767
Peggy J Schmitz, *Ch of Bd*
James Rvansickle II, *President*
Myron L Swartzentruber, *CFO*
EMP: 114

SALES: 17.5MM **Publicly Held**
SIC: **6035** Savings institutions, federally chartered

(G-19780)
WAYNE SAVINGS COMMUNITY BANK (HQ)
151 N Market St (44691-4809)
P.O. Box 858 (44691-0858)
PHONE..................330 264-5767
James Rvansickle II, *President*
EMP: 66
SQ FT: 12,500
SALES: 18.5MM **Publicly Held**
WEB: www.waynesavings.com
SIC: **6022** State commercial banks

(G-19781)
WEAVER CUSTOM HOMES INC
124 E Liberty St Ste A (44691-4421)
PHONE..................330 264-5444
Merle Stutzman, *President*
Ron Wenger, *Vice Pres*
Diann Miller, *Treasurer*
EMP: 40
SQ FT: 2,300
SALES (est): 7.1MM **Privately Held**
SIC: **1531** 1521 1542 Speculative builder, single-family houses; new construction, single-family houses; commercial & office building, new construction

(G-19782)
WEST VIEW MANOR INC
Also Called: WEST VIEW MANOR RETIREMENT CEN
1715 Mechanicsburg Rd (44691-2640)
PHONE..................330 264-8640
Robert Wetter, *CFO*
Mike Jackson, *Director*
Robert Griggs, *Administration*
Carole Van Pelt, *Administration*
EMP: 225
SQ FT: 126,000
SALES: 13.1MM **Privately Held**
WEB: www.westviewmanor.org
SIC: **8051** 8361 Convalescent home with continuous nursing care; geriatric residential care

(G-19783)
WESTERN RESERVE GROUP (PA)
1685 Cleveland Rd (44691-2335)
P.O. Box 36 (44691-0036)
PHONE..................330 262-9060
Michael Reardon, *Ch of Bd*
F Emerson Logee, *Vice Ch Bd*
David Chandler, *President*
Kevin W Day, *President*
Randy Donnamiller, *President*
EMP: 255
SQ FT: 46,100
SALES (est): 333.5MM **Privately Held**
SIC: **6331** Fire, marine & casualty insurance: mutual

(G-19784)
WOLFF BROS SUPPLY INC
565 N Applecreek Rd (44691-9599)
PHONE..................330 264-5900
Michael Huttinger, *Vice Pres*
Mike Huttinger, *Vice Pres*
Tina Sentelik, *Opers Mgr*
EMP: 40
SQ FT: 1,632
SALES (corp-wide): 114.4MM **Privately Held**
WEB: www.wolffbros.com
SIC: **5074** 5063 Plumbing fittings & supplies; electrical supplies
PA: Wolff Bros. Supply, Inc
6078 Wolff Rd
Medina OH 44256
330 725-3451

(G-19785)
WOOSTER COUNTRY CLUB INC
1251 Oak Hill Rd (44691-2600)
PHONE..................330 263-1890
Eric Rhodes, *Principal*
Gabriel Ward, *Project Mgr*
Michelle Kane, *Manager*
Kelly Kranstuber, *Senior Mgr*
EMP: 25

SALES: 1.6MM **Privately Held**
SIC: **7997** Country club, membership

(G-19786)
WOOSTER MOTOR WAYS INC (PA)
3501 W Old Lincoln Way (44691-3253)
P.O. Box 19 (44691-0019)
PHONE..................330 264-9557
Paul M Williams, *President*
Keith Thigpen, *Business Mgr*
Jack Simmons, *Vice Pres*
Hochstetler David, *CFO*
David W Hochstetler, *CFO*
EMP: 140
SQ FT: 40,000
SALES (est): 34.7MM **Privately Held**
WEB: www.woostermotorways.com
SIC: **4214** 4226 4212 Local trucking with storage; special warehousing & storage; local trucking, without storage

(G-19787)
WOOSTER OPHTHALMOLOGISTS INC
Also Called: Eye Surgery Center of Wooster
3519 Friendsville Rd (44691-1241)
PHONE..................330 345-7800
Harry A Zink, *President*
John W Thomas, *Vice Pres*
Thomas C Fenzl, *Treasurer*
Jeffrey W Perkins, *Admin Sec*
Lisa McGinty, *Ophthalmic Tech*
EMP: 45
SQ FT: 20,000
SALES (est): 5.2MM **Privately Held**
SIC: **8011** Ophthalmologist

(G-19788)
WWST CORPORATION LLC
Also Called: Wqkt/Wkvx
186 S Hillcrest Dr (44691-3727)
PHONE..................330 264-5122
Craig Walton, *General Mgr*
EMP: 1634 EST: 1996
SALES: 36.6MM
SALES (corp-wide): 528.2MM **Privately Held**
SIC: **4833** Television broadcasting stations
PA: Dix 1898, Inc.
212 E Liberty St
Wooster OH
330 264-3511

(G-19789)
YOUNG MENS CHRISTIAN ASSOC
Also Called: YMCA OF THE USA
680 Woodland Ave (44691-2743)
PHONE..................330 264-3131
Jeff Vincent, *Office Mgr*
W Robert Johnston, *Director*
EMP: 60
SQ FT: 30,000
SALES: 2.2MM **Privately Held**
SIC: **7999** 8641 7997 7991 Recreation center; youth organizations; membership sports & recreation clubs; physical fitness facilities

---

Worthington
Franklin County

(G-19790)
AAA OHIO AUTO CLUB
90 E Wilson Bridge Rd (43085-2325)
PHONE..................614 431-7800
Ronald Carr, *President*
EMP: 60
SALES (est): 9.1MM **Privately Held**
SIC: **7549** Automotive maintenance services

(G-19791)
AJM WORTHINGTON INC
Also Called: Primrose School of Worthington
6902 N High St (43085-2510)
PHONE..................614 888-5800
Dam Simonds, *President*
Dan Simonds, *President*
Tobie Simonds, *Vice Pres*
EMP: 30

SALES (est): 651.2K **Privately Held**
SIC: **8351** Preschool center

(G-19792)
ALLIEDBARTON SECURITY SVCS LLC
57 E Wilson Bridge Rd # 300 (43085-2368)
PHONE..................614 225-9061
Gary Jones, *Principal*
Jim Soden, *Business Mgr*
EMP: 139
SALES (corp-wide): 3.2B **Privately Held**
SIC: **7381** Security guard service
HQ: Alliedbarton Security Services Llc
8 Tower Bridge 161 Wshgtn
Conshohocken PA 19428
610 239-1100

(G-19793)
AMERIPRISE FINANCIAL SVCS INC
250 W Old Wlsn Brg Rd # 150 (43085-2215)
PHONE..................614 846-8723
Ray Jones, *Opers-Prdtn-Mfg*
EMP: 67
SALES (corp-wide): 12.8B **Publicly Held**
WEB: www.amps.com
SIC: **6211** 6411 6282 Mutual funds, selling by independent salesperson; insurance agents; investment advice
HQ: Ameriprise Financial Services Inc.
707 2nd Ave S
Minneapolis MN 55402
612 671-2733

(G-19794)
ASSOCIATION OF PROSTHODONTICS
Also Called: Worthington Dental Group
7227 N High St Ste 1 (43085-2575)
PHONE..................614 885-2022
Bob Toottle, *Partner*
Richard P Cunningham, *Partner*
EMP: 26
SALES (est): 2.1MM **Privately Held**
SIC: **8021** Dentists' office

(G-19795)
CAPITAL PARTNERS REALTY LLC
Keller Williams Commercial
100 E Wilson Bridge Rd # 100 (43085-2326)
PHONE..................614 888-1000
Jamie Keller, *Broker*
Orr Olson, *Broker*
Teresa Santmyer, *Sales Staff*
Judy Ackerman, *Manager*
Lynn Nadler, *Consultant*
EMP: 39
SALES (est): 1MM
SALES (corp-wide): 1.2MM **Privately Held**
SIC: **6531** Real estate agent, residential
PA: Capital Partners Realty, Llc
100 E Wilson Bridge Rd # 100
Worthington OH 43085
614 888-1000

(G-19796)
CENTRAL OHIO PRIMARY CARE
760 Lakeview Plaza Blvd # 500 (43085-4734)
PHONE..................614 540-7339
EMP: 54 **Privately Held**
SIC: **8011** General & family practice, physician/surgeon
PA: Central Ohio Primary Care Physicians, Inc.
570 Polaris Pkwy Ste 250
Westerville OH 43082

(G-19797)
CHILLER LLC
401 E Wilson Bridge Rd (43085-2320)
PHONE..................614 433-9600
Brian Kvitko, *Branch Mgr*
EMP: 33
SALES (corp-wide): 12.8MM **Privately Held**
SIC: **7999** Ice skating rink operation

PA: Chiller Llc
7001 Dublin Park Dr
Dublin OH 43016
614 764-1000

(G-19798)
CHOICES FOR VCTIMS DOM VOLENCE
500 W Wilson Bridge Rd (43085-2238)
PHONE..................614 224-6617
Larry Cowell, *CEO*
Gail Heller, *Director*
EMP: 29
SALES: 11.4MM **Privately Held**
SIC: **8399** 8322 Advocacy group; emergency shelters

(G-19799)
COMMERCIAL PAINTING INC
530 Lkview Plz Blvd Ste F (43085)
PHONE..................614 298-9963
Greg Scott, *President*
Doug Lovelace, *Vice Pres*
Kevin Kobbeman, *VP Sales*
EMP: 25
SQ FT: 2,000
SALES: 2.1MM **Privately Held**
WEB: www.commercialpaintingohio.com
SIC: **1721** Residential painting

(G-19800)
COMPASSIONATE IN HOME CARE
7100 N High St Ste 200 (43085-2535)
PHONE..................614 888-5683
Joe Govern, *President*
EMP: 40
SALES (est): 1.2MM **Privately Held**
WEB: www.compinhomecare.com
SIC: **8082** Home health care services

(G-19801)
COUGHLIN HOLDINGS LTD PARTNR
Also Called: Coughlin Realty
71 E Wilson Bridge Rd (43085-2358)
PHONE..................614 847-1002
Al Coughlin Jr, *President*
Joe Grundey, *Real Est Agnt*
EMP: 50
SALES (est): 2MM **Privately Held**
SIC: **6512** Nonresidential building operators

(G-19802)
CSI INTERNATIONAL INC
690 Lkview Plz Blvd Ste C (43085)
PHONE..................614 781-1571
J Espinosa, *President*
EMP: 779
SALES (corp-wide): 53MM **Privately Held**
SIC: **7349** Janitorial service, contract basis
PA: Csi International, Inc.
6700 N Andrews Ave # 400
Fort Lauderdale FL 33309
954 308-4300

(G-19803)
DATAFIELD INC
Also Called: A P T
25 W New England Ave (43085-3582)
PHONE..................614 847-9600
Courtland Bishop, *CEO*
Michael F Mizesko, *Principal*
Britney Showalter, *CFO*
Erin Ziegler, *Human Res Mgr*
Brad Haarala, *Director*
EMP: 126
SQ FT: 8,000
SALES (est): 14.1MM **Privately Held**
WEB: www.appliedperformance.com
SIC: **7379** Computer related consulting services

(G-19804)
DAYHUFF GROUP LLC (PA)
740 Lakeview Plaza Blvd Ste # 300 (43085-6724)
PHONE..................614 854-9999
Corey Dayhuff, *President*
EMP: 32
SALES (est): 4.2MM **Privately Held**
WEB: www.dayhuffgroup.com
SIC: **7379**

(G-19805)
ECS HOLDCO INC
705 Lkview Plz Blvd Ste A (43085)
PHONE..................................614 433-0170
Dave Zappa, *Manager*
EMP: 33
SALES (corp-wide): 34MM **Privately Held**
SIC: 8748 Environmental consultant
PA: Ecs Holdco, Inc.

Agawam MA 01001

(G-19806)
ELITE EXPEDITING CORP (PA)
450 W Wilson Bridge Rd # 345
(43085-5226)
PHONE..................................614 279-1181
D Jay Floyd, *President*
EMP: 75
SALES: 5.1MM **Privately Held**
WEB: www.eliteexp.com
SIC: 4215 Package delivery, vehicular

(G-19807)
EPIQURIAN INNS
Also Called: Worthington Inn, The
649 High St (43085-4105)
PHONE..................................614 885-2600
Burke Showe, *Owner*
Hugh Showe II, *Manager*
EMP: 80
SQ FT: 28,000
SALES: 3MM **Privately Held**
SIC: 7011 5812 5813 Hotels; American
restaurant; drinking places

(G-19808)
EVEREST TECHNOLOGIES INC
740 Lakeview Plaza Blvd # 250
(43085-4784)
PHONE..................................614 436-3120
Vineet Arya, *President*
Punnet Arya, *Vice Pres*
Anil Bakhshi, *Vice Pres*
Bob Malik, *Treasurer*
Kapil Malik, *Treasurer*
EMP: 30
SALES (est): 5.3MM **Privately Held**
WEB: www.everesttech.com
SIC: 7379

(G-19809)
**EXCEL ELECTRICAL
CONTRACTOR**
7484 Reliance St (43085-1703)
PHONE..................................740 965-3795
Kenneth B White, *President*
Daniel R Howard, *Vice Pres*
Daniel Howard, *Vice Pres*
EMP: 28 EST: 1997
SQ FT: 2,700
SALES: 1.7MM **Privately Held**
SIC: 1731 Electrical work

(G-19810)
FARRIS ENTERPRISES INC (PA)
Also Called: Mammoth Restoration and Clg
7465 Worthington Galena (43085-6714)
PHONE..................................614 367-9611
Matthew Farris, *President*
EMP: 36
SQ FT: 2,700
SALES: 4.6MM **Privately Held**
SIC: 1521 Repairing fire damage, single-
family houses

(G-19811)
**FRANKLIN COUNTY
RESIDENTIAL S**
445 E Dublin Granville Rd G (43085-3183)
PHONE..................................614 844-5847
Lori Sontag, *Finance*
Gaines Strouse, *Manager*
Margaret Padgett, *Asst Mgr*
Tamika Bailey, *Info Tech Dir*
Todd Mitchell, *Technology*
EMP: 285
SALES: 21.7MM **Privately Held**
WEB: www.fcres.com
SIC: 8361 Home for the mentally handi-
capped

(G-19812)
HE HARI INC
Also Called: Holiday Inn
7007 N High St (43085-2329)
PHONE..................................614 436-0700
Vijay Phapha, *Branch Mgr*
EMP: 89
SALES (est): 3.7MM
SALES (corp-wide): 1.8MM **Privately
Held**
SIC: 7011 Motels
PA: He Hari Inc
600 Enterprise Dr
Lewis Center OH 43035
614 846-6600

(G-19813)
HECO OPERATIONS INC
Also Called: SERVPRO
7440 Pingue Dr (43085-1741)
PHONE..................................614 888-5700
Patricia Heid, *Owner*
Robert Heid, *Owner*
Richard Cottrill, *Vice Pres*
EMP: 36
SQ FT: 19,150
SALES (est): 1.8MM **Privately Held**
WEB: www.spohio.com
SIC: 7349 Building maintenance services

(G-19814)
HER INC
Also Called: H E R Realtors
681 High St (43085-4105)
PHONE..................................614 888-7400
Paul Bean, *Manager*
EMP: 60
SALES (corp-wide): 14.3MM **Privately
Held**
WEB: www.eassent.com
SIC: 6531 Real estate agent, residential
PA: Her, Inc
4261 Morse Rd
Columbus OH 43230
614 221-7400

(G-19815)
**HOME HEALTH CONNECTION
INC**
6797 N High St Ste 113 (43085-2533)
PHONE..................................614 839-4545
Shirine Mafi, *President*
Shawn Mafi, *Vice Pres*
EMP: 30 EST: 2000
SALES: 15.4MM **Privately Held**
SIC: 8059 8011 Personal care home, with
health care; offices & clinics of medical
doctors

(G-19816)
HOMEREACH INC (HQ)
404 E Wilson Bridge Rd (43085-2369)
PHONE..................................614 566-0850
Frances Baby, *President*
EMP: 125
SALES (est): 10.9MM
SALES (corp-wide): 4B **Privately Held**
WEB: www.homereach.net
SIC: 8082 Home health care services
PA: Ohiohealth Corporation
180 E Broad St
Columbus OH 43215
614 788-8860

(G-19817)
**KINDERCARE LEARNING CTRS
INC**
Also Called: Kindercare Child Care Network
77 Caren Ave (43085-2513)
PHONE..................................614 888-9696
Charles Freed, *Manager*
Laura Walker, *Director*
EMP: 25
SALES (corp-wide): 1.2B **Privately Held**
WEB: www.kindercare.com
SIC: 8351 Group day care center
HQ: Kindercare Learning Centers, Llc
650 Ne Holladay St # 1400
Portland OR 97232
503 872-1300

(G-19818)
**KLINGBEIL CAPITAL MGT LLC
(PA)**
500 W Wilson Bridge Rd (43085-2238)
P.O. Box 1474, Centreville VA (20122-
8474)
PHONE..................................614 396-4919
James D Klingbeil Jr, *CEO*
Kevin Kaz,
Mark M Mullen,
James D Schrim III,
EMP: 55
SALES (est): 154.3MM **Privately Held**
SIC: 6799 8741 Real estate investors, ex-
cept property operators; management
services

(G-19819)
LAKES VENTURE LLC
Also Called: Fresh Thyme Farmers Market
933 High St (43085-4020)
PHONE..................................614 681-7050
Ray Simpson, *Manager*
EMP: 100
SALES (corp-wide): 254.3MM **Privately
Held**
SIC: 5141 Groceries, general line
PA: Lakes Venture, Llc
2650 Warrenville Rd # 700
Downers Grove IL 60515
331 251-7100

(G-19820)
**LAUREL HEALTH CARE
COMPANY**
Also Called: Laurels of Norworth
6830 N High St (43085-2510)
PHONE..................................614 888-4553
Rylie Hacker, *Chf Purch Ofc*
Don Appericio, *Director*
Tracy Aitken, *Food Svc Dir*
Jami Young, *Executive*
EMP: 115 **Privately Held**
WEB: www.laurelsofnorworth.com
SIC: 8741 8051 Nursing & personal care
facility management; skilled nursing care
facilities
HQ: Laurel Health Care Company
8181 Worthington Rd Uppr
Westerville OH 43082

(G-19821)
**LAUREL HEALTH CARE
COMPANY**
Also Called: Worlds of Worthington
1030 High St (43085-4014)
PHONE..................................614 885-0408
Chris Hudson, *Manager*
EMP: 200 **Privately Held**
WEB: www.laurelsofnorworth.com
SIC: 8741 8051 8059 Nursing & personal
care facility management; hotel or motel
management; skilled nursing care facili-
ties; convalescent home
HQ: Laurel Health Care Company
8181 Worthington Rd Uppr
Westerville OH 43082

(G-19822)
LEADERS MOVING COMPANY
Also Called: Leaders Moving & Storage Co
7455 Alta View Blvd (43085-5891)
PHONE..................................614 785-9595
Craig Crotinger, *Owner*
Steve Lambert, *COO*
Jason Farley, *Opers Staff*
Macee Pham, *Human Res Mgr*
Candace Gardner, *Consultant*
EMP: 50
SQ FT: 30,000
SALES (est): 8.1MM **Privately Held**
WEB: www.leadersmoving.com
SIC: 4212 4214 Moving services; furniture
moving & storage, local

(G-19823)
LEI CBUS LLC
7492 Sancus Blvd (43085-4923)
PHONE..................................614 302-8830
Matthew Jackson,
EMP: 50
SALES (est): 1.8MM **Privately Held**
SIC: 1521 Single-family housing construc-
tion

(G-19824)
**LIBERTY CAPITAL SERVICES
LLC**
438 E Wilson Bridge Rd (43085-2382)
PHONE..................................614 505-0620
Kenneth Wichman, *CEO*
EMP: 25 EST: 2011
SALES (est): 2.8MM **Privately Held**
SIC: 6162 Mortgage bankers

(G-19825)
**LUTHERAN SCIAL SVCS CENTL
OHIO (PA)**
500 W Wilson Bridge Rd (43085-2238)
PHONE..................................419 289-3523
Larry Crowell, *President*
Leah Schwalbe, *President*
Rose Craig, *Vice Pres*
Rick Davis, *Vice Pres*
Phil D Helser, *Vice Pres*
EMP: 40
SQ FT: 9,000
SALES: 49.2MM **Privately Held**
SIC: 8322 Outreach program

(G-19826)
**LUTHERAN SOCIAL SERVICES
OF**
500 W Wilson Bridge Rd # 245
(43085-2283)
PHONE..................................614 228-5200
Larry Crowell, *CEO*
Henry Kassab, *Accounting Mgr*
EMP: 25
SQ FT: 8,000
SALES (est): 247.3K **Privately Held**
SIC: 8082 Home health care services

(G-19827)
MEDVET ASSOCIATES INC (PA)
Also Called: Med Vet Associates
300 E Wilson Bridge Rd # 100
(43085-2300)
PHONE..................................614 846-5800
Eric Schertel, *President*
Roger Veliz, *Opers Staff*
Linda Lehmkuhl, *Chief Mktg Ofcr*
William Dehoff Dvm Ms, *Shareholder*
EMP: 696
SALES (est): 57.6MM **Privately Held**
WEB: www.medvetassociates.com
SIC: 0742 Veterinarian, animal specialties

(G-19828)
MIDWEST LIQUIDATORS INC
6827 N High St Ste 109 (43085-2517)
PHONE..................................614 433-7355
Robert Cassel, *President*
Deborah R Cassel, *Vice Pres*
EMP: 40
SQ FT: 2,400
SALES: 7.5MM **Privately Held**
WEB: www.casselauctions.com
SIC: 7389 6531 Merchandise liquidators;
auctioneers, fee basis; real estate agents
& managers

(G-19829)
MILE INC (PA)
Also Called: Lion's Den
110 E Wilson Bridge Rd # 100
(43085-2317)
PHONE..................................614 794-2203
Michael R Moran, *President*
Patricia Dixon, *Executive*
EMP: 70
SALES (est): 13.7MM **Privately Held**
SIC: 7841 5942 Video tape rental; book
stores

(G-19830)
NEW ENGLAND RMS INC
402 E Wilson Bridge Rd A (43085-2366)
PHONE..................................401 384-6759
Dixon Buehler, *CEO*
Joseph Cozzolino, *President*
EMP: 40
SQ FT: 8,000
SALES (est): 1.5MM **Privately Held**
SIC: 8361 Residential care for the handi-
capped

(G-19831)
OHIO AUTOMOBILE CLUB (PA)
Also Called: AAA
90 E Wilson Bridge Rd # 1 (43085-2387)
PHONE................................614 431-7901
Mark Shaw, *President*
Tom Keyes, *COO*
EMP: 200
SQ FT: 1,172
SALES (est): 59.9MM **Privately Held**
SIC: 8699 Automobile owners' association

(G-19832)
ORGANIZATIONAL HORIZONS INC
5721 N High St Ste Lla (43085-3978)
P.O. Box 14425, Columbus (43214-0425)
PHONE................................614 268-6013
Sandra Shullman, *President*
EMP: 40
SQ FT: 2,600
SALES: 1.7MM **Privately Held**
SIC: 8742 Business consultant

(G-19833)
PAYCHEX INC
600 Lkview Plz Blvd Ste G (43085)
PHONE................................614 781-6143
Dale Warcewicz, *Branch Mgr*
EMP: 37
SALES (corp-wide): 3.3B **Publicly Held**
SIC: 8721 Payroll accounting service
PA: Paychex, Inc.
911 Panorama Trl S
Rochester NY 14625
585 385-6666

(G-19834)
PAYCOR INC
250 E Wilson Bridge Rd # 110
(43085-2323)
PHONE................................614 985-6140
Becky Fusco, *Branch Mgr*
EMP: 27
SALES (corp-wide): 105.2MM **Privately Held**
SIC: 8721 Payroll accounting service
PA: Paycor, Inc.
4811 Montgomery Rd
Cincinnati OH 45212
513 381-0505

(G-19835)
PHIL GIESSLER
Also Called: Camtaylor Co Realtors
882 High St Ste A (43085-4159)
PHONE................................614 888-0307
Phil Giessler, *Owner*
EMP: 30
SALES (est): 1.2MM **Privately Held**
WEB: www.cam-taylor.com
SIC: 6531 6512 Real estate brokers & agents; nonresidential building operators

(G-19836)
PREMIER CARE
500 W Wilson Bridge Rd # 235
(43085-2287)
PHONE................................614 431-0599
Debbie Ittikraichereon, *Principal*
EMP: 55
SALES (est): 755K **Privately Held**
SIC: 8082 Home health care services

(G-19837)
PRIORITY MORTGAGE CORP
150 E Wilson Bridge Rd # 350
(43085-6302)
PHONE................................614 431-1141
Samuel J Hill, *CEO*
Gary W Erler, *President*
Lisa Kendle, *Assistant VP*
Marianne Viola, *Assistant VP*
David McKee, *Vice Pres*
EMP: 28
SQ FT: 6,000
SALES (est): 5.1MM **Privately Held**
SIC: 6162 Mortgage bankers & correspondents

(G-19838)
PSP OPERATIONS INC
7440 Pingue Dr (43085-1741)
PHONE................................614 888-5700
Kenneth Parker, *Principal*

EMP: 27 **EST:** 2014
SALES (est): 660.5K **Privately Held**
SIC: 7349 Building maintenance services

(G-19839)
QUALITY AERO INC (PA)
Also Called: Acquisition Logistics Engrg
6797 N High St Ste 324 (43085-2598)
PHONE................................614 436-1609
Renee Coogan, *President*
Stephen Brunner, *Vice Pres*
Joseph Coogan, *Vice Pres*
Darryl Kellner, *Engineer*
Tom Autseher, *Info Tech Mgr*
EMP: 25
SQ FT: 5,000
SALES (est): 3.5MM **Privately Held**
WEB: www.ale.com
SIC: 8711 Consulting engineer

(G-19840)
R DORSEY & COMPANY INC
Also Called: R.dorsey & Company
400 W Wilson Bridge Rd # 105
(43085-2259)
P.O. Box 12328, Columbus (43212-0328)
PHONE................................614 486-8900
Robert J Dorsey, *President*
EMP: 50
SQ FT: 2,000
SALES: 4MM **Privately Held**
WEB: www.dorseyplus.com
SIC: 7379 Computer related consulting services

(G-19841)
R P CUNNINGHAM DDS INC
7227 N High St Ste 1 (43085-2575)
PHONE................................614 885-2022
R Cunningham DDS, *Principal*
Richard Cunningham DDS, *Principal*
Robert Tootle DDS, *Vice Pres*
EMP: 25 **EST:** 1975
SALES (est): 751K **Privately Held**
SIC: 8021 Offices & clinics of dentists

(G-19842)
RECYCLED SYSTEMS FURNITURE INC
Also Called: Rsfi Office Furniture
401 E Wilson Bridge Rd (43085-2320)
PHONE................................614 880-9110
Ron Morris, *President*
Jim Ellison, *Vice Pres*
EMP: 25
SQ FT: 100,000
SALES (est): 4.4MM **Privately Held**
WEB: www.rsfi.com
SIC: 7641 5712 2522 Office furniture repair & maintenance; furniture upholstery repair; office furniture; office furniture, except wood

(G-19843)
RESIDENTIAL MANAGEMENT SYSTEMS (PA)
402 E Wilson Bridge Rd (43085-2366)
PHONE................................614 880-6014
Joseph Cozzolino, *President*
Anita Allen, *COO*
Dixon Buehler, *CFO*
Joe McCain, *Accountant*
Rose Childers, *Manager*
EMP: 41
SQ FT: 8,325
SALES: 4.5MM **Privately Held**
SIC: 8361 Home for the mentally handicapped

(G-19844)
RESOURCE ONE CMPT SYSTEMS INC
651 Lkview Plz Blvd Ste E (43085)
PHONE................................614 485-4800
Stampp W Corbin, *President*
EMP: 100
SALES (est): 12.6MM **Privately Held**
SIC: 5734 7378 Computer & software stores; computer maintenance & repair

(G-19845)
RICOH USA INC
300 W Wilson Bridge Rd # 110
(43085-2235)
PHONE................................614 310-6500

Georg Shannon, *Manager*
Marcia Vanderstel, *Information Mgr*
EMP: 70
SALES (corp-wide): 19.3B **Privately Held**
WEB: www.ikon.com
SIC: 5044 Photocopy machines
HQ: Ricoh Usa, Inc.
70 Valley Stream Pkwy
Malvern PA 19355
610 296-8000

(G-19846)
SAFELITE GLASS CORP
Guardian Auto Glass
600 Lkview Plz Blvd Ste A (43085)
P.O. Box 29167, Columbus (43229-0167)
PHONE................................614 431-4936
Paul Janisse, *Director*
EMP: 25
SALES (corp-wide): 2.6MM **Privately Held**
SIC: 7536 Automotive glass replacement shops
HQ: Safelite Glass Corp
7400 Safelite Way
Columbus OH 43235
614 210-9000

(G-19847)
SECURE TRNSP CO OHIO LLC
777 Dearborn Park Ln S (43085-5716)
PHONE................................800 856-9994
David Kurtz, *CFO*
Steve Dobbs,
Anne Marin,
EMP: 25
SALES (est): 534.7K **Privately Held**
SIC: 4789 Pipeline terminal facilities, independently operated

(G-19848)
SERVICES ON MARK INC
705 Lkview Plz Blvd Ste L (43085)
PHONE................................614 846-5400
Mark Stuntz, *President*
EMP: 40
SALES (est): 1.5MM **Privately Held**
SIC: 8322 Child related social services

(G-19849)
SIEMENS INDUSTRY INC
530 Lkview Plz Blvd Ste D (43085)
PHONE................................614 846-9540
Joe Kaiser, *CEO*
Neil Williams, *Manager*
Michael Zarzour, *Manager*
Jim Salerno, *Consultant*
Scott Arnette, *Technician*
EMP: 80
SALES (est): 14.5MM **Privately Held**
SIC: 5063 Electrical apparatus & equipment

(G-19850)
SOUTHAST CMNTY MENTAL HLTH CTR
Also Called: Southeast Counseling
445 E Granville Rd (43085-3192)
PHONE................................614 293-9613
Amy Price, *Branch Mgr*
EMP: 25
SALES (corp-wide): 12.5MM **Privately Held**
WEB: www.southeastinc.com
SIC: 8093 8322 Mental health clinic, outpatient; general counseling services
PA: Southeast Community Mental Health Center Inc
16 W Long St
Columbus OH 43215
614 225-0980

(G-19851)
SOUTHERNTIER TELECOM (PA)
651 Lkview Plz Blvd Ste E (43085)
PHONE................................614 505-6365
Marina Miller, *CEO*
Alex Borodyanskiy, *CFO*
EMP: 40
SQ FT: 4,000
SALES (est): 14.6MM **Privately Held**
SIC: 4813 Telephone communication, except radio

(G-19852)
ST MORITZ SECURITY SVCS INC
705 Lkview Plz Blvd Ste G (43085)
PHONE................................614 351-8798
Gary Harney, *Branch Mgr*
EMP: 45
SALES (corp-wide): 61.2MM **Privately Held**
WEB: www.smssi.com
SIC: 7381 Security guard service; detective services
PA: St. Moritz Security Services, Inc.
4600 Clairton Blvd
Pittsburgh PA 15236
412 885-3144

(G-19853)
STAT EXPRESS DELIVERY LLC (PA)
705 Lkview Plz Blvd Ste M (43085)
PHONE................................614 880-7828
Kathy Rittenhouse,
EMP: 47
SQ FT: 8,600
SALES (est): 2.1MM **Privately Held**
WEB: www.statexpress.com
SIC: 4215 Package delivery, vehicular

(G-19854)
SUNRISE SENIOR LIVING INC
Also Called: Sunrise PI For Memory Impaired
6525 N High St (43085-4045)
PHONE................................614 846-6500
Debra Guzman, *Principal*
EMP: 43
SALES (corp-wide): 4.7B **Publicly Held**
WEB: www.sunrise.com
SIC: 8361 8059 8051 Home for the aged; nursing home, except skilled & intermediate care facility; skilled nursing care facilities
HQ: Sunrise Senior Living, Llc
7902 Westpark Dr
Mc Lean VA 22102

(G-19855)
SWIM INCORPORATED
Also Called: WORTHINGTON SWIMMING POOL
400 W Dublin Granville Rd (43085-3590)
PHONE................................614 885-1619
Tom Bubenik, *President*
Ron Lemerech, *President*
Rob Schmidt, *President*
Dan McCarthy, *Asst Mgr*
Chris Hadden, *Director*
EMP: 50 **EST:** 1953
SALES: 1MM **Privately Held**
WEB: www.worthingtonswimclub.org
SIC: 7997 5812 7991 Swimming club, membership; concessionaire; physical fitness facilities

(G-19856)
THOMAS GLASS COMPANY INC (PA)
400 E Wilson Bridge Rd A (43085-2363)
PHONE................................614 268-8611
Andrew T Gum, *President*
EMP: 43
SQ FT: 4,000
SALES (est): 4.5MM **Privately Held**
WEB: www.thomasglass.com
SIC: 1793 Glass & glazing work

(G-19857)
VERISK CRIME ANALYTICS INC
Also Called: Netmap Analytics
250 Old Wilson Brg (43085-2285)
PHONE................................614 865-6000
Joseph Hirt, *Branch Mgr*
Buzz Hirt, *Director*
EMP: 33 **Publicly Held**
SIC: 7375 Information retrieval services
HQ: Verisk Crime Analytics, Inc.
545 Washington Blvd
Jersey City NJ 07310
201 469-3000

(G-19858)
WARD & WERNER CO
6620 Plesenton Dr W (43085-2945)
P.O. Box 340497, Columbus (43234-0497)
PHONE................................614 885-0741
Anthony Werner, *President*

Cheryl Werner, *Corp Secy*
Randy Ward, *Vice Pres*
EMP: 120
SALES (est): 2.4MM **Privately Held**
SIC: 7349 Building maintenance services

(G-19859)
WEST OHIO CONFERENCE OF (PA)
Also Called: United Methodist Camps
32 Wesley Blvd (43085-3585)
PHONE..............................614 844-6200
Gregory V Palmer, *Principal*
Barb Sholis, *Principal*
Bruce R Ouch, *Bishop*
Bill Brownson, *CFO*
R Stanley Sutton, *Treasurer*
EMP: 39
SQ FT: 16,587
SALES (est): 5.6MM **Privately Held**
WEB: www.cliftonumc.com
SIC: 7032 8661 Recreational camps; Methodist Church

(G-19860)
WHALEN AND COMPANY INC
Also Called: Whalen & Co CPA
250 W Old Wlsn Brg Rd # 300 (43085-2215)
PHONE..............................614 396-4200
Richard D Crabtree, *Partner*
Linda Hickey, *Partner*
Lisa G Shuneson, *Partner*
Laura B Wojciechowski, *Partner*
Jessica Distel, *Accounting Mgr*
EMP: 32
SQ FT: 7,500
SALES (est): 3.2MM **Privately Held**
SIC: 8721 Certified public accountant

(G-19861)
WHITING-TURNER CONTRACTING CO
250 W Old Wilson Bridge R (43085-5227)
PHONE..............................614 459-6515
Tom Garske, *Regional Mgr*
EMP: 255
SALES (corp-wide): 6.1B **Privately Held**
SIC: 1542 Nonresidential construction
PA: The Whiting-Turner Contracting Company
    300 E Joppa Rd Ste 800
    Baltimore MD 21286
    410 821-1100

(G-19862)
WORTHINGTON PUBLIC LIBRARY
820 High St (43085-3182)
PHONE..............................614 807-2626
Margaret Doone, *Business Mgr*
Phyllis Winfield, *Human Res Mgr*
Marietta Brits, *Manager*
Allison Scheuering, *Manager*
Debbie Zimmerman, *Manager*
EMP: 130
SALES: 54.9K **Privately Held**
WEB: www.worthingtonmemory.net
SIC: 8231 8742 Public library; management consulting services

---

Wshngtn CT Hs
Fayette County

(G-19863)
ADENA HEALTH SYSTEM
308 Highland Ave Unit C (43160-1993)
PHONE..............................740 779-7500
Adedoyin Adetoro, *Principal*
EMP: 213
SALES (corp-wide): 470.6MM **Privately Held**
SIC: 8062 General medical & surgical hospitals
PA: Adena Health System
    272 Hospital Rd
    Chillicothe OH 45601
    740 779-7360

(G-19864)
CLARK ROYSTER INC
717 Robinson Rd Se (43160-8630)
PHONE..............................740 335-3810

Steve Emery, *President*
EMP: 30
SALES (est): 672.8K **Privately Held**
SIC: 0711 Soil chemical treatment services

(G-19865)
COMMU ACT COMM OF FAYETTE CNTY (PA)
1400 Us Highway 22 Nw (43160-8604)
PHONE..............................740 335-7282
Mekia Rhoades, *Manager*
Bill Davis, *Supervisor*
Lucinda Baughn, *Exec Dir*
EMP: 95
SQ FT: 2,000
SALES: 7.1MM **Privately Held**
SIC: 8322 Social service center

(G-19866)
COUNTY OF FAYETTE
Also Called: County Engineer
1600 Robinson Rd Se (43160-9205)
PHONE..............................740 335-1541
Ron Longberry, *Superintendent*
Valerie Robinette, *Supervisor*
Karla Morrison, *Admin Sec*
Julie Hidy, *Administration*
EMP: 36 **Privately Held**
SIC: 8711 Engineering services
PA: County Of Fayette
    133 S Main St Rm 401
    Wshngtn Ct Hs OH 43160
    740 335-0720

(G-19867)
COX PAVING INC
2754 Us Highway 22 Nw (43160-9510)
PHONE..............................937 780-3075
Fred B Cox Jr, *President*
Fred B Cox III, *Vice Pres*
Gregory R Cox, *Vice Pres*
Misty Lawson, *Manager*
Cindy Cox, *Admin Sec*
EMP: 93
SALES (est): 12.3MM **Privately Held**
WEB: www.coxpavinginc.com
SIC: 1794 7631 1771 Excavation & grading, building construction; watch repair; driveway contractor

(G-19868)
CUSTOM LAWN CARE & LDSCPG LLC
2411 Us Highway 22 Sw (43160-8652)
PHONE..............................740 333-1669
Jaret L Bishop,
EMP: 25
SALES (est): 3.5MM **Privately Held**
SIC: 0781 Landscape services

(G-19869)
DOUG MARINE MOTORS INC
1120 Clinton Ave (43160-1215)
PHONE..............................740 335-3700
Doug Marine, *President*
Bill D Marine, *Admin Sec*
EMP: 31
SQ FT: 8,000
SALES (est): 10.4MM **Privately Held**
WEB: www.dougmarinemotors.com
SIC: 5511 5538 5531 5012 Automobiles, new & used; general automotive repair shops; automotive & home supply stores; automobiles & other motor vehicles; motor vehicle parts & accessories

(G-19870)
FAYETTE COUNTY FAMILY YMCA
Also Called: Fayette County Family YMCA
100 Civic Dr (43160-9186)
P.O. Box 1021 (43160-8021)
PHONE..............................740 335-0477
Douglas Saunders, *CEO*
Jerrod Ralph, *Director*
EMP: 85 EST: 2000
SQ FT: 35,000
SALES: 1.5MM **Privately Held**
SIC: 8641 Youth organizations

(G-19871)
FAYETTE COUNTY MEMORIAL HOSP (PA)
1430 Columbus Ave (43160-1791)
P.O. Box 310 (43160-0310)
PHONE..............................740 335-1210
Tammie Wilson, *Vice Pres*
Jane Bissel, *CFO*
Melissa Lemle, *Pharmacist*
Lori Blackburn, *Director*
Michael Diener, *Director*
EMP: 224
SALES: 42MM **Privately Held**
SIC: 8062 General medical & surgical hospitals

(G-19872)
FAYETTE PROGRESSIVE INDUSTRIES
Also Called: Fayette County Mrdd
1330 Robinson Rd Se (43160-9201)
PHONE..............................740 335-7453
Steve Hilgeman, *Superintendent*
Mark Schwartz, *Director*
EMP: 40
SALES: 300.2K **Privately Held**
WEB: www.fayettemrdd.com
SIC: 8322 Individual & family services

(G-19873)
FOUR SEASONS WASHINGTON LLC
201 Courthouse Pkwy (43160-6001)
PHONE..............................740 895-6101
Tim A Ross, *Mng Member*
Tracy Ross,
EMP: 80 EST: 2014
SALES (est): 1.7MM **Privately Held**
SIC: 8051 Convalescent home with continuous nursing care

(G-19874)
HCF OF COURT HOUSE INC
Also Called: Court House Manor
555 N Glenn Ave (43160-2711)
PHONE..............................740 335-9290
Belinda Ross, *Executive*
India Williamson, *Administration*
Jo Sanborn, *Administration*
EMP: 224
SALES: 1,000K
SALES (corp-wide): 154.8MM **Privately Held**
SIC: 8051 Convalescent home with continuous nursing care
PA: Hcf Management, Inc.
    1100 Shawnee Rd
    Lima OH 45805
    419 999-2010

(G-19875)
HCF OF WASHINGTON INC
Also Called: St. Cthrnes Manor Wash Crt Hse
555 N Glenn Ave (43160-2711)
PHONE..............................419 999-2010
Barbara Masella, *Vice Pres*
EMP: 33 **Privately Held**
SIC: 8059 Nursing home, except skilled & intermediate care facility
PA: Hcf Of Washington, Inc.
    250 Glenn Ave
    Wshngtn Ct Hs OH 43160

(G-19876)
HUNTINGTON NATIONAL BANK
Also Called: Advantage Bank
134 E Court St (43160-1358)
PHONE..............................740 335-3771
Ann Lenzer, *Branch Mgr*
EMP: 27
SALES (corp-wide): 5.2B **Publicly Held**
SIC: 6036 Savings & loan associations, not federally chartered
HQ: The Huntington National Bank
    17 S High St Fl 1
    Columbus OH 43215
    614 480-4293

(G-19877)
KROGER CO
548 Clinton Ave (43160-1299)
PHONE..............................740 335-4030
William Drum, *Manager*
EMP: 110

SALES (corp-wide): 121.1B **Publicly Held**
WEB: www.kroger.com
SIC: 5411 5122 2051 Supermarkets, chain; drugs, proprietaries & sundries; bread, cake & related products
PA: The Kroger Co
    1014 Vine St Ste 1000
    Cincinnati OH 45202
    513 762-4000

(G-19878)
MCKESSON CORPORATION
3000 Kenskill Ave (43160-8615)
PHONE..............................740 636-3500
Becky Pitakos, *Manager*
Karla Stokley, *Supervisor*
Robert Kearney, *Director*
EMP: 150
SALES (corp-wide): 208.3B **Publicly Held**
WEB: www.imckesson.com
SIC: 5122 Pharmaceuticals
PA: Mckesson Corporation
    1 Post St Fl 18
    San Francisco CA 94104
    415 983-8300

(G-19879)
MERRILL LYNCH PIERCE FENNER
209 E Court St (43160-1301)
PHONE..............................740 335-2930
John Bryan, *Branch Mgr*
George Smith, *Administration*
EMP: 55
SALES (corp-wide): 110.5B **Publicly Held**
SIC: 6211 Security brokers & dealers
HQ: Merrill Lynch, Pierce, Fenner & Smith Incorporated
    111 8th Ave
    New York NY 10011
    800 637-7455

(G-19880)
MID ATLANTIC STOR SYSTEMS INC
1551 Robinson Rd Se (43160-9201)
PHONE..............................740 335-2019
Jerry Morris, *President*
Jeanette Morris, *Corp Secy*
John Fox, *Vice Pres*
EMP: 75
SQ FT: 25,000
SALES (est): 23.9MM **Privately Held**
SIC: 1791 Storage tanks, metal: erection

(G-19881)
RITEN INDUSTRIES
1110 Lakeview Ave (43160-1037)
P.O. Box 340 (43160-0340)
PHONE..............................740 335-5353
J Andrew Lachat, *President*
Patricia Simon, *Manager*
EMP: 60 EST: 1971
SALES (est): 11.7MM **Privately Held**
SIC: 5085 Industrial supplies

(G-19882)
ROSE & DOBYNS AN OHIO PARTNR
298 N Fayette St (43160)
PHONE..............................740 335-4700
EMP: 30 **Privately Held**
SIC: 8111 General practice attorney, lawyer
PA: Rose & Dobyns An Ohio Partnership
    97 N South St
    Wilmington OH 45177

(G-19883)
SCIOTO PNT VLY MENTAL HLTH CTR
Also Called: Scioto Pnt Vly Mental Hlth Ctr
1300 E Paint St (43160-1676)
PHONE..............................740 335-6935
Ed Sipe, *Manager*
EMP: 25
SALES (corp-wide): 14.2MM **Privately Held**
SIC: 8093 8322 8069 Mental health clinic, outpatient; crisis intervention center; drug addiction rehabilitation hospital

GEOGRAPHIC

(PA)=Parent Co (HQ)=Headquarters (DH)=Div Headquarters
✪ = New Business established in last 2 years
    2019 Harris Ohio
    Services Directory
    801

PA: Scioto Paint Valley Mental Health Center
4449 State Route 159
Chillicothe OH 45601
740 775-1260

(G-19884)
SEED CONSULTANTS INC (DH)
648 Miami Trace Rd Sw (43160-9661)
P.O. Box 370 (43160-0370)
PHONE.................................740 333-8644
Chris Jeffries, *General Mgr*
EMP: 50
SQ FT: 32,500
SALES (est): 11MM
SALES (corp-wide): 85.9B **Publicly Held**
WEB: www.seedconsultants.com
SIC: 5261 5191 Nursery stock, seeds &
bulbs; seeds: field, garden & flower
HQ: Pioneer Hi-Bred International, Inc.
7100 Nw 62nd Ave
Johnston IA 50131
515 535-3200

(G-19885)
**WASHINGTON COURT HSE
HOLDG LLC**
Also Called: G K Packaging
1850 Lowes Blvd (43160-8611)
PHONE.................................614 873-7733
Wyane Whitaker, *General Mgr*
EMP: 35
SALES (corp-wide): 24.1MM **Privately
Held**
WEB: www.gkpackaging.com
SIC: 6719 Personal holding companies,
except banks
PA: Gk Packaging, Inc.
7680 Commerce Pl
Plain City OH 43064
614 873-3900

(G-19886)
WESTROCK CP LLC
1010 Mead St (43160-9310)
PHONE.................................770 448-2193
Mark Badgley, *Branch Mgr*
EMP: 93
SALES (corp-wide): 16.2B **Publicly Held**
WEB: www.smurfit-stone.com
SIC: 2653 5113 3412 Boxes, corrugated:
made from purchased materials; corru-
gated & solid fiber boxes; metal barrels,
drums & pails
HQ: Westrock Cp, Llc
1000 Abernathy Rd
Atlanta GA 30328

Xenia
Greene County

(G-19887)
A-1 BAIL BONDS INC
20 S Detroit St (45385-3502)
P.O. Box 771 (45385-0771)
PHONE.................................937 372-2400
Judy Miller, *President*
Jeff Brown, *President*
EMP: 50
SALES (est): 1.3MM **Privately Held**
WEB: www.a-1bailbonds.net
SIC: 7389 Bail bonding

(G-19888)
AK GROUP HOTELS INC
Also Called: Ramada Xenia
300 Xenia Towne Sq (45385-2949)
PHONE.................................937 372-9921
Rajesh Agrawala, *President*
Ketan Kadkia, *Vice Pres*
EMP: 25
SQ FT: 40,000
SALES (est): 1.3MM **Privately Held**
SIC: 7011 5812 Hotels; restaurant, family:
independent

(G-19889)
**AMERICAN NATIONAL RED
CROSS**
Also Called: Green County Housing Program
1080 E Main St (45385-3310)
PHONE 937 376-3111
Tom Foder, *Branch Mgr*

EMP: 29
SALES (corp-wide): 2.5B **Privately Held**
SIC: 8322 Social service center
PA: The American National Red Cross
430 17th St Nw
Washington DC 20006
202 737-8300

(G-19890)
AT&T CORP
767 Industrial Blvd (45385-4031)
PHONE.................................937 372-9945
EMP: 107
SALES (corp-wide): 170.7B **Publicly
Held**
SIC: 4813 Telephone communication, ex-
cept radio
HQ: At&T Corp.
1 At&T Way
Bedminster NJ 07921
800 403-3302

(G-19891)
**ATHLETES IN ACTION SPORTS
(HQ)**
651 Taylor Dr (45385-7246)
PHONE.................................937 352-1000
Mark Householder, *President*
Sonny Mounts, *Maint Spvr*
Beth Morter, *Finance*
Pat Lower, *Human Resources*
Tim Pitcher, *Comms Dir*
EMP: 100
SQ FT: 5,227,200
SALES (est): 16.5MM
SALES (corp-wide): 598.4MM **Privately
Held**
WEB: www.aia.com
SIC: 8699 Charitable organization
PA: Campus Crusade For Christ Inc
100 Lake Hart Dr
Orlando FL 32832
407 826-2000

(G-19892)
**BALANCED CARE
CORPORATION**
Also Called: Outlook Point At Xenia
60 Paceline Cir (45385-1281)
PHONE.................................937 372-7205
Ana Ellen, *Manager*
EMP: 50 **Privately Held**
SIC: 8741 8051 Nursing & personal care
facility management; skilled nursing care
facilities
PA: Balanced Care Corporation
5000 Ritter Rd Ste 202
Mechanicsburg PA 17055

(G-19893)
CITY OF XENIA
Also Called: Xenia Waster Water
779 Ford Rd (45385-9538)
PHONE.................................937 376-7271
Chris Burger, *Principal*
EMP: 25 **Privately Held**
SIC: 4953
PA: City Of Xenia
101 N Detroit St
Xenia OH 45385
937 376-7231

(G-19894)
CITY OF XENIA
Sanitation Division
966 Towler Rd (45385-2412)
PHONE.................................937 376-7260
Jim Jones, *Director*
EMP: 40
SQ FT: 730 **Privately Held**
SIC: 8744 Base maintenance (providing
personnel on continuing basis)
PA: City Of Xenia
101 N Detroit St
Xenia OH 45385
937 376-7231

(G-19895)
COUNTRY CLUB OF NORTH
1 Club North Dr (45385-9399)
PHONE.................................937 374-5000
Michael A Mess, *President*
EMP: 37
SALES (est): 2.3MM **Privately Held**
SIC: 7997 Country club, membership

(G-19896)
**CREATIVE DIVERSIFIED
SERVICES**
335 E Market St (45385-3114)
PHONE.................................937 376-7810
James Wickline, *President*
EMP: 30
SALES: 446.5K **Privately Held**
SIC: 8322 Individual & family services

(G-19897)
DAVITA INC
215 S Allison Ave Ste B (45385-3694)
PHONE.................................937 376-1453
Kim White, *Administration*
EMP: 26 **Publicly Held**
SIC: 8092 Kidney dialysis centers
PA: Davita Inc.
2000 16th St
Denver CO 80202

(G-19898)
DIAMOND COMPANY INC
Also Called: Cricket
823 W 2nd St (45385-3617)
PHONE.................................937 374-1111
Sam Kasen, *Branch Mgr*
EMP: 192
SALES (corp-wide): 8.1MM **Privately
Held**
SIC: 5999 5065 4812 Mobile telephones
& equipment; telephone & telegraphic
equipment; cellular telephone services
PA: The Diamond Company Inc
27600 Chagrin Blvd # 400
Cleveland OH
216 514-1000

(G-19899)
**FILE SHARPENING COMPANY
INC**
Also Called: Save Edge USA
360 W Church St (45385-2900)
PHONE.................................937 376-8268
George Whyde, *President*
▲ **EMP:** 25
SALES (est): 7.8MM **Privately Held**
SIC: 5085 7699 3423 3315 Industrial
tools; knife, saw & tool sharpening & re-
pair; hand & edge tools; steel wire & re-
lated products

(G-19900)
**FOUR OAKS EARLY
INTERVENTION**
245 N Valley Rd (45385-9301)
PHONE.................................937 562-6779
Mary Ann Campbell, *Principal*
EMP: 38
SALES (est): 696.3K **Privately Held**
SIC: 8351 Child day care services

(G-19901)
**GREENE CNTY CHLD SVC BRD
FRBRN**
601 Ledbetter Rd Ste A (45385-5363)
PHONE.................................937 878-1415
Rhonda Reagh, *Administration*
EMP: 75 **EST:** 2001
SALES (est): 1.2MM **Privately Held**
SIC: 8399 Social service information ex-
change

(G-19902)
**GREENE CNTY COMBINED HLTH
DST**
Also Called: Greene County Public Health
360 Wilson Dr (45385-1810)
PHONE.................................937 374-5600
Melissa Branum, *CEO*
Robert Dillaplain, *Commissioner*
Jeff Webb, *Director*
EMP: 69
SQ FT: 13,000
SALES: 4MM **Privately Held**
WEB: www.gcchd.org
SIC: 8322 Social service center

(G-19903)
GREENE COUNTY
Also Called: Green County Engineer
615 Dayton Xenia Rd (45385-2605)
PHONE.................................937 562-7500
Robert Geyer, *Branch Mgr*

Ken Hunley, *Supervisor*
EMP: 40 **Privately Held**
SIC: 8711 9221 Engineering services;
state highway patrol
PA: Greene County
35 Greene St
Xenia OH 45385
937 562-5006

(G-19904)
GREENE COUNTY
Also Called: Human Services
541 Ledbetter Rd (45385-5334)
PHONE.................................937 562-6000
Philip Mastn, *Director*
EMP: 140 **Privately Held**
WEB: www.greeneworks.com
SIC: 8322 Public welfare center
PA: Greene County
35 Greene St
Xenia OH 45385
937 562-5006

(G-19905)
GREENE COUNTY
Also Called: Greene County Services
641 Dayton Xenia Rd (45385-2605)
PHONE.................................937 562-7800
Carl Geisler, *Director*
EMP: 32 **Privately Held**
WEB: www.greeneworks.com
SIC: 8744 Base maintenance (providing
personnel on continuing basis)
PA: Greene County
35 Greene St
Xenia OH 45385
937 562-5006

(G-19906)
**GREENE COUNTY CAREER
CENTER**
2960 W Enon Rd (45385-9545)
PHONE.................................937 372-6941
Matt Lindley, *Principal*
EMP: 40
SALES (est): 1.1MM **Privately Held**
SIC: 8399 Fund raising organization, non-
fee basis

(G-19907)
GREENE INC
Also Called: DOCUMENT SOLUTIONS
121 Fairground Rd (45385-9543)
PHONE.................................937 562-4200
Mary Nissen, *Business Mgr*
Myra Jackson, *Financial Exec*
Dennis Rhodes, *Sales Mgr*
Greg Geyer, *Info Tech Mgr*
Sean Fox, *IT/INT Sup*
EMP: 100
SQ FT: 2,086
SALES: 3.3MM **Privately Held**
WEB: www.greeneinc.org
SIC: 8331 Sheltered workshop

(G-19908)
**GREENE MEMORIAL HOSPITAL
INC (DH)**
1141 N Monroe Dr (45385-1600)
PHONE.................................937 352-2000
Michael R Stephens, *CEO*
Timothy Pollard, *CFO*
Glenda Glavic, *Director*
EMP: 600
SALES: 48.4MM
SALES (corp-wide): 1.7B **Privately Held**
WEB: www.greenememorialhospital.com
SIC: 8062 Hospital, affiliated with AMA res-
idency
HQ: Greene Health Partners
1141 N Monroe Dr
Xenia OH 45385
937 352-2000

(G-19909)
GREENE OAKS
Also Called: Greene Oaks Health Center
164 Office Park Dr (45385-1647)
PHONE.................................937 352-2800
Frannita Porter, *Sls & Mktg Exec*
Dwayne Tracy, *Information Mgr*
John Flannigan, *Exec Dir*
Katie Dickens, *Hlthcr Dir*
EMP: 100
SQ FT: 18,000

SALES: 6.8MM
SALES (corp-wide): 1.7B Privately Held
SIC: 8062 General medical & surgical hospitals
HQ: Kettering Affiliated Health Services, Inc
3535 Southern Blvd
Dayton OH 45429
937 298-4331

(G-19910)
HOME RUN INC (PA)
1299 Lavelle Dr (45385-7402)
PHONE..............................800 543-9198
Gary Harlow, *President*
Thomas Baker, *Vice Pres*
Dennis Harlow, *Vice Pres*
Grant Harlow, *Vice Pres*
Kent Stevens, *Vice Pres*
EMP: 35
SQ FT: 12,800
SALES: 31.4MM Privately Held
WEB: www.homeruninc.com
SIC: 4213 4212 Building materials transport; local trucking, without storage

(G-19911)
HOMETOWN URGENT CARE
101 S Orange St (45385-3603)
PHONE..............................937 372-6012
Ritu Singla, *Principal*
EMP: 123
SALES (corp-wide): 73.2MM Privately Held
SIC: 8031 8011 Offices & clinics of osteopathic physicians; clinic, operated by physicians
PA: Hometown Urgent Care
2400 Corp Exchange Dr # 102
Columbus OH 43231
614 505-7633

(G-19912)
HOSPICE OF MIAMI VALLEY LLC (PA)
46 N Detroit St Ste B (45385-2984)
PHONE..............................937 458-6028
Carol L Brad, *CEO*
EMP: 25
SALES: 16MM Privately Held
SIC: 8052 Personal care facility

(G-19913)
JAMES ADVANTAGE FUNDS
1349 Fairground Rd (45385-9514)
PHONE..............................937 426-7640
Frank James, *Owner*
Barry James, *Vice Pres*
Diane M Rose, *Vice Pres*
Ann Shaw, *CFO*
Michelle Sarmiento, *Marketing Staff*
EMP: 25
SALES (est): 2.1MM Privately Held
SIC: 6722 Management investment, open-end

(G-19914)
KIL KARE INC
Also Called: Kil-Kare Speedway & Drag Strip
1166 Dayton Xenia Rd (45385-7107)
PHONE..............................937 429-2961
David Cotereo, *President*
EMP: 80
SQ FT: 2,000
SALES (est): 2.5MM Privately Held
WEB: www.kilkare.com
SIC: 7948 Automotive race track operation

(G-19915)
KINETIC RENOVATIONS LLC
2299 Jasper Rd (45385-7850)
PHONE..............................937 321-1576
Mark Ernst, *Mng Member*
EMP: 40
SALES: 10MM Privately Held
SIC: 7299 Home improvement & renovation contractor agency

(G-19916)
KROGER CO
1700 W Park Sq (45385-2667)
PHONE..............................937 376-7962
Paul Fullencamb, *Manager*
EMP: 260

SALES (corp-wide): 121.1B Publicly Held
WEB: www.kroger.com
SIC: 5411 5141 Supermarkets, chain; supermarkets, 66,000-99,000 square feet; convenience stores, chain; groceries, general line
PA: The Kroger Co
1014 Vine St Ste 1000
Cincinnati OH 45202
513 762-4000

(G-19917)
LIBERTY NURSING HOME INC
Also Called: Heathergreene Nursing Homes
126 Wilson Dr (45385-1899)
PHONE..............................937 376-2121
Linda Black-Kurek, *President*
Maryann La Vigne, *Vice Pres*
Gretchen Hobbs, *Director*
EMP: 75
SALES (est): 3.9MM Privately Held
SIC: 8051 Extended care facility

(G-19918)
LOWES HOME CENTERS LLC
126 Hospitality Dr (45385-2777)
PHONE..............................937 347-4000
Kimberly Leeper, *Store Mgr*
Jeremy Austin, *Manager*
EMP: 150
SALES (corp-wide): 68.6B Publicly Held
SIC: 5211 5031 5722 5064 Home centers; building materials, exterior; building materials, interior; household appliance stores; electrical appliances, television & radio
HQ: Lowe's Home Centers, Llc
1605 Curtis Bridge Rd
Wilkesboro NC 28697
336 658-4000

(G-19919)
MACAIR AVIATION LLC
140 N Valley Rd (45385-9301)
PHONE..............................937 347-1302
Ross McNutt, *Med Doctor*
EMP: 32 EST: 2012
SALES (est): 1.1MM Privately Held
SIC: 8299 7363 7997 4581 Airline training; pilot service, aviation; flying field, maintained by aviation clubs; airports & flying fields; confinement surveillance systems maintenance & monitoring

(G-19920)
MIAMI VLY JVNILE RHBLTTION CTR
2100 Greene Way Blvd (45385-2677)
PHONE..............................937 562-4000
Amanda Opicka, *Technology*
Gary Neidenthal, *Director*
Michael Higgins, *Director*
EMP: 30
SALES (est): 559.2K Privately Held
SIC: 8322 Rehabilitation services

(G-19921)
NATIONWIDE BIWEEKLY ADM INC
Also Called: Nba
855 Lower Bellbrook Rd (45385-7306)
PHONE..............................937 376-5800
Daniel Lipsky, *President*
Sherry A Scott, *General Mgr*
Sarah Eubank, *Admin Asst*
EMP: 105
SQ FT: 25,000
SALES (est): 51.5MM Privately Held
WEB: www.nbabiweekly.com
SIC: 6099 Clearinghouse associations, bank or check

(G-19922)
REDDY ELECTRIC CO
1145 Bellbrook Ave (45385-4061)
PHONE..............................937 372-8205
Robert L La Freniere, *President*
Shaun Gannon, *COO*
Jeff Eldridge, *Vice Pres*
Jeffrey Eldridge, *Vice Pres*
Steve Stanek, *Vice Pres*
EMP: 140
SQ FT: 7,000

SALES (est): 22MM Privately Held
WEB: www.reddyelectric.com
SIC: 1731 General electrical contractor

(G-19923)
REPTILES BY MACK LLC
1332 Burnett Dr (45385-5680)
PHONE..............................937 372-9570
John Mack, *Principal*
Amy Mack, *Vice Pres*
Dee Kuns, *Controller*
EMP: 50
SALES (est): 2.8MM Privately Held
SIC: 0752 Animal specialty services

(G-19924)
ROGOSIN INSTITUTE INC
740 Birch Rd (45385-9606)
PHONE..............................937 374-3116
Albert L Rubin, *President*
EMP: 25
SALES (corp-wide): 100MM Privately Held
WEB: www.thf.org
SIC: 8733 8731 Medical research; commercial physical research
PA: The Rogosin Institute Inc
505 E 70th St Fl 2
New York NY 10021
212 746-1551

(G-19925)
SENIOR CARE INC
Elmcroft Assisted Living
60 Paceline Cir (45385-1281)
PHONE..............................937 372-1530
Diana Alan, *Branch Mgr*
EMP: 50 Privately Held
SIC: 8361 8051 Home for the aged; skilled nursing care facilities
PA: Senior Care, Inc.
700 N Hurstbourne Pkwy # 200
Louisville KY 40222

(G-19926)
SHOUPES CONSTUCTION
1410 Ludlow Rd (45385-7900)
PHONE..............................937 352-6457
Roger L Shoupes, *Owner*
EMP: 25 EST: 1986
SALES: 850K Privately Held
SIC: 1521 Single-family housing construction

(G-19927)
TCN BEHAVIORAL HEALTH SVCS INC (PA)
Also Called: COMMUNITY NETWORK THE
452 W Market St (45385-2815)
PHONE..............................937 376-8700
Lynn West, *CEO*
Tasha Strcikland, *Property Mgr*
Nathan Wilson, *Manager*
Kate Williamson, *Asst Mgr*
Bobbie Fussichen, *Info Tech Dir*
EMP: 190
SALES: 13.6MM Privately Held
SIC: 8322 8093 Individual & family services; specialty outpatient clinics

(G-19928)
TEAM GREEN LAWN LLC
1070 Union Rd (45385-7216)
PHONE..............................937 673-4315
Josh Anderson, *Mng Member*
EMP: 40 EST: 2009
SALES: 3.5MM Privately Held
SIC: 0782 Lawn care services

(G-19929)
TOWARD INDEPENDENCE INC (PA)
81 E Main St (45385-3201)
PHONE..............................937 376-3996
Robert L Archer, *Exec Dir*
EMP: 250 EST: 1975
SQ FT: 2,000
SALES: 13.9MM Privately Held
WEB: www.ti-inc.org
SIC: 8361 Home for the mentally retarded; home for the mentally handicapped

(G-19930)
TRIAD GOVERNMENTAL SYSTEMS
358 S Monroe St (45385-3442)
PHONE..............................937 376-5446
Tod A Rapp, *President*
EMP: 27
SALES (est): 2.6MM Privately Held
WEB: www.triadgsi.com
SIC: 7371 7372 Computer software development; prepackaged software

(G-19931)
TWIST INC
Also Called: ACC-U-Coil
1380 Lavelle Dr (45385-5676)
P.O. Box 356 (45385-0356)
PHONE..............................937 675-9581
Jill Eright, *President*
Tammy Dinnen, *Executive*
EMP: 35
SALES (corp-wide): 34.2MM Privately Held
SIC: 4225 General warehousing & storage
PA: Twist Inc.
47 S Limestone St
Jamestown OH 45335
937 675-9581

(G-19932)
US ONCOLOGY INC
Also Called: Ruth McMillan Cancer Center
1141 N Monroe Dr (45385-1619)
PHONE..............................937 352-2140
Mark Collins, *Manager*
EMP: 36
SALES (corp-wide): 208.3B Publicly Held
WEB: www.mohpa.com
SIC: 8011 Oncologist
HQ: Us Oncology, Inc.
10101 Woodloch Forest Dr
The Woodlands TX 77380

(G-19933)
WICKLINE LANDSCAPING INC (PA)
Also Called: Wickline Floral & Garden Ctr
1625 N Detroit St (45385-1200)
PHONE..............................937 372-0521
James Wickline, *President*
Helen B Wickline, *Vice Pres*
Mark Wickline, *Vice Pres*
Doug Wickline, *Admin Sec*
EMP: 32
SQ FT: 3,936
SALES (est): 1.8MM Privately Held
SIC: 5992 0782 5261 Ret Florist Lawn/Garden Services Ret Nursery/Garden Supplies

(G-19934)
WOMENS RECOVERY CENTER
515 Martin Dr (45385-1615)
PHONE..............................937 562-2400
Michelle Cox, *Director*
EMP: 40
SALES (est): 2.2MM Privately Held
SIC: 8361 Halfway home for delinquents & offenders

(G-19935)
XENIA AREA CMNTY THEATER INC
Also Called: Xact
45 E 2nd St (45385-3415)
PHONE..............................937 372-0516
Alan King, *President*
Allan King, *President*
EMP: 99 EST: 2010
SALES: 58.9K Privately Held
SIC: 7922 Legitimate live theater producers

(G-19936)
XENIA EAST MANAGEMENT SYSTEMS
Also Called: Hospitality Home East
1301 N Monroe Dr (45385-1623)
PHONE..............................937 372-4495
Grace Mc Cormick, *Social Dir*
John Flanagan, *Administration*
EMP: 95

SALES: 7.5MM **Privately Held**
SIC: 8051 Convalescent home with continuous nursing care

(G-19937)
XENIA WEST MANAGEMENT SYSTEMS
Also Called: Hospitality Home West
1384 N Monroe Dr (45385-1653)
PHONE...............................937 372-8081
Anthony Deaton, *Administration*
EMP: 100
SALES (est): 1.9MM **Privately Held**
SIC: 8051 Skilled nursing care facilities

Yellow Springs
Greene County

(G-19938)
ANTIOCH UNIVERSITY
1 Morgan Pl (45387-1683)
PHONE...............................937 769-1366
Joan Straumanis, *Principal*
EMP: 100
SALES (corp-wide): 65.7MM **Privately Held**
WEB: www.antiochla.edu
SIC: 8731 8221 Commercial physical research; colleges universities & professional schools
PA: Antioch University
　　900 Dayton St
　　Yellow Springs OH 45387
　　937 769-1370

(G-19939)
FRIENDS HEALTH CARE ASSN (PA)
Also Called: FRIENDS CARE CENTER
150 E Herman St (45387-1601)
PHONE...............................937 767-7363
Cindy Willis, *Chf Purch Ofc*
Karl Zalar, *Director*
Olivia Chandler, *Director*
Patrick Horn, *Executive*
EMP: 140
SQ FT: 25,000
SALES: 7.4MM **Privately Held**
WEB: www.friendshealthcare.org
SIC: 8051 Skilled nursing care facilities

(G-19940)
LAYH & ASSOCIATES
416 Xenia Ave (45387-1836)
PHONE...............................937 767-9171
John Layh, *Owner*
EMP: 30
SQ FT: 1,967
SALES (est): 833.9K **Privately Held**
SIC: 8049 8011 Psychologist, psychotherapist & hypnotist; offices & clinics of medical doctors

(G-19941)
YOUNGS JERSEY DAIRY INC
Also Called: Golden Jersey Inn
6880 Springfield Xenia Rd (45387-9610)
PHONE...............................937 325-0629
C Daniel Young, *President*
C Robert Young, *President*
Brian Patterson, *General Mgr*
William H Young, *Vice Pres*
Debra Whittaker, *Treasurer*
EMP: 300
SQ FT: 35,000
SALES (est): 12.1MM **Privately Held**
SIC: 5812 5451 5947 7999 Ice cream stands or dairy bars; family restaurants; dairy products stores; gift shop; golf driving range; miniature golf course operation; dairy farms; ice cream & frozen desserts

Yorkshire
Darke County

(G-19942)
ROBERT WINNER SONS INC (PA)
Also Called: Winner's Meat Service
8544 State Route 705 (45388-9784)
P.O. Box 39, Osgood (45351-0039)
PHONE...............................419 582-4321
Brian K Winner, *President*
Alan Winner, *Senior VP*
Ted Winner, *Vice Pres*
Terrance Winner, *Vice Pres*
Steven Winner, *Treasurer*
EMP: 40 **EST:** 1928
SQ FT: 6,500
SALES: 33.9MM **Privately Held**
SIC: 0213 0751 5154 5147 Hog feedlot; slaughtering: custom livestock services; hogs; meats & meat products; sausages & other prepared meats; meat packing plants

Youngstown
Mahoning County

(G-19943)
A A S AMELS SHEET META L INC
222 Steel St (44509-2547)
P.O. Box 2407 (44509-0407)
PHONE...............................330 793-9326
Andrew A Samuels Jr, *President*
George Timar, *Admin Sec*
EMP: 40
SQ FT: 12,000
SALES (est): 6.7MM **Privately Held**
SIC: 1711 3585 3564 3444 Ventilation & duct work contractor; warm air heating & air conditioning contractor; refrigeration & heating equipment; blowers & fans; sheet metalwork; fabricated plate work (boiler shop)

(G-19944)
A P OHORO COMPANY
3130 Belmont Ave (44505-1802)
P.O. Box 2228 (44504-0228)
PHONE...............................330 759-9317
Daniel P O Horo, *President*
Daniel J O Horo, *Chairman*
Fred Leunis, *Corp Secy*
Thomas P Metzinger, *Vice Pres*
Duane C Thompson, *Vice Pres*
EMP: 90 **EST:** 1948
SQ FT: 6,000
SALES: 52MM **Privately Held**
WEB: www.apohoro.com
SIC: 1629 1622 1623 1611 Waste water & sewage treatment plant construction; bridge construction; sewer line construction; highway & street construction

(G-19945)
ABM PARKING SERVICES INC
20 W Federal St Ste M9 (44503-1430)
PHONE...............................330 747-7678
Dan Strong, *Principal*
EMP: 26
SALES (corp-wide): 6.4B **Publicly Held**
SIC: 7521 Parking garage
HQ: Abm Parking Services, Inc.
　　1150 S Olive St Fl 19
　　Los Angeles CA 90015
　　213 284-7600

(G-19946)
ADO HEALTH SERVICES INC
Also Called: Anesthesiologists, D.O., Inc.
1011 Boardman Canfield Rd (44512-4226)
PHONE...............................330 629-2888
Tracy Neuendorf, *President*
EMP: 70
SQ FT: 14,000
SALES (est): 1.4MM **Privately Held**
SIC: 8062 General medical & surgical hospitals

(G-19947)
ADVANCED DERMATOLOGY AND SKIN
987 Boardman Canfield Rd (44512-4222)
PHONE...............................330 965-8760
Tonia Alsano, *Mng Member*
EMP: 25
SALES (est): 2.6MM **Privately Held**
SIC: 8011 Dermatologist

(G-19948)
ADVANCED UROLOGY INC (PA)
904 Sahara Trl Ste 1 (44514-3695)
PHONE...............................330 758-9787
Richard D Nord MD, *President*
EMP: 27
SQ FT: 10,000
SALES (est): 3.2MM **Privately Held**
SIC: 8011 Urologist; surgeon

(G-19949)
AEY ELECTRIC INC
801 N Meridian Rd (44509-1008)
PHONE...............................330 792-5745
Robert Aey, *President*
Richard J Aey, *Admin Sec*
EMP: 25 **EST:** 1964
SQ FT: 10,000
SALES (est): 4MM **Privately Held**
WEB: www.aeyelectric.com
SIC: 1731 General electrical contractor

(G-19950)
ALLIANCE HOSPITALITY
Also Called: Fairfield Inn
801 N Canfield Niles Rd (44515-1106)
PHONE...............................330 505-2173
Naresh Patel, *President*
EMP: 30
SALES (est): 1.2MM **Privately Held**
WEB: www.alliancehospitalityinc.com
SIC: 7011 Hotels & motels

(G-19951)
ALLIED ERCT & DISMANTLING CO
2100 Poland Ave (44502-2775)
PHONE...............................330 744-0808
John R Ramun, *President*
Louise Ramun, *Admin Sec*
▲ **EMP:** 200
SQ FT: 24,000
SALES (est): 27.8MM
SALES (corp-wide): 29MM **Privately Held**
SIC: 1796 1795 Installing building equipment; wrecking & demolition work
PA: Allied Consolidated Industries Inc
　　2100 Poland Ave
　　Youngstown OH 44502
　　330 744-0808

(G-19952)
ALTA CARE GROUP INC
711 Belmont Ave (44502-1039)
PHONE...............................330 793-2487
Meg Harris, *Opers Spvr*
Joseph Shorokey, *Exec Dir*
Vicci Polish, *Director*
William F D, *Medical Dir*
EMP: 50
SQ FT: 7,428
SALES: 9.4MM **Privately Held**
WEB: www.dandecenter.com
SIC: 8093 Mental health clinic, outpatient

(G-19953)
AMERICAN BULK COMMODITIES INC (PA)
Also Called: R & J Trucking
8063 Southern Blvd (44512-6306)
P.O. Box 9454 (44513-0454)
PHONE...............................330 758-0841
Ronald Carrocce, *President*
Mark Carrocce, *Vice Pres*
Troy Carrocce, *Treasurer*
Gary Carrocce, *Admin Sec*
EMP: 200
SQ FT: 50,000
SALES (est): 55.1MM **Privately Held**
SIC: 7532 6531 7363 4212 Paint shop, automotive; body shop, automotive; body shop, trucks; real estate managers; truck driver services; dump truck haulage

(G-19954)
AMERICAN MAINTENANCE SVCS INC
20 W Federal St Fl 2b (44503-1432)
PHONE...............................330 744-3400
Rodney Turner, *CEO*
EMP: 30
SALES (est): 890K **Privately Held**
SIC: 7349 Janitorial service, contract basis

(G-19955)
AMERISTATE BANCORP INC (PA)
725 Boardman Canfield Rd (44512-4380)
PHONE...............................330 965-9551
Kevin B Powell, *President*
Daniel G Dorko, *Vice Pres*
EMP: 37
SQ FT: 2,000
SALES (est): 4.1MM **Privately Held**
SIC: 6162 Mortgage bankers & correspondents

(G-19956)
ASHLEY PLACE HEALTH CARE INC
5291 Ashley Cir (44515-1160)
PHONE...............................330 793-3010
Patricia Andrews, *President*
Maryann Barnett, *Vice Pres*
EMP: 160
SALES (est): 8.8MM **Privately Held**
SIC: 8051 Skilled nursing care facilities

(G-19957)
AT&T MOBILITY LLC
Also Called: Dobson Cellular Call Center
8089 South Ave (44512-6154)
PHONE...............................330 565-5000
Lynn Gherrardi, *Manager*
EMP: 200
SALES (corp-wide): 170.7B **Publicly Held**
WEB: www.dobsoncellular.com
SIC: 4812 Cellular telephone services
HQ: At&T Mobility Llc
　　1025 Lenox Park Blvd Ne
　　Brookhaven GA 30319
　　800 331-0500

(G-19958)
AUSTIN WOODS NURSING CENTER
Also Called: Austin Wods Rehabilitation Ctr
4780 Kirk Rd (44515-5403)
PHONE...............................330 792-7681
Karapini Prasad MD, *President*
Kathy Prasad, *Exec Dir*
Andy Douglas, *Director*
EMP: 250
SQ FT: 90,000
SALES (est): 14.1MM **Privately Held**
WEB: www.austinwoods.com
SIC: 8051 Convalescent home with continuous nursing care

(G-19959)
AUSTINTOWN DAIRY INC
780 Bev Rd (44512-6424)
P.O. Box 9484 (44513-0484)
PHONE...............................330 629-6170
Joseph Creighton, *President*
Thomas Creighton, *Vice Pres*
EMP: 40 **EST:** 1963
SALES (est): 15.4MM **Privately Held**
WEB: www.austintowndairy.com
SIC: 5143 5451 Milk; ice cream & ices; ice cream (packaged)

(G-19960)
B & B CONTRS & DEVELOPERS INC
2781 Salt Springs Rd (44509-1035)
PHONE...............................330 270-5020
Philip M Beshara, *President*
Donald D'Andrea, *President*
Darren Cesario, *Superintendent*
Dominic Cappibianca, *Vice Pres*
Joseph Tahos, *Vice Pres*
EMP: 80
SQ FT: 12,000

SALES: 24.4MM **Privately Held**
SIC: 1542 1541 Commercial & office building, new construction; shopping center construction; hospital construction; institutional building construction; industrial buildings, new construction

(G-19961)
BALOG STEINES HENDRICKS & MANC
15 Central Sq Ste 300 (44503-1517)
PHONE.................................330 744-4401
Gary G Balog, *President*
Byron Manchester, *Vice Pres*
Randall Reger, *Associate*
Michael Vala, *Associate*
Stephen Zerefos, *Associate*
EMP: 27 **EST:** 1960
SQ FT: 2,500
SALES (est): 3.1MM **Privately Held**
SIC: 8712 Architectural engineering

(G-19962)
BEECHER CARLSON INSUR SVCS LLC
7600 Market St (44512-6078)
PHONE.................................330 726-8177
EMP: 75
SALES (corp-wide): 2B **Publicly Held**
SIC: 6411 Insurance agents
HQ: Beecher Carlson Insurance Services, Llc
6 Concourse Pkwy Ste 2300
Atlanta GA 30328
404 460-1426

(G-19963)
BEL-PARK ANESTHESIA
1044 Belmont Ave (44504-1006)
PHONE.................................330 480-3658
Steve Scharf, *Principal*
Tom Deascentis, *Manager*
Linda Berry, *Anesthesiology*
Luz Gotham, *Anesthesiology*
Carla Pallotta, *Anesthesiology*
EMP: 29
SALES (est): 4.4MM **Privately Held**
SIC: 8011 Anesthesiologist

(G-19964)
BELMONT BHC PINES HOSPITAL INC
615 Churchill Hubbard Rd (44505-1332)
PHONE.................................330 759-2700
George Perry, *President*
EMP: 175
SQ FT: 32,000
SALES (est): 11.7MM **Privately Held**
WEB: www.belmontpines.com
SIC: 8063 8011 8093 8062 Psychiatric hospitals; offices & clinics of medical doctors; mental health clinic, outpatient; general medical & surgical hospitals

(G-19965)
BLAKEMANS VALLEY OFF EQP INC
8534 South Ave (44514-3620)
PHONE.................................330 729-1000
Steve A Blakeman, *President*
Kathy L Blakeman, *Vice Pres*
Steven Blakeman, *Info Tech Dir*
EMP: 37
SQ FT: 8,000
SALES (est): 5.1MM **Privately Held**
SIC: 5999 7629 5044 Business machines & equipment; facsimile equipment; business machine repair, electric; copying equipment; calcvlators, electronic; typewriters

(G-19966)
BLUE CROSS & BLUE SHIELD MICH
2405 Market St (44507-1432)
PHONE.................................330 783-3841
EMP: 620
SALES (corp-wide): 10.1B **Privately Held**
SIC: 6321 Health insurance carriers
PA: Blue Cross And Blue Shield Of Michigan Foundation
600 E Lafayette Blvd
Detroit MI 48226
313 225-9000

(G-19967)
BOAK & SONS INC
75 Victoria Rd (44515-2023)
PHONE.................................330 793-5646
Samuel G Boak, *President*
EMP: 200 **EST:** 1974
SQ FT: 38,000
SALES: 18.9MM **Privately Held**
WEB: www.boakandsons.com
SIC: 1761 1742 1542 1541 Roofing contractor; sheet metalwork; insulation, buildings; nonresidential construction; industrial buildings & warehouses

(G-19968)
BOARD MAN FRST UNTD METHDST CH
Also Called: Boardman Methodist Daycare
6809 Market St (44512-4504)
PHONE.................................330 758-4527
Peg Welch, *Pastor*
Rev Peg Ash Welch, *Pastor*
EMP: 27
SALES (est): 392.5K **Privately Held**
SIC: 8661 8351 Methodist Church; child day care services

(G-19969)
BOARDMAN LOCAL SCHOOLS
Also Called: Boardman School Bus Garage
7410 Market St (44512-5612)
PHONE.................................330 726-3409
Ryan Dunn, *Supervisor*
EMP: 53
SALES (est): 1.1MM
SALES (corp-wide): 34.1MM **Privately Held**
SIC: 4151 8211 School buses; public elementary & secondary schools
PA: Boardman Local Schools
7410 Market St
Youngstown OH 44512
330 726-3400

(G-19970)
BOLT CONSTRUCTION INC
Also Called: BOLT CONSTRUCTION CO
10422 South Ave (44514-3459)
P.O. Box 5470 (44514-0470)
PHONE.................................330 549-0349
Bruno Miletta, *President*
John T Miller Jr, *Vice Pres*
Shirley Miletta, *Treasurer*
Deanna Maker, *Office Mgr*
Melinda Miletta-Mill, *Admin Sec*
EMP: 90 **EST:** 1981
SQ FT: 15,000
SALES: 21.2MM **Privately Held**
SIC: 1623 Pipeline construction; oil & gas pipeline construction

(G-19971)
BOSTON RETAIL PRODUCTS INC
Boston Group
225 Hubbard Rd (44505-3120)
PHONE.................................330 744-8100
James Bellstrom, *Office Mgr*
Sandford Kessler, *Manager*
EMP: 60
SALES (est): 4.7MM
SALES (corp-wide): 21.7MM **Privately Held**
WEB: www.bostonretail.com
SIC: 5051 Metals service centers & offices
PA: Boston Retail Products, Inc.
400 Riverside Ave
Medford MA 02155
781 395-7417

(G-19972)
BRIAN BROCKER DR
1616 Covington St (44510-1244)
PHONE.................................330 747-9215
Dr Brian Brocker, *Owner*
Linda J Eisenbraun, *Manager*
EMP: 30
SALES (est): 1MM **Privately Held**
SIC: 8011 Physicians' office, including specialists

(G-19973)
BRIARFIELD MANOR LLC
461 S Canfield Niles Rd (44515-4089)
PHONE.................................330 270-3468

Joe Vince,
EMP: 150 **EST:** 2000
SQ FT: 1,330
SALES (est): 588.1K **Privately Held**
WEB: www.briarfield.net
SIC: 8051 Skilled nursing care facilities

(G-19974)
BRINKS INCORPORATED
6971 Southern Blvd Ste F (44512-4652)
PHONE.................................330 758-7379
Cathy Pannunzio, *Manager*
EMP: 35
SALES (corp-wide): 3.4B **Publicly Held**
SIC: 7381 Armored car services
HQ: Brink's, Incorporated
1801 Bayberry Ct Ste 400
Richmond VA 23226
804 289-9600

(G-19975)
BROCK & ASSOCIATES BUILDERS
118 Heron Bay Dr (44514-4234)
PHONE.................................330 757-7150
Paul Brock, *President*
Jane Brock, *Corp Secy*
Brian Brock, *Vice Pres*
EMP: 30
SALES: 1.5MM **Privately Held**
SIC: 1521 1751 Single-family housing construction; carpentry work

(G-19976)
BROOKDALE SNIOR LVING CMMNTIES
Also Called: Sterling House of Youngstown
2300 Canfield Rd Ofc (44511-2981)
PHONE.................................330 793-0085
Doug Love, *Director*
EMP: 25
SALES (corp-wide): 4.5B **Publicly Held**
WEB: www.assisted.com
SIC: 8059 Rest home, with health care
HQ: Brookdale Senior Living Communities, Inc.
6737 W Wa St Ste 2300
Milwaukee WI 53214
414 918-5000

(G-19977)
BROWNING-FERRIS INDS OF OHIO (DH)
Also Called: Allied Wste Svcs Yngstown Coml
3870 Hendricks Rd (44515-1528)
PHONE.................................330 793-7676
James E Oconnor, *CEO*
Thomas Van Weelden, *President*
EMP: 54
SQ FT: 5,300
SALES (est): 57.4MM
SALES (corp-wide): 10B **Publicly Held**
SIC: 4953 Garbage: collecting, destroying & processing; sanitary landfill operation

(G-19978)
BUCKEYE LEASING INC
8063 Southern Blvd (44512-6306)
PHONE.................................330 758-0841
Ronald Carrocce, *President*
Gary Carrocce, *Corp Secy*
Mark Carrocce, *Vice Pres*
EMP: 50
SQ FT: 50,000
SALES (est): 1.3MM **Privately Held**
SIC: 7363 Truck driver services
PA: American Bulk Commodities Inc
8063 Southern Blvd
Youngstown OH 44512

(G-19979)
BUTLER INSTITUTE AMERICAN ART (PA)
524 Wick Ave (44502-1213)
PHONE.................................330 743-1711
Louis A Zona, *Exec Dir*
EMP: 30
SQ FT: 80,000
SALES: 3.2MM **Privately Held**
WEB: www.butlerart.com
SIC: 8412 Museum

(G-19980)
CALLOS RESOURCE LLC (PA)
Also Called: Callos Prof Employment II
755 Boardman Canfield Rd N2 (44512-4300)
PHONE.................................330 788-3033
Thomas Walsh, *President*
John Callos, *Chairman*
Eric Sutton, *Senior VP*
Mary Beth Dipaolo, *Vice Pres*
Laura Sherman, *Branch Mgr*
EMP: 30
SQ FT: 8,200
SALES (est): 24.2MM **Privately Held**
SIC: 7363 Temporary help service

(G-19981)
CARDIOVASCULAR ASSOCIATES INC
Also Called: Ohio Heart Instit
1001 Belmont Ave (44504-1003)
PHONE.................................330 747-6446
Sadiq Husain MD, *President*
Shawki Habib MD, *Vice Pres*
Ates Labib MD, *Vice Pres*
Paul Wright, *Admin Sec*
EMP: 27 **EST:** 1973
SQ FT: 23,000
SALES (est): 1.3MM **Privately Held**
SIC: 8011 Cardiologist & cardio-vascular specialist

(G-19982)
CATHOLIC CHRTIES REGIONAL AGCY
319 W Rayen Ave (44502-1119)
PHONE.................................330 744-3320
John Edwards, *Principal*
Nancy Voitus, *Exec Dir*
EMP: 52
SALES (est): 2.1MM **Privately Held**
SIC: 8322 Individual & family services

(G-19983)
CELTIC HEALTHCARE NE OHIO INC
299 Edwards St (44502-1504)
PHONE.................................724 742-4360
Arnold E Burchianti, *Principal*
EMP: 30
SALES (est): 356.4K
SALES (corp-wide): 2.7B **Publicly Held**
SIC: 8099 Health & allied services
HQ: Celtic Healthcare, Inc.
150 Scharberry Ln
Mars PA 16046
724 742-4360

(G-19984)
CERNI MOTOR SALES INC (PA)
5751 Cerni Pl (44515-1174)
P.O. Box 4176 (44515-0176)
PHONE.................................330 652-9917
John P Cerni, *President*
Jeanne Cerni Et Al, *Principal*
Charles Cerni, *Principal*
William Thompson, *Parts Mgr*
Joe Notarianni, *CFO*
EMP: 72 **EST:** 1961
SQ FT: 37,000
SALES (est): 22.9MM **Privately Held**
WEB: www.cernimotors.com
SIC: 5012 Trucks, commercial

(G-19985)
CHANDER M KOHLI MD FACS INC
540 Parmalee Ave Ste 310 (44510-1605)
PHONE.................................330 759-6978
Chander M Kohli MD, *President*
Karen Kohli, *Corp Secy*
EMP: 25
SALES (est): 1.8MM **Privately Held**
SIC: 8011 Neurosurgeon

(G-19986)
CHEMICAL BANK
476 Boardman Canfield Rd (44512-4790)
PHONE.................................330 965-5806
Trisha Minnie, *Branch Mgr*
EMP: 100
SALES (corp-wide): 924.5MM **Publicly Held**
SIC: 6099 Check clearing services

HQ: Chemical Bank
333 E Main St
Midland MI 48640
989 631-9200

(G-19987)
CHEMICAL BANK
3900 Market St (44512-1111)
PHONE..................................330 314-1380
Steven R Lewis, *Branch Mgr*
EMP: 80
SALES (corp-wide): 924.5MM **Publicly Held**
WEB: www.dlkbank.com
SIC: 6022 State commercial banks
HQ: Chemical Bank
333 E Main St
Midland MI 48640
989 631-9200

(G-19988)
CHILDRENS HOSP MED CTR AKRON
8423 Market St Ste 300 (44512-6778)
PHONE..................................330 629-6085
Patrick J Doherty, *Branch Mgr*
EMP: 40
SALES (corp-wide): 747.4MM **Privately Held**
SIC: 8069 Children's hospital
PA: Childrens Hospital Medical Center Of Akron
1 Perkins Sq
Akron OH 44308
330 543-1000

(G-19989)
CINEMARK USA INC
Also Called: Cinemark Tinseltown 7
7401 Market St Rear (44512-5624)
PHONE..................................330 965-2335
Greg Wigley, *Manager*
EMP: 25 **Publicly Held**
SIC: 7832 Motion picture theaters, except drive-in
HQ: Cinemark Usa, Inc.
3900 Dallas Pkwy Ste 500
Plano TX 75093
972 665-1000

(G-19990)
CITY MACHINE TECHNOLOGIES INC
Electric Machinery Division
825 Martin Luther King Jr (44502-1105)
P.O. Box 1466 (44501-1466)
PHONE..................................330 740-8186
Michael J Kovach, *President*
Natalie Jenyk, *Office Mgr*
EMP: 40
SALES (corp-wide): 13.7MM **Privately Held**
WEB: www.cmtcompanies.com
SIC: 3599 7694 3621 3568 Machine shop, jobbing & repair; armature rewinding shops; motors & generators; power transmission equipment
PA: City Machine Technologies, Inc.
773 W Rayen Ave
Youngstown OH 44502
330 747-2639

(G-19991)
CITY OF YOUNGSTOWN (PA)
26 S Phelps St Bsmt (44503-1318)
PHONE..................................330 742-8700
Jamael Tito Brown, *Mayor*
EMP: 300
SQ FT: 45,000
SALES: 75.2MM **Privately Held**
WEB: www.cityofyoungstown.com
SIC: 8741 Administrative management

(G-19992)
CITY OF YOUNGSTOWN
Also Called: Youngstown Water Dept
26 S Phelps St Fl 3a (44503-1318)
P.O. Box 6219 (44501-6219)
PHONE..................................330 742-8749
John Casciano, *Manager*
EMP: 30
SALES (corp-wide): 75.2MM **Privately Held**
WEB: www.cityofyoungstown.com
SIC: 4941 9111 Water supply; mayors' offices

(G-19993)
COCCA DEVELOPMENT LTD
100 Debartolo Pl Ste 400 (44512-6099)
PHONE..................................330 729-1010
Anthony L Cocca, *CEO*
Marc Barca, *Vice Pres*
Jim Shipley, *Vice Pres*
Lynn E Davenport, *CFO*
Lynn Davenport, *CFO*
EMP: 70
SQ FT: 20,000
SALES (est): 20.1MM **Privately Held**
SIC: 1542 Nonresidential construction

(G-19994)
COHEN & COMPANY LTD
Also Called: COHEN & COMPANY,LTD
201 E Commerce St Ste 400 (44503-1690)
PHONE..................................330 743-1040
Nicole Rococi, *Accountant*
Frank J Dixon, *Manager*
EMP: 35
SALES (corp-wide): 36MM **Privately Held**
WEB: www.cohencpa.com
SIC: 8721 Certified public accountant
PA: Cohen & Company, Ltd.
1350 Euclid Ave Ste 800
Cleveland OH 44115
216 579-1040

(G-19995)
COMMERCE TITLE AGCY YOUNGSTOWN
201 E Commerce St (44503-1659)
PHONE..................................330 743-1171
Martha Bushey, *President*
Jeffrey Heintz, *Manager*
EMP: 30
SALES (est): 960.3K **Privately Held**
SIC: 6541 Title & trust companies

(G-19996)
COMMUNICARE HEALTH SVCS INC
Also Called: Greenbriar Healthcare Center
8064 South Ave (44512-6153)
PHONE..................................330 726-3700
EMP: 99
SALES (corp-wide): 125.8MM **Privately Held**
SIC: 8051 Skilled nursing care facilities
PA: Communicare Health Services, Inc.
4700 Ashwood Dr Ste 200
Blue Ash OH 45241
513 530-1654

(G-19997)
COMMUNICARE HEALTH SVCS INC
Also Called: Austintown Healthcare Center
650 S Meridian Rd (44509-2932)
PHONE..................................330 792-7799
Toni Fuzo, *Administration*
EMP: 80
SALES (corp-wide): 125.8MM **Privately Held**
WEB: www.atriumlivingcenters.com
SIC: 6531 8051 Real estate agents & managers; skilled nursing care facilities
PA: Communicare Health Services, Inc.
4700 Ashwood Dr Ste 200
Blue Ash OH 45241
513 530-1654

(G-19998)
COMMUNICARE HEALTH SVCS INC
Also Called: Canfield Healthcare Center
2958 Canfield Rd (44511-2805)
PHONE..................................330 792-5511
Rick Cook, *Manager*
EMP: 80
SALES (corp-wide): 125.8MM **Privately Held**
WEB: www.atriumlivingcenters.com
SIC: 6531 8051 Real estate agents & managers; skilled nursing care facilities

PA: City Of Youngstown
26 S Phelps St Bsmt
Youngstown OH 44503
330 742-8700

(G-19999)
COMMUNITY CAREGIVERS
888 Boardman Canfield Rd D (44512-4276)
PHONE..................................330 533-3427
Barbara E Scott, *Branch Mgr*
EMP: 71
SALES (corp-wide): 2.2MM **Privately Held**
SIC: 8322 Senior citizens' center or association
PA: Community Caregivers
66 S Miller Rd Ste 200
Fairlawn OH 44333
330 836-8585

(G-20000)
COMMUNITY CENTER
Also Called: Help Hotline Crisis Center
1344 5th Ave (44504-1703)
PHONE..................................330 746-7721
Vince Brancaccio, *CEO*
Paul Guggenheim, *Manager*
EMP: 52 EST: 2010
SALES (est): 368.4K **Privately Held**
SIC: 8322 Crisis center

(G-20001)
COMMUNITY CORRECTIONS ASSN (PA)
Also Called: Community Crrctions Facilities
1608 Market St (44507-1130)
PHONE..................................330 744-5143
George Stephens, *Sales Executive*
Richard J Billak, *Director*
EMP: 100
SALES: 6.9MM **Privately Held**
SIC: 8361 Rehabilitation center, residential: health care incidental

(G-20002)
COMPASS FAMILY AND CMMNTY SVCS (PA)
Also Called: FAMILY SERVICE AGENCY
535 Marmion Ave (44502-2323)
PHONE..................................330 743-9275
Joseph F Caruso, *CEO*
David Arnold, *COO*
Mark Wingert, *CFO*
EMP: 34
SQ FT: 9,600
SALES: 9.4MM **Privately Held**
WEB: www.familyserviceagency.com
SIC: 8322 Family (marriage) counseling; child guidance agency; emergency shelters

(G-20003)
COMPASS FAMILY AND CMMNTY SVCS
284 Broadway Ave (44504-1752)
PHONE..................................330 743-9275
Mark Wingert, *CFO*
Kathe Klem, *Human Resources*
Joseph F Caruso, *Branch Mgr*
EMP: 96
SALES (corp-wide): 9.4MM **Privately Held**
SIC: 8322 Family (marriage) counseling
PA: Compass Family And Community Services
535 Marmion Ave
Youngstown OH 44502
330 743-9275

(G-20004)
COMPCO LAND COMPANY (DH)
85 E Hylda Ave (44507-1762)
PHONE..................................330 482-0200
Gregory B Smith Sr, *President*
Clarence R Smith Jr, *Chairman*
Douglas A Hagy, *CFO*
EMP: 60
SQ FT: 42,000
SALES (est): 6.3MM
SALES (corp-wide): 22.9MM **Privately Held**
SIC: 6512 Commercial & industrial building operation

PA: Communicare Health Services, Inc.
4700 Ashwood Dr Ste 200
Blue Ash OH 45241
513 530-1654

HQ: Compco Industries, Inc.
400 W Railroad St Ste 1
Columbiana OH 44408
330 482-6488

(G-20005)
COMPENSATION PROGRAMS OF OHIO
33 Fitch Blvd (44515-2202)
PHONE..................................330 652-9821
Tim Myers, *Owner*
EMP: 25 EST: 2001
SALES: 1.3MM **Privately Held**
SIC: 8721 Billing & bookkeeping service

(G-20006)
COMPREHENSIVE BEHAVIORAL HLTH (PA)
104 Javit Ct Ste A (44515-2439)
P.O. Box 4174 (44515-0174)
PHONE..................................330 797-4050
Kotes Wara Kaza, *Director*
Bob Roth, *Administration*
EMP: 29
SQ FT: 3,000
SALES (est): 3.4MM **Privately Held**
SIC: 8093 Mental health clinic, outpatient

(G-20007)
COMPREHENSIVE LOGISTICS CO INC
365 Victoria Rd (44515-2027)
PHONE..................................330 793-0504
Doug Caswell, *Branch Mgr*
EMP: 50 **Privately Held**
SIC: 8742 4226 3714 3711 Mgmt Consulting Svcs Special Warehse/Storage Mfg Motor Vehicle Parts Mfg Motor Vehicle Bodies
PA: Comprehensive Logistics, Co., Inc.
4944 Belmont Ave Ste 202
Youngstown OH 44505

(G-20008)
COMPREHENSIVE LOGISTICS CO INC (PA)
4944 Belmont Ave Ste 202 (44505-1055)
PHONE..................................800 734-0372
Brad Constantini, *Exec VP*
Fred Callihan, *Opers Mgr*
Tony Sammarco, *Engineer*
Greg Grimm, *Accountant*
Chris Bilski, *Finance*
EMP: 28
SQ FT: 1,200
SALES: 173.4MM **Privately Held**
WEB: www.complog.com
SIC: 4225 4731 General warehousing; customs clearance of freight

(G-20009)
CONCORD HEALTH CARE INC (PA)
202 Churchill Hubbard Rd (44505-1325)
PHONE..................................330 759-2357
Debra Ifft, *President*
EMP: 50
SALES (est): 5.2MM **Privately Held**
SIC: 8051 8052 Skilled nursing care facilities; intermediate care facilities

(G-20010)
CONSTELLATIONS ENTERPRISE LLC (PA)
1775 Logan Ave (44505-2622)
PHONE..................................330 740-8208
Steve Witter,
Jan Doughty,
EMP: 199
SALES (est): 125.8MM **Privately Held**
SIC: 8741 Management services

(G-20011)
CORECIVIC INC
Also Called: Northeast Ohio Corrections
2240 Hubbard Rd (44505-3157)
P.O. Box 1857 (44501-1857)
PHONE..................................330 746-3777
D Bryan Gardner, *Principal*
Latosia Austin, *Manager*
Christopher Chestnut, *Officer*
Derek Rosado, *Officer*
EMP: 450

▲ = Import ▼=Export
◆ =Import/Export

SALES (corp-wide): 1.8B **Publicly Held**
WEB: www.correctionscorp.com
SIC: 8744 Correctional facility
PA: Corecivic, Inc.
　　10 Burton Hills Blvd
　　Nashville TN 37215
　　615 263-3000

(G-20012)
CUMULUS BROADCASTING LLC
Also Called: Wyfm FM
4040 Simon Rd (44512-1362)
PHONE...................................330 783-1000
Clyde Bass, *Manager*
EMP: 80
SALES (corp-wide): 1.1B **Publicly Held**
WEB: www.rockofsavannah.com
SIC: 4832 Radio broadcasting stations, music format
HQ: Cumulus Broadcasting, Llc
　　3280 Peachtree Rd Nw Ste
　　Atlanta GA 30305
　　404 949-0700

(G-20013)
CUSTOM MAINT
73 Country Green Dr (44515-2214)
PHONE...................................330 793-2523
Dennis Gagne, *Owner*
EMP: 52
SALES (est): 564.4K **Privately Held**
SIC: 7349 Building maintenance services

(G-20014)
DANIEL A TERRERI & SONS INC
1091 N Meridian Rd (44509-1016)
PHONE...................................330 538-2950
Daniel Terreri, *President*
Thomas Corroto, *Principal*
Karen Augustine, *Controller*
EMP: 40
SQ FT: 5,000
SALES (est): 2MM **Privately Held**
SIC: 1791 1795 1799 Storage tanks, metal: erection; demolition, buildings & other structures; asbestos removal & encapsulation

(G-20015)
DANRIDGE NURSING HOME INC
31 Maranatha Ct (44505-4970)
PHONE...................................330 746-5157
Julius Blunt, *President*
Leigh Greene, *Vice Pres*
Joanne Blunt, *Administration*
EMP: 80
SQ FT: 29,000
SALES (est): 2.5MM **Privately Held**
SIC: 8051 Convalescent home with continuous nursing care

(G-20016)
DEMPSEY INC
Also Called: ServiceMaster
2803 South Ave (44502-2409)
PHONE...................................330 758-2309
Donald F Dempsey Jr, *CEO*
Tony Dimpsey, *Owner*
EMP: 100
SALES (est): 2.4MM **Privately Held**
SIC: 7349 Building maintenance services

(G-20017)
DEYOR PERFORMING ARTS CENTER
260 W Federal St (44503-1206)
PHONE...................................330 744-4269
Patricia Syak, *President*
EMP: 35
SALES (est): 442.2K **Privately Held**
SIC: 7299 7922 8412 Banquet hall facilities; performing arts center production; arts or science center

(G-20018)
DIRECT MAINTENANCE LLC
100 E Federal St Ste 600 (44503-1811)
PHONE...................................330 744-5211
Daniel P Dascenzo, *Principal*
EMP: 35 EST: 2007
SALES (est): 3.5MM **Privately Held**
SIC: 6282 Investment advice

(G-20019)
DISTRICT BOARD HEALTH MAHONING
50 Westchester Dr (44515-3991)
PHONE...................................330 270-2855
Matthew Stefanak, *Commander*
Matthew A Stefanak, *Commissioner*
Edward J Janik, *Director*
EMP: 49 EST: 2010
SALES (est): 1.6MM **Privately Held**
SIC: 8099 Health & allied services

(G-20020)
DIVER STEEL CITY AUTO CRUSHERS
590 Himrod Ave (44506-1414)
P.O. Box 1293 (44501-1293)
PHONE...................................330 744-5083
John Diver, *President*
EMP: 31
SQ FT: 5,000
SALES (est): 4.1MM **Privately Held**
SIC: 5093 Automotive wrecking for scrap; metal scrap & waste materials

(G-20021)
DON WALTER KITCHEN DISTRS (PA)
260 Victoria Rd (44515-2024)
PHONE...................................330 793-9338
Gary Walter, *President*
Randy Walter, *Vice Pres*
EMP: 30 EST: 1973
SQ FT: 60,000
SALES (est): 19.6MM **Privately Held**
SIC: 5064 5031 Electrical appliances, major; kitchen cabinets

(G-20022)
DRYWALL BARN INC
Also Called: Drywall Barn, The
408 N Meridian Rd (44509-1224)
PHONE...................................330 750-6155
Mark Markota, *CEO*
Jordan Markota, *Vice Pres*
Dickey Schneider, *Sales Staff*
EMP: 25
SALES (est): 14.8MM **Privately Held**
SIC: 5032 Drywall materials

(G-20023)
DUTCHESS DRY CLEANERS
Also Called: Dutchess Cleaner
2710 Belmont Ave Ste D (44505-1835)
PHONE...................................330 759-9382
George Rondinelli, *President*
Jeno Pondinelli, *Owner*
EMP: 30
SALES (est): 304.2K **Privately Held**
SIC: 7216 Curtain cleaning & repair

(G-20024)
EAST OHIO GAS COMPANY
Also Called: Dominion Energy Ohio
1165 W Rayen Ave (44502-1394)
PHONE...................................330 742-8121
EMP: 176
SQ FT: 224
SALES (corp-wide): 13.3B **Publicly Held**
SIC: 4924 Natural gas distribution
HQ: The East Ohio Gas Company
　　1201 E 55th St
　　Cleveland OH 44103
　　800 362-7557

(G-20025)
EASTER SEAL SOCIETY OF (PA)
Also Called: EASTER SEALS
299 Edwards St (44502-1599)
PHONE...................................330 743-1168
Kenan Sklenar, *CEO*
Diane Hardenbrook, *CFO*
EMP: 75
SQ FT: 26,265
SALES: 4.4MM **Privately Held**
SIC: 8322 8093 Individual & family services; rehabilitation center, outpatient treatment; speech defect clinic

(G-20026)
EDM MANAGEMENT INC
1419 Boardman Poland Rd # 500 (44514)
PHONE...................................330 726-5790
Edward Reese, *CEO*
Diane Reese, *President*

Rob Rupeka, *CFO*
EMP: 50
SQ FT: 5,000
SALES (est): 5.5MM **Privately Held**
SIC: 8741 Business management

(G-20027)
EINSTRUCTION CORPORATION (HQ)
255 W Federal St (44503-1207)
PHONE...................................330 746-3015
Rich Fennessy, *CEO*
Tim Torno, *CFO*
▼ EMP: 100
SQ FT: 8,000
SALES: 35.8MM
SALES (corp-wide): 125.9MM **Privately Held**
WEB: www.einstruction.com
SIC: 7371 7379 5045 7372 Computer software development; computer related consulting services; computers, peripherals & software; prepackaged software
PA: Turning Technologies, Llc
　　255 W Federal St
　　Youngstown OH 44503
　　330 746-3015

(G-20028)
ELIZABETH H FARBMAN
100 E Federal St (44503-1838)
PHONE...................................330 744-5211
David Barbee, *Principal*
Elizabeth Farbman,
EMP: 31
SALES (est): 804.9K **Privately Held**
SIC: 8111 General practice attorney, lawyer

(G-20029)
ELLIOTT HELLER MAAS MORROW LPA
Also Called: Heller Mass Morrow and Migue
54 Westchester Dr Ste 10 (44515-3903)
PHONE...................................330 792-6611
Robert Heller, *President*
Rush Elliott, *President*
EMP: 26
SALES (est): 1.6MM **Privately Held**
SIC: 8111 General practice attorney, lawyer

(G-20030)
ESEC CORPORATION (PA)
44 Victoria Rd (44515-2022)
PHONE...................................330 799-1536
David Hutter, *President*
Robert Savich, *Vice Pres*
Mary C Hutter, *Treasurer*
Georgetta Darr, *Admin Sec*
EMP: 34
SALES (est): 7.6MM **Privately Held**
SIC: 5084 5012 Materials handling machinery; trucks, commercial

(G-20031)
EVENTS ON TOP
143 Boardman Canfield Rd (44512-4804)
PHONE...................................330 757-3786
EMP: 45 EST: 2008
SALES (est): 597.6K **Privately Held**
SIC: 7922 Theatrical Producers/Services

(G-20032)
EYE CARE ASSOCIATES INC (PA)
10 Dutton Dr (44502-1899)
PHONE...................................330 746-7691
H S Wang MD, *President*
Robert J Gerberry MD, *Vice Pres*
Sergul Erzurum MD, *Vice Pres*
Keith Wilson MD, *Vice Pres*
Diane Volosin, *Controller*
EMP: 55
SQ FT: 10,000
SALES (est): 8.1MM **Privately Held**
WEB: www.eyecareassociates.com
SIC: 8011 Ophthalmologist

(G-20033)
FAB LIMOUSINES INC
Also Called: Fab Tours & Travel
3681 Connecticut Ave (44515-3002)
PHONE...................................330 792-6700
Mark Bagnoli, *CEO*

EMP: 47
SQ FT: 10,000
SALES (est): 2.3MM **Privately Held**
WEB: www.fablimo.com
SIC: 4119 Limousine rental, with driver

(G-20034)
FALCON TRANSPORT CO (PA)
4944 Belmont Ave Ste 201 (44505-1055)
P.O. Box 6147 (44501-6147)
PHONE...................................330 793-1345
Barbara Takach, *President*
Brad Constantini, *Exec VP*
James Bradley, *Vice Pres*
Steve Olender, *Vice Pres*
Lee Simmerman, *Vice Pres*
EMP: 229
SQ FT: 10,000
SALES (est): 348.7MM **Privately Held**
WEB: www.falcontransport.com
SIC: 4213 Trucking Operator-Nonlocal

(G-20035)
FALCON TRANSPORT CO
4944 Belmont Ave Ste 201 (44505-1055)
PHONE...................................330 793-1345
John Serich, *Branch Mgr*
EMP: 80
SALES (corp-wide): 348.7MM **Privately Held**
WEB: www.falcontransport.com
SIC: 4212 7521 4213 Local Trucking Operator Automobile Parking Trucking Operator-Nonlocal
PA: Falcon Transport Co.
　　4944 Belmont Ave Ste 201
　　Youngstown OH 44505
　　330 793-1345

(G-20036)
FAMILY STATIONS INC
3930 Sunset Blvd (44512-1307)
PHONE...................................330 783-9986
Harold Camping, *President*
EMP: 49
SALES (corp-wide): 5.4MM **Privately Held**
SIC: 4832 Radio broadcasting stations
PA: Family Stations, Inc.
　　1350 S Loop Rd
　　Alameda CA 94502
　　510 568-6200

(G-20037)
FIRST ACCEPTANCE CORPORATION
4774 Mahoning Ave Ste 5 (44515-1643)
PHONE...................................330 792-7181
Annette Kelley, *Principal*
EMP: 27
SALES (corp-wide): 347.5MM **Publicly Held**
SIC: 6411 Insurance agents, brokers & service
PA: First Acceptance Corporation
　　3813 Green Hills Vlg Dr
　　Nashville TN 37215
　　615 844-2800

(G-20038)
FIRST NATIONAL BANK PA
1 W Federal St (44503-1438)
PHONE...................................330 747-0292
Gary J Roberts, *Principal*
EMP: 25
SALES (corp-wide): 1.4B **Publicly Held**
SIC: 6021 6022 National commercial banks; state commercial banks
HQ: First National Bank Of Pennsylvania
　　166 Main St
　　Greenville PA 16125
　　724 588-6770

(G-20039)
FOR KIDS SAKE INC
1245 Boardman Canfield Rd (44512-4004)
PHONE...................................330 726-6878
Cindy Alagretto, *President*
EMP: 30
SALES: 225K **Privately Held**
SIC: 8351 Preschool center

(G-20040)
FORGE INDUSTRIES INC (PA)
4450 Market St (44512-1512)
PHONE...................................330 782-8301

William T James II, *Ch of Bd*
Carl G James, *President*
W Thomas James III, *Vice Pres*
Dan Maisonville, *CFO*
Gary Davis, *Asst Sec*
▲ EMP: 1250 EST: 1900
SQ FT: 1,500
SALES (est): 549.3MM **Privately Held**
WEB: www.forgeindustries.com
SIC: 5085 3566 3599 3531 Bearings; power transmission equipment & apparatus; gears, power transmission, except automotive; machine shop, jobbing & repair; road construction & maintenance machinery; insurance brokers; industrial equipment services

(G-20041)
FYDA FREIGHTLINER YOUNGSTOWN
Also Called: Fyda Truck & Equipment
5260 76 Dr (44515-1148)
PHONE..........................330 797-0224
Walter R Fyda, *President*
Elizabeth Fyda, *Admin Sec*
EMP: 70
SQ FT: 60,000
SALES (est): 18MM **Privately Held**
SIC: 5012 7538 Trucks, commercial; general truck repair

(G-20042)
GALAXIE INDUSTRIAL SVCS LLC
837 E Western Reserve Rd (44514-3360)
P.O. Box 11140 (44511-0140)
PHONE..........................330 503-2334
Cortland Love, *Mng Member*
Donald Myler,
Timothy Potts,
EMP: 34
SQ FT: 20,000
SALES (est): 1.5MM **Privately Held**
SIC: 7349 Cleaning service, industrial or commercial

(G-20043)
GATEWAYS TO BETTER LIVING INC
945 W Rayen Ave (44502-1314)
PHONE..........................330 480-9870
Gail Reiss, *Principal*
EMP: 44
SALES (corp-wide): 18.3MM **Privately Held**
SIC: 8361 Home for the mentally retarded
PA: Gateways To Better Living Inc
6000 Mahoning Ave Ste 234
Youngstown OH 44515
330 792-2854

(G-20044)
GATEWAYS TO BETTER LIVING INC
230 Idaho Rd (44515-3702)
PHONE..........................330 270-0952
Chris Ellis, *Branch Mgr*
EMP: 34
SALES (corp-wide): 18.3MM **Privately Held**
WEB: www.gatewaystbl.com
SIC: 8361 Home for the mentally retarded
PA: Gateways To Better Living Inc
6000 Mahoning Ave Ste 234
Youngstown OH 44515
330 792-2854

(G-20045)
GATEWAYS TO BETTER LIVING INC (PA)
6000 Mahoning Ave Ste 234 (44515-2225)
PHONE..........................330 792-2854
Gail Riess, *Exec Dir*
EMP: 30
SQ FT: 3,000
SALES: 18.3MM **Privately Held**
WEB: www.gatewaystbl.com
SIC: 8361 Home for the mentally retarded

(G-20046)
GBS CORP
Also Called: Computer Solutions
1035 N Meridian Rd (44509-1016)
PHONE..........................330 797-2700
Gregg Fine, *Marketing Staff*

Bob Goricki, *Branch Mgr*
Joe Calabria, *Manager*
Vince Ingles, *Admin Sec*
EMP: 50
SQ FT: 1,100
SALES (corp-wide): 72.8MM **Privately Held**
SIC: 5045 Computer software
PA: Gbs Corp.
7233 Freedom Ave Nw
North Canton OH 44720
330 494-5330

(G-20047)
GENEVA LIBERTY STEEL LTD (PA)
Also Called: GENMAK GENEVA LIBERTY
947 Martin Luther King Jr (44502-1106)
P.O. Box 6124 (44501-6124)
PHONE..........................330 740-0103
David T McLeroy, *President*
EMP: 47
SQ FT: 85,000
SALES: 43.2MM **Privately Held**
SIC: 3316 7389 Strip steel, flat bright, cold-rolled; purchased hot-rolled; scrap steel cutting

(G-20048)
GEORGE G ELLIS JR MD
910 Boardman Canfield Rd (44512-4218)
PHONE..........................330 965-0832
George G Ellis Jr, *Owner*
George Ellis Jr, *Internal Med*
EMP: 35 EST: 1999
SALES (est): 2.4MM **Privately Held**
SIC: 8011 General & family practice, physician/surgeon

(G-20049)
GIFFIN MANAGEMENT GROUP INC
Also Called: Chelsea Court Apartments
6300 South Ave Apt 1200 (44512-3639)
PHONE..........................330 758-4695
Dale Giffin, *President*
EMP: 47
SALES (corp-wide): 4.4MM **Privately Held**
SIC: 6513 Apartment building operators
PA: Giffin Management Group Inc
2725 Airview Blvd Ste 204
Portage MI 49002
269 743-4181

(G-20050)
GIRARD TECHNOLOGIES INC
1101 E Indianola Ave (44502-2643)
PHONE..........................330 783-2495
Alex C Bugno, *President*
Alex Bugno, *President*
EMP: 25
SQ FT: 4,500
SALES: 5.5MM **Privately Held**
SIC: 7379 Computer related consulting services

(G-20051)
GOLD CROSS AMBULANCE SVCS INC
1122 E Midlothian Blvd (44502-2839)
PHONE..........................330 744-4161
Daniel H Becker, *Principal*
EMP: 200
SALES (est): 300.8K
SALES (corp-wide): 643.1MM **Privately Held**
SIC: 4119 Ambulance service; automobile rental, with driver
HQ: Rural/Metro Corporation
8465 N Pima Rd
Scottsdale AZ 85258
480 606-3886

(G-20052)
GOLDEN STRING INC
16 S Phelps St (44503-1316)
PHONE..........................330 503-3894
James F Sutman, *Exec Dir*
EMP: 25
SALES: 374.3K **Privately Held**
SIC: 8322 Individual & family services

(G-20053)
GRAYBAR ELECTRIC COMPANY INC
Also Called: Graybar Youngstown Nat Zone
1100 Ohio Works Dr (44510-1072)
PHONE..........................330 799-3220
Dennis Daloisio, *Branch Mgr*
EMP: 43
SALES (corp-wide): 7.2B **Privately Held**
WEB: www.graybar.com
SIC: 5063 Electrical supplies
PA: Graybar Electric Company, Inc.
34 N Meramec Ave
Saint Louis MO 63105
314 573-9200

(G-20054)
GREAT EXPECTATIONS D CA CENTER
755 Boardman Canfield Rd F8 (44512-4300)
PHONE..........................330 782-9500
Linda Beraduce, *President*
EMP: 25
SALES (est): 546.1K **Privately Held**
SIC: 8351 Child day care services

(G-20055)
GREAT LAKES TELCOM LTD
Also Called: Broadband Hospitality
590 E Western Reserve Rd (44514-3354)
PHONE..........................330 629-8848
Vincent Lucci, *Partner*
EMP: 30
SQ FT: 9,200
SALES (est): 8.7MM **Privately Held**
WEB: www.broadbandhospitality.com
SIC: 4813 3663 ; satellites, communications

(G-20056)
GREEN HAINES SGAMBATI LPA
100 E Federal St Ste 800 (44503-1871)
P.O. Box 849 (44501-0849)
PHONE..........................330 743-5101
Richard Abrams, *President*
Patricia Gruver, *Admin Sec*
EMP: 28
SALES (corp-wide): 5.9MM **Privately Held**
SIC: 8111 General practice law office
PA: Green, Haines Sgambati Lpa
100 E Federal St Ste 800
Youngstown OH 44503
330 743-5101

(G-20057)
GREENWOOD CHEVROLET INC
4695 Mahoning Ave (44515-1687)
PHONE..........................330 270-1299
Gregory Greenwood, *President*
Dave Roberts, *General Mgr*
Jessica Jewell, *Business Mgr*
Wayne C Greenwood Jr, *Vice Pres*
Nick Amendola, *Sales Mgr*
EMP: 146
SQ FT: 50,000
SALES (est): 67MM **Privately Held**
WEB: www.greenwoodchevy.com
SIC: 5511 7538 5521 Automobiles, new & used; trucks, tractors & trailers: new & used; general automotive repair shops; used car dealers

(G-20058)
GROUND TECH INC
240 Sinter Ct (44510-1076)
PHONE..........................330 270-0700
Mathew Frontino, *President*
Joseph Bianco, *Vice Pres*
EMP: 30
SQ FT: 40,000
SALES (est): 3.1MM **Privately Held**
WEB: www.groundtech-inc.com
SIC: 1794 Excavation work

(G-20059)
GUARDIAN PROTECTION SVCS INC
Also Called: Guardian Home Technology
5401 Ashley Cir Ste A (44515-1176)
PHONE..........................330 797-1570
Al Cochran, *Branch Mgr*
EMP: 30 **Privately Held**
WEB: www.guardianprotection.com

SIC: 1731 5999 7382 Safety & security specialization; fire detection & burglar alarm systems specialization; alarm signal systems; security systems services
HQ: Guardian Protection Services, Inc.
174 Thorn Hill Rd
Warrendale PA 15086
412 788-2580

(G-20060)
HARDROCK EXCAVATING LLC
2761 Salt Springs Rd (44509-1035)
PHONE..........................330 792-9524
Ben Lupo, *Mng Member*
EMP: 68
SALES (est): 5.1MM **Privately Held**
SIC: 1794 Excavation work

(G-20061)
HARRINGTON HOPPE MITCHELL LTD
26 Market St Ste 1200 (44503-1769)
P.O. Box 6077 (44501-6077)
PHONE..........................330 744-1111
James L Blomstrom, *Partner*
Frederick S Coombs, *Partner*
Paul M Dutton, *Partner*
Robert A Lenga, *Partner*
Beth Bacon, *Corp Counsel*
EMP: 25
SALES (est): 2.5MM **Privately Held**
SIC: 8111 Specialized law offices, attorneys

(G-20062)
HEART CENTER OF N EASTRN OHIO (PA)
Also Called: Heart Center Northeastern Ohio
250 Debartolo Pl Ste 2750 (44512-6026)
PHONE..........................330 758-7703
Paula Peterson, *Administration*
EMP: 47
SALES (est): 3.1MM **Privately Held**
SIC: 8011 Cardiologist & cardio-vascular specialist

(G-20063)
HELLER MAAS MORO & MAGILL
54 Westchester Dr Ste 10 (44515-3903)
PHONE..........................330 393-6602
Robert Heller, *Partner*
Richard L Magill, *Partner*
Joseph Moro, *Partner*
C Douglas Ames,
Rush E Elliott,
EMP: 26
SQ FT: 7,000
SALES (est): 3.2MM **Privately Held**
WEB: www.hmmmcolpa.com
SIC: 8111 General practice attorney, lawyer

(G-20064)
HELP HOTLINE CRISIS CENTER
Also Called: Help Network of Northeast Ohio
261 E Wood St (44503-1629)
P.O. Box 46 (44501-0046)
PHONE..........................330 747-5111
Dean Wennerstrom, *CFO*
Duane Piccirilli, *Director*
EMP: 34
SALES: 2.5MM **Privately Held**
SIC: 8322 Crisis intervention center

(G-20065)
HILLTRUX TANK LINES INC
6331 Southern Blvd (44512-3313)
P.O. Box 696, North Jackson (44451-0696)
PHONE..........................330 965-1103
Brad G Hille, *President*
Bob Johnson, *Vice Pres*
EMP: 35
SQ FT: 1,600
SALES (est): 3.3MM **Privately Held**
WEB: www.hilltrux.com
SIC: 4212 Petroleum haulage, local

(G-20066)
HOME INSTEAD SENIOR CARE
5437 Mahoning Ave Ste 22 (44515-2421)
PHONE..........................330 729-1233
Carol Haus, *President*
EMP: 100 EST: 2001

SALES (est): 2.3MM **Privately Held**
WEB: www.homecarealternatives.com
SIC: 8082 Home health care services

(G-20067)
HOMETOWN URGENT CARE
1305 Boardman Poland Rd (44514-1935)
PHONE..................................330 629-2300
Tammy Russell, *Branch Mgr*
EMP: 173
SALES (corp-wide): 73.2MM **Privately Held**
SIC: 8049 8011 7291 Occupational therapist; medical centers; tax return preparation services
PA: Hometown Urgent Care
2400 Corp Exchange Dr # 102
Columbus OH 43231
614 505-7633

(G-20068)
HOPES DRAMS CHILDCARE LRNG CTR
33 N Wickliffe Cir (44515-2926)
PHONE..................................330 793-8260
EMP: 29
SALES (est): 1.1MM
SALES (corp-wide): 811K **Privately Held**
SIC: 8351 Group day care center
PA: Hopes And Dreams Childcare & Learning Center
4490 Norquest Blvd
Austintown OH 44515
330 793-3535

(G-20069)
HOSPICE OF THE VALLEY INC (PA)
5190 Market St (44512-2198)
PHONE..................................330 788-1992
Terry Kilbury, *Director*
Lesley Groubert, *Nurse*
EMP: 75
SQ FT: 4,700
SALES: 21.7MM **Privately Held**
SIC: 8069 8322 Specialty hospitals, except psychiatric; individual & family services

(G-20070)
HUMILITY HOUSE
755 Ohltown Rd (44515-1075)
PHONE..................................330 505-0144
Roco Parrell, *Director*
EMP: 100
SALES: 7.2MM **Privately Held**
SIC: 8051 8052 Skilled nursing care facilities; intermediate care facilities

(G-20071)
HUMILITY OF MARY INFO SYSTEMS
250 E Federal St Ste 200 (44503-1814)
PHONE..................................330 884-6600
Charles Folkwein, *CIO*
EMP: 82
SQ FT: 14,000
SALES (est): 3.2MM
SALES (corp-wide): 4.7B **Privately Held**
SIC: 7299 Personal document & information services
PA: Mercy Health
1701 Mercy Health Pl
Cincinnati OH 45237
513 639-2800

(G-20072)
HUNTINGTON NATIONAL BANK
23 Federal Plaza Central (44503-1503)
PHONE..................................330 742-7013
Walter Tomich, *Manager*
EMP: 30
SALES (corp-wide): 5.2B **Publicly Held**
WEB: www.huntingtonnationalbank.com
SIC: 6029 6022 Commercial banks; state commercial banks
HQ: The Huntington National Bank
17 S High St Fl 1
Columbus OH 43215
614 480-4293

(G-20073)
HYNES INDUSTRIES INC (PA)
Also Called: Roll Formed Products Co Div
3805 Hendricks Rd Ste A (44515-3046)
PHONE..................................330 799-3221
William W Bresnahan, *Ch of Bd*
William J Bresnahan, *President*
D R Golding, *President*
C A Covington Jr, *Principal*
Joseph S Donchess, *Principal*
▲ EMP: 124
SQ FT: 154,000
SALES (est): 75MM **Privately Held**
WEB: www.hynesind.com
SIC: 5051 3449 3316 3441 Steel; strip, metal; custom roll formed products; wire, flat, cold-rolled strip: not made in hot-rolled mills; fabricated structural metal

(G-20074)
ICE ZONE LTD
2445 Belmont Ave (44505-2405)
PHONE..................................330 965-1423
Thomas Hutch,
Bruce Zoldan,
EMP: 25
SALES (est): 996.8K **Privately Held**
WEB: www.icezone.com
SIC: 7999 Ice skating rink operation; skating rink operation services

(G-20075)
IDEXX LABORATORIES INC
945 Boardman Canfield Rd (44512-4239)
PHONE..................................330 629-6076
EMP: 100
SALES (corp-wide): 2.2B **Publicly Held**
SIC: 8734 Testing laboratories
PA: Idexx Laboratories, Inc.
1 Idexx Dr
Westbrook ME 04092
207 556-0300

(G-20076)
IHEARTCOMMUNICATIONS INC
7461 South Ave (44512-5789)
PHONE..................................330 965-0057
Bill Kelly, *General Mgr*
EMP: 80 **Publicly Held**
SIC: 4832 Radio broadcasting stations
HQ: Iheartcommunications, Inc.
20880 Stone Oak Pkwy
San Antonio TX 78258
210 822-2828

(G-20077)
INDEPENDENT RADIO TAXI INC
308 And One Half W (44503)
PHONE..................................330 746-8844
Carl Pasternack, *President*
Randall Park, *Manager*
EMP: 35
SALES (est): 1.1MM **Privately Held**
SIC: 4121 Taxicabs

(G-20078)
INDUSTRIAL MILL MAINTENANCE
1609 Wilson Ave Ste 2 (44506-1838)
P.O. Box 1465 (44501-1465)
PHONE..................................330 746-1155
Michael McCarthy Sr, *President*
Kathy McCarthy, *Vice Pres*
EMP: 50
SQ FT: 5,600
SALES: 4MM **Privately Held**
SIC: 3471 1721 3444 3441 Sand blasting of metal parts; industrial painting; sheet metalwork; fabricated structural metal

(G-20079)
INDUSTRIAL WASTE CONTROL INC
240 Sinter Ct (44510-1076)
PHONE..................................330 270-9900
Bobbi J Frontino, *President*
Joseph Bianco, *Principal*
Matt Frontino, *Principal*
EMP: 75
SQ FT: 40,000
SALES (est): 9.2MM **Privately Held**
WEB: www.iwc-inc.com
SIC: 1799 4953 Exterior cleaning, including sandblasting; refuse collection & disposal services

(G-20080)
INFOCISION MANAGEMENT CORP
6951 Southern Blvd Ste E (44512-4655)
PHONE..................................330 726-0872
Carl Albright, *Manager*
EMP: 272
SALES (corp-wide): 242.3MM **Privately Held**
WEB: www.infocision.com
SIC: 7389 Telemarketing services
PA: Infocision Management Corporation
325 Springside Dr
Akron OH 44333
330 668-1411

(G-20081)
INFOCISION MANAGEMENT CORP
5740 Interstate Blvd (44515-1170)
PHONE..................................330 544-1400
Diane Walker, *Manager*
EMP: 423
SALES (corp-wide): 242.3MM **Privately Held**
WEB: www.infocision.com
SIC: 7389 8732 Telemarketing services; commercial nonphysical research
PA: Infocision Management Corporation
325 Springside Dr
Akron OH 44333
330 668-1411

(G-20082)
INN AT CHRISTINE VALLEY
3150 S Schenley Ave (44511-2862)
PHONE..................................330 270-3347
Ed Reese, *Owner*
EMP: 40
SALES (est): 945.9K **Privately Held**
WEB: www.theinnatchristinevalley.com
SIC: 8361 8322 Home for the aged; adult day care center

(G-20083)
INTERNTIONAL TOWERS I OHIO LTD
25 Market St (44503-1731)
PHONE..................................216 520-1250
Frank Sinito, *General Ptnr*
EMP: 99
SALES (est): 868K **Privately Held**
SIC: 6513 Apartment building operators

(G-20084)
IVAN LAW INC
2200 Hubbard Rd (44505-3191)
P.O. Box 14459 (44514-7459)
PHONE..................................330 533-5000
Daniel Garver, *President*
Carol Lynn Price, *Corp Secy*
Cynthia Garver, *Vice Pres*
EMP: 50
SQ FT: 9,000
SALES: 3MM **Privately Held**
WEB: www.ivanlaw.com
SIC: 1771 Concrete work

(G-20085)
JOHN BROWN TRUCKING INC
8063 Southern Blvd (44512-6306)
PHONE..................................330 758-0841
Anne Marie Naples, *Principal*
EMP: 50
SALES (est): 5.1MM **Privately Held**
SIC: 4212 Local trucking, without storage

(G-20086)
JOHN ZIDIAN CO INC (PA)
574 Mcclurg Rd (44512-6405)
PHONE..................................330 743-6050
Tom Zidian, *President*
Jim Zidian, *Treasurer*
Paula Van Cure, *Supervisor*
John Grossman, *Director*
John Angelilli, *Officer*
◆ EMP: 71
SQ FT: 29,000
SALES (est): 55.8MM **Privately Held**
WEB: www.giarussa.com
SIC: 5141 Groceries, general line

(G-20087)
JOHNSON CONTROLS INC
1044 N Meridian Rd Ste A (44509-1070)
PHONE..................................330 270-4385
Edward Dunkerley, *Manager*
EMP: 40 **Privately Held**
SIC: 1711 Plumbing, heating, air-conditioning contractors
HQ: Johnson Controls, Inc.
5757 N Green Bay Ave
Milwaukee WI 53209
414 524-1200

(G-20088)
JPMORGAN CHASE BANK NAT ASSN
3999 Belmont Ave (44505-1409)
PHONE..................................330 759-1750
Jeanette Howell, *Manager*
EMP: 26
SQ FT: 5,185
SALES (corp-wide): 131.4B **Publicly Held**
WEB: www.chase.com
SIC: 6021 National commercial banks
HQ: Jpmorgan Chase Bank, National Association
1111 Polaris Pkwy
Columbus OH 43240
614 436-3055

(G-20089)
JVC SPORTS CORP
Also Called: Sportsworld
8249 South Ave (44512-6416)
PHONE..................................330 726-1757
Joe Corroto, *President*
Eugene Pirko, *Corp Secy*
Chuck Duke, *Vice Pres*
EMP: 40
SALES (est): 3MM **Privately Held**
SIC: 6512 Commercial & industrial building operation

(G-20090)
KIDNEY CENTER PARTNERSHIP
139 Javit Ct (44515-2410)
PHONE..................................330 799-1150
Guss Biscardi, *Partner*
Chester Amedia, *Partner*
Diane Crafton, *Partner*
Leon G Vassilaros, *Partner*
EMP: 75
SALES (est): 1.2MM **Privately Held**
SIC: 8092 Kidney dialysis centers

(G-20091)
KIDNEY GROUP INC
1340 Belmont Ave Ste 2300 (44504-1129)
PHONE..................................330 746-1488
Nathaniel DOE, *President*
Anup Bains, *Vice Pres*
Kathleen Padgitt, *Vice Pres*
Kathlyn Padgitt, *Vice Pres*
Ramish Soundararajan, *Vice Pres*
EMP: 35
SALES (est): 4.7MM **Privately Held**
WEB: www.kidneygroup.com
SIC: 8011 8092 Nephrologist; kidney dialysis centers

(G-20092)
KIDSTOWN LLC
55 Stadium Dr (44512-5519)
PHONE..................................330 502-4484
Prisha Couche,
EMP: 25
SALES (est): 447.6K **Privately Held**
SIC: 8351 Preschool center

(G-20093)
KING COLLISION (PA)
8020 Market St (44512-6239)
PHONE..................................330 729-0525
Douglas J Fenstermaker, *Owner*
EMP: 25
SALES (est): 2.9MM **Privately Held**
SIC: 7532 Collision shops, automotive; body shop, automotive

(G-20094)
KOMAR PLUMBING CO
49 Roche Way (44512-6214)
P.O. Box 3279 (44513-3279)
PHONE..................................330 758-5073

James Grantz, *President*
EMP: 35
SQ FT: 5,000
SALES (est): 4.5MM **Privately Held**
SIC: 1711 Plumbing contractors; warm air heating & air conditioning contractor

(G-20095)
LA FRANCE SOUTH INC (PA)
Also Called: La France Crystal Dry Cleaners
2607 Glenwood Ave (44511-2401)
PHONE...................................330 782-1400
Steven Weiss, *President*
EMP: 25
SALES (est): 1.5MM **Privately Held**
SIC: 7216 Cleaning & dyeing, except rugs

(G-20096)
LAKESIDE REALTY LLC
1749 S Raccoon Rd (44515-4703)
PHONE...................................330 793-4200
George Berick, *Mng Member*
EMP: 50 EST: 2009
SALES (est): 1.4MM **Privately Held**
SIC: 6531 Real estate agent, residential

(G-20097)
LANE LIFE CORP (PA)
Also Called: Lane Life Trans
5801 Mahoning Ave (44515-2222)
PHONE...................................330 799-1002
Joseph Lane, *President*
Dave Knarr, *Purch Agent*
EMP: 34
SALES (est): 7.4MM **Privately Held**
WEB: www.lanelifetrans.com
SIC: 4119 Ambulance service

(G-20098)
LENCYK MASONRY CO INC
7671 South Ave (44512-5724)
PHONE...................................330 729-9780
Lawrence Lencyk, *President*
Jacquelyn Lencyk, *Treasurer*
Dave Detwiler, *Manager*
EMP: 30
SALES (est): 3.5MM **Privately Held**
SIC: 1741 Tuckpointing or restoration

(G-20099)
LIBERTY MAINTENANCE INC
777 N Meridian Rd (44509-1006)
P.O. Box 631, Campbell (44405-0631)
PHONE...................................330 755-7711
Emanouel Frangos, *President*
Nikolaos Frangos, *Vice Pres*
John Frangos, *Treasurer*
Michele Lasko, *Admin Sec*
EMP: 70
SQ FT: 7,900
SALES (est): 10.1MM **Privately Held**
SIC: 1721 Bridge painting

(G-20100)
LOVING HANDS HOME CARE INC
4179 Nottingham Ave (44511-1017)
PHONE...................................330 792-7032
Kathy Stelluto, *President*
EMP: 30
SALES (est): 613.6K **Privately Held**
SIC: 8082 Home health care services

(G-20101)
LOWES HOME CENTERS LLC
1100 Doral Dr (44514-1904)
PHONE...................................330 965-4500
Bran Heckert, *Branch Mgr*
EMP: 150
SALES (corp-wide): 68.6B **Publicly Held**
SIC: 5211 5031 5722 5064 Lumber & other building materials; building materials, exterior; building materials, interior; household appliance stores; electrical appliances, television & radio
HQ: Lowe's Home Centers, Llc
1605 Curtis Bridge Rd
Wilkesboro NC 28697
336 658-4000

(G-20102)
LYDEN OIL COMPANY
3711 Leharps Dr Ste A (44515-1457)
PHONE...................................330 792-1100
Paul Lyden, *Branch Mgr*
EMP: 38

SALES (est): 11.7MM **Privately Held**
WEB: www.spartanoilcorp.com
SIC: 5172 Crude oil
PA: Lyden Oil Company
30692 Tracy Rd
Walbridge OH 43465

(G-20103)
MACK COMMUNICATIONS LLC
2994 Roosevelt Dr Ste B (44504-1204)
PHONE...................................330 347-4020
Natashia McCaskey,
EMP: 25
SALES (est): 382K **Privately Held**
SIC: 8999 Communication services

(G-20104)
MAHONING CLMBANA TRAINING ASSN
20 W Federal St Ste 604 (44503-1423)
PHONE...................................330 747-5639
Denise Yoho, *CFO*
Bert R Cene, *Director*
EMP: 40 EST: 2000
SALES (est): 2.2MM **Privately Held**
WEB: www.mctaworkforce.org
SIC: 8611 Business associations

(G-20105)
MAHONING COUNTY
Sanitary Engineering Dept
761 Industrial Rd (44509-2921)
PHONE...................................330 793-5514
Joseph Warinf, *Manager*
EMP: 35 **Privately Held**
WEB: www.mahoningcountygov.com
SIC: 9511 4953 Sanitary engineering agency, government; garbage: collecting, destroying & processing
PA: The Mahoning County
21 W Boardman St Ste 200
Youngstown OH 44503
330 740-2130

(G-20106)
MAHONING COUNTY
Also Called: Mahoning County Engineers
940 Bears Den Rd (44511-1218)
PHONE...................................330 799-1581
Richard Marsico, *Principal*
Richard A Marsico, *Manager*
EMP: 150 **Privately Held**
WEB: www.mahoningcountygov.com
SIC: 8711 4959 Engineering services; road, airport & parking lot maintenance services
PA: The Mahoning County
21 W Boardman St Ste 200
Youngstown OH 44503
330 740-2130

(G-20107)
MAHONING COUNTY
Also Called: Transportatin Office
4795 Woodridge Dr (44515-5115)
PHONE...................................330 797-2837
Jeffrey Thompson, *Superintendent*
Waymond Grace, *Supervisor*
EMP: 70 **Privately Held**
WEB: www.mahoningcountygov.com
SIC: 4151 9111 8322 4119 School buses; county supervisors' & executives' offices; individual & family services; local passenger transportation
PA: The Mahoning County
21 W Boardman St Ste 200
Youngstown OH 44503
330 740-2130

(G-20108)
MAHONING COUNTY CHILDRENS SVCS
222 W Federal St Fl 4 (44503-1222)
PHONE...................................330 941-8888
Denise Stewart, *Director*
EMP: 135
SALES (est): 2.8MM **Privately Held**
SIC: 8322 Adoption services; child related social services

(G-20109)
MAHONING VALLEY DENTAL SERVICE (PA)
Also Called: Castilla, Dr David DDS
5100 Belmont Ave Ste 1 (44505-1043)
PHONE...................................330 759-1771
Robert Sabatini, *President*
EMP: 30
SALES (est): 3.4MM **Privately Held**
WEB: www.warrenfamilydental.com
SIC: 8021 Dentists' office

(G-20110)
MAHONING VLY HMTLGY ONCLGY ASO
Also Called: Cancer Care Center
500 Gypsy Ln (44504-1315)
P.O. Box 240 (44501-0240)
PHONE...................................330 318-1100
Kathy Clark, *Manager*
EMP: 25
SALES (est): 780.7K **Privately Held**
SIC: 8011 8093 Hematologist; specialty outpatient clinics

(G-20111)
MAHONING VLY INFUSIONCARE INC (PA)
Also Called: Mvi Home Care
4891 Belmont Ave (44505-1015)
PHONE...................................330 759-9487
Kevin McGuire, *President*
EMP: 120
SQ FT: 16,200
SALES (est): 3.5MM **Privately Held**
WEB: www.mvihomecare.com
SIC: 8059 8082 Personal care home, with health care; home health care services

(G-20112)
MAHONING YOUNGSTOWN COMMUNITY (PA)
Also Called: MYCAP
1325 5th Ave (44504-1702)
PHONE...................................330 747-7921
Anthony B Flask, *Principal*
Harry Meshel, *Principal*
J Ronald Pittman, *Principal*
Richard A Roller II, *Exec Dir*
EMP: 51
SALES: 3MM **Privately Held**
WEB: www.my-cap.org
SIC: 8732 8399 8322 Economic research; advocacy group; community center

(G-20113)
MALL PARK SOUTHERN
7401 Market St Rm 267 (44512-5650)
PHONE...................................330 758-4511
David Simon, *President*
John Sabino, *Manager*
EMP: 60
SALES (est): 3.1MM **Privately Held**
SIC: 6512 Shopping center, regional (300,000 - 1,000,000 sq ft)

(G-20114)
MAMMOVAN INC
61 Midgewood Dr (44512-5960)
PHONE...................................330 726-2064
EMP: 30
SALES (est): 1.4MM **Privately Held**
SIC: 8011 Medical Doctor's Office

(G-20115)
MANCHESTER BENNETT TOWERS & UL
201 E Commerce St Ste 200 (44503-1657)
PHONE...................................330 743-1171
Stephen Bolton, *President*
Joseph Houser, *COO*
Mark Beatrice, *Vice Pres*
Timothy J Jacob, *Vice Pres*
John F Zimmerman Jr, *Vice Pres*
EMP: 30
SALES (est): 4MM **Privately Held**
WEB: www.mbpu.com
SIC: 8111 General practice law office

(G-20116)
MARCUS THOMAS LLC
5212 Mahoning Ave Ste 311 (44515-1857)
PHONE...................................330 793-3000
James Nash, *Manager*

EMP: 60
SALES (est): 6.6MM
SALES (corp-wide): 22.3MM **Privately Held**
WEB: www.marcusthomasad.com
SIC: 7311 8743 Advertising consultant; public relations services
PA: Marcus Thomas, Llc.
4781 Richmond Rd
Cleveland OH 44128
216 292-4700

(G-20117)
MARUCCI AND GAFFNEY EXCVTG CO (PA)
18 Hogue St (44502-1425)
PHONE...................................330 743-8170
William Gaffney Sr, *President*
William Thornton, *Project Mgr*
Scott Marucci, *Treasurer*
Linda Booth, *Office Mgr*
EMP: 50
SQ FT: 700
SALES (est): 8.9MM **Privately Held**
WEB: www.maruccigaffney.com
SIC: 1794 1795 1623 Excavation & grading, building contractor; demolition, buildings & other structures; sewer line construction; water main construction

(G-20118)
MASCO INC
160 Marwood Cir (44512-6215)
PHONE...................................330 797-2904
George Winsen, *Manager*
EMP: 25
SALES (est): 843.4K
SALES (corp-wide): 601.6K **Privately Held**
SIC: 8322 Individual & family services
PA: Masco Inc
160 Marwood Cir
Youngstown OH

(G-20119)
MEADOWBROOK MALL COMPANY (PA)
2445 Belmont Ave (44505-2405)
P.O. Box 2186 (44504-0186)
PHONE...................................330 747-2661
Anthony M Cafaro, *Partner*
EMP: 45 EST: 1980
SQ FT: 12,000
SALES (est): 1.9MM **Privately Held**
SIC: 6512 6531 Commercial & industrial building operation; real estate agents & managers

(G-20120)
MEANDER INN INC
Also Called: Best Western Meander Inn
870 N Canfield Niles Rd (44515-1105)
P.O. Box 6428, Delray Beach FL (33482-6428)
PHONE...................................330 544-2378
Bill Kovass, *President*
EMP: 35
SALES (est): 1.3MM **Privately Held**
SIC: 7011 Hotels

(G-20121)
MEANDER INN INCORPORATED
Also Called: Hampton Inn Youngstown West
880 N Canfield Niles Rd (44515-1105)
PHONE...................................330 544-0660
Sheree Moore, *Principal*
Janet Perry, *Manager*
EMP: 35
SALES: 950K **Privately Held**
SIC: 7011 Hotels

(G-20122)
MERCY HEALTH
250 Debartolo Pl (44512-7004)
P.O. Box 1854 (44501-1854)
PHONE...................................330 729-1372
EMP: 136
SALES (corp-wide): 4.7B **Privately Held**
SIC: 8062 General medical & surgical hospitals
PA: Mercy Health
1701 Mercy Health Pl
Cincinnati OH 45237
513 639-2800

▲ = Import ▼=Export
◆ =Import/Export

(G-20123)
MERCY HEALTH
6252 Mahoning Ave (44515-2003)
PHONE.................................330 792-7418
EMP: 33
SALES (corp-wide): 4.7B Privately Held
SIC: 8011 8062 Clinic, operated by physicians; general medical & surgical hospitals
PA: Mercy Health
1701 Mercy Health Pl
Cincinnati OH 45237
513 639-2800

(G-20124)
MERCY HEALTH
Also Called: St. Elizabeth Youngstown Hosp
1044 Belmont Ave (44504-1006)
PHONE.................................330 746-7211
EMP: 133
SALES (corp-wide): 4.7B Privately Held
SIC: 8062 General medical & surgical hospitals
PA: Mercy Health
1701 Mercy Health Pl
Cincinnati OH 45237
513 639-2800

(G-20125)
MERCY HEALTH YOUNGSTOWN LLC
Also Called: St Elizabeth Boardman Hospital
8401 Market St (44512-6725)
PHONE.................................330 729-1420
Margaret Baker, Manager
EMP: 800
SALES (corp-wide): 4.7B Privately Held
SIC: 8011 8071 Freestanding emergency medical center; medical laboratories
HQ: Mercy Health Youngstown Llc
1044 Belmont Ave
Youngstown OH 44504

(G-20126)
MERCY HEALTH YOUNGSTOWN LLC (HQ)
Also Called: St Elizabeth Health Center
1044 Belmont Ave (44504-1006)
P.O. Box 1790 (44501-1790)
PHONE.................................330 746-7211
Robert Shroder, President
Genie Aubel, President
Sarah Quinn, Principal
Arthur H Smith, Emerg Med Spec
EMP: 2500
SALES: 309.7MM
SALES (corp-wide): 4.7B Privately Held
SIC: 8062 8071 Hospital, affiliated with AMA residency; ultrasound laboratory
PA: Mercy Health
1701 Mercy Health Pl
Cincinnati OH 45237
513 639-2800

(G-20127)
MERIDIAN HEALTHCARE (PA)
Also Called: McCdp
527 N Meridian Rd (44509-1227)
PHONE.................................330 797-0070
Lawrence J Moliterno, CEO
Darla S Gallagher, COO
EMP: 60
SALES: 10.6MM Privately Held
WEB: www.meridianservices.org
SIC: 8093 Substance abuse clinics (outpatient)

(G-20128)
MIDWEST MOTORS INC
Also Called: J D Byrider
7871 Market St (44512-5970)
PHONE.................................330 758-5800
Robert Palmer, President
EMP: 35
SALES (est): 5.6MM Privately Held
SIC: 5521 5012 Automobiles, used cars only; automobiles

(G-20129)
MILL CREEK METROPOLITAN PARK
Also Called: Fellows Riverside Gardens
123 Mckinley Ave (44509-2859)
PHONE.................................330 740-7116
Keith Kaiser, Director

EMP: 35
SALES (est): 762K
SALES (corp-wide): 6.7MM Privately Held
WEB: www.millcreekmetroparks.com
SIC: 7999 Recreation services
PA: Mill Creek Metropolitan Park
7574 Clmbiana Canfield Rd
Canfield OH 44406
330 702-3000

(G-20130)
MILL CREEK METROPOLITAN PARK
Also Called: Mill Creek Golf Course
Boardman Canfield Rd (44502)
P.O. Box 596, Canfield (44406-0596)
PHONE.................................330 740-7112
Dennis Miller, Director
EMP: 60
SALES (corp-wide): 6.7MM Privately Held
WEB: www.millcreekmetroparks.com
SIC: 7992 Public golf courses
PA: Mill Creek Metropolitan Park
7574 Clmbiana Canfield Rd
Canfield OH 44406
330 702-3000

(G-20131)
MODERN BUILDERS SUPPLY INC
500 Victoria Rd (44515-2030)
PHONE.................................330 726-7000
Jack Narstellar, President
EMP: 100
SALES (corp-wide): 347.7MM Privately Held
WEB: www.polaristechnologies.com
SIC: 5032 Brick, stone & related material
PA: Modern Builders Supply, Inc.
3500 Phillips Ave
Toledo OH 43608
419 241-3961

(G-20132)
MS CONSULTANTS INC (PA)
333 E Federal St (44503-1821)
PHONE.................................330 744-5321
Thomas E Mosure, President
David Kiraly, COO
Michael D Kratofil, COO
Don Killmeyer, Vice Pres
Brian Szuch, Vice Pres
EMP: 105
SQ FT: 20,000
SALES (est): 43.8MM Privately Held
WEB: www.moshsolutions.com
SIC: 8711 8712 Consulting engineer; architectural services

(G-20133)
MURPHY CONTRACTING CO
285 Andrews Ave (44505-3059)
P.O. Box 1833 (44501-1833)
PHONE.................................330 743-8915
Donald Gubany, President
Len Summers, Vice Pres
Jason Mays, Project Mgr
Michael A Gentile, Admin Sec
EMP: 30
SQ FT: 7,000
SALES (est): 9.4MM Privately Held
SIC: 1542 1541 Commercial & office building, new construction; industrial buildings, new construction

(G-20134)
NANNICOLA WHOLESALE CO
Also Called: Bingo Division
2750 Salt Springs Rd (44509-4001)
PHONE.................................330 799-0888
Charles Nannicola, Manager
EMP: 70
SALES (est): 2.7MM
SALES (corp-wide): 7.9MM Privately Held
SIC: 5092 5199 Bingo games & supplies; gifts & novelties
PA: Nannicola Wholesale Co.
2750 Salt Springs Rd
Youngstown OH 44509
330 799-0888

(G-20135)
NASCO ROOFING AND CNSTR INC
1900 Mccartney Rd (44505-5033)
PHONE.................................330 746-3566
Iraj Nasseri, Principal
EMP: 28
SALES (est): 1.8MM Privately Held
SIC: 1521 1761 Single-family housing construction; roofing contractor

(G-20136)
NATIO ASSOC FOR THE ADVAN OF
Also Called: N A A C P
1350 5th Ave (44504-1728)
P.O. Box 6103 (44501-6103)
PHONE.................................330 782-9777
Willie R Oliver, President
EMP: 28
SALES (corp-wide): 27.6MM Privately Held
WEB: www.detroitnaacp.org
SIC: 8641 Social associations
PA: National Association For The Advancement Of Colored People
4805 Mount Hope Dr
Baltimore MD 21215
410 580-5777

(G-20137)
NATIONAL HEAT EXCH CLG CORP
8397 Southern Blvd (44512-6319)
PHONE.................................330 482-0893
Carroll Joseph, President
Paul Erickson, General Mgr
Brian Antal, Vice Pres
Bill James, Sales Staff
Sherri Provided, Sales Staff
EMP: 40
SQ FT: 52,000
SALES: 9.6MM
SALES (corp-wide): 3.3MM Privately Held
WEB: www.nationalheatexchange.com
SIC: 7699 Industrial equipment cleaning
PA: Gbhx Holding Corporation
131 Varick St Rm 1034
New York NY 10013
212 929-0358

(G-20138)
NATIONAL HERITG ACADEMIES INC
Also Called: Stambaugh Charter Academy
2420 Donald Ave (44509-1306)
PHONE.................................330 792-4806
EMP: 59 Privately Held
SIC: 8741 Management services
PA: National Heritage Academies, Inc.
3850 Broadmoor Ave Se # 201
Grand Rapids MI 49512

(G-20139)
NATIONAL MULTIPLE SCLEROSIS
4300 Belmont Ave (44505-1084)
PHONE.................................330 759-9066
Janet Kramer, Director
EMP: 40
SALES (est): 584.8K Privately Held
SIC: 8399 Fund raising organization, non-fee basis

(G-20140)
NICHALEX INC
Also Called: Wee Care Day Care Lrng Centre
801 Kentwood Dr (44512-5004)
PHONE.................................330 726-1422
Donna McGrath, President
EMP: 27
SALES (est): 587.5K Privately Held
SIC: 8351 Preschool center

(G-20141)
NORTH STAR PAINTING CO INC
3526 Mccartney Rd (44505-5006)
PHONE.................................330 743-2333
Irene Kalouris, President
Nick Kalouris, Corp Secy
EMP: 50
SALES (est): 6MM Privately Held
SIC: 1721 Bridge painting

(G-20142)
NORTH WOOD REALTY (PA)
1315 Boardman Poland Rd # 7 (44514-1935)
PHONE.................................330 423-0837
Richard Salata, President
Audrey Geskey, Consultant
Theresa Goldner, Real Est Agnt
EMP: 105
SALES (est): 5.5MM Privately Held
WEB: www.mikeshomecenter.com
SIC: 6531 Real estate agent, residential

(G-20143)
OHIO EDISON COMPANY
730 South Ave (44502-2011)
PHONE.................................330 740-7754
Daniel Knupp, Engineer
Jeff Elser, Branch Mgr
EMP: 150 Publicly Held
SIC: 4911 Electric services
HQ: Ohio Edison Company
76 S Main St Bsmt
Akron OH 44308
800 736-3402

(G-20144)
OHIO HEART INSTITUTE INC (PA)
1001 Belmont Ave (44504-1088)
PHONE.................................330 747-6446
Wahoub Hout, President
EMP: 32
SQ FT: 23,000
SALES (est): 1.6MM Privately Held
SIC: 8093 Specialty outpatient clinics

(G-20145)
OHIO NORTH E HLTH SYSTEMS INC
One Health Ohio
726 Wick Ave (44505-2827)
PHONE.................................330 747-9551
Dionna Slagle, Branch Mgr
EMP: 25
SALES (est): 1.4MM Privately Held
WEB: www.ychcinc.com
SIC: 8011 Offices & clinics of medical doctors
PA: Ohio North East Health Systems, Inc.
726 Wick Ave
Youngstown OH 44505

(G-20146)
OHIO NORTH E HLTH SYSTEMS INC (PA)
Also Called: Youngstown Community Hlth Ctr
726 Wick Ave (44505-2827)
PHONE.................................330 747-9551
Ronald Dwinnells, CEO
Dionna Slagle, General Mgr
William Addington, COO
Beth Haddle, COO
Maxine Speer, CFO
EMP: 32
SALES: 13.7MM Privately Held
SIC: 8099 8082 Physical examination & testing services; home health care services

(G-20147)
OHIO PRESBT RETIREMENT SVCS
Also Called: Park Vista Retirement Cmnty
1216 5th Ave (44504-1605)
PHONE.................................330 746-2944
Mary L Cochran, Branch Mgr
EMP: 300 Privately Held
WEB: www.nwo.oprs.org
SIC: 8051 8052 6513 Skilled nursing care facilities; intermediate care facilities; apartment building operators
PA: Ohio Living
1001 Kingsmill Pkwy
Columbus OH 43229

(G-20148)
OMNI MANOR INC
Also Called: Omni Nursing Home
3245 Vestal Rd (44509-1069)
PHONE.................................330 793-5648
Amy Croake, QA Dir
Paul Fabian, Manager
David Del Liquadri, Director
Mandi Rust, Hlthcr Dir

EMP: 200
SALES (corp-wide): 57.8K **Privately Held**
SIC: 8051 Convalescent home with continuous nursing care
PA: Omni Manor, Inc
　　101 W Liberty St
　　Girard OH 44420
　　330 545-1550

(G-20149)
P-AMERICAS LLC
Also Called: Pepsico
500 Pepsi Pl (44502-1432)
PHONE................................330 746-7652
Richard Dripps, *Plant Mgr*
Kennneth Kemmer, *Warehouse Mgr*
Kathryn Frantz, *Buyer*
Richard Plant, *Manager*
EMP: 105
SALES (corp-wide): 64.6B **Publicly Held**
SIC: 2086 5149 4225 Carbonated soft drinks, bottled & canned; groceries & related products; general warehousing & storage
HQ: P-Americas Llc
　　1 Pepsi Way
　　Somers NY 10589
　　336 896-5740

(G-20150)
PAISLEY HOUSE FOR AGED WOMEN
1408 Mahoning Ave (44509-2595)
PHONE................................330 799-9431
Audene Patterson, *Director*
Jill Cox, *Nurse*
EMP: 26
SALES: 693.1K **Privately Held**
SIC: 8361 Home for the aged

(G-20151)
PANELMATIC INC
Also Called: Panelmatic Youngstown
1125 Meadowbrook Ave (44512-1884)
PHONE................................330 782-8007
Rod Fellows, *General Mgr*
Gary M Urso, *Branch Mgr*
EMP: 29
SALES (corp-wide): 38MM **Privately Held**
WEB: www.panelmatic.com
SIC: 3613 8711 Control panels, electric; cubicles (electric switchboard equipment); designing: ship, boat, machine & product
PA: Panelmatic, Inc.
　　258 Donald Dr
　　Fairfield OH 45014
　　513 829-3666

(G-20152)
PATELLAS FLOOR CENTER INC
Also Called: Patella Carpet & Tile
6620 Market St (44512-3401)
PHONE................................330 758-4099
Anthony Patella, *President*
Thomas Patella, *Vice Pres*
Karen Patella, *Treasurer*
Maryann Patella, *Admin Sec*
EMP: 25
SQ FT: 3,500
SALES (est): 4.9MM **Privately Held**
SIC: 5713 1752 Carpets; floor tile; carpet laying; vinyl floor tile & sheet installation; ceramic floor tile installation

(G-20153)
PENNSYLVANIA TL SLS & SVC INC (PA)
Also Called: Penn Tool
625 Bev Rd (44512-6421)
P.O. Box 5557, Poland (44514-0557)
PHONE................................330 758-0845
Robert Baxter, *President*
Shawn Baxter, *Sales Staff*
▲ EMP: 93
SQ FT: 100,000
SALES (est): 110MM **Privately Held**
SIC: 7699 5085 5084 Tool repair services; industrial tools; hoists

(G-20154)
PETSMART INC
1101 Doral Dr (44514-1962)
PHONE................................330 629-2479
David Beemf, *Manager*
EMP: 30

SALES (corp-wide): 12.1B **Privately Held**
WEB: www.petsmart.com
SIC: 5999 0752 Pet food; animal specialty services
HQ: Petsmart, Inc.
　　19601 N 27th Ave
　　Phoenix AZ 85027
　　623 580-6100

(G-20155)
PHARMACY DATA MANAGEMENT INC (PA)
Also Called: Pharmacy Benefit Direct
1170 E Western Reserve Rd (44514-3245)
P.O. Box 5300, Poland (44514-0300)
PHONE................................330 757-1500
Douglas Wittenauer, *President*
Richard Pavelick, *Controller*
Karen Cessna, *Sales Dir*
Dana Hughes, *Accounts Mgr*
Kimberly Marsico, *Accounts Mgr*
EMP: 41
SQ FT: 14,000
SALES: 6MM **Privately Held**
WEB: www.pdmi.com
SIC: 6371 Pension, health & welfare funds

(G-20156)
PHOENIX SYSTEMS GROUP INC
Also Called: P S G
755 Brdmn Cnfeld Rd Ste G (44512)
PHONE................................330 726-6500
Jeffrey White, *President*
Constance While, *Treasurer*
Bryan Holsinger, *Admin Sec*
EMP: 25
SQ FT: 2,900
SALES (est): 2.5MM **Privately Held**
WEB: www.phoenix-sys.com
SIC: 7379 ; computer related consulting services

(G-20157)
PLANNED PRENTHOOD GREATER OHIO
Also Called: Youngstown Health Center
77 E Midlothian Blvd (44507-2021)
PHONE................................330 788-2487
Stephanie Kight, *CEO*
EMP: 35
SALES (corp-wide): 20.7MM **Privately Held**
SIC: 8093 Family planning clinic; family planning & birth control clinics
PA: Planned Parenthood Of Greater Ohio
　　206 E State St
　　Columbus OH 43215
　　614 224-2235

(G-20158)
PLANNED PRNTHOOD OF MHNING VLY
77 E Midlothian Blvd (44507-2021)
PHONE................................330 788-6506
Roberta Antoniotti, *Director*
EMP: 28 EST: 1938
SALES (est): 712K **Privately Held**
SIC: 8093 Birth control clinic

(G-20159)
PLEVNIAK CONSTRUCTION INC
1235 Townsend Ave (44505-1293)
PHONE................................330 718-1600
Christopher Plevniak, *CEO*
EMP: 31
SALES (est): 1.2MM **Privately Held**
SIC: 1542 Commercial & office buildings, renovation & repair; shopping center construction; hospital construction; custom builders, non-residential

(G-20160)
PLY-TRIM ENTERPRISES INC
550 N Meridian Rd (44509-1226)
PHONE................................330 799-7876
Harry Hoffman, *Ch of Bd*
Robin Kempf, *President*
Cheryl Dunn, *Treasurer*
EMP: 25
SALES (est): 1.4MM **Privately Held**
SIC: 8748 8742 Business consulting; manufacturing management consultant

(G-20161)
PLY-TRIM SOUTH INC
550 N Meridian Rd (44509-1226)
PHONE................................330 799-7876
Robin D Kempf, *President*
Kathleen A Hoffman, *Principal*
Wayne Johnson, *Vice Pres*
EMP: 25
SQ FT: 4,000
SALES (est): 3MM **Privately Held**
SIC: 5031 Building materials, exterior

(G-20162)
PNC BANK NATIONAL ASSOCIATION
100 E Federal St Ste 100 # 100 (44503-1800)
PHONE................................330 742-4426
Brian George, *President*
EMP: 149
SALES (corp-wide): 19.9B **Publicly Held**
SIC: 6029 6021 Commercial banks; national commercial banks
HQ: Pnc Bank, National Association
　　222 Delaware Ave
　　Wilmington DE 19801
　　877 762-2000

(G-20163)
POLAND MIDDLE SCHOOL PTO
47 College St (44514-2099)
PHONE................................330 757-7003
Ray Vitullo, *Principal*
EMP: 40
SALES (est): 471K **Privately Held**
SIC: 8641 Parent-teachers' association

(G-20164)
POSTAL MAIL SORT INC
1024 Mahoning Ave Ste 8 (44502-1449)
P.O. Box 6542 (44501-6542)
PHONE................................330 747-1515
Jeff Hill, *President*
EMP: 35
SQ FT: 13,000
SALES: 3MM **Privately Held**
WEB: www.postalmailsort.com
SIC: 7331 Mailing service

(G-20165)
PROGRESSIVE MAX INSURANCE CO
Also Called: Progressive Insurance
120 Westchester Dr Ste 1 (44515-3989)
PHONE................................330 533-8733
Rodney Brady, *Branch Mgr*
Lou Deluca, *Senior Mgr*
EMP: 45
SALES (corp-wide): 31.9B **Publicly Held**
SIC: 6331 Fire, marine & casualty insurance
HQ: Progressive Max Insurance Company
　　6300 Wilson Mills Rd
　　Cleveland OH 44143
　　440 461-5000

(G-20166)
PROGRESSIVE WOMENS CARE
6505 Market St Ste C112 (44512-3467)
PHONE................................330 629-8466
Joni S Candi, *President*
Charles Demario, *Co-Owner*
EMP: 25
SALES (est): 1.3MM **Privately Held**
WEB: www.progressivewomenscare.com
SIC: 8011 Obstetrician

(G-20167)
PROUT BOILER HTG & WLDG INC
3124 Temple St (44510-1048)
PHONE................................330 744-0293
Wes Prout, *President*
Richard Dalleske, *Vice Pres*
Linda Prout, *Shareholder*
Donald Raybuck, *Admin Sec*
EMP: 50 EST: 1945
SQ FT: 3,000
SALES (est): 10.1MM **Privately Held**
WEB: www.proutboiler.com
SIC: 1711 7692 3443 Boiler maintenance contractor; heating & air conditioning contractors; plumbing contractors; mechanical contractor; welding repair; fabricated plate work (boiler shop)

(G-20168)
PSYCARE INC (PA)
2980 Belmont Ave (44505-1834)
PHONE................................330 759-2310
Douglas Darnall, *CEO*
Mary Wargo, *Office Mgr*
Anthony Brine, *Psychologist*
Steven Dreyer, *Director*
Tonia Jones, *Director*
EMP: 122
SALES (est): 4.7MM **Privately Held**
SIC: 8049 Clinical psychologist; hypnotist; psychiatric social worker

(G-20169)
PSYCHIATRIC SOLUTIONS INC
615 Churchill Hubbard Rd (44505-1332)
PHONE................................330 759-2700
Krishna Devulapalli, *Branch Mgr*
EMP: 137
SALES (corp-wide): 10.7B **Publicly Held**
WEB: www.intermountainhospital.com
SIC: 8011 Psychiatric clinic
HQ: Psychiatric Solutions, Inc.
　　6640 Carothers Pkwy # 500
　　Franklin TN 37067
　　615 312-5700

(G-20170)
QUADAX INC
17 Colonial Dr Ste 101 (44505-2163)
PHONE................................330 759-4600
Sharon Lloyd, *Branch Mgr*
Nelson Laracuente, *Manager*
Benjamin Frayser, *Representative*
EMP: 50
SALES (corp-wide): 38.1MM **Privately Held**
WEB: www.quadax.net
SIC: 8721 7389 7363 Billing & bookkeeping service; automobile recovery service; medical help service
PA: Quadax, Inc.
　　7500 Old Oak Blvd
　　Middleburg Heights OH 44130
　　440 777-6300

(G-20171)
R & J TRUCKING INC (HQ)
8063 Southern Blvd (44512-6306)
P.O. Box 9454 (44513-0454)
PHONE................................800 262-9365
Ronald Carrocce, *President*
Ron Carrocce, *President*
Gary Carrocce, *Vice Pres*
Mark Carrocce, *Vice Pres*
Rob Reed, *Vice Pres*
EMP: 40 EST: 1981
SQ FT: 7,800
SALES (est): 47.1MM **Privately Held**
WEB: www.rjtrucking.com
SIC: 4212 Dump truck haulage

(G-20172)
R & L TRANSFER INC
5550 Dunlap Rd (44515-2042)
PHONE................................330 743-3609
Jim Laronde, *Manager*
EMP: 78 **Privately Held**
SIC: 4213 Automobiles, transport & delivery
HQ: R & L Transfer, Inc.
　　600 Gilliam Rd
　　Wilmington OH 45177
　　937 382-1494

(G-20173)
R & M FLUID POWER INC
7953 Southern Blvd (44512-6091)
PHONE................................330 758-2766
Robert Gustafson Sr, *Ch of Bd*
Robert Gustafson II, *Vice Pres*
Jennifer Kenetz, *Treasurer*
Melissa Ricciardi, *Admin Sec*
EMP: 25
SQ FT: 40,000
SALES (est): 5.6MM **Privately Held**
WEB: www.rmfluidpower.com
SIC: 3593 5084 Fluid power cylinders, hydraulic or pneumatic; hydraulic systems equipment & supplies

(G-20174)
R & R INC (PA)
Also Called: R & R Cleveland Mack Sales
44 Victoria Rd (44515-2022)
PHONE................330 799-1536
Daniel Ralich, *President*
David Hutter, *Corp Secy*
Evelyn Savich, *Vice Pres*
Jeremy Brown, *Department Mgr*
Christopher Reese, *Manager*
EMP: 29
SQ FT: 24,000
SALES (est): 38.1MM **Privately Held**
SIC: 5511 5012 7538 5013 Trucks, tractors & trailers: new & used; trucks, commercial; general truck repair; truck parts & accessories

(G-20175)
R C ENTERPRISES INC
Also Called: Remco Security
5234 Southern Blvd Ste C (44512-2245)
P.O. Box 2633 (44507-0633)
PHONE................330 782-2111
Richard P Clautti, *President*
Gina Clautti, *Vice Pres*
EMP: 55
SQ FT: 1,200
SALES (est): 1.1MM **Privately Held**
SIC: 7381 Security guard service

(G-20176)
R W SIDLEY INCORPORATED
3424 Oregon Ave (44509-1075)
PHONE................330 793-7374
Gary Hawkins, *Manager*
EMP: 25
SALES (corp-wide): 132.6MM **Privately Held**
WEB: www.rwsidleyinc.com
SIC: 5032 3273 Brick, stone & related material; ready-mixed concrete
PA: R. W. Sidley Incorporated
436 Casement Ave
Painesville OH 44077
440 352-9343

(G-20177)
RAPE INFORMATION & COUNSELING
Also Called: Family Service Agency
535 Marmion Ave (44502-2323)
PHONE................330 782-3936
Dave Arnold, *CEO*
Patricia Jones, *Owner*
Linda Diehl, *Admin Dir*
EMP: 50
SALES (est): 468.2K **Privately Held**
SIC: 8322 Crisis intervention center

(G-20178)
REGAL CINEMAS INC
Also Called: Regal Cinema South 10
7420 South Ave (44512-5719)
PHONE................330 758-0503
Stacy Allsop, *Manager*
EMP: 25 **Privately Held**
WEB: www.regalcinemas.com
SIC: 7832 Motion picture theaters, except drive-in
HQ: Regal Cinemas, Inc.
101 E Blount Ave Ste 100
Knoxville TN 37920
865 922-1123

(G-20179)
REGIONAL IMAGING CONS CORP
Also Called: Boardman X-Ray & Mri
819 Mckay Ct Ste B103 (44512-5796)
PHONE................330 726-9006
Albert M Bleggi, *President*
EMP: 30
SALES (est): 937.9K **Privately Held**
SIC: 8071 X-ray laboratory, including dental

(G-20180)
RENTOKIL NORTH AMERICA INC
Also Called: Rentokil Initial PLC
5560 W Webb Rd (44515-1137)
PHONE................330 797-9090
Dennis Kopelic, *District Mgr*
Michael Griffith, *Branch Mgr*

EMP: 26
SALES (corp-wide): 3.1B **Privately Held**
SIC: 7342 Pest control services
HQ: Rentokil North America, Inc.
1125 Berkshire Blvd # 150
Wyomissing PA 19610
610 372-9700

(G-20181)
REPUBLIC SERVICES INC
450 Thacher Ln (44515-1509)
PHONE................330 793-7676
Lorie Olexo, *President*
EMP: 34
SALES (corp-wide): 10B **Publicly Held**
PA: Republic Services, Inc.
18500 N Allied Way # 100
Phoenix AZ 85054
480 627-2700

(G-20182)
REPUBLIC SERVICES INC
3870 Hendricks Rd (44515-1528)
PHONE................330 793-7676
Robert E Dak, *Branch Mgr*
EMP: 34
SALES (corp-wide): 10B **Publicly Held**
SIC: 4953 Sanitary landfill operation
PA: Republic Services, Inc.
18500 N Allied Way # 100
Phoenix AZ 85054
480 627-2700

(G-20183)
REPUBLIC SERVICES INC
Also Called: Allied Waste Division
3870 Hendricks Rd (44515)
PHONE................330 793-7676
EMP: 34
SALES (corp-wide): 10B **Publicly Held**
SIC: 4953 Refuse collection & disposal services
PA: Republic Services, Inc.
18500 N Allied Way # 100
Phoenix AZ 85054
480 627-2700

(G-20184)
RESCUE MISSION OF MAHONING VAL (PA)
962 Martin L King Jr Blvd (44510-1686)
P.O. Box 298 (44501-0298)
PHONE................330 744-5485
David Sherrard, *Exec Dir*
Ron Starcher, *Director*
Lynn Wyant, *Director*
EMP: 36
SQ FT: 22,000
SALES: 3.1MM **Privately Held**
SIC: 8322 Social service center; emergency shelters

(G-20185)
RESCUE MISSION OF MAHONING VAL
2246 Glenwood Ave (44511-1574)
P.O. Box 298 (44501-0298)
PHONE................330 744-5485
David Sherrard, *Pastor*
EMP: 30
SALES (est): 379.3K
SALES (corp-wide): 3.1MM **Privately Held**
SIC: 8322 Social service center
PA: Rescue Mission Of Mahoning Valley, The (Inc)
962 Martin L King Jr Blvd
Youngstown OH 44510
330 744-5485

(G-20186)
RGIS LLC
5423 Mahoning Ave Ste C (44515-2435)
PHONE................330 799-1566
Carl Fisher, *Manager*
EMP: 100
SALES (corp-wide): 6.8B **Publicly Held**
WEB: www.rgisinv.com
SIC: 7389 Inventory computing service
HQ: Rgis, Llc
2000 Taylor Rd
Auburn Hills MI 48326
248 651-2511

(G-20187)
RNW HOLDINGS INC
200 Division Street Ext (44510-1000)
P.O. Box 478 (44501-0478)
PHONE................330 792-0600
Major Hammond, *Branch Mgr*
EMP: 40
SALES (corp-wide): 64.4MM **Privately Held**
SIC: 5093 1795 3341 Scrap & waste materials; wrecking & demolition work; secondary nonferrous metals
HQ: Rnw Holdings, Inc.
26949 Chagrin Blvd # 305
Cleveland OH 44122
216 831-0510

(G-20188)
ROBERT HALF INTERNATIONAL INC
Also Called: Account Temps
970 Windham Ct Ste 1a (44512-5082)
PHONE................330 629-9494
Carrie Votino, *Branch Mgr*
EMP: 92
SALES (corp-wide): 5.8B **Publicly Held**
WEB: www.rhii.com
SIC: 7361 Executive placement
PA: Robert Half International Inc.
2884 Sand Hill Rd Ste 200
Menlo Park CA 94025
650 234-6000

(G-20189)
ROCKNSTARR HOLDINGS LLC
112 S Meridian Rd (44509-2640)
PHONE................330 509-9086
Ray Starr,
EMP: 28
SQ FT: 52,000
SALES: 12MM **Privately Held**
SIC: 5013 3312 Wheels, motor vehicle; wheels

(G-20190)
ROGER KREPS DRYWALL & PLST INC
939 Augusta Dr (44512-7923)
PHONE................330 726-6090
Roger R Kreps, *President*
Mary Ann Kreps, *Corp Secy*
EMP: 76
SQ FT: 2,500
SALES (est): 7.8MM **Privately Held**
WEB: www.rogerkrepsdrywall.com
SIC: 1751 1742 Carpentry work; drywall; plastering, plain or ornamental; acoustical & ceiling work

(G-20191)
ROMAN CTHLIC DOCESE YOUNGSTOWN
Also Called: Calvary Cemetery
248 S Belle Vista Ave (44509-2252)
PHONE................330 792-4721
Don Goncy, *Superintendent*
EMP: 25
SALES (corp-wide): 23.6MM **Privately Held**
WEB: www.stjosephmantua.com
SIC: 6553 Cemeteries, real estate operation
PA: Roman Catholic Diocese Of Youngstown
144 W Wood St
Youngstown OH 44503
330 744-8451

(G-20192)
RON CARROCCE TRUCKING COMPANY
8063 Southern Blvd (44512-6306)
P.O. Box 9454 (44513-0454)
PHONE................330 758-0841
Ronald Carrocce, *President*
Mark Carrocce, *Corp Secy*
Gary Carrocce, *Vice Pres*
EMP: 110
SQ FT: 50,000
SALES (est): 6.4MM **Privately Held**
SIC: 4212 Dump truck haulage
PA: American Bulk Commodities Inc
8063 Southern Blvd
Youngstown OH 44512

(G-20193)
RON KREPS DRYWALL PLST COMPANG
6042 Market St (44512-2918)
PHONE................330 726-8252
Sean Kreps, *President*
Karen Kreps, *Admin Sec*
EMP: 35
SALES: 1.5MM **Privately Held**
WEB: www.ronkreps.com
SIC: 1742 Drywall

(G-20194)
RONDINELLI COMPANY INC (PA)
Also Called: Dutchess Cleaners
207 Boardman Canfield Rd (44514-4806)
PHONE................330 726-7643
Gino Rondinelli, *President*
EMP: 75
SALES (est): 5.5MM **Privately Held**
SIC: 7216 7299 Cleaning & dyeing, except rugs; tuxedo rental

(G-20195)
RONDINELLIS TUXEDO
207 Boardman Canfield Rd (44514-4806)
PHONE................330 726-7768
Gino Rondinelli, *President*
George Rondinelli, *Vice Pres*
EMP: 35
SQ FT: 6,000
SALES (est): 3.7MM
SALES (corp-wide): 5.5MM **Privately Held**
SIC: 5136 5699 7299 Men's & boys' clothing; formal wear; tuxedo rental
PA: The Rondinelli Company Inc
207 Boardman Canfield Rd
Youngstown OH 44512
330 726-7643

(G-20196)
ROTH BLAIR ROBERTS (PA)
Also Called: Roth Blair
100 E Federal St Ste 600 (44503-1811)
PHONE................330 744-5211
Daniel B Roth, *Chairman*
Richard B Blair, *Vice Pres*
Thomas Lodge, *Treasurer*
James E Roberts, *Treasurer*
Stuart Strasfeld, *Admin Sec*
EMP: 25 **EST:** 1969
SQ FT: 5,000
SALES (est): 2.6MM **Privately Held**
WEB: www.roth-blair.com
SIC: 8111 General practice attorney, lawyer

(G-20197)
ROTH BROS INC (DH)
3847 Crum Rd (44515-1414)
P.O. Box 4209 (44515-0209)
PHONE................330 793-5571
Thomas E Froelich, *Exec VP*
Stephen P Koneval, *Exec VP*
Richard M Wardle, *Exec VP*
Michael A Wardle, *Vice Pres*
Rob Bodnar, *Foreman/Supr*
EMP: 240
SQ FT: 120,000
SALES (est): 83.7MM
SALES (corp-wide): 133.3MM **Privately Held**
SIC: 1711 1761 Warm air heating & air conditioning contractor; roofing contractor; sheet metalwork
HQ: Sodexo, Inc.
9801 Washingtonian Blvd # 1
Gaithersburg MD 20878
301 987-4000

(G-20198)
RUKH BOARDMAN PROPERTIES LLC
Also Called: Holiday Inn
7410 South Ave (44512-5719)
PHONE................330 726-5472
Brent Reynolds, *General Mgr*
Darolyn Boivin, *Controller*
Edward J Debartolo Jr,
EMP: 95
SALES: 1,000K **Privately Held**
WEB: www.hiboardman.com
SIC: 7011 Inns

GEOGRAPHIC

(G-20199)
RURAL/METRO CORPORATION
1122 E Midlothian Blvd (44502-2839)
PHONE....................................216 749-2211
Kurt Narron, *Branch Mgr*
EMP: 165
SALES (corp-wide): 643.1MM **Privately Held**
WEB: www.ruralmetro.com
SIC: 4119 Ambulance service
HQ: Rural/Metro Corporation
　8465 N Pima Rd
　Scottsdale AZ 85258
　480 606-3886

(G-20200)
RURAL/METRO CORPORATION
Also Called: Gold Cross
1122 E Midlothian Blvd (44502-2839)
PHONE....................................330 744-4161
Patrick Sullivan, *Manager*
EMP: 200
SALES (corp-wide): 643.1MM **Privately Held**
WEB: www.ruralmetro.com
SIC: 4119 Ambulance service
HQ: Rural/Metro Corporation
　8465 N Pima Rd
　Scottsdale AZ 85258
　480 606-3886

(G-20201)
RYAN SHERIDAN
45 N Canfield Niles Rd (44515-2343)
PHONE....................................330 270-2380
Ryan Sheridan, *Owner*
EMP: 29 EST: 2015
SALES (est): 392.7K **Privately Held**
SIC: 8322 8093 8099 General counseling
　services; detoxification center, outpatient;
　health screening service

(G-20202)
SAMI S RAFIDI
Also Called: Sfr Group
2000 Canfield Rd (44511-2984)
PHONE....................................330 799-9508
Sami S Rafidi, *Owner*
EMP: 175
SQ FT: 1,000
SALES (est): 4.2MM **Privately Held**
WEB: www.sfrgroup.com
SIC: 6531 6519 Real estate agents &
　managers; real property lessors

(G-20203)
SAMRON INC
Also Called: Stanley Steamer
674 Bev Rd (44512-6422)
PHONE....................................330 782-6539
Ronald Zockle, *President*
Dominic Zockle, *Corp Secy*
Jeff Opencar, *Executive*
EMP: 28 EST: 1974
SQ FT: 6,500
SALES (est): 1.6MM **Privately Held**
WEB: www.samron.net
SIC: 7217 5713 1752 Carpet & furniture
　cleaning on location; floor covering
　stores; floor laying & floor work

(G-20204)
SATERI HOME INC (PA)
7246 Ronjoy Pl (44512-4357)
PHONE....................................330 758-8106
Felix S Savon, *President*
EMP: 100
SQ FT: 26,000
SALES (est): 39.1MM **Privately Held**
SIC: 6513 8051 5999 7352 Apartment
　building operators; skilled nursing fa-
　cilities; medical apparatus & supplies;
　medical equipment rental; individual &
　family services; intermediate care facili-
　ties

(G-20205)
SEARS ROEBUCK AND CO
Also Called: Sears Product Service 1474
7401 Market St Rm 7 (44512-5619)
PHONE....................................330 629-7700
EMP: 41
SALES (corp-wide): 16.7B **Publicly Held**
SIC: 7699 5722 Repair Services Ret
　Household Appliances

HQ: Sears, Roebuck And Co.
　3333 Beverly Rd
　Hoffman Estates IL 60179
　847 286-2500

(G-20206)
SECOND PHASE INC
191 S Four Mile Run Rd (44515-3123)
PHONE....................................330 797-9930
Candy Palmer, *President*
EMP: 49
SQ FT: 1,596
SALES (est): 1.8MM **Privately Held**
WEB: www.secondphase.net
SIC: 8361 Home for the mentally handi-
　capped

(G-20207)
SENIOR INDEPENDENCE
1110 5th Ave (44504-1604)
PHONE....................................330 744-5071
Karen Ambrose, *Director*
EMP: 35
SALES (est): 259K **Privately Held**
WEB: www.parkvista.oprs.org
SIC: 8082 Home health care services

(G-20208)
SEREX CORPORATION (PA)
55 Victoria Rd (44515-2023)
P.O. Box 9022 (44513-0022)
PHONE....................................330 726-6062
Russel Hodge, *President*
Leonard Morris, *Vice Pres*
Gregory Pastore, *VP Sales*
EMP: 34
SQ FT: 14,900
SALES (est): 6.7MM **Privately Held**
SIC: 7699 Vending machine repair

(G-20209)
**SHEPHERD OF THE VALLEY
LUTHERA (PA)**
Also Called: SHEPHERDS WOODS
5525 Silica Rd (44515-1002)
PHONE....................................330 530-4038
Tj Eisenbraun, *Purch Mgr*
Victoria Brown, *CFO*
Victorua Brown, *CFO*
Lynn Miller, *Marketing Staff*
Don Wilson, *Manager*
EMP: 60 EST: 1972
SALES (est): 33MM **Privately Held**
WEB: www.shepherdofthevalley.com
SIC: 8051 Skilled nursing care facilities

(G-20210)
**SHEPHERD OF THE VALLEY
LUTHERA**
Also Called: Shepards Wood Nursing
7148 West Blvd (44512-4336)
PHONE....................................330 726-9061
Richard Limongi, *Manager*
Jennifer Joseph, *Hlthcr Dir*
EMP: 170
SALES (est): 2.6MM
SALES (corp-wide): 33MM **Privately
Held**
WEB: www.shepherdofthevalley.com
SIC: 8051 Skilled nursing care facilities
PA: Shepherd Of The Valley Lutheran Re-
　tirement Services, Inc.
　5525 Silica Rd
　Youngstown OH 44515
　330 530-4038

(G-20211)
SIFFRIN RESIDENTIAL ASSN
Also Called: Bridge The
136 Westchester Dr Ste 1 (44515-3965)
PHONE....................................330 799-8932
EMP: 165
SALES (corp-wide): 11.1MM **Privately
Held**
SIC: 8322 8051 7361 5047 Social serv-
　ices for the handicapped; mental retarda-
　tion hospital; placement agencies;
　technical aids for the handicapped
PA: Siffrin Inc.
　3688 Dressler Rd Nw
　Canton OH 44718
　330 478-0263

(G-20212)
**SIMON ROOFING AND SHTMTL
CORP (PA)**
70 Karago Ave (44512-5949)
P.O. Box 951109, Cleveland (44193-0005)
PHONE....................................330 629-7392
Stephen Manser, *President*
Roberto Morales, *Regional Mgr*
Rocco Augustine, *Vice Pres*
Alex J Simon Jr, *CFO*
Marian Vross, *Regl Sales Mgr*
EMP: 105
SQ FT: 30,000
SALES (est): 86.2MM **Privately Held**
WEB: www.simonroofing.com
SIC: 1761 2952 Roofing contractor; as-
　phalt felts & coatings

(G-20213)
SOUTH MILL PET CARE CENTER
8105 South Ave (44512-6414)
PHONE....................................330 758-6479
Robert Renolds, *President*
EMP: 25
SQ FT: 2,000
SALES (est): 850.9K **Privately Held**
WEB: www.southmillpetcare.com
SIC: 0752 0742 Grooming services, pet &
　animal specialties; veterinarian, animal
　specialties

(G-20214)
SOUTHWOOD AUTO SALES
5334 South Ave (44512-2450)
PHONE....................................330 788-8822
Joseph Mileto III, *Owner*
EMP: 34
SALES (est): 646.4K **Privately Held**
SIC: 7521 7549 Automobile parking; tow-
　ing service, automotive

(G-20215)
**SPRINGFIELD LITTLE TIGERS
FOOT**
49 Philrose Ln (44514-3242)
PHONE....................................330 549-2359
David Billock, *President*
EMP: 85
SALES (est): 100K **Privately Held**
SIC: 8641 Youth organizations

(G-20216)
ST MORITZ SECURITY SVCS INC
Also Called: Saint Moritz Security Services
32 N Four Mile Run Rd (44515-3003)
PHONE....................................330 270-5922
Joe Bonacci, *Branch Mgr*
EMP: 73
SQ FT: 741
SALES (corp-wide): 61.2MM **Privately
Held**
SIC: 7381 Security guard service
PA: St. Moritz Security Services, Inc.
　4600 Clairton Blvd
　Pittsburgh PA 15236
　412 885-3144

(G-20217)
STATE ALARM INC (PA)
Also Called: State Alarm Systems
5956 Market St (44512-2916)
PHONE....................................888 726-8111
Donald P Shury, *President*
Brenda Dull, *Corp Secy*
Jim Wiseman, *Sales Associate*
Christine McFerren, *Manager*
Michael Gorgacz, *Technology*
EMP: 35 EST: 1953
SQ FT: 2,300
SALES (est): 20MM **Privately Held**
WEB: www.state-alarm.com
SIC: 5999 5063 7382 1731 Alarm signal
　systems; burglar alarm systems; fire
　alarm systems; burglar alarm mainte-
　nance & monitoring; fire alarm mainte-
　nance & monitoring; fire detection &
　burglar alarm systems specialization;
　closed circuit television services

(G-20218)
STROLLO ARCHITECTS INC
201 W Federal St (44503-1203)
PHONE....................................330 743-1177
Gregg Strollo, *President*
Robert Hanahan, *Principal*

Rodney Lamberson, *Exec VP*
Joseph Yank, *Vice Pres*
Dave Roose, *Project Mgr*
EMP: 30 EST: 1956
SALES (est): 4.7MM **Privately Held**
SIC: 8712 Architectural engineering

(G-20219)
**SUTTON MOTOR COACH TOURS
INC**
Also Called: Southern Park Limo Service
7338 Southern Blvd (44512-5627)
P.O. Box 3335 (44513-3335)
PHONE....................................330 726-2800
Lorraine Sutton Parnell, *President*
EMP: 30
SQ FT: 4,000
SALES (est): 1.3MM **Privately Held**
SIC: 4111 4142 Airport transportation
　services, regular route; bus charter serv-
　ice, except local

(G-20220)
**TAYLOR - WINFIELD
CORPORATION**
Portage Transformer Co Div
3200 Innovation Pl (44509-4025)
PHONE....................................330 797-0300
Blake Rhein, *Vice Pres*
Duane Bittner, *Safety Mgr*
Robert Comstock, *Engineer*
Mike Hauck, *Engineer*
Loyd Miller, *Engineer*
EMP: 90
SALES (est): 7.9MM
SALES (corp-wide): 20.3MM **Privately
Held**
WEB: www.coil-joining.com
SIC: 5084 Welding machinery & equipment
PA: The Taylor - Winfield Corporation
　3200 Innovation Pl
　Hubbard OH 44425
　330 259-8500

(G-20221)
TELE-SOLUTIONS INC (PA)
6001 Suthern Blvd Ste 102 (44512)
PHONE....................................330 782-2888
Deane Wurst, *President*
Jason Wurst, *Vice Pres*
John Antonucci, *Shareholder*
EMP: 27
SQ FT: 4,200
SALES (est): 5.4MM **Privately Held**
WEB: www.tele-solutions.net
SIC: 5065 1731 Telephone equipment;
　telephone & telephone equipment instal-
　lation

(G-20222)
TIME WARNER CABLE INC
755 Wick Ave (44505-2826)
PHONE....................................330 633-9203
James Manning, *Branch Mgr*
EMP: 42
SALES (corp-wide): 43.6B **Publicly Held**
SIC: 4841 Cable television services; sub-
　scription television services
HQ: Spectrum Management Holding Com-
　pany, Llc
　400 Atlantic St
　Stamford CT 06901
　203 905-7801

(G-20223)
TRANSIT SERVICE COMPANY
1130 Prfmce Pl Unit A (44502)
PHONE....................................330 782-3343
EMP: 50
SALES (est): 3.1MM **Privately Held**
SIC: 4141 Local Bus Charter Service

(G-20224)
**TRAVELCENTERS OF AMERICA
LLC**
I 80 Rte 46 Exit 223 A Rt 46 (44515)
P.O. Box 4296 (44515-0296)
PHONE....................................330 793-4426
Mary Ault, *Principal*
EMP: 100 **Publicly Held**
WEB: www.iowa80group.com
SIC: 5172 Petroleum products
PA: Travelcenters Of America Llc
　24601 Center Ridge Rd # 200
　Westlake OH 44145

(G-20225)
TRI AREA ELECTRIC CO INC
37 Wayne Ave (44502-1900)
PHONE.................................330 744-0151
William T Leone, *President*
Andrea Leone, *Corp Secy*
Tammy Leone, *Office Mgr*
EMP: 50 EST: 1976
SQ FT: 8,000
SALES (est): 7.7MM **Privately Held**
SIC: 1731 General electrical contractor

(G-20226)
TRUMBULL INDUSTRIES INC
1040 N Meridian Rd (44509-1090)
PHONE.................................330 270-7800
Carol London, *Buyer*
Chuck Bidinger, *Purchasing*
Duane Myers, *Design Engr*
Vic Dasbach, *Regl Sales Mgr*
Rick Koch, *Regl Sales Mgr*
EMP: 65
SALES (corp-wide): 150.3MM **Privately Held**
SIC: 5074 Plumbing fittings & supplies
PA: Trumbull Industries, Inc.
300 Dietz Rd Ne
Warren OH 44483
330 393-6624

(G-20227)
TURNING PT COUNSELING SVCS INC (PA)
611 Belmont Ave (44502-1037)
PHONE.................................330 744-2991
J H Wanamaker Et Al, *Principal*
S M Berkowitz, *Principal*
B P Massman, *Principal*
David Polis, *Finance Dir*
Jannie Tagger, *Bookkeeper*
EMP: 80
SALES: 4MM **Privately Held**
WEB: www.turningpointcs.com
SIC: 8322 Alcoholism counseling, nontreatment; general counseling services

(G-20228)
TURNING TECHNOLOGIES LLC (PA)
255 W Federal St (44503-1207)
PHONE.................................330 746-3015
Mike Broderick, *CEO*
Dave Kauer, *President*
Ethan Cohen, *COO*
Sheila Hura, *Vice Pres*
Kevin Owens, *Vice Pres*
◆ EMP: 140
SQ FT: 26,200
SALES (est): 125.9MM **Privately Held**
WEB: www.turningtechnologies.com
SIC: 7372 Business oriented computer software; educational computer software

(G-20229)
TVC HOME HEALTH CARE
70 W Mckinley Way Ste 8 (44514-1967)
PHONE.................................330 755-1110
Jerry Melillo, *Owner*
EMP: 27
SALES (est): 673.9K **Privately Held**
SIC: 8082 8099 Visiting nurse service; health & allied services

(G-20230)
U S WEATHERFORD L P
1100 Performance Pl (44502-4001)
PHONE.................................330 746-2502
EMP: 250 **Privately Held**
SIC: 1389 Oil field services
HQ: U S Weatherford L P
179 Weatherford Dr
Schriever LA 70395
985 493-6100

(G-20231)
UNITED COMMUNITY FINCL CORP (PA)
275 W Federal St (44503-1200)
PHONE.................................330 742-0500
Richard J Schiraldi, *Ch of Bd*
Gary M Small, *President*
Zahid Afzal, *COO*
Matthew T Garrity, *Exec VP*
Barbara J Radis, *Exec VP*
EMP: 200

SALES: 133.9MM **Publicly Held**
WEB: www.ucfcorp.com
SIC: 6036 State savings banks, not federally chartered; savings & loan associations, not federally chartered

(G-20232)
UNITED PARCEL SERVICE INC OH
Also Called: UPS
95 Karago Ave Ste 4 (44512-5951)
PHONE.................................800 742-5877
Stacy Craley, *Business Mgr*
EMP: 158
SALES (corp-wide): 71.8B **Publicly Held**
WEB: www.upsscs.com
SIC: 4215 Package delivery, vehicular; parcel delivery, vehicular
HQ: United Parcel Service, Inc. (Oh)
55 Glenlake Pkwy
Atlanta GA 30328
404 828-6000

(G-20233)
V AND V APPLIANCE PARTS INC (PA)
27 W Myrtle Ave (44507-1193)
PHONE.................................330 743-5144
Victor Lazar, *Ch of Bd*
Bruce Lazar, *President*
Albert E Brennan, *Principal*
Vincent Rypien, *Principal*
Judy Lazar, *Treasurer*
EMP: 40
SQ FT: 16,000
SALES: 210MM **Privately Held**
WEB: www.vvapplianceparts.com
SIC: 5064 Appliance parts, household

(G-20234)
VALLEY ACOUSTICS INC
1203 N Meridian Rd (44509-1020)
PHONE.................................330 799-1894
David Olsavsky, *President*
Tom Olsavsky, *Vice Pres*
EMP: 30 EST: 1960
SQ FT: 3,200
SALES (est): 3.1MM **Privately Held**
SIC: 1751 1742 Carpentry work; acoustical & ceiling work

(G-20235)
VALLEY INDUSTRIAL TRUCKS INC (PA)
1152 Meadowbrook Ave (44512-1887)
PHONE.................................330 788-4081
James E Hammond, *President*
Mark Evans, *VP Opers*
Mike Ladesic, *Warehouse Mgr*
Patricia Wilson, *Controller*
Anthony Farris, *Accounts Mgr*
EMP: 32
SQ FT: 45,000
SALES (est): 10.7MM **Privately Held**
SIC: 7359 5084 Equipment rental & leasing; materials handling machinery

(G-20236)
VETERANS HEALTH ADMINISTRATION
Also Called: Youngstown V A Otpient Clinic
2031 Belmont Ave (44505-2401)
PHONE.................................330 740-9200
Mukesh Jain, *Branch Mgr*
John J Nemes, *Internal Med*
EMP: 30 **Publicly Held**
WEB: www.veterans-ru.org
SIC: 8011 9451 Clinic, operated by physicians; administration of veterans' affairs;
HQ: Veterans Health Administration
810 Vermont Ave Nw
Washington DC 20420

(G-20237)
VIBRA HOSP MAHONING VLY LLC
Also Called: Mahoning Valley Hospital
8049 South Ave (44512-6154)
PHONE.................................330 726-5000
Kirsten Cheeks, *Human Resources*
Mary Jane Larmon, *Mng Member*
Catherine Cardelein, *Manager*
Mark Hunyadi, *Director*
Cindy Wetzel, *Nursing Dir*
EMP: 96

SALES (est): 18.1MM
SALES (corp-wide): 325.2MM **Privately Held**
WEB: www.mahoningvalleyhospital.com
SIC: 8069 Specialty hospitals, except psychiatric
PA: Vibra Healthcare, Llc
4600 Lena Dr Ste 100
Mechanicsburg PA 17055
717 591-5700

(G-20238)
VLP INC
Also Called: Panache Hair Salon
7301 West Blvd Ste A3 (44512-5268)
PHONE.................................330 758-8811
Frank Lucurell, *President*
Nancy Vasu, *Vice Pres*
Francie Patoella, *Admin Sec*
EMP: 30
SALES (est): 810K **Privately Held**
SIC: 7231 Cosmetology & personal hygiene salons

(G-20239)
W H O T INC (PA)
4040 Simon Rd Ste 1 (44512-1362)
PHONE.................................330 783-1000
Brad Marshall, *President*
EMP: 80
SQ FT: 4,000
SALES (est): 2.8MM **Privately Held**
SIC: 4832 Radio broadcasting stations

(G-20240)
WALDON MANAGEMENT CORP (PA)
111 Westchester Dr (44515-3964)
PHONE.................................330 792-7688
Walter Terlecky, *President*
EMP: 30
SALES (est): 2.5MM **Privately Held**
WEB: www.waldonmanagement.com
SIC: 6531 6512 Cooperative apartment manager; commercial & industrial building operation

(G-20241)
WEDGEWOOD LANES INC
1741 S Raccoon Rd (44515-4785)
PHONE.................................330 792-1949
Ed Zitnick, *President*
EMP: 37
SQ FT: 46,000
SALES (est): 951.2K **Privately Held**
SIC: 7933 5813 Ten pin center; cocktail lounge

(G-20242)
WESTERN & SOUTHERN LF INSUR CO
320 S Canfield Niles Rd (44515-4019)
PHONE.................................330 792-6818
Tina Scarpaci, *Manager*
EMP: 25 **Privately Held**
SIC: 6311 Life insurance
HQ: The Western & Southern Life Insurance Company
400 Broadway St
Cincinnati OH 45202
513 629-1800

(G-20243)
WESTERN RESERVE TRANSIT AUTH (PA)
604 Mahoning Ave (44502-1491)
PHONE.................................330 744-8431
James Ferraro, *General Mgr*
Maryann Vaughn, *CFO*
Rich McFadden, *Human Resources*
Judy Saccomen, *Info Tech Mgr*
Jim Ferraro, *Director*
EMP: 82
SALES: 11.1MM **Privately Held**
WEB: www.wrtaonline.com
SIC: 4111 Bus line operations

(G-20244)
WESTVIEW APARTMENTS OHIO LLC
3111 Leo Ave (44509-1051)
PHONE.................................216 520-1250
Frank Sinito,
EMP: 385

SALES (est): 6.9MM **Privately Held**
SIC: 6513 Apartment building operators

(G-20245)
WESTVIEW-YOUNGSTOWN LTD
3111 Leo Ave (44509-1051)
PHONE.................................330 799-2787
Leeann Morein, *Partner*
Paul Phleger, *Partner*
EMP: 99
SALES (est): 3MM **Privately Held**
SIC: 6514 Dwelling operators, except apartments

(G-20246)
WFMJ TELEVISION INC
101 W Boardman St (44503-1305)
P.O. Box 689 (44501-0689)
PHONE.................................330 744-8611
Betty Brown, *President*
John Grdic, *General Mgr*
Mark Brown, *Admin Sec*
EMP: 105
SALES (est): 11.9MM **Privately Held**
WEB: www.wfmj.com
SIC: 4833 Television broadcasting stations

(G-20247)
WINDSOR HOUSE INC
Also Called: Liberty Health Care Center
1355 Churchill Hubbard Rd (44505-1346)
PHONE.................................330 759-7858
Joseph Lambert, *Administration*
EMP: 150
SALES (corp-wide): 14.1MM **Privately Held**
SIC: 8059 8051 Nursing home, except skilled & intermediate care facility; skilled nursing care facilities
PA: Windsor House, Inc.
101 W Liberty St
Girard OH
330 545-1550

(G-20248)
WINDSOR HOUSE INC
Also Called: Windsor Health Care
1735 Belmont Ave (44504-1111)
PHONE.................................330 743-1393
Laurie Forence, *Manager*
Marc Masternick, *Administration*
EMP: 100
SALES (corp-wide): 14.1MM **Privately Held**
SIC: 8051 Skilled nursing care facilities
PA: Windsor House, Inc.
101 W Liberty St
Girard OH
330 545-1550

(G-20249)
WINKLE ELECTRIC COMPANY INC (PA)
1900 Hubbard Rd (44505-3128)
P.O. Box 6014 (44501-6014)
PHONE.................................330 744-5303
Larry A Teaberry Jr, *Exec VP*
Robert J Conger, *Vice Pres*
Brian Vennetti, *Vice Pres*
Gary Connors, *Prdtn Mgr*
Alex Forte, *Sales Engr*
EMP: 35
SQ FT: 50,000
SALES: 40MM **Privately Held**
WEB: www.winkle.com
SIC: 5063 Motor controls, starters & relays; electric

(G-20250)
XA TECHNOLOGIES LLC
22 Early Rd (44505-4705)
PHONE.................................330 787-7846
Arvind Sangwan,
EMP: 25
SALES: 100K **Privately Held**
SIC: 7379 Computer related consulting services

(G-20251)
Y TOWN REALTY INC
1641 5th Ave (44504-1859)
P.O. Box 6482 (44501-6482)
PHONE.................................330 743-8844
Jerome Williams, *President*
EMP: 47

(PA)=Parent Co (HQ)=Headquarters (DH)=Div Headquarters
✪ = New Business established in last 2 years

2019 Harris Ohio
Services Directory

SALES (est): 2MM Privately Held
SIC: 6531 Real estate agent, residential

(G-20252)
YORK-MAHONING MECH CONTRS INC
724 Canfield Rd (44511-2399)
P.O. Box 3077 (44511-0077)
PHONE................................330 788-7011
Michael Fagert, *President*
Ron Fagert, *Vice Pres*
Jeremy Smith, *Project Mgr*
Mary Jo Fagert, *Treasurer*
EMP: 80
SQ FT: 22,000
SALES: 20MM Privately Held
WEB: www.yorkmahoning.com
SIC: 1761 1711 Sheet metalwork; mechanical contractor

(G-20253)
YOUNG MENS CHRISTIAN ASSN (PA)
Also Called: YMCA of Youngstown
17 N Champion St (44503-1602)
P.O. Box 1287 (44501-1287)
PHONE................................330 744-8411
Kenneth Rudge, *CEO*
Tom Lodge, *President*
Kathleen Thomas, *Finance*
Eric K Buckingham, *Director*
EMP: 80
SALES: 11.9MM Privately Held
SIC: 8641 8322 7997 Youth organizations; youth center; membership sports & recreation clubs

(G-20254)
YOUNGSTOWN ARC ENGRAVING CO
Also Called: Youngstown Lithographing Co
380 Victoria Rd (44515-2026)
PHONE................................330 793-2471
E Craig Olsen, *President*
Tim Merrifield, *Exec VP*
George B Snyder, *Vice Pres*
Ken Baytosh, *Purchasing*
EMP: 26 EST: 1900
SQ FT: 30,000
SALES (est): 2.6MM Privately Held
WEB: www.youngstownwholesale.com
SIC: 2796 7335 2791 2789 Photoengraving plates, linecuts or halftones; commercial photography; typesetting; bookbinding & related work; commercial printing; commercial printing, offset

(G-20255)
YOUNGSTOWN AREA GOODWILL INDS (PA)
2747 Belmont Ave (44505-1819)
PHONE................................330 759-7921
Toby Mirto, *Vice Pres*
Michael Mc Bride, *Director*
EMP: 180
SQ FT: 84,000
SALES (est): 5.9MM Privately Held
WEB: www.goodwillyoungstown.org
SIC: 8331 5932 Vocational rehabilitation agency; vocational training agency; clothing & shoes, secondhand

(G-20256)
YOUNGSTOWN AREA JWISH FDRATION (PA)
Also Called: HERITAGE MANOR JEWISH HOME FOR
505 Gypsy Ln (44504-1314)
PHONE................................330 746-3251
William Benedikt, *President*
Sam Kooperman, *Exec VP*
Gerald Peskin, *Vice Pres*
David Stauffer, *CFO*
Amy Hendricks, *Treasurer*
EMP: 120
SQ FT: 100,000
SALES: 12.6MM Privately Held
SIC: 8322 Social service center

(G-20257)
YOUNGSTOWN AREA JWISH FDRATION
Also Called: Heritage Manor
517 Gypsy Ln (44504-1314)
PHONE................................330 746-1076

Gary Weiss, *Director*
EMP: 80
SALES (corp-wide): 12.6MM Privately Held
SIC: 8059 8322 8051 4119 Nursing home, except skilled & intermediate care facility; individual & family services; general counseling services; skilled nursing care facilities; local passenger transportation
PA: Youngstown Area Jewish Federation Inc
505 Gypsy Ln
Youngstown OH 44504
330 746-3251

(G-20258)
YOUNGSTOWN AUTOMATIC DOOR CO
1223 Gibson St (44502-2051)
PHONE................................330 747-3135
EMP: 25
SALES (est): 779.7K Privately Held
SIC: 1751 Carpentry Contractor

(G-20259)
YOUNGSTOWN CLUB
201 E Commerce St Ste 400 (44503-1660)
PHONE................................330 744-3111
Ted Thronton, *Corp Secy*
Stacy Renzel, *Manager*
EMP: 35
SALES (est): 1.8MM Privately Held
SIC: 8641 Social club, membership

(G-20260)
YOUNGSTOWN COMMITTEE ON ALCHOL
Also Called: NEIL KENNEDY RECOVERY CLINIC
2151 Rush Blvd (44507-1535)
PHONE................................330 744-1181
Jerry Carter, *Exec Dir*
EMP: 94
SALES: 5MM Privately Held
SIC: 8069 8322 Alcoholism rehabilitation hospital; individual & family services

(G-20261)
YOUNGSTOWN COUNTRY CLUB
1402 Country Club Dr (44505-2299)
PHONE................................330 759-1040
Jim Dibacco, *President*
Karl Schroedel, *Treasurer*
EMP: 90
SALES: 2.1MM Privately Held
WEB: www.youngstowncountryclub.com
SIC: 7997 5941 5812 Country club, membership; sporting goods & bicycle shops; eating places

(G-20262)
YOUNGSTOWN HEARING SPEECH CTR (PA)
299 Edwards St (44502-1504)
PHONE................................330 726-8391
Alfred Pasini, *Director*
EMP: 43 EST: 1927
SQ FT: 7,000
SALES: 1MM Privately Held
SIC: 8093 Speech defect clinic

(G-20263)
YOUNGSTOWN NEIGHBORHOOD DEV
Also Called: YNDC
820 Canfield Rd (44511-2345)
PHONE................................330 480-0423
Thomas Hull, *Treasurer*
June Johnson, *Treasurer*
Dave Bozanich, *Finance Dir*
Michael Dulay, *Manager*
Tammi Neuscheler, *Manager*
EMP: 30
SQ FT: 1,200
SALES: 2.4MM Privately Held
SIC: 8322 8699 Social service center; charitable organization

(G-20264)
YOUNGSTOWN OHIO OTPATIENT SVCS
6426 Market St (44512-3434)
PHONE................................330 884-2020
David Fikse, *CEO*

EMP: 37
SALES (est): 580K Privately Held
SIC: 8049 Offices of health practitioner

(G-20265)
YOUNGSTOWN PLASTIC TOOLING (PA)
1209 Velma Ct (44512-1829)
PHONE................................330 782-7222
Donald J Liga, *President*
Janet Liga, *Admin Sec*
EMP: 35
SQ FT: 20,000
SALES (est): 6.8MM Privately Held
WEB: www.yptm.com
SIC: 3559 8711 Plastics working machinery; machine tool design; mechanical engineering

(G-20266)
YOUNGSTOWN PROPANE INC (PA)
Also Called: Yp
810 N Meridian Rd (44509-4003)
P.O. Box 2447 (44509-0447)
PHONE................................330 792-6571
Robert Jones, *President*
Albert E Brennan, *Principal*
Richard Jones, *Vice Pres*
Vernon Jones, *Vice Pres*
Kathie Puncekar, *Office Mgr*
EMP: 26
SQ FT: 4,000
SALES (est): 10.6MM Privately Held
WEB: www.youngstownpropane.com
SIC: 5984 5172 5719 Propane gas, bottled; gases, liquefied petroleum (propane); fireplace equipment & accessories

(G-20267)
YOUNGSTOWN-WARREN REG CHAMBER (PA)
11 Central Sq Ste 1600 (44503-1512)
PHONE................................330 744-2131
Thomas Humphries, *President*
Rachel Flickinger, *Vice Pres*
Kim Gonda, *Vice Pres*
Helen Paes, *Vice Pres*
Anthony Paglia, *Vice Pres*
EMP: 32 EST: 1905
SQ FT: 7,000
SALES: 502.5K Privately Held
SIC: 8611 Chamber of Commerce

(G-20268)
YSD INDUSTRIES INC
3710 Henricks Rd (44515)
PHONE................................330 792-6521
Jerome D Hines, *President*
Bruce Wylie, *Vice Pres*
Michael Feschak, *CFO*
Karen Flavell, *Human Resources*
Ralph Boland, *Director*
▲ EMP: 100
SQ FT: 30,000
SALES (est): 20.3MM Privately Held
SIC: 5088 3444 3441 Railroad equipment & supplies; sheet metalwork; fabricated structural metal

(G-20269)
YWCA MAHONING VALLEY
25 W Rayen Ave (44503-1000)
PHONE................................330 746-6361
Varanda Bhide, *Corp Comm Staff*
Leah Brooks, *Exec Dir*
Connie Schaffer, *Director*
Leah Merritt, *Director*
EMP: 45
SALES: 1.3MM Privately Held
WEB: www.ywcaofyoungstown.org
SIC: 8641 7991 8351 7032 Youth organizations; physical fitness facilities; child day care services; youth camps; individual & family services

(G-20270)
ZINZ CNSTR & RESTORATION
6487 Mahoning Ave (44515-2039)
PHONE................................330 332-7939
Bruce L Zinz, *President*
EMP: 30

SALES (est): 4.3MM Privately Held
WEB: www.zinzconstruction.com
SIC: 1521 General remodeling, single-family houses

(G-20271)
ZION CHRISTIAN SCHOOL
3300 Canfield Rd (44511-2701)
PHONE................................330 792-4066
Rachel Gonatas, *Principal*
Dale Giffin, *Pastor*
Geniene Hankey, *Director*
Cathy Diemer, *Admin Asst*
EMP: 25
SALES (est): 399.8K Privately Held
SIC: 8351 8211 Preschool center; private elementary & secondary schools

---

Zanesfield
Logan County

(G-20272)
MAD RIVER MOUNTAIN RESORT
1000 Snow Valley Rd (43360-9774)
P.O. Box 22, Bellefontaine (43311-0022)
PHONE................................937 303-3646
Bruce Mowrey, *Owner*
EMP: 45
SALES (est): 2.8MM Privately Held
SIC: 7011 Resort hotel

Zanesville
Muskingum County

(G-20273)
AG-PRO OHIO LLC
Also Called: John Deere Authorized Dealer
4394 Northpointe Dr (43701-5968)
PHONE................................740 450-7446
EMP: 60
SALES (corp-wide): 232.6MM Privately Held
SIC: 5999 5082 Farm equipment & supplies; construction & mining machinery
HQ: Ag-Pro Ohio, Llc
19595 Us Highway 84 E
Boston GA 31626
229 498-8833

(G-20274)
ALLWELL BEHAVIORAL HEALTH SVCS (PA)
2845 Bell St (43701-1720)
PHONE................................740 454-9766
James A McDonald, *President*
Robert R Santos, *COO*
Tim Llewellyn, *Senior VP*
Sue Foraker, *CFO*
Sue Ellen Foraker, *Controller*
EMP: 26
SQ FT: 10,000
SALES: 14.2MM Privately Held
SIC: 8093 8322 Mental health clinic, outpatient; individual & family services

(G-20275)
AMERICAN NURSING CARE INC
1206 Brandywine Blvd A (43701-1755)
PHONE................................614 847-0555
Diana Phelps, *Manager*
EMP: 200 Privately Held
WEB: www.americannursingcare.com
SIC: 8051 8361 Skilled nursing care facilities; residential care
HQ: American Nursing Care, Inc.
1700 Edison Dr Ste 300
Milford OH 45150
513 576-0262

(G-20276)
AMERICAN NURSING CARE INC
1206 Brandywine Blvd A (43701-1755)
PHONE................................740 452-0569
Diana Phelps, *Director*
EMP: 100
SALES (est): 1.7MM Privately Held
SIC: 8049 8082 Nurses, registered & practical; home health care services

▲ = Import ▼=Export
◆ =Import/Export

(G-20277)
ASSISTED LIVING CONCEPTS LLC
Also Called: Clay House
3784 Frazeysburg Rd Ofc (43701-7576)
PHONE..............................740 450-2744
Shawna Milatodich, *Manager*
Barbie Wilson, *Manager*
EMP: 25
SALES (corp-wide): 380.7MM **Privately Held**
WEB: www.assistedlivingconcepts.com
SIC: 8361 Residential care
HQ: Assisted Living Concepts, Llc
330 N Wabash Ave Ste 3700
Chicago IL 60611

(G-20278)
AT&T CORP
3575 Maple Ave Ste 502 (43701-7020)
PHONE..............................740 455-3042
EMP: 69
SALES (corp-wide): 170.7B **Publicly Held**
SIC: 4812 Cellular telephone services
HQ: At&T Corp.
1 At&T Way
Bedminster NJ 07921
800 403-3302

(G-20279)
AVI FOOD SYSTEMS INC
333 Richards Rd (43701-4643)
PHONE..............................740 452-9363
Donald Hormann, *Manager*
EMP: 50
SALES (corp-wide): 609.6MM **Privately Held**
WEB: www.avifoodsystems.com
SIC: 5962 5812 5046 Merchandising machine operators; eating places; commercial equipment
PA: Avi Food Systems, Inc.
2590 Elm Rd Ne
Warren OH 44483
330 372-6000

(G-20280)
BALLAS EGG PRODUCTS CORP
40 N 2nd St (43701-3402)
P.O. Box 2217 (43702-2217)
PHONE..............................614 453-0386
Leonard Ballas, *President*
Joseph G Saliba, *Vice Pres*
Craig Ballas, *Admin Sec*
▼ EMP: 100 EST: 1961
SQ FT: 200,000
SALES (est): 14.5MM **Privately Held**
SIC: 2015 5144 Egg processing; eggs, processed: desiccated (dried); eggs, processed: frozen; eggs

(G-20281)
BETHESDA HOSPITAL ASSOCIATION
2951 Maple Ave (43701-1465)
PHONE..............................740 454-4000
Thomas Sieber, *President*
Charles Hunter, *COO*
Paul Masterson, *CFO*
EMP: 1100
SQ FT: 400,000
SALES: 187.4K
SALES (corp-wide): 462MM **Privately Held**
SIC: 8062 8063 8082 General medical & surgical hospitals; psychiatric hospitals; home health care services
PA: Genesis Healthcare System
2951 Maple Ave
Zanesville OH 43701
740 454-5000

(G-20282)
BLOOMBERG ROSS MD
2935 Maple Ave (43701-1487)
PHONE..............................740 454-1216
Ross Bloomberg, *Owner*
EMP: 30
SALES (est): 102.7K **Privately Held**
SIC: 8011 Ophthalmologist

(G-20283)
BRENWOOD INC
Also Called: Hairitage, The
1709 Maple Ave (43701-2207)
PHONE..............................740 452-7533
Brenda Atwood, *President*
EMP: 35
SQ FT: 2,100
SALES (est): 629.4K **Privately Held**
SIC: 7231 Manicurist, pedicurist

(G-20284)
BUCKEYE COMPANIES (PA)
999 Zane St (43701-3863)
P.O. Box 1480 (43702-1480)
PHONE..............................740 452-3641
C E Straker, *President*
Stephen R Straker, *President*
M Dean Cole, *Corp Secy*
EMP: 31
SALES (est): 15.5MM **Privately Held**
SIC: 3533 5083 Drill rigs; agricultural machinery & equipment

(G-20285)
BUCKEYE SUPPLY COMPANY (HQ)
999 Zane St Ste A (43701-3863)
P.O. Box 1480 (43702-1480)
PHONE..............................740 452-3641
C E Straker, *CEO*
Stephen R Straker, *President*
George French, *Vice Pres*
Larry Messner, *CFO*
Don Starr, *Benefits Mgr*
▼ EMP: 30
SQ FT: 50,000
SALES (est): 14.6MM
SALES (corp-wide): 15.5MM **Privately Held**
SIC: 5083 5084 Lawn & garden machinery & equipment; farm implements; pumps & pumping equipment; petroleum industry machinery; oil well machinery, equipment & supplies
PA: Buckeye Companies
999 Zane St
Zanesville OH 43701
740 452-3641

(G-20286)
CALICO COURT
1101 Colony Dr (43701-6442)
PHONE..............................740 455-2541
Cynthia Stiverson, *Owner*
EMP: 30
SALES (est): 910K **Privately Held**
SIC: 7231 Beauty shops

(G-20287)
CAMBRIDGE COUNSELING CENTER
Also Called: Zanesville
326 Main St (43701-3426)
PHONE..............................740 450-7790
Susan Lynch, *Owner*
EMP: 150
SALES (corp-wide): 3.9MM **Privately Held**
SIC: 8322 General counseling services
PA: Cambridge Counseling Center
317 Highland Ave
Cambridge OH 43725
740 435-9766

(G-20288)
CARESERVE (HQ)
Also Called: Sunny View Nursing Home
2991 Maple Ave (43701-1499)
PHONE..............................740 454-4000
Thomas Sieber, *President*
Paul Masterson, *Treasurer*
Shelly Fuller, *Admin Sec*
EMP: 151
SQ FT: 25,000
SALES (est): 2.7MM
SALES (corp-wide): 462MM **Privately Held**
SIC: 8051 Skilled nursing care facilities
PA: Genesis Healthcare System
2951 Maple Ave
Zanesville OH 43701
740 454-5000

(G-20289)
CELLCO PARTNERSHIP
Also Called: Verizon Wireless
3575 Maple Ave (43701-7019)
PHONE..............................740 588-0018
EMP: 76
SALES (corp-wide): 130.8B **Publicly Held**
SIC: 4812 Cellular telephone services
HQ: Cellco Partnership
1 Verizon Way
Basking Ridge NJ 07920

(G-20290)
CELLCO PARTNERSHIP
Also Called: Verizon Wireless
2359 Maple Ave (43701-2028)
PHONE..............................740 450-1525
Derric Matz, *Manager*
EMP: 25
SALES (corp-wide): 130.8B **Publicly Held**
SIC: 4813 4812 Telephone communication, except radio; cellular telephone services
HQ: Cellco Partnership
1 Verizon Way
Basking Ridge NJ 07920

(G-20291)
CENTRAL OHIO BANDAG LP
1600 S Point Dr (43701-7366)
PHONE..............................740 454-9728
Steven Dickerson, *Partner*
Wayne Anderson, *Partner*
Bob Sumerel, *Partner*
EMP: 30 EST: 1971
SQ FT: 19,000
SALES (est): 2.9MM **Privately Held**
SIC: 7534 5014 Tire recapping; truck tires & tubes

(G-20292)
CENTURY NATIONAL BANK (HQ)
14 S 5th St (43701-3526)
PHONE..............................740 454-2521
Tom Lyall, *CEO*
William A Phillips, *Ch of Bd*
Jim Blythe, *Senior VP*
Barbara Gibbs, *Senior VP*
Patrick Nash, *Senior VP*
EMP: 39
SQ FT: 25,000
SALES (est): 5.2MM
SALES (corp-wide): 411.9MM **Publicly Held**
WEB: www.centurynationalbank.com
SIC: 6021 National commercial banks
PA: Park National Corporation
50 N 3rd St
Newark OH 43055
740 349-8451

(G-20293)
CENTURY NATIONAL BANK
33 S 5th St (43701-3510)
P.O. Box 1515 (43702-1515)
PHONE..............................800 548-3557
Michael Whiteman, *Senior VP*
EMP: 50
SALES (corp-wide): 411.9MM **Publicly Held**
WEB: www.centurynationalbank.com
SIC: 6021 National commercial banks
HQ: Century National Bank
14 S 5th St
Zanesville OH 43701
740 454-2521

(G-20294)
CENTURY NATIONAL BANK
505 Market St (43701-3610)
PHONE..............................740 455-7330
Jenny Snoud, *Branch Mgr*
EMP: 45
SALES (corp-wide): 411.9MM **Publicly Held**
WEB: www.centurynationalbank.com
SIC: 6035 Federal savings & loan associations
HQ: Century National Bank
14 S 5th St
Zanesville OH 43701
740 454-2521

(G-20295)
CHILD CARE RESOURCES INC (PA)
Also Called: MUSKINGUM COUNTY HEADSTART
1580 Adams Ln Lbby (43701-2606)
PHONE..............................740 454-6251
Jeri Johnson, *Director*
Rachel Morris, *Officer*
Cheryl Bennett, *Assistant*
EMP: 80
SALES: 3.1MM **Privately Held**
WEB: www.ccri.org
SIC: 8351 Head start center, except in conjunction with school

(G-20296)
CITY OF ZANESVILLE
Also Called: Waste Water Treatment Plant
401 Market St Rm 1 (43701-3520)
PHONE..............................740 455-0641
Dan Smith, *Superintendent*
EMP: 30 **Privately Held**
SIC: 4952 Sewerage systems
PA: City Of Zanesville
401 Market St Rm 1
Zanesville OH 43701
740 455-0601

(G-20297)
COMFORT INN
500 Monroe St (43701-3884)
P.O. Box 160 (43702-0160)
PHONE..............................740 454-4144
Timothy Longstreth, *President*
Larry L Wade, *Vice Pres*
EMP: 25
SALES (est): 1.6MM **Privately Held**
SIC: 7011 8661 Hotel, franchised; religious organizations

(G-20298)
COMMUNITY AMBULANCE SERVICE
952 Linden Ave (43701-3062)
PHONE..............................740 454-6800
Greg Beauchemin, *President*
Paul Masterson, *Treasurer*
EMP: 88
SQ FT: 8,000
SALES: 8.6MM
SALES (corp-wide): 462MM **Privately Held**
SIC: 4119 8661 Ambulance service; religious organizations
PA: Genesis Healthcare System
2951 Maple Ave
Zanesville OH 43701
740 454-5000

(G-20299)
DOLGENCORP LLC
Also Called: Dollar General
2505 E Pointe Dr (43701-7761)
PHONE..............................740 588-5700
Sandra Byers, *Human Res Mgr*
Ron Dennis, *Manager*
EMP: 600
SALES (corp-wide): 25.6B **Publicly Held**
SIC: 4225 General warehousing & storage
HQ: Dolgencorp, Llc
100 Mission Rdg
Goodlettsville TN 37072
615 855-4000

(G-20300)
DOWNTHEROAD INC
3625 Maple Ave (43701-1193)
P.O. Box 8071 (43702-8071)
PHONE..............................740 452-4579
Timothy J Hoffer, *President*
Jeff Drennen, *President*
EMP: 33
SALES (est): 7.2MM **Privately Held**
SIC: 5511 7538 Automobiles, new & used; general automotive repair shops

(G-20301)
DUTRO FORD LINCOLN-MERCURY INC (PA)
Also Called: Dutro Nissan
132 S 5th St (43701-3513)
P.O. Box 1265 (43702-1265)
PHONE..............................740 452-6334
James F Graham, *President*

Kenneth D Williams, *Vice Pres*
Doug Roberts, *Manager*
Bryan Graham, *Admin Sec*
EMP: 91
SQ FT: 30,000
SALES (est): 34.8MM **Privately Held**
SIC: 5511 7538 5012 7532 Automobiles,
new & used; pickups, new & used; vans,
new & used; general automotive repair
shops; automobiles & other motor vehi-
cles; top & body repair & paint shops; au-
tomobile & truck equipment & parts

(G-20302)
DVA RENAL HEALTHCARE INC
Also Called: Zanesville Dialysis
3120 Newark Rd (43701-9659)
PHONE...................................740 454-2911
Dave Davis, *Branch Mgr*
EMP: 36 **Publicly Held**
SIC: 8092 Kidney dialysis centers
HQ: Dva Renal Healthcare, Inc.
2000 16th St
Denver CO 80202
253 258-9501

(G-20303)
ECLIPSE RESOURCES - OHIO LLC
4900 Boggs Rd (43701-9491)
P.O. Box 910 (43702-0910)
PHONE...................................740 452-4503
Kristen Heavilin, *Buyer*
Tj Blizzard, *Engineer*
Drew Gray, *Engineer*
Benjamin W Hulburt, *Mng Member*
Bruce Carpenter, *Manager*
EMP: 42
SALES (est): 8.9MM
SALES (corp-wide): 515.1MM **Publicly Held**
SIC: 1381 Drilling oil & gas wells
HQ: Eclipse Resources I, Lp
2121 Old Gatesburg Rd # 110
State College PA 16803
814 308-9754

(G-20304)
ECONOMY LINEN & TOWEL SVC INC
508 Howard St (43701-3637)
PHONE...................................740 454-6888
George Dube, *Manager*
EMP: 200
SALES (corp-wide): 12.5MM **Privately Held**
SIC: 7213 7211 Uniform supply; power
laundries, family & commercial
PA: Economy Linen & Towel Service, Inc.
80 Mead St
Dayton OH 45402
937 222-4625

(G-20305)
ENGLEFIELD INC
Also Called: Zanesville Bulk
1400 Moxahala Ave (43701-5947)
PHONE...................................740 452-2707
EMP: 61
SALES (corp-wide): 615.5MM **Privately Held**
SIC: 5171 Petroleum bulk stations
PA: Englefield, Inc.
447 James Pkwy
Heath OH 43056
740 928-8215

(G-20306)
ENVIRO-FLOW COMPANIES LTD
4830 Northpointe Dr (43701-7273)
PHONE...................................740 453-7980
Jeff Tanner, *President*
Brent Musselman, *Manager*
▲ **EMP:** 31
SQ FT: 30,000
SALES (est): 3.9MM **Privately Held**
WEB: www.enviro-flow.com
SIC: 1711 1623 Plumbing contractors;
heating & air conditioning contractors;
septic system construction; pipeline con-
struction

(G-20307)
FEDEX FREIGHT CORPORATION
1705 Moxahala Ave (43701-5952)
PHONE...................................800 354-9489

EMP: 25
SALES (corp-wide): 65.4B **Publicly Held**
SIC: 4213 4212 Trucking, except local;
local trucking, without storage
HQ: Fedex Freight Corporation
1715 Aaron Brenner Dr
Memphis TN 38120

(G-20308)
FLOW-LINER SYSTEMS LTD
4830 Northpointe Dr (43701-7273)
PHONE...................................800 348-0020
Jeff Tanner, *CEO*
Rick Boles, *Superintendent*
Pam Davis, *Sales Staff*
Brent Musselman, *Manager*
▲ **EMP:** 28 **EST:** 2000
SQ FT: 30,000
SALES (est): 5.8MM **Privately Held**
WEB: www.flow-liner.com
SIC: 3589 1799 Sewage & water treat-
ment equipment; epoxy application

(G-20309)
G & J PEPSI-COLA BOTTLERS INC
Also Called: Pepsico
335 N 6th St (43701-3636)
PHONE...................................740 452-2721
Rick Stone, *Branch Mgr*
EMP: 85
SALES (corp-wide): 418.3MM **Privately Held**
WEB: www.gjpepsi.com
SIC: 2086 5149 Soft drinks: packaged in
cans, bottles, etc.; groceries & related
products
PA: G & J Pepsi-Cola Bottlers Inc
9435 Waterstone Blvd # 390
Cincinnati OH 45249
513 785-6060

(G-20310)
GENESIS HEALTHCARE SYSTEM (PA)
Also Called: Bethesda Care
2951 Maple Ave (43701-1406)
PHONE...................................740 454-5000
Matthew Perry, *President*
Mark Gressley, *General Mgr*
Al Burns, *COO*
Kathy Brock, *Project Dir*
Ron Chaffin, *Opers Staff*
EMP: 1500
SALES: 462MM **Privately Held**
SIC: 8062 General medical & surgical hos-
pitals

(G-20311)
GENESIS HEALTHCARE SYSTEM
Also Called: Kiddie Kollege & Academy
1238 Pfeifer Dr (43701-1354)
PHONE...................................740 453-4959
Barbara Fisher, *Exec Dir*
EMP: 50
SALES (corp-wide): 462MM **Privately Held**
SIC: 8351 Child day care services
PA: Genesis Healthcare System
2951 Maple Ave
Zanesville OH 43701
740 454-5000

(G-20312)
GOSS SUPPLY COMPANY (PA)
620 Marietta St (43701-3633)
P.O. Box 2580 (43702-2580)
PHONE...................................740 454-2571
Terry L Goss, *President*
Pasquale Gallina, *Principal*
Clarence A Goss, *Principal*
Don J Hollingsworth, *Principal*
Andy Goss, *Vice Pres*
EMP: 55 **EST:** 1954
SQ FT: 40,000
SALES (est): 39.6MM **Privately Held**
WEB: www.gosssupply.com
SIC: 5085 Hose, belting & packing

(G-20313)
GOTTLIEB JOHNSON BEAM DAL P
320 Main St (43701-3426)
P.O. Box 190 (43702-0190)
PHONE...................................740 452-7555
Toll Free:...................................888 -
Cole Gerzner, *Managing Prtnr*
Jeff R Beam, *Partner*
Miles D Fries, *Partner*
James R Krischak, *Partner*
Don Dal Ponte, *Partner*
EMP: 26
SQ FT: 3,500
SALES (est): 2.5MM **Privately Held**
SIC: 8111 General practice attorney,
lawyer; general practice law office

(G-20314)
HALLIBURTON ENERGY SVCS INC
4999 E Pointe Dr (43701-7680)
PHONE...................................740 617-2917
EMP: 101 **Publicly Held**
SIC: 1389 Oil field services
HQ: Halliburton Energy Services, Inc.
3000 N Sam Houston Pkwy E
Houston TX 77032
281 871-4000

(G-20315)
HARTLAND PETROLEUM LLC
4560 West Pike (43701-7175)
PHONE...................................740 452-3115
William Snedegar,
EMP: 50
SALES (est): 12.8MM **Privately Held**
SIC: 5172 Fuel oil

(G-20316)
HEALTH CARE SPECIALISTS
945 Bethesda Dr Ste 300 (43701-1880)
PHONE...................................740 454-4530
Myron Knell, *President*
Diane Decenso, *Med Doctor*
EMP: 32
SALES (est): 1.8MM **Privately Held**
SIC: 8062 General medical & surgical hos-
pitals

(G-20317)
HELEN PURCELL HOME
1854 Norwood Blvd (43701-2337)
PHONE...................................740 453-1745
Robert Moehrman Jr, *President*
Nancy Rutledge, *Mktg Dir*
Gina Dilly, *Director*
R Moehrman Jr, *Administration*
EMP: 50
SQ FT: 55,000
SALES: 2.3MM **Privately Held**
SIC: 8361 Home for the aged

(G-20318)
HOSPICE OF GENESIS HEALTH
Also Called: Genesis Hspces Pallitaive Care
713 Forest Ave (43701-2819)
PHONE...................................740 454-5381
Renee Sparks, *Manager*
Sally Scheffler, *Director*
EMP: 43
SALES (est): 1MM **Privately Held**
SIC: 8062 8082 8051 General medical &
surgical hospitals; home health care serv-
ices; skilled nursing care facilities

(G-20319)
HUNTINGTON NATIONAL BANK
422 Main St (43701-3516)
P.O. Box 4658 (43702)
PHONE...................................740 452-8444
Mark Carpenter, *Manager*
EMP: 50
SALES (corp-wide): 5.2B **Publicly Held**
WEB: www.huntingtonnationalbank.com
SIC: 6029 6021 Commercial banks; na-
tional commercial banks
HQ: The Huntington National Bank
17 S High St Fl 1
Columbus OH 43215
614 480-4293

(G-20320)
INTER HEALT CARE OF NORTH OH I
Also Called: Interim Healthcare
2809 Bell St Ste D (43701-1741)
PHONE...................................740 453-5130
Deb Studer, *Manager*
EMP: 100
SALES (corp-wide): 19.8MM **Privately Held**
SIC: 8082 Home health care services
HQ: Interim Health Care Of Northwestern
Ohio, Inc
3100 W Central Ave # 250
Toledo OH 43606

(G-20321)
JOE MCCLELLAND INC (PA)
Also Called: O K Coal & Concrete
98 E La Salle St (43701-6281)
P.O. Box 1815 (43702-1815)
PHONE...................................740 452-3036
Joe Mc Clelland, *President*
Jack Mc Clelland, *Vice Pres*
Michael McClelland, *Vice Pres*
Richard Mc Clelland, *Treasurer*
Gala Lemon, *Admin Sec*
EMP: 25 **EST:** 1934
SQ FT: 1,500
SALES (est): 6.7MM **Privately Held**
WEB: www.okcoalandconcrete.com
SIC: 3273 7992 1442 Ready-mixed con-
crete; public golf courses; construction
sand & gravel

(G-20322)
JUVENILE COURT CNTY MUSKINGUM
1860 East Pike (43701-4619)
PHONE...................................740 453-0351
Joseph A Gormley, *Principal*
EMP: 25
SALES (est): 808.1K **Privately Held**
SIC: 8322 Child related social services

(G-20323)
KESSLER SIGN COMPANY (PA)
Also Called: Kessler Outdoor Advertising
2669 National Rd (43701-8257)
P.O. Box 785 (43702-0785)
PHONE...................................740 453-0668
Robert Kessler, *President*
Rodger Kessler, *Vice Pres*
Dave Kessler, *VP Opers*
Elaine Kessler, *Treasurer*
Elaine Kessler-Kuntz, *Treasurer*
EMP: 50
SQ FT: 25,000
SALES (est): 7.4MM **Privately Held**
WEB: www.kesslersignco.com
SIC: 3993 7312 Signs, not made in cus-
tom sign painting shops; outdoor advertis-
ing services

(G-20324)
LEPI ENTERPRISES INC
630 Gw Morse St (43701-3304)
P.O. Box 457 (43702-0457)
PHONE...................................740 453-2980
James Lepi, *President*
Cathy L George, *Principal*
Kenneth M Mortimer, *Principal*
Jeff Lepi, *Corp Secy*
Michael Lepi, *Vice Pres*
EMP: 100
SQ FT: 20,000
SALES (est): 16.7MM **Privately Held**
WEB: www.lepienterprises.com
SIC: 1799 1541 Asbestos removal & en-
capsulation; lead burning; industrial build-
ings & warehouses

(G-20325)
LOVE N COMFORT HOME CARE
2814 Maple Ave (43701-1716)
PHONE...................................740 450-7658
Mick Buck, *Branch Mgr*
EMP: 50 **EST:** 2008
SALES (est): 596.6K **Privately Held**
SIC: 8082 Home health care services

(G-20326)
LOWES HOME CENTERS LLC
3755 Frazeysburg Rd (43701-1015)
PHONE...................................740 450-5500

Edmund Wanat, *Store Mgr*
Chapman Joe, *Manager*
EMP: 150
SALES (corp-wide): 68.6B **Publicly Held**
SIC: 5211 5031 5722 5064 Home centers; building materials, exterior; building materials, interior; household appliance stores; electrical appliances, television & radio
HQ: Lowe's Home Centers, Llc
    1605 Curtis Bridge Rd
    Wilkesboro NC 28697
    336 658-4000

(G-20327)
LUBURGH INC (PA)
4174 East Pike (43701-8425)
PHONE.................................740 452-3668
Otto Luburgh, *President*
Henry Luburgh, *Vice Pres*
Andrew Luburgh, *Admin Sec*
EMP: 30
SALES (est): 10.2MM **Privately Held**
SIC: 1794 Excavation work

(G-20328)
MAN-TANSKY INC
Also Called: Tansky Honda
3260 Maple Ave (43701-1313)
PHONE.................................740 454-2512
James Kobunski, *Vice Pres*
James J Kobunski, *Vice Pres*
EMP: 38
SQ FT: 20,000
SALES (est): 11.7MM **Privately Held**
WEB: www.tansky.com
SIC: 5511 7538 5531 Automobiles, new & used; general automotive repair shops; automotive parts

(G-20329)
MATTINGLY FOODS INC (PA)
302 State St (43701-3200)
P.O. Box 760 (43702-0760)
PHONE.................................740 454-0136
Rick Barnes, *CEO*
Barbara Callahan, *President*
Angie Schmidt, *Exec VP*
Andrew Hess, *Vice Pres*
Benjamin Hess, *Vice Pres*
EMP: 235
SQ FT: 225,000
SALES (est): 104.9MM **Privately Held**
WEB: www.mattinglyfoods.com
SIC: 5149 5142 5141 Canned goods: fruit, vegetables, seafood, meats, etc.; milk, canned or dried; fruit juices, frozen; vegetables, frozen; fish, frozen: packaged; meat, frozen: packaged; groceries, general line

(G-20330)
MERRILL LYNCH PIERCE FENNER
905 Zane St Ste 3 (43701-3840)
PHONE.................................740 452-3681
Merrill Lhancock, *Branch Mgr*
Mark Moyer, *Agent*
EMP: 27
SALES (corp-wide): 110.5B **Publicly Held**
SIC: 6211 Security brokers & dealers
HQ: Merrill Lynch, Pierce, Fenner & Smith Incorporated
    111 8th Ave
    New York NY 10011
    800 637-7455

(G-20331)
MIDWEST RETINA INC
2935 Maple Ave (43701-1487)
PHONE.................................614 233-9500
EMP: 27
SALES (corp-wide): 2.9MM **Privately Held**
SIC: 8011 Ophthalmologist
PA: Midwest Retina, Inc.
    6655 Post Rd
    Dublin OH 43016
    614 339-8500

(G-20332)
MODERN GLASS PNT & TILE CO INC
933 Linden Ave (43701-3049)
PHONE.................................740 454-1253

John W Melsheimer, *President*
James D Spargrove, *Corp Secy*
Robert R Melsheimer, *Vice Pres*
EMP: 31 **EST:** 1951
SQ FT: 12,000
SALES (est): 9.1MM **Privately Held**
SIC: 1793 5713 5231 Glass & glazing work; floor covering stores; paint; wallcoverings

(G-20333)
MUSKINGUM CNTY CTR FOR SENIORS
160 Nth St (43701)
PHONE.................................740 454-9761
Ann Combs, *Exec Dir*
Kurt Ufholz, *Officer*
Cindy Sheppard, *Receptionist*
EMP: 30
SQ FT: 36,000
SALES: 1.8MM **Privately Held**
SIC: 8322 Senior citizens' center or association

(G-20334)
MUSKINGUM COUNTY ADULT AND CHI
Also Called: Avondale Youth Center
4155 Roseville Rd (43701-8224)
PHONE.................................740 849-2344
Gary King, *Director*
EMP: 25
SALES (est): 901.3K **Privately Held**
SIC: 8322 Youth center

(G-20335)
MUSKINGUM COUNTY OHIO
Also Called: Senior Nutrition
160 N 4th St (43701-3518)
PHONE.................................740 452-0678
Carol Morgan, *Supervisor*
Jodi Paul, *Supervisor*
Ann Combs, *Exec Dir*
Terry Dunn, *Director*
Earl Stapleton, *Food Svc Dir*
EMP: 60 **Privately Held**
SIC: 8322 4119 Senior citizens' center or association; meal delivery program; local passenger transportation
PA: Muskingum County, Ohio
    401 Main St
    Zanesville OH 43701
    740 455-7100

(G-20336)
MUSKINGUM COUNTY OHIO
Also Called: Muskingum County Home
401 Main St (43701-3519)
PHONE.................................740 454-1911
Rebecca Cooper, *Director*
EMP: 100 **Privately Held**
SIC: 8051 8052 Convalescent home with continuous nursing care; intermediate care facilities
PA: Muskingum County, Ohio
    401 Main St
    Zanesville OH 43701
    740 455-7100

(G-20337)
MUSKINGUM COUNTY OHIO
Also Called: Muskingum County Engineers Off
155 Rehl Rd (43701-2730)
PHONE.................................740 453-0381
Dug Davis, *Manager*
EMP: 40 **Privately Held**
SIC: 8711 Engineering services
PA: Muskingum County, Ohio
    401 Main St
    Zanesville OH 43701
    740 455-7100

(G-20338)
MUSKINGUM IRON & METAL CO
345 Arthur St (43701-5850)
P.O. Box 815 (43702-0815)
PHONE.................................740 452-9351
Jack Joseph, *President*
Arthur L Joseph, *Principal*
Shirley L Joseph, *Principal*
Stanley I Joseph, *Principal*
Josh Joseph, *Vice Pres*
EMP: 36 **EST:** 1929
SQ FT: 30,000

SALES (est): 17.4MM **Privately Held**
WEB: www.muskingumiron.com
SIC: 5093 Nonferrous metals scrap; ferrous metal scrap & waste

(G-20339)
MUSKINGUM LIVESTOCK SALES INC
Also Called: Muskingum Livestock Auction
944 Malinda St (43701-3854)
P.O. Box 2003 (43702-2003)
PHONE.................................740 452-9984
David Dailey, *CEO*
Dennis Ruff, *President*
Eloise Barnett, *Corp Secy*
EMP: 35
SQ FT: 20,000
SALES (est): 4.9MM **Privately Held**
WEB: www.muskingumlivestock.com
SIC: 5154 Auctioning livestock; hogs; sheep

(G-20340)
MUSKINGUM RESIDENTIALS INC
1900 Montgomery Ave (43701-2617)
P.O. Box 2415 (43702-2415)
PHONE.................................740 453-5350
Jerri Elson, *Exec Dir*
EMP: 25
SALES: 1.1MM **Privately Held**
SIC: 8361 Home for the mentally handicapped

(G-20341)
MUSKINGUM STARLIGHT INDUSTRIES (PA)
1304 Newark Rd (43701-2621)
PHONE.................................740 453-4622
Mary Thompson Sufferd, *Director*
Larry Wheeler, *Director*
EMP: 175 **EST:** 1959
SQ FT: 11,500
SALES (est): 673.3K **Privately Held**
SIC: 8331 Sheltered workshop

(G-20342)
MUSKINGUM STARLIGHT INDUSTRIES
Also Called: Starlight Special School
1330 Newark Rd (43701-2623)
PHONE.................................740 453-4622
Larry Wheeler, *General Mgr*
Nancy Goff, *Principal*
EMP: 70
SALES (est): 3.3MM
SALES (corp-wide): 673.3K **Privately Held**
SIC: 8731 8211 Commercial physical research; private special education school
PA: Muskingum Starlight Industries Inc
    1304 Newark Rd
    Zanesville OH 43701
    740 453-4622

(G-20343)
NATIONAL GAS & OIL CORPORATION
1423 Lake Dr (43701-5922)
PHONE.................................740 454-7252
Dan Price, *Manager*
EMP: 31
SALES (corp-wide): 65.2MM **Privately Held**
WEB: www.theenergycoop.com
SIC: 4923 4924 4922 Gas transmission & distribution; natural gas distribution; natural gas transmission
HQ: The National Gas & Oil Corporation
    1500 Granville Rd
    Newark OH 43055
    740 344-2102

(G-20344)
NEFF MACHINERY AND SUPPLIES
Also Called: Neff Parts
112 S Shawnee Ave (43701-6221)
P.O. Box 1822 (43702-1822)
PHONE.................................740 454-0128
Robert Neff, *President*
EMP: 30
SQ FT: 20,000

SALES (est): 3.8MM **Privately Held**
SIC: 3599 5084 5013 Machine & other job shop work; machine tools & accessories; motor vehicle supplies & new parts

(G-20345)
NEFF PAVING LTD (PA)
6575 West Pike (43701-8163)
PHONE.................................740 453-3063
Clint Berkfield, *President*
Krysta Berkfield, *Treasurer*
EMP: 25
SALES (est): 5.3MM **Privately Held**
SIC: 1611 Highway & street paving contractor; surfacing & paving

(G-20346)
NORTH HILLS MANAGEMENT COMPANY
Also Called: Inn At North Hills
1575 Bowers Ln Apt C13 (43701-7021)
PHONE.................................740 450-9999
Jerry McClain, *President*
Debbie Booth, *Vice Pres*
Joann Butcher, *Vice Pres*
Diane Katon, *Admin Sec*
EMP: 82
SQ FT: 55,000
SALES (est): 2.3MM **Privately Held**
SIC: 8361 8052 Residential care; intermediate care facilities

(G-20347)
NORTH VALLEY BANK (PA)
2775 Maysville Pike (43701-9772)
P.O. Box 1115 (43702-1115)
PHONE.................................740 452-7920
Carl Raines, *President*
Jesse Rollins, *President*
Julie Paxton, *General Mgr*
Greg Ashby, *Vice Pres*
Theresa Barnhart, *Vice Pres*
EMP: 25 **EST:** 1904
SQ FT: 6,000
SALES: 9.9MM **Privately Held**
WEB: www.nvboh.com
SIC: 6022 State commercial banks

(G-20348)
OHIO MACHINERY CO
Also Called: Caterpillar Authorized Dealer
3415 East Pike (43701-8419)
PHONE.................................740 453-0563
Rick Hensel, *Manager*
Rick Hinsle, *Manager*
Cody Sprankle, *Supervisor*
EMP: 50
SQ FT: 18,000
SALES (corp-wide): 222.7MM **Privately Held**
WEB: www.enginesnow.com
SIC: 5082 7629 General construction machinery & equipment; electrical repair shops
PA: Ohio Machinery Co.
    3993 E Royalton Rd
    Broadview Heights OH 44147
    440 526-6200

(G-20349)
OHIO TEXTILE SERVICE INC
2270 Fairview Rd (43701-8810)
P.O. Box 8048 (43702-8048)
PHONE.................................740 450-4900
David M Struminger, *President*
Donald L Struminger, *Chairman*
EMP: 45
SALES (est): 3.2MM
SALES (corp-wide): 22.3MM **Privately Held**
WEB: www.mohenis.com
SIC: 7213 Linen supply
PA: Mohenis Services, Inc.
    875 E Bank St
    Petersburg VA 23803
    800 879-3315

(G-20350)
ORIGINAL HARTSTONE POTTERY INC
1719 Dearborn St (43701-5299)
PHONE.................................740 452-9999
John McMillan, *President*
Wess Foltz, *Vice Pres*
EMP: 30

GEOGRAPHIC

SALES (est): 6MM Privately Held
WEB: www.hartstonepottery.com
SIC: 5023 Pottery

(G-20351)
ORTHOPEDIC ASSOC OF ZANESVILLE
2854 Bell St (43701-1721)
PHONE.................................740 454-3273
Karl C Saunders, *President*
Deb Apperson, *Administration*
Casey Daugherty,
EMP: 45
SALES (est): 6.2MM Privately Held
SIC: 8011 Orthopedic physician

(G-20352)
P & D TRANSPORTATION INC (PA)
Also Called: Putnam Truck Load Direct
1705 Moxahala Ave (43701-5952)
P.O. Box 2909 (43702-2909)
PHONE.................................740 454-1221
Patrick L Hennessey, *President*
Dan Hennessey, *Vice Pres*
Ronald J Kunkel, *Treasurer*
EMP: 115
SALES (est): 21.3MM Privately Held
SIC: 4213 Contract haulers

(G-20353)
PEABODY COAL COMPANY
2810 East Pike Apt 3 (43701-9197)
PHONE.................................740 450-2420
J T Kneen, *Principal*
EMP: 312
SALES (corp-wide): 5.5B Publicly Held
SIC: 1241 Coal mining services
HQ: Peabody Coal Company
    701 Market St
    Saint Louis MO 63101
    314 342-3400

(G-20354)
PHILO BAND BOOSTERS
1359 Wheeling Ave (43701-4538)
PHONE.................................740 221-3023
Chad Stemm, *Finance Dir*
EMP: 30
SALES (est): 96.3K Privately Held
SIC: 7929 Entertainers & entertainment groups

(G-20355)
PRIMECARE SUTHEASTERN OHIO INC
1210 Ashland Ave (43701-2883)
PHONE.................................740 454-8551
Daniel Sher, *Vice Pres*
EMP: 45 Privately Held
SIC: 8011 Group health association
PA: Primecare Of Southeastern Ohio, Inc.
    860 Bethesda Dr Ste 3
    Zanesville OH 43701

(G-20356)
PROFESSIONAL PLUMBING SERVICES
3570 Old Wheeling Rd (43701-9684)
PHONE.................................740 454-1066
Michael L Burkhart, *President*
Catherine Nash Burkhart, *Treasurer*
Sandra Findeiss, *Info Tech Mgr*
EMP: 28
SQ FT: 5,200
SALES: 2.7MM Privately Held
SIC: 1711 Plumbing contractors; warm air heating & air conditioning contractor

(G-20357)
RANKIN & RANKIN INC
806 Market St (43701-3718)
P.O. Box 2547 (43702-2547)
PHONE.................................740 452-7575
Robert S Glass, *President*
Lisa Curby, *Manager*
Matt Joseph, *Agent*
Billi Parker, *Agent*
EMP: 25
SALES (est): 4.6MM Privately Held
WEB: www.rankininsurance.com
SIC: 6411 Insurance agents

(G-20358)
RESIDENTIAL HOME FOR THE DEVLP
Also Called: Rhdd
3484 Old Wheeling Rd (43701-0904)
PHONE.................................740 452-5133
Lisa Reed, *Director*
Tricia Rasor, *Nursing Dir*
EMP: 30
SALES (corp-wide): 8.4MM Privately Held
WEB: www.reliabledist.com
SIC: 8361 Home for the mentally handicapped
PA: Residential Home For The Developmentally Disabled Incorporated
    925 Chestnut St
    Coshocton OH 43812
    740 622-9778

(G-20359)
ROBERT NEFF & SON INC
132 S Shawnee Ave (43701-6221)
P.O. Box 1822 (43702-1822)
PHONE.................................740 454-0128
Robert G Neff, *President*
EMP: 40 EST: 1939
SQ FT: 7,000
SALES: 2MM Privately Held
SIC: 4212 4213 Coal haulage, local; mail carriers, contract; trucking, except local

(G-20360)
SHELLY AND SANDS INC
3570 S River Rd (43701-9052)
PHONE.................................740 453-0721
Matt Kelley, *Vice Pres*
EMP: 35
SALES (corp-wide): 276.3MM Privately Held
WEB: www.shellyandsands.com
SIC: 1611 2951 1442 1771 Highway & street paving contractor; asphalt & asphaltic paving mixtures (not from refineries); construction sand & gravel; concrete work
PA: Shelly And Sands, Inc.
    3570 S River Rd
    Zanesville OH 43701
    740 453-0721

(G-20361)
SIDWELL MATERIALS INC
4200 Maysville Pike (43701-9372)
P.O. Box 192, White Cottage (43791-0192)
PHONE.................................740 849-2394
Jeffrey R Sidwell, *President*
EMP: 130
SALES (est): 21.3MM Privately Held
SIC: 1795 4953 2951 1422 Demolition, buildings & other structures; rubbish collection & disposal; asphalt paving mixtures & blocks; crushed & broken limestone; brick, stone & related material

(G-20362)
SOUTHEAST AREA TRANSIT (PA)
Also Called: Z-Bus
375 Fairbanks St (43701-3043)
PHONE.................................740 454-8574
Mark McClanan, *General Mgr*
Rich Wood, *Maintenance Dir*
Arlene Johnson, *Supervisor*
Dianne Gill, *Director*
Holly Grimes, *Admin Asst*
EMP: 26
SQ FT: 9,974
SALES (est): 3MM Privately Held
SIC: 4111 Local & suburban transit

(G-20363)
SOUTHEASTERN OHIO BRDCSTG SYS
Also Called: Whiz Am-Fm
629 Downard Rd (43701-5108)
PHONE.................................740 452-5431
Norma Littick, *Ch of Bd*
Henry Littick, *President*
Barbara Saunders, *Corp Secy*
Jay Benson, *Sales Staff*
EMP: 25
SQ FT: 10,000

SALES (est): 1.8MM Privately Held
SIC: 4832 Radio broadcasting stations, music format

(G-20364)
SOUTHEASTERN OHIO TV SYS (PA)
Also Called: Whiz-TV
629 Downard Rd (43701-5108)
PHONE.................................740 452-5431
Henry Littick, *Partner*
Barbara Saunders, *Partner*
Brian Wagner, *Program Dir*
EMP: 26 EST: 1953
SQ FT: 10,000
SALES (est): 10.4MM Privately Held
WEB: www.whizamfmtv.com
SIC: 4832 4833 Radio broadcasting stations, music format; television broadcasting stations

(G-20365)
SPECTRUM MGT HOLDG CO LLC
Also Called: Time Warner
737 Howard St (43701-3757)
PHONE.................................740 455-9705
Terry Oconnell, *President*
EMP: 83
SALES (corp-wide): 43.6B Publicly Held
SIC: 4841 Cable television services
HQ: Spectrum Management Holding Company, Llc
    400 Atlantic St
    Stamford CT 06901
    203 905-7801

(G-20366)
THOMAS E ROJEWSKI MD INC
Also Called: Booth, Jack B MD
2945 Maple Ave (43701-1762)
PHONE.................................740 454-0158
Thomas E Rojewski MD, *President*
Brenda Halberstadp, *Office Mgr*
EMP: 28
SALES (est): 1MM Privately Held
SIC: 8011 Surgeon

(G-20367)
TOWN HOUSE MOTOR LODGE CORP
Also Called: Best Western
135 N 7th St (43701-3707)
P.O. Box 160 (43702-0160)
PHONE.................................740 452-4511
Larry Wade, *President*
Timothy Longstreth, *Corp Secy*
EMP: 32
SQ FT: 40,000
SALES: 500K Privately Held
SIC: 7011 5812 5813 Bed & breakfast inn; American restaurant; cocktail lounge

(G-20368)
TRILOGY REHAB SERVICES LLC
2991 Maple Ave (43701-1499)
PHONE.................................740 452-3000
EMP: 1165
SALES (corp-wide): 149MM Privately Held
SIC: 8051 Skilled nursing care facilities
PA: Trilogy Rehab Services, Llc
    303 N Hurstbourne Pkwy # 200
    Louisville KY 40222
    800 335-1060

(G-20369)
U S XPRESS INC
2705 E Pointe Dr (43701-7294)
PHONE.................................740 452-4153
Duane Stare, *Manager*
EMP: 124 Publicly Held
SIC: 4213 Contract haulers
HQ: U. S. Xpress, Inc.
    4080 Jenkins Rd
    Chattanooga TN 37421
    866 266-7270

(G-20370)
UNITED PARCEL SERVICE INC OH
Also Called: UPS
1507 Augusta St (43701-4155)
PHONE.................................800 742-5877

EMP: 158
SALES (corp-wide): 71.8B Publicly Held
WEB: www.upsscs.com
SIC: 4215 Package delivery, vehicular; parcel delivery, vehicular
HQ: United Parcel Service, Inc. (Oh)
    55 Glenlake Pkwy
    Atlanta GA 30328
    404 828-6000

(G-20371)
VALLEY VIEW PLACE
3200 Shale Dr (43701)
PHONE.................................740 454-7720
EMP: 200 EST: 2014
SQ FT: 40,524
SALES (est): 2MM Privately Held
SIC: 6531 Real Estate Agent/Manager

(G-20372)
VICTOR MCKENZIE DRILLING CO
3596 Maple Ave Ste A (43701-1686)
P.O. Box 3323 (43702-3323)
PHONE.................................740 453-0834
Victor McKenzie, *President*
Sandy McKenzie, *Corp Secy*
EMP: 27
SALES (est): 1.5MM Privately Held
SIC: 1381 Drilling oil & gas wells

(G-20373)
ZANDEX INC (PA)
Also Called: Zandex Health Care
1122 Taylor St (43701-2658)
P.O. Box 730 (43702-0730)
PHONE.................................740 454-1400
Douglas L Ramsay, *President*
Stoey Stout, *Vice Pres*
Lyle Clark, *CFO*
Starla Peterson, *Admin Sec*
EMP: 25
SQ FT: 1,500
SALES (est): 34MM Privately Held
SIC: 8052 8051 Intermediate care facilities; skilled nursing care facilities

(G-20374)
ZANDEX INC
Also Called: Apartments of Cedar Hill
1126 Adair Ave (43701-2804)
PHONE.................................740 452-2087
Cindy Clark, *Manager*
EMP: 30
SALES (corp-wide): 34MM Privately Held
SIC: 8361 Home for the aged
PA: Zandex, Inc.
    1122 Taylor St
    Zanesville OH 43701
    740 454-1400

(G-20375)
ZANDEX INC
Also Called: Adams Lane Care Center
1856 Adams Ln (43701-2612)
PHONE.................................740 454-9769
Dave Wilson, *Branch Mgr*
EMP: 180
SALES (corp-wide): 34MM Privately Held
SIC: 8052 8051 Intermediate care facilities; skilled nursing care facilities
PA: Zandex, Inc.
    1122 Taylor St
    Zanesville OH 43701
    740 454-1400

(G-20376)
ZANDEX INC
Also Called: Cedar Hill Care Center
1136 Adair Ave (43701-2804)
PHONE.................................740 454-6823
Rich Stephens, *Branch Mgr*
EMP: 90
SALES (corp-wide): 34MM Privately Held
SIC: 8052 8051 Personal care facility; skilled nursing care facilities
PA: Zandex, Inc.
    1122 Taylor St
    Zanesville OH 43701
    740 454-1400

(G-20377)
**ZANDEX HEALTH CARE
CORPORATION**
Also Called: Ceder Hill
1136 Adair Ave (43701-2804)
PHONE...................................740 452-4636
Linda Calindine, *President*
Dr Kurt Southam, *President*
Rich Stephens, *Manager*
EMP: 155
SALES (corp-wide): 34MM **Privately
Held**
SIC: **8052** 8051 Intermediate care facili-
ties; skilled nursing care facilities
HQ: Zandex Health Care Corporation
1122 Taylor St
Zanesville OH 43701

(G-20378)
**ZANDEX HEALTH CARE
CORPORATION**
Also Called: Adams Lane Care Center
1856 Adams Ln (43701-2612)
P.O. Box 638 (43702-0638)
PHONE...................................740 454-9769
Cathy Kocher, *Administration*
EMP: 175
SQ FT: 20,000
SALES (corp-wide): 34MM **Privately
Held**
SIC: **8052** 8051 Intermediate care facili-
ties; skilled nursing care facilities
HQ: Zandex Health Care Corporation
1122 Taylor St
Zanesville OH 43701

(G-20379)
**ZANDEX HEALTH CARE
CORPORATION (HQ)**
Also Called: Cedar Hill Care Center
1122 Taylor St (43701-2658)
P.O. Box 730 (43702-0730)
PHONE...................................740 454-1400
Douglas Ramsey, *President*
Stoey Stout, *Vice Pres*
Lyle Clark, *CFO*
EMP: 25
SQ FT: 1,000
SALES (est): 34MM **Privately Held**
SIC: **8052** 8059 8051 Intermediate care
facilities; rest home, with health care;
skilled nursing care facilities; extended
care facility
PA: Zandex, Inc.
1122 Taylor St
Zanesville OH 43701
740 454-1400

(G-20380)
**ZANDEX HEALTH CARE
CORPORATION**
Also Called: Willow Haven Nursing Home
1020 Taylor St (43701-2656)
P.O. Box 2038 (43702-2038)
PHONE...................................740 454-9747
Mary Anne Whickham, *Office Mgr*
Mark Richard, *Manager*
EMP: 120
SALES (corp-wide): 34MM **Privately
Held**
SIC: **8051** 8052 8059 Convalescent home
with continuous nursing care; intermedi-
ate care facilities; rest home, with health
care
HQ: Zandex Health Care Corporation
1122 Taylor St
Zanesville OH 43701

(G-20381)
**ZANESVILLE CHEVROLET
CADILLAC**
3657 Maple Ave (43701-1193)
PHONE...................................740 452-3611
Derek A Truss, *President*
Henry Walters, *Treasurer*
EMP: 27 EST: 1922
SQ FT: 50,000
SALES: 12MM **Privately Held**
SIC: **5511** 7538 Automobiles, new & used;
pickups, new & used; general automotive
repair shops

(G-20382)
ZANESVILLE COUNTRY CLUB
1300 Country Club Dr (43701-1464)
P.O. Box 2490 (43702-2490)
PHONE...................................740 452-2726
Michael Micheli, *President*
Michael Barron, *General Mgr*
Ken Corbin, *Vice Pres*
EMP: 35 EST: 1931
SQ FT: 15,000
SALES: 2.6MM **Privately Held**
SIC: **7997** Country club, membership;
swimming club, membership; tennis club,
membership; golf club, membership

(G-20383)
**ZANESVILLE METRO HSING
AUTH (PA)**
407 Pershing Rd (43701-6871)
PHONE...................................740 454-9714
Steven G Randles, *Exec Dir*
EMP: 59
SALES: 12.8MM **Privately Held**
WEB: www.zanesvillehousing.org
SIC: **6513** Apartment building operators

(G-20384)
ZANESVILLE NH LLC
Also Called: ZANESVILLE HEALTH AND RE-
HABILI
4200 Harrington Dr (43701-6022)
PHONE...................................740 452-4351
Mordecai Rosenberg, *President*
Ronald Swartz, *CFO*
Lisa Schwartz, *Admin Sec*
EMP: 54 EST: 2015
SALES (est): 373.2K **Privately Held**
SIC: **8051** Skilled nursing care facilities

(G-20385)
**ZANESVILLE SURGERY CENTER
LLC**
2907 Bell St (43701-1720)
PHONE...................................740 453-5713
Glenda Rogers, *Administration*
EMP: 55
SALES (est): 3.5MM **Privately Held**
SIC: **8011** Ambulatory surgical center; sur-
geon

(G-20386)
**ZANESVILLE WELFARE
ORGANIZATIO**
3610 West Pike (43701-9335)
PHONE...................................740 450-6060
Lou Cventic, *President*
EMP: 285
SALES: 7.3MM **Privately Held**
SIC: **8699** 8331 Charitable organization;
job training & vocational rehabilitation
services; vocational training agency

(G-20387)
**ZANESVLLE WELFRE
ORGNZTN/GOODW (PA)**
Also Called: Goodwill Retail Store
3610 West Pike (43701-9335)
PHONE...................................740 450-6060
Louis Cvetnic, *CEO*
EMP: 30 EST: 1914
SQ FT: 40,000
SALES: 10.3MM **Privately Held**
SIC: **8331** 5932 Sheltered workshop; used
merchandise stores

(G-20388)
ZEMBA BROS INC
3401 East Pike (43701-8419)
P.O. Box 1270 (43702-1270)
PHONE...................................740 452-1880
Scott M Zemba, *President*
Susan Zemba, *Administration*
EMP: 47
SQ FT: 36,000
SALES (est): 11.2MM **Privately Held**
SIC: **1794** 1711 1623 4212 Excavation &
grading, building construction; septic sys-
tem construction; sewer line construction;
local trucking, without storage

(PA)=Parent Co (HQ)=Headquarters (DH)=Div Headquarters
✪ = New Business established in last 2 years   2019 Harris Ohio
Services Directory

821

SIC INDEX

Standard Industrial Classification Alphabetical Index

SIC NO	PRODUCT

A

6321 Accident & Health Insurance
8721 Accounting, Auditing & Bookkeeping Svcs
7322 Adjustment & Collection Svcs
7311 Advertising Agencies
7319 Advertising, NEC
4513 Air Courier Svcs
4522 Air Transportation, Nonscheduled
4512 Air Transportation, Scheduled
4581 Airports, Flying Fields & Terminal Svcs
7999 Amusement & Recreation Svcs, NEC
7996 Amusement Parks
0291 Animal Production, NEC
0752 Animal Specialty Svcs, Exc Veterinary
1231 Anthracite Mining
8422 Arboreta, Botanical & Zoological Gardens
8712 Architectural Services
7694 Armature Rewinding Shops
7521 Automobile Parking Lots & Garages
5012 Automobiles & Other Motor Vehicles Wholesale
7533 Automotive Exhaust System Repair Shops
7536 Automotive Glass Replacement Shops
7539 Automotive Repair Shops, NEC
7549 Automotive Svcs, Except Repair & Car Washes
7537 Automotive Transmission Repair Shops

B

7929 Bands, Orchestras, Actors & Entertainers
7241 Barber Shops
7231 Beauty Shops
0211 Beef Cattle Feedlots
5181 Beer & Ale Wholesale
0171 Berry Crops
1221 Bituminous Coal & Lignite: Surface Mining
1222 Bituminous Coal: Underground Mining
5192 Books, Periodicals & Newspapers Wholesale
7933 Bowling Centers
5032 Brick, Stone & Related Construction Mtrls Wholesale
1622 Bridge, Tunnel & Elevated Hwy Construction
7349 Building Cleaning & Maintenance Svcs, NEC
4142 Bus Charter Service, Except Local
4173 Bus Terminal & Svc Facilities
8611 Business Associations
8748 Business Consulting Svcs, NEC
7389 Business Svcs, NEC

C

4841 Cable & Other Pay TV Svcs
7542 Car Washes
1751 Carpentry Work
7217 Carpet & Upholstery Cleaning
0119 Cash Grains, NEC
6553 Cemetery Subdividers & Developers
1479 Chemical & Fertilizer Mining
5169 Chemicals & Allied Prdts, NEC Wholesale
0251 Chicken & Poultry Farms
0252 Chicken Egg Farms
8351 Child Day Care Svcs
8641 Civic, Social & Fraternal Associations
1459 Clay, Ceramic & Refractory Minerals, NEC
5052 Coal & Other Minerals & Ores Wholesale
1241 Coal Mining Svcs
7215 Coin Operated Laundries & Cleaning
7993 Coin-Operated Amusement Devices & Arcades
4939 Combination Utilities, NEC
7336 Commercial Art & Graphic Design
6029 Commercial Banks, NEC
8732 Commercial Economic, Sociological & Educational Research
5046 Commercial Eqpt, NEC Wholesale
7335 Commercial Photography
8731 Commercial Physical & Biological Research
6221 Commodity Contracts Brokers & Dealers
4899 Communication Svcs, NEC
7376 Computer Facilities Management Svcs
7373 Computer Integrated Systems Design
7378 Computer Maintenance & Repair
7379 Computer Related Svcs, NEC
7377 Computer Rental & Leasing
5045 Computers & Peripheral Eqpt & Software Wholesale
1771 Concrete Work
5145 Confectionery Wholesale
5082 Construction & Mining Mach & Eqpt Wholesale

5039 Construction Materials, NEC Wholesale
1442 Construction Sand & Gravel
1021 Copper Ores
0115 Corn
0724 Cotton Ginning
4215 Courier Svcs, Except Air
6159 Credit Institutions, Misc Business
6153 Credit Institutions, Short-Term Business
7323 Credit Reporting Svcs
0191 Crop Farming, Misc
0723 Crop Preparation, Except Cotton Ginning
1311 Crude Petroleum & Natural Gas
4612 Crude Petroleum Pipelines
1423 Crushed & Broken Granite
1422 Crushed & Broken Limestone
1429 Crushed & Broken Stone, NEC
7371 Custom Computer Programming Svcs

D

0241 Dairy Farms
5143 Dairy Prdts, Except Dried Or Canned Wholesale
7911 Dance Studios, Schools & Halls
7374 Data & Computer Processing & Preparation
0175 Deciduous Tree Fruits
4412 Deep Sea Foreign Transportation Of Freight
4481 Deep Sea Transportation Of Passengers
8072 Dental Laboratories
7381 Detective & Armored Car Svcs
1411 Dimension Stone
7331 Direct Mail Advertising Svcs
7342 Disinfecting & Pest Control Svcs
1381 Drilling Oil & Gas Wells
5122 Drugs, Drug Proprietaries & Sundries Wholesale
7216 Dry Cleaning Plants, Except Rug Cleaning
5099 Durable Goods: NEC Wholesale

E

6732 Education, Religious & Charitable Trusts
4931 Electric & Other Svcs Combined
4911 Electric Svcs
7629 Electrical & Elex Repair Shop, NEC
5064 Electrical Appliances, TV & Radios Wholesale
1731 Electrical Work
5063 Electrl Apparatus, Eqpt, Wiring Splys Wholesale
5065 Electronic Parts & Eqpt Wholesale
7361 Employment Agencies
8711 Engineering Services
7359 Equipment Rental & Leasing, NEC
1794 Excavating & Grading Work

F

8744 Facilities Support Mgmt Svcs
5083 Farm & Garden Mach & Eqpt Wholesale
0762 Farm Management Svcs
4221 Farm Product Warehousing & Storage
5191 Farm Splys Wholesale
5159 Farm-Prdt Raw Mtrls, NEC Wholesale
6111 Federal Credit Agencies
6061 Federal Credit Unions
6011 Federal Reserve Banks
6035 Federal Savings Institutions
4482 Ferries
1061 Ferroalloy Ores, Except Vanadium
6331 Fire, Marine & Casualty Insurance
5146 Fish & Seafood Wholesale
4785 Fixed Facilities, Inspection, Weighing Svcs Transptn
1752 Floor Laying & Other Floor Work, NEC
5193 Flowers, Nursery Stock & Florists' Splys Wholesale
0182 Food Crops Grown Under Cover
5139 Footwear Wholesale
0851 Forestry Svcs
4731 Freight Forwarding & Arrangement
4432 Freight Transportation On The Great Lakes
5148 Fresh Fruits & Vegetables Wholesale
6099 Functions Related To Deposit Banking, NEC
7261 Funeral Svcs & Crematories
5021 Furniture Wholesale

G

7212 Garment Pressing & Cleaners' Agents
4932 Gas & Other Svcs Combined
4925 Gas Production &/Or Distribution
7538 General Automotive Repair Shop
1541 General Contractors, Indl Bldgs & Warehouses

1542 General Contractors, Nonresidential & Non-indl Bldgs
1522 General Contractors, Residential Other Than Single Family
1521 General Contractors, Single Family Houses
0219 General Livestock, NEC
8062 General Medical & Surgical Hospitals
4225 General Warehousing & Storage
1793 Glass & Glazing Work
5153 Grain & Field Beans Wholesale
0172 Grapes
5149 Groceries & Related Prdts, NEC Wholesale
5141 Groceries, General Line Wholesale

H

5072 Hardware Wholesale
8099 Health & Allied Svcs, NEC
5075 Heating & Air Conditioning Eqpt & Splys Wholesale
7353 Heavy Construction Eqpt Rental & Leasing
1629 Heavy Construction, NEC
7363 Help Supply Svcs
1611 Highway & Street Construction
0213 Hogs
5023 Home Furnishings Wholesale
8082 Home Health Care Svcs
6324 Hospital & Medical Svc Plans Carriers
7011 Hotels, Motels & Tourist Courts
0971 Hunting & Trapping

I

8322 Individual & Family Social Svcs
5113 Indl & Personal Svc Paper Wholesale
7218 Industrial Launderers
5084 Industrial Mach & Eqpt Wholesale
1446 Industrial Sand
5085 Industrial Splys Wholesale
7375 Information Retrieval Svcs
1796 Installation Or Erection Of Bldg Eqpt & Machinery, NEC
6411 Insurance Agents, Brokers & Svc
6399 Insurance Carriers, NEC
4131 Intercity & Rural Bus Transportation
8052 Intermediate Care Facilities
6282 Investment Advice
6799 Investors, NEC
0134 Irish Potatoes
1011 Iron Ores
4971 Irrigation Systems

J

5094 Jewelry, Watches, Precious Stones Wholesale
8331 Job Training & Vocational Rehabilitation Svcs

K

8092 Kidney Dialysis Centers

L

8631 Labor Unions & Similar Organizations
6552 Land Subdividers & Developers
0781 Landscape Counseling & Planning
7219 Laundry & Garment Svcs, NEC
0782 Lawn & Garden Svcs
8111 Legal Svcs
6519 Lessors Of Real Estate, NEC
6311 Life Insurance Carriers
7213 Linen Sply
0751 Livestock Svcs, Except Veterinary
5154 Livestock Wholesale
6163 Loan Brokers
4111 Local & Suburban Transit
4141 Local Bus Charter Svc
4119 Local Passenger Transportation: NEC
4214 Local Trucking With Storage
4212 Local Trucking Without Storage
5031 Lumber, Plywood & Millwork Wholesale

M

8742 Management Consulting Services
6722 Management Investment Offices
8741 Management Services
4493 Marinas
4491 Marine Cargo Handling
1741 Masonry & Other Stonework
5147 Meats & Meat Prdts Wholesale
7352 Medical Eqpt Rental & Leasing
8071 Medical Laboratories
5047 Medical, Dental & Hospital Eqpt & Splys Wholesale

SIC NO	PRODUCT
8699	Membership Organizations, NEC
7997	Membership Sports & Recreation Clubs
7041	Membership-Basis Hotels
5136	Men's & Boys' Clothing & Furnishings Wholesale
1081	Metal Mining Svcs
5051	Metals Service Centers
1499	Miscellaneous Nonmetallic Mining
7299	Miscellaneous Personal Svcs, NEC
6162	Mortgage Bankers & Loan Correspondents
7822	Motion Picture & Video Tape Distribution
7812	Motion Picture & Video Tape Production
7832	Motion Picture Theaters, Except Drive-In
5015	Motor Vehicle Parts, Used Wholesale
5013	Motor Vehicle Splys & New Parts Wholesale
8412	Museums & Art Galleries

N

SIC NO	PRODUCT
6021	National Commercial Banks
4924	Natural Gas Distribution
1321	Natural Gas Liquids
4922	Natural Gas Transmission
4923	Natural Gas Transmission & Distribution
7383	News Syndicates
8733	Noncommercial Research Organizations
5199	Nondurable Goods, NEC Wholesale
1481	Nonmetallic Minerals Svcs, Except Fuels
8059	Nursing & Personal Care Facilities, NEC

O

SIC NO	PRODUCT
5044	Office Eqpt Wholesale
8041	Offices & Clinics Of Chiropractors
8021	Offices & Clinics Of Dentists
8011	Offices & Clinics Of Doctors Of Medicine
8031	Offices & Clinics Of Doctors Of Osteopathy
8049	Offices & Clinics Of Health Practitioners, NEC
8042	Offices & Clinics Of Optometrists
8043	Offices & Clinics Of Podiatrists
6712	Offices Of Bank Holding Co's
6719	Offices Of Holding Co's, NEC
1382	Oil & Gas Field Exploration Svcs
1389	Oil & Gas Field Svcs, NEC
6792	Oil Royalty Traders
1531	Operative Builders
6513	Operators Of Apartment Buildings
6514	Operators Of Dwellings, Except Apartments
6512	Operators Of Nonresidential Bldgs
6515	Operators of Residential Mobile Home Sites
5048	Ophthalmic Goods Wholesale
0181	Ornamental Floriculture & Nursery Prdts
0783	Ornamental Shrub & Tree Svc
7312	Outdoor Advertising Svcs

P

SIC NO	PRODUCT
5142	Packaged Frozen Foods Wholesale
4783	Packing & Crating Svcs
1721	Painting & Paper Hanging Contractors
5198	Paints, Varnishes & Splys Wholesale
7515	Passenger Car Leasing
7514	Passenger Car Rental
4729	Passenger Transportation Arrangement, NEC
6794	Patent Owners & Lessors
6371	Pension, Health & Welfare Funds
6141	Personal Credit Institutions
5172	Petroleum & Petroleum Prdts Wholesale
5171	Petroleum Bulk Stations & Terminals
7334	Photocopying & Duplicating Svcs

SIC NO	PRODUCT
7384	Photofinishing Labs
5043	Photographic Eqpt & Splys Wholesale
7221	Photographic Studios, Portrait
7991	Physical Fitness Facilities
5131	Piece Goods, Notions & Dry Goods Wholesale
1742	Plastering, Drywall, Acoustical & Insulation Work
5162	Plastics Materials & Basic Shapes Wholesale
5074	Plumbing & Heating Splys Wholesale
1711	Plumbing, Heating & Air Conditioning Contractors
8651	Political Organizations
5144	Poultry & Poultry Prdts Wholesale
0254	Poultry Hatcheries
7211	Power Laundries, Family & Commercial
7372	Prepackaged Software
5111	Printing & Writing Paper Wholesale
5049	Professional Eqpt & Splys, NEC Wholesale
8621	Professional Membership Organizations
7941	Professional Sports Clubs & Promoters
8063	Psychiatric Hospitals
7992	Public Golf Courses
8743	Public Relations Svcs

R

SIC NO	PRODUCT
7948	Racing & Track Operations
7622	Radio & TV Repair Shops
4832	Radio Broadcasting Stations
7313	Radio, TV & Publishers Adv Reps
4812	Radiotelephone Communications
4741	Railroad Car Rental
6517	Railroad Property Lessors
4011	Railroads, Line-Hauling Operations
6531	Real Estate Agents & Managers
6798	Real Estate Investment Trusts
4613	Refined Petroleum Pipelines
4222	Refrigerated Warehousing & Storage
7623	Refrigeration & Air Conditioning Svc & Repair Shop
5078	Refrigeration Eqpt & Splys Wholesale
4953	Refuse Systems
7699	Repair Shop & Related Svcs, NEC
8361	Residential Care
7641	Reupholstery & Furniture Repair
5033	Roofing, Siding & Insulation Mtrls Wholesale
1761	Roofing, Siding & Sheet Metal Work
7021	Rooming & Boarding Houses

S

SIC NO	PRODUCT
4959	Sanitary Svcs, NEC
6036	Savings Institutions, Except Federal
4151	School Buses
5093	Scrap & Waste Materials Wholesale
7338	Secretarial & Court Reporting Svcs
6289	Security & Commodity Svcs, NEC
6211	Security Brokers & Dealers
7382	Security Systems Svcs
5087	Service Establishment Eqpt & Splys Wholesale
7829	Services Allied To Motion Picture Distribution
7819	Services Allied To Motion Picture Prdtn
8999	Services Not Elsewhere Classified
4952	Sewerage Systems
8051	Skilled Nursing Facilities
8399	Social Services, NEC
0711	Soil Preparation Svcs
0721	Soil Preparation, Planting & Cultivating Svc
0116	Soybeans
1799	Special Trade Contractors, NEC
4226	Special Warehousing & Storage, NEC

SIC NO	PRODUCT
8069	Specialty Hospitals, Except Psychiatric
8093	Specialty Outpatient Facilities, NEC
7032	Sporting & Recreational Camps
5091	Sporting & Recreational Goods & Splys Wholesale
6022	State Commercial Banks
6062	State Credit Unions
5112	Stationery & Office Splys Wholesale
4961	Steam & Air Conditioning Sply
1791	Structural Steel Erection
6351	Surety Insurance Carriers
8713	Surveying Services
4013	Switching & Terminal Svcs

T

SIC NO	PRODUCT
7291	Tax Return Preparation Svcs
4121	Taxi Cabs
4822	Telegraph & Other Message Communications
4813	Telephone Communications, Except Radio
4833	Television Broadcasting Stations
4231	Terminal & Joint Terminal Maint Facilities
1743	Terrazzo, Tile, Marble & Mosaic Work
8734	Testing Laboratories
7922	Theatrical Producers & Misc Theatrical Svcs
0811	Timber Tracts
7534	Tire Retreading & Repair Shops
5014	Tires & Tubes Wholesale
6541	Title Abstract Offices
6361	Title Insurance
5194	Tobacco & Tobacco Prdts Wholesale
7532	Top, Body & Upholstery Repair & Paint Shops
4725	Tour Operators
4492	Towing & Tugboat Svcs
5092	Toys & Hobby Goods & Splys Wholesale
7033	Trailer Parks & Camp Sites
5088	Transportation Eqpt & Splys, Except Motor Vehicles Wholesale
4789	Transportation Svcs, NEC
4724	Travel Agencies
7513	Truck Rental & Leasing, Without Drivers
4213	Trucking, Except Local
6733	Trusts Except Educational, Religious & Charitable
0253	Turkey & Turkey Egg Farms

U

SIC NO	PRODUCT
6726	Unit Investment Trusts, Face-Amount Certificate Offices
7519	Utility Trailers & Recreational Vehicle Rental

V

SIC NO	PRODUCT
0161	Vegetables & Melons
0742	Veterinary Animal Specialties
0741	Veterinary Livestock Svcs
7841	Video Tape Rental

W

SIC NO	PRODUCT
7631	Watch, Clock & Jewelry Repair
4941	Water Sply
4449	Water Transportation Of Freight, NEC
4499	Water Transportation Svcs, NEC
1781	Water Well Drilling
1623	Water, Sewer & Utility Line Construction
7692	Welding Repair
0111	Wheat
5182	Wine & Distilled Alcoholic Beverages Wholesale
5137	Women's, Children's & Infants Clothing Wholesale
1795	Wrecking & Demolition Work

SIC INDEX

Standard Industrial Classification Numerical Index

SIC NO	PRODUCT

01 agricultural production-crops
0111 Wheat
0115 Corn
0116 Soybeans
0119 Cash Grains, NEC
0134 Irish Potatoes
0161 Vegetables & Melons
0171 Berry Crops
0172 Grapes
0175 Deciduous Tree Fruits
0181 Ornamental Floriculture & Nursery Prdts
0182 Food Crops Grown Under Cover
0191 Crop Farming, Misc

02 agricultural production-livestock and animal specialties
0211 Beef Cattle Feedlots
0213 Hogs
0219 General Livestock, NEC
0241 Dairy Farms
0251 Chicken & Poultry Farms
0252 Chicken Egg Farms
0253 Turkey & Turkey Egg Farms
0254 Poultry Hatcheries
0291 Animal Production, NEC

07 agricultural services
0711 Soil Preparation Svcs
0721 Soil Preparation, Planting & Cultivating Svc
0723 Crop Preparation, Except Cotton Ginning
0724 Cotton Ginning
0741 Veterinary Livestock Svcs
0742 Veterinary Animal Specialties
0751 Livestock Svcs, Except Veterinary
0752 Animal Specialty Svcs, Exc Veterinary
0762 Farm Management Svcs
0781 Landscape Counseling & Planning
0782 Lawn & Garden Svcs
0783 Ornamental Shrub & Tree Svc

08 forestry
0811 Timber Tracts
0851 Forestry Svcs

09 fishing, hunting, and trapping
0971 Hunting & Trapping

10 metal mining
1011 Iron Ores
1021 Copper Ores
1061 Ferroalloy Ores, Except Vanadium
1081 Metal Mining Svcs

12 coal mining
1221 Bituminous Coal & Lignite: Surface Mining
1222 Bituminous Coal: Underground Mining
1231 Anthracite Mining
1241 Coal Mining Svcs

13 oil and gas extraction
1311 Crude Petroleum & Natural Gas
1321 Natural Gas Liquids
1381 Drilling Oil & Gas Wells
1382 Oil & Gas Field Exploration Svcs
1389 Oil & Gas Field Svcs, NEC

14 mining and quarrying of nonmetallic minerals, except fuels
1411 Dimension Stone
1422 Crushed & Broken Limestone
1423 Crushed & Broken Granite
1429 Crushed & Broken Stone, NEC
1442 Construction Sand & Gravel
1446 Industrial Sand
1459 Clay, Ceramic & Refractory Minerals, NEC
1479 Chemical & Fertilizer Mining
1481 Nonmetallic Minerals Svcs, Except Fuels
1499 Miscellaneous Nonmetallic Mining

15 building construction-general contractors and operative builders
1521 General Contractors, Single Family Houses
1522 General Contractors, Residential Other Than Single Family
1531 Operative Builders
1541 General Contractors, Indl Bldgs & Warehouses
1542 General Contractors, Nonresidential & Non-indl Bldgs

16 heavy construction other than building construction-contractors
1611 Highway & Street Construction
1622 Bridge, Tunnel & Elevated Hwy Construction
1623 Water, Sewer & Utility Line Construction
1629 Heavy Construction, NEC

17 construction-special trade contractors
1711 Plumbing, Heating & Air Conditioning Contractors
1721 Painting & Paper Hanging Contractors
1731 Electrical Work
1741 Masonry & Other Stonework
1742 Plastering, Drywall, Acoustical & Insulation Work
1743 Terrazzo, Tile, Marble & Mosaic Work
1751 Carpentry Work
1752 Floor Laying & Other Floor Work, NEC
1761 Roofing, Siding & Sheet Metal Work
1771 Concrete Work
1781 Water Well Drilling
1791 Structural Steel Erection
1793 Glass & Glazing Work
1794 Excavating & Grading Work
1795 Wrecking & Demolition Work
1796 Installation Or Erection Of Bldg Eqpt & Machinery, NEC
1799 Special Trade Contractors, NEC

40 railroad transportation
4011 Railroads, Line-Hauling Operations
4013 Switching & Terminal Svcs

41 local and suburban transit and interurban highway passenger transportation
4111 Local & Suburban Transit
4119 Local Passenger Transportation: NEC
4121 Taxi Cabs
4131 Intercity & Rural Bus Transportation
4141 Local Bus Charter Svc
4142 Bus Charter Service, Except Local
4151 School Buses
4173 Bus Terminal & Svc Facilities

42 motor freight transportation and warehousing
4212 Local Trucking Without Storage
4213 Trucking, Except Local
4214 Local Trucking With Storage
4215 Courier Svcs, Except Air
4221 Farm Product Warehousing & Storage
4222 Refrigerated Warehousing & Storage
4225 General Warehousing & Storage
4226 Special Warehousing & Storage, NEC
4231 Terminal & Joint Terminal Maint Facilities

44 water transportation
4412 Deep Sea Foreign Transportation Of Freight
4432 Freight Transportation On The Great Lakes
4449 Water Transportation Of Freight, NEC
4481 Deep Sea Transportation Of Passengers
4482 Ferries
4491 Marine Cargo Handling
4492 Towing & Tugboat Svcs
4493 Marinas
4499 Water Transportation Svcs, NEC

45 transportation by air
4512 Air Transportation, Scheduled
4513 Air Courier Svcs
4522 Air Transportation, Nonscheduled
4581 Airports, Flying Fields & Terminal Svcs

46 pipelines, except natural gas
4612 Crude Petroleum Pipelines
4613 Refined Petroleum Pipelines

47 transportation services
4724 Travel Agencies
4725 Tour Operators
4729 Passenger Transportation Arrangement, NEC
4731 Freight Forwarding & Arrangement
4741 Railroad Car Rental
4783 Packing & Crating Svcs
4785 Fixed Facilities, Inspection, Weighing Svcs Transptn
4789 Transportation Svcs, NEC

48 communications
4812 Radiotelephone Communications
4813 Telephone Communications, Except Radio
4822 Telegraph & Other Message Communications
4832 Radio Broadcasting Stations
4833 Television Broadcasting Stations
4841 Cable & Other Pay TV Svcs
4899 Communication Svcs, NEC

49 electric, gas, and sanitary services
4911 Electric Svcs
4922 Natural Gas Transmission
4923 Natural Gas Transmission & Distribution
4924 Natural Gas Distribution
4925 Gas Production &/Or Distribution
4931 Electric & Other Svcs Combined
4932 Gas & Other Svcs Combined
4939 Combination Utilities, NEC
4941 Water Sply
4952 Sewerage Systems
4953 Refuse Systems
4959 Sanitary Svcs, NEC
4961 Steam & Air Conditioning Sply
4971 Irrigation Systems

50 wholesale trade¨durable goods
5012 Automobiles & Other Motor Vehicles Wholesale
5013 Motor Vehicle Splys & New Parts Wholesale
5014 Tires & Tubes Wholesale
5015 Motor Vehicle Parts, Used Wholesale
5021 Furniture Wholesale
5023 Home Furnishings Wholesale
5031 Lumber, Plywood & Millwork Wholesale
5032 Brick, Stone & Related Construction Mtrls Wholesale
5033 Roofing, Siding & Insulation Mtrls Wholesale
5039 Construction Materials, NEC Wholesale
5043 Photographic Eqpt & Splys Wholesale
5044 Office Eqpt Wholesale
5045 Computers & Peripheral Eqpt & Software Wholesale
5046 Commercial Eqpt, NEC Wholesale
5047 Medical, Dental & Hospital Eqpt & Splys Wholesale
5048 Ophthalmic Goods Wholesale
5049 Professional Eqpt & Splys, NEC Wholesale
5051 Metals Service Centers
5052 Coal & Other Minerals & Ores Wholesale
5063 Electrl Apparatus, Eqpt, Wiring Splys Wholesale
5064 Electrical Appliances, TV & Radios Wholesale
5065 Electronic Parts & Eqpt Wholesale
5072 Hardware Wholesale
5074 Plumbing & Heating Splys Wholesale
5075 Heating & Air Conditioning Eqpt & Splys Wholesale
5078 Refrigeration Eqpt & Splys Wholesale
5082 Construction & Mining Mach & Eqpt Wholesale
5083 Farm & Garden Mach & Eqpt Wholesale
5084 Industrial Mach & Eqpt Wholesale
5085 Industrial Splys Wholesale
5087 Service Establishment Eqpt & Splys Wholesale
5088 Transportation Eqpt & Splys, Except Motor Vehicles Wholesale
5091 Sporting & Recreational Goods & Splys Wholesale
5092 Toys & Hobby Goods & Splys Wholesale
5093 Scrap & Waste Materials Wholesale
5094 Jewelry, Watches, Precious Stones Wholesale
5099 Durable Goods: NEC Wholesale

51 wholesale trade¨nondurable goods
5111 Printing & Writing Paper Wholesale
5112 Stationery & Office Splys Wholesale
5113 Indl & Personal Svc Paper Wholesale
5122 Drugs, Drug Proprietaries & Sundries Wholesale
5131 Piece Goods, Notions & Dry Goods Wholesale
5136 Men's & Boys' Clothing & Furnishings Wholesale
5137 Women's, Children's & Infants Clothing Wholesale
5139 Footwear Wholesale
5141 Groceries, General Line Wholesale
5142 Packaged Frozen Foods Wholesale
5143 Dairy Prdts, Except Dried Or Canned Wholesale
5144 Poultry & Poultry Prdts Wholesale
5145 Confectionery Wholesale
5146 Fish & Seafood Wholesale
5147 Meats & Meat Prdts Wholesale

SIC NO	PRODUCT

5148 Fresh Fruits & Vegetables Wholesale
5149 Groceries & Related Prdts, NEC Wholesale
5153 Grain & Field Beans Wholesale
5154 Livestock Wholesale
5159 Farm-Prdt Raw Mtrls, NEC Wholesale
5162 Plastics Materials & Basic Shapes Wholesale
5169 Chemicals & Allied Prdts, NEC Wholesale
5171 Petroleum Bulk Stations & Terminals
5172 Petroleum & Petroleum Prdts Wholesale
5181 Beer & Ale Wholesale
5182 Wine & Distilled Alcoholic Beverages Wholesale
5191 Farm Splys Wholesale
5192 Books, Periodicals & Newspapers Wholesale
5193 Flowers, Nursery Stock & Florists' Splys Wholesale
5194 Tobacco & Tobacco Prdts Wholesale
5198 Paints, Varnishes & Splys Wholesale
5199 Nondurable Goods, NEC Wholesale

60 depository institutions

6011 Federal Reserve Banks
6021 National Commercial Banks
6022 State Commercial Banks
6029 Commercial Banks, NEC
6035 Federal Savings Institutions
6036 Savings Institutions, Except Federal
6061 Federal Credit Unions
6062 State Credit Unions
6099 Functions Related To Deposit Banking, NEC

61 nondepository credit institutions

6111 Federal Credit Agencies
6141 Personal Credit Institutions
6153 Credit Institutions, Short-Term Business
6159 Credit Institutions, Misc Business
6162 Mortgage Bankers & Loan Correspondents
6163 Loan Brokers

62 security and commodity brokers, dealers, exchanges, and services

6211 Security Brokers & Dealers
6221 Commodity Contracts Brokers & Dealers
6282 Investment Advice
6289 Security & Commodity Svcs, NEC

63 insurance carriers

6311 Life Insurance Carriers
6321 Accident & Health Insurance
6324 Hospital & Medical Svc Plans Carriers
6331 Fire, Marine & Casualty Insurance
6351 Surety Insurance Carriers
6361 Title Insurance
6371 Pension, Health & Welfare Funds
6399 Insurance Carriers, NEC

64 insurance agents, brokers, and service

6411 Insurance Agents, Brokers & Svc

65 real estate

6512 Operators Of Nonresidential Bldgs
6513 Operators Of Apartment Buildings
6514 Operators Of Dwellings, Except Apartments
6515 Operators of Residential Mobile Home Sites
6517 Railroad Property Lessors
6519 Lessors Of Real Estate, NEC
6531 Real Estate Agents & Managers
6541 Title Abstract Offices
6552 Land Subdividers & Developers
6553 Cemetery Subdividers & Developers

67 holding and other investment offices

6712 Offices Of Bank Holding Co's
6719 Offices Of Holding Co's, NEC
6722 Management Investment Offices
6726 Unit Investment Trusts, Face-Amount Certificate Offices
6732 Education, Religious & Charitable Trusts
6733 Trusts Except Educational, Religious & Charitable
6792 Oil Royalty Traders
6794 Patent Owners & Lessors
6798 Real Estate Investment Trusts
6799 Investors, NEC

70 hotels, rooming houses, camps, and other lodging places

7011 Hotels, Motels & Tourist Courts

7021 Rooming & Boarding Houses
7032 Sporting & Recreational Camps
7033 Trailer Parks & Camp Sites
7041 Membership-Basis Hotels

72 personal services

7211 Power Laundries, Family & Commercial
7212 Garment Pressing & Cleaners' Agents
7213 Linen Sply
7215 Coin Operated Laundries & Cleaning
7216 Dry Cleaning Plants, Except Rug Cleaning
7217 Carpet & Upholstery Cleaning
7218 Industrial Launderers
7219 Laundry & Garment Svcs, NEC
7221 Photographic Studios, Portrait
7231 Beauty Shops
7241 Barber Shops
7261 Funeral Svcs & Crematories
7291 Tax Return Preparation Svcs
7299 Miscellaneous Personal Svcs, NEC

73 business services

7311 Advertising Agencies
7312 Outdoor Advertising Svcs
7313 Radio, TV & Publishers Adv Reps
7319 Advertising, NEC
7322 Adjustment & Collection Svcs
7323 Credit Reporting Svcs
7331 Direct Mail Advertising Svcs
7334 Photocopying & Duplicating Svcs
7335 Commercial Photography
7336 Commercial Art & Graphic Design
7338 Secretarial & Court Reporting Svcs
7342 Disinfecting & Pest Control Svcs
7349 Building Cleaning & Maintenance Svcs, NEC
7352 Medical Eqpt Rental & Leasing
7353 Heavy Construction Eqpt Rental & Leasing
7359 Equipment Rental & Leasing, NEC
7361 Employment Agencies
7363 Help Supply Svcs
7371 Custom Computer Programming Svcs
7372 Prepackaged Software
7373 Computer Integrated Systems Design
7374 Data & Computer Processing & Preparation
7375 Information Retrieval Svcs
7376 Computer Facilities Management Svcs
7377 Computer Rental & Leasing
7378 Computer Maintenance & Repair
7379 Computer Related Svcs, NEC
7381 Detective & Armored Car Svcs
7382 Security Systems Svcs
7383 News Syndicates
7384 Photofinishing Labs
7389 Business Svcs, NEC

75 automotive repair, services, and parking

7513 Truck Rental & Leasing, Without Drivers
7514 Passenger Car Rental
7515 Passenger Car Leasing
7519 Utility Trailers & Recreational Vehicle Rental
7521 Automobile Parking Lots & Garages
7532 Top, Body & Upholstery Repair & Paint Shops
7533 Automotive Exhaust System Repair Shops
7534 Tire Retreading & Repair Shops
7536 Automotive Glass Replacement Shops
7537 Automotive Transmission Repair Shops
7538 General Automotive Repair Shop
7539 Automotive Repair Shops, NEC
7542 Car Washes
7549 Automotive Svcs, Except Repair & Car Washes

76 miscellaneous repair services

7622 Radio & TV Repair Shops
7623 Refrigeration & Air Conditioning Svc & Repair Shop
7629 Electrical & Elex Repair Shop, NEC
7631 Watch, Clock & Jewelry Repair
7641 Reupholstery & Furniture Repair
7692 Welding Repair
7694 Armature Rewinding Shops
7699 Repair Shop & Related Svcs, NEC

78 motion pictures

7812 Motion Picture & Video Tape Production
7819 Services Allied To Motion Picture Prdtn

7822 Motion Picture & Video Tape Distribution
7829 Services Allied To Motion Picture Distribution
7832 Motion Picture Theaters, Except Drive-In
7841 Video Tape Rental

79 amusement and recreation services

7911 Dance Studios, Schools & Halls
7922 Theatrical Producers & Misc Theatrical Svcs
7929 Bands, Orchestras, Actors & Entertainers
7933 Bowling Centers
7941 Professional Sports Clubs & Promoters
7948 Racing & Track Operations
7991 Physical Fitness Facilities
7992 Public Golf Courses
7993 Coin-Operated Amusement Devices & Arcades
7996 Amusement Parks
7997 Membership Sports & Recreation Clubs
7999 Amusement & Recreation Svcs, NEC

80 health services

8011 Offices & Clinics Of Doctors Of Medicine
8021 Offices & Clinics Of Dentists
8031 Offices & Clinics Of Doctors Of Osteopathy
8041 Offices & Clinics Of Chiropractors
8042 Offices & Clinics Of Optometrists
8043 Offices & Clinics Of Podiatrists
8049 Offices & Clinics Of Health Practitioners, NEC
8051 Skilled Nursing Facilities
8052 Intermediate Care Facilities
8059 Nursing & Personal Care Facilities, NEC
8062 General Medical & Surgical Hospitals
8063 Psychiatric Hospitals
8069 Specialty Hospitals, Except Psychiatric
8071 Medical Laboratories
8072 Dental Laboratories
8082 Home Health Care Svcs
8092 Kidney Dialysis Centers
8093 Specialty Outpatient Facilities, NEC
8099 Health & Allied Svcs, NEC

81 legal services

8111 Legal Svcs

83 social services

8322 Individual & Family Social Svcs
8331 Job Training & Vocational Rehabilitation Svcs
8351 Child Day Care Svcs
8361 Residential Care
8399 Social Services, NEC

84 museums, art galleries, and botanical and zoological gardens

8412 Museums & Art Galleries
8422 Arboreta, Botanical & Zoological Gardens

86 membership organizations

8611 Business Associations
8621 Professional Membership Organizations
8631 Labor Unions & Similar Organizations
8641 Civic, Social & Fraternal Associations
8651 Political Organizations
8699 Membership Organizations, NEC

87 engineering, accounting, research, management, and related services

8711 Engineering Services
8712 Architectural Services
8713 Surveying Services
8721 Accounting, Auditing & Bookkeeping Svcs
8731 Commercial Physical & Biological Research
8732 Commercial Economic, Sociological & Educational Research
8733 Noncommercial Research Organizations
8734 Testing Laboratories
8741 Management Services
8742 Management Consulting Services
8743 Public Relations Svcs
8744 Facilities Support Mgmt Svcs
8748 Business Consulting Svcs, NEC

89 services, not elsewhere classified

8999 Services Not Elsewhere Classified

SIC SECTION

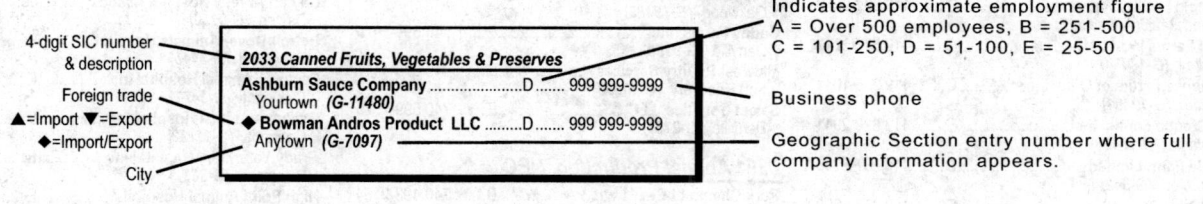

Indicates approximate employment figure
A = Over 500 employees, B = 251-500
C = 101-250, D = 51-100, E = 25-50

4-digit SIC number & description

Foreign trade
▲=Import ▼=Export
◆=Import/Export

City

2033 Canned Fruits, Vegetables & Preserves
Ashburn Sauce Company ....D...... 999 999-9999
Yourtown *(G-11480)*
◆ Bowman Andros Product LLC ....D...... 999 999-9999
Anytown *(G-7097)*

Business phone

Geographic Section entry number where full company information appears.

See footnotes for symbols and codes identification.

- The SIC codes in this section are from the latest Standard Industrial Classification manual published by the U.S. Government's Office of Management and Budget. For more information regarding SICs, see the Explanatory Notes.
- Companies may be listed under multiple classifications.

01 AGRICULTURAL PRODUCTION-CROPS

0111 Wheat
Molyet Crop Production Inc .... E 419 992-4288
Tiffin *(G-17526)*
Schlessman Seed Co .... E 419 499-2572
Milan *(G-14367)*
Stokes Fruit Farm .... E 937 382-4004
Wilmington *(G-19649)*

0115 Corn
George Darr .... E 740 498-5400
Newcomerstown *(G-15132)*
Hartung Brothers Inc .... E 419 352-3000
Bowling Green *(G-1734)*
Molyet Crop Production Inc .... E 419 992-4288
Tiffin *(G-17526)*
Schlessman Seed Co .... E 419 499-2572
Milan *(G-14367)*
Stokes Fruit Farm .... E 937 382-4004
Wilmington *(G-19649)*
Tom Langhals .... E 419 659-5629
Columbus Grove *(G-8942)*

0116 Soybeans
George Darr .... E 740 498-5400
Newcomerstown *(G-15132)*
Molyet Crop Production Inc .... E 419 992-4288
Tiffin *(G-17526)*
Schlessman Seed Co .... E 419 499-2572
Milan *(G-14367)*

0119 Cash Grains, NEC
Ayers Farms Inc .... E 419 938-7707
Perrysville *(G-15939)*
Drw Packing Inc .... D 419 744-2427
North Fairfield *(G-15245)*
Hertzfeld Poultry Farms Inc .... D 419 832-2070
Grand Rapids *(G-11326)*
McMaster Farms .... D 330 482-2913
Columbiana *(G-6790)*

0134 Irish Potatoes
John F Stambaugh & Co .... E 419 687-6833
Plymouth *(G-16077)*
McMaster Farms .... D 330 482-2913
Columbiana *(G-6790)*

0161 Vegetables & Melons
Brenckle Farms Inc .... E 330 877-4426
Hartville *(G-11683)*
Drw Packing Inc .... D 419 744-2427
North Fairfield *(G-15245)*
George Darr .... E 740 498-5400
Newcomerstown *(G-15132)*
George Knick .... E 937 548-2832
Greenville *(G-11379)*
Holthouse Farms of Ohio Inc .... C 419 935-1041
Willard *(G-19481)*
John F Stambaugh & Co .... E 419 687-6833
Plymouth *(G-16077)*
McMaster Farms .... D 330 482-2913
Columbiana *(G-6790)*
Molyet Crop Production Inc .... E 419 992-4288
Tiffin *(G-17526)*

Rothert Farm Inc .... D 419 467-0095
Elmore *(G-10474)*
Suter Produce Inc .... E 419 384-3665
Pandora *(G-15755)*
White Pond Gardens Inc .... E 330 836-2727
Akron *(G-500)*

0171 Berry Crops
James Recker .... E 419 837-5378
Genoa *(G-11257)*
Stokes Fruit Farm .... E 937 382-4004
Wilmington *(G-19649)*
Suter Produce Inc .... D 419 384-3665
Pandora *(G-15755)*

0172 Grapes
Ferrante Wine Farm Inc .... E 440 466-8466
Geneva *(G-11240)*
Mapleside Valley LLC .... D 330 225-5576
Brunswick *(G-1937)*

0175 Deciduous Tree Fruits
Bauman Orchards Inc .... E 330 925-6861
Rittman *(G-16404)*
George Darr .... E 740 498-5400
Newcomerstown *(G-15132)*
Mac Queen Orchards Inc .... E 419 865-2916
Holland *(G-11894)*
Mapleside Valley LLC .... D 330 225-5576
Brunswick *(G-1937)*
Quality Plant Productions Inc .... E 440 526-8711
Richfield *(G-16371)*
Scenic Ridge Fruit Farms .... E 419 368-3353
Jeromesville *(G-12194)*

0181 Ornamental Floriculture & Nursery Prdts
A Brown & Sons Nursery .... E 937 836-5826
Brookville *(G-1909)*
▲ Acorn Farms Inc .... C 614 891-9348
Galena *(G-11153)*
▲ Aris Horticulture Inc .... D 330 745-2143
Barberton *(G-942)*
Barnes Nursery Inc .... E 800 421-8722
Huron *(G-12021)*
Beroske Farms & Greenhouse Inc .... E 419 826-4547
Delta *(G-10041)*
Cottage Gardens Inc .... D 440 259-2900
Perry *(G-15822)*
▲ Cuthbert Greenhouse Inc .... E 614 836-3866
Groveport *(G-11505)*
Davey Tree Expert Company .... C 330 673-9511
Kent *(G-12226)*
Deckers Nursery Inc .... E 614 836-2130
Groveport *(G-11506)*
▲ Dummen Group .... E 614 850-9551
Columbus *(G-7475)*
▲ Dummen Na Inc .... D 614 850-9551
Columbus *(G-7476)*
◆ Green Circle Growers Inc .... C 440 775-1411
Oberlin *(G-15503)*
Green Circle Growers Inc .... B 440 775-1411
Oberlin *(G-15504)*
Henderson Turf Farm Inc .... E 937 748-1559
Franklin *(G-11032)*
Hirts Greenhouse Inc .... E 440 238-8200
Strongsville *(G-17310)*
HJ Benken Flor & Greenhouses .... D 513 891-1040
Cincinnati *(G-3713)*

Jeff Creque Farms Inc .... E 419 829-2941
Sylvania *(G-17433)*
K W Zellers & Son Inc .... E 330 877-9371
Hartville *(G-11693)*
Knollwood Florists Inc .... E 937 426-0861
Beavercreek *(G-1163)*
▲ Lakewood Greenhouse Inc .... E 419 691-3541
Northwood *(G-15397)*
Lowes Grnhse & Gift Sp Inc .... E 440 543-5123
Chagrin Falls *(G-2670)*
Maria Gardens LLC .... E 440 238-7637
Strongsville *(G-17328)*
Mike Ward Landscaping Inc .... E 513 683-6436
Maineville *(G-13116)*
North Branch Nursery Inc .... E 419 287-4679
Pemberville *(G-15805)*
Pennington Seed Inc .... D 513 642-8980
Fairfield *(G-10770)*
Quality Plant Productions Inc .... E 440 526-8711
Richfield *(G-16371)*
R & S Halley & Co Inc .... E 614 771-0388
Hilliard *(G-11810)*
Ridge Manor Nuseries Inc .... C 440 466-5781
Madison *(G-13108)*
Rosby Brothers Inc .... E 216 351-0850
Cleveland *(G-6339)*
Scarffs Nursery Inc .... C 937 845-3130
New Carlisle *(G-14897)*
▲ Schmidt Bros Inc .... E 419 826-3671
Swanton *(G-17406)*
Schusters Greenhouse Ltd .... E 440 235-2440
Cleveland *(G-6377)*
Studebaker Nurseries Inc .... D 800 845-0584
New Carlisle *(G-14898)*
Sunny Border Ohio Inc .... D 440 858-9660
Jefferson *(G-12192)*
▲ Thorsens Greenhouse LLC .... E 740 363-5069
Delaware *(G-10009)*
Wade & Gatton Nurseries .... D 419 883-3191
Bellville *(G-1393)*
White Pond Gardens Inc .... E 330 836-2727
Akron *(G-500)*
Whiteford Greenhouse .... E 419 882-4110
Toledo *(G-18156)*
▲ Willoway Nurseries Inc .... C 440 934-4435
Avon *(G-906)*
▲ Willowbend Nurseries LLC .... C 440 259-3121
Perry *(G-15829)*
Wilsons Hillview Farm Inc .... E 740 763-2873
Newark *(G-15110)*

0182 Food Crops Grown Under Cover
Nature Fresh Farms Usa Inc .... E 419 330-5080
Delta *(G-10047)*
Sunny Border Ohio Inc .... D 440 858-9660
Jefferson *(G-12192)*
White Pond Gardens Inc .... E 330 836-2727
Akron *(G-500)*

0191 Crop Farming, Misc
Circle S Farms Inc .... E 614 878-9462
Grove City *(G-11420)*
Deerfield Farms .... E 330 584-4715
Deerfield *(G-9903)*
George Knick .... E 937 548-2832
Greenville *(G-11379)*
Heimerl Farms Ltd .... E 740 967-0063
Johnstown *(G-12200)*
Henderson Turf Farm Inc .... E 937 748-1559
Franklin *(G-11032)*

Herb Thyme Farms Inc ....B...... 866 386-0854
Perrysburg *(G-15873)*

Hertzfeld Poultry Farms Inc ....D...... 419 832-2070
Grand Rapids *(G-11326)*

Hirzel Farms Inc ....E...... 419 837-2710
Luckey *(G-13054)*

Holthouse Farms of Ohio Inc ......C...... 419 935-1041
Willard *(G-19481)*

Jeff Creque Farms Inc ....E...... 419 829-2941
Sylvania *(G-17433)*

Kunkle Farm Limited ....D...... 419 237-2748
Alvordton *(G-562)*

Ringler Inc ....E...... 419 253-5300
Marengo *(G-13305)*

Rk Family Inc ....C...... 419 443-1663
Tiffin *(G-17534)*

Rohrs Farms ....E...... 419 757-0110
Mc Guffey *(G-13898)*

S&D Farms Inc ....E...... 419 859-3785
Mount Cory *(G-14722)*

Suter Produce Inc ....D...... 419 384-3665
Pandora *(G-15755)*

02 AGRICULTURAL PRODUCTION-LIVESTOCK AND ANIMAL SPECIALTIES

0211 Beef Cattle Feedlots

Ayers Farms Inc ....E...... 419 938-7707
Perrysville *(G-15939)*

Dairy Farmers America Inc ....E...... 330 670-7800
Medina *(G-13929)*

0213 Hogs

Robert Winner Sons Inc ....E...... 419 582-4321
Yorkshire *(G-19942)*

0219 General Livestock, NEC

Pork Champ LLC ....D...... 740 493-2164
Lucasville *(G-13052)*

0241 Dairy Farms

Ayers Farms Inc ....E...... 419 938-7707
Perrysville *(G-15939)*

Bridgewater Dairy LLC ....E...... 419 485-8157
Montpelier *(G-14608)*

Calvary Christian Ch of Ohio ......E...... 740 828-9000
Frazeysburg *(G-11048)*

Dovin Dairy Farms LLC ....E...... 440 653-7009
Oberlin *(G-15501)*

Falling Star Farm Ltd ....E...... 419 945-2651
Polk *(G-16092)*

▲ Miceli Dairy Products Co ....D...... 216 791-6222
Cleveland *(G-5975)*

Springdale Ice Cream Beverage ...E...... 513 699-4984
Cincinnati *(G-4522)*

Stoll Farms Inc ....E...... 330 682-5786
Marshallville *(G-13475)*

Youngs Jersey Dairy Inc ....B...... 937 325-0629
Yellow Springs *(G-19941)*

0251 Chicken & Poultry Farms

Chicn Fixins Inc ....E...... 614 929-8431
Columbus *(G-7184)*

0252 Chicken Egg Farms

Cal-Maine Foods Inc ....E...... 937 337-9576
Rossburg *(G-16457)*

Cal-Maine Foods Inc ....E...... 937 968-4874
Union City *(G-18352)*

▲ Heartland Quality Egg Farm ......E...... 937 355-5103
West Mansfield *(G-19124)*

Ohio Fresh Eggs LLC ....E...... 937 354-2233
Mount Victory *(G-14796)*

▲ Weaver Bros Inc ....D...... 937 526-3907
Versailles *(G-18573)*

Weaver Bros Inc ....E...... 937 526-4777
Versailles *(G-18574)*

0253 Turkey & Turkey Egg Farms

Cooper Hatchery Inc ....C...... 419 594-3325
Oakwood *(G-15483)*

V H Cooper & Co Inc ....E...... 419 375-4116
Fort Recovery *(G-10994)*

0254 Poultry Hatcheries

Cooper Hatchery Inc ....C...... 419 594-3325
Oakwood *(G-15483)*

Cuddy Farms Inc ....E...... 740 599-7979
Danville *(G-9150)*

Midwest Poultry Services Lp ......E...... 419 375-4417
Fort Recovery *(G-10993)*

Select Genetics LLC ....E...... 740 599-7979
Danville *(G-9151)*

0291 Animal Production, NEC

Pork Champ LLC ....D...... 740 493-2164
Lucasville *(G-13052)*

07 AGRICULTURAL SERVICES

0711 Soil Preparation Svcs

Blanchard Tree and Lawn Inc ......D...... 419 865-7071
Holland *(G-11874)*

Clark Royster Inc ....E...... 740 335-3810
Wshngtn CT Hs *(G-19864)*

Henderson Turf Farm Inc ....E...... 937 748-1559
Franklin *(G-11032)*

S & D Application LLC ....E...... 419 288-3660
Wayne *(G-18826)*

0721 Soil Preparation, Planting & Cultivating Svc

Georgetown Vineyards Inc ....E...... 740 435-3222
Cambridge *(G-2069)*

0723 Crop Preparation, Except Cotton Ginning

Andersons Inc ....C...... 419 893-5050
Maumee *(G-13754)*

Case Farms LLC ....D...... 330 832-0030
Massillon *(G-13668)*

Custom Agri Systems Inc ....E...... 419 209-0940
Upper Sandusky *(G-18405)*

Freshealth LLC ....E...... 614 231-3601
Columbus *(G-7625)*

Great Lakes Packers Inc ....E...... 419 483-2956
Bellevue *(G-1379)*

Ohigro Inc ....E...... 740 726-2429
Waldo *(G-18630)*

Schlessman Seed Co ....E...... 419 499-2572
Milan *(G-14367)*

0724 Cotton Ginning

▼ Compass Systems & Sales LLC ...D...... 330 733-2111
Norton *(G-15418)*

0741 Veterinary Livestock Svcs

Howland Corners Twn & Ctry Vet ...E...... 330 856-1862
Warren *(G-18714)*

0742 Veterinary Animal Specialties

Amherst Animal Hospital Inc ......E...... 440 282-5220
Amherst *(G-578)*

Animal Care Unlimited Inc ....E...... 614 766-2317
Columbus *(G-6950)*

Animal Hospital Inc ....E...... 440 946-2800
Willoughby Hills *(G-19586)*

Animal Hospital Polaris LLC ....E...... 614 888-4050
Lewis Center *(G-12524)*

Animal Protective League ....E...... 216 771-4616
Cleveland *(G-4982)*

Annehurst Veterinary Hospital ....E...... 614 818-4221
Westerville *(G-19220)*

Avon Lake Animal Clinic Inc ......E...... 440 933-5297
Avon Lake *(G-909)*

Beechmont Pet Hospital Inc ....E...... 513 232-0300
Cincinnati *(G-3032)*

Beechwold Veterinary Hospital ....E...... 614 268-8666
Columbus *(G-7024)*

Beechwold Veterinary Hospital ....E...... 614 766-1222
Dublin *(G-10143)*

Bigger Road Veterinary Clinic .....E...... 937 435-3262
Dayton *(G-9252)*

Cedar Creek Vterinary Svcs Inc ...E...... 740 467-2949
Millersport *(G-14502)*

Cincinnati Anml Rfrrl ....D...... 513 530-0911
Cincinnati *(G-3221)*

Countryside Veterinary Service ....E...... 330 847-7337
Warren *(G-18691)*

County Animal Hospital ....E...... 513 398-8000
Mason *(G-13568)*

Daniels Boarding Kennels ....E...... 440 238-7179
Strongsville *(G-17296)*

Dayton Animal Hospital Assoc ....E...... 937 890-4744
Dayton *(G-9350)*

Detroit Dover Animals Hospital ...E...... 440 871-5220
Cleveland *(G-5418)*

Eastgate Animal Hospital Inc ......E...... 513 528-0700
Cincinnati *(G-3477)*

Gahanna Animal Hospital Inc ......E...... 614 471-2201
Gahanna *(G-11122)*

Grady Veterinary Hospital Inc .....E...... 513 931-8675
Cincinnati *(G-3632)*

High Point Animal Hospital ....E...... 419 865-3611
Maumee *(G-13801)*

Howland Corners Twn & Ctry Vet ...E...... 330 856-1862
Warren *(G-18714)*

Kettering Animal Hospital Inc ......E...... 937 294-5211
Dayton *(G-9536)*

Knapp Veterinary Hospital Inc .....E...... 614 267-3124
Columbus *(G-7915)*

Medvet Associates Inc ....B...... 937 293-2714
Moraine *(G-14676)*

Medvet Associates Inc ....A...... 614 846-5800
Worthington *(G-19827)*

Metropltan Vterinary Med Group ...E...... 330 253-2544
Copley *(G-8971)*

Michael T Lee Dvm ....E...... 330 722-5076
Medina *(G-13979)*

Midpark Animal Hospital ....E...... 216 362-6622
Cleveland *(G-5987)*

National Veterinary Assoc Inc .....D...... 330 652-0055
Niles *(G-15161)*

North Ridge Veterinary Hosp ......E...... 440 428-5166
Madison *(G-13106)*

Obetz Animal Hospital ....E...... 614 491-5676
Columbus *(G-8223)*

Ohio State University ....C...... 614 292-6661
Columbus *(G-8334)*

Paws Inn Inc ....E...... 937 435-1500
Dayton *(G-9689)*

Petsmart Inc ....D...... 614 418-9389
Columbus *(G-8443)*

Riverside Drv Animal Care Ctr .....E...... 614 414-2668
Dublin *(G-10323)*

RMS Aquaculture Inc ....E...... 216 433-1340
Cleveland *(G-6331)*

Shawnee Animal Clinic Inc ....E...... 740 353-5758
Portsmouth *(G-16169)*

South Mill Pet Care Center ....E...... 330 758-6479
Youngstown *(G-20213)*

Steven L Sawdai ....E...... 513 829-3830
Fairfield *(G-10787)*

Stow-Kent Animal Hospital Inc ....E...... 330 673-0049
Kent *(G-12259)*

Stow-Kent Animal Hospital Inc ....E...... 330 673-1002
Kent *(G-12260)*

Suburban Veterinarian Clinic ......E...... 937 433-2160
Dayton *(G-9798)*

Sylvania Veterinary Hospital ....E...... 419 885-4421
Sylvania *(G-17456)*

Tipp City Veterinary Hosp Inc .....D...... 937 667-8489
Tipp City *(G-17568)*

Tri Zob Inc ....E...... 216 252-4500
Cleveland *(G-6547)*

VCA Animal Hospitals Inc ....E...... 419 423-7232
Findlay *(G-10973)*

VCA Green Animal Medical Ctr .....E...... 330 896-4040
Uniontown *(G-18389)*

Veterinary RFRrl&emer Ctr of ......E...... 330 665-4996
Copley *(G-8979)*

Woodland Run Equin Vet Facilty ...E...... 614 871-4919
Grove City *(G-11490)*

0751 Livestock Svcs, Except Veterinary

Hertzfeld Poultry Farms Inc ....D...... 419 832-2070
Grand Rapids *(G-11326)*

Landes Fresh Meats Inc ....E...... 937 836-3613
Clayton *(G-4859)*

Poultry Service Associates ....E...... 937 968-3339
Dayton *(G-9152)*

Robert Winner Sons Inc ....E...... 419 582-4321
Yorkshire *(G-19942)*

Rubin Erb ....E...... 330 852-4423
Sugarcreek *(G-17380)*

0752 Animal Specialty Svcs, Exc Veterinary

4 Paws Sake Inc ....E...... 419 304-7139
Grand Rapids *(G-11323)*

Anark Inc ....E...... 513 825-7387
Cincinnati *(G-2958)*

Animal Care Unlimited Inc ....E 614 766-2317
Columbus (G-6950)

Annehurst Veterinary Hospital ....E 614 818-4221
Westerville (G-19220)

Avon Lake Animal Clinic Inc ....E 440 933-5297
Avon Lake (G-909)

Barkley of Cleveland LLC ....E 440 248-2275
Chagrin Falls (G-2639)

Birchwood Genetics Inc ....E 937 678-9313
West Manchester (G-19123)

Cleveland All Breed Trning CLB ....D 216 398-1118
Cleveland (G-5229)

Coba/Select Sires Inc ....D 614 878-5333
Columbus (G-7239)

Csa Animal Nutrition LLC ....E 866 615-8084
Dayton (G-9341)

Dayton Animal Hospital Assoc ....E 937 890-4744
Dayton (G-9350)

Dayton Dog Training Club Inc ....E 937 293-5219
Moraine (G-14642)

Foxridge Farms Corp ....E 740 965-1369
Galena (G-11158)

Kettering Animal Hospital Inc ....E 937 294-5211
Dayton (G-9536)

Lake Erie Nature & Science Ctr ....E 440 871-2900
Bay Village (G-1022)

◆ Miraclecorp Products ....D 937 293-9994
Moraine (G-14680)

Orville Pet Spa & Resort ....E 330 683-3335
Orrville (G-15642)

Paws Inn Inc ....E 937 435-1500
Dayton (G-9689)

Pet Central Lodge & Grooming ....E 440 282-1811
Amherst (G-595)

Petsmart Inc ....E 513 336-0365
Mason (G-13626)

Petsmart Inc ....E 513 248-4954
Milford (G-14422)

Petsmart Inc ....E 513 752-8463
Cincinnati (G-2865)

Petsmart Inc ....E 937 236-1335
Huber Heights (G-11957)

Petsmart Inc ....D 614 418-9389
Columbus (G-8443)

Petsmart Inc ....E 330 922-4114
Cuyahoga Falls (G-9117)

Petsmart Inc ....E 330 629-2479
Youngstown (G-20154)

Petsmart Inc ....E 330 544-1499
Niles (G-15167)

Petsmart Inc ....E 614 497-3001
Groveport (G-11529)

Petsmart Inc ....E 440 974-1100
Mentor (G-14096)

Petsuites of America Inc ....E 513 554-4408
Cincinnati (G-4238)

Pups Paradise ....E 419 873-6115
Perrysburg (G-15908)

Red Dog Pet Resort & Spa ....E 513 733-3647
Cincinnati (G-4348)

Reptiles By Mack LLC ....E 937 372-9570
Xenia (G-19923)

Skyview Baptist Ranch Inc ....E 330 674-7511
Millersburg (G-14493)

South Mill Pet Care Center ....E 330 758-6479
Youngstown (G-20213)

0762 Farm Management Svcs

D H I Cooperative Inc ....D 614 545-0460
Columbus (G-7408)

0781 Landscape Counseling & Planning

Aaron Landscape Inc ....E 440 838-8875
North Royalton (G-15345)

▲ Acro Tool & Die Company ....D 330 773-5173
Akron (G-17)

Bladecutters Lawn Service Inc ....E 937 274-3861
Dayton (G-9255)

Blanchard Tree and Lawn Inc ....D 419 865-7071
Holland (G-11874)

Blendon Gardens Inc ....E 614 840-0500
Lewis Center (G-12529)

Brightview Landscape Svcs Inc ....E 614 801-1712
Columbus (G-7068)

Brightview Landscape Svcs Inc ....D 614 478-2085
Columbus (G-7069)

Brightview Landscape Svcs Inc ....D 740 369-4800
Columbus (G-7070)

Brightview Landscapes LLC ....D 513 874-6484
West Chester (G-19047)

Brightview Landscapes LLC ....E 216 398-1289
Oakwood Village (G-15486)

Brightview Landscapes LLC ....E 440 937-5126
Avon (G-869)

Brightview Landscapes LLC ....E 301 987-9200
Columbus (G-7071)

Brightview Landscapes LLC ....D 614 276-5500
Columbus (G-7072)

Brightview Landscapes LLC ....E 440 729-2302
Chesterland (G-2737)

Brightview Landscapes LLC ....D 614 741-8233
New Albany (G-14844)

▲ Buckeye Landscape Service Inc ......D 614 866-0088
Blacklick (G-1475)

Bzak Landscaping Inc ....E 513 831-0907
Milford (G-14375)

Civil & Environmental Cons Inc ....E 513 985-0226
Milford (G-14380)

Collaborative Inc ....E 419 242-7405
Toledo (G-17667)

Country Gardens ....E 740 522-8810
Granville (G-11339)

Custom Lawn Care & Ldscpg LLC ....E 740 333-1669
Wshngtn CT Hs (G-19868)

Dayton City Parks Golf Maint ....E 937 333-3378
Dayton (G-9359)

Detillion Landscaping Co Inc ....E 740 775-5305
Chillicothe (G-2777)

Eastside Landscaping Inc ....E 216 381-0070
Cleveland (G-5460)

Eastside Nursery Inc ....E 513 934-1661
Lebanon (G-12462)

Ever Green Lawn Care Inc ....E 937 335-6418
Troy (G-18201)

Family Entertainment Services ....E 740 286-8587
Jackson (G-12173)

Five Seasons Landscape MGT Inc ....D 740 964-2915
Etna (G-10609)

Floralandscape Inc ....D 419 536-7640
Toledo (G-17744)

Garmann/Miller & Assoc Inc ....E 419 628-4240
Minster (G-14533)

Green Impressions LLC ....E 440 240-8508
Sheffield Village (G-16734)

Greenpro Services Inc ....E 937 748-1559
Franklin (G-11030)

Greenscapes Landscape Company .....D 614 837-1869
Columbus (G-7696)

H A M Landscaping Inc ....E 216 663-6666
Cleveland (G-5650)

Hemlock Landscapes Inc ....E 440 247-3631
Chagrin Falls (G-2667)

Horticultural Management Inc ....E 937 427-8835
Beavercrk Twp (G-1265)

HWH Archtcts-Ngnrs-Plnners Inc ....D 216 875-4000
Cleveland (G-5727)

Impullitti Landscaping Inc ....D 440 834-1866
Burton (G-2017)

Joes Ldscpg Beavercreek Inc ....E 937 427-1133
Beavercreek Township (G-1251)

Kleingers Group Inc ....D 513 779-7851
West Chester (G-18957)

Lanhan Contractors Inc ....E 440 918-1099
Willoughby (G-19542)

Lifestyle Landscaping Inc ....E 440 353-0333
North Ridgeville (G-15334)

Louderback Fmly Invstments Inc ....E 937 845-1762
New Carlisle (G-14893)

Madison Tree & Landscape Co ....E 614 207-5422
West Jefferson (G-19111)

Maslyk Landscaping Inc ....E 440 748-3635
Columbia Station (G-6778)

Mc Clurg & Creamer Inc ....E 419 866-7080
Holland (G-11896)

McGill Smith Punshon Inc ....E 513 759-0004
Cincinnati (G-3987)

Meyers Ldscp Svcs & Nurs Inc ....E 614 210-1194
Lewis Center (G-12551)

MJ Design Associates Inc ....E 614 873-7333
Plain City (G-16061)

Mjs Snow & Landscape LLC ....D 419 656-6724
Port Clinton (G-16113)

Mksk Inc ....D 614 621-2796
Columbus (G-8093)

Mortons Lawn Service Inc ....E 440 236-3550
Columbia Station (G-6779)

Myers/Schmalenberger Inc ....E 614 621-2796
Columbus (G-8125)

▲ Oakland Nursery Inc ....E 614 268-3834
Columbus (G-8221)

Oasis Turf & Tree Inc ....E 513 697-9090
Loveland (G-13018)

Oberlanders Tree & Ldscp Ltd ....E 419 562-8733
Bucyrus (G-1998)

Ohio Valley Group Inc ....E 440 543-0500
Chagrin Falls (G-2676)

Pattie Group Inc ....D 440 338-1288
Novelty (G-15466)

Personal Lawn Care Inc ....E 440 934-5296
Avon (G-900)

Rentokil North America Inc ....E 614 837-0099
Groveport (G-11534)

Scarffs Nursery Inc ....C 937 845-3130
New Carlisle (G-14897)

Schill Landscaping and Lawn CA ....D 440 327-3030
North Ridgeville (G-15343)

Schoenbrunn Landscaping Inc ....E 330 364-3688
Dover (G-10098)

Seacrist Landscaping and Cnstr ....E 440 946-2731
Mentor (G-14107)

Shining Company LLC ....C 614 588-4115
Columbus (G-8634)

Southside Envmtl Group LLC ....E 330 299-0027
Niles (G-15170)

Suncrest Gardens Inc ....C 330 650-4969
Peninsula (G-15813)

Thornton Landscape Inc ....E 513 683-8100
Maineville (G-13119)

Tim Mundy ....E 937 862-8686
Spring Valley (G-16959)

Tucker Landscaping Inc ....D 440 786-9840
Bedford (G-1312)

Vance Property Management LLC ....D 419 467-9548
Toledo (G-18135)

Yardmaster of Columbus Inc ....E 614 863-4510
Blacklick (G-1485)

0782 Lawn & Garden Svcs

A Ressler Inc ....E 216 518-1804
Cleveland (G-4880)

Abbruzzese Brothers Inc ....E 614 873-1550
Plain City (G-16042)

Able Contracting Group Inc ....E 440 951-0880
Painesville (G-15691)

Ameriscape Inc ....E 614 863-5400
Blacklick (G-1473)

Barnes Nursery Inc ....E 800 421-8722
Huron (G-12021)

Bauer Lawn Maintenance Inc ....E 419 893-5296
Maumee (G-13761)

Benchmark Landscape Cnstr Inc ....E 614 873-8080
Plain City (G-16045)

Berns Grnhse & Grdn Ctr Inc ....E 513 423-5306
Middletown (G-14293)

Bladecutters Lawn Service Inc ....E 937 274-3861
Dayton (G-9255)

Blanchard Tree and Lawn Inc ....D 419 865-7071
Holland (G-11874)

Brian-Kyles Construction Inc ....E 440 242-0298
Lorain (G-12887)

Brightview Landscapes LLC ....E 937 235-9595
Dayton (G-9261)

Brightview Landscapes LLC ....E 440 729-2302
Chesterland (G-2737)

Brightview Landscapes LLC ....D 614 741-8233
New Albany (G-14844)

Buck and Sons Ldscp Svc Inc ....E 614 876-5359
Hilliard (G-11750)

▲ Buckeye Landscape Service Inc ......D 614 866-0088
Blacklick (G-1475)

Bzak Landscaping Inc ....E 513 831-0907
Milford (G-14375)

C & B Buck Bros Asp Maint LLC ....E 419 536-7325
Toledo (G-17633)

Camco Inc ....E 740 477-3682
Circleville (G-4827)

Castle Care ....E 440 327-3700
North Ridgeville (G-15323)

Chores Unlimited Inc ....D 440 439-5455
Bedford Heights (G-1320)

Como Inc ....E 614 830-2666
Pickerington (G-15954)

County of Gallia ....E 740 446-2665
Gallipolis (G-11188)

County of Portage ....D 330 296-6411
Ravenna (G-16238)

County of Warren ....E 513 695-1109
Lebanon (G-12458)

Croys Mowing LLC ....E 419 523-5884
Ottawa (G-15658)

Davey Tree Expert Company ....E 330 928-4911
Stow (G-17199)

Davey Tree Expert Company ....D 614 471-4144
Columbus (G-7419)

Davey Tree Expert Company ....E 440 439-4770
Cleveland (G-5407)

Davey Tree Expert Company ....C 330 673-9511
Kent (G-12226)

Dennis Top Soil & Landscaping ....E 419 865-5656
Toledo (G-17697)

Detillion Landscaping Co Inc ....E 740 775-5305
Chillicothe (G-2777)

Disanto Companies ....E 440 442-0600
Cleveland (G-5426)

Dohner Ltd ....E 330 814-4144
Hudson (G-11975)

Dta Inc ....E 419 529-2920
Ontario (G-15548)

Eastside Nursery Inc ....E 513 934-1661
Lebanon (G-12462)

Eds Tree & Turf ....E 740 881-5800
Delaware (G-9972)

Emsi Inc ....E 614 876-9988
Plain City (G-16051)

Envircare Lawn Landscacape LLC ....E 419 874-6779
Perrysburg (G-15864)

Enviroscapes ....E 330 875-0768
Louisville (G-12966)

Ever Green Lawn Care Inc ....E 937 335-6418
Troy (G-18201)

Fackler Country Gardens Inc ....E 740 522-3128
Granville (G-11341)

Floralandscape Inc ....D 419 536-7640
Toledo (G-17744)

Forevergreen Lawn Care ....E 440 327-8987
North Ridgeville (G-15330)

Fredericks Landscaping Inc ....E 513 821-9407
Cincinnati (G-3587)

Gears Garden Center Inc ....E 513 931-3800
Cincinnati (G-3606)

Gonda Lawn Care LLC ....E 330 701-7232
Masury (G-13740)

Grandmas Gardens Inc ....E 937 885-2973
Waynesville (G-18831)

Green Impressions LLC ....E 440 240-8508
Sheffield Village (G-16734)

Green King Company Inc ....E 614 861-4132
Reynoldsburg (G-16308)

Greenleaf Landscapes Inc ....D 740 373-1639
Marietta (G-13332)

Greenscapes Landscape Company ....D 614 837-1869
Columbus (G-7696)

Greentech Corporation ....E 937 339-4758
Troy (G-18204)

Grizzly Golf Center Inc ....B 513 398-5200
Mason (G-13590)

Groundspro LLC ....C 513 242-1700
West Chester (G-18936)

Groundsystems Inc ....E 800 570-0213
Blue Ash (G-1573)

Groundsystems Inc ....E 937 903-5325
Moraine (G-14665)

H A M Landscaping Inc ....E 216 663-6666
Cleveland (G-5650)

Hemlock Landscapes Inc ....E 440 247-3631
Chagrin Falls (G-2667)

Henderson Turf Farm Inc ....E 937 748-1559
Franklin (G-11032)

Hopewell Industries Inc ....D 740 622-3563
Coshocton (G-9018)

Horticultural Management Inc ....E 937 427-8835
Beavercrk Twp (G-1265)

Hyde Park Ldscp & Tree Svc Inc ....E 513 731-1334
Cincinnati (G-3745)

Igh II Inc ....E 419 874-3575
Mansfield (G-13184)

J Gilmore Design Limited ....E 330 638-8224
Cortland (G-8988)

Keller Group Limited ....E 614 866-9551
Columbus (G-7887)

Kgk Gardening Design Corp ....E 330 656-1709
Hudson (G-11990)

Land Art Inc ....E 419 666-5296
Perrysburg (G-15888)

Lewis Landscaping Inc ....E 330 666-2655
Copley (G-8968)

Lockes Garden Center Inc ....E 440 774-6981
Oberlin (G-15507)

M J Lanese Landscaping Inc ....E 440 942-3444
Willoughby (G-19547)

Mc Clurg & Creamer Inc ....E 419 866-7080
Holland (G-11896)

McCallisters Landscaping & Sup ....E 440 259-3348
Painesville (G-15725)

McCoy Landscape Services Inc ....E 740 375-2730
Marion (G-13447)

Miami Valley Memory Grdns Assn ....E 937 885-7779
Dayton (G-9624)

Mike Ward Landscaping Inc ....E 513 683-6436
Maineville (G-13116)

Mortons Lawn Service Inc ....E 440 236-3550
Columbia Station (G-6779)

▲ Motz Group Inc ....E 513 533-6452
Cincinnati (G-4077)

Natrop Inc ....D 513 242-1375
Cincinnati (G-4099)

North Branch Nursery Inc ....E 419 287-4679
Pemberville (G-15805)

Ohio Tpk & Infrastructure Comm ....E 419 826-4831
Swanton (G-17403)

Ohio Tpk & Infrastructure Comm ....C 440 234-2081
Berea (G-1433)

Ohio Tpk & Infrastructure Comm ....E 440 234-2081
Richfield (G-16369)

Pace Sankar Landscaping Inc ....E 330 343-0858
Dover (G-10092)

Paramount Lawn Service Inc ....E 513 984-5200
Loveland (G-13020)

Peabody Landscape Cnstr Inc ....D 614 488-2877
Columbus (G-8431)

Personal Lawn Care Inc ....E 440 934-5296
Avon (G-900)

Peter A Wimberg Company Inc ....E 513 271-2332
Cincinnati (G-4234)

Prusa Inc ....E 330 688-8500
Stow (G-17225)

R & S Halley & Co Inc ....E 614 771-0388
Hilliard (G-11810)

R B Stout Inc ....E 330 666-8811
Akron (G-396)

Richland Newhope Industries ....C 419 774-4400
Mansfield (G-13237)

Richter Landscaping ....E 513 539-0300
Monroe (G-14581)

Riepenhoff Landscape Ltd ....E 614 876-4683
Hilliard (G-11813)

River City Furniture LLC ....D 513 612-7303
West Chester (G-18994)

Robiden Inc ....E 513 421-0000
Fairfield Township (G-10814)

Rwc Inc ....E 614 890-0600
Westerville (G-19208)

Scherzinger Corp ....D 513 531-7848
Cincinnati (G-4435)

Schill Landscaping and Lawn CA ....D 440 327-3030
North Ridgeville (G-15343)

Schoenbrunn Landscaping Inc ....E 330 364-3688
Dover (G-10098)

◆ Scotts Company LLC ....B 937 644-0011
Marysville (G-13528)

▲ Scotts Miracle-Gro Company ....B 937 644-0011
Marysville (G-13529)

Seacrist Landscaping and Cnstr ....E 440 946-2731
Mentor (G-14107)

Sharp Edge LLC ....E 440 255-5917
Mentor (G-14108)

Siebenthaler Company ....D 937 427-4110
Dayton (G-9767)

South Star Corp ....E 330 239-5466
Medina (G-14004)

Spray A Tree Inc ....E 614 457-8257
Columbus (G-8674)

Suncrest Gardens Inc ....C 330 650-4969
Peninsula (G-15813)

Supers Landscaping Inc ....E 440 775-0027
Oberlin (G-15520)

T L C Landscaping Inc ....E 440 248-4852
Cleveland (G-6495)

Team Green Lawn LLC ....E 937 673-4315
Xenia (G-19928)

Tersigni Cargill Entps LLC ....E 330 351-0942
Stow (G-17235)

Thomsons Landscaping ....E 740 374-9353
Marietta (G-13386)

Thornton Landscape Inc ....E 513 683-8100
Maineville (G-13119)

Tim Mundy ....E 937 862-8686
Spring Valley (G-16959)

Todds Enviroscapes Inc ....E 330 875-0768
Louisville (G-12974)

Toledo Memorial Pk & Mausoleum ....E 419 882-7151
Sylvania (G-17460)

Trugreen Limited Partnership ....D 614 527-7070
Hilliard (G-11824)

Trugreen Limited Partnership ....E 937 557-0060
Springboro (G-16986)

Trugreen Limited Partnership ....E 419 884-3636
Mansfield (G-13256)

Trugreen Limited Partnership ....D 440 786-7200
Bedford (G-1311)

Trugreen Limited Partnership ....E 513 223-3707
Fairfield (G-10794)

Trugreen Limited Partnership ....E 440 290-3340
Mentor (G-14116)

Trugreen Limited Partnership ....C 614 285-3721
Lewis Center (G-12564)

Trugreen Limited Partnership ....E 419 516-4200
Lima (G-12771)

Trugreen Limited Partnership ....D 440 540-4209
Elyria (G-10568)

Trugreen Limited Partnership ....E 614 610-4142
Groveport (G-11544)

Trugreen Limited Partnership ....E 330 409-2861
Canton (G-2515)

Trugreen Limited Partnership ....E 740 598-4724
Brilliant (G-1823)

Trugreen Limited Partnership ....E 937 866-8399
Dayton (G-9824)

Trugreen Limited Partnership ....D 937 410-4055
Vandalia (G-18545)

Trugreen-Chem Lawn ....D 330 533-2839
Poland (G-16091)

Turfscape Inc ....C 330 405-0741
Twinsburg (G-18330)

Turnpike and Infrastructure Co ....D 330 527-2169
Windham (G-19664)

Tuttle Landscaping & Grdn Ctr ....E 419 756-7555
Mansfield (G-13257)

University of Cincinnati ....A 513 556-6381
Cincinnati (G-4707)

Upscale Lawncre & Prprty Maint ....E 513 266-1165
Cincinnati (G-4731)

Vizmeg Landscape Inc ....E 330 686-0901
Stow (G-17238)

Walden Turf Center ....E 330 995-0023
Aurora (G-850)

Warstler Brothers Landscaping ....E 330 492-9500
Canton (G-2531)

Weed Man Lawncare LLC ....E 513 683-6310
Cincinnati (G-4772)

Wickline Landscaping Inc ....E 937 372-0521
Xenia (G-19933)

Wilson Enterprises Inc ....E 614 444-8873
Columbus (G-8909)

Winn-Scapes Inc ....D 614 866-9466
Gahanna (G-11151)

Woody Tree Medics ....E 937 298-5316
Dayton (G-9886)

Yardmaster Inc ....D 440 357-8400
Painesville (G-15749)

0783 Ornamental Shrub & Tree Svc

Asplundh Tree Expert LLC ....C 740 467-1028
Millersport (G-14501)

Barberton Tree Service Inc ....E 330 848-2344
Norton (G-15417)

Blanchard Tree and Lawn Inc ....D 419 865-7071
Holland (G-11874)

Care of Trees Inc ....E 800 445-8733
Kent (G-12216)

Davey Resource Group Inc ....D 330 673-9511
Kent (G-12225)

Davey Tree Expert Company ....E 330 908-0833
Macedonia (G-13067)

Davey Tree Expert Company ....E 330 628-1499
Mogadore (G-14546)

Davey Tree Expert Company ....C 330 673-9511
Kent (G-12226)

Davey Tree Expert Company ....D 330 673-9511
Columbus (G-7418)

Davey Tree Expert Company ....E 513 575-1733
Milford (G-14383)

Davey Tree Expert Company ....E 330 928-4911
Stow (G-17199)

Davey Tree Expert Company ....D 614 471-4144
Columbus (G-7419)

Davey Tree Expert Company ....E 440 439-4770
Cleveland (G-5407)

Dbi Services LLC ....E 410 590-4181
South Point (G-16930)

Edwards Land Clearing Inc ....E 440 988-4477
  Amherst (G-585)

Fdc Enterprises Inc ....E 614 774-9182
  Springfield (G-17037)

Forevergreen Lawn Care ....E 440 327-8987
  North Ridgeville (G-15330)

Hyde Park Ldscp & Tree Svc Inc ....E 513 731-1334
  Cincinnati (G-3745)

Land Art Inc ....E 419 666-5296
  Perrysburg (G-15888)

Madison Tree Care & Ldscpg Inc ....E 513 576-6391
  Milford (G-14406)

MBI Tree Service LLC ....E 513 926-9857
  Waynesville (G-18834)

Merciers Incorporated ....C 410 590-4181
  South Point (G-16942)

Metrohealth System ....C 216 957-2100
  Cleveland (G-5972)

Nelson Tree Service Inc ....E 937 294-1313
  Dayton (G-9656)

Oberlanders Tree & Ldscp Ltd ....E 419 562-8733
  Bucyrus (G-1998)

Woody Tree Medics ....E 937 298-5316
  Dayton (G-9886)

08 FORESTRY

0811 Timber Tracts

▲ Acro Tool & Die Company ....D 330 773-5173
  Akron (G-17)

Davey Tree Expert Company ....C 330 673-9511
  Kent (G-12226)

0851 Forestry Svcs

Belmont Cnty Fire & Squad Offi ....E 740 312-5058
  Bridgeport (G-1813)

Cgh-Global Emerg Mngmt Strateg ......E 800 376-0655
  Cincinnati (G-2843)

Middletown City Divison Fire ....D 513 425-7996
  Middletown (G-14309)

09 FISHING, HUNTING, AND TRAPPING

0971 Hunting & Trapping

Miami Valley Gaming & Racg LLC ....D 513 934-7070
  Lebanon (G-12485)

10 METAL MINING

1011 Iron Ores

Cleveland-Cliffs Inc ....D 216 694-5700
  Cleveland (G-5299)

Cliffs Minnesota Minerals Co ....A 216 694-5700
  Cleveland (G-5303)

International Steel Group ....C 330 841-2800
  Warren (G-18715)

The Cleveland-Cliffs Iron Co ....C 216 694-5700
  Cleveland (G-6520)

Tilden Mining Company LC ....A 216 694-5700
  Cleveland (G-6530)

Wabush Mines Cliffs Mining Co ....A 216 694-5700
  Cleveland (G-6647)

1021 Copper Ores

◆ Warrenton Copper LLC ....E 636 456-3488
  Cleveland (G-6654)

1061 Ferroalloy Ores, Except Vanadium

▲ Rhenium Alloys Inc ....D 440 365-7388
  North Ridgeville (G-15340)

1081 Metal Mining Svcs

Alloy Metal Exchange LLC ....E 216 478-0200
  Bedford Heights (G-1315)

Hahs Factory Outlet ....E 330 405-4227
  Twinsburg (G-18277)

Hopedale Mining LLC ....E 740 937-2225
  Hopedale (G-11937)

12 COAL MINING

1221 Bituminous Coal & Lignite: Surface Mining

B&N Coal Inc ....D 740 783-3575
  Dexter City (G-10059)

Coal Services Inc ....D 740 795-5220
  Powhatan Point (G-16214)

J & D Mining Inc ....E 330 339-4935
  New Philadelphia (G-14967)

Marietta Coal Co ....E 740 695-2197
  Saint Clairsville (G-16494)

Murray American Energy Inc ....A 740 338-3100
  Saint Clairsville (G-16496)

Nacco Industries Inc ....E 440 229-5151
  Cleveland (G-6034)

Ohio Valley Coal Company ....B 740 926-1351
  Saint Clairsville (G-16498)

Oxford Mining Company Inc ....D 740 342-7666
  New Lexington (G-14924)

Rosebud Mining Company ....E 740 768-2097
  Bergholz (G-1444)

Rosebud Mining Company ....E 740 922-9122
  Uhrichsville (G-18343)

Sands Hill Coal Hauling Co Inc ....C 740 384-4211
  Hamden (G-11553)

1222 Bituminous Coal: Underground Mining

Coal Services Inc ....D 740 795-5220
  Powhatan Point (G-16214)

Rosebud Mining Company ....E 740 658-4217
  Freeport (G-11055)

Rosebud Mining Company ....E 740 768-2097
  Bergholz (G-1444)

Rosebud Mining Company ....E 740 922-9122
  Uhrichsville (G-18343)

Western KY Coal Resources LLC ....B 740 338-3100
  Saint Clairsville (G-16510)

1231 Anthracite Mining

Coal Services Inc ....D 740 795-5220
  Powhatan Point (G-16214)

1241 Coal Mining Svcs

Coal Services Inc ....D 740 795-5220
  Powhatan Point (G-16214)

Harrison County Coal Company ....E 740 338-3100
  Saint Clairsville (G-16488)

Ohio Valley Resources Inc ....E 740 795-5220
  Saint Clairsville (G-16499)

Ohio Valley Transloading Co ....A 740 795-4967
  Saint Clairsville (G-16500)

Peabody Coal Company ....B 740 450-2420
  Zanesville (G-20353)

Suncoke Energy Nc ....E 513 727-5571
  Middletown (G-14333)

13 OIL AND GAS EXTRACTION

1311 Crude Petroleum & Natural Gas

AB Resources LLC ....E 440 922-1098
  Brecksville (G-1766)

Alliance Petroleum Corporation ....D 330 493-0440
  Canton (G-2180)

Belden & Blake Corporation ....E 330 602-5551
  Dover (G-10066)

Chevron Ae Resources LLC ....E 330 654-4343
  Deerfield (G-9902)

City of Lancaster ....E 740 687-6670
  Lancaster (G-12380)

Columbia Energy Group ....A 614 460-4683
  Columbus (G-7247)

Gulfport Energy Corporation ....E 740 251-0407
  Saint Clairsville (G-16487)

Interstate Gas Supply Inc ....D 614 659-5000
  Dublin (G-10258)

Kenoil Inc ....E 330 262-1144
  Wooster (G-19738)

◆ Koch Knight LLC ....D 330 488-1651
  East Canton (G-10387)

M3 Midstream LLC ....D 740 945-1170
  Scio (G-16663)

M3 Midstream LLC ....E 330 679-5580
  Salineville (G-16571)

M3 Midstream LLC ....E 330 223-2220
  Kensington (G-12210)

M3 Midstream LLC ....E 740 431-4168
  Dennison (G-10052)

Williams Partners LP ....C 330 966-3674
  North Canton (G-15244)

Xto Energy Inc ....D 740 671-9901
  Bellaire (G-1337)

1321 Natural Gas Liquids

Husky Marketing and Supply Co ....E 614 210-2300
  Dublin (G-10250)

1381 Drilling Oil & Gas Wells

Decker Drilling Inc ....E 740 749-3939
  Vincent (G-18585)

Eclipse Resources - Ohio LLC ....E 740 452-4503
  Zanesville (G-20303)

J D Drilling Co ....E 740 949-2512
  Racine (G-16229)

Kilbarger Construction Inc ....C 740 385-6019
  Logan (G-12843)

Qes Pressure Control LLC ....E 740 489-5721
  Lore City (G-12953)

Stratagraph Ne Inc ....E 740 373-3091
  Marietta (G-13384)

Victor McKenzie Drilling Co ....E 740 453-0834
  Zanesville (G-20372)

Warren Drilling Co Inc ....C 740 783-2775
  Dexter City (G-10060)

1382 Oil & Gas Field Exploration Svcs

Alliance Petroleum Corporation ....D 330 493-0440
  Canton (G-2180)

Antero Resources Corporation ....D 740 760-1000
  Marietta (G-13312)

Bakerwell Inc ....D 614 898-7590
  Westerville (G-19146)

Belden & Blake Corporation ....E 330 602-5551
  Dover (G-10066)

Chevron Ae Resources LLC ....E 330 654-4343
  Deerfield (G-9902)

Dlz Ohio Inc ....C 614 888-0040
  Columbus (G-7462)

Enervest Ltd ....D 330 877-6747
  Hartville (G-11685)

Husky Marketing and Supply Co ....E 614 210-2300
  Dublin (G-10250)

New World Energy Resources ....B 740 344-4087
  Newark (G-15081)

Precision Geophysical Inc ....E 330 674-2198
  Millersburg (G-14488)

Range Rsurces - Appalachia LLC ....E 330 866-3301
  Dover (G-10094)

Triad Energy Corporation ....E 740 374-2940
  Marietta (G-13387)

True North Energy LLC ....E 440 442-0060
  Mayfield Heights (G-13883)

1389 Oil & Gas Field Svcs, NEC

Acuren Inspection Inc ....D 937 228-9729
  Dayton (G-9206)

▲ Bdi Inc ....C 216 642-9100
  Cleveland (G-5045)

Belden & Blake Corporation ....E 330 602-5551
  Dover (G-10066)

Cgh-Global Emerg Mngmt Strateg ......E 800 376-0655
  Cincinnati (G-2843)

Clearfield Ohio Holdings Inc ....D 740 947-5121
  Waverly (G-18816)

Express Energy Svcs Oper LP ....E 740 337-4530
  Toronto (G-18184)

Fishburn Tank Truck Service ....D 419 253-6031
  Marengo (G-13303)

Fts International Inc ....A 330 754-2375
  East Canton (G-10386)

Greer & Whitehead Cnstr Inc ....E 513 202-1757
  Harrison (G-11668)

Halliburton Energy Svcs Inc ....C 740 617-2917
  Zanesville (G-20314)

Ingle-Barr Inc ....C 740 702-6117
  Chillicothe (G-2793)

Kelchner Inc ....C 937 704-9890
  Springboro (G-16971)

Siler Excavation Services ....E 513 400-8628
  Milford (G-14432)

Stallion Oilfield Cnstr LLC ....E 330 868-2083
  Paris (G-15757)

▲ Stingray Pressure Pumping LLC ....E 405 648-4177
  Belmont (G-1396)

Stratagraph Ne Inc ....E 740 373-3091
  Marietta (G-13384)

SIC

Terra Star Inc .... E 405 200-1336
Waynesburg (G-18830)

Timothy Sinfield .... E 740 685-3684
Pleasant City (G-16072)

Tk Gas Services Inc .... E 740 826-0303
New Concord (G-14904)

U S Weatherford L P .... C 330 746-2502
Youngstown (G-20230)

Varco LP .... E 440 277-8696
Lorain (G-12950)

14 MINING AND QUARRYING OF NONMETALLIC MINERALS, EXCEPT FUELS

1411 Dimension Stone

Heritage Marble of Ohio Inc .... E 614 436-1464
Columbus (G-7745)

Irg Operating LLC .... E 440 963-4008
Vermilion (G-18554)

National Lime and Stone Co .... D 419 562-0771
Bucyrus (G-1997)

Stoneco Inc .... D 419 422-8854
Findlay (G-10964)

1422 Crushed & Broken Limestone

Acme Company .... D 330 758-2313
Poland (G-16079)

Allgeier & Son Inc .... E 513 574-3735
Cincinnati (G-2925)

Carmeuse Lime Inc .... E 419 638-2511
Millersville (G-14504)

Carmeuse Lime Inc .... E 419 986-5200
Bettsville (G-1458)

Chesterhill Stone Co .... E 740 849-2338
East Fultonham (G-10388)

Conag Inc .... E 419 394-8870
Saint Marys (G-16522)

◆ Covia Holdings Corporation .... D 440 214-3284
Independence (G-12063)

Hanson Aggregates East LLC .... E 937 587-2671
Peebles (G-15802)

Hanson Aggregates East LLC .... D 419 483-4390
Castalia (G-2578)

Hanson Aggregates East LLC .... E 937 442-6009
Winchester (G-19662)

▲ Lang Stone Company Inc .... D 614 235-4099
Columbus (G-7951)

Martin Marietta Materials Inc .... D 513 353-1400
North Bend (G-15182)

Martin Marietta Materials Inc .... E 513 701-1140
West Chester (G-18970)

National Lime and Stone Co .... C 419 396-7671
Carey (G-2545)

National Lime and Stone Co .... E 740 548-4206
Delaware (G-9997)

National Lime and Stone Co .... E 419 423-3400
Findlay (G-10948)

National Lime and Stone Co .... D 419 562-0771
Bucyrus (G-1997)

◆ Omya Industries Inc .... D 513 387-4600
Blue Ash (G-1625)

Piqua Materials Inc .... E 937 773-4824
Piqua (G-16019)

Piqua Materials Inc .... D 513 771-0820
Cincinnati (G-4251)

R W Sidley Incorporated .... E 440 352-9343
Painesville (G-15736)

Shelly Materials Inc .... E 740 666-5841
Ostrander (G-15655)

Shelly Materials Inc .... D 740 246-6315
Thornville (G-17506)

Sidwell Materials Inc .... C 740 849-2394
Zanesville (G-20361)

Stoneco Inc .... E 419 393-2555
Oakwood (G-15484)

Wagner Quarries Company .... E 419 625-8141
Sandusky (G-16655)

White Rock Quarry L P .... A 419 855-8388
Clay Center (G-4855)

1423 Crushed & Broken Granite

Martin Marietta Materials Inc .... E 513 701-1140
West Chester (G-18970)

1429 Crushed & Broken Stone, NEC

Great Lakes Crushing Ltd .... E 440 944-5500
Wickliffe (G-19461)

1442 Construction Sand & Gravel

Barrett Paving Materials Inc .... C 513 271-6200
Middletown (G-14343)

Carl E Oeder Sons Sand & Grav .... E 513 494-1555
Lebanon (G-12454)

Central Ready Mix LLC .... E 513 402-5001
Cincinnati (G-3157)

◆ Covia Holdings Corporation .... D 440 214-3284
Independence (G-12063)

Fleming Construction Co .... E 740 494-2177
Prospect (G-16223)

FML Resin LLC .... E 440 214-3200
Independence (G-12074)

Hanson Aggregates East LLC .... E 740 773-2172
Chillicothe (G-2784)

Hilltop Basic Resources Inc .... E 513 621-1500
Cincinnati (G-3709)

J P Sand & Gravel Company .... E 614 497-0083
Lockbourne (G-12822)

Joe McClelland Inc .... E 740 452-3036
Zanesville (G-20321)

Kenmore Construction Co Inc .... E 330 832-8888
Massillon (G-13702)

Lakeside Sand & Gravel Inc .... E 330 274-2569
Mantua (G-13271)

Martin Marietta Materials Inc .... E 513 701-1140
West Chester (G-18970)

Mecco Inc .... E 513 422-3651
Middletown (G-14307)

National Lime and Stone Co .... E 614 497-0083
Lockbourne (G-12823)

National Lime and Stone Co .... C 419 396-7671
Carey (G-2545)

Oeder Carl E Sons Sand & Grav .... E 513 494-1238
Lebanon (G-12488)

▼ Osborne Materials Company .... E 440 357-7026
Grand River (G-11333)

Phillips Ready Mix Co .... D 937 426-5151
Beavercreek Township (G-1259)

Pioneer Sands LLC .... E 740 599-7773
Howard (G-11940)

Rjw Trucking Company Ltd .... E 740 363-5343
Delaware (G-10004)

Shelly and Sands Inc .... E 740 453-0721
Zanesville (G-20360)

Shelly Materials Inc .... D 740 246-6315
Thornville (G-17506)

Small Sand & Gravel Inc .... E 740 427-3130
Gambier (G-11226)

Smith Concrete Co .... E 740 373-7441
Dover (G-10101)

Stansley Mineral Resources Inc .... E 419 843-2813
Sylvania (G-17453)

Stocker Sand & Gravel Co .... E 740 254-4635
Gnadenhutten (G-11312)

Tri County Concrete Inc .... E 330 425-4464
Twinsburg (G-18328)

Watson Gravel Inc .... D 513 863-0070
Hamilton (G-11654)

Welch Holdings Inc .... E 513 353-3220
Cincinnati (G-4774)

1446 Industrial Sand

◆ Covia Holdings Corporation .... D 440 214-3284
Independence (G-12063)

Fairmount Minerals LLC .... C 269 926-9450
Independence (G-12072)

Pioneer Sands LLC .... E 740 659-2241
Glenford (G-11308)

Pioneer Sands LLC .... E 740 599-7773
Howard (G-11940)

1459 Clay, Ceramic & Refractory Minerals, NEC

◆ Covia Holdings Corporation .... D 440 214-3284
Independence (G-12063)

1479 Chemical & Fertilizer Mining

Cargill Incorporated .... C 216 651-7200
Cleveland (G-5127)

◆ Everris NA Inc .... E 614 726-7100
Dublin (G-10221)

1481 Nonmetallic Minerals Svcs, Except Fuels

Barr Engineering Incorporated .... E 614 714-0299
Columbus (G-7019)

Longyear Company .... E 740 373-2190
Marietta (G-13344)

M G Q Inc .... E 419 992-4236
Tiffin (G-17522)

1499 Miscellaneous Nonmetallic Mining

◆ Covia Holdings Corporation .... D 440 214-3284
Independence (G-12063)

Graftech Holdings Inc .... B 216 676-2000
Independence (G-12077)

15 BUILDING CONSTRUCTION-GENERAL CONTRACTORS AND OPERATIVE BUILDERS

1521 General Contractors, Single Family Houses

1522 Hess Street LLC .... E 614 291-6876
Columbus (G-6840)

50 X 20 Holding Company Inc .... E 740 238-4262
Belmont (G-1394)

50 X 20 Holding Company Inc .... D 330 478-4500
Canton (G-2168)

50 X 20 Holding Company Inc .... E 330 865-4663
Akron (G-10)

A & R Builders Ltd .... E 330 893-2111
Millersburg (G-14453)

AAA Standard Services Inc .... D 419 535-0274
Toledo (G-17578)

Airko Inc .... E 440 333-0133
Cleveland (G-4922)

Alexander and Bebout Inc .... D 419 238-9567
Van Wert (G-18471)

Allan Hunter Construction LLC .... E 330 634-9882
Akron (G-65)

Apco Industries Inc .... D 614 224-2345
Columbus (G-6956)

Apex Restoration Contrs Ltd .... E 513 489-1795
Cincinnati (G-2974)

Arnolds Home Improvement LLC .... E 734 847-9600
Toledo (G-17600)

Asplundh Construction Corp .... C 614 532-5224
Columbus (G-6980)

Behal Sampson Dietz Inc .... E 614 464-1933
Columbus (G-7025)

Belfor USA Group Inc .... E 330 916-6468
Peninsula (G-15809)

Berlin Construction Ltd .... E 330 893-2003
Millersburg (G-14458)

Bernard Busson Builder .... E 330 929-4926
Akron (G-95)

Bob Webb Builders Inc .... E 740 548-5577
Lewis Center (G-12531)

Brady Homes Inc .... E 440 937-6255
Avon (G-867)

Brayman Construction Corp .... E 740 237-0000
Ironton (G-12146)

Brian-Kyles Construction Inc .... E 440 242-0298
Lorain (G-12887)

Brock & Associates Builders .... E 330 757-7150
Youngstown (G-19975)

Buckeye Cmnty Hope Foundation .... D 614 942-2014
Columbus (G-7087)

Burge Building Co Inc .... E 440 245-6871
Lorain (G-12889)

Burkhart Trucking Inc .... E 740 896-2244
Lowell (G-13037)

Bzak Landscaping Inc .... E 513 831-0907
Milford (G-14375)

C V Perry & Co .... E 614 221-4131
Columbus (G-7105)

Cardinal Builders Inc .... E 614 237-1000
Columbus (G-7119)

Clarke Contractors Corp .... E 513 285-7844
West Chester (G-18893)

Cleveland Construction Inc .... E 440 255-8000
Mason (G-13563)

Columbus Drywall & Insulation .... D 614 257-0257
Columbus (G-7276)

Columbus Drywall Inc .... E 614 257-0257
Columbus (G-7277)

Combs Interior Specialties Inc .... D 937 879-2047
Fairborn (G-10665)

Community Improvement Corp ....E....... 440 466-4675
Geneva *(G-11238)*
Cork Inc ....E....... 614 253-8400
Columbus *(G-7370)*
Craftsmen Restoration LLC ....E....... 877 442-3424
Akron *(G-168)*
Crapsey & Gillis Contractors ....E....... 513 891-6333
Loveland *(G-12985)*
Crock Construction Co ....E....... 740 732-2306
Caldwell *(G-2038)*
Cy Schwieterman Inc ....E....... 419 753-2566
Wapakoneta *(G-18641)*
Dan Marchetta Cnstr Co Inc ....E....... 330 668-4800
Akron *(G-180)*
Daugherty Construction Inc ....E....... 216 731-9444
Euclid *(G-10628)*
David W Milliken ....E....... 740 998-5023
Frankfort *(G-11018)*
Davis Paul Restoration Dayton ....E....... 937 436-3411
Moraine *(G-14639)*
Dayton Roof & Remodeling Co ....E....... 937 224-7667
Beavercreek *(G-1146)*
Deerfield Farms ....E....... 330 584-4715
Deerfield *(G-9903)*
Design Homes & Development Co ....E....... 937 438-3667
Dayton *(G-9389)*
Disaster Reconstruction Inc ....E....... 440 918-1523
Eastlake *(G-10428)*
Dixon Builders & Developers ....D....... 513 887-6400
West Chester *(G-18915)*
Dold Homes Inc ....E....... 419 874-2535
Perrysburg *(G-15860)*
Dominion Homes Inc ....D....... 614 356-5000
Dublin *(G-10202)*
Drees Company ....E....... 330 899-9554
Uniontown *(G-18368)*
Dry It Rite LLC ....E....... 614 295-8135
Columbus *(G-7472)*
Dublin Building Systems Co ....E....... 614 760-5831
Dublin *(G-10204)*
Dun Rite Home Improvement Inc ....E....... 330 650-5322
Macedonia *(G-13068)*
E A Zicka Co ....E....... 513 451-1440
Cincinnati *(G-3464)*
Edrich Supply Co ....E....... 440 238-9440
Strongsville *(G-17299)*
Elite Home Remodeling Inc ....E....... 614 785-6700
Columbus *(G-7512)*
Endeavor Construction Ltd ....E....... 513 469-1900
Pleasant Plain *(G-16073)*
Enterprise Construction Inc ....E....... 440 349-3443
Solon *(G-16845)*
Equity Central LLC ....E....... 614 861-7777
Gahanna *(G-11118)*
Erie Construction Mid-West Inc ....E....... 937 898-4688
Dayton *(G-9417)*
Etech-Systems LLC ....D....... 216 221-6600
Lakewood *(G-12342)*
Evans Construction ....E....... 330 305-9355
North Canton *(G-15201)*
Farris Enterprises Inc ....E....... 614 367-9611
Worthington *(G-19810)*
Farrow Cleaners Co ....E....... 216 561-2355
Cleveland *(G-5514)*
Fetters Construction Inc ....C....... 419 542-0944
Hicksville *(G-11727)*
G & G Concrete Cnstr LLC ....E....... 614 475-4151
Columbus *(G-7637)*
GCI Construction LLC ....E....... 216 831-6100
Beachwood *(G-1061)*
Goettle Co ....D....... 513 825-8100
Cincinnati *(G-3622)*
Gold Star Insulation L P ....E....... 614 221-3241
Columbus *(G-7676)*
Great Lakes Companies Inc ....C....... 513 554-0720
Cincinnati *(G-3643)*
Great Traditions Homes ....E....... 513 759-7444
West Chester *(G-18935)*
Greater Dayton Cnstr Ltd ....D....... 937 426-3577
Beavercreek *(G-1220)*
H&H Custom Homes LLC ....E....... 419 994-4070
Loudonville *(G-12956)*
Handy Hubby ....E....... 419 754-1150
Toledo *(G-17777)*
Harrison Construction Inc ....E....... 740 373-7000
Marietta *(G-13333)*
Hays & Sons Construction Inc ....E....... 513 671-9110
Cincinnati *(G-3686)*
Hersh Construction Inc ....E....... 330 877-1515
Hartville *(G-11690)*

HMS Construction & Rental Co ....D....... 330 628-4811
Mogadore *(G-14551)*
Hochstedler Construction Ltd ....E....... 740 427-4880
Gambier *(G-11224)*
▲ **Hoge Lumber Company** ....E....... 419 753-2263
New Knoxville *(G-14917)*
Homes America Inc ....E....... 614 848-8551
Columbus *(G-7766)*
Hometown Improvement Co ....E....... 614 846-1060
Columbus *(G-7767)*
Hoppes Construction LLC ....E....... 580 310-0090
Malvern *(G-13124)*
Icon Environmental Group LLC ....E....... 513 426-6767
Milford *(G-14396)*
Improve It Home Remodeling ....C....... 614 297-5121
Columbus *(G-7804)*
Ingle-Barr Inc ....C....... 740 702-6117
Chillicothe *(G-2793)*
Investmerica limited ....D....... 216 618-3296
Chagrin Falls *(G-2650)*
Ivan Weaver Construction Co ....E....... 330 695-3461
Fredericksburg *(G-11051)*
J & D Home Improvement Inc ....D....... 740 927-0722
Reynoldsburg *(G-16310)*
J A A Interior & Coml Cnstr ....E....... 216 431-7633
Cleveland *(G-5769)*
J Russell Construction ....E....... 330 633-6462
Tallmadge *(G-17479)*
J W Enterprises Inc ....E....... 740 774-4500
Chillicothe *(G-2796)*
Jack Gray ....D....... 216 688-0466
Cincinnati *(G-3799)*
▲ **Joshua Investment Company Inc** ....E....... 614 428-5555
Columbus *(G-7869)*
Jtf Construction Inc ....D....... 513 860-9835
Fairfield *(G-10740)*
K Hovnanian Summit Homes LLC ....E....... 330 454-4048
Canton *(G-2364)*
Kf Construction and Excvtg LLC ....E....... 419 547-7555
Clyde *(G-6747)*
Kokosing Construction Co Inc ....E....... 440 323-9346
Elyria *(G-10522)*
Kopf Construction Corporation ....C....... 440 933-6908
Avon Lake *(G-921)*
Lei Cbus LLC ....E....... 614 302-8830
Worthington *(G-19823)*
Lemmon & Lemmon Inc ....C....... 330 497-8686
North Canton *(G-15218)*
Luke Theis Enterprises Inc ....D....... 419 422-2040
Findlay *(G-10936)*
M M Construction ....E....... 513 553-0106
Bethel *(G-1453)*
Manufactured Housing Entps Inc ....C....... 419 636-4511
Bryan *(G-1963)*
Maronda Homes Inc Florida ....D....... 937 472-3907
Eaton *(G-10451)*
Marous Brothers Cnstr Inc ....B....... 440 951-3904
Willoughby *(G-19550)*
Menard Inc ....C....... 937 630-3550
Miamisburg *(G-14187)*
Menard Inc ....C....... 513 737-2204
Fairfield Township *(G-10813)*
Midwest Roofing & Furnace Co ....E....... 614 252-5241
Columbus *(G-8084)*
Miller Contracting Group Inc ....E....... 419 453-3825
Ottoville *(G-15670)*
Miller Homes of Kidron LLC ....E....... 330 857-0161
Kidron *(G-12309)*
Miracle Renovations ....E....... 513 371-0750
Cincinnati *(G-4060)*
Moyer Industries Inc ....E....... 937 832-7283
Clayton *(G-4860)*
Mural & Son Inc ....E....... 216 267-3322
Cleveland *(G-6025)*
Nasco Roofing and Cnstr Inc ....E....... 330 746-3566
Youngstown *(G-20135)*
Neals Construction Company ....E....... 513 489-7700
Cincinnati *(G-4101)*
New NV Co LLC ....C....... 330 896-7611
Uniontown *(G-18381)*
Nextt Corp ....E....... 513 813-6398
Cincinnati *(G-4115)*
Nhs - Totco Inc ....E....... 419 691-2900
Toledo *(G-17942)*
North Branch Nursery Inc ....E....... 419 287-4679
Pemberville *(G-15805)*
Northern Style Cnstr LLC ....D....... 330 412-9594
Akron *(G-352)*
Nrp Contractors LLC ....E....... 216 475-8900
Cleveland *(G-6102)*

Nrp Group LLC ....D....... 216 475-8900
Cleveland *(G-6103)*
Nvr Inc ....E....... 440 933-7734
Avon *(G-898)*
Nvr Inc ....E....... 440 584-4200
Kent *(G-12252)*
Nvr Inc ....E....... 440 639-0525
Painesville *(G-15729)*
Nvr Inc ....E....... 513 494-0167
South Lebanon *(G-16927)*
Nvr Inc ....E....... 440 584-4250
Brecksville *(G-1794)*
Oberer Development Co ....E....... 937 910-0851
Miamisburg *(G-14199)*
Oberer Residential Cnstr ....C....... 937 278-0851
Miamisburg *(G-14200)*
Ohio Builders Resources LLC ....E....... 614 865-0306
Westerville *(G-19194)*
Olde Towne Windows Inc ....E....... 419 626-9613
Milan *(G-14364)*
Park Group Co of America Inc ....E....... 440 238-9440
Strongsville *(G-17338)*
Petros Homes Inc ....E....... 440 546-9000
Cleveland *(G-6202)*
Phil Wagler Construction Inc ....E....... 330 899-0316
Uniontown *(G-18382)*
Pirhl Contractors LLC ....E....... 216 378-9690
Cleveland *(G-6214)*
R A Hermes Inc ....E....... 513 251-5200
Cincinnati *(G-4329)*
Ram Restoration LLC ....E....... 937 347-7418
Dayton *(G-9726)*
RE Middleton Cnstr LLC ....E....... 513 398-9255
Mason *(G-13632)*
Registered Contractors Inc ....E....... 440 205-0873
Mentor *(G-14102)*
Residence Artists Inc ....E....... 440 286-8822
Chardon *(G-2710)*
Residntial Coml Rnovations Inc ....E....... 330 815-1476
Clinton *(G-6737)*
Robert Lucke Homes Inc ....E....... 513 683-3300
Cincinnati *(G-4392)*
Rockford Homes Inc ....D....... 614 785-0015
Columbus *(G-6834)*
Romanelli & Hughes Building Co ....E....... 614 891-2042
Westerville *(G-19299)*
Rubber City Realty Inc ....D....... 330 745-9034
Akron *(G-413)*
Runyon & Sons Roofing Inc ....D....... 440 974-6810
Mentor *(G-14105)*
Rycon Construction Inc ....D....... 440 481-3770
Parma *(G-15774)*
▲ **Season Contractors Inc** ....E....... 440 717-0188
Broadview Heights *(G-1845)*
Services On Deck Inc ....E....... 513 759-2854
Liberty Township *(G-12585)*
▲ **Shade Tree Cool Living LLC** ....E....... 614 844-5990
Columbus *(G-8626)*
Shoupes Constuction ....E....... 937 352-6457
Xenia *(G-19926)*
Simonson Construction Svcs Inc ....D....... 419 281-8299
Ashland *(G-691)*
Smb Construction Co Inc ....E....... 419 269-1473
Toledo *(G-18038)*
Snavely Building Company ....E....... 440 585-9091
Chagrin Falls *(G-2654)*
Snavely Development Company ....E....... 440 585-9091
Chagrin Falls *(G-2655)*
Society Handicapped Citz Medin ....D....... 330 722-1710
Medina *(G-14003)*
Steel Valley Construction Co ....E....... 330 392-8391
Warren *(G-18746)*
Sure Home Improvments LLC ....E....... 614 586-0610
Columbus *(G-8720)*
Swartz Enterprises Inc ....E....... 419 331-1024
Lima *(G-12758)*
Sws Environmental Services ....E....... 254 629-1718
Findlay *(G-10967)*
Toth Renovation LLC ....E....... 614 542-9683
Columbus *(G-8764)*
Towne Development Group Ltd ....E....... 513 381-8696
Cincinnati *(G-4615)*
Trimat Construction Inc ....E....... 740 388-9515
Bidwell *(G-1470)*
Trinity Home Builders Inc ....E....... 614 889-7830
Columbus *(G-8783)*
Tusing Builders Ltd ....E....... 419 465-3100
Monroeville *(G-14591)*
Two-X Engners Constructers LLC ....E....... 330 995-0592
Aurora *(G-845)*

SIC

US Home Center LLC..................E...... 614 737-9000
Columbus (G-8834)

Vibo Construction Inc.................E...... 614 210-6780
Dublin (G-10365)

Weaver Custom Homes Inc.........E...... 330 264-5444
Wooster (G-19781)

Wh Midwest LLC......................C...... 330 896-7611
Uniontown (G-18390)

Wingler Construction Corp..........E...... 614 626-8546
Columbus (G-8910)

Woda Construction Inc...............E...... 614 396-3200
Columbus (G-8912)

Zinz Cnstr & Restoration............E...... 330 332-7939
Youngstown (G-20270)

1522 General Contractors, Residential Other Than Single Family

Abco Contracting LLC................E...... 419 973-4772
Toledo (G-17580)

Advocate Property Servic...........E...... 330 952-1313
Medina (G-13906)

Ahv Development LLC................D...... 614 890-1440
Westerville (G-19143)

Al Neyer LLC............................D...... 513 271-6400
Cincinnati (G-2918)

Amsdell Construction Inc...........C...... 216 458-0670
Cleveland (G-4974)

Asbuilt Construction Ltd.............E...... 937 550-4900
Franklin (G-11022)

Behal Sampson Dietz Inc...........E...... 614 464-1933
Columbus (G-7025)

Bernard Busson Builder.............E...... 330 929-4926
Akron (G-95)

Cardinal Builders Inc................E...... 614 237-1000
Columbus (G-7119)

Central Ohio Contractors Inc......D...... 740 369-7700
Delaware (G-9958)

CFS Construction Inc.................E...... 513 559-4500
Cincinnati (G-3163)

Community Management Corp.....D...... 513 761-6339
Cincinnati (G-3341)

Cy Schwieterman Inc................E...... 419 753-2566
Wapakoneta (G-18641)

D C Curry Lumber Company........E...... 330 264-5223
Dundee (G-10383)

Danis Industrial Cnstr Co...........D...... 937 228-1225
Miamisburg (G-14161)

Dixon Builders & Developers.......D...... 513 887-6400
West Chester (G-18915)

Donald R Kenney & Company......E...... 614 540-2404
Westerville (G-19159)

Douglas Company......................E...... 419 865-8600
Holland (G-11883)

Douglas Construction Company....E...... 419 865-8600
Holland (G-11884)

Dr Michael J Hulit.......................E...... 330 863-7173
Malvern (G-13122)

Dugan & Meyers Construction Co..C...... 513 891-4300
Blue Ash (G-1546)

Dugan & Meyers Interests Inc......E...... 513 891-4300
Blue Ash (G-1547)

Endeavor Construction Ltd..........E...... 513 469-1900
Pleasant Plain (G-16073)

Equity Central LLC....................E...... 614 861-7777
Gahanna (G-11118)

Etech-Systems LLC...................D...... 216 221-6600
Lakewood (G-12342)

Fairfield Homes Inc...................E...... 740 653-3583
Lancaster (G-12396)

Fairfield Homes Inc...................C...... 614 873-3533
Plain City (G-16053)

Fc 1346 LLC.............................E...... 330 864-8170
Akron (G-216)

Forest City Residential Dev.........E...... 216 621-6060
Cleveland (G-5561)

G III Reitter Walls LLC................E...... 614 545-4444
Columbus (G-7638)

G J Goudreau & Co....................E...... 216 351-5233
Cleveland (G-5586)

Garland Group Inc.....................E...... 614 294-4411
Columbus (G-7650)

GCI Construction LLC................E...... 216 831-6100
Beachwood (G-1061)

Great Lakes Contractors LLC......E...... 216 631-7777
Cleveland (G-5626)

Greater Dayton Cnstr Ltd............D...... 937 426-3577
Beavercreek (G-1220)

Habitat For Humanity-Midohio......E...... 614 422-4828
Columbus (G-7708)

Hills Communities Inc................C...... 513 984-0300
Blue Ash (G-1579)

Homewood Corporation..............C...... 614 898-7200
Columbus (G-7771)

I & M J Gross Company..............E...... 440 237-1681
Cleveland (G-5731)

Iacovetta Builders Inc................E...... 614 272-6464
Columbus (G-7797)

Installed Building Pdts Inc..........C...... 614 221-3399
Columbus (G-7828)

Interstate Construction Inc..........E...... 614 539-1188
Grove City (G-11444)

K-Y Residential Coml Indus Dev...D...... 330 448-4055
Brookfield (G-1852)

Klingbeil Management Group Co...E...... 614 220-8900
Columbus (G-7911)

Kopf Construction Corporation.....C...... 440 933-6908
Avon Lake (G-921)

L R G Inc..................................D...... 937 890-0510
Dayton (G-9553)

Lake Erie Home Repair...............E...... 419 871-0687
Norwalk (G-15442)

Lemmon & Lemmon Inc.............C...... 330 497-8686
North Canton (G-15218)

Lifestyle Communities Ltd...........D...... 614 918-2000
Columbus (G-7976)

Messer Construction Co.............E...... 513 242-1541
Cincinnati (G-4040)

Mv Residential Cnstr Inc.............A...... 513 588-1000
Cincinnati (G-4087)

National Housing Corporation......E...... 614 481-8106
Columbus (G-8134)

Nrp Contractors LLC.................E...... 216 475-8900
Cleveland (G-6102)

Oberer Development Co..............E...... 937 910-0851
Miamisburg (G-14199)

Oberer Residential Cnstr............C...... 937 278-0851
Miamisburg (G-14200)

Oliver House Rest Complex.........D...... 419 243-1302
Toledo (G-17960)

Otterbein Snior Lfstyle Chices.....B...... 513 933-5400
Lebanon (G-12492)

◆ Pivotek LLC..........................E...... 513 372-6205
Milford (G-14424)

Property Estate Management LLC..E...... 513 684-0418
Cincinnati (G-4298)

Pulte Homes Inc.......................E...... 330 239-1587
Medina (G-13991)

Ram Restoration LLC.................E...... 937 347-7418
Dayton (G-9726)

Residntial Coml Rnovations Inc....E...... 330 815-1476
Clinton (G-6737)

Rockford Homes Inc..................D...... 614 785-0015
Columbus (G-6834)

Rubber City Realty Inc...............D...... 330 745-9034
Akron (G-413)

Runyon & Sons Roofing Inc........D...... 440 974-6810
Mentor (G-14105)

Safeguard Properties MGT LLC....A...... 216 739-2900
Cleveland (G-6362)

Schnippel Construction Inc.........E...... 937 693-3831
Botkins (G-1709)

◆ Schroeder Company...............E...... 419 473-3139
Toledo (G-18021)

Showe Builders Inc...................E...... 614 481-8106
Columbus (G-8636)

Snavely Building Company..........E...... 440 585-9091
Chagrin Falls (G-2654)

Snavely Development Company....E...... 440 585-9091
Chagrin Falls (G-2655)

Strawser Construction Inc..........E...... 614 276-5501
Columbus (G-8705)

Superior Kraft Homes LLC...........D...... 740 947-7710
New Boston (G-14884)

T O J Inc.................................E...... 440 352-1900
Mentor (G-14114)

Topmind/Planex Construction......E...... 248 719-0474
Middletown (G-14338)

Towne Building Group Inc............D...... 513 381-8696
Cincinnati (G-4614)

Transcon Builders Inc................E...... 440 439-3400
Cleveland (G-6540)

Turner Construction Company......C...... 513 721-4224
Cincinnati (G-4652)

Upgrade Homes.........................E...... 614 975-8532
Columbus (G-8822)

Wb Services Inc........................D...... 330 390-5722
Millersburg (G-14500)

Wirtzberger Enterprises Corp.......E...... 440 428-1901
Madison (G-13110)

Woda Construction Inc...............E...... 614 396-3200
Columbus (G-8912)

1531 Operative Builders

American Prservation Bldrs LLC...D...... 216 236-2007
Cleveland (G-4963)

Bernard Busson Builder.............E...... 330 929-4926
Akron (G-95)

Dixon Builders & Developers.......D...... 513 887-6400
West Chester (G-18915)

Dold Homes Inc........................E...... 419 874-2535
Perrysburg (G-15860)

Douglas Construction Company....E...... 419 865-8600
Holland (G-11884)

Epcon Cmmnties Franchising Inc..D...... 614 761-1010
Dublin (G-10218)

Epcon Communities Inc.............D...... 614 761-1010
Dublin (G-10219)

Glencoe Restoration Group LLC...E...... 330 752-1244
Akron (G-236)

M/I Homes Inc..........................B...... 614 418-8000
Columbus (G-8006)

M/I Homes of Austin LLC............E...... 614 418-8000
Columbus (G-8007)

Mainthia Technologies Inc..........D...... 216 433-2198
Cleveland (G-5899)

Multicon Construction Co............E...... 614 351-2683
Columbus (G-8123)

Nrp Holdings LLC......................C...... 216 475-8900
Cleveland (G-6104)

Nvr Inc....................................C...... 513 202-0323
Harrison (G-11675)

Nvr Inc....................................C...... 937 529-7000
Dayton (G-9661)

▲ P R Machine Works Inc...........D...... 419 529-5748
Ontario (G-15570)

Phil Wagler Construction Inc........E...... 330 899-0316
Uniontown (G-18382)

Plus Realty Cincinnati Inc...........E...... 513 575-4500
Milford (G-14425)

Spartan Construction Co Inc........E...... 419 389-1854
Monclova (G-14559)

Weaver Custom Homes Inc.........E...... 330 264-5444
Wooster (G-19781)

Zicka Walker Builders Ltd...........E...... 513 247-3500
Cincinnati (G-4818)

1541 General Contractors, Indl Bldgs & Warehouses

AA Boos & Sons Inc..................D...... 419 691-2329
Oregon (G-15580)

Adena Corporation....................C...... 419 529-4456
Ontario (G-15542)

Adolph Johnson & Son Co..........E...... 330 544-8900
Mineral Ridge (G-14508)

Aecom Energy & Cnstr Inc..........B...... 216 622-2300
Cleveland (G-4906)

Agridry LLC..............................E...... 419 459-4399
Edon (G-10470)

Akron Public Schools.................B...... 330 761-1660
Akron (G-52)

Al Neyer LLC............................D...... 513 271-6400
Cincinnati (G-2918)

Albert M Higley Co LLC..............C...... 216 861-2050
Cleveland (G-4926)

Allen-Keith Construction Co.........D...... 330 266-2220
Canton (G-2178)

Amsdell Construction Inc...........C...... 216 458-0670
Cleveland (G-4974)

Austin Building and Design Inc.....C...... 440 544-2600
Cleveland (G-5023)

Ayrshire Inc.............................E...... 440 286-9507
Chardon (G-2687)

B & B Contrs & Developers Inc....D...... 330 270-5020
Youngstown (G-19960)

Beem Construction Inc...............E...... 937 693-3176
Botkins (G-1707)

Belfor USA Group Inc.................E...... 330 916-6468
Peninsula (G-15809)

Bell Hensley Inc.......................E...... 937 498-1718
Sidney (G-16761)

Ben D Imhoff Inc.......................E...... 330 683-4498
Orrville (G-15625)

Bilfinger Westcon Inc.................E...... 330 818-9734
Canton (G-2212)

Boak & Sons Inc.......................C...... 330 793-5646
Youngstown (G-19967)

Burkshire Construction Company..E...... 440 885-9700
Cleveland (G-5103)

Butt Construction Company Inc..........E....... 937 426-1313
  Dayton (G-9163)

C Tucker Cope & Assoc Inc ....E....... 330 482-4472
  Columbiana (G-6782)

Canaan Companies Inc ....E....... 419 842-8373
  Toledo (G-17634)

Central Ohio Building Co Inc ....E....... 614 475-6392
  Columbus (G-7157)

Chapman Industrial Cnstr Inc..........D....... 330 343-1632
  Louisville (G-12961)

Chemsteel Construction Company ......E....... 440 234-3930
  Middleburg Heights (G-14249)

Cm-Gc LLC ....E....... 513 527-4141
  Cincinnati (G-3313)

▲ Compak Inc..........E....... 419 207-8888
  Ashland (G-668)

Continental Building Company ....D....... 614 221-1800
  Columbus (G-7356)

Continental RE Companies ....C....... 614 221-1800
  Columbus (G-7361)

▲ Corna Kokosing Construction Co ....C....... 614 901-8844
  Westerville (G-19247)

D & G Focht Construction Co ....E....... 419 732-2412
  Port Clinton (G-16105)

DAG Construction Co Inc ....E....... 513 542-8597
  Cincinnati (G-3397)

Danis Building Construction Co..........B....... 937 228-1225
  Miamisburg (G-14159)

Dawn Incorporated ....E....... 330 652-7711
  Warren (G-18700)

DE Huddleston Inc..........E....... 740 773-2130
  Chillicothe (G-2776)

Deerfield Construction Co Inc ....E....... 513 984-4096
  Loveland (G-12990)

Delventhal Company ....E....... 419 244-5570
  Millbury (G-14447)

Desalvo Construction Company ....E....... 330 759-8145
  Hubbard (G-11944)

DKM Construction Inc ....E....... 740 289-3006
  Piketon (G-15974)

Dotson Company ....E....... 419 877-5176
  Whitehouse (G-19446)

Dugan & Meyers Construction Co........C....... 513 891-4300
  Blue Ash (G-1546)

Dugan & Meyers Construction Co........E....... 614 257-7430
  Columbus (G-6812)

Dugan & Meyers Interests Inc ....E....... 513 891-4300
  Blue Ash (G-1547)

Dunlop and Johnston Inc..........E....... 330 220-2700
  Valley City (G-18461)

Dynamic Structures Inc..........E....... 330 892-0164
  New Waterford (G-15004)

Elford Inc ....C....... 614 488-4000
  Columbus (G-7511)

▲ Enerfab Inc ....B....... 513 641-0500
  Cincinnati (G-3498)

Equity Inc..........E....... 614 802-2900
  Hilliard (G-11766)

Exxcel Project Management LLC .....E....... 614 621-4500
  Columbus (G-7549)

Farrow Cleaners Co ....E....... 216 561-2355
  Cleveland (G-5514)

Ferguson Construction Company........C....... 937 498-2243
  Sidney (G-16777)

Ferguson Construction Company........D....... 937 274-1173
  Dayton (G-9432)

Ferrous Metal Transfer ....E....... 216 671-8500
  Brooklyn (G-1861)

Fleming Construction Co ....E....... 740 494-2177
  Prospect (G-16223)

Floyd P Bucher & Son Inc ....E....... 419 867-8792
  Toledo (G-17745)

Fortney & Weygandt Inc ....E....... 440 716-4000
  North Olmsted (G-15288)

Fryman-Kuck General Contrs Inc........E....... 937 274-2892
  Dayton (G-9452)

Geis Construction Inc..........D....... 330 528-3500
  Streetsboro (G-17253)

Genco of Lebanon Inc ....A....... 330 837-0561
  Massillon (G-13688)

Grunwell-Cashero Co ....E....... 419 476-2426
  Toledo (G-17774)

H A Dorsten Inc ....E....... 419 628-2327
  Minster (G-14535)

Hammond Construction Inc..........D....... 330 455-7039
  Canton (G-2335)

Head Inc..........E....... 614 338-8501
  Columbus (G-7723)

Helm and Associates Inc ....E....... 419 893-1480
  Maumee (G-13799)

Higgins Building Company Inc..........E....... 740 439-5553
  Cambridge (G-2074)

Hume Supply Inc..........E....... 419 991-5751
  Lima (G-12661)

Icon Environmental Group LLC..........E....... 513 426-6767
  Milford (G-14396)

Ingle-Barr Inc..........C....... 740 702-6117
  Chillicothe (G-2793)

J & F Construction and Dev Inc ....E....... 419 562-6662
  Bucyrus (G-1995)

J & J General Maintenance Inc ....E....... 740 533-9729
  Ironton (G-12158)

Jack Gibson Construction Co..........D....... 330 394-5280
  Warren (G-18717)

Justice & Business Svcs LLC ....E....... 740 423-5005
  Belpre (G-1406)

Kapp Construction Inc ....E....... 937 324-0134
  Springfield (G-17059)

Knoch Corporation ....D....... 330 244-1440
  Canton (G-2370)

▲ Kokosing Construction Co Inc ....C....... 614 228-1029
  Westerville (G-19270)

Koroseal Interior Products LLC..........E....... 855 753-5474
  Marietta (G-13343)

Kramer & Feldman Inc ....E....... 513 821-7444
  Cincinnati (G-3889)

Lathrop Company Inc ....E....... 419 893-7000
  Toledo (G-17849)

Lcs Inc..........E....... 419 678-8600
  Saint Henry (G-16516)

Lepi Enterprises Inc..........D....... 740 453-2980
  Zanesville (G-20324)

Liebel-Flarsheim Company LLC........C....... 513 761-2700
  Cincinnati (G-3926)

Link Construction Group Inc ....E....... 937 292-7774
  Bellefontaine (G-1354)

Lm Constrction Trry Lvrini Inc..........E....... 740 695-9604
  Saint Clairsville (G-16492)

Luke Theis Enterprises Inc..........D....... 419 422-2040
  Findlay (G-10936)

M&W Construction Entps LLC ....E....... 419 227-2000
  Lima (G-12697)

Maco Construction Services..........E....... 330 482-4472
  Columbiana (G-6789)

Maintenance Unlimited Inc ....E....... 440 238-1162
  Strongsville (G-17325)

Matt Construction Services ....E....... 216 641-0030
  Cleveland (G-5923)

Mc Meechan Construction Co ....E....... 216 581-9373
  Cleveland (G-5928)

McDonalds Design & Build Inc..........E....... 419 782-4191
  Defiance (G-9928)

McGraw/Kokosing Inc ....B....... 614 212-5700
  Monroe (G-14576)

McNerney & Son Inc ....E....... 419 666-0200
  Toledo (G-17899)

McTech Corp ....E....... 216 391-7700
  Cleveland (G-5938)

Mel Lanzer Co..........E....... 419 592-2801
  Napoleon (G-14811)

Messer Construction Co ....D....... 937 291-1300
  Dayton (G-9609)

Messer Construction Co ....D....... 513 242-1541
  Cincinnati (G-4040)

Mid-Continent Construction Co..........E....... 440 439-6100
  Oakwood Village (G-15491)

Miencorp Inc ....E....... 330 978-8511
  Niles (G-15159)

Mike Coates Cnstr Co Inc ....C....... 330 652-0190
  Niles (G-15160)

Miles-Mcclellan Cnstr Co Inc ....E....... 614 487-7744
  Columbus (G-8086)

Miller-Valentine Construction ....D....... 937 293-0900
  Dayton (G-9637)

Monarch Construction Company ....C....... 513 351-6900
  Cincinnati (G-4070)

Mowry Construction & Engrg Inc ....E....... 419 289-2262
  Ashland (G-682)

Mullett Company ....E....... 440 564-9000
  Newbury (G-15123)

Mural & Son Inc..........E....... 216 267-3322
  Cleveland (G-6025)

Murphy Contracting Co ....E....... 330 743-8915
  Youngstown (G-20133)

Nicolozakes Trckg & Cnstr Inc ....E....... 740 432-5648
  Cambridge (G-2078)

Norris Brothers Co Inc ....C....... 216 771-2233
  Cleveland (G-6074)

Nyman Construction Co..........E....... 216 475-7800
  Cleveland (G-6108)

Ors Nasco Inc..........E....... 918 781-5300
  West Chester (G-19071)

Palmetto Construction Svcs LLC..........E....... 614 503-7150
  Columbus (G-8417)

Pawnee Maintenance Inc..........D....... 740 373-6861
  Marietta (G-13366)

Pepper Cnstr Co Ohio LLC ....E....... 614 793-4477
  Dublin (G-10307)

Protective Coatings Inc ....E....... 937 275-7711
  Dayton (G-9721)

QBS Inc..........E....... 330 821-8801
  Alliance (G-544)

Quantum Construction Company ....E....... 513 351-6903
  Cincinnati (G-4311)

R G Smith Company ....E....... 419 524-4778
  Mansfield (G-13231)

Ram Construction Services of ....D....... 513 297-1857
  West Chester (G-18990)

Ray Fogg Building Methods Inc ....E....... 216 351-7976
  Cleveland (G-6287)

Refrigeration Systems Company ....D....... 614 263-0913
  Columbus (G-8502)

Registered Contractors Inc ....E....... 440 205-0873
  Mentor (G-14102)

Reinnovations Contracting Inc ....E....... 330 505-9035
  Mineral Ridge (G-14511)

Resers Fine Foods Inc ....E....... 216 231-7112
  Cleveland (G-6313)

Righter Construction Svcs Inc ....E....... 614 272-9700
  Columbus (G-8532)

Robertson Cnstr Svcs Inc ....D....... 740 929-1000
  Heath (G-11708)

Rudolph Libbe Inc..........C....... 419 241-5000
  Walbridge (G-18624)

Rudolph/Libbe Companies Inc ....D....... 419 241-5000
  Walbridge (G-18625)

Ruhlin Company ....E....... 330 239-2800
  Sharon Center (G-16724)

Ruscilli Construction Co Inc..........D....... 614 876-9484
  Columbus (G-8560)

Schirmer Construction Co ....E....... 440 716-4900
  North Olmsted (G-15309)

Schnippel Construction Inc ....E....... 937 693-3831
  Botkins (G-1709)

Simmons Brothers Corporation ....E....... 330 722-1415
  Medina (G-14001)

Skanska USA Building Inc ....E....... 513 421-0082
  Cincinnati (G-4492)

Spieker Company..........E....... 419 872-7000
  Perrysburg (G-15924)

Stamm Contracting Co Inc ....E....... 330 274-8230
  Mantua (G-13276)

Standard Contg & Engrg Inc ....D....... 440 243-1001
  Brookpark (G-1906)

Stanley Miller Construction Co..........E....... 330 484-2229
  East Sparta (G-10424)

Star Builders Inc ....E....... 440 986-5951
  Amherst (G-599)

Structural Building Systems ....D....... 330 656-9353
  Hudson (G-12007)

Studer-Obringer Inc..........E....... 419 492-2121
  New Washington (G-15003)

Sunrush Construction Co Inc ....E....... 740 775-1300
  Chillicothe (G-2830)

Suresite Consulting Group LLC ....E....... 216 593-0400
  Beachwood (G-1110)

Technical Assurance Inc ....D....... 440 953-3147
  Willoughby (G-19575)

Testa Enterprises Inc..........E....... 330 926-9060
  Cuyahoga Falls (G-9130)

Tradesmen Group Inc ....E....... 614 799-0889
  Plain City (G-16070)

Tri State Corporation ....E....... 513 763-0215
  Cincinnati (G-4631)

Trisco Systems Incorporated ....C....... 419 339-9912
  Lima (G-12769)

Troy Built Building LLC ....D....... 419 425-1093
  Findlay (G-10971)

Turner Construction Company ....C....... 513 721-4224
  Cincinnati (G-4652)

TWC Concrete Services LLC..........D....... 513 771-8192
  Cincinnati (G-4656)

Union Industrial Contractors ....E....... 440 998-7871
  Ashtabula (G-757)

Universal Contracting Corp ....E....... 513 482-2700
  Cincinnati (G-4694)

▲ Universal Fabg Cnstr Svcs Inc ....D....... 614 274-1128
  Columbus (G-8815)

Van Tassel Construction Corp..........E....... 419 873-0188
  Perrysburg (G-15931)

S
I
C

Wenco Inc ....C 937 849-6002
New Carlisle (G-14899)

Whiting-Turner Contracting Co ....D 440 449-9200
Cleveland (G-6681)

Williams Bros Builders Inc...................E 440 365-3261
Elyria (G-10575)

1542 General Contractors, Nonresidential & Non-indl Bldgs

A & A Wall Systems Inc ....E 513 489-0086
Cincinnati (G-2887)

A P & P Dev & Cnstr Co ....D 330 833-8886
Massillon (G-13658)

A2 Services LLC...................................D 440 466-6611
Geneva (G-11236)

AA Boos & Sons Inc ....D 419 691-2329
Oregon (G-15580)

Abco Contracting LLC...........................E 419 973-4772
Toledo (G-17580)

Adena Corporation ....C 419 529-4456
Ontario (G-15542)

Adolph Johnson & Son Co ....E 330 544-8900
Mineral Ridge (G-14508)

Advanced Intgrted Slutions LLC ....E 313 724-8600
Blue Ash (G-1497)

Aecom Energy & Cnstr Inc ....C 419 698-6277
Oregon (G-15582)

Aecom Energy & Cnstr Inc ....B 216 622-2300
Cleveland (G-4906)

Airko Inc..E 440 333-0133
Cleveland (G-4922)

Al Neyer LLC ....D 513 271-6400
Cincinnati (G-2918)

Albert M Higley Co LLC ....C 216 861-2050
Cleveland (G-4926)

Alpine Structures LLC ....E 330 359-5708
Dundee (G-10382)

Alvada Const Inc ....C 419 595-4224
Alvada (G-560)

Amsdell Construction Inc ....C 216 458-0670
Cleveland (G-4974)

Apex Restoration Contrs Ltd ....E 513 489-1795
Cincinnati (G-2974)

Arbor Construction Co ....E 216 360-8989
Cleveland (G-5000)

Armcorp Construction Inc ....E 419 778-7024
Celina (G-2583)

Arnolds Home Improvement LLC...........E 734 847-9600
Toledo (G-17600)

Austin Building and Design Inc..............C 440 544-2600
Cleveland (G-5023)

B & B Contrs & Developers Inc ....D 330 270-5020
Youngstown (G-19960)

Becker Construction Inc ....E 937 859-8308
Dayton (G-9247)

Behal Sampson Dietz Inc ....E 614 464-1933
Columbus (G-7025)

Belfor USA Group Inc ....E 330 916-6468
Peninsula (G-15809)

Ben D Imhoff Inc ....E 330 683-4498
Orrville (G-15625)

Berlin Construction Ltd ....E 330 893-2003
Millersburg (G-14458)

Boak & Sons Inc...................................C 330 793-5646
Youngstown (G-19967)

Bogner Construction Company..............D 330 262-6730
Wooster (G-19693)

Boyas Excavating Inc ....E 216 524-3620
Cleveland (G-5072)

Brackett Builders Inc ....E 937 339-7505
Troy (G-18197)

Brenmar Construction Inc....................D 740 286-2151
Jackson (G-12169)

Brocon Construction Inc ....E 614 871-7300
Grove City (G-11412)

▲ Brumbaugh Construction Inc ....E 937 692-5107
Arcanum (G-623)

Burge Building Co Inc ....E 440 245-6871
Lorain (G-12889)

Burkshire Construction Company ....E 440 885-9700
Cleveland (G-5103)

Butt Construction Company Inc.............E 937 426-1313
Dayton (G-9163)

C Tucker Cope & Assoc Inc ....E 330 482-4472
Columbiana (G-6782)

Calvary Contracting Inc.......................E 937 754-0300
Tipp City (G-17550)

Camargo Construction Company ....E 513 248-1500
Cincinnati (G-3107)

Campbell Construction Inc ....D 330 262-5186
Wooster (G-19696)

Canaan Companies Inc ....E 419 842-8373
Toledo (G-17634)

Canton Floors Inc ....E 330 492-1121
Canton (G-2233)

Cattrell Companies Inc ....D 740 537-2481
Toronto (G-18183)

Cedarwood Construction Company ....D 330 836-9971
Akron (G-121)

Central Ohio Building Co Inc ....E 614 475-6392
Columbus (G-7157)

CFS Construction Inc ....E 513 559-4500
Cincinnati (G-3163)

Chaney Roofing Maintenance ....E 419 639-2761
Clyde (G-6741)

Cincinnati Coml Contg LLC ....E 513 561-6633
Cincinnati (G-3235)

▲ Cleveland Construction Inc ....E 440 255-8000
Mentor (G-14031)

Cleveland Construction Inc ....E 740 927-9000
Columbus (G-7224)

Cleveland Construction Inc ....E 440 255-8000
Mason (G-13563)

Cm-Gc LLC ....E 513 527-4141
Cincinnati (G-3313)

Cocca Development Ltd.........................D 330 729-1010
Youngstown (G-19993)

Colaianni Construction Inc ....E 740 769-2362
Dillonvale (G-10062)

Columbus City Trnsp Div ....C 614 645-3182
Columbus (G-7267)

Combs Interior Specialties Inc ....D 937 879-2047
Fairborn (G-10665)

Conger Construction Group Inc ....E 513 932-1206
Lebanon (G-12456)

Construction One Inc ....E 614 961-1140
Columbus (G-7353)

Continental RE Companies ....C 614 221-1800
Columbus (G-7361)

▲ Corna Kokosing Construction Co ......C 614 901-8844
Westerville (G-19247)

Corporate Cleaning Inc ....E 614 203-6051
Columbus (G-7371)

Crapsey & Gillis Contractors ....E 513 891-6333
Loveland (G-12985)

Crock Construction Co ....E 740 732-2306
Caldwell (G-2038)

D & G Focht Construction Co ....E 419 732-2412
Port Clinton (G-16105)

◆ Da Vinci Group Inc ....E 614 419-2393
Reynoldsburg (G-16295)

DAG Construction Co Inc ....E 513 542-8597
Cincinnati (G-3397)

Dan Marchetta Cnstr Co Inc ....E 330 668-4800
Akron (G-180)

Danis Building Construction Co..............B 937 228-1225
Miamisburg (G-14159)

Daugherty Construction Inc ....E 216 731-9444
Euclid (G-10628)

Daytep Inc ....E 937 456-5860
Eaton (G-10442)

DE Huddleston Inc ....E 740 773-2130
Chillicothe (G-2776)

Deerfield Construction Co Inc ....E 513 984-4096
Loveland (G-12990)

Delventhal Company ....E 419 244-5570
Millbury (G-14447)

Desalvo Construction Company ....D 330 759-8145
Hubbard (G-11944)

Design Homes & Development Co ....E 937 438-3667
Dayton (G-9389)

Disaster Reconstruction Inc ....E 440 918-1523
Eastlake (G-10428)

DKM Construction Inc ....E 740 289-3006
Piketon (G-15974)

Donleys Inc ....C 216 524-6800
Cleveland (G-5440)

Dotson Company ....E 419 877-5176
Whitehouse (G-19446)

Douglas Company ....E 419 865-8600
Holland (G-11883)

Dugan & Meyers Construction Co ....C 513 891-4300
Blue Ash (G-1546)

Dugan & Meyers Construction Co ....E 614 257-7430
Columbus (G-6812)

Dugan & Meyers Interests Inc.............E 513 891-4300
Blue Ash (G-1547)

Dugan & Meyers LLC ....C 513 891-4300
Blue Ash (G-1548)

Duncan Oil Co ....E 937 426-5945
Dayton (G-9171)

Dunlop and Johnston Inc ....E 330 220-2700
Valley City (G-18461)

Dynamic Structures Inc........................E 330 892-0164
New Waterford (G-15004)

Early Construction Co ....E 740 894-5150
South Point (G-16933)

Eckinger Construction Company ....E 330 453-2566
Canton (G-2296)

Elford Inc ....E 614 488-4000
Columbus (G-7511)

Enterprise Construction Inc ....E 440 349-3443
Solon (G-16845)

Equity Inc ....E 614 802-2900
Hilliard (G-11766)

Ernest Fritsch ....E 614 436-5995
Columbus (G-7530)

Etech-Systems LLC ....D 216 221-6600
Lakewood (G-12342)

Exxcel Project Management LLC ....E 614 621-4500
Columbus (G-7549)

Fairfield Homes Inc ....C 614 873-3533
Plain City (G-16053)

Feick Contractors Inc ....E 419 625-3241
Sandusky (G-16603)

Ferguson Construction Company ....C 937 498-2243
Sidney (G-16777)

Ferguson Construction Company ....D 937 274-1173
Dayton (G-9432)

Finneytown Contracting Corp ....E 513 482-2700
Cincinnati (G-3552)

Fiorilli Construction Co Inc ....E 216 696-5845
Medina (G-13938)

Fleming Construction Co ....E 740 494-2177
Prospect (G-16223)

Floyd P Bucher & Son Inc ....E 419 867-8792
Toledo (G-17745)

Ford Development Corp ....D 513 772-1521
Cincinnati (G-3577)

Forest City Residential Dev ....E 216 621-6060
Cleveland (G-5561)

Fortney & Weygandt Inc ....E 440 716-4000
North Olmsted (G-15288)

Foti Construction Company LLP ....E 440 347-0728
Wickliffe (G-19459)

Foti Contracting LLC ....C 330 656-3454
Wickliffe (G-19460)

▲ Fred Olivieri Construction Co ....C 330 494-1007
North Canton (G-15205)

Fryman-Kuck General Contrs Inc ....E 937 274-2892
Dayton (G-9452)

G III Reitter Walls LLC ....E 614 545-4444
Columbus (G-7638)

G J Goudreau & Co ....E 216 351-5233
Cleveland (G-5586)

Gem Interiors Inc ....E 513 831-6535
Milford (G-14392)

Gilbane Building Company ....E 614 948-4000
Columbus (G-7668)

Gold Star Insulation L P ....E 614 221-3241
Columbus (G-7676)

Goliath Contracting Ltd..........................E 614 568-7878
Reynoldsburg (G-16306)

Gowdy Partners LLC ....E 614 488-4424
Columbus (G-7682)

Grae-Con Construction Inc ....D 740 282-6830
Steubenville (G-17157)

Great Lakes Contractors LLC ....E 216 631-7777
Cleveland (G-5626)

Greater Dayton Cnstr Ltd ....D 937 426-3577
Beavercreek (G-1220)

Gutknecht Construction Company ....E 614 532-5410
Columbus (G-7705)

H A Dorsten Inc ....E 419 628-2327
Minster (G-14535)

Hal Homes Inc ....E 513 984-5360
Blue Ash (G-1574)

Hammond Construction Inc ....D 330 455-7039
Canton (G-2335)

Hanlin-Rainaldi Construction ....E 614 436-4204
Columbus (G-7715)

Head Inc ....E 614 338-8501
Columbus (G-7723)

Hi-Five Development Svcs Inc................E 513 336-9280
Mason (G-13594)

Higgins Building Company Inc...............E 740 439-5553
Cambridge (G-2074)

▲ Homan Inc ....E 419 925-4349
Maria Stein (G-13307)

Hughes & Knollman Construction ....D....... 614 237-6167
  Columbus (G-7778)

Hummel Construction Company ....E..... 330 274-8584
  Ravenna (G-16246)

Icon Environmental Group LLC ....E..... 513 426-6767
  Milford (G-14396)

Ideal Company Inc ....E..... 937 836-8683
  Clayton (G-4858)

Ingle-Barr Inc ....C....... 740 702-6117
  Chillicothe (G-2793)

Interstate Construction Inc ....E..... 614 539-1188
  Grove City (G-11444)

Ivan Weaver Construction Co ....E..... 330 695-3461
  Fredericksburg (G-11051)

J & F Construction and Dev Inc ....E..... 419 562-6662
  Bucyrus (G-1995)

J & R Associates ....A....... 440 250-4080
  Brookpark (G-1898)

J D Williamson Cnstr Co Inc ....D....... 330 633-1258
  Tallmadge (G-17478)

J&H Rnfrcing Strl Erectors Inc ....C....... 740 355-0141
  Portsmouth (G-16151)

Jack Gibson Construction Co ....D....... 330 394-5280
  Warren (G-18717)

James Hunt Construction Co Inc ....E..... 513 721-0559
  Cincinnati (G-3807)

Jeffrey Carr Construction Inc ....E..... 330 879-5210
  Massillon (G-13701)

Jhi Group Inc ....C....... 419 465-4611
  Monroeville (G-14589)

JJO Construction Inc ....E..... 440 255-1515
  Mentor (G-14067)

JKL Construction Inc ....E..... 513 553-3333
  New Richmond (G-14995)

Justice & Business Svcs LLC ....E..... 740 423-5005
  Belpre (G-1406)

K-Y Residential Coml Indus Dev ....D....... 330 448-4055
  Brookfield (G-1852)

Kapp Construction Inc ....E..... 937 324-0134
  Springfield (G-17059)

Kenny Obayashi Joint Venture V ....C....... 703 969-0611
  Akron (G-300)

Knoch Corporation ....D....... 330 244-1440
  Canton (G-2370)

▲ Kokosing Construction Co Inc ....C....... 614 228-1029
  Westerville (G-19270)

Kramer & Feldman Inc ....E..... 513 821-7444
  Cincinnati (G-3889)

Krumroy-Cozad Cnstr Corp ....E..... 330 376-4136
  Akron (G-305)

▲ L Brands Store Dsign Cnstr Inc ....C....... 614 415-7000
  Columbus (G-7934)

L Jack Ruscilli ....E..... 614 876-9484
  Columbus (G-7936)

L R G Inc ....D....... 937 890-0510
  Dayton (G-9553)

Lathrop Company Inc ....E..... 419 893-7000
  Toledo (G-17849)

Link Construction Group Inc ....E..... 937 292-7774
  Bellefontaine (G-1354)

Lm Constrction Trry Lvrini Inc ....E..... 740 695-9604
  Saint Clairsville (G-16492)

Ludy Greenhouse Mfg Corp ....D....... 800 255-5839
  New Madison (G-14937)

Luke Theis Enterprises Inc ....D....... 419 422-2040
  Findlay (G-10936)

M&W Construction Entps LLC ....E..... 419 227-2000
  Lima (G-12697)

M-A Building and Maint Co ....E..... 216 391-5577
  Independence (G-12096)

Marietta Silos LLC ....E..... 740 373-2822
  Marietta (G-13356)

Mark-L Inc ....E..... 614 863-8832
  Gahanna (G-11134)

Mattlin Construction Inc ....E..... 513 598-5402
  Cleves (G-6733)

Mc Meechan Construction Co ....E..... 216 581-9373
  Cleveland (G-5928)

McDonalds Design & Build Inc ....E..... 419 782-4191
  Defiance (G-9928)

McNerney & Son Inc ....E..... 419 666-0200
  Toledo (G-17899)

MCR Services Inc ....E..... 614 421-0860
  Columbus (G-8047)

Mel Lanzer Co ....E..... 419 592-2801
  Napoleon (G-14811)

Messer Construction Co ....E..... 513 672-5000
  Cincinnati (G-4039)

Messer Construction Co ....E..... 513 242-1541
  Cincinnati (G-4040)

Messer Construction Co ....D....... 614 275-0141
  Columbus (G-8062)

MI - De - Con Inc ....D....... 740 532-2277
  Ironton (G-12164)

Mid-Continent Construction Co ....E..... 440 439-6100
  Oakwood Village (G-15491)

Midland Contracting Inc ....E..... 440 439-4571
  Cleveland (G-5985)

Midwest Church Cnstr Ltd ....E..... 419 874-0838
  Perrysburg (G-15894)

Midwest Contracting Inc ....E..... 419 866-4560
  Holland (G-11897)

Midwest Roofing & Furnace Co ....E..... 614 252-5241
  Columbus (G-8084)

Mike Coates Cnstr Co Inc ....C....... 330 652-0190
  Niles (G-15160)

Miles-Mcclellan Cnstr Co Inc ....E..... 614 487-7744
  Columbus (G-8086)

Miller Contracting Group Inc ....E..... 419 453-3825
  Ottoville (G-15670)

Miller Industrial Svc Team Inc ....D....... 513 877-2708
  Pleasant Plain (G-16075)

Miller-Valentine Construction ....D....... 937 293-0900
  Dayton (G-9637)

Monarch Construction Company ....E..... 513 351-6900
  Cincinnati (G-4070)

Mowry Construction & Engrg Inc ....E..... 419 289-2262
  Ashland (G-682)

Mpower Inc ....E..... 614 783-0478
  Gahanna (G-11136)

Muha Construction Inc ....E..... 937 435-0678
  Dayton (G-9647)

Mullett Company ....E..... 440 564-9000
  Newbury (G-15123)

Multicon Builders Inc ....E..... 614 241-2070
  Columbus (G-8121)

Multicon Builders Inc ....E..... 614 463-1142
  Columbus (G-8122)

Mural & Son Inc ....E..... 216 267-3322
  Cleveland (G-6025)

Murphy Contracting Co ....E..... 330 743-8915
  Youngstown (G-20133)

N Cook Inc ....E..... 513 275-9872
  Cincinnati (G-4089)

National Housing Corporation ....E..... 614 481-8106
  Columbus (G-8134)

Nordmann Roofing Co Inc ....E..... 419 691-5737
  Toledo (G-17944)

Nyman Construction Co ....E..... 216 475-7800
  Cleveland (G-6108)

Oberer Development Co ....E..... 937 910-0851
  Miamisburg (G-14199)

Ohio Maint & Renovation Inc ....E..... 330 315-3101
  Akron (G-360)

Ohio Technical Services Inc ....E..... 614 372-0829
  Columbus (G-8356)

Oliver House Rest Complex ....E..... 419 243-1302
  Toledo (G-17960)

Ozanne Construction Co Inc ....E..... 216 696-2876
  Cleveland (G-6153)

Palmetto Construction Svcs LLC ....E..... 614 503-7150
  Columbus (G-8417)

Pepper Cnstr Co Ohio LLC ....E..... 614 793-4477
  Dublin (G-10307)

Peterson Construction Company ....C....... 419 941-2233
  Wapakoneta (G-18652)

◆ Pivotek LLC ....E..... 513 372-6205
  Milford (G-14424)

Plevniak Construction Inc ....E..... 330 718-1600
  Youngstown (G-20159)

Prestige Interiors Inc ....E..... 330 425-1690
  Twinsburg (G-18307)

Property Estate Management LLC ....E..... 513 684-0418
  Cincinnati (G-4298)

QBS Inc ....E..... 330 821-8801
  Alliance (G-544)

Quandel Construction Group Inc ....E..... 717 657-0909
  Westerville (G-19297)

Quantum Construction Company ....E..... 513 351-6903
  Cincinnati (G-4311)

R A Hermes Inc ....E..... 513 251-5200
  Cincinnati (G-4329)

R B Development Company Inc ....B....... 513 829-8100
  Fairfield (G-10772)

R L Fortney Management Inc ....C....... 440 716-4000
  North Olmsted (G-15307)

Ram Construction Services of ....D....... 513 297-1857
  West Chester (G-18990)

Ray Fogg Building Methods Inc ....E..... 216 351-7976
  Cleveland (G-6287)

Reece-Campbell Inc ....D....... 513 542-4600
  Cincinnati (G-4349)

Registered Contractors Inc ....E..... 440 205-0873
  Mentor (G-14102)

Renier Construction Corp ....E..... 614 866-4580
  Columbus (G-8514)

Residence Artists Inc ....E..... 440 286-8822
  Chardon (G-2710)

Residntial Coml Rnovations Inc ....E..... 330 815-1476
  Clinton (G-6737)

Restaurant Specialties Inc ....E..... 614 885-9707
  Sunbury (G-17394)

Retail Renovations Inc ....E..... 330 334-4501
  Wadsworth (G-18615)

Righter Co Inc ....E..... 614 272-9700
  Columbus (G-8531)

Righter Construction Svcs Inc ....E..... 614 272-9700
  Columbus (G-8532)

Romanelli & Hughes Building Co ....E..... 614 891-2042
  Westerville (G-19299)

◆ Rough Brothers Mfg Inc ....D....... 513 242-0310
  Cincinnati (G-4402)

Rudolph Libbe Inc ....C....... 419 241-5000
  Walbridge (G-18624)

Rudolph/Libbe Companies Inc ....E..... 419 241-5000
  Walbridge (G-18625)

Ruhlin Company ....C....... 330 239-2800
  Sharon Center (G-16724)

Runyon & Sons Roofing Inc ....D....... 440 974-6810
  Mentor (G-14105)

Rupp/Rosebrock Inc ....E..... 419 533-7999
  Liberty Center (G-12575)

Ruscilli Construction Co Inc ....D....... 614 876-9484
  Columbus (G-8560)

Schirmer Construction Co ....E..... 440 716-4900
  North Olmsted (G-15309)

Schnippel Construction Inc ....E..... 937 693-3831
  Botkins (G-1709)

Scs Construction Services Inc ....E..... 513 929-0260
  Cincinnati (G-4441)

▲ Season Contractors Inc ....E..... 440 717-0188
  Broadview Heights (G-1845)

Shelly and Sands Inc ....D....... 740 859-2104
  Rayland (G-16273)

Shelly and Sands Inc ....E..... 614 444-5100
  Columbus (G-8632)

Shook Construction Co ....D....... 440 838-5400
  Dayton (G-9763)

Simonson Construction Svcs Inc ....D....... 419 281-8299
  Ashland (G-691)

Site Worx LLC ....E..... 513 229-0295
  Lebanon (G-12503)

Skanska USA Building Inc ....E..... 513 421-0082
  Cincinnati (G-4492)

Smb Construction Co Inc ....E..... 419 269-1473
  Toledo (G-18038)

Smith Construction Group Inc ....E..... 937 426-0500
  Beavercreek Township (G-1262)

Snavely Building Company ....E..... 440 585-9091
  Chagrin Falls (G-2654)

Spieker Company ....E..... 419 872-7000
  Perrysburg (G-15924)

Stamm Contracting Co Inc ....E..... 330 274-8230
  Mantua (G-13276)

Stanley Miller Construction Co ....E..... 330 484-2229
  East Sparta (G-10424)

Star Builders Inc ....E..... 440 986-5951
  Amherst (G-599)

Stockmeister Enterprises Inc ....E..... 740 286-1619
  Jackson (G-12179)

Studer-Obringer Inc ....E..... 419 492-2121
  New Washington (G-15003)

Sunrush Construction Co Inc ....E..... 740 775-1300
  Chillicothe (G-2830)

Swartz Enterprises Inc ....E..... 419 331-1024
  Lima (G-12758)

T Allen Inc ....E..... 440 234-2366
  Berea (G-1440)

T O J Inc ....E..... 440 352-1900
  Mentor (G-14114)

Tab Construction Company Inc ....E..... 330 454-5228
  Canton (G-2506)

Tri State Corporation ....E..... 513 763-0215
  Cincinnati (G-4631)

Tri-Con Incorporated ....E..... 513 530-9844
  Blue Ash (G-1663)

Trisco Systems Incorporated ....C....... 419 339-9912
  Lima (G-12769)

Trubuilt Construction Svcs LLC ....E..... 614 279-4800
  Columbus (G-8785)

Turner Construction Company ....E 216 522-1180
Cleveland *(G-6556)*

Turner Construction Company ....D 513 363-0883
Cincinnati *(G-4653)*

Turner Construction Company ....D 614 984-3000
Columbus *(G-8788)*

Turner Construction Company ....C 513 721-4224
Cincinnati *(G-4652)*

Tusing Builders Ltd ....E 419 465-3100
Monroeville *(G-14591)*

Twok General Co ....E 740 417-9195
Delaware *(G-10011)*

Union Industrial Contractors ....E 440 998-7871
Ashtabula *(G-757)*

Universal Contracting Corp ....E 513 482-2700
Cincinnati *(G-4694)*

Universal Development MGT Inc ....E 330 759-7017
Girard *(G-11303)*

Valley View Fire Dept ....E 216 524-7200
Cleveland *(G-6619)*

Van Tassel Construction Corp ....E 419 873-0188
Perrysburg *(G-15931)*

VIP Restoration Inc ....E 216 426-9500
Cuyahoga Falls *(G-9136)*

Wallick Construction LLC ....E 614 863-4640
New Albany *(G-14876)*

Watertown Steel Company LLC ....E 740 749-3512
Waterford *(G-18787)*

Weaver Custom Homes Inc ....E 330 264-5444
Wooster *(G-19781)*

Welty Building Company Ltd ....D 330 867-2400
Fairlawn *(G-10855)*

Wenco Inc ....C 937 849-6002
New Carlisle *(G-14899)*

Wenger Temperature Control ....E 614 586-4016
Columbus *(G-8887)*

▲ West Roofing Systems Inc ....E 800 356-5748
Lagrange *(G-12327)*

Whiting-Turner Contracting Co ....B 614 459-6515
Worthington *(G-19861)*

Whiting-Turner Contracting Co ....D 440 449-9200
Cleveland *(G-6681)*

Williams Bros Builders Inc ....E 440 365-3261
Elyria *(G-10575)*

Wingler Construction Corp ....E 614 626-8546
Columbus *(G-8910)*

Winsupply Inc ....D 937 294-5331
Moraine *(G-14707)*

Wise Services Inc ....E 937 854-0281
Dayton *(G-9883)*

Witmers Inc ....E 330 427-2147
Salem *(G-16567)*

Woodward Construction Inc ....E 513 247-9241
Blue Ash *(G-1682)*

Xtreme Contracting Ltd ....E 614 568-7030
Reynoldsburg *(G-16341)*

16 HEAVY CONSTRUCTION OTHER THAN BUILDING CONSTRUCTION-CONTRACTORS

1611 Highway & Street Construction

A & A Safety Inc ....E 513 943-6100
Amelia *(G-563)*

A P OHoro Company ....D 330 759-9317
Youngstown *(G-19944)*

Able Contracting Group Inc ....E 440 951-0880
Painesville *(G-15691)*

Aecom Energy & Cnstr Inc ....B 216 622-2300
Cleveland *(G-4906)*

Akil Incorporated ....E 419 625-0857
Sandusky *(G-16573)*

Allied Paving Inc ....E 419 666-3100
Holland *(G-11869)*

Altruism Society Inc ....D 877 283-4001
Beachwood *(G-1028)*

American Precast Refractories ....B 614 876-8416
Columbus *(G-6934)*

Anthony Allega Cement Contr ....E 216 447-0814
Cleveland *(G-4985)*

Armor Paving & Sealing ....E 614 751-6900
Reynoldsburg *(G-16284)*

◆ Baker Concrete Cnstr Inc ....A 513 539-4000
Monroe *(G-14561)*

Barbicas Construction Co ....E 330 733-9101
Akron *(G-86)*

Barrett Paving Materials Inc ....C 513 271-6200
Middletown *(G-14343)*

Beaver Constructors Inc ....D 330 478-2151
Canton *(G-2210)*

Becdir Construction Company ....E 330 547-2134
Berlin Center *(G-1449)*

Belmont County of Ohio ....E 740 695-1580
Saint Clairsville *(G-16476)*

Brock & Sons Inc ....E 513 874-4555
Fairfield *(G-10701)*

Butler Asphalt Co LLC ....E 937 890-1141
Vandalia *(G-18511)*

C J & L Construction Inc ....E 513 769-3600
Cincinnati *(G-3099)*

C Tucker Cope & Assoc Inc ....E 330 482-4472
Columbiana *(G-6782)*

Camargo Construction Company ....E 513 248-1500
Cincinnati *(G-3107)*

Canton Public Works ....E 330 489-3030
Canton *(G-2240)*

Chemcote Inc ....C 614 792-2683
Dublin *(G-10171)*

Cincinnati Asphalt Corporation ....D 513 367-0250
Cleves *(G-6726)*

Cincinnati Fill Inc ....E 513 242-7526
Cincinnati *(G-3244)*

City of Aurora ....D 330 562-8662
Aurora *(G-825)*

City of Avon ....E 440 937-5740
Avon *(G-876)*

City of Brecksville ....E 440 526-1384
Brecksville *(G-1774)*

City of Cuyahoga Falls ....E 330 971-8030
Cuyahoga Falls *(G-9083)*

City of Euclid ....E 216 289-2800
Cleveland *(G-5200)*

City of Kent ....D 330 678-8105
Kent *(G-12222)*

City of Lima ....E 419 221-5165
Lima *(G-12613)*

City of North Ridgeville ....E 440 327-8326
North Ridgeville *(G-15326)*

City of North Royalton ....E 440 582-3002
Cleveland *(G-5210)*

City of Norwalk ....E 419 663-6715
Norwalk *(G-15426)*

City of Portsmouth ....E 740 353-5419
Portsmouth *(G-16129)*

City of Streetsboro ....E 330 626-2856
Streetsboro *(G-17250)*

City of Westerville ....E 614 901-6500
Westerville *(G-19236)*

City of Willoughby ....D 440 953-4111
Willoughby *(G-19511)*

Colas Solutions Inc ....E 513 272-5348
Cincinnati *(G-3321)*

Columbus Asphalt Paving Inc ....E 614 759-9800
Gahanna *(G-11113)*

Cook Paving and Cnstr Co ....E 216 267-7705
Independence *(G-12062)*

County of Ashtabula ....E 440 576-2816
Jefferson *(G-12191)*

County of Clinton ....E 937 382-2078
Wilmington *(G-19620)*

County of Delaware ....D 740 833-2400
Delaware *(G-9963)*

County of Holmes ....E 330 674-5076
Millersburg *(G-14469)*

County of Monroe ....E 740 472-0760
Woodsfield *(G-19673)*

County of Portage ....D 330 296-6411
Ravenna *(G-16238)*

County of Seneca ....E 419 447-3863
Tiffin *(G-17513)*

County of Shelby ....E 937 498-7244
Sidney *(G-16770)*

County of Summit ....C 330 643-2860
Akron *(G-165)*

County of Trumbull ....D 330 675-2640
Warren *(G-18692)*

Crp Contracting ....E 614 338-8501
Columbus *(G-7398)*

Cunningham Paving Company ....E 216 581-8600
Bedford *(G-1275)*

D B Bentley Inc ....E 440 352-8495
Painesville *(G-15707)*

D G M Inc ....D 740 226-1950
Beaver *(G-1120)*

D&M Carter LLC ....E 513 831-8843
Miamiville *(G-14245)*

Decorative Paving Company ....E 513 576-1222
Loveland *(G-12989)*

Don S Cisle Contractor Inc ....D 513 867-1400
Hamilton *(G-11592)*

Double Z Construction Company ....D 614 274-9334
Columbus *(G-7468)*

E S Wagner Company ....D 419 691-8651
Oregon *(G-15592)*

Eaton Construction Co Inc ....D 740 474-3414
Circleville *(G-4832)*

Ebony Construction Co ....E 419 841-3455
Sylvania *(G-17421)*

Erie Blacktop Inc ....E 419 625-7374
Sandusky *(G-16598)*

Erie Construction Group Inc ....E 419 625-7374
Sandusky *(G-16599)*

Fabrizi Trucking & Pav Co Inc ....C 330 483-3291
Cleveland *(G-5504)*

Ferrous Metal Transfer ....E 216 671-8500
Brooklyn *(G-1861)*

Franklin Cnty Bd Commissioners ....C 614 462-3030
Columbus *(G-7603)*

Fred A Nemann Co ....E 513 467-9400
Cincinnati *(G-3585)*

Fryman-Kuck General Contrs Inc ....E 937 274-2892
Dayton *(G-9452)*

George Kuhn Enterprises Inc ....E 614 481-8838
Columbus *(G-7660)*

Great Lakes Crushing Ltd ....E 440 944-5500
Wickliffe *(G-19461)*

Hardin County Engineer ....E 419 673-2232
Kenton *(G-12278)*

Hi-Way Paving Inc ....D 614 876-1700
Hilliard *(G-11775)*

Hicon Inc ....D 513 242-3612
Cincinnati *(G-3701)*

Image Pavement Maintenance ....E 937 833-9200
Brookville *(G-1914)*

▲ Independence Excavating Inc ....E 216 524-1700
Independence *(G-12082)*

J A Donadee Corporation ....E 330 533-3305
Canfield *(G-2144)*

J K Enterprises Inc ....D 614 481-8838
Columbus *(G-7850)*

J K Meurer Corp ....E 513 831-7500
Loveland *(G-13003)*

J&B Steel Erectors Inc ....C 513 874-1722
West Chester *(G-18951)*

K & M Construction Company ....C 330 723-3681
Medina *(G-13963)*

K West Group LLC ....E 972 722-3874
Perrysburg *(G-15884)*

Ken Heiberger Paving Inc ....E 614 837-0290
Canal Winchester *(G-2112)*

▲ Kenmore Construction Co Inc ....C 330 762-8936
Akron *(G-299)*

Kenmore Construction Co Inc ....E 330 832-8888
Massillon *(G-13702)*

Kirila Contractors Inc ....D 330 448-4055
Brookfield *(G-1853)*

▲ Kokosing Construction Inc ....A 330 263-4168
Wooster *(G-19739)*

▲ Kokosing Construction Co Inc ....C 614 228-1029
Westerville *(G-19270)*

Kokosing Construction Co Inc ....E 614 228-1029
Westerville *(G-19271)*

Kokosing Inc ....D 614 212-5700
Westerville *(G-19272)*

Lake Erie Construction Co ....C 419 668-3302
Norwalk *(G-15441)*

Lash Paving Inc ....D 740 635-4335
Bridgeport *(G-1818)*

Lyndco Inc ....E 740 671-9098
Shadyside *(G-16696)*

M P Dory Co ....D 614 444-2138
Columbus *(G-8004)*

Maco Construction Services ....E 330 482-4472
Columbiana *(G-6789)*

Maintenance Systerms of N Ohio ....E 440 323-1291
Elyria *(G-10532)*

MBC Holdings Inc ....E 419 445-1015
Archbold *(G-632)*

McDaniels Cnstr Corp Inc ....D 614 252-5852
Columbus *(G-8043)*

Miller Bros Const Inc ....E 419 445-1015
Archbold *(G-633)*

Moyer Industries Inc ....E 937 832-7283
Clayton *(G-4860)*

Nas Ventures ....D 614 338-8501
Columbus *(G-8127)*

Neff Paving Ltd ....E 740 453-3063
Zanesville *(G-20345)*

Nerone & Sons Inc ....E 216 662-2235
Cleveland (G-6057)

Northstar Asphalt Inc ....E 330 497-0936
North Canton (G-15224)

Ohio Department Transportation ....C 740 363-1251
Delaware (G-9999)

Ohio Department Transportation ....E 937 548-3015
Greenville (G-11391)

Ohio Department Transportation ....E 419 738-4214
Wapakoneta (G-18651)

Ohio Department Transportation ....E 330 533-4351
Canfield (G-2153)

Ohio Paving & Cnstr Co Inc ....E 440 975-8929
Willoughby (G-19559)

Ohio Tpk & Infrastructure Comm ......E 419 826-4831
Swanton (G-17403)

Ohio Tpk & Infrastructure Comm ......C 440 234-2081
Berea (G-1433)

Ohio Tpk & Infrastructure Comm ......E 440 234-2081
Richfield (G-16369)

Paul Peterson Company ....E 614 486-4375
Columbus (G-8427)

Pdk Construction Inc ....E 740 992-6451
Pomeroy (G-16096)

Perk Company Inc ....E 216 391-1444
Cleveland (G-6195)

Perrysburg Rsdntial Seal Cting ....E 419 872-7325
Perrysburg (G-15904)

Pinnacle Paving & Sealing Inc ....E 513 474-4900
Milford (G-14423)

Precision Paving Inc ....E 419 499-7281
Milan (G-14366)

Premier Asphalt Paving Co Inc ....E 440 237-6600
North Royalton (G-15364)

Prime Polymers Inc ....E 330 662-4200
Medina (G-13988)

Queen City Blacktop Company ....E 513 251-8400
Cincinnati (G-4312)

R B Jergens Contractors Inc ....D 937 669-9799
Vandalia (G-18538)

R D Jergens Contractors Inc ....E 937 669-9799
Vandalia (G-18539)

R T Vernal Paving Inc ....E 330 549-3189
North Lima (G-15274)

Rack Seven Paving Co Inc ....E 513 271-4863
Cincinnati (G-4334)

Ray Bertolini Trucking Co ....E 330 867-0666
Akron (G-397)

Rick Eplion Paving ....E 740 446-3000
Gallipolis (G-11214)

Ruhlin Company ....C 330 239-2800
Sharon Center (G-16724)

S & K Asphalt & Concrete ....E 330 848-6284
Akron (G-414)

Samples Chuck-General Contr ....E 419 586-1434
Celina (G-2610)

Scot Burton Contractors LLC ....E 440 564-1011
Newbury (G-15125)

Security Fence Group Inc ....E 513 681-3700
Cincinnati (G-4444)

Sheedy Paving Inc ....E 614 252-2111
Columbus (G-8631)

Shelly and Sands Inc ....E 614 444-5100
Columbus (G-8632)

Shelly and Sands Inc ....D 419 529-8455
Ontario (G-15572)

Shelly and Sands Inc ....E 740 453-0721
Zanesville (G-20360)

Shelly Company ....E 419 396-7641
Carey (G-2547)

Shelly Company ....E 740 441-1714
Circleville (G-4849)

Shelly Company ....E 330 425-7861
Twinsburg (G-18320)

Shelly Materials Inc ....E 740 666-5841
Ostrander (G-15655)

Smalls Asphalt Paving Inc ....E 740 427-4096
Gambier (G-11227)

Spieker Company ....E 419 872-7000
Perrysburg (G-15924)

Springboro Service Center ....E 937 748-0020
Springboro (G-16984)

Stonegate Construction Inc ....D 740 423-9170
Belpre (G-1410)

Sunesis Construction Company ....C 513 326-6000
West Chester (G-19014)

Superior Paving & Materials ....E 330 499-5849
Canton (G-2504)

Tab Construction Company Inc ....E 330 454-5228
Canton (G-2506)

▲ Terminal Ready-Mix Inc ....E 440 288-0181
Lorain (G-12947)

Township of Copley ....D 330 666-1853
Copley (G-8978)

Trafftech Inc ....E 216 361-8808
Cleveland (G-6538)

Transportation Ohio Department ....E 740 773-3191
Chillicothe (G-2832)

Tri State Corporation ....E 513 763-0215
Cincinnati (G-4631)

Trucco Construction Co Inc ....C 740 417-9010
Delaware (G-10010)

Tucson Inc ....E 330 339-4935
New Philadelphia (G-14985)

Turnpike and Infrastructure Co ....D 330 527-2169
Windham (G-19664)

Unicustom Inc ....E 513 874-9806
Fairfield (G-10795)

Vandalia Blacktop Seal Coating ....E 937 454-0571
Dayton (G-9850)

Velotta Company ....E 330 239-1211
Sharon Center (G-16727)

Virginia Ohio-West Excvtg Co ....C 740 676-7464
Shadyside (G-16698)

W G Lockhart Construction Co ....D 330 745-6520
Akron (G-492)

Waltek Inc ....E 614 469-0156
Columbus (G-8873)

Westpatrick Corp ....E 614 875-8200
Columbus (G-8891)

1622 Bridge, Tunnel & Elevated Hwy Construction

A P OHoro Company ....D 330 759-9317
Youngstown (G-19944)

Aecom Energy & Cnstr Inc ....B 216 622-2300
Cleveland (G-4906)

Akil Incorporated ....E 419 625-0857
Sandusky (G-16573)

Armstrong Steel Erectors Inc ....E 740 345-4503
Newark (G-15012)

Becdir Construction Company ....E 330 547-2134
Berlin Center (G-1449)

▲ Brumbaugh Construction Inc ....E 937 692-5107
Arcanum (G-623)

CJ Mahan Construction Co LLC ....E 614 277-4545
Columbus (G-7215)

Clayton Railroad Cnstr LLC ....E 937 549-2952
West Union (G-19134)

Colas Solutions Inc ....E 513 272-5348
Cincinnati (G-3321)

Complete General Cnstr Co ....C 614 258-9515
Columbus (G-7342)

E S Wagner Company ....D 419 691-8651
Oregon (G-15592)

Eagle Bridge Co ....D 937 492-5654
Sidney (G-16775)

▲ Fenton Rigging & Contg Inc ....C 513 631-5500
Cincinnati (G-3542)

Foundation Steel LLC ....D 419 402-4241
Swanton (G-17397)

Fryman-Kuck General Contrs Inc ....E 937 274-2892
Dayton (G-9452)

J & J Schlaegel Inc ....E 937 652-2045
Urbana (G-18437)

K M & M ....C 216 651-3333
Cleveland (G-5811)

▲ Kokosing Construction Co Inc ....C 614 228-1029
Westerville (G-19270)

Kokosing Construction Co Inc ....E 614 228-1029
Westerville (G-19271)

MBC Holdings Inc ....E 419 445-1015
Archbold (G-632)

National Engrg & Contg Co ....A 440 238-3331
Cleveland (G-6044)

▼ Ohio Bridge Corporation ....C 740 432-6334
Cambridge (G-2079)

Prus Construction Company ....D 513 321-7774
Cincinnati (G-4303)

Righter Co Inc ....E 614 272-9700
Columbus (G-8531)

Righter Construction Svcs Inc ....E 614 272-9700
Columbus (G-8532)

Ruhlin Company ....C 330 239-2800
Sharon Center (G-16724)

Rwb Properties and Cnstr LLC ....D 513 541-0900
Cincinnati (G-4415)

Sunesis Construction Company ....C 513 326-6000
West Chester (G-19014)

Tri State Corporation ....E 513 763-0215
Cincinnati (G-4631)

Velotta Company ....E 330 239-1211
Sharon Center (G-16727)

Westpatrick Corp ....E 614 875-8200
Columbus (G-8891)

1623 Water, Sewer & Utility Line Construction

A Crano Excavating Inc ....E 330 630-1061
Akron (G-11)

A P OHoro Company ....D 330 759-9317
Youngstown (G-19944)

AAA Flexible Pipe Cleaning ....E 216 341-2900
Cleveland (G-4887)

ABC Piping Co ....E 216 398-4000
Brooklyn Heights (G-1863)

Adams-Robinson Enterprises Inc ....C 937 274-5318
Dayton (G-9208)

Adleta Inc ....E 513 554-1469
Cincinnati (G-2908)

Aecom Energy & Cnstr Inc ....B 216 622-2300
Cleveland (G-4906)

Amboy Contractors LLc ....D 419 644-2111
Metamora (G-14131)

American Boring Inc ....E 740 969-8000
Carroll (G-2555)

Anderzack-Pitzen Cnstr Inc ....E 419 553-7015
Metamora (G-14132)

Bitzel Excavating Inc ....E 330 477-9653
Canton (G-2214)

Bluefoot Industrial LLC ....E 740 314-5299
Steubenville (G-17141)

Bolt Construction Inc ....D 330 549-0349
Youngstown (G-19970)

Boone Coleman Construction Inc ....E 740 858-6661
Portsmouth (G-16126)

Broadband Express LLC ....D 419 536-9127
Toledo (G-17626)

Brock & Sons Inc ....E 513 874-4555
Fairfield (G-10701)

Capitol Tunneling Inc ....E 614 444-0255
Columbus (G-7117)

Charles H Hamilton Co ....D 513 683-2442
Maineville (G-13113)

City of Dayton ....E 937 333-3725
Dayton (G-9304)

City of Englewood ....E 937 836-2434
Englewood (G-10582)

Cook Paving and Cnstr Co ....E 216 267-7705
Independence (G-12062)

County of Clermont ....E 513 732-7970
Batavia (G-994)

County of Delaware ....E 740 833-2240
Delaware (G-9962)

County of Union ....D 937 645-4145
Marysville (G-13492)

Darby Creek Excavating Inc ....D 740 477-8600
Circleville (G-4831)

Dave Sugar Excavating LLC ....E 330 542-1100
Petersburg (G-15943)

Davey Resource Group Inc ....E 859 630-9879
Cincinnati (G-3401)

Digioia/Suburban Excvtg LLC ....D 440 237-1978
North Royalton (G-15353)

Don Wartko Construction Co ....D 330 673-5252
Kent (G-12229)

Dynamic Construction Inc ....D 740 927-8898
Pataskala (G-15785)

E S Wagner Company ....D 419 691-8651
Oregon (G-15592)

Edgar Trent Cnstr Co LLC ....D 419 683-4939
Crestline (G-9054)

▲ Enviro-Flow Companies Ltd ....E 740 453-7980
Zanesville (G-20306)

Fabrizi Trucking & Pav Co Inc ....C 330 483-3291
Cleveland (G-5504)

Finlaw Construction Inc ....E 330 889-2074
Bristolville (G-1825)

Fishel Company ....D 614 274-8100
Columbus (G-7588)

Fishel Company ....C 614 850-9012
Columbus (G-7589)

Fishel Company ....C 937 233-2268
Dayton (G-9439)

Fishel Company ....D 614 850-4400
Columbus (G-7590)

Fleming Construction Co ....E 740 494-2177
Prospect (G-16223)

Ford Development Corp ....D 513 772-1521
Cincinnati *(G-3577)*

Fred A Nemann Co ....E 513 467-9400
Cincinnati *(G-3585)*

George J Igel & Co Inc ....A 614 445-8421
Columbus *(G-7659)*

Geotex Construction Svcs Inc ......E 614 444-5690
Columbus *(G-7662)*

Gleason Construction Co Inc ....D 419 865-7480
Holland *(G-11886)*

Gradient Corporation ....E 513 779-0000
Cincinnati *(G-3631)*

Great Lakes Crushing Ltd ....E 440 944-5500
Wickliffe *(G-19461)*

Gudenkauf Corporation ....C 614 488-1776
Columbus *(G-7704)*

H & W Contractors Inc ....E 330 833-0982
Massillon *(G-13691)*

H M Miller Construction Co ....D 330 628-4811
Mogadore *(G-14549)*

Inliner American Inc ....E 614 529-6440
Hilliard *(G-11778)*

J & J General Maintenance Inc ......E 740 533-9729
Ironton *(G-12158)*

J B Express Inc ....D 740 702-9830
Chillicothe *(G-2794)*

J Daniel & Company Inc ....D 513 575-3100
Loveland *(G-13002)*

Jack Conie & Sons Corp ....D 614 291-5931
Columbus *(G-7852)*

JS Bova Excavating LLC ....E 234 254-4040
Struthers *(G-17365)*

Kenneth G Myers Cnstr Co Inc ......D 419 639-2051
Green Springs *(G-11354)*

Kirk Bros Co Inc ....D 419 595-4020
Alvada *(G-561)*

▲ Kokosing Construction Co Inc .....C 614 228-1029
Westerville *(G-19270)*

Kokosing Industrial Inc ....B 614 212-5700
Westerville *(G-19273)*

Larry Smith Contractors Inc ....E 513 367-0218
Cleves *(G-6732)*

Main Lite Electric Co Inc ....E 330 369-8333
Warren *(G-18726)*

Maintenance Unlimited Inc ....E 440 238-1162
Strongsville *(G-17325)*

Majaac Inc ....E 419 636-5678
Bryan *(G-1962)*

Mannon Pipeline LLC ....E 740 643-1534
Willow Wood *(G-19595)*

Mark Schaffer Excvtg Trckg Inc .....D 419 668-5990
Norwalk *(G-15443)*

Marucci and Gaffney Excvtg Co .....E 330 743-8170
Youngstown *(G-20117)*

Microwave Leasing Services LLC .....E 614 308-5433
Columbus *(G-8072)*

Mid-Ohio Contracting Inc ....C 330 343-2925
Dover *(G-10089)*

Mid-Ohio Pipeline Company Inc .....E 419 884-3772
Mansfield *(G-13222)*

Mike Enyart & Sons Inc ....D 740 523-0235
South Point *(G-16943)*

Miller Pipeline LLC ....B 937 506-8837
Tipp City *(G-17562)*

Miller Pipeline LLC ....B 614 777-8377
Hilliard *(G-11799)*

Miracle Plumbing & Heating Co .....E 330 477-2402
Canton *(G-2406)*

Municpal Cntrs Saling Pdts Inc ......E 513 482-3300
Cincinnati *(G-4085)*

National Engrg & Contg Co ....A 440 238-3331
Cleveland *(G-6044)*

Nelson Stark Company ....C 513 489-0866
Cincinnati *(G-4106)*

Nerone & Sons Inc ....E 216 662-2235
Cleveland *(G-6057)*

North Bay Construction Inc ....E 440 835-1898
Westlake *(G-19380)*

O C I Construction Co Inc ....E 440 338-3166
Novelty *(G-15465)*

Ohio Utilities Protection Svc ....D 800 311-3692
North Jackson *(G-15250)*

Ots-NJ LLC ....D 732 833-0600
Butler *(G-2021)*

Parallel Technologies Inc ....D 614 798-9700
Dublin *(G-10304)*

Precision Pipeline Svcs LLC ....E 740 652-1679
Lancaster *(G-12426)*

Quality Lines Inc ....C 740 815-1165
Findlay *(G-10957)*

R & R Pipeline Inc ....D 740 345-3692
Newark *(G-15094)*

R D Jergens Contractors Inc ....D 937 669-9799
Vandalia *(G-18539)*

Rla Investments Inc ....E 513 554-1470
Cincinnati *(G-4384)*

Russell Hawk Enterprises Inc ....E 330 343-4612
Dover *(G-10097)*

Six C Fabrication Inc ....D 330 296-5594
Ravenna *(G-16267)*

Sky Climber Twr Solutions LLC ......D 740 203-3900
Delaware *(G-10007)*

South Shore Cable Cnstr Inc ....D 440 816-0033
Cleveland *(G-6424)*

Southtown Heating & Cooling ....E 937 320-9900
Moraine *(G-14699)*

Steelial Wldg Met Fbrction Inc ....E 740 669-5300
Vinton *(G-18586)*

Stg Communication Services Inc .....E 330 482-0500
Columbiana *(G-6793)*

Sunesis Construction Company ......C 513 326-6000
West Chester *(G-19014)*

Sunesis Environmental LLC ....E 513 326-6000
Fairfield *(G-10788)*

Teasdale Fenton Carpet Cleanin .....C 513 797-0900
Cincinnati *(G-4578)*

Terrace Construction Co Inc ....D 216 739-3170
Cleveland *(G-6515)*

Thayer Pwr Comm Line Cnstr LLC ...D 330 922-4950
Cuyahoga Falls *(G-9131)*

Thayer Pwr Comm Line Cnstr LLC ...E 740 927-0021
Pataskala *(G-15788)*

Todd Alspaugh & Associates ....E 419 476-8126
Toledo *(G-18071)*

▼ Tri County Tower Service ....E 330 538-9874
North Jackson *(G-15255)*

Tribute Contracting & Cons LLC .....E 740 451-1010
South Point *(G-16946)*

Trucco Construction Co Inc ....C 740 417-9010
Delaware *(G-10010)*

Underground Utilities Inc ....D 419 465-2587
Monroeville *(G-14592)*

Universal Recovery Systems ....D 614 299-0184
Columbus *(G-8817)*

Usic Locating Services LLC ....E 419 874-9988
North Baltimore *(G-15180)*

Usic Locating Services LLC ....E 513 554-0456
Cincinnati *(G-4745)*

Utilicon Corporation ....E 216 391-8500
Cleveland *(G-6614)*

Vallejo Company ....E 216 741-3933
Cleveland *(G-6616)*

Wachter Inc ....C 513 777-0701
West Chester *(G-19099)*

Wenger Excavating Inc ....E 330 837-4767
Dalton *(G-9148)*

Woodward Excavating Co ....E 614 866-4384
Reynoldsburg *(G-16340)*

Zemba Bros Inc ....E 740 452-1880
Zanesville *(G-20388)*

1629 Heavy Construction, NEC

A P OHoro Company ....D 330 759-9317
Youngstown *(G-19944)*

Aecom Energy & Cnstr Inc ....B 216 622-2300
Cleveland *(G-4906)*

Amtrac of Ohio Inc ....D 330 683-7206
Orrville *(G-15622)*

Apex Environmental LLC ....D 740 543-4389
Amsterdam *(G-600)*

Aquarius Marine LLC ....E 614 875-8200
Columbus *(G-6961)*

Babcock & Wilcox Cnstr Co Inc .....D 330 860-6301
Barberton *(G-943)*

◆ Babcock & Wilcox Company ....A 330 753-4511
Barberton *(G-944)*

▲ Buckeye Landscape Service Inc ...D 614 866-0088
Blacklick *(G-1475)*

C & B Buck Bros Asp Maint LLC .....E 419 536-7325
Toledo *(G-17633)*

Danis Companies ....B 937 228-1225
Miamisburg *(G-14160)*

▲ Delta Railroad Cnstr Inc ....D 440 992-2997
Ashtabula *(G-736)*

E S Wagner Company ....D 419 691-8651
Oregon *(G-15592)*

Edwards Land Clearing Inc ....E 440 988-4477
Amherst *(G-585)*

▲ Enerfab Inc ....B 513 641-0500
Cincinnati *(G-3498)*

Fritz-Rumer-Cooke Co Inc ....E 614 444-8844
Columbus *(G-7630)*

Fryman-Kuck General Contrs Inc .....E 937 274-2892
Dayton *(G-9452)*

▲ Goette Holding Company Inc ....C 513 825-8100
Cincinnati *(G-3623)*

Great Lakes Crushing Ltd ....E 440 944-5500
Wickliffe *(G-19461)*

Image Pavement Maintenance ....E 937 833-9200
Brookville *(G-1914)*

▲ Independence Excavating Inc ....E 216 524-1700
Independence *(G-12082)*

ISI Systems Inc ....E 740 942-0050
Cadiz *(G-2030)*

J Way Leasing Ltd ....E 440 934-1020
Avon *(G-887)*

Jack Conie & Sons Corp ....D 614 291-5931
Columbus *(G-7852)*

Jack Gibson Construction Co ....D 330 394-5280
Warren *(G-18717)*

Jacobs Constructors Inc ....D 419 226-1344
Lima *(G-12667)*

Jacobs Constructors Inc ....E 513 595-7900
Cincinnati *(G-3800)*

Kirk Bros Co Inc ....D 419 595-4020
Alvada *(G-561)*

Kokosing Construction Co Inc ....E 440 323-9346
Elyria *(G-10522)*

▲ Kokosing Construction Co Inc .....C 614 228-1029
Westerville *(G-19270)*

Kokosing Industrial Inc ....B 614 212-5700
Westerville *(G-19273)*

Landscping Rclmtion Spcialists ......E 330 339-4900
New Philadelphia *(G-14970)*

M T Golf Course Managmnt Inc ......E 513 923-1188
Cincinnati *(G-3955)*

Maintenance Unlimited Inc ....E 440 238-1162
Strongsville *(G-17325)*

McDermott International Inc ....C 740 687-4292
Lancaster *(G-12415)*

Metropolitan Envmtl Svcs Inc ....D 614 771-1881
Hilliard *(G-11793)*

Miller Logging Inc ....E 330 279-4721
Holmesville *(G-11932)*

Mollett Seamless Gutter Co ....E 513 825-0500
West Chester *(G-18976)*

Ohio Irrigation Lawn Sprinkler ....E 937 432-9911
Dayton *(G-9670)*

Pae & Associates Inc ....E 937 833-0013
Dayton *(G-9682)*

Parks Drilling Company ....E 614 761-7707
Dublin *(G-10305)*

Peterson Construction Company .....C 419 941-2233
Wapakoneta *(G-18652)*

Petro Environmental Tech ....E 513 489-6789
Cincinnati *(G-4237)*

Platinum Restoration Inc ....E 440 327-0699
Elyria *(G-10556)*

Railworks Track Services Inc ....B 330 538-2261
North Jackson *(G-15253)*

Riepenhoff Landscape Ltd ....E 614 876-4683
Hilliard *(G-11813)*

Righter Construction Svcs Inc ....E 614 272-9700
Columbus *(G-8532)*

Scg Fields LLC ....E 440 546-1200
Brecksville *(G-1804)*

Scherzinger Drilling Inc ....E 513 738-2000
Harrison *(G-11676)*

Shook Construction Co ....D 440 838-5400
Dayton *(G-9763)*

Siemens Energy Inc ....B 740 393-8897
Mount Vernon *(G-14790)*

Sports Surfaces Cnstr LLC ....E 440 546-1200
Brecksville *(G-1807)*

Sunesis Environmental LLC ....D 513 326-6000
Fairfield *(G-10788)*

Todd Alspaugh & Associates ....E 419 476-8126
Toledo *(G-18071)*

Toledo Refining Company LLC ....C 419 698-6600
Oregon *(G-15611)*

Tri-America Contractors Inc ....E 740 574-0148
Wheelersburg *(G-19441)*

Ulliman Schutte Cnstr LLC ....B 937 247-0375
Miamisburg *(G-14233)*

Uranium Disposition Svcs LLC ....C 740 289-3620
Piketon *(G-15991)*

W Pol Contracting Inc ....E 330 325-7177
Ravenna *(G-16270)*

Whiting-Turner Contracting Co ....D 440 449-9200
Cleveland *(G-6681)*

17 CONSTRUCTION-SPECIAL TRADE CONTRACTORS

1711 Plumbing, Heating & Air Conditioning Contractors

A A S Amels Sheet Meta L Inc...........E..... 330 793-9326
Youngstown (G-19943)

A A Astro Service Inc...........................D..... 216 459-0363
Cleveland (G-4873)

A AAA H Jacks Plumbing Htg Co.........E..... 440 946-1166
Wickliffe (G-19453)

A J Stockmeister Inc.........................E..... 740 286-2106
Jackson (G-12168)

A To Zoff Co Inc...............................E..... 330 733-7902
Akron (G-12)

A-1 Advanced Plumbing Inc.................E..... 614 873-0548
Plain City (G-16040)

A-Team LLC....................................E..... 216 271-7223
Cleveland (G-4885)

AAA Pipe Cleaning Corporation...........C..... 216 341-2900
Cleveland (G-4888)

ABC Fire Inc...................................E..... 440 237-6677
North Royalton (G-15346)

ABC Piping Co.................................E..... 216 398-4000
Brooklyn Heights (G-1863)

Accurate Heating & Cooling...............E..... 740 775-5005
Chillicothe (G-2749)

Accurate Mechanical Inc...................E..... 740 353-4328
Wheelersburg (G-19427)

Accurate Mechanical Inc...................E..... 937 382-1436
Wilmington (G-19602)

Accurate Mechanical Inc...................E..... 740 681-1332
Lancaster (G-12368)

Adelmos Electric Sewer Clg Co...........E..... 216 641-2301
Brooklyn Heights (G-1864)

▲ Advanced Mechanical Svcs Inc.........E..... 937 879-7426
Fairborn (G-10662)

Aetna Building Maintenance Inc...........B..... 614 476-1818
Columbus (G-6881)

Aggressive Mechanical Inc.................E..... 614 443-3280
Columbus (G-6884)

Air Comfort Systems Inc....................E..... 216 587-4125
Cleveland (G-4915)

Air Conditioning Entps Inc.................E..... 440 729-0900
Cleveland (G-4917)

Air-Temp Climate Control Inc..............E..... 216 579-1552
Cleveland (G-4918)

Aire-Tech Inc.................................E..... 614 836-5670
Groveport (G-11492)

Airtron LP.....................................D..... 614 274-2345
Columbus (G-6888)

▲ Alan Manufacturing Inc..................E..... 330 262-1555
Wooster (G-19684)

All About Heating Cooling..................E..... 513 621-4620
Cincinnati (G-2921)

All Temp Refrigeration Inc.................E..... 419 692-5016
Delphos (G-10019)

Allied Restaurant Svc Ohio Inc............E..... 419 589-4759
Mansfield (G-13134)

American Air Furnace Company............D..... 614 876-1702
Grove City (G-11404)

American Mechanical Group Inc............E..... 614 575-3720
Columbus (G-6930)

American Residential Svcs LLC............D..... 216 561-8880
Cleveland (G-4964)

American Residential Svcs LLC............E..... 888 762-7752
Columbus (G-6937)

Apollo Heating and AC Inc..................E..... 513 271-3600
Cincinnati (G-2975)

Apple Heating Inc............................E..... 440 997-1212
Barberton (G-941)

Applied Mechanical Systems Inc...........D..... 513 825-1800
Cincinnati (G-2976)

Arco Heating & AC Co.......................E..... 216 663-3211
Solon (G-16821)

Area Energy & Electric Inc.................C..... 937 498-4784
Sidney (G-16759)

Arise Incorporated...........................E..... 440 746-8860
Brecksville (G-1770)

ARS Rescue Rooter Inc.....................E..... 440 842-8494
Cleveland (G-5009)

Ashland Comfort Control Inc...............E..... 419 281-0144
Ashland (G-650)

Atlas Capital Services Inc..................D..... 614 294-7373
Columbus (G-6997)

Ayers-Sterrett Inc...........................E..... 419 238-5480
Van Wert (G-18473)

Ayrshire Inc...................................D..... 440 992-0743
Ashtabula (G-721)

Aztec Plumbing Inc..........................E..... 513 732-3320
Milford (G-14373)

◆ Babcock & Wilcox Company.............A..... 330 753-4511
Barberton (G-944)

Bachmans Inc..................................E..... 513 943-5300
Batavia (G-983)

Bay Furnace Sheet Metal Co...............E..... 440 871-3777
Westlake (G-19320)

Bay Mechanical & Elec Corp...............D..... 440 282-6816
Lorain (G-12885)

Bayes Inc......................................E..... 419 661-3933
Perrysburg (G-15835)

Bellman Plumbing Inc.......................E..... 440 324-4477
Elyria (G-10481)

Best Plumbing Limited.......................E..... 614 855-1919
New Albany (G-14843)

Blind & Son LLC..............................D..... 330 753-7711
Barberton (G-948)

Blue Chip Plumbing Inc.....................D..... 513 941-4010
Cincinnati (G-3062)

Brady Plumbing & Heating Inc.............E..... 440 324-4261
Elyria (G-10484)

Brennan & Associates Inc..................E..... 216 391-4822
Cleveland (G-5076)

Brewer-Garrett Co...........................C..... 440 243-3535
Middleburg Heights (G-14248)

Bruner Corporation...........................C..... 614 334-9000
Hilliard (G-11749)

Buck and Sons Ldscp Svc Inc..............E..... 614 876-5359
Hilliard (G-11750)

▲ Buckeye Landscape Service Inc.........D..... 614 866-0088
Blacklick (G-1475)

Buckeye Mechanical Contg Inc.............E..... 740 282-0089
Toronto (G-18181)

Budde Sheet Metal Works Inc..............E..... 937 224-0868
Dayton (G-9268)

Building Integrated Svcs LLC..............D..... 330 733-9191
Oakwood Village (G-15487)

Burrier Service Company Inc...............E..... 440 946-6019
Mentor (G-14023)

Cahill Corporation............................E..... 330 724-1224
Uniontown (G-18359)

Campbell Inc...................................E..... 419 476-4444
Northwood (G-15391)

Castle Heating & Air Inc....................E..... 216 696-3940
Solon (G-16833)

Cattrell Companies Inc......................E..... 740 537-2481
Toronto (G-18183)

Century Mech Solutions Inc.................E..... 513 681-5700
Cincinnati (G-3161)

Chemed Corporation.........................D..... 513 762-6690
Cincinnati (G-3175)

Chemsteel Construction Company..........E..... 440 234-3930
Middleburg Heights (G-14249)

◆ Chick Master Incubator Company........C..... 330 722-5591
Medina (G-13917)

Cincinnati Air Conditioning Co.............D..... 513 721-5622
Cincinnati (G-3220)

Clearcreek Construction.....................E..... 740 420-3568
Stoutsville (G-17186)

Coleman Spohn Corporation................E..... 216 431-8070
Cleveland (G-5311)

Colonial Heating & Cooling Co.............E..... 614 837-6100
Pickerington (G-15953)

Columbs/Worthington Htg AC Inc..........E..... 614 771-5381
Columbus (G-7252)

Columbus Heating & Vent Co...............C..... 614 274-1177
Columbus (G-7286)

Comfort Systems USA Ohio Inc.............E..... 440 703-1600
Bedford (G-1273)

Commercial Comfort Systems Inc..........E..... 419 481-4444
Perrysburg (G-15849)

Commercial Hvac Inc........................E..... 513 396-6100
Cincinnati (G-3338)

Complete Mechanical Svcs LLC............E..... 513 489-3080
Blue Ash (G-1536)

Corcoran and Harnist Htg & AC...........E..... 513 921-2227
Cincinnati (G-3361)

Crane Heating & AC Co.....................E..... 513 641-4700
Cincinnati (G-3378)

Crawford Mechanical Svcs Inc.............D..... 614 478-9424
Columbus (G-7385)

Crown Heating & Cooling Inc...............D..... 330 499-4988
Uniontown (G-18365)

Custom AC & Htg Co.........................D..... 614 552-4822
Gahanna (G-11116)

D C Minnck Contracting Ltd.................E..... 937 322-1012
Springfield (G-17028)

Dar Plumbing.................................E..... 614 445-8243
Columbus (G-7417)

Dave Pinkerton...............................E..... 740 477-8888
Chillicothe (G-2775)

David R White Services Inc.................E..... 740 594-8381
Athens (G-775)

Debra-Kuempel Inc...........................D..... 513 271-6500
Cincinnati (G-3414)

Del Monde Inc................................E..... 859 371-7780
Miamisburg (G-14165)

Detmer & Sons Inc...........................E..... 937 879-2373
Fairborn (G-10671)

Dickson Industrial Park Inc.................E..... 740 377-9162
South Point (G-16931)

Diewald & Pope Inc..........................E..... 614 861-6160
Reynoldsburg (G-16298)

Dimech Services Inc.........................E..... 419 727-0111
Toledo (G-17701)

Dival Inc.......................................D..... 216 831-4200
Warrensville Heights (G-18777)

Division Drnking Ground Waters...........D..... 614 644-2752
Columbus (G-7457)

Dooley Heating and AC LLC.................E..... 614 278-9944
Columbus (G-7467)

Dovetail Construction Co Inc...............E..... 740 592-1800
Cleveland (G-5445)

Drake State Air...............................E..... 937 472-3740
Eaton (G-10443)

Drake State Air Systems Inc................E..... 937 472-0640
Eaton (G-10444)

Dunbar Mechanical Inc......................D..... 734 856-6601
Toledo (G-17706)

Dynamic Mechanical Systems...............E..... 513 858-6722
Fairfield (G-10720)

Eaton Plumbing Inc...........................E..... 614 891-7005
Westerville (G-19251)

Eckert Fire Protection Systems............E..... 513 948-1030
Cincinnati (G-3481)

Ecoplumbers Inc..............................E..... 614 299-9903
Hilliard (G-11765)

Edwards Electrical & Mech..................E..... 614 485-2003
Columbus (G-7507)

Ellerbrock Heating & AC....................E..... 419 782-1834
Defiance (G-9912)

Emcor Fclities Svcs N Amer Inc............D..... 614 430-5078
Columbus (G-7513)

▲ Enerfab Inc.................................B..... 513 641-0500
Cincinnati (G-3498)

Energy MGT Specialists Inc.................E..... 216 676-9045
Cleveland (G-5479)

Enervise Incorporated.......................C..... 513 761-6000
Blue Ash (G-1552)

Enervise Incorporated.......................E..... 614 885-9800
Columbus (G-7515)

Engineering Excellence......................D..... 972 535-3756
Blue Ash (G-1553)

Envirnmental Engrg Systems Inc............E..... 937 228-6492
Dayton (G-9415)

▲ Enviro-Flow Companies Ltd..............E..... 740 453-7980
Zanesville (G-20306)

Euclid Heat Treating Co.....................D..... 216 481-8444
Euclid (G-10632)

Excellence Alliance Group Inc..............E..... 513 619-4800
Cincinnati (G-3524)

Falls Heating & Cooling Inc.................E..... 330 929-8777
Cuyahoga Falls (G-9090)

Family Entertainment Services..............D..... 740 286-8587
Jackson (G-12173)

▲ Farber Corporation.......................E..... 614 294-1626
Columbus (G-7561)

Favret Company..............................D..... 614 488-5211
Columbus (G-7566)

Feldkamp Enterprises Inc...................C..... 513 347-4500
Cincinnati (G-3540)

Fire Guard LLC...............................E..... 740 625-5181
Sunbury (G-17388)

Fitzenrider Inc................................E..... 419 784-0828
Defiance (G-9915)

Flickinger Piping Company Inc..............E..... 330 364-4224
Dover (G-10078)

Fowler Electric Co...........................D..... 440 735-2385
Bedford (G-1281)

Franck and Fric Incorporated...............E..... 216 524-4451
Cleveland (G-5572)

Freeland Contracting Co.....................E..... 614 443-2718
Columbus (G-7623)

G Mechanical Inc.............................E..... 614 844-6750
Columbus (G-7639)

Gardiner Service Company LLC.............C..... 440 248-3400
Solon (G-16850)

Geauga Mechanical Company...............D..... 440 285-2000
Chardon (G-2696)

SIC

Gem Industrial Inc	D	419 666-6554
Walbridge (G-18622)
Gene Tolliver Corp	D	440 324-7727
Medina (G-13941)
General Temperature Ctrl Inc	E	614 837-3888
Canal Winchester (G-2109)
Genes Refrigeration Htg & AC	E	330 723-4104
Medina (G-13942)
Gilbert Heating & AC	E	419 625-8875
Sandusky (G-16610)
Glennco Systems Inc	E	740 353-4328
Portsmouth (G-16140)
Gorjanc Comfort Services Inc	E	440 449-4411
Cleveland (G-5617)
Grabill Plumbing & Heating	E	330 756-2075
Beach City (G-1024)
Greer & Whitehead Cnstr Inc	E	513 202-1757
Harrison (G-11668)
Gross Plumbing Incorporated	E	440 324-9999
Elyria (G-10514)
Guenther Mechanical Inc	C	419 289-6900
Ashland (G-674)
Gundlach Sheet Metal Works Inc	D	419 626-4525
Sandusky (G-16614)
Gundlach Sheet Metal Works Inc	E	419 734-7351
Port Clinton (G-16108)
H & M Plumbing Co	E	614 491-4880
Columbus (G-7707)
Haslett Heating & Cooling Inc	E	614 299-2133
Dublin (G-10239)
Hattenbach Company	D	216 881-5200
Cleveland (G-5666)
Havsco Inc	E	440 439-8900
Bedford (G-1284)
HEat Ttal Fclty Slutions Inc	E	740 965-3005
Galena (G-11159)
Helm and Associates Inc	E	419 893-1480
Maumee (G-13799)
Horizon Mechanical and Elec	E	419 529-2738
Mansfield (G-13183)
Houston Dick Plbg & Htg Inc	E	740 763-3961
Newark (G-15043)
Imperial Heating and Coolg Inc	D	440 498-1788
Solon (G-16860)
Industrial Power Systems Inc	C	419 531-3121
Rossford (G-16461)
Inloes Mechanical Inc	E	513 896-9499
Hamilton (G-11612)
J & D Home Improvement Inc	D	740 927-0722
Reynoldsburg (G-16310)
J & J General Maintenance Inc	E	740 533-9729
Ironton (G-12158)
J A Guy Inc	E	937 642-3415
Marysville (G-13508)
J F Bernard Inc	E	330 785-3830
Akron (G-283)
J Feldkamp Design Build Ltd	E	513 870-0601
Cincinnati (G-3795)
J W Geopfert Co Inc	E	330 762-2293
Akron (G-285)
Jackson Comfort Systems Inc	E	330 468-3111
Northfield (G-15381)
Jacobs Mechanical Co	C	513 681-6800
Cincinnati (G-3803)
Jarvis Mechanical Constrs Inc	E	513 831-0055
Milford (G-14398)
Jeff Plumber Inc	E	330 940-2600
Akron (G-289)
Jennings Heating Company Inc	E	330 784-1286
Akron (G-290)
John F Gallagher Plumbing Co	E	440 946-4256
Eastlake (G-10430)
Johnson Controls	D	513 874-1227
West Chester (G-18953)
Johnson Controls	D	614 717-9079
Dublin (G-10261)
Johnson Controls	C	440 268-1160
Strongsville (G-17317)
Johnson Controls	D	614 895-6600
Westerville (G-19266)
Johnson Controls Inc	E	330 270-4385
Youngstown (G-20087)
Johnson Controls Inc	D	513 489-0950
Cincinnati (G-3827)
Jonle Co Inc	E	513 662-2282
Cincinnati (G-3831)
Julian Speer Co	D	614 261-6331
Columbus (G-7876)
K Company Incorporated	C	330 773-5125
Coventry Township (G-9037)
▼ KA Bergquist Inc	E	419 865-4196
Toledo (G-17835)
Ken Neyer Plumbing Inc	C	513 353-3311
Cleves (G-6730)
Kessler Heating & Cooling	E	614 837-9961
Canal Winchester (G-2113)
Kidron Electric Inc	E	330 857-2871
Kidron (G-12308)
Kirk Williams Company Inc	D	614 875-9023
Grove City (G-11445)
Komar Plumbing Co	E	330 758-5073
Youngstown (G-20094)
Kuempel Service Inc	E	513 271-6500
Cincinnati (G-3894)
Kusan Inc	E	614 262-1818
Columbus (G-7931)
Lakes Heating and AC	E	330 644-7811
Coventry Township (G-9038)
▲ Langdon Inc	E	513 733-5955
Cincinnati (G-3909)
Lawn Management Sprinkler Co	E	513 272-3808
Cincinnati (G-3913)
Limbach Company LLC	E	614 299-2175
Columbus (G-7977)
Limbach Company LLC	E	614 299-2175
Columbus (G-7978)
Lippincott Plumbing-Heating AC	E	419 222-0856
Lima (G-12689)
Litter Bob Fuel & Heating Co	E	740 773-2196
Chillicothe (G-2801)
Lochard Inc	D	937 492-8811
Sidney (G-16784)
Lucas Plumbing & Heating Inc	E	440 282-4567
Lorain (G-12925)
Luxury Heating Co	E	440 366-0971
Sheffield Village (G-16738)
M K Moore & Sons Inc	E	937 236-1812
Dayton (G-9579)
M&M Heating & Cooling Inc	E	419 243-3005
Toledo (G-17876)
Mack Industries	C	419 353-7081
Bowling Green (G-1740)
Mansfield Plumbing Pdts LLC	E	330 496-2301
Big Prairie (G-1472)
Marlin Mechanical LLC	E	800 669-2645
Cleveland (G-5910)
Marvin W Mielke Inc	D	330 725-8845
Medina (G-13969)
Mc Clurg & Creamer Inc	E	419 866-7080
Holland (G-11896)
Mc Phillips Plbg & AC Co	E	216 481-1400
Cleveland (G-5929)
McAfee Heating & AC Co Inc	E	937 438-1976
Dayton (G-9593)
Mechancal/Industrial Contg Inc	E	513 489-8282
Cincinnati (G-3991)
Mechanical Cnstr Managers LLC	E	937 274-1987
Dayton (G-9597)
Mechanical Construction Co	E	740 353-5668
Portsmouth (G-16154)
Mechanical Systems Dayton Inc	E	937 254-3235
Dayton (G-9181)
Metal Masters Inc	E	330 343-3515
Dover (G-10088)
Metro Heating and AC Co	E	614 777-1237
Hilliard (G-11792)
Mid-Ohio Mechanical Inc	E	740 587-3362
Granville (G-11346)
Midwest Roofing & Furnace Co	E	614 252-5241
Columbus (G-8084)
Midwestern Plumbing Service	E	513 753-0050
Cincinnati (G-4051)
Miracle Plumbing & Heating Co	E	330 477-2402
Canton (G-2406)
Mj Baumann Co Inc	E	614 759-7100
Columbus (G-8092)
Monroe Mechanical Incorporated	E	513 539-7555
Monroe (G-14577)
Morrison Inc	E	740 373-5869
Marietta (G-13361)
Muetzel Plumbing & Heating Co	D	614 299-7700
Columbus (G-8120)
Naragon Companies Inc	E	330 745-7700
Norton (G-15420)
Nbw Co Inc	E	216 377-1700
Cleveland (G-6051)
Nelson Stark Company	C	513 489-0866
Cincinnati (G-4106)
Neptune Plumbing & Heating Co	D	216 475-9100
Cleveland (G-6056)
Nieman Plumbing Inc	D	513 851-5588
Cincinnati (G-4119)
Noron Inc	E	419 726-2677
Toledo (G-17947)
North Bay Construction Inc	E	440 835-1898
Westlake (G-19380)
North East Mechanical Inc	E	440 871-7525
Westlake (G-19381)
Northern Ohio Plumbing Co	E	440 951-3370
Eastlake (G-10433)
Northern Plumbing Systems	E	513 831-5111
Goshen (G-11313)
Ohio Heating & AC Inc	E	614 863-6666
Columbus (G-8264)
Ohio Irrigation Lawn Sprinkler	E	937 432-9911
Dayton (G-9670)
Osterfeld Champion Service	E	937 254-8437
Dayton (G-9679)
Osterwisch Company Inc	D	513 791-3282
Cincinnati (G-4189)
Overcashier and Horst Htg & AC	E	419 841-3333
Sylvania (G-17441)
P K Wadsworth Heating & Coolg	E	440 248-4821
Solon (G-16880)
◆ Park Corporation	B	216 267-4870
Cleveland (G-6163)
Peck-Hannaford Briggs Svc Corp	D	513 681-1200
Cincinnati (G-4220)
Perfection Group Inc	C	513 772-7545
Cincinnati (G-4230)
Perfection Services Inc	E	513 772-7545
Cincinnati (G-4231)
Perry Kelly Plumbing Inc	E	513 528-6554
Cincinnati (G-4232)
Peterman Plumbing and Htg Inc	E	330 364-4497
Dover (G-10093)
▲ Pioneer Pipe Inc	A	740 376-2400
Marietta (G-13370)
Piper Plumbing Inc	E	330 274-0160
Mantua (G-13275)
Pre-Fore Inc	E	740 467-2206
Millersport (G-14503)
Premier Rstrtion Mech Svcs LLC	E	513 420-1600
Middletown (G-14322)
Process Construction Inc	D	513 251-2211
Cincinnati (G-4289)
Professional Plumbing Services	E	740 454-1066
Zanesville (G-20356)
Prout Boiler Htg & Wldg Inc	E	330 744-0293
Youngstown (G-20167)
Quality Electrical & Mech Inc	E	419 294-3591
Lima (G-12726)
Queen City Mechanicals Inc	E	513 353-1430
Cincinnati (G-4316)
R & R Hvac Systems	E	419 861-0266
Holland (G-11907)
R Kelly Inc	E	513 631-8488
Cincinnati (G-4331)
Rapid Plumbing Inc	D	513 575-1509
Loveland (G-13023)
▲ Recker & Boerger Inc	D	513 942-9663
West Chester (G-19076)
Regal Plumbing & Heating Co	E	937 492-2894
Sidney (G-16795)
Relmec Mechanical LLC	C	216 391-1030
Cleveland (G-6302)
Reupert Heating and AC Co Inc	E	513 922-5050
Cincinnati (G-4365)
Rexs Air Conditioning Company	E	330 499-8733
Canton (G-2460)
Rmf Nooter Inc	D	419 727-1970
Toledo (G-18009)
Robinson Htg Air-Conditioning	E	513 422-6812
Middletown (G-14326)
Roman Plumbing Company	D	330 455-5155
Canton (G-2462)
Ron Johnson Plumbing and Htg	E	419 433-5365
Norwalk (G-15455)
Roth Bros Inc	C	330 793-5571
Youngstown (G-20197)
Roto-Rooter Development Co	D	513 762-6690
Cincinnati (G-4398)
Roto-Rooter Services Company	D	513 762-6690
Cincinnati (G-4400)
Roto-Rooter Services Company	D	513 541-3840
Cincinnati (G-4401)
RPC Mechanical Services	C	513 733-1641
Cincinnati (G-4405)
S&D/Osterfeld Mech Contrs Inc	E	937 277-1700
Dayton (G-9746)

Sals Heating and Cooling Inc ....E 216 676-4949
Cleveland *(G-6366)*

Sauer Group Inc ....C 614 853-2500
Columbus *(G-8592)*

Sauer Incorporated ....D 614 853-2500
Columbus *(G-8593)*

Schibi Heating & Cooling Corp ....E 513 385-3344
Cincinnati *(G-4436)*

Schmid Mechanical Inc ....E 330 264-3633
Wooster *(G-19765)*

Schmid Mechanical Co ....E 614 261-6331
Columbus *(G-8601)*

Schmids Service Now Inc ....E 330 264-2040
Wooster *(G-19766)*

Schneller Heating and AC Co 859 341-1200
Cincinnati *(G-2867)*

Schumm Richard A Plbg & Htg 419 238-4994
Van Wert *(G-18488)*

Schweizer Dipple Inc ....D 440 786-8090
Cleveland *(G-6378)*

Scioto Services Llc ....E 937 644-0888
Marysville *(G-13527)*

Service Experts Htg & AC LLC ....E 937 426-3444
Springfield *(G-17112)*

Service Experts Htg & AC LLC ....E 513 489-3361
Blue Ash *(G-1650)*

Service Experts Htg & AC LLC ....E 614 859-6993
Columbus *(G-8622)*

Service Experts LLC ....E 330 577-3918
Akron *(G-425)*

Sexton Industrial Inc ....C 513 530-5555
West Chester *(G-19080)*

Sisler Heating & Cooling Inc ....E 330 722-7101
Medina *(G-14002)*

Slagle Mechanical Contractors ....E 937 492-4151
Sidney *(G-16801)*

Smith & Oby Company ....D 440 735-5333
Walton Hills *(G-18638)*

Smith & Oby Service Co ....E 440 735-5322
Bedford *(G-1306)*

Smylie One Heating & Cooling ....E 440 449-4328
Bedford *(G-1307)*

Southtown Heating & Cooling ....E 937 320-9900
Moraine *(G-14699)*

Speer Industries Incorporated ....C 614 261-6331
Columbus *(G-8671)*

Standard Plumbing & Heating Co ......D 330 453-5150
Canton *(G-2485)*

Steel Valley Construction Co ....E 330 392-8391
Warren *(G-18746)*

Steingass Mechanical Contg ....E 330 725-6090
Medina *(G-14005)*

Superior Mechanical Svcs Inc ....E 937 259-0082
Dayton *(G-9187)*

Supply Network Inc ....E 614 527-5800
Columbus *(G-8715)*

Tanner Heating & AC Inc ....E 937 299-2500
Moraine *(G-14701)*

Tfh-Eb Inc ....D 614 253-7246
Columbus *(G-8741)*

TH Martin Inc ....D 216 741-2020
Cleveland *(G-6518)*

The Peck-Hannaford Briggs Co ....D 513 681-4600
Cincinnati *(G-4595)*

Thomas J Dyer Company ....C 513 321-8100
Cincinnati *(G-4602)*

Thompson Heating & Cooling ....E 513 242-4450
Cincinnati *(G-4605)*

Thompson Heating Corporation ....D 513 769-7696
Cincinnati *(G-4606)*

Tilton Corporation ....C 419 227-6421
Lima *(G-12762)*

Timmerman John P Heating AC Co ....E 419 229-4015
Lima *(G-12764)*

Tom Schaefer Plumbing Inc ....E 440 602-7300
Willoughby *(G-19576)*

TP Mechanical Contractors Inc ....C 614 253-8556
Columbus *(G-8768)*

Trame Mechanical Inc ....E 937 258-1000
Dayton *(G-9820)*

Trane Inc ....E 440 946-7823
Cleveland *(G-6539)*

Trep Ltd ....E 419 717-5624
Napoleon *(G-14818)*

Triton Services Inc ....C 513 679-6800
Mason *(G-13650)*

U S A Plumbing Company ....E 614 882-6402
Columbus *(G-8792)*

United Group Services Inc ....C 800 633-9690
West Chester *(G-19094)*

Universal Enterprises Inc ....C 419 529-3500
Ontario *(G-15577)*

V M Systems Inc ....D 419 535-1044
Toledo *(G-18133)*

▲ Vaughn Industries LLC ....B 419 396-3900
Carey *(G-2548)*

Vaughn Industries LLC ....E 740 548-7100
Lewis Center *(G-12566)*

Volpone Enterprises Inc ....E 440 969-1141
Ashtabula *(G-759)*

Vulcan Enterprises Inc ....E 419 396-3535
Carey *(G-2549)*

Wadsworth Service Inc ....E 419 861-8181
Middleburg Heights *(G-14265)*

Warner Mechanical Corporation ....E 419 332-7116
Fremont *(G-11106)*

Watkins Mechanical Inc ....E 937 748-0220
Springboro *(G-16987)*

Wells Brothers Inc ....D 937 394-7559
Anna *(G-611)*

Wenger Temperature Control ....E 614 586-4016
Columbus *(G-8887)*

West Jefferson Plumbing Htg ....E 614 879-9606
West Jefferson *(G-19113)*

Western Reserve Mechanical Inc ......E 330 652-3888
Niles *(G-15175)*

Whisler Plumbing & Heating Inc ....E 330 833-2875
Massillon *(G-13735)*

Whitt Inc ....E 513 753-7707
Amelia *(G-577)*

Wilkes & Company Inc ....E 419 433-2325
Huron *(G-12035)*

Willis One Hour Heating & AC ....D 513 752-2512
Cincinnati *(G-2875)*

Wojos Heating & AC Inc ....E 419 693-3220
Northwood *(G-15415)*

York-Mahoning Mech Contrs Inc ......D 330 788-7011
Youngstown *(G-20252)*

Zemba Bros Inc ....E 740 452-1880
Zanesville *(G-20388)*

1721 Painting & Paper Hanging Contractors

A & A Safety Inc ....E 513 943-6100
Amelia *(G-563)*

A B Industrial Coatings ....E 614 228-0383
Columbus *(G-6846)*

Aero-Mark Inc ....E 330 995-0100
Streetsboro *(G-17244)*

Allstate Painting & Contg Co ....D 330 220-5533
Brunswick *(G-1919)*

American Star Painting Co LLC ....E 740 373-5634
Marietta *(G-13311)*

Apbn Inc ....E 724 964-8252
Campbell *(G-2090)*

August Groh & Sons Inc ....E 513 821-0090
Cincinnati *(G-3004)*

Barbara Gheens Painting Inc ....E 740 949-0405
Long Bottom *(G-12877)*

Cipriano Painting ....E 440 892-1827
Cleveland *(G-5181)*

Classic Papering & Painting ....E 614 221-0505
Columbus *(G-7221)*

Cleveland Construction Inc ....E 440 255-8000
Mason *(G-13563)*

Clubhouse Pub N Grub ....E 440 884-2582
Cleveland *(G-5310)*

Commercial Painting Inc ....E 614 298-9963
Worthington *(G-19799)*

Costello Pntg Bldg Restoration ....E 513 321-3326
Cincinnati *(G-3366)*

Cummins Building Maint Inc ....D 740 726-9800
Prospect *(G-16221)*

David W Steinbach Inc ....E 330 497-5959
Canton *(G-2279)*

Dennis Todd Painting Inc ....E 614 879-7952
West Jefferson *(G-19106)*

Dependable Painting Co ....E 216 431-4470
Cleveland *(G-5417)*

Eagle Industrial Painting LLC ....E 330 866-5965
Magnolia *(G-13111)*

Flamos Enterprises Inc ....E 330 478-0009
Canton *(G-2315)*

Frank Novak & Sons Inc ....D 216 475-2495
Cleveland *(G-5573)*

Gpc Contracting Company ....E 740 264-6060
Steubenville *(G-17156)*

Gradient Corporation ....E 513 779-0000
Cincinnati *(G-3631)*

Industrial Mill Maintenance ....E 330 746-1155
Youngstown *(G-20078)*

Ionno Properties s Corp ....E 330 479-9267
Dennison *(G-10051)*

Johnson & Fischer Inc ....E 614 276-8868
Columbus *(G-7862)*

Kendrick-Mollenauer Pntg Co ....E 614 443-7037
Columbus *(G-7892)*

Kneisel Contracting Corp ....E 513 615-8816
Cincinnati *(G-3882)*

Lehn Painting Inc ....E 513 732-1515
Batavia *(G-1003)*

Liberty Maintenance Inc ....D 330 755-7711
Youngstown *(G-20099)*

Liberty-Alpha III JV ....E 330 755-7711
Campbell *(G-2091)*

Lou Ritenour Decorators Inc ....D 330 425-3232
Twinsburg *(G-18294)*

Mark Dura Inc ....E 330 995-0883
Aurora *(G-836)*

Masterpiece Painting Company ....E 330 395-9900
Warren *(G-18727)*

Mike Morris ....E 330 767-4122
Brewster *(G-1811)*

Mrap LLC ....E 614 545-3190
Columbus *(G-8117)*

Muha Construction Inc ....E 937 435-0678
Dayton *(G-9647)*

Napoleon Machine LLC ....E 419 591-7010
Napoleon *(G-14813)*

▲ National Electro-Coatings Inc ....D 216 898-0080
Cleveland *(G-6043)*

North Star Painting Co Inc ....E 330 743-2333
Youngstown *(G-20141)*

P & W Painting Contractors Inc ....E 419 698-2209
Toledo *(G-17969)*

Painting Company ....C 614 873-1334
Plain City *(G-16063)*

Performance Painting LLC ....E 440 735-3340
Oakwood Village *(G-15492)*

Perry Interiors Inc ....E 513 761-9333
Batavia *(G-1006)*

Preferred Acquisition Co LLC ....D 216 587-0957
Cleveland *(G-6229)*

Protective Coatings Inc ....E 937 275-7711
Dayton *(G-9721)*

Reilly Painting Co ....E 216 371-8160
Cleveland Heights *(G-6723)*

Residence Artists Inc ....E 440 286-8822
Chardon *(G-2710)*

RI Painting and Mfg Inc ....E 937 968-5526
Union City *(G-18354)*

South Town Painting Inc ....E 937 847-1600
Miamisburg *(G-14225)*

Unique Construction Svcs Inc ....E 513 608-1363
Blue Ash *(G-1673)*

Vimas Painting Company Inc ....E 330 536-2222
Lowellville *(G-13044)*

W F Bolin Company Inc ....E 614 276-6397
Columbus *(G-8868)*

Yerman & Young Painting Inc ....E 330 861-0022
Barberton *(G-973)*

1731 Electrical Work

A J Goulder Electric Co ....E 440 942-4026
Willoughby *(G-19501)*

Abbott Electric ....D 330 452-6601
Canton *(G-2170)*

ABC Fire Inc ....E 440 237-6677
North Royalton *(G-15346)*

Accurate Electric Cnstr Inc ....C 614 863-1844
Reynoldsburg *(G-16279)*

Acpi Systems Inc ....E 513 738-3840
Hamilton *(G-11554)*

Advanced Service Tech LLC ....E 937 435-4376
Miamisburg *(G-14137)*

AE Electric Inc ....E 419 392-8468
Grand Rapids *(G-11324)*

Aero Electrical Contractors ....E 614 834-8181
Canal Winchester *(G-2103)*

Aetna Building Maintenance Inc ....B 614 476-1818
Columbus *(G-6881)*

Aey Electric Inc ....E 330 792-5745
Youngstown *(G-19949)*

Akron Foundry Co ....E 330 745-3101
Barberton *(G-939)*

All Phase Power and Ltg Inc ....E 419 624-9640
Sandusky *(G-16574)*

Allcan Global Services Inc ....E 513 825-1655
Cincinnati *(G-2924)*

American Electric Power Co Inc ....E 740 295-3070
Coshocton *(G-8998)*

American Electric Power Co Inc ....E 614 716-1000
Columbus *(G-6918)*

AMS Construction Inc ....C 513 398-6689
Maineville *(G-13112)*

AMS Construction Inc ....E 513 794-0410
Loveland *(G-12977)*

Apollo Heating and AC Inc ....E 513 271-3600
Cincinnati *(G-2975)*

Archiable Electric Company ....D 513 621-1307
Cincinnati *(G-2982)*

Area Energy & Electric Inc ....E 937 642-0386
Marysville *(G-13483)*

Area Energy & Electric Inc ....C 937 498-4784
Sidney *(G-16759)*

Atkins & Stang Inc ....D 513 242-8300
Cincinnati *(G-2997)*

Atlas Electrical Construction ....E 440 323-5418
Elyria *(G-10480)*

Atlas Industrial Contrs LLC ....B 614 841-4500
Columbus *(G-7000)*

B & J Electrical Company Inc ....E 513 351-7100
Cincinnati *(G-3014)*

Bansal Construction Inc ....E 513 874-5410
Fairfield *(G-10698)*

Banta Electrical Contrs Inc ....D 513 353-4446
Cleves *(G-6725)*

Bay Mechanical & Elec Corp ....D 440 282-6816
Lorain *(G-12885)*

BCU Electric Inc ....E 419 281-8944
Ashland *(G-656)*

Beacon Electric Company ....D 513 851-0711
Cincinnati *(G-3029)*

Becdel Controls Incorporated ....E 330 652-1386
Niles *(G-15147)*

Benevento Enterprises Inc ....D 216 621-5890
Cleveland *(G-5054)*

Berwick Electric Company ....E 614 834-2301
Canal Winchester *(G-2104)*

Biz Com Electric Inc ....E 513 961-7200
Cincinnati *(G-3052)*

Bodie Electric Inc ....E 419 435-3672
Fostoria *(G-10997)*

Bp-Ls-Pt Co ....D 614 841-4500
Columbus *(G-7057)*

Brennan Electric LLC ....E 513 353-2229
Miamitown *(G-14240)*

Broadband Express LLC ....E 513 834-8085
Cincinnati *(G-3076)*

Broadband Express LLC ....E 614 823-6464
Westerville *(G-19149)*

Broadband Express LLC ....D 419 536-9127
Toledo *(G-17626)*

Brush Contractors Inc ....D 614 850-8500
Columbus *(G-7083)*

Bryan Electric Inc ....E 740 695-9834
Saint Clairsville *(G-16481)*

Buckeye Cable Systems Inc ....E 419 724-2539
Toledo *(G-17631)*

Busy Bee Electric Inc ....E 513 353-3553
Hooven *(G-11934)*

Butchko Electric Inc ....E 440 985-3180
Amherst *(G-582)*

Cable TV Services Inc.....................E 440 816-0033
Cleveland *(G-5112)*

Calvin Electric LLC ....E 937 670-2558
Arcanum *(G-624)*

Capital City Electric LLC ....E 614 933-8700
New Albany *(G-14847)*

Carey Electric Co ....E 937 669-3399
Vandalia *(G-18512)*

Cattrell Companies Inc ....D 740 537-2481
Toronto *(G-18183)*

Chapel Electric Co LLC ....C 937 222-2290
Dayton *(G-9291)*

Chapel-Romanoff Tech LLC ....E 937 222-9840
Dayton *(G-9292)*

Cincinnati Voice and Data ....D 513 683-4127
Loveland *(G-12983)*

Claypool Electric Inc ....C 740 653-5683
Lancaster *(G-12381)*

Cls Facilities MGT Svcs Inc ....E 440 602-4600
Mentor *(G-14032)*

Cochran Electric Inc ....E 614 847-0035
Powell *(G-16189)*

Colgan-Davis Inc ....E 419 893-6116
Maumee *(G-13771)*

Columbia Energy Group ....A 614 460-4683
Columbus *(G-7247)*

Commercial Electric Pdts Corp ....E 216 241-2886
Cleveland *(G-5318)*

Controls Inc ....E 330 239-4345
Medina *(G-13923)*

Converse Electric Inc ....D 614 808-4377
Grove City *(G-11422)*

Copp Systems Inc ....E 937 228-4188
Dayton *(G-9320)*

Corporate Electric Company LLC ....E 330 331-7517
Barberton *(G-951)*

Countryside Electric Inc ....E 614 478-7960
Columbus *(G-7380)*

▲ Craftsman Electric Inc ....E 513 891-4426
Cincinnati *(G-3377)*

CTS Construction Inc ....D 513 489-8290
Cincinnati *(G-3385)*

D B A Inc ....E 513 541-6600
Cincinnati *(G-3394)*

D C Minnick Contracting Ltd ....E 937 322-1012
Springfield *(G-17028)*

D E Williams Electric Inc ....E 440 543-1222
Chagrin Falls *(G-2644)*

▲ Darana Hybrid Inc ....E 513 785-7540
Hamilton *(G-11589)*

Davis H Elliot Cnstr Co Inc ....C 937 847-8025
Miamisburg *(G-14162)*

Davis Pickering & Company Inc ....D 740 373-5896
Marietta *(G-13324)*

Delta Electrical Contrs Ltd ....E 513 421-7744
Cincinnati *(G-3421)*

Denier Electric Co Inc ....C 513 738-2641
Harrison *(G-11665)*

Denier Electric Co Inc ....E 614 338-4664
Grove City *(G-11425)*

DIA Electric Inc ....E 513 281-0783
Cincinnati *(G-3427)*

Diebold Incorporated ....C 330 588-3619
Canton *(G-2285)*

Diebold Nixdorf Incorporated ....D 513 682-6216
Hamilton *(G-11590)*

Dillard Electric Inc ....E 937 836-5381
Union *(G-18350)*

Dovetail Construction Co Inc ....E 740 592-1800
Cleveland *(G-5445)*

Dss Installations Ltd ....E 513 761-7000
Cincinnati *(G-3446)*

Dynalectric Company ....E 614 529-7500
Columbus *(G-7480)*

Dynamic Currents Corp ....E 419 861-2036
Holland *(G-11885)*

Dynamic Mechanical Systems ....E 513 858-6722
Fairfield *(G-10720)*

E S I Inc ....D 513 454-3741
West Chester *(G-19048)*

Efficient Electric Corp ....E 614 552-0200
Columbus *(G-7510)*

▲ Eighth Day Sound Systems Inc ....E 440 995-2647
Cleveland *(G-5469)*

Elect General Contractors Inc ....E 740 420-3437
Circleville *(G-4833)*

Electric Connection Inc ....D 614 436-1121
Westerville *(G-19252)*

Electrical Corp America Inc ....D 440 245-3007
Lorain *(G-12903)*

▲ Enertech Electrical Inc ....E 330 536-2131
Lowellville *(G-13040)*

Enviroserve Inc ....C 330 966-0910
North Canton *(G-15200)*

Erb Electric Co ....C 740 633-5055
Bridgeport *(G-1816)*

Excel Electrical Contractor ....E 740 965-3795
Worthington *(G-19809)*

Fishel Company ....E 614 274-8100
Columbus *(G-7588)*

Fishel Company ....D 614 850-4400
Columbus *(G-7590)*

Fowler Electric Co ....D 440 735-2385
Bedford *(G-1281)*

Fresch Electric Inc ....E 419 626-2535
Sandusky *(G-16609)*

Frey Electric Inc ....D 513 385-0700
Cincinnati *(G-3593)*

Frontier Security LLC ....E 937 247-2824
Miamisburg *(G-14172)*

GA Business Purchaser LLC ....D 419 255-8400
Toledo *(G-17752)*

Garber Electrical Contrs Inc ....D 937 771-5202
Englewood *(G-10587)*

▲ Gatesair Inc ....D 513 459-3400
Mason *(G-13583)*

Gateway Electric Incorporated ....C 216 518-5500
Cleveland *(G-5594)*

Gem Electric ....E 440 286-6200
Chardon *(G-2697)*

Gem Industrial Inc. ....D 419 666-6554
Walbridge *(G-18622)*

Gene Ptacek Son Fire Eqp Inc ....E 216 651-8300
Cleveland *(G-5602)*

General Electric Company ....D 330 256-5331
Cuyahoga Falls *(G-9099)*

General Electric Company ....E 614 527-1078
Hilliard *(G-11768)*

General Electric Company ....E 513 583-3500
Cincinnati *(G-3610)*

Genric Inc ....B 937 553-9250
Marysville *(G-13500)*

Gillmore Security Systems Inc ....E 440 232-1000
Cleveland *(G-5608)*

Goodin Electric Inc ....E 740 522-3113
Newark *(G-15038)*

Gorjanc Comfort Services Inc ....E 440 449-4411
Cleveland *(G-5617)*

Guardian Protection Svcs Inc ....E 330 797-1570
Youngstown *(G-20059)*

Habitec Security Inc. ....D 419 537-6768
Holland *(G-11887)*

Harrington Electric Company ....E 216 361-5101
Cleveland *(G-5662)*

Hatzel & Buehler Inc ....E 740 420-3088
Circleville *(G-4834)*

Helm and Associates Inc. ....E 419 893-1480
Maumee *(G-13799)*

Hilscher-Clarke Electric Co ....E 330 452-9806
Canton *(G-2345)*

Hilscher-Clarke Electric Co ....D 740 622-5557
Coshocton *(G-9017)*

Horizon Mechanical and Elec ....E 419 529-2738
Mansfield *(G-13183)*

Hoskins International LLC ....E 419 628-6015
Minster *(G-14536)*

Ies Infrstrcture Solutions LLC ....D 330 830-3500
Massillon *(G-13698)*

Indrolect Co ....E 513 821-4788
Cincinnati *(G-3758)*

Industrial Comm & Sound Inc ....E 614 276-8123
Cincinnati *(G-3759)*

Industrial Power Systems Inc ....C 419 531-3121
Rossford *(G-16461)*

Insight Communications of Co ....C 614 236-1200
Columbus *(G-7825)*

▲ Instrmntation Ctrl Systems Inc ....E 513 662-2600
Cincinnati *(G-3765)*

Intercnnect Cbling Netwrk Svcs ....E 440 891-0465
Berea *(G-1428)*

J & J General Maintenance Inc ....E 740 533-9729
Ironton *(G-12158)*

J W Didado Electric Inc ....C 330 374-0070
Akron *(G-284)*

Jess Howard Electric Company ....C 614 864-2167
Blacklick *(G-1481)*

Jims Electric Inc. ....E 440 327-8800
North Ridgeville *(G-15331)*

Joe Dickey Electric Inc ....D 330 549-3976
North Lima *(G-15270)*

John A Becker Co ....E 614 272-8800
Columbus *(G-7861)*

John H Cooper Elec Contg Co ....E 513 471-9900
Cincinnati *(G-3823)*

John P Novatny Electric Co ....E 330 630-8900
Akron *(G-293)*

JZE Electric Inc ....C 440 243-7600
Cleveland *(G-5810)*

Kal Electric Inc ....E 740 593-8720
Athens *(G-788)*

Kastle Electric Co LLC ....D 937 254-2681
Moraine *(G-14666)*

Kastle Electric Company ....C 937 254-2681
Moraine *(G-14667)*

Kastle Electric Company ....E 513 360-2901
Monroe *(G-14572)*

Kastle Technologies Co LLC ....E 513 360-2901
Monroe *(G-14573)*

Kastle Technologies Co LLC ....E 614 433-9860
Columbus *(G-7885)*

Kathman Electric Co Inc ....E 513 353-3365
Cleves *(G-6729)*

Kenmarc Inc ....E 513 541-2791
Cincinnati *(G-3859)*

Kidron Electric Inc ....E 330 857-2871
Kidron *(G-12308)*

Koorsen Fire & Security Inc ....E 937 324-9405
Vandalia *(G-18530)*

Kraft Electrical Contg Inc ....E 513 467-0500
Cincinnati (G-3888)

Kween Industries Inc ....E 513 932-2293
Lebanon (G-12477)

Laibe Electric Co ....D 419 724-8200
Toledo (G-17847)

Lake Erie Electric Inc ....D 440 835-5565
Westlake (G-19366)

Lake Erie Electric Inc ....E 330 724-1241
Akron (G-308)

Lake Erie Electric Inc ....E 419 529-4611
Ontario (G-15558)

Lake Horry Electric ....D 440 808-8791
Chagrin Falls (G-2651)

Lawn Management Sprinkler Co ....E 513 272-3808
Cincinnati (G-3913)

Legrand North America LLC ....B 937 224-0639
Dayton (G-9561)

Legrand North America LLC ....C 937 224-0639
Dayton (G-9562)

Lin R Rogers Elec Contrs Inc ....B ...... 614 876-9336 ·
Hilliard (G-11785)

Lippincott Plumbing-Heating AC ....E 419 222-0856
Lima (G-12689)

Live Technologies LLC ....D 614 278-7777
Columbus (G-7986)

Lowry Controls Inc ....E 513 583-0182
Loveland (G-13009)

M & L Electric Inc ....E 937 833-5154
Lewisburg (G-12570)

Main Lite Electric Co Inc ....E 330 369-8333
Warren (G-18726)

▲ Mayers Electric Co Inc ....C 513 272-2900
Cincinnati (G-3982)

Mc Phillips Plbg Htg & AC Co ....E 216 481-1400
Cleveland (G-5929)

Mc Sign LLC ....C 440 209-6200
Mentor (G-14079)

McClintock Electric Inc ....E 330 264-6380
Wooster (G-19743)

McKeever & Niekamp Elc Inc ....E 937 431-9363
Beavercreek (G-1169)

MDU Resources Group Inc ....E 937 424-2550
Moraine (G-14673)

Megacity Fire Protection Inc ....E 937 335-0775
Dayton (G-9605)

Miller Cable Company ....D 419 639-2091
Green Springs (G-11355)

Mills Security Alarm Systems ....E 513 921-4600
Cincinnati (G-4058)

Mitel (delaware) Inc ....E 513 733-8000
West Chester (G-18974)

Nationwide Energy Partners LLC ....E 614 918-2031
Columbus (G-8153)

New River Electrical Corp ....E 614 891-1142
Westerville (G-19285)

Newcome Corp ....E 614 848-5688
Columbus (G-6826)

▼ Ngn Electric Corp ....E 330 923-2777
Brecksville (G-1793)

North Electric Inc ....E 216 331-4141
Cleveland (G-6077)

▼ Northeast Ohio Electric LLC ....B 216 587-9510
Cleveland (G-6093)

▲ Northwest Electrical Contg Inc ....E 419 865-4757
Holland (G-11901)

Northwestern Ohio SEC Systems ....E 419 227-1655
Lima (G-12708)

O D Miller Electric Co Inc ....E 330 875-1651
Louisville (G-12969)

Ohio Power Company ....E 888 216-3523
Canton (G-2429)

Ohio Power Company ....E 419 443-4634
Tiffin (G-17529)

Ohio Valley Elec Svcs LLC ....D 513 771-2410
Blue Ash (G-1623)

Osterwisch Company Inc ....D 513 791-3282
Cincinnati (G-4189)

Oyer Electric Inc ....E 740 773-2828
Chillicothe (G-2809)

Paladin Protective Systems Inc ....E 216 441-6500
Cleveland (G-6158)

Palazzo Brothers Electric Inc ....E 419 668-1100
Norwalk (G-15451)

Penn-Ohio Electrical Company ....E 330 448-1234
Masury (G-13742)

Perram Electric Inc ....E 330 239-2661
Wadsworth (G-18612)

Pomeroy It Solutions Sls Inc ....E 440 717-1364
Brecksville (G-1798)

Positive Electric Inc ....E 937 428-0606
Dayton (G-9700)

Precision Broadbnd Installatns ....C 614 523-2917
Westerville (G-19201)

Precision Electrical Services ....E 740 474-4490
Circleville (G-4846)

Primetech Communications Inc ....D 513 942-6000
West Chester (G-18986)

Professional Telecom Svcs ....E 513 232-7700
Cincinnati (G-4294)

Proline Electric Inc ....E 740 687-4571
Lancaster (G-12428)

Protech Security Inc ....E 330 499-3555
Canton (G-2442)

Quebe Holdings Inc ....D 937 222-2290
Dayton (G-9723)

Queen City Electric Inc ....E 513 591-2600
Cincinnati (G-4313)

R & R Wiring Contractors Inc ....E 513 752-6304
Batavia (G-1007)

R J Martin Elec Svcs Inc ....D 216 662-7100
Bedford Heights (G-1326)

Rapier Electric Inc ....E 513 868-9087
Hamilton (G-11636)

Reddy Electric Co ....C 937 372-8205
Xenia (G-19922)

Regent Electric Inc ....D 419 476-8333
Toledo (G-17998)

Rei Telecom Inc ....E 614 255-3100
Canal Winchester (G-2116)

Reliable Contractors Inc ....D 937 433-0262
Dayton (G-9730)

Research & Investigation Assoc ....E 419 526-1299
Mansfield (G-13234)

Reynolds Electric Company Inc ....D 419 228-5448
Lima (G-12731)

Riverside Electric Inc ....E 513 936-0100
Cincinnati (G-4381)

RJ Runge Company Inc ....E 419 740-5781
Port Clinton (G-16116)

Rmf Nooter Inc ....D 419 727-1970
Toledo (G-18009)

Robinson Htg Air-Conditioning ....E 513 422-6812
Middletown (G-14326)

Roehrenbeck Electric Inc ....E 614 443-9709
Columbus (G-8545)

Romanoff Electric Inc ....C 614 755-4500
Gahanna (G-11143)

Romanoff Electric Co LLC ....B 937 640-7925
Toledo (G-18013)

Royal Electric Cnstr Corp ....E 614 253-6600
Columbus (G-8556)

Ruhl Electric Co ....E 330 823-7230
Alliance (G-551)

S & E Electric Inc ....E 330 425-7866
Twinsburg (G-18315)

Sabroske Electric Inc ....E 419 332-6444
Fremont (G-11092)

Safeway Electric Company Inc ....E 614 443-7672
Columbus (G-8579)

Saturn Electric Inc ....E 937 278-2580
Dayton (G-9752)

Schneder Elc Bldngs Amrcas Inc ....D 513 398-9800
Lebanon (G-12499)

Security Fence Group Inc ....E 513 681-3700
Cincinnati (G-4444)

Servall Electric Company Inc ....E 513 771-5584
Cincinnati (G-4455)

Settle Muter Electric Ltd ....C 614 866-7554
Columbus (G-8625)

Shawntech Communications Inc ....E 937 898-4900
Miamisburg (G-14220)

Shiver Security Systems Inc ....E 513 719-4000
Mason (G-13639)

Sidney Electric Company ....D 419 222-1109
Sidney (G-16799)

Siemens Energy Inc ....B 740 393-8897
Mount Vernon (G-14790)

Simplex Time Recorder LLC ....E 800 746-7539
West Chester (G-19007)

Simplex Time Recorder LLC ....D 937 291-0355
Miamisburg (G-14221)

Simplex Time Recorder LLC ....E 513 874-1227
West Chester (G-19081)

Smink Electric Inc ....E 440 322-5518
Elyria (G-10563)

South Shore Electric Inc ....E 440 366-6289
Elyria (G-10564)

Southeast Security Corporation ....E 330 239-4600
Sharon Center (G-16726)

Southtown Heating & Cooling ....E 937 320-9900
Moraine (G-14699)

Speelman Electric Inc ....D 330 633-1410
Tallmadge (G-17488)

Staley Inc ....E 614 552-2333
Plain City (G-16067)

Star Dist & Manufacturring LLC ....D 513 860-3573
West Chester (G-19083)

State Alarm Inc ....E 888 726-8111
Youngstown (G-20217)

Studebaker Electric Company ....D 937 890-9510
Dayton (G-9797)

Superior Group ....C 614 488-8035
Columbus (G-8714)

Supply Tech of Columbus LLC ....E 614 299-0184
Columbus (G-8716)

T & B Electric Ltd ....E 740 881-5696
Ostrander (G-15656)

T J Williams Electric Co ....E 513 738-5366
Harrison (G-11677)

Taylor Telecommunications Inc ....D 330 628-5501
Mogadore (G-14557)

Tele-Solutions Inc ....E 330 782-2888
Youngstown (G-20221)

Telecom Expertise Inds Inc ....D 937 548-5254
Greenville (G-11397)

Telephone & Cmpt Contrs Inc ....E 419 726-8142
Toledo (G-18062)

Thompson Electric Inc ....C 330 686-2300
Munroe Falls (G-14799)

Timmerman John P Heating AC Co ....E 419 229-4015
Lima (G-12764)

Transtar Electric Inc ....D 419 385-7573
Toledo (G-18108)

Tri Area Electric Co Inc ....E 330 744-0151
Youngstown (G-20225)

Triec Electrical Services Inc ....E 937 323-3721
Springfield (G-17128)

Unicustom Inc ....E 513 874-9806
Fairfield (G-10795)

United Electric Company Inc ....E 502 459-5242
Cincinnati (G-4679)

Universal Recovery Systems ....E 614 299-0184
Columbus (G-8817)

US Communications and Elc Inc ....D 440 519-0880
Cleveland (G-6610)

US Utility Electrical Svcs ....E 419 837-9753
Perrysburg (G-15930)

USI Inc ....E 513 954-4561
Cleves (G-6735)

Valley Electrical Cnsld Inc ....C 330 539-4044
Girard (G-11304)

▲ Vaughn Industries LLC ....B 419 396-3900
Carey (G-2548)

Vaughn Industries LLC ....E 740 548-7100
Lewis Center (G-12566)

Vec Inc ....D 330 539-4044
Girard (G-11305)

Vector Security Inc ....E 440 466-7233
Geneva (G-11249)

Vector Security Inc ....E 330 726-9841
Canfield (G-2164)

VIP Electric Company ....E 440 255-0180
Mentor (G-14123)

W W Schaub Electric Co ....E 330 494-3560
Canton (G-2530)

Wachter Inc ....C 513 777-0701
West Chester (G-19099)

Wagner Industrial Electric Inc ....E 937 298-7481
Moraine (G-14705)

Wells Brothers Inc ....D 937 394-7559
Anna (G-611)

Westfield Electric Inc ....E 419 862-0078
Gibsonburg (G-11280)

▲ Wireless Environment LLC ....E 216 455-0192
Mayfield Village (G-13888)

Wood Electric Inc ....D 330 339-7002
New Philadelphia (G-14989)

Woolace Electric Corp ....E 419 428-3161
Stryker (G-17372)

X F Construction Svcs Inc ....E 614 575-2700
Columbus (G-8923)

Yeck Brothers Company ....E 937 294-4000
Moraine (G-14708)

Zender Electric ....E 419 436-1538
Fostoria (G-11015)

Zenith Systems LLC ....B 216 587-9510
Cleveland (G-6712)

1741 Masonry & Other Stonework

Able Company Ltd Partnership ....D...... 614 444-7663
Columbus *(G-6853)*

Albert Freytag Inc ....E...... 419 628-2018
Minster *(G-14531)*

Allen Refractories Company ....C...... 740 927-8000
Pataskala *(G-15782)*

American International Cnstr ....E...... 440 243-5535
Berea *(G-1411)*

Bama Masonry Inc ....E...... 440 834-4175
Burton *(G-2014)*

Beaver Constructors Inc ....D...... 330 478-2151
Canton *(G-2210)*

Benchmark Masonry Contractors ....D...... 937 228-1225
Middletown *(G-14292)*

Buckner and Sons Masonry Inc ....E...... 614 279-9777
Columbus *(G-7092)*

Canaan Companies Inc ....E...... 419 842-8373
Toledo *(G-17634)*

Casagrande Masonry Inc ....E...... 740 964-0781
New Albany *(G-14849)*

Centennial Prsrvtion Group LLC ....E...... 614 238-0730
Columbus *(G-7150)*

▲ Cleveland Marble Mosaic Co ....C...... 216 749-2840
Cleveland *(G-5265)*

Duer Construction Co Inc ....D...... 330 848-9930
Akron *(G-197)*

Empire Masonry Company Inc ....D...... 440 230-2800
North Royalton *(G-15354)*

F B and S Masonry Inc ....E...... 330 608-3442
Silver Lake *(G-16807)*

Foti Construction Company LLP ....E...... 440 347-0728
Wickliffe *(G-19459)*

Giambrone Masonry Inc ....D...... 216 475-1200
Hudson *(G-11980)*

Hester Masonry Co Inc ....E...... 937 890-2283
Vandalia *(G-18528)*

Hicon Inc ....D...... 513 242-3612
Cincinnati *(G-3701)*

Hovest Construction ....E...... 419 456-3426
Ottawa *(G-15659)*

Hummel Industries Incorporated ....E...... 513 242-1321
Cincinnati *(G-3741)*

Industrial First Inc ....C...... 216 991-8605
Bedford *(G-1286)*

International Masonry Inc ....D...... 614 469-8338
Columbus *(G-7837)*

J & D Home Improvement Inc ....D...... 740 927-0722
Reynoldsburg *(G-16310)*

Jess Hauer Masonry Inc ....E...... 513 521-2178
Cincinnati *(G-3812)*

Kapton Caulking & Building ....E...... 440 526-0670
Cleveland *(G-5814)*

Karst & Sons Inc ....E...... 614 501-9530
Reynoldsburg *(G-16313)*

Kurzhals Inc ....E...... 513 941-4624
Cincinnati *(G-3896)*

Lang Masonry Contractors Inc ....D...... 740 749-3512
Waterford *(G-18786)*

Lencyk Masonry Co Inc ....E...... 330 729-9780
Youngstown *(G-20098)*

Medhurst Mason Contractors Inc ....C...... 440 543-8885
Chagrin Falls *(G-2674)*

Miter Masonry Contractors ....E...... 513 821-3334
Arlington Heights *(G-643)*

Mural & Son Inc ....E...... 216 267-3322
Cleveland *(G-6025)*

Ohio State Home Services Inc ....D...... 614 850-5600
Hilliard *(G-11803)*

▲ Onex Construction Inc ....E...... 330 995-9015
Streetsboro *(G-17264)*

Pioneer Cldding Glzing Systems ....E...... 216 816-4242
Cleveland *(G-6213)*

Platinum Restoration Inc ....E...... 440 327-0699
Elyria *(G-10556)*

Protective Coatings Inc ....E...... 937 275-7711
Dayton *(G-9721)*

Quality Masonry Company Inc ....E...... 740 387-6720
Marion *(G-13453)*

Ray St Clair Roofing Inc ....E...... 513 874-1234
Fairfield *(G-10773)*

S A Storer and Sons Company ....D...... 419 843-3133
Sylvania *(G-17450)*

▲ S P S & Associates Inc ....E...... 330 283-4267
Silver Lake *(G-16808)*

Spartan Construction Co Inc ....E...... 419 389-1854
Monclova *(G-14559)*

Steven H Byerly Inc ....E...... 614 882-0092
Columbus *(G-8699)*

Technical Construction Spc ....E...... 330 929-1088
Cuyahoga Falls *(G-9129)*

Van Ness Stone Inc ....E...... 440 564-1111
Newbury *(G-15127)*

VIP Restoration Inc ....E...... 216 426-9500
Cuyahoga Falls *(G-9136)*

Warren Guillard Bricklayers ....E...... 330 633-3855
Tallmadge *(G-17499)*

Wasiniak Construction Inc ....D...... 419 668-8624
Norwalk *(G-15459)*

Whitaker Masonry Inc ....E...... 330 225-7970
Brunswick *(G-1946)*

William Kerfoot Masonry Inc ....E...... 330 772-6460
Burghill *(G-2010)*

Zavarella Brothers Cnstr Co ....E...... 440 232-2243
Cleveland *(G-6711)*

1742 Plastering, Drywall, Acoustical & Insulation Work

All Construction Services Inc ....E...... 330 225-1653
Brunswick *(G-1918)*

Alloyd Insulation Co Inc ....E...... 937 890-7900
Dayton *(G-9218)*

Anstine Drywall Inc ....E...... 330 784-3867
Akron *(G-75)*

Apex Interiors Inc ....E...... 330 327-2226
Avon *(G-862)*

Architectural Intr Restoration ....E...... 216 241-2255
Cleveland *(G-5006)*

Blackstar Drywall Inc ....E...... 614 242-4242
Sunbury *(G-17383)*

Boak & Sons Inc ....C...... 330 793-5646
Youngstown *(G-19967)*

Buckholz Wall Systems LLC ....E...... 614 870-1775
Hilliard *(G-11751)*

Builder Services Group Inc ....D...... 614 263-9378
Columbus *(G-7095)*

Builder Services Group Inc ....E...... 513 942-2204
Hamilton *(G-11560)*

Central Insulation Systems Inc ....E...... 513 242-0600
Cincinnati *(G-3155)*

Certanteed Gyps Ciling Mfg Inc ....E...... 800 233-8990
Aurora *(G-824)*

Cincinnati Drywall Inc ....E...... 513 321-7322
Cincinnati *(G-3240)*

▲ Cleveland Construction Inc ....D...... 440 255-8000
Mentor *(G-14031)*

Cleveland Construction Inc ....D...... 740 927-9000
Columbus *(G-7224)*

Cleveland Construction Inc ....D...... 440 255-8000
Mason *(G-13563)*

Clubhouse Pub N Grub ....E...... 440 884-2582
Cleveland *(G-5310)*

Columbus Drywall & Insulation ....D...... 614 257-0257
Columbus *(G-7276)*

Columbus Drywall Inc ....E...... 614 257-0257
Columbus *(G-7277)*

Community Action Comsn Belmont ....E...... 740 695-0293
Saint Clairsville *(G-16483)*

Compass Construction Inc ....D...... 614 761-7800
Dublin *(G-10186)*

Competitive Interiors Inc ....C...... 330 297-1281
Ravenna *(G-16237)*

Construction Systems Inc ....D...... 614 252-0708
Columbus *(G-7354)*

Dayton Walls & Ceilings Inc ....D...... 937 277-0531
Dayton *(G-9384)*

Edwards Mooney & Moses ....D...... 614 351-1439
Columbus *(G-7505)*

Fairfield Insul & Drywall LLC ....E...... 740 654-8811
Lancaster *(G-12398)*

Frank Novak & Sons Inc ....D...... 216 475-2495
Cleveland *(G-5573)*

Global Insulation Inc ....E...... 330 479-3100
Canton *(G-2327)*

Halker Drywall Inc ....E...... 419 646-3679
Columbus Grove *(G-8941)*

Hughes & Knollman Construction ....D...... 614 237-6167
Columbus *(G-7778)*

Immaculate Interiors ....E...... 440 324-9300
Elyria *(G-10518)*

Industrial Insul Coatings LLC ....E...... 800 506-1399
Girard *(G-11288)*

Installed Building Pdts II LLC ....D...... 626 812-6070
Columbus *(G-7827)*

Installed Building Pdts LLC ....E...... 614 308-9900
Columbus *(G-7829)*

Installed Building Pdts LLC ....E...... 330 798-9640
Akron *(G-278)*

Installed Building Pdts LLC ....E...... 419 662-4524
Northwood *(G-15396)*

Insulating Sales Co Inc ....E...... 513 742-2600
Cincinnati *(G-3766)*

Integrity Wall & Ceiling Inc ....E...... 419 381-1855
Toledo *(G-17823)*

Knollman Construction LLC ....C...... 614 841-0130
Columbus *(G-7918)*

Larry L Minges ....E...... 513 738-4901
Hamilton *(G-11622)*

Liberty Insulation Co Inc ....D...... 513 621-0108
Beavercreek *(G-1166)*

Lm Constrction Trry Lvrini Inc ....E...... 740 695-9604
Saint Clairsville *(G-16492)*

M & S Drywall Inc ....E...... 513 738-1510
Harrison *(G-11673)*

M K Moore & Sons Inc ....E...... 937 236-1812
Dayton *(G-9579)*

Newark Drywall Inc ....E...... 740 763-3572
Nashport *(G-14820)*

OCP Contractors Inc ....E...... 419 865-7168
Holland *(G-11903)*

OK Interiors Corp ....C...... 513 742-3278
Cincinnati *(G-4164)*

Omni Fireproofing Co LLC ....D...... 513 870-9115
West Chester *(G-18980)*

Overhead Door Co- Cincinnati ....E...... 513 346-4000
West Chester *(G-18981)*

Pedersen Insulation Company ....E...... 614 471-3788
Columbus *(G-8434)*

Porter Drywall Inc ....D...... 614 890-2111
Westerville *(G-19293)*

Priority 1 Construction Svcs ....E...... 513 922-0203
Cincinnati *(G-4282)*

R E Kramig & Co Inc ....C...... 513 761-4010
Cincinnati *(G-4330)*

Rak Corrosion Control Inc ....E...... 440 985-2171
Amherst *(G-596)*

Robinson Insulation Co Inc ....E...... 937 323-9599
Springfield *(G-17102)*

Roger Kreps Drywall & Plst Inc ....D...... 330 726-6090
Youngstown *(G-20190)*

Ron Kreps Drywall Plst Compang ....E...... 330 726-8252
Youngstown *(G-20193)*

Roofing By Insulation Inc ....E...... 937 315-5024
New Carlisle *(G-14896)*

Roricks Inc ....E...... 330 497-6888
Canton *(G-2463)*

Sandel Corp ....E...... 614 475-5898
Gahanna *(G-11144)*

Sports Facility Acoustics Inc ....E...... 440 323-1400
Elyria *(G-10565)*

Synthetic Stucco Corporation ....E...... 513 897-9227
Waynesville *(G-18836)*

T and D Interiors Incorporated ....E...... 419 331-4372
Lima *(G-12760)*

Thermal Solutions Inc ....D...... 513 742-2836
Fairfield *(G-10790)*

Thermal Solutions Inc ....D...... 740 886-2861
Proctorville *(G-16220)*

Thermo-TEC Insulation Inc ....E...... 216 663-3842
Euclid *(G-10659)*

Truteam LLC ....E...... 513 942-2204
Hamilton *(G-11649)*

Unified Cnstr Systems Ltd ....D...... 330 773-2511
Akron *(G-475)*

Valley Acoustics Inc ....E...... 330 799-1894
Youngstown *(G-20234)*

Valley Interior Systems Inc ....E...... 937 890-7319
Dayton *(G-9847)*

Valley Interior Systems Inc ....B...... 513 961-0400
Cincinnati *(G-4747)*

Valley Interior Systems Inc ....C...... 614 351-8440
Columbus *(G-8840)*

Western Reserve Interiors Inc ....E...... 216 447-1081
Cleveland *(G-6676)*

1743 Terrazzo, Tile, Marble & Mosaic Work

▲ Cleveland Marble Mosaic Co ....C...... 216 749-2840
Cleveland *(G-5265)*

▼ Cutting Edge Countertops Inc ....E...... 419 873-9500
Perrysburg *(G-15853)*

Legacy Ntral Stone Srfaces LLC ....E...... 419 420-7440
Findlay *(G-10934)*

Midwest Mosaic Inc ....E...... 419 377-3894
Toledo *(G-17915)*

OCP Contractors Inc ....E...... 419 865-7168
Holland *(G-11903)*

Southwestern Tile and MBL Co ....E...... 614 464-1257
Columbus *(G-8667)*

▲ T H Winston Company E 513 271-2123
Cincinnati *(G-4566)*

1751 Carpentry Work

Advance Door Company E 216 883-2424
Cleveland *(G-4903)*
Airko Inc E 440 333-0133
Cleveland *(G-4922)*
Brock & Associates Builders E 330 757-7150
Youngstown *(G-19975)*
Builders Firstsource Inc E 937 898-1358
Vandalia *(G-18510)*
Burbank Inc E 419 698-3434
Toledo *(G-17632)*
Casegoods Inc E 330 825-2461
Barberton *(G-949)*
Castle Construction Co Inc E 419 289-1122
Ashland *(G-662)*
Combs Interior Specialties Inc D 937 879-2047
Fairborn *(G-10665)*
Command Roofing Co C 937 298-1155
Moraine *(G-14633)*
Competitive Interiors Inc C 330 297-1281
Ravenna *(G-16237)*
Contract Lumber Inc C 740 964-3147
Pataskala *(G-15783)*
Countertop Alternatives Inc E 937 254-3334
Dayton *(G-9324)*
Dayton Door Sales Inc E 937 253-9181
Dayton *(G-9364)*
Door Shop & Service Inc E 614 423-8043
Westerville *(G-19160)*
Dortronic Service Inc E 216 739-3667
Cleveland *(G-5443)*
Dynamic Structures Inc E 330 892-0164
New Waterford *(G-15004)*
Erie Construction Mid-West Inc E 419 472-4200
Toledo *(G-17716)*
▲ Fortune Brands Windows Inc C 614 532-3500
Columbus *(G-7602)*
▲ Forum Manufacturing Inc E 937 349-8685
Milford Center *(G-14445)*
Goliath Contracting Ltd E 614 568-7878
Reynoldsburg *(G-16306)*
Graf and Sons Inc E 614 481-2020
Columbus *(G-7683)*
Hgc Construction Co D 513 861-8866
Cincinnati *(G-3700)*
J & B Equipment & Supply Inc D 419 884-1155
Mansfield *(G-13188)*
Mammana Custom Woodworking Inc E 216 581-9059
Maple Heights *(G-13289)*
Marous Brothers Cnstr Inc B 440 951-3904
Willoughby *(G-19550)*
Metal Framing Enterprises LLC E 216 433-7080
Cleveland *(G-5962)*
Midwest Curtainwalls Inc D 216 641-7900
Cleveland *(G-5989)*
Mjr-Construction Co E 216 523-8050
Cleveland *(G-6002)*
▼ Nofziger Door Sales Inc C 419 337-9900
Wauseon *(G-18808)*
OCP Contractors Inc E 419 865-7168
Holland *(G-11903)*
Ohio Builders Resources LLC E 614 865-0306
Westerville *(G-19194)*
OK Interiors Corp C 513 742-3278
Cincinnati *(G-4164)*
Overhead Door Co- Cincinnati C 513 346-4000
West Chester *(G-18981)*
Overhead Door Corporation D 330 674-7015
Mount Hope *(G-14738)*
Overhead Inc E 419 476-7811
Toledo *(G-17967)*
Premier Construction Company E 513 874-2611
Fairfield *(G-10771)*
Ray St Clair Roofing Inc E 513 874-1234
Fairfield *(G-10773)*
Regency Windows Corporation D 330 963-4077
Twinsburg *(G-18310)*
Riverside Cnstr Svcs Inc E 513 723-0900
Cincinnati *(G-4380)*
Roger Kreps Drywall & Plst Inc D 330 726-6090
Youngstown *(G-20190)*
Ryans All-Glass Incorporated E 513 771-4440
Cincinnati *(G-4417)*
Schlabach Wood Design Inc E 330 897-2600
Baltic *(G-936)*
▲ Season Contractors Inc E 440 717-0188
Broadview Heights *(G-1845)*
Thiels Replacement Systems Inc D 419 289-6139
Ashland *(G-694)*
Traichal Construction Company E 800 255-3667
Niles *(G-15172)*
Valley Acoustics Inc E 330 799-1894
Youngstown *(G-20234)*
Window Factory of America D 440 439-3050
Bedford *(G-1314)*
Youngstown Automatic Door Co E 330 747-3135
Youngstown *(G-20258)*

1752 Floor Laying & Other Floor Work, NEC

American Star Painting Co LLC E 740 373-5634
Marietta *(G-13311)*
Andover Floor Covering E 440 293-5339
Newbury *(G-15118)*
▲ Axis Interior Systems Inc E 513 642-0039
West Chester *(G-18870)*
Centimark Corporation C 330 920-3560
Stow *(G-17194)*
Cincinnati Floor Company Inc E 513 641-4500
Cincinnati *(G-3245)*
Clays Heritage Carpet Inc E 330 497-1280
Canton *(G-2257)*
▲ Cleveland Construction Inc E 440 255-8000
Mentor *(G-14031)*
Cleveland Construction Inc E 740 927-9000
Columbus *(G-7224)*
Command Carpet D 330 673-7404
Kent *(G-12224)*
Company Inc E 216 431-2334
Cleveland *(G-5329)*
◆ Continental Office Furn Corp C 614 262-5010
Columbus *(G-7358)*
Corporate Floors Inc E 216 475-3232
Cleveland *(G-5350)*
Dominguez Inc E 513 425-9955
Monroe *(G-14566)*
▲ Done-Rite Bowling Service Co E 440 232-3280
Bedford *(G-1278)*
Florline Group Inc E 330 830-3380
Massillon *(G-13682)*
Frank Novak & Sons Inc D 216 475-2495
Cleveland *(G-5573)*
Hoover & Wells Inc C 419 691-9220
Toledo *(G-17807)*
JD Music Tile Co E 740 420-9611
Circleville *(G-4837)*
K H F Inc E 330 928-0694
Cuyahoga Falls *(G-9106)*
Legacy Commercial Flooring Ltd B 614 476-1043
Columbus *(G-7962)*
▲ Marble Restoration Inc D 419 865-9000
Maumee *(G-13813)*
OCP Contractors Inc E 419 865-7168
Holland *(G-11903)*
OK Interiors Corp C 513 742-3278
Cincinnati *(G-4164)*
Patellas Floor Center Inc E 330 758-4099
Youngstown *(G-20152)*
Preferred Acquisition Co LLC D 216 587-0957
Cleveland *(G-6229)*
Prime Polymers Inc E 330 662-4200
Medina *(G-13988)*
Progressive Flooring Svcs Inc E 614 868-9005
Etna *(G-10619)*
Protective Coatings Inc E 937 275-7711
Dayton *(G-9721)*
Regal Carpet Center Inc E 216 475-1844
Cleveland *(G-6296)*
Rite Rug Co E 937 318-9197
Fairborn *(G-10681)*
River City Furniture LLC D 513 612-7303
West Chester *(G-18994)*
Samron Inc E 330 782-6539
Youngstown *(G-20203)*
Schoch Tile & Carpet Inc E 513 922-3466
Cincinnati *(G-4439)*
Schumacher & Co Inc E 859 655-9000
Milford *(G-14430)*
Stedman Floor Co Inc E 614 836-3190
Groveport *(G-11539)*
T and D Interiors Incorporated E 419 331-4372
Lima *(G-12760)*
◆ Tremco Incorporated B 216 292-5000
Beachwood *(G-1114)*
W R Shepherd Inc E 614 889-2896
Powell *(G-16212)*
Weiffenbach Marble & Tile Co E 937 832-7055
Englewood *(G-10605)*

1761 Roofing, Siding & Sheet Metal Work

1st Choice Roofing Company E 216 227-7755
Cleveland *(G-4868)*
Able Company Ltd Partnership D 614 444-7663
Columbus *(G-6853)*
Able Roofing LLC E 614 444-7663
Columbus *(G-6854)*
Advanced Industrial Roofg Inc D 330 837-1999
Massillon *(G-13660)*
AH Sturgill Roofing Inc E 937 254-2955
Dayton *(G-9155)*
Airko Inc E 440 333-0133
Cleveland *(G-4922)*
▲ Alan Manufacturing Inc E 330 262-1555
Wooster *(G-19684)*
All-Type Welding & Fabrication E 440 439-3990
Cleveland *(G-4936)*
Ameridian Specialty Services E 513 769-0150
Cincinnati *(G-2952)*
Anchor Metal Processing Inc E 216 362-1850
Cleveland *(G-4978)*
Apco Industries Inc D 614 224-2345
Columbus *(G-6956)*
Architectural Systems Inc D 614 873-2057
Plain City *(G-16044)*
Atlas Roofing Company E 330 467-7683
Cleveland *(G-5021)*
Avon Lake Sheet Metal Co E 440 933-3505
Avon Lake *(G-910)*
Aw Farrell Son Inc E 513 334-0715
Milford *(G-14372)*
B & B Roofing Inc E 740 772-4759
Chillicothe *(G-2757)*
Beck Company E 216 883-0909
Cleveland *(G-5050)*
Boak & Sons Inc C 330 793-5646
Youngstown *(G-19967)*
▲ Bruns Building & Dev Corp Inc D 419 925-4095
Saint Henry *(G-16515)*
Budde Sheet Metal Works Inc E 937 224-0868
Dayton *(G-9268)*
Building Technicians Corp E 440 466-1651
Geneva *(G-11237)*
Burbank Inc E 419 698-3434
Toledo *(G-17632)*
Burns & Scalo Roofing Co Inc E 740 383-4639
Marion *(G-13408)*
Campeon Roofg & Waterproofing E 513 271-8972
Cincinnati *(G-3112)*
Cardinal Builders Inc E 614 237-1000
Columbus *(G-7119)*
Cardinal Maintenance & Svc Co C 330 252-0282
Akron *(G-118)*
Centimark Corporation E 614 536-1960
Reynoldsburg *(G-16288)*
Centimark Corporation E 937 704-9909
Franklin *(G-11026)*
Centimark Corporation C 330 920-3560
Stow *(G-17194)*
▲ Champion Opco LLC B 513 327-7338
Cincinnati *(G-3168)*
Chaney Roofing Maintenance E 419 639-2761
Clyde *(G-6741)*
Chemcote Roofing Company D 614 792-2683
Dublin *(G-10172)*
Christen & Sons Company E 419 243-4161
Toledo *(G-17652)*
Command Roofing Co C 937 298-1155
Moraine *(G-14633)*
Contract Lumber Inc C 740 964-3147
Pataskala *(G-15783)*
▼ Custom Seal Inc E 419 334-1020
Fremont *(G-11068)*
Dahm Brothers Company Inc E 937 461-5627
Dayton *(G-9343)*
Dalton Roofing Co D 513 871-2800
Cincinnati *(G-3398)*
Damschroder Roofing Inc E 419 332-5000
Fremont *(G-11069)*
Daugherty Construction Inc E 216 731-9444
Euclid *(G-10628)*
Dayton Roof & Remodeling Co E 937 224-7667
Beavercreek *(G-1146)*
Deer Park Roofing Inc E 513 891-9151
Cincinnati *(G-3416)*
Detmer & Sons Inc E 937 879-2373
Fairborn *(G-10671)*
Diamond Roofing Systems LLP E 330 856-2500
Warren *(G-18701)*

SIC

Dimensional Metals Inc ....D 740 927-3633
 Reynoldsburg (G-16299)
Division 7 Inc ....E 740 965-1970
 Galena (G-11157)
Ducts Inc ....E 216 391-2400
 Cleveland (G-5448)
Dun Rite Home Improvement Inc ....E 330 650-5322
 Macedonia (G-13068)
▲ Durable Slate Co ....D 614 299-5522
 Columbus (G-7478)
Durable Slate Co ....E 216 751-0151
 Shaker Heights (G-16707)
Eastside Roofg Restoration Co ....E 513 471-0434
 Cincinnati (G-3479)
Eckstein Roofing Company ....E 513 941-1511
 Cincinnati (G-3482)
Erie Construction Mid-West Inc ....E 419 472-4200
 Toledo (G-17716)
Erie Construction Mid-West Inc ....E 937 898-4688
 Dayton (G-9417)
Facility Products & Svcs LLC ....E 330 533-8943
 Canfield (G-2136)
Feazel Roofing Company ....E 614 898-7663
 Westerville (G-19164)
Franck and Fric Incorporated ....D 216 524-4451
 Cleveland (G-5572)
Fred Christen & Sons Company ....D 419 243-4161
 Toledo (G-17747)
Frost Roofing Inc ....D 419 739-2701
 Wapakoneta (G-18643)
Geauga Mechanical Company ....D 440 285-2000
 Chardon (G-2696)
Global Insulation Inc ....E 330 479-3100
 Canton (G-2327)
Harold J Becker Company Inc ....E 614 279-1414
 Beavercreek (G-1222)
Hart Roofing Inc ....E 330 452-4055
 Canton (G-2341)
▲ Hickey Metal Fabrication Roofg ....E 330 337-9329
 Salem (G-16546)
Hicks Roofing Inc ....E 330 364-7737
 New Philadelphia (G-14964)
Hinckley Roofing Inc ....E 330 722-7663
 Medina (G-13949)
Holland Roofing Inc ....E 330 963-0237
 Twinsburg (G-18280)
Holland Roofing Inc ....E 614 430-3724
 Columbus (G-7761)
Holmes Siding Contractors ....D 330 674-2867
 Millersburg (G-14476)
Hwz Contracting LLC ....D 513 671-3300
 West Chester (G-18945)
Industrial Energy Systems Inc ....E 216 267-9590
 Cleveland (G-5747)
Industrial First Inc ....C 216 991-8605
 Bedford (G-1286)
J A Guy Inc ....E 937 642-3415
 Marysville (G-13508)
K & W Roofing Inc ....E 740 927-3122
 Etna (G-10616)
Kelley Brothers Roofing Inc ....D 513 829-7717
 Fairfield (G-10742)
Kerkan Roofing Inc ....D 513 821-0556
 Cincinnati (G-3863)
◆ Kirk & Blum Manufacturing Co .....C 513 458-2600
 Cincinnati (G-3875)
Korman Construction Corp ....E 614 274-2170
 Columbus (G-7924)
Leaffilter North LLC ....C 330 655-7950
 Hudson (G-11994)
M&W Construction Entps LLC ....E 419 227-2000
 Lima (G-12697)
Meade Construction Inc ....E 740 694-5525
 Lexington (G-12574)
Mechanical Cnstr Managers LLC ......C 937 274-1987
 Dayton (G-9597)
Mechanical Construction Co ....E 740 353-5668
 Portsmouth (G-16154)
Mid-America Gutters Inc ....E 513 671-4000
 West Chester (G-19067)
Midwest Roofing & Furnace Co ....E 614 252-5241
 Columbus (G-8084)
Moisture Guard Corporation ....E 330 928-7200
 Stow (G-17220)
Mollett Seamless Gutter Co ....E 513 825-0500
 West Chester (G-18976)
Molloy Roofing Company ....E 513 791-7400
 Blue Ash (G-1614)
N F Mansuetto & Sons Inc ....E 740 633-7320
 Martins Ferry (G-13477)

Nasco Roofing and Cnstr Inc ....E 330 746-3566
 Youngstown (G-20135)
National Blanking LLC ....E 419 385-0636
 Toledo (G-17928)
Nations Roof of Ohio LLC ....E 937 439-4160
 Springboro (G-16978)
Nordmann Roofing Co Inc ....E 419 691-5737
 Toledo (G-17944)
Northern Ohio Roofg Shtmtl Inc ......E 440 322-8262
 Elyria (G-10549)
Ohio & Indiana Roofing ....E 937 339-8768
 Troy (G-18218)
Olde Towne Windows Inc ....E 419 626-9613
 Milan (G-14364)
Ontario Mechanical LLC ....E 419 529-2578
 Ontario (G-15569)
Overhead Door Co- Cincinnati ....C 513 346-4000
 West Chester (G-18981)
◆ Owens Corning Sales LLC ....A 419 248-8000
 Toledo (G-17968)
Pcy Enterprises Inc ....E 513 241-5566
 Cincinnati (G-4219)
▼ Phinney Industrial Roofing ....D 614 308-9000
 Columbus (G-8445)
Preferred Roofing Ohio Inc ....E 216 587-0957
 Cleveland (G-6231)
Preferred Roofing Services LLC ....E 216 587-0957
 Cleveland (G-6232)
Promanco Inc ....E 740 374-2120
 Marietta (G-13373)
Protective Coatings Inc ....E 937 275-7711
 Dayton (G-9721)
Quality Electrical & Mech Inc ....E 419 294-3591
 Lima (G-12726)
R & B Contractors LLC ....E 513 738-0954
 Shandon (G-16721)
Ray St Clair Roofing Inc ....E 513 874-1234
 Fairfield (G-10773)
Regency Roofing Companies Inc ......E 330 468-1021
 Macedonia (G-13081)
Regency Windows Corporation ....D 330 963-4077
 Twinsburg (G-18310)
Reilly Painting Co ....E 216 371-8160
 Cleveland Heights (G-6723)
Residntial Coml Rnovations Inc ....E 330 815-1476
 Clinton (G-6737)
Richland Co & Associates Inc ....E 419 782-0141
 Defiance (G-9937)
Roofing By Insulation Inc ....E 937 315-5024
 New Carlisle (G-14896)
Roth Bros Inc ....C 330 793-5571
 Youngstown (G-20197)
Scs Construction Services Inc ....E 513 929-0260
 Cincinnati (G-4441)
Simon Roofing and Shtmtl Corp ....C 330 629-7392
 Youngstown (G-20212)
Slagle Mechanical Contractors ....E 937 492-4151
 Sidney (G-16801)
Summit Enterprises Contg Corp ....E 513 426-1623
 Lebanon (G-12507)
T & F Systems Inc ....E 216 881-3525
 Cleveland (G-6492)
Tecta America Corp ....D 419 447-1716
 Tiffin (G-17541)
Tecta America Zero Company LLC .....D 513 541-1848
 Cincinnati (G-4582)
Tendon Manufacturing Inc ....E 216 663-3200
 Cleveland (G-6512)
Terik Roofing Inc ....E 330 785-0060
 Coventry Township (G-9044)
Thiels Replacement Systems Inc ....D 419 289-6139
 Ashland (G-694)
Tilton Corporation ....E 419 227-6421
 Lima (G-12762)
◆ Tremco Incorporated ....B 216 292-5000
 Beachwood (G-1114)
Tycor Roofing Inc ....E 330 452-8150
 Canton (G-2516)
United GL & Panl Systems Inc ....E 330 244-9745
 Canton (G-2518)
Valley Roofing LLC ....E 513 831-9444
 Milford (G-14441)
Weatherproofing Tech Inc ....D 216 292-5000
 Beachwood (G-1117)
▲ West Roofing Systems Inc ....E 800 356-5748
 Lagrange (G-12327)
Wm Kramer and Sons Inc ....D 513 353-1142
 Cleves (G-6736)
Wolfes Roofing Inc ....E 419 666-6233
 Walbridge (G-18628)

York-Mahoning Mech Contrs Inc ......D 330 788-7011
 Youngstown (G-20252)

1771 Concrete Work

21st Century Con Cnstr Inc ....E 216 362-0900
 Cleveland (G-4870)
Adleta Inc ....E 513 554-1469
 Cincinnati (G-2908)
Aerodynamic Concrete & Cnstr ....E 330 906-7477
 Akron (G-21)
Akron Concrete Corp ....E 330 864-1188
 Akron (G-35)
Allied Paving Inc ....E 419 666-3100
 Holland (G-11869)
American Coatings Corporation ....E 614 335-1000
 Plain City (G-16043)
Architctural Con Solutions Inc ....E 614 940-5399
 Columbus (G-6968)
Arledge Construction Inc ....E 614 732-4258
 Columbus (G-6969)
Atlas Construction Company ....D 614 475-4705
 Columbus (G-6998)
B & D Concrete Footers Inc ....E 740 964-2294
 Etna (G-10612)
B G Trucking & Construction ....E 234 759-3440
 North Lima (G-15266)
◆ Baker Concrete Cnstr Inc ....A 513 539-4000
 Monroe (G-14561)
Barbicas Construction Co ....D 330 733-9101
 Akron (G-86)
Barrett Paving Materials Inc ....C 513 271-6200
 Middletown (G-14343)
Berlin Contractors ....E 330 893-2904
 Berlin (G-1445)
Bradcorp Ohio II LLC ....D 513 671-3300
 Fairfield (G-10700)
Brown County Asphalt Inc ....E 937 446-2481
 Georgetown (G-11264)
Buckholz Wall Systems LLC ....E 614 870-1775
 Hilliard (G-11751)
Ceco Concrete Cnstr Del LLC ....D 513 874-6953
 West Chester (G-18881)
Cem-Base Inc ....E 330 963-3101
 Twinsburg (G-18251)
Central Ohio Poured Walls Inc ....E 614 889-0505
 Dublin (G-10166)
Charles H Hamilton Co ....D 513 683-2442
 Maineville (G-13113)
Cincinnati Asphalt Corporation ....D 513 367-0250
 Cleves (G-6726)
Cioffi & Son Construction ....D 330 794-9448
 Akron (G-132)
Cleveland Concrete Cnstr Inc ....D 216 741-3954
 Brooklyn Heights (G-1868)
Concrete Coring Company Inc ....E 937 864-7325
 Enon (G-10607)
Cook Paving and Cnstr Co ....E 216 267-7705
 Independence (G-12062)
Cornerstone Concrete Cnstr Inc ....E 937 442-2805
 Sardinia (G-16658)
Cox Paving Inc ....E 937 780-3075
 Wshngtn CT Hs (G-19867)
Day Precision Wall Inc ....E 513 353-2999
 Cleves (G-6727)
Depuy Paving Inc ....E 614 272-0256
 Columbus (G-7437)
Donley Concrete Cutting ....D 614 834-0300
 Pickerington (G-15956)
DOT Diamond Core Drilling Inc ....E 440 322-6466
 Elyria (G-10502)
Dwyer Concrete Lifting Inc ....E 614 501-0998
 Groveport (G-11508)
E&I Construction LLC ....E 513 421-2045
 Cincinnati (G-3466)
Elastizell Systems Inc ....E 937 298-1313
 Moraine (G-14652)
Engineered Con Structures Corp ....E 216 520-2000
 Cleveland (G-5480)
Foor Concrete Co Inc ....D 740 513-4346
 Delaware (G-9978)
Formwork Services LLC ....E 513 539-4000
 Monroe (G-14567)
Freisthler Paving Inc ....E 937 498-4802
 Sidney (G-16779)
G Big Inc ....E 740 867-5758
 Chesapeake (G-2729)
Gardner Cement Contractors ....D 419 389-0768
 Toledo (G-17756)
Gateway Concrete Forming Svcs ......D 513 353-2000
 Miamitown (G-14241)

Geddis Paving & Excavating Inc ....E 419 536-8501
Toledo (G-17757)

George Kuhn Enterprises Inc ....E 614 481-8838
Columbus (G-7660)

Gironda Vito & Bros Inc ....E 330 630-9399
Akron (G-235)

▲ Goettle Holding Company Inc ....C 513 825-8100
Cincinnati (G-3623)

H & M Precision Concrete LLC ....E 937 547-0012
Greenville (G-11385)

H & R Concrete Inc ....E 937 885-2910
Dayton (G-9480)

Halcomb Concrete Construction ....E 513 829-3576
Fairfield (G-10733)

Hanson Concrete Products Ohio ....E 614 443-4846
Columbus (G-7716)

Hayes Concrete Construction ....E 513 648-9400
Cincinnati (G-3685)

Hovest Construction ....E 419 456-3426
Ottawa (G-15659)

Hoyer Poured Walls Inc ....E 937 642-6148
Marysville (G-13507)

Image Pavement Maintenance ....E 937 833-9200
Brookville (G-1914)

▲ Independence Excavating Inc ....E 216 524-1700
Independence (G-12082)

Ivan Law Inc ....E 330 533-5000
Youngstown (G-20084)

J & D Home Improvement Inc ....D 740 927-0722
Reynoldsburg (G-16310)

J K Enterprises Inc ....E 614 481-8838
Columbus (G-7850)

Jennite Co ....E 419 531-1791
Toledo (G-17830)

Jostin Construction Inc ....E 513 559-9390
Cincinnati (G-3835)

K & M Construction Company ....D 330 723-3681
Medina (G-13963)

Keim Concrete LLC ....E 330 264-5313
Wooster (G-19736)

L & I Custom Walls Inc ....E 513 683-2045
Loveland (G-13005)

Latorre Concrete Cnstr Inc ....E 614 257-1401
Columbus (G-7956)

Lavy Concrete Construction ....E 937 606-4754
Covington (G-9047)

Lithko Contracting LLC ....C 614 733-0300
Plain City (G-16057)

Lithko Contracting LLC ....C 513 564-2000
West Chester (G-18963)

Lithko Contracting LLC ....D 513 863-5100
Monroe (G-14574)

Lithko Restoration Tech LLC ....D 513 863-5500
Monroe (G-14575)

Lithko Restoration Tech LLC ....E 614 221-0711
Columbus (G-7984)

Lockhart Concrete Co ....D 330 745-6520
Akron (G-319)

Lucas County Asphalt Inc ....E 419 476-0705
Toledo (G-17867)

Maintenance Systerms of N Ohio ....E 440 323-1291
Elyria (G-10532)

Mattlin Construction Inc ....E 513 598-5402
Cleves (G-6733)

Menke Bros Construction Co ....E 419 286-2086
Delphos (G-10031)

Metcon Ltd ....E 937 447-9200
Bradford (G-1762)

Milcon Concrete Inc ....E 937 339-6274
Troy (G-18216)

Miller Yount Paving Inc ....E 330 372-4408
Cortland (G-8991)

Modern Day Concrete Cnstr ....E 513 738-1026
Harrison (G-11674)

Modern Poured Walls Inc ....D 440 647-6661
Wellington (G-18843)

MPW Construction Services ....E 440 647-6661
Wellington (G-18844)

Newcomer Concrete Services Inc ....D 419 668-2789
Norwalk (G-15445)

Norris Brothers Co Inc ....C 216 771-2233
Cleveland (G-6074)

North Coast Concrete Inc ....E 216 642-1114
Cleveland (G-6076)

Northeast Concrete & Cnstr ....D 614 898-5728
Westerville (G-19191)

Northstar Asphalt Inc ....E 330 497-0936
North Canton (G-15224)

Ohio Con Sawing & Drlg Inc ....E 419 841-1330
Sylvania (G-17440)

Ohio Con Sawing & Drlg Inc ....E 614 252-1122
Columbus (G-8233)

Ohio Paving Group LLC ....E 216 475-1700
Cleveland (G-6122)

Pavement Protectors Inc ....E 614 875-9989
Grove City (G-11464)

Perrin Asphalt Co Inc ....D 330 253-1020
Akron (G-379)

Phillips Companies ....E 937 426-5461
Beavercreek Township (G-1258)

Phillips Ready Mix Co ....E 937 426-5151
Beavercreek Township (G-1259)

Platform Cement Inc ....E 440 602-9750
Mentor (G-14097)

Premier Asphalt Paving Co Inc ....E 440 237-6600
North Royalton (G-15364)

Prime Polymers Inc ....E 330 662-4200
Medina (G-13988)

Prus Construction Company ....C 513 321-7774
Cincinnati (G-4303)

Queen City Blacktop Company ....E 513 251-8400
Cincinnati (G-4312)

▲ R W Sidley Incorporated ....E 440 352-9343
Painesville (G-15735)

Reitter Stucco Inc ....E 614 291-2212
Columbus (G-8508)

Reitter Wall Systems Inc ....E 614 545-4444
Columbus (G-8509)

S & K Asphalt & Concrete ....E 330 848-6284
Akron (G-414)

Scioto-Darby Concrete Inc ....E 614 876-3114
Hilliard (G-11814)

Shelly and Sands Inc ....E 614 444-5100
Columbus (G-8632)

Shelly and Sands Inc ....E 740 453-0721
Zanesville (G-20360)

Shepherd Excavating Inc ....D 614 889-1115
Dublin (G-10333)

Signature Concrete Inc ....E 937 723-8435
Dayton (G-9769)

Smalls Asphalt Paving Inc ....E 740 427-4096
Gambier (G-11227)

Sowder Concrete Corporation ....E 937 890-1633
Dayton (G-9780)

Spano Brothers Cnstr Co ....E 330 645-1544
Akron (G-436)

Spaulding Construction Co Inc ....D 330 494-1776
Canton (G-2481)

◆ Spillman Company ....E 614 444-2184
Columbus (G-8672)

Staarmann Concrete Inc ....E 513 756-9191
Hamilton (G-11643)

Stamm Contracting Co Inc ....D 330 274-8230
Mantua (G-13276)

Standard Contg & Engrg Inc ....D 440 243-1001
Brookpark (G-1906)

Suburban Maint & Cnstr Inc ....E 440 237-7765
North Royalton (G-15368)

Tallmadge Asphalt & Pav Co Inc ....D 330 677-0000
Kent (G-12262)

Technical Construction Spc ....D 330 929-1088
Cuyahoga Falls (G-9129)

Thompson Concrete Ltd ....B 740 756-7256
Carroll (G-2558)

Towne Construction Svcs LLC ....C 513 561-3700
Batavia (G-1012)

Tri-Mor Corp ....C 330 963-3101
Twinsburg (G-18329)

Triple Q Foundations Co Inc ....E 513 932-3121
Lebanon (G-12511)

Trucco Construction Co Inc ....C 740 417-9010
Delaware (G-10010)

Tscs Inc ....E 419 644-3921
Metamora (G-14133)

U S A Concrete Specialists ....E 330 482-9150
Columbiana (G-6794)

Vandra Bros Construction Inc ....E 440 232-3030
Cleveland (G-6621)

Wasiniak Construction Inc ....D 419 668-8624
Norwalk (G-15459)

Wenger Asphalt Inc ....E 330 837-4767
Dalton (G-9147)

Williams Concrete Cnstr Co Inc ....E 330 745-6388
Norton (G-15423)

1781 Water Well Drilling

Collector Wells Intl Inc ....E 614 888-6263
Columbus (G-7246)

Moodys of Dayton Inc ....E 614 443-3898
Miamisburg (G-14194)

Ohio Drilling Company ....E 330 832-1521
Massillon (G-13718)

1791 Structural Steel Erection

Akron Erectors Inc ....E 330 745-7100
Akron (G-39)

Black Swamp Steel Inc ....E 419 867-8050
Holland (G-11873)

◆ Columbiana Boiler Company LLC ......E 330 482-3373
Columbiana (G-6784)

Columbus Steel Erectors Inc ....E 614 876-5050
Columbus (G-7317)

Daniel A Terreri & Sons Inc ....E 330 538-2950
Youngstown (G-20014)

Dublin Building Systems Co ....E 614 760-5831
Dublin (G-10204)

Evers Welding Co Inc ....E 513 385-7352
Cincinnati (G-3521)

Forest City Erectors Inc ....D 330 425-2345
Twinsburg (G-18268)

Foundation Steel LLC ....D 419 402-4241
Swanton (G-17397)

Frameco Inc ....E 216 433-7080
Cleveland (G-5570)

Frederick Steel Company LLC ....D 513 821-6400
Cincinnati (G-3586)

FSRc Tanks Inc ....E 234 221-2015
Bolivar (G-1703)

GL Nause Co Inc ....E 513 722-9500
Loveland (G-12996)

Henry Gurtzweiler Inc ....D 419 729-3955
Toledo (G-17801)

Hovest Construction ....E 419 456-3426
Ottawa (G-15659)

Industrial First Inc ....C 216 991-8605
Bedford (G-1286)

J & B Interests Inc ....D 513 874-1722
West Chester (G-18950)

J&H Rnfrcing Strl Erectors Inc ....C 740 355-0141
Portsmouth (G-16151)

Kelley Steel Erectors Inc ....D 440 232-1573
Cleveland (G-5821)

Legacy Industrial Services LLC ....E 606 584-8953
Ripley (G-16400)

Marysville Steel Inc ....E 937 642-5971
Marysville (G-13515)

Mason Steel Erecting Inc ....E 440 439-1040
Cleveland (G-5921)

Mid Atlantic Stor Systems Inc ....D 740 335-2019
Wshngtn CT Hs (G-19880)

Midwest Reinforcing Contrs ....E 937 390-8998
Springfield (G-17085)

Mohawk RE-Bar Services Inc ....E 440 268-0780
Strongsville (G-17334)

Mound Technologies Inc ....E 937 748-2937
Springboro (G-16977)

▲ Northbend Archtctural Pdts Inc ....E 513 577-7988
Cincinnati (G-4128)

Ontario Mechanical LLC ....E 419 529-2578
Ontario (G-15569)

Orbit Movers & Erectors Inc ....E 937 277-8080
Dayton (G-9677)

R&F Erectors Inc ....E 513 574-8273
Cincinnati (G-4333)

▼ Reading Rock Residential LLC ....E 513 874-4770
West Chester (G-19075)

Rittman Inc ....D 330 927-6855
Rittman (G-16409)

Sawyer Steel Erectors Inc ....E 419 867-8050
Holland (G-11910)

Seneca Steel Erectors Inc ....E 740 385-0517
Logan (G-12853)

Smith Brothers Erection Inc ....E 740 373-3575
Marietta (G-13382)

Sofco Erectors Inc ....C 513 771-1600
Cincinnati (G-4502)

Stein Inc ....E 216 883-4277
Cleveland (G-6464)

Vmi Group Inc ....D 330 405-4146
Macedonia (G-13088)

1793 Glass & Glazing Work

A E D Inc ....E 419 661-9999
Northwood (G-15388)

▲ Advanced Auto Glass Inc ....E 412 373-6675
Akron (G-19)

▲ AGC Automotive Americas ....E 937 599-3131
Bellefontaine (G-1343)

Anderson Aluminum Corporation ....D 614 476-4877
Columbus (G-6946)

SIC

E J Robinson Glass Co ....E 513 242-9250
Cincinnati (G-3465)
J & B Equipment & Supply Inc ....D 419 884-1155
Mansfield (G-13188)
Lakeland Glass Co ....E 440 277-4527
Lorain (G-12912)
Lorain Glass Co Inc ....D 440 277-6004
Lorain (G-12920)
▲ Medina Glass Block Inc ....E 330 239-0239
Medina (G-13974)
Modern Glass Pnt & Tile Co Inc........E 740 454-1253
Zanesville (G-20332)
Pioneer Cldding Glzing Systems........E 216 816-4242
Cleveland (G-6213)
▲ Pioneer Cldding Glzing Systems......D 513 583-5925
Mason (G-13627)
R C Hemm Glass Shops Inc.............E 937 773-5591
Piqua (G-16025)
Richardson Glass Service Inc ....D 740 366-5090
Newark (G-15096)
Ryans All-Glass Incorporated ....E 513 771-4440
Cincinnati (G-4417)
Thomas Glass Company Inc ....E 614 268-8611
Worthington (G-19856)
Toledo Glass LLC ....E 419 241-3151
Toledo (G-18084)
United GL & Panl Systems Inc ....E 330 244-9745
Canton (G-2518)
Wiechart Enterprises Inc ....E 419 227-0027
Lima (G-12784)

1794 Excavating & Grading Work

A Crano Excavating Inc ....E 330 630-1061
Akron (G-11)
Allard Excavation LLC ....D 740 778-2242
South Webster (G-16950)
Allgeier & Son Inc ....E 513 574-3735
Cincinnati (G-2925)
Alliance Crane & Rigging Inc ....E 330 823-8823
Deerfield (G-9901)
Anderzack-Pitzen Cnstr Inc ....E 419 553-7015
Metamora (G-14132)
B & B Wrecking & Excvtg Inc ....E 216 429-1700
Cleveland (G-5031)
Bansal Construction Inc ....E 513 874-5410
Fairfield (G-10698)
Bontrager Excavating Co Inc ....E 330 499-8775
Uniontown (G-18358)
Boyas Excavating Inc ....E 216 524-3620
Cleveland (G-5072)
Burkhart Excavating Inc ....E 740 896-3312
Lowell (G-13036)
C & J Contractors Inc ....E 216 391-5700
Cleveland (G-5109)
Camargo Construction Company........E 513 248-1500
Cincinnati (G-3107)
Charles F Jergens Cnstr Inc ....E 937 233-1830
Dayton (G-9293)
Charles H Hamilton Co ....D 513 683-2442
Maineville (G-13113)
Charles Jergens Contractor ....E 937 233-1830
Dayton (G-9294)
Chieftain Trucking & Excav Inc ....E 216 485-8034
Cleveland (G-5176)
Cincinnati Asphalt Corporation........D 513 367-0250
Cleves (G-6726)
Cox Paving Inc ....D 937 780-3075
Wshngtn CT Hs (G-19867)
D B Bentley Inc ....E 440 352-8495
Painesville (G-15707)
Darby Creek Excavating Inc ....D 740 477-8600
Circleville (G-4831)
Dave Sugar Excavating LLC ....E 330 542-1100
Petersburg (G-15943)
Digioia/Suburban Excvtg LLC ....D 440 237-1978
North Royalton (G-15353)
Don Wartko Construction Co ....D 330 673-5252
Kent (G-12229)
E S Wagner Company ....D 419 691-8651
Oregon (G-15592)
Elite Excavating Company Inc ....E 419 683-4200
Mansfield (G-13172)
Eslich Wrecking Company ....E 330 488-8300
Louisville (G-12967)
Facemyer Backhoe and Dozer Svc .....E 740 965-1137
Sunbury (G-17387)
Fechko Excavating Inc ....D 330 722-2890
Medina (G-13936)
Fechko Excavating LLC ....D 330 722-2890
Medina (G-13937)

Fishel Company ....C 937 233-2268
Dayton (G-9439)
Fleming Construction Co ....E 740 494-2177
Prospect (G-16223)
Ford Development Corp ....D 513 772-1521
Cincinnati (G-3577)
◆ Gayston Corporation ....C 937 743-6050
Miamisburg (G-14173)
Geddis Paving & Excavating Inc ....E 419 536-8501
Toledo (G-17757)
Geo Gradel Co ....D 419 691-7123
Toledo (G-17759)
George J Igel & Co Inc ....A 614 445-8421
Columbus (G-7659)
Geotex Construction Svcs Inc ....E 614 444-5690
Columbus (G-7662)
GMC Excavation & Trucking ....E 419 468-0121
Galion (G-11177)
▲ Goettle Holding Company Inc ....C 513 825-8100
Cincinnati (G-3623)
Ground Tech Inc ....E 330 270-0700
Youngstown (G-20058)
H & R Concrete Inc ....E 937 885-2910
Dayton (G-9480)
Hardrock Excavating LLC ....D 330 792-9524
Youngstown (G-20060)
Harris & Heavener Excavating ....E 740 927-1423
Etna (G-10610)
▲ Independence Excavating Inc ....E 216 524-1700
Independence (G-12082)
Indian Nation Inc ....E 740 532-6143
North Canton (G-15212)
J & J General Maintenance Inc ....E 740 533-9729
Ironton (G-12158)
John Eramo & Sons Inc.................D 614 777-0020
Hilliard (G-11781)
John F Gallagher Plumbing Co ....E 440 946-4256
Eastlake (G-10430)
JS Bova Excavating LLC ....E 234 254-4040
Struthers (G-17365)
JS Paris Excavating Inc.................E 330 538-3048
North Jackson (G-15247)
Kelchner Inc ....C 937 704-9890
Springboro (G-16971)
KMu Trucking & Excvtg Inc ....E 440 934-1008
Avon (G-890)
Larry Lang Excavating Inc ....E 740 984-4750
Beverly (G-1463)
Law Excavating Inc....................E 740 745-3420
Saint Louisville (G-16519)
Layton Inc ....E 740 349-7101
Newark (G-15048)
Loveland Excavating Inc ....E 513 965-6600
Fairfield (G-10748)
Luburgh Inc ....E 740 452-3668
Zanesville (G-20327)
Maintenance Unlimited Inc ....E 440 238-1162
Strongsville (G-17325)
Mark Schaffer Excvtg Trckg Inc ....D 419 668-5990
Norwalk (G-15443)
Martin Greg Excavating Inc ....E 513 727-9300
Middletown (G-14306)
Marucci and Gaffney Excvtg Co ....D 330 743-8170
Youngstown (G-20117)
McConnell Excavating Ltd ....E 440 774-4578
Oberlin (G-15508)
Menke Bros Construction Co ....E 419 286-2086
Delphos (G-10031)
Metropolitan Envmtl Svcs Inc ....D 614 771-1881
Hilliard (G-11793)
Mike Enyart & Sons Inc ....E 740 523-0235
South Point (G-16943)
Mike George Excavating ....E 419 855-4147
Genoa (G-11259)
Mike Pusateri Excavating Inc ....E 330 385-5221
East Liverpool (G-10407)
Miller Yount Paving Inc.................E 330 372-4408
Cortland (G-8991)
Modern Poured Walls Inc ....D 440 647-6661
Wellington (G-18843)
Mr Excavator Inc ....D 440 256-2008
Kirtland (G-12323)
Nelson Stark Company..................C 513 489-0866
Cincinnati (G-4106)
Newcomer Concrete Services Inc ....D 419 668-2789
Norwalk (G-15445)
Nicolozakes Trckg & Cnstr Inc ....D 740 432-5648
Cambridge (G-2078)
Northast Ohio Trnching Svc Inc ....E 216 663-6006
Cleveland (G-6086)

Nuway Incorporated ....E 740 587-2452
Heath (G-11707)
Ohio Heavy Equipment Lsg LLC ....E 513 965-6600
Fairfield (G-10764)
Ohio State Home Services Inc ....D 614 850-5600
Hilliard (G-11803)
Osborne Co ....D 440 942-7000
Mentor (G-14094)
Otto Falkenberg Excavating ....E 330 626-4215
Mantua (G-13274)
Phillips Ready Mix Co...................D 937 426-5151
Beavercreek Township (G-1259)
R D Jones Excavating Inc ....E 419 648-5870
Harrod (G-11681)
R T Vernal Paving Inc..................E 330 549-3189
North Lima (G-15274)
Rack & Ballauer Excvtg Co Inc ....E 513 738-7000
Hamilton (G-11635)
Ray Bertolini Trucking Co ....E 330 867-0666
Akron (G-397)
Rbm Environmental and Cnstr ....E 419 693-5840
Oregon (G-15607)
Ricketts Excavating Inc.................E 740 687-0338
Lancaster (G-12430)
Rudzik Excavating Inc ....E 330 755-1540
Struthers (G-17367)
S E T Inc ....E 330 536-6724
Lowellville (G-13043)
Schumm Richard A Plbg & Htg...........E 419 238-4994
Van Wert (G-18488)
Seals Construction Inc ....E 614 836-7200
Canal Winchester (G-2119)
Sehlhorst Equipment Svcs Inc ....E 513 353-9300
Hooven (G-11935)
Siler Excavation Services ....E 513 400-8628
Milford (G-14432)
Sisler Heating & Cooling Inc ....E 330 722-7101
Medina (G-14002)
Smith & Associates Excavating ....E 740 362-3355
Columbus (G-8655)
Spano Brothers Cnstr Co ....E 330 645-1544
Akron (G-436)
Stahlheber & Sons Inc ....E 513 726-4446
Hamilton (G-11644)
Standard Contg & Engrg Inc ....D 440 243-1001
Brookpark (G-1906)
Star-Ex Inc ....E 937 473-2397
Covington (G-9048)
Steingass Mechanical Contg ....E 330 725-6090
Medina (G-14005)
Stonegate Construction Inc ....D 740 423-9170
Belpre (G-1410)
Stover Excavating Inc ....E 614 873-5865
Plain City (G-16068)
Sws Environmental Services ....E 254 629-1718
Findlay (G-10967)
Taylor Construction Company ....E 330 628-9310
Mogadore (G-14556)
Thompson Concrete Ltd ....B 740 756-7256
Carroll (G-2558)
Todd Alspaugh & Associates ....E 419 476-8126
Toledo (G-18071)
Trafzer Excavating Inc ....E 740 383-2616
Marion (G-13465)
Trimat Construction Inc ....E 740 388-9515
Bidwell (G-1470)
Trucco Construction Co Inc ....C 740 417-9010
Delaware (G-10010)
Utter Construction Inc ....C 513 876-2246
Bethel (G-1455)
Vandalia Blacktop Seal Coating ....E 937 454-0571
Dayton (G-9850)
Wenger Excavating Inc ....E 330 837-4767
Dalton (G-9148)
Zemba Bros Inc ....E 740 452-1880
Zanesville (G-20388)

1795 Wrecking & Demolition Work

Allgeier & Son Inc ....E 513 574-3735
Cincinnati (G-2925)
▲ Allied Erct & Dismantling Co ....C 330 744-0808
Youngstown (G-19951)
Aztec Services Group Inc ....D 513 541-2002
Cincinnati (G-3012)
B & B Wrecking & Excvtg Inc ....E 216 429-1700
Cleveland (G-5031)
Bladecutters Lawn Service Inc ....E 937 274-3861
Dayton (G-9255)
Boyas Excavating Inc ....E 216 524-3620
Cleveland (G-5072)

C & J Contractors Inc ....E 216 391-5700
  Cleveland *(G-5109)*
Charles F Jergens Cnstr Inc ....E 937 233-1830
  Dayton *(G-9293)*
Cook Paving and Cnstr Co ....E 216 267-7705
  Independence *(G-12062)*
Daniel A Terreri & Sons Inc ....E 330 538-2950
  Youngstown *(G-20014)*
Dave Sugar Excavating LLC ....E 330 542-1100
  Petersburg *(G-15943)*
Eslich Wrecking Company ....E 330 488-8300
  Louisville *(G-12967)*
Fluor-Bwxt Portsmouth LLC ....A 866 706-6992
  Piketon *(G-15975)*
▲ Independence Excavating Inc ....E 216 524-1700
  Independence *(G-12082)*
JS Paris Excavating Inc ....E 330 538-3048
  North Jackson *(G-15247)*
Mark Schaffer Excvtg Trckg Inc ....D 419 668-5990
  Norwalk *(G-15443)*
Marucci and Gaffney Excvtg Co ....E 330 743-8170
  Youngstown *(G-20117)*
Miller Brothers Cnstr Dem LLC ....E 513 257-1082
  Oxford *(G-15684)*
Mosier Industrial Services ....E 419 683-4000
  Crestline *(G-9058)*
ORourke Wrecking Company ....D 513 871-1400
  Cincinnati *(G-4184)*
Ray Bertolini Trucking Co ....E 330 867-0666
  Akron *(G-397)*
Rnw Holdings Inc ....E 330 792-0600
  Youngstown *(G-20187)*
S G Loewendick and Sons Inc ....E 614 539-2582
  Grove City *(G-11467)*
Sidwell Materials Inc ....C 740 849-2394
  Zanesville *(G-20361)*
Sunesis Environmental LLC ....D 513 326-6000
  Fairfield *(G-10788)*

1796 Installation Or Erection Of Bldg Eqpt & Machinery, NEC

A and A Mllwright Rigging Svcs ....E 513 396-6212
  Cincinnati *(G-2888)*
▲ Allied Erct & Dismantling Co ....C 330 744-0808
  Youngstown *(G-19951)*
Atlas Industrial Contrs LLC ....B 614 841-4500
  Columbus *(G-7000)*
▲ Canton Erectors Inc ....E 330 453-7363
  Canton *(G-2232)*
▲ Clopay Corporation ....C 800 282-2260
  Mason *(G-13564)*
CTS Construction Inc ....D 513 489-8290
  Cincinnati *(G-3385)*
Expert Crane Inc ....E 216 451-9900
  Cleveland *(G-5502)*
▲ Fenton Rigging & Contg Inc ....C 513 631-5500
  Cincinnati *(G-3542)*
Gem Industrial Inc ....D 419 666-6554
  Walbridge *(G-18622)*
Glt Inc ....E 937 395-0508
  Moraine *(G-14663)*
Grubb Construction Inc ....E 419 293-2316
  Mc Comb *(G-13894)*
Hensley Industries Inc ....E 513 769-6666
  Cincinnati *(G-3698)*
Hgc Construction Co ....D 513 861-8866
  Cincinnati *(G-3700)*
▲ Hy-Tek Material Handling Inc ....D 614 497-2500
  Columbus *(G-7790)*
Industrial Power Systems Inc ....C 419 531-3121
  Rossford *(G-16461)*
◆ Intertec Corporation ....B 419 537-9711
  Toledo *(G-17824)*
J R Mead Industrial Contrs ....E 614 891-4466
  Galena *(G-11160)*
K F T Inc ....D 513 241-5910
  Cincinnati *(G-3843)*
◆ McGill Airclean LLC....................D 614 829-1200
  Columbus *(G-8045)*
Myers Machinery Movers Inc ....E 614 871-5052
  Grove City *(G-11455)*
Nbw Inc ....E 216 377-1700
  Cleveland *(G-6051)*
Norris Brothers Co Inc ....C 216 771-2233
  Cleveland *(G-6074)*
North Bay Construction Inc ....E 440 835-1898
  Westlake *(G-19380)*
Orbit Movers & Erectors Inc ....E 937 277-8080
  Dayton *(G-9677)*

Otis Elevator Company ....D 513 531-7888
  Cincinnati *(G-4190)*
Otis Elevator Company ....D 216 573-2333
  Cleveland *(G-6147)*
Piqua Steel Co 937 773-3632
  Piqua *(G-16020)*
Schindler Elevator Corporation ....E 614 573-2777
  Columbus *(G-8599)*
▲ Sk Rigging Co Inc ....E 513 771-7766
  Cincinnati *(G-4490)*
▲ Spallinger Millwright Svc Co ....D 419 225-5830
  Lima *(G-12742)*
Standard Contg & Engrg Inc ....D 440 243-1001
  Brookpark *(G-1906)*
Tesar Industrial Contrs Inc ....E 216 741-8008
  Cleveland *(G-6517)*
Thyssenkrupp Elevator Corp ....E 513 241-6000
  Cincinnati *(G-4609)*
Thyssenkrupp Elevator Corp ....E 614 895-8930
  Westerville *(G-19302)*

1799 Special Trade Contractors, NEC

AAA Amrican Abatement Asb Corp ....D 216 281-9400
  Cleveland *(G-4886)*
Adelmos Electric Sewer Clg Co ....E 216 641-2301
  Brooklyn Heights *(G-1864)*
Aerco Sandblasting Company ....E 419 224-2464
  Lima *(G-12593)*
▲ AGC Automotive Americas ....D 937 599-3131
  Bellefontaine *(G-1343)*
Allied Builders Inc ....E 937 226-0311
  Dayton *(G-9215)*
Allied Environmental Svcs Inc ....E 419 227-4004
  Lima *(G-12599)*
Allstate Painting & Contg Co ....D 330 220-5533
  Brunswick *(G-1919)*
Alumina Rling Cstm Ir Wrks Inc ....E 513 353-1116
  Cleves *(G-6724)*
▲ AM Industrial Group LLC ....E 216 433-7171
  Brookpark *(G-1890)*
American International Cnstr ....E 440 243-5535
  Berea *(G-1411)*
American Star Painting Co LLC ....E 740 373-5634
  Marietta *(G-13311)*
Apco Aluminum Awning Co ....E 614 334-2726
  Columbus *(G-6955)*
Aquarian Pools Inc ....E 513 576-9771
  Loveland *(G-12978)*
Archer Corporation ....D 330 455-9995
  Canton *(G-2193)*
Architectural Metal Erectors ....E 513 242-5106
  Cincinnati *(G-2983)*
Barr Engineering Incorporated ....E 614 714-0299
  Columbus *(G-7019)*
Basement Systems Ohio Inc ....C 330 423-4430
  Twinsburg *(G-18249)*
Bathroom Alternatives Inc ....E 937 434-1984
  Dayton *(G-9245)*
Belfor USA Group Inc ....E 513 860-3111
  West Chester *(G-19043)*
Bogie Industries Inc Ltd ....D 330 745-3105
  Akron *(G-102)*
Boyas Excavating Inc ....E 216 524-3620
  Cleveland *(G-5072)*
Brilliant Electric Sign Co Ltd ....D 216 741-3800
  Brooklyn Heights *(G-1866)*
Brown Contracting & Dev LLC ....E 419 341-3939
  Port Clinton *(G-16100)*
Buckeye Cable Systems Inc ....E 419 724-2539
  Toledo *(G-17631)*
Buckeye Pool Inc ....E 937 434-7916
  Dayton *(G-9266)*
Burbank Inc ....E 419 698-3434
  Toledo *(G-17632)*
Burdens Machine & Welding ....E 740 345-9246
  Newark *(G-15019)*
Burnett Pools Inc ....E 330 372-1725
  Cortland *(G-8985)*
C M S Enterprises Inc ....E 740 653-1940
  Lancaster *(G-12374)*
Camco Inc ....E 740 477-3682
  Circleville *(G-4827)*
Canaan Companies Inc ....E 419 842-8373
  Toledo *(G-17634)*
Capital Fire Protection Co ....E 614 279-9448
  Columbus *(G-7112)*
Cardinal Builders Inc ....E 614 237-1000
  Columbus *(G-7119)*
Cardinal Environmental Svc Inc ....E 330 252-0220
  Akron *(G-117)*

Carpe Diem Industries LLC ....D 419 659-5639
  Columbus Grove *(G-8940)*
Carpe Diem Industries LLC ....E 419 358-0129
  Bluffton *(G-1689)*
Ceco Concrete Cnstr Del LLC ....D 513 874-6953
  West Chester *(G-18881)*
Central Fire Protection Co Inc ....E 937 322-0713
  Springfield *(G-17006)*
Central Insulation Systems Inc ....E 513 242-0600
  Cincinnati *(G-3155)*
Central Ohio Custom Contg LLC ....E 614 579-4971
  Mount Vernon *(G-14753)*
Chemsteel Construction Company ....E 440 234-3930
  Middleburg Heights *(G-14249)*
Complete Services Inc ....E 513 770-5575
  Mason *(G-13566)*
Coon Caulking & Sealants Inc ....E 330 875-2100
  Louisville *(G-12964)*
Corporate Environments of Ohio ....E 614 358-3375
  Columbus *(G-7372)*
Countertop Alternatives Inc ....E 937 254-3334
  Dayton *(G-9324)*
Crafted Surface and Stone LLC ....E 440 658-3799
  Bedford Heights *(G-1321)*
Curtiss-Wright Flow Control ....D 513 735-2538
  Batavia *(G-995)*
◆ Custom Fabricators Inc ....E 216 831-2266
  Cleveland *(G-5391)*
Daniel A Terreri & Sons Inc ....E 330 538-2950
  Youngstown *(G-20014)*
Daniels Basement Waterproofing ....E 440 965-4332
  Berlin Heights *(G-1450)*
Danite Holdings Ltd ....E 614 444-3333
  Columbus *(G-7416)*
Decoating Inc ....E 419 347-9191
  Shelby *(G-16745)*
Deerfield Farms ....E 330 584-4715
  Deerfield *(G-9903)*
Design Rstrtion Reconstruction ....E 330 563-0010
  North Canton *(G-15196)*
Disaster Reconstruction Inc ....E 440 918-1523
  Eastlake *(G-10428)*
Early Construction Co ....E 740 894-5150
  South Point *(G-16933)*
Empaco Equipment Corporation ....E 330 659-9393
  Richfield *(G-16354)*
Erie Construction Mid-West Inc ....E 937 898-4688
  Dayton *(G-9417)*
Euclid Indus Maint Clg Contrs ....C 216 361-0288
  Cleveland *(G-5493)*
Extreme Detail Clg Cnstr Svcs ....E 419 392-3243
  Toledo *(G-17721)*
Feecorp Corporation ....E 614 837-3010
  Canal Winchester *(G-2108)*
Flamos Enterprises Inc ....E 330 478-0009
  Canton *(G-2315)*
▲ Flow-Liner Systems Ltd ....E 800 348-0020
  Zanesville *(G-20308)*
Gem City Waterproofing....................E 937 220-6800
  Dayton *(G-9457)*
▲ Goettle Holding Company Inc ....C 513 825-8100
  Cincinnati *(G-3623)*
Gradient Corporation ....E 513 779-0000
  Cincinnati *(G-3631)*
Gus Holthaus Signs Inc ....E 513 861-0060
  Cincinnati *(G-3664)*
Harold J Becker Company Inc ....E 614 279-1414
  Beavercreek *(G-1222)*
▲ High-Tech Pools Inc ....E 440 979-5070
  North Olmsted *(G-15292)*
Hughes Kitchens and Bath LLC ....E 330 455-5269
  Canton *(G-2351)*
Hummel Industries Incorporated...........E 513 242-1321
  Cincinnati *(G-3741)*
Identitek Systems Inc ....D 330 832-9844
  Massillon *(G-13697)*
Image Pavement Maintenance ....E 937 833-9200
  Brookville *(G-1914)*
Industrial Fiberglass Spc Inc ....E 937 222-9000
  Dayton *(G-9514)*
Industrial Waste Control Inc ....D 330 270-9900
  Youngstown *(G-20079)*
Ionno Properties s Corp ....E 330 479-9267
  Dennison *(G-10051)*
J & D Home Improvement Inc ....D 740 927-0722
  Reynoldsburg *(G-16310)*
J R Mead Industrial Contrs ....E 614 891-4466
  Galena *(G-11160)*
Jaco Waterproofing LLC ....E 513 738-0084
  Fairfield *(G-10739)*

Janson Industries ....D 330 455-7029
Canton *(G-2360)*

Jtc Contracting Inc ....E 216 635-0745
Cleveland *(G-5807)*

Kapton Caulking & Building ....E 440 526-0670
Cleveland *(G-5814)*

Keen & Cross Envmtl Svcs Inc.................E 513 674-1700
Cincinnati *(G-3851)*

Kens Beverage Inc.................E 513 874-8200
Fairfield *(G-10743)*

Korman Construction Corp.................E 614 274-2170
Columbus *(G-7924)*

L B Foster Company.................E 330 652-1461
Mineral Ridge *(G-14510)*

Lawn Management Sprinkler Co.................E 513 272-3808
Cincinnati *(G-3913)*

▲ Lefeld Welding & Stl Sups Inc.................E 419 678-2397
Coldwater *(G-6762)*

Lepi Enterprises Inc.................D 740 453-2980
Zanesville *(G-20324)*

Lighting Maint Harmon Sign.................D 419 841-6658
Toledo *(G-17855)*

Lincoln Moving & Storage Co.................D 216 741-5500
Cleveland *(G-5871)*

▲ Lorad LLC.................E 216 265-2862
Westlake *(G-19370)*

M K Moore & Sons Inc.................E 937 236-1812
Dayton *(G-9579)*

M T Golf Course Managment Inc.................E 513 923-1188
Cincinnati *(G-3955)*

Marsam Metalfab Inc.................E 330 405-1520
Twinsburg *(G-18295)*

◆ Master Builders LLC.................E 216 831-5500
Beachwood *(G-1076)*

Maxwell Lightning Protection.................E 937 228-7250
Dayton *(G-9590)*

Mc Fadden Construction Inc.................E 419 668-4165
Norwalk *(G-15444)*

Metropolitan Pool Service Co.................E 216 741-9451
Parma *(G-15768)*

Midwest Industrial Supply Inc.................E 800 321-0699
Toledo *(G-17914)*

Mike Morris.................E 330 767-4122
Brewster *(G-1811)*

▲ Mills Fence Co Inc.................E 513 631-0333
Cincinnati *(G-4057)*

▲ Modlich Stoneworks Inc.................E 614 276-2848
Columbus *(G-8094)*

Modular Systems Technicians.................E 216 459-2630
Cleveland *(G-6005)*

▲ Motz Group Inc.................E 513 533-6452
Cincinnati *(G-4077)*

MPS Group Inc.................D 937 746-2117
Carlisle *(G-2552)*

Mrap LLC.................E 614 545-3190
Columbus *(G-8117)*

MRM Construction Inc.................E 740 388-0079
Gallipolis *(G-11205)*

Multi Cntry SEC Slutions Group.................E 216 973-0291
Cleveland *(G-6023)*

Mural & Son Inc.................E 216 267-3322
Cleveland *(G-6025)*

North Bay Construction Inc.................E 440 835-1898
Westlake *(G-19380)*

Northpointe Property MGT LLC.................C 614 579-9712
Columbus *(G-8204)*

Northwest Firestop Inc.................E 419 517-4777
Toledo *(G-17948)*

OCP Contractors Inc.................E 419 865-7168
Holland *(G-11903)*

Ohio Concrete Resurfacing Inc.................E 440 786-9100
Bedford *(G-1297)*

▲ Ohio Pools & Spas Inc.................E 330 494-7755
Canton *(G-2428)*

Ohio State Home Services Inc.................C 330 467-1055
Macedonia *(G-13079)*

Ohio State Home Services Inc.................D 614 850-5600
Hilliard *(G-11803)*

Omni Construction Company Inc.................E 216 514-6664
Beachwood *(G-1091)*

Omni Fireproofing Co LLC.................D 513 870-9115
West Chester *(G-18980)*

▲ Organized Living Ltd.................C 513 674-5484
Cincinnati *(G-4182)*

P-N-D Communications Inc.................E 419 683-1922
Crestline *(G-9059)*

Palazzo Brothers Electric Inc.................E 419 668-1100
Norwalk *(G-15451)*

Paul Peterson Company.................E 614 486-4375
Columbus *(G-8427)*

Paulo Products Company.................E 440 942-0153
Willoughby *(G-19561)*

Pedersen Insulation Company.................E 614 471-3788
Columbus *(G-8434)*

Precision Environmental Co.................B 216 642-6040
Independence *(G-12109)*

Prime Polymers Inc.................E 330 662-4200
Medina *(G-13988)*

Priority 1 Construction Svcs.................E 513 922-0203
Cincinnati *(G-4282)*

Priority III Contracting Inc.................E 513 922-0203
Cincinnati *(G-4283)*

◆ Ptmj Enterprises.................C 440 543-8000
Solon *(G-16886)*

Pucher Paint Co Inc.................E 440 234-0991
Berea *(G-1435)*

Purple Marlin Inc.................E 440 323-1291
Elyria *(G-10557)*

Quality Fabricated Metals Inc.................E 330 332-7008
Salem *(G-16555)*

R E Kramig & Co Inc.................E 513 761-4010
Cincinnati *(G-4330)*

Rak Corrosion Control Inc.................E 440 985-2171
Amherst *(G-596)*

Ram Construction Services.................E 440 740-0100
Broadview Heights *(G-1844)*

Ram Construction Services of.................D 513 297-1857
West Chester *(G-18990)*

Ram Restoration LLC.................E 937 347-7418
Dayton *(G-9726)*

Regency Roofing Companies Inc.................E 330 468-1021
Macedonia *(G-13081)*

Resource International Inc.................C 614 823-4949
Columbus *(G-8523)*

Riverfront Diversified Inc.................D 513 874-7200
West Chester *(G-18995)*

Rudzik Excavating Inc.................E 330 755-1540
Struthers *(G-17367)*

Rusk Industries Inc.................D 419 841-6055
Toledo *(G-18015)*

Safety Grooving & Grinding LP.................E 419 592-8666
Napoleon *(G-14817)*

Sayles Company LLC.................E 614 801-0432
Columbus *(G-8595)*

Security Fence Group Inc.................E 513 681-3700
Cincinnati *(G-4444)*

Signature Control Systems LLC.................E 614 864-2222
Columbus *(G-8639)*

Six C Fabrication Inc.................D 330 296-5594
Ravenna *(G-16267)*

Southway Fence Company.................E 330 477-5251
Canton *(G-2480)*

Stachler Concrete Inc.................E 419 678-3867
Saint Henry *(G-16517)*

Stanley Stemer of Akron Canton.................E 330 785-5005
Coventry Township *(G-9043)*

Style-Line Incorporated.................E 614 291-0600
Columbus *(G-8707)*

Suburban Maint & Cnstr Inc.................E 440 237-7765
North Royalton *(G-15368)*

◆ Sws Equipment Services Inc.................E 330 806-2767
Akron *(G-462)*

Systems Jay LLC Nanogate.................A 419 524-3778
Mansfield *(G-13248)*

Terrafirm Construction LLC.................E 913 433-2998
Columbus *(G-8740)*

Thermal Solutions Inc.................D 740 886-2861
Proctorville *(G-16220)*

Thiels Replacement Systems Inc.................D 419 289-6139
Ashland *(G-694)*

TNT Mobile Powerwash Inc.................E 614 402-7474
Canal Winchester *(G-2121)*

Toledo Area Insulator Wkrs Jac.................D 419 531-5911
Toledo *(G-18073)*

Trinity Contracting Inc.................E 614 905-4410
Columbus *(G-8780)*

U S A Waterproofing Inc.................E 330 425-2440
Twinsburg *(G-18332)*

Unified Cnstr Systems Ltd.................E 330 773-2511
Akron *(G-475)*

United-Maier Signs Inc.................E 513 681-6600
Cincinnati *(G-4690)*

▲ Universal Fabg Cnstr Svcs Inc.................D 614 274-1128
Columbus *(G-8815)*

Vwc Liquidation Company LLC.................C 330 372-6776
Warren *(G-18767)*

Wegman Construction Company.................E 513 381-1111
Cincinnati *(G-4773)*

Wmk LLC.................E 440 951-4335
Mentor *(G-14125)*

X F Construction Svcs Inc.................E 614 575-2700
Columbus *(G-8923)*

40 RAILROAD TRANSPORTATION

4011 Railroads, Line-Hauling Operations

Ann Arbor Railroad Inc.................E 419 726-4181
Toledo *(G-17594)*

Ashland Railway Inc.................E 419 525-2822
Mansfield *(G-13137)*

Cleveland Works Railway Co.................D 216 429-7267
Cleveland *(G-5297)*

Cliffs Resources Inc.................C 216 694-5700
Cleveland *(G-5304)*

Columbus & Ohio River RR Co.................D 740 622-8092
Coshocton *(G-9003)*

◆ Covia Holdings Corporation.................D 440 214-3284
Independence *(G-12063)*

CSX Corporation.................C 419 225-4121
Lima *(G-12628)*

CSX Corporation.................C 419 933-5027
Willard *(G-19479)*

CSX Transportation Inc.................E 440 992-0871
Ashtabula *(G-735)*

CSX Transportation Inc.................E 513 369-5514
Cincinnati *(G-3384)*

CSX Transportation Inc.................E 614 898-3651
Westerville *(G-19155)*

CSX Transportation Inc.................E 937 642-2221
Marysville *(G-13493)*

CSX Transportation Inc.................E 419 257-1225
North Baltimore *(G-15176)*

CSX Transportation Inc.................E 513 422-2031
Middletown *(G-14298)*

CSX Transportation Inc.................D 419 697-2323
Oregon *(G-15588)*

Illinois & Midland RR Inc.................D 217 670-1242
Columbus *(G-7801)*

Illinois Central Railroad Co.................E 419 726-6028
Toledo *(G-17817)*

Indiana & Ohio Central RR.................C 740 385-3127
Logan *(G-12842)*

Indiana & Ohio Rail Corp.................E 513 860-1000
Cincinnati *(G-3756)*

Indiana & Ohio Rail Corp.................E 419 229-1010
Lima *(G-12665)*

Indiana & Ohio Railway Company.................D 513 860-1000
Cincinnati *(G-3757)*

Nimishillen & Tuscarawas LLC.................E 330 438-5821
Canton *(G-2418)*

Norfolk Southern Corporation.................D 419 436-2408
Fostoria *(G-11009)*

Norfolk Southern Corporation.................D 614 251-2684
Columbus *(G-8193)*

Norfolk Southern Corporation.................E 419 381-5505
Toledo *(G-17945)*

Norfolk Southern Corporation.................D 419 254-1562
Toledo *(G-17946)*

Norfolk Southern Corporation.................E 440 992-2274
Ashtabula *(G-749)*

Norfolk Southern Corporation.................D 440 992-2215
Ashtabula *(G-750)*

Norfolk Southern Corporation.................E 216 362-6087
Cleveland *(G-6071)*

Norfolk Southern Corporation.................E 419 529-4574
Ontario *(G-15566)*

Norfolk Southern Corporation.................C 419 483-1423
Bellevue *(G-1382)*

Norfolk Southern Corporation.................E 419 485-3510
Montpelier *(G-14617)*

Norfolk Southern Corporation.................E 216 518-8407
Maple Heights *(G-13290)*

Norfolk Southern Corporation.................E 216 362-6087
Cleveland *(G-6072)*

Norfolk Southern Corporation.................D 740 353-4529
Portsmouth *(G-16155)*

Norfolk Southern Corporation.................E 937 297-5420
Moraine *(G-14685)*

Norfolk Southern Corporation.................D 513 977-3246
Cincinnati *(G-4123)*

Norfolk Southern Corporation.................E 740 574-8491
Wheelersburg *(G-19436)*

Norfolk Southern Railway Co.................D 440 439-1827
Bedford *(G-1294)*

Ohi-Rail Corp.................E 740 765-5083
Richmond *(G-16386)*

Republic N&T Railroad Inc.................C 330 438-5826
Canton *(G-2455)*

Wheeling & Lake Erie Rlwy Co.................B 330 767-3401
Brewster *(G-1812)*

4013 Switching & Terminal Svcs

Ashland Railway Inc ....E 419 525-2822
  Mansfield (G-13137)
National Railroad Pass Corp ....E 419 246-0159
  Toledo (G-17933)
Tidewater River Rail Oper LLC ......D 817 659-0091
  Steubenville (G-17174)

41 LOCAL AND SUBURBAN TRANSIT AND INTERURBAN HIGHWAY PASSENGER TRANSPORTATION

4111 Local & Suburban Transit

Allen Cnty Regional Trnst Auth ....E 419 222-2782
  Lima (G-12594)
Anthony Wayne Local Schools ....D 419 877-0451
  Whitehouse (G-19443)
Butler Cnty Rgional Trnst Auth ....C 513 785-5237
  Hamilton (G-11566)
Central Ohio Transit Authority ....C 614 275-5800
  Columbus (G-7169)
Central Ohio Transit Authority ....A 614 275-5800
  Columbus (G-7170)
Charter Vans Inc ....E 937 898-4043
  Vandalia (G-18513)
City of Wilmington ....E 937 382-7961
  Wilmington (G-19608)
City Taxicab & Transfer Co ....E 440 992-2156
  Ashtabula (G-727)
Columbus Public School Dst ....C 614 365-6542
  Columbus (G-7309)
First Group Investment Partnr ....D 513 241-2200
  Cincinnati (G-3558)
First Transit Inc ....D 513 732-1206
  Batavia (G-999)
First Transit Inc ....D 937 652-4175
  Urbana (G-18433)
Firstgroup America Inc ....D 513 241-2200
  Cincinnati (G-3566)
Firstgroup America Inc ....D 513 241-2200
  Cincinnati (G-3568)
Firstgroup Usa Inc ....B 513 241-2200
  Cincinnati (G-3569)
Greater Cleveland ....A 216 566-5107
  Cleveland (G-5633)
Greater Cleveland Regional ....D 216 575-3932
  Cleveland (G-5638)
Greater Dyton Rgnal Trnst Auth ....D 937 425-8310
  Dayton (G-9474)
Intercoastal Trnsp Systems ....D 513 829-1287
  Fairfield (G-10737)
Ironton and Lawrence County ....B 740 532-3534
  Ironton (G-12155)
Ironton and Lawrence County ....E 740 532-7855
  Ironton (G-12156)
Laidlaw Transit Services Inc ....E 513 241-2200
  Cincinnati (G-3908)
Laketran ....C 440 350-1000
  Painesville (G-15721)
Led Transportation ....E 330 484-2772
  Canton (G-2373)
Lifecare Ambulance Inc ....E 440 323-6111
  Elyria (G-10526)
Metro Regional Transit Auth ....B 330 762-0341
  Akron (G-334)
Metro Regional Transit Auth ....D 330 762-0341
  Akron (G-335)
Mv Transportation Inc ....D 419 627-0740
  Sandusky (G-16628)
Mv Transportation Inc ....D 740 681-5086
  Cincinnati (G-4088)
Park-N-Go Inc ....E 937 890-7275
  Dayton (G-9686)
Pickaway County Community Acti ....D 740 477-1655
  Circleville (G-4839)
Portage Area Rgonal Trnsp Auth ....D 330 678-1287
  Kent (G-12254)
South Transportation ....E 216 691-2040
  Cleveland (G-6425)
Southeast Area Transit ....E 740 454-8574
  Zanesville (G-20362)
Southwest OH Trans Auth ....A 513 621-4455
  Cincinnati (G-4506)
Southwest OH Trans Auth ....A 513 632-7511
  Cincinnati (G-4507)

Stark Area Regional Trnst Auth ....C 330 477-2782
  Canton (G-2487)
Sutton Motor Coach Tours Inc ....E 330 726-2800
  Youngstown (G-20219)
Toledo Area Rgional Trnst Auth ....D 419 243-7433
  Toledo (G-18074)
United Scoto Senior Activities ....E 740 354-6672
  Portsmouth (G-16176)
Universal Transportation Syste ....C 513 829-1287
  Fairfield (G-10796)
Universal Transportation Syste ....E 513 539-9491
  Monroe (G-14585)
Universal Work and Power LLC ....E 513 981-1111
  Cincinnati (G-4696)
Western Reserve Transit Auth ....D 330 744-8431
  Youngstown (G-20243)

4119 Local Passenger Transportation: NEC

1st Advanced Ems LLC ....D 614 348-9991
  Columbus (G-6841)
A1 Mr Limo Inc ....E 440 943-5466
  Wickliffe (G-19454)
Above & Beyond Caregivers LLC ....E 614 478-1700
  Columbus (G-6855)
Aladdins Enterprises Inc ....E 614 891-3440
  Westerville (G-19218)
American Livery Service Inc ....E 216 221-9330
  Cleveland (G-4956)
American Med ....B 330 762-8999
  Akron (G-69)
American Medical Response Inc ....E 330 455-3579
  Canton (G-2186)
Anna Rescue Squad ....E 937 394-7377
  Anna (G-610)
Asv Services LLC ....E 216 797-1701
  Euclid (G-10623)
Athens County Emrgncy Med Svcs ......D 740 797-9560
  The Plains (G-17502)
Bedford Township ....E 740 992-6617
  Pomeroy (G-16093)
Bellevue Four Cnty Ems N Centl ....D 419 483-3322
  Milan (G-14359)
Bkp Ambulance District ....E 419 674-4574
  Kenton (G-12271)
Brookeside Ambulance Services ....E 419 476-7442
  Toledo (G-17628)
Buckeye Ambulance LLC ....D 937 435-1584
  Dayton (G-9263)
C C & S Ambulance Service Inc ....E 330 868-4114
  Minerva (G-14516)
Capital Transportation Inc ....C 614 258-0400
  Columbus (G-7113)
Carlson Ambince Trnspt Svc Inc ....E 330 225-2400
  Brunswick (G-1923)
Catholic Charities of SW Ohio ....D 513 241-7745
  Cincinnati (G-3132)
City of Cleveland ....B 216 664-2555
  Cleveland (G-5189)
City of Cleveland ....B 216 664-2555
  Cleveland (G-5190)
City of Eaton ....E 937 456-5361
  Eaton (G-10438)
City of Lakewood ....E 216 521-1288
  Cleveland (G-5209)
Clark County Board of Developm ....D 937 328-5240
  Springfield (G-17010)
Clemente-Mc Kay Ambulance Inc ....E 330 755-1401
  Struthers (G-17361)
Cleveland Auto Livery Inc ....E 216 421-1101
  Cleveland (G-5231)
Cloverleaf Transport Co ....E 419 599-5015
  Napoleon (G-14801)
Community Ambulance Service ....D 740 454-6800
  Zanesville (G-20298)
Community Care Amblance Netwrk ....D 440 992-1401
  Ashtabula (G-728)
Community Emrgcy Med Svcs Ohio ......C 614 751-6651
  Columbus (G-7331)
Contract Transport Services ....E 216 524-8435
  Cleveland (G-5345)
Coshocton Cnty Emrgncy Med Svc ....D 740 622-4294
  Coshocton (G-9005)
County of Hardin ....E 419 634-7729
  Ada (G-4)
County of Lorain ....E 440 647-5803
  Wellington (G-18838)
County of Ottawa ....E 419 898-7433
  Oak Harbor (G-15469)
County of Seneca ....E 419 937-2340
  Bascom (G-981)

Courtesy Ambulance Inc ....E 740 522-8588
  Newark (G-15029)
Cremation Service Inc ....E 216 861-2334
  Cleveland (G-5378)
Critical Care Transport Inc ....D 614 775-0564
  Columbus (G-7393)
Critical Life Inc ....E 419 525-0502
  Mansfield (G-13160)
Cusa LI Inc ....C 216 267-8810
  Brookpark (G-1895)
Direct Expediting LLC ....E 513 459-0100
  Mason (G-13574)
Donty Horton HM Care Dhhc LLC ....E 513 463-3442
  Cincinnati (G-3440)
Eastern Horizon Inc ....E 614 253-7000
  Columbus (G-7489)
Elite Ambulance Service LLC ....E 888 222-1356
  Loveland (G-12992)
Emergency Medical Transport ....D 330 484-4000
  North Canton (G-15198)
Eric Boeppler Fmly Ltd Partnr ....D 513 336-8108
  Fairfield (G-10725)
Fab Limousines Inc ....E 330 792-6700
  Youngstown (G-20033)
Firelands Ambulance Service ....E 419 929-1487
  New London (G-14932)
First Class Limos Inc ....E 440 248-1114
  Cleveland (G-5533)
Firstgroup America Inc ....D 513 241-2200
  Cincinnati (G-3566)
Firstgroup America Inc ....D 513 241-2200
  Cincinnati (G-3568)
Franklin Township Fire and Ems ....E 513 876-2996
  Felicity (G-10859)
Georgetown Life Squad ....E 937 378-3082
  Georgetown (G-11271)
Gold Cross Ambulance Svcs Inc ....C 330 744-4161
  Youngstown (G-20051)
Gold Cross Limousine Service ....E 330 757-3053
  Struthers (G-17364)
Greater Cleveland Regional ....C 216 781-1110
  Cleveland (G-5639)
Greenville Township Rescue ....E 937 548-9339
  Greenville (G-11384)
Guernsey Health Enterprises ....A 740 439-3561
  Cambridge (G-2072)
Guernsey Health Systems ....A 740 439-3561
  Cambridge (G-2073)
Hanco Ambulance Inc ....E 419 423-2912
  Findlay (G-10916)
Harter Ventures Inc ....D 419 224-4075
  Lima (G-12651)
Henderson Road Rest Systems ....E 614 442-3310
  Columbus (G-7739)
Hillcrest Ambulance Svc Inc ....C 216 797-4000
  Euclid (G-10640)
Homecare Service Inc ....E 513 655-5022
  Blue Ash (G-1582)
Hopkin Arprt Lmsine Shttle Svc ....E 216 267-8282
  Cleveland (G-5703)
Hopkins Airport Limousine Svc ....C 216 267-8810
  Cleveland (G-5704)
Hustead Emergency Medical Svc ....E 937 324-3031
  Springfield (G-17049)
Intercoastal Trnsp Systems ....D 513 829-1287
  Fairfield (G-10737)
J & C Ambulance Services Inc ....C 330 899-0022
  North Canton (G-15213)
Jls Enterprises Inc ....E 513 769-1888
  West Chester (G-18952)
Kare Medical Trnspt Svcs LLP ....E 937 578-0263
  Marysville (G-13509)
Lacp St Ritas Medical Ctr LLC ....D 419 324-4075
  Lima (G-12673)
Lakefront Lines Inc ....C 216 267-8810
  Brookpark (G-1900)
Lakefront Lines Inc ....E 419 537-0677
  Toledo (G-17848)
Lakefront Lines Inc ....E 614 476-1113
  Columbus (G-7944)
Lakefront Lines Inc ....D 513 829-8290
  Fairfield (G-10746)
Lane Life Corp ....E 330 799-1002
  Youngstown (G-20097)
Liberty Ems Services LLC ....E 216 630-6626
  Cleveland (G-5866)
Lifecare Ambulance Inc ....D 440 323-2527
  Elyria (G-10525)
Lifecare Ambulance Inc ....E 440 323-6111
  Elyria (G-10526)

Lifecare Medical Services ....E 614 258-2545
Columbus *(G-7975)*
Lifestar Ambulance Inc ....C 419 245-6210
Toledo *(G-17854)*
Lifeteam Ems Inc ....E 330 386-9284
East Liverpool *(G-10405)*
Lorain Life Care Ambulance Svc ....D 440 244-6467
Lorain *(G-12921)*
Mahoning County ....D 330 797-2837
Youngstown *(G-20107)*
Mansfield Ambulance Inc ....E 419 525-3311
Mansfield *(G-13204)*
Martens Donald & Sons ....D 216 265-4211
Cleveland *(G-5917)*
Med Ride Ems ....D 614 747-9744
Columbus *(G-8051)*
Med Star Emgncy Mdcl Srv ....E 330 394-6611
Warren *(G-18728)*
Med-Trans Inc ....D 937 325-4926
Springfield *(G-17069)*
Med-Trans Inc ....E 937 293-9771
Moraine *(G-14674)*
Meda-Care Transportation Inc ....E 513 521-4799
Cincinnati *(G-3992)*
Medcorp Inc ....C 419 425-9700
Findlay *(G-10942)*
Medcorp Inc ....D 419 727-7000
Toledo *(G-17900)*
Medic Response Service Inc ....E 419 522-1998
Mansfield *(G-13218)*
Medical Transport Systems Inc ....D 330 837-9818
North Canton *(G-15219)*
Medpro LLC ....D 937 336-5586
Eaton *(G-10452)*
Mercy Health ....E 440 775-1211
Oberlin *(G-15510)*
Metrohealth System ....E 216 778-3867
Cleveland *(G-5971)*
Metrohealth System ....C 216 957-4000
Cleveland *(G-5968)*
Mid County Ems ....E 419 898-9366
Oak Harbor *(G-15474)*
Morgan County Public Transit ....E 740 962-1322
McConnelsville *(G-13903)*
Morrow County Fire Fighter ....D 419 946-7976
Mount Gilead *(G-14730)*
Mt Orab Fire Department Inc ....E 937 444-3945
Mount Orab *(G-14743)*
Muskingum County Ohio ....D 740 452-0678
Zanesville *(G-20335)*
Mycity Transporatation Co ....E 216 591-1900
Shaker Heights *(G-16711)*
National Express Transit Corp ....D 513 322-6214
Cincinnati *(G-4091)*
Non Emergency Ambulance Svc ......E 330 296-4541
Ravenna *(G-16251)*
North Star Critical Care LLC ....E 330 386-9110
East Liverpool *(G-10410)*
Northwest Fire Ambulance ....E 937 437-8354
New Paris *(G-14944)*
Northwest Limousine Inc ....E 440 322-5804
Elyria *(G-10550)*
Norwalk Area Health Services ....C 419 499-2515
Milan *(G-14363)*
Norwalk Area Health Services ....C 419 668-8101
Norwalk *(G-15447)*
Ohio Medical Trnsp Inc ....E 937 747-3540
Marysville *(G-13521)*
Ohio Medical Trnsp Inc ....D 740 962-2055
McConnelsville *(G-13904)*
Ohio Medical Trnsp Inc ....D 614 791-4400
Columbus *(G-8274)*
Patriot Emergency Med Svcs Inc .....E 740 532-2222
Ironton *(G-12165)*
Physicians Ambulance Svc Inc ....E 216 332-1667
Cleveland *(G-6210)*
Pickaway County Community Acti ....D 740 477-1655
Circleville *(G-4839)*
Pickaway Plains Ambulance Svc ......C 740 474-4180
Circleville *(G-4845)*
Portage Path Behavorial Health ....D 330 762-6110
Akron *(G-391)*
Portsmouth Ambulance ....C 740 289-2932
Portsmouth *(G-16158)*
Portsmuth Emrgncy Amblance Svc ...B 740 354-3122
Portsmouth *(G-16162)*
Precious Cargo Transportation ....E 440 564-8039
Newbury *(G-15124)*
Professional Transportation ....C 419 661-0576
Walbridge *(G-18623)*

Pymatuning Ambulance Service ....E 440 293-7991
Andover *(G-607)*
Quad Ambulance District ....E 330 866-9847
Waynesburg *(G-18829)*
Rittman City of Inc ....E 330 925-2065
Rittman *(G-16408)*
Rural/Metro Corporation ....C 216 749-2211
Youngstown *(G-20199)*
Rural/Metro Corporation ....C 330 744-4161
Youngstown *(G-20200)*
Rural/Metro Corporation ....C 440 543-3313
Chagrin Falls *(G-2681)*
Sardinia Life Squad ....E 937 446-2178
Sardinia *(G-16660)*
Seneca-Crawford Area Trnsp ....E 419 937-2428
Tiffin *(G-17540)*
Senior Outreach Services ....E 216 421-6900
Cleveland *(G-6397)*
Shima Limousine Services Inc ....E 440 918-6400
Mentor *(G-14109)*
Smith Ambulance Service Inc ....E 330 825-0205
Dover *(G-10099)*
Smith Ambulance Service Inc ....E 330 602-0050
Dover *(G-10100)*
Spirit Medical Transport LLC ....D 937 548-2800
Greenville *(G-11396)*
Sterling Joint Ambulance Dst ....E 740 869-3006
Mount Sterling *(G-14747)*
Stofcheck Ambulance Inc ....C 740 383-2787
Marion *(G-13460)*
Stofcheck Ambulance Svc Inc ....E 740 499-2200
La Rue *(G-12324)*
Toronto Emergency Medical Svc ....E 740 537-3891
Toronto *(G-18186)*
Tri Village Rescue Service ....E 937 996-3155
New Madison *(G-14938)*
Tri-State Amblnce Pramedic Svc ......E 304 233-2331
North Canton *(G-15240)*
Tricounty Ambulance Service ....D 440 951-4600
Mentor *(G-14115)*
United Amblnce Svc of Cmbridge .....E 740 439-7787
Cambridge *(G-2086)*
United Ambulance Service ....E 740 732-5653
Caldwell *(G-2046)*
United Scoto Senior Activities ....E 740 354-6672
Portsmouth *(G-16176)*
Universal Work and Power LLC ....E 513 981-1111
Cincinnati *(G-4696)*
Utica Volunteer Emrgncy Squad ....E 740 892-2369
Utica *(G-18458)*
Village of Antwerp ....E 419 258-6631
Antwerp *(G-616)*
Youngstown Area Jwish Fdration ......D 330 746-1076
Youngstown *(G-20257)*

4121 Taxi Cabs

Americab Inc ....E 216 429-1134
Cleveland *(G-4946)*
City Taxicab & Transfer Co ....E 440 992-2156
Ashtabula *(G-727)*
City Yellow Cab Company ....E 330 253-3141
Akron *(G-140)*
Columbus Green Cabs Inc ....E 614 444-4444
Columbus *(G-7284)*
Independent Radio Taxi Inc ....E 330 746-8844
Youngstown *(G-20077)*
Knox Area Transit ....E 740 392-7433
Mount Vernon *(G-14770)*
Pickaway County Community Acti .....D 740 477-1655
Circleville *(G-4839)*
Shamrock Taxi Ltd ....E 614 263-8294
Columbus *(G-8630)*
United Garage & Service Corp ....D 216 623-1550
Cleveland *(G-6572)*
Westlake Cab Service ....D 440 331-5000
Cleveland *(G-6677)*

4131 Intercity & Rural Bus Transportation

Firstgroup America Inc ....D 513 241-2200
Cincinnati *(G-3566)*
Greater Dyton Rgnal Trnst Auth ....A 937 425-8400
Dayton *(G-9476)*
Greyhound Lines Inc ....E 513 421-7442
Cincinnati *(G-3657)*
Greyhound Lines Inc ....E 614 221-0577
Columbus *(G-7697)*
Muskingum Coach Company ....E 740 622-2545
Coshocton *(G-9023)*
Precious Cargo Transportation ....E 440 564-8039
Newbury *(G-15124)*

Stark Area Regional Trnst Auth ....C 330 477-2782
Canton *(G-2487)*

4141 Local Bus Charter Svc

A T V Inc ....C 614 252-5060
Columbus *(G-6848)*
Charter Vans Inc ....E 937 898-4043
Vandalia *(G-18513)*
Croswell of Williamsburg LLC ....E 513 724-2206
Williamsburg *(G-19492)*
Cusa LI Inc ....C 216 267-8810
Brookpark *(G-1895)*
Cuyahoga Marketing Service ....E 440 526-5350
Cleveland *(G-5400)*
Firstgroup America Inc ....E 513 241-2200
Cincinnati *(G-3566)*
Lakefront Lines Inc ....D 513 829-8290
Fairfield *(G-10746)*
Lakefront Lines Inc ....C 216 267-8810
Brookpark *(G-1900)*
Marfre Inc ....C 513 321-3377
Cincinnati *(G-3969)*
Precious Cargo Transportation ....E 440 564-8039
Newbury *(G-15124)*
Queen City Transportation LLC ....B 513 941-8700
Cincinnati *(G-4322)*
S B S Transit Inc ....B 440 288-2222
Lorain *(G-12942)*
Transit Service Company ....E 330 782-3343
Youngstown *(G-20223)*

4142 Bus Charter Service, Except Local

Buckeye Charter Service Inc ....D 419 222-2455
Lima *(G-12610)*
Buckeye Charter Service Inc ....E 937 879-3000
Dayton *(G-9264)*
Croswell of Williamsburg LLC ....E 513 724-2206
Williamsburg *(G-19492)*
Croswell of Williamsburg LLC ....D 800 782-8747
Dayton *(G-9340)*
Cusa LI Inc ....C 216 267-8810
Brookpark *(G-1895)*
Cuyahoga Marketing Service ....E 440 526-5350
Cleveland *(G-5400)*
Garfield Hts Coach Line Inc ....D 440 232-4550
Chagrin Falls *(G-2646)*
Greyhound Lines Inc ....E 614 221-0577
Columbus *(G-7697)*
Hat White Management LLC ....E 800 525-7967
Akron *(G-255)*
Lakefront Lines Inc ....C 216 267-8810
Brookpark *(G-1900)*
Lakefront Lines Inc ....E 419 537-0677
Toledo *(G-17848)*
Lakefront Lines Inc ....E 614 476-1113
Columbus *(G-7944)*
Pioneer Trails Inc ....E 330 674-1234
Millersburg *(G-14487)*
Put In Bay Transportation ....E 419 285-4855
Put In Bay *(G-16228)*
Queen City Transportation LLC ....E 513 941-8700
Cincinnati *(G-4322)*
S B S Transit Inc ....B 440 288-2222
Lorain *(G-12942)*
Starforce National Corporation ....C 513 979-3600
Cincinnati *(G-4540)*
Sutton Motor Coach Tours Inc ....E 330 726-2800
Youngstown *(G-20219)*
Tesco-Transportion Eqp Sls ....E 419 836-2835
Oregon *(G-15610)*

4151 School Buses

Akron School Trnsp Svcs ....D 330 761-1390
Akron *(G-55)*
Anthony Wayne Local Schools ....D 419 877-0451
Whitehouse *(G-19443)*
Beachwood City Schools ....E 216 464-6609
Cleveland *(G-5047)*
Benton-Carroll-Salem ....E 419 898-6214
Oak Harbor *(G-15468)*
Berea B O E Trnsp Dept ....D 216 898-8300
Berea *(G-1414)*
Boardman Local Schools ....D 330 726-3409
Youngstown *(G-19969)*
Canton City School District ....D 330 456-6710
Canton *(G-2230)*
Chillicothe City School Dst ....E 740 775-2936
Chillicothe *(G-2760)*
Clark Shawnee Schl Transprtn ....E 937 328-5382
Springfield *(G-17014)*

Cleveland Municipal School Dst..........B....... 216 634-7005
Cleveland (G-5273)

Cleveland Municipal School Dst..........B....... 216 432-4600
Cleveland (G-5274)

Community Bus Services Inc..........E....... 330 369-6060
Warren (G-18686)

Dublin City Schools..........C....... 614 764-5926
Dublin (G-10205)

First Group Investment Partnr..........D....... 513 241-2200
Cincinnati (G-3558)

First Student Inc..........E....... 513 531-6888
Cincinnati (G-3560)

First Student Inc..........E....... 937 645-0201
Dayton (G-9438)

First Student Inc..........D....... 513 761-6100
Cincinnati (G-3561)

First Student Inc..........B....... 513 761-5136
Cincinnati (G-3562)

First Student Inc..........E....... 419 382-9915
Toledo (G-17741)

First Student Inc..........E....... 513 241-2200
Cincinnati (G-3563)

Firstgroup America Inc..........D....... 513 241-2200
Cincinnati (G-3566)

Firstgroup America Inc..........B....... 513 419-8611
Cincinnati (G-3567)

Firstgroup America Inc..........D....... 513 241-2200
Cincinnati (G-3568)

Firstgroup Usa Inc..........B....... 513 241-2200
Cincinnati (G-3569)

Gahanna-Jefferson Pub Schl Dst..........D....... 614 751-7581
Columbus (G-7644)

Geneva Area City School Dst..........E....... 440 466-2684
Geneva (G-11241)

Lakota Local School District..........C....... 513 777-2150
Liberty Township (G-12582)

Lima City School District..........E....... 419 996-3450
Lima (G-12676)

Mahoning County..........D....... 330 797-2837
Youngstown (G-20107)

Marfre Inc..........C....... 513 321-3377
Cincinnati (G-3969)

Massillon City School Bus Gar..........E....... 330 830-1849
Massillon (G-13711)

Mentor Exempted Vlg Schl Dst..........C....... 440 974-5260
Mentor (G-14080)

Miamisburg City School Dst..........D....... 937 866-1283
Miamisburg (G-14191)

Middletown School Vhcl Svc Ctr..........D....... 513 420-4568
Middletown (G-14310)

New Albany Plain Loc SC Transp..........E....... 614 855-2033
New Albany (G-14866)

North Canton City School Dst..........D....... 330 497-5615
Canton (G-2420)

Northmont Service Center..........D....... 937 832-5050
Englewood (G-10594)

Ontario Local School District..........E....... 419 529-3814
Ontario (G-15568)

Palmer Express Incorporated..........E....... 440 942-3333
Willoughby (G-19560)

Pauls Bus Service Inc..........E....... 513 851-5089
Cincinnati (G-4215)

Perry Transportation Dept..........E....... 440 259-3005
Perry (G-15827)

Perrysburg Board of Education..........E....... 419 874-3127
Perrysburg (G-15902)

Peterman..........E....... 513 722-2229
Goshen (G-11314)

Petermann..........E....... 513 539-0324
Monroe (G-14580)

Petermann Ltd..........D....... 330 653-3323
Hudson (G-12003)

Petermann Northeast LLC..........A....... 513 351-7383
Cincinnati (G-4236)

Queen City Transportation LLC..........B....... 513 941-8700
Cincinnati (G-4322)

S B S Transit Inc..........B....... 440 288-2222
Lorain (G-12942)

SC Madison Bus Garage..........D....... 419 589-3373
Mansfield (G-13241)

Streetsboro Board Education..........E....... 330 626-4909
Streetsboro (G-17272)

Suburban Transportation Co Inc..........E....... 440 846-9291
Brunswick (G-1940)

Vermilion Board of Education..........E....... 440 204-1700
Vermilion (G-18561)

Washington Local Schools..........D....... 419 473-8356
Toledo (G-18146)

4173 Bus Terminal & Svc Facilities

City of Willoughby..........E....... 440 942-0215
Willoughby (G-19510)

Hans Truck and Trlr Repr Inc..........E....... 216 581-0046
Cleveland (G-5660)

Lakota Local School District..........C....... 513 777-2150
Liberty Township (G-12582)

Meigs Local School District..........E....... 740 742-2990
Middleport (G-14282)

Ottawa County Transit Board..........E....... 419 898-7433
Oak Harbor (G-15477)

Reynoldsburg City Schools..........E....... 614 501-1041
Reynoldsburg (G-16326)

Washington Local Schools..........D....... 419 473-8356
Toledo (G-18146)

42 MOTOR FREIGHT TRANSPORTATION AND WAREHOUSING

4212 Local Trucking Without Storage

1st Carrier Corp..........D....... 740 477-2587
Circleville (G-4821)

44444 LLC..........E....... 330 502-2023
Austintown (G-855)

A L Smith Trucking Inc..........E....... 937 526-3651
Versailles (G-18565)

Accelerated Moving & Stor Inc..........E....... 614 836-1007
Columbus (G-6859)

Aci Const Co Inc..........E....... 419 595-4284
Alvada (G-559)

Advantage Tank Lines Inc..........C....... 330 427-1010
Leetonia (G-12518)

AG Trucking Inc..........E....... 937 497-7770
Sidney (G-16757)

Aim Integrated Logistics Inc..........B....... 330 759-0438
Girard (G-11281)

Aim Leasing Company..........E....... 330 759-0438
Girard (G-11282)

Alan Woods Trucking Inc..........E....... 513 738-3314
Hamilton (G-11556)

All My Sons Moving & Storge of..........E....... 614 405-7202
Hilliard (G-11740)

Allan Hunter Construction LLC..........E....... 330 634-9882
Akron (G-65)

American Bulk Commodities Inc..........C....... 330 758-0841
Youngstown (G-19953)

American Waste MGT Svcs Inc..........E....... 330 856-8800
Warren (G-18664)

Arrowhead Transport Co..........E....... 330 638-2900
Cortland (G-8983)

Atlantic Coastal Trucking..........C....... 201 438-6500
Delaware (G-9953)

Autumn Industries Inc..........E....... 330 372-5002
Warren (G-18671)

B & H Industries Inc..........E....... 419 485-8373
Montpelier (G-14605)

B & L Transport Inc..........E....... 866 848-2888
Millersburg (G-14457)

B D Transportation Inc..........E....... 937 773-9280
Piqua (G-15996)

Back In Black Co..........E....... 419 425-5555
Findlay (G-10866)

Bell Moving and Storage Inc..........E....... 513 942-7500
Fairfield (G-10699)

Berner Trucking..........E....... 419 476-0207
Toledo (G-17612)

Berner Trucking Inc..........C....... 330 343-5812
Dover (G-10067)

Besl Transfer Co..........E....... 513 242-3456
Cincinnati (G-3042)

Best Way Motor Lines Inc..........C....... 419 485-8373
Montpelier (G-14606)

BFI Waste Services LLC..........E....... 800 437-1123
Salem (G-16537)

Big Blue Trucking Inc..........E....... 330 372-1421
Warren (G-18680)

Blatt Trucking Co Inc..........E....... 419 898-0002
Rocky Ridge (G-16419)

Blb Transport Inc..........E....... 740 474-1341
Circleville (G-4825)

Blood Courier Inc..........E....... 216 251-3050
Cleveland (G-5063)

Bob Miller Rigging Inc..........E....... 419 422-7477
Findlay (G-10880)

Bowling Transportation Inc..........D....... 419 436-9590
Fostoria (G-10998)

Brookside Holdings LLC..........E....... 419 224-7019
Lima (G-12609)

Brookside Holdings LLC..........E....... 419 925-4457
Maria Stein (G-13306)

Browning-Ferris Industries LLC..........D....... 330 393-0385
Warren (G-18682)

Bryan Truck Line Inc..........E....... 419 485-8373
Montpelier (G-14609)

Building Systems Trnsp Co..........C....... 740 852-9700
London (G-12861)

Burch Hydro Inc..........E....... 740 694-9146
Fredericktown (G-11052)

Burch Hydro Trucking Inc..........E....... 740 694-9146
Fredericktown (G-11053)

Burkhart Trucking Inc..........E....... 740 896-2244
Lowell (G-13037)

BWC Trucking Company Inc..........E....... 740 532-5188
Ironton (G-12148)

C & G Transportation Inc..........E....... 419 288-2653
Wayne (G-18825)

C-Z Trucking Co..........D....... 330 758-2313
Poland (G-16081)

Capitol Express Entps Inc..........D....... 614 279-2819
Columbus (G-7116)

Carl E Oeder Sons Sand & Grav..........E....... 513 494-1555
Lebanon (G-12454)

Carrier Industries Inc..........B....... 614 851-6363
Columbus (G-7131)

Century Lines Inc..........E....... 216 271-0700
Cleveland (G-5160)

Certified Oil Inc..........D....... 614 421-7500
Columbus (G-7171)

Chapin Logistics Inc..........E....... 440 327-1360
North Ridgeville (G-15325)

Charles D McIntosh Trckg Inc..........E....... 937 378-3803
Georgetown (G-11266)

Cheeseman LLC..........E....... 419 375-4132
Fort Recovery (G-10988)

Circle S Transport Inc..........E....... 614 207-2184
Columbus (G-7203)

City Dash LLC..........C....... 513 562-2000
Cincinnati (G-3298)

City of Dayton..........C....... 937 333-4860
Dayton (G-9303)

City of Marion..........D....... 740 382-1479
Marion (G-13412)

Clary Trucking Inc..........E....... 740 702-4242
Chillicothe (G-2769)

Clayton Weaver Trucking Inc..........E....... 513 896-6932
Fairfield (G-10714)

Competitive Transportation..........E....... 419 529-5300
Bellville (G-1388)

Containerport Group Inc..........D....... 216 692-3124
Euclid (G-10627)

Containerport Group Inc..........E....... 440 333-1330
Columbus (G-7355)

Continental Express Inc..........B....... 937 497-2100
Sidney (G-16767)

Continental Office Furn Corp..........E....... 614 781-0080
Columbus (G-7359)

Continental Transport Inc..........E....... 513 360-2960
Monroe (G-14564)

Corrigan Moving Systems-Ann AR..........E....... 419 874-2900
Perrysburg (G-15850)

Coshocton Trucking South Inc..........C....... 740 622-1311
Coshocton (G-9009)

Cotter Moving & Storage Co..........E....... 330 535-5115
Akron (G-161)

Cousins Waste Control LLC..........D....... 419 726-1500
Toledo (G-17686)

Cowen Truck Line Inc..........D....... 419 938-3401
Perrysville (G-15940)

Custom Movers Services Inc..........E....... 330 564-0507
Stow (G-17196)

D & V Trucking Inc..........E....... 330 482-9440
Columbiana (G-6786)

D&D Trucking and Services Inc..........E....... 419 692-3205
Delphos (G-10023)

Dale Ross Trucking Inc..........E....... 937 981-2168
Greenfield (G-11360)

Daves Sand & Stone Inc..........E....... 419 445-9256
Wauseon (G-18798)

Davidson Trucking Inc..........E....... 419 288-2318
Bradner (G-1764)

Dearman Moving & Storage Co..........E....... 419 524-3456
Mansfield (G-13166)

Dedicated Logistics Inc..........D....... 513 275-1135
West Chester (G-18909)

Dedicated Transport LLC..........C....... 216 641-2500
Brooklyn Heights (G-1869)

Dill-Elam Inc ....E   513 575-0017
 Loveland *(G-12991)*

Dingledine Trucking Company ....E   937 652-3454
 Urbana *(G-18431)*

Direct Express Delivery Svc ....E   513 541-0600
 Cincinnati *(G-3431)*

Disttech LLC ....D   800 321-3143
 Cleveland *(G-5429)*

DOT Smith LLC ....E   740 245-5105
 Thurman *(G-17508)*

Drasc Enterprises Inc ....E   330 852-3254
 Sugarcreek *(G-17377)*

Drivers On Call LLC C   330 867-5193
 Norton *(G-15419)*

Dyno Nobel Transportation ....E   740 439-5050
 Cambridge *(G-2065)*

E & V Ventures Inc ....E   330 794-6683
 Akron *(G-198)*

Early Express Services Inc ....E   937 223-5801
 Dayton *(G-9400)*

Ed Wilson & Son Trucking Inc ....E   330 549-9287
 New Springfield *(G-14996)*

Edw C Levy Co ....E   419 822-8288
 Delta *(G-10042)*

Emory Rothenbuhler & Sons ....E   740 458-1432
 Beallsville *(G-1119)*

Energy Power Services Inc ....E   330 343-2312
 New Philadelphia *(G-14958)*

Expeditus Transport LLC ....E   419 464-9450
 Sylvania *(G-17424)*

Falcon Transport Co ....D   330 793-1345
 Youngstown *(G-20035)*

Federal Express Corporation C   800 463-3339
 Bedford *(G-1280)*

Fedex Freight Inc ....D   330 645-0879
 Akron *(G-218)*

Fedex Freight Corporation ....E   800 354-9489
 Zanesville *(G-20307)*

Fedex Ground Package Sys Inc C   412 859-2653
 Steubenville *(G-17154)*

Fedex Ground Package Sys Inc ....B   800 463-3339
 Toledo *(G-17731)*

Fedex Ground Package Sys Inc ....D   513 942-4330
 West Chester *(G-19052)*

Fedex Ground Package Sys Inc ....B   800 463-3339
 Grove City *(G-11432)*

Ferrous Metal Transfer ....E   216 671-8500
 Brooklyn *(G-1861)*

Findlay Truck Line Inc ....D   419 422-1945
 Findlay *(G-10906)*

First Group Investment Partnr ....D   513 241-2200
 Cincinnati *(G-3558)*

Firstgroup Usa Inc ....B   513 241-2200
 Cincinnati *(G-3569)*

Five Star Trucking Inc ....E   440 953-9300
 Willoughby *(G-19524)*

Forrest Trucking Company ....E   614 879-7347
 London *(G-12864)*

Forrest Trucking Company ....E   614 879-8642
 West Jefferson *(G-19109)*

Fraley & Schilling Inc C   740 598-4118
 Brilliant *(G-1822)*

Fultz & Son Inc ....E   419 547-9365
 Clyde *(G-6743)*

G & S Transfer Inc ....E   330 673-3899
 Kent *(G-12233)*

Garber Ag Freight Inc ....E   937 548-8400
 Greenville *(G-11378)*

Garner Trucking Inc C   419 422-5742
 Findlay *(G-10912)*

Glm Transport Inc ....E   419 363-2041
 Rockford *(G-16415)*

GMC Excavation & Trucking ....E   419 468-0121
 Galion *(G-11177)*

Golden Hawk Inc ....D   419 683-3304
 Crestline *(G-9055)*

Greater Dayton Mvg & Stor Co ....E   937 235-0011
 Dayton *(G-9471)*

H & W Holdings LLC ....E   800 826-3560
 South Point *(G-16935)*

H L C Trucking Inc ....D   740 676-6181
 Shadyside *(G-16695)*

H T I Express ....E   419 423-9555
 Findlay *(G-10915)*

Hc Transport Inc ....E   513 574-1800
 Cincinnati *(G-3687)*

Henderson Trucking Inc ....E   740 369-6100
 Delaware *(G-9985)*

Henderson Turf Farm Inc ....E   937 748-1559
 Franklin *(G-11032)*

Hilltrux Tank Lines Inc ....E   330 965-1103
 Youngstown *(G-20065)*

Hirzel Transfer Co ....E   419 287-3288
 Pemberville *(G-15804)*

Hofstetter Orran Inc ....E   330 683-8070
 Orrville *(G-15634)*

Home Run Inc ....E   800 543-9198
 Xenia *(G-19910)*

Howland Logistics LLC ....E   513 469-5263
 Cincinnati *(G-3734)*

Huntley Trucking Co ....E   740 385-7615
 New Plymouth *(G-14991)*

Hyway Trucking Company ....D   419 423-7145
 Findlay *(G-10926)*

Imperial Express Inc ....E   937 399-9400
 Springfield *(G-17050)*

Innovative Logistics Svcs Inc ....D   330 468-6422
 Northfield *(G-15380)*

Integrity Ex Logistics LLC ....B   888 374-5138
 Cincinnati *(G-3771)*

International Truck & Eng Corp ....A   937 390-4045
 Springfield *(G-17055)*

J M T Cartage Inc ....E   330 478-2430
 Canton *(G-2359)*

J M Towning Inc ....E   614 876-7335
 Hilliard *(G-11779)*

J P Jenks Inc ....E   440 428-4500
 Madison *(G-13098)*

J P Transportation Company ....E   513 424-6978
 Middletown *(G-14304)*

J T Express Inc ....E   513 727-8185
 Monroe *(G-14570)*

J-Trac Inc ....E   419 524-3456
 Mansfield *(G-13189)*

James Air Cargo Inc ....E   440 243-9095
 Cleveland *(G-5779)*

James H Alvis Trucking Inc ....E   513 623-8121
 Harrison *(G-11671)*

Jet Express Inc ....D   937 274-7033
 Dayton *(G-9524)*

John Brown Trucking Inc ....E   330 758-0841
 Youngstown *(G-20085)*

K R Drenth Trucking Inc ....D   708 983-6340
 Cincinnati *(G-3844)*

Kace Logistics LLC ....E   419 273-3388
 Toledo *(G-17836)*

Kenan Advantage Group Inc C   800 969-5419
 North Canton *(G-15216)*

KF Express LLC ....E   614 258-8858
 Powell *(G-16201)*

Klingshirn & Sons Trucking ....E   937 338-5000
 Burkettsville *(G-2012)*

KMu Trucking & Excvtg Inc ....E   440 934-1008
 Avon *(G-890)*

Knight Transportation Inc ....E   614 308-4900
 Columbus *(G-7916)*

Ktib Inc ....E   330 722-7935
 Medina *(G-13967)*

Kuhnle Brothers Inc C   440 564-7168
 Newbury *(G-15122)*

Kuntzman Trucking Inc ....E   330 821-9160
 Alliance *(G-536)*

L V Trucking Inc ....E   614 275-4994
 Columbus *(G-7937)*

Lairson Trucking LLC ....E   513 894-0452
 Hamilton *(G-11621)*

Leaders Moving Company ....E   614 785-9595
 Worthington *(G-19822)*

Lesaint Logistics Inc C   513 874-3900
 West Chester *(G-18958)*

Locker Moving & Storage Inc ....E   330 784-0477
 Canton *(G-2380)*

LT Harnett Trucking Inc ....E   440 997-5528
 Ashtabula *(G-746)*

M C Trucking Company LLC ....E   937 584-2486
 Wilmington *(G-19632)*

Mail Contractors America Inc ....E   513 769-5967
 Cincinnati *(G-3962)*

Martin Trnsp Systems Inc ....D   419 726-1348
 Toledo *(G-17898)*

Masur Trucking Inc ....E   513 860-9600
 Cincinnati *(G-3978)*

Mid America Trucking Company ....E   216 447-0814
 Cleveland *(G-5981)*

Midway Delivery Service ....E   216 391-0700
 Cleveland *(G-5988)*

Midwest Logistics Systems ....B   419 584-1414
 Celina *(G-2605)*

Mikes Trucking Ltd ....E   614 879-8808
 Galloway *(G-11223)*

Moeller Trucking Inc ....D   419 925-4799
 Maria Stein *(G-13308)*

Monesi Trucking & Eqp Repr Inc ....E   614 921-9183
 Columbus *(G-8097)*

Montgomery Trucking Company ....E   740 384-2138
 Wellston *(G-18853)*

Murray Leasing Inc C   330 386-4757
 East Liverpool *(G-10408)*

Mwd Logistics Inc ....D   440 266-2500
 Mentor *(G-14091)*

Myers Machinery Movers Inc ....E   614 871-5052
 Grove City *(G-11455)*

National Highway Equipment Co ....D   614 459-4900
 Columbus *(G-8133)*

National Trnsp Solutions Inc ....D   330 405-2660
 Twinsburg *(G-18300)*

Nb Trucking Inc ....E   740 335-9331
 Washington Court Hou *(G-18784)*

▲ Neighborhood Logistics Co Inc ....E   440 466-0020
 Geneva *(G-11244)*

Nest Tenders Limited ....D   614 901-1570
 Columbus *(G-8170)*

Nicholas Carney-Mc Inc ....E   440 243-8560
 Sheffield Village *(G-16741)*

Nicolozakes Trckg & Cnstr Inc ....E   740 432-5648
 Cambridge *(G-2078)*

Northcoast Moving Enterprising ....E   440 943-3900
 Wickliffe *(G-19471)*

Northcutt Trucking Inc ....E   440 458-5139
 Elyria *(G-10548)*

Ohio Oil Gathering Corporation ....E   740 828-2892
 Nashport *(G-14821)*

Ohio Transport Corporation ....E   513 539-0576
 Middletown *(G-14316)*

One Way Express Incorporated ....E   440 439-9182
 Cleveland *(G-6135)*

Otis Wright & Sons Inc ....E   419 227-4400
 Lima *(G-12715)*

P & D Transportation Inc ....E   614 577-1130
 Columbus *(G-8405)*

P I & I Motor Express Inc C   330 448-4035
 Masury *(G-13741)*

Panther II Transportation Inc C   800 685-0657
 Medina *(G-13985)*

Panther Premium Logistics Inc ....B   800 685-0657
 Medina *(G-13986)*

Peak Transportation Inc ....D   419 874-5201
 Perrysburg *(G-15899)*

▲ Peoples Services Inc ....E   330 453-3709
 Canton *(G-2437)*

PGT Trucking Inc ....E   419 943-3437
 Leipsic *(G-12521)*

Pierceton Trucking Co Inc ....E   740 446-0114
 Gallipolis *(G-11211)*

Pitt-Ohio Express LLC ....D   513 860-3424
 West Chester *(G-19073)*

Pitt-Ohio Express LLC ....B   216 433-9000
 Cleveland *(G-6215)*

Powers Equipment ....E   740 746-8220
 Sugar Grove *(G-17375)*

Prestige Delivery Systems LLC ....E   614 836-8980
 Groveport *(G-11531)*

Pride Transportation Inc ....E   419 424-2145
 Findlay *(G-10956)*

Priority Dispatch Inc ....E   513 791-3900
 Blue Ash *(G-1631)*

Priority Dispatch Inc ....E   216 332-9852
 Solon *(G-16885)*

Professional Drivers GA Inc ....E   614 529-8282
 Columbus *(G-8467)*

Proline Xpress Inc ....E   440 777-8120
 North Olmsted *(G-15306)*

Quick Delivery Service Inc ....E   330 453-3709
 Canton *(G-2447)*

R & J Trucking Inc ....E   800 262-9365
 Youngstown *(G-20171)*

R & J Trucking Inc ....D   330 758-0841
 Shelby *(G-16750)*

R & J Trucking Inc ....D   740 374-3050
 Marietta *(G-13374)*

R & J Trucking Inc ....D   440 960-1508
 Lorain *(G-12939)*

R & J Trucking Inc ....E   419 837-9937
 Perrysburg *(G-15910)*

R & L Transfer Inc C   216 531-3324
 Norwalk *(G-15453)*

R & L Transfer Inc C   330 482-5800
 Columbiana *(G-6791)*

R & M Delivery ....E   740 574-2113
 Franklin Furnace *(G-11047)*

R & R Sanitation Inc .... E 330 325-2311
Mogadore (G-14555)
R E Watson Inc .... E 513 863-0070
Hamilton (G-11634)
Rainbow Express Inc .... D 614 444-5600
Columbus (G-8485)
Ramos Trucking Corporation ...... E 216 781-0770
Cleveland (G-6285)
Rapid Delivery Service Co Inc ..... E 513 733-0500
Cincinnati (G-4337)
Ray Bertolini Trucking Co .... E 330 867-0666
Akron (G-397)
Ray Hamilton Companies .... E 513 641-5400
Blue Ash (G-1640)
Reis Trucking Inc .... E 513 353-1960
Cleves (G-6734)
Reliable Appl Installation Inc ...... E 614 817-1801
Columbus (G-8511)
Reliable Appl Installation Inc ...... E 614 246-6840
Columbus (G-8512)
Reliable Appl Installation Inc ...... E 330 784-7474
Akron (G-401)
Rick Kuntz Trucking Inc .... E 330 296-9311
Windham (G-9663)
Ricketts Excavating Inc .... E 740 687-0338
Lancaster (G-12430)
Rising Sun Express LLC .... D 937 596-6167
Jackson Center (G-12185)
River City Furniture LLC .... D 513 612-7303
West Chester (G-18994)
Rjw Trucking Company Ltd .... D 740 363-5343
Delaware (G-10004)
Rmx Freight Systems Inc .... E 740 849-2374
Roseville (G-16455)
Robert M Neff Inc .... D 614 444-1562
Columbus (G-8543)
Robert Neff & Son Inc .... E 740 454-0128
Zanesville (G-20359)
Ron Carrocce Trucking Company ... C 330 758-0841
Youngstown (G-20192)
Rood Trucking Company Inc .... D 330 652-3519
Mineral Ridge (G-14512)
Rose Transport Inc .... E 614 864-4004
Reynoldsburg (G-16330)
Ross Consolidated Corp .... D 440 748-5800
Grafton (G-11320)
Rt80 Express Inc .... E 330 706-0900
Barberton (G-966)
Rumpke Waste Inc .... D 937 378-4126
Georgetown (G-11274)
Rumpke Waste Inc .... D 513 242-4401
Cincinnati (G-4412)
Rumpke Waste Inc .... C 937 548-1939
Greenville (G-11393)
Rush Package Delivery Inc .... E 937 224-7874
Dayton (G-9742)
Rush Package Delivery Inc .... D 937 297-6182
Dayton (G-9743)
Rush Package Delivery Inc .... E 513 771-7874
Cincinnati (G-4413)
S B Morabito Trucking Inc .... D 216 441-3070
Cleveland (G-6355)
Sanfrey Freight Services Inc ...... E 330 372-1883
Warren (G-18740)
Santmyer Oil Co Inc .... D 330 262-6501
Wooster (G-19764)
Schindewolf Express Inc .... D 937 585-5919
De Graff (G-9900)
Schroeder Associates Inc .... E 419 258-5075
Antwerp (G-614)
SDS Earth Moving Inc .... E 330 358-2132
Diamond (G-10061)
Sebastiani Trucking Inc .... D 330 286-0059
Canfield (G-2158)
▲ Sewell Leasing Corporation ..... D 937 382-3847
Wilmington (G-19648)
Shoreline Transportation Inc ...... C 440 878-2000
Strongsville (G-17345)
Sidle Transit Service Inc .... E 330 683-2807
Orrville (G-15647)
Slay Transportation Co Inc .... C 740 865-2910
Sardis (G-16661)
Spears Transf & Expediting Inc .... E 937 275-2443
Dayton (G-9782)
Spring Grove Rsrce Rcovery Inc ... D 513 681-6242
Cincinnati (G-4519)
Stack Container Service Inc .... D 216 531-7555
Euclid (G-10657)
State-Wide Express Inc .... D 216 676-4600
Cleveland (G-6460)

Strawser Equipment & Lsg Inc .... D 614 444-2521
Columbus (G-8706)
Style Crest Transport Inc .... D 419 332-7369
Fremont (G-11101)
Su-Jon Enterprises .... E 330 372-1100
Warren (G-18749)
Sylvester Materials Co .... E 419 841-3874
Sylvania (G-17457)
T R L Inc .... C 330 448-4071
Brookfield (G-1856)
T&T Enterprises of Ohio Inc .... E 513 942-1141
West Chester (G-19088)
Ted Ruck Co Inc .... E 419 738-2613
Wapakoneta (G-18655)
Tesar Industrial Contrs Inc .... E 216 741-8008
Cleveland (G-6517)
Tfh-Eb Inc .... D 614 253-7246
Columbus (G-8741)
Thomas Transport Delivery Inc .... E 330 908-3100
Macedonia (G-13084)
Todd A Ruck Inc .... E 614 527-9927
Hilliard (G-11822)
Top Dawg Group LLC .... E 216 398-1066
Brooklyn Heights (G-1883)
Total Package Express Inc .... E 513 741-5500
Cincinnati (G-4611)
Trans Vac Inc .... E 419 229-8192
Lima (G-12767)
Trans-States Express Inc .... D 513 679-7100
Cincinnati (G-4627)
Transmerica Svcs Technical Sup ... E 740 282-3695
Steubenville (G-17175)
Transportation Unlimited Inc .... A 216 426-0088
Cleveland (G-6544)
Tricont Trucking Company .... E 614 527-7398
Columbus (G-8778)
Trio Trucking Inc .... E 513 679-7100
Cincinnati (G-4649)
Triple Ladys Agency Inc .... E 330 274-1100
Mantua (G-13277)
Tsm Logistics LLC .... E 419 234-6074
Rockford (G-16418)
TV Minority Company Inc .... E 937 226-1559
Dayton (G-9826)
Two Men & Truck Inc .... E 419 882-1002
Toledo (G-18113)
U-Haul Neighborhood Dealer -Ce ... E 419 929-3724
New London (G-14936)
Universal Disposal Inc .... C 440 286-3153
Chardon (G-2720)
UPS Ground Freight Inc .... C 330 659-6693
Richfield (G-16382)
UPS Ground Freight Inc .... E 937 236-4700
Dayton (G-9843)
USF Holland Inc .... D 740 441-1200
Gallipolis (G-11216)
USF Holland LLC .... C 937 233-7600
Dayton (G-9845)
USF Holland LLC .... C 513 874-8960
West Chester (G-19097)
USF Holland LLC .... D 614 529-9300
Columbus (G-8836)
USF Holland LLC .... C 216 941-4340
Cleveland (G-6612)
Vallejo Company .... E 216 741-3933
Cleveland (G-6616)
Van Howards Lines Inc .... E 937 235-0007
Dayton (G-9848)
Van Mills Lines Inc .... C 440 846-0200
Strongsville (G-17357)
Varney Dispatch Inc .... E 513 682-4200
Cincinnati (G-4751)
Veritas Enterprises Inc .... E 513 578-2748
Cincinnati (G-2874)
▲ Vexor Technology Inc .... E 330 721-9773
Medina (G-14013)
Veyance Industrial Svcs Inc .... E 307 682-7855
Fairlawn (G-10854)
Vin Devers 888 847-9535
Sylvania (G-17462)
Vision Express Inc .... E 740 922-8848
Uhrichsville (G-18348)
W L Logan Trucking Company ..... C 330 478-1404
Canton (G-2529)
Waste Management Ohio Inc ...... D 440 201-1235
Solon (G-16913)
Waste Management Ohio Inc ...... D 800 343-6047
Fairborn (G-10688)
Waste Management Ohio Inc ...... E 440 286-7116
Chardon (G-2724)

Waste Management Ohio Inc ...... C 800 343-6047
Fairborn (G-10689)
Wendel Poultry Service Inc .... E 419 375-2439
Fort Recovery (G-10995)
Werlor Inc .... E 419 784-4285
Defiance (G-9946)
Westhafer Trucking Inc .... E 330 698-3030
Apple Creek (G-622)
William Hafer Drayage Inc .... E 513 771-5000
Cincinnati (G-4796)
Wnb Group LLC .... E 513 641-5400
Cincinnati (G-4801)
Wooster Motor Ways Inc .... C 330 264-9557
Wooster (G-19786)
Wright Brothers Aero Inc .... E 937 454-8475
Dayton (G-9887)
Wright Material Solutions Ltd ...... E 614 530-6999
Columbus (G-8920)
Xpo Logistics Freight Inc .... C 513 870-0044
West Chester (G-19100)
Xpo Logistics Freight Inc .... C 216 433-1000
Parma (G-15780)
Xpo Logistics Freight Inc .... C 614 876-7100
Columbus (G-8924)
Xpo Logistics Freight Inc .... D 330 896-7300
Uniontown (G-18391)
Yrc Inc .... D 330 659-4151
Richfield (G-16385)
Yrc Inc .... B 419 729-0631
Toledo (G-18174)
Zeiter Trucking Inc .... E 419 668-2229
Norwalk (G-15460)
Zemba Bros Inc .... E 740 452-1880
Zanesville (G-20388)
Zone Transportation Co .... D 440 324-3544
Elyria (G-10577)

4213 Trucking, Except Local

1st Carrier Corp .... D 740 477-2587
Circleville (G-4821)
A C Leasing Company .... E 513 771-3676
Cincinnati (G-2890)
A L Smith Trucking Inc .... E 937 526-3651
Versailles (G-18565)
A&R Logistics Inc .... D 614 444-4111
Columbus (G-6849)
ABF Freight System Inc .... D 440 843-4600
Cleveland (G-4893)
ABF Freight System Inc .... E 614 294-3537
Columbus (G-6852)
ABF Freight System Inc .... E 937 236-2210
Dayton (G-9202)
ABF Freight System Inc .... E 513 779-7888
West Chester (G-18858)
ABF Freight System Inc .... E 330 549-3800
North Lima (G-15261)
Accelerated Moving & Stor Inc .... E 614 836-1007
Columbus (G-6859)
Ace Doran Hauling & Rigging Co ... D 513 681-7900
Cincinnati (G-2903)
Advantage Tank Lines Inc .... E 330 491-0474
North Canton (G-15185)
Advantage Tank Lines Inc .... C 330 427-1010
Leetonia (G-12518)
AG Trucking Inc .... E 937 497-7770
Sidney (G-16757)
Akron Centl Engrv Mold Mch Inc ... E 330 794-8704
Akron (G-30)
All Industrial Group Inc .... E 216 441-2000
Newburgh Heights (G-15113)
All Pro Freight Systems Inc .... D 440 934-2222
Westlake (G-19313)
Alpha Freight Systems Inc .... D 800 394-9001
Hudson (G-11965)
Ameri-Line Inc .... E 440 316-4500
Columbia Station (G-6769)
American Power LLC .... E 937 235-0418
Dayton (G-9229)
Arctic Express Inc .... C 614 876-4008
Hilliard (G-11743)
Arms Trucking Co Inc .... E 800 362-1343
Huntsburg (G-12016)
◆ As Logistics Inc .... D 513 863-4627
Liberty Township (G-12577)
Autumn Industries Inc .... E 330 372-5002
Warren (G-18671)
Awl Transport Inc .... E 330 899-3444
Mantua (G-13264)
Awrs LLC .... E 888 611-2292
Cincinnati (G-3009)

B & H Industries Inc E 419 485-8373 Montpelier *(G-14605)*

B & T Express Inc D 330 549-0000 North Lima *(G-15265)*

B D Transportation Inc E 937 773-9280 Piqua *(G-15996)*

Bantam Leasing Inc E 513 734-6696 Amelia *(G-570)*

Barnets Inc E 937 452-3275 Camden *(G-2088)*

Bell Moving and Storage Inc E 513 942-7500 Fairfield *(G-10699)*

Berlin Transportaion LLC E 330 674-3395 Millersburg *(G-14459)*

Besl Transfer Co E 513 242-3456 Cincinnati *(G-3042)*

Best Way Motor Lines Inc C 419 485-8373 Montpelier *(G-14606)*

Bestway Transport Co E 419 687-2000 Plymouth *(G-16076)*

Black Horse Carriers Inc C 330 225-2250 Hinckley *(G-11858)*

Blatt Trucking Co Inc E 419 898-0002 Rocky Ridge *(G-16419)*

Blb Transport Inc E 740 474-1341 Circleville *(G-4825)*

Bobs Moraine Trucking Inc E 937 746-8420 Franklin *(G-11024)*

Bowling Transportation Inc D 419 436-9590 Fostoria *(G-10998)*

Brendamour Moving & Stor Inc D 800 354-9715 Cincinnati *(G-3071)*

Brent Burris Trucking LLC E 419 759-2020 Ada *(G-2)*

Brookside Holdings LLC E 419 925-4457 Maria Stein *(G-13306)*

Bryan Truck Line Inc D 419 485-8373 Montpelier *(G-14609)*

Building Systems Trnsp Co C 740 852-9700 London *(G-12861)*

Bulk Transit Corporation E 614 873-4632 Plain City *(G-16047)*

Bulk Transit Corporation E 937 497-9573 Sidney *(G-16763)*

Bulkmatic Transport Company E 614 497-2372 Columbus *(G-7097)*

Burd Brothers Inc E 800 538-2873 Batavia *(G-984)*

By-Line Transit Inc E 937 642-2500 Marysville *(G-13486)*

C&K Trucking LLC E 440 657-5249 Elyria *(G-10485)*

Carrier Industries Inc B 614 851-6363 Columbus *(G-7131)*

Carry Transport Inc E 937 236-0026 Dayton *(G-9283)*

Cassens Transport Company C 937 644-8886 Marysville *(G-13488)*

Cassens Transport Company C 419 727-0520 Toledo *(G-17639)*

Cavins Trucking & Garage LLC E 419 661-9947 Perrysburg *(G-15847)*

Century Lines Inc E 216 271-0700 Cleveland *(G-5160)*

Chambers Leasing Systems E 937 547-9777 Greenville *(G-11369)*

Chambers Leasing Systems Corp E 419 726-9747 Toledo *(G-17646)*

Cimarron Express Inc D 419 855-7713 Genoa *(G-11252)*

Circle S Transport Inc E 614 207-2184 Columbus *(G-7203)*

Circle T Logistics Inc E 740 262-5096 Marion *(G-13411)*

City Dash LLC C 513 562-2000 Cincinnati *(G-3298)*

Clark Trucking Inc C 937 642-0335 East Liberty *(G-10390)*

Classic Carriers Inc E 937 604-8118 Versailles *(G-18567)*

Clayton Weaver Trucking Inc E 513 896-6932 Fairfield *(G-10714)*

Cle Transportation Company D 567 805-4008 Norwalk *(G-15428)*

Cleveland Express Trckg Co Inc D 216 348-0922 Cleveland *(G-5253)*

Competitive Transportation E 419 529-5300 Bellville *(G-1388)*

Concept Freight Service Inc E 330 784-1134 New Franklin *(G-14908)*

Containerport Group Inc E 440 333-1330 Columbus *(G-7355)*

Containerport Group Inc E 216 341-4800 Cleveland *(G-5343)*

Continental Express Inc B 937 497-2100 Sidney *(G-16767)*

Contract Freighters Inc A 614 577-0447 Reynoldsburg *(G-16294)*

Cooper Brothers Trucking LLC E 330 784-1717 Akron *(G-158)*

Corrigan Moving Systems-Ann AR E 419 874-2900 Perrysburg *(G-15850)*

Cotter Moving & Storage Co E 330 535-5115 Akron *(G-161)*

Covenant Transport Inc D 423 821-1212 Columbus *(G-7383)*

Cowan Systems LLC C 513 769-4774 Cincinnati *(G-3376)*

Cowan Systems LLC C 513 721-6444 West Chester *(G-18903)*

Cowan Systems LLC E 330 963-8483 Twinsburg *(G-18257)*

Cowen Truck Line Inc D 419 938-3401 Perrysville *(G-15940)*

Coy Brothers Inc E 330 533-6864 Canfield *(G-2134)*

Craig Transportation Co E 419 874-7981 Maumee *(G-13777)*

Crescent Park Corporation C 513 759-7000 West Chester *(G-18906)*

Crete Carrier Corporation C 614 853-4500 Columbus *(G-7391)*

CRST International Inc D 740 599-0008 Danville *(G-9149)*

Crw Inc D 330 264-3785 Shreve *(G-16753)*

D L Belknap Trucking Inc D 330 868-7766 Paris *(G-15756)*

Dart Trucking Company Inc E 330 549-0994 North Lima *(G-15268)*

Daves Sand & Stone Inc E 419 445-9256 Wauseon *(G-18798)*

Davidson Trucking Inc E 419 288-2318 Bradner *(G-1764)*

Dayton Freight Lines Inc E 419 661-8600 Perrysburg *(G-15854)*

Dayton Freight Lines Inc E 614 860-1080 Columbus *(G-7422)*

Dayton Freight Lines Inc D 937 236-4880 Dayton *(G-9366)*

Dayton Freight Lines Inc E 330 346-0750 Kent *(G-12227)*

Dedicated Logistics Inc D 513 275-1135 West Chester *(G-18909)*

Dedicated Transport LLC C 216 641-2500 Brooklyn Heights *(G-1869)*

Dhl Supply Chain (usa) E 614 492-6614 Lockbourne *(G-12814)*

Dhl Supply Chain (usa) E 513 942-1575 Cincinnati *(G-3426)*

Diamond Heavy Haul Inc E 330 677-8061 Kent *(G-12228)*

Dick Lavy Trucking Inc C 937 448-2104 Bradford *(G-1761)*

Dill-Elam Inc E 513 575-0017 Loveland *(G-12991)*

Dingledine Trucking Company E 937 652-3454 Urbana *(G-18431)*

Dist-Trans Inc C 614 497-1660 Columbus *(G-7453)*

Distribution and Trnsp Svc Inc E 937 295-3343 Fort Loramie *(G-10985)*

Disttech LLC D 800 321-3143 Cleveland *(G-5429)*

Dlc Transport Inc E 740 282-1763 Steubenville *(G-17152)*

Drasc Enterprises Inc E 330 852-3254 Sugarcreek *(G-17377)*

Drew Ag-Transport Inc D 937 548-3200 Greenville *(G-11376)*

Dworkin Inc E 216 271-5318 Cleveland *(G-5452)*

Elmco Trucking Inc E 419 983-2010 Bloomville *(G-1492)*

Erie Trucking Inc E 419 625-7374 Sandusky *(G-16602)*

Estes Express Lines Inc D 440 327-3884 North Ridgeville *(G-15329)*

Estes Express Lines Inc C 614 275-6000 Columbus *(G-7538)*

Estes Express Lines Inc E 419 531-1500 Toledo *(G-17718)*

Estes Express Lines Inc D 937 237-7536 Huber Heights *(G-11954)*

Estes Express Lines Inc D 419 522-2641 Mansfield *(G-13173)*

Estes Express Lines Inc D 513 779-9581 West Chester *(G-18920)*

Estes Express Lines Inc E 740 401-0410 Belpre *(G-1403)*

Excel Trucking LLC E 614 826-1988 Columbus *(G-7542)*

Exel Holdings (usa) Inc C 614 865-8500 Westerville *(G-19161)*

◆ **Exel Inc** B 614 865-8500 Westerville *(G-19163)*

Express Twing Recovery Svc Inc E 513 881-1900 West Chester *(G-19051)*

F S T Express Inc D 614 529-7900 Columbus *(G-7551)*

Falcon Transport Co C 330 793-1345 Youngstown *(G-20034)*

Falcon Transport Co D 330 793-1345 Youngstown *(G-20035)*

FANTON Logistics Inc D 216 341-2400 Cleveland *(G-5512)*

Federal Express Corporation B 614 492-6106 Columbus *(G-7568)*

Fedex Freight Inc D 330 645-0879 Akron *(G-218)*

Fedex Freight Inc C 937 233-4826 Dayton *(G-9430)*

Fedex Freight Corporation E 877 661-8956 Mentor *(G-14047)*

Fedex Freight Corporation E 419 729-1755 Toledo *(G-17730)*

Fedex Freight Corporation E 800 390-0159 Mansfield *(G-13175)*

Fedex Freight Corporation E 800 521-3505 Lima *(G-12641)*

Fedex Freight Corporation D 800 344-6448 West Jefferson *(G-19107)*

Fedex Freight Corporation C 800 728-8190 Northwood *(G-15394)*

Fedex Freight Corporation E 800 354-9489 Zanesville *(G-20307)*

Fedex Ground Package Sys Inc C 800 463-3339 Columbus *(G-7571)*

Fedex Ground Package Sys Inc D 513 942-4330 West Chester *(G-19052)*

Fedex Ground Package Sys Inc B 800 463-3339 Grove City *(G-11432)*

Ferrous Metal Transfer E 216 671-8500 Brooklyn *(G-1861)*

Fetter and Son LLC E 740 465-2961 Morral *(G-14711)*

Fetter Son Farms Ltd Lblty Co E 740 465-2961 Morral *(G-14712)*

First Group Investment Partnr D 513 241-2200 Cincinnati *(G-3558)*

Firstenterprises Inc B 740 369-5100 Delaware *(G-9976)*

Firstgroup Usa Inc B 513 241-2200 Cincinnati *(G-3569)*

Five Star Trucking Inc E 440 953-9300 Willoughby *(G-19524)*

Fleetmaster Express Inc D 419 420-1835 Findlay *(G-10909)*

Foodliner Inc E 937 898-0075 Dayton *(G-9443)*

Foodliner Inc E 563 451-1047 Dayton *(G-9444)*

Foster Sales & Delivery Inc D 740 245-0200 Bidwell *(G-1468)*

Fraley & Schilling Inc C 740 598-4118 Brilliant *(G-1822)*

Franklin Specialty Trnspt Inc E 614 529-7900 Columbus *(G-7620)*

G & S Transfer Inc E 330 673-3899 Kent *(G-12233)*

Garber Ag Freight Inc E 937 548-8400 Greenville *(G-11378)*

Garner Trucking Inc C 419 422-5742 Findlay *(G-10912)*

General Transport Incorporated E 330 786-3400 Akron *(G-233)*

Glm Transport Inc E 419 363-2041 Rockford *(G-16415)*

Global Workplace Solutions LLC E 513 759-6000 West Chester *(G-18933)*

Globe Trucking Inc..................D...... 419 727-8307
  Toledo (G-17765)
GMC Excavation & Trucking..........E...... 419 468-0121
  Galion (G-11177)
Golden Hawk Transportation Co..........D...... 419 683-3304
  Crestline (G-9056)
Greater Dayton Mvg & Stor Co..........E...... 937 235-0011
  Dayton (G-9471)
Green Lines Transportation Inc..........E...... 330 863-2111
  Malvern (G-13123)
Guenther & Sons Inc..........E...... 513 738-1448
  Ross (G-16456)
H O C J Inc..........E...... 614 539-4601
  Grove City (G-11439)
Harris Distributing Co..........E...... 513 541-4222
  Cincinnati (G-3681)
Hillandale Farms Trnsp..........D...... 740 893-2232
  Johnstown (G-12201)
Hillsboro Transportation Co..........E...... 513 772-9223
  Cincinnati (G-3707)
Hilltrux Tank Lines Inc..........E...... 330 538-3700
  North Jackson (G-15246)
Hofstetter Orran Inc..........E...... 330 683-8070
  Orrville (G-15634)
Homan Transportation Inc..........D...... 419 465-2626
  Monroeville (G-14588)
Home Run Inc..........E...... 800 543-9198
  Xenia (G-19910)
Hoosier Express Inc..........E...... 419 436-9590
  Fostoria (G-11006)
Horizon Freight System Inc..........E...... 216 341-7410
  Cleveland (G-5706)
Horizon Mid Atlantic Inc..........D...... 800 480-6829
  Cleveland (G-5707)
Horizon South Inc..........D...... 800 480-6829
  Cleveland (G-5708)
Hs Express LLC..........D...... 419 729-2400
  Toledo (G-17810)
HTI - Hall Trucking Inc..........E...... 419 423-9555
  Findlay (G-10924)
Huntley Trucking Co..........E...... 740 385-7615
  New Plymouth (G-14991)
Hyway Trucking Company..........D...... 419 423-7145
  Findlay (G-10926)
Integres Global Logistics Inc..........D...... 866 347-2101
  Medina (G-13955)
J & B Leasing Inc of Ohio..........E...... 419 269-1440
  Toledo (G-17826)
J & J Carriers LLC..........E...... 614 447-2615
  Columbus (G-7849)
J B Hunt Transport Inc..........C...... 419 547-2777
  Clyde (G-6746)
J M T Cartage Inc..........E...... 330 478-2430
  Canton (G-2359)
J P Jenks Inc..........E...... 440 428-4500
  Madison (G-13098)
J P Transportation Company..........E...... 513 424-6978
  Middletown (G-14304)
J T Express Inc..........E...... 513 727-8185
  Monroe (G-14570)
J-Trac Inc..........E...... 419 524-3456
  Mansfield (G-13189)
Jack Cooper Transport Co Inc..........C...... 440 949-2044
  Sheffield Village (G-16736)
Jaro Transportation Svcs Inc..........D...... 330 393-5659
  Warren (G-18718)
Jarrells Moving & Transport Co..........D...... 330 764-4333
  Seville (G-16686)
JB Hunt Transport Svcs Inc..........A...... 614 335-6681
  Columbus (G-7855)
Jet Express Inc..........D...... 937 274-7033
  Dayton (G-9524)
K & L Trucking Inc..........E...... 419 822-3836
  Delta (G-10046)
K & P Trucking LLC..........D...... 419 935-8646
  Willard (G-19482)
K-Limited Carrier Ltd..........C...... 419 269-0002
  Toledo (G-17834)
Kaplan Trucking Company..........D...... 216 341-3322
  Cleveland (G-5813)
Kenan Advantage Group Inc..........C...... 800 969-5419
  North Canton (G-15216)
Keystone Freight Corp..........E...... 614 542-0320
  Columbus (G-7899)
KF Express LLC..........E...... 614 258-8858
  Powell (G-16201)
Klingshirn & Sons Trucking..........E...... 937 338-5000
  Burkettsville (G-2012)
Kllee Trucking Inc..........D...... 740 867-6454
  Chesapeake (G-2730)

Kmj Leasing Ltd..........E...... 614 871-3883
  Orient (G-15620)
Knight Transportation Inc..........D...... 614 308-4900
  Columbus (G-7916)
Knight-Swift Trnsp Hldings Inc..........D...... 614 274-5204
  Columbus (G-7917)
Kuhnle Brothers Inc..........C...... 440 564-7168
  Newbury (G-15122)
Kuntzman Trucking Inc..........E...... 330 821-9160
  Alliance (G-536)
L A King Trucking Inc..........E...... 419 727-9398
  Toledo (G-17845)
L J Navy Trucking Company..........E...... 614 754-8929
  Columbus (G-7935)
L O G Transportation Inc..........E...... 440 891-0850
  Berea (G-1429)
L V Trucking Inc..........E...... 614 275-4994
  Columbus (G-7937)
La King Trucking Inc..........E...... 419 225-9039
  Lima (G-12672)
Lewis & Michael Inc..........E...... 937 252-6683
  Dayton (G-9564)
Lincoln Moving & Storage Co..........D...... 216 741-5500
  Cleveland (G-5871)
Liquid Transport Corp..........E...... 513 769-4777
  Cincinnati (G-3937)
Locker Moving & Storage Inc..........E...... 330 784-0477
  Canton (G-2380)
Logos Logistics Inc..........E...... 734 304-1777
  Toledo (G-17857)
LT Harnett Trucking Inc..........E...... 440 997-5528
  Ashtabula (G-746)
Lt Trucking Inc..........E...... 440 997-5528
  Ashtabula (G-747)
Luckey Transfer LLC..........D...... 800 435-4371
  Lima (G-12694)
Lyden Company..........E...... 419 868-6800
  Toledo (G-17874)
Lykins Companies Inc..........E...... 513 831-8820
  Milford (G-14403)
Lykins Transportation Inc..........D...... 513 831-8820
  Milford (G-14405)
M & B Trucking Express Corp..........E...... 440 236-8820
  Columbia Station (G-6777)
Maines Collision Repr & Bdy Sp..........E...... 937 322-4618
  Springfield (G-17066)
Mansfield Whsng & Dist Inc..........E...... 419 522-3510
  Ontario (G-15560)
Martin Trnsp Systems Inc..........D...... 419 726-1348
  Toledo (G-17898)
Mast Trucking Inc..........D...... 330 674-8913
  Millersburg (G-14482)
Material Suppliers Inc..........E...... 419 298-2440
  Edgerton (G-10468)
McFarland Truck Lines Inc..........E...... 937 854-2200
  Dayton (G-9594)
McMullen Transportation LLC..........E...... 937 981-4455
  Greenfield (G-11364)
Merchants 5 Star Ltd..........D...... 740 373-0313
  Marietta (G-13358)
Miami Valley Bekins Inc..........E...... 937 278-4296
  Dayton (G-9615)
Midfitz Inc..........E...... 216 663-8816
  Cleveland (G-5984)
Midwest Logistics Systems..........B...... 419 584-1414
  Celina (G-2605)
Miller Transfer and Rigging Co..........D...... 330 325-2521
  Rootstown (G-16452)
Millis Transfer Inc..........E...... 513 863-0222
  Hamilton (G-11630)
Mitchell & Sons Moving & Stor..........E...... 419 289-3311
  Ashland (G-681)
Mizar Motors Inc..........D...... 419 729-2400
  Toledo (G-17919)
Moeller Trucking Inc..........E...... 419 925-4799
  Maria Stein (G-13308)
Montgomery Trucking Company..........E...... 740 384-2138
  Wellston (G-18853)
Moore Transport of Tulsa LLC..........D...... 419 726-4499
  Toledo (G-17923)
Motor Carrier Service Inc..........E...... 419 693-6207
  Northwood (G-15399)
Murray Leasing Inc..........C...... 330 386-4757
  East Liverpool (G-10408)
Myers Machinery Movers Inc..........E...... 614 871-5052
  Grove City (G-11455)
National Highway Equipment Co..........D...... 614 459-4900
  Columbus (G-8133)
National Trnsp Solutions Inc..........D...... 330 405-2660
  Twinsburg (G-18300)

Nationwide Truck Brokers Inc..........E...... 937 335-9229
  Troy (G-18217)
New World Van Lines Ohio Inc..........E...... 614 836-5720
  Groveport (G-11527)
Nick Strimbu Inc..........D...... 330 448-4046
  Brookfield (G-1855)
Nick Strimbu Inc..........D...... 330 448-4046
  Dover (G-10091)
Nicolozakes Trckg & Cnstr Inc..........E...... 740 432-5648
  Cambridge (G-2078)
Noramco Transport Corp..........E...... 513 245-9050
  Cincinnati (G-4122)
Oeder Carl E Sons Sand & Grav..........E...... 513 494-1238
  Lebanon (G-12488)
Ohio Auto Delivery Inc..........E...... 614 277-1445
  Grove City (G-11461)
Ohio Oil Gathering Corporation..........E...... 740 828-2892
  Nashport (G-14821)
Old Dominion Freight Line Inc..........E...... 330 545-8628
  Girard (G-11296)
Old Dominion Freight Line Inc..........E...... 937 235-1596
  Dayton (G-9674)
Old Dominion Freight Line Inc..........E...... 513 771-1486
  West Chester (G-18979)
Old Dominion Freight Line Inc..........E...... 419 726-4032
  Toledo (G-17959)
Old Dominion Freight Line Inc..........B...... 614 491-3903
  Columbus (G-8369)
Old Dominion Freight Line Inc..........E...... 216 641-5566
  Cleveland (G-6127)
One Way Express Incorporated..........E...... 440 439-9182
  Cleveland (G-6135)
Osborne Trucking Company..........D...... 513 874-2090
  Fairfield (G-10766)
Otis Wright & Sons Inc..........E...... 419 227-4400
  Lima (G-12715)
P & D Transportation Inc..........E...... 614 577-1130
  Columbus (G-8405)
P & D Transportation Inc..........C...... 740 454-1221
  Zanesville (G-20352)
P C C Refrigerated Ex Inc..........E...... 614 754-8929
  Columbus (G-8406)
P I & I Motor Express Inc..........C...... 330 448-4035
  Masury (G-13741)
PAm Transportation Svcs Inc..........D...... 419 935-9501
  Willard (G-19485)
Panther II Transportation Inc..........C...... 800 685-0657
  Medina (G-13985)
Panther Premium Logistics Inc..........B...... 800 685-0657
  Medina (G-13986)
Partnership LLC..........E...... 440 471-8310
  Cleveland (G-6178)
Peak Transportation Inc..........D...... 419 874-5201
  Perrysburg (G-15899)
Penske Logistics LLC..........D...... 216 765-5475
  Beachwood (G-1095)
Penske Logistics LLC..........D...... 330 626-7623
  Streetsboro (G-17265)
▲ Peoples Services Inc..........E...... 330 453-3709
  Canton (G-2437)
PGT Trucking Inc..........E...... 419 943-3437
  Leipsic (G-12521)
Piqua Transfer & Storage Co..........D...... 937 773-3743
  Piqua (G-16021)
Pitt-Ohio Express LLC..........C...... 614 801-1064
  Grove City (G-11465)
Pitt-Ohio Express LLC..........C...... 419 726-6523
  Toledo (G-17978)
Pitt-Ohio Express LLC..........D...... 513 860-3424
  West Chester (G-19073)
Pitt-Ohio Express LLC..........D...... 419 729-8173
  Toledo (G-17979)
Pitt-Ohio Express LLC..........B...... 216 433-9000
  Cleveland (G-6215)
Planes Moving & Storage Inc..........C...... 513 759-6000
  West Chester (G-18982)
Planes Mvg & Stor Co Columbus..........D...... 614 777-9090
  Columbus (G-8451)
Platinum Express Inc..........D...... 937 235-9540
  Dayton (G-9695)
Ploger Transportation LLC..........E...... 419 465-2100
  Bellevue (G-1383)
Predator Trucking Company..........E...... 419 849-2601
  Woodville (G-19682)
Premium Trnsp Logistics LLC..........D...... 419 861-3430
  Toledo (G-17985)
Pride Transportation Inc..........E...... 419 424-2145
  Findlay (G-10956)
Pros Freight Corporation..........E...... 440 543-7555
  Chagrin Falls (G-2679)

Quality Carriers Inc ....E 419 222-6800
Lima (G-12725)

R & J Trucking Inc ....D 740 374-3050
Marietta (G-13374)

R & L Carriers Inc ....E 419 874-5976
Perrysburg (G-15911)

R & L Transfer Inc ....C 216 531-3324
Norwalk (G-15453)

R & L Transfer Inc ....D 330 743-3609
Youngstown (G-20172)

R & L Transfer Inc ....C 330 482-5800
Columbiana (G-6791)

R & S Lines Inc ....E 419 682-7807
Stryker (G-17371)

R E Watson Inc ....E 513 863-0070
Hamilton (G-11634)

R K Campf Corp ....E 330 332-7089
Salem (G-16556)

R+l Pramount Trnsp Systems Inc ......B 937 382-1494
Wilmington (G-19642)

Rainbow Express Inc ....D 614 444-5600
Columbus (G-8485)

Ray Bertolini Trucking Co ....E 330 867-0666
Akron (G-397)

RDF Trucking Corporation ....D 440 282-9060
Lorain (G-12940)

Richard Wolfe Trucking Inc ....E 740 392-2445
Mount Vernon (G-14787)

Rising Sun Express LLC ....E 937 596-6167
Jackson Center (G-12185)

Robert G Owen Trucking Inc ....E 330 756-1013
Navarre (G-14825)

Robert M Neff Inc ....D 614 444-1562
Columbus (G-8543)

Robert Neff & Son Inc ....E 740 454-0128
Zanesville (G-20359)

Roeder Cartage Company Inc ....D 419 221-1600
Lima (G-12733)

Rollins Moving and Storage Inc ....E 937 525-4013
Springfield (G-17105)

Ron Burge Trucking Inc ....E 330 624-5373
Burbank (G-2009)

Rood Trucking Company Inc ....C 330 652-3519
Mineral Ridge (G-14512)

Roseville Motor Express Inc ....E 614 921-2121
Columbus (G-8553)

Ross Transportation Svcs Inc ....C 440 748-5900
Grafton (G-11322)

Rrr Express LLC ....C 800 723-3424
West Chester (G-18996)

Rt80 Express Inc ....E 330 706-0900
Barberton (G-966)

Ryder Last Mile Inc ....D 866 711-3129
New Albany (G-14873)

S & T Truck and Auto Svc Inc ....E 614 272-8163
Columbus (G-8569)

Saia Motor Freight Line LLC ....E 419 726-9761
Toledo (G-18017)

Saia Motor Freight Line LLC ....E 330 659-4277
Richfield (G-16377)

Saia Motor Freight Line LLC ....D 614 870-8778
Columbus (G-8582)

Sanfrey Freight Services Inc ....E 330 372-1883
Warren (G-18740)

Saro Truck Dispatch Inc ....E 419 873-1358
Perrysburg (G-15918)

Scheiderer Transport Inc ....D 614 873-5103
Plain City (G-16064)

Schindewolf Express Inc ....D 937 585-5919
De Graff (G-9900)

Schneider Nat Carriers Inc ....E 740 362-6910
Delaware (G-10006)

Schneider National Inc ....B 419 673-0254
Kenton (G-12287)

Schroeder Associates Inc ....E 419 258-5075
Antwerp (G-614)

Security Storage Co Inc ....D 513 961-2700
Cincinnati (G-4445)

▲ Sewell Leasing Corporation ....D 937 382-3847
Wilmington (G-19648)

Shetler Moving & Stor of Ohio ....E 513 755-0700
West Chester (G-19004)

Shippers Consolidated Dist ....E 216 579-9303
Cleveland (G-6405)

Shoreline Express Inc ....E 440 878-3750
Strongsville (G-17344)

Shoreline Transportation Inc ....C 440 878-2000
Strongsville (G-17345)

Short Freight Lines Inc ....E 419 729-1691
Toledo (G-18031)

Slay Transportation Co Inc ....C 740 865-2910
Sardis (G-16661)

Smith Trucking Inc ....E 419 841-8676
Sylvania (G-17452)

SMS Transport LLC ....E 937 813-8897
Dayton (G-9772)

Spader Freight Carriers Inc ....D 419 547-1117
Clyde (G-6753)

Spader Freight Services Inc ....D 419 547-1117
Clyde (G-6754)

State-Wide Express Inc ....E 216 676-4600
Cleveland (G-6460)

Store & Haul Inc ....E 419 238-4284
Van Wert (G-18489)

Style Crest Transport Inc ....D 419 332-7369
Fremont (G-11101)

Superior Bulk Logistics Inc ....E 513 874-3440
West Chester (G-19085)

Swx Enterprises Inc ....E 216 676-4600
Brookpark (G-1907)

T & L Transport Inc ....E 330 674-0655
Millersburg (G-14494)

Tersher Corporation ....D 440 439-8383
Strongsville (G-17352)

Tesar Industrial Contrs Inc ....E 216 741-8008
Cleveland (G-6517)

Tfi Transportation Inc ....E 330 332-4655
Salem (G-16564)

Thoman Weil Moving & Stor Co ....E 513 251-5000
Cincinnati (G-4601)

Thomas E Keller Trucking Inc ....E 419 784-4805
Defiance (G-9944)

Thomas Trucking Inc ....E 513 731-8411
Cincinnati (G-4603)

Three-D Transport Inc ....E 419 924-5368
West Unity (G-19141)

Thyssenkrupp Logistics Inc ....D 419 662-1800
Northwood (G-15407)

Titan Transfer Inc ....D 513 458-4233
West Chester (G-19016)

Tkx Logistics ....E 419 662-1800
Northwood (G-15409)

Total Package Express Inc ....E 513 741-5500
Cincinnati (G-4611)

Tpg Noramco LLC ....E 513 245-9050
Cincinnati (G-4624)

Trans-States Express Inc ....D 513 679-7100
Cincinnati (G-4627)

Transport Corp America Inc ....E 330 538-3328
North Jackson (G-15254)

Transportation Unlimited Inc ....A 216 426-0088
Cleveland (G-6544)

Triad Transport Inc ....E 614 491-9497
Columbus (G-8777)

Trio Trucking Inc ....E 513 679-7100
Cincinnati (G-4649)

Triple Ladys Agency Inc ....E 330 274-1100
Mantua (G-13277)

U S Xpress Inc ....E 937 328-4100
Springfield (G-17129)

U S Xpress Inc ....D 740 363-0700
Delaware (G-10012)

U S Xpress Inc ....C 740 452-4153
Zanesville (G-20369)

United Road Services Inc ....D 419 837-2703
Toledo (G-18120)

UPS Ground Freight Inc ....C 330 659-6693
Richfield (G-16382)

UPS Ground Freight Inc ....E 937 236-4700
Dayton (G-9843)

UPS Ground Freight Inc ....E 330 448-0440
Masury (G-13743)

USF Holland Inc ....D 740 441-1200
Gallipolis (G-11216)

USF Holland LLC ....E 513 874-8960
West Chester (G-19097)

USF Holland LLC ....D 419 354-6633
Bowling Green (G-1750)

USF Holland LLC ....C 614 529-9300
Columbus (G-8836)

USF Holland LLC ....D 330 549-2917
North Lima (G-15275)

USF Holland LLC ....E 937 233-7600
Dayton (G-9845)

USF Holland LLC ....E 216 941-4340
Cleveland (G-6612)

Valley Transportation Inc ....C 419 289-6200
Ashland (G-696)

Van Howards Lines Inc ....E 937 235-0007
Dayton (G-9848)

Van Mayberrys & Storage Inc ....E 937 298-8800
Moraine (G-14704)

Van Mills Lines Inc ....C 440 846-0200
Strongsville (G-17357)

Van Stevens Lines Inc ....E 419 729-8871
Toledo (G-18134)

Vance Road Enterprises Inc ....E 937 268-6953
Dayton (G-9849)

Venezia Transport Service Inc ....E 330 542-9735
New Middletown (G-14939)

Vision Express Inc ....E 740 922-8848
Uhrichsville (G-18348)

Vitran Express Inc ....C 614 870-2255
Columbus (G-8857)

Vitran Express Inc ....D 216 426-8584
Cleveland (G-6638)

Vitran Express Inc ....E 513 771-4894
West Chester (G-19033)

W L Logan Trucking Company ....C 330 478-1404
Canton (G-2529)

Wannemacher Enterprises Inc ....E 419 225-9060
Lima (G-12775)

Ward Trucking LLC ....E 330 659-6658
Richfield (G-16383)

Ward Trucking LLC ....E 614 275-3800
Columbus (G-8874)

Werner Enterprises Inc ....D 937 325-5403
Springfield (G-17134)

William R Morse ....E 440 352-2600
Painesville (G-15748)

World Shipping Inc ....E 440 356-7676
Cleveland (G-6690)

Xpo Cnw Inc ....C 440 716-8971
North Olmsted (G-15317)

Xpo Logistics Freight Inc ....C 513 870-0044
West Chester (G-19100)

Xpo Logistics Freight Inc ....E 937 898-9808
Dayton (G-9888)

Xpo Logistics Freight Inc ....E 419 499-8888
Milan (G-14368)

Xpo Logistics Freight Inc ....C 216 433-1000
Parma (G-15780)

Xpo Logistics Freight Inc ....E 740 894-3859
South Point (G-16947)

Xpo Logistics Freight Inc ....C 330 824-2242
Warren (G-18775)

Xpo Logistics Freight Inc ....E 419 294-5728
Upper Sandusky (G-18418)

Xpo Logistics Freight Inc ....D 419 666-3022
Perrysburg (G-15937)

Xpo Logistics Freight Inc ....E 937 364-2361
Hillsboro (G-11856)

Xpo Logistics Freight Inc ....E 740 922-5614
Uhrichsville (G-18349)

Xpo Logistics Freight Inc ....D 330 896-7300
Uniontown (G-18391)

Xpo Logistics Freight Inc ....E 937 492-3899
Sidney (G-16806)

Xpo Logistics Freight Inc ....C 614 876-7100
Columbus (G-8924)

Yowell Transportation Svc Inc ....D 937 294-5933
Moraine (G-14709)

Yrc Inc ....C 513 874-9320
West Chester (G-19101)

Yrc Inc ....D 330 659-4151
Richfield (G-16385)

Yrc Inc ....B 419 729-0631
Toledo (G-18174)

Yrc Inc ....C 330 665-0274
Copley (G-8981)

Yrc Inc ....E 614 878-9281
Columbus (G-8933)

Zartran LLC ....D 513 870-4800
Hamilton (G-11656)

Zone Transportation Co ....D 440 324-3544
Elyria (G-10577)

4214 Local Trucking With Storage

A C Leasing Company ....E 513 771-3676
Cincinnati (G-2890)

Abco Contracting LLC ....E 419 973-4772
Toledo (G-17580)

Accelerated Moving & Stor Inc ....E 614 836-1007
Columbus (G-6859)

All My Sons Business Dev Corp ....C 469 461-5000
Cleveland (G-4934)

All Pro Freight Systems Inc ....D 440 934-2222
Westlake (G-19313)

American Way Van and Stor Inc ....E 937 898-7294
Vandalia (G-18503)

Arms Trucking Co Inc	E	800 362-1343	
Huntsburg (G-12016)			
Atlas Home Moving & Storage	E	614 445-8831	
Columbus (G-6999)			
Bell Moving and Storage Inc	E	513 942-7500	
Fairfield (G-10699)			
Brendamour Moving & Stor Inc	D	800 354-9715	
Cincinnati (G-3071)			
Bridge Logistics Inc	E	513 874-7444	
West Chester (G-19046)			
Clark Trucking Inc	C	937 642-0335	
East Liberty (G-10390)			
Cleveland Express Trckg Co Inc	D	216 348-0922	
Cleveland (G-5253)			
Containerport Group Inc	E	216 341-4800	
Cleveland (G-5343)			
Corrigan Moving Systems-Ann AR	E	419 874-2900	
Perrysburg (G-15850)			
County of Hancock	E	419 422-7433	
Findlay (G-10893)			
Dhl Supply Chain (usa)	E	419 727-4318	
Toledo (G-17700)			
Distribution and Trnsp Svc Inc	E	937 295-3343	
Fort Loramie (G-10985)			
Getgo Transportation Co LLC	E	419 666-6850	
Millbury (G-14449)			
Greater Dayton Mvg & Stor Co	E	937 235-0011	
Dayton (G-9471)			
Gws FF&e LLC	E	513 759-6000	
West Chester (G-18939)			
Henderson Trucking Inc	E	740 369-6100	
Delaware (G-9985)			
J-Trac Inc	E	419 524-3456	
Mansfield (G-13189)			
King Tut Logistics LLC	E	614 538-0509	
Columbus (G-7908)			
Lanes Transfer Inc	E	419 222-8692	
Lima (G-12674)			
Leaders Moving Company	E	614 785-9595	
Worthington (G-19822)			
Lewis & Michael Inc	E	937 252-6683	
Dayton (G-9564)			
Lewis & Michael Mvg & Stor Co	E	614 275-2997	
Columbus (G-7968)			
Lincoln Moving & Storage Co	D	216 741-5500	
Cleveland (G-5871)			
Locker Moving & Storage Inc	E	330 784-0477	
Canton (G-2380)			
M G Q Inc	E	419 992-4236	
Tiffin (G-17522)			
Mano Logistics LLC	E	330 454-1307	
Canton (G-2385)			
Marietta Industrial Entps Inc	D	740 373-2252	
Marietta (G-13353)			
Miami Valley Bekins Inc	E	937 278-4296	
Dayton (G-9615)			
Midfitz Inc	E	216 663-8816	
Cleveland (G-5984)			
Mitchell & Sons Moving & Stor	E	419 289-3311	
Ashland (G-681)			
Moving Solutions Inc	D	440 946-9300	
Mentor (G-14090)			
▲ Neighborhood Logistics Co Inc	E	440 466-0020	
Geneva (G-11244)			
Picklesimer Trucking Inc	E	937 642-1091	
Marysville (G-13522)			
Piqua Transfer & Storage Co	D	937 773-3743	
Piqua (G-16021)			
Planes Moving & Storage Inc	C	513 759-6000	
West Chester (G-18982)			
Planes Mvg & Stor Co Columbus	D	614 777-9090	
Columbus (G-8451)			
Proterra Inc	E	216 383-8449	
Wickliffe (G-19474)			
R K Campf Corp	E	330 332-7089	
Salem (G-16556)			
Rainbow Express Inc	D	614 444-5600	
Columbus (G-8485)			
Ray Hamilton Companies	E	513 641-5400	
Blue Ash (G-1640)			
River City Furniture LLC	E	513 612-7303	
West Chester (G-18994)			
Rmb Enterprises Inc	D	513 539-3431	
Middletown (G-14325)			
Rollins Moving and Storage Inc	E	937 525-4013	
Springfield (G-17105)			
Security Storage Co Inc	D	513 961-2700	
Cincinnati (G-4445)			
Shetler Moving & Stor of Ohio	E	513 755-0700	
West Chester (G-19004)			

Shippers Consolidated Dist	E	216 579-9303	
Cleveland (G-6405)			
Spears Transf & Expediting Inc	E	937 275-2443	
Dayton (G-9782)			
State-Wide Express Inc	E	216 676-4600	
Cleveland (G-6460)			
T & B Transportation Inc	E	330 495-0316	
Canton (G-2505)			
▲ Taylor Distributing Company	D	513 771-1850	
West Chester (G-19089)			
Tersher Corporation	D	440 439-8383	
Strongsville (G-17352)			
Thoman Weil Moving & Stor Co	E	513 251-5000	
Cincinnati (G-4601)			
Tri Modal Service Inc	E	614 876-6325	
Columbus (G-8776)			
University Moving & Storage Co	E	248 615-7000	
West Chester (G-19027)			
Van Howards Lines Inc	E	937 235-0007	
Dayton (G-9848)			
Van Mayberrys & Storage Inc	E	937 298-8800	
Moraine (G-14704)			
Van Mills Lines Inc	C	440 846-0200	
Strongsville (G-17357)			
Van Stevens Lines Inc	E	419 729-8871	
Toledo (G-18134)			
Vance Property Management LLC	D	419 467-9548	
Toledo (G-18135)			
William R Morse	E	440 352-2600	
Painesville (G-15748)			
Willis Day Management Inc	E	419 476-8000	
Toledo (G-18159)			
Wnb Group LLC	C	513 641-5400	
Cincinnati (G-4801)			
Wooster Motor Ways Inc	E	330 264-9557	
Wooster (G-19786)			
Yowell Transportation Svc Inc	E	937 294-5933	
Moraine (G-14709)			

4215 Courier Svcs, Except Air

Barberton Laundry & Cleaning	D	330 825-6911	
Barberton (G-947)			
Centaur Mail Inc	E	419 887-5857	
Maumee (G-13769)			
City Dash LLC	C	513 562-2000	
Cincinnati (G-3298)			
City Taxicab & Transfer Co	E	440 992-2156	
Ashtabula (G-727)			
Clockwork Logistics Inc	E	216 587-5371	
Garfield Heights (G-11228)			
Elite Expediting Corp	D	614 279-1181	
Worthington (G-19806)			
Fed Ex Rob Carpenter	E	419 260-1889	
Maumee (G-13790)			
Federal Express Corporation	D	800 463-3339	
Miamisburg (G-14170)			
Federal Express Corporation	D	937 898-3474	
Vandalia (G-18523)			
Federal Express Corporation	B	614 492-6106	
Columbus (G-7568)			
Fedex Freight Corporation	E	800 521-3505	
Lima (G-12641)			
Fedex Ground Package Sys Inc	E	330 244-1534	
Canton (G-2312)			
Fedex Ground Package Sys Inc	D	800 463-3339	
Richfield (G-16357)			
Fedex Ground Package Sys Inc	B	800 463-3339	
Toledo (G-17731)			
Firelands Security Services	E	419 627-0562	
Sandusky (G-16606)			
Keller Logistics Group Inc	E	419 784-4805	
Defiance (G-9922)			
Palmer Express Incorporated	E	440 942-3333	
Willoughby (G-19560)			
Prime Time Enterprises Inc	E	440 891-8855	
Cleveland (G-6236)			
Priority Dispatch Inc	E	216 332-9852	
Solon (G-16885)			
Robert M Neff Inc	D	614 444-1562	
Columbus (G-8543)			
SMS Transport LLC	E	937 813-8897	
Dayton (G-9772)			
Stat Express Delivery LLC	E	614 880-7828	
Worthington (G-19853)			
United Parcel Service Inc	B	440 826-2591	
Cleveland (G-6576)			
United Parcel Service Inc	D	937 859-2314	
West Carrollton (G-18857)			
United Parcel Service Inc	E	800 742-5877	
Chillicothe (G-2833)			

United Parcel Service Inc	E	614 431-0600	
Columbus (G-8806)			
United Parcel Service Inc	E	440 846-6000	
Strongsville (G-17355)			
United Parcel Service Inc OH	C	419 747-3080	
Mansfield (G-13259)			
United Parcel Service Inc OH	C	513 852-6135	
Cincinnati (G-4683)			
United Parcel Service Inc OH	C	800 742-5877	
Cleveland (G-6577)			
United Parcel Service Inc OH	C	740 373-0772	
Marietta (G-13393)			
United Parcel Service Inc OH	D	419 222-7399	
Lima (G-12772)			
United Parcel Service Inc OH	C	440 826-3320	
Wooster (G-19775)			
United Parcel Service Inc OH	A	419 891-6776	
Maumee (G-13865)			
United Parcel Service Inc OH	C	419 424-9494	
Findlay (G-10972)			
United Parcel Service Inc OH	C	330 545-0177	
Girard (G-11302)			
United Parcel Service Inc OH	D	440 275-3301	
Austinburg (G-854)			
United Parcel Service Inc OH	C	330 339-6281	
New Philadelphia (G-14987)			
United Parcel Service Inc OH	C	740 598-4293	
Brilliant (G-1824)			
United Parcel Service Inc OH	E	740 592-4570	
Athens (G-809)			
United Parcel Service Inc OH	E	740 968-3508	
Saint Clairsville (G-16508)			
United Parcel Service Inc OH	C	614 841-7159	
Columbus (G-8807)			
United Parcel Service Inc OH	C	800 742-5877	
Zanesville (G-20370)			
United Parcel Service Inc OH	D	419 891-6841	
Toledo (G-18119)			
United Parcel Service Inc OH	C	330 478-1007	
Canton (G-2520)			
United Parcel Service Inc OH	C	419 586-8556	
Celina (G-2613)			
United Parcel Service Inc OH	C	513 241-5289	
Cincinnati (G-4684)			
United Parcel Service Inc OH	C	614 383-4580	
Marion (G-13472)			
United Parcel Service Inc OH	C	513 782-4000	
Cincinnati (G-4685)			
United Parcel Service Inc OH	C	513 241-5316	
Cincinnati (G-4686)			
United Parcel Service Inc OH	C	419 872-0211	
Perrysburg (G-15928)			
United Parcel Service Inc OH	C	614 272-8500	
Obetz (G-15531)			
United Parcel Service Inc OH	D	513 863-1681	
Hamilton (G-11651)			
United Parcel Service Inc OH	C	937 773-4762	
Piqua (G-16032)			
United Parcel Service Inc OH	D	419 782-3552	
Defiance (G-9945)			
United Parcel Service Inc OH	C	937 382-0658	
Wilmington (G-19652)			
United Parcel Service Inc OH	C	800 742-5877	
Youngstown (G-20232)			
United Parcel Service Inc OH	B	740 363-0636	
Delaware (G-10013)			
United States Cargo & Courier	E	216 325-0483	
Cleveland (G-6579)			

4221 Farm Product Warehousing & Storage

Consolidated Grain & Barge Co	E	513 941-4805	
Cincinnati (G-3351)			
Consolidated Grain & Barge Co	D	419 785-1941	
Defiance (G-9907)			
Deerfield Farms Service Inc	D	330 584-4715	
Deerfield (G-9904)			

4222 Refrigerated Warehousing & Storage

Americold Logistics LLC	D	330 834-1742	
Massillon (G-13661)			
Cloverleaf Cold Storage Co	E	330 833-9870	
Massillon (G-13672)			
Cloverleaf Cold Storage Co	C	419 599-5015	
Napoleon (G-14800)			
Crescent Park Corporation	E	513 759-7000	
West Chester (G-18906)			
D & D Investment Co	E	614 272-6567	
Columbus (G-7405)			
Exel N Amercn Logistics Inc	C	937 854-7900	
Dayton (G-9422)			

SIC

Fresh Mark Inc ....B 330 833-9870
Massillon (G-13686)

Gorbett Enterprises of Solon ....E 440 248-3950
Solon (G-16853)

Interstate Warehousing VA LLC ....D 513 874-6500
Fairfield (G-10738)

RLR Investments LLC ....D 937 382-1494
Wilmington (G-19645)

Woodruff Enterprises Inc ....E 937 399-9300
Springfield (G-17138)

4225 General Warehousing & Storage

A Duie Pyle Inc ....D 330 342-7750
Streetsboro (G-17243)

Aero Fulfillment Services Corp ....D 800 225-7145
Mason (G-13536)

Aero Fulfillment Services Corp ....D 513 874-4112
West Chester (G-18861)

Akron Porcelain & Plastics Co ....E 330 745-2159
Barberton (G-940)

Al-Mar Lanes ....E 419 352-4637
Bowling Green (G-1713)

Albring Vending Company ....E 419 726-8059
Toledo (G-17585)

Aldi Inc ....D 330 273-7351
Hinckley (G-11857)

All Pro Freight Systems Inc ....D 440 934-2222
Westlake (G-19313)

AM Industrial Group LLC ....E 216 267-6783
Cleveland (G-4944)

Andersons Inc ....C 419 891-6479
Maumee (G-13752)

Andersons Inc ....C 419 893-5050
Maumee (G-13755)

Arett Sales Corp ....D 937 552-2005
Troy (G-18195)

Asw Global LLC ....D 330 733-6291
Mogadore (G-14541)

Asw Global LLC ....D 330 899-1003
Canton (G-2196)

Asw Global LLC ....D 330 798-5184
Mogadore (G-14542)

Atotech USA Inc ....D 216 398-0550
Cleveland (G-5022)

Bartram & Sons Groceries ....E 740 532-5216
Ironton (G-12145)

Basista Furniture Inc ....E 216 398-5900
Cleveland (G-5040)

BDS Inc ....E 513 921-8441
Cincinnati (G-3028)

Big Sandy Distribution Inc ....C 740 574-2113
Franklin Furnace (G-11042)

▲ Big Sandy Furniture Inc ....D 740 574-2113
Franklin Furnace (G-11043)

Big Sandy Furniture Inc ....E 740 354-3193
Portsmouth (G-16125)

Big Sandy Furniture Inc ....E 740 775-4244
Chillicothe (G-2758)

Big Sandy Furniture Inc ....E 740 894-4242
Chesapeake (G-2727)

Briar-Gate Realty Inc ....E 614 299-2121
Columbus (G-7062)

Building Systems Trnsp Co ....C 740 852-9700
London (G-12861)

Burd Brothers Inc ....E 800 538-2873
Batavia (G-984)

Childrens Hospital Medical Ctr ....A 513 636-4200
Cincinnati (G-3191)

Cloverleaf Cold Storage Co ....C 419 599-5015
Napoleon (G-14800)

Commercial Warehouse & Cartage ....D 614 409-3901
Groveport (G-11502)

Compak Inc ....E 330 345-5666
Wooster (G-19711)

Compass Self Storage LLC ....E 216 458-0670
Cleveland (G-5330)

Comprehensive Logistics Co Inc ....E 330 233-0805
Parma (G-15762)

Comprehensive Logistics Co Inc ....E 440 934-0870
Lorain (G-12898)

Comprehensive Logistics Co Inc ....E 800 734-0372
Youngstown (G-20008)

Containerport Group Inc ....E 216 341-4800
Cleveland (G-5343)

Cotter Mdse Stor of Ohio ....E 330 773-9177
Akron (G-160)

Cotter Moving & Storage Co ....E 330 535-5115
Akron (G-161)

Crescent Park Corporation ....C 513 759-7000
West Chester (G-18906)

D & D Investment Co ....E 614 272-6567
Columbus (G-7405)

D M I Distribution Inc ....E 765 584-3234
Columbus (G-7410)

Daikin Applied Americas Inc ....E 763 553-5009
Dayton (G-9344)

Daniel Logistics Inc ....D 614 367-9442
Columbus (G-7415)

Dayton Heidelberg Distrg Co ....C 419 666-9783
Perrysburg (G-15855)

Dedicated Logistics Inc ....D 513 275-1135
West Chester (G-18909)

Dhl Supply Chain (usa) ....E 419 727-4318
Toledo (G-17700)

Dhl Supply Chain (usa) ....D 513 482-6015
Cincinnati (G-3425)

Dhl Supply Chain (usa) ....D 614 895-1959
Westerville (G-19158)

Dhl Supply Chain (usa) ....E 513 942-1575
Cincinnati (G-3426)

Dhl Supply Chain (usa) ....D 513 745-7445
Blue Ash (G-1545)

Dolgencorp LLC ....A 740 588-5700
Zanesville (G-20299)

Doylestown Telephone Company ....E 330 658-6666
Doylestown (G-10114)

DSC Logistics LLC ....D 847 390-6800
Toledo (G-17704)

E and P Warehouse Services Ltd ....E 330 898-4800
Warren (G-18704)

Efco Corp ....E 614 876-1226
Columbus (G-7509)

Enterprise Vending Inc ....E 513 772-1373
Cincinnati (G-3500)

Essilor of America Inc ....C 614 492-0888
Groveport (G-11510)

Exel Inc ....D 419 996-7703
Lima (G-12634)

Exel Inc ....D 419 226-5500
Lima (G-12635)

Exel Inc ....E 614 865-8294
Westerville (G-19162)

Exel Inc ....D 740 927-1762
Etna (G-10615)

Exel Inc ....E 614 670-6473
Lockbourne (G-12815)

◆ Exel Inc ....B 614 865-8500
Westerville (G-19163)

Faro Services Inc ....C 614 497-1700
Groveport (G-11513)

Federal Express Corporation ....B 614 492-6106
Columbus (G-7568)

Fedex Sup Chain Dist Sys Inc ....B 412 820-3700
Lockbourne (G-12818)

First Group Investment Partnr ....D 513 241-2200
Cincinnati (G-3558)

Firstgroup Usa Inc ....B 513 241-2200
Cincinnati (G-3569)

Fremont Logistics LLC ....D 419 333-0669
Fremont (G-11077)

Fuchs Lubricants Co ....E 330 963-0400
Twinsburg (G-18270)

▲ Fulfillment Technologies LLC ....C 513 346-3100
West Chester (G-19055)

Fusion Ceramics Inc ....E 330 627-5821
Carrollton (G-2569)

G & J Pepsi-Cola Bottlers Inc ....D 740 593-3366
Athens (G-781)

G & J Pepsi-Cola Bottlers Inc ....E 937 393-5744
Wilmington (G-19624)

G & S Metal Products Co Inc ....C 216 831-2388
Cleveland (G-5585)

Gateway Distribution Inc ....E 513 891-4477
Cincinnati (G-3604)

General Motors LLC ....C 513 874-0535
West Chester (G-18931)

Getgo Transportation Co LLC ....E 419 666-6850
Millbury (G-14449)

GMI Holdings Inc ....D 330 794-0846
Akron (G-238)

Goodwill Ester Seals Miami Vly ....B 937 461-4800
Dayton (G-9465)

Graham Investment Co ....D 740 382-0902
Marion (G-13422)

Great Value Storage ....E 614 848-8420
Columbus (G-7690)

Handl-It Inc ....C 330 468-0734
Macedonia (G-13073)

Hofstetter Orran Inc ....E 330 683-8070
Orrville (G-15634)

Home City Ice Company ....C 513 574-1800
Cincinnati (G-3718)

Hyperlogistics Group Inc ....E 614 497-0800
Columbus (G-7793)

Ieh Auto Parts LLC ....E 216 351-2560
Cleveland (G-5735)

Impact Fulfillment Svcs LLC ....C 614 262-8911
Columbus (G-7803)

Ingersoll-Rand Company ....E 419 633-6800
Bryan (G-1960)

Inter Distr Svcs of Cleve ....E 330 468-4949
Macedonia (G-13075)

J B Express Inc ....D 740 702-9830
Chillicothe (G-2794)

J-Trac Inc ....E 419 524-3456
Mansfield (G-13189)

Jacobson Warehouse Company Inc ....E 614 409-0003
Groveport (G-11523)

Jacobson Warehouse Company Inc ....D 614 497-6300
Groveport (G-11524)

Keller Logistics Group Inc ....E 866 276-9486
Defiance (G-9923)

Keller Warehousing & Dist LLC ....C 419 784-4805
Defiance (G-9924)

King Tut Logistics LLC ....E 614 538-0509
Columbus (G-7908)

Kuehne + Nagel Inc ....E 419 635-4051
Port Clinton (G-16111)

Lakota Local School District ....C 513 777-2150
Liberty Township (G-12582)

Lesaint Logistics Inc ....E 513 874-3900
West Chester (G-18958)

Lesaint Logistics LLC ....E 513 874-3900
West Chester (G-18959)

Lesaint Logistics LLC ....D 513 988-0101
Trenton (G-18188)

Lewis & Michael Inc ....E 937 252-6683
Dayton (G-9564)

Liberty Insulation Co Inc ....E 513 621-0108
Milford (G-14400)

Liverpool Coil Processing Inc ....C 330 558-2600
Valley City (G-18465)

Locker Moving & Storage Inc ....E 330 784-0477
Canton (G-2380)

M A Folkes Company Inc ....E 513 785-4200
Hamilton (G-11626)

Malleys Candies Inc ....E 216 529-6262
Cleveland (G-5903)

Mansfield Whsng & Dist Inc ....C 419 522-3510
Ontario (G-15560)

Marc Glassman Inc ....C 216 265-7700
Cleveland (G-5906)

Matandy Steel & Metal Pdts LLC ....D 513 844-2277
Hamilton (G-11627)

McM Electronics Inc ....D 937 434-0031
Dayton (G-9596)

Menlo Logistics Inc ....D 740 963-1154
Etna (G-10617)

Micro Electronics Inc ....D 614 334-1430
Columbus (G-8071)

Mid State Systems Inc ....D 740 928-1115
Hebron (G-11717)

Mid-Ohio Mechanical Inc ....E 740 587-3362
Granville (G-11346)

Midwest Trmnals Tledo Intl Inc ....E 419 897-6868
Toledo (G-17917)

Midwest Trmnals Tledo Intl Inc ....E 419 698-8171
Toledo (G-17918)

▲ Millwood Inc ....E 330 393-4400
Vienna (G-18582)

Mwd Logistics Inc ....E 419 342-6253
Shelby (G-16748)

▲ Neighborhood Logistics Co Inc ....E 440 466-0020
Geneva (G-11244)

New Age Logistics LLC ....E 440 439-0846
Cleveland (G-6059)

Nifco America Corporation ....C 614 836-8733
Groveport (G-11528)

North Coast Logistics Inc ....E 216 362-7159
Brookpark (G-1903)

Oatey Supply Chain Svcs Inc ....E 216 267-7100
Cleveland (G-6111)

Odw Logistics Inc ....B 614 549-5000
Columbus (G-8225)

Ohio Desk Co ....E 216 623-0600
Brooklyn Heights (G-1877)

Osborne Trucking Company ....D 513 874-2090
Fairfield (G-10766)

P-Americas LLC ....C 330 746-7652
Youngstown (G-20149)

Parker-Hannifin Corporation.............D...... 419 878-7000
 Waterville (G-18790)
Parker-Hannifin Corporation.............A...... 216 531-3000
 Cleveland (G-6171)
PC Connection Sales Corp ....C...... 937 382-4800
 Wilmington (G-19638)
Peoples Cartage Inc ....E...... 330 833-8571
 Massillon (G-13719)
▲ Peoples Services Inc ....E...... 330 453-3709
 Canton (G-2437)
Pepsi-Cola Metro Btlg Co Inc ....E...... 330 336-3553
 Wadsworth (G-18611)
Pepsi-Cola Metro Btlg Co Inc ....E...... 440 323-5524
 Elyria (G-10554)
Piqua Steel Co.............................D...... 937 773-3632
 Piqua (G-16020)
Precision Strip Inc ....D...... 937 667-6255
 Tipp City (G-17565)
▲ Precision Strip Inc ....C...... 419 628-2343
 Minster (G-14540)
Precision Strip Inc ....C...... 419 674-4186
 Kenton (G-12286)
Precision Strip Inc ....D...... 419 661-1100
 Perrysburg (G-15905)
Precision Strip Inc ....D...... 513 423-4166
 Middletown (G-14321)
Prime Time Enterprises Inc ....E...... 440 891-8855
 Cleveland (G-6236)
Public Storage ....E...... 216 220-7978
 Bedford Heights (G-1325)
Reliable Rnners Curier Svc Inc ....E...... 440 578-1011
 Mentor (G-14103)
Restaurant Depot LLC ....E...... 216 525-0101
 Cleveland (G-6316)
Restaurant Equippers Inc ....E...... 614 358-6622
 Columbus (G-8526)
Roppe Holding Company ....E...... 419 435-9335
 Fostoria (G-11011)
RR Donnelley & Sons Company ....E...... 614 539-5527
 Grove City (G-11466)
Ryder Last Mile Inc ....E...... 614 801-0621
 Columbus (G-8566)
Safelite Fulfillment Inc ....E...... 614 781-5449
 Columbus (G-8573)
Safelite Fulfillment Inc ....E...... 216 475-7781
 Cleveland (G-6363)
Sally Beauty Supply LLC..................C...... 937 548-7684
 Greenville (G-11394)
Sally Beauty Supply LLC..................C...... 614 278-1691
 Columbus (G-8584)
SH Bell Company ....E...... 412 963-9910
 East Liverpool (G-10417)
South E Harley Davidson Sls Co ....E...... 440 439-3013
 Cleveland (G-6423)
▲ Spartan Whse & Dist Co Inc..........D...... 614 497-1777
 Columbus (G-8668)
▲ Specialty Logistics Inc ....E...... 513 421-2041
 Cincinnati (G-4512)
Springfield Cartage LLC..................D...... 937 222-2120
 Dayton (G-9785)
Springs Window Fashions LLC ....C...... 614 492-6770
 Groveport (G-11538)
Surface Combustion Inc ....E...... 419 878-8444
 Waterville (G-18794)
Sygma Network Inc.......................B...... 614 734-2500
 Dublin (G-10348)
Synnex Corporation.......................E...... 614 539-6995
 Grove City (G-11475)
Taylor Warehouse Corporation............E...... 513 771-2956
 West Chester (G-19091)
▲ Terminal Warehouse Inc ....D...... 330 773-2056
 Canton (G-2508)
The C-Z Company ....E...... 740 432-6334
 Cambridge (G-2085)
The Maple City Ice Company ....E...... 419 747-4777
 Mansfield (G-13252)
Tmarzetti Company........................C...... 614 277-3577
 Grove City (G-11477)
Top Dawg Group LLC ....E...... 216 398-1066
 Brooklyn Heights (G-1883)
Total Warehousing Services...............D...... 419 562-2878
 Bucyrus (G-2002)
Triple Ladys Agency Inc ....E...... 330 274-1100
 Mantua (G-13277)
TRT Management Corporation ....E...... 419 661-1233
 Perrysburg (G-15927)
Twist Inc ....E...... 937 675-9581
 Xenia (G-19931)
United Retail Logistics Svcs ....C...... 937 332-1500
 Troy (G-18235)

Utility Trailer Mfg Co ....E...... 513 436-2600
 Batavia (G-1015)
Ventra Salem LLC ....E...... 330 337-3240
 Salem (G-16565)
Verst Group Logistics Inc ....C...... 513 782-1725
 Cincinnati (G-4756)
Verst Group Logistics Inc ....C...... 513 772-2494
 Cincinnati (G-4757)
Victory White Metal Company ....E...... 216 271-1400
 Cleveland (G-6629)
Walmart Inc ....B...... 937 843-3681
 Belle Center (G-1342)
Wannemacher Enterprises Inc ....D...... 419 225-9060
 Lima (G-12775)
Warehouse Services Group Llc ....E...... 419 868-6400
 Holland (G-2021)
Westway Trml Cincinnati LLC..............E...... 513 921-8441
 Cincinnati (G-4793)
Whirlpool Corporation......................C...... 419 547-2610
 Clyde (G-6755)
Willis Day Management Inc ....E...... 419 476-8000
 Toledo (G-18159)
Wright Distribution Ctrs Inc ....E...... 419 227-7621
 Lima (G-12785)
WW Grainger Inc ....C...... 330 425-8387
 Macedonia (G-13090)

4226 Special Warehousing & Storage, NEC

Andreas Furniture Company ....E...... 330 852-2494
 Sugarcreek (G-17376)
Auto Warehousing Co Inc ....E...... 419 727-1534
 Toledo (G-17603)
Ballreich Bros Inc ....C...... 419 447-1814
 Tiffin (G-17510)
BDS Inc ....E...... 513 921-8441
 Cincinnati (G-3028)
Briar-Gate Realty Inc ....E...... 614 299-2122
 Grove City (G-11410)
Briar-Gate Realty Inc ....D...... 614 299-2121
 Grove City (G-11411)
Comprehensive Logistics Co Inc ....E...... 330 793-0504
 Youngstown (G-20007)
Distribution and Trnsp Svc Inc ....E...... 937 295-3343
 Fort Loramie (G-10985)
Exel Holdings (usa) Inc ....C...... 614 865-8500
 Westerville (G-19161)
General Motors LLC.........................C...... 513 603-6600
 West Chester (G-18932)
Great Value Storage ....E...... 614 848-8420
 Columbus (G-7690)
High Line Corporation ....C...... 330 848-8800
 Akron (G-261)
Honda Logistics North Amer Inc ....A...... 937 642-0335
 East Liberty (G-10391)
Infostore LLC ....E...... 216 749-4636
 Cleveland (G-5752)
Interstate Warehousing VA LLC ....D...... 513 874-6500
 Fairfield (G-10738)
Iron Mountain Incorporated ....D...... 513 874-3535
 West Chester (G-18948)
Iron Mountain Incorporated ....D...... 614 801-0151
 Urbancrest (G-18449)
Iron Mountain Info MGT LLC ....E...... 513 297-3268
 Cincinnati (G-3787)
Iron Mountain Info MGT LLC ....E...... 513 942-7300
 Hamilton (G-11616)
Iron Mountain Info MGT LLC ....E...... 513 297-1906
 West Chester (G-18949)
Iron Mountain Info MGT LLC ....E...... 614 840-9321
 Columbus (G-7842)
Iron Mountain Info MGT LLC ....C...... 440 248-0999
 Solon (G-16862)
Iron Mountain Info MGT LLC ....E...... 513 247-2183
 Blue Ash (G-1586)
Jacobson Warehouse Company Inc .....C...... 614 314-1091
 Obetz (G-15527)
Kitchen Collection LLC ....E...... 740 773-9150
 Chillicothe (G-2799)
▲ Kuhlman Corporation ....C...... 419 897-6000
 Maumee (G-13808)
Lefco Worthington LLC ....E...... 216 432-4422
 Cleveland (G-5860)
Locker Moving & Storage Inc ....E...... 330 784-0477
 Canton (G-2380)
Midwest Express Inc.......................A...... 937 642-0335
 East Liberty (G-10392)
Nex Transport Inc..........................E...... 937 645-3761
 East Liberty (G-10394)
PC Connection Inc ....C...... 937 382-4800
 Wilmington (G-19637)

Radial South LP ....C...... 678 584-4047
 Groveport (G-11533)
Ray Hamilton Companies ....E...... 513 641-5400
 Blue Ash (G-1640)
SH Bell Company ....E...... 412 963-9910
 East Liverpool (G-10417)
Ship Shape Marine Inc.....................E...... 419 734-1554
 Port Clinton (G-16117)
Target Corporation ....B...... 614 801-6700
 West Jefferson (G-19112)
Thirty-One Gifts LLC ....A...... 614 414-4300
 Columbus (G-8745)
Vista Industrial Packaging LLC ....E...... 800 454-6117
 Columbus (G-8855)
Warren City Board Education ....E...... 330 841-2265
 Warren (G-18768)
Wooster Motor Ways Inc ....C...... 330 264-9557
 Wooster (G-19786)

4231 Terminal & Joint Terminal Maint Facilities

Chieftain Trucking & Excav Inc ....E...... 216 485-8034
 Cleveland (G-5176)
Dayton Freight Lines Inc ....D...... 937 236-4880
 Dayton (G-9366)
Disttech LLC ....D...... 800 321-3143
 Cleveland (G-5429)
Eab Truck Service ....D...... 216 525-0020
 Cleveland (G-5454)
Fedex Freight Corporation ....E...... 877 661-8956
 Mentor (G-14047)
PAm Transportation Svcs Inc ....D...... 419 935-9501
 Willard (G-19485)
Pitt-Ohio Express LLC ....B...... 216 433-9000
 Cleveland (G-6215)
Short Freight Lines Inc ....E...... 419 729-1691
 Toledo (G-18031)
Slay Transportation Co Inc ....C...... 740 865-2910
 Sardis (G-16661)
Stover Transportation Inc ....E...... 614 777-4184
 Hilliard (G-11818)
STS Logistics Inc ....E...... 419 294-1498
 Upper Sandusky (G-18413)
Xpo Logistics Freight Inc ....C...... 614 876-7100
 Columbus (G-8924)
Xpo Logistics Freight Inc ....D...... 330 896-7300
 Uniontown (G-18391)
Yrc Inc ....D...... 614 878-9281
 Columbus (G-8933)

44 WATER TRANSPORTATION

4412 Deep Sea Foreign Transportation Of Freight

APL Logistics Ltd ....C...... 440 930-2822
 Avon Lake (G-908)
Toula Industries Ltd LLC...................C...... 937 689-1818
 Dayton (G-9818)

4432 Freight Transportation On The Great Lakes

The Interlake Steamship Co................E...... 440 260-6900
 Middleburg Heights (G-14261)

4449 Water Transportation Of Freight, NEC

Consolidated Grain & Barge Co ....E...... 513 941-4805
 Cincinnati (G-3351)
Midland Company ....A...... 513 947-5503
 Amelia (G-574)

4481 Deep Sea Transportation Of Passengers

AAA Allied Group Inc.......................D...... 513 228-0866
 Lebanon (G-12447)

4482 Ferries

Kelleys Isle Ferry Boat Lines ....E...... 419 798-9763
 Marblehead (G-13301)
Miller Boat Line Inc ....D...... 419 285-2421
 Put In Bay (G-16227)

4491 Marine Cargo Handling

A-1 Quality Labor Services LLC ....E...... 513 353-0173
 Cincinnati (G-2893)
Bellaire Harbor Service LLC ....E...... 740 676-4305
 Bellaire (G-1329)

Employee Codes: A=Over 500 employees, B=251-500
C=101-250, D=51-100, E=25-50 2019 Harris Ohio
Services Directory 863

S I C

Cincinnati Bulk Terminals LLC ....E ... 513 621-4800
  Cincinnati (G-3231)
Consolidated Grain & Barge Co ....E ... 513 941-4805
  Cincinnati (G-3351)
Cooper/T Smith Corporation ....E ... 419 626-0801
  Sandusky (G-16594)
Hofstetter Orran Inc ....E ... 330 683-8070
  Orrville (G-15634)
Marietta Industrial Entps Inc ....D ... 740 373-2252
  Marietta (G-13353)
McGinnis Inc ....C ... 740 377-4391
  South Point (G-16940)
McGinnis Inc ....E ... 513 941-8070
  Cincinnati (G-3988)
McNational Inc ....E ... 740 377-4391
  South Point (G-16941)
Midwest Trmnals Tldeo Intl Inc ....E ... 419 897-6868
  Toledo (G-17917)
◆ Pinney Dock & Transport LLC ....E ... 440 964-7186
  Ashtabula (G-752)
Reserve Ftl LLC ....E ... 440 519-1768
  Twinsburg (G-18311)
Tidewater River Rail Oper LLC ....D ... 817 659-0091
  Steubenville (G-17174)
Toledo-Lucas County Port Auth ....E ... 419 243-8251
  Toledo (G-18103)

4492 Towing & Tugboat Svcs

A M & O Towing Inc ....E ... 330 385-0639
  Negley (G-14827)
Great Lakes Group ....C ... 216 621-4854
  Cleveland (G-5627)
Shelly Materials Inc ....D ... 740 246-6315
  Thornville (G-17506)

4493 Marinas

Catawba-Cleveland Dev Corp ....D ... 419 797-4424
  Port Clinton (G-16101)
Containerport Group Inc ....E ... 513 771-0275
  West Chester (G-18896)
Erie Island Resort and Marina ....E ... 419 734-9117
  Warren (G-18707)
Island Service Company ....C ... 419 285-3695
  Put In Bay (G-16226)
S B S Transit Inc ....B ... 440 288-2222
  Lorain (G-12942)
Sandusky Harbor Marina Inc ....E ... 419 627-1201
  Sandusky (G-16638)
Saw Mill Creek Ltd ....C ... 419 433-3800
  Huron (G-12030)
Sima Marine Sales Inc ....E ... 440 269-3200
  Willoughby (G-19572)
Tack-Anew Inc ....E ... 419 734-4212
  Port Clinton (G-16119)
Tappan Lake Marina Inc ....E ... 740 269-2031
  Scio (G-16664)
Vermilion Boat Club Inc ....E ... 440 967-6634
  Vermilion (G-18562)

4499 Water Transportation Svcs, NEC

MPW Industrial Water Svcs Inc ....C ... 800 827-8790
  Hebron (G-11720)
Ship Shape Marine Inc ....E ... 419 734-1554
  Port Clinton (G-16117)
South Shore Marine Services ....E ... 419 433-5798
  Huron (G-12033)

45 TRANSPORTATION BY AIR

4512 Air Transportation, Scheduled

American Airlines Inc ....E ... 216 706-0702
  Cleveland (G-4947)
American Airlines Inc ....D ... 937 454-7472
  Vandalia (G-18501)
American Airlines Inc ....E ... 937 890-6668
  Vandalia (G-18502)
American Airlines Inc ....E ... 216 898-1347
  Cleveland (G-4948)
Champlain Enterprises LLC ....C ... 440 779-4588
  North Olmsted (G-15280)
City of Dayton ....C ... 937 454-8200
  Vandalia (G-18515)
Delta Air Lines Inc ....D ... 614 239-4440
  Columbus (G-7434)
Distribution and Trnsp Svc Inc ....E ... 937 295-3343
  Fort Loramie (G-10985)
Envoy Air Inc ....D ... 614 231-4391
  Columbus (G-7523)

Executive Jet Management Inc ....B ... 513 979-6600
  Cincinnati (G-3525)
Federal Express Corporation ....B ... 614 492-6106
  Columbus (G-7568)
Flight Express Inc ....D ... 305 379-8686
  Columbus (G-7596)
Lane Aviation Corporation ....C ... 614 237-3747
  Columbus (G-7950)
Psa Airlines Inc ....D ... 937 454-9338
  Vandalia (G-18536)
Psa Airlines Inc ....C ... 937 454-1116
  Vandalia (G-18537)
United Airlines Inc ....E ... 937 454-2009
  Vandalia (G-18546)
United Airlines Inc ....C ... 216 501-4700
  Cleveland (G-6566)
United Parcel Service Inc OH ....B ... 740 363-0636
  Delaware (G-10013)

4513 Air Courier Svcs

Abx Air Inc ....B ... 937 382-5591
  Wilmington (G-19600)
Abx Air Inc ....A ... 937 366-2282
  Wilmington (G-19601)
Air Transport Svcs Group Inc ....B ... 937 382-5591
  Wilmington (G-19603)
Ames Material Services Inc ....A ... 937 382-5591
  Wilmington (G-19606)
Dhl Express (usa) Inc ....E ... 614 865-8325
  Westerville (G-19157)
Dhl Express (usa) Inc ....E ... 800 225-5345
  Lockbourne (G-12813)
Federal Express Corporation ....D ... 800 463-3339
  Miamisburg (G-14170)
Federal Express Corporation ....E ... 800 463-3339
  Mansfield (G-13174)
Federal Express Corporation ....B ... 614 492-6106
  Columbus (G-7568)
Federal Express Corporation ....E ... 800 463-3339
  Lima (G-12640)
Federal Express Corporation ....E ... 800 463-3339
  Northwood (G-15393)
Federal Express Corporation ....C ... 800 463-3339
  Columbus (G-7569)
Federal Express Corporation ....C ... 800 463-3339
  Columbus (G-7570)
Federal Express Corporation ....D ... 800 463-3339
  Vandalia (G-18522)
Federal Express Corporation ....E ... 800 463-3339
  Canton (G-2311)
Federal Express Corporation ....D ... 937 898-3474
  Vandalia (G-18523)
Fedex Corporation ....E ... 440 234-0315
  Cleveland (G-5524)
Fedex Corporation ....E ... 614 801-0953
  Grove City (G-11431)
Fedex Ground Package Sys Inc ....E ... 800 463-3339
  Chillicothe (G-2778)
Fedex Ground Package Sys Inc ....E ... 800 463-3339
  Richfield (G-16356)
Fedex Smartpost Inc ....D ... 800 463-3339
  Grove City (G-11433)
Garda CL Technical Svcs Inc ....D ... 937 294-4099
  Moraine (G-14660)
Lgstx Services Inc ....E ... 866 931-2337
  Wilmington (G-19627)
Prime Time Enterprises Inc ....E ... 440 891-8855
  Cleveland (G-6236)
United Parcel Service Inc ....D ... 614 385-9100
  Columbus (G-8805)
United Parcel Service Inc OH ....D ... 419 222-7399
  Lima (G-12772)
United Parcel Service Inc OH ....D ... 330 339-6281
  New Philadelphia (G-14987)
United Parcel Service Inc OH ....D ... 419 782-3552
  Defiance (G-9945)
United States Cargo & Courier ....E ... 216 325-0483
  Cleveland (G-6579)

4522 Air Transportation, Nonscheduled

Airnet Systems Inc ....C ... 614 409-4900
  Columbus (G-6886)
Business Aircraft Group Inc ....D ... 216 348-1415
  Cleveland (G-5105)
Executive Jet Management Inc ....B ... 513 979-6600
  Cincinnati (G-3525)
Federal Express Corporation ....B ... 614 492-6106
  Columbus (G-7568)
Jetselect LLC ....D ... 614 338-4380
  Columbus (G-7857)

◆ Jilco Industries Inc ....E ... 330 698-0280
  Kidron (G-12306)
Lane Aviation Corporation ....C ... 614 237-3747
  Columbus (G-7950)
McKinley Air Transport Inc ....E ... 330 497-6956
  Canton (G-2394)
Netjets Inc ....E ... 614 239-5500
  Columbus (G-8174)
Netjets International Inc ....A ... 614 239-5500
  Columbus (G-8175)
Netjets Sales Inc ....C ... 614 239-5500
  Columbus (G-8177)
Ohio Medical Trnsp Inc ....D ... 614 791-4400
  Columbus (G-8274)
One Sky Flight LLC ....A ... 877 703-2348
  Cleveland (G-6133)
Options Flight Support Inc ....C ... 216 261-3500
  Cleveland (G-6139)
Panther II Transportation Inc ....C ... 800 685-0657
  Medina (G-13985)

4581 Airports, Flying Fields & Terminal Svcs

ABM Aviation Inc ....B ... 859 767-7507
  Cincinnati (G-2897)
Abx Air Inc ....B ... 937 382-5591
  Wilmington (G-19600)
Aitheras Aviation Group LLC ....E ... 216 298-9060
  Cleveland (G-4923)
Akron-Canton Regional Airport ....E ... 330 499-4059
  North Canton (G-15186)
American Airlines Inc ....E ... 216 898-1347
  Cleveland (G-4948)
ATI Aviation Services LLC ....E ... 216 268-4888
  Cleveland (G-5019)
Aviation Manufacturing Co Inc ....D ... 419 435-7448
  Fostoria (G-10996)
Cessna Aircraft Company ....D ... 419 866-6761
  Swanton (G-17395)
City of Dayton ....C ... 937 454-8200
  Vandalia (G-18515)
City of Dayton ....E ... 937 454-8231
  Vandalia (G-18516)
Columbus Regional Airport Auth ....E ... 614 239-4000
  Columbus (G-7310)
Columbus Regional Airport Auth ....B ... 614 239-4015
  Columbus (G-7311)
Constant Aviation LLC ....C ... 800 440-9004
  Cleveland (G-5338)
Corporate Wngs - Cleveland LLC ....E ... 216 261-9000
  Cleveland (G-5352)
Duncan Aviation Inc ....D ... 513 873-7523
  Cincinnati (G-3455)
Executive Jet Management Inc ....B ... 513 979-6600
  Cincinnati (G-3525)
◆ Exel Inc ....B ... 614 865-8500
  Westerville (G-19163)
GE Aviation Systems LLC ....B ... 513 786-4555
  West Chester (G-18930)
General Electric Company ....A ... 513 552-2000
  Cincinnati (G-3609)
Huntleigh USA Corporation ....B ... 216 265-3707
  Cleveland (G-5726)
James Air Cargo Inc ....E ... 440 243-9095
  Cleveland (G-5779)
Lane Aviation Corporation ....C ... 614 237-3747
  Columbus (G-7950)
Legndary Cleaners LLC ....E ... 216 374-1205
  Cleveland (G-5864)
Macair Aviation LLC ....E ... 937 347-1302
  Xenia (G-19919)
McKinley Air Transport Inc ....E ... 330 497-6956
  Canton (G-2394)
Menzies Aviation (texas) Inc ....E ... 216 362-6565
  Cleveland (G-5954)
National Flight Services Inc ....D ... 419 865-2311
  Swanton (G-17402)
Netjets Large Aircraft Inc ....D ... 614 239-4853
  Columbus (G-8176)
Park-N-Go Inc ....E ... 937 890-7275
  Dayton (G-9686)
Plane Detail LLC ....E ... 614 734-1201
  Galena (G-11163)
Servisair LLC ....C ... 216 267-9910
  Cleveland (G-6400)
Stevens Aviation Inc ....D ... 937 890-0189
  Vandalia (G-18541)
Toledo-Lucas County Port Auth ....E ... 419 865-2351
  Swanton (G-17408)
Ultimate Jetcharters LLC ....D ... 330 497-3344
  North Canton (G-15242)

Unison Industries LLC..............................B......904 667-9904
  Dayton (G-9188)
Unison Industries LLC..............................B......937 427-0550
  Beavercreek (G-1192)
Winner Aviation Corporation ....D......330 856-5000
  Vienna (G-18584)
Wright Brothers Aero Inc ....D......937 890-8900
  Vandalia (G-18550)

46 PIPELINES, EXCEPT NATURAL GAS

4612 Crude Petroleum Pipelines

Bluefoot Industrial LLC ....E......740 314-5299
  Steubenville (G-17141)
▲ Marathon Pipe Line LLC ....C......419 422-2121
  Findlay (G-10939)
Mplx LP ....E......419 421-2414
  Findlay (G-10946)
Ohio Oil Gathering Corporation ....E......740 828-2892
  Nashport (G-14821)

4613 Refined Petroleum Pipelines

Buckeye Pipe Line Services Co............E......419 698-8770
  Oregon (G-15584)
Integrity Kokosing Pipeline Sv ....C......740 694-6315
  Fredericktown (G-11054)
▲ Marathon Pipe Line LLC ....C......419 422-2121
  Findlay (G-10939)
Mplx LP ....E......419 421-2414
  Findlay (G-10946)
Three Rivers Energy LLC ....E......740 623-3035
  Coshocton (G-9029)

47 TRANSPORTATION SERVICES

4724 Travel Agencies

AAA Allied Group Inc..............................E......419 228-1022
  Lima (G-12591)
AAA Allied Group Inc..............................B......513 762-3301
  Cincinnati (G-2894)
AAA Miami Valley ....D......937 224-2896
  Dayton (G-9201)
AAA Shelby County Motor Club ....E......937 492-3167
  Sidney (G-16756)
Action Travel Center Inc ....E......440 248-8388
  Cleveland (G-4900)
Allstars Travel Group Inc ....C......614 901-4100
  New Albany (G-14842)
Avalon Holdings Corporation ....D......330 856-8800
  Warren (G-18673)
Central Travel & Ticket Inc ....E......419 897-2070
  Toledo (G-17644)
Chima Travel Bureau Inc ....E......330 867-4770
  Fairlawn (G-10819)
Independence Travel ....E......216 447-9950
  Cleveland (G-5744)
Khm Consulting Inc ....E......330 460-5635
  Brunswick (G-1935)
Kollander World Travel Inc....................E......216 692-1000
  Cleveland (G-5838)
Maritz Travel Company ....B......660 626-1501
  Maumee (G-13814)
Muskingum Coach Company..................E......740 622-2545
  Coshocton (G-9023)
Pier n Port Travel Inc ....E......513 841-9900
  Cincinnati (G-4247)
Professional Travel Inc..........................D......440 734-8800
  North Olmsted (G-15305)
Provident Travel Corporation ....D......513 247-1100
  Cincinnati (G-4300)
Travel Authority ....E......513 272-2887
  Cincinnati (G-4629)
West Enterprises Inc ....E......614 237-4488
  Columbus (G-8889)

4725 Tour Operators

Newport Walking Tours LLC ....E......859 951-8560
  Cincinnati (G-4112)
Tours of Black Heritage Inc..................D......440 247-2737
  Cleveland (G-6536)
Trolley Tours of Cleveland ....E......216 771-4484
  Cleveland (G-6550)

4729 Passenger Transportation Arrangement, NEC

Daugwood Inc ....E......937 429-9465
  Beavercreek (G-1144)
Delta Air Lines Inc ....E......216 265-2400
  Cleveland (G-5416)
Rush Expediting Inc ....E......937 885-0894
  Dayton (G-9741)

4731 Freight Forwarding & Arrangement

A Plus Expediting & Logistics ....E......937 424-0220
  Dayton (G-9199)
ABF Freight System Inc ....C......419 525-0118
  Mansfield (G-13132)
Advance Trnsp Systems Inc ....E......513 818-4311
  Cincinnati (G-2910)
Airnet Systems Inc................................C......614 409-4900
  Columbus (G-6886)
Alpha Freight Systems Inc....................D......800 394-9001
  Hudson (G-11965)
Ameri-Line Inc ....E......440 316-4500
  Columbia Station (G-6769)
American Marine Express Inc................E......216 268-3005
  Cleveland (G-4957)
Ardmore Power Logistics LLC ....E......216 502-0640
  Westlake (G-19318)
Bleckmann USA LLC ....E......740 809-2645
  Johnstown (G-12197)
Blood Courier Inc ....E......216 251-3050
  Cleveland (G-5063)
Bnsf Logistics LLC ....E......937 526-3141
  Versailles (G-18566)
Bolt Express LLC ....D......419 729-6698
  Toledo (G-17619)
Burd Brothers Inc ....E......513 708-7787
  Dayton (G-9269)
C & M Express Logistics Inc ....E......440 350-0802
  Painesville (G-15697)
Ceva Freight LLC ....E......614 482-5100
  Groveport (G-11500)
Ceva Freight LLC ....E......216 898-6765
  Cleveland (G-5162)
Ceva Logistics LLC ....B......614 482-5000
  Groveport (G-11501)
Ceva Logistics US Inc ....E......614 482-5107
  Columbus (G-7172)
CH Robinson Company Inc....................E......614 933-5100
  Columbus (G-7175)
CH Robinson Freight Svcs Ltd ....E......440 234-7811
  Cleveland (G-5164)
Colonial Courier Service Inc ....E......419 891-0922
  Maumee (G-13772)
Colonial Courier Service Inc ....E......419 891-0922
  Maumee (G-13773)
Commercial Traffic Company ....D......216 267-2000
  Cleveland (G-5319)
Commercial Traffic Company ....D......216 267-2000
  Cleveland (G-5320)
Complete Qlty Trnsp Sltons LLC ....E......513 914-4882
  Cincinnati (G-3344)
Comprehensive Logistics Co Inc ....E......800 734-0372
  Youngstown (G-20008)
◆ Concord Express Inc ....E......718 656-7821
  Groveport (G-11503)
Containerport Group Inc ....D......440 333-1330
  Cleveland (G-5342)
Containerport Group Inc ....D......216 692-3124
  Euclid (G-10627)
Contech Trckg & Logistics LLC............D......513 645-7000
  West Chester (G-18897)
Cos Express Inc ....D......614 276-9000
  Columbus (G-7376)
County of Medina ....E......330 723-9670
  Medina (G-13927)
Craig Transportation Co........................E......419 874-7981
  Maumee (G-13777)
Dash Services LLC ....D......216 273-9133
  Cleveland (G-5405)
Dayton Freight Lines Inc ....C......937 236-4880
  Dayton (G-9366)
Dhl Supply Chain (usa) ....D......614 836-1265
  Groveport (G-11507)
Dick Lavy Trucking Inc ....C......937 448-2104
  Bradford (G-1761)
Distribution Data Incorporated ....E......216 362-3009
  Brookpark (G-1896)
DSV Solutions LLC ....D......740 989-1200
  Little Hocking (G-12807)
Eckel Logistics Inc ....E......419 349-3118
  Perrysburg (G-15862)

Elite Transportation Svcs LLC..............E......330 769-5830
  Seville (G-16684)
Esj Carrier Corporation ....E......513 728-7388
  Fairfield (G-10726)
Exel Freight Connect Inc......................D......855 393-5378
  Columbus (G-7544)
Exel Global Logistics Inc ....D......440 243-5900
  Cleveland (G-5500)
Exel Global Logistics Inc ....E......614 409-4500
  Columbus (G-7545)
Exel Inc ....D......740 929-2113
  Hebron (G-11713)
Exel Inc ....B......614 662-9247
  Groveport (G-11511)
Exel Inc ....D......800 426-8434
  Lockbourne (G-12816)
Exel N Amercn Logistics Inc ....C......800 272-1052
  Westerville (G-19253)
Expeditors Intl Wash Inc ....D......440 243-9900
  Cleveland (G-5501)
Expeditors Intl Wash Inc ....E......614 492-9840
  Lockbourne (G-12817)
Faf Inc ....B......800 496-4696
  Groveport (G-11512)
Faro Services Inc....................................C......614 497-1700
  Groveport (G-11513)
FCA US LLC ....E......419 729-5959
  Toledo (G-17729)
Fedex Custom Critical Inc....................B......800 463-3339
  Uniontown (G-18369)
Fedex Freight Corporation ....C......800 521-3505
  Lima (G-12641)
Fedex Freight Corporation ....C......800 728-8190
  Northwood (G-15394)
Fedex Supply Chain................................C......614 491-1518
  Lockbourne (G-12819)
Fedex Truckload Brokerage Inc............C......800 463-3339
  Uniontown (G-18370)
Freedom Enterprises Inc......................E......419 675-1192
  Kenton (G-12275)
Freight Rite Inc ....E......419 478-7400
  Toledo (G-17748)
Freshway Foods Inc ....C......937 498-4664
  Sidney (G-16781)
Garner Trucking Inc ....C......419 422-5742
  Findlay (G-10912)
Garys Pharmacy Inc ....C......937 456-5777
  Eaton (G-10446)
◆ GKN Freight Services Inc ....E......419 232-5623
  Van Wert (G-18478)
Global Transportation Services............E......614 409-0770
  Reynoldsburg (G-16305)
Globaltranz Enterprises Inc ....C......513 745-0138
  Blue Ash (G-1571)
Haid Acquisitions LLC ....D......513 941-8700
  Cincinnati (G-3672)
Hub City Terminals Inc ....D......440 779-2226
  Westlake (G-19354)
Hub City Terminals Inc ....E......419 217-5200
  Toledo (G-17811)
IHS Enterprise Inc ....C......216 588-9078
  Independence (G-12081)
Innovative Logistics Group Inc ....E......937 832-9350
  Englewood (G-10591)
Innovel Solutions Inc ....D......614 878-2092
  Columbus (G-7821)
Innovel Solutions Inc ....A......614 492-5304
  Columbus (G-7822)
Integrity Ex Logistics LLC ....B......888 374-5138
  Cincinnati (G-3771)
J B Express Inc ....D......740 702-9830
  Chillicothe (G-2794)
J Rayl Transport Inc..............................E......330 940-1668
  Euclid (G-10646)
Jarrett Logistics Systems Inc ....C......330 682-0099
  Orrville (G-15636)
JB Hunt Transport Svcs Inc ....A......614 335-6681
  Columbus (G-7855)
Keller Logistics Group Inc ....E......866 276-9486
  Defiance (G-9923)
Kgbo Holdings Inc ....E......513 831-2600
  Cincinnati (G-2859)
Krakowski Trucking Inc..........................E......330 722-7935
  Medina (G-13966)
Lesaint Logistics LLC ....D......513 988-0101
  Trenton (G-18188)
Logikor LLC ....E......513 762-7678
  Cincinnati (G-3941)
Martin Logistics Inc ....D......330 456-8000
  Canton (G-2391)

Mid Ohio Vly Bulk Trnspt Inc ....E 740 373-2481
  Marietta (G-13359)
▲ Millwood Inc ....E 330 393-4400
  Vienna (G-18582)
Millwood Natural LLC ....C 330 393-4400
  Vienna (G-18583)
Moving Solutions Inc ....D 440 946-9300
  Mentor (G-14090)
Nationwide Transport Llc ....E 513 554-0203
  Cincinnati (G-4097)
Newark Parcel Service Company ....E 614 253-3777
  Columbus (G-8187)
Nippon Express USA Inc ....D 614 801-5695
  Grove City (G-11459)
Nissin Intl Trnspt USA Inc ....D 937 644-2644
  Marysville (G-13520)
Noramco Transport Corp ....E 513 245-9050
  Cincinnati (G-4122)
Nutrition Trnsp Svcs LLC ....C 937 962-2661
  Lewisburg (G-12571)
Ohio Transport Inc ....E 216 741-8000
  Cleveland (G-6125)
Omni Interglobal Inc ....E 216 239-3833
  Cleveland (G-6131)
Overland Xpress LLC ....E 513 528-1158
  Cincinnati (G-4193)
Packship Usa Inc ....D 330 682-7225
  Orrville (G-15643)
Pride Transportation Inc ....E 419 424-2145
  Findlay (G-10956)
Ray Hamilton Companies ....E 513 641-5400
  Blue Ash (G-1640)
Regional Express Inc ....D 516 458-3514
  Richfield (G-16374)
Reliable Trnsp Solutions LLC ....E 937 378-2700
  Georgetown (G-11273)
Ringler Feedlots LLC ....E 419 253-5300
  Marengo (G-13304)
Rk Express International LLC ....D 513 574-2400
  Cincinnati (G-4383)
Roadrunner Trnsp Systems Inc ....E 330 920-4101
  Peninsula (G-15812)
Rondy Fleet Services Inc ....C 330 745-9016
  Barberton (G-965)
Ryan Logistics Inc ....D 937 642-4158
  Marysville (G-13526)
Schenker Inc ....E 419 866-6390
  Swanton (G-17405)
Schneider Nat Carriers Inc ....E 740 362-6910
  Delaware (G-10006)
Shoreline Transportation Inc ....C 440 878-2000
  Strongsville (G-17345)
SMS Transport LLC ....E 937 813-8897
  Dayton (G-9772)
Stack Container Service Inc ....D 216 531-7555
  Euclid (G-10657)
Taylor Logistics Inc ....E 513 771-1850
  West Chester (G-19090)
Tazmanian Freight Fwdg Inc ....E 216 265-7881
  Middleburg Heights (G-14260)
Tersher Corporation ....E 440 439-8383
  Strongsville (G-17352)
Tgs International Inc ....E 330 893-4828
  Millersburg (G-14495)
Tier One Distribution LLC ....D 937 323-6325
  Springfield (G-17126)
Tjm Express Inc ....E 216 385-4164
  Berea (G-1441)
Total Package Express Inc ....E 513 741-5500
  Cincinnati (G-4611)
Total Quality Logistics LLC ....E 513 831-2600
  Milford (G-14437)
Total Quality Logistics LLC ....D 513 831-2600
  Cincinnati (G-4612)
Total Quality Logistics LLC ....C 513 831-2600
  Milford (G-14438)
Total Quality Logistics LLC ....B 513 831-2600
  Cincinnati (G-2873)
Tpg Noramco LLC ....E 513 245-9050
  Cincinnati (G-4624)
Trans-Continental Systems Inc ....E 513 769-4774
  Cincinnati (G-4626)
Transfreight Inc ....E 937 332-0366
  Troy (G-18232)
Triple T Transport Inc ....D 740 657-3244
  Lewis Center (G-12563)
Trx Great Plains Inc ....D 855 259-9259
  Cleveland (G-6551)
TV Minority Company Inc ....E 937 832-9350
  Englewood (G-10603)

United Parcel Service Inc OH ....B 740 363-0636
  Delaware (G-10013)
United States Cargo & Courier ....E 614 449-2854
  Columbus (G-8810)
US Expediting Logistics LLC ....E 937 235-1014
  Vandalia (G-18547)
USF Holland LLC ....C 216 941-4340
  Cleveland (G-6612)
Verst Group Logistics Inc ....E 513 772-2494
  Cincinnati (G-4757)
William R Morse ....E 440 352-2600
  Painesville (G-15748)
Wnb Group LLC ....E 513 641-5400
  Cincinnati (G-4801)
World Ex Shipg Trnsp Fwdg Svcs ....E 440 826-5055
  Middleburg Heights (G-14266)
World Shipping Inc ....E 440 356-7676
  Cleveland (G-6690)
Wright Distribution Ctrs Inc ....E 419 227-7621
  Lima (G-12785)
Xpo Intermodal Inc ....D 614 923-1400
  Dublin (G-10377)
Xpo Intermodal Solutions Inc ....A 614 923-1400
  Dublin (G-10378)
Xpo Stacktrain LLC ....E 614 923-1400
  Dublin (G-10379)
Yrc Inc ....E 913 344-5174
  Copley (G-8982)
Zipline Logistics LLC ....D 888 469-4754
  Columbus (G-8938)

4741 Railroad Car Rental

Andersons Inc ....C 419 893-5050
  Maumee (G-13754)
▼ Djj Holding Corporation ....C 513 621-8770
  Cincinnati (G-3437)

4783 Packing & Crating Svcs

Amerisource Health Svcs LLC ....D 614 492-8177
  Columbus (G-6941)
Bates Metal Products Inc ....D 740 498-8371
  Port Washington (G-16121)
Containerport Group Inc ....E 440 333-1330
  Columbus (G-7355)
Crescent Park Corporation ....C 513 759-7000
  West Chester (G-18906)
Deufol Worldwide Packaging LLC ....D 440 232-1100
  Bedford (G-1276)
Deufol Worldwide Packaging LLC ....D 414 967-8000
  Fairfield (G-10717)
Flick Lumber Co Inc ....E 419 468-6278
  Galion (G-11172)
Hcg Inc ....E 513 539-9269
  Monroe (G-14569)
Impact Fulfillment Svcs LLC ....C 614 262-8911
  Columbus (G-7803)
Inquiry Systems Inc ....E 614 464-3800
  Columbus (G-7824)
Lefco Worthington LLC ....E 216 432-4422
  Cleveland (G-5860)
◆ McNerney & Associates LLC ....E 513 241-9951
  Cincinnati (G-3990)
Morral Companies LLC ....E 740 465-3251
  Morral (G-14713)
Packship Usa Inc ....D 330 682-7225
  Orrville (G-15643)
Reynolds Industries Inc ....E 330 889-9466
  West Farmington (G-19102)
Southeast Diversified Inds ....D 740 432-4241
  Cambridge (G-2082)
Star Packaging Inc ....E 614 564-9936
  Columbus (G-8688)
Sugar Creek Packing Co ....C 513 551-5255
  Blue Ash (G-1653)
Vista Industrial Packaging LLC ....D 800 454-6117
  Columbus (G-8855)

4785 Fixed Facilities, Inspection, Weighing Svcs Transptn

Argus International Inc ....E 513 852-1010
  Cincinnati (G-2985)
Johnson Mirmiran Thompson Inc ....D 614 714-0270
  Columbus (G-7863)
▲ Magnum Management Corporation ....A 419 627-2334
  Sandusky (G-16626)
Ohio Tpk & Infrastructure Comm ....C 440 234-2081
  Berea (G-1432)
Pti Qlity Cntnment Sltions LLC ....D 313 304-8677
  Toledo (G-17994)

4789 Transportation Svcs, NEC

Access Home Care LLC ....E 937 224-9991
  Dayton (G-9205)
Age Line Inc ....E 216 941-9990
  Cleveland (G-4912)
Ahoy Transport LLC ....E 740 596-0536
  Creola (G-9050)
All American Trnsp Svcs LLC ....E 419 589-7433
  Ontario (G-15544)
Alstom Signaling Operation LLC ....B 513 552-6485
  Cincinnati (G-2933)
American Linehaul Corporation ....E 614 409-8568
  Columbus (G-6929)
Ameripro Logistics LLC ....E 410 375-3469
  Dayton (G-9231)
Andersons Inc ....E 419 891-6634
  Maumee (G-13753)
Andersons Inc ....C 419 893-5050
  Maumee (G-13754)
Ashtabula Chemical Corp ....E 440 998-0100
  Ashtabula (G-707)
Bob Evans Transportation ....A 937 322-4447
  Springfield (G-17001)
Brothers Auto Transport LLC ....E 330 824-0082
  Warren (G-18681)
Coldliner Express Inc ....D 614 570-0836
  Columbus (G-7243)
CSX Corporation ....A 614 242-3932
  Columbus (G-7402)
CT Logistics Inc ....C 216 267-1636
  Cleveland (G-5387)
Dayton Freight Lines Inc ....C 419 589-0350
  Mansfield (G-13165)
Euclid SC Transportation ....D 216 797-7600
  Cleveland (G-5494)
Fidelitone Inc ....E 440 260-6523
  Middleburg Heights (G-14252)
Genox Transportation Inc ....E 419 837-2023
  Perrysburg (G-15868)
Great Lakes Cold Logistics ....E 216 520-0930
  Independence (G-12078)
Haggerty Logistics Inc ....E 734 713-9800
  Cincinnati (G-3671)
Health Care Logistics Inc ....D 800 848-1633
  Galloway (G-11220)
Hoc Transport Company ....E 330 630-0100
  Akron (G-264)
Hogan Services Inc ....E 614 491-8402
  Columbus (G-7758)
Jarrells Moving & Transport Co ....E 330 952-1240
  Medina (G-13960)
▼ Jk-Co LLC ....E 419 422-5240
  Findlay (G-10928)
Jti Transportation Inc ....E 419 661-9360
  Stony Ridge (G-17184)
Kettering City School District ....D 937 499-1770
  Dayton (G-9538)
Lake Local Board of Education ....B 330 877-9383
  Hartville (G-11694)
Marietta Transfer Company ....E 740 896-3565
  Lowell (G-13038)
Midwest Trmnals Tledo Intl Inc ....E 419 698-8171
  Toledo (G-17918)
Mikesell Transportation Broker ....E 937 996-5731
  Arcanum (G-625)
Mkm Distribution Services Inc ....D 330 549-9670
  North Lima (G-15272)
Multi Flow Transport Inc ....E 216 641-0200
  Brooklyn Heights (G-1875)
Niese Transport Inc ....E 419 523-4400
  Ottawa (G-15661)
Nobel County Engineers Office ....E 740 732-4400
  Caldwell (G-2041)
Nye F A & Sons Enterprises ....E 419 986-5400
  Tiffin (G-17527)
OH St Trans Dist 02 Outpost ....E 419 693-8870
  Northwood (G-15404)
Ohio State University ....E 614 292-6122
  Columbus (G-8332)
PAm Transportation Svcs Inc ....B 330 270-7900
  North Jackson (G-15251)
Parsec Inc ....E 513 621-6111
  Cincinnati (G-4206)
Precision Vhcl Solutions LLC ....E 513 651-9444
  Cincinnati (G-4268)
R W Godbey Railroad Services ....E 513 651-3800
  Cincinnati (G-4332)
Schenker Inc ....E 614 662-7217
  Groveport (G-11537)

School Transportation ....E 937 855-3897
Germantown *(G-11277)*

Schroeder Associates Inc ....E 419 258-5075
Antwerp *(G-614)*

Secure Trnsp Co Ohio LLC ....E 800 856-9994
Worthington *(G-19847)*

Tmt Inc ....C 419 592-1041
Perrysburg *(G-15926)*

Total Quality Logistics LLC ....E 800 580-3101
Centerville *(G-2635)*

Total Quality Logistics LLC ....E 800 580-3101
West Chester *(G-19017)*

Total Transportation Trckg Inc ....E 216 398-6090
Cleveland *(G-6534)*

Universal Transportation Syste ....E 513 539-9491
Monroe *(G-14585)*

Village Transport Corp ....C 440 461-5000
Cleveland *(G-6633)*

Water Transport LLC ....E 740 937-2199
Hopedale *(G-11938)*

Williams Freight Logistics ....E 614 333-9173
Columbus *(G-8906)*

Wmk Inc ....E 630 782-1900
Richfield *(G-16384)*

Woodruff Enterprises Inc ....E 937 399-9300
Springfield *(G-17138)*

World Trck Towing Recovery Inc ....E 330 723-1116
Seville *(G-16693)*

48 COMMUNICATIONS

4812 Radiotelephone Communications

ABC Phones North Carolina Inc ....E 440 290-4262
Mentor On The Lake *(G-14128)*

ABC Phones North Carolina Inc ....E 440 319-3654
Ashtabula *(G-703)*

ABC Phones North Carolina Inc ....E 330 752-0009
Macedonia *(G-13057)*

ABC Phones North Carolina Inc ....E 440 328-4331
Sheffield Village *(G-16731)*

Aka Wireless Inc ....E 440 572-5777
Strongsville *(G-17282)*

Aka Wireless Inc ....E 216 213-8040
Hartville *(G-11682)*

Alltel Communications Corp ....D 740 349-8551
Newark *(G-15008)*

Answering Service Inc ....E 440 473-1200
Cleveland *(G-4984)*

AT&T Corp ....D 937 320-9648
Beavercreek *(G-1203)*

AT&T Corp ....D 614 798-3898
Dublin *(G-10140)*

AT&T Corp ....D 614 539-0165
Grove City *(G-11407)*

AT&T Corp ....D 740 455-3042
Zanesville *(G-20278)*

AT&T Corp ....D 740 549-4546
Lewis Center *(G-12525)*

AT&T Corp ....D 330 665-3100
Akron *(G-80)*

AT&T Corp ....D 440 951-5309
Willoughby *(G-19507)*

AT&T Corp ....D 614 575-3044
Columbus *(G-6991)*

AT&T Corp ....D 614 851-2400
Columbus *(G-6992)*

AT&T Corp ....D 513 741-1700
Cincinnati *(G-2993)*

AT&T Corp ....D 330 723-1717
Medina *(G-13911)*

AT&T Corp ....E 330 505-4200
Niles *(G-15145)*

AT&T Corp ....A 513 629-5000
Cincinnati *(G-2994)*

AT&T Inc ....E 937 320-9648
Beavercreek *(G-1204)*

AT&T Mobility LLC ....E 614 291-2500
Columbus *(G-6994)*

AT&T Mobility LLC ....C 330 565-5000
Youngstown *(G-19957)*

AT&T Mobility LLC ....E 440 846-3232
Strongsville *(G-17287)*

AT&T Mobility LLC ....E 216 382-0825
Cleveland *(G-5018)*

AT&T Mobility LLC ....E 419 516-0602
Lima *(G-12603)*

AT&T Mobility LLC ....E 513 381-6800
Cincinnati *(G-2995)*

AT&T Mobility LLC ....E 937 439-4900
Centerville *(G-2622)*

AT&T Services Inc ....C 937 456-2330
Eaton *(G-10437)*

Cellco Partnership ....B 614 560-2000
Dublin *(G-10162)*

Cellco Partnership ....D 513 923-2700
Cincinnati *(G-3143)*

Cellco Partnership ....D 330 823-7758
Alliance *(G-523)*

Cellco Partnership ....D 419 333-1009
Fremont *(G-11061)*

Cellco Partnership ....D 740 652-9540
Lancaster *(G-12377)*

Cellco Partnership ....D 740 695-3600
Saint Clairsville *(G-16482)*

Cellco Partnership ....D 740 432-7785
Cambridge *(G-2057)*

Cellco Partnership ....D 330 376-8275
Akron *(G-122)*

Cellco Partnership ....D 513 755-1666
West Chester *(G-18883)*

Cellco Partnership ....D 513 697-1190
Cincinnati *(G-3144)*

Cellco Partnership ....D 440 934-0576
Avon *(G-872)*

Cellco Partnership ....D 419 381-1726
Toledo *(G-17640)*

Cellco Partnership ....C 216 765-1444
Beachwood *(G-1042)*

Cellco Partnership ....D 440 998-3111
Ashtabula *(G-724)*

Cellco Partnership ....D 513 422-3437
Middletown *(G-14345)*

Cellco Partnership ....D 740 588-0018
Zanesville *(G-20289)*

Cellco Partnership ....E 513 688-1300
Cincinnati *(G-3145)*

Cellco Partnership ....E 419 424-2351
Findlay *(G-10886)*

Cellco Partnership ....D 419 897-9133
Maumee *(G-13768)*

Cellco Partnership ....E 440 953-1155
Mentor *(G-14027)*

Cellco Partnership ....E 440 646-9625
Cleveland *(G-5147)*

Cellco Partnership ....E 440 846-8881
Strongsville *(G-17289)*

Cellco Partnership ....E 740 397-6609
Mount Vernon *(G-14752)*

Cellco Partnership ....E 614 459-7200
Columbus *(G-7148)*

Cellco Partnership ....E 937 429-4000
Beavercreek *(G-1138)*

Cellco Partnership ....E 513 671-2200
Cincinnati *(G-3146)*

Cellco Partnership ....E 513 697-0222
Cincinnati *(G-3147)*

Cellco Partnership ....E 419 843-2995
Toledo *(G-17641)*

Cellco Partnership ....E 330 493-7979
Canton *(G-2247)*

Cellco Partnership ....E 216 573-5880
Independence *(G-12056)*

Cellco Partnership ....D 937 578-0022
Marysville *(G-13489)*

Cellco Partnership ....D 440 542-9631
Solon *(G-16834)*

Cellco Partnership ....D 330 626-0524
Streetsboro *(G-17248)*

Cellco Partnership ....D 330 308-0549
New Philadelphia *(G-14948)*

Cellco Partnership ....D 614 793-8989
Dublin *(G-10163)*

Cellco Partnership ....E 440 324-9479
Elyria *(G-10486)*

Cellco Partnership ....E 614 793-8989
Dublin *(G-10164)*

Cellco Partnership ....D 614 277-2900
Grove City *(G-11418)*

Cellco Partnership ....E 740 522-6446
Newark *(G-15021)*

Cellco Partnership ....D 330 345-6465
Wooster *(G-19698)*

Cellco Partnership ....E 330 722-6622
Medina *(G-13916)*

Cellco Partnership ....E 440 984-5200
Amherst *(G-583)*

Cellco Partnership ....E 740 450-1525
Zanesville *(G-20290)*

Cellular Sales Knoxville Inc ....E 614 322-9975
Columbus *(G-7149)*

Diamond Company Inc ....C 937 374-1111
Xenia *(G-19898)*

Horizon Pcs Inc ....C 740 772-8200
Chillicothe *(G-2790)*

Lima Radio Hospital Inc ....E 419 229-6010
Lima *(G-12686)*

Maximum Communications Inc ....E 513 489-3414
Cincinnati *(G-3981)*

Nextel Communications Inc ....D 513 891-9200
Cincinnati *(G-4113)*

Nextel Communications Inc ....D 614 801-9267
Grove City *(G-11458)*

Nextel Partners Operating Corp ....E 330 305-1365
North Canton *(G-15223)*

Nextel Partners Operating Corp ....E 419 380-2000
Toledo *(G-17941)*

Sprint Spectrum LP ....E 614 575-5500
Columbus *(G-8675)*

Sprint Spectrum LP ....E 614 428-2300
Columbus *(G-8677)*

Supermedia LLC ....D 740 369-2391
Marion *(G-13462)*

TSC Communications Inc ....E 419 739-2200
Wapakoneta *(G-18657)*

Twin Comm Inc ....E 740 774-4701
Marietta *(G-13390)*

Verizon Communications Inc ....C 330 334-1268
Wadsworth *(G-18617)*

Verizon Communications Inc ....C 440 892-4504
Westlake *(G-19420)*

Verizon New York Inc ....E 614 301-2498
Hilliard *(G-11827)*

Verizon Wireless ....E 330 963-1300
Twinsburg *(G-18336)*

Verizon Wireless Inc ....D 937 434-2355
Dayton *(G-9853)*

Wireless Center Inc ....B 216 503-3777
Cleveland *(G-6686)*

4813 Telephone Communications, Except Radio

1 Community ....E 216 923-2272
Cleveland *(G-4863)*

▲ 4mybenefits Inc ....E 513 891-6648
Blue Ash *(G-1494)*

Advanced Cmpt Connections LLC ....E 419 668-4080
Norwalk *(G-15424)*

Alltel Communications Corp ....D 740 349-8551
Newark *(G-15008)*

Alltel Communications Corp ....E 330 656-8000
Chardon *(G-2686)*

Armstrong Utilities Inc ....E 740 894-3886
South Point *(G-16928)*

At T Broadband & Intern ....E 614 839-4271
Columbus *(G-6988)*

AT&T Corp ....D 330 337-3505
Salem *(G-16535)*

AT&T Corp ....D 614 223-5318
Westerville *(G-19224)*

AT&T Corp ....C 614 271-8911
Powell *(G-16185)*

AT&T Corp ....D 614 223-6513
Columbus *(G-6989)*

AT&T Corp ....C 937 372-9945
Xenia *(G-19890)*

AT&T Corp ....C 330 752-7776
Akron *(G-81)*

AT&T Corp ....C 216 672-0809
Cleveland *(G-5017)*

AT&T Corp ....A 513 629-5000
Cincinnati *(G-2994)*

AT&T Corp ....D 614 337-3902
Columbus *(G-6993)*

AT&T Corp ....A 614 223-8236
Columbus *(G-6990)*

AT&T Datacomm LLC ....E 614 223-5799
Westerville *(G-19225)*

AT&T Mobility LLC ....E 614 291-2500
Columbus *(G-6994)*

AT&T Services Inc ....C 937 456-2330
Eaton *(G-10437)*

AVI-Spl Employee ....E 937 836-4787
Englewood *(G-10579)*

Block Communications Inc ....B 419 724-2539
Northwood *(G-15389)*

Broadvox LLC ....E 216 373-4600
Cleveland *(G-5083)*

Buckeye Telesystem Inc ....C 419 724-9898
Northwood *(G-15390)*

C T Wireless ....D 937 653-2208
Urbana *(G-18420)*

Cass Information Systems Inc............E 614 839-4503
Columbus *(G-7134)*

Cellco Partnership ....E 440 984-5200
Amherst *(G-583)*

Cellco Partnership ....E 740 450-1525
Zanesville *(G-20290)*

Centurylink Inc ....A 614 215-4223
Dublin *(G-10167)*

Champaign Telephone Company ....E 937 653-4000
Urbana *(G-18426)*

Chillicothe Telephone Company ....C 740 772-8200
Chillicothe *(G-2767)*

Chillicothe Telephone Company ....D 740 772-8361
Chillicothe *(G-2768)*

▲ Cincinnati Bell Inc ....D 513 397-9900
Cincinnati *(G-3226)*

Cincinnati Bell Tele Co LLC ....C 513 565-9402
Cincinnati *(G-3228)*

Cinciti Bl Etd Trts LLC ....D 513 397-0963
Cincinnati *(G-3283)*

Com Net Inc ....D 419 739-3100
Wapakoneta *(G-18639)*

Community Isp Inc ....E 419 867-6060
Toledo *(G-17672)*

Conneaut Telephone Company ....E 440 593-7140
Conneaut *(G-8953)*

Connect Call Global LLC ....E 513 348-1800
Mason *(G-13567)*

Construction Biddingcom LLC ....E 440 716-4087
North Olmsted *(G-15284)*

Cox Communications Inc ....D 937 222-5700
Dayton *(G-9336)*

Cox Ohio Telcom LLC ....D 216 535-3500
Parma *(G-15764)*

Cypress Communications Inc ....C 404 965-7248
Cleveland *(G-5402)*

Datzap LLC ....E 330 785-2100
Akron *(G-181)*

Dct Telecom Group Inc ....E 440 892-0300
Westlake *(G-19339)*

Deliass Assets Corp ....D 614 891-0101
Westerville *(G-19248)*

Doylestown Telephone Company........E 330 658-2121
Doylestown *(G-10113)*

Doylestown Telephone Company ....E 330 658-6666
Doylestown *(G-10114)*

Echo 24 Inc ....E 740 964-7081
Reynoldsburg *(G-16302)*

▲ F+w Media Inc. ....B 513 531-2690
Blue Ash *(G-1559)*

First Communications LLC ....E 330 835-2323
Fairlawn *(G-10830)*

▲ First Communications LLC ....D 330 835-2323
Fairlawn *(G-10831)*

Great Lakes Telcom Ltd ....E 330 629-8848
Youngstown *(G-20055)*

Horizon Telcom Inc ....B 740 772-8200
Chillicothe *(G-2791)*

Infotelecom Holdings LLC ....B 216 373-4811
Cleveland *(G-5753)*

Intellinet Corporation ....D 216 289-4100
Cleveland *(G-5759)*

Intgrted Bridge Communications ....E 513 381-1380
Cincinnati *(G-3782)*

J E Davis Corporation ....E 440 377-4700
Sheffield Village *(G-16735)*

Jumplinecom Inc ....E 614 859-1170
Columbus *(G-7877)*

Kraft Electrical Contg Inc ....E 614 836-9300
Groveport *(G-11526)*

Kraftmaid Trucking Inc ....D 440 632-2531
Middlefield *(G-14271)*

Level 3 Communications Inc ....E 330 256-8999
Akron *(G-310)*

Level 3 Telecom LLC ....E 234 542-6279
Akron *(G-311)*

Level 3 Telecom LLC ....E 513 841-0000
Cincinnati *(G-3919)*

Level 3 Telecom LLC ....E 513 841-0000
Cincinnati *(G-3920)*

Level 3 Telecom LLC ....E 513 682-7806
West Chester *(G-18960)*

Level 3 Telecom LLC ....E 513 682-7806
West Chester *(G-18961)*

Level 3 Telecom LLC ....E 513 682-7806
West Chester *(G-18962)*

Level 3 Telecom LLC ....E 513 841-0000
Cincinnati *(G-3921)*

Link Iq LLC ....E 859 983-6080
Dayton *(G-9569)*

Making Evrlasting Memories LLC ....E 513 864-0100
Cincinnati *(G-3964)*

Marietta College ....E 740 376-4790
Marietta *(G-13350)*

Massillon Cable TV Inc ....D 330 833-4134
Massillon *(G-13710)*

MCI Communications Svcs Inc ....B 216 265-9953
Cleveland *(G-5934)*

MCI Communications Svcs Inc ....E 440 635-0418
Chardon *(G-2704)*

Mitel (delaware) Inc ....E 513 733-8000
West Chester *(G-18974)*

Morelia Group LLC ....E 513 469-1500
Cincinnati *(G-4073)*

Mvd Communications LLC ....D 513 683-4711
Mason *(G-13621)*

Ohio Bell Telephone Company ....A 216 822-3439
Cleveland *(G-6115)*

Ohio State University ....E 614 292-6291
Columbus *(G-8322)*

Oxcyon Inc ....E 440 239-3345
Cleveland *(G-6152)*

Pearl Interactive Network Inc ....B 614 258-2943
Columbus *(G-8432)*

Png Telecommunications Inc ....D 513 942-7900
Cincinnati *(G-4260)*

Premier System Integrators Inc ....D 513 217-7294
Middletown *(G-14323)*

Primax Marketing Group ....E 513 443-2797
Cincinnati *(G-4279)*

Professional Telecom Svcs ....E 513 232-7700
Cincinnati *(G-4294)*

Profit Recovery of Ohio ....C 440 243-1743
Cleveland *(G-6240)*

Quanexus Inc ....E 937 885-7272
Dayton *(G-9722)*

Qwest Corporation ....D 614 793-9258
Dublin *(G-10316)*

Raco Wireless LLC ....E 513 870-6480
Blue Ash *(G-1637)*

Revolution Group Inc ....D 614 212-1111
Westerville *(G-19207)*

Round Room LLC ....E 330 880-0660
Massillon *(G-13726)*

Round Room LLC ....E 937 429-2230
Beavercreek *(G-1184)*

Roundtable Online Learning LLC ....E 440 220-5252
Chagrin Falls *(G-2680)*

Rxp Ohio LLC ....D 614 937-2844
Columbus *(G-8564)*

Rxp Wireless LLC ....E 330 264-1500
Wooster *(G-19763)*

▼ Skycasters LLC ....E 330 785-2100
Akron *(G-431)*

Southerntier Telecom ....E 614 505-6365
Worthington *(G-19851)*

Spectrum Networks Inc ....E 513 697-2000
Cincinnati *(G-4514)*

Sprint Communications Co LP ....E 419 725-2444
Toledo *(G-18043)*

Sprint Spectrum LP ....E 440 686-2600
North Olmsted *(G-15311)*

Sprint Spectrum LP ....E 614 575-5500
Columbus *(G-8675)*

Sprint Spectrum LP ....E 614 793-2500
Columbus *(G-8676)*

Sprint Spectrum LP ....E 614 428-2300
Columbus *(G-8677)*

Sprint Spectrum LP ....E 330 470-4614
Canton *(G-2484)*

Suite 224 Internet ....E 440 593-7113
Conneaut *(G-8959)*

Swn Communications Inc ....E 877 698-3262
Dayton *(G-9803)*

Time Warner Cable Inc ....E 330 800-3874
Akron *(G-470)*

Tremor LLC ....E 513 983-1100
Blue Ash *(G-1662)*

TSC Communications Inc ....E 419 739-2200
Wapakoneta *(G-18657)*

TSC Television Inc ....D 419 941-6001
Wapakoneta *(G-18658)*

TW Telecom Inc ....E 234 542-6279
Akron *(G-474)*

United Telephone Company Ohio ....B 419 227-1660
Lima *(G-12773)*

Verizon Bus Netwrk Svcs Inc ....E 513 897-1501
Waynesville *(G-18837)*

Verizon Business Global LLC ....E 614 219-2317
Hilliard *(G-11826)*

Verizon Communications Inc ....C 330 334-1268
Wadsworth *(G-18617)*

Verizon Communications Inc ....C 440 892-4504
Westlake *(G-19420)*

Verizon North Inc ....E 740 942-2566
Cadiz *(G-2033)*

Vox Mobile ....E 800 536-9030
Independence *(G-12139)*

West Central Ohio Internet ....E 419 229-2645
Lima *(G-12779)*

Xo Communications LLC ....E 216 619-3200
Cleveland *(G-6698)*

4822 Telegraph & Other Message Communications

AT&T Corp ....A 513 629-5000
Cincinnati *(G-2994)*

Maximum Communications Inc ....E 513 489-3414
Cincinnati *(G-3981)*

▲ Stratacache Inc ....C 937 224-0485
Dayton *(G-9796)*

Verizon Business Global LLC ....E 614 219-2317
Hilliard *(G-11826)*

Verizon Select Services Inc ....E 908 559-2054
North Royalton *(G-15370)*

4832 Radio Broadcasting Stations

Alpha Media LLC ....E 937 294-5858
Dayton *(G-9220)*

Ashtabula Broadcasting Station ....E 440 993-2126
Ashtabula *(G-706)*

Bonneville International Corp............D 513 699-5102
Cincinnati *(G-3067)*

Bowling Green State University ....D 419 372-8657
Bowling Green *(G-1723)*

CBS Corporation ....C 513 749-1035
Cincinnati *(G-3135)*

CBS Radio Inc ....D 513 699-5105
Cincinnati *(G-3136)*

CBS Radio Inc ....E 216 861-0100
Cleveland *(G-5144)*

Cd1025 ....E 614 221-9923
Columbus *(G-7145)*

Cincinnati Public Radio Inc............E 513 241-8282
Cincinnati *(G-3262)*

City Casters ....E 937 224-1137
Dayton *(G-9301)*

Cumulus Broadcasting LLC............E 850 243-7676
Cincinnati *(G-3387)*

Cumulus Broadcasting LLC............D 330 783-1000
Youngstown *(G-20012)*

Cumulus Media Inc ....D 419 725-5700
Toledo *(G-17690)*

Cumulus Media Inc ....D 513 241-9898
Cincinnati *(G-3388)*

Cumulus Media Inc ....D 419 240-1000
Toledo *(G-17691)*

D A Peterson Inc ....E 330 821-1111
Alliance *(G-529)*

Dayton Public School District............D 937 542-3000
Dayton *(G-9379)*

Educational and Community Rdo ....E 513 724-3939
Batavia *(G-997)*

Elyria-Lorain Broadcasting Co ....E 440 322-3761
Elyria *(G-10507)*

Fairborn Sftball Offcials Assn ....E 937 902-9920
Dayton *(G-9425)*

Family Stations Inc ....E 330 783-9986
Youngstown *(G-20036)*

Findlay Publishing Company ....E 419 422-4545
Findlay *(G-10905)*

Franklin Communications Inc............D 614 451-2191
Columbus *(G-7613)*

Franklin Communications Inc............D 614 459-9769
Columbus *(G-7614)*

Hubbard Radio Cincinnati LLC............D 513 699-5102
Cincinnati *(G-3737)*

Iheartcommunications Inc ....E 419 625-1010
Sandusky *(G-16618)*

Iheartcommunications Inc ....E 937 224-1137
Dayton *(G-9511)*

Iheartcommunications Inc ....D 614 486-6101
Columbus *(G-7799)*

Iheartcommunications Inc ....C 937 224-1137
Dayton *(G-9512)*

Iheartcommunications Inc ....C 513 241-1550
Cincinnati *(G-3750)*

Iheartcommunications Inc ....E 440 992-9700
Ashtabula (G-742)

Iheartcommunications Inc ....C 216 520-2600
Cleveland (G-5736)

Iheartcommunications Inc ....E 419 289-2605
Ashland (G-676)

Iheartcommunications Inc ....E 419 529-2211
Mansfield (G-13185)

Iheartcommunications Inc ....D 330 965-0057
Youngstown (G-20076)

Iheartcommunications Inc ....E 216 409-9673
Cleveland (G-5737)

Iheartcommunications Inc ....B 513 763-5500
Cincinnati (G-3751)

Iheartcommunications Inc ....D 419 782-9336
Defiance (G-9920)

Iheartcommunications Inc ....D 419 223-2060
Lima (G-12664)

Ingleside Investments Inc ....E 614 221-1025
Columbus (G-7818)

Johnny Appleseed Broadcasting ....E 419 529-5900
Ontario (G-15556)

Kent State University ....E 330 672-3114
Kent (G-12243)

Lorain City School District ....E 440 233-2239
Lorain (G-12913)

Marietta College ....E 740 376-4790
Marietta (G-13350)

Maverick Media ....E 419 331-1600
Lima (G-12700)

Media-Com Inc ....E 330 673-2323
Kent (G-12249)

Miami Valley Broadcasting Corp ....C 937 259-2111
Dayton (G-9616)

North American Broadcasting ....D 614 481-7800
Columbus (G-8196)

Ohio State University ....C 614 292-4510
Columbus (G-8312)

Ohio University ....E 740 593-1771
Athens (G-797)

Ohio University ....E 740 593-1771
Athens (G-796)

Pillar of Fire ....E 513 542-1212
Cincinnati (G-4249)

Public Broadcasting Found NW ....E 419 380-4600
Toledo (G-17995)

Radio Promotions ....C 513 381-5000
Cincinnati (G-4335)

Radio Seaway Inc ....E 216 916-6100
Cleveland (G-6277)

Radiohio Incorporated ....D 614 460-3850
Columbus (G-8484)

Rubber City Radio Group ....D 330 869-9800
Akron (G-412)

Saga Communications Neng Inc ....D 614 451-2191
Columbus (G-8580)

Salem Media Group Inc ....D 216 901-0921
Cleveland (G-6365)

Sandusky Newspapers Inc ....C 419 625-5500
Sandusky (G-16639)

Southeastern Ohio Brdcstg Sys ....E 740 452-5431
Zanesville (G-20363)

Southeastern Ohio TV Sys ....E 740 452-5431
Zanesville (G-20364)

Sunrise Television Corp ....E 419 244-2197
Toledo (G-18054)

Urban One Inc ....D 216 579-1111
Cleveland (G-6607)

Urban One Inc ....E 513 749-1009
Cincinnati (G-4734)

Urban One Inc ....E 614 487-1444
Columbus (G-8828)

Urban One Inc ....D 216 861-0100
Cleveland (G-6608)

Urban One Inc ....E 513 679-6000
Cincinnati (G-4735)

W H O T Inc ....D 330 783-1000
Youngstown (G-20239)

W K H R Radio ....E 440 708-0915
Bainbridge (G-932)

W M V O 1300 AM ....E 740 397-1000
Mount Vernon (G-14791)

Weol ....E 440 236-9283
Elyria (G-10571)

Wqio 93q Request ....D 740 392-9370
Mount Vernon (G-14793)

Wqmx Love Fund ....D 330 869-9800
Akron (G-504)

Wrwk 1065 ....E 419 725-5700
Toledo (G-18162)

Wzrx ....E 419 223-2060
Lima (G-12787)

Xavier University ....E 513 745-3335
Cincinnati (G-4810)

4833 Television Broadcasting Stations

Barrington Toledo LLC ....E 419 535-0024
Toledo (G-17605)

Bowling Green State University ....E 419 372-2700
Bowling Green (G-1725)

Dispatch Printing Company ....A 614 461-5000
Columbus (G-7451)

Dispatch Printing Company ....C 740 548-5331
Lewis Center (G-12541)

Fox Television Stations Inc ....C 216 431-8888
Cleveland (G-5568)

Gray Media Group Inc ....C 216 367-7300
Cleveland (G-5624)

Gray Media Group Inc ....C 513 421-1919
Cincinnati (G-3636)

Gray Television Group Inc ....D 419 531-1313
Toledo (G-17768)

Greater Cincinnati TV Educ Fnd ....D 513 381-4033
Cincinnati (G-3654)

Greater Dayton Public TV ....E 937 220-1600
Dayton (G-9472)

▲ Ideastream ....C 216 916-6100
Cleveland (G-5734)

Iheartcommunications Inc ....C 216 520-2600
Cleveland (G-5736)

Johnny Appleseed Broadcasting ....E 419 529-5900
Ontario (G-15556)

Lima Communications Corp ....E 419 228-8835
Lima (G-12678)

Nexstar Broadcasting Inc ....E 614 263-4444
Columbus (G-8188)

Nexstar Broadcasting Inc ....D 937 293-2101
Moraine (G-14683)

Northastern Eductl TV Ohio Inc ....E 330 677-4549
Kent (G-12251)

Ohio News Network ....D 216 367-7493
Cleveland (G-6121)

Ohio State University ....C 614 292-4510
Columbus (G-8312)

Ohio University ....E 740 593-1771
Athens (G-796)

Ohio University ....E 740 593-1771
Athens (G-797)

Ohio/Oklahoma Hearst TV Inc ....C 513 412-5000
Cincinnati (G-4163)

Public Broadcasting Found NW ....E 419 380-4600
Toledo (G-17995)

Sinclair Broadcast Group Inc ....E 513 641-4400
Cincinnati (G-4484)

Sinclair Broadcast Group Inc ....C 513 641-4400
Cincinnati (G-4485)

Sinclair Media II Inc ....C 614 481-6666
Columbus (G-8646)

Sinclair Media II Inc ....C 614 481-6666
Columbus (G-8647)

Sinclair Media II Inc ....C 614 481-6666
Columbus (G-8648)

Southeastern Ohio TV Sys ....E 740 452-5431
Zanesville (G-20364)

Sunrise Television Corp ....C 937 293-2101
Moraine (G-14700)

Sunrise Television Corp ....D 740 282-9999
Mingo Junction (G-14530)

Sunrise Television Corp ....E 419 244-2197
Toledo (G-18054)

Tegna Inc ....C 419 248-1111
Toledo (G-18061)

Thinktv Network ....E 937 220-1600
Dayton (G-9813)

Toledo Television Investors LP ....D 419 535-0024
Toledo (G-18100)

W B N X T V 55 ....E 330 922-5500
Cuyahoga Falls (G-9138)

W L W TT V 5 ....C 513 412-5000
Cincinnati (G-4766)

Wbns Tv Inc ....C 614 460-3700
Columbus (G-8881)

Wfmj Television Inc ....C 330 744-8611
Youngstown (G-20246)

Wfts ....C 216 431-5555
Cleveland (G-6680)

Wfts ....C 513 721-9900
Cincinnati (G-4794)

Winston Brdcstg Netwrk Inc ....E 330 928-5711
Cuyahoga Falls (G-9140)

Wkyc-Tv Inc ....C 216 344-3300
Cleveland (G-6687)

Wupw LLC ....E 419 244-3600
Toledo (G-18163)

Wwst Corporation LLC ....A 330 264-5122
Wooster (G-19788)

4841 Cable & Other Pay TV Svcs

Armstrong Utilities Inc ....E 330 758-6411
North Lima (G-15262)

ASC of Cincinnati Inc ....E 513 886-7100
Lebanon (G-12450)

Block Communications Inc ....B 419 724-2539
Northwood (G-15389)

C T Wireless ....D 937 653-2208
Urbana (G-18420)

Chillicothe Telephone Company ....C 740 772-8200
Chillicothe (G-2767)

Coaxial Communications of Sout ....D 513 797-4400
Columbus (G-7238)

Comcast Cble Cmmunications LLC ......C 503 372-9144
Steubenville (G-17149)

Comcast Corporation ....D 740 633-3437
Bridgeport (G-1815)

Comcast Spotlight ....E 440 617-2280
Westlake (G-19335)

Comcast Spotlight Inc ....B 216 575-8016
Cleveland (G-5315)

Conneaut Telephone Company ....E 440 593-7140
Conneaut (G-8953)

Cox Cable Cleveland Area Inc ....C 216 676-8300
Cleveland (G-5374)

Cox Communications Inc ....D 216 712-4500
Parma (G-15763)

Dish Network Corporation ....D 614 534-2001
Hilliard (G-11761)

Doylestown Communications ....E 330 658-7000
Doylestown (G-10111)

Erie County Cablevision Inc ....E 419 627-0800
Sandusky (G-16600)

▲ Fulfillment Technologies LLC ....C 513 346-3100
West Chester (G-19055)

Insight Communications of Co ....C 614 236-1200
Columbus (G-7825)

Marrik Dish Company LLC ....E 419 475-6538
Toledo (G-17895)

Massillon Cable TV Inc ....D 330 833-4134
Massillon (G-13710)

Ohio News Network ....D 614 460-3700
Columbus (G-8275)

Pioneer North America Inc ....E 614 771-1050
Columbus (G-8448)

Satcom Service LLC ....D 614 863-6470
Reynoldsburg (G-16331)

Spectrum MGT Holdg Co LLC ....D 614 481-5408
Columbus (G-8669)

Spectrum MGT Holdg Co LLC ....D 740 455-9705
Zanesville (G-20365)

Spectrum MGT Holdg Co LLC ....D 330 856-2343
Warren (G-18745)

Spectrum MGT Holdg Co LLC ....D 419 386-0040
Port Clinton (G-16118)

Spectrum MGT Holdg Co LLC ....D 740 762-0291
Chillicothe (G-2829)

Spectrum MGT Holdg Co LLC ....D 513 469-1112
Cincinnati (G-4513)

Spectrum MGT Holdg Co LLC ....E 614 344-4159
Columbus (G-8670)

Spectrum MGT Holdg Co LLC ....D 937 552-5760
Springfield (G-17114)

Spectrum MGT Holdg Co LLC ....D 740 200-3385
Athens (G-803)

Spectrum MGT Holdg Co LLC ....D 614 503-4153
Hilliard (G-11816)

Spectrum MGT Holdg Co LLC ....D 440 319-3271
Ashtabula (G-756)

Spectrum MGT Holdg Co LLC ....D 419 775-9292
Mansfield (G-13245)

Spectrum MGT Holdg Co LLC ....E 330 208-9028
Akron (G-437)

Spectrum MGT Holdg Co LLC ....D 937 684-8891
Dayton (G-9783)

Spectrum MGT Holdg Co LLC ....E 740 772-7809
Lancaster (G-12437)

Spectrum MGT Holdg Co LLC ....D 937 294-6800
Dayton (G-9784)

Spectrum MGT Holdg Co LLC ....D 937 306-6082
Piqua (G-16029)

State Alarm Inc ....E 888 726-8111
Youngstown (G-20217)

Time Warner Cable Entps LLC..............A 614 255-6289
Columbus *(G-8754)*

Time Warner Cable Entps LLC..............A 513 489-5000
Blue Ash *(G-1658)*

Time Warner Cable Entps LLC..............E 614 481-5072
Columbus *(G-8755)*

Time Warner Cable Inc ....E 614 236-1200
Columbus *(G-8756)*

Time Warner Cable Inc ....D 440 366-0416
Elyria *(G-10567)*

Time Warner Cable Inc ....D 419 331-1111
Lima *(G-12763)*

Time Warner Cable Inc ....D 614 481-5050
Columbus *(G-8757)*

Time Warner Cable Inc ....E 330 800-3874
Akron *(G-470)*

Time Warner Cable Inc ....A 614 481-5000
Columbus *(G-8758)*

Time Warner Cable Inc ....D 330 494-9200
Canton *(G-2511)*

Time Warner Cable Inc ....E 330 633-9203
Youngstown *(G-20222)*

Time Warner Cable Inc ....D 513 489-5000
Blue Ash *(G-1660)*

Time Warner Cable Inc ....E 937 471-1572
Eaton *(G-10462)*

Time Warner Cable Inc ....D 513 523-6333
Oxford *(G-15690)*

Time Warner Cable Inc ....E 937 483-5152
Troy *(G-18230)*

Time Warner Cable Inc ....D 937 667-8302
Tipp City *(G-17567)*

Time Warner Cable Inc ....D 937 492-4145
Sidney *(G-16802)*

TSC Television Inc ....D 419 941-6001
Wapakoneta *(G-18658)*

USI Cable Corp ....E 937 606-2636
Piqua *(G-16036)*

Verizon Communications Inc ....C 440 892-4504
Westlake *(G-19420)*

4899 Communication Svcs, NEC

A M Communications Ltd...................D 419 528-3051
Vandalia *(G-18500)*

Allied Communications Corp..............E 614 275-2075
Columbus *(G-6896)*

Armstrong Utilities Inc ....E 740 894-3886
South Point *(G-16928)*

Brand Technologies Inc ....E 419 873-6600
Perrysburg *(G-15841)*

◆ Calvert Wire & Cable Corp...............E 216 433-7600
Cleveland *(G-5115)*

Cincinnati Voice and Data ....D 513 683-4127
Loveland *(G-12983)*

Communication Svc For Deaf Inc........C 937 299-0917
Moraine *(G-14635)*

Inet Interactive LLC...........................E 513 322-5600
West Chester *(G-18947)*

Jay Blue Communications ....E 216 661-2828
Cleveland *(G-5783)*

Oovoo LLC......................................D 917 515-2074
Kettering *(G-12298)*

Springdot Inc ....D 513 542-4000
Cincinnati *(G-4523)*

Telcom Construction Svcs Inc............D 330 239-6900
Medina *(G-14010)*

Time Warner Cable Inc ....E 513 354-1100
Blue Ash *(G-1659)*

Velocity Grtest Phone Ever Inc...........B 419 868-9983
Holland *(G-11924)*

Vox Mobile ....E 800 536-9030
Independence *(G-12139)*

49 ELECTRIC, GAS, AND SANITARY SERVICES

4911 Electric Svcs

Adams Rural Electric Coop Inc ....E 937 544-2305
West Union *(G-19132)*

AEP Energy Partners Inc ....E 614 716-1000
Columbus *(G-6877)*

AEP Energy Services Inc ....B 614 583-2900
Columbus *(G-6878)*

AEP Generating Company ....A 614 223-1000
Columbus *(G-6879)*

AEP Power Marketing Inc ....A 614 716-1000
Columbus *(G-6880)*

American Electric Power Co Inc...........E 419 420-3011
Findlay *(G-10864)*

American Electric Power Co Inc...........E 740 829-4129
Conesville *(G-8947)*

American Electric Power Co Inc...........E 740 594-1988
Athens *(G-763)*

American Electric Power Co Inc...........C 330 438-7024
Canton *(G-2184)*

American Electric Power Co Inc...........E 419 998-5106
Lima *(G-12600)*

American Electric Power Co Inc...........E 740 779-5261
Chillicothe *(G-2756)*

American Electric Power Co Inc...........E 614 856-2750
Columbus *(G-6916)*

American Electric Power Co Inc...........D 614 351-3715
Columbus *(G-6917)*

American Electric Power Co Inc...........E 740 384-7981
Wellston *(G-18847)*

American Electric Power Co Inc...........E 330 580-5085
Canton *(G-2185)*

American Electric Power Co Inc...........E 740 598-4164
Brilliant *(G-1819)*

▲ American Electric Pwr Svc Corp .....B 614 716-1000
Columbus *(G-6919)*

American Electric Pwr Svc Corp ....E 614 582-1742
Columbus *(G-6920)*

◆ American Municipal Power Inc.......C 614 540-1111
Columbus *(G-6931)*

▲ Appalachian Power Company.........C 614 716-1000
Columbus *(G-6958)*

Appalachian Power Company ....D 330 438-7102
Canton *(G-2192)*

Buckeye Power Inc ....B 740 598-6534
Brilliant *(G-1820)*

Buckeye Power Inc ....E 614 781-0573
Columbus *(G-7089)*

Buckeye Rural Elc Coop Inc ....E 740 379-2025
Patriot *(G-15789)*

Butler Rural Electric Coop ....E 513 867-4400
Oxford *(G-15674)*

Butterfly Inc ....E 440 892-7777
Independence *(G-12051)*

Cardinal Operating Company ....E 740 598-4164
Brilliant *(G-1821)*

Carroll Electric Coop Inc ....E 330 627-2116
Carrollton *(G-2560)*

▲ Cinergy Corp ....A 513 421-9500
Cincinnati *(G-3289)*

City of Cuyahoga Falls ....D 330 971-8000
Cuyahoga Falls *(G-9080)*

City of Dublin ....E 614 410-4750
Dublin *(G-10175)*

City of Hamilton ....E 513 785-7450
Hamilton *(G-11580)*

City of Hudson Village ....D 330 650-1052
Hudson *(G-11973)*

City of Painesville ....E 440 392-5954
Painesville *(G-15699)*

City of Toledo ....D 419 245-1800
Toledo *(G-17654)*

City of Westerville ....E 614 901-6700
Westerville *(G-19237)*

Cleveland Elc Illuminating Co............D 800 589-3101
Akron *(G-143)*

Cleveland Elc Illuminating Co............D 440 953-7650
Painesville *(G-15702)*

Columbus Southern Power Co ....D 614 716-1000
Columbus *(G-7314)*

Columbus Southern Power Co ....D 740 829-2378
Conesville *(G-8948)*

Consolidated Electric Coop ....E 740 363-2641
Delaware *(G-9961)*

Consolidated Electric Coop Inc...........D 419 947-3055
Mount Gilead *(G-14725)*

Dayton Power and Light Company ....C 937 331-4063
Dayton *(G-9168)*

Dayton Power and Light Company ....B 937 549-2641
Manchester *(G-13127)*

Dayton Power and Light Company ....E 937 331-3032
Miamisburg *(G-14163)*

Dayton Power and Light Company ....E 937 549-2641
Manchester *(G-13128)*

Dayton Power and Light Company ....E 937 331-4123
Moraine *(G-14647)*

DPL Inc...E 937 331-4063
Dayton *(G-9170)*

Duke Energy Beckjord LLC................A 513 287-2561
Cincinnati *(G-3448)*

Duke Energy Ohio Inc.......................C 800 544-6900
Cincinnati *(G-3451)*

Duke Energy Ohio Inc.......................E 513 287-1120
Cincinnati *(G-3452)*

Duke Energy Ohio Inc.......................C 513 467-5000
New Richmond *(G-14994)*

▲ Duke Energy Ohio Inc..................D 704 382-3853
Cincinnati *(G-3450)*

Duquesne Light Company ....C 330 385-6103
East Liverpool *(G-10401)*

Dynegy Zimmer LLC ....E 713 767-0483
Moscow *(G-14720)*

▲ Echogen Power Systems Del Inc ....E 234 542-4379
Akron *(G-201)*

Energy Cooperative Inc ....E 740 348-1206
Newark *(G-15031)*

First Energy Linde ....D 330 384-4959
Akron *(G-220)*

Firstenergy Corp ....E 419 321-7114
Oak Harbor *(G-15472)*

Firstenergy Corp ....A 800 736-3402
Akron *(G-221)*

Firstenergy Nuclear Oper Co ....A 800 646-0400
Akron *(G-222)*

Firstenergy Solutions Corp ....E 800 736-3402
Akron *(G-223)*

Frontier Power Company ....E 740 622-6755
Coshocton *(G-9015)*

Gavin AEP Plant ....E 740 925-3166
Cheshire *(G-2735)*

Great Lakes Energy ....E 440 582-4662
Broadview Heights *(G-1834)*

Guernsy-Muskingum Elc Coop Inc.....E 740 826-7661
New Concord *(G-14900)*

Hancock-Wood Electric Coop Inc........E 419 257-3241
North Baltimore *(G-15177)*

Hearthstone Utilities Inc...................D 440 974-3770
Cleveland *(G-5679)*

Holmes-Wayne Electric Coop ....E 330 674-1055
Millersburg *(G-14477)*

Igs Solar LLC ....E 844 447-7652
Dublin *(G-10253)*

Indiana Michigan Power Company.......C 614 716-1000
Columbus *(G-7807)*

▲ Jersey Central Pwr & Light Co.......C 800 736-3402
Akron *(G-291)*

Jersey Central Pwr & Light Co ....D 440 994-8271
Ashtabula *(G-744)*

Jersey Central Pwr & Light Co ....D 419 366-2915
Sandusky *(G-16619)*

Jersey Central Pwr & Light Co ....E 330 315-6713
Fairlawn *(G-10836)*

Jersey Central Pwr & Light Co ....D 937 327-1218
Springfield *(G-17056)*

Jersey Central Pwr & Light Co ....C 740 537-6308
Stratton *(G-17242)*

Jersey Central Pwr & Light Co ....D 440 326-3222
Elyria *(G-10520)*

Jersey Central Pwr & Light Co ....D 216 432-6330
Cleveland *(G-5791)*

Jersey Central Pwr & Light Co ....A 440 546-8609
Brecksville *(G-1785)*

Jersey Central Pwr & Light Co ....D 330 336-9884
Wadsworth *(G-18601)*

Jersey Central Pwr & Light Co ....D 216 479-1132
Cleveland *(G-5792)*

Jersey Central Pwr & Light Co ....D 440 953-7651
Painesville *(G-15716)*

Licking Rural Electrification ....D 740 892-2071
Utica *(G-18456)*

Metropolitan Edison Company ....C 800 736-3402
Akron *(G-336)*

Mid-Ohio Energy Cooperative ....E 419 568-5321
Kenton *(G-12284)*

National Gas & Oil Corporation ....E 740 344-2102
Newark *(G-15079)*

Nisource Inc ....E 614 460-4878
Columbus *(G-8190)*

North Central Elc Coop Inc ....E 800 426-3072
Attica *(G-814)*

NRG Power Midwest LP ....D 440 930-6401
Avon Lake *(G-925)*

NRG Power Midwest LP ....D 330 505-4327
Niles *(G-15165)*

Ohio Edison Company ....A 800 736-3402
Akron *(G-358)*

Ohio Edison Company ....C 740 671-2900
Shadyside *(G-16697)*

Ohio Edison Company ....C 330 740-7754
Youngstown *(G-20143)*

Ohio Edison Company ....C 330 336-9880
Wadsworth *(G-18610)*

Ohio Power Company ....C 614 716-1000
Columbus *(G-8279)*

Ohio Power Company.................D....... 740 695-7800
Saint Clairsville **(G-16497)**

Ohio Valley Electric Corp.................D....... 740 289-7200
Piketon **(G-15981)**

Ohio Valley Electric Corp.................D....... 740 289-7225
Piketon **(G-15982)**

Paulding-Putnam Electric Coop.................E....... 419 399-5015
Paulding **(G-15798)**

Pennsylvania Electric Company.................D....... 800 545-7741
Akron **(G-375)**

Pennsylvania Power Company.................C....... 800 720-3600
Akron **(G-376)**

Pioneer Rural Electric Coop.................D....... 800 762-0997
Piqua **(G-16016)**

Public Service Company Okla.................C....... 614 716-1000
Columbus **(G-8479)**

Reliability First Corporation.................E....... 216 503-0600
Cleveland **(G-6301)**

South Central Power Company.................E....... 740 474-6045
Circleville **(G-4850)**

▲ South Central Power Company.................C....... 740 653-4422
Lancaster **(G-12436)**

South Central Power Company.................E....... 614 837-4351
Canal Winchester **(G-2120)**

South Central Power Company.................E....... 740 425-4018
Barnesville **(G-979)**

Southwestern Electric Power Co.................C....... 614 716-1000
Columbus **(G-8666)**

Toledo Edison Company.................D....... 800 447-3333
Akron **(G-471)**

Toledo Edison Company.................E....... 419 321-8488
Oak Harbor **(G-15479)**

Toledo Edison Company.................D....... 419 249-5364
Holland **(G-11920)**

Union Rural Electric Coop Inc.................E....... 937 642-1826
Marysville **(G-13535)**

Vistra Energy Corp.................C....... 513 467-5289
Moscow **(G-14721)**

Vistra Energy Corp.................C....... 513 467-4900
North Bend **(G-15183)**

Volunteer Energy Services Inc.................E....... 614 856-3128
Pickerington **(G-15969)**

Walleye Power LLC.................D....... 567 298-7400
Oregon **(G-15614)**

4922 Natural Gas Transmission

Belden & Blake Corporation.................E....... 330 602-5551
Dover **(G-10066)**

Columbia Energy Group.................A....... 614 460-4683
Columbus **(G-7247)**

Columbia Gas Transmission LLC.................E....... 614 460-6000
Columbus **(G-7250)**

Columbia Gas Transmission LLC.................E....... 740 397-8242
Mount Vernon **(G-14754)**

Columbia Gas Transmission LLC.................E....... 614 460-4704
Columbus **(G-7251)**

Columbia Gas Transmission LLC.................E....... 740 892-2552
Homer **(G-11933)**

Columbia Gulf Transmission LLC.................E....... 740 746-9105
Sugar Grove **(G-17373)**

Consumers Gas Cooperative.................E....... 330 682-4144
Orrville **(G-15627)**

Dominion Energy Transm Inc.................E....... 513 932-5793
Lebanon **(G-12460)**

▲ Duke Energy Ohio Inc.................D....... 704 382-3853
Cincinnati **(G-3450)**

Eureka Midstream LLC.................E....... 740 868-1325
Marietta **(G-13327)**

Kinder Mrgan Lqds Trminals LLC.................E....... 513 841-0500
Cincinnati **(G-3870)**

◆ Koch Knight LLC.................D....... 330 488-1651
East Canton **(G-10387)**

National Gas & Oil Corporation.................E....... 740 344-2102
Newark **(G-15079)**

National Gas & Oil Corporation.................E....... 740 454-7252
Zanesville **(G-20343)**

Ohio Gas Company.................E....... 419 636-3642
Bryan **(G-1967)**

Texas Eastern Transmission LP.................E....... 513 932-1816
Lebanon **(G-12510)**

Utica East Ohio Midstream LLC.................A....... 740 431-4168
Dennison **(G-10056)**

4923 Natural Gas Transmission & Distribution

Aspire Energy of Ohio LLC.................E....... 330 682-7726
Orrville **(G-15623)**

Columbia Gas Transmission LLC.................E....... 740 432-1612
Cambridge **(G-2059)**

Dayton Power and Light Company.................D....... 937 331-4123
Moraine **(G-14647)**

East Ohio Gas Company.................C....... 330 478-1700
Canton **(G-2293)**

National Gas & Oil Corporation.................E....... 740 454-7252
Zanesville **(G-20343)**

4924 Natural Gas Distribution

Bay State Gas Company.................B....... 614 460-4292
Columbus **(G-7021)**

▲ Cinergy Corp.................A....... 513 421-9500
Cincinnati **(G-3289)**

City of Lancaster.................E....... 740 687-6670
Lancaster **(G-12380)**

City of Toledo.................D....... 419 245-1800
Toledo **(G-17654)**

Columbia Gas of Ohio Inc.................E....... 614 460-6000
Columbus **(G-7248)**

Columbia Gas of Ohio Inc.................D....... 440 891-2458
Cleveland **(G-5314)**

Columbia Gas of Ohio Inc.................E....... 419 435-7725
Findlay **(G-10890)**

Columbia Gas of Ohio Inc.................E....... 740 264-5577
Steubenville **(G-17148)**

Columbia Gas of Ohio Inc.................C....... 614 481-1000
Columbus **(G-7249)**

Columbia Gas of Ohio Inc.................E....... 419 539-6046
Toledo **(G-17668)**

Delta Energy LLC.................E....... 614 761-3603
Dublin **(G-10198)**

▲ Duke Energy Ohio Inc.................D....... 704 382-3853
Cincinnati **(G-3450)**

East Ohio Gas Company.................A....... 800 362-7557
Cleveland **(G-5457)**

East Ohio Gas Company.................C....... 330 742-8121
Youngstown **(G-20024)**

East Ohio Gas Company.................B....... 330 266-2169
New Franklin **(G-14909)**

East Ohio Gas Company.................C....... 330 477-9411
Canton **(G-2291)**

East Ohio Gas Company.................E....... 216 736-6959
Cleveland **(G-5458)**

East Ohio Gas Company.................D....... 216 736-6120
Ashtabula **(G-737)**

East Ohio Gas Company.................D....... 330 499-2501
Canton **(G-2292)**

East Ohio Gas Company.................C....... 330 478-1700
Canton **(G-2293)**

East Ohio Gas Company.................C....... 216 736-6917
Wickliffe **(G-19457)**

Energy Cooperative Inc.................E....... 740 348-1206
Newark **(G-15031)**

Hearthstone Utilities Inc.................D....... 440 974-3770
Cleveland **(G-5679)**

National Gas & Oil Corporation.................E....... 740 344-2102
Newark **(G-15079)**

National Gas & Oil Corporation.................E....... 740 454-7252
Zanesville **(G-20343)**

National Gas Oil Corp.................E....... 740 348-1243
Hebron **(G-11721)**

Nwo Resources Inc.................C....... 419 636-1117
Bryan **(G-1965)**

Ohio Gas Company.................E....... 419 636-1117
Bryan **(G-1966)**

Stand Energy Corporation.................E....... 513 621-1113
Cincinnati **(G-4532)**

4925 Gas Production &/Or Distribution

Heritage Cooperative Inc.................D....... 419 294-2371
West Mansfield **(G-19125)**

4931 Electric & Other Svcs Combined

AEP Dresden Plant.................E....... 740 450-1964
Dresden **(G-10115)**

City of Columbus.................C....... 614 645-7627
Columbus **(G-7205)**

Cliffs Minnesota Minerals Co.................A....... 216 694-5700
Cleveland **(G-5303)**

Dayton Power and Light Company.................D....... 937 549-2641
Manchester **(G-13128)**

Dayton Power and Light Company.................D....... 937 331-4123
Moraine **(G-14647)**

Dayton Power and Light Company.................C....... 937 331-4063
Dayton **(G-9168)**

Dayton Power and Light Company.................E....... 937 331-3032
Miamisburg **(G-14163)**

Duke Energy Kentucky Inc.................C....... 704 594-6200
Cincinnati **(G-3449)**

▲ Duke Energy Ohio Inc.................D....... 704 382-3853
Cincinnati **(G-3450)**

Medical Center Co (inc).................E....... 216 368-4256
Cleveland **(G-5942)**

Stockport Mill Country Inn Inc.................E....... 740 559-2822
Stockport **(G-17183)**

4932 Gas & Other Svcs Combined

Dayton Power and Light Company.................D....... 937 549-2641
Manchester **(G-13128)**

Dayton Power and Light Company.................E....... 937 331-3032
Miamisburg **(G-14163)**

Dayton Power and Light Company.................D....... 937 331-4123
Moraine **(G-14647)**

Duke Energy Kentucky Inc.................C....... 704 594-6200
Cincinnati **(G-3449)**

G & O Resources Ltd.................D....... 330 253-2525
Akron **(G-231)**

Heritage Cooperative Inc.................D....... 419 294-2371
West Mansfield **(G-19125)**

National Gas & Oil Corporation.................E....... 740 344-2102
Newark **(G-15079)**

4939 Combination Utilities, NEC

City of Lorain.................C....... 440 204-2500
Lorain **(G-12891)**

City of Painesville.................B....... 440 392-5795
Painesville **(G-15700)**

Jersey Central Pwr & Light Co.................E....... 330 315-6713
Fairlawn **(G-10836)**

Ohio Edison Company.................C....... 740 671-2900
Shadyside **(G-16697)**

Universal Green Energy Solutio.................E....... 844 723-7768
Reynoldsburg **(G-16335)**

University of Cincinnati.................D....... 513 558-1799
Cincinnati **(G-4719)**

4941 Water Sply

Aqua Ohio Inc.................E....... 440 255-3984
Mentor **(G-14019)**

Aqua Ohio Inc.................E....... 330 832-5764
Massillon **(G-13663)**

Aqua Pennsylvania Inc.................E....... 614 882-6586
Westerville **(G-19221)**

Belmont County of Ohio.................E....... 740 695-3144
Saint Clairsville **(G-16473)**

City Alliance Water Sewer Dst.................E....... 330 823-5216
Alliance **(G-525)**

City of Akron.................E....... 330 678-0077
Kent **(G-12221)**

City of Akron.................C....... 330 375-2420
Akron **(G-135)**

City of Avon Lake.................E....... 440 933-6226
Avon Lake **(G-912)**

City of Celina.................E....... 419 586-2451
Celina **(G-2588)**

City of Cleveland.................E....... 216 664-3121
Cleveland **(G-5191)**

City of Cleveland Heights.................E....... 216 291-5995
Cleveland Heights **(G-6717)**

City of Columbus.................E....... 614 645-7490
Columbus **(G-7206)**

City of Columbus.................E....... 614 645-8297
Columbus **(G-7212)**

City of Columbus.................D....... 614 645-8270
Columbus **(G-7210)**

City of Cuyahoga Falls.................E....... 330 971-8130
Cuyahoga Falls **(G-9082)**

City of Dayton.................C....... 937 333-6070
Dayton **(G-9306)**

City of Dayton.................E....... 937 333-3725
Dayton **(G-9304)**

City of Huron.................D....... 419 433-5000
Huron **(G-12023)**

City of Lorain.................E....... 440 288-0281
Lorain **(G-12890)**

City of Lorain.................C....... 440 204-2500
Lorain **(G-12891)**

City of Massillon.................E....... 330 833-3304
Massillon **(G-13671)**

City of Toledo.................D....... 419 245-1800
Toledo **(G-17654)**

City of Troy.................C....... 937 335-1914
Troy **(G-18198)**

City of Westerville.................E....... 614 901-6500
Westerville **(G-19236)**

City of Youngstown.................E....... 330 742-8749
Youngstown **(G-19992)**

Clearwater Services Inc.................D....... 330 836-4946
Akron **(G-142)**

Cleveland Water Department.................A....... 216 664-3168
Cleveland **(G-5296)**

S I C

County of Licking..............E....740 967-5951
  Johnstown (G-12199)
County of Warren..............D...*513 925-1377
  Lebanon (G-12459)
Del-Co Water Company Inc..............D...740 548-7746
  Delaware (G-9966)
East Liverpool Water Dept..............E....330 385-8812
  East Liverpool (G-10402)
Employment Relations Board..............E....513 863-0828
  Hamilton (G-11594)
Hecla Water Association..............E....740 533-0526
  Ironton (G-12154)
Highland County Water Co Inc..............E....937 393-4281
  Hillsboro (G-11844)
Medical Center Co (inc)..............E....216 368-4256
  Cleveland (G-5942)
Muskingum Wtrshed Cnsrvncy Dst..............B...330 343-6647
  New Philadelphia (G-14974)
New Lexington City of..............E....740 342-1633
  New Lexington (G-14922)
Northast Ohio Rgonal Sewer Dst..............C...216 881-6600
  Cleveland (G-6081)
Northern Ohio Rural Water..............E....419 668-7213
  Norwalk (G-15446)
Northwestern Water & Sewer Dst..............E....419 354-9090
  Bowling Green (G-1742)
Ohio-American Water Co Inc..............E....740 382-3993
  Marion (G-13451)
Ross County Water Company Inc..............E....740 774-4117
  Chillicothe (G-2822)
Rural Lorain County Water Auth..............D...440 355-5121
  Lagrange (G-12326)
Scioto County Region Wtr Dst 1..............E....740 259-2301
  Lucasville (G-13053)
Syracuse Water Dept..............E....740 992-7777
  Pomeroy (G-16097)
The Mahoning Valley Sani Dst..............D...330 799-6315
  Mineral Ridge (G-14514)
Toledo Cy Pub Utlity Wtr Distr..............E....419 936-2506
  Toledo (G-18082)
Twin City Water and Sewer Dst..............E....740 922-1460
  Dennison (G-10055)
Victory White Metal Company..............E....216 271-1400
  Cleveland (G-6629)

4952 Sewerage Systems

Belmont County of Ohio..............E....740 695-3144
  Saint Clairsville (G-16473)
City of Akron..............E....330 375-2666
  Akron (G-137)
City of Avon Lake..............E....440 933-6226
  Avon Lake (G-912)
City of Columbus..............D...614 645-3248
  Lockbourne (G-12811)
City of Dayton..............D...937 333-1837
  Dayton (G-9305)
City of Findlay..............E....419 424-7179
  Findlay (G-10889)
City of Hamilton..............E....513 785-7551
  Hamilton (G-11578)
City of Hamilton..............E....513 868-5971
  Hamilton (G-11579)
City of Kent..............D...330 678-8105
  Kent (G-12222)
City of Lima..............E....419 221-5175
  Lima (G-12615)
City of Lorain..............C...440 204-2500
  Lorain (G-12891)
City of Sandusky..............E....419 627-5907
  Sandusky (G-16585)
City of Toledo..............C...419 936-2924
  Toledo (G-17657)
City of Toledo..............D...419 245-1800
  Toledo (G-17654)
City of Westerville..............E....614 901-6500
  Westerville (G-19236)
City of Zanesville..............E....740 455-0641
  Zanesville (G-20296)
Clermont Cnty Wtr Rsurces Dept..............D...513 732-7970
  Batavia (G-987)
County of Lorain..............D...440 329-5584
  Elyria (G-10494)
County of Stark..............A...330 451-2303
  Canton (G-2268)
County of Warren..............D...513 925-1377
  Lebanon (G-12459)
Metropolitan Sewer District..............A...513 244-1300
  Cincinnati (G-4042)
New Lexington City of..............E....740 342-1633
  New Lexington (G-14922)

Northast Ohio Rgonal Sewer Dst..............C...216 641-6000
  Cleveland (G-6084)
Northast Ohio Rgonal Sewer Dst..............D...216 531-4892
  Cleveland (G-6085)
Northast Ohio Rgonal Sewer Dst..............D...216 641-3200
  Cleveland (G-6082)
Northwestern Water & Sewer Dst..............E....419 354-9090
  Bowling Green (G-1742)

4953 Refuse Systems

Allied Waste Industries LLC..............E....440 774-3100
  Oberlin (G-15498)
Allied Waste Systems Inc..............E....937 268-8110
  Dayton (G-9217)
Allied Waste Systems Inc..............E....419 925-4592
  Celina (G-2581)
Allied Waste Systems Inc..............D...937 593-3566
  Bellefontaine (G-1344)
Allied Waste Systems Inc..............E....419 636-2242
  Bryan (G-1951)
American Landfill Inc..............E....330 866-3265
  Waynesburg (G-18828)
Appliance Recycl Ctrs Amer Inc..............D...614 876-8771
  Hilliard (G-11742)
Athens-Hcking Cnty Recycl Ctrs..............E....740 594-5312
  Athens (G-770)
Atlas Recycling Inc..............E....800 837-1520
  Warren (G-18668)
Avalon Holdings Corporation..............D...330 856-8800
  Warren (G-18673)
B & B Plastics Recyclers Inc..............C...614 409-2880
  Columbus (G-7009)
BFI Waste Services LLC..............E....800 437-1123
  Salem (G-16537)
Big O Refuse Inc..............E....740 344-7544
  Granville (G-11334)
Boral Resources LLC..............D...740 622-8042
  Coshocton (G-8999)
Browning-Ferris Inds of Ohio..............D...330 793-7676
  Youngstown (G-19977)
Browning-Ferris Inds of Ohio..............E....330 536-8013
  Lowellville (G-13039)
Browning-Ferris Industries Inc..............E....513 899-2942
  Morrow (G-14715)
Browning-Ferris Industries LLC..............E....440 786-9390
  Solon (G-16830)
Browning-Ferris Industries LLC..............D...330 393-0385
  Warren (G-18682)
Buckeye Waste Industries Inc..............E....330 645-9900
  Coventry Township (G-9033)
Builders Trash Service..............E....614 444-7060
  Columbus (G-7096)
Caraustar Industries Inc..............E....937 298-9969
  Moraine (G-14631)
Cecos International Inc..............E....513 724-6114
  Williamsburg (G-19490)
Central Ohio Contractors Inc..............D...614 539-2579
  Grove City (G-11419)
Central Ohio Contractors Inc..............D...740 369-7700
  Delaware (G-9958)
Chemtron Corporation..............E....440 937-6348
  Avon (G-875)
City of Canton..............E....330 489-3080
  Canton (G-2256)
City of Cleveland Heights..............E....216 691-7300
  Cleveland (G-5199)
City of Dayton..............C...937 333-4860
  Dayton (G-9303)
City of Elyria..............D...440 366-2211
  Elyria (G-10489)
City of Lakewood..............E....216 252-4322
  Cleveland (G-5205)
City of Perrysburg..............E....419 872-8020
  Perrysburg (G-15848)
City of Xenia..............E....937 376-7271
  Xenia (G-19893)
Clean Harbors Envmtl Svcs Inc..............D...216 429-2402
  Cleveland (G-5222)
Clean Harbors Envmtl Svcs Inc..............D...216 429-2401
  Cleveland (G-5223)
Clean Harbors Envmtl Svcs Inc..............E....513 681-6242
  Cincinnati (G-3303)
Clean Harbors Envmtl Svcs Inc..............E....740 929-3532
  Hebron (G-11711)
Clean Hrbors Es Indus Svcs Inc..............C...937 425-0512
  Dayton (G-9308)
Clean Water Environmental LLC..............E....937 268-6501
  Dayton (G-9309)
Clm Pallet Recycling Inc..............E....614 272-5761
  Columbus (G-7233)

Counts Container Corporation..............E....216 433-4336
  Cleveland (G-5360)
County of Erie..............D...419 433-0617
  Milan (G-14360)
County of Montgomery..............E....937 781-3046
  Moraine (G-14637)
County of Portage..............E....330 297-3670
  Ravenna (G-16239)
Crispin Iron & Metal Co LLC..............E....740 616-6213
  Granville (G-11340)
Eco Global Corp..............E....419 363-2681
  Rockford (G-16414)
Envirite of Ohio Inc..............E....330 456-6238
  Canton (G-2302)
Environmental Enterprises Inc..............D...513 541-1823
  Cincinnati (G-3501)
Envirosafe Services of Ohio..............E....419 698-3500
  Oregon (G-15594)
Envision Waste Services LLC..............D...216 831-1818
  Cleveland (G-5487)
▲ Fpt Cleveland LLC..............C...216 441-3800
  Cleveland (G-5569)
Fultz & Son Inc..............E....419 547-9365
  Clyde (G-6743)
▲ Garden Street Iron & Metal..............E....513 853-3700
  Cincinnati (G-3603)
Gateway Products Recycling Inc..............E....216 341-8777
  Cleveland (G-5596)
▼ Grasan Equipment Company Inc....D...419 526-4440
  Mansfield (G-13180)
Greenstar Mid-America LLC..............E....330 784-1167
  Akron (G-246)
Hpj Industries Inc..............E....419 278-1000
  Deshler (G-10058)
Hpj Industries Inc..............D...419 278-1000
  North Baltimore (G-15178)
◆ I-Tran Inc..............E....330 659-0801
  Richfield (G-16360)
▲ Imco Recycling of Ohio LLC..............C...740 922-2373
  Uhrichsville (G-18342)
In-Plas Recycling Inc..............E....513 541-9800
  Cincinnati (G-3755)
Industrial Waste Control Inc..............D...330 270-9900
  Youngstown (G-20079)
▲ Interstate Shredding LLC..............E....330 545-5477
  Girard (G-11289)
▼ Jasar Recycling Inc..............D...864 233-5421
  East Palestine (G-10420)
Jee Foods..............E....513 917-1712
  Hamilton (G-11617)
Kimble Companies Inc..............E....330 963-5493
  Twinsburg (G-18288)
Kimble Recycl & Disposal Inc..............C...330 343-1226
  Dover (G-10084)
Liquid Wste Solidification LLC..............E....440 285-4648
  Chardon (G-2703)
M W Recycling LLC..............E....440 753-5400
  Mayfield Heights (G-13877)
Mahoning County..............E....330 793-5514
  Youngstown (G-20105)
Metal Management Ohio Inc..............E....419 782-7791
  Defiance (G-9930)
Metalico Akron Inc..............E....330 376-1400
  Akron (G-333)
Micro Construction LLC..............E....740 862-0751
  Baltimore (G-937)
Miles Alloy Inc..............E....216 245-8893
  Cleveland (G-5991)
Milliron Recycling Inc..............D...419 747-6522
  Mansfield (G-13223)
Mondo Polymer Technologies Inc..............E....740 376-9396
  Reno (G-16277)
Montgomery Iron & Paper Co Inc..............D...937 222-4059
  Dayton (G-9643)
Novotec Recycling LLC..............E....614 231-8326
  Columbus (G-8210)
Pinnacle Recycling LLC..............E....330 745-3700
  Akron (G-383)
Plastic Recycling Tech Inc..............E....937 615-9286
  Piqua (G-16023)
Plastic Recycling Tech Inc..............E....419 238-9395
  Van Wert (G-18486)
Polychem Corporation..............D...419 547-1400
  Clyde (G-6750)
R & R Sanitation Inc..............E....330 325-2311
  Mogadore (G-14555)
Republic Services Inc..............E....937 593-3566
  Bellefontaine (G-1361)
Republic Services Inc..............E....330 536-8013
  Lowellville (G-13042)

Republic Services Inc ....E 419 925-4592
Celina (G-2609)

Republic Services Inc ....E 419 626-2454
Sandusky (G-16635)

Republic Services Inc ....E 216 741-4013
Cleveland (G-6310)

Republic Services Inc ....D 216 741-4013
Cleveland (G-6311)

Republic Services Inc ....E 440 458-5191
Elyria (G-10559)

Republic Services Inc ....E 330 830-9050
Massillon (G-13722)

Republic Services Inc ....E 330 793-7676
Youngstown (G-20181)

Republic Services Inc ....E 330 793-7676
Youngstown (G-20182)

Republic Services Inc ....E 330 793-7676
Youngstown (G-20183)

Republic Services Inc ....E 419 636-5109
Bryan (G-1973)

Republic Services Inc ....E 440 774-4060
Oberlin (G-15518)

Republic Services Inc ....E 513 554-0237
Cincinnati (G-4360)

Republic Services Inc ....E 937 268-8110
Dayton (G-9733)

Republic Services Inc ....E 567 712-6634
Lima (G-12729)

Republic Services Inc ....E 614 308-3000
Columbus (G-8515)

Republic Services Inc ....D 740 969-4487
Columbus (G-8516)

Republic Services Inc ....E 800 247-3644
Massillon (G-13723)

Republic Services Inc ....E 330 434-9183
Akron (G-404)

Republic Services Inc ....E 800 331-0988
Gallipolis (G-11212)

Republic Services Inc ....E 419 396-3581
Carey (G-2546)

Republic Services Inc ....E 419 635-2367
Port Clinton (G-16115)

Republic Services Inc ....E 419 726-9465
Toledo (G-18003)

Republic Services Inc ....E 937 492-3470
Sidney (G-16796)

Rls Disposal Company Inc ....E 740 773-1440
Chillicothe (G-2815)

Ross Consolidated Corp ....D 440 748-5800
Grafton (G-11320)

▼ Ross Incineration Services Inc ....C 440 366-2000
Grafton (G-11321)

Royal Paper Stock Company Inc ....D 614 851-4714
Columbus (G-8557)

Royal Paper Stock Company Inc ....E 513 870-5780
West Chester (G-19077)

Rpg Inc ....D 419 289-2757
Ashland (G-687)

RSR Partners LLC ....B 440 248-3991
Solon (G-16894)

Rumpke Cnsld Companies Inc ....C 513 738-0800
Hamilton (G-11640)

Rumpke Sanitary Landfill Inc ....C 513 851-0122
Cincinnati (G-4409)

Rumpke Transportation Co LLC ....E 937 461-0004
Dayton (G-9740)

Rumpke Transportation Co LLC ....C 513 242-4600
Cincinnati (G-4410)

Rumpke Waste Inc ....D 513 851-0122
Cincinnati (G-4411)

Rumpke Waste Inc ....C 937 548-1939
Greenville (G-11393)

Rumpke Waste Inc ....D 937 378-4126
Georgetown (G-11274)

Rumpke Waste Inc ....D 513 242-2401
Cincinnati (G-4412)

Rumpke Waste Inc ....D 740 474-9790
Circleville (G-4847)

Safety-Kleen Systems Inc ....D 740 929-3532
Hebron (G-11724)

Shredded Bedding Corporation ....E 740 893-3567
Centerburg (G-2616)

Sidwell Materials Inc ....C 740 849-2394
Zanesville (G-20361)

Solid Waste Auth Cntl Ohio ....C 614 871-5100
Grove City (G-11471)

Spring Grove Rsrce Rcovery Inc ....D 513 681-6242
Cincinnati (G-4519)

Stericycle Inc ....D 330 393-0370
Warren (G-18747)

Stericycle Inc ....E 419 729-1934
Toledo (G-18048)

T C Rumpke Waste Collection ....E 513 385-7627
Cincinnati (G-4565)

Triad Transport Inc ....E 614 491-9497
Columbus (G-8777)

Veolia Es Tchncal Slutions LLC ....D 937 859-6101
Miamisburg (G-14234)

▲ Vexor Technology Inc ....E 330 721-9773
Medina (G-14013)

Waste Management Ohio Inc ....D 440 201-1235
Solon (G-16913)

Waste Management Ohio Inc ....E 800 910-2831
Wooster (G-19777)

Waste Management Ohio Inc ....E 330 452-9000
Canton (G-2532)

Waste Management Ohio Inc ....E 614 382-6342
Canal Winchester (G-2125)

Waste Management Ohio Inc ....E 419 547-7791
Vickery (G-18576)

Waste Management Ohio Inc ....E 866 797-9018
North Jackson (G-15256)

Waste Management Ohio Inc ....D 866 409-4671
Northwood (G-15413)

Waste Management Ohio Inc ....E 440 286-7116
Chardon (G-2724)

Waste Management Ohio Inc ....D 740 345-1212
Newark (G-15108)

Waste Management Ohio Inc ....D 419 221-3644
Lima (G-12776)

Waste Management Ohio Inc ....E 614 833-5290
Canal Winchester (G-2126)

Waste Management Ohio Inc ....C 800 343-6047
Fairborn (G-10689)

Waste Management Ohio Inc ....E 440 285-6767
Geneva (G-11250)

Waste Management Ohio Inc ....E 419 221-2029
Lima (G-12777)

Waste Parchment Inc ....E 330 674-6868
Millersburg (G-14499)

4959 Sanitary Svcs, NEC

AST Environmental Inc ....E 937 743-0002
Springboro (G-16962)

Bauer Lawn Maintenance Inc ....E 419 893-5296
Maumee (G-13761)

Bladecutters Lawn Service Inc ....E 937 274-3861
Dayton (G-9255)

Board Amercn Township Trustees ....E 419 331-8651
Elida (G-10471)

C & B Buck Bros Asp Maint LLC ....E 419 536-7325
Toledo (G-17633)

C & K Industrial Services Inc ....D 216 642-0055
Independence (G-12052)

C & K Industrial Services Inc ....E 513 829-5353
Fairfield (G-10705)

Chemtron Corporation ....E 440 937-6348
Avon (G-875)

City of Lima ....E 419 221-5294
Lima (G-12614)

City of Toledo ....E 419 936-2924
Toledo (G-17657)

Contract Sweepers & Eqp Co ....E 614 221-7441
Columbus (G-7366)

Cousins Waste Control LLC ....D 419 726-1500
Toledo (G-17686)

Cuyahoga County Sani Engrg Svc ....C 216 443-8211
Cleveland (G-5399)

▼ Diproinduca (usa) Limited LLC ....D 330 722-4442
Medina (G-13930)

Dun Rite Home Improvement Inc ....E 330 650-5322
Macedonia (G-13068)

Environment Control of Greater ....D 614 868-9788
Columbus (G-7521)

Green Impressions LLC ....E 440 240-8508
Sheffield Village (G-16734)

Greenscapes Landscape Company ....D 614 837-1869
Columbus (G-7696)

H A M Landscaping Inc ....E 216 663-6666
Cleveland (G-5650)

Image Pavement Maintenance ....E 937 833-9200
Brookville (G-1914)

Interdyne Corporation ....E 419 229-8192
Lima (G-12666)

Los Alamos Technical Assoc Inc ....E 614 508-1200
Westerville (G-19275)

Mahoning County ....C 330 799-1581
Youngstown (G-20106)

Mc Clurg & Creamer Inc ....E 419 866-7080
Holland (G-11896)

Northast Ohio Rgonal Sewer Dst ....C 216 641-3200
Cleveland (G-6082)

Ohio Irrigation Lawn Sprinkler ....E 937 432-9911
Dayton (G-9670)

Ohio State University ....E 614 293-8732
Columbus (G-8327)

Paramount Lawn Service Inc ....E 513 984-5200
Loveland (G-13020)

Petro Environmental Tech ....E 513 489-6789
Cincinnati (G-4237)

Progrssive Sweeping Contrs Inc ....E 419 464-0130
Toledo (G-17990)

Reilly Sweeping Inc ....E 440 786-8400
Cleveland (G-6299)

▲ Samsel Rope & Marine Supply Co ...E 216 241-0333
Cleveland (G-6370)

Schill Landscaping and Lawn CA ....D 440 327-3030
North Ridgeville (G-15343)

Superior Envmtl Solutions LLC ....C 513 874-8355
West Chester (G-19087)

Supers Landscaping Inc ....E 440 775-0027
Oberlin (G-15520)

T J D Industrial Clg & Maint ....E 419 425-5025
Findlay (G-10968)

T L C Landscaping Inc ....E 440 248-4852
Cleveland (G-6495)

T O J Inc ....E 440 352-1900
Mentor (G-14114)

Warstler Brothers Landscaping ....E 330 492-9500
Canton (G-2531)

Wastren Advantage Inc ....E 970 254-1277
Piketon (G-15993)

Yardmaster of Columbus Inc ....E 614 863-4510
Blacklick (G-1485)

Z Snow Removal Inc ....E 513 683-7719
Maineville (G-13120)

4961 Steam & Air Conditioning Sply

Akron Energy Systems LLC ....D 330 374-0600
Akron (G-38)

Brewer-Garrett Co ....C 440 243-3535
Middleburg Heights (G-14248)

Cleveland Thermal LLC ....E 216 241-3636
Cleveland (G-5293)

Honeywell International Inc ....D 216 459-6053
Cleveland (G-5702)

Marketing Comm Resource Inc ....D 440 484-3010
Willoughby (G-19549)

Medical Center Co (inc) ....E 216 368-4256
Cleveland (G-5942)

4971 Irrigation Systems

City of Dayton ....D 937 333-7138
Dayton (G-9307)

City of Westerville ....E 614 901-6500
Westerville (G-19236)

◆ Pentair Rsdntial Fltration LLC ....E 440 286-4116
Chardon (G-2708)

Warstler Brothers Landscaping ....E 330 492-9500
Canton (G-2531)

50 WHOLESALE TRADE¨DURABLE GOODS

5012 Automobiles & Other Motor Vehicles Wholesale

1106 West Main Inc ....E 330 673-2122
Kent (G-12212)

ABC Detroit/Toledo Auto Auctn ....E 419 872-0872
Perrysburg (G-15832)

Abers Garage Inc ....E 419 281-5500
Ashland (G-644)

Ace Truck Body Inc ....E 614 871-3100
Grove City (G-11403)

Adesa Corporation LLC ....C 937 746-5361
Franklin (G-11021)

Adesa-Ohio Llc ....C 330 467-8280
Northfield (G-15372)

Akron Auto Auction Inc ....C 330 724-7708
Coventry Township (G-9032)

▼ Albert Mike Leasing Inc ....C 513 563-1400
Cincinnati (G-2919)

Auction Broadcasting Co LLC ....C 419 872-0872
Perrysburg (G-15833)

Baker Vehicle Systems Inc ....E 330 467-2250
Macedonia (G-13061)

Beechmont Motors Inc ....E 513 388-3883
Cincinnati (G-3031)

Beechmont Toyota Inc ....D.... 513 388-3800
Cincinnati (G-3034)

Bob Sumerel Tire Co Inc ....E.... 513 792-6600
Cincinnati (G-3065)

Bobb Automotive Inc ....E.... 614 853-3000
Columbus (G-7052)

Broadvue Motors Inc ....D.... 440 845-6000
Cleveland (G-5084)

Brown Industrial Inc ....E.... 937 693-3838
Botkins (G-1708)

Buckeye Truck Equipment Inc ....E.... 614 299-1136
Columbus (G-7091)

Bulk Carrier Trnsp Eqp Co ....E.... 330 339-3333
New Philadelphia (G-14947)

Bulldawg Holdings LLC ....E.... 419 423-3131
Findlay (G-10885)

Central Hummr East ....E.... 216 514-2700
Cleveland (G-5155)

Cerni Motor Sales Inc ....D.... 330 652-9917
Youngstown (G-19984)

Chuck Nicholson Pntc-GMC Trcks ....E.... 330 343-7781
Dover (G-10069)

Columbus Fair Auto Auction Inc ....A.... 614 497-2000
Obetz (G-15525)

Copart Inc ....E.... 614 497-1590
Columbus (G-7367)

Coughlin Chevrolet Inc ....D.... 740 964-9191
Pataskala (G-15784)

Cox Automotive Inc ....C.... 513 874-9310
West Chester (G-18904)

Cox Automotive Inc ....B.... 614 871-2771
Grove City (G-11423)

Dave Knapp Ford Lincoln Inc ....E.... 937 547-3000
Greenville (G-11373)

Donley Ford-Lincoln Inc ....E.... 419 281-3673
Ashland (G-672)

Dons Automotive Group LLC ....E.... 419 337-3010
Wauseon (G-18799)

Dons Brooklyn Chevrolet Inc ....E.... 216 741-1500
Cleveland (G-5441)

Doug Bigelow Chevrolet Inc ....D.... 330 644-7500
Akron (G-192)

Doug Marine Motors Inc ....E.... 740 335-3700
Wshngtn CT Hs (G-19869)

Downtown Ford Lincoln Inc ....D.... 330 456-2781
Canton (G-2290)

Dutro Ford Lincoln-Mercury Inc ....D.... 740 452-6334
Zanesville (G-20301)

Ed Schmidt Auto Inc ....C.... 419 874-4331
Perrysburg (G-15863)

Ed Tomko Chryslr Jep Dge Inc ....E.... 440 835-5900
Avon Lake (G-916)

Esec Corporation ....E.... 330 799-1536
Youngstown (G-20030)

Esec Corporation ....E.... 614 875-3732
Grove City (G-11430)

Freightlner Trcks of Cncinnati ....E.... 513 772-7171
Cincinnati (G-3591)

Fyda Freightliner Youngstown ....D.... 330 797-0224
Youngstown (G-20041)

Gallipolis Auto Auction Inc ....E.... 740 446-1576
Gallipolis (G-11193)

Gene Stevens Auto & Truck Ctr ....E.... 419 429-2000
Findlay (G-10913)

George P Ballas Buick GMC Trck ....E.... 419 535-1000
Toledo (G-17760)

Graham Chevrolet-Cadillac Co ....D.... 419 989-4012
Ontario (G-15551)

Great Dane Columbus Inc ....E.... 614 876-0666
Hilliard (G-11770)

Greater Cleveland Auto Auction ....D.... 216 433-7777
Cleveland (G-5634)

Haydocy Automotive Inc ....D.... 614 279-8880
Columbus (G-7719)

Helton Enterprises Inc ....E.... 419 423-4180
Findlay (G-10922)

Hidy Motors Inc ....D.... 937 426-9564
Dayton (G-9176)

▼ Honda North America Inc ....E.... 937 642-5000
Marysville (G-13504)

Interstate Truckway Inc ....E.... 614 771-1220
Columbus (G-7839)

Interstate Truckway Inc ....E.... 513 542-5500
Cincinnati (G-3781)

Kenworth of Cincinnati Inc ....D.... 513 771-5831
Cincinnati (G-3862)

Klaben Lincoln Ford Inc ....D.... 330 673-3139
Kent (G-12246)

▲ Ktm North America Inc ....E.... 855 215-6360
Amherst (G-591)

Laria Chevrolet-Buick Inc ....E.... 330 925-2015
Rittman (G-16406)

Liberty Ford Southwest Inc ....D.... 440 888-2600
Cleveland (G-5867)

Life Star Rescue Inc ....E.... 419 238-2507
Van Wert (G-18482)

Lower Great Lakes Kenworth Inc ....E.... 419 874-3511
Perrysburg (G-15890)

M H EBY Inc ....E.... 614 879-6901
West Jefferson (G-19110)

▲ Mac Manufacturing Inc ....A.... 330 823-9900
Alliance (G-539)

Mac Manufacturing Inc ....C.... 330 829-1680
Salem (G-16552)

▲ Mac Trailer Manufacturing Inc ....C.... 330 823-9900
Alliance (G-540)

Mansfield Truck Sls & Svc Inc ....E.... 419 522-9811
Mansfield (G-13211)

McCluskey Chevrolet Inc ....C.... 513 761-1111
Cincinnati (G-3986)

Medina Management Company LLC ....D.... 330 723-3291
Medina (G-13976)

Midwest Motors Inc ....E.... 330 758-5800
Youngstown (G-20128)

Montpelier Auto Auction Ohio ....C.... 419 485-1691
Montpelier (G-14614)

Mullinax East LLC ....D.... 440 296-3020
Wickliffe (G-19470)

▼ National Car Mart III Inc ....E.... 216 398-2228
Cleveland (G-6038)

Nollenberger Truck Center ....E.... 419 837-5996
Stony Ridge (G-17185)

Peterbilt of Cincinnati ....E.... 513 772-1740
Cincinnati (G-4235)

Peterbilt of Northwest Ohio ....E.... 419 423-3441
Findlay (G-10952)

R & R Inc ....E.... 330 799-1536
Youngstown (G-20174)

R & R Truck Sales Inc ....E.... 330 784-5881
Akron (G-395)

Rush Truck Centers Ohio Inc ....E.... 513 733-8500
Cincinnati (G-4414)

Rush Truck Centers Ohio Inc ....E.... 419 224-6045
Lima (G-12735)

Schodorf Truck Body & Eqp Co ....E.... 614 228-6793
Columbus (G-8603)

Sharron Group Inc ....E.... 614 873-5856
Plain City (G-16066)

Sims Buick-G M C Truck Inc ....E.... 330 372-3500
Warren (G-18744)

Slimans Sales & Service Inc ....E.... 440 988-4484
Amherst (G-597)

South East Chevrolet Co ....E.... 440 585-9300
Willoughby Hills (G-19594)

State Park Motors Inc ....E.... 740 264-3113
Steubenville (G-17170)

Stoops Frghtlnr-Qlity Trlr Inc ....E.... 937 236-4092
Dayton (G-9795)

Stoops of Lima Inc ....E.... 419 228-4334
Lima (G-12757)

Stratton Chevrolet Co ....E.... 330 537-3151
Beloit (G-1398)

Stykemain Pntiac-Buick-Gmc Ltd ....D.... 419 784-5252
Defiance (G-9942)

Tesco-Transportion Eqp Sls ....E.... 419 836-2835
Oregon (G-15610)

Tri-State Trailer Sales Inc ....E.... 412 747-7777
West Chester (G-19093)

Truck Country Indiana Inc ....E.... 419 228-4334
Lima (G-12770)

◆ Valley Ford Truck Inc ....D.... 216 524-2400
Cleveland (G-6617)

Value Auto Auction LLC ....D.... 740 982-3030
Crooksville (G-9064)

▲ Venco Venturo Industries LLC ....E.... 513 772-8448
Cincinnati (G-4753)

Village Motors Inc ....D.... 330 674-2055
Millersburg (G-14498)

Voss Auto Network Inc ....E.... 937 428-2447
Dayton (G-9860)

Voss Chevrolet Inc ....E.... 937 428-2500
Dayton (G-9862)

Voss Dodge ....E.... 937 435-7800
Dayton (G-9863)

Warner Buick-Nissan Inc ....E.... 419 423-7161
Findlay (G-10974)

White Family Companies Inc ....C.... 937 222-3701
Dayton (G-9879)

Whites Service Center Inc ....E.... 937 653-5279
Urbana (G-18446)

◆ Wholecycle Inc ....E.... 330 929-8123
Peninsula (G-15815)

Youngstown-Kenworth Inc ....E.... 330 534-9761
Hubbard (G-11952)

5013 Motor Vehicle Splys & New Parts Wholesale

▲ Accel Performance Group LLC ....C.... 216 658-6413
Independence (G-12036)

Ace Truck Body Inc ....E.... 614 871-3100
Grove City (G-11403)

◆ Adelmans Truck Parts Corp ....E.... 330 456-0206
Canton (G-2173)

Advance Stores Company Inc ....C.... 740 369-4491
Delaware (G-9950)

Alex Products Inc ....C.... 419 399-4500
Paulding (G-15790)

All Lift Service Company Inc ....E.... 440 585-1542
Willoughby (G-19503)

Allied Truck Parts Co ....E.... 330 477-8127
Canton (G-2181)

Atlas Industries Inc ....B.... 419 637-2117
Tiffin (G-17509)

▲ Auto Aftermarket Concepts ....E.... 513 942-2535
Cincinnati (G-3005)

Automotive Distributors Co Inc ....C.... 614 476-1315
Columbus (G-7005)

Automotive Distributors Co Inc ....E.... 330 785-7290
Akron (G-82)

Automotive Distributors Co Inc ....E.... 216 398-2014
Cleveland (G-5025)

Beechmont Ford Inc ....C.... 513 752-6611
Cincinnati (G-2842)

Beechmont Motors Inc ....E.... 513 388-3883
Cincinnati (G-3031)

Beechmont Toyota Inc ....D.... 513 388-3800
Cincinnati (G-3034)

◆ Bendix Coml Vhcl Systems LLC ....B.... 440 329-9000
Elyria (G-10482)

◆ Better Brake Parts Inc ....E.... 419 227-0685
Lima (G-12607)

Bills Battery Company Inc ....E.... 513 922-0100
Cincinnati (G-3050)

Bridgeport Auto Parts Inc ....E.... 740 635-0441
Bridgeport (G-1814)

Brookville Roadster Inc ....E.... 937 833-4605
Brookville (G-1912)

▲ Building 8 Inc ....E.... 513 771-8000
Cincinnati (G-3088)

▲ Buyers Products Company ....D.... 440 974-8888
Mentor (G-14024)

▲ Cadna Rubber Company Inc ....E.... 901 566-9090
Fairlawn (G-10818)

Car Parts Warehouse Inc ....E.... 440 259-2991
Perry (G-15821)

▲ Car Parts Warehouse Inc ....E.... 216 281-4500
Brookpark (G-1892)

Cedar Elec Holdings Corp ....D.... 773 804-6288
West Chester (G-18882)

Certified Power Inc ....D.... 419 355-1200
Fremont (G-11062)

Columbus Diesel Supply Co Inc ....E.... 614 445-8391
Reynoldsburg (G-16292)

Columbus Public School Dst ....C.... 614 365-5263
Columbus (G-7305)

Cornwell Quality Tools Company ....E.... 330 335-2933
Wadsworth (G-18594)

Cross Truck Equipment Co Inc ....E.... 330 477-8151
Canton (G-2274)

Crown Dielectric Inds Inc ....E.... 614 224-5161
Columbus (G-7397)

D-G Custom Chrome LLC ....D.... 513 531-1881
Cincinnati (G-3396)

Dana Heavy Vehicle Systems ....D.... 419 866-3900
Holland (G-11881)

Denso International Amer Inc ....B.... 937 393-6800
Hillsboro (G-11837)

◆ Durable Corporation ....D.... 800 537-1603
Norwalk (G-15433)

▼ East Manufacturing Corporation ....B.... 330 325-9921
Randolph (G-16230)

▲ Faurecia Emissions Control Sys ....C.... 812 341-2000
Toledo (G-17727)

Fayette Parts Service Inc ....C.... 740 282-4547
Steubenville (G-17153)

Finishmaster Inc ....D.... 614 228-4328
Columbus (G-7578)

◆ Four Wheel Drive Hardware LLC ....C.... 330 482-4733
Columbiana (G-6788)

Freudenberg-Nok General Partnr B 419 499-2502
Milan *(G-14361)*

Frontier Tank Center Inc E 330 659-3888
Richfield *(G-16358)*

Fuyao Glass America Inc C 937 496-5777
Dayton *(G-9454)*

▲ G S Wiring Systems Inc B 419 423-7111
Findlay *(G-10911)*

▼ G-Cor Automotive Corp E 614 443-6735
Columbus *(G-7641)*

General Motors LLC C 513 874-0535
West Chester *(G-18931)*

General Motors LLC C 513 603-6600
West Chester *(G-18932)*

General Parts Inc D 330 220-6500
Brunswick *(G-1931)*

General Parts Inc E 614 267-5197
Columbus *(G-7653)*

◆ Goodyear Tire & Rubber Company A 330 796-2121
Akron *(G-242)*

Greenleaf Auto Recyclers LLC E 330 832-6001
Massillon *(G-13689)*

GTM Service Inc E 440 944-5099
Wickliffe *(G-19462)*

H & H Auto Parts Inc D 330 456-4778
Canton *(G-2332)*

H & H Auto Parts Inc E 330 494-2975
Canton *(G-2333)*

Hahn Automotive Warehouse Inc E 937 223-1068
Dayton *(G-9483)*

Hamilton Automotive Warehouse D 513 896-4100
Hamilton *(G-11607)*

Hankook Tire America Corp E 330 896-6199
Uniontown *(G-18373)*

Hebco Products Inc A 419 562-7987
Bucyrus *(G-1992)*

Herbert E Orr Company C 419 399-4866
Paulding *(G-15794)*

Hite Parts Exchange Inc E 614 272-5115
Columbus *(G-7756)*

Honda Trading America Corp C 937 644-8004
Marysville *(G-13506)*

▲ Hy-Tek Material Handling Inc D 614 497-2500
Columbus *(G-7790)*

Ieh Auto Parts LLC E 740 373-8327
Marietta *(G-13336)*

Ieh Auto Parts LLC E 740 732-2395
Caldwell *(G-2040)*

Ieh Auto Parts LLC E 740 373-8151
Marietta *(G-13337)*

◆ Interstate Diesel Service Inc B 216 881-0015
Cleveland *(G-5765)*

▲ Jegs Automotive Inc C 614 294-5050
Delaware *(G-9990)*

Jim Hayden Inc D 513 563-8828
Cincinnati *(G-3819)*

Joseph Russo E 440 748-2690
Grafton *(G-11317)*

Jr Engineering Inc C 330 848-0960
Barberton *(G-957)*

K - O - I Warehouse Inc E 937 323-5585
Springfield *(G-17058)*

▲ K - O - I Warehouse Inc E 513 357-2400
Cincinnati *(G-3842)*

◆ Kaffenbarger Truck Eqp Co C 937 845-3804
New Carlisle *(G-14892)*

◆ Keihin Thermal Tech Amer Inc B 740 869-3000
Mount Sterling *(G-14745)*

Kenton Auto and Truck Wrecking E 419 673-8234
Kenton *(G-12283)*

Kenworth of Cincinnati Inc D 513 771-5831
Cincinnati *(G-3862)*

Keystone Automotive Inds Inc D 513 961-5500
Cincinnati *(G-3866)*

Keystone Automotive Inds Inc E 330 759-8019
Girard *(G-11293)*

Klase Enterprises Inc E 330 452-6300
Canton *(G-2369)*

Knox Auto LLC E 330 701-5266
Mount Vernon *(G-14771)*

▲ KOI Enterprises Inc D 513 357-2400
Cincinnati *(G-3886)*

Lower Great Lakes Kenworth Inc E 419 874-3511
Perrysburg *(G-15890)*

◆ Luk-Aftermarket Service Inc D 330 273-4383
Valley City *(G-18466)*

▲ Mac Trailer Manufacturing Inc C 330 823-9900
Alliance *(G-540)*

▲ Matco Tools Corporation B 330 929-4949
Stow *(G-17219)*

▲ McBee Supply Corporation D 216 881-0015
Cleveland *(G-5930)*

◆ MJ Auto Parts Inc E 440 205-6272
Mentor *(G-14088)*

Myers Industries Inc E 330 253-5592
Akron *(G-342)*

National Marketshare Group E 513 921-0800
Cincinnati *(G-4094)*

Neff Machinery and Supplies E 740 454-0128
Zanesville *(G-20344)*

Nk Parts Industries Inc E 937 493-4651
Sidney *(G-16787)*

Nu-Di Products Co Inc D 216 251-9070
Cleveland *(G-6106)*

▲ Ohashi Technica USA Inc E 740 965-5115
Sunbury *(G-17393)*

Ohio Auto Supply Company E 330 454-5105
Canton *(G-2424)*

Ohio Automotive Supply Co E 419 422-1655
Findlay *(G-10951)*

OReilly Automotive Inc D 330 494-0042
North Canton *(G-15226)*

OReilly Automotive Inc E 419 630-0811
Bryan *(G-1968)*

OReilly Automotive Inc E 330 318-3136
Boardman *(G-1700)*

P & M Exhaust Systems Whse E 513 825-2660
Cincinnati *(G-4195)*

▼ Par International Inc E 614 529-1300
Obetz *(G-15528)*

Pat Young Service Co Inc E 440 891-1550
Avon *(G-899)*

▲ Pat Young Service Co Inc E 216 447-8550
Cleveland *(G-6180)*

Perkins Motor Service Ltd E 440 277-1256
Lorain *(G-12938)*

Peterbilt of Cincinnati E 513 772-1740
Cincinnati *(G-4235)*

▲ Pioneer Automotive Tech Inc C 937 746-2293
Springboro *(G-16982)*

▲ Power Train Components Inc D 419 636-4430
Bryan *(G-1971)*

Premier Truck Parts Inc E 216 642-5000
Cleveland *(G-6233)*

R & R Inc E 330 799-1536
Youngstown *(G-20174)*

▲ R L Morrissey & Assoc Inc E 440 498-3730
Solon *(G-16889)*

Rockstarr Holdings LLC E 330 509-9086
Youngstown *(G-20189)*

Shiloh Manufacturing LLC E 330 558-2693
Valley City *(G-18469)*

▲ Shrader Tire & Oil Inc E 419 472-2128
Toledo *(G-18032)*

Smyth Automotive Inc D 513 528-2800
Cincinnati *(G-4496)*

Smyth Automotive Inc D 513 528-0061
Cincinnati *(G-4497)*

Smyth Automotive Inc E 513 575-2000
Milford *(G-14434)*

Smyth Automotive Inc E 513 777-6400
West Chester *(G-19010)*

Smyth Automotive Inc E 513 734-7800
Bethel *(G-1454)*

▲ Snyders Antique Auto Parts Inc E 330 549-5313
New Springfield *(G-14998)*

▲ Stellar Srkg Acquisition LLC E 330 769-8484
Seville *(G-16692)*

▲ Stoddard Imported Cars Inc D 440 951-1040
Mentor *(G-14112)*

Thyssenkrupp Bilstein Amer Inc E 513 881-7600
West Chester *(G-19015)*

◆ Thyssenkrupp Bilstein Amer Inc C 513 881-7600
Hamilton *(G-11647)*

Tk Holdings Inc E 937 778-9713
Piqua *(G-16031)*

Transport Services Inc D 440 582-4900
Cleveland *(G-6543)*

Truckomat Corporation E 740 467-2818
Hebron *(G-11725)*

Turbo Parts LLC E 740 223-1695
Marion *(G-13466)*

◆ Valley Ford Truck Inc D 216 524-2400
Cleveland *(G-6617)*

▲ Ventra Salem LLC A 330 337-8002
Salem *(G-16566)*

Voss Toyota Inc E 937 431-2100
Beavercreek *(G-1195)*

W W Williams Company LLC D 419 837-5067
Perrysburg *(G-15933)*

W W Williams Company LLC E 419 837-5067
Perrysburg *(G-15932)*

◆ Western Tradewinds Inc E 937 859-4300
Miamisburg *(G-14238)*

Whites Service Center Inc E 937 653-5279
Urbana *(G-18446)*

▲ Winston Products LLC D 440 478-1418
Cleveland *(G-6685)*

World Auto Parts Inc E 216 781-8418
Cleveland *(G-6689)*

◆ Wz Management Inc E 330 628-4881
Akron *(G-506)*

Young Truck Sales Inc E 330 477-6271
Canton *(G-2541)*

Youngstown-Kenworth Inc E 330 534-9761
Hubbard *(G-11952)*

5014 Tires & Tubes Wholesale

▲ American Kenda Rbr Indus Ltd E 866 536-3287
Reynoldsburg *(G-16283)*

Belle Tire Distributors Inc E 419 473-1393
Toledo *(G-17610)*

▲ Best One Tire & Svc Lima Inc E 419 229-2380
Lima *(G-12606)*

Bob Sumerel Tire Co Inc E 513 792-6600
Cincinnati *(G-3065)*

Bob Sumerel Tire Co Inc E 614 527-9700
Columbus *(G-7051)*

▲ Capital Tire Inc E 419 241-5111
Toledo *(G-17635)*

Capital Tire Inc E 419 865-7151
Toledo *(G-17636)*

Central Ohio Bandag LP E 740 454-9728
Zanesville *(G-20291)*

Conrads Tire Service Inc E 216 941-3333
Cleveland *(G-5334)*

Dayton Marshall Tire Sales Co E 937 293-8330
Moraine *(G-14646)*

◆ Dealer Tire LLC B 216 432-0088
Cleveland *(G-5413)*

▲ Grismer Tire Company E 937 643-2526
Centerville *(G-2626)*

Hankook Tire America Corp E 330 896-6199
Uniontown *(G-18373)*

Hercules Tire & Rubber Company D 419 425-6400
Findlay *(G-10923)*

Joseph Russo E 440 748-2690
Grafton *(G-11317)*

▲ K & M Tire Inc C 419 695-1061
Delphos *(G-10029)*

K & M Tire Inc E 419 695-1060
Delphos *(G-10030)*

▲ Millersburg Tire Service Inc E 330 674-1085
Millersburg *(G-14483)*

Myers Industries Inc E 330 253-5592
Akron *(G-342)*

North Gateway Tire Co Inc E 330 725-8473
Medina *(G-13982)*

Reville Tire Co D 330 468-1900
Northfield *(G-15385)*

Rush Truck Centers Ohio Inc D 513 733-8500
Cincinnati *(G-4414)*

Rush Truck Centers Ohio Inc E 419 224-6045
Lima *(G-12735)*

▲ Shrader Tire & Oil Inc E 419 472-2128
Toledo *(G-18032)*

Shrader Tire & Oil Inc E 614 445-6601
Columbus *(G-8637)*

▲ Speck Sales Incorporated E 419 353-8312
Bowling Green *(G-1749)*

▲ Stoney Hollow Tire Inc D 740 635-5200
Martins Ferry *(G-13478)*

◆ Technical Rubber Company Inc B 740 967-9015
Johnstown *(G-12204)*

Thyssenkrupp Bilstein Amer Inc D 513 881-7600
Hamilton *(G-11648)*

Tire Waste Transport Inc B 419 363-2681
Rockford *(G-16417)*

▲ W D Tire Warehouse Inc E 614 461-8944
Columbus *(G-8867)*

Ziegler Tire and Supply Co E 330 353-1499
Massillon *(G-13739)*

5015 Motor Vehicle Parts, Used Wholesale

Beheydts Auto Wrecking E 330 658-6109
Doylestown *(G-10108)*

Bob Sumerel Tire Co Inc E 614 527-9700
Columbus *(G-7051)*

Cedar Elec Holdings Corp D 773 804-6288
West Chester *(G-18882)*

▼ Dales Truck Parts Inc ....E 937 766-2551
   Cedarville (G-2580)

▼ G-Cor Automotive Corp ....E 614 443-6735
   Columbus (G-7641)

General Motors LLC ....C 513 603-6600
   West Chester (G-18932)

Greenleaf Ohio LLC ....E 330 832-6001
   Massillon (G-13690)

Lkq Triplettasap Inc ....C 330 733-6333
   Akron (G-317)

▲ Mac Trailer Manufacturing Inc ...C 330 823-9900
   Alliance (G-540)

Myers Bus Parts and Sups Co ....E 330 533-2275
   Canfield (G-2150)

Nk Parts Industries Inc ....E 937 493-4651
   Sidney (G-16787)

Speedie Auto Salvage Ltd ....E 330 878-9961
   Dover (G-10102)

▼ Stricker Bros Inc ....E 513 732-1152
   Batavia (G-1010)

5021 Furniture Wholesale

◆ American Interiors Inc ....E 419 324-0365
   Toledo (G-17590)

Apg Office Furnishings Inc ....E 216 621-4590
   Cleveland (G-4989)

▲ Big Lots Stores Inc ....A 614 278-6800
   Columbus (G-7035)

Business Furniture LLC ....E 937 293-1010
   Dayton (G-9271)

Cbf Industries Inc ....E 216 229-9300
   Bedford (G-1271)

Central Business Equipment Co .....E 513 891-4430
   Cincinnati (G-3150)

Collaborative Inc ....E 419 242-7405
   Toledo (G-17667)

◆ Continental Office Furn Corp .....C 614 262-5010
   Columbus (G-7358)

◆ Cornerstone Brands Inc ....A 513 603-1000
   West Chester (G-18898)

◆ Custom Fabricators Inc ....E 216 831-2266
   Cleveland (G-5391)

Ebo Inc ....E 216 229-9300
   Bedford (G-1279)

Everybodys Inc ....E 937 293-1010
   Moraine (G-14654)

Federated Logistics ....E 937 294-3074
   Moraine (G-14656)

Friends Service Co Inc ....D 419 427-1704
   Findlay (G-10910)

Indepndence Office Bus Sup Inc ....D 216 398-8880
   Cleveland (G-5746)

Jones Group Interiors Inc ....E 330 253-9180
   Akron (G-294)

King Business Interiors Inc ....E 614 430-0020
   Columbus (G-7906)

La-Z-Boy Incorporated ....C 614 478-0898
   Columbus (G-7939)

Loth Inc ....D 614 487-4000
   Columbus (G-7989)

◆ Mantua Manufacturing Co ....C 800 333-8333
   Solon (G-16870)

McNerney & Son Inc ....E 419 666-0200
   Toledo (G-17899)

▲ Mill Distributors Inc ....D 330 995-9200
   Aurora (G-837)

Office Furniture Resources Inc ......E 216 781-8200
   Cleveland (G-6113)

Patterson Pope Inc ....D 513 891-4430
   Cincinnati (G-4213)

▲ Progressive Furniture Inc ....E 419 446-4500
   Archbold (G-635)

▲ Regency Seating Inc ....E 330 848-3700
   Akron (G-400)

S P Richards Company ....E 614 497-2270
   Obetz (G-15529)

◆ Sauder Woodworking Co ....A 419 446-2711
   Archbold (G-639)

Seagate Office Products Inc ....E 419 861-6161
   Holland (G-11913)

Signal Office Supply Inc ....E 513 821-2280
   Cincinnati (G-4482)

Springfield Business Eqp Co ....E 937 322-3828
   Springfield (G-17117)

Staples Inc ....E 614 472-2014
   Columbus (G-8685)

Thomas W Ruff and Company ....B 800 828-0234
   Columbus (G-8747)

Veritas Enterprises Inc ....E 513 578-2748
   Cincinnati (G-2874)

W B Mason Co Inc ....D 216 267-5000
   Cleveland (G-6644)

◆ Wasserstrom Company ....B 614 228-6525
   Columbus (G-8878)

Workshops of David T Smith ....E 513 932-2472
   Morrow (G-14718)

5023 Home Furnishings Wholesale

Accent Drapery Co Inc ....E 614 488-0741
   Columbus (G-6860)

▲ American Frame Corporation ......E 419 893-5595
   Maumee (G-13748)

▲ Americas Floor Source LLC ....D 614 808-3915
   Columbus (G-6940)

▲ Bostwick-Braun Company ....D 419 259-3600
   Toledo (G-17620)

Business Furniture LLC ....E 937 293-1010
   Dayton (G-9271)

◆ Cinmar LLC ....C 513 603-1000
   West Chester (G-18888)

Creative Products Inc ....E 419 866-5501
   Holland (G-11880)

▲ Culver Art & Frame Co ....C 740 548-6868
   Lewis Center (G-12536)

D & S Crtive Cmmunications Inc ...E 419 524-4312
   Mansfield (G-13164)

▲ Dealers Supply North Inc ....E 614 274-6285
   Lockbourne (G-12812)

Dwa Mrkting Prmtional Pdts LLC ...E 216 476-0635
   Strongsville (G-17298)

Everybodys Inc ....E 937 293-1010
   Moraine (G-14654)

Famous Distribution Inc ....D 330 762-9621
   Akron (G-210)

▲ G G Marck & Associates Inc .....E 419 478-0900
   Toledo (G-17751)

Ghp II LLC ....B 740 681-6825
   Lancaster (G-12406)

▲ Hayward Distributing Co ....E 614 272-5953
   Columbus (G-7720)

Hobby Lobby Stores Inc ....E 330 686-1508
   Stow (G-17209)

◆ Interdesign Inc ....B 440 248-0136
   Solon (G-16861)

JP Flooring Systems Inc ....E 513 346-4300
   West Chester (G-18954)

Lumenomics Inc ....E 614 798-3500
   Lewis Center (G-12550)

Luminex Home Decor ....A 513 563-1113
   Blue Ash (G-1601)

◆ Marketing Results Ltd ....E 614 575-9300
   Columbus (G-8021)

▲ Mill Distributors Inc ....D 330 995-9200
   Aurora (G-837)

National Marketshare Group ....E 513 921-0800
   Cincinnati (G-4094)

Newell Brands Inc ....C 419 662-2225
   Bowling Green (G-1741)

▲ Norwood Hardware & Supply Co ..E 513 733-1175
   Cincinnati (G-4134)

▲ Ohio Valley Flooring Inc ....D 513 271-3434
   Cincinnati (G-4160)

Old Time Pottery Inc ....D 513 825-5211
   Cincinnati (G-4167)

Old Time Pottery Inc ....D 440 842-1244
   Cleveland (G-6128)

Old Time Pottery Inc ....E 614 337-1258
   Columbus (G-8370)

Original Hartstone Pottery Inc ....E 740 452-9999
   Zanesville (G-20350)

Pfpc Enterprises Inc ....B 513 941-6200
   Cincinnati (G-4240)

Pottery Barn Inc ....E 614 478-3154
   Columbus (G-8456)

Regal Carpet Center Inc ....E 216 475-1844
   Cleveland (G-6296)

◆ State Crest Carpet & Flooring ....E 440 232-3980
   Bedford (G-1309)

Style-Line Incorporated ....E 614 291-0600
   Columbus (G-8707)

Ten Thusand Villages Cleveland .....E 216 575-1058
   Cleveland (G-6510)

Walter F Stephens Jr Inc ....E 937 746-0521
   Franklin (G-11041)

Workshops of David T Smith ....E 513 932-2472
   Morrow (G-14718)

▲ World Tableware Inc ....D 419 325-2608
   Toledo (G-18161)

5031 Lumber, Plywood & Millwork Wholesale

Acord Rk Lumber Company ....E 740 289-3761
   Piketon (G-15970)

Adkins Timber Products Inc ....E 740 984-2768
   Beverly (G-1459)

Advance Door Company ....E 216 883-2424
   Cleveland (G-4903)

Allied Building Products Corp ....E 216 362-1764
   Cleveland (G-4938)

Allied Building Products Corp ....E 513 784-9090
   Cincinnati (G-2926)

American Warming and Vent ....D 419 288-2703
   Bradner (G-1763)

Apco Industries Inc ....D 614 224-2345
   Columbus (G-6956)

Appalachia Wood Inc ....E 740 596-2551
   Mc Arthur (G-13889)

▲ Appalachian Hardwood Lumber Co .E 440 232-6767
   Cleveland (G-4990)

▲ Associated Materials LLC ....B 330 929-1811
   Cuyahoga Falls (G-9070)

Associated Materials Group Inc ......E 330 929-1811
   Cuyahoga Falls (G-9071)

Associated Mtls Holdings LLC ....A 330 929-1811
   Cuyahoga Falls (G-9072)

Baillie Lumber Co LP ....E 419 462-2000
   Galion (G-11168)

▼ Bennett Supply of Ohio LLC ......E 800 292-5577
   Macedonia (G-13062)

Bluelinx Corporation ....E 330 794-1141
   Akron (G-101)

Bluelinx Corporation ....E 513 874-6770
   West Chester (G-19045)

Boise Cascade Company ....E 513 451-5700
   Cincinnati (G-3066)

Boise Cascade Company ....E 740 382-6766
   Marion (G-13406)

▼ Brenneman Lumber Co ....E 740 397-0573
   Mount Vernon (G-14750)

Brower Products Inc ....D 937 563-1111
   Cincinnati (G-3082)

Buckeye Components LLC ....E 330 482-5163
   Columbiana (G-6781)

Builders Firstsource Inc ....E 937 898-1358
   Vandalia (G-18510)

Builders Firstsource Inc ....E 513 874-9950
   Cincinnati (G-3087)

Carter-Jones Companies Inc ....E 330 673-6100
   Kent (G-12217)

Carter-Jones Companies Inc ....C 330 674-0047
   Millersburg (G-14462)

Carter-Jones Lumber Company ....C 330 674-9060
   Millersburg (G-14463)

▲ Carter-Jones Lumber Company ...C 330 673-6100
   Kent (G-12218)

Carter-Jones Lumber Company ....D 330 784-5441
   Akron (G-119)

Carter-Jones Lumber Company ....A 330 673-6000
   Kent (G-12219)

Clark Son Actn Liquidation Inc ....E 330 837-9710
   Canal Fulton (G-2094)

▲ Clem Lumber and Distrg Co ....D 330 821-2130
   Alliance (G-526)

Contract Lumber Inc ....D 614 751-1109
   Columbus (G-7365)

Daniels Lumber Co Inc ....D 330 533-2211
   Canfield (G-2135)

Dayton Door Sales Inc ....E 937 253-9181
   Dayton (G-9364)

▲ Direct Import Home Decor Inc ....E 216 898-9758
   Cleveland (G-5424)

Don Walter Kitchen Distrs ....E 330 793-9338
   Youngstown (G-20021)

Dortronic Service Inc ....E 216 739-3667
   Cleveland (G-5443)

Dublin Millwork Co Inc ....E 614 889-7776
   Dublin (G-10211)

▼ Eagle Hardwoods Inc ....E 330 339-8838
   Newcomerstown (G-15130)

Edrich Supply Co ....E 440 238-9440
   Strongsville (G-17299)

▲ Enclosure Suppliers LLC ....E 513 782-3900
   Cincinnati (G-3496)

Famous Enterprises Inc ....E 330 762-9621
   Akron (G-212)

Fifth Avenue Lumber Co ....D 614 294-0068
   Columbus (G-7575)

Francis-Schulze Co ....E 937 295-3941
   Russia (G-16466)

Garick LLC ....E..... 937 462-8350
South Charleston (G-16924)

Gorell Enterprises Inc ....B..... 724 465-1800
Streetsboro (G-17254)

Graf and Sons Inc ....E..... 614 481-2020
Columbus (G-7683)

Gross Lumber Inc ....E..... 330 683-2055
Apple Creek (G-619)

Gunton Corporation ....C..... 216 831-2420
Cleveland (G-5647)

▲ Hamilton-Parker Company ....D..... 614 358-7800
Columbus (G-7713)

▼ Hartzell Hardwoods Inc ....D..... 937 773-7054
Piqua (G-16006)

Hd Supply Inc ....E..... 614 771-4849
Groveport (G-11516)

Holmes Lumber & Bldg Ctr Inc ....C..... 330 674-9060
Millersburg (G-14475)

Huttig Building Products Inc ....E..... 614 492-8248
Obetz (G-15526)

J McCoy Lumber Co Ltd ....E..... 937 587-3423
Peebles (G-15803)

Kansas City Hardwood Corp ....E..... 913 621-1975
Lakewood (G-12349)

Keidel Supply Company Inc ....E..... 513 351-1600
Cincinnati (G-3852)

Keim Lumber Company ....E..... 330 893-2251
Baltic (G-935)

Khempco Bldg Sup Co Ltd Partnr ....D..... 740 549-0465
Delaware (G-9993)

Koch Aluminum Mfg Inc ....E..... 419 625-5956
Sandusky (G-16622)

La Force Inc ....E..... 513 772-0783
Cincinnati (G-3902)

◆ Litco International Inc ....E..... 330 539-5433
Vienna (G-18581)

Lowes Home Centers LLC ....C..... 216 351-4723
Cleveland (G-5882)

Lowes Home Centers LLC ....C..... 419 739-1300
Wapakoneta (G-18649)

Lowes Home Centers LLC ....C..... 937 235-2920
Dayton (G-9574)

Lowes Home Centers LLC ....C..... 740 574-6200
Wheelersburg (G-19435)

Lowes Home Centers LLC ....C..... 330 665-9356
Akron (G-321)

Lowes Home Centers LLC ....C..... 330 829-2700
Alliance (G-538)

Lowes Home Centers LLC ....C..... 937 599-4000
Bellefontaine (G-1357)

Lowes Home Centers LLC ....C..... 419 420-7531
Findlay (G-10935)

Lowes Home Centers LLC ....C..... 330 832-1901
Massillon (G-13704)

Lowes Home Centers LLC ....C..... 513 741-0585
Cincinnati (G-3945)

Lowes Home Centers LLC ....C..... 614 433-9957
Columbus (G-6822)

Lowes Home Centers LLC ....C..... 740 389-9737
Marion (G-13430)

Lowes Home Centers LLC ....C..... 740 450-5500
Zanesville (G-20326)

Lowes Home Centers LLC ....C..... 513 598-7050
Cincinnati (G-3946)

Lowes Home Centers LLC ....C..... 614 769-9940
Reynoldsburg (G-16317)

Lowes Home Centers LLC ....C..... 614 853-6200
Columbus (G-7990)

Lowes Home Centers LLC ....C..... 440 937-3500
Avon (G-893)

Lowes Home Centers LLC ....C..... 513 445-1000
South Lebanon (G-16926)

Lowes Home Centers LLC ....B..... 216 831-2860
Bedford (G-1290)

Lowes Home Centers LLC ....C..... 937 327-6000
Springfield (G-17065)

Lowes Home Centers LLC ....C..... 419 331-3598
Lima (G-12693)

Lowes Home Centers LLC ....C..... 740 681-3464
Lancaster (G-12413)

Lowes Home Centers LLC ....C..... 614 659-0530
Dublin (G-10275)

Lowes Home Centers LLC ....C..... 614 238-2601
Columbus (G-7991)

Lowes Home Centers LLC ....C..... 740 522-0003
Newark (G-15063)

Lowes Home Centers LLC ....C..... 740 773-7777
Chillicothe (G-2803)

Lowes Home Centers LLC ....C..... 440 998-6555
Ashtabula (G-745)

Lowes Home Centers LLC ....B..... 513 753-5094
Cincinnati (G-2861)

Lowes Home Centers LLC ....C..... 614 497-6170
Columbus (G-7992)

Lowes Home Centers LLC ....C..... 513 731-6127
Cincinnati (G-3947)

Lowes Home Centers LLC ....C..... 330 287-2261
Wooster (G-19742)

Lowes Home Centers LLC ....C..... 937 339-2544
Troy (G-18211)

Lowes Home Centers LLC ....C..... 440 392-0027
Mentor (G-14078)

Lowes Home Centers LLC ....C..... 440 942-2759
Willoughby (G-19546)

Lowes Home Centers LLC ....C..... 740 374-2151
Marietta (G-13345)

Lowes Home Centers LLC ....C..... 419 874-6758
Perrysburg (G-15891)

Lowes Home Centers LLC ....C..... 330 626-2980
Streetsboro (G-17259)

Lowes Home Centers LLC ....C..... 419 389-9464
Toledo (G-17864)

Lowes Home Centers LLC ....C..... 419 843-9758
Toledo (G-17865)

Lowes Home Centers LLC ....C..... 614 447-2851
Columbus (G-7993)

Lowes Home Centers LLC ....C..... 330 245-4300
Akron (G-322)

Lowes Home Centers LLC ....C..... 513 965-3280
Milford (G-14402)

Lowes Home Centers LLC ....C..... 330 908-2750
Northfield (G-15382)

Lowes Home Centers LLC ....C..... 419 470-2491
Toledo (G-17866)

Lowes Home Centers LLC ....C..... 513 336-9741
Mason (G-13612)

Lowes Home Centers LLC ....C..... 937 498-8400
Sidney (G-16785)

Lowes Home Centers LLC ....C..... 740 699-3000
Saint Clairsville (G-16493)

Lowes Home Centers LLC ....C..... 330 920-9280
Stow (G-17218)

Lowes Home Centers LLC ....C..... 740 589-3750
Athens (G-791)

Lowes Home Centers LLC ....C..... 740 393-5350
Mount Vernon (G-14779)

Lowes Home Centers LLC ....C..... 937 547-2400
Greenville (G-11389)

Lowes Home Centers LLC ....C..... 330 335-1900
Wadsworth (G-18606)

Lowes Home Centers LLC ....C..... 937 347-4000
Xenia (G-19918)

Lowes Home Centers LLC ....C..... 440 239-2630
Strongsville (G-17324)

Lowes Home Centers LLC ....C..... 513 755-4300
West Chester (G-18966)

Lowes Home Centers LLC ....C..... 513 671-2093
Cincinnati (G-3948)

Lowes Home Centers LLC ....C..... 440 331-1027
Rocky River (G-16440)

Lowes Home Centers LLC ....C..... 330 677-3040
Kent (G-12247)

Lowes Home Centers LLC ....C..... 419 747-1920
Ontario (G-15559)

Lowes Home Centers LLC ....C..... 330 339-1936
New Philadelphia (G-14971)

Lowes Home Centers LLC ....C..... 440 985-5700
Lorain (G-12924)

Lowes Home Centers LLC ....C..... 419 447-4101
Tiffin (G-17521)

Lowes Home Centers LLC ....C..... 937 578-4440
Marysville (G-13511)

Lowes Home Centers LLC ....C..... 440 324-5004
Elyria (G-10531)

Lowes Home Centers LLC ....C..... 937 438-4900
Dayton (G-9575)

Lowes Home Centers LLC ....C..... 937 427-1110
Beavercreek (G-1168)

Lowes Home Centers LLC ....C..... 937 848-5600
Dayton (G-9576)

Lowes Home Centers LLC ....C..... 614 529-5900
Hilliard (G-11786)

Lowes Home Centers LLC ....C..... 513 737-3700
Hamilton (G-11625)

Lowes Home Centers LLC ....C..... 419 355-0221
Fremont (G-11084)

Lowes Home Centers LLC ....C..... 419 624-6000
Sandusky (G-16625)

Lowes Home Centers LLC ....C..... 419 782-9000
Defiance (G-9926)

Lowes Home Centers LLC ....C..... 330 609-8000
Warren (G-18725)

Lowes Home Centers LLC ....C..... 740 894-7120
South Point (G-16939)

Lowes Home Centers LLC ....C..... 513 727-3900
Middletown (G-14305)

Lowes Home Centers LLC ....C..... 330 497-2720
Canton (G-2381)

Lowes Home Centers LLC ....C..... 740 266-3500
Steubenville (G-17164)

Lowes Home Centers LLC ....C..... 330 965-4500
Youngstown (G-20101)

Lowes Home Centers LLC ....C..... 937 383-7000
Wilmington (G-19630)

Lowes Home Centers LLC ....C..... 937 854-8200
Dayton (G-9577)

Lowes Home Centers LLC ....C..... 614 476-7100
Columbus (G-7994)

Lumberjacks Inc ....E..... 330 762-2401
Akron (G-323)

Lute Supply Inc ....E..... 740 353-1447
Portsmouth (G-16153)

Mae Holding Company ....E..... 513 751-2424
Cincinnati (G-3959)

Marsh Building Products Inc ....E..... 937 222-3321
Dayton (G-9586)

Mason Structural Steel Inc ....D..... 440 439-1040
Walton Hills (G-18637)

Mentor Lumber and Supply Co ....C..... 440 255-8814
Mentor (G-14082)

▲ Meyer Decorative Surfaces USA ....E..... 800 776-3900
Hudson (G-11996)

Milestone Ventures LLC ....E..... 317 908-2093
Newark (G-15072)

Milliken Millwork Inc ....D..... 513 874-6771
West Chester (G-19069)

Modern Builders Supply Inc ....E..... 513 531-1000
Cincinnati (G-4069)

Nilco LLC ....E..... 888 248-5151
Hartville (G-11695)

Nilco LLC ....E..... 330 538-3386
North Jackson (G-15249)

Norandex Bldg Mtls Dist Inc ....A..... 330 656-8924
Hudson (G-11999)

North Shore Door Co Inc ....E..... 800 783-6112
Elyria (G-10547)

Northwest Bldg Resources Inc ....E..... 419 286-5400
Fort Jennings (G-10984)

▲ Norwood Hardware & Supply Co ....E..... 513 733-1175
Cincinnati (G-4134)

OK Interiors Corp ....E..... 513 742-3278
Cincinnati (G-4164)

Olde Towne Windows Inc ....E..... 419 626-9613
Milan (G-14364)

Orrville Trucking & Grading Co ....E..... 330 682-4010
Orrville (G-15641)

Pallet Distributors Inc ....E..... 888 805-9670
Lakewood (G-12359)

Palmer-Donavin Mfg Co ....D..... 614 277-2777
Urbancrest (G-18451)

Paxton Hardwoods LLC ....E..... 513 984-8200
Cincinnati (G-4216)

Pella Corporation ....D..... 513 948-8480
Cincinnati (G-4224)

Ply-Trim South Inc ....E..... 330 799-7876
Youngstown (G-20161)

Premier Construction Company ....E..... 513 874-2611
Fairfield (G-10771)

▼ Price Woods Products Inc ....E..... 513 722-1200
Loveland (G-13021)

▲ Professional Laminate Mllwk Inc ....E..... 513 891-7858
Milford (G-14427)

Provia Holdings Inc ....C..... 330 852-4711
Sugarcreek (G-17379)

S R Door Inc ....C..... 740 927-3558
Hebron (G-11723)

Schneider Home Equipment Co ....E..... 513 522-1200
Cincinnati (G-4438)

▲ Sims-Lohman Inc ....E..... 513 651-3510
Cincinnati (G-4483)

Southern Ohio Door Contrls Inc ....E..... 513 353-4793
Miamitown (G-14243)

▲ Stephen M Trudick ....E..... 440 834-1891
Burton (G-2019)

◆ Style Crest Inc ....B..... 419 332-7369
Fremont (G-11099)

◆ T J Ellis Enterprises Inc ....E..... 419 999-5026
Lima (G-12761)

Toledo Molding & Die Inc ....D..... 419 692-6022
Delphos (G-10036)

S I C (side tab)

Traichal Construction Company ....E 800 255-3667
Niles *(G-15172)*

Tri-County Pallet Recycl Inc ....E 330 848-0313
Akron *(G-473)*

▲ Tri-State Forest Products Inc ....E 937 323-6325
Springfield *(G-17127)*

◆ Usavinyl LLC ....E 614 771-4805
Groveport *(G-11547)*

Vwc Liquidation Company LLC ....C 330 372-6776
Warren *(G-18767)*

Wappoo Wood Products Inc ....E 937 492-1166
Sidney *(G-16805)*

Window Factory of America ....D 440 439-3050
Bedford *(G-1314)*

5032 Brick, Stone & Related Construction Mtrls Wholesale

▲ Accco Inc ....E 740 697-2005
Roseville *(G-16453)*

Acme Company ....D 330 758-2313
Poland *(G-16079)*

Allega Recycled Mtls & Sup Co ....E 216 447-0814
Cleveland *(G-4937)*

Arrowhead Transport Co ....E 330 638-2900
Cortland *(G-8983)*

Barrett Paving Materials Inc ....C 513 271-6200
Middletown *(G-14343)*

Boral Resources LLC ....D 740 622-8042
Coshocton *(G-8999)*

▼ Bruder Inc ....E 216 791-9800
Maple Heights *(G-13282)*

C & B Buck Bros Asp Maint LLC ....E 419 536-7325
Toledo *(G-17633)*

CCI Supply Inc ....C 440 953-0045
Mentor *(G-14026)*

▲ Clay Burley Products Co ....E 740 452-3633
Roseville *(G-16454)*

Columbus Coal & Lime Co ....E 614 224-9241
Columbus *(G-7269)*

Digeronimo Aggregates LLC ....E 216 524-2950
Independence *(G-12067)*

▲ Direct Import Home Decor Inc ....E 216 898-9758
Cleveland *(G-5424)*

Drywall Barn Inc ....E 330 750-6155
Youngstown *(G-20022)*

Glen-Gery Corporation ....D 419 468-4890
Galion *(G-11176)*

Gms Inc ....E 937 222-4444
Dayton *(G-9463)*

▲ Hamilton-Parker Company ....D 614 358-7800
Columbus *(G-7713)*

Hull Builders Supply Inc ....E 440 967-3159
Vermilion *(G-18553)*

Huron Cement Products Company ....E 419 433-4161
Huron *(G-12026)*

Hy-Grade Corporation ....E 216 341-7711
Cleveland *(G-5728)*

▲ Indus Trade & Technology LLC ....E 614 527-0257
Columbus *(G-7811)*

J & B Equipment & Supply Inc ....D 419 884-1155
Mansfield *(G-13188)*

▲ Jainco International Inc ....C 440 519-0100
Solon *(G-16863)*

Janell Inc ....E 513 489-9111
Blue Ash *(G-1589)*

▲ Justice & Co Inc ....E 330 225-6000
Medina *(G-13962)*

▲ Kenmore Construction Co Inc ....C 330 762-8936
Akron *(G-299)*

Koltcz Concrete Block Co ....E 440 232-3630
Bedford *(G-1287)*

▲ Konkus Marble & Granite Inc ....C 614 876-4000
Columbus *(G-7921)*

▲ Kuhlman Corporation ....C 419 897-6000
Maumee *(G-13808)*

L & W Supply Corporation ....E 614 276-6391
Columbus *(G-7932)*

L & W Supply Corporation ....E 513 723-1150
Cincinnati *(G-3899)*

▲ Lang Stone Company Inc ....D 614 235-4099
Columbus *(G-7951)*

Martin Marietta Materials Inc ....E 513 829-6446
Fairfield *(G-10750)*

Martin Marietta Materials Inc ....E 614 871-6708
Grove City *(G-11451)*

▲ Maza Inc ....E 614 760-0003
Plain City *(G-16059)*

▲ Mees Distributors Inc ....E 513 541-2311
Cincinnati *(G-4002)*

Micro Construction LLC ....E 740 862-0751
Baltimore *(G-937)*

Mid-Ohio Valley Lime Inc ....E 740 373-1006
Marietta *(G-13360)*

Mintek Resources Inc ....E 937 431-0218
Beavercreek *(G-1171)*

Modern Builders Supply Inc ....D 330 726-7000
Youngstown *(G-20131)*

Modern Builders Supply Inc ....E 419 241-3961
Toledo *(G-17922)*

◆ Pinney Dock & Transport LLC ....E 440 964-7186
Ashtabula *(G-752)*

Proterra Inc ....E 216 383-8449
Wickliffe *(G-19474)*

Quality Block & Supply Inc ....E 330 364-4411
Mount Eaton *(G-14723)*

R W Sidley Incorporated ....E 330 793-7374
Youngstown *(G-20176)*

Robinson Insulation Co Inc ....E 937 323-9599
Springfield *(G-17102)*

Sewer Rodding Equipment Co ....E 419 991-2065
Lima *(G-12739)*

Sidwell Materials Inc ....C 740 849-2394
Zanesville *(G-20361)*

▲ Snyder Concrete Products Inc ....E 937 885-5176
Moraine *(G-14697)*

Stamm Contracting Co Inc ....E 330 274-8230
Mantua *(G-13276)*

Stone Coffman Company LLC ....E 614 861-4668
Gahanna *(G-11147)*

Sylvester Materials Co ....C 419 841-3874
Sylvania *(G-17457)*

Virginia Tile Company ....E 216 741-8400
Brooklyn Heights *(G-1886)*

Westfall Aggregate & Mtls Inc ....D 740 420-9090
Circleville *(G-4852)*

5033 Roofing, Siding & Insulation Mtrls Wholesale

Allied Building Products Corp ....E 513 784-9090
Cincinnati *(G-2926)*

Allied Building Products Corp ....E 614 488-0717
Columbus *(G-6895)*

Alpine Insulation I LLC ....A 614 221-3399
Columbus *(G-6904)*

Apco Industries Inc ....D 614 224-2345
Columbus *(G-6956)*

Associated Materials LLC ....E 614 985-4611
Columbus *(G-6983)*

▲ Associated Materials LLC ....B 330 929-1811
Cuyahoga Falls *(G-9070)*

Associated Materials Group Inc ....E 330 929-1811
Cuyahoga Falls *(G-9071)*

Associated Mtls Holdings LLC ....A 330 929-1811
Cuyahoga Falls *(G-9072)*

Beacon Sales Acquisition Inc ....C 330 425-3359
Twinsburg *(G-18250)*

CCI Supply Inc ....C 440 953-0045
Mentor *(G-14026)*

◆ Great Lakes Textiles Inc ....E 440 914-1122
Solon *(G-16854)*

Hd Supply Inc ....E 614 771-4849
Groveport *(G-11516)*

Installed Building Pdts Inc ....C 614 221-3399
Columbus *(G-7828)*

Johns Manville Corporation ....D 419 784-7000
Defiance *(G-9921)*

Lindsey Cnstr & Design Inc ....E 330 785-9931
Akron *(G-316)*

Modern Builders Supply Inc ....E 216 273-3605
Cleveland *(G-6004)*

Modern Builders Supply Inc ....E 937 222-2627
Dayton *(G-9641)*

Modern Builders Supply Inc ....E 513 531-1000
Cincinnati *(G-4069)*

Norandex Bldg Mtls Dist Inc ....A 330 656-8924
Hudson *(G-11999)*

▲ Palmer-Donavin Mfg Co ....C 800 652-1234
Columbus *(G-8416)*

R E Kramig & Co Inc ....C 513 761-4010
Cincinnati *(G-4330)*

Roofing Supply Group LLC ....E 614 239-1111
Columbus *(G-8548)*

Vinyl Design Corporation ....E 419 283-4009
Holland *(G-11925)*

5039 Construction Materials, NEC Wholesale

▲ Agratronix LLC ....E 330 562-2222
Streetsboro *(G-17245)*

American Warming and Vent ....D 419 288-2703
Bradner *(G-1763)*

Anderson Glass Co Inc ....E 614 476-4877
Columbus *(G-6947)*

Apco Industries Inc ....D 614 224-2345
Columbus *(G-6956)*

▼ Cleveland Glass Block Inc ....E 216 531-6363
Cleveland *(G-5256)*

Cleveland Glass Block Inc ....E 614 252-5888
Columbus *(G-7225)*

D & S Crtive Cmmunications Inc ....E 419 524-4312
Mansfield *(G-13164)*

Efficient Services Ohio Inc ....E 330 627-4440
Carrollton *(G-2568)*

Eger Products Inc ....D 513 753-4200
Amelia *(G-572)*

Harmon Inc ....E 513 645-1550
West Chester *(G-18942)*

Marysville Steel Inc ....E 937 642-5971
Marysville *(G-13515)*

▲ Medina Glass Block Inc ....E 330 239-0239
Medina *(G-13974)*

▲ Mills Fence Co Inc ....E 513 631-0333
Cincinnati *(G-4057)*

Morton Buildings Inc ....D 419 675-2311
Kenton *(G-12285)*

Olde Towne Windows Inc ....E 419 626-9613
Milan *(G-14364)*

Palmer-Donavin Mfg Co ....E 419 692-5000
Delphos *(G-10032)*

Real America Inc ....B 216 261-1177
Cleveland *(G-6289)*

▲ Richards Whl Fence Co Inc ....E 330 773-0423
Akron *(G-407)*

Schneider Home Equipment Co ....E 513 522-1200
Cincinnati *(G-4438)*

Security Fence Group Inc ....E 513 681-3700
Cincinnati *(G-4444)*

Six C Fabrication Inc ....D 330 296-5594
Ravenna *(G-16267)*

▲ Valicor Environmental Svcs LLC ....D 513 733-4666
Monroe *(G-14586)*

▲ Will-Burt Company ....B 330 682-7015
Orrville *(G-15649)*

Will-Burt Company ....E 330 682-7015
Orrville *(G-15650)*

5043 Photographic Eqpt & Splys Wholesale

Collins KAO Inc ....E 513 948-9000
Cincinnati *(G-3329)*

▲ KAO Collins Inc ....D 513 948-9000
Cincinnati *(G-3847)*

Technicolor Thomson Group ....C 937 383-6000
Wilmington *(G-19651)*

5044 Office Eqpt Wholesale

American Copy Equipment Inc ....C 330 722-9555
Cleveland *(G-4952)*

Andrew Belmont Sargent ....E 513 769-7800
Cincinnati *(G-2965)*

Apg Office Furnishings Inc ....E 216 621-4590
Cleveland *(G-4989)*

▲ Big Lots Stores Inc ....A 614 278-6800
Columbus *(G-7035)*

Blakemans Valley Off Eqp Inc ....E 330 729-1000
Youngstown *(G-19965)*

Blue Technologies Inc ....C 216 271-4800
Cleveland *(G-5066)*

Blue Technologies Inc ....E 330 499-9300
Canton *(G-2215)*

Business Data Systems Inc ....E 330 633-1221
Tallmadge *(G-17470)*

Canon Solutions America Inc ....D 937 260-4495
Miamisburg *(G-14148)*

Canon Solutions America Inc ....D 216 446-3830
Independence *(G-12053)*

Collaborative Inc ....E 419 242-7405
Toledo *(G-17667)*

Comdoc Inc ....E 330 539-4822
Girard *(G-11285)*

Comdoc Inc ....E 330 896-2346
Uniontown *(G-18363)*

Continuum Inc ....E 614 891-9200
Westerville *(G-19246)*

David Francis Corporation ....C 216 524-0900
Cleveland *(G-5408)*

Document Imging Spcialists LLC ....E 614 868-9008
Hilliard *(G-11762)*

Document Solutions Ohio LLC ....E 614 846-2400
Columbus *(G-7465)*

Donnellon Mc Carthy Inc	E	937 299-3564	
Moraine (G-14648)			
Donnellon Mc Carthy Inc	E	513 681-3200	
Cincinnati (G-3439)			
Essendant Co	C	330 425-4001	
Twinsburg (G-18264)			
Essendant Co	D	614 876-7774	
Columbus (G-7534)			
Franklin Imaging Llc	E	614 885-6894	
Columbus (G-7618)			
Friends Service Co Inc	D	419 427-1704	
Findlay (G-10910)			
Giesecke & Devrient Amer Inc	C	330 425-1515	
Twinsburg (G-18274)			
Goodremonts	E	419 476-1492	
Toledo (G-17766)			
Gordon Flesch Company Inc	E	419 884-2031	
Mansfield (G-13179)			
▲ Graphic Enterprises Inc	D	800 553-6616	
North Canton (G-15207)			
Graphic Entps Off Slutions Inc	D	800 553-6616	
North Canton (G-15208)			
Konica Minolta Business Soluti	E	614 766-7800	
Dublin (G-10264)			
Konica Minolta Business Soluti	E	910 990-5837	
Cleveland (G-5840)			
Konica Minolta Business Soluti	D	440 546-5795	
Broadview Heights (G-1837)			
Konica Minolta Business Soluti	E	419 536-7720	
Toledo (G-17843)			
Lorain Cnty Sty Off Eqp Co Inc	E	440 960-7070	
Amherst (G-592)			
M T Business Technologies	E	440 933-7682	
Avon Lake (G-924)			
Meritech Inc	D	216 459-8333	
Cleveland (G-5956)			
Modern Office Methods Inc	D	513 791-0909	
Blue Ash (G-1613)			
Mt Business Technologies Inc	C	419 529-6100	
Mansfield (G-13225)			
Neopost USA Inc	E	440 526-3196	
Brecksville (G-1792)			
Northcoast Duplicating Inc	C	216 573-6681	
Cleveland (G-6087)			
Office Concepts Inc	E	419 221-2679	
Lima (G-12710)			
Office Depot Inc	E	800 463-3768	
Cleveland (G-6112)			
Office Products Toledo Inc	E	419 865-7001	
Holland (G-11904)			
Office World Inc	E	419 991-4694	
Lima (G-12791)			
Ohio Business Machines LLC	E	216 485-2000	
Cleveland (G-6117)			
P-N-D Communications Inc	E	419 683-1922	
Crestline (G-9059)			
Perry Pro Tech Inc	E	419 475-9030	
Perrysburg (G-15901)			
Perry Pro Tech Inc	D	419 228-1360	
Lima (G-12720)			
Ricoh Usa Inc	D	513 984-9898	
Sharonville (G-16730)			
Ricoh Usa Inc	D	614 310-6500	
Worthington (G-19845)			
Ricoh Usa Inc	D	216 574-9111	
Cleveland (G-6324)			
Ricoh Usa Inc	D	330 523-3900	
Richfield (G-16376)			
Ricoh Usa Inc	E	330 384-9111	
Akron (G-408)			
Schenker Inc	D	614 257-8365	
Lockbourne (G-12824)			
Springfield Business Eqp Co	E	937 322-3828	
Springfield (G-17117)			
Symatic Inc	E	330 225-1510	
Brunswick (G-1941)			
▲ Tameran Graphic Systems Inc	E	440 349-7100	
Solon (G-16908)			
Viking Office Products Inc	B	513 881-7200	
West Chester (G-19032)			
Visual Edge Technology Inc	C	330 494-9694	
Canton (G-2528)			
W B Mason Co Inc	D	216 267-5000	
Cleveland (G-6644)			
Xerox Corporation	D	740 592-5609	
Athens (G-812)			
Xerox Corporation	D	216 642-7806	
Cleveland (G-6697)			
Xerox Corporation	B	513 554-3200	
Blue Ash (G-1684)			

5045 Computers & Peripheral Eqpt & Software Wholesale

3sg Corporation	C	614 309-3600	
Dublin (G-10117)			
Advanced Cmpt Connections LLC	E	419 668-4080	
Norwalk (G-15424)			
Advantech Corporation	D	513 742-8895	
Blue Ash (G-1501)			
Agilysys Inc	E	440 519-6262	
Solon (G-16816)			
Arrow Globl Asset Dspstion Inc	D	614 328-4100	
Gahanna (G-11110)			
Ascendtech Inc	E	216 458-1101	
Willoughby (G-19506)			
Avid Technologies Inc	E	330 487-0770	
Twinsburg (G-18248)			
Blue Tech Smart Solutions LLC	E	216 271-4800	
Cleveland (G-5065)			
Blue Technologies Inc	D	330 499-9300	
Canton (G-2215)			
Bsl - Applied Laser Tech LLC	E	216 663-8181	
Cleveland (G-5097)			
Business Data Systems Inc	D	330 633-1221	
Tallmadge (G-17470)			
Canon Solutions America Inc	D	937 260-4495	
Miamisburg (G-14148)			
Cdw Technologies LLC	D	513 677-4100	
Cincinnati (G-3138)			
Cincinnati Bell Techno	E	513 841-6700	
Cincinnati (G-3227)			
Cisco Systems Inc	E	614 764-4987	
Dublin (G-10174)			
Commercial Time Sharing Inc	E	330 644-3059	
Akron (G-148)			
Computer Helper Publishing	E	614 939-9094	
Columbus (G-7345)			
Cranel Incorporated	D	614 431-8000	
Columbus (G-6811)			
Datavantage Corporation	B	440 498-4414	
Cleveland (G-5406)			
Digital Controls Corporation	D	513 746-8118	
Miamisburg (G-14166)			
DMC Technology Group	E	419 535-2900	
Toledo (G-17703)			
Dolbey Systems Inc	E	440 392-9900	
Painesville (G-15710)			
Eci Macola/Max LLC	C	978 539-6186	
Dublin (G-10213)			
▼ Einstruction Corporation	D	330 746-3015	
Youngstown (G-20027)			
Enhanced Software Inc	E	877 805-8388	
Columbus (G-7518)			
Environmental Systems Research	D	614 933-8698	
Columbus (G-7522)			
Evanhoe & Associates Inc	E	937 235-2995	
Dayton (G-9173)			
▲ GBS Corp	C	330 494-5330	
North Canton (G-15206)			
GBS Corp	E	330 797-2700	
Youngstown (G-20046)			
Global Gvrnment Edcatn Sltions	D	937 368-2308	
Dayton (G-9462)			
Global Mall Unlimited	E	740 533-7203	
Delaware (G-9981)			
Gordon Flesch Company Inc	E	419 884-2031	
Mansfield (G-13179)			
Government Acquisitions Inc	E	513 721-8700	
Cincinnati (G-3628)			
Horizon Payroll Services Inc	B	937 434-8244	
Dayton (G-9506)			
Indico LLC	E	440 775-7777	
Oberlin (G-15505)			
Insight Direct Usa Inc	D	614 456-0423	
Columbus (G-7826)			
Isqft Inc	C	513 645-8004	
Cincinnati (G-3788)			
▲ King Memory LLC	E	614 418-6044	
Columbus (G-7907)			
Kiwiplan Inc	E	513 554-1500	
Cincinnati (G-3878)			
Legrand North America LLC	B	937 224-0639	
Dayton (G-9561)			
Manatron Inc	E	937 431-4000	
Beavercreek (G-1228)			
Manatron Sabre Systems and Svc	E	937 431-4000	
Beavercreek (G-1229)			
Mapsys Inc	E	614 255-7258	
Columbus (G-8014)			
McPc Inc	C	440 238-0102	
Brookpark (G-1902)			

Mediquant Inc	E	440 746-2300	
Brecksville (G-1789)			
▼ Meyer Hill Lynch Corporation	E	419 897-9797	
Maumee (G-13821)			
Micro Center Inc	B	614 850-3000	
Hilliard (G-11794)			
Micro Center Online Inc	C	614 326-8500	
Columbus (G-8069)			
Micro Electronics Inc	D	614 326-8500	
Columbus (G-8070)			
Micro Electronics Inc	D	614 334-1430	
Columbus (G-8071)			
▲ Micro Electronics Inc	B	614 850-3000	
Hilliard (G-11795)			
Micro Electronics Inc	D	614 850-3500	
Hilliard (G-11796)			
Micro Electronics Inc	C	440 449-7000	
Cleveland (G-5979)			
Micro Electronics Inc	C	513 782-8500	
Cincinnati (G-4048)			
Microplex Inc	E	330 498-0600	
North Canton (G-15220)			
Mitel (delaware) Inc	E	513 733-8000	
West Chester (G-18974)			
Mtm Technologies (texas) Inc	E	513 786-6600	
Cincinnati (G-4084)			
Netwave Corporation	E	614 850-6300	
Dublin (G-10289)			
Office Depot Inc	E	800 463-3768	
Cleveland (G-6112)			
Office World Inc	E	419 991-4694	
Lima (G-12791)			
Oracle Systems Corporation	D	216 328-9100	
Beachwood (G-1093)			
Park Place International LLC	D	877 991-1991	
Chagrin Falls (G-2677)			
PC Connection Inc	C	937 382-4800	
Wilmington (G-19637)			
Pcm Sales Inc	E	501 342-1000	
Cleveland (G-6185)			
Pcm Sales Inc	C	513 842-3500	
Blue Ash (G-1628)			
Pcm Sales Inc	E	740 548-2222	
Lewis Center (G-12558)			
Pcm Sales Inc	D	937 885-6444	
Miamisburg (G-14204)			
Pomeroy It Solutions Sls Inc	E	440 717-1364	
Brecksville (G-1798)			
Positive Bus Solutions Inc	D	513 772-2255	
Cincinnati (G-4265)			
▼ Provantage LLC	D	330 494-3781	
North Canton (G-15228)			
Quilalea Corporation	E	330 487-0777	
Richfield (G-16372)			
Raco Industries LLC	D	513 984-2101	
Blue Ash (G-1636)			
Radial South LP	C	678 584-4047	
Groveport (G-11533)			
S & P Solutions Inc	C	440 918-9111	
Willoughby Hills (G-19593)			
Sadler-Necamp Financial Svcs	E	513 489-5477	
Cincinnati (G-4421)			
Software Info Systems LLC	E	513 791-7777	
Cincinnati (G-4503)			
Software Solutions Inc	E	513 932-6667	
Lebanon (G-12504)			
Sophisticated Systems Inc	D	614 418-4600	
Columbus (G-8660)			
▲ Systemax Manufacturing Inc	C	937 368-2300	
Dayton (G-9805)			
Total Loop Inc	D	888 614-5667	
Uniontown (G-18388)			
Transcriptiongear Inc	E	888 834-2392	
Painesville (G-15743)			
▲ Vecmar Corporation	E	440 953-1119	
Mentor (G-14121)			
Virtual Technologies Group	E	419 991-4694	
Lima (G-12794)			
Xerox Corporation	D	216 642-7806	
Cleveland (G-6697)			

5046 Commercial Eqpt, NEC Wholesale

Access Catalog Company LLC	E	440 572-5377	
Strongsville (G-17279)			
Acorn Distributors Inc	E	614 294-6444	
Columbus (G-6867)			
AVI Food Systems Inc	E	740 452-9363	
Zanesville (G-20279)			
Bakemark USA LLC	D	513 870-0880	
West Chester (G-18872)			

SIC

Employee Codes: A=Over 500 employees, B=251-500
C=101-250, D=51-100, E=25-50   2019 Harris Ohio
Services Directory   879

Brechbuhler Scales Inc	E	330 458-3060	
Canton *(G-2217)*			
▼ Burkett and Sons Inc	E	419 242-7377	
Perrysburg *(G-15844)*			
Business Data Systems Inc	E	330 633-1221	
Tallmadge *(G-17470)*			
Captive-Aire Systems Inc	E	614 777-7378	
Gahanna *(G-11111)*			
▲ Carroll Manufacturing & Sales	E	440 937-3900	
Avon *(G-871)*			
Cbf Industries Inc	E	216 229-9300	
Bedford *(G-1271)*			
▼ Century Marketing Corporation	C	419 354-2591	
Bowling Green *(G-1727)*			
Cleveland Coin Mch Exch Inc	D	847 842-6310	
Willoughby *(G-19514)*			
Cmbb LLC	C	937 652-2151	
Urbana *(G-18428)*			
▲ CMC Daymark Corporation	C	419 354-2591	
Bowling Green *(G-1728)*			
▲ Door Fabrication Services Inc	E	937 454-9207	
Vandalia *(G-18520)*			
Dtv Inc	E	216 226-5465	
Mayfield Heights *(G-13873)*			
Ebo Inc	E	216 229-9300	
Bedford *(G-1279)*			
Filing Scale Company Inc	E	330 425-3092	
Twinsburg *(G-18266)*			
▲ General Data Company Inc	C	513 752-7978	
Cincinnati *(G-2853)*			
▲ Globe Food Equipment Company	E	937 299-5493	
Moraine *(G-14662)*			
▲ Harry C Lobalzo & Sons Inc	E	330 666-6758	
Akron *(G-251)*			
◆ Hubert Company LLC	B	513 367-8600	
Harrison *(G-11670)*			
◆ ITW Food Equipment Group LLC	A	937 332-2396	
Troy *(G-18208)*			
John H Kappus Co	E	216 367-6677	
Cleveland *(G-5799)*			
◆ N Wasserstrom & Sons Inc	C	614 228-5550	
Columbus *(G-8126)*			
Nemco Inc	D	419 542-7751	
Hicksville *(G-11730)*			
OK Interiors Corp	C	513 742-3278	
Cincinnati *(G-4164)*			
Productivity Qulty Systems Inc	E	937 885-2255	
Dayton *(G-9717)*			
Quality Supply Co	E	937 890-6114	
Cincinnati *(G-4310)*			
Restaurant Depot LLC	E	513 542-3000	
Cincinnati *(G-4364)*			
Restaurant Depot LLC	E	614 272-6670	
Columbus *(G-8525)*			
Restaurant Equippers Inc	E	614 358-6622	
Columbus *(G-8526)*			
◆ Russell T Bundy Associates Inc	D	937 652-2151	
Urbana *(G-18444)*			
S S Kemp & Company	C	216 271-7062	
Cleveland *(G-6357)*			
Shearer Farm Inc	E	419 465-4622	
Monroeville *(G-14590)*			
Sign America Incorporated	E	740 765-5555	
Richmond *(G-16387)*			
▲ Specialty Equipment Sales Co	E	216 351-2559	
Brooklyn Heights *(G-1882)*			
Sprayworks Equipment Group LLC	E	330 587-4141	
Canton *(G-2483)*			
▲ Takkt America Holding Inc	C	513 367-8600	
Harrison *(G-11678)*			
The Cottingham Paper Co	E	614 294-6444	
Columbus *(G-8742)*			
Trimark Usa LLC	D	216 271-7700	
Cleveland *(G-6549)*			
Vulcan Feg	D	937 332-2763	
Troy *(G-18239)*			
◆ Wasserstrom Company	B	614 228-6525	
Columbus *(G-8878)*			
▲ Zink Foodservice Group	E	800 492-7400	
Columbus *(G-8937)*			

5047 Medical, Dental & Hospital Eqpt & Splys Wholesale

Advanced Medical Equipment Inc	E	937 534-1080	
Kettering *(G-12290)*			
Advantage Appliance Services	C	330 498-8101	
Canton *(G-2174)*			
Alpha Imaging LLC	E	440 953-3800	
Willoughby *(G-19504)*			

American Home Health Care Inc	E	614 237-1133	
Columbus *(G-6925)*			
Americas Best Medical Eqp Co	E	330 928-0884	
Akron *(G-71)*			
Amerimed	E	513 942-3670	
West Chester *(G-18866)*			
Apria Healthcare LLC	D	419 471-1919	
Maumee *(G-13758)*			
Ardus Medical Inc	D	855 592-7387	
Blue Ash *(G-1507)*			
Asd Specialty Healthcare LLC	D	513 682-3600	
West Chester *(G-18869)*			
Assuramed Inc	E	330 963-6998	
Twinsburg *(G-18246)*			
Benco Dental Supply Co	D	513 874-2990	
Cincinnati *(G-3040)*			
Benco Dental Supply Co	E	614 761-1053	
Dublin *(G-10144)*			
Benco Dental Supply Co	D	317 845-5356	
West Chester *(G-19044)*			
Biorx LLC	C	866 442-4679	
Cincinnati *(G-3051)*			
◆ Biotech Medical Inc	A	330 494-5504	
Canton *(G-2213)*			
▲ Blatchford Inc	D	937 291-3636	
Miamisburg *(G-14145)*			
▲ Bound Tree Medical LLC	D	614 760-5000	
Dublin *(G-10149)*			
Braden Med Services Inc	E	740 732-2356	
Caldwell *(G-2036)*			
◆ Butler Animal Health Sup LLC	E	614 761-9095	
Dublin *(G-10154)*			
▼ Butler Animal Hlth Holdg LLC	E	614 761-9095	
Dublin *(G-10155)*			
Cando Pharmaceutical	E	513 354-2694	
Loveland *(G-12980)*			
◆ Cardinal Health Inc	A	614 757-5000	
Dublin *(G-10156)*			
Cardinal Health Inc	D	614 497-9552	
Obetz *(G-15524)*			
Cardinal Health 100 Inc	B	614 757-5000	
Dublin *(G-10157)*			
Cardinal Health 200 LLC	E	440 349-1247	
Cleveland *(G-5122)*			
Cardinal Health 200 LLC	C	614 491-0050	
Columbus *(G-7122)*			
▲ Cardinal Health 301 LLC	A	614 757-5000	
Dublin *(G-10159)*			
Centura Inc	E	216 593-0226	
Cleveland *(G-5156)*			
Cintas Corporation No 2	D	513 459-1200	
Mason *(G-13559)*			
Clinical Specialties Inc	C	614 659-6580	
Columbus *(G-7228)*			
Clinical Technology Inc	E	440 526-0160	
Brecksville *(G-1777)*			
Columbus Prescr Phrms Inc	C	614 294-1600	
Westerville *(G-19243)*			
Community Srgl Sply Toms Rvr	E	614 307-2975	
Columbus *(G-7338)*			
Community Srgl Sply Toms Rvr	C	216 475-8440	
Cleveland *(G-5328)*			
◆ Compass Health Brands Corp	C	800 947-1728	
Middleburg Heights *(G-14250)*			
Concordnce Hlthcare Sltons LLC	D	419 455-2153	
Tiffin *(G-17512)*			
Cornerstone Medical Associates	E	330 374-0229	
Akron *(G-159)*			
CT Medical Electronics Co	C	440 526-3551	
Broadview Heights *(G-1829)*			
▲ Demarius Corporation	E	760 957-5500	
Dublin *(G-10199)*			
Dentronix Inc	D	330 916-7300	
Cuyahoga Falls *(G-9086)*			
▲ Dermamed Coatings Company LLC	E	330 634-9449	
Tallmadge *(G-17474)*			
Espt Liquidation Inc	D	330 698-4711	
Apple Creek *(G-618)*			
▲ Ethicon Endo-Surgery Inc	A	513 337-7000	
Blue Ash *(G-1558)*			
◆ Ferno-Washington Inc	C	877 733-0911	
Wilmington *(G-19623)*			
Full Range Rehab LLC	E	513 330-5995	
West Chester *(G-19056)*			
Garys Pharmacy Inc	E	937 456-5777	
Eaton *(G-10446)*			
▲ Gem Edwards Inc	D	330 342-8300	
Hudson *(G-618)*			
Gulf South Medical Supply Inc	E	614 501-9080	
Gahanna *(G-11123)*			

Haag-Streit USA Inc	E	513 336-7255	
Mason *(G-13591)*			
Haag-Streit USA Inc	C	513 336-7255	
Mason *(G-13592)*			
Hardy Diagnostics	D	937 550-2768	
Springboro *(G-16968)*			
Henry Schein Inc	E	440 349-0891	
Cleveland *(G-5685)*			
▲ Hitachi Hlthcare Americas Corp	B	330 425-1313	
Twinsburg *(G-18279)*			
Homereach Inc	E	614 566-0850	
Lewis Center *(G-12545)*			
Institutional Care Pharmacy	D	419 447-6216	
Tiffin *(G-17520)*			
Jones Metal Products Company	E	740 545-6341	
West Lafayette *(G-19114)*			
▲ Julius Zorn Inc	D	330 923-4999	
Cuyahoga Falls *(G-9105)*			
Keysource Acquisition LLC	E	513 469-7881	
Cincinnati *(G-3865)*			
Kunkel Pharmaceuticals Inc	E	513 231-1943	
Cincinnati *(G-3895)*			
Lake Erie Med Surgical Sup Inc	E	734 847-3847	
Holland *(G-11892)*			
Lima Medical Supplies Inc	E	419 226-9581	
Lima *(G-12682)*			
M & R Fredericktown Ltd Inc	E	440 801-1563	
Akron *(G-324)*			
Marquis Mobility Inc	D	330 497-5373	
Canton *(G-2389)*			
McKesson Medical-Surgical Inc	C	614 539-2600	
Urbancrest *(G-18450)*			
McKesson Medical-Surgical Top	E	513 985-0525	
Cincinnati *(G-3989)*			
▲ Medline Diamed LLC	E	330 484-1450	
Canton *(G-2398)*			
Medpace Inc	A	513 579-9911	
Cincinnati *(G-4000)*			
▲ Mill Rose Laboratories Inc	E	440 974-6730	
Mentor *(G-14086)*			
▲ Mobility Revolution LLC	E	909 980-2259	
Cleveland *(G-6003)*			
Modern Medical Inc	C	800 547-3330	
Westerville *(G-19186)*			
Neighborcare Inc	A	513 719-2600	
Cincinnati *(G-4103)*			
Nightngl-Alan Med Eqp Svcs LLC	E	513 247-8200	
Blue Ash *(G-1621)*			
▲ O E Meyer Co	C	419 625-1256	
Sandusky *(G-16631)*			
Ohio State University	E	614 293-8588	
Columbus *(G-8328)*			
Omnicare Inc	C	513 719-2600	
Cincinnati *(G-4168)*			
Partssource Inc	C	330 562-9900	
Aurora *(G-838)*			
▲ Pdi Communication Systems Inc	D	937 743-6010	
Springboro *(G-16979)*			
Pel LLC	E	216 267-5775	
Cleveland *(G-6191)*			
◆ Perio Inc	E	614 791-1207	
Dublin *(G-10308)*			
Pharmed Corporation	C	440 250-5400	
Westlake *(G-19391)*			
◆ Philips Medical Systems Clevel	B	440 247-2652	
Cleveland *(G-6203)*			
Phoenix Resource Network LLC	E	800 990-4948	
Cincinnati *(G-4244)*			
Precision Products Group Inc	D	330 698-4711	
Apple Creek *(G-620)*			
Professional Sales Associates	E	330 299-7343	
Seville *(G-16687)*			
Radebaugh-Fetzer Company	E	440 878-4700	
Strongsville *(G-17340)*			
Radiometer America Inc	D	440 871-8900	
Westlake *(G-19396)*			
Riverain Technologies LLC	E	937 425-6811	
Miamisburg *(G-14215)*			
S L Klabunde Corp	E	614 508-6012	
Columbus *(G-8570)*			
▲ Safety Today Inc	E	614 409-7200	
Grove City *(G-11468)*			
Sarnova Inc	D	614 760-5000	
Dublin *(G-10328)*			
Seeley Medical Oxygen Co	E	440 255-7163	
Andover *(G-609)*			
▲ Seneca Medical LLC	C	419 447-0236	
Tiffin *(G-17539)*			
Siffrin Residential Assn	C	330 799-8932	
Youngstown *(G-20211)*			

Sourceone Healthcare Tech Inc............C...... 440 701-1200
Mentor *(G-14111)*

Therapy Support Inc ....!.D...... 513 469-6999
Blue Ash *(G-1657)*

Thermo Fisher Scientific Inc...............C...... 800 871-8909
Oakwood Village *(G-15495)*

▲ Tosoh America Inc ....B...... 614 539-8622
Grove City *(G-11478)*

▲ Tri-Anim Health Services Inc ....E...... 614 760-5000
Dublin *(G-10357)*

Twin Med LLC ....E...... 440 973-4555
Middleburg Heights *(G-14262)*

United Seating & Mobility LLC............E...... 567 302-4000
Maumee *(G-13866)*

▲ United States Endoscopy...............C...... 440 639-4494
Mentor *(G-14118)*

▲ Viewray Technologies Inc ....D...... 440 703-3210
Oakwood Village *(G-15496)*

▲ Wbc Group LLC..............................D...... 866 528-2144
Hudson *(G-12012)*

Ziks Family Pharmacy 100 ....E...... 937 225-9350
Dayton *(G-9898)*

5048 Ophthalmic Goods Wholesale

Haag-Streit USA Inc ....C...... 513 336-7255
Mason *(G-13592)*

▲ Interstate Optical Co.....................D...... 419 529-6800
Ontario *(G-15555)*

Sight Resource Corporation ....D...... 513 942-4423
West Chester *(G-19006)*

Toledo Optical Laboratory Inc ....D...... 419 248-3384
Toledo *(G-18094)*

Walman Optical Company....................D...... 419 248-3384
Toledo *(G-18145)*

Walmart Inc...B...... 740 286-8203
Jackson *(G-12182)*

5049 Professional Eqpt & Splys, NEC Wholesale

Champion Optical Network ....E...... 216 831-1800
Beachwood *(G-1043)*

Diebold Incorporated ....C...... 330 588-3619
Canton *(G-2285)*

Diebold Nixdorf Incorporated ....D...... 513 682-6216
Hamilton *(G-11590)*

▲ Diebold Self Service Systems.........A...... 330 490-5099
Canton *(G-2286)*

Essilor Laboratories Amer Inc.............E...... 614 274-0840
Columbus *(G-7537)*

Euclid City Schools ....E...... 216 261-2900
Euclid *(G-10631)*

Franklin Imaging Llc ....E...... 614 885-6894
Columbus *(G-7618)*

Hamilton Safe Products Co Inc ....E...... 614 268-5530
Hilliard *(G-11771)*

▼ ICM Distributing Company Inc.........E...... 234 212-3030
Twinsburg *(G-18281)*

▲ Key Blue Prints Inc ....D...... 614 228-3285
Columbus *(G-7898)*

▲ Lorenz Corporation ....D...... 937 228-6118
Dayton *(G-9573)*

▲ Monarch Steel Company Inc ....E...... 216 587-8000
Cleveland *(G-6007)*

▲ Panini North America Inc ....E...... 937 291-2195
Dayton *(G-9684)*

Perkinelmer Hlth Sciences Inc............E...... 330 825-4525
Akron *(G-378)*

Queen City Reprographics....................C...... 513 326-2300
Cincinnati *(G-4321)*

▲ S&V Industries Inc ....E...... 330 666-1986
Medina *(G-13997)*

Shawnee Optical Inc ....D...... 440 997-2020
Ashtabula *(G-754)*

Teledyne Instruments Inc ....E...... 513 229-7000
Mason *(G-13645)*

Teledyne Tekmar Company ....E...... 513 229-7000
Mason *(G-13646)*

US Tsubaki Power Transm LLC ....C...... 419 626-4560
Sandusky *(G-16653)*

Zaner-Bloser Inc ....D...... 614 486-0221
Columbus *(G-8935)*

5051 Metals Service Centers

▲ A J Oster Foils LLC ....D...... 330 823-1700
Alliance *(G-512)*

Advanced Graphite Machining US ....E...... 216 658-6521
Parma *(G-15759)*

Albco Sales Inc ....E...... 330 424-9446
Lisbon *(G-12795)*

◆ All Foils Inc ....D...... 440 572-3645
Strongsville *(G-17283)*

▲ All Metal Sales Inc ....E...... 440 617-1234
Westlake *(G-19312)*

Alro Steel Corporation 330 929-4660
Cuyahoga Falls *(G-9069)*

Alro Steel Corporation ....D...... 513 769-9999
Cincinnati *(G-2932)*

Alro Steel Corporation ....E...... 419 720-5300
Toledo *(G-17586)*

Alro Steel Corporation ....E...... 614 878-7271
Columbus *(G-6905)*

Alro Steel Corporation ....E...... 937 253-6121
Dayton *(G-9221)*

Alumalloy Metalcasting Company.......D...... 440 930-2222
Avon Lake *(G-907)*

▲ Aluminum Line Products Company .D...... 440 835-8880
Westlake *(G-19316)*

AM Castle & Co 330 425-7000
Bedford *(G-1269)*

◆ American Consolidated Inds Inc......D...... 216 587-8000
Cleveland *(G-4951)*

American Posts LLC............................E...... 419 720-0652
Toledo *(G-17593)*

▲ American Tank & Fabricating Co......E...... 216 252-1500
Cleveland *(G-4967)*

Anchor Bronze and Metals Inc ....E...... 440 549-5653
Cleveland *(G-4976)*

Associated Steel Company Inc.............C...... 216 475-8000
Cleveland *(G-5015)*

Atlas Bolt & Screw Company LLC ......E...... 419 289-6171
Ashland *(G-653)*

◆ Atlas Steel Products Co ....D...... 330 425-1600
Twinsburg *(G-18247)*

▲ Avalon Precision Cast Co LLC ....C...... 216 362-4100
Brookpark *(G-1891)*

Benjamin Steel Company Inc...............E...... 937 233-1212
Springfield *(G-16998)*

Benjamin Steel Company Inc...............E...... 419 229-8045
Lima *(G-12605)*

Benjamin Steel Company Inc...............E...... 419 522-5500
Mansfield *(G-13140)*

▲ Bico Akron Inc ....D...... 330 794-1716
Mogadore *(G-14543)*

Blackburns Fabrication Inc ....E...... 614 875-0784
Columbus *(G-7046)*

Boston Retail Products Inc ....E...... 330 744-8100
Youngstown *(G-19971)*

Burger Iron Company ....C...... 330 794-1716
Mogadore *(G-14544)*

Butler Processing Inc ....E...... 513 874-1400
Hamilton *(G-11572)*

Central Steel and Wire Company ....C...... 513 242-2233
Cincinnati *(G-3158)*

Chapel Steel Corp ....E...... 800 570-7674
Bedford Heights *(G-1319)*

Chatham Steel Corporation ....D...... 740 377-9310
South Point *(G-16929)*

Cincinnati Steel Products Co................E...... 513 871-4444
Cincinnati *(G-3270)*

▲ Clifton Steel Company ....D...... 216 662-6111
Maple Heights *(G-13283)*

▲ Clinton Aluminum Dist Inc ....C...... 330 882-6743
New Franklin *(G-14902)*

◆ Cme Acquisitions LLC......................E...... 216 464-4480
Twinsburg *(G-18255)*

Coilplus Inc ....D...... 614 866-1338
Columbus *(G-7242)*

Coilplus Inc ....E...... 937 322-4455
Springfield *(G-17016)*

Coilplus Inc ....E...... 937 778-8884
Piqua *(G-16000)*

▲ Concast Metal Products Co ....D...... 440 965-4455
Wakeman *(G-18620)*

▲ Contractors Materials Company ....E...... 513 733-3000
Cincinnati *(G-3353)*

Contractors Steel Company..................E...... 330 425-3050
Twinsburg *(G-18744)*

Diamond Metals Dist Inc ....E...... 216 898-7900
Cleveland *(G-5421)*

Earle M Jorgensen Company ....E...... 513 771-3223
Cincinnati *(G-3470)*

Earle M Jorgensen Company ....E...... 330 425-1500
Twinsburg *(G-18259)*

Efco Corp ....E...... 614 876-1226
Columbus *(G-7509)*

▲ F I L US Inc ....E...... 440 248-9500
Solon *(G-16847)*

▲ Fay Industries Inc ....D...... 440 572-5030
Strongsville *(G-17304)*

▲ Ferralloy Inc ....E...... 440 250-1900
Cleveland *(G-5525)*

▲ Fisher Cast Steel Products Inc ....E...... 614 879-8325
West Jefferson *(G-19108)*

▲ Flack Steel LLC ....E...... 216 456-0700
Cleveland *(G-5542)*

▲ Fpt Cleveland LLC ....C...... 216 441-3800
Cleveland *(G-5569)*

Freedom Steel Inc ....E...... 440 266-6800
Mentor *(G-14048)*

Gnw Aluminum Inc ....E...... 330 821-7955
Alliance *(G-533)*

Graber Metal Works Inc ....E...... 440 237-8422
North Royalton *(G-15356)*

◆ Greer Steel Company ....C...... 330 343-8811
Dover *(G-10080)*

H & D Steel Service Inc ....E...... 440 237-3390
North Royalton *(G-15357)*

▲ Haverhill Coke Company LLC...........D...... 740 355-9819
Franklin Furnace *(G-11046)*

Heidtman Steel Products ....A...... 419 691-4646
Toledo *(G-17799)*

Heidtman Steel Products Inc ....D...... 216 641-6995
Cleveland *(G-5681)*

Heidtman Steel Products Inc ....E...... 419 385-0636
Toledo *(G-17800)*

Holub Iron & Steel Company ....E...... 330 252-5655
Akron *(G-267)*

◆ Howmet Corporation ....E...... 757 825-7086
Newburgh Heights *(G-15114)*

▲ Hynes Industries Inc ....E...... 330 799-3221
Youngstown *(G-20073)*

▲ Independent Steel Company LLC......E...... 330 225-7741
Valley City *(G-18463)*

▲ Industrial Tube and Steel Corp ....E...... 330 474-5530
Kent *(G-12237)*

Infra-Metals Co ....E...... 740 353-1350
Portsmouth *(G-16149)*

▲ Is Acquisition Inc ....E...... 440 287-0150
Streetsboro *(G-17257)*

▲ Jade-Sterling Steel Co Inc ....E...... 330 425-3141
Twinsburg *(G-18285)*

Joseph T Ryerson & Son Inc ....E...... 513 896-4600
Hamilton *(G-11618)*

Jsw Steel USA Ohio Inc.......................D...... 740 535-8172
Mingo Junction *(G-14528)*

Kloeckner Metals Corporation ....D...... 513 769-4000
Cincinnati *(G-3879)*

L B Industries Inc................................E...... 330 750-1002
Struthers *(G-17366)*

Lapham-Hickey Steel Corp ....E...... 614 443-4881
Columbus *(G-7952)*

◆ Latrobe Spcialty Mtls Dist Inc ....D...... 330 609-5137
Vienna *(G-18580)*

Liberty Steel Industries Inc.................C...... 330 372-6363
Warren *(G-18724)*

◆ Liberty Steel Products Inc ....E...... 330 538-2236
North Jackson *(G-15248)*

Liberty Steel Products Inc...................C...... 330 534-7998
Hubbard *(G-11948)*

◆ Loveman Steel Corporation ....D...... 440 232-6200
Bedford *(G-1289)*

▲ Majestic Steel Usa Inc ....C...... 440 786-2666
Cleveland *(G-5902)*

Major Metals Company ....E...... 419 886-4600
Mansfield *(G-13202)*

Master-Halco Inc ....E...... 513 869-7600
Fairfield *(G-10751)*

Mazzella Holding Company Inc ....D...... 513 772-4466
Cleveland *(G-5926)*

McWane Inc ....B...... 740 622-6651
Coshocton *(G-9022)*

▲ Metal Conversions Ltd ....E...... 419 525-0011
Mansfield *(G-13219)*

Metals USA Crbn Flat Rlled Inc ....D...... 937 882-6354
Springfield *(G-17082)*

Metals USA Flat Rlled Cntl Inc ....E...... 618 451-4700
Wooster *(G-19744)*

▼ Miami Valley Steel Service Inc.........C...... 937 773-7127
Piqua *(G-16014)*

Mid-America Steel Corp ....D...... 800 282-3466
Cleveland *(G-5982)*

Mid-West Materials Inc ....E...... 440 259-5200
Perry *(G-15826)*

Miller Consolidated Industries............E...... 937 294-2681
Moraine *(G-14678)*

Modern Welding Co Ohio Inc................E...... 740 344-9425
Newark *(G-15073)*

▲ Monarch Steel Company Inc ....E...... 216 587-8000
Cleveland *(G-6007)*

S I C

▲ National Bronze Mtls Ohio Inc ....E 440 277-1226
　Lorain (G-12929)

National Metal Trading LLC ....E 440 487-9771
　Willoughby (G-19553)

New Technology Steel LLC ....D 419 385-0636
　Toledo (G-17939)

▲ New Technology Steel LLC ....E 419 385-0636
　Toledo (G-17940)

Northstar Alloys & Machine Co ....E 440 234-3069
　Berea (G-1431)

Ohio Metal Processing Inc ....E 740 286-6457
　Jackson (G-12178)

Ohio Steel Sheet & Plate Inc ....E 800 827-2401
　Hubbard (G-11949)

Ohio-Kentucky Steel Corp ....E 937 743-4600
　Franklin (G-11035)

Olympic Steel Inc ....D 216 292-3800
　Cleveland (G-6129)

Olympic Steel Inc ....D 216 292-3800
　Cleveland (G-6130)

Olympic Steel Inc ....E 440 287-0150
　Streetsboro (G-17263)

Olympic Steel Inc ....C 216 292-3800
　Bedford (G-1298)

◆ Panacea Products Corporation ....E 614 850-7000
　Columbus (G-8418)

▲ Parker Steel International Inc ....E 419 473-2481
　Maumee (G-13832)

Phoenix Corporation ....E 513 727-4763
　Middletown (G-14320)

Phoenix Steel Service Inc ....E 216 332-0600
　Cleveland (G-6206)

Precesion Finning Bending Inc ....E 330 382-9351
　East Liverpool (G-10416)

Precision Steel Services Inc ....D 419 476-5702
　Toledo (G-17984)

Quality Steels Corp ....E 937 294-4133
　Moraine (G-14690)

▲ R L Morrissey & Assoc Inc ....E 440 498-3730
　Solon (G-16889)

Radix Wire Co ....D 216 731-9191
　Cleveland (G-6279)

◆ Remelt Sources Incorporated ....E 216 289-4555
　Cleveland (G-6303)

▲ Samsel Rope & Marine Supply Co ...E 216 241-0333
　Cleveland (G-6370)

Samuel Son & Co (usa) Inc ....D 419 470-7070
　Toledo (G-18018)

Samuel Steel Pickling Company ....D 330 963-3777
　Twinsburg (G-18317)

Scot Industries Inc ....E 330 262-7585
　Wooster (G-19767)

Scott Steel LLC ....E 937 552-9670
　Piqua (G-16028)

Select Steel Inc ....E 330 652-1756
　Niles (G-15169)

▲ Shadco Inc ....E 310 217-8777
　Toronto (G-18185)

Shells Inc ....D 330 808-5558
　Copley (G-8974)

Singer Steel Company ....E 330 562-7200
　Streetsboro (G-17269)

SL Wellspring LLC ....D 513 948-2339
　Cincinnati (G-4494)

◆ Special Metals Corporation ....B 216 755-3030
　Warrensville Heights (G-18781)

Specialty Steel Co Inc ....E 800 321-8500
　Cleveland (G-6444)

St Lawrence Holdings LLC ....E 330 562-9000
　Maple Heights (G-13297)

Stark Metal Sales Inc ....E 330 823-7383
　Alliance (G-554)

Steel Plate LLC ....E 888 894-8818
　Twinsburg (G-18324)

Steel Warehouse Cleveland LLC .....E 888 225-3760
　Cleveland (G-6461)

Steel Warehouse Company LLC ....E 216 206-2800
　Cleveland (G-6462)

Steel Warehouse of Ohio LLC ....D 888 225-3760
　Cleveland (G-6463)

Steelsummit Holdings Inc ....E 513 825-8550
　Cincinnati (G-4542)

Swagelok Company ....D 440 349-5934
　Solon (G-16905)

Symcox Grinding & Steele Co ....E 330 678-1080
　Kent (G-12261)

The Mansfield Strl & Erct Co ....E 419 522-5911
　Mansfield (G-13251)

▲ Thomas Steel Strip Corporation .....B 330 841-6429
　Warren (G-18751)

▲ Three D Metals Inc ....D 330 220-0451
　Valley City (G-18470)

Thyssenkrupp Materials NA Inc ....D 216 883-8100
　Independence (G-12131)

Thyssenkrupp Materials NA Inc ....E 937 898-7400
　Miamisburg (G-14231)

Thyssenkrupp Materials NA Inc ....C 440 234-7500
　Cleveland (G-6529)

Thyssenkrupp Onlinemetals LLC ....E 206 285-8603
　Northwood (G-15408)

◆ Timken Corporation ....D 330 471-3378
　North Canton (G-15239)

Tomson Steel Company ....E 513 420-8600
　Middletown (G-14337)

Tri-State Aluminium Inc ....E 419 666-0100
　Toledo (G-18109)

◆ Tricor Industrial Inc ....D 330 264-3299
　Wooster (G-19773)

◆ Tylinter Inc ....D 800 321-6188
　Mentor (G-14117)

◆ United Performance Metals Inc ....C 513 860-6500
　Hamilton (G-11652)

▲ United Steel Service LLC ....C 330 448-4057
　Brookfield (G-1857)

▲ Universal Steel Company ....E 216 883-4972
　Cleveland (G-6583)

Van Pelt Corporation ....E 513 242-6000
　Cincinnati (G-4750)

◆ Voestlpine Precision Strip LLC ....E 330 220-7800
　Brunswick (G-1944)

▲ Waelzholz North America LLC ....E 216 267-5500
　Cleveland (G-6649)

◆ Watteredge LLC ....D 440 933-6110
　Avon Lake (G-929)

Westfield Steel Inc ....E 937 322-2414
　Springfield (G-17136)

William Wood ....E 740 543-4052
　Bloomingdale (G-1491)

Witt Glvnzing - Cincinnati Inc ....E 513 871-5700
　Cincinnati (G-4800)

Worthington Industries Inc ....C 513 539-9291
　Monroe (G-14587)

Worthngton Stelpac Systems LLC .....C 614 438-3205
　Columbus (G-8919)

5052 Coal & Other Minerals & Ores Wholesale

Graphel Corporation ....C 513 779-6166
　West Chester (G-18934)

▲ Tosoh America Inc ....B 614 539-8622
　Grove City (G-11478)

5063 Electrl Apparatus, Eqpt, Wiring Splys Wholesale

ABB Inc ....C 614 818-6300
　Westerville (G-19142)

Accurate Mechanical Inc ....E 740 681-1332
　Lancaster (G-12368)

Afc Cable Systems Inc ....D 740 435-3340
　Cambridge (G-2047)

Akron Electric Inc ....D 330 745-8891
　Akron (G-37)

Akron Foundry Co ....C 330 745-3101
　Akron (G-40)

Ametek Tchnical Indus Pdts Inc ....D 330 677-3754
　Kent (G-12214)

Anixter Inc ....E 513 881-4600
　West Chester (G-18868)

▲ Applied Indus Tech - CA LLC ....B 216 426-4000
　Cleveland (G-4994)

Asset Protection Corporation ....E 419 531-3400
　Toledo (G-17601)

Associated Mtls Holdings LLC ....A 330 929-1811
　Cuyahoga Falls (G-9072)

Belting Company of Cincinnati ....E 937 498-2104
　Sidney (G-16762)

▲ Belting Company of Cincinnati ....C 513 621-9050
　Cincinnati (G-3039)

▲ Best Lighting Products Inc ....D 740 964-0063
　Etna (G-10613)

▲ Bostwick-Braun Company ....D 419 259-3600
　Toledo (G-17620)

Buckeye Power Sales Co Inc ....E 937 346-8322
　Moraine (G-14628)

◆ Calvert Wire & Cable Corp ....E 216 433-7600
　Cleveland (G-5115)

▲ Capital Lighting Inc ....D 614 841-1200
　Columbus (G-6802)

Cincinnati Belt and Transm...........D 513 621-9050
　Cincinnati (G-3229)

Cls Facilities MGT Svcs Inc ....E 440 602-4600
　Mentor (G-14032)

Consolidated Elec Distrs Inc ....E 614 445-8871
　Columbus (G-7351)

◆ Current Lighting Solutions LLC ....E 800 435-4448
　Cleveland (G-5390)

Dickman Supply Inc ....C 937 492-6166
　Sidney (G-16773)

Dickman Supply Inc ....E 937 492-6166
　Sidney (G-16774)

Dickman Supply Inc ....E 937 492-6166
　Greenville (G-11375)

Dxp Enterprises Inc ....E 513 242-2227
　Cincinnati (G-3459)

Eaton Corporation ....E 614 839-4387
　Columbus (G-7495)

Eaton Corporation ....E 888 402-1915
　Cleveland (G-5463)

Edison Equipment ....E 614 883-5710
　Columbus (G-7501)

Electric Motor Tech LLC ....E 513 821-9999
　Cincinnati (G-3486)

Fenton Bros Electric Co ....E 330 343-0093
　New Philadelphia (G-14959)

◆ Filnor Inc ....E 330 821-8731
　Alliance (G-532)

Furbay Electric Supply Co ....E 330 454-3033
　Canton (G-2319)

GA Business Purchaser LLC ....D 419 255-8400
　Toledo (G-17752)

Gene Ptacek Son Fire Eqp Inc ....E 216 651-8300
　Cleveland (G-5602)

Graybar Electric Company Inc ....E 216 573-6144
　Cleveland (G-5625)

Graybar Electric Company Inc ....D 513 719-7400
　Cincinnati (G-3637)

Graybar Electric Company Inc ....E 614 486-4391
　Columbus (G-7688)

Graybar Electric Company Inc ....E 330 799-3220
　Youngstown (G-20053)

Gross Electric Inc ....E 419 537-1818
　Toledo (G-17773)

H Leff Electric Company ....C 216 325-0941
　Cleveland (G-5651)

Handl-It Inc ....D 440 439-9400
　Bedford (G-1283)

◆ Hinkley Lighting Inc ....D 440 653-5500
　Avon Lake (G-920)

Horner Industrial Services Inc ....E 937 390-6667
　Springfield (G-17047)

Hubbell Power Systems Inc ....D 330 335-2361
　Wadsworth (G-18600)

Hughes Corporation ....E 440 238-2550
　Strongsville (G-17312)

Iewc Corp ....E 440 835-5601
　Westlake (G-19356)

John A Becker Co ....D 937 226-1341
　Dayton (G-9527)

John A Becker Co ....D 513 771-2550
　Cincinnati (G-3822)

John A Becker Co ....E 614 272-8800
　Columbus (G-7861)

Johnson Cntrls SEC Sltions LLC ....D 440 262-1084
　Brecksville (G-1786)

Johnson Electric Supply Co ....E 513 421-3700
　Cincinnati (G-3828)

▲ Kirk Key Interlock Company LLC .....E 330 833-8223
　North Canton (G-15217)

Laughlin Music & Vending Svc ....E 740 593-7778
　Athens (G-790)

Legrand North America LLC ....B 937 224-0639
　Dayton (G-9561)

Lighting Services Inc ....E 330 405-4879
　Twinsburg (G-18293)

▲ Loeb Electric Company ....D 614 294-6351
　Columbus (G-7987)

LSI Industries Inc ....C 913 281-1100
　Blue Ash (G-1600)

M & R Electric Motor Svc Inc ....E 937 222-6282
　Dayton (G-9578)

▲ Major Electronix Corp ....E 440 942-0054
　Eastlake (G-10431)

Mars Electric Company ....D 440 946-2250
　Cleveland (G-5913)

Matlock Electric Co Inc...........E 513 731-9600
　Cincinnati (G-3979)

▲ McNaughton-Mckay Elc Ohio Inc .....D 614 476-2800
　Columbus (G-8046)

McNaughton-Mckay Elc Ohio Inc ....E 419 422-2984
  Findlay *(G-10941)*
McNaughton-Mckay Elc Ohio Inc ....E 419 891-0262
  Maumee *(G-13820)*
Mid-Ohio Electric Co. ....E 614 274-8000
  Columbus *(G-8076)*
◆ Monarch Electric Service Co ....D 216 433-7800
  Cleveland *(G-6006)*
▲ Multilink Inc ....C 440 366-6966
  Elyria *(G-10540)*
New Haven Estates Inc ....E 419 933-2181
  New Haven *(G-14916)*
Newark Electronics Corporation ....C 330 523-4912
  Richfield *(G-16366)*
Nimers & Woody II Inc ....D 937 898-2060
  Vandalia *(G-18533)*
◆ Noco Company ....B 216 464-8131
  Solon *(G-16879)*
◆ Noland Company ....C 937 396-7980
  Moraine *(G-14684)*
Ohio Alarm Inc ....E 216 692-1204
  Independence *(G-12105)*
Ohio Rural Electric Coops Inc ....E 614 846-5757
  Columbus *(G-8283)*
▲ Osburn Associates Inc ....E 740 385-5732
  Logan *(G-12852)*
Powell Electrical Systems Inc.............D 330 966-1750
  Canton *(G-2438)*
Professional Electric Pdts Co ....E 419 269-3790
  Toledo *(G-17989)*
Research & Investigation Assoc ....E 419 526-1299
  Mansfield *(G-13234)*
Rexel Usa Inc ....E 216 778-6400
  Cleveland *(G-6318)*
Rexel Usa Inc. ....D 440 248-3800
  Solon *(G-16892)*
Rexel Usa Inc. ....E 419 625-6761
  Sandusky *(G-16636)*
Rexel Usa Inc. ....E 614 771-7373
  Hilliard *(G-11812)*
▲ Richards Electric Sup Co Inc ....C 513 242-8800
  Cincinnati *(G-4370)*
▼ Riverside Drives Inc ....E 216 362-1211
  Cleveland *(G-6329)*
Sabroske Electric Inc. ....E 419 332-6444
  Fremont *(G-11092)*
Schneider Electric Usa Inc ....E 440 526-9070
  Richfield *(G-16378)*
Schneider Electric Usa Inc..................D 513 755-5000
  West Chester *(G-18997)*
Scott Fetzer Company ....C 216 267-9000
  Cleveland *(G-6379)*
▲ Shoemaker Electric Company ....E 614 294-5626
  Columbus *(G-8635)*
Siemens Industry Inc ....D 614 846-9540
  Worthington *(G-19849)*
Siemens Industry Inc ....D 513 742-5590
  Cincinnati *(G-4480)*
Signature Control Systems LLC ....E 614 864-2222
  Columbus *(G-8639)*
Simplex Time Recorder LLC ....E 513 874-1227
  West Chester *(G-19081)*
State Alarm Inc ....E 888 726-8111
  Youngstown *(G-20217)*
Stock Fairfield Corporation..................C 440 543-6000
  Chagrin Falls *(G-2684)*
Sumitomo Elc Wirg Systems Inc ....E 937 642-7579
  Marysville *(G-13531)*
▲ Technical Consumer Pdts Inc...........B 800 324-1496
  Aurora *(G-844)*
▲ Thomas Door Controls Inc...............E 614 263-1756
  Columbus *(G-8746)*
▲ TPC Wire & Cable Corp ....D 800 521-7935
  Macedonia *(G-13085)*
◆ Venture Lighting Intl Inc ....D 800 451-2606
  Twinsburg *(G-18335)*
Vincent Ltg Systems Co Inc..................E 216 475-7600
  Solon *(G-16912)*
W W Williams Company LLC ....E 419 837-5067
  Perrysburg *(G-15932)*
Wesco Distribution Inc ....E 216 741-0441
  Cleveland *(G-6665)*
Wesco Distribution Inc ....E 937 228-9668
  Dayton *(G-9874)*
Western Branch Diesel Inc...................E 330 454-8800
  Canton *(G-2534)*
Westfield Electric Inc..........................E 419 862-0078
  Gibsonburg *(G-11280)*
Winkle Electric Company Inc ....E 330 744-5303
  Youngstown *(G-20249)*

▲ Winkle Industries Inc ....D 330 823-9730
  Alliance *(G-557)*
Wolff Bros Supply Inc.........................E 419 425-8511
  Findlay *(G-10976)*
Wolff Bros Supply Inc ....E 330 786-4140
  Akron *(G-503)*
Wolff Bros Supply Inc ....E 330 264-5900
  Wooster *(G-19784)*
Wright State University ....A 937 775-3333
  Beavercreek *(G-1199)*
WW Grainger Inc ....E 614 276-5231
  Columbus *(G-8921)*
WW Grainger Inc ....E 513 563-7100
  Blue Ash *(G-1683)*

5064 Electrical Appliances, TV & Radios Wholesale

C C Mitchell Supply Company ....E 440 526-2040
  Cleveland *(G-5110)*
◆ Danby Products Inc..........................E 419 425-8627
  Findlay *(G-10895)*
Dayton Appliance Parts Co ....E 937 224-0487
  Dayton *(G-9352)*
Don Walter Kitchen Distrs ....E 330 793-9338
  Youngstown *(G-20021)*
Lowes Home Centers LLC ....C 216 351-4723
  Cleveland *(G-5882)*
Lowes Home Centers LLC ....C 419 739-1300
  Wapakoneta *(G-18649)*
Lowes Home Centers LLC ....C 937 235-2920
  Dayton *(G-9574)*
Lowes Home Centers LLC ....C 740 574-6200
  Wheelersburg *(G-19435)*
Lowes Home Centers LLC ....C 330 665-9356
  Akron *(G-321)*
Lowes Home Centers LLC ....C 330 829-2700
  Alliance *(G-538)*
Lowes Home Centers LLC ....C 937 599-4000
  Bellefontaine *(G-1357)*
Lowes Home Centers LLC ....C 419 420-7531
  Findlay *(G-10935)*
Lowes Home Centers LLC ....C 330 832-1901
  Massillon *(G-13704)*
Lowes Home Centers LLC ....C 513 741-0585
  Cincinnati *(G-3945)*
Lowes Home Centers LLC ....C 614 433-9957
  Columbus *(G-6822)*
Lowes Home Centers LLC ....C 740 389-9737
  Marion *(G-13430)*
Lowes Home Centers LLC ....C 740 450-5500
  Zanesville *(G-20326)*
Lowes Home Centers LLC ....C 513 598-7050
  Cincinnati *(G-3946)*
Lowes Home Centers LLC ....C 614 769-9940
  Reynoldsburg *(G-16317)*
Lowes Home Centers LLC ....C 614 853-6200
  Columbus *(G-7990)*
Lowes Home Centers LLC ....C 440 937-3500
  Avon *(G-893)*
Lowes Home Centers LLC ....C 513 445-1000
  South Lebanon *(G-16926)*
Lowes Home Centers LLC ....B 216 831-2860
  Bedford *(G-1290)*
Lowes Home Centers LLC ....C 937 327-6000
  Springfield *(G-17065)*
Lowes Home Centers LLC ....C 419 331-3598
  Lima *(G-12693)*
Lowes Home Centers LLC ....C 740 681-3464
  Lancaster *(G-12413)*
Lowes Home Centers LLC ....C 614 659-0530
  Dublin *(G-10275)*
Lowes Home Centers LLC ....C 614 238-2601
  Columbus *(G-7991)*
Lowes Home Centers LLC ....C 740 522-0003
  Newark *(G-15063)*
Lowes Home Centers LLC ....C 740 773-7777
  Chillicothe *(G-2803)*
Lowes Home Centers LLC ....C 440 998-6555
  Ashtabula *(G-745)*
Lowes Home Centers LLC ....B 513 753-5094
  Cincinnati *(G-2861)*
Lowes Home Centers LLC ....C 614 497-6170
  Columbus *(G-7992)*
Lowes Home Centers LLC ....C 513 731-6127
  Cincinnati *(G-3947)*
Lowes Home Centers LLC ....C 330 287-2261
  Wooster *(G-19742)*
Lowes Home Centers LLC ....C 937 339-2544
  Troy *(G-18211)*

Lowes Home Centers LLC ....C 440 392-0027
  Mentor *(G-14078)*
Lowes Home Centers LLC ....C 440 942-2759
  Willoughby *(G-19546)*
Lowes Home Centers LLC ....C 740 374-2151
  Marietta *(G-13345)*
Lowes Home Centers LLC ....C 419 874-6758
  Perrysburg *(G-15891)*
Lowes Home Centers LLC ....C 330 626-2980
  Streetsboro *(G-17259)*
Lowes Home Centers LLC ....C 419 389-9464
  Toledo *(G-17864)*
Lowes Home Centers LLC ....C 419 843-9758
  Toledo *(G-17865)*
Lowes Home Centers LLC ....C 614 447-2851
  Columbus *(G-7993)*
Lowes Home Centers LLC ....C 330 245-4300
  Akron *(G-322)*
Lowes Home Centers LLC ....C 513 965-3280
  Milford *(G-14402)*
Lowes Home Centers LLC ....C 330 908-2750
  Northfield *(G-15382)*
Lowes Home Centers LLC ....C 419 470-2491
  Toledo *(G-17866)*
Lowes Home Centers LLC ....C 513 336-9741
  Mason *(G-13612)*
Lowes Home Centers LLC ....C 937 498-8400
  Sidney *(G-16785)*
Lowes Home Centers LLC ....C 740 699-3000
  Saint Clairsville *(G-16493)*
Lowes Home Centers LLC ....C 330 920-9280
  Stow *(G-17218)*
Lowes Home Centers LLC ....C 740 589-3750
  Athens *(G-791)*
Lowes Home Centers LLC ....C 740 393-5350
  Mount Vernon *(G-14779)*
Lowes Home Centers LLC ....C 937 547-2400
  Greenville *(G-11389)*
Lowes Home Centers LLC ....C 330 335-1900
  Wadsworth *(G-18606)*
Lowes Home Centers LLC ....C 937 347-4000
  Xenia *(G-19918)*
Lowes Home Centers LLC ....C 440 239-2630
  Strongsville *(G-17324)*
Lowes Home Centers LLC ....C 513 755-4300
  West Chester *(G-18966)*
Lowes Home Centers LLC ....C 513 671-2093
  Cincinnati *(G-3948)*
Lowes Home Centers LLC ....C 440 331-1027
  Rocky River *(G-16440)*
Lowes Home Centers LLC ....C 330 677-3040
  Kent *(G-12247)*
Lowes Home Centers LLC ....C 419 747-1920
  Ontario *(G-15559)*
Lowes Home Centers LLC ....C 330 339-1936
  New Philadelphia *(G-14971)*
Lowes Home Centers LLC ....C 440 985-5700
  Lorain *(G-12924)*
Lowes Home Centers LLC ....C 419 447-4101
  Tiffin *(G-17521)*
Lowes Home Centers LLC ....C 937 578-4440
  Marysville *(G-13511)*
Lowes Home Centers LLC ....C 937 438-4900
  Dayton *(G-9575)*
Lowes Home Centers LLC ....C 937 427-1110
  Beavercreek *(G-1168)*
Lowes Home Centers LLC ....C 937 848-5600
  Dayton *(G-9576)*
Lowes Home Centers LLC ....C 614 529-5900
  Hilliard *(G-11786)*
Lowes Home Centers LLC ....C 513 737-3700
  Hamilton *(G-11625)*
Lowes Home Centers LLC ....C 419 355-0221
  Fremont *(G-11084)*
Lowes Home Centers LLC ....C 419 624-6000
  Sandusky *(G-16625)*
Lowes Home Centers LLC ....C 419 782-9000
  Defiance *(G-9926)*
Lowes Home Centers LLC ....C 330 609-8000
  Warren *(G-18725)*
Lowes Home Centers LLC ....C 740 894-7120
  South Point *(G-16939)*
Lowes Home Centers LLC ....C 513 727-3900
  Middletown *(G-14305)*
Lowes Home Centers LLC ....C 330 497-2720
  Canton *(G-2381)*
Lowes Home Centers LLC ....C 740 266-3500
  Steubenville *(G-17164)*
Lowes Home Centers LLC ....C 330 965-4500
  Youngstown *(G-20101)*

S I C

Lowes Home Centers LLC ....C 937 383-7000
Wilmington (G-19630)

Lowes Home Centers LLC ....C 937 854-8200
Dayton (G-9577)

Lowes Home Centers LLC ....C 614 476-7100
Columbus (G-7994)

◆ Mas Inc ....E 330 659-3333
Richfield (G-16362)

▲ Merc Acquisitions Inc ....E 216 925-5918
Twinsburg (G-18298)

Mobilcomm Inc ....D 513 742-5555
Cincinnati (G-4066)

Panasonic Corp North America ....D 513 770-9294
Mason (G-13625)

Panasonic Corp North America ....E 201 392-6872
Troy (G-18221)

Rieman Arszman Cstm Distrs Inc ....E 513 874-5444
Fairfield (G-10774)

◆ Royal Appliance Mfg Co ....C 440 996-2000
Cleveland (G-6344)

RPC Electronics Inc ....E 877 522-7927
Cleveland (G-6348)

V and V Appliance Parts Inc ....E 330 743-5144
Youngstown (G-20233)

W W W M ....E 419 240-1055
Toledo (G-18143)

Whirlpool Corporation ....D 419 423-6097
Findlay (G-10975)

Whirlpool Corporation ....C 740 383-7122
Marion (G-13473)

5065 Electronic Parts & Eqpt Wholesale

21st Century Solutions Ltd ....E 877 439-5377
Miamisburg (G-14134)

ABC Appliance Inc ....E 419 693-4414
Oregon (G-15581)

Acadia Solutions Inc ....E 614 505-6135
Dublin (G-10118)

Access Catalog Company LLC ....E 440 572-5377
Strongsville (G-17279)

Acuative Corporation ....D 440 202-4500
Strongsville (G-17280)

Agilysys Inc ....E 440 519-6262
Solon (G-16816)

Airborn Electronics Inc ....E 330 245-2630
Akron (G-25)

▲ Allied Enterprises Inc ....E 440 808-8760
Westlake (G-19314)

Arrow Electronics Inc ....D 800 722-5273
Solon (G-16822)

Arrow Electronics Inc ....D 440 498-6400
Solon (G-16823)

Asset Protection Corporation ....E 419 531-3400
Toledo (G-17601)

AT&T Corp ....E 330 505-4200
Niles (G-15145)

▲ Audio-Technica US Inc ....D 330 686-2600
Stow (G-17191)

Avnet Inc ....E 440 479-3607
Eastlake (G-10427)

Avnet Inc ....E 614 865-1400
Columbus (G-7006)

Avnet Inc ....E 440 349-7600
Beachwood (G-1033)

Aysco Security Consultants Inc ....E 330 733-8183
Kent (G-12215)

Bear Communications Inc ....E 216 642-1670
Independence (G-12049)

C A E C Inc ....E 614 337-1091
Columbus (G-7102)

Cellco Partnership ....E 330 722-6622
Medina (G-13916)

Cellco Partnership ....E 440 779-1313
North Olmsted (G-15279)

Cincinnati Voice and Data ....D 513 683-4127
Loveland (G-12983)

▲ Clercom Inc ....D 513 724-6101
Williamsburg (G-19491)

Commercial Electronics Inc ....E 740 281-0180
Newark (G-15023)

Communications III Inc ....E 614 901-7720
Westerville (G-19244)

Comproducts Inc ....D 614 276-5552
Columbus (G-7344)

Consolidated Communications ....E 330 896-3905
Canton (G-2266)

Convergint Technologies LLC ....C 513 771-1717
Cincinnati (G-3357)

Copp Systems Inc ....E 937 228-4188
Dayton (G-9320)

Cornerstone Controls Inc ....E 937 263-6429
Dayton (G-9322)

Diamond Company Inc ....C 937 374-1111
Xenia (G-19898)

Donnellon Mc Carthy Inc ....E 937 299-0200
Moraine (G-14649)

▲ DSI Systems Inc ....E 614 871-1456
Grove City (G-11429)

E-Cycle LLC ....D 614 832-7032
Hilliard (G-11763)

Electra Sound Inc ....D 216 433-9600
Parma (G-15766)

Enviro It LLC ....E 614 453-0709
Columbus (G-7520)

Exonic Systems LLC ....D 330 315-3100
Akron (G-207)

Famous Industries Inc ....E 330 535-1811
Akron (G-214)

▼ Fox International Limited Inc ....E 216 454-1001
Beachwood (G-1058)

▲ Funai Service Corporation ....E 614 409-2600
Groveport (G-11514)

Gordon Flesch Company Inc ....E 419 884-2031
Mansfield (G-13179)

Graybar Electric Company Inc ....D 216 573-6144
Cleveland (G-5625)

Honeywell International Inc ....E 614 717-2270
Columbus (G-7772)

Hughes Corporation ....E 440 238-2550
Strongsville (G-17313)

Keithley Instruments Intl Corp ....E 440 248-0400
Cleveland (G-5819)

Killer Spotscom Inc ....D 513 201-1380
Cincinnati (G-3869)

▲ Koehlke Components Inc ....E 937 435-5435
Franklin (G-11034)

▲ Ladd Distribution LLC ....D 937 438-2646
Kettering (G-12296)

◆ Mace Personal Def & SEC Inc ....E 440 424-5321
Cleveland (G-5893)

▲ Major Electronix Corp ....D 440 942-0054
Eastlake (G-10431)

◆ Mark Feldstein & Assoc Inc ....E 419 867-9500
Sylvania (G-17437)

McM Electronics Inc ....D 937 434-0031
Dayton (G-9596)

▲ McM Electronics Inc ....D 888 235-4692
Centerville (G-2630)

Mega Techway Inc ....C 440 605-0700
Cleveland (G-5947)

Mendelson Electronics Co Inc ....E 937 461-3525
Dayton (G-9606)

Midwest Communications Inc ....D 800 229-4756
North Canton (G-15221)

Midwest Digital Inc ....D 330 966-4744
North Canton (G-15222)

Mitel (delaware) Inc ....E 513 733-8000
West Chester (G-18974)

Mobilcomm Inc ....D 513 742-5555
Cincinnati (G-4066)

Neteam Systems LLC ....E 330 523-5100
Cleveland (G-6058)

Newark Corporation ....B 330 523-4457
Richfield (G-16365)

Newark Electronics Corporation ......C 330 523-4912
Richfield (G-16366)

P & R Communications Svc Inc ....E 937 222-0861
Dayton (G-9680)

Pager Plus One Inc ....C 513 748-3788
Milford (G-14417)

▲ Pepperl + Fuchs Inc ....E 330 425-3555
Twinsburg (G-18302)

Pepperl + Fuchs Americas Inc ....D 330 425-3555
Twinsburg (G-18303)

Polycom Inc ....E 937 245-1853
Englewood (G-10597)

▲ Pro Oncall Technologies LLC ....D 513 489-7660
Cincinnati (G-4287)

Quasonix Inc ....E 513 942-1287
West Chester (G-18988)

REM Electronics Supply Co Inc ....E 330 373-1300
Warren (G-18738)

Ricoh Usa Inc ....D 513 984-9898
Sharonville (G-16730)

▲ RPC Electronics Inc ....E 440 461-4700
Highland Heights (G-11736)

Schuster Electronics Inc ....E 330 425-8134
Twinsburg (G-18319)

Shawntech Communications Inc ......E 937 898-4900
Miamisburg (G-14220)

Sound Com Corporation ....D 440 234-2604
Berea (G-1437)

▲ Standex Electronics Inc ....D 513 871-3777
Cincinnati (G-4534)

Tele-Solutions Inc ....E 330 782-2888
Youngstown (G-20221)

Teletronic Services Inc ....E 216 778-6500
Strongsville (G-17351)

Visual Edge Technology Inc ....C 330 494-9694
Canton (G-2528)

Warwick Communications Inc ....E 216 787-0300
Broadview Heights (G-1850)

◆ Western Tradewinds Inc ....E 937 859-4300
Miamisburg (G-14238)

◆ Wholesale House Inc ....D 419 542-1315
Hicksville (G-11731)

◆ Winncom Technologies Corp ....E 440 498-9510
Solon (G-16916)

◆ Wurtec Incorporated ....D 419 726-1066
Toledo (G-18164)

5072 Hardware Wholesale

◆ A M Leonard Inc ....D 937 773-2694
Piqua (G-15994)

Ace Hardware Corporation ....C 440 333-4223
Rocky River (G-16421)

Akron Hardware Consultants Inc ......E 330 644-7167
Akron (G-47)

▲ Atlas Bolt & Screw Company LLC ....C 419 289-6171
Ashland (G-653)

Barnes Group Inc ....E 419 891-9292
Maumee (G-13760)

▲ Bostwick-Braun Company ....D 419 259-3600
Toledo (G-17620)

Brighton-Best Intl Inc ....E 440 238-1350
Strongsville (G-17288)

▲ Country Saw and Knife Inc ....E 330 332-1611
Salem (G-16540)

Do Cut Sales & Service Inc ....E 330 533-9878
Warren (G-18703)

Do It Best Corp ....C 330 725-3859
Medina (G-13933)

Elliott Tool Technologies Ltd ....D 937 253-6133
Dayton (G-9412)

◆ F & M Mafco Inc ....E 513 367-2151
Harrison (G-11666)

◆ Facil North America Inc ....C 330 487-2500
Twinsburg (G-18265)

Fastener Corp of America Inc ....E 440 835-5100
Westlake (G-19343)

Gemini Advertising Associates ....D 513 896-3541
Hamilton (G-11600)

GMI Holdings Inc ....D 330 794-0846
Akron (G-238)

Hd Supply Facilities Maint Ltd ....E 440 542-9188
Solon (G-16857)

Hillman Companies Inc ....D 513 851-4900
Cincinnati (G-3703)

Hillman Companies Inc ....B 513 851-4900
Cincinnati (G-3704)

◆ Hillman Companies Inc ....E 513 851-4900
Cincinnati (G-3705)

◆ Hillman Group Inc ....C 513 851-4900
Cincinnati (G-3706)

▲ Hodell-Natco Industries Inc ....E 773 472-2305
Cleveland (G-5699)

Khempco Bldg Sup Co Ltd Partnr .....D 740 549-0465
Delaware (G-9993)

La Force Inc ....D 614 875-2545
Grove City (G-11446)

▲ LE Smith Company ....D 419 636-4555
Bryan (G-1961)

Mae Holding Company ....E 513 751-2424
Cincinnati (G-3959)

▲ Matco Tools Corporation ....B 330 929-4949
Stow (G-17219)

Mazzella Holding Company Inc ....D 513 772-4466
Cleveland (G-5926)

Menard Inc ....E 419 726-4029
Toledo (G-17903)

▲ Mid-State Bolt and Nut Co Inc ....E 614 253-8631
Columbus (G-8078)

◆ Noco Company ....B 216 464-8131
Solon (G-16879)

▲ Norwood Hardware & Supply Co .....E 513 733-1175
Cincinnati (G-4134)

▲ Ohashi Technica USA Inc ....E 740 965-5115
Sunbury (G-17393)

▲ Omni Fasteners Inc ....E 440 838-1800
Broadview Heights (G-1842)

Reitter Stucco Inc ....E 614 291-2212
Columbus *(G-8508)*

▲ Saw Service and Supply Company ..E 216 252-5600
Cleveland *(G-6372)*

▲ Serv-A-Lite Products Inc ....C 309 762-7741
Cincinnati *(G-4454)*

▼ State Industrial Products Corp ....B 877 747-6986
Cleveland *(G-6458)*

▼ The Mau-Sherwood Supply Co ....E 330 405-1200
Twinsburg *(G-18326)*

▲ TTI Floor Care North Amer Inc..........B 440 996-2000
Solon *(G-16909)*

▲ Waxman Consumer Pdts Group Inc.D 440 439-1830
Cleveland *(G-6656)*

Waxman Consumer Pdts Group Inc ......E 614 491-0500
Groveport *(G-11551)*

◆ Waxman Industries Inc ....C 440 439-1830
Cleveland *(G-6657)*

WW Grainger Inc.................................E 614 276-5231
Columbus *(G-8921)*

Ziegler Bolt & Parts Co........................D 330 478-2542
Canton *(G-2544)*

5074 Plumbing & Heating Splys Wholesale

Accurate Mechanical Inc......................E 740 681-1332
Lancaster *(G-12368)*

▲ Chandler Systems Incorporated.........D 888 363-9434
Ashland *(G-666)*

▲ Corrosion Fluid Products Corp ....E 248 478-0100
Columbus *(G-7375)*

Dayton Windustrial Co ....E 937 461-2603
Dayton *(G-9385)*

Eastway Supplies Inc ....E 614 252-3650
Columbus *(G-7494)*

Edelman Plumbing Supply Inc ....E 216 591-0150
Bedford Heights *(G-1322)*

▲ Empire Brass Co ....E 216 431-6565
Cleveland *(G-5477)*

▲ Enting Water Conditioning Inc............E 937 294-5100
Moraine *(G-14653)*

Famous Distribution Inc.........................D 330 762-9621
Akron *(G-210)*

Famous Distribution Inc.........................E 330 434-5194
Akron *(G-211)*

Famous Enterprises Inc ....E 330 938-6350
Sebring *(G-16669)*

Famous Enterprises Inc ....E 330 762-9621
Akron *(G-212)*

Famous II Inc ....D 330 762-9621
Akron *(G-213)*

Famous Industries Inc ....E 330 535-1811
Akron *(G-215)*

Famous Industries Inc ....E 330 535-1811
Akron *(G-214)*

Ferguson Enterprises Inc........................E 513 771-6566
West Chester *(G-18923)*

Ferguson Enterprises Inc........................E 614 876-8555
Hilliard *(G-11767)*

Gordon Brothers Inc ....E 800 331-7611
Salem *(G-16545)*

Habegger Corporation............................E 330 499-4328
North Canton *(G-15209)*

Habegger Corporation............................D 513 612-4700
Cincinnati *(G-3669)*

Hague Water Conditioning Inc.................E 614 482-8121
Groveport *(G-11515)*

Hajoca Corporation................................E 216 447-0050
Cleveland *(G-5657)*

Industrial Controls Distrs LLC.................E 513 733-5200
West Chester *(G-18946)*

Keidel Supply Company Inc....................E 513 351-1600
Cincinnati *(G-3852)*

L B Brunk & Sons Inc ....E 330 332-0359
Salem *(G-16550)*

Lakeside Supply Co...............................E 216 941-6800
Cleveland *(G-5849)*

Lute Supply Inc ....E 740 353-1447
Portsmouth *(G-16153)*

◆ Mansfield Plumbing Pdts LLC.............A 419 938-5211
Perrysville *(G-15941)*

Mason Structural Steel Inc.....................D 440 439-1040
Walton Hills *(G-18637)*

Maumee Plumbing & Htg Sup Inc...........E 419 874-7991
Perrysburg *(G-15892)*

Morrow Control and Supply Inc...............E 330 452-9791
Canton *(G-2408)*

Mussun Sales Inc ....E 216 431-5088
Cleveland *(G-6029)*

New Haven Estates Inc ....E 419 933-2181
New Haven *(G-14916)*

◆ Noland Company ....C 937 396-7980
Moraine *(G-14684)*

▲ Oatey Supply Chain Svcs Inc ....C 216 267-7100
Cleveland *(G-6110)*

Palmer-Donavin Mfg Co ....E 419 692-5000
Delphos *(G-10032)*

Parker-Hannifin Corporation....................B 937 456-5571
Eaton *(G-10457)*

Parker-Hannifin Corporation....................C 614 279-7070
Columbus *(G-8421)*

Pickrel Brothers Inc ....E 937 461-5960
Dayton *(G-9691)*

▼ Reading Rock Residential LLC............E 513 874-4770
West Chester *(G-19075)*

Rexel Usa Inc.......................................E 419 625-6761
Sandusky *(G-16636)*

River Plumbing Inc ....E 440 934-3720
Avon *(G-903)*

Robertson Heating Sup Co Ohio..............E 800 433-9532
Alliance *(G-545)*

▲ Robertson Htg Sup Alliance Ohio ....C 330 821-9180
Alliance *(G-546)*

Robertson Htg Sup Canton Ohio..............E 330 821-9180
Alliance *(G-547)*

Ssi Fabricated Inc.................................E 513 217-3535
Middletown *(G-14330)*

The Famous Manufacturing Co ....E 330 762-9621
Akron *(G-469)*

Trumbull Industries Inc ....E 330 393-6624
Warren *(G-18758)*

Trumbull Industries Inc ....E 330 270-7800
Youngstown *(G-20226)*

▲ Trumbull Manufacturing Inc................D 330 393-6624
Warren *(G-18759)*

United Atmtc Htng Spply of Clv...............E 216 621-5571
Cleveland *(G-6567)*

Waxman Consumer Pdts Group Inc ......D 614 491-0500
Groveport *(G-11551)*

▲ Waxman Consumer Pdts Group Inc.D 440 439-1830
Cleveland *(G-6656)*

◆ Waxman Industries Inc ....C 440 439-1830
Cleveland *(G-6657)*

▲ Wayne/Scott Fetzer Company.............C 800 237-0987
Harrison *(G-11680)*

Winsupply Inc.......................................E 937 865-0796
Miamisburg *(G-14239)*

Winsupply Inc.......................................D 937 294-5331
Moraine *(G-14707)*

Wolff Bros Supply Inc............................E 419 425-8511
Findlay *(G-10976)*

Wolff Bros Supply Inc............................E 330 400-5990
Sandusky *(G-16656)*

Wolff Bros Supply Inc............................E 330 264-5900
Wooster *(G-19784)*

Wolff Bros Supply Inc............................E 330 786-4140
Akron *(G-503)*

Woodhill Supply Inc..............................E 440 269-1100
Willoughby *(G-19585)*

Worly Plumbing Supply Inc ....E 614 445-1000
Columbus *(G-8918)*

Zekelman Industries Inc.........................E 740 432-2146
Cambridge *(G-2087)*

5075 Heating & Air Conditioning Eqpt & Splys Wholesale

Air Systems of Ohio Inc.........................E 216 741-1700
Brooklyn Heights *(G-1865)*

Airtron LP ....D 614 274-2345
Columbus *(G-6888)*

Allied Supply Company Inc.....................E 937 224-9833
Dayton *(G-9216)*

American Hood Systems Inc ....E 440 365-4567
Elyria *(G-10478)*

Best Aire Compressor Service ....D 419 726-0055
Millbury *(G-14446)*

Buckeye Heating and AC Sup Inc ....E 216 831-0066
Bedford Heights *(G-1318)*

Controls and Sheet Metal Inc..................E 513 721-3610
Cincinnati *(G-3355)*

Controls Center Inc...............................D 513 772-2665
Cincinnati *(G-3356)*

◆ Copeland Access + Inc ....E 937 498-3802
Sidney *(G-16768)*

Daikin Applied Americas Inc...................E 763 553-5009
Dayton *(G-9344)*

Diversified Air Systems Inc.....................E 330 784-3366
Akron *(G-903)*

Famous Distribution Inc.........................E 330 434-5194
Akron *(G-211)*

Famous Distribution Inc........................D 330 762-9621
Akron *(G-210)*

Famous Enterprises Inc ....E 330 762-9621
Akron *(G-212)*

Famous Enterprises Inc ....E 216 529-1010
Cleveland *(G-5511)*

Famous Enterprises Inc ....E 419 478-0343
Toledo *(G-17726)*

Famous II Inc ....D 330 762-9621
Akron *(G-213)*

Gardiner Service Company LLC...............C 440 248-3400
Solon *(G-16850)*

▲ Habegger Corporation........................E 513 853-6644
Cincinnati *(G-3668)*

Habegger Corporation............................D 513 612-4700
Cincinnati *(G-3669)*

▲ Hamilton-Parker Company ....D 614 358-7800
Columbus *(G-7713)*

Honeywell International Inc ....D 216 459-6053
Cleveland *(G-5702)*

Honeywell International Inc ....E 614 717-2270
Columbus *(G-7772)*

Industrial Controls Distrs LLC.................E 513 733-5200
West Chester *(G-18946)*

Lakeside Supply Co...............................E 216 941-6800
Cleveland *(G-5849)*

Lennox Industries Inc............................E 614 871-3017
Grove City *(G-11447)*

Lute Supply Inc ....E 740 353-1447
Portsmouth *(G-16153)*

Luxury Heating Co................................D 440 366-0971
Sheffield Village *(G-16738)*

Monroe Mechanical Incorporated............E 513 539-7555
Monroe *(G-14577)*

◆ Noland Company ....C 937 396-7980
Moraine *(G-14684)*

OEM Parts Outlet ....E 419 472-2237
Toledo *(G-17957)*

Robertson Heating Sup Co Ohio..............E 800 433-9532
Alliance *(G-545)*

Robertson Htg Sup Clumbus Ohio...........C 330 821-9180
Alliance *(G-548)*

Slawson Equipment Co Inc.....................E 216 391-7263
Cleveland *(G-6416)*

Style Crest Inc.....................................C 419 332-7369
Fremont *(G-11098)*

◆ Style Crest Inc ....B 419 332-7369
Fremont *(G-11099)*

Style Crest Enterprises Inc ....D 419 355-8586
Fremont *(G-11100)*

Swift Filters Inc ....E 440 735-0995
Oakwood Village *(G-15494)*

The Famous Manufacturing Co ....E 330 762-9621
Akron *(G-469)*

Thompson Heating Corporation...............D 513 769-7696
Cincinnati *(G-4606)*

United Atmtc Htng Spply of Clv...............E 216 621-5571
Cleveland *(G-6567)*

▼ Verantis Corporation ....E 440 243-0700
Middleburg Heights *(G-14264)*

Wadsworth-Slawson Inc.........................E 216 391-7263
Perrysburg *(G-15934)*

Wolff Bros Supply Inc............................E 419 425-8511
Findlay *(G-10976)*

Wolff Bros Supply Inc............................E 330 786-4140
Akron *(G-503)*

WW Grainger Inc.................................E 614 276-5231
Columbus *(G-8921)*

Yanfeng US Automotive ....D 419 662-4905
Northwood *(G-15416)*

5078 Refrigeration Eqpt & Splys Wholesale

Allied Supply Company Inc.....................E 937 224-9833
Dayton *(G-9216)*

Buckeye Heating and AC Sup Inc ....E 216 831-0066
Bedford Heights *(G-1318)*

Controls Center Inc...............................D 513 772-2665
Cincinnati *(G-3356)*

Gordon Brothers Inc ....E 800 331-7611
Salem *(G-16545)*

Hattenbach Company.............................D 216 881-5200
Cleveland *(G-5666)*

Scotts Towing Co..................................E 419 729-7888
Toledo *(G-18022)*

Slush Puppie ....D 513 771-0940
West Chester *(G-19082)*

WW Grainger Inc.................................E 614 276-5231
Columbus *(G-8921)*

5082 Construction & Mining Mach & Eqpt Wholesale

▼ Advanced Specialty Products............D...... 419 882-6528
Bowling Green *(G-1712)*

Ag-Pro Ohio LLC ....D...... 740 450-7446
Zanesville *(G-20273)*

American Crane Inc ....E...... 614 496-2268
Reynoldsburg *(G-16281)*

▲ American Producers Sup Co Inc ..D...... 740 373-5050
Marietta *(G-13310)*

Baker & Sons Equipment Co ....E...... 740 567-3317
Lewisville *(G-12573)*

Bauer Corporation ....E...... 800 321-4760
Wooster *(G-19689)*

Belden & Blake Corporation ....E...... 330 602-5551
Dover *(G-10066)*

▲ Bobcat Enterprises Inc ....D...... 513 874-8945
West Chester *(G-18877)*

Brandsafway Services LLC ....E...... 513 860-2626
West Chester *(G-18879)*

Carmichael Equipment Inc ....E...... 740 446-2412
Bidwell *(G-1467)*

Cecil I Walker Machinery Co ....E...... 740 286-7566
Jackson *(G-12170)*

▼ Columbus Equipment Company .....E...... 614 437-0352
Columbus *(G-7281)*

Columbus Equipment Company ....E...... 513 771-3922
Cincinnati *(G-3330)*

Columbus Equipment Company ....E...... 330 659-6681
Richfield *(G-16351)*

Columbus Equipment Company ....E...... 614 443-6541
Columbus *(G-7282)*

Cope Farm Equipment Inc ....E...... 330 821-5867
Alliance *(G-528)*

D&M Sales & Solutions LLC ....E...... 937 667-8713
Tipp City *(G-17554)*

Dover Investments Inc ....E...... 440 235-5511
Olmsted Falls *(G-15533)*

E T B Ltd ....E...... 740 373-6686
Marietta *(G-13326)*

Ebony Construction Co ....E...... 419 841-3455
Sylvania *(G-17421)*

Equipment Maintenance Inc ....E...... 513 353-3518
Cleves *(G-6728)*

EZ Grout Corporation Inc ....E...... 740 962-2024
Malta *(G-13121)*

◆ F & M Mafco Inc ....C...... 513 367-2151
Harrison *(G-11666)*

Fabco Inc ....D...... 419 427-0872
Findlay *(G-10899)*

Findlay Implement Co ....E...... 419 424-0471
Findlay *(G-10903)*

▲ Hartville Hardware Inc ....C...... 330 877-4690
Hartville *(G-11688)*

Janell Inc ....E...... 513 489-9111
Blue Ash *(G-1589)*

K & M Contracting Ohio Inc ....E...... 330 759-1090
Girard *(G-11292)*

Kuester Implement Company Inc ......E...... 740 944-1502
Bloomingdale *(G-1490)*

▲ Lefeld Implement Inc ....E...... 419 678-2375
Coldwater *(G-6761)*

Leppo Inc ....C...... 330 633-3999
Tallmadge *(G-17480)*

◆ Mesa Industries Inc ....D...... 513 321-2950
Cincinnati *(G-4038)*

Murphy Tractor & Eqp Co Inc ....E...... 513 772-3232
Cincinnati *(G-4086)*

◆ Npk Construction Equipment Inc....D...... 440 232-7900
Bedford *(G-1295)*

Ohio Machinery Co ....C...... 419 874-7975
Perrysburg *(G-15897)*

Ohio Machinery Co ....E...... 740 942-4626
Cadiz *(G-2032)*

Ohio Machinery Co ....E...... 330 478-6525
Canton *(G-2427)*

Ohio Machinery Co ....E...... 740 453-0563
Zanesville *(G-20348)*

Ohio Machinery Co ....C...... 513 771-0515
Cincinnati *(G-4157)*

Ohio Machinery Co ....B...... 614 878-2287
Columbus *(G-8273)*

Ohio Machinery Co ....D...... 440 526-0520
Broadview Heights *(G-1841)*

Ohio Machinery Co ....E...... 937 335-7660
Troy *(G-18220)*

Ohio Machinery Co ....E...... 330 530-9010
Girard *(G-11295)*

Ohio Machinery Co ....E...... 330 874-1003
Bolivar *(G-1705)*

◆ Ohio Machinery Co ....C...... 440 526-6200
Broadview Heights *(G-1840)*

▲ Reco Equipment Inc ....E...... 740 619-8071
Belmont *(G-1395)*

◆ Richard Goettle Inc ....D...... 513 825-8100
Cincinnati *(G-4369)*

Seal Aftermarket Products LLC ......E...... 419 355-1200
Fremont *(G-11094)*

Shearer Farm Inc ....E...... 330 345-9023
Wooster *(G-19768)*

Shearer Farm Inc ....E...... 419 465-4622
Monroeville *(G-14590)*

Shetlers Sales & Service Inc ....E...... 330 760-3358
Copley *(G-8975)*

Simpson Strong-Tie Company Inc .....C...... 614 876-8060
Columbus *(G-8645)*

Southeastern Equipment Co Inc ....E...... 614 889-1073
Dublin *(G-10338)*

▼ Stone Products Inc ....E...... 800 235-6088
Canton *(G-2500)*

Terry Asphalt Materials Inc ....E...... 513 874-6192
Hamilton *(G-11646)*

TNT Equipment Company ....E...... 614 882-1549
Columbus *(G-8761)*

Vermeer Sales & Service Inc ....E...... 330 723-8383
Medina *(G-14012)*

▲ Wrench Ltd Company ....D...... 740 654-5304
Carroll *(G-2559)*

Yoder Drilling and Geothermal ....E...... 330 852-4342
Sugarcreek *(G-17381)*

5083 Farm & Garden Mach & Eqpt Wholesale

Ag-Pro Ohio LLC ....C...... 614 879-6620
London *(G-12858)*

▲ Agrinomix LLC ....E...... 440 774-2981
Oberlin *(G-15497)*

Apple Farm Service Inc ....E...... 937 526-4851
Covington *(G-9045)*

Baker & Sons Equipment Co ....E...... 740 567-3317
Lewisville *(G-12573)*

▲ Bostwick-Braun Company ....D...... 419 259-3600
Toledo *(G-17620)*

Buckeye Companies ....E...... 740 452-3641
Zanesville *(G-20284)*

▼ Buckeye Supply Company ....E...... 740 452-3641
Zanesville *(G-20285)*

Bzak Landscaping Inc ....E...... 513 831-0907
Milford *(G-14375)*

Cahall Bros Inc ....E...... 937 378-4439
Georgetown *(G-11265)*

Century Equipment Inc ....E...... 419 865-7400
Toledo *(G-17645)*

Century Equipment Inc ....E...... 513 285-1800
Hamilton *(G-11575)*

Century Equipment Inc ....E...... 216 292-6911
Cleveland *(G-5158)*

◆ Clarke Power Services Inc ....D...... 513 771-2200
Cincinnati *(G-3302)*

Coughlin Chevrolet Inc ....E...... 740 852-1122
London *(G-12862)*

Crouse Implement ....E...... 740 892-2086
Utica *(G-18455)*

Deerfield Farms Service Inc ....D...... 330 584-4715
Deerfield *(G-9904)*

Dta Inc ....E...... 419 529-2920
Ontario *(G-15548)*

Evolution Ag LLC ....E...... 740 363-1341
Plain City *(G-16052)*

Fackler Country Gardens Inc ....E...... 740 522-3128
Granville *(G-11341)*

Farmers Equipment Inc ....E...... 419 339-7000
Lima *(G-12638)*

Farmers Equipment Inc ....E...... 419 339-7000
Urbana *(G-18432)*

◆ Fort Recovery Equipment Inc ....E...... 419 375-1006
Fort Recovery *(G-10990)*

Gardner-Connell LLC ....E...... 614 456-4000
Columbus *(G-7649)*

▲ Hawthorne Hydroponics LLC ....D...... 480 777-2000
Marysville *(G-13501)*

▲ Hayward Distributing Co ....E...... 614 272-5953
Columbus *(G-7720)*

Homier & Sons Inc ....E...... 419 596-3965
Continental *(G-8961)*

Hull Bros Inc ....E...... 419 375-2827
Fort Recovery *(G-10992)*

Kenmar Lawn & Grdn Care Co LLC ...E...... 330 239-2924
Medina *(G-13965)*

Kenn-Feld Group LLC.....................E...... 419 678-2375
Coldwater *(G-6760)*

Krystowski Tractor Sales Inc ....E...... 440 647-2015
Wellington *(G-18842)*

▼ Lesco Inc ....C...... 216 706-9250
Cleveland *(G-5865)*

Liechty Inc ....E...... 419 445-1565
Archbold *(G-631)*

▼ Myers Equipment Corporation ......E...... 330 533-5556
Canfield *(G-2151)*

Ohio Irrigation Lawn Sprinkler ....E...... 937 432-9911
Dayton *(G-9670)*

Pax Steel Products Inc ....E...... 419 678-1481
Coldwater *(G-6764)*

Rk Family Inc ....B...... 513 737-0436
Hamilton *(G-11639)*

Roger Shawn Houck ....E...... 513 933-0563
Oregonia *(G-15617)*

Schmidt Machine Company ....E...... 419 294-3814
Upper Sandusky *(G-18412)*

Shearer Farm Inc ....E...... 419 529-6160
Ontario *(G-15571)*

Shearer Farm Inc ....E...... 440 237-4806
North Royalton *(G-15367)*

▲ Speck Sales Incorporated ....E...... 419 353-8312
Bowling Green *(G-1749)*

Streacker Tractor Sales Inc ....E...... 419 422-6973
Findlay *(G-10965)*

Wellington Implement Co Inc ....E...... 440 647-3725
Wellington *(G-18846)*

◆ Western Tradewinds Inc ....E...... 937 859-4300
Miamisburg *(G-14238)*

▲ Wolf Creek Company Inc ....D...... 937 854-2694
Dayton *(G-9884)*

Wyandot Tractor & Implement Co .....E...... 419 294-2349
Upper Sandusky *(G-18417)*

5084 Industrial Mach & Eqpt Wholesale

▲ 2828 Clinton Inc ....E...... 216 241-7157
Leetonia *(G-12517)*

A & A Safety Inc ....E...... 513 943-6100
Amelia *(G-563)*

A P O Holdings Inc ....D...... 330 650-1330
Hudson *(G-11960)*

▲ Absolute Machine Tools Inc ....D...... 440 839-9696
Lorain *(G-12878)*

▲ Addisonmckee Inc ....C...... 513 228-7000
Lebanon *(G-12448)*

Aerocontrolex Group Inc ....E...... 440 352-6182
Painesville *(G-15692)*

▲ Agrinomix LLC ....E...... 440 774-2981
Oberlin *(G-15497)*

Air Systems of Ohio Inc ....E...... 216 741-1700
Brooklyn Heights *(G-1865)*

Airgas Inc....................................B...... 866 935-3370
Cleveland *(G-4919)*

Airgas Inc....................................D...... 937 222-8312
Moraine *(G-14619)*

Airgas Usa LLC ....E...... 513 563-8070
Cincinnati *(G-2916)*

Airgas Usa LLC ....B...... 216 642-6600
Independence *(G-12042)*

Alba Manufacturing Inc ....D...... 513 874-0551
Fairfield *(G-10694)*

Albright Welding Supply Co Inc ....E...... 330 264-2021
Wooster *(G-19685)*

Aldrich Chemical ....D...... 937 859-1808
Miamisburg *(G-14138)*

▲ Alfons Haar Inc ....E...... 937 560-2031
Springboro *(G-16961)*

▲ Alkon Corporation ....D...... 419 355-9111
Fremont *(G-11058)*

Alkon Corporation ....E...... 614 799-6650
Dublin *(G-10126)*

All Lift Service Company Inc ....E...... 440 585-1542
Willoughby *(G-19503)*

▲ AM Industrial Group LLC.............E...... 216 433-7171
Brookpark *(G-1890)*

Andersen & Associates Inc ....E...... 330 425-8500
Twinsburg *(G-18244)*

Anderson & Vreeland Inc ....D...... 419 636-5002
Bryan *(G-1952)*

▲ Argo-Hytos Inc ....A...... 419 353-6070
Bowling Green *(G-1714)*

Atlas Machine and Supply Inc ....E...... 502 584-7262
West Chester *(G-19041)*

▲ Ats Systems Oregon Inc ....B...... 541 738-0932
Lewis Center *(G-12527)*

▲ Becker Pumps Corporation ....E...... 330 928-9966
Cuyahoga Falls *(G-9074)*

▲ Best & Donovan N A Inc ....E...... 513 791-9180
Blue Ash *(G-1513)*

▲ Bettcher Industries Inc ....C...... 440 965-4422
Wakeman (G-18619)

▲ Bevcorp LLC ....D...... 440 954-3500
Willoughby (G-19508)

Bionix Safety Technologies Ltd ....E...... 419 727-0552
Toledo (G-17615)

◆ Blastmaster Holdings Usa LLC ....D...... 877 725-2781
Columbus (G-7047)

Bobcat of Dayton Inc ....E...... 937 293-3176
Moraine (G-14627)

Bohl Crane Inc ....D...... 419 476-7525
Toledo (G-17616)

▲ Bohl Equipment Company ....D...... 419 476-7525
Toledo (G-17617)

Bollin & Sons Inc ....E...... 419 693-6573
Toledo (G-17618)

Bosch Rexroth Corporation ....E...... 614 527-7400
Grove City (G-11409)

▲ Bostwick-Braun Company ....D...... 419 259-3600
Toledo (G-17620)

Breathing Air Systems Inc ....E...... 614 864-1235
Reynoldsburg (G-16286)

Brennan Industrial Truck Co ....E...... 419 867-6000
Holland (G-11875)

Brown Industrial Inc ....E...... 937 693-3838
Botkins (G-1708)

▼ Buckeye Supply Company ....E...... 740 452-3641
Zanesville (G-20285)

Burns Industrial Equipment Inc ....E...... 330 425-2476
Macedonia (G-13063)

C H Bradshaw Co ....E...... 614 871-2087
Grove City (G-11417)

Casey Equipment Corporation ....E...... 330 750-1005
Struthers (G-17360)

Cecil I Walker Machinery Co ....E...... 740 286-7566
Jackson (G-12170)

◆ Cintas Corporation ....A...... 513 459-1200
Cincinnati (G-3291)

Cintas Corporation ....D...... 513 631-5750
Cincinnati (G-3292)

Cintas Corporation No 2..................A...... 513 459-1200
Mason (G-13557)

▲ Cintas Corporation No 2 ....A...... 513 459-1200
Mason (G-13558)

Clarke Power Services Inc ....E...... 937 684-4402
Huber Heights (G-11953)

Cleveland Tank & Supply Inc ....E...... 216 771-8265
Cleveland (G-5291)

Columbus Equipment Company ....E...... 513 771-3922
Cincinnati (G-3330)

Contract Sweepers & Eqp Co ....E...... 614 221-7441
Columbus (G-7366)

▲ Corrosion Fluid Products Corp .....E...... 248 478-0100
Columbus (G-7375)

▲ CPI - Cnstr Polymers Inc ....E...... 330 861-5200
North Canton (G-15193)

Cross Truck Equipment Co Inc ....E...... 330 477-8151
Canton (G-2274)

◆ Crown Equipment Corporation ......A...... 419 629-2311
New Bremen (G-14887)

Crown Equipment Corporation ....D...... 419 629-2311
New Bremen (G-14888)

Ctm Integration Incorporated ....E...... 330 332-1800
Salem (G-16541)

Cummins Bridgeway Columbus LLC ..D...... 614 771-1000
Hilliard (G-11758)

Cummins Inc ....E...... 614 771-1000
Hilliard (G-11759)

Cummins Inc ....E...... 513 563-6670
West Chester (G-18907)

D M I Distribution Inc ....E...... 765 584-3234
Columbus (G-7410)

▲ Daihen Inc ....E...... 937 667-0800
Tipp City (G-17555)

▼ Decker Equipment Company Inc ....E...... 866 252-4395
Cleveland (G-5414)

Detroit Diesel Corporation ....B...... 330 430-4300
Canton (G-2284)

▼ Devirsified Material Handling ......E...... 419 865-8025
Holland (G-11882)

Dickman Supply Inc ....C...... 937 492-6166
Sidney (G-16773)

Dickman Supply Inc ....E...... 937 492-6166
Greenville (G-11375)

▲ Double A Trailer Sales Inc ....E...... 419 692-7626
Delphos (G-10025)

Dreier & Maller Inc ....E...... 614 575-0065
Reynoldsburg (G-16300)

Dxp Enterprises Inc ....E...... 513 242-2227
Cincinnati (G-3459)

E F Bavis & Associates Inc ....E...... 513 677-0500
Maineville (G-13115)

Eaton Corporation ....B...... 216 523-5000
Beachwood (G-1054)

Eaton Corporation ....B...... 216 920-2000
Cleveland (G-5462)

Ellison Technologies Inc ....E...... 440 546-1920
Brecksville (G-1780)

▲ EMI Corp ....D...... 937 596-5511
Jackson Center (G-12183)

Equipment Depot Ohio Inc ....E...... 513 934-2121
Lebanon (G-12463)

▲ Equipment Depot Ohio Inc ....E...... 513 891-0600
Blue Ash (G-1557)

Equipment Depot Ohio Inc ....E...... 513 934-2121
Lebanon (G-12464)

▲ Equipment Manufacturers Intl ......E...... 216 651-6700
Cleveland (G-5488)

Esec Corporation ....E...... 330 799-1536
Youngstown (G-20030)

Esec Corporation ....E...... 614 875-3732
Grove City (G-11430)

▲ Esko-Graphics Inc ....D...... 937 454-1721
Miamisburg (G-14168)

Estabrook Corporation ....E...... 440 234-8566
Berea (G-1424)

▲ Eurolink Inc ....E...... 740 392-1549
Mount Vernon (G-14765)

Expert Crane Inc ....E...... 216 451-9900
Cleveland (G-5502)

Fairborn Equipment Company Inc ....D...... 419 209-0760
Upper Sandusky (G-18406)

▲ Fallsway Equipment Co Inc ....C...... 330 633-6000
Akron (G-209)

Fastener Industries Inc ....E...... 440 891-2031
Berea (G-1426)

▲ Fcx Performance Inc ....E...... 614 324-6050
Columbus (G-7567)

◆ Federal Machinery & Eqp Co ....E...... 800 652-2466
Cleveland (G-5522)

◆ Feintool Equipment Corporation ...E...... 513 791-1118
Blue Ash (G-1561)

▲ Fischer Pump & Valve Company .....E...... 513 583-4800
Loveland (G-12994)

Fluid Line Products Inc ....C...... 440 946-9470
Willoughby (G-19525)

Fluid Mechanics LLC ....E...... 216 362-7800
Avon Lake (G-917)

Forte Indus Eqp Systems Inc ....E...... 513 398-2800
Mason (G-13581)

Freeman Manufacturing & Sup Co ...E...... 440 934-1902
Avon (G-881)

Gardner Inc ....C...... 614 456-4000
Columbus (G-7648)

Gateway Products Recycling Inc ......E...... 216 341-8777
Cleveland (G-5596)

Ged Holdings Inc ....E...... 330 963-5401
Twinsburg (G-18272)

▲ General Data Company Inc ....C...... 513 752-7978
Cincinnati (G-2853)

General Electric Company ....E...... 513 530-7107
Blue Ash (G-1567)

General Electric Intl Inc ....E...... 330 963-2066
Twinsburg (G-18273)

Genesis Rescue Systems ....E...... 937 293-6240
Kettering (G-12293)

▲ Giant Industries Inc ....E...... 419 531-4600
Toledo (G-17762)

Glavin Industries Inc ....E...... 440 349-0049
Solon (G-16851)

◆ Goettsch International Inc ....E...... 513 563-6500
Blue Ash (G-1572)

◆ Gosiger Inc ....C...... 937 228-5174
Dayton (G-9466)

Gosiger Inc ....E...... 937 228-5174
Dayton (G-9467)

Graco Ohio Inc ....D...... 330 494-1313
Canton (G-2331)

▲ Great Lakes Power Products Inc ....D...... 440 951-5111
Mentor (G-14056)

Great Lakes Water Treatment ....E...... 216 464-8292
Cleveland (G-5631)

Hannon Company ....D...... 330 456-4728
Canton (G-2339)

Heidelberg USA Inc ....E...... 937 492-1281
Sidney (G-16782)

Hendrickson International Corp ....D...... 740 929-5600
Hebron (G-11714)

Henry P Thompson Company ....E...... 513 248-3200
Milford (G-14394)

◆ Heritage Equipment Company ....E...... 614 873-3941
Plain City (G-16054)

▼ Hgr Industrial Surplus Inc ....E...... 216 486-4567
Euclid (G-10639)

◆ Hiab USA Inc ....D...... 419 482-6000
Perrysburg (G-15874)

Hirsch International Holdings ....C...... 513 733-4111
Cincinnati (G-3710)

▲ Hy-Tek Material Handling Inc ....D...... 614 497-2500
Columbus (G-7790)

Hydraulic Parts Store Inc ....E...... 330 364-6667
New Philadelphia (G-14966)

Imco Carbide Tool Inc ....D...... 419 661-6313
Perrysburg (G-15877)

▲ Impact Products LLC ....C...... 419 841-2891
Toledo (G-17818)

◆ IMS Company ....D...... 440 543-1615
Chagrin Falls (G-2668)

Industrial Air Centers Inc ....E...... 614 274-9171
Columbus (G-7812)

Industrial Financial Svcs Inc ....E...... 614 777-0000
Columbus (G-7813)

Industrial Maint Svcs Inc ....E...... 440 729-2068
Chagrin Falls (G-2669)

◆ Industrial Parts & Service Co ....E...... 330 966-5025
Canton (G-2355)

Innovative Enrgy Solutions LLC ......E...... 937 228-3044
Hamilton (G-11613)

▲ Intelligrated Systems Inc ....A...... 866 936-7300
Mason (G-13598)

Intelligrated Systems LLC ....E...... 513 701-7300
Mason (G-13599)

◆ Intelligrated Systems Ohio LLC .....A...... 513 701-7300
Mason (G-13600)

Iwi Incorporated ....E...... 440 585-5900
Wickliffe (G-19466)

J and S Tool Incorporated ....E...... 216 676-8330
Cleveland (G-5770)

Jed Industries Inc ....E...... 440 639-9973
Grand River (G-11332)

▲ Jergens Inc ....C...... 216 486-5540
Cleveland (G-5790)

▲ Joseph Industries Inc ....D...... 330 528-0091
Streetsboro (G-17258)

Jr Engineering Inc ....C...... 330 848-0960
Barberton (G-957)

▲ JWF Technologies Llc ....E...... 513 769-9611
Fairfield (G-10741)

▼ KA Bergquist Inc ....E...... 419 865-4196
Toledo (G-17835)

◆ Ken Miller Supply Inc ....D...... 330 264-9146
Wooster (G-19737)

Kmh Systems Inc ....E...... 513 469-9400
Cincinnati (G-3881)

▲ Kolbus America Inc ....E...... 216 931-5100
Cleveland (G-5837)

▲ Kyocera SGS Precision Tools ....E...... 330 688-6667
Munroe Falls (G-14797)

◆ Lawrence Industries Inc ....C...... 216 518-7000
Cleveland (G-5858)

▲ Lefeld Welding & Stl Sups Inc ......E...... 419 678-2397
Coldwater (G-6762)

Linden Industries Inc ....E...... 330 928-4064
Cuyahoga Falls (G-9109)

▲ LNS America Inc ....D...... 513 528-5674
Cincinnati (G-2860)

M Conley Company ....C...... 330 456-8243
Canton (G-2383)

Maag Automatik Inc ....E...... 330 677-2225
Kent (G-12248)

Maple Mountain Industries Inc ....C...... 330 948-2510
Lodi (G-12828)

Marcy Industries Company LLC ....E...... 740 943-2343
Marion (G-13433)

Matheson Tri-Gas Inc ....E...... 614 771-1311
Hilliard (G-11788)

McCormick Equipment Co Inc ....E...... 513 677-8888
Loveland (G-13012)

▲ Met-Chem Inc ....E...... 216 881-7900
Cleveland (G-5961)

Mh Equipment Company ....E...... 937 890-6800
Dayton (G-9613)

Mh Equipment Company ....E...... 614 871-1571
Grove City (G-11452)

Mh Equipment Company ....D...... 513 681-2200
Cincinnati (G-4043)

MH Logistics Corp ....D...... 513 681-2200
West Chester (G-19066)

MH Logistics Corp ....E...... 330 425-2476
Hudson (G-11997)

Miami Industrial Trucks Inc ....D...... 937 293-4194
Moraine *(G-14677)*

Miami Industrial Trucks Inc ....E...... 419 424-0042
Findlay *(G-10944)*

Mid-Ohio Forklifts Inc ....E...... 330 633-1230
Akron *(G-338)*

▲ Midlands Millroom Supply Inc ......E...... 330 453-9100
Canton *(G-2403)*

▲ Midwest Industrial Supply Inc ......D...... 330 456-3121
Canton *(G-2404)*

▲ Miller Supply of WvA Inc ....E...... 330 264-9146
Wooster *(G-19748)*

Mine Equipment Services LLC ....E...... 740 936-5427
Sunbury *(G-17390)*

Minerva Welding and Fabg Inc ....E...... 330 868-7731
Minerva *(G-14522)*

Modal Shop Inc ....D...... 513 351-9919
Cincinnati *(G-4067)*

Monode Marking Products Inc ....D...... 440 975-8802
Mentor *(G-14089)*

▲ Multi Products Company ....E...... 330 674-5981
Millersburg *(G-14484)*

Neff Group Distributors Inc ....E...... 440 835-7010
Westlake *(G-19378)*

Neff Machinery and Supplies ....E...... 740 454-0128
Zanesville *(G-20344)*

◆ Nelsen Corporation ....E...... 330 745-6000
Norton *(G-15421)*

Nelson Stud Welding Inc ....E...... 440 250-9242
Elyria *(G-10543)*

▲ Newtown Nine Inc ....D...... 440 781-0623
Macedonia *(G-13078)*

Newtown Nine Inc ....E...... 330 376-7741
Akron *(G-345)*

Nfm/Welding Engineers Inc ....E...... 330 837-3868
Massillon *(G-13717)*

Nordson Corporation ....B...... 440 985-4496
Amherst *(G-594)*

North Coast Lift Trck Ohio LLC ......E...... 419 836-2100
Curtice *(G-9066)*

▲ O E Meyer Co ....C...... 419 625-1256
Sandusky *(G-16631)*

Ohio Hydraulics Inc ....E...... 513 771-2590
Cincinnati *(G-4155)*

Ohio Transmission Corporation ......E...... 419 468-7866
Galion *(G-11181)*

◆ Ohio Transmission Corporation ....C...... 614 342-6247
Columbus *(G-8357)*

Otis Elevator Company ....E...... 614 777-6500
Columbus *(G-8402)*

◆ Park Corporation ....B...... 216 267-4870
Cleveland *(G-6163)*

Parker-Hannifin Corporation ....E...... 216 896-3000
Cleveland *(G-6170)*

Paul Peterson Company ....E...... 614 486-4375
Columbus *(G-8427)*

▲ Pennsylvania TI Sls & Svc Inc ......D...... 330 758-0845
Youngstown *(G-20153)*

Pfpc Enterprises Inc ....B...... 513 941-6200
Cincinnati *(G-4240)*

▲ Pines Manufacturing Inc ....E...... 440 835-5553
Westlake *(G-19392)*

▲ Power Distributors LLC ....D...... 614 876-3533
Columbus *(G-8457)*

Power-Pack Conveyor Company ......E...... 440 975-9955
Willoughby *(G-19563)*

Praxair Distribution Inc ....E...... 330 376-2242
Akron *(G-393)*

Precision Supply Company Inc ....D...... 330 225-5530
Brunswick *(G-1938)*

Primetals Technologies USA LLC ......E...... 419 929-1554
New London *(G-14935)*

Process Pump & Seal Inc ....E...... 513 988-7000
Trenton *(G-18190)*

▲ Prospect Mold & Die Company ......D...... 330 929-3311
Cuyahoga Falls *(G-9119)*

▼ Questar Solutions LLC ....E...... 330 966-2070
North Canton *(G-15229)*

R & M Fluid Power Inc ....E...... 330 758-2766
Youngstown *(G-20173)*

R and J Corporation ....E...... 440 871-6009
Westlake *(G-19394)*

▼ R&M Materials Handling Inc ....E...... 937 328-5100
Springfield *(G-17099)*

▲ Raymond Storage Concepts Inc ....D...... 513 891-7290
Blue Ash *(G-1641)*

Rde System Corp ....C...... 513 933-8000
Lebanon *(G-12496)*

Reid Asset Management Company ....E...... 216 642-3223
Cleveland *(G-6298)*

Remtec Engineering ....E...... 513 860-4299
Mason *(G-13635)*

Rilco Industrial Controls Inc ....E...... 513 530-0055
Cincinnati *(G-4374)*

▲ Robeck Fluid Power Co ....D...... 330 562-1140
Aurora *(G-840)*

▲ Rodem Inc ....E...... 513 922-6140
Cincinnati *(G-4394)*

▲ Rubber City Machinery Corp ....E...... 330 434-3500
Akron *(G-411)*

▲ Rumpke/Kenworth Contract ....E...... 740 774-5111
Chillicothe *(G-2824)*

S & S Inc ....E...... 216 383-1880
Cleveland *(G-6354)*

Safety Solutions Inc ....D...... 614 799-9900
Columbus *(G-8578)*

▲ Safety Today Inc ....E...... 614 409-7200
Grove City *(G-11468)*

▲ Salvagnini America Inc ....E...... 513 874-8284
Hamilton *(G-11641)*

Samuel Strapping Systems Inc ....D...... 740 522-2500
Heath *(G-11709)*

Schindler Elevator Corporation ......E...... 614 573-2777
Columbus *(G-8599)*

Scott Industrial Systems Inc ....D...... 937 233-8146
Dayton *(G-9753)*

Select Industries Corp ....E...... 937 233-9191
Dayton *(G-9758)*

Sentinel Fluid Controls LLC ....E...... 419 478-9086
Toledo *(G-18025)*

▼ Sgl Carbon Technic LLC ....E...... 440 572-3600
Strongsville *(G-17343)*

Shawcor Pipe Protection LLC ....E...... 513 683-7800
Loveland *(G-13027)*

Shearer Farm Inc ....E...... 440 237-4806
North Royalton *(G-15367)*

Siemens Industry Inc ....E...... 440 526-2770
Brecksville *(G-1805)*

Simco Supply Co ....E...... 614 253-1999
Columbus *(G-8641)*

South Shore Controls Inc ....E...... 440 259-2500
Perry *(G-15828)*

◆ Spillman Company ....E...... 614 444-2184
Columbus *(G-8672)*

Staufs Coffee Roasters II Inc ....E...... 614 487-6050
Columbus *(G-8696)*

Stolle Machinery Company LLC ......E...... 330 493-0444
Canton *(G-2498)*

Stolle Machinery Company LLC ......D...... 330 453-2015
North Canton *(G-15235)*

Sumitomo Demag Plstc Machinery ....E...... 440 876-8960
Strongsville *(G-17350)*

Super Systems Inc ....E...... 513 772-0060
Cincinnati *(G-4555)*

▲ System Seals Inc ....D...... 440 735-0200
Cleveland *(G-6491)*

T J Automation Inc ....E...... 419 267-5687
Archbold *(G-641)*

Tank Leasing Corp ....E...... 330 339-3333
New Philadelphia *(G-14984)*

▲ Tape Products Company ....D...... 513 489-8840
Cincinnati *(G-4577)*

Taylor - Winfield Corporation ....D...... 330 797-0300
Youngstown *(G-20220)*

Tech Products Corporation ....E...... 937 438-1100
Miamisburg *(G-14227)*

Thyssenkrupp Elevator Corp ....E...... 440 717-0080
Broadview Heights *(G-1848)*

Thyssenkrupp Elevator Corp ....D...... 513 241-0222
Cincinnati *(G-4608)*

Thyssenkrupp Elevator Corp ....E...... 614 895-8930
Westerville *(G-19302)*

Tiffin Loader Crane Company ....D...... 419 448-8156
Tiffin *(G-17543)*

Tom Langhals ....E...... 419 659-5629
Columbus Grove *(G-8942)*

▲ Tomita USA Inc ....E...... 614 873-6509
Plain City *(G-16069)*

▲ Total Fleet Solutions LLC ....E...... 419 868-8853
Holland *(G-11921)*

▲ Towlift Inc ....E...... 216 749-6800
Brooklyn Heights *(G-1884)*

Towlift Inc ....E...... 419 666-1333
Northwood *(G-15411)*

Towlift Inc ....E...... 614 851-1001
Columbus *(G-8765)*

Towlift Inc ....E...... 419 531-6110
Toledo *(G-18106)*

Toyota Industrial Eqp Dlr ....E...... 419 865-8025
Holland *(G-11922)*

Toyota Industries N Amer Inc ....E...... 513 779-7500
West Chester *(G-19018)*

Toyota Industries N Amer Inc ....E...... 937 237-0976
Dayton *(G-9819)*

Toyota Material Hdlg Ohio Inc ....D...... 216 328-0970
Independence *(G-12132)*

Triad Technologies LLC ....E...... 937 832-2861
Vandalia *(G-18544)*

▲ Tripack LLC ....E...... 513 248-1255
Milford *(G-14439)*

Union Supply Group Inc ....E...... 614 409-1444
Groveport *(G-11545)*

US Safetygear Inc ....E...... 330 898-1344
Warren *(G-18764)*

V & P Hydraulic Products LLC ....D...... 740 203-3600
Delaware *(G-10014)*

Valley Industrial Trucks Inc ....E...... 330 788-4081
Youngstown *(G-20235)*

Vargo Inc ....E...... 614 876-1163
Hilliard *(G-11825)*

▲ Venco Venturo Industries LLC ......E...... 513 772-8448
Cincinnati *(G-4753)*

Venturo Manufacturing Inc ....E...... 513 772-8448
Cincinnati *(G-4754)*

Veritiv Operating Company ....D...... 216 901-5700
Cleveland *(G-6623)*

W W Williams Company LLC ....E...... 330 534-1161
Hubbard *(G-11951)*

W W Williams Company LLC ....D...... 800 336-6651
West Chester *(G-19098)*

W W Williams Company LLC ....E...... 419 837-5067
Perrysburg *(G-15932)*

W W Williams Company LLC ....E...... 330 225-7751
Brunswick *(G-1945)*

◆ Wardjet LLC ....D...... 330 677-9100
Tallmadge *(G-17498)*

Weld Plus Inc ....E...... 513 941-4411
Cincinnati *(G-4775)*

Western Branch Diesel Inc ....E...... 330 454-8800
Canton *(G-2534)*

◆ Western Tradewinds Inc ....E...... 937 859-4300
Miamisburg *(G-14238)*

Wilkris Company ....E...... 513 271-9344
Terrace Park *(G-17501)*

Williams Super Service Inc ....E...... 330 733-7750
East Sparta *(G-10425)*

Willis Day Management Inc ....E...... 419 476-8000
Toledo *(G-18159)*

Winelco Inc ....E...... 513 755-8050
West Chester *(G-19038)*

Wolf Machine Company ....C...... 513 791-5194
Blue Ash *(G-1679)*

Woodcraft Supply LLC ....D...... 513 407-8371
Cincinnati *(G-4805)*

Wright Brothers Inc ....E...... 513 731-2222
Cincinnati *(G-4807)*

◆ Wurtec Incorporated ....D...... 419 726-1066
Toledo *(G-18164)*

WW Grainger Inc ....E...... 513 563-7100
Blue Ash *(G-1683)*

WW Grainger Inc ....E...... 614 276-5231
Columbus *(G-8921)*

▲ Xigent Automation Systems Inc ....D...... 740 548-3700
Lewis Center *(G-12567)*

Yoder Machinery Sales Company ......E...... 419 865-5555
Holland *(G-11927)*

5085 Industrial Splys Wholesale

3b Holdings Inc ....D...... 800 791-7124
Cleveland *(G-4871)*

▲ A-T Controls Inc ....E...... 513 530-5175
West Chester *(G-19039)*

▲ Advanced Elastomer Systems LP ....C...... 800 352-7866
Akron *(G-20)*

▲ Afc Industries Inc ....E...... 513 874-7456
Fairfield *(G-10692)*

◆ Air Supply Co ....E...... 704 732-8034
Twinsburg *(G-18242)*

Albright Welding Supply Co Inc ....E...... 330 264-2021
Wooster *(G-19685)*

▲ Alkon Corporation ....D...... 419 355-9111
Fremont *(G-11058)*

Alkon Corporation ....E...... 614 799-6650
Dublin *(G-10126)*

▲ All Ohio Threaded Rod Co Inc ......E...... 216 426-1800
Cleveland *(G-4935)*

Allen Refractories Company ....C...... 740 927-8000
Pataskala *(G-15782)*

Allied Supply Company Inc ....E...... 937 224-9833
Dayton *(G-9216)*

Alro Steel Corporation	E	419 720-5300	
Toledo *(G-17586)*			
Alro Steel Corporation	E	614 878-7271	
Columbus *(G-6905)*			
▲ American Producers Sup Co Inc	D	740 373-5050	
Marietta *(G-13310)*			
Andre Corporation	E	574 293-0207	
Mason *(G-13540)*			
▲ Applied Industrial Tech Inc	B	216 426-4000	
Cleveland *(G-4996)*			
Applied Mint Sups Slutions LLC	E	216 456-3600	
Strongsville *(G-17285)*			
▲ ARC Abrasives Inc	D	800 888-4885	
Troy *(G-18194)*			
▲ Atlas Bolt & Screw Company LLC	C	419 289-6171	
Ashland *(G-653)*			
B W Grinding Co	E	419 923-1376	
Lyons *(G-13056)*			
◆ Bearing Distributors Inc	C	216 642-9100	
Cleveland *(G-5048)*			
▲ Bearing Technologies Ltd	D	440 937-4770	
Avon *(G-866)*			
▲ Belting Company of Cincinnati	C	513 621-9050	
Cincinnati *(G-3039)*			
Binkelman Corporation	E	419 537-9333	
Toledo *(G-17613)*			
Blackhawk Industries	E	918 610-4719	
Brunswick *(G-1920)*			
▲ Bordner and Associates Inc	E	614 552-6905	
Columbus *(G-7054)*			
Brand Energy & Infrastructure	E	419 324-1305	
Toledo *(G-17623)*			
▲ Brennan Industries Inc	E	440 248-1880	
Cleveland *(G-5077)*			
Brennan Industries Inc	E	440 248-7088	
Solon *(G-16829)*			
▲ Buckeye Rubber & Packing Co	E	216 464-8900	
Beachwood *(G-1039)*			
▲ C B Mfg & Sls Co Inc	D	937 866-5986	
Miamisburg *(G-14147)*			
Chandler Products LLC	E	216 481-4400	
Cleveland *(G-5167)*			
Chardon Tool & Supply Co Inc	E	440 286-6440	
Chardon *(G-2690)*			
Ci Disposition Co	E	216 587-5200	
Brooklyn Heights *(G-1867)*			
◆ Clippard Instrument Lab Inc	C	513 521-4261	
Cincinnati *(G-3309)*			
Commercial Electric Pdts Corp	E	216 241-2886	
Cleveland *(G-5318)*			
Cornerstone Controls Inc	E	937 263-6429	
Dayton *(G-9322)*			
Cornwell Quality Tools Company	D	330 628-2627	
Mogadore *(G-14545)*			
Cornwell Quality Tools Company	E	330 335-2933	
Wadsworth *(G-18594)*			
Crane Pumps & Systems Inc	B	937 773-2442	
Piqua *(G-16003)*			
▲ Creative Plastic Concepts LLC	E	419 927-9588	
Sycamore *(G-17410)*			
◆ Datwyler Sling Sltions USA Inc	D	937 387-2800	
Vandalia *(G-18519)*			
Dayton Industrial Drum Inc	E	937 253-8933	
Dayton *(G-9167)*			
Delille Oxygen Company	E	614 444-1177	
Columbus *(G-7432)*			
Dolin Supply Co	E	304 529-4171	
South Point *(G-16932)*			
◆ Duramax Marine LLC	D	440 834-5400	
Hiram *(G-11864)*			
Dynatech Systems Inc	E	440 365-1774	
Elyria *(G-10503)*			
Eagle Equipment Corporation	E	937 746-0510	
Franklin *(G-11028)*			
◆ Eagle Industrial Truck Mfg LLC	E	734 442-1000	
Swanton *(G-17396)*			
▲ Earnest Machine Products Co	E	440 895-8400	
Rocky River *(G-16431)*			
Edward W Daniel LLC	E	440 647-1960	
Wellington *(G-18839)*			
Ellison Technologies Inc	E	310 323-2121	
Hamilton *(G-11593)*			
Evans Adhesive Corporation	E	614 451-2665	
Columbus *(G-7540)*			
◆ F & M Mafco Inc	C	513 367-2151	
Harrison *(G-11666)*			
F B Wright Co Cincinnati	E	513 874-9100	
West Chester *(G-18921)*			
◆ Facil North America Inc	C	330 487-2500	
Twinsburg *(G-18265)*			
Famous Distribution Inc	D	330 762-9621	
Akron *(G-210)*			
▲ Faster Inc	E	419 868-8197	
Maumee *(G-13789)*			
▲ Fcx Performance Inc	E	614 324-6050	
Columbus *(G-7567)*			
Federal-Mogul Powertrain LLC	C	740 432-2393	
Cambridge *(G-2067)*			
▲ File Sharpening Company Inc	E	937 376-8268	
Xenia *(G-19899)*			
First Francis Company Inc	E	440 352-8927	
Painesville *(G-15714)*			
▲ Fischer Pump & Valve Company	E	513 583-4800	
Loveland *(G-12994)*			
Flodraulic Group Incorporated	E	614 276-8141	
Columbus *(G-7597)*			
▲ Forge Industries Inc	A	330 782-8301	
Youngstown *(G-20040)*			
General Factory Sups Co Inc	E	513 681-6300	
Cincinnati *(G-3615)*			
◆ Ges Graphite Inc	E	216 658-6660	
Parma *(G-15767)*			
◆ Gorilla Glue Company	E	513 271-3300	
Cincinnati *(G-3627)*			
Goss Supply Company	E	740 454-2571	
Zanesville *(G-20312)*			
▲ Great Lakes Fasteners Inc	E	330 425-4488	
Twinsburg *(G-18276)*			
▲ Great Lakes Power Products Inc	E	440 951-5111	
Mentor *(G-14056)*			
▲ Great Lakes Textiles Inc	E	440 914-1122	
Solon *(G-16854)*			
▲ H & D Steel Service Inc	E	440 237-3390	
North Royalton *(G-15357)*			
▲ Hart Industries Inc	E	513 541-4278	
Middletown *(G-14301)*			
Hd Supply Facilities Maint Ltd	E	440 542-9188	
Solon *(G-16857)*			
Ishikawa Gasket America Inc	E	419 353-7300	
Bowling Green *(G-1738)*			
J & J Entps Westerville Inc	E	614 898-5997	
Sunbury *(G-17389)*			
Jet Rubber Company	E	330 325-1821	
Rootstown *(G-16450)*			
JIT Packaging Inc	E	330 562-8080	
Aurora *(G-831)*			
Kaman Corporation	E	330 468-1811	
Macedonia *(G-13077)*			
▲ Kaufman Container Company	C	216 898-2000	
Cleveland *(G-5817)*			
Lakeside Supply Co	E	216 941-6800	
Cleveland *(G-5849)*			
◆ Lancaster Commercial Pdts LLC	E	740 286-5081	
Columbus *(G-7945)*			
◆ Lawrence Industries Inc	E	216 518-7000	
Cleveland *(G-5858)*			
Liberty Casting Company LLC	E	740 363-1941	
Delaware *(G-9996)*			
▲ Logan Clutch Corporation	E	440 808-4258	
Cleveland *(G-5879)*			
Lute Supply Inc	E	740 353-1447	
Portsmouth *(G-16153)*			
Macomb Group Inc	E	419 666-6899	
Northwood *(G-15398)*			
◆ Main Line Supply Co Inc	E	937 254-6910	
Dayton *(G-9581)*			
Mauser Usa LLC	E	740 397-1762	
Mount Vernon *(G-14781)*			
Mazzella Holding Company Inc	D	513 772-4466	
Cleveland *(G-5926)*			
Mc Neal Industries Inc	E	440 721-0400	
Painesville *(G-15724)*			
▲ McNeil Industries Inc	E	440 951-7756	
Painesville *(G-15726)*			
McWane Inc	B	740 622-6651	
Coshocton *(G-9022)*			
Megacity Fire Protection Inc	E	937 335-0775	
Dayton *(G-9605)*			
▼ Merchandise Inc	E	513 353-2200	
Miamitown *(G-14242)*			
▲ Mesa Industries Inc	E	513 321-2950	
Cincinnati *(G-4038)*			
▲ Miba Bearings US LLC	B	740 962-4242	
McConnelsville *(G-13902)*			
◆ Mid-State Bolt and Nut Co Inc	E	614 253-8631	
Columbus *(G-8078)*			
◆ Midwest Fasteners Inc	D	937 866-0463	
Miamisburg *(G-14193)*			
▲ Mill-Rose Company	C	440 255-9171	
Mentor *(G-14087)*			
▲ Mirka USA Inc	D	330 963-6421	
Twinsburg *(G-18299)*			
Motion Industries Inc	D	513 860-8400	
West Chester *(G-19070)*			
MRC Global (us) Inc	E	419 324-0039	
Toledo *(G-17925)*			
MRC Global (us) Inc	E	513 489-6922	
West Chester *(G-18977)*			
▲ Mullins International Sls Corp	D	937 233-4213	
Dayton *(G-9648)*			
New Haven Estates Inc	E	419 933-2181	
New Haven *(G-14916)*			
◆ Noland Company	C	937 396-7980	
Moraine *(G-14684)*			
▲ North Coast Bearings LLC	E	440 930-7600	
Avon *(G-896)*			
◆ Ohio Transmission Corporation	C	614 342-6247	
Columbus *(G-8357)*			
Ohio Transmission Corporation	E	419 468-7866	
Galion *(G-11181)*			
Ors Nasco Inc	E	918 781-5300	
West Chester *(G-19071)*			
Otp Holding LLC	E	614 342-6123	
Columbus *(G-8403)*			
Pallet Distributors Inc	C	888 805-9670	
Lakewood *(G-12359)*			
▲ Pennsylvania TI Sls & Svc Inc	D	330 758-0845	
Youngstown *(G-20153)*			
Permatex Inc	E	440 914-3100	
Solon *(G-16882)*			
Precision Supply Company Inc	D	330 225-5530	
Brunswick *(G-1938)*			
Process Pump & Seal Inc	E	513 988-7000	
Trenton *(G-18190)*			
▲ R L Morrissey & Assoc Inc	E	440 498-3730	
Solon *(G-16889)*			
Riten Industries	D	740 335-5353	
Wshngtn CT Hs *(G-19881)*			
Roger Zatkoff Company	E	248 478-2400	
Twinsburg *(G-18313)*			
Ruthman Pump and Engineering	E	937 783-2411	
Blanchester *(G-1489)*			
▲ Sabco Industries Inc	E	419 531-5347	
Toledo *(G-18016)*			
▲ Samsel Rope & Marine Supply Co	E	216 241-0333	
Cleveland *(G-6370)*			
Samuel Strapping Systems Inc	D	740 522-2500	
Heath *(G-11709)*			
Scioto Services LLc	E	937 644-0888	
Marysville *(G-13527)*			
Selinsky Force LLC	C	330 477-4527	
Canton *(G-2473)*			
Shan-Rod Inc	E	419 588-2066	
Berlin Heights *(G-1451)*			
Sign Source USA Inc	D	419 224-1130	
Lima *(G-12741)*			
▲ SSP Fittings Corp	C	330 425-4250	
Twinsburg *(G-18323)*			
▲ Stafast Products Inc	E	440 357-5546	
Painesville *(G-15741)*			
▼ Stark Industrial LLC	E	330 493-9773	
North Canton *(G-15234)*			
State Industrial Products Corp	C	216 861-6363	
Cleveland *(G-6459)*			
▲ Summers Acquisition Corp	E	216 941-7700	
Cleveland *(G-6474)*			
Superior Products LLC	D	216 651-9400	
Cleveland *(G-6484)*			
◆ Superior Products Llc	E	216 651-9400	
Cleveland *(G-6483)*			
▲ Supply Technologies LLC	C	440 947-2100	
Cleveland *(G-6485)*			
Swagelok Company	E	440 542-1250	
Solon *(G-16906)*			
▼ The Mau-Sherwood Supply Co	E	330 405-1200	
Twinsburg *(G-18326)*			
Timken Company	C	330 471-2121	
Canton *(G-2512)*			
Timken Company	D	234 262-3000	
Niles *(G-15171)*			
◆ Timken Corporation	C	330 471-3378	
North Canton *(G-15239)*			
▲ Tolco Corporation	D	419 241-1113	
Toledo *(G-18072)*			
◆ Tricor Industrial Inc	D	330 264-3299	
Wooster *(G-19773)*			
Tricor Metals	D	330 264-3299	
Wooster *(G-19774)*			
Vallen Distribution Inc	D	513 942-9100	
West Chester *(G-19028)*			

▲ Victory White Metal Company ....D 216 271-1400
Cleveland *(G-6628)*

◆ Watteredge LLC ....D 440 933-6110
Avon Lake *(G-929)*

Wesco Distribution Inc ....E 419 666-1670
Northwood *(G-15414)*

Wesco Distribution Inc ....E 216 741-0441
Cleveland *(G-6665)*

Wesco Distribution Inc ....E 937 228-9668
Dayton *(G-9874)*

Winsupply Inc ....D 937 294-5331
Moraine *(G-14707)*

▲ Wulco Inc ....D 513 679-2600
Cincinnati *(G-4808)*

WW Grainger Inc ....C 330 425-8387
Macedonia *(G-13090)*

WW Grainger Inc ....E 614 276-5231
Columbus *(G-8921)*

Ziegler Bolt & Parts Co ....D 330 478-2542
Canton *(G-2544)*

5087 Service Establishment Eqpt & Splys Wholesale

A-1 Sprinkler Company Inc ....D 937 859-6198
Miamisburg *(G-14136)*

Acorn Distributors Inc ....E 614 294-6444
Columbus *(G-6867)*

▲ Action Coupling & Eqp Inc ....D 330 279-4242
Holmesville *(G-11928)*

Airgas Usa LLC ....B 216 642-6600
Independence *(G-12042)*

▲ Alco-Chem Inc ....E 330 253-3535
Akron *(G-63)*

Alco-Chem Inc ....E 330 833-8551
Canton *(G-2177)*

American Sales Inc ....E 937 253-9520
Dayton *(G-9159)*

Baxter Burial Vault Service ....E 513 641-1010
Cincinnati *(G-3024)*

Brakefire Incorporated ....E 330 535-4343
Akron *(G-103)*

Captive-Aire Systems Inc ....E 614 777-7378
Gahanna *(G-11111)*

Century Equipment Inc ....E 513 285-1800
Hamilton *(G-11575)*

Clean Innovations ....E 614 299-1187
Columbus *(G-7222)*

Cleveland Coin Mch Exch Inc ....D 847 842-6310
Willoughby *(G-19514)*

Commercial Parts & Ser ....D 614 221-0057
Columbus *(G-7327)*

Dawnchem Inc ....E 440 943-3332
Willowick *(G-19597)*

Envirochemical Inc ....E 440 287-2200
Solon *(G-16846)*

Finley Fire Equipment Co ....E 740 962-4328
McConnelsville *(G-13900)*

▼ Fox International Limited Inc ....E 216 454-1001
Beachwood *(G-1058)*

▲ Fredrics Corporation ....C 513 874-2226
West Chester *(G-18926)*

Friends Service Co Inc ....D 419 427-1704
Findlay *(G-10910)*

H P Products Corporation ....D 513 683-8553
Cincinnati *(G-3667)*

Hd Supply Facilities Maint Ltd ....E 440 542-9188
Solon *(G-16857)*

Hillside Maint Sup Co Inc ....E 513 751-4100
Cincinnati *(G-3708)*

I Supply Co ....C 937 878-5240
Fairborn *(G-10676)*

▲ Impact Products LLC ....C 419 841-2891
Toledo *(G-17818)*

Laughlin Music & Vending Svc ....E 740 593-7778
Athens *(G-790)*

Lute Supply Inc ....E 740 353-1447
Portsmouth *(G-16153)*

M Conley Company ....C 330 456-8243
Canton *(G-2383)*

▲ Majestic Manufacturing Inc ....E 330 457-2447
New Waterford *(G-15005)*

Mansfield City Building Maint ....E 419 755-9698
Mansfield *(G-13205)*

Mapp Building Service LLC ....E 513 253-3990
Blue Ash *(G-1602)*

Mark Humrichouser ....E 614 324-5231
Westerville *(G-19184)*

Martin-Brower Company LLC ....B 513 773-2301
West Chester *(G-18971)*

Mougianis Industries Inc ....D 740 264-6372
Steubenville *(G-17167)*

MSA Group Inc ....B 614 334-0400
Columbus *(G-8119)*

National Marketshare Group ....E 513 921-0800
Cincinnati *(G-4094)*

▲ Norm Sharlotte Inc ....E 336 788-7705
Fairfield *(G-10760)*

North Central Sales Inc ....E 216 481-2418
Cleveland *(G-6075)*

◆ Perio Inc ....E 614 791-1207
Dublin *(G-10308)*

▲ Phillips Supply Company ....D 513 579-1762
Cincinnati *(G-4242)*

Powell Company Ltd ....D 419 228-3552
Lima *(G-12723)*

Pro-Touch Inc ....C 614 586-0303
Columbus *(G-8465)*

Rde System Corp ....C 513 933-8000
Lebanon *(G-12496)*

Rdp Foodservice Ltd ....D 614 261-5661
Hilliard *(G-11811)*

Rhiel Supply Co Inc ....E 330 799-7777
Austintown *(G-861)*

Rose Products and Services Inc ....E 614 443-7647
Columbus *(G-8551)*

Sally Beauty Supply LLC ....C 937 548-7684
Greenville *(G-11394)*

Sally Beauty Supply LLC ....C 614 278-1691
Columbus *(G-8584)*

Salon Ware Inc ....E 330 665-2244
Copley *(G-8972)*

Seaway Sponge & Chamois Co ....E 419 691-4694
Toledo *(G-18023)*

ServiceMaster of Defiance Inc ....D 419 784-5570
Defiance *(G-9940)*

▲ Shaffer Distributing Company ....D 614 421-6800
Columbus *(G-8628)*

◆ Sutphen Corporation ....E 800 726-7030
Dublin *(G-10347)*

The Cottingham Paper Co ....E 614 294-6444
Columbus *(G-8742)*

◆ Tranzonic Companies ....C 216 535-4300
Richmond Heights *(G-16395)*

◆ Wasserstrom Company ....B 614 228-6525
Columbus *(G-8878)*

5088 Transportation Eqpt & Splys, Except Motor Vehicles Wholesale

A & K Railroad Materials Inc ....E 419 537-9470
Toledo *(G-17574)*

Abx Air Inc ....B 937 382-5591
Wilmington *(G-19600)*

◆ Aim Mro Holdings Inc ....D 513 831-2938
Miamiville *(G-14244)*

Airborne Maint Engrg Svcs Inc ....A 937 366-2559
Wilmington *(G-19604)*

Airborne Maint Engrg Svcs Inc ....D 937 382-5591
Wilmington *(G-19605)*

Amsted Industries Incorporated ....C 614 836-2323
Groveport *(G-11493)*

▲ Buck Equipment Inc ....E 614 539-3039
Grove City *(G-11414)*

Century Equipment Inc ....E 419 865-7400
Toledo *(G-17645)*

Century Equipment Inc ....E 216 292-6911
Cleveland *(G-5158)*

Cleveland Wheels ....D 440 937-6211
Avon *(G-877)*

▼ Djj Holding Corporation ....C 513 621-8770
Cincinnati *(G-3437)*

▲ Eleet Cryogenics Inc ....E 330 874-4009
Bolivar *(G-1702)*

GE Engine Services LLC ....B 513 977-1500
Cincinnati *(G-3605)*

▲ Greenfield Products Inc ....D 937 981-2696
Greenfield *(G-11362)*

Grimes Aerospace Company ....D 937 484-2001
Urbana *(G-18436)*

◆ Jilco Industries Inc ....E 330 698-0280
Kidron *(G-12306)*

Mazzella Holding Company Inc ....D 513 772-4466
Cleveland *(G-5926)*

Netjets Inc ....E 614 239-5500
Columbus *(G-8174)*

Netjets Sales Inc ....C 614 239-5500
Columbus *(G-8177)*

NJ Executive Services Inc ....E 614 239-2996
Columbus *(G-8191)*

Schuster Electronics Inc ....E 330 425-8134
Twinsburg *(G-18319)*

▲ Sportsmans Market Inc ....C 513 735-9100
Batavia *(G-1009)*

Transdigm Group Incorporated ....C 216 706-2960
Cleveland *(G-6542)*

▲ Ysd Industries Inc ....D 330 792-6521
Youngstown *(G-20268)*

5091 Sporting & Recreational Goods & Splys Wholesale

21st Century Health Spa Inc ....E 419 476-5585
Toledo *(G-17573)*

4th and Goal Distribution LLC ....E 440 212-0769
Burbank *(G-2008)*

A K Athletic Equipment Inc ....E 614 920-3069
Canal Winchester *(G-2102)*

AB Marketing LLC ....E 513 385-6158
Fairfield *(G-10691)*

Air Venturi Ltd ....D 216 292-2570
Solon *(G-16818)*

Aspc Corp ....C 937 593-7010
Bellefontaine *(G-1345)*

◆ Ball Bounce and Sport Inc ....B 419 289-9310
Ashland *(G-654)*

Beaver-Vu Bowl ....E 937 426-6771
Beavercreek *(G-1130)*

Brennan-Eberly Team Sports Inc ....E 419 865-8326
Holland *(G-11876)*

Cherry Valley Lodge ....D 740 788-1200
Newark *(G-15022)*

Coachs Sports Corner Inc ....E 419 609-3737
Sandusky *(G-16588)*

Competitor Swim Products Inc ....D 800 888-7946
Columbus *(G-7341)*

▲ Done-Rite Bowling Service Co ....E 440 232-3280
Bedford *(G-1278)*

Dtv Inc ....E 216 226-5465
Mayfield Heights *(G-13873)*

Durga Llc ....D 513 771-2080
Cincinnati *(G-3457)*

Dwa Mrkting Prmtional Pdts LLC ....E 216 476-0635
Strongsville *(G-17298)*

Emsco ....E 440 238-2100
Strongsville *(G-17300)*

▲ Golf Galaxy Golfworks Inc ....C 740 328-4193
Newark *(G-15037)*

▲ Kohlmyer Sporting Goods Inc ....E 440 277-8296
Lorain *(G-12910)*

Lmn Development LLC ....D 419 433-7200
Sandusky *(G-16623)*

Mc Alarney Pool Spas and Billd ....E 740 373-6698
Marietta *(G-13357)*

Mc Gregor Family Enterprises ....E 513 583-0040
Cincinnati *(G-3984)*

Metropolitan Pool Service Co ....E 216 741-9451
Parma *(G-15768)*

▲ Miami Corporation ....E 800 543-0448
Cincinnati *(G-4044)*

▲ Micnan Inc ....E 330 920-6200
Cuyahoga Falls *(G-9113)*

R & A Sports Inc ....E 216 289-2254
Euclid *(G-10654)*

Riddell Inc ....E 440 366-8225
North Ridgeville *(G-15341)*

▲ Schneider Saddlery LLC ....E 440 543-2700
Chagrin Falls *(G-2682)*

Suarez Corporation Industries ....D 330 494-4282
Canton *(G-2502)*

Willow and Cane LLC ....E 609 280-1150
Springboro *(G-16988)*

Wilson Sporting Goods Co ....C 419 634-9901
Ada *(G-6)*

▲ Zebec of North America Inc ....E 513 829-5533
Fairfield *(G-10800)*

Zide Sport Shop of Ohio Inc ....D 740 373-6446
Marietta *(G-13403)*

5092 Toys & Hobby Goods & Splys Wholesale

▲ AW Faber-Castell Usa Inc ....D 216 643-4660
Cleveland *(G-5028)*

Ball Bounce and Sport Inc ....E 419 759-3838
Dunkirk *(G-10384)*

Ball Bounce and Sport Inc ....E 614 662-5381
Columbus *(G-7015)*

◆ Ball Bounce and Sport Inc ....B 419 289-9310
Ashland *(G-654)*

Ball Bounce and Sport Inc ....E 419 289-9310
Ashland (G-655)

▲ Bendon Inc ....D 419 207-3600
Ashland (G-657)

▲ Closeout Distribution Inc ....A 614 278-6800
Columbus (G-7234)

▼ Craft Wholesalers Inc ....C 740 964-6210
Groveport (G-11504)

▲ CSC Distribution Inc ....E 614 278-6800
Columbus (G-7400)

Dwa Mrkting Prmtional Pdts LLC ....E 216 476-0635
Strongsville (G-17298)

Flower Factory Inc ....D 614 275-6220
Columbus (G-7598)

▲ Galaxy Balloons Incorporated ....E 216 476-3360
Cleveland (G-5589)

▼ ICM Distributing Company Inc ......E 234 212-3030
Twinsburg (G-18281)

◆ K & K Interiors Inc ....D 419 627-0039
Sandusky (G-16620)

▲ K & M International Inc ....D 330 425-2550
Twinsburg (G-18286)

Lamrite West Inc ....E 440 268-0634
Strongsville (G-17323)

▲ Lamrite West Inc ....C 440 238-9150
Strongsville (G-17321)

▲ Lancaster Bingo Company Inc ......D 740 681-4759
Lancaster (G-12410)

◆ Mas Inc ....E 330 659-3333
Richfield (G-16362)

▲ Miller Fireworks Company Inc ....E 419 865-7329
Holland (G-11899)

Nannicola Wholesale Co ....D 330 799-0888
Youngstown (G-20134)

National Marketshare Group ....E 513 921-0800
Cincinnati (G-4094)

◆ Neil Kravitz Group Sales Inc ....E 513 961-8697
Cincinnati (G-4105)

▲ Pyramyd Air Ltd ....E 216 896-0893
Solon (G-16887)

R and G Enterprises of Ohio ....E 440 845-6870
Cleveland (G-6271)

5093 Scrap & Waste Materials Wholesale

◆ Aci Industries Ltd ....E 740 368-4160
Delaware (G-9948)

▲ Agmet LLC ....E 440 439-7400
Cleveland (G-4913)

Agmet LLC ....E 216 662-6939
Maple Heights (G-13280)

Allen County Recyclers Inc ....E 419 223-5010
Lima (G-12596)

Ascendtech Inc ....E 216 458-1101
Willoughby (G-19506)

Associated Paper Stock Inc ....E 330 549-5311
North Lima (G-15263)

Brims Imports ....E 419 674-4137
Kenton (G-12272)

Byer Steel Recycling Inc ....E 513 948-0300
Cincinnati (G-3098)

Carpenter Metal Solutions Inc ....E 330 829-2771
Alliance (G-522)

City Scrap & Salvage Co ....E 330 753-5051
Akron (G-139)

Cohen Electronics Inc ....D 513 425-6911
Middletown (G-14296)

▼ Diproinduca (usa) Limited LLC .....D 330 722-4442
Medina (G-13930)

Diver Steel City Auto Crushers ....E 330 744-5083
Youngstown (G-20020)

▼ Djj Holding Corporation ....C 513 621-8770
Cincinnati (G-3437)

▲ Fpt Cleveland LLC ....C 216 441-3800
Cleveland (G-5569)

Frankes Wood Products LLC ....E 937 642-0706
Marysville (G-13497)

▲ Franklin Iron & Metal Corp ....C 937 253-8184
Dayton (G-9449)

▼ G-Cor Automotive Corp ....E 614 443-6735
Columbus (G-7641)

Hamilton Scrap Processors ....E 513 863-3474
Hamilton (G-11609)

Harry Rock & Company ....E 330 644-3748
Cleveland (G-5663)

Holub Iron & Steel Company ....E 330 252-5655
Akron (G-267)

I H Schlezinger Inc ....E 614 252-1188
Columbus (G-7794)

Imperial Alum - Minerva LLC ....D 330 868-7765
Minerva (G-14520)

▼ Intex Supply Company ....E 216 535-4300
Richmond Heights (G-16391)

Kenton Auto and Truck Wrecking ....E 419 673-8234
Kenton (G-12283)

▲ Legend Smelting and Recycl Inc ....D 740 928-0139
Hebron (G-11716)

M & M Metals International Inc ....E 513 221-4411
Cincinnati (G-3954)

Mauser Usa LLC ....E 740 397-1762
Mount Vernon (G-14780)

Metalico Akron Inc ....E 330 376-1400
Akron (G-333)

Midwest Iron and Metal Co ....D 937 222-5992
Dayton (G-9633)

Muskingum Iron & Metal Co ....E 740 452-9351
Zanesville (G-20338)

Niles Iron & Metal Company LLC ....E 330 652-2262
Niles (G-15163)

Omnisource LLC ....D 419 537-1631
Toledo (G-17961)

Omnisource LLC ....E 419 784-5669
Defiance (G-9933)

Omnisource LLC ....E 419 227-3411
Lima (G-12712)

Omnisource LLC ....E 419 394-3351
Saint Marys (G-16529)

Omnisource LLC ....E 419 537-9400
Toledo (G-17962)

PSC Metals Inc ....E 330 455-0212
Canton (G-2443)

PSC Metals Inc ....E 614 299-4175
Columbus (G-8477)

PSC Metals Inc ....D 234 208-2331
Barberton (G-963)

PSC Metals Inc ....E 330 745-4437
Barberton (G-964)

PSC Metals Inc ....E 330 484-7610
Canton (G-2444)

PSC Metals Inc ....E 216 341-3400
Cleveland (G-6266)

PSC Metals - Wooster LLC ....D 330 264-8956
Wooster (G-19760)

PSC Metals Inc ....A 330 879-5001
Navarre (G-14824)

◆ Quantum Metals Inc ....E 513 573-0144
Lebanon (G-12494)

R L S Corporation ....E 740 773-1440
Chillicothe (G-2812)

Reserve Ftl LLC ....E 773 721-8740
Canton (G-2459)

▼ River Recycling Entps Ltd ....E 216 459-2100
Cleveland (G-6328)

Rm Advisory Group Inc ....E 513 242-2100
Cincinnati (G-4385)

Rnw Holdings Inc ....E 330 792-0600
Youngstown (G-20187)

Scrap Yard LLC ....E 216 271-5825
Cleveland (G-6381)

Shredded Bedding Corporation ....E 740 893-3567
Centerburg (G-2616)

Slesnick Iron & Metal Co ....D 330 453-8475
Canton (G-2479)

Tms International LLC ....E 419 747-5500
Mansfield (G-13254)

◆ Unico Alloys & Metals Inc ....D 614 299-0545
Columbus (G-8797)

W R G Inc ....E 216 351-8494
Cleveland (G-6645)

Wilmington Iron and Met Co Inc ....E 937 382-3867
Wilmington (G-19654)

5094 Jewelry, Watches, Precious Stones Wholesale

▲ Cas-Ker Company Inc ....E 513 674-7700
Cincinnati (G-3128)

Equity Diamond Brokers Inc ....E 513 793-4760
Cincinnati (G-3511)

J L Swaney Inc ....E 740 884-4450
Chillicothe (G-2795)

Marfo Company ....D 614 276-3352
Columbus (G-8019)

Toledo Jewelers Supply Co ....E 419 241-4181
Toledo (G-18088)

United States Commemrtv Art GA .....E 330 494-5504
Canton (G-2521)

5099 Durable Goods: NEC Wholesale

3s Incorporated ....E 513 202-5070
Harrison (G-11659)

77 Coach Supply Ltd ....E 330 674-1454
Millersburg (G-14452)

ABC Fire Inc ....E 440 237-6677
North Royalton (G-15346)

Abco Fire LLC ....E 800 875-7200
Cincinnati (G-2896)

Abco Fire Protection Inc ....E 800 875-7200
Cleveland (G-4891)

▼ Abco Holdings LLC ....D 216 433-7200
Cleveland (G-4892)

Andrew Distribution Inc ....B 614 824-3123
Columbus (G-6948)

Bladecutters Lawn Service Inc ....E 937 274-3861
Dayton (G-9255)

◆ Dualite Sales & Service Inc ....C 513 724-7100
Williamsburg (G-19493)

Earth n Wood Products Inc ....E 330 644-1858
Akron (G-199)

Gene Ptacek Son Fire Eqp Inc ....E 216 651-8300
Cleveland (G-5602)

Gia USA Inc ....E 216 831-8678
Cleveland (G-5606)

Gross Lumber Inc ....E 330 683-2055
Apple Creek (G-619)

◆ Hanser Music Group Inc ....D 859 817-7100
West Chester (G-19058)

Keidel Supply Company Inc ....E 513 351-1600
Cincinnati (G-3852)

Koorsen Fire & Security Inc ....E 614 878-2228
Columbus (G-7923)

Live Technologies LLC ....D 614 278-7777
Columbus (G-7986)

▼ Merchandise Inc ....D 513 353-2200
Miamitown (G-14242)

▲ Midwest Tape LLC ....B 419 868-9370
Holland (G-11898)

▲ Pipeline Packaging Corporation .....E 440 349-3200
Solon (G-16884)

▲ Premium Beverage Supply Ltd .....E 614 777-1007
Hilliard (G-11807)

▲ Recaro Child Safety LLC ....E 248 904-1570
Cincinnati (G-4344)

Rk Family Inc ....B 740 389-2674
Marion (G-13457)

Rk Family Inc ....B 419 355-8230
Fremont (G-11090)

Rk Family Inc ....B 330 264-5475
Wooster (G-19761)

Rk Family Inc ....B 513 934-0015
Lebanon (G-12498)

▲ Safety Today Inc ....E 614 409-7200
Grove City (G-11468)

Southern Ohio Gun Distrs Inc ....E 513 932-8148
Lebanon (G-12505)

Superr-Spdie Portable Svcs Inc ....E 330 733-9000
Akron (G-461)

Telarc International Corp ....E 216 464-2313
Beachwood (G-1111)

TS Tech Americas Inc ....E 740 593-5958
Athens (G-808)

▲ TS Tech Americas Inc ....B 614 575-4100
Reynoldsburg (G-16334)

U-Haul Neighborhood Dealer -Ce ......E 419 929-3724
New London (G-14936)

Union Tank Car Company ....C 419 864-7216
Marion (G-13468)

Vinifera Imports Ltd ....E 440 942-9463
Mentor (G-14122)

▲ West Chester Holdings LLC ....C 800 647-1900
Cincinnati (G-4781)

Windy Hill Ltd Inc ....D 216 391-4800
Cleveland (G-6684)

51 WHOLESALE TRADE¨NONDURABLE GOODS

5111 Printing & Writing Paper Wholesale

Catalyst Paper (usa) Inc ....E 937 528-3800
Dayton (G-9286)

▲ Millcraft Group LLC ....D 216 441-5500
Cleveland (G-5993)

▲ Millcraft Paper Company ....C 216 441-5505
Cleveland (G-5994)

Millcraft Paper Company ....E 937 222-7829
Dayton (G-9636)

Millcraft Paper Company ....E 614 675-4800
Columbus (G-8087)

Millcraft Paper Company ....E 216 441-5500
Cleveland (G-5995)

Ohio & Michigan Paper Company ......E 419 666-1500
Perrysburg *(G-15896)*
Rosemark Paper Inc ......D 614 443-0303
Columbus *(G-8552)*
▲ Sterling Paper Co ......E 614 443-0303
Columbus *(G-8697)*
The Cincinnati Cordage Ppr Co ......E 513 242-3600
Cincinnati *(G-4590)*
Veritiv Operating Company ......E 419 243-6100
Toledo *(G-18137)*
◆ Veritiv Pubg & Print MGT Inc ......E 330 650-5522
Hudson *(G-12011)*

5112 Stationery & Office Splys Wholesale

American Future Systems Inc ......E 330 394-1555
Warren *(G-18662)*
▲ AW Faber-Castell Usa Inc ......D 216 643-4660
Cleveland *(G-5028)*
Business Stationery LLC ......D 216 514-1192
Cleveland *(G-5107)*
Canon Solutions America Inc ......E 216 750-2980
Independence *(G-12054)*
▲ Dexxxon Digital Storage Inc ......E 740 548-7179
Lewis Center *(G-12538)*
Electronic Printing Pdts Inc ......E 330 689-3930
Stow *(G-17200)*
EMI Enterprises Inc ......E 419 666-0012
Northwood *(G-15392)*
Envelope Mart of North E Ohio ......E 440 322-8862
Elyria *(G-10511)*
Envelope Mart of Ohio Inc ......E 440 365-8177
Elyria *(G-10512)*
Essendant Co ......D 330 650-9361
Hudson *(G-11977)*
Essendant Co ......C 330 425-4001
Twinsburg *(G-18264)*
Essendant Co ......D 513 942-1354
West Chester *(G-19049)*
Essendant Co ......D 614 876-7774
Columbus *(G-7534)*
Friends Service Co Inc ......D 419 427-1704
Findlay *(G-10910)*
▲ GBS Corp ......C 330 494-5330
North Canton *(G-15206)*
Indepndence Office Bus Sup Inc ......D 216 398-8880
Cleveland *(G-5746)*
Med-Pass Incorporated ......E 937 438-8884
Dayton *(G-9599)*
Ohio & Michigan Paper Company ......E 419 666-1500
Perrysburg *(G-15896)*
Optimum System Products Inc ......E 614 885-4464
Westerville *(G-19288)*
Pac Worldwide Corporation ......D 800 610-9367
Middletown *(G-14319)*
Pfg Ventures LP ......D 216 520-8400
Independence *(G-12107)*
Powell Company Ltd ......D 419 228-3552
Lima *(G-12723)*
▼ Quick Tab II Inc ......D 419 448-6622
Tiffin *(G-17533)*
Ricoh Usa Inc ......D 513 984-9898
Sharonville *(G-16730)*
S P Richards Company ......E 614 497-2270
Obetz *(G-15529)*
Seagate Office Products Inc ......E 419 861-6161
Holland *(G-11913)*
▲ Shamrock Companies Inc ......D 440 899-9510
Westlake *(G-19405)*
Signal Office Supply Inc ......E 513 821-2280
Cincinnati *(G-4482)*
Staples Inc ......E 740 845-5600
London *(G-12875)*
W B Mason Co Inc ......D 216 267-5000
Cleveland *(G-6644)*
◆ Wasserstrom Company ......B 614 228-6525
Columbus *(G-8878)*
Western States Envelope Co ......D 419 666-7480
Walbridge *(G-18627)*

5113 Indl & Personal Svc Paper Wholesale

◆ Aci Industries Converting Ltd ......E 740 368-4160
Delaware *(G-9949)*
Acorn Distributors Inc ......E 614 294-6444
Columbus *(G-6867)*
Alco-Chem Inc ......E 330 833-8551
Canton *(G-2177)*
▲ Atlapac Corp ......D 614 252-2121
Columbus *(G-6995)*
Avalon Foodservice Inc ......C 330 854-4551
Canal Fulton *(G-2092)*

▲ Berk Enterprises Inc ......D 330 369-1192
Warren *(G-18679)*
Buckeye Boxes Inc ......E 614 274-8484
Columbus *(G-7085)*
▼ Buckeye Paper Co Inc ......D 330 477-5925
Canton *(G-2220)*
Bunzl Usa Inc ......E 513 891-9010
Blue Ash *(G-1518)*
▲ Cannon Group Inc ......E 614 890-0343
Westerville *(G-19230)*
Commerce Paper Company ......E 419 241-9101
Toledo *(G-17669)*
Dawnchem Inc ......E 440 943-3332
Willowick *(G-19597)*
Dayton Industrial Drum Inc ......E 937 253-8933
Dayton *(G-9167)*
Deufol Worldwide Packaging LLC ......D 440 232-1100
Bedford *(G-1276)*
Deufol Worldwide Packaging LLC ......D 414 967-8000
Fairfield *(G-10717)*
Espt Liquidation Inc ......D 330 698-4711
Apple Creek *(G-618)*
Food Distributors Inc ......E 740 439-2764
Cambridge *(G-2068)*
I Supply Co ......C 937 878-5240
Fairborn *(G-10676)*
Impressive Packaging Inc ......E 419 368-6808
Hayesville *(G-11701)*
J V Hansel Inc ......E 330 716-0806
Warren *(G-18716)*
JIT Packaging Inc ......E 330 562-8080
Aurora *(G-831)*
◆ Joshen Paper & Packaging Co ......C 216 441-5600
Cleveland *(G-5804)*
Keystone Foods LLC ......D 419 843-3009
Toledo *(G-17839)*
Lynk Packaging Inc ......E 330 562-8080
Aurora *(G-833)*
M Conley Company ......C 330 456-8243
Canton *(G-2383)*
▲ Mailender Inc ......D 513 942-5453
West Chester *(G-18968)*
Maines Paper & Food Svc Inc ......E 216 643-7500
Bedford *(G-1291)*
▲ Mast Logistics Services Inc ......C 614 415-7500
Columbus *(G-8035)*
▲ Millcraft Group LLC ......D 216 441-5500
Cleveland *(G-5993)*
▲ Millcraft Paper Company ......E 216 441-5505
Cleveland *(G-5994)*
Millcraft Paper Company ......D 937 222-7829
Dayton *(G-9636)*
Millcraft Paper Company ......E 614 675-4800
Columbus *(G-8087)*
Millcraft Paper Company ......E 216 441-5500
Cleveland *(G-5995)*
Millers Textile Services Inc ......D 419 738-3552
Wapakoneta *(G-18650)*
North American Plas Chem Inc ......E 330 627-2210
Carrollton *(G-2573)*
Ohio & Michigan Paper Company ......E 419 666-1500
Perrysburg *(G-15896)*
▲ Peck Distributors Inc ......E 216 587-6814
Maple Heights *(G-13291)*
Pollak Distributing Co Inc ......E 216 851-9911
Euclid *(G-10653)*
▲ Polymer Packaging Inc ......D 330 832-2000
Massillon *(G-13720)*
Precision Products Group Inc ......D 330 698-4711
Apple Creek *(G-620)*
▲ Ranpak Corp ......C 440 354-4445
Concord Township *(G-8944)*
Ricking Paper and Specialty Co ......E 513 825-3551
Cincinnati *(G-4372)*
Sonoco Products Company ......E 937 429-0040
Beavercreek Township *(G-1263)*
Sysco Cincinnati LLC ......B 513 563-6300
Cincinnati *(G-4562)*
Systems Pack Inc ......E 330 467-5729
Macedonia *(G-13083)*
▲ Tape Products Company ......E 513 489-8840
Canton *(G-4577)*
The Cincinnati Cordage Ppr Co ......E 513 242-3600
Cincinnati *(G-4590)*
The Cottingham Paper Co ......E 614 294-6444
Columbus *(G-8742)*
Tiffin Paper Company ......E 419 447-2121
Tiffin *(G-17544)*
Veritiv Operating Company ......C 513 242-0800
Fairfield *(G-10798)*

Veritiv Operating Company ......E 614 251-7100
Grove City *(G-11480)*
Veritiv Operating Company ......E 216 573-7400
Independence *(G-12137)*
Veritiv Operating Company ......C 513 285-0999
Fairfield *(G-10799)*
Westrock Cp LLC ......D 770 448-2193
Wshngtn CT Hs *(G-19886)*

5122 Drugs, Drug Proprietaries & Sundries Wholesale

ACS Acqco Corp ......C 513 719-2600
Cincinnati *(G-2905)*
▲ American Cutting Edge Inc ......C 937 866-5986
Miamisburg *(G-14140)*
American Regent Inc ......D 614 436-2222
Hilliard *(G-11741)*
Amerisourcebergen Corporation ......C 610 727-7000
Columbus *(G-6942)*
Amerisourcebergen Corporation ......D 614 497-3665
Lockbourne *(G-12808)*
Amerisourcebergen Drug Corp ......D 614 409-0741
Lockbourne *(G-12809)*
Basic Drugs Inc ......E 937 898-4010
Vandalia *(G-18507)*
Beiersdorf Inc ......C 513 682-7300
West Chester *(G-19042)*
Biolife Plasma Services LP ......D 419 425-8680
Findlay *(G-10868)*
Biorx LLC ......C 866 442-4679
Cincinnati *(G-3051)*
Braden Med Services Inc ......E 740 732-2356
Caldwell *(G-2036)*
◆ Brothers Trading Co Inc ......C 937 746-1010
Springboro *(G-16964)*
Butler Animal Health Sup LLC ......E 614 718-2000
Columbus *(G-7100)*
◆ Butler Animal Health Sup LLC ......C 614 761-9095
Dublin *(G-10154)*
▼ Butler Animal Hlth Holdg LLC ......E 614 761-9095
Dublin *(G-10155)*
Capital Wholesale Drug Company ......D 614 297-8225
Columbus *(G-7114)*
◆ Cardinal Health Inc ......A 614 757-5000
Dublin *(G-10156)*
Cardinal Health Inc ......D 614 497-9552
Obetz *(G-15524)*
Cardinal Health Inc ......E 614 409-6770
Groveport *(G-11499)*
Cardinal Health Inc ......D 614 757-7690
Columbus *(G-7121)*
Cardinal Health 100 Inc ......B 614 757-5000
Dublin *(G-10157)*
Cardinal Health 201 Inc ......E 614 757-5000
Dublin *(G-10158)*
Cardinal Health 414 LLC ......E 419 867-1077
Holland *(G-11877)*
Cardinal Health 414 LLC ......E 937 438-1888
Moraine *(G-14632)*
Catamaran Home Dlvry Ohio Inc ......D 440 930-5520
Avon Lake *(G-911)*
Columbus Serum Company ......C 614 444-5211
Columbus *(G-7313)*
▲ Cosmax USA Inc Cosmax USA CorpE 440 600-5738
Solon *(G-16839)*
▲ Discount Drug Mart Inc ......C 330 725-2340
Medina *(G-13931)*
EBY-Brown Company LLC ......D 937 324-1036
Springfield *(G-17032)*
Equitas Health Inc ......E 937 424-1440
Dayton *(G-9416)*
Evergreen Pharmaceutical LLC ......B 513 719-2600
Cincinnati *(G-3519)*
Evergreen Phrm Cal Inc ......E 513 719-2600
Cincinnati *(G-3520)*
F Dohmen Co ......C 614 757-5000
Dublin *(G-10223)*
▲ Fredrics Corporation ......C 513 874-2226
West Chester *(G-18926)*
G E G Enterprises Inc ......E 330 477-3133
Canton *(G-2321)*
▲ Gem Edwards Inc ......D 330 342-8300
Hudson *(G-11979)*
Greenfield Hts Oper Group LLC ......E 312 877-1153
Lima *(G-12648)*
Heartland Healthcare Svcs LLC ......C 419 535-8435
Toledo *(G-17794)*
▼ ICM Distributing Company Inc ......E 234 212-3030
Twinsburg *(G-18281)*

Imagepace LLC ....B 513 579-9911
  Cincinnati *(G-3753)*

Institutional Care Pharmacy ....D 419 447-6216
  Tiffin *(G-17520)*

Keysource Acquisition LLC ....E 513 469-7881
  Cincinnati *(G-3865)*

Kroger Co ....C 740 335-4030
  Wshngtn CT Hs *(G-19877)*

Kroger Co ....B 614 898-3200
  Westerville *(G-19274)*

Masters Drug Company Inc ....B 800 982-7922
  Lebanon *(G-12284)*

McKesson Corporation ....C 740 636-3500
  Wshngtn CT Hs *(G-19878)*

Medpace Inc ....A 513 579-9911
  Cincinnati *(G-4000)*

▼ Merchandise Inc ....D 513 353-2200
  Miamitown *(G-14242)*

▲ Mhc Medical Products LLC ....E 877 358-4342
  Fairfield *(G-10757)*

Miami-Luken Inc ....D 937 743-7775
  Springboro *(G-16974)*

Mimrx Co Inc ....B 614 850-6672
  Columbus *(G-8088)*

▲ Mitsubshi Intl Fd Ingrdnts Inc ....E 614 652-1111
  Dublin *(G-10281)*

MSA Group Inc ....B 614 334-0400
  Columbus *(G-8119)*

Ncs Healthcare of Ohio LLC ....E 330 364-5011
  Wadsworth *(G-18609)*

Ncs Healthcare of Ohio LLC ....D 513 719-2600
  Cincinnati *(G-4100)*

Ncs Healthcare of Ohio LLC ....E 614 534-0400
  Columbus *(G-8167)*

▲ Nehemiah Manufacturing Co LLC ....E 513 351-5700
  Cincinnati *(G-4102)*

Neighborcare Inc ....A 513 719-2600
  Cincinnati *(G-4103)*

Omnicare Inc ....C 513 719-2600
  Cincinnati *(G-4168)*

Omnicare Distribution Ctr LLC ....D 419 720-8200
  Cincinnati *(G-4169)*

Omnicare Phrm of Midwest LLC ....D 513 719-2600
  Cincinnati *(G-4171)*

Orchard Phrm Svcs LLC ....C 330 491-4200
  North Canton *(G-15225)*

Pca-Corrections LLC ....E 614 297-8244
  Columbus *(G-8430)*

Pharmed Corporation ....C 440 250-5400
  Westlake *(G-19391)*

Physicians Weight Ls Ctr Amer ....E 330 666-7952
  Akron *(G-382)*

Prescription Supply Inc ....D 419 661-6600
  Northwood *(G-15405)*

Raisin Rack Inc ....E 614 882-5886
  Westerville *(G-19298)*

Remedi Seniorcare of Ohio LLC ....E 800 232-4239
  Troy *(G-18227)*

Riser Foods Company ....D 216 292-7000
  Bedford Heights *(G-1327)*

River City Pharma ....D 513 870-1680
  Fairfield *(G-10775)*

▲ Robert J Matthews Company ....D 330 834-3000
  Massillon *(G-13724)*

Samuels Products Inc ....E 513 891-4456
  Blue Ash *(G-1649)*

Schaaf Drugs LLC ....E 419 879-4327
  Lima *(G-12736)*

Specialized Pharmacy Svcs LLC ....E 513 719-2600
  Cincinnati *(G-4511)*

Suarez Corporation Industries ....D 330 494-4282
  Canton *(G-2502)*

Superior Care Pharmacy Inc ....C 513 719-2600
  Cincinnati *(G-4556)*

Teva Womens Health Inc ....C 513 731-9900
  Cincinnati *(G-4589)*

Trickeration Inc ....E 216 360-9966
  Warrensville Heights *(G-18782)*

▲ Triplefin LLC ....D 855 877-5346
  Blue Ash *(G-1665)*

Walter F Stephens Jr Inc ....E 937 746-0521
  Franklin *(G-11041)*

▲ Wbc Group LLC ....D 866 528-2144
  Hudson *(G-12012)*

Westhaven Services Co LLC ....B 419 661-2200
  Perrysburg *(G-15935)*

5131 Piece Goods, Notions & Dry Goods Wholesale

▲ Checker Notions Company Inc ....D 419 893-3636
  Maumee *(G-13770)*

▲ Custom Products Corporation ....D 440 528-7100
  Solon *(G-16842)*

Electronic Printing Pdts Inc ....E 330 689-3930
  Stow *(G-17200)*

◆ Great Lakes Textiles Inc ....E 440 914-1122
  Solon *(G-16854)*

▲ Miami Corporation ....E 800 543-0448
  Cincinnati *(G-4044)*

R S Sewing Inc ....E 330 478-3360
  Canton *(G-2449)*

Style-Line Incorporated ....E 614 291-0600
  Columbus *(G-8707)*

Welspun Usa Inc ....E 614 945-5100
  Grove City *(G-11484)*

Zincks In Berlin Inc ....E 330 893-2071
  Berlin *(G-1447)*

5136 Men's & Boys' Clothing & Furnishings Wholesale

▼ Abercrombie & Fitch Trading Co ....E 614 283-6500
  New Albany *(G-14839)*

Barbs Graffiti Inc ....D 216 881-5550
  Cleveland *(G-5035)*

▲ Barbs Graffiti Inc ....E 216 881-5550
  Cleveland *(G-5036)*

Brennan-Eberly Team Sports Inc ....E 419 865-8326
  Holland *(G-11876)*

◆ Cintas Corporation No 1 ....A 513 459-1200
  Mason *(G-13556)*

Cintas Sales Corporation ....B 513 459-1200
  Cincinnati *(G-3295)*

◆ For Women Like Me Inc ....E 407 848-7339
  Chagrin Falls *(G-2645)*

Gymnastic World Inc ....E 440 526-2970
  Cleveland *(G-5649)*

Heritage Sportswear Inc ....D 740 928-7771
  Hebron *(G-11715)*

▲ J Peterman Company LLC ....E 888 647-2555
  Blue Ash *(G-1588)*

▼ Lion-Vallen Ltd Partnership ....E 937 898-1949
  Dayton *(G-9571)*

▲ Mast Industries Inc ....C 614 415-7000
  Columbus *(G-8034)*

Mast Industries Inc ....D 614 856-6000
  Reynoldsburg *(G-16319)*

▲ McCc Sportswear Inc ....E 513 583-9210
  West Chester *(G-19065)*

▲ MGF Sourcing Us LLC ....D 614 904-3300
  Columbus *(G-8066)*

R & A Sports Inc ....E 216 289-2254
  Euclid *(G-10654)*

▲ R G Barry Corporation ....D 614 864-6400
  Pickerington *(G-15966)*

Rassak LLC ....E 513 791-9453
  Cincinnati *(G-4339)*

Rondinellis Tuxedo ....E 330 726-7768
  Youngstown *(G-20195)*

Safety Solutions Inc ....D 614 799-9900
  Columbus *(G-8578)*

◆ Standard Textile Co Inc ....B 513 761-9256
  Cincinnati *(G-4533)*

Walter F Stephens Jr Inc ....E 937 746-0521
  Franklin *(G-11041)*

▲ West Chester Holdings LLC ....C 800 647-1900
  Cincinnati *(G-4781)*

5137 Women's, Children's & Infants Clothing Wholesale

▼ Abercrombie & Fitch Trading Co ....E 614 283-6500
  New Albany *(G-14839)*

▲ Atrium Buying Corporation ....D 740 966-8200
  Blacklick *(G-1474)*

Barbs Graffiti Inc ....D 216 881-5550
  Cleveland *(G-5035)*

▲ Barbs Graffiti Inc ....E 216 881-5550
  Cleveland *(G-5036)*

Brennan-Eberly Team Sports Inc ....E 419 865-8326
  Holland *(G-11876)*

Cheek-O Inc ....E 513 942-4880
  Cincinnati *(G-3174)*

◆ Cintas Corporation No 1 ....A 513 459-1200
  Mason *(G-13556)*

Cintas Sales Corporation ....B 513 459-1200
  Cincinnati *(G-3295)*

▲ Classic Imports Inc ....E 330 262-5277
  Wooster *(G-19706)*

◆ For Women Like Me Inc ....E 407 848-7339
  Chagrin Falls *(G-2645)*

Gymnastic World Inc ....E 440 526-2970
  Cleveland *(G-5649)*

Heritage Sportswear Inc ....D 740 928-7771
  Hebron *(G-11715)*

▲ J Peterman Company LLC ....E 888 647-2555
  Blue Ash *(G-1588)*

▼ Lion-Vallen Ltd Partnership ....E 937 898-1949
  Dayton *(G-9571)*

▲ Mast Industries Inc ....C 614 415-7000
  Columbus *(G-8034)*

Mast Industries Inc ....D 614 856-6000
  Reynoldsburg *(G-16319)*

▲ McCc Sportswear Inc ....E 513 583-9210
  West Chester *(G-19065)*

▲ MGF Sourcing Us LLC ....D 614 904-3300
  Columbus *(G-8066)*

◆ Philips Medical Systems Clevel ....B 440 247-2652
  Cleveland *(G-6203)*

R & A Sports Inc ....E 216 289-2254
  Euclid *(G-10654)*

▲ R G Barry Corporation ....D 614 864-6400
  Pickerington *(G-15966)*

Rassak LLC ....E 513 791-9453
  Cincinnati *(G-4339)*

▲ TSC Apparel LLC ....D 513 771-1138
  Cincinnati *(G-4651)*

▲ West Chester Holdings LLC ....C 800 647-1900
  Cincinnati *(G-4781)*

▲ Zimmer Enterprises Inc ....E 937 428-1057
  Dayton *(G-9899)*

5139 Footwear Wholesale

Brennan-Eberly Team Sports Inc ....E 419 865-8326
  Holland *(G-11876)*

▲ Drew Ventures Inc ....E 740 653-4271
  Lancaster *(G-12390)*

Ebuys Inc ....E 858 831-0839
  Columbus *(G-7496)*

Georgia-Boot Inc ....D 740 753-1951
  Nelsonville *(G-14832)*

◆ Lehigh Outfitters LLC ....C 740 753-1951
  Nelsonville *(G-14834)*

M & R Fredericktown Ltd Inc ....E 440 801-1563
  Akron *(G-324)*

▲ R G Barry Corporation ....D 614 864-6400
  Pickerington *(G-15966)*

Safety Solutions Inc ....D 614 799-9900
  Columbus *(G-8578)*

5141 Groceries, General Line Wholesale

Acosta Inc ....D 440 498-7370
  Solon *(G-16815)*

Advantage Sales & Mktg LLC ....D 513 841-0500
  Blue Ash *(G-1500)*

Advantage Waypoint LLC ....E 248 919-3144
  Twinsburg *(G-18241)*

Albert Guarnieri & Co ....D 330 794-9834
  Hudson *(G-11962)*

Anderson and Dubose Inc ....D 440 248-8800
  Warren *(G-18665)*

Atlantic Fish & Distrg Co ....E 330 454-1307
  Canton *(G-2197)*

Blue Line Distribution ....E 614 497-9610
  Groveport *(G-11496)*

◆ Brothers Trading Co Inc ....C 937 746-1010
  Springboro *(G-16964)*

Cantrell Oil Company ....E 937 695-8003
  Winchester *(G-19660)*

Chas G Buchy Packing Company ....E 800 762-1060
  Cincinnati *(G-3172)*

Circle S Farms Inc ....E 614 878-9462
  Grove City *(G-11420)*

Dwa Mrktng Prmtional Pdts LLC ....E 216 476-0635
  Strongsville *(G-17298)*

EBY-Brown Company LLC ....C 937 324-1036
  Springfield *(G-17032)*

Euclid Fish Company ....D 440 951-6448
  Mentor *(G-14044)*

Food Sample Express LLc ....D 330 225-3550
  Brunswick *(G-1930)*

Forths Foods Inc ....E 740 886-9769
  Proctorville *(G-16216)*

General Mills Inc ....D 513 770-0558
  Mason *(G-13585)*

S
I
C

Gordon Food Service Inc ....E 440 953-1785
Mentor *(G-14052)*

Greeneview Foods LLC ....E 937 675-4161
Jamestown *(G-12187)*

Gummer Wholesale Inc ....D 740 928-0415
Heath *(G-11704)*

Hillandale Farms Corporation ....E 330 724-3199
Akron *(G-262)*

Impact Sales Inc ....D 937 274-1905
Dayton *(G-9513)*

J V Hansel Inc ....E 330 716-0806
Warren *(G-18716)*

Jetro Cash and Carry Entps LLC ....D 216 525-0101
Cleveland *(G-5794)*

◆ John Zidian Co Inc ....D 330 743-6050
Youngstown *(G-20086)*

Kcbs LLC ....E 513 421-9422
Cincinnati *(G-3849)*

Keystone Foods LLC ....C 419 843-3009
Toledo *(G-17839)*

Kroger Co ....D 740 363-4398
Delaware *(G-9994)*

Kroger Co ....C 614 759-2745
Columbus *(G-7928)*

Kroger Co ....B 937 376-7962
Xenia *(G-19916)*

Kroger Co ....D 937 848-5990
Dayton *(G-9552)*

Lakes Venture LLC ....D 614 681-7050
Worthington *(G-19819)*

Larosas Inc ....A 513 347-5660
Cincinnati *(G-3911)*

Mattingly Foods Inc ....C 740 454-0136
Zanesville *(G-20329)*

Mds Foods Inc ....E 330 879-9780
Navarre *(G-14823)*

Meadowbrook Meat Company Inc ......C 614 771-9660
Columbus *(G-8049)*

◆ Mountain Foods Inc ....E 440 286-7177
Chardon *(G-2705)*

Mpf Sales and Mktg Group LLC ....C 513 793-6241
Blue Ash *(G-1616)*

Nestle Usa Inc ....E 513 576-4930
Loveland *(G-13015)*

Novelart Manufacturing Company ....D 513 351-7700
Cincinnati *(G-4136)*

Ovations Food Services LP ....D 513 419-7254
Cincinnati *(G-4192)*

Physicians Weight Ls Ctr Amer ....E 330 666-7952
Akron *(G-382)*

Pollak Distributing Co Inc ....E 216 851-9911
Euclid *(G-10653)*

Queensgate Food Group LLC ....D 513 721-5503
Cincinnati *(G-4325)*

R G Sellers Company ....E 937 299-1545
Moraine *(G-14691)*

Reinhart Foodservice LLC ....C 513 421-9184
Cincinnati *(G-4353)*

Restaurant Depot LLC ....E 216 525-0101
Cleveland *(G-6316)*

Ricking Paper and Specialty Co ....E 513 825-3551
Cincinnati *(G-4372)*

Riser Foods Company ....D 216 292-7000
Bedford Heights *(G-1327)*

Sandridge Food Corporation ....C 330 725-8883
Medina *(G-13999)*

Shaker Valley Foods Inc ....E 216 961-8600
Cleveland *(G-6403)*

Sherwood Food Distributors LLC ....B 216 662-6794
Maple Heights *(G-13296)*

Sommers Market LLC ....D 330 352-7470
Hartville *(G-11699)*

Spartannash Company ....A 937 599-1110
Bellefontaine *(G-1366)*

Spartannash Company ....B 419 228-3141
Lima *(G-12744)*

Spartannash Company ....D 419 998-2562
Lima *(G-12745)*

Spartannash Company ....D 937 599-1110
Bellefontaine *(G-1367)*

Spartannash Company ....D 513 793-6300
Cincinnati *(G-4510)*

Sygma Network Inc ....C 614 771-3801
Columbus *(G-8723)*

Sysco Central Ohio Inc ....B 614 272-0658
Columbus *(G-8725)*

Tasty Pure Food Company ....E 330 434-8141
Akron *(G-464)*

Total Wholesale Inc ....E 216 361-5757
Cleveland *(G-6535)*

▼ Tusco Grocers Inc ....D 740 922-8721
Dennison *(G-10054)*

US Foods Inc ....C 330 963-6789
Twinsburg *(G-18334)*

US Foods Inc ....A 614 539-7993
West Chester *(G-19096)*

Valley Wholesale Foods Inc ....E 740 354-5216
Portsmouth *(G-16180)*

Vendors Supply Inc ....E 513 755-2111
West Chester *(G-19030)*

Wrightway Fd Svc Rest Sup Inc ....E 419 222-7911
Lima *(G-12786)*

5142 Packaged Frozen Foods Wholesale

A To Z Portion Ctrl Meats Inc ....E 419 358-2926
Bluffton *(G-1686)*

Anderson and Dubose Inc ....D 440 248-8800
Warren *(G-18665)*

Avalon Foodservice Inc ....C 330 854-4551
Canal Fulton *(G-2092)*

Best Express Foods Inc ....D 513 531-2378
Cincinnati *(G-3043)*

Blue Ribbon Meats Inc ....D 216 631-8850
Cleveland *(G-5064)*

Euclid Fish Company ....D 440 951-6448
Mentor *(G-14044)*

Food Distributors Inc ....E 740 439-2764
Cambridge *(G-2068)*

Gordon Food Service Inc ....E 419 747-1212
Ontario *(G-15550)*

Gordon Food Service Inc ....E 419 225-8983
Lima *(G-12646)*

Gordon Food Service Inc ....E 216 573-4900
Cleveland *(G-5616)*

Hillcrest Egg & Cheese Co ....D 216 361-4625
Cleveland *(G-5691)*

Instantwhip Foods Inc ....E 330 688-8825
Stow *(G-17213)*

Jetro Cash and Carry Entps LLC ....D 216 525-0101
Cleveland *(G-5794)*

King Kold Inc ....E 937 836-2731
Englewood *(G-10592)*

Koch Meat Co Inc ....B 513 874-3500
Fairfield *(G-10745)*

Lori Holding Co ....E 740 342-3230
New Lexington *(G-14920)*

Maines Paper & Food Svc Inc ....E 216 643-7500
Bedford *(G-1291)*

Mattingly Foods Inc ....C 740 454-0136
Zanesville *(G-20329)*

Northern Frozen Foods Inc ....C 440 439-0600
Cleveland *(G-6096)*

▲ Peck Distributors Inc ....E 216 587-6814
Maple Heights *(G-13291)*

Pinata Foods Inc ....E 216 281-8811
Cleveland *(G-6211)*

Powell Company Ltd ....D 419 228-3552
Lima *(G-12723)*

Produce One Inc ....D 931 253-4749
Dayton *(G-9715)*

Ritchies Food Distributors Inc ....E 740 443-6303
Piketon *(G-15988)*

Sherwood Food Distributors LLC ....B 216 662-6794
Maple Heights *(G-13296)*

Spartannash Company ....D 513 793-6300
Cincinnati *(G-4510)*

Swd Corporation ....E 419 227-2436
Lima *(G-12759)*

Sysco Central Ohio Inc ....B 614 272-0658
Columbus *(G-8725)*

Tasty Pure Food Company ....E 330 434-8141
Akron *(G-464)*

US Foods Inc ....A 614 539-7993
West Chester *(G-19096)*

◆ White Castle System Inc ....B 614 228-5781
Columbus *(G-8896)*

Z Produce Co Inc ....E 614 224-4373
Columbus *(G-8934)*

5143 Dairy Prdts, Except Dried Or Canned Wholesale

Auburn Dairy Products Inc ....E 614 488-2536
Columbus *(G-7001)*

Austintown Dairy Inc ....E 330 629-6170
Youngstown *(G-19959)*

Barkett Fruit Co Inc ....E 330 364-6645
Dover *(G-10065)*

Borden Dairy Co Cincinnati LLC ....C 513 948-8811
Cincinnati *(G-3068)*

Coblentz Distributing Inc ....C 330 852-2888
Walnut Creek *(G-18631)*

Euclid Fish Company ....D 440 951-6448
Mentor *(G-14044)*

◆ Great Lakes Cheese Co Inc ....B 440 834-2500
Hiram *(G-11865)*

▲ Hans Rothenbuhler & Son Inc ....E 440 632-6000
Middlefield *(G-14270)*

Hillandale Farms Corporation ....E 330 724-3199
Akron *(G-262)*

Hillcrest Egg & Cheese Co ....D 216 361-4625
Cleveland *(G-5691)*

Instantwhip Foods Inc ....E 330 688-8825
Stow *(G-17213)*

Instantwhip-Akron Inc ....E 614 488-2536
Stow *(G-17214)*

Instantwhip-Columbus Inc ....E 614 871-9447
Grove City *(G-11443)*

Lori Holding Co ....E 740 342-3230
New Lexington *(G-14920)*

Louis Trauth Dairy LLC ....B 859 431-7553
West Chester *(G-19064)*

Prairie Farms Dairy Inc ....D 937 235-5930
Huber Heights *(G-11958)*

S and S Gilardi Inc ....D 740 397-2751
Mount Vernon *(G-14788)*

Siemer Distributing Company ....E 740 342-3230
New Lexington *(G-14928)*

Smithfoods Orrville Inc ....D 330 683-8710
Orrville *(G-15648)*

Sysco Cincinnati LLC ....B 513 563-6300
Cincinnati *(G-4562)*

Troyer Cheese Inc ....E 330 893-2479
Millersburg *(G-14497)*

United Dairy Farmers Inc ....C 513 396-8700
Cincinnati *(G-4678)*

US Foods Inc ....A 614 539-7993
West Chester *(G-19096)*

▲ Weaver Bros Inc ....D 937 526-3907
Versailles *(G-18573)*

5144 Poultry & Poultry Prdts Wholesale

▼ Ballas Egg Products Corp ....D 614 453-0386
Zanesville *(G-20280)*

Barkett Fruit Co Inc ....E 330 364-6645
Dover *(G-10065)*

Borden Dairy Co Cincinnati LLC ....C 513 948-8811
Cincinnati *(G-3068)*

C W Egg Products LLC ....E 419 375-5800
Fort Recovery *(G-10987)*

Cooper Frms Spring Madow Farms ......E 419 375-4119
Rossburg *(G-16458)*

Di Feo & Sons Poultry Inc ....E 330 564-8172
Akron *(G-185)*

Euclid Fish Company ....D 440 951-6448
Mentor *(G-14044)*

Hillandale Farms Inc ....E 740 968-3597
Flushing *(G-10979)*

Hillandale Farms Corporation ....E 330 724-3199
Akron *(G-262)*

Hillcrest Egg & Cheese Co ....D 216 361-4625
Cleveland *(G-5691)*

Koch Meat Co Inc ....B 513 874-3500
Fairfield *(G-10745)*

▲ Ohio Fresh Eggs LLC ....C 740 893-7200
Croton *(G-9065)*

Ohio Fresh Eggs LLC ....E 937 354-2233
Mount Victory *(G-14796)*

R W Sauder Inc ....E 330 359-5440
Winesburg *(G-19666)*

Sherwood Food Distributors LLC ....D 216 662-8000
Maple Heights *(G-13295)*

Sysco Cincinnati LLC ....B 513 563-6300
Cincinnati *(G-4562)*

5145 Confectionery Wholesale

Albert Guarnieri & Co ....D 330 794-9834
Hudson *(G-11962)*

EBY-Brown Company LLC ....C 937 324-1036
Springfield *(G-17032)*

Frito-Lay North America Inc ....C 513 759-1000
West Chester *(G-18927)*

Frito-Lay North America Inc ....D 513 874-0112
West Chester *(G-19054)*

Frito-Lay North America Inc ....C 216 491-4000
Cleveland *(G-5583)*

Frito-Lay North America Inc ....E 937 224-8716
Dayton *(G-9451)*

Frito-Lay North America Inc ....E 330 786-6000
Akron *(G-230)*

Gorant Chocolatier LLC C 330 726-8821
Boardman *(G-1698)*
Grippo Foods Inc E 513 923-1900
Cincinnati *(G-3658)*
Gummer Wholesale Inc D 740 928-0415
Heath *(G-11704)*
JE Carsten Company E 330 794-4440
Hudson *(G-11987)*
Jones Potato Chip Co E 419 529-9424
Mansfield *(G-13191)*
Lobby Shoppes Inc C 937 324-0002
Springfield *(G-17063)*
Mike-Sells Potato Chip Co E 937 228-9400
Dayton *(G-9635)*
Multi-Flow Dispensers Ohio Inc D 216 641-0200
Brooklyn Heights *(G-1876)*
Novelart Manufacturing Company D 513 351-7700
Cincinnati *(G-4136)*
Ohio Hickory Harvest Brand Pro E 330 644-6266
Coventry Township *(G-9040)*
Robert E McGrath Inc E 440 572-7747
Strongsville *(G-17341)*
S-L Distribution Company LLC D 740 676-6932
Bellaire *(G-1335)*
◆ **Shearers Foods LLC** A 330 834-4030
Massillon *(G-13730)*
Snyders-Lance Inc C 419 289-0787
Ashland *(G-692)*
Tarrier Foods Corp E 614 876-8594
Columbus *(G-8732)*
The Anter Brothers Company E 216 252-4555
Cleveland *(G-6519)*
Tiffin Paper Company E 419 447-2121
Tiffin *(G-17544)*

5146 Fish & Seafood Wholesale

101 River Inc E 440 352-6343
Grand River *(G-11331)*
Farm House Food Distrs Inc E 216 791-6948
Cleveland *(G-5513)*
Midwest Seafood Inc D 937 746-8856
Springboro *(G-16975)*
Ocean Wide Seafood Company E 937 610-5740
Cincinnati *(G-4146)*
◆ **Omega Sea LLC** E 440 639-2372
Painesville *(G-15731)*
Riser Foods Company D 216 292-7000
Bedford Heights *(G-1327)*
Ritchies Food Distributors Inc E 740 443-6303
Piketon *(G-15988)*
Sherwood Food Distributors LLC B 216 662-6794
Maple Heights *(G-13296)*
Sherwood Food Distributors LLC D 216 662-8000
Maple Heights *(G-13295)*

5147 Meats & Meat Prdts Wholesale

Blue Ribbon Meats Inc D 216 631-8850
Cleveland *(G-5064)*
Boars Head Provisions Co Inc B 614 662-5300
Groveport *(G-11497)*
Carfagnas Incorporated E 614 846-6340
Columbus *(G-7127)*
Carles Bratwurst Inc E 419 562-7741
Bucyrus *(G-1981)*
Dutch Creek Foods Inc E 330 852-2631
Sugarcreek *(G-17378)*
Fresh Mark Inc B 330 832-7491
Massillon *(G-13687)*
◆ **Fresh Mark Inc** B 330 834-3669
Massillon *(G-13685)*
Hillandale Farms Corporation E 330 724-3199
Akron *(G-262)*
Hillcrest Egg & Cheese Co D 216 361-4625
Cleveland *(G-5691)*
Hormel Foods Corp Svcs LLC E 513 563-0211
Cincinnati *(G-3726)*
Jetro Cash and Carry Entps LLC D 216 525-0101
Cleveland *(G-5794)*
Kenosha Beef International Ltd C 614 771-1330
Columbus *(G-7894)*
Landes Fresh Meats Inc E 937 836-3613
Clayton *(G-4859)*
Lori Holding Co E 740 342-3230
New Lexington *(G-14920)*
Marshallville Packing Co Inc E 330 855-2871
Marshallville *(G-13474)*
Meadowbrook Meat Company Inc C 614 771-9660
Columbus *(G-8049)*
Northern Frozen Foods Inc C 440 439-0600
Cleveland *(G-6096)*
Pioneer Packing Co D 419 352-5283
Bowling Green *(G-1745)*
Produce One Inc D 931 253-4749
Dayton *(G-9715)*
Ritchies Food Distributors Inc E 740 443-6303
Piketon *(G-15988)*
Robert Winner Sons Inc E 419 582-4321
Yorkshire *(G-19942)*
S and S Gilardi Inc D 740 397-2751
Mount Vernon *(G-14788)*
Sherwood Food Distributors LLC D 216 662-8000
Maple Heights *(G-13295)*
Sherwood Food Distributors LLC B 216 662-6794
Maple Heights *(G-13296)*
Siemer Distributing Company E 740 342-3230
New Lexington *(G-14928)*
Spartannash Company D 513 793-6300
Cincinnati *(G-4510)*
Tasty Pure Food Company E 330 434-8141
Akron *(G-464)*
Tri-State Beef Co Inc E 513 579-1722
Cincinnati *(G-4633)*
Troyer Cheese Inc E 330 893-2479
Millersburg *(G-14497)*
Tsg-Cincinnati LLC D 513 793-6241
Blue Ash *(G-1669)*
Weilands Fine Meats Inc E 614 267-9910
Columbus *(G-8883)*

5148 Fresh Fruits & Vegetables Wholesale

Al Peake & Sons Inc E 419 243-9284
Toledo *(G-17584)*
Anselmo Rssis Premier Prod Ltd E 800 229-5517
Cleveland *(G-4983)*
Barkett Fruit Co Inc E 330 364-6645
Dover *(G-10065)*
Bowman Organic Farms Ltd E 740 246-3936
Thornville *(G-17504)*
Cabbage Inc E 440 899-9171
Vermilion *(G-18551)*
▲ **Caruso Inc** C 513 860-9200
Cincinnati *(G-3127)*
Chariott Foods Inc E 419 243-1101
Toledo *(G-17648)*
Chefs Garden Inc C 419 433-4947
Huron *(G-12022)*
Circle S Farms Inc E 614 878-9462
Grove City *(G-11420)*
Del Monte Fresh Produce NA Inc E 614 527-7398
Columbus *(G-7431)*
Dno Inc D 614 231-3601
Columbus *(G-7463)*
Dole Fresh Vegetables Inc C 937 525-4300
Springfield *(G-17030)*
Economy Prod Vegetable Co Inc E 216 431-2800
Cleveland *(G-5466)*
Farris Produce Inc E 330 837-4607
Massillon *(G-13681)*
Freshway Foods Inc C 937 498-4664
Sidney *(G-16780)*
Greenline Foods Inc D 419 354-1149
Bowling Green *(G-1732)*
Hillcrest Egg & Cheese Co D 216 361-4625
Cleveland *(G-5691)*
JES Foods Inc E 216 883-8987
Cleveland *(G-5793)*
Joe Lasita & Sons Inc E 513 241-5288
Cincinnati *(G-3821)*
Midwest Fresh Foods Inc E 614 469-1492
Columbus *(G-8081)*
Miles Farmers Market Inc C 440 248-5222
Solon *(G-16872)*
Mrs Dennis Potato Farm Inc E 419 335-2778
Wauseon *(G-18807)*
Powell Company Ltd D 419 228-3552
Lima *(G-12723)*
Produce One Inc D 931 253-4749
Dayton *(G-9715)*
Sanfillipo Produce Co Inc E 614 237-3300
Columbus *(G-8591)*
Sirna & Sons Inc C 330 298-2222
Ravenna *(G-16266)*
Spartannash Company D 513 793-6300
Cincinnati *(G-4510)*
US Foods Inc A 614 539-7993
West Chester *(G-19096)*
Vermilion Farm Market E 440 967-9666
Vermilion *(G-18564)*
Z Produce Co Inc E 614 224-4373
Columbus *(G-8934)*

5149 Groceries & Related Prdts, NEC Wholesale

▲ **Akron Coca-Cola Bottling Co** A 330 784-2653
Akron *(G-34)*
Aladdins Baking Company Inc E 216 861-0317
Cleveland *(G-4925)*
Alfred Nickles Bakery Inc E 419 332-6418
Fremont *(G-11057)*
American Bottling Company D 614 237-4201
Columbus *(G-6913)*
▲ **Antonio Sofo Son Importing Co** C 419 476-4211
Toledo *(G-17596)*
▲ **Atlantic Foods Corp** D 513 772-3535
Cincinnati *(G-2998)*
Avalon Foodservice Inc C 330 854-4551
Canal Fulton *(G-2092)*
Bagel Place Inc E 419 885-1000
Toledo *(G-17604)*
Bakemark USA LLC D 513 870-0880
West Chester *(G-18872)*
▲ **Bellas Co** E 740 598-4171
Mingo Junction *(G-14527)*
Berardis Fresh Roast Inc E 440 582-4303
North Royalton *(G-15348)*
Bimbo Bakeries Usa Inc E 614 868-7565
Columbus *(G-7038)*
◆ **Brothers Trading Co Inc** C 937 746-1010
Springboro *(G-16964)*
Busken Bakery Inc D 513 871-2114
Cincinnati *(G-3097)*
▼ **Butler Animal Hlth Holdg LLC** E 614 761-9095
Dublin *(G-10155)*
Cassanos Inc E 937 294-8400
Dayton *(G-9285)*
Central Coca-Cola Btlg Co Inc C 419 476-6622
Toledo *(G-17643)*
Cleveland Sysco Inc A 216 201-3000
Cleveland *(G-5290)*
Clintonville Community Mkt E 614 261-3663
Columbus *(G-7231)*
Coca-Cola Bottling Co Cnsld D 937 878-5000
Dayton *(G-9311)*
Coffee Break Corporation E 513 841-1100
Cincinnati *(G-3318)*
Dayton Heidelberg Distrg Co C 937 220-6450
Moraine *(G-14645)*
Distillata Company D 216 771-2900
Cleveland *(G-5428)*
Ditsch Usa LLC E 513 782-8888
Cincinnati *(G-3433)*
Dutch Cntry Apple Dmplings Inc D 330 683-0646
Orrville *(G-15629)*
Dutchman Hospitality Group Inc C 614 873-3414
Plain City *(G-16050)*
EBY-Brown Company LLC C 937 324-1036
Springfield *(G-17032)*
▲ **Esber Beverage Company** E 330 456-4361
Canton *(G-2306)*
▲ **Euro Usa Inc** D 216 714-0500
Cleveland *(G-5495)*
Flavorfresh Dispensers Inc E 216 641-0200
Brooklyn Heights *(G-1871)*
Food Distributors Inc E 740 439-2764
Cambridge *(G-2068)*
Frito-Lay North America Inc C 216 491-4000
Cleveland *(G-5583)*
Frito-Lay North America Inc D 419 893-8171
Maumee *(G-13794)*
G & J Pepsi-Cola Bottlers Inc E 740 774-2148
Chillicothe *(G-2782)*
G & J Pepsi-Cola Bottlers Inc B 740 354-9191
Franklin Furnace *(G-11045)*
G & J Pepsi-Cola Bottlers Inc D 740 593-3366
Athens *(G-781)*
G & J Pepsi-Cola Bottlers Inc D 740 452-2721
Zanesville *(G-20309)*
Gordon Food Service Inc E 419 747-1212
Ontario *(G-15550)*
Gordon Food Service Inc E 419 225-8983
Lima *(G-12646)*
Gordon Food Service Inc E 216 573-4900
Cleveland *(G-5616)*
▲ **Gust Gallucci Co** E 216 881-0045
Cleveland *(G-5648)*
Hiland Group Incorporated D 330 499-8404
Canton *(G-2344)*
▲ **Hill Distributing Company** D 614 276-6533
Dublin *(G-10242)*
Hillcrest Egg & Cheese Co D 216 361-4625
Cleveland *(G-5691)*

S
I
C

Interbake Foods LLC ....C...... 614 294-4931
Columbus (G-7833)
Interbake Foods LLC ....A...... 614 294-4931
Columbus (G-7834)
▲ Interntional Molasses Corp Ltd ....E...... 937 276-7980
Dayton (G-9519)
Klosterman Baking Co ....D...... 513 242-1004
Cincinnati (G-3880)
▲ Knall Beverage Inc ....D...... 216 252-2500
Cleveland (G-5834)
▲ Leo A Dick & Sons Co ....D...... 330 452-5010
Canton (G-2374)
Louis Trauth Dairy LLC ....B...... 859 431-7553
West Chester (G-19064)
Luxfer Magtech Inc ....E...... 513 772-3066
Cincinnati (G-3952)
M & M Wine Cellar Inc ....E...... 330 536-6450
Lowellville (G-13041)
Made From Scratch Inc ....E...... 614 873-3344
Plain City (G-16058)
Magnetic Springs Water Company ......D...... 614 421-1780
Columbus (G-8009)
Maines Paper & Food Svc Inc ....E...... 216 643-7500
Bedford (G-1291)
Mattingly Foods Inc ....C...... 740 454-0136
Zanesville (G-20329)
Michaels Bakery Inc ....E...... 216 351-7530
Cleveland (G-5978)
Michaels Gourmet Catering ....E...... 419 698-2988
Toledo (G-17912)
Mondelez Global LLC ....D...... 330 626-6500
Streetsboro (G-17262)
Morton Salt Inc ....C...... 330 925-3015
Rittman (G-16407)
National Marketshare Group ....E...... 513 921-0800
Cincinnati (G-4094)
▼ Natural Foods Inc ....E...... 419 537-1713
Toledo (G-17934)
Norcia Bakery ....E...... 330 454-1077
Canton (G-2419)
Northern Frozen Foods Inc ....C...... 440 439-0600
Cleveland (G-6096)
Ohio Citrus Juices Inc ....E...... 614 539-0030
Grove City (G-11463)
Ohio Hickory Harvest Brand Pro ....E...... 330 644-6266
Coventry Township (G-9040)
Ohio Pizza Products Inc ....D...... 937 294-6969
Monroe (G-14578)
Osf International Inc ....D...... 513 942-6620
Fairfield (G-10767)
Osmans Pies Inc ....E...... 330 607-9083
Stow (G-17222)
P-Americas LLC ....E...... 419 227-3541
Lima (G-12716)
P-Americas LLC ....D...... 216 252-7377
Cleveland (G-6156)
P-Americas LLC ....C...... 330 746-7652
Youngstown (G-20149)
▲ Peck Distributors Inc ....E...... 216 587-6814
Maple Heights (G-13291)
Pepsi-Cola Metro Btlg Co Inc ....D...... 937 328-6750
Springfield (G-17097)
Pepsi-Cola Metro Btlg Co Inc ....E...... 330 336-3553
Wadsworth (G-18611)
Pepsi-Cola Metro Btlg Co Inc ....B...... 937 461-4664
Dayton (G-9690)
Pepsi-Cola Metro Btlg Co Inc ....E...... 440 323-5524
Elyria (G-10554)
Pepsi-Cola Metro Btlg Co Inc ....B...... 330 963-0426
Twinsburg (G-18304)
Perfection Bakeries Inc ....D...... 937 492-2220
Sidney (G-16793)
Powell Company Ltd ....D...... 419 228-3552
Lima (G-12723)
Produce One Inc ....D...... 931 253-4749
Dayton (G-9715)
▲ R L Lipton Distributing Co ....D...... 216 475-4150
Maple Heights (G-13292)
Rdp Foodservice Ltd ....D...... 614 261-5661
Hilliard (G-11811)
Ritchies Food Distributors Inc ....E...... 740 443-6303
Piketon (G-15988)
Schwebel Baking Company ....C...... 440 248-1500
Solon (G-16895)
Servatii Inc ....D...... 513 271-5040
Cincinnati (G-4456)
Sherwood Food Distributors LLC ....B...... 216 662-6794
Maple Heights (G-13296)
Skallys Old World Bakery Inc ....E...... 513 931-1411
Cincinnati (G-4491)

▲ Skidmore Sales & Distrg Co Inc ......E...... 513 755-4200
West Chester (G-19009)
◆ Skyline Chili Inc ....C...... 513 874-1188
Fairfield (G-10785)
Staufs Coffee Roasters II Inc ....E...... 614 487-6050
Columbus (G-8696)
Superior Beverage Group Ltd ....D...... 614 294-3555
Lewis Center (G-12562)
▲ Superior Beverage Group Ltd ....C...... 440 703-4580
Solon (G-16904)
▲ Sygma Network Inc ....C...... 614 734-2500
Dublin (G-10349)
Sysco Cincinnati LLC ....B...... 513 563-6300
Cincinnati (G-4562)
Tarrier Foods Corp ....E...... 614 876-8594
Columbus (G-8732)
Thurns Bakery & Deli ....E...... 614 221-9246
Columbus (G-8753)
Tiffin Paper Company ....E...... 419 447-2121
Tiffin (G-17544)
Tony Packos Toledo LLC ....D...... 419 691-6054
Toledo (G-18105)
Troyer Cheese Inc ....E...... 330 893-2479
Millersburg (G-14497)
Troyers Home Pantry ....E...... 330 698-4182
Apple Creek (G-621)
US Foods Inc ....E...... 330 963-6789
Twinsburg (G-18334)
US Foods Inc ....A...... 614 539-7993
West Chester (G-19096)
Veritas Enterprises Inc ....E...... 513 578-2748
Cincinnati (G-2874)
Walnut Creek Chocolate Company ......E...... 330 893-2995
Walnut Creek (G-18632)
Wasserstrom Company ....E...... 614 228-6525
Columbus (G-8879)
◆ Wine-Art of Ohio Inc ....E...... 330 678-7733
Kent (G-12269)
Z Produce Co Inc ....E...... 614 224-4373
Columbus (G-8934)

5153 Grain & Field Beans Wholesale

Andersons Inc ....C...... 419 893-5050
Maumee (G-13754)
Andersons Marathon Ethanol LLC ....E...... 937 316-3700
Greenville (G-11365)
Archbold Elevator Inc ....E...... 419 445-2451
Archbold (G-626)
Barnets Inc ....E...... 937 452-3275
Camden (G-2088)
Bunge North America Foundation ....D...... 419 692-6010
Delphos (G-10020)
Champaign Landmark Inc ....E...... 937 652-2135
Urbana (G-18423)
Consolidated Grain & Barge Co ....D...... 419 785-1941
Defiance (G-9907)
Consolidated Grain & Barge Co ....E...... 513 941-4805
Cincinnati (G-3351)
Cooper Hatchery Inc ....C...... 419 594-3325
Oakwood (G-15483)
Deerfield Farms Service Inc ....D...... 330 584-4715
Deerfield (G-9904)
Farmers Elev Grn & Sply Assoc ....E...... 419 653-4132
New Bavaria (G-14879)
Fort Recovery Equity Inc ....C...... 419 375-4119
Fort Recovery (G-10991)
Granville Milling Co ....E...... 740 587-0221
Granville (G-11343)
Hanby Farms Inc ....E...... 740 763-3554
Nashport (G-14819)
Hansen-Mueller Co ....E...... 419 729-5535
Toledo (G-17778)
Heritage Cooperative Inc ....E...... 419 294-2371
West Mansfield (G-19125)
Mercer Landmark Inc ....E...... 419 586-7443
Celina (G-2602)
Pioneer Hi-Bred Intl Inc ....E...... 419 748-8051
Grand Rapids (G-11328)
Sunrise Cooperative Inc ....B...... 937 575-6780
Piqua (G-16030)

5154 Livestock Wholesale

Barnesville Livestock Sales Co ....E...... 740 425-3611
Barnesville (G-976)
Hord Livestock Company Inc ....E...... 419 562-0277
Bucyrus (G-1994)
Kalmbach Pork Finishing LLC ....D...... 419 294-3838
Upper Sandusky (G-18409)
Mt Hope Auction Inc ....E...... 330 674-6188
Mount Hope (G-14737)

Muskingum Livestock Sales Inc ....E...... 740 452-9984
Zanesville (G-20339)
Robert Winner Sons Inc ....E...... 419 582-4321
Yorkshire (G-19942)
United Producers Inc ....E...... 937 456-4161
Eaton (G-10464)
United Producers Inc ....C...... 614 433-2150
Columbus (G-8809)

5159 Farm-Prdt Raw Mtrls, NEC Wholesale

Altria Group Distribution Co ....C...... 804 274-2000
Mason (G-13538)
Hills Supply Inc ....E...... 740 477-8994
Circleville (G-4835)
Inland Products Inc ....E...... 614 443-3425
Columbus (G-7819)

5162 Plastics Materials & Basic Shapes Wholesale

▲ Advanced Elastomer Systems LP ....C...... 800 352-7866
Akron (G-20)
Alro Steel Corporation ....E...... 419 720-5300
Toledo (G-17586)
Alro Steel Corporation ....E...... 614 878-7271
Columbus (G-6905)
Ampacet Corporation ....E...... 513 247-5400
Cincinnati (G-2956)
▲ Blade-Tech Industries Inc ....D...... 877 331-5793
Streetsboro (G-17247)
Bprex Plastic Packaging Inc ....E...... 419 423-3271
Findlay (G-10882)
▲ Cannon Group Inc ....E...... 614 890-0343
Westerville (G-19230)
▲ Checker Notions Company Inc ....D...... 419 893-3636
Maumee (G-13770)
F B Wright Co Cincinnati ....E...... 513 874-9100
West Chester (G-18921)
Florline Group Inc ....E...... 330 830-3380
Massillon (G-13682)
Hexpol Compounding LLC ....C...... 440 834-4644
Burton (G-2016)
HP Manufacturing Company Inc ....D...... 216 361-6500
Cleveland (G-5721)
Ilpea Industries Inc ....C...... 330 562-2916
Aurora (G-830)
◆ Multi-Plastics Inc ....D...... 740 548-4894
Lewis Center (G-12552)
Plastics R Unique Inc ....E...... 330 334-4820
Wadsworth (G-18613)
▲ Polymer Packaging Inc ....D...... 330 832-2000
Massillon (G-13720)
Polymershapes LLC ....E...... 937 877-1903
Tipp City (G-17564)
◆ Polyone Corporation ....D...... 440 930-1000
Avon Lake (G-926)
Queen City Polymers Inc ....E...... 513 779-0990
West Chester (G-18989)
▲ Surreal Entertainment LLC ....E...... 330 262-5277
Wooster (G-19772)
Tahoma Enterprises Inc ....D...... 330 745-9016
Barberton (G-969)
▼ Tahoma Rubber & Plastics Inc ....D...... 330 745-9016
Barberton (G-970)

5169 Chemicals & Allied Prdts, NEC Wholesale

Airgas Inc ....B...... 440 632-1758
Middlefield (G-14268)
Airgas Inc ....D...... 937 222-8312
Moraine (G-14619)
▲ Airgas Merchant Gases LLC ....B...... 800 242-0105
Cleveland (G-4920)
Airgas Safety Inc ....E...... 513 942-1465
Hamilton (G-11555)
Airgas Usa LLC ....E...... 216 642-6600
Independence (G-12042)
Airgas Usa LLC ....D...... 440 786-2864
Oakwood Village (G-15485)
Airgas Usa LLC ....E...... 513 563-8070
Cincinnati (G-2916)
Akrochem Corporation ....E...... 330 535-2108
Barberton (G-938)
Americas Best Medical Eqp Co ....E...... 330 928-0884
Akron (G-71)
Anatrace Products LLC ....E...... 419 740-6600
Maumee (G-13751)
▲ Applied Indus Tech - Dixie Inc ....C...... 216 426-4000
Cleveland (G-4995)

▲ Applied Industrial Tech Inc ....B 216 426-4000
Cleveland (G-4996)

Ashland LLC ....D 614 232-8510
Columbus (G-6977)

Ashland LLC ....E 614 276-6144
Columbus (G-6978)

Ashland LLC ....C 614 839-4503
Dublin (G-10138)

Ashland LLC ....D 216 961-4690
Cleveland (G-5012)

Ashland LLC ....E 216 883-8200
Cleveland (G-5013)

Ashland LLC ....D 419 289-9588
Ashland (G-652)

Ashland LLC ....C 614 790-3333
Dublin (G-10139)

Avalon Foodservice Inc ....C 330 854-4551
Canal Fulton (G-2092)

Bleachtech LLC ....E 216 921-1980
Seville (G-16683)

▲ Bonded Chemicals Inc ....E 614 777-9240
Columbus (G-7053)

Braden Med Services Inc ....E 740 732-2356
Caldwell (G-2036)

◆ Budenheim Usa Inc ....E 614 345-2400
Columbus (G-7093)

▲ Calvary Industries Inc ....D 513 874-1113
Fairfield (G-10706)

Cantrell Oil Company ....E 937 695-8003
Winchester (G-19660)

Cargill Incorporated ....D 440 716-4664
North Olmsted (G-15278)

Chemical Services Inc ....E 937 898-5566
Dayton (G-9295)

▲ Chemical Solvents Inc ....E 216 741-9310
Cleveland (G-5173)

Chemical Solvents Inc ....D 216 741-9310
Cleveland (G-5174)

▲ Cimcool Industrial Pdts LLC ....D 888 246-2665
Cincinnati (G-3216)

▲ CL Zimmerman Delaware LLC ....E 513 860-9300
West Chester (G-18890)

▼ Cr Brands Inc ....D 513 860-5039
West Chester (G-18905)

Custom Chemical Solutions ....E 800 291-1057
Loveland (G-12987)

D & D Investment Co ....E 614 272-6567
Columbus (G-7405)

D W Dickey and Son Inc ....D 330 424-1441
Lisbon (G-12799)

Dawnchem Inc ....E 440 943-3332
Willowick (G-19597)

▼ Dubois Chemicals Inc ....C 513 731-6350
Cincinnati (G-3447)

Dupont Inc ....D 937 268-3411
Dayton (G-9398)

▲ Electro Prime Group LLC ....D 419 476-0100
Toledo (G-17710)

▲ Eliokem Inc ....D 330 734-1100
Fairlawn (G-10824)

▲ Emerald Hilton Davis LLC ....D 513 841-0057
Cincinnati (G-3493)

Flex Technologies Inc ....E 330 897-6311
Baltic (G-934)

Flow Polymers LLC ....C 216 249-4900
Cleveland (G-5549)

Formlabs Ohio Inc ....E 419 837-9783
Millbury (G-14448)

Galaxy Associates Inc ....E 513 731-6350
Cincinnati (G-3600)

GFS Chemicals Inc ....D 740 881-5501
Columbus (G-7667)

◆ Gorilla Glue Company ....E 513 271-3300
Cincinnati (G-3627)

◆ Harwick Standard Dist Corp ....D 330 798-9300
Akron (G-253)

Hillside Maint Sup Co Inc ....E 513 751-4100
Cincinnati (G-3708)

▲ Imcd Us LLC ....E 216 228-8900
Lakewood (G-12348)

▲ Industrial Chemical Corp ....E 330 725-0800
Medina (G-13953)

◆ Joshen Paper & Packaging Co ....C 216 441-5600
Cleveland (G-5804)

◆ Koch Knight LLC ....D 330 488-1651
East Canton (G-10387)

Kraton Polymers US LLC ....B 740 423-7571
Belpre (G-1407)

Lanxess Corporation ....C 440 279-2367
Chardon (G-2701)

Maines Paper & Food Svc Inc ....E 216 643-7500
Bedford (G-1291)

Mantaline Corporation ....D 330 274-2264
Mantua (G-13273)

Matheson Tri-Gas Inc ....E 614 771-1311
Hilliard (G-11788)

Medi Home Health Agency Inc ....E 740 266-3977
Steubenville (G-17165)

Midwest Industrial Supply Inc ....E 800 321-0699
Toledo (G-17914)

▲ Mitsubshi Intl Fd Ingrdnts Inc ....E 614 652-1111
Dublin (G-10281)

▲ National Colloid Company ....E 740 282-1171
Steubenville (G-17168)

Nexeo Solutions LLC ....D 330 405-0461
Twinsburg (G-18301)

Nexeo Solutions LLC ....D 330 405-0461
Whipple (G-19442)

▲ Palmer Holland Inc ....D 440 686-2300
North Olmsted (G-15304)

▲ Phoenix Technologies Intl LLC ....E 419 353-7738
Bowling Green (G-1744)

Polymer Additives Holdings Inc ....C 216 875-7200
Independence (G-12108)

Polyone Corporation ....D 440 930-1000
North Baltimore (G-15179)

Procter & Gamble Distrg LLC ....E 513 945-7960
Cincinnati (G-4291)

Procter & Gamble Distrg LLC ....C 937 387-5189
Union (G-18351)

Rde System Corp ....C 513 933-8000
Lebanon (G-12496)

Rhiel Supply Co Inc ....E 330 799-7777
Austintown (G-861)

Rudolph Brothers & Co ....E 614 833-0707
Canal Winchester (G-2118)

Rwc Inc ....E 614 890-0600
Westerville (G-19208)

◆ Sea-Land Chemical Co ....D 440 871-7887
Westlake (G-19404)

Sika Corporation ....D 740 387-9224
Marion (G-13459)

▲ Skidmore Sales & Distrg Co Inc ....E 513 755-4200
West Chester (G-19009)

◆ Struktol Company America LLC ....C 330 928-5188
Stow (G-17233)

T&L Global Management LLC ....D 614 586-0303
Columbus (G-8727)

▲ Tembec Btlsr Inc ....E 419 244-5856
Toledo (G-18063)

Texo International Inc ....D 513 731-6350
Norwood (G-15463)

▼ The Mau-Sherwood Supply Co ....E 330 405-1200
Twinsburg (G-18326)

▲ Tosoh America Inc ....B 614 539-8622
Grove City (G-11478)

◆ Tricor Industrial Inc ....D 330 264-3299
Wooster (G-19773)

▲ United McGill Corporation ....E 614 829-1200
Groveport (G-11546)

Univar Inc ....E 440 510-1259
Eastlake (G-10435)

Univar USA Inc ....C 513 714-5264
West Chester (G-19095)

Univar USA Inc ....E 419 666-7880
Walbridge (G-18626)

Univar USA Inc ....E 330 425-4330
Twinsburg (G-18333)

Univar USA Inc ....E 513 870-4050
Hamilton (G-11653)

Univar USA Inc ....D 440 238-8550
Strongsville (G-17356)

Viking Explosives LLC ....E 218 263-8845
Cleveland (G-6630)

VWR Chemicals LLC ....E 330 425-2522
Aurora (G-847)

Wampum Hardware Co ....E 740 685-2585
Salesville (G-16569)

Wampum Hardware Co ....C 419 273-2542
Forest (G-10982)

▼ Washing Systems LLC ....C 800 272-1974
Loveland (G-13032)

Young Chemical Co LLC ....E 330 486-4210
Twinsburg (G-18338)

Zep Inc ....E 440 239-1580
Cleveland (G-6713)

5171 Petroleum Bulk Stations & Terminals

Cincinnati - Vulcan Company ....D 513 242-5300
Cincinnati (G-3219)

Englefield Inc ....D 740 452-2707
Zanesville (G-20305)

New Vulco Mfg & Sales Co LLC ....D 513 242-2672
Cincinnati (G-4109)

Universal Oil Inc ....E 216 771-4300
Cleveland (G-6582)

5172 Petroleum & Petroleum Prdts Wholesale

Afm East Archwood Oil Inc ....E 330 786-1000
Akron (G-23)

▲ Applied Indus Tech - Dixie Inc ....C 216 426-4000
Cleveland (G-4995)

Bazell Oil Co Inc ....E 740 385-5420
Logan (G-12831)

Bd Oil Gathering Corp ....E 740 374-9355
Marietta (G-13315)

Blue Star Lubrication Tech LLC ....E 847 285-1888
Cincinnati (G-3064)

Centerra Co-Op ....E 800 362-9598
Jefferson (G-12190)

Centerra Co-Op ....E 419 281-2153
Ashland (G-665)

Champaign Landmark Inc ....E 937 652-2135
Urbana (G-18423)

Circleville Oil Co ....D 740 474-7568
Circleville (G-4828)

Clay Distributing Co ....E 419 426-3051
Attica (G-813)

▲ Coolants Plus Inc ....E 513 892-4000
Hamilton (G-11587)

Cuyahoga Landmark Inc ....E 440 238-3900
Strongsville (G-17295)

D W Dickey and Son Inc ....D 330 424-1441
Lisbon (G-12799)

Duncan Oil Co ....E 937 426-5945
Dayton (G-9171)

Free Enterprises Incorporated ....D 330 722-2031
Medina (G-13940)

Hartland Petroleum LLC ....E 740 452-3115
Zanesville (G-20315)

Hearthstone Utilities Inc ....D 440 974-3770
Cleveland (G-5679)

Heartland Petroleum LLC ....E 614 441-4001
Columbus (G-7733)

Hightowers Petroleum Company ....E 513 423-4272
Middletown (G-14349)

Holland Oil Company ....D 330 835-1815
Akron (G-266)

Knisely Inc ....D 330 343-5812
Dover (G-10085)

◆ Koch Knight LLC ....D 330 488-1651
East Canton (G-10387)

Krebs Steve BP Oil Co ....E 513 641-0150
Cincinnati (G-3890)

Lyden Oil Company ....D 330 832-7800
Massillon (G-13705)

Lyden Oil Company ....E 330 792-1100
Youngstown (G-20102)

Lykins Companies Inc ....E 513 831-8820
Milford (G-14403)

Lykins Oil Company ....E 513 831-8820
Milford (G-14404)

Marathon Petroleum Company LP ....B 330 479-5688
Canton (G-2387)

Marathon Petroleum Company LP ....E 614 274-1125
Columbus (G-8015)

Marathon Petroleum Company LP ....E 513 932-6007
Lebanon (G-12483)

Marathon Petroleum Corporation ....B 419 422-2121
Findlay (G-10938)

McKinley Air Transport Inc ....E 330 497-6956
Canton (G-2394)

Melzers Fuel Service Inc ....E 800 367-0203
Painesville (G-15727)

Mighty Mac Investments Inc ....E 937 335-2928
Troy (G-18215)

Mplx Terminals LLC ....E 440 526-4653
Cleveland (G-6017)

Mplx Terminals LLC ....B 330 479-5539
Canton (G-2409)

Mplx Terminals LLC ....E 504 252-8064
Heath (G-11706)

Mplx Terminals LLC ....E 513 451-0485
Cincinnati (G-4079)

Northeast Lubricants Ltd ....C 216 478-0507
Cleveland (G-6088)

Nzr Retail of Toledo Inc ....D 419 724-0005
Toledo (G-17955)

Employee Codes: A=Over 500 employees, B=251-500
C=101-250, D=51-100, E=25-50   2019 Harris Ohio
Services Directory   897

SIC

Santmyer Oil Co Inc......................D....330 262-6501
Wooster (G-19764)
▲ Shrader Tire & Oil Inc.................E....419 472-2128
Toledo (G-18032)
Sines Inc......................................E....440 352-6572
Painesville (G-15740)
◆ Specialty Lubricants Corp.............E....330 425-2567
Macedonia (G-13082)
The Columbia Oil Co.......................D....513 868-8700
Liberty Twp (G-12589)
Travelcenters of America LLC.........D....330 793-4426
Youngstown (G-20224)
Triumph Energy Corporation...........E....513 367-9900
Harrison (G-11679)
True North Energy LLC...................E....877 245-9336
Brecksville (G-1808)
Ull Inc...E....440 543-5195
Chagrin Falls (G-2685)
Vesco Oil Corporation...................E....614 367-1412
Blacklick (G-1484)
Winner Aviation Corporation...........D....330 856-5000
Vienna (G-18584)
X F Construction Svcs Inc..............E....614 575-2700
Columbus (G-8923)
Youngstown Propane Inc................E....330 792-6571
Youngstown (G-20266)

5181 Beer & Ale Wholesale

Anheuser-Busch LLC......................C....513 381-3927
Cincinnati (G-2970)
Anheuser-Busch LLC......................D....330 438-2036
Canton (G-2189)
▲ Bellas Co...................................E....740 598-4171
Mingo Junction (G-14527)
▲ Beverage Distributors Inc............C....216 431-1600
Cleveland (G-5061)
▲ Bonbright Distributors Inc...........C....937 222-1001
Dayton (G-9258)
▲ Brown Distributing Inc.................D....740 349-7999
Newark (G-15017)
▲ Cavalier Distributing Company......D....513 247-9222
Blue Ash (G-1520)
Cdc Management Co........................C....614 781-0216
Columbus (G-7146)
▲ Central Beverage Group Ltd.........C....614 294-3555
Lewis Center (G-12532)
▲ City Beverage Company...............E....419 782-7065
Defiance (G-9906)
▲ Columbus Distributing Company.....B....614 846-1000
Columbus (G-7275)
Columbus Distributing Company........E....740 726-2211
Waldo (G-18629)
▲ Dayton Heidelberg Distrg Co........C....937 222-8692
Moraine (G-14643)
Dayton Heidelberg Distrg Co...........C....216 520-2626
Cleveland (G-5412)
Dayton Heidelberg Distrg Co...........D....419 666-9783
Perrysburg (G-15856)
Dayton Heidelberg Distrg Co...........C....937 220-6450
Moraine (G-14645)
Dayton Heidelberg Distrg Co...........D....513 421-5000
Cincinnati (G-3406)
Dayton Heidelberg Distrg Co...........C....614 308-0400
Columbus (G-7423)
Dayton Heidelberg Distrg Co...........C....419 666-9783
Perrysburg (G-15855)
▲ Dickerson Distributing Company....D....513 539-8483
Monroe (G-14565)
▲ Donzells Flower & Grdn Ctr Inc.....E....330 724-0550
Akron (G-191)
▲ Esber Beverage Company.............E....330 456-4361
Canton (G-2306)
Glazers Distributors Ohio Inc..........E....440 542-7000
Solon (G-16852)
▲ Goodman Beverage Co Inc...........D....440 787-2255
Lorain (G-12905)
Hanson Distributing Co Inc.............D....419 435-3214
Fostoria (G-11004)
Heidelberg Distributing Co..............E....614 308-0400
Columbus (G-7734)
▲ Heritage Beverage Company LLC...D....440 255-5550
Mentor (G-14060)
▲ Hill Distributing Company.............D....614 276-6533
Dublin (G-10242)
House of La Rose Cleveland............C....440 746-7500
Brecksville (G-1783)
Jetro Cash and Carry Entps LLC......D....216 525-0101
Cleveland (G-5794)
▲ Knall Beverage Inc.....................D....216 252-2500
Cleveland (G-5834)

Litter Distributing Co Inc................D....740 774-2831
Chillicothe (G-2802)
M & A Distributing Co Inc................E....440 703-4580
Solon (G-16868)
▲ Matesich Distributing Co.............D....740 349-8686
Newark (G-15065)
Nwo Beverage Inc..........................E....419 725-2162
Northwood (G-15403)
◆ Ohio Valley Wine Company...........D....513 771-9370
Cincinnati (G-4161)
R L Lipton Distributing LLC.............E....800 321-6553
Austintown (G-860)
▲ R L Lipton Distributing Co............D....216 475-4150
Maple Heights (G-13292)
▲ Rhinegeist LLC...........................D....513 381-1367
Cincinnati (G-4368)
Southern Glazers Wine and Sp.........D....330 422-9463
Streetsboro (G-17271)
▲ Southern Glzers Dstrs Ohio LLC....D....614 552-7900
Columbus (G-8664)
Superior Beverage Company Inc.......D....440 703-4580
Solon (G-16903)
The Maple City Ice Company............E....419 668-2531
Norwalk (G-15457)
Treu House of Munch Inc.................E....419 666-7770
Northwood (G-15412)
▲ Warsteiner Importers Agency.......D....513 942-9872
West Chester (G-19034)

5182 Wine & Distilled Alcoholic Beverages Wholesale

August Food & Wine LLC.................E....513 421-2020
Cincinnati (G-3003)
▲ Bellas Co...................................E....740 598-4171
Mingo Junction (G-14527)
Dayton Heidelberg Distrg Co...........C....614 308-0400
Columbus (G-7423)
Dayton Heidelberg Distrg Co...........C....419 666-9783
Perrysburg (G-15855)
Dayton Heidelberg Distrg Co...........C....937 220-6450
Moraine (G-14645)
▲ Esber Beverage Company.............D....330 456-4361
Canton (G-2306)
Fredericks Wine & Dine...................E....216 581-5299
Cleveland (G-5576)
Glazers Distributors Ohio Inc..........E....440 542-7000
Solon (G-16852)
▲ Goodman Beverage Co Inc...........D....440 787-2255
Lorain (G-12905)
▲ H Dennert Distributing Corp.........C....513 871-7272
Cincinnati (G-3666)
M & A Distributing Co Inc................E....440 703-4580
Solon (G-16868)
M & A Distributing Co Inc................D....614 294-3555
Columbus (G-8002)
M & M Wine Cellar Inc....................E....330 536-6450
Lowellville (G-13041)
▲ Mid-Ohio Wines Inc.....................E....440 989-1011
Lorain (G-12927)
◆ Ohio Valley Wine Company...........D....513 771-9370
Cincinnati (G-4161)
▲ R L Lipton Distributing Co............D....216 475-4150
Maple Heights (G-13292)
Southern Glazers Wine and Sp.........D....330 422-9463
Streetsboro (G-17271)
Southern Glazers Wine and Sp.........D....513 755-7082
Fairfield (G-10786)
▲ Southern Glzers Dstrs Ohio LLC....D....614 552-7900
Columbus (G-8664)
Superior Beverage Company Inc.......D....440 703-4580
Solon (G-16903)
▲ Vanguard Wines LLC....................D....614 291-3493
Columbus (G-8844)
Vintage Wine Distributor Inc...........E....614 876-2580
Columbus (G-8852)
▲ Wine Trends Inc.........................E....216 520-2626
Independence (G-12141)

5191 Farm Splys Wholesale

◆ A M Leonard Inc.........................E....937 773-2694
Piqua (G-15994)
Alabama Farmers Coop Inc..............E....419 655-2289
Cygnet (G-9142)
Andersons Inc...............................C....419 893-5050
Maumee (G-13754)
◆ Andersons Agriculture Group LP....E....419 893-5050
Maumee (G-13756)
Archbold Elevator Inc.....................E....419 445-2451
Archbold (G-626)

Berns Grnhse & Grdn Ctr Inc...........E....513 423-5306
Middletown (G-14293)
▲ Bfg Supply Co Llc......................E....440 834-1883
Burton (G-2015)
Centerra Co-Op.............................E....800 362-9598
Jefferson (G-12190)
Champaign Landmark Inc.................E....937 652-2135
Urbana (G-18423)
Cooper Farms Inc..........................D....419 375-4116
Fort Recovery (G-10989)
Cover Crop Shop LLC.....................D....937 417-3972
Sidney (G-16772)
Deerfield Farms Service Inc............D....330 584-4715
Deerfield (G-9904)
Do Cut Sales & Service Inc.............E....330 533-9878
Warren (G-18703)
▲ Express Seed Company...............D....440 774-2259
Oberlin (G-15502)
Farmers Elev Grn & Sply Assoc.......E....419 653-4132
New Bavaria (G-14879)
Gardenlife Inc...............................E....800 241-7333
Concord Twp (G-8945)
Gardner-Connell LLC......................E....614 456-4000
Columbus (G-7649)
Gerber Feed Service Inc.................E....330 857-4421
Dalton (G-9145)
Granville Milling Co.......................E....740 587-0221
Granville (G-11343)
Hanby Farms Inc...........................E....740 763-3554
Nashport (G-14819)
◆ Jiffy Products America Inc...........E....440 282-2818
Lorain (G-12908)
K M B Inc.....................................E....330 889-3451
Bristolville (G-1826)
Land OLakes Inc............................E....330 879-2158
Massillon (G-13703)
▼ Lesco Inc..................................C....216 706-9250
Cleveland (G-5865)
▲ Mac Kenzie Nursery Supply Inc....E....440 259-3517
Perry (G-15825)
Mennel Milling Company.................E....740 385-6824
Logan (G-12849)
Mennel Milling Company.................D....740 385-6824
Logan (G-12850)
Morral Companies LLC....................E....740 465-3251
Morral (G-14713)
Noxious Vegetation Control Inc........D....614 486-8994
Ashville (G-762)
Ohigro Inc....................................E....740 726-2429
Waldo (G-18630)
Phillips Ready Mix Co.....................D....937 426-5151
Beavercreek Township (G-1259)
Pioneer Hi-Bred Intl Inc.................E....740 657-6120
Delaware (G-10000)
Pioneer Hi-Bred Intl Inc.................E....419 748-8051
Grand Rapids (G-11328)
Premier Feeds LLC.........................E....937 584-2411
Wilmington (G-19641)
◆ Provimi North America Inc...........B....937 770-2400
Brookville (G-1916)
S & D Application LLC.....................E....419 288-3660
Wayne (G-18826)
Schlessman Seed Co......................E....419 499-2572
Milan (G-14367)
Seed Consultants Inc.....................E....740 333-8644
Wshngtn CT Hs (G-19884)
Sunrise Cooperative Inc..................E....937 462-8341
South Charleston (G-16925)
Sunrise Cooperative Inc..................E....419 683-7340
Crestline (G-9060)
Sunrise Cooperative Inc..................E....937 382-1633
Wilmington (G-19650)
Sunrise Cooperative Inc..................E....937 323-7536
Springfield (G-17122)
Sunrise Cooperative Inc..................B....937 575-6780
Piqua (G-16030)
United States Dept Agriculture........D....419 626-8439
Sandusky (G-16652)
Waterworks America Inc..................C....440 526-4815
Cleveland (G-6655)

5192 Books, Periodicals & Newspapers Wholesale

Afit Ls Usaf..................................E....937 255-3636
Dayton (G-9154)
◆ Barbour Publishing Inc................E....740 922-1321
Uhrichsville (G-18339)
◆ Bookmasters Inc........................C....419 281-1802
Ashland (G-658)

CSS Publishing Co Inc ....E 419 227-1818
Lima *(G-12627)*

Ed Map Inc ....D....... 740 753-3439
Nelsonville *(G-14830)*

▲ Findaway World LLC ....D....... 440 893-0808
Solon *(G-16849)*

Friends of The Lib Cyahoga FLS ....C 330 928-2117
Cuyahoga Falls *(G-9097)*

▲ H & M Patch Company ....D....... 614 339-8950
Columbus *(G-7706)*

Hecks Direct Mail & Prtg Svc ....E 419 661-6028
Toledo *(G-17798)*

Hubbard Company............................E 419 784-4455
Defiance *(G-9917)*

Indico LLC ....D....... 440 775-7777
Oberlin *(G-15505)*

Mackin Book Company ....E 330 854-0099
Massillon *(G-13706)*

McGraw-Hill School Education H ....B 419 207-7400
Ashland *(G-679)*

Media Source Inc ....D....... 614 873-7635
Plain City *(G-16060)*

Scholastic Book Fairs Inc ....D....... 513 714-1000
West Chester *(G-18998)*

Windy Hill Ltd Inc ....E 216 391-4800
Cleveland *(G-6684)*

Zaner-Bloser Inc ....D....... 614 486-0221
Columbus *(G-8935)*

5193 Flowers, Nursery Stock & Florists' Splys Wholesale

▲ August Corso Sons Inc ....C....... 419 626-0765
Sandusky *(G-16576)*

Autograph Inc ....E 216 881-1911
Cleveland *(G-5024)*

Beroske Farms & Greenhouse Inc .....E 419 826-4547
Delta *(G-10041)*

C M Brown Nurseries Inc ....E 440 259-5403
Perry *(G-15820)*

Claprood Roman J Co ....E 614 221-5515
Columbus *(G-7217)*

Cottage Gardens Inc ....D....... 440 259-2900
Perry *(G-15822)*

◆ Darice Inc ....C....... 440 238-9150
Strongsville *(G-17297)*

Davis Tree Farm & Nursery Inc ....E 330 483-3324
Valley City *(G-18460)*

Dennis Top Soil & Landscaping ....E 419 865-5656
Toledo *(G-17697)*

Denver Wholesale Florists Co ....C....... 419 241-7241
Toledo *(G-17698)*

▲ Dummen Group ....E 614 850-9551
Columbus *(G-7475)*

▲ Express Seed Company ....D....... 440 774-2259
Oberlin *(G-15502)*

Flower Factory Inc ....D....... 614 275-6220
Columbus *(G-7598)*

▲ Flowerland Garden Centers ....E 440 439-8636
Oakwood Village *(G-15489)*

Giant Eagle Inc ....D....... 330 364-5301
Dover *(G-10079)*

Gs Ohio Inc ....D....... 614 885-5350
Powell *(G-16196)*

Kens Flower Shop Inc ....E 419 841-9590
Perrysburg *(G-15885)*

Lcn Holdings Inc ....E 440 259-5571
Madison *(G-13101)*

▲ Mac Kenzie Nursery Supply Inc......E 440 259-3517
Perry *(G-15825)*

Maria Gardens LLC ....E 440 238-7637
Strongsville *(G-17328)*

◆ New Diamond Line Cont Corp ....E 330 644-9993
Coventry Township *(G-9039)*

North Branch Nursery Inc ....E 419 287-4679
Pemberville *(G-15805)*

North Coast Perennials Inc ....E 440 428-1277
Madison *(G-13105)*

▲ Oberers Flowers Inc ....E 937 223-1253
Dayton *(G-9665)*

Plantscaping Inc ....D....... 216 367-1200
Cleveland *(G-6216)*

Rentokil North America Inc ....E 614 837-0099
Groveport *(G-11534)*

Rusty Oak Nursery Ltd ....E 330 225-7704
Valley City *(G-18468)*

Scarffs Nursery Inc ....C....... 937 845-3130
New Carlisle *(G-14897)*

▲ Schmidt Bros Inc ....E 419 826-3671
Swanton *(G-17406)*

Siebenthaler Company ....D....... 937 427-4110
Dayton *(G-9767)*

▲ Straders Garden Centers Inc ....C....... 614 889-1314
Columbus *(G-8703)*

▲ Thorsens Greenhouse LLC ....C....... 740 363-5069
Delaware *(G-10009)*

5194 Tobacco & Tobacco Prdts Wholesale

Albert Guarnieri & Co ....D....... 330 794-9834
Hudson *(G-11962)*

Core-Mark Ohio ....D....... 650 589-9445
Solon *(G-16837)*

Dittman-Adams Company ....E 513 870-7530
West Chester *(G-18914)*

EBY-Brown Company LLC ....C....... 937 324-1036
Springfield *(G-17032)*

Gummer Wholesale Inc ....D....... 740 928-0415
Heath *(G-11704)*

JE Carsten Company ....E 330 794-4440
Hudson *(G-11987)*

Jetro Cash and Carry Entps LLC ....C....... 216 525-0101
Cleveland *(G-5794)*

Novelart Manufacturing Company ....D....... 513 351-7700
Cincinnati *(G-4136)*

Swd Corporation ....E 419 227-2436
Lima *(G-12759)*

The Anter Brothers Company ....E 216 252-4555
Cleveland *(G-6519)*

5198 Paints, Varnishes & Splys Wholesale

Carlisle Fluid Tech Inc ....E 419 825-5186
Toledo *(G-17637)*

◆ Comex North America Inc ....D....... 303 307-2100
Cleveland *(G-5316)*

Continental Products Company ....E 216 531-0710
Cleveland *(G-5344)*

Fashion Architectural Designs ....D....... 216 432-1600
Cleveland *(G-5515)*

Finishmaster Inc ....D....... 614 228-4328
Columbus *(G-7578)*

Matrix Sys Auto Finishes LLC ....D....... 248 668-8135
Massillon *(G-13713)*

Miller Bros Wallpaper Company ....E 513 231-4470
Cincinnati *(G-4052)*

Systems Jay LLC Nanogate ....E 419 747-6639
Mansfield *(G-13249)*

▲ Teknol Inc ....D....... 937 264-0190
Dayton *(G-9808)*

5199 Nondurable Goods, NEC Wholesale

▲ A-Roo Company LLC ....D....... 440 238-8850
Strongsville *(G-17278)*

▲ Ameri Interntl Trade Grp Inc...........E 419 586-6433
Celina *(G-2582)*

▼ Armaly LLC ....D....... 740 852-3621
London *(G-12859)*

Aunties Attic ....E 740 548-5059
Lewis Center *(G-12528)*

◆ Aurora Wholesalers LLC..................D....... 440 248-5200
Solon *(G-16825)*

Avery Dennison Corporation ....D....... 440 534-6000
Mentor *(G-14020)*

◆ B D G Wrap-Tite Inc ....E 440 349-5400
Solon *(G-16826)*

Bag-Pack Inc ....E 513 346-3900
West Chester *(G-18871)*

Boost Technologies LLC ....D....... 800 223-2203
Dayton *(G-9259)*

▲ Bottomline Ink Corporation ....E 419 897-8000
Perrysburg *(G-15840)*

Bprex Closures LLC ....E 812 424-2904
Maumee *(G-13764)*

Buy Below Retail Inc ....E 216 292-7805
Cleveland *(G-5108)*

Cambridge Packaging Inc ....E 740 432-3351
Cambridge *(G-2055)*

Cannell Graphics LLC ....E 614 781-9760
Columbus *(G-7110)*

▼ Century Marketing Corporation ....E 419 354-2591
Bowling Green *(G-1727)*

▲ Checker Notions Company Inc ....D....... 419 893-3636
Maumee *(G-13770)*

▲ Clercom Inc ....D....... 513 724-6101
Williamsburg *(G-19491)*

Columbus Serum Company ....C....... 614 444-5211
Columbus *(G-7313)*

▲ Compass Packaging LLC ....E 330 274-2001
Mantua *(G-13266)*

▲ Corporate Imageworks LLC ....E 216 292-8800
Streetsboro *(G-17251)*

▲ Custom Products Corporation ....D....... 440 528-7100
Solon *(G-16842)*

D & D Advertising Enterprises............E 513 921-6827
Cincinnati *(G-3393)*

▲ Dayton Bag & Burlap Co ....E 937 258-8000
Dayton *(G-9355)*

Dayton Heidelberg Distrg Co ....D....... 937 220-6450
Moraine *(G-14644)*

Distribution Data Incorporated ....E 216 362-3009
Brookpark *(G-1896)*

Diversified Products & Svcs ....D....... 740 393-6202
Mount Vernon *(G-14763)*

Dollar Paradise ....E 216 432-0421
Cleveland *(G-5436)*

Don Drumm Studios & Gallery ....E 330 253-6840
Akron *(G-190)*

Dwa Mrkting Prmtional Pdts LLC ....E 216 476-0635
Strongsville *(G-17298)*

Eastgate Graphics LLC ....E 513 228-5522
Lebanon *(G-12461)*

▲ Esc and Company Inc ....E 614 794-0568
Columbus *(G-7532)*

Evolution Crtive Solutions LLC ....E 513 681-4450
Cincinnati *(G-3523)*

▲ First 2 Market Products LLC ....E 419 874-5444
Perrysburg *(G-15865)*

Flower Factory Inc ....D....... 614 275-6220
Columbus *(G-7598)*

▲ G R B Inc ....D....... 800 628-9195
West Chester *(G-18929)*

▲ Galaxy Balloons Incorporated ....C....... 216 476-3360
Cleveland *(G-5589)*

Glen Surplus Sales Inc ....E 419 347-1212
Shelby *(G-16746)*

▲ Global-Pak Inc ....D....... 330 482-1993
Lisbon *(G-12802)*

◆ Glow Industries Inc ....E 419 872-4772
Perrysburg *(G-15869)*

Gordon Bernard Company LLC ....E 513 248-7600
Milford *(G-14393)*

Gpax Ltd ....E 614 501-7622
Reynoldsburg *(G-16307)*

Graham Packaging Holdings Co ....E 419 628-1070
Minster *(G-14534)*

Graham Packg Plastic Pdts Inc ....C....... 419 423-3271
Findlay *(G-10914)*

Gummer Wholesale Inc ....D....... 740 928-0415
Heath *(G-11704)*

Hammacher Schlemmer & Co Inc ......C....... 513 860-4570
West Chester *(G-18941)*

Harold Tatman & Sons Entps Inc ....E 740 655-2880
Kingston *(G-12315)*

Hays Enterprises Inc ....E 330 392-2278
Warren *(G-18711)*

▲ Hi-Way Distributing Corp Amer ....D....... 330 645-6633
Coventry Township *(G-9035)*

Home City Ice Company ....E 614 836-2877
Groveport *(G-11518)*

IAMS Company ....D....... 937 962-7782
Lewisburg *(G-12568)*

▼ ICM Distributing Company Inc ....E 234 212-3030
Twinsburg *(G-18281)*

Impressive Packaging Inc ....E 419 368-6808
Hayesville *(G-11701)*

▲ Inno-Pak LLC ....E 740 363-0090
Delaware *(G-9989)*

▲ Innovtive Lbling Solutions Inc ....D....... 513 860-2457
Hamilton *(G-11614)*

Jlt Packaging Cincinnati Inc ....D....... 513 933-0250
Lebanon *(G-12474)*

▲ Johnson Bros Rubber Co Inc ....D....... 419 853-4122
West Salem *(G-19128)*

Johnson Bros Rubber Co Inc ....E 419 752-4814
Greenwich *(G-11402)*

▲ K & M International Inc ....D....... 330 425-2550
Twinsburg *(G-18286)*

Kapstone Container Corporation ....C....... 330 562-6111
Aurora *(G-832)*

L M Berry and Company ....D....... 513 768-7700
Cincinnati *(G-3900)*

Labelle News Agency Inc ....E 740 282-9731
Steubenville *(G-17161)*

Lamrite West Inc ....E 440 572-9946
Strongsville *(G-17322)*

▲ Lamrite West Inc ....C....... 440 238-9150
Strongsville *(G-17321)*

▲ Leader Promotions Inc ....D....... 614 416-6565
Columbus *(G-7961)*

▲ Leather Gallery Inc ....E 513 312-1722
Lebanon *(G-12479)*

Liqui-Box Corporation	E	614 888-9280	
Columbus *(G-7982)*			
Lori Holding Co	E	740 342-3230	
New Lexington *(G-14920)*			
M & M Wintergreens Inc	D	216 398-1288	
Cleveland *(G-5891)*			
Marathon Mfg & Sup Co	D	330 343-2656	
New Philadelphia *(G-14972)*			
◆ **Mark Feldstein & Assoc Inc**	E	419 867-9500	
Sylvania *(G-17437)*			
Media Advertising Cons LLC	E	614 615-1398	
Columbus *(G-8052)*			
▼ **Merchandise Inc**	D	513 353-2200	
Miamitown *(G-14242)*			
Mid-States Packaging Inc	E	937 843-3243	
Lewistown *(G-12572)*			
▲ **Millennium Leather LLC**	E	201 541-7121	
Mason *(G-13620)*			
▲ **Mosser Glass Incorporated**	E	740 439-1827	
Cambridge *(G-2077)*			
Nannicola Wholesale Co	D	330 799-0888	
Youngstown *(G-20134)*			
◆ **Novelty Advertising Co Inc**	E	740 622-3113	
Coshocton *(G-9024)*			
▼ **Nutis Press Inc**	C	614 237-8626	
Columbus *(G-8218)*			
Pac Worldwide Corporation	D	800 535-0039	
Cincinnati *(G-4196)*			
▼ **Pacific MGT Holdings LLC**	E	440 324-3339	
Elyria *(G-10552)*			
Packaging & Pads R Us LLC	E	419 499-2905	
Milan *(G-14365)*			
Pactiv LLC	C	614 777-4019	
Columbus *(G-8411)*			
▼ **Pakmark LLC**	E	513 285-1040	
Fairfield *(G-10768)*			
▼ **Par International Inc**	E	614 529-1300	
Obetz *(G-15528)*			
▲ **Peter Graham Dunn Inc**	E	330 816-0035	
Dalton *(G-9146)*			
Petland Inc	E	740 775-2464	
Chillicothe *(G-2811)*			
Plastipak Packaging Inc	C	330 725-0205	
Medina *(G-13987)*			
▲ **Potter Inc**	E	419 636-5624	
Bryan *(G-1970)*			
Printpack Inc	C	513 891-7886	
Cincinnati *(G-4281)*			
▼ **Questar Solutions LLC**	E	330 966-2070	
North Canton *(G-15229)*			
Raco Industries LLC	D	513 984-2101	
Blue Ash *(G-1636)*			
▲ **Relay Gear Ltd**	E	888 735-2943	
Columbus *(G-8510)*			
Riser Foods Company	D	216 292-7000	
Bedford Heights *(G-1327)*			
Rosemark Paper Inc	D	614 443-0303	
Columbus *(G-8552)*			
Rrp Packaging	E	419 666-6119	
Perrysburg *(G-15915)*			
S & S Inc	E	216 383-1880	
Cleveland *(G-6354)*			
▲ **S S T Enterprises Inc**	D	330 343-2656	
New Philadelphia *(G-14979)*			
Samuel Strapping Systems Inc	D	740 522-2500	
Heath *(G-11709)*			
Scholastic Book Fairs Inc	D	513 714-1000	
West Chester *(G-18998)*			
Scioto Packaging Inc	E	614 491-1500	
Columbus *(G-8612)*			
Screen Works Inc	E	937 264-9111	
Dayton *(G-9754)*			
▲ **Shamrock Companies Inc**	D	440 899-9510	
Westlake *(G-19405)*			
▲ **Ship-Paq Inc**	E	513 860-0700	
Fairfield *(G-10780)*			
▲ **Shumsky Enterprises Inc**	D	937 223-2203	
Dayton *(G-9765)*			
Siemer Distributing Company	E	740 342-3230	
New Lexington *(G-14928)*			
SJS Packaging Group Inc	E	513 841-1351	
Cincinnati *(G-4489)*			
Skybox Packaging LLC	D	419 525-7209	
Mansfield *(G-13243)*			
Star Packaging Inc	E	614 564-9936	
Columbus *(G-8688)*			
▲ **Sterling Paper Co**	E	614 443-0303	
Columbus *(G-8697)*			
▲ **Storopack Inc**	E	513 874-0314	
West Chester *(G-19084)*			

Superior Packaging Toledo LLC	E	419 380-3335	
Toledo *(G-18056)*			
Systems Pack Inc	E	330 467-5729	
Macedonia *(G-13083)*			
Tahoma Enterprises Inc	E	330 745-9016	
Barberton *(G-969)*			
▼ **Tahoma Rubber & Plastics Inc**	E	330 745-9016	
Barberton *(G-970)*			
Third Dimension Inc		877 926-3223	
Geneva *(G-11247)*			
▲ **Trademark Global LLC**	D	440 960-6200	
Lorain *(G-12948)*			
Traichal Construction Company	E	800 255-3667	
Niles *(G-15172)*			
Two Happy Frogs Incorporated	E	330 633-1666	
Tallmadge *(G-17495)*			
US Safetygear Inc	E	330 898-1344	
Warren *(G-18764)*			
▲ **Waterbeds n Stuff Inc**	E	614 871-1171	
Grove City *(G-11483)*			
Welch Packaging LLC	E	937 223-3958	
Dayton *(G-9872)*			
Welch Packaging Group Inc	C	419 726-3491	
Toledo *(G-18148)*			
Welch Packaging Group Inc	D	216 447-9800	
Cleveland *(G-6660)*			
White Barn Candle Co	A	614 856-6000	
Reynoldsburg *(G-16338)*			
Wolverton Inc	E	330 220-3320	
Brunswick *(G-1949)*			
◆ **X-S Merchandise Inc**	E	216 524-5620	
Independence *(G-12142)*			

60 DEPOSITORY INSTITUTIONS

6011 Federal Reserve Banks

Federal Rsrve Bnk of Cleveland	A	216 579-2000	
Cleveland *(G-5523)*			
Federal Rsrve Bnk of Cleveland	C	513 721-4787	
Cincinnati *(G-3539)*			

6021 National Commercial Banks

Bank of America	C	614 882-4319	
Westerville *(G-19148)*			
Century National Bank	E	740 454-2521	
Zanesville *(G-20292)*			
Century National Bank	E	800 548-3557	
Zanesville *(G-20293)*			
Champaign National Bank Urbana	E	937 653-1100	
Urbana *(G-18424)*			
Champaign National Bank Urbana	E	614 798-1321	
Dublin *(G-10168)*			
Chase Equipment Finance Inc	C	800 678-2601	
Columbus *(G-6807)*			
Chase Equipment Finance Inc	C	614 213-2246	
Columbus *(G-6808)*			
Citizens Nat Bnk of Bluffton	E	419 358-8040	
Bluffton *(G-1690)*			
Citizens Nat Bnk of Bluffton	E	419 224-0400	
Lima *(G-12612)*			
Citizens Nat Bnk Urbana Ohio	E	937 653-1200	
Urbana *(G-18427)*			
Citizens National Bank	E	740 472-1696	
Woodsfield *(G-19672)*			
Civista Bank	E	419 744-3100	
Norwalk *(G-15427)*			
Colonial Banc Corp	E	937 456-5544	
Eaton *(G-10439)*			
Congressional Bank	E	614 441-9230	
Columbus *(G-7348)*			
Consumers Bancorp Inc	C	330 868-7701	
Minerva *(G-14517)*			
Consumers National Bank	E	330 868-7701	
Minerva *(G-14518)*			
Credit First NA	C	216 362-5000	
Brookpark *(G-1894)*			
Croghan Bancshares Inc	D	419 794-9399	
Maumee *(G-13778)*			
Eastern Ohio P-16	E	330 675-7623	
Warren *(G-18705)*			
Fairfield National Bank	E	740 653-7242	
Lancaster *(G-12400)*			
Farmers Bank & Savings Co Inc	E	740 992-0088	
Pomeroy *(G-16094)*			
Farmers National Bank	D	330 533-3341	
Canfield *(G-2137)*			
Farmers National Bank	D	330 544-7447	
Niles *(G-15156)*			
Farmers National Bank	D	330 682-1010	
Orrville *(G-15631)*			

Farmers National Bank	D	330 385-9200	
East Liverpool *(G-10403)*			
Farmers National Bank	D	330 682-1030	
Orrville *(G-15632)*			
First Capital Bancshares Inc	D	740 775-6777	
Chillicothe *(G-2779)*			
First Citizens Nat Bnk Inc	E	419 294-2351	
Upper Sandusky *(G-18407)*			
First Commonwealth Bank	E	740 548-3340	
Delaware *(G-9974)*			
First Commonwealth Bank	E	740 369-0048	
Delaware *(G-9975)*			
First Commonwealth Bank	E	614 336-2280	
Powell *(G-16194)*			
First Financial Bancorp	C	513 551-5640	
Cincinnati *(G-3555)*			
First Financial Bank	E	513 979-5800	
Cincinnati *(G-3556)*			
First Nat Bnk of Nelsonville	E	740 753-1941	
Nelsonville *(G-14831)*			
First National Bank Bellevue	E	419 483-7340	
Bellevue *(G-1378)*			
First National Bank of Pandora	E	419 384-3221	
Pandora *(G-15751)*			
First National Bank of Waverly	E	740 947-2136	
Waverly *(G-18818)*			
First National Bank PA	E	330 747-0292	
Youngstown *(G-20038)*			
First National Bnk of Dennison	E	740 922-2532	
Dennison *(G-10049)*			
First-Knox National Bank	C	740 399-5500	
Mount Vernon *(G-14766)*			
FNB Corporation	C	330 721-7484	
Medina *(G-13939)*			
FNB Corporation	E	440 439-2200	
Cleveland *(G-5550)*			
FNB Corporation	D	330 425-1818	
Twinsburg *(G-18267)*			
Futura Banc Corp	D	937 653-1167	
Urbana *(G-18434)*			
Greenville National Bank	E	937 548-1114	
Greenville *(G-11383)*			
Huntington Bancshares Inc	C	614 480-8300	
Columbus *(G-7781)*			
Huntington National Bank	A	330 996-6300	
Akron *(G-271)*			
Huntington National Bank	A	330 384-7201	
Akron *(G-272)*			
Huntington National Bank	E	330 384-7092	
Akron *(G-273)*			
Huntington National Bank	D	614 480-8300	
Columbus *(G-7788)*			
Huntington National Bank	E	330 343-6611	
Dover *(G-10083)*			
Huntington National Bank	E	740 452-8444	
Zanesville *(G-20319)*			
Huntington National Bank	E	216 515-6401	
Cleveland *(G-5725)*			
Huntington National Bank	C	513 762-1860	
Cincinnati *(G-3742)*			
Huntington National Bank	E	740 773-2681	
Chillicothe *(G-2792)*			
Huntington National Bank	E	419 226-8200	
Lima *(G-12662)*			
Huntington Technology Finance	C	614 480-5169	
Columbus *(G-7789)*			
Icx Corporation	E	330 656-3611	
Cleveland *(G-5733)*			
Jpmorgan Chase Bank Nat Assn	E	614 248-2410	
Reynoldsburg *(G-16312)*			
Jpmorgan Chase Bank Nat Assn	E	614 476-1910	
Columbus *(G-7870)*			
Jpmorgan Chase Bank Nat Assn	E	513 221-1040	
Cincinnati *(G-3836)*			
Jpmorgan Chase Bank Nat Assn	E	419 358-4055	
Bluffton *(G-1692)*			
Jpmorgan Chase Bank Nat Assn	E	513 985-5120	
Cincinnati *(G-3837)*			
Jpmorgan Chase Bank Nat Assn	A	740 363-8032	
Delaware *(G-9992)*			
Jpmorgan Chase Bank Nat Assn	E	419 394-2358	
Saint Marys *(G-16526)*			
Jpmorgan Chase Bank Nat Assn	E	419 294-4944	
Upper Sandusky *(G-18408)*			
Jpmorgan Chase Bank Nat Assn	E	740 676-2671	
Bellaire *(G-1334)*			
Jpmorgan Chase Bank Nat Assn	E	330 972-1905	
Cuyahoga Falls *(G-9104)*			
Jpmorgan Chase Bank Nat Assn	E	513 985-5350	
Milford *(G-14399)*			

Jpmorgan Chase Bank Nat Assn ....E 513 595-6450
Cincinnati (G-3839)

Jpmorgan Chase Bank Nat Assn ....E 440 442-7800
Cleveland (G-5805)

Jpmorgan Chase Bank Nat Assn ....E 330 972-1735
New Franklin (G-14910)

Jpmorgan Chase Bank Nat Assn ....E 330 287-5101
Wooster (G-19733)

Jpmorgan Chase Bank Nat Assn ....E 440 352-5491
Perry (G-15823)

Jpmorgan Chase Bank Nat Assn ....E 419 424-7570
Findlay (G-10929)

Jpmorgan Chase Bank Nat Assn ....A 937 534-8218
Dayton (G-9530)

Jpmorgan Chase Bank Nat Assn ....E 330 287-5101
Wooster (G-19734)

Jpmorgan Chase Bank Nat Assn ....E 419 946-3015
Mount Gilead (G-14727)

Jpmorgan Chase Bank Nat Assn ....E 419 586-6668
Celina (G-2596)

Jpmorgan Chase Bank Nat Assn ....B 440 352-5969
Painesville (G-15717)

Jpmorgan Chase Bank Nat Assn ....E 330 545-2551
Girard (G-11290)

Jpmorgan Chase Bank Nat Assn ....E 440 286-6111
Chardon (G-2699)

Jpmorgan Chase Bank Nat Assn ....E 330 972-1915
Akron (G-295)

Jpmorgan Chase Bank Nat Assn ....E 330 759-1750
Youngstown (G-20088)

Jpmorgan Chase Bank Nat Assn ....E 419 424-7512
Findlay (G-10930)

Jpmorgan Chase Bank Nat Assn ....D 614 248-5800
Westerville (G-19267)

Jpmorgan Chase Bank Nat Assn ....E 740 374-2263
Marietta (G-13341)

Jpmorgan Chase Bank Nat Assn ....E 614 248-7505
Westerville (G-19268)

Jpmorgan Chase Bank Nat Assn ....C 614 248-5800
Westerville (G-19269)

Jpmorgan Chase Bank Nat Assn ....E 419 739-3600
Wapakoneta (G-18647)

Jpmorgan Chase Bank Nat Assn ....E 614 759-8955
Reynoldsburg (G-16311)

Keybanc Capital Markets Inc ....B 800 553-2240
Cleveland (G-5826)

Keybank National Association ....B 800 539-2968
Cleveland (G-5827)

Keybank National Association ....E 216 689-8481
Cleveland (G-5828)

Kingston National Bank Inc ....E 740 642-2191
Kingston (G-12316)

Lcnb National Bank ....D 513 932-1414
Lebanon (G-12478)

Lcnb National Bank ....E 740 775-6777
Chillicothe (G-2800)

Lcnb National Bank ....D 937 456-5544
Eaton (G-10450)

Lorain National Bank ....C 440 244-6000
Lorain (G-12922)

Merchants National Bank ....E 937 393-1134
Hillsboro (G-11851)

Merrill Lynch Business ....E 513 791-5700
Blue Ash (G-1611)

National City Mortgage ....E 614 401-5030
Dublin (G-10286)

One Main Financial Services ....C 419 841-0785
Toledo (G-17963)

Pandora Bancshares Inc ....E 419 384-3221
Pandora (G-15754)

Park National Bank ....C 740 349-8451
Newark (G-15089)

Park National Bank ....E 614 228-0063
Columbus (G-8420)

Park National Bank ....C 740 349-8451
Newark (G-15090)

Park National Bank ....E 937 324-6800
Springfield (G-17094)

Peoples Bancorp Inc ....E 740 373-3155
Marietta (G-13367)

Peoples Bank ....E 937 748-0067
Springboro (G-16980)

Peoples Bank ....C 937 382-1441
Wilmington (G-19640)

Peoples Bank ....E 740 439-2767
Cambridge (G-2080)

Peoples Bank National Assn ....E 937 746-5733
Franklin (G-11037)

Peoples Nat Bnk of New Lxngton .....E 740 342-5111
New Lexington (G-14925)

PNC Bank National Association ....C 330 375-8342
Akron (G-387)

PNC Bank National Association ....E 740 349-8431
Newark (G-15092)

PNC Bank National Association ....B 513 721-2500
Cincinnati (G-4257)

PNC Bank National Association ....E 513 455-9522
Cincinnati (G-4258)

PNC Bank National Association ....E 419 621-2930
Sandusky (G-16632)

PNC Bank National Association ....C 330 854-0974
Canal Fulton (G-2096)

PNC Bank National Association ....B 419 259-5466
Toledo (G-17981)

PNC Bank National Association ....C 330 742-4426
Youngstown (G-20162)

PNC Bank National Association ....C 330 562-9700
Aurora (G-839)

Second National Bank ....E 937 548-2122
Greenville (G-11395)

Security National Bank & Tr Co ....C 740 426-6384
Newark (G-15097)

Security National Bank & Tr Co ....C 937 324-6800
Springfield (G-17110)

Standing Stone National Bank ....E 740 653-5115
Lancaster (G-12438)

State Bank and Trust Company ....E 419 485-5521
Montpelier (G-14618)

The First Central National Bnk ....E 937 663-4186
Saint Paris (G-16534)

The Liberty Nat Bankof Ada ....E 419 673-1217
Kenton (G-12288)

United Bank National Assn ....E 419 562-3040
Bucyrus (G-2003)

Unity National Bank ....E 937 773-0752
Piqua (G-16033)

◆ US Bank National Association ....A 513 632-4234
Cincinnati (G-4738)

US Bank National Association ....E 740 353-4151
Portsmouth (G-16178)

US Bank National Association ....E 513 979-1000
Cincinnati (G-4739)

US Bank National Association ....E 513 458-2844
Cincinnati (G-4740)

US Bank National Association ....D 937 873-7845
Fairborn (G-10685)

US Bank National Association ....E 937 335-8351
Troy (G-18236)

US Bank National Association ....E 937 498-1131
Sidney (G-16803)

Waterford Bank National Assn ....D 419 720-3900
Toledo (G-18147)

Wells Fargo Bank National Assn ....D 513 424-6640
Middletown (G-14339)

6022 State Commercial Banks

Andover Bancorp Inc ....E 440 293-7605
Andover (G-603)

Apple Creek Banking Co (inc) ....E 330 698-2631
Apple Creek (G-617)

Buckeye Community Bank ....E 440 233-8800
Lorain (G-12888)

Chemical Bank ....E 440 779-0807
North Olmsted (G-15281)

Chemical Bank ....D 330 314-1380
Youngstown (G-19987)

Citizens Bank Company ....E 740 984-2381
Beverly (G-1461)

Citizens Bank National Assn ....D 330 580-1913
Canton (G-2255)

Citizens Bank of Ashville Ohio ....E 740 983-2511
Ashville (G-761)

Citizens Bnk of Logan Ohio Inc ....E 740 380-2561
Logan (G-12833)

Civista Bank ....D 419 625-4121
Sandusky (G-16586)

Civista Bank ....E 419 744-3100
Norwalk (G-15427)

CNB Bank ....E 419 562-7040
Bucyrus (G-1983)

Commercial Svgs Bank Millersbu ......E 330 674-9015
Millersburg (G-14466)

Crogan Colonial Bank ....E 419 483-2541
Bellevue (G-1375)

Croghan Colonial Bank ....E 419 332-7301
Fremont (G-11067)

CSB Bancorp Inc ....E 330 674-9015
Millersburg (G-14473)

Farmers & Merchants State Bank ......E 419 446-2501
Archbold (G-630)

Farmers Citizens Bank ....E 419 562-7040
Bucyrus (G-1990)

Farmers National Bank ....D 330 544-7447
Niles (G-15156)

Federal Home Ln Bnk Cincinnati ....D 513 852-5719
Cincinnati (G-3537)

▲ Fifth Third Bancorp ....D 800 972-3030
Cincinnati (G-3546)

Fifth Third Bank ....C 513 574-4457
Cincinnati (G-3547)

Fifth Third Bank ....C 440 984-2402
Amherst (G-587)

▲ Fifth Third Bank ....A 513 579-5203
Cincinnati (G-3548)

Fifth Third Bank ....E 419 259-7820
Toledo (G-17733)

Fifth Third Bank ....D 513 579-5203
Cincinnati (G-3549)

Fifth Third Bank ....D 330 686-0511
Cuyahoga Falls (G-9095)

Fifth Third Bank of NW Ohio ....B 419 259-7820
Toledo (G-17734)

Fifth Third Bank of Sthrn OH ....E 937 840-5353
Hillsboro (G-11839)

Fifth Third Bnk of Columbus OH ....A 614 744-7553
Columbus (G-7576)

First Commonwealth Bank ....C 740 657-7000
Lewis Center (G-12542)

First Federal Bank of Midwest ....E 419 695-1055
Delphos (G-10026)

First Financial Bank ....C 877 322-9530
Cincinnati (G-3557)

First National Bank PA ....E 330 747-0292
Youngstown (G-20038)

First State Bank ....E 937 695-0331
Winchester (G-19661)

Fort Jennings State Bank ....E 419 286-2527
Fort Jennings (G-10983)

Genoa Banking Company ....E 419 855-8381
Genoa (G-11255)

Heartland Bank ....E 614 337-4600
Gahanna (G-11125)

Henry County Bank ....E 419 599-1065
Napoleon (G-14808)

Hicksville Bank Inc ....E 419 542-7726
Hicksville (G-11729)

Hocking Vly Bnk of Athens Co ....E 740 592-4441
Athens (G-784)

Hometown Bank ....E 330 673-9827
Kent (G-12236)

Huntington National Bank ....E 330 742-7013
Youngstown (G-20072)

Huntington National Bank ....E 740 695-3323
Saint Clairsville (G-16489)

Huntington National Bank ....E 419 782-5050
Defiance (G-9918)

Independence Bank ....E 216 447-1444
Cleveland (G-5742)

◆ Jpmorgan Chase Bank Nat Assn ......A 614 436-3055
Columbus (G-6818)

Jpmorgan Chase Bank Nat Assn ....E 513 826-2317
Blue Ash (G-1591)

Jpmorgan Chase Bank Nat Assn ....E 216 781-2127
Columbus (G-7871)

Jpmorgan Chase Bank Nat Assn ....E 740 423-4111
Belpre (G-1405)

Jpmorgan Chase Bank Nat Assn ....E 614 248-5391
Columbus (G-7872)

Jpmorgan Chase Bank Nat Assn ....E 614 248-2083
Columbus (G-7874)

Jpmorgan Chase Bank Nat Assn ....E 216 781-4437
Cleveland (G-5806)

Jpmorgan Chase Bank Nat Assn ....E 614 759-8955
Reynoldsburg (G-16311)

Keybank National Association ....B 800 539-2968
Cleveland (G-5827)

Killbuck Savings Bank Co Inc ....E 330 276-4881
Killbuck (G-12310)

Liberty Savings Bank FSB ....C 937 382-1000
Wilmington (G-19629)

Mechanics Bank ....E 419 524-0831
Mansfield (G-13213)

Minster Bank ....E 419 628-2351
Minster (G-14538)

North Side Bank and Trust Co ....D 513 542-7800
Cincinnati (G-4126)

North Side Bank and Trust Co ....D 513 533-8000
Cincinnati (G-4127)

North Valley Bank ....E 740 452-7920
Zanesville (G-20347)

SIC

Northwest Bank ....B 330 342-4018
  Hudson *(G-12000)*

Northwest Ohio Chapter Cfma ....E 419 891-1040
  Maumee *(G-13824)*

Ohio Valley Bank Company ....D 740 446-2168
  Gallipolis *(G-11206)*

Ohio Valley Bank Company ....C 740 446-2631
  Gallipolis *(G-11207)*

Ohio Valley Bank Company ....E 740 446-1646
  Gallipolis *(G-11208)*

Ohio Valley Bank Company ....E 740 446-2631
  Gallipolis *(G-11209)*

Old Fort Banking Company ....D 419 447-4790
  Tiffin *(G-17530)*

Osgood State Bank (inc) ....E 419 582-2681
  Osgood *(G-15653)*

Peoples Bank ....C 740 373-3155
  Marietta *(G-13368)*

Peoples Bank ....E 740 286-6773
  Wellston *(G-18854)*

Portage Community Bank Inc ....D 330 296-8090
  Ravenna *(G-16254)*

Richland Trust Company ....D 419 525-8700
  Mansfield *(G-13240)*

Richwood Banking Company ....E 740 943-2317
  Richwood *(G-16397)*

Savings Bank ....E 740 474-3191
  Circleville *(G-4848)*

Sb Financial Group Inc ....C 419 783-8950
  Defiance *(G-9939)*

◆ State Bank and Trust Company ......E 419 783-8950
  Defiance *(G-9941)*

State Bank and Trust Company ....E 419 485-5521
  Montpelier *(G-14618)*

The Cortland Sav & Bnkg Co ....D 330 637-8040
  Cortland *(G-8994)*

The Liberty Nat Bankof Ada ....E 419 673-1217
  Kenton *(G-12288)*

The Middlefield Banking Co ....E 440 632-1666
  Middlefield *(G-14277)*

The Peoples Bank Co Inc ....E 419 678-2385
  Coldwater *(G-6765)*

The Peoples Bank Co Inc ....E 419 678-2385
  Coldwater *(G-6766)*

Unified Bank ....E 740 633-0445
  Martins Ferry *(G-13479)*

Union Bank Company ....E 740 387-2265
  Marion *(G-13467)*

Vinton County Nat Bnk McArthur ....E 740 596-2525
  Mc Arthur *(G-13892)*

Wayne Savings Community Bank ....D 330 264-5767
  Wooster *(G-19780)*

Wesbanco Inc ....E 740 532-0263
  Ironton *(G-12167)*

Wesbanco Bank Inc ....D 740 425-1927
  Barnesville *(G-980)*

Wesbanco Bank Inc ....E 513 741-5766
  Cincinnati *(G-4778)*

6029 Commercial Banks, NEC

Croghan Bancshares Inc ....D 419 794-9399
  Maumee *(G-13778)*

Farm Credit Mid-America ....E 740 441-9312
  Albany *(G-510)*

Farmers Savings Bank ....E 330 648-2441
  Spencer *(G-16954)*

First Merchants Bank ....E 614 486-9000
  Columbus *(G-7587)*

FNB Corporation ....D 330 425-1818
  Twinsburg *(G-18267)*

Huntington Capital I ....C 614 480-4038
  Columbus *(G-7782)*

Huntington Insurance Inc ....E 419 429-4627
  Findlay *(G-10925)*

Huntington National Bank ....C 513 762-1860
  Cincinnati *(G-3742)*

Huntington National Bank ....E 330 742-7013
  Youngstown *(G-20072)*

Huntington National Bank ....E 330 343-6611
  Dover *(G-10083)*

Huntington National Bank ....E 740 773-2681
  Chillicothe *(G-2792)*

Huntington National Bank ....E 614 480-4293
  Columbus *(G-7786)*

Huntington National Bank ....E 740 452-8444
  Zanesville *(G-20319)*

▲ Huntington National Bank ....B 614 480-4293
  Columbus *(G-7787)*

Huntington National Bank ....E 740 695-3323
  Saint Clairsville *(G-16489)*

Huntington National Bank ....E 419 226-8200
  Lima *(G-12662)*

Huntington National Bank ....E 216 621-1717
  Cleveland *(G-5724)*

Huntington National Bank ....E 216 515-6401
  Cleveland *(G-5725)*

Huntington National Bank ....E 419 782-5050
  Defiance *(G-9918)*

Jpmorgan Chase Bank Nat Assn ......E 614 759-8955
  Reynoldsburg *(G-16311)*

Jpmorgan Chase Bank Nat Assn ......E 513 784-0770
  Cincinnati *(G-3838)*

Jpmorgan Chase Bank Nat Assn ......E 330 364-7242
  New Philadelphia *(G-14968)*

Jpmorgan Chase Bank Nat Assn ......E 740 382-7362
  Marion *(G-13426)*

Jpmorgan Chase Bank Nat Assn ......E 330 650-0476
  Hudson *(G-11989)*

Jpmorgan Chase Bank Nat Assn ......B 843 679-3653
  Columbus *(G-7873)*

Jpmorgan Chase Bank Nat Assn ......E 330 325-7855
  Randolph *(G-16231)*

Jpmorgan Chase Bank Nat Assn ......E 614 920-4182
  Canal Winchester *(G-2111)*

Jpmorgan Chase Bank Nat Assn ......E 614 834-3120
  Pickerington *(G-15960)*

Jpmorgan Chase Bank Nat Assn ......E 614 853-2999
  Galloway *(G-11221)*

Jpmorgan Chase Bank Nat Assn ......E 614 248-3315
  Powell *(G-16199)*

Jpmorgan Chase Bank Nat Assn ......E 740 657-8906
  Lewis Center *(G-12547)*

Jpmorgan Chase Bank Nat Assn ......E 216 524-0600
  Seven Hills *(G-16676)*

Jpmorgan Chase Bank Nat Assn ......E 440 277-1038
  Lorain *(G-12909)*

Jpmorgan Chase Bank Nat Assn ......E 330 722-6626
  Medina *(G-13961)*

MB Financial Inc ....D 937 283-2027
  Wilmington *(G-19634)*

PNC Bank National Association ....E 330 742-4426
  Youngstown *(G-20162)*

PNC Bank National Association ....C 330 562-9700
  Aurora *(G-839)*

Raymond James Fincl Svcs Inc ....E 419 586-5121
  Celina *(G-2608)*

Republic Bank ....B 513 793-7666
  Blue Ash *(G-1644)*

UBS Financial Services Inc ....E 440 414-2740
  Westlake *(G-19416)*

Wesbanco Inc ....E 614 208-7298
  Columbus *(G-8888)*

Westfield Bank Fsb ....E 800 368-8930
  Westfield Center *(G-19309)*

6035 Federal Savings Institutions

Belmont Federal Sav & Ln Assn ....E 740 676-1165
  Bellaire *(G-1331)*

Century National Bank ....E 740 455-7330
  Zanesville *(G-20294)*

Chemical Bank ....E 513 232-0800
  Cincinnati *(G-3176)*

Chemical Bank ....E 440 926-2191
  Grafton *(G-11316)*

Chemical Bank ....E 330 314-1395
  Poland *(G-16082)*

Chemical Bank ....E 440 323-7451
  Elyria *(G-10488)*

Chemical Bank ....D 330 298-0510
  Ravenna *(G-16235)*

Cheviot Mutual Holding Company ......E 513 661-0457
  Cincinnati *(G-3179)*

Cincinnatus Savings & Loan ....E 513 661-6903
  Cincinnati *(G-3281)*

Citizens Federal Sav & Ln Assn ....E 937 593-0015
  Bellefontaine *(G-1348)*

Eagle Financial Bancorp Inc ....E 513 574-0700
  Cincinnati *(G-3468)*

Fairfield Federal Sav Ln Assn ....E 740 653-3863
  Lancaster *(G-12395)*

Ffd Financial Corporation ....D 330 364-7777
  Dover *(G-10077)*

First Defiance Financial Corp ....E 419 353-8611
  Bowling Green *(G-1731)*

First Fdral Sav Ln Assn Galion ....D 419 468-1518
  Galion *(G-11170)*

First Fdral Sav Ln Assn Lkwood ....C 216 221-7300
  Lakewood *(G-12343)*

First Fdral Sav Ln Assn Lorain ....D 440 282-6188
  Lorain *(G-12904)*

First Fdral Sav Ln Assn Newark ....E 740 345-3494
  Newark *(G-15033)*

First Fdral Sving Ln Assn Dlta ....E 419 822-3131
  Delta *(G-10043)*

First Federal Bank of Midwest ....E 419 782-5015
  Defiance *(G-9914)*

First Federal Bank of Midwest ....E 419 695-1055
  Delphos *(G-10026)*

First Federal Bank of Midwest ....D 419 855-8326
  Genoa *(G-11253)*

First Federal Bank of Ohio ....D 419 468-1518
  Galion *(G-11171)*

First Financial Bancorp ....C 513 551-5640
  Cincinnati *(G-3555)*

Greenville Federal ....E 937 548-4158
  Greenville *(G-11381)*

Guardian Savings Bank ....E 513 942-3535
  West Chester *(G-18938)*

Guardian Savings Bank ....E 513 528-8787
  Cincinnati *(G-3661)*

Harrison Building and Ln Assn ....E 513 367-2015
  Harrison *(G-11669)*

Liberty Capital Inc ....D 937 382-1000
  Wilmington *(G-19628)*

New York Community Bank ....E 440 734-7040
  North Olmsted *(G-15300)*

New York Community Bank ....E 216 741-7333
  Cleveland *(G-6063)*

New York Community Bank ....A 216 736-3480
  Cleveland *(G-6064)*

Peoples Bancorp Inc ....E 740 947-4372
  Waverly *(G-18819)*

Peoples Bancorp Inc ....D 740 574-9100
  Wheelersburg *(G-19437)*

Peoples Bancorp Inc ....D 513 793-2422
  Cincinnati *(G-4228)*

Peoples Bancorp Inc ....E 513 271-9100
  Cincinnati *(G-4229)*

Peoples Bank ....D 740 354-3177
  Portsmouth *(G-16157)*

Peoples Federal Sav & Ln Assn ....E 937 492-6129
  Sidney *(G-16791)*

Peoples Savings and Loan Co ....E 419 562-6896
  Bucyrus *(G-2000)*

Peoples-Sidney Financial Corp ....E 937 492-6129
  Sidney *(G-16792)*

Richwood Banking Company ....E 937 390-0470
  Springfield *(G-17101)*

Talmer Bank and Trust ....E 330 726-3396
  Canfield *(G-2159)*

Third Federal Savings ....B 800 844-7333
  Cleveland *(G-6522)*

Third Federal Savings ....E 440 716-1865
  North Olmsted *(G-15314)*

Third Federal Savings ....E 440 843-6300
  Cleveland *(G-6524)*

Union Savings Bank ....D 937 434-1254
  Dayton *(G-9829)*

Wayne Savings Bancshares Inc ....C 330 264-5767
  Wooster *(G-19779)*

Wesbanco Inc ....E 740 532-0263
  Ironton *(G-12167)*

6036 Savings Institutions, Except Federal

Belmont Savings Bank ....E 740 695-0140
  Saint Clairsville *(G-16478)*

Fort Jennings State Bank ....E 419 286-2527
  Fort Jennings *(G-10983)*

Geauga Savings Bank ....E 440 564-9441
  Newbury *(G-15121)*

Harrison Building and Ln Assn ....E 513 367-2015
  Harrison *(G-11669)*

Home Savings Bank ....D 330 499-1900
  North Canton *(G-15211)*

Huntington National Bank ....E 740 335-3771
  Wshngtn CT Hs *(G-19876)*

Resolute Bank ....D 419 868-1750
  Maumee *(G-13844)*

The Peoples Savings and Ln Co ....E 937 653-1600
  Urbana *(G-18445)*

Union Savings Bank ....D 937 434-1254
  Dayton *(G-9829)*

United Community Fincl Corp ....C 330 742-0500
  Youngstown *(G-20231)*

6061 Federal Credit Unions

Advantage Credit Union Inc ....E 419 529-5603
  Ontario *(G-15543)*

American Chem Soc Fderal Cr Un ......A 614 447-3675
  Columbus *(G-6914)*

Aur Group Financial Credit Un ....E 513 737-0508
  Hamilton *(G-11558)*
Aurgroup Financial Credit Un ....D 513 942-4422
  Fairfield *(G-10697)*
B F G Federal Credit Union ....D 330 374-2990
  Akron *(G-84)*
Bayer Heritage Federal Cr Un ....E 740 929-2015
  Hebron *(G-11710)*
Best Reward Credit Union ....E 216 367-8000
  Cleveland *(G-5059)*
Bmi Federal Credit Union ....D 614 707-4000
  Dublin *(G-10147)*
Bmi Federal Credit Union ....D 614 298-8527
  Columbus *(G-7049)*
C E S Credit Union Inc ....E 740 397-1136
  Mount Vernon *(G-14751)*
Canton School Employees Fed Cr ....D 330 452-9801
  Canton *(G-2243)*
Century Federal Credit Union ....E 216 535-3600
  Cleveland *(G-5159)*
Chaco Credit Union Inc ....E 513 785-3500
  Hamilton *(G-11576)*
Cincinnati Central Cr Un Inc ....D 513 241-2050
  Cincinnati *(G-3232)*
Cinco Credit Union ....E 513 281-9988
  Cincinnati *(G-3284)*
Cinfed Federal Credit Union ....D 513 333-3800
  Cincinnati *(G-3290)*
Clyde-Findlay Area Cr Un Inc ....E 419 547-7781
  Clyde *(G-6742)*
Columbus Municipal Employees ....E 614 224-8890
  Columbus *(G-7300)*
Corporate One Fed Cr Un ....D 614 825-9314
  Columbus *(G-6810)*
Day Air Credit Union Inc ....E 937 643-2160
  Dayton *(G-9348)*
Day-Met Credit Union Inc ....E 937 236-2562
  Moraine *(G-14640)*
Desco Federal Credit Union ....D 740 354-7791
  Portsmouth *(G-16135)*
Dover Phila Federal Cr Un ....E 330 364-8874
  Dover *(G-10076)*
Fairview Hlth Sys Fderal Cr Un ....A 216 476-7000
  Cleveland *(G-5507)*
Firelands Federal Credit Union ....E 419 483-4180
  Bellevue *(G-1377)*
First Day Fincl Federal Cr Un ....E 937 222-4546
  Dayton *(G-9435)*
First Miami Student Credit Un ....E 513 529-1251
  Oxford *(G-15677)*
Fremont Federal Credit Union ....C 419 334-4434
  Fremont *(G-11076)*
General Electric Credit Union ....D 513 243-4328
  Cincinnati *(G-3612)*
Glass City Federal Credit Un ....E 419 887-1000
  Maumee *(G-13797)*
Honda Federal Credit Union ....E 937 642-6000
  Marysville *(G-13503)*
Lima Superior Federal Cr Un ....C 419 223-9746
  Lima *(G-12688)*
Miami University ....E 513 529-1251
  Oxford *(G-15682)*
Midwest Cmnty Federal Cr Un ....E 419 782-9856
  Defiance *(G-9931)*
Ohio Catholic Federal Cr Un ....E 216 663-6800
  Cleveland *(G-6118)*
Ohio Educational Credit Union ....E 216 621-6296
  Seven Hills *(G-16678)*
Ohio Healthcare Federal Cr Un ....E 614 737-6034
  Dublin *(G-10297)*
River Valley Credit Union Inc ....E 937 859-1970
  Miamisburg *(G-14214)*
Saint Francis De Sales Church ....E 440 884-2319
  Cleveland *(G-6364)*
School Employees Lorain County ......E 440 324-3400
  Elyria *(G-10561)*
Sun Federal Credit Union ....E 800 786-0945
  Maumee *(G-13856)*
Sun Federal Credit Union ....D 419 537-0200
  Toledo *(G-18052)*
Superior Credit Union Inc ....E 419 738-4512
  Wapakoneta *(G-18654)*
Telhio Credit Union Inc ....E 614 221-3233
  Columbus *(G-8737)*
Telhio Credit Union Inc ....E 614 221-3233
  Columbus *(G-8738)*
True Core Federal Credit Union ....E 740 345-6608
  Newark *(G-15104)*
Vacationland Federal Credit Un ....E 440 967-5155
  Sandusky *(G-16654)*

6062 State Credit Unions

Atomic Credit Union Inc ....E 740 289-5060
  Piketon *(G-15971)*
Aur Group Financial Credit Un ....E 513 737-0508
  Hamilton *(G-11558)*
Buckeye State Credit Union ....D 330 253-9197
  Akron *(G-113)*
C E S Credit Union Inc ....E 561 203-5443
  Loudonville *(G-12954)*
C E S Credit Union Inc ....E 740 892-3323
  Utica *(G-18454)*
Cme Federal Credit Union ....E 614 224-4388
  Columbus *(G-7235)*
Credit Union of Ohio Inc ....E 614 487-6650
  Hilliard *(G-11757)*
Cuso Corporation ....D 513 984-2876
  Cincinnati *(G-3390)*
Directions Credit Union Inc ....D 419 720-4769
  Sylvania *(G-17419)*
Directions Credit Union Inc ....E 419 524-7113
  Mansfield *(G-13167)*
Erie Shores Credit Union Inc ....E 419 897-8110
  Maumee *(G-13787)*
Firefighters Cmnty Cr Un Inc ....E 216 621-4644
  Cleveland *(G-5527)*
Greater Cincinnati Credit Un ....E 513 559-1234
  Mason *(G-13589)*
Hancock Federal Credit Union ....E 419 420-0338
  Findlay *(G-10917)*
Homeland Credit Union Inc ....D 740 775-3024
  Chillicothe *(G-2787)*
Homeland Credit Union Inc ....E 740 775-3331
  Chillicothe *(G-2788)*
Kemba Credit Union Inc ....D 513 762-5070
  West Chester *(G-18955)*
Kemba Financial Credit Union ....D 614 235-2395
  Columbus *(G-7890)*
Midusa Credit Union ....D 513 420-8640
  Middletown *(G-14313)*
Midusa Credit Union ....E 513 420-8640
  Middletown *(G-14351)*
Seven Seventeen Credit Un Inc ....C 330 372-8100
  Warren *(G-18741)*
Seven Seventeen Credit Un Inc ....E 330 372-8100
  Warren *(G-18742)*
Sun Federal Credit Union ....D 419 537-0200
  Toledo *(G-18052)*
Taleris Credit Union Inc ....E 216 739-2300
  Independence *(G-12128)*
Universal 1 Credit Union Inc ....D 800 762-9555
  Dayton *(G-9835)*
Wright-Patt Credit Union Inc ....B 937 912-7000
  Beavercreek *(G-1200)*

6099 Functions Related To Deposit Banking, NEC

Allied Cash Holdings LLC ....D 305 371-3141
  Cincinnati *(G-2928)*
Bannockburn Global Forex LLC ....E 513 386-7400
  Cincinnati *(G-3016)*
Buckeye Check Cashing Inc ....C 614 798-5900
  Dublin *(G-10152)*
Cashland Financial Svcs Inc ....E 937 253-7842
  Dayton *(G-9284)*
Checksmart Financial Company ....E 614 798-5900
  Dublin *(G-10170)*
Chemical Bank ....D 330 965-5806
  Youngstown *(G-19986)*
CNG Financial Corporation ....B 513 336-7735
  Cincinnati *(G-3316)*
Community Choice Financial Inc ....D 440 602-9922
  Willoughby *(G-19515)*
Community Choice Financial Inc ....E 614 798-5900
  Dublin *(G-10185)*
First Data Gvrnment Sltions LP ....D 513 489-9599
  Blue Ash *(G-1562)*
Huntington National Bank ....D 614 480-0067
  Columbus *(G-7785)*
Huntington National Bank ....D 614 336-4620
  Columbus *(G-10249)*
◆ Jpmorgan Chase Bank Nat Assn ......A 614 436-3055
  Columbus *(G-6818)*
Klarna Inc ....E 614 615-4705
  Columbus *(G-7909)*
Mary C Enterprises Inc ....D 937 253-6169
  Dayton *(G-9588)*
National Consumer Coop Bnk ....E 937 393-4246
  Hillsboro *(G-11852)*
Nationwide Biweekly ADM Inc ....C 937 376-5800
  Xenia *(G-19921)*

PNC Bank-Atm ....E 937 865-6800
  Miamisburg *(G-14206)*
Ptc Holdings Inc ....B 216 771-6960
  Cleveland *(G-6267)*
Sack n Save Inc ....E 740 382-2464
  Marion *(G-13458)*
Southwstern PCF Spclty Fin Inc ....E 513 336-7735
  Cincinnati *(G-4508)*

61 NONDEPOSITORY CREDIT INSTITUTIONS

6111 Federal Credit Agencies

Columbus Metro Federal Cr Un ....E 614 239-0210
  Columbus *(G-7297)*
Columbus Metro Federal Cr Un ....E 614 239-0210
  Columbus *(G-7298)*
Federal Home Ln Bnk Cincinnati ....A 513 852-7500
  Cincinnati *(G-3536)*
Hanna Holdings Inc ....E 440 971-5600
  North Royalton *(G-15358)*
National Cooperative Bank NA ....D 937 393-4246
  Hillsboro *(G-11853)*

6141 Personal Credit Institutions

722 Redemption Funding Inc ....E 513 679-8302
  Cincinnati *(G-2885)*
Affordable Cars & Finance Inc ....E 440 777-2424
  North Olmsted *(G-15277)*
Caliber Home Loans Inc ....E 937 435-5363
  Dayton *(G-9272)*
Central Credit Corp ....D 614 856-5840
  Reynoldsburg *(G-16289)*
Citizens Capital Markets Inc ....E 216 589-0900
  Cleveland *(G-5184)*
Dfs Corporate Services LLC ....E 614 283-2499
  New Albany *(G-14851)*
Education Loan Servicing Corp ....D 216 706-8130
  Cleveland *(G-5467)*
Farm Credit Mid-America ....E 740 441-9312
  Albany *(G-510)*
General Electric Company ....A 330 433-5163
  Canton *(G-2324)*
General Revenue Corporation ....B 513 469-1472
  Mason *(G-13586)*
Homeland Credit Union Inc ....E 740 775-3331
  Chillicothe *(G-2788)*
Howard Hanna Smythe Cramer ....D 330 725-4137
  Medina *(G-13952)*
Macys Cr & Customer Svcs Inc ....A 513 398-5221
  Mason *(G-13613)*
▼ Mtd Holdings Inc ....B 330 225-2600
  Valley City *(G-18467)*
PNC Bank National Association ....D 440 546-6760
  Brecksville *(G-1797)*
Security Nat Auto Accptnce LLC ....C 513 459-8118
  Mason *(G-13637)*
Security National Bank & Tr Co ....C 937 324-6800
  Springfield *(G-17110)*
Student Loan Strategies LLC ....E 513 645-5400
  Cincinnati *(G-4550)*
Tebo Financial Services Inc ....E 234 207-2500
  Canton *(G-2507)*
United Consumer Fincl Svcs Co ....C 440 835-3230
  Cleveland *(G-6570)*

6153 Credit Institutions, Short-Term Business

Ally Financial Inc ....E 330 533-7300
  Canfield *(G-2130)*
Business Backer LLC ....E 513 792-6866
  Cincinnati *(G-3095)*
General Electric Company ....C 440 255-0930
  Mentor *(G-14050)*
General Electric Company ....E 937 534-2000
  Dayton *(G-9459)*
General Electric Company ....A 937 534-6920
  Dayton *(G-9458)*
Lakewood Acceptance Corp ....E 216 658-1234
  Cleveland *(G-5850)*
Morgan Stanley ....E 330 670-4600
  Akron *(G-341)*
Preferred Capital Lending Inc ....E 216 472-1391
  Cleveland *(G-6230)*
Relentless Recovery Inc ....D 216 621-8333
  Cleveland *(G-6300)*
Scott Fetzer Financial Group ....E 440 892-3000
  Cleveland *(G-6380)*

S I C

Sears Roebuck and Co ....C 440 845-0120
Cleveland **(G-6385)**
Sherman Financial Group LLC ....E 513 707-3000
Cincinnati **(G-4470)**
Unifund Ccr LLC ....D 513 489-8877
Blue Ash **(G-1671)**
Unifund Corporation ....E 513 489-8877
Blue Ash **(G-1672)**

6159 Credit Institutions, Misc Business

BMW Financial Services Na LLC ....E 614 718-6900
Hilliard **(G-11747)**
BMW Financial Services Na LLC ....C 614 718-6900
Dublin **(G-10148)**
Ford Motor Company ....E 513 573-1101
Mason **(G-13580)**
Kempthorn Motors Inc ....D 330 452-6511
Canton **(G-2366)**
Keybank National Association ....B 800 539-2968
Cleveland **(G-5827)**
Kings Cove Automotive LLC ....D 513 677-0177
Fairfield **(G-10744)**
Klaben Leasing and Sales Inc ....D 330 673-9971
Kent **(G-12245)**
Lancaster Pollard Mrtg Co LLC ....D 614 224-8800
Columbus **(G-7947)**
N C B International Department ....D 216 488-7990
Cleveland **(G-6033)**
◆ Ohio Machinery Co ....C 440 526-6200
Broadview Heights **(G-1840)**
PNC Equipment Finance LLC ....D 513 421-9191
Cincinnati **(G-4259)**
Reynolds and Reynolds Company ....A 937 485-2000
Kettering **(G-12299)**
Ricoh Usa Inc ....D 513 984-9898
Sharonville **(G-16730)**
Security Nat Auto Accptnce LLC ....C 513 459-8118
Mason **(G-13637)**
Summit Funding Group Inc ....D 513 489-1222
Mason **(G-13642)**

6162 Mortgage Bankers & Loan Correspondents

American Eagle Mortgage Co LLC ....E 440 988-2900
Lorain **(G-12879)**
American Midwest Mortgage Corp.......E 440 882-5210
Cleveland **(G-4958)**
Amerifirst Financial Corp.......................D 216 452-5120
Lakewood **(G-12335)**
Ameristate Bancorp Inc..........................E 330 965-9551
Youngstown **(G-19955)**
Bank England Mortgage Corp ....D 440 327-5626
North Ridgeville **(G-15321)**
Broadview Mortgage Company ....D 614 854-7000
Powell **(G-16187)**
Chase Manhattan Mortgage Corp.........C 614 422-7982
Columbus **(G-7180)**
Chase Manhattan Mortgage Corp.........A 614 422-6900
Columbus **(G-7181)**
Equitable Mortgage Corporation ....E 614 764-1232
Columbus **(G-7524)**
Fairway Independent Mrtg Corp ....E 513 367-6344
Harrison **(G-11667)**
Fairway Independent Mrtg Corp ....E 614 930-6552
Columbus **(G-7556)**
Farm Credit Mid-America ....E 740 441-9312
Albany **(G-510)**
Fifth Third Bank of Sthrn OH ....E 937 840-5353
Hillsboro **(G-11839)**
First Day Fincl Federal Cr Un ....E 937 222-4564
Dayton **(G-9435)**
First Federal Bank of Midwest...............E 419 695-1055
Delphos **(G-10026)**
First Ohio Banc & Lending Inc ....B 216 642-8900
Cleveland **(G-5537)**
First Ohio Home Finance Inc ....E 937 322-3396
Springfield **(G-17039)**
First Union Banc Corp ....E 330 896-1222
Uniontown **(G-18371)**
Firstmerit Mortgage Corp.......................D 330 478-3400
Canton **(G-2314)**
FNB Corporation ....D 330 425-1818
Twinsburg **(G-18267)**
G & G Investment LLC ....D 513 984-0300
Blue Ash **(G-1566)**
Hallmark Home Mortgage LLC...............E 614 568-1960
Columbus **(G-7711)**
Huntington National Bank ....C 513 762-1860
Cincinnati **(G-3742)**

Huntington National Bank ....E 740 773-2681
Chillicothe **(G-2792)**
Huntington National Bank ....E 419 226-8200
Lima **(G-12662)**
◆ Jpmorgan Chase Bank Nat Assn ....A 614 436-3055
Columbus **(G-6818)**
Lancaster Pollard Mrtg Co LLC ....D 614 224-8800
Columbus **(G-7947)**
Liberty Capital Services LLC ....E 614 505-0620
Worthington **(G-19824)**
Liberty Mortgage Company Inc ....E 614 224-4000
Columbus **(G-7971)**
M/I Financial LLC ....D 614 418-8650
Columbus **(G-8005)**
M/I Homes Inc ....B 614 418-8000
Columbus **(G-8006)**
MB Financial Inc ....E 937 283-2027
Wilmington **(G-19634)**
Mortgage Now Inc ....E 800 245-1050
Cleveland **(G-6013)**
National City Mortgage Inc ....A 937 910-1200
Miamisburg **(G-14196)**
Nations Lending Corporation ....E 440 842-4817
Westlake **(G-19377)**
Nations Lending Corporation ....E 440 842-4817
Independence **(G-12102)**
Nationstar Mortgage LLC ....E 614 985-9500
Columbus **(G-8142)**
Nfgm Inc ....D 800 236-2600
Dublin **(G-10290)**
Northern Ohio Investment Co ....D 419 885-8300
Sylvania **(G-17438)**
Old Rpblic Ttle Nthrn Ohio LLC ....B 216 524-5700
Independence **(G-12106)**
Pgim Inc ....E 419 331-6604
Lima **(G-12721)**
PNC Mortgage Company ....D 412 762-2000
Miamisburg **(G-14207)**
Precision Funding Corp ....E 330 405-1313
Twinsburg **(G-18306)**
Primero Home Loans LLC ....C 877 959-2921
Dublin **(G-10312)**
Priority Mortgage Corp ....E 614 431-1141
Worthington **(G-19837)**
Quicken Loans Inc ....E 216 586-8900
Cleveland **(G-6270)**
Rapid Mortgage Company ....E 937 748-8888
Cincinnati **(G-4338)**
Realty Corporation of America ....E 216 522-0020
Cleveland Heights **(G-6722)**
Red Mortgage Capital LLC ....E 614 857-1400
Columbus **(G-8499)**
Residential Finance Corp.......................B 614 324-4700
Columbus **(G-8520)**
Security Savings Mortgage Corp ....D 330 455-2833
Canton **(G-2472)**
Sibcy Cline Inc ....D 513 777-8100
West Chester **(G-19005)**
Sirva Mortgage Inc ....D 800 531-3837
Independence **(G-12121)**
Sunrise Mortgage Services Inc.............D 614 989-5412
Gahanna **(G-11148)**
Third Federal Savings ....E 440 885-4900
Cleveland **(G-6523)**
Union Home Mortgage Corp ....E 440 234-4300
Strongsville **(G-17353)**
Vinton County Nat Bnk McArthur ....E 740 596-2525
Mc Arthur **(G-13892)**
Wells Fargo Home Mortgage Inc ....E 614 781-8847
Dublin **(G-10373)**

6163 Loan Brokers

Appalachian Development Corp.............D 740 374-9436
Marietta **(G-13313)**
Best Reward Credit Union ....E 216 367-8000
Cleveland **(G-5059)**
Board of Dir of Wittenbe ....E 937 327-6310
Springfield **(G-17000)**
Caliber Home Loans Inc ....E 937 435-5363
Dayton **(G-9272)**
Clyde-Findlay Area Cr Un Inc ....E 419 547-7781
Clyde **(G-6742)**
Columbus Metro Federal Cr Un ....E 614 239-0210
Columbus **(G-7298)**
Commonwealth Financial Svcs ....D 440 449-7709
Cleveland **(G-5321)**
Directions Credit Union Inc ....E 419 524-7113
Mansfield **(G-13167)**
Equity Consultants LLC ....D 330 659-7600
Seven Hills **(G-16674)**

Firefighters Cmnty Cr Un Inc ....E 216 621-4644
Cleveland **(G-5527)**
Firelands Federal Credit Union ....E 419 483-4180
Bellevue **(G-1377)**
First Merchants Bank ....E 614 486-9000
Columbus **(G-7587)**
Forest City Residential Dev ....E 216 621-6060
Cleveland **(G-5561)**
Fremont Federal Credit Union ....C 419 334-4434
Fremont **(G-11076)**
George W Mc Cloy ....D 614 457-6233
Columbus **(G-7661)**
Guardian Savings Bank..........................E 513 942-3535
West Chester **(G-18938)**
Guardian Savings Bank..........................E 513 528-8787
Cincinnati **(G-3661)**
Henry County Bank.................................E 419 599-1065
Napoleon **(G-14808)**
Manhattan Mortgage Group Ltd ....D 614 933-8955
Blacklick **(G-1482)**
Multi-Fund Inc ....E 216 750-2331
Cleveland **(G-6024)**
Nations Lending Corporation ....D 440 842-4817
Independence **(G-12102)**
Nationstar Mortgage LLC ....D 614 985-9500
Columbus **(G-8142)**
Ohio Equity Fund Inc ....E 614 469-1797
Columbus **(G-8254)**
Osgood State Bank (inc) ....E 419 582-2681
Osgood **(G-15653)**
Precision Funding Corp ....E 330 405-1313
Twinsburg **(G-18306)**
Premiere Service Mortgage Corp ....E 513 546-9895
West Chester **(G-18984)**
Randall Mortgage Services ....C 614 336-7948
Dublin **(G-10318)**
Real Estate Mortgage Corp ....D 440 356-5373
Chagrin Falls **(G-2653)**
Second National Bank ....E 937 548-2122
Greenville **(G-11395)**
Seven Seventeen Credit Un Inc ....C 330 372-8100
Warren **(G-18741)**
Seven Seventeen Credit Un Inc ....E 330 372-8100
Warren **(G-18742)**
Sibcy Cline Mortgage Services..............E 513 984-6776
Cincinnati **(G-4478)**
◆ State Bank and Trust Company ....E 419 783-8950
Defiance **(G-9941)**
The Peoples Savings and Ln Co ....E 937 653-1600
Urbana **(G-18445)**
Trio Limited ....E 614 898-5463
Columbus **(G-8784)**
Union Mortgage Services Inc.................E 614 457-4815
Columbus **(G-8799)**
Welles Bowen Realty Inc........................D 419 535-0011
Toledo **(G-18149)**
William D Taylor Sr Inc ....D 614 653-6683
Etna **(G-10621)**

62 SECURITY AND COMMODITY BROKERS, DEALERS, EXCHANGES, AND SERVICES

6211 Security Brokers & Dealers

Ameriprise Financial Svcs Inc ....D 614 846-8723
Worthington **(G-19793)**
Axa Advisors LLC ....C 614 985-3015
Columbus **(G-7007)**
Bowers Insurance Agency Inc ....E 330 638-6146
Cortland **(G-8984)**
Brown Gibbons Lang & Co LLC ....E 216 241-2800
Cleveland **(G-5092)**
Cadle Company II Inc..............................C 330 872-0918
Newton Falls **(G-15136)**
Charles Schwab & Co Inc ....E 330 908-4478
Richfield **(G-16349)**
Charles Schwab Corporation.................E 440 617-2301
Westlake **(G-19330)**
Charles Schwab Corporation.................E 216 291-9333
Cleveland **(G-5170)**
Cincinnati Financial Corp.......................A 513 870-2000
Fairfield **(G-10710)**
Citigroup Global Markets Inc ....D 860 291-4181
Beavercreek **(G-1210)**
Citigroup Global Markets Inc ....D 513 579-8300
Cincinnati **(G-3296)**
Citigroup Global Markets Inc ....E 419 842-5383
Toledo **(G-17653)**

Citigroup Global Markets Inc ....E 440 617-2000
  Cleveland (G-5183)

Columbus Metro Federal Cr Un ....E 614 239-0210
  Columbus (G-7297)

Corporate Fin Assoc of Clumbus ....D 614 457-9219
  Columbus (G-7374)

Cowen and Company LLC ....E 440 331-3531
  Rocky River (G-16429)

Deutsche Bank Securities Inc..............E 440 237-0188
  Broadview Heights (G-1831)

Equity Resources Inc ....D 513 518-6318
  Cincinnati (G-3512)

Haven Financial Enterprise..................E 800 265-2401
  Cleveland (G-5667)

Hbi Payments Ltd............................D 614 944-5788
  Columbus (G-7721)

Huntington Insurance Inc ....E 614 480-3800
  Columbus (G-7783)

Ifs Financial Services Inc ....E 513 362-8000
  Westerville (G-19264)

Jdel Inc......................................E 614 436-2418
  Columbus (G-7856)

◆ Jpmorgan Chase Bank Nat Assn ......A 614 436-3055
  Columbus (G-6818)

Keybanc Capital Markets Inc ....B 800 553-2240
  Cleveland (G-5826)

Kidney & Hypertension Cons ....E 330 649-9400
  Canton (G-2367)

Lancaster Pollard & Co LLC ....E 614 224-8800
  Columbus (G-7946)

Linsalata Capital Partners Fun ....C 440 684-1400
  Cleveland (G-5873)

MAI Capital Management LLC ....E 216 920-4913
  Columbus (G-5897)

Mc Cloy Financial Services ....D 614 457-6233
  Columbus (G-8042)

Merrill Lynch Pierce Fenner ....D 614 225-3152
  Columbus (G-8059)

Merrill Lynch Pierce Fenner ....E 419 891-2091
  Perrysburg (G-15893)

Merrill Lynch Pierce Fenner ....D 740 335-2930
  Wshngtn CT Hs (G-19879)

Merrill Lynch Pierce Fenner ....E 614 475-2798
  Columbus (G-8060)

Merrill Lynch Pierce Fenner ....E 740 452-3681
  Zanesville (G-20330)

Merrill Lynch Pierce Fenner ....E 614 225-3197
  Springfield (G-17081)

Merrill Lynch Pierce Fenner ....E 937 847-4000
  Miamisburg (G-14189)

Merrill Lynch Pierce Fenner ....D 614 225-3000
  Columbus (G-8061)

Merrill Lynch Pierce Fenner ....E 330 670-2400
  Akron (G-331)

Merrill Lynch Pierce Fenner ....C 216 363-6500
  Cleveland (G-5959)

Merrill Lynch Pierce Fenner ....D 330 670-2400
  Akron (G-332)

Merrill Lynch Pierce Fenner ....E 614 825-0350
  Columbus (G-6824)

Merrill Lynch Pierce Fenner ....C 513 579-3600
  Cincinnati (G-4036)

Merrill Lynch Pierce Fenner ....E 216 292-8000
  Cleveland (G-5960)

Merrill Lynch Pierce Fenner ....E 513 562-2100
  Cincinnati (G-4037)

Merrill Lynch Pierce Fenner ....E 614 798-4354
  Dublin (G-10278)

Merrill Lynch Pierce Fenner ....E 330 497-6600
  Canton (G-2401)

Merrill Lynch Pierce Fenner ....E 330 702-7300
  Canfield (G-2147)

Merrill Lynch Pierce Fenner ....E 330 702-0535
  Canfield (G-2148)

Merrill Lynch Pierce Fenner ....E 330 655-2312
  Hudson (G-11995)

Merrill Lynch Pierce Fenner ....E 330 670-2400
  Bath (G-1017)

Morgan Stanley ....E 513 721-2000
  Cincinnati (G-4074)

Morgan Stanley ....E 440 835-6750
  Westlake (G-19376)

Morgan Stanley ....E 216 523-3000
  Cleveland (G-6010)

Morgan Stanley ....D 614 473-2086
  Columbus (G-8102)

Morgan Stanley & Co LLC..................E 614 798-3100
  Dublin (G-10282)

Morgan Stanley & Co LLC..................E 614 228-0600
  Columbus (G-8103)

Morgan Stnley Smith Barney LLC ....E 216 360-4900
  Cleveland (G-6011)

Nationwide Fin Inst Dis Agency ....D 614 249-6825
  Columbus (G-8154)

Nationwide Inv Svcs Corp ....D 614 249-7111
  Columbus (G-8157)

Nationwide Life Insur Co Amer ....A 800 688-5177
  Columbus (G-8158)

O N Equity Sales Company ....A 513 794-6794
  Montgomery (G-14597)

Ohio Department of Commerce ....E 614 644-7381
  Columbus (G-8237)

Old Rpblic Ttle Nthrn Ohio LLC ....B 216 524-5700
  Independence (G-12106)

R B C Apollo Equity Partners ....E 216 875-2626
  Cleveland (G-6272)

Raymond James Fincl Svcs Inc ....E 419 586-5121
  Celina (G-2608)

Red Capital Markets LLC...................C 614 857-1400
  Columbus (G-8497)

Riversidecompanycom ....E 216 344-1040
  Cleveland (G-6330)

Robert W Baird & Co Inc ....E 216 737-7330
  Cleveland (G-6334)

Ross Sinclaire & Assoc LLC ....E 513 381-3939
  Cincinnati (G-4396)

Shane Security Services Inc ....D 330 757-4001
  Poland (G-16088)

Sirak Financial Services Inc...............D 330 493-0642
  Canton (G-2477)

Southwest Financial Svcs Ltd ....E 513 621-6699
  Cincinnati (G-4505)

Stateco Financial Services.................C 614 464-5000
  Columbus (G-8695)

The Cadle Company ....C 330 872-0918
  Newton Falls (G-15141)

The Huntington Investment Co ....E 614 480-3600
  Columbus (G-8744)

The Huntington Investment Co ....E 513 351-2555
  Cincinnati (G-4593)

UBS Financial Services Inc ....D 513 576-5000
  Cincinnati (G-4661)

UBS Financial Services Inc ....D 419 318-5525
  Sylvania (G-17461)

UBS Financial Services Inc ....E 937 428-1300
  Dayton (G-9827)

UBS Financial Services Inc ....E 513 792-2146
  Cincinnati (G-4662)

UBS Financial Services Inc ....E 216 831-3400
  Cleveland (G-6560)

UBS Financial Services Inc ....E 614 460-6559
  Columbus (G-8793)

UBS Financial Services Inc ....E 614 442-6240
  Columbus (G-8794)

UBS Financial Services Inc ....E 937 223-3141
  Miamisburg (G-14232)

UBS Financial Services Inc ....E 513 792-2100
  Cincinnati (G-4663)

Ultimus Fund Solutions LLC ....E 513 587-3400
  Cincinnati (G-4672)

Valmark Financial Group LLC.............D 330 576-1234
  Akron (G-483)

Valmark Securities Inc ....E 330 576-1234
  Akron (G-484)

Van Dyk Mortgage Corporation ....E 513 429-2122
  Mason (G-13653)

Wells Fargo Clearing Svcs LLC ....E 614 764-2040
  Dublin (G-10372)

Wells Fargo Clearing Svcs LLC ....E 216 378-2722
  Cleveland (G-6661)

Wells Fargo Clearing Svcs LLC ....E 614 221-8371
  Columbus (G-8885)

Wells Fargo Clearing Svcs LLC ....E 419 356-3272
  Toledo (G-18150)

Wells Fargo Clearing Svcs LLC ....E 440 835-9250
  Westlake (G-19422)

Wells Fargo Clearing Svcs LLC ....E 419 720-9700
  Toledo (G-18151)

Wells Fargo Clearing Svcs LLC ....E 513 241-9900
  Cincinnati (G-4776)

Wells Fargo Clearing Svcs LLC ....E 216 574-7300
  Cleveland (G-6662)

Western & Southern Lf Insur Co ....A 513 629-1800
  Cincinnati (G-4786)

Western Southern Mutl Holdg Co ....A 866 832-7719
  Cincinnati (G-4791)

Western Sthern Fincl Group Inc ....A 866 832-7719
  Cincinnati (G-4792)

Westmnster Fncl Securities Inc...........E 937 898-5010
  Dayton (G-9878)

Wunderlich Securities Inc ....E 440 646-1400
  Cleveland (G-6694)

6221 Commodity Contracts Brokers & Dealers

Merrill Lynch Pierce Fenner ....E 937 847-4000
  Miamisburg (G-14189)

Merrill Lynch Pierce Fenner ....D 330 670-2400
  Akron (G-332)

Wells Fargo Clearing Svcs LLC ....D 216 574-7300
  Cleveland (G-6662)

6282 Investment Advice

American Money Management Corp.....E 513 579-2592
  Cincinnati (G-2946)

Ameriprise Financial Svcs Inc ....E 330 494-9300
  Akron (G-72)

Ameriprise Financial Svcs Inc ....E 614 934-4057
  Dublin (G-10135)

Ameriprise Financial Svcs Inc ....D 614 846-8723
  Worthington (G-19793)

Bartlett & Co LLC ....D 513 621-4612
  Cincinnati (G-3023)

Brown WD General Agency Inc ....D 216 241-5840
  Cleveland (G-5094)

C H Dean Inc ....D 937 222-9531
  Beavercreek (G-1136)

Carnegie Capital Asset MGT LLC ....E 216 595-1349
  Cleveland (G-5128)

Centaurus Financial Inc ....D 419 756-9747
  Mansfield (G-13149)

Cleveland Research Company LLC .....E 216 649-7250
  Cleveland (G-5284)

CNG Financial Corp ....A 513 336-7735
  Cincinnati (G-3315)

Crestview Partners II Gp LP ....B 216 898-2400
  Brooklyn (G-1860)

Cw Financial LLC ....B 941 907-9490
  Beachwood (G-1050)

Diamond Hill Capital MGT Inc ....E 614 255-3333
  Columbus (G-7444)

Diamond Hill Funds ....E 614 255-3333
  Columbus (G-7445)

Direct Maintenance LLC ....E 330 744-5211
  Youngstown (G-20018)

Eubel Brady Suttman Asset Mgt ....E 937 291-1223
  Miamisburg (G-14169)

Financial Engines Inc ....E 330 726-3100
  Boardman (G-1697)

Financial Plnners of Cleveland ....E 440 473-1115
  Cleveland (G-5526)

Fiserv Solutions LLC ....C 412 577-3000
  Dublin (G-10228)

Fort Wash Inv Advisors Inc ....D 513 361-7600
  Cincinnati (G-3579)

Fund Evaluation Group LLC ....E 513 977-4400
  Cincinnati (G-3597)

Hanson McClain Inc ....E 513 469-7500
  Cincinnati (G-3680)

Ifs Financial Services Inc ....E 513 362-8000
  Westerville (G-19264)

Johnson Trust Co ....C 513 598-8859
  Cincinnati (G-3830)

Jpmorgan Inv Advisors Inc ....A 614 248-5800
  Columbus (G-6820)

Kemba Financial Credit Un Inc ....D 614 235-2395
  Columbus (G-7889)

Lancaster Pollard Mrtg Co LLC ....D 614 224-8800
  Columbus (G-7947)

Lang Financial Group Inc ....E 513 699-2966
  Blue Ash (G-1596)

Lassiter Corporation ....E 216 391-4800
  Cleveland (G-5856)

Lincoln Fincl Advisors Corp ....E 216 765-7400
  Beachwood (G-1074)

Longbow Research LLC...................D 216 986-0700
  Independence (G-12095)

MAI Capital Management LLC ....D 216 920-4800
  Cleveland (G-5896)

Mc Cormack Advisors Intl ....E 216 522-1200
  Cleveland (G-5927)

Meeder Asset Management Inc ....D 614 760-2112
  Dublin (G-10277)

Merrill Lynch Pierce Fenner ....C 216 363-6500
  Cleveland (G-5959)

Merrill Lynch Pierce Fenner ....E 937 847-4000
  Miamisburg (G-14189)

Merrill Lynch Pierce Fenner ....D 614 225-3000
  Columbus (G-8061)

S I C

Merrill Lynch Pierce Fenner ....D 330 670-2400
Akron (G-332)
Morgan Stanley ....D 614 473-2086
Columbus (G-8102)
Morgan Stanley ....E 513 721-2000
Cincinnati (G-4074)
Mt Washington Care Center Inc ...C 513 231-4561
Cincinnati (G-4083)
Mutual Shareholder Svcs LLC ......E 440 922-0067
Broadview Heights (G-1838)
Oak Associates Ltd ....E 330 666-5263
Akron (G-354)
Parkwood Corporation ....E 216 875-6500
Cleveland (G-6174)
Red Capital Partners LLC ....D 614 857-1400
Columbus (G-8498)
Richard Allen Group LLC ....D 614 623-2654
Powell (G-16206)
Roulston & Company Inc ....E 216 431-3000
Cleveland (G-6342)
S&P Global Inc ....C 614 835-2444
Groveport (G-11536)
S&P Global Inc ....C 330 482-9544
Leetonia (G-12519)
Sena Weller Rohs Williams ....E 513 241-6443
Cincinnati (G-4451)
Standard Retirement Svcs Inc .....E 440 808-2724
Westlake (G-19409)
Stepstone Group Real Estate LP ...E 216 522-0330
Cleveland (G-6467)
Stonehenge Capital Company LLC ...E 614 246-2456
Columbus (G-8701)
Stratos Wealth Partners Ltd ....D 440 519-2500
Beachwood (G-1108)
Summit Financial Strategies ....E 614 885-1115
Columbus (G-8710)
The Cadle Company ....C 330 872-0918
Newton Falls (G-15141)
Westminster Financial Company ...E 937 898-5010
Dayton (G-9877)
William D Taylor Sr Inc ....D 614 653-6683
Etna (G-10621)

6289 Security & Commodity Svcs, NEC

Flex Fund Inc ....E 614 766-7000
Dublin (G-10229)

63 INSURANCE CARRIERS

6311 Life Insurance Carriers

21st Century Financial Inc ....E 330 668-9065
Akron (G-9)
Allstate Insurance Company ....E 330 650-2917
Hudson (G-11963)
Alpha Investment Partnership ......D 513 621-1826
Cincinnati (G-2931)
American Financial Group Inc ......C 513 579-2121
Cincinnati (G-2943)
American Income Life Insur Co ....D 440 582-0040
Cleveland (G-4954)
American Mutual Life Assn ....E 216 531-1900
Cleveland (G-4960)
American Security Insurance Co ...E 937 327-7700
Springfield (G-16995)
Ameritas Life Insurance Corp ....E 513 595-2334
Cincinnati (G-2953)
Bankers Life & Casualty Co ....E 614 987-0590
Columbus (G-6801)
Cigna Corporation ....C 216 642-1700
Independence (G-12058)
Cincinnati Financial Corp ....A 513 870-2000
Fairfield (G-10710)
Cincinnati Life Insurance Co ....A 513 870-2000
Fairfield (G-10713)
Colonial Lf Accident Insur Co ......B 614 793-8622
Dublin (G-10180)
Columbus Financial Gr ....E 614 785-5100
Columbus (G-6809)
Columbus Life Insurance Co ....D 513 361-6700
Cincinnati (G-3331)
Employers Mutual Casualty Co ....D 513 221-6010
Blue Ash (G-1551)
Family Heritg Lf Insur Co Amer ...E 440 922-5200
Broadview Heights (G-1832)
Great American Life Insur Co ....E 513 357-3300
Cincinnati (G-3640)
Guardian Life Insur Co of Amer ...E 513 579-1114
Cincinnati (G-3660)
Howard Hanna Smythe Cramer .....D 330 725-4137
Medina (G-13952)

Irongate Inc ....C 937 433-3300
Centerville (G-2628)
J P Farley Corporation ....E 440 250-4300
Westlake (G-19360)
Kelley Companies ....D 330 668-6100
Copley (G-8967)
Lafayette Life Insurance Co ....C 800 443-8793
Cincinnati (G-3907)
Loyal American Life Insur Co ....C 800 633-6752
Cincinnati (G-3949)
Massachusetts Mutl Lf Insur Co ...E 513 579-8555
Cincinnati (G-3977)
Massachusetts Mutl Lf Insur Co ...E 216 592-7359
Cleveland (G-5922)
Midland-Guardian Co ....A 513 943-7100
Amelia (G-575)
Motorists Life Insurance Co ....E 614 225-8211
Columbus (G-8106)
Nationwide Financial Svcs Inc .....C 614 249-7111
Columbus (G-8155)
Nationwide General Insur Co ....E 614 249-7111
Columbus (G-8156)
◆ Nationwide Mutual Insurance Co ...A 614 249-7111
Columbus (G-8160)
Northwestern Mutl Lf Insur Co .....E 614 221-5287
Columbus (G-8209)
Ohio Casualty Insurance Co ....A 800 843-6446
Fairfield (G-10763)
Ohio Nat Mutl Holdings Inc ....A 513 794-6100
Montgomery (G-14598)
Ohio National Fincl Svcs Inc ....A 513 794-6100
Montgomery (G-14599)
Ohio Pia Service Corporation ....E 614 552-8000
Gahanna (G-11108)
Penn Mutual Life Insurance Co .....E 330 668-9065
Akron (G-374)
State Farm Mutl Auto Insur Co .....A 614 775-2001
New Albany (G-14875)
Summa Insurance Company Inc ...B 800 996-8411
Akron (G-453)
Transamerica Premier Lf Insur .....E 614 488-5983
Columbus (G-8773)
Transamerica Premier Lf Insur .....E 216 524-1436
Independence (G-12133)
Ulysses Caremark Holding Corp ...C 440 542-4214
Solon (G-16910)
Union Central Life Insur Co ....A 866 696-7478
Cincinnati (G-4673)
United American Insurance Co ......E 440 265-9200
Strongsville (G-17354)
United Omaha Life Insurance Co ...E 216 573-6900
Cleveland (G-6575)
UNUM Life Insurance Co Amer .....E 614 807-2500
Columbus (G-8821)
Voya Financial Inc ....E 614 431-5000
Columbus (G-8863)
Western & Southern Lf Insur Co ...E 614 277-4800
Grove City (G-11486)
Western & Southern Lf Insur Co ...E 330 792-6818
Youngstown (G-20242)
Western & Southern Lf Insur Co ...E 937 435-1964
Miamisburg (G-14237)
Western & Southern Lf Insur Co ...A 513 629-1800
Cincinnati (G-4786)
Western & Southern Lf Insur Co ...E 234 380-4525
Hudson (G-12013)

6321 Accident & Health Insurance

1-888 Ohio Comp LLC ....D 216 426-0646
Cleveland (G-4864)
American Financial Group Inc ......C 513 579-2121
Cincinnati (G-2943)
American Modern Home Svc Co ...E 513 943-7100
Amelia (G-567)
American Modrn Insur Group Inc ...C 800 543-2644
Amelia (G-568)
Aultcare Insurance Company ....B 330 363-6360
Canton (G-2199)
Blue Cross & Blue Shield Mich .....A 330 783-3841
Youngstown (G-19966)
Caresource Management Group Co ...A 937 224-3300
Dayton (G-9278)
Caresource Management Group Co ...A 614 221-3370
Hilliard (G-11753)
Caresource Management Group Co ...E 937 224-3300
Dayton (G-9279)
Cincinnati Equitable Insur Co ......E 513 621-1826
Cincinnati (G-3242)
Dawson Companies ....D 440 333-9000
Richfield (G-16352)

Employers Mutual Casualty Co ....D 513 221-6010
Blue Ash (G-1551)
J P Farley Corporation ....E 440 250-4300
Westlake (G-19360)
James B Oswald Company ....E 330 723-3637
Medina (G-13959)
Liberty Mutual Insurance Co ....E 614 855-6193
Westerville (G-19183)
Medical Bnfits Admnstrtors Inc ...D 740 522-8425
Newark (G-15070)
Medical Mutual of Ohio ....B 216 292-0400
Beachwood (G-1078)
◆ Nationwide Corporation ....E 614 249-7111
Columbus (G-8152)
◆ Nationwide Mutual Insurance Co ...A 614 249-7111
Columbus (G-8160)
Paramount Care Inc ....B 419 887-2500
Maumee (G-13830)
Progressive Casualty Insur Co .....D 440 603-4033
Cleveland (G-6244)
▼ Progressive Casualty Insur Co ...A 440 461-5000
Mayfield Village (G-13886)
Signature Healthcare LLC ....C 440 232-1800
Bedford (G-1305)
State Farm Mutl Auto Insur Co .....A 614 775-2001
New Albany (G-14875)
Summa Insurance Company Inc ...B 800 996-8411
Akron (G-453)
Superior Dental Care Inc ....E 937 438-0283
Dayton (G-9802)
Transamerica Premier Lf Insur .....E 614 488-5983
Columbus (G-8773)
Union Central Life Insur Co ....A 866 696-7478
Cincinnati (G-4673)

6324 Hospital & Medical Svc Plans Carriers

1-888 Ohio Comp LLC ....D 216 426-0646
Cleveland (G-4864)
Aetna Health California Inc ....E 614 933-6000
New Albany (G-14841)
Aetna Life Insurance Company .....E 330 659-8000
Richfield (G-16342)
Amerigroup Ohio Inc ....E 513 733-2300
Blue Ash (G-1504)
Anthem Insurance Companies Inc ...D 614 438-3542
Columbus (G-6799)
Anthem Insurance Companies Inc ...E 330 492-2151
Canton (G-2191)
Aultcare Corp ....B 330 363-6360
Canton (G-2198)
Aultman Hospital ....A 330 363-6262
Canton (G-2204)
Benefit Services Inc ....D 330 666-0337
Copley (G-8963)
Caresource Management Group Co ...A 216 839-1001
Cleveland (G-5126)
Centene Corporation ....C 513 469-4500
Blue Ash (G-1523)
Clinical Research Center ....D 513 636-4412
Cincinnati (G-3308)
Close to Home Health Care Ctr ....E 614 932-9013
Dublin (G-10176)
Community Insurance Company ...E 859 282-7888
Cincinnati (G-3340)
Custom Design Benefits Inc ....E 513 598-2929
Cincinnati (G-3391)
Dcp Holding Company ....D 513 554-1100
Sharonville (G-16728)
Deaconess Associations Inc ....B 513 559-2100
Cincinnati (G-3409)
Ebso Inc ....E 419 423-3823
Findlay (G-10898)
Ebso Inc ....E 440 262-1133
Cleveland (G-5464)
Family Health Plan Inc ....C 419 241-6501
Toledo (G-17724)
Firelands Regional Health Sys ......C 419 626-7400
Sandusky (G-16605)
Health Plan of Ohio Inc ....C 330 837-6880
Massillon (G-13693)
Healthspan Integrated Care ....E 440 937-2350
Avon (G-885)
Healthspan Integrated Care ....D 216 362-2000
Cleveland (G-5675)
Healthspan Integrated Care ....E 216 524-7377
Cleveland (G-5676)
Healthspan Integrated Care ....C 216 621-5600
Cleveland (G-5677)
Healthspan Integrated Care ....E 440 572-1000
Cleveland (G-5678)

Healthspan Integrated Care ....E 330 767-3436
  Brewster (G-1810)
Healthspan Integrated Care ....E 330 486-2800
  Twinsburg (G-18278)
Healthspan Integrated Care ....E 330 877-4018
  Hartville (G-11689)
Healthspan Integrated Care ....E 330 334-1549
  Wadsworth (G-18597)
Healthspan Integrated Care ....E 216 362-2277
  Lakewood (G-12346)
Humana Health Plan Ohio Inc ....D 513 784-5200
  Cincinnati (G-3739)
Humana Inc ....E 330 877-5464
  Hartville (G-11692)
Humana Inc ....E 216 328-2047
  Independence (G-12080)
Humana Inc ....E 614 210-1038
  Dublin (G-10248)
J P Farley Corporation ....E 440 250-4300
  Westlake (G-19360)
Kelley Companies ....D 330 668-6100
  Copley (G-8967)
Medical Mutual of Ohio ....A 216 687-7000
  Cleveland (G-5943)
Medical Mutual of Ohio ....B 419 473-7100
  Toledo (G-17902)
Metrohealth System ....E 216 778-3867
  Cleveland (G-5971)
Miami Valley Hospitalist Group ....D 937 208-8394
  Dayton (G-9622)
Molina Healthcare Inc ....A 800 642-4168
  Columbus (G-8096)
Nextrx LLC ....A 317 532-6000
  Mason (G-13622)
Ohio Health Choice Inc ....D 800 554-0027
  Cleveland (G-6120)
Oxford Blazer Company Inc ....E 614 792-2220
  Dublin (G-10302)
Promedica Health Systems Inc ....A 567 585-7454
  Toledo (G-17993)
Uc Health Llc ....E 513 585-7600
  Cincinnati (G-4665)
United Healthcare Ohio Inc ....D 216 694-4080
  Cleveland (G-6573)
United Healthcare Ohio Inc ....B 614 410-7000
  Columbus (G-8801)
United Healthcare Ohio Inc ....C 513 603-6200
  Cincinnati (G-4680)
Unitedhealth Group Inc ....B 513 603-6200
  Cincinnati (G-4691)

6331 Fire, Marine & Casualty Insurance

Affiliated FM Insurance Co ....E 216 362-4820
  North Olmsted (G-15276)
American Commerce Insurance Co ....C 614 272-6951
  Columbus (G-6915)
American Empire Surplus Lines ....E 513 369-3000
  Cincinnati (G-2939)
American Emprie Srpls Lines In ....D 513 369-3000
  Cincinnati (G-2940)
American Financial Group Inc ....C 513 579-2121
  Cincinnati (G-2943)
American Modern Home Insur Co ....D 513 943-7100
  Amelia (G-566)
American Select Insurance Co ....A 330 887-0101
  Westfield Center (G-19307)
American Western Home Insur Co ....B 513 943-7100
  Amelia (G-569)
Amica Mutual Insurance Company ....E 866 942-6422
  West Chester (G-18867)
Amtrust North America Inc ....C 216 328-6100
  Cleveland (G-4975)
Artisan and Truckers Cslty Co ....A 440 461-5000
  Cleveland (G-5011)
Broadspire Services Inc ....E 614 436-8990
  Columbus (G-7077)
Buckeye State Mutual Insur Co ....D 937 778-5000
  Piqua (G-15999)
Carrara Companies Inc ....D 330 659-2800
  Richfield (G-16348)
Celina Mutual Insurance Co ....C 419 586-5181
  Celina (G-2587)
Central Mutual Insurance Co ....B 419 238-1010
  Van Wert (G-18474)
Cincinnati Equitable Insur Co ....E 513 621-1826
  Cincinnati (G-3242)
Cincinnati Financial Corp ....A 513 870-2000
  Fairfield (G-10710)
Cincinnati Indemnity Co ....A 513 870-2000
  Fairfield (G-10712)

Erie Insurance Exchange ....D 330 568-1802
  Hubbard (G-11945)
Erie Insurance Exchange ....D 330 479-1010
  Canton (G-2304)
Erie Insurance Exchange ....C 614 436-0224
  Columbus (G-7529)
Erie Insurance Exchange ....D 330 433-1925
  Canton (G-2305)
Factory Mutual Insurance Co ....C 440 779-0651
  North Olmsted (G-15287)
Factory Mutual Insurance Co ....D 513 742-9516
  Cincinnati (G-3527)
Foremost Insurance Company ....D 216 674-7000
  Independence (G-12075)
Grange Mutual Casualty Company ....A 614 445-2900
  Columbus (G-7687)
Grange Mutual Casualty Company ....E 513 671-3722
  Cincinnati (G-3633)
◆ Great American Insurance Co ....A 513 369-5000
  Cincinnati (G-3639)
Great American Insurance Co ....D 513 603-2570
  Fairfield (G-10731)
Home and Farm Insurance Co ....D 937 778-5000
  Piqua (G-16010)
James B Oswald Company ....E 330 723-3637
  Medina (G-13959)
L Calvin Jones & Company ....E 330 533-1195
  Canfield (G-2145)
Lancer Insurance Company ....E 440 473-1634
  Cleveland (G-5854)
Liberty Mutual Insurance Co ....D 614 864-4100
  Gahanna (G-11131)
Liberty Mutual Insurance Co ....D 513 984-0550
  Fairfield (G-10747)
Liberty Mutual Insurance Co ....E 614 855-6193
  Westerville (G-19183)
Midland Company ....A 513 947-5503
  Amelia (G-574)
Midland-Guardian Co ....A 513 943-7100
  Amelia (G-575)
Motorists Coml Mutl Insur Co ....E 614 225-8211
  Columbus (G-8105)
Motorists Mutual Insurance Co ....A 614 225-8211
  Columbus (G-8107)
Motorists Mutual Insurance Co ....E 440 779-8900
  North Olmsted (G-15299)
Motorists Mutual Insurance Co ....E 330 896-9311
  Uniontown (G-18379)
Motorists Mutual Insurance Co ....E 937 435-5540
  Columbus (G-8108)
Mountain Laurel Assurance Co ....C 440 461-5000
  Cleveland (G-6015)
Munich Reinsurance America Inc ....E 614 221-7123
  Columbus (G-8124)
National Continental Insur Co ....B 631 320-2405
  Cleveland (G-6041)
National Interstate Corp ....D 330 659-8900
  Richfield (G-16363)
National Interstate Insur Co ....C 330 659-8900
  Richfield (G-16364)
Nationwide General Insur Co ....D 614 249-7111
  Columbus (G-8156)
◆ Nationwide Mutual Insurance Co ....A 614 249-7111
  Columbus (G-8160)
Occupational Health Link ....E 614 885-0039
  Columbus (G-8224)
Ohic Insurance Company ....D 614 221-7777
  Columbus (G-8227)
Ohio Casualty Insurance Co ....C 513 867-3000
  Hamilton (G-11631)
Ohio Casualty Insurance Co ....A 800 843-6446
  Fairfield (G-10763)
Ohio Fair Plan Undwrt Assn ....E 614 839-6446
  Columbus (G-8257)
Ohio Farmers Insurance Company ....A 800 243-0210
  Westfield Center (G-19308)
Ohio Indemnity Company ....E 614 228-1601
  Columbus (G-8269)
Ohio Mutual Insurance Company ....C 419 562-3011
  Bucyrus (G-1999)
Ohio National Life Insur Co ....D 513 794-6100
  Montgomery (G-14601)
Permanent Gen Asrn Corp Ohio ....E 216 986-3000
  Cleveland (G-6196)
Personal Service Insurance Co ....B 800 282-9416
  Columbus (G-8441)
Platinum Restoration Contrs ....E 440 327-0699
  Elyria (G-10555)
Progressive Advanced Insur Co ....C 440 461-5000
  Cleveland (G-6242)

Progressive Casualty Insur Co ....E 440 683-8164
  Cleveland (G-6243)
Progressive Casualty Insur Co ....D 440 603-4033
  Cleveland (G-6244)
▼ Progressive Casualty Insur Co ....A 440 461-5000
  Mayfield Village (G-13886)
Progressive Choice Insur Co ....B 440 461-5000
  Cleveland (G-6245)
Progressive Corporation ....B 440 461-5000
  Cleveland (G-6247)
Progressive Express Insur Co ....C 440 461-5000
  Cleveland (G-6248)
Progressive Freedom Insur Co ....C 440 461-5000
  Cleveland (G-6249)
Progressive Grdn State Insur ....C 440 461-5000
  Cleveland (G-6250)
Progressive Max Insurance Co ....E 330 533-8733
  Youngstown (G-20165)
Progressive Northwestern Insur ....E 440 461-5000
  Cleveland (G-6251)
Progressive Paloverde Insur Co ....C 440 461-5000
  Cleveland (G-6252)
Progressive Rsc Inc ....C 440 461-5000
  Cleveland (G-6255)
Progressive Select Insur Co ....C 440 461-5000
  Cleveland (G-6256)
Progressive Universal Insur Co ....C 440 461-5000
  Cleveland (G-6257)
Progressive Vehicle Service Co ....C 440 461-5000
  Cleveland (G-6258)
Progressive West Insurance Co ....B 440 446-5100
  Cleveland (G-6259)
Rtw Inc ....E 614 594-9217
  Columbus (G-8559)
Rtw Inc ....D 952 893-0403
  Minerva (G-14523)
Safe Auto Insurance Company ....E 740 472-1900
  Woodsfield (G-19678)
Safe Auto Insurance Group Inc ....D 614 231-0200
  Columbus (G-8572)
Seven Hills Fireman Assn ....E 216 524-3321
  Seven Hills (G-16681)
State Auto Financial Corp ....D 614 464-5000
  Columbus (G-8691)
State Automobile Mutl Insur Co ....A 833 724-3577
  Columbus (G-8692)
Verti Insurance Company ....D 844 448-3784
  Columbus (G-8845)
Wayne Mutual Insurance Co ....E 330 345-8100
  Wooster (G-19778)
Western Reserve Group ....B 330 262-9060
  Wooster (G-19783)
Workers Compensation Ohio Bur ....E 800 644-6292
  Columbus (G-8917)
Zurich American Insurance Co ....E 216 328-9400
  Independence (G-12143)

6351 Surety Insurance Carriers

American Commerce Insurance Co ....C 614 272-6951
  Columbus (G-6915)
▼ Progressive Casualty Insur Co ....A 440 461-5000
  Mayfield Village (G-13886)
Progressive Corporation ....B 440 461-5000
  Cleveland (G-6247)
State Automobile Mutl Insur Co ....A 833 724-3577
  Columbus (G-8692)

6361 Title Insurance

A R E A Title Agency Inc ....E 419 242-5485
  Toledo (G-17576)
Accurate Group Holdings Inc ....D 216 520-1740
  Independence (G-12037)
Barristers of Ohio LLC ....E 330 898-5600
  Warren (G-18678)
Chicago Title Insurance Co ....D 330 873-9393
  Akron (G-128)
Chicago Title Insurance Co ....E 216 241-6045
  Cleveland (G-5175)
Fidelity National Fincl Inc ....E 614 865-1562
  Westerville (G-19256)
First American Equity Ln Svcs ....C 800 221-8683
  Cleveland (G-5528)
First American Title Insur Co ....E 216 241-1278
  Cleveland (G-5529)
First American Title Insur Co ....E 419 625-8505
  Sandusky (G-16607)
First American Title Insur Co ....E 740 450-0006
  South Zanesville (G-16951)
First Amrcn Cash Advnce SC LLC ....D 330 644-9144
  Akron (G-219)

Howard Hanna Smythe Cramer ....D 330 725-4137
Medina *(G-13952)*

Landsel Title Agency Inc ....E 614 337-1928
Gahanna *(G-11130)*

Lawyers Title Cincinnati Inc ....D 513 421-1313
Cincinnati *(G-3914)*

Louisvlle Title Agcy For NW OH ....D 419 248-4611
Toledo *(G-17862)*

Midland Title Security Inc ....D 216 241-6045
Cleveland *(G-5986)*

Mortgage Information Services ....D 216 514-7480
Cleveland *(G-6012)*

Northwest Hts Title Agcy LLC ....E 614 451-6313
Columbus *(G-8206)*

Northwest Ttl Agy of OH MI In ....D 419 241-8195
Toledo *(G-17951)*

Ohio Bar Title Insurance Co ....D 614 310-8098
Columbus *(G-6827)*

Ohio Real Title Agency LLC ....E 216 373-9900
Cleveland *(G-6123)*

Omega Title Agency LLC ....D 330 436-0600
Stow *(G-17221)*

Port Lawrence Title and Tr Co ....E 419 244-4605
Toledo *(G-17982)*

Resource Title Agency Inc ....D 216 520-0050
Cleveland *(G-6315)*

Resource Title Nat Agcy Inc ....D 216 520-0050
Independence *(G-12113)*

Service Center Title Agency ....E 937 312-3080
Dayton *(G-9761)*

Southern Title of Ohio Ltd ....E 419 525-4600
Mansfield *(G-13244)*

Sterling Land Title Agency ....E 513 755-3700
West Chester *(G-19013)*

Stewart Advnced Land Title Ltd ....E 513 753-2800
Cincinnati *(G-2870)*

Stewart Title Company ....E 440 520-7130
Willoughby *(G-19574)*

Title First Agency Inc ....E 614 224-9207
Columbus *(G-8759)*

U S Title Agency Inc ....E 216 621-1424
Cleveland *(G-6559)*

Valmer Land Title Agency ....E 614 860-0005
Reynoldsburg *(G-16336)*

Valmer Land Title Agency ....E 614 875-7001
Grove City *(G-11479)*

6371 Pension, Health & Welfare Funds

Clinton County Dept Jobs/Fmly ....D 937 382-0963
Wilmington *(G-19612)*

County of Ashtabula ....D 440 994-1206
Ashtabula *(G-734)*

County of Gallia ....D 740 446-3222
Gallipolis *(G-11187)*

County of Seneca ....D 419 447-5011
Tiffin *(G-17514)*

Great Amrcn Fncl Resources Inc ......C 513 333-5300
Cincinnati *(G-3641)*

Great Amrcn Plan Admin Inc ....D 513 412-2316
Cincinnati *(G-3642)*

Nationwide Rtrment Sltions Inc ....C 614 854-8300
Dublin *(G-10287)*

Ohio Pub Employees Rtrement Sys ......B 614 228-8471
Columbus *(G-8282)*

Pharmacy Data Management Inc ....E 330 757-1500
Youngstown *(G-20155)*

School Employees Retirement ....C 614 222-5853
Columbus *(G-8606)*

Sheet Metal Workers Local No ....E 216 267-1645
Parma *(G-15776)*

State Tchers Rtrement Sys Ohio ....C 614 227-4090
Columbus *(G-8694)*

6399 Insurance Carriers, NEC

American Contrs Indemnity Co ....E 513 688-0800
Cincinnati *(G-2938)*

American Mutl Share Insur Corp ....E 614 764-1900
Dublin *(G-10133)*

Dimension Service Corporation ....C 614 226-7455
Dublin *(G-10200)*

Excess Share Insurance Corp ....E 614 764-1900
Dublin *(G-10222)*

Hartville Group Inc ....E 330 484-8166
Akron *(G-252)*

Heritage Wrranty Insur Rrg Inc ....D 800 753-5236
Dublin *(G-10241)*

Ohio Farmers Insurance Company ......C 330 484-5660
Canton *(G-2425)*

64 INSURANCE AGENTS, BROKERS, AND SERVICE

6411 Insurance Agents, Brokers & Svc

A A Hammersmith Insurance Inc ....E 330 832-7411
Massillon *(G-13657)*

A-1 General Insurance Agency ....D 216 986-3000
Cleveland *(G-4883)*

AAA Cincinnati Insurance Svc ....E 513 345-5600
Cincinnati *(G-2895)*

AAA Club Alliance Inc ....C 937 427-5884
Beavercreek *(G-1123)*

Aba Insurance Services Inc ....D 800 274-5222
Shaker Heights *(G-16702)*

Ability Network Inc ....E 513 943-8888
Cincinnati *(G-2840)*

Accurate Group Holdings Inc ....D 216 520-1740
Independence *(G-12037)*

Advanced Group Corp ....E 216 431-8800
Cleveland *(G-4904)*

AFLAC Incorporated ....C 614 410-1696
Columbus *(G-6882)*

Alex N Sill Company ....E 216 524-9999
Seven Hills *(G-16671)*

All America Insurance Company ....B 419 238-1010
Van Wert *(G-18472)*

Allan Peace & Associates Inc ....E 513 579-1700
Cincinnati *(G-2923)*

Allen Gardiner Deroberts ....E 614 221-1500
Columbus *(G-6892)*

Allstate Insurance Company ....E 330 650-2917
Hudson *(G-11963)*

Allstate Insurance Company ....D 330 656-6000
Hudson *(G-11964)*

Alternative Care Mgt Systems ....E 614 761-0035
Dublin *(G-10127)*

Althans Insurance Agency Inc ....E 440 247-6422
Chagrin Falls *(G-2638)*

American Family Home Insur Co ....D 513 943-7100
Amelia *(G-565)*

American Fidelity Assurance Co ....A 800 437-1011
Columbus *(G-6921)*

American Gen Lf Insur Co Del ....E 513 762-7807
Cincinnati *(G-2944)*

American Highways Insur Agcy ....C 330 659-8900
Richfield *(G-16345)*

American Income Life Insur Co ....D 440 582-0040
Cleveland *(G-4954)*

American Insur Administrators ....E 614 486-5388
Dublin *(G-10131)*

American Intl Group Inc ....C 216 479-8800
Cleveland *(G-4955)*

American Modrn Insur Group Inc ....C 800 543-2644
Amelia *(G-568)*

American Risk Services LLC ....E 513 772-3712
Cincinnati *(G-2951)*

American Title of Ohio LLC ....E 303 868-2250
Cleveland *(G-4968)*

Ameriprise Financial Svcs Inc ....D 614 846-8723
Worthington *(G-19793)*

Amtrust North America Inc ....C 216 328-6100
Cleveland *(G-4975)*

Anthem Midwest Inc ....A 614 433-8350
Mason *(G-13541)*

AON Consulting Inc ....E 614 436-8100
Columbus *(G-6952)*

AON Consulting Inc ....D 614 847-4670
Columbus *(G-6953)*

AON Consulting Inc ....E 216 621-8100
Cleveland *(G-4987)*

AON Risk Svcs Northeast Inc ....A 216 621-8100
Cleveland *(G-4988)*

Archer-Meek-Weiler Agency Inc ....E 614 212-1009
Westerville *(G-19145)*

Art Hauser Insurance Inc ....D 513 745-9200
Cincinnati *(G-2990)*

Arthur J Gallagher & Co ....E 513 977-3100
Cincinnati *(G-2991)*

Auto-Owners Insurance Company ....D 937 432-6740
Miamisburg *(G-14143)*

Auto-Owners Life Insurance Co ....D 419 227-1452
Lima *(G-12604)*

Axa Advisors LLC ....E 513 762-7700
Cincinnati *(G-3010)*

Beecher Carlson Insur Svcs LLC ....D 330 726-8177
Youngstown *(G-19962)*

Benefit ADM Agcy LLC ....E 614 791-1143
Dublin *(G-10145)*

Bowers Insurance Agency Inc ....E 330 638-6146
Cortland *(G-8984)*

Brands Insurance Agency Inc ....E 513 777-7775
West Chester *(G-18878)*

Britton-Gallagher & Assoc Inc ....D 216 658-7100
Cleveland *(G-5082)*

Brooks & Stafford Co ....E 216 696-3000
Cleveland *(G-5089)*

Brown & Brown of Ohio LLC ....C 419 874-1974
Perrysburg *(G-15842)*

Brown WD General Agency Inc ....D 216 241-5840
Cleveland *(G-5094)*

Bruce Klinger ....E 419 473-2270
Toledo *(G-17630)*

▲ Brunswick Companies ....D 330 864-8800
Cleveland *(G-5095)*

Buren Insurance Group Inc ....E 419 281-8060
Ashland *(G-661)*

Business Admnstrators Cons Inc ....E 614 863-8780
Reynoldsburg *(G-16287)*

Cai/Insurance Agency Inc ....E 513 221-1140
Cincinnati *(G-3104)*

Careworks of Ohio Inc ....B 614 792-1085
Dublin *(G-10161)*

Carriage Town Chrysler Plymouth ......D 740 369-9611
Delaware *(G-9957)*

Cbiz Inc ....D 330 644-2044
Uniontown *(G-18361)*

Central Bnfits Admnstrtors Inc ....D 614 797-5200
Westerville *(G-19232)*

Chapman & Chapman Inc ....E 440 934-4102
Avon *(G-874)*

Cincinnati Casualty Company ....D 513 870-2000
Fairfield *(G-10709)*

Cincinnati Equitable Insur Co ....E 440 349-2210
Solon *(G-16835)*

Cincinnati Financial Corp ....A 513 870-2000
Fairfield *(G-10710)*

Clark Theders Insurance Agency ....E 513 779-2800
West Chester *(G-18891)*

Cobos Insurance Centre LLC ....E 440 324-3732
Elyria *(G-10491)*

Columbus Life Insurance Co ....D 513 361-6700
Cincinnati *(G-3331)*

Combined Insurance Co Amer ....D 614 210-6209
Columbus *(G-7323)*

Compmanagement Inc ....E 614 376-5300
Dublin *(G-10187)*

Cornerstone Broker Ins Svcs AG ....E 513 241-7675
Cincinnati *(G-3363)*

Corporate Health Benefits ....E 740 348-1401
Newark *(G-15027)*

Corporate Plans Inc ....E 440 542-7800
Solon *(G-16838)*

Crawford & Company ....E 440 243-8710
Cleveland *(G-5375)*

CSC Insurance Agency Inc ....D 614 895-2000
Westerville *(G-19154)*

Cumberland Mutl Fire Insur Co ....E 419 525-4443
Mansfield *(G-13163)*

Defense Info Systems Agcy ....C 614 692-4433
Columbus *(G-7430)*

Ebso Inc ....E 419 423-3823
Findlay *(G-10898)*

Employee Benefit Management ....E 614 766-5800
Dublin *(G-10217)*

Employers Mutual Casualty Co ....D 513 221-6010
Blue Ash *(G-1551)*

Envision Phrm Svcs LLC ....B 330 405-8080
Twinsburg *(G-18263)*

Erie Indemnity Company ....D 330 433-6300
Canton *(G-2303)*

Erie Insurance Exchange ....D 614 430-8530
Columbus *(G-7528)*

Executive Insurance Agency ....E 330 576-1234
Akron *(G-205)*

Explorer Rv Insurance Agcy Inc ....C 330 659-8900
Richfield *(G-16355)*

F W Arnold Agency Co Inc ....E 330 832-1556
Massillon *(G-13679)*

Farmers Financial Services ....E 937 424-0643
Beavercreek *(G-1217)*

Farmers Group Inc ....E 330 467-6575
Northfield *(G-15378)*

Farmers Group Inc ....E 614 766-6005
Columbus *(G-7562)*

Farmers Group Inc ....E 614 799-3200
Columbus *(G-7563)*

Farmers Group Inc ....E 216 750-4010
Independence *(G-12073)*

Farmers Insurance of Columbus..........B....... 614 799-3200
  Columbus (G-7564)

Fedeli Group Inc.............................D....... 216 328-8080
  Cleveland (G-5520)

Federal Insurance Company............E....... 216 687-1700
  Cleveland (G-5521)

Federal Insurance Company............D....... 513 721-0601
  Cincinnati (G-3538)

Financial Design Group Inc ....E....... 419 843-4737
  Toledo (G-17736)

Financial PInners of Cleveland ....E....... 440 473-1115
  Cleveland (G-5526)

First Acceptance Corporation ....E....... 614 237-9700
  Columbus (G-7580)

First Acceptance Corporation ....E....... 937 778-8888
  Piqua (G-16004)

First Acceptance Corporation ....E....... 513 741-0811
  Cincinnati (G-3553)

First Acceptance Corporation ....E....... 614 492-1446
  Columbus (G-7581)

First Acceptance Corporation ....E....... 330 792-7181
  Youngstown (G-20037)

First Acceptance Corporation ....E....... 614 853-3344
  Columbus (G-7582)

First Defiance Financial Corp ....E....... 419 353-8611
  Bowling Green (G-1731)

▲ Forge Industries Inc......................A....... 330 782-8301
  Youngstown (G-20040)

▲ Freedom Specialty Insurance Co .....C....... 614 249-1545
  Columbus (G-7622)

Gallagher Bassett Services...............E....... 614 764-7616
  Dublin (G-10233)

Gallagher Benefit Services Inc ....E....... 216 623-2600
  Cleveland (G-5590)

Galt Enterprises Inc ....E....... 216 464-6744
  Moreland Hills (G-14710)

Geico General Insurance Co ....B....... 513 794-3426
  Cincinnati (G-3607)

George W Mc Cloy ....D....... 614 457-6233
  Columbus (G-7661)

German Mutual Insurance Co ....E....... 419 599-3993
  Napoleon (G-14806)

Grange Indemnity Insurance Co........D....... 614 445-2900
  Columbus (G-7685)

Grange Life Insurance Company.........E....... 800 445-3030
  Columbus (G-7686)

Grange Mutual Casualty Company ......E....... 614 337-4400
  Cleveland (G-5622)

Great American Advisors Inc ....E....... 513 357-3300
  Cincinnati (G-3638)

Guardian Business Services ....E....... 614 416-6090
  Columbus (G-7699)

Hanover Insurance Company ....D....... 614 408-9000
  Dublin (G-10237)

Hanover Insurance Company ....D....... 513 829-4555
  Fairfield (G-10734)

Harrington Health Services Inc.........C....... 614 212-7000
  Westerville (G-19259)

Hartford Fire Insurance Co ....C....... 216 447-1000
  Cleveland (G-5664)

Health Design Plus Inc ....D....... 330 656-1072
  Hudson (G-11981)

Home and Farm Insurance Co ....D....... 937 778-5000
  Piqua (G-16010)

Hummel Group Inc ....E....... 330 683-1050
  Orrville (G-15635)

Huntington Insurance Inc ....C....... 419 720-7900
  Toledo (G-17813)

Huntington Insurance Inc..................E....... 614 480-3800
  Columbus (G-7783)

Huntington Insurance Inc..................E....... 216 206-1787
  Cleveland (G-5723)

Huntington Insurance Inc..................E....... 330 262-6611
  Wooster (G-19732)

Huntington Insurance Inc..................D....... 614 899-8500
  Columbus (G-7784)

Huntington Insurance Inc..................E....... 330 337-9933
  Salem (G-16548)

Huntington Insurance Inc..................E....... 330 674-2931
  Millersburg (G-14479)

Huntington Insurance Inc..................E....... 330 430-1300
  Canton (G-2353)

Hyatt Legal Plans Inc.......................D....... 216 241-0022
  Cleveland (G-5729)

Hylant Administrative Services ....E....... 419 255-1020
  Toledo (G-17814)

Hylant Group Inc ....E....... 513 985-2400
  Cincinnati (G-3747)

Hylant Group Inc ....E....... 614 932-1200
  Dublin (G-10251)

Hylant Group Inc ....C....... 419 255-1020
  Toledo (G-17815)

Hylant Group Inc ....D....... 216 447-1050
  Cleveland (G-5730)

Hylant-Maclean Inc ....E....... 614 932-1200
  Dublin (G-10252)

Infoquest Information Services ....E....... 614 761-3003
  Columbus (G-7815)

Insurance Claims MGT Inc ....C....... 937 328-4300
  Springfield (G-17053)

Insurance Intermediaries Inc ....D...... 614 846-1111
  Columbus (G-7831)

International Healthcare Corp............D....... 513 731-3338
  Cincinnati (G-3779)

James B Oswald Company ....E....... 330 723-3637
  Medina (G-13959)

Kellison & Co ....D....... 216 464-5160
  Cleveland (G-5822)

Keybank National Association ....C....... 216 813-0000
  Cleveland (G-5829)

Knight Crockett Miller Ins ....E....... 419 254-2400
  Toledo (G-17841)

Lang Financial Group Inc ....E....... 513 699-2966
  Blue Ash (G-1596)

Leonard Insur Svcs Agcy Inc ....E....... 330 266-1904
  Canton (G-2375)

Licking Memorial Hlth Systems..........A....... 220 564-4000
  Newark (G-15056)

Life Insurance Mktg Co Inc ....E....... 330 867-1707
  Akron (G-313)

Lighthouse Insurance Group LLC........D....... 216 503-2439
  Independence (G-12093)

Louieville Title Agncy For Nrt ....D....... 419 248-4611
  Toledo (G-17861)

LP Insurance Services LLC................C....... 877 369-5121
  Solon (G-16866)

Luce Smith & Scott Inc.....................E....... 440 746-1700
  Brecksville (G-1788)

Marsh & McLennan Agency LLC ....E....... 513 248-4888
  Loveland (G-13010)

Marsh & McLennan Agency LLC ....D....... 937 228-4135
  Dayton (G-9585)

Marsh USA Inc ....B....... 216 937-1700
  Cleveland (G-5914)

Marsh USA Inc ....D....... 513 287-1600
  Cincinnati (G-3976)

Marsh USA Inc ....D....... 614 227-6200
  Columbus (G-8029)

Marsh USA Inc ....D....... 216 830-8000
  Cleveland (G-5915)

Masters Agency Inc ....E....... 330 805-5985
  Wadsworth (G-18607)

Mc Cloy Financial Services ....D....... 614 457-6233
  Columbus (G-8042)

McGohan/Brabender Agency Inc ....D....... 937 293-1600
  Moraine (G-14672)

McGowan & Company Inc ....D....... 800 545-1538
  Cleveland (G-5932)

Medical Benefits Mutl Lf Insur ....C....... 740 522-8425
  Newark (G-15069)

Medical Mutual of Ohio......................D....... 440 878-4800
  Strongsville (G-17330)

Medical Mutual of Ohio......................B....... 216 292-0400
  Beachwood (G-1078)

MetLife Auto HM Insur Agcy Inc..........A....... 815 266-5301
  Dayton (G-9610)

Metropolitan Life Insur Co ....D....... 614 792-1463
  Dublin (G-10279)

Motorists Mutual Insurance Co ....E....... 440 779-8900
  North Olmsted (G-15299)

Motorists Mutual Insurance Co ....E....... 937 435-5540
  Columbus (G-8108)

National Auto Care Corporation ....D....... 800 548-1875
  Westerville (G-19187)

National General Insurance ....B....... 212 380-9462
  Cleveland (G-6045)

National Interstate Corp ....D....... 330 659-8900
  Richfield (G-16363)

Nations Title Agency of Ohio ....E....... 614 839-3848
  Columbus (G-8141)

◆ Nationwide Corporation ....E....... 614 249-7111
  Columbus (G-8152)

Nationwide Corporation ....A....... 330 452-8705
  Canton (G-2415)

Nationwide Corporation ....B....... 614 277-5103
  Grove City (G-11456)

Nationwide Financial Svcs Inc.............C....... 614 249-7111
  Columbus (G-8155)

Nationwide Life Insur Co Amer............A....... 800 688-5177
  Columbus (G-8158)

Nationwide Mutl Fire Insur Co ....E....... 614 249-7111
  Columbus (G-8159)

Nationwide Mutual Insurance Co ....C....... 402 420-6153
  Grove City (G-11457)

Nationwide Mutual Insurance Co ....A....... 330 489-5000
  Canton (G-2416)

Nationwide Mutual Insurance Co ....E....... 614 948-4153
  Westerville (G-19189)

Nationwide Mutual Insurance Co ....E....... 614 430-3047
  Lewis Center (G-12553)

Nationwide Rtrment Sltions Inc...........C....... 614 854-8300
  Dublin (G-10287)

Neace Assoc Insur Agcy of Ohio.........E....... 614 224-0772
  Columbus (G-8168)

New England Life Insurance Co ....E....... 614 457-6233
  Columbus (G-8185)

New York Life Insurance Co................C....... 216 520-1345
  Independence (G-12103)

New York Life Insurance Co................D....... 513 621-9999
  Cincinnati (G-4110)

New York Life Insurance Co................D....... 216 221-1100
  Lakewood (G-12357)

NI of Ky Inc ....E....... 740 689-9876
  Lancaster (G-12423)

NI of Ky Inc ....E....... 216 643-7100
  Rocky River (G-16442)

NI of Ky Inc ....E....... 614 224-0772
  Columbus (G-8192)

Noble-Davis Consulting Inc ....E....... 440 519-0850
  Solon (G-16878)

Norman-Spencer Agency Inc ....E....... 800 543-3248
  Dayton (G-9659)

Northwestern Mutl Lf Insur Co............D....... 513 366-3600
  Cincinnati (G-4132)

Northwestern Ohio Admnistrators ....E....... 419 248-2401
  Holland (G-11902)

Ohic Insurance Company....................D....... 614 221-7777
  Columbus (G-8227)

Ohio Farmers Insurance Company ....A....... 800 243-0210
  Westfield Center (G-19308)

Ohio Farmers Insurance Company ....C....... 330 484-5660
  Canton (G-2425)

Ohio Farmers Insurance Company ....D....... 614 848-6174
  Columbus (G-6828)

Ohio Indemnity Company ....E....... 614 228-1601
  Columbus (G-8269)

Ohio Mutual Insurance Company.........C....... 419 562-3011
  Bucyrus (G-1999)

Ohio National Life Assurance ....A....... 513 794-6100
  Montgomery (G-14600)

Old Rpblic Ttle Nthrn Ohio LLC............B....... 216 524-5700
  Independence (G-12106)

Optumrx Inc.....................................A....... 614 794-3300
  Westerville (G-19196)

Pasco Inc ....B....... 330 650-0613
  Hudson (G-12001)

Paul Moss LLC..................................E....... 216 765-1580
  Solon (G-16881)

Phelan Insurance Agency Inc ....E....... 800 843-3069
  Versailles (G-18570)

Postema Insurance & Investment ....E....... 419 782-2500
  Defiance (G-9934)

Producer Group LLC..........................E....... 440 871-7700
  Rocky River (G-16444)

Progressive Spclty Ins Agcy Inc ....C....... 440 461-5000
  Cleveland (G-6241)

▼ Progressive Casualty Insur Co ....A....... 440 461-5000
  Mayfield Village (G-13886)

Progressive Casualty Insur Co.............E....... 440 683-8164
  Cleveland (G-6243)

Progressive Corporation ....A....... 800 925-2886
  Cleveland (G-6246)

Progressive Premier Insurance............C....... 440 461-5000
  Cleveland (G-6254)

Prudential Insur Co of Amer ....E....... 513 612-6400
  Cincinnati (G-4302)

Prudential Insur Co of Amer ....E....... 330 896-7200
  Uniontown (G-18383)

Prudential Insur Co of Amer ....E....... 440 684-4409
  Cleveland (G-6264)

Prudential Insur Co of Amer ....E....... 419 893-6227
  Maumee (G-13836)

Qualchoice Inc ....B....... 330 656-1231
  Beachwood (G-1098)

R L King Insurance Agency ....E....... 419 255-9947
  Holland (G-11908)

Rankin & Rankin Inc ....E....... 740 452-7575
  Zanesville (G-20357)

Richfield Financial Group Inc ....E....... 440 546-4288
  Brecksville (G-1802)

Employee Codes: A=Over 500 employees, B=251-500
C=101-250, D=51-100, E=25-50   2019 Harris Ohio
Services Directory   909

Rick Allman ....E 330 699-1660
Canton *(G-2461)*

Rick Blazing Insurance Agency ....E 513 677-8300
Cincinnati *(G-4371)*

Rod Lightning Mutual Insur Co ....B 330 262-9060
Wooster *(G-19762)*

Root Insurance Company ....C 866 980-9431
Columbus *(G-8549)*

Royalton Financial Group ....E 440 582-3020
Cleveland *(G-6347)*

S & S Halthcare Strategies Ltd ....C 513 772-8866
Cincinnati *(G-4420)*

Safe Auto Insurance Company ....B 614 231-0200
Columbus *(G-8571)*

Safe Auto Insurance Group Inc ....D 614 231-0200
Columbus *(G-8572)*

▲ Safelite Group Inc ....A 614 210-9000
Columbus *(G-8576)*

Savage and Associates Inc ....C 419 475-8665
Maumee *(G-13849)*

Sbm Business Services Inc ....E 330 396-7000
Akron *(G-419)*

Schauer Group Incorporated ....E 330 453-7721
Canton *(G-2471)*

Schiff John J & Thomas R & Co ....E 513 870-2580
Fairfield *(G-10778)*

Schwendeman Agency Inc ....E 740 373-6793
Marietta *(G-13378)*

Sedgwick CMS Holdings Inc ....A 614 658-0900
Hilliard *(G-11815)*

Sedgwick CMS Holdings Inc ....A 800 825-6755
Dublin *(G-10331)*

Seibert-Keck Insurance Agency ....E 330 867-3140
Fairlawn *(G-10849)*

Self-Funded Plans Inc ....E 216 566-1455
Cleveland *(G-6395)*

Selman & Company ....D 440 646-9336
Cleveland *(G-6396)*

Seymour & Associates ....E 419 517-7079
Maumee *(G-13850)*

Sirak Financial Services Inc ....D 330 493-0642
Canton *(G-2477)*

Sirak-Moore Insurance Agcy Inc ....E 330 493-3211
Canton *(G-2478)*

Smart ....C 216 228-9400
North Olmsted *(G-15310)*

Stammen Insurance Agency LLC ....E 419 586-7500
Celina *(G-2611)*

State Automobile Mutl Insur Co ....A 833 724-3577
Columbus *(G-8692)*

State Farm General Insur Co ....D 740 364-5000
Newark *(G-15100)*

State Farm Life Insurance Co ....D 937 276-1900
Dayton *(G-9791)*

State Farm Mutl Auto Insur Co ....D 419 873-0100
Perrysburg *(G-15925)*

State Farm Mutl Auto Insur Co ....D 216 621-3723
Cleveland *(G-6456)*

State Farm Mutl Auto Insur Co ....A 614 775-2001
New Albany *(G-14875)*

State Farm Mutl Auto Insur Co ....A 740 364-5000
Newark *(G-15101)*

State Farm Mutl Auto Insur Co ....D 216 321-1422
Cleveland *(G-6457)*

Steele W W Jr Agency Inc ....E 330 453-7721
Canton *(G-2497)*

Stephens-Matthews Mktg Inc ....E 740 984-8011
Beverly *(G-1466)*

Stolly Insurance Agency Inc ....E 419 227-2570
Lima *(G-12756)*

Strategic Research Group Inc ....E 614 220-8860
Columbus *(G-8704)*

Summit Claim Services LLC ....D 330 706-9898
New Franklin *(G-14915)*

Supreme Court of Ohio ....E 614 387-9800
Columbus *(G-8718)*

The Sheakley Group Inc ....E 513 771-2277
Cincinnati *(G-4596)*

Todd Associates Inc ....D 440 461-1101
Beachwood *(G-1113)*

Travelers Property Cslty Corp ....E 513 639-5300
Cincinnati *(G-4630)*

Travelers Property Cslty Corp ....C 216 643-2100
Cleveland *(G-6546)*

Uct Property Inc ....E 614 228-3276
Columbus *(G-8795)*

Ues Metals Group ....E 937 255-9340
Beavercreek *(G-1191)*

Union Security Insurance Co ....E 513 621-1924
Cincinnati *(G-4674)*

United Agencies Inc ....E 216 696-8044
Cleveland *(G-6565)*

United American Insurance Co ....E 440 265-9200
Strongsville *(G-17354)*

United Insurance Company Amer ....E 513 771-6771
Cincinnati- *(G-4681)*

United Insurance Company Amer ....E 419 531-4289
Toledo *(G-18118)*

United Insurance Company Amer ....E 216 514-1904
Beachwood *(G-1115)*

United Ohio Insurance Company ....C 419 562-3011
Bucyrus *(G-2004)*

Usi Inc ....D 419 243-1191
Toledo *(G-18132)*

USI Insurance Services Nat Inc ....E 614 228-5565
Columbus *(G-8837)*

▲ USI Midwest LLC ....C 513 852-6300
Cincinnati *(G-4744)*

Utica National Insurance Group ....E 614 823-5300
Columbus *(G-8838)*

Valmark Financial Group LLC ....D 330 576-1234
Akron *(G-483)*

Vision Service Plan ....C 614 471-7511
Columbus *(G-8854)*

Voya Financial Inc ....E 614 431-5000
Columbus *(G-8863)*

W P Dolle LLC ....E 513 421-6515
Cincinnati *(G-4767)*

Wabe Maquaw Holdings Inc ....D 419 243-1191
Toledo *(G-18144)*

Wallace & Turner Insurance Inc ....E 937 324-8492
Springfield *(G-17131)*

Western & Southern Lf Insur Co ....E 234 380-4525
Hudson *(G-12013)*

Western & Southern Lf Insur Co ....E 440 324-2626
Elyria *(G-10574)*

Western & Southern Lf Insur Co ....E 330 825-9935
Barberton *(G-972)*

Western & Southern Lf Insur Co ....E 740 653-3210
Lancaster *(G-12444)*

Western & Southern Lf Insur Co ....E 513 891-0777
Loveland *(G-13034)*

Western & Southern Lf Insur Co ....E 614 898-1066
Columbus *(G-6838)*

Western & Southern Lf Insur Co ....E 937 773-5303
Piqua *(G-16039)*

Western & Southern Lf Insur Co ....E 937 399-7696
Springfield *(G-17135)*

Western & Southern Lf Insur Co ....E 740 354-2848
Portsmouth *(G-16181)*

Western & Southern Lf Insur Co ....E 937 393-1969
Hillsboro *(G-11855)*

Western & Southern Lf Insur Co ....E 419 524-1800
Ontario *(G-15579)*

Westfield Services Inc ....E 614 796-7700
Columbus *(G-6839)*

William D Taylor Sr Inc ....D 614 653-6683
Etna *(G-10621)*

Willis of Ohio Inc ....E 614 457-7000
Columbus *(G-8907)*

Wilmared Inc ....E 513 891-6615
Loveland *(G-13035)*

Workers Compensation Ohio Bur ....A 800 644-6292
Columbus *(G-8916)*

York Risk Services Group Inc ....C 866 391-9675
Dublin *(G-10380)*

York Risk Services Group Inc ....E 440 863-2500
Cleveland *(G-6700)*

65 REAL ESTATE

6512 Operators Of Nonresidential Bldgs

127 PS Fee Owner LLC ....D 216 520-1250
Cleveland *(G-4865)*

Ad Investments LLC ....E 614 857-2340
Columbus *(G-6870)*

American Maritime Officers ....E 419 255-3940
Toledo *(G-17591)*

Americas Best Value Inn ....E 419 626-9890
Sandusky *(G-16575)*

Anderson Jeffery R RE Inc ....E 513 241-5800
Cincinnati *(G-2961)*

Ashtabula Chemical Corp ....E 440 998-0100
Ashtabula *(G-707)*

Assembly Center ....E 800 582-1099
Monroe *(G-14560)*

At Holdings Corporation ....A 216 692-6000
Cleveland *(G-5016)*

Barcus Company Inc ....E 614 451-9000
Columbus *(G-7017)*

Best Western Columbus N Hotel ....E 614 888-8230
Columbus *(G-7030)*

C M Limited ....E 614 888-4567
Columbus *(G-7103)*

Canal Road Partners ....E 216 447-0814
Cleveland *(G-5118)*

Cararo Co Inc ....E 330 652-6980
Niles *(G-15150)*

Carew Realty Inc ....E 513 241-3888
Cincinnati *(G-3123)*

Carnegie Management & Dev Corp ......E 440 892-6800
Westlake *(G-19327)*

Casto Communities Cnstr Ltd ....B 614 228-8545
Columbus *(G-7137)*

Catholic Diocese of Cleveland ....E 419 289-7224
Ashland *(G-664)*

Cavaliers Holdings LLC ....E 216 420-2000
Cleveland *(G-5136)*

Cbl & Associates Prpts Inc ....E 513 424-8517
Middletown *(G-14344)*

Central Ohio Associates Ltd ....E 419 342-2045
Shelby *(G-16743)*

Centro Properties Group LLC ....E 440 324-6610
Elyria *(G-10487)*

Ch Relty Iv/Clmbus Partners LP ....D 614 885-3334
Columbus *(G-7174)*

Chapel Hill Management Inc ....E 330 633-7100
Akron *(G-125)*

Cincinnati Sports Mall Inc ....D 513 527-4000
Cincinnati *(G-3269)*

City of Cleveland ....E 216 621-4231
Cleveland *(G-5193)*

Coldwell Bnkr Hritg Rltors LLC ....E 937 434-7600
Dayton *(G-9313)*

Columbian Corporation Mantua ....E 330 274-2576
Mantua *(G-13265)*

Compco Land Company ....D 330 482-0200
Youngstown *(G-20004)*

Continental Properties ....B 614 221-1800
Columbus *(G-7360)*

Cornerstone Managed Prpts LLC ....E 440 263-7708
Lorain *(G-12899)*

Coughlin Holdings Ltd Partnr ....E 614 847-1002
Worthington *(G-19801)*

Court Stret Center Associates ....E 513 241-0415
Cincinnati *(G-3375)*

Daniel Maury Construction Co ....E 513 984-4096
Loveland *(G-12988)*

Dayton Hcri Place Denver ....E 419 247-2800
Toledo *(G-17693)*

Duke Realty Corporation ....D 614 932-6000
Dublin *(G-10212)*

Easton Town Center II LLC ....D 614 416-7000
Columbus *(G-7492)*

Easton Town Center LLC ....C 614 337-2560
Columbus *(G-7493)*

Emmett Dan House Ltd Partnr ....E 740 392-6886
Mount Vernon *(G-14764)*

Equity Residential Properties ....E 216 861-2700
Cleveland *(G-5489)*

F H Bonn ....E 937 323-7024
Springfield *(G-17035)*

Fairfield Homes Inc ....C 614 873-3533
Plain City *(G-16053)*

Fairlawn Associates Ltd ....C 330 867-5000
Fairlawn *(G-10826)*

Findlay Inn & Conference Ctr ....D 419 422-5682
Findlay *(G-10904)*

First Interstate Properties ....E 216 381-2900
Cleveland *(G-5536)*

▲ Forest City Enterprises LP ....B 216 621-6060
Cleveland *(G-5553)*

Forest City Enterprises LP ....E 216 416-3756
Cleveland *(G-5554)*

Forest City Enterprises LP ....E 440 888-8664
Cleveland *(G-5555)*

Forest City Enterprises LP ....E 216 416-3780
Cleveland *(G-5556)*

Forest City Enterprises LP ....D 216 416-3766
Cleveland *(G-5557)*

Forest City Properties LLC ....E 216 621-6060
Cleveland *(G-5559)*

Friedman Management Company ....D 614 224-2424
Columbus *(G-7626)*

Gardner Inc ....C 614 456-4000
Columbus *(G-7648)*

Garland/Dbs Inc ....C 216 641-7500
Cleveland *(G-5592)*

Glemsure Realty Trust ....E 740 522-6620
Heath *(G-11703)*

Glen Arbors Ltd Partnership ....D 937 293-0900
Moraine *(G-14661)*

Glimcher Realty Trust ....E 614 861-3232
Columbus *(G-7674)*

Gms Management Co Inc ....E 216 766-6000
Cleveland *(G-5612)*

Goldberg Companies Inc ....E 216 475-2600
Cleveland *(G-5613)*

Goodall Properties Ltd ....E 513 621-5522
Cincinnati *(G-3626)*

Goodman Properties Inc ....E 740 264-7781
Steubenville *(G-17155)*

Graham Investment Co ....D 740 382-0902
Marion *(G-13422)*

Great Lakes Management Inc ....E 216 883-6500
Cleveland *(G-5628)*

Greater Clumbus Convention Ctr ....C 614 827-2500
Columbus *(G-7691)*

Hadler-Zimmerman Inc ....E 614 457-6650
Columbus *(G-7710)*

Hall Nazareth Inc ....D 419 832-2900
Grand Rapids *(G-11325)*

Highland Village Ltd Partnr ....D 614 863-4640
New Albany *(G-14856)*

Hills Property Management Inc ....E 513 984-0300
Blue Ash *(G-1581)*

Hit Portfolio I Misc Trs LLC ....C 614 228-1234
Columbus *(G-7753)*

Holland Management Inc ....B 330 239-4474
Sharon Center *(G-16722)*

Hotel 50 S Front Opco L P ....D 614 885-3334
Columbus *(G-7774)*

Hoty Enterprises Inc ....E 419 609-7000
Sandusky *(G-16617)*

I-X Center Corporation ....C 216 265-2675
Cleveland *(G-5732)*

Islander Company ....E 440 243-0593
Cleveland *(G-5767)*

Jacobs Real Estate Services ....E 216 514-9830
Beachwood *(G-1068)*

Jade Investments ....E 330 425-3141
Twinsburg *(G-18284)*

Judy Mills Company Inc ....E 513 271-4241
Cincinnati *(G-3841)*

Jvc Sports Corp ....E 330 726-1757
Youngstown *(G-20089)*

King Group Inc ....E 216 831-9330
Beachwood *(G-1073)*

King James Group IV Ltd ....E 440 250-1851
Westlake *(G-19363)*

King James Park Ltd ....E 440 835-1100
Westlake *(G-19364)*

Kingsmason Properties Ltd ....E 513 932-6010
Lebanon *(G-12476)*

Kohr Royer Griffith Dev Co LLC ....E 614 228-2471
Columbus *(G-7920)*

L and M Investment Co ....E 740 653-3583
Lancaster *(G-12409)*

L Brands Service Company LLC ......D 614 415-7000
Columbus *(G-7933)*

Ladera Healthcare Company ....E 614 459-1313
Columbus *(G-7943)*

Laudan Properties LLC ....E 234 212-3225
Twinsburg *(G-18290)*

Lewis Price Realty Co ....E 330 856-1911
Warren *(G-18723)*

Lima Mall Inc ....E 419 331-6255
Lima *(G-12681)*

Lmt Enterprises Maumee Inc ....E 419 891-7325
Maumee *(G-13810)*

Lofinos Inc ....D 937 431-1662
Dayton *(G-9572)*

M & L Leasing Co ....E 330 343-8910
Mineral City *(G-14506)*

Majestic Steel Properties Inc ....D 440 786-2666
Cleveland *(G-5901)*

Makoy Center Inc ....E 614 777-1211
Hilliard *(G-11787)*

Mall Park Southern ....D 330 758-4511
Youngstown *(G-20113)*

Manleys Manor Nursing Home Inc ...C 419 424-0402
Findlay *(G-10937)*

Marion Road Enterprises ....C 614 228-6525
Columbus *(G-8020)*

Matco Properties Inc ....D 440 366-5501
Elyria *(G-10533)*

McM General Properties Ltd ....E 216 851-8000
Cleveland *(G-5937)*

Meadowbrook Mall Company ....E 330 747-2661
Youngstown *(G-20119)*

MEI Hotels Incorporated ....C 216 589-0441
Cleveland *(G-5949)*

Mendelson Realty Ltd ....E 937 461-3525
Dayton *(G-9607)*

Miller-Valentine Partners ....C 937 293-0900
Moraine *(G-14679)*

Mills Corporation ....E 513 671-2882
Cincinnati *(G-4056)*

▲ Musical Arts Association ....C 216 231-7300
Cleveland *(G-6028)*

Oak Health Care Investor ....E 614 794-8800
Westerville *(G-19192)*

Ohio State University ....A 614 688-3939
Columbus *(G-8159)*

Olentangy Village Associates ....E 614 515-4680
Columbus *(G-8371)*

Oliver House Rest Complex ....D 419 243-1302
Toledo *(G-17960)*

Park Cincinnati Board ....D 513 421-4086
Cincinnati *(G-4201)*

◆ Park Corporation ....B 216 267-4870
Cleveland *(G-6163)*

Phil Giessler ....E 614 888-0307
Worthington *(G-19835)*

Polaris Towne Center LLC ....E 614 456-0123
Columbus *(G-6830)*

Power Management Inc ....E 937 222-2909
Dayton *(G-9701)*

Primo Properties LLC ....C 330 606-6746
Austintown *(G-859)*

◆ Pubco Corporation ....E 216 881-5300
Cleveland *(G-6268)*

Quincy Mall Inc ....E 614 228-5331
Columbus *(G-8482)*

Raf Celina LLC ....E 216 464-6626
Celina *(G-2607)*

Reed Hartman Corporate Center ....E 513 984-3030
Blue Ash *(G-1642)*

Ricco Enterprises Incorporated ......E 216 883-7775
Cleveland *(G-6319)*

Richard E Jacobs Group LLC ....E 440 871-4800
Cleveland *(G-6320)*

Robinson Investments Ltd ....E 937 593-1849
Bellefontaine *(G-1362)*

Roemer Land Investment Co ....E 419 475-5151
Toledo *(G-18012)*

Rootstown Township ....E 330 296-8240
Ravenna *(G-16265)*

Rose Properties Inc ....E 216 881-6000
Cleveland *(G-6341)*

Sanico Inc ....D 440 439-5686
Cleveland *(G-6371)*

Saw Mill Creek Ltd ....C 419 433-3800
Huron *(G-12030)*

Schottenstein Realty LLC ....E 614 445-8461
Columbus *(G-8609)*

Simon Property Group ....E 614 717-9300
Dublin *(G-10335)*

Smg Holdings Inc ....C 614 827-2500
Columbus *(G-8654)*

Southwest Associates ....C 440 243-7888
Cleveland *(G-6426)*

Stranahan Theatre Trust ....D 419 381-8851
Toledo *(G-18050)*

Ted Graham ....E 740 223-3509
Marion *(G-13463)*

The C-Z Company ....E 740 432-6334
Cambridge *(G-2085)*

Thompson Hall & Jordan Fnrl HM ....E 513 761-8881
Cincinnati *(G-4604)*

Three M Associates ....D 330 674-9646
Millersburg *(G-14496)*

U S Development Corp ....E 330 673-6900
Kent *(G-12264)*

United Fd Coml Wkrs Local 880 ......E 216 241-5930
Cleveland *(G-6571)*

United Management Inc ....D 614 228-5331
Columbus *(G-8803)*

Universal Veneer Mill Corp ....C 740 522-1147
Newark *(G-15106)*

Valley Title & Escro Agency ....D 330 392-6171
Warren *(G-18765)*

Visconsi Management Inc ....E 216 464-5550
Cleveland *(G-6635)*

Waldon Management Corp ....E 330 792-7688
Youngstown *(G-20240)*

Washington PRI ....C 614 621-9000
Columbus *(G-8875)*

Washington Prime Group Inc ....D 614 621-9000
Columbus *(G-8877)*

Waterfront & Associates Inc ....B 859 581-1414
Cincinnati *(G-4770)*

Wernli Realty Inc ....D 937 258-7878
Beavercreek *(G-1240)*

Weston Inc ....E 440 349-9000
Cleveland *(G-6679)*

White & Chambers Partnership ....E 740 594-8381
Athens *(G-811)*

Whitford Woods Co Inc ....E 440 693-4344
Middlefield *(G-14279)*

Wickliffe Associates Partnr ....E 440 585-3505
Wickliffe *(G-19477)*

Willis Day Management Inc ....E 419 476-8000
Toledo *(G-18159)*

Zaremba LLC ....D 216 221-6600
Cleveland *(G-6709)*

Zucker Building Company ....D 216 861-7114
Cleveland *(G-6714)*

Zvn Properties Inc ....D 330 854-5890
Canal Fulton *(G-2100)*

6513 Operators Of Apartment Buildings

12000 Edgewater Drive LLC ....D 216 520-1250
Lakewood *(G-12333)*

A P & P Dev & Cnstr Co ....D 330 833-8886
Massillon *(G-13658)*

Akron Metropolitan Hsing Auth ....C 330 920-1652
Stow *(G-17189)*

Allen Metropolitan Hsing Auth ....E 419 228-6065
Lima *(G-12598)*

Alliance Towers LLC ....A 330 823-1063
Alliance *(G-517)*

Alpha PHI Alpha Homes Inc ....D 330 376-2115
Akron *(G-68)*

Andrews Apartments Ltd ....C 440 946-3600
Willoughby *(G-19505)*

Arbor Park Phase Two Assoc ....E 561 998-0700
Cleveland *(G-5001)*

Arbor Pk Phase Three Assoc LP ......E 561 998-0700
Cleveland *(G-5002)*

Aurora Hotel Partners LLC ....E 330 562-0767
Aurora *(G-817)*

Azalea Alabama Investment LLC .....D 216 520-1250
Cleveland *(G-5030)*

Baptist Home and Center ....C 513 662-5880
Cincinnati *(G-3018)*

Barcus Company Inc ....E 614 451-9000
Columbus *(G-7017)*

Belmont Metro Hsing Auth ....E 740 633-5085
Martins Ferry *(G-13476)*

Biltmore Apartments Ltd ....D 937 461-9695
Dayton *(G-9254)*

Brethren Care Inc ....C 419 289-0803
Ashland *(G-659)*

Brodhead Village Ltd ....D 614 863-4640
New Albany *(G-14845)*

Brookdale Lving Cmmunities Inc .....E 330 666-4545
Akron *(G-109)*

Brookdale Senior Living Inc ....E 330 262-1615
Wooster *(G-19695)*

Buckeye Cmnty Eighty One LP ....E 614 942-2020
Columbus *(G-7086)*

Buckeye Cmnty Thirty Five LP ....D 614 942-2020
Akron *(G-112)*

Buckingham Management LLC ....C 844 361-5559
Perrysburg *(G-15843)*

Burton Carol Management ....E 216 464-5130
Cleveland *(G-5104)*

C I E Inc ....B 419 986-5566
Burgoon *(G-2011)*

Capital Senior Living Corp ....C 419 874-2564
Perrysburg *(G-15845)*

Capital Senior Living Corp ....C 216 289-9800
Richmond Heights *(G-16388)*

Capital Senior Living Corp ....C 513 829-6200
Fairfield *(G-10707)*

Cardinal Retirement Village ....E 330 928-7888
Cuyahoga Falls *(G-9076)*

Cassady Vlg Aprtments Ohio LLC ....D 216 520-1250
Columbus *(G-7136)*

Chelmsford Apartments Ltd ....E 419 389-0800
Toledo *(G-17649)*

Cincinnati Metro Hsing Auth ....E 513 421-2642
Cincinnati *(G-3254)*

Cincinnati Metro Hsing Auth ....E 513 333-0670
Cincinnati *(G-3256)*

City of Akron ....D 330 564-4075
Akron *(G-133)*

Claremont Retirement Village ....D 614 761-2011
Columbus *(G-7218)*

Commons of Providence..........D 419 624-1171	Holland Management Inc............B 330 239-4474	Ohio Eastern Star Home...........C 740 397-1706
Sandusky *(G-16590)*	Sharon Center *(G-16722)*	Mount Vernon *(G-14785)*
Community Prpts Ohio III LLC.........D 614 253-0984	Horizon House Apartments LLC.........D 740 354-6393	Ohio Living ....B 614 224-1651
Columbus *(G-7334)*	Portsmouth *(G-16147)*	Columbus *(G-8271)*
Community Prpts Ohio MGT Svcs ....D 614 253-0984	Huber Investment Corporation ....E 937 233-1122	Ohio Presbt Retirement Svcs ....B 330 746-2944
Columbus *(G-7335)*	Dayton *(G-9509)*	Youngstown *(G-20147)*
Copeland Oaks.............................B 330 938-1050	Iacovetta Builders Inc ....E 614 272-6464	Olentangy Village Associates ....E 614 515-4680
Sebring *(G-16666)*	Columbus *(G-7797)*	Columbus *(G-8371)*
Copeland Oaks.............................E 330 938-6126	Indian Hills Senior Community ....E 216 486-7700	Oliver House Rest Complex ....D 419 243-1302
Sebring *(G-16667)*	Euclid *(G-10643)*	Toledo *(G-17960)*
Creative Living Inc ....E 614 421-1131	Interntional Towers I Ohio Ltd ....D 216 520-1250	Olmsted Mnor Rtrment Cmnty Ltd .....E 440 779-8886
Columbus *(G-7386)*	Youngstown *(G-20083)*	North Olmsted *(G-15303)*
Creative Living Housing Corp ....E 614 421-1226	Intown Suites Management Inc ....E 937 433-9038	One Lincoln Park ....D 937 298-0594
Columbus *(G-7387)*	Dayton *(G-9520)*	Dayton *(G-9675)*
Crestview Manor Nursing Home.........C 740 654-2634	Islander Company........................E 440 243-0593	Original Partners Ltd Partnr ....C 513 381-8696
Lancaster *(G-12386)*	Cleveland *(G-5767)*	Cincinnati *(G-4183)*
Cwb Property Managment Inc ....E 614 793-2244	Judson ....B 216 791-2004	Orrvilla Inc ....E 330 683-4455
Dublin *(G-10195)*	Cleveland *(G-5808)*	Orrville *(G-15637)*
D & S Properties..........................E 614 224-6663	K & D Enterprises Inc ....E 440 946-3600	Otterbein Portage Valley Inc ....C 888 749-4950
Columbus *(G-7407)*	Willoughby *(G-19531)*	Pemberville *(G-15806)*
E A Zicka Co ....E 513 451-1440	K&D Group Inc ....E 440 946-3600	Overbrook Park Ltd ....D 740 773-1159
Cincinnati *(G-3464)*	Willoughby *(G-19532)*	Chillicothe *(G-2808)*
Ea Vica Co ....E 513 481-3500	Kensington Place Inc ....E 614 252-5276	Owners Management Company ....E 440 439-3800
Cincinnati *(G-3467)*	Columbus *(G-7895)*	Parma *(G-15770)*
Eaglewood Care Center ....C 937 399-7195	Kettering Medical Center ....D 937 866-2984	Parklane Manor of Akron Inc ....E 330 724-3315
Springfield *(G-17031)*	Miamisburg *(G-14182)*	Akron *(G-370)*
Ebenezer Road Corp ....C 513 941-0099	Kingsbury Tower I Ltd ....D 216 795-3950	Paul Dennis ....E 440 746-8600
Cincinnati *(G-3480)*	Cleveland *(G-5832)*	Brecksville *(G-1795)*
Edward Rose Associates Inc ....E 513 752-2727	Klingbeil Multifamilty Fund IV ....D 415 398-0106	Phoenix Residential Centers ....D 440 887-6097
Batavia *(G-998)*	Columbus *(G-7912)*	Cleveland *(G-6205)*
Emerald Dev Ecnomic Netwrk Inc ....D 216 961-9690	Kopf Construction Corporation ....D 440 933-0250	Pickaway County Community Acti ....D 740 477-1655
Cleveland *(G-5473)*	Avon Lake *(G-922)*	Circleville *(G-4839)*
Englewood Square Ltd ....D 937 836-4117	L S C Service Corp ....E 216 521-7260	Pinewood Place Apartments ....A 419 243-1413
Englewood *(G-10586)*	Lakewood *(G-12350)*	Toledo *(G-17977)*
Episcopal Retirement Homes ....D 513 271-9610	L W Limited ....E 513 721-2744	Plaza Properties Inc ....E 614 237-3726
Cincinnati *(G-3507)*	Cincinnati *(G-3901)*	Columbus *(G-8455)*
Equity Residential Properties ....E 216 861-2700	Lakewoods II Ltd ....D 937 254-6141	Pleasant Lake Apartments Ltd ....E 440 845-2694
Cleveland *(G-5489)*	Dayton *(G-9556)*	Cleveland *(G-6220)*
Evangelical Retirement ....C 937 837-5581	Links ....E 937 644-9988	Power Management Inc ....E 937 222-2909
Dayton *(G-9419)*	Marysville *(G-13510)*	Dayton *(G-9701)*
Fairfield Homes Inc ....E 740 653-3583	Little Bark View Limited ....E 216 520-1250	Primrose Rtrment Cmmnities LLC .....E 419 224-1200
Lancaster *(G-12397)*	Cleveland *(G-5874)*	Lima *(G-12724)*
Fairfield Homes Inc ....C 614 873-3533	Mansfield Memorial Homes...........C 419 774-5100	Province Kent OH LLC ....E 330 673-3808
Plain City *(G-16053)*	Mansfield *(G-13208)*	Kent *(G-12255)*
Fay Limited Partnership ....E 513 542-8333	Marsol Apartments ....E 440 449-5800	Rahf IV Kent LLC ....E 216 621-6060
Cincinnati *(G-3534)*	Cleveland *(G-5916)*	Kent *(G-12256)*
Fay Limited Partnership ....E 513 241-1911	Menorah Park Center For Senio ....E 216 831-6515	Real Estate Investors Mgt Inc ....E 614 777-2444
Cincinnati *(G-3535)*	Beachwood *(G-1079)*	Columbus *(G-8494)*
Fieldstone Limited Partnership ....C 937 293-0900	Menorah Park Center For Senio ....A 216 831-6500	Riverside Commons Ltd Partnr ....D 614 863-4640
Moraine *(G-14658)*	Cleveland *(G-5952)*	Reynoldsburg *(G-16329)*
Fish Creek Plaza Ltd ....D 330 688-0450	Mercy Health West Park ....C 513 451-8900	Saint Edward Housing Corp ....E 330 668-2828
Stow *(G-17204)*	Cincinnati *(G-4033)*	Fairlawn *(G-10846)*
▲ Forest City Enterprises LP ....B 216 621-6060	Miami Cnty Cmnty Action Cuncil ....E 937 335-7921	Sateri Home Inc...........................D 330 758-8106
Cleveland *(G-5553)*	Troy *(G-18212)*	Youngstown *(G-20204)*
Forest City Properties LLC ....C 216 621-6060	Millennia Housing MGT Ltd.............E 216 520-1250	Senior Lifestyle Corporation ....D 513 777-4457
Cleveland *(G-5559)*	Cleveland *(G-5996)*	West Chester *(G-19002)*
Fort Austin Ltd Partnership ....C 440 892-4200	Mrn Limited Partnership...............E 216 589-5631	Sh-91 Limited Partnership ....E 330 535-1581
Cleveland *(G-5564)*	Cleveland *(G-6019)*	Akron *(G-426)*
FTM Associates LLC ....D 614 846-1834	Mulberry Garden A L S ....E 330 630-3980	Shaker House ....D 216 991-6000
Columbus *(G-7632)*	Munroe Falls *(G-14798)*	Cleveland *(G-6402)*
G J Goudreau Operating Co ....E 216 741-7524	Murray Guttman ....D 513 984-0300	Shepherd of The Valley Luthera ....E 330 726-7110
Cleveland *(G-5587)*	Blue Ash *(G-1617)*	Poland *(G-16089)*
Galion East Ohio I LP ....D 216 520-1250	National Church Residences ....C 614 451-2151	Sherman Thompson Oh Tc LP.........D 216 520-1250
Galion *(G-11175)*	Columbus *(G-8130)*	Ironton *(G-12166)*
Garland Group Inc ....E 614 294-4411	National Housing Corporation ....E 614 481-8106	SKW Management LLC..................E 937 382-7938
Columbus *(G-7650)*	Columbus *(G-8134)*	Lynchburg *(G-13055)*
Gemini Properties ....E 419 531-9211	Neighborhood Properties Inc ....E 419 473-2604	Slaters Inc ....E 740 654-2204
Toledo *(G-17758)*	Toledo *(G-17937)*	Lancaster *(G-12435)*
Gemini Properties ....E 614 764-2800	Network Restorations II ....D 614 253-0984	Smb Construction Co Inc ....E 419 269-1473
Dublin *(G-10234)*	Columbus *(G-8179)*	Toledo *(G-18038)*
Giffin Management Group Inc ....E 330 758-4695	Network Restorations III LLC.........D 614 253-0984	Smith Tandy Company ....E 614 224-9255
Youngstown *(G-20049)*	Columbus *(G-8180)*	Columbus *(G-8656)*
Glen Wesley Inc ....D 614 888-7492	New Birch Manor I Assoc LLC ....D 330 723-3404	South Franklin Circle ....C 440 247-1300
Columbus *(G-7673)*	Medina *(G-13980)*	Chagrin Falls *(G-2683)*
Gms Management Co Inc ....E 216 766-6000	▲ Northeast Cincinnati Hotel LLC ....C 513 459-9800	Spruce Bough Homes LLC.............D 614 253-0984
Cleveland *(G-5612)*	Mason *(G-13623)*	Columbus *(G-8678)*
Goldberg Companies Inc ....E 216 475-2600	Northwesterly Ltd ....E 216 228-2266	St Regis Investment LLC...............D 216 520-1250
Cleveland *(G-5613)*	Cleveland *(G-6098)*	Cleveland *(G-6449)*
Harvest Facility Holdings LP ....E 419 472-7115	Notre Dame Academy Apartments ....E 216 707-1590	Stautberg Family LLC ....E 513 941-5070
Toledo *(G-17784)*	Cleveland *(G-6100)*	Cincinnati *(G-4541)*
Harvest Facility Holdings LP ....E 440 268-9555	Npa Associates ....D 614 258-4053	Summerfield Homes LLC...............E 614 253-0984
Cleveland *(G-5665)*	Beachwood *(G-1088)*	Columbus *(G-8709)*
Hcf Management Inc ....D 419 999-2010	Oak Brook Gardens ....D 440 237-3613	Summit Management Services Inc.........E 330 723-0864
Lima *(G-12652)*	North Royalton *(G-15363)*	Medina *(G-14007)*
Highland Village Ltd Partnr ....D 614 863-4640	Oakleaf Toledo Ltd Partnership ....E 419 885-3934	Sunpoint Senior Living Hamlet.........E 440 247-4200
New Albany *(G-14856)*	Toledo *(G-17956)*	Chagrin Falls *(G-2657)*
Hills Property Management Inc ....D 513 984-0300	Oakwood Management Company ....E 740 774-3570	Sunset Rtrment Communities Inc ....D 419 724-1200
Blue Ash *(G-1581)*	Chillicothe *(G-2806)*	Ottawa Hills *(G-15669)*
Hilltop Village ....E 216 261-8383	Oberer Development Co ....E 937 910-0851	Superior Apartments ....E 216 861-6405
Cleveland *(G-5693)*	Miamisburg *(G-14199)*	Cleveland *(G-6482)*

Tm Wallick Rsdntl Prpts I Ltd ....D....... 614 863-4640
Reynoldsburg (G-16333)
Towne Properties Asset MGT ....A....... 513 381-8696
Cincinnati (G-4617)
Towne Properties Assoc Inc ....E....... 513 874-3737
Cincinnati (G-4620)
Townhomes Management Inc ....E....... 614 228-3578
Columbus (G-8767)
Transcon Builders Inc ....E....... 440 439-3400
Cleveland (G-6540)
Unite Churc Resid of Oxfor Mis ....E....... 740 382-4885
Marion (G-13469)
United Church Homes ....D....... 740 382-4885
Marion (G-13470)
United Church Res of Kenton ....D....... 740 382-4885
Kenton (G-12289)
United Church Residences of ....D....... 614 837-2008
Canal Winchester (G-2123)
Universal Development MGT Inc ....E....... 330 759-7017
Girard (G-11303)
Uptown Rental Properties LLC ....E....... 513 861-9394
Cincinnati (G-4732)
Urbancrest Affrdbl Hsing LLC ....D....... 614 228-3578
Columbus (G-8829)
Victory Sq Aprtmnts Ltd Partnr ....D....... 330 455-8035
Canton (G-2527)
Wallace F Ackley Co ....D....... 614 231-3661
Columbus (G-8871)
Wallick Construction Co ....E....... 937 399-7009
Springfield (G-17132)
Walnut Hills Preservation LP ....D....... 513 281-1288
Cincinnati (G-4768)
Washington Square Apartments ....E....... 740 349-8353
Newark (G-15107)
▲ Welltower Inc ....B....... 419 247-2800
Toledo (G-18152)
Westgate Limited Partnership ....C....... 419 535-7070
Toledo (G-18155)
Westlake Village Inc ....C....... 440 892-4200
Cleveland (G-6678)
Westview Apartments Ohio LLC ....B....... 216 520-1250
Youngstown (G-20244)
Whitehurst Company ....E....... 419 865-0799
Maumee (G-13868)
Windsorwood Place Inc ....E....... 740 623-4600
Coshocton (G-9031)
Zanesville Metro Hsing Auth ....D....... 740 454-9714
Zanesville (G-20383)
Zepf Housing Corp One Inc ....C....... 419 531-0019
Toledo (G-18180)

6514 Operators Of Dwellings, Except Apartments

Birchaven Village ....B....... 419 424-3000
Findlay (G-10870)
Cincinnati Metro Hsing Auth ....E....... 513 421-8190
Cincinnati (G-3255)
Cincinnati Metro Hsing Auth ....E....... 513 333-0670
Cincinnati (G-3256)
Cwb Property Managmnt Inc ....E....... 614 793-2244
Dublin (G-10195)
Huber Investment Corporation ....E....... 937 233-1122
Dayton (G-9509)
J & R Associates ....A....... 440 250-4080
Brookpark (G-1898)
Kent Place Housing ....D....... 614 942-2020
Columbus (G-7896)
L and M Investment Co ....E....... 740 653-3583
Lancaster (G-12409)
North Park Care Center LLC ....D....... 440 250-4080
Brookpark (G-1904)
Norwalk Golf Properties Inc ....E....... 419 668-8535
Norwalk (G-15450)
Original Partners Ltd Partnr ....C....... 513 381-8696
Cincinnati (G-4183)
Our House Inc ....E....... 440 835-2110
Westlake (G-19390)
Rv Properties LLC ....E....... 330 928-7888
Cuyahoga Falls (G-9123)
Towne Properties Assoc Inc ....E....... 513 874-3737
Cincinnati (G-4620)
Westview-Youngstown Ltd ....D....... 330 799-2787
Youngstown (G-20245)

6515 Operators of Residential Mobile Home Sites

Mercelina Mobile Home Park ....D....... 419 586-5407
Celina (G-2599)

Park Management Specialist ....D....... 419 893-4879
Maumee (G-13831)

6517 Railroad Property Lessors

Feridean Group Inc ....E....... 614 898-7488
Westerville (G-19166)

6519 Lessors Of Real Estate, NEC

Baker Bnngson Rlty Auctioneers ....E....... 419 547-7777
Clyde (G-6740)
Bessemer and Lake Erie RR Co ....C....... 440 593-1102
Conneaut (G-8951)
Catawba-Cleveland Dev Corp ....D....... 419 797-4424
Port Clinton (G-16101)
Cutler Real Estate Inc ....E....... 614 339-4664
Dublin (G-10194)
Darfus ....E....... 740 380-1710
Logan (G-12834)
Employers Mutual Casualty Co ....D....... 513 221-6010
Blue Ash (G-1551)
Etb University Properties LLC ....C....... 440 826-2212
Berea (G-1425)
Fairlawn Associates Ltd ....C....... 330 867-5000
Fairlawn (G-10826)
Hertz Clvland 600 Superior LLC ....E....... 310 584-8108
Cleveland (G-5687)
J & E LLC ....E....... 513 241-0429
Cincinnati (G-3793)
James Lafontaine ....E....... 740 474-5052
Circleville (G-4836)
Mapleview Farms Inc ....E....... 419 826-3671
Swanton (G-17401)
Midway Realty Company ....E....... 440 324-2404
Elyria (G-10538)
Mwa Enterprises Ltd ....E....... 419 599-3835
Napoleon (G-14812)
Ohio Living ....A....... 330 638-2420
Cortland (G-8993)
Sami S Rafidi ....C....... 330 799-9508
Youngstown (G-20202)
Schottenstein Realty LLC ....E....... 614 445-8461
Columbus (G-8609)
Select Hotels Group LLC ....E....... 513 754-0003
Mason (G-13638)
Stranahan Theatre Trust ....E....... 419 381-8851
Toledo (G-18050)
Weston Inc ....E....... 440 349-9001
Solon (G-16914)

6531 Real Estate Agents & Managers

0714 Inc ....E....... 440 327-2123
North Ridgeville (G-15318)
1440 Corporation Inc ....E....... 513 424-2421
Middletown (G-14284)
2780 Airport Drive LLC ....E....... 513 563-7555
Cincinnati (G-2881)
36 E Seventh LLC ....E....... 513 699-2279
Cincinnati (G-2882)
AA Green Realty Inc ....E....... 419 352-5331
Bowling Green (G-1711)
Abco Contracting LLC ....E....... 419 973-4772
Toledo (G-17580)
Adena Commercial LLC ....E....... 614 436-9800
Columbus (G-6798)
Al Neyer LLC ....D....... 513 271-6400
Cincinnati (G-2917)
Al-Mar Lanes ....E....... 419 352-4637
Bowling Green (G-1713)
Allen Est Mangement Ltd ....E....... 419 526-6505
Mansfield (G-13133)
Allen Metro Hsing MGT Dev Corp ....E....... 419 228-6065
Lima (G-12597)
Altobelli Realestate ....E....... 330 652-0200
Niles (G-15143)
American Bulk Commodities Inc ....C....... 330 758-0841
Youngstown (G-19953)
American Title Services Inc ....E....... 330 652-1609
Niles (G-15144)
Amsdell Construction Inc ....E....... 216 458-0670
Cleveland (G-4974)
Appraisal Research Corporation ....E....... 419 423-3582
Findlay (G-10865)
Arena Management Holdings LLC ....A....... 513 421-4111
Cincinnati (G-2984)
Baker Bnngson Rlty Auctioneers ....E....... 419 547-7777
Clyde (G-6740)
Baur Leo Century 21 Realty ....E....... 440 585-2300
Willowick (G-19596)
Bellwether Entp RE Capitl LLC ....E....... 216 820-4500
Cleveland (G-5052)

Best Realty Inc ....E....... 513 932-3948
Lebanon (G-12451)
Beyond 2000 Realty Inc ....E....... 440 842-7200
Cleveland (G-5062)
Big Hill Realty Corp ....D....... 937 426-4420
Beavercreek (G-1206)
Big Hill Realty Corp ....C....... 937 435-1177
Dayton (G-9251)
Big Hill Realty Corp ....E....... 937 429-2200
Beavercreek (G-1207)
Blossom Hill Elderly Housing L ....D....... 330 385-4310
East Liverpool (G-10398)
Blue Ash Distribution Ctr LLC ....E....... 513 699-2279
Cincinnati (G-3059)
Brg Realty Group LLC ....C....... 513 936-5960
Cincinnati (G-3072)
Brookwood Management Company ....E....... 330 497-6565
Canton (G-2219)
Buckeye Cmnty Twenty Six LP ....E....... 614 942-2020
Columbus (G-7088)
Butler County of Ohio ....D....... 513 887-3154
Hamilton (G-11562)
C V Perry & Co ....E....... 614 221-4131
Columbus (G-7105)
Calabresem Racek & Markos Inc ....E....... 216 696-5442
Cleveland (G-5113)
Capital Partners Realty LLC ....E....... 614 888-1000
Worthington (G-19795)
Capital Properties MGT Ltd ....E....... 216 991-3057
Cleveland (G-5120)
Capital Senior Living ....E....... 440 356-5444
Rocky River (G-16425)
Carleton Realty Inc ....E....... 740 653-5200
Lancaster (G-12375)
Carnegie Companies Inc ....E....... 440 232-2300
Solon (G-16831)
Cassidy Trley Coml RE Svcs Inc ....E....... 513 771-2580
Cincinnati (G-3130)
Cbre Inc ....D....... 513 369-1300
Cincinnati (G-3134)
Cbre Inc ....E....... 216 687-1800
Cleveland (G-5142)
Cbre Inc ....E....... 614 419-7429
Blacklick (G-1476)
Cbre Inc ....D....... 614 438-5488
Columbus (G-7144)
Century 21 Elite Performance ....E....... 937 438-8221
Spring Valley (G-16957)
Century 21 Trammell Odonnell ....D....... 440 888-6800
Cleveland (G-5157)
Century 21-Joe Walker & Assoc ....E....... 614 899-1400
Columbus (G-6804)
Chartwell Group LLC ....E....... 216 360-0009
Cleveland (G-5171)
Cincinnati Coml Contg LLC ....E....... 513 561-6633
Cincinnati (G-3235)
City of Willoughby ....B....... 440 953-4111
Willoughby (G-19512)
Classic Real Estate Co ....E....... 937 393-3416
Hillsboro (G-11833)
Cleveland Real Estate Partners ....E....... 216 623-1600
Cleveland (G-5283)
Coffman Family Partnership ....E....... 614 864-5400
Columbus (G-7241)
Coldwell Banker ....E....... 513 321-9944
Cincinnati (G-3323)
Coldwell Banker First Place RE ....D....... 330 726-8161
Poland (G-16083)
Coldwell Banker King Thompson ....D....... 614 759-0808
Pickerington (G-15952)
Coldwell Banker West Shell ....E....... 513 829-4000
West Chester (G-18894)
Coldwell Banker West Shell ....D....... 513 922-9400
Cincinnati (G-3324)
Coldwell Banker West Shell ....E....... 513 385-9300
Cincinnati (G-3325)
Coldwell Banker West Shell ....D....... 513 777-7900
West Chester (G-18895)
Coldwell Banker West Shell ....E....... 513 271-7200
Cincinnati (G-3326)
Coldwell Bnkr Hritg Rltors LLC ....E....... 937 304-8500
Dayton (G-9312)
Coldwell Bnkr Hritg Rltors LLC ....E....... 937 748-5500
Springboro (G-16966)
Coldwell Bnkr Hritg Rltors LLC ....E....... 937 434-7600
Dayton (G-9313)
Coldwell Bnkr Hritg Rltors LLC ....E....... 937 426-6060
Beavercreek Township (G-1244)
Coldwell Bnkr Hritg Rltors LLC ....E....... 937 890-2200
Vandalia (G-18518)

Comey & Shepherd LLC ....E 513 489-2100
Cincinnati *(G-3332)*

Comey & Shepherd LLC ....E 513 321-4343
Cincinnati *(G-3333)*

Comey & Shepherd LLC ....E 513 231-2800
Cincinnati *(G-3334)*

Comey & Shepherd LLC ....E 513 891-4444
Cincinnati *(G-3335)*

Communicare Health Svcs Inc ....D 330 792-7799
Youngstown *(G-19997)*

Communicare Health Svcs Inc ....D 419 394-7611
Saint Marys *(G-16521)*

Communicare Health Svcs Inc ....D 330 792-5511
Youngstown *(G-19998)*

Communicare Health Svcs Inc ....C 330 454-2152
Canton *(G-2263)*

Communicare Health Svcs Inc ....D 330 630-9780
Tallmadge *(G-17472)*

Connor Group A RE Inv Firm LLC ....B 937 434-3095
Miamisburg *(G-14154)*

Continental Realty Ltd ....E 614 221-6260
Columbus *(G-7362)*

County of Allen ....E 419 228-6065
Lima *(G-12621)*

Crawford Hoying Ltd ....C 614 335-2020
Dublin *(G-10192)*

Croxton Realty Company ....E 330 492-1697
Canton *(G-2275)*

Cushman & Wakefield Inc ....E 513 631-1121
Norwood *(G-15461)*

Cushman & Wakefield Inc ....E 937 222-7884
Moraine *(G-14638)*

Cutler and Associates Inc ....D 330 896-1680
Akron *(G-177)*

Cutler and Associates Inc ....E 330 688-2100
Stow *(G-17197)*

Cutler and Associates Inc ....E 330 493-9323
Canton *(G-2276)*

Cutler Real Estate ....D 330 499-9922
North Canton *(G-15195)*

Cutler Real Estate ....C 330 836-9141
Fairlawn *(G-10820)*

Cutler Real Estate ....E 330 688-2100
Stow *(G-17198)*

Cutler Real Estate ....D 330 733-7575
Ravenna *(G-16241)*

Cutler Real Estate ....D 330 492-7230
Canton *(G-2277)*

Cutler Real Estate Inc ....E 614 339-4664
Dublin *(G-10194)*

Cwb Property Managmnt Inc ....E 614 793-2244
Dublin *(G-10195)*

Danberry Co ....D 419 866-8888
Maumee *(G-13779)*

Darfus ....E 740 380-1710
Logan *(G-12834)*

Dari Pizza Enterprises II Inc ....C 419 534-3000
Maumee *(G-13780)*

David Campbell ....E 937 266-7064
Dayton *(G-9345)*

Ddr Corp ....E 216 755-5547
Canton *(G-2282)*

Deed Realty Co ....E 330 225-5220
Brunswick *(G-1926)*

Deerfield Estates Inc ....E 440 838-1400
Brecksville *(G-1779)*

Design Homes & Development Co ....E 937 438-3667
Dayton *(G-9389)*

Di Salle Real Estate Co ....E 419 885-4475
Sylvania *(G-17418)*

Duke Realty Corporation ....D 513 651-3900
Mason *(G-13576)*

E A Zicka Co ....E 513 451-1440
Cincinnati *(G-3464)*

E M Columbus LLC ....E 614 861-3232
Columbus *(G-7484)*

Eagle Realty Group LLC ....E 513 361-7700
Cincinnati *(G-3469)*

Eastgate Professional Off Pk V ....E 513 943-0050
Cincinnati *(G-2851)*

Eaton Group GMAC Real Estate ....E 330 726-9999
Warren *(G-18706)*

Echoing Hills Village Inc ....C 740 327-2311
Warsaw *(G-18783)*

Elden Properties Ltd Partnr ....E 440 967-0521
Vermilion *(G-18552)*

Ellis Richard CB Reichle Klein ....E 419 861-1100
Toledo *(G-17711)*

Equity Central LLC ....E 614 861-7777
Gahanna *(G-11118)*

Erhal Inc ....E 513 272-5555
Cincinnati *(G-3513)*

Essex Healthcare Corporation ....E 614 416-0600
Columbus *(G-7536)*

Executive Properties Inc ....E 330 376-4037
Akron *(G-206)*

Fairfield Homes Inc ....E 740 653-3583
Lancaster *(G-12396)*

Fairfield Homes Inc ....C 614 873-3533
Plain City *(G-16053)*

Fay Limited Partnership ....E 513 241-1911
Cincinnati *(G-3535)*

Fc Continental Landlord LLC ....A 216 621-6060
Cleveland *(G-5519)*

First Realty Property MGT Ltd ....E 440 720-0100
Mayfield Village *(G-13885)*

Fleetwood Management Inc ....E 614 538-1277
Columbus *(G-7595)*

Flex Realty ....E 419 841-6208
Toledo *(G-17743)*

Forest City Commercial MGT Inc ....C 216 621-6060
Cleveland *(G-5552)*

Forest Cy Residential MGT Inc ....C 216 621-6060
Cleveland *(G-5563)*

Fujiyama International Inc ....E 614 891-2224
Columbus *(G-7633)*

G H A Inc ....E 440 729-2130
Chesterland *(G-2739)*

G J Goudreau & Co ....E 216 351-5233
Cleveland *(G-5586)*

Garland Group Inc ....E 614 294-4411
Columbus *(G-7650)*

Geneva Chervenic Realty Inc ....D 330 686-8400
Stow *(G-17208)*

Giammarco Properties LLC ....E 419 885-4844
Toledo *(G-17761)*

Gideon ....D 800 395-6014
Cleveland *(G-5607)*

Green Springs Residential Ltd ....C 419 639-2581
Green Springs *(G-11353)*

Greene Town Center LLC ....D 937 490-4990
Beavercreek *(G-1221)*

Hadler Realty Company ....E 614 457-6650
Columbus *(G-7709)*

Hallmark Management Associates ....E 216 681-0080
Cleveland *(G-5658)*

Hanna Holdings Inc ....E 440 971-5600
North Royalton *(G-15358)*

Hanna Holdings Inc ....E 440 933-6195
Avon *(G-884)*

Hanna Holdings Inc ....D 330 707-1000
Poland *(G-16085)*

Henkle-Schueler & Associates ....E 513 932-6070
Lebanon *(G-12471)*

Her Inc ....E 614 240-7400
Columbus *(G-7740)*

Her Inc ....E 614 221-7400
Columbus *(G-7741)*

Her Inc ....D 614 888-7400
Worthington *(G-19814)*

Her Inc ....E 614 239-7400
Columbus *(G-7742)*

Her Inc ....E 614 878-4734
Columbus *(G-7743)*

Her Inc ....E 614 864-7400
Pickerington *(G-15957)*

Her Inc ....C 614 889-7400
Dublin *(G-10240)*

Her Inc ....E 614 771-7400
Hilliard *(G-11772)*

Her Inc ....C 614 890-7400
Westerville *(G-19172)*

Hidden Lake Condominiums ....D 614 488-1131
Columbus *(G-7746)*

Hmshost Corporation ....C 419 547-8667
Clyde *(G-6744)*

Hoeting Inc ....D 513 451-4800
Cincinnati *(G-3715)*

Home Town Realtors LLC ....D 937 890-9111
Dayton *(G-9502)*

Homelife Companies Inc ....E 740 369-1297
Delaware *(G-9986)*

Howard Hanna Smythe Cramer ....E 440 237-8888
North Royalton *(G-15361)*

Howard Hanna Smythe Cramer ....E 330 345-2244
Wooster *(G-19731)*

Howard Hanna Smythe Cramer ....E 440 248-3000
Solon *(G-16858)*

Howard Hanna Smythe Cramer ....E 800 656-7356
Canfield *(G-2142)*

Howard Hanna Smythe Cramer ....E 216 831-0210
Beachwood *(G-1064)*

Howard Hanna Smythe Cramer ....C 216 447-4477
Cleveland *(G-5716)*

Howard Hanna Smythe Cramer ....E 440 333-6500
Rocky River *(G-16436)*

Howard Hanna Smythe Cramer ....D 216 447-4477
Akron *(G-270)*

Howard Hanna Smythe Cramer ....E 330 468-6833
Macedonia *(G-13074)*

Howard Hanna Smythe Cramer ....D 330 725-4137
Medina *(G-13952)*

Howard Hanna Smythe Cramer ....E 440 835-2800
Cleveland *(G-5717)*

Howard Hanna Smythe Cramer ....E 440 282-8002
Amherst *(G-590)*

Howard Hanna Smythe Cramer ....E 330 686-1166
Stow *(G-17212)*

Howard Hanna Smythe Cramer ....E 440 516-4444
Willoughby *(G-19530)*

Howard Hanna Smythe Cramer ....E 440 248-3380
Cleveland *(G-5718)*

Howard Hanna Smythe Cramer ....E 216 751-8550
Beachwood *(G-1065)*

Howard Hanna Smythe Cramer ....D 216 831-9310
Pepper Pike *(G-15818)*

Howard Hanna Smythe Cramer ....E 330 562-6188
Aurora *(G-829)*

Howard Hanna Smythe Cramer ....E 440 428-1818
Madison *(G-13097)*

Howard Hanna Smythe Cramer ....E 330 493-6555
Canton *(G-2350)*

Howard Hanna Smythe Cramer ....E 440 526-1800
Cleveland *(G-5719)*

Howard Hanna Smythe Cramer ....E 330 896-3333
Uniontown *(G-18374)*

Hunt Club LLC ....E 419 885-4647
Sylvania *(G-17431)*

Hunter Realty Inc ....E 216 831-2911
Cleveland *(G-5722)*

Hunter Realty Inc ....E 440 466-9177
Geneva *(G-11243)*

I H S Services Inc ....E 419 224-8811
Lima *(G-12663)*

Inc/Ballew A Head Joint Ventr ....D 614 338-5801
Columbus *(G-7806)*

Integra Cncinnati/Columbus Inc ....E 614 764-8040
Dublin *(G-10257)*

Investek Realty LLC ....E 419 873-1236
Perrysburg *(G-15881)*

Irg Realty Advisors LLC ....E 330 659-4060
Richfield *(G-16361)*

Irongate Inc ....C 937 433-3300
Centerville *(G-2628)*

Irongate Inc ....E 937 298-6000
Dayton *(G-9521)*

Irongate Inc ....D 937 432-3432
Dayton *(G-9522)*

J W Enterprises Inc ....E 740 774-4500
Chillicothe *(G-2796)*

Jacob Real Estate Services ....E 216 687-0500
Cleveland *(G-5777)*

Jacobs Real Estate Services ....E 216 514-9830
Beachwood *(G-1068)*

Jobar Enterprise Inc ....E 216 561-5184
Cleveland *(G-5798)*

John Dellagnese & Assoc Inc ....E 330 668-4000
Akron *(G-292)*

John Stewart Company ....D 513 703-5412
Cincinnati *(G-3824)*

Jones Lang Lsalle Americas Inc ....E 216 447-5276
Brecksville *(G-1787)*

Jordan Realtors Inc ....E 513 791-0281
Cincinnati *(G-3832)*

Joseph Schmidt Realty Inc ....E 330 225-6688
Brunswick *(G-1934)*

Joseph Walker Inc ....E 614 895-3840
Columbus *(G-6817)*

Karam & Simon Realty Inc ....E 330 929-0707
Cuyahoga Falls *(G-9107)*

Kaval-Levine Management Co ....E 440 944-5402
Willoughby Hills *(G-19590)*

Keller Williams Advisors LLC ....E 513 766-9200
Cincinnati *(G-3853)*

Keller Williams Advisory Rlty ....E 513 372-6500
Cincinnati *(G-3854)*

Keller Williams Classic Pro ....D 614 451-8500
Columbus *(G-7888)*

Keller Williams Rlty M Walker ....E 330 571-2020
Stow *(G-17215)*

Company	Code	Phone
Kencor Properties Inc	E	513 984-3870
Cincinnati *(G-3857)*		
Kettering Medical Center	D	937 866-2984
Miamisburg *(G-14182)*		
Key Realty Ltd	C	419 270-7445
Holland *(G-11891)*		
Klingbeil Management Group Co	E	614 220-8900
Columbus *(G-7911)*		
Knoxbi Company LLC	D	440 892-6800
Westlake *(G-19365)*		
Kramer & Kramer Inc	E	937 456-1101
Eaton *(G-10448)*		
Kwik Parking	E	419 246-0454
Toledo *(G-17844)*		
L J F Management Inc	E	513 688-0104
Blue Ash *(G-1593)*		
L O M Inc	E	216 363-6009
Cleveland *(G-5843)*		
Lakeside Realty LLC	E	330 793-4200
Youngstown *(G-20096)*		
Lee & Associates Inc	E	614 923-3300
Dublin *(G-10269)*		
Lenz Inc	E	937 277-9364
Dayton *(G-9563)*		
Lewis Price Realty Co	E	330 856-1911
Warren *(G-18723)*		
Linn Street Holdings LLC	E	513 699-8825
Cincinnati *(G-3936)*		
Longwood Phase One Assoc LP	E	561 998-0700
Cleveland *(G-5880)*		
Lt Land Development LLC	E	937 382-0072
Wilmington *(G-19631)*		
Lucien Realty	D	440 331-8500
Cleveland *(G-5888)*		
Mall Realty Inc	E	937 866-3700
Dayton *(G-9582)*		
Manatron Sabre Systems and Svc	D	937 431-4000
Beavercreek *(G-1229)*		
Marcus Mlichap RE Inv Svcs Inc	E	614 360-9800
Columbus *(G-8017)*		
Marion Plaza Inc	D	330 747-2661
Niles *(G-15158)*		
Martin + WD Apprisal Group Ltd	E	419 241-4998
Toledo *(G-17897)*		
Maryann McEowen	D	330 638-6385
Cortland *(G-8990)*		
Mc Mahon Realestate Co	E	740 344-2250
Newark *(G-15067)*		
Meadowbrook Mall Company	E	330 747-2661
Youngstown *(G-20119)*		
Mendelson Realty Ltd	E	937 461-3525
Dayton *(G-9607)*		
Midland Atlantic Prpts LLC	E	513 792-5000
Cincinnati *(G-4049)*		
Midwest Liquidators Inc	E	614 433-7355
Worthington *(G-19828)*		
Millennia Housing MGT Ltd	E	216 520-1250
Cleveland *(G-5996)*		
Miller-Valentine Partners Ltd	E	513 588-1000
Cincinnati *(G-4054)*		
Miller-Vlentine Operations Inc	E	937 293-0900
Dayton *(G-9638)*		
Miller-Vlentine Operations Inc	A	513 771-0900
Dayton *(G-9639)*		
Miller-Vlntine Partners Ltd Lc	E	513 588-1000
Cincinnati *(G-4055)*		
Model Group Inc	E	513 559-0048
Cincinnati *(G-4068)*		
Morelia Consultants LLC	D	513 469-1500
Cincinnati *(G-4072)*		
Mortgage Information Services	D	216 514-7480
Cleveland *(G-6012)*		
Mrap LLC	E	614 545-3190
Columbus *(G-8117)*		
Mri Software LLC	C	800 321-8770
Solon *(G-16874)*		
Murwood Real Estate Group LLC	E	216 839-5500
Beachwood *(G-1085)*		
Mv Land Development Company	B	937 293-0900
Dayton *(G-9649)*		
National Church Residences	C	614 451-2151
Columbus *(G-8130)*		
National Realty Services Inc	E	614 798-0971
Columbus *(G-8136)*		
◆ Nationwide Mutual Insurance Co	A	614 249-7111
Columbus *(G-8160)*		
Neighborhood Properties Inc	E	419 473-2604
Toledo *(G-17937)*		
Newmark & Company RE Inc	E	216 453-3000
Cleveland *(G-6065)*		
Neyer Real Estate MGT LLC	E	513 618-6000
Cincinnati *(G-4117)*		
Nisbet Corporation	C	513 563-1111
Cincinnati *(G-4120)*		
Noakes Rooney Rlty & Assoc Co	E	419 423-4861
Findlay *(G-10949)*		
Noneman Real Estate Company	E	419 531-4020
Toledo *(G-17943)*		
NOR Corp	E	440 366-0099
Elyria *(G-10544)*		
Normandy Office Associates	D	513 381-8696
Cincinnati *(G-4124)*		
North American Properties Inc	E	513 721-2744
Cincinnati *(G-4125)*		
North Star Realty Incorporated	E	513 737-1700
Fairfield *(G-10761)*		
North Wood Realty	E	330 423-0837
Youngstown *(G-20142)*		
North Wood Realty	E	330 856-3915
Warren *(G-18734)*		
Northpointe Plaza	D	614 744-2229
Columbus *(G-8203)*		
Nrt Commercial Utah LLC	D	614 239-0808
Columbus *(G-8211)*		
Nrt Commercial Utah LLC	E	614 889-0808
Dublin *(G-10293)*		
Nwd Arena District II LLC	E	614 857-2330
Columbus *(G-8219)*		
Oak Brook Gardens	D	440 237-3613
North Royalton *(G-15363)*		
Oakwood Management Company	E	614 866-8702
Reynoldsburg *(G-16322)*		
Oberer Residential Cnstr	C	937 278-0851
Miamisburg *(G-14200)*		
Ohio Equities LLC	D	614 469-0058
Columbus *(G-8253)*		
Olmsted Residence Corporation	C	440 235-7100
Olmsted Twp *(G-15539)*		
One Lincoln Park	D	937 298-0594
Dayton *(G-9675)*		
Owners Management Company	E	440 439-3800
Parma *(G-15770)*		
Pache Management Company Inc	E	614 451-5919
Columbus *(G-8409)*		
Paran Management Company Ltd	E	216 921-5663
Cleveland *(G-6162)*		
Petros Homes Inc	E	440 546-9000
Columbus *(G-6202)*		
Pfh Partners LLC	E	513 241-5800
Cincinnati *(G-4239)*		
Phil Giessler	E	614 888-0307
Worthington *(G-19835)*		
Phillips Edison & Company LLC	E	513 554-1110
Cincinnati *(G-4241)*		
Pizzuti Inc	E	614 280-4000
Columbus *(G-8450)*		
Platinum RE Professionals LLC	E	440 942-2100
Willoughby *(G-19562)*		
Plaza Properties Inc	E	614 237-3726
Columbus *(G-8455)*		
Plus Realty Cincinnati Inc	E	513 575-4500
Milford *(G-14425)*		
Port Lawrence Title and Tr Co	E	419 244-4605
Toledo *(G-17982)*		
Preferred RE Investments LLC	E	614 901-2400
Westerville *(G-19202)*		
Preferred Real Estate Group	E	513 533-4111
Cincinnati *(G-4269)*		
Prudential Calhoon Co Realtors	E	614 777-1000
Hilliard *(G-11808)*		
Prudential Lucien Realty	E	216 226-4673
Lakewood *(G-12360)*		
Prudential Select Properties	D	440 255-1111
Mentor *(G-14098)*		
Prudential Welsh Realty	E	440 974-3100
Mentor *(G-14099)*		
R A Hermes Inc	E	513 251-5200
Cincinnati *(G-4329)*		
Randolph and Associates RE	E	614 269-8418
Columbus *(G-8489)*		
Re/Max	E	937 477-4997
Beavercreek *(G-1234)*		
Re/Max Consultant Group	D	614 855-2822
New Albany *(G-14869)*		
RE/Max Experts Realty	E	330 364-7355
Dover *(G-10095)*		
RE/Max Real Estate Experts	E	440 255-6505
Mentor *(G-14101)*		
Real Estate Capital Fund LLC	E	216 491-3990
Cleveland *(G-6290)*		
Real Estate II Inc	E	937 390-3119
Springfield *(G-17100)*		
Real Estate Showcase	E	740 389-2000
Marion *(G-13454)*		
Real Living Title Agency Ltd	E	440 974-7810
Painesville *(G-15737)*		
Real Living Title Agency Ltd	D	614 459-7400
Columbus *(G-8495)*		
Real Property Management Inc	E	614 766-6500
Dublin *(G-10320)*		
Red Brick Property MGT LLC	E	513 524-9340
Oxford *(G-15689)*		
Remax Homesource	E	440 951-2500
Willoughby *(G-19567)*		
REO Network Inc	E	740 374-8900
Marietta *(G-13376)*		
Residential Hm Assn of Marion	C	740 387-9999
Marion *(G-13455)*		
Residential One Realty Inc	E	614 436-9830
Columbus *(G-8521)*		
Resource Title Agency Inc	E	216 520-0050
Cleveland *(G-6315)*		
Resource Title Nat Agcy Inc	D	216 520-0050
Independence *(G-12113)*		
Reuben Co	E	419 241-3400
Toledo *(G-18005)*		
Richard H Freyhof	E	937 653-5837
Urbana *(G-18443)*		
Richland Mall Shopping Ctr	E	419 529-4003
Mansfield *(G-13236)*		
Rlj Management Co Inc	E	614 942-2020
Columbus *(G-8540)*		
Robert F Lindsay Co	D	419 476-6221
Toledo *(G-18010)*		
Roediger Realty Inc	E	937 322-0352
Springfield *(G-17104)*		
Rolls Realty	E	614 792-5662
Powell *(G-16207)*		
Ron Neff Real Estate	E	740 773-4670
Chillicothe *(G-2816)*		
Rose Community Management LLC	C	917 542-3600
Independence *(G-12118)*		
RPM Midwest LLC	E	513 762-9000
Cincinnati *(G-4407)*		
Rubber City Realty Inc	D	330 745-9034
Akron *(G-413)*		
Rybac Inc	E	614 228-3578
Columbus *(G-8565)*		
Sami S Rafidi	C	330 799-9508
Youngstown *(G-20202)*		
Sawmill Road Management Co LLC	E	937 342-9071
Springfield *(G-17108)*		
Sawyer Realtors	E	513 423-6521
Middletown *(G-14327)*		
Saxton Real Estate Co	D	614 875-2327
Grove City *(G-11469)*		
Schottenstein RE Group LLC	E	614 418-8900
Columbus *(G-8608)*		
◆ Schroeder Company	E	419 473-3139
Toledo *(G-18021)*		
Sibcy Cline Inc	E	937 610-3404
Dayton *(G-9766)*		
Sibcy Cline Inc	E	513 752-4000
Cincinnati *(G-2868)*		
Sibcy Cline Inc	D	513 793-2121
Cincinnati *(G-4474)*		
Sibcy Cline Inc	E	513 385-3330
Fairfield *(G-10783)*		
Sibcy Cline Inc	D	513 984-4100
Cincinnati *(G-4475)*		
Sibcy Cline Inc	D	513 829-0044
Fairfield *(G-10784)*		
Sibcy Cline Inc	D	513 777-8100
West Chester *(G-19005)*		
Sibcy Cline Inc	E	513 793-2700
Cincinnati *(G-4476)*		
Sibcy Cline Inc	E	513 931-7700
Cincinnati *(G-4477)*		
Sibcy Cline Inc	D	513 677-1830
Mason *(G-13640)*		
Sibcy Cline Inc	E	937 429-2101
Beavercreek *(G-1186)*		
Sibcy Cline Inc	D	513 932-6334
Lebanon *(G-12501)*		
Siena Springs II	E	513 639-2800
Dayton *(G-9768)*		
Signature Associates Inc	E	419 244-7505
Toledo *(G-18034)*		
Skye Development Company LLC	E	216 223-0160
Cleveland *(G-6412)*		

Springcar Company LLC ......E 440 892-6800
Westlake *(G-19408)*

Star One Holdings Inc ......E 513 474-9100
Cincinnati *(G-4538)*

Star One Holdings Inc ......E 513 779-9500
West Chester *(G-19012)*

Star One Holdings Inc ......E 513 300-6663
Cincinnati *(G-4539)*

Sterling Heights Gsa Prpts Ltd ......E 419 609-7000
Sandusky *(G-16648)*

Steve Brown ......D 937 436-2700
Dayton *(G-9793)*

Stickelman Schneider Assoc LLC ......E 513 475-6000
Fairborn *(G-10682)*

Stouffer Realty Inc ......E 330 835-4900
Fairlawn *(G-10852)*

STS Restaurant Management Inc ......D 419 246-0730
Toledo *(G-18051)*

Sue Smedley ......E 937 399-5155
Springfield *(G-17120)*

Sweeney Team Inc ......E 513 934-0700
Lebanon *(G-12508)*

Sweeney Team Inc ......E 513 241-3400
Cincinnati *(G-4559)*

T & R Properties ......E 614 923-4000
Dublin *(G-10351)*

Tiger 2010 LLC ......E 330 236-5100
North Canton *(G-15238)*

Tolson Enterprises Inc ......E 419 843-6465
Toledo *(G-18104)*

Tom Baier & Assoc Inc ......E 330 497-3115
Canton *(G-2513)*

Tom Properties LLC ......D 614 781-0055
Columbus *(G-8762)*

Towne Properties Assoc Inc ......E 513 489-4059
Cincinnati *(G-4619)*

Towne Properties Assoc Inc ......E 513 874-3737
Cincinnati *(G-4620)*

Townhomes Management Inc ......E 614 228-3578
Columbus *(G-8767)*

Township of Fowler ......D 330 637-2653
Fowler *(G-11017)*

Triad Pll ......E 740 374-2940
Marietta *(G-13389)*

Triangle Office Park LLC ......E 513 563-7555
Cincinnati *(G-4634)*

U S Associates Realty Inc ......E 216 663-3400
Cleveland *(G-6557)*

U S Title Agency Inc ......E 216 621-1424
Cleveland *(G-6559)*

Ufcw 75 Real Estate Corp ......E 937 677-0075
Dayton *(G-9828)*

United Management Inc ......E 513 936-8568
Cincinnati *(G-4682)*

University Circle Incorporated ......E 216 791-3900
Cleveland *(G-6586)*

Valley View Place ......C 740 454-7720
Zanesville *(G-20371)*

Village Communities LLC ......C 614 540-2400
Westerville *(G-19216)*

Visconsi Companies Ltd ......E 216 464-5550
Cleveland *(G-6634)*

Waldon Management Corp ......E 330 792-7688
Youngstown *(G-20240)*

Wallick Properties Midwest LLC ......C 614 539-9041
Grove City *(G-11482)*

Wallick Properties Midwest LLC ......A 419 381-7477
New Albany *(G-14878)*

Ward Realestate Inc ......E 419 281-2000
Ashland *(G-698)*

Washington Square Apartments ......E 740 349-8353
Newark *(G-15107)*

Welles Bowen Realty Inc ......D 419 535-0011
Toledo *(G-18149)*

West Shell Commercial Inc ......D 513 721-4200
Cincinnati *(G-4784)*

West Shell Gale Schnetzer ......E 513 683-3833
Loveland *(G-13033)*

West-Way Management Company ......E 440 250-1851
Westlake *(G-19423)*

Western Reserve Realty LLC ......E 440 247-3707
Chagrin Falls *(G-2659)*

Weston Inc ......E 440 349-9001
Solon *(G-16914)*

Whitehurst Company ......E 419 865-0799
Maumee *(G-13868)*

Wilbur Realty Inc ......E 330 673-5883
Kent *(G-12268)*

William Zamarelli Realtors ......E 330 856-2299
Warren *(G-18772)*

Williams Homes LLC ......E 419 472-1005
Toledo *(G-18158)*

Y Town Realty Inc ......E 330 743-8844
Youngstown *(G-20251)*

Yocum Realty Company ......E 419 222-3040
Lima *(G-12788)*

Your Home Court Advantage LLC ......E 330 364-6602
New Philadelphia *(G-14990)*

Zaremba Group Incorporated ......E 216 221-6600
Cleveland *(G-6708)*

Zaremba Group LLC ......C 216 221-6600
Lakewood *(G-12366)*

Zaremba LLC ......D 216 221-6600
Cleveland *(G-6709)*

Zaremba Zanesville LLC ......E 216 221-6600
Lakewood *(G-12367)*

6541 Title Abstract Offices

A R E A Title Agency Inc ......E 419 242-5485
Toledo *(G-17576)*

American Title Services Inc ......E 330 652-1609
Niles *(G-15144)*

Commerce Title Agcy Youngstown ......E 330 743-1171
Youngstown *(G-19995)*

County of Delaware ......E 740 657-3945
Lewis Center *(G-12535)*

First Fincl Title Agcy of Ohio ......E 216 664-1920
Cleveland *(G-5535)*

Intitle Agency Inc ......D 513 241-8780
Cincinnati *(G-3783)*

Lakeside Title Escrow Agcy Inc ......E 216 503-5600
Westlake *(G-19367)*

Landsel Title Agency Inc ......E 614 337-1928
Gahanna *(G-11130)*

Real Living Title Agency Ltd ......D 614 459-7400
Columbus *(G-8495)*

Search 2 Close Columbus Ltd ......E 614 389-5353
Powell *(G-16210)*

Security Title Guarantee Agcy ......C 513 651-3393
Cincinnati *(G-4446)*

Sterling Land Title Agency ......E 937 438-2000
Dayton *(G-9792)*

Talon Title Agency LLC ......E 614 818-0500
Westerville *(G-19213)*

Valley Title & Escrow Agency ......E 440 632-9833
Middlefield *(G-14278)*

Weston Inc ......E 440 349-9000
Cleveland *(G-6679)*

6552 Land Subdividers & Developers

Al Neyer LLC ......D 513 271-6400
Cincinnati *(G-2918)*

Breezy Point Ltd Partnership ......C 440 247-3363
Solon *(G-16828)*

C V Perry & Co ......E 614 221-4131
Columbus *(G-7105)*

Cardida Corporation ......E 740 439-4359
Kimbolton *(G-12311)*

Carnegie Management & Dev Corp ......E 440 892-6800
Westlake *(G-19327)*

Carter-Jones Companies Inc ......E 330 673-6100
Kent *(G-12217)*

Columbus Housing Partnr Inc ......D 614 221-8889
Columbus *(G-7289)*

Coral Company ......E 216 932-8822
Cleveland *(G-5349)*

Creekside II LLC ......E 614 280-4000
Columbus *(G-7389)*

Duke Realty Corporation ......D 513 651-3900
Mason *(G-13576)*

Eagle Realty Group LLC ......E 513 361-7700
Cincinnati *(G-3469)*

Edwards Land Company ......E 614 241-2070
Columbus *(G-7508)*

Equity Inc ......E 614 802-2900
Hilliard *(G-11766)*

▲ Forest City Enterprises LP ......B 216 621-6060
Cleveland *(G-5553)*

Forest City Washington LLC ......E 261 621-6060
Cleveland *(G-5562)*

Forest Cy Residential MGT Inc ......C 216 621-6060
Cleveland *(G-5563)*

Forrer Development Ltd ......E 937 431-6489
Dayton *(G-9445)*

George J Igel & Co Inc ......A 614 445-8421
Columbus *(G-7659)*

Goodman Properties Inc ......E 740 264-7781
Steubenville *(G-17155)*

Great Traditions Dev Group Inc ......E 513 563-4070
Cincinnati *(G-3646)*

Henkle-Schueler & Associates ......E 513 932-6070
Lebanon *(G-12471)*

Highland Som Development ......E 330 528-3500
Streetsboro *(G-17256)*

Jack Gray ......D 216 688-0466
Cincinnati *(G-3799)*

Laurel Development Corporation ......E 614 794-8800
Westerville *(G-19179)*

Lha Developments ......E 330 785-3219
Akron *(G-312)*

Lt Land Development LLC ......E 937 382-0072
Wilmington *(G-19631)*

▲ Magnum Management Corporation ......A 419 627-2334
Sandusky *(G-16626)*

Midwestern Plumbing Service ......E 513 753-0050
Cincinnati *(G-4051)*

Miller-Vlentine Operations Inc ......E 937 293-0900
Dayton *(G-9638)*

Miller-Vlentine Operations Inc ......A 513 771-0900
Dayton *(G-9639)*

Multicon Builders Inc ......E 614 241-2070
Columbus *(G-8121)*

Multicon Builders Inc ......E 614 463-1142
Columbus *(G-8122)*

Mv Residential Development LLC ......E 937 293-0900
Moraine *(G-14682)*

Nationwide Rlty Investors Ltd ......E 614 857-2330
Columbus *(G-8161)*

North American Properties Inc ......E 513 721-2744
Cincinnati *(G-4125)*

Oberer Development Co ......E 937 910-0851
Miamisburg *(G-14199)*

Ostendorf-Morris Properties ......D 216 861-7200
Cleveland *(G-6146)*

Phillips Edison & Company LLC ......E 513 554-1110
Cincinnati *(G-4241)*

Piatt Park Ltd Partnership ......D 513 381-8696
Cincinnati *(G-4246)*

Pizzuti Builders LLC ......E 614 280-4000
Columbus *(G-8449)*

Pizzuti Inc ......E 614 280-4000
Columbus *(G-8450)*

Rama Tika Developers LLC ......E 419 806-6446
Mansfield *(G-13232)*

Req/Jqh Holdings Inc ......D 513 891-1066
Blue Ash *(G-1645)*

Richland Mall Shopping Ctr ......E 419 529-4003
Mansfield *(G-13236)*

Robert L Stark Enterprises Inc ......E 216 292-0242
Cleveland *(G-6333)*

Rockford Homes Inc ......D 614 785-0015
Columbus *(G-6834)*

Sawyer Realtors ......E 513 423-6521
Middletown *(G-14327)*

Seg of Ohio Inc ......E 614 414-7300
Columbus *(G-8617)*

Signature Associates Inc ......E 419 244-7505
Toledo *(G-18034)*

Slavic Village Development ......E 216 429-1182
Cleveland *(G-6415)*

Soho Development Company ......D 614 207-3261
Johnstown *(G-12203)*

Sommerset Development Ltd ......C 440 286-6194
Chardon *(G-2715)*

Southgate Corp ......E 740 522-2151
Newark *(G-15098)*

Sunrise Land Co ......E 216 621-6060
Cleveland *(G-6478)*

T O J Inc ......E 440 352-1900
Mentor *(G-14114)*

The Daimler Group Inc ......E 614 488-4424
Columbus *(G-8743)*

Towne Development Group Ltd ......E 513 381-8696
Cincinnati *(G-4615)*

TP Mechanical Contractors Inc ......A 513 851-8881
Cincinnati *(G-4623)*

Urban Retail Properties LLC ......E 513 346-4482
Cincinnati *(G-4736)*

Visconsi Companies Ltd ......E 216 464-5550
Cleveland *(G-6634)*

Wallick Enterprises Inc ......D 614 863-4640
New Albany *(G-14877)*

Warren Housing Development ......D 330 369-1533
Warren *(G-18770)*

Windsor Companies ......E 740 653-8822
Lancaster *(G-12445)*

Wryneck Development LLC ......E 419 354-2535
Bowling Green *(G-1760)*

Zaremba Group Incorporated ......E 216 221-6600
Cleveland *(G-6708)*

Zaremba Group LLC ....C 216 221-6600
Lakewood (G-12366)

6553 Cemetery Subdividers & Developers

Arlington Memorial Grdns Assn ....E 513 521-7003
Cincinnati (G-2987)
Catholic Association of The Di ....D 216 641-7575
Cleveland (G-5131)
Catholic Cemeteries ....E 614 491-2751
Lockbourne (G-12810)
Catholic Diocese of Cleveland ....E 216 267-2850
Cleveland (G-5135)
City of Cleveland ....E 216 348-7210
Cleveland (G-5196)
Green Haven Memorial Gardens ....E 330 533-6811
Canfield (G-2139)
Green Lawn Cemetery Assn ....E 614 444-1123
Columbus (G-7695)
Miami Valley Memory Grdns Assn ....E 937 885-7779
Dayton (G-9624)
Ottawa Hills Memorial Park ....E 419 539-0218
Ottawa Hills (G-15668)
Roman Cthlic Docese Youngstown ....E 330 792-4721
Youngstown (G-20191)
Spring Grove Cmtry & Arboretum ....D 513 681-7526
Cincinnati (G-4517)
Stonemor Partners LP ....E 330 491-8001
Canton (G-2501)
Stonemor Partners LP ....E 937 866-4135
Dayton (G-9794)
Stonemor Partners LP ....E 330 425-8128
Twinsburg (G-18325)
Sunset Hills Cemetery Corp ....E 330 494-2051
Canton (G-2503)
Sunset Memorial Park Assn ....E 440 777-0450
North Olmsted (G-15313)
Toledo Memorial Pk & Mausoleum ....E 419 882-7151
Sylvania (G-17460)

67 HOLDING AND OTHER INVESTMENT OFFICES

6712 Offices Of Bank Holding Co's

Community Invstors Bancorp Inc ....E 419 562-7055
Bucyrus (G-1985)
Comunibanc Corp ....D 419 599-1065
Napoleon (G-14802)
First Capital Bancshares Inc ....D 740 775-6777
Chillicothe (G-2779)
Genbanc ....E 419 855-8381
Genoa (G-11254)
Greenville National Bancorp ....E 937 548-1114
Greenville (G-11382)
Muskingum Vly Bancshares Inc ....E 740 984-2381
Beverly (G-1464)
Portage Bancshares Inc ....D 330 296-8090
Ravenna (G-16253)

6719 Offices Of Holding Co's, NEC

A and S Ventures Inc ....E 419 376-3934
Toledo (G-17575)
◆ Ampac Holdings LLC ....A 513 671-1777
Cincinnati (G-2955)
Amrstrong Distributors Inc ....E 419 483-4840
Bellevue (G-1371)
Aprecia Pharmaceuticals Co ....C 513 864-4107
Blue Ash (G-1506)
AWH Holdings Inc ....D 513 241-2614
Cincinnati (G-3008)
Betco Corporation ....C 419 241-2156
Bowling Green (G-1719)
Bleux Holdings LLC ....E 859 414-5060
Cincinnati (G-3056)
Ce Power Holdings Inc ....D 513 563-6150
Cincinnati (G-3140)
Drb Holdings LLC ....D 330 645-3299
Akron (G-194)
Drt Holdings Inc ....D 937 298-7391
Dayton (G-9395)
Eci Macola/Max Holding LLC ....E 614 410-2712
Dublin (G-10214)
Elyria Foundry Holdings LLC ....B 440 322-4657
Elyria (G-10506)
Entelco Corporation ....D 419 872-4620
Maumee (G-13785)
Global Cnsld Holdings Inc ....D 513 703-0965
Mason (G-13588)
Global Graphene Group Inc ....E 937 331-9884
Dayton (G-9461)

Going Home Medical Holding Co ....E 305 340-1034
Strongsville (G-17306)
Hartzell Industries Inc ....D 937 773-6295
Piqua (G-16007)
Jbo Holding Company ....C 216 367-8787
Cleveland (G-5785)
Jo-Ann Stores Holdings Inc ....D 888 739-4120
Hudson (G-11988)
Lion Group Inc ....D 937 898-1949
Dayton (G-9570)
Liqui-Box International Inc ....E 614 888-9280
Columbus (G-7983)
M J S Holding ....E 614 410-2512
Columbus (G-8003)
Mssl Consolidated Inc ....B 330 766-5510
Warren (G-18732)
Nationwide Life Insur Co Amer ....A 800 688-5177
Columbus (G-8158)
Norse Dairy Systems Inc ....C 614 294-4931
Columbus (G-8195)
Nri Global Inc ....E 905 790-2828
Delta (G-10048)
Nwo Resources Inc ....C 419 636-1117
Bryan (G-1965)
Ocr Services Corporation ....C 513 719-2600
Cincinnati (G-4148)
Pet Food Holdings Inc ....E 419 394-3374
Saint Marys (G-16531)
Pf Holdings LLC ....D 740 549-3558
Lewis Center (G-12559)
PMC Acquisitions Inc ....D 419 429-0042
Findlay (G-10955)
Premix Holding Company ....B 330 666-3751
Fairlawn (G-10843)
Qsr Parent Co ....A 330 425-8472
Twinsburg (G-18309)
Sca Acquisitions Inc ....A 216 777-2750
Seven Hills (G-16680)
Towne Investment Company LP ....D 513 381-8696
Cincinnati (G-4616)
Washington Court Hse Holdg LLC ....E 614 873-7733
Wshngtn CT Hs (G-19885)
Wasserstrom Holdings Inc ....C 614 228-6525
Columbus (G-8880)

6722 Management Investment Offices

James Advantage Funds ....E 937 426-7640
Xenia (G-19913)
Jpmorgan High Yield Fund ....E 614 248-7017
Columbus (G-6819)
Stonehenge Fincl Holdings Inc ....D 614 246-2500
Columbus (G-8702)
Victory Capital Management Inc ....C 216 898-2400
Brooklyn (G-1862)

6726 Unit Investment Trusts, Face-Amount Certificate Offices

National Housing Tr Ltd Partnr ....E 614 451-9929
Columbus (G-8135)
Rockbridge Capital LLC ....E 614 246-2400
Columbus (G-8544)
Rockwood Equity Partners LLC ....E 216 342-1760
Cleveland (G-6337)

6732 Education, Religious & Charitable Trusts

Altruism Society Inc ....D 877 283-4001
Beachwood (G-1028)
Cleveland Foundation ....D 216 861-3810
Cleveland (G-5255)
Golden Endings Golden Ret Resc ....E 614 486-0773
Columbus (G-7677)
Mercy Health Foundation ....B 937 523-6670
Springfield (G-17079)
Miami Valley Community Action ....D 937 222-1009
Dayton (G-9617)
Shawnee Weekday Early Lrng Ctr ....E 419 991-4806
Lima (G-12793)

6733 Trusts Except Educational, Religious & Charitable

Charles V Francis Trust ....E 513 528-5600
Cincinnati (G-3170)
Cleveland Clinic Foundation ....D 330 505-2280
Niles (G-15151)
Cleveland Clinic Foundation ....D 614 451-0489
Columbus (G-7223)

Cleveland Clinic Foundation ....D 216 444-2820
Cleveland (G-5237)
Cleveland Clinic Foundation ....E 216 445-8585
Cleveland (G-5238)
Cleveland Clinic Foundation ....B 216 444-5000
Cleveland (G-5239)
Cleveland Clinic Foundation ....D 330 287-4500
Wooster (G-19708)
Cleveland Clinic Foundation ....D 216 444-2200
Cleveland (G-5243)
Cleveland Clinic Foundation ....D 440 930-6800
Avon Lake (G-913)
Cleveland Clinic Foundation ....D 440 366-9444
Elyria (G-10490)
Cleveland Clinic Foundation ....D 440 204-7800
Lorain (G-12894)
Cleveland Clinic Foundation ....D 216 986-4000
Independence (G-12061)
Cleveland Clinic Foundation ....D 216 445-6439
Cleveland (G-5244)
Clinton Memorial Hospital ....E 937 383-3402
Wilmington (G-19614)
County of Preble ....D 937 839-5845
West Alexandria (G-18855)
Huntington Auto Trust 2015-1 ....C 302 636-5401
Columbus (G-7779)
Huntington Auto Trust 2016-1 ....C 302 636-5401
Columbus (G-7780)
Kaiser Foundation Hospitals ....B 216 524-7377
Willoughby (G-19533)
Raymond James Fincl Svcs Inc ....E 419 586-5121
Celina (G-2608)
Sky Financial Capital Tr III ....C 614 480-3278
Columbus (G-8650)

6792 Oil Royalty Traders

Exchangebase LLC ....E 440 331-3600
Rocky River (G-16432)

6794 Patent Owners & Lessors

Cassanos Inc ....E 937 294-8400
Dayton (G-9285)
Clark Brands LLC ....A 330 723-9886
Medina (G-13920)
Cleveland Rest Oper Ltd Partnr ....C 216 328-1121
Cleveland (G-5285)
Convenient Food Mart Inc ....E 800 860-4844
Mentor (G-14035)
Covelli Family Ltd Partnership ....E 330 856-3176
Warren (G-18694)
Diet Center Worldwide Inc ....E 330 665-5861
Akron (G-186)
East of Chicago Pizza Inc ....E 419 225-7116
Lima (G-12630)
Epcon Cmmnties Franchising Inc ....D 614 761-1010
Dublin (G-10218)
Escape Enterprises Inc ....E 614 224-0300
Columbus (G-7533)
Gold Star Chili Inc ....E 513 231-4541
Cincinnati (G-3624)
Gosh Enterprises Inc ....E 614 923-4700
Columbus (G-7681)
Howley Bread Group Ltd ....D 440 808-1600
Westlake (G-19352)
Larosas Inc ....A 513 347-5660
Cincinnati (G-3911)
Marcos Inc ....C 419 885-4844
Toledo (G-17894)
McDonalds Corporation ....E 614 682-1128
Columbus (G-8044)
Moto Franchise Corporation ....E 937 291-1900
Dayton (G-9646)
Ohio Valley Acquisition Inc ....B 513 553-0768
Cincinnati (G-4159)
Petland Inc ....E 740 775-2464
Chillicothe (G-2811)
Physicians Weight Ls Ctr Amer ....E 330 666-7952
Akron (G-382)
Premier Broadcasting Co Inc ....E 614 866-0700
Columbus (G-8458)
Red Robin Gourmet Burgers Inc ....D 330 305-1080
Canton (G-2452)
ServiceMaster of Defiance Inc ....D 419 784-5570
Defiance (G-9940)
▲ Skyline Chili Inc ....C 513 874-1188
Fairfield (G-10785)
▲ Stanley Steemer Intl Inc ....C 614 764-2007
Dublin (G-10341)
Ta Operating LLC ....B 440 808-9100
Westlake (G-19411)

Travelcenters of America LLC ....B 724 981-9464
  Westlake *(G-19414)*
Tuffy Associates Corp ....E 419 865-6900
  Toledo *(G-18112)*
United Mercantile Corporation ....E 513 831-1300
  Milford *(G-14440)*
◆ Wendys Company ....B 614 764-3100
  Dublin *(G-10374)*
Wendys Restaurants LLC ....C 614 764-3100
  Dublin *(G-10375)*

6798 Real Estate Investment Trusts

845 Yard Street LLC ....D 614 857-2330
  Columbus *(G-6845)*
Bre Ddr Parker Pavilions LLC ....E 216 755-6451
  Beachwood *(G-1036)*
Ddr Corp ....E 614 785-6445
  Columbus *(G-7425)*
Ddr Tucson Spectrum I LLC ....E 216 755-5500
  Beachwood *(G-1051)*
Forest City Realty Trust Inc ....E 216 621-6060
  Cleveland *(G-5560)*
Investmerica limited ....D 216 618-3296
  Chagrin Falls *(G-2650)*
Morelia Consultants LLC ....D 513 469-1500
  Cincinnati *(G-4072)*
Moskowitz Family Ltd ....D 513 729-2300
  Cincinnati *(G-4076)*
Site Centers Corp ....C 216 755-5500
  Beachwood *(G-1107)*
Washington Prime Group LP ....A 614 621-9000
  Columbus *(G-8876)*
Washington Prime Group Inc ....D 614 621-9000
  Columbus *(G-8877)*

6799 Investors, NEC

Arthur Middleton Capital Holdn ....C 330 966-3033
  Canton *(G-2194)*
Blackbird Capital Group LLC ....C 513 762-7890
  Cincinnati *(G-3055)*
Camelot Realty Investments ....E 740 357-5291
  Lucasville *(G-13045)*
Capital Investment Group Inc ....E 513 241-5090
  Cincinnati *(G-3113)*
Ctd Investments LLC ....E 614 570-9949
  Columbus *(G-7403)*
Ibi Group Engrg Svcs USA Inc ....D 614 818-4900
  Westerville *(G-19263)*
◆ Jpmorgan Chase Bank Nat Assn ....A 614 436-3055
  Columbus *(G-6818)*
K M Clemens DDS Inc ....E 419 228-4036
  Lima *(G-12668)*
Klingbeil Capital MGT LLC ....D 614 396-4919
  Worthington *(G-19818)*
Lti Inc ....D 614 278-7777
  Columbus *(G-7996)*
McM Capital Partners ....B 216 514-1840
  Beachwood *(G-1077)*
Natl City Coml Capitol LLC ....E 513 455-9746
  Cincinnati *(G-4098)*
Newmark & Company RE Inc ....E 216 453-3000
  Cleveland *(G-6065)*
Oakdale Estates II Inv LLC ....D 216 520-1250
  West Union *(G-19137)*
Rev1 Ventures ....E 614 487-3700
  Columbus *(G-8529)*
Rightway Investments LLC ....E 216 854-7697
  Twinsburg *(G-18312)*
Rjb Acquisitions LLC ....E 513 314-2711
  Cincinnati *(G-4382)*
Roulston Research Corp ....E 216 431-3000
  Cleveland *(G-6343)*
Rse Group Inc ....D 937 596-6167
  Jackson Center *(G-12186)*
Shancliff Investments Ltd ....E 330 883-5560
  West Chester *(G-19003)*
Shields Capital Corporation ....D 216 767-1340
  Beachwood *(G-1104)*
Styx Acquisition LLC ....A 330 264-9900
  Wooster *(G-19770)*
Superior Street Partners LLC ....D 216 862-0058
  Shaker Heights *(G-16716)*
The Huntington Investment Co ....E 513 351-2555
  Cincinnati *(G-4593)*
Wings Investors Company Ltd ....E 513 241-5800
  Cincinnati *(G-4799)*
Ws One Investment Usa LLC ....D 855 895-3728
  Aurora *(G-852)*

70 HOTELS, ROOMING HOUSES, CAMPS, AND OTHER LODGING PLACES

7011 Hotels, Motels & Tourist Courts

1460 Ninth St Assoc Ltd Partnr ....E 216 241-6600
  Cleveland *(G-4866)*
16644 Snow Rd LLC ....E 216 676-5200
  Brookpark *(G-1889)*
1st Stop Inc ....E 937 695-0318
  Winchester *(G-19658)*
21c Cincinnati LLC ....D 513 578-6600
  Cincinnati *(G-2879)*
5 Star Hotel Management IV LP ....D 614 431-1819
  Columbus *(G-6842)*
50 S Front LLC ....D 614 224-4600
  Columbus *(G-6843)*
506 Phelps Holdings LLC ....E 513 651-1234
  Cincinnati *(G-2883)*
5901 Pfffer Rd Htels Sites LLC ....D 513 793-4500
  Blue Ash *(G-1495)*
6300 Sharonville Assoc LLC ....C 513 489-3636
  Cincinnati *(G-2884)*
631 South Main Street Dev LLC ....D 419 423-0631
  Findlay *(G-10861)*
A C Management Inc ....E 440 461-9200
  Cleveland *(G-4876)*
Aimbridge Hospitality LLC ....A 330 668-9090
  Akron *(G-24)*
AIR Management Group LLC ....D 330 856-1900
  Warren *(G-18660)*
Airport Core Hotel LLC ....E 614 536-0500
  Columbus *(G-6887)*
AK Group Hotels Inc ....E 937 372-9921
  Xenia *(G-19888)*
Akron Inn Limited Partnership ....E 330 336-7692
  Wadsworth *(G-18587)*
Alexander House Inc ....E 513 523-4569
  Oxford *(G-15672)*
Alliance Hospitality ....E 330 505-2173
  Youngstown *(G-19950)*
Alliance Hospitality Inc ....E 440 951-7333
  Mentor *(G-14016)*
Alsan Corporation ....D 330 385-3636
  East Liverpool *(G-10396)*
American Prprty-Mnagement Corp ....D 330 454-5000
  Canton *(G-2187)*
Americas Best Value Inn ....E 419 626-9890
  Sandusky *(G-16575)*
Amish Door Inc ....B 330 359-5464
  Wilmot *(G-19657)*
Amitel Beachwood Ltd Partnr ....E 216 707-9839
  Cleveland *(G-4970)*
Amitel Beachwood Ltd Partnr ....E 216 831-3030
  Cleveland *(G-4971)*
Amitel Rockside Ltd Partnr ....E 216 520-1450
  Cleveland *(G-4972)*
Ap/Aim Dublin Suites Trs LLC ....D 614 790-9000
  Dublin *(G-10136)*
Ap/Aim Indpndnce Sites Trs LLC ....D 216 986-9900
  Independence *(G-12045)*
Apple Gate Operating Co Inc ....E 330 405-4488
  Twinsburg *(G-18245)*
Army & Air Force Exchange Svc ....C 937 257-2928
  Dayton *(G-9160)*
Arvind Sagar Inc ....E 614 428-8800
  Columbus *(G-6975)*
Ashford Trs Lessee LLC ....E 937 436-2400
  Miamisburg *(G-14142)*
At Hospitality LLC ....D 513 527-9962
  Cincinnati *(G-2992)*
Athens OH 1013 LLC ....E 740 589-5839
  Athens *(G-769)*
Aurora Hotel Partners LLC ....E 330 562-0767
  Aurora *(G-817)*
Avalon Inn Services Inc ....C 330 856-1900
  Warren *(G-18674)*
Avalon Resort and Spa LLC ....E 330 856-1900
  Warren *(G-18676)*
Awe Hospitality Group LLC ....D 330 888-8836
  Macedonia *(G-13060)*
B & I Hotel Management LLC ....C 330 995-0200
  Aurora *(G-819)*
Bass Lake Tavern Inc ....D 440 285-3100
  Chardon *(G-2688)*
Bellville Hotel Company ....E 419 886-7000
  Bellville *(G-1387)*
Bennett Enterprises Inc ....E 419 874-3111
  Perrysburg *(G-15838)*

Bennett Enterprises Inc ....E 419 893-1004
  Maumee *(G-13762)*
Best Western Columbus N Hotel ....E 614 888-8230
  Columbus *(G-7030)*
Best Western Executive Inn ....E 330 794-1050
  Akron *(G-97)*
Best Wooster Inc ....E 330 264-7750
  Wooster *(G-19690)*
Beverly Hills Inn La Llc ....E 859 494-9151
  Aberdeen *(G-1)*
Bindu Associates LLC ....E 440 324-0099
  Elyria *(G-10483)*
Bird Enterprises LLC ....E 330 674-1457
  Millersburg *(G-14460)*
Black Sapphire C Columbus Univ ....D 614 297-9912
  Columbus *(G-7045)*
Blue-Kenwood LLC ....E 513 469-6900
  Blue Ash *(G-1515)*
Bob Mor Inc ....C 419 485-5555
  Montpelier *(G-14607)*
Boulevard Motel Corp ....E 440 234-3131
  Cleveland *(G-5070)*
Broad Street Hotel Assoc LP ....D 614 861-0321
  Columbus *(G-7076)*
Brothers Properties Corp ....C 513 381-3000
  Cincinnati *(G-3081)*
Buffalo-Gtb Associates LLC ....E 216 831-3735
  Beachwood *(G-1040)*
Buxton Inn Inc ....E 740 587-0001
  Granville *(G-11335)*
Ca-Mj Hotel Associates Ltd ....D 330 494-6494
  Canton *(G-2223)*
Cabin Restaurant ....E 330 562-9171
  Aurora *(G-823)*
Cafaro Peachcreek Co Ltd ....D 419 625-6280
  Sandusky *(G-16579)*
Cambria Green Management LLC ....E 330 899-1263
  Uniontown *(G-18360)*
Cambridge Associates Ltd ....E 740 432-7313
  Cambridge *(G-2051)*
Cambridge Property Investors ....E 740 432-7313
  Cambridge *(G-2056)*
Canter Inns Inc ....E 740 354-7711
  Portsmouth *(G-16127)*
Canton Hotel Holdings Inc ....E 330 492-1331
  Canton *(G-2234)*
Canus Hospitality LLC ....E 937 323-8631
  Springfield *(G-17003)*
Cardida Corporation ....E 740 439-4359
  Kimbolton *(G-12311)*
Carlisle Hotels Inc ....E 614 851-5599
  Columbus *(G-7129)*
Carlson Hotels Ltd Partnership ....D 740 386-5451
  Marion *(G-13409)*
Carol Burton Management LLC ....E 419 666-5120
  Toledo *(G-17638)*
Carroll Properties ....E 513 398-8075
  Mason *(G-13549)*
CD Block K Hotel LLC ....E 440 871-3100
  Westlake *(G-19328)*
Cedar Point Park LLC ....E 419 627-2500
  Sandusky *(G-16583)*
CER Hotels LLC ....E 330 422-1855
  Streetsboro *(G-17249)*
Ceres Enterprises LLC ....D 440 617-9385
  Westlake *(G-19329)*
Ch Relty Iv/Clmbus Partners LP ....D 614 885-3334
  Columbus *(G-7174)*
Charter Hotel Group Ltd Partnr ....E 216 772-4538
  Mentor *(G-14028)*
Cherry Valley Lodge ....E 740 788-1200
  Newark *(G-15022)*
Chillicothe Motel LLC ....E 740 773-3903
  Chillicothe *(G-2764)*
Chimneys Inn ....E 937 567-7850
  Dayton *(G-9297)*
Cincinnati Netherland Ht LLC ....B 513 421-9100
  Cincinnati *(G-3259)*
Cincinnatian Hotel ....C 513 381-3000
  Cincinnati *(G-3279)*
Claire De Leigh Corp ....E 614 459-6575
  Columbus *(G-7216)*
Clermont Hills Co LLC ....D 513 752-4400
  Cincinnati *(G-2846)*
Cleveland Airport Hospitality ....D 440 871-6000
  Westlake *(G-19333)*
Cleveland Bchwood Hsptlity LLC ....D 216 464-5950
  Beachwood *(G-1044)*
Cleveland Crowne Plaza Airport ....E 440 243-4040
  Cleveland *(G-5251)*

Cleveland East Hotel LLC ....D...... 216 378-9191
Cleveland (G-5252)
Cleveland S Hospitality LLC ....E...... 216 447-1300
Cleveland (G-5286)
Cleveland Westlake ....E...... 440 892-0333
Westlake (G-19334)
Clinic Care Inc ....D...... 216 707-4200
Cleveland (G-5306)
Cmp I Blue Ash Owner LLC ....E...... 513 733-4334
Blue Ash (G-1531)
Cmp I Columbus I Owner LLC ....E...... 614 764-9393
Dublin (G-10177)
Cmp I Columbus II Owner LLC ....E...... 614 436-7070
Columbus (G-7236)
Cni Thl Ops LLC ....E...... 937 890-6112
Dayton (G-9310)
Cni Thl Ops LLC ....E...... 614 791-8675
Dublin (G-10179)
Columbia Properties Lima LLC ....D...... 419 222-0004
Lima (G-12616)
Columbus Airport Ltd Partnr ....C...... 614 475-7551
Columbus (G-7253)
Columbus Concord Ltd Partnr ....D...... 614 228-3200
Columbus (G-7271)
Columbus Easton Hotel LLC ....E...... 614 414-1000
Columbus (G-7278)
Columbus Easton Hotel LLC ....D...... 614 414-5000
Columbus (G-7279)
Columbus Easton Hotel LLC ....E...... 614 383-2005
Columbus (G-7280)
Columbus Hospitality ....E...... 614 461-2648
Columbus (G-7287)
Columbus Hotel Partners ....E...... 513 891-1066
Blue Ash (G-1534)
Columbus Hotel Partnership LLC ....D...... 614 890-8600
Columbus (G-7288)
Columbus Leasing LLC ....D...... 614 885-1885
Columbus (G-7292)
Columbus Oh-16 Airport Gahanna ......E...... 614 501-4770
Gahanna (G-11114)
Columbus Worthington Hospitali ....D...... 614 885-3334
Columbus (G-7321)
Comfort Inn ....E...... 740 454-4144
Zanesville (G-20297)
Comfort Inn Northeast ....E...... 513 683-9700
Cincinnati (G-3336)
Comfort Inns ....E...... 614 885-4084
Columbus (G-7325)
Commodore Prry Inns Suites LLC ......D...... 419 732-2645
Port Clinton (G-16102)
Commodore Resorts Inc ....E...... 419 285-3101
Port Clinton (G-16103)
Commonwealth Hotels LLC ....D...... 216 524-5814
Cleveland (G-5322)
Commonwealth Hotels LLC ....C...... 614 790-9000
Dublin (G-10184)
Concord Dayton Hotel II LLC ....D...... 937 223-1000
Dayton (G-9316)
Concord Hamiltonian Rvrfrnt Ho ....D...... 513 896-6200
Hamilton (G-11586)
Concord Testa Hotel Assoc LLC ....D...... 330 252-9228
Akron (G-156)
▲ Continental GL Sls & Inv Group ......B...... 614 679-1201
Powell (G-16192)
Continental/Olentangy Ht LLC ....D...... 614 297-9912
Columbus (G-7363)
Corporate Exchange Hotel Assoc ....C...... 614 890-8600
Columbus (G-7373)
Coshocton Village Inn Suites ....E...... 740 622-9455
Coshocton (G-9010)
Courtyard By Marriott ....E...... 216 765-1900
Cleveland (G-5372)
Courtyard By Marriott ....E...... 513 341-4140
West Chester (G-18901)
Courtyard By Marriott ....E...... 440 871-3756
Westlake (G-19338)
Courtyard By Marriott ....D...... 937 433-3131
Miamisburg (G-14156)
Courtyard By Marriott Dayton ....E...... 937 220-9060
Dayton (G-9335)
Courtyard By Marriott Rossford ....E...... 419 872-5636
Rossford (G-16460)
Courtyard Management Corp ....E...... 614 475-8530
Columbus (G-7381)
Courtyard Management Corp ....E...... 216 901-9988
Cleveland (G-5373)
CPX Canton Airport LLC ....C...... 330 305-0500
North Canton (G-15194)
CPX Carrollton Es LLC ....D...... 330 627-1200
Carrollton (G-2566)

Crefiii Waramaug ....D...... 937 322-3600
Springfield (G-17027)
Crowne Plaza Toledo ....D...... 419 241-1411
Toledo (G-17689)
Cs Hotels Limited Partnership ....D...... 614 771-8999
Columbus (G-7399)
Cumberland Gap LLC ....E...... 513 681-9300
Cincinnati (G-3386)
Cwb Property Managment Inc ....E...... 614 793-2244
Dublin (G-10195)
Das Dutch Village Inn ....E...... 330 482-5050
Columbiana (G-6787)
Days Inn ....E...... 740 695-0100
Saint Clairsville (G-16486)
Dayton Hotels LLC ....E...... 937 832-2222
Englewood (G-10584)
DB&p Logistics Inc ....E...... 614 491-4035
Columbus (G-7424)
Dbp Enterprises LLC ....E...... 740 513-2399
Sunbury (G-17386)
Detroit Westfield LLC ....D...... 330 666-4131
Akron (G-184)
Dino Persichetti ....E...... 330 821-9600
Alliance (G-530)
Dixie Management II Inc ....D...... 937 832-1234
Englewood (G-10585)
Donlen Inc ....D...... 216 961-6767
Cleveland (G-5439)
Doubletree Guest Suites Dayton ....D...... 937 436-2400
Miamisburg (G-14167)
Drury Hotels Company LLC ....E...... 614 798-8802
Dublin (G-10203)
Drury Hotels Company LLC ....E...... 513 336-0108
Mason (G-13575)
Drury Hotels Company LLC ....E...... 614 221-7008
Columbus (G-7471)
Drury Hotels Company LLC ....E...... 937 454-5200
Dayton (G-9396)
Drury Hotels Company LLC ....E...... 513 771-5601
Cincinnati (G-3444)
Drury Hotels Company LLC ....E...... 614 798-8802
Grove City (G-11428)
Dublin Hotel Ltd Liability Co ....C...... 513 891-1066
Dublin (G-10208)
Dure Investments LLC ....E...... 419 697-7800
Oregon (G-15591)
Durga Llc ....D...... 513 771-2080
Cincinnati (G-3457)
East End Ro Burton Inc ....E...... 440 942-2742
Willoughby (G-19519)
Eastlake Lodging LLC ....E...... 440 953-8000
Eastlake (G-10429)
Econo Lodge ....D...... 419 627-8000
Sandusky (G-16597)
Edmond Hotel Investors LLC ....D...... 614 891-2900
Columbus (G-7503)
Elbe Properties ....A...... 513 489-1955
Cincinnati (G-3485)
Emmett Dan House Ltd Partnr ....E...... 740 392-6886
Mount Vernon (G-14764)
Epiqurian Inns ....D...... 614 885-2600
Worthington (G-19807)
Fairfeld Inn Stes Clmbus Arprt ....E...... 614 237-2100
Columbus (G-7554)
Fairfield Inn ....D...... 614 267-1111
Columbus (G-7555)
Fairlawn Associates Ltd ....C...... 330 867-5000
Fairlawn (G-10826)
Falcon Plaza LLC ....E...... 419 352-4671
Bowling Green (G-1730)
Findlay Inn & Conference Ctr ....D...... 419 422-5682
Findlay (G-10904)
First Hospitality Company LLC ....E...... 614 864-4555
Reynoldsburg (G-16304)
First Hotel Associates LP ....D...... 614 228-3800
Columbus (G-7586)
Fmw Rri Opco LLC ....E...... 614 744-2659
Columbus (G-7599)
Frog & Toad Inc ....E...... 419 877-1180
Whitehouse (G-19447)
Gallipolis Hospitality Inc ....E...... 740 446-0090
Gallipolis (G-11195)
Gateway Hospitality Group Inc ....C...... 330 405-9800
Twinsburg (G-18271)
Geeta Hospitality Inc ....E...... 937 642-3777
Marysville (G-13499)
Glenlaurel Inc ....E...... 740 385-4070
Rockbridge (G-16413)
Glidden House Associates Ltd ....E...... 216 231-8900
Cleveland (G-5610)

Golden Lamb ....C...... 513 932-5065
Lebanon (G-12468)
Goodnight Inn Inc ....E...... 419 334-9551
Fremont (G-11078)
Grand Heritage Hotel Portland ....E...... 440 734-4477
North Olmsted (G-15291)
Grand View Inn Inc ....D...... 740 377-4388
South Point (G-16934)
Grandview Ht Ltd Partnr Ohio ....D...... 937 766-5519
Springfield (G-17043)
Granville Hospitality Llc ....D...... 740 587-3333
Granville (G-11342)
Great Bear Lodge Sandusky LLC ....B...... 419 609-6000
Sandusky (G-16613)
Green Township Hospitality LLC ....B...... 513 574-6000
Cincinnati (G-3656)
Hampton Inn & Suite Inc ....E...... 440 234-0206
Middleburg Heights (G-14253)
Hampton Inns LLC ....E...... 330 492-0151
Canton (G-2337)
Hampton Inns LLC ....E...... 330 422-0500
Streetsboro (G-17255)
Hardage Hotels I LLC ....E...... 614 766-7762
Dublin (G-10238)
Haribol Haribol Inc ....E...... 330 339-7731
New Philadelphia (G-14963)
Hauck Hospitality LLC ....D...... 513 563-8330
Cincinnati (G-3684)
Hawkeye Hotels Inc ....E...... 614 782-8292
Grove City (G-11440)
Hdi Ltd ....C...... 937 224-0800
Dayton (G-9488)
He Hari Inc ....D...... 614 436-0700
Worthington (G-19812)
He Hari Inc ....D...... 614 846-6600
Lewis Center (G-12544)
Hide-A-Way Hills Club ....E...... 740 746-9589
Sugar Grove (G-17374)
Hilton Garden Inn ....D...... 614 263-7200
Columbus (G-7751)
Hilton Garden Inn Akron ....E...... 330 966-4907
Canton (G-2346)
Hilton Garden Inn Beavercreek ....D...... 937 458-2650
Dayton (G-9177)
Hilton Grdn Inn Clmbus Polaris ....E...... 614 846-8884
Columbus (G-6814)
Hilton Grdn Inn Columbus Arprt ....D...... 614 231-2869
Columbus (G-7752)
Hilton Polaris ....E...... 614 885-1600
Columbus (G-6815)
Hit Portfolio I Hil Trs LLC ....E...... 614 235-0717
Dublin (G-10243)
Hit Portfolio I Misc Trs LLC ....C...... 216 575-1234
Cleveland (G-5694)
Hit Portfolio I Misc Trs LLC ....C...... 513 241-3575
Cincinnati (G-3711)
Hit Portfolio I Misc Trs LLC ....C...... 614 228-1234
Columbus (G-7753)
Hit Portfolio I Trs LLC ....E...... 614 846-4355
Columbus (G-7754)
Hit Swn Trs LLC ....E...... 614 228-3200
Columbus (G-7755)
Hmshost Corporation ....C...... 419 547-8667
Clyde (G-6744)
Holiday Inn ....E...... 419 691-8800
Oregon (G-15598)
Holiday Inn Express ....E...... 419 332-7700
Fremont (G-11080)
Holiday Inn Express ....E...... 937 424-5757
Dayton (G-9497)
Holiday Inn Express ....E...... 614 447-1212
Columbus (G-7759)
Hollywood Casino Toledo ....D...... 419 661-5200
Toledo (G-17804)
Home2 By Hilton ....E...... 513 422-3454
West Chester (G-18944)
Honey Run Retreats LLC ....E...... 330 674-0011
Millersburg (G-14478)
Hopkins Partners ....C...... 216 267-1500
Cleveland (G-5705)
Horseshoe Cleveland MGT LLC ....E...... 216 297-4777
Cleveland (G-5709)
Host Cincinnati Hotel LLC ....C...... 513 621-7700
Cincinnati (G-3731)
Hoster Hotels LLC ....E...... 419 931-8900
Perrysburg (G-15876)
Hotel 1100 Carnegie Opco L P ....D...... 216 658-6400
Cleveland (G-5715)
Hotel 2345 LLC ....E...... 614 766-7762
Dublin (G-10245)

S
I
C

Hotel 50 S Front Opco L P	D	614 885-3334	Columbus (G-7774)
Hotel 50 S Front Opco LP	D	614 228-4600	Columbus (G-7775)
Hotel 75 E State Opco L P	E	614 365-4500	Columbus (G-7776)
Hotel Stow LP	E	330 945-9722	Stow (G-17211)
Howard Johnson	C	513 825-3129	Cincinnati (G-3733)
Hst Lessee Cincinnati LLC	C	513 852-2702	Cincinnati (G-3736)
Hyatt Corporation	B	614 463-1234	Columbus (G-7791)
Hyatt Regency Columbus	B	614 463-1234	Columbus (G-7792)
IA Urban Htels Bchwood Trs LLC	D	216 765-8066	Beachwood (G-1066)
Ihg Management (maryland) LLC	C	614 461-4100	Columbus (G-7800)
Independent Hotel Partners LLC	D	216 524-0700	Cleveland (G-5745)
Indus Airport Hotel II LLC	D	614 235-0717	Columbus (G-7808)
Indus Airport Hotels I LLC	D	614 231-2869	Columbus (G-7809)
Indus Hilliard Hotel LLC	E	614 334-1800	Hilliard (G-11777)
Indus Newark Hotel LLC	D	740 322-6455	Columbus (G-7810)
Inn At Marietta Ltd	D	740 373-9600	Marietta (G-13338)
Inn At Wickliffe LLC	E	440 585-0600	Wickliffe (G-19465)
Integrated CC LLC	E	216 707-4132	Cleveland (G-5757)
Integrity Hotel Group	C	937 224-0800	Dayton (G-9517)
Intercntnntal Ht Group Rsurces	D	216 707-4300	Cleveland (G-5760)
Intercontinental Hotels Group	E	216 707-4100	Cleveland (G-5761)
Island Hospitality MGT LLC	E	614 864-8844	Columbus (G-7847)
Island House Inc	E	419 734-0100	Port Clinton (G-16110)
Jack Cincinnati Casino LLC	E	513 252-0777	Cincinnati (G-3798)
Jackson I-94 Ltd Partnership	E	614 793-2244	Dublin (G-10259)
Jagi Clveland Independence LLC	C	216 524-8050	Cleveland (G-5778)
Jagi Juno LLC	E	513 489-1955	Cincinnati (G-3804)
Jagi Springhill LLC	E	216 264-4190	Independence (G-12084)
Janus Hotels and Resorts Inc	E	513 631-8500	Lewisburg (G-12569)
Johnson Howard International	E	513 401-8683	Cincinnati (G-3829)
Kenyon College	E	740 427-2202	Gambier (G-11225)
Kiwi Hospitality - Cincinnati	E	513 241-8660	Cincinnati (G-3877)
Kribha LLC	E	740 788-8991	Newark (G-15046)
Lancaster Host LLC	E	740 654-4445	Lancaster (G-12412)
Lawnfield Properties LLC	E	440 974-3572	Mentor (G-14076)
Legacy Village Hospitality LLC	E	216 382-3350	Cleveland (G-5861)
Levis Commons Hotel LLC	D	419 873-3573	Perrysburg (G-15889)
Liberty Ashtabula Holdings	E	330 872-6000	Newton Falls (G-15140)
Liberty Ctr Lodging Assoc LLC	E	608 833-4100	Liberty Township (G-12583)
Lieben Wooster LP	E	330 390-5722	Millersburg (G-14481)
Lmn Development LLC	D	419 433-7200	Sandusky (G-16623)
Lodging Industry Inc	E	440 323-7488	Sandusky (G-16624)
Lodging Industry Inc	E	419 732-2929	Port Clinton (G-16112)
Lodging Industry Inc	E	440 324-3911	Elyria (G-10529)
Lq Management LLC	E	614 866-6456	Reynoldsburg (G-16318)

Lq Management LLC	D	513 771-0300	Cincinnati (G-3951)
Lq Management LLC	E	216 447-1133	Cleveland (G-5883)
Lq Management LLC	E	216 251-8500	Cleveland (G-5884)
M&C Hotel Interests Inc	E	937 778-8100	Piqua (G-16012)
Mad River Mountain Resort	E	937 303-3646	Zanesfield (G-20272)
Mansfield Hotel Partnership	E	419 529-2100	Mansfield (G-13206)
Mansfield Hotel Partnership	D	419 529-1000	Mansfield (G-13207)
March Investors Ltd	E	740 373-5353	Marietta (G-13346)
Marcus Hotels Inc	E	614 228-3800	Columbus (G-8016)
Marios International Spa & Ht	E	330 562-5141	Aurora (G-835)
Marriott	E	440 542-2375	Solon (G-16871)
Marriott Hotel Services Inc	C	216 252-5333	Cleveland (G-5911)
Marriott International Inc	C	614 861-1400	Columbus (G-8022)
Marriott International Inc	E	330 484-0300	Canton (G-2390)
Marriott International Inc	C	513 487-3800	Cincinnati (G-3973)
Marriott International Inc	E	513 487-3800	Cincinnati (G-3974)
Marriott International Inc	B	216 696-9200	Cleveland (G-5912)
Marriott International Inc	B	614 228-5050	Columbus (G-8023)
Marriott International Inc	E	614 436-7070	Columbus (G-8024)
Marriott International Inc	E	614 475-8530	Columbus (G-8025)
Marriott International Inc	E	614 864-8844	Columbus (G-8026)
Marriott International Inc	C	614 222-2610	Columbus (G-8027)
Marriott International Inc	E	614 885-0799	Columbus (G-8028)
Marriott International Inc	E	330 666-4811	Copley (G-8970)
Marriott International Inc	E	419 866-1001	Holland (G-11895)
Marriott International Inc	E	440 716-9977	North Olmsted (G-15297)
Marriott International Inc	C	513 530-5060	Blue Ash (G-1605)
Mason Family Resorts LLC	B	513 339-0141	Mason (G-13615)
Maumee Lodging Enterprises	D	419 865-1380	Maumee (G-13818)
McPaul Corp	E	419 447-6313	Tiffin (G-17523)
Meander Hospitality Group Inc	E	330 702-0226	Canfield (G-2146)
Meander Hsptality Group II LLC	E	330 422-0500	Streetsboro (G-17260)
Meander Inn Inc	E	330 544-2378	Youngstown (G-20120)
Meander Inn Incorporated	E	330 544-0660	Youngstown (G-20121)
Middletown Innkeepers Inc	E	513 942-3440	Fairfield (G-10758)
Moody Nat Cy Dt Clumbus Mt LLC	E	614 228-3200	Columbus (G-8100)
Moody Nat Cy Willoughby Mt LLC	E	440 530-1100	Willoughby (G-19551)
Motel 6 Operating LLC	E	614 431-2525	Columbus (G-8104)
Motel Investments Marietta Inc	E	740 374-8190	Marietta (G-13362)
Moti Corporation	E	440 734-4500	Cleveland (G-6014)
Mrn-Newgar Hotel Ltd	E	216 443-1000	Cleveland (G-6020)
Msk Hospitality Inc	E	513 771-0370	Cincinnati (G-4080)
N P Motel System Inc	E	330 339-7731	New Philadelphia (G-14975)
Natural Resources Ohio Dept	D	419 938-5411	Perrysville (G-15942)
Newark Management Partners LLC	D	740 322-6455	Newark (G-15084)

Nf II Cleveland Op Co LLC	E	216 443-9043	Cleveland (G-6068)
Norstar Aluminum Molds Inc	D	440 632-0853	Middlefield (G-14273)
▲ Northeast Cincinnati Hotel LLC	C	513 459-9800	Mason (G-13623)
Northern Tier Hospitality LLC	D	570 888-7711	Westlake (G-19383)
Northland Hotel Inc	E	614 885-1601	Columbus (G-8202)
Northtown Square Ltd Partnr	E	419 691-8911	Oregon (G-15601)
Ntk Hotel Group II LLC	D	614 559-2000	Columbus (G-8212)
Oakwood Hospitality Corp	E	440 786-1998	Bedford (G-1296)
Oberlin College	D	440 935-1475	Oberlin (G-15515)
Oh-16 Cleveland Westlake	E	440 892-4275	Westlake (G-19385)
Oh-16 Clvlnd Arprt S Prprty Su	E	440 243-8785	Middlburg Heights (G-14255)
Ohio Inns Inc	E	937 440-9303	Troy (G-18219)
Ohio State Parks Inc	D	513 664-3504	College Corner (G-6768)
Ohio State University	E	614 247-4000	Columbus (G-8310)
Ohio State University	B	614 292-3238	Columbus (G-8333)
Olshan Hotel Management Inc	E	614 414-1000	Columbus (G-8373)
Olshan Hotel Management Inc	E	614 416-8000	Columbus (G-8374)
Optima 777 LLC	E	216 771-7700	Cleveland (G-6138)
Oxford Hospitality Group Inc	E	513 524-0114	Oxford (G-15687)
Pacific Heritg Inn Polaris LLC	E	614 880-9080	Columbus (G-6829)
Park Hotels & Resorts Inc	C	216 447-0020	Cleveland (G-6165)
Park Hotels & Resorts Inc	E	513 421-9100	Cincinnati (G-4202)
Park Hotels & Resorts Inc	B	216 464-5950	Cleveland (G-6166)
Park Hotels & Resorts Inc	E	937 436-2400	Miamisburg (G-14202)
Park Inn	E	419 241-3000	Toledo (G-17970)
Parkins Incorporated	E	614 334-1800	Hilliard (G-11805)
Peitro Properties Ltd Partnr	E	216 328-7777	Cleveland (G-6190)
PH Fairborn Ht Owner 2800 LLC	D	937 426-7800	Beavercreek (G-1176)
Pinecraft Land Holdings LLC	E	330 390-5722	Millersburg (G-14486)
Playhouse Square Foundation	C	216 615-7500	Cleveland (G-6217)
Polaris Innkeepers Inc	E	614 568-0770	Westerville (G-19199)
Primary Dayton Innkeepers LLC	E	937 938-9550	Dayton (G-9711)
Qh Management Company LLC	D	440 497-1100	Concord Twp (G-8946)
Quail Hollow Management Inc	D	440 639-4000	Painesville (G-15734)
R & H Service Inc	E	330 626-2888	Streetsboro (G-17267)
R & K Gorby LLC	E	419 222-0004	Lima (G-12728)
R & Y Holding	E	419 353-3464	Bowling Green (G-1747)
R P L Corporation	C	937 335-0021	Troy (G-18223)
Radisson Hotel Cleve	E	440 734-5060	North Olmsted (G-15308)
Radisson Hotel Cleveland Gtwy	D	216 377-9000	Cleveland (G-6278)
Rama Inc	E	614 473-9888	Columbus (G-8488)
Red Roof Inns Inc	A	614 744-2600	New Albany (G-14871)
Red Roof Inns Inc	E	614 224-6539	Columbus (G-8500)
Red Roof Inns Inc	E	440 892-7920	Cleveland (G-6294)
Red Roof Inns Inc	E	740 695-4057	Saint Clairsville (G-16503)

Red Roof Inns Inc ....E.... 440 243-5166
Cleveland *(G-6295)*
Renaissance Hotel Operating Co ....A.... 216 696-5600
Cleveland *(G-6305)*
Renthotel Dayton LLC ....D.... 937 461-4700
Dayton *(G-9731)*
Req/Jqh Holdings Inc ....D.... 937 432-0000
Miamisburg *(G-14211)*
Residence Inn ....E.... 614 222-2610
Columbus *(G-8519)*
Residence Inn By Marriott Beav ....E.... 937 427-3914
Beavercreek *(G-1182)*
Richfield Banquet & Confer ....E.... 330 659-6151
Richfield *(G-16375)*
Riders 1812 Inn ....E.... 440 354-0922
Painesville *(G-15738)*
Ridgehills Hotel Ltd Partnr ....D.... 440 585-0600
Wickliffe *(G-19475)*
River Road Hotel Corp ....E.... 614 267-7461
Columbus *(G-8535)*
Riverside Cmnty Urban Redev ....C.... 330 929-3000
Cuyahoga Falls *(G-9120)*
Riverview Hotel LLC ....E.... 614 268-8700
Columbus *(G-8538)*
Rlj III - Em Clmbus Lessee LLC ....D.... 614 890-8600
Columbus *(G-8539)*
Roce Group LLC ....E.... 330 969-2627
Stow *(G-17227)*
Rockside Hospitality LLC ....D.... 216 524-0700
Independence *(G-12115)*
Roschmans Restaurant ADM ....E.... 419 225-8300
Lima *(G-12734)*
Rose Gracias ....E.... 614 785-0001
Columbus *(G-8550)*
Rossford Hospitality Group Inc ....E.... 419 874-2345
Rossford *(G-16464)*
Rukh Boardman Properties LLC ....D.... 330 726-5472
Youngstown *(G-20198)*
Rukh-Jagi Holdings LLC ....D.... 330 494-2770
Canton *(G-2465)*
S & S Management Inc ....E.... 937 382-5858
Wilmington *(G-19647)*
S & S Management Inc ....E.... 937 235-2000
Dayton *(G-9745)*
S & S Management Inc ....E.... 567 356-4151
Wapakoneta *(G-18653)*
S P S Inc ....E.... 937 339-7801
Troy *(G-18228)*
Sadguru Krupa LLC ....E.... 330 644-2111
Akron *(G-416)*
Sage Hospitality Resources LLC ....D.... 513 771-2080
Cincinnati *(G-4424)*
Salt Fork Resort Club Inc ....A.... 740 498-8116
Kimbolton *(G-12312)*
Sar Biren ....E.... 419 865-0407
Maumee *(G-13848)*
Sauder Heritage Inn ....E.... 419 445-6408
Archbold *(G-637)*
Saw Mill Creek Ltd ....C.... 419 433-3800
Huron *(G-12030)*
Sawmill Creek Resort Ltd ....C.... 419 433-3800
Huron *(G-12031)*
Sb Hotel LLC ....E.... 614 793-2244
Dublin *(G-10329)*
SBS of Canton Jv LLC ....E.... 330 966-6620
Canton *(G-2470)*
Seagate Hospitality Group LLC ....E.... 216 252-7700
Cleveland *(G-6383)*
Seal Mayfield LLC ....E.... 440 684-4100
Mayfield Heights *(G-13881)*
Select Hotels Group LLC ....E.... 513 754-0003
Mason *(G-13638)*
Select Hotels Group LLC ....E.... 216 328-1060
Cleveland *(G-6393)*
Select Hotels Group LLC ....E.... 614 799-1913
Dublin *(G-10332)*
Shaker House ....D.... 216 991-6000
Cleveland *(G-6402)*
Shiv Hotels LLC ....E.... 740 374-8190
Marietta *(G-13381)*
Shree Shankar LLC ....E.... 440 734-4477
Richfield *(G-16379)*
Signature Boutique Hotel LP ....E.... 216 595-0900
Beachwood *(G-1106)*
Six Continents Hotels Inc ....C.... 513 563-8330
Cincinnati *(G-4487)*
Skyline Clvland Rnaissance LLC ....D.... 216 696-5600
Cleveland *(G-6414)*
Skyline CM Portfolio LLC ....E.... 937 433-3131
Miamisburg *(G-14222)*
Skyline CM Portfolio LLC ....E.... 419 866-1001
Holland *(G-11914)*
SM Double Tree Hotel Lake ....E.... 216 241-5100
Cleveland *(G-6418)*
Sojourn Lodging Inc ....E.... 330 422-1855
Streetsboro *(G-17270)*
Solon Lodging Associates LLC ....E.... 440 248-9600
Solon *(G-16899)*
Somnus Corporation ....E.... 740 695-3961
Saint Clairsville *(G-16505)*
Son-Rise Hotels Inc ....E.... 330 769-4949
Seville *(G-16691)*
Sonesta Intl Hotels Corp ....C.... 614 791-8554
Dublin *(G-10337)*
Sortino Management & Dev Co ....E.... 419 626-6761
Sandusky *(G-16643)*
South Beach Resort ....E.... 419 798-4900
Lakeside Marblehead *(G-12331)*
Spread Eagle Tavern Inc ....E.... 330 223-1583
Hanoverton *(G-11658)*
Spring Hill Suites ....E.... 513 381-8300
Cincinnati *(G-4520)*
Sree Hotels LLC ....E.... 513 354-2430
Cincinnati *(G-4525)*
Star Group Ltd ....E.... 614 428-8678
Gahanna *(G-11146)*
Starwood Hotels & Resorts ....C.... 614 345-9291
Columbus *(G-8689)*
Starwood Hotels & Resorts ....C.... 614 888-8230
Columbus *(G-8690)*
Sterling Lodging LLC ....E.... 419 879-4000
Lima *(G-12755)*
Stockport Mill Country Inn Inc ....E.... 740 559-2822
Stockport *(G-17183)*
Stoney Lodge Inc ....D.... 419 837-6409
Millbury *(G-14451)*
Strang Corporation ....E.... 216 961-6767
Cleveland *(G-6472)*
Strongsville Lodging Assoc 1 ....C.... 440 238-8800
Strongsville *(G-17348)*
Summit Associates Inc ....D.... 216 831-3300
Cleveland *(G-6475)*
Summit Hotel ....D.... 513 527-9900
Cincinnati *(G-4552)*
Summit Hotel Trs 144 LLC ....E.... 216 443-9043
Cleveland *(G-6476)*
Sunrise Hospitality Inc ....D.... 419 332-7650
Fremont *(G-11102)*
Sycamore Lake Inc ....C.... 440 729-9775
Chesterland *(G-2746)*
Synergy Hotels LLC ....E.... 614 492-9000
Obetz *(G-15530)*
Tharaldson Hospitality MGT ....E.... 513 947-9402
Cincinnati *(G-2872)*
Toledo Inns Inc ....E.... 440 243-4040
Cleveland *(G-6531)*
Town House Motor Lodge Corp ....E.... 740 452-4511
Zanesville *(G-20367)*
Town Inn Co LLC ....D.... 614 221-3281
Columbus *(G-8766)*
TownePlace Suites By Marriott ....E.... 513 774-0610
Cincinnati *(G-4621)*
Tramz Hotels LLC ....D.... 440 975-9922
Willoughby *(G-19577)*
Travelcenters of America LLC ....D.... 330 769-2053
Lodi *(G-12829)*
TW Recreational Services Inc ....E.... 440 564-9144
Newbury *(G-15126)*
Union Centre Hotel LLC ....C.... 513 874-7335
West Chester *(G-19026)*
United Hsptality Solutions LLC ....A.... 800 238-0487
Buffalo *(G-2007)*
Uph Holdings LLC ....D.... 614 447-9777
Columbus *(G-8823)*
Valley Hospitality Inc ....E.... 740 374-9660
Marietta *(G-13395)*
Valleyview Management Co Inc ....E.... 419 886-4000
Bellville *(G-1392)*
Visicon Inc ....D.... 937 879-2696
Fairborn *(G-10687)*
Vjp Hospitality Ltd ....E.... 614 475-8383
Columbus *(G-8858)*
W & H Realty Inc ....E.... 513 891-1066
Blue Ash *(G-1677)*
West Montrose Properties ....D.... 330 867-4013
Fairlawn *(G-10856)*
Westgate Limited Partnership ....C.... 419 535-7070
Toledo *(G-18155)*
Westlake Marriott ....E.... 440 892-6887
Westlake *(G-19424)*
Westpost Columbus LLC ....D.... 614 885-1885
Columbus *(G-8892)*
Willoughby Lodging LLC ....E.... 440 530-1100
Willoughby *(G-19583)*
Winegardner & Hammons Inc ....C.... 614 791-1000
Dublin *(G-10376)*
Winegrdner Hmmons Ht Group LLC ....E.... 513 891-1066
Blue Ash *(G-1678)*
Wm Columbus Hotel LLC ....C.... 614 228-3800
Columbus *(G-8911)*
Wph Cincinnati LLC ....C.... 513 771-2080
Cincinnati *(G-4806)*
Wright Executive Ht Ltd Partnr ....C.... 937 283-3200
Wilmington *(G-19656)*
Wright Executive Ht Ltd Partnr ....C.... 937 426-7800
Beavercreek *(G-1196)*
Wright Executive Ht Ltd Partnr ....C.... 937 429-0600
Beavercreek *(G-1197)*
Wyndham International Inc ....E.... 330 666-9300
Copley *(G-8980)*
Zincks Inn ....E.... 330 893-6600
Berlin *(G-1448)*

7021 Rooming & Boarding Houses

A M Management Inc ....E.... 937 426-6500
Beavercreek *(G-1122)*
Lodging First LLC ....E.... 614 792-2770
Dublin *(G-10273)*

7032 Sporting & Recreational Camps

Archdiocese of Cincinnati ....D.... 513 729-1725
Cincinnati *(G-2980)*
Camp Patmos Inc ....E.... 419 746-2214
Kelleys Island *(G-12209)*
Camp Pinecliff Inc ....D.... 614 236-5698
Columbus *(G-7109)*
Classroom Antics Inc ....E.... 800 595-3776
North Royalton *(G-15350)*
Columbus Frkln Cnty Pk ....E.... 614 891-0700
Westerville *(G-19242)*
Community Services Inc ....D.... 937 667-8631
Tipp City *(G-17553)*
Echoing Hills Village Inc ....D.... 740 594-3541
Athens *(G-778)*
Echoing Hills Village Inc ....C.... 740 327-2311
Warsaw *(G-18783)*
Echoing Hills Village Inc ....D.... 937 854-5151
Dayton *(G-9406)*
Echoing Hills Village Inc ....E.... 937 237-7881
Dayton *(G-9407)*
Echoing Hills Village Inc ....D.... 440 989-1400
Lorain *(G-12902)*
Echoing Hills Village Inc ....D.... 440 986-3085
South Amherst *(G-16921)*
Family YMCA of LANcstr&fairfld ....D.... 740 277-7373
Lancaster *(G-12403)*
Findlay Y M C A Child Dev ....E.... 419 422-3174
Findlay *(G-10908)*
First Community Church ....E.... 740 385-3827
Logan *(G-12835)*
Friars Club Inc ....D.... 513 488-8777
Cincinnati *(G-3594)*
Galion Community Center YMCA ....E.... 419 468-7754
Galion *(G-11173)*
Great Miami Valley YMCA ....A.... 513 887-0001
Hamilton *(G-11602)*
Great Miami Valley YMCA ....C.... 513 892-9622
Fairfield Township *(G-10808)*
Great Miami Valley YMCA ....D.... 513 887-0014
Hamilton *(G-11604)*
Great Miami Valley YMCA ....D.... 513 868-9622
Hamilton *(G-11605)*
Great Miami Valley YMCA ....D.... 513 829-3091
Fairfield *(G-10732)*
Hardin County Family YMCA ....E.... 419 673-6131
Kenton *(G-12279)*
Highland County Family YMCA ....E.... 937 840-9622
Hillsboro *(G-11842)*
Huber Heights YMCA ....D.... 937 236-9622
Dayton *(G-9508)*
Lake County YMCA ....C.... 440 352-3303
Painesville *(G-15718)*
Lake County YMCA ....C.... 440 946-1160
Willoughby *(G-19538)*
Lake County YMCA ....E.... 440 259-2724
Perry *(G-15824)*
Lake County YMCA ....D.... 440 428-5125
Madison *(G-13099)*
Lutheran Outdr Ministries OH ....E.... 614 890-2267
Westerville *(G-19276)*

S
I
C

Mideast Baptist Conference........E 440 834-8984		
Burton *(G-2018)*		
Ohio Camp Cherith Inc........E 330 725-4202		
Medina *(G-13984)*		
Ohio F F A Camps Inc........E 330 627-2208		
Carrollton *(G-2574)*		
Pike County YMCA........E 740 947-8862		
Waverly *(G-18822)*		
Procamps Inc........E 513 745-5855		
Blue Ash *(G-1632)*		
Red Oak Camp........E 440 256-0716		
Willoughby *(G-19565)*		
Rockwell Springs Trout Club........E 419 684-7971		
Clyde *(G-6751)*		
Salvation Army........D 330 735-2671		
Carrollton *(G-2577)*		
Scribes & Scrbblr Chld Dev Ctr........E 440 884-5437		
Cleveland *(G-6382)*		
Sheldon Harry E Calvary Camp........D 440 593-4381		
Conneaut *(G-8958)*		
Skyview Baptist Ranch Inc........E 330 674-7511		
Millersburg *(G-14493)*		
Springfield Family Y M C A........D 937 323-3781		
Springfield *(G-17119)*		
Sycamore Board of Education........D 513 489-3937		
Cincinnati *(G-4560)*		
Ucc Childrens Center........E 513 217-5501		
Middletown *(G-14356)*		
West Ohio Conference of........E 614 844-6200		
Worthington *(G-19859)*		
Y M C A Central Stark County........E 330 305-5437		
Canton *(G-2539)*		
Y M C A Central Stark County........E 330 875-1611		
Louisville *(G-12975)*		
Y M C A Central Stark County........E 330 877-8933		
Uniontown *(G-18392)*		
Y M C A Central Stark County........E 330 830-6275		
Massillon *(G-13736)*		
Y M C A Central Stark County........E 330 498-4082		
Canton *(G-2540)*		
Y M C A of Ashland Ohio Inc........D 419 289-0626		
Ashland *(G-700)*		
YMCA........E 330 823-1930		
Alliance *(G-558)*		
YMCA of Clermont County Inc........E 513 724-9622		
Batavia *(G-1016)*		
YMCA of Massillon........E 330 879-0800		
Navarre *(G-14826)*		
Young Mens Christian........B 513 932-1424		
Lebanon *(G-12516)*		
Young Mens Christian Assn........E 419 238-0443		
Van Wert *(G-18498)*		
Young Mens Christian Assoc........D 513 932-3756		
Oregonia *(G-15618)*		
Young Mens Christian Assoc........C 614 885-4252		
Columbus *(G-8927)*		
Young Mens Christian Assoc........E 419 729-8135		
Toledo *(G-18167)*		
Young Mens Christian Assoc........C 614 871-9622		
Grove City *(G-11491)*		
Young Mens Christian Assoc........E 937 223-5201		
Dayton *(G-9892)*		
Young Mens Christian Assoc........D 330 923-5223		
Cuyahoga Falls *(G-9141)*		
Young Mens Christian Assoc........E 330 467-8366		
Macedonia *(G-13091)*		
Young Mens Christian Assoc........E 330 784-0408		
Akron *(G-507)*		
Young Mens Christian Assoc........C 614 416-9622		
Gahanna *(G-11152)*		
Young Mens Christian Assoc........C 614 334-9622		
Hilliard *(G-11832)*		
Young Mens Christian Assoc........E 937 312-1810		
Dayton *(G-9893)*		
Young Mens Christian Assoc........E 614 539-1770		
Urbancrest *(G-18453)*		
Young Mens Christian Assoc........D 614 252-3166		
Columbus *(G-8929)*		
Young Mens Christian Assoc........E 937 593-9001		
Bellefontaine *(G-1370)*		
Young Mens Christian Associat........D 513 241-9622		
Cincinnati *(G-4815)*		
Young Mens Christian Associat........D 513 923-4466		
Cincinnati *(G-4816)*		
Young Mens Christian Associat........E 419 474-3995		
Toledo *(G-18169)*		
Young Mens Christian Associat........D 419 866-9622		
Maumee *(G-13871)*		
Young Mens Christian Associat........E 419 475-3496		
Toledo *(G-18170)*		

Young Mens Christian Associat........D 419 691-3523
Oregon *(G-15615)*
Young Mens Christian Mt Vernon........D 740 392-9622
Mount Vernon *(G-14794)*
Young MNS Chrstn Assn Clveland........E 216 521-8400
Lakewood *(G-12364)*
Young MNS Chrstn Assn Clveland........E 216 731-7454
Cleveland *(G-6703)*
Young MNS Chrstn Assn Clveland........D 440 285-7543
Chardon *(G-2726)*
Young MNS Chrstn Assn Grter NY........D 740 392-9622
Mount Vernon *(G-14795)*
Young Womens Christian........D 419 241-3235
Toledo *(G-18172)*
Young Womens Christian........E 419 238-6639
Van Wert *(G-18499)*
Young Womens Christian Assn........E 614 224-9121
Columbus *(G-8931)*
Young Womens Christian Associ........E 216 881-6878
Cleveland *(G-6705)*
Young Womns Chrstn Assc Canton........D 330 453-0789
Canton *(G-2543)*
YWCA Dayton........D 937 461-5550
Dayton *(G-9896)*
YWCA Mahoning Valley........E 330 746-6361
Youngstown *(G-20269)*
YWCA of Greater Cincinnati........D 513 241-7090
Cincinnati *(G-4817)*
YWCA Shelter & Housing Network........E 937 222-6333
Dayton *(G-9897)*

7033 Trailer Parks & Camp Sites

Big Broth and Big Siste of Cen........E 614 839-2447
Columbus *(G-7034)*
Clare-Mar Camp Inc........E 440 647-3318
New London *(G-14931)*
Dayton Tall Timbers Resort........E 937 833-3888
Brookville *(G-1913)*
Elbe Properties........A 513 489-1955
Cincinnati *(G-3485)*
Great Miami Valley YMCA........E 513 867-0600
Hamilton *(G-11603)*
Muskingum Wtrshed Cnsrvncy Dst........E 330 343-6780
Mineral City *(G-14507)*
Natural Resources Ohio Dept........E 419 394-3611
Saint Marys *(G-16528)*
Parks Recreation Athens........E 740 592-0046
Athens *(G-801)*
Real America Inc........B 216 261-1177
Cleveland *(G-6289)*

7041 Membership-Basis Hotels

Air Force US Dept of........D 937 257-6068
Dayton *(G-9157)*
Alpha CHI Omega........E 614 291-3871
Columbus *(G-6901)*
Alpha Epsilon PHI........E 614 294-5243
Columbus *(G-6902)*
CHI Omega Sorority........E 937 325-9323
Springfield *(G-17007)*
Cincinnati Fifth Street Ht LLC........D 513 579-1234
Cincinnati *(G-3243)*
Ohio State University........E 614 294-2635
Columbus *(G-8336)*
Rockwell Springs Trout Club........E 419 684-7971
Clyde *(G-6751)*
Sigma CHI Frat........E 614 297-8783
Columbus *(G-8638)*

72 PERSONAL SERVICES

7211 Power Laundries, Family & Commercial

Buckeye Launderer and Clrs LLC........D 419 592-2941
Sylvania *(G-17413)*
Dee Jay Cleaners Inc........E 216 731-7060
Euclid *(G-10630)*
Economy Linen & Towel Svc Inc........C 740 454-6888
Zanesville *(G-20304)*
Evergreen Cooperative Ldry Inc........E 216 268-3548
Cleveland *(G-5497)*
George Gardner........D 419 636-4277
Bryan *(G-1958)*
Heights Laundry & Dry Cleaning........E 216 932-9666
Cleveland Heights *(G-6718)*
Midwest Laundry Inc........D 513 563-5560
Cincinnati *(G-4050)*

7212 Garment Pressing & Cleaners' Agents

Apc2 Inc........D 513 231-5540
Cincinnati *(G-2972)*
C&C Clean Team Enterprises LLC........C 513 321-5100
Cincinnati *(G-3102)*
R & E Joint Venture Inc........E 614 891-9404
Westerville *(G-19206)*

7213 Linen Sply

Aramark Unf & Career AP LLC........D 937 223-6667
Dayton *(G-9236)*
Aramark Unf & Career AP LLC........C 614 445-8341
Columbus *(G-6962)*
Aramark Unf & Career AP LLC........C 216 341-7400
Cleveland *(G-4999)*
Barberton Laundry & Cleaning........D 330 825-6911
Barberton *(G-947)*
Buckeye Linen Service Inc........D 740 345-4046
Newark *(G-15018)*
◆ **Cintas Corporation No 1**........A 513 459-1200
Mason *(G-13556)*
Cintas Corporation No 2........D 614 878-7313
Columbus *(G-7201)*
Cintas Corporation No 2........C 440 352-4003
Painesville *(G-15698)*
Cintas Corporation No 2........E 740 687-6230
Lancaster *(G-12379)*
Cintas Corporation No 2........C 614 860-9152
Blacklick *(G-1477)*
Cintas Corporation No 2........C 513 965-0800
Milford *(G-14379)*
Economy Linen & Towel Svc Inc........C 740 454-6888
Zanesville *(G-20304)*
◆ **G&K Services LLC**........B 952 912-5500
Mason *(G-13582)*
Kimmel Cleaners Inc........D 419 294-1959
Upper Sandusky *(G-18410)*
Kramer Enterprises Inc........D 419 422-7924
Findlay *(G-10932)*
Midwest Laundry Inc........D 513 563-5560
Cincinnati *(G-4050)*
Millers Textile Services Inc........D 419 738-3552
Wapakoneta *(G-18650)*
Millers Textile Services Inc........E 614 262-1206
Springfield *(G-17086)*
Morgan Services Inc........E 419 243-2214
Toledo *(G-17924)*
Morgan Services Inc........C 216 241-3107
Cleveland *(G-6009)*
Morgan Services Inc........D 937 223-5241
Dayton *(G-9645)*
Nucentury Textile Services LLC........D 419 241-2267
Toledo *(G-17952)*
Ohio Textile Service Inc........E 740 450-4900
Zanesville *(G-20349)*
Paris Cleaners Inc........C 330 296-3300
Ravenna *(G-16252)*
Springfeld Unfrm-Linen Sup Inc........D 937 323-5544
Springfield *(G-17116)*
Superior Linen & AP Svcs Inc........D 513 751-1345
Cincinnati *(G-4557)*
Synergy Health North Amer Inc........D 513 398-6406
Mason *(G-13643)*
Unifirst Corporation........E 614 575-9999
Blacklick *(G-1483)*
Unifirst Corporation........D 937 746-0531
Franklin *(G-11040)*
Van Dyne-Crotty Co........E 614 684-0048
Columbus *(G-8842)*
Van Dyne-Crotty Co........C 614 491-3903
Columbus *(G-8843)*
Van Dyne-Crotty Co........E 440 248-6935
Solon *(G-16911)*

7215 Coin Operated Laundries & Cleaning

American Sales Inc........E 937 253-9520
Dayton *(G-9159)*
Fox Cleaners Inc........D 937 276-4171
Dayton *(G-9447)*
Joseph S Mischell........E 513 542-9800
Cincinnati *(G-3834)*
St Clair 60 Minute Clrs Inc........E 740 695-3100
Saint Clairsville *(G-16506)*
Super Laundry Inc........E 614 258-5147
Columbus *(G-8713)*

7216 Dry Cleaning Plants, Except Rug Cleaning

A One Fine Dry Cleaners Inc ....D 513 351-2663
Cincinnati **(G-2892)**

Apc2 Inc ....D 513 231-5540
Cincinnati **(G-2972)**

Aramark Unf & Career AP LLC ....D 937 223-6667
Dayton **(G-9236)**

Caskey Cleaning Co ....D 614 443-7448
Columbus **(G-7132)**

Dee Jay Cleaners Inc ....E 216 731-7060
Euclid **(G-10630)**

Dublin Cleaners Inc ....D 614 764-9934
Columbus **(G-7474)**

Dutchess Dry Cleaners ....E 330 759-9382
Youngstown **(G-20023)**

Edco Cleaners Inc ....E 330 477-3357
Canton **(G-2297)**

Farrow Cleaners Co ....E 216 561-2355
Cleveland **(G-5514)**

Fox Cleaners Inc ....D 937 276-4171
Dayton **(G-9447)**

George Gardner ....D 419 636-4277
Bryan **(G-1958)**

Heider Cleaners Inc ....E 937 298-6631
Dayton **(G-9494)**

Heights Laundry & Dry Cleaning ......E 216 932-9666
Cleveland Heights **(G-6718)**

Kimmel Cleaners Inc ....D 419 294-1959
Upper Sandusky **(G-18410)**

Kramer Enterprises Inc ....D 419 422-7924
Findlay **(G-10932)**

La France South Inc ....E 330 782-1400
Youngstown **(G-20095)**

Midwest Laundry Inc ....D 513 563-5560
Cincinnati **(G-4050)**

Miles Cleaning Services Inc ....D 330 633-8562
Cleveland **(G-5992)**

Pierce Cleaners Inc ....E 614 888-4225
Columbus **(G-8446)**

Quality Cleaners of Ohio Inc ....D 330 688-5616
Stow **(G-17226)**

Rentz Corp ....E 937 434-2774
Dayton **(G-9732)**

Rockwood Dry Cleaners Corp ....E 614 471-3700
Gahanna **(G-11142)**

Rondinelli Company Inc ....D 330 726-7643
Youngstown **(G-20194)**

St Clair 60 Minute Clrs Inc ....E 740 695-3100
Saint Clairsville **(G-16506)**

Sunset Carpet Cleaning ....E 937 836-5531
Englewood **(G-10602)**

Velco Inc ....E 513 772-4226
Cincinnati **(G-4752)**

Widmers LLC ....C 513 321-5100
Cincinnati **(G-4795)**

7217 Carpet & Upholstery Cleaning

Allen-Keith Construction Co ....D 330 266-2220
Canton **(G-2178)**

Americas Floor Source LLC ....E 216 342-4929
Bedford Heights **(G-1316)**

Arslanian Bros Crpt Rug Clg Co ....E 216 271-6888
Warrensville Heights **(G-18776)**

C M S Enterprises Inc ....E 740 653-1940
Lancaster **(G-12374)**

C&C Clean Team Enterprises LLC .....C 513 321-5100
Cincinnati **(G-3102)**

Carpet Services Plus Inc ....E 330 458-2409
Canton **(G-2246)**

D & J Master Clean Inc ....D 614 847-1181
Columbus **(G-7406)**

Farrow Cleaners Co ....E 216 561-2355
Cleveland **(G-5514)**

Icon Environmental Group LLC ....D 513 426-6767
Milford **(G-14396)**

Image By J & K LLC ....B 888 667-6929
Maumee **(G-13802)**

Lazar Brothers Inc ....E 440 585-9333
Wickliffe **(G-19468)**

Marks Cleaning Service Inc ....E 330 725-5702
Medina **(G-13968)**

Martin Carpet Cleaning Company ......E 614 443-4655
Columbus **(G-8031)**

Merlene Enterprises Inc ....E 440 593-6771
Conneaut **(G-8956)**

Miles Cleaning Services Inc ....D 330 633-8562
Cleveland **(G-5992)**

New Albany Cleaning Services ....E 614 855-9990
New Albany **(G-14863)**

Ohio Building Service Inc ....E 513 761-0268
Cincinnati **(G-4151)**

Samron Inc ....E 330 782-6539
Youngstown **(G-20203)**

Springfeld Unfrm-Linen Sup Inc ....D 937 323-5544
Springfield **(G-17116)**

▲ Stanley Steemer Intl Inc ....C 614 764-2007
Dublin **(G-10341)**

Stanley Steemer Intl Inc ....E 419 227-1212
Lima **(G-12754)**

Stanley Steemer Intl Inc ....E 513 771-0213
Cincinnati **(G-4536)**

Stanley Steemer Intl Inc ....E 614 652-2241
Dublin **(G-10342)**

Stanley Stemer of Akron Canton ....E 330 785-5005
Coventry Township **(G-9043)**

Sunset Carpet Cleaning ....E 937 836-5531
Englewood **(G-10602)**

Teasdale Fenton Carpet Cleanin ....C 513 797-0900
Cincinnati **(G-4578)**

Velco Inc ....E 513 772-4226
Cincinnati **(G-4752)**

Widmers LLC ....C 513 321-5100
Cincinnati **(G-4795)**

Wiggins Clg & Crpt Svc Inc ....D 937 279-9080
Dayton **(G-9881)**

7218 Industrial Launderers

Aramark Unf & Career AP LLC ....C 513 533-1000
Cincinnati **(G-2978)**

Aramark Unf & Career AP LLC ....D 937 223-6667
Dayton **(G-9236)**

Aramark Unf & Career AP LLC ....C 614 445-8341
Columbus **(G-6962)**

Aramark Unf & Career AP LLC ....C 216 341-7400
Cleveland **(G-4999)**

Brent Industries Inc ....E 419 382-8693
Toledo **(G-17624)**

◆ Cintas Corporation ....A 513 459-1200
Cincinnati **(G-3291)**

Cintas Corporation ....D 330 821-2220
Alliance **(G-524)**

Cintas Corporation ....D 513 671-7717
Cincinnati **(G-3293)**

Cintas Corporation ....D 513 631-5750
Cincinnati **(G-3292)**

Cintas Corporation No 2 ....D 440 746-7777
Girard **(G-11284)**

Cintas Corporation No 2 ....D 440 746-7777
Brecksville **(G-1773)**

Cintas Corporation No 2 ....C 513 965-0800
Milford **(G-14379)**

Cintas Corporation No 2 ....C 330 966-7800
Canton **(G-2254)**

Cintas Corporation No 2 ....D 614 878-7313
Columbus **(G-7201)**

Cintas Corporation No 2 ....C 614 860-9152
Blacklick **(G-1477)**

Cintas R US Inc ....A 513 459-1200
Cincinnati **(G-3294)**

Cintas Sales Corporation ....B 513 459-1200
Cincinnati **(G-3295)**

Cintas-Rus LP ....E 513 459-1200
Mason **(G-13561)**

Duckworth Enterprises LLC ....E 614 575-2900
Reynoldsburg **(G-16301)**

◆ G&K Services LLC ....B 952 912-5500
Mason **(G-13582)**

G&K Services LLC ....D 937 873-4500
Fairborn **(G-10675)**

Kimmel Cleaners Inc ....D 419 294-1959
Upper Sandusky **(G-18410)**

Leef Bros Inc ....C 952 912-5500
Mason **(G-13609)**

Midwest Laundry Inc ....D 513 563-5560
Cincinnati **(G-4050)**

Morgan Services Inc ....E 419 243-2214
Toledo **(G-17924)**

Morgan Services Inc ....C 216 241-3107
Cleveland **(G-6009)**

Rentwear Inc ....D 330 535-2301
Canton **(G-2453)**

Runt Ware & Sanitary Service ....E 330 494-5776
Canton **(G-2466)**

Springfeld Unfrm-Linen Sup Inc ....D 937 323-5544
Springfield **(G-17116)**

Unifirst Corporation ....E 614 575-9999
Blacklick **(G-1483)**

Unifirst Corporation ....D 216 658-6900
Independence **(G-12134)**

Unifirst Corporation ....D 937 746-0531
Franklin **(G-11040)**

Van Dyne-Crotty Co ....E 614 684-0048
Columbus **(G-8842)**

Van Dyne-Crotty Co ....C 614 491-3903
Columbus **(G-8843)**

Van Dyne-Crotty Co ....E 440 248-6935
Solon **(G-16911)**

7219 Laundry & Garment Svcs, NEC

Central Ohio Medical Textiles ....C 614 453-9274
Columbus **(G-7159)**

Clean Living Laundry LLC ....E 513 569-0439
Cincinnati **(G-3304)**

◆ G&K Services LLC ....B 952 912-5500
Mason **(G-13582)**

Pins & Needles Inc ....E 440 243-6400
Cleveland **(G-6212)**

Quality Cleaners of Ohio Inc ....E 330 688-5616
Stow **(G-17226)**

Springfeld Unfrm-Linen Sup Inc ....D 937 323-5544
Springfield **(G-17116)**

Van Dyne-Crotty Co ....E 614 684-0048
Columbus **(G-8842)**

7221 Photographic Studios, Portrait

Childers Photography ....E 937 256-0501
Dayton **(G-9165)**

Lifetouch Inc ....E 419 435-2646
Fostoria **(G-11008)**

Lifetouch Inc ....E 937 298-6275
Dayton **(G-9567)**

Lifetouch Nat Schl Studios Inc ....E 419 483-8200
Bellevue **(G-1380)**

Lifetouch Nat Schl Studios Inc ....E 330 497-1291
Canton **(G-2379)**

Lifetouch Nat Schl Studios Inc ....E 513 772-2110
Cincinnati **(G-3928)**

Pam Johnsonident ....D 419 946-4551
Mount Gilead **(G-14733)**

Peters Main Street Photography ....E 740 852-2731
London **(G-12872)**

Rapid Mortgage Company ....E 937 748-8888
Cincinnati **(G-4338)**

Ripcho Studio ....E 216 631-0664
Cleveland **(G-6327)**

Royal Color Inc ....B 440 234-1337
Bellevue **(G-1385)**

Universal Technology Corp ....D 937 426-2808
Beavercreek **(G-1193)**

Usam Inc ....D 330 244-8782
Canton **(G-2525)**

Woodard Photographic Inc ....E 419 483-3364
Bellevue **(G-1386)**

7231 Beauty Shops

Alsan Corporation ....D 330 385-3636
East Liverpool **(G-10396)**

Anthony David Salon & Spa ....E 440 233-8570
Lorain **(G-12881)**

Attitudes New Inc ....E 330 856-1143
Warren **(G-18669)**

Attractions ....E 740 592-5600
Athens **(G-771)**

Beauty Bar LLC ....E 419 537-5400
Toledo **(G-17609)**

Bella Capelli Inc ....E 440 899-1225
Westlake **(G-19322)**

Best Cuts Inc ....E 440 884-6300
Cleveland **(G-5058)**

Beverly Hills Inn La Llc ....E 859 494-9151
Aberdeen **(G-1)**

Brenwood Inc ....E 740 452-7533
Zanesville **(G-20283)**

Calico Court ....E 740 455-2541
Zanesville **(G-20286)**

Casals Hair Salon Inc ....E 330 533-6766
Canfield **(G-2132)**

Castilian & Co ....E 937 836-9671
Englewood **(G-10581)**

Changes Hair Designers Inc ....E 614 846-6666
Columbus **(G-6806)**

Collins Salon Inc ....E 513 683-1700
Loveland **(G-12984)**

Cookie Cutters Haircutters ....E 614 522-0220
Pickerington **(G-15955)**

Creative Images College of B ....E 937 478-7922
Dayton **(G-9337)**

Dana Lauren Salon & Spa ....E 440 262-1092
Broadview Heights **(G-1830)**

SIC

Employee Codes: A=Over 500 employees, B=251-500
C=101-250, D=51-100, E=25-50   2019 Harris Ohio
Services Directory   923

David Scott Salon .... E 440 734-7595
North Olmsted (G-15285)

Definitions of Design Inc .... E 419 891-0188
Maumee (G-13781)

Dino Palmieri Beauty Salon .... D 440 498-9411
Bedford (G-1277)

Ecotage .... E 513 782-2229
Cincinnati (G-3484)

Edge Hair Design & Spa .... E 330 477-2300
Canton (G-2298)

Englefield Inc .... D 740 323-2077
Thornville (G-17505)

Esbi International Salon .... E 330 220-3724
Brunswick (G-1929)

Flux A Salon By Hazelton .... E 419 841-5100
Perrysburg (G-15866)

Frank Santo LLC .... E 216 831-9374
Pepper Pike (G-15817)

G E G Enterprises Inc .... E 330 494-9160
Canton (G-2320)

G E G Enterprises Inc .... E 330 477-3133
Canton (G-2321)

Hair Forum .... E 513 245-0800
Cincinnati (G-3673)

Hair Shoppe Inc .... D 330 497-1651
Canton (G-2334)

Hairy Cactus Salon Inc .... E 513 771-9335
West Chester (G-18940)

Head Quarters Inc .... E 440 233-8508
Lorain (G-12906)

Image Engineering Inc .... E 513 541-8544
Cincinnati (G-3752)

Intl Europa Salon & Spa .... E 216 292-6969
Cleveland (G-5766)

Intrigue Salon & Day Spa .... E 330 493-7003
Canton (G-2358)

Jbentley Studio & Spa LLC .... D 614 790-8828
Powell (G-16198)

Jbj Enterprises Inc .... E 440 992-6051
Ashtabula (G-743)

JC Penney Corporation Inc .... B 330 633-7700
Akron (G-288)

John Rbrts Hair Studio Spa Inc .... D 216 839-1430
Cleveland (G-5800)

Karen Funke Inc .... E 216 464-4311
Beachwood (G-1072)

Kenneths Hair Salons & Day Sp .... B 614 457-7712
Columbus (G-7893)

Kerr House Inc .... E 419 832-1733
Grand Rapids (G-11327)

Kristie Warner .... E 330 650-4450
Hudson (G-11992)

L A Hair Force .... E 419 756-3101
Mansfield (G-13196)

Laser Hair Removal Center .... D 937 433-7536
Dayton (G-9559)

Le Nails .... E 440 846-1866
Cleveland (G-5859)

Legrand Services Inc .... E 740 682-6046
Oak Hill (G-15481)

M C Hair Consultants Inc .... E 234 678-3987
Cuyahoga Falls (G-9110)

Marios International Spa & Ht .... C 330 562-5141
Aurora (G-835)

Marios International Spa & Ht .... E 440 845-7373
Cleveland (G-5908)

Mark Luikart Inc .... E 330 339-9141
New Philadelphia (G-14973)

Mato Inc .... E 440 729-9008
Chesterland (G-2740)

Merle-Holden Enterprises Inc .... E 216 661-6887
Cleveland (G-5957)

Mfh Inc .... E 937 435-4701
Dayton (G-9611)

Mfh Inc .... E 937 435-4701
Dayton (G-9612)

Michael A Garcia Salon .... E 614 235-1605
Columbus (G-8067)

Michael Christopher Salon Inc .... E 440 449-0999
Cleveland (G-5977)

Mitchells Salon & Day Spa .... D 513 793-0900
Cincinnati (G-4061)

Mitchells Salon & Day Spa .... C 513 793-0900
West Chester (G-18973)

Mitchells Salon & Day Spa .... E 513 772-3200
Cincinnati (G-4062)

Mitchells Salon & Day Spa .... D 513 731-0600
Cincinnati (G-4063)

Mzf Inc .... E 216 464-3910
Cleveland (G-6032)

Noggins Hair Design Inc .... E 513 474-4405
Cincinnati (G-4121)

Nurtur Holdings LLC .... E 614 487-3033
Loveland (G-13016)

Nutur Holdings LLC .... C 513 576-9333
Loveland (G-13017)

P JS Hair Styling Shoppe .... E 440 333-1244
Cleveland (G-6155)

Paragon Salons Inc .... E 513 651-4600
Cincinnati (G-4199)

Paragon Salons Inc .... E 513 683-6700
Cincinnati (G-4200)

Philip Icuss Jr .... E 740 264-4647
Steubenville (G-17169)

Phyllis At Madison .... E 513 321-1300
Cincinnati (G-4245)

Picasso For Nail LLC .... E 440 308-4470
Solon (G-16883)

PS Lifestyle LLC .... A 440 600-1595
Cleveland (G-6265)

Pure Concept Salon Inc .... E 513 770-2120
Mason (G-13630)

Pure Concept Salon Inc .... D 513 794-0202
Cincinnati (G-4305)

R L O Inc .... E 937 620-9998
Dayton (G-9724)

Reflections Hair Studio Inc .... E 330 725-5782
Medina (G-13995)

Reves Salon & Spa .... E 419 885-1140
Sylvania (G-17447)

Rometrics Too Hair Nail Gllery .... E 440 808-1391
Westlake (G-19402)

Salon Alexandre Inc .... E 513 207-8406
West Chester (G-19078)

Salon Communication Services .... E 614 233-8500
Columbus (G-8586)

Salon Hazelton .... E 419 874-9404
Perrysburg (G-15917)

Salon La .... E 513 784-1700
Cincinnati (G-4428)

Salon Ware Inc .... E 330 665-2244
Copley (G-8972)

Shamas Ltd .... E 419 872-9908
Perrysburg (G-15920)

Sheer Professionals Inc .... E 330 345-8666
Wooster (G-19769)

Skyland Columbus LLC .... E 614 478-0922
Columbus (G-8651)

Soto Salon & Spa .... E 419 872-5555
Perrysburg (G-15922)

Star Beauty Plus LLC .... E 216 662-9750
Maple Heights (G-13298)

Tanos Salon .... E 216 831-7880
Cleveland (G-6498)

Tara Flaherty .... E 419 565-1334
Mansfield (G-13250)

Uptown Hair Studio Inc .... E 937 832-2111
Englewood (G-10604)

Urban Oasis Inc .... E 614 766-9946
Dublin (G-10361)

Vlp Inc .... E 330 758-8811
Youngstown (G-20238)

Walmart Inc .... C 937 399-0370
Springfield (G-17133)

Yearwood Corporation .... E 937 223-3572
Dayton (G-9889)

Z A F Inc .... E 216 291-1234
Cleveland (G-6707)

7241 Barber Shops

Attractions .... E 740 592-5600
Athens (G-771)

Head Quarters Inc .... E 440 233-8508
Lorain (G-12906)

Lucas Metropolitan Hsing Auth .... D 419 259-9457
Toledo (G-17869)

Mfh Inc .... E 937 435-4701
Dayton (G-9611)

Ricks Hair Center .... E 330 545-5120
Girard (G-11299)

7261 Funeral Svcs & Crematories

Cole Selby Funeral Inc .... E 330 856-4695
Vienna (G-18578)

Cremation Service Inc .... E 216 861-2334
Cleveland (G-5378)

Cremation Service Inc .... E 216 621-6222
Cleveland (G-5379)

Cummings and Davis Fnrl HM Inc .... E 216 541-1111
Cleveland (G-5389)

Davidson Becker Inc .... E 330 755-2111
Struthers (G-17363)

Domajaparo Inc .... E 513 742-3600
Cincinnati (G-3438)

E F Boyd & Son Inc .... E 216 791-0770
Cleveland (G-5453)

Ferfolia Funeral Homes Inc .... E 216 663-4222
Northfield (G-15379)

Keller Ochs Koch Inc .... E 419 332-8288
Fremont (G-11082)

Lucas Funeral Homes Inc .... E 419 294-1985
Upper Sandusky (G-18411)

Martin Altmeyer Funeral Home .... E 330 385-3650
East Liverpool (G-10406)

Newcomer Funeral Svc Group Inc .... B 513 521-1971
Cincinnati (G-4111)

Paul R Young Funeral Homes .... E 513 521-9303
Cincinnati (G-4214)

Rutherford Funeral Home Inc .... E 614 451-0593
Columbus (G-8563)

Spring Grove Funeral Homes Inc .... C 513 681-7526
Cincinnati (G-4518)

7291 Tax Return Preparation Svcs

Barnes Wendling Cpas Inc .... E 216 566-9000
Cleveland (G-5037)

Colonial Banc Corp .... E 937 456-5544
Eaton (G-10439)

Damon Tax Service .... E 513 574-9087
Cincinnati (G-3399)

Delaneys Tax Accunting Svc Ltd .... E 513 248-2829
Milford (G-14384)

Deloitte & Touche LLP .... B 513 784-7100
Cincinnati (G-3420)

Dw Together LLC .... E 330 225-8200
Brunswick (G-1928)

E T Financial Service Inc .... E 937 716-1726
Trotwood (G-18193)

H & R Block Inc .... E 419 352-9467
Bowling Green (G-1733)

H & R Block Inc .... E 330 345-1040
Wooster (G-19726)

H & R Block Inc .... E 513 868-1818
Hamilton (G-11606)

H&R Block Inc .... E 440 282-4288
Amherst (G-589)

H&R Block Inc .... E 216 861-1185
Cleveland (G-5653)

Hometown Urgent Care .... C 330 629-2300
Youngstown (G-20067)

Hometown Urgent Care .... D 740 363-3133
Delaware (G-9987)

Hometown Urgent Care .... C 937 252-2000
Wooster (G-19728)

Jennings & Associates .... E 740 369-4426
Delaware (G-9991)

Phillip Mc Guire .... E 740 482-2701
Nevada (G-14838)

Regional Income Tax Agency .... C 800 860-7482
Brecksville (G-1801)

Skoda Minotti Holdings LLC .... E 440 449-6800
Cleveland (G-6411)

Village of Coldwater .... D 419 678-2685
Coldwater (G-6767)

7299 Miscellaneous Personal Svcs, NEC

3sg Plus LLC .... E 614 652-0019
Columbus (G-6797)

A Tara Tiffanys Property .... E 330 448-0778
Brookfield (G-1851)

Action For Children Inc .... E 614 224-0222
Columbus (G-6868)

Administrative Svcs Ohio Dept .... D 614 466-5090
Columbus (G-6872)

Akron Metropolitan Hsing Auth .... C 330 920-1652
Stow (G-17189)

Alpha PHI Alpha Homes Inc .... D 330 376-2115
Akron (G-68)

American Commodore Tu .... D 216 291-4601
Cleveland (G-4950)

Assembly Center .... E 800 582-1099
Monroe (G-14560)

Attractions .... E 740 592-5600
Athens (G-771)

Banquets Unlimited .... E 859 689-4000
Cincinnati (G-3017)

Barberton Laundry & Cleaning .... D 330 825-6911
Barberton (G-947)

Best Upon Request Corp Inc .... D 513 605-7800
Cincinnati (G-3044)

Black Tie Affair Inc ....E 330 345-8333
  Wooster (G-19691)
Blue Chip Mailing Services Inc ....E 513 541-4800
  Blue Ash (G-1514)
Brown Derby Roadhouse ....E 330 528-3227
  Hudson (G-11968)
Buffalo Jacks ....E 937 473-2524
  Covington (G-9046)
Buns of Delaware Inc ....E 740 363-2867
  Delaware (G-9956)
Cabin Restaurant ....E 330 562-9171
  Aurora (G-823)
Camargo Rental Center Inc ....E 513 271-6510
  Cincinnati (G-3109)
Camden FLS Rcption Cnfrnce Ctr .....E 419 448-7699
  Tiffin (G-17511)
Carol Scudere ....E 614 839-4357
  New Albany (G-14848)
Carrie Cerino Restaurants Inc ....C 440 237-3434
  Cleveland (G-5129)
Cec Entertainment Inc ....D 937 439-1108
  Miamisburg (G-14149)
Cheers Chalet ....E 740 654-9036
  Lancaster (G-12378)
Child & Elder Care Insights ....E 440 356-2900
  Rocky River (G-16426)
Cincinnati Circus Company LLC ......D 513 921-5454
  Cincinnati (G-3233)
Cintas Document Management LLC .....E 800 914-1960
  Mason (G-13560)
City Life Inc ....E 216 523-5899
  Cleveland (G-5186)
City of Beavercreek ....D 937 320-0742
  Beavercreek (G-1141)
City of Centerville ....E 937 438-3585
  Dayton (G-9302)
City of Vandalia ....E 937 890-1300
  Vandalia (G-18517)
Cleveland Metroparks ....C 216 661-6500
  Cleveland (G-5267)
Connor Concepts Inc ....E 937 291-1661
  Dayton (G-9317)
Consumer Credit Coun ....E 614 552-2222
  Gahanna (G-11115)
Continntal Mssage Solution Inc ......D 614 224-4534
  Columbus (G-7364)
Coshocton Village Inn Suites ....E 740 622-9455
  Coshocton (G-9010)
Costume Specialists Inc ....E 614 464-2115
  Columbus (G-7378)
Cuyahoga County ....D 216 443-8920
  Cleveland (G-5397)
Delaware Golf Club Inc ....E 740 362-2582
  Delaware (G-9969)
Deyor Performing Arts Center ....D 330 744-4269
  Youngstown (G-20017)
Diet Center Worldwide Inc ....E 330 665-5861
  Akron (G-186)
Dinos Catering Inc ....E 440 943-1010
  Wickliffe (G-19455)
Eagle Industries Ohio Inc ....E 513 247-2900
  Fairfield (G-10721)
Emmys Bridal Inc ....E 419 628-7555
  Minster (G-14532)
Engle Management Group ....D 513 232-9729
  Cincinnati (G-3499)
Eventions Ltd ....E 216 952-9898
  Cleveland (G-5496)
Excel Decorators Inc ....C 614 522-0056
  Columbus (G-7541)
▲ Farm Inc ....E 513 922-7020
  Cincinnati (G-3532)
Findlay Inn & Conference Ctr ....D 419 422-5682
  Findlay (G-10904)
Formu3 International Inc ....E 330 668-1461
  Akron (G-227)
Fun Day Events LLC ....E 740 549-9000
  Gahanna (G-11121)
G E G Enterprises Inc ....E 330 477-3133
  Canton (G-2321)
German Family Society Inc ....E 330 678-8229
  Kent (G-12234)
Goldfish Swim School ....E 216 364-9090
  Warrensville Heights (G-18778)
Grandview Ht Ltd Partnr Ohio ....D 937 766-5519
  Springfield (G-17043)
Great Southern Video Inc ....E 216 642-8855
  Cleveland (G-5632)
Guys Party Center ....E 330 724-6373
  Akron (G-247)

Hall Nazareth Inc ....D 419 832-2900
  Grand Rapids (G-11325)
Haribol Haribol Inc ....E 330 339-7731
  New Philadelphia (G-14963)
Healthquest Blanchester Inc ....E 937 783-4535
  Blanchester (G-1487)
Heatherwoode Golf Course ....C 937 748-3222
  Springboro (G-16969)
Hkt Teleservices Inc ....C 614 652-6300
  Grove City (G-11441)
Humility of Mary Info Systems ......D 330 884-6600
  Youngstown (G-20071)
Iacominis Papa Joes Inc ....D 330 923-7999
  Akron (G-274)
Informa Business Media Inc ....E 216 696-7000
  Cleveland (G-5751)
Intelisol Inc ....D 614 409-0052
  Lockbourne (G-12820)
Irish Envy LLC ....E 440 808-8000
  Westlake (G-19358)
Jack & Jill Babysitting Svc ....E 513 731-5261
  Cincinnati (G-3797)
Kiddie Party Company LLC ....E 440 273-7680
  Mayfield Heights (G-13875)
Kinane Inc ....D 513 459-0177
  Mason (G-13605)
Kinetic Renovations LLC ....E 937 321-1576
  Xenia (G-19915)
Kitchen Katering Inc ....E 216 481-8080
  Euclid (G-10647)
Kohler Foods Inc ....E 937 291-3600
  Dayton (G-9550)
La Villa Cnference Banquet Ctr .....E 216 265-9305
  Cleveland (G-5844)
Lees Roby Inc ....E 330 872-0983
  Newton Falls (G-15139)
Leos La Piazza Inc ....E 937 339-5553
  Troy (G-18210)
Life Time Inc ....C 614 428-6000
  Columbus (G-7973)
Little Miami River Catering Co .....E 937 848-2464
  Bellbrook (G-1341)
Longworth Enterprises Inc ....B 513 738-4663
  West Chester (G-18965)
Lorain Party Center ....E 440 282-5599
  Lorain (G-12923)
Mackil Inc ....E 937 833-3310
  Brookville (G-1915)
Makoy Center Inc ....E 614 777-1211
  Hilliard (G-11787)
Mandalay Inc ....E 937 294-6600
  Moraine (G-14671)
Mark Luikart Inc ....E 330 339-9141
  New Philadelphia (G-14973)
Mason Family Resorts LLC ....B 513 339-0141
  Mason (G-13615)
Massage Envy ....E 440 878-0500
  Strongsville (G-17329)
Menard Inc ....C 614 501-1654
  Columbus (G-8056)
Mercy Health ....E 419 407-3990
  Toledo (G-17906)
Michaels Inc ....D 440 357-0384
  Mentor (G-14085)
Mocha House Inc ....E 330 392-3020
  Warren (G-18731)
Mustard Seed Health Fd Mkt Inc .....E 440 519-3663
  Solon (G-16875)
Nelson Financial Group ....E 513 686-7800
  Dayton (G-9182)
New Jersey Aquarium LLC ....D 614 414-7300
  Columbus (G-8186)
Noggins Hair Design Inc ....E 513 474-4405
  Cincinnati (G-4121)
Occasions Party Centre ....E 330 882-5113
  New Franklin (G-14911)
Old Barn Out Back Inc ....D 419 999-3989
  Lima (G-12711)
Parking Solutions Inc ....A 614 469-7000
  Columbus (G-8422)
Pines Golf Club ....E 330 684-1414
  Orrville (G-15644)
Public Safety Ohio Department ......A 614 752-7600
  Columbus (G-8478)
Pure Romance LLC ....D 513 248-8656
  Cincinnati (G-4306)
Queens Tower Restaurant Inc ....E 513 251-6467
  Cincinnati (G-4324)
Raymond Recepton House ....E 614 276-6127
  Columbus (G-8490)

Refectory Restaurant Inc ....E 614 451-9774
  Columbus (G-8501)
Research Associates Inc ....D 440 892-1000
  Cleveland (G-6312)
Riverside Cmnty Urban Redev ....C 330 929-3000
  Cuyahoga Falls (G-9120)
Rondinelli Company Inc ....D 330 726-7643
  Youngstown (G-20194)
Rondinellis Tuxedo ....E 330 726-7768
  Youngstown (G-20195)
Roscoe Village Foundation ....D 740 622-2222
  Coshocton (G-9026)
Sam BS Restaurant ....E 419 353-2277
  Bowling Green (G-1748)
Sauder Village ....B 419 446-2541
  Archbold (G-638)
Snpj Recreation Farm ....E 440 256-3423
  Willoughby (G-19573)
Spagnas ....E 740 376-9245
  Marietta (G-13383)
Sr Improvements Services LLC ....E 567 207-6488
  Vickery (G-18575)
Super Tan ....E 330 722-2799
  Medina (G-14008)
Teasdale Fenton Carpet Cleanin .....C 513 797-0900
  Cincinnati (G-4578)
The Oaks Lodge ....E 330 769-2601
  Chippewa Lake (G-2838)
Toris Station ....E 513 829-7815
  Fairfield (G-10791)
Twin Haven Reception Hall ....E 330 425-1616
  Twinsburg (G-18331)
Ussa Inc ....E 740 354-6672
  Portsmouth (G-16179)
Valley Hospitality Inc ....E 740 374-9660
  Marietta (G-13395)
Villa Milano Inc ....E 614 882-2058
  Columbus (G-8851)
Vulcan Machinery Corporation ....E 330 376-6025
  Akron (G-491)
Winking Lizard Inc ....D 330 467-1002
  Peninsula (G-15816)
Winking Lizard Inc ....D 330 220-9944
  Brunswick (G-1948)

73 BUSINESS SERVICES

7311 Advertising Agencies

▲ Airmate Company ....D 419 636-3184
  Bryan (G-1950)
▲ Albrecht Inc ....E 513 576-9900
  Milford (G-14369)
AMG Marketing Resources Inc ....E 216 621-1835
  Solon (G-16820)
AMP Advertising Inc ....E 513 333-4100
  Cincinnati (G-2954)
Barefoot LLC ....E 513 861-3668
  Cincinnati (G-3020)
BBDO Worldwide Inc ....E 513 861-3668
  Cincinnati (G-3026)
Bbs & Associates Inc ....E 330 665-5227
  Akron (G-89)
Black River Group Inc ....D 419 524-6699
  Mansfield (G-13142)
Brokaw Inc ....E 216 241-8003
  Cleveland (G-5085)
Charles W Powers & Assoc Inc ....E 513 721-5353
  Cincinnati (G-3171)
Commerce Holdings Inc ....E 513 579-1950
  Cincinnati (G-3337)
Cooper-Smith Advertising LLC ....E 419 470-5900
  Toledo (G-17679)
Curiosity LLC ....D 513 744-6000
  Cincinnati (G-3389)
Deanhouston Creative Group Inc .....E 513 421-6622
  Cincinnati (G-3413)
Detroit Royalty Incorporated ....D 216 771-5700
  Cleveland (G-5419)
Dix & Eaton Incorporated ....E 216 241-0405
  Cleveland (G-5431)
Epipheo Incorporated ....E 888 687-7620
  Cincinnati (G-3506)
Fahlgren Inc ....E 614 383-1500
  Columbus (G-7552)
Fahlgren Inc ....E 614 383-1500
  Columbus (G-7553)
Guardian Enterprise Group Inc ......E 614 416-6080
  Columbus (G-7702)
Gypc Inc ....C 309 677-0405
  Dayton (G-9479)

Hart Associates Inc	D	419 893-9600	Toledo (G-17783)
Hitchcock Fleming & Assoc Inc	D	330 376-2111	Akron (G-263)
Hsr Marketing Communications	E	513 671-3811	Cincinnati (G-3735)
Inquiry Systems Inc	E	614 464-3800	Columbus (G-7824)
Kreber Graphics Inc	D	614 529-5701	Columbus (G-7926)
Kuno Creative Group LLC	E	440 225-4144	Avon (G-891)
L M Berry and Company	A	937 296-2121	Moraine (G-14670)
Madison Avenue Mktg Group Inc	E	419 473-9000	Toledo (G-17878)
Marcus Thomas Llc	D	216 292-4700	Cleveland (G-5907)
Marcus Thomas Llc	D	330 793-3000	Youngstown (G-20116)
Marketing Support Services Inc	E	513 752-1200	Cincinnati (G-3972)
Matrix Media Services Inc	E	614 228-2200	Columbus (G-8039)
Melamed Riley Advertising LLC	D	216 241-2141	Cleveland (G-5950)
Monster Worldwide Inc	E	513 719-3331	Cincinnati (G-4071)
Nas Rcrtment Cmmunications LLC	C	216 478-0300	Cleveland (G-6036)
National Yllow Pages Media LLC	E	216 447-9400	Independence (G-12101)
People To My Site LLC	E	614 452-8179	Columbus (G-8437)
Real Art Design Group Inc	E	937 223-9955	Dayton (G-9728)
Rockfish Interactive Corp	D	513 381-1583	Cincinnati (G-4393)
Ron Foth Retail Inc	D	614 888-7771	Columbus (G-8547)
Sgk LLC	D	513 569-9900	Cincinnati (G-4461)
Stern Advertising Inc	E	216 331-5827	Cleveland (G-6468)
Thread Information Design Inc	E	419 887-6801	Toledo (G-18065)
▲ Touchstone Mdse Group LLC	D	513 741-0400	Mason (G-13648)
Universal Advertising Assoc	E	513 522-5000	Cincinnati (G-4693)
Vivial Media LLC	D	937 610-4100	Dayton (G-9857)
Wern-Rausch Locke Advertising	E	330 493-8866	Canton (G-2533)
Whitespace Design Group Inc	E	330 762-9320	Akron (G-501)
Wyse Advertising Inc	D	216 696-2424	Cleveland (G-6695)
Young & Rubicam Inc	C	513 419-2300	Cincinnati (G-4811)

7312 Outdoor Advertising Svcs

Kessler Sign Company	E	740 453-0668	Zanesville (G-20323)
Lamar Advertising Company	E	216 676-4321	Cleveland (G-5853)
Lamar Advertising Company	E	740 699-0000	Saint Clairsville (G-16490)
Matrix Media Services Inc	E	614 228-2200	Columbus (G-8039)
Orange Barrel Media LLC	E	614 294-4898	Columbus (G-8383)

7313 Radio, TV & Publishers Adv Reps

Agri Communicators Inc	E	614 273-0465	Columbus (G-6885)
American City Bus Journals Inc	E	937 528-4400	Dayton (G-9226)
B G News	E	419 372-2601	Bowling Green (G-1715)
Copley Ohio Newspapers Inc	C	330 364-5577	New Philadelphia (G-14951)
Creative Crafts Group LLC	D	303 215-5600	Blue Ash (G-1540)
Ctv Media Inc	E	614 848-5800	Powell (G-16193)
Iheartcommunications Inc	C	937 224-1137	Dayton (G-9512)
Killer Spotscom Inc	D	513 201-1380	Cincinnati (G-3869)

Madison Avenue Mktg Group Inc	E	419 473-9000	Toledo (G-17878)
Manta Media Inc	E	888 875-5833	Columbus (G-6823)
Maverick Media	E	419 331-1600	Lima (G-12700)
Sandusky Register	E	419 625-5500	Sandusky (G-16640)
Segmint Inc	E	330 594-5379	Akron (G-421)
Thinktv Network	E	937 220-1600	Dayton (G-9813)

7319 Advertising, NEC

Berry Network LLC	C	800 366-1264	Moraine (G-14625)
Ctv Media Inc	E	614 848-5800	Powell (G-16193)
Digital Color Intl LLC	E	330 762-6959	Akron (G-187)
Dispatch Consumer Services	D	740 687-1893	Lancaster (G-12389)
Dispatch Consumer Services	D	740 548-5555	Columbus (G-7450)
▲ Downing Displays Inc	D	513 248-9800	Milford (G-14386)
Elyria-Lorain Broadcasting Co	E	440 322-3761	Elyria (G-10508)
Empower Mediamarketing Inc	C	513 871-7779	Cincinnati (G-3495)
Groupcle LLC	E	216 251-9641	Cleveland (G-5645)
Harmon Media Group	E	330 478-5325	Canton (G-2340)
Hillman Group Inc	E	513 874-5905	West Chester (G-19060)
Innomark Communications LLC	E	937 425-6152	Sharonville (G-16729)
Ohs LLC	E	513 252-2249	Blue Ash (G-1624)
Paul Werth Associates Inc	E	614 224-8114	Columbus (G-8429)
Signum LLC	D	440 248-2233	Solon (G-16897)
Team Management Inc	C	614 486-0864	Columbus (G-8735)

7322 Adjustment & Collection Svcs

Allied Interstate LLC	D	715 386-1810	Columbus (G-6898)
Apelles LLC	E	614 899-7322	Columbus (G-6957)
Axcess Rcvery Cr Solutions Inc	E	513 229-6700	Cincinnati (G-3011)
C & S Associates Inc	E	440 461-9661	Highland Heights (G-11732)
Celco Ltd	E	330 655-7000	Hudson (G-11969)
Choice Recovery Inc	D	614 358-9900	Columbus (G-7193)
Controlled Credit Corporation	E	513 921-2600	Cincinnati (G-3354)
Credit Adjustments Inc	D	419 782-3709	Defiance (G-9908)
Credit Bur Collectn Svcs Inc	E	614 223-0688	Columbus (G-7388)
Credit Bur Collectn Svcs Inc	E	937 496-2577	Dayton (G-9338)
Dfs Corporate Services LLC	B	614 777-7020	Hilliard (G-11760)
Estate Information Svcs LLC	D	614 729-1700	Gahanna (G-11119)
Fidelity Properties Inc	E	330 821-9700	Alliance (G-531)
Finance System of Toledo Inc	E	419 578-4300	Toledo (G-17735)
First Federal Credit Control	E	216 360-2000	Cleveland (G-5534)
General Audit Corp	E	419 993-2900	Lima (G-12642)
General Revenue Corporation	B	513 469-1472	Mason (G-13586)
Guardian Water & Power Inc	D	614 291-3141	Columbus (G-7703)
Head Mercantile Co Inc	D	440 847-2700	Westlake (G-19349)
HMC Group Inc	E	440 847-2720	Westlake (G-19350)
Hs Financial Group LLC	E	440 871-8484	Westlake (G-19353)

Innovtive Cllectn Concepts Inc	E	513 489-5500	Blue Ash (G-1584)
JP Recovery Services Inc	D	440 331-2200	Rocky River (G-16438)
Macys Cr & Customer Svcs Inc	A	513 398-5221	Mason (G-13613)
McCarthy Burgess & Wolff Inc	C	440 735-5100	Bedford (G-1292)
Media Collections Inc	D	216 831-5626	Twinsburg (G-18297)
Medical Administrators Inc	E	440 899-2229	Westlake (G-19372)
Medical Care PSC Inc	E	513 281-4400	Cincinnati (G-3993)
National Entp Systems Inc	C	440 542-1360	Solon (G-16876)
Ncs Incorporated	C	440 684-9455	Cleveland (G-6052)
Oriana House Inc	C	419 447-1444	Tiffin (G-17531)
PRC Medical LLC	D	330 493-9004	Cuyahoga Falls (G-9118)
Receivable MGT Svcs Corp	D	330 659-1000	Richfield (G-16373)
Recovery One LLC	D	614 336-4207	Columbus (G-8496)
Reliant Capital Solutions LLC	C	614 452-6100	Gahanna (G-11141)
Revenue Assistance Corporation	C	216 763-2100	Cleveland (G-6317)
Roddy Group Inc	E	216 763-0088	Beachwood (G-1102)
Rossman	E	614 523-4150	New Albany (G-14872)
Security Check LLC	C	614 944-5788	Columbus (G-8615)
Spartan Asset Rcvery Group Inc	D	786 930-0188	Cincinnati (G-4509)
Tek-Collect Incorporated	E	614 299-2766	Columbus (G-8736)
United Collection Bureau Inc	C	419 866-6227	Toledo (G-18117)
United Collection Bureau Inc	E	419 866-6227	Maumee (G-13864)

7323 Credit Reporting Svcs

Cbc Companies Inc	E	614 222-4343	Columbus (G-7141)
Cbc Companies Inc	D	614 538-6100	Columbus (G-7142)
Cbcinnovis International Inc	E	614 222-4343	Columbus (G-7143)
Credit Infonet Inc	E	866 218-1003	Dayton (G-9339)
Innovis Data Solutions Inc	E	614 222-4343	Columbus (G-7823)
Kreller Bus Info Group Inc	E	513 723-8900	Cincinnati (G-3891)
Open Online LLC	E	614 481-6999	Columbus (G-8376)
Pasco Inc	B	330 650-0613	Hudson (G-12001)

7331 Direct Mail Advertising Svcs

A W S Inc	C	440 333-1791	Rocky River (G-16420)
A W S Inc	B	216 749-0356	Cleveland (G-4881)
Aero Fulfillment Services Corp	D	800 225-7145	Mason (G-13536)
Amerimark Holdings LLC	B	440 325-2000	Cleveland (G-4969)
Angstrom Graphics Inc Midwest	E	330 225-8950	Cleveland (G-4981)
Angstrom Graphics Inc Midwest	B	216 271-5300	Cleveland (G-4980)
▲ Atco Inc	C	740 592-6659	Athens (G-765)
Bindery & Spc Pressworks Inc	D	614 873-4623	Plain City (G-16046)
Blue Chip Mailing Services Inc	E	513 541-4800	Blue Ash (G-1514)
Bpm Realty Inc	E	614 221-6811	Columbus (G-7058)
Brothers Publishing Co LLC	E	937 548-3330	Greenville (G-11368)
Case Western Reserve Univ	E	216 368-2560	Cleveland (G-5130)
Centurion of Akron Inc	D	330 645-6699	Copley (G-8964)

Clipper Magazine LLC ....D 513 794-4100
Blue Ash (G-1529)
▲ Consolidated Graphics Group Inc......C 216 881-9191
Cleveland (G-5335)
Ctrac Inc....................................E 440 572-1000
Cleveland (G-5388)
Dayton Mailing Services Inc ....E 937 222-5056
Dayton (G-9371)
Ddm-Digital Imaging Data ....D 740 928-1110
Hebron (G-11712)
Deepwood Industries Inc ....C 440 350-5231
Mentor (G-14040)
Digital Color Intl LLC ....E 330 762-6959
Akron (G-187)
Directconnectgroup Ltd ....A 216 281-2866
Cleveland (G-5425)
Early Express Services Inc ....E 937 223-5801
Dayton (G-9400)
▲ Fine Line Graphics Corp ....C 614 486-0276
Columbus (G-7577)
▲ Haines & Company Inc ....C 330 494-9111
North Canton (G-15210)
▲ Hecks Direct Mail & Prtg Svc ....E 419 697-3505
Toledo (G-17797)
Hecks Direct Mail & Prtg Svc ....E 419 661-6028
Toledo (G-17798)
Hkm Drect Mkt Cmmnications Inc......C 216 651-9500
Cleveland (G-5696)
J C Direct Mail Inc ....C 614 836-4848
Groveport (G-11522)
Literature Fulfillment Svcs ....E 513 774-8600
Blue Ash (G-1598)
Macke Brothers Inc ....D 513 771-7500
Cincinnati (G-3956)
Macys Cr & Customer Svcs Inc ....D 513 881-9950
West Chester (G-18967)
Mail It Corp ....E 419 249-4848
Toledo (G-17879)
Patented Acquisition Corp ....C 937 353-2299
Miamisburg (G-14203)
Pickaway Diversfied Industries ....D 740 474-1522
Circleville (G-4842)
Popper & Associates Msrp LLC ....E 614 798-8991
Dublin (G-10309)
Postal Mail Sort Inc ....E 330 747-1515
Youngstown (G-20164)
Power Management Inc ....E 937 222-2909
Dayton (G-9701)
Presort America Ltd ....D 614 836-5120
Groveport (G-11530)
Resource Interactive.......................E 614 621-2888
Columbus (G-8522)
Sourcelink Ohio LLC ....C 937 885-8000
Miamisburg (G-14224)
TMR Inc ....C 330 220-8564
Brunswick (G-1942)
Traxium LLC ....E 330 572-8200
Stow (G-17236)
W C National Mailing Corp ....B 614 836-5703
Groveport (G-11550)
Weekleys Mailing Service Inc ....D 440 234-4325
Berea (G-1443)
Yeck Brothers Company ....E 937 294-4000
Moraine (G-14708)

7334 Photocopying & Duplicating Svcs

A-A Blueprint Co Inc ....E 330 794-8803
Akron (G-13)
American Reprographics Co LLC ....E 614 224-5149
Columbus (G-6936)
ARC Document Solutions Inc ....D 216 281-1234
Cleveland (G-5003)
ARC Document Solutions Inc ....E 513 326-2300
Cincinnati (G-2979)
ARC Document Solutions Inc ....E 937 277-7930
Dayton (G-9237)
Cannell Graphics LLC ....E 614 781-9760
Columbus (G-7110)
Fedex Office & Print Svcs Inc ....E 440 946-6353
Willoughby (G-19523)
Fedex Office & Print Svcs Inc ....E 937 436-0677
Dayton (G-9431)
Fedex Office & Print Svcs Inc ....E 614 621-1100
Columbus (G-7572)
Fedex Office & Print Svcs Inc ....E 614 898-0000
Westerville (G-19255)
Fedex Office & Print Svcs Inc ....E 216 292-2679
Beachwood (G-1057)
Franklin Imaging Llc ....E 614 885-6894
Columbus (G-7618)

▲ Key Blue Prints Inc ....D 614 228-3285
Columbus (G-7898)
Mike Rennie ....E 513 830-0020
Dayton (G-9634)
Profile Digital Printing LLC ....E 937 866-4241
Dayton (G-9719)
Queen City Reprographics................C 513 326-2300
Cincinnati (G-4321)
Ricoh Usa Inc ....D 513 984-9898
Sharonville (G-16730)
TMR Inc ....C 330 220-8564
Brunswick (G-1942)

7335 Commercial Photography

Aerocon Photogrammetric Svcs ....E 440 946-6277
Willoughby (G-19502)
AG Interactive Inc ....C 216 889-5000
Cleveland (G-4911)
Childers Photography ....E 937 256-0501
Dayton (G-9165)
◆ Ideal Image Inc ....D 937 832-1660
Englewood (G-10590)
Interphace Phtgrphy Cmmnctions ....E 254 289-6270
Amelia (G-573)
Kucera International Inc ....D 440 975-4230
Willoughby (G-19536)
Marsh Inc ....E 513 421-1234
Cincinnati (G-3975)
Queen City Reprographics................C 513 326-2300
Cincinnati (G-4321)
Rapid Mortgage Company ....E 937 748-8888
Cincinnati (G-4338)
Tj Metzgers Inc ....D 419 861-8611
Toledo (G-18066)
Woodard Photographic Inc ....E 419 483-3364
Bellevue (G-1386)
Youngstown ARC Engraving Co.........E 330 793-2471
Youngstown (G-20254)

7336 Commercial Art & Graphic Design

Academy Graphic Comm Inc ....E 216 661-2550
Cleveland (G-4897)
Adcom Group Inc ....C 216 574-9100
Cleveland (G-4901)
Art-American Printing Plates ....E 216 241-4420
Cleveland (G-5010)
Austin Foam Plastics Inc ....E 614 921-0824
Columbus (G-7003)
Container Graphics Corp ....D 419 531-5133
Toledo (G-17678)
Coyne Graphic Finishing Inc ....E 740 397-6232
Mount Vernon (G-14759)
Digital Color Intl LLC ....E 330 762-6959
Akron (G-187)
Diversipak Inc ....C 513 321-7884
Cincinnati (G-3436)
Don Drumm Studios & Gallery ....E 330 253-6840
Akron (G-190)
Edward Howard & Co ....E 216 781-2400
Cleveland (G-5468)
Evolution Crtive Solutions LLC ....E 513 681-4450
Cincinnati (G-3523)
Exhibitpro Inc ....E 614 885-9541
New Albany (G-14853)
Fisher Design Inc ....E 513 417-8235
Cincinnati (G-3570)
Fitch Inc ....E 614 885-3453
Columbus (G-7591)
Fx Digital Media Inc ....E 216 241-4040
Cleveland (G-5584)
▲ Galaxy Balloons Incorporated ....C 216 476-3360
Cleveland (G-5589)
General Theming Contrs LLC ....C 614 252-6342
Columbus (G-7655)
Graffiti Inc ....E 216 881-5550
Cleveland (G-5621)
▲ Graphic Publications Inc ....D 330 674-2300
Millersburg (G-14474)
Haney Inc ....D 513 561-1441
Cincinnati (G-3679)
Innovtive Crtive Solutions LLC ....E 614 491-9638
Groveport (G-11520)
Interbrand Hulefeld Inc ....E 513 421-2210
Cincinnati (G-3778)
Libby Przszyk Kthman Hldngs Inc ......B 513 241-6401
Cincinnati (G-3923)
Marsh Inc ....E 513 421-1234
Cincinnati (G-3975)
Mlp Interent Enterprises LLC ....E 614 917-8705
Mansfield (G-13224)

Mitosis LLC...................................E 937 557-3440
Dayton (G-9640)
Mueller Art Cover & Binding Co ....E 440 238-3303
Strongsville (G-17335)
Northeast Scene Inc ....E 216 241-7550
Cleveland (G-6095)
Nottingham-Spirk Des ....E 216 800-5782
Cleveland (G-6101)
ONeil & Associates Inc ....B 937 865-0800
Miamisburg (G-14201)
Real Art Design Group Inc ....E 937 223-9955
Dayton (G-9728)
Screen Works Inc ....E 937 264-9111
Dayton (G-9754)
Sfc Graphics Inc ....E 419 255-1283
Toledo (G-18027)
▲ Shamrock Companies Inc ....D 440 899-9510
Westlake (G-19405)
▲ Suntwist Corp 800 935-3534
Maple Heights (G-13300)
Taylor Made Graphics ....E 440 882-6318
Cleveland (G-6501)
Third Dimension Inc ....E 877 926-3223
Geneva (G-11247)
▲ Univenture Inc ....D 937 645-4600
Dublin (G-10359)
Visual Art Graphic Services ....E 330 274-2775
Mantua (G-13278)
Whitespace Design Group Inc ....E 330 762-9320
Akron (G-501)
Woodrow Manufacturing Co ....E 937 399-9333
Springfield (G-17137)
Young Mens Christian Associat ....C 513 791-5000
Blue Ash (G-1685)

7338 Secretarial & Court Reporting Svcs

Ace-Merit LLC................................E 513 241-3200
Cincinnati (G-2904)
Chase Transcriptions Inc ....E 330 650-0539
Hudson (G-11972)
Mehler and Hagestrom Inc ....E 216 621-4984
Cleveland (G-5948)
National Service Information ....E 740 387-6806
Marion (G-13448)
Premier Transcription Service ....E 513 741-1800
Cincinnati (G-4274)
Robert Erney 312 788-9005
Brookpark (G-1905)

7342 Disinfecting & Pest Control Svcs

All Gone Termite & Pest Ctrl ....E 513 874-7500
West Chester (G-18863)
Corporate Cleaning Inc ....E 614 203-6051
Columbus (G-7371)
DCS Sanitation Management Inc..........D 513 891-4980
Cincinnati (G-3407)
General Pest Control Company ....E 216 252-7140
Cleveland (G-5604)
Image By J & K LLC ....B 888 667-6929
Maumee (G-13802)
◆ J T Eaton & Co Inc ....E 330 425-7801
Twinsburg (G-18283)
Living Matters LLC 866 587-8074
Cleveland (G-5876)
Ohio Exterminating Co Inc ....E 614 294-6311
Columbus (G-8256)
Orkin LLC ....E 614 888-5811
Columbus (G-8386)
Rentokil North America Inc ....E 330 797-9090
Youngstown (G-20180)
Rentokil North America Inc ....E 216 328-0700
Brooklyn Heights (G-1879)
Rentokil North America Inc ....E 216 328-0700
Brooklyn Heights (G-1880)
Rentokil North America Inc ....E 614 837-0099
Canal Winchester (G-2117)
Scherzinger Corp ....D 513 531-7848
Cincinnati (G-4435)
▲ Scotts Miracle-Gro Company ....B 937 644-0011
Marysville (G-13529)
Steve Shaffer ....E 614 276-6355
Columbus (G-8698)
Terminix Intl Co Ltd Partnr ....E 513 942-6670
Fairfield (G-10789)
Terminix Intl Co Ltd Partnr................E 216 518-1091
Cleveland (G-6514)
Terminix Intl Co Ltd Partnr................E 419 868-8290
Maumee (G-13861)
Terminix Intl Co Ltd Partnr ....E 513 539-7846
Middletown (G-14335)

S
I
C

Terminix Intl Co Ltd Partnr	E	978 744-2402
Canton *(G-2509)*		
Terminix Intl Coml Xenia	E	513 539-7846
Middletown *(G-14336)*		

7349 Building Cleaning & Maintenance Svcs, NEC

A 1 Janitorial Cleaning Svc	E	513 932-8003
Lebanon *(G-12446)*		
A B M Inc	E	419 421-2292
Findlay *(G-10862)*		
A Bee C Service Inc	E	440 735-1505
Cleveland *(G-4875)*		
AAA Standard Services Inc	D	419 535-0274
Toledo *(G-17578)*		
ABM Facility Services Inc	E	859 767-4393
Cincinnati *(G-2898)*		
ABM Janitorial Services Inc	C	216 861-1199
Cleveland *(G-4894)*		
ABM Janitorial Services Inc	C	513 731-1418
Cincinnati *(G-2899)*		
Absolute Cleaning Services	D	440 542-1742
Solon *(G-16813)*		
Academic Support Services LLC	E	740 274-6138
Columbus *(G-6857)*		
Access Cleaning Service Inc	E	937 276-2605
Dayton *(G-9204)*		
Ace Building Maintenance LLC	E	614 471-2223
Columbus *(G-6864)*		
Advanced Facilities Maint Corp	E	614 389-3495
Columbus *(G-6874)*		
Aetna Building Maintenance Inc	B	614 476-1818
Columbus *(G-6881)*		
Aetna Building Maintenance Inc	D	937 324-5711
Springfield *(G-16992)*		
Aetna Building Maintenance Inc	C	866 238-6201
Dayton *(G-9211)*		
Ajax Cleaning Contractors Co	D	216 881-8484
Cleveland *(G-4924)*		
Ajax Commercial Cleaning Inc	D	330 928-4543
Cuyahoga Falls *(G-9067)*		
Akron Public School Maint Svcs	D	330 761-2640
Akron *(G-51)*		
All Pro Cleaning Services Inc	D	440 519-0055
Solon *(G-16819)*		
Allen-Keith Construction Co	D	330 266-2220
Canton *(G-2178)*		
Alpha & Omega Bldg Svcs Inc	E	513 429-5082
Blue Ash *(G-1502)*		
Alpha & Omega Bldg Svcs Inc	E	937 298-2125
Dayton *(G-9219)*		
American Maintenance Svcs Inc	E	330 744-3400
Youngstown *(G-19954)*		
AMF Facility Services Inc	E	800 991-2273
Dayton *(G-9232)*		
Anchor Cleaning Contractors	E	216 961-7343
Cleveland *(G-4977)*		
Any Domest Work Inc	D	440 845-9911
Cleveland *(G-4986)*		
Apex Environmental Svcs LLC	D	513 772-2739
Cincinnati *(G-2973)*		
Aramark Facility Services LLC	E	216 687-5000
Cleveland *(G-4998)*		
Ashland Cleaning LLC	E	419 281-1747
Ashland *(G-647)*		
Ashland Cleaning LLC	E	419 281-1747
Ashland *(G-648)*		
Atlantis Co Inc	D	888 807-3272
Cleveland *(G-5020)*		
Ats Group LLC	C	216 744-5757
Solon *(G-16824)*		
August Groh & Sons Inc	E	513 821-0090
Cincinnati *(G-3004)*		
Basol Maintenance Service Inc	D	419 422-0946
Findlay *(G-10867)*		
Belfor USA Group Inc	E	513 860-3111
West Chester *(G-19043)*		
Beneficial Building Services	D	330 848-2556
Akron *(G-94)*		
Bkg Services Inc	E	614 476-1800
Columbus *(G-7043)*		
Blanchard Valley Health System	A	419 423-4500
Findlay *(G-10871)*		
Bleachtech LLC	E	216 921-1980
Seville *(G-16683)*		
Blue Chip 2000 Coml Clg Inc	B	513 561-2999
Cincinnati *(G-3061)*		
Buckeye Commercial Cleaning	E	614 866-4700
Pickerington *(G-15949)*		

Butchko Electric Inc	E	440 985-3180
Amherst *(G-582)*		
Butterfield Co Inc	D	330 832-1282
Massillon *(G-13666)*		
C & K Industrial Services Inc	D	216 642-0055
Independence *(G-12052)*		
C M S Enterprises Inc	E	740 653-1940
Lancaster *(G-12374)*		
Camco Inc	E	740 477-3682
Circleville *(G-4827)*		
Cardinal Maintenance & Svc Co	C	330 252-0282
Akron *(G-118)*		
Carol Scudere	E	614 839-4357
New Albany *(G-14848)*		
Carrara Companies Inc	D	330 659-2800
Richfield *(G-16348)*		
Caveney Inc	D	330 497-4600
North Canton *(G-15192)*		
Champion Clg Specialists Inc	E	513 871-2333
Cincinnati *(G-3167)*		
▲ **Chemical Solvents Inc**	E	216 741-9310
Cleveland *(G-5173)*		
Circle Building Services Inc	D	614 228-6090
Columbus *(G-7202)*		
Clean All Services Inc	C	937 498-4146
Sidney *(G-16766)*		
Clean Break Inc	E	330 638-5648
Warren *(G-18684)*		
Clean Care Inc	C	419 725-2100
Toledo *(G-17663)*		
Cleaner Carpet & Jantr Inc	E	513 469-2070
Mason *(G-13562)*		
Clearview Cleaning Contractors	E	216 621-6688
Cleveland *(G-5224)*		
Clinton-Carvell Inc	E	614 351-8858
Columbus *(G-7229)*		
CMS Business Services LLC	D	740 687-0577
Lancaster *(G-12383)*		
Coleman Professional Svcs Inc	C	330 673-1347
Kent *(G-12223)*		
Columbus Public School Dst	B	614 365-5043
Columbus *(G-7307)*		
Commercial Cleaning Solutions	E	937 981-4870
Greenfield *(G-11359)*		
Complete Building Maint LLC	E	513 235-7511
Cincinnati *(G-3343)*		
Contract Lumber Inc	D	614 751-1109
Columbus *(G-7365)*		
Control Cleaning Solutions	D	330 220-3333
Brunswick *(G-1925)*		
Corporate Cleaning Inc	E	614 203-6051
Columbus *(G-7371)*		
County of Cuyahoga	A	216 443-6954
Cleveland *(G-7379)*		
Crystal Clear Bldg Svcs Inc	D	440 439-2288
Oakwood Village *(G-15488)*		
Csi International Inc	A	614 781-1571
Worthington *(G-19802)*		
Cummins Building Maint Inc	D	740 726-9800
Prospect *(G-16221)*		
Cummins Facility Services LLC	B	740 726-9800
Prospect *(G-16222)*		
Custom Cleaning and Maint	E	440 946-7028
Willoughby *(G-19517)*		
Custom Cleaning Service LLC	E	440 774-1222
Oberlin *(G-15500)*		
Custom Maid Cleaning Services	E	513 351-6571
Cincinnati *(G-3392)*		
Custom Maint	D	330 793-2523
Youngstown *(G-20013)*		
D & J Master Clean Inc	D	614 847-1181
Columbus *(G-7406)*		
Dave & Barb Enterprises Inc	D	513 553-0050
New Richmond *(G-14992)*		
DCS Sanitation Management Inc	D	513 891-4980
Cincinnati *(G-3407)*		
Dempsey Inc	D	330 758-2309
Youngstown *(G-20016)*		
Dependable Cleaning Contrs	D	440 953-9191
Willoughby *(G-19518)*		
Dove Building Services Inc	D	614 299-4700
Columbus *(G-7469)*		
Dublin Coml Property Svcs Inc	E	419 732-6732
Port Clinton *(G-16106)*		
E Wynn Inc	D	614 444-5288
Columbus *(G-7487)*		
Emcor Facilities Services Inc	D	888 846-9462
Cincinnati *(G-3492)*		
Environment Control of Greater	D	614 868-9788
Columbus *(G-7521)*		

Environment Ctrl Beachwood Inc	D	330 405-6201
Twinsburg *(G-18260)*		
Environment Ctrl of Miami Cnty	D	937 669-9900
Tipp City *(G-17556)*		
Ermc II LP	E	513 424-8517
Middletown *(G-14346)*		
Essentialprofile1corp	D	614 805-4794
Columbus *(G-7535)*		
Euclid Indus Maint Clg Contrs	C	216 361-0288
Cleveland *(G-5493)*		
Executive Management Services	C	419 529-8800
Ontario *(G-15549)*		
Extreme Detail Clg Cnstr Svcs	E	419 392-3243
Toledo *(G-17721)*		
Facility Svc Maint Systems Inc	D	513 422-7060
Middletown *(G-14347)*		
Family Entertainment Services	D	740 286-8587
Jackson *(G-12173)*		
Feecorp Industrial Services	C	740 533-1445
Ironton *(G-12152)*		
Four Corners Cleaning Inc	E	330 644-0834
Barberton *(G-952)*		
G J Goudreau & Co	E	216 351-5233
Cleveland *(G-5586)*		
G7 Services Inc	E	937 256-3473
Dayton *(G-9455)*		
Galaxie Industrial Svcs LLC	E	330 503-2334
Youngstown *(G-20042)*		
Gca Services Group Inc	D	800 422-8760
Cleveland *(G-5598)*		
General Building Maintenance	D	330 682-2238
Orrville *(G-15633)*		
General Services Cleaning Co	E	614 840-0562
Columbus *(G-7654)*		
George Gardner	D	419 636-4277
Bryan *(G-1958)*		
Green Impressions LLC	E	440 240-8508
Sheffield Village *(G-16734)*		
Gsf North American Jantr Svc	C	513 733-1451
West Chester *(G-19057)*		
Guardian Care Services	E	614 436-8500
Columbus *(G-7700)*		
H & B Window Cleaning Inc	E	440 934-6158
Avon Lake *(G-918)*		
Harrison Industries Inc	D	740 942-2988
Cadiz *(G-2029)*		
Heco Operations Inc	E	614 888-5700
Worthington *(G-19813)*		
Heits Building Svcs Cnkd LLC	D	855 464-3487
Cincinnati *(G-3697)*		
High Power Inc	E	937 667-1772
Tipp City *(G-17557)*		
High-TEC Industrial Services	C	937 667-1772
Tipp City *(G-17558)*		
Hopewell Industries Inc	D	740 622-3563
Coshocton *(G-9018)*		
Image By J & K LLC	B	888 667-6929
Maumee *(G-13802)*		
Industrial Air Control Inc	D	330 772-6422
Hubbard *(G-11947)*		
Inovative Facility Svcs LLC	B	419 861-1710
Maumee *(G-13803)*		
Ivory Services Inc	E	216 344-3094
Cleveland *(G-5768)*		
J B M Cleaning & Supply Co	E	330 837-8805
Massillon *(G-13700)*		
J Rutledge Enterprises Inc	E	502 241-4100
Cincinnati *(G-3796)*		
J V Janitorial Services Inc	E	216 749-1150
Cleveland *(G-5774)*		
Jacob Real Estate Services	E	216 687-0500
Cleveland *(G-5777)*		
Jancoa Janitorial Services Inc	B	513 351-7200
Cincinnati *(G-3808)*		
Jani-Source LLC	E	740 374-6298
Marietta *(G-13340)*		
Janitorial Services Inc	B	216 341-8601
Cleveland *(G-5781)*		
Jantech Building Services Inc	C	216 661-6102
Brooklyn Heights *(G-1872)*		
Jdd Inc	E	216 464-8855
Cleveland *(G-5786)*		
Jenkins Enterprises LLC	E	513 752-7896
Cincinnati *(G-2857)*		
John O Bostock Jr	E	937 263-8540
Dayton *(G-9528)*		
Jordan Kyli Enterprises Inc	E	216 256-3773
Westlake *(G-19361)*		
K & L Floormasters LLC	E	330 493-0869
Canton *(G-2363)*		

K & M Kleening Service Inc	D	614 737-3750	
Groveport (G-11525)			
Kellermyer Bergensons Svcs LLC	D	419 867-4300	
Maumee (G-13807)			
Kelli Woods Management Inc	C	419 478-1200	
Toledo (G-17838)			
Kettering City School District	D	937 297-1990	
Dayton (G-9537)			
Kleman Services LLC	E	419 339-0871	
Lima (G-12671)			
Ktm Enterprises Inc	E	937 548-8357	
Greenville (G-11388)			
Lake Side Building Maintenance	E	216 589-9900	
Cleveland (G-5848)			
Larue Enterprises Inc	E	937 438-5711	
Beavercreek (G-1225)			
▲ Leadec Corp	E	513 731-3590	
Blue Ash (G-1597)			
Lima Sheet Metal Machine & Mfg	E	419 229-1161	
Lima (G-12687)			
Living Matters LLC	E	866 587-8074	
Cleveland (G-5876)			
Logan-Hocking School District	E	740 385-7844	
Logan (G-12848)			
Louderback Fmly Invstments Inc	E	937 845-1762	
New Carlisle (G-14893)			
Lucas Building Mainenance LLC	A	740 479-1800	
Ironton (G-12162)			
Maids Home Service of Cincy	E	513 396-6900	
Cincinnati (G-3961)			
Mapp Building Service LLC	E	513 253-3990	
Blue Ash (G-1602)			
Marks Cleaning Service Inc	E	330 725-5702	
Medina (G-13968)			
Mathews Josiah	E	567 204-8818	
Lima (G-12699)			
Metropolitan Envmtl Svcs Inc	D	614 771-1881	
Hilliard (G-11793)			
Mid-American Clg Contrs Inc	C	419 429-6222	
Findlay (G-10945)			
Mid-American Clg Contrs Inc	D	419 229-3899	
Lima (G-12703)			
Mid-American Clg Contrs Inc	C	614 291-7170	
Columbus (G-8074)			
Milford Coml Clg Svcs Inc	E	513 575-5678	
Milford (G-14411)			
Molly Maid of Lorain County	E	440 327-0000	
Elyria (G-10539)			
Mougianis Industries Inc	D	740 264-6372	
Steubenville (G-17167)			
MPW Industrial Services Inc	D	330 454-1898	
Canton (G-2410)			
▲ MPW Industrial Services Inc	A	800 827-8790	
Hebron (G-11718)			
MPW Industrial Services Inc	D	740 774-5251	
Chillicothe (G-2805)			
MPW Industrial Services Inc	D	937 644-0200	
East Liberty (G-10393)			
MPW Industrial Services Inc	E	440 277-9072	
Lorain (G-12928)			
MPW Industrial Svcs Group Inc	D	740 927-8790	
Hebron (G-11719)			
Mrap LLC	E	614 545-3190	
Columbus (G-8117)			
N Services Inc	D	513 793-2000	
Blue Ash (G-1619)			
New Albany Cleaning Services	E	614 855-9990	
New Albany (G-14863)			
Nicholas D Starr Inc	C	419 229-3192	
Lima (G-12706)			
North Coast Sales	E	440 632-0793	
Middlefield (G-14274)			
Northpointe Property MGT LLC	C	614 579-9712	
Columbus (G-8204)			
Nortone Service Inc	E	740 527-2057	
Buckeye Lake (G-1975)			
Ohio Building Service Inc	E	513 761-0268	
Cincinnati (G-4151)			
Ohio Custodial Maintenance	C	614 443-1232	
Columbus (G-8235)			
Ohio State University	A	614 292-6158	
Columbus (G-8352)			
Ohio Window Cleaning Inc	D	937 877-0832	
Tipp City (G-17563)			
Perry Contract Services Inc	D	614 274-4350	
Columbus (G-8440)			
Priority Building Services Inc	D	937 233-7030	
Beavercreek Township (G-1260)			
Pro Care Janitor Supply	E	937 778-2275	
Piqua (G-16024)			

Pro-Touch Inc	C	614 586-0303	
Columbus (G-8465)			
Professional Hse Clg Svcs Inc	E	440 729-7866	
Chesterland (G-2743)			
Professional Maint Dayton	D	937 461-5259	
Dayton (G-9718)			
Professional Maint of Columbus	C	614 443-6528	
Columbus (G-8469)			
Professional Maint of Columbus	B	513 579-1762	
Cincinnati (G-4293)			
Professional Restoration Svc	D	330 825-1803	
Medina (G-13989)			
Professnl Mint Cincinnati Inc	A	513 579-1161	
Cincinnati (G-4295)			
Promanco Inc	E	740 374-2120	
Marietta (G-13373)			
Psp Operations Inc	E	614 888-5700	
Worthington (G-19838)			
Putman Janitorial Service Inc	E	513 942-1900	
West Chester (G-19074)			
Quality Assured Cleaning Inc	D	614 798-1505	
Columbus (G-8480)			
Quality Cleaning Systems LLC	E	330 567-2050	
Shreve (G-16754)			
Quality Clg Svc of NW Ohio	D	419 335-9105	
Wauseon (G-18809)			
R K Hydro-Vac Inc	E	937 773-8600	
Piqua (G-16026)			
R T Industries Inc	C	937 335-5784	
Troy (G-18224)			
Rcs Enterprises Inc	D	614 337-8520	
Columbus (G-8492)			
Rde System Corp	C	513 933-8000	
Lebanon (G-12496)			
Rde System Corporation	D	513 933-8000	
Dayton (G-9727)			
Red Carpet Janitorial Service	B	513 242-7575	
Cincinnati (G-4347)			
Restoration Resources Inc	D	330 650-4486	
Hudson (G-12004)			
Richland Newhope Industries	E	419 774-4400	
Mansfield (G-13237)			
Romaster Corp	D	330 825-1945	
Norton (G-15422)			
Rwk Services Inc	E	440 526-2144	
Cleveland (G-6351)			
Saftek Industrial Service Inc	E	937 667-1772	
Tipp City (G-17566)			
Scarlet & Gray Cleaning Svc	C	513 661-4483	
Cincinnati (G-4434)			
Schenker Inc	E	419 491-1055	
Swanton (G-17404)			
Scioto Services Llc	E	937 644-0888	
Marysville (G-13527)			
Seaway Sponge & Chamois Co	E	419 691-4694	
Toledo (G-18023)			
Service Master Co	E	330 864-7300	
Eastlake (G-10434)			
ServiceMaster By Sidwell Inc	E	740 687-1077	
Lancaster (G-12434)			
ServiceMaster By Steinbach	E	330 497-5959	
Canton (G-2474)			
ServiceMaster of Defiance Inc	D	419 784-5570	
Defiance (G-9940)			
Shining Company LLC	C	614 588-4115	
Columbus (G-8634)			
Southtown Heating & Cooling	E	937 320-9900	
Moraine (G-14699)			
Sparkle Wash of Lima	E	419 224-9274	
Lima (G-12743)			
Sr Improvements Services LLC	E	567 207-6488	
Vickery (G-18575)			
Stanley Stemer of Akron Canton	E	330 785-5005	
Coventry Township (G-9043)			
Star Inc	C	740 354-1517	
Portsmouth (G-16174)			
Starlight Enterprises Inc	C	330 339-2020	
New Philadelphia (G-14983)			
Stb Enterprises	D	330 478-0044	
Canton (G-2496)			
Stout Lori Cleaning & Such	E	419 637-7644	
Gibsonburg (G-11279)			
Suburban Maintenance & Contrs	E	440 237-7765	
North Royalton (G-15369)			
Super Shine Inc	E	513 423-8999	
Middletown (G-14334)			
Sylvania Lighting Svcs Corp	E	440 742-8208	
Solon (G-16907)			
T & L Enterprises Inc	E	440 234-5900	
Berea (G-1439)			

T N C Construction Inc	E	614 554-5330	
Grove City (G-11476)			
T&L Global Management LLC	D	614 586-0303	
Columbus (G-8727)			
Tdg Facilities LLC	C	513 834-6105	
Blue Ash (G-1655)			
The Maids	D	440 735-6243	
Bedford Heights (G-1328)			
TNT Power Wash Inc	E	614 662-3110	
Groveport (G-11541)			
TNT Power Wash Inc	E	614 662-3110	
Groveport (G-11542)			
Toledo Building Services Co	A	419 241-3101	
Toledo (G-18075)			
Toledo Public Schools	D	419 243-6422	
Toledo (G-18095)			
Trg Maintenance LLC	A	614 891-4850	
Westerville (G-19214)			
Tri Tech Service Systems Inc	C	937 787-4664	
Somerville (G-16919)			
Turn Around Group Inc	D	330 372-0064	
Warren (G-18762)			
Twin Cedars Services Inc	D	513 932-0399	
Lebanon (G-12512)			
Two Men & A Vacuum LLC	D	614 300-7970	
Columbus (G-8791)			
Ultimate Building Maintenance	D	330 369-9771	
Warren (G-18763)			
United Scoto Senior Activities	E	740 354-6672	
Portsmouth (G-16176)			
University of Cincinnati	A	513 556-6381	
Cincinnati (G-4707)			
Vadakin Inc	E	740 373-7518	
Marietta (G-13394)			
W David Maupin Inc	E	419 389-0458	
Toledo (G-18141)			
Ward & Werner Co	C	614 885-0741	
Worthington (G-19858)			
Wells & Sons Janitorial Svc	E	937 878-4375	
Fairborn (G-10690)			
White Glove Executive Services	E	614 226-2553	
Grove City (G-11488)			
Wiggins Clg & Crpt Svc Inc	D	937 279-9080	
Dayton (G-9881)			
Wj Service Co Inc	E	330 372-5040	
Warren (G-18773)			
York Building Maintenance Inc	C	216 398-8100	
Cleveland (G-6699)			
Youngstown Window Cleaning Co	C	330 743-3880	
Girard (G-11306)			

7352 Medical Eqpt Rental & Leasing

American Home Health Care Inc	E	614 237-1133	
Columbus (G-6925)			
Americas Best Medical Eqp Co	E	330 928-0884	
Akron (G-71)			
Ancillary Medical Investments	E	937 456-5520	
Eaton (G-10436)			
Apria Healthcare LLC	E	614 351-5920	
Columbus (G-6960)			
Apria Healthcare LLC	E	216 485-1180	
Cleveland (G-4997)			
Apria Healthcare LLC	D	419 471-1919	
Maumee (G-13758)			
▲ Boardman Medical Supply Co	C	330 545-6700	
Girard (G-11283)			
Braden Med Services Inc	E	740 732-2356	
Caldwell (G-2036)			
Cornerstone Med Svcs Midwest	E	513 554-0222	
Blue Ash (G-1537)			
Cornerstone Medical Associates	E	330 374-0229	
Akron (G-159)			
Cornerstone Medical Services	E	513 554-0222	
Blue Ash (G-1538)			
Fairfield Medical Center	A	740 687-8000	
Lancaster (G-12399)			
Fortec Medical Inc	E	330 463-1265	
Hudson (G-11978)			
Fortec Medical Inc	E	513 742-9100	
Cincinnati (G-3580)			
Medical Service Company	D	440 232-3000	
Bedford (G-1293)			
Medical Specialties Distrs LLC	E	440 232-0320	
Oakwood Village (G-15490)			
Mercy Health - St R	A	419 227-3361	
Lima (G-12702)			
Millers Rental and Sls Co Inc	D	330 753-8600	
Akron (G-339)			
Pharmerica Long-Term Care Inc	E	330 425-4450	
Twinsburg (G-18305)			

Sateri Home Inc ....D...... 330 758-8106
Youngstown *(G-20204)*

Seeley Enterprises Company ....E...... 440 293-6600
Andover *(G-608)*

Seeley Medical Oxygen Co ....E...... 440 255-7163
Andover *(G-609)*

Toledo Medical Equipment Co ....E...... 419 866-7120
Maumee *(G-13862)*

7353 Heavy Construction Eqpt Rental & Leasing

1st Choice LLC ....D...... 877 564-6658
Cleveland *(G-4867)*

A and A Mllwright Rigging Svcs ....E...... 513 396-6212
Cincinnati *(G-2888)*

▼ All Aerials LLC ....E...... 330 659-9600
Richfield *(G-16343)*

All Crane Rental Corp ....D...... 614 261-1800
Columbus *(G-6891)*

All Erection & Crane Rental ....C...... 216 524-6550
Cleveland *(G-4930)*

All Erection & Crane Rental ....D...... 216 524-6550
Cleveland *(G-4931)*

All Erection Crane Rentl Corp ....E...... 216 524-6550
Cleveland *(G-4932)*

American Crane Inc ....E...... 614 496-2268
Reynoldsburg *(G-16281)*

Bluefoot Industrial LLC ....E...... 740 314-5299
Steubenville *(G-17141)*

▲ Bobcat Enterprises Inc ....D...... 513 874-8945
West Chester *(G-18877)*

▲ Canton Erectors Inc ....E...... 330 453-7363
Canton *(G-2232)*

Capital City Group Inc ....E...... 419 931-6757
Oregon *(G-15586)*

Cecil I Walker Machinery Co ....E...... 740 286-7566
Jackson *(G-12170)*

Charles Jergens Contractor ....E...... 937 233-1830
Dayton *(G-9294)*

▼ Columbus Equipment Company ....E...... 614 437-0352
Columbus *(G-7281)*

Columbus Equipment Company ....E...... 614 443-6541
Columbus *(G-7282)*

Construction Eqp & Sup Ltd ....E...... 419 625-7192
Sandusky *(G-16593)*

Dolin Supply Co ....E...... 304 529-4171
South Point *(G-16932)*

Eastland Crane Service Inc ....E...... 614 868-9750
Columbus *(G-7490)*

Efco Corp ....E...... 614 876-1226
Columbus *(G-7509)*

▲ Eleet Cryogenics Inc ....E...... 330 874-4009
Bolivar *(G-1702)*

◆ F & M Mafco Inc ....C...... 513 367-2151
Harrison *(G-11666)*

General Crane Rental LLC ....E...... 330 908-0001
Macedonia *(G-13070)*

Grady Rentals LLC ....E...... 330 627-2022
Carrollton *(G-2570)*

H M Miller Construction Co ....D...... 330 628-4811
Mogadore *(G-14549)*

Holt Rental Services ....E...... 513 771-0515
Cincinnati *(G-3716)*

Indian Nation Inc ....E...... 740 532-6143
North Canton *(G-15212)*

JBK Group Inc ....E...... 216 901-0000
Cleveland *(G-5784)*

Jeffers Crane Service Inc ....D...... 419 693-0421
Oregon *(G-15599)*

Kelley Steel Erectors Inc ....D...... 440 232-1573
Cleveland *(G-5821)*

▲ Lefeld Welding & Stl Sups Inc ....E...... 419 678-2397
Coldwater *(G-6762)*

Leppo Inc ....E...... 330 456-2930
Canton *(G-2376)*

Leppo Inc ....C...... 330 633-3999
Tallmadge *(G-17480)*

Malavite Excavating Inc ....E...... 330 484-1274
East Sparta *(G-10423)*

Midwest Equipment Co ....E...... 216 441-1400
Cleveland *(G-5990)*

Ohio Machinery Co ....E...... 330 530-9010
Girard *(G-11295)*

◆ Ohio Machinery Co ....C...... 440 526-6200
Broadview Heights *(G-1840)*

Phillips Ready Mix Co ....D...... 937 426-5151
Beavercreek Township *(G-1259)*

Piqua Steel Co ....D...... 937 773-3632
Piqua *(G-16020)*

Pollock Research & Design Inc ....E...... 330 332-3300
Salem *(G-16554)*

RELAM Inc ....E...... 440 232-3354
Solon *(G-16891)*

Sommerset Development Ltd ....C...... 440 286-6194
Chardon *(G-2715)*

Sunbelt Rentals Inc ....E...... 216 362-0300
Cleveland *(G-6477)*

TNT Equipment Company ....E...... 614 882-1549
Columbus *(G-8761)*

Towlift Inc ....E...... 419 666-1333
Northwood *(G-15411)*

▲ Trimble Engineering & Cnstr ....E...... 937 233-8921
Dayton *(G-9823)*

United Rentals North Amer Inc ....E...... 800 877-3687
Perrysburg *(G-15929)*

7359 Equipment Rental & Leasing, NEC

A & A Safety Inc ....E...... 513 943-6100
Amelia *(G-563)*

A B C Rental Center East Inc ....E...... 216 475-8240
Cleveland *(G-4874)*

Aarons Inc ....E...... 330 823-1879
Alliance *(G-513)*

Aarons Inc ....E...... 216 251-4500
Cleveland *(G-4889)*

Aarons Inc ....E...... 330 385-7201
East Liverpool *(G-10395)*

Aarons Inc ....E...... 937 778-3577
Piqua *(G-15995)*

Aarons Inc ....E...... 216 587-2745
Maple Heights *(G-13279)*

Ace Rental Place ....D...... 937 642-2891
Marysville *(G-13482)*

Advanced Tenting Solutions ....E...... 216 291-3300
Newbury *(G-15117)*

Ahern Rentals Inc ....E...... 440 498-0869
Solon *(G-16817)*

All Erection & Crane Rental ....C...... 216 524-6550
Cleveland *(G-4930)*

All Erection & Crane Rental ....D...... 216 524-6550
Cleveland *(G-4931)*

All Lift Service Company Inc ....E...... 440 585-1542
Willoughby *(G-19503)*

All Occasions Event Rental ....E...... 513 563-0600
Cincinnati *(G-2922)*

All Temp Refrigeration Inc ....E...... 419 692-5016
Delphos *(G-10019)*

American Roadway Logistics Inc ....E...... 330 659-2003
Richfield *(G-16346)*

Ayrshire Inc ....D...... 440 992-0743
Ashtabula *(G-721)*

Baker Bnngson Rlty Auctioneers ....E...... 419 547-7777
Clyde *(G-6740)*

Baker Equipment and Mtls Ltd ....E...... 513 422-6697
Monroe *(G-14562)*

Baker Vehicle Systems Inc ....E...... 330 467-2250
Macedonia *(G-13061)*

Beacon Company ....E...... 330 733-8322
Akron *(G-92)*

Bkg Holdings LLC ....E...... 614 252-7455
Columbus *(G-7042)*

Black Swamp Equipment LLC ....E...... 419 445-0030
Archbold *(G-627)*

Bluefoot Industrial LLC ....E...... 740 314-5299
Steubenville *(G-17141)*

Bnd Rentals Inc ....E...... 937 898-5061
Vandalia *(G-18508)*

Bobcat of Dayton Inc ....E...... 937 293-3176
Moraine *(G-14627)*

Brennan Industrial Truck Co ....E...... 419 867-6000
Holland *(G-11875)*

Budco Group Inc ....E...... 513 621-6111
Cincinnati *(G-3086)*

Budget Dumpster LLC ....E...... 866 284-6164
Westlake *(G-19325)*

Camargo Rental Center Inc ....E...... 513 271-6510
Cincinnati *(G-3109)*

Chase Phipps ....E...... 330 754-0467
Canton *(G-2248)*

Cleveland Corporate Svcs Inc ....C...... 216 397-1492
Cleveland *(G-5250)*

Colortone Audio Visual ....E...... 216 928-1530
Cleveland *(G-5313)*

Columbus AAA Corp ....E...... 614 889-2840
Dublin *(G-10181)*

Comdoc Inc ....C...... 330 896-2346
Uniontown *(G-18363)*

Continuum Inc ....E...... 614 891-9200
Westerville *(G-19246)*

Cort Business Services Corp ....D...... 513 759-8181
West Chester *(G-18900)*

▲ Countryside Rentals Inc ....E...... 740 634-2666
Bainbridge *(G-930)*

Cuyahoga Vending Co Inc ....B...... 216 663-1457
Maple Heights *(G-13284)*

David Francis Corporation ....C...... 216 524-0900
Cleveland *(G-5408)*

◆ De Nora Tech LLC ....D...... 440 710-5300
Painesville *(G-15708)*

Diane Sauer Chevrolet Inc ....C...... 330 373-1600
Warren *(G-18702)*

E T B Ltd ....E...... 740 373-6686
Marietta *(G-13326)*

Elliott Tool Technologies Ltd ....D...... 937 253-6133
Dayton *(G-9412)*

Equipment Depot Ohio Inc ....E...... 513 934-2121
Lebanon *(G-12464)*

▲ Fallsway Equipment Co Inc ....C...... 330 633-6000
Akron *(G-209)*

Fern Exposition Services LLC ....E...... 513 621-6111
Cincinnati *(G-3543)*

Fifth Third Equipment Fin Co ....E...... 800 972-3030
Cincinnati *(G-3550)*

Filing Scale Company Inc ....E...... 330 425-3092
Twinsburg *(G-18266)*

Flight Options Inc ....B...... 216 261-3880
Richmond Heights *(G-16389)*

Flight Options LLC ....C...... 216 261-3500
Cleveland *(G-5547)*

Flight Options Intl Inc ....E...... 216 261-3500
Richmond Heights *(G-16390)*

Garda CL Great Lakes Inc ....B...... 561 939-7000
Columbus *(G-7647)*

Gordon Brothers Inc ....E...... 800 331-7611
Salem *(G-16545)*

Gordon Flesch Company Inc ....E...... 419 884-2031
Mansfield *(G-13179)*

Great Lakes Crushing Ltd ....E...... 440 944-5500
Wickliffe *(G-19461)*

HEat Ttal Fclty Slutions Inc ....E...... 740 965-3005
Galena *(G-11159)*

Home Depot USA Inc ....C...... 614 523-0600
Columbus *(G-7762)*

Home Depot USA Inc ....C...... 330 965-4790
Boardman *(G-1699)*

Home Depot USA Inc ....C...... 330 497-1810
Canton *(G-2347)*

Home Depot USA Inc ....C...... 513 688-1654
Cincinnati *(G-3719)*

Home Depot USA Inc ....C...... 330 922-3448
Cuyahoga Falls *(G-9100)*

Home Depot USA Inc ....C...... 937 312-9053
Dayton *(G-9499)*

Home Depot USA Inc ....C...... 937 312-9076
Dayton *(G-9500)*

Home Depot USA Inc ....C...... 216 692-2780
Euclid *(G-10642)*

Home Depot USA Inc ....C...... 216 676-9969
Cleveland *(G-5700)*

Home Depot USA Inc ....C...... 216 581-6611
Maple Heights *(G-13287)*

Home Depot USA Inc ....D...... 937 431-7346
Beavercreek *(G-1156)*

Home Depot USA Inc ....C...... 330 245-0280
Akron *(G-268)*

Home Depot USA Inc ....D...... 937 837-1551
Dayton *(G-9501)*

Home Depot USA Inc ....C...... 216 297-1303
Cleveland Heights *(G-6719)*

Home Depot USA Inc ....C...... 513 661-2413
Cincinnati *(G-3720)*

Home Depot USA Inc ....C...... 513 887-1450
Fairfield Township *(G-10810)*

Home Depot USA Inc ....C...... 419 476-4573
Toledo *(G-17805)*

Home Depot USA Inc ....C...... 440 357-0428
Mentor *(G-14061)*

Home Depot USA Inc ....C...... 513 631-1705
Cincinnati *(G-3721)*

Home Depot USA Inc ....C...... 440 684-1343
Highland Heights *(G-11734)*

Home Depot USA Inc ....C...... 419 537-1920
Toledo *(G-17806)*

Home Depot USA Inc ....C...... 614 878-9150
Columbus *(G-7763)*

Home Depot USA Inc ....C...... 440 826-9092
Strongsville *(G-17311)*

Home Depot USA Inc ....C...... 614 939-5036
Columbus *(G-7764)*

Home Depot USA Inc ....D 440 937-2240
  Avon (G-886)
Home Depot USA Inc ....C 614 577-1601
  Reynoldsburg (G-16309)
Home Depot USA Inc ....C 330 220-2654
  Brunswick (G-1932)
Home Depot USA Inc ....C 419 626-6493
  Sandusky (G-16616)
Home Depot USA Inc ....C 614 876-5558
  Hilliard (G-11776)
Home Depot USA Inc ....C 440 324-7222
  Elyria (G-10515)
Home Depot USA Inc ....C 419 529-0015
  Ontario (G-15552)
Home Depot USA Inc ....C 216 251-3091
  Cleveland (G-5701)
J Way Leasing Ltd ....E 440 934-1020
  Avon (G-887)
Janell Inc ....E 513 489-9111
  Blue Ash (G-1589)
Jbjs Acquisitions LLC ....E 513 769-0393
  Cincinnati (G-3810)
JBK Group Inc ....E 216 901-0000
  Cleveland (G-5784)
Lasting Impressions Event ....D 614 252-5400
  Columbus (G-7955)
Live Technologies LLC ....D 614 278-7777
  Columbus (G-7986)
M & L Leasing Co ....E 330 343-8910
  Mineral City (G-14506)
Made From Scratch Inc ....E 614 873-3344
  Plain City (G-16058)
Maloney & Associates Inc ....E 330 479-7084
  Canton (G-2384)
Mapleview Farms Inc ....E 419 826-3671
  Swanton (G-17401)
MH Logistics Corp ....E 330 425-2476
  Hudson (G-11997)
Miami Industrial Trucks Inc ....D 937 293-4194
  Moraine (G-14677)
Miller & Co Portable Toil Svcs ......E 330 453-9472
  Canton (G-2405)
Millers Rental and Sls Co Inc ....E 216 642-1447
  Cleveland (G-5997)
Mitel (delaware) Inc ....E 513 733-8000
  West Chester (G-18974)
Mobilcomm Inc ....D 513 742-5555
  Cincinnati (G-4066)
Modal Shop Inc ....D 513 351-9919
  Cincinnati (G-4067)
Modern Office Methods Inc ....D 513 791-0909
  Blue Ash (G-1613)
Multi-Flow Dispensers Ohio Inc ....D 216 641-0200
  Brooklyn Heights (G-1876)
Netjets Inc ....E 614 239-5500
  Columbus (G-8174)
Northeast Projections Inc ....E 216 514-5023
  Cleveland (G-6094)
Office Products Toledo Inc ....E 419 865-7001
  Holland (G-11904)
Ohio Machinery Co ....C 419 874-7975
  Perrysburg (G-15897)
ONeil Awning and Tent Inc ....D 614 837-6352
  Canal Winchester (G-2115)
Paul Peterson Company ....E 614 486-4375
  Columbus (G-8427)
Paul Peterson Safety Div Inc ....E 614 486-4375
  Columbus (G-8428)
Piqua Steel Co ....D 937 773-3632
  Piqua (G-16020)
Pitney Bowes Inc ....D 203 426-7025
  Brecksville (G-1796)
Pitney Bowes Inc ....D 740 374-5535
  Marietta (G-13371)
Prestige Audio Visual Inc ....D 513 641-1600
  Cincinnati (G-4276)
Prime Time Party Rental Inc ....E 937 296-9262
  Moraine (G-14687)
Pro-Kleen Industrial Svcs Inc ....E 740 689-1886
  Lancaster (G-12427)
Rent-A-Center Inc ....D 330 337-1107
  Salem (G-16557)
Rent-A-Center Inc ....D 419 382-8585
  Toledo (G-18002)
Rent-N-Roll ....D 513 528-6929
  Cincinnati (G-4359)
Rentech Solutions Inc ....D 216 398-1111
  Willoughby (G-19568)
Ricoh Usa Inc ....D 513 984-9898
  Sharonville (G-16730)

Rumpke Transportation Co LLC .....E 937 461-0004
  Dayton (G-9740)
Rumpke Waste Inc ....C 937 548-1939
  Greenville (G-11393)
S and R Leasing ....E 330 276-3061
  Millersburg (G-14491)
Setiawan Associates LLC ....E 614 285-5815
  Columbus (G-8624)
Stout Lori Cleaning & Such ....E 419 637-7644
  Gibsonburg (G-11279)
Sunbelt Rentals Inc ....E 216 362-0300
  Cleveland (G-6477)
Superr-Spdie Portable Svcs Inc ....E 330 733-9000
  Akron (G-461)
▲ Thomas Do-It Center Inc ....D 740 446-2002
  Gallipolis (G-11215)
▲ Towlift Inc ....C 216 749-6800
  Brooklyn Heights (G-1884)
Two Men & A Vacuum LLC ....D 614 300-7970
  Columbus (G-8791)
U Haul Co of Northwestern Ohio ...E 419 478-1101
  Toledo (G-18114)
United Rentals North Amer Inc .....E 800 877-3687
  Perrysburg (G-15929)
Valley Industrial Trucks Inc ....E 330 788-4081
  Youngstown (G-20235)
Vincent Ltg Systems Co Inc ....E 216 475-7600
  Solon (G-16912)
Waids Rainbow Rental Inc ....E 216 524-3736
  Akron (G-493)
Warwick Communications Inc ....E 216 787-0300
  Broadview Heights (G-1850)
Waste Management Ohio Inc ....D 800 343-6047
  Fairborn (G-10688)
Winner Aviation Corporation ....D 330 856-5000
  Vienna (G-18584)
Yockey Group Inc ....E 513 899-2188
  Morrow (G-14719)

7361 Employment Agencies

56 Plus Management LLC ....E 937 323-4114
  Springfield (G-16991)
A-1 Healthcare Staffing LLC ....C 216 862-0906
  Cleveland (G-4884)
A-1 Healthcare Staffing LLC ....D 216 862-0906
  Lakewood (G-12334)
A-1 Nursing Care Inc ....C 614 268-3800
  Columbus (G-6850)
Abacus Corporation ....B 614 367-7000
  Reynoldsburg (G-16278)
Abilities First Foundation Inc ....D 513 423-9496
  Middletown (G-14285)
Accentcare Home Health Cal Inc ...C 740 387-4568
  Circleville (G-4822)
Accountants To You LLC ....E 513 651-2855
  Cincinnati (G-2902)
Advantage Resourcing Amer Inc ....E 781 472-8900
  Cincinnati (G-2912)
Advantage Rn LLC ....D 866 301-4045
  West Chester (G-18859)
Alexander Mann Solutions Corp ....B 216 336-6756
  Cleveland (G-4928)
Allcan Global Services Inc ....E 513 825-1655
  Cincinnati (G-2924)
Alliance Legal Solutions LLC ....D 216 525-0100
  Independence (G-12043)
Alliance Solutions Group LLC ....E 216 503-1690
  Independence (G-12044)
Alternate Solutions First LLC ....C 937 298-1111
  Dayton (G-9223)
American Bus Personnel Svcs ....E 513 770-3300
  Mason (G-13539)
Amotec Inc ....E 440 250-4600
  Cleveland (G-4973)
Aspen Community Living ....E 614 880-6000
  Columbus (G-6979)
Assured Health Care Inc ....E 937 294-2803
  Dayton (G-9242)
Atterro Inc ....E 800 938-9675
  Cincinnati (G-3002)
B & B Employment Resource LLC ...B 513 370-5542
  Cincinnati (G-3013)
Belflex Staffing Network LLC ....C 513 488-8588
  Cincinnati (G-3038)
Berns Oneill SEC & Safety LLC ......E 330 374-9133
  Akron (G-96)
Blanchard Valley Health System ....D 419 424-3000
  Findlay (G-10872)
Blanchard Valley Industries ....D 419 422-6386
  Findlay (G-10874)

Cardinalcommerce Corporation .....D 877 352-8444
  Mentor (G-14025)
Career Cnnctions Staffing Svcs .....E 440 471-8210
  Westlake (G-19326)
Carestar Inc ....C 513 618-8300
  Cincinnati (G-3122)
Careworks of Ohio Inc ....B 614 792-1085
  Dublin (G-10161)
Chad Downing ....E 614 532-5127
  Columbus (G-7177)
Childrens Home Care Dayton ....D 937 641-4663
  Dayton (G-9296)
Cleveland Job Corps Center ....C 216 541-2500
  Cleveland (G-5264)
Cnsld Humacare- Employee MGT ...E 513 605-3522
  Cincinnati (G-3317)
Collier Nursing Service Inc ....C 513 791-4357
  Montgomery (G-14594)
Community Hlth Prfssionals Inc .....C 419 238-9223
  Van Wert (G-18475)
Community Hlth Prfssionals Inc .....D 419 586-6266
  Celina (G-2590)
Community Home Care ....E 330 971-7011
  Cuyahoga Falls (G-9084)
Compass Professional Svcs LLC ....D 216 705-2233
  Columbus (G-7339)
Construction Labor Contrs LLC .....D 614 932-9937
  Columbus (G-7352)
Corporate Ladder Search ....E 330 776-4390
  Uniontown (G-18364)
County of Guernsey ....D 740 432-2381
  Cambridge (G-2062)
County of Holmes ....E 330 674-5035
  Millersburg (G-14468)
County of Huron ....D 419 668-8126
  Norwalk (G-15431)
County of Wayne ....E 330 264-5060
  Wooster (G-19716)
Csu/Career Services Center ....E 216 687-2233
  Cleveland (G-5386)
Ctpartners Exec Search Inc ....D 216 464-8710
  Beachwood (G-1049)
Custom Hlthcare Proffesional ....E 216 381-1010
  Cleveland (G-5392)
Custom Staffing Inc ....E 419 221-3097
  Lima (G-12629)
Daily Services LLC ....C 614 431-5100
  Columbus (G-7411)
Damascus Staffing LLC ....D 513 954-8941
  Maineville (G-13114)
Dawson Resources ....E 614 255-1400
  Columbus (G-7420)
Dawson Resources ....B 614 274-8900
  Columbus (G-7421)
Dedicated Nursing Assoc Inc ....D 937 886-4559
  Miamisburg (G-14164)
Dedicated Nursing Assoc Inc ....E 866 450-5550
  Cincinnati (G-3415)
Dedicated Nursing Assoc Inc ....E 877 411-8350
  Galloway (G-11219)
Dedicated Nursing Assoc Inc ....E 877 547-9144
  Parma (G-15765)
Dedicated Nursing Assoc Inc ....C 888 465-6929
  Beavercreek (G-1214)
Dedicated Technologies Inc ....E 614 460-3200
  Columbus (G-7427)
Discover Training Inc ....D 614 871-0010
  Grove City (G-11426)
Diversfied Emplyee Sltions Inc .....B 330 764-4125
  Medina (G-13932)
Diversity Search Group LLC ....B 614 352-2988
  Columbus (G-7455)
E & L Premier Corporation ....C 330 836-9901
  Fairlawn (G-10823)
Employbridge Holding Company ....C 419 874-7125
  Toledo (G-17713)
Employment Network ....E 440 324-5244
  Elyria (G-10510)
Endevis LLc ....E 419 482-4848
  Toledo (G-17715)
Epilogue Inc ....D 440 582-5555
  North Royalton (G-15355)
Exodus Integrity Service ....D 440 918-0140
  Willoughby (G-19522)
Experis Us Inc ....E 614 223-2300
  Columbus (G-7547)
Fast Switch Ltd ....B 614 336-1122
  Dublin (G-10226)
First Choice Med Staff of Ohio ......D 419 521-2700
  Mansfield (G-13177)

First Choice Medical Staffing......B......216 521-2222
  Cleveland *(G-5532)*
First Diversity Staffing Group......B......937 323-4114
  Springfield *(G-17038)*
Firstat Nursing Services......D......216 295-1500
  Cleveland *(G-5538)*
Gallery Holdings LLC......D......773 693-6220
  Independence *(G-12076)*
Global Exec Slutions Group LLC......E......330 666-3354
  Akron *(G-237)*
Global Tchnical Recruiters Inc......E......216 251-9560
  Westlake *(G-19344)*
Global Tchnical Recruiters Inc......D......440 365-1670
  Westlake *(G-19345)*
Goodwill Industries Inc......E......330 724-6995
  Akron *(G-240)*
Greater Dyton Rgnal Trnst Auth......A......937 425-8400
  Dayton *(G-9475)*
Gus Perdikakis Associates......D......513 583-0900
  Cincinnati *(G-3665)*
Health Care Plus......C......614 340-7587
  Westerville *(G-19170)*
Heitmeyer Group LLC......B......614 573-5571
  Westerville *(G-19171)*
HJ Ford Associates Inc......C......937 429-9711
  Beavercreek *(G-1155)*
Home Care Network Inc......D......937 435-1142
  Dayton *(G-9498)*
Horizon Personnel Resources......C......440 585-0031
  Wickliffe *(G-19464)*
Horizons Employment Svcs LLC......B......419 254-9644
  Toledo *(G-17808)*
Hospice of Darke County Inc......E......419 678-4808
  Coldwater *(G-6759)*
Hr Services Inc......E......419 224-2462
  Lima *(G-12660)*
Human Resources Services......E......740 587-3484
  Westerville *(G-19173)*
I-Force LLC......C......614 431-5100
  Columbus *(G-7796)*
Integrity Enterprizes......E......216 289-8801
  Euclid *(G-10645)*
Interim Halthcare Columbus Inc......E......330 836-5571
  Fairlawn *(G-10834)*
Its Technologies Inc......D......419 842-2100
  Holland *(G-11890)*
Jacor LLC......A......330 441-4182
  Medina *(G-13958)*
Job Center LLC......E......440 499-1000
  Elyria *(G-10521)*
Job1usa Inc......D......419 255-5005
  Toledo *(G-17831)*
Key Career Place......D......216 987-3029
  Cleveland *(G-5825)*
Kforce Inc......E......614 436-4027
  Columbus *(G-7900)*
Kforce Inc......E......216 643-8141
  Independence *(G-12085)*
Kilgore Group Inc......E......513 684-3721
  Cincinnati *(G-3868)*
Lane Wood Industries......B......419 352-5059
  Bowling Green *(G-1739)*
Management Recruiters Intl Inc......E......614 252-6200
  Columbus *(G-8012)*
Management Recruiters Intl Inc......D......440 543-1284
  Chagrin Falls *(G-2672)*
Mancan Inc......A......440 884-9675
  Strongsville *(G-17326)*
Marvel Consultants......E......216 292-2855
  Cleveland *(G-5918)*
Medi Home Health Agency Inc......E......740 266-3977
  Steubenville *(G-17165)*
Medical Solutions LLC......D......513 936-3468
  Blue Ash *(G-1607)*
Mid Ohio Employment Services......E......419 747-5466
  Ontario *(G-15564)*
Midwest Emergency Services LLC......E......586 294-2700
  Fairlawn *(G-10841)*
Mj-6 LLC......E......419 517-7725
  Toledo *(G-17920)*
Murtech Consulting LLC......D......216 328-8580
  Cleveland *(G-6026)*
National Staffing Group Ltd......E......440 546-0800
  Brecksville *(G-1791)*
Nurses Care Inc......E......513 791-0233
  Cincinnati *(G-4141)*
Nurses Heart Med Staffing LLC......E......614 648-5111
  Columbus *(G-8217)*
Ohio Dept of Job & Fmly Svcs......D......330 484-5402
  Akron *(G-357)*

Ohio State University......A......614 293-2494
  Columbus *(G-8318)*
Onestaff Inc......E......859 815-1345
  Cincinnati *(G-4175)*
P E Miller & Assoc......D......614 231-4743
  Columbus *(G-8407)*
Pathway Inc......E......419 242-7304
  Toledo *(G-17974)*
Pearl Interactive Network Inc......B......614 258-2943
  Columbus *(G-8432)*
Per Diem Nurse Staffing LLT......E......419 878-8880
  Waterville *(G-18791)*
Personal Touch HM Care IPA Inc......E......937 456-4447
  Eaton *(G-10458)*
Pps Holding LLC......D......513 985-6400
  Cincinnati *(G-4267)*
Private Practice Nurses Inc......E......216 481-1305
  Cleveland *(G-6237)*
Prn Health Services Inc......D......513 792-2217
  Cincinnati *(G-4286)*
Prn Nurse Inc......B......614 864-9292
  Columbus *(G-8464)*
Professional Contract Systems......C......513 469-8800
  Cincinnati *(G-4292)*
Professional Data Resources Inc......C......513 792-5100
  Blue Ash *(G-1633)*
Promedica Physcn Cntinuum Svcs......C......419 824-7200
  Sylvania *(G-17444)*
PSI Associates Inc......B......330 425-8474
  Twinsburg *(G-18308)*
Psychpros Inc......E......513 651-9500
  Cincinnati *(G-4304)*
R E Richards Inc......E......330 499-1001
  Canton *(G-2448)*
Randstad Professional Us LP......E......513 792-6658
  Blue Ash *(G-1638)*
Randstad Technologies LLC......D......614 436-0961
  Columbus *(G-6832)*
Randstad Technologies LLC......D......216 520-0206
  Independence *(G-12111)*
Reserves Network Inc......E......440 779-1400
  Cleveland *(G-6314)*
Rightthing LLC......B......419 420-1830
  Findlay *(G-10958)*
Rkpl Inc......D......419 224-2121
  Lima *(G-12732)*
Robert Half International Inc......D......937 224-7376
  Dayton *(G-9738)*
Robert Half International Inc......D......330 629-9494
  Youngstown *(G-20188)*
Robert Half International Inc......D......513 563-0770
  Blue Ash *(G-1647)*
Robert Half International Inc......D......614 221-8326
  Columbus *(G-8541)*
Robert Half International Inc......D......614 602-0505
  Dublin *(G-10324)*
Robert Half International Inc......D......513 621-8367
  Cincinnati *(G-4391)*
Robert Half International Inc......D......216 621-4253
  Cleveland *(G-6332)*
Robert Half International Inc......D......614 221-1544
  Columbus *(G-8542)*
Rumpf Corporation......E......419 255-5005
  Toledo *(G-18014)*
Rvet Operating LLC......E......513 683-5020
  Loveland *(G-13025)*
S & H Risner Inc......D......937 778-8563
  Piqua *(G-16027)*
Safegard Bckgrund Screening LLC......C......216 370-7345
  Cleveland *(G-6360)*
Seifert & Group Inc......D......330 833-2700
  Massillon *(G-13727)*
Siffrin Residential Assn......C......330 799-8932
  Youngstown *(G-20211)*
St Ritas Medical Center......C......419 538-7025
  Lima *(G-12751)*
Staffmark Holdings Inc......D......513 651-1111
  Cincinnati *(G-4528)*
Staffmark Investment LLC......C......513 651-3600
  Cincinnati *(G-4529)*
Stearns Companies LLC......E......419 422-0241
  Findlay *(G-10963)*
Tailored Management Services......D......614 859-1500
  Columbus *(G-8729)*
Talemed LLC......B......513 774-7300
  Loveland *(G-13031)*
Taylors Staffing LLC......D......740 446-3305
  Pomeroy *(G-16098)*
Tech Center Inc......E......330 762-6212
  Akron *(G-465)*

Telamon Corporation......E......937 254-2004
  Dayton *(G-9809)*
Telecmmnctons Stffing Slutions......E......614 799-9300
  Dublin *(G-10355)*
Thinkpath Engineering Svcs LLC......E......937 291-8374
  Miamisburg *(G-14229)*
Tradesmen International LLC......C......419 502-9140
  Sandusky *(G-16649)*
Tradesmen International LLC......D......513 771-1115
  Blue Ash *(G-1661)*
Tradesmen International LLC......E......440 349-3432
  Macedonia *(G-13086)*
Tradesmen Services LLC......D......440 349-3432
  Macedonia *(G-13087)*
Tradesource Inc......C......216 801-4944
  Parma *(G-15778)*
Tradesource Inc......C......614 824-3883
  Columbus *(G-8771)*
Trak Staffing Services Inc......E......513 333-4199
  Cincinnati *(G-4625)*
Trustaff Management Inc......A......513 272-3999
  Blue Ash *(G-1668)*
Ulrich Professional Group......E......330 673-9501
  Kent *(G-12265)*
United Steelworkers......E......440 244-1358
  Lorain *(G-12949)*
Vector Technical Inc......C......440 946-8800
  Willoughby *(G-19581)*
Vishnia & Associates Inc......D......330 929-5512
  Cuyahoga Falls *(G-9137)*
Willory LLC......E......330 576-5486
  Bath *(G-1020)*
Wood County Ohio......E......419 352-5059
  Bowling Green *(G-1758)*
Work Solutions Group LLC......E......440 205-8297
  Mentor *(G-14126)*
Wtw Delaware Holdings LLC......C......216 937-4000
  Cleveland *(G-6693)*
Youth Opportunities Unlimited......E......216 566-5445
  Cleveland *(G-6706)*

7363 Help Supply Svcs

A B S Temps Inc......E......937 252-9888
  Dayton *(G-9198)*
A Jacobs Inc......E......614 774-6757
  Hilliard *(G-11738)*
Acloche LLC......E......888 608-0889
  Columbus *(G-6865)*
Act I Temporaries Findlay Inc......B......419 423-0713
  Findlay *(G-10863)*
Adecco Usa Inc......E......419 720-0111
  Toledo *(G-17582)*
Ado Staffing Inc......E......419 222-8395
  Lima *(G-12592)*
Advantage Human Resourcing Inc......D......318 324-8060
  Cincinnati *(G-2911)*
Advantage Tchncal Rsurcing Inc......B......513 651-1111
  Cincinnati *(G-2913)*
Aerotek Inc......E......330 517-7330
  Akron *(G-22)*
Aerotek Inc......E......216 573-5520
  Independence *(G-12040)*
Aldo Peraza......D......614 804-0403
  Galloway *(G-11218)*
Alliance Solutions Group LLC......E......216 503-1690
  Independence *(G-12044)*
Alternate Solutions Healthcare......D......937 299-1111
  Dayton *(G-9224)*
American Bulk Commodities Inc......C......330 758-0841
  Youngstown *(G-19953)*
Amerimed Inc......E......513 942-3670
  West Chester *(G-18866)*
Arcadia Services Inc......D......330 869-9520
  Akron *(G-77)*
Arcadia Services Inc......D......937 912-5800
  Beavercreek *(G-1126)*
Area Temps Inc......A......216 227-8200
  Lakewood *(G-12336)*
Area Temps Inc......E......216 781-5350
  Independence *(G-12046)*
Area Temps Inc......A......216 518-2000
  Maple Heights *(G-13281)*
Ashtabula Stevedore Company......E......440 964-7186
  Ashtabula *(G-720)*
Aspen Community Living......C......614 880-6000
  Columbus *(G-6979)*
Atterro Inc......E......800 938-9675
  Cincinnati *(G-3002)*
Belcan LLC......A......513 985-7777
  Blue Ash *(G-1509)*

Belcan LLC ....A...... 513 645-1509
West Chester *(G-18875)*

Belcan LLC ....A...... 513 891-0972
Blue Ash *(G-1510)*

Belcan LLC ....A...... 513 217-4562
Middletown *(G-14291)*

Belcan LLC ....A...... 740 393-8888
Mount Vernon *(G-14749)*

Belcan LLC ....D...... 513 891-0972
Solon *(G-16827)*

Belcan Corporation ....A...... 614 224-6080
Columbus *(G-7026)*

Belcan Svcs Group Ltd Partnr ....C...... 937 586-5053
Dayton *(G-9248)*

Belcan Svcs Group Ltd Partnr ....C...... 513 891-0972
Blue Ash *(G-1512)*

Belcan Svcs Group Ltd Partnr ....D...... 937 859-8880
Miamisburg *(G-14144)*

Belflex Staffing Network LLC ....C...... 513 488-8588
Cincinnati *(G-3038)*

Buckeye Leasing Inc ....E...... 330 758-0841
Youngstown *(G-19978)*

Callos Resource LLC ....E...... 330 788-3033
Youngstown *(G-19980)*

Carol Scudere ....E...... 614 839-4357
New Albany *(G-14848)*

Cbiz Inc ....C...... 216 447-9000
Cleveland *(G-5139)*

Central Ohio Hospitalists ....E...... 614 255-6900
Columbus *(G-7158)*

CHI Health At Home ....E...... 513 576-0262
Milford *(G-14377)*

▲ Cima Inc ....E...... 513 382-8976
Hamilton *(G-11577)*

Columbiana Service Company LLC ...D...... 330 482-5511
Columbiana *(G-6785)*

Constant Aviation LLC ....C...... 800 440-9004
Cleveland *(G-5338)*

CPC Logistics Inc ....D...... 513 874-5787
Fairfield *(G-10715)*

Custom Staffing Inc ....E...... 419 221-3097
Lima *(G-12629)*

D C Transportation Service ....C...... 440 237-0900
North Royalton *(G-15351)*

Dawson Resources ....E...... 614 255-1400
Columbus *(G-7420)*

Dedicated Nursing Assoc Inc ....E...... 866 450-5550
Cincinnati *(G-3415)*

Dedicated Nursing Assoc Inc ....E...... 877 411-8350
Galloway *(G-11219)*

Dedicated Nursing Assoc Inc ....E...... 877 547-9144
Parma *(G-15765)*

Dedicated Nursing Assoc Inc ....C...... 888 465-6929
Beavercreek *(G-1214)*

Dedicated Tech Services Inc ....E...... 614 309-0059
Dublin *(G-10197)*

Diversified Employment Grp II ....E...... 513 428-6525
Cincinnati *(G-3435)*

Diversified Labor Support LLC ....B...... 440 234-3090
Cleveland *(G-5430)*

Doepker Group Inc ....E...... 419 355-1409
Fremont *(G-11070)*

E & L Premier Corporation ....C...... 330 836-9901
Fairlawn *(G-10823)*

Edge Plastics Inc ....E...... 419 522-6696
Mansfield *(G-13171)*

Emily Management Inc ....D...... 440 354-6713
Painesville *(G-15712)*

Emp Holdings Ltd ....A...... 330 493-4443
Canton *(G-2300)*

Everstaff LLC ....E...... 440 992-0238
Mentor *(G-14045)*

Firstat Nursing Services ....D...... 216 295-1500
Cleveland *(G-5538)*

Flex Temp Employment Services ......C...... 419 355-9675
Fremont *(G-11074)*

Flex-Team Inc ....B...... 330 745-3838
Akron *(G-224)*

Focus Solutions Inc ....E...... 513 376-8349
Cincinnati *(G-3575)*

Franklin Cnty Crt Common Pleas ......E...... 614 525-5775
Columbus *(G-7612)*

Frontline National LLC ....D...... 513 528-7823
Milford *(G-14390)*

Health Carousel LLC ....D...... 866 665-4544
Cincinnati *(G-3693)*

Heartland Employment Svcs LLC ......A...... 419 252-5500
Toledo *(G-17792)*

Heiser Staffing Services LLC ....E...... 614 800-4188
Columbus *(G-7737)*

Hogan Truck Leasing Inc ....E...... 513 454-3500
Fairfield *(G-10736)*

Horizon Personnel Resources ....C...... 440 585-0031
Wickliffe *(G-19464)*

Hr Services Inc ....E...... 419 224-2462
Lima *(G-12660)*

▲ Industrial Repair & Mfg Inc ....D...... 419 822-4232
Delta *(G-10045)*

Innovtive Sltons Unlimited LLC ....E...... 740 289-3282
Piketon *(G-15978)*

Innovtive Sltons Unlimited LLC ....D...... 740 289-3282
Piketon *(G-15979)*

▲ Integrated Marketing Tech Inc ....D...... 330 225-3550
Brunswick *(G-1933)*

Interim Halthcare Columbus Inc ....E...... 614 888-3130
Gahanna *(G-11127)*

Interim Halthcare Columbus Inc ....E...... 330 836-5571
Fairlawn *(G-10834)*

Its Technologies Inc ....D...... 419 842-2100
Holland *(G-11890)*

JB Management Inc ....D...... 419 841-2596
Toledo *(G-17829)*

Jet Mintenance Consulting Corp ....E...... 937 205-2406
Wilmington *(G-19625)*

Job1usa Inc ....D...... 419 255-5005
Toledo *(G-17831)*

Kilgore Group Inc ....E...... 513 684-3721
Cincinnati *(G-3868)*

Larue Enterprises Inc ....E...... 937 438-5711
Beavercreek *(G-1225)*

Lee Personnel Inc ....E...... 513 744-6780
Cincinnati *(G-3916)*

Locum Medical Group LLC ....D...... 216 464-2125
Independence *(G-12094)*

Macair Aviation LLC ....E...... 937 347-1302
Xenia *(G-19919)*

Maxim Healthcare Services Inc ....D...... 216 606-3000
Independence *(G-12097)*

Maxim Healthcare Services Inc ....D...... 614 986-3001
Gahanna *(G-11135)*

Medlink of Ohio Inc ....B...... 330 773-9434
Akron *(G-330)*

Medport Inc ....D...... 216 244-6832
Cleveland *(G-5945)*

Medsearch Staffing Svcs Inc ....D...... 440 243-6363
Cleveland *(G-5946)*

Minute Men Inc ....D...... 216 426-2225
Cleveland *(G-5999)*

MPW Industrial Services Inc ....D...... 937 644-0200
East Liberty *(G-10393)*

Msstaff LLC ....C...... 419 868-8536
Toledo *(G-17926)*

Neo-Pet LLC ....E...... 440 893-9949
Cleveland *(G-6055)*

Netjets Assn Shred Arcft Plots ....D...... 614 532-0555
Columbus *(G-8173)*

Nursing Resources Corp ....E...... 419 333-3000
Maumee *(G-13825)*

Ohio Dept of Job & Fmly Svcs ....E...... 419 334-3891
Fremont *(G-11089)*

P E Miller & Associates Inc ....D...... 614 231-4743
Columbus *(G-8408)*

Paradigm Industrial LLC ....E...... 937 224-4415
Dayton *(G-9685)*

Patrick Staffing Inc ....E...... 937 743-5585
Franklin *(G-11036)*

Physician Staffing Inc ....B...... 440 542-5000
Cleveland *(G-6209)*

Pontoon Solutions Inc ....D...... 855 881-1533
Maumee *(G-13833)*

Preferred Temporary Services ....E...... 330 494-5502
Canton *(G-2439)*

Prestige Technical Svcs Inc ....E...... 513 779-6800
West Chester *(G-18985)*

Prn Nurse Inc ....B...... 614 864-9292
Columbus *(G-8464)*

Production Design Services Inc ....D...... 937 866-3377
Dayton *(G-9716)*

Professional Transportation ....C...... 419 661-0576
Walbridge *(G-18623)*

Prueter Enterprises Ltd ....C...... 419 872-5343
Perrysburg *(G-15907)*

Quadax Inc ....E...... 330 759-4600
Youngstown *(G-20170)*

Randstad Professionals Us LLC ....E...... 419 893-2400
Maumee *(G-13840)*

Randstad Professionals Us LP ....E...... 513 791-8600
Blue Ash *(G-1639)*

Renhill Stffing Srvces-America ....E...... 419 254-2800
Perrysburg *(G-15912)*

Reserves Network Inc ....E...... 440 779-1400
Cleveland *(G-6314)*

Rkpl Inc ....D...... 419 224-2121
Lima *(G-12732)*

Rumpf Corporation ....E...... 419 255-5005
Toledo *(G-18014)*

S & B Trucking Inc ....E...... 614 554-4090
Hubbard *(G-11950)*

Salo Inc ....A...... 740 623-2331
Coshocton *(G-9027)*

Select Staffing ....D...... 513 247-9772
West Chester *(G-19001)*

Sequent Inc ....D...... 614 436-5880
Columbus *(G-6836)*

Sfn Group Inc ....E...... 419 727-4104
Toledo *(G-18028)*

Spherion of Lima Inc ....A...... 419 224-8367
Lima *(G-12747)*

Staffmark Holdings Inc ....D...... 513 651-1111
Cincinnati *(G-4528)*

Stage Works ....E...... 513 522-3118
Cincinnati *(G-4530)*

Super Shine Inc ....E...... 513 423-8999
Middletown *(G-14334)*

Taylors Staffing LLC ....D...... 740 446-3305
Pomeroy *(G-16098)*

Top Echelon Contracting Inc ....B...... 330 454-3508
Canton *(G-2514)*

Township of Chester ....E...... 440 729-9951
Chesterland *(G-2747)*

Transportation Unlimited Inc ....A...... 216 426-0088
Cleveland *(G-6544)*

Trueblue Inc ....E...... 740 282-1079
Steubenville *(G-17182)*

Tsl Ltd ....A...... 419 843-3200
Toledo *(G-18110)*

Verified Person Inc ....E...... 901 767-6121
Independence *(G-12136)*

Volt Management Corp ....D...... 513 791-2600
Cincinnati *(G-4764)*

Wayne Industries Inc ....E...... 937 548-6025
Greenville *(G-11401)*

Waypoint Aviation LLC ....E...... 800 769-4765
Cincinnati *(G-4771)*

7371 Custom Computer Programming Svcs

1 Edi Source Inc ....C...... 440 519-7800
Solon *(G-16812)*

22nd Century Technologies Inc ....C...... 866 537-9191
Beavercreek *(G-1121)*

Acadia Solutions Inc ....E...... 614 505-6135
Dublin *(G-10118)*

Aclara Technologies LLC ....E...... 440 528-7200
Solon *(G-16814)*

Advanced Prgrm Resources Inc ....E...... 614 761-9994
Dublin *(G-10119)*

Advantage Technology Group ....E...... 513 563-3560
West Chester *(G-18860)*

Aktion Associates Incorporated ....E...... 419 893-7001
Maumee *(G-13747)*

Alien Technology LLC ....C...... 408 782-3900
Miamisburg *(G-14139)*

Alonovus Corp ....D...... 330 674-2300
Millersburg *(G-14454)*

American Systems Cnsulting Inc ....C...... 614 282-7180
Dublin *(G-10134)*

Assured Information SEC Inc ....D...... 937 427-9720
Beavercreek *(G-1127)*

Astute Inc ....E...... 614 508-6100
Columbus *(G-6986)*

Auto Des Sys Inc ....E...... 614 488-7984
Upper Arlington *(G-18394)*

◆ B-Tek Scales LLC ....E...... 330 471-8900
Canton *(G-2208)*

Batch Labs Inc ....D...... 216 901-9366
Cleveland *(G-5041)*

Big Red Rooster ....E...... 614 255-0200
Columbus *(G-7036)*

Billback Systems LLC ....E...... 937 433-1844
Dayton *(G-9253)*

Boundless Flight Inc ....E...... 440 610-3683
Rocky River *(G-16424)*

Briteskies LLC ....E...... 216 369-3600
Cleveland *(G-5081)*

Btas Inc ....C...... 937 431-9431
Beavercreek *(G-1135)*

Business Equipment Co Inc ....E...... 513 948-1500
Cincinnati *(G-3096)*

Camgen Ltd ....D...... 330 204-8636
Cleveland *(G-5116)*

Camgen Ltd	E	330 204-8636
Canal Winchester *(G-2105)*		
Campuseai Inc	C	216 589-9626
Cleveland *(G-5117)*		
Care Information Systems LLC	D	614 496-4338
Dublin *(G-10160)*		
Cbiz Operations Inc	D	216 447-9000
Cleveland *(G-5140)*		
Cdo Technologies Inc	D	937 258-0022
Dayton *(G-9164)*		
Cengage Learning Inc	B	513 229-1000
Mason *(G-13552)*		
Centergrid LLC	E	513 712-1212
Hamilton *(G-11574)*		
Certified SEC Solutions Inc	E	216 785-2986
Independence *(G-12057)*		
Cimx LLC	E	513 248-7700
Cincinnati *(G-3217)*		
Cincom Intrnational Operations	B	513 612-2300
Cincinnati *(G-3285)*		
Click4care Inc	D	614 431-3700
Powell *(G-16188)*		
Cloudroute LLC	E	216 373-4601
Cleveland *(G-5307)*		
Clubessential LLC	E	800 448-1475
Blue Ash *(G-1530)*		
Cochin Technologies LLC	E	440 941-4856
Avon *(G-878)*		
Coleman Professional Svcs Inc	C	330 673-1347
Kent *(G-12223)*		
Command Alkon Incorporated	D	614 799-0600
Dublin *(G-10183)*		
Commercial Time Sharing Inc	E	330 644-3059
Akron *(G-148)*		
Commsys Inc	E	937 220-4990
Moraine *(G-14634)*		
Computer Helper Publishing	E	614 939-9094
Columbus *(G-7345)*		
Comtech Global Inc	D	614 796-1148
Columbus *(G-7347)*		
Connectivity Systems Inc	E	740 420-5400
Williamsport *(G-19498)*		
Cott Systems Inc	D	614 847-4405
Columbus *(G-7379)*		
County of Montgomery	B	937 496-3103
Dayton *(G-9333)*		
Critical Business Analysis Inc	E	419 874-0800
Perrysburg *(G-15852)*		
▲ Crosschx Inc	D	800 501-3161
Columbus *(G-7395)*		
CT Logistics Inc	C	216 267-1636
Cleveland *(G-5387)*		
Dassault Systemes Simulia Corp	E	513 275-1430
Mason *(G-13572)*		
Datavantage Corporation	B	440 498-4414
Cleveland *(G-5406)*		
Dedicated Tech Services Inc	E	614 309-0059
Dublin *(G-10197)*		
Deemsys Inc	D	614 322-9928
Gahanna *(G-11117)*		
Devcare Solutions Ltd	E	614 221-2277
Columbus *(G-7439)*		
▲ Dexxxon Digital Storage Inc	E	740 548-7179
Lewis Center *(G-12538)*		
Digiknow Inc	E	888 482-4455
Cleveland *(G-5422)*		
Digitek Software Inc	E	614 764-8875
Lewis Center *(G-12540)*		
Diskcopy Duplication Services	E	440 460-0800
Cleveland *(G-5427)*		
Distribution Data Incorporated	E	216 362-3009
Brookpark *(G-1896)*		
Diversified Systems Inc	E	614 476-9939
Westerville *(G-19249)*		
Dizer Corp	E	440 368-0200
Painesville *(G-15709)*		
DMC Technology Group	E	419 535-2900
Toledo *(G-17703)*		
Dotloop LLC	E	513 257-0550
Cincinnati *(G-3441)*		
Drb Systems LLC	C	330 645-3299
Akron *(G-195)*		
Drs Signal Technologies Inc	E	937 429-7470
Beavercreek *(G-1148)*		
Dynamite Technologies LLC	D	614 538-0095
Columbus *(G-7481)*		
Eci Macola/Max LLC	C	978 539-6186
Dublin *(G-10213)*		
Eclipse Blind Systems Inc	C	330 296-0112
Ravenna *(G-16242)*		

Edaptive Computing Inc	D	937 433-0477
Dayton *(G-9408)*		
▼ Einstruction Corporation	D	330 746-3015
Youngstown *(G-20027)*		
Electronic Registry Systems	E	513 771-7330
Cincinnati *(G-3489)*		
Eliassen Group LLC		781 205-8100
Blue Ash *(G-1550)*		
Epsilon	C	513 248-2882
Milford *(G-14387)*		
Erp Analysts Inc	B	614 718-9222
Dublin *(G-10220)*		
Evanhoe & Associates Inc	E	937 235-2995
Dayton *(G-9173)*		
Everyone Counts Inc	D	858 427-4673
Cleveland *(G-5498)*		
Exodus Integrity Service	D	440 918-0140
Willoughby *(G-19522)*		
Fascor Inc	E	513 421-1777
Cincinnati *(G-3533)*		
Fastems LLC	E	513 779-4614
West Chester *(G-18922)*		
First Data Gvrnmnt Solutns Inc	C	513 489-9599
Blue Ash *(G-1563)*		
Flairsoft Ltd	E	614 888-0700
Columbus *(G-7594)*		
Flexnova Inc	E	216 288-6961
Broadview Heights *(G-1833)*		
Foresight Corporation	E	614 791-1600
Dublin *(G-10230)*		
Fortis North Canton LLC	D	330 682-5984
North Canton *(G-15204)*		
Foundation Software Inc	D	330 220-8383
Strongsville *(G-17305)*		
Fraternal Order of Eagles BR	E	419 636-7812
Bryan *(G-1957)*		
Frontier Technology Inc	E	937 429-3302
Beavercreek Township *(G-1248)*		
Fund Evaluation Group LLC	E	513 977-4400
Cincinnati *(G-3597)*		
Gannett Media Tech Intl	E	513 665-3777
Cincinnati *(G-3602)*		
▲ Gatesair Inc	D	513 459-3400
Mason *(G-13583)*		
Gb Liquidating Company Inc	E	513 248-7600
Milford *(G-14391)*		
Genomoncology LLC	E	216 496-4216
Cleveland *(G-5605)*		
▲ Gensuite LLC	D	513 774-1000
Mason *(G-13587)*		
▼ Gracie Plum Investments Inc	E	740 355-9029
Portsmouth *(G-16141)*		
Hab Inc	E	608 785-7650
Solon *(G-16856)*		
Harley-Dvidson Dlr Systems Inc	D	216 573-1393
Cleveland *(G-5661)*		
Health Care Dataworks Inc	D	614 255-5400
Columbus *(G-7724)*		
Henry Call Inc	C	216 433-5609
Cleveland *(G-5684)*		
Holo Pundits Inc	E	614 707-5225
Dublin *(G-10244)*		
Horizon Payroll Services Inc	B	937 434-8244
Dayton *(G-9506)*		
Icr Inc	D	513 900-7007
Mason *(G-13596)*		
Ils Technology LLC	E	800 695-8650
Cleveland *(G-5738)*		
Imflux Inc	E	513 488-1017
Hamilton *(G-11611)*		
Incubit LLC	D	740 362-1401
Delaware *(G-9988)*		
Indecon Solutions LLC	E	614 799-1850
Dublin *(G-10254)*		
Indigo Group	E	513 557-8794
Liberty Twp *(G-12587)*		
Inet Interactive LLC	E	513 322-5600
West Chester *(G-18947)*		
Infor (us) Inc	B	678 319-8000
Columbus *(G-7816)*		
Infovision 21 Inc	E	614 761-8844
Dublin *(G-10256)*		
Inreality LLC	E	513 218-9603
Cincinnati *(G-3763)*		
Integrated Telehealth Inc	E	216 373-2221
Hudson *(G-11985)*		
▲ Intelligrated Systems Inc	A	866 936-7300
Mason *(G-13598)*		
Intelligrated Systems LLC	A	513 701-7300
Mason *(G-13599)*		

International Technegroup Inc	D	513 576-3900
Milford *(G-14397)*		
Iq Innovations LLC	E	614 222-0882
Columbus *(G-7841)*		
Irth Solutions Inc	E	614 459-2328
Columbus *(G-7843)*		
Isqft Inc	C	513 645-8004
Cincinnati *(G-3788)*		
Itcube LLC	D	513 891-7300
Blue Ash *(G-1587)*		
▲ Jenne Inc	C	440 835-0040
Avon *(G-888)*		
Jjr Solutions LLC	E	937 912-0288
Beavercreek *(G-1159)*		
Jyg Innovations LLC	E	937 630-3858
Dayton *(G-9531)*		
▲ Keithley Instruments LLC	C	440 248-0400
Solon *(G-16864)*		
Keystone Technology Cons	E	330 666-6200
Akron *(G-302)*		
Kiwiplan Inc	E	513 554-1500
Cincinnati *(G-3878)*		
Kmi Inc	E	614 326-6304
Columbus *(G-7914)*		
Knowledge MGT Interactive Inc	E	614 224-0664
Columbus *(G-7919)*		
Lakeland Foundation	E	440 525-7094
Willoughby *(G-19541)*		
Lap Technology LLC	E	937 415-5794
Dayton *(G-9558)*		
Leader Technologies Inc	E	614 890-1986
Lewis Center *(G-12549)*		
Leidos Inc	D	937 431-2270
Beavercreek *(G-1164)*		
Liberty Comm Sftwr Sltions Inc	E	614 318-5000
Columbus *(G-7970)*		
Lifecycle Solutions Jv LLC	D	937 938-1321
Beavercreek *(G-1167)*		
Lisnr Inc	E	513 322-8400
Cincinnati *(G-3938)*		
Logic Soft Inc	E	614 884-5544
Dublin *(G-10274)*		
London Computer Systems Inc	D	513 583-0840
Cincinnati *(G-3942)*		
Main Sequence Technology Inc	E	440 946-5214
Mentor On The Lake *(G-14129)*		
Managed Technology Svcs LLC	D	937 247-8915
Miamisburg *(G-14186)*		
Manhattan Associates Inc	D	440 878-0771
Strongsville *(G-17327)*		
Manifest Solutions Corp	E	614 930-2800
Upper Arlington *(G-18401)*		
Mapsys Inc	E	614 255-7258
Columbus *(G-8014)*		
Marshall Information Svcs LLC	E	614 430-0355
Columbus *(G-8030)*		
Marxent Labs LLC	D	937 999-5005
Kettering *(G-12297)*		
Matrix Pointe Software LLC	E	216 333-1263
Westlake *(G-19371)*		
Mirifex Systems LLC	C	440 891-1210
Cleveland *(G-6001)*		
Mitosis LLC	E	937 557-3440
Dayton *(G-9640)*		
Montpelier Exempted Vlg Schl	D	419 485-3676
Montpelier *(G-14615)*		
Morphick Inc	E	844 506-6774
Blue Ash *(G-1615)*		
Mri Software LLC	C	800 321-8770
Solon *(G-16874)*		
MSI International LLC	E	330 869-6459
Cleveland *(G-6022)*		
Neumeric Technologies Corp	D	248 204-0652
Westerville *(G-19190)*		
New Innovations Inc	E	330 899-9954
Uniontown *(G-18380)*		
Noble Technologies Corp	E	330 287-1530
Wooster *(G-19752)*		
Northwods Cnslting Prtners Inc	C	614 781-7800
Dublin *(G-10292)*		
Nsb Retail Systems Inc	D	614 840-1421
Lewis Center *(G-12554)*		
Ntt Data Inc	D	513 794-1400
Cincinnati *(G-4137)*		
Odyssey Consulting Services	C	614 523-4248
Columbus *(G-8226)*		
Oeconnection LLC	D	888 776-5792
Richfield *(G-16367)*		
Office World Inc	E	419 991-4694
Lima *(G-12791)*		

Ohio University ....D 740 593-1000
  Athens (G-795)
Online Mega Sellers Corp ....D 888 384-6468
  Toledo (G-17964)
Parker-Hannifin Corporation ....D 513 831-2340
  Milford (G-14419)
Path Robotics Inc ....E 330 808-2788
  Cleveland (G-6181)
Patterson Pope Inc ....D 513 891-4430
  Cincinnati (G-4213)
Pcms Datafit Inc ....D 513 587-3100
  Blue Ash (G-1629)
Pegasus Technical Services Inc ....E 513 793-0094
  Cincinnati (G-4223)
Plumbline Solutions Inc ....E 419 581-2963
  Findlay (G-10954)
Positive Bus Solutions Inc ....D 513 772-2255
  Cincinnati (G-4265)
Primatech Inc ....E 614 841-9800
  Columbus (G-8462)
Primax Marketing Group ....E 513 443-2797
  Cincinnati (G-4279)
Productivity Qulty Systems Inc ....E 937 885-2255
  Dayton (G-9717)
Qvidian Corporation ....E 513 631-1155
  Blue Ash (G-1634)
Raco Wireless LLC ....E 513 870-6480
  Blue Ash (G-1637)
Rainbow Data Systems Inc ....E 937 431-8000
  Beavercreek (G-1180)
Resource International Inc ....C 614 823-4949
  Columbus (G-8523)
Retalix Usa Inc ....C 937 384-2277
  Miamisburg (G-14213)
Rippe & Kingston Systems Inc ....D 513 977-4578
  Cincinnati (G-4375)
Roadtrippers Inc ....E 917 688-9887
  Cincinnati (G-4387)
Sadler-Necamp Financial Svcs ....E 513 489-5477
  Cincinnati (G-4421)
Saec/Kinetic Vision Inc ....C 513 793-4959
  Cincinnati (G-4422)
Sanctuary Software Studio Inc ....E 330 666-9690
  Fairlawn (G-10847)
Sap America Inc ....E 513 762-7630
  Cincinnati (G-4433)
Sawdey Solution Services Inc ....E 937 490-4060
  Beavercreek (G-1236)
Scientific Forming Tech Corp ....E 614 451-8330
  Columbus (G-8610)
Seapine Software Inc ....E 513 754-1655
  Mason (G-13636)
Seifert & Group Inc ....D 330 833-2700
  Massillon (G-13727)
Service Pronet Inc ....E 614 874-4300
  Columbus (G-8623)
Shoptech Industrial Sftwr ....D 513 985-9900
  Cincinnati (G-4471)
Siemens Product Life Mgmt Sftw ....D 513 576-2400
  Milford (G-14431)
Software Answers Inc ....E 440 526-0095
  Brecksville (G-1806)
Solutions Through Innovative T ....D 937 320-9994
  Beavercreek (G-1187)
Sordyl & Associates Inc ....E 419 866-6811
  Maumee (G-13854)
Srinsoft Inc ....E 614 893-6535
  Dublin (G-10339)
Staid Logic LLC. ....E 309 807-0575
  Columbus (G-8682)
Strategic Data Systems Inc ....E 513 772-7374
  Cincinnati (G-4549)
Streamlink Software Inc ....E 216 377-5500
  Cleveland (G-6473)
Sumaria Systems Inc ....D 937 429-6070
  Beavercreek (G-1188)
Sumtotal Systems LLC ....C 352 264-2800
  Columbus (G-8711)
Sunstorm Games LLC ....E 216 403-4820
  Beachwood (G-1109)
Synoran ....E 614 236-4014
  Columbus (G-8724)
Systems Alternatives Intl ....E 419 891-1100
  Maumee (G-13860)
Systems Evolution Inc ....D 513 459-1992
  Cincinnati (G-4564)
T-Cetra LLC. ....E 877 956-2359
  Dublin (G-10352)
Tata America Intl Corp ....B 513 677-6500
  Milford (G-14435)

Tech Mahindra (americas) Inc ....D 216 912-2002
  Cleveland (G-6508)
Thinkware Incorporated ....E 513 598-3300
  Cincinnati (G-4600)
Timeware Inc ....D 330 963-2700
  Twinsburg (G-18327)
TOA Technologies Inc ....D 216 360-8106
  Beachwood (G-1112)
Tour De Force Inc ....E 419 425-4800
  Findlay (G-10970)
Tradeglobal LLC ....D 866 345-5835
  West Chester (G-19092)
Triad Governmental Systems ....E 937 376-5446
  Xenia (G-19930)
Tridec Technologies LLC ....E 937 938-8160
  Huber Heights (G-11959)
Tyco International MGT Co LLC ....E 888 787-8324
  Cincinnati (G-4658)
Unicon International Inc ....C 614 861-7070
  Columbus (G-8798)
Vediscovery LLC ....E 216 241-3443
  Cleveland (G-6622)
▼ Ventech Solutions Inc ....D 614 757-1167
  Cleveland (G-6837)
Virtual Hold Technology LLC ....D 330 670-2200
  Akron (G-489)
Widepint Intgrted Sltions Corp ....E 614 410-1587
  Columbus (G-8901)
Wtw Delaware Holdings LLC ....C 216 937-4000
  Cleveland (G-6693)
Yashco Systems Inc ....E 614 467-4600
  Hilliard (G-11831)

7372 Prepackaged Software

Advanced Prgrm Resources Inc ....E 614 761-9994
  Dublin (G-10119)
Agile Global Solutions Inc ....E 916 655-7745
  Independence (G-12041)
Air Force US Dept of ....B 937 656-2354
  Dayton (G-9156)
Auto Des Sys Inc ....E 614 488-7984
  Upper Arlington (G-18394)
Besttransportcom Inc ....E 614 888-2378
  Columbus (G-7031)
Cimx LLC ....E 513 248-7700
  Cincinnati (G-3217)
Cincom Systems Inc ....C 513 459-1470
  Mason (G-13555)
Citynet Ohio LLC. ....E 614 364-7881
  Columbus (G-7214)
Clinicl Otcms Mngmnt Syst LLC ....D 330 650-9900
  Broadview Heights (G-1828)
Creative Microsystems Inc ....D 937 836-4499
  Englewood (G-10583)
Dakota Software Corporation ....D 216 765-7100
  Cleveland (G-5403)
Datatrak International Inc ....E 440 443-0082
  Mayfield Heights (G-13872)
Delta Media Group Inc ....D 330 493-0350
  Canton (G-2283)
Digital Controls Corporation ....D 513 746-8118
  Miamisburg (G-14166)
Drb Systems LLC ....D 330 645-3299
  Akron (G-195)
Eci Macola/Max LLC ....C 978 539-6186
  Dublin (G-10213)
Edict Systems Inc ....E 937 429-4288
  Beavercreek (G-1151)
▼ Einstruction Corporation ....D 330 746-3015
  Youngstown (G-20027)
EMC Corporation ....E 216 606-2000
  Independence (G-12069)
▲ Esko-Graphics Inc ....D 937 454-1721
  Miamisburg (G-14168)
Estreamz Inc ....E 513 278-7836
  Cincinnati (G-3516)
Explorys Inc ....D 216 767-4700
  Cleveland (G-5503)
Exponentia US Inc ....E 614 944-5103
  Columbus (G-7548)
Finastra USA Corporation ....E 937 435-2335
  Miamisburg (G-14171)
Flexnova Inc ....E 216 288-6961
  Cleveland (G-5546)
Flypaper Studio Inc ....E 602 801-2208
  Cincinnati (G-3574)
Foundation Software Inc ....D 330 220-8383
  Strongsville (G-17305)
▼ Gracie Plum Investments Inc ....E 740 355-9029
  Portsmouth (G-16141)

Hab Inc ....E 608 785-7650
  Solon (G-16856)
Honeywell International Inc ....D 513 745-7200
  Cincinnati (G-3724)
Hyland Software Inc ....A 440 788-5000
  Westlake (G-19355)
Infoaccessnet LLC ....E 216 328-0100
  Cleveland (G-5750)
Juniper Networks Inc ....D 614 932-1432
  Dublin (G-10262)
Mapsys Inc ....E 614 255-7258
  Columbus (G-8014)
Matrix Management Solutions ....C 330 470-3700
  Canton (G-2392)
Microsoft Corporation ....E 614 719-5900
  Columbus (G-6825)
Microsoft Corporation ....E 216 986-1440
  Cleveland (G-5980)
Microsoft Corporation ....D 513 339-2800
  Mason (G-13619)
Mim Software Inc ....E 216 896-9798
  Beachwood (G-1082)
Netsmart Technologies Inc ....E 440 942-4040
  Solon (G-16877)
Nextmed Systems Inc ....E 216 674-0511
  Cincinnati (G-4114)
Nsa Technologies LLC ....C 330 576-4600
  Akron (G-353)
Ohio Cllbrtive Lrng Sltons Inc ....E 216 595-5289
  Beachwood (G-1089)
Onx USA LLC ....E 440 569-2300
  Cleveland (G-6136)
Open Text Inc ....E 614 658-3588
  Hilliard (G-11804)
Oracle Corporation ....C 513 826-5632
  Beavercreek (G-1174)
Oracle Systems Corporation ....E 513 826-6000
  Beavercreek (G-1092)
Parallel Technologies Inc ....D 614 798-9700
  Dublin (G-10304)
Patrick J Burke & Co ....D 513 455-8200
  Cincinnati (G-4212)
Patriot Software LLC ....D 877 968-7147
  Canton (G-2436)
Peco II Inc ....D 614 431-0694
  Columbus (G-8433)
Preemptive Solutions LLC ....E 440 443-7200
  Cleveland (G-6228)
Quest Software Inc ....D 614 336-9223
  Dublin (G-10315)
Rebiz LLC ....E 844 467-3249
  Cleveland (G-6291)
Retalix Inc ....C 937 384-2277
  Miamisburg (G-14212)
Revolution Group Inc ....D 614 212-1111
  Westerville (G-19207)
Rivals Sports Grille LLC ....E 216 267-0005
  Middleburg Heights (G-14258)
Sanctuary Software Studio Inc ....E 330 666-9690
  Fairlawn (G-10847)
Seapine Software Inc ....E 513 754-1655
  Mason (G-13636)
Sigmatek Systems LLC ....D 513 674-0005
  Cincinnati (G-4481)
Skillsoft Corporation ....D 216 524-5200
  Independence (G-12123)
Software Management Group ....E 513 618-2165
  Cincinnati (G-4504)
Software Solutions Inc ....E 513 932-6667
  Lebanon (G-12504)
Starwin Industries LLC ....E 937 293-8568
  Dayton (G-9790)
Symantec Corporation ....D 216 643-6700
  Independence (G-12127)
Tata America Intl Corp ....B 513 677-6500
  Milford (G-14435)
Thinkware Incorporated ....E 513 598-3300
  Cincinnati (G-4600)
Tmw Systems Inc ....C 216 831-6606
  Mayfield Heights (G-13882)
Triad Governmental Systems ....E 937 376-5446
  Xenia (G-19930)
◆ Turning Technologies LLC ....C 330 746-3015
  Youngstown (G-20228)
Virtual Hold Technology LLC ....D 330 670-2200
  Akron (G-489)
Workspeed Management LLC ....E 917 369-9025
  Solon (G-16917)
Zipscene LLC ....D 513 201-5174
  Cincinnati (G-4819)

S I C

7373 Computer Integrated Systems Design

Acadia Solutions Inc ....E 614 505-6135
Dublin *(G-10118)*

Aclara Technologies LLC ....C 440 528-7200
Solon *(G-16814)*

Advanced Prgrm Resources Inc ....E 614 761-9994
Dublin *(G-10119)*

Advanced Service Tech LLC ....E 937 435-4376
Miamisburg *(G-14137)*

Afidence Inc ....E 513 234-5822
Mason *(G-13537)*

Aisling Enterprises LLC ....E 937 203-1757
Centerville *(G-2619)*

Altamira Technologies Corp ....C 937 490-4804
Beavercreek *(G-1124)*

Assured Information SEC Inc ....D 937 427-9720
Beavercreek *(G-1127)*

▲ Ats Carolina Inc ....D 803 324-9300
Lewis Center *(G-12526)*

Attevo Inc ....D 216 928-2800
Beachwood *(G-1032)*

Axia Consulting Inc ....D 614 675-4050
Columbus *(G-7008)*

Baxter Hodell Donnelly Preston ....C 513 271-1634
Cincinnati *(G-3025)*

Bpi Infrmtion Systems Ohio Inc ....E 440 717-4112
Brecksville *(G-1771)*

Brandmuscle Inc ....C 216 464-4342
Cleveland *(G-5074)*

Cameo Solutions Inc ....E 513 645-4220
West Chester *(G-18880)*

Cdo Technologies Inc ....D 937 258-0022
Dayton *(G-9164)*

▲ Cincinnati Bell Inc ....D 513 397-9900
Cincinnati *(G-3226)*

Cincinnati Training Trml Svcs ....E 513 563-4474
Cincinnati *(G-3273)*

Cincom Intrnational Operations ....B 513 612-2300
Cincinnati *(G-3285)*

Cincom Systems Inc ....B 513 612-2300
Cincinnati *(G-3286)*

Cisco Systems Inc ....C 330 523-2000
Richfield *(G-16350)*

Commercial Time Sharing Inc ....E 330 644-3059
Akron *(G-148)*

Commsys Inc ....E 937 220-4990
Moraine *(G-14634)*

Concentrix Cvg Corporation ....A 513 723-7000
Cincinnati *(G-3348)*

Cott Systems Inc ....D 614 847-4405
Columbus *(G-7379)*

Courtview Justice Solutions ....E 330 497-0033
Canton *(G-2271)*

Creative Microsystems Inc ....D 937 836-4499
Englewood *(G-10583)*

Dedicated Tech Services Inc ....E 614 309-0059
Dublin *(G-10197)*

Deemsys Inc ....D 614 322-9928
Gahanna *(G-11117)*

Definitive Solutions Co Inc ....D 513 719-9100
Cincinnati *(G-3417)*

Devcare Solutions Ltd ....E 614 221-2277
Columbus *(G-7439)*

Document Tech Systems Ltd ....D 330 928-5311
Cuyahoga Falls *(G-9088)*

Drb Systems LLC ....C 330 645-3299
Akron *(G-195)*

Dyncorp ....C 513 942-6500
West Chester *(G-18916)*

Dyncorp ....D 513 569-7415
Cincinnati *(G-3460)*

E&I Solutions LLC ....E 937 912-0288
Beavercreek *(G-1150)*

Easy2 Technologies Inc ....E 216 479-0482
Cleveland *(G-5461)*

Evanhoe & Associates Inc ....E 937 235-2995
Dayton *(G-9173)*

Honeywell International Inc ....D 513 745-7200
Cincinnati *(G-3724)*

ID Networks Inc ....E 440 992-0062
Ashtabula *(G-741)*

Infor (us) Inc ....B 678 319-8000
Columbus *(G-7816)*

Infotelecom Holdings LLC ....B 216 373-4811
Cleveland *(G-5753)*

Juniper Networks Inc ....D 614 932-1432
Dublin *(G-10262)*

Knotice LLC ....D 800 801-4194
Akron *(G-304)*

Leidos Inc ....D 937 431-2270
Beavercreek *(G-1164)*

Manatron Inc ....E 937 431-4000
Beavercreek *(G-1228)*

Manifest Solutions Corp ....D 614 930-2800
Upper Arlington *(G-18401)*

Matrix Management Solutions ....C 330 470-3700
Canton *(G-2392)*

Microman Inc ....E 614 923-8000
Dublin *(G-10280)*

Millenium Control Systems LLC ....D 440 510-0050
Eastlake *(G-10432)*

Natural Resources Ohio Dept ....E 614 265-6852
Columbus *(G-8163)*

Northern Datacomm Corp ....E 330 665-0344
Akron *(G-351)*

Northrop Grumman Systems Corp ....E 937 429-6450
Beavercreek *(G-1232)*

Northrop Grumman Technical ....D 937 320-3100
Beavercreek Township *(G-1255)*

Ohio State University ....E 614 728-8100
Columbus *(G-8338)*

Online Mega Sellers Corp ....D 888 384-6468
Toledo *(G-17964)*

Onx Entrprise Solutions US Inc ....D 440 569-2300
Mayfield Heights *(G-13878)*

Pcms Datafit Inc ....D 513 587-3100
Blue Ash *(G-1629)*

Peerless Technologies Corp ....D 937 490-5000
Beavercreek Township *(G-1257)*

Pegasus Technical Services Inc ....E 513 793-0094
Cincinnati *(G-4223)*

Pomeroy It Solutions Sls Inc ....E 937 439-9682
Dayton *(G-9698)*

Pomeroy It Solutions Sls Inc ....E 440 717-1364
Brecksville *(G-1798)*

Presidio Infrastructure ....D 419 241-8303
Toledo *(G-17986)*

Presidio Infrastructure ....D 614 381-1400
Dublin *(G-10310)*

Rainbow Data Systems Inc ....E 937 431-8000
Beavercreek *(G-1180)*

Ranac Computer Corporation ....E 317 844-0141
Moraine *(G-14692)*

Reynolds and Reynolds Company ....A 937 485-2000
Kettering *(G-12299)*

Robots and Pencils LP ....D 587 350-4095
Beachwood *(G-1101)*

Rockwell Automation Ohio Inc ....D 513 576-6151
Milford *(G-14428)*

Rolta Advizex Technologies LLC ....E 216 901-1818
Independence *(G-12117)*

Rovisys Building Tech LLC ....E 330 954-7600
Aurora *(G-841)*

Sgi Matrix LLC ....D 937 438-9033
Miamisburg *(G-14219)*

Soaring Eagle Inc ....D 330 385-5579
East Liverpool *(G-10418)*

Software Solutions Inc ....E 513 932-6667
Lebanon *(G-12504)*

Sogeti USA LLC ....D 614 847-4477
Westerville *(G-19210)*

Sterling Buying Group LLC ....E 513 564-9000
Cincinnati *(G-4543)*

Suite 224 Internet ....E 440 593-7113
Conneaut *(G-8959)*

Sumaria Systems Inc ....D 937 429-6070
Dayton *(G-1188)*

▲ Systemax Manufacturing Inc ....C 937 368-2300
Dayton *(G-9805)*

Sytronics Inc ....E 937 431-6100
Beavercreek *(G-1189)*

Talx Corporation ....E 614 527-9404
Hilliard *(G-11819)*

Tata America Intl Corp ....B 513 677-6500
Milford *(G-14435)*

Teknobility LLC ....E 216 255-9433
Medina *(G-14009)*

Telligen Tech Inc ....E 614 934-1554
Columbus *(G-8739)*

Thinkpath Engineering Svcs LLC ....E 937 291-8374
Miamisburg *(G-14229)*

Tsi Inc ....E 419 468-1855
Galion *(G-11184)*

Twism Enterprises LLC ....E 513 800-1098
Cincinnati *(G-4657)*

Tyco International MGT Co LLC ....E 888 787-8324
Cincinnati *(G-4658)*

United Technical Support Svcs ....D 330 562-3330
Streetsboro *(G-17275)*

Velocity Grtest Phone Ever Inc ....B 419 868-9983
Holland *(G-11924)*

▼ Ventech Solutions Inc ....D 614 757-1167
Columbus *(G-6837)*

Warnock Tanner & Assoc Inc ....E 419 897-6999
Maumee *(G-13867)*

Wescom Solutions Inc ....E 513 831-1207
Milford *(G-14443)*

7374 Data & Computer Processing & Preparation

1st All File Recovery Usa ....E 800 399-7150
Shaker Heights *(G-16701)*

Aero Fulfillment Services Corp ....D 800 225-7145
Mason *(G-13536)*

Alliance Data Systems Corp ....B 614 729-4000
Columbus *(G-6894)*

Aurora Imaging Company ....E 614 761-1390
Dublin *(G-10141)*

Automatic Data Processing Inc ....C 216 447-1980
Independence *(G-12048)*

Automatic Data Processing Inc ....C 614 895-7700
Westerville *(G-19226)*

Btas Inc ....C 937 431-9431
Beavercreek *(G-1135)*

Cache Next Generation LLC ....E 614 850-9444
Hilliard *(G-11752)*

Cbc Companies Inc ....D 614 538-6100
Columbus *(G-7142)*

Central Command Inc ....E 330 723-2062
Columbia Station *(G-6771)*

Change Hlthcare Operations LLC ....E 330 405-0001
Hudson *(G-11970)*

Change Hlthcare Operations LLC ....E 216 589-5878
Cleveland *(G-5168)*

Checkfree Services Corporation ....A 614 564-3000
Dublin *(G-10169)*

▲ Cincinnati Bell Inc ....D 513 397-9900
Cincinnati *(G-3226)*

City of Cleveland ....D 216 664-2430
Cleveland *(G-5194)*

Cleveland State University ....E 216 687-3786
Cleveland *(G-5289)*

Clubessential LLC ....E 800 448-1475
Blue Ash *(G-1530)*

Coleman Professional Svcs Inc ....C 330 628-2275
Akron *(G-147)*

Coleman Professional Svcs Inc ....C 330 673-1347
Kent *(G-12223)*

Concentrix Cvg Corporation ....A 513 723-7000
Cincinnati *(G-3348)*

Convergys Gvrnment Sltions LLC ....D 513 723-7006
Cincinnati *(G-3359)*

County of Cuyahoga ....C 216 443-8011
Cleveland *(G-5364)*

Csi Complete Inc ....E 800 343-0641
Plain City *(G-16048)*

Ctrac Inc ....E 440 572-1000
Cleveland *(G-5388)*

Datatrak International Inc ....E 440 443-0082
Mayfield Heights *(G-13872)*

Decisionone Corporation ....E 614 883-0228
Urbancrest *(G-18448)*

Definitive Solutions Co Inc ....D 513 719-9100
Cincinnati *(G-3417)*

Early Express Services Inc ....E 937 223-5801
Dayton *(G-9400)*

Eliassen Group LLC ....E 781 205-8100
Blue Ash *(G-1550)*

Enterprise Data Management Inc ....E 513 791-7272
Blue Ash *(G-1554)*

Enterprise Services LLC ....D 740 423-9501
Belpre *(G-1402)*

Expedata LLC ....E 937 439-6767
Dayton *(G-9423)*

Fiserv Inc ....D 412 577-3326
Dublin *(G-10227)*

▼ Gracie Plum Investments Inc ....E 740 355-9029
Portsmouth *(G-16141)*

Great Lakes Publishing Company ....D 216 771-2833
Cleveland *(G-5630)*

Hyperquake LLC ....E 513 563-6555
Cincinnati *(G-3748)*

Illumination Works LLC ....D 937 938-1321
Beavercreek *(G-1157)*

Infovision 21 Inc ....E 614 761-8844
Dublin *(G-10256)*

Integrated Data Services Inc ....D 937 656-5496
Dayton *(G-9515)*

▲ Integrated Marketing Tech Inc ....D 330 225-3550
Brunswick *(G-1933)*

Interact One Inc ....E 513 469-7042
Blue Ash *(G-1585)*

International Data MGT Inc ....E 330 869-8500
Fairlawn *(G-10835)*

Karcher Group Inc ....E 330 493-6141
North Canton *(G-15215)*

Kuno Creative Group LLC ....E 440 225-4144
Avon *(G-891)*

Lake Data Center Inc ....D 440 944-2020
Wickliffe *(G-19467)*

Lou-Ray Associates Inc ....E 330 220-1999
Brunswick *(G-1936)*

Mast Technology Services Inc ....A 614 415-7000
Columbus *(G-8036)*

Medical Mutual Services LLC ....C 440 878-4800
Strongsville *(G-17331)*

Merchant Data Service Inc ....C 937 847-6585
Miamisburg *(G-14188)*

Midland Council Governments ....E 330 264-6047
Wooster *(G-19745)*

▲ Midwest Tape LLC ....B 419 868-9370
Holland *(G-11898)*

Mri Software LLC ....E 800 321-8770
Solon *(G-16874)*

Northwest Ohio Computer Assn ....D 419 267-5565
Archbold *(G-634)*

Office World Inc ....E 419 991-4694
Lima *(G-12791)*

Personalized Data Corporation ....E 216 289-2200
Cleveland *(G-6198)*

Quadax Inc ....E 614 882-1200
Westerville *(G-19296)*

Racksquared LLC ....E 614 737-8812
Columbus *(G-8483)*

Rebiz LLC ....E 844 467-3249
Cleveland *(G-6291)*

Record Express LLC ....E 513 685-7329
Batavia *(G-1008)*

Rgis LLC ....D 248 651-2511
Reynoldsburg *(G-16328)*

Rurbanc Data Services Inc ....D 419 782-2530
Defiance *(G-9938)*

Sedlak Management Consultants ....E 216 206-4700
Cleveland *(G-6391)*

Service Pronet Inc ....E 614 874-4300
Columbus *(G-8623)*

Sourcelink Ohio LLC ....C 937 885-8000
Miamisburg *(G-14224)*

Speedeon Data LLC ....E 440 264-2100
Cleveland *(G-6446)*

Sumaria Systems Inc ....D 937 429-6070
Beavercreek *(G-1188)*

Thinkware Incorporated ....E 513 598-3300
Cincinnati *(G-4600)*

Universal Enterprises Inc ....C 419 529-3500
Ontario *(G-15577)*

Vediscovery LLC ....E 216 241-3443
Cleveland *(G-6622)*

Worldpay LLC ....B 877 713-5964
Symmes Twp *(G-17468)*

7375 Information Retrieval Svcs

Acxiom Corporation ....E 216 520-3181
Independence *(G-12038)*

AGS Custom Graphics Inc ....D 330 963-7770
Macedonia *(G-13058)*

Amaxx Inc ....E 614 486-3481
Dublin *(G-10128)*

Cobalt Group Inc ....D 614 876-4013
Hilliard *(G-11756)*

Com Net Inc ....D 419 739-3100
Wapakoneta *(G-18639)*

Community Isp Inc ....E 419 867-6060
Toledo *(G-17672)*

Doylestown Communications ....E 330 658-7000
Doylestown *(G-10111)*

Ecommerce LLC ....D 800 861-9394
Columbus *(G-7499)*

Hkm Drect Mkt Cmmnications Inc ....C 216 651-9500
Cleveland *(G-5696)*

Innovative Technologies Corp ....D 937 252-2145
Dayton *(G-9179)*

Intellicorp Records Inc ....D 216 450-5200
Beachwood *(G-1067)*

▲ Lexisnexis Group ....C 937 865-6800
Miamisburg *(G-14185)*

Medical Mutual Services LLC ....C 440 878-4800
Strongsville *(G-17331)*

Mirifex Systems LLC ....C 440 891-1210
Cleveland *(G-6001)*

Oclc Inc ....A 614 764-6000
Dublin *(G-10295)*

One Source Technology LLC ....E 216 420-1700
Cleveland *(G-6134)*

Png Telecommunications Inc ....D 513 942-7900
Cincinnati *(G-4260)*

Relx Inc ....B 937 865-6800
Miamisburg *(G-14209)*

▲ Repro Acquisition Company LLC ....E 216 738-3800
Cleveland *(G-6309)*

Salvagedata Recovery LLC ....E 914 600-2434
Cleveland *(G-6367)*

Seifert & Group LLC ....D 330 833-2700
Massillon *(G-13727)*

Simplified Logistics LLC ....E 440 250-8912
Westlake *(G-19406)*

Title First Agency Inc ....E 614 224-9207
Columbus *(G-8759)*

TSC Communications Inc ....E 419 739-2200
Wapakoneta *(G-18657)*

Verisk Crime Analytics Inc ....E 614 865-6000
Worthington *(G-19857)*

Verizon Business Global LLC ....E 614 219-2317
Hilliard *(G-11826)*

Webmd Health Corp 330 425-3241
Twinsburg *(G-18337)*

7376 Computer Facilities Management Svcs

Ability Network Inc ....E 513 943-8888
Cincinnati *(G-2840)*

Change Hlth Prac MGT Solns Grp ....E 937 291-7850
Miamisburg *(G-14151)*

City of Cleveland ....E 216 664-2941
Cleveland *(G-5192)*

Computer Sciences Corporation ....E 937 904-5113
Dayton *(G-9166)*

Computer Sciences Corporation ....C 614 801-2343
Grove City *(G-11421)*

Dedicated Tech Services Inc ....E 614 309-0059
Dublin *(G-10197)*

Dyn Marine Services Inc ....E 937 427-2663
Beavercreek *(G-1149)*

E&I Solutions LLC ....E 937 912-0288
Beavercreek *(G-1150)*

Evanhoe & Associates Inc ....E 937 235-2995
Dayton *(G-9173)*

General Electric Company ....C 513 583-3500
Cincinnati *(G-3610)*

Jjr Solutions LLC ....E 937 912-0288
Beavercreek *(G-1159)*

Jyg Innovations LLC ....E 937 630-3858
Dayton *(G-9531)*

Selecttech Services Corp ....C 937 438-9905
Centerville *(G-2633)*

Technical Assurance Inc ....E 440 953-3147
Willoughby *(G-19575)*

7377 Computer Rental & Leasing

Information Builders Inc ....E 513 891-2338
Montgomery *(G-14595)*

Pomeroy It Solutions Sls Inc ....E 440 717-1364
Brecksville *(G-1798)*

7378 Computer Maintenance & Repair

Ascendtech Inc ....E 216 458-1101
Willoughby *(G-19506)*

Bpi Infrmtion Systems Ohio Inc ....E 440 717-4112
Brecksville *(G-1771)*

Bsl - Applied Laser Tech LLC ....E 216 663-8181
Cleveland *(G-5097)*

Butler County of Ohio ....E 513 887-3418
Hamilton *(G-11571)*

Cincinnati Copiers Inc ....C 513 769-0606
Blue Ash *(G-1525)*

Cincinnati Voice and Data ....D 513 683-4127
Loveland *(G-12983)*

County of Montgomery ....B 937 496-3103
Dayton *(G-9333)*

CTS Construction Inc ....D 513 489-8290
Cincinnati *(G-3385)*

Datatech Depot (east) Inc ....E 513 860-5651
West Chester *(G-18908)*

Decisionone Corporation ....E 614 883-0228
Urbancrest *(G-18448)*

Diebold Nixdorf Incorporated ....D 513 682-6216
Hamilton *(G-11590)*

DMC Technology Group ....E 419 535-2900
Toledo *(G-17703)*

Efix Computer Repair & Svc LLC ....E 937 985-4447
Kettering *(G-12292)*

Enterprise Data Management Inc ....E 513 791-7272
Blue Ash *(G-1554)*

Evanhoe & Associates Inc ....E 937 235-2995
Dayton *(G-9173)*

Fiserv Solutions LLC ....C 412 577-3000
Dublin *(G-10228)*

Government Acquisitions Inc ....E 513 721-8700
Cincinnati *(G-3628)*

Great Lakes Computer Corp ....D 440 937-1100
Avon *(G-883)*

Intelligent Information Inc ....E 513 860-4233
West Chester *(G-19061)*

Mt Business Technologies Inc ....C 419 529-6100
Mansfield *(G-13225)*

Northcoast Duplicating Inc ....C 216 573-6681
Cleveland *(G-6087)*

Park Place Technologies LLC ....E 603 617-7123
Cleveland *(G-6169)*

Park Place Technologies LLC ....B 610 544-0571
Mayfield Heights *(G-13879)*

Park Place Technologies LLC ....C 877 778-8707
Mayfield Heights *(G-13880)*

Perry Pro Tech Inc ....D 419 228-1360
Lima *(G-12720)*

Pomeroy It Solutions Sls Inc ....E 440 717-1364
Brecksville *(G-1798)*

Positive Bus Solutions Inc ....D 513 772-2255
Cincinnati *(G-4265)*

Realm Technologies LLC ....E 513 297-3095
Lebanon *(G-12497)*

Resource One Cmpt Systems Inc ....D 614 485-4800
Worthington *(G-19844)*

Sjn Data Center LLC ....E 513 386-7871
Cincinnati *(G-4488)*

Systems Alternatives Intl ....E 419 891-1100
Maumee *(G-13860)*

Uptime Corporation ....E 216 661-1655
Brooklyn Heights *(G-1885)*

Vertiv Corporation ....E 614 841-6400
Westerville *(G-19215)*

Wellington Technologies Inc ....E 440 238-4377
Westlake *(G-19421)*

Xerox Corporation ....D 216 642-7806
Cleveland *(G-6697)*

7379 Computer Related Svcs, NEC

1 Edi Source Inc ....C 440 519-7800
Solon *(G-16812)*

Advanced Prgrm Resources Inc ....E 614 761-9994
Dublin *(G-10119)*

Advantage Technology Group ....E 513 563-3560
West Chester *(G-18860)*

Affiliated Resource Group Inc ....D 614 889-6555
Dublin *(G-10121)*

American Bus Solutions Inc ....D 614 888-2227
Lewis Center *(G-12522)*

American Systems Cnsulting Inc ....D 614 282-7180
Dublin *(G-10134)*

Arszman & Lyons LLC ....E 513 527-4900
Blue Ash *(G-1508)*

Ascendtech Inc ....E 216 458-1101
Willoughby *(G-19506)*

Atos It Solutions and Svcs Inc ....B 513 336-1000
Mason *(G-13543)*

Attevo Inc ....D 216 928-2800
Beachwood *(G-1032)*

Baseline Consulting LLC ....D 440 336-5382
Cleveland *(G-5038)*

Bcg Systems That Work Inc ....E 330 864-4816
Akron *(G-90)*

Blue Chip Consulting Group LLC ....E 216 503-6001
Seven Hills *(G-16672)*

Cache Next Generation LLC ....D 614 850-9444
Hilliard *(G-11752)*

Cadre Computer Resources Co ....E 513 762-7350
Cincinnati *(G-3103)*

Capgemini America Inc ....B 678 427-6642
Dayton *(G-9274)*

Cardinal Solutions Group Inc ....D 513 984-6700
Cincinnati *(G-3118)*

Cbiz Operations Inc ....D 216 447-9000
Cleveland *(G-5140)*

Cbiz Technologies LLC ....E 216 447-9000
Independence *(G-12055)*

▼ Cbts Technology Solutions LLC ....B 513 841-2287
Cincinnati *(G-3137)*

Cgi Technologies Solutions Inc ....C 216 687-1480
Cleveland *(G-5163)*

Cgi Technologies Solutions Inc....D....614 228-2245
Columbus (G-7173)
Cgi Technologies Solutions Inc....D....614 880-2200
Columbus (G-6805)
▲ Cincinnati Bell Inc....D....513 397-9900
Cincinnati (G-3226)
Cincinnati Bell Techno....D....513 841-6700
Cincinnati (G-3227)
Cincinnati Training Trml Svcs....D....513 563-4474
Cincinnati (G-3273)
Cincom Systems Inc....E....513 389-2344
Cincinnati (G-3287)
Cisco Systems Inc....A....937 427-4264
Beavercreek (G-1140)
Comptech Computer Tech Inc....E....937 228-2667
Dayton (G-9314)
Comresource Inc....E....614 221-6348
Columbus (G-7346)
Creek Technologies Company....C....937 272-4581
Beavercreek (G-1142)
CSRA LLC....B....937 429-9774
Beavercreek (G-1143)
Datacomm Tech....E....614 755-5100
Reynoldsburg (G-16296)
Datafield Inc....C....614 847-9600
Worthington (G-19803)
Datalysys LLC....E....614 495-0260
Dublin (G-10196)
Dayhuff Group LLC....E....614 854-9999
Worthington (G-19804)
Dedicated Tech Services Inc....E....614 309-0059
Dublin (G-10197)
Definitive Solutions Co Inc....D....513 719-9100
Cincinnati (G-3417)
Digital Controls Corporation....D....513 746-8118
Miamisburg (G-14166)
Digital Management Inc....D....240 223-4800
Mason (G-13573)
Diversified Systems Inc....E....614 476-9939
Westerville (G-19249)
DMC Technology Group....E....419 535-2900
Toledo (G-17703)
E&I Solutions LLC....E....937 912-0288
Beavercreek (G-1150)
E-Mek Technologies LLC....D....937 424-3163
Dayton (G-9399)
E2b Teknologies Inc....E....440 352-4700
Chardon (G-2693)
Echo-Tape LLC....E....614 892-3246
Columbus (G-7498)
▼ Einstruction Corporation....D....330 746-3015
Youngstown (G-20027)
Enterprise Data Management Inc....E....513 791-7272
Blue Ash (G-1554)
Enterprise Systems Sftwr LLC....D....419 841-3179
Sylvania (G-17423)
Entrust Solutions LLC....E....614 504-4900
Columbus (G-7519)
Entrypoint Consulting LLC....D....216 674-9070
Cleveland (G-5484)
Enviro It LLC....E....614 453-0709
Columbus (G-7520)
Estreamz Inc....E....513 278-7836
Cincinnati (G-3516)
Evanhoe & Associates Inc....E....937 235-2995
Dayton (G-9173)
Everest Technologies Inc....E....614 436-3120
Worthington (G-19808)
Fhc Enterprises LLC....E....614 271-3513
Columbus (G-7574)
Fit Technologies LLC....E....216 583-5000
Cleveland (G-5540)
Forsythe Technology LLC....D....513 697-5100
Cincinnati (G-3578)
Franklin Cmpt Svcs Group Inc....E....614 431-3327
New Albany (G-14854)
Genesis Corp....D....330 597-4100
Akron (G-234)
Genesis Corp....E....614 934-1211
Columbus (G-7657)
Girard Technologies Inc....E....330 783-2495
Youngstown (G-20050)
GP Strategies Corporation....E....513 583-8810
Cincinnati (G-3629)
Great Nthrn Cnsulting Svcs Inc....E....614 890-9999
Columbus (G-7689)
Greentree Group Inc....D....937 490-5500
Dayton (G-9477)
Illumination Works LLC....D....937 938-1321
Beavercreek (G-1157)
Indecon Solutions LLC....E....614 799-1850
Dublin (G-10254)
Information Control Co LLC....B....614 523-3070
Columbus (G-7817)
Infovision 21 Inc....E....614 761-8844
Dublin (G-10256)
Integrated Solutions and....E....513 826-1932
Dayton (G-9516)
Integrity Information Tech Inc....E....937 846-1769
New Carlisle (G-14891)
Interactive Bus Systems Inc....E....513 984-2205
Cincinnati (G-3775)
International Association of....E....330 628-3012
Canton (G-2357)
International Bus Mchs Corp....B....917 406-7400
Beavercreek (G-1158)
Intralot Inc....E....440 268-2900
Strongsville (G-17316)
Itelligence Inc....C....513 956-2000
Cincinnati (G-3790)
Itelligence Outsourcing Inc....D....513 956-2000
Cincinnati (G-3791)
Jaekle Group Inc....E....330 405-9353
Macedonia (G-13076)
Jjr Solutions LLC....E....937 912-0288
Beavercreek (G-1159)
Jyg Innovations LLC....E....937 630-3858
Dayton (G-9531)
Kristi Britton....E....614 868-7612
Reynoldsburg (G-16315)
Laketec Communications Inc....E....440 892-2001
North Olmsted (G-15295)
Lan Solutions Inc....E....513 469-6500
Blue Ash (G-1594)
Lanco Global Systems Inc....D....937 660-8090
Dayton (G-9557)
Leadership Circle LLC....E....801 518-2980
Whitehouse (G-19450)
Leading Edje LLC....E....614 636-3353
Dublin (G-10268)
Lightwell Inc....D....614 310-2700
Dublin (G-10272)
Link Iq LLC....E....859 983-6080
Dayton (G-9569)
London Computer Systems Inc....D....513 583-0840
Cincinnati (G-3942)
Main Sail LLC....D....216 472-5100
Cleveland (G-5898)
Maxim Technologies Inc....E....614 457-6325
Hilliard (G-11789)
Mt Business Technologies Inc....C....419 529-6100
Mansfield (G-13225)
Myca Mltmdia Trning Sltons LLC....E....513 544-2379
Blue Ash (G-1618)
Natural Resources Ohio Dept....E....614 265-6852
Columbus (G-8163)
Navigtor MGT Prtners Ltd Lblty....E....614 796-0090
Columbus (G-8164)
Netsmart Technologies Inc....E....440 942-4040
Solon (G-16877)
Netwave Corporation....E....614 850-6300
Dublin (G-10289)
Nova Technology Solutions LLC....E....937 426-2596
Beavercreek (G-1173)
Oasis Systems Inc....E....937 426-1295
Beavercreek Township (G-1256)
Ohio State University....C....614 292-4843
Columbus (G-8313)
Onx USA LLC....D....440 569-2300
Cleveland (G-6136)
Optimum Technology Inc....E....614 785-1110
Columbus (G-8380)
PC Connection Services....C....937 382-4800
Wilmington (G-19639)
Perceptis LLC....C....216 458-4122
Cleveland (G-6194)
Phoenix Systems Group Inc....E....330 726-6500
Youngstown (G-20156)
Platinum Technologies....E....216 926-1080
Akron (G-385)
Plus One Communications LLC....B....330 255-4500
Akron (G-386)
Prime Prodata Inc....E....330 497-2578
North Canton (G-15227)
Professional Data Resources Inc....C....513 792-5100
Blue Ash (G-1633)
Qbase LLC....E....888 458-0345
Beavercreek (G-1179)
Quanexus Inc....E....937 885-7272
Dayton (G-9722)
Quest Def Systems Slutions Inc....D....860 573-5950
Cincinnati (G-4326)
R Dorsey & Company Inc....E....614 486-8900
Worthington (G-19840)
R Square Inc....E....216 328-2077
Cleveland (G-6274)
Rainbow Data Systems Inc....E....937 431-8000
Beavercreek (G-1180)
Recker Consulting LLC....D....513 924-5500
Cincinnati (G-4345)
Regent Systems Inc....E....937 640-8010
Dayton (G-9729)
Resolvit Resources LLC....E....703 734-3330
Cincinnati (G-4361)
Revolution Group Inc....D....614 212-1111
Westerville (G-19207)
Rippe & Kingston Systems Inc....D....513 977-4578
Cincinnati (G-4375)
Rockwell Automation Ohio Inc....D....513 576-6151
Milford (G-14428)
Roundtower Technologies LLC....D....513 247-7900
Cincinnati (G-4403)
S & P Solutions Inc....C....440 918-9111
Willoughby Hills (G-19593)
Sjn Data Center LLC....E....513 386-7871
Cincinnati (G-4488)
Snapblox Hosted Solutions LLC....E....866 524-7707
Cincinnati (G-4498)
Sogeti USA LLC....E....614 847-4477
Westerville (G-19210)
Sogeti USA LLC....D....937 433-3334
Dayton (G-9773)
Sogeti USA LLC....C....937 291-8100
Miamisburg (G-14223)
Sogeti USA LLC....E....216 654-2230
Cleveland (G-6419)
Sogeti USA LLC....E....513 824-3000
Blue Ash (G-1651)
Sonit Systems LLC....E....419 446-2151
Archbold (G-640)
Sophisticated Systems Inc....D....614 418-4600
Columbus (G-8660)
Speedeon Data LLC....E....440 264-2100
Cleveland (G-6446)
Staid Logic LLC....E....309 807-0575
Columbus (G-8682)
Strategic Systems Inc....C....614 717-4774
Dublin (G-10343)
Sudhi Infomatics Inc....E....614 882-7309
Westerville (G-19212)
Technology Recovery Group Ltd....D....440 250-9970
Westlake (G-19412)
Techsoft Systems Inc....E....513 772-5010
Cincinnati (G-4580)
Teksystems Inc....E....216 606-3600
Independence (G-12129)
Teksystems Inc....E....513 719-3950
Cincinnati (G-4583)
Telligen Tech Inc....E....614 934-1554
Columbus (G-8739)
Teradata Operations Inc....D....937 242-4030
Miamisburg (G-14228)
Top Gun Sales Performance Inc....E....513 770-0870
Mason (G-13647)
Unicon International Inc....C....614 861-7070
Columbus (G-8798)
United Software Group Inc....C....614 791-3223
Dublin (G-10358)
Vana Solutions LLC....E....937 242-6399
Beavercreek (G-1194)
▼ Ventech Solutions Inc....D....614 757-1167
Columbus (G-6837)
Vertical Knowledge LLC....E....216 920-7790
Chagrin Falls (G-2658)
Vital Resources Inc....E....440 614-5150
Huron (G-12034)
Vitalyst....D....216 201-9070
Cleveland (G-6637)
Warnock Tanner & Assoc Inc....E....419 897-6999
Maumee (G-13867)
Web Yoga Inc....E....937 428-0000
Dayton (G-9870)
Wolcott Group....E....330 666-5900
Medina (G-14015)
Wolters Kluwer Clinical Drug....D....330 650-6506
Hudson (G-12014)
XA Technologies LLC....E....330 787-7846
Youngstown (G-20250)
Zin Technologies Inc....C....440 625-2200
Middleburg Heights (G-14267)

7381 Detective & Armored Car Svcs

1st Advnce SEC Invstgtions Inc E 937 317-4433
Dayton *(G-9194)*
1st Advnce SEC Invstgtions Inc D 937 210-9010
Dayton *(G-9153)*
1st Choice Security Inc C 513 381-6789
Cincinnati *(G-2877)*
Acrux Investigation Agency B 937 842-5780
Lakeview *(G-12332)*
Allied Security LLC B 513 771-3776
Cincinnati *(G-2929)*
Alliedbarton Security Svcs LLC C 614 225-9061
Worthington *(G-19792)*
Alliedbarton Security Svcs LLC E 419 874-9005
Rossford *(G-16459)*
Alpha Security LLC D 330 406-2181
Poland *(G-16080)*
American Svcs & Protection LLC D 614 884-0177
Columbus *(G-6939)*
Anderson SEC & Fire Systems E 937 294-1478
Moraine *(G-14620)*
Anderson Security Inc D 937 294-1478
Moraine *(G-14621)*
Andy Frain Services Inc B 419 897-7909
Maumee *(G-13757)*
Area Wide Protective Inc E 513 321-9889
Fairfield *(G-10696)*
Aset Corporation E 937 890-8881
Vandalia *(G-18504)*
Atlantis Co Inc D 888 807-3272
Cleveland *(G-5020)*
Awp Inc A 330 677-7401
North Canton *(G-15191)*
Brinks Incorporated E 419 729-5389
Toledo *(G-17625)*
Brinks Incorporated E 614 291-1268
Columbus *(G-7073)*
Brinks Incorporated E 614 291-0624
Columbus *(G-7074)*
Brinks Incorporated D 216 621-7493
Cleveland *(G-5080)*
Brinks Incorporated E 330 633-5351
Akron *(G-108)*
Brinks Incorporated D 513 621-9310
Cincinnati *(G-3075)*
Brinks Incorporated E 937 253-9777
Dayton *(G-9162)*
Brinks Incorporated E 330 832-6130
Massillon *(G-13665)*
Brinks Incorporated E 330 758-7379
Youngstown *(G-19974)*
Cal Crim Inc C 513 563-5500
Trenton *(G-18187)*
Cefaratti Investigation & Prcs E 216 696-1161
Cleveland *(G-5145)*
Celebrity Security Inc E 216 671-6425
Cleveland *(G-5146)*
Community Crime Patrol E 614 247-1765
Columbus *(G-7329)*
Cooperate Screening Services E 440 816-0500
Cleveland *(G-5348)*
Corporate Screening Svcs Inc D 440 816-0500
Cleveland *(G-5351)*
D B A Inc E 513 541-6600
Cincinnati *(G-3394)*
Danson Inc C 513 948-0066
Cincinnati *(G-3400)*
Darke County Sheriffs Patrol D 937 548-3399
Greenville *(G-11372)*
Deacon 10 D 216 731-4000
Euclid *(G-10629)*
Donty Horton HM Care Dhhc LLC E 513 463-3442
Cincinnati *(G-3440)*
Dunbar Armored Inc E 513 381-8000
Cincinnati *(G-3454)*
Dunbar Armored Inc E 614 475-1969
Columbus *(G-7477)*
Dunbar Armored Inc E 216 642-5700
Cleveland *(G-5449)*
Dusk To Dawn Protective Svcs E 330 837-9992
Massillon *(G-13676)*
Elite Isg E 937 668-6858
Dayton *(G-9409)*
Falu Corporation E 502 641-8106
Cincinnati *(G-3528)*
Firelands Security Services E 419 627-0562
Sandusky *(G-16606)*
G4s Secure Solutions (usa) C 513 874-0941
Cincinnati *(G-3599)*
G4s Secure Solutions USA Inc C 614 322-5100
Columbus *(G-7642)*
Garda CL Great Lakes Inc E 614 863-4044
Columbus *(G-7646)*
Garda CL Great Lakes Inc E 419 385-2411
Toledo *(G-17754)*
Garda CL Great Lakes Inc B 561 939-7000
Columbus *(G-7647)*
Garda CL Technical Svcs Inc E 937 294-4099
Moraine *(G-14660)*
Genric Inc B 937 553-9250
Marysville *(G-13500)*
Guardsmark LLC C 513 851-5523
Cincinnati *(G-3662)*
Guardsmark LLC E 419 229-9300
Lima *(G-12650)*
Highway Patrol E 740 354-2888
Lucasville *(G-13051)*
Home State Protective Svcs LLC E 513 253-3095
Cincinnati *(G-3722)*
Infinite SEC Solutions LLC E 419 720-5678
Toledo *(G-17820)*
Info Trak Incorporated E 419 747-9296
Mansfield *(G-13186)*
Jefferson Invstgtors Scurities D 740 283-3681
Steubenville *(G-17160)*
Job1usa Inc D 419 255-5005
Toledo *(G-17831)*
Key II Security Inc E 937 339-8530
Troy *(G-18209)*
Kreller Bus Info Group Inc E 513 723-8900
Cincinnati *(G-3891)*
Marshall & Associates Inc E 513 683-6396
Loveland *(G-13011)*
McKeen Security Inc D 740 699-1301
Saint Clairsville *(G-16495)*
Merchants Scrty Srvc of Dayton B 937 256-9373
Dayton *(G-9608)*
Metro Safety and Security LLC D 614 792-2770
Columbus *(G-8064)*
Metropolitan Security Svcs Inc A 216 298-4076
Cleveland *(G-5973)*
Metropolitan Security Svcs Inc B 330 253-6459
Akron *(G-337)*
Moonlight Security Inc D 937 252-1600
Moraine *(G-14681)*
NASA-Trmi Group Inc D 937 387-6517
Dayton *(G-9652)*
Official Investigations Inc D 844 263-3424
Cincinnati *(G-4149)*
Ohio Entertainment Security D 937 325-7216
South Vienna *(G-16948)*
Ohio Support Services Corp E 614 443-0291
Columbus *(G-8353)*
Ohio Tctcal Enfrcment Svcs LLC D 614 989-9485
Columbus *(G-8355)*
Patrol Urban Services LLC E 614 620-4672
Westerville *(G-19291)*
Pennington International Inc E 513 631-2130
Cincinnati *(G-4225)*
Pls Protective Services E 513 521-3581
Cincinnati *(G-4256)*
Professional Investigating D 614 228-7422
Columbus *(G-8468)*
Public Safety Ohio Department E 419 768-3955
Mount Gilead *(G-14734)*
R C Enterprises Inc D 330 782-2111
Youngstown *(G-20175)*
R-Cap Security LLC C 216 761-6355
Cleveland *(G-6275)*
Rmi International Inc D 937 642-5032
Marysville *(G-13525)*
Rumpf Corporation E 419 255-5005
Toledo *(G-18014)*
Ryno 24 Inc E 440 946-7700
Willoughby *(G-19569)*
Safeguard Properties LLC A 216 739-2900
Cleveland *(G-6361)*
Sam-Tom Inc C 216 426-7752
Cleveland *(G-6369)*
Securitas SEC Svcs USA Inc C 216 431-3139
Cleveland *(G-6388)*
Securitas SEC Svcs USA Inc D 513 639-7615
Cincinnati *(G-4443)*
Securitas SEC Svcs USA Inc C 937 224-7432
Dayton *(G-9757)*
Securitas SEC Svcs USA Inc C 614 871-6051
Grove City *(G-11470)*
Securitas SEC Svcs USA Inc A 440 887-6800
Cleveland *(G-6389)*
Securitas SEC Svcs USA Inc C 216 503-2021
Cleveland *(G-6390)*
Seven Secured Inc E 281 362-2887
Strongsville *(G-17342)*
Shane Security Services Inc D 330 757-4001
Poland *(G-16088)*
Shield Security Service E 330 650-2001
Hudson *(G-12006)*
St Moritz Security Svcs Inc D 330 270-5922
Youngstown *(G-20216)*
St Moritz Security Svcs Inc E 614 351-8798
Worthington *(G-19852)*
Start-Black Servicesjv LLC D 740 598-4891
Mingo Junction *(G-14529)*
Sterling Infosystems Inc E 216 685-7600
Independence *(G-12125)*
Tenable Protective Svcs Inc A 216 361-0002
Cleveland *(G-6511)*
Tenable Protective Svcs Inc A 513 741-3560
Cincinnati *(G-4584)*
US Protection Service LLC D 513 422-7910
Cincinnati *(G-4742)*
US Security Associates Inc C 513 381-7033
Cincinnati *(G-4743)*
US Security Associates Inc C 937 454-9035
Vandalia *(G-18548)*
US Security Holdings Inc D 614 488-6110
Columbus *(G-8835)*
Veteran Security Patrol Co E 937 222-7333
Dayton *(G-9855)*
Veteran Security Patrol Co C 513 381-4482
Cincinnati *(G-4758)*
Whitestone Group Inc B 614 501-7007
Reynoldsburg *(G-16339)*
Whittguard Security Services C 440 288-7233
Avon *(G-904)*
Willo Security Inc C 614 481-9456
Columbus *(G-8908)*
Willo Security Inc E 440 953-9191
Willoughby *(G-19582)*

7382 Security Systems Svcs

ABC Fire Inc E 440 237-6677
North Royalton *(G-15346)*
ADT Security D 440 397-5751
Strongsville *(G-17281)*
American Svcs & Protection LLC D 614 884-0177
Columbus *(G-6939)*
Anderson Security Inc D 937 294-1478
Moraine *(G-14621)*
Area Wide Protective Inc E 513 321-9889
Fairfield *(G-10696)*
Asset Protection Corporation E 419 531-3400
Toledo *(G-17601)*
Bass Security Services Inc C 216 755-1200
Bedford Heights *(G-1317)*
Brawnstone Security LLC D 330 800-9006
Canton *(G-2216)*
Brentley Institute Inc E 216 225-0087
Cleveland *(G-5078)*
Bureau Workers Compensation E 614 466-5109
Pickerington *(G-15950)*
D B A Inc E 513 541-6600
Cincinnati *(G-3394)*
Electra Sound Inc C 216 433-1050
Cleveland *(G-5471)*
GA Business Purchaser LLC D 419 255-8400
Toledo *(G-17752)*
Gene Ptacek Son Fire Eqp Inc E 216 651-8300
Cleveland *(G-5602)*
Genric Inc B 937 553-9250
Marysville *(G-13500)*
Gillmore Security Systems Inc E 440 232-1000
Cleveland *(G-5608)*
Guardian Protection Svcs Inc D 513 422-5319
West Chester *(G-18937)*
Guardian Protection Svcs Inc E 330 797-1570
Youngstown *(G-20059)*
Henley & Assoc SEC Group LLC E 614 378-3727
Blacklick *(G-1479)*
Honeywell International Inc E 614 717-2270
Columbus *(G-7772)*
Integrated Protection Svcs Inc D 513 631-5505
Cincinnati *(G-3770)*
Integrted Prcision Systems Inc E 330 963-0064
Twinsburg *(G-18282)*
▲ **Jenne Inc** C 440 835-0040
Avon *(G-888)*
Johnson Cntrls SEC Sltions LLC C 330 497-0850
Canton *(G-2362)*

SIC

Johnson Cntrls SEC Sltions LLC ....D 440 262-1084
Brecksville *(G-1786)*
Johnson Cntrls SEC Sltions LLC ....C 561 988-3600
Dublin *(G-10260)*
Johnson Cntrls SEC Sltions LLC ....E 513 277-4966
Cincinnati *(G-3826)*
Johnson Cntrls SEC Sltions LLC ....E 419 243-8400
Maumee *(G-13806)*
Koorsen Fire & Security Inc ....E 614 878-2228
Columbus *(G-7922)*
Koorsen Fire & Security Inc ....E 419 526-2212
Mansfield *(G-13195)*
Koorsen Fire & Security Inc ....E 937 324-9405
Vandalia *(G-18530)*
Kst Security Inc ....E 614 878-2228
Columbus *(G-7930)*
Macair Aviation LLC ....E 937 347-1302
Xenia *(G-19919)*
Metro Safety and Security LLC ....D 614 792-2770
Columbus *(G-8064)*
Mills Security Alarm Systems ....E 513 921-4600
Cincinnati *(G-4058)*
Northwestern Ohio SEC Systems ....E 419 227-1655
Lima *(G-12708)*
OGara Group Inc ....D 513 338-0660
Cincinnati *(G-4150)*
Ohio Tctcal Enfrcment Svcs LLC ....D 614 989-9485
Columbus *(G-8355)*
Ohio Valley Integration Svcs ....E 937 492-0008
Sidney *(G-16790)*
Protech Security Inc ....E 330 499-1540
Canton *(G-2442)*
Research & Investigation Assoc ......E 419 526-1299
Mansfield *(G-13234)*
Safe-N-Sound Security Inc ....D 330 491-1148
Millersburg *(G-14492)*
Safeguard Properties LLC ....A 216 739-2900
Cleveland *(G-6361)*
Securestate LLC ....E 216 927-0115
Cleveland *(G-6387)*
Securitas Electronic SEC Inc ....C 855 331-0359
Uniontown *(G-18386)*
Security Investments LLC ....D 614 441-4601
Columbus *(G-8616)*
Sievers Security Systems Inc ....E 216 383-1234
Cleveland *(G-6408)*
State Alarm Inc ....E 888 726-8111
Youngstown *(G-20217)*
Tacg LLC ....C 937 203-8201
Beavercreek *(G-1237)*
United States Protective ....E 216 475-8550
Independence *(G-12135)*
Universal Green Energy Solutio ....E 844 723-7768
Reynoldsburg *(G-16335)*
Vector Security Inc ....E 440 466-7233
Geneva *(G-11249)*
Vector Security Inc ....E 330 726-9841
Canfield *(G-2164)*
Vigilant Defense ....E 513 309-0672
West Chester *(G-19031)*
Wj Service Co Inc ....E 330 372-5040
Warren *(G-18773)*

7383 News Syndicates

Associated Press ....E 614 885-3444
Columbus *(G-6984)*
Ohio News Network ....D 614 460-3700
Columbus *(G-8275)*

7384 Photofinishing Labs

Buckeye Prof Imaging Inc ....E 800 433-1292
Canton *(G-2221)*
Buehler Food Markets Inc ....C 330 364-3079
Dover *(G-10068)*
▲ Digico Imaging Inc ....D 614 239-5200
Columbus *(G-7446)*
Discount Drug Mart Inc ....E 330 343-7700
Dover *(G-10072)*
Fred W Albrecht Grocery Co ....C 330 645-6222
Coventry Township *(G-9034)*
Fred W Albrecht Grocery Co ....C 330 666-6781
Akron *(G-229)*
Kroger Co ....C 937 294-7210
Dayton *(G-9551)*
Marc Glassman Inc ....C 330 995-9246
Aurora *(G-834)*
Marco Photo Service Inc ....D 419 529-9010
Ontario *(G-15561)*
Solar Imaging LLC ....E 614 626-8536
Gahanna *(G-11145)*

Target Stores Inc ....C 614 279-4224
Columbus *(G-8731)*
Vista Color Imaging Inc ....E 216 651-2830
Brooklyn Heights *(G-1887)*
Walgreen Co ....E 937 433-5314
Dayton *(G-9864)*
Walgreen Co ....E 614 236-8622
Columbus *(G-8869)*
Walgreen Co ....E 330 677-5650
Kent *(G-12267)*
Walgreen Co ....E 330 745-2674
Barberton *(G-971)*
Walgreen Co ....E 937 396-1358
Kettering *(G-12303)*
Walgreen Co ....E 937 781-9561
Dayton *(G-9865)*
Walgreen Co ....E 330 733-4237
Akron *(G-494)*
Walgreen Co ....E 937 277-6022
Dayton *(G-9866)*
Walgreen Co ....E 740 368-9380
Delaware *(G-10015)*
Walgreen Co ....E 614 336-0431
Dublin *(G-10369)*
Walgreen Co ....E 937 859-3879
Miamisburg *(G-14235)*
Walgreen Co ....E 330 928-5444
Cuyahoga Falls *(G-9139)*

7389 Business Svcs, NEC

1 Financial Corporation ....E 513 936-1400
Blue Ash *(G-1493)*
3-D Technical Services Company .....E 937 746-2901
Franklin *(G-11020)*
6200 Rockside LLC ....D 216 642-8004
Cleveland *(G-4872)*
A Sainato Enterprises Inc ....E 216 795-5167
Brecksville *(G-1765)*
A-1 Bail Bonds Inc ....E 937 372-2400
Xenia *(G-19887)*
A2z Field Services LLC ....C 614 873-0211
Plain City *(G-16041)*
AA Fire Protection LLC ....E 440 327-0060
Elyria *(G-10475)*
Abco Fire LLC ....E 216 433-7200
Cleveland *(G-4890)*
Abco Fire LLC ....E 800 875-7200
Cincinnati *(G-2896)*
▼ Abco Holdings LLC ....D 216 433-7200
Cleveland *(G-4892)*
Ability Works Inc ....C 419 626-1048
Sandusky *(G-16572)*
Abraham Ford LLC ....E 440 233-7402
Elyria *(G-10477)*
Academy Answering Service Inc .....E 440 442-8500
Cleveland *(G-4896)*
▲ Accel Inc ....C 614 656-1100
New Albany *(G-14840)*
Accurate Inventory and C ....B 800 777-9414
Columbus *(G-6863)*
Ace Assembly Packaging Inc ....E 330 866-9117
Waynesburg *(G-18827)*
Acuren Inspection Inc ....E 937 228-9729
Dayton *(G-9207)*
Acxiom Info SEC Svcs Inc ....E 216 685-7600
Independence *(G-12039)*
ADS Manufacturing Ohio LLC ....D 513 217-4502
Middletown *(G-14286)*
▼ Advanced Specialty Products ....D 419 882-6528
Bowling Green *(G-1712)*
Advanced Translation/Cnsltng ....E 440 716-0820
Westlake *(G-19311)*
Adventure Cmbat Operations LLC ...E 330 818-1029
Canton *(G-2175)*
Aecom Energy & Cnstr Inc ....A 216 523-5600
Cleveland *(G-4907)*
Aecom Energy & Cnstr Inc ....A 216 523-5600
Cleveland *(G-4908)*
Aerocon Photogrammetric Svcs ......E 440 946-6277
Willoughby *(G-19502)*
Affinity Disp Expositions Inc ....C 513 771-2339
Cincinnati *(G-2915)*
◆ Affinity Specialty Apparel Inc ....D 866 548-8434
Fairborn *(G-10663)*
▲ Akron-Summit Convention ....E 330 374-7560
Akron *(G-62)*
Al-Mar Lanes ....E 419 352-4637
Bowling Green *(G-1713)*
Alliance Data Systems Corp ....B 614 729-5000
Westerville *(G-19219)*

Alliance Data Systems Corp ....C 614 729-5800
Reynoldsburg *(G-16280)*
Allied Infotech Corporation ....D 330 745-8529
Akron *(G-66)*
Allstate Insurance Company ....E 330 650-2917
Hudson *(G-11963)*
Almost Family Inc ....E 513 662-3400
Cincinnati *(G-2930)*
Alorica Customer Care Inc ....A 216 525-3311
Cleveland *(G-4940)*
Alternative Services Inc ....E 419 861-2121
Holland *(G-11870)*
American Crane Inc ....E 614 496-2268
Reynoldsburg *(G-16281)*
American Publishers LLC ....D 419 626-0623
Huron *(G-12020)*
Ameridial Inc ....B 800 445-7128
Canton *(G-2188)*
Ameridial Inc ....D 330 479-8044
North Canton *(G-15188)*
Ameridial Inc ....B 330 497-4888
North Canton *(G-15189)*
Ameridial Inc ....D 330 339-7222
New Philadelphia *(G-14946)*
Ameridial Inc ....D 330 868-2000
Minerva *(G-14515)*
▲ Amos Media Company ....C 937 498-2111
Sidney *(G-16758)*
Ampersand Group LLC ....E 330 379-0044
Akron *(G-73)*
Another Chance Inc ....E 614 868-3541
Pickerington *(G-15946)*
Answering Service Inc ....E 440 473-1200
Cleveland *(G-4984)*
Argus International Inc ....E 513 852-1010
Cincinnati *(G-2985)*
ARS Ohio LLC ....E 513 327-7645
Cincinnati *(G-2989)*
▲ Asm International ....D 440 338-5151
Novelty *(G-15464)*
Atrium Apparel Corporation ....E 740 966-8200
Johnstown *(G-12195)*
Auction Services Inc ....A 614 497-2000
Obetz *(G-15522)*
Avery Dennison Corporation ....C 440 534-6000
Mentor *(G-14020)*
Baker Bnngson Rlty Auctioneers .....E 419 547-7777
Clyde *(G-6740)*
Banc Certified Merch Svcs LLC ....E 614 850-2740
Hilliard *(G-11744)*
Banc One Services Corporation ....A 614 248-5800
Columbus *(G-6800)*
Barnett Associates Inc ....D 516 877-2860
Hilliard *(G-11745)*
▲ Baumfolder Corporation ....E 937 492-1281
Sidney *(G-16760)*
Bay Mechanical & Elec Corp ....D 440 282-6816
Lorain *(G-12885)*
Bbs & Associates Inc ....E 330 665-5227
Akron *(G-89)*
Bdo Usa LLP ....E 513 592-2400
Cincinnati *(G-3027)*
BDS Packaging Inc ....D 937 643-0530
Moraine *(G-14624)*
Beheydts Auto Wrecking ....E 330 658-6109
Doylestown *(G-10108)*
Benchmark Craftsman Inc ....E 330 975-4214
Seville *(G-16682)*
Bermex Inc ....B 330 945-7500
Stow *(G-17192)*
Best Payment Solutions Inc ....E 630 321-0117
Symmes Twp *(G-17465)*
Biotest Pharmaceuticals Corp ....E 419 819-3068
Bowling Green *(G-1720)*
Board of Dir of Wittenbe ....E 937 327-6231
Springfield *(G-16999)*
Bollin & Sons Inc ....E 419 693-6573
Toledo *(G-17618)*
◆ Bookmasters Inc ....C 419 281-1802
Ashland *(G-658)*
Bpf Enterprises Inc ....D 419 855-2545
Maumee *(G-13763)*
Bst & G Joint Fire District ....E 740 965-3841
Sunbury *(G-17384)*
Buckeye Mechanical Contg Inc ....E 740 282-0089
Toronto *(G-18181)*
Buckeye Pool Inc ....E 937 434-7916
Dayton *(G-9266)*
Burgess & Niple-Heapy LLC ....D 614 459-2050
Columbus *(G-7099)*

Business Backer LLC	E	513 792-6866	
Cincinnati (G-3095)			
Calvin Lanier	E	937 952-4221	
Dayton (G-9273)			
Camargo Rental Center Inc	E	513 271-6510	
Cincinnati (G-3109)			
Canton Inventory Service	E	330 453-1633	
Canton (G-2235)			
Canton S-Group Ltd	B	419 625-7003	
Sandusky (G-16580)			
Carol Reese	E	513 347-0252	
Cincinnati (G-3126)			
Cass Information Systems Inc	C	614 766-2277	
Columbus (G-7135)			
Catsi Inc	E	800 922-0468	
Wheelersburg (G-19429)			
Cbiz Inc	C	216 447-9000	
Cleveland (G-5139)			
Cdd LLC	B	905 829-2794	
Mason (G-13551)			
Cec Combustion Safety LLC	E	216 749-2992	
Brookpark (G-1893)			
Ceiba Enterprises Incorporated	C	614 818-3220	
Westerville (G-19231)			
Cgh-Global Security LLC	E	800 376-0655	
Cincinnati (G-3164)			
Chapel Hl Chrstn Schl Endwment	D	330 929-1901	
Cuyahoga Falls (G-9078)			
Chardon Laboratories Inc	E	614 860-1000	
Reynoldsburg (G-16291)			
Chute Gerdeman Inc	E	614 469-1001	
Columbus (G-7198)			
Cincilingua Inc	E	513 721-8782	
Cincinnati (G-3218)			
Cincinnati Financial Corp	A	513 870-2000	
Fairfield (G-10710)			
▼ Cincinnati Indus Actoneers Inc	E	513 241-9701	
Cincinnati (G-3250)			
Cintas Corporation No 2	D	440 838-8611	
Cleveland (G-5180)			
CIP International Inc	D	513 874-9925	
West Chester (G-18889)			
Citicorp Credit Services Inc	B	212 559-1000	
Columbus (G-7204)			
Citigroup Inc	B	740 548-0594	
Delaware (G-9960)			
Citizens Financial Svcs Inc	D	513 385-3200	
Cincinnati (G-3297)			
City of Cleveland	E	216 664-2620	
Cleveland (G-5195)			
City of Cleveland	E	216 664-3922	
Cleveland (G-5198)			
City of North Olmsted	E	440 777-0678	
North Olmsted (G-15283)			
City of Solon	E	440 248-6939	
Solon (G-16836)			
City of Wooster	E	330 263-5266	
Wooster (G-19704)			
Clearwater Services Inc	D	330 836-4946	
Akron (G-142)			
Cleveland Clinic Foundation	B	216 444-5000	
Cleveland (G-5239)			
Clgt Solutions LLC	E	740 920-4795	
Granville (G-11338)			
Clovernook Center For The Bli	C	513 522-3860	
Cincinnati (G-3311)			
Coast To Coast Studios LLC	E	614 861-9800	
Blacklick (G-1478)			
Colerain Volunteer Fire Co	E	740 738-0735	
Dillonvale (G-10063)			
Collaborative Inc	E	419 242-7405	
Toledo (G-17667)			
Collections Acquisition Co LLC	C	614 944-5788	
Columbus (G-7245)			
Columbus Bride	D	614 888-4567	
Columbus (G-7263)			
Comenity Servicing LLC	C	614 729-4000	
Columbus (G-7324)			
Compliant Healthcare Tech LLC	E	216 255-9607	
Cleveland (G-5331)			
Continental Business Services	E	614 224-4534	
Columbus (G-7357)			
Controls Inc	E	330 239-4345	
Medina (G-13923)			
Convention & Vistors Bureau of	E	216 875-6603	
Cleveland (G-5347)			
▼ Convergys Cstmer MGT Group Inc	B	513 723-6104	
Cincinnati (G-3358)			
Conversa Language Center Inc	E	513 651-5679	
Cincinnati (G-3360)			

▲ Conversion Tech Intl Inc	E	419 924-5566	
West Unity (G-19140)			
Convivo Network LLC	E	216 631-9000	
Rocky River (G-16428)			
Corporate Fin Assoc of Clumbus	D	614 457-9219	
Columbus (G-7374)			
Corporate Support Inc	E	419 221-3838	
Lima (G-12620)			
Corporate United Inc	E	440 895-0938	
Westlake (G-19337)			
Covelli Enterprises Inc	D	614 889-7802	
Dublin (G-10191)			
Crain Communications Inc	D	330 836-9180	
Akron (G-169)			
Crane 1 Services Inc	E	937 704-9900	
Miamisburg (G-14157)			
Credit First National Assn	B	216 362-5300	
Cleveland (G-5377)			
Crescent Park Corporation	C	513 759-7000	
West Chester (G-18906)			
Cronins Inc	E	513 851-5900	
Cincinnati (G-3380)			
Csa Amrica Tstg Crtfcation LLC	B	216 524-4990	
Independence (G-12064)			
Custom Pkg & Inspecting Inc	D	330 399-8961	
Warren (G-18697)			
▲ Custom Products Corporation	D	440 528-7100	
Solon (G-16842)			
Custom-Pak Inc	D	330 725-0800	
Medina (G-13928)			
Cwm Envronmental Cleveland LLC	E	216 663-0808	
Cleveland (G-5401)			
Dash Logistics Inc	E	937 382-9110	
Wilmington (G-19621)			
Dasher Lawless Automation LLC	E	855 755-7275	
Warren (G-18699)			
Dayton Cvb	E	937 226-8211	
Dayton (G-9361)			
Dayton Digital Media Inc	E	937 223-8335	
Dayton (G-9362)			
Definitive Solutions Co Inc	D	513 719-9100	
Cincinnati (G-3417)			
Dennis & Carol Liederbach	E	256 582-6200	
Northfield (G-15377)			
Design Central Inc	E	614 890-0202	
Columbus (G-7438)			
Dfs Corporate Services LLC	B	614 777-7020	
Hilliard (G-11760)			
Dialamerica Marketing Inc	C	330 836-5293	
Fairlawn (G-10822)			
Dialamerica Marketing Inc	C	440 234-4410	
Cleveland (G-5420)			
Division 7 Inc	E	740 965-1970	
Galena (G-11157)			
DMR Management Inc	E	513 771-1700	
Avon Lake (G-915)			
Document Concepts Inc	E	330 575-5685	
North Canton (G-15197)			
Domino Foods Inc	D	216 432-3222	
Cleveland (G-5437)			
Douglas R Denny	E	216 236-2400	
Independence (G-12068)			
Dreier & Maller Inc	E	614 575-0065	
Reynoldsburg (G-16300)			
Dwellworks LLC	D	216 682-4200	
Cleveland (G-5450)			
E & A Pedco Services Inc	D	513 782-4920	
Cincinnati (G-3461)			
E T Financial Service Inc	E	937 716-1726	
Trotwood (G-18193)			
Ebsco Industries Inc	B	330 478-0281	
Canton (G-2295)			
Electrovations Inc	E	330 274-3558	
Aurora (G-826)			
Elevar Design Group Inc	E	513 721-0600	
Cincinnati (G-3490)			
Emersion Design LLC	E	513 841-9100	
Cincinnati (G-3494)			
Empire One LLC	E	330 628-9310	
Mogadore (G-14548)			
Employeescreeniq Inc	D	216 514-2800	
Independence (G-12070)			
Enesco Properties LLC	A	440 473-2000	
Highland Heights (G-11733)			
Essilor of America Inc	C	614 492-0888	
Groveport (G-11510)			
Etransmedia Technology Inc	E	724 743-5960	
Columbus (G-7539)			
Evanston Bulldogs Youth Footba	E	513 254-9500	
Cincinnati (G-3518)			

Eventions Ltd	E	216 952-9898	
Cleveland (G-5496)			
Evolution Crtive Solutions LLC	E	513 681-4450	
Cincinnati (G-3523)			
Exhibitpro Inc	E	614 885-9541	
New Albany (G-14853)			
Express Packaging Ohio Inc	B	740 498-4700	
Newcomerstown (G-15131)			
Facts Management Company	E	440 892-4272	
Westlake (G-19340)			
Ferguson Hills Inc	E	513 539-4497	
Dayton (G-9433)			
Filterfresh Coffee Service Inc	E	513 681-8911	
West Chester (G-19053)			
Finastra USA Corporation	E	937 435-2335	
Miamisburg (G-14171)			
▲ First Choice Packaging Inc	C	419 333-4100	
Fremont (G-11073)			
Flamos Enterprises Inc	E	330 478-0009	
Canton (G-2315)			
Flight Services & Systems Inc	D	216 328-0090	
Cleveland (G-5548)			
Fnb Inc	E	740 922-2532	
Dennison (G-10050)			
FNB Corporation	D	330 425-1818	
Twinsburg (G-18267)			
▼ Fox International Limited Inc	E	216 454-1001	
Beachwood (G-1058)			
Frankes Unlimited Inc	E	937 642-0706	
Marysville (G-13496)			
Franklin Cnty Bd Commissioners	E	614 525-3322	
Columbus (G-7604)			
Freudenberg-Nok General Partnr	B	419 499-2502	
Milan (G-14361)			
Future Poly Tech Inc	E	614 942-1209	
Columbus (G-7636)			
Fx Facility Group LLC	E	513 639-2509	
Cincinnati (G-3598)			
▼ G Robert Toney & Assoc Inc	E	216 391-1900	
Cleveland (G-5588)			
Garda CL Great Lakes Inc	B	561 939-7000	
Columbus (G-7647)			
Gateway Distribution Inc	E	513 891-4477	
Cincinnati (G-3604)			
General Electric Company	A	937 534-6920	
Dayton (G-9458)			
General Theming Contrs LLC	C	614 252-6342	
Columbus (G-7655)			
Geneva Liberty Steel Ltd	E	330 740-0103	
Youngstown (G-20047)			
Gerdau Macsteel Atmosphere Ann	D	330 478-0314	
Canton (G-2325)			
Greater Cincinnati Cnvntn/Vstr	E	513 621-2142	
Cincinnati (G-3650)			
Greatr Columbus Conventn & Vis	E	614 221-6623	
Columbus (G-7694)			
Greenspace Enterprise Tech Inc	E	888 309-8517	
Franklin (G-11031)			
Greentown Volunteer Fire Dept	E	330 494-3002	
Uniontown (G-18372)			
Guardian Water & Power Inc	D	614 291-3141	
Columbus (G-7703)			
Gws FF&e LLC	E	513 759-6000	
West Chester (G-18939)			
Hague Water Conditioning Inc	E	614 482-8121	
Groveport (G-11515)			
Hamilton Cnty Auditor Office	C	513 946-4000	
Cincinnati (G-3674)			
Hanco International	D	330 456-9407	
Canton (G-2338)			
Hastings Water Works Inc	E	440 832-7700	
Brecksville (G-1782)			
Haven Financial Enterprise	E	800 265-2401	
Cleveland (G-5667)			
Heartland Payment Systems LLC	D	513 518-6125	
Loveland (G-12998)			
High Line Corporation	E	330 848-8800	
Akron (G-261)			
Hkt Teleservices Inc	C	614 652-6300	
Grove City (G-11441)			
Hochstedler Construction Ltd	E	740 427-4880	
Gambier (G-11224)			
Horter Investment MGT LLC	E	513 984-9933	
Cincinnati (G-3727)			
▲ Hrm Enterprises Inc	C	330 877-9353	
Hartville (G-11691)			
Human Resource Profile Inc	E	513 388-4300	
Cincinnati (G-3738)			
Hunt Products Inc	E	440 667-2457	
Newburgh Heights (G-15115)			

Company		Phone	Location (ref)

I-X Center Corporation .... C 216 265-2675
  Cleveland (G-5732)
Ies Systems Inc .... E 330 533-6683
  Canfield (G-2143)
Improvedge LLC .... E 614 793-1738
  Powell (G-16197)
In Terminal Services Corp .... E 216 518-8407
  Maple Heights (G-13288)
Incept Corporation .... C 330 649-8000
  Canton (G-2354)
▲ Independent Steel Company LLC .... E 330 225-7741
  Valley City (G-18463)
▲ Industrial Chemical Corp .... E 330 725-0800
  Medina (G-13953)
Industrial Insul Coatings LLC .... E 800 506-1399
  Girard (G-11288)
Infocision Management Corp .... B 330 668-1411
  Akron (G-276)
Infocision Management Corp .... B 330 726-0872
  Youngstown (G-20080)
Infocision Management Corp .... D 419 529-8685
  Mansfield (G-13187)
Infocision Management Corp .... C 330 668-6615
  Akron (G-277)
Infocision Management Corp .... B 330 544-1400
  Youngstown (G-20081)
Innovairre Communications LLC .... D 330 869-8500
  Fairlawn (G-10833)
Inquiry Systems Inc .... E 614 464-3800
  Columbus (G-7824)
Inspection Group Incorporated .... E 614 891-3606
  Westerville (G-19175)
Interbrand Design Forum LLC .... C 513 421-2210
  Cincinnati (G-3777)
Interior Supply Cincinnati LLC .... E 614 424-6611
  Columbus (G-7835)
◆ Interscope Manufacturing Inc .... E 513 423-8866
  Middletown (G-14303)
J & B Systems Company Inc .... C 513 732-2000
  Batavia (G-1002)
J Schoen Enterprises Inc .... E 419 536-0970
  Toledo (G-17828)
James Ray Lozier .... E 419 884-2656
  Mansfield (G-13190)
Jason Wilson .... E 937 604-8209
  Tipp City (G-17561)
Jbjs Acquisitions LLC .... E 513 769-0393
  Cincinnati (G-3810)
JLW Marketing LLC .... D 513 260-8418
  Cincinnati (G-3820)
Jones Group Interiors Inc .... E 330 253-9180
  Akron (G-294)
◆ Jpmorgan Chase Bank Nat Assn .... A 614 436-3055
  Columbus (G-6818)
Juice Technologies Inc .... E 800 518-5576
  Columbus (G-7875)
K & R Distributors Inc .... E 937 864-5495
  Fairborn (G-10677)
Karlsberger Companies .... C 614 461-9500
  Columbus (G-7883)
Keller Logistics Group Inc .... E 866 276-9486
  Defiance (G-9923)
▼ Kent Adhesive Products Co .... D 330 678-1626
  Kent (G-12239)
Kidron Auction Inc .... E 330 857-2641
  Kidron (G-12307)
King Tut Logistics LLC .... E 614 538-0509
  Columbus (G-7908)
Knisely Inc .... D 330 343-5812
  Dover (G-10085)
Kns Financial Inc .... E 800 215-1136
  Toledo (G-17842)
Koorsen Fire & Security Inc .... E 937 324-9405
  Vandalia (G-18530)
Kramer & Kramer Inc .... E 937 456-1101
  Eaton (G-10448)
Kucera International Inc .... D 440 975-4230
  Willoughby (G-19536)
L Van & Associates Corporation .... E 419 208-9145
  Toledo (G-17846)
Landmark America Inc .... E 330 372-6800
  Warren (G-18721)
Laser Craft Inc .... E 440 327-4300
  North Ridgeville (G-15333)
Laserflex Corporation .... D 614 850-9600
  Hilliard (G-11783)
Lawnview Industries Inc .... C 937 653-5217
  Urbana (G-18438)
Legacy Industrial Services LLC .... E 606 584-8953
  Ripley (G-16400)

Legend Equities Corporation .... D 216 741-3113
  Independence (G-12087)
Liberty Healthshare Inc .... E 855 585-4237
  Canton (G-2377)
Lighthouse Youth Services Inc .... D 513 861-1111
  Cincinnati (G-3930)
Limitless Solutions Inc .... E 614 577-1550
  Columbus (G-7979)
Lindsey Cnstr & Design Inc .... E 330 785-9931
  Akron (G-316)
Lions Gate SEC Solutions Inc .... E 440 539-8382
  Euclid (G-10648)
Logistics Inc .... E 419 478-1514
  Toledo (G-17856)
Loth Inc .... C 513 554-4900
  Cincinnati (G-3944)
Ltd Productions LLC .... D 440 688-1905
  Cleveland (G-5885)
M A Folkes Company Inc .... E 513 785-4200
  Hamilton (G-11626)
M P & A Fibers Inc .... E 440 926-1074
  Grafton (G-11318)
Macys Cr & Customer Svcs Inc .... D 513 881-9950
  West Chester (G-18967)
Macys Cr & Customer Svcs Inc .... A 513 398-5221
  Mason (G-13613)
Marcums Don Pool Care Inc .... E 513 561-7050
  Cincinnati (G-3968)
Matvest Inc .... E 614 487-8720
  Columbus (G-8040)
Maximum Communications Inc .... E 513 489-3414
  Cincinnati (G-3981)
McConnell Excavating Ltd .... E 440 774-4578
  Oberlin (G-15508)
McDonalds 3490 .... E 330 762-7747
  Akron (G-326)
Medigistics Inc .... D 614 430-5700
  Columbus (G-8054)
Megacity Fire Protection Inc .... E 937 335-0775
  Dayton (G-9605)
Merchant Data Service Inc .... C 937 847-6585
  Miamisburg (G-14188)
Metal Shredders Inc .... E 937 866-0777
  Miamisburg (G-14190)
Metropolitan Pool Service Co .... E 216 741-9451
  Parma (G-15768)
Metzenbaum Sheltered Inds Inc .... E 440 729-1919
  Chesterland (G-2741)
Miami University .... D 513 529-1230
  Oxford (G-15683)
Miami University .... D 513 529-6911
  Oxford (G-15681)
Michael Schuster Associates .... E 513 241-5666
  Cincinnati (G-4047)
Micro Products Co Inc .... D 440 943-0258
  Willoughby Hills (G-19591)
Microanalysis Society Inc .... B 614 256-8063
  Hilliard (G-11797)
Midwest Liquidators Inc .... E 614 433-7355
  Worthington (G-19828)
▲ Midwest Tape LLC .... B 419 868-9370
  Holland (G-11898)
Miencorp Inc .... E 330 978-8511
  Niles (G-15159)
Military Resources LLC .... E 330 263-1040
  Wooster (G-19746)
▼ Military Resources LLC .... D 330 309-9970
  Wooster (G-19747)
Millennium Cpitl Recovery Corp .... E 330 528-1450
  Hudson (G-11998)
Miller Products Inc .... E 330 238-4200
  Alliance (G-541)
Mission Essntial Personnel LLC .... C 614 416-2345
  New Albany (G-14859)
Mistras Group Inc .... E 419 227-4100
  Lima (G-12704)
Mt Hope Auction Inc .... E 330 674-6188
  Mount Hope (G-14737)
Mt Washington Care Center Inc .... C 513 231-4561
  Cincinnati (G-4083)
N Safe Sound Security Inc .... E 888 317-7233
  Millersburg (G-14485)
National Board of Boiler .... D 614 888-8320
  Columbus (G-8129)
National Weather Service .... E 937 383-0031
  Wilmington (G-19636)
Nationwide General Insur Co .... D 614 249-7111
  Columbus (G-8156)
Neighborcare Inc .... A 513 719-2600
  Cincinnati (G-4103)

Nelson Packaging Company Inc .... D 419 229-3471
  Lima (G-12705)
▲ New Path International LLC .... E 614 410-3974
  Powell (G-16204)
Nexxtshow Exposition Svcs LLC .... E 877 836-3131
  Cincinnati (G-4116)
Ngm Inc .... E 513 821-7363
  Cincinnati (G-4118)
North Bay Construction Inc .... E 440 835-1898
  Westlake (G-19380)
Notoweega Nation Inc .... D 740 777-1480
  Logan (G-12851)
Npc Group Inc .... A 312 627-6000
  Symmes Twp (G-17466)
Official Investigations Inc .... D 844 263-3424
  Cincinnati (G-4149)
Ohio Design Centre .... D 216 831-1245
  Beachwood (G-1090)
▲ Ohio Gasket and Shim Co Inc .... E 330 630-0626
  Akron (G-359)
▲ Ohio Laminating & Binding Inc .... E 614 771-4868
  Hilliard (G-11802)
Ohio Metal Processing Inc .... E 740 286-6457
  Jackson (G-12178)
Ohio Presbyterian Rtr Svcs .... E 614 888-7800
  Columbus (G-8281)
Ohio Steel Slitters Inc .... E 330 477-6741
  Canton (G-2432)
Oki Auction LLC .... D 513 679-7910
  Cincinnati (G-4165)
One Main Financial Services .... C 419 841-0785
  Toledo (G-17963)
Onyx Creative Inc .... D 216 223-3200
  Cleveland (G-6137)
Orbit Industries Inc .... D 440 243-3311
  Cleveland (G-6141)
P C Workshop Inc .... D 419 399-4805
  Paulding (G-15795)
P3 Infrastructure Inc .... A 330 686-1129
  Stow (G-17223)
Packship Usa Inc .... D 330 682-7225
  Orrville (G-15643)
Pactiv LLC .... C 614 771-5400
  Columbus (G-8410)
▲ Pak Lab .... E 513 735-4777
  Batavia (G-1005)
Pandora Manufacturing Llc .... D 419 384-3241
  Ottawa (G-15663)
Passprt Accept Fclty Mansfld P .... C 419 755-4621
  Mansfield (G-13230)
Patented Acquisition Corp .... C 937 353-2299
  Miamisburg (G-14203)
Pathway House LLC .... E 872 223-9797
  Cleveland (G-6182)
Penske Logistics LLC .... E 419 547-2615
  Clyde (G-6749)
Perceptionist Inc .... E 614 384-7500
  Westerville (G-19292)
Perfect Cut-Off Inc .... E 440 943-0000
  Wickliffe (G-19473)
Piqua Industrial Cut & Sew .... E 937 773-7397
  Piqua (G-16018)
Pitney Bowes Presort Svcs Inc .... D 513 860-3607
  West Chester (G-19072)
Platinum Prestige Property .... E 614 705-2251
  Columbus (G-8453)
Pmwi LLC .... D 614 975-5004
  Hilliard (G-11806)
Polaris Automation Inc .... D 614 431-0170
  Lewis Center (G-12560)
Pollock Research & Design Inc .... E 330 332-3300
  Salem (G-16554)
Popper & Associates Msrp LLC .... E 614 798-8991
  Dublin (G-10309)
Predictive Service LLC .... D 866 772-6770
  Cleveland (G-6227)
Printing Services .... E 440 708-1999
  Chagrin Falls (G-2678)
Priority Designs Inc .... D 614 337-9979
  Columbus (G-8463)
Progressive Quality Care Inc .... A 330 875-7866
  Louisville (G-12972)
Progressive Quality Care Inc .... E 216 661-6800
  Parma (G-15773)
Project Packaging Inc .... E 216 451-7878
  Cleveland (G-6260)
Pucher Paint Co Inc .... E 440 234-0991
  Berea (G-1435)
Pxp Ohio .... E 614 575-4242
  Reynoldsburg (G-16324)

Quadax Inc ....E 330 759-4600
Youngstown (G-20170)

Quality Control Inspection ....D 440 359-1900
Cleveland (G-6269)

Quality Lines Inc ....C 740 815-1165
Findlay (G-10957)

Quintus Technologies LLC ....E 614 891-2732
Lewis Center (G-12561)

Quotient Technology Inc ....E 513 229-8659
Mason (G-13631)

R and J Corporation ....E 440 871-6009
Westlake (G-19394)

R D D Inc ....C 216 781-5858
Cleveland (G-6273)

R P Marketing Public Relations ....E 419 241-2221
Holland (G-11909)

Raco Industries LLC ....D 513 984-2101
Blue Ash (G-1636)

Rainbow Flea Market Inc ....E 614 291-3133
Columbus (G-8486)

Rapid Mortgage Company ....E 937 748-8888
Cincinnati (G-4338)

Rdi Corporation ....D 513 524-3320
Oxford (G-15688)

Rdl Architects Inc ....E 216 752-4300
Cleveland (G-6288)

Recording Workshop ....E 740 663-1000
Chillicothe (G-2813)

Recycling Services Inc ....E 419 381-7762
Maumee (G-13842)

Reid Asset Management Company .....E 216 642-3223
Cleveland (G-6298)

▲ Relay Gear Ltd ....E 888 735-2943
Columbus (G-8510)

Reliable Polymer Services LP ....E 800 321-0954
Wadsworth (G-18614)

Reliance Financial Services NA ....E 419 783-8007
Defiance (G-9936)

Relx Inc ....E 937 865-6800
Miamisburg (G-14210)

Renaissance Hotel Operating Co ....A 216 696-5600
Cleveland (G-6305)

Republic Telcom Worldwide LLC ....D 330 244-8285
North Canton (G-15230)

Republic Telcom Worldwide LLC ....C 330 966-4586
Canton (G-2456)

Resource Interactive ....E 614 621-2888
Columbus (G-8522)

Restaurant Finance Corporation ....D 614 764-3100
Dublin (G-10321)

Return Polymers Inc ....D 419 289-1998
Ashland (G-686)

Rgis LLC ....D 216 447-1744
Independence (G-12114)

Rgis LLC ....D 330 799-1566
Youngstown (G-20186)

Rgis LLC ....D 248 651-2511
Reynoldsburg (G-16328)

Rgis LLC ....D 330 896-9802
Akron (G-406)

Rgis LLC ....C 513 772-5990
Cincinnati (G-4366)

Richard Allen Group LLC ....D 614 623-2654
Powell (G-16206)

▲ Richardson Printing Corp ....D 740 373-5362
Marietta (G-13377)

Richland Newhope Industries ....C 419 774-4400
Mansfield (G-13237)

Rite Rug Co ....E 614 478-3365
Columbus (G-8533)

River City Furniture LLC ....D 513 612-7303
West Chester (G-18994)

Roy J Miller ....E 330 674-2405
Millersburg (G-14490)

Rudolph Brothers & Co ....E 614 833-0707
Canal Winchester (G-2118)

Rush Package Delivery Inc ....D 937 297-6182
Dayton (G-9743)

Rvet Operating LLC ....E 513 683-5020
Loveland (G-13025)

Ryder Last Mile Inc ....D 866 711-3129
New Albany (G-14873)

S&P Data Ohio LLC ....B 216 965-0018
Cleveland (G-6358)

Safety-Kleen Systems Inc ....D 740 929-3532
Hebron (G-11724)

Samuel Steel Pickling Company ....D 330 963-3777
Twinsburg (G-18317)

Sander Woody Ford ....D 513 541-5586
Cincinnati (G-4431)

Sanese Services Inc ....B 614 436-1234
Warren (G-18739)

Sb Capital Group LLC ....E 516 829-2400
Columbus (G-8597)

Scot Industries Inc ....E 330 262-7585
Wooster (G-19767)

Screen Works Inc ....E 937 264-9111
Dayton (G-9754)

Security Check LLC ....C 614 944-5788
Columbus (G-8615)

Seifert Technologies Inc ....E 330 833-2700
Massillon (G-13728)

Service Pronet Inc ....E 614 874-4300
Columbus (G-8623)

Servicelink Field Services LLC ....A 440 424-0058
Solon (G-16896)

▲ Shamrock Companies Inc ....E 440 899-9510
Westlake (G-19405)

Shotstop Ballistics LLC ....E 330 686-0020
Stow (G-17230)

Shred-It USA LLC ....D 847 288-0377
Fairfield (G-10781)

Shred-It USA LLC ....E 800 697-4733
Fairfield (G-10782)

Shredded Bedding Corporation ....E 740 893-3567
Centerburg (G-2616)

Side Effects Inc ....E 937 704-9696
Franklin (G-11039)

Silco Fire Protection Company ....E 330 535-4343
Akron (G-429)

Sirva Inc ....E 216 606-4000
Independence (G-12120)

Sirva Relocation LLC ....B 216 606-4000
Independence (G-12122)

Six Sigma Logistics Inc ....E 440 666-6026
Vermilion (G-18559)

Skipco Financial Adjusters ....D 330 854-4800
Canal Fulton (G-2097)

Snapblox Hosted Solutions LLC ....E 866 524-7707
Cincinnati (G-4498)

Snl Designs Ltd ....E 440 247-2344
Chagrin Falls (G-2656)

Solomon Lei & Associates Inc ....E 419 246-6931
Toledo (G-18039)

Solupay Consulting Inc ....D 216 535-9016
Twinsburg (G-18322)

Sonoco Prtective Solutions Inc ....E 937 890-7628
Dayton (G-9774)

Sotera Health LLC ....D 440 262-1410
Broadview Heights (G-1846)

Soundtrack Printing ....C 330 606-7117
Cuyahoga Falls (G-9124)

Southern Graphic Systems Inc ....B 419 662-9873
Perrysburg (G-15923)

Sparkbase Inc ....E 216 867-0877
Cleveland (G-6442)

◆ Specialty Lubricants Corp ....E 330 425-2567
Macedonia (G-13082)

Spectrum Networks Inc ....E 513 697-2000
Cincinnati (G-4514)

Springleaf Fincl Holdings LLC ....A 419 334-9748
Fremont (G-11097)

Stamper Staffing LLC ....E 937 938-7010
Kettering (G-12300)

Stark County Federation of Con ....E 330 268-1652
Canton (G-2492)

Startek Inc ....C 419 528-7801
Ontario (G-15576)

Steriltek Inc ....E 615 627-0241
Painesville (G-15742)

Sterling Buying Group LLC ....E 513 564-9000
Cincinnati (G-4543)

Sterling Infosystems Inc ....E 216 685-7600
Independence (G-12125)

Streamline Technical Svcs LLC ....D 614 441-7448
Lockbourne (G-12825)

Summit Advantage LLC ....D 330 835-2453
Fairlawn (G-10853)

Summit Claim Services LLC ....D 330 706-9898
New Franklin (G-14915)

▲ Superior Abrasives LLC ....E 937 278-9123
Vandalia (G-18542)

Systems Pack Inc ....E 330 467-5729
Macedonia (G-13083)

T W I International Inc ....C 440 439-1830
Cleveland (G-6496)

Tan Products ....E 513 288-9264
Cincinnati (G-4576)

Tbn Acquisition LLC ....D 740 653-2091
Lancaster (G-12441)

TDS Document Management Ltd ....E 614 367-9633
Columbus (G-8734)

Technical Assurance Inc ....E 440 953-3147
Willoughby (G-19575)

Tekni-Plex Inc ....E 419 491-2399
Holland (G-11918)

Telarc International Corp ....E 216 464-2313
Beachwood (G-1111)

Telemessaging Services Inc ....E 440 845-5400
Cleveland (G-6509)

Telinx Solutions LLC ....E 330 819-0657
Medina (G-14011)

Terminix Intl Co Ltd Partnr ....E 513 539-7846
Middletown (G-14335)

Teva Womens Health Inc ....C 513 731-9900
Cincinnati (G-4589)

Third Dimension Inc ....E 877 926-3223
Geneva (G-11247)

Tim Mundy ....E 937 862-8686
Spring Valley (G-16959)

Tm Capture Services LLC ....E 937 728-1781
Beavercreek (G-1238)

◆ Toledo Shredding LLC ....E 419 698-1153
Toledo (G-18097)

Toledo Sign Company Inc ....E 419 244-4444
Toledo (G-18098)

Tommy Bahama Group Inc ....C 614 750-9668
Columbus (G-8763)

Toms Installation Co Inc ....E 419 584-1218
Celina (G-2612)

Top Tier Soccer LLC ....E 937 903-6114
Dayton (G-9816)

Tpusa Inc ....B 330 374-1232
Akron (G-472)

Tpusa Inc ....A 614 621-5512
Columbus (G-8769)

Traffic Ctrl Safety Svcs LLC ....E 330 904-2732
Alliance (G-556)

▼ Tri County Tower Service ....E 330 538-9874
North Jackson (G-15255)

Tri Green Interstate Equipment ....E 614 879-7731
London (G-12876)

Tricor Emplyment Screening Ltd ....E 800 818-5116
Berea (G-1442)

▲ Tripack LLC ....E 513 248-1255
Milford (G-14439)

Triplefin LLC ....E 513 794-9870
Blue Ash (G-1666)

Truechoicepack Corp ....E 937 630-3832
Mason (G-13651)

Trumbull Special Courier Inc ....E 330 841-0074
Warren (G-18761)

Turtles Envmtl Abatement Co ....E 614 603-9439
Columbus (G-8790)

Twin Comm Inc ....E 740 774-4701
Marietta (G-13390)

Tyler Technologies Inc ....C 937 276-5261
Moraine (G-14703)

UBS Financial Services Inc ....E 330 655-8319
Hudson (G-12009)

UBS Financial Services Inc ....E 440 414-2740
Westlake (G-19416)

UBS Financial Services Inc ....E 419 624-6800
Sandusky (G-16650)

UBS Financial Services Inc ....E 740 336-7823
Marietta (G-13391)

Uhhs/Csahs - Cuyahoga Inc ....D 440 746-3401
Cleveland (G-6561)

▲ Ultra Tech Machinery Inc ....E 330 929-5544
Cuyahoga Falls (G-9134)

Unirush LLC ....D 866 766-2229
Blue Ash (G-1674)

United Art and Education Inc ....E 800 322-3247
Dayton (G-9830)

United Parcel Service Inc ....E 440 243-3344
Middleburg Heights (G-14263)

United Parcel Service Inc OH ....B 216 676-4560
Cleveland (G-6578)

United Parcel Service Inc OH ....B 740 363-0636
Delaware (G-10013)

United Parcel Service Inc OH ....B 614 277-3300
Urbancrest (G-18452)

United Parcel Service Inc OH ....B 614 870-4111
Columbus (G-8808)

United Parcel Service Inc OH ....B 740 962-7971
Portsmouth (G-16175)

▲ Univenture Inc ....D 937 645-4600
Dublin (G-10359)

Univenture Inc ....E 937 645-4600
Dublin (G-10360)

▼ Universal Grinding Corporation ....E 216 631-9410
Cleveland *(G-6581)*

Universal Packg Systems Inc ....B 513 732-2000
Batavia *(G-1013)*

Universal Packg Systems Inc ....E 513 735-4777
Batavia *(G-1014)*

Universal Packg Systems Inc ....B 513 674-9400
Cincinnati *(G-4695)*

US Bronco Services Inc ....E 513 829-9880
Fairfield *(G-10797)*

US Protection Service LLC ....D 513 422-7910
Cincinnati *(G-4742)*

◆ Veritiv Pubg & Print MGT Inc ....E 330 650-5522
Hudson *(G-12011)*

Vigilant Global Trade Svcs LLC ....E 260 417-1825
Shaker Heights *(G-16719)*

Vista Industrial Packaging LLC ....D 800 454-6117
Columbus *(G-8855)*

Vocalink Inc ....B 937 223-1415
Dayton *(G-9858)*

Vocon Design Inc 216 588-0800
Cleveland *(G-6641)*

Walter Alexander Entps Inc ....E 513 841-1100
Cincinnati *(G-4769)*

Weaver Industries Inc ....C 330 379-3606
Akron *(G-496)*

Weaver Industries Inc ....E 330 379-3660
Akron *(G-497)*

Weaver Industries Inc ....C 330 666-5114
Akron *(G-498)*

Weaver Industries Inc ....C 330 745-2400
Akron *(G-499)*

Wegman Construction Company ....E 513 381-1111
Cincinnati *(G-4773)*

Welch Packaging Group Inc ....C 614 870-2000
Columbus *(G-8884)*

West Corporation ....B 330 574-0510
Niles *(G-15174)*

◆ Western Rserve Wtr Systems Inc ....D 216 341-9797
Newburgh Heights *(G-15116)*

▲ White Oak Investments Inc ....D 614 491-1000
Columbus *(G-8897)*

Wiegands Lake Park Inc ....E 440 338-5795
Novelty *(G-15467)*

Worldpay Inc ....C 513 900-5250
Symmes Twp *(G-17467)*

Wtb Inc ....E 216 298-1895
Cleveland *(G-6692)*

Zebu Compliance Solutions LLC.......E 740 355-9029
Portsmouth *(G-16182)*

75 AUTOMOTIVE REPAIR, SERVICES, AND PARKING

7513 Truck Rental & Leasing, Without Drivers

Aim Integrated Logistics Inc ....B 330 759-0438
Girard *(G-11281)*

Aim Leasing Company ....D 330 759-0438
Girard *(G-11282)*

▼ Albert Mike Leasing Inc ....C 513 563-1400
Cincinnati *(G-2919)*

Benedict Enterprises Inc ....E 513 539-9216
Monroe *(G-14563)*

Best Way Motor Lines Inc ....C 419 485-8373
Montpelier *(G-14606)*

Diane Sauer Chevrolet Inc ....D 330 373-1600
Warren *(G-18702)*

E H Schmidt Executive ....D 419 874-4331
Perrysburg *(G-15861)*

First Group Investment Partnr ....D 513 241-2200
Cincinnati *(G-3558)*

Firstgroup Usa Inc ....B 513 241-2200
Cincinnati *(G-3569)*

Fountain City Leasing Inc ....D 419 785-3100
Defiance *(G-9916)*

Geo Byers Sons Holding Inc ....E 614 239-1084
Columbus *(G-7658)*

Graham Chevrolet-Cadillac Co ....D 419 989-4012
Ontario *(G-15551)*

▼ Grogans Towne Chrysler Inc ....D 419 476-0761
Toledo *(G-17772)*

Helton Enterprises Inc ....E 419 423-4180
Findlay *(G-10922)*

Hogan Truck Leasing Inc ....E 513 454-3500
Fairfield *(G-10736)*

▲ Hy-Tek Material Handling Inc ....D 614 497-2500
Columbus *(G-7790)*

Interstate Truckway Inc ....D 513 542-5500
Cincinnati *(G-3781)*

Kempthorn Motors Inc ....C 800 451-3877
Canton *(G-2365)*

Kenworth of Cincinnati Inc ....D 513 771-5831
Cincinnati *(G-3862)*

Kirk NationaLease Co ....E 937 498-1151
Sidney *(G-16783)*

Knisely Inc ....D 330 343-5812
Dover *(G-10085)*

▲ Krieger Ford Inc ....C 614 888-3320
Columbus *(G-7927)*

McCluskey Chevrolet Inc ....C 513 761-1111
Cincinnati *(G-3986)*

Miami Valley Intl Trcks Inc ....D 513 733-8500
Cincinnati *(G-4045)*

Montrose Ford Inc ....D 330 666-0711
Fairlawn *(G-10842)*

Murray Leasing Inc ....E 330 386-4757
East Liverpool *(G-10408)*

Northern Management & Leasing........D 216 676-4600
Cleveland *(G-6097)*

◆ Ohio Machinery Co ....C 440 526-6200
Broadview Heights *(G-1840)*

Os Hill Leasing Inc ....E 330 386-6440
East Liverpool *(G-10414)*

Paccar Leasing Corporation ....E 937 235-2589
Dayton *(G-9681)*

Penske Logistics LLC ....D 440 232-5811
Cleveland *(G-6192)*

Penske Truck Leasing Co LP ....E 419 873-8611
Perrysburg *(G-15900)*

Penske Truck Leasing Co LP ....E 614 658-0000
Columbus *(G-8436)*

Penske Truck Leasing Co LP ....E 513 771-7701
Cincinnati *(G-4227)*

Penske Truck Leasing Co LP ....E 330 645-3100
Akron *(G-377)*

Penske Truck Leasing Co LP ....E 440 232-5811
Bedford *(G-1300)*

Predator Trucking Company ....E 330 530-0712
Mc Donald *(G-13897)*

Premier Truck Parts Inc ....E 216 642-5000
Cleveland *(G-6233)*

▼ Premier Truck Sls & Rentl Inc.........E 800 825-1255
Cleveland *(G-6234)*

Roger Bettis Trucking Inc ....C 330 863-2111
Malvern *(G-13126)*

Rouen Chrysler Plymouth Dodge........E 419 837-6228
Woodville *(G-19683)*

Roush Equipment Inc ....E 614 882-1535
Westerville *(G-19300)*

Rush Truck Centers Ohio Inc ....D 513 733-8500
Cincinnati *(G-4414)*

Rush Truck Centers Ohio Inc ....E 419 224-6045
Lima *(G-12735)*

Ryder Truck Rental Inc ....E 614 846-6780
Columbus *(G-8567)*

Ryder Truck Rental Inc ....E 513 241-7736
Cincinnati *(G-4418)*

Ryder Truck Rental Inc ....E 419 666-9833
Perrysburg *(G-15916)*

Ryder Truck Rental Inc ....E 614 876-0405
Columbus *(G-8568)*

Ryder Truck Rental Inc ....E 937 236-1650
Dayton *(G-9744)*

Ryder Truck Rental Inc ....E 513 772-0223
Cincinnati *(G-4419)*

Ryder Truck Rental Inc ....E 216 433-4700
Cleveland *(G-6353)*

Schoner Chevrolet Inc ....E 330 877-6731
Hartville *(G-11698)*

South East Chevrolet Co ....E 440 585-9300
Willoughby Hills *(G-19594)*

Star Leasing Co ....D 614 278-9999
Columbus *(G-8687)*

U Haul Co of Northwestern Ohio ....E 419 478-1101
Toledo *(G-18114)*

U-Haul Neighborhood Dealer -Ce ....E 419 929-3724
New London *(G-14936)*

Vin Devers ....C 888 847-9535
Sylvania *(G-17462)*

Voss Auto Network Inc ....E 937 428-2447
Dayton *(G-9860)*

White Family Companies Inc ....C 937 222-3701
Dayton *(G-9879)*

7514 Passenger Car Rental

Afford-A-Car Inc ....E 937 235-2700
Tipp City *(G-17548)*

Avis Administration ....D 937 898-2581
Vandalia *(G-18505)*

Budget Rent A Car System Inc ....D 216 267-2080
Cleveland *(G-5101)*

Budget Rent A Car System Inc ....E 937 898-1396
Vandalia *(G-18509)*

Cartemp USA Inc ....C 440 715-1000
Solon *(G-16832)*

Clerac LLC ....E 440 345-3999
Strongsville *(G-17290)*

Crawford Group Inc ....D 419 873-7360
Perrysburg *(G-15851)*

Crawford Group Inc ....D 330 665-5432
Akron *(G-170)*

Dealers Group Limited ....E 440 352-4970
Beachwood *(G-1052)*

Edison Local School District ....E 740 543-4011
Amsterdam *(G-601)*

Enterprise Holdings Inc ....D 614 866-1480
Reynoldsburg *(G-16303)*

Enterprise Holdings Inc ....E 937 879-0023
Blue Ash *(G-1555)*

Falls Motor City Inc ....D 330 929-3066
Cuyahoga Falls *(G-9091)*

Family Ford Lincoln Inc ....D 740 373-9127
Marietta *(G-13328)*

Geo Byers Sons Holding Inc ....E 614 239-1084
Columbus *(G-7658)*

George P Ballas Buick GMC Trck ....D 419 535-1000
Toledo *(G-17760)*

Hertz Corporation ....D 216 267-8900
Cleveland *(G-5688)*

Hertz Corporation ....E 513 533-3161
Cincinnati *(G-3699)*

Hertz Corporation ....E 937 890-2721
Vandalia *(G-18526)*

Hertz Corporation ....E 937 898-5806
Vandalia *(G-18527)*

Leikin Motor Companies Inc ....D 440 946-6900
Willoughby *(G-19544)*

Lincoln Mrcury Kings Auto Mall ....C 513 683-3800
Cincinnati *(G-3933)*

National Rental (us) Inc ....E 937 890-0100
Vandalia *(G-18532)*

National Rental (us) Inc ....E 614 239-3270
Columbus *(G-8137)*

Precision Coatings Systems ....E 937 642-4727
Marysville *(G-13523)*

Rental Concepts Inc ....E 216 525-3870
Cleveland *(G-6308)*

Schmidt Daily Rental Inc ....D 419 874-4331
Perrysburg *(G-15919)*

Schoner Chevrolet Inc ....E 330 877-6731
Hartville *(G-11698)*

Spitzer Chevrolet Company ....E 330 966-9524
Canton *(G-2482)*

Taylor Chevrolet Inc ....C 740 653-2091
Lancaster *(G-12440)*

Thrifty Rent-A-Car System Inc ....E 440 842-1660
Cleveland *(G-6528)*

U Save Auto Rental ....E 330 925-2015
Rittman *(G-16410)*

7515 Passenger Car Leasing

1106 West Main Inc ....E 330 673-2122
Kent *(G-12212)*

▼ Albert Mike Leasing Inc ....C 513 563-1400
Cincinnati *(G-2919)*

Auto Center USA Inc ....E 513 683-4900
Cincinnati *(G-3006)*

Beechmont Ford Inc ....C 513 752-6611
Cincinnati *(G-2842)*

Bob Pulte Chevrolet Inc ....E 513 932-0303
Lebanon *(G-12453)*

Bobb Automotive Inc ....E 614 853-3000
Columbus *(G-7052)*

Brondes All Makes Auto Leasing ....D 419 887-1511
Maumee *(G-13767)*

▼ Brondes Ford ....D 419 473-1411
Toledo *(G-17627)*

Brown Motor Sales Co ....E 419 531-0151
Toledo *(G-17629)*

Budget Rent A Car System Inc ....E 937 898-1396
Vandalia *(G-18509)*

▼ Carcorp Inc ....C 877 857-2801
Columbus *(G-7118)*

Chesrown Oldsmobile GMC Inc ....E 614 846-3040
Columbus *(G-7182)*

City Yellow Cab Company ....E 330 253-3141
Akron *(G-140)*

Classic Buick Olds Cadillac ....D 440 639-4500
Painesville *(G-15701)*

Clerac LLC ....E 440 345-3999
Strongsville (G-17290)

Columbus SAI Motors LLC ....E 614 851-3273
Columbus (G-7312)

Dave White Chevrolet Inc ....C 419 885-4444
Sylvania (G-17417)

Dunning Motor Sales Inc ....E 740 439-4465
Cambridge (G-2064)

E H Schmidt Executive ....D 419 874-4331
Perrysburg (G-15861)

Ed Schmidt Chevrolet Inc ....E 419 897-8600
Maumee (G-13783)

Ed Tomko Chryslr Jep Dge Inc ....E 440 835-5900
Avon Lake (G-916)

Enterprise Holdings Inc ....E 937 879-0023
Blue Ash (G-1555)

Germain On Scarborough LLC ....C 614 868-0300
Columbus (G-7665)

Graham Chevrolet-Cadillac Co ....D 419 989-4012
Ontario (G-15551)

Greenwoods Hubbard Chevy-Olds ....E 330 568-4335
Hubbard (G-11946)

▼ Grogans Towne Chrysler Inc ....D 419 476-0761
Toledo (G-17772)

Hidy Motors Inc ....D 937 426-9564
Dayton (G-9176)

Jake Sweeney Automotive Inc ....C 513 782-2800
Cincinnati (G-3805)

Jim Brown Chevrolet Inc ....C 440 255-5511
Mentor (G-14065)

Joe Dodge Kidd Inc ....E 513 752-1804
Cincinnati (G-2858)

Kempthorn Motors Inc ....C 800 451-3877
Canton (G-2365)

Kent Automotive Inc ....E 330 678-5520
Kent (G-12240)

Kerns Chevrolet-Buick-Gmc Inc ....E 419 586-5131
Celina (G-2597)

Kerry Ford Inc ....D 513 671-6400
Cincinnati (G-3864)

Kings Toyota Inc ....D 513 583-4333
Cincinnati (G-3874)

Klaben Family Dodge Inc ....E 330 673-9971
Kent (G-12244)

Klaben Lincoln Ford Inc ....D 330 673-3139
Kent (G-12246)

▲ Krieger Ford Inc ....C 614 888-3320
Columbus (G-7927)

Lakewood Chrysler-Plymouth ....E 216 521-1000
Brookpark (G-1901)

Lang Chevrolet Co ....D 937 426-2313
Beavercreek Township (G-1253)

Lariche Subaru Inc ....D 419 422-1855
Findlay (G-10933)

Lavery Chevrolet-Buick Inc ....D 330 823-1100
Alliance (G-537)

Lebanon Chrysler - Plymuth Inc ......E 513 932-2717
Lebanon (G-12480)

Lima Auto Mall Inc ....D 419 993-6000
Lima (G-12675)

Lincoln Mrcury Kings Auto Mall ....C 513 683-3800
Cincinnati (G-3933)

Mathews Dodge Chrysler Jeep ....E 740 389-2341
Marion (G-13444)

Mathews Kennedy Ford L-M Inc ....D 740 387-3673
Marion (G-13445)

Mc Daniel Motor Co (Inc) ....E 740 389-2355
Marion (G-13446)

McCluskey Chevrolet Inc ....C 513 761-1111
Cincinnati (G-3986)

Medina World Cars Inc ....E 330 725-4901
Strongsville (G-17332)

Merrick Chevrolet Co ....D 440 878-6700
Strongsville (G-17333)

Montrose Ford Inc ....D 330 666-0711
Fairlawn (G-10842)

Mullinax Ford North Canton Inc ....C 330 238-3206
Canton (G-2411)

Nick Mayer Lincoln-Mercury Inc ....E 440 835-3700
Westlake (G-19379)

Northgate Chrysler Jeep Inc ....D 513 385-3900
Cincinnati (G-4129)

Oregon Ford Inc ....C 419 698-4444
Oregon (G-15605)

Partners Auto Group Bdford Inc ....D 440 439-2323
Bedford (G-1299)

Ron Marhofer Automall Inc ....E 330 923-5059
Cuyahoga Falls (G-9122)

Rouen Chrysler Plymouth Dodge ....E 419 837-6228
Woodville (G-19683)

Roush Equipment Inc ....C 614 882-1535
Westerville (G-19300)

Saturn of Toledo Inc ....E 419 841-9070
Toledo (G-18020)

Schoner Chevrolet Inc ....E 330 877-6731
Hartville (G-11698)

Sonic Automotive ....D 614 870-8200
Columbus (G-8658)

Sonic Automotive-1495 Automall ......E 614 317-4326
Columbus (G-8659)

Sorbir Inc ....D 440 449-1000
Cleveland (G-6421)

South East Chevrolet Co ....E 440 585-9300
Willoughby Hills (G-19594)

Spitzer Auto World Amherst ....E 440 988-4444
Amherst (G-598)

Sunnyside Toyota Inc ....D 440 777-9911
North Olmsted (G-15312)

Tansky Motors Inc ....E 650 322-7069
Logan (G-12855)

Team Rahal of Dayton Inc ....E 937 438-3800
Dayton (G-9807)

Tom Ahl Chryslr-Plymouth-Dodge ......C 419 227-0202
Lima (G-12765)

Toyota of Bedford ....D 440 439-8600
Bedford (G-1310)

Van Devere Inc ....D 330 253-6137
Akron (G-485)

Vin Devers ....C 888 847-9535
Sylvania (G-17462)

Yark Automotive Group Inc ....A 419 841-7771
Toledo (G-18166)

7519 Utility Trailers & Recreational Vehicle Rental

A Duie Pyle Inc ....D 330 342-7750
Streetsboro (G-17243)

Ample Trailer Leasing & Sales ....E 513 563-2550
Cincinnati (G-2957)

Benedict Enterprises Inc ....E 513 539-9216
Monroe (G-14563)

Brown Gibbons Lang Ltd Ptrship ....C 216 241-2800
Cleveland (G-5093)

E & J Trailer Leasing Inc ....E 513 563-7366
Cincinnati (G-3462)

E & J Trailer Sales & Service ....E 513 563-2550
Cincinnati (G-3463)

▲ Eleet Cryogenics Inc ....E 330 874-4009
Bolivar (G-1702)

Ryder Truck Rental Inc ....E 614 846-6780
Columbus (G-8567)

Ryder Truck Rental Inc ....E 513 772-0223
Cincinnati (G-4419)

Transport Services Inc ....D 440 582-4900
Cleveland (G-6543)

U Haul Co of Northwestern Ohio ....E 419 478-1101
Toledo (G-18114)

U-Haul Neighborhood Dealer -Ce ......E 419 929-3724
New London (G-14936)

7521 Automobile Parking Lots & Garages

ABM Parking Services Inc ....E 937 461-2113
Dayton (G-9203)

ABM Parking Services Inc ....E 330 747-7678
Youngstown (G-19945)

ABM Parking Services Inc ....E 216 621-6600
Cleveland (G-4895)

Allpro Parking Ohio LLC ....E 614 221-9696
Columbus (G-6899)

Amherst Exempted Vlg Schools ....E 440 988-2633
Amherst (G-579)

Asv Services LLC ....E 216 797-1701
Euclid (G-10623)

Central Parking System Inc ....E 513 381-2621
Cincinnati (G-3156)

Chillicothe City School Dst ....D 740 775-2936
Chillicothe (G-2760)

City of Garfield Heights ....E 216 475-1107
Cleveland (G-5201)

City of Lakewood ....D 216 941-1116
Cleveland (G-5208)

City of New Philadelphia ....E 330 339-2121
New Philadelphia (G-14950)

City of Parma ....D 440 885-8983
Cleveland (G-5211)

City of Portsmouth ....E 740 353-3459
Portsmouth (G-16130)

County of Holmes ....C 330 674-5916
Millersburg (G-14470)

Dasher Lawless Automation LLC ....E 855 755-7275
Warren (G-18699)

Falcon Transport Co ....D 330 793-1345
Youngstown (G-20035)

Kwik Parking ....E 419 246-0454
Toledo (G-17844)

Ohio Department Transportation ....E 330 637-5951
Cortland (G-8992)

Park n Fly Inc ....E 404 264-1000
Cleveland (G-6167)

Park Place Management Inc ....E 216 362-1080
Cleveland (G-6168)

Park-N-Go Inc ....E 937 890-7275
Dayton (G-9686)

Parking Company America Inc ....B 513 241-0415
Cincinnati (G-4204)

Parking Company America Inc ....E 216 265-0500
Cleveland (G-6173)

Parking Company America Inc ....E 513 381-2179
Cincinnati (G-4205)

Prestige Valet Inc ....D 513 871-4220
Cincinnati (G-4277)

Republic Parking System Inc ....E 937 415-0016
Vandalia (G-18540)

Shaias Parking Inc ....E 216 621-0328
Cleveland (G-6401)

Sharps Valet Parking ....E 513 863-1777
Fairfield (G-10779)

Southwood Auto Sales ....D 330 788-8822
Youngstown (G-20214)

Sp Plus Corporation ....D 216 444-2255
Cleveland (G-6436)

Sp Plus Corporation ....E 216 687-0141
Cleveland (G-6437)

Sp Plus Corporation ....D 216 267-7275
Cleveland (G-6438)

Sp Plus Corporation ....D 216 267-5030
Cleveland (G-6439)

United Parcel Service Inc OH ....C 419 424-9494
Findlay (G-10972)

USA Parking Systems Inc ....D 216 621-9255
Cleveland (G-6611)

Yark Automotive Group Inc ....A 419 841-7771
Toledo (G-18166)

7532 Top, Body & Upholstery Repair & Paint Shops

Advantage Ford Lincoln Mercury ....E 419 334-9751
Fremont (G-11056)

American Bulk Commodities Inc ....C 330 758-0841
Youngstown (G-19953)

American Nat Fleet Svc Inc ....D 216 447-6060
Cleveland (G-4961)

Arch Abraham Susuki Ltd ....E 440 934-6001
Elyria (G-10479)

Auto Body North Inc ....D 614 436-3700
Columbus (G-7004)

Bakers Cllsion Repr Specialist ....E 419 524-1350
Mansfield (G-13138)

Bauman Chrysler Jeep Dodge ....E 419 332-8291
Fremont (G-11059)

Bobbart Industries Inc ....E 419 350-5477
Sylvania (G-17412)

▼ Brondes Ford ....D 419 473-1411
Toledo (G-17627)

Brown Motor Sales Co ....D 419 531-0151
Toledo (G-17629)

Buddies Inc ....E 216 642-3362
Cleveland (G-5100)

Burtons Collision ....E 513 984-3396
Cincinnati (G-3094)

Busam Fairfield LLC ....E 513 771-8100
Fairfield (G-10702)

Carls Body Shop Inc ....E 937 253-5166
Dayton (G-9280)

Chesrown Oldsmobile GMC Inc ....E 614 846-3040
Columbus (G-7182)

Cincinnati Collision Center ....E 513 984-4445
Blue Ash (G-1524)

Coughlin Chevrolet Inc ....E 740 852-1122
London (G-12862)

Coughlin Chevrolet Inc ....D 740 964-9191
Pataskala (G-15784)

Coughlin Chevrolet Toyota Inc ....D 740 366-1381
Newark (G-15028)

Dan Tobin Pontiac Buick GMC ....E 614 889-6300
Columbus (G-7412)

Dave Dnnis Chrysler Jeep Dodge ....D 937 429-5566
Beavercreek Township (G-1245)

Dave White Chevrolet Inc ....C 419 885-4444
　Sylvania (G-17417)
Decorative Paint Incorporated ....D 419 485-0632
　Montpelier (G-14613)
Dent Magic ....E 614 864-3368
　Columbus (G-7435)
Donnell Ford-Lincoln ....E 330 332-0031
　Salem (G-16542)
Doug Bigelow Chevrolet Inc ....D 330 644-7500
　Akron (G-192)
Downtown Ford Lincoln Inc ....D 330 456-2781
　Canton (G-2290)
Dutro Ford Lincoln-Mercury Inc ....D 740 452-6334
　Zanesville (G-20301)
Eastside Body Shop ....E 513 624-1145
　Cincinnati (G-3478)
Ed Mullinax Ford LLC ....C 440 984-2431
　Amherst (G-584)
Ed Schmidt Auto Inc ....C 419 874-4331
　Perrysburg (G-15863)
Excalibur Auto Body Inc ....E 440 942-5550
　Willowick (G-19598)
Family Ford Lincoln Inc ....D 740 373-9127
　Marietta (G-13328)
Franks Auto Body Shop Inc ....E 513 829-8282
　Fairfield (G-10729)
George P Ballas Buick GMC Trck ....D 419 535-1000
　Toledo (G-17760)
▼ Grogans Towne Chrysler Inc ....D 419 476-0761
　Toledo (G-17772)
Haydocy Automotive Inc ....D 614 279-8880
　Columbus (G-7719)
I-75 Pierson Automotive Inc ....E 513 424-1881
　Middletown (G-14350)
Jake Sweeney Automotive Inc ....C 513 782-2800
　Cincinnati (G-3805)
Jake Sweeney Body Shop ....E 513 782-1100
　Cincinnati (G-3806)
Jeff Wyler Ft Thomas Inc ....D 513 752-7450
　Cincinnati (G-2856)
Jim Brown Chevrolet Inc ....E 440 255-5511
　Mentor (G-14066)
Joe Dodge Kidd Inc ....E 513 752-1804
　Cincinnati (G-2858)
Joseph Chevrolet Oldsmobile Co ....C 513 741-6700
　Cincinnati (G-3833)
Joyce Buick Inc ....E 419 529-3211
　Ontario (G-15557)
Kallas Enterprises Inc ....E 330 253-6893
　Akron (G-297)
Kerry Ford Inc ....D 513 671-6400
　Cincinnati (G-3864)
King Collision ....E 330 729-0525
　Youngstown (G-20093)
King Collision Inc ....E 330 372-3242
　Warren (G-18720)
Kumler Collision Inc ....E 740 653-4301
　Lancaster (G-12408)
Lang Chevrolet Co ....D 937 426-2313
　Beavercreek Township (G-1253)
Lavery Chevrolet-Buick Inc ....E 330 823-1100
　Alliance (G-537)
Leikin Motor Companies Inc ....D 440 946-6900
　Willoughby (G-19544)
Lennys Auto Sales Inc ....E 330 848-2993
　Barberton (G-959)
Lima Auto Mall Inc ....D 419 993-6000
　Lima (G-12675)
Magic Industries Inc ....E 614 759-8422
　Columbus (G-8008)
Maines Collision Repr & Bdy Sp ....D 937 322-4618
　Springfield (G-17066)
Mark Thomas Ford Inc ....E 330 638-1010
　Cortland (G-8989)
Mathews Ford Inc ....D 740 522-2181
　Newark (G-15066)
Mathews Kennedy Ford L-M Inc ....D 740 387-3673
　Marion (G-13445)
Matia Motors Inc ....E 440 365-7311
　Elyria (G-10534)
Medina World Cars Inc ....E 330 725-4901
　Strongsville (G-17332)
Merrick Body Shop ....E 440 243-6700
　Berea (G-1430)
Mike Castrucci Ford ....C 513 831-7010
　Milford (G-14410)
Montrose Ford Inc ....D 330 666-0711
　Fairlawn (G-10842)
Mowerys Collision Inc ....E 614 274-6072
　Columbus (G-8116)

Mullinax East LLC ....D 440 296-3020
　Wickliffe (G-19470)
Northgate Chrysler Jeep Inc ....D 513 385-3900
　Cincinnati (G-4129)
Oregon Ford Inc ....C 419 698-4444
　Oregon (G-15605)
Palmer Trucks Inc ....E 937 235-3318
　Dayton (G-9683)
Paul Hrnchar Ford-Mercury Inc ....E 330 533-3673
　Canfield (G-2155)
Precision Coatings Systems ....E 937 642-4727
　Marysville (G-13523)
▼ QT Equipment Company ....D 330 724-3055
　Akron (G-394)
Ron Marhofer Automall Inc ....B 330 835-6707
　Cuyahoga Falls (G-9121)
Ron Marhofer Automall Inc ....E 330 923-5059
　Cuyahoga Falls (G-9122)
Ron Marhofer Collision Center ....E 330 686-2262
　Stow (G-17228)
Roush Equipment Inc ....C 614 882-1535
　Westerville (G-19300)
Service King Holdings LLC ....D 216 362-1600
　Cleveland (G-6399)
Service King Holdings LLC ....E 330 926-0100
　Stow (G-17229)
Sharonville Car Wash ....E 513 769-4219
　Cincinnati (G-4464)
Sharpnack Chvrlet Bick Cdillac ....D 419 935-0194
　Willard (G-19487)
Skinner Diesel Services Inc ....E 614 491-8785
　Columbus (G-8649)
Sonic Automotive-1495 Automall ....E 614 317-4326
　Columbus (G-8659)
St Clair Auto Body ....E 216 531-7300
　Cleveland (G-6448)
Suburban Collision Centers ....E 440 243-5533
　Berea (G-1438)
Sunnyside Toyota Inc ....E 440 777-9911
　North Olmsted (G-15312)
Surfside Motors Inc ....E 419 462-1746
　Galion (G-11183)
Tallmadge Collision Center ....E 330 630-2188
　Tallmadge (G-17494)
Tansky Motors Inc ....E 650 322-7069
　Logan (G-12855)
Target Auto Body Inc ....E 216 391-1942
　Cleveland (G-6499)
Three C Body Shop Inc ....D 614 274-9700
　Columbus (G-8751)
Three C Body Shop Inc ....E 614 885-0900
　Columbus (G-8752)
▲ Transitworks LLC ....D 330 861-1118
　Richfield (G-16381)
True2form Collision Repair Ctr ....E 330 399-6659
　Warren (G-18752)
Voss Auto Network Inc ....B 937 433-1444
　Dayton (G-9861)
Walker Auto Group Inc ....D 937 433-4950
　Miamisburg (G-14236)
Warner Buick-Nissan Inc ....E 419 423-7161
　Findlay (G-10974)
Wayside Body Shop Inc ....E 937 233-3182
　Dayton (G-9869)
White Family Collision Center ....E 419 885-8885
　Sylvania (G-17464)
Wmk LLC ....E 440 951-4335
　Mentor (G-14125)

7533 Automotive Exhaust System Repair Shops

Dayton-Dixie Mufflers Inc ....E 419 243-7281
　Toledo (G-17694)
Midas Auto Systems Experts ....E 419 243-7281
　Toledo (G-17913)
Monro Inc ....D 937 999-3202
　Springboro (G-16976)
Monro Inc ....D 614 360-3883
　Columbus (G-8099)
Monro Inc ....D 440 835-2393
　Westlake (G-19375)
Tuffy Associates Corp ....E 419 865-6900
　Toledo (G-18112)

7534 Tire Retreading & Repair Shops

▲ Best One Tire & Svc Lima Inc ....E 419 229-2380
　Lima (G-12606)
Bob Sumerel Tire Co Inc ....E 937 235-0062
　Dayton (G-9256)

Bob Sumerel Tire Co Inc ....E 614 527-9700
　Columbus (G-7051)
Bridgestone Ret Operations LLC ....E 513 367-7888
　Harrison (G-11662)
Bridgestone Ret Operations LLC ....E 419 586-1600
　Celina (G-2585)
Central Ohio Bandag LP ....E 740 454-9728
　Zanesville (G-20291)
Goodyear Tire & Rubber Company ....E 440 735-9910
　Walton Hills (G-18636)
◆ Goodyear Tire & Rubber Company ....A 330 796-2121
　Akron (G-242)
▲ Grismer Tire Company ....E 937 643-2526
　Centerville (G-2626)
H & H Retreading Inc ....D 740 682-7721
　Oak Hill (G-15480)
K S Bandag Inc ....E 330 264-9237
　Wooster (G-19735)
Liberty Tire Recycling LLC ....E 614 871-8097
　Grove City (G-11448)

7536 Automotive Glass Replacement Shops

▲ Advanced Auto Glass Inc ....E 412 373-6675
　Akron (G-19)
▲ Belletech Corp ....D 937 599-3774
　Bellefontaine (G-1347)
▲ C-Auto Glass Inc ....E 216 351-2193
　Cleveland (G-5111)
Mels Auto Glass Inc ....E 513 563-7771
　Cincinnati (G-4005)
Ryans All-Glass Incorporated ....E 513 771-4440
　Cincinnati (G-4417)
Safelite Fulfillment Inc ....E 614 781-5449
　Columbus (G-8573)
Safelite Fulfillment Inc ....E 216 475-7781
　Cleveland (G-6363)
Safelite Fulfillment Inc ....E 614 210-9050
　Columbus (G-8574)
▲ Safelite Glass Corp ....A 614 210-9000
　Columbus (G-8575)
Safelite Glass Corp ....E 614 431-4936
　Worthington (G-19846)
▲ Safelite Group Inc ....A 614 210-9000
　Columbus (G-8576)
Wiechart Enterprises Inc ....E 419 227-0027
　Lima (G-12784)

7537 Automotive Transmission Repair Shops

Ohio Transmission Corporation ....E 614 342-6247
　Columbus (G-8358)
W W Williams Company LLC ....D 614 228-5000
　Dublin (G-10368)
W W Williams Company LLC ....E 330 225-7751
　Brunswick (G-1945)

7538 General Automotive Repair Shop

Abers Garage Inc ....E 419 281-5500
　Ashland (G-644)
Abraham Ford LLC ....E 440 233-7402
　Elyria (G-10477)
Advantage Ford Lincoln Mercury ....E 419 334-9751
　Fremont (G-11056)
Aim Leasing Company ....D 330 759-0438
　Girard (G-11282)
Allied Truck Parts Co ....E 330 477-8127
　Canton (G-2181)
Allstate Trk Sls of Estrn OH ....E 330 339-5555
　New Philadelphia (G-14945)
American Nat Fleet Svc Inc ....D 216 447-6060
　Cleveland (G-4961)
Ashtabula Area City School Dst ....E 440 992-1221
　Ashtabula (G-705)
Auto Center USA Inc ....E 513 683-4900
　Cincinnati (G-3006)
Beaverdam Fleet Services Inc ....E 419 643-8880
　Beaverdam (G-1266)
Beechmont Ford Inc ....C 513 752-6611
　Cincinnati (G-2842)
Benedict Enterprises Inc ....E 513 539-9216
　Monroe (G-14563)
Bill Delord Autocenter Inc ....D 513 932-3000
　Lebanon (G-12452)
Bob-Boyd Ford Inc ....D 614 860-0606
　Lancaster (G-12372)
Bowling Green Lncln-Mrcury Inc ....E 419 352-2553
　Bowling Green (G-1722)
▲ Brentlinger Enterprises ....C 614 889-2571
　Dublin (G-10150)
▼ Brondes Ford ....D 419 473-1411
　Toledo (G-17627)

Brown Motor Sales Co .... E 419 531-0151
Toledo *(G-17629)*
Burtons Collision .... E 513 984-3396
Cincinnati *(G-3094)*
Cain Motors Inc .... E 330 494-5588
Canton *(G-2225)*
Carl E Oeder Sons Sand & Grav .... E 513 494-1555
Lebanon *(G-12454)*
Cascade Group Inc .... E 330 929-1861
Cuyahoga Falls *(G-9077)*
Central Cadillac Limited .... D 216 861-5800
Cleveland *(G-5153)*
Chillicothe City School Dst .... E 740 775-2936
Chillicothe *(G-2760)*
City of Berea .... E 440 826-5853
Berea *(G-1418)*
City of Toledo .... D 419 936-2507
Toledo *(G-17659)*
Classic International Inc .... D 440 975-1222
Mentor *(G-14030)*
Cole-Valley Motor Co .... D 330 372-1665
Warren *(G-18685)*
Columbus Col-Weld Corporation .... E 614 276-5303
Columbus *(G-7270)*
Columbus Diesel Supply Co Inc .... E 614 445-8391
Reynoldsburg *(G-16292)*
Columbus SAI Motors LLC .... E 614 851-3273
Columbus *(G-7312)*
Conrads Tire Service Inc .... E 216 941-3333
Cleveland *(G-5334)*
Coughlin Chevrolet Inc .... D 740 964-9191
Pataskala *(G-15784)*
County Engineering Office .... E 419 334-9731
Fremont *(G-11064)*
County Engineers Office .... E 740 702-3130
Chillicothe *(G-2771)*
County of Lorain .... D 440 326-5880
Elyria *(G-10500)*
Crestmont Cadillac Corporation .... E 216 831-5300
Cleveland *(G-5380)*
Cummins Inc .... E 614 771-1000
Hilliard *(G-11759)*
Dan Tobin Pontiac Buick GMC .... D 614 889-6300
Columbus *(G-7412)*
Dave Dnnis Chrysler Jeep Dodge .... D 937 429-5566
Beavercreek Township *(G-1245)*
Dave White Chevrolet Inc .... C 419 885-4444
Sylvania *(G-17417)*
Dcr Systems LLC .... E 440 205-9900
Mentor *(G-14039)*
Decosky Motor Holdings Inc .... E 740 397-9122
Mount Vernon *(G-14762)*
Delaware City School District .... E 740 363-5901
Delaware *(G-9967)*
Dickinson Fleet Services LLC .... E 513 772-3629
Cincinnati *(G-3429)*
Don Wood Inc .... D 740 593-6641
Athens *(G-776)*
Don Wood Inc .... D 740 593-6641
Athens *(G-777)*
Donnell Ford-Lincoln .... E 330 332-0031
Salem *(G-16542)*
Doug Bigelow Chevrolet Inc .... D 330 644-7500
Akron *(G-192)*
Doug Marine Motors Inc .... E 740 335-3700
Wshngtn CT Hs *(G-19869)*
Downtheroad Inc .... E 740 452-4579
Zanesville *(G-20300)*
Downtown Ford Lincoln Inc .... D 330 456-2781
Canton *(G-2290)*
Dunning Motor Sales Inc .... E 740 439-4465
Cambridge *(G-2064)*
Dutro Ford Lincoln-Mercury Inc .... D 740 452-6334
Zanesville *(G-20301)*
Ed Mullinax Ford LLC .... C 440 984-2431
Amherst *(G-584)*
Ed Schmidt Auto Inc .... C 419 874-4331
Perrysburg *(G-15863)*
Ed Tomko Chryslr Jep Dge Inc .... E 440 835-5900
Avon Lake *(G-916)*
Family Ford Lincoln Inc .... D 740 373-9127
Marietta *(G-13328)*
FCA US LLC .... E 419 727-2800
Toledo *(G-17728)*
Flagship Services of Ohio Inc .... D 740 533-1657
Ironton *(G-12153)*
Fyda Freightliner Youngstown .... D 330 797-0224
Youngstown *(G-20041)*
Germain On Scarborough LLC .... C 614 868-0300
Columbus *(G-7665)*
Giles Marathon Inc .... E 440 974-8815
Mentor *(G-14051)*
Glenway Automotive Service .... E 513 921-2117
Cincinnati *(G-3620)*
◆ **Goodyear Tire & Rubber Company** .... A 330 796-2121
Akron *(G-242)*
Greenwood Chevrolet Inc .... C 330 270-1299
Youngstown *(G-20057)*
Greenwoods Hubbard Chevy-Olds .... E 330 568-4335
Hubbard *(G-11946)*
Greg Ford Sweet Inc .... E 440 593-7714
North Kingsville *(G-15257)*
▲ **Grismer Tire Company** .... E 937 643-2526
Centerville *(G-2626)*
▼ **Grogans Towne Chrysler Inc** .... D 419 476-0761
Toledo *(G-17772)*
Guess Motors Inc .... E 866 890-0522
Carrollton *(G-2571)*
Hartwig Transit Inc .... E 513 563-1765
Cincinnati *(G-3683)*
Haydocy Automotive Inc .... D 614 279-8880
Columbus *(G-7719)*
▼ **Hill Intl Trcks NA LLC** .... D 330 386-6440
East Liverpool *(G-10404)*
Hoss Value Cars & Trucks Inc .... E 937 428-2400
Dayton *(G-9507)*
▲ **Hy-Tek Material Handling Inc** .... D 614 497-2500
Columbus *(G-7790)*
I-75 Pierson Automotive Inc .... E 513 424-1881
Middletown *(G-14350)*
Irace Inc .... E 330 836-7247
Akron *(G-281)*
J D S Leasing Inc .... E 440 236-6575
Columbia Station *(G-6776)*
Jake Sweeney Automotive Inc .... C 513 782-2800
Cincinnati *(G-3805)*
Jerry Haag Motors Inc .... E 937 402-2090
Hillsboro *(G-11848)*
Jim Brown Chevrolet Inc .... E 440 255-5511
Mentor *(G-14066)*
Jim Keim Ford .... D 614 888-3333
Columbus *(G-7859)*
Joe Dodge Kidd Inc .... E 513 752-1804
Cincinnati *(G-2858)*
Joseph Chevrolet Oldsmobile Co .... C 513 741-6700
Cincinnati *(G-3833)*
Joseph Russo .... E 440 748-2690
Grafton *(G-11317)*
▲ **Jtekt Auto Tenn Morristown** .... C 440 835-1000
Westlake *(G-19362)*
Kaffenbarger Truck Eqp Co .... E 513 772-6800
Cincinnati *(G-3846)*
Kempthorn Motors Inc .... C 800 451-3877
Canton *(G-2365)*
Kennedy Mint Inc .... D 440 572-3222
Cleveland *(G-5824)*
Kent Automotive Inc .... E 330 678-5520
Kent *(G-12240)*
Kenworth of Cincinnati Inc .... D 513 771-5831
Cincinnati *(G-3862)*
Kerns Chevrolet-Buick-Gmc Inc .... E 419 586-5131
Celina *(G-2597)*
Kerry Ford Inc .... D 513 671-6400
Cincinnati *(G-3864)*
Kings Toyota Inc .... D 513 583-4333
Cincinnati *(G-3874)*
Kirk NationaLease Co .... E 937 498-1151
Sidney *(G-16783)*
Klaben Family Dodge Inc .... E 330 673-9971
Kent *(G-12244)*
Knox Auto LLC .... E 330 701-5266
Mount Vernon *(G-14771)*
▲ **Krieger Ford Inc** .... C 614 888-3320
Columbus *(G-7927)*
Lakewood Chrysler-Plymouth .... E 216 521-1000
Brookpark *(G-1901)*
Lakota Bus Garage .... E 419 986-5558
Kansas *(G-12208)*
Lane Chevrolet .... D 937 426-2313
Beavercreek Township *(G-1252)*
Lang Chevrolet Co .... D 937 426-2313
Beavercreek Township *(G-1253)*
Lariche Subaru Inc .... D 419 422-1855
Findlay *(G-10933)*
Lavery Chevrolet-Buick Inc .... E 330 823-1100
Alliance *(G-537)*
Lebanon Chrysler - Plymouth Inc .... E 513 932-2717
Lebanon *(G-12480)*
Lima Auto Mall Inc .... D 419 993-6000
Lima *(G-12675)*
Lima City School District .... E 419 996-3450
Lima *(G-12676)*
Lincoln Mrcury Kings Auto Mall .... C 513 683-3800
Cincinnati *(G-3933)*
Lindsey Accura Inc .... E 800 980-8199
Columbus *(G-7981)*
Lower Great Lakes Kenworth Inc .... E 419 874-3511
Perrysburg *(G-15890)*
Madison Motor Service Inc .... E 419 332-0727
Fremont *(G-11085)*
Maines Collision Repr & Bdy Sp .... D 937 322-4618
Springfield *(G-17066)*
Man-Tansky Inc .... E 740 454-2512
Zanesville *(G-20328)*
Mansfield Truck Sls & Svc Inc .... E 419 522-9811
Mansfield *(G-13211)*
Mark Thomas Ford Inc .... E 330 638-1010
Cortland *(G-8989)*
Martin Chevrolet Inc .... E 937 849-1381
Dayton *(G-9587)*
Mathews Dodge Chrysler Jeep .... E 740 389-2341
Marion *(G-13444)*
Mathews Ford Inc .... D 740 522-2181
Newark *(G-15066)*
Mathews Kennedy Ford L-M Inc .... D 740 387-3673
Marion *(G-13445)*
Matia Motors Inc .... E 440 365-7311
Elyria *(G-10534)*
May Jim Auto Sales LLC .... E 419 422-9797
Findlay *(G-10940)*
Medina World Cars Inc .... E 330 725-4901
Strongsville *(G-17332)*
Midway Garage Inc .... E 740 345-0699
Newark *(G-15071)*
Midwest Trailer Sales & Svc .... E 513 772-2818
West Chester *(G-18972)*
Mike Castrucci Ford .... C 513 831-7010
Milford *(G-14410)*
Mizar Motors Inc .... D 419 729-2400
Toledo *(G-17919)*
Monro Inc .... D 440 835-2393
Westlake *(G-19375)*
Montrose Ford Inc .... D 330 666-0711
Fairlawn *(G-10842)*
Morris Cadillac Buick GMC .... D 440 327-4181
North Olmsted *(G-15298)*
Mullinax East LLC .... D 440 296-3020
Wickliffe *(G-19470)*
Nassief Automotive Inc .... E 440 997-5151
Austinburg *(G-853)*
National Auto Experts LLC .... E 440 274-5114
Strongsville *(G-17336)*
Navistar Intl Trnsp Corp .... C 937 390-4242
Springfield *(G-17087)*
Newtown Nine Inc .... E 330 376-7741
Akron *(G-345)*
Nick Mayer Lincoln-Mercury Inc .... E 440 835-3700
Westlake *(G-19379)*
Northern Automotive Inc .... E 614 436-2001
Columbus *(G-8200)*
Northgate Chrysler Jeep Inc .... D 513 385-3900
Cincinnati *(G-4129)*
Ohio Automobile Club .... E 614 559-0000
Columbus *(G-8231)*
Oregon Ford Inc .... C 419 698-4444
Oregon *(G-15605)*
OReilly Automotive Inc .... E 513 783-1343
Middletown *(G-14317)*
OReilly Automotive Inc .... E 330 267-4383
Hartville *(G-11696)*
OReilly Automotive Inc .... E 513 800-1169
Cincinnati *(G-4180)*
OReilly Automotive Inc .... E 513 818-4166
Cincinnati *(G-4181)*
Palmer Trucks Inc .... E 937 235-3318
Dayton *(G-9683)*
Parrish Tire Company of Akron .... E 330 628-6800
Mogadore *(G-14554)*
Pep Boys - Manny Moe & Jack .... E 614 864-2092
Columbus *(G-8438)*
Peterbilt of Cincinnati .... E 513 772-1740
Cincinnati *(G-4235)*
PGT Trucking Inc .... E 419 943-3437
Leipsic *(G-12521)*
Progrssive Oldsmobile Cadillac .... E 330 833-8585
Massillon *(G-13721)*
R & R Inc .... E 330 799-1536
Youngstown *(G-20174)*
Rebman Truck Service Inc .... E 419 589-8161
Mansfield *(G-13233)*

Employee Codes: A=Over 500 employees, B=251-500
C=101-250, D=51-100, E=25-50
2019 Harris Ohio
Services Directory
947

▲ Ricart Ford Inc ....B 614 836-5321
　Groveport *(G-11535)*
Ron Marhofer Automall Inc ....E 330 923-5059
　Cuyahoga Falls *(G-9122)*
Rondy Fleet Services Inc ....C 330 745-9016
　Barberton *(G-965)*
Roush Equipment Inc ....C 614 882-1535
　Westerville *(G-19300)*
Rush Motor Sales Inc ....E 614 471-9980
　Columbus *(G-8561)*
Rush Truck Centers Ohio Inc ....D 513 733-8500
　Cincinnati *(G-4414)*
Rush Truck Centers Ohio Inc ....E 419 224-6045
　Lima *(G-12735)*
Schoner Chevrolet Inc ....E 330 877-6731
　Hartville *(G-11698)*
Scotts Towing Co ....E 419 729-7888
　Toledo *(G-18022)*
Skinner Diesel Services Inc ....E 614 491-8785
　Columbus *(G-8649)*
Sonic Automotive ....D 614 870-8200
　Columbus *(G-8658)*
Spires Motors Inc ....E 614 771-2345
　Hilliard *(G-11817)*
Spitzer Chevrolet Inc ....D 330 467-4141
　Northfield *(G-15386)*
Spitzer Motor City Inc ....E 567 307-7119
　Ontario *(G-15575)*
Spurlock Truck Service ....E 937 268-6100
　Dayton *(G-9787)*
Steubenville Truck Center Inc ....E 740 282-2711
　Steubenville *(G-17173)*
Stoops Frghtlnr-Qlity Trlr Inc ....E 937 236-4092
　Dayton *(G-9795)*
Stratton Chevrolet Co ....E 330 537-3151
　Beloit *(G-1398)*
Sunnyside Toyota Inc ....D 440 777-9911
　North Olmsted *(G-15312)*
Surfside Motors Inc ....E 419 462-1746
　Galion *(G-11183)*
Ta Operating LLC ....B 440 808-9100
　Westlake *(G-19411)*
Tallmadge Board of Education ....E 330 633-2215
　Tallmadge *(G-17493)*
Tansky Motors Inc ....E 650 322-7069
　Logan *(G-12855)*
Taylor Chevrolet Inc ....C 740 653-2091
　Lancaster *(G-12440)*
Ted Ruck Co Inc ....E 419 738-2613
　Wapakoneta *(G-18655)*
Trader Buds Westside Dodge ....D 614 272-0000
　Columbus *(G-8770)*
Travelcenters America Inc ....A 440 808-9100
　Westlake *(G-19413)*
Travelcenters of America LLC ....A 440 808-9100
　Westlake *(G-19415)*
Travelcenters of America LLC ....D 330 769-2053
　Lodi *(G-12829)*
Trepanier Daniels & Trepanier ....D 740 286-1288
　Jackson *(G-12180)*
United Parcel Service Inc OH ....C 419 872-0211
　Perrysburg *(G-15928)*
Valentine Buick Gmc Inc ....D 937 878-7371
　Fairborn *(G-10686)*
Vin Devers ....C 888 847-9535
　Sylvania *(G-17462)*
Volvo BMW Dyton Evans Volkswag .E 937 890-6200
　Dayton *(G-9859)*
Voss Auto Network Inc ....E 937 428-2447
　Dayton *(G-9860)*
Voss Toyota Inc ....E 937 431-2100
　Beavercreek *(G-1195)*
W W Williams Company LLC ....E 419 837-5067
　Perrysburg *(G-15932)*
W W Williams Company LLC ....E 216 252-9977
　Cleveland *(G-6646)*
W W Williams Company LLC ....D 614 228-5000
　Dublin *(G-10368)*
W W Williams Company LLC ....E 330 225-7751
　Brunswick *(G-1945)*
W W Williams Company LLC ....E 614 527-9400
　Hilliard *(G-11828)*
W W Williams Company LLC ....E 614 527-9400
　Hilliard *(G-11829)*
Wagner Lincoln-Mercury Inc ....E 419 435-8131
　Carey *(G-2550)*
Walker Auto Group Inc ....D 937 433-4950
　Miamisburg *(G-14236)*
Warner Buick-Nissan Inc ....E 419 423-7161
　Findlay *(G-10974)*

Workforce Services Inc ....E 330 484-2566
　Canton *(G-2538)*
Young Truck Sales Inc ....E 330 477-6271
　Canton *(G-2541)*
Youngstown-Kenworth Inc ....E 330 534-9761
　Hubbard *(G-11952)*
Zanesville Chevrolet Cadillac ....E 740 452-3611
　Zanesville *(G-20381)*
Zender Electric ....E 419 436-1538
　Fostoria *(G-11015)*

7539 Automotive Repair Shops, NEC

Bbt Fleet Services LLC ....E 419 462-7722
　Mansfield *(G-13139)*
Beechmont Motors Inc ....E 513 388-3883
　Cincinnati *(G-3031)*
Beechmont Toyota Inc ....D 513 388-3800
　Cincinnati *(G-3034)*
Bobby Layman Cadillac GMC Inc ...E 740 654-9590
　Carroll *(G-2556)*
Bridgestone Ret Operations LLC ....E 330 929-3391
　Cuyahoga Falls *(G-9075)*
Broad & James Inc ....E 614 231-8697
　Columbus *(G-7075)*
Burtons Collision ....E 513 984-3396
　Cincinnati *(G-3094)*
Capitol City Trailers Inc ....D 614 491-2616
　Obetz *(G-15523)*
Certified Power Inc ....D 419 355-1200
　Fremont *(G-11062)*
Coates Car Care Inc ....E 330 652-4180
　Niles *(G-15152)*
▲ Double A Trailer Sales Inc ....E 419 692-7626
　Delphos *(G-10025)*
▼ East Manufacturing Corporation ..B 330 325-9921
　Randolph *(G-16230)*
First Services Inc ....A 513 241-2200
　Cincinnati *(G-3559)*
First Transit Inc ....B 513 241-2200
　Cincinnati *(G-3564)*
Fleetpride West Inc ....E 419 243-3161
　Toledo *(G-17742)*
Fred Martin Nissan LLC ....E 330 644-8888
　Akron *(G-228)*
Germain Ford LLC ....C 614 889-7777
　Columbus *(G-7664)*
◆ Goodyear Tire & Rubber Company ..A 330 796-2121
　Akron *(G-242)*
Haasz Automall LLC ....E 330 296-2866
　Ravenna *(G-16245)*
Hans Truck and Trlr Repr Inc ....E 216 581-0046
　Cleveland *(G-5660)*
Hoss II Inc ....E 937 669-4300
　Tipp City *(G-17560)*
Irace Inc ....E 330 836-7247
　Akron *(G-281)*
Jones Truck & Spring Repr Inc ....D 614 443-4619
　Columbus *(G-7868)*
Kings Cove Automotive LLC ....D 513 677-0177
　Fairfield *(G-10744)*
▲ Mac Trailer Manufacturing Inc .....C 330 823-9900
　Alliance *(G-540)*
Marmon Highway Tech LLC ....E 330 878-5595
　Dover *(G-10087)*
Monro Inc ....E 614 235-3684
　Columbus *(G-8098)*
Montrose Sheffield LLC ....D 440 934-6699
　Sheffield Village *(G-16740)*
▼ Nelson Manufacturing Company ...E 419 523-5321
　Ottawa *(G-15660)*
Paul Hrnchar Ford-Mercury Inc ......E 330 533-3673
　Canfield *(G-2155)*
Perkins Motor Service Ltd ....E 440 277-1256
　Lorain *(G-12938)*
Professional Transit Mgt ....E 513 677-6000
　Loveland *(G-13022)*
◆ RL Best Company ....E 330 758-8601
　Boardman *(G-1701)*
S&S Car Care Inc ....E 330 494-9535
　Canton *(G-2468)*
Sanoh America Inc ....C 740 392-9200
　Mount Vernon *(G-14789)*
▲ Speck Sales Incorporated ....E 419 353-8312
　Bowling Green *(G-1749)*
Spitzer Chevrolet Inc ....D 330 467-4141
　Northfield *(G-15386)*
Star Leasing Co ....D 614 278-9999
　Columbus *(G-8687)*
Stoops Frghtlnr-Qlity Trlr Inc ....E 937 236-4092
　Dayton *(G-9795)*

Three C Body Shop Inc ....D 614 274-9700
　Columbus *(G-8751)*
Transport Services Inc ....D 440 582-4900
　Cleveland *(G-6543)*
Tuffy Associates Corp ....E 419 865-6900
　Toledo *(G-18112)*
United Garage & Service Corp ....D 216 623-1550
　Cleveland *(G-6572)*

7542 Car Washes

3 B Ventures LLC ....E 419 236-9461
　Lima *(G-12590)*
Allied Car Wash Inc ....E 513 559-1733
　Cincinnati *(G-2927)*
Beheydts Auto Wrecking ....E 330 658-6109
　Doylestown *(G-10108)*
Blue Beacon of Hubbard Inc ....E 330 534-4419
　Hubbard *(G-11941)*
Blue Beacon USA LP II ....E 330 534-4419
　Hubbard *(G-11942)*
Blue Beacon USA LP II ....E 419 643-8146
　Beaverdam *(G-1267)*
Blue Beacon USA LP II ....E 937 437-5533
　New Paris *(G-14940)*
Bp ....E 216 731-3826
　Euclid *(G-10625)*
Car Wash ....E 216 662-6289
　Cleveland *(G-5121)*
Car Wash Plus Ltd ....E 513 683-4228
　Cincinnati *(G-3114)*
Coates Car Care Inc ....E 330 652-4180
　Niles *(G-15152)*
Consumer Foods ....E 440 284-5972
　Elyria *(G-10493)*
Covington Car Wash Inc ....E 513 831-6164
　Milford *(G-14382)*
Elliott Auto Bath Inc ....E 513 422-3700
　Middletown *(G-14299)*
Expresso Car Wash Systems Inc ....D 419 536-7540
　Toledo *(G-17719)*
Expresso Car Wash Systems Inc ....E 419 866-7099
　Toledo *(G-17720)*
Falls Supersonic Car Wash Inc ......E 330 928-1657
　Cuyahoga Falls *(G-9093)*
Henderson Road Rest Systems ....E 614 442-3310
　Columbus *(G-7739)*
JKL Development Company ....E 937 390-0358
　Springfield *(G-17057)*
John Atwood Inc ....E 440 777-4147
　North Olmsted *(G-15294)*
Johnnys Carwash ....D 513 474-6603
　Cincinnati *(G-3825)*
Klean A Kar Inc ....E 614 221-3145
　Columbus *(G-7910)*
Lawnview Industries Inc ....C 937 653-5217
　Urbana *(G-18438)*
Mikes Carwash Inc ....C 513 677-4700
　Loveland *(G-13013)*
Moo Moo North Hamilton LLC ....D 614 751-9274
　Etna *(G-10611)*
Mr Magic Carnegie Inc ....E 440 461-7572
　Beachwood *(G-1084)*
Napoleon Wash-N-Fill Inc ....C 419 422-7216
　Findlay *(G-10947)*
Napoleon Wash-N-Fill Inc ....D 419 592-0851
　Napoleon *(G-14814)*
North Lima Dairy Queen Inc ....E 330 549-3220
　North Lima *(G-15273)*
Red Carpet Car Wash Inc ....E 330 477-5772
　Canton *(G-2451)*
Robert Stough Ventures Corp ....E 419 882-4073
　Toledo *(G-18011)*
Royal Car Wash Inc ....E 513 385-2777
　Cincinnati *(G-4404)*
Royal Sheen Service Center ....E 330 966-7200
　Canton *(G-2464)*
Sax 5th Ave Car Wash Inc ....E 614 486-9093
　Columbus *(G-8594)*
Sharonville Car Wash ....E 513 769-4219
　Cincinnati *(G-4464)*
Standard Oil Company ....E 330 530-8049
　Girard *(G-11301)*
Susan A Smith Crystal Care ....E 419 747-2666
　Butler *(G-2022)*
Truckomat Corporation ....E 740 467-2818
　Hebron *(G-11725)*
Waterway Gas & Wash Company ....E 330 995-2900
　Aurora *(G-851)*
Yund Inc ....E 330 837-9358
　Massillon *(G-13738)*

7549 Automotive Svcs, Except Repair & Car Washes

AAA Ohio Auto Club ....D.... 614 431-7800
Worthington *(G-19790)*
Abers Garage Inc ....E.... 419 281-5500
Ashland *(G-644)*
▲ **AGC Automotive Americas** ....D.... 937 599-3131
Bellefontaine *(G-1343)*
Aptiv Services Us LLC ....E.... 330 373-3568
Warren *(G-18666)*
Arlington Towing Inc ....E.... 614 488-2006
Columbus *(G-6971)*
Atlas Towing Service ....E.... 513 451-1854
Cincinnati *(G-2999)*
Auto Concepts Cincinnatti LLC ....E.... 513 769-4540
Cincinnati *(G-3007)*
Auto Warehousing Co Inc ....E.... 330 824-5149
Warren *(G-18670)*
B & D Auto & Towing Inc ....E.... 440 237-3737
North Royalton *(G-15347)*
Beaverdam Fleet Services Inc ....E.... 419 643-8880
Beaverdam *(G-1266)*
Broad & James Inc ....E.... 614 231-8697
Columbus *(G-7075)*
Buddies Inc ....E.... 216 642-3362
Cleveland *(G-5100)*
Charlie Towing Service Inc ....E.... 440 234-5300
Berea *(G-1417)*
Chesrown Oldsmobile Cadillac ....E.... 740 366-7373
Granville *(G-11337)*
◆ **Cintas Corporation No 1** ....A.... 513 459-1200
Mason *(G-13556)*
Cleveland Pick-A-Part Inc ....E.... 440 236-5031
Columbia Station *(G-6772)*
Coates Car Care Inc ....E.... 330 652-4180
Niles *(G-15152)*
Cresttek LLC ....E.... 248 602-2083
Dublin *(G-10193)*
Dave Marshall Inc ....D.... 937 878-9135
Fairborn *(G-10668)*
Dealer Supply and Eqp Ltd ....E.... 419 724-8473
Toledo *(G-17695)*
Dutys Towing ....E.... 614 252-3336
Columbus *(G-7479)*
Eastland Crane Service Inc ....E.... 614 868-9750
Columbus *(G-7490)*
Eaton Corporation ....B.... 440 523-5000
Beachwood *(G-1053)*
Eitel Towing Service Inc ....E.... 614 877-4139
Orient *(G-15619)*
Englewood Truck Inc ....E.... 937 836-5109
Clayton *(G-4857)*
Envirotest Systems Corp ....E.... 330 963-4464
Twinsburg *(G-18261)*
Envirotest Systems Corp ....E.... 330 963-4464
Berea *(G-1423)*
Envirotest Systems Corp ....E.... 330 963-4464
Cleveland *(G-5485)*
Envirotest Systems Corp ....E.... 330 963-4464
Kent *(G-12231)*
Envirotest Systems Corp ....E.... 330 963-4464
Elyria *(G-10513)*
Envirotest Systems Corp ....E.... 330 963-4464
Cleveland *(G-5486)*
Envirotest Systems Corp ....E.... 330 963-4464
Chagrin Falls *(G-2665)*
Envirotest Systems Corp ....E.... 330 963-4464
Painesville *(G-15713)*
Envirotest Systems Corp ....E.... 330 963-4464
Medina *(G-13935)*
Envirotest Systems Corp ....E.... 330 963-4464
Chardon *(G-2694)*
Envirotest Systems Corp ....E.... 330 963-4464
Amherst *(G-586)*
Envirotest Systems Corp ....E.... 330 963-4464
Spencer *(G-16953)*
Envirotest Systems Corp ....E.... 330 963-4464
Twinsburg *(G-18262)*
Fayette Parts Service Inc ....C.... 724 880-3616
Wintersville *(G-19670)*
First Vehicle Services Inc ....C.... 513 241-2200
Cincinnati *(G-3565)*
Genicon Inc ....E.... 419 491-4478
Swanton *(G-17398)*
Ground Effects LLC ....E.... 440 565-5925
Westlake *(G-19346)*
Herrnstein Chrysler Inc ....D.... 740 773-2203
Chillicothe *(G-2786)*
Industrial Sorting Services ....E.... 513 772-6501
Cincinnati *(G-3760)*
Jo Lynn Inc ....D.... 419 994-3204
Loudonville *(G-12958)*
Madison Motor Service Inc ....E.... 419 332-0727
Fremont *(G-11085)*
Maines Collision Repr & Bdy Sp ....D.... 937 322-4618
Springfield *(G-17066)*
Mathews Ford Inc ....D.... 740 522-2181
Newark *(G-15066)*
Pete Baur Buick Gmc Inc ....E.... 440 238-5600
Cleveland *(G-6200)*
Precision Coatings Systems ....E.... 937 642-4727
Marysville *(G-13523)*
Pro-Tow Inc ....E.... 614 444-8697
Columbus *(G-8466)*
Quest Quality Services LLC ....D.... 419 704-7407
Maumee *(G-13839)*
Reladyne LLC ....E.... 513 489-6000
Cincinnati *(G-4355)*
Richs Towing & Service Inc ....E.... 440 234-3435
Middleburg Heights *(G-14257)*
Rustys Towing Service Inc ....D.... 614 491-6288
Columbus *(G-8562)*
Sandys Auto & Truck Svc Inc ....D.... 937 461-4980
Moraine *(G-14694)*
Sandys Towing ....E.... 937 461-4980
Moraine *(G-14695)*
Scotts Towing Co ....E.... 419 729-7888
Toledo *(G-18022)*
Sears Roebuck and Co ....C.... 614 797-2095
Columbus *(G-6835)*
Sears Roebuck and Co ....E.... 937 427-8528
Beavercreek *(G-1185)*
Sears Roebuck and Co ....D.... 419 226-4172
Lima *(G-12737)*
Sears Roebuck and Co ....D.... 614 760-7195
Dublin *(G-10330)*
Sears Roebuck and Co ....C.... 330 652-5128
Niles *(G-15168)*
Sears Roebuck and Co ....C.... 440 846-3595
Cleveland *(G-6386)*
SGS North America Inc ....E.... 513 674-7048
Cincinnati *(G-4462)*
Shamrock Towing Inc ....E.... 614 882-3555
Westerville *(G-19209)*
Southern Express Lubes Inc ....E.... 937 278-5807
Dayton *(G-9778)*
Southwood Auto Sales ....E.... 330 788-8822
Youngstown *(G-20214)*
Sprandel Enterprises Inc ....E.... 513 777-6622
West Chester *(G-19011)*
Spurlock Truck Service ....E.... 937 268-6100
Dayton *(G-9787)*
Star Leasing Co ....D.... 614 278-9999
Columbus *(G-8687)*
Steve Austin Auto Group ....E.... 937 592-3015
Bellefontaine *(G-1368)*
Steve S Towing and Recovery ....E.... 513 422-0254
Middletown *(G-14332)*
TSS Acquisition Company ....D.... 513 772-7000
Cleveland *(G-6552)*
Valvoline Inc ....D.... 513 451-1753
Cincinnati *(G-4748)*
Valvoline Instant Oil Change ....C.... 937 548-0123
Greenville *(G-11398)*
Valvoline LLC ....D.... 513 557-3100
Cincinnati *(G-4749)*
Van Wert County Engineers ....E.... 419 238-0210
Van Wert *(G-18493)*
Westfall Towing LLC ....E.... 740 371-5185
Marietta *(G-13401)*
World Trck Towing Recovery Inc ....E.... 330 723-1116
Seville *(G-16693)*
Yund Inc ....E.... 330 837-9358
Massillon *(G-13738)*

76 MISCELLANEOUS REPAIR SERVICES

7622 Radio & TV Repair Shops

Central USA Wireless LLC ....E.... 513 469-1500
Cincinnati *(G-3159)*
Comproducts Inc ....D.... 614 276-5552
Columbus *(G-7344)*
Consolidated Communications ....E.... 330 896-3905
Canton *(G-2266)*
Dss Installations Ltd ....E.... 513 761-7000
Cincinnati *(G-3446)*
Electra Sound Inc ....C.... 216 433-1050
Cleveland *(G-5471)*
Electra Sound Inc ....D.... 216 433-9600
Parma *(G-15766)*
Household Centralized Svc Inc ....E.... 419 474-5754
Toledo *(G-17809)*
K M T Service ....E.... 614 777-7770
Hilliard *(G-11782)*
Mobilcomm Inc ....D.... 513 742-5555
Cincinnati *(G-4066)*
Office World Inc ....E.... 419 991-4694
Lima *(G-12791)*
P & R Communications Svc Inc ....E.... 937 222-0861
Dayton *(G-9680)*
Professional Telecom Svcs ....E.... 513 232-7700
Cincinnati *(G-4294)*
Staley Technologies Inc ....E.... 330 339-2898
New Philadelphia *(G-14982)*
Sunrise Television Corp ....D.... 740 282-9999
Mingo Junction *(G-14530)*

7623 Refrigeration & Air Conditioning Svc & Repair Shop

Columbs/Worthington Htg AC Inc ....E.... 614 771-5381
Columbus *(G-7252)*
Cov-Ro Inc ....E.... 330 856-3176
Warren *(G-18693)*
Dickson Industrial Park Inc ....E.... 740 377-9162
South Point *(G-16931)*
Electrical Appl Repr Svc Inc ....E.... 216 459-8700
Brooklyn Heights *(G-1870)*
Gardiner Service Company LLC ....C.... 440 248-3400
Solon *(G-16850)*
Honeywell International Inc ....D.... 216 459-6053
Cleveland *(G-5702)*
Mid-Ohio Air Conditioning ....E.... 614 291-4664
Columbus *(G-8075)*
Osterfeld Champion Service ....E.... 937 254-8437
Dayton *(G-9679)*
Refrigeration Systems Company ....D.... 614 263-0913
Columbus *(G-8502)*
Roto-Rooter Services Company ....D.... 513 541-3840
Cincinnati *(G-4401)*
Smith & Oby Service Co ....E.... 440 735-5322
Bedford *(G-1306)*
▲ **Transport Specialists Inc** ....E.... 513 771-2220
Cincinnati *(G-4628)*

7629 Electrical & Elex Repair Shop, NEC

Alco-Chem Inc ....E.... 330 833-8551
Canton *(G-2177)*
▲ **Amko Service Company** ....E.... 330 364-8857
Midvale *(G-14357)*
Ascendtech Inc ....E.... 216 458-1101
Willoughby *(G-19506)*
AT&T Corp ....A.... 614 223-8236
Columbus *(G-6990)*
▲ **Automation & Control Tech Ltd** ....E.... 419 661-6400
Perrysburg *(G-15834)*
Blakemans Valley Off Eqp Inc ....E.... 330 729-1000
Youngstown *(G-19965)*
Blue Technologies Inc ....E.... 330 499-9300
Canton *(G-2215)*
Boeing Company ....E.... 740 788-4000
Newark *(G-15014)*
Ce Power Engineered Svcs LLC ....D.... 513 563-6150
Cincinnati *(G-3139)*
Ce Power Holdings Inc ....D.... 513 563-6150
Cincinnati *(G-3140)*
Cellco Partnership ....E.... 440 779-1313
North Olmsted *(G-15279)*
Central Repair Service Inc ....E.... 513 943-0500
Point Pleasant *(G-16078)*
City of Wadsworth ....E.... 330 334-1581
Wadsworth *(G-18592)*
DTE Inc ....E.... 419 522-3428
Mansfield *(G-13170)*
Electric Motor Tech LLC ....E.... 513 821-9999
Cincinnati *(G-3486)*
Electric Service Co Inc ....E.... 513 271-6387
Cincinnati *(G-3487)*
Electrical Appl Repr Svc Inc ....E.... 216 459-8700
Brooklyn Heights *(G-1870)*
▲ **Enprotech Industrial Tech LLC** ....C.... 216 883-3220
Cleveland *(G-5482)*
Fak Group Inc ....E.... 440 498-8465
Solon *(G-16848)*
◆ **Fosbel Inc** ....C.... 216 362-3900
Cleveland *(G-5565)*
General Electric Company ....D.... 216 883-1000
Cleveland *(G-5603)*

General Electric Company ....B 513 977-1500
Cincinnati *(G-3608)*

High Line Corporation ....E 330 848-8800
Akron *(G-261)*

Household Centralized Svc Inc ....E 419 474-5754
Toledo *(G-17809)*

▲ Instrmntation Ctrl Systems Inc .....E 513 662-2600
Cincinnati *(G-3765)*

Internash Global Svc Group LLC ......D 513 772-0430
West Chester *(G-19062)*

▲ J-C-R Tech Inc ....E 937 783-2296
Blanchester *(G-1488)*

Jacobs Telephone Contrs Inc ....E 614 527-8977
Hilliard *(G-11780)*

Jersey Central Pwr & Light Co ....E 419 321-7207
Oak Harbor *(G-15473)*

Kiemle-Hankins Company ....E 419 661-2430
Perrysburg *(G-15886)*

Leppo Inc ....C 330 633-3999
Tallmadge *(G-17480)*

▲ Magnetech Industrial Svcs Inc .....D 330 830-3500
Massillon *(G-13707)*

Mid-Ohio Electric Co ....E 614 274-8000
Columbus *(G-8076)*

Mmi-Cpr LLC ....E 216 674-0645
Independence *(G-12098)*

Modern Office Methods Inc ....D 513 791-0909
Blue Ash *(G-1613)*

Modern Office Methods Inc ....E 614 891-3693
Westerville *(G-19281)*

Narrow Way Custom Technology ....E 937 743-1611
Carlisle *(G-2553)*

NCR Corporation ....D 330 497-7300
Canton *(G-2417)*

Ohio Business Machines LLC ....E 216 485-2000
Cleveland *(G-6117)*

Ohio Machinery Co ....E 740 453-0563
Zanesville *(G-20348)*

Ohio State University ....A 614 292-6158
Columbus *(G-8352)*

Professional Telecom Svcs ....E 513 232-7700
Cincinnati *(G-4294)*

▲ Rubber City Machinery Corp ....E 330 434-3500
Akron *(G-411)*

S D Myers Inc ....C 330 630-7000
Tallmadge *(G-17486)*

Sage Sustainable Elec LLC ....E 844 472-4373
Columbus *(G-8581)*

Star Dist & Manufacturing LLC ....D 513 860-3573
West Chester *(G-19083)*

▲ Steel Eqp Specialists Inc ....D 330 823-8260
Alliance *(G-555)*

Tegam Inc ....E 440 466-6100
Geneva *(G-11246)*

Terex Utilities Inc ....D 513 539-9770
Monroe *(G-14584)*

Toshiba Amer Bus Solutions Inc ......E 216 642-7555
Cleveland *(G-6533)*

Vertiv Corporation ....D 614 841-6104
Columbus *(G-8848)*

◆ Vertiv Corporation ....A 614 888-0246
Columbus *(G-8848)*

◆ Vertiv Energy Systems Inc ....A 440 288-1122
Lorain *(G-12951)*

▲ Wauseon Machine & Mfg Inc ....D 419 337-0940
Wauseon *(G-18812)*

7631 Watch, Clock & Jewelry Repair

Cox Paving Inc ....D 937 780-3075
Wshngtn CT Hs *(G-19867)*

Sdr Services LLC ....E 513 625-0695
Goshen *(G-11315)*

7641 Reupholstery & Furniture Repair

Business Furniture LLC ....E 937 293-1010
Dayton *(G-9271)*

▲ Casco Mfg Solutions Inc ....D 513 681-0003
Cincinnati *(G-3129)*

Everybodys Inc ....E 937 293-1010
Moraine *(G-14654)*

OfficeMax North America Inc ....E 614 899-6186
Westerville *(G-19286)*

Recycled Systems Furniture Inc ......E 614 880-9110
Worthington *(G-19842)*

Soft Touch Wood LLC ....E 330 545-4204
Girard *(G-11300)*

7692 Welding Repair

A & C Welding Inc ....E 330 762-4777
Peninsula *(G-15808)*

▲ A & G Manufacturing Co Inc ....E 419 468-7433
Galion *(G-11164)*

Abbott Tool Inc ....E 419 476-6742
Toledo *(G-17579)*

All-Type Welding & Fabrication ......E 440 439-3990
Cleveland *(G-4936)*

Allied Fabricating & Wldg Co ....E 614 751-6664
Columbus *(G-6897)*

ARC Gas & Supply LLC ....E 216 341-5882
Cleveland *(G-5004)*

Arctech Fabricating Inc ....E 937 525-9353
Springfield *(G-16997)*

Athens Mold and Machine Inc ....D 740 593-6613
Athens *(G-768)*

Bayloff Stmped Pdts Knsman Inc ......D 330 876-4511
Kinsman *(G-12317)*

Blevins Metal Fabrication Inc ....E 419 522-6082
Mansfield *(G-13143)*

Breitinger Company ....E 419 526-4255
Mansfield *(G-13145)*

Brown Industrial Inc ....E 937 693-3838
Botkins *(G-1708)*

▲ Byron Products Inc ....D 513 870-9111
Fairfield *(G-10704)*

C & R Inc ....E 614 497-1130
Groveport *(G-11498)*

C-N-D Industries Inc ....E 330 478-8811
Massillon *(G-13667)*

Carter Manufacturing Co Inc ....E 513 398-7303
Mason *(G-13550)*

Chipmatic Tool & Machine Inc ....D 419 862-2737
Elmore *(G-10472)*

Cleveland Jsm Inc ....D 440 876-3050
Strongsville *(G-17291)*

Compton Metal Products Inc ....D 937 382-2403
Wilmington *(G-19618)*

Creative Mold and Machine Inc ....E 440 338-5146
Newbury *(G-15119)*

Crest Bending Inc ....E 419 492-2108
New Washington *(G-15001)*

Custom Machine Inc ....E 419 986-5122
Tiffin *(G-17515)*

Dynamic Weld Corporation ....E 419 582-2900
Osgood *(G-15652)*

▲ East End Welding Company ....E 330 677-6000
Kent *(G-12230)*

Falls Stamping & Welding Co ....C 330 928-1191
Cuyahoga Falls *(G-9092)*

◆ Fosbel Inc ....C 216 362-3900
Cleveland *(G-5565)*

Fosbel Holding Inc ....E 216 362-3900
Cleveland *(G-5566)*

Gaspar Inc ....D 330 477-2222
Canton *(G-2322)*

▲ General Tool Company ....C 513 733-5500
Cincinnati *(G-3616)*

George Steel Fabricating Inc ....E 513 932-2887
Lebanon *(G-12466)*

▲ Glenridge Machine Co ....E 440 975-1055
Willoughby *(G-19526)*

Habco Tool and Dev Co Inc ....E 440 946-5546
Mentor *(G-14058)*

HI Tecmetal Group Inc ....E 440 946-2280
Willoughby *(G-19528)*

HI Tecmetal Group Inc ....E 440 373-5101
Wickliffe *(G-19463)*

▲ Hi-Tek Manufacturing Inc ....C 513 459-1094
Mason *(G-13595)*

Hobart Bros Stick Electrode ....E 937 332-5375
Troy *(G-18206)*

▲ Industry Products Co ....B 937 778-0585
Piqua *(G-16011)*

J & S Industrial Mch Pdts Inc ....D 419 691-1380
Toledo *(G-17827)*

Jerl Machine Inc ....D 419 873-0270
Perrysburg *(G-15882)*

JMw Welding and Mfg ....E 330 484-2428
Canton *(G-2361)*

K-M-S Industries Inc ....E 440 243-6680
Brookpark *(G-1899)*

Kings Welding and Fabg Inc ....E 330 738-3592
Mechanicstown *(G-13905)*

▲ Kottler Metal Products Co Inc ....E 440 946-7473
Willoughby *(G-19535)*

L B Industries Inc ....E 330 750-1002
Struthers *(G-17366)*

Laserflex Corporation ....D 614 850-9600
Hilliard *(G-11783)*

Liberty Casting Company LLC ....E 740 363-1941
Delaware *(G-9996)*

Lima Sheet Metal Machine & Mfg ......E 419 229-1161
Lima *(G-12687)*

▲ Long-Stanton Mfg Company ....E 513 874-8020
West Chester *(G-18964)*

Majestic Tool and Machine Inc ....E 440 248-5058
Solon *(G-16869)*

Marsam Metalfab Inc ....E 330 405-1520
Twinsburg *(G-18295)*

Meta Manufacturing Corporation ......E 513 793-6382
Blue Ash *(G-1612)*

Norman Noble Inc ....C 216 761-2133
Cleveland *(G-6073)*

Northwind Industries Inc ....E 216 433-0666
Cleveland *(G-6099)*

Ohio Hydraulics Inc ....E 513 771-2590
Cincinnati *(G-4155)*

Ohio State University ....E 614 292-4139
Columbus *(G-8306)*

Paulo Products Company ....E 440 942-0153
Willoughby *(G-19561)*

◆ Pentaflex Inc ....C 937 325-5551
Springfield *(G-17096)*

Perkins Motor Service Ltd ....E 440 277-1256
Lorain *(G-12938)*

Phillips Mfg and Tower Co ....D 419 347-1720
Shelby *(G-16749)*

Precision Mtal Fabrication Inc ......E 937 235-9261
Dayton *(G-9702)*

Precision Welding Corporation ....E 216 524-6110
Cleveland *(G-6226)*

Prout Boiler Htg & Wldg Inc ....E 330 744-0293
Youngstown *(G-20167)*

Quality Welding Inc ....E 419 483-6067
Bellevue *(G-1384)*

Quality Wldg & Fabrication LLC ......D 419 225-6208
Lima *(G-12727)*

▲ R K Industries Inc ....E 419 523-5001
Ottawa *(G-15666)*

Rbm Environmental and Cnstr ....E 419 693-5840
Oregon *(G-15607)*

▲ Rose City Manufacturing Inc ......D 937 325-5561
Springfield *(G-17106)*

Schmidt Machine Company ....E 419 294-3814
Upper Sandusky *(G-18412)*

Steubenville Truck Center Inc ....E 740 282-2711
Steubenville *(G-17173)*

Tendon Manufacturing Inc ....E 216 663-3200
Cleveland *(G-6512)*

Triangle Precision Industries ....D 937 299-6776
Dayton *(G-9822)*

Turn-Key Industrial Svcs LLC ....D 614 274-1128
Columbus *(G-8787)*

Two M Precision Co Inc ....E 440 946-2120
Willoughby *(G-19578)*

Valley Machine Tool Co Inc ....E 513 899-2737
Morrow *(G-14717)*

Viking Fabricators Inc ....E 740 374-5246
Marietta *(G-13397)*

Wayne Trail Technologies Inc ....D 937 295-2120
Fort Loramie *(G-10986)*

7694 Armature Rewinding Shops

▲ 3-D Service Ltd ....C 330 830-3500
Massillon *(G-13656)*

City Machine Technologies Inc ....E 330 740-8186
Youngstown *(G-19990)*

Dolin Supply Co ....E 304 529-4171
South Point *(G-16932)*

Fenton Bros Electric Co ....E 330 343-0093
New Philadelphia *(G-14959)*

Horner Industrial Services Inc ......E 937 390-6667
Springfield *(G-17047)*

Integrated Power Services LLC ....E 216 433-7808
Cleveland *(G-5758)*

Integrated Power Services LLC ....E 513 863-8816
Hamilton *(G-11615)*

Kiemle-Hankins Company ....E 419 661-2430
Perrysburg *(G-15886)*

M & R Electric Motor Svc Inc ....E 937 222-6282
Dayton *(G-9578)*

Magnetech Industrial Svcs Inc ....C 330 830-3500
Massillon *(G-13708)*

Matlock Electric Co Inc ....E 513 731-9600
Cincinnati *(G-3979)*

Mid-Ohio Electric Co ....E 614 274-8000
Columbus *(G-8076)*

◆ National Electric Coil Inc ....B 614 488-1151
Columbus *(G-8131)*

▲ Setco Sales Company ....D 513 941-5110
Cincinnati *(G-4457)*

▲ Shoemaker Electric Company ....E 614 294-5626
Columbus *(G-8635)*

Whelco Industrial Ltd ....E 419 873-6134
Perrysburg *(G-15936)*

7699 Repair Shop & Related Svcs, NEC

1157 Design Concepts LLC ....E 937 497-1157
Sidney *(G-16755)*

▲ 3-D Service Ltd ....C 330 830-3500
Massillon *(G-13656)*

A and A Millwright Rigging Svcs ....E 513 396-6212
Cincinnati *(G-2888)*

A P O Holdings Inc ....D 330 650-1330
Hudson *(G-11960)*

AAA Pipe Cleaning Corporation ....C 216 341-2900
Cleveland *(G-4888)*

AD Farrow LLC ....E 614 228-6353
Columbus *(G-6869)*

Adelmos Electric Sewer Clg Co ....E 216 641-2301
Brooklyn Heights *(G-1864)*

Advance Door Company ....E 216 883-2424
Cleveland *(G-4903)*

Adventure Harley Davidson ....E 330 343-2295
Dover *(G-10064)*

Airborne Maint Engrg Svcs Inc ....A 937 366-2559
Wilmington *(G-19604)*

Airborne Maint Engrg Svcs Inc.........D 937 382-5591
Wilmington *(G-19605)*

◆ Ajax Tocco Magnethermic Corp ....C 330 372-8511
Warren *(G-18661)*

Akil Incorporated ....E 419 625-0857
Sandusky *(G-16573)*

Akron Area Commercial Cleaning ....E 330 434-0767
Akron *(G-26)*

▲ All American Sports Corp ....A 440 366-8225
North Ridgeville *(G-15319)*

All Lift Service Company Inc ....E 440 585-1542
Willoughby *(G-19503)*

Alpha Imaging LLC ....E 440 953-3800
Willoughby *(G-19504)*

Altaquip LLC.............E 513 674-6464
Harrison *(G-11660)*

▲ American Frame Corporation ....E 419 893-5595
Maumee *(G-13748)*

American Frame Corporation ....E 419 893-5595
Maumee *(G-13749)*

▲ Amko Service Company ....E 330 364-8857
Midvale *(G-14357)*

Andrew Belmont Sargent ....E 513 769-7800
Cincinnati *(G-2965)*

Apple Farm Service Inc ....E 937 526-4851
Covington *(G-9045)*

▲ Applied Industrial Tech Inc ....B 216 426-4000
Cleveland *(G-4996)*

Atm Solutions Inc ....D 513 742-4900
Cincinnati *(G-3000)*

◆ Babcock & Wilcox Company ....A 330 753-4511
Barberton *(G-944)*

Bedford Heights City Waste ....E 440 439-5343
Bedford *(G-1270)*

Benchmark Technologies Corp ....E 419 843-6691
Toledo *(G-17611)*

Best Aire Compressor Service ....D 419 726-0055
Millbury *(G-14446)*

Boc Water Hydraulics Inc.............E 330 332-4444
Salem *(G-16539)*

Brechbuhler Scales Inc ....E 330 458-3060
Canton *(G-2217)*

Burch Hydro Inc ....E 740 694-9146
Fredericktown *(G-11052)*

C & W Tank Cleaning Company.........D 419 691-1995
Oregon *(G-15585)*

C H Bradshaw Co ....E 614 871-2087
Grove City *(G-11417)*

Capitol Varsity Sports Inc ....E 513 523-4126
Oxford *(G-15675)*

Cbord Group Inc ....C 330 498-2702
Uniontown *(G-18362)*

Cecil I Walker Machinery Co ....E 740 286-7566
Jackson *(G-12170)*

Chemed Corporation ....D 513 762-6690
Cincinnati *(G-3175)*

Cincinnati Hydraulic Svc Inc.............E 513 874-0540
West Chester *(G-18887)*

Cleveland Electric Labs Co ....E 800 447-2207
Twinsburg *(G-18253)*

Cleveland Jsm Inc.............D 440 876-3050
Strongsville *(G-17291)*

Cleveland Pump Repr & Svcs LLC ....E 330 963-3100
Twinsburg *(G-18254)*

Cmbb LLC ....C 937 652-2151
Urbana *(G-18428)*

Columbs/Worthington Htg AC Inc ....E 614 771-5381
Columbus *(G-7252)*

Comdoc Inc ....C 330 896-2346
Uniontown *(G-18363)*

Commercial Electric Pdts Corp ....E 216 241-2886
Cleveland *(G-5318)*

▲ Compak Inc ....E 419 207-8888
Ashland *(G-668)*

Compton Metal Products Inc ....D 937 382-2403
Wilmington *(G-19618)*

Consolidated Rail Corporation ....D 440 786-3014
Macedonia *(G-13066)*

Constant Aviation LLC ....E 216 261-7119
Cleveland *(G-5337)*

Convergint Technologies LLC ....C 513 771-1717
Cincinnati *(G-3357)*

Cope Farm Equipment Inc ....E 330 821-5867
Alliance *(G-528)*

Corporate Cleaning Inc ....E 614 203-6051
Columbus *(G-7371)*

Corrotec Inc ....E 937 325-3585
Springfield *(G-17021)*

▲ Country Saw and Knife Inc ....E 330 332-1611
Salem *(G-16540)*

County of Stark ....E 330 477-3609
Massillon *(G-13674)*

Cov-Ro Inc ....E 330 856-3176
Warren *(G-18693)*

Damarc Inc.............E 330 454-6171
Canton *(G-2278)*

Dayton Door Sales Inc ....E 937 253-9181
Dayton *(G-9364)*

Dayton Industrial Drum Inc ....E 937 253-8933
Dayton *(G-9167)*

Diversified Air Systems Inc.............E 330 784-3366
Akron *(G-188)*

Document Imging Spcialists LLC ....E 614 868-9008
Hilliard *(G-11762)*

Dortronic Service Inc.............E 216 739-3667
Cleveland *(G-5443)*

▲ Dover Hydraulics Inc ....D 330 364-1617
Dover *(G-10074)*

Dreier & Maller Inc ....E 614 575-0065
Reynoldsburg *(G-16300)*

Dtv Inc ....E 216 226-5465
Mayfield Heights *(G-13873)*

Elmco Engineering Oh Inc ....E 419 238-1100
Van Wert *(G-18477)*

▲ Emsco Inc ....E 330 830-7125
Massillon *(G-13677)*

Emsco Inc ....E 330 833-5600
Massillon *(G-13678)*

Enterprise Vending Inc ....E 513 772-1373
Cincinnati *(G-3500)*

Equipment Maintenance Inc ....E 513 353-3518
Cleves *(G-6728)*

▲ Equipment MGT Svc & Repr Inc ....E 937 383-1052
Wilmington *(G-19622)*

Estabrook Corporation ....E 440 234-8566
Berea *(G-1424)*

Expert Crane Inc ....E 216 451-9900
Cleveland *(G-5502)*

▲ Fallsway Equipment Co Inc ....C 330 633-6000
Akron *(G-209)*

Famous Enterprises Inc ....E 330 762-9621
Akron *(G-212)*

▲ File Sharpening Company Inc ....E 937 376-8268
Xenia *(G-19899)*

Filing Scale Company Inc ....E 330 425-3092
Twinsburg *(G-18266)*

Fire Foe Corp ....E 330 759-9834
Girard *(G-11287)*

Forge Industries Inc.............A 330 782-8301
Youngstown *(G-20040)*

Freedom Harley-Davidson Inc ....E 330 494-2453
Canton *(G-2317)*

French Company LLC.............D 330 963-4344
Twinsburg *(G-18269)*

Frontier Tank Center Inc ....E 330 659-3888
Richfield *(G-16358)*

▲ Fusion Interior Services Ltd ....E 513 759-4100
West Chester *(G-18928)*

General Plastex Inc ....E 330 745-7775
Barberton *(G-953)*

GL Nause Co Inc ....E 513 722-9500
Loveland *(G-12996)*

Graphic Systems Services Inc.............E 937 746-0708
Springboro *(G-16967)*

Grimes Aerospace Company ....B 937 484-2001
Urbana *(G-18436)*

◆ Grob Systems Inc ....C 419 358-9015
Bluffton *(G-1691)*

▲ Hall Contracting Services Inc ....D 440 930-0050
Avon Lake *(G-919)*

Hans Truck and Trlr Repr Inc ....E 216 581-0046
Cleveland *(G-5660)*

▲ Harry C Lobalzo & Sons Inc ....E 330 666-6758
Akron *(G-251)*

Hays Enterprises Inc ....E 330 392-2278
Warren *(G-18711)*

Henry P Thompson Company ....E 513 248-3200
Milford *(G-14394)*

◆ Hillman Companies Inc ....E 513 851-4900
Cincinnati *(G-3705)*

Honeywell International Inc ....D 216 459-6053
Cleveland *(G-5702)*

House Calls LLC ....E 513 841-9800
Cincinnati *(G-3732)*

Hydraulic Specialists Inc.............E 740 922-3343
Midvale *(G-14358)*

Industrial Air Control Inc ....D 330 772-6422
Hubbard *(G-11947)*

Industrial Maint Svcs Inc ....E 440 729-2068
Chagrin Falls *(G-2669)*

◆ Industrial Parts & Service Co ....E 330 966-5025
Canton *(G-2355)*

▲ Industrial Repair & Mfg Inc ....D 419 822-4232
Delta *(G-10045)*

Inertial Airline Services Inc ....E 440 995-6555
Cleveland *(G-5749)*

Inner-Space Cleaning Corp ....C 440 646-0701
Cleveland *(G-5755)*

Integrity Processing LLC ....E 330 285-6937
Barberton *(G-955)*

J and J Environmental Inc ....E 513 398-4521
Mason *(G-13602)*

J&J Precision Machine Ltd ....E 330 923-5783
Cuyahoga Falls *(G-9103)*

Kens Beverage Inc.............E 513 874-8200
Fairfield *(G-10743)*

Kig Enterprises LLC ....E 937 263-6429
Dayton *(G-9544)*

Kone Inc.............E 330 762-8886
Cleveland *(G-5839)*

Kone Inc.............E 614 866-1751
Gahanna *(G-11129)*

Lance A1 Cleaning Services LLC ....D 614 370-0550
Columbus *(G-7948)*

Laserflex Corporation.............D 614 850-9600
Hilliard *(G-11783)*

◆ Lawrence Industries Inc ....C 216 518-7000
Cleveland *(G-5858)*

Leppo Inc.............E 330 456-2930
Canton *(G-2376)*

Liberty Casting Company LLC ....E 740 363-1941
Delaware *(G-9996)*

▲ Lucas Precision LLC ....E 216 451-5588
Cleveland *(G-5887)*

Magnetech Industrial Svcs Inc ....E 330 830-3500
Massillon *(G-13708)*

Marsh Building Products Inc ....E 937 222-3321
Dayton *(G-9586)*

McNational Inc.............E 740 377-4391
South Point *(G-16941)*

Med Clean ....C 614 207-3317
Columbus *(G-8050)*

Miami Industrial Trucks Inc.............D 937 293-4194
Moraine *(G-14677)*

Mid-American Clg Contrs Inc.............C 937 859-6222
Dayton *(G-9631)*

Mid-Ohio Harley-Davidson Inc ....E 937 322-3590
Springfield *(G-17084)*

Mine Equipment Services LLC ....E 740 936-5427
Sunbury *(G-17390)*

Mispace Inc.............E 614 626-2602
Columbus *(G-8091)*

Mmic Inc.............D 513 697-0445
Loveland *(G-13014)*

Mobile Instr Svc & Repr Inc ....C 937 592-5025
Bellefontaine *(G-1360)*

◆ Monarch Electric Service Co.............D 216 433-7800
Cleveland *(G-6006)*

MPW Container Management Corp.........D 216 362-8400
Cleveland *(G-6018)*

▲ Mr Rooter Plumbing Corporation ....E 419 625-4444
Independence *(G-12100)*

Mt Texas LLC.............E 513 853-4400
Cincinnati *(G-4082)*

S
I
C

National Compressor Svcs LLC ....E 419 868-4980
Holland *(G-11900)*

National Heat Exch Clg Corp ....E 330 482-0893
Youngstown *(G-20137)*

Nbw Inc ....E 216 377-1700
Cleveland *(G-6051)*

No Cages Harley-Davidson ....E 614 764-2453
Plain City *(G-16062)*

Norris Brothers Co Inc ....C 216 771-2233
Cleveland *(G-6074)*

Nurotoco Massachusetts Inc ....C 513 762-6690
Cincinnati *(G-4140)*

Obr Cooling Towers Inc ....E 419 243-3443
Rossford *(G-16463)*

▼ Ohio Broach & Machine Company ....E 440 946-1040
Willoughby *(G-19557)*

Ohio Hydraulics Inc ....E 513 771-2590
Cincinnati *(G-4155)*

Ohio Machinery Co ....E 330 530-9010
Girard *(G-11295)*

Ohio Machinery Co ....E 330 874-1003
Bolivar *(G-1705)*

◆ Ohio Machinery Co ....C 440 526-6200
Broadview Heights *(G-1840)*

◆ OKL Can Line Inc ....E 513 825-1655
Cincinnati *(G-4166)*

Omni Cart Services Inc ....E 440 205-8363
Mentor *(G-14093)*

Oregon Clean Energy Center ....E 419 566-9466
Oregon *(G-15604)*

Osterfeld Champion Service ....E 937 254-8437
Dayton *(G-9679)*

Otis Elevator Company ....D 216 573-2333
Cleveland *(G-6147)*

Otis Elevator Company ....E 513 531-7888
Cincinnati *(G-4190)*

Otis Elevator Company ....E 614 777-6500
Columbus *(G-8402)*

Paradigm Industrial LLC ....E 937 224-4415
Dayton *(G-9685)*

Pas Technologies Inc ....D 937 840-1000
Hillsboro *(G-11854)*

Patriot Indus Contg Svcs LLC ....E 513 248-8222
Milford *(G-14421)*

▲ Pennsylvania TI Sls & Svc Inc ....D 330 758-0845
Youngstown *(G-20153)*

Perkins Motor Service Ltd ....E 440 277-1256
Lorain *(G-12938)*

Petro-Com Corp ....E 440 327-6900
North Ridgeville *(G-15339)*

Precision Endoscopy Amer Inc ....E 410 527-9598
Stow *(G-17224)*

Premier Cleaning Services Inc ....E 513 831-2492
Milford *(G-14426)*

Primetals Technologies USA LLC ....E 419 929-1554
New London *(G-14935)*

Pro-Kleen Industrial Svcs Inc ....E 740 689-1886
Lancaster *(G-12427)*

Providian Med Field Svc LLC ....E 440 833-0460
Highland Heights *(G-11735)*

Quintus Technologies LLC ....E 614 891-2732
Lewis Center *(G-12561)*

Randy L Fork Inc ....E 419 891-1230
Maumee *(G-13841)*

▲ Raymond Storage Concepts Inc ....D 513 891-7290
Blue Ash *(G-1641)*

Rbm Environmental and Cnstr ....E 419 693-5840
Oregon *(G-15607)*

Reladyne LLC ....E 513 489-6000
Cincinnati *(G-4355)*

Riverside Marine Inds Inc ....D 419 729-1621
Toledo *(G-18008)*

Rmf Nooter Inc ....D 419 727-1970
Toledo *(G-18009)*

Roto Rt Inc ....E 513 762-6690
Cincinnati *(G-4397)*

Roto-Rooter Development Co ....D 513 762-6690
Cincinnati *(G-4398)*

Roto-Rooter Group Inc ....C 513 762-6690
Cincinnati *(G-4399)*

Roto-Rooter Services Company ....E 614 238-8006
Columbus *(G-8555)*

Roto-Rooter Services Company ....D 513 762-6690
Cincinnati *(G-4400)*

Roto-Rooter Services Company ....D 513 541-3840
Cincinnati *(G-4401)*

Roto-Rooter Services Company ....E 216 429-1928
Solon *(G-16893)*

◆ Russell T Bundy Associates Inc ....D 937 652-2151
Urbana *(G-18444)*

S & S Inc ....E 216 383-1880
Cleveland *(G-6354)*

▲ Sabco Industries Inc ....E 419 531-5347
Toledo *(G-18016)*

▲ Saw Service and Supply Company ..E 216 252-5600
Cleveland *(G-6372)*

Saw Systems Inc ....E 330 963-2992
Twinsburg *(G-18318)*

Schindler Elevator Corporation ....D 216 391-8600
Cleveland *(G-6374)*

Schindler Elevator Corporation ....E 513 341-2600
West Chester *(G-19079)*

Schindler Elevator Corporation ....C 419 867-5100
Holland *(G-11911)*

Schindler Elevator Corporation ....E 614 573-2777
Columbus *(G-8599)*

Schindler Elevator Corporation ....E 216 370-9524
Cleveland *(G-6375)*

Schindler Elevator Corporation ....E 419 861-5900
Holland *(G-11912)*

▲ Scott Fetzer Company ....E 440 892-3000
Westlake *(G-19403)*

Sears Roebuck and Co ....E 330 629-7700
Youngstown *(G-20205)*

Seilkop Industries Inc ....E 513 761-1035
Cincinnati *(G-4448)*

Serex Corporation ....E 330 726-6062
Youngstown *(G-20208)*

Sharron Group Inc ....E 614 873-5856
Plain City *(G-16066)*

Siemens Industry Inc ....E 800 879-8079
Lebanon *(G-12502)*

Sirpilla Recrtl Vhcl Ctr Inc ....D 330 494-2525
Akron *(G-430)*

Smith & Oby Service Co ....E 440 735-5322
Bedford *(G-1306)*

SMS Group Inc ....E 330 426-4126
East Palestine *(G-10421)*

Southern Ohio Door Contrls Inc ....E 513 353-4793
Miamitown *(G-14243)*

Spartan Supply Co Inc ....E 513 932-6954
Lebanon *(G-12506)*

Ssi Fabricated Inc ....E 513 217-3535
Middletown *(G-14330)*

St Marys City Board Education ....E 419 394-1116
Saint Marys *(G-16532)*

Standrdaero Component Svcs Inc ......A 513 618-9588
Cincinnati *(G-4535)*

▲ Steel Eqp Specialists Inc ....D 330 823-8260
Alliance *(G-555)*

Steven H Byerly Inc ....E 614 882-0092
Columbus *(G-8699)*

Superior Marine Ways Inc ....C 740 894-6224
Proctorville *(G-16219)*

Supers Landscaping Inc ....E 440 775-0027
Oberlin *(G-15520)*

Team Industrial Services Inc ....E 440 498-9494
Cleveland *(G-6506)*

▲ Tech Pro Inc ....D 330 923-3546
Akron *(G-466)*

Terex Utilities Inc ....E 614 444-7373
Etna *(G-10620)*

Terex Utilities Inc ....C 937 293-6526
Springfield *(G-17125)*

Tfh-Eb Inc ....D 614 253-7246
Columbus *(G-8741)*

▲ Thomas Door Controls Inc ....E 614 263-1756
Columbus *(G-8746)*

Thyssenkrupp Elevator Corp ....E 440 717-0080
Broadview Heights *(G-1848)*

Thyssenkrupp Elevator Corp ....E 513 241-6000
Cincinnati *(G-4609)*

Thyssenkrupp Elevator Corp ....E 614 895-8930
Westerville *(G-19302)*

TNT Equipment Company ....E 614 882-1549
Columbus *(G-8761)*

▲ Towlift Inc ....E 216 749-6800
Brooklyn Heights *(G-1884)*

Towlift Inc ....D 614 851-1001
Columbus *(G-8765)*

Towlift Inc ....E 419 666-1333
Northwood *(G-15411)*

Toyota Industries N Amer Inc ....E 937 237-0976
Dayton *(G-9819)*

Tracy Refrigeration Inc ....E 419 223-4786
Lima *(G-12766)*

Transco Railway Products Inc ....E 419 726-3383
Toledo *(G-18107)*

Transforce Inc ....E 513 860-4402
West Chester *(G-19019)*

United Technical Support Svcs ....E 330 562-3330
Aurora *(G-846)*

US Molding Machinery Co Inc ....E 440 918-1701
Willoughby *(G-19580)*

Valley Harley Davidson Co ....E 740 695-9591
Belmont *(G-1397)*

Vermeer Sales & Service Inc ....E 330 723-8383
Medina *(G-14012)*

Victory Machine and Fab ....E 937 693-3171
Sidney *(G-16804)*

◆ Walker National Inc ....E 614 492-1614
Columbus *(G-8870)*

Williams Super Service Inc ....E 330 733-7750
East Sparta *(G-10425)*

Winelco Inc ....E 513 755-8050
West Chester *(G-19038)*

▲ Winkle Industries Inc ....D 330 823-9730
Alliance *(G-557)*

Witmers Inc ....E 330 427-2147
Salem *(G-16567)*

◆ Wood Graphics Inc ....E 513 771-6300
Cincinnati *(G-4804)*

Woodhull LLC ....E 937 294-5311
Springboro *(G-16989)*

Xerox Corporation ....E 419 418-6500
Toledo *(G-18165)*

Xerox Corporation ....D 216 642-7806
Cleveland *(G-6697)*

78 MOTION PICTURES

7812 Motion Picture & Video Tape Production

Bkg Holdings LLC ....E 614 252-7455
Columbus *(G-7042)*

Estreamz Inc ....E 513 278-7836
Cincinnati *(G-3516)*

Fastball Spt Productions LLC ....E 440 746-8000
Cleveland *(G-5516)*

For Women Like Me Inc ....E 407 848-7339
Cleveland *(G-5551)*

◆ For Women Like Me Inc ....E 407 848-7339
Chagrin Falls *(G-2645)*

Fox Television Stations Inc ....C 216 431-8888
Cleveland *(G-5568)*

Greater Cincinnati TV Educ Fnd ....D 513 381-4033
Cincinnati *(G-3654)*

Intgrted Bridge Communications ....E 513 381-1380
Cincinnati *(G-3782)*

Killer Spotscom Inc ....D 513 201-1380
Cincinnati *(G-3869)*

Madison Avenue Mktg Group Inc ....E 419 473-9000
Toledo *(G-17878)*

Mills/James Inc ....C 614 777-9933
Hilliard *(G-11800)*

Mitosis LLC ....E 937 557-3440
Dayton *(G-9640)*

Pagetech Ltd ....D 614 238-0518
Columbus *(G-8412)*

Province of St John The Baptis ....D 513 241-5615
Cincinnati *(G-4301)*

Ron Foth Retail Inc ....D 614 888-7771
Columbus *(G-8547)*

Shalom Ministries Intl Inc ....E 614 504-6052
Plain City *(G-16065)*

Universal Technology Corp ....D 937 426-2808
Beavercreek *(G-1193)*

▲ Video Duplication Services Inc ....E 614 871-3827
Columbus *(G-8850)*

World Harvest Church Inc ....B 614 837-1990
Canal Winchester *(G-2128)*

7819 Services Allied To Motion Picture Prdtn

Litigation Support Svcs Inc ....E 513 241-5605
Cincinnati *(G-3940)*

Live Technologies LLC ....D 614 278-7777
Columbus *(G-7986)*

Mills/James Inc ....C 614 777-9933
Hilliard *(G-11800)*

Signal Productions Inc ....E 323 382-0000
Cleveland *(G-6409)*

Technicolor Thomson Group ....C 937 383-6000
Wilmington *(G-19651)*

University of Dayton ....C 937 229-5432
Dayton *(G-9838)*

7822 Motion Picture & Video Tape Distribution

▲ Midwest Tape LLC ....B 419 868-9370
Holland *(G-11898)*

Nunn Productions LLC ....E 614 695-5350
Columbus *(G-8216)*
Technicolor Thomson Group ....C 937 383-6000
Wilmington *(G-19651)*
Zebo Productions ....D 937 339-0397
Troy *(G-18240)*

7829 Services Allied To Motion Picture Distribution

Technicolor Thomson Group ....C 937 383-6000
Wilmington *(G-19651)*

7832 Motion Picture Theaters, Except Drive-In

AMC Entertainment Inc ....E 614 846-6575
Columbus *(G-6910)*
AMC Entertainment Inc ....E 614 428-5716
Columbus *(G-6911)*
AMC Entertainment Inc ....E 614 429-0100
Columbus *(G-6912)*
AMC Entertainment Inc ....E 216 749-0260
Brooklyn *(G-1859)*
American Multi-Cinema Inc ....D 614 801-9130
Grove City *(G-11406)*
American Multi-Cinema Inc ....E 614 889-0580
Dublin *(G-10132)*
American Multi-Cinema Inc ....E 216 749-0260
Cleveland *(G-4959)*
American Multi-Cinema Inc ....E 440 331-2826
Rocky River *(G-16422)*
B and D Investment Partnership ....E 937 233-6698
Dayton *(G-9244)*
Carmike Cinemas Inc ....E 740 264-1680
Steubenville *(G-17143)*
Cincinnati Museum Center ....B 513 287-7000
Cincinnati *(G-3258)*
Cinemark Usa Inc ....E 330 965-2335
Youngstown *(G-19989)*
Cinemark Usa Inc ....C 216 447-8820
Cleveland *(G-5179)*
Cinemark Usa Inc ....E 330 908-1005
Macedonia *(G-13065)*
Cinemark Usa Inc ....E 419 589-7300
Ontario *(G-15546)*
Cinemark Usa Inc ....E 614 538-0403
Columbus *(G-7199)*
Cinemark Usa Inc ....E 330 497-9118
Canton *(G-2253)*
Cinemark Usa Inc ....E 614 527-3773
Hilliard *(G-11755)*
Cinemark Usa Inc ....E 614 471-7620
Gahanna *(G-11112)*
Cinemark Usa Inc ....E 330 345-2610
Wooster *(G-19702)*
Cinemark Usa Inc ....E 614 529-8547
Columbus *(G-7200)*
Danbarry Linemas Inc ....E 740 779-6115
Chillicothe *(G-2774)*
Drc Holdings Inc ....E 419 230-0188
Pandora *(G-15750)*
Great Eastern Theatre Company ....D 419 691-9668
Oregon *(G-15596)*
M E Theaters Inc ....E 937 596-6424
Jackson Center *(G-12184)*
Marcus Theatres Corporation ....E 614 759-6500
Pickerington *(G-15963)*
Marcus Theatres Corporation ....D 614 436-9818
Columbus *(G-8018)*
National Amusements Inc ....E 513 699-1500
Milford *(G-14413)*
National Amusements Inc ....E 513 699-1500
Cincinnati *(G-4090)*
National Amusements Inc ....D 419 215-3095
Maumee *(G-13823)*
Ohio Light Opera ....D 330 263-2345
Wooster *(G-19753)*
Quincy Amusements Inc ....E 419 874-2154
Perrysburg *(G-15909)*
Regal Cinemas Inc ....E 614 853-0850
Columbus *(G-8503)*
Regal Cinemas Inc ....E 330 723-4416
Medina *(G-13996)*
Regal Cinemas Inc ....E 440 975-8820
Willoughby *(G-19566)*
Regal Cinemas Inc ....E 937 431-9418
Beavercreek *(G-1181)*
Regal Cinemas Inc ....E 440 934-3356
Elyria *(G-10558)*
Regal Cinemas Inc ....E 330 666-9373
Akron *(G-398)*
Regal Cinemas Inc ....E 440 871-4546
Westlake *(G-19399)*
Regal Cinemas Inc ....E 330 758-0503
Youngstown *(G-20178)*
Regal Cinemas Inc ....E 330 633-7668
Akron *(G-399)*
Regal Cinemas Corporation ....E 513 770-0713
Mason *(G-13633)*
Regal Cinemas Corporation ....E 440 720-0500
Richmond Heights *(G-16393)*
Regal Cinemas Inc ....E 440 891-9845
Cleveland *(G-6297)*
Seminole Theater Co LLC ....E 440 934-6998
Avon Lake *(G-927)*
Theatre Management Corporation ....E 513 723-1180
Cincinnati *(G-4597)*

7841 Video Tape Rental

Emerge Ministries Inc ....E 330 865-8351
Akron *(G-203)*
Mile Inc ....C 614 252-6724
Columbus *(G-8085)*
Mile Inc ....D 614 794-2203
Worthington *(G-19829)*

79 AMUSEMENT AND RECREATION SERVICES

7911 Dance Studios, Schools & Halls

Applause Talent Presentation ....E 513 844-6788
Hamilton *(G-11557)*
Artistic Dance Enterprises ....E 614 761-2882
Columbus *(G-6974)*
Ballet Metropolitan Inc ....C 614 229-4860
Columbus *(G-7016)*
Cincinnati Ballet Company Inc ....E 513 621-5219
Cincinnati *(G-3224)*
Cleveland Mus Schl Settlement ....C 216 421-5806
Cleveland *(G-5280)*
Eldora Enterprises Inc ....E 937 338-3815
New Weston *(G-15007)*
Ohio Chamber Ballet ....E 330 972-7900
Akron *(G-356)*
Piqua Country Club Holding Co ....E 937 773-7744
Piqua *(G-16017)*
Truenorth Cultural Arts ....E 440 949-5200
Avon Lake *(G-928)*

7922 Theatrical Producers & Misc Theatrical Svcs

Ballet Metropolitan Inc ....C 614 229-4860
Columbus *(G-7016)*
Beck Center For Arts ....C 216 521-2540
Cleveland *(G-5049)*
Cincinnati Opera Association ....E 513 768-5500
Cincinnati *(G-3260)*
Cincinnati Shakespeare Company ....E 513 381-2273
Cincinnati *(G-3267)*
City of Cleveland ....D 216 664-6800
Cleveland *(G-5197)*
▲ Columbus Association For The P ....A 614 469-1045
Columbus *(G-7259)*
Columbus Association For The P ....D 614 469-0939
Columbus *(G-7260)*
Deyor Performing Arts Center ....E 330 744-4269
Youngstown *(G-20017)*
Events On Top ....E 330 757-3786
Youngstown *(G-20031)*
Funny Bone Comedy Club & Cafe ....E 614 471-5653
Columbus *(G-7634)*
Hanson Productions Inc ....E 419 327-6100
Maumee *(G-13798)*
◆ International Management Group ....B 216 522-1200
Cleveland *(G-5762)*
Interntonal Aliance Thea Stage ....E 440 734-4883
North Olmsted *(G-15293)*
Licking County Players Inc ....E 740 349-2287
Newark *(G-15054)*
Little Theater Off Broadway ....E 614 875-3919
Grove City *(G-11450)*
Ohio Chamber Ballet ....E 330 972-7900
Akron *(G-356)*
Ohio Light Opera ....D 330 263-2345
Wooster *(G-19753)*
Ovations ....E 216 687-9292
Cleveland *(G-6149)*
Playhouse Square Foundation ....D 216 771-4444
Cleveland *(G-6218)*
Playhouse Square Holdg Co LLC ....C 216 771-4444
Cleveland *(G-6219)*
Rock and Roll of Fame and Muse ....D 216 781-7625
Cleveland *(G-6336)*
Shadoart Productions Inc ....D 614 416-7625
Columbus *(G-8627)*
Stranahan Theatre Trust ....D 419 381-8851
Toledo *(G-18050)*
The In Cincinnati Playhouse ....D 513 421-3888
Cincinnati *(G-4594)*
Xenia Area Cmnty Theater Inc ....D 937 372-0516
Xenia *(G-19935)*

7929 Bands, Orchestras, Actors & Entertainers

A To Z Golf Managment Co ....E 937 434-4911
Dayton *(G-9200)*
Adventure Cmbat Operations LLC ....E 330 818-1029
Canton *(G-2175)*
Bird Enterprises LLC ....E 330 674-1457
Millersburg *(G-14460)*
Blue Water Chamber Orchestra ....E 440 781-6215
Cleveland *(G-5067)*
Catholic Diocese of Columbus ....D 614 276-5263
Columbus *(G-7138)*
Cincinnati Symphony Orchestra ....C 513 621-1919
Cincinnati *(G-3271)*
Cleveland Phlhrmonic Orchestra ....D 216 556-1800
Rocky River *(G-16427)*
Columbus Association For The P ....D 614 469-0939
Columbus *(G-7260)*
Columbus Symphony Orchestra ....D 614 228-9600
Columbus *(G-7318)*
Dayton Performing Arts Aliance ....D 937 224-3521
Dayton *(G-9375)*
Food Concepts Intl Inc ....D 513 336-7449
Mason *(G-13579)*
Fountain Square MGT Group LLC ....E 513 621-4400
Cincinnati *(G-3582)*
Henrys King Touring Company ....E 330 628-1886
Mogadore *(G-14550)*
Ingram Entrmt Holdings Inc ....E 419 662-3132
Perrysburg *(G-15879)*
J S P A Inc ....E 407 957-6664
Columbus *(G-7851)*
Know Theatre of Cincinnati ....E 513 300-5669
Cincinnati *(G-3883)*
▲ Musical Arts Association ....C 216 231-7300
Cleveland *(G-6028)*
Muskingum Vly Symphonic Winds ....E 740 826-8095
New Concord *(G-14901)*
Northeast Ohio Dukes ....E 330 360-0968
Warren *(G-18736)*
Philo Band Boosters ....E 740 221-3023
Zanesville *(G-20354)*
Radio Seaway Inc ....E 216 916-6100
Cleveland *(G-6277)*
Rcwc Col Inc ....D 614 564-9344
Columbus *(G-8493)*
▲ Rock House Entrmt Group Inc ....C 440 232-7625
Oakwood Village *(G-15493)*
Run Jump-N-Play ....E 513 701-7529
Blue Ash *(G-1648)*
Sliddy Ent LLC ....E 419 376-1797
Toledo *(G-18037)*
Southeastern Ohio Symphony Orc ....E 740 826-8197
New Concord *(G-14903)*
Toledo Swiss Singers ....E 419 693-4110
Oregon *(G-15612)*
▲ Zink Calls ....E 419 732-6171
Port Clinton *(G-16120)*

7933 Bowling Centers

Al-Mar Lanes ....E 419 352-4637
Bowling Green *(G-1713)*
AMF Bowling Centers Inc ....E 330 725-4548
Medina *(G-13910)*
AMF Bowling Centers Inc ....E 614 889-0880
Columbus *(G-6944)*
Beaver-Vu Bowl ....E 937 426-6771
Beavercreek *(G-1130)*
Big Western Operating Co Inc ....E 614 274-1169
Columbus *(G-7037)*
Bigelow Corporation ....E 937 339-3315
Troy *(G-18196)*
Bowlero Corp ....E 440 327-1190
North Ridgeville *(G-15322)*

Brookpark Freeway Lanes LLC ....E... 216 267-2150
  Cleveland *(G-5088)*
Capri Bowling Lanes Inc ....E... 937 832-4000
  Dayton *(G-9276)*
Cherry Grove Sports Center ....E... 513 232-7199
  Cincinnati *(G-3177)*
Chillicothe Bowling Lanes Inc ....E... 740 773-3300
  Chillicothe *(G-2759)*
Cloverleaf Bowling Center Inc ....E... 216 524-4833
  Cleveland *(G-5308)*
Columbus Square Bowling Palace........E... 614 895-1122
  Columbus *(G-7316)*
Coshocton Bowling Center................E... 740 622-6332
  Coshocton *(G-9004)*
Crossgate Lanes Inc ....E... 513 891-0310
  Blue Ash *(G-1542)*
East Mentor Recreation Inc..............E... 440 354-2000
  Mentor *(G-14042)*
Eastbury Bowling Center ....E... 330 452-3700
  Canton *(G-2294)*
Eastland Lanes Inc ....E... 614 868-9866
  Columbus *(G-7491)*
Freeway Lanes Bowl Group LLC........E... 440 946-5131
  Mentor *(G-14049)*
Holiday Lanes Inc ....E... 614 861-1600
  Columbus *(G-7760)*
Interstate Lanes of Ohio Ltd ....E... 419 666-2695
  Rossford *(G-16462)*
Madison Bowl Inc..............E... 513 271-2700
  Cincinnati *(G-3958)*
Mahalls 20 Lanes ....E... 216 521-3280
  Cleveland *(G-5895)*
Midway Bowling Lanes Inc ....E... 330 762-7477
  Cuyahoga Falls *(G-9114)*
Northland Lanes Inc ....E... 419 224-1961
  Lima *(G-12707)*
Olmsted Lanes Inc ....E... 440 777-6363
  North Olmsted *(G-15301)*
Park Centre Lanes Inc ....E... 330 499-0555
  Canton *(G-2434)*
Plaz-Way Inc..............E... 330 264-9025
  Wooster *(G-19759)*
Poelking Bowling Centers..............E... 937 435-3855
  Dayton *(G-9696)*
Poelking Lanes Inc ....D... 937 299-5573
  Dayton *(G-9697)*
Rainbow Lanes Inc ....E... 614 491-7155
  Columbus *(G-8487)*
Rebman Recreation Inc ....E... 440 282-6761
  Lorain *(G-12941)*
Roseland Lanes Inc ....D... 440 439-0097
  Bedford *(G-1302)*
Sequoia Pro Bowl ....E... 614 885-7043
  Columbus *(G-8620)*
Skylane LLC ....E... 330 527-9999
  Garrettsville *(G-11230)*
Sortino Management & Dev Co ....E... 419 626-6761
  Sandusky *(G-16643)*
Stonehedge Enterprises Inc ....E... 330 928-2161
  Akron *(G-442)*
Suburban Gala Lanes Inc ....E... 419 468-7488
  Bucyrus *(G-2001)*
Thompson Capri Lanes Inc ....E... 614 888-3159
  Columbus *(G-8748)*
Tiki Bowling Lanes Inc ....E... 740 654-4513
  Lancaster *(G-12442)*
Toledo Sports Center Inc ....E... 419 693-0687
  Toledo *(G-18099)*
United Sttes Bowl Congress Inc...........D... 440 327-0102
  North Ridgeville *(G-15344)*
Victory Lanes Inc ....E... 937 323-8684
  Springfield *(G-17130)*
Wedgewood Lanes Inc ....E... 330 792-1949
  Youngstown *(G-20241)*
Westgate Lanes Incorporated............E... 419 229-3845
  Lima *(G-12783)*

7941 Professional Sports Clubs & Promoters

Alliance Hot Stove Baseball L ....E... 330 823-7034
  Alliance *(G-516)*
Ap23 Sports Complex LLC ....E... 614 452-0760
  Columbus *(G-6954)*
Arena Management Holdings LLC ....A....... 513 421-4111
  Cincinnati *(G-2984)*
Brixx Ice Company..............E... 937 222-2257
  Dayton *(G-9262)*
Cascia LLC ....E... 440 975-8085
  Willoughby *(G-19509)*
Cavaliers Holdings LLC............C... 216 420-2000
  Cleveland *(G-5136)*

Cavaliers Operating Co LLC ....A... 216 420-2000
  Cleveland *(G-5137)*
Cincinnati Bengals Inc ....C... 513 621-3550
  Cincinnati *(G-3230)*
▼ Cincinnati Reds LLC ....C... 513 765-7000
  Cincinnati *(G-3263)*
Cincinnati Reds LLC ....E... 513 765-7923
  Cincinnati *(G-3264)*
Cleveland Browns Football LLC...........C... 440 891-5000
  Berea *(G-1419)*
Cleveland Indians Baseball Com ....D... 216 420-4487
  Cleveland *(G-5262)*
▲ Colhoc Limited Partnership ....C... 614 246-4625
  Columbus *(G-7244)*
▲ Columbus Team Soccer LLC ....C... 614 447-1301
  Columbus *(G-7319)*
Crew Soccer Stadium LLC ....C... 614 447-2739
  Columbus *(G-7392)*
Dayton Prof Basbal CLB LLC ....E... 937 228-2287
  Dayton *(G-9378)*
Five Seasons Spt Cntry CLB Inc ....D... 937 848-9200
  Dayton *(G-9441)*
◆ International Management Group ....B... 216 522-1200
  Cleveland *(G-5762)*
International Mdsg Corp ....B... 216 522-1200
  Cleveland *(G-5763)*
National Football Museum Inc ....C... 330 456-8207
  Canton *(G-2414)*
Ohio High School Football Coac...........E... 419 673-1286
  Etna *(G-10618)*
Ohio State University ....E... 614 292-2624
  Columbus *(G-8307)*
Palisdes Bsbal A Cal Ltd Prtnr ....C... 330 505-0000
  Niles *(G-15166)*
Phoenix ....D... 513 721-8901
  Cincinnati *(G-4243)*
Toledo Mud Hens Basbal CLB Inc........D... 419 725-4367
  Toledo *(G-18091)*
Towne Properties Assoc Inc ....E... 513 489-9700
  Cincinnati *(G-4618)*
Wall2wall Soccer LLC ....E... 513 573-9898
  Mason *(G-13655)*
Windwood Swim & Tennis Club ....E... 513 777-2552
  West Chester *(G-19037)*

7948 Racing & Track Operations

Brush Creek Motorsports ....E... 937 515-1353
  West Union *(G-19133)*
Eldora Enterprises Inc ....E... 937 338-3815
  New Weston *(G-15007)*
Fast Traxx Promotions LLC ....E... 740 767-3740
  Millfield *(G-14505)*
Kil Kare Inc ....D... 937 429-2961
  Xenia *(G-19914)*
National Hot Rod Association ....C... 740 928-5706
  Hebron *(G-11722)*
Pnk (ohio) LLC ....E... 513 232-8000
  Cincinnati *(G-4261)*
Raceway Foods Inc............E... 513 932-2457
  Lebanon *(G-12495)*
River Downs Turf Club Inc ....E... 513 232-8000
  Cincinnati *(G-4377)*
Scioto Downs Inc ....A... 614 295-4700
  Columbus *(G-8611)*
Stonehedge Enterprises Inc ....E... 330 928-2161
  Akron *(G-442)*
◆ Team Rahal Inc ....E... 614 529-7000
  Hilliard *(G-11820)*
Thistledown Inc ....C... 216 662-8600
  Cleveland *(G-6525)*

7991 Physical Fitness Facilities

Akron General Medical Center.................C... 330 665-8000
  Akron *(G-46)*
Alsan Corporation ....D... 330 385-3636
  East Liverpool *(G-10396)*
Aussiefit I LLC ....E... 614 755-4400
  Columbus *(G-7002)*
Avalon Holdings Corporation ....D... 330 856-8800
  Warren *(G-18673)*
B & I Hotel Management LLC ....C... 330 995-0200
  Aurora *(G-819)*
Beechmont Racquet Club Inc ....E... 513 528-5700
  Cincinnati *(G-3033)*
Bellazio Salon & Day Spa ....E... 937 432-6722
  Dayton *(G-9249)*
Bennett Enterprises Inc............B... 419 874-3111
  Perrysburg *(G-15838)*
Best Western Columbus N Hotel ....E... 614 888-8230
  Columbus *(G-7030)*

Breezy Point Ltd Partnership..............E... 330 995-0600
  Aurora *(G-822)*
Broad Street Hotel Assoc LP ....D... 614 861-0321
  Columbus *(G-7076)*
Carroll Properties............E... 513 398-8075
  Mason *(G-13549)*
Centerville Fitness Inc ....E... 937 291-7990
  Centerville *(G-2623)*
Chalk Box Get Fit LLC ....E... 440 992-9619
  Ashtabula *(G-725)*
Changes Hair Designers Inc ....E... 614 846-6666
  Columbus *(G-6806)*
Chillicothe Motel LLC ....E... 740 773-3903
  Chillicothe *(G-2764)*
Chillicothe Racquet Club ....E... 740 773-4928
  Chillicothe *(G-2766)*
Cincinnati Sports Mall Inc ....E... 513 527-4000
  Cincinnati *(G-3269)*
City of Brecksville ....D... 440 526-4109
  Brecksville *(G-1775)*
Columbus Country Club ....E... 614 861-0800
  Columbus *(G-7272)*
Compel Fitness LLC ....C... 216 965-5694
  Cincinnati *(G-3342)*
Coshocton Village Inn Suites ....E... 740 622-9455
  Coshocton *(G-9010)*
Courtyard Ltd ....E... 513 777-5530
  West Chester *(G-18902)*
Emh Regional Medical Center ....D... 440 988-6800
  Avon *(G-880)*
Family YMCA of LANcstr&fairfld ....C... 740 654-0616
  Lancaster *(G-12404)*
Family YMCA of LANcstr&fairfld ....D... 740 277-7373
  Lancaster *(G-12403)*
Findlay Country Club ....E... 419 422-9263
  Findlay *(G-10902)*
Findlay Y M C A Child Dev ....E... 419 422-3174
  Findlay *(G-10908)*
Fitness International LLC ....E... 513 298-0134
  West Chester *(G-18924)*
Fitness International LLC ....E... 937 427-0700
  Beavercreek *(G-1152)*
Fitness International LLC ....E... 419 482-7740
  Maumee *(G-13792)*
Fitworks Holding LLC ....E... 330 688-2329
  Stow *(G-17205)*
Fitworks Holding LLC ....B... 513 923-9931
  Cincinnati *(G-3571)*
Fitworks Holding LLC ....E... 440 333-4141
  Rocky River *(G-16433)*
Fitworks Holding LLC ....D... 513 531-1500
  Cincinnati *(G-3572)*
Flexeco Incorporated............E... 216 812-3304
  Cleveland *(G-5545)*
Frans Child Care-Mansfield ....C... 419 775-2500
  Mansfield *(G-13178)*
Friars Club Inc ....D... 513 488-8777
  Cincinnati *(G-3594)*
Galion Community Center YMCA ....E... 419 468-7754
  Galion *(G-11173)*
Geeta Hospitality Inc ....E... 937 642-3777
  Marysville *(G-13499)*
General Electric Company ....E... 513 243-9404
  Cincinnati *(G-3611)*
Grandview Ht Ltd Partnr Ohio ....D... 937 766-5519
  Springfield *(G-17043)*
Great Miami Valley YMCA ....A... 513 887-0001
  Hamilton *(G-11602)*
Great Miami Valley YMCA ....C... 513 892-9622
  Fairfield Township *(G-10808)*
Great Miami Valley YMCA ....D... 513 887-0014
  Hamilton *(G-11604)*
Great Miami Valley YMCA ....D... 513 868-9622
  Hamilton *(G-11605)*
Great Miami Valley YMCA ....D... 513 829-3091
  Fairfield *(G-10732)*
Grooveryde Cle ....E... 323 595-1701
  Cleveland *(G-5644)*
Hardin County Family YMCA ....E... 419 673-6131
  Kenton *(G-12279)*
Highland County Family YMCA ....E... 937 840-9622
  Hillsboro *(G-11842)*
Holzer Clinic LLC ....E... 740 446-5412
  Gallipolis *(G-11199)*
Huber Heights YMCA ....D... 937 236-9622
  Dayton *(G-9508)*
Island Hospitality MGT LLC ....E... 614 864-8844
  Columbus *(G-7847)*
Jbentley Studio & Spa LLC............D... 614 790-8828
  Powell *(G-16198)*

Jto Club Corp .... D 440 352-1900
  Mentor (G-14068)
Karen Funke Inc .... E 216 464-4311
  Beachwood (G-1072)
Kerr House Inc .... E 419 832-1733
  Grand Rapids (G-11327)
Kettering Recreation Center .... E 937 296-2587
  Dayton (G-9542)
Kinsale Golf & Fitnes CLB LLC ...... C 740 881-6500
  Powell (G-16202)
Kristie Warner .... E 330 650-4450
  Hudson (G-11992)
L A Fitness Intl LLC .... E 937 439-2795
  Washington Township (G-18785)
Lake County YMCA .... C 440 352-3303
  Painesville (G-15718)
Lake County YMCA .... C 440 946-1160
  Willoughby (G-19538)
Lake County YMCA .... E 440 259-2724
  Perry (G-15824)
Lake County YMCA .... D 440 428-5125
  Madison (G-13099)
Life Time Inc .... C 614 428-6000
  Columbus (G-7973)
Life Time Fitness Inc .... C 513 234-0660
  Mason (G-13611)
Life Time Fitness Inc .... C 952 229-7158
  Dublin (G-10271)
Lima Family YMCA .... E 419 223-6045
  Lima (G-12680)
Mansfield Hotel Partnership .... D 419 529-1000
  Mansfield (G-13207)
Marios International Spa & Ht .... C 330 562-5141
  Aurora (G-835)
Medallion Club .... C 614 794-6999
  Westerville (G-19185)
Midwest Fitness LLC .... E 216 965-5694
  Westlake (G-19374)
Mitchells Salon & Day Spa .... D 513 793-0900
  Cincinnati (G-4061)
Mitchells Salon & Day Spa .... D 513 731-0600
  Cincinnati (G-4063)
N C R Employee Benefit Assn .... C 937 299-3571
  Dayton (G-9651)
New Carlisle Spt & Fitnes Ctr .... E 937 846-1000
  New Carlisle (G-14895)
Ohio State University .... E 614 293-2800
  Columbus (G-8298)
Ohio State University .... B 614 292-3238
  Columbus (G-8333)
Oid Associates .... E 330 666-3161
  Akron (G-363)
Paragon Salons Inc .... E 513 574-7610
  Cincinnati (G-4198)
Pike County YMCA .... E 740 947-8862
  Waverly (G-18822)
Queen City Racquet Club LLC .... E 513 771-2835
  Cincinnati (G-4320)
Redefine Enterprises LLC .... E 330 952-2024
  Medina (G-13994)
Ross County YMCA .... D 740 772-4340
  Chillicothe (G-2823)
S P S Inc .... E 937 339-7801
  Troy (G-18228)
Scioto Reserve Inc .... D 740 881-9082
  Powell (G-16208)
Select Hotels Group LLC .... E 614 799-1913
  Dublin (G-10332)
Shady Hollow Cntry CLB Co Inc ..... D 330 832-1581
  Massillon (G-13729)
Southwest General Health Ctr .... D 440 816-4202
  Cleveland (G-6430)
Spa Fitness Centers Inc .... E 419 476-6018
  Toledo (G-18040)
Springfield Family Y M C A .... D 937 323-3781
  Springfield (G-17119)
Swim Incorporated .... E 614 885-1619
  Worthington (G-19855)
Sycamore Board of Education .... D 513 489-3937
  Cincinnati (G-4560)
Synergy Hotels LLC .... E 614 492-9000
  Obetz (G-15530)
T O J Inc .... E 440 352-1900
  Mentor (G-14114)
Tippecanoe Country Club Inc .... E 330 758-7518
  Canfield (G-2161)
TLC Health Wellness & Fitness ...... E 330 527-4852
  Garrettsville (G-11232)
Tom Tise Golf Professional .... D 937 836-5186
  Clayton (G-4862)

Tuscany Spa Salon .... E 513 489-8872
  Cincinnati (G-4655)
Ucc Childrens Center .... E 513 217-5501
  Middletown (G-14356)
Uptown Hair Studio Inc 937 832-2111
  Englewood (G-10604)
Vermilion Family YMCA .... E 440 967-4208
  Vermilion (G-18563)
W T Sports Inc .... E 740 654-0035
  Dublin (G-10367)
Washington Twnship Mntgomery .... C 937 433-0130
  Dayton (G-9868)
Wyandotte Athletic Club .... E 614 861-6303
  Columbus (G-8922)
Y M C A Central Stark County .... E 330 305-5437
  Canton (G-2539)
Y M C A Central Stark County .... E 330 875-1611
  Louisville (G-12975)
Y M C A Central Stark County .... E 330 877-8933
  Uniontown (G-18392)
Y M C A Central Stark County .... E 330 830-6275
  Massillon (G-13736)
Y M C A Central Stark County .... E 330 498-4082
  Canton (G-2540)
Y M C A of Ashland Ohio Inc .... D 419 289-0626
  Ashland (G-700)
YMCA .... E 330 823-1930
  Alliance (G-558)
YMCA .... D 937 653-9622
  Urbana (G-18447)
YMCA of Clermont County Inc .... E 513 724-9622
  Batavia (G-1016)
YMCA of Massillon .... E 330 879-0800
  Navarre (G-14826)
Young Mens Christian .... B 513 932-1424
  Lebanon (G-12516)
Young Mens Christian Assn .... E 419 238-0443
  Van Wert (G-18498)
Young Mens Christian Assoc .... E 419 729-8135
  Toledo (G-18167)
Young Mens Christian Assoc .... C 614 871-9622
  Grove City (G-11491)
Young Mens Christian Assoc .... E 937 223-5201
  Dayton (G-9892)
Young Mens Christian Assoc .... D 330 923-5223
  Cuyahoga Falls (G-9141)
Young Mens Christian Assoc .... E 330 467-8366
  Macedonia (G-13091)
Young Mens Christian Assoc .... E 330 784-0408
  Akron (G-507)
Young Mens Christian Assoc .... C 614 416-9622
  Gahanna (G-11152)
Young Mens Christian Assoc .... C 614 334-9622
  Hilliard (G-11832)
Young Mens Christian Assoc .... E 937 312-1810
  Dayton (G-9893)
Young Mens Christian Assoc .... E 614 539-1770
  Urbancrest (G-18453)
Young Mens Christian Assoc .... D 614 252-3166
  Columbus (G-8929)
Young Mens Christian Assoc .... E 937 593-9001
  Bellefontaine (G-1370)
Young Mens Christian Assoc .... D 740 477-1661
  Circleville (G-4854)
Young Mens Christian Assoc .... D 330 264-3131
  Wooster (G-19789)
Young Mens Christian Assoc .... E 937 228-9622
  Dayton (G-9895)
Young Mens Christian Assoc .... C 937 223-5201
  Springboro (G-16990)
Young Mens Christian Assoc .... E 614 834-9622
  Canal Winchester (G-2129)
Young Mens Christian Associat ..... D 513 241-9622
  Cincinnati (G-4815)
Young Mens Christian Associat ..... D 513 923-4466
  Cincinnati (G-4816)
Young Mens Christian Associat ..... E 419 474-3995
  Toledo (G-18169)
Young Mens Christian Associat ..... D 419 866-9622
  Maumee (G-13871)
Young Mens Christian Associat ..... C 419 475-3496
  Toledo (G-18170)
Young Mens Christian Associat ..... D 419 691-3523
  Oregon (G-15615)
Young Mens Christian Associat ..... D 513 731-0115
  Cincinnati (G-4813)
Young Mens Christian Associat ..... E 513 474-1400
  Cincinnati (G-4814)
Young Mens Christian Mt Vernon ... D 740 392-9622
  Mount Vernon (G-14794)

Young Mens Christn Assn Shelby ... D 419 347-1312
  Shelby (G-16751)
Young MNS Christn Assn Findlay .... D 419 422-4424
  Findlay (G-10977)
Young MNS Chrstn Assn Clveland ... E 216 521-8400
  Lakewood (G-12364)
Young MNS Chrstn Assn Clveland ... E 216 731-7454
  Cleveland (G-6703)
Young MNS Chrstn Assn Clveland ... D 440 285-7543
  Chardon (G-2726)
Young MNS Chrstn Assn Clveland ... D 216 382-4300
  Cleveland (G-6704)
Young MNS Chrstn Assn Clveland ... D 440 808-8150
  Westlake (G-19426)
Young MNS Chrstn Assn Grter NY ... D 740 392-9622
  Mount Vernon (G-14795)
Young Womens Christian .... E 419 238-6639
  Van Wert (G-18499)
Young Womens Christian Assn .... D 614 224-9121
  Columbus (G-8931)
Young Womens Christian Associ ..... E 216 881-6878
  Cleveland (G-6705)
Young Womns Chrstn Assc Canton ... D 330 453-0789
  Canton (G-2543)
YWCA Dayton .... E 937 461-5550
  Dayton (G-9896)
YWCA Mahoning Valley .... E 330 746-6361
  Youngstown (G-20269)
YWCA of Greater Cincinnati .... D 513 241-7090
  Cincinnati (G-4817)
YWCA Shelter & Housing Network ... E 937 222-6333
  Dayton (G-9897)

7992 Public Golf Courses

797 Elks Golf Club Inc .... E 937 382-2666
  Wilmington (G-19599)
A To Z Golf Managment Co .... D 937 434-4911
  Dayton (G-9200)
▲ Aboutgolf Limited .... D 419 482-9095
  Maumee (G-13745)
American Golf Corporation .... E 740 965-5122
  Galena (G-11154)
American Golf Corporation .... E 419 693-1991
  Toledo (G-17589)
Amix Inc .... E 513 539-7220
  Middletown (G-14288)
Ashland Golf Club .... E 419 289-2917
  Ashland (G-651)
Aston Oaks Golf Club .... E 513 467-0070
  North Bend (G-15181)
Avalon Golf & Country Club .... D 330 539-5008
  Vienna (G-18577)
Avalon Lakes Golf Inc .... E 330 856-8898
  Warren (G-18675)
Avon Properties Inc .... E 440 934-6217
  Avon (G-864)
Avondale Golf Club .... E 440 934-4398
  Avon (G-865)
Bayview Retirees Golf Course .... D 419 726-8081
  Toledo (G-17607)
Beckett Ridge Country Club .... D 513 874-2710
  West Chester (G-18873)
Black Diamond Golf Course .... E 330 674-6110
  Millersburg (G-14461)
Blackbrook Country Club Inc .... E 440 951-0010
  Mentor (G-14022)
Bramarjac Inc .... E 419 884-3434
  Mansfield (G-13144)
Brandywine Country Club Inc .... E 330 657-2525
  Peninsula (G-15810)
Brentwood Golf Club Inc .... E 440 322-9254
  Sheffield Village (G-16733)
Bw Enterprises Inc .... E 937 568-9660
  South Charleston (G-16923)
Cambridge Country Club Company ... E 740 439-2744
  Byesville (G-2023)
Caravon Golf Company Ltd .... D 440 937-6018
  Avon (G-870)
Championship Management Co .... D 740 524-4653
  Sunbury (G-17385)
Chardon Lakes Golf Course Inc ..... E 440 285-4653
  Chardon (G-2689)
Chgc Inc .... D 330 225-6122
  Valley City (G-18459)
Chippewa Golf Corp .... E 330 658-2566
  Doylestown (G-10109)
Circling Hills Golf Course .... E 513 367-5858
  Harrison (G-11664)
City of Akron .... E 330 864-0020
  Akron (G-134)

City of Beavercreek ....D 937 320-0742
Beavercreek (G-1141)

City of Blue Ash ....E 513 745-8577
Blue Ash (G-1528)

City of Cuyahoga Falls ....E 330 971-8416
Cuyahoga Falls (G-9081)

City of Miamisburg ....E 937 866-4653
Miamisburg (G-14153)

City of Parma ....E 440 885-8876
Cleveland (G-5212)

City of Pickerington ....E 614 645-8474
Pickerington (G-15951)

City of Vandalia ....E 937 890-1300
Vandalia (G-18517)

City of Westlake ....E 440 835-6442
Westlake (G-19332)

City of Willoughby ....E 440 953-4280
Willoughby (G-19513)

Cleveland Metroparks ....D 440 526-4285
Brecksville (G-1776)

Cleveland Metroparks ....E 440 232-7184
Cleveland (G-5271)

Cleveland Metroparks ....E 440 331-1070
Cleveland (G-5272)

Columbus Frkln Cnty Pk ....E 614 861-3193
Reynoldsburg (G-16293)

Columbus Zoological Park Assn ....C 614 645-3400
Powell (G-16190)

Creekside Golf Ltd ....E 513 785-2999
Fairfield Township (G-10806)

Creekside Ltd LLC ....D 513 583-4977
Loveland (G-12986)

Crooked Tree Golf Course ....E 513 398-3933
Cincinnati (G-3381)

Cumberland Trail Golf CLB Crse ....E 740 964-9336
Etna (G-10614)

Darby Creek Golf Course Inc ....E 937 349-7491
Marysville (G-13494)

Dorlon Golf Club ....E 440 236-8234
Columbia Station (G-6774)

E J Links Co The Inc ....E 440 235-0501
Olmsted Twp (G-15535)

Emerald Woods Golf Course ....E 440 236-8940
Columbia Station (G-6775)

Fox Den Fairways Inc ....E 330 678-6792
Stow (G-17206)

Ganzfair Investment Inc ....E 614 792-6630
Delaware (G-9980)

Gc At Stonelick Hills ....E 513 735-4653
Batavia (G-1000)

Golf Club of Dublin LLC ....E 614 792-3825
Dublin (G-10235)

Grizzly Golf Center Inc ....B 513 398-5200
Mason (G-13590)

Hawkins Markets Inc ....E 330 435-4611
Creston (G-9061)

Heatherwoode Golf Course ....C 937 748-3222
Springboro (G-16969)

Heritage Golf Club Ltd Partnr ....D 614 777-1690
Hilliard (G-11773)

Hickory Woods Golf Course Inc ....E 513 575-3900
Loveland (G-12999)

Homestead Golf Course Inc ....E 937 698-4876
Tipp City (G-17559)

Indian Ridge Golf Club L L C ....E 513 524-4653
Oxford (G-15678)

Joe McClelland Inc ....E 740 452-3036
Zanesville (G-20321)

Kinsale Golf & Fitnes CLB LLC ....C 740 881-6500
Powell (G-16202)

Link & Reneissance Inc ....E 440 235-0501
Olmsted Twp (G-15538)

Links At Windy Knoll LLC ....D 937 631-3744
Springfield (G-17062)

Locust Hills Golf Inc ....E 937 265-5152
Springfield (G-17064)

Loyal Oak Golf Course Inc ....E 330 825-2904
Barberton (G-960)

Madison Route 20 LLC ....E 440 358-7888
Painesville (G-15723)

Mahoning Country Club Inc ....E 330 545-2517
Girard (G-11294)

Mayfair Country Club Inc ....D 330 699-2209
Uniontown (G-18378)

Meadowlake Corporation ....E 330 492-2010
Canton (G-2397)

Mental Memorial Golf Course ....E 614 645-8453
Galloway (G-11222)

Miami Valley Golf Club ....D 937 278-7381
Dayton (G-9618)

Michael Brothers Inc ....E 419 332-5716
Fremont (G-11087)

Mill Creek Golf Course Corp ....E 740 666-7711
Ostrander (G-15654)

Mill Creek Metropolitan Park ....D 330 740-7112
Youngstown (G-20130)

Mohican Hills Golf Club Inc ....E 419 368-4700
Jeromesville (G-12193)

Moundbuilders Country Club Co ....D 740 344-4500
Newark (G-15076)

Norwalk Golf Properties Inc ....E 419 668-8535
Norwalk (G-15450)

Ohio State Parks Inc ....D 513 664-3504
College Corner (G-6768)

Park Arrowhead Golf Club Inc ....E 419 628-2444
Minster (G-14539)

Pine Brook Golf Club Inc ....E 440 748-2939
Grafton (G-11319)

Pine Hills Golf Club Inc ....E 330 225-4477
Hinckley (G-11860)

Pines Golf Club ....E 330 684-1414
Orrville (G-15644)

Quail Hollow Management Inc ....D 440 639-4000
Painesville (G-15734)

Rawiga Country Club Inc ....D 330 336-2220
Seville (G-16688)

Reserve Run Golf Club LLC ....D 330 758-1017
Poland (G-16087)

River Greens Golf Course Inc ....E 740 545-7817
West Lafayette (G-19116)

Sable Creek Golf Course Inc ....E 330 877-9606
Hartville (G-11697)

Scioto Reserve Inc ....D 740 881-9082
Powell (G-16208)

Scioto Reserve Inc ....D 740 881-6500
Powell (G-16209)

Shady Hollow Cntry CLB Co Inc ....D 330 832-1581
Massillon (G-13729)

Shaker Run Golf Club ....D 513 727-0007
Lebanon (G-12500)

Silver Lake Country Club ....D 330 688-6066
Silver Lake (G-16809)

Split Rock Golf Club Inc ....E 614 877-9755
Orient (G-15621)

Spring Hills Golf Club ....E 330 825-2439
New Franklin (G-14912)

Sugarbush Golf Inc ....E 330 527-4202
Garrettsville (G-11231)

Table Rock Golf Club Inc ....E 740 625-6859
Centerburg (G-2617)

Tamaron Golf LLC ....D 419 474-5067
Toledo (G-18058)

TW Recreational Services ....E 419 836-1466
Oregon (G-15613)

Valleywood Golf Club Inc ....E 419 826-3991
Swanton (G-17409)

Vieira Inc ....E 937 599-3221
Bellefontaine (G-1369)

Wicked Woods Gulf Club Inc ....E 440 564-7960
Newbury (G-15128)

Win Tamer Corporation ....E 330 637-2881
Cortland (G-8996)

Wmvh LLC ....D 513 425-7886
Middletown (G-14340)

Yankee Run Golf Course ....D 330 448-8096
Brookfield (G-1858)

7993 Coin-Operated Amusement Devices & Arcades

16 Bit Bar ....E 513 381-1616
Cincinnati (G-2876)

Bell Music Company ....E 330 376-6337
Akron (G-93)

Entertrainment Inc ....E 513 898-8000
West Chester (G-18919)

Jack Thistledown Racino LLC ....E 216 662-8600
Cleveland (G-5775)

Magic Castle Inc ....E 937 434-4911
Dayton (G-9580)

Pnk (ohio) LLC ....A 513 232-8000
Cincinnati (G-4261)

S & B Enterprises LLC ....E 740 753-2646
Nelsonville (G-14836)

Stonehedge Enterprises Inc ....E 330 928-2161
Akron (G-442)

Strike Zone Inc ....D 440 235-4420
Olmsted Twp (G-15541)

7996 Amusement Parks

CCJ Enterprises Inc ....E 330 345-4386
Wooster (G-19697)

▲ Cedar Fair LP ....A 419 626-0830
Sandusky (G-16582)

Cedar Point Park LLC ....D 419 627-2500
Sandusky (G-16583)

Columbus Frkln Cnty Pk ....E 614 895-6219
Westerville (G-19240)

▲ Fun n Stuff Amusements Inc ....D 330 467-0821
Macedonia (G-13069)

Funtime Parks Inc ....C 330 562-7131
Aurora (G-827)

▲ Kings Island Company ....C 513 754-5700
Kings Mills (G-12313)

Kings Island Park LLC ....C 513 754-5901
Kings Mills (G-12314)

Lazer Kraze ....E 513 339-1030
Galena (G-11162)

Linwood Park Company ....E 440 963-0481
Vermilion (G-18556)

Little Squirt Sports Park ....E 419 227-6200
Lima (G-12690)

Lmn Development LLC ....D 419 433-7200
Sandusky (G-16623)

Lodge Stone Wood ....E 513 769-4325
Blue Ash (G-1599)

Lost Nation Sports Park ....E 440 602-4000
Willoughby (G-19545)

▲ Magnum Management Corporation ....A 419 627-2334
Sandusky (G-16626)

Muskingum Wtrshed Cnsrvncy Dst ....E 740 685-6013
Senecaville (G-16670)

Muskingum Wtrshed Cnsrvncy Dst ....E 330 343-6780
Mineral City (G-14507)

Rumpke Amusements Inc ....E 513 738-2646
Cincinnati (G-4408)

Seaworld Entertainment Inc ....E 330 562-8101
Aurora (G-843)

Strongville Recreation Complex ....C 440 580-3230
Strongsville (G-17349)

Y & E Entertainment Group LLC ....E 440 385-5500
Parma (G-15781)

7997 Membership Sports & Recreation Clubs

797 Elks Golf Club Inc ....E 937 382-2666
Wilmington (G-19599)

Akron Management Corp ....B 330 644-8441
Akron (G-48)

Akron Womans City Club Inc ....E 330 762-6261
Akron (G-59)

Alano Club Inc ....D 419 335-6211
Wauseon (G-18796)

American Golf Corporation ....D 440 286-9544
Chesterland (G-2736)

American Golf Corporation ....E 419 726-9353
Toledo (G-17588)

American Golf Corporation ....E 740 965-5122
Galena (G-11154)

American Golf Corporation ....E 310 664-4278
Grove City (G-11405)

American Golf Corporation ....E 419 693-1991
Toledo (G-17589)

Armco Association Park ....E 513 695-3980
Lebanon (G-12449)

Athens Golf & Country Club ....D 740 592-1655
Athens (G-767)

Atwood Yacht Club Inc ....E 330 735-2135
Sherrodsville (G-16752)

Avalon Golf & Country Club ....D 330 539-5008
Vienna (G-18577)

Avalon Golf and Cntry CLB Inc ....D 330 856-8898
Warren (G-18672)

Avon Oaks Country Club ....E 440 892-0660
Avon (G-863)

Avondale Golf Club ....E 440 934-4398
Avon (G-865)

Barrington Golf Club Inc ....D 330 995-0600
Aurora (G-820)

Barrington Golf Club Inc ....D 330 995-0821
Aurora (G-821)

Beechmont Inc ....D 216 831-9100
Cleveland (G-5051)

Beechmont Racquet Club Inc ....E 513 528-5700
Cincinnati (G-3033)

Bel-Wood Country Club Inc ....D 513 899-3361
Morrow (G-14714)

Belmont Country Club ....D 419 666-1472
Perrysburg (G-15837)

Belmont Hills Country Club ....D.... 740 695-2181
Saint Clairsville *(G-16477)*
Big Red LP ....D.... 740 548-7799
Galena *(G-11156)*
Blennerhassett Yacht Club Inc ....E.... 740 423-9062
Belpre *(G-1400)*
Boys & Girls CLB Hamilton Inc ....E.... 513 893-0071
Hamilton *(G-11559)*
Brass Ring Golf Club Ltd ....E.... 740 385-8966
Logan *(G-12832)*
Breezy Point Ltd Partnership ....E.... 330 995-0600
Aurora *(G-822)*
Breezy Point Ltd Partnership ....C.... 440 247-3363
Solon *(G-16828)*
Brook Plum Country Club ....D.... 419 625-5394
Sandusky *(G-16578)*
Brookside Country Club Inc ....D.... 330 477-6505
Canton *(G-2218)*
Brookside Golf & Cntry CLB Co ....C.... 614 889-2581
Columbus *(G-7081)*
Browns Run Country Club ....D.... 513 423-6291
Middletown *(G-14294)*
Buckeye Golf Club Co Inc ....E.... 419 636-6984
Bryan *(G-1953)*
Buckeye Lake Yacht Club Inc ....E.... 740 929-4466
Buckeye Lake *(G-1974)*
Camargo Club ....C.... 513 561-9292
Cincinnati *(G-3106)*
Cambridge Country Club Company ....E.... 740 439-2744
Byesville *(G-2023)*
Cambridge Country Club Corp ....E.... 740 432-2107
Byesville *(G-2024)*
Canterbury Golf Club Inc ....D.... 216 561-1914
Cleveland *(G-5119)*
Cascia LLC ....E.... 440 975-8085
Willoughby *(G-19509)*
Catawba-Cleveland Dev Corp ....D.... 419 797-4424
Port Clinton *(G-16101)*
Chagrin Valley Athletic Club ....D.... 440 543-5141
Chagrin Falls *(G-2662)*
Chagrin Valley Country Club Co ....D.... 440 248-4310
Chagrin Falls *(G-2641)*
Chagrin Valley Hunt Club ....E.... 440 423-4414
Gates Mills *(G-11234)*
Chillicothe Country Club Co ....E.... 740 775-0150
Chillicothe *(G-2761)*
Chillicothe Racquet Club ....E.... 740 773-4928
Chillicothe *(G-2766)*
Cincinnati Country Club ....C.... 513 533-5200
Cincinnati *(G-3236)*
Cincinnati Sports Mall Inc ....D.... 513 527-4000
Cincinnati *(G-3269)*
City of Parma ....E.... 440 885-8876
Cleveland *(G-5212)*
City of Sylvania ....E.... 419 885-1167
Sylvania *(G-17415)*
Cleveland Hts Tigers Youth Spo ....E.... 216 906-4168
Cleveland *(G-5260)*
Cleveland Racquet Club Inc ....D.... 216 831-2155
Cleveland *(G-5282)*
Cleveland Skating Club ....C.... 216 791-2800
Cleveland *(G-5287)*
Cleveland Yachting Club Inc ....D.... 440 333-1155
Cleveland *(G-5298)*
Clovernook Country Club ....D.... 513 521-0333
Cincinnati *(G-3312)*
Club At Hillbrook Inc ....E.... 440 247-4940
Chagrin Falls *(G-2643)*
Clubcorp Usa Inc ....E.... 330 724-4444
Akron *(G-145)*
Clubcorp Usa Inc ....E.... 216 851-2582
Cleveland *(G-5309)*
Coldstream Country Club ....E.... 513 231-3900
Cincinnati *(G-3322)*
Columbia Hills Country CLB Inc ....E.... 440 236-5051
Columbia Station *(G-6773)*
Columbia Recreation Assn ....E.... 740 849-2466
East Fultonham *(G-10389)*
Columbus Club Co ....E.... 614 224-4131
Columbus *(G-7268)*
Columbus Country Club ....E.... 614 861-0800
Columbus *(G-7272)*
Columbus Sail and Pwr Squadron ....C.... 614 384-0245
Lewis Center *(G-12534)*
Congress Lake Club Company ....E.... 330 877-9318
Hartville *(G-11684)*
Corporex Realty & Inv LLC ....B.... 859 292-5500
Cincinnati *(G-3364)*
Country Club Inc ....C.... 216 831-9200
Cleveland *(G-5359)*

Country Club At Muirfield Vlg ....E.... 614 764-1714
Dublin *(G-10190)*
Country Club of Hudson ....E.... 330 650-1188
Hudson *(G-11974)*
Country Club of North ....E.... 937 374-5000
Xenia *(G-19895)*
County of Perry ....E.... 740 342-0416
New Lexington *(G-14918)*
Courtyard Ltd ....E.... 513 777-5530
West Chester *(G-18902)*
Dayton Country Club Company ....D.... 937 294-3352
Dayton *(G-9360)*
Dayton Mdowbrook Cntry CLB LLC ....D.... 937 836-5186
Clayton *(G-4856)*
Dayton Toro Motorcycle Club ....D.... 937 723-9133
Dayton *(G-9382)*
Dornoch Golf Club Inc ....E.... 740 369-0863
Delaware *(G-9971)*
Dry Run Limited Partnership ....E.... 513 561-9119
Cincinnati *(G-3445)*
Dunsiane Swim Club ....E.... 937 433-7946
Dayton *(G-9397)*
Elm Valley Fishing Club Inc ....D.... 937 845-0584
New Carlisle *(G-14890)*
Elms Country Club Inc ....E.... 330 833-2668
North Lawrence *(G-15258)*
Elms of Massillon Inc ....E.... 330 833-2668
North Lawrence *(G-15259)*
Elyria Country Club Company ....C.... 440 322-6391
Elyria *(G-10505)*
Fairfield Tempo Club ....E.... 513 863-2081
Fairfield *(G-10727)*
Fairlawn Country Club Company ....D.... 330 836-5541
Akron *(G-208)*
Family YMCA of LANcstr&fairfld ....C.... 740 654-0616
Lancaster *(G-12404)*
Field & Stream Bowhunters ....D.... 419 423-9861
Findlay *(G-10901)*
Findlay Country Club ....E.... 419 422-9263
Findlay *(G-10902)*
Fitworks Holding LLC ....E.... 440 333-4141
Rocky River *(G-16433)*
Five Seasons Spt Cntry CLB Inc ....D.... 513 842-1188
Cincinnati *(G-3573)*
Five Seasons Spt Cntry CLB Inc ....D.... 937 848-9200
Dayton *(G-9441)*
Five Seasons Spt Cntry CLB Inc ....D.... 440 899-4555
Cleveland *(G-5541)*
Four Bridges Country Club Ltd ....D.... 513 759-4620
Liberty Township *(G-12581)*
Frontier Bassmasters Inc ....E.... 740 423-9293
Belpre *(G-1404)*
Ganzfair Investment Inc ....E.... 614 792-6630
Delaware *(G-9980)*
General Electric Employees ....E.... 513 243-2129
Cincinnati *(G-3613)*
Geneva Area Recreational ....E.... 440 466-1002
Geneva *(G-11242)*
German Family Society Inc ....E.... 330 678-8229
Kent *(G-12234)*
Glenmoor Country Club Inc ....C.... 330 966-3600
Canton *(G-2326)*
Golf Club Co ....E.... 614 855-7326
New Albany *(G-14855)*
Golf Course Maintenance ....D.... 330 262-9141
Wooster *(G-19724)*
Grove City Community Club ....E.... 614 875-6074
Grove City *(G-11437)*
Grove Walnut Country Club Inc ....E.... 937 253-3109
Dayton *(G-9174)*
Hawthorne Valley Country Club ....D.... 440 232-1400
Bedford *(G-1285)*
Heritage Club ....D.... 513 459-7711
Mason *(G-13593)*
Heritage Golf Club Ltd Partnr ....D.... 614 777-1690
Hilliard *(G-11773)*
Hillbrook Club Inc ....E.... 440 247-4940
Cleveland *(G-5690)*
Hyde Park Golf & Country Club ....D.... 513 321-3721
Cincinnati *(G-3743)*
Inverness Club ....D.... 419 578-9000
Toledo *(G-17825)*
Island Service Company ....C.... 419 285-3695
Put In Bay *(G-16226)*
Jefferson Golf & Country Club ....E.... 614 759-7500
Blacklick *(G-1480)*
Kenwood Country Club Inc ....C.... 513 527-3590
Cincinnati *(G-3860)*
Kettering Tennis Center ....E.... 937 434-6602
Dayton *(G-9543)*

Kirtland Country Club Company ....D.... 440 942-4400
Willoughby *(G-19534)*
Lake Club ....C.... 330 549-3996
Poland *(G-16086)*
Lake Front II Inc ....E.... 330 337-8033
Salem *(G-16551)*
Lakes Country Club Inc ....C.... 614 882-4167
Galena *(G-11161)*
Lakes Golf & Country Club Inc ....E.... 614 882-2582
Westerville *(G-19178)*
Lakewood Country Club Company ....D.... 440 871-0400
Cleveland *(G-5851)*
Lancaster Country Club ....D.... 740 654-3535
Lancaster *(G-12411)*
Legend Lake Golf Club Inc ....E.... 440 285-3110
Chardon *(G-2702)*
Leisure Sports Inc ....E.... 419 829-2891
Sylvania *(G-17436)*
Lenau Park ....E.... 440 235-2646
Olmsted Twp *(G-15537)*
Losantiville Country Club ....D.... 513 631-4133
Cincinnati *(G-3943)*
Lost Creek Country Club Inc ....E.... 419 229-2026
Lima *(G-12691)*
M&C Hotel Interests Inc ....E.... 440 543-1331
Chagrin Falls *(G-2671)*
Macair Aviation LLC ....E.... 937 347-1302
Xenia *(G-19919)*
Madison Route 20 LLC ....E.... 440 358-7888
Painesville *(G-15723)*
Maketewah Country Club Company ....D.... 513 242-9333
Cincinnati *(G-3963)*
Marietta Bantam Baseball Leag ....E.... 740 350-9844
Marietta *(G-13348)*
Marietta Country Club Inc ....E.... 740 373-7722
Marietta *(G-13351)*
Marion Country Club Company ....E.... 740 387-0974
Marion *(G-13436)*
Mayfield Sand Ridge Club ....D.... 216 381-0826
Cleveland *(G-5924)*
Medallion Club ....C.... 614 794-6999
Westerville *(G-19185)*
Mentor Lagoons Yacht Club Inc ....D.... 440 205-3625
Mentor *(G-14081)*
Miami Rifle Pistol Club ....D.... 513 732-9943
Milford *(G-14409)*
Mill Creek Golf Course Corp ....E.... 740 666-7711
Ostrander *(G-15654)*
Mohawk Golf Club ....E.... 419 447-5876
Tiffin *(G-17525)*
Montgomery Swim & Tennis Club ....E.... 513 793-6433
Montgomery *(G-14596)*
Moraine Country Club ....E.... 937 294-6200
Dayton *(G-9644)*
Moundbuilders Country Club Co ....D.... 740 344-4500
Newark *(G-15076)*
Muirfield Village Golf Club ....E.... 614 889-6700
Dublin *(G-10284)*
N C R Employee Benefit Assn ....C.... 937 299-3571
Dayton *(G-9651)*
National Exchange Club ....E.... 419 535-3232
Toledo *(G-17929)*
New Albany Athc Booster CLB ....E.... 614 413-8325
New Albany *(G-14862)*
New Albany Country Club Comm A ....C.... 614 939-8500
New Albany *(G-14864)*
New Albany Links Dev Co Ltd ....D.... 614 939-5914
New Albany *(G-14865)*
New Wembley LLC ....E.... 440 543-8171
Chagrin Falls *(G-2675)*
Newlex Classic Riders Inc ....D.... 740 342-3885
New Lexington *(G-14923)*
Northwest Swim Club Inc ....E.... 614 442-8716
Columbus *(G-8208)*
Oak Hills Swim & Racquet ....E.... 513 922-1827
Cincinnati *(G-4143)*
Oakland Pk Cnservation CLB Inc ....D.... 614 989-8739
Dublin *(G-10294)*
OBannon Creek Golf Club ....E.... 513 683-5657
Loveland *(G-13019)*
Oberlin College ....C.... 440 775-8519
Oberlin *(G-15513)*
Ohio Automobile Club ....E.... 614 277-1310
Grove City *(G-11462)*
Ohio Automobile Club ....E.... 513 870-0951
West Chester *(G-18978)*
Opcc LLC ....D.... 904 276-7660
Johnstown *(G-12202)*
Orchard Hill Swim Club ....D.... 513 385-0211
Cincinnati *(G-4179)*

SIC

Oxford Country Club Inc ....E ... 513 524-0801
　Oxford (G-15686)

Pepper Pike Club Company Inc ....D ... 216 831-9400
　Cleveland (G-6193)

Pike Run Golf Club Inc ....E ... 419 538-7000
　Ottawa (G-15664)

Piqua Country Club Holding Co ....E ... 937 773-7744
　Piqua (G-16017)

Portage Country Club Company ....D ... 330 836-8565
　Akron (G-389)

Progressive Fishing Assn ....D ... 419 877-9909
　Whitehouse (G-19451)

Quail Hollow Management Inc ....D ... 440 639-4000
　Painesville (G-15734)

Raintree Country Club Inc ....D ... 330 699-3232
　Uniontown (G-18384)

Reynoldsburg Swim Club Inc ....E ... 614 866-3211
　Reynoldsburg (G-16327)

Safari Club International ....E ... 440 247-8614
　North Ridgeville (G-15342)

Salt Fork Resort Club Inc ....A ... 740 498-8116
　Kimbolton (G-12312)

Sand Ridge Golf Club ....D ... 440 285-8088
　Chardon (G-2713)

Sandusky Rotary Club Charitabl ....E ... 419 625-1707
　Huron (G-12029)

Sandusky Yacht Club Inc ....D ... 419 625-6567
　Sandusky (G-16641)

Sawmill Greek Golf Racquet CLB ....D ... 419 433-3789
　Huron (G-12032)

Scarbrough E Tennis Fitnes Ctr ....E ... 614 751-2597
　Columbus (G-8598)

Scioto Reserve Inc ....D ... 740 881-9082
　Powell (G-16208)

Shadow Valley Tennis & Fitness ....E ... 419 861-3986
　Toledo (G-18029)

Shadow Valley Tennis Club ....E ... 419 865-1141
　Maumee (G-13851)

Shady Hollow Cntry CLB Co Inc ....D ... 330 832-1581
　Massillon (G-13729)

Shaker Heights Country Club Co ....C ... 216 991-3324
　Shaker Heights (G-16712)

Shawnee Country Club ....D ... 419 227-7177
　Lima (G-12740)

Silver Lake Country Club ....D ... 330 688-6066
　Silver Lake (G-16809)

Silver Lake Management Corp ....C ... 330 688-6066
　Silver Lake (G-16810)

Snow Hill Country Club Inc ....E ... 937 987-2491
　New Vienna (G-14999)

Soccer Centre Inc ....E ... 419 893-5419
　Maumee (G-13852)

Sportsman Gun & Reel Club Inc ....C ... 440 233-8287
　Lorain (G-12944)

Spring Valley Golf & Athc CLB ....D ... 440 365-1411
　Westlake (G-19407)

Springfield Country Club Co ....E ... 937 399-4215
　Springfield (G-17118)

Steubenville Country Club Inc ....D ... 740 264-0521
　Steubenville (G-17172)

Stone Oak Country Club ....D ... 419 867-0969
　Holland (G-11917)

Swim Incorporated ....E ... 614 885-1619
　Worthington (G-19855)

Sycamore Creek Country Club ....C ... 937 748-0791
　Springboro (G-16985)

Sylvania Country Club ....E ... 419 392-0530
　Sylvania (G-17455)

Tartan Fields Golf Club Ltd ....D ... 614 792-0900
　Dublin (G-10353)

Tennis Unlimited Inc ....E ... 330 928-8763
　Akron (G-467)

Terrace Park Country Club Inc ....D ... 513 965-4061
　Milford (G-14436)

Tiffin Cmnty YMCA Rcration Ctr ....D ... 419 447-8711
　Tiffin (G-17542)

Tippecanoe Country Club Inc ....E ... 330 758-7518
　Canfield (G-2161)

Toledo Club ....D ... 419 243-2200
　Toledo (G-18081)

Tom Tise Golf Professional ....D ... 937 836-5186
　Clayton (G-4862)

Tri County Nite Hunter Assn Ci ....E ... 740 385-7341
　Logan (G-12856)

Troy Country Club Inc ....E ... 937 335-5691
　Troy (G-18234)

Turpin Hills Swim Racquet CLB ....E ... 513 231-3242
　Cincinnati (G-4654)

Turtle Golf Management Ltd ....E ... 614 882-5920
　Westerville (G-19303)

Union Country Club ....E ... 330 343-5544
　Dover (G-10105)

US Swimming Lake Erie Swimming .....E ... 330 423-0485
　Bay Village (G-1023)

Valleaire Golf Club Inc ....D ... 440 237-9191
　Hinckley (G-11862)

Vermilion Boat Club Inc ....D ... 440 967-6634
　Vermilion (G-18562)

Vermilion Family YMCA ....E ... 440 967-4208
　Vermilion (G-18563)

Vertical Adventures Inc ....D ... 614 888-8393
　Columbus (G-8846)

Walden Club ....D ... 330 995-7162
　Aurora (G-848)

Walden Company Ltd ....C ... 330 562-7145
　Aurora (G-849)

Wedgewood Golf & Country Club ....C ... 614 793-9600
　Powell (G-16213)

West Denison Baseball League ....E ... 216 251-5790
　Cleveland (G-6666)

Western Hills Country Club ....D ... 513 922-0011
　Cincinnati (G-4789)

Western Hills Sportsplex Inc ....D ... 513 451-4900
　Cincinnati (G-4790)

Western Reserve Racquet Club ....E ... 330 653-3103
　Streetsboro (G-17277)

Westwood Country Club Company ......D ... 440 331-3016
　Rocky River (G-16448)

Wetherngton Golf Cntry CLB Inc ......E ... 513 755-2582
　West Chester (G-19036)

Weymouth Valley Inc ....E ... 440 498-8888
　Solon (G-16915)

Wickertree Tnnis Ftnes CLB LLC ....E ... 614 882-5724
　Columbus (G-8900)

Wildwood Yacht Club Inc ....D ... 216 531-9052
　Cleveland (G-6683)

Wooster Country Club Inc ....E ... 330 263-1890
　Wooster (G-19785)

YMCA of Ashtabula County Inc ....D ... 440 997-5321
　Ashtabula (G-760)

York Temple Country Club Inc ....E ... 614 885-5459
　Columbus (G-8925)

Young Mens Christian Assn ....E ... 419 332-9622
　Fremont (G-11108)

Young Mens Christian Assn ....D ... 330 744-8411
　Youngstown (G-20253)

Young Mens Christian Assoc ....D ... 740 477-1661
　Circleville (G-4854)

Young Mens Christian Assoc ....D ... 937 426-9622
　Dayton (G-9894)

Young Mens Christian Assoc ....E ... 614 878-7269
　Columbus (G-8930)

Young Mens Christian Assoc ....D ... 330 264-3131
　Wooster (G-19789)

Young Mens Christian Assoc ....D ... 937 836-9622
　Englewood (G-10606)

Young Mens Christian Assoc ....E ... 937 228-9622
　Dayton (G-9895)

Young Mens Christian Assoc ....C ... 937 223-5201
　Springboro (G-16990)

Young Mens Christian Assoc ....C ... 614 834-9622
　Canal Winchester (G-2129)

Young Mens Christian Associat ....E ... 513 521-7112
　Cincinnati (G-4812)

Young Mens Christian Associat ....E ... 513 731-0115
　Cincinnati (G-4813)

Young Mens Christian Associat ....C ... 513 474-1400
　Cincinnati (G-4814)

Young Mens Christian Associat ....C ... 513 791-5000
　Blue Ash (G-1685)

Young Mens Christn Assn Shelby ....E ... 419 347-1312
　Shelby (G-16751)

Young MNS Christn Assn Findlay ....D ... 419 422-4424
　Findlay (G-10977)

Young MNS Chrstn Assn Clveland ......D ... 216 382-4300
　Cleveland (G-6704)

Young MNS Chrstn Assn Clveland ......E ... 216 941-4654
　Cleveland (G-6702)

Youngstown Country Club ....D ... 330 759-1040
　Youngstown (G-20261)

Zanesville Country Club ....E ... 740 452-2726
　Zanesville (G-20382)

7999 Amusement & Recreation Svcs, NEC

797 Elks Golf Club Inc ....E ... 937 382-2666
　Wilmington (G-19599)

Alice Noble Ice Arena ....E ... 330 345-8686
　Wooster (G-19686)

Alliance Hospitality Inc ....E ... 440 951-7333
　Mentor (G-14016)

Amusements of America Inc ....C ... 614 297-8863
　Columbus (G-6945)

Anderson Township Park Dst ....E ... 513 474-0003
　Cincinnati (G-2963)

Army & Air Force Exchange Svc ....A ... 937 257-7736
　Dayton (G-9161)

▲ Asm International ....D ... 440 338-5151
　Novelty (G-15464)

Avalon Holdings Corporation ....D ... 330 856-8800
　Warren (G-18673)

Baldwin Wallace University ....E ... 440 826-2285
　Berea (G-1413)

Bates Bros Amusement Co ....D ... 740 266-2950
　Wintersville (G-19668)

Beaver-Vu Bowl ....E ... 937 426-6771
　Beavercreek (G-1130)

Bramarjac Inc ....E ... 419 884-3434
　Mansfield (G-13144)

Centennial Terrace & Quarry ....E ... 419 885-7106
　Sylvania (G-17414)

Central Ohio Ice Rinks Inc ....E ... 614 475-7575
　Dublin (G-10165)

Chiller LLC ....D ... 614 764-1000
　Dublin (G-10173)

Chiller LLC ....E ... 740 549-0009
　Lewis Center (G-12533)

Chiller LLC ....E ... 614 433-9600
　Worthington (G-19797)

Chiller LLC ....E ... 614 475-7575
　Columbus (G-7192)

Christian Twigs Gymnastics CLB ....E ... 937 866-8356
　Dayton (G-9299)

Cincinnati Gymnastics Academy ....E ... 513 860-3082
　Fairfield (G-10711)

Cincinnati Pool Management Inc ....A ... 513 777-1444
　Cincinnati (G-3261)

Cincinnati Tae Kwon Do Inc ....E ... 513 271-6900
　Cincinnati (G-3272)

Circle S Farms Inc ....E ... 614 878-9462
　Grove City (G-11420)

City of Brook Park ....E ... 216 433-1545
　Cleveland (G-5188)

City of Gallipolis ....E ... 740 441-6003
　Gallipolis (G-11186)

City of Independence ....E ... 216 524-3262
　Cleveland (G-5203)

City of Miamisburg ....E ... 937 866-4532
　Miamisburg (G-14152)

City of North Olmsted ....D ... 440 734-8200
　North Olmsted (G-15282)

City of Rocky River ....E ... 440 356-5656
　Cleveland (G-5214)

City of Seven Hills ....C ... 216 524-6262
　Seven Hills (G-16673)

City of South Euclid ....E ... 216 291-3902
　Cleveland (G-5216)

City of Sylvania ....E ... 419 885-1167
　Sylvania (G-17415)

Cleveland Metroparks ....D ... 440 331-5530
　Cleveland (G-5268)

Cleveland Metroparks ....B ... 216 635-3200
　Cleveland (G-5269)

Cleveland Metroparks ....B ... 216 739-6040
　Strongsville (G-17292)

Cleveland Metroparks ....E ... 440 572-9990
　Strongsville (G-17293)

Cloverleaf Bowling Center Inc ....E ... 216 524-4833
　Cleveland (G-5308)

Columbus Frkln Cnty Pk ....E ... 614 891-0700
　Westerville (G-19241)

Community Action Columbiana CT ......E ... 330 385-7251
　East Liverpool (G-10400)

▲ Coney Island Inc ....E ... 513 232-8230
　Cincinnati (G-3350)

County of Hancock ....E ... 419 425-7275
　Findlay (G-10894)

Creekside Golf Dome ....E ... 330 545-5000
　Girard (G-11286)

Cuyahoga County AG Soc ....E ... 440 243-0090
　Berea (G-1421)

Darby Creek Golf Course Inc ....E ... 937 349-7491
　Marysville (G-13494)

Daves Running Shop Inc ....E ... 567 525-4767
　Findlay (G-10896)

David Barber Civic Center ....E ... 740 498-4383
　Newcomerstown (G-15129)

Dayton History ....C ... 937 293-2841
　Dayton (G-9368)

Delaware Golf Club Inc ....E ... 740 362-2582
　Delaware (G-9969)

Dutch Heritage Farms Inc ....E 330 893-3232
Berlin *(G-1446)*
Edgewood Skate Arena ....E 419 331-0647
Lima *(G-12631)*
Fat Jacks Pizza II Inc ....E 419 227-1813
Lima *(G-12639)*
Fieldstone Farm Therapeutic Rl ....E 440 708-0013
Chagrin Falls *(G-2666)*
Flash Seats LLC ....E 216 420-2000
Cleveland *(G-5543)*
Flytz Gymnastics Inc ....E 330 926-2900
Cuyahoga Falls *(G-9096)*
Foxridge Farms Corp ....E 740 965-1369
Galena *(G-11158)*
Goldfish Swim School ....E 216 364-9090
Warrensville Heights *(G-18778)*
Goodrich Gnnett Nghborhood Ctr ....E 216 432-1717
Cleveland *(G-5614)*
Goofy Golf II Inc ....D 419 732-6671
Port Clinton *(G-16107)*
Goofy Golf Inc ....E 419 625-1308
Sandusky *(G-16612)*
Gymnastic World Inc ....E 440 526-2970
Cleveland *(G-5649)*
Hamilton County Parks District ....E 513 825-3701
Cincinnati *(G-3676)*
Heaven Bound Ascensions ....E 330 633-3288
Tallmadge *(G-17477)*
Huntington Hlls Recreation CLB ....E 614 837-0293
Pickerington *(G-15959)*
Ice Land USA Lakewood ....E 216 529-1200
Lakewood *(G-12347)*
Ice Land USA Ltd ....D 440 268-2800
Strongsville *(G-17314)*
Ice Zone Ltd ....E 330 965-1423
Youngstown *(G-20074)*
▲ Integrity Global Marketing LLC ....E 330 492-9989
Canton *(G-2356)*
Integrity Gymnstics Chrleading ....E 614 733-0818
Plain City *(G-16055)*
◆ International Management Group ....B 216 522-1200
Cleveland *(G-5762)*
International Mdsg Corp ....B 216 522-1200
Cleveland *(G-5763)*
Island Bike Rental Inc ....E 419 285-2016
Put In Bay *(G-16225)*
Iticketscom ....E 614 410-4140
Columbus *(G-7848)*
J&B Sprafka Enterprises Inc ....E 330 733-4212
Akron *(G-286)*
Kettering Recreation Center ....E 937 296-2587
Dayton *(G-9542)*
Kissel Bros Shows Inc ....E 513 741-1080
Cincinnati *(G-3876)*
Kissel Entertainment LLC ....E 513 266-4505
Okeana *(G-15532)*
Lake Metroparks ....B 440 639-7275
Painesville *(G-15720)*
Lake Metroparks ....E 440 428-3164
Madison *(G-13100)*
Lake Metroparks ....D 440 256-2122
Kirtland *(G-12322)*
Lake Metroparks ....E 440 256-1404
Willoughby *(G-19540)*
Lakewood City School District ....E 216 529-4400
Lakewood *(G-12352)*
Leaders Family Farms ....E 419 599-1570
Napoleon *(G-14810)*
Leo Yannenoff Jewish Community ....C 614 231-2731
Columbus *(G-7966)*
Magic Castle Inc ....E 937 434-4911
Dayton *(G-9580)*
Makoy Center Inc ....E 614 777-1211
Hilliard *(G-11787)*
Man Golf Ohio LLC ....E 440 635-5178
Huntsburg *(G-12018)*
Marietta Aquatic Center ....E 740 373-2445
Marietta *(G-13347)*
Max Dixons Expressway Park ....E 513 831-2273
Milford *(G-14407)*
Metropolitan Pool Service Co ....E 216 741-9451
Parma *(G-15768)*
Miami Valley Gaming & Racg LLC ....D 513 934-7070
Lebanon *(G-12485)*
Mill Creek Metropolitan Park ....D 330 702-3000
Canfield *(G-2149)*
Mill Creek Metropolitan Park ....E 330 740-7116
Youngstown *(G-20129)*
National Concession Company ....E 216 881-9911
Cleveland *(G-6040)*

Oberlin College ....C 440 775-8519
Oberlin *(G-15513)*
Ohio Dept Natural Resources ....E 740 869-3124
Mount Sterling *(G-14746)*
Ohio Exposition Center ....D 614 644-4000
Columbus *(G-8255)*
Ohio Skate Inc ....E 419 476-2808
Toledo *(G-17958)*
Our Lady Prptul Hlp Cnmty Bngo ....E 513 742-3200
Cincinnati *(G-4191)*
◆ Park Corporation ....B 216 267-4870
Cleveland *(G-6163)*
Paul A Ertel ....D 216 696-8888
Cleveland *(G-6183)*
Rec Center ....E 330 721-6900
Medina *(G-13993)*
Recreational Golf Inc ....E 513 677-0347
Loveland *(G-13024)*
Relx Inc ....E 937 865-6800
Miamisburg *(G-14210)*
Roto Group LLC ....D 614 760-8690
Dublin *(G-10325)*
S & S Management Inc ....E 567 356-4151
Wapakoneta *(G-18653)*
Skate Town U S A ....E 513 874-9855
West Chester *(G-19008)*
Skateworld Inc ....E 937 294-4032
Dayton *(G-9771)*
Sky Zone Indoor Trampoline Pk ....D 614 302-6093
Cincinnati *(G-4493)*
Snows Lakeside Tavern ....E 513 954-5626
Cincinnati *(G-4499)*
Soccer Centre Owners Ltd ....E 419 893-5425
Maumee *(G-13853)*
Society of The Transfiguration ....E 513 771-7462
Cincinnati *(G-4501)*
South E Harley Davidson Sls Co ....E 440 439-5300
Cleveland *(G-6422)*
Spring Hills Golf Club ....E 740 543-3270
East Springfield *(G-10426)*
Stark County Park District ....D 330 477-3552
Canton *(G-2494)*
Stockport Mill Country Inn Inc ....E 740 559-2822
Stockport *(G-17183)*
Stonehedge Enterprises Inc ....E 330 928-2161
Akron *(G-442)*
Strike Zone Inc ....D 440 235-4420
Olmsted Twp *(G-15541)*
Three D Golf LLC ....E 513 732-0295
Batavia *(G-1011)*
Tom Tise Golf Professional ....D 937 836-5186
Clayton *(G-4862)*
United Skates America Inc ....E 440 944-5300
Wickliffe *(G-19476)*
Valley Riding ....E 216 267-2525
Cleveland *(G-6618)*
Vertical Adventures Inc ....D 614 888-8393
Columbus *(G-8846)*
Washington Township Park Dst ....E 937 433-5155
Centerville *(G-2636)*
Washington Twnship Mntgomery ....E 937 433-0130
Dayton *(G-9868)*
Western Hills Sportsplex Inc ....D 513 451-4900
Cincinnati *(G-4790)*
Wiegands Lake Park Inc ....E 440 338-5795
Novelty *(G-15467)*
Wonderworker Inc ....D 234 249-3030
Hudson *(G-12015)*
Wyandot County AG Soc ....E 419 294-4320
Upper Sandusky *(G-18415)*
YMCA ....D 937 653-9622
Urbana *(G-18447)*
Young Mens Christian Assoc ....D 330 264-3131
Wooster *(G-19789)*
Young Mens Christian Assoc ....E 614 276-8224
Columbus *(G-8928)*
Young Mens Christian Assoc ....D 740 477-1661
Circleville *(G-4854)*
Young Mens Christian Assoc ....E 614 885-4252
Columbus *(G-8927)*
Young Mens Christian Assoc ....E 937 228-9622
Dayton *(G-9895)*
Youngs Jersey Dairy Inc ....B 937 325-0629
Yellow Springs *(G-19941)*
YWCA of Hamilton ....E 513 856-9800
Hamilton *(G-11655)*

80 HEALTH SERVICES

8011 Offices & Clinics Of Doctors Of Medicine

3rd Street Community Clinic ....D 419 522-6191
Mansfield *(G-13130)*
A Thomas Dalagiannis MD ....E 419 887-7000
Maumee *(G-13744)*
A-1 Healthcare Staffing LLC ....C 216 862-0906
Cleveland *(G-4884)*
A-1 Healthcare Staffing LLC ....D 216 862-0906
Lakewood *(G-12334)*
Access Ohio ....E 614 367-7700
Columbus *(G-6862)*
Adena Pckwy-Ross Fmly Physcans ....E 740 779-4500
Chillicothe *(G-2755)*
Adrian M Schnall MD ....D 216 291-4300
Cleveland *(G-4902)*
Advanced Dermatology and Skin ....E 330 965-8760
Youngstown *(G-19947)*
Advanced Urology Inc ....E 330 758-9787
Youngstown *(G-19948)*
Advocate Radiology Bil ....C 614 210-1885
Powell *(G-16183)*
Affiliates In Oral & Maxlofcl ....E 513 829-8080
West Chester *(G-18862)*
Akron General Health System ....E 330 665-8200
Akron *(G-42)*
Akron Neonatology Inc ....E 330 379-9473
Akron *(G-49)*
Akron Plastic Surgeons Inc ....E 330 253-9161
Akron *(G-50)*
Allergy & Asthma Inc ....E 740 654-8623
Lancaster *(G-12369)*
Allergy & Asthma Centre Dayton ....E 937 435-8999
Centerville *(G-2621)*
Alta Partners LLC ....E 440 808-3654
Westlake *(G-19315)*
Ambulatory Medical Care Inc ....E 513 831-8555
Milford *(G-14370)*
American Health Network Inc ....E 614 794-4500
Columbus *(G-6922)*
American Hlth Netwrk Ohio LLC ....D 614 794-4500
Columbus *(G-6924)*
American Hlth Ntwrk & Fmly PRC ....E 419 524-2212
Mansfield *(G-13135)*
American Para Prof Systems Inc ....E 513 531-2900
Cincinnati *(G-2949)*
Amherst Hospital Association ....C 440 988-6000
Amherst *(G-580)*
Anderson Hills Pediatrics Inc ....D 513 232-8100
Cincinnati *(G-2960)*
Anesthesia Associates Inc ....E 440 350-0832
Painesville *(G-15693)*
Anesthesiology Assoc of Akron ....E 330 344-6401
Akron *(G-74)*
Anesthesiology Services Netwrk ....E 937 208-6173
Dayton *(G-9234)*
Anesthsia Assoc Cincinnati Inc ....D 513 585-0577
Cincinnati *(G-2966)*
AP Cchmc ....E 513 636-4200
Cincinnati *(G-2971)*
▲ Arlington Contact Lens Svc Inc ....E 614 921-9894
Columbus *(G-6970)*
Ashtabula Clinic Inc ....D 440 997-6980
Ashtabula *(G-708)*
Ashtabula County Medical Ctr ....C 440 997-6960
Ashtabula *(G-716)*
Associated Specialists ....E 937 208-7272
Dayton *(G-9241)*
Associates In Dermatology Inc ....E 440 249-0274
Westlake *(G-19319)*
Assocted Ctract Laser Surgeons ....E 419 693-4444
Oregon *(G-15583)*
Aultman Health Foundation ....E 330 452-9911
Canton *(G-2201)*
Aultman North Canton Med Group ....B 330 433-1200
Canton *(G-2206)*
Aultman North Inc ....E 330 305-6999
Canton *(G-2207)*
Avita Health System ....C 419 468-7059
Galion *(G-11166)*
Avita Health System ....C 419 468-4841
Galion *(G-11167)*
Axesspointe Cmnty Hlth Ctr Inc ....E 330 724-5471
Akron *(G-83)*
Barb Linden ....E 440 233-1068
Lorain *(G-12884)*
Barberton Area Family Practice ....E 330 615-3205
Barberton *(G-945)*

Bel-Park Anesthesia ....E 330 480-3658
Youngstown (G-19963)
Belmont Bhc Pines Hospital Inc ......C 330 759-2700
Youngstown (G-19964)
Belmont Professional Assoc Inc ......C 740 425-5140
Barnesville (G-977)
Bernstein Allergy Group Inc ....E 513 931-0775
Cincinnati (G-3041)
Bethesda Hospital Inc ....E 513 563-1505
Cincinnati (G-3049)
Big Run Urgent Care Center ....E 614 871-7130
Grove City (G-11408)
Bio-Mdical Applications RI Inc ....E 740 389-4111
Marion (G-13405)
Blanchard Valley Hospital ....E 419 423-4335
Findlay (G-10873)
Blanchard Valley Medical Assoc ......D 419 424-0380
Findlay (G-10875)
Blanchard Vly Rgional Hlth Ctr ....C 419 358-9010
Bluffton (G-1687)
Bloomberg Ross MD ....E 740 454-1216
Zanesville (G-20282)
Brian Brocker Dr ....E 330 747-9215
Youngstown (G-19972)
Bruce R Bracken ....E 513 558-3700
Cincinnati (G-3084)
Buckeye Drmtlogy Drmthphthlogy .....E 614 389-6331
Dublin (G-10153)
Buckeye Drmtlogy Drmthphthlogy .....E 614 317-9630
Grove City (G-11415)
Bucyrus Community Physicians ....D 419 492-2200
New Washington (G-15000)
Butler Cnty Cmnty Hlth Cnsrtm ....D 513 454-1460
Hamilton (G-11565)
Campolo Michael MD ....E 740 522-7600
Newark (G-15020)
Canal Physician Group ....E 330 344-4000
Akron (G-116)
Canton Ophthalmology Assoc ....E 330 994-1286
Canton (G-2239)
Canyon Medical Center Inc ....E 614 864-6010
Columbus (G-7111)
Capitol City Cardiology Inc ....E 614 464-0884
Columbus (G-7115)
Cardiac Vsclar Thrcic Surgeons ....E 513 421-3494
Cincinnati (G-3116)
Cardinal Orthopaedic Group Inc ....E 614 759-1186
Columbus (G-7124)
Cardio Thoracic Surgery ....E 614 293-4509
Columbus (G-7125)
Cardiologist ....D 440 882-0075
Cleveland (G-5123)
Cardiologist Clark & Champaign ....E 937 653-8897
Urbana (G-18421)
Cardiologist of Clark & Champ ....E 937 323-1404
Springfield (G-17004)
Cardiology Consultants Inc ....D 330 454-8076
Canton (G-2244)
Cardiology Ctr of Cincinnati ....E 513 745-9800
Cincinnati (G-3119)
Cardiology Specialists Inc ....E 330 297-6110
Ravenna (G-16234)
Cardiovascular Associates Inc ....E 330 747-6446
Youngstown (G-19981)
Cardiovascular Clinic Inc ....D 440 882-0075
Cleveland (G-5124)
Cardiovascular Consultants Inc ....D 330 454-8076
Canton (G-2245)
Cardiovascular Medicine Assoc ....E 440 816-2708
Cleveland (G-5125)
Cei Physicians Inc ....B 513 984-5133
Blue Ash (G-1521)
Cei Physicians PSC Inc ....E 513 233-2700
Cincinnati (G-3141)
Cei Physicians PSC Inc ....E 513 531-2020
Cincinnati (G-3142)
Cei Physicians PSC LLC ....C 513 984-5133
Blue Ash (G-1522)
Center For Dagnstc Imaging Inc ....C 614 841-0800
Columbus (G-6803)
Center For Srgcal Drmtlogy Inc ....D 614 847-4100
Westerville (G-19150)
Center For Urologic Health LLC ....E 330 375-0924
Akron (G-124)
Centers For Dialysis Care Inc ....C 216 295-7000
Shaker Heights (G-16705)
Central Ohio Geriatrics LLC ....E 614 530-4077
Granville (G-11336)
Central Ohio Primary Care ....E 614 459-3687
Columbus (G-7162)

Central Ohio Primary Care ....E 614 451-1551
Columbus (G-7163)
Central Ohio Primary Care ....E 614 473-1300
Columbus (G-7165)
Central Ohio Primary Care ....D 614 508-0110
Westerville (G-19234)
Central Ohio Primary Care ....E 614 552-2300
Reynoldsburg (G-16290)
Central Ohio Primary Care ....E 614 891-9505
Westerville (G-19151)
Central Ohio Primary Care ....E 614 882-0708
Westerville (G-19235)
Central Ohio Primary Care ....D 614 268-8164
Columbus (G-7166)
Central Ohio Primary Care ....E 614 834-8042
Canal Winchester (G-2106)
Central Ohio Primary Care ....D 614 540-7339
Worthington (G-19796)
Central Ohio Primary Care ....D 614 326-2672
Westerville (G-19152)
Central Ohio Primary Care ....E 614 818-9550
Westerville (G-19233)
Central Ohio Primary Care ....E 614 442-7550
Columbus (G-7167)
Central Ohio Surgical Assoc ....E 614 222-8000
Columbus (G-7168)
Chander M Kohli MD Facs Inc ....E 330 759-6978
Youngstown (G-19985)
Charles L Maccallum MD Inc ....E 330 655-2161
Hudson (G-11971)
Chester West Dentistry ....E 330 753-7734
Akron (G-127)
Child & Adolescent Speciality ....E 937 667-7711
Tipp City (G-17552)
Childrens Hosp Med Ctr Akron ....E 330 543-8004
Akron (G-131)
Childrens Hospital Medical Ctr ....A 513 636-8778
Cincinnati (G-3192)
Childrens Hospital Medical Ctr ....A 513 803-9600
Liberty Township (G-12580)
Childrens Hospital Medical Ctr ....A 513 636-4200
Cincinnati (G-3190)
Childrens Hospital Medical Ctr ....E 513 636-6800
Mason (G-13554)
Childrens Physician Inc ....E 330 494-5600
Canton (G-2251)
Childrens Surgery Center Inc ....D 614 722-2920
Columbus (G-7191)
Chillicothe Family Physicians ....E 740 779-4100
Chillicothe (G-2762)
Christ Hospital ....E 513 564-4000
Cincinnati (G-3200)
Christ Hospital ....C 513 561-7809
Cincinnati (G-3201)
▲ Christian Community Hlth Svcs ....E 513 381-2247
Cincinnati (G-3213)
Christian Healthcare ....E 330 848-1511
Barberton (G-950)
Christopher C Kaeding ....E 614 293-3600
Columbus (G-7197)
Cincinnati Hand Surgery Cons ....E 513 961-4263
Cincinnati (G-3246)
Cincinnati Head and Neck Inc ....E 513 232-3277
Cincinnati (G-3247)
City of Columbus ....E 614 645-1600
Columbus (G-7207)
City of Whitehall ....E 614 237-5478
Columbus (G-7213)
Clevelan Clinic Hlth Sys W Reg ....E 216 476-7606
Cleveland (G-5227)
Clevelan Clinic Hlth Sys W Reg ....D 216 476-7007
Cleveland (G-5228)
Cleveland Anesthesia Group ....E 216 901-5706
Independence (G-12059)
Cleveland Clinic Cole Eye Inst ....E 216 444-4508
Cleveland (G-5235)
Cleveland Clinic Community Onc ....E 216 447-9747
Independence (G-12060)
Cleveland Clinic Foundation ....E 330 287-4930
Wooster (G-19707)
Cleveland Clinic Foundation ....B 216 448-4325
Cleveland (G-5242)
▲ Cleveland Clinic Foundation ....A 216 636-8335
Cleveland (G-5236)
Cleveland Clinic Foundation ....D 419 609-2812
Sandusky (G-16587)
Cleveland Preterm ....E 216 991-4577
Cleveland (G-5281)
Clevelnd Clnc Chagrn Flls Fmly ....E 440 893-9393
Chagrin Falls (G-2642)

Clinton Memorial Hospital ....E 937 283-2273
Wilmington (G-19615)
Clinton Memorial Hospital ....E 937 383-3402
Wilmington (G-19614)
Clyo Internal Medicine Inc ....D 937 435-5857
Centerville (G-2624)
Coleman Professional Svcs Inc ....C 330 673-1347
Kent (G-12223)
Columbus Arthritis Center Inc ....E 614 486-5200
Columbus (G-7258)
Columbus Cardiology Cons Inc ....C 614 224-2281
Columbus (G-7264)
Columbus Cardiology Cons Inc ....C 614 224-2281
Columbus (G-7265)
Columbus Gstrntrlogy Group Inc ....D 614 457-1213
Columbus (G-7285)
Columbus Neighborhood Health C ......C 614 445-0685
Columbus (G-7302)
Columbus Obsttrcans Gynclgists ....E 614 434-2400
Columbus (G-7303)
▲ Columbus Oncology Assoc Inc ....E 614 442-3130
Columbus (G-7304)
Columbus Surgical Center LLP ....E 614 932-9503
Dublin (G-10182)
Community Action Comm Pike CNT ....E 740 947-7726
Waverly (G-18817)
Community Health & Wellness PA ....D 937 599-1411
West Liberty (G-19118)
Community Health Partners Regi ....E 440 960-4000
Lorain (G-12895)
Community Mental Health Svc ....D 740 695-9344
Saint Clairsville (G-16484)
Compass Community Health ....E 740 355-7102
Portsmouth (G-16133)
Comprehensive Health Care Inc ....E 419 238-7777
Van Wert (G-18476)
Comprehensive Pediatrics ....E 440 835-8270
Westlake (G-19336)
Concorde Therapy Group Inc ....E 330 493-4210
Alliance (G-527)
Consolidated Care Inc ....E 937 465-8065
West Liberty (G-19120)
Consultnts In Gastroenterology ....E 440 386-2250
Painesville (G-15705)
Corporate Health Dimensions ....E 740 775-6119
Chillicothe (G-2770)
County of Delaware ....D 740 203-2040
Delaware (G-9964)
County of Lucas ....C 419 213-4018
Toledo (G-17683)
County of Montgomery ....E 937 225-4156
Dayton (G-9334)
Covenant Care Ohio Inc ....D 937 526-5570
Versailles (G-18569)
Cranley Surgical Associates ....E 513 961-4335
Cincinnati (G-3379)
Crossroads Lake County Adole ....C 440 255-1700
Mentor (G-14037)
Crystal Arthritis Center Inc ....E 330 668-4045
Akron (G-171)
Crystal Clinic Surgery Ctr Inc ....A 330 668-4040
Akron (G-172)
David Lee Grossman MD ....E 419 843-8150
Toledo (G-17692)
David M Schneider MD Inc ....E 513 752-5700
Cincinnati (G-2849)
Davis Eye Center ....E 330 923-5676
Cuyahoga Falls (G-9085)
Davue Ob-Gyn Associates Inc ....D 937 277-8988
Dayton (G-9347)
Dayton Cardiology Consultants ....E 937 223-3053
Dayton (G-9356)
Dayton Childrens Hospital ....E 937 641-3376
Dayton (G-9357)
Dayton Eye Surgery Center ....E 937 431-9531
Beavercreek (G-1213)
Dayton Heart Center Inc ....D 937 277-4274
Dayton (G-9367)
Dayton Medical Imaging ....D 937 439-0390
Dayton (G-9372)
Dayton Ob Gyn ....E 937 439-7550
Centerville (G-2625)
Dayton Physicians LLC ....C 937 280-8400
Dayton (G-9376)
Dayton Physicians LLC ....C 937 547-0563
Greenville (G-11374)
Dayton Primary & Urgent Care ....E 937 461-0800
Dayton (G-9377)
Dayton Regional Dialysis Inc ....E 937 898-5526
Dayton (G-9380)

Defiance Family Physicians.............E......419 785-3281
Defiance *(G-9910)*

Dennis C McCluskey MD & Assoc....E......330 628-2686
Mogadore *(G-14547)*

Dermatlgists of Southwest Ohio.......E......937 435-2094
Dayton *(G-9388)*

Digestive Care Inc..............D......937 320-5050
Beavercreek *(G-1215)*

Digestive Disease Consultants.......E......330 225-6468
Brunswick *(G-1927)*

▲ Digestive Specialists Inc........E......937 534-7330
Dayton *(G-9391)*

Dignity Health..............C......330 493-4443
Canton *(G-2287)*

Doctors Hosp Physcn Svcs LLC......E......330 834-4725
Massillon *(G-13675)*

Doctors Ohiohealth Corporation.......A......614 544-5424
Columbus *(G-7464)*

Doctors Urgent Care..............E......419 586-1611
Celina *(G-2594)*

Drs Hill & Thomas Co..............E......440 944-8887
Cleveland *(G-5446)*

Drs Paul Boyles & Kennedy.......E......614 734-3347
Columbus *(G-7470)*

Dublin Family Care Inc..............E......614 761-2244
Dublin *(G-10206)*

Dunlap Family Physicians Inc.......E......330 684-2015
Orrville *(G-15628)*

E N T Toledo Inc..............E......419 578-7555
Toledo *(G-17707)*

Eastern Hill Internal Medicine.......E......513 232-3500
Cincinnati *(G-3475)*

Eastern Hills Pediatric Assoc.......E......513 231-3345
Cincinnati *(G-3476)*

Elizabeth Place Holdings LLC.......E......323 300-3700
Dayton *(G-9410)*

Emerald Pediatrics..............E......614 932-5050
Dublin *(G-10216)*

Emergency Medical Group Inc.......E......419 866-6009
Toledo *(G-17712)*

Emergency Medicine Specialists.......D......937 438-8910
Dayton *(G-9414)*

Emergency Services Inc..............E......614 224-6420
Columbus *(G-7514)*

Emp Management Group Ltd........D......330 493-4443
Canton *(G-2301)*

Endo-Surgical Center Fla LLC.......B......440 708-0582
Chagrin Falls *(G-2664)*

Endoscopy Center..............E......419 843-7993
Sylvania *(G-17422)*

Endoscopy Center of Dayton.......E......937 320-5050
Beavercreek *(G-1216)*

▲ ENt and Allergy Health Svcs.......E......440 779-1112
North Olmsted *(G-15286)*

Equitas Health Inc..............D......614 340-6700
Columbus *(G-7526)*

Equitas Health Inc..............D......614 299-2437
Columbus *(G-7527)*

Eric Hasemeier Do..............E......740 594-7979
Athens *(G-780)*

Erieside Medical Group..............E......440 918-6270
Willoughby *(G-19521)*

Evokes LLC..............E......513 947-8433
Mason *(G-13578)*

Eye Care Associates Inc..............D......330 746-7691
Youngstown *(G-20032)*

Eye Centers of Ohio Inc..............E......330 966-1111
North Canton *(G-15202)*

Eye Centers of Ohio Inc..............E......330 966-1111
Canton *(G-2308)*

Eye Inst of Northwestern OH In.......E......419 865-3866
Toledo *(G-17722)*

Eye Surgery Center Ohio Inc.......E......614 228-3937
Columbus *(G-7550)*

Fairview Eye Center Inc..............E......440 333-3060
Cleveland *(G-5506)*

Fairview Hospital..............E......216 476-7000
Cleveland *(G-5508)*

Fallen Timbers Fmly Physicians.......D......419 893-3321
Maumee *(G-13788)*

Falls Family Practice Inc..............E......330 923-9585
Cuyahoga Falls *(G-9089)*

Family Health Care Center Inc.......E......614 274-4171
Columbus *(G-7684)*

Family Health Partners Inc..............E......419 935-0196
Willard *(G-19480)*

Family Health Plan Inc..............C......419 241-6501
Toledo *(G-17724)*

Family Hlth Svcs Drke Cnty Inc.......C......937 548-3806
Greenville *(G-11377)*

Family Medical Group..............E......513 389-1400
Cincinnati *(G-3529)*

Family Medicine Center Minerva.......E......330 868-4184
Minerva *(G-14519)*

Family Medicine Stark County.......E......330 499-5600
Canton *(G-2309)*

Family Physician Associates.......E......614 901-2273
Westerville *(G-19254)*

Family Physicians Associates.......E......440 442-3866
Cleveland *(G-5510)*

Family Physicians Inc..............E......330 494-7099
Canton *(G-2310)*

Family Physicians of Coshocton.......E......740 622-0332
Coshocton *(G-9014)*

Family Physicians of Gahanna.......E......614 471-9654
Columbus *(G-7560)*

Family Practice & Associates.......E......937 399-6650
Springfield *(G-17036)*

Family Practice Ctr Salem Inc.......E......330 332-9961
Salem *(G-16543)*

Far Oaks Orthopedists Inc..............E......937 433-5309
Dayton *(G-9426)*

Far Oaks Orthopedists Inc..............E......937 298-0452
Vandalia *(G-18521)*

Far Oaks Orthopedists Inc..............E......937 433-5309
Dayton *(G-9427)*

Fauster-Cameron Inc..............B......419 784-1414
Defiance *(G-9913)*

Findlay Womens Care LLC.......E......419 420-0904
Findlay *(G-10907)*

First Med Urgent & Fmly Ctr.......E......740 756-9238
Lancaster *(G-12405)*

First Settlement Orthopaedics.......E......740 373-8756
Marietta *(G-13329)*

Fisher-Titus Medical Center.......C......419 663-6464
Norwalk *(G-15436)*

Fisher-Titus Medical Center.......E......440 839-2226
Wakeman *(G-18621)*

Five Rivers Health Centers.......E......937 734-6841
Dayton *(G-9440)*

Flowers Family Practice Inc.......E......614 277-9631
Grove City *(G-11434)*

Fortunefavorsthe Bold LLC.......E......216 469-2845
Lakewood *(G-12344)*

Foundations Hlth Solutions Inc.......D......440 793-0200
North Olmsted *(G-15289)*

Franklin & Seidelmann Inc.......E......216 255-5700
Beachwood *(G-1059)*

Frederick C Smith Clinic Inc.......B......740 383-7000
Marion *(G-13421)*

Frederick C Smith Clinic Inc.......E......740 363-9021
Delaware *(G-9979)*

Fresenius Medical Care..............E......614 855-3677
Gahanna *(G-11120)*

Gastrntrlogy Assoc Clvland Inc.......E......216 593-7700
Cleveland *(G-5593)*

Gastroenterology Associates.......E......330 493-1480
Canton *(G-2323)*

Gem City Urologist Inc..............E......937 832-8400
Englewood *(G-10588)*

George G Ellis Jr MD..............D......330 965-0832
Youngstown *(G-20048)*

George P Pettit MD Inc..............E......740 354-1434
Portsmouth *(G-16139)*

Good Samaritan Hosp Cincinnati.......E......513 569-6251
Cincinnati *(G-3625)*

Goudy Internal Medicine Inc.......D......419 468-8323
Galion *(G-11178)*

Grandview Family Practice.......E......740 258-9267
Columbus *(G-7684)*

Greater Cin Cardi Consults In.......E......513 751-4222
Cincinnati *(G-3649)*

Greater Cincinnati Gastro Assc.......D......513 336-8636
Cincinnati *(G-3652)*

Greater Cincinnati Ob/Gyn Inc.......E......513 245-3103
Cincinnati *(G-3653)*

Greater Dayton Surgery Ctr LLC.......E......937 535-2200
Dayton *(G-9473)*

GTE Internet..............D......614 508-6000
Columbus *(G-7698)*

Gw Sutherland MD..............E......419 578-7200
Toledo *(G-17775)*

Gyneclgic Onclgists of Ne Ohio.......E......330 384-6041
Akron *(G-248)*

H M T Dermatology Inc..............E......330 725-0569
Medina *(G-13946)*

Hand Ctr At Orthopaedic Inst.......D......937 298-4417
Dayton *(G-9484)*

Hand Rehabilitation Associates.......E......330 668-4055
Akron *(G-249)*

Hans Zwart MD & Associates.......E......937 433-4183
Dayton *(G-9485)*

Health Collaborative..............D......513 618-3600
Cincinnati *(G-3694)*

Health Works Mso Inc..............E......740 368-5366
Delaware *(G-9983)*

Healthsource of Ohio Inc..............E......937 392-4381
Georgetown *(G-11272)*

Healthsource of Ohio Inc..............E......937 981-7707
Greenfield *(G-11363)*

Heart Care..............D......614 533-5000
Gahanna *(G-11124)*

Heart Center of N Eastrn Ohio.......E......330 758-7703
Youngstown *(G-20062)*

Heart Ohio Family Health Ctrs.......E......614 235-5555
Columbus *(G-7728)*

Heart Specialists of Ohio..............E......614 538-0527
Columbus *(G-7729)*

Hector A Buch Jr MD..............E......419 227-7399
Lima *(G-12658)*

Hernando Zegarra..............E......216 831-5700
Cleveland *(G-5686)*

Herzig-Krall Medical Group.......E......513 896-9595
Fairfield *(G-10735)*

Hickman Cancer Center..............D......419 824-1952
Sylvania *(G-17430)*

Hillsboro Health Center Inc.......E......937 393-5781
Hillsboro *(G-11846)*

Hmt Dermatology Associates Inc.......E......330 725-0569
Medina *(G-13950)*

Holzer Clinic LLC..............C......304 746-3701
Gallipolis *(G-11196)*

Holzer Clinic LLC..............A......740 446-5411
Gallipolis *(G-11197)*

Holzer Clinic LLC..............C......304 744-2300
Gallipolis *(G-11198)*

Holzer Clinic LLC..............E......740 886-9403
Proctorville *(G-16217)*

Holzer Clinic LLC..............E......740 446-5412
Gallipolis *(G-11199)*

Holzer Clinic LLC..............C......740 589-3100
Athens *(G-785)*

Home Health Connection Inc.......E......614 839-4545
Worthington *(G-19815)*

Hometown Urgent Care..............C......614 263-4400
Columbus *(G-7768)*

Hometown Urgent Care..............C......330 505-9400
Warren *(G-18712)*

Hometown Urgent Care..............C......614 472-2880
Columbus *(G-7769)*

Hometown Urgent Care..............C......614 272-1100
Columbus *(G-7770)*

Hometown Urgent Care..............C......937 236-8630
Dayton *(G-9504)*

Hometown Urgent Care..............C......937 322-6222
Springfield *(G-17046)*

Hometown Urgent Care..............C......614 835-0400
Groveport *(G-11519)*

Hometown Urgent Care..............C......937 372-6012
Xenia *(G-19911)*

Hometown Urgent Care..............C......330 629-2300
Youngstown *(G-20067)*

Hometown Urgent Care..............D......740 363-3133
Delaware *(G-9987)*

Hometown Urgent Care..............C......937 252-2000
Wooster *(G-19728)*

Hometown Urgent Care..............C......513 831-5900
Milford *(G-14395)*

Hometown Urgent Care..............C......937 342-9520
Springfield *(G-17045)*

Hope Ctr For Cncer Care Warren.......D......330 856-8600
Warren *(G-18713)*

Hopewell Health Centers Inc.......E......740 596-5249
Mc Arthur *(G-13890)*

HRP Capital Inc..............E......419 865-3111
Holland *(G-11889)*

Immediate Health Associates.......E......614 794-0481
Westerville *(G-19265)*

Immediate Medical Service Inc.......E......330 823-0400
Alliance *(G-534)*

Independence Oncology..............E......216 524-7979
Cleveland *(G-5743)*

Institute/Reproductive Health.......E......513 585-2355
Cincinnati *(G-3764)*

Internal Mdcine Cons of Clmbus.......E......614 878-6413
Columbus *(G-7836)*

Ironton and Lawrence County.......B......740 532-3534
Ironton *(G-12155)*

Johnson Adams & Protrouski.......E......419 238-6251
Van Wert *(G-18481)*

S I C

Joint Emergency Med Svc Inc ....E 937 746-3471
Franklin *(G-11033)*

Joint Implant Surgeons Inc ....E 614 221-6331
New Albany *(G-14858)*

Jon R Dvorak MD ....E 419 872-7700
Perrysburg *(G-15883)*

Joseph A Girgis MD Inc ....E 440 930-6095
Sheffield Village *(G-16737)*

Joslin Diabetes Center Inc ....E 937 401-7575
Dayton *(G-9529)*

Jyg Innovations LLC ....E 937 630-3858
Dayton *(G-9531)*

Kaiser Foundation Hospitals ....A 440 350-3614
Concord Township *(G-8943)*

Kaiser Foundation Hospitals ....A 330 633-8400
Akron *(G-296)*

Kaiser Foundation Hospitals ....A 216 524-7377
Avon *(G-889)*

Kaiser Foundation Hospitals ....A 800 524-7377
Cleveland Heights *(G-6721)*

Kaiser Foundation Hospitals ....A 216 524-7377
Brooklyn Heights *(G-1873)*

Kaiser Foundation Hospitals ....A 800 524-7377
North Canton *(G-15214)*

Kaiser Foundation Hospitals ....A 800 524-7377
Medina *(G-13964)*

Kaiser Foundation Hospitals ....A 800 524-7377
Fairlawn *(G-10837)*

Kaiser Foundation Hospitals ....A 800 524-7377
Mentor *(G-14069)*

Kaiser Foundation Hospitals ....A 800 524-7377
Kent *(G-12238)*

Kaiser Foundation Hospitals ....A 216 524-7377
Rocky River *(G-16439)*

Kaiser Foundation Hospitals ....A 800 524-7377
Brooklyn Heights *(G-1874)*

Kaiser Foundation Hospitals ....A 216 524-7377
Strongsville *(G-17318)*

Kaiser Foundation Hospitals ....A 330 486-2800
Twinsburg *(G-18287)*

Kathleen K Karol MD ....D 419 878-7992
Toledo *(G-17837)*

Kentucky Heart Institute Inc ....E 740 353-8100
Portsmouth *(G-16152)*

Kettering Anesthesia Assoc Inc ....D 937 298-4331
Dayton *(G-9535)*

Kevin C McDonnell MD ....D 330 344-6401
Akron *(G-301)*

Kiddie West Pediatric Center ....E 614 276-7733
Columbus *(G-7901)*

Kidney & Hypertension Center ....E 513 861-0800
Cincinnati *(G-3867)*

Kidney Group Inc ....E 330 746-1488
Youngstown *(G-20091)*

Kindred Healthcare Inc ....D 937 222-5963
Dayton *(G-9546)*

Kolczun & Kolczun Orthopedics ....E 440 985-3113
Lorain *(G-12911)*

Kunesh Eye Center Inc ....E 937 298-1703
Oakwood *(G-15482)*

Labcare ....E 330 753-3649
Barberton *(G-958)*

Lake County Family Practice ....E 440 352-4880
Mentor *(G-14072)*

Lake Hospital System Inc ....A 440 632-3024
Middlefield *(G-14272)*

Lake Urgent & Family Med Ctr ....E 440 255-6400
Mentor *(G-14074)*

Lakewood Clveland Fmly Med Ctr .....E 216 227-2162
Lakewood *(G-12353)*

Lakewood Hospital Association ....E 216 228-5437
Cleveland *(G-5852)*

Laser Hair Removal Center ....D 937 433-7536
Dayton *(G-9559)*

Lasik Plus Vision Center ....D 513 794-9964
Cincinnati *(G-3912)*

Lawrence A Cervino MD ....E 330 668-4065
Akron *(G-309)*

Layh & Associates ....E 937 767-9171
Yellow Springs *(G-19940)*

Lca-Vision Inc ....C 513 792-9292
Cincinnati *(G-3915)*

Libbey Inc ....A 419 671-6000
Toledo *(G-17853)*

Life Line Screening ....D 216 581-6556
Independence *(G-12090)*

Lifecare Fmly Hlth & Dntl Ctr ....E 330 454-2000
Canton *(G-2378)*

Lifestges Smrtan Ctr For Women ......E 937 277-8988
Dayton *(G-9566)*

Lu-Jean Feng Clinic LLC ....E 216 831-7007
Cleveland *(G-5886)*

Luis F Soto MD ....E 330 649-9400
Canton *(G-2382)*

Luke Immediate Care Center ....E 419 227-2245
Lima *(G-12695)*

Lutheran Medical Center ....B 216 696-4300
Solon *(G-16867)*

Magnum Medical Overseas JV LLC ...D 979 848-8169
Cincinnati *(G-3960)*

Mahoning Vly Hmtlgy Onclgy Aso .....E 330 318-1100
Youngstown *(G-20110)*

Mammovan Inc ....E 330 726-2064
Youngstown *(G-20114)*

Margaret B Shipley Child Hlth ....E 330 478-6333
Canton *(G-2388)*

Marietta Gynecologic Assoc ....D 740 374-3622
Marietta *(G-13352)*

Mark E Grosinger ....E 937 382-2000
Wilmington *(G-19633)*

Markowitz Rosenberg Assoc Drs ......E 440 646-2200
Cleveland *(G-5909)*

Marysvlle Ohio Srgical Ctr LLC ....A 937 578-4200
Marysville *(G-13517)*

Matern Ohio Management Inc ....D 614 457-7660
Columbus *(G-8037)*

Maumee Ob Gyn Assoc ....E 419 891-6201
Maumee *(G-13819)*

Mayfield Clinic Inc ....D 513 221-1100
Cincinnati *(G-3983)*

MBC Cardiologist Inc ....D 937 223-4461
Dayton *(G-9591)*

Med -Center/Med Partners ....E 440 349-6400
Cleveland *(G-5940)*

Med Center One Streetsboro ....E 330 626-3455
Streetsboro *(G-17261)*

Medcentral Health System ....E 419 526-8900
Ontario *(G-15562)*

Medical Arts Physician Center ....D 216 431-1500
Cleveland *(G-5941)*

Medical Assoc Cambridge Inc ....E 740 439-3515
Cambridge *(G-2076)*

Medical College of Ohio ....E 419 383-7100
Toledo *(G-17901)*

Medical Diagnostic Lab Inc ....E 440 333-1375
Avon *(G-894)*

Medical Group Associates Inc ....E 740 283-4773
Steubenville *(G-17166)*

Medical Mutual of Ohio ....E 614 621-4585
Columbus *(G-8053)*

Medical Onclgy-Hematology Assn ....E 937 223-2183
Dayton *(G-9602)*

Mentor Surgery Center Ltd ....E 440 205-5725
Mentor *(G-14083)*

Mercer Cnty Joint Townshp Hosp ......E 419 586-1611
Celina *(G-2601)*

Mercy Health ....E 419 935-0187
Willard *(G-19484)*

Mercy Health ....E 330 792-7418
Youngstown *(G-20123)*

Mercy Health ....E 513 829-1700
Fairfield *(G-10754)*

Mercy Health ....E 419 492-1300
New Washington *(G-15002)*

Mercy Health ....E 513 248-0100
Milford *(G-14408)*

Mercy Health ....E 513 686-8100
Blue Ash *(G-1609)*

Mercy Health ....E 513 985-0741
Cincinnati *(G-4017)*

Mercy Health ....E 440 336-2239
Elyria *(G-10535)*

Mercy Health ....E 440 775-1881
Oberlin *(G-15509)*

Mercy Health ....E 440 934-8344
Sheffield Village *(G-16739)*

Mercy Health ....E 440 967-8713
Vermilion *(G-18557)*

Mercy Health ....D 513 233-6736
Cincinnati *(G-4020)*

Mercy Health ....D 419 251-2659
Toledo *(G-17905)*

Mercy Health ....E 513 924-8200
Cincinnati *(G-4021)*

Mercy Health ....E 513 339-0800
Mason *(G-13618)*

Mercy Health ....E 440 366-5577
North Ridgeville *(G-15336)*

Mercy Health ....E 513 585-9600
Cincinnati *(G-4022)*

Mercy Health ....E 419 475-4666
Toledo *(G-17907)*

Mercy Health ....E 419 264-5800
Holgate *(G-11866)*

Mercy Health - Springfield C ....E 937 323-5001
Springfield *(G-17078)*

Mercy Health Youngstown LLC ....A 330 729-1420
Youngstown *(G-20125)*

Mercy Hlth - Clermont Hosp LLC ....D 513 732-8200
Batavia *(G-1004)*

Mercy Hlth St Vincent Med LLC ....A 419 251-0580
Toledo *(G-17910)*

Mercy Medical Associates ....E 513 686-4840
Cincinnati *(G-4034)*

Mercy Medical Center Inc ....E 330 627-7641
Carrollton *(G-2572)*

Mercy Professional Care ....D 330 832-2280
Massillon *(G-13715)*

Metro Health System ....D 330 669-2249
Smithville *(G-16811)*

Metrohealth System ....D 216 778-8446
Cleveland *(G-5969)*

Metropolitian Family Care Inc ....E 614 237-1067
Reynoldsburg *(G-16320)*

Miamisburg Family Practice ....E 937 866-2494
Miamisburg *(G-14192)*

Mid-Ohio Pdiatrics Adolescents ....E 614 899-0000
Westerville *(G-19280)*

Middltown Crdvscular Assoc Inc ....E 513 217-6400
Middletown *(G-14312)*

Midohio Crdiolgy Vascular Cons ....E 614 262-6772
Columbus *(G-8079)*

Midwest Allergy Associates ....E 614 846-5944
Columbus *(G-8080)*

Midwest Cmnty Hlth Assoc Inc ....C 419 633-4034
Bryan *(G-1964)*

Midwest Physcans Ansthsia Svcs ......D 614 884-0641
Columbus *(G-8083)*

Midwest Retina Inc ....E 614 233-9500
Zanesville *(G-20331)*

Miller-Valentine Construction ....D 937 293-0900
Dayton *(G-9637)*

Mobile Cardiac Imaging LLC ....E 419 251-3711
Toledo *(G-17921)*

Monroe Family Health Center ....E 740 472-0757
Woodsfield *(G-19677)*

Mount Auburn Obstetrics & Gyne ......E 513 241-4774
Cincinnati *(G-4078)*

Mount Carmel Central Ohio ....D 614 268-9561
Westerville *(G-19282)*

Moyal and Petroff MD ....E 440 461-6477
Cleveland *(G-6016)*

Mrp Inc ....E 513 965-9700
Milford *(G-14412)*

Mt Carmel Medical Group ....E 614 277-9631
Grove City *(G-11454)*

Mvhe Inc ....E 937 499-8211
Dayton *(G-9650)*

My Community Health Center ....E 330 363-6242
Canton *(G-2413)*

National Guard Ohio ....D 614 492-3166
Columbus *(G-8132)*

National Rgstry Emrgncy Mdcl ....E 614 888-4484
Columbus *(G-8138)*

Neighborhood Health Care Inc ....E 216 281-8945
Cleveland *(G-6053)*

Nelson & Bold Inc ....E 440 975-1422
Willoughby *(G-19554)*

Neurological Associates Inc ....D 614 544-4455
Columbus *(G-8181)*

Neurology Nroscience Assoc Inc ....E 330 572-1011
Akron *(G-344)*

Neurosurgical Network Inc ....E 419 251-1155
Toledo *(G-17938)*

New Beginnings Pediatrics Inc ....E 419 483-4122
Bellevue *(G-1381)*

New Horizons Surgery Center ....E 740 375-5854
Marion *(G-13449)*

North Coast Prof Co LLC ....C 419 557-5541
Sandusky *(G-16629)*

North Ohio Heart Center ....D 440 204-4000
Lorain *(G-12936)*

North Ohio Heart Center Inc ....E 440 414-9500
Cleveland *(G-6078)*

North Ohio Heart Center Inc ....E 440 366-3600
Elyria *(G-10545)*

North Ohio Heart Center Inc ....E 440 204-4000
Avon *(G-897)*

North Ohio Heart Center Inc ....E 440 204-4000
Lorain *(G-12937)*

North Ohio Heart Center Inc ....E 440 326-4120
Elyria (G-10546)

North Shore Gstrenterology Inc ....D...... 440 808-1212
Westlake (G-19382)

Northast Ohio Eye Surgeons Inc............E 330 678-0201
Kent (G-12250)

Northast Ohio Eye Surgeons Inc............E 330 836-8545
Akron (G-347)

Northast Ohio Orthpedics Assoc ....E 330 344-1980
Akron (G-348)

Northast Srgical Assoc of Ohio ....E 216 643-2780
Independence (G-12104)

Northeast Family Health Care................E 330 630-2332
Tallmadge (G-17482)

Northeast OH Neighborhood Heal........C....... 216 231-7700
Cleveland (G-6090)

Northeast Ohio Cardiology Svcs ....D...... 330 253-8195
Akron (G-350)

Northern Ohio Med Spclists LLC...........E 419 625-2841
Sandusky (G-16630)

Northwest Columbus Urology ....E 937 342-9260
Springfield (G-17090)

Northwest Eye Surgeons Inc ....E 614 451-7550
Columbus (G-8205)

Northwest Ohio Cardiology Cons ....D...... 419 842-3000
Toledo (G-17949)

Northwest Ohio Orthopedics ....E 419 885-2553
Sylvania (G-17439)

Northwest Ohio Urgent Care Inc ....E 419 720-7363
Toledo (G-17950)

Norwalk Clinic Inc ....E 419 668-4851
Norwalk (G-15449)

Norwood Endoscopy Center ....E 513 731-5600
Cincinnati (G-4133)

Nuerocare Center Inc ....D...... 330 494-2917
Canton (G-2423)

Nuerological & Sleep Disorders ....E 513 721-7533
Cincinnati (G-4138)

Nueterra Holdings LLC ....E 614 451-0500
Columbus (G-8214)

Nuray Radiologists Inc ....E 513 965-8059
Cincinnati (G-4139)

Nwo Gastroenterology Assoc Inc ....E 419 471-1317
Toledo (G-17954)

Oakhill Medical Associates ....E 937 599-1411
West Liberty (G-19121)

Ob Gyn Associates of Lancaster...........E 740 653-5088
Lancaster (G-12424)

Ob-Gyn Specialists Lima Inc ....E 419 227-0610
Lima (G-12709)

Oberlin Clinic Inc ....C....... 440 774-7337
Oberlin (G-15512)

Obstetrics & Gynecology Assoc ....D...... 513 221-3800
Fairfield (G-10762)

Obstetrics & Gynecology S Inc ....E 937 296-0167
Dayton (G-9666)

Obstetrics Gynclogy of Reserve ....E 330 666-1166
Akron (G-355)

Occupational Health Services ....E 937 492-7296
Sidney (G-16788)

Ohio Cancer Specialists.......................E 419 756-2122
Mansfield (G-13228)

Ohio Eye Alliance ....E 330 823-1680
Alliance (G-542)

Ohio Eye Associates Inc ....D...... 800 423-0694
Mansfield (G-13229)

Ohio Eye Specialists Inc ....E 800 948-3937
Chillicothe (G-2807)

Ohio Gstoenterology Group Inc.............E 614 221-8355
Columbus (G-8259)

Ohio Gstroenterology Group Inc............E 614 754-5500
Columbus (G-8260)

Ohio Gstroenterology Group Inc...........D...... 614 754-5500
Columbus (G-8261)

Ohio Head & Neck Surgeons Inc ....E 330 492-2844
Canton (G-2426)

Ohio Health Group LLC ....E 614 566-0010
Columbus (G-8263)

Ohio Heart ....E 513 206-1320
Cincinnati (G-4152)

Ohio Heart and Vascular ....E 513 206-1800
Cincinnati (G-4153)

Ohio Heart Health Center Inc ....C....... 513 351-9900
Cincinnati (G-4154)

Ohio Hills Health Services ....D...... 740 425-5165
Barnesville (G-978)

Ohio Institute of Cardiac Care ....E 937 322-1700
Dayton (G-9184)

Ohio Medical Group.............................E 440 414-9400
Westlake (G-19386)

Ohio Minority Medical..........................E 513 400-5011
East Liverpool (G-10411)

Ohio North E Hlth Systems Inc ....E 330 747-9551
Youngstown (G-20145)

Ohio Orthpd Surgery Inst LLC...............E 614 827-8777
Columbus (G-8277)

Ohio Pediatrics Inc ....E 937 299-2339
Dayton (G-9671)

Ohio Pediatrics Inc ....E 937 299-2743
Dayton (G-9672)

Ohio Retina Associates Inc ....E 330 966-9800
Canton (G-2430)

Ohio State Univ Wexner Med Ctr ....C....... 614 293-2663
Columbus (G-8291)

Ohio State Univ Wexner Med Ctr ....A 614 293-6255
Columbus (G-8294)

Ohio State University ....E 614 366-3692
Columbus (G-8295)

Ohio State University ....A 614 293-8045
Columbus (G-8297)

Ohio State University ....A 614 293-7417
Columbus (G-8301)

Ohio State University ....A 614 293-8116
Columbus (G-8303)

Ohio State University ....A 614 293-3860
Columbus (G-8309)

Ohio State University ....E 614 293-4997
Columbus (G-8317)

Ohio State University ....E 614 293-8732
Columbus (G-8321)

Ohio State University ....E 614 293-2222
Columbus (G-8339)

Ohio State University ....B 614 293-8133
Columbus (G-8340)

Ohio State University ....A 614 293-5066
Columbus (G-8342)

Ohio State University ....E 614 293-4967
Columbus (G-8351)

Ohio State University ....A 614 257-3000
Columbus (G-8300)

Ohio Surgery Center Ltd ....D...... 614 451-0500
Columbus (G-8354)

Ohio University ....D...... 740 593-2195
Athens (G-798)

Ohio University ....E 740 593-1660
Athens (G-799)

Ohio Valley Ambulatory Surgery ....E 740 423-4684
Belpre (G-1409)

Ohiocare Ambulatory Surgery ....E 419 897-5501
Maumee (G-13826)

Oncolgy/Hmatology Care Inc PSC ....D...... 513 751-2145
Cincinnati (G-4174)

Ophthalmology Associates of ....E 419 865-3866
Maumee (G-13828)

Ophthlmic Srgeons Cons of Ohio ....E 614 221-7464
Columbus (G-8378)

Optivue Inc ....C....... 419 891-1391
Oregon (G-15602)

Orthoneuro ....E 614 890-6555
Westerville (G-19289)

Orthoneuro ....D...... 614 890-6555
Columbus (G-8387)

Orthoneuro ....D...... 614 890-6555
Columbus (G-8388)

Orthopaedic & Spine Center At ....E 614 468-0300
Dublin (G-10300)

Orthopaedic Institute Ohio Inc ....D...... 419 222-6622
Lima (G-12714)

Orthopaedic Offices Inc ....E 513 221-5500
Blue Ash (G-1626)

Orthopdic Spt Mdicine Cons Inc ....E 513 777-7714
Middletown (G-14318)

Orthopedic Assoc of Zanesville ....E 740 454-3273
Zanesville (G-20351)

Orthopedic Associates ....D...... 800 824-9861
Liberty Township (G-12584)

Orthopedic Associates ....E 937 415-9100
Centerville (G-2631)

Orthopedic Associates Dayton...............E 937 280-4988
Dayton (G-9678)

Orthopedic Associates Inc ....E 440 892-1440
Westlake (G-19388)

▲ Orthopedic Cons Cincinnati ....C....... 513 733-8894
Blue Ash (G-1627)

Orthopedic Cons Cincinnati ....E 513 753-7488
Cincinnati (G-2863)

Orthopedic Cons Cincinnati ....E 513 232-6677
Cincinnati (G-4185)

Orthopedic Cons Cincinnati ....E 513 245-2500
Cincinnati (G-4186)

Orthopedic Cons Cincinnati ....E 513 347-9999
Cincinnati (G-4187)

Orthopedic Diagnstc Trtmnt Ctr ....E 513 791-6611
Montgomery (G-14602)

Orthopedic Diagnstc Trtmnt Ctr ....E 513 221-4848
Cincinnati (G-4188)

Orthopedic One Inc.............................D...... 614 827-8700
Columbus (G-8389)

Orthopedic One Inc.............................D...... 614 545-7900
Columbus (G-8390)

Orthorpdics Mltspcialty Netwrk ....E 330 493-1630
Canton (G-2433)

Osu Emergency Medicine LLC ....D...... 614 947-3700
Columbus (G-8391)

Osu Physical Medicine LLC ....E 614 366-6398
Columbus (G-8395)

Osu Psychiatry LLC ....E 614 794-1818
Columbus (G-8396)

Osu Radiology LLC ....E 614 293-8315
Columbus (G-8397)

OSu Spt Mdcine Physcians Inc ....E 614 293-3600
Columbus (G-8398)

Osu Surgery LLC ....E 614 293-8116
Columbus (G-8399)

Osu Surgery LLC ....C....... 614 261-1141
Columbus (G-8400)

Osup Community Outreach LLC ....E 614 685-1542
Columbus (G-8401)

P C Vpa ....E 937 293-2133
Moraine (G-14686)

Pain Control Consultants Inc................E 614 430-5727
Columbus (G-8413)

Pain Net Inc ....D...... 614 481-5960
Columbus (G-8414)

Pajka Eye Center Inc...........................E 419 228-7432
Lima (G-12717)

Patricia A Dickerson MD ....E 937 436-1117
Dayton (G-9688)

Pediatric Assoc Cincinnati ....E 513 791-1222
Cincinnati (G-4221)

Pediatric Assoc of Fairfield ....E 513 874-9460
Fairfield (G-10769)

Pediatric Assoc of Springfield ....D...... 937 328-2320
Springfield (G-17095)

Pediatric Associates Inc ....E 614 501-7337
Columbus (G-8435)

Pediatric Associates of Dayton ....E 937 832-7337
Englewood (G-10596)

Pediatric Care Inc ....E 513 931-6357
Cincinnati (G-4222)

Pediatric Services Inc ....E 440 845-1500
Cleveland (G-6189)

Pediatrics Assoc of Mt Carmel ....E 513 752-3650
Cincinnati (G-2864)

Pediatrics of Akron Inc ....E 330 253-7753
Akron (G-373)

Pediatrics of Lima Inc ....E 419 222-4045
Lima (G-12719)

Perrysburg Pediatrics ....E 419 872-7700
Perrysburg (G-15903)

Physicians Care of Marietta ....D...... 740 373-2519
Marietta (G-13369)

Physicians In Family Practice ....E 440 775-1881
Oberlin (G-15517)

Physicians Surgeons For Women ....E 937 323-7340
Springfield (G-17098)

Pioneer Physicians Networking ....E 330 633-6601
Tallmadge (G-17484)

Plastic Surgery Group Inc.....................E 513 791-4440
Cincinnati (G-4253)

Portage Family Medicine......................E 330 626-5566
Streetsboro (G-17266)

Portage Pediatrics ....E 330 297-8824
Ravenna (G-16258)

Portsmouth Hospital Corp ....A 740 991-4000
Portsmouth (G-16159)

Preble County General Hlth Dst ....E 937 472-0087
Eaton (G-10460)

Premier Health Group LLC ....E 937 535-4100
Dayton (G-9703)

Premier Health Partners ....D...... 937 526-3235
Versailles (G-18571)

Premier Health Specialists Inc...............E 937 223-4518
Dayton (G-9705)

Premier Heart Associates Inc ....E 937 832-2425
Dayton (G-9706)

Premier Heart Inc ....E 937 832-2425
Englewood (G-10598)

Premier Integrated Med Assoc ....D...... 937 291-6813
Centerville (G-2632)

Premier Physicians Centers Inc ....E 440 895-5085
Westlake *(G-19393)*

Premier Radiology Group Inc ....E 937 431-9729
Beavercreek *(G-1177)*

Primary Care Nursing Services ....D 614 764-0960
Dublin *(G-10311)*

Primary Care Physicians Assn ....E 330 499-9944
Canton *(G-2440)*

Primary Cr Ntwrk Prmr Hlth Prt ....E 513 492-5940
Mason *(G-13628)*

Primary Cr Ntwrk Prmr Hlth Prt ....E 937 890-6644
Vandalia *(G-18535)*

Primary Cr Ntwrk Prmr Hlth Prt ....E 937 278-5854
Dayton *(G-9707)*

Primary Cr Ntwrk Prmr Hlth Prt ....D 937 208-9090
Dayton *(G-9708)*

Primary Cr Ntwrk Prmr Hlth Prt ....D 937 208-7000
Beavercreek *(G-1178)*

Primary Cr Ntwrk Prmr Hlth Prt ....E 937 743-5965
Franklin *(G-11038)*

Primary Cr Ntwrk Prmr Hlth Prt ....E 513 420-5233
Middletown *(G-14354)*

Primary Cr Ntwrk Prmr Hlth Prt ....E 937 226-7085
Dayton *(G-9709)*

Primary Cr Ntwrk Prmr Hlth Prt ....D 937 424-9800
Dayton *(G-9710)*

Primary Eyecare Associates ....E 937 492-2351
Sidney *(G-16794)*

Primecare Sutheastern Ohio Inc ....E 740 454-8551
Zanesville *(G-20355)*

Primed ....E 937 435-9013
Dayton *(G-9712)*

Primed Physicians ....E 937 298-8058
Dayton *(G-9713)*

Primed Premier Integrated Med ....C 937 291-6893
Dayton *(G-9714)*

Primehalth Wns Hlth Specialist ....E 440 918-4630
Willoughby Hills *(G-19592)*

Professionals For Womens Hlth ....E 614 268-8800
Columbus *(G-8471)*

Progressive Womens Care ....E 330 629-8466
Youngstown *(G-20166)*

Promedica ....D 419 291-3450
Maumee *(G-13834)*

Promedica GI Physicians LLC ....E 419 843-7996
Toledo *(G-17991)*

Promedica Gnt-Urinary Surgeons ....E 419 531-8558
Toledo *(G-17992)*

Promedica Health Systems Inc ....E 419 891-6201
Maumee *(G-13835)*

Proscan Imaging LLC ....E 513 759-7350
West Chester *(G-18987)*

Provider Physicians Inc ....D 614 755-3000
Columbus *(G-8475)*

Psy-Care Inc ....E 330 856-6663
Warren *(G-18737)*

Psychiatric Solutions Inc ....C 440 953-3000
Willoughby *(G-19564)*

Psychiatric Solutions Inc ....C 330 759-2700
Youngstown *(G-20169)*

Psychiatric Solutions Inc ....C 419 891-9333
Maumee *(G-13837)*

Psychiatric Solutions Inc ....C 740 695-2131
Saint Clairsville *(G-2156)*

Public Safety Ohio Department ....E 937 335-6209
Troy *(G-18222)*

Pulmonary & Medicine Dayton ....E 937 439-3600
Miamisburg *(G-14208)*

Pulmonary Crtcal Care Spcalist ....E 419 843-7800
Maumee *(G-13838)*

Queen City General & Vascular ....E 513 232-8181
Cincinnati *(G-4314)*

Queen City Medical Group ....E 513 528-5600
Cincinnati *(G-4317)*

Queen City Physicians ....D 513 872-2061
Cincinnati *(G-4318)*

Queen City Physicians Ltd ....E 513 791-6992
Cincinnati *(G-4319)*

Queen Cy Spt Mdcine Rhbltation ....E 513 561-1111
Cincinnati *(G-4323)*

R I D Inc ....E 419 251-4790
Toledo *(G-17996)*

Radiology Physicians Inc ....E 614 717-9840
Delaware *(G-10001)*

Rakesh Ranjan MD & Assoc Inc ....E 216 375-9897
Cleveland *(G-6284)*

Reading Family Practice ....E 513 563-6934
Cincinnati *(G-4343)*

Reconstructive Orthopedics ....E 513 793-3933
Cincinnati *(G-4346)*

Regency Park Eye Associates ....E 419 882-0588
Toledo *(G-17997)*

Rehab Continuum Inc ....E 513 984-8070
Blue Ash *(G-1643)*

Reid Physician Associates Inc ....B 937 456-4400
Eaton *(G-10461)*

Reproductive Gynecology Inc ....E 330 375-7722
Akron *(G-403)*

Reproductive Gynecology Inc ....E 330 452-6010
Canton *(G-2454)*

Reserve ....E 330 666-1166
Akron *(G-405)*

Retina Associate of Cleveland ....E 216 831-5700
Beachwood *(G-1100)*

Retina Associate of Cleveland ....E 216 221-2878
Westlake *(G-19400)*

Retina Group Inc ....E 614 464-3937
Columbus *(G-8528)*

Reynolds Road Surgical Ctr LLC ....D 419 578-7500
Toledo *(G-18006)*

Richard J Nelson MD ....E 419 578-7555
Maumee *(G-13845)*

Richard L Liston MD ....D 937 320-2020
Beavercreek *(G-1235)*

Richard Tomm MD ....D 216 297-3060
Cleveland *(G-6323)*

Richmond Medical Center ....B 440 585-6500
Richmond Heights *(G-16394)*

River Road Family Physicians ....E 419 872-7745
Perrysburg *(G-15913)*

River Vly Orthpdics Spt Mdcine ....E 740 687-3346
Lancaster *(G-12431)*

Riverhills Healthcare Inc ....E 513 241-2370
Cincinnati *(G-4378)*

Riverhills Healthcare Inc ....E 513 791-6400
Cincinnati *(G-4379)*

Riverside Nephrology Assoc Inc ....E 614 538-2250
Columbus *(G-8536)*

Riverside Radiology and ....C 614 340-7747
Columbus *(G-8537)*

Riverview Health Institute ....E 937 222-5390
Dayton *(G-9736)*

Riverview Surgery Center ....E 740 681-2700
Lancaster *(G-12432)*

Robert E Kose ....E 419 843-7800
Maumee *(G-13847)*

Robert E Lubow MD ....E 513 961-8861
Cincinnati *(G-4389)*

Robert Ellis ....E 513 821-0275
Cincinnati *(G-4390)*

Robert F Arrom Md Inc ....E 513 893-4107
Fairfield *(G-10776)*

Robert Wiley MD Inc ....E 216 621-3211
Cleveland *(G-6335)*

Robinson Health System Inc ....A 330 297-0811
Ravenna *(G-16263)*

Robinson Memorial Hospital ....E 330 626-3455
Streetsboro *(G-17268)*

Rocking Horse Chld Hlth Ctr ....E 937 328-7266
Springfield *(G-17103)*

Roger S Palutsis MD ....E 330 821-0201
Alliance *(G-549)*

Roholt Vision Institute Inc ....E 330 702-8755
Canfield *(G-2156)*

Russell D Ens Do ....E 330 499-5700
Canton *(G-2467)*

Russell Weisman Jr MD ....C 216 844-3127
Cleveland *(G-6350)*

Sabry Hospital ....E 216 476-7052
Cleveland *(G-6359)*

Sagar Satyavolu MD ....E 937 323-1404
Springfield *(G-17107)*

Salem Internal Medicine Assoc ....E 330 332-5232
Salem *(G-16563)*

Saras Garden ....E 419 335-7272
Wauseon *(G-18810)*

Schoenbrunn Healthcare ....D 330 339-3595
New Philadelphia *(G-14980)*

Schuster Cardiology ....E 937 866-0637
Miamisburg *(G-14216)*

Senior Lifestyle Corporation ....D 513 777-4457
West Chester *(G-19002)*

Seven Hills Obgyn Associates ....E 513 922-6666
Cincinnati *(G-4458)*

Seven Hills Womens Health Ctrs ....C 513 721-3200
Cincinnati *(G-4459)*

Shawneespring Hlth Cre Cntr RI ....B 513 943-4000
Loveland *(G-13028)*

Signature Healthcare LLC ....C 440 232-1800
Bedford *(G-1305)*

Somc Foundation Inc ....D 740 356-5000
Portsmouth *(G-16170)*

South Dayton Acute Care Cons ....E 937 433-8990
Dayton *(G-9776)*

South Dyton Urlgcal Asscations ....E 937 294-1489
Dayton *(G-9777)*

Southast Cmnty Mental Hlth Ctr ....C 614 225-0980
Columbus *(G-8661)*

Southern Ohio Eye Assoc LLC ....E 740 773-6347
Chillicothe *(G-2827)*

Southern Ohio Wns Cancer Prj ....D 740 775-7332
Chillicothe *(G-2828)*

Southwest Cleveland Sleep Ctr ....E 440 239-7533
Cleveland *(G-6427)*

Southwest Family Physicians ....E 440 816-2750
Cleveland *(G-6429)*

Southwest General Health Ctr ....C 440 816-4900
Strongsville *(G-17347)*

Southwest Ohio Amblatry Srgery ....E 513 425-0930
Middletown *(G-14329)*

Southwest Ohio Ent Spclsts Inc ....E 937 496-2600
Dayton *(G-9779)*

Southwest Urology LLC ....E 440 845-0900
Cleveland *(G-6435)*

Southwestern Obstetricians & G ....E 614 875-0444
Grove City *(G-11473)*

Spectrum Eye Care Inc ....E 419 423-8665
Findlay *(G-10961)*

Spectrum Orthpedics Inc Canton ....E 330 455-5367
North Canton *(G-15233)*

Sports Care Rehabilitation ....E 419 578-7530
Toledo *(G-18042)*

Springdale Family Medicine PC ....E 513 771-7213
Cincinnati *(G-4521)*

St Ritas Medical Center ....D 419 227-3361
Lima *(G-12752)*

St Ritas Medical Center ....E 419 996-5895
Lima *(G-12753)*

Stark County Neurologists Inc ....D 330 494-2097
Canton *(G-2493)*

Stark County Womens Clinic Inc ....D 330 493-0313
Canton *(G-2495)*

Stark Medical Specialties Inc ....E 330 837-1111
Massillon *(G-13732)*

Stephen A Rudolph Inc ....E 216 381-1367
Cleveland *(G-6466)*

Suburban Pediatrics Inc ....E 513 336-6700
Cincinnati *(G-4551)*

Summa Health System ....D 330 375-3584
Akron *(G-450)*

Summa Health System ....E 330 375-3000
Akron *(G-452)*

Summa Health System ....C 330 375-3315
Akron *(G-451)*

Summit Cnty Internists & Assoc ....E 330 375-3690
Akron *(G-457)*

Summit Hand Center Inc ....E 330 668-4055
Akron *(G-458)*

Summit Opthomology Optical ....E 330 864-8060
Akron *(G-459)*

Sunforest Ob Gyn Associates ....E 419 473-6622
Toledo *(G-18053)*

Superior Med LLC ....E 740 439-8839
Cambridge *(G-2084)*

Superior Medical Care Inc ....E 440 282-7420
Lorain *(G-12946)*

Surgery Center Cincinnati LLC ....D 513 947-1130
Cincinnati *(G-2871)*

Surgery Center Howland Ltd ....E 330 609-7874
Warren *(G-18750)*

Surgery Ctr An Ohio Ltd Partnr ....D 440 826-3240
Cleveland *(G-6488)*

Surgicenter Ltd ....E 740 522-3937
Newark *(G-15102)*

System Optics Csmt Srgcal Arts ....E 330 630-9699
Tallmadge *(G-17491)*

System Optics Laser Vision Ctr ....E 330 630-2451
Tallmadge *(G-17492)*

Talmage N Porter MD ....E 937 435-9013
Dayton *(G-9806)*

Taylor Stn Surgical Ctr Ltd ....D 614 751-4466
Columbus *(G-8733)*

Teater Orthopedic Surgeons ....E 330 343-3335
Dover *(G-10103)*

Terence Isakov MD ....D 440 449-1014
Cleveland *(G-6513)*

The Healthcare Connection Inc ....E 513 588-3623
Cincinnati *(G-4592)*

Thomas E Rojewski MD Inc ....E 740 454-0158
Zanesville *(G-20366)*

Thomas L Stover Inc ....E 330 665-8060
Mogadore (G-14558)
TLC Eyecare ....E 419 882-2020
Toledo (G-18069)
Toledo Cardiology Cons Inc ....D 419 251-6183
Toledo (G-18076)
Toledo Cardiology Inc ....E 419 479-5690
Toledo (G-18077)
▲ Toledo Clinic Inc ....B 419 473-3561
Toledo (G-18078)
Toledo Clinic Inc ....C 419 841-1600
Toledo (G-18080)
Toledo Family Health Center ....D 419 241-1554
Toledo (G-18083)
Toledo Hospital ....E 419 291-2051
Toledo (G-18085)
Toledo Hospital ....A 419 291-4000
Toledo (G-18086)
Total Renal Care Inc ....E 937 294-6711
Kettering (G-12301)
Township of Colerain ....C 513 741-7551
Cincinnati (G-4622)
Tri County Family Physicians ....E 614 837-6363
Canal Winchester (G-2122)
Tri County Mental Health Svcs ....C 740 592-3091
Athens (G-806)
Tri State Urlogic Svcs PSC Inc ....C 513 841-7400
Cincinnati (G-4632)
Trihealth Inc ....E 513 891-1627
Blue Ash (G-1664)
Trihealth G LLC ....D 513 732-0700
Cincinnati (G-4641)
Trihealth G LLC ....D 513 624-5535
Cincinnati (G-4643)
Trihealth G LLC ....E 513 346-5000
Cincinnati (G-4642)
Trihealth G LLC ....D 513 922-1200
Cincinnati (G-4644)
Trihealth Inc ....C 513 985-0900
Montgomery (G-14603)
Trihealth Oncology Inst LLC ....E 513 451-4033
Cincinnati (G-4645)
Trinity Health System ....B 740 283-7000
Steubenville (G-17179)
Trinity Hospital Twin City ....B 740 922-2800
Dennison (G-10053)
Trumbull Mem Hosp Foundation ....A 330 841-9376
Warren (G-18760)
Trumbull-Mahoning Med Group ....D 330 372-8800
Cortland (G-8995)
Uc Health Llc ....E 513 584-6999
Mason (G-13652)
Uc Health Llc ....D 513 475-7458
West Chester (G-19020)
Uc Health Llc ....D 513 475-7880
Cincinnati (G-4664)
Uc Health Llc ....D 513 475-8881
West Chester (G-19022)
Uc Health Llc ....E 513 475-7777
West Chester (G-19024)
Uc Health Llc ....D 513 648-9077
Cincinnati (G-4666)
Uc Health Llc ....D 513 475-7500
West Chester (G-19025)
Uhmg Department of Urologist ....E 216 844-3009
Cleveland (G-6562)
Union Hospital Association ....D 330 343-3311
Dover (G-10106)
United Health Network Ltd ....E 330 492-2102
Canton (G-2519)
United Srgcal Prtners Intl Inc ....E 330 702-1489
Canfield (G-2163)
Unity Health Network LLC ....E 330 678-7782
Kent (G-12266)
Unity Health Network LLC ....E 330 626-0549
Streetsboro (G-17276)
Univ Dermatology ....D 513 475-7630
Cincinnati (G-4692)
University Anesthesiologists ....E 216 844-3777
Cleveland (G-6585)
University Dermatology Cons ....E 513 584-4775
Cincinnati (G-4698)
University Dermatology Cons ....E 513 475-7630
Cincinnati (G-4699)
University Eye Surgeons ....C 614 293-5635
Columbus (G-8818)
University Family Physicians ....E 513 929-0104
Cincinnati (G-4700)
University Family Physicians ....D 513 475-7505
Cincinnati (G-4701)

University GYN&ob Cnsltnts Inc ....E 614 293-8697
Columbus (G-8819)
▲ University Hospitals ....A 216 767-8900
Shaker Heights (G-16717)
University Hospitals ....A 440 743-3000
Parma (G-15779)
University Hospitals ....D 216 844-8797
Cleveland (G-6590)
University Hospitals Cleveland ....E 440 205-5755
Mentor (G-14119)
University Hospitals Cleveland ....D 216 342-5556
Beachwood (G-1116)
University Medical Assoc Inc ....C 740 593-0753
Athens (G-810)
University Mednet ....C 440 255-0800
Mentor (G-14120)
University Mednet ....E 440 285-9079
Bedford (G-1313)
University Neurology Inc ....D 513 475-8730
Cincinnati (G-4702)
University of Cincinnati ....E 513 558-4194
Cincinnati (G-4703)
University of Cincinnati ....E 513 475-8771
Cincinnati (G-4705)
University of Cincinnati ....B 513 558-1200
Cincinnati (G-4706)
University of Cincinnati ....E 513 558-5471
Cincinnati (G-4721)
University of Cincinnati ....D 513 475-8524
Cincinnati (G-4722)
University of Cincinnati ....E 513 558-4831
Cincinnati (G-4724)
University of Cncnnati Srgeons ....E 513 245-3300
Cincinnati (G-4727)
University of Toledo ....D 419 534-3770
Toledo (G-18125)
University of Toledo ....E 419 383-3556
Toledo (G-18126)
University of Toledo ....E 419 383-5322
Toledo (G-18128)
University Ophthalmology Assoc ....E 216 382-8022
Cleveland (G-6600)
University Orthopaedic Cnsltnt ....E 513 475-8690
Cincinnati (G-4728)
University Orthpedic Assoc Inc ....E 216 844-1000
Cleveland (G-6601)
University Otolaryngologists ....E 614 273-2241
Columbus (G-8820)
University Prmry Care Prctices ....E 440 946-7391
Willoughby (G-19579)
University Radiology Assoc ....D 513 475-8760
Cincinnati (G-4729)
University Rdlgsts of Clveland ....D 216 844-1700
Cleveland (G-6602)
University Suburban Health Ctr ....C 216 382-8920
Cleveland (G-6604)
Upper Valley Family Care ....E 937 339-5355
Piqua (G-16034)
Urological Associates Inc ....E 614 221-5189
Columbus (G-8830)
US Dept of the Air Force ....D 937 257-0837
Dayton (G-9190)
US Oncology Inc ....E 937 352-2140
Xenia (G-19932)
Ushc Physicians Inc ....E 216 382-2036
Cleveland (G-6613)
Valley Regional Surgery Center ....E 877 858-5029
Piqua (G-16037)
Van Wert County Hospital Assn ....C 419 232-2077
Van Wert (G-18495)
Vanguard Imaging Partners ....D 937 236-4780
Dayton (G-9851)
Veterans Affairs US Dept ....A 937 268-6511
Dayton (G-9856)
Veterans Health Administration ....B 740 568-0412
Marietta (G-13396)
Veterans Health Administration ....D 740 773-1141
Chillicothe (G-2836)
Veterans Health Administration ....A 513 861-3100
Cincinnati (G-4759)
Veterans Health Administration ....B 513 943-3680
Cincinnati (G-4760)
Veterans Health Administration ....A 216 791-3800
Cleveland (G-6625)
Veterans Health Administration ....C 614 257-5524
Columbus (G-8849)
Veterans Health Administration ....B 866 463-0912
Ashtabula (G-758)
Veterans Health Administration ....B 740 695-9321
Saint Clairsville (G-16509)

Veterans Health Administration ....D 419 259-2000
Toledo (G-18138)
Veterans Health Administration ....E 330 740-9200
Youngstown (G-20236)
Veterans Health Administration ....B 216 939-0699
Cleveland (G-6626)
Veterans Health Administration ....D 330 489-4600
Canton (G-2526)
Veterinary RFRrl&emer Ctr of ....E 330 665-4996
Copley (G-8979)
▲ Volk Optical Inc ....D 440 942-6161
Mentor (G-14124)
Warren Drmatology Allergies PC ....E 330 856-6365
Warren (G-18769)
West Central Ohio Group Ltd ....E 419 224-7586
Lima (G-12778)
West Central Ohio Surgery & En ....E 419 226-8700
Lima (G-12780)
West Park Family Physician ....E 419 472-1124
Toledo (G-18153)
West Side Cardiology Assoc ....E 440 333-8600
Cleveland (G-6668)
West Side Cardiology Assoc ....E 440 333-8600
Cleveland (G-6669)
West Side Pediatrics Inc ....E 513 922-8200
Cincinnati (G-4785)
Western Family Physicians ....E 513 853-4900
Cincinnati (G-4787)
Westerville Dermatology Inc ....E 614 895-0400
Westerville (G-19305)
Westshore Prmry Care Assoc Inc ....D 440 934-0276
Sheffield Village (G-16742)
Westside Family Practice Inc ....E 614 878-4541
Columbus (G-8893)
Wheeling Hospital Inc ....E 740 695-2090
Saint Clairsville (G-16511)
Wheeling Hospital Inc ....E 740 633-4765
Martins Ferry (G-13481)
Whole Health Management Inc ....E 216 921-8601
Cleveland (G-6682)
Wilmington Medical Associates ....D 937 382-1616
Wilmington (G-19655)
Women Health Partners ....E 740 363-9021
Delaware (G-10017)
Women Physicians of Ob/Gyn Inc ....E 614 734-3340
Columbus (G-8913)
Womens Care Inc ....D 419 756-6000
Mansfield (G-13263)
Wood Health Company LLC ....D 419 353-7069
Bowling Green (G-1759)
Wooster Ophthalmologists Inc ....E 330 345-7800
Wooster (G-19787)
Wright State Physcans Drmtlogy ....E 937 224-7546
Beavercreek (G-1198)
Yeater Alene K MD ....E 740 348-4694
Newark (G-15112)
Youngstown Orthopaedic Assoc ....E 330 726-1466
Canfield (G-2166)
Zanesville Surgery Center LLC ....D 740 453-5713
Zanesville (G-20385)
Zepf Center ....E 419 255-4050
Toledo (G-18178)

8021 Offices & Clinics Of Dentists

Advance Implant Dentistry Inc ....E 513 271-0821
Cincinnati (G-2909)
Affiliates In Oral & Maxlofcl ....E 513 829-8080
West Chester (G-18862)
▲ Ashtabula Dental Associates ....E 440 992-3146
Ashtabula (G-717)
Association of Prosthodontics ....E 614 885-2022
Worthington (G-19794)
C Ted Forsberg ....E 440 992-3145
Ashtabula (G-723)
Charles C Smith DDS Inc ....E 937 667-2417
Tipp City (G-17551)
Chester West Dental Group Inc ....E 513 942-8181
West Chester (G-18884)
Chester West Dentistry ....E 330 753-7734
Akron (G-127)
Cincinnati Dental Services ....E 513 753-6446
Cincinnati (G-2845)
Cincinnati Dental Services ....E 513 741-7779
Cincinnati (G-3238)
Cincinnati Dental Services ....D 513 721-8888
Cincinnati (G-3239)
Cincinnati Dental Services ....E 513 774-8800
Loveland (G-12982)
Concorde Therapy Group Inc ....C 330 493-4210
Canton (G-2264)

S
I
C

Dental Center Northwest Ohio..........E...... 419 422-7664
  Findlay (G-10897)
Dental Facility..........E...... 614 292-1472
  Columbus (G-7436)
Dental Health Group PA..........E...... 330 630-9222
  Akron (G-183)
▲ Dental Health Services..........E...... 330 864-9090
  Fairlawn (G-10821)
Dental One Inc..........E...... 216 584-1000
  Independence (G-12066)
Dental Servics of Ohio Daniel..........D...... 614 863-2222
  Reynoldsburg (G-16297)
Donald Bowen and Assoc DDS..........E...... 614 274-0454
  Columbus (G-7466)
Dr Michael J Hulit..........E...... 330 863-7173
  Malvern (G-13122)
Equitas Health Inc..........D...... 614 299-2437
  Columbus (G-7527)
Eric W Warnock..........E...... 419 228-2233
  Lima (G-12633)
Family Dental Team Inc..........E...... 330 733-7911
  Fairlawn (G-10828)
Family Dentistry Inc..........E...... 513 932-6991
  Lebanon (G-12465)
Fixari Family Dental Inc..........E...... 614 866-7445
  Columbus (G-7593)
Greiner Dental Association..........E...... 440 255-2600
  Mentor (G-14057)
Health Smile Center..........E...... 440 992-2700
  Ashtabula (G-739)
Hopewell Dental Care..........E...... 740 522-5000
  Newark (G-15041)
Hudec Dental Associates Inc..........D...... 216 485-5788
  Brecksville (G-1784)
Lawrence M Shell DDS..........E...... 614 235-3444
  Columbus (G-7959)
Lima Dental Assoc Risolvato Lt..........E...... 419 228-4036
  Lima (G-12679)
Locust Dental Center..........E...... 330 535-7876
  Akron (G-320)
▲ Lucas & Clark Family Dentistry..........E...... 937 393-3494
  Hillsboro (G-11850)
Mahoning Valley Dental Service..........E...... 330 759-1771
  Youngstown (G-20109)
Martin Ls DDS Ms..........E...... 513 829-8999
  Fairfield (G-10749)
Metro Health Dental Associates..........E...... 216 778-4982
  Cleveland (G-5964)
Metrohealth Dept of Dentistry..........E...... 216 778-4739
  Cleveland (G-5965)
Metrohealth System..........E...... 216 957-1500
  Cleveland (G-5970)
Ohio State University..........D...... 614 292-5578
  Columbus (G-8299)
Ohio State University..........E...... 614 292-5144
  Columbus (G-8326)
Ohio State University..........D...... 614 292-1472
  Columbus (G-8344)
Ohio State University..........D...... 614 292-2751
  Columbus (G-8350)
Oral & Maxillofacial Surgeons..........E...... 419 385-5743
  Toledo (G-17965)
Oral & Maxillofacial Surgeons..........E...... 419 471-0300
  Toledo (G-17966)
Orthodontic Associates LLC..........E...... 419 229-8771
  Lima (G-12713)
Orthodontic Association..........E...... 419 523-4014
  Ottawa (G-15662)
Osu Orthodontic Clinic..........E...... 614 292-1058
  Columbus (G-8393)
Painesville Dental Group Inc..........E...... 440 354-2183
  Painesville (G-15732)
R P Cunningham DDS Inc..........E...... 614 885-2022
  Worthington (G-19841)
Rahn Dental Group Inc..........E...... 937 435-0324
  Dayton (G-9725)
Raymond A Greiner DDS Inc..........E...... 440 951-6688
  Mentor (G-14100)
Shelley Elizabeth Blum..........E...... 440 964-0542
  Ashtabula (G-755)
Smile Brands Inc..........E...... 419 627-1255
  Sandusky (G-16642)
Smile Development Inc..........E...... 419 882-7187
  Sylvania (G-17451)
State Valley Dental Center..........E...... 330 920-8060
  Cuyahoga Falls (G-9125)
Stow Dental Group Inc..........E...... 330 688-6456
  Stow (G-17231)
Thomas and Associates..........E...... 330 494-2111
  Canton (G-2510)

Thomas E Anderson DDS Inc..........E...... 330 467-6466
  Northfield (G-15387)
US Dental Care/M D Gelender..........E...... 614 252-3181
  Columbus (G-8833)
Van Buren Dental Associates..........E...... 937 253-9115
  Kettering (G-12302)

8031 Offices & Clinics Of Doctors Of Osteopathy

Access Ohio..........E...... 614 367-7700
  Columbus (G-6862)
Adena Health System..........E...... 740 779-7201
  Chillicothe (G-2750)
Allergy & Asthma Centre Dayton..........E...... 937 435-8999
  Centerville (G-2621)
Christ Hospital..........C...... 513 561-7809
  Cincinnati (G-3201)
Davis Eye Center..........E...... 330 923-5676
  Cuyahoga Falls (G-9085)
Doctors Hospital Health Center..........E...... 614 544-0101
  Grove City (G-11427)
Eric Hasemeier Do..........E...... 740 594-7979
  Athens (G-780)
Family Practice Center Inc..........E...... 330 682-3075
  Orrville (G-15630)
Grandview Family Practice..........E...... 740 258-9267
  Columbus (G-7684)
Hometown Urgent Care..........C...... 937 372-6012
  Xenia (G-19911)
Internal Mdcine Cons of Clmbus..........E...... 614 878-6413
  Columbus (G-7836)
Medical and Surgical Assoc..........E...... 740 522-7600
  Newark (G-15068)
Mercy Health..........E...... 419 264-5800
  Holgate (G-11866)
Metro Health System..........D...... 330 669-2249
  Smithville (G-16811)
Michael G Lawley..........E...... 513 793-3933
  Cincinnati (G-4046)
Physicians In Family Practice..........E...... 440 775-1881
  Oberlin (G-15517)
R I D Inc..........E...... 419 251-4790
  Toledo (G-17996)
Sports Medicine Grant Inc..........D...... 614 461-8174
  Columbus (G-8673)
Ulrich Professional Group..........E...... 330 673-9501
  Kent (G-12265)

8041 Offices & Clinics Of Chiropractors

Active Chiropractic..........E...... 440 893-8800
  Chagrin Falls (G-2637)
Healthquest Blanchester Inc..........E...... 937 783-4535
  Blanchester (G-1487)
Lbi Starbucks DC 3..........C...... 614 415-6363
  Columbus (G-7960)

8042 Offices & Clinics Of Optometrists

James D Egbert Optometrist..........E...... 937 236-1770
  Huber Heights (G-11955)
Optivue Inc..........C...... 419 891-1391
  Oregon (G-15602)
Ottivue..........D...... 419 693-4444
  Oregon (G-15606)
Primary Eyecare Associates..........E...... 937 492-2351
  Sidney (G-16794)
Shawnee Optical Inc..........E...... 440 997-2020
  Ashtabula (G-754)
Sight Resource Corporation..........D...... 513 942-4423
  West Chester (G-19006)
Thomas R Truitt Od..........E...... 937 644-8637
  Marysville (G-13533)
Vision Associates Inc..........D...... 419 578-7598
  Toledo (G-18139)

8043 Offices & Clinics Of Podiatrists

Ankle and Foot Care Center..........E...... 330 385-2413
  East Liverpool (G-10397)
Foot & Ankle Care Center..........E...... 937 492-1211
  Sidney (G-16778)
Medicine Midwest LLC..........D...... 513 533-1199
  Cincinnati (G-3996)
Medicine Midwest LLC..........E...... 937 435-8786
  Dayton (G-9603)
Toledo Clinic Inc..........D...... 419 381-9977
  Toledo (G-18079)
Unity Health Network LLC..........E...... 330 626-0549
  Streetsboro (G-17276)

8049 Offices & Clinics Of Health Practitioners, NEC

A+ Solutions LLC..........E...... 216 896-0111
  Beachwood (G-1025)
Abilities First Foundation Inc..........D...... 513 423-9496
  Middletown (G-14285)
Accurate Nurse Staffing..........E...... 419 475-2424
  Toledo (G-17581)
Amedisys Inc..........E...... 740 373-8549
  Marietta (G-13309)
American Nursing Care Inc..........D...... 740 452-0569
  Zanesville (G-20276)
Appleseed Cmnty Mntal Hlth Ctr..........E...... 419 281-3716
  Ashland (G-645)
Around Clock Home Care..........D...... 440 350-2547
  Painesville (G-15694)
Atrium Medical Center..........E...... 513 420-5013
  Middletown (G-14289)
Aultman Health Foundation..........B...... 330 875-6050
  Louisville (G-12960)
Bellefontaine Physical Therapy..........E...... 937 592-1625
  Bellefontaine (G-1346)
Carington Health Systems..........C...... 513 961-8881
  Cincinnati (G-3124)
Center For Cognitive and Beh..........E...... 614 459-4490
  Columbus (G-7151)
Central Ohio Nutrition Center..........E...... 614 864-7225
  Columbus (G-7160)
Central Ohio Primary Care..........D...... 614 818-9550
  Westerville (G-19233)
Central Ohio Primary Care..........E...... 614 268-6555
  Columbus (G-7164)
Central Ohio Primary Care..........E...... 614 442-7550
  Columbus (G-7167)
Central Ohio Sleep Medicine..........E...... 614 475-6700
  Westerville (G-19153)
Chcc Home Health Care..........E...... 330 759-4069
  Austintown (G-857)
Childrens Aid Society..........E...... 216 521-6511
  Cleveland (G-5178)
Christ Hospital..........B...... 513 688-1111
  Cincinnati (G-3202)
Cincinnati Occupational Therap..........E...... 513 791-5688
  Blue Ash (G-1526)
City of Blue Ash..........E...... 513 745-8534
  Blue Ash (G-1527)
Coleman Professional Svcs Inc..........D...... 330 296-8313
  Ravenna (G-16236)
Colerain Volunteer Fire Co..........E...... 740 738-0735
  Dillonvale (G-10063)
Concorde Therapy Group Inc..........C...... 330 493-4210
  Canton (G-2264)
Concorde Therapy Group Inc..........E...... 330 478-1752
  Canton (G-2265)
Concorde Therapy Group Inc..........E...... 330 493-4210
  Louisville (G-12963)
Concorde Therapy Group Inc..........E...... 330 493-4210
  Alliance (G-527)
Consolidated Care Inc..........E...... 937 465-8065
  West Liberty (G-19120)
▲ Cora Health Services Inc..........E...... 419 221-3004
  Lima (G-12619)
County of Cuyahoga..........D...... 216 721-5610
  Cleveland (G-5363)
Crisis Intervention & Rcvy Ctr..........D...... 330 455-9407
  Canton (G-2272)
Dietary Solutions Inc..........E...... 614 985-6567
  Lewis Center (G-12539)
Emerge Counseling Service..........E...... 330 865-8351
  Akron (G-202)
Equitas Health Inc..........D...... 614 299-2437
  Columbus (G-7527)
First Settlement Orthopaedics..........E...... 740 373-8756
  Marietta (G-13329)
George W Arensberg Phrm Inc..........E...... 740 344-2195
  Newark (G-15036)
Health Services Inc..........E...... 330 837-7678
  Massillon (G-13694)
Healthquest Blanchester Inc..........E...... 937 783-4535
  Blanchester (G-1487)
Herman Bair Enterprise..........E...... 330 262-4449
  Wooster (G-19727)
Hilty Memorial Home Inc..........C...... 419 384-3218
  Pandora (G-15753)
Holzer Clinic LLC..........E...... 740 886-9403
  Proctorville (G-16217)
Hometown Urgent Care..........C...... 330 629-2300
  Youngstown (G-20067)
Hometown Urgent Care..........D...... 740 363-3133
  Delaware (G-9987)

Hometown Urgent Care ....C 937 252-2000
Wooster *(G-19728)*
Hometown Urgent Care ....D 513 831-5900
Milford *(G-14395)*
Hometown Urgent Care ....C 937 342-9520
Springfield *(G-17045)*
Inter Healt Care of Cambr Zane ....E 513 984-1110
Cincinnati *(G-3773)*
Jewish Home of Cincinnati ....B 513 754-3100
Mason *(G-13603)*
Just In Time Care Inc ....E 614 985-3555
Columbus *(G-7879)*
Layh & Associates ....E 937 767-9171
Yellow Springs *(G-19940)*
Licking Rhabilitation Svcs Inc ....E 740 345-2837
Newark *(G-15059)*
Lifeteam Ems Inc ....E 330 386-9284
East Liverpool *(G-10405)*
Maxim Healthcare Services Inc ....D 740 772-4100
Chillicothe *(G-2804)*
Medcentral Health System ....C 419 342-5015
Shelby *(G-16747)*
Medcentral Health System ....C 419 683-1040
Crestline *(G-9057)*
Medlink of Ohio Inc ....B 216 751-5900
Cleveland *(G-5944)*
Medlink of Ohio Inc ....B 330 773-9434
Akron *(G-330)*
Medwork LLC ....D 937 449-0800
Dayton *(G-9604)*
Mercy Health ....E 937 390-5075
Springfield *(G-17077)*
Midwest Behavioral Care Ltd ....E 937 454-0092
Dayton *(G-9632)*
Milan Skilled Nursing LLC ....D 216 727-3996
Milan *(G-14362)*
Msstaff LLC ....E 419 868-8536
Toledo *(G-17926)*
Netcare Corporation ....E 614 274-9500
Columbus *(G-8172)*
Newcomerstown Progress Corp ....C 740 498-5165
Newcomerstown *(G-15134)*
Nexstep Healthcare LLC ....C 216 797-4040
Cleveland *(G-6066)*
Occupational Health Services ....E 937 492-7296
Sidney *(G-16788)*
Ohio HI Point Career Center ....E 937 599-3010
Urbana *(G-18442)*
Ohio Presbt Retirement Svcs ....C 614 228-8888
Columbus *(G-8280)*
Ohio State University ....D 614 292-6741
Columbus *(G-8325)*
Ohio State University ....A 614 366-3692
Columbus *(G-8295)*
Ohio State University ....A 614 257-3000
Columbus *(G-8300)*
Orthoneuro ....D 614 890-6555
Columbus *(G-8387)*
Pastoral Counseling Svc Summit ....C 330 996-4600
Akron *(G-371)*
Prohealth Partners Inc ....E 419 491-7150
Perrysburg *(G-15906)*
PSI Associates Inc ....B 330 425-8474
Twinsburg *(G-18308)*
Psycare Inc ....C 330 759-2310
Youngstown *(G-20168)*
Psychiatric Solutions Inc ....C 440 953-3000
Willoughby *(G-19564)*
R & F Inc ....E 419 868-2909
Holland *(G-11906)*
Rehab Center ....E 330 297-2770
Ravenna *(G-16261)*
Rehab Continuum Inc ....E 513 984-8070
Blue Ash *(G-1643)*
Rehabilitation Aquatics ....E 419 843-2500
Toledo *(G-17999)*
Reverse Center Clinic ....E 419 885-8800
Sylvania *(G-17446)*
River Rock Rehabilitation ....E 740 382-4035
Marion *(G-13456)*
Samaritan Regional Health Sys ....E 419 281-1330
Ashland *(G-689)*
Sandy Creek Joint Fire Dst ....E 330 868-5193
Minerva *(G-14524)*
Selby General Hospital ....C 740 568-2037
Marietta *(G-13379)*
Sisters of Mercy Amer Reg Comm ....D 419 696-7203
Oregon *(G-15609)*
Society For Rehabilitation ....E 440 209-0135
Mentor *(G-14110)*

Sports Therapy Inc ....E 513 671-5841
Cincinnati *(G-4515)*
Sports Therapy Inc ....E 513 531-1698
Cincinnati *(G-4516)*
St Lukes Hospital ....A 419 441-1002
Waterville *(G-18793)*
Stephen R Saddemi MD ....E 419 578-7200
Toledo *(G-18047)*
Steward Trumbull Mem Hosp Inc ....A 330 841-9011
Warren *(G-18748)*
Summa Rehab Hospital LLC ....D 330 572-7300
Akron *(G-454)*
Summit Psychological Assoc Inc ....E 330 535-8181
Akron *(G-460)*
Therapy In Motion LLC ....C 216 459-2846
Independence *(G-12130)*
Tky Associates LLC ....D 419 535-7777
Toledo *(G-18068)*
Toledo District Nurses Assn ....E 419 255-0983
Sylvania *(G-17458)*
Total Rhabilitation Specialist ....E 440 236-8527
Columbia Station *(G-6780)*
Trihealth G LLC ....D 513 922-1200
Cincinnati *(G-4644)*
United Rehabilitation Services ....D 937 233-1230
Dayton *(G-9832)*
Walnut Hills Physical Therapy ....E 614 234-8000
Columbus *(G-8872)*
Weinstein Donald Jay PHD ....E 216 831-1040
Painesville *(G-15747)*
Wsb Rehabilitation Svcs Inc ....D 330 533-1338
Canfield *(G-2165)*
Youngstown Ohio Otpatient Svcs ....E 330 884-2020
Youngstown *(G-20264)*

8051 Skilled Nursing Facilities

10 Wilmington Place ....D 937 253-1010
Dayton *(G-9193)*
204 W Main Street Oper Co LLC ....D 419 929-1563
New London *(G-14930)*
3g Operating Company LLC ....B 440 944-9400
Parma *(G-15758)*
5440 Charlesgate Rd Oper LLC ....D 937 236-6707
Dayton *(G-9195)*
A L K Inc ....D 740 369-8741
Delaware *(G-9947)*
A M Mc Gregor Home ....B 216 851-8200
Cleveland *(G-4878)*
A Provide Care Inc ....C 330 828-2278
Dalton *(G-9143)*
Adams County Manor ....D 937 544-2205
West Union *(G-19131)*
Adena NH LLC ....E 740 546-3620
Adena *(G-7)*
Ahf Ohio Inc ....D 330 725-4123
Medina *(G-13907)*
Ahf Ohio Inc ....D 740 532-6188
Ironton *(G-12144)*
Ahf Ohio Inc ....D 614 760-8870
Dublin *(G-10122)*
Ahf Ohio Inc ....D 937 256-4663
Dayton *(G-9212)*
Ahf/Central States Inc ....D 615 383-3570
Dublin *(G-10123)*
Alexson Services Inc ....B 513 874-0423
Fairfield *(G-10695)*
Alpha Nursing Homes Inc ....D 740 345-9197
Newark *(G-15009)*
Altenheim Foundation Inc ....E 440 238-3361
Strongsville *(G-17284)*
Altercare Inc ....C 330 335-2555
Wadsworth *(G-18588)*
Altercare Inc ....E 440 327-5285
North Ridgeville *(G-15320)*
Altercare Nobles Pond Inc ....D 330 834-4800
Canton *(G-2182)*
Altercare of Bucyrus Inc ....D 419 562-7644
Bucyrus *(G-1976)*
Altercare of Louisville Center ....C 330 875-4224
Louisville *(G-12959)*
Altercare of Mentor Center ....D 440 953-4421
Mentor *(G-14017)*
Altercare of Millersburg ....D 330 674-4444
Millersburg *(G-14455)*
Amedisys Inc ....E 740 373-8549
Marietta *(G-13309)*
American Eagle Hlth Care Svcs ....C 440 428-5103
Madison *(G-13092)*
American Nursing Care Inc ....E 513 731-4600
Cincinnati *(G-2947)*

American Nursing Care Inc ....D 513 245-1500
Cincinnati *(G-2948)*
American Nursing Care Inc ....D 513 576-0262
Milford *(G-14371)*
American Nursing Care Inc ....E 937 438-3844
Dayton *(G-9228)*
American Nursing Care Inc ....C 614 847-0555
Zanesville *(G-20275)*
American Nursing Care Inc ....D 419 228-0888
Lima *(G-12601)*
American Retirement Corp ....D 216 291-6140
Cleveland *(G-4965)*
American Retirement Corp ....D 216 321-6331
Cleveland *(G-4966)*
Anchor Lodge Nursing Home Inc ....C 440 244-2019
Lorain *(G-12880)*
Anderson Healthcare Ltd ....D 513 474-6200
Cincinnati *(G-2959)*
Andover Vlg Retirement Cmnty ....C 440 293-5416
Andover *(G-604)*
Anna Maria of Aurora Inc ....C 330 562-6171
Aurora *(G-815)*
Anna Maria of Aurora Inc ....D 330 562-3120
Aurora *(G-816)*
Apostolic Christian Home Inc ....D 330 927-1010
Rittman *(G-16403)*
Appalachian Respite Care Ltd ....D 740 984-4262
Beverly *(G-1460)*
April Enterprises Inc ....B 937 293-7703
Moraine *(G-14623)*
Arbors East LLC ....C 614 575-9003
Columbus *(G-6963)*
Arbors West LLC ....D 614 879-7661
West Jefferson *(G-19103)*
Aristocrat W Nursing Hm Corp ....C 440 835-0660
Cleveland *(G-5007)*
Aristocrat W Nursing Hm Corp ....C 216 252-7730
Cleveland *(G-5008)*
Arlington Care Ctr ....C 740 344-0303
Newark *(G-15011)*
Arlington Court Nursing ....C 614 545-5502
Upper Arlington *(G-18393)*
Ashley Enterprises LLC ....D 330 726-5790
Boardman *(G-1695)*
Ashley Place Health Care Inc ....C 330 793-3010
Youngstown *(G-19956)*
Assisted Living Concepts LLC ....E 419 586-2484
Celina *(G-2584)*
Assisted Living Concepts LLC ....E 419 224-6327
Lima *(G-12602)*
Assumption Village ....C 330 549-2434
North Lima *(G-15264)*
Astoria Healthcare Group LLC ....B 937 855-2363
Germantown *(G-11276)*
Astoria Place Columbus LLC ....D 614 228-5900
Columbus *(G-6985)*
Astoria Place of Clyde LLC ....D 419 547-9595
Clyde *(G-6739)*
Aurora Manor Ltd Partnership ....E 330 562-5000
Aurora *(G-818)*
Austin Woods Nursing Center ....C 330 792-7681
Youngstown *(G-19958)*
Autumn Aegis Inc ....D 440 282-6768
Lorain *(G-12883)*
Autumn Hills Care Center Inc ....C 330 652-2053
Niles *(G-15146)*
Balanced Care Corporation ....E 330 908-1166
Northfield *(G-15373)*
Balanced Care Corporation ....E 937 372-7205
Xenia *(G-19892)*
Baltic Health Care Corp ....D 330 897-4311
Baltic *(G-933)*
Baptist Home and Center ....C 513 662-5880
Cincinnati *(G-3018)*
Barnesville Healthcare Rehab ....D 740 425-3648
Barnesville *(G-974)*
Bath Manor Limited Partnership ....E 330 836-1006
Akron *(G-87)*
Beacon of Light Ltd ....E 419 531-9060
Toledo *(G-17608)*
Beechwood Home ....C 513 321-9294
Cincinnati *(G-3035)*
Beechwood Terrace Care Ctr Inc ....C 513 578-6200
Cincinnati *(G-3036)*
Bel Air Care Center ....D 330 821-3939
Alliance *(G-518)*
Bellbrook Rhbltion Healthcare ....D 937 848-8421
Bellbrook *(G-1338)*
Bellevue Healthcare Group LLC ....E 419 483-6225
Bellevue *(G-1372)*

S
I
C

Belmont County Home D 740 695-4925
Saint Clairsville *(G-16472)*
Belmore Leasing Co LLC C 216 268-3600
Cleveland *(G-5053)*
Bentley Leasing Co LLC A 330 337-9503
Salem *(G-16536)*
Best Care Nrsing Rhbltion Ctr C 740 574-2558
Wheelersburg *(G-19428)*
Bethany Nursing Home Inc E 330 492-7171
Canton *(G-2211)*
Bethesda Foundation Inc E 513 569-6575
Cincinnati *(G-3046)*
Biorx LLC C 866 442-4679
Cincinnati *(G-3051)*
Birchaven Village B 419 424-3000
Findlay *(G-10870)*
Blanchard Vly Residential Ctr D 419 422-6503
Findlay *(G-10877)*
Blossom Hills Nursing Home D 440 635-5567
Huntsburg *(G-12017)*
Blossom Nursing & Rehab Center C 330 337-3033
Salem *(G-16538)*
Blue Ash Healthcare Group Inc E 513 793-3362
Cincinnati *(G-3060)*
Blue Creek Healthcare LLC D 419 877-5338
Whitehouse *(G-19445)*
Bluesky Healthcare Inc C 330 345-9050
Wooster *(G-19692)*
Braeview Manor Inc C 216 486-9300
Cleveland *(G-5073)*
Brecksville Leasing Co LLC C 330 659-6166
Richfield *(G-16347)*
Brenn Field Nursing Center C 330 683-4075
Orrville *(G-15626)*
Brentwood Life Care Company C 330 468-2273
Northfield *(G-15375)*
Brethren Care Inc C 419 289-0803
Ashland *(G-659)*
Brewster Parke Inc D 330 767-4179
Brewster *(G-1809)*
Briar Hl Hlth Care Rsdence Inc D 440 632-5241
Middlefield *(G-14269)*
Briarfield Manor LLC C 330 270-3468
Youngstown *(G-19973)*
Briarwood Ltd D 330 688-1828
Stow *(G-17193)*
Bridges To Independence Inc E 740 375-5533
Marion *(G-13407)*
Broadview NH LLC D 614 337-1066
Columbus *(G-7078)*
Broadview Nursing Home Inc C 216 661-5084
Parma *(G-15761)*
Brook Willow Chrstn Cmmunities D 614 885-3300
Columbus *(G-7079)*
Brookdale Senior Living Inc E 614 336-3677
Dublin *(G-10151)*
Brookdale Senior Living Inc D 937 203-8596
Beavercreek Township *(G-1264)*
Brookdale Senior Living Inc E 216 321-6331
Cleveland *(G-5087)*
Brookdale Senior Living Inc D 419 422-8657
Findlay *(G-10883)*
Brookdale Snior Lving Cmmnties E 330 249-1071
Austintown *(G-856)*
Brookview Healthcare Ctr D 419 784-1014
Defiance *(G-9905)*
Brookville Enterprises Inc B 937 833-2133
Brookville *(G-1911)*
Bryant Eliza Village B 216 361-6141
Cleveland *(G-5096)*
Bryant Health Center Inc C 740 532-6188
Ironton *(G-12147)*
Bryden Place Inc C 614 258-6623
Beachwood *(G-1038)*
Burchwood Care Center E 513 868-3300
Fairfield Township *(G-10802)*
Burlington House Inc D 513 851-7888
Cincinnati *(G-3093)*
Butler County of Ohio C 513 887-3728
Fairfield Township *(G-10803)*
C Micah Rand Inc C 513 605-2000
Cincinnati *(G-3101)*
Camargo Manor Inc D 513 605-3000
Cincinnati *(G-3108)*
Cambridge Home Healthcare E 740 432-6191
Cambridge *(G-2053)*
Cambridge NH LLC D 740 432-7717
Cambridge *(G-2054)*
Camillus Villa Inc D 440 236-5091
Columbia Station *(G-6770)*
Canterbury Vlla Oprations Corp D 330 821-4000
Alliance *(G-520)*
Canton Assisted Living C 330 492-7131
Canton *(G-2227)*
Capital Health Services Inc E 937 278-0404
Dayton *(G-9275)*
Caprice Health Care Inc C 330 965-9200
North Lima *(G-15267)*
Care One LLC C 937 236-6707
Dayton *(G-9277)*
Careserve C 740 454-4000
Zanesville *(G-20288)*
Careserve Inc C 740 962-3761
McConnelsville *(G-13899)*
Carington Health Systems B 513 732-6500
Batavia *(G-985)*
Carington Health Systems C 513 961-8881
Cincinnati *(G-3124)*
Carington Health Systems C 937 743-2754
Franklin *(G-11025)*
Carington Health Systems E 513 682-2700
Hamilton *(G-11573)*
Caritas Inc E 419 332-2589
Fremont *(G-11060)*
Carlisle Health Care Inc E 937 746-2662
Carlisle *(G-2551)*
Carriage Court Company Inc E 740 654-4422
Lancaster *(G-12376)*
Carriage Inn of Bowerston Inc D 740 269-8001
Bowerston *(G-1710)*
Carriage Inn of Cadiz Inc E 740 942-8084
Cadiz *(G-2027)*
Carriage Inn of Steubenville C 740 264-7161
Steubenville *(G-17145)*
Carriage Inn of Trotwood Inc C 937 854-1180
Trotwood *(G-18192)*
Carriage Inn of Trotwood Inc D 937 277-0505
Dayton *(G-9281)*
Carriage Inn Retirement Cmnty C 937 278-0404
Dayton *(G-9282)*
Carroll Health Care Center C 330 627-5501
Carrollton *(G-2562)*
Castle Nursing Homes Inc C 330 674-0015
Millersburg *(G-14464)*
Casto Health Care D 419 884-6400
Mansfield *(G-13148)*
Catherines Care Center Inc D 740 282-3605
Steubenville *(G-17146)*
Center Ridge Nursing Home Inc C 440 808-5500
North Ridgeville *(G-15324)*
Centerburg Two LLC D 740 625-5774
Centerburg *(G-2614)*
CHI Living Communities D 567 455-0414
Toledo *(G-17651)*
Childs Investment Co E 330 837-2100
Massillon *(G-13669)*
Chillicothe Long Term Care C 740 773-6161
Chillicothe *(G-2763)*
Chillicothe Long Term Care C 513 793-8804
Cincinnati *(G-3194)*
Chillicothe Opco LLC D 740 772-5900
Chillicothe *(G-2765)*
Christian Worthington Vlg Inc E 614 846-6076
Columbus *(G-7196)*
CHS Miami Valley Inc E 330 204-1040
Sidney *(G-16765)*
CHS Norwood Inc D 513 242-1360
Cincinnati *(G-3214)*
CHS of Bowerston Oper Co Inc D 937 277-0505
Dayton *(G-9300)*
CHS-Lake Erie Inc C 440 964-8446
Ashtabula *(G-726)*
Chs-Norwood Inc C 513 351-7007
Cincinnati *(G-3215)*
Church of God Retirement Cmnty C 513 422-5600
Middletown *(G-14295)*
Cincinnati Senior Care LLC E 513 272-0600
Cincinnati *(G-3266)*
City View Nursing & Rehab LLC C 216 361-1414
Cleveland *(G-5218)*
Clermont Care Inc C 513 831-1770
Milford *(G-14381)*
Clifton Care Center Inc C 513 530-1600
Cincinnati *(G-3307)*
Clime Leasing Co LLC D 614 276-4400
Columbus *(G-7226)*
Clovernook Inc C 513 605-4000
Cincinnati *(G-3310)*
Coal Grove Long Term Care Inc D 740 532-0449
Ironton *(G-12151)*
Colonial Manor Health Care Ctr C 419 994-4191
Loudonville *(G-12955)*
Columbus Alzheimers Care Ctr C 614 459-7050
Columbus *(G-7254)*
Columbus Area D 614 251-6561
Columbus *(G-7255)*
Columbus Clny For Elderly Care C 614 891-5055
Westerville *(G-19239)*
Communi Care Inc E 419 382-2200
Toledo *(G-17670)*
Communicare Health Svcs Inc D 440 234-0454
Berea *(G-1420)*
Communicare Health Svcs Inc D 330 726-3700
Youngstown *(G-19996)*
Communicare Health Svcs Inc D 419 485-8307
Montpelier *(G-14610)*
Communicare Health Svcs Inc E 330 454-6508
Canton *(G-2262)*
Communicare Health Svcs Inc C 937 399-9217
Springfield *(G-17018)*
Communicare Health Svcs Inc C 877 366-5306
Wintersville *(G-19669)*
Communicare Health Svcs Inc D 740 264-1155
Steubenville *(G-17150)*
Communicare Health Svcs Inc D 330 792-7799
Youngstown *(G-19997)*
Communicare Health Svcs Inc D 330 792-5511
Youngstown *(G-19998)*
Communicare Health Svcs Inc C 330 454-2152
Canton *(G-2263)*
Communicare Health Svcs Inc D 330 630-9780
Tallmadge *(G-17472)*
Communicare Health Svcs Inc D 419 394-7611
Saint Marys *(G-16521)*
Community Hlth Prfssionals Inc E 419 634-7443
Ada *(G-3)*
Community Mercy Hlth Partners C 937 653-5432
Urbana *(G-18429)*
Community Skilled Health Care C 330 373-1160
Warren *(G-18689)*
Concord Care Center of Toledo D 419 385-6616
Toledo *(G-17676)*
Concord Health Care Inc E 330 759-2357
Youngstown *(G-20009)*
Concord Health Care Inc E 419 626-5373
Sandusky *(G-16592)*
Concord Hlth Rhabilitation Ctr E 740 574-8441
Wheelersburg *(G-19432)*
Congregate Living of America D 513 899-2801
Morrow *(G-14716)*
Congregate Living of America E 937 393-6700
Hillsboro *(G-11834)*
Consulate Healthcare Inc E 419 865-1248
Maumee *(G-13775)*
Consulate Management Co LLC D 330 837-1001
Massillon *(G-13673)*
Consulate Management Co LLC D 419 886-3922
Bellville *(G-1389)*
Consulate Management Co LLC D 440 237-7966
Cleveland *(G-5340)*
Consulate Management Co LLC C 419 683-3255
Crestline *(G-9052)*
Consulate Management Co LLC D 419 867-7926
Maumee *(G-13776)*
Consulate Management Co LLC D 740 259-2351
Lucasville *(G-13046)*
Continent Hlth Co Cortland LLC E 330 637-7906
Cortland *(G-8986)*
Contining Hlthcare Sltions Inc D 440 466-1181
Geneva *(G-11239)*
Copley Health Center Inc C 330 666-0980
Copley *(G-8965)*
Cortland Healthcare Group Inc E 330 638-4015
Cortland *(G-8987)*
Coshocton Opco LLC D 740 622-1220
Coshocton *(G-9008)*
Cottingham Retirement Cmnty C 513 563-3600
Cincinnati *(G-3367)*
Country Club Center Homes Inc D 330 343-6351
Dover *(G-10071)*
Country Club Center II Ltd C 740 397-2350
Mount Vernon *(G-14756)*
Country Club Retirement Center C 740 671-9330
Bellaire *(G-1333)*
Country Court Ltd C 740 397-4125
Mount Vernon *(G-14757)*
Country Mdow Fclty Oprtons LLC D 419 886-3922
Bellville *(G-1390)*
Country Pointe Skilled Nursing E 330 264-7881
Wooster *(G-19714)*

County of Allen ....C 419 221-1103
Lima (G-12622)
County of Erie ....C 419 627-8733
Huron (G-12024)
County of Logan ....C 937 592-2901
Bellefontaine (G-1351)
County of Lucas ....D 419 385-6021
Toledo (G-17685)
County of Marion ....D 740 389-4624
Marion (G-13414)
County of Monroe ....D 740 472-0144
Woodsfield (G-19674)
County of Montgomery ....B 937 264-0460
Dayton (G-9328)
County of Ottawa ....C 419 898-6459
Oak Harbor (G-15470)
County of Perry ....E 740 342-0416
New Lexington (G-14918)
County of Sandusky ....D 419 334-2602
Fremont (G-11066)
County of Shelby ....C 937 492-6900
Sidney (G-16771)
County of Van Wert ....E 419 968-2141
Middle Point (G-14246)
County of Williams ....C 419 636-4508
Bryan (G-1956)
Covenant Care Ohio Inc ....D 419 898-5506
Port Clinton (G-16104)
Covenant Care Ohio Inc ....D 419 531-4201
Toledo (G-17687)
Covenant Care Ohio Inc ....D 937 378-0188
Georgetown (G-11269)
Covenant Care Ohio Inc ....D 937 399-5551
Springfield (G-17026)
Covenant Care Ohio Inc ....D 937 526-5570
Versailles (G-18569)
Covenant Care Ohio Inc ....D 937 878-7046
Fairborn (G-10666)
Covington Snf Inc ....E 330 426-2920
East Palestine (G-10419)
Crandall Medical Center Inc ....C 330 938-6126
Sebring (G-16668)
Creative Foundations Inc ....E 614 832-2121
Mount Vernon (G-14760)
Crestline Nursing Home Inc ....E 419 683-3255
Crestline (G-9053)
Crestmont Nursing Home N Corp ....C 216 228-9550
Lakewood (G-12340)
Crestmont Nursing Home N Corp ....D 216 228-9550
Lakewood (G-12341)
Crestview Health Care Center ....D 740 695-2500
Saint Clairsville (G-16485)
Crestview Manor Nursing Home ....C 740 654-2634
Lancaster (G-12386)
Crestview Manor Nursing Home ....C 740 654-2634
Lancaster (G-12387)
Crestview Ridge Nursing ....E 937 393-6700
Hillsboro (G-11836)
Cridersville Health Care Ctr ....E 419 645-4468
Cridersville (G-9062)
Crotinger Nursing Home Inc ....D 937 968-5284
Union City (G-18353)
Crystal Care Center Portsmouth ....E 740 354-6619
Portsmouth (G-16134)
Crystal Care Centers Inc ....E 419 281-9595
Ashland (G-670)
Crystal Care Centers Inc ....E 419 747-2666
Mansfield (G-13161)
Crystal Care Centers Inc ....D 419 747-2666
Mansfield (G-13162)
D James Incorporated ....C 513 574-4550
Cincinnati (G-3395)
Danridge Nursing Home Inc ....D 330 746-5157
Youngstown (G-20015)
Day Spring Health Care Corp ....D 740 984-4262
Beverly (G-1462)
Dayspring Health Care Center ....C 937 864-5800
Fairborn (G-10670)
Dayton Dmh Inc ....C 937 436-2273
Dayton (G-9363)
Dayton Nwborn Care Spclsts Inc ....A 937 641-3329
Dayton (G-9373)
Deaconess Long Term Care of MI ....A 513 487-3600
Cincinnati (G-3412)
Dearth Management Company ....C 419 253-0144
Marengo (G-13302)
Dearth Management Company ....E 740 389-1214
Marion (G-13418)
Dearth Management Company ....C 330 339-3595
New Philadelphia (G-14956)
Dedicated Nursing Assoc Inc ....C 888 465-6929
Beavercreek (G-1214)
Dedicated Nursing Assoc Inc ....E 866 450-5550
Cincinnati (G-3415)
Dedicated Nursing Assoc Inc ....E 877 411-8350
Galloway (G-11219)
Dedicated Nursing Assoc Inc ....E 877 547-9144
Parma (G-15765)
Delaware Opco LLC ....D 502 429-8062
Delaware (G-9970)
Diverscare Healthcare Svcs Inc ....E 513 271-7010
Cincinnati (G-3434)
Diverscare Healthcare Svcs Inc ....E 937 278-8211
Dayton (G-9392)
Diversicare Leasing Corp ....D 615 771-7575
Wheelersburg (G-19433)
Diversicare of Avon LLC ....C 440 937-6201
Avon (G-879)
Diversicare of Mansfield LLC ....D 419 529-6447
Ontario (G-15547)
DMD Management Inc ....E 330 405-6040
Twinsburg (G-18258)
DMD Management Inc ....A 216 371-3600
Cleveland (G-5435)
Doctors Hospital Cleveland Inc ....C 740 753-7300
Nelsonville (G-14829)
Dover Nursing Center ....D 330 364-4436
Dover (G-10075)
Doylestown Health Care Center ....C 330 658-1533
Doylestown (G-10112)
Drake Center LLC ....A 513 418-2500
Cincinnati (G-3442)
Dublin Geriatric Care Co LP ....E 614 761-1188
Dublin (G-10207)
Eagle Creek Hlthcare Group Inc ....E 937 544-5531
West Union (G-19136)
Eaglewood Care Center ....C 937 399-7195
Springfield (G-17031)
East Carroll Nursing Home ....D 330 627-6900
Carrollton (G-2567)
East Galbraith Nursing Home ....C 513 984-5220
Cincinnati (G-3472)
East Water Leasing Co LLC ....D 419 278-6921
Deshler (G-10057)
Eastern Star Hm of Cyhoga Cnty ....D 216 761-0170
Cleveland (G-5459)
Eastgate Health Care Center ....C 513 752-3710
Cincinnati (G-2850)
Eastside Multi Care Inc ....C 216 662-3343
Maple Heights (G-13286)
Eaton Gardens Rehabilitation A ....D 937 456-5537
Eaton (G-10445)
Ebenezer Road Corp ....C 513 941-0099
Cincinnati (G-3480)
Echoing Hills Village Inc ....C 740 327-2311
Warsaw (G-18783)
Echoing Hills Village Inc ....D 937 854-5151
Dayton (G-9406)
Echoing Hills Village Inc ....D 440 989-1400
Lorain (G-12902)
Edgewood Manor of Lucasville ....C 740 259-5536
Lucasville (G-13048)
Elms Retirement Village Inc ....D 440 647-2414
Wellington (G-18840)
Elmwood Center Inc ....D 419 639-2626
Green Springs (G-11351)
Embassy Autumnwood MGT LLC ....D 330 927-2060
Rittman (G-16405)
Embassy Healthcare Inc ....D 513 868-6500
Fairfield (G-10724)
Emeritus Corporation ....D 440 201-9200
Cleveland (G-5475)
Emery Leasing Co LLC ....B 216 475-8880
Cleveland (G-5476)
Encore Healthcare LLC ....C 330 769-2015
Seville (G-16685)
Episcopal Retirement Homes Inc ....E 513 271-9610
Cincinnati (G-3508)
Es3 Management Inc ....D 440 593-6266
Conneaut (G-8954)
Euclid Health Care Inc ....C 513 561-4105
Cincinnati (G-3517)
Evangelical Lutheran ....D 419 365-5115
Arlington (G-642)
Ezra Health Care Inc ....C 440 498-3000
Beachwood (G-1056)
Fairchild MD Leasing Co LLC ....C 330 678-4912
Kent (G-12232)
Fairhope Hospice and Palliativ ....D 740 654-7077
Lancaster (G-12402)
Fairlawn Opco LLC ....D 502 429-8062
Fairlawn (G-10827)
Fairmont Nursing Home Inc ....D 440 338-8220
Newbury (G-15120)
Fairport Enterprises Inc ....C 330 830-9988
Massillon (G-13680)
Falling Leasing Co LLC ....C 440 238-1100
Strongsville (G-17303)
Falls Village Retirement Cmnty ....D 330 945-9797
Cuyahoga Falls (G-9094)
First Community Village ....B 614 324-4455
Columbus (G-7585)
First Louisville Arden LLC ....E 419 252-5500
Toledo (G-17740)
First Richmond Corp ....D 937 783-4949
Blanchester (G-1486)
Five Star Senior Living Inc ....D 614 451-6793
Columbus (G-7592)
Flower Hospital ....B 419 824-1000
Sylvania (G-17425)
Fountainhead Nursing Home Inc ....E 740 354-9113
Franklin Furnace (G-11044)
Four Seasons Washington LLC ....D 740 895-6101
Wshngtn CT Hs (G-19873)
Franciscan Care Ctr Sylvania ....C 419 882-2087
Toledo (G-17746)
Franciscan Sisters of Chicago ....C 440 843-7800
Cleveland (G-5571)
Franklin Blvd Nursing HM Inc ....C 216 651-1600
Cleveland (G-5574)
Franklin Shcp Inc ....D 440 614-0160
Columbus (G-7619)
Friendly Nursing Home Inc ....E 937 855-2363
Franklin (G-11029)
Friends Health Care Assn ....C 937 767-7363
Yellow Springs (G-19939)
Friendship Vlg of Clumbus Ohio ....D 614 890-8287
Columbus (G-7628)
Friendship Vlg of Clumbus Ohio ....C 614 890-8282
Columbus (G-7629)
Friendship Vlg of Dublin Ohio ....C 614 764-1600
Dublin (G-10232)
Front Leasing Co LLC ....C 440 243-4000
Berea (G-1427)
Fulton County Health Center ....C 419 335-2017
Wauseon (G-18801)
Gables At Green Pastures ....C 937 642-3893
Marysville (G-13498)
Gables Care Center Inc ....C 740 937-2900
Hopedale (G-11936)
Gahanna Health Care Center ....E 614 475-7222
Columbus (G-7643)
Galion Community Hospital ....B 419 468-4841
Galion (G-11174)
Gallipolis Care LLC ....C 740 446-7112
Gallipolis (G-11194)
Garden Manor Extended Care Cen ....C 513 420-5972
Middletown (G-14300)
Gardens At Wapakoneta ....E 419 738-0725
Wapakoneta (G-18644)
Gateway Family House ....E 216 531-5400
Euclid (G-10636)
Gateway Health Care Center ....C 216 486-4949
Cleveland (G-5595)
Gaymont Nursing Homes Inc ....D 419 668-8258
Norwalk (G-15439)
Generation Health & Rehab Cntr ....D 740 344-9465
Newark (G-15035)
Generation Health Corp ....C 614 337-1066
Columbus (G-7656)
GFS Leasing Inc ....D 330 296-6415
Kent (G-12235)
GFS Leasing Inc ....D 330 877-2666
Hartville (G-11687)
Gibsonburg Health Llc ....C 419 637-2104
Gibsonburg (G-11278)
Gillette Nursing Home Inc ....D 330 372-1960
Warren (G-18710)
Glen Wesley Inc ....D 614 888-7492
Columbus (G-7673)
Glendale Place Care Center LLC ....E 513 771-1779
Cincinnati (G-3619)
Glendora Health Care Center ....D 330 264-0912
Wooster (G-19723)
Glenn View Manor Inc ....C 330 652-9901
Mineral Ridge (G-14509)
Glenward Inc ....C 513 863-3100
Fairfield Township (G-10807)
Golden Living LLC ....D 419 599-4070
Napoleon (G-14807)

Golden Living LLC ... C ... 330 762-6486
Akron (G-239)
Golden Living LLC ... D ... 330 725-3393
Medina (G-13944)
Golden Living LLC ... D ... 419 227-2154
Lima (G-12644)
Golden Living LLC ... C ... 614 861-6666
Columbus (G-7678)
Golden Living LLC ... C ... 330 297-5781
Ravenna (G-16244)
Golden Living LLC ... D ... 330 335-1558
Wadsworth (G-18596)
Golden Years Nursing Home Inc ... E ... 513 893-0471
Hamilton (G-11601)
Good Shepard Village LLC ... D ... 937 322-1911
Springfield (G-17042)
Good Shepherd Home ... C ... 419 937-1801
Fostoria (G-11003)
Good Shepherd Home For Aged ... C ... 614 228-5200
Ashland (G-673)
Governors Village LLC ... E ... 440 449-8788
Cleveland (G-5618)
Grace Brethren Village Inc ... E ... 937 836-4011
Englewood (G-10589)
Graceworks Lutheran Services ... A ... 937 433-2140
Dayton (G-9469)
Greenbrier Senior Living Cmnty ... C ... 440 888-5900
Cleveland (G-5641)
Greenbrier Senior Living Cmnty ... D ... 440 888-0400
Cleveland (G-5642)
Greens of Lyndhurst The Inc ... C ... 440 460-1000
Cleveland (G-5643)
Guardian Elder Care LLC ... C ... 330 549-0898
North Lima (G-15269)
Hackensack Meridian Health Inc ... D ... 513 792-9697
Cincinnati (G-3670)
Hamlet Village In Chagrin FLS ... D ... 216 263-6033
Chagrin Falls (G-2649)
Hampton Woods Nursing Ctr Inc ... E ... 330 707-1400
Poland (G-16084)
Hanover House Inc ... C ... 330 837-1741
Massillon (G-13692)
Harborside Clveland Ltd Partnr ... D ... 440 871-5900
Westlake (G-19347)
Harborside Clveland Ltd Partnr ... C ... 440 526-4770
Broadview Heights (G-1835)
Harborside Healthcare Corp ... C ... 419 825-1111
Swanton (G-17399)
Harborside Healthcare NW Ohio ... C ... 419 636-5071
Bryan (G-1959)
Harborside Pointe Place LLC ... C ... 419 727-7870
Toledo (G-17782)
Harborside Sylvania LLC ... D ... 419 882-1875
Sylvania (G-17429)
Harborside Troy LLC ... D ... 937 335-7161
Troy (G-18205)
Havar Inc ... E ... 740 373-7175
Marietta (G-13334)
Hcf Management Inc ... C ... 740 289-2394
Piketon (G-15977)
Hcf Management Inc ... D ... 419 435-8112
Fostoria (G-11005)
Hcf Management Inc ... D ... 419 999-2010
Lima (G-12652)
Hcf Management Inc ... C ... 419 999-2055
Lima (G-12653)
Hcf of Bowl Green Care Ctr Inc ... D ... 419 352-7558
Bowling Green (G-1735)
Hcf of Bowling Green Inc ... B ... 419 352-4694
Bowling Green (G-1736)
Hcf of Briarwood Inc ... C ... 419 678-2311
Coldwater (G-6758)
Hcf of Court House Inc ... C ... 740 335-9290
Wshngtn CT Hs (G-19874)
Hcf of Crestview Inc ... D ... 937 426-5033
Beavercreek (G-1223)
Hcf of Fox Run Inc ... D ... 419 424-0832
Findlay (G-10921)
Hcf of Lima Inc ... D ... 419 999-2010
Lima (G-12654)
Hcf of Perrysburg Inc ... D ... 419 874-0306
Perrysburg (G-15870)
Hcf of Piqua Inc ... D ... 937 773-0040
Piqua (G-16008)
Hcf of Roselawn Inc ... C ... 419 647-4115
Spencerville (G-16956)
Hcf of Shawnee Inc ... D ... 419 999-2055
Lima (G-12655)
Hcf of Van Wert Inc ... D ... 419 999-2010
Van Wert (G-18479)

Hcf of Wapakoneta Inc ... D ... 419 738-3711
Wapakoneta (G-18645)
Hcr Manor Care Svc Fla III Inc ... E ... 419 252-5500
Toledo (G-17785)
Hcr Manorcare Med Svcs Fla LLC ... E ... 513 745-9600
Cincinnati (G-3688)
Hcr Manorcare Med Svcs Fla LLC ... D ... 513 233-0831
Cincinnati (G-3689)
Hcr Manorcare Med Svcs Fla LLC ... C ... 419 252-5500
Portsmouth (G-16142)
Hcr Manorcare Med Svcs Fla LLC ... C ... 419 531-2127
Toledo (G-17786)
Hcr Manorcare Med Svcs Fla LLC ... C ... 330 753-5005
Barberton (G-954)
Hcr Manorcare Med Svcs Fla LLC ... C ... 513 561-4111
Cincinnati (G-3690)
Hcr Manorcare Med Svcs Fla LLC ... C ... 614 882-1511
Westerville (G-19260)
Hcr Manorcare Med Svcs Fla LLC ... D ... 330 668-6889
Akron (G-257)
Hcr Manorcare Med Svcs Fla LLC ... C ... 419 252-5500
Toledo (G-17787)
Hcr Manorcare Med Svcs Fla LLC ... C ... 216 251-3300
Cleveland (G-5670)
Hcr Manorcare Med Svcs Fla LLC ... D ... 440 473-0090
Cleveland (G-5671)
Hcr Manorcare Med Svcs Fla LLC ... C ... 216 486-2300
Cleveland (G-5672)
Hcr Manorcare Med Svcs Fla LLC ... C ... 937 436-9700
Centerville (G-2627)
Hcr Manorcare Med Svcs Fla LLC ... C ... 419 691-3088
Oregon (G-15597)
Hcr Manorcare Med Svcs Fla LLC ... E ... 440 808-9275
Westlake (G-19348)
Hcr Manorcare Med Svcs Fla LLC ... C ... 513 591-0400
Cincinnati (G-3691)
Hcr Manorcare Med Svcs Fla LLC ... D ... 440 887-1442
North Royalton (G-15360)
Health Care Opportunities Inc ... E ... 513 932-0300
Lebanon (G-12469)
Health Care Opportunities Inc ... E ... 513 932-4861
Lebanon (G-12470)
Health Care Retirement Corp ... B ... 419 252-5500
Toledo (G-17788)
Health Care Rtrement Corp Amer ... C ... 419 252-5500
Toledo (G-17789)
Health Care Rtrement Corp Amer ... D ... 419 474-6021
Toledo (G-17790)
Health Care Rtrement Corp Amer ... D ... 740 286-5026
Jackson (G-12174)
Health Care Rtrement Corp Amer ... D ... 419 562-9907
Bucyrus (G-1991)
Health Care Rtrement Corp Amer ... C ... 937 298-8084
Dayton (G-9490)
Health Care Rtrement Corp Amer ... D ... 740 373-8920
Marietta (G-13335)
Health Care Rtrement Corp Amer ... C ... 937 429-1106
Dayton (G-9175)
Health Care Rtrement Corp Amer ... D ... 937 456-5537
Eaton (G-10447)
Health Care Rtrement Corp Amer ... D ... 740 773-5000
Chillicothe (G-2785)
Health Care Rtrement Corp Amer ... C ... 740 354-4505
Portsmouth (G-16143)
Health Care Rtrement Corp Amer ... D ... 614 882-3782
Westerville (G-19261)
Health Care Rtrement Corp Amer ... D ... 937 599-5123
Bellefontaine (G-1353)
Health Care Rtrement Corp Amer ... D ... 614 464-2273
Columbus (G-7725)
Health Care Rtrement Corp Amer ... C ... 937 390-0005
Springfield (G-17044)
Health Care Rtrement Corp Amer ... D ... 740 894-3287
South Point (G-16936)
Health Care Rtrement Corp Amer ... D ... 937 393-5766
Hillsboro (G-11841)
Health Care Rtrement Corp Amer ... C ... 440 946-1912
Mentor (G-14059)
Health Care Rtrement Corp Amer ... D ... 740 635-4600
Bridgeport (G-1817)
Health Care Rtrement Corp Amer ... D ... 937 773-9346
Piqua (G-16009)
Health Care Rtrement Corp Amer ... C ... 419 874-3578
Perrysburg (G-15871)
Health Care Rtrement Corp Amer ... C ... 937 866-8885
Miamisburg (G-14176)
Health Care Rtrement Corp Amer ... C ... 937 548-3141
Greenville (G-11386)
Health Care Rtrement Corp Amer ... E ... 419 337-3050
Wauseon (G-18806)

Health Care Rtrement Corp Amer ... C ... 419 878-8523
Waterville (G-18789)
Health Care Rtrement Corp Amer ... C ... 513 751-0880
Cincinnati (G-3692)
Healthcare Facility MGT LLC ... D ... 419 382-2200
Toledo (G-17791)
Healthcare Facility MGT LLC ... C ... 330 836-7953
Akron (G-258)
Healthcare Walton Group LLC ... C ... 440 439-4433
Cleveland (G-5673)
Heartland Fort Myers Fl LLC ... E ... 419 252-5500
Toledo (G-17793)
Heartlnd-Riverview S Pt OH LLC ... C ... 740 894-3287
South Point (G-16937)
Heath Nursing Care Center ... C ... 740 522-1171
Newark (G-15040)
Heather Knoll Retirement Vlg ... C ... 330 688-8600
Tallmadge (G-17476)
Heatherhill Care Communities ... E ... 440 285-4040
Chardon (G-2698)
Hempstead Manor ... C ... 740 354-8150
Portsmouth (G-16145)
Hennis Nursing Home ... C ... 330 364-8849
Dover (G-10081)
Heritage Park Rehabilita ... E ... 937 437-2311
New Paris (G-14943)
Hgcc of Allentown Inc ... D ... 419 252-5500
Toledo (G-17803)
Hickory Creek Healthcare ... D ... 419 542-7795
Hicksville (G-11728)
Hickory Health Care Inc ... D ... 330 762-6486
Akron (G-260)
Highbanks Care Center LLC ... D ... 614 888-2021
Columbus (G-7747)
Hill Side Plaza ... D ... 216 486-6300
Cleveland (G-5689)
Hill View Retirement Center ... C ... 740 354-3135
Portsmouth (G-16146)
Hillandale Healthcare Inc ... D ... 513 813-5595
West Chester (G-18943)
Hillspring Health Care Center ... E ... 937 748-1100
Springboro (G-16970)
Hilty Memorial Home Inc ... C ... 419 384-3218
Pandora (G-15753)
Holzer Senior Care Center ... E ... 740 446-5001
Bidwell (G-1469)
Home Echo Club Inc ... C ... 614 864-1718
Pickerington (G-15958)
Home The Friends Inc ... C ... 513 897-6050
Waynesville (G-18832)
Homestead II Healthcare Group ... B ... 440 352-0788
Painesville (G-15715)
Hooberry Associates Inc ... D ... 330 872-1991
Newton Falls (G-15137)
Horizon Health Management LLC ... D ... 513 793-5220
Cincinnati (G-3725)
Horn Nursing and Rehab Center ... D ... 330 262-2951
Wooster (G-19730)
Hospice Cincinnati Inc ... E ... 513 862-1100
Cincinnati (G-3728)
Hospice Cincinnati Inc ... D ... 513 891-7700
Cincinnati (G-3729)
Hospice of Genesis Health ... E ... 740 454-5381
Zanesville (G-20318)
Hospice of North Central Ohio ... E ... 419 281-7107
Ashland (G-675)
Hospice of The Western Reserve ... D ... 440 951-8692
Willoughby Hills (G-19588)
Hosser Assisted Living ... E ... 740 286-8785
Jackson (G-12176)
House of Loreto ... D ... 330 453-8137
Canton (G-2349)
Huffman Health Care Inc ... C ... 937 476-1000
Dayton (G-9510)
Humility House ... D ... 330 505-0144
Youngstown (G-20070)
Huron Health Care Center Inc ... C ... 419 433-4990
Huron (G-12027)
Huston Nursing Home ... D ... 740 384-3485
Hamden (G-11552)
Hyde Park Health Center ... E ... 513 272-0600
Cincinnati (G-3744)
I Vrable Inc ... C ... 614 545-5500
Columbus (G-7795)
Independence Care Community ... D ... 419 435-8505
Fostoria (G-11007)
Indian Hlls Hlthcare Group Inc ... A ... 216 486-8880
Euclid (G-10644)
Isabelle Ridgway Care Ctr Inc ... C ... 614 252-4931
Columbus (G-7846)

Ivy Health Care Inc ....C...... 513 251-2557
Cincinnati *(G-3792)*

J W J Investments Inc ....C...... 419 643-3161
Delphos *(G-10028)*

Jackson County Hlth Facilities ...D...... 740 384-0722
Wellston *(G-18851)*

Jacobs Dwelling Nursing Home .....E...... 740 824-3635
Coshocton *(G-9020)*

Jennings Eliza Home Inc ....C...... 216 226-0282
Cleveland *(G-5788)*

Jennings Eliza Senior Care ....A...... 216 226-5000
Olmsted Twp *(G-15536)*

Jennings Ctr For Older Adults ....B...... 216 581-2900
Cleveland *(G-5789)*

Jewish Fdrtion of Grter Dayton ...D...... 937 837-2651
Dayton *(G-9525)*

Jewish Home of Cincinnati ....B...... 513 754-3100
Mason *(G-13603)*

Jma Healthcare LLC ....C...... 440 439-7976
Cleveland *(G-5797)*

Jo Lin Health Center Inc ....C...... 740 532-0860
Ironton *(G-12160)*

Joint Township Dst Mem Hosp ......B...... 419 394-3335
Saint Marys *(G-16524)*

Judson Care Center Inc ....E...... 513 662-5880
Cincinnati *(G-3840)*

Karl Hc LLC ....B...... 614 846-5420
Columbus *(G-7882)*

Kendal At Granville ....C...... 740 321-0400
Granville *(G-11344)*

Kendal At Oberlin ....C...... 440 775-0094
Oberlin *(G-15506)*

Kenwood Ter Hlth Care Ctr Inc ....C...... 513 793-2255
Cincinnati *(G-3861)*

Kimes Convalescent Center ....E...... 740 593-3391
Athens *(G-789)*

Kindred Healthcare Inc ....D...... 937 222-5963
Dayton *(G-9546)*

Kindred Healthcare Oper Inc ......D...... 740 545-6355
West Lafayette *(G-19115)*

Kindred Healthcare Oper Inc ......C...... 740 439-4437
Cambridge *(G-2075)*

Kindred Healthcare Operating .....C...... 330 762-0901
Akron *(G-303)*

Kindred Healthcare Operating .....D...... 419 877-5338
Whitehouse *(G-19449)*

Kindred Nursing Centers E LLC ....C...... 740 772-5900
Chillicothe *(G-2798)*

Kindred Nursing Centers E LLC ....C...... 513 932-0105
Lebanon *(G-12475)*

Kindred Nursing Centers E LLC ....D...... 614 276-8222
Columbus *(G-7905)*

Kindred Nursing Centers E LLC ....C...... 614 837-9666
Canal Winchester *(G-2114)*

Kindred Nursing Centers E LLC ....C...... 314 631-3000
Pickerington *(G-15961)*

Kindred Nursing Centers E LLC ....C...... 502 596-7300
Logan *(G-12844)*

King Tree Leasing Co LLC ....D...... 937 278-0723
Dayton *(G-9548)*

Kingston Healthcare Company ......C...... 937 866-9089
Miamisburg *(G-14183)*

Kingston Healthcare Company ......C...... 440 967-1800
Vermilion *(G-18555)*

Kingston Healthcare Company ......C...... 419 289-3859
Ashland *(G-677)*

Kingston Rsdnce Perrysburg LLC ...D...... 419 872-6200
Perrysburg *(G-15887)*

Lakewood Health Care Center ......C...... 216 226-3103
Lakewood *(G-12355)*

Lancia Nursing Home Inc ....E...... 740 695-4404
Saint Clairsville *(G-16491)*

Lancia Nursing Home Inc ....E...... 740 264-7101
Steubenville *(G-17162)*

Larchwood Health Group LLC ....E...... 216 941-6100
Cleveland *(G-5855)*

Laurel Health Care Company ....D...... 740 264-5042
Steubenville *(G-17163)*

Laurel Health Care Company ....D...... 614 794-8800
Westerville *(G-19180)*

Laurel Health Care Company ....C...... 614 888-4553
Worthington *(G-19820)*

Laurel Health Care Company ....C...... 614 885-0408
Worthington *(G-19821)*

Laurel Healthcare ....C...... 419 782-7879
Defiance *(G-9925)*

Laurel Hlth Care Battle Creek ....E...... 614 794-8800
Westerville *(G-19181)*

Laurel Hlth Care of Mt Plasant ...D...... 614 794-8800
Westerville *(G-19182)*

Laurel Lk Retirement Cmnty Inc ...B...... 330 650-0681
Hudson *(G-11993)*

Laurels of Hillsboro ....D...... 937 393-1925
Hillsboro *(G-11849)*

Leader Nuring & Rehabilitation ...C...... 419 252-5718
Toledo *(G-17850)*

Lebanon Nursing & Rehab Ctr ......D...... 513 932-1121
Lebanon *(G-12481)*

Levering Management Inc ....B...... 740 397-3897
Mount Vernon *(G-14778)*

Levering Management Inc ....D...... 419 756-4747
Mansfield *(G-13198)*

Levering Management Inc ....D...... 740 387-9545
Marion *(G-13429)*

Levering Management Inc ....D...... 740 369-6400
Delaware *(G-9995)*

Lexington Court Care Center ......D...... 419 884-2000
Mansfield *(G-13199)*

Liberty Health Care Center Inc ...E...... 937 296-1550
Bellbrook *(G-1340)*

Liberty Nrsing Ctr of Jmestown ...D...... 937 675-3311
Jamestown *(G-12188)*

Liberty Nrsing Ctr Rvrside LLC ...D...... 513 557-3621
Cincinnati *(G-3924)*

Liberty Nursing Center ....D...... 937 836-5143
Englewood *(G-10593)*

Liberty Nursing Home Inc ....D...... 937 376-2121
Xenia *(G-19917)*

Liberty Nursing of Willard ....D...... 419 935-0148
Willard *(G-19483)*

Life Care Centers America Inc ....C...... 440 365-5200
Elyria *(G-10524)*

Life Care Centers America Inc ....C...... 440 871-3030
Westlake *(G-19369)*

Life Care Centers America Inc ....D...... 614 889-6320
Columbus *(G-7972)*

Life Care Centers America Inc ....C...... 330 483-3131
Valley City *(G-18464)*

Lima Cnvlscent HM Fndation Inc ...C...... 419 227-5450
Lima *(G-12677)*

Lincoln Crawford Nrsg/Rehab CT ...E...... 513 861-2044
Cincinnati *(G-3932)*

Lincoln Park Associates II LP ....C...... 937 297-4300
Dayton *(G-9568)*

Livin Care Alter of Kirke Inc ....D...... 740 927-3209
Kirkersville *(G-12320)*

Living Care Alternatives ....E...... 740 927-3209
Kirkersville *(G-12321)*

Locust Ridge Nursing Home Inc ....D...... 937 444-2920
Williamsburg *(G-19494)*

Lodge Care Center Inc ....C...... 513 683-9966
Loveland *(G-13007)*

Logan Health Care Center ....C...... 740 385-2155
Logan *(G-13616)*

Logan Healthcare Leasing LLC .....D...... 216 367-1214
Logan *(G-12847)*

Longterm Lodging Inc ....C...... 614 224-0614
Columbus *(G-7988)*

Lorantffy Care Center Inc ....D...... 330 666-2631
Copley *(G-8969)*

Lost Creek Health Care ....B...... 419 225-9040
Lima *(G-12692)*

Loveland Health Care Center ......C...... 513 605-6000
Loveland *(G-13008)*

Lutheran Home ....B...... 440 871-0090
Cleveland *(G-5889)*

Lutheran Scial Svcs Centl Ohio ...C...... 419 289-3523
Ashland *(G-678)*

Lutheran Senior City Inc ....B...... 614 228-5200
Columbus *(G-8000)*

Lutheran Village At Wolf Creek ...C...... 419 861-2233
Holland *(G-11893)*

Lynnhaven V LLC ....C...... 440 272-5600
Windsor *(G-19665)*

Lynnhaven Xii LLC ....C...... 419 756-7111
Mansfield *(G-13200)*

Madeira Health Care Center ....C...... 513 561-4105
Cincinnati *(G-3957)*

Madison Care Inc ....D...... 440 428-1492
Madison *(G-13102)*

Main Street Terrace Care Ctr .....D...... 740 653-8767
Lancaster *(G-12414)*

Mallard Cove Senior Dev LLC ......C...... 513 772-6655
Cincinnati *(G-3966)*

Manleys Manor Nursing Home Inc ...C...... 419 424-0402
Findlay *(G-10937)*

Manor Care Inc ....D...... 419 252-5500
Toledo *(G-17880)*

Manor Care Nursing Center ....E...... 419 252-5500
Toledo *(G-17881)*

Manor Care of America Inc ....D...... 440 543-6766
Chagrin Falls *(G-2673)*

Manor Care of America Inc ....D...... 330 867-8530
Akron *(G-325)*

Manor Care of America Inc ....C...... 330 492-7835
Canton *(G-2386)*

Manor Care of America Inc ....C...... 440 779-6900
North Olmsted *(G-15296)*

Manor Care of America Inc ....C...... 440 951-5551
Willoughby *(G-19548)*

Manor Care of America Inc ....C...... 440 345-9300
North Royalton *(G-15362)*

Manor Care of Boynton Beach ......C...... 419 252-5500
Toledo *(G-17882)*

Manor Care of Kansas Inc ....C...... 419 252-5500
Toledo *(G-17883)*

Manor Care of North Olmsted ......B...... 419 252-5500
Toledo *(G-17884)*

Manor Care of Plantation Inc .....C...... 419 252-5500
Toledo *(G-17885)*

Manor Care of York North Inc .....C...... 419 252-5500
Toledo *(G-17886)*

Manor Care Wilmington Inc ....E...... 419 252-5500
Toledo *(G-17887)*

Manor Care York (south) Inc ......C...... 419 252-5500
Toledo *(G-17888)*

Manor Cr-Mprial Rchmond VA LLC ...D...... 419 252-5000
Toledo *(G-17889)*

Manorcare Health Services LLC ....E...... 419 252-5500
Toledo *(G-17890)*

Manorcare Health Svcs VA Inc .....C...... 419 252-5500
Toledo *(G-17891)*

Manorcare of Kingston Court ......C...... 419 252-5500
Toledo *(G-17892)*

Manorcare of Willoughby Inc ......C...... 419 252-5500
Toledo *(G-17893)*

Mansfield Memorial Homes LLC .....C...... 419 774-5100
Mansfield *(G-13209)*

Mansfield Opco LLC ....D...... 502 429-8062
Mansfield *(G-13210)*

Maple Knoll Communities Inc ......E...... 513 524-7990
Oxford *(G-15679)*

Maple Knoll Communities Inc ......A...... 513 782-2400
Cincinnati *(G-3967)*

Maplewood Nursing Center Inc .....E...... 740 383-2126
Marion *(G-13431)*

Marietta Center For Health & .....C...... 740 373-1867
Marietta *(G-13349)*

Marion Manor ....D...... 740 387-9545
Marion *(G-13443)*

▲ **Marymount Hospital Inc** ....B...... 216 581-0500
Cleveland *(G-5920)*

Mason Health Care Center ....D...... 513 398-2881
Mason *(G-13616)*

Masonic Healthcare Inc ....B...... 937 525-3001
Springfield *(G-17067)*

Mayfair Nursing Care Centers .....D...... 614 889-6320
Columbus *(G-8041)*

Mayflower Nursing Home Inc ....C...... 330 492-7131
Canton *(G-2393)*

Mc Auley Center ....C...... 937 653-5432
Urbana *(G-18439)*

McClellan Management Inc ....C...... 419 855-7755
Genoa *(G-11258)*

McGregor Senior Ind Hsing ....D...... 216 851-8200
Cleveland *(G-5933)*

McKinley Hall Inc ....E...... 937 328-5300
Springfield *(G-17068)*

McKinley Life Care Center LLC ....D...... 330 456-1014
Canton *(G-2396)*

McV Health Care Facilities ....C...... 513 398-1486
Mason *(G-13617)*

Meadow Wind Hlth Care Ctr Inc ....C...... 330 833-2026
Massillon *(G-13714)*

Meadowbrook Manor of Hartford ....D...... 330 772-5253
Fowler *(G-11016)*

Medina Meadows ....D...... 330 725-1550
Medina *(G-13977)*

Medina Medical Investors Ltd .....C...... 330 483-3131
Medina *(G-13978)*

Megco Management Inc ....C...... 330 874-9999
Bolivar *(G-1704)*

Meigs Center Ltd ....C...... 740 992-6472
Middleport *(G-14281)*

Mennonite Memorial Home ....E...... 419 358-7654
Bluffton *(G-1694)*

Mennonite Memorial Home ....B...... 419 358-1015
Bluffton *(G-1693)*

Menorah Park Center For Senio ....A...... 216 831-6500
Cleveland *(G-5952)*

Mental Rtrdtion Preble Cnty Bd..........D...... 937 456-5891
  Eaton (G-10453)

Mentor Way Nursing & Rehab Cen......C...... 440 255-9309
  Mentor (G-14084)

Mercy Health West Park..........C...... 513 451-8900
  Cincinnati (G-4033)

Mercy St Theresa Center Inc..........C...... 513 271-7010
  Cincinnati (G-4035)

Merit House LLC..........C...... 419 478-5131
  Toledo (G-17911)

Merit Leasing Co LLC..........C...... 216 261-9592
  Cleveland (G-5955)

Mff Somerset LLC..........E...... 216 752-5600
  Shaker Heights (G-16710)

Mill Creek Nursing..........E...... 419 468-4046
  Galion (G-11179)

Mill Manor Nursing Home Inc..........E...... 440 967-6614
  Vermilion (G-18558)

Mill Run Care Center LLC..........D...... 614 527-3000
  Hilliard (G-11798)

Minerva Elder Care Inc..........E...... 330 868-4147
  Minerva (G-14521)

Mkjb Inc..........C...... 513 851-8400
  West Chester (G-18975)

Montefiore Home..........B...... 216 360-9080
  Beachwood (G-1083)

Mount Vernon NH LLC..........E...... 740 392-1099
  Mount Vernon (G-14783)

Mt Washington Care Center Inc..........C...... 513 231-4561
  Cincinnati (G-4083)

Multi-Care Inc..........D...... 440 352-0788
  Painesville (G-15728)

Multicare Management Group..........C...... 513 868-6500
  Fairfield (G-10759)

Muskingum County Ohio..........D...... 740 454-1911
  Zanesville (G-20336)

Muskingum Vly Nrsing Rhblttion..........D...... 740 984-4262
  Beverly (G-1465)

Myocare Nursing Home Inc..........C...... 216 252-7555
  Cleveland (G-6031)

National Church Residences..........C...... 614 451-2151
  Columbus (G-8130)

Ncop LLC..........D...... 419 599-4070
  Napoleon (G-14815)

Nentwick Convalescent Home..........C...... 330 385-5001
  East Liverpool (G-10409)

New Albany Care Center LLC..........C...... 614 855-8866
  Columbus (G-8183)

New Dawn Health Care Inc..........C...... 330 343-5521
  Dover (G-10090)

New Life Hospice Inc..........E...... 440 934-1458
  Lorain (G-12930)

New Life Hospice Inc..........D...... 440 934-1458
  Lorain (G-12931)

Newark Care Center LLC..........D...... 740 366-2321
  Newark (G-15082)

Newark Leasing LLC..........C...... 740 344-0357
  Newark (G-15083)

Newark NH LLC..........D...... 740 345-9197
  Newark (G-15085)

Newcomerstown Development Inc......C...... 740 498-5165
  Newcomerstown (G-15133)

Newcomerstown Progress Corp..........C...... 740 498-5165
  Newcomerstown (G-15134)

Nightingale Holdings LLC..........B...... 330 645-0200
  Akron (G-346)

Normandy Manor of Rocky River..........C...... 440 333-5401
  Rocky River (G-16443)

Northpoint Senior Services LLC..........D...... 740 369-9614
  Delaware (G-9998)

Northpoint Senior Services LLC..........C...... 740 373-3597
  Marietta (G-13363)

Northpoint Senior Services LLC..........D...... 513 248-1655
  Milford (G-14414)

Norwalk Area Hlth Systems Inc..........A...... 419 668-8101
  Norwalk (G-15448)

Norwood Health Care Center LLC..........D...... 513 351-0153
  Cincinnati (G-4135)

Nursing Care MGT Amer Inc..........C...... 419 385-3958
  Toledo (G-17953)

Nursing Care MGT Amer Inc..........D...... 740 927-9888
  Pataskala (G-15786)

Nursing Care MGT Amer Inc..........D...... 513 793-5092
  Cincinnati (G-4142)

Oak Creek Terrace Inc..........C...... 937 439-1454
  Dayton (G-9662)

Oak Grove Manor Inc..........C...... 419 589-6222
  Mansfield (G-13227)

Oak Health Care Investors..........D...... 740 397-3200
  Mount Vernon (G-14784)

Oak Health Care Investors..........E...... 614 794-8800
  Westerville (G-19193)

Oakhill Manor Care Center..........C...... 330 875-5060
  Louisville (G-12970)

Oaks of West Kettering Inc..........C...... 937 293-1152
  Dayton (G-9664)

Oaktree LLC..........D...... 513 598-8000
  Cincinnati (G-4145)

October Enterprises Inc..........C...... 937 456-9535
  Eaton (G-10456)

Ohio Department Veterans Svcs..........A...... 614 644-0898
  Columbus (G-8243)

Ohio Eastern Star Home..........C...... 740 397-1706
  Mount Vernon (G-14785)

Ohio Living..........B...... 614 224-1651
  Columbus (G-8271)

Ohio Living..........C...... 513 681-4230
  Cincinnati (G-4156)

Ohio Presbt Retirement Svcs..........B...... 330 746-2944
  Youngstown (G-20147)

Ohio Presbt Retirement Svcs..........C...... 330 867-2150
  Akron (G-361)

Ohio Presbt Retirement Svcs..........B...... 937 498-2391
  Sidney (G-16789)

Ohio Presbt Retirement Svcs..........C...... 513 539-7391
  Monroe (G-14579)

Ohio Valley Manor Inc..........C...... 937 392-4318
  Ripley (G-16401)

Ohioguidestone..........E...... 440 234-2006
  Berea (G-1434)

Ohiohealth Corporation..........A...... 614 788-8860
  Columbus (G-8362)

Olmsted Manor Nursing Home..........C...... 440 250-4080
  North Olmsted (G-15302)

Olmsted Mnor Rtrment Cmnty Ltd......C...... 440 779-8886
  North Olmsted (G-15303)

Omni Manor Inc..........C...... 330 545-1550
  Girard (G-11297)

Omni Manor Inc..........C...... 330 793-5648
  Youngstown (G-20148)

Orchard Villa Inc..........C...... 419 697-4100
  Oregon (G-15603)

Orion Care Services LLC..........C...... 216 752-3600
  Cleveland (G-6144)

Otterbein Lebanon..........E...... 513 933-5465
  Lebanon (G-12491)

Otterbein Portage Valley Inc..........C...... 888 749-4950
  Pemberville (G-15806)

Otterbein Snior Lfstyle Chices..........B...... 513 933-5400
  Lebanon (G-12492)

Otterbein Snior Lfstyle Chices..........C...... 419 645-5114
  Cridersville (G-9063)

Otterbein Snior Lfstyle Chices..........C...... 513 260-7690
  Middletown (G-14352)

Otterbein Snior Lfstyle Chices..........C...... 419 394-2366
  Saint Marys (G-16530)

Ovm Investment Group LLC..........C...... 937 392-0145
  Ripley (G-16402)

Parkcliffe Development..........D...... 419 381-9447
  Toledo (G-17971)

Parkview Manor Inc..........C...... 419 243-5191
  Toledo (G-17972)

Parkview Manor Inc..........D...... 937 296-1550
  Englewood (G-10595)

Parma Care Center Inc..........C...... 216 661-6800
  Cleveland (G-6175)

Pebble Creek Cnvlscnt Ctr..........C...... 330 645-0200
  Akron (G-372)

Peregrine Health Services Inc..........D...... 330 823-9005
  Alliance (G-543)

Phyllis Wheatley Assn Dev..........E...... 216 391-4443
  Cleveland (G-6208)

Pickaway Manor Inc..........C...... 740 474-5400
  Circleville (G-4844)

Piketon Nursing Center Inc..........C...... 740 289-4074
  Piketon (G-15986)

Pleasant Hill Leasing LLC..........C...... 740 289-2394
  Piketon (G-15987)

Pleasant Lake Nursing Home..........B...... 440 842-2273
  Cleveland (G-6221)

Pleasant Ridge Care Center Inc..........C...... 513 631-1310
  Cincinnati (G-4255)

Pleasant View Nursing Home..........D...... 330 745-6028
  Barberton (G-961)

Premier Estates 521 LLC..........D...... 765 288-2488
  Cincinnati (G-4271)

Premier Health Care MGT Inc..........E...... 248 644-5522
  Blue Ash (G-961)

Progressive Green Meadows LLC......C...... 330 875-1456
  Louisville (G-12971)

Progressive Macedonia LLC..........E...... 330 908-1260
  Macedonia (G-13080)

Progressive Park LLC..........C...... 330 434-4514
  Cleveland (G-6253)

Quaker Heights Nursing HM Inc..........D...... 513 897-6050
  Waynesville (G-18835)

Quality Care Nursing Svcs LLC..........C...... 740 377-9095
  South Point (G-16944)

R & F Inc..........E...... 419 868-2909
  Holland (G-11906)

R & J Investment Co Inc..........C...... 440 934-5204
  Avon (G-902)

Rae-Ann Holdings Inc..........D...... 440 871-5181
  Cleveland (G-6281)

Rae-Ann Holdings Inc..........D...... 440 871-0500
  Westlake (G-19397)

Rae-Ann Suburban Inc..........C...... 440 871-5181
  Westlake (G-19398)

Raeann Inc..........E...... 440 871-5181
  Cleveland (G-6282)

Raeann Inc..........D...... 440 466-5733
  Geneva (G-11245)

Rapids Nursing Homes Inc..........E...... 216 292-5706
  Grand Rapids (G-11329)

Rcr East Inc..........C...... 513 793-2090
  Cincinnati (G-4341)

Rcr East Inc..........C...... 513 231-8292
  Cincinnati (G-4342)

Red Carpet Health Care Center..........C...... 740 439-4401
  Cambridge (G-2081)

Regency Leasing Co LLC..........B...... 614 542-3100
  Columbus (G-8505)

Rescare Ohio Inc..........E...... 740 625-6873
  Centerburg (G-1803)

Rest Haven Nursing Home Inc..........C...... 937 548-1138
  Greenville (G-11392)

Ridge Murray Prod Ctr Oberlin......E...... 440 774-7400
  Oberlin (G-15519)

Ridge Pleasant Valley Inc..........C...... 440 845-0200
  Cleveland (G-6325)

Rivers Bend Health Care LLC..........D...... 740 894-3476
  South Point (G-16945)

Riverside Care Center LLC..........D...... 740 962-5303
  Mc Connelsville (G-13895)

Rocky River Leasing Co LLC..........C...... 440 243-5688
  Berea (G-1436)

Rolling Hlls Rhab Wellness Ctr..........C...... 330 225-9121
  Brunswick (G-1939)

Roman Cthlic Docese Youngstown......C...... 330 875-5562
  Louisville (G-12973)

Rosary Care Center..........D...... 419 824-3600
  Sylvania (G-17449)

Rose Ln Hlth Rhabilitation Inc..........C...... 330 833-3174
  Massillon (G-13725)

Rossford Grtric Care Ltd Prtnr..........C...... 614 459-0445
  Columbus (G-8554)

Royal Manor Health Care Inc..........E...... 216 752-3600
  Cleveland (G-6345)

Royal Oak Nrsing Rhblttion Ctr..........D...... 440 884-9191
  Cleveland (G-6346)

Royce Leasing Co LLC..........D...... 740 354-1240
  Portsmouth (G-16165)

Rwdop LLC..........C...... 330 666-3776
  Fairlawn (G-10845)

Saber Healthcare Group LLC..........E...... 440 546-0643
  Brecksville (G-1803)

Saber Healthcare Group LLC..........E...... 216 486-5736
  Euclid (G-10655)

Saber Healthcare Group LLC..........E...... 216 662-3343
  Maple Heights (G-13294)

Saber Healthcare Group LLC..........E...... 937 826-3351
  Woodstock (G-19680)

Saber Healthcare Group LLC..........C...... 937 779-4150
  West Union (G-19138)

Saber Healthcare Group LLC..........E...... 419 484-1111
  Grand Rapids (G-11330)

Saber Healthcare Group LLC..........E...... 216 292-5706
  Bedford (G-1303)

Saber Healthcare Group LLC..........B...... 740 852-3100
  London (G-12874)

Salem Community Hospital..........A...... 330 332-1551
  Salem (G-16560)

Salutary Providers Inc..........C...... 440 964-8446
  Ashtabula (G-753)

Samaritan Care Center & Villa..........D...... 330 725-4123
  Medina (G-13998)

Sanctuary At Tuttle Crossing..........D...... 614 408-0182
  Dublin (G-10327)

Sanctuary At Wilmington Place..........D...... 937 256-4663
  Dayton (G-9751)

Sarah Jane Living Center Ltd ....E 419 692-6618
Delphos (G-10034)
Sateri Home Inc ....D 330 758-8106
Youngstown (G-20204)
Schoenbrunn Healthcare ....D 330 339-3595
New Philadelphia (G-14980)
Schroer Properties Inc ....D 740 687-5100
Lancaster (G-12433)
Schroer Properties Inc ....C 440 357-7900
Mentor (G-14106)
Select Spclty Hsptal-Akron LLC ....D 330 761-7500
Akron (G-423)
Semma Enterprises Inc ....C 513 863-7775
Middletown (G-14328)
Senior Care Inc ....E 937 372-1530
Xenia (G-19925)
Senior Care Inc ....E 937 291-3211
Miamisburg (G-14217)
Sensi Care 3 ....E 440 323-6310
Elyria (G-10562)
Shelby County Mem Hosp Assn ....D 937 492-9591
Sidney (G-16798)
Shepherd of The Valley Luthera ....D 330 530-4038
Youngstown (G-20209)
Shepherd of The Valley Luthera ....C 330 726-9061
Youngstown (G-20210)
Shg Whitehall Holdings LLC ....C 614 501-8271
Columbus (G-8633)
Sienna Hills Nursing & Rehab ....E 740 546-3013
Adena (G-8)
Siffrin Residential Assn ....C 330 799-8932
Youngstown (G-20211)
Singleton Health Care Center ....E 216 231-0076
Cleveland (G-6410)
Sisters Od Saint Joseph of SAI ....B 216 531-7426
Euclid (G-10656)
Sisters of Charity of Cinc ....D 513 347-5200
Mount Saint Joseph (G-14744)
Sisters of Little ....C 216 464-1222
Warrensville Heights (G-18780)
Sisters of Little ....C 419 698-4331
Oregon (G-15608)
Slovene Home For The Aged ....C 216 486-0268
Cleveland (G-6417)
Snf Wadsworth LLC ....D 330 336-3472
Solon (G-16898)
Solon Pnte At Emrald Ridge LLC ....E 440 498-3000
Solon (G-16900)
Somerset NH LLC ....D 740 743-2924
Somerset (G-16918)
South Broadway ....D 330 339-2151
New Philadelphia (G-14981)
Southbrook Health Care Ctr Inc ....C 937 322-3436
Springfield (G-17113)
Sprenger Enterprises Inc ....A 440 244-2019
Lorain (G-12945)
Spring Meadow Extended Care Ce ....D 419 866-6124
Holland (G-11916)
Springhills LLC ....C 937 274-1400
Dayton (G-9786)
Springhills LLC ....D 513 424-9999
Middletown (G-14355)
Springview Manor Nursing Home ....E 419 227-3661
Lima (G-12748)
St Augustine Corporation ....B 216 939-7600
Lakewood (G-12363)
St Catherines Care Centers O ....C 419 435-8112
Fostoria (G-11013)
St Catherines Care Ctr Findlay ....C 419 422-3978
Findlay (G-10962)
St Edward Home ....C 330 668-2828
Fairlawn (G-10851)
St Joseph Leasing Co LLC ....D 513 530-1654
Blue Ash (G-1652)
Stone Crossing Assisted Living ....C 330 492-7131
Canton (G-2499)
Stow Opco LLC ....D 502 429-8062
Stow (G-17232)
Streetsboro Opco LLC ....D 502 429-8062
Streetsboro (G-17273)
Summit Facility Operations LLC ....D 330 633-0555
Tallmadge (G-17490)
Summitt Ohio Leasing Co LLC ....C 937 436-2273
Dayton (G-9800)
Sumner Home For The Aged Inc ....C 330 666-2952
Copley (G-8976)
Sun Healthcare Group Inc ....C 419 784-1450
Defiance (G-9943)
Sunbrdge Marion Hlth Care Corp ....D 740 389-6306
Marion (G-13461)
Sunbridge Care Enterprises Inc ....D 740 653-8630
Lancaster (G-12439)
Sunbridge Circleville ....E 740 477-1695
Circleville (G-4851)
Sunbridge Healthcare LLC ....C 740 342-5161
New Lexington (G-14929)
Sunrise Connecticut Avenue Ass ....E 614 451-6766
Columbus (G-8712)
Sunrise Healthcare Group LLC ....C 216 662-3343
Maple Heights (G-13299)
Sunrise Manor Convalescent Ctr ....D 513 797-5144
Amelia (G-576)
Sunrise Senior Living Inc ....D 937 438-0054
Dayton (G-9801)
Sunrise Senior Living Inc ....E 614 418-9775
Gahanna (G-11149)
Sunrise Senior Living Inc ....D 440 895-2383
Rocky River (G-16446)
Sunrise Senior Living Inc ....D 440 808-0074
Westlake (G-19410)
Sunrise Senior Living Inc ....D 216 751-0930
Cleveland (G-6479)
Sunrise Senior Living Inc ....D 614 457-3500
Upper Arlington (G-18402)
Sunrise Senior Living Inc ....E 614 846-6500
Worthington (G-19854)
Sunrise Senior Living LLC ....E 937 836-9617
Englewood (G-10601)
Sunrise Senior Living LLC ....E 330 262-1615
Wooster (G-19771)
Sunrise Senior Living LLC ....E 419 425-3440
Findlay (G-10966)
Sunrise Senior Living LLC ....E 330 707-1313
Poland (G-16090)
Sunrise Senior Living LLC ....E 513 729-5233
Cincinnati (G-4554)
Sunrise Senior Living LLC ....D 330 929-8500
Cuyahoga Falls (G-9128)
Sunrise Senior Living LLC ....E 216 447-8909
Cleveland (G-6480)
Sunrise Senior Living LLC ....E 513 893-9000
Hamilton (G-11645)
Sunset Mnor Hlthcare Group Inc ....E 216 795-5710
Cleveland (G-6481)
Swa Inc ....C 440 243-7888
Cleveland (G-6489)
Swan Pnte Fclty Operations LLC ....D 419 867-7926
Maumee (G-13858)
Swanton Hlth Care Rtrement Ctr ....D 419 825-1145
Swanton (G-17407)
Tender Nursing Care ....E 614 856-3508
Reynoldsburg (G-16332)
The Maria-Joseph Center ....B 937 278-2692
Dayton (G-9812)
Thornville NH LLC ....D 740 246-5253
Thornville (G-17507)
Tlevay Inc ....C 419 385-3958
Toledo (G-18070)
Toledo Opco LLC ....D 502 429-8062
Toledo (G-18093)
Traditions At Bath Rd Inc ....C 330 929-6272
Cuyahoga Falls (G-9132)
Traditions At Stygler Road ....E 614 475-8778
Columbus (G-8772)
Tri County Extended Care Ctr ....C 513 829-3555
Fairfield (G-10793)
Trilogy Health Services LLC ....D 419 935-6511
Willard (G-19489)
Trilogy Healthcare Allen LLC ....D 419 643-3161
Delphos (G-10037)
Trilogy Healthcare Putnam LLC ....C 419 532-2961
Kalida (G-12207)
Trilogy Rehab Services LLC ....A 740 452-3000
Zanesville (G-20368)
Trinity Health Corporation ....B 614 846-5420
Columbus (G-8781)
Trinity Healthcare Corporation ....C 513 489-2444
Cincinnati (G-4648)
Twilight Gardens Healthcare ....E 419 668-2086
Norwalk (G-15458)
Twin Maples Nursing Home ....E 740 596-5955
Mc Arthur (G-13891)
Twin Oaks Care Center Inc ....E 419 524-1205
Mansfield (G-13258)
U C M Residential Services ....D 937 643-3757
Union City (G-18355)
Uhrichsville Health Care Ctr ....D 740 922-2208
Uhrichsville (G-18346)
Union Christel Manor Inc ....D 937 968-6265
Union City (G-18356)
United Church Homes Inc ....C 513 922-1440
Cincinnati (G-4677)
United Church Homes Inc ....C 330 854-4177
Canal Fulton (G-2099)
United Church Homes Inc ....C 937 426-8481
Beavercreek (G-1239)
United Church Homes Inc ....D 740 382-4885
Marion (G-13471)
United Church Homes Inc ....C 419 621-1900
Sandusky (G-16651)
United Church Homes Inc ....C 937 878-0262
Fairborn (G-10684)
United Church Homes Inc ....D 740 376-5600
Marietta (G-13392)
United Church Homes Inc ....D 740 286-7551
Jackson (G-12181)
University Hospitals Health ....E 440 285-4040
Chardon (G-2722)
University Manor Healthcare ....C 216 721-1400
Cleveland (G-6598)
University Manor Hlth Care Ctr ....C 216 721-1400
Cleveland (G-6599)
Uvmc Management Corporation ....D 937 440-4000
Troy (G-18237)
Uvmc Nursing Care Inc ....C 937 440-7663
Troy (G-18238)
Uvmc Nursing Care Inc ....C 937 667-7500
Tipp City (G-17572)
Uvmc Nursing Care Inc ....C 937 473-2075
Covington (G-9049)
V Clew LLC ....E 740 687-2273
Lancaster (G-12443)
V Vrable Inc ....C 614 545-5500
Columbus (G-8839)
Valley Hospice Inc ....E 740 859-5041
Rayland (G-16274)
Valley View Alzhimers Care Ctr ....D 740 998-2948
Frankfort (G-11019)
Van Rue Incorporated ....C 419 238-0715
Van Wert (G-18491)
Vancare Inc ....C 937 898-4202
Vandalia (G-18549)
Vancrest Ltd ....C 419 695-2871
Delphos (G-10038)
Vancrest Ltd ....C 419 749-2194
Convoy (G-8962)
Vancrest Ltd ....D 937 456-3010
Eaton (G-10465)
Vancrest Apts ....E 419 695-7335
Delphos (G-10039)
Vancrest Health Care Center ....D 419 264-0700
Holgate (G-11867)
Vienna Enterprises Inc ....E 937 568-4524
South Vienna (G-16949)
Village Green Healthcare Ctr ....D 937 548-1993
Greenville (G-11399)
Vista Centre ....D 330 424-5852
Lisbon (G-12806)
Volunters Amer Care Facilities ....C 419 447-7151
Tiffin (G-17546)
Volunters Amer Care Facilities ....C 419 225-9040
Lima (G-12774)
Volunters Amer Care Facilities ....C 419 334-9521
Fremont (G-11103)
Vrable Healthcare Inc ....E 614 545-5500
Columbus (G-8864)
Vrable II Inc ....D 614 545-5502
Columbus (G-8865)
Vrable IV Inc ....D 614 545-5502
Columbus (G-8866)
Walnut Hills Inc ....C 330 852-2457
Walnut Creek (G-18633)
Walton Manor Health Care Ctr ....C 440 439-4433
Cleveland (G-6652)
Washington Manor Inc ....E 937 433-3441
Dayton (G-9867)
Water Leasing Co LLC ....C 440 285-9400
Chardon (G-2725)
Waterville Care LLC ....D 419 878-3901
Waterville (G-18795)
Waverly Care Center Inc ....E 740 947-2113
Waverly (G-18824)
Wayside Farms Inc ....D 330 666-7716
Peninsula (G-15814)
Weber Health Care Center Inc ....C 440 647-2088
Wellington (G-18845)
Wessell Generations Inc ....C 440 775-1491
Oberlin (G-15521)
West Liberty Care Center Inc ....C 937 465-5065
West Liberty (G-19122)

SIC

West Park Retirement Community ....C 513 451-8900
  Cincinnati (G-4783)
West Side Dtscher Fruen Verein ....B 440 238-3361
  Strongsville (G-17359)
West View Manor Inc ....C 330 264-8640
  Wooster (G-19782)
Western Hills Care Center ....C 513 941-0099
  Cincinnati (G-4788)
Western Rsrve Msonic Cmnty Inc ....C 330 721-3000
  Medina (G-14014)
Wexner Heritage Village ....B 614 231-4900
  Columbus (G-8894)
Whetstone Care Center LLC ....C 614 875-7700
  Grove City (G-11487)
Whetstone Care Center LLC ....C 614 457-1100
  Columbus (G-8895)
Whetstone Care Center LLC ....C 740 474-6036
  Circleville (G-4853)
Wickliffe Country Place Ltd ....C 440 944-9400
  Wickliffe (G-19478)
Widows Home of Dayton Ohio ....D 937 252-1661
  Dayton (G-9880)
Willow Brook Chrstn Cmmunities ....C 740 369-0048
  Delaware (G-10016)
Willowood Care Center ....C 330 225-3156
  Brunswick (G-1947)
Wilmington Halthcare Group Inc ....D 937 382-1621
  Wilmington (G-19653)
Winchester Place Leasing LLC ....D 614 834-2273
  Canal Winchester (G-2127)
Windsong Healthcare Group LLC ....E 216 292-5706
  Akron (G-502)
Windsor House Inc ....D 330 743-1393
  Youngstown (G-20248)
Windsor House Inc ....D 330 482-1375
  Columbiana (G-6795)
Windsor House Inc ....C 330 549-9259
  Columbiana (G-6796)
Windsor House Inc ....C 330 759-7858
  Youngstown (G-20247)
Windsor House Inc ....E 440 834-0544
  Burton (G-2020)
Windsor Medical Center Inc ....D 330 499-8300
  Canton (G-2536)
Womens Welsh Clubs of America ....D 440 331-0420
  Rocky River (G-16449)
Wood County Ohio ....C 419 353-8411
  Bowling Green (G-1756)
Woodland Assisted Living Resi ....E 614 755-7591
  Columbus (G-8914)
Woodland Country Manor Inc ....E 513 523-4449
  Somerville (G-16920)
Woodlands Healthcare Group LLC ....E 330 297-4564
  Ravenna (G-16271)
Woodsfield Opco LLC ....D 502 429-8062
  Woodsfield (G-19679)
Woodside Village Care Center ....D 419 947-2015
  Mount Gilead (G-14736)
Woodstock Healthcare Group Inc ....E 937 826-3351
  Woodstock (G-19681)
Wyant Leasing Co LLC ....B 330 836-7953
  Akron (G-505)
Xenia East Management Systems ....D 937 372-4495
  Xenia (G-19936)
Xenia West Management Systems ....D 937 372-8081
  Xenia (G-19937)
Yorkland Health Care Inc ....D 614 751-2525
  Columbus (G-8926)
Youngstown Area Jwish Fdration ....D 330 746-1076
  Youngstown (G-20257)
Zandex Inc ....E 740 676-8381
  Shadyside (G-16700)
Zandex Inc ....E 740 454-1400
  Zanesville (G-20373)
Zandex Inc ....C 740 872-0809
  New Concord (G-14905)
Zandex Inc ....C 740 454-9769
  Zanesville (G-20375)
Zandex Inc ....C 740 695-7233
  Saint Clairsville (G-16513)
Zandex Inc ....D 740 967-1111
  Johnstown (G-12205)
Zandex Inc ....D 740 454-6823
  Zanesville (G-20376)
Zandex Health Care Corporation ....C 740 454-9747
  Zanesville (G-20380)
Zandex Health Care Corporation ....C 740 452-4636
  Zanesville (G-20377)
Zandex Health Care Corporation ....C 740 454-9769
  Zanesville (G-20378)

Zandex Health Care Corporation ....C 740 695-7233
  Saint Clairsville (G-16514)
Zandex Health Care Corporation ....C 740 454-1400
  New Concord (G-14906)
Zandex Health Care Corporation ....E 740 454-1400
  Zanesville (G-20379)
Zanesville NH LLC ....D 740 452-4351
  Zanesville (G-20384)

8052 Intermediate Care Facilities

10 Wilmington Place ....D 937 253-1010
  Dayton (G-9193)
599 W Main Corporation ....E 440 466-5901
  Geneva (G-11235)
A Provide Care Inc ....C 330 828-2278
  Dalton (G-9143)
Adams County Manor ....D 937 544-2205
  West Union (G-19131)
Alexson Services Inc ....B 513 874-0423
  Fairfield (G-10695)
Algart Health Care Inc ....D 216 631-1550
  Cleveland (G-4929)
Alpha Nursing Homes Inc ....D 740 345-9197
  Newark (G-15009)
Alpha Nursing Homes Inc ....D 740 622-2074
  Coshocton (G-8997)
Altercare Inc ....C 330 335-2555
  Wadsworth (G-18588)
Altercare Nobles Pond Inc ....D 330 834-4800
  Canton (G-2182)
Alternative Residences Two ....D 740 526-0514
  Saint Clairsville (G-16468)
Alternative Residences Two ....E 330 453-0200
  Canton (G-2183)
American Retirement Corp ....D 216 291-6140
  Cleveland (G-4965)
Amherst Manor Nursing Home ....D 440 988-4415
  Amherst (G-581)
Anchor Lodge Nursing Home Inc ....D 440 244-2019
  Lorain (G-12880)
Angels 4 Life LLC ....E 513 474-5683
  Cincinnati (G-2968)
Anne Grady Corporation ....C 419 380-8985
  Holland (G-11872)
Apostolic Christian Home Inc ....D 330 927-1010
  Rittman (G-16403)
Arbors At Clide Asssted Living ....E 419 547-7746
  Clyde (G-6738)
Arbors East LLC ....C 614 575-9003
  Columbus (G-6963)
Arlington Care Ctr ....C 740 344-0303
  Newark (G-15011)
Arlington Court Nursing ....C 614 545-5502
  Upper Arlington (G-18393)
Asana Hospice Cleveland LLC ....E 419 903-0300
  Berea (G-1412)
Baptist Home and Center ....C 513 662-5880
  Cincinnati (G-3018)
Beeghly Oaks Operating LLC ....C 330 884-2300
  Boardman (G-1696)
Bel Air Care Center ....D 330 821-3939
  Alliance (G-518)
Bittersweet Inc ....D 419 875-6986
  Whitehouse (G-19444)
Blossom Hills Nursing Home ....D 440 635-5567
  Huntsburg (G-12017)
Bluesky Healthcare Inc ....C 330 345-9050
  Wooster (G-19692)
Boyds Kinsman Home Inc ....E 330 876-5581
  Kinsman (G-12318)
Braeview Manor Inc ....C 216 486-9300
  Cleveland (G-5073)
Brethren Care Inc ....C 419 289-0803
  Ashland (G-659)
Brewster Parke Inc ....D 330 767-4179
  Brewster (G-1809)
Brook Willow Chrstn Cmmunities ....D 614 885-3300
  Columbus (G-7079)
Brookdale Senior Living Inc ....E 740 373-9600
  Marietta (G-13316)
Brookville Enterprises Inc ....B 937 833-2133
  Brookville (G-1911)
Brown Memorial Home Inc ....D 740 474-6238
  Circleville (G-4826)
Butler County of Ohio ....C 513 887-3728
  Fairfield Township (G-10803)
Butler County Board of Develop ....E 513 867-5913
  Fairfield (G-10703)
C R G Health Care Systems ....E 330 498-8107
  Niles (G-15148)

Camargo Manor Inc ....D 513 605-3000
  Cincinnati (G-3108)
Canton Assisted Living ....C 330 492-7131
  Canton (G-2227)
Caprice Health Care Inc ....C 330 965-9200
  North Lima (G-15267)
Cardinal Retirement Village ....E 330 928-7888
  Cuyahoga Falls (G-9076)
Carington Health Systems ....C 937 743-2754
  Franklin (G-11025)
Carriage Crt Mrysvlle Ltd Prtn ....E 937 642-2202
  Marysville (G-13487)
Carroll Golden Age Retreat ....E 330 627-4665
  Carrollton (G-2561)
Carroll Health Care Center ....C 330 627-5501
  Carrollton (G-2562)
Center For Eating Disorders ....E 614 896-8222
  Columbus (G-7153)
Center Ridge Nursing Home Inc ....C 440 808-5500
  North Ridgeville (G-15324)
Chelmsford Apartments Ltd ....E 419 389-0800
  Toledo (G-17649)
Childrens Forever Haven Inc ....E 440 652-6749
  North Royalton (G-15349)
Childrens Forever Haven Inc ....E 440 250-9182
  Westlake (G-19331)
Childs Investment Co ....E 330 837-2100
  Massillon (G-13669)
Choices In Community Living ....C 937 898-3655
  Dayton (G-9298)
Church of God Retirement Cmnty ....C 513 422-5600
  Middletown (G-14295)
Co Open Options Inc ....E 513 932-0724
  Lebanon (G-12455)
Columbus Area Integrated Healt ....D 614 252-0711
  Columbus (G-7257)
Commons of Providence ....D 419 624-1171
  Sandusky (G-16590)
Communicare Health Svcs Inc ....D 419 394-7611
  Saint Marys (G-16521)
Concord Health Care Inc ....C 330 759-2357
  Youngstown (G-20009)
Concord Hlth Rhabilitation Ctr ....E 740 574-8441
  Wheelersburg (G-19432)
Congregate Living of America ....E 937 393-6700
  Hillsboro (G-11834)
Congregate Living of America ....D 513 899-2801
  Morrow (G-14716)
Consulate Healthcare Inc ....E 419 865-1248
  Maumee (G-13775)
Consulate Management Co LLC ....D 440 237-7966
  Cleveland (G-5340)
Country Club Center Homes Inc ....D 330 343-6351
  Dover (G-10071)
Country Club Center II Ltd ....C 740 397-2350
  Mount Vernon (G-14756)
Country Club Retirement Center ....C 740 671-9330
  Bellaire (G-1333)
County of Lorain ....E 440 282-3074
  Lorain (G-12900)
County of Montgomery ....B 937 264-0460
  Dayton (G-9328)
County of Shelby ....C 937 492-6900
  Sidney (G-16771)
County of Wood ....B 419 686-6951
  Portage (G-16122)
Covenant Care Ohio Inc ....D 937 878-7046
  Fairborn (G-10666)
Cred-Kap Inc ....D 330 755-1466
  Struthers (G-17362)
Cridersville Health Care Ctr ....E 419 645-4468
  Cridersville (G-9062)
Crystal Care Centers Inc ....E 419 747-2666
  Mansfield (G-13161)
Crystalwood Inc ....D 513 605-1000
  Cincinnati (G-3383)
Cypress Hospice LLC ....E 440 973-0250
  Berea (G-1422)
Dayspring Health Care Center ....C 937 864-5800
  Fairborn (G-10670)
Deaconess Long Term Care of MI ....A 513 487-3600
  Cincinnati (G-3412)
Dearth Management Company ....E 740 389-1214
  Marion (G-13418)
Dearth Management Company ....C 614 847-1070
  Columbus (G-7426)
Dearth Management Company ....C 330 339-3595
  New Philadelphia (G-14956)
Dearth Management Company ....C 419 253-0144
  Marengo (G-13302)

Develpmntal Dsblties Ohio Dept .... A 740 446-1642
Gallipolis *(G-11190)*
Develpmntal Dsblties Ohio Dept .... B 614 272-0509
Columbus *(G-7441)*
Dover Nursing Center .... D 330 364-4436
Dover *(G-10075)*
Doylestown Health Care Center .... C 330 658-1533
Doylestown *(G-10112)*
Eagle Creek Hlthcare Group Inc .... E 937 544-5531
West Union *(G-19136)*
Earley & Ross Ltd .... D 740 634-3301
Sabina *(G-16467)*
East Galbraith Nursing Home .... C 513 984-5220
Cincinnati *(G-3472)*
Eastern Star Hm of Cyhoga Cnty .... D 216 761-0170
Cleveland *(G-5459)*
Ebenezer Road Corp .... C 513 941-0099
Cincinnati *(G-3480)*
Echoing Hills Village Inc .... D 440 989-1400
Lorain *(G-12902)*
Edgewood Manor of Wellston .... E 740 384-5611
Wellston *(G-18849)*
Elms Retirement Village Inc .... D 440 647-2414
Wellington *(G-18840)*
Elmwood Center Inc .... D 419 639-2581
Green Springs *(G-11350)*
Elmwood Center Inc .... D 419 447-6885
Tiffin *(G-17516)*
Emeritus Corporation .... E 330 342-0934
Stow *(G-17201)*
Emeritus Corporation .... E 614 836-5990
Groveport *(G-11509)*
Fairmont Nursing Home Inc .... D 440 338-8220
Newbury *(G-15120)*
Falls Village Retirement Cmnty .... D 330 945-9797
Cuyahoga Falls *(G-9094)*
Filling Memorial Home of Mercy .... B 419 592-6451
Napoleon *(G-14804)*
Fisher-Titus Medical Center .... E 419 668-4228
Norwalk *(G-15437)*
▲ **Fisher-Titus Medical Center** .... A 419 668-8101
Norwalk *(G-15438)*
Flower Hospital .... B 419 824-1000
Sylvania *(G-17425)*
Fort Austin Ltd Partnership .... C 440 892-4200
Cleveland *(G-5564)*
Foundations .... D 937 437-2311
New Paris *(G-14942)*
Foundations Hlth Solutions Inc .... D 440 793-0200
North Olmsted *(G-15289)*
Franciscan At St Leonard .... B 937 433-0480
Dayton *(G-9448)*
Friends of Good Shepherd Manor .... D 740 289-2861
Lucasville *(G-13049)*
Furney Group Home .... E 419 389-0152
Toledo *(G-17750)*
Garbry Ridge Assisted Living .... E 937 778-9385
Piqua *(G-16005)*
Gaslite Villa Convalescent Ctr .... D 330 494-4500
Canal Fulton *(G-2095)*
Gateway Health Care Center .... C 216 486-4949
Cleveland *(G-5595)*
Gaymont Nursing Homes Inc .... D 419 668-8258
Norwalk *(G-15439)*
Generation Health & Rehab Cntr .... D 740 344-9465
Newark *(G-15035)*
Gillette Nursing Home Inc .... D 330 372-1960
Warren *(G-18710)*
Golden Living LLC .... D 419 227-2154
Lima *(G-12644)*
Golden Living LLC .... C 614 861-6666
Columbus *(G-7678)*
Golden Living LLC .... C 330 297-5781
Ravenna *(G-16244)*
Golden Living LLC .... D 330 335-1558
Wadsworth *(G-18596)*
Good Shepherd Home .... C 419 937-1801
Fostoria *(G-11003)*
Grace Hospice LLC .... C 513 458-5545
Cincinnati *(G-3630)*
Grace Hospice LLC .... C 937 293-1381
Moraine *(G-14664)*
Grace Hospice LLC .... C 216 288-7413
Mentor *(G-14054)*
Greater Arms Holistic Health .... E 513 970-2767
Cincinnati *(G-3648)*
Greens of Lyndhurst The Inc .... C 440 460-1000
Cleveland *(G-5643)*
Guardian Elde .... D 419 225-9040
Lima *(G-12649)*

Guernsey Health Systems .... A 740 439-3561
Cambridge *(G-2073)*
Harbor .... E 800 444-3353
Toledo *(G-17781)*
Harborside Sylvania LLC .... D 419 882-1875
Sylvania *(G-17429)*
Hattie Larlham Center For .... C 330 274-2272
Mantua *(G-13267)*
Healthcare Facility MGT LLC .... C 330 836-7953
Akron *(G-258)*
Healthcare Management Cons .... E 419 363-2193
Rockford *(G-16416)*
Heinzerling Foundation .... C 614 272-8888
Columbus *(G-7735)*
Hempstead Manor .... C 740 354-8150
Portsmouth *(G-16145)*
Hennis Nursing Home .... C 330 364-8849
Dover *(G-10081)*
Heritage Park Rehabilita .... E 937 437-2311
New Paris *(G-14943)*
Heritage Professional Services .... E 740 456-8245
New Boston *(G-14880)*
Hill Side Plaza .... D 216 486-6300
Cleveland *(G-5689)*
Home Echo Club Inc .... C 614 864-1718
Pickerington *(G-15958)*
Horn Nursing and Rehab Center .... D 330 262-2951
Wooster *(G-19730)*
Hospice of Darke County Inc .... E 937 548-2999
Greenville *(G-11387)*
Hospice of Hamilton .... E 513 895-1270
Hamilton *(G-11610)*
Hospice of Hope Inc .... D 937 444-4900
Mount Orab *(G-14741)*
Hospice of Miami Valley LLC .... E 937 458-6028
Xenia *(G-19912)*
Hospice of Northwest Ohio .... B 419 661-4001
Perrysburg *(G-15875)*
Hospice of Ohio LLC .... D 440 286-2500
Cleveland *(G-5710)*
Hospice of The Western Reserve .... E 440 787-2080
Lorain *(G-12907)*
Hospice of The Western Reserve .... C 216 383-2222
Cleveland *(G-5712)*
Hospice of The Western Reserve .... D 800 707-8922
Cleveland *(G-5713)*
Humility House .... D 330 505-0144
Youngstown *(G-20070)*
Indian Hlls Hlthcare Group Inc .... A 216 486-8880
Euclid *(G-10644)*
Inn At Marietta Ltd .... D 740 373-9600
Marietta *(G-13338)*
Inn At Univ Vlg MGT Co LLC .... E 330 837-3000
Massillon *(G-13699)*
Inner City Nursing Home .... C 216 795-1363
Cleveland *(G-5754)*
Isabelle Ridgway Care Ctr Inc .... C 614 252-4931
Columbus *(G-7846)*
Jennings Eliza Home Inc .... C 216 226-0282
Cleveland *(G-5788)*
Jennings Ctr For Older Adults .... B 216 581-2900
Cleveland *(G-5789)*
Judson .... D 216 791-2004
Cleveland *(G-5808)*
Judson Care Center Inc .... E 513 662-5880
Cincinnati *(G-3840)*
Kendal At Oberlin .... C 440 775-0094
Oberlin *(G-15506)*
Kindred Healthcare Oper Inc .... D 740 545-6355
West Lafayette *(G-19115)*
Kindred Healthcare Operating .... D 419 877-5338
Whitehouse *(G-19449)*
Kingston Healthcare Company .... D 419 824-4200
Sylvania *(G-17435)*
Lakeside Manor Inc .... E 330 549-2545
North Lima *(G-15271)*
Laurels of Hillsboro .... D 937 393-1925
Hillsboro *(G-11849)*
Leeda Services Inc .... E 330 392-6006
Warren *(G-18722)*
Levering Management Inc .... D 740 369-6400
Delaware *(G-9995)*
Lexington Court Care Center .... D 419 884-2000
Mansfield *(G-13199)*
Liberty Nursing Center .... E 937 836-5143
Englewood *(G-10593)*
Liberty Nursing Center of Thre .... C 513 941-0787
Cincinnati *(G-3925)*
Liberty Nursing of Willard .... D 419 935-0148
Willard *(G-19483)*

Liberty Residence II .... E 330 334-3262
Wadsworth *(G-18603)*
Life Care Centers America Inc .... C 330 483-3131
Valley City *(G-18464)*
Lifeservices Development Corp .... E 440 257-3866
Mentor *(G-14077)*
Light of Hearts Villa .... D 440 232-1991
Cleveland *(G-5869)*
Lincoln Park Associates II LP .... C 937 297-4300
Dayton *(G-9568)*
Living Care Altrntves of Utica .... E 740 892-3414
Utica *(G-18457)*
Longmeadow Care Center Inc .... C 330 297-5781
Ravenna *(G-16249)*
Luther Home of Mercy .... B 419 836-3918
Williston *(G-19500)*
Lutheran Home .... B 440 871-0090
Cleveland *(G-5889)*
Lutheran Memorial Home Inc .... D 419 502-5700
Toledo *(G-17873)*
Lutheran Village At Wolf Creek .... C 419 861-2233
Holland *(G-11893)*
Lynnhaven V LLC .... C 440 272-5600
Windsor *(G-19665)*
Main Street Terrace Care Ctr .... D 740 653-8767
Lancaster *(G-12414)*
Manorcare of Willoughby Inc .... C 419 252-5500
Toledo *(G-17893)*
Mansfield Memorial Homes LLC .... C 419 774-5100
Mansfield *(G-13209)*
Maple Knoll Communities Inc .... A 513 782-2400
Cincinnati *(G-3967)*
Mary Scott Nursing Home Inc .... D 937 278-0761
Dayton *(G-9589)*
McClellan Management Inc .... C 419 855-7755
Genoa *(G-11258)*
McV Health Care Facilities .... C 513 398-1486
Mason *(G-13617)*
Meigs Center Ltd .... C 740 992-6472
Middleport *(G-14281)*
Mennonite Memorial Home .... B 419 358-1015
Bluffton *(G-1693)*
Mental Health Service .... E 937 399-9500
Springfield *(G-17070)*
Mercer Residential Svcs Inc .... D 419 586-4709
Celina *(G-2604)*
Mercy Health .... C 937 390-9665
Springfield *(G-17075)*
Miami Valley Hsing Assn I Inc .... E 937 263-4449
Dayton *(G-9623)*
Mill Manor Nursing Home Inc .... E 440 967-6614
Vermilion *(G-18558)*
Mill Run Care Center LLC .... D 614 527-3000
Hilliard *(G-11798)*
Mount Aloysius Corp .... C 740 342-3343
New Lexington *(G-14921)*
Muskingum County Ohio .... D 740 454-1911
Zanesville *(G-20336)*
New Dawn Health Care Inc .... C 330 343-5521
Dover *(G-10090)*
New Hope & Horizons .... E 513 761-7999
Cincinnati *(G-4107)*
North Hills Management Company .... D 740 450-9999
Zanesville *(G-20346)*
North Point Eductl Svc Ctr .... E 440 967-0904
Huron *(G-12028)*
Northpoint Senior Services LLC .... C 740 373-3597
Marietta *(G-13363)*
Northpoint Senior Services LLC .... D 513 248-1655
Milford *(G-14414)*
Norwood Health Care Center LLC .... D 513 351-0153
Cincinnati *(G-4135)*
Oak Health Care Investors .... D 740 397-3200
Mount Vernon *(G-14784)*
October Enterprises Inc .... C 937 456-9535
Eaton *(G-10456)*
Ohio Eastern Star Home .... C 740 397-1706
Mount Vernon *(G-14785)*
Ohio Living .... C 513 681-4230
Cincinnati *(G-4156)*
Ohio Living .... B 614 224-1651
Columbus *(G-8271)*
Ohio Presbt Retirement Svcs .... B 330 746-2944
Youngstown *(G-20147)*
Ohio Presbt Retirement Svcs .... C 513 539-7391
Monroe *(G-14579)*
Ohio Presbt Retirement Svcs .... B 937 498-2391
Sidney *(G-16789)*
Ohio Valley Manor Inc .... C 937 392-4318
Ripley *(G-16401)*

S I C

Olmsted Manor Nursing Home ....C...... 440 250-4080
North Olmsted (G-15302)
On-Call Nursing Inc ....D...... 216 577-8890
Lakewood (G-12358)
Orchard Villa Inc ....C...... 419 697-4100
Oregon (G-15603)
Orion Care Services LLC............C...... 216 752-3600
Cleveland (G-6144)
Otterbein Portage Valley Inc ....C...... 888 749-4950
Pemberville (G-15806)
Otterbein Snior Lfstyle Chices ....B...... 513 933-5400
Lebanon (G-12492)
Palm Crest East Inc ....E...... 440 322-0726
Elyria (G-10553)
Park Creek Rtirement Cmnty Inc ....E...... 440 842-5100
Cleveland (G-6164)
Parkview Manor Inc ....D...... 937 296-1550
Englewood (G-10595)
Parma Care Center Inc ....C...... 216 661-6800
Cleveland (G-6175)
◆ Perio Inc ....E...... 614 791-1207
Dublin (G-10308)
Personacare of Ohio Inc............C...... 440 357-1311
Painesville (G-15733)
Pickaway Manor Inc............C...... 740 474-5400
Circleville (G-4844)
Places Inc ....D...... 937 461-4300
Dayton (G-9693)
Pleasant Lake Nursing Home ....B...... 440 842-2273
Cleveland (G-6221)
Pleasant View Nursing Home ....E...... 330 848-5028
Barberton (G-962)
Queen City Hospice LLC............E...... 513 510-4406
Cincinnati (G-4315)
Rae-Ann Holdings Inc............D...... 440 871-0500
Westlake (G-19397)
Raeann Inc............D...... 440 466-5733
Geneva (G-11245)
Renaissance House Inc............D...... 419 626-1110
Sandusky (G-16634)
RES-Care Inc ....E...... 740 968-0181
Flushing (G-10981)
RES-Care Inc ....E...... 330 627-7552
Carrollton (G-2575)
RES-Care Inc ....E...... 740 941-1178
Waverly (G-18823)
RES-Care Inc ....E...... 419 435-6620
Fostoria (G-11010)
RES-Care Inc ....D...... 740 446-7549
Gallipolis (G-11213)
RES-Care Inc ....E...... 330 453-4144
Canton (G-2457)
Rescare Ohio Inc............E...... 513 724-1177
Williamsburg (G-19496)
Residence of Chardon............D...... 440 286-2277
Chardon (G-2711)
Residential Concepts Inc ....E...... 513 724-6067
Williamsburg (G-19497)
Rest Haven Nursing Home Inc............C...... 937 548-1138
Greenville (G-11392)
Ridge Pleasant Valley Inc............C...... 440 845-0200
Cleveland (G-6325)
Ridgewood At Friendship Vlg............E...... 614 890-8285
Columbus (G-8530)
Rivers Bend Health Care LLC ....D...... 740 894-3476
South Point (G-16945)
Roman Cthlic Docese Youngstown......C...... 330 875-5562
Louisville (G-12973)
Rose Mary Johanna Grassell............C...... 216 481-4823
Cleveland (G-6340)
Royal Manor Health Care Inc ....E...... 216 752-3600
Cleveland (G-6345)
Saint Johns Villa ....C...... 330 627-4662
Carrollton (G-2576)
Salutary Providers Inc............C...... 440 964-8446
Ashtabula (G-753)
Samaritan Care Center & Villa ....D...... 330 725-4123
Medina (G-13998)
Sarah Moore Hlth Care Ctr Inc............D...... 740 362-9641
Delaware (G-10005)
Sateri Home Inc............D...... 330 758-8106
Youngstown (G-20204)
Senior Care Inc............D...... 330 721-2000
Medina (G-14000)
Sensi Care 3 ....E...... 440 323-6310
Elyria (G-10562)
Singleton Health Care Center ....E...... 216 231-0076
Cleveland (G-6410)
Sisters of Little ....C...... 216 464-1222
Warrensville Heights (G-18780)
Sisters of Little ....C...... 513 281-8001
Cincinnati (G-4486)
Society Handicapped Citz Medin............E...... 330 722-1900
Seville (G-16689)
Sociey For Handicapped Citizen ....C...... 330 725-7041
Seville (G-16690)
Spring Meadow Extended Care Ce......D...... 419 866-6124
Holland (G-11916)
Spring Meadow Extended Care Ce......D...... 419 866-6124
Mansfield (G-13246)
St Augustine Corporation ....B...... 216 939-7600
Lakewood (G-12363)
St Joseph Infant Maternity Hm ....C...... 513 563-2520
Cincinnati (G-4527)
St Luke Lutheran Community............D...... 330 644-3914
New Franklin (G-14913)
St Luke Lutheran Community............D...... 330 644-3914
New Franklin (G-14914)
Stein Hospice Services Inc ....D...... 419 663-3222
Norwalk (G-15456)
Stratford Commons Inc............C...... 440 914-0900
Solon (G-16902)
Summit Acres Inc............C...... 740 732-2364
Caldwell (G-2044)
Summit Facility Operations LLC ....D...... 330 633-0555
Tallmadge (G-17490)
Sunbridge Healthcare LLC............C...... 740 342-5161
New Lexington (G-14929)
Sunset House Inc............C...... 419 536-4645
Toledo (G-18055)
Sunshine Communities ....B...... 419 865-0251
Maumee (G-13857)
Supportcare Inc............C...... 216 446-2650
Independence (G-12126)
Swanton Hlth Care Rtrement Ctr ....D...... 419 825-1145
Swanton (G-17407)
The Maria-Joseph Center............B...... 937 278-2692
Dayton (G-9812)
The Villa At Lake MGT Co............D...... 440 599-1999
Conneaut (G-8960)
Triad Residential ....E...... 419 482-0711
Maumee (G-13863)
Twilight Gardens Healthcare............E...... 419 668-2086
Norwalk (G-15458)
Twin Maples Nursing Home ....E...... 740 596-5955
Mc Arthur (G-13891)
Twin Pines Retreat Care Center............E...... 330 688-5553
Stow (G-17237)
United Cerebral Palsy............D...... 216 381-9993
Cleveland (G-6569)
United Church Homes Inc............C...... 937 878-0262
Fairborn (G-10684)
United Church Homes Inc............D...... 740 286-7551
Jackson (G-12181)
United Church Homes Inc............C...... 513 922-1440
Cincinnati (G-4677)
United Church Homes Inc............C...... 937 426-8481
Beavercreek (G-1239)
United Church Homes Inc............C...... 419 294-4973
Upper Sandusky (G-18414)
University Hospitals Health ....E...... 440 285-4040
Chardon (G-2722)
University Manor Hlth Care Ctr............C...... 216 721-1400
Cleveland (G-6599)
Vancare Inc............C...... 937 898-4202
Vandalia (G-18549)
Vienna Enterprises Inc ....E...... 937 568-4524
South Vienna (G-16949)
Vista Centre ....D...... 330 424-5852
Lisbon (G-12806)
Vitas Healthcare Corporation ....D...... 513 742-6310
Cincinnati (G-4762)
Voca of Ohio ....E...... 419 435-5836
Fostoria (G-11014)
Voiers Enterprises Inc ....E...... 740 259-2838
Mc Dermott (G-13896)
Volunters Amer Care Facilities ....C...... 419 225-9040
Lima (G-12774)
Walnut Hills Inc ....C...... 330 852-2457
Walnut Creek (G-18633)
Warren County Board Devlpmntal ....E...... 513 925-1813
Lebanon (G-12514)
Washington Manor Inc ....E...... 937 433-3441
Dayton (G-9867)
Weber Health Care Center Inc ....C...... 440 647-2088
Wellington (G-18845)
Wedgewood Estates............E...... 419 756-7400
Mansfield (G-13262)
Wellington Place LLC ....D...... 440 734-9933
North Olmsted (G-15316)
Wesley Ridge Inc............C...... 614 759-0023
Reynoldsburg (G-16337)
West Liberty Care Center Inc............C...... 937 465-5065
West Liberty (G-19122)
West Park Retirement Community............C...... 513 451-8900
Cincinnati (G-4783)
Western Rsrve Msonic Cmnty Inc............C...... 330 721-3000
Medina (G-14014)
Wexner Heritage Village............B...... 614 231-4900
Columbus (G-8894)
Willglo Services Inc............E...... 614 443-3020
Columbus (G-8903)
Willow Brook Chrstn Cmmunities............C...... 740 369-0048
Delaware (G-10016)
Windsor House Inc ....C...... 330 549-9259
Columbiana (G-6796)
Windsor Medical Center Inc............D...... 330 499-8300
Canton (G-2536)
Woodside Village Care Center............D...... 419 947-2015
Mount Gilead (G-14736)
Zandex Inc ....E...... 740 695-3281
Saint Clairsville (G-16512)
Zandex Inc ....E...... 740 454-1400
Zanesville (G-20373)
Zandex Inc ....C...... 740 872-0809
New Concord (G-14905)
Zandex Inc ....C...... 740 454-9769
Zanesville (G-20375)
Zandex Inc ....C...... 740 695-7233
Saint Clairsville (G-16513)
Zandex Inc ....D...... 740 967-1111
Johnstown (G-12205)
Zandex Inc ....D...... 740 454-6823
Zanesville (G-20376)
Zandex Health Care Corporation............C...... 740 452-4636
Zanesville (G-20377)
Zandex Health Care Corporation............C...... 740 454-9769
Zanesville (G-20378)
Zandex Health Care Corporation............C...... 740 695-7233
Saint Clairsville (G-16514)
Zandex Health Care Corporation............E...... 740 454-1400
Zanesville (G-20379)
Zandex Health Care Corporation............D...... 740 454-1400
Johnstown (G-12206)
Zandex Health Care Corporation............C...... 740 454-1400
New Concord (G-14906)
Zandex Health Care Corporation............C...... 740 454-9747
Zanesville (G-20380)
Zusman Community Hospice ....E...... 614 559-0350
Columbus (G-8939)

8059 Nursing & Personal Care Facilities, NEC

Ability Matters LLC ....E...... 614 214-9652
Hilliard (G-11739)
Access Home Care LLC ....E...... 937 224-9991
Dayton (G-9205)
Accurate Healthcare Inc............E...... 513 208-6988
West Chester (G-19040)
Age Line Inc............E...... 216 941-9990
Cleveland (G-4912)
Alpha Nursing Homes Inc ....D...... 740 622-2074
Coshocton (G-8997)
Angel Hearts Home Health Inc............C...... 937 263-6194
Moraine (G-14622)
Antioch Cnnction Canton Ml LLC............E...... 614 531-9285
Pickerington (G-15947)
Antioch Salem Fields Frederick ....E...... 614 531-9285
Pickerington (G-15948)
Apostolic Christian Home Inc............D...... 330 927-1010
Rittman (G-16403)
Arbors West LLC............D...... 614 879-7661
West Jefferson (G-19103)
Bel Air Care Center ....D...... 330 821-3939
Alliance (G-518)
Berea Lk Twers Rtirement Cmnty............E...... 440 243-9050
Berea (G-1416)
Birchaven Village............C...... 419 424-3000
Findlay (G-10869)
Blue Ash Healthcare Group Inc ....E...... 513 793-3362
Cincinnati (G-3060)
Boy-Ko Management Inc ....E...... 513 677-4900
Loveland (G-12979)
Boyds Kinsman Home Inc............E...... 330 876-5581
Kinsman (G-12318)
Brethren Care Village LLC ....D...... 419 289-1585
Ashland (G-660)
Brewster Parke Inc............D...... 330 767-4179
Brewster (G-1809)
Briarwood Ltd............D...... 330 688-1828
Stow (G-17193)

Bristol Village Homes	E	740 947-2118	
Waverly (G-18814)			
Broken Arrow Inc	E	419 562-3480	
Bucyrus (G-1977)			
Brookdale Deer Park	D	513 745-7600	
Cincinnati (G-3077)			
Brookdale Lving Cmmunities Inc	E	937 399-1216	
Springfield (G-17002)			
Brookdale Senior Living Commun	E	330 829-0180	
Alliance (G-519)			
Brookdale Senior Living Commun	E	937 203-8443	
Beavercreek (G-1208)			
Brookdale Senior Living Commun	E	937 548-6800	
Greenville (G-11367)			
Brookdale Senior Living Inc	E	419 756-5599	
Mansfield (G-13146)			
Brookdale Senior Living Inc	D	855 308-2438	
Cincinnati (G-3078)			
Brookdale Senior Living Inc	E	513 745-9292	
Cincinnati (G-3079)			
Brookdale Senior Living Inc	D	330 666-7011	
Akron (G-110)			
Brookdale Senior Living Inc	E	440 892-4200	
Westlake (G-19324)			
Brookdale Senior Living Inc	D	513 745-7600	
Cincinnati (G-3080)			
Brookdale Snior Lving Cmmnties	E	740 366-0005	
Newark (G-15015)			
Brookdale Snior Lving Cmmnties	E	937 832-8500	
Englewood (G-10580)			
Brookdale Snior Lving Cmmnties	E	419 354-5300	
Bowling Green (G-1726)			
Brookdale Snior Lving Cmmnties	E	740 681-9903	
Lancaster (G-12373)			
Brookdale Snior Lving Cmmnties	E	419 423-4440	
Findlay (G-10884)			
Brookdale Snior Lving Cmmnties	E	330 249-1071	
Austintown (G-856)			
Brookdale Snior Lving Cmmnties	E	419 756-5599	
Mansfield (G-13147)			
Brookdale Snior Lving Cmmnties	E	937 773-0500	
Piqua (G-15998)			
Brookdale Snior Lving Cmmnties	E	330 793-0085	
Youngstown (G-19976)			
Brookside Extended Care Center	C	513 398-1020	
Mason (G-13547)			
Brookview Healthcare Ctr	D	419 784-1014	
Defiance (G-9905)			
Bryant Health Center Inc	C	740 532-6188	
Ironton (G-12147)			
Buckeye Community Services Inc	C	740 941-1639	
Waverly (G-18815)			
Capital Health Services Inc	E	937 278-0404	
Dayton (G-9275)			
Capital Senior Living	E	440 356-5444	
Rocky River (G-16425)			
Careworks of Ohio Inc	B	614 792-1085	
Dublin (G-10161)			
Carriage Court Company Inc	E	740 654-4422	
Lancaster (G-12376)			
Carroll Golden Age Retreat	E	330 627-4665	
Carrollton (G-2561)			
Center Ridge Nursing Home Inc	C	440 808-5500	
North Ridgeville (G-15324)			
Center Street Cmnty Clinic Inc	E	740 751-6380	
Marion (G-13410)			
Chcc Home Health Care	E	330 759-4069	
Austintown (G-857)			
Columbus Alzheimers Care Ctr	C	614 459-7050	
Columbus (G-7254)			
Columbus Ctr For Humn Svcs Inc	E	614 245-8180	
New Albany (G-14850)			
Columbus Ctr For Humn Svcs Inc	C	614 641-2904	
Columbus (G-7273)			
Community Concepts Inc	C	513 398-8181	
Mason (G-13565)			
Concord Hlth Rhabilitation Ctr	E	740 574-8441	
Wheelersburg (G-19432)			
Consulate Management Co LLC	D	740 259-2351	
Lucasville (G-13046)			
Consumer Support Services Inc	B	740 788-8257	
Newark (G-15024)			
Consumer Support Services Inc	D	330 764-4785	
Medina (G-13922)			
Contining Hlthcare Sltions Inc.	E	216 772-1105	
Middleburg Heights (G-14251)			
Country Acres of Wayne County	E	330 698-2031	
Wooster (G-19713)			
Country Club Center Homes Inc.	D	330 343-6351	
Dover (G-10071)			

Country Club Retirement Center	D	440 992-0022	
Ashtabula (G-731)			
Country Club Retirement Center	C	740 671-9330	
Bellaire (G-1333)			
Country Meadow Care Center LLC	E	419 886-3922	
Bellville (G-1391)			
Countryview Assistant Living	E	740 489-5351	
Lore City (G-12952)			
County of Auglaize	C	419 738-3816	
Wapakoneta (G-18640)			
County of Henry	E	419 592-8075	
Napoleon (G-14803)			
County of Richland	B	419 774-4200	
Mansfield (G-13159)			
County of Shelby	C	937 492-6900	
Sidney (G-16771)			
County of Wayne	D	330 262-1786	
Wooster (G-19715)			
County of Wood	B	419 686-6951	
Portage (G-16122)			
County of Wyandot	D	419 294-1714	
Upper Sandusky (G-18404)			
Crystal Care Centers Inc	D	419 747-2666	
Mansfield (G-13162)			
Crystalwood Inc	D	513 605-1000	
Cincinnati (G-3383)			
Csi Managed Care Inc	D	440 717-1700	
Brecksville (G-1778)			
Deaconess Long Term Care of MI	A	513 487-3600	
Cincinnati (G-3412)			
Dobbins Nursing Home Inc	C	513 553-4139	
New Richmond (G-14993)			
Dublin Geriatric Care Co LP	E	614 761-1188	
Dublin (G-10207)			
East Carroll Nursing Home	D	330 627-6900	
Carrollton (G-2567)			
East Galbraith Health Care Ctr	B	513 984-5220	
Cincinnati (G-3471)			
Echoing Hills Village Inc	E	937 237-7881	
Dayton (G-9407)			
Echoing Hills Village Inc	D	440 986-3085	
South Amherst (G-16921)			
Elizabeth Scott Inc	C	419 865-3002	
Maumee (G-13784)			
Elms Retirement Village Inc	D	440 647-2414	
Wellington (G-18840)			
Encore Healthcare LLC	D	330 769-2015	
Seville (G-16685)			
Evangelical Lutheran	D	419 365-5115	
Arlington (G-642)			
First Choice Medical Staffing	C	216 521-2222	
Cleveland (G-5531)			
First Community Village	B	614 324-4455	
Columbus (G-7585)			
Franciscan At St Leonard	B	937 433-0480	
Dayton (G-9448)			
Friendship Vlg of Dublin Ohio	D	614 764-1600	
Dublin (G-10232)			
Gardens Western Reserve Inc	D	330 342-9100	
Streetsboro (G-17252)			
Gaslite Villa Convalescent Ctr	D	330 494-4500	
Canal Fulton (G-2095)			
Gentiva Health Services Inc	D	419 887-6700	
Maumee (G-13795)			
Gillette Associates LP	D	330 372-1960	
Warren (G-18709)			
Golden Living LLC	D	419 599-4070	
Napoleon (G-14807)			
Golden Living LLC	D	419 227-2154	
Lima (G-12644)			
Golden Living LLC	C	440 247-4200	
Chagrin Falls (G-2647)			
Golden Living LLC	C	614 861-6666	
Columbus (G-7678)			
Golden Living LLC	C	440 256-8100	
Willoughby (G-19527)			
Golden Living LLC	D	330 297-5781	
Ravenna (G-16244)			
Golden Living LLC	C	330 762-6486	
Akron (G-239)			
Golden Living LLC	D	330 335-1558	
Wadsworth (G-18596)			
Golden Living LLC	D	330 725-3393	
Medina (G-13944)			
Governors Pointe LLC	E	440 205-1570	
Mentor (G-14053)			
Guardian Elder Care Columbus	D	614 868-9306	
Columbus (G-7701)			
Guernsey Health Enterprises	A	740 439-3561	
Cambridge (G-2072)			

H C F Inc	C	740 289-2528	
Piketon (G-15976)			
H C R Corp	D	419 472-0076	
Toledo (G-17776)			
Hamlet Village In Chagrin FLS	D	440 247-4200	
Chagrin Falls (G-2648)			
Hampton Woods Nursing Ctr Inc	E	330 707-1400	
Poland (G-16084)			
Harborside Healthcare NW Ohio	C	419 636-5071	
Bryan (G-1959)			
Hardin County Home	E	419 673-0961	
Kenton (G-12280)			
Harrison Pavilion	E	513 662-5800	
Cincinnati (G-3682)			
Hcf of Findlay Inc	D	419 999-2010	
Findlay (G-10920)			
Hcf of Fox Run Inc	D	419 424-0832	
Findlay (G-10921)			
Hcf of Washington Inc	E	419 999-2010	
Wshngtn CT Hs. (G-19875)			
Heartland Home Care LLC	D	419 252-5500	
Toledo (G-17795)			
Heath Nursing Care Center	C	740 522-1171	
Newark (G-15040)			
Heinzerling Foundation	C	614 272-8888	
Columbus (G-7735)			
Heinzerling Foundation	E	614 272-2000	
Columbus (G-7736)			
Home Health Connection Inc	E	614 839-4545	
Worthington (G-19815)			
Hospice of North Central Ohio	E	419 281-7107	
Ashland (G-675)			
Hospice of The Western Reserve	D	440 357-5833	
Willoughby Hills (G-19589)			
Hospice of The Western Reserve	E	440 414-7349	
Westlake (G-19351)			
Hospice Tuscarawas County Inc	C	330 343-7605	
New Philadelphia (G-14965)			
Inn At Hillenvale Ltd	D	740 392-8245	
Mount Vernon (G-14769)			
J E F Inc	D	513 921-4130	
Cincinnati (G-3794)			
J W J Investments Inc	C	419 643-3161	
Delphos (G-10028)			
Jacobs Dwelling Nursing Home	E	740 824-3635	
Coshocton (G-9020)			
Jennings Ctr For Older Adults	B	216 581-2900	
Cleveland (G-5789)			
Judson	D	216 791-2004	
Cleveland (G-5808)			
Judson Palmer Home Corp	E	419 422-9656	
Findlay (G-10931)			
Just In Time Care Inc	E	614 985-3555	
Columbus (G-7879)			
Karrington Operating Co Inc	D	614 324-5951	
Columbus (G-7884)			
Kingston Healthcare Company	E	419 247-2880	
Toledo (G-17840)			
Kingston Healthcare Company	C	440 967-1800	
Vermilion (G-18555)			
Koinonia Homes Inc	C	216 351-5361	
Cleveland (G-5836)			
L JC Home Care LLC	D	614 495-0276	
Dublin (G-10265)			
Laurel Health Care Company	C	614 885-0408	
Worthington (G-19821)			
Lcd Home Health Agency LLC	E	513 497-0441	
Hamilton (G-11623)			
Levering Management Inc	D	740 369-6400	
Delaware (G-9995)			
Levering Management Inc	E	419 768-2401	
Chesterville (G-2748)			
Liberty Vlg Senior Communities	E	614 889-5002	
Dublin (G-10270)			
Lima Cnvlscent HM Fndation Inc	C	419 227-5450	
Lima (G-12677)			
Lincoln Park Associates II LP	C	937 297-4300	
Dayton (G-9568)			
Lutheran Memorial Home Inc	C	419 502-5700	
Toledo (G-17873)			
Lutheran Village At Wolf Creek	C	419 861-2233	
Holland (G-11893)			
Mahoning Vly Infusioncare Inc	C	330 759-9487	
Youngstown (G-20111)			
Maplewood At Bath Creek LLC	D	234 208-9872	
Cuyahoga Falls (G-9111)			
Marion Manor	D	740 387-9545	
Marion (G-13443)			
Marymount Health Care Systems	E	216 332-1100	
Cleveland (G-5919)			

Mayflower Nursing Home Inc	C	330 492-7131	Canton (G-2393)

Mayflower Nursing Home Inc ....C....... 330 492-7131
  Canton (G-2393)
McV Health Care Facilities ....C....... 513 398-1486
  Mason (G-13617)
Medina Medical Investors Ltd.............C....... 330 483-3131
  Medina (G-13978)
Mennonite Memorial Home ....B....... 419 358-1015
  Bluffton (G-1693)
Mercer Residential Services ....E....... 419 586-4709
  Celina (G-2603)
Mercy Health West Park ....C....... 513 451-8900
  Cincinnati (G-4033)
Miami Valley Urgent Care..................E....... 937 252-2000
  Dayton (G-9627)
Mikouis Enterprise Inc ....D....... 330 424-1418
  Lisbon (G-12804)
Mill Run Care Center LLC ....D....... 614 527-3000
  Hilliard (G-11798)
Minamyer Residential Mr/Dd Svc ......E....... 614 802-0190
  Columbus (G-8089)
Minford Retirement Center LLC..........E....... 740 820-2821
  Minford (G-14526)
Mkjb Inc ....C....... 513 851-8400
  West Chester (G-18975)
Mohun Health Care Center ....E....... 614 416-6132
  Columbus (G-8095)
Morning View Delaware Inc...............C....... 740 965-3984
  Sunbury (G-17391)
Msab Park Creek LLC ....E....... 440 842-5100
  Rocky River (G-16441)
Mt Healthy Christian Home Inc ....C....... 513 931-5000
  Cincinnati (G-4081)
National Church Residences ....C....... 614 451-2151
  Columbus (G-8130)
Nentwick Convalescent Home.............E....... 330 385-5001
  East Liverpool (G-10409)
New Concord Health Center ....C....... 740 826-4135
  New Concord (G-14902)
Niles Residential Care LLC ....D....... 216 727-3996
  Niles (G-15164)
North Park Retirement Cmnty.............E....... 216 267-0555
  Cleveland (G-6079)
Norwood Health Care Center LLC.......D....... 513 351-0153
  Cincinnati (G-4135)
Nursing Care MGT Amer Inc ....D....... 740 927-9888
  Pataskala (G-15786)
Nursing Care MGT Amer Inc ....D....... 513 793-5092
  Cincinnati (G-4142)
Nursing Resources Corp ....C....... 419 333-3000
  Maumee (G-13825)
Oakwood Health Care Svcs Inc ....C....... 440 439-7976
  Cleveland (G-6109)
Ohio Presbt Retirement Svcs ....B....... 937 498-2391
  Sidney (G-16789)
Ohio Presbt Retirement Svcs ....C....... 937 415-5666
  Dayton (G-9673)
Ohio Valley Manor Inc........................C....... 937 392-4318
  Ripley (G-16401)
Olmsted Manor Retirement Prpts........E....... 440 250-4080
  Westlake (G-19387)
On-Call Nursing Inc ....D....... 216 577-8890
  Lakewood (G-12358)
Orchard Villa Inc ....C....... 419 697-4100
  Oregon (G-15603)
Otterbein Snior Lfstyle Chices ....C....... 513 260-7690
  Middletown (G-14352)
Overlook House ....E....... 216 795-3550
  Cleveland (G-6150)
Park Haven Inc ....E....... 440 992-9441
  Ashtabula (G-751)
Partners of City View LLC ....C....... 216 361-1414
  Cleveland (G-6177)
Prime Home Care LLC ....E....... 419 535-1414
  Toledo (G-17988)
Pristine Senior Living of ....D....... 419 935-0148
  Willard (G-19486)
Provider Services Inc ....D....... 614 888-2021
  Columbus (G-8476)
Rae-Ann Enterprises Inc ....D....... 440 249-5092
  Cleveland (G-6280)
Rae-Ann Holdings Inc ....D....... 440 871-0500
  Westlake (G-19397)
Rae-Ann Holdings Inc ....D....... 440 871-5181
  Cleveland (G-6281)
Red Carpet Health Care Center ....C....... 740 439-4401
  Cambridge (G-2081)
Regency Park ....D....... 330 682-2273
  Orrville (G-15645)
Regency Park Nursing & Rehab...........D....... 330 682-2273
  Orrville (G-15646)

Residence At Kensington Place ....C....... 513 863-4218
  Hamilton (G-11638)
Rest Haven Nursing Home Inc............C....... 937 548-1138
  Greenville (G-11392)
Rittenhouse ....E....... 513 423-2322
  Middletown (G-14324)
RMS of Ohio Inc ....E....... 513 841-0990
  Cincinnati (G-4386)
Roselawn Health Services Corp ....E....... 330 823-0618
  Alliance (G-550)
Royalton Senior Living Inc ....E....... 440 582-4111
  North Royalton (G-15366)
Salutary Providers Inc ....C....... 440 964-8446
  Ashtabula (G-753)
Samaritan Care Center & Villa ....D....... 330 725-4123
  Medina (G-13998)
Sarah Moore Hlth Care Ctr Inc ....D....... 740 362-9641
  Delaware (G-10005)
Schoenbrunn Healthcare ....D....... 330 339-3595
  New Philadelphia (G-14980)
Senior Care Inc ....E....... 937 291-3211
  Miamisburg (G-14217)
Senior Lifestyle Corporation..............D....... 513 777-4457
  West Chester (G-19002)
Serenity Center Inc ....C....... 614 891-1111
  Columbus (G-8621)
Shiloh Group ....C....... 937 833-2219
  Brookville (G-1917)
Society of The Transfiguration ....E....... 513 771-7462
  Cincinnati (G-4501)
Steubenville Country CLB Manor.........D....... 740 266-6118
  Steubenville (G-17171)
Stewart Lodge Inc ....D....... 440 417-1898
  Madison (G-13109)
Stratford Commons Inc ....C....... 440 914-0900
  Solon (G-16902)
Summit At Park Hills LLC ....E....... 317 462-8048
  Fairborn (G-10683)
Sumner On Ridgewood ....E....... 330 664-1360
  Copley (G-8977)
Sunrise Senior Living Inc ....D....... 614 457-3500
  Upper Arlington (G-18402)
Sunrise Senior Living Inc ....E....... 614 846-6500
  Worthington (G-19854)
Susan A Smith Crystal Care ....E....... 419 747-2666
  Butler (G-2022)
The Villa At Lake MGT Co ....D....... 440 599-1999
  Conneaut (G-8960)
Traditions At Mill Run ....E....... 614 771-0100
  Hilliard (G-11823)
Traditions of Chillicothe ....E....... 740 773-8107
  Chillicothe (G-2831)
United Cerebral Palsy ....D....... 216 381-9993
  Cleveland (G-6559)
United Church Homes Inc ....C....... 419 294-4973
  Upper Sandusky (G-18414)
United Rest Homes Inc ....E....... 440 354-2131
  Painesville (G-15745)
University Hospitals Health ....E....... 440 285-4040
  Chardon (G-2722)
Uvmc Nursing Care Inc ....C....... 937 473-2075
  Covington (G-9049)
Valley View Alzhimers Care Ctr ....D....... 740 998-2948
  Frankfort (G-11019)
Viaquest Home Health LLC ....E....... 800 645-3267
  Dublin (G-10364)
Vienna Enterprises Inc ....E....... 937 568-4524
  South Vienna (G-16949)
Wedgewood Estates ....E....... 419 756-7400
  Mansfield (G-13262)
Wesley Ridge Inc ....C....... 614 759-0023
  Reynoldsburg (G-16337)
Western Rsrve Msonic Cmnty Inc ....C....... 330 721-3000
  Medina (G-14014)
Whetstone Care Center LLC ....C....... 614 457-1100
  Columbus (G-8895)
Whetstone Care Center LLC ....C....... 740 474-6036
  Circleville (G-4853)
Whispering Hills Care Center ....E....... 740 392-3982
  Mount Vernon (G-14792)
Williamsburg of Cincinnati Mgt ....C....... 513 948-2308
  Cincinnati (G-4798)
Windsor House Inc ....C....... 330 759-7858
  Youngstown (G-20247)
Windsor Medical Center Inc ....D....... 330 499-8300
  Canton (G-2536)
Windsorwood Place Inc ....E....... 740 623-4600
  Coshocton (G-9031)
Youngstown Area Jwish Fdration ....D....... 330 746-1076
  Youngstown (G-20257)

Zandex Health Care Corporation ....E....... 740 454-1400
  Zanesville (G-20379)
Zandex Health Care Corporation ....D....... 740 454-1400
  Johnstown (G-12206)
Zandex Health Care Corporation ....C....... 740 695-7233
  Saint Clairsville (G-16514)
Zandex Health Care Corporation ....C....... 740 454-9747
  Zanesville (G-20380)

8062 General Medical & Surgical Hospitals

Acute Care Specialty Hospital ....A....... 330 363-4860
  Canton (G-2172)
Adams County Regional Med Ctr ....C....... 937 386-3001
  Seaman (G-16665)
Adena Health System ....E....... 740 779-7201
  Chillicothe (G-2750)
Adena Health System ....A....... 740 779-7360
  Chillicothe (G-2751)
Adena Health System ....C....... 740 779-7500
  Wshngtn CT Hs (G-19863)
Adena Health System ....C....... 740 420-3000
  Circleville (G-4824)
Adena Health System ....C....... 937 981-9444
  Greenfield (G-11358)
Adena Health System ....C....... 740 779-8995
  Chillicothe (G-2752)
Adena Health System ....E....... 740 779-4801
  Chillicothe (G-2753)
Ado Health Services Inc ....D....... 330 629-2888
  Youngstown (G-19946)
Affiliates In Oral & Maxlofcl ....E....... 513 829-8080
  Fairfield (G-10693)
Akron City Hospital Inc ....A....... 330 253-5046
  Akron (G-32)
Akron General Medical Center.............C....... 330 344-1980
  Akron (G-44)
Akron General Medical Center.............C....... 330 344-1444
  Akron (G-45)
Akron General Medical Center.............C....... 330 665-8000
  Akron (G-46)
Akron Radiology Inc ....C....... 330 375-3043
  Akron (G-53)
Allianalce Hospitalist Group ....E....... 330 823-5626
  Alliance (G-514)
Alliance Citizens Health Assn..............A....... 330 596-6000
  Alliance (G-515)
Anesthesiology Consultant Inc ....E....... 614 566-9983
  Columbus (G-6949)
Ashtabula County Medical Ctr ....A....... 440 997-2262
  Ashtabula (G-715)
Ashtabula County Medical Ctr ....C....... 440 997-6960
  Ashtabula (G-716)
Atrium Medical Center ....E....... 513 420-5013
  Middletown (G-14289)
Aultman Health Foundation ....C....... 330 305-6999
  Canton (G-2200)
Aultman Health Foundation ....A....... 330 682-3010
  Orrville (G-15624)
Aultman Hospital ....A....... 330 452-9911
  Canton (G-2202)
Aultman Hospital ....B....... 330 452-9911
  Canton (G-2203)
Aultman Hospital ....A....... 330 363-6262
  Canton (G-2204)
Aultman Hospital ....E....... 330 452-2273
  Canton (G-2205)
Aultman North Inc ....E....... 330 305-6999
  Canton (G-2207)
Auxiliary Bd Fairview Gen Hosp...........A....... 216 476-7000
  Cleveland (G-5026)
Barberton Healthcare Group LLC...........E....... 330 615-3717
  Wadsworth (G-18591)
Barnesville Hospital Assn Inc ....D....... 740 425-3941
  Barnesville (G-975)
Bay Park Community Hospital................D....... 567 585-9600
  Toledo (G-17606)
Beavercreek Medical Center ....D....... 937 558-3000
  Beavercreek (G-1132)
Beavercreek Medical Center ....D....... 937 558-3000
  Beavercreek (G-1133)
Beckett Springs LLC ....E....... 513 942-9500
  West Chester (G-18874)
Bellevue Hospital ....B....... 419 483-4040
  Bellevue (G-1373)
Bellevue Hospital ....B....... 419 547-0074
  Bellevue (G-1374)
Belmont Bhc Pines Hospital Inc...........C....... 330 759-2700
  Youngstown (G-19964)
Belmont Community Hospital.................B....... 740 671-1200
  Bellaire (G-1330)

Bethesda Hospital Inc	E	513 894-8888	Fairfield Township *(G-10801)*
Bethesda Hospital Inc	A	513 569-6100	Cincinnati *(G-3047)*
Bethesda Hospital Inc	A	513 745-1111	Cincinnati *(G-3048)*
Bethesda Hospital Inc	E	513 563-1505	Cincinnati *(G-3049)*
Bethesda Hospital Association	A	740 454-4000	Zanesville *(G-20281)*
Blanchard Vly Rgional Hlth Ctr	C	419 427-0809	Findlay *(G-10878)*
▲ **Blanchard Vly Rgional Hlth Ctr**	A	419 423-4500	Findlay *(G-10879)*
Blue Chp Srgcl Ctr Ptns LLC	D	513 561-8900	Cincinnati *(G-3063)*
Bon Secours Health System	E	740 966-3116	Johnstown *(G-12198)*
Bridgeshome Health Care	E	330 764-1000	Medina *(G-13913)*
Brown Memorial Hospital	B	440 593-1131	Conneaut *(G-8952)*
Bucyrus Community Hospital Inc	C	419 562-4677	Bucyrus *(G-1979)*
Bucyrus Community Hospital LLC	D	419 562-4677	Bucyrus *(G-1980)*
Butler Cnty Ancillary Svcs LLC	E	513 454-1400	Fairfield Township *(G-10804)*
Caep-Dunlap LLC	E	330 456-2695	Canton *(G-2224)*
Canton Altman Emrgncy Physcans	E	330 456-2695	Canton *(G-2226)*
Center For Health Affairs	D	800 362-2628	Cleveland *(G-5152)*
Center For Spinal Disorders	E	419 383-4878	Toledo *(G-17642)*
Change Healthcare Tech Enabled	D	614 566-5861	Columbus *(G-7179)*
Charles Mercy Hlth-St Hospita	D	419 696-7200	Oregon *(G-15587)*
Chester West Medical Center	A	513 298-3000	West Chester *(G-18885)*
Childrens Hosp Med Ctr Akron	A	330 425-3344	Twinsburg *(G-18252)*
Childrens Hosp Med Ctr Akron	E	330 676-1020	Kent *(G-12220)*
Childrens Hosp Med Ctr Akron	A	330 308-5432	New Philadelphia *(G-14949)*
Childrens Hospital	E	513 636-4051	Cincinnati *(G-3183)*
Childrens Hospital Medical Ctr	A	513 541-4500	Cincinnati *(G-3184)*
Childrens Hospital Medical Ctr	A	513 803-9600	Liberty Township *(G-12580)*
Childrens Hospital Medical Ctr	A	513 636-4200	Cincinnati *(G-3185)*
Childrens Hospital Medical Ctr	A	513 803-1751	Cincinnati *(G-3186)*
Childrens Hospital Medical Ctr	A	513 636-4200	Cincinnati *(G-3187)*
Childrens Hospital Medical Ctr	A	513 636-4366	Cincinnati *(G-3188)*
Childrens Hospital Medical Ctr	A	513 636-8778	Cincinnati *(G-3193)*
Chirst Hospital Surgery Center	E	513 272-3448	Cincinnati *(G-3195)*
Christ Hospital	C	513 347-2300	Cincinnati *(G-3198)*
Christ Hospital	E	513 721-8272	Cincinnati *(G-3199)*
Christ Hospital	E	513 564-4000	Cincinnati *(G-3200)*
Christ Hospital	C	513 561-7809	Cincinnati *(G-3201)*
Christ Hospital	B	513 688-1111	Cincinnati *(G-3202)*
Christ Hospital	C	513 564-1340	Cincinnati *(G-3203)*
Christ Hospital	C	513 651-0094	Cincinnati *(G-3204)*
Christ Hospital	B	513 272-3448	Cincinnati *(G-3205)*
Christ Hospital	E	513 585-0050	Cincinnati *(G-3206)*
Christ Hospital	C	513 755-4700	West Chester *(G-18886)*
Christ Hospital	A	513 585-2000	Cincinnati *(G-3207)*
Christ Hospital	D	513 631-3300	Cincinnati *(G-3208)*
Christ Hospital	D	513 351-0800	Cincinnati *(G-3209)*
Christ Hospital	C	513 791-5200	Cincinnati *(G-3210)*
Christ Hospital Spine Surgery	E	513 619-5899	Cincinnati *(G-3211)*
City Hospital Association	A	330 385-7200	East Liverpool *(G-10399)*
City of Wooster	A	330 263-8100	Wooster *(G-19705)*
▲ **Cleveland Clinic Foundation**	A	216 636-8335	Cleveland *(G-5236)*
Cleveland Clinic Foundation	A	440 282-6669	Lorain *(G-12892)*
Cleveland Clinic Foundation	A	800 223-2273	Cleveland *(G-5240)*
Cleveland Clinic Foundation	D	419 609-2812	Sandusky *(G-16587)*
Cleveland Clinic Foundation	A	216 444-5755	Cleveland *(G-5241)*
Cleveland Clinic Foundation	A	440 327-1050	North Ridgeville *(G-15327)*
Cleveland Clinic Foundation	A	216 448-0116	Beachwood *(G-1046)*
Cleveland Clinic Foundation	A	440 986-4000	Broadview Heights *(G-1827)*
Cleveland Clinic Foundation	D	216 444-5757	Cleveland *(G-5245)*
Cleveland Clinic Foundation	A	216 444-2200	Cleveland *(G-5246)*
Cleveland Clinic Foundation	E	330 287-4930	Wooster *(G-19707)*
Cleveland Clinic Foundation	D	216 444-2820	Cleveland *(G-5237)*
Cleveland Clinic Foundation	D	440 988-5651	Lorain *(G-12893)*
Cleveland Clinic Health System	E	440 449-4500	Cleveland *(G-5247)*
Cleveland Clinic Health System	E	216 692-7555	Cleveland *(G-5248)*
Cleveland Clinic Lerner Colleg	D	216 445-3853	Cleveland *(G-5249)*
Clevelnd Clnc Hlth Systm East	E	330 287-4830	Wooster *(G-19709)*
Clevelnd Clnc Hlth Systm East	E	330 468-0190	Northfield *(G-15376)*
Clinical Research Center	D	513 636-4412	Cincinnati *(G-3308)*
Clinton Memorial Hospital	A	937 382-6611	Wilmington *(G-19613)*
Columbia-Csa/Hs Greater Canton	A	330 489-1000	Canton *(G-2260)*
Community Health Ptnrs Reg Fou	A	440 960-4000	Lorain *(G-12896)*
Community Hlth Ptnr Reg Hlth S	A	440 960-4000	Lorain *(G-12897)*
Community Hospital of Bedford	B	440 735-3900	Bedford *(G-1274)*
Community Hospitals	B	419 636-1131	Bryan *(G-1954)*
Community Hsptals Wllness Ctrs	D	419 485-3154	Montpelier *(G-14611)*
Community Hsptals Wllness Ctrs	D	419 445-2015	Archbold *(G-629)*
Community Hsptals Wllness Ctrs	C	419 636-1131	Bryan *(G-1955)*
Community Memorial Hospital	C	419 542-6692	Hicksville *(G-11726)*
Community Mercy Hlth Partners	E	937 523-6670	Springfield *(G-17019)*
Copc Hospitals	E	614 268-8164	Columbus *(G-7368)*
County of Holmes	C	330 674-1015	Millersburg *(G-14471)*
Dayton Osteopathic Hospital	A	937 762-1629	Dayton *(G-9374)*
Deaconess Hospital of Cincinna	D	513 559-2100	Cincinnati *(G-3410)*
Defiance Hospital Inc	B	419 782-6955	Defiance *(G-9911)*
Delphos Ambulatory Care Center	E	419 692-2662	Delphos *(G-10024)*
Doctors Hospital Cleveland Inc	C	740 753-7300	Nelsonville *(G-14829)*
Doctors Ohiohealth Corporation	A	614 544-5424	Columbus *(G-7464)*
Elmwood of Green Springs Ltd	D	419 639-2626	Green Springs *(G-11352)*
Emh Regional Medical Center	D	440 988-6800	Avon *(G-880)*
Encompass Health Corporation	E	205 970-4869	Springfield *(G-17034)*
Euclid Hospital	D	216 531-9000	Euclid *(G-10633)*
Fairfield Medical Center	A	740 687-8000	Lancaster *(G-12399)*
Fairview Hospital	E	216 476-7000	Cleveland *(G-5508)*
Fairview Hospital	D	440 871-1063	Westlake *(G-19341)*
Fayette County Memorial Hosp	C	740 335-1210	Wshngtn CT Hs *(G-19871)*
Firelands Regional Health Sys	A	419 557-7400	Sandusky *(G-16604)*
Firelands Regional Health Sys	E	419 332-5524	Fremont *(G-11072)*
▲ **Fisher-Titus Medical Center**	A	419 668-8101	Norwalk *(G-15438)*
Flower Hospital	A	419 824-1444	Sylvania *(G-17426)*
Fort Hamilton Hospital	D	513 867-2000	Hamilton *(G-11597)*
Fort Hmltn-Hghes Hlthcare Corp	A	513 867-2000	Hamilton *(G-11598)*
Fostoria Hospital Association	B	419 435-7734	Fostoria *(G-11000)*
Fulton County Health Center	C	419 335-2017	Wauseon *(G-18801)*
Fulton County Health Center	A	419 335-2015	Wauseon *(G-18803)*
G M A Surgery Inc	E	937 429-7350	Beavercreek *(G-1153)*
Galion Community Hospital	B	419 468-4841	Galion *(G-11174)*
Gamble Elzbeth Dcness HM Assn	A	513 751-4224	Cincinnati *(G-3601)*
Garden II Leasing Co LLC	D	419 381-0037	Toledo *(G-17755)*
Genesis Healthcare System	A	740 454-5000	Zanesville *(G-20310)*
Glenmont	E	614 876-0084	Hilliard *(G-11769)*
Good Samaritan Hosp Cincinnati	E	513 569-6251	Cincinnati *(G-3625)*
Grace Hospital	D	216 476-2704	Cleveland *(G-5620)*
Grace Hospital	D	216 687-1500	Bedford *(G-1282)*
Grace Hospital	D	216 687-1500	Warrensville Heights *(G-18779)*
Grace Hospital	D	216 687-4013	Amherst *(G-588)*
Grady Memorial Hospital	E	740 615-1000	Delaware *(G-9982)*
Greene Memorial Hosp Svcs Inc	E	937 352-2000	Miamisburg *(G-14174)*
Greene Memorial Hospital Inc	A	937 352-2000	Xenia *(G-19908)*
Greene Memorial Hospital Inc	E	937 458-4500	Beavercreek *(G-1154)*
Greene Oaks	D	937 352-2800	Xenia *(G-19909)*
Greenfield Area Medical Ctr	D	937 981-9400	Greenfield *(G-11361)*
Guernsey Health Systems	A	740 439-3561	Cambridge *(G-2073)*
H B Magruder Memorial Hospital	B	419 734-4539	Port Clinton *(G-16109)*
Hardin Memorial Hospital	D	419 673-0761	Kenton *(G-12281)*
Hcl of Dayton Inc	C	937 384-8300	Miamisburg *(G-14175)*
Health Care Specialists	E	740 454-4530	Zanesville *(G-20316)*
Henry County Hospital Inc	B	419 592-4015	Napoleon *(G-14809)*
Highland County Joint	B	937 393-6100	Hillsboro *(G-11843)*
Hillcrest Hospital Auxiliary	D	440 449-4500	Cleveland *(G-5692)*
Hocking Valley Community Ho	B	740 380-8336	Logan *(G-12837)*
Holzer Health System	E	740 446-5060	Gallipolis *(G-11200)*
Holzer Hospital Foundation	A	740 446-5000	Gallipolis *(G-11201)*
Holzer Hospital Foundation	B	740 446-5000	Gallipolis *(G-11202)*
Holzer Medical Ctr - Jackson	B	740 288-4625	Jackson *(G-12175)*

SIC

Hometown Urgent Care	C	937 342-9520	
Springfield (G-17045)			
Hospice of Genesis Health	E	740 454-5381	
Zanesville (G-20318)			
Hospice of Southern Ohio	D	740 356-2567	
Portsmouth (G-16148)			
Humana Inc	A	330 498-0537	
Canton (G-2352)			
Internal Medicine of Akron	E	330 376-2728	
Akron (G-279)			
▲ Jewish Hospital LLC	A	513 686-3000	
Cincinnati (G-3817)			
▲ Jewish Hospital Cincinnati Inc	A	513 686-3303	
Cincinnati (G-3818)			
Joel Pomerene Memorial Hosp	B	330 674-1015	
Millersburg (G-14480)			
Joint Township Dst Mem Hosp	D	419 394-9959	
Saint Marys (G-16523)			
Joint Township Dst Mem Hosp	B	419 394-3335	
Saint Marys (G-16524)			
Kettering Adventist Healthcare	E	937 426-0049	
Beavercreek (G-1160)			
Kettering Adventist Healthcare	D	937 534-4651	
Moraine (G-14668)			
Kettering Adventist Healthcare	E	937 298-3399	
Kettering (G-12294)			
Kettering Adventist Healthcare	E	937 878-8644	
Fairborn (G-10678)			
Kettering Adventist Healthcare	E	937 401-6306	
Centerville (G-2629)			
Kettering Adventist Healthcare	E	937 294-1658	
Dayton (G-9532)			
Kettering Adventist Healthcare	D	937 298-4331	
Dayton (G-9533)			
Kettering Adventist Healthcare	D	937 762-1361	
Miamisburg (G-14179)			
Kettering Adventist Healthcare	E	937 298-4331	
Dayton (G-9534)			
Kettering Adventist Healthcare	D	937 395-8816	
Miamisburg (G-14180)			
Kettering Medical Center	D	937 702-4000	
Beavercreek (G-1161)			
Kettering Medical Center	E	937 298-4331	
Kettering (G-12295)			
Kettering Medical Center	B	937 866-0551	
Miamisburg (G-14181)			
Kettering Medical Center	E	937 298-4331	
Dayton (G-9539)			
Kettering Medical Center	E	937 299-0099	
Dayton (G-9540)			
Kettering Medical Center	E	937 384-8750	
Dayton (G-9541)			
Kindred Healthcare Inc	D	937 222-5963	
Dayton (G-9546)			
Kindred Healthcare Inc	D	937 222-5963	
Dayton (G-9547)			
Kindred Hospital Central Ohio	E	419 526-0777	
Lima (G-12670)			
Knox Community Hosp Foundation	E	740 393-9814	
Mount Vernon (G-14772)			
Knox Community Hospital	A	740 393-9000	
Mount Vernon (G-14773)			
Lake Hospital System Inc	A	440 953-9600	
Willoughby (G-19539)			
Lake Hospital System Inc	A	440 632-3024	
Middlefield (G-14272)			
Lake Hospital System Inc	A	440 375-8100	
Painesville (G-15719)			
Lakewood Hospital Association	A	216 529-7160	
Lakewood (G-12356)			
Lakewood Hospital Association	E	216 228-5437	
Cleveland (G-5852)			
Licking Memorial Hospital	D	740 348-4137	
Newark (G-15057)			
Life Line Screening	D	216 581-6556	
Independence (G-12090)			
Lima Memorial Hospital	D	419 228-3335	
Lima (G-12683)			
Lima Memorial Hospital La	B	419 738-5151	
Wapakoneta (G-18648)			
Lima Memorial Joint Oper Co	A	419 228-5165	
Lima (G-12684)			
Lodi Community Hospital	C	330 948-1222	
Lodi (G-12827)			
Lutheran Medical Center	B	216 696-4300	
Solon (G-16867)			
Madison Family Health Corp	C	740 845-7000	
London (G-12868)			
Madison Medical Campus	E	440 428-6800	
Madison (G-13104)			

Manor Care Inc	D	419 252-5500	
Toledo (G-17880)			
Marietta Memorial Hospital	B	740 401-0362	
Belpre (G-1408)			
Marietta Memorial Hospital	A	740 374-1400	
Marietta (G-13354)			
Marietta Memorial Hospital	E	740 373-8549	
Marietta (G-13355)			
Marion Gen Social Work Dept	E	740 383-8788	
Marion (G-13438)			
Marion General Hosp HM Hlth	E	740 383-8770	
Marion (G-13439)			
Marion General Hospital Inc	D	740 383-8400	
Marion (G-13440)			
Mary Rutan Hospital	A	937 592-4015	
Bellefontaine (G-1359)			
▲ Marymount Hospital Inc	B	216 581-0500	
Cleveland (G-5920)			
Marysvlle Ohio Srgical Ctr LLC	C	937 642-6622	
Marysville (G-13516)			
Massillon Health System LLC	A	330 837-7200	
Massillon (G-13712)			
McCullough-Hyde Mem Hosp Inc	B	513 523-2111	
Oxford (G-15680)			
McCullough-Hyde Mem Hosp Inc	B	513 863-2215	
Hamilton (G-11628)			
Med America Hlth Systems Corp	A	937 223-6192	
Dayton (G-9598)			
Medcath Intermediate Holdings	B	937 221-8016	
Dayton (G-9600)			
Medcentral Health System	E	419 526-8900	
Ontario (G-15562)			
Medcentral Health System	E	419 526-8442	
Mansfield (G-13214)			
Medcentral Health System	D	419 526-8000	
Mansfield (G-13215)			
Medcentral Health System	D	419 526-8970	
Mansfield (G-13216)			
Medcentral Health System	C	419 683-1040	
Crestline (G-9057)			
Medcentral Health System	C	419 342-5015	
Shelby (G-16747)			
Medcentral Health System	E	419 526-8043	
Mansfield (G-13217)			
Medical Associates of Mid-Ohio	E	419 289-1331	
Ashland (G-680)			
Medical Center At Elizabeth Pl	C	937 223-6237	
Dayton (G-9601)			
Medina Hospital	E	330 723-3117	
Medina (G-13975)			
Medone Hospital Physicians	E	314 255-6900	
Columbus (G-8055)			
Memorial Hospital	B	419 334-6657	
Fremont (G-11086)			
Memorial Hospital	E	419 547-6419	
Clyde (G-6748)			
Memorial Hospital Union County	C	937 644-1001	
Marysville (G-13518)			
Memorial Hospital Union County	A	937 644-6115	
Marysville (G-13519)			
Mental Health and Addi Serv	C	614 752-0333	
Columbus (G-8058)			
Mercer Cnty Joint Townshp Hosp	B	419 678-2341	
Coldwater (G-6763)			
Mercer Cnty Joint Townshp Hosp	A	419 586-1611	
Celina (G-2601)			
Mercy Franciscan Hosp Mt Airy	C	513 853-5101	
Cincinnati (G-4008)			
Mercy Frncscan Hosp Wstn Hills	A	513 389-5000	
Cincinnati (G-4009)			
Mercy Hamilton Hospital	E	513 603-8600	
Fairfield (G-10753)			
Mercy Health	C	330 729-1372	
Youngstown (G-20122)			
Mercy Health	E	513 686-5392	
Cincinnati (G-4010)			
Mercy Health	D	513 981-4700	
Mount Orab (G-14742)			
Mercy Health	D	513 639-0250	
Cincinnati (G-4011)			
Mercy Health	C	513 981-5750	
Cincinnati (G-4012)			
Mercy Health	E	440 355-4206	
Lagrange (G-12325)			
Mercy Health	D	937 390-1700	
Springfield (G-17074)			
Mercy Health	E	513 639-2800	
Cincinnati (G-4013)			
Mercy Health	D	513 232-7100	
Cincinnati (G-4014)			

Mercy Health	E	440 988-1009	
Amherst (G-593)			
Mercy Health	E	937 653-3445	
Urbana (G-18440)			
Mercy Health	D	561 358-1619	
Cincinnati (G-4015)			
Mercy Health	D	513 981-5463	
Cincinnati (G-4016)			
Mercy Health	E	440 937-4600	
Avon (G-895)			
Mercy Health	E	440 327-7372	
North Ridgeville (G-15335)			
Mercy Health	E	513 639-2800	
Cincinnati (G-4018)			
Mercy Health	D	513 979-2999	
Cincinnati (G-4019)			
Mercy Health	E	513 870-7008	
Fairfield (G-10755)			
Mercy Health	C	330 746-7211	
Youngstown (G-20124)			
Mercy Health	D	937 328-8700	
Springfield (G-17076)			
Mercy Health	D	440 774-6800	
Oberlin (G-15511)			
Mercy Health	E	513 741-8200	
Cincinnati (G-4023)			
Mercy Health	E	330 792-7418	
Youngstown (G-20123)			
Mercy Health	A	440 233-1000	
Lorain (G-12926)			
Mercy Health - St	E	419 696-7465	
Oregon (G-15600)			
Mercy Health - St R	A	419 227-3361	
Lima (G-12702)			
Mercy Health - Tiffin Hosp LLC	C	419 455-7000	
Tiffin (G-17524)			
Mercy Health Anderson Hospital	A	513 624-4500	
Cincinnati (G-4024)			
Mercy Health Anderson Hospital	E	513 624-1950	
Cincinnati (G-4025)			
Mercy Health Anderson Hospital	E	513 624-4025	
Cincinnati (G-4026)			
Mercy Health Cincinnati LLC	D	513 952-5000	
Cincinnati (G-4027)			
Mercy Health Partners	D	513 233-2444	
Cincinnati (G-4028)			
Mercy Health Partners	D	513 389-5000	
Cincinnati (G-4029)			
Mercy Health Partners	C	513 853-5101	
Cincinnati (G-4030)			
Mercy Health Partners	D	513 981-5056	
Blue Ash (G-1610)			
Mercy Health Partners	D	513 686-4800	
Cincinnati (G-4032)			
Mercy Health Sys - Nthrn Reg	B	419 251-1359	
Toledo (G-17908)			
Mercy Health Youngstown LLC	A	330 746-7211	
Youngstown (G-20126)			
Mercy Health Youngstown LLC	A	330 841-4000	
Warren (G-18730)			
Mercy Hlth - Clermont Hosp LLC	D	513 732-8200	
Batavia (G-1004)			
Mercy Hlth St Vincent Med LLC	A	419 251-3232	
Toledo (G-17909)			
Mercy Hospital of Defiance	C	419 782-8444	
Defiance (G-9929)			
Mercy Medical Center	A	937 390-5000	
Springfield (G-17080)			
Mercy Medical Center Inc	D	330 649-4380	
Canton (G-2399)			
Mercy Medical Center Inc	E	330 489-1000	
Canton (G-2400)			
Metrohealth System	A	216 398-6000	
Cleveland (G-5967)			
Metrohealth System	C	216 957-4000	
Cleveland (G-5968)			
Metrohealth System	E	216 957-1500	
Cleveland (G-5970)			
Metrohealth System	E	216 765-0733	
Beachwood (G-1080)			
Metrohealth System	E	216 957-3200	
Westlake (G-19373)			
Metrohealth System	E	216 591-0523	
Beachwood (G-1081)			
Miami Valley Hospital	C	937 436-5200	
Dayton (G-9619)			
Miami Valley Hospital	A	937 208-7065	
Vandalia (G-18531)			
Miami Valley Hospital	A	937 208-8000	
Dayton (G-9620)			

Mid-Ohio Heart Clinic Inc .....E..... 419 524-8151
Mansfield (G-13221)

Mill Pond Family Physicians.....E..... 330 928-3111
Cuyahoga Falls (G-9115)

Morrow County Hospital .....B..... 419 949-3085
Mount Gilead (G-14731)

Morrow County Hospital .....B..... 419 946-5015
Mount Gilead (G-14732)

Mount Carmel East Hospital.....A..... 614 234-6000
Columbus (G-8110)

Mount Carmel Health.....A..... 614 234-5000
Columbus (G-8111)

Mount Carmel Health.....E..... 614 855-4878
New Albany (G-14860)

Mount Carmel Health.....D..... 614 234-0100
Westerville (G-19283)

Mount Carmel Health System.....A..... 614 234-6000
Columbus (G-8113)

Mount Carmel Health System.....E..... 614 775-6600
New Albany (G-14861)

Nationwide Childrens Hospital.....B..... 614 722-5750
Columbus (G-8144)

◆ Nationwide Childrens Hospital .....A..... 614 722-2000
Columbus (G-8145)

Nationwide Childrens Hospital.....B..... 513 636-6000
Cincinnati (G-2862)

Nationwide Childrens Hospital.....B..... 614 355-8100
Columbus (G-8149)

Neuroscience Center Inc.....D..... 614 293-8930
Columbus (G-8182)

New Albany Surgery Center LLC.....C..... 614 775-1616
New Albany (G-14867)

New Lfcare Hspitals Dayton LLC.....B..... 937 384-8300
Miamisburg (G-14197)

Niagara Health Corporation.....A..... 614 898-4000
Columbus (G-8189)

Norwalk Area Hlth Systems Inc.....A..... 419 668-8101
Norwalk (G-15448)

Ohio Osteopathic Hospital Assn.....E..... 614 299-2107
Columbus (G-8278)

Ohio State Univ Wexner Med Ctr.....A..... 614 293-8000
Columbus (G-8292)

Ohio State Univ Wexner Med Ctr.....C..... 614 366-3687
Columbus (G-8293)

Ohio State University.....A..... 614 257-3000
Columbus (G-8300)

Ohio State University.....C..... 614 293-8750
Columbus (G-8302)

Ohio State University.....E..... 614 293-8158
Columbus (G-8323)

Ohio State University.....C..... 614 292-6251
Columbus (G-8337)

Ohio State University.....E..... 614 293-8419
Columbus (G-8343)

Ohio State University.....E..... 614 293-8196
Columbus (G-8345)

Ohio State University.....E..... 614 293-8333
Columbus (G-8346)

Ohio State University.....A..... 614 293-8000
Columbus (G-8347)

Ohio Valley Medical Center LLC.....D..... 937 521-3900
Springfield (G-17093)

Ohiohealth Corporation.....C..... 614 566-5456
Columbus (G-8359)

Ohiohealth Corporation.....B..... 614 544-8000
Dublin (G-10299)

Ohiohealth Corporation.....C..... 614 566-2124
Columbus (G-8360)

Ohiohealth Corporation.....A..... 614 788-8860
Columbus (G-8362)

Ohiohealth Corporation.....D..... 614 566-5977
Columbus (G-8363)

Ohiohealth Corporation.....C..... 614 566-9000
Columbus (G-8364)

Ohiohealth Corporation.....C..... 614 566-4800
Columbus (G-8365)

Ohiohealth Corporation.....E..... 614 566-5414
Columbus (G-8366)

Ohiohealth Research Institute.....E..... 614 566-4297
Columbus (G-8367)

Ohiohlth Rverside Methdst Hosp.....A..... 614 566-5000
Columbus (G-8368)

Orrville Hospital Foundation.....C..... 330 684-4700
Orrville (G-15640)

Osu Nephrology Medical Ctr.....E..... 614 293-8300
Columbus (G-8392)

Parma Community General Hosp.....A..... 440 743-3000
Parma (G-15771)

Paulding County Hospital.....C..... 419 399-4080
Paulding (G-15796)

Physician Hospital Alliance.....E..... 937 558-3456
Miamisburg (G-14205)

Pine Hills Continuing Care Ctr.....E..... 740 753-1931
Nelsonville (G-14835)

Poison Information Center.....E..... 513 636-5111
Cincinnati (G-4262)

Promedica Defiance Regional.....E..... 419 783-6802
Defiance (G-9935)

Promedica Health Systems Inc.....A..... 567 585-7454
Toledo (G-17993)

Providence Care Center.....E..... 419 627-2273
Sandusky (G-16633)

Rchp - Wilmington LLC.....D..... 937 382-6611
Wilmington (G-19643)

Regency Hospital Cincinnati.....E..... 513 862-4700
Cincinnati (G-4350)

Regency Hospital Toledo LLC.....E..... 419 318-5700
Sylvania (G-17445)

Research Institute At Nation.....C..... 614 722-2700
Columbus (G-8518)

Richmond Medical Center.....B..... 440 585-6500
Richmond Heights (G-16394)

Robinson Health System Inc.....E..... 330 678-4100
Ravenna (G-16262)

Robinson Health System Inc.....A..... 330 297-0811
Ravenna (G-16263)

Robinson Health System Inc.....E..... 330 297-0811
Kent (G-12257)

Robinson Memorial Hospital.....A..... 330 626-3455
Streetsboro (G-17268)

Salem Community Hospital.....A..... 330 332-1551
Salem (G-16560)

Samaritan Health Partners.....A..... 937 208-8400
Dayton (G-9749)

Samaritan N Surgery Ctr Ltd.....E..... 937 567-6100
Englewood (G-10600)

Samaritan Professional Corp.....E..... 419 289-0491
Ashland (G-688)

Samaritan Regional Health Sys.....E..... 419 281-1330
Ashland (G-689)

Samaritan Regional Health Sys.....B..... 419 289-0491
Ashland (G-690)

Selby General Hospital.....C..... 740 568-2000
Marietta (G-13380)

Select Medical Corporation.....C..... 216 983-8030
Cleveland (G-6394)

Select Medical Corporation.....D..... 330 761-7500
Akron (G-422)

Select Specialty Hosp Columbus.....D..... 614 291-8467
Columbus (G-8618)

Select Specialty Hospital.....D..... 513 862-4700
Cincinnati (G-4449)

Select Specty Hospi- Colmbus.....C..... 614 293-6931
Columbus (G-8619)

Shelby County Mem Hosp Assn.....A..... 937 498-2311
Sidney (G-16797)

Shelby County Mem Hosp Assn.....B..... 937 492-9591
Sidney (G-16798)

Sheltering Arms Hospital Found.....B..... 740 592-9300
Athens (G-802)

Shriners Hspitals For Children.....B..... 513 872-6000
Cincinnati (G-4473)

Sisters of Mrcy of Wllard Ohio.....C..... 419 964-5000
Willard (G-19488)

▲ Southern Ohio Medical Center.....C..... 740 354-5000
Portsmouth (G-16171)

Southern Ohio Medical Center.....E..... 740 356-5000
Portsmouth (G-16172)

Southern Ohio Medical Center.....A..... 740 354-5000
Portsmouth (G-16173)

Southstern Ohio Rgonal Med Ctr.....E..... 740 439-3561
Cambridge (G-2083)

Southwest Cmnty Hlth Systems.....A..... 440 816-8000
Cleveland (G-6428)

Southwest General Health Ctr.....D..... 440 816-4202
Cleveland (G-6430)

Southwest General Health Ctr.....C..... 440 816-4900
Strongsville (G-17347)

Southwest General Health Ctr.....D..... 440 816-8200
Cleveland (G-6431)

Southwest General Health Ctr.....A..... 440 816-8000
Cleveland (G-6432)

Southwest General Health Ctr.....A..... 440 816-8005
Cleveland (G-6433)

Southwest General Med Group.....A..... 440 816-8000
Middleburg Heights (G-14259)

Southwest Healthcare of Brown.....D..... 937 378-7800
Georgetown (G-11275)

Southwest Internal Medicine.....E..... 440 816-2777
Cleveland (G-6434)

Specialty Hosp Cleveland Inc.....D..... 216 592-2830
Cleveland (G-6443)

St Anne Mercy Hospital.....E..... 419 407-2663
Toledo (G-18045)

St Lukes Hospital.....D..... 419 893-5911
Maumee (G-13855)

St Ritas Medical Center.....E..... 419 538-6288
Glandorf (G-11307)

St Vincent Charity Med Ctr.....A..... 216 861-6200
Cleveland (G-6450)

Steward Trumbull Mem Hosp Inc.....A..... 330 841-9011
Warren (G-18748)

Suburban Pediatrics Inc.....E..... 440 498-0065
Shaker Heights (G-16715)

Summa Health.....A..... 330 873-1518
Akron (G-443)

Summa Health.....A..... 330 836-9023
Akron (G-444)

Summa Health.....B..... 330 252-0095
Akron (G-445)

Summa Health.....B..... 330 926-0384
Cuyahoga Falls (G-9126)

Summa Health.....E..... 330 630-9726
Tallmadge (G-17489)

Summa Health.....D..... 330 753-3649
Barberton (G-967)

Summa Health.....C..... 330 375-3315
Akron (G-446)

Summa Health.....E..... 330 688-4531
Stow (G-17234)

Summa Health.....B..... 330 864-8060
Akron (G-447)

Summa Health Center Lk Medina.....E..... 330 952-0014
Medina (G-14006)

Summa Health System.....D..... 330 535-7319
Akron (G-448)

Summa Health System.....C..... 330 375-3000
Akron (G-449)

Summa Health System.....A..... 330 334-1504
Wadsworth (G-18616)

Summa Health System.....D..... 330 375-3584
Akron (G-450)

Summa Health System.....C..... 330 375-3315
Akron (G-451)

Summa Health System.....E..... 330 375-3000
Akron (G-452)

Summa Health System.....A..... 330 615-3000
Barberton (G-968)

Surgery and Gynecology Inc.....E..... 614 294-1603
Columbus (G-8721)

Sylvania Franciscan Health.....E..... 419 882-8373
Maumee (G-13859)

Taussig Cancer Center.....E..... 866 223-8100
Cleveland (G-6500)

Toledo Hospital.....D..... 419 291-8701
Toledo (G-18087)

Toledo Hospital.....A..... 419 291-4000
Toledo (G-18086)

Trihealth Inc.....E..... 513 569-6111
Cincinnati (G-4638)

Trihealth Evendale Hospital.....C..... 513 454-2222
Cincinnati (G-4640)

Trinity Health System.....B..... 740 283-7000
Steubenville (G-17179)

Trinity Health System.....A..... 740 264-8000
Steubenville (G-17177)

Trinity Health System.....E..... 740 264-8101
Steubenville (G-17178)

Trinity Hospital Holding Co.....A..... 740 264-8000
Steubenville (G-17180)

Trinity Hospital Twin City.....B..... 740 922-2800
Dennison (G-10053)

Trinity West.....A..... 740 264-8000
Steubenville (G-17181)

Tripoint Medical Center.....A..... 440 375-8100
Painesville (G-15744)

Triumph Hospital Mansfield.....E..... 419 526-0777
Mansfield (G-13255)

Uc Health Llc.....E..... 513 584-8600
Cincinnati (G-4667)

Uhhs Westlake Medical Center.....C..... 440 250-2070
Westlake (G-19417)

Uhhs-Memorial Hosp of Geneva.....C..... 440 466-1141
Geneva (G-11248)

Union Hospital Association.....D..... 330 343-3311
Dover (G-10106)

University Hospitals.....B..... 440 250-2001
Westlake (G-19418)

University Hospitals.....B..... 216 593-5500
Cleveland (G-6587)

S
I
C

University Hospitals	E	216 536-3020
Cleveland *(G-6588)*
University Hospitals	A	440 285-6000
Chardon *(G-2721)*
▲ University Hospitals	A	216 767-8900
Shaker Heights *(G-16717)*
University Hospitals	A	440 743-3000
Parma *(G-15779)*
University Hospitals	E	216 844-6400
Cleveland *(G-6589)*
University Hospitals	E	216 767-8500
Cleveland *(G-6591)*
University Hospitals Cleveland	A	216 844-1000
Cleveland *(G-6592)*
University Hospitals Cleveland	E	440 205-5755
Mentor *(G-14119)*
▲ University Hospitals Cleveland	A	216 844-1000
Cleveland *(G-6593)*
University Hospitals Cleveland	D	216 844-4663
Cleveland *(G-6594)*
University Hospitals Cleveland	A	216 844-3323
Shaker Heights *(G-16718)*
University Hospitals Cleveland	D	216 342-5556
Beachwood *(G-1116)*
University Hospitals Cleveland	E	216 844-3528
Cleveland *(G-6595)*
University Hospitals Health Sy	E	216 844-4663
Cleveland *(G-6597)*
University Hospitals St John	A	440 835-8000
Westlake *(G-19419)*
University of Cincinnati	E	513 584-7522
Cincinnati *(G-4704)*
University of Cincinnati	E	513 584-4396
Cincinnati *(G-4710)*
University of Cincinnati	E	513 584-1000
Cincinnati *(G-4723)*
University of Cincinnati	E	513 584-1000
Cincinnati *(G-4725)*
University of Toledo	A	419 383-4000
Toledo *(G-18127)*
University of Toledo	A	419 383-3759
Toledo *(G-18129)*
University of Toledo	B	419 383-4229
Toledo *(G-18130)*
University Surgeons Inc	E	216 844-3021
Cleveland *(G-6605)*
▲ Universty of Cincinnti Medcl C	E	513 584-1000
Cincinnati *(G-4730)*
Uvmc Management Corporation	D	937 440-4000
Troy *(G-18237)*
VA Medical Center Automated RE	E	740 772-7118
Chillicothe *(G-2835)*
Van Wert County Hospital Assn	D	419 238-2390
Van Wert *(G-18494)*
Van Wert Medical Services Ltd	B	419 238-7727
Van Wert *(G-18496)*
Vibra Healthcare LLC	D	330 675-5555
Warren *(G-18766)*
Wayne Healthcare	B	937 548-1141
Greenville *(G-11400)*
Wheeling Hospital Inc	C	740 942-4631
Cadiz *(G-2034)*
Wheeling Hospital Inc	D	740 942-4116
Cadiz *(G-2035)*
Wood County Hospital Assoc	A	419 354-8900
Bowling Green *(G-1754)*
Wright Center	E	216 382-1868
Cleveland *(G-6691)*
Wyandot Memorial Hospital	C	419 294-4991
Upper Sandusky *(G-18416)*

8063 Psychiatric Hospitals

Adriel School Inc	D	937 465-0010
West Liberty *(G-19117)*
Belmont Bhc Pines Hospital Inc	C	330 759-2700
Youngstown *(G-19964)*
Bethesda Hospital Association	A	740 454-4000
Zanesville *(G-20281)*
Bhc Fox Run Hospital Inc	C	740 695-2131
Saint Clairsville *(G-16479)*
Cambridge Behavioral Hospital	C	740 432-4906
Cambridge *(G-2052)*
Center For Addiction Treatment	D	513 381-6672
Cincinnati *(G-3148)*
Central Commnty Hlth Brd of Ha	D	513 559-2000
Cincinnati *(G-3152)*
Central Commnty Hlth Brd of Ha	D	513 559-2000
Cincinnati *(G-3153)*
County of Paulding	E	419 399-3636
Paulding *(G-15793)*

Develpmntal Dsblties Ohio Dept	A	740 446-1642
Gallipolis *(G-11190)*
Develpmntal Dsblties Ohio Dept	B	614 272-0509
Columbus *(G-7441)*
Eastway Corporation	C	937 496-2000
Dayton *(G-9404)*
Eastway Corporation	C	937 531-7000
Dayton *(G-9405)*
Focus Healthcare of Ohio LLC	E	419 891-9333
Maumee *(G-13793)*
Heartland Bhavioral Healthcare	B	330 833-3135
Massillon *(G-13695)*
Laurelwood Hospital	B	440 953-3000
Willoughby *(G-19543)*
▲ Marymount Hospital Inc	B	216 581-0500
Cleveland *(G-5920)*
Mental Health and Addi Serv	C	419 381-1881
Toledo *(G-17904)*
Mental Health and Addi Serv	B	513 948-3600
Cincinnati *(G-4006)*
Mental Health and Addi Serv	D	614 752-0333
Columbus *(G-8057)*
Mental Health and Addi Serv	B	330 467-7131
Northfield *(G-15383)*
Mental Hlth Serv For CL & Mad	E	937 390-7980
Springfield *(G-17071)*
Mental Hlth Serv For CL & Mad	C	937 399-9500
Springfield *(G-17072)*
Mental Hlth Serv For CL & Mad	E	740 852-6256
London *(G-12871)*
Mercy Health	A	440 233-1000
Lorain *(G-12926)*
Oglethorpe Middlepoint LLC	E	419 968-2950
Middle Point *(G-14247)*
Ohio Hospital For Psychiatry	E	877 762-9026
Columbus *(G-8267)*
Rehab Continuum Inc	E	513 984-8070
Blue Ash *(G-1643)*
Rescue Incorporated	C	419 255-9585
Toledo *(G-18004)*
Southast Cmnty Mental Hlth Ctr	E	614 444-0800
Columbus *(G-8662)*
St Ritas Medical Center	E	419 226-9067
Lima *(G-12749)*

8069 Specialty Hospitals, Except Psychiatric

Affiliates In Oral & Maxlofcl	E	513 829-8080
Fairfield *(G-10693)*
Affiliates In Oral & Maxlofcl	E	513 829-8080
West Chester *(G-18862)*
Akron Gen Edwin Shaw Rhblttion	D	330 375-1300
Fairlawn *(G-10816)*
Alcohol Drug Addction & Mental	E	937 443-0416
Dayton *(G-9213)*
Anderson Healthcare Ltd	D	513 474-6200
Cincinnati *(G-2959)*
Arthur G James Cance	A	614 293-4878
Columbus *(G-6972)*
Arthur G James Cancer Hospital	E	614 293-3300
Columbus *(G-6973)*
Aultman Hospital	A	330 452-9911
Canton *(G-2202)*
Aultman Hospital	B	330 452-9911
Canton *(G-2203)*
Behavral Cnnctions WD Cnty Inc	E	419 352-5387
Bowling Green *(G-1717)*
Cambridge Behavioral Hospital	C	740 432-4906
Cambridge *(G-2052)*
Center For Addiction Treatment	D	513 381-6672
Cincinnati *(G-3148)*
Charity Hospice Inc	E	740 264-2280
Steubenville *(G-17147)*
Childrens Hosp Med Ctr Akron	A	330 308-5432
New Philadelphia *(G-14949)*
Childrens Hosp Med Ctr Akron	E	330 629-6085
Youngstown *(G-19988)*
Childrens Hosp Med Ctr Akron	A	330 543-1000
Akron *(G-130)*
Childrens Hosp Med Ctr Akron	D	330 543-8004
Akron *(G-131)*
Childrens Hospital Medical Ctr	E	513 636-6036
Cincinnati *(G-2844)*
Childrens Hospital Medical Ctr	A	513 636-4200
Cincinnati *(G-3190)*
Childrens Hospital Medical Ctr	E	513 636-6800
Mason *(G-13554)*
Community Care Hospice	E	937 382-5400
Wilmington *(G-19617)*
Community Counseling Services	E	419 468-8211
Bucyrus *(G-1984)*

Compass Corp For Recovery Svcs	D	419 241-8827
Toledo *(G-17673)*
Cornell Companies Inc	C	419 747-3322
Shelby *(G-16744)*
County of Stark	E	330 455-6644
Canton *(G-2270)*
Covenant Care Ohio Inc	D	937 878-7046
Fairborn *(G-10666)*
Crossroads Center	C	513 475-5300
Cincinnati *(G-3382)*
Crystal Clnic Orthpdic Ctr LLC	D	330 668-4040
Akron *(G-173)*
Crystal Clnic Orthpdic Ctr LLC	D	330 535-3396
Akron *(G-174)*
▲ Dayton Childrens Hospital	A	937 641-3000
Dayton *(G-9358)*
Encompass Health Corporation	C	513 418-5600
Cincinnati *(G-3497)*
Firelands Regional Health Sys	E	419 332-5524
Fremont *(G-11072)*
Frs Counseling Inc	E	937 393-0585
Hillsboro *(G-11840)*
Glenbeigh	E	440 563-3400
Rock Creek *(G-16411)*
Glenbeigh Health Sources Inc	C	440 951-7000
Rock Creek *(G-16412)*
Greenbrier Senior Living Cmnty	C	440 888-5900
Cleveland *(G-5641)*
Hcr Manorcare Med Svcs Fla LLC	C	614 882-1511
Westerville *(G-19260)*
Health Recovery Services Inc	C	740 592-6720
Athens *(G-783)*
HealthSouth	C	937 424-8200
Dayton *(G-9491)*
Hospice of Central Ohio	C	740 344-0311
Newark *(G-15042)*
Hospice of Miami Valley LLC	E	937 521-1444
Springfield *(G-17048)*
Hospice of Middletown	E	513 424-2273
Middletown *(G-14302)*
Hospice of The Valley Inc	D	330 788-1992
Youngstown *(G-20069)*
Hospice of The Western Reserve	D	330 800-2240
Medina *(G-13951)*
Laurelwood Hospital	B	440 953-3000
Willoughby *(G-19543)*
Liberty Nrsing Ctr Rvrside LLC	D	513 557-3621
Cincinnati *(G-3924)*
Lorain County Alcohol and Drug	E	440 989-4900
Lorain *(G-12917)*
Lutheran Medical Center	B	216 696-4300
Solon *(G-16867)*
Marietta Memorial Hospital	A	740 374-1400
Marietta *(G-13354)*
Maryhaven Inc	B	614 449-1530
Columbus *(G-8032)*
McKinley Hall Inc	E	937 328-5300
Springfield *(G-17068)*
Medcath Intermediate Holdings	B	937 221-8016
Dayton *(G-9600)*
Mental Health & Recovery Ctr	E	937 383-3031
Wilmington *(G-19635)*
Mercy Health	E	419 226-9064
Lima *(G-12701)*
Mercy Health Anderson Hospital	E	513 624-4025
Cincinnati *(G-4026)*
Metrohealth System	C	216 957-2100
Cleveland *(G-5972)*
Metrohealth System	E	216 778-3867
Cleveland *(G-5971)*
Morrow County Council On Drugs	E	419 947-4055
Mount Gilead *(G-14729)*
Nationwide Childrens Hospital	C	614 722-2700
Columbus *(G-8143)*
Nationwide Childrens Hospital	E	330 253-5200
Akron *(G-343)*
Nationwide Childrens Hospital	A	614 722-2000
Columbus *(G-8146)*
Nationwide Childrens Hospital	E	614 355-8300
Westerville *(G-19188)*
Nationwide Childrens Hospital	B	614 722-8200
Columbus *(G-8147)*
Nationwide Childrens Hospital	A	614 864-9216
Pickerington *(G-15964)*
Nationwide Childrens Hospital	A	614 355-0802
Columbus *(G-8148)*
Nationwide Childrens Hospital	B	614 355-9200
Columbus *(G-8150)*
Nationwide Childrens Hospital	B	614 355-8000
Columbus *(G-8151)*

Newark Sleep Diagnostic Center..........E 740 522-9499
  Newark (G-15087)
Nord Center Associates Inc ....E 440 233-7232
  Lorain (G-12935)
Northwest Ohio Orthopedic & Sp......C 419 427-1984
  Findlay (G-10950)
Ohio Department Youth Services ....E 740 881-3337
  Columbus (G-8244)
Ohio State University......................E 614 293-4925
  Columbus (G-8348)
Oriana House Inc ....C 216 361-9655
  Cleveland (G-6143)
Oriana House Inc ....D 330 996-7730
  Akron (G-367)
Parkside Behavioral Healthcare ....E 614 471-2552
  Gahanna (G-11140)
Parma Clinic Cancer Center..............C 440 743-4747
  Cleveland (G-6176)
Pike Cnty Recovery Council Inc..........E 740 835-8437
  Waverly (G-18821)
Recovery Works Healing Ctr LLC........E 937 384-0580
  West Carrollton (G-18856)
Salvation Army.............................C 330 773-3331
  Akron (G-418)
Scioto Pnt Vly Mental Hlth Ctr...........E 740 335-6935
  Wshngtn CT Hs (G-19883)
Select Spclty Hsptal-Akron LLC.........D 330 761-7500
  Akron (G-423)
Southast Cmnty Mental Hlth Ctr........E 614 444-0800
  Columbus (G-8662)
Southwest General Health Ctr ....D 440 816-8200
  Cleveland (G-6431)
Stein Hospice Services Inc ....D 419 447-0475
  Sandusky (G-16645)
Stein Hospice Services Inc ....D 419 502-0019
  Sandusky (G-16646)
▲ Stein Hospice Services Inc ....B 800 625-5269
  Sandusky (G-16647)
Stein Hospice Services Inc ....D 419 663-3222
  Norwalk (G-15456)
Stella Maris Inc ....E 216 781-0550
  Cleveland (G-6465)
Syntero Inc ....E 614 889-5722
  Dublin (G-10350)
Talbert House ....C 513 751-7747
  Cincinnati (G-4571)
Talbert House ....D 513 684-7968
  Cincinnati (G-4574)
Transitional Living Inc ....D 513 863-6383
  Fairfield Township (G-10815)
Trihealth Os LLC ....D 513 791-6611
  Montgomery (G-14604)
Trinity Health Corporation ....B 614 846-5420
  Columbus (G-8781)
Twin Oaks Care Center Inc...............E 419 524-1205
  Mansfield (G-13258)
▲ University Hospitals Cleveland ....A 216 844-1000
  Cleveland (G-6593)
University Hospitals Health ....E 440 285-4040
  Chardon (G-2722)
University Mednet.........................B 216 383-0100
  Euclid (G-10660)
Uvmc Nursing Care Inc ....C 937 473-2075
  Covington (G-9049)
Vibra Hosp Mahoning Vly LLC...........D 330 726-5000
  Youngstown (G-20237)
Whetstone Care Center LLC ....C 614 875-7700
  Grove City (G-11487)
Youngstown Committee On Alchol......D 330 744-1181
  Youngstown (G-20260)

8071 Medical Laboratories

Alliance Imaging Inc ....C 330 493-5100
  Canton (G-2179)
Amerathon LLC ....B 513 752-7300
  Cincinnati (G-2841)
Ameripath Cincinnati Inc ....E 513 745-8330
  Blue Ash (G-1505)
Arbor View Family Medicine Inc ....E 740 687-3386
  Lancaster (G-12371)
Associated Imaging Corporation ....E 419 517-0500
  Toledo (G-17602)
Bayless Pathmark Inc.....................E 440 274-2494
  Cleveland (G-5044)
Berkebile Russell & Associates ....E 440 989-4480
  Lorain (G-12886)
Blossom Nursing & Rehab Center ....C 330 337-3033
  Salem (G-16538)
Brook Haven Home Health Care ....E 937 833-6945
  Brookville (G-1910)

Cadx Systems Inc ....D 937 431-1464
  Beavercreek (G-1137)
Cellular Technology Limited ....E 216 791-5084
  Shaker Heights (G-16704)
Childrens Hospital Medical Ctr ....E 513 636-6400
  Fairfield (G-10708)
▼ Cleveland Heartlab Inc ....D 866 358-9828
  Cleveland (G-5258)
Cols Health & Wellness Testing ....E 614 839-2781
  Westerville (G-19238)
Compunet Clinical Labs LLC ....D 937 427-2655
  Beavercreek (G-1211)
Compunet Clinical Labs LLC ....D 937 342-0015
  Springfield (G-17020)
Compunet Clinical Labs LLC ....D 937 296-0844
  Moraine (G-14636)
Compunet Clinical Labs LLC ....B 937 208-3555
  Dayton (G-9315)
Connie Parks ....E 330 759-8334
  Hubbard (G-11943)
Consultants Laboratory Medici ....E 419 535-9629
  Toledo (G-17677)
Dayton Medical Imaging ....D 937 439-0390
  Dayton (G-9372)
Dna Diagnostics Center Inc ....C 513 881-7800
  Fairfield (G-10719)
Drew Medical Inc ....E 407 363-6700
  Hudson (G-11976)
Drs Hill & Thomas Co ....E 440 944-8887
  Cleveland (G-5446)
Ecg Scanning & Medical Svcs ....E 888 346-5837
  Moraine (G-14651)
Gloria Gadmack Do ....C 216 363-2353
  Cleveland (G-5611)
Heart To Heart Home Health ....E 330 335-9999
  Wadsworth (G-18598)
Labcare ....E 330 753-3649
  Barberton (G-958)
Labone Inc ....A 513 585-9000
  Cincinnati (G-3903)
Laboratory Corporation America ....E 614 475-7852
  Columbus (G-7940)
Laboratory Corporation America ....E 937 383-6964
  Wilmington (G-19626)
Laboratory Corporation America ....E 330 865-3624
  Akron (G-307)
Laboratory Corporation America ....E 440 951-6841
  Willoughby (G-19537)
Laboratory Corporation America ....E 614 882-6278
  Columbus (G-7941)
Laboratory Corporation America ....E 513 242-6800
  Cincinnati (G-3904)
Laboratory Corporation America ....E 937 866-8188
  Miamisburg (G-14184)
Laboratory Corporation America ....A 614 336-3993
  Dublin (G-10267)
Laboratory Corporation America ....E 440 328-3275
  Mansfield (G-13197)
Laboratory Corporation America ....E 440 884-1591
  Cleveland (G-5846)
Laboratory Corporation America ....E 740 522-2034
  Newark (G-15047)
Laboratory Corporation America ....E 330 686-0194
  Stow (G-17216)
Laboratory Corporation America ....E 440 205-8299
  Mentor (G-14070)
Laboratory Corporation America ....E 440 838-0404
  Cleveland (G-5847)
Laboratory of Dermatopathology ....E 937 434-2351
  Dayton (G-9554)
Lima Pathology Associates Labs ....E 419 226-9595
  Lima (G-12685)
Maternohio Clinical Assoicates ....E 614 457-7660
  Columbus (G-8038)
Medcentral Workable ....E 419 526-8444
  Ontario (G-15563)
Medical Diagnostic Lab Inc ....E 440 333-1375
  Avon (G-894)
Medpace Inc ....A 513 366-3220
  Cincinnati (G-3999)
Medpace Bioanalytical Labs LLC ....E 513 366-3260
  Cincinnati (G-4001)
Mercy Health Youngstown LLC ....A 330 729-1420
  Youngstown (G-20125)
Mercy Health Youngstown LLC ....A 330 746-7211
  Youngstown (G-20126)
Monroe Family Health Center ....E 740 472-0757
  Woodsfield (G-19677)
Mount Carmel Imaging & Therapy ....E 614 234-8080
  Columbus (G-8114)

Mp Biomedicals LLC ....C 440 337-1200
  Solon (G-16873)
Nationwide Childrens Hospital ....C 614 722-2700
  Columbus (G-8143)
Northeast OH Neighborhood Heal.......C 216 231-7700
  Cleveland (G-6090)
Oncodiagnostic Laboratory Inc ....E 216 861-5846
  Cleveland (G-6132)
Osu Pathology Services LLC ....D 614 247-6461
  Columbus (G-8394)
Pathology Laboratories Inc ....C 419 255-4600
  Toledo (G-17973)
Proscan Imaging LLC ....D 513 281-3400
  Cincinnati (G-4299)
Regional Imaging Cons Corp ....E 330 726-9006
  Youngstown (G-20179)
Ridgepark Medical Associates ....E 216 749-8256
  Cleveland (G-6326)
Shared PET Imaging Llc ....C 330 491-0480
  Canton (G-2475)
Southwest Urology LLC ....E 440 845-0900
  Cleveland (G-6435)
St Lukes Hospital ....A 419 441-1002
  Waterville (G-18793)
St Ritas Medical Center ....D 419 226-9229
  Lima (G-12750)
▲ Standards Testing Labs Inc ....E 330 833-8548
  Massillon (G-13731)
Stembanc Inc ....E 440 332-4279
  Chardon (G-2717)
Stork Studios Inc ....E 419 841-7766
  Toledo (G-18049)
Suburban Medical Laboratory ....C 330 929-7992
  Euclid (G-10658)
Summa Health ....D 330 753-3649
  Barberton (G-967)
Summa Health ....E 330 688-4531
  Stow (G-17234)
Superior Medical Care Inc ....E 440 282-7420
  Lorain (G-12946)
Triad Group Inc ....D 419 228-8800
  Lima (G-12768)
Trident USA Health Svcs LLC ....E 614 888-2226
  Columbus (G-8779)
University of Cincinnati...................E 513 558-4444
  Cincinnati (G-4708)
University of Cincinnati...................E 513 558-5439
  Cincinnati (G-4713)
University of Cincinnati...................E 513 584-5331
  Cincinnati (G-4716)
Vet Path Services Inc ....E 513 469-0777
  Mason (G-13654)
Womens Centers-Dayton ....E 937 228-2222
  Dayton (G-9885)
X-Ray Industries Inc ....E 216 642-0100
  Cleveland (G-6696)
Zak Enterprises Ltd ....D 216 261-9700
  Euclid (G-10661)

8072 Dental Laboratories

Classic Dental Labs Inc ....E 614 443-0328
  Columbus (G-7220)
Dental Ceramics Inc ....E 330 523-5240
  Richfield (G-16353)
Doling & Associates Dental Lab ....E 937 254-0075
  Dayton (G-9393)
Dresch Tolson Dental Labs ....D 419 842-6730
  Sylvania (G-17420)
Greater Cincinnati Dental Labs ....E 513 385-4222
  Cincinnati (G-3651)
Health Smile Center ....E 440 992-2700
  Ashtabula (G-739)
National Dentex LLC ....E 216 671-0577
  Cleveland (G-6042)
Roe Dental Laboratory Inc ....D 216 663-2233
  Independence (G-12116)
Sentage Corporation ....E 937 865-5900
  Miamisburg (G-14218)
State Valley Dental Center ....E 330 920-8060
  Cuyahoga Falls (G-9125)
United Dental Laboratories ....E 330 253-1810
  Tallmadge (G-17496)

8082 Home Health Care Svcs

1st Class Home Health Care Ser ....E 216 678-0213
  Northfield (G-15371)
A Touch of Grace Inc ....D 567 560-2350
  Mansfield (G-13131)
A Touch of Grace Inc ....D 740 397-7971
  Mount Vernon (G-14748)

S
I
C

A-1 Nursing Care Inc ....C 614 268-3800
Columbus (G-6850)

Ability Matters LLC ....E 614 214-9652
Hilliard (G-11739)

Above & Beyond Caregivers LLC ....E ... 614 478-1700
Columbus (G-6855)

Accentcare Home Health Cal Inc ....C ... 740 387-4568
Circleville (G-4822)

Accentcare Home Health Cal Inc ....C ... 740 474-7826
Circleville (G-4823)

Addus Homecare Corporation ....A ... 866 684-0385
Wintersville (G-19667)

Advance Home Care LLC ....D 614 436-3611
Columbus (G-6873)

Advance Home Care LLC ....D 937 723-6335
Dayton (G-9209)

Advantage Home Health Care ....D 800 636-2330
Portsmouth (G-16124)

Advantage Home Health Svcs Inc ....E ... 330 491-8161
North Canton (G-15184)

All About Home Care Svcs LLC ....E ... 937 222-2980
Dayton (G-9214)

All Heart Home Care LLC ....E 419 298-0034
Edgerton (G-10466)

All Hearts Home Health Care ....E 440 342-2026
Cleveland (G-4933)

Almost Family Inc ....E 614 457-1900
Columbus (G-6900)

Almost Family Inc ....E 330 724-7545
Akron (G-67)

Almost Family Inc ....E 216 464-0443
Cleveland (G-4939)

Alpine Nursing Care ....E 216 650-6295
Cleveland (G-4942)

Alternacare Home Health Inc ....E 740 689-1589
Lancaster (G-12370)

Alternate Sltions Private Duty ....D ... 937 298-1111
Dayton (G-9222)

Alternate Solutions First LLC ....C 937 298-1111
Dayton (G-9223)

Alternative Home Care & Stffng ....E ... 513 794-0571
Cincinnati (G-2934)

Alternative Home Health Care ....E 513 794-0555
Cincinnati (G-2935)

Altimate Care LLC ....E 614 794-9600
Columbus (G-6906)

Amandacare Inc ....C 614 884-8880
Columbus (G-6908)

Amber Home Care LLC ....E 614 523-0668
Columbus (G-6909)

Amedisys Inc ....E 740 373-8549
Marietta (G-13309)

Amenity Home Health Care LLC ....E ... 513 931-3689
Cincinnati (G-2937)

American Nursing Care Inc ....E 513 731-4600
Cincinnati (G-2947)

American Nursing Care Inc ....E 937 438-3844
Dayton (G-9228)

American Nursing Care Inc ....D 419 228-0888
Lima (G-12601)

American Nursing Care Inc ....D 740 452-0569
Zanesville (G-20276)

Angel Above Byond Hm Hlth Svcs ....E ... 513 553-9955
Cincinnati (G-2967)

Angels 4 Life LLC ....E 513 474-5683
Cincinnati (G-2968)

Angels Home Care LLC ....E 419 947-9373
Mount Gilead (G-14724)

Angels In Waiting Home Care ....E 440 946-0349
Mentor (G-14018)

Angels Touch Nursing Care ....E 513 661-4111
Cincinnati (G-2969)

Angels Visiting ....D 419 298-0034
Edgerton (G-10467)

Answercare LLC ....D 855 213-1511
Canton (G-2190)

Appalachian Community Visi ....D 740 594-8226
Athens (G-764)

Apria Healthcare LLC ....E 937 291-2842
Miamisburg (G-14141)

Arcadia Services Inc ....D 330 869-9520
Akron (G-77)

Arcadia Services Inc ....D 937 912-5800
Beavercreek (G-1126)

Area Agency On Aging Planni ....C 800 258-7277
Dayton (G-9239)

Area Office On Aging of Nwstrn ....D ... 419 382-0624
Toledo (G-17599)

Arlingworth Home Health Inc ....E 614 659-0961
Dublin (G-10137)

Around Clock Home Care ....D 440 350-2547
Painesville (G-15694)

ASAP Homecare Inc ....D 330 674-3306
Millersburg (G-14456)

ASAP Homecare Inc ....D 330 491-0700
Canton (G-2195)

ASAP Homecare Inc ....E 330 334-7027
Wadsworth (G-18590)

ASAP Homecare Inc ....C 330 263-4733
Wooster (G-19688)

Ashtabula Rgional Hm Hlth Svcs ....D ... 440 992-4663
Ashtabula (G-719)

Assured Health Care Inc ....E 937 294-2803
Dayton (G-9242)

Atrium Health System ....A 937 499-5606
Middletown (G-14342)

B & L Agency LLC ....E 740 373-8272
Marietta (G-13314)

B H C Services Inc ....A 216 289-5300
Euclid (G-10624)

Benjamin Rose Institute ....D 216 791-8000
Cleveland (G-5057)

Bethesda Hospital Association ....A 740 454-4000
Zanesville (G-20281)

Beyond The Horizons Home Healt ....E ... 608 630-0617
Columbus (G-7033)

Black Stone Cincinnati LLC ....D 937 424-1370
Moraine (G-14626)

Black Stone Cincinnati LLC ....E 513 924-1370
Cincinnati (G-3054)

Blanchard Valley Health System ....D ... 419 424-3000
Findlay (G-10872)

Bracor Inc ....E 216 289-5300
Euclid (G-10625)

Braden Med Services Inc ....E 740 732-2356
Caldwell (G-2036)

Bradley Bay Assisted Living ....E 440 871-4509
Bay Village (G-1021)

Bridgeshome Health Care ....E 330 764-1000
Medina (G-13913)

Brightstar Healthcare ....E 513 321-4688
Blue Ash (G-1516)

Brook Haven Home Health Care ....E ... 937 833-6945
Brookville (G-1910)

Brookdale Senior Living Commun ....E ... 937 548-6800
Greenville (G-11367)

Buckeye Hills-Hck Vly Reg Dev ....E ... 740 373-6400
Reno (G-16276)

Buckeye Home Health Care ....C 513 791-6446
Blue Ash (G-1517)

Buckeye Home Health Care ....E 937 291-3780
Dayton (G-9265)

Buckeye Home Healthcare Inc ....E 614 776-3372
Westerville (G-19229)

Buckeye Homecare Services Inc ....D ... 216 321-9300
Cleveland (G-5098)

Buckeye Rsdntial Solutions LLC ....D ... 330 235-9183
Ravenna (G-16233)

C K of Cincinnati Inc ....C 513 752-5533
Cincinnati (G-3100)

C R G Health Care Systems ....E 330 498-8107
Niles (G-15148)

Capital Health Homecare ....E 740 264-8815
Steubenville (G-17142)

Capital Senior Living Corp ....C 330 748-4204
Macedonia (G-13064)

Caprice Health Care Inc ....C 330 965-9200
North Lima (G-15267)

Care Connection of Cincinnati ....D ... 513 842-1101
Cincinnati (G-3120)

Caregivers Health Network Inc ....D ... 513 662-3400
Cincinnati (G-3121)

Carestar Inc ....C 513 618-8300
Columbus (G-3122)

Caring Hands Inc ....C 330 821-6310
Alliance (G-521)

Caring Hands Home Health Care ....E ... 740 532-9020
Ironton (G-12149)

Caring Hearts Home Health Care ....B ... 513 339-1237
Mason (G-13548)

Carl Mills ....D 740 282-2382
Toronto (G-18182)

Central Star ....C 419 756-9449
Ontario (G-15545)

Chcc Home Health Care ....D 330 759-4069
Austintown (G-857)

Chemed Corporation ....D 513 762-6690
Cincinnati (G-3175)

Chestnut Hill Management Co ....D 614 855-3700
Columbus (G-7183)

CHI Health At Home ....D 513 576-0262
Milford (G-14376)

Childrens Home Care Dayton ....D 937 641-4663
Dayton (G-9296)

Childrens Home Care Group ....B 330 543-5000
Akron (G-129)

Childrens Homecare Services ....C 614 355-1100
Columbus (G-7188)

Choice Healthcare Limited ....D 937 254-6220
Beavercreek (G-1139)

Circle J Home Health Care ....D 330 482-0877
Salineville (G-16570)

City of Wooster ....E 330 263-8636
Wooster (G-19703)

Clearpath HM Hlth Hospice LLC ....D ... 330 784-2162
Akron (G-141)

Clovvr LLC ....E 740 653-2224
Lancaster (G-12382)

Colt Enterprises Inc ....E 567 336-6062
Maumee (G-13774)

Columbus Behavioral Health LLC ....E ... 732 747-1800
Columbus (G-7262)

Comfort Healthcare ....E 216 281-9999
Cleveland (G-5317)

Comfort Keepers ....E 419 229-1031
Lima (G-12617)

Comfort Keepers ....E 440 721-0100
Painesville (G-15703)

Comfort Keepers Inc ....E 937 322-6288
Springfield (G-17017)

Committed To Care Inc ....E 513 245-1190
Cincinnati (G-3339)

Community Caregivers ....E 330 725-9800
Wadsworth (G-18593)

Community Choice Home Care ....E ... 740 574-9900
Wheelersburg (G-19431)

Community Concepts Inc ....C 513 398-8181
Mason (G-13565)

Community Health Systems Inc ....D ... 330 841-9011
Warren (G-18688)

Community Hlth Prfssionals Inc ....E ... 419 634-7443
Ada (G-3)

Community Hlth Prfssionals Inc ....E ... 419 445-5128
Archbold (G-628)

Community Hlth Prfssionals Inc ....C ... 419 238-9223
Van Wert (G-18475)

Community Hlth Prfssionals Inc ....E ... 419 399-4708
Paulding (G-15791)

Community Hlth Prfssionals Inc ....E ... 419 991-1822
Lima (G-12789)

Community Hlth Prfssionals Inc ....E ... 419 586-1999
Celina (G-2589)

Community Hlth Prfssionals Inc ....D ... 419 586-6266
Celina (G-2590)

Community Hlth Prfssionals Inc ....E ... 419 695-8101
Delphos (G-10022)

Community Home Care ....E 330 971-7011
Cuyahoga Falls (G-9084)

Companions of Ashland LLC ....E 419 281-2273
Ashland (G-669)

Compassionate In Home Care ....E 614 888-5683
Worthington (G-19800)

Concord Hlth Rhabilitation Ctr ....E ... 740 574-8441
Wheelersburg (G-19432)

Consumer Support Services Inc ....C ... 330 652-8800
Niles (G-15153)

Consumer Support Services Inc ....B ... 740 788-8257
Newark (G-15024)

Continued Care Inc ....E 419 222-2273
Lima (G-12618)

Continuum Home Care Inc ....E 440 964-3332
Ashtabula (G-730)

Cori Care Inc ....D 614 848-4357
Columbus (G-7369)

Cottages of Clayton ....E 937 280-0300
Dayton (G-9323)

County of Knox ....E 740 392-2200
Mount Vernon (G-14758)

County of Washington ....E 740 373-2028
Marietta (G-13322)

County of Williams ....E 419 485-3141
Montpelier (G-14612)

Covenant Home Health Care LLC ....E ... 614 465-2017
Columbus (G-7382)

Covington Square Senior APT ....E ... 740 623-4603
Coshocton (G-9013)

Crawford Cnty Shared Hlth Svcs ....E ... 419 468-7985
Galion (G-11169)

Dacas Nursing Systems Inc ....C 330 884-2530
Warren (G-18698)

Daugwood Inc ....E 937 429-9465
Beavercreek (G-1144)

Daynas Homecare LLC ....E 216 323-0323
Maple Heights (G-13285)

Dayton Hospice Incorporated.......B 937 256-4490
Dayton (G-9369)

Dayton Hospice Incorporated.......C 513 422-0300
Franklin (G-11027)

Decahealth Inc ....D 866 908-3514
Toledo (G-17696)

Detox Health Care Corp Ohio ......B 513 742-6310
Cincinnati (G-3424)

Diane Vishnia Rn and Assoc........D 330 929-1113
Cuyahoga Falls (G-9087)

Dillon Holdings LLC ....C 513 942-5600
West Chester (G-18911)

▲ Discount Drug Mart Inc ....C 330 725-2340
Medina (G-13931)

Diversified Health Management.....E 614 338-8888
Columbus (G-7454)

EJq Home Health Care Inc ....D 440 323-7004
Elyria (G-10504)

Eldercare Services Inst LLC ......D 216 791-8000
Cleveland (G-5470)

Ember Complete Care ....C 740 922-6888
Uhrichsville (G-18340)

Ember Home Care...................B 740 922-6968
Uhrichsville (G-18341)

Emh Regional Homecare Agency .....E 440 329-7519
Elyria (G-10509)

Enhanced Home Health Care LLC ....D 614 433-7266
Columbus (G-7517)

Enhanced Homecare Medina Inc......E 330 952-2331
Medina (G-13934)

Every Child Succeeds ....C 513 636-2830
Cincinnati (G-3522)

Everyday Homecare.................E 937 444-1672
Mount Orab (G-14740)

Excel Health Services LLC ....D 614 794-0006
Delaware (G-9973)

Exclusive Homecare Services ......D 937 236-6750
Dayton (G-9421)

Fairfield Community Health Ctr ...E 740 277-6043
Lancaster (G-12392)

Fairhope Hospice and Palliativ ...D 740 654-7077
Lancaster (G-12402)

Faithful Companions Inc ....E 440 255-4357
Mentor (G-14046)

Family Senior Care Inc ....E 740 441-1428
Gallipolis (G-11191)

Family Service of NW Ohio ....D 419 321-6455
Toledo (G-17725)

Fidelity Health Care ....B 937 208-6400
Moraine (G-14657)

First Choice Medical Staffing.....D 419 861-2722
Toledo (G-17739)

First Community Hlth Svcs LLC ....E 937 247-0400
Dayton (G-9434)

First Community Village ....B 614 324-4455
Columbus (G-7585)

Fns Inc ....E 740 775-5463
Chillicothe (G-2781)

Frencor Inc ....D 330 332-1203
Salem (G-16544)

Gamble Elzbeth Dcness HM Assn.....A 513 751-4224
Cincinnati (G-3601)

Good Samaritan Hosp Cincinnati ...E 513 569-6251
Cincinnati (G-3625)

Graceworks Lutheran Services .....B 937 436-6850
Dayton (G-9468)

Great Lakes Home Hlth Svcs Inc ...E 888 260-9835
Toledo (G-17769)

Great Lakes Home Hlth Svcs Inc ...E 888 260-9835
Akron (G-244)

Great Lakes Home Hlth Svcs Inc ...E 888 260-9835
Mentor (G-14055)

Guardian Angls Home Hlth Svcs ....D 419 517-7797
Sylvania (G-17428)

Hamilton Homecare Inc ....E 614 221-0022
Columbus (G-7712)

Hanson Services Inc ....C 216 226-5425
Lakewood (G-12345)

Hastings Home Health Ctr Inc .....E 216 898-3300
Medina (G-13947)

Hattie Larlham Community Svcs.....D 330 274-2272
Mantua (G-13270)

Hcr Manorcare Med Svcs Fla LLC ...D 513 233-0831
Cincinnati (G-3689)

Healing Hands Home Health Ltd ....E 740 385-0710
Logan (G-12836)

Healing Touch Healthcare ....E 937 610-5555
Dayton (G-9489)

Health & HM Care Concepts Inc ....E 740 383-4968
Marion (G-13423)

Health Care Facility MGT LLC .....D 513 489-7100
Blue Ash (G-1576)

Health Care Plus ....C 614 340-7587
Westerville (G-19170)

Health Services Coshocton Cnty ...E 740 622-7311
Coshocton (G-9016)

Healthcare Circle Inc ....D 440 331-7347
Strongsville (G-17308)

Healthcare Holdings Inc ....D 513 530-1600
Blue Ash (G-1577)

Healthlinx Inc ....E 513 402-2018
Cincinnati (G-3695)

Healthsource of Ohio Inc ....E 937 981-7707
Greenfield (G-11363)

Healthy Life HM Healthcare LLC ...E 614 865-3368
Columbus (G-7727)

Heart To Heart Home Health ....E 330 335-9999
Wadsworth (G-18598)

Heartland Home Care LLC ....E 614 433-0423
Columbus (G-7731)

Heartland Hospice Services LLC ...D 614 433-0423
Columbus (G-7732)

Heartland Hospice Services LLC ...D 740 351-0575
Portsmouth (G-16144)

Heartland Hospice Services LLC ...D 740 259-0281
Lucasville (G-13050)

Heartland Hospice Services LLC ...D 419 531-0440
Perrysburg (G-15872)

Heartland Hospice Services LLC ...E 937 299-6980
Dayton (G-9492)

Heartland Hospice Services LLC ...D 216 901-1464
Independence (G-12079)

Heavenly Home Health ....E 740 859-4735
Rayland (G-16272)

Helping Hands Health Care Inc ....C 513 755-4181
West Chester (G-19059)

Heritage Day Health Centers ......E 614 451-2151
Columbus (G-7744)

Heritage Health Care Services ....D 419 222-2404
Lima (G-12659)

Heritage Health Care Services ....C 419 867-2002
Maumee (G-13800)

Heritage Home Health Care ....E 440 333-1925
Rocky River (G-16435)

Highpoint Home Healthcare Agcy ...E 330 491-1805
Canton (G-2343)

Hillebrand Home Health Inc ....E 513 598-6648
Cincinnati (G-3702)

Home Care Advantage..............D 330 337-4663
Salem (G-16547)

Home Care Network Inc ....D 937 435-1142
Dayton (G-9498)

Home Care Relief Inc ....D 216 692-2270
Euclid (G-10641)

Home Helper Direct Link ....D 330 865-5730
Akron (G-269)

Home Helpers ....D 937 393-8600
Hillsboro (G-11847)

Home Instead Senior Care ....D 330 334-4664
Wadsworth (G-18599)

Home Instead Senior Care ....E 740 393-2500
Mount Vernon (G-14767)

Home Instead Senior Care ....D 330 729-1233
Youngstown (G-20066)

Home Instead Senior Care ....D 614 432-8524
Upper Arlington (G-18398)

Homecare Mtters HM Hlth Hspice ...D 419 562-2001
Bucyrus (G-1993)

Homecare Service Inc ....E 513 655-5022
Blue Ash (G-1582)

Homereach Inc ....C 614 566-0850
Worthington (G-19816)

Hope Homes Inc ....E 330 688-4935
Stow (G-17210)

Horizon HM Hlth Care Agcy LLC ....E 614 279-2933
Columbus (G-7773)

Hospice Care Ohio ....D 330 665-1455
Fairlawn (G-10832)

Hospice Caring Way ....D 419 238-9223
Van Wert (G-18480)

Hospice Cincinnati Inc ....E 513 862-1100
Cincinnati (G-3728)

Hospice Cincinnati Inc ....D 513 891-7700
Cincinnati (G-3729)

Hospice of Genesis Health ....E 740 454-5381
Zanesville (G-20318)

Hospice of Knox County ....E 740 397-5188
Mount Vernon (G-14768)

Hospice of Memorial Hospita L ....E 419 334-6626
Clyde (G-6745)

Hospice of Miami County Inc ......E 937 335-5191
Troy (G-18207)

Hospice of Miami Valley LLC ......E 937 521-1444
Springfield (G-17048)

Hospice of North Central Ohio ....E 419 524-9200
Ontario (G-15553)

Hospice of North Central Ohio ....E 419 281-7107
Ashland (G-675)

Hospice of The Western Reserve ...D 330 800-2240
Medina (G-13951)

Hospice of The Western Reserve ...E 800 707-8921
Cleveland (G-5711)

Hospice of The Western Reserve ...E 440 997-6619
Ashtabula (G-740)

Hospice of The Western Reserve ...C 216 227-9048
Cleveland (G-5714)

Hospice Southwest Ohio Inc ....D 513 770-0820
Cincinnati (G-3730)

Huntsey Corporation ....E 614 568-5030
Westerville (G-19174)

In Home Health LLC ....E 419 531-0440
Toledo (G-17819)

In Home Health LLC ....D 513 831-5800
Cincinnati (G-3754)

In Home Health LLC ....D 419 355-9209
Fremont (G-11081)

Independent Living of Ohio ....E 937 323-8400
Springfield (G-17051)

Infinity Health Services Inc .....D 440 614-0145
Westlake (G-19357)

▲ Infusion Partners Inc ....E 513 396-6060
Cincinnati (G-3761)

Inter Healt Care of Cambr Zane ...E 614 436-9404
Columbus (G-7832)

Inter Healt Care of Cambr Zane ...E 513 984-1110
Cincinnati (G-3773)

Inter Healt Care of North OH I ...D 740 453-5130
Zanesville (G-20320)

Inter Healt Care of North OH I ...E 419 422-5328
Findlay (G-10927)

Interim Halthcare Columbus Inc ...D 330 836-5571
Fairlawn (G-10834)

Interim Healthcare Columbus Inc ..A 740 349-8700
Newark (G-15044)

Interim Healthcare................D 740 354-5550
Portsmouth (G-16150)

Interim Healthcare of Dayton .....B 937 291-5330
Dayton (G-9518)

Interim Healthcare SE Ohio Inc ...D 740 373-3800
Marietta (G-13339)

International Healthcare Corp .....D 513 731-3338
Cincinnati (G-3779)

Intervention For Peace Inc ....D 330 725-1298
Medina (G-13957)

Jag Healthcare Inc ....A 440 385-4370
Rocky River (G-16437)

Joint Township Home Health ....E 419 394-3335
Saint Marys (G-16525)

Kaiser-Wells Inc ....E 419 668-7651
Norwalk (G-15440)

Karopa Incorporate ....E 513 860-1616
Hamilton (G-11619)

Khc Inc ....D 740 775-5463
Chillicothe (G-2797)

Labelle Hmhealth Care Svcs LLC ...D 440 842-3005
Cleveland (G-5845)

Labelle Hmhealth Care Svcs LLC ...D 740 392-1405
Mount Vernon (G-14777)

Laurie Ann Home Health Care ......E 330 872-7512
Newton Falls (G-15138)

Lbs International Inc ....D 614 866-3688
Pickerington (G-15962)

Lifecare Alliance ....C 614 278-3130
Columbus (G-7974)

Lighthouse Medical Staffing ......D 614 937-6259
Hilliard (G-11784)

Little Miami Home Care Inc ....E 513 248-8988
Milford (G-14401)

Living Assistance Services ....D 330 733-1532
Tallmadge (G-17481)

Love N Comfort Home Care ....E 740 450-7658
Zanesville (G-20325)

Loving Care Hospice Inc ....E 740 852-7755
London (G-12866)

Loving Family Home Care Inc.......D 888 469-2178
Toledo (G-17863)

Loving Hands Home Care Inc ....E 330 792-7032	Omni Park Health Care LLC ....C 216 289-8963	RES-Care Inc ....E 513 858-4550
Youngstown *(G-20100)*	Euclid *(G-10651)*	West Chester *(G-18992)*
Lutheran Social Services of ....E 614 228-5200	Omnicare Inc ....C 513 719-2600	Rescare Ohio Inc ....E 740 867-4568
Worthington *(G-19826)*	Cincinnati *(G-4168)*	Chesapeake *(G-2732)*
Mahoning Vly Infusioncare Inc ....C 330 759-9487	On-Call Nursing Svc ....D 216 577-8890	Richard Health Systems LLC ....C 419 534-2371
Youngstown *(G-20111)*	Lakewood *(G-12358)*	Toledo *(G-18007)*
Majastan Group LLC ....D 216 231-6400	Open Arms Health Systems Llc ....E 614 385-8354	Right At Home ....D 937 291-2244
Cleveland *(G-5900)*	Columbus *(G-8375)*	Springboro *(G-16983)*
Manor Care Inc ....D 419 252-5500	Option Care Enterprises Inc ....C 513 576-8400	Right At Home LLC ....E 614 734-1110
Toledo *(G-17880)*	Milford *(G-14415)*	Columbus *(G-6833)*
Maple Knoll Communities Inc ....A 513 782-2400	Option Care Infusion Svcs Inc ....E 614 431-6453	RMS of Ohio Inc ....E 937 291-3622
Cincinnati *(G-3967)*	Columbus *(G-8381)*	Dayton *(G-9737)*
Maplecrst Asistd Lvg Intl Ordr ....E 419 562-4988	Option Care Infusion Svcs Inc ....D 513 576-8400	Robinson Visitn Nrs Asoc/Hospc ......E 330 297-8899
Bucyrus *(G-1996)*	Milford *(G-14416)*	Ravenna *(G-16264)*
Marietta Memorial Hospital ....E 740 373-8549	P E Miller & Assoc ....E 614 231-4743	Ross County Health District ....C 740 775-1114
Marietta *(G-13355)*	Columbus *(G-8407)*	Chillicothe *(G-2820)*
▲ Marymount Hospital Inc ....B 216 581-0500	P E Miller & Associates Inc ....D 614 231-4743	RWS Enterprises LLC ....D 513 598-6770
Cleveland *(G-5920)*	Columbus *(G-8408)*	Cincinnati *(G-4416)*
Mch Services Inc ....C 260 432-9699	Palladium Healthcare LLC ....C 216 644-4383	Rx Home Health Care Inc ....D 216 295-0056
Dayton *(G-9595)*	Cleveland *(G-6159)*	Cleveland *(G-6352)*
Med America Hlth Systems Corp ......A 937 223-6192	Paramount Support Service ....D 740 526-0540	Salem Area Vsiting Nurse Assoc ......E 330 332-9986
Dayton *(G-9598)*	Saint Clairsville *(G-16501)*	Salem *(G-16558)*
Medcentral Health System ....E 419 526-8442	Parkside Care Corporation ....D 440 286-2273	Salo Inc ....D 614 436-9404
Mansfield *(G-13214)*	Chardon *(G-2707)*	Columbus *(G-8585)*
Medcorp Inc ....D 419 727-7000	Passion To Heal Healthcare ....E 216 849-0180	Salo Inc ....A 740 964-2904
Toledo *(G-17900)*	Cleveland *(G-6179)*	Pataskala *(G-15787)*
Medcorp Inc ....C 419 425-9700	Paula Jo Moore ....E 330 894-2910	Sand Run Supports LLC ....E 330 256-2127
Findlay *(G-10942)*	Kensington *(G-12211)*	Fairlawn *(G-10848)*
Medi Home Health Agency Inc ....E 740 266-3977	Personal Touch HM Care IPA Inc ......C 216 986-0885	Sar Enterprises LLC ....D 419 472-8181
Steubenville *(G-17165)*	Cleveland *(G-6197)*	Toledo *(G-18019)*
Medi Home Health Agency Inc ....E 740 441-1779	Personal Touch HM Care IPA Inc ......D 937 456-4447	Schroer Properties Inc ....D 330 498-8200
Gallipolis *(G-11204)*	Eaton *(G-10458)*	North Canton *(G-15231)*
Medlink of Ohio Inc ....B 216 751-5900	Personal Touch HM Care IPA Inc ......C 513 868-2272	Sdx Home Care Operations LLC ......D 937 322-6288
Cleveland *(G-5944)*	Hamilton *(G-11632)*	Springfield *(G-17109)*
Memorial Hospital ....E 419 547-6419	Personal Touch HM Care IPA Inc ......D 513 984-9600	Selective Networking Inc ....D 740 574-2682
Clyde *(G-6748)*	Cincinnati *(G-4233)*	Wheelersburg *(G-19440)*
Menorah Park Center For Senio ....D 330 867-2143	Personal Touch HM Care IPA Inc ......E 614 227-6952	Senior Care Management Inc ....D 419 578-7000
Cuyahoga Falls *(G-9112)*	Columbus *(G-8442)*	Toledo *(G-18024)*
Mercer Cnty Joint Townshp Hosp ......E 419 584-0143	Personal Touch HM Care IPA Inc ......A 330 263-1112	Senior Independence ....E 330 744-5071
Celina *(G-2600)*	Wooster *(G-19758)*	Youngstown *(G-20207)*
Mid Ohio Home Health Ltd ....E 419 529-3883	Phoenix Homes Inc ....E 419 692-2421	Senior Independence ....D 330 873-3468
Ontario *(G-15565)*	Delphos *(G-10033)*	Fairlawn *(G-10850)*
Mircale Health Care ....C 614 237-7702	Physicians Choice Inc ....E 513 844-1608	Senior Independence Adult ....E 513 539-2697
Columbus *(G-8090)*	Liberty Twp *(G-12588)*	Monroe *(G-14583)*
Mount Crmel Hospice Evrgrn Ctr ......D 614 234-0200	Preferred Medical Group Inc ....C 404 403-8310	Senior Select Home Health Care ......E 330 665-4663
Columbus *(G-8115)*	Beachwood *(G-1096)*	Copley *(G-8973)*
Multicare Home Health Services ....D 216 731-8900	Premier Care ....E 614 431-0599	Serenity HM Halthcare Svcs LLC ......D 937 222-0002
Euclid *(G-10649)*	Worthington *(G-19836)*	Dayton *(G-9760)*
Nationwide Childrens Hospital ....E 614 355-8300	Premier Health Partners ....A 937 499-9596	Simone Health Management Inc ......E 614 224-1347
Westerville *(G-19188)*	Dayton *(G-9704)*	Columbus *(G-8643)*
Nationwide Health MGT LLC ....D 440 888-8888	Premierfirst Home Health Care ....E 614 443-3110	Source Diagnostics LLC ....D 440 542-9481
Parma *(G-15769)*	Columbus *(G-8459)*	Solon *(G-16901)*
NC Hha Inc ....D 216 593-7750	Primary Care Nursing Services ....D 614 764-0960	Southern Care Inc ....E 419 774-0555
Elyria *(G-10542)*	Dublin *(G-10311)*	Ontario *(G-15574)*
NCR At Home Health & Wellness ......D 614 451-2151	Prime Home Care LLC ....E 513 340-4183	Special Touch Homecare LLC ....E 937 549-1843
Columbus *(G-8166)*	Maineville *(G-13117)*	Manchester *(G-13129)*
New Life Hospice Inc ....E 440 934-1458	Prime Home Care LLC ....E 419 535-1414	Ssth LLC ....D 614 884-0793
Lorain *(G-12930)*	Toledo *(G-17988)*	Columbus *(G-8679)*
New Life Hospice Inc ....D 440 934-1458	Private Duty Services Inc ....C 419 238-3714	St Augustine Manor ....B 440 888-7722
Lorain *(G-12931)*	Van Wert *(G-18487)*	Parma *(G-15777)*
Nightingale Home Healthcare ....E 614 408-0104	Private HM Care Foundation Inc ....E 513 662-8999	St Augustine Towers ....E 216 634-7444
Dublin *(G-10291)*	Cincinnati *(G-4285)*	Cleveland *(G-6447)*
Northeast Professional Hm Care ....E 330 966-2311	Pro Health Care Services Ltd ....E 614 856-9111	St Ritas Medical Center ....C 419 538-7025
Canton *(G-2421)*	Groveport *(G-11532)*	Lima *(G-12751)*
Nurse Medicial Healthcare Svcs ....D 614 801-1300	Proactive Occpational Medicine ....E 740 574-8728	Summit Acres Inc ....C 740 732-2364
Grove City *(G-11460)*	Wheelersburg *(G-19438)*	Caldwell *(G-2044)*
Nurses Care Inc ....D 513 424-1141	Prome Conti Care Serv Corpo ....A 419 885-1715	Sunshine Homecare ....E 419 207-9900
Miamisburg *(G-14198)*	Sylvania *(G-17493)*	Ashland *(G-693)*
Nursing Resources Corp ....C 419 333-3000	Protem Homecare LLC ....E 216 663-8188	Supportcare Inc ....E 614 889-5837
Maumee *(G-13825)*	Cleveland *(G-6261)*	Dublin *(G-10346)*
Odyssey Healthcare Inc ....E 614 414-0500	Putnam Cnty Homecare & Hospice ......D 419 523-4449	Supreme Touch Home Health Svcs ......D 614 783-1115
Gahanna *(G-11138)*	Ottawa *(G-15665)*	Columbus *(G-8719)*
Ohio Home Health Care Inc ....E 937 853-0271	Quality Care Nursing Svcs LLC ....C 740 377-9095	Svh Holdings LLC ....D 844 560-7775
Dayton *(G-9669)*	South Point *(G-16944)*	Columbus *(G-8722)*
Ohio North E Hlth Systems Inc ....E 330 747-9551	Quality Life Providers LLC ....E 614 527-9999	Synergy Homecare ....D 937 610-0555
Youngstown *(G-20146)*	Hilliard *(G-11809)*	Dayton *(G-9804)*
Ohio Senior Home Hlth Care LLC ......D 614 470-6070	Quantum Health Inc ....D 614 846-4318	Think-Ability LLC ....E 419 589-2238
Columbus *(G-8286)*	Columbus *(G-8481)*	Mansfield *(G-13253)*
Ohio Valley Home Care LLC ....E 330 385-2333	R & F Inc ....E 419 868-2909	Tk Homecare Llc ....C 419 517-7000
East Liverpool *(G-10412)*	Holland *(G-11906)*	Toledo *(G-18067)*
Ohio Valley Home Health Inc ....E 740 249-4219	Rainbow Residentials LLC ....E 330 819-4202	Tky Associates LLC ....D 419 535-7777
Athens *(G-800)*	Tallmadge *(G-17485)*	Toledo *(G-18068)*
Ohio Valley Home Health Inc ....D 740 441-1393	Reflektions Ltd ....E 614 560-6994	TLC Home Health Care Inc ....E 740 732-5211
Gallipolis *(G-11210)*	Delaware *(G-10003)*	Caldwell *(G-2045)*
Ohio Valley Home Hlth Svcs Inc ....E 330 385-2333	REM Corp ....E 740 828-2601	Toledo District Nurses Assn ....E 419 255-0983
East Liverpool *(G-10413)*	Frazeysburg *(G-11050)*	Sylvania *(G-17458)*
Ohioans Home Health Care Inc ....D 419 843-4422	RES-Care Inc ....E 740 782-1476	Toledo Hospital ....C 419 291-2273
Perrysburg *(G-15898)*	Bethesda *(G-1457)*	Sylvania *(G-17459)*
Ohiohealth Corporation ....A 614 788-8860	RES-Care Inc ....E 440 729-2432	Tri County Visitng Nrs Prvt ....E 419 738-7430
Columbus *(G-8362)*	Chesterland *(G-2744)*	Wapakoneta *(G-18656)*

Trusted Homecare Solutions ....E 937 506-7063
Dayton (G-9825)
Tsk Assisted Living Services ....E 330 297-2000
Ravenna (G-16269)
TVC Home Health Care ....E 330 755-1110
Youngstown (G-20229)
Uahs Heather Hill Home Health ....E 440 285-5098
Chardon (G-2719)
Union Hospital Home Hlth Care ....E 330 343-6909
Dover (G-10107)
United Home Health Services ....D 614 880-8686
Columbus (G-8802)
Unity I Home Healthcare LLC ....E 740 351-0500
Portsmouth (G-16177)
Universal Health Care Svcs Inc ....C 614 547-0282
Columbus (G-8816)
Universal Nursing Services ....E 330 434-7318
Akron (G-478)
University Hospitals Cleveland ....D 216 844-4663
Cleveland (G-6594)
University Hospitals He ....B 216 844-4663
Cleveland (G-6596)
University Mednet ....B 216 383-0100
Euclid (G-10660)
Ussa Inc ....E 740 354-6672
Portsmouth (G-16179)
Viaquest Behavioral Health LLC ....E 614 339-0868
Dublin (G-10363)
VIP Homecare Inc ....D 330 929-2838
Akron (G-488)
Vishnia & Associates Inc ....D 330 929-5512
Cuyahoga Falls (G-9137)
Visions Matter LLC ....D 513 934-1934
Lebanon (G-12513)
Visiting Nrse Assn of Clveland ....B 419 281-2480
Ashland (G-697)
Visiting Nrse Assn of Clveland ....E 419 522-4969
Mansfield (G-13260)
Visiting Nrse Assn of Mid-Ohio ....E 216 931-1300
Cleveland (G-6636)
Visiting Nurse Associat ....C 513 345-8000
Cincinnati (G-4761)
Visiting Nurse Service Inc ....B 330 745-1601
Akron (G-490)
Visiting Nurse Service Inc ....E 440 286-9461
Chardon (G-2723)
Vistacare USA Inc ....E 614 975-3230
Columbus (G-8856)
Vrable III Inc ....D 740 446-7150
Bidwell (G-1471)
Western Reserve Area Agency ....C 216 621-0303
Cleveland (G-6673)
Ziks Family Pharmacy 100 ....E 937 225-9350
Dayton (G-9898)

8092 Kidney Dialysis Centers

Alomie Dialysis LLC ....E 740 941-1688
Waverly (G-18813)
Amelia Davita Dialysis Center ....E 513 797-0713
Amelia (G-564)
Barrington Dialysis LLC ....E 740 346-2740
Steubenville (G-17140)
Basin Dialysis LLC ....E 937 643-2337
Kettering (G-12291)
Beck Dialysis LLC ....E 513 422-6879
Middletown (G-14290)
Bio-Mdcal Applcations Ohio Inc ....E 937 279-3120
Trotwood (G-18191)
Bio-Mdcal Applcations Ohio Inc ....E 419 874-3447
Perrysburg (G-15839)
Bio-Mdcal Applcations Ohio Inc ....E 614 538-1060
Columbus (G-7040)
Bio-Mdcal Applcations Ohio Inc ....E 330 376-4905
Akron (G-98)
Bio-Mdcal Applcations Ohio Inc ....E 419 774-0180
Mansfield (G-13141)
Bio-Mdcal Applcations Ohio Inc ....E 330 896-6311
Uniontown (G-18357)
Bio-Mdcal Applcations Ohio Inc ....E 614 338-8202
Columbus (G-7041)
Bio-Mdcal Applications RI Inc ....E 740 389-4111
Marion (G-13405)
Center For Dlysis Cre of Cnfld ....E 330 702-3040
Canfield (G-2133)
Centers For Dialysis Care Inc ....C 216 295-7000
Shaker Heights (G-16705)
Columbus Med Partners LLC ....E 614 538-1060
Columbus (G-7295)
Columbus-Rna-Davita LLC ....E 614 985-1732
Columbus (G-7322)

Community Dialysis Center ....E 216 295-7000
Cleveland (G-5325)
Community Dialysis Center ....C 216 229-6170
Cleveland (G-5326)
Community Dialysis Center ....E 330 609-0370
Warren (G-18687)
Community Dialysis Center ....B 216 295-7000
Shaker Heights (G-16706)
Community Dialysis Ctr Mentor ....E 440 255-5999
Mentor (G-14033)
Court Dialysis LLC ....E 740 773-3733
Chillicothe (G-2773)
Crestview Health Care Center ....D 740 695-2500
Saint Clairsville (G-16485)
Davita Healthcare Partners Inc ....E 216 961-6498
Cleveland (G-5410)
Davita Healthcare Partners Inc ....E 440 353-0114
North Ridgeville (G-15328)
Davita Inc ....E 513 939-1110
Fairfield (G-10716)
Davita Inc ....E 216 712-4700
Rocky River (G-16430)
Davita Inc ....E 440 891-5645
Cleveland (G-5411)
Davita Inc ....E 740 376-2622
Marietta (G-13325)
Davita Inc ....E 937 456-1174
Eaton (G-10441)
Davita Inc ....E 330 494-2091
Canton (G-2280)
Davita Inc ....E 216 525-0990
Independence (G-12065)
Davita Inc ....E 937 879-0433
Fairborn (G-10669)
Davita Inc ....E 937 426-6475
Beavercreek (G-1145)
Davita Inc ....E 937 435-4030
Dayton (G-9346)
Davita Inc ....E 937 376-1453
Xenia (G-19897)
Davita Inc ....E 440 293-6028
Andover (G-605)
Davita Inc ....E 513 784-1800
Cincinnati (G-3403)
Davita Inc ....E 740 401-0607
Belpre (G-1401)
Davita Inc ....E 330 335-2300
Wadsworth (G-18595)
Davita Inc ....E 440 251-6237
Madison (G-13094)
Davita Inc ....E 615 341-6311
Georgetown (G-11270)
Davita Inc ....E 330 733-1861
Akron (G-182)
Davita Inc ....E 419 697-2191
Oregon (G-15589)
Davita Inc ....E 513 624-0400
Cincinnati (G-3404)
Dayton Regional Dialysis Inc ....E 937 898-5526
Dayton (G-9380)
Desoto Dialysis LLC ....E 419 691-1514
Oregon (G-15590)
Dialysis Center of Dayton East ....E 937 252-1867
Dayton (G-9390)
Dialysis Clinic Inc ....D 513 281-0091
Cincinnati (G-3428)
Dialysis Clinic Inc ....E 740 351-0596
Portsmouth (G-16136)
Dialysis Clinic Inc ....E 513 777-0855
West Chester (G-18910)
Dialysis Clinic Inc ....E 740 264-6687
Steubenville (G-17151)
Dialysis Specialists Fairfield ....E 513 863-6331
Fairfield (G-10718)
Dome Dialysis LLC ....E 614 882-1734
Westerville (G-19250)
DSI East ....E 330 733-1861
Akron (G-196)
Dva Healthcare - South ....E 513 347-0444
Cincinnati (G-3458)
Dva Renal Healthcare Inc ....E 740 454-2911
Zanesville (G-20302)
Fort Dialysis LLC ....E 330 837-7730
Massillon (G-13683)
Fresenius Med Care Butler Cty ....E 513 737-1415
Hamilton (G-11599)
Fresenius Med Care Hldings Inc ....E 216 267-1451
Cleveland (G-5578)
Fresenius Med Care Hldings Inc ....E 800 881-5101
Columbus (G-7624)

Fresenius Med Care Milford LLC ....E 513 248-1690
Milford (G-14389)
Fresenius Medical Care Vro LLC ....E 614 875-2349
Grove City (G-11435)
Fresenius Usa Inc ....E 330 837-2575
Massillon (G-13684)
Fresenius Usa Inc ....E 419 691-2475
Oregon (G-15595)
Fresenius Usa Inc ....E 440 734-7474
North Olmsted (G-15290)
Goza Dialysis LLC ....E 513 738-0276
Fairfield (G-10730)
Greater Columbus Regional ....D 614 228-9114
Columbus (G-7693)
Greenfield Health Systems Corp ....E 419 389-9681
Toledo (G-17771)
Hemodialysis Services Inc ....E 216 378-2691
Beachwood (G-1063)
Heyburn Dialysis LLC ....E 614 876-3610
Hilliard (G-11774)
Innovative Dialysis ....E 419 473-9900
Toledo (G-17822)
Isd Renal Inc ....D 330 375-6848
Akron (G-282)
Kidney Center of Bexley LLC ....D 614 231-2200
Columbus (G-7902)
Kidney Center Partnership ....D 330 799-1150
Youngstown (G-20090)
Kidney Group Inc ....E 330 746-1488
Youngstown (G-20091)
Kidney Services W Centl Ohio ....E 419 227-0918
Lima (G-12669)
Kinswa Dialysis LLC ....E 419 332-0310
Fremont (G-11083)
Lakeshore Dialysis LLC ....E 937 278-0516
Dayton (G-9555)
Lory Dialysis LLC ....E 740 522-2955
Newark (G-15062)
Mahoney Dialysis LLC ....E 937 642-0676
Marysville (G-13512)
Manzano Dialysis LLC ....E 937 879-0433
Fairborn (G-10680)
Mesilla Dialysis LLC ....E 937 484-4600
Urbana (G-18441)
Morro Dialysis LLC ....E 937 865-0633
Miamisburg (G-14195)
Mount Carmel E Dialysis Clnc ....E 614 322-0433
Columbus (G-8109)
Ohio Renal Care Group LLC ....D 440 974-3459
Mentor (G-14092)
Ohio Renal Care Group LLC ....E 330 928-4511
Cuyahoga Falls (G-9116)
Pendster Dialysis LLC ....E 937 237-0769
Huber Heights (G-11956)
Renal Life Link Inc ....E 937 383-3338
Wilmington (G-19644)
Seneca Dialysis LLC ....D 419 443-1051
Tiffin (G-17538)
Steele Dialysis LLC ....E 419 462-1028
Galion (G-11182)
Tonka Bay Dialysis LLC ....E 740 375-0849
Marion (G-13464)
Total Renal Care Inc ....E 937 294-6711
Kettering (G-12301)
Total Renal Care Inc ....E 937 252-1867
Dayton (G-9817)
Trinity Health Corporation ....B 614 846-5420
Columbus (G-8781)
Vogel Dialysis LLC ....E 614 834-3564
Canal Winchester (G-2124)
Wakoni Dialysis LLC ....E 937 294-7188
Moraine (G-14706)
Wallowa Dialysis LLC ....E 419 747-4039
Ontario (G-15578)
Wauseon Dialysis LLC ....E 419 335-0695
Wauseon (G-18811)

8093 Specialty Outpatient Facilities, NEC

A W S Inc ....D 216 941-8800
Cleveland (G-4882)
A+ Solutions LLC ....E 216 896-0111
Beachwood (G-1025)
Aaris Therapy Group Inc ....E 330 505-1606
Niles (G-15142)
Access Ohio ....E 614 367-7700
Columbus (G-6862)
Akron General Medical Center ....C 330 665-8000
Akron (G-46)
Alcohol Drug Addction & Mental ....E 937 443-0416
Dayton (G-9213)

S I C

Allwell Behavioral Health Svcs............E 740 454-9766
Zanesville *(G-20274)*

Allwell Behavioral Health Svcs............E 740 439-4428
Cambridge *(G-2049)*

Alta Care Group Inc............E 330 793-2487
Youngstown *(G-19952)*

Alternative Paths Inc............E 330 725-9195
Medina *(G-13909)*

Ambulatory Care Solutions LLC............C 740 695-3721
Saint Clairsville *(G-16469)*

American Kidney Stone MGT Ltd............E 800 637-5188
Columbus *(G-6928)*

Amethyst Inc............D 614 242-1284
Columbus *(G-6943)*

Anazao Community Partners............E 330 264-9597
Wooster *(G-19687)*

Appleseed Cmnty Mntal Hlth Ctr............E 419 281-3716
Ashland *(G-645)*

Aurora Manor Ltd Partnership............E 330 562-5000
Aurora *(G-818)*

Bayshore Counseling Svc Inc............E 419 626-9156
Sandusky *(G-16577)*

Beacon Health............C 440 354-9924
Mentor *(G-14021)*

Behavioral Healthcare............E 740 522-8477
Newark *(G-15013)*

Behavral Cnnctions WD Cnty Inc............C 419 352-5387
Bowling Green *(G-1716)*

Behavral Cnnctions WD Cnty Inc............E 419 872-2419
Perrysburg *(G-15836)*

Behavral Cnnctions WD Cnty Inc............C 419 352-5387
Bowling Green *(G-1717)*

Behavral Cnnctions WD Cnty Inc............C 419 352-5387
Bowling Green *(G-1718)*

Belmont Bhc Pines Hospital Inc............C 330 759-2700
Youngstown *(G-19964)*

Best Care Nrsing Rhblttion Ctr............E 740 574-2558
Wheelersburg *(G-19428)*

Bhc Fox Run Hospital Inc............C 740 695-2131
Saint Clairsville *(G-16479)*

Blick Clinic Inc............C 330 762-5425
Akron *(G-99)*

Blick Clinic Inc............D 330 762-5425
Akron *(G-100)*

Brecksvlle Halthcare Group Inc............D 440 546-0643
Brecksville *(G-1772)*

Bridgeway Inc............B 216 688-4114
Cleveland *(G-5079)*

Butler Bhavioral Hlth Svcs Inc............E 513 896-7887
Hamilton *(G-11564)*

Cancer Ntwk of W Cent............E 419 226-9085
Lima *(G-12611)*

Caprice Health Care Inc............C 330 965-9200
North Lima *(G-15267)*

Center 5............D 330 379-5900
Akron *(G-123)*

Center For Addiction Treatment............D 513 381-6672
Cincinnati *(G-3148)*

Center For Families & Children............E 216 252-5800
Cleveland *(G-5151)*

Center For Individual and Fmly............C 419 522-4357
Mansfield *(G-13150)*

Central Commnty Hlth Brd of Ha............E 513 559-2981
Cincinnati *(G-3154)*

Central Commnty Hlth Brd of Ha............E 513 559-2000
Cincinnati *(G-3152)*

Central Ohio Mental Health Ctr............C 740 368-7831
Delaware *(G-9959)*

Century Health Inc............D 419 425-5050
Findlay *(G-10887)*

CHI Health At Home............E 513 576-0262
Milford *(G-14377)*

Child Adlscent Behavioral Hlth............E 330 454-7917
Canton *(G-2249)*

Child Focus Inc............D 513 752-1555
Cincinnati *(G-3180)*

Childrens Hospital Medical Ctr............E 513 636-6100
Cincinnati *(G-3189)*

Childrens Hospital Medical Ctr............E 513 636-6800
Mason *(G-13554)*

Childrens Rehabilitation Ctr............E 330 856-2107
Warren *(G-18683)*

Christ Hospital Spine Surgery............E 513 619-5899
Cincinnati *(G-3211)*

Christian Chld HM Ohio Inc............D 330 345-7949
Wooster *(G-19700)*

Cincinnati Speech Hearing Ctr............E 513 221-0527
Cincinnati *(G-3268)*

Clermont Recovery Center Inc............E 513 735-8100
Batavia *(G-991)*

Cleveland Clinic Foundation............D 440 988-5651
Lorain *(G-12893)*

Cleveland Preterm............E 216 991-4577
Cleveland *(G-5281)*

Cleveland Treatment Center............E 216 861-4246
Cleveland *(G-5294)*

Clevelnd Clnc Hlth Systm East............C 330 287-4830
Wooster *(G-19709)*

Clevelnd Clnc Hlth Systm East............C 330 468-0190
Northfield *(G-15376)*

Clinton County Board of Dd............E 937 382-7519
Wilmington *(G-19609)*

Clinton Memorial Hospital............E 937 383-3402
Wilmington *(G-19614)*

Coleman Professional Svcs Inc............C 330 673-1347
Kent *(G-12223)*

Coleman Professional Svcs Inc............D 330 296-8313
Ravenna *(G-16236)*

Columbus Area............D 614 251-6561
Columbus *(G-7255)*

Columbus Area Inc............E 614 252-0711
Columbus *(G-7256)*

Columbus Area Integrated Healt............D 614 252-0711
Columbus *(G-7257)*

Community Action Against Addic............E 216 881-0765
Cleveland *(G-5323)*

Community Assesment and Treatm............E 216 441-0200
Cleveland *(G-5324)*

Community Behavioral Hlth Inc............C 513 887-8500
Hamilton *(G-11585)*

Community Counseling Services............E 419 468-8211
Bucyrus *(G-1984)*

Community Counsing Ctr Ashtabu............D 440 998-4210
Ashtabula *(G-729)*

Community Drug Board Inc............D 330 315-5590
Akron *(G-149)*

Community Health Centers Ohio............E 216 831-1494
Beachwood *(G-1047)*

Community Mental Health Svc............D 740 695-9344
Saint Clairsville *(G-16484)*

Community Mental Healthcare............E 330 343-1811
Dover *(G-10070)*

Community Solutions Assn............E 330 394-9090
Warren *(G-18690)*

Community Support Services Inc............C 330 253-9388
Akron *(G-153)*

Community Support Services Inc............D 330 253-9675
Akron *(G-154)*

Community Support Services Inc............D 330 733-6203
Akron *(G-155)*

Compass Community Health............E 740 355-7102
Portsmouth *(G-16133)*

Comprehensive Addiction Svc Sy............D 419 241-8827
Toledo *(G-17674)*

Comprehensive Behavioral Hlth............E 330 797-4050
Youngstown *(G-20006)*

Comprehensive Counseling Svc............E 513 424-0921
Middletown *(G-14297)*

Concept Rehab Inc............D 419 843-6002
Toledo *(G-17675)*

Consolidated Care Inc............E 937 465-8065
West Liberty *(G-19120)*

Cornerstone Support Services............D 330 339-7850
New Philadelphia *(G-14952)*

Counseling Center Huron County............E 419 663-3737
Norwalk *(G-15430)*

Counseling Source Inc............E 513 984-9838
Blue Ash *(G-1539)*

Country Meadow Care Center LLC............E 419 886-3922
Bellville *(G-1391)*

County of Allen............E 419 221-1226
Lima *(G-12625)*

County of Carroll............E 330 627-7651
Carrollton *(G-2565)*

County of Cuyahoga............E 216 443-7035
Cleveland *(G-5361)*

County of Geauga............C 440 286-6264
Chesterland *(G-2738)*

County of Hamilton............B 513 598-2965
Cincinnati *(G-3372)*

County of Lorain............E 440 989-4900
Elyria *(G-10499)*

Craig and Frances Lindner Cent............C 513 536-4673
Mason *(G-13569)*

Crossroads Center............C 513 475-5300
Cincinnati *(G-3382)*

Crossroads Lake County Adole............C 440 255-1700
Mentor *(G-14037)*

Darke Cnty Mental Hlth Clinic............E 937 548-1635
Greenville *(G-11371)*

Day-Mont Bhvoral Hlth Care Inc............D 937 222-8111
Moraine *(G-14641)*

East Way Behavioral Hlth Care............C 937 222-4900
Dayton *(G-9403)*

Easter Seal Society of............D 330 743-1168
Youngstown *(G-20025)*

Eastway Corporation............C 937 531-7000
Dayton *(G-9405)*

Education Alternatives............D 216 332-9360
Brookpark *(G-1897)*

Emerge Counseling Service............E 330 865-8351
Akron *(G-202)*

Empowered For Excellence............E 567 316-7253
Toledo *(G-17714)*

Equitas Health Inc............E 614 926-4132
Columbus *(G-7525)*

Equitas Health Inc............D 614 299-2437
Columbus *(G-7527)*

F R S Connections............E 937 393-9662
Hillsboro *(G-11838)*

Family Planning Center............E 740 439-3340
Cambridge *(G-2066)*

Family Recovery Center Inc............E 330 424-1468
Lisbon *(G-12801)*

Family Rsource Ctr NW Ohio Inc............E 419 222-1168
Lima *(G-12637)*

Family Rsource Ctr NW Ohio Inc............E 419 422-8616
Findlay *(G-10900)*

Fieldstone Farm Therapeutic RI............E 440 708-0013
Chagrin Falls *(G-2666)*

Firelands Regional Health Sys............E 419 332-5524
Fremont *(G-11072)*

Firelands Regional Health Sys............E 419 663-3737
Norwalk *(G-15435)*

First Call For Help Inc............E 419 599-1660
Napoleon *(G-14805)*

Formu3 International Inc............E 330 668-1461
Akron *(G-227)*

Foundtion Behavioral Hlth Svcs............E 419 584-1000
Celina *(G-2595)*

Frs Counseling Inc............E 937 393-0585
Hillsboro *(G-11840)*

Fulton County Health Center............E 419 337-8661
Wauseon *(G-18802)*

Fulton County Health Dept............E 419 337-0915
Wauseon *(G-18804)*

Genesis Respiratory Svcs Inc............C 740 354-4363
Portsmouth *(G-16138)*

Greater Cincinnati Behavioral............C 513 354-7000
Walnut Hills *(G-18634)*

Harbor............D 419 479-3233
Toledo *(G-17779)*

Harbor............D 419 241-6191
Toledo *(G-17780)*

Harbor............E 800 444-3353
Toledo *(G-17781)*

HCA Holdings Inc............D 440 826-3240
Cleveland *(G-5669)*

Hcf of Roselawn Inc............C 419 647-4115
Spencerville *(G-16956)*

▲ Health Partners Health Clinic............E 937 645-8488
Marysville *(G-13502)*

Healthsource of Ohio Inc............E 513 707-1997
Batavia *(G-1001)*

Healthsource of Ohio Inc............E 937 981-7707
Greenfield *(G-11363)*

Heartland Rhblitation Svcs Inc............D 419 537-0764
Toledo *(G-17796)*

Heartlnd-Riverview S Pt OH LLC............C 740 894-3287
South Point *(G-16937)*

Hill Manor 1 Inc............E 740 972-3227
Columbus *(G-7750)*

Hitchcock Center For Women Inc............E 216 421-0662
Cleveland *(G-5695)*

Hope Ctr For Cncer Care Warren............D 330 856-8600
Warren *(G-18713)*

Hopewell Health Centers Inc............C 740 385-8468
Logan *(G-12840)*

Hopewell Health Centers Inc............E 740 773-1006
Chillicothe *(G-2789)*

Hopewell Health Centers Inc............E 740 385-6594
Logan *(G-12841)*

Hospice of Darke County Inc............E 419 678-4808
Coldwater *(G-6759)*

Integrated Youth Services Inc............E 937 427-3837
Springfield *(G-17054)*

Ironton and Lawrence County............B 740 532-3534
Ironton *(G-12155)*

Jac-Lin Manor............D 419 994-5700
Loudonville *(G-12957)*

Kindred Healthcare Oper Inc ....D 740 545-6355
West Lafayette *(G-19115)*

Kindred Nursing Centers E LLC ....C 502 596-7300
Logan *(G-12844)*

Legacy Freedom Treatment Ctr ....E 614 741-2100
Columbus *(G-7963)*

Lorain County Alcohol and Drug...........D 440 246-0109
Lorain *(G-12916)*

Lorain County Alcohol and Drug...........E 440 989-4900
Lorain *(G-12917)*

Lorain County Board ....E 440 329-3734
Elyria *(G-10530)*

Lutheran Social ....E 419 229-2222
Lima *(G-12696)*

Mahoning Vly Hmtlgy Onclgy Aso ....E 330 318-1100
Youngstown *(G-20110)*

Main Place Inc ....E 740 345-6246
Newark *(G-15064)*

Manor Care of Kansas Inc ....D 419 252-5500
Toledo *(G-17883)*

Marca Terrace Widows ....D 937 252-1661
Dayton *(G-9584)*

Marietta Center For Health & ....C 740 373-1867
Marietta *(G-13349)*

Marion Area Counseling Ctr ....C 740 387-5210
Marion *(G-13434)*

Maryhaven Inc ....E 937 644-9192
Marysville *(G-13513)*

Maumee Valley Guidance Center..........E 419 782-8856
Defiance *(G-9927)*

McKinley Hall Inc ....E 937 328-5300
Springfield *(G-17068)*

Medcentral Health System ....C 419 683-1040
Crestline *(G-9057)*

Medcentral Health System ....E 419 526-8442
Mansfield *(G-13214)*

Meigs Center Ltd ....C 740 992-6472
Middleport *(G-14281)*

Melrose Rehab LLC ....E 419 424-9625
Findlay *(G-10943)*

Mental Health & Recovery Ctr..............E 937 383-3031
Wilmington *(G-19635)*

Mental Health and Addi Serv ....E 740 594-5000
Athens *(G-792)*

Mental Health and Addi Serv ....C 614 752-0333
Columbus *(G-8058)*

Mental Health Services ....E 216 623-6555
Cleveland *(G-5953)*

Mental Hlth Serv For CL & Mad ....E 740 852-6256
London *(G-12871)*

Mercy Healthplexm LLC ....E 513 870-7101
Fairfield *(G-10756)*

Mercy Medical Center Inc.....................E 330 627-7641
Carrollton *(G-2572)*

Meridian Healthcare.............................D 330 797-0070
Youngstown *(G-20127)*

Met Group ....E 330 864-1916
Fairlawn *(G-10840)*

Metrohealth System ....E 216 957-5000
Cleveland *(G-5966)*

Metrohealth System ....D 216 778-8446
Cleveland *(G-5969)*

Mid-Ohio Psychlogical Svcs Inc ....D 740 687-0042
Lancaster *(G-12419)*

Midwest Behavioral Care Ltd ....E 937 454-0092
Dayton *(G-9632)*

Midwest Rehab Inc ....D 419 692-3405
Ada *(G-5)*

Moundbuilders Guidance Ctr Inc ....E 740 397-0442
Mount Vernon *(G-14782)*

Nationwide Childrens Hospital ....B 614 355-8000
Columbus *(G-8151)*

Neighborhood Health Asso....................D 419 720-7883
Toledo *(G-17935)*

Neighborhood House ....D 614 252-4941
Columbus *(G-8169)*

Netcare Corporation ....D 614 274-9500
Columbus *(G-8171)*

Noble Cnty Nble Cnty Cmmsoners ....E 740 732-4958
Caldwell *(G-2043)*

Norcare Enterprises Inc ....B 440 233-7232
Lorain *(G-12932)*

Nord Center ....E 440 233-7232
Lorain *(G-12933)*

▲ Nord Center Associates Inc ....C 440 233-7232
Lorain *(G-12934)*

North Cntl Mntal Hlth Svcs Inc ....D 614 227-6865
Columbus *(G-8198)*

North Community Counseling Ctr..........E 614 846-2588
Columbus *(G-8199)*

North East Ohio Health Svcs ....D 216 831-6466
Beachwood *(G-1086)*

Northpoint Senior Services LLC............D 740 369-9614
Delaware *(G-9998)*

Northwest Mental Health Svcs ....E 614 457-7876
Columbus *(G-8207)*

Odyssey Healthcare Inc ....E 937 298-2800
Dayton *(G-9667)*

Ohio Heart Institute Inc ....E 330 747-6446
Youngstown *(G-20144)*

Ohio State University ....A 614 257-3000
Columbus *(G-8300)*

Opportunities For Ohioans ....E 513 852-3260
Cincinnati *(G-4177)*

Oral & Maxillofacial Surgeons ....E 419 385-5743
Toledo *(G-17965)*

Orca House ....E 216 231-3772
Cleveland *(G-6142)*

Pain Management Associates Inc ....E 937 252-2000
Dayton *(G-9186)*

Peak Performance Center Inc ....E 440 838-5600
Broadview Heights *(G-1843)*

Peregrine Health Services Inc ....D 330 823-9005
Alliance *(G-543)*

Philio Inc ....E 419 531-5544
Toledo *(G-17976)*

Piqua Village Rehab LLC ....E 937 773-9537
Piqua *(G-16022)*

Planned Parenthood Association............E 937 226-0780
Dayton *(G-9694)*

Planned Parenthood NW Ohio Inc..........E 419 255-1115
Toledo *(G-17980)*

Planned Parenthood of SW OH ....E 513 721-7635
Cincinnati *(G-4252)*

Planned Prenthood Greater Ohio ....E 614 224-2235
Columbus *(G-8452)*

Planned Prenthood Greater Ohio ....D 330 535-2671
Akron *(G-384)*

Planned Prenthood Greater Ohio ....E 216 961-8804
Bedford Heights *(G-1324)*

Planned Prenthood Greater Ohio ....E 330 788-2487
Youngstown *(G-20157)*

Planned Prnthood of Mhning Vly ....E 330 788-6506
Youngstown *(G-20158)*

Plastic Surgery Group Inc ....E 513 791-4440
Cincinnati *(G-4253)*

Portage Path Behavorial Health ....D 330 253-3100
Akron *(G-390)*

Portage Path Behavorial Health ....D 330 762-6110
Akron *(G-391)*

Positive Education Program ....E 440 471-8200
Cleveland *(G-6224)*

Pregnancy Care of Cincinnati ....E 513 487-7777
Cincinnati *(G-4270)*

Project C U R E Inc ....E 937 262-3500
Dayton *(G-9720)*

Psy-Care Inc ....E 330 856-6663
Warren *(G-18737)*

Psychlgcal Behavioral Cons LLC...........E 216 456-8123
Beachwood *(G-1097)*

Ravenwood Mental Health Center ....E 440 632-5355
Middlefield *(G-14275)*

Ravenwood Mental Hlth Ctr Inc ....E 440 285-3568
Chardon *(G-2709)*

Recovery & Prevention Resource ....E 740 369-6811
Delaware *(G-10002)*

Recovery Center ....E 740 687-4500
Lancaster *(G-12429)*

Recovery Resources ....E 216 431-4131
Cleveland *(G-6292)*

Recovery Resources ....E 216 431-4131
Cleveland *(G-6293)*

Rehab Center ....E 330 297-2770
Ravenna *(G-16261)*

Rehab Medical Inc ....D 513 381-3740
Cincinnati *(G-4351)*

Rehabcare Group MGT Svcs Inc ....E 740 779-6732
Chillicothe *(G-2814)*

Rehabcare Group MGT Svcs Inc ....D 740 356-6160
Portsmouth *(G-16163)*

Rehablttion Ctr At Mrietta Mem ....D 740 374-1407
Marietta *(G-13375)*

Rescue Incorporated ....C 419 255-9585
Toledo *(G-18004)*

Robinson Health System Inc ....E 330 678-4100
Ravenna *(G-16262)*

Ryan Sheridan ....E 330 270-2380
Youngstown *(G-20201)*

Samaritan Behavioral Health ....E 937 276-8333
Dayton *(G-9748)*

Scioto Pnt Vly Mental Hlth Ctr ....E 740 335-6935
Wshngtn CT Hs *(G-19883)*

Scioto Pnt Vly Mental Hlth Ctr ....C 740 775-1260
Chillicothe *(G-2825)*

Shr Management Resources Corp ....E 937 274-1546
Dayton *(G-9764)*

Signature Health Inc ....B 440 953-9999
Willoughby *(G-19571)*

Sleep Care Inc ....E 614 901-8989
Columbus *(G-8652)*

Society For Rehabilitation.....................E 440 209-0135
Mentor *(G-14110)*

South Community Inc ....C 937 293-8300
Moraine *(G-14698)*

South Community Inc ....E 937 252-0100
Dayton *(G-9775)*

Southast Cmnty Mental Hlth Ctr ....E 614 225-0980
Columbus *(G-8661)*

Southast Cmnty Mental Hlth Ctr ....E 614 445-6832
Columbus *(G-8663)*

Southast Cmnty Mental Hlth Ctr ....E 614 293-9613
Worthington *(G-19850)*

Southast Cmnty Mental Hlth Ctr ....E 614 444-0800
Columbus *(G-8662)*

Springfeld Rgnal Otpatient Ctr ....E 937 390-8310
Springfield *(G-17115)*

St Aloysius Services Inc ....E 513 482-1745
Cincinnati *(G-4526)*

St Ritas Medical Center ....E 419 226-9067
Lima *(G-12749)*

St Vincent Family Centers ....C 614 252-0731
Columbus *(G-8681)*

Stark County Board of Developm...........A 330 477-5200
Canton *(G-2490)*

Summa Health System ....C 330 375-3315
Akron *(G-451)*

Summit Acres Inc ....C 740 732-2364
Caldwell *(G-2044)*

Sunbrdge Marion Hlth Care Corp ....D 740 389-6306
Marion *(G-13461)*

Surgicenter of Mansfield ....E 419 774-9410
Mansfield *(G-13247)*

Syntero Inc ....E 614 889-5722
Dublin *(G-10350)*

Taylor Murtis Human Svcs Sys ....D 216 283-4400
Cleveland *(G-6503)*

Taylor Murtis Human Svcs Sys ....E 216 283-4400
Cleveland *(G-6505)*

Taylor Murtis Human Svcs Sys ....D 216 281-7192
Cleveland *(G-6504)*

Tcn Behavioral Health Svcs Inc ....C 937 376-8700
Xenia *(G-19927)*

Theratrust ....E 740 345-7688
Newark *(G-15103)*

Thompkins Child Adlescent Svcs ....D 740 622-4470
Coshocton *(G-9028)*

Tri County Mental Health Svcs ....C 740 592-3091
Athens *(G-806)*

Tri County Mental Health Svcs ....D 740 594-5045
Athens *(G-807)*

Trihealth Inc ....E 513 569-6777
Cincinnati *(G-4637)*

Trihealth G LLC ....E 513 346-5000
Cincinnati *(G-4642)*

Ultimate Rehab Ltd ....D 513 563-8777
Blue Ash *(G-1670)*

Unison Behavioral Health Group............C 419 693-0631
Toledo *(G-18115)*

Unison Bhvioral Hlth Group Inc ....D 419 214-4673
Toledo *(G-18116)*

United Disability Services Inc ....E 330 374-1169
Akron *(G-476)*

United Rehabilitation Services ....D 937 233-1230
Dayton *(G-9832)*

Univ Dermatology ....D 513 475-7630
Cincinnati *(G-4692)*

University Mednet................................C 440 255-0800
Mentor *(G-14120)*

University of Cincinnati ....C 513 584-3200
Cincinnati *(G-4720)*

University Radiology Assoc ....D 513 475-8760
Cincinnati *(G-4729)*

Upper Arlington Surgery Center............E 614 442-6515
Columbus *(G-8826)*

Wendt-Bristol Health Services...............E 614 403-9966
Columbus *(G-8886)*

West End Health Center Inc ....E 513 621-2726
Cincinnati *(G-4782)*

Westwood Behavioral Health Ctr ....E 419 238-3434
Van Wert *(G-18497)*

S
I
C

Wood County Chld Svcs Assn	D	419 352-7588	Bowling Green (G-1752)
Woodland Centers Inc	D	740 446-5500	Gallipolis (G-11217)
Wsb Rehabilitation Svcs Inc	A	330 847-7819	Warren (G-18774)
Youngstown Hearing Speech Ctr	E	330 726-8391	Youngstown (G-20262)
Zepf Center	E	419 255-4050	Toledo (G-18175)
Zepf Center	D	419 841-7701	Toledo (G-18176)
Zepf Center	E	419 213-5627	Toledo (G-18177)
Zepf Center	E	419 255-4050	Toledo (G-18178)
Zepf Center	E	419 213-5627	Toledo (G-18179)

8099 Health & Allied Svcs, NEC

24 - Seven Home Hlth Care LLC	E	614 794-0325	Hilliard (G-11737)
Abbott Laboratories	A	614 624-3191	Columbus (G-6851)
Advantage Imaging LLC	E	216 292-9998	Beachwood (G-1027)
Aksm/Genesis Medical Svcs Inc	E	614 447-0281	Columbus (G-6889)
Alveo Health LLC	E	513 557-3502	Cincinnati (G-2936)
American National Red Cross	E	330 469-6403	Warren (G-18663)
American National Red Cross	E	614 334-0425	Columbus (G-6933)
Bio-Blood Components Inc	E	614 294-3183	Columbus (G-7039)
Biolife Plasma Services LP	E	419 224-0117	Lima (G-12608)
Biolife Plasma Services LP	D	419 425-8680	Findlay (G-10868)
Biomat Usa Inc	E	419 531-3332	Toledo (G-17614)
Black Stone Cincinnati LLC	E	937 773-8573	Piqua (G-15997)
Blood Services Centl Ohio Reg	C	614 253-7981	Columbus (G-7048)
Brecksvlle Hlthcare Group Inc	D	440 546-0643	Brecksville (G-1772)
Broadspire Services Inc	E	614 436-8990	Columbus (G-7077)
Cardinal Health Inc	C	614 473-0786	Columbus (G-7120)
Cardinal Healthcare	E	954 202-1883	Columbus (G-7123)
Carespring Health Care MGT LLC	E	513 943-4000	Loveland (G-12981)
Celtic Healthcare Ne Ohio Inc	E	724 742-4360	Youngstown (G-19983)
Central Clinic Outpatient Svcs	D	513 558-9005	Cincinnati (G-3151)
Central Ohio Poison Center	E	800 222-1222	Columbus (G-7161)
Cincinnati Speech Hearing Ctr	E	513 221-0527	Cincinnati (G-3268)
Clinic5	E	614 598-9960	Columbus (G-7227)
Cols Health & Wellness Testing	E	614 839-2781	Westerville (G-19238)
Community and Rural Hlth Svcs	D	419 334-8943	Fremont (G-11063)
Consulate Management Co LLC	D	740 259-5536	Lucasville (G-13047)
County of Carroll	E	330 627-4866	Carrollton (G-2564)
County of Clark	D	937 390-5600	Springfield (G-17022)
Csl Plasma Inc	D	937 331-9186	Dayton (G-9342)
Csl Plasma Inc	D	614 267-4982	Columbus (G-7401)
Csl Plasma Inc	D	330 535-4338	Akron (G-175)
Csl Plasma Inc	D	216 398-0440	Cleveland (G-5385)
District Board Health Mahoning	E	330 270-2855	Youngstown (G-20019)
Diverscare Healthcare Svcs Inc	E	513 867-4100	Hamilton (G-11591)
Divine Healthcare Services LLC	E	614 899-6767	Columbus (G-7456)

Engaged Health Care Bus Svcs	E	614 457-8180	Columbus (G-7516)
Excelas LLC	E	440 442-7310	Cleveland (G-5499)
F R S Connections	E	937 393-9662	Hillsboro (G-11838)
Fairfield Diagnstc Imaging LLC	E	740 654-7559	Lancaster (G-12394)
Family Birth Center Lima Mem	E	419 998-4570	Lima (G-12636)
First Choice Med Staff of Ohio	E	330 867-1409	Fairlawn (G-10829)
First Choice Medical Staffing	D	513 631-5656	Cincinnati (G-3554)
Foundation For Communit	C	937 461-3450	Dayton (G-9446)
Franklin County Adamh Board	E	614 224-1057	Columbus (G-7616)
Good Night Medical Ohio LLC	E	614 384-7433	Columbus (G-6813)
Greater Clvland Hlthcare Assn	D	216 696-6900	Cleveland (G-5640)
Harter Ventures Inc	E	419 224-4075	Lima (G-12651)
Health Data MGT Solutions Inc	E	216 595-1232	Beachwood (G-1062)
Health Partners Western Ohio	E	419 679-5994	Kenton (G-12282)
Heartspring Home Hlth Care LLC	D	937 531-6920	Dayton (G-9493)
Hopewell Health Centers Inc	E	740 596-5249	Mc Arthur (G-13890)
Horizon Home Health Care	E	937 264-3155	Vandalia (G-18529)
Ironton and Lawrence County	E	740 532-7855	Ironton (G-12156)
Ironton and Lawrence County	B	740 532-3534	Ironton (G-12155)
Joint Emergency Med Svc Inc	E	937 746-3471	Franklin (G-11033)
Kindred Healthcare Inc	E	513 336-0178	Mason (G-13606)
Larlham Care Hattie Group	D	330 274-2272	Mantua (G-13272)
Leroy Twp Fire Dept	E	440 254-4124	Painesville (G-15722)
Life Connection of Ohio	E	419 893-4891	Maumee (G-13809)
Life Connection of Ohio Inc	E	937 223-8223	Dayton (G-9565)
Life Line Screening Amer Ltd	C	216 581-6556	Independence (G-12091)
Life Line Screening Amer Ltd	C	216 581-6556	Independence (G-12092)
Lifebanc	D	216 752-5433	Cleveland (G-5868)
Lifecenter Organ Donor Network	E	513 558-5555	Cincinnati (G-3927)
Lifeshare Cmnty Blood Svcs Inc	E	440 322-6159	Elyria (G-10527)
Lifeshare Community Blood Svcs	E	440 322-6573	Elyria (G-10528)
Lifestges Smrtan Ctr For Women	E	937 277-8988	Dayton (G-9566)
London Health & Rehab Ctr LLC	C	740 852-3100	London (G-12865)
Madison Cnty Lndon Cy Hlth Dst	E	740 852-3065	London (G-12867)
Maxim Healthcare Services Inc	D	740 772-4100	Chillicothe (G-2804)
Medical Arts Physician Center	D	216 431-1500	Cleveland (G-5941)
Mercy Health	E	937 323-4585	Springfield (G-17073)
Mercy Health	E	440 324-0400	Elyria (G-10536)
Metro Health System	D	330 669-2249	Smithville (G-16811)
Metrohealth System	E	216 957-5000	Cleveland (G-5966)
Molina Healthcare Inc	B	216 606-1400	Independence (G-12099)
Mount Crmel Hospice Evrgrn Ctr	D	614 234-0200	Columbus (G-12867)
Mutual Health Services Company	D	216 687-7000	Cleveland (G-6030)
Mvhe Inc	D	937 499-8211	Dayton (G-9650)
New Carlisle Spt & Fitnes Ctr	E	937 846-1000	New Carlisle (G-14895)

Northast Ohio Med Rserve Corps	E	216 789-6653	Broadview Heights (G-1839)
Northeast OH Neighborhood Heal	E	216 231-7700	Cleveland (G-6089)
Northeast OH Neighborhood Heal	C	216 231-7700	Cleveland (G-6090)
Novus Clinic	E	330 630-9699	Tallmadge (G-17483)
Ohio Health Physician Group	D	740 594-8819	Athens (G-793)
Ohio Kepro Inc	E	216 447-9604	Seven Hills (G-16679)
Ohio North E Hlth Systems Inc	E	330 747-9551	Youngstown (G-20146)
Ohio State University	E	614 292-5504	Columbus (G-8304)
Ohio State University	D	614 257-5200	Columbus (G-8314)
Ohio State University	D	614 292-0110	Columbus (G-8324)
Ohio State University	D	614 293-8074	Columbus (G-8349)
P C Vpa	E	440 826-0500	Cleveland (G-6154)
P N P Inc	D	330 386-1231	East Liverpool (G-10415)
Palestine Chld Relief Fund	D	330 678-2645	Kent (G-12253)
Peregrine Health Services Inc	D	419 586-4135	Celina (G-2606)
Peregrine Health Services Inc	D	419 298-2321	Edgerton (G-10469)
Primary Cr Ntwrk Prmr Hlth Prt	E	513 204-5785	Mason (G-13629)
Proactive Occptnal Mdicine Inc	E	740 574-8728	Wheelersburg (G-19439)
Prosperity Care Service	E	614 430-8626	Columbus (G-8473)
Regensis Stna Training Program	E	614 849-0115	Columbus (G-8506)
Renaissance Home Health Care	D	216 662-8702	Bedford (G-1301)
Ryan Sheridan	E	330 270-2380	Youngstown (G-20201)
Saber Healthcare Group LLC	C	440 352-0788	Painesville (G-15739)
Seneca County Ems	C	419 447-0266	Tiffin (G-17536)
Signature Healthcare LLC	D	330 372-1977	Warren (G-18743)
Sports Medicine Grant Inc	E	614 461-8199	Pickerington (G-15968)
Spryance Inc	E	678 808-0600	Toledo (G-18044)
Sterling Medical Associates	D	513 984-1800	Cincinnati (G-4544)
Summacare Inc	B	330 996-8410	Akron (G-455)
Taylor Murtis Human Svcs Sys	C	216 283-4400	Cleveland (G-6502)
Toledo Clinic Inc	C	419 865-3111	Holland (G-11919)
Trihealth Hf LLC	E	513 398-3445	Mason (G-13649)
TVC Home Health Care	E	330 755-1110	Youngstown (G-20229)
Unity Health Network LLC	E	330 655-3820	Hudson (G-12010)
Unity Health Network LLC	D	330 923-5899	Cuyahoga Falls (G-9135)
Unity Health Network LLC	E	330 633-7782	Tallmadge (G-17497)
University Womens Healthcare	E	937 208-2948	Dayton (G-9842)
Wheeling Hospital Inc	D	740 671-0850	Shadyside (G-16699)
Wheeling Hospital Inc	D	740 676-4623	Bellaire (G-1336)

81 LEGAL SERVICES

8111 Legal Svcs

Advoctes For Bsic Lgal Eqality	E	419 255-0814	Toledo (G-17583)
Agee Clymer Mtchll & Prtman	E	614 221-3318	Columbus (G-6883)
Allen Khnle Stovall Neuman LLP	E	614 221-8500	Columbus (G-6893)
Altick & Corwin Co Lpa	E	937 223-1201	Dayton (G-9225)

American Financial Corporation ....D 513 579-2121
Cincinnati *(G-2942)*
American Title Services Inc ....E 330 652-1609
Niles *(G-15144)*
Amin Turocy & Watson LLP ....E 216 696-8730
Beachwood *(G-1029)*
Anspach Meeks Ellenberger LLP ....E 614 745-8350
Columbus *(G-6951)*
Anspach Meeks Ellenberger LLP ....E 419 447-6181
Toledo *(G-17595)*
Arthur Middleton Capital Holdn ....E 330 966-9000
North Canton *(G-15190)*
Auman Mahan & Furry A Legal ....E 937 223-6003
Dayton *(G-9243)*
Bailey Cavalieri LLC ....D 614 221-3258
Columbus *(G-7013)*
Baker & Hostetler LLP ....B 216 861-7587
Cleveland *(G-5033)*
Baker & Hostetler LLP ....B 216 621-0200
Cleveland *(G-5034)*
Baker & Hostetler LLP ....C 614 228-1541
Columbus *(G-7014)*
Baker & Hostetler LLP ....E 513 929-3400
Cincinnati *(G-3015)*
Baker Dblkar Beck Wley Mathews ....E 330 499-6000
Canton *(G-2209)*
Barkan & Neff Co Lpa ....E 614 221-4221
Columbus *(G-7018)*
Bavan & Associates ....E 330 650-0088
Northfield *(G-15374)*
Benesch Friedlander Coplan & ....E 614 223-9300
Columbus *(G-7027)*
Bhatti Enterprises Inc ....E 513 886-6000
West Chester *(G-18876)*
Bieser Greer & Landis LLP ....E 937 223-3277
Dayton *(G-9250)*
Bigmar Inc ....E 740 966-5800
Johnstown *(G-12196)*
Bolotin Law Offices ....E 419 424-9800
Findlay *(G-10881)*
Bonezzi Swtzer Polito Hupp Lpa ....E 216 875-2767
Cleveland *(G-5068)*
Bordas & Bordas Pllc ....E 740 695-8141
Saint Clairsville *(G-16480)*
Brennan Manna & Diamond LLC ....E 330 253-5060
Akron *(G-105)*
Bricker & Eckler LLP ....B 614 227-2300
Columbus *(G-7063)*
Bricker & Eckler LLP ....C 513 870-6700
Cincinnati *(G-3073)*
Brouse McDowell Lpa ....E 216 830-6830
Cleveland *(G-5090)*
Brown and Margolius Co Lpa ....E 216 621-2034
Cleveland *(G-5091)*
Bruce M Allman ....D 513 352-6712
Cincinnati *(G-3083)*
Buckingham Dlttle Brroughs LLC ....C 330 376-5300
Akron *(G-114)*
Buckingham Dlttle Brroughs LLC ....D 330 492-8717
Canton *(G-2222)*
Buckingham Dlttle Brroughs LLC ....D 216 621-5300
Cleveland *(G-5099)*
Burke Manley Lpa ....E 513 721-5525
Cincinnati *(G-3092)*
Butler County of Ohio ....D 513 887-3282
Hamilton *(G-11561)*
Butler Cincione and Dicuccio ....E 614 221-3151
Columbus *(G-7101)*
Butler County of Ohio ....E 513 887-3090
Hamilton *(G-11570)*
C T Corporation System ....E 614 473-9749
Columbus *(G-7104)*
Calfee Halter & Griswold LLP ....B 216 831-2732
Cleveland *(G-5114)*
Calfee Halter & Griswold LLP ....C 513 693-4880
Cincinnati *(G-3105)*
Calfee Halter & Griswold LLP ....E 614 621-1500
Columbus *(G-7106)*
Calfee Halgerr Griswold LLC ....E 614 621-7003
Columbus *(G-7107)*
Carlile Patchen & Murphy LLP ....D 614 228-6135
Columbus *(G-7128)*
Carlisle McNellie Rini Kram ....E 216 360-7200
Beachwood *(G-1041)*
Carpenter Lipps & Leland LLP ....E 614 365-4100
Columbus *(G-7130)*
Cavitch Familo & Durkin Co Lpa ....E 216 621-7860
Cleveland *(G-5138)*
Chamberlain Hr ....C 216 589-9280
Avon *(G-873)*
City of Columbus ....E 614 645-6624
Columbus *(G-7211)*
City of Lakewood ....C 216 529-6170
Cleveland *(G-5207)*
City of Marion ....D 740 382-1479
Marion *(G-13412)*
Cleveland Metro Bar Assn ....E 216 696-3525
Cleveland *(G-5266)*
Cleveland Teachers Union Inc ....E 216 861-7676
Cleveland *(G-5292)*
Climaco Lefkwtz Peca Wlcox & ....D 216 621-8484
Cleveland *(G-5305)*
Cohen Todd Kite Stanford LLC ....E 513 205-7286
Cincinnati *(G-3319)*
Community Legal Aid Services ....E 330 725-1231
Medina *(G-13921)*
Community Legal Aid Services ....D 330 535-4191
Akron *(G-152)*
Connor Evans Hafenstein LLP ....E 614 464-2025
Columbus *(G-7350)*
Coolidge Law ....D 937 223-8177
Dayton *(G-9318)*
Coolidge Wall Co LPA ....C 937 223-8177
Dayton *(G-9319)*
Cors & Bassett LLC ....D 513 852-8200
Cincinnati *(G-3365)*
County of Lucas ....C 419 213-4700
Toledo *(G-17681)*
County of Montgomery ....C 937 225-5623
Dayton *(G-9331)*
County of Ottawa ....C 419 898-6459
Oak Harbor *(G-15470)*
County of Ottawa ....E 419 898-2089
Oak Harbor *(G-15471)*
County of Portage ....E 330 297-3850
Ravenna *(G-16240)*
Crabbe Brown & James LLP ....E 614 229-4587
Columbus *(G-7384)*
Criminal Jstice Crdnting Cncil ....E 567 200-6850
Toledo *(G-17688)*
Critchfeld Crtchfield Johnston ....D 330 264-4444
Wooster *(G-19720)*
Dagger Johnston Miller ....E 740 653-6464
Lancaster *(G-12388)*
Dana & Pariser Attys ....E 614 253-1010
Columbus *(G-7413)*
David L Barth Lwyr ....D 513 852-8228
Cincinnati *(G-3402)*
Davis Young A Legal Prof Assn ....E 216 348-1700
Cleveland *(G-5409)*
Day Ketterer Ltd ....D 330 455-0173
Canton *(G-2281)*
Dinn Hochman and Potter LLC ....E 440 446-1100
Cleveland *(G-5423)*
Dinsmore & Shohl LLP ....B 513 977-8200
Cincinnati *(G-3430)*
Douglass & Associates Co Lpa ....E 216 362-7777
Cleveland *(G-5444)*
Duane Morris LLP ....E 202 577-3075
Cleveland *(G-5447)*
Duane Morris LLP ....E 937 424-7086
Columbus *(G-7473)*
Dungan & Lefevre Co Lpa ....E 937 339-0511
Troy *(G-18200)*
Dworken & Bernstein Co Lpa ....E 216 861-4211
Cleveland *(G-5451)*
Dworken & Bernstein Co Lpa ....E 440 352-3391
Painesville *(G-15711)*
E S Gallon & Associates ....E 937 586-3100
Moraine *(G-14650)*
Eastman & Smith Ltd ....C 419 241-6000
Toledo *(G-17709)*
Elizabeth H Farbman ....E 330 744-5211
Youngstown *(G-20028)*
Elk & Elk Co Lpa ....D 800 355-6446
Mayfield Heights *(G-13874)*
Elliott Heller Maas Morrow Lpa ....E 330 792-6611
Youngstown *(G-20029)*
Epiq Systems Inc ....C 513 794-0400
Loveland *(G-12993)*
Ernest V Thomas Jr ....E 513 961-5311
Cincinnati *(G-3514)*
Executives Agencies ....E 614 466-2980
Columbus *(G-7543)*
Fairfield Federal Sav Ln Assn ....E 740 653-3863
Lancaster *(G-12395)*
Faruki Ireland & Cox Pllc ....E 937 227-3700
Dayton *(G-9428)*
Faulkner Grmhsen Keister Shenk ....E 937 492-1271
Sidney *(G-16776)*
Fay Sharpe LLP ....D 216 363-9000
Cleveland *(G-5518)*
Firm Hahn Law ....E 614 221-0240
Columbus *(G-7579)*
Flanagan Lberman Hoffman Swaim ....E 937 223-5200
Dayton *(G-9442)*
Franklin Cnty Bd Commissioners ....C 614 462-3194
Columbus *(G-7610)*
Frantz Ward LLP ....C 216 515-1660
Cleveland *(G-5575)*
Freeze/Arnold A Freund Legal ....D 937 222-2424
Dayton *(G-9450)*
Freking Betz ....E 513 721-1975
Cincinnati *(G-3592)*
Friedberg Meyers Roman ....E 216 831-0042
Cleveland *(G-5579)*
Friedman Domiano Smith Co Lpa ....E 216 621-0070
Cleveland *(G-5580)*
Frost Brown Todd LLC ....B 513 651-6800
Cincinnati *(G-3596)*
Frost Brown Todd LLC ....E 614 464-1211
Columbus *(G-7631)*
Fuller & Henry Ltd ....E 419 247-2500
Toledo *(G-17749)*
Gallagher Gams Pryor Tallan ....E 614 228-5151
Columbus *(G-7645)*
Gallagher Sharp ....C 216 241-5310
Cleveland *(G-5591)*
Gallon Takacs Boissoneault & S ....D 419 843-2001
Toledo *(G-17753)*
General Audit Corp ....E 419 993-2900
Lima *(G-12642)*
Gottlieb Johnson Beam Dal P ....E 740 452-7555
Zanesville *(G-20313)*
Green Haines Sgambati Lpa ....E 330 743-5101
Youngstown *(G-20056)*
Hahmooeser & Parks ....E 330 864-5550
Cleveland *(G-5655)*
Hahn Loeser & Parks LLP ....C 216 621-0150
Cleveland *(G-5656)*
Hammond Law Group LLC ....E 513 381-2011
Cincinnati *(G-3678)*
Hanna Cambell & Powell ....E 330 670-7300
Akron *(G-250)*
Harrington Hoppe Mitchell Ltd ....E 330 744-1111
Youngstown *(G-20061)*
Harris & Burgin ....E 513 891-3270
Blue Ash *(G-1575)*
Hawkins & Co Lpa Ltd ....E 216 861-1365
Cleveland *(G-5668)*
Heller Maas Moro & Magill ....E 330 393-6602
Youngstown *(G-20063)*
Heyman Ralph E Attorney At Law ....D 937 449-2820
Dayton *(G-9495)*
Hoglund Chwlkowski Mrozik Pllc ....C 330 252-8009
Akron *(G-265)*
Horenstein Nicho & Blume A L ....E 937 224-7200
Dayton *(G-9505)*
Ice Miller LLP ....D 614 462-2700
Columbus *(G-7798)*
International Paper Compa ....D 513 248-6000
Loveland *(G-13001)*
Isaac Brant Ledman Teetor LLP ....D 614 221-2121
Columbus *(G-7844)*
Isaac Wiles Burkholder & Teeto ....D 614 221-5216
Columbus *(G-7845)*
Jackson Kelly Pllc ....D 330 252-9060
Akron *(G-287)*
Jackson Kohrman & Pll Krantz ....D 216 696-8700
Cleveland *(G-5776)*
James C Sass Atty ....E 419 843-3545
Swanton *(G-17400)*
James L Jacobson ....E 937 223-1130
Dayton *(G-9523)*
Janik LLP ....D 440 838-7600
Cleveland *(G-5780)*
Javitch Block LLC ....E 513 381-3051
Cincinnati *(G-3809)*
Javitch Block LLC ....C 216 623-0000
Cleveland *(G-5782)*
Javitch Block LLC ....D 216 623-0000
Columbus *(G-7854)*
Jefferson Medical Co ....E 216 443-9000
Cleveland *(G-5787)*
Jeffrey W Smith ....E 740 532-9000
Ironton *(G-12159)*
Jones Day Limited Partnership ....C 614 469-3939
Columbus *(G-7866)*
Jones Day Limited Partnership ....A 216 586-3939
Cleveland *(G-5803)*

SIC

Jones Law Group LLC ....E 614 545-9998	Marshall & Associates Inc ....E 513 683-6396	Richard A Broock ....E 937 449-2840
Columbus (G-7867)	Loveland (G-13011)	Dayton (G-9735)
Joseph R Harrison Company Lpa ....E 330 666-6900	Marshall & Melhorn LLC ....D 419 249-7100	Rickerier and Eckler ....E 513 870-6565
Barberton (G-956)	Toledo (G-17896)	West Chester (G-18993)
Jurus Stanley R Atty At Law ....E 614 486-0297	Mazanec Raskin & Ryder Co Lpa ....D 440 248-7906	Ritter & Randolph LLC ....E 513 381-5700
Columbus (G-7878)	Cleveland (G-5925)	Cincinnati (G-4376)
Kademenos Wisehart Hines ....E 419 524-6011	▲ McCaslin Imbus & Mccaslin Lpa ....E 513 421-4646	Robbins Kelly Patterson Tucker ....E 513 721-3330
Mansfield (G-13192)	Cincinnati (G-3985)	Cincinnati (G-4388)
Katz Teller Brant Hild Co Lpa ....D 513 721-4532	MCDONALD HOPKINS LLC ....E 216 348-5400	Roderick Linton Belfance LLP ....E 330 434-3000
Cincinnati (G-3848)	Cleveland (G-5931)	Akron (G-409)
Keating Muething & Klekamp Pll ....B 513 579-6400	Micha Ltd ....E 740 653-6464	Roetzel and Andress A Legal P ....C 330 376-2700
Cincinnati (G-3850)	Lancaster (G-12418)	Akron (G-410)
Kegler Brown Hl Ritter Co Lpa ....C 614 462-5400	Miller Cnfeld Pddock Stone PLC ....D 513 394-5252	Roetzel and Andress A Legal P ....E 614 463-9489
Columbus (G-7886)	Cincinnati (G-4053)	Columbus (G-8546)
Kegler Brown Hl Ritter Co Lpa ....D 216 586-6650	Millikin and Fitton Law Firm ....E 513 829-6700	Roetzel and Andress A Legal P ....E 216 623-0150
Cleveland (G-5818)	Hamilton (G-11629)	Cleveland (G-6338)
Kelley & Ferraro LLP ....D 216 575-0777	Morris Schneider Wittstadt LLC ....D 440 942-5168	Rose & Dobyns An Ohio Partnr ....E 740 335-4700
Cleveland (G-5820)	Willoughby (G-19552)	Wshngtn CT Hs (G-19882)
Kelly Farrish Lpa ....E 513 621-8700	Murray & Murray Co Lpa ....E 419 624-3000	Rose & Dobyns An Ohio Partnr ....D 937 382-2838
Cincinnati (G-3855)	Sandusky (G-16627)	Wilmington (G-19646)
Kendis & Associates Co Lpa ....E 216 579-1818	Nadler Nadler & Burdman Co Lpa ....D 330 533-6195	Ross Brittain Schonberg Lpa ....E 216 447-1551
Cleveland (G-5823)	Canfield (G-2152)	Independence (G-12119)
Kenneth Zerrusen ....D 330 869-9007	National Labor Relations Board ....E 216 522-3716	Roth Blair Roberts ....E 330 744-5211
Fairlawn (G-10838)	Cleveland (G-6047)	Youngstown (G-20196)
Kohnen & Patton ....E 513 381-0656	National Service Information ....E 740 387-6806	Schimpf Ginocchio Mullins Lpa ....E 513 977-5570
Cincinnati (G-3885)	Marion (G-13448)	Cincinnati (G-4437)
Krugliak Wilkins Grifiyhd & ....E 330 364-3472	Nicholas E Davis ....E 937 228-2838	Scott D Phillips ....E 513 870-8200
New Philadelphia (G-14969)	Dayton (G-9657)	West Chester (G-19000)
Krugliak Wilkins Grifiyhd & ....D 330 497-0700	Nicola Gudbranson & Cooper LLC ....E 216 621-7227	Scott Scriven & Wahoff LLP ....E 614 222-8686
Canton (G-2372)	Cleveland (G-6069)	Columbus (G-8613)
Lane Alton & Horst LLC ....E 614 228-6885	Northwest Ttl Agy of OH Ml In ....D 419 241-8195	Sebaly Shillito & Dyer Lpa ....E 937 222-2500
Columbus (G-7949)	Toledo (G-17951)	Dayton (G-9755)
Larrimer & Larrimer LLC ....E 419 222-6266	Nurenberg Plevin Heller ....D 440 423-0750	Seeley Svdge Ebert Gourash Lpa ....E 216 566-8200
Columbus (G-7953)	Cleveland (G-6107)	Cleveland (G-6392)
Larrimer & Larrimer LLC ....E 614 221-7548	OBrien Law Firm Company Lpa ....E 216 685-7500	Shapiro Shapiro & Shapiro ....E 216 927-2030
Columbus (G-7954)	Westlake (G-19384)	Cleveland (G-6404)
Larrimer & Larrimer LLC ....E 740 366-0184	OConnor Acciani & Levy LLC ....E 513 241-7111	Shared Services LLC ....D 513 821-4278
Granville (G-11345)	Cincinnati (G-4147)	Cincinnati (G-4463)
Laurito & Laurito LLC ....E 937 743-4878	Ohio Disability Rights Law Pol ....E 614 466-7264	Shindler Neff Holmes Schlag ....E 419 243-6281
Dayton (G-9560)	Columbus (G-8249)	Toledo (G-18030)
Law Offces Rbert A Schrger Lpa ....E 614 824-5731	Ohio State Bar Association ....E 614 487-2050	Shumaker Loop & Kendrick LLP ....C 419 241-9000
Columbus (G-7957)	Columbus (G-8288)	Toledo (G-18033)
Law Offices of John D Clunk C ....D 330 436-0300	Opers Legal Dept ....E 614 227-0550	Siegel Siegel J & Jennings Co ....E 216 763-1004
Stow (G-17217)	Columbus (G-8377)	Beachwood (G-1105)
Lawrence Cnty Hstorical Museum ....E 740 532-1222	Palmer Volkema Thomas Inc ....E 614 221-4400	Smith Peter Kalail Co Lpa ....E 216 503-5055
Ironton (G-12161)	Columbus (G-8415)	Independence (G-12124)
Legal Aid Society Cincinnati ....D 513 241-9400	Pappas Leah ....E 614 621-7007	Smith Rolfes & Skazdahl Lpa ....E 513 579-0080
Cincinnati (G-3917)	Columbus (G-8419)	Cincinnati (G-4495)
Legal Aid Society of Cleveland ....D 216 861-5500	Pearne & Gordon LLP ....E 216 579-1700	Sottile & Barile LLC ....E 513 345-0592
Cleveland (G-5863)	Cleveland (G-6187)	Loveland (G-13030)
Legal Aid Society of Columbus ....D 614 737-0139	Peter M Kostoff ....D 330 849-6681	Spangenberg Shibley Liber LLP ....E 216 215-7445
Columbus (G-7964)	Akron (G-380)	Cleveland (G-6440)
Legal Aid Western Ohio Inc ....D 419 724-0030	Peterj Brodhead ....E 216 696-3232	Spengler Nathanson PLL ....D 419 241-2201
Toledo (G-17851)	Cleveland (G-6041)	Toledo (G-18041)
Lerner Sampson & Rothfuss ....B 513 241-3100	Pickrel Schaeffer Ebeling Lpa ....D 937 223-1130	Squire Patton Boggs (us) LLP ....E 513 361-1200
Cincinnati (G-3918)	Dayton (G-9692)	Cincinnati (G-4524)
Levine Arnold S Law Offices ....E 513 241-6748	Porter Wrght Morris Arthur LLP ....E 513 381-4700	Stagnaro Saba Patterson Co Lpa ....E 513 533-2700
Cincinnati (G-3922)	Cincinnati (G-4264)	Cincinnati (G-4531)
Levy & Associates LLC ....E 614 898-5200	Porter Wrght Morris Arthur LLP ....D 216 443-2506	Standley Law Group LLP ....E 614 792-5555
Columbus (G-7967)	Cleveland (G-6222)	Dublin (G-10340)
Lewis P C Jackson ....E 216 750-0404	Porter Wrght Morris Arthur LLP ....E 937 449-6810	Stark Knoll ....E 330 376-3300
Independence (G-12089)	Dayton (G-9699)	Akron (G-441)
Lewis P C Jackson ....E 937 306-6304	Rathbone Group LLC ....D 800 870-5521	Supreme Court of Ohio ....E 937 898-3996
Beavercreek (G-1226)	Cleveland (G-6286)	Vandalia (G-18543)
Lindhorst & Dreidame Co Lpa ....D 513 421-6630	Recovery One LLC ....D 614 336-4207	Sweeney Robert E Co Lpa ....E 216 696-0606
Cincinnati (G-3934)	Columbus (G-8496)	Cleveland (G-6490)
Litigation Management Inc ....B 440 484-2000	Reese Pyle Drake & Meyer ....E 740 345-3431	Tafaro John ....D 513 381-0656
Mayfield Heights (G-13876)	Newark (G-15095)	Cincinnati (G-4567)
Litigation Support Svcs Inc ....E 513 241-5605	Reimer Law Co ....E 440 600-5500	Taft Stettinius Hollister LLP ....B 513 381-2838
Cincinnati (G-3940)	Solon (G-16890)	Cincinnati (G-4569)
Littler Mendelson PC ....D 216 696-7600	Reisenfeld & Assoc Lpa LLC ....C 513 322-7000	Taft Stettinius Hollister LLP ....D 614 221-4000
Cleveland (G-5875)	Cincinnati (G-4354)	Columbus (G-8728)
LLP Ziegler Metzger ....E 216 781-5470	Reminger Co LPA ....C 216 687-1311	Taft Stettinius Hollister LLP ....D 216 241-3141
Cleveland (G-5877)	Cleveland (G-6304)	Cleveland (G-6497)
Luper Neidental & Logan A Leg ....E 614 221-7663	Reminger Co LPA ....D 419 254-1311	Thompson Hine LLP ....C 614 469-3200
Columbus (G-7998)	Toledo (G-18001)	Columbus (G-8749)
Lyons Doughty & Veldhuis PC ....E 614 229-3888	Reminger Co LPA ....D 614 228-1311	Thompson Hine LLP ....C 614 469-3200
Columbus (G-8001)	Columbus (G-8513)	Columbus (G-8750)
Macmillan Sobanski & Todd LLC ....E 419 255-5900	Reminger Co LPA ....E 513 721-1311	Thompson Hine LLP ....C 937 443-6859
Toledo (G-17877)	Cincinnati (G-4356)	Miamisburg (G-14230)
Magolius Margolius & Assoc Lpa ....D 216 621-2034	Rendigs Fry Kiely & Dennis LLP ....D 513 381-9200	Thompson Hine LLP ....B 216 566-5500
Cleveland (G-5894)	Cincinnati (G-4357)	Cleveland (G-6526)
Maguire & Schneider LLP ....E 614 224-1222	Renner Kenner Grieve Bobak ....E 330 376-1242	Thos A Lupica ....D 419 252-6298
Columbus (G-8010)	Akron (G-402)	Toledo (G-18064)
Manchester Bennett Towers & Ul ....E 330 743-1171	Renner Otto Boiselle & Sklar ....E 216 621-1113	Thrasher Dinsmore & Dolan ....E 440 285-2242
Youngstown (G-20115)	Cleveland (G-6306)	Chardon (G-2718)
Manley Deas & Kochalski LLC ....D 614 220-5611	Rennie & Jonson Montgomery ....E 513 241-4722	Toledo Legal Aid Society ....E 419 720-3048
Columbus (G-8013)	Cincinnati (G-4357)	Toledo (G-18089)
Mannion & Gray Co LpA ....E 216 344-9422	Rich Crites & Dittmer LLC ....E 614 228-5822	Tucker Ellis LLP ....D 720 897-4400
Cleveland (G-5905)	Dublin (G-10322)	Cleveland (G-6553)

Tucker Ellis LLP ....C 216 592-5000
  Cleveland *(G-6554)*
Tucker Ellis LLP ....D 614 358-9717
  Columbus *(G-8786)*
Ulmer & Berne LLP ....D 513 698-5000
  Cincinnati *(G-4669)*
Ulmer & Berne LLP ....B 216 583-7000
  Cleveland *(G-6563)*
Ulmer & Berne LLP ....D 513 698-5000
  Cincinnati *(G-4670)*
Ulmer & Berne LLP ....C 513 698-5058
  Cincinnati *(G-4671)*
Ulmer & Berne LLP ....E 614 229-0000
  Columbus *(G-8796)*
United Scoto Senior Activities ......E 740 354-6672
  Portsmouth *(G-16176)*
Value Recovery Group Inc ....E 614 324-5959
  Columbus *(G-8841)*
Village of Strasburg ....E 330 878-7115
  Strasburg *(G-17241)*
Vorys Sater Seymour Pease LLP .....E 216 479-6100
  Cleveland *(G-6643)*
Vorys Sater Seymour Pease LLP .....C 513 723-4000
  Cincinnati *(G-4765)*
Walter Haverfield LLP ....D 216 781-1212
  Cleveland *(G-6650)*
Warner Dennehey Marshall ....D 216 912-3787
  Cleveland *(G-6653)*
Wegman Hessler Vanderburg ....D 216 642-3342
  Cleveland *(G-6658)*
Weiner Keith D Co L P A Inc ....E 216 771-6500
  Cleveland *(G-6659)*
Weltman Weinberg & Reis Co Lpa .....C 216 739-5100
  Brooklyn Heights *(G-1888)*
Weltman Weinberg & Reis Co Lpa .....C 216 685-1000
  Cleveland *(G-6663)*
Weltman Weinberg & Reis Co Lpa .....C 614 801-2600
  Grove City *(G-11485)*
Weltman Weinberg & Reis Co Lpa .....C 513 723-2200
  Cincinnati *(G-4777)*
Weltman Weinberg & Reis Co Lpa .....C 216 459-8633
  Cleveland *(G-6664)*
Wickens Hrzer Pnza Cook Btista .....D 440 695-8000
  Avon *(G-905)*
Wiles Boyle Burkholder & ....D 614 221-5216
  Columbus *(G-8902)*
Wilmer Cutler Pick Hale Dorr ....B 937 395-2100
  Dayton *(G-9882)*
Wong Margaret W Assoc Co Lpa .....E 313 527-9989
  Cleveland *(G-6688)*
Wood Herron & Evans LLP ....E 513 241-2324
  Cincinnati *(G-4802)*
Wood & Lamping LLP ....D 513 852-6000
  Cincinnati *(G-4803)*
Young & Alexander Co Lpa ....D 937 224-9291
  Dayton *(G-9891)*
Zaremba Group Incorporated ....E 216 221-6600
  Cleveland *(G-6708)*
Zaremba Group LLC ....C 216 221-6600
  Lakewood *(G-12366)*
Zashin & Rich Co LPA ....E 216 696-4441
  Cleveland *(G-6710)*
Zeiger Tigges & Little LLP ....E 614 365-9900
  Columbus *(G-8936)*

83 SOCIAL SERVICES

8322 Individual & Family Social Svcs

2100 Lakeside Shelter For Men ......E 216 566-0047
  Cleveland *(G-4869)*
6th Circuit Court ....E 614 719-3100
  Columbus *(G-6844)*
6th Circuit Court ....E 614 719-3100
  Dayton *(G-9196)*
A Better Choice Child Care LLC ......E 614 268-8503
  Columbus *(G-6847)*
A Renewed Mind ....D 419 214-0606
  Perrysburg *(G-15831)*
A W S Inc ....E 216 486-0600
  Euclid *(G-10622)*
A-Team LLC ....E 216 271-7223
  Cleveland *(G-4885)*
Ability Works Inc ....C 419 626-1048
  Sandusky *(G-16572)*
Absolute Care Management Llc ....E 614 846-8053
  Columbus *(G-6856)*
Access Inc ....E 330 535-2999
  Akron *(G-16)*
Access Counseling Services LLC ....C 513 649-8008
  Middletown *(G-14341)*

Achievement Ctrs For Children ......D 216 292-9700
  Cleveland *(G-4899)*
Achievement Ctrs For Children ......E 440 250-2520
  Westlake *(G-19310)*
Action For Children Inc ....E 614 224-0222
  Columbus *(G-6868)*
Adams Cnty Snior Ctzens Cuncil ....E 937 544-7459
  West Union *(G-19130)*
Addiction Services Council ....E 513 281-7880
  Cincinnati *(G-2907)*
Adena Health System ....E 740 779-4888
  Chillicothe *(G-2754)*
Adena NH LLC ....E 740 546-3620
  Adena *(G-7)*
Aids Tskfrce Grter Clvland Inc ....D 216 357-3131
  Cleveland *(G-4914)*
Akron General Foundation ....E 330 344-6888
  Akron *(G-41)*
Akron General Medical Center ....D 330 344-6000
  Akron *(G-43)*
Alexson Services Inc ....E 614 889-5837
  Dublin *(G-10125)*
All Star Training Club ....E 330 352-5602
  Akron *(G-64)*
Allwell Behavioral Health Svcs ....E 740 454-9766
  Zanesville *(G-20274)*
Allwell Behavioral Health Svcs ....E 740 439-4428
  Cambridge *(G-2049)*
Alternative Paths Inc ....E 330 725-9195
  Medina *(G-13909)*
Altruism Society Inc ....D 877 283-4001
  Beachwood *(G-1028)*
American Cancer Society East ....E 800 227-2345
  Cleveland *(G-4949)*
American National Red Cross ....E 216 303-5476
  Parma *(G-15760)*
American National Red Cross ....E 937 631-9315
  Springfield *(G-16994)*
American National Red Cross ....C 419 382-2707
  Toledo *(G-17592)*
American National Red Cross ....E 330 535-6131
  Akron *(G-70)*
American National Red Cross ....E 614 436-3862
  Lewis Center *(G-12523)*
American National Red Cross ....E 614 473-3783
  Gahanna *(G-11109)*
American National Red Cross ....E 800 448-3543
  Columbus *(G-6932)*
American National Red Cross ....E 740 344-2510
  Newark *(G-15010)*
American National Red Cross ....E 419 524-0311
  Mansfield *(G-13136)*
American National Red Cross ....E 937 376-3111
  Xenia *(G-19889)*
American Red Cross ....E 513 579-3000
  Cincinnati *(G-2950)*
American Red Cross ....E 937 222-0124
  Dayton *(G-9230)*
American Red Cross of Grtr Col ......E 614 253-7981
  Columbus *(G-6935)*
Amethyst Inc ....E 614 242-1284
  Columbus *(G-6943)*
Anazao Community Partners ....E 330 264-9597
  Wooster *(G-19687)*
Ansonia Area Emergency Service ...E 937 337-2651
  Ansonia *(G-612)*
Applewood Centers Inc ....D 216 696-6815
  Cleveland *(G-4991)*
Applewood Centers Inc ....E 216 521-6511
  Cleveland *(G-4992)*
Applewood Centers Inc ....E 440 324-1300
  Lorain *(G-12882)*
Applewood Centers Inc ....C 216 741-2241
  Cleveland *(G-4993)*
Arbor Rehabilitation & Healtcr ....B 440 423-0206
  Gates Mills *(G-11233)*
ARC Industries Incorporated O ....B 614 836-0700
  Groveport *(G-11494)*
Archdiocese of Cincinnati ....E 937 323-6507
  Springfield *(G-16996)*
Area Agency On Aging Planni ....E 800 258-7277
  Dayton *(G-9239)*
Area Agency On Aging Dst 7 Inc ......C 800 582-7277
  Rio Grande *(G-16399)*
Area Agency On Aging Dst 7 Inc ......E 740 446-7000
  Gallipolis *(G-11185)*
Area Agency On Aging Reg 9 Inc ......D 740 439-4478
  Cambridge *(G-2050)*
Area Office On Aging of Nwstrn ....D 419 382-0624
  Toledo *(G-17599)*

Artis Senior Living ....E 513 229-7450
  Mason *(G-13542)*
Ashland Cnty Council On Aging ......E 419 281-1477
  Ashland *(G-710)*
Ashtabula Community Counseling ....D 440 998-6032
  Ashtabula *(G-710)*
Ashtabula County Commnty Actn .....D 440 593-6441
  Conneaut *(G-8949)*
Ashtabula County Commnty Actn .....D 440 576-6911
  Jefferson *(G-12189)*
Ashtabula County Community ....C 440 997-1721
  Ashtabula *(G-714)*
Ashtabula Job and Family Svcs ....C 440 994-2020
  Ashtabula *(G-718)*
Assoc Dvlpmtly Disabled ....E 614 486-4361
  Westerville *(G-19222)*
Athens County Board of Dev ....D 740 594-3539
  Athens *(G-766)*
Aultman Hospital ....A 330 363-6262
  Canton *(G-2204)*
Avalon Foodservice Inc ....C 330 854-4551
  Canal Fulton *(G-2092)*
Battered Womens Shelter ....C 330 723-3900
  Medina *(G-13912)*
Battered Womens Shelter ....D 330 374-0740
  Akron *(G-88)*
Battle Bullying Hotline Inc ....E 216 731-1976
  Cleveland *(G-5042)*
Beatitude House ....E 440 992-0265
  Ashtabula *(G-722)*
Beavercreek YMCA ....E 937 426-9622
  Dayton *(G-9246)*
Bedford Township ....E 740 992-2117
  Middleport *(G-14280)*
Beech Acres Parenting Center ....D 513 231-6630
  Cincinnati *(G-3030)*
Beeghly Oaks Operating LLC ....C 330 884-2300
  Boardman *(G-1696)*
Behavioral Treatments ....E 614 558-1968
  Hilliard *(G-11746)*
Behavral Cnnctions WD Cnty Inc .....E 419 872-2419
  Perrysburg *(G-15836)*
Bellefaire Jewish Chld Bur ....B 216 932-2800
  Shaker Heights *(G-16703)*
Belmont County of Ohio ....E 740 695-3813
  Saint Clairsville *(G-16474)*
Belmont County of Ohio ....D 740 695-0460
  Saint Clairsville *(G-16475)*
Ben El Child Development Ctr ....E 937 465-0010
  Urbana *(G-18419)*
Benjamin Rose Institute ....D 216 791-8000
  Cleveland *(G-5057)*
Benjamin Rose Institute ....D 216 791-3580
  Cleveland *(G-5056)*
Beth-El Agape Christian Center ....E 614 445-0674
  Columbus *(G-7032)*
Big Broth and Big Siste of Cen ....E 614 839-2447
  Columbus *(G-7034)*
Blanchard Vlly Crt Case Mngmnt .....D 419 422-6387
  Findlay *(G-10876)*
Blick Clinic Inc ....C 330 762-5425
  Akron *(G-99)*
Bluebird Retirement Community ....E 740 845-1880
  London *(G-12860)*
Board Mental Retardation Dvlpm .....E 740 472-1712
  Woodsfield *(G-19671)*
Board of Delaware County ....D 740 201-3600
  Lewis Center *(G-12530)*
Bobby Tripodi Foundation Inc ....E 216 524-3787
  Independence *(G-12050)*
Box 21 Rescue Squad Inc ....E 937 223-2821
  Dayton *(G-9260)*
Brenn Field Nursing Center ....C 330 683-4075
  Orrville *(G-15626)*
Bridges To Independence Inc ....C 740 362-1996
  Delaware *(G-9955)*
Bridgeway Inc ....B 216 688-4114
  Cleveland *(G-5079)*
Broken Arrow Inc ....E 419 562-3480
  Bucyrus *(G-1977)*
Brook Beech ....E 216 831-2255
  Cleveland *(G-5086)*
Brookdale Place Wooster LLC ....E 330 262-1615
  Wooster *(G-19694)*
Brown Cnty Snior Ctzen Council ......E 937 378-6603
  Georgetown *(G-11262)*
Bryant Eliza Village ....B 216 361-6141
  Cleveland *(G-5096)*
Butler County of Ohio ....C 513 887-3728
  Fairfield Township *(G-10803)*

CA Group	E	419 586-2137	
Celina (G-2586)			
Cambridge Counseling Center	C	740 450-7790	
Zanesville (G-20287)			
Canton Christian Home Inc	C	330 456-0004	
Canton (G-2228)			
Canton Jewish Community Center	D	330 452-6444	
Canton (G-2236)			
Caracole Inc	E	513 761-1480	
Cincinnati (G-3115)			
Care & Share of Erie Count	D	419 624-1411	
Sandusky (G-16581)			
Carriage Inn of Cadiz Inc	E	740 942-8084	
Cadiz (G-2027)			
Casleo Corporation	E	614 252-6508	
Columbus (G-7133)			
Casto Health Care	D	419 884-6400	
Mansfield (G-13148)			
Catholic Charities Corporation	B	330 723-9615	
Medina (G-13915)			
Catholic Charities Corporation	E	216 939-3713	
Cleveland (G-5132)			
Catholic Charities Corporation	E	216 268-4006	
Cleveland (G-5133)			
Catholic Charities Corporation	E	419 289-1903	
Ashland (G-663)			
Catholic Charities of Southwst	D	937 325-8715	
Springfield (G-17005)			
Catholic Charities of SW Ohio	D	513 241-7745	
Cincinnati (G-3132)			
Catholic Chrties Regional Agcy	D	330 744-3320	
Youngstown (G-19982)			
Catholic Diocese of Columbus	E	614 221-5891	
Columbus (G-7139)			
Catholic Residential Service	E	513 784-0400	
Cincinnati (G-3133)			
Catholic Social Services Inc	D	614 221-5891	
Columbus (G-7140)			
Catholic Social Svc Miami Vly	E	937 223-7217	
Dayton (G-9287)			
Center For Cognitv Behav Psych	E	614 459-4490	
Columbus (G-7152)			
Center For Families & Children	E	440 888-0300	
Cleveland (G-5149)			
Center For Families & Children	E	216 432-7200	
Cleveland (G-5150)			
Center For Families & Children	E	216 932-9497	
Cleveland Heights (G-6715)			
Center For Families & Children	E	216 252-5800	
Cleveland (G-5151)			
Center For Individual and Fmly	C	419 522-4357	
Mansfield (G-13150)			
Central Cmnty Hse of Columbus	E	614 253-7267	
Columbus (G-7155)			
Central OH Area Agency On Agng	C	614 645-7250	
Columbus (G-7156)			
Cgh-Global Emerg Mngmt Strateg	E	800 376-0655	
Cincinnati (G-2843)			
Chagrin Valley Dispatch	E	440 247-7321	
Bedford (G-1272)			
Champaign Cnty Board of Dd	E	937 653-5217	
Urbana (G-18422)			
Champaign Residential Services	E	614 481-5550	
Columbus (G-7178)			
Child Adlscent Behavioral Hlth	D	330 433-6075	
Canton (G-2250)			
Child Focus Inc	E	513 732-8800	
Batavia (G-986)			
Child Focus Inc	D	513 752-1555	
Cincinnati (G-3180)			
Child Focus Inc	D	937 444-1613	
Mount Orab (G-14739)			
Childrens Advocacy Center	E	740 432-6581	
Cambridge (G-2058)			
Childrens Cmprhensive Svcs Inc	D	419 589-5511	
Mansfield (G-13151)			
Childrens HM of Cncinnati Ohio	C	513 272-2800	
Cincinnati (G-3182)			
Childrens Homecare Services	C	614 355-1100	
Columbus (G-7188)			
Childrens Hosp Med Ctr Akron	E	330 633-2055	
Tallmadge (G-17471)			
Childrens Hunger Alliance	E	614 341-7700	
Columbus (G-7190)			
Chmc Cmnty Hlth Svcs Netwrk	A	513 636-8778	
Cincinnati (G-3196)			
CHN Inc - Adult Day Care	E	937 548-0506	
Greenville (G-11370)			
Choices For Vctims Dom Volence	D	614 258-6080	
Columbus (G-7194)			
Choices For Vctims Dom Volence	E	614 224-6617	
Worthington (G-19798)			
◆ Christian Aid Ministries	E	330 893-2428	
Millersburg (G-14465)			
Christian Chld HM Ohio Inc	D	330 345-7949	
Wooster (G-19700)			
Cincinnati Area Senior Svcs	C	513 721-4330	
Cincinnati (G-3222)			
▲ Cincinnati Assn For The Blind	C	513 221-8558	
Cincinnati (G-3223)			
Cincinnati Ctr/Psychoanalysis	E	513 961-8484	
Cincinnati (G-3237)			
Cincinnati Youth Collaborative	E	513 475-4165	
Cincinnati (G-3275)			
Cincinnati-Hmltn Cnty Comm Act	E	513 569-1840	
Cincinnati (G-3276)			
Cincinnati-Hmltn Cnty Comm Act	E	513 569-4510	
Cincinnati (G-3277)			
Cincinnati-Hmltn Cnty Comm Act	E	513 354-3900	
Cincinnati (G-3278)			
Cincysmiles Foundation Inc	E	513 621-0248	
Cincinnati (G-3288)			
Circle Health Services	E	216 721-4010	
Cleveland (G-5182)			
City Gospel Mission	E	513 241-5525	
Cincinnati (G-3299)			
City Mission	D	216 431-3510	
Cleveland (G-5187)			
City of Brecksville	D	440 526-4109	
Brecksville (G-1775)			
City of Bucyrus	E	419 562-3050	
Bucyrus (G-1982)			
City of Canal Winchester	E	614 837-8276	
Canal Winchester (G-2107)			
City of Highland Heights	D	440 461-2441	
Cleveland (G-5202)			
City of Independence	E	216 524-7373	
Cleveland (G-5204)			
City of Lakewood	E	216 521-1515	
Lakewood (G-12338)			
City of Parma	E	440 888-4514	
Cleveland (G-5213)			
City of Willoughby Hills	E	440 942-7207	
Willoughby Hills (G-19587)			
Clark County Board of Developm	E	937 328-2675	
Springfield (G-17009)			
Cleaners Extraordinaire Inc	D	937 324-8488	
Springfield (G-17015)			
Clermont Counseling Center	E	513 345-8555	
Cincinnati (G-3305)			
Clermont Counseling Center	E	513 947-7000	
Amelia (G-571)			
Clermont County Community Svcs	E	513 732-2277	
Batavia (G-988)			
Clermont Senior Services Inc	C	513 724-1255	
Batavia (G-992)			
Cleveland Center For Etng Dsor	E	216 765-2535	
Beachwood (G-1045)			
Cleveland Christian Home Inc	C	216 671-0977	
Cleveland (G-5234)			
Cleveland Municipal School Dst	D	216 521-6511	
Cleveland (G-5278)			
Cleveland Soc For The Blind	C	216 791-8118	
Cleveland (G-5288)			
Clinton County Board of Dd	E	937 382-7519	
Wilmington (G-19609)			
Clintonville Beechwold Communi	E	614 268-3539	
Columbus (G-7230)			
Clossman Catering Incorporated	E	513 942-7744	
Hamilton (G-11581)			
Clovernook Center For The Bli	E	513 522-3860	
Cincinnati (G-3311)			
College Now Grter Clveland Inc	D	216 241-5587	
Cleveland (G-5312)			
Columbus Speech & Hearing Ctr	D	614 263-5151	
Columbus (G-7315)			
Commquest Services Inc	C	330 455-0374	
Canton (G-2261)			
Commu Act Comm of Fayette Cnty	C	740 335-7282	
Wshngtn CT Hs (G-19865)			
Community Action Comm Pike CNT	C	740 289-2371	
Piketon (G-15973)			
Community Action Comm Pike CNT	E	740 961-4011	
Portsmouth (G-16131)			
Community Action Comm Pike CNT	E	740 286-2826	
Jackson (G-12172)			
Community Action Comsn Belmont	E	740 695-0293	
Saint Clairsville (G-16483)			
Community Action Organization	C	740 354-7541	
Portsmouth (G-16132)			
Community Action Program Comm	C	740 653-1711	
Lancaster (G-12384)			
Community Action Program Corp	E	740 373-6016	
Marietta (G-13320)			
Community Action-Wayne/Medina	D	330 264-8677	
Wooster (G-19710)			
Community Caregivers	D	330 533-3427	
Youngstown (G-19999)			
Community Center	D	330 746-7721	
Youngstown (G-20000)			
Community Counseling Services	E	419 468-8211	
Bucyrus (G-1984)			
Community Drug Board Inc	D	330 996-5114	
Akron (G-150)			
Community Drug Board Inc	D	330 315-5590	
Akron (G-149)			
Community Ems District	E	330 527-4100	
Garrettsville (G-11229)			
Community Refugee & Immigation	D	614 235-5747	
Columbus (G-7336)			
Community Services Inc	D	937 667-8631	
Tipp City (G-17553)			
Community Solutions Assn	E	330 394-9090	
Warren (G-18690)			
Compass Family and Cmnty Svcs	E	330 743-9275	
Youngstown (G-20002)			
Compass Family and Cmnty Svcs	E	330 743-9275	
Youngstown (G-20003)			
Compdrug	D	614 224-4506	
Columbus (G-7340)			
Comprehensive Cmnty Child Care	E	513 221-0033	
Cincinnati (G-3345)			
Comprehensive Services Inc	E	614 442-0664	
Columbus (G-7343)			
Concord	E	614 882-9338	
Westerville (G-19245)			
Concordia Care	D	216 791-3580	
Cleveland (G-5333)			
Consolidated Care Inc	E	937 465-8065	
West Liberty (G-19119)			
Consolidated Care Inc	E	937 465-8065	
West Liberty (G-19120)			
Consumer Support Services Inc	D	740 522-5464	
Newark (G-15025)			
Consumer Support Services Inc	D	740 344-3600	
Newark (G-15026)			
Consumer Support Services Inc	B	740 788-8257	
Newark (G-15024)			
Consumer Support Services Inc	D	330 764-4785	
Medina (G-13922)			
Corporation For OH Appalachian	E	740 594-8499	
Athens (G-772)			
Coshocton Drug Alcohol Council	E	740 622-0033	
Coshocton (G-9007)			
Council For Economic Opport	D	216 696-9077	
Cleveland (G-5355)			
Council On Aging of Southweste	C	513 721-1025	
Cincinnati (G-3368)			
Council On Rur Svc Prgrams Inc	E	937 773-0773	
Piqua (G-16002)			
Counseling Center Huron County	E	419 663-3737	
Norwalk (G-15430)			
Counseling Ctr Wayne Holmes CT	C	330 264-9029	
Wooster (G-19712)			
Country Neighbor Program Inc	E	440 437-6311	
Orwell (G-15651)			
County of Adams	E	937 544-5067	
West Union (G-19135)			
County of Allen	C	419 228-2120	
Lima (G-12623)			
County of Allen	E	419 227-8590	
Lima (G-12624)			
County of Allen	E	419 996-7050	
Lima (G-12626)			
County of Ashtabula	C	440 224-2157	
Ashtabula (G-732)			
County of Ashtabula	D	440 998-1811	
Ashtabula (G-733)			
County of Brown	E	937 378-6104	
Georgetown (G-11268)			
County of Clark	C	937 327-1700	
Springfield (G-17023)			
County of Clark	B	937 327-1700	
Springfield (G-17024)			
County of Clark	B	937 327-1700	
Springfield (G-17025)			
County of Clinton	E	937 382-2449	
Wilmington (G-19619)			
County of Columbiana	C	330 424-1386	
Lisbon (G-12798)			

County of Coshocton ....D..... 740 622-1020
 Coshocton (G-9012)
County of Cuyahoga ....A..... 419 399-8260
 Paulding (G-15792)
County of Cuyahoga ....A..... 216 432-2621
 Cleveland (G-5370)
County of Cuyahoga ....E..... 216 443-5100
 Cleveland (G-5365)
County of Cuyahoga ....D..... 216 681-4433
 Cleveland (G-5368)
County of Darke ....E..... 937 526-4488
 Versailles (G-18568)
County of Erie ....C..... 419 626-6781
 Sandusky (G-16595)
County of Geauga ....D..... 440 285-9141
 Chardon (G-2692)
County of Geauga ....D..... 440 564-2246
 Chardon (G-2691)
County of Guernsey ....E..... 740 439-6681
 Cambridge (G-2063)
County of Guernsey ....D..... 740 432-2381
 Cambridge (G-2062)
County of Hamilton ....E..... 513 821-6946
 Cincinnati (G-3373)
County of Hamilton ....B..... 513 742-1576
 Cincinnati (G-3369)
County of Highland ....E..... 937 393-4278
 Hillsboro (G-11835)
County of Holmes ....E..... 330 674-1111
 Millersburg (G-14472)
County of Holmes ....E..... 330 674-1926
 Millersburg (G-14467)
County of Huron ....D..... 419 668-8126
 Norwalk (G-15431)
County of Huron ....D..... 419 663-5437
 Norwalk (G-15432)
County of Lake ....D..... 440 269-2193
 Willoughby (G-19516)
County of Logan ....E..... 937 599-7290
 Bellefontaine (G-1352)
County of Lorain ....E..... 440 329-3734
 Elyria (G-10495)
County of Lorain ....E..... 440 326-4700
 Elyria (G-10496)
County of Lorain ....D..... 440 284-1830
 Elyria (G-10498)
County of Lorain ....C..... 440 329-5340
 Elyria (G-10501)
County of Lucas ....C..... 419 213-3000
 Toledo (G-17680)
County of Lucas ....B..... 419 213-8999
 Toledo (G-17682)
County of Marion ....E..... 740 387-6688
 Marion (G-13413)
County of Marion ....E..... 740 389-2317
 Marion (G-13415)
County of Mercer ....D..... 419 586-2369
 Celina (G-2591)
County of Mercer ....E..... 419 586-5106
 Celina (G-2592)
County of Mercer ....E..... 419 678-8071
 Coldwater (G-6757)
County of Montgomery ....B..... 937 224-5437
 Dayton (G-9326)
County of Montgomery ....D..... 937 224-5437
 Dayton (G-9332)
County of Montgomery ....B..... 937 225-4804
 Dayton (G-9330)
County of Ottawa ....E..... 419 898-2089
 Oak Harbor (G-15471)
County of Paulding ....E..... 419 399-3636
 Paulding (G-15793)
County of Pickaway ....D..... 740 474-7588
 Circleville (G-4830)
County of Preble ....E..... 937 456-2085
 Eaton (G-10440)
County of Richland ....E..... 419 774-5894
 Mansfield (G-13154)
County of Richland ....C..... 419 774-5400
 Mansfield (G-13156)
County of Richland ....C..... 419 774-4100
 Mansfield (G-13155)
County of Summit ....D..... 330 643-2300
 Akron (G-162)
County of Summit ....B..... 330 643-7217
 Akron (G-166)
County of Summit ....A..... 330 634-8193
 Tallmadge (G-17473)
County of Tuscarawas ....E..... 330 343-0099
 New Philadelphia (G-14954)

County of Tuscarawas ....D..... 330 339-7791
 New Philadelphia (G-14955)
County of Union ....D..... 937 645-6733
 Marysville (G-13491)
County of Warren ....E..... 513 695-1420
 Lebanon (G-12457)
County of Washington ....D..... 740 373-5513
 Marietta (G-13323)
County of Wayne ....E..... 330 287-5600
 Wooster (G-19718)
Couple To Couple Leag Intl Inc ....E..... 513 471-2000
 Cincinnati (G-3374)
Crawford County Children Svcs ....E..... 419 562-1200
 Bucyrus (G-1988)
Crawford County Council On Agi ....E..... 419 562-3050
 Bucyrus (G-1989)
Creative Diversified Services ....E..... 937 376-7810
 Xenia (G-19896)
Creative Foundations Inc ....D..... 740 362-5102
 Delaware (G-9965)
Crisis Intervention & Rcvy Ctr ....D..... 330 455-9407
 Canton (G-2272)
Crisis Intvntn Ctr Stark Cnty ....D..... 330 452-9812
 Canton (G-2273)
Crittenton Family Services ....E..... 614 251-0103
 Columbus (G-7394)
Crossroads Lake County Adole ....C..... 440 255-1700
 Mentor (G-14037)
Cuyahoga County ....A..... 216 431-4500
 Cleveland (G-5395)
Cuyahoga County ....D..... 216 420-6750
 Cleveland (G-5393)
Cyo & Community Services Inc ....E..... 330 762-2961
 Akron (G-178)
Danbury Woods of Wooster ....E..... 330 264-0355
 Wooster (G-19721)
Day Share Ltd ....E..... 513 451-1100
 Cincinnati (G-3405)
Dayton Urban League ....E..... 937 226-1513
 Dayton (G-9383)
Deepwood Industries Inc ....C..... 440 350-5231
 Mentor (G-14040)
Defiance Cnty Bd Commissioners ....E..... 419 782-3233
 Defiance (G-9909)
Delhi Township ....D..... 513 922-0060
 Cincinnati (G-3419)
Developmental Disabilities ....D..... 513 732-7015
 Owensville (G-15671)
Develpmntal Dsblties Ohio Dept ....C..... 937 233-8108
 Columbus (G-7442)
Develpmntal Dsblties Ohio Dept ....C..... 513 732-9200
 Batavia (G-996)
Direction Home Akron Canton AR ....C..... 330 896-9172
 Uniontown (G-18367)
Directions For Youth Families ....E..... 614 258-8043
 Columbus (G-7447)
Directions For Youth Families ....E..... 614 694-0203
 Columbus (G-7448)
Directions For Youth Families ....E..... 614 294-2661
 Columbus (G-7449)
Diverscare Healthcare Svcs Inc ....E..... 937 278-8211
 Dayton (G-9392)
DMD Management Inc ....A..... 216 371-3600
 Cleveland (G-5435)
Domestic Violence Project Inc ....E..... 330 445-2000
 Canton (G-2289)
Don Bosco Community Center Inc ....E..... 816 421-3160
 Cleveland (G-5438)
East End Neighborhood Hse Assn ....E..... 216 791-9378
 Cleveland (G-5456)
East Toledo Family Center ....D..... 419 691-1429
 Toledo (G-17708)
Easter Seal Society of ....D..... 330 743-1168
 Youngstown (G-20025)
Easter Seals Center ....D..... 614 228-5523
 Hilliard (G-11764)
Easter Seals Metro Chicago Inc ....E..... 419 332-3016
 Fremont (G-11071)
Easter Seals Tristate ....C..... 513 985-0515
 Blue Ash (G-1549)
Easter Seals Tristate LLC ....C..... 513 475-6791
 Cincinnati (G-3474)
Eastway Corporation ....C..... 937 496-2000
 Dayton (G-9404)
Echoing Hills Village Inc ....C..... 740 327-2311
 Warsaw (G-18783)
Elderly United of Springfield ....D..... 937 323-4948
 Springfield (G-17033)
Emerge Counseling Service ....E..... 330 865-8041
 Akron (G-202)

Emerge Ministries Inc ....E..... 330 865-8351
 Akron (G-203)
Episcopal Retirement Homes Inc ....E..... 513 271-9610
 Cincinnati (G-3508)
Equitas Health Inc ....D..... 614 299-2437
 Columbus (G-7527)
F R S Connections ....E..... 937 393-9662
 Hillsboro (G-11838)
Fairborn Fish ....E..... 937 879-1313
 Fairborn (G-10672)
Fairborn YMCA ....E..... 937 754-9622
 Fairborn (G-10674)
Fairfld Ctr For Disablts & CER ....E..... 740 653-1186
 Lancaster (G-12401)
Faith Mission Inc ....E..... 614 224-6617
 Columbus (G-7557)
Faith Mission Inc ....E..... 614 224-6617
 Columbus (G-7558)
Family & Child Abuse ....E..... 419 244-3053
 Toledo (G-17723)
Family Cmnty Svcs Portage Cnty ....C..... 330 297-0078
 Ravenna (G-16243)
Family Senior Care Inc ....E..... 740 441-1428
 Gallipolis (G-11191)
Family Service ....E..... 513 381-6300
 Cincinnati (G-3531)
Family Service Association ....E..... 937 222-9481
 Moraine (G-14655)
Family Service of NW Ohio ....D..... 419 321-6455
 Toledo (G-17725)
Family YMCA of LANcstr&fairfld ....D..... 740 277-7373
 Lancaster (G-12403)
Far West Center ....E..... 440 835-6212
 Westlake (G-19342)
Fayette Progressive Industries ....D..... 740 335-7453
 Wshngtn CT Hs (G-19872)
Feed Lucas County Children Inc ....D..... 419 260-1556
 Toledo (G-17732)
Findlay Y M C A Child Dev ....E..... 419 422-3174
 Findlay (G-10908)
Firelands Regional Health Sys ....E..... 419 663-3737
 Norwalk (G-15435)
First Community Village ....B..... 614 324-4455
 Columbus (G-7585)
Focus On Youth Inc ....E..... 513 644-1030
 West Chester (G-18925)
For Specialized Alternatives ....D..... 419 695-8010
 Delphos (G-10027)
Foundations Hlth Solutions Inc ....D..... 440 793-0200
 North Olmsted (G-15289)
Four County Family Center ....E..... 800 693-6000
 Wauseon (G-18800)
Franklin Cnty Bd Commissioners ....C..... 614 275-2571
 Columbus (G-7605)
Franklin Cnty Bd Commissioners ....B..... 614 462-3275
 Columbus (G-7607)
Franklin Cnty Bd Commissioners ....B..... 614 229-7100
 Columbus (G-7609)
Frans Child Care-Mansfield ....C..... 419 775-2500
 Mansfield (G-13178)
Free Store/Food Bank Inc ....E..... 513 482-4526
 Cincinnati (G-3588)
Free Store/Food Bank Inc ....E..... 513 241-1064
 Cincinnati (G-3589)
Freestore Foodbank Inc ....E..... 513 482-4500
 Cincinnati (G-3590)
Friend To Friend Program ....E..... 216 861-1838
 Cleveland (G-5581)
Friendly Inn Settlement House ....E..... 216 431-7656
 Cleveland (G-5582)
Frs Counseling Inc ....E..... 937 393-0585
 Hillsboro (G-11840)
Fulton County Senior Center ....E..... 419 337-9299
 Wauseon (G-18805)
Furniture Bank Central Ohio ....E..... 614 272-9544
 Columbus (G-7635)
G M N Tri Cnty Commnty Action ....C..... 740 732-2388
 Caldwell (G-2039)
Galion Community Center YMCA ....E..... 419 468-7754
 Galion (G-11173)
Gallia-Meigs Community Action ....E..... 740 367-7341
 Cheshire (G-2734)
Ganzhorn Suites Inc ....D..... 614 356-9810
 Powell (G-16195)
Gardens Western Reserve Inc ....D..... 330 342-9100
 Streetsboro (G-17252)
Gerlach John J Center For Sen ....E..... 614 566-5858
 Columbus (G-7663)
Girl Scuts Appleseed Ridge Inc ....E..... 419 225-4085
 Lima (G-12643)

Gladden Community House	E	614 221-7801
Columbus (G-7671)		
Godman Guild	E	614 294-5476
Columbus (G-7675)		
Golden String Inc	E	330 503-3894
Youngstown (G-20052)		
Good Smaritan Netwrk Ross Cnty	E	740 774-6303
Chillicothe (G-2783)		
Goodrich Gnnett Nghborhood Ctr	E	216 432-1717
Cleveland (G-5614)		
Goodwill Inds Rhbilitation Ctr	C	330 454-9461
Canton (G-2330)		
Goodwill Industries Inc	E	330 724-6995
Akron (G-240)		
Goodwill Industries of Erie	E	419 625-4744
Sandusky (G-16611)		
Goodwill Industries of Erie	D	419 334-7566
Fremont (G-11079)		
Grace Resurrection Association	E	937 548-2595
Greenville (G-11380)		
Graceworks Lutheran Services	C	937 433-2110
Dayton (G-9470)		
Great Miami Valley YMCA	A	513 887-0001
Hamilton (G-11602)		
Great Miami Valley YMCA	C	513 892-9622
Fairfield Township (G-10808)		
Great Miami Valley YMCA	D	513 887-0014
Hamilton (G-11604)		
Great Miami Valley YMCA	D	513 868-9622
Hamilton (G-11605)		
Great Miami Valley YMCA	D	513 829-3091
Fairfield (G-10732)		
Greater Cincinnati Behavioral	D	513 755-2203
Walnut Hills (G-18635)		
Greater Cleveland Food Bnk Inc	C	216 738-2265
Cleveland (G-5635)		
Greene Cnty Combined Hlth Dst	D	937 374-5600
Xenia (G-19902)		
Greene County	C	937 562-6000
Xenia (G-19904)		
Greenleaf Family Center	E	330 376-9494
Akron (G-245)		
Grove Cy Chrstn Child Care Ctr	D	614 875-2551
Grove City (G-11438)		
Hancock Job & Family Services	D	419 424-7022
Findlay (G-10919)		
Handson Central Ohio Inc	E	614 221-2255
Columbus (G-7714)		
Harbor House Inc	E	740 498-7213
New Philadelphia (G-14960)		
Harcatus Tri-County Community	E	740 922-0933
New Philadelphia (G-14961)		
Hardin Cnty Cncil On Aging Inc	E	419 673-1102
Kenton (G-12277)		
Hardin County Family YMCA	E	419 673-6131
Kenton (G-12279)		
Harrison Pavilion	E	513 662-5800
Cincinnati (G-3682)		
Hattie Larlham Center For	C	330 274-2272
Mantua (G-13267)		
Hattie Larlham Community Svcs	E	330 274-2272
Mantua (G-13269)		
Havar Inc	D	740 594-3533
Athens (G-782)		
Haven Bhavioral Healthcare Inc	B	937 234-0100
Dayton (G-9487)		
Haven Rest Ministries Inc	D	330 535-1563
Akron (G-256)		
Hcf Management Inc	C	740 289-2394
Piketon (G-15977)		
Hcf of Roselawn Inc	C	419 647-4115
Spencerville (G-16956)		
Hcr Manorcare Med Svcs Fla LLC	D	440 887-1442
North Royalton (G-15360)		
Healing Hrts Cunseling Ctr Inc	E	419 528-5993
Mansfield (G-13181)		
Heap Home Energy Assistance	D	419 626-6540
Sandusky (G-16615)		
Hearing Spch Deaf Ctr Grtr Cnc	E	513 221-0527
Cincinnati (G-3696)		
Heartbeat International Inc	E	614 885-7577
Columbus (G-7730)		
Help Hotline Crisis Center	E	330 747-5111
Youngstown (G-20064)		
Help Line of Dlware Mrrow Cnty	E	740 369-3316
Delaware (G-9984)		
Help ME Grow	E	419 738-4773
Wapakoneta (G-18646)		
Highland County Family YMCA	E	937 840-9622
Hillsboro (G-11842)		
Highlnd Cnty Commnty Action or	E	937 393-3060
Hillsboro (G-11845)		
Hilty Memorial Home Inc	C	419 384-3218
Pandora (G-15753)		
Hocking College Addc	E	740 541-2221
Glouster (G-11309)		
Hockingthensperry Cmnty Action	E	740 385-6813
Logan (G-12839)		
Hockingthensperry Cmnty Action	E	740 767-4500
Glouster (G-11310)		
Home Instead Senior Care	D	330 334-4664
Wadsworth (G-18599)		
Homefull	D	937 293-1945
Dayton (G-9503)		
Homeless Families Foundation	E	614 461-9427
Columbus (G-7765)		
Homes For Kids of Ohio Inc	E	330 544-8005
Niles (G-15157)		
Hospice of Knox County	E	740 397-5188
Mount Vernon (G-14768)		
Hospice of The Valley Inc	D	330 788-1992
Youngstown (G-20069)		
Hospice of The Western Reserve	D	440 997-6619
Ashtabula (G-740)		
Huber Heights YMCA	D	937 236-9622
Dayton (G-9508)		
Huckleberry House	D	614 294-5553
Columbus (G-7777)		
Hudson City Engineering Dept	E	330 342-1770
Hudson (G-11982)		
Impact Community Action	E	614 252-2799
Columbus (G-7802)		
Info Line Inc	E	330 252-8064
Akron (G-275)		
Inn At Christine Valley	E	330 270-3347
Youngstown (G-20082)		
Inn At Medina Limited LLC	D	330 723-0110
Medina (G-13954)		
Inside Out	D	937 525-7880
Springfield (G-17052)		
Integrated Services of Appala	D	740 594-6807
Athens (G-786)		
Interfaith Hosptlty Ntwrk of W	D	513 934-5250
Lebanon (G-12473)		
Jackson County Board On Aging	E	740 286-2909
Jackson (G-12177)		
James Powers	E	614 566-9397
Columbus (G-7853)		
Jewish Cmnty Ctr of Toledo	D	419 885-4485
Sylvania (G-17434)		
Jewish Community Ctr Cleveland	E	216 831-0700
Beachwood (G-1069)		
Jewish Family Service of	E	513 469-1188
Cincinnati (G-3815)		
Jewish Family Services	E	614 231-1890
Columbus (G-7858)		
Jewish Family Services Associa	B	216 292-3999
Cleveland (G-5795)		
Jewish Family Services Associa	E	216 292-3999
Cleveland (G-5796)		
Jewish Fderation of Cincinnati	E	513 985-1500
Cincinnati (G-3816)		
Jewish Fdrtion of Grter Dayton	D	937 837-2651
Dayton (G-9525)		
Juvenile Court Cnty Muskingum	E	740 453-0351
Zanesville (G-20322)		
KElly Youth Services Inc	E	513 761-0700
Cincinnati (G-3856)		
Kettering Recreation Center	E	937 296-2587
Dayton (G-9542)		
Kinnect	E	216 692-1161
Cleveland (G-5833)		
Kno-Ho-Co- Ashland Community A	C	740 622-9801
Coshocton (G-9021)		
Lake County Council On Aging	E	440 205-8111
Mentor (G-14071)		
Lake County YMCA	C	440 352-3303
Painesville (G-15718)		
Lake County YMCA	C	440 946-1160
Willoughby (G-19538)		
Lake County YMCA	C	440 259-2724
Perry (G-15824)		
Lake County YMCA	D	440 428-5125
Madison (G-13099)		
Lawrence Cnty Bd Dev Dsblities	E	740 377-2356
South Point (G-16938)		
Leads Inc	E	740 349-8606
Newark (G-15049)		
Leeda Services Inc	E	330 325-1560
Rootstown (G-16451)		
Liberty Nursing Center of Thre	C	513 941-0787
Cincinnati (G-3925)		
Licco Inc	C	740 522-8345
Newark (G-15050)		
Licking Cnty Alcoholism Prvntn	E	740 281-3639
Newark (G-15051)		
Licking County Aging Program	D	740 345-0821
Newark (G-15052)		
Licking County Board of Mrdd	C	740 349-6588
Newark (G-15053)		
Life Center Adult Day Care	E	614 866-7212
Reynoldsburg (G-16316)		
Lifecare Hospice	E	330 264-4899
Wooster (G-19741)		
Lifecare Hospice	D	330 336-6595
Wadsworth (G-18604)		
Lifespan Incorporated	D	513 868-3210
Hamilton (G-11624)		
Light of Hearts Villa	D	440 232-1991
Cleveland (G-5869)		
Lighthouse Youth Services Inc	D	513 221-1017
Cincinnati (G-3929)		
Lighthouse Youth Services Inc	D	513 221-3350
Cincinnati (G-3931)		
Lighthouse Youth Services Inc	D	740 634-3094
Bainbridge (G-931)		
Lima Family YMCA	E	419 223-6045
Lima (G-12680)		
Living In Family Environment	D	614 475-5305
Gahanna (G-11133)		
Lucas County Board of Developm	D	419 380-4000
Toledo (G-17868)		
Lutheran Scial Svcs Centl Ohio	E	419 289-3523
Worthington (G-19825)		
Lyman W Liggins Urban Affairs	D	419 385-2532
Toledo (G-17875)		
Maco Inc	E	740 472-5445
Woodsfield (G-19675)		
Mahoning County	D	330 797-2837
Youngstown (G-20107)		
Mahoning County Childrens Svcs	C	330 941-8888
Youngstown (G-20108)		
Mahoning Youngstown Community	D	330 747-7921
Youngstown (G-20112)		
Marion Area Counseling Ctr	C	740 387-5210
Marion (G-13434)		
Marion Family YMCA	D	740 725-9622
Marion (G-13437)		
Marsh Foundation	E	419 238-1695
Van Wert (G-18484)		
Masco Inc	E	330 797-2904
Youngstown (G-20118)		
Matco Industries Inc	E	740 852-7054
London (G-12870)		
Meals On Wheels-Older Adult Al	E	740 681-5050
Lancaster (G-12416)		
Medina Creative Accessibility	D	330 591-4434
Medina (G-13973)		
Meigs County Council On Aging	E	740 992-2161
Pomeroy (G-16095)		
Menorah Park Center For Senio	A	216 831-6500
Cleveland (G-5952)		
Mental Health & Recovery Ctr	E	937 383-3031
Wilmington (G-19635)		
Mental Hlth Serv For CL & Mad	E	937 390-7980
Springfield (G-17071)		
Mercy Health	A	440 233-1000
Lorain (G-12926)		
Mercy Health	E	440 324-0400
Elyria (G-10536)		
Mercy Health - St	E	419 696-7465
Oregon (G-15600)		
Mercy Health Partners	B	513 451-8900
Cincinnati (G-4031)		
Merrick House	E	216 771-5077
Cleveland (G-5958)		
Miami County Childrens Svcs Bd	E	937 335-4103
Troy (G-18213)		
Miami Valley Community Action	E	937 456-2800
Eaton (G-10454)		
Miami Valley Community Action	E	937 548-8143
Greenville (G-11390)		
Miami Valley Community Action	D	937 222-1009
Dayton (G-9617)		
Miami Vly Jvnile Rhbltion Ctr	E	937 562-4000
Xenia (G-19920)		
Mid-Ohio Foodbank	C	614 317-9400
Grove City (G-11453)		
Mid-Ohio Psychological Svcs Inc	D	740 687-0042
Lancaster (G-12419)		

Middltown Area Senior Citizens D 513 423-1734 Middletown *(G-14311)*
Midwest Behavioral Care Ltd E 937 454-0092 Dayton *(G-9632)*
Miracle Spirtl Retrst Orgnsizn E 216 324-4287 Cleveland *(G-6000)*
Mobile Meals D 330 376-7717 Akron *(G-340)*
Mobile Meals of Salem Inc E 330 332-2160 Salem *(G-16553)*
Mound Builders Guidance Center D 740 522-2828 Newark *(G-15075)*
Mount Carmel Health C 614 234-8170 Columbus *(G-8112)*
Mt Washington Care Center Inc C 513 231-4561 Cincinnati *(G-4083)*
Murray Ridge Production Center B 440 329-3734 Elyria *(G-10541)*
Muskingum Cnty Ctr For Seniors E 740 454-9761 Zanesville *(G-20333)*
Muskingum County Adult and CHI E 740 849-2344 Zanesville *(G-20334)*
Muskingum County Ohio D 740 452-0678 Zanesville *(G-20335)*
Nami of Preble County Ohio E 937 456-4947 Eaton *(G-10455)*
National Exchange Club Foundat E 419 535-3232 Toledo *(G-17930)*
National Youth Advocate Progra E 740 349-7511 Newark *(G-15080)*
National Youth Advocate Progra E 614 487-8758 Columbus *(G-8139)*
National Youth Advocate Progra D 614 252-6927 Columbus *(G-8140)*
Neighborhood House D 614 252-4941 Columbus *(G-8169)*
New Horizon Youth Center Co E 740 782-0092 Bethesda *(G-1456)*
New Horizon Youth Family Ctr E 740 687-0835 Lancaster *(G-12421)*
Nick Amster Inc D 330 264-9667 Wooster *(G-19751)*
North East Ohio Health Svcs D 216 831-6466 Beachwood *(G-1086)*
Northeast Ohio Chapter Natnl E 216 696-8220 Cleveland *(G-6092)*
Northland Brdg Franklin Cnty E 614 846-2588 Columbus *(G-8201)*
Northwest Mental Health Svcs E 614 457-7876 Columbus *(G-8207)*
Northwestrn OH Communty Action C 419 784-2150 Defiance *(G-9932)*
Ohio Association of Foodbanks E 614 221-4336 Columbus *(G-8229)*
Ohio Department of Health B 330 792-2397 Austintown *(G-858)*
Ohio Department of Health B 614 645-3621 Columbus *(G-8239)*
Ohio Department of Health D 937 285-6250 Dayton *(G-9668)*
Ohio Department of Health A 614 438-1255 Columbus *(G-8241)*
Ohio Dept of Job & Fmly Svcs C 614 466-1213 Columbus *(G-8247)*
Ohio Dept Rhbilitation Corectn B 614 274-9000 Columbus *(G-8248)*
Ohio District 5 Area C 419 522-5612 Ontario *(G-15567)*
Ohio Hrtland Cmnty Action Comm E 419 468-5121 Galion *(G-11180)*
Ohio State University A 614 366-3692 Columbus *(G-8295)*
Ohioguidestone E 440 234-2006 Berea *(G-1434)*
Ohioguidestone C 440 260-8900 Cleveland *(G-6126)*
Older Wiser Life Services LLC E 330 659-2111 Richfield *(G-16370)*
Olmsted Residence Corporation C 440 235-7100 Olmsted Twp *(G-15539)*
Oneeighty Inc D 330 263-6021 Wooster *(G-19756)*
ONeill Senior Center Inc E 740 373-3914 Marietta *(G-13365)*
Opportunities For Ohioans E 614 438-1200 Columbus *(G-8379)*
Option Line E 614 586-1380 Columbus *(G-8382)*
Options For Family & Youth E 216 267-7070 Strongsville *(G-17337)*
Oriana House Inc A 330 374-9610 Akron *(G-365)*
Oriana House Inc D 330 535-8116 Akron *(G-366)*
Oriana House Inc D 330 996-7730 Akron *(G-367)*
Oriana House Inc C 330 643-2171 Akron *(G-368)*
Ottawa County Board M R D D E 419 734-6650 Oak Harbor *(G-15476)*
Otterbein Snior Lfstyle Chices C 419 394-2366 Saint Marys *(G-16530)*
Outreach Community Living Svcs E 330 263-0862 Wooster *(G-19757)*
Pastoral Care Management Svcs E 513 205-1398 Cincinnati *(G-4207)*
Pastoral Counseling Svc Summit C 330 996-4600 Akron *(G-371)*
Pathway Inc E 419 242-7304 Toledo *(G-17974)*
Pathway 2 Hope Inc E 866 491-3040 Cincinnati *(G-4208)*
Pathways Inc D 440 918-1000 Mentor *(G-14095)*
Pathways of Central Ohio E 740 345-6166 Newark *(G-15091)*
Personal & Fmly Counseling Svc E 330 343-8171 New Philadelphia *(G-14976)*
Phillis Wheatley E 216 391-4443 Cleveland *(G-6204)*
Pickaway County Community Acti D 740 477-1655 Circleville *(G-4839)*
Pickaway County Community Acti E 740 474-7411 Circleville *(G-4840)*
Pickaway County Community Acti E 740 477-1655 Circleville *(G-4841)*
Pickaway Diversified E 740 474-1522 Circleville *(G-4843)*
Pike County YMCA E 740 947-8862 Waverly *(G-18822)*
Planned Parenthood Association E 937 226-0780 Dayton *(G-9694)*
Portage County Board D 330 678-2400 Ravenna *(G-16255)*
Portsmouth Metro Housing Auth E 740 354-4547 Portsmouth *(G-16161)*
Positive Education Program E 216 227-2730 Cleveland *(G-6223)*
Preble County Council On Aging E 937 456-4947 Eaton *(G-10459)*
Pregnancy Care of Cincinnati E 513 487-7777 Cincinnati *(G-4270)*
Pressley Ridge Foundation A 513 752-4548 Cincinnati *(G-2866)*
Pressley Ridge Foundation E 513 737-0400 Hamilton *(G-11633)*
Pressley Ridge Pryde E 513 559-1402 Cincinnati *(G-4275)*
Private Duty Services Inc C 419 238-3714 Van Wert *(G-18487)*
Pro Seniors Inc E 513 345-4160 Cincinnati *(G-4288)*
Prokids Inc E 513 281-2000 Cincinnati *(G-4297)*
Providence House Inc E 216 651-5982 Cleveland *(G-6263)*
Pump House Ministries E 419 207-3900 Ashland *(G-684)*
Quest Recovery Prevention Svcs C 330 453-8252 Canton *(G-2446)*
Rape Information & Counseling E 330 782-3936 Youngstown *(G-20177)*
Rehab Resources E 513 474-4123 Cincinnati *(G-4352)*
Rehabltation Corectn Ohio Dept D 614 752-0800 Columbus *(G-8507)*
Rescue Mission of Mahoning Val E 330 744-5485 Youngstown *(G-20184)*
Rescue Mission of Mahoning Val E 330 744-5485 Youngstown *(G-20185)*
Richland County Child Support E 419 774-5700 Mansfield *(G-13235)*
Rocking Horse Chld Hlth Ctr E 937 328-7266 Springfield *(G-17103)*
Ronald McDonald Hse Grtr Cinci E 513 636-7642 Cincinnati *(G-4395)*
Ross Cnty Cmmittee For Elderly E 740 773-3544 Chillicothe *(G-2817)*
Ross County Children Svcs Ctr D 740 773-2651 Chillicothe *(G-2818)*
Ross County YMCA D 740 772-4340 Chillicothe *(G-2823)*
Royal Redeemer Lutheran Church E 440 237-7958 North Royalton *(G-15365)*
Ryan Sheridan E 330 270-2380 Youngstown *(G-20201)*
Safely Home Inc E 440 232-9310 Bedford *(G-1304)*
Salem Community Center Inc D 330 332-5885 Salem *(G-16559)*
Saline Township E 330 532-2195 Hammondsville *(G-11657)*
Salvation Army D 614 252-7171 Columbus *(G-8587)*
Salvation Army E 937 528-5100 Dayton *(G-9747)*
Salvation Army D 859 255-5791 Cincinnati *(G-4429)*
Salvation Army D 800 728-7825 Columbus *(G-8588)*
Salvation Army D 513 762-5600 Cincinnati *(G-4430)*
Salvation Army D 216 861-8185 Cleveland *(G-6368)*
Santa Maria Community Svcs Inc E 513 557-2720 Cincinnati *(G-4432)*
Santantonio Diana and Assoc E 440 323-5121 Elyria *(G-10560)*
Sateri Home Inc D 330 758-8106 Youngstown *(G-20204)*
Scioto County Counseling Ctr D 740 354-6685 Portsmouth *(G-16167)*
Scioto County Ohio E 740 456-4164 New Boston *(G-14882)*
Scioto Pnt Vly Mental Hlth Ctr C 740 775-1260 Chillicothe *(G-2825)*
Scioto Pnt Vly Mental Hlth Ctr E 740 335-6935 Wshngtn CT Hs *(G-19883)*
Seamans Services E 216 621-4107 Cleveland *(G-6384)*
Sechkar Company E 740 385-8900 Nelsonville *(G-14837)*
Self Reliance Inc E 937 525-0809 Springfield *(G-17111)*
Senior Independence Adult E 440 954-8372 Willoughby *(G-19570)*
Senior Independence Adult E 513 681-8174 Monroe *(G-14582)*
Senior Independence Adult E 513 539-2697 Monroe *(G-14583)*
Senior Outreach Services E 216 421-6900 Cleveland *(G-6397)*
Senior Resource Connection C 937 223-8246 Dayton *(G-9759)*
Senior Star Management Company B 513 271-1747 Cincinnati *(G-4453)*
Services On Mark Inc E 614 846-5400 Worthington *(G-19848)*
Seven Hlls Neighborhood Houses D 513 407-5362 Cincinnati *(G-4460)*
Shaw Jewish Community Center C 330 867-7850 Akron *(G-427)*
Sheakley Cente E 513 487-7106 Cincinnati *(G-4466)*
Shelter House Volunteer Group E 513 721-0643 Cincinnati *(G-4469)*
Sickle Cell Awaremess Grp E 513 281-4450 Cincinnati *(G-4479)*
Sidney-Shelby County YMCA E 937 492-9134 Sidney *(G-16800)*
Siffrin Residential Assn C 330 799-8932 Youngstown *(G-20211)*
Simply Youth LLC D 330 284-2537 Canton *(G-2476)*
Sioto Paintsville Mental Hlth E 740 775-1260 Chillicothe *(G-2826)*
Skyview Baptist Ranch Inc E 330 674-7511 Millersburg *(G-14493)*
Society For Handicapped Citzns E 937 746-4201 Carlisle *(G-2554)*
Society of St Vincent De Paul E 513 421-2273 Cincinnati *(G-4500)*
Sojourner Recovery Services D 513 868-7654 Hamilton *(G-11642)*
Sourcepoint D 740 363-6677 Delaware *(G-10008)*
Southast Cmnty Mental Hlth Ctr E 614 444-0800 Columbus *(G-8662)*
Southast Cmnty Mental Hlth Ctr E 614 445-6832 Columbus *(G-8663)*

Southeast Cmnty Mental Hlth Ctr........E 614 293-9613	Transformation Network.................E 419 207-1188	Westcare Ohio Inc.................E 937 259-1898
Worthington (G-19850)	Ashland (G-695)	Dayton (G-9876)
Southeast Diversified Inds.................D 740 432-4241	Tri County Help Center Inc.................E 740 695-5441	Western Reserve Area Agency ....C 216 621-0303
Cambridge (G-2082)	Saint Clairsville (G-16507)	Cleveland (G-6673)
Southeastern Rehabilitation ....E 740 679-2111	Tri-County Community Act ....E 740 385-6812	Western Reserve Area Agency ....E 216 621-0303
Salesville (G-16568)	Logan (G-12857)	Cleveland (G-6674)
Southstern Ohio Rgional Fd Ctr ....E 740 385-6813	Trihealth Rehabilitation Hosp ....C 513 601-0600	Whetstone Industries Inc ....E 419 947-9222
Logan (G-12854)	Cincinnati (G-4646)	Mount Gilead (G-14735)
Spanish American Committee ....E 216 961-2100	Trillium Family Solutions Inc ....D 330 454-7066	Wood County Chld Svcs Assn.........D 419 352-7588
Cleveland (G-6441)	Cuyahoga Falls (G-9133)	Bowling Green (G-1752)
Specialized Alternatives For F ....C 216 295-7239	Trinity Action Partnership ....E 937 456-2800	Wood County Committee On Aging ......E 419 353-5661
Shaker Heights (G-16714)	Eaton (G-10463)	Bowling Green (G-1753)
Specialized Alternatives For F ....C 419 222-1527	Trumball Cnty Fire Chiefs Assn.........D 330 675-6602	Wood County Ohio ....C 419 354-9201
Lima (G-12746)	Warren (G-18753)	Bowling Green (G-1755)
Specialized Alternatives For F ....E 419 695-8010	Trumbull County One Stop ....D 330 675-2000	WoodInds Srving Centl Ohio Inc ....E 740 349-7051
Delphos (G-10035)	Warren (G-18756)	Newark (G-15111)
Spectrum Supportive Services ....E 216 875-0460	Turning Pt Counseling Svcs Inc ....D 330 744-2991	Y M C A Central Stark County ....E 330 305-5437
Cleveland (G-6445)	Youngstown (G-20227)	Canton (G-2539)
Springfield Family Y M C A ....D 937 323-3781	Tuscarawas County Commitee ....D 330 364-6611	Y M C A Central Stark County ....E 330 875-1611
Springfield (G-17119)	Dover (G-10104)	Louisville (G-12975)
St Joseph Infant Maternity Hm ....C 513 563-2520	Tuscarawas County Help ME Grow ....E 330 339-3493	Y M C A Central Stark County ....E 330 877-8933
Cincinnati (G-4527)	New Philadelphia (G-14986)	Uniontown (G-18392)
St Pauls Community Center.................D 419 255-5520	Twelve Inc ....E 330 837-3555	Y M C A Central Stark County ....E 330 830-6275
Toledo (G-18046)	Massillon (G-13733)	Massillon (G-13736)
St Stephens Community House ....D 614 294-6347	Ucc Childrens Center ....E 513 217-5501	Y M C A Central Stark County ....E 330 498-4082
Columbus (G-8680)	Middletown (G-14356)	Canton (G-2540)
St Vincent De Paul Scl Svs ....D 937 222-7349	United Disability Services Inc ....C 330 374-1169	Y M C A of Ashland Ohio Inc ....D 419 289-0626
Dayton (G-9789)	Akron (G-476)	Ashland (G-700)
St Vincent Family Centers ....C 614 252-0731	United Methodist Childrens ....C 614 885-5020	YMCA ....D 937 653-9622
Columbus (G-8681)	Columbus (G-8804)	Urbana (G-18447)
Stark Cnty Dept Job Fmly Svcs ....B 330 451-8400	United Rehabilitation Services ....D 937 233-1230	YMCA ....E 330 823-1930
Canton (G-2488)	Dayton (G-9832)	Alliance (G-558)
Summit Cnty Dept Job Fmly Svcs ....D 330 643-8200	United Scoto Senior Activities ....E 740 354-6672	YMCA of Clermont County Inc ....E 513 724-9622
Akron (G-456)	Portsmouth (G-16176)	Batavia (G-1016)
Sunshine Communities ....B 419 865-0251	United Way Greater Cincinnati ....D 513 762-7100	YMCA of Massillon ....E 330 879-0800
Maumee (G-13857)	Cincinnati (G-4689)	Navarre (G-14826)
Support To At Risk Teens ....E 216 696-5507	United Way of Greater Toledo ....D 419 254-4742	Young Mens Christian ....B 513 932-1424
Cleveland (G-6486)	Toledo (G-18122)	Lebanon (G-12516)
Supreme Court United States ....E 419 213-5800	United Way of The Greater Dayt ....E 937 225-3060	Young Mens Christian Assn ....E 419 332-9622
Toledo (G-18057)	Dayton (G-9834)	Fremont (G-11108)
Supreme Court United States ....D 614 719-3107	University of Cincinnati.................D 513 556-3803	Young Mens Christian Assn ....D 330 744-8411
Columbus (G-8717)	Cincinnati (G-4726)	Youngstown (G-20253)
Supreme Court United States ....E 513 564-7575	Upreach LLC.................B 614 442-7702	Young Mens Christian Assn ....E 419 238-0443
Cincinnati (G-4558)	Columbus (G-8827)	Van Wert (G-18498)
Supreme Court United States ....E 216 357-7300	Ussa Inc ....E 740 354-6672	Young Mens Christian Assoc.................C 614 885-4252
Cleveland (G-6487)	Portsmouth (G-16179)	Columbus (G-8927)
Sycamore Board of Education.................D 513 489-3937	Vantage Aging ....A 440 324-3588	Young Mens Christian Assoc.................D 614 276-8224
Cincinnati (G-4560)	Elyria (G-10569)	Columbus (G-8928)
Sycamore Senior Center.................D 513 984-1234	Vantage Aging ....D 330 253-4597	Young Mens Christian Assoc.................C 614 834-9622
Blue Ash (G-1654)	Akron (G-486)	Canal Winchester (G-2129)
Sylvania Community Svcs Ctr ....E 419 885-2451	Vasconcellos Inc ....E 513 576-1250	Young Mens Christian Assoc.................E 419 729-8135
Sylvania (G-17454)	Milford (G-14442)	Toledo (G-18167)
Syntero Inc ....E 614 889-5722	Venture Productions Inc.................D 937 544-2823	Young Mens Christian Assoc.................C 614 871-9622
Dublin (G-10350)	West Union (G-19139)	Grove City (G-11491)
Talbert House ....E 513 541-0127	Vermilion Family YMCA ....E 440 967-4208	Young Mens Christian Assoc.................E 937 223-5201
Cincinnati (G-4570)	Vermilion (G-18563)	Dayton (G-9892)
Talbert House ....E 513 541-1184	Village of Groveport.................E 614 830-2060	Young Mens Christian Assoc.................D 330 923-5223
Cincinnati (G-4572)	Groveport (G-11549)	Cuyahoga Falls (G-9141)
Talbert House ....D 513 872-5863	Volunteers America Ohio & Ind ....C 614 253-6100	Young Mens Christian Assoc.................E 330 467-8366
Cincinnati (G-4573)	Columbus (G-8859)	Macedonia (G-13091)
Talbert House ....D 513 933-9304	Volunteers of America NW Ohio ....E 419 248-3733	Young Mens Christian Assoc.................E 330 784-0408
Lebanon (G-12509)	Toledo (G-18140)	Akron (G-507)
Talbert House Health ....E 513 541-7577	Volunters of Amer Greater Ohio ....E 614 861-8551	Young Mens Christian Assoc.................C 614 416-9622
Cincinnati (G-4575)	Columbus (G-8860)	Gahanna (G-11152)
Tarry House Inc ....E 330 253-6689	Volunters of Amer Greater Ohio ....D 216 541-9000	Young Mens Christian Assoc.................C 614 334-9622
Akron (G-463)	Cleveland (G-6642)	Hilliard (G-11832)
Tasc New Town LLC ....E 419 242-9955	Volunters of Amer Greater Ohio ....E 614 372-3120	Young Mens Christian Assoc.................E 937 312-1810
Toledo (G-18059)	Columbus (G-8861)	Dayton (G-9893)
Tasc of Northwest Ohio Inc ....E 419 242-9955	Volunters of Amer Greater Ohio ....E 419 524-5013	Young Mens Christian Assoc.................E 614 539-1770
Toledo (G-18060)	Mansfield (G-13261)	Urbancrest (G-18453)
Tasc of Southeast Ohio ....E 740 594-2276	Volunters of Amer Greater Ohio ....E 614 263-9134	Young Mens Christian Assoc.................E 614 252-3166
Athens (G-805)	Columbus (G-8862)	Columbus (G-8929)
Taylor Corporation ....E 419 420-0790	Volunters of America Cntl Ohio ....D 614 801-1655	Young Mens Christian Assoc.................C 937 223-5201
Findlay (G-10969)	Grove City (G-11481)	Springboro (G-16990)
Taylor Murtis Human Svcs Sys.........D 216 281-7192	W S O S Community A.................D 419 333-6068	Young Mens Christian Assoc.................E 937 593-9001
Cleveland (G-6504)	Fremont (G-11104)	Bellefontaine (G-1370)
Taylor Murtis Human Svcs Sys.........D 216 283-4400	WEBa Outreach Food Pantry ....E 740 543-3227	Young Mens Christian Associat ....D 513 241-9622
Cleveland (G-6503)	Amsterdam (G-602)	Cincinnati (G-4815)
Taylor Murtis Human Svcs Sys.........D 216 283-4400	Wesley Community Services LLC ....D 513 661-2777	Young Mens Christian Associat ....D 513 923-4466
Cleveland (G-6505)	Cincinnati (G-4779)	Cincinnati (G-4816)
Tcn Behavioral Health Svcs Inc.........C 937 376-8700	West Ohio Cmnty Action Partnr ....C 419 227-2586	Young Mens Christian Associat ....E 419 474-3995
Xenia (G-19927)	Lima (G-12781)	Toledo (G-18169)
Tender Mercies Inc.................D 513 721-8666	West Ohio Cmnty Action Partnr ....C 419 227-2586	Young Mens Christian Associat ....D 419 866-9622
Cincinnati (G-4585)	Lima (G-12782)	Maumee (G-13871)
The Foodbank Inc ....E 937 461-0265	West Side Community House ....E 216 771-7297	Young Mens Christian Associat ....C 419 475-3496
Dayton (G-9810)	Cleveland (G-6670)	Toledo (G-18170)
Tom Paige Catering Company ....E 216 431-4236	West Side Ecumenical Ministry ....C 216 325-9369	Young Mens Christian Associat ....D 419 691-3523
Cleveland (G-6532)	Cleveland (G-6671)	Oregon (G-15615)
Townhall 2 ....E 330 678-3006	Westark Family Services Inc ....E 330 832-5043	Young Mens Christian Mt Vernon ....D 740 392-9622
Kent (G-12263)	Massillon (G-13734)	Mount Vernon (G-14794)

Young MNS Chrstn Assn Clveland.......E 216 941-4654
  Cleveland (G-6702)
Young MNS Chrstn Assn Clveland.......D 440 808-8150
  Westlake (G-19426)
Young MNS Chrstn Assn Clveland.......E 216 521-8400
  Lakewood (G-12364)
Young MNS Chrstn Assn Clveland.......E 216 731-7454
  Cleveland (G-6703)
Young MNS Chrstn Assn Clveland.......D 440 285-7543
  Chardon (G-2726)
Young MNS Chrstn Assn Grter NY.......D 740 392-9622
  Mount Vernon (G-14795)
Young Womens Christian ....D 419 241-3235
  Toledo (G-18172)
Young Womens Christian ....E 419 238-6639
  Van Wert (G-18499)
Young Womens Christian Assn ....D 614 224-9121
  Columbus (G-8931)
Young Womens Christian Associ ....E 216 881-6878
  Cleveland (G-6705)
Young Womns Chrstn Assc Canton.....D 330 453-0789
  Canton (G-2543)
Youngstown Area Jwish Fdration ......C 330 746-3251
  Youngstown (G-20256)
Youngstown Area Jwish Fdration ......D 330 746-1076
  Youngstown (G-20257)
Youngstown Committee On Alchol .....D 330 744-1181
  Youngstown (G-20260)
Youngstown Neighborhood Dev ....E 330 480-0423
  Youngstown (G-20263)
Youth Advocate Services ....E 614 258-9927
  Columbus (G-8932)
Youth Mntrng & At Rsk Intrvntn.........E 216 324-2451
  Richmond Heights (G-16396)
Youth Services Ohio Department ....C 419 875-6965
  Liberty Center (G-12576)
YWCA Dayton ....D 937 461-5550
  Dayton (G-9896)
YWCA Mahoning Valley ....E 330 746-6361
  Youngstown (G-20269)
YWCA of Greater Cincinnati ....D 513 241-7090
  Cincinnati (G-4817)
YWCA Shelter & Housing Network .....E 937 222-6333
  Dayton (G-9897)

8331 Job Training & Vocational Rehabilitation Svcs

A W S Inc ....C 440 333-1791
  Rocky River (G-16420)
A W S Inc ....B 216 749-0356
  Cleveland (G-4881)
A W S Inc ....E 216 486-0600
  Euclid (G-10622)
A W S Inc ....D 216 941-8800
  Cleveland (G-4882)
Abilities First Foundation Inc ....D 513 423-9496
  Middletown (G-14285)
Ability Works Inc ....C 419 626-1048
  Sandusky (G-16572)
Akron Blind Center & Workshop ....D 330 253-2555
  Akron (G-29)
Alpha Group of Delaware Inc ....D 614 222-1855
  Columbus (G-6903)
Alpha Group of Delaware Inc ....D 740 368-5810
  Delaware (G-9951)
Alpha Group of Delaware Inc ....E 740 368-5820
  Delaware (G-9952)
Angeline Industries Inc ....E 419 294-4488
  Upper Sandusky (G-18403)
Anne Grady Corporation ....E 419 867-7501
  Holland (G-11871)
ARC Industries Incorporated O ....C 614 479-2500
  Columbus (G-6964)
ARC Industries Incorporated O ....B 614 436-4800
  Columbus (G-6965)
ARC Industries Incorporated O ....B 614 864-2406
  Columbus (G-6966)
ARC Industries Incorporated O ....D 614 267-1207
  Columbus (G-6967)
ARC Industries Incorporated O ....B 614 836-0700
  Groveport (G-11494)
Ash Craft Industries Inc ....C 440 224-2177
  Ashtabula (G-704)
▲ Atco Inc ....C 740 592-6659
  Athens (G-765)
Belco Works Inc ....B 740 695-0500
  Saint Clairsville (G-16470)
Brookhill Center Industries...............C 419 876-3932
  Ottawa (G-15657)

Brown Cnty Bd Mntal Rtardation........E 937 378-4891
  Georgetown (G-11261)
Butler County of Ohio.....................E 513 785-6500
  Hamilton (G-11563)
Butler County Bd of Mental RE.........C 513 785-2870
  Fairfield Township (G-10805)
Capabilities Inc.............................E 419 394-0003
  Saint Marys (G-16520)
Capano & Associates LLC ....E 513 403-6000
  Liberty Township (G-12578)
Carroll Hills Industries Inc ....D 330 627-5524
  Carrollton (G-2563)
Center of Voctnl Altrntvs Mntl...........D 614 294-7117
  Columbus (G-7154)
▲ Cincinnati Assn For The Blind.......D 513 221-8558
  Cincinnati (G-3223)
Cleveland Christian Home Inc ....E 216 671-0977
  Cleveland (G-5234)
CLI Incorporated ....C 419 668-8840
  Norwalk (G-15429)
Collins Career Center ....D 740 867-6641
  Chesapeake (G-2728)
Community Action Organization ....C 740 354-7541
  Portsmouth (G-16132)
Community Support Services Inc ....C 330 253-9388
  Akron (G-153)
Cornucopia Inc.............................E 216 521-4600
  Lakewood (G-12339)
County of Crawford ....D 419 562-0015
  Bucyrus (G-1986)
County of Cuyahoga ....D 216 475-7066
  Cleveland (G-5362)
County of Geauga ....D 440 564-2246
  Chardon (G-2691)
County of Hamilton ....B 513 742-1576
  Cincinnati (G-3369)
County of Hancock ....E 419 422-6387
  Findlay (G-10891)
County of Hardin ....E 419 674-4158
  Kenton (G-12274)
County of Holmes ....E 330 674-1111
  Millersburg (G-14472)
County of Lake ....A 440 350-5100
  Mentor (G-14036)
County of Lake ....D 440 269-2193
  Willoughby (G-19516)
County of Marion ....D 740 387-1035
  Marion (G-13416)
County of Mercer ....D 419 586-2369
  Celina (G-2591)
County of Montgomery ....E 937 225-4804
  Dayton (G-9330)
County of Sandusky ....D 419 637-2243
  Fremont (G-11065)
County of Seneca ....D 419 435-0729
  Fostoria (G-10999)
County of Stark ....D 330 484-4814
  Canton (G-2267)
Creative Learning Workshop ....E 330 393-5929
  Warren (G-18696)
Creative Learning Workshop ....E 937 437-0146
  New Paris (G-14941)
Cuyahoga County ....D 216 265-3030
  Cleveland (G-5394)
D-R Training Center & Workshop ....C 419 289-0470
  Ashland (G-671)
Dayton Urban League ....E 937 226-1513
  Dayton (G-9383)
Deepwood Industries Inc ....C 440 350-5231
  Mentor (G-14040)
Easter Seals Tristate......................E 513 985-0515
  Blue Ash (G-1549)
Easter Seals Tristate LLC ....C 513 281-2316
  Cincinnati (G-3473)
Employment Development Inc...........C 330 424-7711
  Lisbon (G-12800)
Esc of Cuyahoga County ....D 216 524-3000
  Independence (G-12071)
Fairhaven Sheltered Workshop ....D 330 652-1116
  Niles (G-15154)
Fairhaven Sheltered Workshop ....C 330 847-7275
  Warren (G-18708)
Fairhaven Sheltered Workshop ....C 330 505-3644
  Niles (G-15155)
▲ Findaway World LLC ....D 440 893-0808
  Solon (G-16849)
First Capital Enterprises Inc ....D 740 773-2166
  Chillicothe (G-2780)
Food For Good Thought Inc ....C 614 447-0424
  Columbus (G-7600)

Gallco Inc....................................D 740 446-3775
  Gallipolis (G-11192)
Goodwill Ester Seals Miami Vly ....C 937 461-4800
  Dayton (G-9464)
Goodwill Idstrs Grtr Clvlnd L ....E 440 783-1168
  Strongsville (G-17307)
Goodwill Idstrs Grtr Clvlnd L ....E 216 581-6320
  Cleveland (G-5615)
Goodwill Idstrs Grtr Clvlnd L ....D 330 454-9461
  Canton (G-2329)
Goodwill Inds Centl Ohio Inc ....B 614 294-5181
  Columbus (G-7679)
Goodwill Inds Centl Ohio Inc ....D 740 373-1304
  Marietta (G-13331)
Goodwill Inds Centl Ohio Inc ....E 614 274-5296
  Columbus (G-7680)
Goodwill Inds Centl Ohio Inc ....E 740 439-7000
  Cambridge (G-2070)
Goodwill Inds NW Ohio Inc ....D 419 255-0070
  Toledo (G-17767)
Goodwill Inds of Ashtabula...............C 440 964-3565
  Ashtabula (G-738)
Goodwill Inds Rhbilitation Ctr ....C 330 454-9461
  Canton (G-2330)
Goodwill Industries ....B 330 264-1300
  Wooster (G-19725)
Goodwill Industries Inc ....B 330 724-6995
  Akron (G-240)
Goodwill Industries of Akron ....C 330 724-6995
  Akron (G-241)
Goodwill Industries of Lima ....D 419 228-4821
  Lima (G-12645)
GP Strategies Corporation ....E 513 583-8810
  Cincinnati (G-3629)
Great Oaks Inst Tech Creer Dev ....D 513 613-3657
  Cincinnati (G-3644)
Great Oaks Inst Tech Creer Dev ....E 513 771-8840
  Cincinnati (G-3645)
Greene Inc ....D 937 562-4200
  Xenia (G-19907)
Gw Business Solutions LLC ....C 740 645-9861
  Newark (G-15039)
Handson Central Ohio Inc ....E 614 221-2255
  Columbus (G-7714)
Harco Industries Inc ....E 419 674-4159
  Kenton (G-12276)
Harrison Industries Inc....................D 740 942-2988
  Cadiz (G-2029)
Hocking Valley Industries Inc ....D 740 385-2118
  Logan (G-12838)
Hockingthensperry Cmnty Action........C 740 767-4500
  Glouster (G-11310)
Holmes County Board of Dd ....D 330 674-8045
  Holmesville (G-11930)
Hopewell Industries Inc...................D 740 622-3563
  Coshocton (G-9018)
▲ Hunter Defense Tech Inc ....E 216 438-6111
  Solon (G-16859)
Integrated Services of Appala ....D 740 594-6807
  Athens (G-786)
Ironton and Lawrence County ....B 740 532-3534
  Ironton (G-12155)
J-Vac Industries Inc ....D 740 384-2155
  Wellston (G-18850)
Jewish Family Services ....D 614 231-1890
  Columbus (G-7858)
Joe and Jill Lewis Inc ....D 937 718-8829
  Dayton (G-9526)
Ken Harper..................................C 740 439-4452
  Byesville (G-2025)
Knox New Hope Industries Inc ....C 740 397-4601
  Mount Vernon (G-14776)
L & M Products Inc ....C 937 456-7141
  Eaton (G-10449)
Licco Inc ....C 740 522-8345
  Newark (G-15050)
Licking-Knox Goodwill Inds Inc ....D 740 345-9861
  Newark (G-15061)
Linking Employment Abilities ....E 216 696-2716
  Cleveland (G-5872)
Lorain County Board ....E 440 329-3734
  Elyria (G-10530)
Lott Industries Incorporated ....B 419 476-2516
  Toledo (G-17858)
Lott Industries Incorporated ....B 419 891-5215
  Maumee (G-13811)
Lott Industries Incorporated ....A 419 534-4980
  Toledo (G-17859)
Lott Industries Incorporated ....B 419 534-4980
  Toledo (G-17860)

Lynn Hope Industries Inc ....D.... 330 674-8045
Holmesville (G-11931)

Marca Industries Inc ....E.... 740 387-1035
Marion (G-13432)

Marimor Industries Inc ....C.... 419 221-1226
Lima (G-12698)

Marion Cnty Bd Dev Dsabilities ....D.... 740 387-1035
Marion (G-13435)

Marion Goodwill Industries ....E.... 740 387-7023
Marion (G-13441)

Mary Hmmond Adult Actvties Ctr ....D.... 740 962-4200
McConnelsville (G-13901)

Matco Industries Inc ....E.... 740 852-7054
London (G-12870)

Medina County Sheltered Inds ....B.... 330 334-4491
Wadsworth (G-18608)

Meigs Industries Inc ....E.... 740 992-6681
Syracuse (G-17469)

Metzenbaum Sheltered Inds Inc ....C.... 440 729-1919
Chesterland (G-2741)

Miami University ....B.... 513 727-3200
Middletown (G-14308)

Mickis Creative Options Inc ....E.... 419 526-4254
Mansfield (G-13220)

Monco Enterprises Inc ....A.... 937 461-0034
Dayton (G-9642)

Murray Ridge Production Center ....B.... 440 329-3734
Elyria (G-10541)

Muskingum Starlight Industries ....C.... 740 453-4622
Zanesville (G-20341)

Nick Amster Inc ....C.... 330 264-9667
Wooster (G-19750)

Ohio Dept of Job & Fmly Svcs ....E.... 614 752-9494
Columbus (G-8246)

Ohio Rehabilitation Svcs Comm ....E.... 330 643-3080
Akron (G-362)

Ohio State University ....D.... 614 292-7788
Columbus (G-8319)

Ohio State University ....D.... 614 292-4353
Columbus (G-8316)

Perco Inc ....D.... 740 342-5156
New Lexington (G-14926)

Pickaway Diversfied Industries ....D.... 740 474-1522
Circleville (G-4842)

Portage Industries Inc ....C.... 330 296-3996
Ravenna (G-16257)

Portage Private Industry ....D.... 330 297-7795
Ravenna (G-16259)

Production Services Unlimited ....D.... 513 695-1658
Lebanon (G-12493)

Project Rebuild Inc ....E.... 330 639-1559
Canton (G-2441)

Quadco Rehabilitation Center ....D.... 419 445-1950
Archbold (G-636)

Quadco Rehabilitation Ctr Inc ....B.... 419 682-1011
Stryker (G-17370)

R T Industries Inc ....C.... 937 339-8313
Troy (G-18225)

R T Industries Inc ....C.... 937 335-5784
Troy (G-18224)

Richcreek Bailey Rehabilitatio ....E.... 440 527-8610
Mentor (G-14104)

Richland Newhope Industries ....E.... 419 774-4200
Mansfield (G-13238)

Richland Newhope Industries ....D.... 419 774-4496
Mansfield (G-13239)

Richland Newhope Industries ....E.... 419 774-4400
Mansfield (G-13237)

Ridge Murray Prod Ctr Oberlin ....E.... 440 774-7400
Oberlin (G-15519)

Riverview Industries Inc ....C.... 419 898-5250
Oak Harbor (G-15478)

Ross Training Center Inc ....D.... 937 592-0025
Bellefontaine (G-1363)

RTC Industries Inc ....E.... 937 592-0534
Bellefontaine (G-1364)

Sandco Industries ....C.... 419 334-9090
Clyde (G-6752)

Southeast Diversified Inds ....D.... 740 432-4241
Cambridge (G-2082)

Spanish American Committee ....E.... 216 961-2100
Cleveland (G-6441)

Spectrum Supportive Services ....E.... 216 875-0460
Cleveland (G-6445)

Star Inc ....C.... 740 354-1517
Portsmouth (G-16174)

Stark County Board of Developm ....A.... 330 477-5200
Canton (G-2490)

Starlight Enterprises Inc ....C.... 330 339-2020
New Philadelphia (G-14983)

Step By Step Emplyment Trining ....E.... 440 967-9042
Vermilion (G-18560)

TAC Industries Inc ....C.... 937 328-5200
Springfield (G-17124)

TAC Industries Inc ....B.... 937 328-5200
Springfield (G-17123)

Tri-State Industries Inc ....C.... 740 532-0406
Coal Grove (G-6756)

Trumbull Cmnty Action Program ....E.... 330 393-2507
Warren (G-18754)

U-Co Industries Inc ....D.... 937 644-3021
Marysville (G-13534)

United Cerebral Palsy ....C.... 216 791-8363
Cleveland (G-6568)

United Disability Services Inc ....C.... 330 374-1169
Akron (G-476)

Vgs Inc ....C.... 216 431-7800
Cleveland (G-6627)

Vision & Vocational Services ....E.... 614 294-5571
Columbus (G-8853)

Voc Works Ltd ....D.... 614 760-3515
Dublin (G-10366)

Vocational Guidance Services ....A.... 216 431-7800
Cleveland (G-6639)

Vocational Guidance Services ....E.... 440 322-1123
Elyria (G-10570)

Vocational Services Inc ....C.... 216 431-8085
Cleveland (G-6640)

W S O S Community A ....E.... 419 639-2802
Green Springs (G-11356)

W S O S Community A ....E.... 419 334-8511
Fremont (G-11105)

W S O S Community A ....E.... 419 333-6068
Fremont (G-11104)

Wasco Inc ....E.... 740 373-3418
Marietta (G-13400)

Waycraft Inc ....C.... 419 563-0550
Bucyrus (G-2005)

Waycraft Inc ....D.... 419 562-3321
Bucyrus (G-2006)

Weaver Industries Inc ....E.... 330 379-3660
Akron (G-497)

Weaver Industries Inc ....C.... 330 666-5114
Akron (G-498)

Wood County Ohio ....E.... 419 352-5059
Bowling Green (G-1758)

Workforce Initiative Assn ....E.... 330 433-9675
Canton (G-2537)

Youngstown Area Goodwill Inds ....C.... 330 759-7921
Youngstown (G-20255)

Zanesville Welfare Organizatio ....B.... 740 450-6060
Zanesville (G-20386)

Zanesvlle Welfre Orgnztn/Goodw ....D.... 740 450-6060
Zanesville (G-20387)

Zepf Center ....E.... 419 213-5627
Toledo (G-18177)

8351 Child Day Care Svcs

1 Amazing Place Co ....E.... 419 420-0424
Findlay (G-10860)

A & D Daycare and Learning Ctr ....E.... 937 263-4447
Dayton (G-9197)

A Better Child Care Corp ....E.... 513 353-5437
Cincinnati (G-2889)

A CCS Day Care Centers Inc ....E.... 513 841-2227
Cincinnati (G-2891)

A Childs Place Nursery School ....D.... 330 493-1333
Canton (G-2169)

A New Beginning Preschool ....D.... 216 531-7465
Cleveland (G-4879)

Abacus Child Care Centers Inc ....E.... 330 773-4200
Akron (G-14)

ABC Child Care & Learning Ctr ....E.... 440 964-8799
Ashtabula (G-702)

Abilities First Foundation Inc ....D.... 513 423-9496
Middletown (G-14285)

Academy Kids Learning Ctr Inc ....E.... 614 258-5437
Columbus (G-6858)

Action For Children Inc ....E.... 614 224-0222
Columbus (G-6868)

Adams Cnty /Ohio Vly Schl Dst ....D.... 937 544-2951
West Union (G-19129)

Agj Kidz LLC ....E.... 937 350-1001
Centerville (G-2618)

Ajm Worthington Inc ....E.... 614 888-5800
Worthington (G-19791)

Akron Summit Cmnty Action Agcy ....D.... 330 733-2290
Akron (G-57)

All About Kids ....E.... 937 885-7480
Centerville (G-2620)

All About Kids Daycare N ....E.... 330 494-8700
North Canton (G-15187)

All Around Children Montessori ....E.... 330 928-1444
Stow (G-17190)

All For Kids Inc ....E.... 740 435-8050
Cambridge (G-2048)

Allen County Eductl Svc Ctr ....E.... 419 222-1836
Lima (G-12595)

Amandas Playroom Inc ....E.... 330 296-3934
Ravenna (G-16232)

Anderson Little ....E.... 513 474-7800
Cincinnati (G-2962)

Angel Care Inc ....E.... 440 736-7267
Brecksville (G-1768)

Angels On Earth Child Care Co ....E.... 216 476-8100
Cleveland (G-4979)

Annas Child Care Lrng Ctr Inc ....D.... 937 667-1903
Tipp City (G-17549)

Arlitt Child Development Ctr ....D.... 513 556-3802
Cincinnati (G-2988)

Ashland City School District ....E.... 419 289-7967
Ashland (G-646)

Assoc Dvlpmtly Disabled ....E.... 614 447-0606
Columbus (G-6982)

Aultman Hospital ....E.... 330 452-2273
Canton (G-2205)

Bailey & Long Inc ....E.... 614 937-9435
Columbus (G-7011)

Bay Village City School Dst ....E.... 440 617-7330
Cleveland (G-5043)

Bay Village Montessori Inc ....E.... 440 871-8773
Westlake (G-19321)

Beachwood City Schools ....D.... 216 464-2600
Beachwood (G-1034)

Beavercreek Church of Nazarene ....E.... 937 426-0079
Beavercreek (G-1131)

Beavercreek YMCA ....D.... 937 426-9622
Dayton (G-9246)

Bethlehem Lutheran Ch Parma ....E.... 440 845-2230
Cleveland (G-5060)

Board Man Frst Untd Methdst Ch ....E.... 330 758-4527
Youngstown (G-19968)

Bombeck Family Learning Center ....E.... 937 229-2158
Dayton (G-9257)

Bowling Green Coop Nurs Schl ....E.... 419 352-8675
Bowling Green (G-1721)

Bright Beginnings ....E.... 937 748-2612
Springboro (G-16963)

Bright Horizons Chld Ctrs LLC ....E.... 614 754-7023
Columbus (G-7064)

Bright Horizons Chld Ctrs LLC ....E.... 614 566-9322
Columbus (G-7065)

Bright Horizons Chld Ctrs LLC ....E.... 614 566-4847
Columbus (G-7067)

Bright Horizons Chld Ctrs LLC ....E.... 330 375-7633
Akron (G-107)

Brooksedge Day Care Center ....E.... 614 529-0077
Hilliard (G-11748)

Brownstone Private Child Care ....E.... 216 221-1470
Lakewood (G-12337)

Brunswick City Schools ....A.... 330 225-7731
Brunswick (G-1921)

Butler County Bd of Mental RE ....E.... 513 785-2815
Hamilton (G-11567)

Butler County Eductl Svc Ctr ....E.... 513 737-2817
Hamilton (G-11568)

Campbell Family Childcare Inc ....E.... 614 855-4780
New Albany (G-14846)

Canton City School District ....E.... 330 456-3167
Canton (G-2229)

Canton Country Day School ....E.... 330 453-8279
Canton (G-2231)

Canton Montessori Association ....E.... 330 452-0148
Canton (G-2238)

Cardinal Pacelli School ....B.... 513 321-1048
Cincinnati (G-3117)

Carol Scudere ....E.... 614 839-4357
New Albany (G-14848)

Catholic Social Svc Miami Vly ....E.... 937 223-7217
Dayton (G-9287)

Centerville Child Development ....E.... 937 434-5949
Dayton (G-9289)

Chal-Ron LLC ....E.... 216 383-9050
Cleveland (G-5166)

Champons In Making Daycare LLC .....E.... 937 728-4886
Wilmington (G-19607)

Child Care Resource Center ....E.... 216 575-0061
Cleveland (G-5177)

Child Care Resources Inc ....D.... 740 454-6251
Zanesville (G-20295)

Child Dev Ctr Jackson Cnty ....E ...... 740 286-3995 Jackson *(G-12171)*	Creative Center For Children ....E ...... 513 867-1118 Hamilton *(G-11588)*	Friend-Ship Child Care Ctr LLC ....E ...... 330 484-2051 Canton *(G-2318)*
Child Dvlpmnt Cncl of Frnkln ....D ...... 614 221-1709 Columbus *(G-7185)*	Creative Childrens World LLC ....E ...... 513 336-7799 Mason *(G-13570)*	Future Advantage Inc ....E ...... 330 686-7707 Stow *(G-17207)*
Child Dvlpmnt Cncl of Frnkln ....E ...... 614 416-5178 Columbus *(G-7186)*	Creative Playroom ....D ...... 216 475-6464 Cleveland *(G-5376)*	Galion Community Center YMCA ....E ...... 419 468-7754 Galion *(G-11173)*
Child Focus Inc ....D ...... 937 444-1613 Mount Orab *(G-14739)*	Creative Playroom ....E ...... 440 248-3100 Solon *(G-16840)*	Gearity Early Child Care Ctr ....E ...... 216 371-7356 Cleveland *(G-5601)*
Child Focus Inc ....D ...... 513 752-1555 Cincinnati *(G-3180)*	Creative Playrooms Inc ....E ...... 440 572-9365 Strongsville *(G-17294)*	Geary Family YMCA Fostria ....E ...... 419 435-6608 Fostoria *(G-11002)*
Child Focus Learning Center ....E ...... 513 528-7224 Cincinnati *(G-3181)*	Creative Playrooms Inc ....E ...... 440 349-9111 Solon *(G-16841)*	Genesis Healthcare ....A ...... 937 875-4604 Troy *(G-18203)*
Children First Inc ....E ...... 614 466-0945 Columbus *(G-7187)*	Creme De La Creme Colorado Inc ....E ...... 513 459-4300 Mason *(G-13571)*	Genesis Healthcare System ....E ...... 740 453-4959 Zanesville *(G-20311)*
Childrens Discovery Center ....E ...... 419 861-1060 Holland *(G-11878)*	Crossroads Lake County Adole ....E ...... 440 358-7370 Painesville *(G-15706)*	Gethsemane Lutheran Church ....E ...... 614 885-4319 Columbus *(G-7666)*
Childrens Rehabilitation Ctr ....E ...... 330 856-2107 Warren *(G-18683)*	Dakota Girls LLC ....E ...... 614 801-2558 Grove City *(G-11424)*	Giggles & Wiggles Inc ....E ...... 740 574-4536 Wheelersburg *(G-19434)*
Childtime Childcare Inc ....E ...... 330 723-8697 Medina *(G-13918)*	Days of Discovery ....E ...... 937 862-4465 Spring Valley *(G-16958)*	Gingerbread Inc ....E ...... 513 793-4122 Blue Ash *(G-1569)*
Childvine Inc ....E ...... 937 748-1260 Springboro *(G-16965)*	Delth Corporation ....E ...... 440 255-7655 Mentor *(G-14041)*	Goddard School ....E ...... 513 697-9663 Loveland *(G-12997)*
Chippewa School District ....E ...... 330 658-4868 Doylestown *(G-10110)*	Diocese of Toledo ....E ...... 419 243-7255 Toledo *(G-17702)*	Goddard School ....E ...... 614 920-9810 Canal Winchester *(G-2110)*
Christian Heartland School ....C ...... 330 482-2331 Columbiana *(G-6783)*	Discovery School ....E ...... 419 756-8880 Mansfield *(G-13169)*	Goddard School ....E ...... 513 271-6311 Cincinnati *(G-3621)*
Christian Missionary Alliance ....E ...... 614 457-4085 Columbus *(G-7195)*	Dover City Schools ....D ...... 330 343-8880 Dover *(G-10073)*	Goddard School of Avon ....E ...... 440 934-3300 Avon *(G-882)*
Christian Perry Pre School ....E ...... 330 477-7262 Canton *(G-2252)*	Dublin Latchkey Inc ....D ...... 614 793-0871 Dublin *(G-10209)*	Goddard School of Twinsburg ....E ...... 330 487-0394 Twinsburg *(G-18275)*
Christian Rivertree School ....E ...... 330 494-1860 Massillon *(G-13670)*	Dublin Learning Academy ....E ...... 614 761-1800 Dublin *(G-10210)*	Golden Key Ctr For Excptnl Chl ....E ...... 330 493-4400 Canton *(G-2328)*
Christian Schools Inc ....D ...... 330 857-7311 Kidron *(G-12305)*	Early Childhood Enrichment Ctr ....E ...... 216 991-9761 Cleveland *(G-5455)*	Grace Baptist Church ....E ...... 937 652-1133 Urbana *(G-18435)*
Christian Wooster School ....E ...... 330 345-6436 Wooster *(G-19701)*	Early Childhood Learning Commu ....D ...... 614 451-6418 Columbus *(G-7488)*	Grace Brthren Ch Columbus Ohio ..,.......C ...... 614 888-7733 Westerville *(G-19168)*
Cincinnati Early Learning Ctr ....E ...... 513 961-2690 Cincinnati *(G-3241)*	Early Learning Tree Chld Ctr ....E ...... 937 276-3221 Dayton *(G-9401)*	Great Expectations D CA Center ....E ...... 330 782-9500 Youngstown *(G-20054)*
Cincinnati Early Learning Ctr ....E ...... 513 367-2129 Harrison *(G-11663)*	Early Learning Tree Chld Ctr ....E ...... 937 293-7907 Dayton *(G-9402)*	Great Miami Valley YMCA ....A ...... 513 887-0001 Hamilton *(G-11602)*
City of Lakewood ....E ...... 216 226-0080 Cleveland *(G-5206)*	East Dayton Christian School ....E ...... 937 252-5400 Dayton *(G-9172)*	Great Miami Valley YMCA ....E ...... 513 892-9622 Fairfield Township *(G-10808)*
Cleveland Child Care Inc ....E ...... 216 631-3211 Cleveland *(G-5233)*	East End Neighborhood Hse Assn ....E ...... 216 791-9378 Cleveland *(G-5456)*	Great Miami Valley YMCA ....D ...... 513 887-0014 Hamilton *(G-11604)*
Cleveland Mus Schl Settlement ....C ...... 216 421-5806 Cleveland *(G-5280)*	Edwards Creative Learning Ctr ....E ...... 614 492-8977 Columbus *(G-7506)*	Great Miami Valley YMCA ....D ...... 513 868-9622 Hamilton *(G-11605)*
Clinton County Community Actn ....E ...... 937 382-5624 Wilmington *(G-19611)*	Elderly Day Care Center ....E ...... 419 228-2688 Lima *(G-12632)*	Great Miami Valley YMCA ....D ...... 513 829-3091 Fairfield *(G-10732)*
Colerain Dry Rdge Chldcare Ltd ....E ...... 513 923-4300 Cincinnati *(G-3328)*	Enrichment Center of Wishing W ....D ...... 440 237-5000 Cleveland *(G-5483)*	Hamilton County Eductl Svc Ctr ....D ...... 513 674-4200 Cincinnati *(G-3675)*
Colonial Senior Services Inc ....C ...... 513 867-4006 Hamilton *(G-11583)*	Epworth Preschool and Daycare ....E ...... 740 387-1062 Marion *(G-13419)*	Hanna Perkins School ....E ...... 216 991-4472 Shaker Heights *(G-16709)*
Colonial Senior Services Inc ....C ...... 513 856-8600 Hamilton *(G-11582)*	Epworth United Methodist Ch ....D ...... 740 387-1062 Marion *(G-13420)*	Harcatus Tri-County Community ....D ...... 330 602-5442 New Philadelphia *(G-14962)*
Columbus Christian Center Inc ....E ...... 614 416-9673 Columbus *(G-7266)*	Erie Huron Cac Headstart Inc ....E ...... 419 663-2623 Norwalk *(G-15434)*	Hardin County Family YMCA ....E ...... 419 673-6131 Kenton *(G-12279)*
Columbus Day Care Center ....E ...... 614 269-8980 Columbus *(G-7274)*	Fairborn St Luke Untd Mthdst ....E ...... 937 878-5042 Fairborn *(G-10673)*	Health Care Plus ....C ...... 614 340-7587 Westerville *(G-19170)*
Columbus Montessori Education ....E ...... 614 231-3790 Columbus *(G-7299)*	Fairmount Montessori Assn ....E ...... 216 321-7571 Cleveland *(G-5505)*	Hewlettco Inc ....E ...... 440 238-4600 Strongsville *(G-17309)*
Columbus Public School Dst ....E ...... 614 365-5456 Columbus *(G-7306)*	Family Lrng Ctr At Sentinel ....E ...... 419 448-5079 Tiffin *(G-17517)*	Highland County Family YMCA ....E ...... 937 840-9622 Hillsboro *(G-11842)*
Community Action Comsn Belmont ....D ...... 740 676-0800 Bellaire *(G-1332)*	Family YMCA of LANcstr&fairfld ....D ...... 740 277-7373 Lancaster *(G-12403)*	Hilty Child Care Center ....E ...... 419 384-3220 Pandora *(G-15752)*
Community Action Comsn Belmont ....E ...... 740 695-0293 Saint Clairsville *(G-16483)*	Findlay Y M C A Child Dev ....E ...... 419 422-3174 Findlay *(G-10908)*	Hopes Drams Childcare Lrng Ctr ....E ...... 330 793-8260 Youngstown *(G-20068)*
Consolidated Learning Ctrs Inc ....C ...... 614 791-0050 Dublin *(G-10189)*	First Apostolic Church ....E ...... 419 885-4888 Toledo *(G-17738)*	Horizon Education Centers ....E ...... 440 322-0288 Elyria *(G-10516)*
Corporation For OH Appalachian ....E ...... 330 364-8882 New Philadelphia *(G-14953)*	First Assembly Child Care ....E ...... 419 529-6501 Mansfield *(G-13176)*	Horizon Education Centers ....E ...... 440 458-5115 Elyria *(G-10517)*
Coshocton County Head Start ....E ...... 740 622-3667 Coshocton *(G-9006)*	First Baptist Day Care Center ....E ...... 216 371-9394 Cleveland *(G-5530)*	Huber Heights YMCA ....D ...... 937 236-9622 Dayton *(G-9508)*
Council For Economic Opport ....C ...... 216 736-2934 Cleveland *(G-5357)*	First Christian Church ....E ...... 330 445-2700 Canton *(G-2313)*	Hudson Montessori Association ....E ...... 330 650-0424 Hudson *(G-11983)*
Council For Economic Opport ....D ...... 216 696-9077 Cleveland *(G-5355)*	First Community Church ....E ...... 614 488-0681 Columbus *(G-7583)*	Hyde Park Play School ....E ...... 513 631-2095 Cincinnati *(G-3746)*
Council of Ecnmc Opprtnts of G ....E ...... 216 651-5154 Cleveland *(G-5358)*	First Community Church ....E ...... 614 488-0681 Columbus *(G-7584)*	Independence Local Schools ....E ...... 216 642-5865 Independence *(G-12083)*
Council On Rur Svc Prgrams Inc ....D ...... 937 452-1090 Camden *(G-2089)*	First Fruits Child Dev Ctr I ....E ...... 216 862-4715 Euclid *(G-10635)*	Ironton and Lawrence County ....B ...... 740 532-3534 Ironton *(G-12155)*
Council On Rur Svc Prgrams Inc ....E ...... 937 492-8787 Sidney *(G-16769)*	First School Corp ....E ...... 937 433-3455 Dayton *(G-9437)*	Israel Adath ....E ...... 513 793-1800 Cincinnati *(G-3789)*
Council On Rur Svc Prgrams Inc ....E ...... 937 773-0773 Piqua *(G-16002)*	Flying Colors Public Preschool ....E ...... 740 349-1629 Newark *(G-15034)*	J Nan Enterprises LLC ....E ...... 330 653-3766 Hudson *(G-11986)*
County of Athens ....D ...... 740 592-3061 Athens *(G-774)*	For Kids Sake Inc ....E ...... 330 726-6878 Youngstown *(G-20039)*	J&B Sprafka Enterprises Inc ....E ...... 330 733-4212 Akron *(G-286)*
County of Guernsey ....E ...... 740 439-5555 Cambridge *(G-2060)*	Four Oaks Early Intervention ....E ...... 937 562-6779 Xenia *(G-19900)*	Jewish Day Schl Assoc Grtr Clv ....D ...... 216 763-1400 Pepper Pike *(G-15819)*
County of Mercer ....D ...... 419 586-2369 Celina *(G-2591)*	Frans Child Care-Mansfield ....E ...... 419 775-2500 Mansfield *(G-13178)*	Jolly Tots Too Inc ....E ...... 614 471-0688 Columbus *(G-7865)*

Joseph and Florence Mandel..............D......216 464-4055
Beachwood (G-1070)

Just 4 Kidz Childcare.....................E......440 285-2221
Chardon (G-2700)

Kandy Kane Childrens Lrng Ctr......E......330 864-6642
Akron (G-298)

Kangaroo Pouch Daycare Inc...........E......440 473-4725
Cleveland (G-5812)

Kare A Lot.................................E......614 298-8933
Columbus (G-7880)

Kare A Lot Infnt Tddlr Dev Ctr.......E......614 481-7532
Columbus (G-7881)

Kiddie Kollege Inc......................E......440 327-5435
North Ridgeville (G-15332)

Kiddle Korral............................E......419 626-9082
Sandusky (G-16621)

Kids Ahead Inc..........................E......330 628-7404
Mogadore (G-14552)

Kids Country.............................E......330 899-0909
Uniontown (G-18375)

Kids First Learning Centers..........D......440 235-2500
Olmsted Falls (G-15534)

Kids Kastle Day Care....................E......419 586-0903
Celina (G-2598)

Kids R Kids 1 Ohio Inc.................E......513 398-9944
Mason (G-13604)

Kids R Kids 2 Ohio.....................E......513 860-3197
West Chester (G-18956)

Kids R Kids Schools Qulty Lrng.....E......937 748-1260
Springboro (G-16972)

Kids World...............................E......614 473-9229
Columbus (G-7903)

Kids-Play Inc............................E......330 896-2400
Uniontown (G-18376)

Kids-Play Inc............................E......330 896-2400
Canton (G-2368)

Kidstown LLC............................E......330 502-4484
Youngstown (G-20092)

Kidz By Riverside Inc..................E......330 392-0700
Warren (G-18719)

Kinder Garden School...................E......513 791-4300
Blue Ash (G-1592)

Kinder Kare Day Nursery...............E......740 886-6905
Proctorville (G-16218)

Kindercare Education LLC..............E......513 896-4769
Fairfield Township (G-10812)

Kindercare Education LLC..............E......330 405-5556
Twinsburg (G-18289)

Kindercare Education LLC..............E......614 337-2035
Gahanna (G-11128)

Kindercare Education LLC..............E......440 442-3360
Cleveland (G-5830)

Kindercare Learning Ctrs Inc.........E......937 435-2353
Dayton (G-9545)

Kindercare Learning Ctrs Inc.........E......614 888-9696
Worthington (G-19817)

Kindercare Learning Ctrs LLC.........E......440 248-5437
Solon (G-16865)

Kindercare Learning Ctrs LLC.........E......513 771-8787
Cincinnati (G-3871)

Kindercare Learning Ctrs LLC.........E......740 549-0264
Lewis Center (G-12548)

Kindercare Learning Ctrs LLC.........E......440 442-8067
Cleveland (G-5831)

Kindercare Learning Ctrs LLC.........E......614 866-4446
Reynoldsburg (G-16314)

Kindercare Learning Ctrs LLC.........E......513 961-3164
Cincinnati (G-3872)

Kindercare Learning Ctrs LLC.........E......614 759-6622
Columbus (G-7904)

Kindercare Learning Ctrs LLC.........E......513 791-4712
Cincinnati (G-3873)

Kindertown Educational Centers......E......859 344-8802
Cleves (G-6731)

Kingdom Kids Inc.......................E......513 851-6400
Hamilton (G-11620)

Knox County Head Start Inc..........E......740 397-1344
Mount Vernon (G-14775)

Kozmic Korner..........................E......330 494-4148
Canton (G-2371)

Krieger Enterprises Inc................E......513 573-9132
Mason (G-13607)

Ladan Learning Center..................E......614 426-4306
Columbus (G-7942)

Lake County YMCA......................C......440 352-3303
Painesville (G-15718)

Lake County YMCA......................C......440 946-1160
Willoughby (G-19538)

Lake County YMCA......................E......440 259-2724
Perry (G-15824)

Lake County YMCA......................D......440 428-5125
Madison (G-13099)

Lakewood Catholic Academy..........E......216 521-4352
Lakewood (G-12351)

Lakewood Community Care Center....E......216 226-0080
Lakewood (G-12354)

Laurel School............................C......216 464-1441
Cleveland (G-5857)

Lawrence Cnty Bd Dev Dsblities......E......740 377-2356
South Point (G-16938)

Le Chaperon Rouge......................E......440 934-0296
Avon (G-892)

Le Chaperon Rouge Company.........E......440 899-9477
Westlake (G-19368)

Learning Tree Childcare Ctr............E......419 229-5484
Lima (G-12790)

Lebanon Presbyterian Church.........E......513 932-0369
Lebanon (G-12482)

Leo Yannenoff Jewish Community....C......614 231-2731
Columbus (G-7966)

Liberty Bible Academy Assn...........E......513 754-1234
Mason (G-13610)

Life Center Adult Day Care.............E......614 866-7212
Reynoldsburg (G-16316)

Lillian and Betty Ratner Schl..........E......216 464-0033
Cleveland (G-5870)

Lima Family YMCA.....................E......419 223-6045
Lima (G-12680)

Little Drmers Big Blievers LLC........E......614 824-4666
Columbus (G-7985)

Little Lambs Childrens Center.........E......614 471-9269
Gahanna (G-11132)

Logan Housing Corp Inc................D......937 592-2009
Bellefontaine (G-1356)

Lorain County Community Action....E......440 246-0480
Lorain (G-12919)

Louis Stokes Head Start................E......216 295-0854
Cleveland (G-5881)

Louisville Child Care Center...........E......330 875-4303
Uniontown (G-18377)

M J J B Ltd..............................E......937 748-4414
Springboro (G-16973)

Madison Local School District.........E......440 428-5111
Madison (G-13103)

Madison Local School District.........B......419 589-2600
Mansfield (G-13201)

Marion Head Start Center...............E......740 382-6858
Marion (G-13442)

McKinley Early Childhood Ctr.........E......330 454-4800
Canton (G-2395)

McKinley Early Childhood Ctr.........E......330 252-2552
Akron (G-327)

Medcentral Health System..............E......419 526-8043
Mansfield (G-13217)

Medina Advantage Inc..................E......330 723-8697
Medina (G-13970)

Merrick House..........................E......216 771-5077
Cleveland (G-5958)

Merry Moppets Early Learning........E......614 529-1730
Hilliard (G-11791)

Miami Valley Hospital..................E......937 224-3916
Dayton (G-9621)

Miami Valley School....................E......937 434-4444
Dayton (G-9626)

Miami Vly Child Dev Ctrs Inc.........D......937 226-5664
Dayton (G-9628)

Miami Vly Child Dev Ctrs Inc.........C......937 325-2559
Springfield (G-17083)

Miami Vly Child Dev Ctrs Inc.........E......937 228-1644
Dayton (G-9629)

Migrant Head Start.....................E......937 846-0699
New Carlisle (G-14894)

Mini University Inc.....................D......513 275-5184
Oxford (G-15685)

Mini University Inc.....................C......937 426-1414
Beavercreek (G-1231)

Ministerial Day Care-Headstart........E......216 881-6924
Cleveland (G-5998)

Miss Pats Day Care Center.............E......440 729-8255
Chesterland (G-2742)

Mk Childcare Warsaw Ave LLC.......E......513 922-6279
Cincinnati (G-4064)

Mlm Childcare LLC.....................E......513 623-8243
Cincinnati (G-4065)

Montessori Community School.........E......740 344-9411
Newark (G-15074)

Montessori High School Assn.........E......216 421-3033
Cleveland (G-6008)

Morrow County Child Care Ctr........D......419 946-5007
Mount Gilead (G-14728)

My First Days Daycare LLC............E......419 466-3354
Toledo (G-17927)

My Place Child Care....................E......740 349-3505
Newark (G-15078)

N & C Active Learning LLC...........E......937 545-1342
Beavercreek (G-1172)

Nanaeles Day Care Inc.................E......216 991-6139
Cleveland (G-6035)

National Benevolent Associatio.......D......216 476-0333
Cleveland (G-6037)

Neighborhood House....................E......614 252-4941
Columbus (G-8169)

New Bgnnngs Assembly of God Ch....E......614 497-2658
Columbus (G-8184)

New Dawn Health Care Inc............C......330 343-5521
Dover (G-10090)

New Hope Christian Academy.........E......740 477-6427
Circleville (G-4838)

New Life Christian Center..............E......740 687-1572
Lancaster (G-12422)

New School Inc..........................E......513 281-7999
Cincinnati (G-4108)

Nichalex Inc.............................E......330 726-1422
Youngstown (G-20140)

Nightingale Montessori Inc............E......937 324-0336
Springfield (G-17089)

Noahs Ark Child Dev Ctr...............E......513 988-0921
Trenton (G-18189)

Noahs Ark Creative Care...............E......740 323-3664
Newark (G-15088)

Noahs Ark Learning Center............E......740 965-1668
Sunbury (G-17392)

Nobel Learning Center..................E......740 732-4722
Caldwell (G-2042)

North Broadway Childrens Ctr........E......614 262-6222
Columbus (G-8197)

Northfield Presbt Day Care Ctr........E......330 467-4411
Northfield (G-15384)

Northside Baptst Child Dev Ctr........E......513 932-5642
Lebanon (G-12487)

Northwest Child Development An.....E......937 559-9565
Dayton (G-9660)

Northwest Local School Dst............D......513 923-1000
Cincinnati (G-4131)

Nurtury................................E......330 723-1800
Medina (G-13983)

Oak Creek United Church..............E......937 434-3941
Dayton (G-9663)

Oberlin Early Childhood Center.......E......440 774-8193
Oberlin (G-15516)

Ohio Dept of Job & Fmly Svcs.........C......614 466-1213
Columbus (G-8247)

Ohio State University...................D......614 292-4453
Columbus (G-8311)

Ohioguidestone.........................E......440 234-2006
Berea (G-1434)

Old Trail School........................D......330 666-1118
Bath (G-1018)

Open Door Christian School...........D......440 322-6386
Elyria (G-10551)

Our Lady of Bethlehem Schools.......E......614 459-8285
Columbus (G-8404)

Ourday At Messiah Preschool.........E......614 882-4416
Westerville (G-19290)

Oxford Blazer Company Inc..........E......614 792-2220
Dublin (G-10302)

P J & R J Connection Inc...............E......513 398-2777
Mason (G-13624)

Paulding Exempted Vlg Schl Dst.......C......419 594-3309
Paulding (G-15797)

Pickaway County Community Acti....E......740 474-7411
Circleville (G-4840)

Pike County Head Start Inc............D......740 289-2371
Piketon (G-15985)

Pike County YMCA......................E......740 947-8862
Waverly (G-18822)

Pilgrim United Church Christ...........E......513 574-4208
Cincinnati (G-4248)

Play Time Day Nursery Inc.............E......513 385-8281
Cincinnati (G-4254)

Playtime Preschool LLC...............E......614 975-1005
Columbus (G-8454)

Portage Private Industry...............D......330 297-7795
Ravenna (G-16259)

Powell Enterprises Inc..................E......614 882-0111
Westerville (G-19200)

Precious Angels Lrng Ctr Inc..........E......440 886-1919
Cleveland (G-6225)

Presbyterian Child Center..............E......740 852-3190
London (G-12873)

Pride -N- Joy Preschool Inc ....E 740 522-3338
Newark *(G-15093)*

Primrose School At Golf Vlg ....E 740 881-5830
Powell *(G-16205)*

Primrose School At Polaris ....E 614 899-2588
Westerville *(G-19203)*

Primrose School of Symmes ....E 513 697-6970
Cincinnati *(G-4280)*

Professional Maint of Columbus ....B 513 579-1762
Cincinnati *(G-4293)*

Promedica Health Systems Inc ....A 567 585-7454
Toledo *(G-17993)*

Pulaski Head Start ....E 419 636-8862
Bryan *(G-1972)*

R & J Investment Co Inc ....C 440 934-5204
Avon *(G-902)*

Rainbow Station Day Care Inc ....E 614 759-8667
Pickerington *(G-15967)*

Ravenna Assembly of God Inc ....E 330 297-1493
Ravenna *(G-16260)*

Ready Set Grow ....E 614 855-5100
New Albany *(G-14870)*

Robert A Kaufmann Inc ....E 216 663-1150
Maple Heights *(G-13293)*

Ross County YMCA ....D 740 772-4340
Chillicothe *(G-2823)*

Royal Redeemer Lutheran Church ....E 440 237-7958
North Royalton *(G-15365)*

Ruffing Montessori School ....E 440 333-2250
Rocky River *(G-16445)*

Saint Cecilia Church ....E 614 878-5353
Columbus *(G-8583)*

Saint James Day Care Center ....E 513 662-2287
Cincinnati *(G-4425)*

Saint Johns Villa ....C 330 627-4662
Carrollton *(G-2576)*

Salem Church of God Inc ....E 937 836-6500
Clayton *(G-4861)*

Samkel Inc ....E 614 491-3270
Columbus *(G-8589)*

Sandusky Area YMCA Foundation ....E 419 621-9622
Sandusky *(G-16637)*

Santas Hide Away Hollow Inc ....E 440 632-5000
Middlefield *(G-14276)*

Scioto County C A O Headstart ....E 740 354-3333
Portsmouth *(G-16166)*

Scribes & Scrbblr Chld Dev Ctr ....E 440 884-5437
Cleveland *(G-6382)*

Seton Catholic School Hudson ....E 330 342-4200
Hudson *(G-12005)*

Sharonville Mthdist Wkdays Nrs ....E 513 563-8278
Cincinnati *(G-4465)*

Sisters of Notre D..............................E 419 471-0170
Toledo *(G-18035)*

Sisters of Notre Dame of Chard...........E 440 279-0575
Chardon *(G-2714)*

Smoky Row Childrens Center...............E 614 766-2122
Powell *(G-16211)*

Something Special Lrng Ctr Inc ....E 419 422-1400
Findlay *(G-10960)*

Something Special Lrng Ctr Inc ....E 419 878-4190
Waterville *(G-18792)*

South- Western City School Dst ....D 614 801-8438
Grove City *(G-11472)*

Southside Learning & Dev Ctr ....E 614 444-1529
Columbus *(G-8665)*

Spanish American Committee ....E 216 961-2100
Cleveland *(G-6441)*

Springfield Family Y M C A ....D 937 323-3781
Springfield *(G-17119)*

St Francis De Sales Church ....D 740 345-9874
Newark *(G-15099)*

St Marys City Board Education ....D 419 394-2616
Saint Marys *(G-16533)*

St Patrick Church Inc..........................E 937 335-2833
Troy *(G-18229)*

St Pauls Catholic Church ....E 330 724-1263
Akron *(G-439)*

St Stephen United Church Chrst ....E 419 624-1814
Sandusky *(G-16644)*

St Stephens Community House ....D 614 294-6347
Columbus *(G-8680)*

St Thomas Episcopal Church ....E 513 831-6908
Terrace Park *(G-17500)*

Success Kidz 24-Hr Enrchmt Ctr ....E 614 419-2276
Columbus *(G-8708)*

Sunny Day Academy LLC ....E 614 718-1717
Dublin *(G-10344)*

Sycamore Board of Education...............D 513 489-3937
Cincinnati *(G-4560)*

Sylvania Community Svcs Ctr ....E 419 885-2451
Sylvania *(G-17454)*

T L C Child Development Center ....E 330 655-2797
Hudson *(G-12008)*

T M C Systems LLC ....E 440 740-1234
Broadview Heights *(G-1847)*

Tiny Tots Day Nursery ....E 330 755-6473
Struthers *(G-17368)*

Tri County Assembly of God ....E 513 874-8575
Fairfield *(G-10792)*

Troy Christian School..........................D 937 339-5692
Troy *(G-18233)*

Twinbrook Hills Baptist Church ....E 513 863-3107
Hamilton *(G-11650)*

U C Child Care Center Inc ....E 513 961-2825
Cincinnati *(G-4659)*

Ucc Childrens Center ....E 513 217-5501
Middletown *(G-14356)*

United Rehabilitation Services ....D 937 233-1230
Dayton *(G-9832)*

United States Enrichment Corp.............A 740 897-2457
Piketon *(G-15990)*

University of Akron ....E 330 972-8210
Akron *(G-480)*

Upper Arlington City Schl Dst ....E 614 487-5133
Columbus *(G-8824)*

Upper Arlington Lutheran Ch ....E 614 451-3736
Columbus *(G-8825)*

Valentour Education Inc ....E 937 434-5949
Dayton *(G-9846)*

Van Wert County Day Care Inc ....E 419 238-9918
Van Wert *(G-18492)*

Vermilion Family YMCA.......................E 440 967-4208
Vermilion *(G-18563)*

W S O S Community A ....E 419 729-8035
Toledo *(G-18142)*

W S O S Community A ....D 419 333-6068
Fremont *(G-11104)*

W S O S Community A ....E 419 334-8511
Fremont *(G-11105)*

Wee Care Daycare ....E 330 856-1313
Warren *(G-18771)*

Wee Care Learning Center ....E 937 454-9363
Dayton *(G-9873)*

Wenzler Daycare Learning Ctr ....E 937 435-8200
Dayton *(G-9873)*

Wesley Educ Cntr For Chldrn ....E 513 569-1840
Cincinnati *(G-4780)*

West Chester Chrstn Chld ....E 513 777-6300
West Chester *(G-19035)*

West Liberty Care Center Inc ....C 937 465-5065
West Liberty *(G-19122)*

West Ohio Cmnty Action Partnr ....C 419 227-2586
Lima *(G-12782)*

West Ohio Conference of ....E 937 773-5313
Piqua *(G-16038)*

West Shore Child Care Center ....E 440 333-2040
Cleveland *(G-6667)*

West Side Montessori ....D 419 866-1931
Toledo *(G-18154)*

Westerville-Worthington Learni ....E 614 891-4105
Westerville *(G-19306)*

Westlake Mntsr Schl & Chld Dv ....E 440 835-5858
Westlake *(G-19425)*

Whitehall City Schools ....E 614 417-5680
Columbus *(G-8898)*

Willoughby Montessori Day Schl ....E 440 942-5602
Willoughby *(G-19584)*

Wise Choices In Learning Ltd ....E 440 324-6056
Elyria *(G-10576)*

Wright State University ....E 937 775-4070
Dayton *(G-9192)*

Wsos Child Development Program ....E 419 334-8511
Fremont *(G-11107)*

Y M C A Central Stark County ....E 330 305-5437
Canton *(G-2539)*

Y M C A Central Stark County ....E 330 875-1611
Louisville *(G-12975)*

Y M C A Central Stark County ....E 330 877-8933
Uniontown *(G-18392)*

Y M C A Central Stark County ....E 330 830-6275
Massillon *(G-13736)*

Y M C A Central Stark County ....E 330 498-4082
Canton *(G-2540)*

Y M C A of Ashland Ohio Inc ....D 419 289-0626
Ashland *(G-700)*

YMCA ....E 330 823-1930
Alliance *(G-558)*

YMCA of Clermont County Inc ....E 513 724-9622
Batavia *(G-1016)*

YMCA of Massillon..............................E 330 879-0800
Navarre *(G-14826)*

Young Mens Christian ....B 513 932-1424
Lebanon *(G-12516)*

Young Mens Christian Assn..................D 740 373-2250
Marietta *(G-13402)*

Young Mens Christian Assn..................E 419 238-0443
Van Wert *(G-18498)*

Young Mens Christian Assoc ....E 330 724-1255
Akron *(G-508)*

Young Mens Christian Assoc ....A 330 376-1335
Akron *(G-509)*

Young Mens Christian Assoc ....D 419 523-5233
Ottawa *(G-15667)*

Young Mens Christian Assoc ....E 937 228-9622
Dayton *(G-9895)*

Young Mens Christian Assoc ....C 937 223-5201
Springboro *(G-16990)*

Young Mens Christian Assoc ....E 419 729-8135
Toledo *(G-18167)*

Young Mens Christian Assoc ....C 614 871-9622
Grove City *(G-11491)*

Young Mens Christian Assoc ....E 937 223-5201
Dayton *(G-9892)*

Young Mens Christian Assoc ....D 330 923-5223
Cuyahoga Falls *(G-9141)*

Young Mens Christian Assoc ....E 330 467-8366
Macedonia *(G-13091)*

Young Mens Christian Assoc ....E 330 784-0408
Akron *(G-507)*

Young Mens Christian Assoc ....E 614 416-9622
Gahanna *(G-11152)*

Young Mens Christian Assoc ....C 614 334-9622
Hilliard *(G-11832)*

Young Mens Christian Assoc ....E 937 312-1810
Dayton *(G-9893)*

Young Mens Christian Assoc ....E 614 539-1770
Urbancrest *(G-18453)*

Young Mens Christian Assoc ....D 614 252-3166
Columbus *(G-8929)*

Young Mens Christian Assoc ....E 937 593-9001
Bellefontaine *(G-1370)*

Young Mens Christian Associat ....E 513 731-0115
Cincinnati *(G-4813)*

Young Mens Christian Associat ....C 513 474-1400
Cincinnati *(G-4814)*

Young Mens Christian Associat ....E 513 791-5000
Blue Ash *(G-1685)*

Young Mens Christian Associat ....D 513 241-9622
Cincinnati *(G-4815)*

Young Mens Christian Associat ....D 513 923-4466
Cincinnati *(G-4816)*

Young Mens Christian Associat ....E 419 474-3995
Toledo *(G-18169)*

Young Mens Christian Associat ....D 419 866-9622
Maumee *(G-13871)*

Young Mens Christian Associat ....C 419 475-3496
Toledo *(G-18170)*

Young Mens Christian Associat ....D 419 691-3523
Oregon *(G-15615)*

Young Mens Christian Mt Vernon ....D 740 392-9622
Mount Vernon *(G-14794)*

Young MNS Chrstn Assn Clveland ....E 216 521-8400
Lakewood *(G-12364)*

Young MNS Chrstn Assn Clveland ....E 216 731-7454
Cleveland *(G-6703)*

Young MNS Chrstn Assn Clveland ....D 440 285-7543
Chardon *(G-2726)*

Young MNS Chrstn Assn Grter NY ....D 740 392-9622
Mount Vernon *(G-14795)*

Young Services Inc ....E 419 704-2009
Toledo *(G-18171)*

Young Womens Christian ....D 419 241-3235
Toledo *(G-18172)*

Young Womens Christian ....E 419 238-6639
Van Wert *(G-18499)*

Young Womens Christian Assn ....D 614 224-9121
Columbus *(G-8931)*

Young Womens Christian Associ ....E 216 881-6878
Cleveland *(G-6705)*

Young Womns Chrstn Assc Canton ....D 330 453-0789
Canton *(G-2543)*

YWCA Dayton ....D 937 461-5550
Dayton *(G-9896)*

YWCA Mahoning Valley ....E 330 746-6361
Youngstown *(G-20269)*

YWCA of Greater Cincinnati ....D 513 241-7090
Cincinnati *(G-4817)*

YWCA Shelter & Housing Network.........E 937 222-6333
Dayton *(G-9897)*

Zion Christian School E 330 792-4066
Youngstown *(G-20271)*
Znm Wecare Corporation E 740 548-2022
Delaware *(G-10018)*

8361 Residential Care

A&L Home Care & Training Ctr C 740 886-7623
Proctorville *(G-16215)*
Abbewood Limited Partnership E 440 366-8980
Elyria *(G-10476)*
Abilities First Foundation Inc D 513 423-9496
Middletown *(G-14285)*
Ability Ctr of Greater Toledo E 419 517-7123
Sylvania *(G-17411)*
Adriel School Inc D 937 465-0010
West Liberty *(G-19117)*
Advanced Geriatric Education & E 888 393-9799
Loveland *(G-12976)*
Ahf Ohio Inc D 330 725-4123
Medina *(G-13907)*
Ahf Ohio Inc D 614 760-8870
Dublin *(G-10122)*
Ahf Ohio Inc D 937 256-4663
Dayton *(G-9212)*
Akron Summit Cmnty Action Agcy C 330 572-8532
Akron *(G-56)*
Aleph Home & Senior Care Inc D 216 382-7689
Cleveland *(G-4927)*
Alexson Services Inc B 513 874-0423
Fairfield *(G-10695)*
Alternative Residences Two C 740 526-0514
Saint Clairsville *(G-16468)*
Alternative Residences Two E 330 453-0200
Canton *(G-2183)*
Alvis Inc C 614 252-1788
Columbus *(G-6907)*
Amedisys Inc E 740 373-8549
Marietta *(G-13309)*
American Nursing Care Inc C 614 847-0555
Zanesville *(G-20275)*
Anne Grady Corporation C 419 380-8985
Holland *(G-11872)*
Antwerp Mnor Asssted Lving LLC E 419 258-1500
Antwerp *(G-613)*
Archdiocese of Cincinnati E 513 231-5010
Cincinnati *(G-2981)*
Ardmore Inc C 330 535-2601
Akron *(G-79)*
Ashtabula County Residential I E 440 593-6404
Conneaut *(G-8950)*
Aspen Woodside Village D 440 439-8666
Cleveland *(G-5014)*
Assisted Living Concepts LLC E 740 450-2744
Zanesville *(G-20277)*
Assoc Dvlpmtly Disabled E 614 486-4361
Westerville *(G-19222)*
Assoc Dvlpmtly Disabled E 614 447-0606
Columbus *(G-6982)*
Atria Senior Living Inc E 513 923-3711
Cincinnati *(G-3001)*
Basinger Lfe Enhncmnt Sprt Svc D 614 557-5461
Marysville *(G-13484)*
Bastin Home Inc E 513 734-2662
Bethel *(G-1452)*
Bellefaire Jewish Chld Bur B 216 932-2800
Shaker Heights *(G-16703)*
Bellmont County E 740 695-9750
Saint Clairsville *(G-16471)*
Benjamin Rose Institute D 216 791-3580
Cleveland *(G-5056)*
Berea Lake Towers Inc E 440 243-9050
Berea *(G-1415)*
Bittersweet Inc D 419 875-6986
Whitehouse *(G-19444)*
Bradley Bay Assisted Living E 440 871-4509
Bay Village *(G-1021)*
Brighter Horizons Residential E 440 417-1751
Madison *(G-13093)*
Broadway Care Ctr Mple Hts LLC E 216 662-0551
Beachwood *(G-1037)*
Brookdale Lving Cmmunities Inc D 614 734-1000
Columbus *(G-7080)*
Brookdale Senior Living Inc D 513 229-3155
Mason *(G-13546)*
Brookdale Senior Living Inc D 614 277-1200
Grove City *(G-11413)*
Brookdale Senior Living Inc D 614 794-2499
Westerville *(G-19228)*
Brookdale Senior Living Inc D 330 723-5825
Medina *(G-13914)*
Brookdale Senior Living Inc D 937 738-7342
Marysville *(G-13485)*
Browning Mesonic Community E 419 878-4055
Waterville *(G-18788)*
Buckeye Ranch Inc D 614 384-7700
Columbus *(G-7090)*
Buckeye Ranch Inc C 614 875-2371
Grove City *(G-11416)*
Butler County Bd of Mental RE E 513 785-2815
Hamilton *(G-11567)*
Butler County Bd of Mental RE C 513 785-2870
Fairfield Township *(G-10805)*
Butler County Board of Develop E 513 867-5913
Fairfield *(G-10703)*
C I E Inc B 419 986-5566
Burgoon *(G-2011)*
Caracole Inc E 513 761-1480
Cincinnati *(G-3115)*
Cardinal Retirement Village E 330 928-7888
Cuyahoga Falls *(G-9076)*
Caritas Inc E 419 332-2589
Fremont *(G-11060)*
Carriage Court Company Inc E 740 654-4422
Lancaster *(G-12376)*
Carriage Crt Mrysvlle Ltd Prtn E 937 642-2202
Marysville *(G-13487)*
Carriage House Assisted Living E 740 264-7667
Steubenville *(G-17144)*
Champaign Residential Svcs Inc D 937 653-1320
Urbana *(G-18425)*
Cherry St Mission Ministries E 419 242-5141
Toledo *(G-17650)*
Childrens Cmprhensive Svcs Inc D 419 589-5511
Mansfield *(G-13151)*
Choices For Vctims Dom Volence D 614 258-6080
Columbus *(G-7194)*
Choices In Community Living C 937 898-3655
Dayton *(G-9298)*
Christian Chld HM Ohio Inc D 330 345-7949
Wooster *(G-19700)*
Church of God Retirement Cmnty C 513 422-5600
Middletown *(G-14295)*
Cincinnatis Optimum RES Envir C 513 771-2673
Cincinnati *(G-3280)*
City Mission D 216 431-3510
Cleveland *(G-5187)*
Clark County Board of Developm C 937 328-5200
Springfield *(G-17011)*
Clark Memorial Home Assn E 937 399-4262
Springfield *(G-17013)*
Cleveland Christian Home Inc C 216 671-0977
Cleveland *(G-5234)*
Cleveland Municipal School Dst C 216 459-9818
Cleveland *(G-5279)*
Close To Home III E 740 534-1100
Ironton *(G-12150)*
College Park Inc E 740 623-4607
Coshocton *(G-9002)*
Commons of Providence D 419 624-1171
Sandusky *(G-16590)*
Community Assisted Living Inc E 740 653-2575
Lancaster *(G-12385)*
Community Corrections Assn D 330 744-5143
Youngstown *(G-20001)*
Community Hbilitation Svcs Inc E 234 334-4288
Akron *(G-151)*
Community Hsing Netwrk Dev Co C 614 487-6700
Columbus *(G-7332)*
Community Living Experiences E 614 588-0320
Columbus *(G-7333)*
Community Support Services Inc C 330 253-9388
Akron *(G-153)*
Compdrug D 614 224-4506
Columbus *(G-7340)*
Comprehensive Addiction Svc Sy D 419 241-8827
Toledo *(G-17674)*
Concepts In Community Living E 740 393-0055
Mount Vernon *(G-14755)*
Contining Hlthcare Sltions Inc E 216 772-1105
Middleburg Heights *(G-14251)*
Cornell Companies Inc C 419 747-3322
Shelby *(G-16744)*
County of Allen C 419 221-1103
Lima *(G-12622)*
County of Auglaize D 419 629-2419
New Bremen *(G-14886)*
County of Cuyahoga C 216 241-8230
Cleveland *(G-5367)*
County of Hamilton C 513 552-1200
Cincinnati *(G-3370)*
County of Hancock E 419 422-6387
Findlay *(G-10891)*
County of Hancock D 419 424-7050
Findlay *(G-10892)*
County of Holmes E 330 279-2801
Holmesville *(G-11929)*
County of Logan C 937 592-2901
Bellefontaine *(G-1351)*
County of Lorain E 440 282-3074
Lorain *(G-12900)*
County of Lorain E 440 329-3734
Elyria *(G-10495)*
County of Lorain C 440 329-5340
Elyria *(G-10501)*
County of Medina E 330 723-9553
Medina *(G-13925)*
County of Richland D 419 774-4300
Mansfield *(G-13152)*
County of Richland C 419 774-4100
Mansfield *(G-13155)*
County of Richland D 419 774-5578
Mansfield *(G-13157)*
County of Ross E 740 773-4169
Chillicothe *(G-2772)*
County of Summit C 330 643-2943
Akron *(G-163)*
County of Wayne D 330 345-5340
Wooster *(G-19717)*
Crestview Health Care Center D 740 695-2500
Saint Clairsville *(G-16485)*
Crossroads Center C 513 475-5300
Cincinnati *(G-3382)*
Crystalwood Inc D 513 605-1000
Cincinnati *(G-3383)*
D-R Training Center & Workshop C 419 289-0470
Ashland *(G-671)*
Deaconess Long Term Care of MI A 513 487-3600
Cincinnati *(G-3412)*
Develpmntal Dsblties Ohio Dept B 419 385-0231
Toledo *(G-17699)*
Develpmntal Dsblties Ohio Dept C 330 544-2231
Columbus *(G-7440)*
Domestic Violence Project Inc E 330 445-2000
Canton *(G-2289)*
Donty Horton HM Care Dhhc LLC E 513 463-3442
Cincinnati *(G-3440)*
Drake Development Inc D 513 418-4370
Cincinnati *(G-3443)*
Eastgate Village E 513 753-4400
Cincinnati *(G-2852)*
Eastwood Residential Living E 440 417-0608
Madison *(G-13095)*
Eastwood Residential Living E 440 428-1588
Madison *(G-13096)*
ECHO Residential Support E 614 210-0944
Columbus *(G-7497)*
Echoing Hills Village Inc D 740 594-3541
Athens *(G-778)*
Echoing Hills Village Inc C 740 327-2311
Warsaw *(G-18783)*
Emeritus Corporation E 330 477-5727
Canton *(G-2299)*
Emeritus Corporation E 440 269-8600
Willoughby *(G-19520)*
Episcopal Retirement Homes Inc E 513 271-9610
Cincinnati *(G-3508)*
Episcopal Retirement Homes Inc E 513 561-6363
Cincinnati *(G-3509)*
Episcopal Retirement Homes Inc C 513 871-2090
Cincinnati *(G-3510)*
Erie Residential Living Inc E 419 625-0060
Sandusky *(G-16601)*
Evant E 330 920-1517
Stow *(G-17203)*
Extended Family Concepts Inc E 330 966-2555
Canton *(G-2307)*
Fairways D 440 943-2050
Wickliffe *(G-19458)*
Feridean Commons LLC E 614 898-7488
Westerville *(G-19165)*
Firelands Regional Health Sys E 419 448-9440
Tiffin *(G-17518)*
First Community Village B 614 324-4455
Columbus *(G-7585)*
First Mental Retardation Corp E 937 262-3077
Dayton *(G-9436)*
Five County Joint Juvenile Det E 937 642-1015
Marysville *(G-13495)*
Flat Rock Care Center C 419 483-7330
Flat Rock *(G-10978)*

Foundations Hlth Solutions Inc ...D... 440 793-0200	Kent Ridge At Golden Pond Ltd ...D... 330 677-4040	Northgate Pk Retirement Cmnty ...D... 513 923-3711
North Olmsted (G-15289)	Kent (G-12241)	Cincinnati (G-4130)
Franklin Cnty Bd Commissioners ...E... 614 462-3429	Kingston Healthcare Company ...D... 419 824-4200	Oakleaf Toledo Ltd Partnership ...E... 419 885-3934
Columbus (G-7608)	Sylvania (G-17435)	Toledo (G-17956)
Franklin County Residential S ...B... 614 844-5847	Kingston Healthcare Company ...D... 740 389-2311	Oakleaf Village Ltd ...D... 614 431-1739
Worthington (G-19811)	Marion (G-13427)	Columbus (G-8222)
Friars Club Inc ...D... 513 488-8777	Kingston Rsdnce Perrysburg LLC ...D... 419 872-6200	Oasis Thrptic Fster Care Ntwrk ...E... 740 698-0340
Cincinnati (G-3594)	Perrysburg (G-15887)	Albany (G-511)
Friedman Vlg Retirement Cmnty ...E... 419 443-1540	Ladd Inc ...E... 513 861-4089	Oesterlen-Services For Youth ...C... 937 399-6101
Tiffin (G-17519)	Cincinnati (G-3906)	Springfield (G-17091)
Friends of Good Shepherd Manor ...D... 740 289-2861	Lakeside Manor Inc ...E... 330 549-2545	Ohio Department of Aging ...E... 614 466-5500
Lucasville (G-13049)	North Lima (G-15271)	Columbus (G-8236)
Friendship Vlg of Clumbus Ohio ...C... 614 890-8282	Larchwood Health Group LLC ...E... 216 941-6100	Ohio Department of Health ...B... 419 447-1450
Columbus (G-7629)	Cleveland (G-5855)	Tiffin (G-17528)
Furney Group Home ...E... 419 389-0152	Laurel Lk Retirement Cmnty Inc ...B... 330 650-0681	Ohio Living ...C... 513 681-4230
Toledo (G-17750)	Hudson (G-11993)	Cincinnati (G-4156)
G & D Alternative Living Inc ...E... 937 446-2803	Life Enriching Communities ...E... 513 719-3510	Ohio Living ...B... 440 942-4342
Sardinia (G-16659)	Loveland (G-13006)	Willoughby (G-19558)
Garden Manor Extended Care Cen ...C... 513 420-5972	Lighthouse Youth Services Inc ...E... 740 634-3094	Ohio Living ...E... 614 888-7800
Middletown (G-14300)	Bainbridge (G-931)	Columbus (G-8272)
Gardens Western Reserve Inc ...D... 330 928-4500	Lindley Inn ...E... 740 797-9701	Ohio Presbt Retirement Svcs ...C... 513 539-7391
Cuyahoga Falls (G-9098)	The Plains (G-17503)	Monroe (G-14579)
Gateways To Better Living Inc ...E... 330 480-9870	Lutheran Home ...D... 419 724-1414	Ohioguidestone ...E... 440 234-2006
Youngstown (G-20043)	Toledo (G-17870)	Berea (G-1434)
Gateways To Better Living Inc ...E... 330 270-0952	Lutheran Homes Society Inc ...E... 419 724-1525	One Way Farm of Fairfield Inc ...E... 513 829-3276
Youngstown (G-20044)	Toledo (G-17871)	Fairfield (G-10765)
Gateways To Better Living Inc ...E... 330 797-1764	Lutheran Village At Wolf Creek ...C... 419 861-2233	Opportunity Homes Inc ...E... 330 424-1411
Canfield (G-2138)	Holland (G-11893)	Lisbon (G-12805)
Gateways To Better Living Inc ...E... 330 792-2854	Madison House Inc ...E... 740 845-0145	Orrvilla Retirement Community ...E... 330 683-4455
Youngstown (G-20045)	London (G-12869)	Orrville (G-15638)
Gentlebrook Inc ...C... 330 877-3694	Manfield Living Center Ltd ...E... 419 512-1711	Otterbein Homes ...D... 513 933-5439
Hartville (G-11686)	Mansfield (G-13203)	Lebanon (G-12490)
Gerspacher Companies ...E... 330 725-1596	Maple Knoll Communities Inc ...E... 513 524-7990	Otterbein Snior Lfstyle Chices ...C... 513 260-7690
Medina (G-13943)	Oxford (G-15679)	Middletown (G-14352)
Glen Wesley Inc ...E... 614 888-7492	Mason Health Care Center ...D... 513 398-2881	Otterbein Snior Lfstyle Chices ...B... 513 933-5400
Columbus (G-7673)	Mason (G-13616)	Lebanon (G-12492)
Glenwood Community Inc ...E... 740 376-9555	McElvain Group Home ...E... 419 589-6697	Otterbein Snior Lfstyle Chices ...E... 419 943-4376
Marietta (G-13330)	Mansfield (G-13212)	Leipsic (G-12520)
Grace Hospice LLC ...C... 440 826-0350	Medina Cnty Jvnile Dtntion Ctr ...E... 330 764-8408	Otterbein Snior Lfstyle Chices ...C... 419 645-5114
Cleveland (G-5619)	Medina (G-13971)	Cridersville (G-9063)
Greenbrier Senior Living Cmnty ...D... 440 888-0400	Mended Reeds Home ...E... 740 533-1883	Otterbein Snior Lfstyle Chices ...E... 419 394-2366
Cleveland (G-5642)	Ironton (G-12163)	Saint Marys (G-16530)
Harbor ...D... 419 241-6191	Miami Vly Hsing Oprtunties Inc ...E... 937 263-4449	Paisley House For Aged Women ...E... 330 799-9431
Toledo (G-17780)	Dayton (G-9630)	Youngstown (G-20150)
Harmony Home Care Inc ...E... 440 877-1977	Mid-Western Childrens Home ...E... 513 877-2141	Parkcliffe Development ...D... 419 381-9447
North Royalton (G-15359)	Pleasant Plain (G-16074)	Toledo (G-17971)
Harrison Co County Home ...E... 740 942-3573	Midwest Health Services Inc ...C... 330 828-0779	Pathway Caring For Children ...D... 330 493-0083
Cadiz (G-2028)	Massillon (G-13716)	Canton (G-2435)
Hattie Larlham Center For ...C... 330 274-2272	Mount Aloysius Corp ...C... 740 342-3343	Paul Dennis ...E... 440 746-8600
Mantua (G-13267)	New Lexington (G-14921)	Brecksville (G-1795)
Hattie Larlham Center For ...D... 330 274-2272	Mulberry Garden A L S ...E... 330 630-3980	Phoenix Residential Ctrs Inc ...E... 440 428-9082
Mantua (G-13268)	Munroe Falls (G-14798)	Madison (G-13107)
Havar Inc ...D... 740 594-3533	Multi County Juvenile Det Ctr ...E... 740 652-1525	Pine Ridge Pine Vllg Resdntl H ...E... 513 724-3460
Athens (G-782)	Lancaster (G-12420)	Williamsburg (G-19495)
Hcf Management Inc ...C... 419 999-2055	Multi-Cnty Jvnile Attntion Sys ...D... 330 484-6471	Portage County Board ...E... 330 297-6209
Lima (G-12653)	Canton (G-2412)	Ravenna (G-16256)
Health Recovery Services Inc ...C... 740 592-6720	Muskingum Residentials Inc ...E... 740 453-5350	Premier Estates 525 LLC ...D... 513 631-6800
Athens (G-783)	Zanesville (G-20340)	Cincinnati (G-4272)
Heinzerling Foundation ...A... 614 272-2000	National Benevolent Associatio ...D... 216 476-0333	Premier Estates 526 LLC ...D... 513 922-1440
Columbus (G-7736)	Cleveland (G-6037)	Cincinnati (G-4273)
Helen Purcell Home ...E... 740 453-1745	National Mentor Inc ...E... 216 525-1885	Pristine Senior Living ...D... 513 471-8667
Zanesville (G-20317)	Cleveland (G-6048)	Cincinnati (G-4284)
Help Foundation Inc ...E... 216 486-5258	Necco Center ...D... 740 534-1386	Pristine Snior Lving Englewood ...C... 937 836-5143
Cleveland (G-5683)	Pedro (G-15800)	Englewood (G-10599)
Hill Manor 1 Inc ...E... 740 972-3227	Network Housing 2005 Inc ...D... 614 487-6700	Providence House Inc ...E... 216 651-5982
Columbus (G-7750)	Columbus (G-8178)	Cleveland (G-6263)
Hill Manor Enterprises ...E... 614 567-7134	New Avenues To Independence ...D... 216 481-1907	R T Industries Inc ...E... 937 335-5784
Groveport (G-11517)	Cleveland (G-6060)	Troy (G-18224)
Hitchcock Center For Women Inc ...E... 216 421-0662	New Avenues To Independence ...E... 216 671-8224	Rchp - Wilmington LLC ...D... 937 382-6611
Cleveland (G-5695)	Cleveland (G-6061)	Wilmington (G-19643)
Hocking Vly Cmnty Rsdntial Ctr ...E... 740 753-4400	New Avenues To Independence ...E... 888 853-8905	Rehablttion Ctr At Mrietta Mem ...D... 740 374-1407
Nelsonville (G-14833)	Ashtabula (G-748)	Marietta (G-13375)
Hopewell ...E... 440 693-4074	New Dawn Health Care Inc ...C... 330 343-5521	REM-Ohio Inc ...E... 937 335-8267
Mesopotamia (G-14130)	Dover (G-10090)	Troy (G-18226)
Horizons Tuscarawas/Carroll ...E... 330 262-4183	New Directions Inc ...D... 216 591-0324	REM-Ohio Inc ...D... 330 644-9730
Wooster (G-19729)	Cleveland (G-6062)	Coventry Township (G-9041)
House of New Hope ...E... 740 345-5437	New England Rms Inc ...E... 401 384-6759	REM-Ohio Inc ...D... 614 367-1370
Saint Louisville (G-16518)	Worthington (G-19830)	Reynoldsburg (G-16325)
Inn At Christine Valley ...E... 330 270-3347	New Nghbors Rsdential Svcs Inc ...E... 937 717-5731	Renaissance House Inc ...E... 419 663-1316
Youngstown (G-20082)	Springfield (G-17088)	Norwalk (G-15454)
Interval Brotherhood Homes ...D... 330 644-4095	Newark Resident Homes Inc ...D... 740 345-7231	RES-Care Inc ...E... 740 526-0285
Coventry Township (G-9036)	Newark (G-15086)	Saint Clairsville (G-16504)
J & R Associates ...A... 440 250-4080	Nickolas Rsidential Trtmnt Ctr ...E... 937 496-7100	Rescare Ohio Inc ...E... 330 479-9841
Brookpark (G-1898)	Dayton (G-9658)	Canton (G-2458)
Jo Lin Health Center Inc ...C... 740 532-0860	North Cntl Mntal Hlth Svcs Inc ...D... 614 227-6865	Rescare Ohio Inc ...E... 513 724-1177
Ironton (G-12160)	Columbus (G-8198)	Williamsburg (G-19496)
Josina Lott Foundation ...E... 419 866-9013	North Hills Management Company ...D... 740 450-9999	Rescare Ohio Inc ...D... 513 829-8992
Toledo (G-17833)	Zanesville (G-20346)	Hamilton (G-11637)
Judson ...D... 216 791-2555	North Shore Retirement Cmnty ...D... 419 798-8203	Rescue Incorporated ...C... 419 255-9585
Cleveland (G-5809)	Lakeside (G-12330)	Toledo (G-18004)

S
I
C

Residential Hm Assn of Marion ....C...... 740 387-9999
  Marion (G-13455)
Residential Home For The Devlp ....C...... 740 622-9778
  Coshocton (G-9025)
Residential Home For The Devlp ....E...... 740 452-5133
  Zanesville (G-20358)
Residential Inc ....E...... 740 342-4158
  New Lexington (G-14927)
Residential Management Systems ....E...... 419 222-8806
  Lima (G-12730)
Residential Management Systems ....E...... 614 880-6014
  Worthington (G-19843)
Residential Management Systems ....D...... 419 255-6060
  Maumee (G-13843)
Rhc Inc ....C...... 513 389-7501
  Cincinnati (G-4367)
Roman Cthlic Docese Youngstown ....C...... 330 875-5562
  Louisville (G-12973)
Rose Mary Johanna Grassell ....C...... 216 481-4823
  Cleveland (G-6340)
Saint Johns Villa ....C...... 330 627-4662
  Carrollton (G-2576)
Saint Joseph Orphanage ....D...... 513 231-5010
  Cincinnati (G-4426)
Saint Joseph Orphanage ....D...... 513 741-3100
  Cincinnati (G-4427)
Sattlerpearson Inc ....E...... 419 698-3822
  Northwood (G-15406)
Scioto Residential Services ....E...... 740 353-0288
  Portsmouth (G-16168)
Second Mental Retardation ....E...... 937 262-3077
  Dayton (G-9756)
Second Phase Inc ....E...... 330 797-9930
  Youngstown (G-20206)
Select Spclty Hsptal-Akron LLC ....D...... 330 761-7500
  Akron (G-423)
SEM Villa Inc ....E...... 513 831-3262
  Loveland (G-13026)
Senior Care Inc ....E...... 937 372-1530
  Xenia (G-19925)
Senior Care Inc ....E...... 937 291-3211
  Miamisburg (G-14217)
Senior Care Inc ....C...... 419 516-4788
  Lima (G-12738)
Senior Lifestyle Corporation ....D...... 513 777-4457
  West Chester (G-19002)
Senior Lifestyle Evergreen Ltd ....C...... 513 948-2308
  Cincinnati (G-4452)
Shalom House Inc ....E...... 614 239-1999
  Columbus (G-8629)
Shurmer Place At Altenheim ....E...... 440 238-9001
  Strongsville (G-17346)
Sisters of Little ....C...... 513 281-8001
  Cincinnati (G-4486)
Sisters of Mercy ....C...... 419 332-8208
  Fremont (G-11096)
Society For Handicapped Citzns ....E...... 937 746-4201
  Carlisle (G-2554)
Society Handicapped Citz Medin ....E...... 330 722-1900
  Seville (G-16689)
Sociey For Handicapped Citizen ....C...... 330 725-7041
  Seville (G-16690)
Southast Cmnty Mental Hlth Ctr ....C...... 614 225-0980
  Columbus (G-8661)
St Edward Home ....C...... 330 668-2828
  Fairlawn (G-10851)
St Luke Lutheran Community ....E...... 330 868-5600
  Minerva (G-14525)
St Vincent Family Centers ....C...... 614 252-0731
  Columbus (G-8681)
Stone Gardens ....D...... 216 292-0070
  Cleveland (G-6469)
Stonewood Residential Inc ....E...... 216 267-9777
  Cleveland (G-6470)
◆ Style Crest Inc ....B...... 419 332-7369
  Fremont (G-11099)
Summerville Senior Living Inc ....D...... 440 354-5499
  Mentor (G-14113)
Sunrise Senior Living Inc ....E...... 614 846-6500
  Worthington (G-19854)
Sunrise Senior Living Inc ....E...... 614 418-9775
  Gahanna (G-11149)
Sunrise Senior Living Inc ....D...... 440 895-2383
  Rocky River (G-16446)
Sunrise Senior Living LLC ....E...... 614 718-2062
  Dublin (G-10345)
Sunrise Senior Living LLC ....E...... 330 262-1615
  Wooster (G-19771)
Sunrise Senior Living LLC ....E...... 419 425-3440
  Findlay (G-10966)

Sunrise Senior Living LLC ....E...... 216 447-8909
  Cleveland (G-6480)
Sunset House Inc ....C...... 419 536-4645
  Toledo (G-18055)
Sunset Rtrment Communities Inc ....D...... 419 724-1200
  Ottawa Hills (G-15669)
Sunshine Communities ....B...... 419 865-0251
  Maumee (G-13857)
T/R Rsdntial Care Fclities Inc ....C...... 740 754-2600
  Dresden (G-10116)
Terre Forme Enterprises Inc ....E...... 330 847-6800
  Mineral Ridge (G-14513)
Threshold Residential Svcs Inc ....C...... 330 426-4553
  East Palestine (G-10422)
Toledo Hospital ....C...... 419 291-2273
  Sylvania (G-17459)
Toward Independence Inc ....C...... 937 376-3996
  Xenia (G-19929)
Traditions At Bath Rd Inc ....C...... 330 929-6272
  Cuyahoga Falls (G-9132)
Tri County Mental Health Svcs ....C...... 740 592-3091
  Athens (G-806)
Trilogy Health Services LLC ....D...... 419 935-6511
  Willard (G-19489)
Twelve Inc ....E...... 330 837-3555
  Massillon (G-13733)
United Cerebral Palsy ....E...... 216 791-8363
  Cleveland (G-6568)
United Cerebral Palsy ....D...... 216 381-9993
  Cleveland (G-6569)
United Cerebral Palsy Gr Cinc ....E...... 513 221-4606
  Cincinnati (G-4676)
United Church Homes Inc ....D...... 740 376-5600
  Marietta (G-13392)
United Church Homes Inc ....C...... 513 922-1440
  Cincinnati (G-4677)
United Church Homes Inc ....C...... 937 426-8481
  Beavercreek (G-1239)
United Methodist Childrens ....C...... 614 885-5020
  Columbus (G-8804)
Ursuline Convent Sacred Heart ....E...... 419 531-8990
  Toledo (G-18131)
Uvmc Nursing Care Inc ....C...... 937 667-7500
  Tipp City (G-17572)
Village Network ....C...... 330 264-0650
  Wooster (G-19776)
Volunteers America Ohio & Ind ....C...... 614 253-6100
  Columbus (G-8859)
Wallick Construction Co ....E...... 937 399-7009
  Springfield (G-17132)
Washington Manor Inc ....E...... 937 433-3441
  Dayton (G-9867)
Wesleyan Senior Living ....C...... 440 284-9000
  Elyria (G-10572)
Wesleyan Village ....B...... 440 284-9000
  Elyria (G-10573)
West View Manor Inc ....C...... 330 264-8640
  Wooster (G-19782)
Whitehouse Operator LLC ....D...... 419 877-5338
  Whitehouse (G-19452)
Widows Home of Dayton Ohio ....D...... 937 252-1661
  Dayton (G-9880)
Wiley Homes Inc ....D...... 419 535-3988
  Toledo (G-18157)
Womens Recovery Center ....E...... 937 562-2400
  Xenia (G-19934)
Womens Welsh Clubs of America ....D...... 440 331-0420
  Rocky River (G-16449)
Wood County Chld Svcs Assn ....D...... 419 352-7588
  Bowling Green (G-1752)
Wynn-Reeth Inc ....E...... 419 639-2094
  Green Springs (G-11357)
Zandex Inc ....E...... 740 452-2087
  Zanesville (G-20374)
Zandex Health Care Corporation ....C...... 740 454-1400
  New Concord (G-14906)

8399 Social Services, NEC

Abcd Inc ....E...... 330 455-6385
  Canton (G-2171)
Adams & Brown Counties Economi ....E...... 937 695-0316
  Winchester (G-19659)
Adams & Brown Counties Economi ....C...... 937 378-6041
  Georgetown (G-11260)
Adams Cnty Snior Ctzens Cuncil ....E...... 937 544-7459
  West Union (G-19130)
Air Frce Museum Foundation Inc ....E...... 937 258-1218
  Dayton (G-9158)
Akron Cmnty Svc Ctr Urban Leag ....E...... 234 542-4141
  Akron (G-33)

Akron Summit Cmnty Action Agcy ....C...... 330 572-8532
  Akron (G-56)
Akron Summit Cmnty Action Agcy ....D...... 330 733-2290
  Akron (G-57)
Akron Summit Cmnty Action Agcy ....B...... 330 376-7730
  Akron (G-58)
ARC Industries Incorporated O ....E...... 614 836-6050
  Groveport (G-11495)
Ashtabula County Commnty Actn ....C...... 440 997-1721
  Ashtabula (G-711)
Ashtabula County Commnty Actn ....D...... 440 593-6441
  Conneaut (G-8949)
Ashtabula County Commnty Actn ....D...... 440 576-6911
  Jefferson (G-12189)
Ashtabula County Commnty Actn ....D...... 440 993-7716
  Ashtabula (G-712)
Ashtabula County Commnty Actn ....D...... 440 997-5957
  Ashtabula (G-713)
Barberton Jaycees ....E...... 330 745-3733
  Barberton (G-946)
Catholic Charities Corporation ....E...... 216 939-3713
  Cleveland (G-5132)
Catholic Charities Corporation ....E...... 216 268-4006
  Cleveland (G-5133)
Catholic Charities Corporation ....E...... 419 289-1903
  Ashland (G-663)
Catholic Charities Corporation ....E...... 216 334-2900
  Cleveland (G-5134)
Center For Community Solutions ....E...... 216 781-2944
  Cleveland (G-5148)
Childrens Hospital Foundation ....E...... 614 355-0888
  Columbus (G-7189)
Childrens Hunger Alliance ....E...... 614 341-7700
  Columbus (G-7190)
Choices For Vctims Dom Violence ....E...... 614 224-6617
  Worthington (G-19798)
Cincinnati Institute Fine Arts ....E...... 513 871-2787
  Cincinnati (G-3251)
City of Columbus ....D...... 614 645-3072
  Columbus (G-7208)
City of Columbus ....D...... 614 645-7417
  Columbus (G-7209)
City of Portsmouth ....E...... 740 353-5153
  Portsmouth (G-16128)
City of Warrensville Heights ....E...... 216 587-1230
  Cleveland (G-5217)
Cleveland Jewish Federation ....C...... 216 593-2900
  Cleveland (G-5263)
Cleveland Municipal School Dst ....B...... 216 838-0000
  Cleveland (G-5276)
Cleveland Municipal School Dst ....E...... 216 838-8700
  Cleveland (G-5277)
Clinton County Community Actn ....D...... 937 382-8365
  Wilmington (G-19610)
Clinton County Community Actn ....E...... 937 382-5624
  Wilmington (G-19611)
Colonial Senior Services Inc ....C...... 513 856-8600
  Hamilton (G-11582)
Columbus Jewish Federation ....E...... 614 237-7686
  Columbus (G-7290)
Columbus Landmarks Foundation ....E...... 614 221-0227
  Columbus (G-7291)
Columbus Surgical Center LLP ....E...... 614 932-9503
  Dublin (G-10182)
Columbus Urban League Inc ....E...... 614 257-6300
  Columbus (G-7320)
Community Action Columbiana CT ....D...... 330 424-7221
  Lisbon (G-12796)
Community Action Commission ....E...... 419 626-6540
  Sandusky (G-16591)
Community Action Program Corp ....B...... 740 373-3745
  Marietta (G-13319)
Community Action Program Corp ....E...... 740 373-6016
  Marietta (G-13320)
Community Action Program Inc ....D...... 937 382-0225
  Wilmington (G-19616)
Community Imprv Corp Nble Cnty ....D...... 740 509-0248
  Caldwell (G-2037)
Community Re-Entry Inc ....E...... 216 696-2717
  Cleveland (G-5327)
Concord ....E...... 614 882-9338
  Westerville (G-19245)
Council For Economic Opport ....D...... 216 541-7878
  Cleveland (G-5353)
Council For Economic Opport ....D...... 216 696-9077
  Cleveland (G-5355)
Council For Economic Opport ....E...... 216 692-4010
  Cleveland (G-5356)
Council On Aging of Southweste ....C...... 513 721-1025
  Cincinnati (G-3368)

Council On Rur Svc Prgrams Inc ....E 937 492-8787
Sidney *(G-16769)*

Council On Rur Svc Prgrams Inc ....E 937 778-5220
Piqua *(G-16001)*

Council On Rur Svc Prgrams Inc ....E 937 773-0773
Piqua *(G-16002)*

County of Medina ....D 330 995-5243
Medina *(G-13926)*

County of Montgomery ....D 937 225-4192
Dayton *(G-9325)*

Daybreak Inc ....E 937 395-4600
Dayton *(G-9349)*

Economic & Cmnty Dev Inst Inc ....E 614 559-0104
Columbus *(G-7500)*

Epilepsy Cncl/Grter Cincinnati ....E 513 721-2905
Cincinnati *(G-3505)*

Epilepsy Cntr of Nrthwstrn OH ....D 419 867-5950
Maumee *(G-13786)*

Fairfield Cnty Job & Fmly Svcs ....D 800 450-8845
Lancaster *(G-12391)*

Fairfield County ....D 740 653-4060
Lancaster *(G-12393)*

Famicos Foundation ....E 216 791-6476
Cleveland *(G-5509)*

Far West Center ....E 440 835-6212
Westlake *(G-19342)*

Fidelity Charitable Gift Fund ....C 800 952-4438
Cincinnati *(G-3544)*

Fort Hamilton Hosp Foundation ....B 513 867-5492
Hamilton *(G-11596)*

Gc Neighborhood Ctrs Assoc Inc ....C 216 298-4440
Cleveland *(G-5597)*

GE Reuter Stokes ....D 216 749-6332
Cleveland *(G-5600)*

Greater Cleveland Food Bnk Inc ....C 216 738-2265
Cleveland *(G-5635)*

Greene Cnty Chld Svc Brd Frbrn ....D 937 878-1415
Xenia *(G-19901)*

Greene County Career Center ....E 937 372-6941
Xenia *(G-19906)*

Guernsey County Cmnty Dev Corp .....C 740 439-0020
Cambridge *(G-2071)*

Habitat For Humanity ....E 216 429-1299
Cleveland *(G-5654)*

Hancock Hardin Wyandot Putnam ....C 419 423-3755
Findlay *(G-10918)*

Health Partners Western Ohio ....D 419 221-3072
Lima *(G-12656)*

Hockingthensperry Cmnty Action ....C 740 767-4500
Glouster *(G-11310)*

Integrated Services of Appala ....D 740 594-6807
Athens *(G-786)*

Interact For Health ....E 513 458-6600
Cincinnati *(G-3774)*

Jackson-Vinton Cmnty Action ....E 740 384-3722
Wellston *(G-18852)*

Jefferson Cnty Cmmnty Action ....C 740 282-0971
Steubenville *(G-17159)*

Jewish Edcatn Ctr of Cleveland ....D 216 371-0446
Cleveland Heights *(G-6720)*

Karamu House Inc ....E 216 795-7070
Cleveland *(G-5815)*

Leads Inc ....E 740 349-8606
Newark *(G-15049)*

Licking County Aging Program ....D 740 345-0821
Newark *(G-15052)*

Lifeline Systems Company ....E 330 762-5627
Akron *(G-314)*

Lifeservices Development Corp ....E 440 257-3866
Mentor *(G-14077)*

Lincare Inc ....E 330 928-0884
Akron *(G-315)*

Lorain County Community Action ....E 440 245-2009
Lorain *(G-12918)*

Lutheran Metropolitan Ministry ....C 216 658-4638
Cleveland *(G-5890)*

Mahoning Youngstown Community ......D 330 747-7921
Youngstown *(G-20112)*

Med Assist Prgram of Info Line ....E 330 762-0609
Akron *(G-328)*

Medill Elemntary Sch of Volntr ....E 740 687-7352
Lancaster *(G-12417)*

Miami Cnty Cmnty Action Cuncil ....E 937 335-7921
Troy *(G-18212)*

Miami Valley Community Action ....D 937 222-1009
Dayton *(G-9617)*

Miami Vly Fandom For Literacy ....E 513 933-0452
Lebanon *(G-12486)*

Montpelier Senior Center ....E 419 485-3218
Montpelier *(G-14616)*

National Affrdbl Hsing Tr Inc ....E 614 451-9929
Columbus *(G-8128)*

National Multiple Sclerosis ....E 330 759-9066
Youngstown *(G-20139)*

National Youth Advocate Progra ....E 614 487-8758
Columbus *(G-8139)*

Nationwide Childrens Hospital ....B 614 722-8200
Columbus *(G-8147)*

Nationwide Childrens Hospital ....C 614 722-2700
Columbus *(G-8143)*

Neighborhood Development Svcs ....E 330 296-2003
Ravenna *(G-16250)*

Neighborhood Health Care Inc ....E 513 221-4949
Cincinnati *(G-4104)*

Neighborhood Hsg Servs Toledo ....E 419 691-2900
Toledo *(G-17936)*

Neighborhood Progress Inc ....E 216 830-2770
Cleveland *(G-6054)*

Northwestrn OH Communty Action ......C 419 784-2150
Defiance *(G-9932)*

Occupational Health Link ....E 614 885-0039
Columbus *(G-8224)*

Ohio Citizen Action ....E 216 861-5200
Cleveland *(G-6119)*

Ohio Hrtland Cmnty Action Comm ....E 740 387-1039
Marion *(G-13450)*

Ohio Hrtland Cmnty Action Comm ....E 419 468-5121
Galion *(G-11180)*

Ohio Legal Rights Service ....E 614 466-7264
Columbus *(G-8270)*

Orphan Foundation of America ....E 571 203-0270
Beachwood *(G-1094)*

Pavilion At Piketon For Nursin ....D 740 289-2394
Piketon *(G-15984)*

Phyllis Wheatley Assn Dev ....E 216 391-4443
Cleveland *(G-6208)*

Pike Cnty Adult Activities Ctr ....E 740 947-7503
Waverly *(G-18820)*

Pilot Dogs Incorporated ....E 614 221-6367
Columbus *(G-8447)*

Playhouse Square Holdg Co LLC ....C 216 771-4444
Cleveland *(G-6219)*

Prescription Hope Inc ....E 877 296-4673
Westerville *(G-19294)*

Prevent Blindness - Ohio ....E 614 464-2020
Columbus *(G-8460)*

Provider Services Inc ....D 614 888-2021
Columbus *(G-8476)*

Randall R Leab ....E 330 689-6263
Ashland *(G-685)*

REM-Ohio Inc ....E 440 986-3337
South Amherst *(G-16922)*

Ross County Community ....D 740 702-7222
Chillicothe *(G-2819)*

Salvation Army ....D 513 762-5600
Cincinnati *(G-4430)*

Salvation Army ....E 614 252-7171
Columbus *(G-8587)*

Salvation Army ....D 800 728-7825
Columbus *(G-8588)*

Senior Independence ....D 330 873-3468
Fairlawn *(G-10850)*

Shafer Confession ....E 419 399-4662
Paulding *(G-15799)*

Sharon Twnship Frfighters Assn ....E 330 239-4992
Sharon Center *(G-16725)*

Solidarity Health Network Inc ....E 216 831-1220
Cleveland *(G-6420)*

St Jude Social Concern Hot ....D 440 365-7971
Elyria *(G-10566)*

Stark County Cmnty Action Agcy ....C 330 454-1676
Canton *(G-2491)*

Stark County Cmnty Action Agcy ....E 330 821-5977
Alliance *(G-553)*

T and J Trnstnal HM For Dsbled ....E 216 703-4673
Cleveland *(G-6493)*

Tipp-Monroe Community Svcs Inc ....E 937 667-8631
Tipp City *(G-17569)*

Tri-County Community Act ....E 740 385-6812
Logan *(G-12857)*

United Labor Agency Inc ....C 216 664-3446
Cleveland *(G-6574)*

United Methodist Community Ctr ....E 330 743-5149
Canfield *(G-2162)*

United Rehabilitation Services ....D 937 233-1230
Dayton *(G-9832)*

United Way Central Ohio Inc ....D 614 227-2700
Columbus *(G-8814)*

United Way Greater Cleveland ....C 216 436-2100
Cleveland *(G-6580)*

United Way Greater Stark Cnty ....E 330 491-0445
Canton *(G-2523)*

United Way of Summit County ....E 330 762-7601
Akron *(G-477)*

United Way of The Greater Dayt ....C 937 225-3060
Dayton *(G-9834)*

University of Tledo Foundation ....E 419 530-7730
Toledo *(G-18124)*

University Settlement Inc ....E 216 641-8948
Cleveland *(G-6603)*

Urban League of Greater Southw ....D 513 281-9955
Cincinnati *(G-4733)*

W T C S A Headstart Niles Ctr ....E 330 652-0338
Niles *(G-15173)*

Warren County Community Svcs ....C 513 695-2100
Lebanon *(G-12515)*

West Ohio Cmnty Action Partnr ....C 419 227-2586
Lima *(G-12782)*

Westcare Ohio Inc ....E 937 259-1898
Dayton *(G-9876)*

Wood County Ohio ....E 419 353-6914
Bowling Green *(G-1757)*

84 MUSEUMS, ART GALLERIES, AND BOTANICAL AND ZOOLOGICAL GARDENS

8412 Museums & Art Galleries

Akron Art Museum ....D 330 376-9185
Akron *(G-27)*

Akron Childrens Museum ....E 330 396-6103
Akron *(G-31)*

Anderson Twnship Hstorical Soc ....E 513 231-2114
Cincinnati *(G-2964)*

Ark Foundation of Dayton ....E 937 256-2759
Dayton *(G-9240)*

Arts and Exhibitions Intl LLC ....D 330 995-9300
Streetsboro *(G-17246)*

Belpre Historical Society ....E 740 423-7588
Belpre *(G-1399)*

Butler Institute American Art ....E 330 743-1711
Youngstown *(G-19979)*

Chagrin Falls Historical Soc ....E 440 247-4695
Chagrin Falls *(G-2640)*

Cincinnati Institute Fine Arts ....E 513 241-0343
Cincinnati *(G-3252)*

▲ Cincinnati Museum Association ....C 513 721-5204
Cincinnati *(G-3257)*

Cincinnati Museum Center ....B 513 287-7000
Cincinnati *(G-3258)*

Cincinnati Nature Center ....E 513 831-1711
Milford *(G-14378)*

Cleveland Hungarian Heritg Soc ....E 216 523-3900
Cleveland *(G-5261)*

▲ Clevelnd Museum of Natural His ....D 216 231-4600
Cleveland *(G-5301)*

▲ Columbus Museum of Art ....D 614 221-6801
Columbus *(G-7301)*

Contemporary Arts Center ....E 513 721-0390
Cincinnati *(G-3352)*

▲ Dayton Art Institute ....D 937 223-5277
Dayton *(G-9354)*

Dayton History ....C 937 293-2841
Dayton *(G-9368)*

Dayton Intl Peace Museum ....E 937 227-3223
Dayton *(G-9370)*

▲ Dayton Society Natural History ....D 937 275-7431
Dayton *(G-9381)*

Dayton Society Natural History ....E 513 932-4421
Oregonia *(G-15616)*

Delaware County Historical Soc ....D 740 369-3831
Delaware *(G-9968)*

Deyor Performing Arts Center ....E 330 744-4269
Youngstown *(G-20017)*

Dumouchelle Art Galleries ....E 419 255-7606
Toledo *(G-17705)*

Fairfield Industries Inc ....E 740 409-1539
Carroll *(G-2557)*

◆ Franklin County Historical Soc ....C 614 228-2674
Columbus *(G-7617)*

▲ Great Lakes Museum of Science ......C 216 694-2000
Cleveland *(G-5629)*

Greater Andrson Premotes Peace ......E 513 588-8391
Cincinnati *(G-3647)*

Kingwood Center ....E 419 522-0211
Mansfield *(G-13194)*

Lake Erie Nature & Science Ctr ....E 440 871-2900
Bay Village *(G-1022)*

Lawrence Cnty Hstorical Museum ....E 740 532-1222
Ironton (G-12161)

▲ Museum Cntmprary Art Cleveland ..E 216 421-8671
Cleveland (G-6027)

National Underground Railroad.........D 513 333-7500
Cincinnati (G-4095)

New London Area Historical Soc ......D 419 929-3674
New London (G-14933)

Norhteast Ohio Museum ....E 330 336-7657
Medina (G-13981)

Ohio Historical Society...................C 614 297-2300
Columbus (G-8265)

Rock and Roll of Fame and Muse.......D 216 781-7625
Cleveland (G-6336)

Rthrford B Hayes Prsdntial Ctr ....E 419 332-2081
Fremont (G-11091)

Salem Historical Soc Museum...........E 330 337-6733
Salem (G-16562)

Sauder Village ....B 419 446-2541
Archbold (G-638)

Stan Hywet Hall and Grdns Inc ....D 330 836-5533
Akron (G-440)

Stark Cnty Historical Soc Inc ....E 330 455-7043
Canton (G-2489)

Taft Museum of Art ....E 513 241-0343
Cincinnati (G-4568)

▲ Toledo Museum of Art ....C 419 255-8000
Toledo (G-18092)

Toledo Science Center ....E 419 244-2674
Toledo (G-18096)

Western Reserve Historical Soc ....D 330 666-3711
Bath (G-1019)

Western Reserve Historical Soc..........D 216 721-5722
Cleveland (G-6675)

8422 Arboreta, Botanical & Zoological Gardens

Akron Zoological Park....................E 330 375-2550
Akron (G-60)

Animal Mgt Svcs Ohio Inc ....E 248 398-6533
Port Clinton (G-16099)

Cleveland Metroparks ....C 216 661-6500
Cleveland (G-5267)

Cleveland Metroparks ....C 216 661-6500
Cleveland (G-5270)

Columbus Zoological Park Assn ....C 614 645-3400
Powell (G-16190)

Dawes Arboretum ....E 740 323-2355
Newark (G-15030)

Holden Arboretum ....D 440 946-4400
Willoughby (G-19529)

Park Cincinnati Board ....D 513 421-4086
Cincinnati (G-4201)

Stan Hywet Hall and Grdns Inc..........D 330 836-5533
Akron (G-440)

Toledo Zoo ....E 419 385-5721
Toledo (G-18101)

Toledo Zoological Society.................B 419 385-4040
Toledo (G-18102)

▲ Zoological Society Cincinnati ....B 513 281-4700
Cincinnati (G-4820)

86 MEMBERSHIP ORGANIZATIONS

8611 Business Associations

A Fox Construction.......................E 614 506-1685
Canal Winchester (G-2101)

Altruism Society Inc ....D 877 283-4001
Beachwood (G-1028)

American Jersey Cattle Assn ....E 614 861-3636
Reynoldsburg (G-16282)

American Legion Post ....E 330 872-5475
Newton Falls (G-15135)

Blue Ash Business Association...........D 513 253-1006
Cincinnati (G-3058)

Bnai Brith Hillel Fdn At Osu ....E 614 294-4797
Columbus (G-7050)

Buckeye Power Inc ....E 614 781-0573
Columbus (G-7089)

Builders Exchange Inc ....E 216 393-6300
Cleveland (G-5102)

Canton Reg Cham of Comm Fdn..........E 330 456-7253
Canton (G-2241)

Canton Rgnal Chmber of Cmmerce ......E 330 456-7253
Canton (G-2242)

Certified Angus Beef LLC ....D 330 345-2333
Wooster (G-19699)

Chamber Commerce New Carlisle ....E 937 845-3911
New Carlisle (G-14889)

Cincinnati USA Rgional Chamber ....D 513 579-3100
Cincinnati (G-3274)

City of Circleville.........................E 740 477-8255
Circleville (G-4829)

City of Kenton ....E 419 674-4850
Kenton (G-12273)

City of Louisville.........................E 330 875-3321
Louisville (G-12962)

City of Montgomery ....D 513 891-2424
Montgomery (G-14593)

City of Oberlin ....E 440 775-1531
Oberlin (G-15499)

City of Toledo ....A 419 245-1001
Toledo (G-17655)

City of Toledo ....D 419 245-1400
Toledo (G-17658)

Consolidated Electric Coop Inc ....D 419 947-3055
Mount Gilead (G-14725)

County of Montgomery ....E 937 225-4010
Dayton (G-9329)

Dayton Area Chamber Commerce ....E 937 226-1444
Dayton (G-9353)

Energy Cooperative Inc..................E 740 348-1206
Newark (G-15031)

Enon Firemans Association ....E 937 864-7429
Enon (G-10608)

Greater Cleveland Partnership ....D 216 621-3300
Cleveland (G-5637)

Greater Clvland Halthcare Assn ....D 216 696-6900
Cleveland (G-5640)

Greater Columbus Chmbr Commrce ....E 614 221-1321
Columbus (G-7692)

Gs1 Us Inc ....D 609 620-0200
Dayton (G-9478)

▲ Hirzel Canning Company ....D 419 693-0531
Northwood (G-15395)

Home Bldrs Assn Grter Cncnnati ....D 513 851-6300
Cincinnati (G-3717)

In His Prsence Ministries Intl ....E 614 516-1812
Columbus (G-7805)

Interstate Contractors LLC ....E 513 372-5393
Mason (G-13601)

Mahoning Clmbana Training Assn ....E 330 747-5639
Youngstown (G-20104)

Mid-Ohio Regional Plg Comm ....D 614 228-2663
Columbus (G-8077)

National All-Jersey Inc ....E 614 861-3636
Reynoldsburg (G-16321)

National Ground Water Assn Inc ....E 614 898-7791
Westerville (G-19284)

National Hot Rod Association ....C 740 928-5706
Hebron (G-11722)

New Waterford Fireman...................E 330 457-2363
New Waterford (G-15006)

Oak Harbor Lions Club ....E 419 898-3828
Oak Harbor (G-15475)

Odd Fellows Hall ....E 440 599-7973
Conneaut (G-8957)

Ohio Assn Pub Treasurers ....C 937 415-2237
Vandalia (G-18534)

Ohio Association Realtors Inc ....E 614 228-6675
Columbus (G-8230)

Ohio Biliffs Crt Officers Assn ....D 419 354-9302
Bowling Green (G-1743)

Ohio Chamber of Commerce ....E 614 228-4201
Columbus (G-8232)

Ohio Civil Service Employees A ....D 614 865-4700
Westerville (G-19195)

Ohio Department of Commerce ....C 614 728-8400
Columbus (G-8238)

Ohio Farm Bur Federation Inc ....D 614 249-2400
Columbus (G-8258)

Ohio Rural Electric Coops Inc ....E 614 846-5757
Columbus (G-8283)

Ohio Utilities Protection Svc.............D 800 311-3692
North Jackson (G-15250)

▲ Precision Metalforming Assn ....E 216 241-1482
Independence (G-12110)

Ross County YMCA ....D 740 772-4340
Chillicothe (G-2823)

Saint Mary Parish ....D 440 285-7051
Chardon (G-2712)

Service Corps Retired Execs ....E 216 522-4194
Cleveland (G-6398)

Service Corps Retired Execs ....E 419 259-7598
Toledo (G-18026)

Southeast Area Law Enforcement ....E 216 475-1234
Bedford (G-1308)

◆ Superior Clay Corp.....................D 740 922-4122
Uhrichsville (G-18344)

Town of Canal Fulton ....E 330 854-9448
Canal Fulton (G-2098)

Union Rural Electric Coop Inc ....E 937 642-1826
Marysville (G-13535)

United States Trotting Assn ....D 614 224-2291
Westerville (G-19304)

Universal Advertising Assoc ....E 513 522-5000
Cincinnati (G-4693)

Vigilant Global Trade Svcs LLC ....E 260 417-1825
Shaker Heights (G-16719)

Village of Antwerp ....E 419 258-7422
Antwerp (G-615)

Village of Versailles ....E 937 526-4191
Versailles (G-18572)

Westfield Belden Village ....E 330 494-5490
Canton (G-2535)

Youngstown-Warren Reg Chamber ....E 330 744-2131
Youngstown (G-20267)

8621 Professional Membership Organizations

Aauw Action Fund Inc ....E 330 833-0520
Massillon (G-13659)

Akron Council of Engineering ....E 330 535-8835
Akron (G-36)

American Ceramic Society ....E 614 890-4700
Westerville (G-19144)

American Cllege Crdlgy Fndtion ....E 614 442-5950
Dublin (G-10130)

American Heart Association Inc ....E 614 848-6676
Columbus (G-6923)

American National Red Cross ....D 937 399-3872
Springfield (G-16993)

American Society For Nondstctv ....E 614 274-6003
Columbus (G-6938)

Association For Middle Lvl Edu ....E 614 895-4730
Westerville (G-19223)

Balanced Care Corporation ....E 330 908-1166
Northfield (G-15373)

Breathing Association ....E 614 457-4570
Columbus (G-7061)

Buckeye Assn Schl Admnstrators ....E 614 846-4080
Columbus (G-7084)

Center School Association ....D 440 995-7400
Mayfield Village (G-13884)

Central Hospital Services Inc ....D 216 696-6900
Cleveland (G-5154)

Chesapeake Research Review LLC ......D 410 884-2900
Cincinnati (G-3178)

Cincinnati Bar Association ....E 513 381-8213
Cincinnati (G-3225)

Clark County Combined Hlth Dst ....D 937 390-5600
Springfield (G-17012)

Cleveland Health Network ....E 216 986-1100
Cleveland (G-5257)

Columbus Bar Association ....E 614 221-4112
Columbus (G-7261)

Columbus Med Assn Foundation ....E 614 240-7420
Columbus (G-7294)

Columbus Medical Association ....E 614 240-7410
Columbus (G-7296)

Community Shelter Board ....E 614 221-9195
Columbus (G-7337)

Consortium For Hlthy & Immunzd...........D 216 201-2001
Cleveland (G-5336)

Dayton Anthem ....D 937 428-8000
Dayton (G-9351)

Deaconis Assocation Inc ....D 419 874-9008
Perrysburg (G-15858)

Dental Support Specialties LLC ....E 330 639-1333
Uniontown (G-18366)

Dignity Health............................C 330 493-4443
Canton (G-2287)

Dnv GL Healthcare Usa Inc ....E 281 396-1610
Milford (G-14385)

Emergency Medical Transport ....D 330 484-4000
North Canton (G-15198)

Geauga County Health District ....E 440 279-1940
Chardon (G-2695)

Greater Cleveland Hosp Assn ....D 216 696-6900
Cleveland (G-5636)

Health Collaborative ....D 513 618-3600
Cincinnati (G-3694)

Jefferson Behavioral Hlth Sys ....C 740 264-7751
Steubenville (G-17158)

Lakeside Association ....E 419 798-4461
Lakeside (G-12329)

Monroe County Association For ....E 740 472-1712
Woodsfield (G-19676)

Ohio Department of Health ....C 614 466-1521
Columbus *(G-8240)*

Ohio Health Council ....D 614 221-7614
Columbus *(G-8262)*

Ohio Hospital Association ....D 614 221-7614
Columbus *(G-8266)*

Ohio School Psychologists Assn ....E 614 414-5980
Columbus *(G-8285)*

Ohio Soc of Crtif Pub Accntnts ....D 614 764-2727
Columbus *(G-8287)*

Ohio State Bar Association ....E 614 487-2050
Columbus *(G-8289)*

Ohio State Medical Association ....D 614 527-6762
Dublin *(G-10298)*

Pain Net Inc ....D 614 481-5960
Columbus *(G-8414)*

Resident Home Association ....D 937 278-0791
Dayton *(G-9734)*

Society Plastics Engineers Inc ....C 419 287-4898
Pemberville *(G-15807)*

State of Ohio ....E 614 466-3834
Grove City *(G-11474)*

Visiting Nurse Association ....E 216 931-1300
Independence *(G-12138)*

Warren Twnship Vlntr Fire Dept ....E 740 373-2424
Marietta *(G-13399)*

William I Notz ....E 614 292-3154
Columbus *(G-8904)*

Wingspan Care Group ....E 216 932-2800
Shaker Heights *(G-16720)*

8631 Labor Unions & Similar Organizations

Amalgamated Transit Union ....E 216 861-3350
Cleveland *(G-4945)*

American Federation of Gov ....E 513 861-6047
Cincinnati *(G-2941)*

American Federation of State ....E 937 461-9983
Dayton *(G-9227)*

Brotherhood of Locomotive Engi ....E 740 345-0978
Newark *(G-15016)*

Cleveland Teachers Union Inc ....E 216 861-7676
Cleveland *(G-5292)*

Healthcare and Social ....E 614 461-1199
Columbus *(G-7726)*

Humaserve Hr LLC ....E 513 605-3522
Cincinnati *(G-3740)*

International Chem Wkrs Cr Un ....E 330 926-1444
Akron *(G-280)*

International Union United Au ....E 216 447-6080
Cleveland *(G-5764)*

International Union United Au ....D 513 897-4939
Waynesville *(G-18833)*

International Union United Au ....D 513 563-1252
Cincinnati *(G-3780)*

International Union United Au ....E 419 893-4677
Maumee *(G-13804)*

Interntional Assn Firefighters ....E 330 823-5222
Alliance *(G-535)*

Lake County Local Hazmat ....E 440 350-5499
Mentor *(G-14073)*

Licking Knox Labor Council ....D 740 345-1765
Newark *(G-15055)*

Local 18 IUOE ....E 216 432-3131
Cleveland *(G-5878)*

Local 911 United Mine Workers ....E 740 256-6083
Gallipolis *(G-11203)*

Local Union 856 Uaw Bldg Corp ....E 330 733-6231
Akron *(G-318)*

National Assn Ltr Carriers ....E 419 289-8359
Ashland *(G-683)*

National Assn Ltr Carriers ....D 419 693-8392
Northwood *(G-15400)*

Ohio Assn Pub Schl Employees ....E 614 890-4770
Columbus *(G-8228)*

Ohio Assn Pub Schl Employees ....E 937 253-5100
Dayton *(G-9183)*

Ohio Assn Pub Schl Employees ....D 330 659-7335
Richfield *(G-16368)*

Ohio Civil Service Employees A ....D 614 865-4700
Westerville *(G-19195)*

Ohio Education Association ....D 614 485-6000
Columbus *(G-8250)*

Ohio Education Association ....D 614 228-4526
Columbus *(G-8251)*

Ohio Lbrers Frnge Bneft Prgram ....E 614 898-9006
Westerville *(G-19287)*

Ohio Operating Engineers Apprn ....E 614 487-6531
Columbus *(G-8276)*

Pace International Union ....E 419 929-1335
New London *(G-14934)*

Pace International Union ....E 740 772-2038
Chillicothe *(G-2810)*

Pace International Union ....E 740 289-2368
Piketon *(G-15983)*

Painters District Council 6 ....E 440 239-4575
Cleveland *(G-6157)*

Painters Local Union 555 ....D 740 353-1431
Portsmouth *(G-16156)*

Smart ....C 216 228-9400
North Olmsted *(G-15310)*

Union Cnstr Wkrs Hlth Plan ....E 419 248-2401
Holland *(G-11923)*

United Fd & Coml Wkrs Intl Un ....E 216 241-2828
Broadview Heights *(G-1849)*

United Fd Coml Wkrs Local 880 ....E 216 241-5930
Cleveland *(G-6571)*

United Food & Commercial Wkr ....D 330 452-4850
Canton *(G-2517)*

United Food and Coml Wkrs ....D 937 665-0075
Dayton *(G-9831)*

United Food Comml Wrkrs Un ....E 614 235-3635
Columbus *(G-8800)*

United Steelworkers ....E 740 772-5988
Chillicothe *(G-2834)*

United Steelworkers ....C 740 928-0157
Newark *(G-15105)*

United Steelworkers ....E 440 979-1050
North Olmsted *(G-15315)*

United Steelworkers ....E 419 238-7980
Van Wert *(G-18490)*

United Steelworkers ....E 740 633-0899
Martins Ferry *(G-13480)*

United Steelworkers ....E 440 244-1358
Lorain *(G-12949)*

United Steelworkers ....E 440 354-2328
Painesville *(G-15746)*

United Steelworkers ....E 614 272-8609
Columbus *(G-8812)*

United Steelworkers ....E 740 622-8860
Coshocton *(G-9030)*

United Steelworkers ....E 513 793-0272
Cincinnati *(G-4687)*

United Steelworkers of America ....C 330 493-7721
Canton *(G-2522)*

8641 Civic, Social & Fraternal Associations

2444 Mdson Rd Cndo Owners Assn ....E 513 871-0100
Cincinnati *(G-2880)*

Aerie Frtnrl Order Egles 2875 ....E 419 433-4611
Huron *(G-12019)*

Akron Roundtable ....D 330 247-8682
Cuyahoga Falls *(G-9068)*

American Heritage Girls Inc ....D 513 771-2025
Cincinnati *(G-2945)*

American Legion ....D 330 488-0119
East Canton *(G-10385)*

American Legion ....E 440 834-8621
Burton *(G-2013)*

American Legion Post ....E 330 393-9858
Southington *(G-16952)*

Amvets Post No 6 Inc ....E 330 833-5935
Massillon *(G-13662)*

Apple Vly Property Owners Assn ....E 740 397-3311
Howard *(G-11939)*

Barrington Elem School Pto ....D 614 487-5180
Upper Arlington *(G-18395)*

Benevolent/Protectv Order Elks ....E 440 357-6943
Painesville *(G-15695)*

Beta RHO House Assoc Kappa ....D 513 221-1280
Cincinnati *(G-3045)*

Beta Theta PI Fraternity ....E 513 523-7591
Oxford *(G-15673)*

Bluffton Family Recreation ....E 419 358-6978
Bluffton *(G-1688)*

Bowling Green State University ....D 419 372-2186
Bowling Green *(G-1724)*

Boy Scouts of America ....E 513 961-2336
Cincinnati *(G-3069)*

Boy Scuts Amer - Lk Erie Cncil ....E 216 861-6060
Cleveland *(G-5071)*

Boys & Girls Club of Columbus ....E 614 221-8830
Columbus *(G-7056)*

Boys & Girls Club of Toledo ....E 419 241-4258
Toledo *(G-17622)*

Boys & Girls Clubs Grtr Cinc ....D 513 421-8909
Cincinnati *(G-3070)*

Bpo Elks of USA ....E 740 622-0794
Coshocton *(G-9000)*

Brandywine Master Assn ....D 419 866-0135
Maumee *(G-13765)*

Bridgetown Middle School Pta ....D 513 574-3511
Cincinnati *(G-3074)*

Buckeye Trls Girl Scout Cncil ....E 937 275-7601
Dayton *(G-9267)*

Buckeye Vly E Elementary Pto ....D 740 747-2266
Ashley *(G-701)*

Burkhardt Springfield Neighbor ....E 937 252-7076
Dayton *(G-9270)*

Cafaro Co ....E 330 652-6980
Niles *(G-15149)*

Change Healthcare Tech Enabled ....D 614 566-5861
Columbus *(G-7179)*

Chester West YMCA ....E 513 779-3917
Liberty Township *(G-12579)*

Cincinnati Scholar House LP ....E 513 559-0048
Cincinnati *(G-3265)*

Clearmount Elementary School ....E 330 497-5640
Canton *(G-2258)*

Cleveland Botanical Garden ....E 216 721-1600
Cleveland *(G-5232)*

Cleveland Heights Highschool ....E 216 691-5452
Cleveland *(G-5259)*

Cleveland Municipal School Dst ....D 216 459-4200
Cleveland *(G-5275)*

Clevelnd Clnc Hlth Systm East ....E 216 761-3300
Cleveland *(G-5300)*

Columbus Foundation ....E 614 251-4000
Columbus *(G-7283)*

Columbus Maennerchor ....E 614 444-3531
Columbus *(G-7293)*

Commodore Denig Post No 83 ....E 419 625-3274
Sandusky *(G-16589)*

Communities In Schools ....D 614 268-2472
Columbus *(G-7328)*

Community Action Columbiana CT ....E 330 385-7251
East Liverpool *(G-10400)*

County of Cuyahoga ....D 216 443-7265
Cleveland *(G-5371)*

County of Darke ....E 937 526-4488
Versailles *(G-18568)*

Cuyahoga County AG Soc ....E 440 243-0090
Berea *(G-1421)*

Delta Gamma Fraternity ....E 614 481-8169
Upper Arlington *(G-18396)*

Delta Gamma Fraternity ....E 614 487-5599
Upper Arlington *(G-18397)*

Delta Kappa Gamma Society ....E 419 586-6016
Celina *(G-2593)*

Disabled American Veterans ....E 330 875-5795
Louisville *(G-12965)*

Disabled American Veterans ....B 419 526-0203
Mansfield *(G-13168)*

Disabled American Veterans ....B 330 364-1204
New Philadelphia *(G-14957)*

Disabled American Veterans ....B 740 367-7973
Cheshire *(G-2733)*

Division Drnking Ground Waters ....D 614 644-2752
Columbus *(G-7457)*

Easter Seals Nothern Ohio Inc ....C 440 324-6600
Lorain *(G-12901)*

EMs Rams Youth Dev Group Inc ....E 216 282-4688
Cleveland *(G-5478)*

Enon Firemans Association ....E 937 864-7429
Enon *(G-10608)*

Fairborn YMCA ....E 937 754-9622
Fairborn *(G-10674)*

Family Motor Coach Assn Inc ....E 513 474-3622
Cincinnati *(G-3530)*

Family YMCA of LANcstr&fairfld ....D 740 277-7373
Lancaster *(G-12403)*

Farmersville Fire Assn Inc ....E 937 696-2863
Farmersville *(G-10857)*

Fayette County Family YMCA ....D 740 335-0477
Wshngtn CT Hs *(G-19870)*

Feldys ....E 513 474-2212
Cincinnati *(G-3541)*

Findlay Y M C A Child Dev ....E 419 422-3174
Findlay *(G-10908)*

For Evers Kids LLC ....E 330 258-9014
Akron *(G-226)*

Frans Child Care-Mansfield ....C 419 775-2500
Mansfield *(G-13178)*

Fraternal Order Eagles Inc ....E 330 477-8059
Canton *(G-2316)*

Fraternal Order Eagles Inc ....E 419 738-2582
Wapakoneta *(G-18642)*

Fraternal Order Eagles Inc ....E 419 332-3961
Fremont *(G-11075)*

Fraternal Order Eagles Inc ....E 440 293-5997
Andover *(G-606)*

SIC

Fraternal Order of Eagles........E....... 937 323-0671
Springfield *(G-17040)*
Fraternal Order of Eagles BR........E....... 419 636-7812
Bryan *(G-1957)*
Fraternal Order of Police of O........E....... 614 224-5700
Columbus *(G-7621)*
Friends of Art For Cultural........E....... 614 888-9929
Columbus *(G-7627)*
Galion Community Center YMCA........E....... 419 468-7754
Galion *(G-11173)*
Gamma PHI Beta Sorority Alpha........D....... 937 324-3436
Springfield *(G-17041)*
Geary Family YMCA Fostria........E....... 419 435-6608
Fostoria *(G-11002)*
Genoa Legion Post 324........E....... 419 855-7049
Genoa *(G-11256)*
Girl Scouts Lake Erie Council........E....... 330 864-9933
Macedonia *(G-13071)*
Girl Scouts North East Ohio........D....... 216 481-1313
Cleveland *(G-5609)*
Girl Scouts North East Ohio........D....... 330 864-9933
Macedonia *(G-13072)*
Girl Scouts of The US Amer........C....... 614 487-8101
Columbus *(G-7669)*
Girl Scouts of Western Ohio........E....... 513 489-1025
Blue Ash *(G-1570)*
Girl Scouts of Western Ohio........E....... 567 225-3557
Toledo *(G-17763)*
Girl Scuts Appleseed Ridge Inc........E....... 419 225-4085
Lima *(G-12643)*
Girl Scuts Ohios Heartland Inc........D....... 614 340-8820
Columbus *(G-7670)*
Girl Scuts Wstn Ohio Tledo Div........E....... 419 243-8216
Toledo *(G-17764)*
Goldwood Primary School Pta........E....... 440 356-6720
Rocky River *(G-16434)*
Grand Aerie of The Fraternal........E....... 614 883-2200
Grove City *(G-11436)*
Grand Aerie of The Fraternal........E....... 419 227-1566
Lima *(G-12647)*
Great Miami Valley YMCA........D....... 513 217-5501
Middletown *(G-14348)*
Great Miami Valley YMCA........A....... 513 887-0001
Hamilton *(G-11602)*
Great Miami Valley YMCA........C....... 513 892-9622
Fairfield Township *(G-10808)*
Great Miami Valley YMCA........E....... 513 867-0600
Hamilton *(G-11603)*
Great Miami Valley YMCA........D....... 513 887-0014
Hamilton *(G-11604)*
Great Miami Valley YMCA........D....... 513 868-9622
Hamilton *(G-11605)*
Great Miami Valley YMCA........D....... 513 829-3091
Fairfield *(G-10732)*
Greater Cnncnati Crime Stopper........E....... 859 468-1310
Cincinnati *(G-3655)*
Grove City Community Club........E....... 614 875-6074
Grove City *(G-11437)*
Hamilton Lodge 93 Benevolant P........E....... 513 887-4384
Liberty Twp *(G-12586)*
Hardin County Family YMCA........E....... 419 673-6131
Kenton *(G-12279)*
Heart of OH Cncl Bsa........E....... 740 389-4615
Marion *(G-13424)*
Heart of OH Cncl Bsa........E....... 419 522-8300
Mansfield *(G-13182)*
Help Foundation Inc........E....... 216 289-7710
Euclid *(G-10637)*
Heritage Pto........E....... 330 636-4400
Medina *(G-13948)*
Hide-A-Way Hills Club........E....... 740 746-9589
Sugar Grove *(G-17374)*
Highland County Family YMCA........E....... 937 840-9622
Hillsboro *(G-11842)*
Highland Relief Organization........E....... 614 843-5152
Columbus *(G-7748)*
Huber Heights YMCA........D....... 937 236-9622
Dayton *(G-9508)*
Independence Foundation Inc........C....... 330 296-2851
Ravenna *(G-16247)*
Independent Order Odd Fellows........E....... 740 548-5038
Lewis Center *(G-12546)*
Intercity Amateur Rdo CLB Inc........E....... 419 989-3429
Ontario *(G-15554)*
International Assn Lions........E....... 740 986-6502
Williamsport *(G-19499)*
International Frat of Del........E....... 330 922-5959
Cuyahoga Falls *(G-9102)*
International Ordr of Rnbow Fo........E....... 419 862-3009
Elmore *(G-10473)*
International Un Elev Constrs........C....... 614 291-5859
Columbus *(G-7838)*
Ioof Home of Ohio Inc........C....... 419 352-3014
Bowling Green *(G-1737)*
Izaak Walton League America........E....... 740 532-2342
Ironton *(G-12157)*
Jewish Community Center Inc........D....... 513 761-7500
Cincinnati *(G-3814)*
Joey Boyle........E....... 216 273-8317
Athens *(G-787)*
Junior Achvment Mhning Vly Inc........E....... 330 539-5268
Girard *(G-11291)*
Kappa Kappa Gamma Foundation........E....... 614 228-6515
Dublin *(G-10263)*
Kiwanis International Inc........E....... 740 385-5887
Logan *(G-12845)*
Knights of Columbus........E....... 937 890-2971
Dayton *(G-9549)*
Knights of Columbus........E....... 419 628-2089
Minster *(G-14537)*
Knights of Columbus........D....... 740 382-3671
Marion *(G-13428)*
Lake County YMCA........C....... 440 352-3303
Painesville *(G-15718)*
Lake County YMCA........C....... 440 946-1160
Willoughby *(G-19538)*
Lake County YMCA........E....... 440 259-2724
Perry *(G-15824)*
Lake County YMCA........D....... 440 428-5125
Madison *(G-13099)*
Lake Mhawk Prperty Owners Assn........E....... 330 863-0000
Malvern *(G-13125)*
Lake Wynoka Prprty Owners Assn........E....... 937 446-3774
Lake Waynoka *(G-12328)*
Lenau Park........E....... 440 235-2646
Olmsted Twp *(G-15537)*
Leo Yannenoff Jewish Community........C....... 614 231-2731
Columbus *(G-7966)*
Lima Family YMCA........E....... 419 223-6045
Lima *(G-12680)*
Lions Club International Inc........E....... 330 424-3490
Lisbon *(G-12803)*
Lithuanian World Community........E....... 513 542-0076
Cincinnati *(G-3939)*
Lorain Cnty Bys Girls CLB Inc........E....... 440 775-2582
Lorain *(G-12914)*
Louisville Frternal Order of E........E....... 330 875-2113
Louisville *(G-12968)*
Marion Family YMCA........D....... 740 725-9622
Marion *(G-13437)*
Maumee Lodge No 1850 Bnvlt........E....... 419 893-7272
Maumee *(G-13817)*
Miami Co YMCA Child Care........E....... 937 778-5241
Piqua *(G-16013)*
Miami County Park District........E....... 937 335-6273
Troy *(G-18214)*
Mills Creek Association........E....... 440 327-5336
North Ridgeville *(G-15337)*
Minature Society Cincinnati........D....... 513 931-9708
Cincinnati *(G-4059)*
Moose International Inc........E....... 513 422-6776
Middletown *(G-14314)*
Muirfield Association Inc........E....... 614 889-0922
Dublin *(G-10283)*
Natio Assoc For The Advan of........E....... 330 782-9777
Youngstown *(G-20136)*
Neighborhood Development Svcs........E....... 330 296-2003
Ravenna *(G-16250)*
New Boston Aerie 2271 FOE........E....... 740 456-0171
New Boston *(G-14881)*
New Pittsburgh Fire & Rescue F........E....... 330 264-1230
Wooster *(G-19749)*
Norwich Elementary Pto........E....... 614 921-6000
Hilliard *(G-11801)*
O S U Faculty Club........E....... 614 292-2262
Columbus *(G-8220)*
Oakdale Elementary Pta........D....... 513 574-1100
Cincinnati *(G-4144)*
Ohio Dept Amvet Svc Foundation........D....... 614 431-6990
Columbus *(G-8245)*
Ohio Masonic Retirement Vlg........D....... 937 525-1743
Springfield *(G-17092)*
Ohio Rver Vly Wtr Snttion Comm........E....... 513 231-7719
Cincinnati *(G-4158)*
Ohio State Univ Alumni Assn........D....... 614 292-2200
Columbus *(G-8290)*
Ohio State University........E....... 614 688-5721
Columbus *(G-8329)*
Optimist International........D....... 419 238-5086
Van Wert *(G-18485)*
Order of Symposiarchs America........E....... 740 387-9713
Marion *(G-13452)*
Order of Unite Commercial Tra........D....... 614 487-9680
Columbus *(G-8385)*
Orrville Boys and Girls Club........E....... 330 683-4888
Orrville *(G-15639)*
Owners Management........E....... 440 439-3800
Cleveland *(G-6151)*
Parks Recreation Division........E....... 937 496-7135
Dayton *(G-9687)*
Pike County YMCA........E....... 740 947-8862
Waverly *(G-18822)*
Poland Middle School Pto........E....... 330 757-7003
Youngstown *(G-20163)*
Polish American Citizens Club........E....... 330 253-0496
Akron *(G-388)*
Port Clnton Bpo Elks Ldge 1718........E....... 419 734-1900
Port Clinton *(G-16114)*
Portsmouth Lodge 154 B P O E........E....... 740 353-1013
Portsmouth *(G-16160)*
Pta OH Cong McVay Elem Pta........D....... 614 797-7230
Westerville *(G-19295)*
Pta Ohio Cngrss - Msn Elem Pta........E....... 330 588-2156
Canton *(G-2445)*
Pta Olms Falls Int Sch........D....... 440 427-6500
Olmsted Twp *(G-15540)*
Ross County YMCA........D....... 740 772-4340
Chillicothe *(G-2823)*
S R Restaurant Corp........E....... 216 781-6784
Cleveland *(G-6356)*
Salvation Army........D....... 216 861-8185
Cleveland *(G-6368)*
Salvation Army........D....... 419 447-2252
Tiffin *(G-17535)*
Sandusky Area YMCA Foundation........E....... 419 621-9622
Sandusky *(G-16637)*
Saxon House Condo........D....... 440 333-8675
Cleveland *(G-6373)*
Schlee Malt House Condo Assn........E....... 614 463-1999
Columbus *(G-8600)*
Seneca County Firemens Assn........D....... 419 447-7909
Tiffin *(G-17537)*
Seven Hills Fireman Assn........E....... 216 524-3321
Seven Hills *(G-16681)*
Sidney-Shelby County YMCA........E....... 937 492-9134
Sidney *(G-16800)*
Sigma CHI Frat........E....... 614 297-8783
Columbus *(G-8638)*
Simon Knton Cncil Byscuts Amer........E....... 614 436-7200
Columbus *(G-8642)*
Springfield Family Y M C A........D....... 937 323-3781
Springfield *(G-17119)*
Springfield Little Tigers Foot........D....... 330 549-2359
Youngstown *(G-20215)*
Star House Foundation........E....... 614 826-5868
Columbus *(G-8686)*
Sycamore Board of Education........D....... 513 489-3937
Cincinnati *(G-4560)*
The Boys and Girls Club of........E....... 330 773-3375
Akron *(G-468)*
The For Cincinnati Association........D....... 513 744-3344
Cincinnati *(G-4591)*
The For National Association........E....... 937 470-1059
Dayton *(G-9811)*
The Nature Conservancy........E....... 614 717-2770
Dublin *(G-10356)*
Three Village Condominium........E....... 440 461-1483
Cleveland *(G-6527)*
Tiffin Cmnty YMCA Rcration Ctr........D....... 419 447-8711
Tiffin *(G-17542)*
Toledo Club........D....... 419 243-2200
Toledo *(G-18081)*
Towards Employment Inc........E....... 216 696-5750
Cleveland *(G-6537)*
Tusco Imaa Chapter No 602........E....... 330 878-7369
Strasburg *(G-17240)*
Ucc Childrens Center........E....... 513 217-5501
Middletown *(G-14356)*
Union Club Company........D....... 216 621-4230
Cleveland *(G-6564)*
University Club Inc........E....... 513 721-2600
Cincinnati *(G-4697)*
Urban Leagu of Greater Clevlnd........E....... 216 622-0999
Cleveland *(G-6606)*
Vermilion Family YMCA........E....... 440 967-4208
Vermilion *(G-18563)*
Veterans Fgn Wars Post 2850........D....... 216 631-2585
Cleveland *(G-6624)*
Vietnam Veterans America Inc........E....... 330 877-6017
Hartville *(G-11700)*

Village of Cuyahoga Heights ....C 216 641-7020
Cleveland (G-6631)

Wapakoneta YMCA ....D 419 739-9622
Wapakoneta (G-18659)

Wesley Community Center Inc ....E 937 263-3556
Dayton (G-9875)

Western Rsrve Girl Scout Cncil ....E 330 864-9933
Macedonia (G-13089)

Western Rsrve Land Conservancy ....E 440 729-9621
Chagrin Falls (G-2660)

Whitehall Frmens Bnvlence Fund ....E 614 237-5478
Columbus (G-8899)

Wolves Club Inc ....E 419 476-4418
Toledo (G-18160)

Y M C A Central Stark County ....E 330 305-5437
Canton (G-2539)

Y M C A Central Stark County ....E 330 875-1611
Louisville (G-12975)

Y M C A Central Stark County ....E 330 877-8933
Uniontown (G-18392)

Y M C A Central Stark County ....E 330 830-6275
Massillon (G-13736)

Y M C A Central Stark County ....E 330 498-4082
Canton (G-2540)

Y M C A of Ashland Ohio Inc ....D 419 289-0626
Ashland (G-700)

YMCA ....E 330 823-1930
Alliance (G-558)

YMCA of Ashtabula County Inc ....D 440 997-5321
Ashtabula (G-760)

YMCA of Clermont County Inc ....E 513 724-9622
Batavia (G-1016)

YMCA of Massillon ....E 330 837-5116
Massillon (G-13737)

YMCA of Massillon ....D 330 879-0800
Navarre (G-14826)

YMCA of Sandusky Ohio Inc ....E 419 621-9622
Sandusky (G-16657)

York Rite ....E 216 751-1417
Cleveland (G-6701)

Young Mens Christian ....B 513 932-1424
Lebanon (G-12516)

Young Mens Christian Assn ....E 419 332-9622
Fremont (G-11108)

Young Mens Christian Assn ....D 330 744-8411
Youngstown (G-20253)

Young Mens Christian Assn ....D 740 373-2250
Marietta (G-13402)

Young Mens Christian Assn ....E 419 238-0443
Van Wert (G-18498)

Young Mens Christian Assoc ....C 614 491-0980
Lockbourne (G-12826)

Young Mens Christian Assoc ....E 419 729-8135
Toledo (G-18167)

Young Mens Christian Assoc ....C 614 871-9622
Grove City (G-11491)

Young Mens Christian Assoc ....E 937 223-5201
Dayton (G-9892)

Young Mens Christian Assoc ....D 330 923-5223
Cuyahoga Falls (G-9141)

Young Mens Christian Assoc ....E 330 467-8366
Macedonia (G-13091)

Young Mens Christian Assoc ....E 330 784-0408
Akron (G-507)

Young Mens Christian Assoc ....D 740 477-1661
Circleville (G-4854)

Young Mens Christian Assoc ....C 614 885-4252
Columbus (G-8927)

Young Mens Christian Assoc ....E 330 724-1255
Akron (G-508)

Young Mens Christian Assoc ....A 330 376-1335
Akron (G-509)

Young Mens Christian Assoc ....C 614 416-9622
Gahanna (G-11152)

Young Mens Christian Assoc ....C 614 334-9622
Hilliard (G-11832)

Young Mens Christian Assoc ....E 937 312-1810
Dayton (G-9893)

Young Mens Christian Assoc ....E 614 539-1770
Urbancrest (G-18453)

Young Mens Christian Assoc ....D 614 276-8224
Columbus (G-8928)

Young Mens Christian Assoc ....D 513 932-3756
Oregonia (G-15618)

Young Mens Christian Assoc ....D 614 252-3166
Columbus (G-8929)

Young Mens Christian Assoc ....D 937 426-9622
Dayton (G-9894)

Young Mens Christian Assoc ....D 937 836-9622
Englewood (G-10606)

Young Mens Christian Assoc ....D 419 523-5233
Ottawa (G-15667)

Young Mens Christian Assoc ....E 937 228-9622
Dayton (G-9895)

Young Mens Christian Assoc ....C 937 223-5201
Springboro (G-16990)

Young Mens Christian Assoc ....E 614 878-7269
Columbus (G-8930)

Young Mens Christian Assoc ....E 937 593-9001
Bellefontaine (G-1370)

Young Mens Christian Assoc ....E 614 834-9622
Canal Winchester (G-2129)

Young Mens Christian Assoc ....D 330 264-3131
Wooster (G-19789)

Young Mens Christian Associat ....E 419 475-3496
Toledo (G-18168)

Young Mens Christian Associat ....E 419 794-7304
Maumee (G-13870)

Young Mens Christian Associat ....D 513 521-7112
Cincinnati (G-4812)

Young Mens Christian Associat ....C 419 251-9622
Perrysburg (G-15938)

Young Mens Christian Associat ....E 513 731-0115
Cincinnati (G-4813)

Young Mens Christian Associat ....E 513 791-5000
Blue Ash (G-1685)

Young Mens Christian Associat ....E 513 474-1400
Cincinnati (G-4814)

Young Mens Christian Associat ....D 513 241-9622
Cincinnati (G-4815)

Young Mens Christian Associat ....D 513 923-4466
Cincinnati (G-4816)

Young Mens Christian Associat ....E 419 474-3995
Toledo (G-18169)

Young Mens Christian Associat ....D 419 866-9622
Maumee (G-13871)

Young Mens Christian Associat ....C 419 475-3496
Toledo (G-18170)

Young Mens Christian Associat ....D 419 691-3523
Oregon (G-15615)

Young Mens Christian Mt Vernon ....D 740 392-9622
Mount Vernon (G-14794)

Young Mens Christian Assn Shelby ....D 419 347-1312
Shelby (G-16751)

Young MNS Christn Assn Findlay ....D 419 422-4424
Findlay (G-10977)

Young MNS Chrstn Assn Clveland ....E 216 521-8400
Lakewood (G-12364)

Young MNS Chrstn Assn Clveland ....E 216 941-4654
Cleveland (G-6702)

Young MNS Chrstn Assn Clveland ....E 216 731-7454
Cleveland (G-6703)

Young MNS Chrstn Assn Clveland ....E 216 382-4300
Cleveland (G-6704)

Young MNS Chrstn Assn Clveland ....D 440 285-7543
Chardon (G-2726)

Young MNS Chrstn Assn Clveland ....D 440 808-8150
Westlake (G-19426)

Young MNS Chrstn Assn Grter NY ....D 740 392-9622
Mount Vernon (G-14795)

Young Wns Chrstn Assn Canton ....D 330 453-7644
Canton (G-2542)

Young Womens Christian ....E 419 238-6639
Van Wert (G-18499)

Young Womens Christian Assn ....D 614 224-9121
Columbus (G-8931)

Young Womens Christian Associ ....E 216 881-6878
Cleveland (G-6705)

Young Womns Chrstn Assc Canton ....D 330 453-0789
Canton (G-2543)

Young Womns Chrstn Assc Lima ....E 419 241-3230
Toledo (G-18173)

Youngstown Club ....E 330 744-3111
Youngstown (G-20259)

YWCA Dayton ....D 937 461-5550
Dayton (G-9896)

YWCA Mahoning Valley ....E 330 746-6361
Youngstown (G-20269)

YWCA of Greater Cincinnati ....D 513 241-7090
Cincinnati (G-4817)

YWCA of Hamilton ....E 513 856-9800
Hamilton (G-11655)

YWCA Shelter & Housing Network ....E 937 222-6333
Dayton (G-9897)

8651 Political Organizations

County of Richland ....E 419 774-5676
Mansfield (G-13153)

Republican Headquarters ....E 330 343-6131
Dover (G-10096)

Republican State Central Execu ....E 614 228-2481
Columbus (G-8517)

8699 Membership Organizations, NEC

AAA Allied Group Inc ....B 513 762-3301
Cincinnati (G-2894)

AAA Club Alliance Inc ....D 419 843-1200
Toledo (G-17577)

AAA Miami Valley ....D 937 224-2896
Dayton (G-9201)

AAA South Central Ohio Inc ....E 740 354-5614
Portsmouth (G-16123)

Affinion Group LLC ....A 614 895-1803
Westerville (G-19217)

Akron Automobile Association ....D 330 762-0631
Akron (G-28)

Akron-Canton Regional Foodbank ....E 330 535-6900
Akron (G-61)

American Motorcycle Assn ....D 614 856-1900
Pickerington (G-15945)

American National Red Cross ....D 937 399-3872
Springfield (G-16993)

Animal Protective League ....E 216 771-4616
Cleveland (G-4982)

Applewood Centers Inc ....D 216 696-6815
Cleveland (G-4991)

Ardmore Inc ....C 330 535-2601
Akron (G-79)

Athletes In Action Sports ....D 937 352-1000
Xenia (G-19891)

Auxiliary St Lukes Hospital ....E 419 893-5911
Maumee (G-13759)

▲ Battelle Memorial Institute ....A 614 424-6424
Columbus (G-7020)

Beachwood Prof Fire Fighters C ....E 216 292-1968
Beachwood (G-1035)

Broken Arrow Inc ....E 419 562-3480
Bucyrus (G-1977)

Brunswick Food Pantry Inc ....E 330 225-0395
Brunswick (G-1922)

Buckeye Drag Racing Assn LLC ....E 419 562-0869
Bucyrus (G-1978)

Carmen Steering Committee ....E 330 756-2066
Navarre (G-14822)

Carol A & Ralp V H US B Fdn Tr ....E 513 632-4426
Cincinnati (G-3125)

Center For Health Affairs ....D 800 362-2628
Cleveland (G-5152)

Cincinnati Health Network Inc ....E 513 961-0600
Cincinnati (G-3248)

Cincinnati Humn Relations Comm ....E 513 352-3237
Cincinnati (G-3249)

City of Brunswick ....C 330 225-9144
Brunswick (G-1924)

City of Compassion ....D 419 422-7800
Findlay (G-10888)

Cleveland America Scores ....E 216 881-7988
Cleveland (G-5230)

Cliffs Cleveland Foundation ....E 216 694-5700
Cleveland (G-5302)

Columbus Landmarks Foundation ....E 614 221-0227
Columbus (G-7291)

Community Dev For All People ....E 614 445-7342
Columbus (G-7330)

Conserv For Cyhg Vlly Nat Prk ....D 330 657-2909
Peninsula (G-15811)

Council For Economic Opport ....D 216 476-3201
Cleveland (G-5354)

County of Summit Board of Mntl ....A 330 634-8100
Akron (G-167)

Dayton Society Natural History ....E 513 932-4421
Oregonia (G-15616)

Downtown Akron Partnership Inc ....E 330 374-7676
Akron (G-193)

East Akron Neighborhood Dev ....E 330 773-6838
Akron (G-200)

Eastern Mumee Bay Arts Council ....E 419 690-5718
Oregon (G-15593)

Elizabeths New Life Center Inc ....D 937 226-7414
Dayton (G-9411)

Ethnic Voice of America ....E 440 845-0922
Cleveland (G-5492)

Fairfield Industries Inc ....E 740 409-1539
Carroll (G-2557)

First Capital Enterprises Inc ....D 740 773-2166
Chillicothe (G-2780)

Franklin Cnty Bd Commissioners ....E 614 462-4360
Columbus (G-7611)

Frazeysburg Lions Club Inc ....E 740 828-2313
Frazeysburg (G-11049)

Free & Accepted Masons ....D...... 419 822-3736
Delta *(G-10044)*
Gideons International ....E...... 513 932-2857
Lebanon *(G-12467)*
Goodwill Inds Centl Ohio Inc ....E...... 740 439-7000
Cambridge *(G-2070)*
Granger Township ....E...... 330 239-2111
Medina *(G-13945)*
Hadassah Dayton Chapter ....E...... 937 275-0227
Dayton *(G-9481)*
Hamilton County Society ....E...... 513 541-6100
Cincinnati *(G-3677)*
Hearing Spch Deaf Ctr Grtr Cnc ......E...... 513 221-0527
Cincinnati *(G-3696)*
Heartbeats To City Inc ....E...... 330 452-4524
Canton *(G-2342)*
Heights Emergency Food Center ......D...... 216 381-0707
Cleveland *(G-5682)*
Jeanne B McCoy Comm ....E...... 614 245-4701
New Albany *(G-14857)*
Kids In Need Foundation ....E...... 937 296-1230
Moraine *(G-14669)*
Koinonia Homes Inc ....B...... 216 588-8777
Cleveland *(G-5835)*
Kroger Co Foundation ....E...... 513 762-4000
Cincinnati *(G-3893)*
Leo Yannenoff Jewish Community .....C...... 614 231-2731
Columbus *(G-7966)*
Licking Valley Lions Club ....C...... 740 763-3733
Newark *(G-15060)*
Marysville Food Pantry ....E...... 937 644-3248
Marysville *(G-13514)*
Massillon Automobile Club ....E...... 330 833-1084
Massillon *(G-13709)*
Mid-Ohio Foodbank ....C...... 614 317-9400
Grove City *(G-11453)*
Nami of Preble County Ohio ....E...... 937 456-4947
Eaton *(G-10455)*
Niles Historical Society ....D...... 330 544-2143
Niles *(G-15162)*
Northast Ohio Sstnble Cmmnties........D...... 216 410-7698
Akron *(G-349)*
Oberlin College ....E...... 440 775-8500
Oberlin *(G-15514)*
Ohio Academy of Science ....E...... 614 488-2228
Dublin *(G-10296)*
Ohio Automobile Club ....C...... 614 431-7901
Worthington *(G-19831)*
Ohio Federation of Soil and WA ....E...... 614 784-1900
Reynoldsburg *(G-16323)*
▲ Ohio School Boards Association ....E...... 614 540-4000
Columbus *(G-8284)*
Parma Community General Hosp ......B...... 440 743-4280
Parma *(G-15772)*
Pepper Pike Club Company Inc ....D...... 216 831-9400
Cleveland *(G-6193)*
Pheasants Forever Inc ....E...... 567 454-6319
Pettisville *(G-15944)*
Professnl Glfers Assn of Amer ....E...... 419 882-3197
Sylvania *(G-17442)*
Recovery Center ....E...... 740 687-4500
Lancaster *(G-12429)*
Ridgeville Community Choir..............E...... 419 267-3820
Ridgeville Corners *(G-16398)*
Ross County Sportsmen and Wild .....E...... 740 649-9614
Chillicothe *(G-2821)*
Royal Arch Masons of Ohio ....E...... 419 762-5565
Napoleon *(G-14816)*
Ruritan ....E...... 330 542-2308
New Springfield *(G-14997)*
School Choice Ohio Inc ....E...... 614 223-1555
Columbus *(G-8605)*
Seneca RE ADS Ind Fostoria Div.......C...... 419 435-0729
Fostoria *(G-11012)*
Shoreby Club Inc ....D...... 216 851-2587
Cleveland *(G-6406)*
Sons of Un Vtrans of Civil War ....D...... 740 992-6144
Middleport *(G-14283)*
Sporty Events ....E...... 440 342-5046
Chesterland *(G-2745)*
Team NEO ....E...... 216 363-5400
Cleveland *(G-6507)*
United Sttes Bowl Congress Inc..........D...... 740 922-3120
Uhrichsville *(G-18347)*
United Sttes Bowl Congress Inc..........D...... 513 761-3338
Cincinnati *(G-4688)*
United Sttes Bowl Congress Inc..........D...... 419 531-4058
Toledo *(G-18121)*
United Sttes Bowl Congress Inc..........D...... 614 237-3716
Columbus *(G-8813)*

University of Cincinnati.....................C...... 513 556-4603
Cincinnati *(G-4718)*
Volunteers of America NW Ohio ....E...... 419 248-3733
Toledo *(G-18140)*
Wapakoneta YMCA ....D...... 419 739-9622
Wapakoneta *(G-18659)*
White Gorilla Corporation ....E...... 202 384-6486
Hilliard *(G-11830)*
Womens Civic Club Grove City ....E...... 614 871-0145
Grove City *(G-11489)*
Youngstown Neighborhood Dev ....E...... 330 480-0423
Youngstown *(G-20263)*
Zanesville Welfare Organizatio ....B...... 740 450-6060
Zanesville *(G-20386)*

87 ENGINEERING, ACCOUNTING, RESEARCH, MANAGEMENT, AND RELATED SERVICES

8711 Engineering Services

7nt Enterprises LLC..........................E...... 614 961-2026
Miamisburg *(G-14135)*
ACC Automation Co Inc ....E...... 330 928-3821
Akron *(G-15)*
Accelerant Technologies LLC..............D...... 419 236-8768
Genoa *(G-11251)*
Acpi Systems Inc ....E...... 513 738-3840
Hamilton *(G-11554)*
Adaptive Corporation ....E...... 440 257-7460
Hudson *(G-11961)*
▲ Advanced Design Industries Inc.......E...... 440 277-4141
Sheffield Village *(G-16732)*
Advanced Engrg Solutions Inc............D...... 937 743-6900
Springboro *(G-16960)*
Advantage Aerotech Inc ....E...... 614 759-8329
Columbus *(G-6875)*
Aecom Energy & Cnstr Inc ....D...... 216 523-5600
Cleveland *(G-4909)*
Aecom Global II LLC ....E...... 937 233-1230
Dayton *(G-9210)*
Aecom Global II LLC ....D...... 216 523-5600
Cleveland *(G-4910)*
Aecom Technical Services Inc ....E...... 937 233-1898
Batavia *(G-982)*
Airgas Usa LLC ....C...... 440 232-1590
Cleveland *(G-4921)*
Alexander & Associates Co ....E...... 513 731-7800
Cincinnati *(G-2920)*
▲ Alfons Haar Inc............................E...... 937 560-2031
Springboro *(G-16961)*
Alphaport Inc ....E...... 216 619-2400
Cleveland *(G-4941)*
Alt & Witzig Engineering Inc ....E...... 513 777-9890
West Chester *(G-18865)*
▲ American Electric Pwr Svc Corp ......B...... 614 716-1000
Columbus *(G-6919)*
American Rock Mechanics Inc ....E...... 330 963-0550
Twinsburg *(G-18243)*
Amg Inc ....E...... 937 260-4646
Dayton *(G-9233)*
Aptim Corp ....E...... 513 782-4700
Cincinnati *(G-2977)*
Aptiv Services Us LLC ....B...... 330 373-7666
Warren *(G-18667)*
Arcadis US Inc ....D...... 330 434-1995
Akron *(G-78)*
Argus International Inc ....E...... 513 852-5110
Cincinnati *(G-2986)*
Atc Group Services LLC ....D...... 513 771-2112
Cincinnati *(G-2996)*
Austin Building and Design Inc...........C...... 440 544-2600
Cleveland *(G-5023)*
Avid Technologies Inc ....E...... 330 487-0770
Twinsburg *(G-18248)*
Azimuth Corporation ....E...... 937 256-8571
Beavercreek Township *(G-1243)*
B&N Coal Inc ....D...... 740 783-3575
Dexter City *(G-10059)*
Barr Engineering Incorporated ....E...... 614 714-0299
Columbus *(G-7019)*
Bayer & Becker Inc ....E...... 513 492-7401
Mason *(G-13545)*
BBC&m Engineering Inc ....D...... 614 793-2226
Dublin *(G-10142)*
Bbs Professional Corporation ....E...... 614 888-3100
Columbus *(G-7022)*
Belcan LLC ....A...... 513 891-0972
Blue Ash *(G-1510)*

Belcan Corporation...........................C...... 513 277-3100
Cincinnati *(G-3037)*
Belcan Engineering Group LLC...........A...... 513 891-0972
Blue Ash *(G-1511)*
◆ Bendix Coml Vhcl Systems LLC........B...... 440 329-9000
Elyria *(G-10482)*
Bertec Corporation ....E...... 614 543-0962
Columbus *(G-7029)*
BHF Incorporated ....E...... 740 945-6410
Scio *(G-16662)*
Black & Veatch Corporation ....E...... 614 473-0921
Columbus *(G-7044)*
Booz Allen Hamilton Inc ....E...... 937 429-5580
Beavercreek *(G-1134)*
Boral Resources LLC........................D...... 740 622-8042
Coshocton *(G-8999)*
Bowen Engineering Corporation ....C...... 614 536-0273
Columbus *(G-7055)*
Bramhall Engrg & Surveying Co ....E...... 440 934-7878
Avon *(G-868)*
Brewer-Garrett Co............................C...... 440 243-3535
Middleburg Heights *(G-14248)*
Brilligent Solutions Inc ....E...... 937 879-4148
Fairborn *(G-10664)*
Brown and Caldwell ....E...... 614 410-6144
Columbus *(G-7082)*
Brumbaugh Engrg Surveying LLC ....E...... 937 698-3000
West Milton *(G-19126)*
BSI Engineering LLC ....C...... 513 201-3100
Cincinnati *(G-3085)*
Burgess & Niple Inc ....B...... 502 254-2344
Columbus *(G-7098)*
Burgess & Niple Inc ....D...... 440 354-9700
Painesville *(G-15696)*
Burgess & Niple Inc ....C...... 513 579-0042
Cincinnati *(G-3089)*
Burgess & Niple-Heapy LLC ....D...... 614 459-2050
Columbus *(G-7099)*
Butler County of Ohio ....D...... 513 867-5744
Hamilton *(G-11569)*
Camgen Ltd ....E...... 330 204-8636
Canal Winchester *(G-2105)*
Capano & Associates LLC ....E...... 513 403-6000
Liberty Township *(G-12578)*
Cbc Engineers & Associates Ltd..........E...... 937 428-6150
Dayton *(G-9288)*
Cbre Heery Inc ....E...... 216 781-1313
Cleveland *(G-5143)*
CDM Smith Inc ....E...... 740 897-2937
Piketon *(G-15972)*
Cec Combustion Safety LLC ....E...... 216 749-2992
Brookpark *(G-1893)*
Ceso Inc ....D...... 937 435-8584
Miamisburg *(G-14150)*
Cetek Ltd ....E...... 216 362-3900
Cleveland *(G-5161)*
Cgh-Global Emerg Mngmt Strateg ......E...... 800 376-0655
Cincinnati *(G-2843)*
Ch2m Hill Inc ....D...... 513 243-5070
Cincinnati *(G-3166)*
Ch2m Hill Inc ....E...... 614 888-3100
Columbus *(G-7176)*
Cha Consulting Inc ....C...... 216 443-1700
Cleveland *(G-5165)*
Chemstress Consultant Company ....C...... 330 535-5591
Akron *(G-126)*
Chipmatic Tool & Machine Inc ....D...... 419 862-2737
Elmore *(G-10472)*
Choice One Engineering Corp ....E...... 937 497-0200
Sidney *(G-16764)*
Circle Prime Manufacturing ....D...... 330 923-0019
Cuyahoga Falls *(G-9079)*
Circuits & Cables Inc ....E...... 937 415-2070
Vandalia *(G-18514)*
City of Akron ....D...... 330 375-2355
Akron *(G-136)*
City of Delphos ....E...... 419 695-4010
Delphos *(G-10021)*
City of Sandusky ....D...... 419 627-5829
Sandusky *(G-16584)*
City of Toledo ....D...... 419 936-2275
Toledo *(G-17660)*
Civil & Environmental Cons Inc............E...... 513 985-0226
Milford *(G-14380)*
Clarkdietrich Engineering Serv ....D...... 513 870-1100
West Chester *(G-18892)*
Clear Vision Engineering LLC ....E...... 419 478-7151
Toledo *(G-17664)*
Cmta Inc ....C...... 502 326-3085
Cincinnati *(G-3314)*

Coal Services Inc ....D 740 795-5220
  Powhatan Point (G-16214)

▼ Corrpro Companies Inc ....E 330 723-5082
  Medina (G-13924)

County Engineering Office ....E 419 334-9731
  Fremont (G-11064)

County Engineers Office ....E 740 702-3130
  Chillicothe (G-2771)

County of Athens ....E 740 593-5514
  Athens (G-773)

County of Brown ....E 937 378-6456
  Georgetown (G-11267)

County of Champaign ....E 937 653-4848
  Urbana (G-18430)

County of Coshocton ....E 740 622-2135
  Coshocton (G-9011)

County of Crawford ....E 419 562-7731
  Bucyrus (G-1987)

County of Delaware ....D 740 833-2400
  Delaware (G-9963)

County of Erie ....E 419 627-7710
  Sandusky (G-16596)

County of Fayette ....E 740 335-1541
  Wshngtn CT Hs (G-19866)

County of Fulton ....E 419 335-3816
  Wauseon (G-18797)

County of Gallia ....E 740 446-4009
  Gallipolis (G-11189)

County of Hamilton ....D 513 946-4250
  Cincinnati (G-3371)

County of Hancock ....E 419 422-7433
  Findlay (G-10893)

County of Lorain ....E 440 326-5884
  Elyria (G-10497)

County of Lucas ....D 419 213-2892
  Holland (G-11879)

County of Madison ....E 740 852-9404
  London (G-12863)

County of Montgomery ....D 937 854-4576
  Dayton (G-9327)

County of Perry ....E 740 342-2191
  New Lexington (G-14919)

County of Portage ....D 330 296-6411
  Ravenna (G-16238)

County of Richland ....E 419 774-5591
  Mansfield (G-13158)

County of Stark ....C 330 477-6781
  Canton (G-2269)

County of Summit ....C 330 643-2850
  Akron (G-164)

County of Union ....E 937 645-3018
  Marysville (G-13490)

County of Washington ....E 740 376-7430
  Marietta (G-13321)

County of Wayne ....D 330 287-5500
  Wooster (G-19719)

Crowne Group LLC ....D 216 589-0198
  Cleveland (G-5383)

CT Consultants Inc ....E 513 791-1700
  Blue Ash (G-1543)

CT Consultants Inc ....C 440 951-9000
  Mentor (G-14038)

CTI Engineers Inc ....D 330 294-5996
  Akron (G-176)

Ctl Engineering Inc ....C 614 276-8123
  Columbus (G-7404)

Curtiss-Wright Controls ....E 937 252-5601
  Fairborn (G-10667)

▲ Custom Materials Inc ....D 440 543-8284
  Chagrin Falls (G-2663)

Cuyahoga County ....A 216 348-3800
  Cleveland (G-5396)

DCS Corporation ....E 937 306-7180
  Beavercreek Township (G-1247)

Denmark Consultants Inc ....E 513 530-9984
  Cincinnati (G-3422)

Design Homes & Development Co ......E 937 438-3667
  Dayton (G-9389)

Design Knowledge Company ....E 937 320-9244
  Beavercreek (G-1147)

Deskey Associates Inc ....D 513 721-6800
  Cincinnati (G-3423)

Dillin Engineered Systems Corp ....E 419 666-6789
  Perrysburg (G-15859)

Dizer Corp ....E 440 368-0200
  Painesville (G-15709)

Dj Neff Enterprises Inc ....E 440 884-3100
  Cleveland (G-5432)

Dkmp Consulting Inc ....C 614 733-0979
  Plain City (G-16049)

◆ Dlhbowles Inc ....B 330 478-2503
  Canton (G-2288)

Dlr Group Inc ....D 216 522-1350
  Cleveland (G-5433)

Dlz American Drilling Inc ....E 614 888-0040
  Columbus (G-7459)

Dlz Construction Services Inc ....E 614 888-0040
  Columbus (G-7460)

Dlz National Inc ....E 614 888-0040
  Columbus (G-7461)

Dlz Ohio Inc ....C 614 888-0040
  Columbus (G-7462)

Dlz Ohio Inc ....E 330 923-0401
  Akron (G-189)

Donald E Didion II ....E 419 483-2226
  Bellevue (G-1376)

Dynamix Engineering Ltd ....D 614 443-1178
  Columbus (G-7482)

Dynotec Inc ....E 614 880-7320
  Columbus (G-7483)

E & A Pedco Services Inc ....D 513 782-4920
  Cincinnati (G-3461)

E P Ferris & Associates Inc ....E 614 299-2999
  Columbus (G-7485)

E-Technologies Group LLC ....E 513 771-7271
  West Chester (G-18917)

Earl Twinam ....E 740 820-2654
  Portsmouth (G-16137)

Early Construction Co ....E 740 894-5150
  South Point (G-16933)

Eaton-Aeroquip Llc ....D 419 891-7775
  Maumee (G-13782)

Electrol Systems Inc ....E 513 942-7777
  Cincinnati (G-3488)

Electrovations Inc ....E 330 274-3558
  Aurora (G-826)

Elevar Design Group Inc ....E 513 721-0600
  Cincinnati (G-3490)

Emersion Design LLC ....E 513 841-9100
  Cincinnati (G-3494)

◆ Emh Inc ....E 330 220-8600
  Valley City (G-18462)

Engineering Associates Inc ....E 330 345-6556
  Wooster (G-19722)

Engineering Design and Testing ....D 440 239-0362
  Cleveland (G-5481)

Engisystems Inc ....D 513 229-8860
  Mason (G-13577)

▲ Enprotech Industrial Tech LLC ....C 216 883-3220
  Cleveland (G-5482)

Equity Engineering Group Inc ....D 216 283-9519
  Shaker Heights (G-16708)

Essig Research Inc ....E 513 942-7100
  West Chester (G-19050)

Euthenics Inc ....E 440 260-1555
  Strongsville (G-17302)

Evans Mechwart Ham ....B 614 775-4500
  New Albany (G-14852)

Fed/Matrix A Joint Venture LLC ....E 863 665-6363
  Dayton (G-9429)

Feller Finch & Associates Inc ....E 419 893-3680
  Maumee (G-13791)

Fishbeck Thmpson Carr Hber Inc ....E 513 469-2370
  Blue Ash (G-1564)

Fishel Company ....D 614 850-4400
  Columbus (G-7590)

Fishel Company ....D 614 274-8100
  Columbus (G-7588)

Forte Indus Eqp Systems Inc ....E 513 398-2800
  Mason (G-13581)

Fosdick & Hilmer Inc ....D 513 241-5640
  Cincinnati (G-3581)

Frontier Technology Inc ....E 937 429-3302
  Beavercreek Township (G-1248)

Futura Design Service Inc ....E 937 890-5252
  Dayton (G-9453)

Gannett Fleming Inc ....E 614 794-9424
  Westerville (G-19257)

Garmann/Miller & Assoc Inc ....E 419 628-4240
  Minster (G-14533)

Gbc Design Inc ....E 330 283-6870
  Akron (G-232)

GE Aviation Systems LLC ....D 937 474-9397
  Dayton (G-9456)

GE Aviation Systems LLC ....B 937 898-5881
  Vandalia (G-18524)

◆ General Electric Intl Inc ....C 617 443-3000
  Cincinnati (G-3614)

Global Military Expert Co ....E 800 738-9795
  Beavercreek (G-1219)

Global Risk Consultants Corp ....E 440 746-8861
  Brecksville (G-1781)

Glowe-Smith Industrial Inc ....C 330 638-5088
  Vienna (G-18579)

Greene County ....E 937 562-7500
  Xenia (G-19903)

Gus Perdikakis Associates ....D 513 583-0900
  Cincinnati (G-3665)

▲ Hamilton Manufacturing Corp ....E 419 867-4858
  Holland (G-11888)

Hammontree & Associates Ltd ....E 330 499-8817
  Canton (G-2336)

Hawa Incorporated ....E 614 451-1711
  Columbus (G-7718)

HDR Engineering Inc ....E 614 839-5770
  Columbus (G-7722)

Henningson Drham Richardson PC .....D 513 984-7500
  Blue Ash (G-1578)

High Voltage Maintenance Corp ....E 937 278-0811
  Dayton (G-9496)

HJ Ford Associates Inc ....C 937 429-9711
  Beavercreek (G-1155)

Hntb Corporation ....E 216 522-1140
  Cleveland (G-5697)

Hockaden & Associates Inc ....E 614 252-0993
  Columbus (G-7757)

Hokuto USA Inc ....E 614 782-6200
  Grove City (G-11442)

Horn Electric Company ....E 330 364-7784
  Dover (G-10082)

Hull & Associates Inc ....E 614 793-8777
  Dublin (G-10247)

Hull & Associates Inc ....E 419 385-2018
  Toledo (G-17812)

▲ Hunter Defense Tech Inc ....E 216 438-6111
  Solon (G-16859)

HWH Archtcts-Ngnrs-Plnners Inc ....D 216 875-4000
  Cleveland (G-5727)

▲ Hydro-Dyne Inc ....E 330 832-5076
  Massillon (G-13696)

I T E LLC ....D 513 576-6200
  Loveland (G-13000)

Ibi Group Engrg Svcs USA Inc ....E 513 942-3141
  Cincinnati (G-3749)

Ibi Group Engrg Svcs USA Inc ....D 614 818-4900
  Westerville (G-19263)

Icr Inc ....E 513 900-7007
  Mason (G-13596)

Iet Inc ....E 419 385-1233
  Toledo (G-17816)

Ijus LLC ....D 614 470-9882
  Gahanna (G-11126)

Illumination Works LLC ....D 937 938-1321
  Beavercreek (G-1157)

Industrial Origami Inc ....E 440 260-0000
  Cleveland (G-5748)

Infoscitex Corporation ....E 937 429-9008
  Beavercreek Township (G-1249)

Innovative Controls Corp ....D 419 691-6684
  Toledo (G-17821)

Innovtive Sltons Unlimited LLC ....E 740 289-3282
  Piketon (G-15978)

Innovtive Sltons Unlimited LLC ....D 740 289-3282
  Piketon (G-15979)

Interbrand Design Forum LLC ....C 513 421-2210
  Cincinnati (G-3777)

Intren Inc ....E 815 482-0651
  Cincinnati (G-3784)

Invotec Engineering Inc ....D 937 886-3232
  Miamisburg (G-14177)

J R Johnson Engineering Inc ....E 440 234-9972
  Cleveland (G-5772)

Jack A Hamilton & Assoc Inc ....E 740 968-4947
  Flushing (G-10980)

Jacobs Constructors Inc ....E 419 226-1344
  Lima (G-12667)

Jacobs Engineering Group Inc ....E 513 595-7500
  Cincinnati (G-3801)

Jacobs Engineering Group Inc ....D 513 595-7500
  Cincinnati (G-3802)

Jacobs Technology Inc ....E 937 429-5056
  Beavercreek Township (G-1250)

Jdi Group Inc ....D 419 725-7161
  Maumee (G-13805)

Jdrm Engineering Inc ....E 419 824-2400
  Sylvania (G-17432)

Jedson Engineering Inc ....D 513 965-5999
  Cincinnati (G-3811)

Jetson Engineering ....D 513 965-5999
  Cincinnati (G-3813)

Jjr Solutions LLC	E	937 912-0288	
Beavercreek (G-1159)			
Jobes Henderson & Assoc Inc	E	740 344-5451	
Newark (G-15045)			
Johnson Mirmiran Thompson Inc	D	614 714-0270	
Columbus (G-7863)			
Johnson Mirmiran Thompson Inc	D	614 714-0270	
Blue Ash (G-1590)			
Johnson Mirmiran Thompson Inc	E	614 714-0270	
Columbus (G-7864)			
Johnson Mirmiran Thompson Inc	D	614 714-0270	
Cleveland (G-5801)			
Jones & Henry Engineers Ltd	E	419 473-9611	
Toledo (G-17832)			
Juice Technologies Inc	E	800 518-5576	
Columbus (G-7875)			
K&K Technical Group Inc	C	513 202-1300	
Harrison (G-11672)			
Karpinski Engineering Inc	E	614 430-9820	
Columbus (G-6821)			
Karpinski Engineering Inc	D	216 391-3700	
Cleveland (G-5816)			
Kemron Environmental Svcs Inc	D	740 373-4071	
Marietta (G-13342)			
▲ Kendall Holdings Ltd	E	614 486-4750	
Columbus (G-7891)			
Kenexis Consulting Corporation	E	614 451-7031	
Upper Arlington (G-18400)			
◆ Keuchel & Associates Inc	E	330 945-9455	
Cuyahoga Falls (G-9108)			
Kevin Kennedy Associates Inc	E	317 536-7000	
Columbus (G-7897)			
Keyw Corporation	E	937 702-9512	
Beavercreek (G-1162)			
Kleingers Group Inc	D	614 882-4311	
Westerville (G-19177)			
Kleingers Group Inc	D	513 779-7851	
West Chester (G-18957)			
Knox County Engineer	E	740 397-1590	
Mount Vernon (G-14774)			
KS Associates Inc	D	440 365-4730	
Elyria (G-10523)			
Kucera International Inc	D	440 975-4230	
Willoughby (G-19536)			
KZF Bwsc Joint Venture	E	513 621-6211	
Cincinnati (G-3897)			
KZF Design Inc	D	513 621-6211	
Cincinnati (G-3898)			
L&T Technology Services Ltd	E	732 688-4402	
Dublin (G-10266)			
L-3 Cmmncations Nova Engrg Inc	C	877 282-1168	
Mason (G-13608)			
L3 Aviation Products Inc	D	614 825-2001	
Columbus (G-7938)			
Land Design Consultants	E	440 255-8463	
Mentor (G-14075)			
Logan County Engineering Off	E	937 592-2791	
Bellefontaine (G-1355)			
Los Alamos Technical Assoc Inc	E	614 508-1200	
Westerville (G-19275)			
Louis Perry & Associates Inc	C	330 334-1585	
Wadsworth (G-18605)			
LSI Adl Techonology LLC	E	614 345-9040	
Columbus (G-7995)			
M Consultants LLC	D	614 839-4639	
Westerville (G-19277)			
M Retail Engineering Inc	E	614 818-2323	
Westerville (G-19278)			
Macaulay-Brown Inc	B	937 426-3421	
Beavercreek (G-1227)			
Macdonald Mott LLC	E	216 535-3640	
Cleveland (G-5892)			
Mahoning County	C	330 799-1581	
Youngstown (G-20106)			
Majidzadeh Enterprises Inc	E	614 823-4949	
Columbus (G-8011)			
Mannik & Smith Group Inc	C	419 891-2222	
Maumee (G-13812)			
Mannik & Smith Group Inc	E	740 942-4222	
Cadiz (G-2031)			
Manufacturing Services Intl	E	937 299-9922	
Dayton (G-9583)			
Matrix Research Inc	D	937 427-8433	
Beavercreek (G-1230)			
Matrix Technologies Inc	D	419 897-7200	
Maumee (G-13816)			
▲ Maval Industries LLC	C	330 405-1600	
Twinsburg (G-18296)			
McGill Smith Punshon Inc	E	513 759-0004	
Cincinnati (G-3987)			
Mechanical Support Svcs Inc	E	614 777-8808	
Hilliard (G-11790)			
Medina County Sanitary	E	330 273-3610	
Medina (G-13972)			
Metamateria Partners LLC	E	614 340-1690	
Columbus (G-8063)			
Metcalf & Eddy Inc	E	216 910-2000	
Cleveland (G-5963)			
Michael Baker Intl Inc	C	330 453-3110	
Canton (G-2402)			
Michael Baker Intl Inc	E	412 269-6300	
Cleveland (G-5976)			
Michael Baker Intl Inc	C	614 418-1773	
Columbus (G-8068)			
Michael Benza and Assoc Inc	E	440 526-4206	
Brecksville (G-1790)			
Micro Industries Corporation	D	740 548-7878	
Westerville (G-19279)			
Mid-Ohio Electric Co	E	614 274-8000	
Columbus (G-8076)			
Middough Inc		216 367-6000	
Cleveland (G-5983)			
Mistras Group Inc	D	330 244-1541	
Canton (G-2407)			
Mkc Associates Inc	E	740 657-3202	
Powell (G-16203)			
Modal Shop Inc	D	513 351-9919	
Cincinnati (G-4067)			
Modern Tech Solutions Inc	E	937 426-9025	
Beavercreek Township (G-1254)			
Moody-Nolan Inc	D	614 461-4664	
Columbus (G-8101)			
Morris Technologies Inc	C	513 733-1611	
Cincinnati (G-4075)			
Ms Consultants Inc	C	330 744-5321	
Youngstown (G-20132)			
Ms Consultants Inc	C	614 898-7100	
Columbus (G-8118)			
Ms Consultants Inc	E	216 522-1926	
Cleveland (G-6021)			
Muskingum County Ohio	E	740 453-0381	
Zanesville (G-20337)			
Natural Resources Ohio Dept	E	614 265-6948	
Columbus (G-8162)			
Neteam Systems LLC	D	330 523-5100	
Cleveland (G-6058)			
Neundorfer Inc	E	440 942-8990	
Willoughby (G-19555)			
▲ New Path International LLC	E	614 410-3974	
Powell (G-16204)			
Nexus Engineering Group LLC	E	216 404-7867	
Cleveland (G-6067)			
Northast Ohio Rgonal Sewer Dst	D	216 961-2187	
Cleveland (G-6083)			
Northrop Grumman Technical	C	937 320-3100	
Beavercreek Township (G-1255)			
Nottingham-Spirk Des	E	216 800-5782	
Cleveland (G-6101)			
Nu Waves Ltd	D	513 360-0800	
Middletown (G-14315)			
Ohio Blow Pipe Company	E	216 681-7379	
Cleveland (G-6116)			
Ohio Structures Inc	E	330 533-0084	
Canfield (G-2154)			
On-Power Inc	E	513 228-2100	
Lebanon (G-12489)			
Onyx Creative Inc	D	216 223-3200	
Cleveland (G-6137)			
Optis Solutions	E	513 948-2070	
Cincinnati (G-4178)			
Osborn Engineering Company	D	216 861-2020	
Cleveland (G-6145)			
P E Systems Inc	D	937 258-0141	
Dayton (G-9185)			
Pakteem Technical Services	E	513 772-1515	
Cincinnati (G-4197)			
Panelmatic Inc	C	330 782-8007	
Youngstown (G-20151)			
Peco II Inc	D	614 431-0694	
Columbus (G-8433)			
Pegasus Technical Services Inc	E	513 793-0094	
Cincinnati (G-4223)			
Peterman Associates Inc	E	419 722-9566	
Findlay (G-10953)			
Peters Tschantz & Assoc Inc	E	330 666-3702	
Akron (G-381)			
Phantom Technical Services Inc	E	614 868-9920	
Columbus (G-8444)			
Phoenix Group Holding Co	C	937 704-9850	
Springboro (G-16981)			
Pioneer Solutions LLC	E	216 383-3400	
Euclid (G-10652)			
PMC Systems Limited	E	330 538-2268	
North Jackson (G-15252)			
Pmwi LLC	D	614 975-5004	
Hilliard (G-11806)			
Poggemeyer Design Group Inc	C	419 244-8074	
Bowling Green (G-1746)			
Poggemeyer Design Group Inc	E	419 748-7438	
Mc Clure (G-13893)			
Polaris Automation Inc	D	614 431-0170	
Lewis Center (G-12560)			
Pollock Research & Design Inc	E	330 332-3300	
Salem (G-16554)			
Power Engineers Incorporated	E	513 326-1500	
Cincinnati (G-4266)			
Power Engineers Incorporated	E	234 678-9875	
Akron (G-392)			
Power System Engineering Inc	E	740 568-9220	
Marietta (G-13372)			
Primatech Inc	E	614 841-9800	
Columbus (G-8462)			
Prime Ae Group Inc	D	614 839-0250	
Columbus (G-6831)			
Prisma Integration Corp	E	330 545-8690	
Girard (G-11298)			
Process Plus LLC	C	513 742-7590	
Cincinnati (G-4290)			
Production Design Services Inc	D	937 866-3377	
Dayton (G-9716)			
Professional Service Inds Inc	E	614 876-8000	
Columbus (G-8470)			
Professional Service Inds Inc	D	216 447-1335	
Cleveland (G-6239)			
Providence Rees Inc	E	614 833-6231	
Columbus (G-8474)			
Pyramid Control Systems Inc	E	513 679-7400	
Cincinnati (G-4307)			
Quality Aero Inc	E	614 436-1609	
Worthington (G-19839)			
Quest Global Services-Na Inc	D	860 787-1600	
Cincinnati (G-4328)			
Quilalea Corporation	E	330 487-0777	
Richfield (G-16372)			
R E Warner & Associates Inc	D	440 835-9400	
Westlake (G-19395)			
Ra Consultants LLC	E	513 469-6600	
Blue Ash (G-1635)			
Racaza International LLC	E	614 973-9266	
Dublin (G-10317)			
RAD-Con Inc	E	440 871-5720	
Lakewood (G-12361)			
RCT Engineering Inc	E	561 684-7534	
Beachwood (G-1099)			
Reps Resource LLC	E	513 874-0500	
West Chester (G-18991)			
Resource International	D	513 769-6998	
Blue Ash (G-1646)			
Resource International Inc	C	614 823-4949	
Columbus (G-8523)			
Richard L Bowen & Assoc Inc	D	216 491-9300	
Cleveland (G-6321)			
River Consulting LLC	D	614 797-2480	
Columbus (G-8534)			
Rovisys Company	C	330 562-8600	
Aurora (G-842)			
S&Me Inc	D	614 793-2226	
Dublin (G-10326)			
Saec/Kinetic Vision Inc	C	513 793-4959	
Cincinnati (G-4422)			
Safran Humn Rsrces Support Inc	D	513 552-3230	
Cincinnati (G-4423)			
Safran Power Usa LLC	C	330 487-2000	
Twinsburg (G-18316)			
Sands Decker Cps Llc	E	614 459-6992	
Columbus (G-8590)			
Sandusky County Engr & Hwy Gar	E	419 334-9731	
Fremont (G-11093)			
Sawdey Solution Services Inc	E	937 490-4060	
Beavercreek (G-1236)			
Scheeser Buckley Mayfield LLC	E	330 896-4664	
Uniontown (G-18385)			
Schomer Glaus Pyle	D	614 210-0751	
Columbus (G-8604)			
Schomer Glaus Pyle	E	216 518-5544	
Cleveland (G-6376)			
Schomer Glaus Pyle	B	330 572-2100	
Akron (G-420)			
Schomer Glaus Pyle	D	330 645-2131	
Coventry Township (G-9042)			

Schooley Caldwell Associates ....D...... 614 628-0300
  Columbus (G-8607)
Sea Ltd ....D...... 614 888-4160
  Columbus (G-8614)
Sebesta Inc ....E...... 216 351-7621
  Parma (G-15775)
Seifert & Group Inc ....D...... 330 833-2700
  Massillon (G-13727)
Sgi Matrix LLC ....D...... 937 438-9033
  Miamisburg (G-14219)
Shaffer Pomeroy Ltd ....E...... 419 756-7302
  Mansfield (G-13242)
Shotstop Ballistics LLC ....E...... 330 686-0020
  Stow (G-17230)
Sierra Lobo Inc ....E...... 419 332-7101
  Fremont (G-11095)
Sigma Technologies Ltd ....E...... 419 874-9262
  Perrysburg (G-15921)
Slick Automated Solutions Inc ....E...... 567 247-1080
  Ontario (G-15573)
Society Plastics Engineers Inc ....C...... 419 287-4898
  Pemberville (G-15807)
Sponseller Group Inc ....E...... 419 861-3000
  Holland (G-11915)
Ssoe Inc ....E...... 330 821-7198
  Alliance (G-552)
Stantec Arch & Engrg PC ....E...... 216 454-2150
  Cleveland (G-6451)
Stantec Arch & Engrg PC ....E...... 614 486-4383
  Columbus (G-8683)
Stantec Architecture Inc ....E...... 216 454-2150
  Cleveland (G-6453)
Stantec Consulting Svcs Inc ....E...... 216 621-2407
  Cleveland (G-6455)
Stantec Consulting Svcs Inc ....E...... 216 454-2150
  Cleveland (G-6454)
Stantec Consulting Svcs Inc ....D...... 513 842-8200
  Cincinnati (G-4537)
Stantec Consulting Svcs Inc ....C...... 614 486-4383
  Columbus (G-8684)
Steven Schaefer Associates Inc ......D...... 513 542-3300
  Cincinnati (G-4547)
Stilson & Associates Inc ....E...... 614 847-0300
  Columbus (G-8700)
Stock Fairfield Corporation ....C...... 440 543-6000
  Chagrin Falls (G-2684)
Straight 72 Inc ....D...... 740 943-5730
  Marysville (G-13530)
Strand Associates Inc ....E...... 513 861-5600
  Cincinnati (G-4548)
Strand Associates Inc ....E...... 614 835-0460
  Groveport (G-11540)
Stress Engineering Svcs Inc ....D...... 513 336-6701
  Mason (G-13641)
Sumaria Systems Inc ....D...... 937 429-6070
  Beavercreek (G-1188)
Sumitomo Elc Wirg Systems Inc ......E...... 937 642-7579
  Marysville (G-13532)
Sunpower Inc ....D...... 740 594-2221
  Athens (G-804)
Superior Mechanical Svcs Inc ....E...... 937 259-0082
  Dayton (G-9187)
T J Neff Holdings Inc ....E...... 440 884-3100
  Cleveland (G-6494)
TEC Engineering Inc ....E...... 513 771-8828
  Mason (G-13644)
Technical Assurance Inc ....E...... 440 953-3147
  Willoughby (G-19575)
Technical Construction Spc ....E...... 330 929-1088
  Cuyahoga Falls (G-9129)
Technical Consultants Inc ....E...... 513 521-2696
  Cincinnati (G-4579)
Technology House Ltd ....E...... 440 248-3025
  Streetsboro (G-17274)
Techsolve Inc ....D...... 513 948-2000
  Cincinnati (G-4581)
Telecom Expertise Inds Inc ....D...... 937 548-5254
  Greenville (G-11397)
Terracon Consultants Inc ....C...... 513 321-5816
  Cincinnati (G-4586)
Terracon Consultants Inc ....E...... 614 863-3110
  Gahanna (G-11150)
Thelen Associates Inc ....E...... 513 825-4350
  Cincinnati (G-4598)
Thermal Treatment Center Inc ....E...... 216 881-8100
  Cleveland (G-6521)
Thermaltech Engineering Inc ....E...... 513 561-2271
  Cincinnati (G-4599)
Thinkpath Engineering Svcs LLC .....E...... 937 291-8374
  Miamisburg (G-14229)

Thomas L Miller ....D...... 740 374-3041
  Marietta (G-13385)
Thorson Baker & Assoc Inc ....C...... 330 659-6688
  Richfield (G-16380)
Thp Limited Inc ....D...... 513 241-3222
  Cincinnati (G-4607)
TL Industries Inc ....E...... 419 666-8144
  Northwood (G-15410)
Transcore Its LLC ....E...... 440 243-2222
  Cleveland (G-6541)
Transystems Corporation ....E...... 614 433-7800
  Columbus (G-8775)
Transystems Corporation ....E...... 216 861-1780
  Columbus (G-6545)
Tri-Tech Associates Inc ....E...... 937 306-1630
  Dayton (G-9821)
Triad Engineering & Contg Co ....E...... 440 786-1000
  Cleveland (G-6548)
Trumbull County Engineering ....D...... 330 675-2640
  Warren (G-18755)
Tsi Inc ....E...... 419 468-1855
  Galion (G-11184)
Ttl Associates Inc ....C...... 419 241-4556
  Toledo (G-18111)
Turnkey Network Solutions LLC ....E...... 614 876-9944
  Columbus (G-8789)
Twism Enterprises LLC ....E...... 513 800-1098
  Cincinnati (G-4657)
U S Army Corps of Engineers ....D...... 740 269-2681
  Uhrichsville (G-18345)
U S Army Corps of Engineers ....D...... 740 767-3527
  Glouster (G-11311)
U S Army Corps of Engineers ....D...... 513 684-3048
  Cincinnati (G-4660)
Universal Technology Corp ....D...... 937 426-2808
  Beavercreek (G-1193)
University of Akron ....D...... 330 972-6008
  Akron (G-479)
University of Cincinnati ....E...... 513 556-3732
  Cincinnati (G-4717)
URS Group Inc ....D...... 216 622-2300
  Cleveland (G-6609)
URS Group Inc ....C...... 614 464-4500
  Columbus (G-8831)
URS Group Inc ....D...... 513 651-3440
  Cincinnati (G-4737)
URS Group Inc ....D...... 330 836-9111
  Akron (G-481)
URS-Smith Group VA Idiq Joint ....E...... 614 464-4500
  Columbus (G-8832)
US Tech Arospc Engrg Corp ....D...... 330 455-1181
  Canton (G-2524)
Utility Technologies Intl Corp ....E...... 614 879-7624
  Groveport (G-11548)
Vantage Partners LLC ....E...... 216 925-1302
  Brookpark (G-1908)
Varo Engineers Inc ....D...... 513 729-9313
  West Chester (G-19029)
Varo Engineers Inc ....E...... 740 587-2228
  Granville (G-11349)
W E Quicksall and Assoc Inc ....E...... 330 339-6676
  New Philadelphia (G-14988)
Wade Trim ....E...... 216 363-0300
  Cleveland (G-6648)
Wastren Advantage Inc ....E...... 970 254-1277
  Piketon (G-15993)
Weastec Incorporated ....E...... 614 734-9645
  Dublin (G-10371)
Wheaton & Sprague Engineering ......E...... 330 923-5560
  Stow (G-17239)
Wilkris Company ....E...... 513 271-9344
  Terrace Park (G-17501)
Wood Environment & ....E...... 513 489-6611
  Blue Ash (G-1681)
Woolpert Inc ....E...... 614 476-6000
  Columbus (G-8915)
Youngstown Plastic Tooling ....E...... 330 782-7222
  Youngstown (G-20265)
Zin Technologies Inc ....C...... 440 625-2200
  Middleburg Heights (G-14267)

8712 Architectural Services

A D A Architects Inc ....E...... 216 521-5134
  Cleveland (G-4877)
Acock Assoc Architects LLC ....E...... 614 228-1586
  Columbus (G-6866)
Aecom Global II LLC ....B...... 614 726-3500
  Dublin (G-10120)
Aecom Global II LLC ....D...... 216 523-5600
  Cleveland (G-4910)

Aptiv Services Us LLC ....E...... 330 373-3568
  Warren (G-18666)
Arcadis US Inc ....E...... 216 781-6177
  Cleveland (G-5005)
ASC Group Inc ....E...... 614 268-2514
  Columbus (G-6976)
Austin Building and Design Inc ....C...... 440 544-2600
  Cleveland (G-5023)
Balog Steines Hendricks & Manc .....E...... 330 744-4401
  Youngstown (G-19961)
Baxter Hodell Donnelly Preston ....C...... 513 271-1634
  Cincinnati (G-3025)
Behal Sampson Dietz Inc ....E...... 614 464-1933
  Columbus (G-7025)
Berardi + Partners ....E...... 614 221-1110
  Columbus (G-7028)
Big Red Rooster ....E...... 614 255-0200
  Columbus (G-7036)
Bostwick Design Partnr Inc ....E...... 216 621-7900
  Cleveland (G-5069)
Braun & Steidl Architects Inc ....E...... 330 864-7755
  Akron (G-104)
Burgess & Niple Inc ....C...... 513 579-0042
  Cincinnati (G-3089)
Burgess & Niple Inc ....B...... 502 254-2344
  Columbus (G-7098)
Burgess & Niple Inc ....D...... 440 354-9700
  Painesville (G-15696)
Burgess & Niple-Heapy LLC ....E...... 614 459-2050
  Columbus (G-7099)
Cbre Heery Inc ....E...... 216 781-1313
  Cleveland (G-5143)
Ceso Inc ....D...... 937 435-8584
  Miamisburg (G-14150)
Cha Consulting Inc ....C...... 216 443-1700
  Cleveland (G-5165)
Champlin Haupt Architects Inc ....E...... 513 241-4474
  Cincinnati (G-3169)
Chemstress Consultant Company .....C...... 330 535-5591
  Akron (G-126)
Chute Gerdeman Inc ....D...... 614 469-1001
  Columbus (G-7198)
City Architecture Inc ....E...... 216 881-2444
  Cleveland (G-5185)
Cole + Russell Architects Inc ....E...... 513 721-8080
  Cincinnati (G-3327)
Collaborative Inc ....E...... 419 242-7405
  Toledo (G-17667)
Cornelia C Hodgson - Architec ....E...... 216 593-0057
  Beachwood (G-1048)
CT Consultants Inc ....E...... 513 791-1700
  Blue Ash (G-1543)
CT Consultants Inc ....C...... 440 951-9000
  Mentor (G-14038)
Dei Incorporated ....D...... 513 825-5800
  Cincinnati (G-3418)
Design Center ....E...... 513 618-3133
  Blue Ash (G-1544)
Dlr Group Inc ....D...... 216 522-1350
  Cleveland (G-5433)
Dlz Ohio Inc ....E...... 614 888-0040
  Columbus (G-7462)
Domokur Architects Inc ....E...... 330 666-7878
  Copley (G-8966)
Dorsky Hodgson + Partners Inc ....D...... 216 464-8600
  Cleveland (G-5442)
E & A Pedco Services Inc ....E...... 513 782-4920
  Cincinnati (G-3461)
Elevar Design Group Inc ....E...... 513 721-0600
  Cincinnati (G-3490)
Emersion Design LLC ....E...... 513 841-9100
  Cincinnati (G-3494)
Fanning/Howey Associates Inc ....D...... 614 764-4661
  Dublin (G-10224)
Fanning/Howey Associates Inc ....E...... 919 831-1831
  Dublin (G-10225)
Fed/Matrix A Joint Venture LLC ....E...... 863 665-6363
  Dayton (G-9429)
Feinknopf Macioce Schappa ARC .....E...... 614 297-1020
  Columbus (G-7573)
Frch Design Worldwide - Cincin ....B...... 513 241-3000
  Cincinnati (G-3584)
Garland/Dbs Inc ....C...... 216 641-7500
  Cleveland (G-5592)
Garmann/Miller & Assoc Inc ....E...... 419 628-4240
  Minster (G-14533)
Gbc Design Inc ....E...... 330 283-6870
  Akron (G-232)
Glavan & Accociates Architects ....E...... 614 205-4060
  Columbus (G-7672)

Gpd Services Company Inc ....D...... 330 572-2100
Akron **(G-243)**

Hardlines Design Company ....E...... 614 784-8733
Columbus **(G-7717)**

Hasenstab Architects Inc ....E...... 330 434-4464
Akron **(G-254)**

Heery International Inc ....E...... 216 510-4701
Cleveland **(G-5680)**

Hixson Incorporated ....C...... 513 241-1230
Cincinnati **(G-3712)**

Holland Professional Group ....D...... 330 239-4474
Sharon Center **(G-16723)**

HWH Archtcts-Ngnrs-Plnners Inc ....D...... 216 875-4000
Cleveland **(G-5727)**

Jdi Group Inc ....D...... 419 725-7161
Maumee **(G-13805)**

Johnson Mirmiran Thompson Inc ....D...... 614 714-0270
Columbus **(G-7863)**

K4 Architecture LLC ....E...... 513 455-5005
Cincinnati **(G-3845)**

Karlsberger Companies ....C...... 614 461-9500
Columbus **(G-7883)**

KZF Bwsc Joint Venture ....E...... 513 621-6211
Cincinnati **(G-3897)**

KZF Design Inc ....D...... 513 621-6211
Cincinnati **(G-3898)**

Lacaisse Inc ....D...... 513 621-6211
Cincinnati **(G-3905)**

Loth Inc ....C...... 513 554-4900
Cincinnati **(G-3944)**

Louis Perry & Associates Inc ....C...... 330 334-1585
Wadsworth **(G-18605)**

Lusk & Harkin Ltd ....E...... 614 221-3707
Columbus **(G-7999)**

McGill Smith Punshon Inc ....E...... 513 759-0004
Cincinnati **(G-3987)**

Meacham & Apel Architects Inc ....D...... 614 764-0407
Columbus **(G-8048)**

Meyers + Associates Arch LLC ....E...... 614 221-9433
Columbus **(G-8065)**

Michael Schuster Associates ....E...... 513 241-5666
Cincinnati **(G-4047)**

Middough Inc ....B...... 216 367-6000
Cleveland **(G-5983)**

Mkc Associates Inc ....E...... 740 657-3202
Powell **(G-16203)**

Moody-Nolan Inc ....C...... 614 461-4664
Columbus **(G-8101)**

Ms Consultants Inc ....C...... 330 744-5321
Youngstown **(G-20132)**

NBBJ LLC ....A...... 206 223-5026
Columbus **(G-8165)**

Nelson ....C...... 216 781-9144
Seven Hills **(G-16677)**

Onyx Creative Inc ....D...... 216 223-3200
Cleveland **(G-6137)**

Orchard Hiltz & McCliment Inc ....D...... 614 418-0600
Columbus **(G-8384)**

Osborn Engineering Company ....D...... 216 861-2020
Cleveland **(G-6145)**

Perkfect Design Solutions ....E...... 614 778-3560
Columbus **(G-8439)**

Perspectus Architecture LLC ....E...... 216 752-1800
Cleveland **(G-6199)**

Poggemeyer Design Group Inc ....C...... 419 244-8074
Bowling Green **(G-1746)**

Pond-Woolpert LLC ....D...... 937 461-5660
Beavercreek **(G-1233)**

Prime Ae Group Inc ....D...... 614 839-0250
Columbus **(G-6831)**

R E Warner & Associates Inc ....D...... 440 835-9400
Westlake **(G-19395)**

Rdl Architects Inc ....E...... 216 752-4300
Cleveland **(G-6288)**

Richard L Bowen & Assoc Inc ....D...... 216 491-9300
Cleveland **(G-6321)**

Richard R Jencen & Associates ....E...... 216 781-0131
Cleveland **(G-6322)**

Schomer Glaus Pyle ....D...... 614 210-0751
Columbus **(G-8604)**

Schomer Glaus Pyle ....E...... 216 518-5544
Cleveland **(G-6376)**

Schomer Glaus Pyle ....B...... 330 572-2100
Akron **(G-420)**

Schooley Caldwell Associates ....D...... 614 628-0300
Columbus **(G-8607)**

Sfa Architects Inc ....E...... 937 281-0600
Dayton **(G-9762)**

Shp Leading Design ....D...... 513 381-2112
Cincinnati **(G-4472)**

Shremshock Architects Inc ....D...... 614 545-4550
New Albany **(G-14874)**

Simonson Construction Svcs Inc ....D...... 419 281-8299
Ashland **(G-691)**

Ssoe Inc ....E...... 330 821-7198
Alliance **(G-552)**

Stantec Arch & Engrg PC ....E...... 216 454-2150
Cleveland **(G-6451)**

Stantec Arch & Engrg PC ....E...... 614 486-4383
Columbus **(G-8683)**

Stantec Architecture Inc ....E...... 216 621-2407
Cleveland **(G-6452)**

Stantec Architecture Inc ....E...... 216 454-2150
Cleveland **(G-6453)**

Stantec Consulting Svcs Inc ....E...... 216 454-2150
Cleveland **(G-6454)**

Stantec Consulting Svcs Inc ....D...... 513 842-8200
Cincinnati **(G-4537)**

Stantec Consulting Svcs Inc ....C...... 614 486-4383
Columbus **(G-8684)**

Stilson & Associates Inc ....E...... 614 847-0300
Columbus **(G-8700)**

Strollo Architects Inc ....E...... 330 743-1177
Youngstown **(G-20218)**

Technical Assurance Inc ....E...... 440 953-3147
Willoughby **(G-19575)**

Trinity Health Group Ltd ....E...... 614 899-4830
Columbus **(G-8782)**

Twism Enterprises LLC ....E...... 513 800-1098
Cincinnati **(G-4657)**

United Architectural Mtls Inc ....E...... 330 433-9220
North Canton **(G-15243)**

URS Group Inc ....D...... 330 836-9111
Akron **(G-481)**

URS Group Inc ....C...... 614 464-4500
Columbus **(G-8831)**

WD Partners Inc ....E...... 614 634-7000
Dublin **(G-10370)**

Woolprt-Mrrick Joint Ventr LLP ....E...... 937 461-5660
Beavercreek **(G-1241)**

8713 Surveying Services

7nt Enterprises LLC ....E...... 614 961-2026
Miamisburg **(G-14135)**

▲ American Electric Pwr Svc Corp ....B...... 614 716-1000
Columbus **(G-6919)**

ASC Group Inc ....E...... 614 268-2514
Columbus **(G-6976)**

Barr Engineering Incorporated ....E...... 614 714-0299
Columbus **(G-7019)**

Bayer & Becker Inc ....E...... 513 492-7297
Mason **(G-13544)**

Bayer & Becker Inc ....E...... 513 492-7401
Mason **(G-13545)**

Bramhall Engrg & Surveying Co ....E...... 440 934-7878
Avon **(G-868)**

Choice One Engineering Corp ....E...... 937 497-0200
Sidney **(G-16764)**

CT Consultants Inc ....C...... 440 951-9000
Mentor **(G-14038)**

CT Consultants Inc ....E...... 513 791-1700
Blue Ash **(G-1543)**

Ctl Engineering Inc ....E...... 614 276-8123
Columbus **(G-7404)**

Division of Geological Survey ....E...... 614 265-6576
Columbus **(G-7458)**

Dj Neff Enterprises Inc ....E...... 440 884-3100
Columbus **(G-5432)**

Dlz Ohio Inc ....C...... 614 888-0040
Columbus **(G-7462)**

E P Ferris & Associates Inc ....E...... 614 299-2999
Columbus **(G-7485)**

Evans Mechwart Ham ....B...... 614 775-4500
New Albany **(G-14852)**

Feller Finch & Associates Inc ....E...... 419 893-3680
Maumee **(G-13791)**

Garcia Surveyors Inc ....E...... 419 877-0400
Whitehouse **(G-19448)**

Hammontree & Associates Ltd ....E...... 330 499-8817
Canton **(G-2336)**

Jack A Hamilton & Assoc Inc ....E...... 740 968-4947
Flushing **(G-10980)**

Jobes Henderson & Assoc Inc ....E...... 740 344-5451
Newark **(G-15045)**

Kleingers Group Inc ....E...... 513 779-7851
West Chester **(G-18957)**

KS Associates Inc ....D...... 440 365-4730
Elyria **(G-10523)**

Kucera International Inc ....D...... 440 975-4230
Willoughby **(G-19536)**

Land Design Consultants ....E...... 440 255-8463
Mentor **(G-14075)**

McGill Smith Punshon Inc ....E...... 513 759-0004
Cincinnati **(G-3987)**

McSteen & Associates Inc ....E...... 440 585-9800
Wickliffe **(G-19469)**

Penetrating R Ground ....E...... 419 843-9804
Toledo **(G-17975)**

Peterman Associates Inc ....E...... 419 722-9566
Findlay **(G-10953)**

Poggemeyer Design Group Inc ....E...... 419 748-7438
Mc Clure **(G-13893)**

Poggemeyer Design Group Inc ....C...... 419 244-8074
Bowling Green **(G-1746)**

R E Warner & Associates Inc ....D...... 440 835-9400
Westlake **(G-19395)**

Resource International Inc ....C...... 614 823-4949
Columbus **(G-8523)**

Sands Decker Cps Llc ....E...... 614 459-6992
Columbus **(G-8590)**

T J Neff Holdings Inc ....E...... 440 884-3100
Cleveland **(G-6494)**

Usic Locating Services LLC ....C...... 330 733-9393
Akron **(G-482)**

Wade Trim ....E...... 216 363-0300
Cleveland **(G-6648)**

8721 Accounting, Auditing & Bookkeeping Svcs

415 Group Inc ....E...... 330 492-0094
Canton **(G-2167)**

Advance Payroll Funding Ltd ....C...... 216 831-8900
Beachwood **(G-1026)**

Ahola Corporation ....D...... 440 717-7620
Brecksville **(G-1767)**

Akron-Canton Regional Airport ....E...... 330 499-4059
North Canton **(G-15186)**

▲ American Electric Pwr Svc Corp ....B...... 614 716-1000
Columbus **(G-6919)**

Apple Growth Partners Inc ....C...... 330 867-7350
Akron **(G-76)**

APS Medical Billing ....D...... 419 866-1804
Toledo **(G-17597)**

Archways Brookville Inc ....D...... 513 367-2649
Harrison **(G-11661)**

Arthur Middleton Capital Holdn ....E...... 330 966-9000
North Canton **(G-15190)**

Barnes Dennig & Co Ltd ....D...... 513 241-8313
Cincinnati **(G-3021)**

Barnes Wendling Cpas Inc ....E...... 216 566-9000
Cleveland **(G-5037)**

Bdo Usa LLP ....E...... 614 488-3126
Columbus **(G-7023)**

Bdo Usa LLP ....E...... 513 592-2400
Cincinnati **(G-3027)**

Bdo Usa LLP ....D...... 216 325-1700
Cleveland **(G-5046)**

Bdo Usa LLP ....D...... 330 668-9696
Akron **(G-91)**

Billing Connection Inc ....E...... 740 964-0043
Reynoldsburg **(G-16285)**

Bkd LLP ....D...... 513 621-8300
Cincinnati **(G-3053)**

Blue & Co LLC ....C...... 513 241-4507
Cincinnati **(G-3057)**

Bober Markey Fedorovich ....D...... 330 762-9785
Fairlawn **(G-10817)**

Bodine Perry LLC ....E...... 330 702-8100
Canfield **(G-2131)**

Brady Ware & Schoenfeld Inc ....E...... 614 885-7407
Columbus **(G-7059)**

Brady Ware & Schoenfeld Inc ....D...... 937 223-5247
Miamisburg **(G-14146)**

Brady Ware & Schoenfeld Inc ....D...... 614 825-6277
Columbus **(G-7060)**

Brott Mardis & Co ....E...... 330 762-5022
Akron **(G-111)**

Burke & Schindler Pllc ....E...... 859 344-8887
Cincinnati **(G-3091)**

C H Dean LLC ....D...... 937 222-9531
Beavercreek **(G-1136)**

Cassady Schiller & Associates ....E...... 513 483-6699
Blue Ash **(G-1519)**

Cbiz Accounting Tax ....D...... 330 668-6500
Akron **(G-120)**

Cbiz Med MGT Professionals Inc ....E...... 614 771-2222
Hilliard **(G-11754)**

Central Accounting Systems ....E...... 513 605-2700
Cincinnati **(G-3149)**

Change Hlth Prac MGT Solns Grp E 937 291-7850
Miamisburg *(G-14151)*

Chard Snyder & Associates LLC C 513 459-9997
Mason *(G-13553)*

Cincinnati Medical Billing Svc E 513 965-8041
Cincinnati *(G-3253)*

City of Wellston D 740 384-2428
Wellston *(G-18848)*

Ciulla Smith & Dale LLP E 440 884-2036
Cleveland *(G-5219)*

Ciuni & Panichi Inc D 216 831-7171
Cleveland *(G-5220)*

Clark Schaefer Hackett & Co E 937 399-2000
Springfield *(G-17008)*

Clark Schaefer Hackett & Co E 513 241-3111
Cincinnati *(G-3301)*

Clark Schaefer Hackett & Co E 216 672-5252
Cleveland *(G-5221)*

Clark Schaefer Hackett & Co D 419 243-0218
Toledo *(G-17662)*

Clark Schaefer Hackett & Co D 614 885-2208
Columbus *(G-7219)*

Cliftonlarsonallen LLP D 330 497-2000
Canton *(G-2259)*

Cliftonlarsonallen LLP E 419 244-3711
Toledo *(G-17665)*

Cliftonlarsonallen LLP E 330 376-0100
Akron *(G-144)*

Cohen & Company Ltd E 330 743-1040
Youngstown *(G-19994)*

Cohen & Company Ltd D 330 374-1040
Akron *(G-146)*

Compensation Programs of Ohio E 330 652-9821
Youngstown *(G-20005)*

Comprehensive Med Data MGT LLC D 614 717-9840
Powell *(G-16191)*

County of Lucas E 419 213-4500
Toledo *(G-17684)*

Crowe LLP C 614 469-0001
Columbus *(G-7396)*

Crowe LLP E 216 623-7500
Cleveland *(G-5382)*

Csh Group E 937 226-0070
Miamisburg *(G-14158)*

Defense Fin & Accounting Svc E 410 436-9740
Columbus *(G-7428)*

Defense Fin & Accounting Svc A 614 693-6700
Columbus *(G-7429)*

Deloitte & Touche LLP D 937 223-8821
Dayton *(G-9386)*

Deloitte & Touche LLP B 513 784-7100
Cincinnati *(G-3420)*

Deloitte & Touche LLP C 614 221-1000
Columbus *(G-7433)*

Deloitte & Touche LLP C 216 589-1300
Cleveland *(G-5415)*

Doctors Consulting Service E 614 793-1980
Dublin *(G-10201)*

E T Financial Service Inc E 937 716-1726
Trotwood *(G-18193)*

Elliott Davis LLC E 513 579-1717
Cincinnati *(G-3491)*

Emergency Medical Svcs Billing E 216 664-2598
Cleveland *(G-5474)*

Ernst & Young LLP D 216 861-5000
Cleveland *(G-5490)*

Ernst & Young LLP C 216 583-1823
Cleveland *(G-5491)*

Ernst & Young LLP C 614 224-5678
Columbus *(G-7531)*

Ernst & Young LLP C 513 612-1400
Cincinnati *(G-3515)*

Ernst & Young LLP C 419 244-8000
Toledo *(G-17717)*

Essex and Associates Inc E 937 432-1040
Dayton *(G-9418)*

Euclid Hospital C 216 445-6440
Euclid *(G-10634)*

Experis Finance Us LLC D 614 223-2300
Columbus *(G-7546)*

Experis Finance Us LLC E 216 621-0200
Seven Hills *(G-16675)*

Fehr Services LLC E 513 829-9333
Fairfield *(G-10728)*

First-Knox National Bank C 740 399-5500
Mount Vernon *(G-14766)*

Flagel Huber Flagel & Co E 937 299-3400
Moraine *(G-14659)*

Flex Fund Inc E 614 766-7000
Dublin *(G-10229)*

Foundations Hlth Solutions Inc D 440 793-0200
North Olmsted *(G-15289)*

Foxx & Company E 513 241-1616
Cincinnati *(G-3583)*

Fruth & Co E 419 435-8541
Fostoria *(G-11001)*

Gbq Holdings LLC E 614 221-1120
Columbus *(G-7652)*

Gilmore Jasion Mahler Ltd D 419 794-2000
Maumee *(G-13796)*

Grant Thornton LLP C 216 771-1400
Cleveland *(G-5623)*

Grant Thornton LLP D 513 762-5000
Cincinnati *(G-3634)*

Healthpro Medical Billing Inc D 419 223-2717
Lima *(G-12657)*

Hill Barth & King LLC E 330 758-8613
Canfield *(G-2140)*

Hill Barth & King LLC D 614 228-4000
Columbus *(G-7749)*

Hill Barth & King LLC E 330 747-1903
Canfield *(G-2141)*

Hobe Lcas Crtif Pub Accntants E 216 524-7167
Cleveland *(G-5698)*

Holbrook & Manter E 740 387-8620
Marion *(G-13425)*

Howard Wershbale & Co D 216 831-1200
Cleveland *(G-5720)*

Hr Butler LLC E 614 923-2900
Dublin *(G-10246)*

Humaserve Hr LLC E 513 605-3522
Cincinnati *(G-3740)*

Jennings & Associates E 740 369-4426
Delaware *(G-9991)*

Jones Cochenour & Co Inc E 740 653-9581
Lancaster *(G-12407)*

Julian & Grube Inc E 614 846-1899
Westerville *(G-19176)*

Kaiser Consulting LLC E 614 378-5361
Powell *(G-16200)*

Kennedy Group Enterprises Inc E 440 879-0078
Strongsville *(G-17320)*

Kent State University D 330 672-2607
Kent *(G-12242)*

Klingbeil Management Group Co E 614 220-8900
Columbus *(G-7911)*

Kpmg LLP C 513 421-6430
Cincinnati *(G-3887)*

Kpmg LLP C 614 249-2300
Columbus *(G-7925)*

Kpmg LLP C 216 696-9100
Cleveland *(G-5841)*

Lassiter Corporation E 216 391-4800
Cleveland *(G-5856)*

Lbk Health Care Inc E 937 296-1550
Bellbrook *(G-1339)*

Maloney + Novotny LLC D 216 363-0100
Cleveland *(G-5904)*

MBI Solutions Inc C 937 619-4000
Dayton *(G-9592)*

McCrate Delaet & Co E 937 492-3161
Sidney *(G-16786)*

MD Business Solutions Inc E 513 872-4500
Blue Ash *(G-1606)*

Meaden & Moore LLP D 216 241-3272
Cleveland *(G-5939)*

Medic Management Group LLC D 330 670-5316
Akron *(G-329)*

Medical Account Services Inc E 937 297-6072
Moraine *(G-14675)*

Medical Care PSC Inc E 513 281-4400
Cincinnati *(G-3993)*

Medical Care Reimbursement E 513 281-4400
Cincinnati *(G-3994)*

Medicount Management Inc E 513 772-4465
Cincinnati *(G-3997)*

Medigistics Inc D 614 430-5700
Columbus *(G-8054)*

Mellott & Mellott Pll E 513 241-2940
Cincinnati *(G-4004)*

Midwest Emergency Services LLC E 586 294-2700
Fairlawn *(G-10841)*

Mosley Pfundt & Glick Inc E 419 861-1120
Maumee *(G-13822)*

Murray Wlls Wndeln Rbnson Cpas E 937 773-6373
Piqua *(G-16015)*

Mutual Shareholder Svcs LLC E 440 922-0067
Broadview Heights *(G-1838)*

Nationwide Childrens Hospital E 330 253-5200
Akron *(G-343)*

Nms Inc Certif Pub Accountants E 440 286-5222
Chardon *(G-2706)*

Norman Jones Enlow & Co E 614 228-4000
Columbus *(G-8194)*

Northcoast Healthcare MGT C 216 591-2000
Beachwood *(G-1087)*

Ohio Bell Telephone Company A 216 822-3439
Cleveland *(G-6115)*

Ohio State University E 614 292-6831
Columbus *(G-8315)*

Omicron Investment Company LLC D 419 891-1040
Maumee *(G-13827)*

Patrick J Burke & Co E 513 455-8200
Cincinnati *(G-4212)*

Paychex Inc E 614 781-6143
Worthington *(G-19833)*

Paychex Inc C 330 342-0530
Hudson *(G-12002)*

Paychex Inc E 513 727-9182
Middletown *(G-14353)*

Paychex Inc D 800 939-2462
Lima *(G-12718)*

Paychex Inc D 614 210-0400
Dublin *(G-10306)*

Paycom Software Inc A 888 678-0796
Cincinnati *(G-4217)*

Paycor Inc E 614 985-6140
Worthington *(G-19834)*

Paycor Inc E 216 447-7913
Cleveland *(G-6184)*

Paycor Inc C 513 381-0505
Cincinnati *(G-4218)*

Payne Nickles & Co CPA E 419 668-2552
Norwalk *(G-15452)*

Payroll Services Unlimited E 740 653-9581
Lancaster *(G-12425)*

Pease & Associates LLC E 216 348-9600
Cleveland *(G-6188)*

Pioneer Physicians Networking E 330 633-6601
Tallmadge *(G-17484)*

Pricewaterhousecoopers LLP B 216 875-3000
Cleveland *(G-6235)*

Pricewaterhousecoopers LLP E 419 254-2500
Toledo *(G-17987)*

Pricewaterhousecoopers LLP D 513 723-4700
Cincinnati *(G-4278)*

Pricewaterhousecoopers LLP C 614 225-8700
Columbus *(G-8461)*

Promedica Physcn Cntinuum Svcs C 419 824-7200
Sylvania *(G-17444)*

Protiviti Inc E 216 696-6010
Cleveland *(G-6262)*

Quadax Inc E 330 759-4600
Youngstown *(G-20170)*

Quadax Inc C 440 777-6300
Middleburg Heights *(G-14256)*

Quadax Inc E 614 882-1200
Westerville *(G-19296)*

Radiology Assoc Canton Inc E 330 363-2842
Canton *(G-2450)*

REA & Associates Inc E 330 722-8222
Medina *(G-13992)*

REA & Associates Inc D 330 339-6651
New Philadelphia *(G-14977)*

REA & Associates Inc E 419 331-1040
Lima *(G-12792)*

REA & Associates Inc E 330 674-6055
Millersburg *(G-14489)*

REA & Associates Inc D 440 266-0077
New Philadelphia *(G-14978)*

REA & Associates Inc E 614 889-8725
Dublin *(G-10319)*

Real Property Management Inc E 614 766-6500
Dublin *(G-10320)*

Rehmann LLC D 419 865-8118
Toledo *(G-18000)*

REM-Ohio Inc D 330 644-9730
Coventry Township *(G-9041)*

Reynolds & Co Inc E 740 353-1040
Portsmouth *(G-16164)*

Richland Trust Company D 419 525-8700
Mansfield *(G-13240)*

Rlj Management Co Inc C 614 942-2020
Columbus *(G-8540)*

RSM US LLP C 937 298-0201
Moraine *(G-14693)*

RSM US LLP E 614 224-7722
Columbus *(G-8558)*

RSM US LLP C 216 523-1900
Cleveland *(G-6349)*

SIC

Schneider Downs & Co Inc ....D...... 614 621-4060
  Columbus (G-8602)
Schroedel Scullin & Bestic LLC ....E...... 330 533-1131
  Canfield (G-2157)
Sheakley-Uniservice Inc ....C...... 513 771-2277
  Cincinnati (G-4468)
Siegfried Group LLP ....E...... 216 522-1910
  Cleveland (G-6407)
Skoda Mntti Crtif Pub Accntnts ....D...... 440 449-6800
  Mayfield Village (G-13887)
Smithpearlman & Co ....E...... 513 248-9210
  Milford (G-14433)
Specialty Medical Services ....E...... 440 245-8010
  Lorain (G-12943)
Terry J Reppa & Associates ....E...... 440 888-8533
  Cleveland (G-6516)
The Peoples Bank Co Inc ....E...... 419 678-2385
  Coldwater (G-6765)
The Sheakley Group Inc ....E...... 513 771-2277
  Cincinnati (G-4596)
Thomas Packer & Co ....E...... 330 533-9777
  Canfield (G-2160)
Thomas Rosser ....C...... 614 890-2900
  Westerville (G-19301)
Top Echelon Contracting Inc ....B...... 330 454-3508
  Canton (G-2514)
Verizon Business Global LLC ....E...... 614 219-2317
  Hilliard (G-11826)
Vernon F Glaser & Associates ....E...... 937 298-5536
  Dayton (G-9854)
Village of Byesville ....E...... 740 685-5901
  Byesville (G-2026)
Vivial Media LLC ....E...... 513 768-7800
  Cincinnati (G-4763)
Walthall LLP ....E...... 216 573-2330
  Cleveland (G-6651)
Warren Bros & Sons Inc ....D...... 740 373-1430
  Marietta (G-13398)
Weber Obrien Ltd ....E...... 419 885-8338
  Sylvania (G-17463)
Whalen and Company Inc ....E...... 614 396-4200
  Worthington (G-19860)
Whitcomb & Hess Inc ....E...... 419 289-7007
  Ashland (G-699)
Whited Seigneur Sams & Rahe ....E...... 740 702-2600
  Chillicothe (G-2837)
William Vaughan Company ....D...... 419 891-1040
  Maumee (G-13869)
Wilson Shannon & Snow Inc ....E...... 740 345-6611
  Newark (G-15109)
Wulff & Associates CPA LLC ....E...... 513 245-1010
  Cincinnati (G-4809)
Zinner & Co ....E...... 216 831-0733
  Beachwood (G-1118)

8731 Commercial Physical & Biological Research

Akron Rubber Dev Lab Inc ....D...... 330 794-6600
  Akron (G-54)
Aktion Associates Incorporated ....E...... 419 893-7001
  Maumee (G-13747)
Alcatel-Lucent USA Inc ....B...... 614 860-2000
  Dublin (G-10124)
Alliance Imaging Inc ....C...... 330 493-5100
  Canton (G-2179)
American Showa Inc ....E...... 740 965-4040
  Sunbury (G-17382)
Antioch University ....D...... 937 769-1366
  Yellow Springs (G-19938)
Applied Medical Technology Inc ....E...... 440 717-4000
  Brecksville (G-1769)
Applied Research Assoc Inc ....E...... 937 435-1016
  Columbus (G-6959)
Applied Research Assoc Inc ....E...... 937 873-8166
  Dayton (G-9235)
Applied Sciences Inc ....E...... 937 766-2020
  Cedarville (G-2579)
Arthur G James Cance ....A...... 614 293-4878
  Columbus (G-6972)
ASC Group Inc ....E...... 614 268-2514
  Columbus (G-6976)
Asymmetric Technologies LLC ....E...... 614 725-5310
  Columbus (G-6987)
Atk Space Systems Inc ....E...... 937 490-4121
  Beavercreek (G-1205)
Azimuth Corporation ....E...... 937 256-8571
  Beavercreek Township (G-1243)
BASF Catalysts LLC ....D...... 216 360-5005
  Cleveland (G-5039)

▲ Battle Memorial Institute ....A...... 614 424-6424
  Columbus (G-7020)
Battelle Memorial Institute ....D...... 937 258-6717
  Beavercreek (G-1129)
Battelle Memorial Institute ....B...... 614 424-5435
  West Jefferson (G-19104)
Battelle Memorial Institute ....B...... 614 424-5435
  West Jefferson (G-19105)
Biosortia Pharmaceuticals Inc ....E...... 614 636-4850
  Dublin (G-10146)
◆ Borchers Americas Inc ....D...... 440 899-2950
  Westlake (G-19323)
Bridgestone Research LLC ....A...... 330 379-7570
  Akron (G-106)
Brilligent Solutions Inc ....E...... 937 879-4148
  Fairborn (G-10664)
Center For Eating Disorders ....E...... 614 896-8222
  Columbus (G-7153)
Champaign Premium Grn Growers ....E...... 937 826-3003
  Milford Center (G-14444)
▲ Champion Spark Plug Company ....E...... 419 535-2567
  Toledo (G-17647)
Charles River Laboratories Inc ....C...... 419 647-4196
  Spencerville (G-16955)
Charles Rver Labs Clveland Inc ....D...... 216 332-1665
  Cleveland (G-5169)
Chemimage Filter Tech LLC ....E...... 330 686-2829
  Stow (G-17195)
Childrens Hospital Medical Ctr ....A...... 513 636-4200
  Cincinnati (G-3190)
Circle Prime Manufacturing ....D...... 330 923-0019
  Cuyahoga Falls (G-9079)
Cleveland F E S Center ....D...... 216 231-3257
  Cleveland (G-5254)
Concord Biosciences LLC ....D...... 440 357-3200
  Painesville (G-15704)
Conwed Plas Acquisition V LLC ....D...... 440 926-2607
  Akron (G-157)
Ctl Engineering Inc ....C...... 614 276-8123
  Columbus (G-7404)
Curtiss-Wright Controls ....E...... 937 252-5601
  Fairborn (G-10667)
Defense Research Assoc Inc ....E...... 937 431-1644
  Dayton (G-9169)
Edison Biotechnology Institute ....E...... 740 593-4713
  Athens (G-779)
Edison Welding Institute Inc ....C...... 614 688-5000
  Columbus (G-7502)
EMD Millipore Corporation ....C...... 513 631-0445
  Norwood (G-15462)
Ensafe Inc ....E...... 513 621-7233
  West Chester (G-18918)
Firstenergy Nuclear Oper Co ....D...... 440 604-9836
  Cleveland (G-5539)
◆ Flexsys America LP ....D...... 330 666-4111
  Akron (G-225)
Fram Group Operations LLC ....D...... 419 661-6700
  Perrysburg (G-15867)
Ftech R&D North America Inc ....D...... 937 339-2777
  Troy (G-18202)
◆ Guild Associates Inc ....D...... 614 798-8215
  Dublin (G-10236)
▲ Heraeus Precious Metals North ....E...... 937 264-1000
  Vandalia (G-18525)
Hydrogeologic Inc ....E...... 330 463-3303
  Hudson (G-11984)
Icon Government ....B...... 330 278-2343
  Hinckley (G-11859)
Illumination Research Inc ....E...... 513 774-9531
  Mason (G-13597)
Kemron Environmental Svcs Inc ....D...... 740 373-4071
  Marietta (G-13342)
Kenmore Research Company ....D...... 330 297-1407
  Ravenna (G-16248)
Laboratory Corporation America ....A...... 614 336-3993
  Dublin (G-10267)
Leidos Inc ....E...... 330 405-9810
  Twinsburg (G-18291)
Leidos Inc ....D...... 937 431-2270
  Beavercreek (G-1164)
Leidos Inc ....B...... 858 826-6000
  Columbus (G-7965)
Leidos Inc ....B...... 937 431-2220
  Beavercreek (G-1165)
Leidos Engineering LLC ....D...... 330 405-9810
  Twinsburg (G-18292)
Leidos Technical Services Inc ....D...... 513 672-8400
  West Chester (G-19063)
Lindner Clinical Trial Center ....E...... 513 585-1777
  Cincinnati (G-3935)

Lubrizol Advanced Mtls Inc ....E...... 440 933-0400
  Avon Lake (G-923)
Lyondell Chemical Company ....D...... 513 530-4000
  Cincinnati (G-3953)
Medpace Inc ....A...... 513 579-9911
  Cincinnati (G-4000)
Midwest Optoelectronics LLC ....C...... 419 724-0565
  Toledo (G-17916)
Modern Tech Solutions Inc ....D...... 937 426-9025
  Beavercreek Township (G-1254)
Morris Technologies Inc ....C...... 513 733-1611
  Cincinnati (G-4075)
Mp Biomedicals LLC ....C...... 440 337-1200
  Solon (G-16873)
Muskingum Starlight Industries ....D...... 740 453-4622
  Zanesville (G-20342)
Nationwide Childrens Hospital ....C...... 614 722-2700
  Columbus (G-8143)
Natural Resources Ohio Dept ....E...... 614 265-6852
  Columbus (G-8163)
North Amercn Science Assoc Inc ....C...... 419 666-9455
  Northwood (G-15401)
North Amercn Science Assoc Inc ....C...... 419 666-9455
  Northwood (G-15402)
Nsa Technologies LLC ....C...... 330 576-4600
  Akron (G-353)
Ohio State University ....A...... 330 263-3700
  Wooster (G-19754)
Ohio State University ....C...... 614 688-8220
  Columbus (G-8331)
Ohio State University ....E...... 330 263-3725
  Canton (G-2431)
Olon Ricerca Bioscience LLC ....D...... 440 357-3300
  Painesville (G-15730)
Omnova Solutions Inc ....D...... 330 794-6300
  Akron (G-364)
Owens Corning Sales LLC ....B...... 740 587-3562
  Granville (G-11347)
Pen Brands LLC ....E...... 216 447-1199
  Brooklyn Heights (G-1878)
Phycal Inc ....E...... 440 460-2477
  Cleveland (G-6207)
▲ Plastic Technologies Inc ....D...... 419 867-5400
  Holland (G-11905)
Potter Technologies LLC ....D...... 419 380-8404
  Toledo (G-17983)
PPG Architectural Finishes Inc ....B...... 440 826-5100
  Strongsville (G-17339)
Promerus LLC ....E...... 440 922-0300
  Brecksville (G-1799)
Q Labs LLC ....C...... 513 471-1300
  Cincinnati (G-4309)
Quest Global Services-Na Inc ....D...... 513 563-8855
  Cincinnati (G-4327)
Quest Global Services-Na Inc ....D...... 860 787-1600
  Cincinnati (G-4328)
▲ R & D Nestle Center Inc ....C...... 937 642-7015
  Marysville (G-13524)
R & D Nestle Center Inc ....D...... 440 349-5757
  Solon (G-16888)
Renovo Neural Inc ....E...... 216 445-4202
  Cleveland (G-6307)
Rogosin Institute Inc ....E...... 937 374-3116
  Xenia (G-19924)
Schneller LLC ....D...... 330 673-1299
  Kent (G-12258)
Sensation Research ....E...... 513 602-1611
  Maineville (G-13118)
Steiner Eoptics Inc ....D...... 937 426-2341
  Miamisburg (G-14226)
Stembanc Inc ....E...... 440 332-4279
  Chardon (G-2717)
Sunpower Inc ....D...... 740 594-2221
  Athens (G-804)
Syneos Health LLC ....C...... 513 381-5550
  Cincinnati (G-4561)
Sytronics Inc ....E...... 937 431-6100
  Beavercreek (G-1189)
Terracon Consultants Inc ....E...... 614 863-3113
  Gahanna (G-11150)
U S Laboratories Inc ....E...... 440 248-1223
  Cleveland (G-6558)
Ues Inc ....C...... 937 426-6900
  Beavercreek (G-1190)
University of Cincinnati ....E...... 513 556-5511
  Cincinnati (G-4709)
Velocys Inc ....D...... 614 733-3300
  Plain City (G-16071)
Work Connections Intl LLC ....E...... 419 448-4655
  Tiffin (G-17547)

Wyle Laboratories Inc..................C...... 937 320-2712
Beavercreek *(G-1242)*

Zin Technologies Inc ....C...... 440 625-2200
Middleburg Heights *(G-14267)*

8732 Commercial Economic, Sociological & Educational Research

8451 LLC *(G-2886)*.......................C...... 513 632-1020
Cincinnati *(G-2886)*

AK Steel Corporation....................C...... 513 425-6541
Middletown *(G-14287)*

Alphamicron Inc...........................E...... 330 676-0648
Kent *(G-12213)*

Applied Research Assoc Inc..........E...... 937 873-8166
Dayton *(G-9235)*

Assistnce In Mktg Columbus Inc....E...... 614 583-2100
Columbus *(G-6981)*

Bionetics Corporation ....E...... 757 873-0900
Heath *(G-11702)*

Burke Inc....................................D...... 513 576-5700
Milford *(G-14374)*

Burke Inc....................................C...... 513 241-5663
Cincinnati *(G-3090)*

Business Research Services ....E...... 216 831-5200
Cleveland *(G-5106)*

Canton Med Educatn Foundation.........D...... 330 363-6783
Canton *(G-2237)*

▼ Convergys Cstmer MGT Group Inc..B... 513 723-6104
Cincinnati *(G-3358)*

Creative Marketing Enterprises ......D...... 419 867-4444
Sylvania *(G-17416)*

Deskey Associates Inc ....D...... 513 721-6800
Cincinnati *(G-3423)*

Directions Research Inc ....C...... 513 651-2990
Cincinnati *(G-3432)*

Fields Marketing Research Inc ....D...... 513 821-6266
Cincinnati *(G-3545)*

Freedonia Publishing LLC ....D...... 440 684-9600
Cleveland *(G-5577)*

Friedman-Swift Associates Inc ......D...... 513 772-9200
Cincinnati *(G-3595)*

Gfk Custom Research LLC ....C...... 513 562-1507
Blue Ash *(G-1568)*

Great Lakes Mktg Assoc Inc ....E...... 419 534-4700
Toledo *(G-17770)*

Honda R&D Americas Inc ....E...... 937 644-0439
Raymond *(G-16275)*

I T E LLC ....D...... 513 576-6200
Loveland *(G-13000)*

Icon Government ....B...... 330 278-2343
Hinckley *(G-11859)*

Illumination Research Inc ....E...... 513 774-9531
Mason *(G-13597)*

Infocision Management Corp ....B...... 330 544-1400
Youngstown *(G-20081)*

Integer Holdings Corporation ....B...... 216 937-2800
Cleveland *(G-5756)*

Intelliq Health ....D...... 513 489-8838
Cincinnati *(G-3772)*

Ipsos-Asi LLC ....D...... 513 872-4300
Cincinnati *(G-3785)*

Ipsos-Insight LLC.........................C...... 513 552-1100
Cincinnati *(G-3786)*

Jobsohio ....D...... 614 224-6446
Columbus *(G-7860)*

Klein Associates Inc ....E...... 937 873-8166
Fairborn *(G-10679)*

Leidos Inc ....B...... 937 431-2220
Beavercreek *(G-1165)*

Lindner Clinical Trial Center ....E...... 513 585-1777
Cincinnati *(G-3935)*

Mahoning Youngstown Community....D...... 330 747-7921
Youngstown *(G-20112)*

Maritzcx Research LLC ....B...... 419 725-4000
Maumee *(G-13815)*

Market Inquiry Llc ....E...... 513 794-1088
Blue Ash *(G-1603)*

Marketing Research Svcs Inc ....D...... 513 772-7580
Cincinnati *(G-3970)*

Marketing Research Svcs Inc ....D...... 513 579-1555
Cincinnati *(G-3971)*

Marketvision Research Inc.............E...... 513 603-6340
West Chester *(G-18969)*

Marketvision Research Inc.............D...... 513 791-3100
Blue Ash *(G-1604)*

National Rgstry Emrgncy Mdcl..........E...... 614 888-4484
Columbus *(G-8138)*

Nielsen Consumer Insights Inc ....D...... 513 489-9000
Blue Ash *(G-1620)*

Northrop Grumman Technical ....C...... 937 320-3100
Beavercreek Township *(G-1255)*

Ohio State University.....................D...... 740 376-7431
Marietta *(G-13364)*

Ohio State University.....................D...... 740 593-2657
Athens *(G-794)*

Ohio State University.....................D...... 614 292-4353
Columbus *(G-8316)*

Ohio State University.....................D...... 614 442-7300
Columbus *(G-8320)*

Ohio State University.....................E...... 614 292-9404
Columbus *(G-8341)*

Ohio State University.....................D...... 614 292-5491
Columbus *(G-8305)*

Opinions Ltd...............................E...... 440 893-0300
Chagrin Falls *(G-2652)*

Orc International Inc.....................E...... 419 893-0029
Maumee *(G-13829)*

Osborn Marketing Research Corp........E...... 440 871-1047
Westlake *(G-19389)*

Parker Marketing Research LLC.......E...... 513 248-8100
Milford *(G-14418)*

Power Management Inc ....E...... 937 222-2909
Dayton *(G-9701)*

Q Fact Marketing Research Inc ....C...... 513 891-2271
Cincinnati *(G-4308)*

Ritter & Associates Inc ....E...... 419 535-5757
Maumee *(G-13846)*

Scanner Applications LLC ....E...... 513 248-5588
Milford *(G-14429)*

SSS Consulting Inc ....E...... 937 259-1200
Dayton *(G-9788)*

Sytronics Inc ....E...... 937 431-6100
Beavercreek *(G-1189)*

Tns North America Inc..................D...... 513 621-7887
Cincinnati *(G-4610)*

University of Cincinnati.................E...... 513 556-4054
Cincinnati *(G-4712)*

Various Views Research Inc ....D...... 513 489-9000
Blue Ash *(G-1675)*

Wolf Sensory Inc.........................E...... 513 891-9100
Blue Ash *(G-1680)*

8733 Noncommercial Research Organizations

Advantage Aerotech Inc ....E...... 614 759-8329
Columbus *(G-6875)*

American Cancer Society East........B...... 888 227-6446
Dublin *(G-10129)*

American Heart Assn Ohio Vly ....E...... 216 791-7500
Cleveland *(G-4953)*

American Institute Research ....B...... 614 221-8717
Columbus *(G-6926)*

American Institute Research ....B...... 614 310-8982
Columbus *(G-6927)*

Applied Optimization Inc................C...... 937 431-5100
Beavercreek *(G-1125)*

Applied Research Solutions Inc ....D...... 937 912-6100
Beavercreek *(G-1202)*

Arthur G James Cance ....A...... 614 293-4878
Columbus *(G-6972)*

ASC Group Inc ....E...... 614 268-2514
Columbus *(G-6976)*

Assured Information SEC Inc ....D...... 937 427-9720
Beavercreek *(G-1127)*

Barrett Center For Cancer Prev ....D...... 513 558-3200
Cincinnati *(G-3022)*

Benjamin Rose Institute................D...... 216 791-8000
Cleveland *(G-5055)*

Charles River Labs Ashland LLC ....C...... 419 282-8700
Ashland *(G-667)*

Childrens Hosp Med Ctr Akron.........E...... 330 633-2055
Tallmadge *(G-17471)*

Childrens Hospital Medical Ctr ....E...... 513 636-6100
Cincinnati *(G-3189)*

Childrens Hospital Medical Ctr ....A...... 513 636-4200
Cincinnati *(G-3190)*

Childrens Hospital Medical Ctr ....E...... 513 636-6400
Fairfield *(G-10708)*

Childrens Hospital Medical Ctr ....E...... 513 636-6800
Mason *(G-13554)*

Cincinnti Educ & RES For Vetrn ....E...... 513 861-3100
Cincinnati *(G-3364)*

Cleveland VA Medical Research ....E...... 216 791-2300
Cleveland *(G-5295)*

Cornerstone Research Group Inc ....E...... 937 320-1877
Miamisburg *(G-14155)*

Dayton Foundation Inc..................E...... 937 222-0410
Dayton *(G-9365)*

Jjr Solutions LLC ....E...... 937 912-0288
Beavercreek *(G-1159)*

Kendle International Inc ....E...... 513 763-1414
Cincinnati *(G-3858)*

Macaulay-Brown Inc ....B...... 937 426-3421
Beavercreek *(G-1227)*

Mp Biomedicals LLC.....................C...... 440 337-1200
Solon *(G-16873)*

Nationwide Childrens Hospital ....A...... 614 722-2000
Columbus *(G-8146)*

Ofeq Institute Inc........................E...... 440 943-1497
Wickliffe *(G-19472)*

Ohio Aerospace Institute ....D...... 440 962-3000
Cleveland *(G-6114)*

Ohio State University.....................E...... 614 292-1681
Columbus *(G-8308)*

Ohio State University.....................B...... 330 263-3701
Wooster *(G-19755)*

Ohio State University.....................C...... 614 292-5990
Columbus *(G-8335)*

Ohio Technical College Inc ....E...... 216 881-1700
Cleveland *(G-6124)*

Prologue Research Intl Inc ....D...... 614 324-1500
Columbus *(G-8472)*

Quasonix Inc ....E...... 513 942-1287
West Chester *(G-18988)*

Research Institute At Nation ....E...... 614 722-2700
Columbus *(G-8518)*

Riverside Research Institute...........D...... 937 431-3810
Beavercreek *(G-1183)*

Rogosin Institute Inc ....E...... 937 374-3116
Xenia *(G-19924)*

Sunpower Inc ....D...... 740 594-2221
Athens *(G-804)*

Truenorth Cultural Arts ....E...... 440 949-5200
Avon Lake *(G-928)*

United States Dept of Navy ....E...... 937 938-3926
Dayton *(G-9189)*

Universities Space Res Assn ....E...... 216 368-0750
Cleveland *(G-6584)*

University Hospitals ....D...... 216 844-8797
Cleveland *(G-6590)*

University of Dayton ....C...... 937 229-2113
Dayton *(G-9839)*

University of Dayton ....B...... 937 229-3822
Dayton *(G-9840)*

▲ University of Dayton ....A...... 937 229-2919
Dayton *(G-9837)*

US Dept of the Air Force ....B...... 937 255-5150
Dayton *(G-9191)*

Wright State University ....E...... 937 298-4331
Kettering *(G-12304)*

8734 Testing Laboratories

Acuren Inspection Inc ....E...... 513 671-7073
Cincinnati *(G-2906)*

Advanced Testing Lab Inc ....C...... 513 489-8447
Blue Ash *(G-1498)*

Advanced Testing MGT Group Inc ....C...... 513 489-8447
Blue Ash *(G-1499)*

Agrana Fruit Us Inc ....C...... 937 693-3821
Botkins *(G-1706)*

Akzo Nobel Coatings Inc................C...... 614 294-3361
Columbus *(G-6890)*

Als Group Usa Corp ....E...... 513 733-5336
Blue Ash *(G-1503)*

Als Services Usa Corp..................D...... 513 582-8277
West Chester *(G-18864)*

Als Services Usa Corp..................E...... 604 998-5311
Cleveland *(G-4943)*

Analytical Pace Services LLC ....E...... 937 832-8242
Englewood *(G-10578)*

Aqua Tech Envmtl Labs Inc ....E...... 740 389-5991
Marion *(G-13404)*

Atc Group Services LLC ....D...... 513 771-2112
Cincinnati *(G-2996)*

Balancing Company Inc ....E...... 937 898-9111
Vandalia *(G-18506)*

Barr Engineering Incorporated ....E...... 614 714-0299
Columbus *(G-7019)*

Bayless Pathmark Inc ....E...... 440 274-2494
Cleveland *(G-5044)*

Bionetics Corporation ....E...... 757 873-0900
Heath *(G-11702)*

Bowser-Morner Inc ....D...... 419 691-4800
Toledo *(G-17621)*

Brookside Laboratories Inc ....E...... 419 977-2766
New Bremen *(G-14885)*

Bwi Chassis Dynamics NA Inc ....E...... 937 455-5230
Moraine *(G-14629)*

SIC

Bwi North America Inc ....E 937 212-2892
  Moraine *(G-14630)*

Certified Pressure Testing LLC ....E 740 374-2071
  Marietta *(G-13318)*

Chemsultants International Inc ....E 440 974-3080
  Mentor *(G-14029)*

Cliff North Consultants Inc ....E 513 251-4930
  Cincinnati *(G-3306)*

Clinton-Carvell Inc ....E 614 351-8858
  Columbus *(G-7229)*

Csa America Inc ....D 216 524-4990
  Cleveland *(G-5384)*

Ctl Engineering Inc ....C 614 276-8123
  Columbus *(G-7404)*

Curtiss-Wright Flow Control ....D 513 528-7900
  Cincinnati *(G-2847)*

Curtiss-Wright Flow Ctrl Corp ....D 513 528-7900
  Cincinnati *(G-2848)*

Daymark Food Safety Systems ....C 419 353-2458
  Bowling Green *(G-1729)*

Electro-Analytical Inc ....E 440 951-3514
  Mentor *(G-14043)*

Element Cincinnati ....E 513 984-4112
  Fairfield *(G-10722)*

Element Mtls Tech Cncnnati Inc ....E 513 771-2536
  Fairfield *(G-10723)*

Element Mtrls Tchnlgy Hntngtn ....E 216 643-1208
  Cleveland *(G-5472)*

Emlab P&K LLC ....D 330 497-9396
  North Canton *(G-15199)*

Envirite of Ohio Inc ....E 330 456-6238
  Canton *(G-2302)*

Enviroscience Inc ....C 330 688-0111
  Stow *(G-17202)*

Firstenergy Nuclear Oper Co ....D 440 604-9836
  Cleveland *(G-5539)*

Food Safety Net Services Ltd ....E 614 274-2070
  Columbus *(G-7601)*

Fram Group Operations LLC ....D 419 661-6700
  Perrysburg *(G-15867)*

General Electric Company ....C 937 587-2631
  Peebles *(G-15801)*

Gentherm Medical LLC ....D 513 326-5252
  Cincinnati *(G-3618)*

Glowe-Smith Industrial Inc ....C 330 638-5088
  Vienna *(G-18579)*

▲ Godfrey & Wing Inc ....E 330 562-1440
  Aurora *(G-828)*

Grace Consulting Inc ....E 440 647-6672
  Wellington *(G-18841)*

Grl Engineers Inc ....E 216 831-6131
  Solon *(G-16855)*

High Voltage Maintenance Corp ....E 937 278-0811
  Dayton *(G-9496)*

Idexx Laboratories Inc ....D 330 629-6076
  Youngstown *(G-20075)*

Intertek Testing Svcs NA Inc ....E 614 279-8090
  Columbus *(G-7840)*

Isomedix Operations Inc ....E 614 836-5757
  Groveport *(G-11521)*

Isomedix Operations Inc ....C 440 354-2600
  Mentor *(G-14064)*

J T Adams Co ....E 216 641-3290
  Cleveland *(G-5773)*

Juice Technologies Inc ....E 800 518-5576
  Columbus *(G-7875)*

Kemron Environmental Svcs Inc ....D 740 373-4071
  Marietta *(G-13342)*

Kenmore Research Company ....D 330 297-1407
  Ravenna *(G-16248)*

Landing Gear Test Facility ....E 937 255-5740
  Dayton *(G-9180)*

Lexamed ....E 419 693-5307
  Toledo *(G-17852)*

McCloy Engineering LLC ....E 513 984-4112
  Fairfield *(G-10752)*

Mercy Health ....E 330 841-4406
  Warren *(G-18729)*

Metcut Research Associates Inc ....D 513 271-5100
  Cincinnati *(G-4041)*

Mistras Group Inc ....D 419 836-5904
  Millbury *(G-14450)*

Mistras Group Inc ....E 740 788-9188
  Heath *(G-11705)*

MPW Industrial Services Inc ....E 740 345-2431
  Newark *(G-15077)*

National Testing Laboratories ....E 440 449-2525
  Cleveland *(G-6049)*

Nestle Usa Inc ....D 614 526-5300
  Dublin *(G-10288)*

North Amercn Science Assoc Inc ....C 419 666-9455
  Northwood *(G-15401)*

Northast Ohio Rgonal Sewer Dst ....C 216 641-6000
  Cleveland *(G-6084)*

Nsl Analytical Services Inc ....D 216 438-5200
  Cleveland *(G-6105)*

Nucon International Inc ....E 614 846-5710
  Columbus *(G-8213)*

Ohio Department Transportation ....D 614 275-1324
  Columbus *(G-8242)*

Ohio Rver Vly Wtr Snttion Comm ......E 513 231-7719
  Cincinnati *(G-4158)*

Omega Laboratories Inc ....D 330 628-5748
  Mogadore *(G-14553)*

Pace Analytical Services Inc ....E 614 486-5421
  Dublin *(G-10303)*

▲ Plastic Technologies Inc ....D 419 867-5400
  Holland *(G-11905)*

Professional Service Inds Inc ....E 614 876-8000
  Columbus *(G-8470)*

Q Labs LLC ....C 513 471-1300
  Cincinnati *(G-4309)*

Raitz Inc ....E 513 769-1200
  Cincinnati *(G-4336)*

Reid Asset Management Company .....E 216 642-3223
  Cleveland *(G-6298)*

Resource International Inc ....E 614 823-4949
  Columbus *(G-8523)*

Rev1 Ventures ....E 614 487-3700
  Columbus *(G-8529)*

S D Myers Inc ....C 330 630-7000
  Tallmadge *(G-17486)*

Sample Machining Inc ....E 937 258-3338
  Dayton *(G-9750)*

SD Myers LLC ....C 330 630-7000
  Tallmadge *(G-17487)*

Sensation Research ....E 513 602-1611
  Maineville *(G-13118)*

Shaw Group Inc ....A 937 593-2022
  Bellefontaine *(G-1365)*

Silliker Laboratories Ohio Inc ....E 614 486-0150
  Columbus *(G-8640)*

Smithers Quality Assessments ....E 330 762-4231
  Akron *(G-433)*

Smithers Rapra Inc ....E 330 297-1495
  Ravenna *(G-16268)*

Smithers Rapra Inc ....C 330 762-7441
  Akron *(G-434)*

Smithers Tire & Auto Testng TX ....E 330 762-7441
  Akron *(G-435)*

Standard Laboratories Inc ....E 513 422-1088
  Middletown *(G-14331)*

▲ Standards Testing Labs Inc ....D 330 833-8548
  Massillon *(G-13731)*

Summit Environmental Tech Inc ....D 330 253-8211
  Cuyahoga Falls *(G-9127)*

Testamerica Laboratories Inc ....C 800 456-9396
  North Canton *(G-15237)*

Testamerica Laboratories Inc ....E 513 733-5700
  Cincinnati *(G-4587)*

Testamerica Laboratories Inc ....D 937 294-6856
  Moraine *(G-14702)*

Tool Testing Lab Inc ....E 937 898-5696
  Tipp City *(G-17570)*

Tool Testing Lab Inc ....D 937 898-5696
  Tipp City *(G-17571)*

Transportation Ohio Department ....E 614 275-1300
  Columbus *(G-8774)*

US Inspection Services Inc ....E 937 660-9879
  Dayton *(G-9844)*

US Inspection Services Inc ....E 513 671-7073
  Cincinnati *(G-4741)*

US Tubular Products Inc ....D 330 832-1734
  North Lawrence *(G-15260)*

Wallover Enterprises Inc ....E 440 238-9250
  Strongsville *(G-17358)*

Wyle Laboratories Inc ....E 937 912-3470
  Beavercreek *(G-1201)*

X-Ray Industries Inc ....E 216 642-0100
  Cleveland *(G-6696)*

Yoder Industries Inc ....C 937 278-5769
  Dayton *(G-9890)*

8741 Management Services

3c Technologies Inc ....D 419 868-8999
  Holland *(G-11868)*

Acuity Healthcare LP ....D 740 283-7499
  Steubenville *(G-17139)*

Advocare Inc ....D 216 514-1451
  Cleveland *(G-4905)*

Aecom Global II LLC ....D 216 523-5600
  Cleveland *(G-4910)*

Aim Integrated Logistics Inc ....B 330 759-0438
  Girard *(G-11281)*

Allcan Global Services Inc ....E 513 825-1655
  Cincinnati *(G-2924)*

Alternative Home Health Care ....E 513 794-0555
  Cincinnati *(G-2935)*

American Hospitality Group Inc ....A 330 336-6684
  Wadsworth *(G-18589)*

American Med ....B 330 762-8999
  Akron *(G-69)*

Ameridian Specialty Services ....E 513 769-0150
  Cincinnati *(G-2952)*

Apollo Property Management LLC ......E 216 468-0050
  Beachwood *(G-1030)*

Arthur Middleton Capital Holdn ....A 330 966-9000
  North Canton *(G-15190)*

Atlantic Hospitality & MGT LLC ....E 216 454-5450
  Beachwood *(G-1031)*

Aultcomp Inc ....E 330 830-4919
  Massillon *(G-13664)*

Authentic Food LLC ....E 740 369-0377
  Delaware *(G-9954)*

◆ Babcock & Wilcox Company ....A 330 753-4511
  Barberton *(G-944)*

Bailey Associates ....C 614 760-7752
  Columbus *(G-7012)*

Balanced Care Corporation ....E 330 908-1166
  Northfield *(G-15373)*

Balanced Care Corporation ....E 937 372-7205
  Xenia *(G-19892)*

Baxter Hodell Donnelly Preston ....C 513 271-1634
  Cincinnati *(G-3025)*

Benchmark Technologies Corp ....E 419 843-6691
  Toledo *(G-17611)*

Benjamin Rose Institute ....D 216 791-3580
  Cleveland *(G-5056)*

Bernard Busson Builder ....E 330 929-4926
  Akron *(G-95)*

Bistro Off Broadway ....E 937 316-5000
  Greenville *(G-11366)*

Blanchard Valley Health System ....A 419 423-4500
  Findlay *(G-10871)*

Blanchard Valley Health System ....D 419 424-3000
  Findlay *(G-10872)*

Bon Appetit Management Co ....E 614 823-1880
  Westerville *(G-19227)*

Bravo Wellness LLC ....C 216 658-9500
  Cleveland *(G-5075)*

Bridgepoint Risk MGT LLC ....E 419 794-1075
  Maumee *(G-13766)*

Brown Co Ed Service Center ....D 937 378-6118
  Georgetown *(G-11263)*

Camden Management Inc ....E 513 383-1635
  Cincinnati *(G-3110)*

Cameron Mitchell Rest LLC ....E 614 621-3663
  Columbus *(G-7108)*

◆ Cardinal Health Inc ....A 614 757-5000
  Dublin *(G-10156)*

Cardinal Health Inc ....D 614 497-9552
  Obetz *(G-15524)*

Carespring Health Care MGT LLC ......E 513 943-4000
  Loveland *(G-12981)*

Careworks of Ohio Inc ....B 614 792-1085
  Dublin *(G-10161)*

Cargotec Services USA Inc ....D 419 482-6000
  Perrysburg *(G-15846)*

Carington Health Systems ....E 513 682-2700
  Hamilton *(G-11573)*

Cbre Heery Inc ....E 216 781-1313
  Cleveland *(G-5143)*

Cdc Management Co ....C 614 781-0216
  Columbus *(G-7146)*

Cedarwood Construction Company .....D 330 836-9971
  Akron *(G-121)*

CFM Religion Pubg Group LLC ....E 513 931-4050
  Cincinnati *(G-3162)*

Chemstress Consultant Company ....C 330 535-5591
  Akron *(G-126)*

Christian Benevolent Assn ....B 513 931-5000
  Cincinnati *(G-3212)*

Chu Management Co Inc ....E 330 725-4571
  Medina *(G-13919)*

Cincinnati Health Network Inc ....E 513 961-0600
  Cincinnati *(G-3248)*

City of Youngstown ....B 330 742-8700
  Youngstown *(G-19991)*

Clermont North East School Dst ....E 513 625-8283
  Batavia *(G-990)*

Clevelan Clinic Hlth Sys W Reg..........B....... 216 518-3444
Cleveland (G-5225)
Clevelan Clinic Hlth Sys W Reg..........A....... 216 476-7000
Cleveland (G-5226)
Clevelan Clinic Hlth Sys W Reg..........E....... 216 476-7606
Cleveland (G-5227)
Clevelan Clinic Hlth Sys W Reg..........D....... 216 476-7007
Cleveland (G-5228)
▲ Cleveland Clinic Foundation..........A....... 216 636-8335
Cleveland (G-5236)
Cleveland Clinic Foundation..........D....... 419 609-2812
Sandusky (G-16587)
Cleveland Health Network..........E....... 216 986-1100
Cleveland (G-5257)
Clk Multi-Family MGT LLC..........C....... 614 891-0011
Columbus (G-7232)
Cmp I Owner-T LLC..........E....... 614 764-9393
Dublin (G-10178)
Cmp I Owner-T LLC..........E....... 614 436-7070
Columbus (G-7237)
Cmp I Owner-T LLC..........E....... 513 733-4334
Blue Ash (G-1532)
Coal Services Inc..........D....... 740 795-5220
Powhatan Point (G-16214)
Collins Assoc Tchncal Svcs Inc..........C....... 740 574-2320
Wheelersburg (G-19430)
Colonial Senior Services Inc..........C....... 513 856-8600
Hamilton (G-11582)
Colonial Senior Services Inc..........C....... 513 867-4006
Hamilton (G-11583)
Colonial Senior Services Inc..........C....... 513 844-8004
Hamilton (G-11584)
Communicare Health Svcs Inc..........E....... 513 530-1654
Blue Ash (G-1535)
Community Mercy Hlth Partners..........C....... 937 653-5432
Urbana (G-18429)
Comprehensive Health Care..........A....... 440 329-7500
Elyria (G-10492)
Comprehensive Managed Care Sys..........E....... 513 533-0021
Cincinnati (G-3347)
Constellations Enterprise LLC..........C....... 330 740-8208
Youngstown (G-20010)
Consulate Management Co LLC..........A....... 419 683-3436
Crestline (G-9051)
Contech-Gdcg..........E....... 937 426-3577
Beavercreek (G-1212)
Continntal Mssage Solution Inc..........D....... 614 224-4534
Columbus (G-7364)
Cook Paving and Cnstr Co..........E....... 216 267-7705
Independence (G-12062)
Core Resources Inc..........D....... 513 731-1771
Cincinnati (G-3362)
Corporate Health Dimensions..........E....... 740 775-6119
Chillicothe (G-2770)
County of Cuyahoga..........B....... 216 443-7181
Cleveland (G-5369)
County of Morrow..........E....... 419 946-2618
Mount Gilead (G-14726)
Crawford & Company..........E....... 330 652-3296
Warren (G-18695)
Crescent Park Corporation..........C....... 513 759-7000
West Chester (G-18906)
Crestline Hotels & Resorts LLC..........E....... 614 846-4355
Columbus (G-7390)
Crestline Hotels & Resorts LLC..........E....... 513 489-3666
Blue Ash (G-1541)
Crestwood Mgmt LLC..........D....... 440 484-2400
Cleveland (G-5381)
Critical Business Analysis Inc..........E....... 419 874-0800
Perrysburg (G-15852)
Cypress Communications Inc..........E....... 404 965-7248
Cleveland (G-5402)
Cypress Companies Inc..........E....... 330 849-6500
Akron (G-179)
D J- Seve Group Inc..........E....... 614 888-6600
Lewis Center (G-12537)
Das Dutch Kitchen Inc..........D....... 330 683-0530
Dalton (G-9144)
Dave Commercial Ground MGT..........E....... 440 237-5394
North Royalton (G-15352)
Dayton Foundation Inc..........E....... 937 222-0410
Dayton (G-9365)
◆ Dco LLC..........B....... 419 931-9086
Perrysburg (G-15857)
DE Foxx & Associates Inc..........B....... 513 621-5522
Cincinnati (G-3408)
Deaconess Long Term Care Inc..........D....... 513 861-0400
Cincinnati (G-3411)
Dearth Management Company..........C....... 614 847-1070
Columbus (G-7426)

Dhl Supply Chain (usa)..........E....... 419 727-4318
Toledo (G-17700)
Dimensionmark Ltd..........E....... 513 305-3525
West Chester (G-18912)
Distribution Data Incorporated..........E....... 216 362-3009
Brookpark (G-1896)
DMD Management Inc..........C....... 440 944-9400
Wickliffe (G-19456)
DMD Management Inc..........E....... 216 898-8399
Cleveland (G-5434)
Early Learning Tree Chld Ctr..........D....... 937 293-7907
Dayton (G-9402)
Eclipse Co LLC..........E....... 440 552-9400
Cleveland (G-5465)
EDM Management Inc..........E....... 330 726-5790
Youngstown (G-20026)
Education Innovations Intl LLC..........C....... 614 339-3676
Dublin (G-10215)
▲ Eleet Cryogenics Inc..........E....... 330 874-4009
Bolivar (G-1702)
Elford Inc..........C....... 614 488-4000
Columbus (G-7511)
Emp Management Group Ltd..........D....... 330 493-4443
Canton (G-2301)
Erie Indemnity Company..........D....... 330 433-6300
Canton (G-2303)
Excellence In Motivation Inc..........E....... 763 445-3000
Dayton (G-9420)
Executive Jet Management Inc..........B....... 513 979-6600
Cincinnati (G-3525)
Facilities Kahn Management..........E....... 313 202-7607
Dayton (G-9424)
FC Schwendler LLC..........E....... 330 733-8715
Akron (G-217)
First Services Inc..........A....... 513 241-2200
Cincinnati (G-3559)
First Transit Inc..........B....... 513 241-2200
Cincinnati (G-3564)
Fisher Foods Marketing Inc..........C....... 330 497-3000
North Canton (G-15203)
Flat Rock Care Center..........C....... 419 483-7330
Flat Rock (G-10978)
Focus Solutions Inc..........C....... 513 376-8349
Cincinnati (G-3575)
Folkers Management Corporation..........E....... 513 421-0230
Cincinnati (G-3576)
Foseco Management Inc..........A....... 440 826-4548
Cleveland (G-5567)
Franklin & Seidelmann LLC..........D....... 216 255-5700
Beachwood (G-1060)
French Company LLC..........D....... 330 963-4344
Twinsburg (G-18269)
Frito-Lay North America Inc..........D....... 419 893-8171
Maumee (G-13794)
Fx Facility Group LLC..........E....... 513 639-2509
Cincinnati (G-3598)
G Stephens Inc..........D....... 614 227-0304
Columbus (G-7640)
Gcha..........D....... 216 696-6900
Cleveland (G-5599)
Genesis Technology Partners..........E....... 513 585-5800
Cincinnati (G-3617)
Gentlebrook Inc..........C....... 330 877-3694
Hartville (G-11686)
Gilbane Building Company..........E....... 614 948-4000
Columbus (G-7668)
Grote Enterprises LLC..........D....... 513 731-5700
Cincinnati (G-3659)
Hammond Construction Inc..........D....... 330 455-7039
Canton (G-2335)
Hanger Prosthetics &..........E....... 330 633-9807
Tallmadge (G-17475)
Harborside Healthcare Corp..........D....... 937 436-6155
Dayton (G-9486)
Hat White Management LLC..........E....... 800 525-7967
Akron (G-255)
Healthcare Management Cons..........E....... 419 363-2193
Rockford (G-16416)
Healthscope Benefits Inc..........E....... 614 797-5200
Westerville (G-19262)
Helmsman Management Svcs LLC..........D....... 614 478-8282
Columbus (G-7738)
Help Foundation Inc..........D....... 216 432-4810
Euclid (G-10638)
Hernandez Cnstr Svcs Inc..........E....... 330 796-0500
Akron (G-259)
Hill Barth & King LLC..........E....... 330 758-8613
Canfield (G-2140)
Hills Developers Inc..........C....... 513 984-0300
Blue Ash (G-1580)

Hmshost Corporation..........C....... 419 547-8667
Clyde (G-6744)
Holzer Clinic LLC..........A....... 740 446-5411
Gallipolis (G-11897)
Holzer Senior Care Center..........E....... 740 446-5001
Bidwell (G-1469)
Hospitalists MGT Group LLC..........A....... 866 464-7497
Canton (G-2348)
HRP Capital Inc..........E....... 419 865-3111
Holland (G-11889)
Ideal Setech LLC..........E....... 419 782-5522
Defiance (G-9919)
Illinois Tool Works Inc..........E....... 513 891-7485
Blue Ash (G-1583)
Illumetek Corp..........E....... 330 342-7582
Cuyahoga Falls (G-9101)
Imflux Inc..........E....... 513 488-1017
Hamilton (G-11611)
Infinite Shares LLC..........E....... 216 317-1601
Mentor (G-14063)
Infocision Management Corp..........C....... 937 259-2400
Dayton (G-9178)
Ingle-Barr Inc..........C....... 740 702-6117
Chillicothe (G-2793)
Innovative Architectural..........E....... 614 416-0614
Columbus (G-7820)
Instantwhip-Columbus Inc..........C....... 614 871-9447
Grove City (G-11443)
Integra Ohio Inc..........B....... 513 378-5214
Cincinnati (G-3768)
Intergrated Consulting..........E....... 216 214-7547
Bedford Heights (G-1323)
Investek Management Svcs F/C..........E....... 419 873-1236
Perrysburg (G-15880)
Island Service Company..........E....... 419 285-3695
Put In Bay (G-16226)
J A G Black Gold Management Co..........D....... 614 565-3246
Lockbourne (G-12821)
Jack Gibson Construction Co..........D....... 330 394-5280
Warren (G-18717)
Jake Sweeney Automotive Inc..........C....... 513 782-2800
Cincinnati (G-3805)
Jeff Wyler Automotive Fmly Inc..........E....... 513 752-7450
Cincinnati (G-2855)
Jtd Health Systems Inc..........A....... 419 394-3335
Saint Marys (G-16527)
Juice Technologies Inc..........E....... 800 518-5576
Columbus (G-7875)
Kaiser Logistics LLC..........D....... 937 534-0213
Monroe (G-14571)
Kappa House Corp of Delta..........E....... 614 487-9461
Upper Arlington (G-18399)
Kerrington Health Systems Inc..........C....... 513 863-0360
Fairfield Township (G-10811)
Kettcor Inc..........B....... 937 458-4949
Miamisburg (G-14178)
Kingston Healthcare Company..........E....... 419 247-2880
Toledo (G-17840)
Klingbeil Capital MGT LLC..........D....... 614 396-4919
Worthington (G-19818)
Kroger Co..........C....... 513 782-3300
Cincinnati (G-3892)
Kross Acquisition Company LLC..........E....... 513 554-0555
Loveland (G-13004)
Kurtz Bros Compost Services..........E....... 330 864-2621
Akron (G-306)
Lathrop Company Inc..........E....... 419 893-7000
Toledo (G-17849)
Laurel Health Care Company..........C....... 614 888-4553
Worthington (G-19820)
Laurel Health Care Company..........C....... 614 885-0408
Worthington (G-19821)
▲ Leadec Corp..........E....... 513 731-3590
Blue Ash (G-1597)
Leatherman Nursing Ctrs Corp..........A....... 330 336-6684
Wadsworth (G-18602)
Legacy Village Management Off..........E....... 216 382-3871
Cleveland (G-5862)
Levering Management Inc..........E....... 419 768-2401
Chesterville (G-2748)
Levering Management Inc..........D....... 740 387-9545
Marion (G-13429)
Licking Memorial Hlth Systems..........A....... 220 564-4000
Newark (G-15056)
Licking-Knox Goodwill Inds Inc..........D....... 740 345-9861
Newark (G-15061)
Lincolnview Local Schools..........C....... 419 968-2226
Van Wert (G-18483)
Lineage Logistics LLC..........E....... 937 328-3349
Springfield (G-17061)

S
I
C

Lott Industries Incorporated ....A..... 419 534-4980
Toledo (G-17859)

Lutheran Housing Services Inc ....E..... 419 861-4990
Toledo (G-17872)

M A Folkes Company Inc ....E..... 513 785-4200
Hamilton (G-11626)

M&C Hotel Interests Inc. ....E..... 440 543-1331
Chagrin Falls (G-2671)

Marsh Berry & Company Inc ....E..... 440 354-3230
Beachwood (G-1075)

Mary Rtan Hlth Assn Logan Cnty ....E..... 937 592-4015
Bellefontaine (G-1358)

Marymount Health Care Systems ....E..... 216 332-1100
Cleveland (G-5919)

McDaniels Cnstr Corp Inc ....D..... 614 252-5852
Columbus (G-8043)

McR LLC ....D..... 937 879-5055
Beavercreek (G-1170)

MD Business Solutions Inc ....E..... 513 872-4500
Blue Ash (G-1606)

Med America Hlth Systems Corp ....A..... 937 223-6192
Dayton (G-9598)

Megen Construction Company Inc........E..... 513 742-9191
Cincinnati (G-4003)

MEI Hotels Incorporated........................C..... 216 589-0441
Cleveland (G-5949)

Mercy Franciscan Hosp Mt Airy ....A..... 513 853-5101
Cincinnati (G-4008)

Mfbusiness Group ....E..... 216 510-0717
Cleveland (G-5974)

Michael Baker Intl Inc ....C..... 330 453-3110
Canton (G-2402)

Michael Baker Intl Inc ....E..... 412 269-6300
Cleveland (G-5976)

▲ Midwest Tape LLC............................B..... 419 868-9370
Holland (G-11898)

Ministerial Day Care-Headstart ....E..... 216 881-6924
Cleveland (G-5998)

National Heritg Academies Inc ....D..... 937 223-2889
Dayton (G-9653)

National Heritg Academies Inc ....D..... 513 251-6000
Cincinnati (G-4092)

National Heritg Academies Inc ....D..... 419 269-2247
Toledo (G-17931)

National Heritg Academies Inc ....D..... 513 751-5555
Cincinnati (G-4093)

National Heritg Academies Inc ....D..... 419 531-3285
Toledo (G-17932)

National Heritg Academies Inc ....D..... 937 235-5498
Dayton (G-9654)

National Heritg Academies Inc ....D..... 937 278-6671
Dayton (G-9655)

National Heritg Academies Inc ....D..... 216 731-0127
Euclid (G-10650)

National Heritg Academies Inc ....D..... 216 451-1725
Cleveland (G-6046)

National Heritg Academies Inc ....D..... 330 792-4806
Youngstown (G-20138)

Nationwide General Insur Co ....D..... 614 249-7111
Columbus (G-8156)

Netjets Aviation Inc ....E..... 614 239-5501
Gahanna (G-11137)

Nexstep Healthcare LLC......................C..... 216 797-4040
Cleveland (G-6066)

Niagara Health Corporation ....C..... 614 898-4000
Columbus (G-8189)

Niederst Management Ltd ....D..... 440 331-8800
Cleveland (G-6070)

North Randall Village ....D..... 216 663-1112
Cleveland (G-6080)

Northcoast Healthcare MGT...................C..... 216 591-2000
Beachwood (G-1087)

Novotec Recycling LLC........................E..... 614 231-8326
Columbus (G-8210)

Nursing Care MGT Amer Inc ....D..... 740 927-9888
Pataskala (G-15786)

Nursing Care MGT Amer Inc ....D..... 513 793-5092
Cincinnati (G-4142)

Ohio Cllbrtive Lrng Sltons Inc ....E..... 216 595-5289
Beachwood (G-1089)

Ohio Department of Education ....E..... 740 289-2908
Piketon (G-15980)

Omnicare Inc ....C..... 513 719-2600
Cincinnati (G-4168)

Omnicare Management Company ....A..... 513 719-1535
Cincinnati (G-4170)

Omnicare Purch Ltd Partner Inc...........C..... 800 990-6664
Cincinnati (G-4172)

Osu Internal Medicine LLC ....D..... 614 293-0080
Dublin (G-10301)

Outreach Professional Svcs Inc ....D..... 216 472-4094
Cleveland (G-6148)

P I & I Motor Express Inc ....C..... 330 448-4035
Masury (G-13741)

Parker-Hannifin Intl Corp ....B..... 216 896-3000
Cleveland (G-6172)

Parkops Columbus LLC 877 499-9155
Columbus (G-8423)

Perduco Group Inc ....E..... 937 401-0271
Beavercreek (G-1175)

Permedion Inc ....D..... 614 895-9900
Westerville (G-19198)

Pk Management LLC...........................C..... 216 472-1870
Richmond Heights (G-16392)

Plus Management Services Inc ....C..... 419 225-9018
Lima (G-12722)

Premier Management Co Inc ....D..... 740 867-2144
Chesapeake (G-2731)

Professional Transit Mgt ....E..... 513 677-6000
Loveland (G-13022)

Promedica Hlth Systems Inc ....A..... 567 585-7454
Toledo (G-17993)

Promedica Physcn Cntinuum Svcs ....C..... 419 824-7200
Sylvania (G-17444)

Providence Health Partners LLC ....E..... 937 297-8999
Moraine (G-14688)

Providence Medical Group Inc ....E..... 937 297-8999
Moraine (G-14689)

Quality Control Inspection ....D..... 440 359-1900
Cleveland (G-6269)

Quality Supply Chain Co-Op Inc ....E..... 614 764-3124
Dublin (G-10314)

Quandel Construction Group Inc ....E..... 717 657-0909
Westerville (G-19297)

Rama Tika Developers LLC..................E..... 419 806-6446
Mansfield (G-13232)

Rbp Atlanta LLC..................................D..... 614 246-2522
Columbus (G-8491)

Regal Hospitality LLC..........................E..... 614 436-0004
Columbus (G-8504)

Renaissance House Inc ....D..... 419 626-1110
Sandusky (G-16634)

Renier Construction Corp ....E..... 614 866-4580
Columbus (G-8514)

Req/Jqh Holdings Inc ....D..... 513 891-1066
Blue Ash (G-1645)

Resource International Inc ....C..... 614 823-4949
Columbus (G-8523)

Rev1 Ventures ....E..... 614 487-3700
Columbus (G-8529)

Revolution Group Inc ....D..... 614 212-1111
Westerville (G-19207)

Ricco Enterprises Incorporated ....E..... 216 883-7775
Cleveland (G-6319)

Richard L Bowen & Assoc Inc ....D..... 216 491-9300
Cleveland (G-6321)

Richland Mall Shopping Ctr ....E..... 419 529-4003
Mansfield (G-13236)

RJ Runge Company Inc........................E..... 419 740-5781
Port Clinton (G-16116)

RMS of Ohio Inc ....B..... 440 617-6605
Westlake (G-19401)

Ross Consolidated Corp ....D..... 440 748-5800
Grafton (G-11320)

Roundstone Management Ltd ....E..... 440 617-0333
Lakewood (G-12362)

Ruscilli Construction Co Inc ....D..... 614 876-9484
Columbus (G-8560)

Saber Healthcare Group LLC ....E..... 216 292-5706
Bedford (G-1303)

Safeguard Properties LLC.....................A..... 216 739-2900
Cleveland (G-6361)

Safran Power Usa LLC ....C..... 330 487-2000
Twinsburg (G-18316)

Salem Healthcare MGT LLC ....E..... 330 332-1588
Salem (G-16561)

Salvation Army ....D..... 419 447-2252
Tiffin (G-17535)

Salvation Army ....C..... 330 773-3331
Akron (G-418)

Sears Roebuck and Co.........................E..... 513 741-6422
Cincinnati (G-4442)

Select Hotels Group LLC ....E..... 513 754-0003
Mason (G-13638)

Signature Inc ....C..... 614 734-0010
Dublin (G-10334)

Simonson Construction Svcs Inc..........D..... 419 281-8299
Ashland (G-691)

Skanska USA Building Inc ....E..... 513 421-0082
Cincinnati (G-4492)

Sleep Network Inc...............................D..... 419 535-9282
Toledo (G-18036)

Smg Holdings Inc ....C..... 614 827-2500
Columbus (G-8654)

Ssoe Inc ....E..... 330 821-7198
Alliance (G-552)

St Augustine Corporation ....B..... 216 939-7600
Lakewood (G-12363)

St George & Co Inc ....E..... 330 733-7528
Akron (G-438)

Standard Retirement Svcs Inc ....E..... 440 808-2724
Westlake (G-19409)

Stat Integrated Tech Inc ....E..... 440 286-7663
Chardon (G-2716)

Sterling Medical Corporation ....D..... 513 984-1800
Cincinnati (G-4545)

Sterling Medical Corporation ....E..... 513 984-1800
Cincinnati (G-4546)

Summit Advantage LLC........................D..... 330 835-2453
Fairlawn (G-10853)

Sylvania Franciscan Health ....E..... 419 882-8373
Maumee (G-13859)

T K Edwards LLC ....E..... 614 406-8064
Columbus (G-8726)

TAC Industries Inc ....B..... 937 328-5200
Springfield (G-17123)

Technical Consultants Inc ....E..... 513 521-2696
Cincinnati (G-4579)

The Sheakley Group Inc ....E..... 513 771-2277
Cincinnati (G-4596)

Thomas Rosser ....C..... 614 890-2900
Westerville (G-19301)

Tjm Clmbus LLC Tjm Clumbus LLC....D..... 614 885-1885
Columbus (G-8760)

Tm Capture Services LLC ....D..... 937 728-1781
Beavercreek (G-1238)

Trihealth Inc ....E..... 513 929-0020
Cincinnati (G-4635)

Trihealth Inc ....E..... 513 865-1111
Cincinnati (G-4636)

Trihealth Inc ....E..... 513 569-6777
Cincinnati (G-4637)

Trihealth Inc ....E..... 513 891-1627
Blue Ash (G-1664)

Trihealth Inc ....E..... 513 569-6111
Cincinnati (G-4638)

Trihealth Inc ....E..... 513 871-2340
Cincinnati (G-4639)

Trihealth Inc.......................................C..... 513 985-0900
Montgomery (G-14603)

Trinity Health System ....C..... 740 283-7848
Steubenville (G-17176)

Trinity Health System ....A..... 740 264-8000
Steubenville (G-17177)

Trinity Health System ....E..... 740 264-8101
Steubenville (G-17178)

Trinity Hospital Holding Co ....A..... 740 264-8000
Steubenville (G-17180)

Triversity Construction Co LLC.............E..... 513 733-0046
Cincinnati (G-4650)

Ttl Associates Inc ....C..... 419 241-4556
Toledo (G-18111)

Tudor Arms Mstr Subtenant LLC...........D..... 216 696-6611
Cleveland (G-6555)

Uc Health Llc ....C..... 513 298-3000
West Chester (G-19023)

Uc Health Llc ....E..... 513 584-8600
Cincinnati (G-4667)

Uc Health Llc ....A..... 513 585-6000
Cincinnati (G-4668)

United Telemanagement Corp ....E..... 937 454-1888
Dayton (G-9833)

▲ University Hospitals ....A..... 216 767-8900
Shaker Heights (G-16717)

University Hospitals ....A..... 440 743-3000
Parma (G-15779)

University Hospitals ....D..... 216 844-8797
Cleveland (G-6590)

University Hospitals Cleveland ....E..... 216 844-3528
Cleveland (G-6595)

University of Cincinnati ....E..... 513 556-4200
Cincinnati (G-4714)

University of Cincinnati ....C..... 513 558-4231
Cincinnati (G-4715)

V Westaar Inc ....E..... 740 803-2803
Lewis Center (G-12565)

Vance Property Management LLC ....D..... 419 887-1878
Toledo (G-18136)

Verst Group Logistics Inc ....E..... 513 772-2494
Cincinnati (G-4757)

Viaquest Inc..................................E.......614 889-5837
Dublin *(G-10362)*

Village of Valley View.....................C.......216 524-6511
Cleveland *(G-6632)*

Voc Works Ltd...............................D.......614 760-3515
Dublin *(G-10366)*

Vora Ventures LLC.........................C.......513 792-5100
Blue Ash *(G-1676)*

Wadsworth Galaxy Rest Inc...........D.......330 334-3663
Wadsworth *(G-18618)*

Walnut Ridge Management..............D.......234 678-3900
Akron *(G-495)*

Western Management Inc...............E.......216 941-3333
Cleveland *(G-6672)*

Westminster Management Company....C.......614 274-5154
Columbus *(G-8890)*

Windsor House Inc........................E.......440 834-0544
Burton *(G-2020)*

Wings Investors Company Ltd.........E.......513 241-5800
Cincinnati *(G-4799)*

Zarcal Zanesville LLC....................D.......216 226-2132
Lakewood *(G-12365)*

8742 Management Consulting Services

0714 Inc.......................................E.......440 327-2123
North Ridgeville *(G-15318)*

1st Advnce SEC Invstgtions Inc.........E.......937 317-4433
Dayton *(G-9194)*

2060 Digital LLC...........................E.......513 699-5012
Cincinnati *(G-2878)*

3sg Plus LLC.................................E.......614 652-0019
Columbus *(G-6797)*

5me LLC..E.......513 719-1600
Cincinnati *(G-2839)*

Accelerant Technologies LLC...........D.......419 236-8768
Genoa *(G-11251)*

Accenture LLP................................C.......216 685-1435
Cleveland *(G-4898)*

Accenture LLP................................C.......614 629-2000
Columbus *(G-6861)*

Accenture LLP................................D.......513 455-1000
Cincinnati *(G-2900)*

Accenture LLP................................D.......513 651-2444
Cincinnati *(G-2901)*

Accurate Inventory and C...............B.......800 777-9414
Columbus *(G-6863)*

Acloche LLC..................................E.......888 608-0889
Columbus *(G-6865)*

Acuity Healthcare LP.....................D.......740 283-7499
Steubenville *(G-17139)*

Adept Marketing Outsourced LLC....E.......614 452-4011
Columbus *(G-6871)*

Advanced Computer Graphics..........E.......513 936-5060
Blue Ash *(G-1496)*

Advanced Prgrm Resources Inc........E.......614 761-9994
Dublin *(G-10119)*

Advocate Solutions LLC.................E.......614 444-5144
Columbus *(G-6876)*

Aeea LLC.......................................E.......330 497-5304
Canton *(G-2176)*

Ake Marketing...............................E.......440 232-1661
Bedford *(G-1268)*

Akron Centl Engrv Mold Mch Inc....E.......330 794-8704
Akron *(G-30)*

Alonovus Corp...............................D.......330 674-2300
Millersburg *(G-14454)*

Alternative Care Mgt Systems.........E.......614 761-0035
Dublin *(G-10127)*

American Health Group Inc.............D.......419 891-1212
Maumee *(G-13750)*

Ameriprise Financial Svcs Inc.........E.......614 934-4057
Dublin *(G-10135)*

▲ Applied Marketing Services.........E.......440 716-9962
Westlake *(G-19317)*

Archway Marketing Services Inc.......C.......440 572-0725
Strongsville *(G-17286)*

Ardmore Power Logistics LLC..........E.......216 502-0640
Westlake *(G-19318)*

Armada Ltd...................................D.......614 505-7256
Powell *(G-16184)*

Arysen Inc....................................D.......440 230-4400
Independence *(G-12047)*

Ascent Global Logistics Holdin........E.......800 689-6255
Hudson *(G-11967)*

AT&T Government Solutions Inc.......D.......937 306-3030
Beavercreek *(G-1128)*

Atlas Advisors LLC........................E.......888 282-0873
Columbus *(G-6996)*

Attevo Inc....................................D.......216 928-2800
Beachwood *(G-1032)*

Austin Building and Design Inc.......C.......440 544-2600
Cleveland *(G-5023)*

Automotive Events Inc..................E.......440 356-1383
Rocky River *(G-16423)*

Avatar Management Services..........E.......330 963-3900
Macedonia *(G-13059)*

AVI Food Systems Inc....................C.......330 372-6000
Warren *(G-18677)*

Axa Advisors LLC..........................D.......216 621-7715
Cleveland *(G-5029)*

Azimuth Corporation......................E.......937 256-8571
Beavercreek Township *(G-1243)*

B&F Capital Markets Inc................E.......216 472-2700
Cleveland *(G-5032)*

Babcox Media Inc..........................D.......330 670-1234
Akron *(G-85)*

Backoffice Associates LLC.............D.......419 660-4600
Norwalk *(G-15425)*

Banc Amer Prctice Slutions Inc........C.......614 794-8247
Westerville *(G-19147)*

Bannockburn Global Forex LLC.......E.......513 386-7400
Cincinnati *(G-3016)*

Barrett & Associates Inc...............E.......330 928-2323
Cuyahoga Falls *(G-9073)*

Baxter Hodell Donnelly Preston......C.......513 271-1634
Cincinnati *(G-3025)*

Beacon of Light Ltd.......................E.......419 531-9060
Toledo *(G-17608)*

Benchmark Technologies Corp.........E.......419 843-6691
Toledo *(G-17611)*

Bionetics Corporation....................E.......757 873-0900
Heath *(G-11702)*

Bodine Perry LLC...........................E.......330 702-8100
Canfield *(G-2131)*

Boenning & Scattergood Inc...........E.......614 336-8851
Powell *(G-16186)*

Brandmuscle Inc...........................C.......216 464-4342
Cleveland *(G-5074)*

Brentley Institute Inc....................E.......216 225-0087
Cleveland *(G-5078)*

Btas Inc..E.......937 431-9431
Beavercreek *(G-1135)*

Budros Ruhlin & Roe Inc................E.......614 481-6900
Columbus *(G-7094)*

Burke Inc......................................C.......513 241-5663
Cincinnati *(G-3090)*

C H Dean Inc.................................D.......937 222-9531
Beavercreek *(G-1136)*

Career Partners Intl LLC................A.......919 401-4260
Columbus *(G-7126)*

Carol Scudere...............................E.......614 839-4357
New Albany *(G-14848)*

Catalina Marketing Corporation.......E.......513 564-8200
Cincinnati *(G-3131)*

Cbiz Inc..C.......216 447-9000
Cleveland *(G-5139)*

Center For Health Affairs...............D.......800 362-2628
Cleveland *(G-5152)*

Change Hlth Prac MGT Solns Grp.....E.......937 291-7850
Miamisburg *(G-14151)*

Chapman & Chapman Inc...............E.......440 934-4102
Avon *(G-874)*

Chartwell Group LLC.....................E.......216 360-0009
Cleveland *(G-5171)*

Chattree and Associates Inc...........D.......216 831-1494
Cleveland *(G-5172)*

Chemsultants International Inc........E.......440 974-3080
Mentor *(G-14029)*

Claritas LLC..................................E.......513 739-6869
Cincinnati *(G-3300)*

Classic Real Estate Co...................E.......937 393-3416
Hillsboro *(G-11833)*

Clear Vision Engineering LLC.........E.......419 478-7151
Toledo *(G-17664)*

Clgt Solutions LLC.........................E.......740 920-4795
Granville *(G-11338)*

Coho Creative LLC.........................E.......513 751-7500
Cincinnati *(G-3320)*

Columbus Public School Dst...........E.......614 365-5000
Columbus *(G-7308)*

◆ Comex North America Inc...........D.......303 307-2100
Cleveland *(G-5316)*

Commercial Debt Cunseling Corp.....D.......614 848-9800
Columbus *(G-7326)*

Commquest Services Inc.................C.......330 455-0374
Canton *(G-2261)*

Communica Inc..............................E.......419 244-7766
Toledo *(G-17671)*

Comprehensive Hr Solutions LLC.....E.......513 771-2277
Cincinnati *(G-3346)*

Comprehensive Logistics Co Inc......E.......330 793-0504
Youngstown *(G-20007)*

Comprehensive Logistics Co Inc......E.......330 233-2627
Avon Lake *(G-914)*

Concordia Properties LLC...............E.......513 671-0120
Cincinnati *(G-3349)*

Consumer Credit Counseling Ser......E.......800 254-4100
Cleveland *(G-5341)*

Contract Marketing Inc..................D.......440 639-9100
Mentor *(G-14034)*

Corbus LLC....................................E.......937 226-7724
Dayton *(G-9321)*

▼ Cornerstone Brands Group Inc.....A.......513 603-1000
West Chester *(G-18899)*

Corporate Fin Assoc of Clumbus.....D.......614 457-9219
Columbus *(G-7374)*

Corporate Plans Inc......................E.......440 542-7800
Solon *(G-16838)*

Cosmic Concepts Ltd.....................D.......614 228-1104
Columbus *(G-7377)*

County of Marion...........................E.......740 382-0624
Marion *(G-13417)*

CPC Logistics Inc..........................D.......513 874-5787
Fairfield *(G-10715)*

Critical Business Analysis Inc.........E.......419 874-0800
Perrysburg *(G-15852)*

D L A Training Center....................D.......614 692-5986
Columbus *(G-7409)*

D L Ryan Companies LLC................E.......614 436-6558
Westerville *(G-19156)*

Dari Pizza Enterprises II Inc...........C.......419 534-3000
Maumee *(G-13780)*

Davis 5 Star Holdings LLC..............E.......954 470-8456
Springfield *(G-17029)*

Dayton Aerospace Inc....................E.......937 426-4300
Beavercreek Township *(G-1246)*

Dayton Digital Media Inc................E.......937 223-8335
Dayton *(G-9362)*

Dayton Foundation Inc...................E.......937 222-0410
Dayton *(G-9365)*

DE Foxx & Associates Inc..............B.......513 621-5522
Cincinnati *(G-3408)*

Dealers Group Limited...................E.......440 352-4970
Beachwood *(G-1052)*

Dedicated Tech Services Inc...........E.......614 309-0059
Dublin *(G-10197)*

Dedicated Technologies Inc............D.......614 460-3200
Columbus *(G-7427)*

Deloitte & Touche LLP....................D.......937 223-8821
Dayton *(G-9386)*

Deloitte & Touche LLP....................C.......216 589-1300
Cleveland *(G-5415)*

Deloitte & Touche LLP....................B.......513 784-7100
Cincinnati *(G-3420)*

Deloitte Consulting LLP..................C.......937 223-8821
Dayton *(G-9387)*

Delta Energy LLC...........................E.......614 761-3603
Dublin *(G-10198)*

Dental One Inc..............................E.......216 584-1000
Independence *(G-12066)*

Devry University Inc......................C.......614 251-6969
Columbus *(G-7443)*

Digital Controls Corporation...........D.......513 746-8118
Miamisburg *(G-14166)*

Direct Options Inc.........................E.......513 779-4416
West Chester *(G-18913)*

Distribution Data Incorporated.......E.......216 362-3009
Brookpark *(G-1896)*

Diversified Systems Inc..................E.......614 476-9939
Westerville *(G-19249)*

Djd Express Inc.............................D.......740 676-7464
Shadyside *(G-16694)*

Duke Energy Ohio Inc....................C.......513 421-9500
Cincinnati *(G-3453)*

Duncan Falls Assoc.......................D.......740 674-7105
Duncan Falls *(G-10381)*

Dunnhumby Inc.............................D.......513 579-3400
Cincinnati *(G-3456)*

East Way Behavioral Hlth Care.......C.......937 222-4900
Dayton *(G-9403)*

Efficient Collaborative Retail.........D.......440 498-0500
Solon *(G-16843)*

Emerald Health Network Inc...........D.......216 479-2030
Fairlawn *(G-10825)*

Enabling Partners LLC....................E.......440 878-9418
Strongsville *(G-17301)*

Engaged Health Care Bus Svcs........E.......614 457-8180
Columbus *(G-7516)*

Enterprise Data Management Inc......E.......513 791-7272
Blue Ash *(G-1554)*

Epiphany Management Group LLC ......E 330 706-4056
Akron *(G-204)*

Epipheo Incorporated ....E 888 687-7620
Cincinnati *(G-3506)*

Equity Resources Inc ....D 513 518-6318
Cincinnati *(G-3512)*

Ernst & Young LLP ....C 614 224-5678
Columbus *(G-7531)*

Ernst & Young LLP ....C 513 612-1400
Cincinnati *(G-3515)*

Excellence Alliance Group Inc ....E 513 619-4800
Cincinnati *(G-3524)*

Facilities MGT Solutions LLC ....E 513 639-2230
Cincinnati *(G-3526)*

Fahlgren Inc ....D 614 383-1500
Columbus *(G-7553)*

Fathom Seo LLC ....D 614 291-8456
Columbus *(G-7565)*

Fathom Seo LLC ....D 216 525-0510
Cleveland *(G-5517)*

Financial Design Group Inc ....E 419 843-4737
Toledo *(G-17736)*

Findley Inc ....D 419 255-1360
Toledo *(G-17737)*

Finit Group LLC ....D 513 793-4648
Cincinnati *(G-3551)*

First Choice Medical Staffing ....E 419 626-9740
Sandusky *(G-16608)*

First Command Fincl Plg Inc ....E 937 429-4490
Beavercreek *(G-1218)*

First Data Gvrnment Sltions LP ....D 513 489-9599
Blue Ash *(G-1562)*

First Transit Inc ....B 513 241-2200
Cincinnati *(G-3564)*

Focus Solutions Inc ....C 513 376-8349
Cincinnati *(G-3575)*

Forest City Enterprises LP ....D 216 621-6060
Cleveland *(G-5558)*

Frank Gates Service Company ....B 614 793-8000
Dublin *(G-10231)*

Frankes Wood Products LLC ....E 937 642-0706
Marysville *(G-13497)*

Fusion Alliance LLC ....E 614 852-8000
Westerville *(G-19167)*

Fusion Alliance LLC ....E 513 563-8444
Blue Ash *(G-1565)*

Garretyson Frm Resolution Grp ....C 513 794-0400
Loveland *(G-12995)*

Gbq Consulting LLC ....D 614 221-1120
Columbus *(G-7651)*

General Fncl Tax Cnsulting LLC ....E 888 496-2679
Cincinnati *(G-2854)*

Genesis Corp ....E 614 934-1211
Columbus *(G-7657)*

Germain & Co Inc ....E 937 885-5827
Dayton *(G-9460)*

Global Cnsld Holdings Inc ....D 513 703-0965
Mason *(G-13588)*

Global Military Expert Co ....E 800 738-9795
Beavercreek *(G-1219)*

GP Strategies Corporation ....E 513 583-8810
Cincinnati *(G-3629)*

Greentree Group Inc ....D 937 490-5500
Dayton *(G-9477)*

Group Management Services Inc ......E 330 659-0100
Richfield *(G-16359)*

Gund Sports Marketing Llc ....E 216 420-2000
Cleveland *(G-5646)*

H T V Industries Inc ....D 216 514-0060
Cleveland *(G-5652)*

Hafenbrack Mktg Cmmnctions Inc .....E 937 424-8950
Dayton *(G-9482)*

Halley Consulting Group LLC ....E 614 899-7325
Westerville *(G-19258)*

Hamilton Parks Conservancy ....E 513 785-7055
Hamilton *(G-11608)*

Hanna Commercial LLC ....D 216 861-7200
Cleveland *(G-5659)*

Hanson McClain Inc ....E 513 469-7500
Cincinnati *(G-3680)*

Harris Mackessy & Brennan ....C 614 221-6831
Westerville *(G-19169)*

HDR Engineering Inc ....E 614 839-5770
Columbus *(G-7722)*

Health and Safety Sciences LLC ....E 513 488-1952
Fairfield Township *(G-10809)*

Healthcomp Inc ....D 216 696-6900
Cleveland *(G-5674)*

Henry Call Inc ....C 216 433-5609
Cleveland *(G-5684)*

HJ Ford Associates Inc ....C 937 429-9711
Beavercreek *(G-1155)*

Hmt Associates Inc ....E 216 369-0109
Broadview Heights *(G-1836)*

Homelife Companies Inc ....E 740 369-1297
Delaware *(G-9986)*

Honda of America Mfg Inc ....C 937 644-0724
Marysville *(G-13505)*

Hr Butler LLC ....E 614 923-2900
Dublin *(G-10246)*

I T E LLC ....D 513 576-6200
Loveland *(G-13000)*

Ilead LLC ....E 440 846-2346
Strongsville *(G-17315)*

Impact Ceramics LLC ....E 440 554-3624
Cleveland *(G-5740)*

Incentisoft Solutions LLC ....D 877 562-4461
Cleveland *(G-5741)*

Incubit LLC ....D 740 362-1401
Delaware *(G-9988)*

Independent Evaluators Inc ....D 419 872-5650
Perrysburg *(G-15878)*

Industry Insights Inc ....E 614 389-2100
Columbus *(G-7814)*

Ingleside Investments Inc ....E 614 221-1025
Columbus *(G-7818)*

Innerworkings Inc ....E 513 984-9500
Cincinnati *(G-3762)*

Innovative Technologies Corp ....D 937 252-2145
Dayton *(G-9179)*

Inquiry Systems Inc ....E 614 464-3800
Columbus *(G-7824)*

Institute For Human Services ....E 614 251-6000
Columbus *(G-7830)*

Integra Group Inc ....E 513 326-5600
Cincinnati *(G-3767)*

Integra Realty Resources - Cin ....B 513 561-2305
Cincinnati *(G-3769)*

Integrated Prj Resources LLC ....E 330 272-0998
Salem *(G-16549)*

Interbrand Design Forum LLC ....C 513 421-2210
Cincinnati *(G-3777)*

Ipsos-Asi LLC ....D 513 872-4300
Cincinnati *(G-3785)*

Iron Mountain Info MGT LLC ....C 440 248-0999
Solon *(G-16862)*

Island Hospitality MGT LLC ....E 614 864-8844
Columbus *(G-7847)*

ITM Marketing Inc ....C 740 295-3575
Coshocton *(G-9019)*

Its Financial LLC ....D 937 425-6889
Beavercreek *(G-1224)*

J G Martin Inc ....E 216 491-1584
Cleveland *(G-5771)*

Jarrett Logistics Systems Inc ....C 330 682-0099
Orrville *(G-15636)*

Jersey Central Pwr & Light Co ....E 330 315-6713
Fairlawn *(G-10836)*

Jjr Solutions LLC ....E 937 912-0288
Beavercreek *(G-1159)*

Johnson Mirmiran Thompson Inc .....D 614 714-0270
Columbus *(G-7863)*

Jonathon R Johnson & Assoc ....E 216 932-6529
Cleveland *(G-5802)*

Jyg Innovations LLC ....E 937 630-3858
Dayton *(G-9531)*

Kaiser Consulting LLC ....E 614 378-5361
Powell *(G-16200)*

Kalypso LP ....D 216 378-4290
Beachwood *(G-1071)*

Karlsberger Companies ....C 614 461-9500
Columbus *(G-7883)*

Kelley Companies ....D 330 668-6100
Copley *(G-8967)*

Kennedy Group Enterprises Inc ....E 440 879-0078
Strongsville *(G-17320)*

Kings Medical Company ....C 330 653-3968
Hudson *(G-11991)*

Kingsley Gate Partners LLC ....D 216 400-9880
Independence *(G-12086)*

Klingbeil Management Group Co ....E 614 220-8900
Columbus *(G-7911)*

Km2 Solutions LLC ....B 610 213-1408
Columbus *(G-7913)*

Knowledgeworks Foundation ....E 513 241-1422
Cincinnati *(G-3884)*

Kroger Refill Center ....E 614 333-5017
Columbus *(G-7929)*

L and C Soft Serve Inc ....E 330 364-3823
Dover *(G-10086)*

Landrum & Brown Incorporated ....E 513 530-5333
Blue Ash *(G-1595)*

Lang Financial Group Inc ....E 513 699-2966
Blue Ash *(G-1596)*

Language Logic ....E 513 241-9112
Cincinnati *(G-3910)*

Leidos Inc ....D 937 431-2270
Beavercreek *(G-1164)*

Lesaint Logistics LLC ....D 513 988-0101
Trenton *(G-18188)*

Level Seven ....D 216 524-9055
Independence *(G-12088)*

Lincoln Fincl Advisors Corp ....D 614 888-6516
Columbus *(G-7980)*

Lpl Financial Holdings Inc ....B 513 772-2592
Cincinnati *(G-3950)*

Madison Avenue Mktg Group Inc ......E 419 473-9000
Toledo *(G-17878)*

Malik Punam ....D 513 636-1333
Cincinnati *(G-3965)*

Managed Technology Svcs LLC ....D 937 247-8915
Miamisburg *(G-14186)*

Mancan Inc ....A 440 884-9675
Strongsville *(G-17326)*

Marketing Indus Solutions Corp ....E 513 703-0965
Mason *(G-13614)*

Marsh Berry & Company Inc ....E 440 354-3230
Beachwood *(G-1075)*

Mas International Mktg LLC ....D 614 446-2003
Columbus *(G-8033)*

Matrix Claims Management Inc ....D 513 351-1222
Cincinnati *(G-3980)*

MB Financial Inc ....D 937 283-2027
Wilmington *(G-19634)*

Mc Cloy Financial Services ....D 614 457-6233
Columbus *(G-8042)*

McKinsey & Company Inc ....E 216 274-4000
Cleveland *(G-5935)*

McKinsey & Company Inc ....D 216 274-4000
Cleveland *(G-5936)*

Med-Pass Incorporated ....E 937 438-8884
Dayton *(G-9599)*

Medco Health Solutions Inc ....A 614 822-2000
Dublin *(G-10276)*

Medical Account Services Inc ....E 937 297-6072
Moraine *(G-14675)*

Medical Recovery Systems Inc..........D 513 872-7000
Cincinnati *(G-3995)*

Medisync Midwest Ltd Lblty Co ....D 513 533-1199
Cincinnati *(G-3998)*

Melo International Inc ....B 440 519-0526
Cleveland *(G-5951)*

Mercer (us) Inc ....E 513 632-2600
Cincinnati *(G-4007)*

Merchandising Services Co ....D 866 479-8246
Blue Ash *(G-1608)*

Merrill Lynch Pierce Fenner ....E 937 847-4000
Miamisburg *(G-14189)*

Merrill Lynch Pierce Fenner ....D 614 225-3000
Columbus *(G-8061)*

Merrill Lynch Pierce Fenner ....D 330 670-2400
Akron *(G-332)*

Merrill Lynch Pierce Fenner ....E 330 655-2312
Hudson *(G-11995)*

Miami University ....B 513 727-3200
Middletown *(G-14308)*

Midwest Mfg Solutions LLC ....E 513 381-7200
West Chester *(G-19068)*

▲ Midwest Motor Supply Co ....C 800 233-1294
Columbus *(G-8082)*

Motion Controls Robotics Inc ....E 419 334-5886
Fremont *(G-11088)*

Murtech Consulting LLC ....D 216 328-8580
Cleveland *(G-6026)*

National Administative Svc LLC ....E 614 358-3607
Dublin *(G-10285)*

National City Cmnty Dev Corp ....C 216 575-2000
Cleveland *(G-6039)*

Nationwide Financial Svcs Inc ....C 614 249-7111
Columbus *(G-8155)*

Nationwide Rtrment Sltions Inc ....C 614 854-8300
Dublin *(G-10287)*

Navigtor MGT Prtners Ltd Lblty ....E 614 796-0090
Columbus *(G-8164)*

Neighborhood Development Svcs ....E 330 296-2003
Ravenna *(G-16250)*

Normandy Group LLC ....E 513 745-0990
Blue Ash *(G-1622)*

Northwest Country Place Inc ....D 440 488-2700
Willoughby *(G-19556)*

Nsa Technologies LLC ....C 330 576-4600
Akron (G-353)

Ohic Insurance Company.................D 614 221-7777
Columbus (G-8227)

Ohio Custodial Maintenance.............C 614 443-1232
Columbus (G-8235)

Ohio Equities LLC ....E 614 207-1805
Columbus (G-8252)

Ohio State University....................E 614 728-8100
Columbus (G-8338)

Ohio-Kentucky-Indiana Regional ....E 513 621-6300
Cincinnati (G-4162)

Ohiohealth Corporation..................D 614 566-3500
Columbus (G-8361)

Ologie LLC ....D 614 221-1107
Columbus (G-8372)

Oncall LLC ....D 513 381-4320
Cincinnati (G-4173)

One10 LLC ....D 763 445-3000
Dayton (G-9676)

Oppenheimer & Co Inc ....E 513 723-9200
Cincinnati (G-4176)

OR Colan Associates LLC ....E 440 827-6116
Cleveland (G-6140)

Orbit Systems Inc ....E 614 504-8011
Lewis Center (G-12556)

Organizational Horizons Inc ....E 614 268-6013
Worthington (G-19832)

Paragon Consulting Inc.................E 440 684-3101
Cleveland (G-6160)

Paragon Tec Inc ....D 216 361-5555
Cleveland (G-6161)

Park International Theme Svcs...........E 513 381-6131
Cincinnati (G-4203)

Parman Group Inc ....E 513 673-0077
Columbus (G-8424)

Pat Henry Group LLC ....E 216 447-0831
Milford (G-14420)

Patient Account MGT Svcs LLC ....E 614 575-0044
Columbus (G-8425)

Patientpint Hosp Solutions LLC ....C 513 936-6800
Cincinnati (G-4209)

Patientpint Ntwrk Slutions LLC ....D 513 936-6800
Cincinnati (G-4210)

Patientpoint LLC ....E 513 936-6800
Cincinnati (G-4211)

Patrick Mahoney ....E 614 292-5766
Columbus (G-8426)

Pcs Cost ....E 216 771-1090
Cleveland (G-6186)

Pension Corporation America ....E 513 281-3366
Cincinnati (G-4226)

Peopleworks Dev of Hr LLC ....E 419 636-4637
Bryan (G-1969)

Perduco Group Inc ....E 937 401-0271
Beavercreek (G-1175)

Phoenix Cosmopolitan Group LLC ....E 814 746-4863
Avon (G-901)

Phoenix Resource Network LLC ....E 800 990-4948
Cincinnati (G-4244)

Piasans Mill Inc ....E 419 448-0100
Tiffin (G-17532)

Pitmark Services Inc ....E 330 876-2217
Kinsman (G-12319)

Plus Management Services Inc ....C 419 225-9018
Lima (G-12722)

Ply-Trim Enterprises Inc ....E 330 799-7876
Youngstown (G-20160)

Pope & Associates Inc ....E 513 671-1277
West Chester (G-18983)

Power Management Inc ....E 937 222-2909
Dayton (G-9701)

Producer Group LLC ....E 440 871-7700
Rocky River (G-16444)

Productivity Qulty Systems Inc ....E 937 885-2255
Dayton (G-9717)

Professnal Mint Cincinnati Inc...........A 513 579-1161
Cincinnati (G-4295)

Progressive Entps Holdings Inc ....A 614 794-3300
Westerville (G-19204)

Projetech Inc ....E 513 481-4900
Cincinnati (G-4296)

Protiviti Inc ....E 216 696-6010
Cleveland (G-6262)

Provenitfinance LLC ....E 888 958-1060
Pickerington (G-15965)

PSI Supply Chain Solutions LLC.........E 614 389-4717
Dublin (G-10313)

Quick Solutions Inc ....C 614 825-8000
Westerville (G-19205)

Quotient Technology Inc ....E 513 229-8659
Mason (G-13631)

R D D Inc ....C 216 781-5858
Cleveland (G-6273)

R P Marketing Public Relations ....E 419 241-2221
Holland (G-11909)

Racksquared LLC ....E 614 737-8812
Columbus (G-8483)

Rahim Inc ....E 216 621-8977
Cleveland (G-6283)

Raymond James Fincl Svcs Inc ....E 513 287-6777
Cincinnati (G-4340)

Real Estate Capital Fund LLC...........E 216 491-3990
Cleveland (G-6290)

Redwood Living Inc ....C 216 360-9441
Independence (G-12112)

Regent Systems Inc ....E 937 640-8010
Dayton (G-9729)

Remtec Automation LLC ....E 877 759-8151
Mason (G-13634)

Residential Hm Assn of Marion ....C 740 387-9999
Marion (G-13455)

Resource Ventures Ltd ....D 614 621-2888
Columbus (G-8524)

Retail Forward Inc ....E 614 355-4000
Columbus (G-8527)

Revlocal Inc ....D 740 392-9246
Mount Vernon (G-14786)

Ride Share Information ....E 513 621-6300
Cincinnati (G-4373)

Risk International Svcs Inc ....E 216 255-3400
Fairlawn (G-10844)

RMS of Ohio Inc ....B 440 617-6605
Westlake (G-19401)

Robex LLC ....D 419 270-0770
Perrysburg (G-15914)

Root Inc ....D 419 874-0077
Sylvania (G-17448)

Royalton Financial Group ....E 440 582-3020
Cleveland (G-6347)

Rpf Consulting LLC ....E 678 494-8030
Cincinnati (G-4406)

Ruralogic Inc ....D 419 630-0500
Beachwood (G-1103)

Rx Options LLC ....D 330 405-8080
Twinsburg (G-18314)

Ryder Last Mile Inc ....E 614 801-0621
Columbus (G-8566)

Sacs Cnslting Training Ctr Inc ....E 330 255-1101
Akron (G-415)

Safelite Solutions LLC ....A 614 210-9000
Columbus (G-8577)

Safety Resources Company Ohio ....E 330 477-1100
Canton (G-2469)

Sb Capital Acquisitions LLC ....A 614 443-4080
Columbus (G-8596)

Schrudder Prfmce Group LLC ....E 513 652-7675
West Chester (G-18999)

SCI Direct LLC ....A 330 494-5504
North Canton (G-15232)

Scrogginsgrear Inc ....C 513 672-4281
Cincinnati (G-4440)

Sedlak Management Consultants ....E 216 206-4700
Cleveland (G-6391)

SEI - Cincinnati LLC ....D 513 459-1992
Cincinnati (G-4447)

Selection MGT Systems Inc ....D 513 522-8764
Cincinnati (G-4450)

Sheakley Unicomp Inc ....C 513 771-2277
Cincinnati (G-4467)

Sheakley-Uniservice Inc ....C 513 771-2277
Cincinnati (G-4468)

Shotstop Ballistics LLC ....E 330 686-0020
Stow (G-17230)

Shp Leading Design ....D 513 381-2112
Cincinnati (G-4472)

Signature Associates Inc ....E 419 244-7505
Toledo (G-18034)

Signet Management Co Ltd ....C 330 762-9102
Akron (G-428)

Silver Spruce Holding LLC ....E 937 259-1200
Dayton (G-9770)

Skylight Financial Group LLC...........E 216 621-5680
Cleveland (G-6413)

Smart Harbor LLC ....E 800 295-4519
Columbus (G-8653)

Smith & English II Inc ....E 513 697-9300
Loveland (G-13029)

Smithers Group Inc ....D 330 762-7441
Akron (G-432)

Smithers Quality Assessments ....E 330 762-4231
Akron (G-433)

Smithers Rapra Inc ....D 330 762-7441
Akron (G-434)

Smoot Construction Co Ohio ....E 614 253-9000
Columbus (G-8657)

Sodexo Inc ....E 330 425-0709
Twinsburg (G-18321)

Solenis LLC ....E 614 336-1101
Dublin (G-10336)

Spirit Women Health Netwrk LLC ....E 561 544-2004
Cincinnati (G-2869)

SSS Consulting Inc ....E 937 259-1200
Dayton (G-9788)

State of Ohio ....D 614 466-3455
Columbus (G-8693)

Stepstone Group Real Estate LP ....E 216 522-0330
Cleveland (G-6467)

Sumner Solutions Inc ....E 513 531-6382
Cincinnati (G-4553)

Sun Valley Infosys LLC ....D 937 267-6435
Springfield (G-17121)

Support Fincl Resources Inc ....E 800 444-5465
Centerville (G-2634)

Surgere Inc ....E 330 526-7971
North Canton (G-15236)

Synergy Consulting Group Inc ....E 330 899-9301
Uniontown (G-18387)

Tacg LLC ....C 937 203-8201
Beavercreek (G-1237)

Techncal Sltons Spcialists Inc ....E 513 792-8930
Blue Ash (G-1656)

Techsolve Inc ....D 513 948-2000
Cincinnati (G-4581)

Tek Systems ....D 614 789-6200
Dublin (G-10354)

Terry J Reppa & Associates ....E 440 888-8533
Cleveland (G-6516)

The Sheakley Group Inc ....E 513 771-2277
Cincinnati (G-4596)

Thomas and King Inc ....C 614 527-0571
Hilliard (G-11821)

Tm Capture Services LLC ....D 937 728-1781
Beavercreek (G-1238)

Toni & Marie Bader ....E 937 339-3621
Troy (G-18231)

Top Echelon Contracting Inc ....B 330 454-3508
Canton (G-2514)

Total Marketing Resources LLC ....E 330 220-1275
Brunswick (G-1943)

Touchstone Group Assoc LLC ....E 513 791-1717
Cincinnati (G-4613)

Triad Oil & Gas Engineering ....D 740 374-2940
Marietta (G-13388)

Trilogy Fulfillment LLC ....E 614 491-0553
Groveport (G-11543)

Trinity Credit Counseling Inc ....E 513 769-0621
Cincinnati (G-4647)

Trinity Health Corporation ....E 419 448-3124
Tiffin (G-17545)

Truepoint Inc ....E 513 792-6648
Blue Ash (G-1667)

Tsg Resources Inc ....A 330 498-8200
North Canton (G-15241)

Turtle Golf Management Ltd ....E 614 882-5920
Westerville (G-19303)

TV Minority Company Inc ....E 937 832-9350
Englewood (G-10603)

United Audit Systems Inc ....C 513 723-1122
Cincinnati (G-4675)

United States Enrichment Corp ....A 740 897-2331
Piketon (G-15989)

United States Enrichment Corp ....A 740 897-2457
Piketon (G-15990)

Universal Marketing Group LLC ....D 419 720-9696
Toledo (G-18123)

Universal Transportation Syste ....C 513 829-1287
Fairfield (G-10796)

University of Dayton ....C 937 255-3141
Dayton (G-9836)

University of Dayton ....C 937 229-3913
Dayton (G-9841)

Upper Valley Financial Inc ....E 937 381-0054
Piqua (G-16035)

Vand Corp ....E 216 481-3788
Cleveland (G-6620)

Vartek Services Inc ....E 937 438-3550
Dayton (G-9852)

Vediscovery LLC ....E 216 241-3443
Cleveland (G-6622)

S I C

Vernon F Glaser & Associates............E......937 298-5536
  Dayton (G-9854)
Versatex LLC............E......513 639-3119
  Cincinnati (G-4755)
Weber Obrien Ltd............E......419 885-8338
  Sylvania (G-17463)
Weber Partners Ltd............E......614 222-6806
  Columbus (G-8882)
Wellington Group LLC............E......216 525-2200
  Independence (G-12140)
William Thomas Group Inc............D......800 582-3107
  Cincinnati (G-4797)
Willowood Care Center............C......330 225-3156
  Brunswick (G-1947)
Wirefree Home Automation............E......440 247-8978
  Chagrin Falls (G-2661)
Worthington Public Library............C......614 807-2626
  Worthington (G-19862)
Wpmi Inc............E......440 392-2171
  Mentor (G-14127)
Wtw Delaware Holdings LLC............C......216 937-4000
  Cleveland (G-6693)
Xzamcorp............E......330 629-2218
  Perry (G-15830)
Young and Associates Inc............E......330 678-0524
  Kent (G-12270)

8743 Public Relations Svcs

Automotive Events Inc............E......440 356-1383
  Rocky River (G-16423)
Babbage-Simmel & Assoc Inc............E......614 481-6555
  Columbus (G-7010)
Campbell Sales Company............E......513 697-2900
  Cincinnati (G-3111)
City of Cleveland Heights............E......216 291-2323
  Cleveland Heights (G-6716)
Code One Communications Inc............E......614 338-0321
  Columbus (G-7240)
County of Guernsey............D......800 307-8422
  Cambridge (G-2061)
County of Logan............E......937 599-7252
  Bellefontaine (G-1349)
D L Ryan Companies LLC............E......614 436-6558
  Westerville (G-19156)
Dix & Eaton Incorporated............E......216 241-0405
  Cleveland (G-5431)
Domestic Relations............E......937 225-4063
  Dayton (G-9394)
Edward Howard & Co............E......216 781-2400
  Cleveland (G-5468)
Fahlgren Inc............D......614 383-1500
  Columbus (G-7553)
Fast Traxx Promotions LLC............E......740 767-3740
  Millfield (G-14505)
Forwith Logistics LLC............E......513 386-8310
  Milford (G-14388)
L Brands Service Company LLC............D......614 415-7000
  Columbus (G-7933)
Marcus Thomas Llc............D......330 793-3000
  Youngstown (G-20116)
Marsh Inc............E......513 421-1234
  Cincinnati (G-3975)
Midway Mall Merchants Assoc............E......440 244-1245
  Elyria (G-10537)
Nugrowth Solutions LLC............E......800 747-9273
  Columbus (G-8215)
Ohio State University............E......614 293-3737
  Columbus (G-8330)
Paul Werth Associates Inc............E......614 224-8114
  Columbus (G-8429)
Quotient Technology Inc............E......513 229-8659
  Mason (G-13631)
RA Staff Company Inc............E......440 891-9900
  Cleveland (G-6276)
United States Trotting Assn............D......614 224-2291
  Columbus (G-8811)
Universal Veneer Sales Corp............E......740 522-2000
  Granville (G-11348)
Ver-A-Fast Corp............E......440 331-0250
  Rocky River (G-16447)
Whitespace Design Group Inc............E......330 762-9320
  Akron (G-501)

8744 Facilities Support Mgmt Svcs

Alco Inc............E......740 527-2991
  Logan (G-12830)
Aramark Facility Services LLC............E......216 687-5000
  Cleveland (G-4998)
Aztec Services Group Inc............D......513 541-2002
  Cincinnati (G-3012)

City of Xenia............E......937 376-7260
  Xenia (G-19894)
Community Education Ctrs Inc............B......330 424-4065
  Lisbon (G-12797)
Corecivic Inc............B......330 746-3777
  Youngstown (G-20011)
Correction Commission NW Ohio............C......419 428-3800
  Stryker (G-17369)
Correctons Comm Sthastern Ohio............D......740 753-4060
  Nelsonville (G-14828)
County of Miami............E......937 335-1314
  Troy (G-18199)
Cuyahoga County Convention Fac............D......216 928-1600
  Cleveland (G-5398)
Environmental Specialists Inc............E......740 788-8134
  Newark (G-15032)
Enviroserve Inc............C......330 966-0910
  North Canton (G-15200)
Firstgroup America Inc............E......513 241-2200
  Cincinnati (G-3566)
Four Seasons Environmental Inc............B......513 539-2978
  Monroe (G-14568)
Franklin Cnty Bd Commissioners............C......614 462-3800
  Columbus (G-7606)
Franklin Community Base Correc............C......614 525-4600
  Columbus (G-7615)
Greene County............E......937 562-7800
  Xenia (G-19905)
Henry Call Inc............C......216 433-5609
  Cleveland (G-5684)
L B & B Associates Inc............E......216 451-2672
  Cleveland (G-5842)
Licking Muskingum Cmnty Correc............E......740 349-6980
  Newark (G-15058)
Management & Training Corp............C......801 693-2600
  Conneaut (G-8955)
Midwest Environmental Inc............E......419 382-9200
  Perrysburg (G-15895)
MPW Industrial Svcs Group Inc............D......740 927-8790
  Hebron (G-11719)
Neocap/Cbcf............D......330 675-2669
  Warren (G-18733)
North Bay Construction Inc............E......440 835-1898
  Westlake (G-19380)
Selecttech Services Corp............C......937 438-9905
  Centerville (G-2633)
Serco Inc............E......937 331-4180
  Moraine (G-14696)
Southside Envmtl Group LLC............E......330 299-0027
  Niles (G-15170)
Space Management Inc............E......937 254-6622
  Dayton (G-9781)
Technical Assurance Inc............E......440 953-3147
  Willoughby (G-19575)
Wastren - Energx Mission............C......740 897-3724
  Piketon (G-15992)
Wastren Advantage Inc............E......970 254-1277
  Piketon (G-15993)

8748 Business Consulting Svcs, NEC

A M Communications Ltd............D......419 528-3051
  Galion (G-11165)
ABC Fire Inc............E......440 237-6677
  North Royalton (G-15346)
Acadia Solutions Inc............E......614 505-6135
  Dublin (G-10118)
Accenture LLP............E......216 685-1435
  Cleveland (G-4898)
Accenture LLP............C......614 629-2000
  Columbus (G-6861)
Accessrn Inc............D......419 698-1988
  Maumee (G-13746)
Acrt Inc............E......800 622-2562
  Stow (G-17187)
Acrt Services Inc............A......330 945-7500
  Stow (G-17188)
Actionlink LLC............A......888 737-8757
  Akron (G-18)
Aecom............D......513 651-3440
  Cincinnati (G-2914)
Aecom Global II LLC............D......419 774-9862
  Delta (G-10040)
Air Compliance Testing Inc............E......216 525-0900
  Cleveland (G-4916)
Alice Training Institute LLC............D......330 661-0106
  Medina (G-13908)
Allied Environmental Svcs Inc............E......419 227-4004
  Lima (G-12599)
◆ Alpha Technologies Svcs LLC............D......330 745-1641
  Hudson (G-11966)

Als Group Usa Corp............E......513 733-5336
  Blue Ash (G-1503)
American Broadband Telecom Co............E......419 824-5800
  Toledo (G-17587)
▲ American Envmtl Group Ltd............B......330 659-5930
  Richfield (G-16344)
American Health Group Inc............E......419 891-1212
  Maumee (G-13750)
Apple Growth Partners Inc............D......330 867-7350
  Akron (G-76)
Arcadis US Inc............D......419 473-1121
  Toledo (G-17598)
Ardent Technologies Inc............C......937 312-1345
  Dayton (G-9238)
Ashtabula Cnty Eductl Svc Ctr............D......440 576-4085
  Ashtabula (G-709)
Attentn Web Administrtr Marjon............E......513 708-9888
  Franklin (G-11023)
Avantia Inc............E......216 901-9366
  Cleveland (G-5027)
B2b Power Partners............E......614 309-6964
  Galena (G-11155)
Barbara S Desalvo Inc............E......513 729-2111
  Cincinnati (G-3019)
Bbs & Associates Inc............E......330 665-5227
  Akron (G-89)
Benchmark Technologies Corp............E......419 843-6691
  Toledo (G-17611)
Big Red Rooster............E......614 255-0200
  Columbus (G-7036)
Biorx LLC............C......866 442-4679
  Cincinnati (G-3051)
Bjaam Environmental Inc............E......330 854-5300
  Canal Fulton (G-2093)
Bkd LLP............D......513 621-8300
  Cincinnati (G-3053)
Bravo Wellness LLC............C......216 658-9500
  Cleveland (G-5075)
Bright Horizons Chld Ctrs LLC............E......614 227-0550
  Columbus (G-7066)
Buckeye Hills-Hck Vly Reg Dev............D......740 373-0087
  Marietta (G-13317)
Bureau Veritas North Amer Inc............E......330 252-5100
  Akron (G-115)
Calabresem Racek & Markos Inc............E......216 696-5442
  Cleveland (G-5113)
Capital City Indus Systems LLC............E......614 519-5047
  Put In Bay (G-16224)
Cardinal Maintenance & Svc Co............C......330 252-0282
  Akron (G-118)
Cash Flow Solutions Inc............D......513 524-2320
  Oxford (G-15676)
Cbiz Inc............D......330 644-2044
  Uniontown (G-18361)
Cbiz Operations Inc............D......216 447-9000
  Cleveland (G-5140)
Cbiz Risk & Advisory Svcs LLC............E......216 447-9000
  Cleveland (G-5141)
CDM SMITH INC............E......614 847-8340
  Columbus (G-7147)
Celebrity Security Inc............E......216 671-6425
  Cleveland (G-5146)
Centric Consulting LLC............D......888 781-7567
  Dayton (G-9290)
Cgh-Global Technologies LLC............E......800 376-0655
  Cincinnati (G-3165)
Check It Out 4 Me LLC............E......513 568-4269
  Cincinnati (G-3173)
Cincinnati Cnslting Consortium............E......513 233-0011
  Cincinnati (G-3234)
City of Akron............E......330 375-2851
  Akron (G-138)
City of Coshocton............D......740 622-1763
  Coshocton (G-9001)
Clermont County Gen Hlth Dst............E......513 732-7499
  Batavia (G-989)
Clgt Solutions LLC............E......740 920-4795
  Granville (G-11338)
Cliff North Consultants Inc............E......513 251-4930
  Cincinnati (G-3306)
Clinton-Carvell Inc............E......614 351-8858
  Columbus (G-7229)
Coact Associates Ltd............E......866 646-4400
  Toledo (G-17666)
Cohesion Consulting LLC............D......513 587-7700
  Blue Ash (G-1533)
Communications III Inc............E......614 901-7720
  Westerville (G-19244)
Compmanagement Health Systems............D......614 766-5223
  Dublin (G-10188)

Composite Tech Amer Inc	E	330 562-5201	Cleveland *(G-5332)*
Connaissance Consulting LLC	C	614 289-5200	Columbus *(G-7349)*
Construction Resources Inc	E	440 248-9800	Cleveland *(G-5339)*
Controlsoft Inc	E	440 443-3900	Cleveland *(G-5346)*
Corbus LLC	D	937 226-7724	Dayton *(G-9321)*
Corporate Ladder Search	E	330 776-4390	Uniontown *(G-18364)*
CTS Construction Inc	D	513 489-8290	Cincinnati *(G-3385)*
Dan-Ray Construction LLC	E	216 518-8484	Cleveland *(G-5404)*
Dancor Inc	E	614 340-2155	Columbus *(G-7414)*
Datavantage Corporation	B	440 498-4414	Cleveland *(G-5406)*
Dedicated Technologies Inc	E	614 460-3200	Columbus *(G-7427)*
Deemsys Inc	D	614 322-9928	Gahanna *(G-11117)*
Deloitte & Touche LLP	B	513 784-7100	Cincinnati *(G-3420)*
Deloitte Consulting LLP	E	937 223-8821	Dayton *(G-9387)*
Devcare Solutions Ltd	E	614 221-2277	Columbus *(G-7439)*
E Retailing Associates LLC	D	614 300-5785	Columbus *(G-7486)*
Eco Engineering Inc	D	513 985-8300	Cincinnati *(G-3483)*
Ecs Holdco Inc	E	614 433-0170	Worthington *(G-19805)*
Educational Solutions Co	D	614 989-4588	Columbus *(G-7504)*
Ellipse Solutions LLC	E	937 312-1547	Dayton *(G-9413)*
Emergency Response & Trnng	E	440 349-2700	Solon *(G-16844)*
Emersion Design LLC	E	513 841-9100	Cincinnati *(G-3494)*
Employee Benefit Management	E	614 766-5800	Dublin *(G-10217)*
Envirnmental Resources MGT Inc	E	216 593-5200	Beachwood *(G-1055)*
Envirnmental Resources MGT Inc	E	513 830-9030	Blue Ash *(G-1556)*
Environmental Quality MGT	D	513 825-7500	Cincinnati *(G-3502)*
Environmental Solutions	E	513 451-1777	Cincinnati *(G-3503)*
Enviroscience Inc	C	330 688-0111	Stow *(G-17202)*
Enviroserve Inc	C	330 966-0910	North Canton *(G-15200)*
Envision Corporation	D	513 772-5437	Cincinnati *(G-3504)*
Excellence In Motivation Inc	C	763 445-3000	Dayton *(G-9420)*
Feg Consulting LLC	E	412 224-2263	Blue Ash *(G-1560)*
Flavik Village Development	E	216 429-1182	Cleveland *(G-5544)*
Flexential Corp	D	513 645-2900	Hamilton *(G-11595)*
Floyd Browne Group Inc	E	740 363-6792	Delaware *(G-9977)*
General Electric Company	C	513 583-3626	Mason *(G-13584)*
Gleaming Systems LLC	E	614 348-7475	Lewis Center *(G-12543)*
Grace Consulting Inc	E	440 647-6672	Wellington *(G-18841)*
Gunning & Assocaites Marketing	E	513 688-1370	Cincinnati *(G-3663)*
Halley Consulting Group LLC	E	614 899-7325	Westerville *(G-19258)*
Healthquest Blanchester Inc	E	937 783-4535	Blanchester *(G-1487)*
Heritage Envmtl Svcs LLC	E	419 729-1321	Toledo *(G-17802)*
Hobsons Inc	C	513 891-5444	Cincinnati *(G-3714)*
Homeland Defense Solutions	E	513 333-7800	Cincinnati *(G-3723)*
Hoskins International LLC	E	419 628-6015	Minster *(G-14536)*
Hull & Associates Inc	E	614 793-8777	Dublin *(G-10247)*
Humantics Innovative Solutions	E	567 265-5200	Huron *(G-12025)*
Hzw Environmental Cons LLC	E	800 804-8484	Mentor *(G-14062)*
Icon Environmental Group LLC	E	513 426-6767	Milford *(G-14396)*
Illumination Works LLC	D	937 938-1321	Beavercreek *(G-1157)*
Image Consulting Services Inc	E	440 951-9919	Cleveland *(G-5739)*
Impact Medical Mgt Group	E	440 365-7014	Elyria *(G-10519)*
Improvedge LLC	E	614 793-1738	Powell *(G-16197)*
Incentisoft Solutions LLC	E	877 562-4461	Cleveland *(G-5741)*
Indecon Solutions LLC	E	614 799-1850	Dublin *(G-10254)*
Industrial Vibrations Cons	E	513 932-4678	Lebanon *(G-12472)*
Infoverity Inc	E	614 310-1709	Dublin *(G-10255)*
Integrated Solutions and	E	513 826-1932	Dayton *(G-9516)*
Interactive Engineering Corp	E	330 239-6888	Medina *(G-13956)*
Interactive Solutions Intl LLC	E	513 619-5100	Cincinnati *(G-3776)*
Interdyne Corporation	E	419 229-8192	Lima *(G-12666)*
Its Traffic Systems Inc	D	440 892-4500	Westlake *(G-19359)*
Jennings & Associates	E	740 369-4426	Delaware *(G-9991)*
Jones Group Interiors Inc	E	330 253-9180	Akron *(G-294)*
Juice Technologies Inc	E	800 518-5576	Columbus *(G-7875)*
Jyg Innovations LLC	E	937 630-3858	Dayton *(G-9531)*
Kemper Company	D	440 846-1100	Strongsville *(G-17319)*
Kemron Environmental Svcs Inc	D	740 373-4071	Marietta *(G-13342)*
Kennedy Group Enterprises Inc	E	440 879-0078	Strongsville *(G-17320)*
Key Office Services	E	419 747-9749	Mansfield *(G-13193)*
Keyw Corporation	E	937 702-9512	Beavercreek *(G-1162)*
Kirila Fire Trning Fclties Inc	E	724 854-5207	Brookfield *(G-1854)*
Klais and Company Inc	E	330 867-8443	Fairlawn *(G-10839)*
Ladder Man Inc	E	614 784-1120	Wooster *(G-19740)*
Landrum & Brown Incorporated	E	513 530-5333	Blue Ash *(G-1595)*
Lateef Elmin Mhammad Inv Group	D	937 450-3388	Springfield *(G-17060)*
Lawhon and Associates Inc	E	614 481-8600	Columbus *(G-7958)*
Legacy Consultant Pharmacy	E	336 760-1670	Bedford *(G-1288)*
Lextant Corporation	E	614 228-9711	Columbus *(G-7969)*
Lorain Cnty Elderly Hsing Corp	D	440 288-1600	Lorain *(G-12915)*
Lumenance LLC	E	319 541-6811	Columbus *(G-7997)*
Mannik & Smith Group Inc	C	419 891-2222	Maumee *(G-13812)*
Massillon Cable TV Inc	D	330 833-4134	Massillon *(G-13710)*
Mediadvertiser Inc	E	513 651-0265	Fayetteville *(G-10858)*
Miami Valley Regional Plg Comm	E	937 223-6323	Dayton *(G-9625)*
Mission Essntial Personnel LLC	C	614 416-2345	New Albany *(G-14859)*
Nas Rcrtment Cmmunications LLC	C	216 478-0300	Cleveland *(G-6036)*
Nationwide Energy Partners LLC	E	614 918-2031	Columbus *(G-8153)*
Nationwide Rtrment Sltions Inc	C	614 854-8300	Dublin *(G-10287)*
Neutral Telecom Corporation	E	440 377-4700	North Ridgeville *(G-15338)*
Northeast Ohio Areawide	E	216 621-3055	Cleveland *(G-6091)*
Northeast Ohio Communic	D	330 399-2700	Warren *(G-18735)*
Northern Indus Enrgy Dev Inc	D	330 498-9130	Canton *(G-2422)*
Nugrowth Solutions LLC	E	800 747-9273	Columbus *(G-8215)*
Occupational Health Services	E	937 492-7296	Sidney *(G-16788)*
Ohio Housing Finance Agency	B	614 466-7970	Columbus *(G-8268)*
Ohio Utilities Protection Svc	D	800 311-3692	North Jackson *(G-15250)*
On Site Instruments LLC	E	614 846-1900	Lewis Center *(G-12555)*
Oracle Systems Corporation	E	216 328-9100	Beachwood *(G-1093)*
Orin Group LLC	E	330 630-3937	Akron *(G-369)*
▼ Orton Edward Jr Crmic Fndation	E	614 895-2663	Westerville *(G-19197)*
Pinnacle Environmental Cons	E	513 533-1823	Cincinnati *(G-4250)*
Ply-Trim Enterprises Inc	E	330 799-7876	Youngstown *(G-20160)*
Poggemeyer Design Group Inc	C	419 244-8074	Bowling Green *(G-1746)*
Port Grter Cincinnati Dev Auth	E	513 621-3000	Cincinnati *(G-4263)*
Primatech Inc	E	614 841-9800	Columbus *(G-8462)*
Pro Ed Communications Inc	E	216 595-7919	Cleveland *(G-6238)*
Qwaide Enterprises LLC	E	614 209-0551	New Albany *(G-14868)*
Resolvit Resources LLC	E	513 619-5900	Cincinnati *(G-4362)*
Resolvit Resources LLC	D	703 564-2100	Cincinnati *(G-4363)*
RJ Runge Company Inc	E	419 740-5781	Port Clinton *(G-16116)*
Romitech Inc	E	937 297-9529	Dayton *(G-9739)*
Root Inc	D	419 874-0077	Sylvania *(G-17448)*
Sadler-Necamp Financial Svcs	E	513 489-5477	Cincinnati *(G-4421)*
Safety-Kleen Systems Inc	E	513 563-0931	Fairfield *(G-10777)*
Saloma Intl Co Since 1978	E	440 941-1527	Akron *(G-417)*
Sawdey Solution Services Inc	E	937 490-4060	Beavercreek *(G-1236)*
Schooley Caldwell Associates	D	614 628-0300	Columbus *(G-8607)*
Seifert & Group Inc	D	330 833-2700	Massillon *(G-13727)*
Sequent Inc	D	614 436-5880	Columbus *(G-6836)*
Service Corps Retired Execs	E	330 379-3163	Akron *(G-424)*
Shotstop Ballistics LLC	E	330 686-0020	Stow *(G-17230)*
Simplifi Eso LLC	C	614 635-8679	Columbus *(G-8644)*
Six Disciplines LLC	E	419 424-6647	Findlay *(G-10959)*
Sjn Data Center LLC	E	513 386-7871	Cincinnati *(G-4488)*
Smith & English II Inc	E	513 697-9300	Loveland *(G-13029)*
Smithers Quality Assessments	E	330 762-4231	Akron *(G-417)*
Software Support Group Inc	D	216 566-0555	Shaker Heights *(G-16713)*
Solar Testing Laboratories Inc	C	216 741-7007	Brooklyn Heights *(G-1881)*
Sordyl & Associates Inc	E	419 866-6811	Maumee *(G-13854)*
South Central Ohio Eductl Ctr	C	740 456-0517	New Boston *(G-14883)*
SSS Consulting Inc	E	937 259-1200	Dayton *(G-9788)*
Star County Home Consortium	E	330 451-7395	Canton *(G-2486)*
Status Solutions LLC	E	866 846-7272	Westerville *(G-19211)*
Stout Risius Ross LLC	E	216 685-5000	Cleveland *(G-6471)*

SIC

Summit Solutions Inc ....E 937 291-4333
Dayton *(G-9799)*

Systems Evolution Inc ....D 513 459-1992
Cincinnati *(G-4563)*

Tangoe Us Inc ....D 614 842-9918
Columbus *(G-8730)*

Team NEO ....E 216 363-5400
Cleveland *(G-6507)*

Techsolve Inc ....D 513 948-2000
Cincinnati *(G-4581)*

Tetra Tech Inc ....E 513 251-2730
Cincinnati *(G-4588)*

Tipharah Group Corp ....C 937 430-6266
Dayton *(G-9814)*

Tipharah Group Corp ....C 937 430-6266
Dayton *(G-9815)*

Toledo Metro Area Cncl Gvrnmnt ......E 419 241-9155
Toledo *(G-18090)*

Towe & Associates Inc ....E 937 275-0900
West Milton *(G-19127)*

Tribute Contracting & Cons LLC ....E 740 451-1010
South Point *(G-16946)*

Truechoicepack Corp ....E 937 630-3832
Mason *(G-13651)*

Trumbull Housing Dev Corp ....D 330 369-1533
Warren *(G-18757)*

Ttl Associates Inc ....C 419 241-4556
Toledo *(G-18111)*

Turnkey Network Solutions LLC ....E 614 876-9944
Columbus *(G-8789)*

Twism Enterprises LLC ....E 513 800-1098
Cincinnati *(G-4657)*

Uc Health Llc ....C 513 475-7630
West Chester *(G-19021)*

Unique Home Solutions Inc ....E 800 800-1971
Hinckley *(G-11861)*

US Home Center LLC ....E 614 737-9000
Columbus *(G-8834)*

Uts Inc ....E 513 332-9000
Cincinnati *(G-4746)*

Vahalla Company Inc ....E 216 326-2245
Cleveland *(G-6615)*

Vans Express Inc ....E 216 224-5388
Hinckley *(G-11863)*

Warstler Brothers Landscaping ....E 330 492-9500
Canton *(G-2531)*

Weber Obrien Ltd ....E 419 885-8338
Sylvania *(G-17463)*

William Sydney Druen ....E 614 444-7655
Columbus *(G-8905)*

Wtb Inc ....E 216 298-1895
Cleveland *(G-6692)*

Yashco Systems Inc ....E 614 467-4600
Hilliard *(G-11831)*

89 SERVICES, NOT ELSEWHERE CLASSIFIED

8999 Services Not Elsewhere Classified

Accelerant Technologies LLC ....D 419 236-8768
Genoa *(G-11251)*

American National Red Cross ....E 216 431-3152
Cleveland *(G-4962)*

ASC Group Inc ....E 614 268-2514
Columbus *(G-6976)*

Central Ohio Primary Care ....E 614 882-0708
Westerville *(G-19235)*

Centre Communications Corp ....E 440 454-3262
Beavercreek *(G-1209)*

Centric Consulting LLC ....E 513 791-3061
Cincinnati *(G-3160)*

Chp AP Shared Services ....E 513 981-6704
Cincinnati *(G-3197)*

City of Rocky River ....E 440 356-5630
Cleveland *(G-5215)*

City of Toledo ....E 419 936-2875
Toledo *(G-17656)*

Civil & Environmental Cons Inc ....E 419 724-5281
Toledo *(G-17661)*

Coleman Professional Svcs Inc ....C 330 673-1347
Kent *(G-12223)*

County of Clermont ....E 513 732-7661
Batavia *(G-993)*

County of Logan ....E 937 599-4221
Bellefontaine *(G-1350)*

Daily Services LLC ....C 740 326-6130
Mount Vernon *(G-14761)*

▼ Diproinduca (usa) Limited LLC ....D 330 722-4442
Medina *(G-13930)*

Dispatch Productions Inc ....D 614 460-3700
Columbus *(G-7452)*

Don Drumm Studios & Gallery ....E 330 253-6840
Akron *(G-190)*

Gray & Pape Inc ....E 513 287-7700
Cincinnati *(G-3635)*

Grenada Stamping Assembly Inc ....E 419 842-3600
Sylvania *(G-17427)*

Htp Inc ....E 614 885-1272
Columbus *(G-6816)*

Lighthouse Youth Services Inc ....D 513 861-1111
Cincinnati *(G-3930)*

Linemaster Services LLC ....E 614 507-9945
Grove City *(G-11449)*

Mack Communications LLC ....E 330 347-4020
Youngstown *(G-20103)*

Madison Avenue Mktg Group Inc ....E 419 473-9000
Toledo *(G-17878)*

Marsden Holding LLC ....D 440 973-7774
Middleburg Heights *(G-14254)*

Miami Conservancy District ....E 937 223-1271
Dayton *(G-9614)*

Miami County Park District ....E 937 335-6273
Troy *(G-18214)*

Mid Ohio Emergency Svcs LLC ....E 614 566-5070
Columbus *(G-8073)*

National Service Information ....E 740 387-6806
Marion *(G-13448)*

National Valuation Consultants ....E 513 929-4100
Cincinnati *(G-4096)*

National Weather Service ....E 937 383-0031
Wilmington *(G-19636)*

National Weather Service ....E 216 265-2370
Cleveland *(G-6050)*

National Weather Service ....E 419 522-1375
Mansfield *(G-13226)*

Ohio Consumers Counsel ....E 614 466-8574
Columbus *(G-8234)*

ONeil & Associates Inc ....B 937 865-0800
Miamisburg *(G-14201)*

P & D Removal Service ....E 513 226-7687
Cincinnati *(G-4194)*

Pcm Inc ....E 614 854-1399
Lewis Center *(G-12557)*

Provato LLC ....E 440 546-0768
Brecksville *(G-1800)*

Psychology Consultants Inc ....E 330 764-7916
Medina *(G-13990)*

Quantech Services Inc ....C 937 490-8461
Beavercreek Township *(G-1261)*

Richland Township Fire Dept ....E 740 536-7313
Rushville *(G-16465)*

Stg Communication Services Inc ....E 330 482-0500
Columbiana *(G-6792)*

Superior Envmtl Sltons SES Inc ....B 513 874-6910
West Chester *(G-19086)*

Thinkpath Engineering Svcs LLC ....E 937 291-8374
Miamisburg *(G-14229)*

University of Cincinnati ....A 513 556-5087
Cincinnati *(G-4711)*

Vantage Aging ....A 330 785-9770
Akron *(G-487)*

Wireless Source Entps LLC ....E 419 266-5556
Bowling Green *(G-1751)*

Wtw Delaware Holdings LLC ....C 216 937-4000
Cleveland *(G-6693)*

ALPHABETIC SECTION

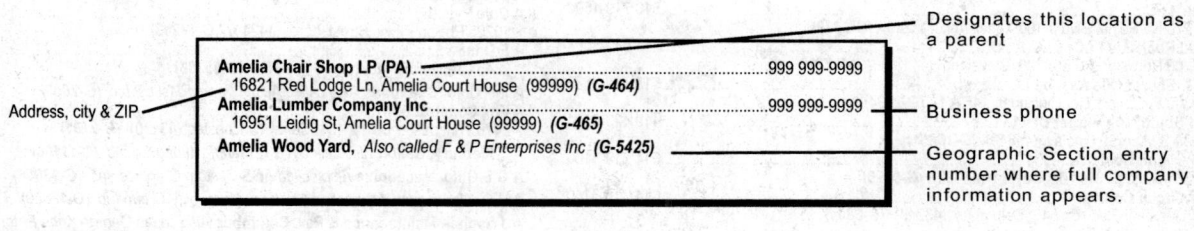

Designates this location as a parent

Amelia Chair Shop LP (PA) 999 999-9999
  16821 Red Lodge Ln, Amelia Court House (99999) *(G-464)*

Address, city & ZIP

Amelia Lumber Company Inc 999 999-9999
  16951 Leidig St, Amelia Court House (99999) *(G-465)*

Business phone

Amelia Wood Yard, *Also called F & P Enterprises Inc (G-5425)*

Geographic Section entry number where full company information appears.

See footnotes for symbols and codes identification.

* Companies listed alphabetically.

* Complete physical or mailing address.

0714 Inc 440 327-2123
32648 Center Ridge Rd North Ridgeville (44039) *(G-15318)*

1 Amazing Place Co 419 420-0424
207 E Foulke Ave Findlay (45840) *(G-10860)*

1 Community 216 923-2272
1375 Euclid Ave Cleveland (44115) *(G-4863)*

1 Edi Source Inc 440 519-7800
31875 Solon Rd Solon (44139) *(G-16812)*

1 Financial Corporation 513 936-1400
10123 Alliance Rd Ste 110 Blue Ash (45242) *(G-1493)*

1-888 Ohio Comp LLC 216 426-0646
2900 Carnegie Ave Cleveland (44115) *(G-4864)*

10 Wilmington Place 937 253-1010
10 Wilmington Ave Dayton (45420) *(G-9193)*

101 River Inc 440 352-6343
101 River St Grand River (44045) *(G-11331)*

1106 West Main Inc 330 673-2122
1106 W Main St Kent (44240) *(G-12212)*

1157 Design Concepts LLC 937 497-1157
210 S Lester Ave Sidney (45365) *(G-16755)*

12000 Edgewater Drive LLC 216 520-1250
12000 Edgewater Dr Lakewood (44107) *(G-12333)*

127 PS Fee Owner LLC 216 520-1250
1300 Key Tower 127 Pub Sq Cleveland (44114) *(G-4865)*

1440 Corporation Inc 513 424-2421
1440 S Breiel Blvd Middletown (45044) *(G-14284)*

1460 Ninth St Assoc Ltd Partnr 216 241-6600
1460 E 9th St Cleveland (44114) *(G-4866)*

1522 Hess Street LLC 614 291-6876
1522 Hess St Columbus (43212) *(G-6840)*

16 Bit Bar 513 381-1616
1331 Walnut St Cincinnati (45202) *(G-2876)*

16644 Snow Rd LLC 216 676-5200
16644 Snow Rd Brookpark (44142) *(G-1889)*

1st Advanced Ems LLC 614 348-9991
723 N James Rd Columbus (43219) *(G-6841)*

1st Advnce SEC Invstgtions Inc 937 317-4433
111 W 1st St Ste 101 Dayton (45402) *(G-9194)*

1st Advnce SEC Invstgtions Inc 937 210-9010
1675 Woodman Dr Dayton (45432) *(G-9153)*

1st All File Recovery Usa 800 399-7150
3570 Warrensville Ctr Rd Shaker Heights (44122) *(G-16701)*

1st Carrier Corp 740 477-2587
177 Neville St Circleville (43113) *(G-4821)*

1st Choice LLC 877 564-6658
600 Superior Ave E # 1300 Cleveland (44114) *(G-4867)*

1st Choice Roofing Company 216 227-7755
10311 Berea Rd Cleveland (44102) *(G-4868)*

1st Choice Security Inc 513 381-6789
2245 Gilbert Ave Ste 400 Cincinnati (45206) *(G-2877)*

1st Class Home Health Care Ser 216 678-0213
10333 Nrthfeld Rd Unit 30 Northfield (44067) *(G-15371)*

1st Class Wellness Healty Eats, Northfield *Also called 1st Class Home Health Care Ser (G-15371)*

1st Stop Inc (PA) 937 695-0318
18856 State Route 136 Winchester (45697) *(G-19658)*

204 W Main Street Oper Co LLC 419 929-1563
204 W Main St New London (44851) *(G-14930)*

2060 Digital LLC 513 699-5012
2060 Reading Rd Cincinnati (45202) *(G-2878)*

2100 Lakeside Shelter For Men 216 566-0047
2100 Lakeside Ave E Cleveland (44114) *(G-4869)*

21c Cincinnati LLC 513 578-6600
609 Walnut St Ste 2 Cincinnati (45202) *(G-2879)*

21c Museum Hotel Cincinnati, Cincinnati *Also called 21c Cincinnati LLC (G-2879)*

21st Century Con Cnstr Inc 216 362-0900
13925 Enterprise Ave Cleveland (44135) *(G-4870)*

21st Century Financial Inc 330 668-9065
130 Springside Dr Ste 100 Akron (44333) *(G-9)*

21st Century Health Spa Inc (PA) 419 476-5585
343 New Towne Square Dr Toledo (43612) *(G-17573)*

21st Century Solutions Ltd 877 439-5377
955 Mound Rd Miamisburg (45342) *(G-14134)*

22nd Century Technologies Inc 866 537-9191
2601 Commons Blvd Ste 130 Beavercreek (45431) *(G-1121)*

24 - Seven Home Hlth Care LLC 614 794-0325
5064 Edgeley Dr Hilliard (43026) *(G-11737)*

2444 Mdson Rd Cndo Owners Assn 513 871-0100
2444 Madison Rd Ste 101 Cincinnati (45208) *(G-2880)*

2780 Airport Drive LLC 513 563-7555
2135 Dana Ave Ste 200 Cincinnati (45207) *(G-2881)*

2828 Clinton Inc (PA) 216 241-7157
600 Cherry Fork Rd Leetonia (44431) *(G-12517)*

3 B Ventures LLC 419 236-9461
980 N Eastown Rd Lima (45807) *(G-12590)*

3-D Service Ltd (PA) 330 830-3500
800 Nave Rd Se Massillon (44646) *(G-13656)*

3-D Technical Services Company 937 746-2901
255 Industrial Dr Franklin (45005) *(G-11020)*

3-Dmed, Franklin *Also called 3-D Technical Services Company (G-11020)*

36 E Seventh LLC 513 699-2279
2135 Dana Ave Ste 200 Cincinnati (45207) *(G-2882)*

3b Holdings Inc (PA) 800 791-7124
11470 Euclid Ave Ste 407 Cleveland (44106) *(G-4871)*

3b Supply, Cleveland *Also called 3b Holdings Inc (G-4871)*

3c Technologies Inc 419 868-8999
6834 Spring Valley Dr # 202 Holland (43528) *(G-11868)*

3g Operating Company LLC 440 944-9400
12380 Plaza Dr Parma (44130) *(G-15758)*

3rd Street Community Clinic 419 522-6191
600 W 3rd St Mansfield (44906) *(G-13130)*

3RD STREET FAMILY HEALTH SERVI, Mansfield *Also called 3rd Street Community Clinic (G-13130)*

3s Incorporated (HQ) 513 202-5070
8686 Southwest Pkwy Harrison (45030) *(G-11659)*

3sg Corporation 614 309-3600
344 Cramer Creek Ct Dublin (43017) *(G-10117)*

3sg Plus LLC 614 652-0019
8415 Pulsar Pl Ste 100 Columbus (43240) *(G-6797)*

4 Paws Sake Inc 419 304-7139
13244 Neowash Rd Grand Rapids (43522) *(G-11323)*

4 Seasons Car Wash, Lima *Also called 3 B Ventures LLC (G-12590)*

415 Group Inc (PA) 330 492-0094
4100 Holiday St Nw # 100 Canton (44718) *(G-2167)*

44444 LLC 330 502-2023
5783 Norquest Blvd Austintown (44515) *(G-855)*

4C FOR CHILDREN, Cincinnati *Also called Comprehensive Cmnty Child Care (G-3345)*

4mybenefits Inc 513 891-6648
4665 Cornell Rd Ste 331 Blue Ash (45241) *(G-1494)*

4th and Goal Distribution LLC 440 212-0769
9911 Avon Lake Rd Burbank (44214) *(G-2008)*

4wd, Columbiana *Also called Four Wheel Drive Hardware LLC (G-6788)*

5 Star Hotel Management IV LP 614 431-1819
6191 Quarter Horse Dr Columbus (43229) *(G-6842)*

50 S Front LLC 614 224-4600
50 S Front St Columbus (43215) *(G-6843)*

50 X 20 Holding Company Inc 740 238-4262
41201 Bond Dr Belmont (43718) *(G-1394)*

50 X 20 Holding Company Inc (PA) 330 478-4500
2715 Wise Ave Nw Canton (44708) *(G-2168)*

50 X 20 Holding Company Inc 330 865-4663
779 White Pond Dr Akron (44320) *(G-10)*

506 Phelps Holdings LLC 513 651-1234
506 E 4th St Cincinnati (45202) *(G-2883)*

5440 Charlesgate Rd Oper LLC 937 236-6707
5440 Charlesgate Rd Dayton (45424) *(G-9195)*

55 Degrees, Streetsboro *Also called Southern Glazers Wine and Sp (G-17271)*

56 Plus Management LLC 937 323-4114
560 E High St Springfield (45505) *(G-16991)*

5901 Pffter Rd Htels Sites LLC 513 793-4500
5901 Pfeiffer Rd Blue Ash (45242) *(G-1495)*

A
L
P
H
A
B
E
T
I
C

---

599 W Main Corporation 440 466-5901
599 W Main St Geneva (44041) *(G-11235)*

5me LLC 513 719-1600
4270 Ivy Pointe Blvd # 100 Cincinnati (45245) *(G-2839)*

6200 Rockside LLC 216 642-8004
6200 Rockside Rd Ste 100 Cleveland (44131) *(G-4872)*

6300 Sharonville Assoc LLC 513 489-3636
6300 E Kemper Rd Cincinnati (45241) *(G-2884)*

631 South Main Street Dev LLC 419 423-0631
631 S Main St Findlay (45840) *(G-10861)*

6th Circuit Court 614 719-3100
200 W 2nd St Ste 702 Dayton (45402) *(G-9196)*

6th Circuit Court 614 719-3100
85 Marconi Blvd Rm 546 Columbus (43215) *(G-6844)*

7 Physcian Fmly Practice Group, Mentor Also called Lake County Family Practice *(G-14072)*

7 Up / R C/Canada Dry Btlg Co, Columbus Also called American Bottling Company *(G-6913)*

722 Redemption Funding Inc 513 679-8302
169 Northland Blvd Ste 2 Cincinnati (45246) *(G-2885)*

77 Coach Supply Ltd 330 674-1454
7426 County Road 77 Millersburg (44654) *(G-14452)*

797 Elks Golf Club Inc 937 382-2666
2593 E Us Highway 22 3 Wilmington (45177) *(G-19599)*

7nt Enterprises LLC (PA) 614 961-2026
3090 S Tech Blvd Miamisburg (45342) *(G-14135)*

845 Yard Street LLC (PA) 614 857-2330
375 N Front St Ste 200 Columbus (43215) *(G-6845)*

8451 LLC (HQ) 513 632-1020
100 W 5th St Cincinnati (45202) *(G-2886)*

94 5 Xkr Rdo Stn Bus & Sls Off, Toledo Also called Wrwk 1065 *(G-18162)*

A A S Amels Sheet Meta L Inc 330 793-9326
222 Steel St Youngstown (44509) *(G-19943)*

A & A Safety Inc (PA) 513 943-6100
1126 Ferris Rd Bldg B Amelia (45102) *(G-563)*

A & A Truck Stop, Jackson Also called Trepanier Daniels & Trepanier *(G-12180)*

A & A Wall Systems Inc 513 489-0086
11589 Deerfield Rd Cincinnati (45242) *(G-2887)*

A & C Welding Inc 330 762-4777
80 Cuyhoga Fls Indus Pkwy Peninsula (44264) *(G-15808)*

A & D Daycare and Learning Ctr 937 263-4447
1049 Infirmary Rd Dayton (45417) *(G-9197)*

A & G Manufacturing Co Inc (PA) 419 468-7433
280 Gelsanliter Rd Galion (44833) *(G-11164)*

A & J Asphalt, Columbus Also called J K Enterprises Inc *(G-7850)*

A & K Railroad Materials Inc 419 537-9470
2750 Hill Ave Toledo (43607) *(G-17574)*

A & R Builders Ltd 330 893-2111
6914 County Road 672 Millersburg (44654) *(G-14453)*

A 1 Janitorial Cleaning Svc 513 932-8003
939 Old 122 Rd Lebanon (45036) *(G-12446)*

A A Angelone, Cleveland Also called Cleveland Auto Livery Inc *(G-5231)*

A A Astro Service Inc 216 459-0363
5283 Pearl Rd Cleveland (44129) *(G-4873)*

A A Hammersmith Insurance Inc (PA) 330 832-7411
210 Erie St N Massillon (44646) *(G-13657)*

A AAA H Jacks Plumbing Htg Co 440 946-1166
29930 Lakeland Blvd Wickliffe (44092) *(G-19453)*

A and A Mllwright Rigging Svcs 513 396-6212
2205 Langdon Farm Rd Cincinnati (45237) *(G-2888)*

A and S Ventures Inc 419 376-3934
4311 Garden Estates Dr Toledo (43623) *(G-17575)*

A B C D, Canton Also called Abcd Inc *(G-2171)*

A B C Rental Center East Inc 216 475-8240
5204 Warrensville Ctr Rd Cleveland (44137) *(G-4874)*

A B Industrial Coatings 614 228-0383
212 N Grant Ave Columbus (43215) *(G-6846)*

A B M Inc 419 421-2292
119 E Sandusky St Findlay (45840) *(G-10862)*

A B S Temps Inc 937 252-9888
2770 Wilmington Pike Dayton (45419) *(G-9198)*

A Bee C Service Inc (PA) 440 735-1505
7589 First Pl Ste 1 Cleveland (44146) *(G-4875)*

A Better Child Care Corp 513 353-5437
6945 Harrison Ave Cincinnati (45247) *(G-2889)*

A Better Choice Child Care LLC 614 268-8503
2572 Cleveland Ave Columbus (43211) *(G-6847)*

A Brown & Sons Nursery (PA) 937 836-5826
11506 Dyton Grnville Pike Brookville (45309) *(G-1909)*

A C Leasing Company 513 771-3676
3023 E Kemper Rd Bldg 9 Cincinnati (45241) *(G-2890)*

A C Management Inc 440 461-9200
780 Beta Dr Cleveland (44143) *(G-4876)*

A C Supply, Strongsville Also called Lamrite West Inc *(G-17322)*

A C Trucking, Cincinnati Also called A C Leasing Company *(G-2890)*

A CCS Day Care Centers Inc 513 841-2227
1705 Section Rd Cincinnati (45237) *(G-2891)*

A Childs Place Nursery School 330 493-1333
4770 Higbee Ave Nw Canton (44718) *(G-2169)*

A Coach USA Company, Brookpark Also called Cusa LI Inc *(G-1895)*

A Crano Excavating Inc 330 630-1061
1505 Industrial Pkwy Akron (44310) *(G-11)*

A D A Architects Inc 216 521-5134
17710 Detroit Ave Cleveland (44107) *(G-4877)*

A D D, Westerville Also called Assoc Dvlpmtly Disabled *(G-19222)*

A D M Crisis Center, Akron Also called Oriana House Inc *(G-367)*

A Duie Pyle Inc 330 342-7750
10225 Philipp Pkwy Streetsboro (44241) *(G-17243)*

A E D Inc 419 661-9999
2845 Crane Way Northwood (43619) *(G-15388)*

A F P Ohio, Columbus Also called Austin Foam Plastics Inc *(G-7003)*

A Fox Construction 614 506-1685
6478 Winchester Blvd # 156 Canal Winchester (43110) *(G-2101)*

A G Mercury, Galion Also called A & G Manufacturing Co Inc *(G-11164)*

A G S Ohio, Macedonia Also called AGS Custom Graphics Inc *(G-13058)*

A H G, Wadsworth Also called American Hospitality Group Inc *(G-18589)*

A J Asphalt Maintenance & Pav, Columbus Also called George Kuhn Enterprises Inc *(G-7660)*

A J Goulder Electric Co 440 942-4026
4307 Hamann Pkwy Willoughby (44094) *(G-19501)*

A J Oster Foils LLC 330 823-1700
2081 Mccrea St Alliance (44601) *(G-512)*

A J Stockmeister Inc (PA) 740 286-2106
702 E Main St Jackson (45640) *(G-12168)*

A J'S Body Shop, Cleveland Also called Buddies Inc *(G-5100)*

A Jacobs Inc 614 774-6757
4410 Hansen Dr Hilliard (43026) *(G-11738)*

A K Athletic Equipment Inc 614 920-3069
8015 Howe Industrial Pkwy Canal Winchester (43110) *(G-2102)*

A L K Inc 740 369-8741
462 W Central Ave Delaware (43015) *(G-9947)*

A L Smith Trucking Inc 937 526-3651
8984 Murphy Rd Versailles (45380) *(G-18565)*

A L T, Cleveland Also called Bsl - Applied Laser Tech LLC *(G-5097)*

A M & O Towing Inc 330 385-0639
11341 State Route 170 Negley (44441) *(G-14827)*

A M Communications Ltd 419 528-3051
4431 Old Springfield Rd Vandalia (45377) *(G-18500)*

A M Communications Ltd (PA) 419 528-3051
5707 State Route 309 Galion (44833) *(G-11165)*

A M Leonard Inc 937 773-2694
241 Fox Dr Piqua (45356) *(G-15994)*

A M Management Inc 937 426-6500
2000 Zink Rd Beavercreek (45324) *(G-1122)*

A M Mc Gregor Home 216 851-8200
14900 Private Dr Ofc Cleveland (44112) *(G-4878)*

A Miracle Home Care, Blue Ash Also called N Services Inc *(G-1619)*

A New Beginning Preschool 216 531-7465
18403 Euclid Ave Cleveland (44112) *(G-4879)*

A O N, Cleveland Also called AON Risk Svcs Northeast Inc *(G-4988)*

A One Fine Dry Cleaners Inc (PA) 513 351-2663
6223 Montgomery Rd Cincinnati (45213) *(G-2892)*

A P & P Dev & Cnstr Co (PA) 330 833-8886
2851 Lincoln Way E Massillon (44646) *(G-13658)*

A P O Holdings Inc (PA) 330 650-1330
6607 Chittenden Rd Hudson (44236) *(G-11960)*

A P O Pumps and Compressors, Hudson Also called A P O Holdings Inc *(G-11960)*

A P OHoro Company 330 759-9317
3130 Belmont Ave Youngstown (44505) *(G-19944)*

A P P S, Cincinnati Also called American Para Prof Systems Inc *(G-2949)*

A P S Medical Billing, Toledo Also called APS Medical Billing *(G-17597)*

A P T, Worthington Also called Datafield Inc *(G-19803)*

A Plus Expediting & Logistics 937 424-0220
2947 Boulder Ave Dayton (45414) *(G-9199)*

A Provide Care Inc 330 828-2278
15028 Old Lincoln Way Dalton (44618) *(G-9143)*

A R C, Troy Also called ARC Abrasives Inc *(G-18194)*

A R C, Cleveland Also called ARC Document Solutions Inc *(G-5003)*

A R E A Title Agency Inc (PA) 419 242-5485
5450 Monroe St Ste 2 Toledo (43623) *(G-17576)*

A Renewed Mind 419 214-0606
885 Commerce Dr Ste D Perrysburg (43551) *(G-15831)*

A Ressler Inc 216 518-1804
12750 Broadway Ave Cleveland (44125) *(G-4880)*

A S I, Dayton Also called American Sales Inc *(G-9159)*

A S I, Plain City Also called Architectural Systems Inc *(G-16044)*

A Sainato Enterprises Inc 216 795-5167
11160 Snowville Rd Brecksville (44141) *(G-1765)*

A Savannah Nite Limousine Svcs, Fairfield Also called Eric Boeppler Fmly Ltd Partnr *(G-10725)*

A T & F Co, Cleveland Also called American Tank & Fabricating Co *(G-4967)*

A T V Inc 614 252-5060
2047 Leonard Ave Columbus (43219) *(G-6848)*

A Tara Tiffanys Property 330 448-0778
601 Bedford Rd Se Brookfield (44403) *(G-1851)*

A Thomas Dalagiannis MD 419 887-7000
1360 Arrowhead Dr Maumee (43537) *(G-13744)*

A To Z Golf Managment Co 937 434-4911
4990 Wilmington Pike Dayton (45440) *(G-9200)*

A To Z Portion Ctrl Meats Inc 419 358-2926
201 N Main St Bluffton (45817) *(G-1686)*

A To Zoff Co Inc 330 733-7902
1105 Canton Rd Akron (44312) *(G-12)*

(G-0000) Company's Geographic Section entry number

A Touch of Grace Inc 567 560-2350
787 Lexington Ave Ste 303 Mansfield (44907) *(G-13131)*
A Touch of Grace Inc (PA) 740 397-7971
809 Coshocton Ave Ste B Mount Vernon (43050) *(G-14748)*
A W S Inc 440 333-1791
20120 Detroit Rd Rocky River (44116) *(G-16420)*
A W S Inc 216 749-0356
4720 Hinckley Indus Pkwy Cleveland (44109) *(G-4881)*
A W S Inc 216 486-0600
1490 E 191st St Euclid (44117) *(G-10622)*
A W S Inc 216 941-8800
10991 Memphis Ave Cleveland (44144) *(G-4882)*
A Wireless, Mentor On The Lake *Also called ABC Phones North Carolina Inc (G-14128)*
A Wireless, Ashtabula *Also called ABC Phones North Carolina Inc (G-703)*
A Wireless, Macedonia *Also called ABC Phones North Carolina Inc (G-13057)*
A&L Home Care & Training Ctr 740 886-7623
6101 County Road 107 Proctorville (45669) *(G-16215)*
A&L Imaging, Blue Ash *Also called Arszman & Lyons LLC (G-1508)*
A&R Logistics Inc 614 444-4111
1230 Harmon Ave Columbus (43223) *(G-6849)*
A+ Solutions LLC 216 896-0111
3659 Green Rd Ste 112 Beachwood (44122) *(G-1025)*
A-1 Advanced Plumbing Inc 614 873-0548
8299 Memorial Dr Plain City (43064) *(G-16040)*
A-1 Bail Bonds Inc 937 372-2400
20 S Detroit St Xenia (45385) *(G-19887)*
A-1 Best Locksmith, Cincinnati *Also called Serv-A-Lite Products Inc (G-4454)*
A-1 General Insurance Agency (HQ) 216 986-3000
9700 Rockside Rd Ste 250 Cleveland (44125) *(G-4883)*
A-1 Healthcare Staffing LLC (PA) 216 862-0906
2991 E 73rd St Cleveland (44104) *(G-4884)*
A-1 Healthcare Staffing LLC 216 862-0906
15644 Madison Ave Lakewood (44107) *(G-12334)*
A-1 Nursing Care Inc 614 268-3800
2500 Corp Exchange Dr # 220 Columbus (43231) *(G-6850)*
A-1 Quality Labor Services LLC 513 353-0173
3055 Blue Rock Rd Cincinnati (45239) *(G-2893)*
A-1 Sprinkler Company Inc 937 859-6198
2383 Northpointe Dr Miamisburg (45342) *(G-14136)*
A-A Blueprint Co Inc 330 794-8803
2757 Gilchrist Rd Akron (44305) *(G-13)*
A-Advnced Mvg Stor Systms-Self, Akron *Also called Cotter Moving & Storage Co (G-161)*
A-Roo Company LLC (HQ) 440 238-8850
22360 Royalton Rd Strongsville (44149) *(G-17278)*
A-T Controls Inc (PA) 513 530-5175
9955 International Blvd West Chester (45246) *(G-19039)*
A-Team LLC 216 271-7223
5280 W 161st St Frnt Cleveland (44142) *(G-4885)*
A1 Drywall Supply, Nashport *Also called Newark Drywall Inc (G-14820)*
A1 Mr Limo Inc 440 943-5466
29555 Lakeland Blvd Wickliffe (44092) *(G-19454)*
A1a Highway & Construction Eqp, Columbus *Also called Industrial Financial Svcs Inc (G-7813)*
A2 Services LLC 440 466-6611
4749 N Ridge Rd E Geneva (44041) *(G-11236)*
A2z Field Services LLC 614 873-0211
7450 Industrial Pkwy # 105 Plain City (43064) *(G-16041)*
AA Boos & Sons Inc 419 691-2329
2015 Pickle Rd Oregon (43616) *(G-15580)*
AA Fire Protection LLC 440 327-0060
620 Sugar Ln Elyria (44035) *(G-10475)*
AA Green Realty Inc 419 352-5331
1045 N Main St Ste 2 Bowling Green (43402) *(G-1711)*
AAA, Worthington *Also called Ohio Automobile Club (G-19831)*
AAA Allied Group Inc 513 228-0866
603 E Main St Lebanon (45036) *(G-12447)*
AAA Allied Group Inc 419 228-1022
2115 Allentown Rd Lima (45805) *(G-12591)*
AAA Allied Group Inc (PA) 513 762-3301
15 W Central Pkwy Cincinnati (45202) *(G-2894)*
AAA Amrican Abatement Asb Corp 216 281-9400
15401 Chatfield Ave Cleveland (44111) *(G-4886)*
AAA Auto Wash, Cincinnati *Also called Allied Car Wash Inc (G-2927)*
AAA Car Care Plus, Columbus *Also called Ohio Automobile Club (G-8231)*
AAA Cincinnati Insurance Svc 513 345-5600
15 W Central Pkwy Cincinnati (45202) *(G-2895)*
AAA Club Alliance Inc (PA) 419 843-1200
3201 Meijer Dr Toledo (43617) *(G-17577)*
AAA Club Alliance Inc 937 427-5884
3321 Dayton Xenia Rd Beavercreek (45432) *(G-1123)*
AAA Flexible Pipe, Cleveland *Also called AAA Pipe Cleaning Corporation (G-4888)*
AAA Flexible Pipe Cleaning 216 341-2900
7277 Bessemer Ave Cleveland (44127) *(G-4887)*
AAA Massillon Automobile Club, Massillon *Also called Massillon Automobile Club (G-13709)*
AAA Miami Valley (PA) 937 224-2896
825 S Ludlow St Dayton (45402) *(G-9201)*
AAA Mid-Atlantic, Toledo *Also called AAA Club Alliance Inc (G-17577)*
AAA Ohio Auto Club 614 431-7800
90 E Wilson Bridge Rd Worthington (43085) *(G-19790)*

AAA Pipe Cleaning Corporation (PA) 216 341-2900
7277 Bessemer Ave Cleveland (44127) *(G-4888)*
AAA Rental & Sales, Dublin *Also called Columbus AAA Corp (G-10181)*
AAA Shelby County Motor Club 937 492-3167
920 Wapakoneta Ave Sidney (45365) *(G-16756)*
AAA South Central Ohio Inc 740 354-5614
1414 12th St Portsmouth (45662) *(G-16123)*
AAA Standard Services Inc 419 535-0274
4117 South Ave Toledo (43615) *(G-17578)*
AAA Travel Agency, Lebanon *Also called AAA Allied Group Inc (G-12447)*
AAA Travel Agency, Dayton *Also called AAA Miami Valley (G-9201)*
Aaris Therapy Group Inc 330 505-1606
950 Youngstown Warren Rd A Niles (44446) *(G-15142)*
Aaron Landscape Inc 440 838-8875
14900 York Rd North Royalton (44133) *(G-15345)*
Aarons Inc 330 823-1879
2102 W State St Alliance (44601) *(G-513)*
Aarons Inc 216 251-4500
11629 Lorain Ave Cleveland (44111) *(G-4889)*
Aarons Inc 330 385-7201
16240 Dresden Ave Ste A East Liverpool (43920) *(G-10395)*
Aarons Inc 937 778-3577
1305 E Ash St Piqua (45356) *(G-15995)*
Aarons Inc 216 587-2745
5420 Northfield Rd Maple Heights (44137) *(G-13279)*
Aauw Action Fund Inc 330 833-0520
8400 Milmont St Nw Massillon (44646) *(G-13659)*
Aaz Galvanizing Cincinnati, Cincinnati *Also called Witt Glvnzing - Cincinnati Inc (G-4800)*
AB Marketing LLC 513 385-6158
1211 Symmes Rd Apt B Fairfield (45014) *(G-10691)*
AB Resources LLC 440 922-1098
6802 W Snowville Rd Ste E Brecksville (44141) *(G-1766)*
AB Tube Company, Twinsburg *Also called Atlas Steel Products Co (G-18247)*
Aba Insurance Services Inc 800 274-5222
3401 Tuttle Rd Ste 300 Shaker Heights (44122) *(G-16702)*
Abaco Rhblttion Nursing Fcilty, Columbus *Also called Longterm Lodging Inc (G-7988)*
Abacus Child Care Centers Inc 330 773-4200
839 S Arlington St Akron (44306) *(G-14)*
Abacus Corporation 614 367-7000
1676 Brice Rd Reynoldsburg (43068) *(G-16278)*
ABB Inc 614 818-6300
579 Executive Campus Dr Westerville (43082) *(G-19142)*
ABB Industrial Systems, Westerville *Also called ABB Inc (G-19142)*
Abbewood Limited Partnership 440 366-8980
1210 Abbe Rd S Ofc Elyria (44035) *(G-10476)*
Abbott Electric (PA) 330 452-6601
1935 Allen Ave Se Canton (44707) *(G-2170)*
Abbott Laboratories 614 624-3191
585 Cleveland Ave Columbus (43215) *(G-6851)*
Abbott Nutrition, Columbus *Also called Abbott Laboratories (G-6851)*
Abbott Tool Inc 419 476-6742
405 Dura Ave Toledo (43612) *(G-17579)*
Abbruzzese Brothers Inc (PA) 614 873-1550
7775 Smith Calhoun Rd Plain City (43064) *(G-16042)*
Abbyshire Place Skilled Nurse, Bidwell *Also called Vrable III Inc (G-1471)*
ABC Appliance Inc 419 693-4414
3012 Navarre Ave Oregon (43616) *(G-15581)*
ABC Child Care & Learning Ctr 440 964-8799
2012 W 11th St Ashtabula (44004) *(G-702)*
ABC Day Care, Ashtabula *Also called ABC Child Care & Learning Ctr (G-702)*
ABC Detroit/Toledo, Perrysburg *Also called Auction Broadcasting Co LLC (G-15833)*
ABC Detroit/Toledo Auto Auctn 419 872-0872
9797 Fremont Pike 3 Perrysburg (43551) *(G-15832)*
ABC Early Childhood Lrng Ctr, Cincinnati *Also called Colerain Dry Rdge Chldcare Ltd (G-3328)*
ABC Fire Inc 440 237-6677
10250 Royalton Rd North Royalton (44133) *(G-15346)*
ABC Phones North Carolina Inc 440 290-4262
5965 Andrews Rd Ste B Mentor On The Lake (44060) *(G-14128)*
ABC Phones North Carolina Inc 440 319-3654
2411 W Prospect Rd Ashtabula (44004) *(G-703)*
ABC Phones North Carolina Inc 330 752-0009
8266 Golden Link Blvd Macedonia (44067) *(G-13057)*
ABC Phones North Carolina Inc 440 328-4331
5255 Detroit Rd Sheffield Village (44054) *(G-16731)*
ABC Piping Co 216 398-4000
1277 E Schaaf Rd Ste 5 Brooklyn Heights (44131) *(G-1863)*
Abcd Inc (PA) 330 455-6385
1225 Gross Ave Ne Canton (44705) *(G-2171)*
Abco Contracting LLC 419 973-4772
947 Belmont Ave Toledo (43607) *(G-17580)*
Abco Fire LLC 800 875-7200
510 W Benson St Cincinnati (45215) *(G-2896)*
Abco Fire LLC (HQ) 216 433-7200
4545 W 160th St Cleveland (44135) *(G-4890)*
Abco Fire Protection, Cleveland *Also called Abco Holdings LLC (G-4892)*
Abco Fire Protection, Cincinnati *Also called Abco Fire LLC (G-2896)*
Abco Fire Protection Inc (PA) 800 875-7200
4545 W 160th St Cleveland (44135) *(G-4891)*

A
L
P
H
A
B
E
T
I
C

Abco Holdings LLC (PA)................................216 433-7200
　4545 W 160th St Cleveland (44135) *(G-4892)*

Aber's Truck Center, Ashland Also called Abers Garage Inc *(G-644)*

Abercrombie & Fitch Trading Co (HQ)................614 283-6500
　6301 Fitch Path New Albany (43054) *(G-14839)*

Aberdeen Business Park, Cleveland Also called Forest City Enterprises LP *(G-5557)*

Abers Garage Inc (PA)................................419 281-5500
　1729 Claremont Ave Ashland (44805) *(G-644)*

ABF Freight System Inc................................440 843-4600
　5630 Chevrolet Blvd Cleveland (44130) *(G-4893)*

ABF Freight System Inc................................614 294-3537
　1720 Joyce Ave Columbus (43219) *(G-6852)*

ABF Freight System Inc................................937 236-2210
　8051 Center Point 70 Blvd Dayton (45424) *(G-9202)*

ABF Freight System Inc................................513 779-7888
　6290 Allen Rd West Chester (45069) *(G-18858)*

ABF Freight System Inc................................419 525-0118
　25 S Mulberry St Mansfield (44902) *(G-13132)*

ABF Freight System Inc................................330 549-3800
　11000 Market St North Lima (44452) *(G-15261)*

ABG Advisors, Cincinnati Also called Pension Corporation America *(G-4226)*

Abilities First Foundation Inc (PA)................513 423-9496
　4710 Timber Trail Dr Middletown (45044) *(G-14285)*

Ability Ctr of Greater Toledo (PA)................419 517-7123
　5605 Monroe St Sylvania (43560) *(G-17411)*

Ability Matters LLC................................614 214-9652
　6058 Heritage View Ct Hilliard (43026) *(G-11739)*

Ability Network Inc................................513 943-8888
　4357 Ferguson Dr Ste 100 Cincinnati (45245) *(G-2840)*

Ability Works Inc................................419 626-1048
　3920 Columbus Ave Sandusky (44870) *(G-16572)*

ABLE, Toledo Also called Advoctes For Bsic Lgal Eqality *(G-17583)*

Able Company Ltd Partnership (PA)................614 444-7663
　4777 Westerville Rd Columbus (43231) *(G-6853)*

Able Contracting Group Inc (PA)................440 951-0880
　11117 Caddie Ln Painesville (44077) *(G-15691)*

Able Fence & Guard Rail Co, Painesville Also called Able Contracting Group Inc *(G-15691)*

Able Roofing, Columbus Also called Able Company Ltd Partnership *(G-6853)*

Able Roofing LLC................................614 444-7663
　4777 Westerville Rd Columbus (43231) *(G-6854)*

ABM Aviation Inc................................859 767-7507
　790 Grenoble Ct Cincinnati (45255) *(G-2897)*

ABM Engineering, Cincinnati Also called ABM Facility Services Inc *(G-2898)*

ABM Facility Services Inc................................859 767-4393
　3087 B Terminal Dr Cincinnati (45275) *(G-2898)*

ABM Janitorial Services Inc................................216 861-1199
　1501 Euclid Ave Ste 320 Cleveland (44115) *(G-4894)*

ABM Janitorial Services Inc................................513 731-1418
　354 Gest St Cincinnati (45203) *(G-2899)*

ABM Parking Services Inc................................937 461-2113
　40 N Main St Ste 1540 Dayton (45423) *(G-9203)*

ABM Parking Services Inc................................330 747-7678
　20 W Federal St Ste M9 Youngstown (44503) *(G-19945)*

ABM Parking Services Inc................................216 621-6600
　1459 Hamilton Ave Cleveland (44114) *(G-4895)*

Aboutgolf Limited (PA)................................419 482-9095
　352 Tomahawk Dr Maumee (43537) *(G-13745)*

Above & Beyond Caregivers LLC................................614 478-1700
　2862 Johnstown Rd Columbus (43219) *(G-6855)*

Abraham Ford LLC................................440 233-7402
　1115 E Broad St Elyria (44035) *(G-10477)*

Abraxas Foundation of Ohio, Shelby Also called Cornell Companies Inc *(G-16744)*

Abror Health Care, Clyde Also called Arbors At Clide Asssted Living *(G-6738)*

ABS Business Products, Cincinnati Also called Andrew Belmont Sargent *(G-2965)*

Absolute Care Management Llc (PA)................614 846-8053
　4618 Sawmill Rd Columbus (43220) *(G-6856)*

Absolute Cleaning Services................................440 542-1742
　5349 Harper Rd Solon (44139) *(G-16813)*

Absolute Health Services, Canton Also called Advantage Appliance Services *(G-2174)*

Absolute Machine Tools Inc (PA)................440 839-9696
　7420 Industrial Pkwy Dr Lorain (44053) *(G-12878)*

Abx Air Inc (HQ)................................937 382-5591
　145 Hunter Dr Wilmington (45177) *(G-19600)*

Abx Air Inc................................937 366-2282
　145 Hunter Dr Wilmington (45177) *(G-19601)*

AC Lens, Columbus Also called Arlington Contact Lens Svc Inc *(G-6970)*

Academic Support Services LLC................................740 274-6138
　2958 Blossom Ave Columbus (43231) *(G-6857)*

Academy Answering Service Inc................................440 442-8500
　30 Alpha Park Cleveland (44143) *(G-4896)*

Academy Communications, Cleveland Also called Academy Answering Service Inc *(G-4896)*

Academy For Young Childrn, Hudson Also called T L C Child Development Center *(G-12008)*

Academy Graphic Comm Inc................................216 661-2550
　1000 Brookpark Rd Cleveland (44109) *(G-4897)*

Academy Kids Learning Ctr Inc................................614 258-5437
　289 Woodland Ave Columbus (43203) *(G-6858)*

Academy Medical Staffing Svcs, Columbus Also called Acloche LLC *(G-6865)*

Acadia Solutions Inc................................614 505-6135
　6751 Burnside Ln Dublin (43016) *(G-10118)*

ACC Automation Co Inc................................330 928-3821
　475 Wolf Ledges Pkwy Akron (44311) *(G-15)*

ACC-U-Coil, Xenia Also called Twist Inc *(G-19931)*

ACCAA, Ashtabula Also called Ashtabula County Commnty Actn *(G-711)*

Accco Inc................................740 697-2005
　451 Gordon St Roseville (43777) *(G-16453)*

Accel Inc................................614 656-1100
　9000 Smiths Mill Rd New Albany (43054) *(G-14840)*

Accel Performance Group LLC (HQ)................216 658-6413
　6100 Oak Tree Blvd # 200 Independence (44131) *(G-12036)*

Accelerant Solutions, Genoa Also called Accelerant Technologies LLC *(G-11251)*

Accelerant Technologies LLC................................419 236-8768
　2257 N Manor Dr Genoa (43430) *(G-11251)*

Accelerated Moving & Stor Inc................................614 836-1007
　4001 Refugee Rd Ste 2 Columbus (43232) *(G-6859)*

Accent Drapery Co Inc................................614 488-0741
　1180 Goodale Blvd Columbus (43212) *(G-6860)*

Accent Drapery Supply Co, Columbus Also called Accent Drapery Co Inc *(G-6860)*

Accentcare Home Health Cal Inc................................740 387-4568
　119 S Court St Ste A Circleville (43113) *(G-4822)*

Accentcare Home Health Cal Inc................................740 474-7826
　119 S Court St Ste A Circleville (43113) *(G-4823)*

Accenture LLP................................216 685-1435
　1400 W 10th St Ste 401 Cleveland (44113) *(G-4898)*

Accenture LLP................................614 629-2000
　400 W Nationwide Blvd # 100 Columbus (43215) *(G-6861)*

Accenture LLP................................513 455-1000
　201 E 4th St Ste 1600 Cincinnati (45202) *(G-2900)*

Accenture LLP................................513 651-2444
　425 Walnut St Ste 1200 Cincinnati (45202) *(G-2901)*

Access Inc................................330 535-2999
　230 W Market St Akron (44303) *(G-16)*

Access Catalog Company LLC................................440 572-5377
　21848 Commerce Pkwy # 100 Strongsville (44149) *(G-17279)*

Access Cleaning Service Inc................................937 276-2605
　5045 N Main St Ste 100 Dayton (45415) *(G-9204)*

Access Counseling Services LLC................................513 649-8008
　4464 S Dixie Hwy Middletown (45005) *(G-14341)*

Access Home Care LLC................................937 224-9991
　2555 S Dixie Dr Ste 100 Dayton (45409) *(G-9205)*

Access Ohio................................614 367-7700
　99 N Brice Rd Ste 360 Columbus (43213) *(G-6862)*

Accessibility, Ashland Also called Randall R Leab *(G-685)*

Accessrn Inc................................419 698-1988
　1540 S Hlland Sylvania Rd Maumee (43537) *(G-13746)*

Accf Accreditation, Dublin Also called American Cllege Crdlgy Fndtion *(G-10130)*

Account Temps, Youngstown Also called Robert Half International Inc *(G-20188)*

Accountants To You LLC................................513 651-2855
　430 Reading Rd Ste 100 Cincinnati (45202) *(G-2902)*

Accounts Payable Department, Columbus Also called Ohio State University *(G-8315)*

Accounts Payable Sso, Cincinnati Also called Mercy Health *(G-4018)*

Accucut, North Royalton Also called Aaron Landscape Inc *(G-15345)*

Accurate Electric Cnstr Inc................................614 863-1844
　6901 Americana Pkwy Reynoldsburg (43068) *(G-16279)*

Accurate Group Holdings Inc (PA)................216 520-1740
　6000 Freedom Square Dr # 300 Independence (44131) *(G-12037)*

Accurate Healthcare Inc................................513 208-6988
　4681 Interstate Dr West Chester (45246) *(G-19040)*

Accurate Heating & Cooling................................740 775-5005
　3001 River Rd Chillicothe (45601) *(G-2749)*

Accurate Inventory and C................................800 777-9414
　4284 N High St Fl 1 Columbus (43214) *(G-6863)*

Accurate It Services, Columbus Also called Enviro It LLC *(G-7520)*

Accurate Mechanical Inc................................740 681-1332
　566 Mill Park Dr Lancaster (43130) *(G-12368)*

Accurate Mechanical Inc................................740 353-4328
　8732 Ohio River Rd Wheelersburg (45694) *(G-19427)*

Accurate Mechanical Inc................................937 382-1436
　363 E Main St Wilmington (45177) *(G-19602)*

Accurate Nurse Staffing................................419 475-2424
　4165 Monroe St Toledo (43606) *(G-17581)*

Accutek Testing Laboratory, Fairfield Also called McCloy Engineering LLC *(G-10752)*

Ace Assembly Packaging Inc................................330 866-9117
　133 N Mill St Waynesburg (44688) *(G-18827)*

Ace Building Maintenance LLC................................614 471-2223
　2565 Mccutcheon Rd Columbus (43219) *(G-6864)*

Ace Disposal, Dover Also called Kimble Recycl & Disposal Inc *(G-10084)*

Ace Doran Hauling & Rigging Co................................513 681-7900
　1601 Blue Rock St Cincinnati (45223) *(G-2903)*

Ace Hardware, Marysville Also called Ace Rental Place *(G-13482)*

Ace Hardware Corporation................................440 333-4223
　20200 Detroit Rd Rocky River (44116) *(G-16421)*

Ace Mitchell Bowlers Mart, Cuyahoga Falls Also called Micnan Inc *(G-9113)*

Ace Rental Place................................937 642-2891
　1299 W 5th St Marysville (43040) *(G-13482)*

Ace Truck Body Inc................................614 871-3100
　1600 Thrailkill Rd Grove City (43123) *(G-11403)*

Ace-Merit LLC................................513 241-3200
　30 Garfield Pl Ste 540 Cincinnati (45202) *(G-2904)*

Achievement Ctrs For Children (PA) ... 216 292-9700
4255 Northfield Rd Cleveland (44128) *(G-4899)*
Achievement Ctrs For Children ... 440 250-2520
24211 Center Ridge Rd Westlake (44145) *(G-19310)*
Aci Const Co Inc ... 419 595-4284
2959 S Us Highway 23 Alvada (44802) *(G-559)*
Aci Industries Ltd (PA) ... 740 368-4160
970 Pittsburgh Dr Delaware (43015) *(G-9948)*
Aci Industries Converting Ltd (HQ) ... 740 368-4160
970 Pittsburgh Dr Delaware (43015) *(G-9949)*
Aclara Technologies LLC ... 440 528-7200
30400 Solon Rd Solon (44139) *(G-16814)*
Acloche LLC (PA) ... 888 608-0889
1800 Watermark Dr Ste 430 Columbus (43215) *(G-6865)*
Acme, Coventry Township *Also called Fred W Albrecht Grocery Co (G-9034)*
Acme, Akron *Also called Fred W Albrecht Grocery Co (G-229)*
Acme Company ... 330 758-2313
9495 Harvard Blvd Poland (44514) *(G-16079)*
Acne Bowling Supply, Cuyahoga Falls *Also called Midway Bowling Lanes Inc (G-9114)*
Acock Assoc Architects LLC ... 614 228-1586
383 N Front St Ste 1 Columbus (43215) *(G-6866)*
Acord Rk Lumber Company ... 740 289-3761
125 W 4th St Piketon (45661) *(G-15970)*
Acorn Distributors Inc ... 614 294-6444
5310 Crosswind Dr Columbus (43228) *(G-6867)*
Acorn Farms Inc ... 614 891-9348
7679 Worthington Rd B Galena (43021) *(G-11153)*
Acosta Inc ... 440 498-7370
30600 Aurora Rd Ste 100 Solon (44139) *(G-16815)*
Acpi Systems Inc ... 513 738-3840
3445 Hmlton New London Rd Hamilton (45013) *(G-11554)*
Acquisition Logistics Engrg, Worthington *Also called Quality Aero Inc (G-19839)*
Acres of Fun, Wooster *Also called CCJ Enterprises Inc (G-19697)*
Acro Tool & Die Company ... 330 773-5173
325 Morgan Ave Akron (44311) *(G-17)*
Acrt Inc (PA) ... 800 622-2562
4500 Courthouse Blvd # 150 Stow (44224) *(G-17187)*
Acrt Services Inc ... 330 945-7500
4500 Courthouse Blvd # 150 Stow (44224) *(G-17188)*
Acrux Investigation Agency (PA) ... 937 842-5780
8823 Township Road 239 Lakeview (43331) *(G-12332)*
ACS Acqco Corp ... 513 719-2600
201 E 4th St Ste 900 Cincinnati (45202) *(G-2905)*
Act I Temporaries Findlay Inc ... 419 423-0713
2017 Tiffin Ave Findlay (45840) *(G-10863)*
Action Coupling & Eqp Inc ... 330 279-4242
8248 County Road 245 Holmesville (44633) *(G-11928)*
Action Door, Cleveland *Also called Dortronic Service Inc (G-5443)*
Action For Children Inc (PA) ... 614 224-0222
78 Jefferson Ave Columbus (43215) *(G-6868)*
Action Travel Center Inc (PA) ... 440 248-8388
5900 Harper Rd Ste 101 Cleveland (44139) *(G-4900)*
Actionlink LLC ... 888 737-8757
286 N Cleveland Massillon Akron (44333) *(G-18)*
Active Chiropractic ... 440 893-8800
1 S Main St Ste 1 # 1 Chagrin Falls (44022) *(G-2637)*
Active Detective Bureau, Cincinnati *Also called D B A Inc (G-3394)*
Activity Training, Cleveland *Also called County of Cuyahoga (G-5368)*
ACTUARIAL & EMPLOYEE BENEFIT S, Cincinnati *Also called Cai/Insurance Agency Inc (G-3104)*
Acuative Corporation ... 440 202-4500
8237 Dow Cir Strongsville (44136) *(G-17280)*
Acuity Healthcare LP ... 740 283-7499
380 Summit Ave Fl 3 Steubenville (43952) *(G-17139)*
Acuren Inspection, Dayton *Also called US Inspection Services Inc (G-9844)*
Acuren Inspection Inc ... 937 228-9729
705 Albany St Dayton (45417) *(G-9206)*
Acuren Inspection Inc ... 513 671-7073
502 W Crescentville Rd Cincinnati (45246) *(G-2906)*
Acuren Inspection Inc ... 937 228-9729
7333 Paragon Rd Ste 240 Dayton (45459) *(G-9207)*
Acusport Corporation, Bellefontaine *Also called Aspc Corp (G-1345)*
Acute Care Specialty Hospital ... 330 363-4860
2600 6th St Sw Canton (44710) *(G-2172)*
Acxiom Corporation ... 216 520-3181
5005 Rockside Rd Ste 600 Independence (44131) *(G-12038)*
Acxiom Info SEC Svcs Inc ... 216 685-7600
6111 Oak Tree Blvd Independence (44131) *(G-12039)*
AD Farrow LLC (PA) ... 614 228-6353
491 W Broad St Columbus (43215) *(G-6869)*
Ad Investments LLC ... 614 857-2340
375 N Front St Ste 200 Columbus (43215) *(G-6870)*
Ada Lberty Joint Ambulance Dst, Ada *Also called County of Hardin (G-4)*
Ada Visiting Nurses, Ada *Also called Community Hlth Prfssionals Inc (G-3)*
Adamhs Bd For Montgomery Cnty, Dayton *Also called Alcohol Drug Addction & Mental (G-9213)*
Adams & Brown Counties Economi ... 937 695-0316
19211 Main St Winchester (45697) *(G-19659)*
Adams & Brown Counties Economi (PA) ... 937 378-6041
406 W Plum St Georgetown (45121) *(G-11260)*

Adams Brown Wthrzation Program, Winchester *Also called Adams & Brown Counties Economi (G-19659)*
Adams Cnty /Ohio Vly Schl Dst ... 937 544-2951
555 Lloyd Rd West Union (45693) *(G-19129)*
Adams Cnty Snior Ctzens Cuncil ... 937 544-7459
10835 State Route 41 West Union (45693) *(G-19130)*
Adams County Manor ... 937 544-2205
10856 State Route 41 West Union (45693) *(G-19131)*
Adams County Regional Med Ctr ... 937 386-3001
230 Medical Center Dr Seaman (45679) *(G-16665)*
Adams Lane Care Center, Zanesville *Also called Zandex Health Care Corporation (G-20378)*
Adams Lane Care Center, Zanesville *Also called Zandex Inc (G-20375)*
Adams Robinson Construction, Dayton *Also called Adams-Robinson Enterprises Inc (G-9208)*
Adams Rural Electric Coop Inc ... 937 544-2305
4800 State Route 125 West Union (45693) *(G-19132)*
Adams Signs, Massillon *Also called Identitek Systems Inc (G-13697)*
Adams-Robinson Enterprises Inc (PA) ... 937 274-5318
2735 Needmore Rd Dayton (45414) *(G-9208)*
Adaptive Corporation (PA) ... 440 257-7460
118 W Streetsboro St # 221 Hudson (44236) *(G-11961)*
Adcom Group Inc ... 216 574-9100
1370 W 6th St Fl 3 Cleveland (44113) *(G-4901)*
Addiction Services Council ... 513 281-7880
2828 Vernon Pl Cincinnati (45219) *(G-2907)*
Addison Hts Hlth Rhbltion Ctr, Maumee *Also called Swan Pnte Fclty Operations LLC (G-13858)*
Addisonmckee Inc (PA) ... 513 228-7000
1637 Kingsview Dr Lebanon (45036) *(G-12448)*
Addus Home Care, Wintersville *Also called Addus Homecare Corporation (G-19667)*
Addus Homecare Corporation ... 866 684-0385
1406 Cadiz Rd Wintersville (43953) *(G-19667)*
Adecco Usa Inc ... 419 720-0111
336 N Superior St 200 Toledo (43604) *(G-17582)*
Adelman's Truck Sales, Canton *Also called Adelmans Truck Parts Corp (G-2173)*
Adelmans Truck Parts Corp (PA) ... 330 456-0206
2000 Waynesburg Dr Se Canton (44707) *(G-2173)*
Adelmos Electric Sewer Clg Co ... 216 641-2301
4917 Van Epps Rd Brooklyn Heights (44131) *(G-1864)*
Adelphia, Westlake *Also called Comcast Spotlight (G-19335)*
Adelphia, Cleveland *Also called Comcast Spotlight Inc (G-5315)*
Adena Commercial LLC ... 614 436-9800
8800 Lyra Dr Ste 650 Columbus (43240) *(G-6798)*
Adena Corporation ... 419 529-4456
1310 W 4th St Ontario (44906) *(G-15542)*
Adena Counseling Center, Chillicothe *Also called Adena Health System (G-2754)*
Adena Dialysis, Chillicothe *Also called Court Dialysis LLC (G-2773)*
Adena Fmly Medicine-Greenfield, Greenfield *Also called Adena Health System (G-11358)*
Adena Health System ... 740 779-7201
4439 State Route 159 # 120 Chillicothe (45601) *(G-2750)*
Adena Health System (PA) ... 740 779-7360
272 Hospital Rd Chillicothe (45601) *(G-2751)*
Adena Health System ... 740 779-7500
308 Highland Ave Unit C Wshngtn CT Hs (43160) *(G-19863)*
Adena Health System ... 740 420-3000
798 N Court St Circleville (43113) *(G-4824)*
Adena Health System ... 937 981-9444
1075 N Washington St Greenfield (45123) *(G-11358)*
Adena Health System ... 740 779-8995
85 River Trce Chillicothe (45601) *(G-2752)*
Adena Health System ... 740 779-4801
445 Shawnee Ln Chillicothe (45601) *(G-2753)*
Adena Health System ... 740 779-4888
455 Shawnee Dr Ln Chillicothe (45601) *(G-2754)*
Adena NH LLC ... 740 546-3620
213 U S Route 250 Adena (43901) *(G-7)*
Adena Pckwy-Ross Fmly Physcans ... 740 779-4500
100 N Walnut St Chillicothe (45601) *(G-2755)*
Adena Rhbltation Wellness Ctr, Chillicothe *Also called Adena Health System (G-2753)*
Adept Marketing Outsourced LLC ... 614 452-4011
855 Grandview Ave Ste 140 Columbus (43215) *(G-6871)*
Adesa Cleveland, Northfield *Also called Adesa-Ohio Llc (G-15372)*
Adesa Corporation LLC ... 937 746-5361
4400 William C Good Blvd Franklin (45005) *(G-11021)*
Adesa-Ohio Llc ... 330 467-8280
210 E Twinsburg Rd Northfield (44067) *(G-15372)*
Adex International, Cincinnati *Also called Affinity Disp Expositions Inc (G-2915)*
ADI, Sheffield Village *Also called Advanced Design Industries Inc (G-16732)*
Adkins Timber Products Inc ... 740 984-2768
22180 State Rte 60 Beverly (45715) *(G-1459)*
Adler Team Sports, Euclid *Also called R & A Sports Inc (G-10654)*
Adleta Construction, Cincinnati *Also called Adleta Inc (G-2908)*
Adleta Inc ... 513 554-1469
389 S Wayne Ave Cincinnati (45215) *(G-2908)*
Administration Services Dept, Cincinnati *Also called University of Cincinnati (G-4707)*
Administrative Service Cons, Findlay *Also called Ebso Inc (G-10898)*
Administrative Service Cons, Cleveland *Also called Ebso Inc (G-5464)*

Administrative Svcs Ohio Dept 614 466-5090
  4200 Surface Rd Columbus (43228) *(G-6872)*

Admirals Pnte Nrsing Rhblttion, Huron *Also called Huron Health Care Center Inc (G-12027)*

Ado Health Services Inc 330 629-2888
  1011 Boardman Canfield Rd Youngstown (44512) *(G-19946)*

Ado Staffing Inc 419 222-8395
  2100 Harding Hwy Lima (45804) *(G-12592)*

Adolph Johnson & Son Co 330 544-8900
  3497 Union St Mineral Ridge (44440) *(G-14508)*

ADP, Independence *Also called Automatic Data Processing Inc (G-12048)*

ADP, Westerville *Also called Automatic Data Processing Inc (G-19226)*

Adrian M Schnall MD 216 291-4300
  1611 S Green Rd Lbby A Cleveland (44121) *(G-4902)*

Adriel School Inc (PA) 937 465-0010
  414 N Detroit St West Liberty (43357) *(G-19117)*

ADS Manufacturing Ohio LLC 513 217-4502
  1701 Reinartz Blvd Middletown (45042) *(G-14286)*

ADT Security 440 397-5751
  13022 Pearl Rd Strongsville (44136) *(G-17281)*

Adult Probation Department, Elyria *Also called County of Lorain (G-10496)*

Advance Auto Parts, Brunswick *Also called General Parts Inc (G-1931)*

Advance Cleaning Contractors, Toledo *Also called Kelli Woods Management Inc (G-17838)*

Advance Door Company 216 883-2424
  4555 Willow Pkwy Cleveland (44125) *(G-4903)*

Advance Home Care LLC (PA) 614 436-3611
  1191 S James Rd Ste D Columbus (43227) *(G-6873)*

Advance Home Care LLC 937 723-6335
  1250 W Dorothy Ln Dayton (45409) *(G-9209)*

Advance Implant Dentistry Inc 513 271-0821
  5823 Wooster Pike Cincinnati (45227) *(G-2909)*

Advance Partners, Beachwood *Also called Advance Payroll Funding Ltd (G-1026)*

Advance Payroll Funding Ltd 216 831-8900
  3401 Entp Pkwy Fl 5 Flr 5 Beachwood (44122) *(G-1026)*

Advance Services, Chillicothe *Also called Dave Pinkerton (G-2775)*

Advance Stores Company Inc 740 369-4491
  1675 Us Highway 42 S Delaware (43015) *(G-9950)*

Advance Trnsp Systems Inc 513 818-4311
  10558 Taconic Ter Cincinnati (45215) *(G-2910)*

Advanced Auto Glass Inc (PA) 412 373-6675
  44 N Union St Akron (44304) *(G-19)*

Advanced Bar Technology, Canton *Also called Gerdau Macsteel Atmosphere Ann (G-2325)*

Advanced Benefit Cons Agcy, Cleveland *Also called Advanced Group Corp (G-4904)*

Advanced Cmpt Connections LLC 419 668-4080
  166 Milan Ave Norwalk (44857) *(G-15424)*

Advanced Computer Graphics 513 936-5060
  10895 Indeco Dr Blue Ash (45241) *(G-1496)*

Advanced Dermatology and Skin 330 965-8760
  987 Boardman Canfield Rd Youngstown (44512) *(G-19947)*

Advanced Design Industries Inc 440 277-4141
  4686 French Creek Rd Sheffield Village (44054) *(G-16732)*

Advanced Elastomer Systems LP (HQ) 800 352-7866
  388 S Main St Ste 600 Akron (44311) *(G-20)*

Advanced Engrg Solutions Inc 937 743-6900
  250 Advanced Dr Springboro (45066) *(G-16960)*

Advanced Facilities Maint Corp (PA) 614 389-3495
  6171 Huntley Rd Ste G Columbus (43229) *(G-6874)*

Advanced Fastener, Fairfield *Also called Afc Industries Inc (G-10692)*

Advanced Geriatric Education & 888 393-9799
  9823 Tulip Tree Ct Loveland (45140) *(G-12976)*

Advanced Graphite Machining US 216 658-6521
  12300 Snow Rd Parma (44130) *(G-15759)*

Advanced Group Corp (PA) 216 431-8800
  3800 Lkside Ave E Ste 400 Cleveland (44114) *(G-4904)*

Advanced Healtcare Center, Toledo *Also called Healthcare Facility MGT LLC (G-17791)*

Advanced Health Care Center, Toledo *Also called Communi Care Inc (G-17670)*

Advanced Industrial Products, Columbus *Also called Otp Holding LLC (G-8403)*

Advanced Industrial Roofg Inc 330 837-1999
  1330 Erie St S Massillon (44646) *(G-13660)*

Advanced Intgrted Slutions LLC 313 724-8600
  11140 Deerfield Rd Blue Ash (45242) *(G-1497)*

Advanced Mechanical Svcs Inc 937 879-7426
  575 Sports St Fairborn (45324) *(G-10662)*

Advanced Medical Equipment Inc (PA) 937 534-1080
  2655 S Dixie Dr Kettering (45409) *(G-12290)*

Advanced Prgrm Resources Inc (PA) 614 761-9994
  2715 Tuller Pkwy Dublin (43017) *(G-10119)*

Advanced Service Tech LLC 937 435-4376
  885 Mound Rd Miamisburg (45342) *(G-14137)*

Advanced Specialty Hosp Toledo, Toledo *Also called Garden II Leasing Co LLC (G-17755)*

Advanced Specialty Products 419 882-6528
  428 Clough St Bowling Green (43402) *(G-1712)*

Advanced Systems Group, Beavercreek Township *Also called Jacobs Technology Inc (G-1250)*

Advanced Tenting Solutions 216 291-3300
  10750 Music St Newbury (44065) *(G-15117)*

Advanced Testing Lab Inc 513 489-8447
  6954 Cornell Rd Ste 200 Blue Ash (45242) *(G-1498)*

Advanced Testing Laboratories, Blue Ash *Also called Advanced Testing Lab Inc (G-1498)*

Advanced Testing MGT Group Inc 513 489-8447
  6954 Cornell Rd Ste 200 Blue Ash (45242) *(G-1499)*

Advanced Translation/Cnsltng 440 716-0820
  3751 Willow Run Westlake (44145) *(G-19311)*

Advanced Urology Inc (PA) 330 758-9787
  904 Sahara Trl Ste 1 Youngstown (44514) *(G-19948)*

Advanced Welding Division, Tipp City *Also called Daihen Inc (G-17555)*

Advantage Aerotech Inc 614 759-8329
  1400 Hollybrier Dr # 121 Columbus (43230) *(G-6875)*

Advantage Appliance Services 330 498-8101
  7235 Whipple Ave Nw Canton (44720) *(G-2174)*

Advantage Bank, Wshngtn CT Hs *Also called Huntington National Bank (G-19876)*

Advantage Credit Union Inc (PA) 419 529-5603
  700 Stumbo Rd Ontario (44906) *(G-15543)*

Advantage Diagnostic, Beachwood *Also called Advantage Imaging LLC (G-1027)*

Advantage Ford Lincoln Mercury 419 334-9751
  885 Hagerty Dr Fremont (43420) *(G-11056)*

Advantage Home Health Care 800 636-2330
  1656 Coles Blvd Portsmouth (45662) *(G-16124)*

Advantage Home Health Svcs Inc 330 491-8161
  7951 Pittsburg Ave Nw North Canton (44720) *(G-15184)*

Advantage Human Resourcing Inc (HQ) 318 324-8060
  201 E 4th St Ste 800 Cincinnati (45202) *(G-2911)*

Advantage Imaging LLC (PA) 216 292-9998
  3733 Park East Dr Ste 100 Beachwood (44122) *(G-1027)*

Advantage Local, West Chester *Also called Advantage Rn LLC (G-18859)*

Advantage Resourcing Amer Inc (HQ) 781 472-8900
  201 E 4th St Ste 800 Cincinnati (45202) *(G-2912)*

Advantage Rn LLC (PA) 866 301-4045
  9021 Meridian Way West Chester (45069) *(G-18859)*

Advantage Sales & Mktg, Blue Ash *Also called Advantage Sales & Mktg LLC (G-1500)*

Advantage Sales & Mktg LLC 513 841-0500
  10300 Alliance Rd Ste 400 Blue Ash (45242) *(G-1500)*

Advantage Staffing, Cincinnati *Also called Advantage Human Resourcing Inc (G-2911)*

Advantage Staffing, Cincinnati *Also called Advantage Resourcing Amer Inc (G-2912)*

Advantage Tank Lines Inc (HQ) 330 491-0474
  4366 Mount Pleasant St Nw North Canton (44720) *(G-15185)*

Advantage Tank Lines Inc 330 427-1010
  404 12 Pearl St Leetonia (44431) *(G-12518)*

Advantage Tchncal Rsurcing Inc 513 651-1111
  201 E 4th St Ste 800 Cincinnati (45202) *(G-2913)*

Advantage Technology Group (PA) 513 563-3560
  7723 Tylers Place Blvd # 132 West Chester (45069) *(G-18860)*

Advantage Waypoint LLC 248 919-3144
  9458 Ravenna Rd Twinsburg (44087) *(G-18241)*

Advantech Corporation 513 742-8895
  11380 Reed Hartman Hwy Blue Ash (45241) *(G-1501)*

Advantech Indus Automtn Group, Blue Ash *Also called Advantech Corporation (G-1501)*

Adventure Cmbat Operations LLC 330 818-1029
  4501 Hlls Dls Rd Nw A Canton (44708) *(G-2175)*

Adventure Harley Davidson 330 343-2295
  1465 State Route 39 Nw Dover (44622) *(G-10064)*

Advocare Inc 216 514-1451
  25001 Emery Rd Cleveland (44128) *(G-4905)*

Advocate Property Servic 330 952-1313
  620 E Smith Rd Medina (44256) *(G-13906)*

Advocate Radiology Bil 614 210-1885
  10567 Swmill Pkwy Ste 100 Powell (43065) *(G-16183)*

Advocate Solutions LLC 614 444-5144
  762 S Pearl St Columbus (43206) *(G-6876)*

Advoctes For Bsic Lgal Eqality (PA) 419 255-0814
  525 Jefferson Ave Toledo (43604) *(G-17583)*

Adw, Cleveland *Also called Any Domest Work Inc (G-4986)*

AE Electric Inc 419 392-8468
  T483 County Road 1 Grand Rapids (43522) *(G-11324)*

Aecom 513 651-3440
  525 Vine St Ste 1800 Cincinnati (45202) *(G-2914)*

Aecom Energy & Cnstr Inc 216 622-2300
  1300 E 9th St Ste 500 Cleveland (44114) *(G-4906)*

Aecom Energy & Cnstr Inc 216 523-5600
  1500 W 3rd St Ste 200 Cleveland (44113) *(G-4907)*

Aecom Energy & Cnstr Inc 216 523-5600
  1500 W 3rd St Ste 200 Cleveland (44113) *(G-4908)*

Aecom Energy & Cnstr Inc 216 523-5600
  1500 W 3rd St Ste 470 Cleveland (44113) *(G-4909)*

Aecom Energy & Cnstr Inc 419 698-6277
  4001 Cedar Point Rd Oregon (43616) *(G-15582)*

Aecom Global II LLC 419 774-9862
  605 Taylor St Delta (43515) *(G-10040)*

Aecom Global II LLC 937 233-1230
  7333 Paragon Rd Ste 175 Dayton (45459) *(G-9210)*

Aecom Global II LLC 614 726-3500
  5550 Blazer Pkwy Ste 175 Dublin (43017) *(G-10120)*

Aecom Global II LLC 216 523-5600
  1500 W 3rd St Fl 2 Cleveland (44113) *(G-4910)*

Aecom Technical Services Inc 937 233-1898
  4386 Haskell Ln Batavia (45103) *(G-982)*

Aeea LLC 330 497-5304
  4383 Executive Cir Nw Canton (44718) *(G-2176)*

Aegco, Columbus *Also called AEP Generating Company (G-6879)*

Aegis Protective Services, Cincinnati *Also called Danson Inc (G-3400)*

AEP, Columbus *Also called Ohio Power Company (G-8279)*

AEP, Columbus *Also called Southwestern Electric Power Co (G-8666)*

AEP, Columbus *Also called Indiana Michigan Power Company* ***(G-7807)***
AEP, Piketon *Also called Ohio Valley Electric Corp* ***(G-15981)***
AEP, Columbus *Also called Public Service Company Okla* ***(G-8479)***
AEP, Canton *Also called American Electric Power Co Inc* ***(G-2185)***
AEP Dresden Plant......740 450-1964
9595 Mcglade School Rd Dresden (43821) ***(G-10115)***
AEP Energy Partners Inc......614 716-1000
1 Riverside Plz Columbus (43215) ***(G-6877)***
AEP Energy Services Inc......614 583-2900
155 W Nationwide Blvd Columbus (43215) ***(G-6878)***
AEP Generating Company (HQ)......614 223-1000
1 Riverside Plz Ste 1600 Columbus (43215) ***(G-6879)***
AEP Power Marketing Inc (HQ)......614 716-1000
1 Riverside Plz Fl 1 # 1 Columbus (43215) ***(G-6880)***
AEP Pro Serv Rso, Columbus *Also called American Electric Power Co Inc* ***(G-6918)***
AEP Service, Columbus *Also called American Electric Pwr Svc Corp* ***(G-6920)***
AEP Texas North Company, Canton *Also called American Electric Power Co Inc* ***(G-2184)***
Aerco Sandblasting Company......419 224-2464
429 N Jackson St Lima (45801) ***(G-12593)***
Aerie Frtnrl Order Egles 2875......419 433-4611
2902 Cleveland Rd W Huron (44839) ***(G-12019)***
Aero Electrical Contractors......614 834-8181
8020 Dove Pkwy Ste A Canal Winchester (43110) ***(G-2103)***
Aero Fulfillment Services Corp (PA)......800 225-7145
3900 Aero Dr Mason (45040) ***(G-13536)***
Aero Fulfillment Services Corp......513 874-4112
6023 Un Centre Blvd Steb West Chester (45069) ***(G-18861)***
Aero-Mark Inc......330 995-0100
10423 Danner Dr Streetsboro (44241) ***(G-17244)***
Aerocon Photogrammetric Svcs (PA)......440 946-6277
4515 Glenbrook Rd Willoughby (44094) ***(G-19502)***
Aerocontrolex Group Inc (HQ)......440 352-6182
313 Gillett St Painesville (44077) ***(G-15692)***
Aerodynamic Concrete & Cnstr......330 906-7477
1726 Massillon Rd Akron (44312) ***(G-21)***
Aerotek Inc......330 517-7330
540 White Pond Dr B Akron (44320) ***(G-22)***
Aerotek Inc......216 573-5520
5990 W Creek Rd Ste 150 Independence (44131) ***(G-12040)***
Aerotek 58, Independence *Also called Aerotek Inc* ***(G-12040)***
AES, Akron *Also called Advanced Elastomer Systems LP* ***(G-20)***
Aesi, Springboro *Also called Advanced Engrg Solutions Inc* ***(G-16960)***
Aetna Building Maintenance Inc (HQ)......614 476-1818
646 Parsons Ave Columbus (43206) ***(G-6881)***
Aetna Building Maintenance Inc......937 324-5711
525 N Yellow Springs St Springfield (45504) ***(G-16992)***
Aetna Building Maintenance Inc......866 238-6201
2044 Wayne Ave Dayton (45410) ***(G-9211)***
Aetna Health California Inc......614 933-6000
7400 W Campus Rd Ste 100 New Albany (43054) ***(G-14841)***
Aetna Integrated Services, Columbus *Also called Aetna Building Maintenance Inc* ***(G-6881)***
Aetna Life Insurance Company......330 659-8000
4059 Kinros Lake Pkwy # 300 Richfield (44286) ***(G-16342)***
Aey Electric Inc......330 792-5745
801 N Meridian Rd Youngstown (44509) ***(G-19949)***
Afc Cable Systems Inc......740 435-3340
829 Georgetown Rd Cambridge (43725) ***(G-2047)***
Afc Industries Inc (PA)......513 874-7456
3795 Port Union Rd Fairfield (45014) ***(G-10692)***
Affiliate of Nations Roof, Springboro *Also called Nations Roof of Ohio LLC* ***(G-16978)***
Affiliated FM Insurance Co......216 362-4820
25050 Country Club Blvd # 400 North Olmsted (44070) ***(G-15276)***
Affiliated Resource Group Inc......614 889-6555
5700 Perimeter Dr Ste H Dublin (43017) ***(G-10121)***
Affiliates In Oral & Maxlofcl (PA)......513 829-8080
5188 Winton Rd Fairfield (45014) ***(G-10693)***
Affiliates In Oral & Maxlofcl......513 829-8080
7795 Discovery Dr Ste C West Chester (45069) ***(G-18862)***
Affinion Group LLC......614 895-1803
300 W Schrock Rd Westerville (43081) ***(G-19217)***
Affinity Apparel, Fairborn *Also called Affinity Specialty Apparel Inc* ***(G-10663)***
Affinity Disp Expositions Inc......513 771-2339
1301 Glendale Milford Rd Cincinnati (45215) ***(G-2915)***
Affinity Family Physicians, Massillon *Also called Doctors Hosp Physcn Svcs LLC* ***(G-13675)***
Affinity Specialty Apparel Inc (PA)......866 548-8434
1202 E Dayton Yllow Spgs Fairborn (45324) ***(G-10663)***
Afford-A-Car Inc......937 235-2700
8973 State 201 Tipp City (45371) ***(G-17548)***
Affordable Cars & Finance Inc (PA)......440 777-2424
27932 Lorain Rd North Olmsted (44070) ***(G-15277)***
Afidence Inc......513 234-5822
5412 Curseview Dr Ste 122 Mason (45040) ***(G-13537)***
Afit Ls Usaf......937 255-3636
2950 Hobson Way Dayton (45433) ***(G-9154)***
AFLAC Incorporated......614 410-1696
30 Northwoods Blvd # 100 Columbus (43235) ***(G-6882)***
Afm East Archwood Oil Inc......330 786-1000
745 E Archwood Ave Akron (44306) ***(G-23)***
African Safari Wildlife Park, Port Clinton *Also called Animal Mgt Svcs Ohio Inc* ***(G-16099)***
After Market Products, Avon *Also called North Coast Bearings LLC* ***(G-896)***
AG Interactive Inc (HQ)......216 889-5000
1 American Rd Cleveland (44144) ***(G-4911)***
AG Trucking Inc......937 497-7770
798 S Vandemark Rd Sidney (45365) ***(G-16757)***
Ag-Pro Ohio LLC......740 450-7446
4394 Northpointe Dr Zanesville (43701) ***(G-20273)***
Ag-Pro Ohio LLC......614 879-6620
1660 Us Highway 42 Ne London (43140) ***(G-12858)***
AGC Automotive Americas......937 599-3131
1465 W Sandusky Ave Bellefontaine (43311) ***(G-1343)***
Age Line Inc......216 941-9990
4350 Rocky River Dr Cleveland (44135) ***(G-4912)***
Agee Clymer Mtchll & Prtman (PA)......614 221-3318
226 N 5th St Ste 501 Columbus (43215) ***(G-6883)***
Aggressive Mechanical Inc......614 443-3280
638 Greenlawn Ave Columbus (43223) ***(G-6884)***
Agile Global Solutions Inc......916 655-7745
5755 Granger Rd Ste 610 Independence (44131) ***(G-12041)***
Agilysys Inc......440 519-6262
6521 Davis Indus Pkwy Solon (44139) ***(G-16816)***
Agj Kidz LLC......937 350-1001
101 E Alexville 1 Rd 110 Centerville (45459) ***(G-2618)***
Agmet LLC (PA)......440 439-7400
7800 Medusa Rd Cleveland (44146) ***(G-4913)***
Agmet LLC......216 662-6939
5463 Dunham Rd Maple Heights (44137) ***(G-13280)***
Agpro, London *Also called Ag-Pro Ohio LLC* ***(G-12858)***
Agrana Fruit Us Inc......937 693-3821
16197 County Road 25a Botkins (45306) ***(G-1706)***
Agratronix LLC......330 562-2222
10375 State Route 43 Streetsboro (44241) ***(G-17245)***
Agri Communicators Inc......614 273-0465
1625 Bethel Rd Ste 203 Columbus (43220) ***(G-6885)***
Agridry LLC......419 459-4399
3460 Us Highway 20 Edon (43518) ***(G-10470)***
Agrinomix LLC......440 774-2981
300 Creekside Dr Oberlin (44074) ***(G-15497)***
AGS Custom Graphics Inc......330 963-7770
8107 Bavaria Rd Macedonia (44056) ***(G-13058)***
AH Sturgill Roofing Inc......937 254-2955
4358 Springfield St B Dayton (45431) ***(G-9155)***
Ahern Rentals Inc......440 498-0869
29001 Solon Rd Ste 17 Solon (44139) ***(G-16817)***
Ahf Ohio Inc......330 725-4123
806 E Washinton St Medina (44256) ***(G-13907)***
Ahf Ohio Inc......740 532-6188
2932 S 5th St Ironton (45638) ***(G-12144)***
Ahf Ohio Inc......614 760-8870
4880 Tuttle Rd Dublin (43017) ***(G-10122)***
Ahf Ohio Inc......937 256-4663
264 Wilmington Ave Dayton (45420) ***(G-9212)***
Ahf/Central States Inc......615 383-3570
5920 Venture Dr Ste 100 Dublin (43017) ***(G-10123)***
Ahola Corporation......440 717-7620
6820 W Snowville Rd Brecksville (44141) ***(G-1767)***
Ahoy Transport LLC......740 596-0536
301 E Main St Creola (45622) ***(G-9050)***
Ahsland Cleaning, Ashland *Also called Ashland Cleaning LLC* ***(G-648)***
Ahv Construction, Westerville *Also called Ahv Development LLC* ***(G-19143)***
Ahv Development LLC......614 890-1440
592 Office Pkwy Westerville (43082) ***(G-19143)***
Aidc Solutions, Dayton *Also called Evanhoe & Associates Inc* ***(G-9173)***
Aids Tskfrce Grter Clvland Inc......216 357-3131
2829 Euclid Ave Cleveland (44115) ***(G-4914)***
AIG, Cincinnati *Also called American Gen Lf Insur Co Del* ***(G-2944)***
Aim Integrated Logistics Inc......330 759-0438
1500 Trumbull Ave Girard (44420) ***(G-11281)***
Aim Leasing Company (PA)......330 759-0438
1500 Trumbull Ave Girard (44420) ***(G-11282)***
Aim Mro Holdings Inc (PA)......513 831-2938
375 Center St 175 Miamiville (45147) ***(G-14244)***
Aimbridge Hospitality LLC......330 668-9090
100 Springside Dr Akron (44333) ***(G-24)***
Air Comfort Systems Inc......216 587-4125
5108 Richmond Rd Cleveland (44146) ***(G-4915)***
Air Compliance Testing Inc (PA)......216 525-0900
5525 Canal Rd Ste 1 Cleveland (44125) ***(G-4916)***
Air Conditioning Entps Inc......440 729-0900
1370 Ontario St Ste 450 Cleveland (44113) ***(G-4917)***
Air Force Morale Welfare Rec, Dayton *Also called Army & Air Force Exchange Svc* ***(G-9161)***
Air Force US Dept of......937 656-2354
4225 Logistics Ave Dayton (45433) ***(G-9156)***
Air Force US Dept of......937 257-6068
5215 Thurlow St 2 Dayton (45433) ***(G-9157)***
Air Frce Museum Foundation Inc......937 258-1218
1100 Spaatz St Bldg 489 Dayton (45433) ***(G-9158)***
AIR Management Group LLC......330 856-1900
1 American Way Ne 20 Warren (44484) ***(G-18660)***
Air National Guard Med Clinic, Columbus *Also called National Guard Ohio* ***(G-8132)***
Air Supply Co (PA)......704 732-8034
2300 E Enterprise Pkwy Twinsburg (44087) ***(G-18242)***

ALPHABETIC

Air Systems of Ohio Inc (PA).................................216 741-1700
  4760 Van Epps Rd Brooklyn Heights (44131) *(G-1865)*
Air Technologies, Columbus Also called Ohio Transmission Corporation *(G-8358)*
Air Transport Svcs Group Inc (PA).............................937 382-5591
  145 Hunter Dr Wilmington (45177) *(G-19603)*
Air Venturi Ltd...216 292-2570
  5135 Naiman Pkwy Solon (44139) *(G-16818)*
Air-Temp Climate Control Inc.................................216 579-1552
  3013 Payne Ave Cleveland (44114) *(G-4918)*
Air-Temp Mechanical, Cleveland Also called Air-Temp Climate Control Inc *(G-4918)*
Airborn Electronics Inc......................................330 245-2630
  2230 Picton Pkwy Akron (44312) *(G-25)*
Airborne Maint Engrg Svcs Inc.................................937 366-2559
  1111 Airport Rd Wilmington (45177) *(G-19604)*
Airborne Maint Engrg Svcs Inc (HQ)............................937 382-5591
  145 Hunter Dr Wilmington (45177) *(G-19605)*
Aircraft Wheels and Breaks, Avon Also called Cleveland Wheels *(G-877)*
Aire-Tech Inc...614 836-5670
  4681 Homer Ohio Ln Groveport (43125) *(G-11492)*
Airgas Inc..866 935-3370
  2020 Train Ave Cleveland (44113) *(G-4919)*
Airgas Inc...440 632-1758
  14943 Madison Rd Middlefield (44062) *(G-14268)*
Airgas Inc...937 222-8312
  2400 Sandridge Dr Moraine (45439) *(G-14619)*
Airgas Merchant Gases LLC (HQ)...............................800 242-0105
  6055 Rckside Woods Blvd N Cleveland (44131) *(G-4920)*
Airgas Safety Inc..513 942-1465
  N Park Business Hamilton (45011) *(G-11555)*
Airgas Usa LLC...216 642-6600
  6055 Rockside Woods Independence (44131) *(G-12042)*
Airgas Usa LLC...440 786-2864
  7600 Oak Leaf Rd Oakwood Village (44146) *(G-15485)*
Airgas Usa LLC...513 563-8070
  10031 Cncnnati Dyton Pike Cincinnati (45241) *(G-2916)*
Airgas Usa LLC...440 232-1590
  6055 Rocksd Woods Blv 400 Cleveland (44131) *(G-4921)*
Airko Inc...440 333-0133
  20160 Center Ridge Rd # 101 Cleveland (44116) *(G-4922)*
Airmate Company...419 636-3184
  16280 County Road D Bryan (43506) *(G-1950)*
Airnet Systems Inc (PA)......................................614 409-4900
  7250 Star Check Dr Columbus (43217) *(G-6886)*
Airplaco Equipment Company, Cincinnati Also called Mesa Industries Inc *(G-4038)*
Airport Core Hotel LLC (PA)...................................614 536-0500
  2886 Airport Dr Columbus (43219) *(G-6887)*
Airport Pass Park, Cleveland Also called Parking Company America Inc *(G-6173)*
Airtron LP..614 274-2345
  3021 International St Columbus (43228) *(G-6888)*
Aisling Enterprises LLC.......................................937 203-1757
  9747 Crooked Creek Dr Centerville (45458) *(G-2619)*
Aitg, Celina Also called Ameri Interntl Trade Grp Inc *(G-2582)*
Aitheras Aviation Group LLC (PA).............................216 298-9060
  2301 N Marginal Rd Cleveland (44114) *(G-4923)*
Ajax Cleaning Contractors Co..................................216 881-8484
  1561 E 40th St Cleveland (44103) *(G-4924)*
Ajax Commercial Cleaning Inc.................................330 928-4543
  3566 State Rd Ste 5 Cuyahoga Falls (44223) *(G-9067)*
Ajax Tocco Magnethermic Corp (HQ).............................330 372-8511
  1745 Overland Ave Ne Warren (44483) *(G-18661)*
Ajm Worthington Inc...614 888-5800
  6902 N High St Worthington (43085) *(G-19791)*
AK Group Hotels Inc...937 372-9921
  300 Xenia Towne Sq Xenia (45385) *(G-19888)*
AK Steel Corporation..513 425-6541
  1801 Crawford St Middletown (45044) *(G-14287)*
Aka Wireless Inc...216 213-8040
  882 W Maple St Hartville (44632) *(G-11682)*
Aka Wireless Inc...440 572-5777
  14150 Pearl Rd Strongsville (44136) *(G-17282)*
Ake Marketing...440 232-1661
  503 Broadway Ave Bedford (44146) *(G-1268)*
Akil Incorporated...419 625-0857
  2525 W Monroe St Sandusky (44870) *(G-16573)*
Akil Industrial Cleaning, Sandusky Also called Akil Incorporated *(G-16573)*
Akro-Plastics, Kent Also called U S Development Corp *(G-12264)*
Akrochem Corporation..330 535-2108
  2845 Newpark Dr Barberton (44203) *(G-938)*
Akron Area Commercial Cleaning................................330 434-0767
  1264 Copley Rd Akron (44320) *(G-26)*
Akron Art Museum..330 376-9185
  1 S High St Akron (44308) *(G-27)*
Akron Auto Auction Inc..330 724-7708
  2471 Ley Dr Coventry Township (44319) *(G-9032)*
Akron Automobile Association (PA).............................330 762-0631
  100 Rosa Parks Dr Akron (44311) *(G-28)*
AKRON AUTOMOBILE CLUB, Akron Also called Akron Automobile Association *(G-28)*
Akron Blind Center & Workshop (PA)............................330 253-2555
  325 E Market St Akron (44304) *(G-29)*
Akron Canton Airport, North Canton Also called Akron-Canton Regional Airport *(G-15186)*

Akron Canton Kidney Center, Uniontown Also called Bio-Mdcal Applcations Ohio Inc *(G-18357)*
Akron Centl Engrv Mold Mch Inc................................330 794-8704
  1625 Massillon Rd Akron (44312) *(G-30)*
Akron Children's Hospital, Akron Also called Childrens Hosp Med Ctr Akron *(G-130)*
Akron Childrens Museum..330 396-6103
  216 S Main St Akron (44308) *(G-31)*
AKRON CITIZEN'S COALITION FOR, Akron Also called Access Inc *(G-16)*
Akron City Hospital, Akron Also called Summa Health *(G-446)*
Akron City Hospital Inc.......................................330 253-5046
  525 E Market St Akron (44304) *(G-32)*
Akron Cmnty Svc Ctr Urban Leag................................234 542-4141
  440 Vernon Odom Blvd Akron (44307) *(G-33)*
Akron Coca-Cola Bottling Co...................................330 784-2653
  1560 Triplett Blvd Akron (44306) *(G-34)*
AKRON COMMUNITY SERV CENTER, Akron Also called Akron Cmnty Svc Ctr Urban Leag *(G-33)*
Akron Concrete Corp...330 864-1188
  910 White Pond Dr Akron (44320) *(G-35)*
Akron Council of Engineering..................................330 535-8835
  411 Wolf Ledges Pkwy Akron (44311) *(G-36)*
Akron Electric, Barberton Also called Akron Foundry Co *(G-939)*
Akron Electric Inc..330 745-8891
  1025 Eaton Ave Akron (44303) *(G-37)*
Akron Energy Systems LLC......................................330 374-0600
  226 Opportunity Pkwy Akron (44307) *(G-38)*
Akron Erectors Inc..330 745-7100
  8098 W Waterloo Rd Akron (44314) *(G-39)*
Akron Foundry Co (PA)...330 745-3101
  2728 Wingate Ave Akron (44314) *(G-40)*
Akron Foundry Co..330 745-3101
  1025 Eagon St Barberton (44203) *(G-939)*
Akron Gen Edwin Shaw Rhblttion................................330 375-1300
  3600 W Market St Ste 102 Fairlawn (44333) *(G-10816)*
Akron Gen Hlth & Wellness Ctr, Akron Also called Akron General Medical Center *(G-46)*
Akron General Foundation......................................330 344-6888
  400 Wabash Ave Akron (44307) *(G-41)*
AKRON GENERAL HEALTH SYSTEM, Akron Also called Akron General Foundation *(G-41)*
Akron General Health System...................................330 665-8200
  4125 Medina Rd Ste 104 Akron (44333) *(G-42)*
Akron General Medical Center (HQ).............................330 344-6000
  1 Akron General Ave Akron (44307) *(G-43)*
Akron General Medical Center..................................330 344-1980
  224 W Exchange St Ste 330 Akron (44302) *(G-44)*
Akron General Medical Center..................................330 344-1444
  1 Akron General Ave Akron (44307) *(G-45)*
Akron General Medical Center..................................330 665-8000
  4125 Medina Rd Ste 1 Akron (44333) *(G-46)*
Akron Hardware Consultants Inc (PA)...........................330 644-7167
  1100 Killian Rd Akron (44312) *(G-47)*
Akron Health Center, Akron Also called Planned Prenthood Greater Ohio *(G-384)*
Akron Inn Limited Partnership.................................330 336-7692
  5 Park Centre Dr Wadsworth (44281) *(G-18587)*
Akron Lead Base Program, Akron Also called East Akron Neighborhood Dev *(G-200)*
Akron Management Corp...330 644-8441
  452 E Warner Rd Akron (44319) *(G-48)*
Akron Metropolitan Hsing Auth.................................330 920-1652
  500 Hardman Dr Stow (44224) *(G-17189)*
Akron Neonatology Inc..330 379-9473
  300 Locust St Akron (44302) *(G-49)*
Akron Plastic Surgeons Inc...................................330 253-9161
  1 Park West Blvd Ste 350 Akron (44320) *(G-50)*
Akron Porcelain & Plastics Co.................................330 745-2159
  83 E State St Barberton (44203) *(G-940)*
Akron Public School Maint Svcs................................330 761-2640
  515 Grant St Akron (44311) *(G-51)*
Akron Public Schools..330 761-1660
  70 N Broadway St Akron (44308) *(G-52)*
Akron Radiology Inc...330 375-3043
  525 E Market St Akron (44304) *(G-53)*
Akron Renal Center, Akron Also called Isd Renal Inc *(G-282)*
Akron Roundtable..330 247-8682
  P.O. Box 1051 Cuyahoga Falls (44223) *(G-9068)*
Akron Rubber Dev Lab Inc (PA).................................330 794-6600
  2887 Gilchrist Rd Akron (44305) *(G-54)*
Akron School Trnsp Svcs.......................................330 761-1390
  500 E North St Akron (44304) *(G-55)*
Akron Summit Cmnty Action Agcy................................330 572-8532
  670 W Exchange St Akron (44302) *(G-56)*
Akron Summit Cmnty Action Agcy................................330 733-2290
  1335 Massillon Rd Akron (44306) *(G-57)*
Akron Summit Cmnty Action Agcy (PA)...........................330 376-7730
  55 E Mill St Akron (44308) *(G-58)*
Akron Water Distribution Div, Akron Also called City of Akron *(G-135)*
Akron Welding & Spring Co, Akron Also called Brakefire Incorporated *(G-103)*
Akron Womans City Club Inc....................................330 762-6261
  732 W Exchange St Akron (44302) *(G-59)*
Akron Zoological Park...330 375-2550
  500 Edgewood Ave Akron (44307) *(G-60)*
Akron-Canton Regional Airport.................................330 499-4059
  5400 Lauby Rd Ste 9 North Canton (44720) *(G-15186)*

(G-0000) Company's Geographic Section entry number

Akron-Canton Regional Foodbank (PA) 330 535-6900
350 Opportunity Pkwy Akron (44307) *(G-61)*

Akron-Summit Convention 330 374-7560
77 E Mill St Akron (44308) *(G-62)*

Aksm, Columbus *Also called American Kidney Stone MGT Ltd (G-6928)*

Aksm/Genesis Medical Svcs Inc 614 447-0281
100 W 3rd Ave Ste 350 Columbus (43201) *(G-6889)*

Aksn, Columbus *Also called Allen Khnle Stovall Neuman LLP (G-6893)*

Aktion Associates Incorporated 419 893-7001
1687 Woodlands Dr Maumee (43537) *(G-13747)*

Akzo Nobel Coatings Inc 614 294-3361
1313 Windsor Ave Columbus (43211) *(G-6890)*

Al Neyer LLC (PA) 513 271-6400
302 W 3rd St Ste 800 Cincinnati (45202) *(G-2917)*

Al Neyer LLC 513 271-6400
302 W 3rd St Ste 800 Cincinnati (45202) *(G-2918)*

Al Peake & Sons Inc 419 243-9284
4949 Stickney Ave Toledo (43612) *(G-17584)*

Al-Mar Lanes 419 352-4637
1010 N Main St Bowling Green (43402) *(G-1713)*

Alabama Farmers Coop Inc 419 655-2289
12419 Jerry City Rd Cygnet (43413) *(G-9142)*

Aladdin Limousines, Westerville *Also called Aladdins Enterprises Inc (G-19218)*

Aladdins Baking Company Inc 216 861-0317
1301 Carnegie Ave Cleveland (44115) *(G-4925)*

Aladdins Enterprises Inc 614 891-3440
3408 E Dblin Granville Rd Westerville (43081) *(G-19218)*

Alan Manufacturing Inc 330 262-1555
3927 E Lincoln Way Wooster (44691) *(G-19684)*

Alan Woods Trucking Inc 513 738-3314
3592 Herman Rd Hamilton (45013) *(G-11556)*

Alano Club Inc 419 335-6211
222 S Brunell St Wauseon (43567) *(G-18796)*

Alba Manufacturing Inc 513 874-0551
8950 Seward Rd Fairfield (45011) *(G-10694)*

Albco Sales Inc (PA) 330 424-9446
230 Maple St Lisbon (44432) *(G-12795)*

Albert Freytag Inc 419 628-2018
306 Executive Dr Minster (45865) *(G-14531)*

Albert Guarnieri & Co 330 794-9834
7481 Herrick Park Dr Hudson (44236) *(G-11962)*

Albert M Higley Co LLC (PA) 216 861-2050
3636 Euclid Ave Fl 3 Cleveland (44115) *(G-4926)*

Albert Mike Leasing Inc (PA) 513 563-1400
10340 Evendale Dr Cincinnati (45241) *(G-2919)*

Albrecht Inc (PA) 513 576-9900
1040 Techne Center Dr Milford (45150) *(G-14369)*

Albrecht & Company, Milford *Also called Albrecht Inc (G-14369)*

Albright Welding Supply Co Inc (PA) 330 264-2021
3132 E Lincoln Way Wooster (44691) *(G-19685)*

Albring Vending Company 419 726-8059
702 Galena St Toledo (43611) *(G-17585)*

Alcatel-Lucent USA Inc 614 860-2000
5475 Rings Rd Ste 101 Dublin (43017) *(G-10124)*

Alco Inc 740 527-2991
36050 Smith Chapel Rd Logan (43138) *(G-12830)*

Alco-Chem Inc 330 833-8551
1303 Park Ave Sw Canton (44706) *(G-2177)*

Alco-Chem Inc (PA) 330 253-3535
45 N Summit St Akron (44308) *(G-63)*

Alcoa Power & Propulsion, Newburgh Heights *Also called Howmet Corporation (G-15114)*

Alcohol and Drug Recovery Ctr, Cleveland *Also called Cleveland Clinic Foundation (G-5238)*

Alcohol Drug Addction & Mental 937 443-0416
409 E Monument Ave # 102 Dayton (45402) *(G-9213)*

Alcohol, Drug Addiction, Akron *Also called City of Akron (G-133)*

Alcohol/Drug Outpatient T, Cleveland *Also called County of Cuyahoga (G-5361)*

ALCOHOLIC DROP-IN CENTER, Cincinnati *Also called Shelter House Volunteer Group (G-4469)*

ALCOHOLISM & CHEMICAL DEPENDEN, Newark *Also called Licking Cnty Alcoholism Prvntn (G-15051)*

Aldi Inc 330 273-7351
1319 W 130th St Hinckley (44233) *(G-11857)*

Aldo Peraza 614 804-0403
308 Eastcreek Dr Galloway (43119) *(G-11218)*

Aldrich Chemical 937 859-1808
3858 Benner Rd Miamisburg (45342) *(G-14138)*

Aleph Home & Senior Care Inc 216 382-7689
2448 Beachwood Blvd Cleveland (44122) *(G-4927)*

Alex N Sill Company (PA) 216 524-9999
6000 Lombardo Ctr Ste 600 Seven Hills (44131) *(G-16671)*

Alex Products Inc 419 399-4500
810 W Gasser Rd Paulding (45879) *(G-15790)*

Alexander & Associates Co (PA) 513 731-7800
360 Mclean Dr Cincinnati (45237) *(G-2920)*

Alexander and Bebout Inc 419 238-9567
10098 Lincoln Hwy Van Wert (45891) *(G-18471)*

Alexander Great Distributing, Steubenville *Also called Mougianis Industries Inc (G-17167)*

Alexander House Inc 513 523-4569
118 Hilltop Rd Oxford (45056) *(G-15672)*

Alexander Mann Solutions Corp 216 336-6756
1301 E 9th St Ste 1200 Cleveland (44114) *(G-4928)*

Alexis Gardens, Toledo *Also called Harvest Facility Holdings LP (G-17784)*

Alexis Medical Center, Toledo *Also called David Lee Grossman MD (G-17692)*

Alexson Services Inc 614 889-5837
525 Metro Pl N Ste 300 Dublin (43017) *(G-10125)*

Alexson Services Inc 513 874-0423
350 Kolb Dr Fairfield (45014) *(G-10695)*

Alfons Haar Inc 937 560-2031
150 Advanced Dr Springboro (45066) *(G-16961)*

Alfred Nickles Bakery Inc 419 332-6418
721 White Rd Fremont (43420) *(G-11057)*

Algart Health Care Inc 216 631-1550
8902 Detroit Ave Cleveland (44102) *(G-4929)*

Alice Noble Ice Arena 330 345-8686
851 Oldman Rd Wooster (44691) *(G-19686)*

Alice Training Institute LLC 330 661-0106
2508 Medina Rd Medina (44256) *(G-13908)*

Alien Technology LLC 408 782-3900
3001 W Tech Blvd Miamisburg (45342) *(G-14139)*

Alkon Corporation (PA) 419 355-9111
728 Graham Dr Fremont (43420) *(G-11058)*

Alkon Corporation 614 799-6650
6750 Crosby Ct Dublin (43016) *(G-10126)*

All About Heating Cooling 513 621-4620
7861 Palace Dr Cincinnati (45249) *(G-2921)*

All About Home Care Svcs LLC 937 222-2980
1307 E 3rd St Dayton (45403) *(G-9214)*

All About Kids 937 885-7480
1300 E Social Row Rd Centerville (45458) *(G-2620)*

All About Kids Daycare N 330 494-8700
6199 Frank Ave Nw North Canton (44720) *(G-15187)*

All Aerials LLC 330 659-9600
4945 Brecksville Rd Richfield (44286) *(G-16343)*

All America Insurance Company (HQ) 419 238-1010
800 S Washington St Van Wert (45891) *(G-18472)*

All American Heating AC, Medina *Also called Gene Tolliver Corp (G-13941)*

All American Sports Corp (HQ) 440 366-8225
7501 Performance Ln North Ridgeville (44039) *(G-15319)*

All American Trnsp Svcs LLC 419 589-7433
575 Beer Rd Ontario (44906) *(G-15544)*

All Around Children Montessori 330 928-1444
4117 Bridgewater Pkwy Stow (44224) *(G-17190)*

All Construction Services Inc 330 225-1653
945 Industrial Pkwy N Brunswick (44212) *(G-1918)*

All Construction/Mooney Moses, Brunswick *Also called All Construction Services Inc (G-1918)*

All Crane Rental Corp (PA) 614 261-1800
683 Oakland Park Ave Columbus (43224) *(G-6891)*

All Erection & Crane Rental (PA) 216 524-6550
4700 Acorn Dr Ste 100 Cleveland (44131) *(G-4930)*

All Erection & Crane Rental 216 524-6550
7809 Old Rockside Rd Cleveland (44131) *(G-4931)*

All Erection Crane Rentl Corp 216 524-6550
4700 Acorn Dr Ste 100 Cleveland (44131) *(G-4932)*

All Foils Inc 440 572-3645
16100 Imperial Pkwy Strongsville (44149) *(G-17283)*

All For Kids Inc 740 435-8050
1405 E Wheeling Ave Cambridge (43725) *(G-2048)*

All Gone Termite & Pest Ctrl 513 874-7500
9037 Sutton Pl West Chester (45011) *(G-18863)*

All Heart Home Care LLC 419 298-0034
143 N Michigan Ave Edgerton (43517) *(G-10466)*

All Hearts Home Health Care 440 342-2026
6009 Landerhaven Dr Ste D Cleveland (44124) *(G-4933)*

All Industrial Engine Service, Willoughby *Also called All Lift Service Company Inc (G-19503)*

All Industrial Group Inc (PA) 216 441-2000
1555 1/2 Harvard Ave Newburgh Heights (44105) *(G-15113)*

All Lift Service Company Inc 440 585-1542
4607 Hamann Pkwy Willoughby (44094) *(G-19503)*

All Metal Sales Inc 440 617-1234
29260 Clemens Rd Ste 3 Westlake (44145) *(G-19312)*

All My Sons Business Dev Corp 469 461-5000
15224 Neo Pkwy Cleveland (44128) *(G-4934)*

All My Sons Moving & Storge of 614 405-7202
4401 Lyman Dr Ste D Hilliard (43026) *(G-11740)*

All Occasions Event Rental 513 563-0600
10629 Reading Rd Cincinnati (45241) *(G-2922)*

All Ohio Threaded Rod Co Inc 216 426-1800
5349 Saint Clair Ave Cleveland (44103) *(G-4935)*

All Phase Power and Ltg Inc 419 624-9640
2122 Campbell St Sandusky (44870) *(G-16574)*

All Pro Cleaning Services Inc 440 519-0055
29500 Aurora Rd Ste 14 Solon (44139) *(G-16819)*

All Pro Freight Systems Inc (PA) 440 934-2222
1006 Crocker Rd Westlake (44145) *(G-19313)*

All Service Glass Company, Lima *Also called Wiechart Enterprises Inc (G-12784)*

All Star Training Club 330 352-5602
3108 Sparrows Crst Akron (44319) *(G-64)*

All Temp Refrigeration Inc 419 692-5016
18996 State Route 66 Delphos (45833) *(G-10019)*

All-Line Truck Sales, Hubbard *Also called Youngstown-Kenworth Inc (G-11952)*

All-Med Medical Supply, Middleburg Heights *Also called Twin Med LLC (G-14262)*

(PA)=Parent Co (HQ)=Headquarters (DH)=Div Headquarters

All-Type Welding & Fabrication................440 439-3990
 7690 Bond St Cleveland (44139) *(G-4936)*

Allan Hunter Construction LLC................330 634-9882
 931 Evans Ave Akron (44305) *(G-65)*

Allan Peace & Associates Inc................513 579-1700
 2035 Reading Rd Cincinnati (45202) *(G-2923)*

Allard Excavation................740 778-2242
 8336 Bennett Schl Hse Rd South Webster (45682) *(G-16950)*

Allcan Global Services Inc (PA)................513 825-1655
 11235 Sebring Dr Cincinnati (45240) *(G-2924)*

Alleen Company, The, Cincinnati Also called Jbjs Acquisitions LLC *(G-3810)*

Allega Recycled Mtls & Sup Co................216 447-0814
 5585 Canal Rd Cleveland (44125) *(G-4937)*

Allen Cnty Regional Trnst Auth................419 222-2782
 200 E High St Ste 2a Lima (45801) *(G-12594)*

Allen County Childrens Svcs Bd, Lima Also called County of Allen *(G-12624)*

Allen County Eductl Svc Ctr................419 222-1836
 1920 Slabtown Rd Lima (45801) *(G-12595)*

Allen County Health Care Ctr, Lima Also called County of Allen *(G-12622)*

Allen County Recyclers Inc................419 223-5010
 541 S Central Ave Lima (45804) *(G-12596)*

Allen County Refuse, Lima Also called Allen County Recyclers Inc *(G-12596)*

Allen Est Mangement Ltd................419 526-6505
 132 Distl Ave Mansfield (44902) *(G-13133)*

Allen Gardiner Deroberts................614 221-1500
 777 Goodale Blvd Ste 200 Columbus (43212) *(G-6892)*

Allen Horizon Center, Elyria Also called Horizon Education Centers *(G-10517)*

Allen Khnle Stovall Neuman LLP................614 221-8500
 17 S High St Ste 1220 Columbus (43215) *(G-6893)*

Allen Metro Housinig Auth, Lima Also called County of Allen *(G-12621)*

Allen Metro Hsing MGT Dev Corp................419 228-6065
 600 S Main St Lima (45804) *(G-12597)*

Allen Metro Tenants Councel, Lima Also called Allen Metropolitan Hsing Auth *(G-12598)*

Allen Metropolitan Hsing Auth................419 228-6065
 600 S Main St Lima (45804) *(G-12598)*

Allen Refractories Company................740 927-8000
 131 Shackelford Rd Pataskala (43062) *(G-15782)*

Allen-Keith Construction Co (PA)................330 266-2220
 2735 Greensburg Rd Canton (44720) *(G-2178)*

Allergy & Asthma Inc................740 654-8623
 2405 N Columbus St # 270 Lancaster (43130) *(G-12369)*

Allergy & Asthma Centre Dayton, Centerville Also called Allergy & Asthma Centre Dayton *(G-2621)*

Allergy & Asthma Centre Dayton (PA)................937 435-8999
 8039 Wash Vlg Dr Ste 100 Centerville (45458) *(G-2621)*

Allgeier & Son Inc (PA)................513 574-3735
 6386 Bridgetown Rd Cincinnati (45248) *(G-2925)*

Allgood Home Improvements, Fairfield Also called Eagle Industries Ohio Inc *(G-10721)*

Allianalce Hospitalist Group................330 823-5626
 200 E State St Alliance (44601) *(G-514)*

Alliance Academy of Cincinnati, Cincinnati Also called National Heritg Academies Inc *(G-4093)*

Alliance Advantage, Columbus Also called Advantage Aerotech Inc *(G-6875)*

Alliance Calibration, Cincinnati Also called Raitz Inc *(G-4336)*

Alliance Citizens Health Assn................330 596-6000
 200 E State St Alliance (44601) *(G-515)*

Alliance Crane & Rigging Inc................330 823-8823
 1370 Alliance Rd Deerfield (44411) *(G-9901)*

Alliance Data Systems Corp................614 729-4000
 3075 Loyalty Cir Columbus (43219) *(G-6894)*

Alliance Data Systems Corp................614 729-5000
 220 W Schrock Rd Westerville (43081) *(G-19219)*

Alliance Data Systems Corp................614 729-5800
 6939 Americana Pkwy Reynoldsburg (43068) *(G-16280)*

Alliance Fire Dept, Alliance Also called Interntional Assn Firefighters *(G-535)*

Alliance Franklin Head Start, Alliance Also called Stark County Cmnty Action Agcy *(G-553)*

Alliance Health, Cincinnati Also called Uc Health Llc *(G-4667)*

Alliance Hospitality................330 505-2173
 801 N Canfield Niles Rd Youngstown (44515) *(G-19950)*

Alliance Hospitality Inc................440 951-7333
 7701 Reynolds Rd Mentor (44060) *(G-14016)*

Alliance Hot Stove Baseball L................330 823-7034
 1127 Forest Ave Alliance (44601) *(G-516)*

Alliance Imaging Inc................330 493-5100
 4825 Higbee Ave Nw # 201 Canton (44718) *(G-2179)*

Alliance Legal Solutions LLC................216 525-0100
 6161 Oak Tree Blvd # 300 Independence (44131) *(G-12043)*

Alliance Petroleum Corporation (HQ)................330 493-0440
 4150 Belden Village Mall Canton (44718) *(G-2180)*

Alliance Solutions Group LLC (PA)................216 503-1690
 6161 Oak Tree Blvd Independence (44131) *(G-12044)*

Alliance Towers LLC................330 823-1063
 350 S Arch Ave Apt 106 Alliance (44601) *(G-517)*

Allied Barton Security Svcs, Rossford Also called Alliedbarton Security Svcs LLC *(G-16459)*

Allied Builders Inc (PA)................937 226-0311
 1644 Kuntz Rd Dayton (45404) *(G-9215)*

Allied Building Products Corp................216 362-1764
 12800 Brookpark Rd Cleveland (44130) *(G-4938)*

Allied Building Products Corp................513 784-9090
 1735 Eastern Ave Cincinnati (45202) *(G-2926)*

Allied Building Products Corp................614 488-0717
 1055 Kinnear Rd Columbus (43212) *(G-6895)*

Allied Car Wash Inc................513 559-1733
 3330 Central Pkwy Cincinnati (45225) *(G-2927)*

Allied Cash Advance, Cincinnati Also called Allied Cash Holdings LLC *(G-2928)*

Allied Cash Holdings LLC (PA)................305 371-3141
 7755 Montgomery Rd # 400 Cincinnati (45236) *(G-2928)*

Allied Communications Corp (PA)................614 275-2075
 755 Georgesville Rd Columbus (43228) *(G-6896)*

Allied Enterprises Inc (PA)................440 808-8760
 26021 Center Ridge Rd Westlake (44145) *(G-19314)*

Allied Environmental Svcs Inc................419 227-4004
 585 Liberty Commons Pkwy Lima (45804) *(G-12599)*

Allied Erct & Dismantling Co................330 744-0808
 2100 Poland Ave Youngstown (44502) *(G-19951)*

Allied Fabricating & Wldg Co................614 751-6664
 5699 Chantry Dr Columbus (43232) *(G-6897)*

Allied Fence Builders, Dayton Also called Allied Builders Inc *(G-9215)*

Allied Home Health Services, Holland Also called R & F Inc *(G-11906)*

Allied Infotech Corporation................330 745-8529
 2170 Romig Rd Akron (44320) *(G-66)*

Allied Interstate LLC................715 386-1810
 P.O. Box 561534 Columbus (43236) *(G-6898)*

Allied Paving Company, Holland Also called Allied Paving Inc *(G-11869)*

Allied Paving Inc................419 666-3100
 8406 Airport Hwy Holland (43528) *(G-11869)*

Allied Restaurant Svc Ohio Inc (PA)................419 589-4759
 187 Illinois Ave S Mansfield (44905) *(G-13134)*

Allied Security LLC................513 771-3776
 110 Boggs Ln Ste 140 Cincinnati (45246) *(G-2929)*

Allied Separation, Twinsburg Also called Air Supply Co *(G-18242)*

Allied Supply Company Inc (PA)................937 224-9833
 1100 E Monument Ave Dayton (45402) *(G-9216)*

Allied Truck Parts Co................330 477-8127
 4216 Southway St Sw Canton (44706) *(G-2181)*

Allied Waste Division, Youngstown Also called Republic Services Inc *(G-20183)*

Allied Waste Division, Dayton Also called Republic Services Inc *(G-9733)*

Allied Waste Division, Lima Also called Republic Services Inc *(G-12729)*

Allied Waste Industries LLC................440 774-3100
 43502 Oberlin Elyria Rd Oberlin (44074) *(G-15498)*

Allied Waste Systems Inc................937 268-8110
 1577 W River Rd Dayton (45417) *(G-9217)*

Allied Waste Systems Inc................419 925-4592
 6141 Depweg Rd Celina (45822) *(G-2581)*

Allied Waste Systems Inc................937 593-3566
 2946 Us Highway 68 N Bellefontaine (43311) *(G-1344)*

Allied Waste Systems Inc................419 636-2242
 12604 County Road G Bryan (43506) *(G-1951)*

Allied Wste Svcs Yngstown Coml, Youngstown Also called Browning-Ferris Inds of Ohio *(G-19977)*

Alliedbarton Security Svcs LLC................614 225-9061
 57 E Wilson Bridge Rd # 300 Worthington (43085) *(G-19792)*

Alliedbarton Security Svcs LLC................419 874-9005
 1001 Dixie Hwy Ste F Rossford (43460) *(G-16459)*

Alloy Metal Exchange LLC................216 478-0200
 26000 Corbin Dr Bedford Heights (44128) *(G-1315)*

Alloyd Insulation Co Inc................937 890-7900
 5734 Webster St Dayton (45414) *(G-9218)*

Allpro Parking Ohio LLC................614 221-9696
 431 E Broad St Columbus (43215) *(G-6899)*

Allshred Services, Maumee Also called Recycling Services Inc *(G-13842)*

Allstars Travel Group Inc................614 901-4100
 7775 Walton Pkwy Ste 100 New Albany (43054) *(G-14842)*

Allstate, Brecksville Also called Luce Smith & Scott Inc *(G-1788)*

Allstate Insurance Company................330 650-2917
 75 Milford Dr Ste 222 Hudson (44236) *(G-11963)*

Allstate Insurance Company................330 656-6000
 75 Executive Pkwy Hudson (44237) *(G-11964)*

Allstate Painting & Contg Co................330 220-5533
 1256 Industrial Pkwy N # 2 Brunswick (44212) *(G-1919)*

Allstate Trk Sls of Estrn OH................330 339-5555
 327 Stonecreek Rd Nw New Philadelphia (44663) *(G-14945)*

Alltel Communications Corp (HQ)................740 349-8551
 66 N 4th St Newark (43055) *(G-15008)*

Alltel Communications Corp................330 656-8000
 205 S Hambden St Chardon (44024) *(G-2686)*

Allwell Behavioral Health Svcs (PA)................740 454-9766
 2845 Bell St Zanesville (43701) *(G-20274)*

Allwell Behavioral Health Svcs................740 439-4428
 2500 Glenn Hwy Cambridge (43725) *(G-2049)*

Ally Financial Inc................330 533-7300
 3731 Boardman Canfield Rd Canfield (44406) *(G-2130)*

Almost Family Inc................614 457-1900
 445 Hutchinson Ave Columbus (43235) *(G-6900)*

Almost Family Inc................330 724-7545
 1225 E Waterloo Rd Akron (44306) *(G-67)*

Almost Family Inc................513 662-3400
 2135 Dana Ave Ste 220 Cincinnati (45207) *(G-2930)*

Almost Family Inc................216 464-0443
 23611 Chagrin Blvd # 130 Cleveland (44122) *(G-4939)*

Alois Alzheimer Center, The, Cincinnati Also called Crystalwood Inc *(G-3383)*

Alomie Dialysis LLC 740 941-1688
  609 W Emmitt Ave Waverly (45690) *(G-18813)*

Alonovus Corp 330 674-2300
  7368 County Road 623 Millersburg (44654) *(G-14454)*

Alorica Customer Care Inc 216 525-3311
  9525 Sweet Valley Dr Cleveland (44125) *(G-4940)*

Alpco, Westlake *Also called Aluminum Line Products Company (G-19316)*

Alpha & Omega Bldg Svcs Inc 513 429-5082
  11319 Grooms Rd Blue Ash (45242) *(G-1502)*

Alpha & Omega Bldg Svcs Inc (PA) 937 298-2125
  2843 Culver Ave Ste B Dayton (45429) *(G-9219)*

Alpha CHI Omega 614 291-3871
  103 E 15th Ave Columbus (43201) *(G-6901)*

Alpha Epsilon PHI 614 294-5243
  200 E 17th Ave Columbus (43201) *(G-6902)*

Alpha Freight Systems Inc 800 394-9001
  5876 Darrow Rd Hudson (44236) *(G-11965)*

Alpha Group of Delaware Inc 614 222-1855
  85 Marconi Blvd Columbus (43215) *(G-6903)*

Alpha Group of Delaware Inc (PA) 740 368-5810
  1000 Alpha Dr Delaware (43015) *(G-9951)*

Alpha Group of Delaware Inc 740 368-5820
  1000 Alpha Dr Delaware (43015) *(G-9952)*

Alpha Imaging LLC (PA) 440 953-3800
  4455 Glenbrook Rd Willoughby (44094) *(G-19504)*

Alpha Investment Partnership (PA) 513 621-1826
  525 Vine St Ste 1925 Cincinnati (45202) *(G-2931)*

Alpha Media LLC 937 294-5858
  717 E David Rd Dayton (45429) *(G-9220)*

Alpha Nursing Homes Inc 740 345-9197
  17 Forry St Newark (43055) *(G-15009)*

Alpha Nursing Homes Inc 740 622-2074
  1991 Otsego Ave Coshocton (43812) *(G-8997)*

Alpha PHI Alpha Homes Inc 330 376-2115
  730 Callis Dr Akron (44311) *(G-68)*

Alpha Security LLC 330 406-2181
  87 W Mckinley Way Ste 1 Poland (44514) *(G-16080)*

Alpha Technologies Svcs LLC (HQ) 330 745-1641
  6279 Hudson Crossing Pkwy Hudson (44236) *(G-11966)*

Alphamicron Inc 330 676-0648
  1950 State Route 59 Kent (44240) *(G-12213)*

Alphaport Inc 216 619-2400
  18013 Cleveland Cleveland (44135) *(G-4941)*

Alphera Financial Services, Hilliard *Also called BMW Financial Services Na LLC (G-11747)*

Alpine Insulation I LLC 614 221-3399
  495 S High St Ste 50 Columbus (43215) *(G-6904)*

Alpine Nursing Care 216 650-6295
  5555 Brecksville Rd Cleveland (44131) *(G-4942)*

Alpine Structures LLC 330 359-5708
  2675 Us Route 62 Dundee (44624) *(G-10382)*

Alpine Valley Ski Area, Chesterland *Also called Sycamore Lake Inc (G-2746)*

Alro Steel Corporation 330 929-4660
  4787 State Rd Cuyahoga Falls (44223) *(G-9069)*

Alro Steel Corporation 513 769-9999
  10310 S Medallion Dr Cincinnati (45241) *(G-2932)*

Alro Steel Corporation 419 720-5300
  3003 Airport Hwy Toledo (43609) *(G-17586)*

Alro Steel Corporation 614 878-7271
  555 Hilliard Rome Rd Columbus (43228) *(G-6905)*

Alro Steel Corporation 937 253-6121
  821 Springfield St Dayton (45403) *(G-9221)*

Als Group Usa Corp 513 733-5336
  4388 Glendale Milford Rd Blue Ash (45242) *(G-1503)*

Als Laboratory Group, Cleveland *Also called Als Services Usa Corp (G-4943)*

Als Services Usa Corp 513 582-8277
  8961 Steeplechase Way West Chester (45069) *(G-18864)*

Als Services Usa Corp 604 998-5311
  6180 Halle Dr Ste D Cleveland (44125) *(G-4943)*

Alsan Corporation 330 385-3636
  900 W 8th St East Liverpool (43920) *(G-10396)*

Alside Supply Center, Columbus *Also called Associated Materials LLC (G-6983)*

Alstate-Peterbilt-Trucks, New Philadelphia *Also called Allstate Trk Sls of Estrn OH (G-14945)*

Alstom Signaling Operation LLC 513 552-6485
  25 Merchant St Cincinnati (45246) *(G-2933)*

Alt & Witzig Engineering Inc 513 777-9890
  6205 Schumacher Park Dr West Chester (45069) *(G-18865)*

Alta Care Group Inc 330 793-2487
  711 Belmont Ave Youngstown (44502) *(G-19952)*

Alta Partners LLC 440 808-3654
  902 Westpoint Pkwy # 320 Westlake (44145) *(G-19315)*

Alta360 Research, Maumee *Also called Ritter & Associates Inc (G-13846)*

Altamira Technologies Corp 937 490-4804
  2850 Presidential Dr # 200 Beavercreek (45324) *(G-1124)*

Altaquip LLC (HQ) 513 674-6464
  100 Production Dr Harrison (45030) *(G-11660)*

Altenheim, Strongsville *Also called West Side Dtscher Fruen Verein (G-17359)*

Altenheim Foundation Inc 440 238-3361
  18627 Shurmer Rd Strongsville (44136) *(G-17284)*

Altercare 330 335-2555
  147 Garfield St Wadsworth (44281) *(G-18588)*

Altercare Inc (PA) 440 327-5285
  35990 Westminister Ave North Ridgeville (44039) *(G-15320)*

Altercare Adena, Adena *Also called Adena NH LLC (G-7)*

Altercare Hartville, Hartville *Also called GFS Leasing Inc (G-11687)*

Altercare Nobles Pond Inc 330 834-4800
  7006 Fulton Dr Nw Canton (44718) *(G-2182)*

Altercare of Bucyrus Inc 419 562-7644
  1929 Whetstone St Bucyrus (44820) *(G-1976)*

Altercare of Louisville Center 330 875-4224
  7187 Saint Francis St Louisville (44641) *(G-12959)*

Altercare of Mentor, Mentor *Also called Schroer Properties Inc (G-14106)*

Altercare of Mentor Center 440 953-4421
  9901 Johnnycake Ridge Rd Mentor (44060) *(G-14017)*

Altercare of Millersburg 330 674-4444
  105 Majora Ln Millersburg (44654) *(G-14455)*

Altercare of Navarre, North Canton *Also called Schroer Properties Inc (G-15231)*

Altercare of Ohio, Canton *Also called Altercare Nobles Pond Inc (G-2182)*

Altercare of Ravenna, Kent *Also called GFS Leasing Inc (G-12235)*

Altercare of Wadsworth, Wadsworth *Also called Altercare (G-18588)*

Altercrest, Cincinnati *Also called Archdiocese of Cincinnati (G-2981)*

Alternacare Home Health Inc 740 689-1589
  1566 Monmouth Dr Ste 103 Lancaster (43130) *(G-12370)*

Alternate Sltions Private Duty (PA) 937 298-1111
  1251 E Dorothy Ln Dayton (45419) *(G-9222)*

Alternate Solutions First LLC 937 298-1111
  1251 E Dorothy Ln Dayton (45419) *(G-9223)*

Alternate Solutions Healthcare 937 299-1111
  1050 Forrer Blvd Dayton (45420) *(G-9224)*

Alternative Care Mgt Systems 614 761-0035
  4789 Rings Rd Dublin (43017) *(G-10127)*

Alternative Care MGT Systs, Dublin *Also called Alternative Care Mgt Systems (G-10127)*

Alternative Home Care & Stffng 513 794-0571
  7759 Montgomery Rd Cincinnati (45236) *(G-2934)*

Alternative Home Health Care 513 794-0555
  5150 E Galbraith Rd # 200 Cincinnati (45236) *(G-2935)*

Alternative Nursing & HM Care, Wheelersburg *Also called Selective Networking Inc (G-19440)*

Alternative Paths Inc 330 725-9195
  246 Northland Dr Ste 200a Medina (44256) *(G-13909)*

Alternative Residences Two (PA) 740 526-0514
  67051 Executive Dr Saint Clairsville (43950) *(G-16468)*

Alternative Residences Two 330 453-0200
  2832 34th St Ne Canton (44705) *(G-2183)*

Alternative Services Inc 419 861-2121
  7710 Hill Ave Holland (43528) *(G-11870)*

Althans Insurance Agency Inc 440 247-6422
  543 Washington St Chagrin Falls (44022) *(G-2638)*

Altick & Corwin Co Lpa 937 223-1201
  1 S Main St Ste 1590 Dayton (45402) *(G-9225)*

Altimate Care LLC (PA) 614 794-9600
  5869 Cleveland Ave Columbus (43231) *(G-6906)*

Altobelli Realestate (PA) 330 652-0200
  304 Vienna Ave Niles (44446) *(G-15143)*

Altria Group Distribution Co. 804 274-2000
  4680 Parkway Dr Ste 450 Mason (45040) *(G-13538)*

Altruism Society Inc 877 283-4001
  3695 Green Rd Unit 22896 Beachwood (44122) *(G-1028)*

Alumalloy Metalcasting Company 440 930-2222
  33665 Walker Rd Avon Lake (44012) *(G-907)*

ALUMINA RAILING PRODUCTS, Cleves *Also called Alumina Rling Cstm Ir Wrks Inc (G-6724)*

Alumina Rling Cstm Ir Wrks Inc. 513 353-1116
  8301 Strimple Rd Cleves (45002) *(G-6724)*

Aluminum Line Products Company (PA) 440 835-8880
  24460 Sperry Cir Westlake (44145) *(G-19316)*

ALUMNI ASSOCIATION, THE, Columbus *Also called Ohio State Univ Alumni Assn (G-8290)*

Alvada Const Inc 419 595-4224
  2959 S Us Highway 23 Alvada (44802) *(G-560)*

Alvada Construction, Alvada *Also called Alvada Const Inc (G-560)*

Alvada Trucking, Alvada *Also called Aci Const Co Inc (G-559)*

Alveo Health LLC 513 557-3502
  700 W Pete Rose Way # 426 Cincinnati (45203) *(G-2936)*

Alvis House, Columbus *Also called Alvis Inc (G-6907)*

Alvis Inc 614 252-1788
  844 Bryden Rd Columbus (43205) *(G-6907)*

Alvis Lndcape Golf Curses Mtls, Harrison *Also called James H Alvis Trucking Inc (G-11671)*

Alzheimer Center, Beachwood *Also called University Hospitals Cleveland (G-1116)*

AM Castle & Co 330 425-7000
  26800 Miles Rd Bedford (44146) *(G-1269)*

AM Industrial Group LLC (PA) 216 433-7171
  16000 Commerce Park Dr Brookpark (44142) *(G-1890)*

AM Industrial Group LLC 216 267-6783
  4680 Grayton Rd Cleveland (44135) *(G-4944)*

Amalgamated Transit Union 216 861-3350
  2428 Saint Clair Ave Ne Cleveland (44114) *(G-4945)*

Amanda House, Lima *Also called Assisted Living Concepts LLC (G-12602)*

Amanda's Garden, Ravenna *Also called Amandas Playroom Inc (G-16232)*

Amandacare Inc 614 884-8880
  2101 S Hamilton Rd # 212 Columbus (43232) *(G-6908)*

Amandacare Home Health, Columbus *Also called Amandacare Inc (G-6908)*

Amandas Playroom Inc (PA) 330 296-3934
  6709 Cleveland Rd Ravenna (44266) *(G-16232)*

Amaxx Inc...614 486-3481
  5975 Wilcox Pl Ste B Dublin (43016) *(G-10128)*

Ambassador Nursing, Hilliard *Also called Lighthouse Medical Staffing (G-11784)*

Amber Gardens, Stow *Also called Tersigni Cargill Entps LLC (G-17235)*

Amber Home Care LLC..................................614 523-0668
  2800 Corp Exchange Dr # 100 Columbus (43231) *(G-6909)*

Amberwood Manor, New Philadelphia *Also called South Broadway (G-14981)*

Ambius, Brooklyn Heights *Also called Rentokil North America Inc (G-1880)*

Amboy Contractors LLc.................................419 644-2111
  424 E Main St Metamora (43540) *(G-14131)*

Ambulatory Care Solutions LLC......................740 695-3721
  103 Plaza Dr Ste A Saint Clairsville (43950) *(G-16469)*

Ambulatory Medical Care Inc (PA)..................513 831-8555
  935 State Route 28 Milford (45150) *(G-14370)*

AMC, Dublin *Also called American Multi-Cinema Inc (G-10132)*

AMC, Cleveland *Also called American Multi-Cinema Inc (G-4959)*

AMC, Rocky River *Also called American Multi-Cinema Inc (G-16422)*

AMC Entertainment Inc..................................614 846-6575
  6360 Busch Blvd Columbus (43229) *(G-6910)*

AMC Entertainment Inc..................................614 428-5716
  275 Easton Town Ctr Columbus (43219) *(G-6911)*

AMC Entertainment Inc..................................614 429-0100
  777 Kinnear Rd Columbus (43212) *(G-6912)*

AMC Entertainment Inc..................................216 749-0260
  4788 Ridge Rd Brooklyn (44144) *(G-1859)*

Amedisys Inc...740 373-8549
  210 N 7th St Marietta (45750) *(G-13309)*

Amelia Davita Dialysis Center........................513 797-0713
  1761 E Ohio Pike Amelia (45102) *(G-564)*

Amenity Home Health Care LLC.....................513 931-3689
  3025 W Galbraith Rd Cincinnati (45239) *(G-2937)*

Amerathon LLC (HQ)....................................513 752-7300
  671 Ohio Pike Ste K Cincinnati (45245) *(G-2841)*

Ameri Interntl Trade Grp Inc..........................419 586-6433
  1 Visions Pkwy Celina (45822) *(G-2582)*

Ameri-Line Inc...440 316-4500
  27060 Royalton Rd Columbia Station (44028) *(G-6769)*

America Electric Power Texas, Columbus *Also called AEP Power Marketing Inc (G-6880)*

America's Best Medical, Akron *Also called Lincare Inc (G-315)*

Americab Inc..216 429-1134
  3380 W 137th St Cleveland (44111) *(G-4946)*

American Air Comfort Tech, Grove City *Also called American Air Furnace Company (G-11404)*

American Air Furnace Company.......................614 876-1702
  3945 Brookham Dr Grove City (43123) *(G-11404)*

American Airlines Inc...................................216 706-0702
  5300 Riverside Dr Ste 8a Cleveland (44135) *(G-4947)*

American Airlines Inc...................................937 454-7472
  10398 Freight Dr Vandalia (45377) *(G-18501)*

American Airlines Inc...................................937 890-6668
  3600 Terminal Rd Ste 1 Vandalia (45377) *(G-18502)*

American Airlines Inc...................................216 898-1347
  5300 Riverside Dr Ste 1a Cleveland (44135) *(G-4948)*

American Benefits Management, Wadsworth *Also called Masters Agency Inc (G-18607)*

American Boring Inc......................................740 969-8000
  6895 Pickerington Rd Carroll (43112) *(G-2555)*

American Bottling Company...........................614 237-4201
  950 Stelzer Rd Columbus (43219) *(G-6913)*

American Brass, Cleveland *Also called Empire Brass Co (G-5477)*

American Broadband Telecom Co....................419 824-5800
  1 Seagate Ste 600 Toledo (43604) *(G-17587)*

American Brzing Div Paulo Pdts, Willoughby *Also called Paulo Products Company (G-19561)*

American Bulk Commodities Inc (PA)...............330 758-0841
  8063 Southern Blvd Youngstown (44512) *(G-19953)*

American Bus Personnel Svcs (PA)..................513 770-3300
  7547 Central Parke Blvd Mason (45040) *(G-13539)*

American Bus Solutions Inc............................614 888-2227
  8850 Whitney Dr Lewis Center (43035) *(G-12522)*

American Business Machines, Richfield *Also called Ricoh Usa Inc (G-16376)*

American Cancer Society East.......................800 227-2345
  10501 Euclid Ave Cleveland (44106) *(G-4949)*

American Cancer Society East.......................888 227-6446
  5555 Frantz Rd Frnt Frnt Dublin (43017) *(G-10129)*

American Ceramic Society (PA).......................614 890-4700
  550 Polaris Pkwy Ste 510 Westerville (43082) *(G-19144)*

American Chem Soc Fderal Cr Un....................614 447-3675
  2540 Olentangy River Rd Columbus (43202) *(G-6914)*

American City Bus Journals Inc......................937 528-4400
  40 N Main St Ste 800 Dayton (45423) *(G-9226)*

American Cllege Crdlgy Fndtion.....................614 442-5950
  5600 Blazer Pkwy 320 Dublin (43017) *(G-10130)*

American Coatings Corporation......................614 335-1000
  7510 Montgomery Rd Plain City (43064) *(G-16043)*

American Commerce Insurance Co (HQ)...........614 272-6951
  3590 Twin Creeks Dr Columbus (43204) *(G-6915)*

American Commodore Tu (PA)........................216 291-4601
  4130 Mayfield Rd Cleveland (44121) *(G-4950)*

American Consolidated Inds Inc (PA)................216 587-8000
  4650 Johnston Pkwy Cleveland (44128) *(G-4951)*

American Contrs Indemnity Co.......................513 688-0800
  7794 5 Mile Rd Cincinnati (45230) *(G-2938)*

American Copy Equipment Inc.......................330 722-9555
  6599 Granger Rd Cleveland (44131) *(G-4952)*

American Crane Inc......................................614 496-2268
  7791 Taylor Rd Sw Ste A Reynoldsburg (43068) *(G-16281)*

American Crane & Lift Trck Svc, Reynoldsburg *Also called American Crane Inc (G-16281)*

American Custom Industries, Sylvania *Also called Bobbart Industries Inc (G-17412)*

American Cutting Edge Inc.............................937 866-5986
  4475 Infirmary Rd Miamisburg (45342) *(G-14140)*

American Diesel, Inc., Cleveland *Also called Interstate Diesel Service Inc (G-5765)*

American Eagle Hlth Care Svcs.......................440 428-5103
  6831 Chapel Rd Madison (44057) *(G-13092)*

American Eagle Mortgage Co LLC (PA).............440 988-2900
  6145 Park Square Dr Ste 4 Lorain (44053) *(G-12879)*

American Electric Power, Brilliant *Also called Cardinal Operating Company (G-1821)*

American Electric Power Co Inc.......................419 420-3011
  430 Emma St Findlay (45840) *(G-10864)*

American Electric Power Co Inc.......................740 829-4129
  47201 County Road 273 Conesville (43811) *(G-8947)*

American Electric Power Co Inc.......................740 594-1988
  9135 State Route 682 Athens (45701) *(G-763)*

American Electric Power Co Inc.......................330 438-7024
  301 Cleveland Ave Sw Canton (44702) *(G-2184)*

American Electric Power Co Inc.......................419 998-5106
  369 E Oconnor Ave Lima (45801) *(G-12600)*

American Electric Power Co Inc.......................740 779-5261
  701 Hardin Dr Chillicothe (45601) *(G-2756)*

American Electric Power Co Inc.......................614 856-2750
  5900 Refugee Rd Columbus (43232) *(G-6916)*

American Electric Power Co Inc.......................614 351-3715
  1759 W Mound St Columbus (43223) *(G-6917)*

American Electric Power Co Inc.......................740 384-7981
  3 W 13th St Wellston (45692) *(G-18847)*

American Electric Power Co Inc.......................740 295-3070
  405 Brewer Ln Coshocton (43812) *(G-8998)*

American Electric Power Co Inc.......................330 580-5085
  5300 Navarre Rd Sw Canton (44706) *(G-2185)*

American Electric Power Co Inc.......................740 598-4164
  306 County Road 7e Brilliant (43913) *(G-1819)*

American Electric Power Co Inc.......................614 716-1000
  1 Riverside Plz Ste 1600 Columbus (43215) *(G-6918)*

American Electric Pwr Svc Corp (HQ)...............614 716-1000
  1 Riverside Plz Fl 1 # 1 Columbus (43215) *(G-6919)*

American Electric Pwr Svc Corp......................614 582-1742
  825 Tech Center Dr Columbus (43230) *(G-6920)*

American Empire Insurance, Cincinnati *Also called American Empire Surplus Lines (G-2939)*

American Empire Surplus Lines.......................513 369-3000
  515 Main St Cincinnati (45202) *(G-2939)*

American Emprie Srpls Lines In (HQ)................513 369-3000
  580 Walnut St Cincinnati (45202) *(G-2940)*

American Envmtl Group Ltd............................330 659-5930
  3600 Brecksville Rd # 100 Richfield (44286) *(G-16344)*

American Family Home Insur Co......................513 943-7100
  7000 Midland Blvd Amelia (45102) *(G-565)*

American Federal Bank, Columbus *Also called Congressional Bank (G-7348)*

American Federation of Gov...........................513 861-6047
  3200 Vine St Cincinnati (45220) *(G-2941)*

American Federation of State.........................937 461-9983
  15 Gates St Dayton (45402) *(G-9227)*

American Fidelity Assurance Co......................800 437-1011
  90 Northwoods Blvd Ste B Columbus (43235) *(G-6921)*

American Financial Corporation......................513 579-2121
  580 Walnut St Fl 9 Cincinnati (45202) *(G-2942)*

American Financial Group Inc (PA).................513 579-2121
  301 E 4th St Fl 8 Cincinnati (45202) *(G-2943)*

American Fleet Services, Cleveland *Also called American Nat Fleet Svc Inc (G-4961)*

American Frame Corporation (PA)....................419 893-5595
  400 Tomahawk Dr Maumee (43537) *(G-13748)*

American Frame Corporation..........................419 893-5595
  1684 Woodlands Dr Ste 400 Maumee (43537) *(G-13749)*

American Future Systems Inc.........................330 394-1555
  5000 E Market St Warren (44484) *(G-18662)*

American Gen Lf Insur Co Del.........................513 762-7807
  250 E 5th St Ste 1500 Cincinnati (45202) *(G-2944)*

American Golf Corporation............................440 286-9544
  13095 Rockhaven Rd Chesterland (44026) *(G-2736)*

American Golf Corporation............................419 726-9353
  4001 N Summit St Toledo (43611) *(G-17588)*

American Golf Corporation............................740 965-5122
  3300 Miller Paul Rd Galena (43021) *(G-11154)*

American Golf Corporation............................310 664-4278
  3223 Norton Rd Grove City (43123) *(G-11405)*

American Golf Corporation............................419 693-1991
  3915 Heatherdowns Blvd Toledo (43614) *(G-17589)*

American Greetings, Cleveland *Also called AG Interactive Inc (G-4911)*

American Health Group Inc............................419 891-1212
  570 Longbow Dr Maumee (43537) *(G-13750)*

American Health Network Inc........................614 794-4500
  2500 Corp Exchange Dr # 100 Columbus (43231) *(G-6922)*

American Health Packaging, Columbus *Also called Amerisource Health Svcs LLC (G-6941)*

American Heart Assn Ohio Vly..........216 791-7500
1375 E 9th St Ste 600 Cleveland (44114) *(G-4953)*
American Heart Association Inc..........614 848-6676
5455 N High St Columbus (43214) *(G-6923)*
American Heritage Girls Inc..........513 771-2025
175 Tri County Pkwy # 100 Cincinnati (45246) *(G-2945)*
American Highways Insur Agcy..........330 659-8900
3250 Interstate Dr Richfield (44286) *(G-16345)*
American Hlth Netwrk Ohio LLC (HQ)..........614 794-4500
2500 Corporate Exchange D Columbus (43231) *(G-6924)*
American Hlth Ntwrk & Fmly PRC..........419 524-2212
248 Blymyer Ave Mansfield (44903) *(G-13135)*
American Home Health Care Inc..........614 237-1133
861 Taylor Rd Unit I Columbus (43230) *(G-6925)*
American Home Health Services,, Westlake *Also called Infinity Health Services Inc (G-19357)*
American Hood Systems Inc..........440 365-4567
177 Reaser Ct Elyria (44035) *(G-10478)*
American Hospitality Group Inc (HQ)..........330 336-6684
200 Smokerise Dr Ste 300 Wadsworth (44281) *(G-18589)*
American Income Life Insur Co..........440 582-0040
12301 Ridge Rd Cleveland (44133) *(G-4954)*
American Institute Research..........614 221-8717
41 S High St Ste 2425 Columbus (43215) *(G-6926)*
American Institute Research..........614 310-8982
820 Freeway Dr N Columbus (43229) *(G-6927)*
American Insur Administrators..........614 486-5388
5455 Rings Rd Ste 200 Dublin (43017) *(G-10131)*
American Interiors Inc (PA)..........419 324-0365
302 S Byrne Rd Bldg 100 Toledo (43615) *(G-17590)*
American International Cnstr..........440 243-5535
1180 Berea Indus Pkwy Berea (44017) *(G-1411)*
American Intl Group Inc..........216 479-8800
1300 E 9th St Ste 1400 Cleveland (44114) *(G-4955)*
American Jersey Cattle Assn (PA)..........614 861-3636
6486 E Main St Reynoldsburg (43068) *(G-16282)*
American Kenda Rbr Indus Ltd (HQ)..........866 536-3287
7095 Americana Pkwy Reynoldsburg (43068) *(G-16283)*
American Kidney Stone MGT Ltd (PA)..........800 637-5188
100 W 3rd Ave Ste 350 Columbus (43201) *(G-6928)*
American Landfill Inc..........330 866-3265
7916 Chapel St Se Waynesburg (44688) *(G-18828)*
American Legacy Tours, Cincinnati *Also called Newport Walking Tours LLC (G-4112)*
American Legion..........330 488-0119
204 Wood St S East Canton (44730) *(G-10385)*
American Legion..........440 834-8621
14052 Goodwin St Burton (44021) *(G-2013)*
American Legion Post..........330 393-9858
4200 Herner Cnty Line Rd Southington (44470) *(G-16952)*
American Legion Post..........330 872-5475
2025 E River Rd Newton Falls (44444) *(G-15135)*
American Legion Post 667, East Canton *Also called American Legion (G-10385)*
American Limousine Service, Cleveland *Also called American Livery Service Inc (G-4956)*
American Linehaul Corporation..........614 409-8568
1860 Williams Rd Columbus (43207) *(G-6929)*
American Livery Service Inc..........216 221-9330
11723 Detroit Ave Cleveland (44107) *(G-4956)*
American Maintenance Svcs Inc..........330 744-3400
20 W Federal St Fl 2b Youngstown (44503) *(G-19954)*
American Marine Express Inc..........216 268-3005
765 E 140th St Ste A Cleveland (44110) *(G-4957)*
American Maritime Officers..........419 255-3940
1 Maritime Plz Fl 2 Toledo (43604) *(G-17591)*
American Mdrn Srpls Lnes Insur, Amelia *Also called American Modern Home Insur Co (G-566)*
American Mechanical Group Inc..........614 575-3720
5729 Westbourne Ave Columbus (43213) *(G-6930)*
American Med..........330 762-8999
1265 Triplett Blvd Akron (44306) *(G-69)*
American Medical Equipment, Columbus *Also called American Home Health Care Inc (G-6925)*
American Medical Response Inc..........330 455-3579
817 3rd St Sw Canton (44707) *(G-2186)*
American Midwest Mortgage Corp (PA)..........440 882-5210
6363 York Rd Ste 300 Cleveland (44130) *(G-4958)*
American Modern Home Insur Co, Amelia *Also called American Modrn Insur Group Inc (G-568)*
American Modern Home Insur Co (HQ)..........513 943-7100
7000 Midland Blvd Amelia (45102) *(G-566)*
American Modern Home Svc Co..........513 943-7100
7000 Midland Blvd Amelia (45102) *(G-567)*
American Modrn Insur Group Inc (HQ)..........800 543-2644
7000 Midland Blvd Amelia (45102) *(G-568)*
American Money Management Corp..........513 579-2592
301 E 4th St Fl 27 Cincinnati (45202) *(G-2946)*
American Motorcycle Assn (PA)..........614 856-1900
13515 Yarmouth Dr Pickerington (43147) *(G-15945)*
AMERICAN MOTORCYCLIST ASSOCIAT, Pickerington *Also called American Motorcycle Assn (G-15945)*
American Multi-Cinema Inc..........614 801-9130
4218 Buckeye Pkwy Grove City (43123) *(G-11406)*
American Multi-Cinema Inc..........614 889-0580
6700 Village Pkwy Dublin (43017) *(G-10132)*
American Multi-Cinema Inc..........216 749-0260
4788 Ridge Rd Cleveland (44144) *(G-4959)*
American Multi-Cinema Inc..........440 331-2826
21653 Center Ridge Rd Rocky River (44116) *(G-16422)*
American Municipal Power Inc..........614 540-1111
1111 Schrock Rd Ste 100 Columbus (43229) *(G-6931)*
American Mutl Share Insur Corp (PA)..........614 764-1900
5656 Frantz Rd Dublin (43017) *(G-10133)*
American Mutual Life Assn (PA)..........216 531-1900
19424 S Waterloo Rd Cleveland (44119) *(G-4960)*
American Nat Fleet Svc Inc..........216 447-6060
7714 Commerce Park Oval Cleveland (44131) *(G-4961)*
American National Red Cross..........937 399-3872
1830 N Limestone St Ste 1 Springfield (45503) *(G-16993)*
American National Red Cross..........216 303-5476
5585 Pearl Rd Parma (44129) *(G-15760)*
American National Red Cross..........937 631-9315
1830 N Limestone St Ste 1 Springfield (45503) *(G-16994)*
American National Red Cross..........216 431-3152
3747 Euclid Ave Cleveland (44115) *(G-4962)*
American National Red Cross..........330 469-6403
126 Valley Cir Ne Warren (44484) *(G-18663)*
American National Red Cross..........419 382-2707
1111 Research Dr Toledo (43614) *(G-17592)*
American National Red Cross..........330 535-6131
501 W Market St Akron (44303) *(G-70)*
American National Red Cross..........614 436-3862
1327 Cameron Ave Lewis Center (43035) *(G-12523)*
American National Red Cross..........614 473-3783
337 Stoneridge Ln Gahanna (43230) *(G-11109)*
American National Red Cross..........800 448-3543
1 W Nationwide Blvd Columbus (43215) *(G-6932)*
American National Red Cross..........740 344-2510
1272 W Main St Bldg 5s Newark (43055) *(G-15010)*
American National Red Cross..........419 524-0311
39 Park St N Mansfield (44902) *(G-13136)*
American National Red Cross..........937 376-3111
1080 E Main St Xenia (45385) *(G-19889)*
American National Red Cross..........614 334-0425
4327 Equity Dr Columbus (43228) *(G-6933)*
American Natl Red CRS-Bld Svcs, Akron *Also called American National Red Cross (G-70)*
American Natl Red CRS-Bld Svcs, Columbus *Also called American National Red Cross (G-6933)*
American Nursing Care Inc..........513 731-4600
4750 Wesley Ave Ste Q Cincinnati (45212) *(G-2947)*
American Nursing Care Inc..........513 245-1500
4460 Red Bank Rd Ste 100 Cincinnati (45227) *(G-2948)*
American Nursing Care Inc (HQ)..........513 576-0262
1700 Edison Dr Ste 300 Milford (45150) *(G-14371)*
American Nursing Care Inc..........937 438-3844
5335 Far Hills Ave # 103 Dayton (45429) *(G-9228)*
American Nursing Care Inc..........614 847-0555
1206 Brandywine Blvd A Zanesville (43701) *(G-20275)*
American Nursing Care Inc..........419 228-0888
658 W Market St Ste 200 Lima (45801) *(G-12601)*
American Nursing Care Inc..........740 452-0569
1206 Brandywine Blvd A Zanesville (43701) *(G-20276)*
American Para Prof Systems Inc..........513 531-2900
6056 Montgomery Rd Cincinnati (45213) *(G-2949)*
American Posts LLC..........419 720-0652
810 Chicago St Toledo (43611) *(G-17593)*
American Power LLC..........937 235-0418
1819 Troy St Dayton (45404) *(G-9229)*
American Precast Refractories..........614 876-8416
2700 Scioto Pkwy Columbus (43221) *(G-6934)*
American Procomm, Marietta *Also called Davis Pickering & Company Inc (G-13324)*
American Producers Sup Co Inc (PA)..........740 373-5050
119 2nd St Marietta (45750) *(G-13310)*
American Prprty-Mnagement Corp..........330 454-5000
320 Market Ave S Canton (44702) *(G-2187)*
American Prservation Bldrs LLC..........216 236-2007
127 Public Sq Ste 1300 Cleveland (44114) *(G-4963)*
American Publishers LLC..........419 626-0623
2401 Sawmill Pkwy Ste 10 Huron (44839) *(G-12020)*
American Red Cross, Lewis Center *Also called American National Red Cross (G-12523)*
American Red Cross, Gahanna *Also called American National Red Cross (G-11109)*
American Red Cross, Columbus *Also called American National Red Cross (G-6932)*
American Red Cross, Newark *Also called American National Red Cross (G-15010)*
American Red Cross, Mansfield *Also called American National Red Cross (G-13136)*
American Red Cross..........513 579-3000
2111 Dana Ave Cincinnati (45207) *(G-2950)*
American Red Cross..........937 222-0124
370 W 1st St Dayton (45402) *(G-9230)*
American Red Cross Med Educa, Warren *Also called American National Red Cross (G-18663)*
American Red Cross of Grtr Col (PA)..........614 253-7981
995 E Broad St Columbus (43205) *(G-6935)*
American Regent Inc..........614 436-2222
4150 Lyman Dr Hilliard (43026) *(G-11741)*

ALPHABETIC

American Reprographics Co LLC 614 224-5149
  1159 Dublin Rd Columbus (43215) *(G-6936)*
American Residential Svcs LLC 216 561-8880
  4547 Hinckley Industrial Cleveland (44109) *(G-4964)*
American Residential Svcs LLC 888 762-7752
  3050 Switzer Ave Columbus (43219) *(G-6937)*
American Response Center, Independence *Also called Ohio Alarm Inc (G-12105)*
American Retirement Corp 216 291-6140
  3 Homewood Way Cleveland (44143) *(G-4965)*
American Retirement Corp 216 321-6331
  3151 Mayfield Rd Apt 1105 Cleveland (44118) *(G-4966)*
American Ring & Tool Co, Solon *Also called R L Morrissey & Assoc Inc (G-16889)*
American Risk Services LLC 513 772-3712
  1130 Congress Ave Ste A Cincinnati (45246) *(G-2951)*
American Roadway Logistics Inc 330 659-2003
  3920 Congress Pkwy Richfield (44286) *(G-16346)*
American Rock Mechanics Inc 330 963-0550
  9241 Ravenna Rd Ste 6 Twinsburg (44087) *(G-18243)*
American Sales Inc 937 253-9520
  1755 Spaulding Rd Dayton (45432) *(G-9159)*
American Sand & Gravel Div, Massillon *Also called Kenmore Construction Co Inc (G-13702)*
American Seaway, Bedford Heights *Also called Riser Foods Company (G-1327)*
American Security Insurance Co 937 327-7700
  1 Assurant Way Springfield (45505) *(G-16995)*
American Select Insurance Co 330 887-0101
  1 Park Cir Westfield Center (44251) *(G-19307)*
AMERICAN SHARE INSURANCE, Dublin *Also called American Mutl Share Insur Corp (G-10133)*
AMERICAN SHARE INSURANCE, Dublin *Also called Excess Share Insurance Corp (G-10222)*
American Showa Inc 740 965-4040
  677 W Cherry St Sunbury (43074) *(G-17382)*
American Society For Nondstctv 614 274-6003
  1711 Arlingate Ln Columbus (43228) *(G-6938)*
American Star Painting Co LLC 740 373-5634
  201 Mitchells Ln Marietta (45750) *(G-13311)*
American Star Pntg & Coatings, Marietta *Also called American Star Painting Co LLC (G-13311)*
American Svcs & Protection LLC 614 884-0177
  2572 Oakstone Dr 8 Columbus (43231) *(G-6939)*
American Systems Cnsulting Inc 614 282-7180
  5777 Frantz Rd Ste 150 Dublin (43017) *(G-10134)*
American Tank & Fabricating Co (PA) 216 252-1500
  12314 Elmwood Ave Cleveland (44111) *(G-4967)*
American Title of Ohio LLC 303 868-2250
  600 Superior Ave E # 1300 Cleveland (44114) *(G-4968)*
American Title Services Inc 330 652-1609
  700 Youngstown Warren Rd Niles (44446) *(G-15144)*
American Warming and Vent 419 288-2703
  120 Plin St Bradner (43406) *(G-1763)*
American Waste MGT Svcs Inc 330 856-8800
  1 American Way Ne Warren (44484) *(G-18664)*
American Way Van & Storage, Vandalia *Also called American Way Van and Stor Inc (G-18503)*
American Way Van and Stor Inc 937 898-7294
  1001 S Brown School Rd Vandalia (45377) *(G-18503)*
American Western Home Insur, Amelia *Also called Midland Company (G-574)*
American Western Home Insur Co 513 943-7100
  7000 Midland Blvd Amelia (45102) *(G-569)*
Americas Best Medical Eqp, Akron *Also called Americas Best Medical Eqp Co (G-71)*
Americas Best Medical Eqp Co 330 928-0884
  1566 Akron Peninsula Rd # 2 Akron (44313) *(G-71)*
Americas Best Value Inn, Streetsboro *Also called R & H Service Inc (G-17267)*
Americas Best Value Inn 419 626-9890
  5608 Milan Rd Sandusky (44870) *(G-16575)*
Americas Floor Source LLC 216 342-4929
  26000 Richmond Rd Ste 1 Bedford Heights (44146) *(G-1316)*
Americas Floor Source LLC (PA) 614 808-3915
  3442 Millennium Ct Columbus (43219) *(G-6940)*
Americoat, Plain City *Also called American Coatings Corporation (G-16043)*
Americold Logistics LLC 330 834-1742
  2140 17th St Sw Massillon (44647) *(G-13661)*
Ameridial Inc 800 445-7128
  4877 Higbee Ave Nw Canton (44718) *(G-2188)*
Ameridial Inc 330 479-8044
  4535 Strasser St Nw North Canton (44720) *(G-15188)*
Ameridial Inc (HQ) 330 497-4888
  4535 Strasser St Nw North Canton (44720) *(G-15189)*
Ameridial Inc 330 339-7222
  521 W High Ave New Philadelphia (44663) *(G-14946)*
Ameridial Inc 330 868-2000
  102 N Market St Minerva (44657) *(G-14515)*
Ameridian Specialty Services 513 769-0150
  11520 Rockfield Ct Cincinnati (45241) *(G-2952)*
Amerifirst Financial Corp 216 452-5120
  14701 Detroit Ave Ste 750 Lakewood (44107) *(G-12335)*
Amerigroup Ohio Inc 513 733-2300
  10123 Alliance Rd Ste 140 Blue Ash (45242) *(G-1504)*
Amerihost Mt. Vernon, Mount Vernon *Also called Emmett Dan House Ltd Partnr (G-14764)*

Amerimark Holdings LLC (PA) 440 325-2000
  6864 Engle Rd Cleveland (44130) *(G-4969)*
Amerimed Inc 513 942-3670
  9961 Cincinnati Dayton Rd West Chester (45069) *(G-18866)*
Ameripath Cincinnati Inc 513 745-8330
  9670 Kenwood Rd Blue Ash (45242) *(G-1505)*
Ameriprise Financial Svcs Inc 330 494-9300
  3333 Massillon Rd Ste 110 Akron (44312) *(G-72)*
Ameriprise Financial Svcs Inc 614 846-8723
  250 W Old Wlsn Brg Rd # 150 Worthington (43085) *(G-19793)*
Ameriprise Financial Svcs Inc 614 934-4057
  655 Metro Pl S Ste 450 Dublin (43017) *(G-10135)*
Ameripro Logistics LLC 410 375-3469
  6754 Stovali Dr Dayton (45424) *(G-9231)*
Ameriscape Inc 614 863-5400
  6751 Taylor Rd Unit D1 Blacklick (43004) *(G-1473)*
Amerisource Health Svcs LLC 614 492-8177
  2550 John Glenn Ave Ste A Columbus (43217) *(G-6941)*
Amerisourcebergen Corporation 610 727-7000
  1200 E 5th Ave Columbus (43219) *(G-6942)*
Amerisourcebergen Corporation 614 497-3665
  6301 Lasalle Dr Lockbourne (43137) *(G-12808)*
Amerisourcebergen Drug Corp 614 409-0741
  6305 Lasalle Dr Lockbourne (43137) *(G-12809)*
Ameristate Bancorp Inc (PA) 330 965-9551
  725 Boardman Canfield Rd Youngstown (44512) *(G-19955)*
Ameristop Food Marts, Cincinnati *Also called Ohio Valley Acquisition Inc (G-4159)*
Ameritas Life Insurance Corp 513 595-2334
  1876 Waycross Rd Cincinnati (45240) *(G-2953)*
Ames Material Services Inc 937 382-5591
  145 Hunter Dr Wilmington (45177) *(G-19606)*
Ametek Electromechanical Group, Kent *Also called Ametek Tchnical Indus Pdts Inc (G-12214)*
Ametek Tchnical Indus Pdts Inc (HQ) 330 677-3754
  100 E Erie St Ste 130 Kent (44240) *(G-12214)*
Amethyst Inc 614 242-1284
  455 E Mound St Columbus (43215) *(G-6943)*
AMF Bowling Centers Inc 330 725-4548
  201 Harding St Medina (44256) *(G-13910)*
AMF Bowling Centers Inc 614 889-0880
  4825 Sawmill Rd Columbus (43235) *(G-6944)*
AMF Facility Services Inc 800 991-2273
  844 Oakleaf Dr Dayton (45417) *(G-9232)*
Amg Inc (PA) 937 260-4646
  1497 Shoup Mill Rd Dayton (45414) *(G-9233)*
AMG Advertising & PR, Solon *Also called AMG Marketing Resources Inc (G-16820)*
AMG Marketing Resources Inc 216 621-1835
  30670 Bnbridge Rd Ste 200 Solon (44139) *(G-16820)*
AMG-Eng, Dayton *Also called Amg Inc (G-9233)*
Amherst Animal Hospital Inc 440 282-5220
  1425 Cooper Foster Pk Rd Amherst (44001) *(G-578)*
Amherst Exempted Vlg Schools 440 988-2633
  225 Washington St Amherst (44001) *(G-579)*
Amherst Hospital Association 440 988-6000
  254 Cleveland Ave Amherst (44001) *(G-580)*
Amherst Maintenance Bldg, Berea *Also called Ohio Tpk & Infrastructure Comm (G-1433)*
Amherst Manor Nursing Home 440 988-4415
  175 N Lake St Amherst (44001) *(G-581)*
AMI, Mayfield Heights *Also called Park Place Technologies LLC (G-13879)*
Amica Mutual Insurance Company 866 942-6422
  9277 Centre Pointe Dr # 230 West Chester (45069) *(G-18867)*
Amin Turocy & Watson LLP (PA) 216 696-8730
  200 Park Ave Ste 300 Beachwood (44122) *(G-1029)*
Amish Door Inc (PA) 330 359-5464
  1210 Winesburg St Wilmot (44689) *(G-19657)*
Amish Door Restaurant, Wilmot *Also called Amish Door Inc (G-19657)*
Amish Farm, The, Berlin *Also called Dutch Heritage Farms Inc (G-1446)*
Amitel Beachwood Ltd Partnr (PA) 216 707-9839
  6000 Rckside Woods Blvd N Cleveland (44131) *(G-4970)*
Amitel Beachwood Ltd Partnr 216 831-3030
  3628 Park Dr Cleveland (44134) *(G-4971)*
Amitel Rockside Ltd Partnr 216 520-1450
  5101 Independence Cleveland (44131) *(G-4972)*
Amix Inc 513 539-7220
  6487 Hankins Rd Middletown (45044) *(G-14288)*
Amko Service Company (HQ) 330 364-8857
  3211 Brightwood Rd Midvale (44653) *(G-14357)*
AMLA, Cleveland *Also called American Mutual Life Assn (G-4960)*
Amos Media Company (PA) 937 498-2111
  911 S Vandemark Rd Sidney (45365) *(G-16758)*
Amotec Inc (PA) 440 250-4600
  1701 E 12th St Apt 10b Cleveland (44114) *(G-4973)*
AMP Advertising Inc 513 333-4100
  700 Walnut St Ste 500 Cincinnati (45202) *(G-2954)*
AMP-Ohio, Columbus *Also called American Municipal Power Inc (G-6931)*
Ampac Holdings LLC (HQ) 513 671-1777
  12025 Tricon Rd Cincinnati (45246) *(G-2955)*
Ampacet Corporation 513 247-5400
  4705 Duke Dr 400 Cincinnati (45249) *(G-2956)*
Ampco System Parking, Cleveland *Also called ABM Parking Services Inc (G-4895)*

Ampersand Group LLC 330 379-0044
1946 S Arlington St Akron (44306) *(G-73)*
Ample Trailer Leasing & Sales 513 563-2550
610 Wayne Park Dr Cincinnati (45215) *(G-2957)*
AMR Eagle, Columbus *Also called Envoy Air Inc (G-7523)*
Amrstrong Distributors Inc 419 483-4840
421 Monroe St Bellevue (44811) *(G-1371)*
AMS, Sidney *Also called Bell Hensley Inc (G-16761)*
AMS Construction Inc 513 398-6689
7431 Windsor Park Dr Maineville (45039) *(G-13112)*
AMS Construction Inc (PA) 513 794-0410
10670 Loveland Madeira Rd Loveland (45140) *(G-12977)*
Amsc, Cleveland *Also called Northast Ohio Rgonal Sewer Dst (G-6084)*
Amsdell Construction Inc (PA) 216 458-0670
20445 Emerald Pkwy # 220 Cleveland (44135) *(G-4974)*
Amstan Logistics, Liberty Township *Also called As Logistics Inc (G-12577)*
Amsted Industries Incorporated 614 836-2323
3900 Bixby Rd Groveport (43125) *(G-11493)*
Amt, Brecksville *Also called Applied Medical Technology Inc (G-1769)*
Amtrac of Ohio Inc 330 683-7206
11842 Lincoln Way E Orrville (44667) *(G-15622)*
Amtrac Railroad Contrs Ohio, Orrville *Also called Amtrac of Ohio Inc (G-15622)*
Amtrak, Toledo *Also called National Railroad Pass Corp (G-17933)*
Amtrust Financial Services, Cleveland *Also called Amtrust North America Inc (G-4975)*
Amtrust North America Inc (HQ) 216 328-6100
800 Superior Ave E # 2100 Cleveland (44114) *(G-4975)*
AMTS, Brookpark *Also called Credit First NA (G-1894)*
Amusements of America Inc 614 297-8863
717 E 17th Ave Columbus (43211) *(G-6945)*
Amvets Post No 6 Inc 330 833-5935
8417 Audubon St Nw Massillon (44646) *(G-13662)*
Amx, Cleveland *Also called American Marine Express Inc (G-4957)*
Analytical Pace Services LLC 937 832-8242
25 Holiday Dr Englewood (45322) *(G-10578)*
Anark Inc 513 825-7387
2150 Struble Rd Cincinnati (45231) *(G-2958)*
Anatrace Products LLC (HQ) 419 740-6600
434 W Dussel Dr Maumee (43537) *(G-13751)*
Anazao Community Partners (PA) 330 264-9597
2587 Back Orrville Rd Wooster (44691) *(G-19687)*
Anchor Bronze and Metals Inc 440 549-5653
11470 Euclid Ave Ste 509 Cleveland (44106) *(G-4976)*
Anchor Cleaning Contractors 216 961-7343
1966 W 52nd St Cleveland (44102) *(G-4977)*
Anchor Lodge, Lorain *Also called Sprenger Enterprises Inc (G-12945)*
Anchor Lodge Nursing Home Inc 440 244-2019
3756 W Erie Ave Ofc Lorain (44053) *(G-12880)*
Anchor Metal Processing Inc (PA) 216 362-1850
11830 Brookpark Rd Cleveland (44130) *(G-4978)*
ANCHOR TRADER, Upper Arlington *Also called Delta Gamma Fraternity (G-18396)*
Ancillary Medical Investments 937 456-5520
125 Amelia Dr Eaton (45320) *(G-10436)*
Ancom Business Products, Brunswick *Also called Symatic Inc (G-1941)*
Andersen & Associates Inc 330 425-8500
1960 Summit Commerce Park Twinsburg (44087) *(G-18244)*
Anderson & Vreeland Inc 419 636-5002
15348 State Rte 127 E Bryan (43506) *(G-1952)*
Anderson Aluminum Corporation 614 476-4877
2816 Morse Rd Columbus (43231) *(G-6946)*
Anderson and Dubose Inc (PA) 440 248-8800
5300 Tod Ave Sw Warren (44481) *(G-18665)*
Anderson Ferry, Cincinnati *Also called Consolidated Grain & Barge Co (G-3351)*
Anderson Glass Co Inc 614 476-4877
2816 Morse Rd Columbus (43231) *(G-6947)*
Anderson Healthcare Ltd 513 474-6200
8139 Beechmont Ave Cincinnati (45255) *(G-2959)*
Anderson Hills Pediatrics Inc 513 232-8100
7400 Jager Ct Cincinnati (45230) *(G-2960)*
Anderson Jeffery R RE Inc 513 241-5800
3805 Edwards Rd Ste 700 Cincinnati (45209) *(G-2961)*
Anderson Little 513 474-7800
8516 Beechmont Ave Cincinnati (45255) *(G-2962)*
Anderson Properties, Columbus *Also called Anderson Aluminum Corporation (G-6946)*
Anderson SEC & Fire Systems 937 294-1478
4600 S Dixie Dr Moraine (45439) *(G-14620)*
Anderson Security & Fire Systs, Moraine *Also called Anderson SEC & Fire Systems (G-14620)*
Anderson Security Inc (PA) 937 294-1478
4600 S Dixie Dr Moraine (45439) *(G-14621)*
Anderson Township Park Dst 513 474-0003
6910 Salem Rd Cincinnati (45230) *(G-2963)*
Anderson Twnship Hstorical Soc 513 231-2114
6550 Clough Pike Cincinnati (45244) *(G-2964)*
Anderson Vreeland Midwest, Bryan *Also called Anderson & Vreeland Inc (G-1952)*
Anderson's Farm, Maumee *Also called Andersons Agriculture Group LP (G-13756)*
Anderson's Rail Car Service, Maumee *Also called Andersons Inc (G-13753)*
Anderson, The, Cincinnati *Also called Anderson Healthcare Ltd (G-2959)*
Anderson-Dubose Co, The, Warren *Also called Anderson and Dubose Inc (G-18665)*
Andersons Inc 419 891-6479
1380 Ford St Maumee (43537) *(G-13752)*
Andersons Inc 419 891-6634
421 Illinois Ave Maumee (43537) *(G-13753)*
Andersons Inc (PA) 419 893-5050
1947 Briarfield Blvd Maumee (43537) *(G-13754)*
Andersons Inc 419 893-5050
533 Illinois Ave Maumee (43537) *(G-13755)*
Andersons Agriculture Group LP (HQ) 419 893-5050
1947 Briarfield Blvd Maumee (43537) *(G-13756)*
Andersons Marathon Ethanol LLC 937 316-3700
5728 Sebring Warner Rd N Greenville (45331) *(G-11365)*
Anderzack-Pitzen Cnstr Inc 419 553-7015
424 E Main St Metamora (43540) *(G-14132)*
Andover Bancorp Inc (PA) 440 293-7605
19 Public Sq Andover (44003) *(G-603)*
Andover Floor Covering 440 293-5339
9950 Belleflower Cir Newbury (44065) *(G-15118)*
Andover Vlg Retirement Cmnty 440 293-5416
486 S Main St Andover (44003) *(G-604)*
Andre Corporation 574 293-0207
4600 N Masn Montgomery Rd Mason (45040) *(G-13540)*
Andreas Furniture Company 330 852-2494
580 Belden Pkwy Ne Sugarcreek (44681) *(G-17376)*
Andrew Belmont Sargent (PA) 513 769-7800
10855 Medallion Dr Cincinnati (45241) *(G-2965)*
Andrew Distribution Inc 614 824-3123
509 Industry Dr Columbus (43204) *(G-6948)*
Andrew Philips Collection, Mason *Also called Millennium Leather LLC (G-13620)*
Andrews Apartments Ltd 440 946-3600
4420 Sherwin Rd Willoughby (44094) *(G-19505)*
Andy Frain Services Inc 419 897-7909
1715 Indian Wood Cir # 200 Maumee (43537) *(G-13757)*
Andy's Mirror and Glass, Cincinnati *Also called E J Robinson Glass Co (G-3465)*
Anesthesia Associates Inc 440 350-0832
7757 Auburn Rd Ste 15 Painesville (44077) *(G-15693)*
Anesthesiologists, D.O., Inc., Youngstown *Also called Ado Health Services Inc (G-19946)*
Anesthesiology Assoc of Akron 330 344-6401
224 W Exchange St Ste 220 Akron (44302) *(G-74)*
Anesthesiology Consultant Inc 614 566-9983
111 S Grant Ave Columbus (43215) *(G-6949)*
Anesthesiology Services Netwrk 937 208-6173
1 Wyoming St Dayton (45409) *(G-9234)*
Anesthsia Assoc Cincinnati Inc 513 585-0577
2139 Auburn Ave Cincinnati (45219) *(G-2966)*
Angel Above Byond Hm Hlth Svcs 513 553-9955
8320 Beechmont Ave Cincinnati (45255) *(G-2967)*
Angel Care Inc 440 736-7267
7033 Oakes Rd Brecksville (44141) *(G-1768)*
Angel Hearts Home Health Inc 937 263-6194
2213 Arbor Blvd Moraine (45439) *(G-14622)*
Angeline Industries Inc 419 294-4488
11028 County Highway 44 Upper Sandusky (43351) *(G-18403)*
Angelo J Colosimo MD, Cincinnati *Also called University Orthopaedic Cnsltnt (G-4728)*
Angels 4 Life LLC 513 474-5683
431 Ohio Pike Ste 182s Cincinnati (45255) *(G-2968)*
Angels Home Care LLC 419 947-9373
4440 State Route 61 Mount Gilead (43338) *(G-14724)*
Angels In Waiting Home Care 440 946-0349
8336 Tyler Blvd Mentor (44060) *(G-14018)*
Angels On Earth Child Care Co 216 476-8100
13439 Lorain Ave Cleveland (44111) *(G-4979)*
Angels Touch Nursing Care 513 661-4111
3619 Harrison Ave Cincinnati (45211) *(G-2969)*
Angels Visiting 419 298-0034
143 N Michigan Ave Edgerton (43517) *(G-10467)*
Angstrom Graphics Inc Midwest (HQ) 216 271-5300
4437 E 49th St Cleveland (44125) *(G-4980)*
Angstrom Graphics Inc Midwest 330 225-8950
4437 E 49th St Cleveland (44125) *(G-4981)*
Anheuser-Busch LLC 513 381-3927
600 Vine St Ste 1002 Cincinnati (45202) *(G-2970)*
Anheuser-Busch LLC 330 438-2036
1611 Marietta Ave Se Canton (44707) *(G-2189)*
Animal Ark Pet Resort, Cincinnati *Also called Anark Inc (G-2958)*
Animal Care Unlimited Inc 614 766-2317
2665 Billingsley Rd Columbus (43235) *(G-6950)*
Animal Hospital Inc 440 946-2800
2735 Som Center Rd Willoughby Hills (44094) *(G-19586)*
Animal Hospital Polaris LLC 614 888-4050
8928 S Old State Rd Lewis Center (43035) *(G-12524)*
Animal Medical Center Medina, Medina *Also called Michael T Lee Dvm (G-13979)*
Animal Mgt Svcs Ohio Inc 248 398-6533
267 S Lightner Rd Port Clinton (43452) *(G-16099)*
Animal Protective League 216 771-4616
1729 Willey Ave Cleveland (44113) *(G-4982)*
Anixter Inc 513 881-4600
4440 Muhlhauser Rd # 200 West Chester (45011) *(G-18868)*
Ankle and Foot Care Center (PA) 330 385-2413
16844 Saint Clair Ave # 2 East Liverpool (43920) *(G-10397)*
Ann Arbor Railroad Inc 419 726-4181
4058 Chrysler Dr Toledo (43608) *(G-17594)*

ALPHABETIC

Anna Maria of Aurora Inc (PA) 330 562-6171
  889 N Aurora Rd Aurora (44202) *(G-815)*
Anna Maria of Aurora Inc 330 562-3120
  849 Rural Rd Aurora (44202) *(G-816)*
Anna Rescue Squad 937 394-7377
  203 S Linden St Anna (45302) *(G-610)*
Annas Child Care Lrng Ctr Inc (PA) 937 667-1903
  4949 S County Road 25a Tipp City (45371) *(G-17549)*
Anne Camm, Psy.d., Company, Middletown *Also called Primary Cr Ntwrk Prmr Hlth Prt (G-14354)*
Anne Grady Corporation 419 867-7501
  1645 Trade Rd Holland (43528) *(G-11871)*
Anne Grady Corporation (PA) 419 380-8985
  1525 Eber Rd Holland (43528) *(G-11872)*
Annehurst Veterinary Hospital 614 818-4221
  25 Collegeview Rd Westerville (43081) *(G-19220)*
Another Chance Inc 614 868-3541
  9866 Haverford Pl Pickerington (43147) *(G-15946)*
Anselmo Rssis Premier Prod Ltd 800 229-5517
  4500 Willow Pkwy Cleveland (44125) *(G-4983)*
Ansonia Area Emergency Service 937 337-2651
  225 W Elroy Ansonia Rd Ansonia (45303) *(G-612)*
Anspach Meeks Ellenberger LLP 614 745-8350
  175 S 3rd St Ste 285 Columbus (43215) *(G-6951)*
Anspach Meeks Ellenberger LLP (PA) 419 447-6181
  300 Madison Ave Ste 1600 Toledo (43604) *(G-17595)*
Anstine Drywall Inc 330 784-3867
  2215 E Waterloo Rd # 403 Akron (44312) *(G-75)*
Answer Group, The, Blue Ash *Also called Nielsen Consumer Insights Inc (G-1620)*
Answercare LLC 855 213-1511
  4150 Belden Village St Nw # 307 Canton (44718) *(G-2190)*
Answering Service Inc 440 473-1200
  5767 Mayfield Rd Rear 1 Cleveland (44124) *(G-4984)*
Antares Management Solutions, Strongsville *Also called Medical Mutual Services LLC (G-17331)*
Antares Management Solutions, Beachwood *Also called Medical Mutual of Ohio (G-1078)*
Antero Resources Corporation 740 760-1000
  2335 State Route 821 Marietta (45750) *(G-13312)*
Anthem, Cincinnati *Also called Community Insurance Company (G-3340)*
Anthem Insurance Companies Inc 614 438-3542
  8940 Lyra Dr Columbus (43240) *(G-6799)*
Anthem Insurance Companies Inc 330 492-2151
  4150 Belden Village St Nw # 506 Canton (44718) *(G-2191)*
Anthem Midwest Inc 614 433-8350
  4361 Irwin Simpson Rd Mason (45040) *(G-13541)*
Anthony Allega, Cleveland *Also called Mid America Trucking Company (G-5981)*
Anthony Allega Cement Contr 216 447-0814
  5585 Canal Rd Cleveland (44125) *(G-4985)*
Anthony David Salon & Spa 440 233-8570
  6401 S Broadway Lorain (44053) *(G-12881)*
Anthony Wayne Local Schools 419 877-0451
  6320 Industrial Pkwy Whitehouse (43571) *(G-19443)*
Anthony Wayne Trnsp Dept, Whitehouse *Also called Anthony Wayne Local Schools (G-19443)*
Antioch Cnnction Canton MI LLC 614 531-9285
  799 Windmiller Dr Pickerington (43147) *(G-15947)*
Antioch Salem Fields Frederick 614 531-9285
  799 Windmiller Dr Pickerington (43147) *(G-15948)*
Antioch University 937 769-1366
  1 Morgan Pl Yellow Springs (45387) *(G-19938)*
Antonio Sofo Son Importing Co (PA) 419 476-4211
  253 Waggoner Blvd Toledo (43612) *(G-17596)*
Antwerp Mnor Asssted Lving LLC 419 258-1500
  204 Archer Dr Antwerp (45813) *(G-613)*
Any Domest Work Inc 440 845-9911
  5735 Pearl Rd Cleveland (44129) *(G-4986)*
Anytime Collect, Chardon *Also called E2b Teknologies Inc (G-2693)*
AON Consulting Inc 614 436-8100
  445 Hutchinson Ave # 900 Columbus (43235) *(G-6952)*
AON Consulting Inc 614 847-4670
  355 E Campus View Blvd Columbus (43235) *(G-6953)*
AON Consulting Inc 216 621-8100
  1660 W 2nd St Ste 650 Cleveland (44113) *(G-4987)*
AON Risk Svcs Northeast Inc (HQ) 216 621-8100
  1660 W 2nd St Cleveland (44113) *(G-4988)*
AP Cchmc 513 636-4200
  3333 Burnet Ave Cincinnati (45229) *(G-2971)*
Ap/Aim Dublin Suites Trs LLC 614 790-9000
  5100 Upper Metro Pl Dublin (43017) *(G-10136)*
Ap/Aim Indpndnce Sites Trs LLC 216 986-9900
  5800 Rckside Woods Blvd N Independence (44131) *(G-12045)*
Ap23 Sports Complex LLC 614 452-0760
  775 Georgesville Rd Columbus (43228) *(G-6954)*
Apartments of Cedar Hill, Zanesville *Also called Zandex Inc (G-20374)*
Apbn Inc 724 964-8252
  670 Robinson Rd Campbell (44405) *(G-2090)*
Apc2 Inc (PA) 513 231-5540
  6812 Clough Pike Cincinnati (45244) *(G-2972)*
Apco Aluminum Awning Co 614 334-2726
  815 Michigan Ave Columbus (43215) *(G-6955)*

Apco Industries Inc 614 224-2345
  777 Michigan Ave Columbus (43215) *(G-6956)*
Apco Window & Door Company, Columbus *Also called Apco Industries Inc (G-6956)*
Apelles LLC 614 899-7222
  3700 Corp Dr 2f Ste 240 2 F Columbus (43231) *(G-6957)*
Apex Academy, Cleveland *Also called National Heritg Academies Inc (G-6046)*
Apex Environmental LLC 740 543-4389
  11 County Road 78 Amsterdam (43903) *(G-600)*
Apex Environmental Svcs LLC 513 772-2739
  295 Northland Blvd Cincinnati (45246) *(G-2973)*
Apex Interiors Inc 330 327-2226
  3233 Waterford Way Avon (44011) *(G-862)*
Apex Restoration Contrs Ltd (PA) 513 489-1795
  6315 Warrick St Cincinnati (45227) *(G-2974)*
Apg Office Furnishings Inc 216 621-4590
  3615 Superior Ave E 4407a Cleveland (44114) *(G-4989)*
APL Logistics Ltd 440 930-2822
  32608 Surrey Ln Avon Lake (44012) *(G-908)*
Apollo Heating and AC Inc 513 271-3600
  1730 Tennessee Ave Cincinnati (45229) *(G-2975)*
Apollo Property Management LLC (PA) 216 468-0050
  200 Park Ave Ste 410 Beachwood (44122) *(G-1030)*
Apostolic Christian Academy, Toledo *Also called First Apostolic Church (G-17738)*
Apostolic Christian Home Inc 330 927-1010
  10680 Steiner Rd Rittman (44270) *(G-16403)*
Appalachia Wood Inc (PA) 740 596-2551
  31310 State Route 93 Mc Arthur (45651) *(G-13889)*
Appalachian Community Visi 740 594-8226
  444 W Union St Ste C Athens (45701) *(G-764)*
Appalachian Development Corp (PA) 740 374-9436
  1400 Pike St Marietta (45750) *(G-13313)*
Appalachian Hardwood Lumber Co 440 232-6767
  5433 Perkins Rd Cleveland (44146) *(G-4990)*
Appalachian Power Company (HQ) 614 716-1000
  1 Riverside Plz Columbus (43215) *(G-6958)*
Appalachian Power Company 330 438-7102
  301 Cleveland Ave Sw Canton (44702) *(G-2192)*
Appalachian Respite Care Ltd 740 984-4262
  501 Pinecrest Dr Beverly (45715) *(G-1460)*
Appalchian Bhvioral Healthcare, Athens *Also called Mental Health and Addi Serv (G-792)*
Appearance Plus, Cincinnati *Also called Apc2 Inc (G-2972)*
Applause Talent Presentation 513 844-6788
  1525 Singer Ave Hamilton (45011) *(G-11557)*
Apple A Day Healthcare Svcs, Toledo *Also called Horizons Employment Svcs LLC (G-17808)*
Apple Creek Banking Co (inc) (PA) 330 698-2631
  3 W Main St Apple Creek (44606) *(G-617)*
Apple Electric, Barberton *Also called Apple Heating Inc (G-941)*
Apple Farm Service Inc (PA) 937 526-4851
  10120 W Versailles Rd Covington (45318) *(G-9045)*
Apple Farm Service Infc, Covington *Also called Apple Farm Service Inc (G-9045)*
Apple Gate Operating Co Inc 330 405-4488
  8971 Wilcox Dr Twinsburg (44087) *(G-18245)*
Apple Growth Partners Inc (PA) 330 867-7350
  1540 W Market St Akron (44313) *(G-76)*
Apple Heating Inc (PA) 440 997-1212
  344 4th St Nw Barberton (44203) *(G-941)*
Apple Vly Property Owners Assn (PA) 740 397-3311
  113 Hasbrouck Cir Howard (43028) *(G-11939)*
Appleseed Cmnty Mntal Hlth Ctr 419 281-3716
  2233 Rocky Ln Ashland (44805) *(G-645)*
APPLESEED COUNSELING, Ashland *Also called Appleseed Cmnty Mntal Hlth Ctr (G-645)*
Applewood Centers Inc (PA) 216 696-6815
  10427 Detroit Ave Cleveland (44102) *(G-4991)*
Applewood Centers Inc 216 521-6511
  10427 Detroit Ave Cleveland (44102) *(G-4992)*
Applewood Centers Inc 440 324-1300
  1865 N Ridge Rd E Ste A Lorain (44055) *(G-12882)*
Applewood Centers Inc 216 741-2241
  3518 W 25th St Cleveland (44109) *(G-4993)*
Appliance Recycl Ctrs Amer Inc 614 876-8771
  3700 Parkway Ln Ste D&G Hilliard (43026) *(G-11742)*
Applied Indus Tech - CA LLC (HQ) 216 426-4000
  1 Applied Plz Cleveland (44115) *(G-4994)*
Applied Indus Tech - Dixie Inc (HQ) 216 426-4000
  1 Applied Plz Cleveland (44115) *(G-4995)*
Applied Industrial Tech Inc (HQ) 216 426-4000
  1 Applied Plz Cleveland (44115) *(G-4996)*
Applied Marketing Services (HQ) 440 716-9962
  28825 Ranney Pkwy Westlake (44145) *(G-19317)*
Applied Mechanical Systems Inc 513 825-1800
  12082 Champion Way Cincinnati (45241) *(G-2976)*
Applied Medical Technology Inc 440 717-4000
  8006 Katherine Blvd Brecksville (44141) *(G-1769)*
Applied Mint Sups Slutions LLC (HQ) 216 456-3600
  14790 Foltz Pkwy Strongsville (44149) *(G-17285)*
Applied Optimization Inc 937 431-5100
  3040 Presidential Dr # 100 Beavercreek (45324) *(G-1125)*
Applied Research Assoc Inc 937 435-1016
  1330 Kinnear Rd Columbus (43212) *(G-6959)*
Applied Research Assoc Inc 937 873-8166
  7735 Paragon Rd Dayton (45459) *(G-9235)*

Applied Research Solutions Inc (HQ)..............937 912-6100
  51 Plum St Ste 240 Beavercreek (45440) *(G-1202)*
Applied Sciences Inc (PA).................................937 766-2020
  141 W Xenia Ave Cedarville (45314) *(G-2579)*
Appraisal Research Corporation (PA)..............419 423-3582
  101 E Sandusky St Ste 408 Findlay (45840) *(G-10865)*
APPRISEN, Gahanna *Also called Consumer Credit Coun (G-11115)*
Aprecia Pharmaceuticals Co............................513 864-4107
  10901 Kenwood Rd Blue Ash (45242) *(G-1506)*
Apria Healthcare LLC..614 351-5920
  4060 Business Park Dr A Columbus (43204) *(G-6960)*
Apria Healthcare LLC..937 291-2842
  2029 Lyons Rd Miamisburg (45342) *(G-14141)*
Apria Healthcare LLC..419 471-1919
  4062 Technology Dr Maumee (43537) *(G-13758)*
Apria Healthcare LLC..216 485-1180
  5480 Cloverleaf Pkwy # 4 Cleveland (44125) *(G-4997)*
April Enterprises Inc...937 293-7703
  5070 Lamme Rd Moraine (45439) *(G-14623)*
APS Medical Billing..419 866-1804
  5620 Southwyck Blvd Toledo (43614) *(G-17597)*
Aptim Corp...513 782-4700
  5050 Section Ave Cincinnati (45212) *(G-2977)*
Aptiv Services Us LLC.......................................330 373-3568
  1265 N River Rd Ne Warren (44483) *(G-18666)*
Aptiv Services Us LLC.......................................330 373-7666
  Larchmond North River Rd Warren (44483) *(G-18667)*
Aqua Doc Lake & Pond MGT, Chardon *Also called Stat Integrated Tech Inc (G-2716)*
Aqua Falls Bottled Watrer, Fairborn *Also called K & R Distributors Inc (G-10677)*
Aqua Marine Luxury Apartments, Avon Lake *Also called Kopf Construction Corporation (G-922)*
Aqua Ohio Inc..440 255-3984
  8644 Station St Mentor (44060) *(G-14019)*
Aqua Ohio Inc..330 832-5764
  870 3rd St Nw Massillon (44647) *(G-13663)*
Aqua Pennsylvania Inc......................................614 882-6586
  5481 Buenos Aires Blvd Westerville (43081) *(G-19221)*
Aqua Tech Envmtl Labs Inc (PA).....................740 389-5991
  1776 Marion Waldo Rd Marion (43302) *(G-13404)*
Aquarian Pools Inc...513 576-9771
  631 Lveland Miamiville Rd Loveland (45140) *(G-12978)*
Aquarius Marine LLC..614 875-8200
  250 N Hartford Ave Columbus (43222) *(G-6961)*
Aquasonic Auto & Van Wash, North Olmsted *Also called John Atwood Inc (G-15294)*
Aquasonic Car Wash, Euclid *Also called Bp (G-10625)*
ARA Staffing Services, Cincinnati *Also called Healthlinx Inc (G-3695)*
Aramark Facility Services LLC.........................216 687-5000
  2121 Euclid Ave Cleveland (44115) *(G-4998)*
Aramark Unf & Career AP LLC.........................513 533-1000
  P.O. Box 12131 Cincinnati (45212) *(G-2978)*
Aramark Unf & Career AP LLC.........................937 223-6667
  1200 Webster St Dayton (45404) *(G-9236)*
Aramark Unf & Career AP LLC.........................614 445-8341
  1900 Progress Ave Columbus (43207) *(G-6962)*
Aramark Unf & Career AP LLC.........................216 341-7400
  3600 E 93rd St Cleveland (44105) *(G-4999)*
Arbor Construction Co......................................216 360-8989
  1350 W 3rd St Cleveland (44113) *(G-5000)*
Arbor Park Phase Two Assoc...........................561 998-0700
  3750 Fleming Ave Cleveland (44115) *(G-5001)*
ARBOR PARK VILLAGE, Cleveland *Also called Arbor Pk Phase Three Assoc LP (G-5002)*
Arbor Park Village, Cleveland *Also called Arbor Park Phase Two Assoc (G-5001)*
Arbor Park Village, Cleveland *Also called Longwood Phase One Assoc LP (G-5880)*
Arbor Pk Phase Three Assoc LP.......................561 998-0700
  3750 Fleming Ave Cleveland (44115) *(G-5002)*
Arbor Rehabilitation & Healtcr........................440 423-0206
  45125 Fairmount Blvd Gates Mills (44040) *(G-11233)*
Arbor View Family Medicine Inc.......................740 687-3386
  2405 N Columbus St # 200 Lancaster (43130) *(G-12371)*
Arbors At Clide Asssted Living.........................419 547-7746
  700 Coulson St Clyde (43410) *(G-6738)*
ARBORS AT DELAWARE, Delaware *Also called Delaware Opco LLC (G-9970)*
Arbors At Fairlawn, Fairlawn *Also called Fairlawn Opco LLC (G-10827)*
Arbors At London, London *Also called Saber Healthcare Group LLC (G-12874)*
Arbors At Marietta, Marietta *Also called Northpoint Senior Services LLC (G-13363)*
Arbors At Mifflin, Mansfield *Also called Mansfield Opco LLC (G-13210)*
Arbors At Milfor, The, Milford *Also called Northpoint Senior Services LLC (G-14414)*
Arbors At Stow, Stow *Also called Stow Opco LLC (G-17232)*
Arbors At Streetsboro, Streetsboro *Also called Streetsboro Opco LLC (G-17273)*
ARBORS AT SYLVANIA, Toledo *Also called Toledo Opco LLC (G-18093)*
ARBORS AT WATERVILLE, Waterville *Also called Waterville Care LLC (G-18795)*
Arbors At Woodsfield, Woodsfield *Also called Woodsfield Opco LLC (G-19679)*
Arbors East LLC..614 575-9003
  5500 E Broad St Columbus (43213) *(G-6963)*
Arbors of Delaware, Delaware *Also called Northpoint Senior Services LLC (G-9998)*
Arbors West LLC...614 879-7661
  375 W Main St West Jefferson (43162) *(G-19103)*

ARBORS WEST SUBACUTE & REHABIL, West Jefferson *Also called Arbors West LLC (G-19103)*
ARC, Columbus *Also called American Reprographics Co LLC (G-6936)*
ARC Abrasives Inc..800 888-4885
  2131 Corporate Dr Troy (45373) *(G-18194)*
ARC Document Solutions Inc...........................216 281-1234
  3666 Carnegie Ave Cleveland (44115) *(G-5003)*
ARC Document Solutions Inc...........................513 326-2300
  7157 E Kemper Rd Cincinnati (45249) *(G-2979)*
ARC Document Solutions Inc...........................937 277-7930
  222 N Saint Clair St Dayton (45402) *(G-9237)*
ARC Gas & Supply LLC....................................216 341-5882
  4560 Nicky Blvd Ste D Cleveland (44125) *(G-5004)*
ARC Industreis East, Columbus *Also called ARC Industries Incorporated O (G-6966)*
ARC Industries Incorporated O (PA)................614 479-2500
  2780 Airport Dr Columbus (43219) *(G-6964)*
ARC Industries Incorporated O.........................614 436-4800
  6633 Doubletree Ave Columbus (43229) *(G-6965)*
ARC Industries Incorporated O.........................614 864-2406
  909 Taylor Station Rd Columbus (43230) *(G-6966)*
ARC Industries Incorporated O.........................614 267-1207
  250 W Dodridge St Columbus (43202) *(G-6967)*
ARC Industries Incorporated O.........................614 836-0700
  4395 Marketing Pl Groveport (43125) *(G-11494)*
ARC Industries Incorporated O.........................614 836-6050
  4200 Bixby Rd Groveport (43125) *(G-11495)*
ARC Industries North, Columbus *Also called ARC Industries Incorporated O (G-6965)*
ARC Industries South, Groveport *Also called ARC Industries Incorporated O (G-11494)*
ARC Industries West, Columbus *Also called ARC Industries Incorporated O (G-6967)*
Arcadia Health Care, Akron *Also called Arcadia Services Inc (G-77)*
Arcadia Services Inc...330 869-9520
  1650 W Market St Ste 27 Akron (44313) *(G-77)*
Arcadia Services Inc...937 912-5800
  2440 Dayton Xenia Rd C Beavercreek (45434) *(G-1126)*
Arcadis US Inc..216 781-6177
  1111 Superior Ave E # 1300 Cleveland (44114) *(G-5005)*
Arcadis US Inc..330 434-1995
  222 S Main St Ste 200 Akron (44308) *(G-78)*
Arcadis US Inc..419 473-1121
  1 Seagate Ste 700 Toledo (43604) *(G-17598)*
Arch Abraham Nissan & Susuki, Elyria *Also called Arch Abraham Susuki Ltd (G-10479)*
Arch Abraham Susuki Ltd.................................440 934-6001
  1111 E Broad St Elyria (44035) *(G-10479)*
Archbishop Leibold Home, Cincinnati *Also called Sisters of Little (G-4486)*
Archbold Elevator Inc.......................................419 445-2451
  3265 County Road 24 Archbold (43502) *(G-626)*
Archbold Hospital, Archbold *Also called Community Hsptals Wllness Ctrs (G-629)*
Archdiocese of Cincinnati................................937 323-6507
  701 E Columbia St Springfield (45503) *(G-16996)*
Archdiocese of Cincinnati................................513 729-1725
  9375 Winton Rd Cincinnati (45231) *(G-2980)*
Archdiocese of Cincinnati................................513 231-5010
  274 Sutton Rd Cincinnati (45230) *(G-2981)*
Archer Corporation...330 455-9995
  1917 Henry Ave Sw Canton (44706) *(G-2193)*
Archer Sign, Canton *Also called Archer Corporation (G-2193)*
Archer-Meek-Weiler Agency Inc.......................614 212-1009
  440 Polaris Pkwy Ste 400 Westerville (43082) *(G-19145)*
Archiable Electric Company.............................513 621-1307
  3803 Ford Cir Cincinnati (45227) *(G-2982)*
Architctural Con Solutions Inc.........................614 940-5399
  1997 Harmon Ave Columbus (43223) *(G-6968)*
Architechs Plus, Blue Ash *Also called Design Center (G-1544)*
Architectural Intr Restoration...........................216 241-2255
  2401 Train Ave Ste 100 Cleveland (44113) *(G-5006)*
Architectural Justice, Medina *Also called Justice & Co Inc (G-13962)*
Architectural Metal Erectors............................513 242-5106
  869 W North Bend Rd Cincinnati (45224) *(G-2983)*
Architectural Systems Inc................................614 873-2057
  8633 Memorial Dr Plain City (43064) *(G-16044)*
Archway Marketing Services Inc......................440 572-0725
  20770 Westwood Dr Strongsville (44149) *(G-17286)*
Archways Brookville Inc....................................513 367-2649
  375 Industrial Dr Harrison (45030) *(G-11661)*
Arco Heating & AC Co (PA)..............................216 663-3211
  5325 Naiman Pkwy Ste J Solon (44139) *(G-16821)*
Arctech Fabricating Inc (PA)............................937 525-9353
  1317 Lagonda Ave Springfield (45503) *(G-16997)*
Arctic Express Inc...614 876-4008
  4277 Lyman Dr Hilliard (43026) *(G-11743)*
Arden Courts of Akron Bath, Akron *Also called Hcr Manorcare Med Svcs Fla LLC (G-257)*
Arden Courts of Anderson Twp., Cincinnati *Also called Hcr Manorcare Med Svcs Fla LLC (G-3689)*
Arden Courts of Bainbridge, Chagrin Falls *Also called Manor Care of America Inc (G-2673)*
Arden Courts of Parma, North Royalton *Also called Hcr Manorcare Med Svcs Fla LLC (G-15360)*
Arden Crts Manorcare Hlth Svcs, Westlake *Also called Hcr Manorcare Med Svcs Fla LLC (G-19348)*

Ardent Technologies Inc 937 312-1345
　6234 Far Hills Ave Dayton (45459) *(G-9238)*
Ardmore Inc 330 535-2601
　981 E Market St Akron (44305) *(G-79)*
Ardmore Logistics, Westlake *Also called Ardmore Power Logistics LLC (G-19318)*
Ardmore Power Logistics LLC 216 502-0640
　24610 Detroit Rd Ste 1200 Westlake (44145) *(G-19318)*
Ardus Medical Inc 855 592-7387
　9407 Kenwood Rd Blue Ash (45242) *(G-1507)*
Area Agency On Aging, Marietta *Also called Buckeye Hills-Hck Vly Reg Dev (G-13317)*
Area Agency On Aging, Reno *Also called Buckeye Hills-Hck Vly Reg Dev (G-16276)*
Area Agency On Aging Planni 800 258-7277
　40 W 2nd St Ste 400 Dayton (45402) *(G-9239)*
Area Agency On Aging Dst 7 Inc (PA) 800 582-7277
　160 Dorsey Dr Rio Grande (45674) *(G-16399)*
Area Agency On Aging Dst 7 Inc 740 446-7000
　1167 State Route 160 Gallipolis (45631) *(G-11185)*
Area Agency On Aging P S A 2, Dayton *Also called Area Agency On Aging Planni (G-9239)*
Area Agency On Aging Reg 9 Inc 740 439-4478
　1730 Southgate Pkwy Cambridge (43725) *(G-2050)*
Area Energy & Electric Inc 937 642-0386
　19255 Smokey Rd Marysville (43040) *(G-13483)*
Area Energy & Electric Inc (PA) 937 498-4784
　2001 Commerce Dr Sidney (45365) *(G-16759)*
Area Office On Aging of Nwstrn 419 382-0624
　2155 Arlington Ave Toledo (43609) *(G-17599)*
Area Temps Inc 216 227-8200
　14801 Detroit Ave Lakewood (44107) *(G-12336)*
Area Temps Inc (PA) 216 781-5350
　4511 Rockside Rd Ste 190 Independence (44131) *(G-12046)*
Area Temps Inc 216 518-2000
　15689 Broadway Ave Maple Heights (44137) *(G-13281)*
Area Wide Protective, North Canton *Also called Awp Inc (G-15191)*
Area Wide Protective Inc 513 321-9889
　9500 Le Saint Dr Fairfield (45014) *(G-10696)*
Arena Eye Surgeons, Columbus *Also called Eye Surgery Center Ohio Inc (G-7550)*
Arena Management Holdings LLC 513 421-4111
　100 Broadway St Cincinnati (45202) *(G-2984)*
Arensberg Home Health, Newark *Also called George W Arensberg Phrm Inc (G-15036)*
Arett Sales Corp 937 552-2005
　1261 Brukner Dr Troy (45373) *(G-18195)*
Argo-Hytos Inc 419 353-6070
　1835 N Research Dr Bowling Green (43402) *(G-1714)*
Argus International Inc 513 852-1010
　4240 Airport Rd Ste 300 Cincinnati (45226) *(G-2985)*
Argus International Inc (PA) 513 852-5110
　4240 Airport Rd Ste 300 Cincinnati (45226) *(G-2986)*
Aris Horticulture Inc (PA) 330 745-2143
　115 3rd St Se Barberton (44203) *(G-942)*
Arise Incorporated 440 746-8860
　7000 S Edgerton Rd # 100 Brecksville (44141) *(G-1770)*
Aristocrat Berea Skilled, Berea *Also called Front Leasing Co LLC (G-1427)*
Aristocrat W Nursing Hm Corp (PA) 440 835-0660
　24340 Sperry Dr Cleveland (44145) *(G-5007)*
Aristocrat W Nursing Hm Corp 216 252-7730
　4401 W 150th St Cleveland (44135) *(G-5008)*
Ark Foundation of Dayton 937 256-2759
　2002 S Smithville Rd Dayton (45420) *(G-9240)*
ARKY BOOK STORE, Dayton *Also called Ark Foundation of Dayton (G-9240)*
Arledge Construction Inc (PA) 614 732-4258
　2460 Performance Way Columbus (43207) *(G-6969)*
Arlette Child Family Rese, Cincinnati *Also called University of Cincinnati (G-4726)*
Arlington Care Ctr 740 344-0303
　98 S 30th St Newark (43055) *(G-15011)*
Arlington Contact Lens Svc Inc (HQ) 614 921-9894
　4265 Diplomacy Dr Columbus (43228) *(G-6970)*
Arlington Court Nursing (PA) 614 545-5502
　1605 Nw Prof Plz Upper Arlington (43220) *(G-18393)*
Arlington Court Skilled, Upper Arlington *Also called Arlington Court Nursing (G-18393)*
Arlington Memorial Grdns Assn 513 521-7003
　2145 Compton Rd Cincinnati (45231) *(G-2987)*
Arlington Towing Inc 614 488-2006
　2354 Wood Ave Columbus (43221) *(G-6971)*
Arlington-Blaine Lumber Co, Delaware *Also called Khempco Bldg Sup Co Ltd Partnr (G-9993)*
Arlingworth Home Health Inc 614 659-0961
　6479 Reflections Dr # 100 Dublin (43017) *(G-10137)*
Arlitt Child Development Ctr 513 556-3802
　44 W Corry St Cincinnati (45219) *(G-2988)*
Arlo Aluminum & Steel, Dayton *Also called Alro Steel Corporation (G-9221)*
Armada Ltd 614 505-7256
　23 Clairedan Dr Powell (43065) *(G-16184)*
Armaly Brands, London *Also called Armaly LLC (G-12859)*
Armaly LLC 740 852-3621
　110 W 1st St London (43140) *(G-12859)*
Armco Association Park 513 695-3980
　1223 N State Route 741 Lebanon (45036) *(G-12449)*
Armco Park, Lebanon *Also called Armco Association Park (G-12449)*
Armcorp Construction Inc 419 778-7024
　8511 State Route 703 C Celina (45822) *(G-2583)*

Armor Paving & Sealing 614 751-6900
　6900 Americana Pkwy Reynoldsburg (43068) *(G-16284)*
Arms Trucking Co Inc (PA) 800 362-1343
　14818 Mayfield Rd Huntsburg (44046) *(G-12016)*
Armstrong Cable Services, North Lima *Also called Armstrong Utilities Inc (G-15262)*
Armstrong Steel Erectors Inc 740 345-4503
　50 S 4th St Newark (43055) *(G-15012)*
Armstrong Utilities Inc 740 894-3886
　9651 County Road 1 South Point (45680) *(G-16928)*
Armstrong Utilities Inc 330 758-6411
　9328 Woodworth Rd North Lima (44452) *(G-15262)*
Army & Air Force Exchange Svc 937 257-2928
　2439 Schlatter Dr Dayton (45433) *(G-9160)*
Army & Air Force Exchange Svc 937 257-7736
　5215 Thurlow St Ste 2 Dayton (45433) *(G-9161)*
Arnold's Landscaping, Ontario *Also called Dta Inc (G-15548)*
Arnolds Home Improvement LLC 734 847-9600
　1770 Premainsville Toledo (43613) *(G-17600)*
Around Clock Home Care 440 350-2547
　7757 Auburn Rd Ste 6 Painesville (44077) *(G-15694)*
Arrow Electronics Inc 800 722-5273
　5440 Naiman Pkwy Solon (44139) *(G-16822)*
Arrow Electronics Inc 440 498-6400
　6675 Parkland Blvd Solon (44139) *(G-16823)*
Arrow Globl Asset Dspstion Inc 614 328-4100
　1120 Morrison Rd Ste A Gahanna (43230) *(G-11110)*
Arrow Industrial Supply, Sunbury *Also called J & J Entps Westerville Inc (G-17389)*
Arrowhead Transport Co 330 638-2900
　2555 Greenville Rd Cortland (44410) *(G-8983)*
ARS Ohio LLC 513 327-7645
　947 Sundance Dr Cincinnati (45233) *(G-2989)*
ARS Rescue Rooter Inc 440 842-8494
　4547 Hinckley Industrial Cleveland (44109) *(G-5009)*
Arslanian Bros Crpt Rug Clg Co 216 271-6888
　19499 Miles Rd Warrensville Heights (44128) *(G-18776)*
Arslanian Brothers Company, Warrensville Heights *Also called Arslanian Bros Crpt Rug Clg Co (G-18776)*
Arszman & Lyons LLC 513 527-4900
　9933 Alliance Rd Ste 2 Blue Ash (45242) *(G-1508)*
Art Hauser Insurance Inc 513 745-9200
　8260 Northcreek Dr # 200 Cincinnati (45236) *(G-2990)*
Art Wall, Strongsville *Also called Dwa Mrkting Prmtional Pdts LLC (G-17298)*
Art-American Printing Plates 216 241-4420
　1138 W 9th St Fl 4 Cleveland (44113) *(G-5010)*
Arthur G James Cance 614 293-4878
　460 W 10th Ave Columbus (43210) *(G-6972)*
Arthur G James Cancer Hospital 614 293-3300
　300 W 10th Ave Columbus (43210) *(G-6973)*
Arthur J Gallagher & Co. 513 977-3100
　201 E 4th St Ste 625 Cincinnati (45202) *(G-2991)*
Arthur Middleton Capital Holdn 330 966-3033
　8000 Freedom Ave Nw Canton (44720) *(G-2194)*
Arthur Middleton Capital Holdn (PA) 330 966-9000
　8000 Freedom Ave Nw North Canton (44720) *(G-15190)*
Artis Senior Living 513 229-7450
　6200 Snider Rd Mason (45040) *(G-13542)*
Artisan and Truckers Cslty Co 440 461-5000
　6300 Wilson Mills Rd Cleveland (44143) *(G-5011)*
Artistic Dance Enterprises 614 761-2882
　2665 Farmers Dr Columbus (43235) *(G-6974)*
Arts and Exhibitions Intl LLC 330 995-9300
　10145 Philipp Pkwy D Streetsboro (44241) *(G-17246)*
ARTSWAVE, Cincinnati *Also called Cincinnati Institute Fine Arts (G-3251)*
Arvind Sagar Inc 614 428-8800
　2880 Airport Dr Columbus (43219) *(G-6975)*
Arysen Inc 440 230-4400
　5005 Rockside Rd Ste 600 Independence (44131) *(G-12047)*
As Automotive Systems, Valley City *Also called Luk-Aftermarket Service Inc (G-18466)*
As Logistics Inc (HQ) 513 863-4627
　7570 Bales St Ste 310 Liberty Township (45069) *(G-12577)*
Asana Hospice Cleveland LLC 419 903-0300
　885 W Bagley Rd Berea (44017) *(G-1412)*
Asana Hospice Palliative Care, Berea *Also called Asana Hospice Cleveland LLC (G-1412)*
ASAP Homecare Inc 330 674-3306
　31 N Mad Anthony St Millersburg (44654) *(G-14456)*
ASAP Homecare Inc 330 491-0700
　4150 Belden Village St Nw Canton (44718) *(G-2195)*
ASAP Homecare Inc (PA) 330 334-7027
　1 Park Centre Dr Ste 107 Wadsworth (44281) *(G-18590)*
ASAP Homecare Inc 330 263-4733
　133 Beall Ave Wooster (44691) *(G-19688)*
Asbuilt Construction Ltd 937 550-4900
　29 Eagle Ct Franklin (45005) *(G-11022)*
ASC Group Inc (PA) 614 268-2514
　800 Freeway Dr N Ste 101 Columbus (43229) *(G-6976)*
ASC of Cincinnati Inc 513 886-7100
　4028 Binion Way Lebanon (45036) *(G-12450)*
Ascendtech Inc 216 458-1101
　4772 E 355th St Willoughby (44094) *(G-19506)*
Ascent Global Logistics Holdin (HQ) 800 689-6255
　5876 Darrow Rd Hudson (44236) *(G-11967)*
Asci, Dublin *Also called American Systems Cnsulting Inc (G-10134)*

(G-0000) Company's Geographic Section entry number

Asd Specialty Healthcare LLC.....513 682-3600
9075 Centre Pointe Dr West Chester (45069) ***(G-18869)***
Aset Corporation (PA).....937 890-8881
407 Corporate Center Dr Vandalia (45377) ***(G-18504)***
Asfoura, Jehad MD, Canton *Also called Luis F Soto MD* ***(G-2382)***
Ash Craft Industries Inc.....440 224-2177
5959 Green Rd Ashtabula (44004) ***(G-704)***
Ashford Trs Lessee LLC.....937 436-2400
300 Prestige Pl Miamisburg (45342) ***(G-14142)***
Ashland City School District.....419 289-7967
850 Jackson Dr Ashland (44805) ***(G-646)***
Ashland Cleaning LLC.....419 281-1747
48 W Main St Ashland (44805) ***(G-647)***
Ashland Cleaning LLC.....419 281-1747
48 W Main St Ashland (44805) ***(G-648)***
Ashland Cnty Council On Aging.....419 281-1477
240 E 3rd St Ashland (44805) ***(G-649)***
Ashland Comfort Control Inc (PA).....419 281-0144
805 E Main St Ashland (44805) ***(G-650)***
Ashland Distribution, Twinsburg *Also called Nexeo Solutions LLC* ***(G-18301)***
Ashland Distribution, Dublin *Also called Ashland LLC* ***(G-10139)***
Ashland Distribution, Cleveland *Also called Ashland LLC* ***(G-5012)***
Ashland Distribution, Ashland *Also called Ashland LLC* ***(G-652)***
Ashland Golf Club.....419 289-2917
1333 Center St Ashland (44805) ***(G-651)***
Ashland LLC.....614 232-8510
802 Harmon Ave Columbus (43223) ***(G-6977)***
Ashland LLC.....614 276-6144
3849 Fisher Rd Columbus (43228) ***(G-6978)***
Ashland LLC.....614 839-4503
5200 Blazer Pkwy Dublin (43017) ***(G-10138)***
Ashland LLC.....614 790-3333
5200 Blazer Pkwy Dublin (43017) ***(G-10139)***
Ashland LLC.....216 961-4690
2191 W 110th St Cleveland (44102) ***(G-5012)***
Ashland LLC.....216 883-8200
4600 E 71st St Cleveland (44125) ***(G-5013)***
Ashland LLC.....419 289-9588
1745 Cottage St Ashland (44805) ***(G-652)***
Ashland Performance Materials, Columbus *Also called Ashland LLC* ***(G-6977)***
Ashland Railway Inc.....419 525-2822
803 N Main St Mansfield (44902) ***(G-13137)***
Ashley Enterprises LLC (PA).....330 726-5790
1419 Boardman Canfield Rd Boardman (44512) ***(G-1695)***
Ashley Place Health Care Inc.....330 793-3010
5291 Ashley Cir Youngstown (44515) ***(G-19956)***
Ashtabula Area City School Dst.....440 992-1221
5921 Gerald Rd Ashtabula (44004) ***(G-705)***
Ashtabula Board of Mental, Ashtabula *Also called County of Ashtabula* ***(G-732)***
Ashtabula Broadcasting Station.....440 993-2126
3226 Jefferson Rd Ashtabula (44004) ***(G-706)***
Ashtabula Chemical Corp.....440 998-0100
4606 State Rd Ashtabula (44004) ***(G-707)***
Ashtabula Clinic Inc (PA).....440 997-6980
2422 Lake Ave Ashtabula (44004) ***(G-708)***
Ashtabula Cnty Chldren Svcs Bd, Ashtabula *Also called County of Ashtabula* ***(G-733)***
Ashtabula Cnty Eductl Svc Ctr.....440 576-4085
2630 W 13th St Ste A Ashtabula (44004) ***(G-709)***
Ashtabula Community Counseling.....440 998-6032
2801 C Ct Unit 2 Ashtabula (44004) ***(G-710)***
Ashtabula County Commnty Actn (PA).....440 997-1721
6920 Austinburg Rd Ashtabula (44004) ***(G-711)***
Ashtabula County Commnty Actn.....440 593-6441
327 Mill St Conneaut (44030) ***(G-8949)***
Ashtabula County Commnty Actn.....440 576-6911
32 E Jefferson St Jefferson (44047) ***(G-12189)***
Ashtabula County Commnty Actn.....440 993-7716
4510 Main Ave Ashtabula (44004) ***(G-712)***
Ashtabula County Commnty Actn.....440 997-5957
3215 Lake Ave Ashtabula (44004) ***(G-713)***
Ashtabula County Community.....440 997-1721
6920 Austinburg Rd Ashtabula (44004) ***(G-714)***
ASHTABULA COUNTY FAMILY Y, Ashtabula *Also called YMCA of Ashtabula County Inc* ***(G-760)***
Ashtabula County Highway Dept, Jefferson *Also called County of Ashtabula* ***(G-12191)***
Ashtabula County Medical Ctr (PA).....440 997-2262
2420 Lake Ave Ashtabula (44004) ***(G-715)***
Ashtabula County Medical Ctr.....440 997-6960
2422 Lake Ave Ashtabula (44004) ***(G-716)***
Ashtabula County Residential I (PA).....440 593-6404
29 Parrish Rd Conneaut (44030) ***(G-8950)***
Ashtabula County V A Clinic, Ashtabula *Also called Veterans Health Administration* ***(G-758)***
Ashtabula Dental Associates.....440 992-3146
5005 State Rd Ashtabula (44004) ***(G-717)***
Ashtabula Job and Family Svcs.....440 994-2020
2924 Donahoe Dr Ashtabula (44004) ***(G-718)***
Ashtabula Rgional Hm Hlth Svcs.....440 992-4663
2131 Lake Ave Ste 2 Ashtabula (44004) ***(G-719)***
Ashtabula Stevedore Company.....440 964-7186
1149 E 5th St Ashtabula (44004) ***(G-720)***
Ashtabula Welfare Department, Ashtabula *Also called County of Ashtabula* ***(G-734)***

Ask Childrens, Akron *Also called Childrens Hosp Med Ctr Akron* ***(G-131)***
Asm International.....440 338-5151
9639 Kinsman Rd Novelty (44073) ***(G-15464)***
Aspc Corp (PA).....937 593-7010
1 Hunter Pl Bellefontaine (43311) ***(G-1345)***
Aspen Community Living.....614 880-6000
2021 E Dublin Granville R Columbus (43229) ***(G-6979)***
Aspen Woodside Village.....440 439-8666
19455 Rockside Rd Ofc Cleveland (44146) ***(G-5014)***
Aspire Energy of Ohio LLC (HQ).....330 682-7726
300 Tracy Bridge Rd Orrville (44667) ***(G-15623)***
Aspire Home Healthcare of Ohio, Dublin *Also called Nightingale Home Healthcare* ***(G-10291)***
Asplundh Construction Corp.....614 532-5224
481 Schrock Rd Columbus (43229) ***(G-6980)***
Asplundh Tree Expert LLC.....740 467-1028
12488 Lancaster St # 94 Millersport (43046) ***(G-14501)***
Assembly Center.....800 582-1099
913 Lebanon St Monroe (45050) ***(G-14560)***
Asset Protection Corporation.....419 531-3400
5211 Renwyck Dr Toledo (43615) ***(G-17601)***
Asset Solutions, Cincinnati *Also called Loth Inc* ***(G-3944)***
Assisted Care By Black Stone, Moraine *Also called Black Stone Cincinnati LLC* ***(G-14626)***
Assisted Care By Black Stone, Cincinnati *Also called Black Stone Cincinnati LLC* ***(G-3054)***
Assisted Living Apartments, Lorain *Also called Autumn Aegis Inc* ***(G-12883)***
Assisted Living Concepts LLC.....419 586-2484
1506 Meadowview Dr Ofc Celina (45822) ***(G-2584)***
Assisted Living Concepts LLC.....740 450-2744
3784 Frazeysburg Rd Ofc Zanesville (43701) ***(G-20277)***
Assisted Living Concepts LLC.....419 224-6327
1070 Gloria Ave Ofc Lima (45805) ***(G-12602)***
Assisted Living Facilities, Chillicothe *Also called Traditions of Chillicothe* ***(G-2831)***
Assistnce In Mktg Columbus Inc.....614 583-2100
1 Easton Oval Ste 100 Columbus (43219) ***(G-6981)***
Assoc Dvlpmtly Disabled (PA).....614 486-4361
769 Brooksedge Blvd Westerville (43081) ***(G-19222)***
Assoc Dvlpmtly Disabled.....614 447-0606
1915 E Cooke Rd Columbus (43224) ***(G-6982)***
Associated Eye Care, Toledo *Also called Regency Park Eye Associates* ***(G-17997)***
Associated Imaging Corporation.....419 517-0500
3830 Woodley Rd Ste A Toledo (43606) ***(G-17602)***
Associated Materials LLC.....614 985-4611
640 Dearborn Park Ln Columbus (43085) ***(G-6983)***
Associated Materials LLC (HQ).....330 929-1811
3773 State Rd Cuyahoga Falls (44223) ***(G-9070)***
Associated Materials Group Inc (PA).....330 929-1811
3773 State Rd Cuyahoga Falls (44223) ***(G-9071)***
Associated Mtls Holdings LLC.....330 929-1811
3773 State Rd Cuyahoga Falls (44223) ***(G-9072)***
Associated Paper Stock Inc (PA).....330 549-5311
11510 South Ave North Lima (44452) ***(G-15263)***
Associated Press.....614 885-3444
1103 Schrock Rd Ste 300 Columbus (43229) ***(G-6984)***
Associated Specialists.....937 208-7272
7707 Paragon Rd Ste 101 Dayton (45459) ***(G-9241)***
Associated Steel Company Inc.....216 475-8000
18200 Miles Rd Cleveland (44128) ***(G-5015)***
Associates In Dermatology Inc (PA).....440 249-0274
26908 Detroit Rd Ste 103 Westlake (44145) ***(G-19319)***
Association For Middle Lvl Edu.....614 895-4730
4151 Executive Pkwy # 300 Westerville (43081) ***(G-19223)***
Association of Prosthodontics.....614 885-2022
7227 N High St Ste 1 Worthington (43085) ***(G-19794)***
Assocted Ctract Laser Surgeons.....419 693-4444
2740 Navarre Ave Oregon (43616) ***(G-15583)***
Assumption Village.....330 549-2434
9800 Market St North Lima (44452) ***(G-15264)***
Assuramed Inc (HQ).....330 963-6998
1810 Summit Commerce Park Twinsburg (44087) ***(G-18246)***
Assurant Employee Benefits, Cincinnati *Also called Union Security Insurance Co* ***(G-4674)***
Assured Health Care Inc.....937 294-2803
1250 W Dorothy Ln Ste 200 Dayton (45409) ***(G-9242)***
Assured Hlth Care HM Care Svcs, Dayton *Also called Assured Health Care Inc* ***(G-9242)***
Assured Information SEC Inc.....937 427-9720
3500 Pentagon Blvd # 310 Beavercreek (45431) ***(G-1127)***
AST, Miamisburg *Also called Advanced Service Tech LLC* ***(G-14137)***
AST Environmental Inc.....937 743-0002
70 Commercial Way Springboro (45066) ***(G-16962)***
Aston Oaks Golf Club.....513 467-0070
1 Aston Oaks Dr North Bend (45052) ***(G-15181)***
ASTORIA HEALTH & REHAB CENTER, Germantown *Also called Astoria Healthcare Group LLC* ***(G-11276)***
Astoria Healthcare Group LLC.....937 855-2363
300 Astoria Rd Germantown (45327) ***(G-11276)***
Astoria Place Columbus LLC.....614 228-5900
44 S Souder Ave Columbus (43222) ***(G-6985)***
Astoria Place of Barnesville, Barnesville *Also called Barnesville Healthcare Rehab* ***(G-974)***
Astoria Place of Clyde LLC.....419 547-9595
700 Helen St Clyde (43410) ***(G-6739)***
Astute Inc (PA).....614 508-6100
4400 Easton Cmns Columbus (43219) ***(G-6986)***
Astute Solutions, Columbus *Also called Astute Inc* ***(G-6986)***

ALPHABETIC

(PA)=Parent Co (HQ)=Headquarters (DH)=Div Headquarters

Asurint, Cleveland *Also called One Source Technology LLC* ***(G-6134)***
Asv Services LLC......216 797-1701
27801 Euclid Ave Ste 420 Euclid (44132) ***(G-10623)***
Asw Akron Logistic, Canton *Also called Asw Global LLC* ***(G-2196)***
Asw Global LLC (PA)......330 733-6291
3375 Gilchrist Rd Mogadore (44260) ***(G-14541)***
Asw Global LLC......330 899-1003
2150 International Pkwy Canton (44720) ***(G-2196)***
Asw Global LLC......330 798-5184
3325 Gilchrist Rd Mogadore (44260) ***(G-14542)***
Asw Supply Chain Service, Mogadore *Also called Asw Global LLC* ***(G-14542)***
Asymmetric Technologies LLC......614 725-5310
1395 Grandview Ave Ste 3 Columbus (43212) ***(G-6987)***
At Holdings Corporation......216 692-6000
23555 Euclid Ave Cleveland (44117) ***(G-5016)***
At Hospitality LLC......513 527-9962
5375 Medpace Way Cincinnati (45227) ***(G-2992)***
At Systems, Columbus *Also called Garda CL Great Lakes Inc* ***(G-7646)***
At T Broadband & Intern......614 839-4271
P.O. Box 182552 Columbus (43218) ***(G-6988)***
AT&T Corp......937 320-9648
4467 Walnut St Beavercreek (45440) ***(G-1203)***
AT&T Corp......330 337-3505
1098 E State St Ste A Salem (44460) ***(G-16535)***
AT&T Corp......614 223-5318
814 Green Crest Dr Westerville (43081) ***(G-19224)***
AT&T Corp......614 798-3898
7497 Sawmill Rd Dublin (43016) ***(G-10140)***
AT&T Corp......614 271-8911
10654 Brettridge Dr Powell (43065) ***(G-16185)***
AT&T Corp......614 539-0165
4108 Buckeye Pkwy Grove City (43123) ***(G-11407)***
AT&T Corp......614 223-6513
3419 Indianola Ave Columbus (43214) ***(G-6989)***
AT&T Corp......740 455-3042
3575 Maple Ave Ste 502 Zanesville (43701) ***(G-20278)***
AT&T Corp......740 549-4546
8601 Columbus Pike Lewis Center (43035) ***(G-12525)***
AT&T Corp......330 665-3100
3890 Medina Rd Ste B Akron (44333) ***(G-80)***
AT&T Corp......330 505-4200
5412 Youngstown Warren Rd Niles (44446) ***(G-15145)***
AT&T Corp......440 951-5309
34808 Euclid Ave Willoughby (44094) ***(G-19507)***
AT&T Corp......937 372-9945
767 Industrial Blvd Xenia (45385) ***(G-19890)***
AT&T Corp......614 223-8236
150 E Gay St Ste 4a Columbus (43215) ***(G-6990)***
AT&T Corp......614 575-3044
2583 S Hamilton Rd Columbus (43232) ***(G-6991)***
AT&T Corp......330 752-7776
45 E Market St Akron (44308) ***(G-81)***
AT&T Corp......614 851-2400
1649 Georgesville Sq Dr Columbus (43228) ***(G-6992)***
AT&T Corp......513 741-1700
3612 Stonecreek Blvd Cincinnati (45251) ***(G-2993)***
AT&T Corp......216 672-0809
3530 Ridge Rd Cleveland (44102) ***(G-5017)***
AT&T Corp......513 629-5000
221 E 4th St Cincinnati (45202) ***(G-2994)***
AT&T Corp......330 723-1717
1088 N Court St Medina (44256) ***(G-13911)***
AT&T Corp......614 337-3902
4300 Appian Way Columbus (43230) ***(G-6993)***
AT&T Datacomm LLC......614 223-5799
814 Green Crest Dr Westerville (43081) ***(G-19225)***
AT&T Government Solutions Inc......937 306-3030
2940 Presidential Dr # 390 Beavercreek (45324) ***(G-1128)***
AT&T Inc......937 320-9648
4467 Walnut St Ste A120 Beavercreek (45440) ***(G-1204)***
AT&T Mobility LLC......614 291-2500
1555 Olentangy River Rd Columbus (43212) ***(G-6994)***
AT&T Mobility LLC......330 565-5000
8089 South Ave Youngstown (44512) ***(G-19957)***
AT&T Mobility LLC......440 846-3232
17970 Royalton Rd Strongsville (44136) ***(G-17287)***
AT&T Mobility LLC......216 382-0825
25309 Cedar Rd Cleveland (44124) ***(G-5018)***
AT&T Mobility LLC......419 516-0602
2421 Elida Rd Lima (45805) ***(G-12603)***
AT&T Mobility LLC......513 381-6800
1605 Western Ave Cincinnati (45214) ***(G-2995)***
AT&T Mobility LLC......937 439-4900
199 E Alex Bell Rd # 418 Centerville (45459) ***(G-2622)***
AT&T Ohio, Cleveland *Also called Ohio Bell Telephone Company* ***(G-6115)***
AT&T Services Inc......937 456-2330
1338 N Barron St Eaton (45320) ***(G-10437)***
Atc Associates, Cincinnati *Also called Atc Group Services LLC* ***(G-2996)***
Atc Group Services LLC......513 771-2112
11121 Canal Rd Cincinnati (45241) ***(G-2996)***
Atco Inc......740 592-6659
1002 E State St Ste 5 Athens (45701) ***(G-765)***
Atel, Marion *Also called Aqua Tech Envmtl Labs Inc* ***(G-13404)***
Athens Bicycle Club, Athens *Also called Joey Boyle* ***(G-787)***
ATHENS COUNTRY CLUB, Athens *Also called Athens Golf & Country Club* ***(G-767)***
Athens County Board of Dev (PA)......740 594-3539
801 W Union St Athens (45701) ***(G-766)***
Athens County Childrens Svcs, Athens *Also called County of Athens* ***(G-774)***
Athens County Emrgncy Med Svcs......740 797-9560
36 N Plains Rd Ste 2 The Plains (45780) ***(G-17502)***
Athens Golf & Country Club (PA)......740 592-1655
7606 Country Club Rd Athens (45701) ***(G-767)***
Athens Health Partners, The Plains *Also called Lindley Inn* ***(G-17503)***
Athens Mold and Machine Inc......740 593-6613
180 Mill St Athens (45701) ***(G-768)***
Athens OH 1013 LLC......740 589-5839
924 E State St Athens (45701) ***(G-769)***
Athens-Hcking Cnty Recycl Ctrs......740 594-5312
5991 Industrial Park Rd Athens (45701) ***(G-770)***
Athletes In Action Sports (HQ)......937 352-1000
651 Taylor Dr Xenia (45385) ***(G-19891)***
Athletic Dept, Oberlin *Also called Oberlin College* ***(G-15514)***
Athletics Dept, Cincinnati *Also called University of Cincinnati* ***(G-4718)***
ATI, Toledo *Also called Abbott Tool Inc* ***(G-17579)***
ATI Aviation Services LLC......216 268-4888
12401 Taft Ave Cleveland (44108) ***(G-5019)***
Atk Space Systems Inc......937 490-4121
1365 Technology Ct Beavercreek (45430) ***(G-1205)***
Atkins & Stang Inc......513 242-8300
1031 Meta Dr Cincinnati (45237) ***(G-2997)***
Atlantic Coastal Trucking......201 438-6500
222 E William St Delaware (43015) ***(G-9953)***
Atlantic Fish & Distrg Co......330 454-1307
430 6th St Se Canton (44702) ***(G-2197)***
Atlantic Food Distributors, Canton *Also called Atlantic Fish & Distrg Co* ***(G-2197)***
Atlantic Foods Corp......513 772-3535
1999 Section Rd Cincinnati (45237) ***(G-2998)***
Atlantic Hospitality & MGT LLC......216 454-5450
26300 Chagrin Blvd Beachwood (44122) ***(G-1031)***
Atlantic Triangle Trucking, Delaware *Also called Atlantic Coastal Trucking* ***(G-9953)***
Atlantis Co Inc (PA)......888 807-3272
105 Ken Mar Indus Pkwy Cleveland (44147) ***(G-5020)***
Atlantis Company, The, Cleveland *Also called Atlantis Co Inc* ***(G-5020)***
Atlapac Corp......614 252-2121
2901 E 4th Ave Ste 5 Columbus (43219) ***(G-6995)***
Atlas Advisors LLC......888 282-0873
1795 S High St Columbus (43207) ***(G-6996)***
Atlas Bolt & Screw Company LLC (HQ)......419 289-6171
1628 Troy Rd Ashland (44805) ***(G-653)***
Atlas Butler Heating & Cooling, Columbus *Also called Atlas Capital Services Inc* ***(G-6997)***
Atlas Capital Services Inc (PA)......614 294-7373
4849 Evanswood Dr Columbus (43229) ***(G-6997)***
Atlas Construction Company......614 475-4705
4672 Friendship Dr Columbus (43230) ***(G-6998)***
Atlas Electrical Construction......440 323-5418
7974 Murray Ridge Rd Elyria (44035) ***(G-10480)***
Atlas Fasteners For Cnstr, Ashland *Also called Atlas Bolt & Screw Company LLC* ***(G-653)***
Atlas Home Moving & Storage......614 445-8831
1570 Integrity Dr E Columbus (43209) ***(G-6999)***
Atlas Industrial Contrs LLC (HQ)......614 841-4500
5275 Sinclair Rd Columbus (43229) ***(G-7000)***
Atlas Industries Inc......419 637-2117
401 Wall St Tiffin (44883) ***(G-17509)***
Atlas Machine and Supply Inc......502 584-7262
4985 Provident Dr West Chester (45246) ***(G-19041)***
Atlas Recycling Inc......800 837-1520
1420 Burton St Se Warren (44484) ***(G-18668)***
Atlas Roofing Company......330 467-7683
4190 E 71st St Cleveland (44105) ***(G-5021)***
Atlas Steel Products Co (PA)......330 425-1600
7990 Bavaria Rd Twinsburg (44087) ***(G-18247)***
Atlas Towing Service......513 451-1854
5675 Glenway Ave Cincinnati (45238) ***(G-2999)***
Atlasbooks, Ashland *Also called Bookmasters Inc* ***(G-658)***
Atm Solutions Inc (PA)......513 742-4900
551 Northland Blvd Cincinnati (45240) ***(G-3000)***
Atomic Credit Union Inc (PA)......740 289-5060
711 Beaver Creek Rd Piketon (45661) ***(G-15971)***
Atos It Solutions and Svcs Inc......513 336-1000
4705 Duke Dr Mason (45040) ***(G-13543)***
Atotech USA Inc......216 398-0550
1000 Harvard Ave Cleveland (44109) ***(G-5022)***
Atria Senior Living Inc......513 923-3711
9191 Round Top Rd Ofc Cincinnati (45251) ***(G-3001)***
Atrium Apparel Corporation......740 966-8200
188 Commerce Blvd Johnstown (43031) ***(G-12195)***
Atrium Buying Corporation......740 966-8200
1010 Jackson Hole Dr # 100 Blacklick (43004) ***(G-1474)***
Atrium Dialysis, Middletown *Also called Beck Dialysis LLC* ***(G-14290)***
Atrium Health System (HQ)......937 499-5606
1 Medical Center Dr Middletown (45005) ***(G-14342)***
Atrium Medical Center......513 420-5013
105 Mcknight Dr Middletown (45044) ***(G-14289)***

Ats Carolina Inc 803 324-9300
425 Enterprise Dr Lewis Center (43035) *(G-12526)*

Ats Group LLC 216 744-5757
5845 Harper Rd Solon (44139) *(G-16824)*

Ats Systems Oregon Inc 541 738-0932
425 Enterprise Dr Lewis Center (43035) *(G-12527)*

Ats Transportation Services, Cincinnati *Also called Advance Trnsp Systems Inc (G-2910)*

Atsg, Wilmington *Also called Air Transport Svcs Group Inc (G-19603)*

ATT, Cleveland *Also called AT&T Corp (G-5017)*

Attentn Web Administrtr Marjon 513 708-9888
3093 N State Route 741 Franklin (45005) *(G-11023)*

Atterro Inc (HQ) 800 938-9675
201 E 4th Ste 800 Cincinnati (45202) *(G-3002)*

Atterro Human Capital Group, Cincinnati *Also called Atterro Inc (G-3002)*

Attevo Inc 216 928-2800
24500 Chagrin Blvd # 300 Beachwood (44122) *(G-1032)*

Attitudes New Inc 330 856-1143
1543 Westview Dr Ne Warren (44483) *(G-18669)*

Attorneys-At-Law, Dayton *Also called Porter Wrght Morris Arthur LLP (G-9699)*

Attractions 740 592-5600
19 N Court St Athens (45701) *(G-771)*

Atwood Lake Park, Mineral City *Also called Muskingum Wtrshed Cnsrvncy Dst (G-14507)*

Atwood Mock Post 459, Burton *Also called American Legion (G-2013)*

Atwood Yacht Club Inc 330 735-2135
2637 Lodge Rd Sw Sherrodsville (44675) *(G-16752)*

Auburn Dairy Products Inc 614 488-2536
2200 Cardigan Ave Columbus (43215) *(G-7001)*

Auction Broadcasting Co LLC 419 872-0872
9797 Fremont Pike Perrysburg (43551) *(G-15833)*

Auction Services Inc 614 497-2000
4700 Groveport Rd Obetz (43207) *(G-15522)*

Audi Willoughby, Mentor *Also called Stoddard Imported Cars Inc (G-14112)*

Audio-Technica US Inc (HQ) 330 686-2600
1221 Commerce Dr Stow (44224) *(G-17191)*

Auditor's Ofiice, Coshocton *Also called City of Coshocton (G-9001)*

Auditors Office, Hamilton *Also called Butler County of Ohio (G-11562)*

Auglaize County Board of Mr/Dd, New Bremen *Also called County of Auglaize (G-14886)*

August Corso Sons Inc 419 626-0765
3404 Milan Rd Sandusky (44870) *(G-16576)*

August Food & Wine LLC 513 421-2020
1214 Vine St Cincinnati (45202) *(G-3003)*

August Groh & Sons Inc 513 821-0090
8832 Reading Rd Cincinnati (45215) *(G-3004)*

Aultcare Corp 330 363-6360
2600 6th St Sw Canton (44710) *(G-2198)*

Aultcare Insurance Company 330 363-6360
2600 6th St Sw Canton (44710) *(G-2199)*

Aultcomp Inc 330 830-4919
2458 Lincoln Way E Massillon (44646) *(G-13664)*

Aultman Health Foundation 330 305-6999
6100 Whipple Ave Nw Canton (44720) *(G-2200)*

Aultman Health Foundation 330 682-3010
832 S Main St Orrville (44667) *(G-15624)*

Aultman Health Foundation 330 875-6050
1925 Williamsburg Way Ne Louisville (44641) *(G-12960)*

Aultman Health Foundation (PA) 330 452-9911
2600 6th St Sw Canton (44710) *(G-2201)*

Aultman Hospital (PA) 330 452-9911
2600 6th St Sw Canton (44710) *(G-2202)*

Aultman Hospital 330 452-9911
2600 6th St Sw Canton (44710) *(G-2203)*

Aultman Hospital 330 363-6262
2600 6th St Sw Canton (44710) *(G-2204)*

Aultman Hospital 330 452-2273
125 Dartmouth Ave Sw Canton (44710) *(G-2205)*

Aultman North Canton Med Group (PA) 330 433-1200
6046 Whipple Ave Nw Canton (44720) *(G-2206)*

Aultman North Inc 330 305-6999
6100 Whipple Ave Nw Canton (44720) *(G-2207)*

Aultman Orrville Hospital, Orrville *Also called Orrville Hospital Foundation (G-15640)*

Auman Mahan & Furry A Legal 937 223-6003
110 N Main St Ste 1000 Dayton (45402) *(G-9243)*

Aunties Attic 740 548-5059
1550 Lewis Center Rd G Lewis Center (43035) *(G-12528)*

Aur Group Financial Credit Un 513 737-0508
1401 Nw Washington Blvd Hamilton (45013) *(G-11558)*

Aurgroup Financial Credit Un 513 942-4422
8811 Holden Blvd Fairfield (45014) *(G-10697)*

Aurora Hotel Partners LLC 330 562-0767
30 Shawnee Trl Aurora (44202) *(G-817)*

Aurora Imaging Company 614 761-1390
344 Cramer Creek Ct Dublin (43017) *(G-10141)*

Aurora Inn Hotel & Event Ctr, Aurora *Also called Aurora Hotel Partners LLC (G-817)*

Aurora Manor Ltd Partnership 330 562-5000
101 S Bissell Rd Aurora (44202) *(G-818)*

Aurora Mnor Spcial Care Centre, Aurora *Also called Aurora Manor Ltd Partnership (G-818)*

Aurora Wholesalers LLC (PA) 440 248-5200
31000 Aurora Rd Solon (44139) *(G-16825)*

Aussiefit I LLC 614 755-4400
5929 E Main St Columbus (43213) *(G-7002)*

Austin Building and Design Inc (HQ) 440 544-2600
6095 Parkland Blvd # 100 Cleveland (44124) *(G-5023)*

Austin Company, The, Cleveland *Also called Austin Building and Design Inc (G-5023)*

Austin Foam Plastics Inc 614 921-0824
2200 International St Columbus (43228) *(G-7003)*

Austin Wods Rehabilitation Ctr, Youngstown *Also called Austin Woods Nursing Center (G-19958)*

Austin Woods Nursing Center 330 792-7681
4780 Kirk Rd Youngstown (44515) *(G-19958)*

Austintown Dairy Inc 330 629-6170
780 Bev Rd Youngstown (44512) *(G-19959)*

Austintown Healthcare Center, Youngstown *Also called Communicare Health Svcs Inc (G-19997)*

Authentic Food LLC 740 369-0377
535 Sunbury Rd Delaware (43015) *(G-9954)*

Auto Aftermarket Concepts 513 942-2535
1031 Redna Ter Cincinnati (45215) *(G-3005)*

Auto Body Mill Run, Columbus *Also called Auto Body North Inc (G-7004)*

Auto Body North Inc (PA) 614 436-3700
8675 N High St Columbus (43235) *(G-7004)*

Auto Center USA Inc 513 683-4900
4544 Kings Water Dr Cincinnati (45249) *(G-3006)*

Auto Concepts Cincinnatti LLC 513 769-4540
3428 Hauck Rd Ste I Cincinnati (45241) *(G-3007)*

Auto Crushers, Canton *Also called Slesnick Iron & Metal Co (G-2479)*

Auto Des Sys Inc 614 488-7984
3518 Riverside Dr Upper Arlington (43221) *(G-18394)*

Auto Plus, Marietta *Also called Ieh Auto Parts LLC (G-13336)*

Auto Warehousing Co Inc 330 824-5149
1950 Hallock Young Warren (44481) *(G-18670)*

Auto Warehousing Co Inc 419 727-1534
4405 Chrysler Dr Toledo (43608) *(G-17603)*

Auto-Owners Insurance Company 937 432-6740
1 Prestige Pl Ste 280 Miamisburg (45342) *(G-14143)*

Auto-Owners Life Insurance Co 419 227-1452
2325 N Cole St Lima (45801) *(G-12604)*

Autobody Supply Company, Columbus *Also called Finishmaster Inc (G-7578)*

Autograph Inc 216 881-1911
4419 Perkins Ave Cleveland (44103) *(G-5024)*

Autograph Foliages, Cleveland *Also called Autograph Inc (G-5024)*

Automated Transaction MGT, Westerville *Also called Continuum Inc (G-19246)*

Automatic Data Processing Inc 216 447-1980
7007 E Pleasant Valley Rd Independence (44131) *(G-12048)*

Automatic Data Processing Inc 614 895-7700
713 Brooksedge Plaza Dr Westerville (43081) *(G-19226)*

Automation & Control Tech Ltd 419 661-6400
28210 Cedar Park Blvd Perrysburg (43551) *(G-15834)*

Automation Tooling Systems, Lewis Center *Also called Ats Carolina Inc (G-12526)*

Automotive Distributors Co Inc (PA) 614 476-1315
2981 Morse Rd Columbus (43231) *(G-7005)*

Automotive Distributors Co Inc 330 785-7290
1329 E Archwood Ave Akron (44306) *(G-82)*

Automotive Distributors Co Inc 216 398-2014
990 Valley Belt Dr Cleveland (44109) *(G-5025)*

Automotive Distributors Whse, Columbus *Also called Automotive Distributors Co Inc (G-7005)*

Automotive Div Of,, Cincinnati *Also called SGS North America Inc (G-4462)*

Automotive Events Inc (PA) 440 356-1383
19111 Detroit Rd Ste 306 Rocky River (44116) *(G-16423)*

Autonation Ford Amherst, Amherst *Also called Ed Mullinax Ford LLC (G-584)*

Autonation Ford East, Wickliffe *Also called Mullinax East LLC (G-19470)*

Autonation Ford North Canton, Canton *Also called Mullinax Ford North Canton Inc (G-2411)*

Autumn, Bedford *Also called Legacy Consultant Pharmacy (G-1288)*

Autumn Aegis Inc 440 282-6768
1130 Tower Blvd Ste A Lorain (44052) *(G-12883)*

Autumn Health Care, Newark *Also called Alpha Nursing Homes Inc (G-15009)*

Autumn Health Care, Coshocton *Also called Alpha Nursing Homes Inc (G-8997)*

Autumn Hills Care Center Inc 330 652-2053
2565 Niles Vienna Rd Niles (44446) *(G-15146)*

Autumn Industries Inc (PA) 330 372-5002
518 Perkins Jones Rd Ne Warren (44483) *(G-18671)*

Autumn Years Nursing Center, Sabina *Also called Earley & Ross Ltd (G-16467)*

Auxiliary Bd Fairview Gen Hosp 216 476-7000
18101 Lorain Ave Cleveland (44111) *(G-5026)*

Auxiliary St Lukes Hospital 419 893-5911
5901 Monclova Rd Maumee (43537) *(G-13759)*

Avalon Foodservice Inc 330 854-4551
1 Avalon Dr Canal Fulton (44614) *(G-2092)*

Avalon Golf & Country Club 330 539-5008
761 Youngstown Kingsvlle Vienna (44473) *(G-18577)*

Avalon Golf and Cntry CLB Inc 330 856-8898
1 American Way Ne Warren (44484) *(G-18672)*

Avalon Holdings Corporation (PA) 330 856-8800
1 American Way Ne Warren (44484) *(G-18673)*

Avalon Inn and Resort, Warren *Also called AIR Management Group LLC (G-18660)*

Avalon Inn Services Inc 330 856-1900
9519 E Market St Warren (44484) *(G-18674)*

A L P H A B E T I C

Avalon Lakes Golf Inc (HQ) 330 856-8898
　1 American Way Ne Warren (44484) *(G-18675)*
Avalon Lakes Pro Shop, Warren Also called Avalon Lakes Golf Inc *(G-18675)*
Avalon Precision Cast Co LLC 216 362-4100
　15583 Brookpark Rd Brookpark (44142) *(G-1891)*
Avalon Precision Metalsmiths, Brookpark Also called Avalon Precision Cast Co
LLC *(G-1891)*
Avalon Resort and Spa LLC 330 856-1900
　9519 E Market St Warren (44484) *(G-18676)*
Avanti Salon, Chesterland Also called Mato Inc *(G-2740)*
Avantia Inc 216 901-9366
　9655 Sweet Valley Dr # 1 Cleveland (44125) *(G-5027)*
Avatar Management Services (PA) 330 963-3900
　8157 Bavaria Dr E Macedonia (44056) *(G-13059)*
Avatar Solutions, Macedonia Also called Avatar Management Services *(G-13059)*
AVENUE AT MACEDONIA, THE, Macedonia Also called Progressive Macedonia
LLC *(G-13080)*
Avery Dennison Corporation 440 534-6000
　8080 Norton Pkwy Mentor (44060) *(G-14020)*
Avery Dennison Materials Group, Mentor Also called Avery Dennison Corporation *(G-14020)*
AVI Food Systems Inc (PA) 330 372-6000
　2590 Elm Rd Ne Warren (44483) *(G-18677)*
AVI Food Systems Inc 740 452-9363
　333 Richards Rd Zanesville (43701) *(G-20279)*
AVI-Spl Employee 937 836-4787
　35 Rockridge Rd Ste B Englewood (45322) *(G-10579)*
Aviation Manufacturing Co Inc 419 435-7448
　901 S Union St Fostoria (44830) *(G-10996)*
Aviation, Department of, Vandalia Also called City of Dayton *(G-18515)*
Avid Technologies Inc 330 487-0770
　2112 Case Pkwy Ste 1 Twinsburg (44087) *(G-18248)*
Avis Administration 937 898-2581
　3300 Valet Dr Vandalia (45377) *(G-18505)*
Avita Health System 419 468-7059
　955 Hosford Rd Galion (44833) *(G-11166)*
Avita Health System (PA) 419 468-4841
　269 Portland Way S Galion (44833) *(G-11167)*
Aviva Metals, Lorain Also called National Bronze Mtls Ohio Inc *(G-12929)*
Avizent, Dublin Also called Frank Gates Service Company *(G-10231)*
Avnet Inc 440 479-3607
　34201 Melinz Pkwy Unit D Eastlake (44095) *(G-10427)*
Avnet Inc 614 865-1400
　2800 Corp Exchange Dr # 160 Columbus (43231) *(G-7006)*
Avnet Inc 440 349-7600
　2000 Auburn Dr Ste 200 Beachwood (44122) *(G-1033)*
Avnet Computers, Eastlake Also called Avnet Inc *(G-10427)*
Avnet Computers, Columbus Also called Avnet Inc *(G-7006)*
Avnet Computers, Beachwood Also called Avnet Inc *(G-1033)*
Avon Lake Animal Care Center, Avon Lake Also called Avon Lake Animal Clinic Inc *(G-909)*
Avon Lake Animal Clinic Inc 440 933-5297
　124 Miller Rd Avon Lake (44012) *(G-909)*
Avon Lake Generating Station, Avon Lake Also called NRG Power Midwest LP *(G-925)*
Avon Lake Sheet Metal Co 440 933-3505
　33574 Pin Oak Pkwy Avon Lake (44012) *(G-910)*
Avon Medical Offices, Avon Also called Kaiser Foundation Hospitals *(G-889)*
Avon Oaks Country Club 440 892-0660
　32300 Detroit Rd Ste A Avon (44011) *(G-863)*
Avon Oaks Nursing Home, Avon Also called R & J Investment Co Inc *(G-902)*
Avon Properties Inc 440 934-6217
　4141 Center Rd Avon (44011) *(G-864)*
Avon Skilled Nursing, Avon Also called Diversicare of Avon LLC *(G-879)*
Avondale Golf Club 440 934-4398
　3111 Moon Rd Avon (44011) *(G-865)*
Avondale Youth Center, Zanesville Also called Muskingum County Adult and CHI *(G-20334)*
AW Faber-Castell Usa Inc 216 643-4660
　9450 Allen Dr Ste B Cleveland (44125) *(G-5028)*
Aw Farrell Son Inc 513 334-0715
　745 Us Route 50 Milford (45150) *(G-14372)*
Awe Hospitality Group LLC 330 888-8836
　9652 N Bedford Rd Macedonia (44056) *(G-13060)*
AWH Holdings Inc 513 241-2614
　125 E 9th St Cincinnati (45202) *(G-3008)*
Awis Designs, Amelia Also called Interphace Phtgrphy Cmmnctions *(G-573)*
Awl Transport Inc 330 899-3444
　4626 State Route 82 Mantua (44255) *(G-13264)*
Awms, Warren Also called American Waste MGT Svcs Inc *(G-18664)*
Awp Inc (PA) 330 677-7401
　4244 Mount Pleasant St Nw # 100 North Canton (44720) *(G-15191)*
Awrs LLC 888 611-2292
　10866 Newmarket Dr Cincinnati (45251) *(G-3009)*
Axa Advisors LLC 513 762-7700
　4000 Smith Rd Ste 300 Cincinnati (45209) *(G-3010)*
Axa Advisors LLC 216 621-7715
　1001 Lakeside Ave E # 1650 Cleveland (44114) *(G-5029)*
Axa Advisors LLC 614 985-3015
　7965 N High St Ste 140 Columbus (43235) *(G-7007)*
Axcess Rcvery Cr Solutions Inc 513 229-6700
　4540 Cooper Rd Ste 305 Cincinnati (45242) *(G-3011)*

Axesspointe Cmnty Hlth Ctr Inc (PA) 330 724-5471
　1400 S Arlington St # 38 Akron (44306) *(G-83)*
Axesspointe Community Hlth Ctr, Akron Also called Axesspointe Cmnty Hlth Ctr Inc *(G-83)*
Axia Consulting 614 675-4050
　1391 W 5th Ave Ste 320 Columbus (43212) *(G-7008)*
Axis Interior Systems Inc (PA) 513 642-0039
　8216 Prnceton Glendale Rd West Chester (45069) *(G-18870)*
Ayers Farms Inc 419 938-7707
　820 State Route 39 Perrysville (44864) *(G-15939)*
Ayers-Sterrett Inc 419 238-5480
　222 N Market St Van Wert (45891) *(G-18473)*
Ayrshire Inc 440 286-9507
　191 Fifth Ave Chardon (44024) *(G-2687)*
Ayrshire Inc 440 992-0743
　1432 E 21st St Ashtabula (44004) *(G-721)*
Aysco Security Consultants Inc 330 733-8183
　4075 Karg Industrial Pkwy B Kent (44240) *(G-12215)*
Azalea Alabama Investment LLC 216 520-1250
　8111 Rockside Rd Ste 200 Cleveland (44125) *(G-5030)*
Azimuth Corporation 937 256-8571
　4027 Colonel Glenn Hwy # 230 Beavercreek Township (45431) *(G-1243)*
Aztec Plumbg, Milford Also called Aztec Plumbing Inc *(G-14373)*
Aztec Plumbing Inc 513 732-3320
　5989 Meijer Dr Ste 8 Milford (45150) *(G-14373)*
Aztec Services Group Inc 513 541-2002
　3814 William P Dooley Byp Cincinnati (45223) *(G-3012)*
B & A, Cuyahoga Falls Also called Barrett & Associates Inc *(G-9073)*
B & B Contrs & Developers Inc 330 270-5020
　2781 Salt Springs Rd Youngstown (44509) *(G-19960)*
B & B Employment Resource LLC 513 370-5542
　260 Northland Blvd # 216 Cincinnati (45246) *(G-3013)*
B & B Industries, Orient Also called Kmj Leasing Ltd *(G-15620)*
B & B Plastics Recyclers Inc 614 409-2880
　3300 Lockbourne Rd Columbus (43207) *(G-7009)*
B & B Roofing Inc 740 772-4759
　150 Cooks Hill Rd Chillicothe (45601) *(G-2757)*
B & B Wrecking & Excvtg Inc 216 429-1700
　4510 E 71st St Ste 6 Cleveland (44105) *(G-5031)*
B & C COMMUNICATIONS, Columbus Also called Comproducts Inc *(G-7344)*
B & D Auto & Towing Inc 440 237-3737
　14290 State Rd Ste 1 North Royalton (44133) *(G-15347)*
B & D Concrete Footers Inc 740 964-2294
　12897 National Rd Sw Etna (43062) *(G-10612)*
B & H Industries Inc 419 485-8373
　14020 Us Highway 20a Montpelier (43543) *(G-14605)*
B & I Hotel Management LLC 330 995-0200
　600 N Aurora Rd Aurora (44202) *(G-819)*
B & J Electrical Company Inc 513 351-7100
　6316 Wiehe Rd Cincinnati (45237) *(G-3014)*
B & L Agency LLC 740 373-8272
　1001 Pike St Ste 4 Marietta (45750) *(G-13314)*
B & L Transport Inc (PA) 866 848-2888
　3149 State Route 39 Millersburg (44654) *(G-14457)*
B & R Railroad Services, Cincinnati Also called R W Godbey Railroad Services *(G-4332)*
B & T Express Inc (PA) 330 549-0000
　400 Miley Rd North Lima (44452) *(G-15265)*
B and D Investment Partnership 937 233-6698
　7650 Waynetowne Blvd Dayton (45424) *(G-9244)*
B C G Systems, Akron Also called Bcg Systems That Work Inc *(G-90)*
B C M, Cleveland Also called Burton Carol Management *(G-5104)*
B D G Wrap-Tite Inc 440 349-5400
　6200 Cochran Rd Solon (44139) *(G-16826)*
B D Transportation Inc 937 773-9280
　9590 Looney Rd Piqua (45356) *(G-15996)*
B F G Federal Credit Union (PA) 330 374-2990
　445 S Main St Ste B Akron (44311) *(G-84)*
B G News 419 372-2601
　214 W Hall Bgsu Bowling Green (43403) *(G-1715)*
B G Trucking & Construction 234 759-3440
　11330 Market St North Lima (44452) *(G-15266)*
B H C Services Inc 216 289-5300
　26250 Euclid Ave Ste 901 Euclid (44132) *(G-10624)*
B I, Cleveland Also called Brennan Industries Inc *(G-5077)*
B S T, London Also called Building Systems Trnsp Co *(G-12861)*
B W Grinding Co 419 923-1376
　15048 County Road 10 3 Lyons (43533) *(G-13056)*
B W S, Akron Also called Battered Womens Shelter *(G-88)*
B&F Capital Markets Inc 216 472-2700
　635 W Lkeside Ave Apt 201 Cleveland (44113) *(G-5032)*
B&N Coal Inc 740 783-3575
　38455 Marietta Rte Dexter City (45727) *(G-10059)*
B-Tek Scales LLC 330 471-8900
　1510 Metric Ave Sw Canton (44706) *(G-2208)*
B2b Power Partners 614 309-6964
　5647 Summer Blvd Galena (43021) *(G-11155)*
Babbage Simmel, Columbus Also called Babbage-Simmel & Assoc Inc *(G-7010)*
Babbage-Simmel & Assoc Inc 614 481-6555
　2780 Airport Dr Ste 160 Columbus (43219) *(G-7010)*
Babcock & Wilcox Cnstr Co Inc (HQ) 330 860-6301
　74 Robinson Ave Barberton (44203) *(G-943)*

(G-0000) Company's Geographic Section entry number

Babcock & Wilcox Company (HQ) 330 753-4511
  20 S Van Buren Ave Barberton (44203) *(G-944)*
Babcox Media Inc 330 670-1234
  3550 Embassy Pkwy Akron (44333) *(G-85)*
Babyphat, Blue Ash Also called Unirush LLC *(G-1674)*
Bachmans Inc 513 943-5300
  4058 Clough Woods Dr Batavia (45103) *(G-983)*
Back In Black Co 419 425-5555
  2100 Fostoria Ave Findlay (45840) *(G-10866)*
Background Information Svcs, Independence Also called Employeescreeniq Inc *(G-12070)*
Backoffice Associates LLC 419 660-4600
  16 Executive Dr Ste 200 Norwalk (44857) *(G-15425)*
Bag, The, Lancaster Also called Dispatch Consumer Services *(G-12389)*
Bag-Pack Inc 513 346-3900
  9486 Sutton Pl West Chester (45011) *(G-18871)*
Bagel Place Inc (PA) 419 885-1000
  3715 King Rd Toledo (43617) *(G-17604)*
Bagpack, West Chester Also called Bag-Pack Inc *(G-18871)*
Bailey & Long Inc 614 937-9435
  101 E Town St Ste 115 Columbus (43215) *(G-7011)*
Bailey Associates 614 760-7752
  6836 Caine Rd Columbus (43235) *(G-7012)*
Bailey Cavalieri LLC (PA) 614 221-3258
  10 W Broad St Ste 2100 Columbus (43215) *(G-7013)*
Baillie Lumber Co LP 419 462-2000
  3953 County Road 51 Galion (44833) *(G-11168)*
Bakemark USA LLC 513 870-0880
  9401 Le Saint Dr West Chester (45014) *(G-18872)*
Baker & Hostetler LLP 216 861-7587
  127 Public Sq Ste 2000 Cleveland (44114) *(G-5033)*
Baker & Hostetler LLP (PA) 216 621-0200
  127 Public Sq Ste 2000 Cleveland (44114) *(G-5034)*
Baker & Hostetler LLP 614 228-1541
  65 E State St Ste 2100 Columbus (43215) *(G-7014)*
Baker & Hostetler LLP 513 929-3400
  312 Walnut St Ste 3200 Cincinnati (45202) *(G-3015)*
Baker & Sons Equipment Co 740 567-3317
  45381 State Route 145 Lewisville (43754) *(G-12573)*
Baker Bnngson Rlty Auctioneers 419 547-7777
  1570 W Mcpherson Hwy Clyde (43410) *(G-6740)*
Baker Concrete Cnstr Inc (PA) 513 539-4000
  900 N Garver Rd Monroe (45050) *(G-14561)*
Baker Dblkar Beck Wley Mathews 330 499-6000
  400 S Main St Canton (44720) *(G-2209)*
Baker Dublikar, Canton Also called Baker Dblkar Beck Wley Mathews *(G-2209)*
Baker Equipment and Mtls Ltd 513 422-6697
  990 N Main St Monroe (45050) *(G-14562)*
Baker Vehicle Systems Inc 330 467-2250
  9035 Freeway Dr Macedonia (44056) *(G-13061)*
Bakers Cllsion Repr Specialist 419 524-1350
  595 5th Ave Mansfield (44905) *(G-13138)*
Bakerwell Inc 614 898-7590
  6295 Maxtown Rd Ste 300 Westerville (43082) *(G-19146)*
Balanced Care Corporation 330 908-1166
  997 W Aurora Rd Northfield (44067) *(G-15373)*
Balanced Care Corporation 937 372-7205
  60 Paceline Cir Xenia (45385) *(G-19892)*
Balancing Company Inc (PA) 937 898-9111
  898 Center Dr Vandalia (45377) *(G-18506)*
Baldwin International, Solon Also called F I L US Inc *(G-16847)*
Baldwin Wallace University 440 826-2285
  136 E Bagley Rd Berea (44017) *(G-1413)*
Ball Bounce and Sport Inc 419 759-3838
  211 W Geneva St Dunkirk (45836) *(G-10384)*
Ball Bounce and Sport Inc 614 662-5381
  3275 Alum Creek Dr Columbus (43207) *(G-7015)*
Ball Bounce and Sport Inc (PA) 419 289-9310
  1 Hedstrom Dr Ashland (44805) *(G-654)*
Ball Bounce and Sport Inc 419 289-9310
  100 Hedstrom Dr Ashland (44805) *(G-655)*
Ballas Egg Products Corp 614 453-0386
  40 N 2nd St Zanesville (43701) *(G-20280)*
Ballet Metropolitan Inc 614 229-4860
  322 Mount Vernon Ave Columbus (43215) *(G-7016)*
BALLETMET COLUMBUS, Columbus Also called Ballet Metropolitan Inc *(G-7016)*
Ballreich Bros Inc 419 447-1814
  186 Ohio Ave Tiffin (44883) *(G-17510)*
Ballreichs Potato Chips Snacks, Tiffin Also called Ballreich Bros Inc *(G-17510)*
Balog Steines Hendricks & Manc 330 744-4401
  15 Central Sq Ste 300 Youngstown (44503) *(G-19961)*
Baltic Health Care Corp 330 897-4311
  130 Buena Vista St Baltic (43804) *(G-933)*
Bama Masonry Inc 440 834-4175
  14379 Aquilla Rd Burton (44021) *(G-2014)*
Banc Amer Prctice Slutions Inc 614 794-8247
  600 N Cleveland Ave # 300 Westerville (43082) *(G-19147)*
Banc Certified Merch Svcs LLC 614 850-2740
  5006 Cemetery Rd Hilliard (43026) *(G-11744)*
Banc One Services Corporation (HQ) 614 248-5800
  1111 Polaris Pkwy Ste B3 Columbus (43240) *(G-6800)*
Bank England Mortgage Corp 440 327-5626
  37723 Center Ridge Rd North Ridgeville (44039) *(G-15321)*

Bank of America 614 882-4319
  600 N Cleveland Ave # 300 Westerville (43082) *(G-19148)*
Bankers Life & Casualty Co 614 987-0590
  8740 Orion Pl Ste 204 Columbus (43240) *(G-6801)*
Bannockburn Global Forex LLC 513 386-7400
  312 Walnut St Ste 3580 Cincinnati (45202) *(G-3016)*
Banquets Unlimited 859 689-4000
  1320 Ethan Ave Cincinnati (45225) *(G-3017)*
Bansal Construction Inc 513 874-5410
  3263 Homeward Way Ste A Fairfield (45014) *(G-10698)*
Banta Electrical Contrs Inc 513 353-4446
  5701 Hamilton Cleves Rd Cleves (45002) *(G-6725)*
Bantam Leasing Inc 513 734-6696
  2291 State Route 125 Amelia (45102) *(G-570)*
Baptist Home and Center 513 662-5880
  2373 Harrison Ave Cincinnati (45211) *(G-3018)*
Bar 145, Columbus Also called Rcwc Col Inc *(G-8493)*
Barb Linden 440 233-1068
  1800 Livingston Ave # 200 Lorain (44052) *(G-12884)*
Barbara Gheens Painting Inc 740 949-0405
  50550 Rainbow Ridge Rd Long Bottom (45743) *(G-12877)*
Barbara S Desalvo Inc 513 729-2111
  800 Compton Rd Unit 18 Cincinnati (45231) *(G-3019)*
Barberton Area Family Practice 330 615-3205
  155 5th St Ne Barberton (44203) *(G-945)*
Barberton Healthcare Group LLC 330 615-3717
  540 Great Oaks Trl Wadsworth (44281) *(G-18591)*
Barberton Jaycees 330 745-3733
  541 W Tuscarawas Ave # 104 Barberton (44203) *(G-946)*
Barberton Laundry & Cleaning 330 825-6911
  1050 Northview Ave Barberton (44203) *(G-947)*
Barberton Tree Service Inc 330 848-2344
  3307 Clark Mill Rd Norton (44203) *(G-15417)*
Barbicas Construction Co 330 733-9101
  124 Darrow Rd Ste 1 Akron (44305) *(G-86)*
Barbour Publishing Inc (PA) 740 922-1321
  1810 Barbour Dr Se Uhrichsville (44683) *(G-18339)*
Barbs Graffiti Inc 216 881-5550
  3111 Carnegie Ave Cleveland (44115) *(G-5035)*
Barbs Graffiti Inc (PA) 216 881-5550
  3111 Carnegie Ave Cleveland (44115) *(G-5036)*
Barcus Company Inc 614 451-9000
  1601 Bethel Rd Ste 100 Columbus (43220) *(G-7017)*
Barefoot LLC 513 861-3668
  700 W Pete Rose Way Cincinnati (45203) *(G-3020)*
Bargain Hunter, Millersburg Also called Graphic Publications Inc *(G-14474)*
Baring Distributors, Cleveland Also called Bdi Inc *(G-5045)*
Barkan & Neff Co Lpa (PA) 614 221-4221
  250 E Broad St Fl 10 Columbus (43215) *(G-7018)*
Barkett Fruit Co Inc (PA) 330 364-6645
  1213 E 3rd St Dover (44622) *(G-10065)*
Barkley of Cleveland LLC 440 248-2275
  27349 Miles Rd Chagrin Falls (44022) *(G-2639)*
Barkley Pet Hotel & Day Spa, Chagrin Falls Also called Barkley of Cleveland LLC *(G-2639)*
Barnes Dennig & Co Ltd (PA) 513 241-8313
  150 E 4th St Ste 300 Cincinnati (45202) *(G-3021)*
Barnes Cope, Dayton Also called Mall Realty Inc *(G-9582)*
Barnes Group Inc 419 891-9292
  370 W Dussel Dr Ste A Maumee (43537) *(G-13760)*
Barnes Nursery Inc (PA) 800 421-8722
  3511 Cleveland Rd W Huron (44839) *(G-12021)*
Barnes Wendling Cpas Inc (PA) 216 566-9000
  1350 Euclid Ave Ste 1400 Cleveland (44115) *(G-5037)*
Barnesville Healthcare Rehab 740 425-3648
  400 Carrie Ave Barnesville (43713) *(G-974)*
Barnesville Hospital Assn Inc (PA) 740 425-3941
  639 W Main St Barnesville (43713) *(G-975)*
Barnesville Live Stock Ofc, Barnesville Also called Barnesville Livestock Sales Co *(G-976)*
Barnesville Livestock Sales Co 740 425-3611
  315 S Gardner St Barnesville (43713) *(G-976)*
Barnets Inc 937 452-3275
  1619 Barnetts Mill Rd Camden (45311) *(G-2088)*
Barnett Associates Inc 516 877-2860
  3455 Mill Run Dr Ste 100 Hilliard (43026) *(G-11745)*
Barr & Prevost, A Jmt Division, Columbus Also called Johnson Mirmiran Thompson Inc *(G-7863)*
Barr Engineering Incorporated (PA) 614 714-0299
  2800 Corp Exchange Dr # 240 Columbus (43231) *(G-7019)*
Barrett & Associates Inc (PA) 330 928-2323
  1060 Graham Rd Ste C Cuyahoga Falls (44224) *(G-9073)*
Barrett Center For Cancer Prev 513 558-3200
  234 Goodman St Cincinnati (45219) *(G-3022)*
Barrett Paving Materials Inc 513 271-6200
  3751 Commerce Dr Middletown (45005) *(G-14343)*
Barrington Dialysis LLC 740 346-2740
  1799 Sinclair Ave Ste 2 Steubenville (43953) *(G-17140)*
Barrington Elem School Pto 614 487-5180
  1780 Barrington Rd Upper Arlington (43221) *(G-18395)*
Barrington Golf Club, Aurora Also called Breezy Point Ltd Partnership *(G-822)*
Barrington Golf Club Inc (PA) 330 995-0600
  350 N Aurora Rd Aurora (44202) *(G-820)*

Barrington Golf Club Inc......330 995-0821
680 N Aurora Rd Aurora (44202) ***(G-821)***
Barrington Toledo LLC......419 535-0024
300 S Byrne Rd Toledo (43615) ***(G-17605)***
Barristers of Ohio LLC......330 898-5600
223 Niles Cortland Rd Se # 1 Warren (44484) ***(G-18678)***
Barry Bagel's Place, Toledo *Also called Bagel Place Inc* ***(G-17604)***
Bartha Audio Visual, Columbus *Also called Bkg Holdings LLC* ***(G-7042)***
Bartlett & Co LLC......513 621-4612
600 Vine St Ste 2100 Cincinnati (45202) ***(G-3023)***
Bartley Ambulance, Minerva *Also called C C & S Ambulance Service Inc* ***(G-14516)***
Bartram & Sons Groceries......740 532-5216
2407 S 6th St Ironton (45638) ***(G-12145)***
Bartram Groceries, Ironton *Also called Bartram & Sons Groceries* ***(G-12145)***
Baseline Consulting LLC......440 336-5382
21298 Endsley Ave Cleveland (44116) ***(G-5038)***
Basement Systems Ohio Inc......330 423-4430
8295 Darrow Rd Twinsburg (44087) ***(G-18249)***
BASF Catalysts LLC......216 360-5005
23800 Mercantile Rd Cleveland (44122) ***(G-5039)***
Basic Drugs Inc......937 898-4010
300 Corporate Center Dr Vandalia (45377) ***(G-18507)***
Basic Vitamins, Vandalia *Also called Basic Drugs Inc* ***(G-18507)***
Basin Dialysis LLC......937 643-2337
3050 S Dixie Dr Kettering (45409) ***(G-12291)***
Basinger Lfe Enhncmnt Sprt Svc (PA)......614 557-5461
941 E 5th St Marysville (43040) ***(G-13484)***
Basista & Associates, Cleveland *Also called Profit Recovery of Ohio* ***(G-6240)***
Basista Furniture Inc......216 398-5900
5340 Brookpark Rd Cleveland (44134) ***(G-5040)***
Basol Maintenance Service Inc......419 422-0946
318 W Sundunsky St Findlay (45840) ***(G-10867)***
Bass Lake Inn, Chardon *Also called Bass Lake Tavern Inc* ***(G-2688)***
Bass Lake Tavern Inc......440 285-3100
426 South St Chardon (44024) ***(G-2688)***
Bass Security Services Inc......216 755-1200
26701 Richmond Rd Bedford Heights (44146) ***(G-1317)***
Bastin Home Inc......513 734-2662
656 W Plane St Bethel (45106) ***(G-1452)***
Batavia Nrsing Cnvalescent Inn, Batavia *Also called Carington Health Systems* ***(G-985)***
Batch Labs Inc......216 901-9366
9655 Sweet Valley Dr # 1 Cleveland (44125) ***(G-5041)***
Bates Bros Amusement Co......740 266-2950
1506 Fernwood Rd Wintersville (43953) ***(G-19668)***
Bates Metal Products Inc......740 498-8371
403 E Mn St Port Washington (43837) ***(G-16121)***
Bath Fitter, Dayton *Also called Bathroom Alternatives Inc* ***(G-9245)***
Bath Manor Limited Partnership......330 836-1006
2330 Smith Rd Akron (44333) ***(G-87)***
BATH MANOR SPECIAL CARE CENTRE, Akron *Also called Bath Manor Limited Partnership* ***(G-87)***
Bathroom Alternatives Inc......937 434-1984
85 Westpark Rd Dayton (45459) ***(G-9245)***
Battelle Memorial Institute (PA)......614 424-6424
505 King Ave Columbus (43201) ***(G-7020)***
Battelle Memorial Institute......937 258-6717
5100 Springfield St Beavercreek (45431) ***(G-1129)***
Battelle Memorial Institute......614 424-5435
Hc 142 West Jefferson (43162) ***(G-19104)***
Battelle Memorial Institute......614 424-5435
1425 State Route 142 Ne West Jefferson (43162) ***(G-19105)***
Battelle W Jfferson Operations, West Jefferson *Also called Battelle Memorial Institute* ***(G-19105)***
Battered Womens Shelter......330 723-3900
120 W Washington St 3e1 Medina (44256) ***(G-13912)***
Battered Womens Shelter (PA)......330 374-0740
974 E Market St Akron (44305) ***(G-88)***
Battle Bullying Hotline Inc......216 731-1976
3185 Warren Rd Cleveland (44111) ***(G-5042)***
Bauer Corporation (PA)......800 321-4760
2540 Progress Dr Wooster (44691) ***(G-19689)***
Bauer Ladder, Wooster *Also called Bauer Corporation* ***(G-19689)***
Bauer Lawn Maintenance Inc......419 893-5296
6341 Monclova Rd Maumee (43537) ***(G-13761)***
Baum USA, Sidney *Also called Heidelberg USA Inc* ***(G-16782)***
Bauman Chrysler Jeep Dodge......419 332-8291
2577 W State St Fremont (43420) ***(G-11059)***
Bauman Orchards Inc......330 925-6861
161 Rittman Ave Rittman (44270) ***(G-16404)***
Baumfolder Corporation......937 492-1281
1660 Campbell Rd Sidney (45365) ***(G-16760)***
Baur Leo Century 21 Realty......440 585-2300
32801 Vine St Ste D Willowick (44095) ***(G-19596)***
Bavan & Associates......330 650-0088
10360 Northfield Rd Northfield (44067) ***(G-15374)***
Baxter Burial Vault Service......513 641-1010
909 E Ross Ave Cincinnati (45217) ***(G-3024)***
Baxter Hodell Donnelly Preston (PA)......513 271-1634
302 W 3rd St Ste 500 Cincinnati (45202) ***(G-3025)***
Baxter-Wilbert Burial Vault, Cincinnati *Also called Baxter Burial Vault Service* ***(G-3024)***
Bay Furnace Sheet Metal Co......440 871-3777
24530 Sperry Dr Westlake (44145) ***(G-19320)***
Bay Heating & Air Conditioning, Westlake *Also called Bay Furnace Sheet Metal Co* ***(G-19320)***
Bay Mechanical & Elec Corp......440 282-6816
2221 W Park Dr Lorain (44053) ***(G-12885)***
Bay Park Community Hospital (HQ)......567 585-9600
100 Madison Ave Toledo (43604) ***(G-17606)***
Bay State Gas Company......614 460-4292
200 Civic Center Dr Columbus (43215) ***(G-7021)***
Bay Village City School Dst......440 617-7330
28727 Wolf Rd Cleveland (44140) ***(G-5043)***
Bay Village Montessori Inc......440 871-8773
28370 Bassett Rd Westlake (44145) ***(G-19321)***
Bayer & Becker Inc......513 492-7297
6900 Tylersville Rd Ste A Mason (45040) ***(G-13544)***
Bayer & Becker Inc (PA)......513 492-7401
6900 Tylersville Rd Ste A Mason (45040) ***(G-13545)***
Bayer Heritage Federal Cr Un......740 929-2015
1111 O Neill Dr Hebron (43025) ***(G-11710)***
Bayes Inc......419 661-3933
7414 Ponderosa Rd Perrysburg (43551) ***(G-15835)***
Bayless Pathmark Inc......440 274-2494
19250 Bagley Rd Ste 101 Cleveland (44130) ***(G-5044)***
Bayloff Stmped Pdts Knsman Inc......330 876-4511
8091 State Route 5 Kinsman (44428) ***(G-12317)***
Baymont Inn & Suites, Maumee *Also called Sar Biren* ***(G-13848)***
Bayshore Counseling Svc Inc (PA)......419 626-9156
1634 Sycamore Line Sandusky (44870) ***(G-16577)***
Bayshore Obgyn, Sandusky *Also called Northern Ohio Med Spclists LLC* ***(G-16630)***
Bayview Retirees Golf Course......419 726-8081
3900 N Summit St Toledo (43611) ***(G-17607)***
Bazell Oil Co Inc......740 385-5420
14371 State Route 328 Logan (43138) ***(G-12831)***
BBC&m Engineering Inc (PA)......614 793-2226
6190 Enterprise Ct Dublin (43016) ***(G-10142)***
BBDO Worldwide Inc......513 861-3668
700 W Pete Rose Way Cincinnati (45203) ***(G-3026)***
Bbs & Associates Inc......330 665-5227
130 Springside Dr Ste 200 Akron (44333) ***(G-89)***
Bbs Professional Corporation (HQ)......614 888-3100
1103 Schrock Rd Ste 400 Columbus (43229) ***(G-7022)***
Bbt Fleet Services LLC......419 462-7722
549 Russell Rd Mansfield (44903) ***(G-13139)***
Bcbd, West Chester *Also called Cameo Solutions Inc* ***(G-18880)***
Bccp, Chillicothe *Also called Southern Ohio Wns Cancer Prj* ***(G-2828)***
Bcg Systems That Work Inc......330 864-4816
1735 Merriman Rd Ste 3000 Akron (44313) ***(G-90)***
Bcrta, Hamilton *Also called Butler Cnty Rgional Trnst Auth* ***(G-11566)***
BCU Electric Inc......419 281-8944
1019 Us Highway 250 N Ashland (44805) ***(G-656)***
Bd Oil Gathering Corp......740 374-9355
649 Mitchells Ln Marietta (45750) ***(G-13315)***
Bdi Inc (PA)......216 642-9100
8000 Hub Pkwy Cleveland (44125) ***(G-5045)***
Bdi-USA, Cleveland *Also called Bearing Distributors Inc* ***(G-5048)***
Bdo Usa LLP......614 488-3126
300 Spruce St Ste 100 Columbus (43215) ***(G-7023)***
Bdo Usa LLP......513 592-2400
221 E 4th St Ste 2600 Cincinnati (45202) ***(G-3027)***
Bdo Usa LLP......216 325-1700
1422 Euclid Ave Ste 1500 Cleveland (44115) ***(G-5046)***
Bdo Usa LLP......330 668-9696
301 Springside Dr Akron (44333) ***(G-91)***
BDS Inc (PA)......513 921-8441
3500 Southside Ave Cincinnati (45204) ***(G-3028)***
BDS Packaging Inc......937 643-0530
3155 Elbee Rd Ste 201 Moraine (45439) ***(G-14624)***
Beach Golf Course, Arcanum *Also called Mikesell Transportation Broker* ***(G-625)***
Beachwood Board of Education, Beachwood *Also called Beachwood City Schools* ***(G-1034)***
Beachwood City Schools......216 464-6609
23757 Commerce Park Cleveland (44122) ***(G-5047)***
Beachwood City Schools......216 464-2600
24601 Fairmount Blvd Beachwood (44122) ***(G-1034)***
Beachwood Nrsing Halthcare Ctr, Beachwood *Also called Ezra Health Care Inc* ***(G-1056)***
Beachwood Prof Fire Fighters C......216 292-1968
P.O. Box 221250 Beachwood (44122) ***(G-1035)***
Beacon Company (PA)......330 733-8322
2350 Gilchrist Rd Akron (44305) ***(G-92)***
Beacon Electric Company......513 851-0711
7815 Redsky Dr Cincinnati (45249) ***(G-3029)***
Beacon Electrical Contractors, Cincinnati *Also called Beacon Electric Company* ***(G-3029)***
Beacon Health......440 354-9924
9220 Mentor Ave Mentor (44060) ***(G-14021)***
Beacon House, The, Saint Clairsville *Also called Zandex Inc* ***(G-16512)***
Beacon of Light Ltd......419 531-9060
242 S Reynolds Rd Ste A Toledo (43615) ***(G-17608)***
Beacon of Light Health Agency, Toledo *Also called Beacon of Light Ltd* ***(G-17608)***
Beacon Point Rehab, Uhrichsville *Also called Uhrichsville Health Care Ctr* ***(G-18346)***

1052 2019 Harris Ohio Services Directory (G-0000) Company's Geographic Section entry number

Beacon Sales Acquisition Inc......................330 425-3359
  2440 Edison Blvd Twinsburg (44087) **(G-18250)**

Beall Rose Crtif Pub Accntants, Dublin *Also called REA & Associates Inc (G-10319)*

Bear Communications Inc..........................216 642-1670
  900 Resource Dr Ste 8 Independence (44131) **(G-12049)**

Bearing Distributors Inc (HQ)...................216 642-9100
  8000 Hub Pkwy Cleveland (44125) **(G-5048)**

Bearing Technologies Ltd (PA)....................440 937-4770
  1141 Jaycox Rd Avon (44011) **(G-866)**

Beary Land, Piqua *Also called Council On Rur Svc Prgrams Inc (G-16002)*

Beatitude House..440 992-0265
  3404 Lake Ave Ashtabula (44004) **(G-722)**

Beauty Bar LLC..419 537-5400
  2919 W Central Ave Toledo (43606) **(G-17609)**

Beauty Systems Group, Greenville *Also called Sally Beauty Supply LLC (G-11394)*

Beaver Clinic, Waverly *Also called Community Action Comm Pike CNT (G-18817)*

Beaver Constructors Inc.............................330 478-2151
  2000 Beaver Place Ave Sw Canton (44706) **(G-2210)**

Beaver-Vu Bowl..937 426-6771
  1238 N Fairfield Rd Beavercreek (45432) **(G-1130)**

Beavercreek Church of Nazarene...................937 426-0079
  1850 N Fairfield Rd Beavercreek (45432) **(G-1131)**

Beavercreek Health Park, Beavercreek *Also called Greene Memorial Hospital Inc (G-1154)*

Beavercreek Medical Center........................937 558-3000
  2510 Commons Blvd Ste 120 Beavercreek (45431) **(G-1132)**

Beavercreek Medical Center........................937 558-3000
  2510 Commons Blvd Ste 120 Beavercreek (45431) **(G-1133)**

Beavercreek YMCA...................................937 426-9622
  111 W 1st St Ste 207 Dayton (45402) **(G-9246)**

Beavercreek YMCA Sch's Out I, Dayton *Also called Young Mens Christian Assoc (G-9894)*

Beaverdam Fleet Services Inc.....................419 643-8880
  424 E Main St Beaverdam (45808) **(G-1266)**

Becdel Controls Incorporated.....................330 652-1386
  1869 Warren Ave Niles (44446) **(G-15147)**

Becdir Construction Company.......................330 547-2134
  15764 W Akron Canfield Rd Berlin Center (44401) **(G-1449)**

Beck Center For Arts................................216 521-2540
  17801 Detroit Ave Cleveland (44107) **(G-5049)**

Beck Company...216 883-0909
  10701 Broadway Ave Cleveland (44125) **(G-5050)**

Beck Dialysis LLC....................................513 422-6879
  4421 Roosevelt Blvd Ste D Middletown (45044) **(G-14290)**

Becker & Becker, Mason *Also called Bayer & Becker Inc (G-13544)*

Becker Construction Inc............................937 859-8308
  525 Gargrave Rd Dayton (45449) **(G-9247)**

Becker Electric Supply, Dayton *Also called John A Becker Co (G-9527)*

Becker Electric Supply, Cincinnati *Also called John A Becker Co (G-3822)*

Becker Electric Supply, Columbus *Also called John A Becker Co (G-7861)*

Becker Pumps Corporation..........................330 928-9966
  100 E Ascot Ln Cuyahoga Falls (44223) **(G-9074)**

Beckett House, New Concord *Also called Zandex Inc (G-14905)*

Beckett House At New Concord, New Concord *Also called Zandex Health Care Corporation (G-14906)*

Beckett Ridge Country Club.........................513 874-2710
  5595 Beckett Ridge Blvd # 2 West Chester (45069) **(G-18873)**

Beckett Springs LLC (PA)...........................513 942-9500
  8614 Shepherd Farm Dr West Chester (45069) **(G-18874)**

Beckett Springs Hospital, West Chester *Also called Beckett Springs LLC (G-18874)*

Beckjord Power Station, New Richmond *Also called Duke Energy Ohio Inc (G-14994)*

Beco Legal Systems, Cincinnati *Also called Business Equipment Co Inc (G-3096)*

Bedford Heights City Waste 440 439-5343
  25301 Solon Rd Bedford (44146) **(G-1270)**

Bedford Heights City Waste Wtr, Bedford *Also called Bedford Heights City Waste (G-1270)*

Bedford Heights Health Center, Bedford Heights *Also called Planned Prenthood Greater Ohio (G-1324)*

Bedford Medical Offices, Brooklyn Heights *Also called Kaiser Foundation Hospitals (G-1873)*

Bedford Township......................................740 992-6617
  Mulburry Heights Stn 11 Pomeroy (45769) **(G-16093)**

Bedford Township......................................740 992-2117
  175 Race St Middleport (45760) **(G-14280)**

Beds N Stuff, Grove City *Also called Waterbeds n Stuff Inc (G-11483)*

Beech Acres Parenting Center (PA).................513 231-6630
  6881 Beechmont Ave Cincinnati (45230) **(G-3030)**

Beech Acres Park, Cincinnati *Also called Anderson Township Park Dst (G-2963)*

Beech Acres Thrptic Fster Care, Cincinnati *Also called Beech Acres Parenting Center (G-3030)*

Beecher Carlson Insur Svcs LLC...................330 726-8177
  7600 Market St Youngstown (44512) **(G-19962)**

Beechmont Inc.......................................216 831-9100
  29600 Chagrin Blvd Cleveland (44122) **(G-5051)**

Beechmont Country Club, Cleveland *Also called Beechmont Inc (G-5051)*

Beechmont Ford Inc (PA)...........................513 752-6611
  600 Ohio Pike Cincinnati (45245) **(G-2842)**

Beechmont Motors Inc (PA).........................513 388-3883
  8639 Beechmont Ave Cincinnati (45255) **(G-3031)**

Beechmont Pet Hospital Inc........................513 232-0300
  6400 Salem Rd Cincinnati (45230) **(G-3032)**

Beechmont Porsche, Cincinnati *Also called Beechmont Motors Inc (G-3031)*

Beechmont Racquet and Fitness, Cincinnati *Also called Beechmont Racquet Club Inc (G-3033)*

Beechmont Racquet Club Inc.......................513 528-5700
  435 Ohio Pike Cincinnati (45255) **(G-3033)**

Beechmont Toyota Inc...............................513 388-3800
  8667 Beechmont Ave Cincinnati (45255) **(G-3034)**

Beechwold Veterinary Hospital (PA)...............614 268-8666
  4590 Indianola Ave Columbus (43214) **(G-7024)**

Beechwold Veterinary Hospital.....................614 766-1222
  6924 Riverside Dr Dublin (43017) **(G-10143)**

Beechwood Home......................................513 321-9294
  2140 Pogue Ave Cincinnati (45208) **(G-3035)**

Beechwood Terrace Care Ctr Inc...................513 578-6200
  8700 Moran Rd Cincinnati (45244) **(G-3036)**

Beeghly Oaks Center For Rehabi, Boardman *Also called Beeghly Oaks Operating LLC (G-1696)*

Beeghly Oaks Operating LLC.......................330 884-2300
  6505 Market St Bldg D Boardman (44512) **(G-1696)**

Beeghly Oaks Skilled, Columbus *Also called V Vrable Inc (G-8839)*

Beem Construction Inc..............................937 693-3176
  225 S Mill St Botkins (45306) **(G-1707)**

Beerco Distributing Co, Fostoria *Also called Hanson Distributing Co Inc (G-11004)*

Behal Sampson Dietz Inc...........................614 464-1933
  990 W 3rd Ave Columbus (43212) **(G-7025)**

Behavioral Treatments...............................614 558-1968
  5275 Norwich St Hilliard (43026) **(G-11746)**

Behavorial Healthcare (PA)..........................740 522-8477
  65 Messimer Dr Newark (43055) **(G-15013)**

Behavral Cnnctions WD Cnty Inc (PA)..............419 352-5387
  280 S Main St Bowling Green (43402) **(G-1716)**

Behavral Cnnctions WD Cnty Inc....................419 872-2419
  27072 Carronade Dr Ste A Perrysburg (43551) **(G-15836)**

Behavral Cnnctions WD Cnty Inc....................419 352-5387
  320 W Gypsy Lane Rd Ste A Bowling Green (43402) **(G-1717)**

Behavral Cnnctions WD Cnty Inc....................419 352-5387
  1010 N Prospect St Bowling Green (43402) **(G-1718)**

Beheydts Auto Wrecking.............................330 658-6109
  15475 Serfass Rd Doylestown (44230) **(G-10108)**

Beiersdorf Inc...513 682-7300
  5232 E Provident Dr West Chester (45246) **(G-19042)**

Bekins Van Lines, Cincinnati *Also called Thoman Weil Moving & Stor Co (G-4601)*

Bel Air Care Center..................................330 821-3939
  2350 Cherry Ave Alliance (44601) **(G-518)**

Bel-Park Anesthesia..................................330 480-3658
  1044 Belmont Ave Youngstown (44504) **(G-19963)**

Bel-Wood Country Club Inc.........................513 899-3361
  5873 Ludlum Rd Morrow (45152) **(G-14714)**

Belcan LLC..513 985-7777
  10200 Anderson Way Blue Ash (45242) **(G-1509)**

Belcan LLC..513 645-1509
  9100 Centre Pointe Dr West Chester (45069) **(G-18875)**

Belcan LLC (PA).....................................513 891-0972
  10200 Anderson Way Blue Ash (45242) **(G-1510)**

Belcan LLC..513 217-4562
  4490 Marie Dr Middletown (45044) **(G-14291)**

Belcan LLC..740 393-8888
  105 N Sandusky St Mount Vernon (43050) **(G-14749)**

Belcan LLC..513 891-0972
  32125 Solon Rd Ste 150 Solon (44139) **(G-16827)**

Belcan Corporation..................................513 277-3100
  7785 E Kemper Rd Cincinnati (45249) **(G-3037)**

Belcan Corporation..................................614 224-6080
  519 S High St Columbus (43215) **(G-7026)**

Belcan Engineering Group LLC (HQ)...............513 891-0972
  10200 Anderson Way Blue Ash (45242) **(G-1511)**

Belcan Engineering Services, Mount Vernon *Also called Belcan LLC (G-14749)*

Belcan Engineering Services, Cincinnati *Also called Belcan Corporation (G-3037)*

Belcan Staffing Services, Dayton *Also called Belcan Svcs Group Ltd Partnr (G-9248)*

Belcan Staffing Solutions, Middletown *Also called Belcan LLC (G-14291)*

Belcan Staffing Solutions, Columbus *Also called Belcan Corporation (G-7026)*

Belcan Svcs Group Ltd Partnr......................937 586-5053
  832 S Ludlow St Ste 1 Dayton (45402) **(G-9248)**

Belcan Svcs Group Ltd Partnr (HQ)................513 891-0972
  10200 Anderson Way Blue Ash (45242) **(G-1512)**

Belcan Svcs Group Ltd Partnr......................937 859-8880
  3494 Technical Dr Miamisburg (45342) **(G-14144)**

Belcan Techservices, Miamisburg *Also called Belcan Svcs Group Ltd Partnr (G-14144)*

Belco Works Inc......................................740 695-0500
  340 Fox Shannon Pl Saint Clairsville (43950) **(G-16470)**

Belcourt Terracenursing Home, Dublin *Also called Ahf/Central States Inc (G-10123)*

Belden & Blake Corporation........................330 602-5551
  1748 Saltwell Rd Nw Dover (44622) **(G-10066)**

Belflex Staffing Network LLC (PA)................513 488-8588
  11591 Goldcoast Dr Cincinnati (45249) **(G-3038)**

Belfor USA Group Inc................................330 916-6468
  79 Cuyahoga Fls Indus Par Peninsula (44264) **(G-15809)**

Belfor USA Group Inc................................513 860-3111
  4710 Interstate Dr Ste L West Chester (45246) **(G-19043)**

Bell Hensley Inc......................................937 498-1718
  804 W Parkwood St Sidney (45365) **(G-16761)**

A
L
P
H
A
B
E
T
I
C

Bell Moving and Storage Inc (PA) 513 942-7500
    4075 Port Union Rd Fairfield (45014) *(G-10699)*
Bell Music Company 330 376-6337
    533 W Market St Akron (44303) *(G-93)*
Bella Capelli Inc 440 899-1225
    24350 Center Ridge Rd Westlake (44145) *(G-19322)*
Bella Capelli Salon, Westlake Also called Bella Capelli Inc *(G-19322)*
Bellaire Harbor Service LLC 740 676-4305
    4102 Jefferson St Bellaire (43906) *(G-1329)*
Bellas Co 740 598-4171
    2670 Commercial Ave Mingo Junction (43938) *(G-14527)*
Bellazio Salon & Day Spa 937 432-6722
    101 E Alex Bell Rd # 127 Dayton (45459) *(G-9249)*
Bellbrook Rhblttion Healthcare, Bellbrook Also called Bellbrook Rhblttion
Healthcare *(G-1338)*
Bellbrook Rhblttion Healthcare 937 848-8421
    1957 N Lakeman Dr Bellbrook (45305) *(G-1338)*
Belle Tire Distributors Inc 419 473-1393
    5253 Secor Rd Toledo (43623) *(G-17610)*
Bellefaire Jewish Chld Bur (PA) 216 932-2800
    22001 Fairmount Blvd Shaker Heights (44118) *(G-16703)*
Bellefontaine Distribution Ctr, Bellefontaine Also called Spartannash Company *(G-1367)*
Bellefontaine Physical Therapy 937 592-1625
    711 Rush Ave Bellefontaine (43311) *(G-1346)*
Belletech Corp (HQ) 937 599-3774
    700 W Lake Ave Bellefontaine (43311) *(G-1347)*
Bellevue Care Center, Bellevue Also called Bellevue Healthcare Group LLC *(G-1372)*
Bellevue Four Cnty Ems N Centl 419 483-3322
    12513 Us Highway 250 N Milan (44846) *(G-14359)*
Bellevue Healthcare Group LLC 419 483-6225
    1 Audrich Sq Bellevue (44811) *(G-1372)*
Bellevue Hospital (PA) 419 483-4040
    1400 W Main St Unit Front Bellevue (44811) *(G-1373)*
Bellevue Hospital 419 547-0074
    811 Northwest St Bellevue (44811) *(G-1374)*
Bellman Plumbing Inc 440 324-4477
    7520 W Ridge Rd Elyria (44035) *(G-10481)*
Bellmont County 740 695-9750
    210 Fox Shannon Pl Saint Clairsville (43950) *(G-16471)*
Bellville Hotel Company 419 886-7000
    1000 Comfort Plaza Dr Bellville (44813) *(G-1387)*
Bellwether Entp RE Capitl LLC (PA) 216 820-4500
    1360 E 9th St Ste 300 Cleveland (44114) *(G-5052)*
Belmont Bhc Pines Hospital Inc 330 759-2700
    615 Churchill Hubbard Rd Youngstown (44505) *(G-19964)*
Belmont Cnty Fire & Squad Offi 740 312-5058
    69604 Sunset Hts Bridgeport (43912) *(G-1813)*
Belmont Community Hlth Ctr, Bellaire Also called Wheeling Hospital Inc *(G-1336)*
Belmont Community Hospital (HQ) 740 671-1200
    4697 Harrison St Bellaire (43906) *(G-1330)*
Belmont Country Club 419 666-1472
    29601 Bates Rd Perrysburg (43551) *(G-15837)*
Belmont County Children Svcs, Saint Clairsville Also called Belmont County of
Ohio *(G-16474)*
Belmont County Engineering, Saint Clairsville Also called Belmont County of
Ohio *(G-16476)*
Belmont County Home 740 695-4925
    100 Pine Ave Saint Clairsville (43950) *(G-16472)*
Belmont County of Ohio 740 695-3144
    67711 Oak View Rd Saint Clairsville (43950) *(G-16473)*
Belmont County of Ohio 740 695-3813
    101 N Market St Ste A Saint Clairsville (43950) *(G-16474)*
Belmont County of Ohio 740 695-0460
    68421 Hammond Rd Saint Clairsville (43950) *(G-16475)*
Belmont County of Ohio 740 695-1580
    101 W Maint St Saint Clairsville (43950) *(G-16476)*
Belmont County Sani Sewer Dst, Saint Clairsville Also called Belmont County of
Ohio *(G-16473)*
Belmont Division, Barnesville Also called South Central Power Company *(G-979)*
Belmont Federal Sav & Ln Assn (PA) 740 676-1165
    3301 Guernsey St Bellaire (43906) *(G-1331)*
Belmont Hills Country Club 740 695-2181
    47080 National Rd Saint Clairsville (43950) *(G-16477)*
Belmont Manor Nursing Home, Saint Clairsville Also called Lancia Nursing Home
Inc *(G-16491)*
Belmont Metro Hsing Auth (PA) 740 633-5085
    100 S 3rd St Martins Ferry (43935) *(G-13476)*
Belmont Metro Hsing Auth A, Martins Ferry Also called Belmont Metro Hsing Auth *(G-13476)*
Belmont Professional Assoc Inc 740 425-5140
    100 Hospital Dr Ste 109 Barnesville (43713) *(G-977)*
Belmont Savings Bank 740 695-0140
    215 W Main St Saint Clairsville (43950) *(G-16478)*
Belmore Leasing Co LLC 216 268-3600
    1835 Belmore Rd Cleveland (44112) *(G-5053)*
Belpre Historical Society 740 423-7588
    509 Ridge St Belpre (45714) *(G-1399)*
Belting Company of Cincinnati (PA) 513 621-9050
    5500 Ridge Ave Cincinnati (45213) *(G-3039)*
Belting Company of Cincinnati 937 498-2104
    301 Stolle Ave Sidney (45365) *(G-16762)*

Ben D Imhoff Inc 330 683-4498
    315 E Market St Orrville (44667) *(G-15625)*
Ben El Child Development Ctr 937 465-0010
    1150 Scioto St Ste 200 Urbana (43078) *(G-18419)*
Benchmark Craftsman Inc 330 975-4214
    4700 Greenwich Rd Seville (44273) *(G-16682)*
Benchmark Craftsmen, Seville Also called Benchmark Craftsman Inc *(G-16682)*
Benchmark Landscape Cnstr Inc 614 873-8080
    9600 Industrial Pkwy Plain City (43064) *(G-16045)*
Benchmark Masonry Contractors 937 228-1225
    2924 Cincinnati Dayton Rd Middletown (45044) *(G-14292)*
Benchmark Outfitters, Cincinnati Also called Rassak LLC *(G-4339)*
Benchmark Technologies Corp 419 843-6691
    3161 N Republic Blvd Toledo (43615) *(G-17611)*
Benco Dental Supply Co 513 874-2990
    10014 Intl Blvd Bldg 9 Cincinnati (45246) *(G-3040)*
Benco Dental Supply Co 614 761-1053
    4333 Tuller Rd Ste E Dublin (43017) *(G-10144)*
Benco Dental Supply Co 317 845-5356
    10014 International Blvd West Chester (45246) *(G-19044)*
Bendix Coml Vhcl Systems LLC (HQ) 440 329-9000
    901 Cleveland St Elyria (44035) *(G-10482)*
Bendon Inc (PA) 419 207-3600
    1840 S Baney Rd Ashland (44805) *(G-657)*
Benedict Enterprises Inc (PA) 513 539-9216
    750 Lakeview Rd Monroe (45050) *(G-14563)*
Beneficial Building Services (PA) 330 848-2556
    1830 13th St Sw Akron (44314) *(G-94)*
Benefit ADM Agcy LLC 614 791-1143
    5880 Venture Dr Dublin (43017) *(G-10145)*
Benefit Services Inc (PA) 330 666-0337
    3636 Copley Rd Ste 201 Copley (44321) *(G-8963)*
Benesch Friedlander Coplan & 614 223-9300
    41 S High St Ste 2600 Columbus (43215) *(G-7027)*
Benevento Enterprises Inc 216 621-5890
    1384 E 26th St Cleveland (44114) *(G-5054)*
Benevolent/Protectv Order Elks 440 357-6943
    723 Liberty St Painesville (44077) *(G-15695)*
Benjamin Rose Institute 216 791-8000
    850 Euclid Ave Ste 1100 Cleveland (44114) *(G-5055)*
Benjamin Rose Institute 216 791-3580
    2373 Euclid Heights Blvd 2f Cleveland (44106) *(G-5056)*
Benjamin Rose Institute (PA) 216 791-8000
    11890 Fairhill Rd Cleveland (44120) *(G-5057)*
Benjamin Steel Company Inc 937 233-1212
    777 Benjamin Dr Springfield (45502) *(G-16998)*
Benjamin Steel Company Inc 419 229-8045
    3111 Saint Johns Rd Lima (45804) *(G-12605)*
Benjamin Steel Company Inc 419 522-5500
    15 Industrial Pkwy Mansfield (44903) *(G-13140)*
Benmit Division, North Lawrence Also called US Tubular Products Inc *(G-15260)*
Bennett Enterprises Inc 419 874-3111
    10630 Fremont Pike Perrysburg (43551) *(G-15838)*
Bennett Enterprises Inc 419 893-1004
    1409 Reynolds Rd Maumee (43537) *(G-13762)*
Bennett Supply of Ohio LLC 800 292-5577
    8170 Roll And Hold Pkwy Macedonia (44056) *(G-13062)*
Bennett Venture Academy, Toledo Also called National Heritg Academies Inc *(G-17931)*
Bennington Glen Nursing Home, Marengo Also called Dearth Management
Company *(G-13302)*
Bentley Excavating, Painesville Also called D B Bentley Inc *(G-15707)*
Bentley Leasing Co LLC 330 337-9503
    2511 Bentley Dr Salem (44460) *(G-16536)*
Benton School Bus Garage, Oak Harbor Also called Benton-Carroll-Salem *(G-15468)*
Benton-Carroll-Salem 419 898-6214
    601 N Benton St Oak Harbor (43449) *(G-15468)*
Berardi + Partners 614 221-1110
    1398 Goodale Blvd Columbus (43212) *(G-7028)*
Berardis Fresh Roast Inc 440 582-4303
    12029 Abbey Rd North Royalton (44133) *(G-15348)*
Berea Alzheimer's Care Center, Berea Also called Communicare Health Svcs Inc *(G-1420)*
Berea B O E Trnsp Dept 216 898-8300
    235 Riveredge Pkwy Berea (44017) *(G-1414)*
Berea Lake Towers Inc 440 243-9050
    4 Berea Cmns Ste 1 Berea (44017) *(G-1415)*
Berea Lk Twers Rtirement Cmnty 440 243-9050
    3 Berea Cmns Berea (44017) *(G-1416)*
Berea Service Garage, Berea Also called City of Berea *(G-1418)*
Bergholz 7, Bergholz Also called Rosebud Mining Company *(G-1444)*
Berk Enterprises Inc (PA) 330 369-1192
    1554 Thomas Rd Se Warren (44484) *(G-18679)*
Berk Paper & Supply, Warren Also called Berk Enterprises Inc *(G-18679)*
Berkebile Russell & Associates 440 989-4480
    1720 Cooper Foster Park R Lorain (44053) *(G-12886)*
Berkeley Square Retirement Ctr, Hamilton Also called Colonial Senior Services
Inc *(G-11582)*
Berkshire Realty Group, Cincinnati Also called Brg Realty Group LLC *(G-3072)*
Berlin Construction Ltd 330 893-2003
    4740 Township Road 356 Millersburg (44654) *(G-14458)*

Berlin Contractors 330 893-2904
  5233 Township Rd 359 Berlin (44610) *(G-1445)*
Berlin Transportaion LLC 330 674-3395
  7576 State Route 241 Millersburg (44654) *(G-14459)*
Berman Moving & Storage, Cleveland *Also called Midfitz Inc (G-5984)*
Bermex, Columbus *Also called Matvest Inc (G-8040)*
Bermex Inc 330 945-7500
  4500 Courthouse Blvd # 150 Stow (44224) *(G-17192)*
Bernard Busson Builder 330 929-4926
  1551 Treetop Trl Akron (44313) *(G-95)*
Bernard Daniels Lumber Co, Canfield *Also called Daniels Lumber Co Inc (G-2135)*
Berner Trucking, Dover *Also called Knisely Inc (G-10085)*
Berner Trucking 419 476-0207
  4310 Lagrange St Toledo (43612) *(G-17612)*
Berner Trucking Inc 330 343-5812
  5885 Crown Rd Nw Dover (44622) *(G-10067)*
Berns Garden Center, Middletown *Also called Berns Grnhse & Grdn Ctr Inc (G-14293)*
Berns Grnhse & Grdn Ctr Inc (PA) 513 423-5306
  825 Greentree Rd Middletown (45044) *(G-14293)*
Berns Oneill SEC & Safety LLC 330 374-9133
  1000 N Main St Akron (44310) *(G-96)*
Bernstein Allergy Group Inc 513 931-0775
  8444 Winton Rd Cincinnati (45231) *(G-3041)*
Beroske Farms & Greenhouse Inc 419 826-4547
  12647 County Road 5 Delta (43515) *(G-10041)*
Berriehill, Columbus *Also called Applied Research Assoc Inc (G-6959)*
Berry Network LLC (HQ) 800 366-1264
  3100 Kettering Blvd Moraine (45439) *(G-14625)*
Bertec Corporation 614 543-0962
  6171 Huntley Rd Ste J Columbus (43229) *(G-7029)*
Bertka, Vicki M MD, Maumee *Also called Fallen Timbers Fmly Physicians (G-13788)*
Bertram Inn, Aurora *Also called B & I Hotel Management LLC (G-819)*
Berwick Electric Company 614 834-2301
  6863 Eliza Dr Canal Winchester (43110) *(G-2104)*
Besl Transfer Co 513 242-3456
  5700 Este Ave Cincinnati (45232) *(G-3042)*
Besse Medical, West Chester *Also called Asd Specialty Healthcare LLC (G-18869)*
Bessemer and Lake Erie RR Co 440 593-1102
  950 Ford Ave Conneaut (44030) *(G-8951)*
Best & Donovan N A Inc 513 791-9180
  5570 Creek Rd Blue Ash (45242) *(G-1513)*
Best Aire Compressor Service (HQ) 419 726-0055
  3648 Rockland Cir Millbury (43447) *(G-14446)*
Best Care Nrsing Rhbltttion Ctr 740 574-2558
  2159 Dogwood Ridge Rd Wheelersburg (45694) *(G-19428)*
Best Controls Company, Ashland *Also called Chandler Systems Incorporated (G-666)*
Best Cuts Inc 440 884-6300
  7541 W Ridgewood Dr Cleveland (44129) *(G-5058)*
Best Express Foods Inc 513 531-2378
  2368 Victory Pkwy Ste 410 Cincinnati (45206) *(G-3043)*
Best Lighting Products Inc (HQ) 740 964-0063
  1213 Etna Pkwy Etna (43062) *(G-10613)*
Best One Tire & Svc Lima Inc (PA) 419 229-2380
  701 E Hanthorn Rd Lima (45804) *(G-12606)*
Best Payment Solutions Inc (HQ) 630 321-0117
  8500 Governors Hill Dr Symmes Twp (45249) *(G-17465)*
Best Plumbing Limited 614 855-1919
  5791 Zarley St Ste A New Albany (43054) *(G-14843)*
Best Realty Inc 513 932-3948
  645 Columbus Ave Ste A Lebanon (45036) *(G-12451)*
Best Reward Credit Union 216 367-8000
  5681 Smith Rd Cleveland (44142) *(G-5059)*
Best Upon Request Corp Inc 513 605-7800
  8170 Corp Pk Dr Ste 300 Cincinnati (45242) *(G-3044)*
Best Way Motor Lines Inc (PA) 419 485-8373
  14020 Us Highway 20a Montpelier (43543) *(G-14606)*
Best Western, Zanesville *Also called Town House Motor Lodge Corp (G-20367)*
Best Western, Englewood *Also called Dayton Hotels LLC (G-10584)*
Best Western Columbus N Hotel 614 888-8230
  888 E Dublin Granville Rd Columbus (43229) *(G-7030)*
Best Western Columbus North, Columbus *Also called Best Western Columbus N Hotel (G-7030)*
Best Western Executive Inn 330 794-1050
  2677 Gilchrist Rd Unit 1 Akron (44305) *(G-97)*
Best Western Falcon Plaza Mtl, Bowling Green *Also called Falcon Plaza LLC (G-1730)*
Best Western Grnd Victoria Inn, Westlake *Also called Northern Tier Hospitality LLC (G-19383)*
Best Western Meander Inn, Youngstown *Also called Meander Inn Inc (G-20120)*
Best Western Wooster Plaza, Wooster *Also called Best Wooster Inc (G-19690)*
Best Wooster Inc 330 264-7750
  243 E Liberty St Ste 11 Wooster (44691) *(G-19690)*
Best Wstn Lawnfield Inn Suites, Mentor *Also called Lawnfield Properties LLC (G-14076)*
Besttransportcom Inc 614 888-2378
  1103 Schrock Rd Ste 100 Columbus (43229) *(G-7031)*
Bestway Transport Co (PA) 419 687-2000
  2040 Sandusky St Plymouth (44865) *(G-16076)*
Beta Lab & Technical Svcs, Cleveland *Also called Firstenergy Nuclear Oper Co (G-5539)*
Beta PHI, Celina *Also called Delta Kappa Gamma Society (G-2593)*

Beta RHO House Assoc Kappa 513 221-1280
  2801 Clifton Ave Cincinnati (45220) *(G-3045)*
Beta Theta PI Fraternity (PA) 513 523-7591
  5134 Bonham Rd Oxford (45056) *(G-15673)*
Betco Corporation (PA) 419 241-2156
  400 Van Camp Rd Bowling Green (43402) *(G-1719)*
Beth-El Agape Christian Center 614 445-0674
  840 Mansfield Ave Columbus (43219) *(G-7032)*
Bethany Nursing Home Inc 330 492-7171
  626 34th St Nw Canton (44709) *(G-2211)*
Bethany Village Linden, Dayton *Also called Graceworks Lutheran Services (G-9468)*
Bethesda Butler Hospital, Fairfield Township *Also called Bethesda Hospital Inc (G-10801)*
Bethesda Care, Zanesville *Also called Genesis Healthcare System (G-20310)*
Bethesda Care Center, Fremont *Also called Volunters Amer Care Facilities (G-11103)*
Bethesda Foundation Inc 513 569-6575
  619 Oak St Cincinnati (45206) *(G-3046)*
Bethesda Hospital Inc 513 894-8888
  3125 Hamilton Mason Rd Fairfield Township (45011) *(G-10801)*
Bethesda Hospital Inc (HQ) 513 569-6100
  4750 Wesley Ave Cincinnati (45212) *(G-3047)*
Bethesda Hospital Inc 513 745-1111
  10500 Montgomery Rd Cincinnati (45242) *(G-3048)*
Bethesda Hospital Inc 513 563-1505
  3801 Hauck Rd Frnt Cincinnati (45241) *(G-3049)*
Bethesda Hospital Association 740 454-4000
  2951 Maple Ave Zanesville (43701) *(G-20281)*
Bethesda North Hospital, Cincinnati *Also called Trihealth Inc (G-4636)*
Bethesda North Hospital, Cincinnati *Also called Bethesda Hospital Inc (G-3047)*
Bethesda North Hospital, Cincinnati *Also called Bethesda Hospital Inc (G-3048)*
Bethlehem Lutheran Ch Parma 440 845-2230
  7500 State Rd Cleveland (44134) *(G-5060)*
Bettcher Industries Inc 440 965-4422
  6801 State Route 60 Wakeman (44889) *(G-18619)*
Better Brake Parts Inc 419 227-0685
  915 Shawnee Rd Lima (45805) *(G-12607)*
Better Homes and Gardens, Beavercreek *Also called Big Hill Realty Corp (G-1207)*
Bevan and Associates Lpa, Northfield *Also called Bavan & Associates (G-15374)*
Bevcorp LLC (PA) 440 954-3500
  4711 E 355th St Willoughby (44094) *(G-19508)*
Beverage Distributors Inc 216 431-1600
  3800 King Ave Cleveland (44114) *(G-5061)*
Beverly, Napoleon *Also called Golden Living LLC (G-14807)*
Beverly, Lima *Also called Golden Living LLC (G-12644)*
Beverly, Columbus *Also called Golden Living LLC (G-7678)*
Beverly, Willoughby *Also called Golden Living LLC (G-19527)*
Beverly, Ravenna *Also called Golden Living LLC (G-16244)*
Beverly, Akron *Also called Golden Living LLC (G-239)*
Beverly, Wadsworth *Also called Golden Living LLC (G-18596)*
Beverly, Medina *Also called Golden Living LLC (G-13944)*
Beverly Hills Inn La Llc 859 494-9151
  1830 Us Highway 52 Aberdeen (45101) *(G-1)*
Bexley, Columbus *Also called Nrt Commercial Utah LLC (G-8211)*
Bexley Plaza Apartments, Columbus *Also called Plaza Properties Inc (G-8455)*
Beyond 2000 Realty Inc 440 842-7200
  18332 Bagley Rd Cleveland (44130) *(G-5062)*
Beyond The Horizons Home Healt 608 630-0617
  2645 Fairwood Ave Columbus (43207) *(G-7033)*
Bfg Supply Co Llc (HQ) 440 834-1883
  14500 Kinsman Rd Burton (44021) *(G-2015)*
BFI Waste Services LLC 800 437-1123
  1717 Pennsylvania Ave Salem (44460) *(G-16537)*
BFR, Bluffton *Also called Bluffton Family Recreation (G-1688)*
Bfs Supply, Cincinnati *Also called Frederick Steel Company LLC (G-3586)*
Bg News, Bowling Green *Also called B G News (G-1715)*
Bhatti Enterprises Inc 513 886-6000
  8045 Vegas Cir West Chester (45069) *(G-18876)*
Bhc Fox Run Hospital Inc 740 695-2131
  67670 Traco Dr Saint Clairsville (43950) *(G-16479)*
BHDP ARCHITECTURE, Cincinnati *Also called Baxter Hodell Donnelly Preston (G-3025)*
BHF Incorporated 740 945-6410
  147 E College St Scio (43988) *(G-16662)*
Bhfi, Scio *Also called BHF Incorporated (G-16662)*
Bico, Mogadore *Also called Burger Iron Company (G-14544)*
Bico Akron Inc 330 794-1716
  3100 Gilchrist Rd Mogadore (44260) *(G-14543)*
Bico Steel Service Centers, Mogadore *Also called Bico Akron Inc (G-14543)*
Biederman Educational Centers, Cleves *Also called Kindertown Educational Centers (G-6731)*
Bieser Greer & Landis LLP 937 223-3277
  6 N Main St Ste 400 Dayton (45402) *(G-9250)*
Big Blue Trucking Inc 330 372-1421
  518 Perkins Jones Rd Ne Warren (44483) *(G-18680)*
Big Broth and Big Siste of Cen (PA) 614 839-2447
  1855 E Dbln Grnvl Rd Fl 1 Flr 1 Columbus (43229) *(G-7034)*
Big Hill Realty Corp 937 426-4420
  4011 Danern Dr Beavercreek (45430) *(G-1206)*

ALPHABETIC

Big Hill Realty Corp (PA) 937 435-1177
5580 Far Hills Ave Dayton (45429) *(G-9251)*
Big Hill Realty Corp 937 429-2200
3944 Indian Ripple Rd Beavercreek (45440) *(G-1207)*
Big Lots Stores Inc (HQ) 614 278-6800
4900 E Dblin Granville Rd Columbus (43081) *(G-7035)*
Big Mat Golf Course, Cleveland *Also called Cleveland Metroparks (G-5272)*
Big O Refuse Inc 740 344-7544
1919 Lancaster Rd Ste B Granville (43023) *(G-11334)*
Big Red LP 740 548-7799
6025 Cheshire Rd Galena (43021) *(G-11156)*
Big Red Rooster (HQ) 614 255-0200
121 Thurman Ave Columbus (43206) *(G-7036)*
Big Run Urgent Care Center 614 871-7130
3000 Meadow Pond Ct # 200 Grove City (43123) *(G-11408)*
Big Sandy Distribution Inc (PA) 740 574-2113
8375 Gallia Pike Franklin Furnace (45629) *(G-11042)*
Big Sandy Furniture Inc (HQ) 740 574-2113
8375 Gallia Pike Franklin Furnace (45629) *(G-11043)*
Big Sandy Furniture Inc 740 354-3193
730 10th St Portsmouth (45662) *(G-16125)*
Big Sandy Furniture Inc 740 775-4244
1404 N Bridge St Chillicothe (45601) *(G-2758)*
Big Sandy Furniture Inc 740 894-4242
45 County Rd 407 Chesapeake (45619) *(G-2727)*
Big Sandy Furniture Store 5, Portsmouth *Also called Big Sandy Furniture Inc (G-16125)*
Big Sandy Service Company, Franklin Furnace *Also called Big Sandy Furniture Inc (G-11043)*
Big Sandy Superstore, Chesapeake *Also called Big Sandy Furniture Inc (G-2727)*
Big Sandy Superstores, Franklin Furnace *Also called Big Sandy Distribution Inc (G-11042)*
Big Western Lanes, Columbus *Also called Big Western Operating Co Inc (G-7037)*
Big Western Operating Co Inc 614 274-1169
500 Georgesville Rd Columbus (43228) *(G-7037)*
Bigelow Corporation (PA) 937 339-3315
1530 Mckaig Ave Troy (45373) *(G-18196)*
Bigger Road Veterinary Clinic (PA) 937 435-3262
5655 Bigger Rd Dayton (45440) *(G-9252)*
Bigmar Inc 740 966-5800
9711 Sportsman Club Rd Johnstown (43031) *(G-12196)*
Bilfinger Westcon Inc 330 818-9734
4525 Vliet St Sw Canton (44710) *(G-2212)*
Bill & Don's Catering, Lorain *Also called Lorain Party Center (G-12923)*
Bill Delord Autocenter Inc 513 932-3000
917 Columbus Ave Lebanon (45036) *(G-12452)*
Billback Systems LLC 937 433-1844
8000 Millers Farm Ln Dayton (45458) *(G-9253)*
Billing Connection Inc 740 964-0043
6422 E Main St Ste 202 Reynoldsburg (43068) *(G-16285)*
Billing Services, Lorain *Also called Specialty Medical Services (G-12943)*
Bills Battery Company Inc 513 922-0100
5221 Crookshank Rd Cincinnati (45238) *(G-3050)*
Billy Royal, Chagrin Falls *Also called Schneider Saddlery LLC (G-2682)*
Biltimore Towers, Dayton *Also called Biltmore Apartments Ltd (G-9254)*
Biltmore Apartments Ltd 937 461-9695
210 N Main St Dayton (45402) *(G-9254)*
Bimbo Bakeries Usa Inc 614 868-7565
1020 Claycraft Rd Ste D Columbus (43230) *(G-7038)*
Bindery & Spc Pressworks Inc 614 873-4623
351 W Bigelow Ave Plain City (43064) *(G-16046)*
Bindley Western Drug, Dublin *Also called Cardinal Health 100 Inc (G-10157)*
Bindu Associates LLC 440 324-0099
645 Griswold Rd Elyria (44035) *(G-10483)*
Bingo Division, Youngstown *Also called Nannicola Wholesale Co (G-20134)*
Binkelman Corporation (PA) 419 537-9333
2601 Hill Ave Toledo (43607) *(G-17613)*
Bio-Blood Components Inc 614 294-3183
1393 N High St Columbus (43201) *(G-7039)*
Bio-Mdcal Applcations Ohio Inc 937 279-3120
4100 Salem Ave Trotwood (45416) *(G-18191)*
Bio-Mdcal Applcations Ohio Inc 419 874-3447
701 Commerce Dr Perrysburg (43551) *(G-15839)*
Bio-Mdcal Applcations Ohio Inc 614 538-1060
758 Communications Pkwy Columbus (43214) *(G-7040)*
Bio-Mdcal Applcations Ohio Inc 330 376-4905
345 Bishop St Akron (44307) *(G-98)*
Bio-Mdcal Applcations Ohio Inc 419 774-0180
680 Bally Row Mansfield (44906) *(G-13141)*
Bio-Mdcal Applcations Ohio Inc 330 896-6311
1575 Corp Woods Pkwy # 100 Uniontown (44685) *(G-18357)*
Bio-Mdcal Applcations Ohio Inc 614 338-8202
4039 E Broad St Columbus (43213) *(G-7041)*
Bio-Mdical Applications Rl Inc 740 389-4111
1730 Marion Waldo Rd Marion (43302) *(G-13405)*
Biolife Plasma Services LP 419 425-8680
1789 E Melrose Ave Findlay (45840) *(G-10868)*
Biolife Plasma Services LP 419 224-0117
4299 Elida Rd Lima (45807) *(G-12608)*
Biomat Usa Inc 419 531-3332
3217 Dorr St Ste B Toledo (43607) *(G-17614)*
Biomedical Laboratory, Hubbard *Also called Connie Parks (G-11943)*
Biomedical Research & Educatn, Cincinnati *Also called Cincinnti Educ & RES For Vetrn (G-3282)*
Bionetics Corporation 757 873-0900
813 Irving Wick Dr W Heath (43056) *(G-11702)*
Bionix Safety Technologies Ltd (HQ) 419 727-0552
5154 Enterprise Blvd Toledo (43612) *(G-17615)*
Biorx LLC (HQ) 866 442-4679
7167 E Kemper Rd Cincinnati (45249) *(G-3051)*
Biosortia Pharmaceuticals Inc 614 636-4850
4266 Tuller Rd Dublin (43017) *(G-10146)*
Biotech Medical Inc 330 494-5504
7800 Whipple Ave Nw Canton (44767) *(G-2213)*
Biotest Pharmaceuticals Corp 419 819-3068
1616 E Wooster St Unit 39 Bowling Green (43402) *(G-1720)*
Biotest Plasma Center, Bowling Green *Also called Biotest Pharmaceuticals Corp (G-1720)*
Birch Manor Apartments I, Medina *Also called New Birch Manor I Assoc LLC (G-13980)*
Birchaven Village 419 424-3000
415 College St Findlay (45840) *(G-10869)*
Birchaven Village (PA) 419 424-3000
15100 Birchaven Ln Ofc C Findlay (45840) *(G-10870)*
Birchwood Genetics Inc (PA) 937 678-9313
465 Stephens Rd West Manchester (45382) *(G-19123)*
Bird Enterprises LLC 330 674-1457
35 W Jackson St Millersburg (44654) *(G-14460)*
Bishop Ready High School, Columbus *Also called Catholic Diocese of Columbus (G-7138)*
Bistro Off Broadway 937 316-5000
117 E 5th St Greenville (45331) *(G-11366)*
Bitec, Dayton *Also called Sample Machining Inc (G-9750)*
BITTERSWEET FARMS, Whitehouse *Also called Bittersweet Inc (G-19444)*
Bittersweet Inc (PA) 419 875-6986
12660 Archbold Whthuse Rd Whitehouse (43571) *(G-19444)*
Bitzel Excavating Inc 330 477-9653
4141 Southway St Sw Canton (44706) *(G-2214)*
Bixby Living Skills Center, Groveport *Also called ARC Industries Incorporated O (G-11495)*
Biz Com Electric Inc 513 961-7200
2867 Stanton Ave Cincinnati (45206) *(G-3052)*
Bjaam Environmental Inc 330 854-5300
472 Elm Ridge Ave Canal Fulton (44614) *(G-2093)*
Bkd LLP 513 621-8300
312 Walnut St Ste 3000 Cincinnati (45202) *(G-3053)*
Bkg Holdings LLC 614 252-7455
600 N Cassady Ave Ofc Columbus (43219) *(G-7042)*
Bkg Services Inc 614 476-1800
3948 Townsfair Way # 230 Columbus (43219) *(G-7043)*
Bkp Ambulance District 419 674-4574
439 S Main St Kenton (43326) *(G-12271)*
Black & Veatch Corporation 614 473-0921
4449 Easton Way Ste 150 Columbus (43219) *(G-7044)*
Black Diamond Golf Course 330 674-6110
7500 Township Road 103 Millersburg (44654) *(G-14461)*
Black Eagle Transfer Company, Ashtabula *Also called City Taxicab & Transfer Co (G-727)*
Black Horse Carriers Inc 330 225-2250
1319 W 130th St Hinckley (44233) *(G-11858)*
Black River Display, Mansfield *Also called D & S Crtive Cmmunications Inc (G-13164)*
Black River Display Group, Mansfield *Also called Black River Group Inc (G-13142)*
Black River Group Inc (PA) 419 524-6699
140 Park Ave E Mansfield (44902) *(G-13142)*
Black Sapphire C Columbus Univ 614 297-9912
1421 Olentangy River Rd Columbus (43212) *(G-7045)*
Black Stone Cincinnati LLC 937 773-8573
106 W Ash St Ste 504 Piqua (45356) *(G-15997)*
Black Stone Cincinnati LLC 937 424-1370
3044 Kettering Blvd Moraine (45439) *(G-14626)*
Black Stone Cincinnati LLC (PA) 513 924-1370
4700 E Galbraith Rd Fl 3 Cincinnati (45236) *(G-3054)*
Black Swamp Equipment LLC (PA) 419 445-0030
700 E Lugbill Rd Archbold (43502) *(G-627)*
Black Swamp Steel Inc 419 867-8050
1761 Commerce Rd Holland (43528) *(G-11873)*
Black Tie Affair Inc 330 345-8333
50 Riffel Rd Wooster (44691) *(G-19691)*
Blackbird Capital Group LLC 513 762-7890
312 Walnut St Ste 1600 Cincinnati (45202) *(G-3055)*
Blackbrook Country Club Inc 440 951-0010
8900 Lake Shore Blvd Mentor (44060) *(G-14022)*
Blackburns Fabrication Inc 614 875-0784
2467 Jackson Pike Columbus (43223) *(G-7046)*
Blackhawk Industries 918 610-4719
2845 Interstate Pkwy Brunswick (44212) *(G-1920)*
Blacklick Wods Mtro Golf Crses, Reynoldsburg *Also called Columbus Frkln Cnty Pk (G-16293)*
Blackstar Drywall Inc 614 242-4242
9821 E State Route 37 Sunbury (43074) *(G-17383)*
Blackwell Inn, The, Columbus *Also called Ohio State University (G-8310)*
Blade-Tech Industries Inc 877 331-5793
10125 Wellman Rd Streetsboro (44241) *(G-17247)*
Bladecutters Lawn and Ldscpg, Dayton *Also called Bladecutters Lawn Service Inc (G-9255)*
Bladecutters Lawn Service Inc 937 274-3861
5440 N Dixie Dr Dayton (45414) *(G-9255)*
Blakemans Valley Off Eqp Inc 330 729-1000
8534 South Ave Youngstown (44514) *(G-19965)*

Blanchard Tree and Lawn Inc..........419 865-7071
1530 Kieswetter Rd Holland (43528) ***(G-11874)***
Blanchard Valley Center, Findlay *Also called Blanchard Vlly Crt Case Mngmnt* ***(G-10876)***
Blanchard Valley Health System (PA)..........419 423-4500
1900 S Main St Findlay (45840) ***(G-10871)***
Blanchard Valley Health System..........419 424-3000
15100 Birchaven Ln Findlay (45840) ***(G-10872)***
BLANCHARD VALLEY HOSPITAL, Findlay *Also called Blanchard Vly Rgional Hlth Ctr* ***(G-10879)***
Blanchard Valley Hospital..........419 423-4335
306 Lima Ave Findlay (45840) ***(G-10873)***
Blanchard Valley Industries, Findlay *Also called County of Hancock* ***(G-10891)***
Blanchard Valley Industries..........419 422-6386
318 W Main Cross St Findlay (45840) ***(G-10874)***
Blanchard Valley Medical Assoc..........419 424-0380
200 W Pearl St Findlay (45840) ***(G-10875)***
Blanchard Valley School, Findlay *Also called Blanchard Vly Residential Ctr* ***(G-10877)***
Blanchard Vlly Crt Case Mngmnt..........419 422-6387
318 W Main Cross St Findlay (45840) ***(G-10876)***
Blanchard Vly Residential Ctr..........419 422-6503
1705 E Main Cross St Findlay (45840) ***(G-10877)***
Blanchard Vly Rgional Hlth Ctr..........419 427-0809
1800 N Blanchard St # 121 Findlay (45840) ***(G-10878)***
Blanchard Vly Rgional Hlth Ctr (HQ)..........419 423-4500
1900 S Main St Findlay (45840) ***(G-10879)***
Blanchard Vly Rgional Hlth Ctr..........419 358-9010
139 Garau St Bluffton (45817) ***(G-1687)***
Blastmaster Holdings Usa LLC..........877 725-2781
4510 Bridgeway Ave Columbus (43219) ***(G-7047)***
Blastone International, Columbus *Also called Blastmaster Holdings Usa LLC* ***(G-7047)***
Blatchford Inc..........937 291-3636
1031 Byers Rd Miamisburg (45342) ***(G-14145)***
Blatt Trucking Co Inc (PA)..........419 898-0002
1205 Main St Rocky Ridge (43458) ***(G-16419)***
Blb Transport Inc..........740 474-1341
20615 Us Highway 23 N Circleville (43113) ***(G-4825)***
Bleachtech LLC..........216 921-1980
320 Ryan Rd Seville (44273) ***(G-16683)***
Bleckmann USA LLC..........740 809-2645
188 Commerce Blvd Ste B Johnstown (43031) ***(G-12197)***
Blendon Gardens Inc..........614 840-0500
9590 S Old State Rd Lewis Center (43035) ***(G-12529)***
Blendonwoods Metro Park, Westerville *Also called Columbus Frkln Cnty Pk* ***(G-19240)***
Blennerhassett Yacht Club Inc..........740 423-9062
800 Oneal St Belpre (45714) ***(G-1400)***
Bless, Marysville *Also called Basinger Lfe Enhncmnt Sprt Svc* ***(G-13484)***
Bleux Holdings LLC..........859 414-5060
7257 Wooster Pike Cincinnati (45227) ***(G-3056)***
Blevins Fabrication, Mansfield *Also called Blevins Metal Fabrication Inc* ***(G-13143)***
Blevins Metal Fabrication Inc..........419 522-6082
288 Illinois Ave S Mansfield (44905) ***(G-13143)***
Blick Clinic Inc (PA)..........330 762-5425
640 W Market St Akron (44303) ***(G-99)***
Blick Clinic Inc..........330 762-5425
682 W Market St Akron (44303) ***(G-100)***
Blind & Son LLC..........330 753-7711
344 4th St Nw Barberton (44203) ***(G-948)***
Block Communications Inc..........419 724-2539
2700 Oregon Rd Northwood (43619) ***(G-15389)***
Blood Center, Cincinnati *Also called University of Cincinnati* ***(G-4706)***
Blood Courier Inc..........216 251-3050
3965 W 130th St Cleveland (44111) ***(G-5063)***
Blood Services Centl Ohio Reg (PA)..........614 253-7981
995 E Broad St Columbus (43205) ***(G-7048)***
Bloomberg Ross MD..........740 454-1216
2935 Maple Ave Zanesville (43701) ***(G-20282)***
BLOOMFIELD COTTAGES, Ashland *Also called Brethren Care Inc* ***(G-659)***
Blooms By Plantscaping, Cleveland *Also called Plantscaping Inc* ***(G-6216)***
Blossom Hill Care Center, Huntsburg *Also called Blossom Hills Nursing Home* ***(G-12017)***
Blossom Hill Elderly Housing L..........330 385-4310
100 Wilbert Ave East Liverpool (43920) ***(G-10398)***
Blossom Hills Nursing Home..........440 635-5567
12496 Princeton Rd Huntsburg (44046) ***(G-12017)***
Blossom Nrsing Rhblitation Ctr, Salem *Also called Blossom Nursing & Rehab Center* ***(G-16538)***
Blossom Nursing & Rehab Center..........330 337-3033
109 Blossom Ln Salem (44460) ***(G-16538)***
Blue & Co LLC..........513 241-4507
720 E Pete Rose Way # 100 Cincinnati (45202) ***(G-3057)***
Blue Ash Business Association..........513 253-1006
P.O. Box 429277 Cincinnati (45242) ***(G-3058)***
Blue Ash Care Center, Cincinnati *Also called Blue Ash Healthcare Group Inc* ***(G-3060)***
Blue Ash Distribution Ctr LLC..........513 699-2279
2135 Dana Ave Ste 200 Cincinnati (45207) ***(G-3059)***
Blue Ash Golf Course, Blue Ash *Also called City of Blue Ash* ***(G-1528)***
Blue Ash Healthcare Group Inc..........513 793-3362
4900 Cooper Rd Cincinnati (45242) ***(G-3060)***
Blue Ash Roofing Co, Blue Ash *Also called Molloy Roofing Company* ***(G-1614)***
Blue Ash YMCA, Blue Ash *Also called Young Mens Christian Associat* ***(G-1685)***
Blue Beacon of Beaverdam, Beaverdam *Also called Blue Beacon USA LP II* ***(G-1267)***
Blue Beacon of Hubbard Inc..........330 534-4419
7044 Truck World Blvd Hubbard (44425) ***(G-11941)***
Blue Beacon Truck Wash, Hubbard *Also called Blue Beacon USA LP II* ***(G-11942)***
Blue Beacon Truck Wash, New Paris *Also called Blue Beacon USA LP II* ***(G-14940)***
Blue Beacon USA LP II..........330 534-4419
7044 Truck World Blvd Hubbard (44425) ***(G-11942)***
Blue Beacon USA LP II..........419 643-8146
413 E Main St Beaverdam (45808) ***(G-1267)***
Blue Beacon USA LP II..........937 437-5533
9787 Us Route 40 W New Paris (45347) ***(G-14940)***
Blue Chip 2000 Coml Clg Inc..........513 561-2999
7250 Edington Dr Cincinnati (45249) ***(G-3061)***
Blue Chip Broadcasting, Cincinnati *Also called Urban One Inc* ***(G-4735)***
Blue Chip Consulting Group LLC..........216 503-6001
6000 Lombardo Ctr Ste 650 Seven Hills (44131) ***(G-16672)***
Blue Chip Mailing Services Inc..........513 541-4800
9933 Alliance Rd Ste 1 Blue Ash (45242) ***(G-1514)***
Blue Chip Plumbing Inc..........513 941-4010
1950 Waycross Rd Cincinnati (45240) ***(G-3062)***
Blue Chip Pros, Cincinnati *Also called Blue Chip 2000 Coml Clg Inc* ***(G-3061)***
Blue Chip, The, Cleveland *Also called Massachusetts Mutl Lf Insur Co* ***(G-5922)***
Blue Chp Srgcl Ctr Ptns LLC..........513 561-8900
4760 Red Bank Rd Ste 222 Cincinnati (45227) ***(G-3063)***
Blue Creek Healthcare LLC..........419 877-5338
11239 Waterville St Whitehouse (43571) ***(G-19445)***
Blue Cross, Columbus *Also called Anthem Insurance Companies Inc* ***(G-6799)***
Blue Cross, Canton *Also called Anthem Insurance Companies Inc* ***(G-2191)***
Blue Cross & Blue Shield Mich..........330 783-3841
2405 Market St Youngstown (44507) ***(G-19966)***
Blue Line Distribution..........614 497-9610
2250 Spiegel Dr Ste P Groveport (43125) ***(G-11496)***
Blue Line Food Service, Groveport *Also called Blue Line Distribution* ***(G-11496)***
Blue Ribbon Meats Inc..........216 631-8850
3316 W 67th Pl Cleveland (44102) ***(G-5064)***
Blue Sky Therapy, Canfield *Also called Wsb Rehabilitation Svcs Inc* ***(G-2165)***
Blue Star Lubrication Tech LLC..........847 285-1888
3630 E Kemper Rd Cincinnati (45241) ***(G-3064)***
Blue Tech Smart Solutions LLC..........216 271-4800
5885 Grant Ave Cleveland (44105) ***(G-5065)***
Blue Technologies Inc..........330 499-9300
5701 Mayfair Rd Canton (44720) ***(G-2215)***
Blue Technologies Inc (PA)..........216 271-4800
5885 Grant Ave Cleveland (44105) ***(G-5066)***
Blue Water Chamber Orchestra..........440 781-6215
3631 Perkins Ave Apt 4cn Cleveland (44114) ***(G-5067)***
Blue-Kenwood LLC..........513 469-6900
5300 Cornell Rd Blue Ash (45242) ***(G-1515)***
Bluebird Retirement Community..........740 845-1880
2260 State Route 56 Sw London (43140) ***(G-12860)***
Bluefin Media, Perrysburg *Also called Brand Technologies Inc* ***(G-15841)***
Bluefoot Energy Services, Steubenville *Also called Bluefoot Industrial LLC* ***(G-17141)***
Bluefoot Industrial LLC..........740 314-5299
224 N 3rd St Steubenville (43952) ***(G-17141)***
Bluelinx Corporation..........330 794-1141
550 Munroe Falls Rd Akron (44305) ***(G-101)***
Bluelinx Corporation..........513 874-6770
400 Circle Freeway Dr West Chester (45246) ***(G-19045)***
Bluesky Healthcare Inc..........330 345-9050
4110 E Smithville Wstn Rd Wooster (44691) ***(G-19692)***
Bluffton Campus, Bluffton *Also called Blanchard Vly Rgional Hlth Ctr* ***(G-1687)***
Bluffton Family Recreation..........419 358-6978
215 Snider Rd Bluffton (45817) ***(G-1688)***
Blumenthal, Barry, Cincinnati *Also called Trihealth G LLC* ***(G-4642)***
Bmf, Fairlawn *Also called Bober Markey Fedorovich* ***(G-10817)***
Bmi Federal Credit Union..........614 707-4000
6165 Emerald Pkwy Dublin (43016) ***(G-10147)***
Bmi Federal Credit Union (PA)..........614 298-8527
760 Kinnear Rd Frnt Columbus (43212) ***(G-7049)***
BMW Financial Services Na LLC (HQ)..........614 718-6900
5550 Britton Pkwy Hilliard (43026) ***(G-11747)***
BMW Financial Services Na LLC..........614 718-6900
5515 Parkcenter Cir Dublin (43017) ***(G-10148)***
Bnai Brith Hillel Fdn At Osu..........614 294-4797
46 E 16th Ave Columbus (43201) ***(G-7050)***
Bnd Rentals Inc..........937 898-5061
950 Engle Rd Vandalia (45377) ***(G-18508)***
Bnsf Logistics LLC..........937 526-3141
611 Marker Rd Versailles (45380) ***(G-18566)***
Boak & Sons Inc..........330 793-5646
75 Victoria Rd Youngstown (44515) ***(G-19967)***
Board Amercn Township Trustees..........419 331-8651
102 Pioneer Rd Elida (45807) ***(G-10471)***
Board Lucas Cnty Commissioners, Toledo *Also called County of Lucas* ***(G-17684)***
Board Man Frst Untd Methdst Ch..........330 758-4527
6809 Market St Youngstown (44512) ***(G-19968)***
Board Mental Retardation Dvlpm..........740 472-1712
47011 State Route 26 Woodsfield (43793) ***(G-19671)***
Board of Delaware County..........740 201-3600
7991 Columbus Pike Lewis Center (43035) ***(G-12530)***

A
L
P
H
A
B
E
T
I
C

Board of Dir of Wittenbe 937 327-6231
134 W Ward St Springfield (45504) ***(G-16999)***
Board of Dir of Wittenbe 937 327-6310
225 N Fountain Ave Springfield (45504) ***(G-17000)***
Board of Mental Retardation, Carrollton *Also called County of Carroll* ***(G-2565)***
Board of Mrdd, Marion *Also called County of Marion* ***(G-13416)***
Boardman Local Schools 330 726-3409
7410 Market St Youngstown (44512) ***(G-19969)***
Boardman Medical Supply Co (HQ) 330 545-6700
300 N State St Girard (44420) ***(G-11283)***
Boardman Methodist Daycare, Youngstown *Also called Board Man Frst Untd Methdst Ch* ***(G-19968)***
Boardman School Bus Garage, Youngstown *Also called Boardman Local Schools* ***(G-19969)***
Boardman X-Ray & Mri, Youngstown *Also called Regional Imaging Cons Corp* ***(G-20179)***
Boars Head Provisions Co Inc 614 662-5300
2225 Spiegel Dr Groveport (43125) ***(G-11497)***
Bob Evans Transportation 937 322-4447
6088 Green Field Dr Springfield (45502) ***(G-17001)***
Bob Miller Rigging Inc 419 422-7477
11758 Township Road 100 Findlay (45840) ***(G-10880)***
Bob Mor Inc 419 485-5555
13508 State Route 15 Montpelier (43543) ***(G-14607)***
Bob O Link Golf Course, Avon *Also called Avon Properties Inc* ***(G-864)***
Bob Pulte Chevrolet Inc 513 932-0303
909 Columbus Ave Lebanon (45036) ***(G-12453)***
Bob Sumerel Tire Co Inc 937 235-0062
7711 Center Point 70 Blvd Dayton (45424) ***(G-9256)***
Bob Sumerel Tire Co Inc 513 792-6600
2540 Annuity Dr Cincinnati (45241) ***(G-3065)***
Bob Sumerel Tire Co Inc 614 527-9700
2807 International St Columbus (43228) ***(G-7051)***
Bob Webb Builders Inc 740 548-5577
7662 N Central Dr Lewis Center (43035) ***(G-12531)***
Bob Webb Homes, Lewis Center *Also called Bob Webb Builders Inc* ***(G-12531)***
Bob-Boyd Ford Inc (PA) 614 860-0606
2840 N Columbus St Lancaster (43130) ***(G-12372)***
Bobb Automotive Inc 614 853-3000
4639 W Broad St Columbus (43228) ***(G-7052)***
Bobb Suzuki, Columbus *Also called Bobb Automotive Inc* ***(G-7052)***
Bobbart Industries Inc 419 350-5477
5035 Alexis Rd Ste 1 Sylvania (43560) ***(G-17412)***
Bobboyd Auto Family, Lancaster *Also called Bob-Boyd Ford Inc* ***(G-12372)***
Bobby Layman Cadillac GMC Inc 740 654-9590
3733 Claypool Dr Carroll (43112) ***(G-2556)***
Bobby Tripodi Foundation Inc (PA) 216 524-3787
5905 Brecksville Rd Independence (44131) ***(G-12050)***
Bobcat Enterprises Inc (PA) 513 874-8945
9605 Prnceton Glendale Rd West Chester (45011) ***(G-18877)***
Bobcat of Dayton Inc (PA) 937 293-3176
2850 E River Rd Unit 1 Moraine (45439) ***(G-14627)***
Bobcat of Pittsburgh, Belmont *Also called Reco Equipment Inc* ***(G-1395)***
Bober Markey Fedorovich (PA) 330 762-9785
3421 Ridgewood Rd Ste 300 Fairlawn (44333) ***(G-10817)***
Bobs Moraine Trucking Inc 937 746-8420
8251 Claude Thomas Rd Franklin (45005) ***(G-11024)***
Boc Water Hydraulics Inc 330 332-4444
12024 Salem Warren Rd Salem (44460) ***(G-16539)***
Bodie Electric Inc 419 435-3672
1109 N Main St Fostoria (44830) ***(G-10997)***
Bodine Perry LLC (PA) 330 702-8100
3711 Strrs Cntre Dr Ste 2 Canfield (44406) ***(G-2131)***
Boeing Company 740 788-4000
801 Irving Wick Dr W Newark (43056) ***(G-15014)***
Boenning & Scattergood Inc 614 336-8851
9922 Brewster Ln Powell (43065) ***(G-16186)***
Bogie Industries Inc Ltd 330 745-3105
1100 Home Ave Akron (44310) ***(G-102)***
Bogner Construction Company 330 262-6730
305 Mulberry St Wooster (44691) ***(G-19693)***
Bohl Crane Inc (PA) 419 476-7525
534 W Laskey Rd Toledo (43612) ***(G-17616)***
Bohl Equipment Company (PA) 419 476-7525
534 W Laskey Rd Toledo (43612) ***(G-17617)***
Boise Cascade Company 513 451-5700
771 Neeb Rd Cincinnati (45233) ***(G-3066)***
Boise Cascade Company 740 382-6766
3007 Harding Hwy E Marion (43302) ***(G-13406)***
Bold, E Luke MD PH D, Willoughby *Also called Nelson & Bold Inc* ***(G-19554)***
Bollin & Sons Inc 419 693-6573
6001 Brent Dr Toledo (43611) ***(G-17618)***
Bollin Label Systems, Toledo *Also called Bollin & Sons Inc* ***(G-17618)***
Bolotin Law Offices 419 424-9800
612 S Main St Ste 201 Findlay (45840) ***(G-10881)***
Bolt Construction Inc 330 549-0349
10422 South Ave Youngstown (44514) ***(G-19970)***
BOLT CONSTRUCTION CO, Youngstown *Also called Bolt Construction Inc* ***(G-19970)***
Bolt Express LLC (PA) 419 729-6698
7255 Crossleigh Ct # 108 Toledo (43617) ***(G-17619)***
Bombeck Family Learning Center 937 229-2158
941 Alberta St Dayton (45409) ***(G-9257)***
Bon Appetit Management Co 614 823-1880
100 W Home St Westerville (43081) ***(G-19227)***
Bon Secours Health System 740 966-3116
8148 Windy Hollow Rd Johnstown (43031) ***(G-12198)***
Bonbright Distributors Inc 937 222-1001
1 Arena Park Dr Dayton (45417) ***(G-9258)***
Bonded Chemicals Inc (HQ) 614 777-9240
2645 Charter St Columbus (43228) ***(G-7053)***
Bonezzi Swtzer Polito Hupp Lpa (PA) 216 875-2767
1300 E 9th St Ste 1950 Cleveland (44114) ***(G-5068)***
Bonneville International Corp 513 699-5102
2060 Reading Rd Ste 400 Cincinnati (45202) ***(G-3067)***
Bonnie Plant Farm, Cygnet *Also called Alabama Farmers Coop Inc* ***(G-9142)***
Bontrager Excavating Co Inc 330 499-8775
11087 Cleveland Ave Nw Uniontown (44685) ***(G-18358)***
Bookmasters Inc (PA) 419 281-1802
30 Amberwood Pkwy Ashland (44805) ***(G-658)***
Boone Coleman Construction Inc 740 858-6661
32 State Route 239 Portsmouth (45663) ***(G-16126)***
Boonshoft Museum of Discovery, Dayton *Also called Dayton Society Natural History* ***(G-9381)***
Boost Technologies, Dayton *Also called Shumsky Enterprises Inc* ***(G-9765)***
Boost Technologies LLC 800 223-2203
811 E 4th St Dayton (45402) ***(G-9259)***
Booth, Jack B MD, Zanesville *Also called Thomas E Rojewski MD Inc* ***(G-20366)***
Booz Allen Hamilton Inc 937 429-5580
3800 Pentagon Blvd # 110 Beavercreek (45431) ***(G-1134)***
Boral Resources LLC 740 622-8042
48699 County Rd 275 Coshocton (43812) ***(G-8999)***
Borchers Americas Inc (HQ) 440 899-2950
811 Sharon Dr Westlake (44145) ***(G-19323)***
Bordas & Bordas Pllc 740 695-8141
106 E Main St Saint Clairsville (43950) ***(G-16480)***
Borden Dairy Co Cincinnati LLC 513 948-8811
415 John St Cincinnati (45215) ***(G-3068)***
Bordner and Associates Inc (PA) 614 552-6905
950 Taylor Station Rd E Columbus (43230) ***(G-7054)***
Bosch Rexroth Corporation 614 527-7400
3940 Gantz Rd Ste F Grove City (43123) ***(G-11409)***
Bosco Centre For Senior, Cleveland *Also called Don Bosco Community Center Inc* ***(G-5438)***
Boss Investigations, Akron *Also called Berns Oneill SEC & Safety LLC* ***(G-96)***
Boston Maintenance Bldg, Richfield *Also called Ohio Tpk & Infrastructure Comm* ***(G-16369)***
Boston Retail Products Inc 330 744-8100
225 Hubbard Rd Youngstown (44505) ***(G-19971)***
Bostwick Design Partnr Inc 216 621-7900
2729 Prospect Ave E Cleveland (44115) ***(G-5069)***
Bostwick-Braun Company (PA) 419 259-3600
7349 Crossleigh Ct Toledo (43617) ***(G-17620)***
Bottomline Ink Corporation 419 897-8000
7829 Ponderosa Rd Perrysburg (43551) ***(G-15840)***
Boulevard Motel Corp 440 234-3131
17550 Rosbough Blvd Cleveland (44130) ***(G-5070)***
Bound Tree Medical LLC (HQ) 614 760-5000
5000 Tuttle Crossing Blvd Dublin (43016) ***(G-10149)***
Boundless Flight Inc (PA) 440 610-3683
20226 Detroit Rd Rocky River (44116) ***(G-16424)***
Bowen Engineering Corporation 614 536-0273
22 E Gay St Ste 700 Columbus (43215) ***(G-7055)***
Bowers Insurance Agency Inc 330 638-6146
339 N High St Cortland (44410) ***(G-8984)***
Bowlero Corp 440 327-1190
38931 Center Ridge Rd North Ridgeville (44039) ***(G-15322)***
Bowling Green Coop Nurs Schl 419 352-8675
315 S College Dr Bowling Green (43402) ***(G-1721)***
Bowling Green Lincoln Auto SL, Bowling Green *Also called Bowling Green Lncln-Mrcury Inc* ***(G-1722)***
Bowling Green Lncln-Mrcury Inc 419 352-2553
1079 N Main St Bowling Green (43402) ***(G-1722)***
Bowling Green State University 419 372-8657
120 W Hall Bowling Green (43403) ***(G-1723)***
Bowling Green State University 419 372-2186
516 Admin Bldg Bowling Green (43403) ***(G-1724)***
Bowling Green State University 419 372-2700
245 Troup Ave Bowling Green (43402) ***(G-1725)***
Bowling Transportation Inc (PA) 419 436-9590
1827 Sandusky St Fostoria (44830) ***(G-10998)***
Bowman Agricultural RES Ctr, Thornville *Also called Bowman Organic Farms Ltd* ***(G-17504)***
Bowman Organic Farms Ltd 740 246-3936
8100 Blackbird Ln Thornville (43076) ***(G-17504)***
Bowser Morner and Associates, Toledo *Also called Bowser-Morner Inc* ***(G-17621)***
Bowser-Morner Inc 419 691-4800
1419 Miami St Toledo (43605) ***(G-17621)***
Box 21 Rescue Squad Inc 937 223-2821
100 E Helena St 120 Dayton (45404) ***(G-9260)***
Boxdrop Mansfield Mattress, Mansfield *Also called Mlp Interent Enterprises LLC* ***(G-13224)***
BOY SCOUTS OF AMERICA, Columbus *Also called Simon Knton Cncil Byscuts Amer* ***(G-8642)***
Boy Scouts of America (PA) 513 961-2336
10078 Reading Rd Cincinnati (45241) ***(G-3069)***

1058 2019 Harris Ohio Services Directory (G-0000) Company's Geographic Section entry number

Boy Scuts Amer - Lk Erie Cncil 216 861-6060
2241 Woodland Ave Cleveland (44115) *(G-5071)*

Boy-Ko Management Inc 513 677-4900
9370 Union Cemetery Rd Loveland (45140) *(G-12979)*

Boyas Excavating Inc (PA) 216 524-3620
11311 Rockside Rd Cleveland (44125) *(G-5072)*

Boyd Funeral Home, Cleveland *Also called E F Boyd & Son Inc (G-5453)*

Boyds Kinsman Home Inc 330 876-5581
7929 State Route 5 Kinsman (44428) *(G-12318)*

Boys & Girls CLB Hamilton Inc (PA) 513 893-0071
958 East Ave Hamilton (45011) *(G-11559)*

Boys & Girls Club of Columbus 614 221-8830
1108 City Park Ave # 301 Columbus (43206) *(G-7056)*

Boys & Girls Club of Toledo (PA) 419 241-4258
2250 N Detroit Ave Toledo (43606) *(G-17622)*

Boys & Girls Clubs Grtr Cinc (PA) 513 421-8909
600 Dalton Ave Cincinnati (45203) *(G-3070)*

Boys Club Camp Association, Toledo *Also called Boys & Girls Club of Toledo (G-17622)*

BP, Aurora *Also called Waterway Gas & Wash Company (G-851)*

BP, Thornville *Also called Englefield Inc (G-17505)*

Bp 216 731-3826
24310 Lakeland Blvd Euclid (44132) *(G-10625)*

Bp-Ls-Pt Co 614 841-4500
5275 Sinclair Rd Columbus (43229) *(G-7057)*

Bpf Enterprises Ltd 419 855-2545
1901 Middlesbrough Ct # 2 Maumee (43537) *(G-13763)*

Bpi Infrmtion Systems Ohio Inc 440 717-4112
6055 W Snowville Rd Brecksville (44141) *(G-1771)*

Bpm Realty Inc 614 221-6811
195 N Grant Ave Fl 2a Columbus (43215) *(G-7058)*

Bpo Elks of USA 740 622-0794
434 Chestnut St Coshocton (43812) *(G-9000)*

Bprex Closures LLC 812 424-2904
1695 Indian Cir Ste 116 Maumee (43537) *(G-13764)*

Bprex Plastic Packaging Inc 419 423-3271
170 Stanford Pkwy Findlay (45840) *(G-10882)*

Brackett Builders Inc (PA) 937 339-7505
185 Marybill Dr S Troy (45373) *(G-18197)*

Bracor Inc 216 289-5300
26250 Euclid Ave Ste 901 Euclid (44132) *(G-10626)*

Bradcorp Ohio II LLC (PA) 513 671-3300
3195 Profit Dr Fairfield (45014) *(G-10700)*

Braden Med Services Inc 740 732-2356
44519 Marietta Rd Caldwell (43724) *(G-2036)*

Bradley Bay Assisted Living 440 871-4509
605 Bradley Rd Bay Village (44140) *(G-1021)*

Brady Ware & Schoenfeld Inc 614 885-7407
4249 Easton Way Ste 100 Columbus (43219) *(G-7059)*

Brady Ware & Schoenfeld Inc (PA) 937 223-5247
3601 Rigby Rd Ste 400 Miamisburg (45342) *(G-14146)*

Brady Ware & Schoenfeld Inc 614 825-6277
4249 Easton Way Ste 175 Columbus (43219) *(G-7060)*

Brady Homes Inc 440 937-6255
36741 Chester Rd Avon (44011) *(G-867)*

Brady Plumbing & Heating Inc 440 324-4261
43191 N Ridge Rd Elyria (44035) *(G-10484)*

Brady Ware, Columbus *Also called Brady Ware & Schoenfeld Inc (G-7060)*

Brady Ware & Company, Miamisburg *Also called Brady Ware & Schoenfeld Inc (G-14146)*

BRADYVIEW MANOR, Lima *Also called Lost Creek Health Care (G-12692)*

Braeview Manor Inc 216 486-9300
20611 Euclid Ave Cleveland (44117) *(G-5073)*

Brakefire Incorporated 330 535-4343
451 Kennedy Rd Akron (44305) *(G-103)*

Bramarjac Inc 419 884-3434
4300 Algire Rd Mansfield (44904) *(G-13144)*

Bramhall Engrg & Surveying Co (PA) 440 934-7878
801 Moore Rd Avon (44011) *(G-868)*

Brampton Inn, Cleveland *Also called 1460 Ninth St Assoc Ltd Partnr (G-4866)*

Branch Clear Chan San Antonio, Mount Vernon *Also called W M V O 1300 AM (G-14791)*

Brand Energy & Infrastructure 419 324-1305
2961 South Ave Toledo (43609) *(G-17623)*

Brand Technologies Inc 419 873-6600
2262 Levis Commons Blvd Perrysburg (43551) *(G-15841)*

Brandmuscle Inc (HQ) 216 464-4342
1100 Superior Ave E # 500 Cleveland (44114) *(G-5074)*

Brands Insurance Agency Inc 513 777-7775
6449 Allen Rd Ste 1 West Chester (45069) *(G-18878)*

Brands' Marina, Port Clinton *Also called Tack-Anew Inc (G-16119)*

Brandsafway Services LLC 513 860-2626
9536 Glades Dr West Chester (45011) *(G-18879)*

Brandywine Country Club Inc 330 657-2525
5555 Akron Peninsula Rd Peninsula (44264) *(G-15810)*

Brandywine Golf Course, Peninsula *Also called Brandywine Country Club Inc (G-15810)*

Brandywine Master Assn 419 866-0135
7705 Pilgrims Lndg Maumee (43537) *(G-13765)*

Brason's Willcare, Euclid *Also called B H C Services Inc (G-10624)*

Brass Ring Golf Club Ltd 740 385-8966
14405 Country Club Ln Logan (43138) *(G-12832)*

Braun & Steidl Architects Inc (HQ) 330 864-7755
450 White Pond Dr Ste 200 Akron (44320) *(G-104)*

Bravo Wellness LLC (PA) 216 658-9500
20445 Emerald Pkwy # 400 Cleveland (44135) *(G-5075)*

Brawnstone Security LLC 330 800-9006
6986 Fenwick Ave Ne Canton (44721) *(G-2216)*

Brayman Construction Corp 740 237-0000
505 S 3rd St Ironton (45638) *(G-12146)*

Bre Ddr Parker Pavilions LLC 216 755-6451
3300 Enterprise Pkwy Beachwood (44122) *(G-1036)*

Breakthrough Media Ministries, Canal Winchester *Also called World Harvest Church Inc (G-2128)*

Breast Consultation Center, Cincinnati *Also called University of Cincinnati (G-4716)*

Breathing Air Systems Inc 614 864-1235
8855 E Broad St Reynoldsburg (43068) *(G-16286)*

Breathing Association 614 457-4570
1520 Old Henderson Rd # 201 Columbus (43220) *(G-7061)*

Brechbuhler Scales Inc (PA) 330 458-3060
1424 Scales St Sw Canton (44706) *(G-2217)*

Breckenridge Village, Willoughby *Also called Ohio Living (G-19558)*

Brecksville City Service Dept, Brecksville *Also called City of Brecksville (G-1774)*

Brecksville Community Center, Brecksville *Also called City of Brecksville (G-1775)*

Brecksville Leasing Co LLC 330 659-6166
4360 Brecksville Rd Richfield (44286) *(G-16347)*

Brecksvlle Halthcare Group Inc 440 546-0643
8757 Brecksville Rd Brecksville (44141) *(G-1772)*

Brecon Distribution Center, Cincinnati *Also called Duke Energy Ohio Inc (G-3452)*

Breezy Point Ltd Partnership (PA) 440 247-3363
30575 Bnbridge Rd Ste 100 Solon (44139) *(G-16828)*

Breezy Point Ltd Partnership 330 995-0600
350 N Aurora Rd Aurora (44202) *(G-822)*

Breitinger Company 419 526-4255
595 Oakenwaldt St Mansfield (44905) *(G-13145)*

Brenckle Farms Inc 330 877-4426
12434 Duquette Ave Ne Hartville (44632) *(G-11683)*

Brendamour Moving & Stor Inc 800 354-9715
2630 Glendale Milford Rd D Cincinnati (45241) *(G-3071)*

Brenmar Construction Inc 740 286-2151
900 Morton St Jackson (45640) *(G-12169)*

Brenn Field Nursing Center 330 683-4075
1980 Lynn Dr Orrville (44667) *(G-15626)*

Brennan Manna & Diamond LLC (PA) 330 253-5060
75 E Market St Akron (44308) *(G-105)*

Brennan & Associates Inc 216 391-4822
1550 E 33rd St Cleveland (44114) *(G-5076)*

Brennan Electric LLC 513 353-2229
6859 Cemetary Dr Miamitown (45041) *(G-14240)*

Brennan Equipment Services, Holland *Also called Brennan Industrial Truck Co (G-11875)*

Brennan Industrial Truck Co 419 867-6000
6940 Hall St Holland (43528) *(G-11875)*

Brennan Industries Inc (PA) 440 248-1880
6701 Cochran Rd Cleveland (44139) *(G-5077)*

Brennan Industries Inc 440 248-7088
30205 Solon Rd Solon (44139) *(G-16829)*

Brennan-Eberly Team Sports Inc 419 865-8326
6144 Merger Dr Holland (43528) *(G-11876)*

Brenneman Lumber Co 740 397-0573
51 Parrott St Mount Vernon (43050) *(G-14750)*

Brent Burris Trucking LLC 419 759-2020
2445 County Road 75 Ada (45810) *(G-2)*

Brent Industries Inc 419 382-8693
2922 South Ave Toledo (43609) *(G-17624)*

Brentley Institute Inc 216 225-0087
3143 W 33rd St Ste 2 Cleveland (44109) *(G-5078)*

Brentlinger Enterprises 614 889-2571
6335 Perimeter Loop Rd Dublin (43017) *(G-10150)*

Brentwood Golf Club Inc 440 322-9254
4456 Abbe Rd Sheffield Village (44054) *(G-16733)*

Brentwood Health Care Center, Northfield *Also called Brentwood Life Care Company (G-15375)*

Brentwood Life Care Company 330 468-2273
907 W Aurora Rd Northfield (44067) *(G-15375)*

Brenwood Inc 740 452-7533
1709 Maple Ave Zanesville (43701) *(G-20283)*

Brethren Care Inc 419 289-0803
2140 Center St Ofc Ashland (44805) *(G-659)*

Brethren Care Village LLC 419 289-1585
2140 Center St Ashland (44805) *(G-660)*

Brewer-Garrett Co (PA) 440 243-3535
6800 Eastland Rd Middleburg Heights (44130) *(G-14248)*

Brewster Convalescent Center, Brewster *Also called Brewster Parke Inc (G-1809)*

Brewster Parke Inc 330 767-4179
264 Mohican St Ne Brewster (44613) *(G-1809)*

Brg Realty Group LLC (PA) 513 936-5960
7265 Kenwood Rd Ste 111 Cincinnati (45236) *(G-3072)*

Brian Brocker Dr 330 747-9215
1616 Covington St Youngstown (44510) *(G-19972)*

Brian-Kyles Construction Inc 440 242-0298
875 N Ridge Rd E Lorain (44055) *(G-12887)*

Briar Hill Hlth Care Residence, Middlefield *Also called Briar HI Hlth Care Rsdence Inc (G-14269)*

Briar HI Hlth Care Rsdence Inc 440 632-5241
15950 Pierce St Middlefield (44062) *(G-14269)*

A
L
P
H
A
B
E
T
I
C

Briar-Gate Realty Inc..614 299-2121
  1675 W Mound St Columbus (43223) *(G-7062)*
Briar-Gate Realty Inc..614 299-2122
  3655 Brookham Dr Grove City (43123) *(G-11410)*
Briar-Gate Realty Inc (PA)....................................614 299-2121
  3827 Brookham Dr Grove City (43123) *(G-11411)*
Briarfield At Ashley Circle, Boardman *Also called Ashley Enterprises LLC (G-1695)*
Briarfield At Glanzman Road, Toledo *Also called Concord Care Center of Toledo (G-17676)*
Briarfield Manor LLC..330 270-3468
  461 S Canfield Niles Rd Youngstown (44515) *(G-19973)*
Briarfield of Sandusky, Sandusky *Also called Concord Health Care Inc (G-16592)*
Briarwood Banquet Center, Cincinnati *Also called Banquets Unlimited (G-3017)*
Briarwood Healthcare Center, Stow *Also called Briarwood Ltd (G-17193)*
Briarwood Ltd..330 688-1828
  3700 Englewood Dr Stow (44224) *(G-17193)*
Briarwood Mano, Coldwater *Also called Hcf of Briarwood Inc (G-6758)*
Bricker & Eckler LLP (PA)....................................614 227-2300
  100 S 3rd St Ste B Columbus (43215) *(G-7063)*
Bricker & Eckler LLP..513 870-6700
  201 E 5th St Ste 1110 Cincinnati (45202) *(G-3073)*
Brickman Facility Services, New Albany *Also called Brightview Landscapes LLC (G-14844)*
Bridge Counseling Center, Columbus *Also called Northland Brdg Franklin Cnty (G-8201)*
Bridge Home Health & Hostice, Findlay *Also called Blanchard Valley Health System (G-10872)*
Bridge Logistics Inc..513 874-7444
  5 Circle Freeway Dr West Chester (45246) *(G-19046)*
Bridge The, Youngstown *Also called Siffrin Residential Assn (G-20211)*
Bridgepoint Risk MGT LLC....................................419 794-1075
  1440 Arrowhead Dr Maumee (43537) *(G-13766)*
Bridgeport Auto Parts Inc (PA)............................740 635-0441
  890 National Rd Bridgeport (43912) *(G-1814)*
Bridgeport Healthcare Center, Portsmouth *Also called Royce Leasing Co LLC (G-16165)*
Bridges To Independence Inc (PA)........................740 362-1996
  61 W William St Delaware (43015) *(G-9955)*
Bridges To Independence Inc............................740 375-5533
  117 N Greenwood St Ste 2 Marion (43302) *(G-13407)*
Bridgeshome Health Care....................................330 764-1000
  5075 Windfall Rd Medina (44256) *(G-13913)*
Bridgestone Americas Center, Akron *Also called Bridgestone Research LLC (G-106)*
Bridgestone Research LLC....................................330 379-7570
  1655 S Main St Akron (44301) *(G-106)*
Bridgestone Ret Operations LLC........................513 367-7888
  10606 New Haven Rd Harrison (45030) *(G-11662)*
Bridgestone Ret Operations LLC........................330 929-3391
  2761 State Rd Cuyahoga Falls (44223) *(G-9075)*
Bridgestone Ret Operations LLC........................419 586-1600
  1109 N Main St Celina (45822) *(G-2585)*
Bridgetown Middle School Pta............................513 574-3511
  3900 Race Rd Cincinnati (45211) *(G-3074)*
Bridgewater Dairy LLC..419 485-8157
  14587 County Road 8 50 Montpelier (43543) *(G-14608)*
Bridgeway Inc (PA)..216 688-4114
  2202 Prame Ave Cleveland (44109) *(G-5079)*
Bridgeway Pointe, Cincinnati *Also called Drake Development Inc (G-3443)*
Bright Beginnings..937 748-2612
  60 E North St Springboro (45066) *(G-16963)*
Bright Beginnings Preschool, Bowling Green *Also called Bowling Green Coop Nurs Schl (G-1721)*
Bright Dental, Sandusky *Also called Smile Brands Inc (G-16642)*
Bright Horizons Battelle, Columbus *Also called Bright Horizons Chld Ctrs LLC (G-7064)*
Bright Horizons Chld Ctrs LLC............................614 754-7023
  835 Thomas Ln Columbus (43214) *(G-7064)*
Bright Horizons Chld Ctrs LLC............................614 566-9322
  111 S Grant Ave Columbus (43215) *(G-7065)*
Bright Horizons Chld Ctrs LLC............................614 227-0550
  277 E Town St Columbus (43215) *(G-7066)*
Bright Horizons Chld Ctrs LLC............................614 566-4847
  835 Thomas Ln Columbus (43214) *(G-7067)*
Bright Horizons Chld Ctrs LLC............................330 375-7633
  475 Ohio St Akron (44304) *(G-107)*
Brighter Horizons Residential............................440 417-1751
  1899 Hubbard Rd Madison (44057) *(G-13093)*
Brighton Gardens of Westlake, Westlake *Also called Sunrise Senior Living Inc (G-19410)*
Brighton Gardens Wash Township, Dayton *Also called Sunrise Senior Living Inc (G-9801)*
Brighton-Best Intl Inc..440 238-1350
  21855 Commerce Pkwy Strongsville (44149) *(G-17288)*
Brightstar Healthcare..513 321-4688
  10999 Reed Hartman Hwy # 209 Blue Ash (45242) *(G-1516)*
Brightview Landscape Svcs Inc............................614 801-1712
  3001 Innis Rd Columbus (43224) *(G-7068)*
Brightview Landscape Svcs Inc............................614 478-2085
  3001 Innis Rd Columbus (43224) *(G-7069)*
Brightview Landscape Svcs Inc............................740 369-4800
  3001 Innis Rd Columbus (43224) *(G-7070)*
Brightview Landscapes LLC................................937 235-9595
  38 Brandt St Dayton (45404) *(G-9261)*
Brightview Landscapes LLC................................513 874-6484
  10139 Transportation Way West Chester (45246) *(G-19047)*

Brightview Landscapes LLC................................216 398-1289
  25072 Broadway Ave Oakwood Village (44146) *(G-15486)*
Brightview Landscapes LLC................................440 937-5126
  1051 Lear Industrial Pkwy A Avon (44011) *(G-869)*
Brightview Landscapes LLC................................301 987-9200
  2323 Performance Way Columbus (43207) *(G-7071)*
Brightview Landscapes LLC................................614 276-5500
  2240 Harper Rd Columbus (43204) *(G-7072)*
Brightview Landscapes LLC................................440 729-2302
  7901 Old Ranger Rd Chesterland (44026) *(G-2737)*
Brightview Landscapes LLC................................614 741-8233
  6530 W Campus Oval # 300 New Albany (43054) *(G-14844)*
Brilliant Electric Sign Co Ltd............................216 741-3800
  4811 Van Epps Rd Brooklyn Heights (44131) *(G-1866)*
Brilligent Solutions Inc (PA)............................937 879-4148
  1130 Channingway Dr Fairborn (45324) *(G-10664)*
Brim's Imports Sales & Service, Kenton *Also called Brims Imports (G-12272)*
Brims Imports (PA)..419 674-4137
  370 W Franklin St Kenton (43326) *(G-12272)*
Brinks Incorporated..419 729-5389
  1265 Matzinger Rd Toledo (43612) *(G-17625)*
Brinks Incorporated..614 291-1268
  1362 Essex Ave Columbus (43211) *(G-7073)*
Brinks Incorporated..614 291-0624
  506 E Starr Ave Columbus (43201) *(G-7074)*
Brinks Incorporated..216 621-7493
  1422 Superior Ave E Cleveland (44114) *(G-5080)*
Brinks Incorporated..330 633-5351
  1601 Industrial Pkwy Akron (44310) *(G-108)*
Brinks Incorporated..513 621-9310
  1105 Hopkins St Cincinnati (45203) *(G-3075)*
Brinks Incorporated..937 253-9777
  4395 Springfield St Dayton (45431) *(G-9162)*
Brinks Incorporated..330 832-6130
  300 Nova Dr Se Massillon (44646) *(G-13665)*
Brinks Incorporated..330 758-7379
  6971 Southern Blvd Ste F Youngstown (44512) *(G-19974)*
Bristol Village Homes..740 947-2118
  660 E 5th St Waverly (45690) *(G-18814)*
Bristol West Casualty Insur Co, Independence *Also called Foremost Insurance Company (G-12075)*
Brite Brazing, Wickliffe *Also called HI Tecmetal Group Inc (G-19463)*
Briteskies LLC..216 369-3600
  2658 Scranton Rd Ste 3 Cleveland (44113) *(G-5081)*
Britton-Gallagher & Assoc Inc............................216 658-7100
  1375 E 9th St Fl 30 Cleveland (44114) *(G-5082)*
Brixx Ice Company..937 222-2257
  500 E 1st St Dayton (45402) *(G-9262)*
Broad & James Inc..614 231-8697
  3502 E 7th Ave Columbus (43219) *(G-7075)*
Broad & James Towing, Columbus *Also called Broad & James Inc (G-7075)*
Broad Street Hotel Assoc LP................................614 861-0321
  4801 E Broad St Columbus (43213) *(G-7076)*
Broadband Express LLC..513 834-8085
  11359 Mosteller Rd Cincinnati (45241) *(G-3076)*
Broadband Express LLC..614 823-6464
  374 Westdale Ave Ste A Westerville (43082) *(G-19149)*
Broadband Express LLC..419 536-9127
  1915 Nebraska Ave Toledo (43607) *(G-17626)*
Broadband Hospitality, Youngstown *Also called Great Lakes Telcom Ltd (G-20055)*
Broadspire Services Inc......................................614 436-8990
  445 Hutchinson Ave # 550 Columbus (43235) *(G-7077)*
Broadview Health Center, Columbus *Also called Generation Health Corp (G-7656)*
Broadview Heights, Broadview Heights *Also called Cleveland Clinic Foundation (G-1827)*
Broadview Mortgage Company (PA)........................614 854-7000
  3982 Powell Rd Ste 230 Powell (43065) *(G-16187)*
Broadview Multi-Care Center, Parma *Also called Broadview Nursing Home Inc (G-15761)*
Broadview NH LLC..614 337-1066
  5151 N Hamilton Rd Columbus (43230) *(G-7078)*
Broadview Nursing Home Inc................................216 661-5084
  5520 Broadview Rd Parma (44134) *(G-15761)*
Broadvox, Cleveland *Also called Infotelecom Holdings LLC (G-5753)*
Broadvox LLC (HQ)..216 373-4600
  75 Erieview Plz Fl 4 Cleveland (44114) *(G-5083)*
Broadvue Motors Inc..440 845-6000
  6930 Pearl Rd Cleveland (44130) *(G-5084)*
Broadway Care Ctr Mple Hts LLC........................216 662-0551
  25201 Chagrin Blvd # 190 Beachwood (44122) *(G-1037)*
Brock & Associates Builders................................330 757-7150
  118 Heron Bay Dr Youngstown (44514) *(G-19975)*
Brock & Sons Inc..513 874-4555
  8731 N Gilmore Rd Fairfield (45014) *(G-10701)*
Brocon Construction Inc......................................614 871-7300
  2120 Hardy Parkway St Grove City (43123) *(G-11412)*
Brodhead Village Ltd (PA)..................................614 863-4640
  160 W Main St New Albany (43054) *(G-14845)*
Brohl & Appell, Sandusky *Also called Rexel Usa Inc (G-16636)*
Brokaw Inc..216 241-8003
  1213 W 6th St Cleveland (44113) *(G-5085)*
Broken Arrow Inc..419 562-3480
  1649 Marion Rd Bucyrus (44820) *(G-1977)*

Brondes All Makes Auto Leasing 419 887-1511
1511 Reynolds Rd Maumee (43537) *(G-13767)*
Brondes Ford (PA) 419 473-1411
5545 Secor Rd Toledo (43623) *(G-17627)*
Brondes Ford Toledo, Toledo *Also called Brondes Ford (G-17627)*
Brook Beech 216 831-2255
3737 Lander Rd Cleveland (44124) *(G-5086)*
Brook Haven Home Health Care 937 833-6945
850 Albert Rd Brookville (45309) *(G-1910)*
Brook Park Recreation Center, Cleveland *Also called City of Brook Park (G-5188)*
Brook Plum Country Club 419 625-5394
3712 Galloway Rd Sandusky (44870) *(G-16578)*
Brook Willow Chrstn Cmmunities 614 885-3300
55 Lazelle Rd Columbus (43235) *(G-7079)*
Brookdale Austintown, Austintown *Also called Brookdale Snior Lving Cmmnties (G-856)*
Brookdale Beavercreek, Beavercreek *Also called Brookdale Senior Living Commun (G-1208)*
Brookdale Deer Park 513 745-7600
3801 E Galbraith Rd Ofc Cincinnati (45236) *(G-3077)*
Brookdale Kettering, Beavercreek Township *Also called Brookdale Senior Living Inc (G-1264)*
Brookdale Living Cmnty Ohio, Columbus *Also called Brookdale Lving Cmmunities Inc (G-7080)*
Brookdale Lving Cmmunities Inc 614 734-1000
3500 Trillium Xing Columbus (43235) *(G-7080)*
Brookdale Lving Cmmunities Inc 330 666-4545
100 Brookmont Rd Ofc Akron (44333) *(G-109)*
Brookdale Lving Cmmunities Inc 937 399-1216
2981 Vester Ave Springfield (45503) *(G-17002)*
Brookdale Place Wooster LLC 330 262-1615
1615 Cleveland Rd Wooster (44691) *(G-19694)*
Brookdale Senior Living Commun 330 829-0180
1277 S Sawburg Ave Alliance (44601) *(G-519)*
Brookdale Senior Living Commun 937 203-8443
3839 Indian Ripple Rd Beavercreek (45440) *(G-1208)*
Brookdale Senior Living Commun 937 548-6800
1401 N Broadway St Greenville (45331) *(G-11367)*
Brookdale Senior Living Inc 614 336-3677
7220 Muirfield Dr Dublin (43017) *(G-10151)*
Brookdale Senior Living Inc 937 203-8596
280 Walden Way Ofc Beavercreek Township (45440) *(G-1264)*
Brookdale Senior Living Inc 419 756-5599
1841 Middle Bellville Rd Mansfield (44904) *(G-13146)*
Brookdale Senior Living Inc 513 229-3155
5535 Irwin Simpson Rd Mason (45040) *(G-13546)*
Brookdale Senior Living Inc 855 308-2438
9101 Winton Rd Cincinnati (45231) *(G-3078)*
Brookdale Senior Living Inc 513 745-9292
9090 Montgomery Rd Cincinnati (45242) *(G-3079)*
Brookdale Senior Living Inc 330 262-1615
1615 Cleveland Rd Wooster (44691) *(G-19695)*
Brookdale Senior Living Inc 330 666-7011
101 N Clvland Mssillon Rd Akron (44333) *(G-110)*
Brookdale Senior Living Inc 614 277-1200
1305 Lamplighter Dr Grove City (43123) *(G-11413)*
Brookdale Senior Living Inc 216 321-6331
3151 Mayfield Rd Cleveland (44118) *(G-5087)*
Brookdale Senior Living Inc 440 892-4200
28550 Westlake Village Dr Westlake (44145) *(G-19324)*
Brookdale Senior Living Inc 740 373-9600
150 Browns Rd Marietta (45750) *(G-13316)*
Brookdale Senior Living Inc 614 794-2499
690 Cooper Rd Apt 514 Westerville (43081) *(G-19228)*
Brookdale Senior Living Inc 330 723-5825
49 Leisure Ln A Medina (44256) *(G-13914)*
Brookdale Senior Living Inc 513 745-7600
3801 E Galbraith Rd Ofc Cincinnati (45236) *(G-3080)*
Brookdale Senior Living Inc 419 422-8657
600 Fox Run Rd Ofc Findlay (45840) *(G-10883)*
Brookdale Senior Living Inc 937 738-7342
1565 London Ave Frnt Marysville (43040) *(G-13485)*
Brookdale Snior Lving Cmmnties 740 366-0005
331 Goosepond Rd Newark (43055) *(G-15015)*
Brookdale Snior Lving Cmmnties 937 832-8500
350 Union Blvd Englewood (45322) *(G-10580)*
Brookdale Snior Lving Cmmnties 419 354-5300
121 N Wintergarden Rd Ofc Bowling Green (43402) *(G-1726)*
Brookdale Snior Lving Cmmnties 740 681-9903
241 Whittier Dr S Lancaster (43130) *(G-12373)*
Brookdale Snior Lving Cmmnties 419 423-4440
725 Fox Run Rd Findlay (45840) *(G-10884)*
Brookdale Snior Lving Cmmnties 330 249-1071
1420 S Canfield Niles Rd Austintown (44515) *(G-856)*
Brookdale Snior Lving Cmmnties 419 756-5599
1841 Middle Bellville Rd Mansfield (44904) *(G-13147)*
Brookdale Snior Lving Cmmnties 937 773-0500
1744 W High St Ofc Piqua (45356) *(G-15998)*
Brookdale Snior Lving Cmmnties 330 793-0085
2300 Canfield Rd Ofc Youngstown (44511) *(G-19976)*
Brookdale Willoughby, Willoughby *Also called Emeritus Corporation (G-19520)*
Brookeside Ambulance Services 419 476-7442
640 Phillips Ave Toledo (43612) *(G-17628)*

Brookhaven Home Health Care, Brookville *Also called Brook Haven Home Health Care (G-1910)*
BROOKHAVEN NURSING & CARE CENT, Brookville *Also called Brookville Enterprises Inc (G-1911)*
Brookhill Center Industries 419 876-3932
7989 State Route 108 Ottawa (45875) *(G-15657)*
Brookledge Golf Club, Cuyahoga Falls *Also called City of Cuyahoga Falls (G-9081)*
Brooklyn Adult Activity Center, Cleveland *Also called A W S Inc (G-4882)*
Brooklyn House, Cleveland *Also called Koinonia Homes Inc (G-5836)*
Brookpark Freeway Lanes LLC 216 267-2150
12859 Brookpark Rd Cleveland (44130) *(G-5088)*
Brooks & Stafford Co 216 696-3000
55 Public Sq Ste 1650 Cleveland (44113) *(G-5089)*
Brooksedge Day Care Center 614 529-0077
2185 Hilliard Rome Rd Hilliard (43026) *(G-11748)*
Brookside Country Club Inc 330 477-6505
1800 Canton Ave Nw Canton (44708) *(G-2218)*
Brookside Extended Care Center 513 398-1020
780 Snider Rd Mason (45040) *(G-13547)*
Brookside Golf & Cntry CLB Co 614 889-2581
2770 W Dblin Granville Rd Columbus (43235) *(G-7081)*
Brookside Holdings LLC 419 224-7019
3211 S Dixie Hwy Lima (45804) *(G-12609)*
Brookside Holdings LLC (PA) 419 925-4457
8022 State Route 119 Maria Stein (45860) *(G-13306)*
Brookside Laboratories Inc 419 977-2766
200 White Mountain Dr New Bremen (45869) *(G-14885)*
Brookside Trucking, Lima *Also called Brookside Holdings LLC (G-12609)*
Brookside Trucking, Maria Stein *Also called Brookside Holdings LLC (G-13306)*
Brookview Healthcare Center, Defiance *Also called Brookview Healthcare Ctr (G-9905)*
Brookview Healthcare Ctr 419 784-1014
214 Harding St Defiance (43512) *(G-9905)*
Brookville Enterprises Inc 937 833-2133
1 Country Ln Brookville (45309) *(G-1911)*
Brookville Roadster Inc 937 833-4605
718 Albert Rd Brookville (45309) *(G-1912)*
Brookwood Management Company (PA) 330 497-6565
1201 S Main St Ste 220 Canton (44720) *(G-2219)*
Brookwood Retirement Community, Cincinnati *Also called C Micah Rand Inc (G-3101)*
Brotherhd Frtrnl Ordr, Coshocton *Also called Bpo Elks of USA (G-9000)*
Brotherhood of Locomotive Engi 740 345-0978
745 Sherman Ave Newark (43055) *(G-15016)*
Brothers Auto Transport LLC 330 824-0082
2188 Lyntz Townline Rd Sw Warren (44481) *(G-18681)*
Brothers Properties Corp 513 381-3000
601 Vine St Ste 1 Cincinnati (45202) *(G-3081)*
Brothers Publishing Co LLC 937 548-3330
100 Washington Ave Greenville (45331) *(G-11368)*
Brothers Trading Co Inc (PA) 937 746-1010
400 Victory Ln Springboro (45066) *(G-16964)*
Brothrhood Lcomotive Engineers, Newark *Also called Brotherhood of Locomotive Engi (G-15016)*
Brott Mardis & Co 330 762-5022
1540 W Market St Akron (44313) *(G-111)*
Broughton International, Cincinnati *Also called Rippe & Kingston Systems Inc (G-4375)*
Brouse McDowell Lpa 216 830-6830
600 Superior Ave E # 1600 Cleveland (44114) *(G-5090)*
Brower Products Inc (HQ) 937 563-1111
401 Northland Blvd Cincinnati (45240) *(G-3082)*
Brown & Brown of Ohio LLC 419 874-1974
360 3 Meadows Dr Perrysburg (43551) *(G-15842)*
Brown and Caldwell 614 410-6144
445 Hutchinson Ave # 540 Columbus (43235) *(G-7082)*
Brown and Margolius Co Lpa 216 621-2034
55 Public Sq Ste 1100 Cleveland (44113) *(G-5091)*
Brown Cnty Bd Mntal Rtardation 937 378-4891
325 W State St Ste A2 Georgetown (45121) *(G-11261)*
Brown Cnty Snior Ctzen Council 937 378-6603
505 N Main St Georgetown (45121) *(G-11262)*
Brown Co Ed Service Center 937 378-6118
9231b Hamer Rd Georgetown (45121) *(G-11263)*
Brown Contracting & Dev LLC 419 341-3939
318 Madison St Port Clinton (43452) *(G-16100)*
Brown County Asphalt Inc 937 446-2481
11254 Hamer Rd Georgetown (45121) *(G-11264)*
Brown County Engineers Office, Georgetown *Also called County of Brown (G-11267)*
Brown Derby Roadhouse 330 528-3227
72 N Main St Ste 208 Hudson (44236) *(G-11968)*
Brown Distributing Inc 740 349-7999
51 Swans Rd Ne Newark (43055) *(G-15017)*
Brown Gibbons Lang & Co LLC (PA) 216 241-2800
1 Cleveland Ctr Cleveland (44114) *(G-5092)*
Brown Gibbons Lang Ltd Ptrship 216 241-2800
1111 Superior Ave E # 900 Cleveland (44114) *(G-5093)*
Brown Industrial Inc 937 693-3838
311 W South St Botkins (45306) *(G-1708)*
Brown Medical Services, Wheelersburg *Also called Proactive Occptnal Mdicine Inc (G-19439)*
Brown Memorial Home Inc 740 474-6238
158 E Mound St Circleville (43113) *(G-4826)*

A
L
P
H
A
B
E
T
I
C

Brown Memorial Hospital 440 593-1131
　158 W Main Rd Conneaut (44030) *(G-8952)*
Brown Motor Sales Co (PA) 419 531-0151
　5625 W Central Ave Toledo (43615) *(G-17629)*
Brown Motors, Toledo *Also called Brown Motor Sales Co (G-17629)*
Brown WD General Agency Inc 216 241-5840
　950 Main Ave Ste 600 Cleveland (44113) *(G-5094)*
Brown, Chris R & Vicki J, Willard *Also called Family Health Partners Inc (G-19480)*
Brown, Frank R & Sons, Silver Lake *Also called F B and S Masonry Inc (G-16807)*
Browning Mesonic Community (PA) 419 878-4055
　8883 Browning Dr Waterville (43566) *(G-18788)*
Browning-Ferris Inds of Ohio (HQ) 330 793-7676
　3870 Hendricks Rd Youngstown (44515) *(G-19977)*
Browning-Ferris Inds of Ohio 330 536-8013
　8100 S State Line Rd Lowellville (44436) *(G-13039)*
Browning-Ferris Industries Inc 513 899-2942
　2420 Mason Morrow Millgro Morrow (45152) *(G-14715)*
Browning-Ferris Industries LLC 440 786-9390
　30300 Pettibone Rd Solon (44139) *(G-16830)*
Browning-Ferris Industries LLC 330 393-0385
　1901 Pine Ave Se Warren (44483) *(G-18682)*
Browns Run Country Club 513 423-6291
　6855 Sloebig Rd Middletown (45042) *(G-14294)*
Brownstone Private Child Care 216 221-1470
　18225 Sloane Ave Lakewood (44107) *(G-12337)*
Bruce Klinger 419 473-2270
　3950 Sunforest Ct Ste 200 Toledo (43623) *(G-17630)*
Bruce M Allman 513 352-6712
　312 Walnut St Ste 1400 Cincinnati (45202) *(G-3083)*
Bruce R Bracken 513 558-3700
　222 Piedmont Ave Cincinnati (45219) *(G-3084)*
Bruder Inc 216 791-9800
　16900 Rockside Rd Maple Heights (44137) *(G-13282)*
Brumbaugh Construction Inc 937 692-5107
　3520 State Route 49 Arcanum (45304) *(G-623)*
Brumbaugh Engrg Surveying LLC 937 698-3000
　1105 S Miami St Ste 1 West Milton (45383) *(G-19126)*
Bruner Corporation (PA) 614 334-9000
　3637 Lacon Rd Hilliard (43026) *(G-11749)*
Brunk's Stoves, Salem *Also called L B Brunk & Sons Inc (G-16550)*
Bruns Building & Dev Corp Inc 419 925-4095
　1429 Cranberry Rd Saint Henry (45883) *(G-16515)*
Brunswick Center Ridge Lanes, North Ridgeville *Also called Bowlero Corp (G-15322)*
Brunswick City Schools (PA) 330 225-7731
　3643 Center Rd Brunswick (44212) *(G-1921)*
Brunswick Companies (PA) 330 864-8800
　5309 Transportation Blvd Cleveland (44125) *(G-5095)*
Brunswick Food Pantry Inc 330 225-0395
　2876 Center Rd Brunswick (44212) *(G-1922)*
Brush Contractors Inc 614 850-8500
　5000 Transamerica Dr Columbus (43228) *(G-7083)*
Brush Creek Motorsports 937 515-1353
　720 E Main St West Union (45693) *(G-19133)*
Brust Pipeline, Bryan *Also called Majaac Inc (G-1962)*
Bryan Electric Inc 740 695-9834
　46139 National Rd Saint Clairsville (43950) *(G-16481)*
Bryan Systems, Montpelier *Also called Bryan Truck Line Inc (G-14609)*
Bryan Systems, Montpelier *Also called Best Way Motor Lines Inc (G-14606)*
Bryan Truck Line Inc 419 485-8373
　14020 Us Hwy 20 Ste A Montpelier (43543) *(G-14609)*
Bryant Eliza Village 216 361-6141
　7201 Wade Park Ave Cleveland (44103) *(G-5096)*
Bryant Health Center Inc 740 532-6188
　2932 S 5th St Ironton (45638) *(G-12147)*
Bryden Place Inc 614 258-6623
　25201 Chagrin Blvd # 190 Beachwood (44122) *(G-1038)*
BSI Engineering LLC (PA) 513 201-3100
　300 E Bus Way Ste 300 Cincinnati (45241) *(G-3085)*
Bsl - Applied Laser Tech LLC (PA) 216 663-8181
　4560 Johnston Pkwy Cleveland (44128) *(G-5097)*
Bst & G Joint Fire District 740 965-3841
　350 W Cherry St Sunbury (43074) *(G-17384)*
Btas Inc (PA) 937 431-9431
　4391 Dayton Xenia Rd Beavercreek (45432) *(G-1135)*
Buchy Food Service, Cincinnati *Also called Chas G Buchy Packing Company (G-3172)*
Buck and Sons Ldscp Svc Inc 614 876-5359
　7147 Hayden Run Rd Hilliard (43026) *(G-11750)*
Buck Equipment Inc 614 539-3039
　1720 Feddern Ave Grove City (43123) *(G-11414)*
Buckeye Ambulance LLC 937 435-1584
　1516 Nicholas Rd Dayton (45417) *(G-9263)*
Buckeye Asphalt Paving Co, Toledo *Also called Lucas County Asphalt Inc (G-17867)*
Buckeye Assn Schl Admnstrators 614 846-4080
　8050 N High St Ste 150 Columbus (43235) *(G-7084)*
Buckeye Body and Equipment, Columbus *Also called Buckeye Truck Equipment Inc (G-7091)*
Buckeye Boxes Inc 614 274-8484
　601 N Hague Ave Columbus (43204) *(G-7085)*
Buckeye Broadband, Northwood *Also called Block Communications Inc (G-15389)*
Buckeye Cable Systems Inc 419 724-2539
　4212 South Ave Toledo (43615) *(G-17631)*

Buckeye Charter Service Inc (PA) 419 222-2455
　1235 E Hanthorn Rd Lima (45804) *(G-12610)*
Buckeye Charter Service Inc 937 879-3000
　8240 Expansion Way Dayton (45424) *(G-9264)*
Buckeye Charters, Dayton *Also called Buckeye Charter Service Inc (G-9264)*
Buckeye Check Cashing Inc (HQ) 614 798-5900
　6785 Bobcat Way Ste 200 Dublin (43016) *(G-10152)*
Buckeye Cmnty Eighty One LP 614 942-2020
　3021 E Dblin Granville Rd Columbus (43231) *(G-7086)*
Buckeye Cmnty Hope Foundation (PA) 614 942-2014
　3021 E Dblin Grndville Rd Columbus (43231) *(G-7087)*
Buckeye Cmnty Thirty Five LP 614 942-2020
　2228 11th St Sw Akron (44314) *(G-112)*
Buckeye Cmnty Twenty Six LP 614 942-2020
　3021 E Dblin Granville Rd Columbus (43231) *(G-7088)*
Buckeye Commercial Cleaning 614 866-4700
　12936 Stonecreek Dr Ste F Pickerington (43147) *(G-15949)*
Buckeye Community Bank 440 233-8800
　105 Sheffield Ctr Lorain (44055) *(G-12888)*
Buckeye Community Forty Four, Columbus *Also called Kent Place Housing (G-7896)*
Buckeye Community Services Inc 740 941-1639
　207 Remy Ct Waverly (45690) *(G-18815)*
Buckeye Companies (PA) 740 452-3641
　999 Zane St Zanesville (43701) *(G-20284)*
Buckeye Components LLC 330 482-5163
　1340 State Route 14 Columbiana (44408) *(G-6781)*
BUCKEYE DIALYSIS, Kettering *Also called Basin Dialysis LLC (G-12291)*
Buckeye Drag Racing Assn LLC 419 562-0869
　201 Penn Ave Bucyrus (44820) *(G-1978)*
Buckeye Drmtlogy Drmthphthlogy (PA) 614 389-6331
　5720 Blazer Pkwy Dublin (43017) *(G-10153)*
Buckeye Drmtlogy Drmthphthlogy 614 317-9630
　1933 Ohio Dr Grove City (43123) *(G-11415)*
BUCKEYE FASTENERS COMPANY, Streetsboro *Also called Joseph Industries
Inc (G-17258)*
Buckeye Golf Club Co Inc 419 636-6984
　10277 County Road D Bryan (43506) *(G-1953)*
Buckeye Heating and AC Sup Inc (PA) 216 831-0066
　5075 Richmond Rd Bedford Heights (44146) *(G-1318)*
Buckeye Hills-Hck Vly Reg Dev (HQ) 740 373-0087
　1400 Pike St Marietta (45750) *(G-13317)*
Buckeye Hills-Hck Vly Reg Dev 740 373-6400
　P.O. Box 368 Reno (45773) *(G-16276)*
Buckeye Home Health Care 513 791-6446
　10921 Reed Hartman Hwy # 310 Blue Ash (45242) *(G-1517)*
Buckeye Home Health Care (PA) 937 291-3780
　7700 Paragon Rd Ste A Dayton (45459) *(G-9265)*
Buckeye Home Healthcare Inc (PA) 614 776-3372
　635 Park Madow Rd Ste 110 Westerville (43081) *(G-19229)*
Buckeye Homecare Services Inc 216 321-9300
　14077 Cedar Rd Ste 103 Cleveland (44118) *(G-5098)*
Buckeye Honda, Hilliard *Also called Spires Motors Inc (G-11817)*
Buckeye Horizon, Mansfield *Also called Horizon Mechanical and Elec (G-13183)*
Buckeye Insurance, Piqua *Also called Home and Farm Insurance Co (G-16010)*
Buckeye Insurance Group, Piqua *Also called Buckeye State Mutual Insur Co (G-15999)*
Buckeye Lake Yacht Club Inc 740 929-4466
　5019 Northbank Rd Buckeye Lake (43008) *(G-1974)*
Buckeye Landscape Service Inc 614 866-0088
　6608 Taylor Rd Blacklick (43004) *(G-1475)*
Buckeye Lanes, North Olmsted *Also called Olmsted Lanes Inc (G-15301)*
Buckeye Launderer and Clrs LLC 419 592-2941
　4930 N Holland Sylvania Sylvania (43560) *(G-17413)*
Buckeye Leasing Inc 330 758-0841
　8063 Southern Blvd Youngstown (44512) *(G-19978)*
Buckeye Linen Service Inc 740 345-4046
　76 Jefferson St Newark (43055) *(G-15018)*
Buckeye Mechanical Contg Inc 740 282-0089
　2325 Township Road 370 Toronto (43964) *(G-18181)*
Buckeye Metals, Cleveland *Also called W R G Inc (G-6645)*
Buckeye Paper Co Inc 330 477-5925
　5233 Southway St Sw # 523 Canton (44706) *(G-2220)*
Buckeye Pipe Line Services Co 419 698-8770
　3321 York St Oregon (43616) *(G-15584)*
Buckeye Pool Inc 937 434-7916
　486 Windsor Park Dr Dayton (45459) *(G-9266)*
Buckeye Power Inc (PA) 614 781-0573
　6677 Busch Blvd Columbus (43229) *(G-7089)*
Buckeye Power Inc 740 598-6534
　306 County Road 7e Brilliant (43913) *(G-1820)*
Buckeye Power Sales Co Inc 937 346-8322
　5238 Cobblegate Blvd Moraine (45439) *(G-14628)*
Buckeye Prof Imaging Inc 800 433-1292
　5143 Stoneham Rd Canton (44720) *(G-2221)*
Buckeye Ranch Inc 614 384-7700
　697 E Broad St Columbus (43215) *(G-7090)*
Buckeye Ranch Inc (PA) 614 875-2371
　5665 Hoover Rd Grove City (43123) *(G-11416)*
Buckeye Real Estate, Columbus *Also called Garland Group Inc (G-7650)*
Buckeye Rsdntial Solutions LLC 330 235-9183
　320 E Main St Ste 301 Ravenna (44266) *(G-16233)*

Buckeye Rubber & Packing Co 216 464-8900
23940 Mercantile Rd Beachwood (44122) *(G-1039)*
Buckeye Rural Elc Coop Inc 740 379-2025
4848 State Route 325 Patriot (45658) *(G-15789)*
Buckeye State Credit Union (PA) 330 253-9197
197 E Thornton St Akron (44311) *(G-113)*
Buckeye State Mutual Insur Co (PA) 937 778-5000
1 Heritage Pl Piqua (45356) *(G-15999)*
Buckeye Supply Company (HQ) 740 452-3641
999 Zane St Ste A Zanesville (43701) *(G-20285)*
Buckeye Telesystem Inc (HQ) 419 724-9898
2700 Oregon Rd Northwood (43619) *(G-15390)*
Buckeye Trils Girl Scout Cncil (PA) 937 275-7601
450 Shoup Mill Rd Dayton (45415) *(G-9267)*
Buckeye Truck Equipment Inc 614 299-1136
939 E Starr Ave Columbus (43201) *(G-7091)*
Buckeye Vly E Elementary Pto 740 747-2266
522 E High St Ashley (43003) *(G-701)*
Buckeye Waste Industries Inc 330 645-9900
2430 S Main St Coventry Township (44319) *(G-9033)*
Buckeye Western Star, Plain City *Also called Sharron Group Inc (G-16066)*
Buckholz Wall Systems, Hilliard *Also called Buckholz Wall Systems LLC (G-11751)*
Buckholz Wall Systems LLC 614 870-1775
4160 Anson Dr Hilliard (43026) *(G-11751)*
Buckingham Dlttle Brroughs LLC (PA) 330 376-5300
3800 Embassy Pkwy Akron (44333) *(G-114)*
Buckingham Dlttle Brroughs LLC 330 492-8717
4277 Munson St Nw Canton (44718) *(G-2222)*
Buckingham Dlttle Brroughs LLC 216 621-5300
1375 E 9th St Ste 1700 Cleveland (44114) *(G-5099)*
Buckingham Doolittle Burroughs, Cleveland *Also called Buckingham Dlttle Brroughs LLC (G-5099)*
Buckingham Management LLC 844 361-5559
1000 Hollister Ln Perrysburg (43551) *(G-15843)*
Buckner and Sons Masonry Inc 614 279-9777
2300 Sullivant Ave Columbus (43204) *(G-7092)*
Bucyrus Community Hospital Inc 419 562-4677
629 N Sandusky Ave Bucyrus (44820) *(G-1979)*
Bucyrus Community Hospital LLC 419 562-4677
629 N Sandusky Ave Bucyrus (44820) *(G-1980)*
Bucyrus Community Physicians 419 492-2200
120 W Main St New Washington (44854) *(G-15000)*
Budco Group Inc (PA) 513 621-6111
1100 Gest St Cincinnati (45203) *(G-3086)*
Budde Sheet Metal Works Inc (PA) 937 224-0868
305 Leo St Dayton (45404) *(G-9268)*
Buddies Inc (PA) 216 642-3362
3888 Pearl Rd Cleveland (44109) *(G-5100)*
Budenheim Usa Inc 614 345-2400
855 Grandview Ave Ste 120 Columbus (43215) *(G-7093)*
Budget Dumpster LLC (PA) 866 284-6164
830 Canterbury Rd Westlake (44145) *(G-19325)*
Budget Dumpster Rental, Westlake *Also called Budget Dumpster LLC (G-19325)*
Budget Rent A Car System Inc 216 267-2080
19719 Maplewood Ave Cleveland (44135) *(G-5101)*
Budget Rent A Car System Inc 937 898-1396
3300 Valet Dr Vandalia (45377) *(G-18509)*
Budget Rent-A-Car, Toledo *Also called George P Ballas Buick GMC Trck (G-17760)*
Budget Rent-A-Car, Cleveland *Also called Budget Rent A Car System Inc (G-5101)*
Budget Rent-A-Car, Vandalia *Also called Budget Rent A Car System Inc (G-18509)*
Budros Ruhlin & Roe Inc 614 481-6900
1801 Watermark Dr Ste 300 Columbus (43215) *(G-7094)*
Buehler 10, Dover *Also called Buehler Food Markets Inc (G-10068)*
Buehler Food Markets Inc 330 364-3079
3000 N Wooster Ave Dover (44622) *(G-10068)*
Buffalo Jacks 937 473-2524
137 S High St Covington (45318) *(G-9046)*
Buffalo Mfg Works BMW, Columbus *Also called Edison Welding Institute Inc (G-7502)*
Buffalo-Gtb Associates LLC 216 831-3735
3840 Orange Pl Beachwood (44122) *(G-1040)*
Builder Services Group Inc 614 263-9378
2365 Scioto Harper Dr Columbus (43204) *(G-7095)*
Builder Services Group Inc 513 942-2204
28 Keisland Ct Hamilton (45015) *(G-11560)*
Builders Exchange Inc (PA) 216 393-6300
9555 Rockside Rd Ste 300 Cleveland (44125) *(G-5102)*
Builders Firstsource Inc 937 898-1358
4173 Old Springfield Rd Vandalia (45377) *(G-18510)*
Builders Firstsource Inc 513 874-9950
10059 Princeton Glendale Cincinnati (45246) *(G-3087)*
Builders Trash Service 614 444-7060
1575 Harmon Ave Columbus (43223) *(G-7096)*
Building 8 Inc 513 771-8000
10995 Canal Rd Cincinnati (45241) *(G-3088)*
Building Blocks Child Care Ctr, Maple Heights *Also called Robert A Kaufmann Inc (G-13293)*
Building Group Division, Dayton *Also called Shook Construction Co (G-9763)*
Building Integrated Svcs LLC 330 733-9191
7777 First Pl Oakwood Village (44146) *(G-15487)*
Building Systems Trnsp Co 740 852-9700
460 E High St London (43140) *(G-12861)*
Building Technicians Corp 440 466-1651
4500 Clay St Geneva (44041) *(G-11237)*
Bulk Carrier Trnsp Eqp Co 330 339-3333
2743 Brightwood Rd Se New Philadelphia (44663) *(G-14947)*
Bulk Carriers and Tank Leasing, New Philadelphia *Also called Tank Leasing Corp (G-14984)*
Bulk Transit Corporation (PA) 614 873-4632
7177 Indl Pkwy Plain City (43064) *(G-16047)*
Bulk Transit Corporation 937 497-9573
1377 Riverside Dr Sidney (45365) *(G-16763)*
Bulkfoods.com, Toledo *Also called Natural Foods Inc (G-17934)*
Bulkmatic Transport Company 614 497-2372
2271 Williams Rd Columbus (43207) *(G-7097)*
Bulldawg Holdings LLC (PA) 419 423-3131
151 Stanford Pkwy Findlay (45840) *(G-10885)*
Bullock, Jos D MD, Columbus *Also called Midwest Allergy Associates (G-8080)*
Bundy Baking Solutions, Urbana *Also called Cmbb LLC (G-18428)*
Bunge North America Foundation 419 692-6010
234 S Jefferson St Delphos (45833) *(G-10020)*
Buns of Delaware Inc 740 363-2867
14 W Winter St Delaware (43015) *(G-9956)*
Buns Restaurant & Bakery, Delaware *Also called Buns of Delaware Inc (G-9956)*
Bunzl Cincinnati, Blue Ash *Also called Bunzl Usa Inc (G-1518)*
Bunzl Usa Inc 513 891-9010
4699 Malsbary Rd Blue Ash (45242) *(G-1518)*
Burbank Inc 419 698-3434
623 Burbank Dr Toledo (43607) *(G-17632)*
Burch Hydro Inc 740 694-9146
17860 Ankneytown Rd Fredericktown (43019) *(G-11052)*
Burch Hydro Trucking Inc 740 694-9146
17860 Ankneytown Rd Fredericktown (43019) *(G-11053)*
Burchwood Care Center 513 868-3300
4070 Hamilton Mason Rd Fairfield Township (45011) *(G-10802)*
Burd Brothers Inc 513 708-7787
1789 Stanley Ave Dayton (45404) *(G-9269)*
Burd Brothers Inc (PA) 800 538-2873
4005 Borman Dr Batavia (45103) *(G-984)*
Burdens Machine & Welding 740 345-9246
94 S 5th St Newark (43055) *(G-15019)*
Bureau Information & Support, Columbus *Also called Ohio Department of Health (G-8240)*
Bureau Labor Market Info, Columbus *Also called Ohio Dept of Job & Fmly Svcs (G-8246)*
Bureau of Sanitation, Perrysburg *Also called City of Perrysburg (G-15848)*
Bureau of Support, Lima *Also called County of Allen (G-12626)*
Bureau Vctional Rehabilitation, Akron *Also called Ohio Rehabilitation Svcs Comm (G-362)*
Bureau Veritas North Amer Inc 330 252-5100
520 S Main St Ste 2444 Akron (44311) *(G-115)*
Bureau Workers Compensation 614 466-5109
13430 Yarmouth Dr Pickerington (43147) *(G-15950)*
Buren Insurance Group Inc (PA) 419 281-8060
1101 Sugarbush Dr Ashland (44805) *(G-661)*
Burge Building Co Inc 440 245-6871
2626 Broadway Lorain (44052) *(G-12889)*
Burge Service, Columbus *Also called Willglo Services Inc (G-8903)*
Burge, Ron, Burbank *Also called Ron Burge Trucking Inc (G-2009)*
Burger Iron Company 330 794-1716
3100 Gilchrist Rd Mogadore (44260) *(G-14544)*
Burger Plant, Shadyside *Also called Ohio Edison Company (G-16697)*
Burgess & Niple Inc (PA) 502 254-2344
5085 Reed Rd Columbus (43220) *(G-7098)*
Burgess & Niple Inc 440 354-9700
100 W Erie St Painesville (44077) *(G-15696)*
Burgess & Niple Inc 513 579-0042
312 Plum St Ste 1210 Cincinnati (45202) *(G-3089)*
Burgess & Niple-Heapy LLC 614 459-2050
5085 Reed Rd Columbus (43220) *(G-7099)*
Burke Inc 513 576-5700
25 Whitney Dr Ste 110 Milford (45150) *(G-14374)*
Burke Inc (PA) 513 241-5663
500 W 7th St Cincinnati (45203) *(G-3090)*
Burke & Company, Cincinnati *Also called Patrick J Burke & Co (G-4212)*
Burke & Schindler Pllc 859 344-8887
901 Evans St Cincinnati (45204) *(G-3091)*
Burke Institute, Cincinnati *Also called Burke Inc (G-3090)*
Burke Manley Lpa 513 721-5525
225 W Court St Cincinnati (45202) *(G-3092)*
Burke Milford, Milford *Also called Burke Inc (G-14374)*
Burkett and Sons Inc 419 242-7377
28740 Glenwood Rd Perrysburg (43551) *(G-15844)*
Burkett Restaurant Equipment, Perrysburg *Also called Burkett and Sons Inc (G-15844)*
Burkhardt Springfield Neighbor 937 252-7076
735 Huffman Ave Dayton (45403) *(G-9270)*
Burkhart Excavating Inc 740 896-3312
9950 State Route 60 Lowell (45744) *(G-13036)*
Burkhart Trucking Inc 740 896-2244
9950 State Route 60 Lowell (45744) *(G-13037)*
Burkhart Trucking & Excavating, Lowell *Also called Burkhart Trucking Inc (G-13037)*
Burkshire Construction Company 440 885-9700
6033 State Rd Cleveland (44134) *(G-5103)*
Burlington House Inc 513 851-7888
2222 Springdale Rd Cincinnati (45231) *(G-3093)*

ALPHABETIC

Burman Wine, Perrysburg *Also called Dayton Heidelberg Distrg Co* (G-15855)

Burnett Pools Inc (PA).............................330 372-1725
2498 State Route 5 Cortland (44410) (G-8985)

Burnett Pools and Spas, Cortland *Also called Burnett Pools Inc* (G-8985)

Burns & Scalo Roofing Co Inc....................740 383-4639
2181 Innovation Dr # 101 Marion (43302) (G-13408)

Burns Industrial Equipment Inc...................330 425-2476
8155 Roll And Hold Pkwy Macedonia (44056) (G-13063)

Burns International Staffing, Mansfield *Also called Lexington Court Care Center* (G-13199)

Burrier Service Company Inc.....................440 946-6019
8669 Twinbrook Rd Mentor (44060) (G-14023)

Burton Carol Management (PA)...................216 464-5130
4832 Richmond Rd Ste 200 Cleveland (44128) (G-5104)

Burton Health Care Center, Burton *Also called Windsor House Inc* (G-2020)

Burton Rubber Processing, Burton *Also called Hexpol Compounding LLC* (G-2016)

Burtons Collision...............................513 984-3396
4384 E Galbraith Rd Cincinnati (45236) (G-3094)

Burtons Collision & Auto Repr, Cincinnati *Also called Burtons Collision* (G-3094)

Bus Garage, Amherst *Also called Amherst Exempted Vlg Schools* (G-579)

Bus Garage, Liberty Township *Also called Lakota Local School District* (G-12582)

Bus Garage, Geneva *Also called Geneva Area City School Dst* (G-11241)

Bus Garage & Maintenance Dept, Toledo *Also called Washington Local Schools* (G-18146)

Bus Transportation Department, Columbus *Also called Gahanna-Jefferson Pub Schl Dst* (G-7644)

Busam Fairfield LLC............................513 771-8100
6195 Dixie Hwy Fairfield (45014) (G-10702)

Busam Subaru/Suzuki, Fairfield *Also called Busam Fairfield LLC* (G-10702)

Business Admnstrators Cons Inc (PA)............614 863-8780
6331 E Livingston Ave Reynoldsburg (43068) (G-16287)

Business Aircraft Group Inc (PA)...............216 348-1415
2301 N Marginal Rd Cleveland (44114) (G-5105)

Business Backer Inc............................513 792-6866
10856 Reed Hartman Hwy # 100 Cincinnati (45242) (G-3095)

Business Community Section, Cincinnati *Also called Universal Advertising Assoc* (G-4693)

Business Consultants Limited, Trenton *Also called Cal Crim Inc* (G-18187)

Business Data Systems Inc......................330 633-1221
1267 Southeast Ave Ste 5 Tallmadge (44278) (G-17470)

Business Equipment Co Inc......................513 948-1500
175 Tri County Pkwy # 120 Cincinnati (45246) (G-3096)

Business Furniture LLC.........................937 293-1010
8 N Main St Dayton (45402) (G-9271)

Business Research Services.....................216 831-5200
26600 Renaissance Pkwy # 150 Cleveland (44128) (G-5106)

Business Stationery LLC........................216 514-1192
4944 Commerce Pkwy Cleveland (44128) (G-5107)

Business Tech & Solutions, Beavercreek *Also called Btas Inc* (G-1135)

Busken Bakery Inc (PA).........................513 871-2114
2675 Madison Rd Cincinnati (45208) (G-3097)

Bussines Air Craft Center, Cleveland *Also called Business Aircraft Group Inc* (G-5105)

Busy Bee Electric Inc..........................513 353-3553
100 Washington St Hooven (45033) (G-11934)

Butchko Electric Inc...........................440 985-3180
7333 S Dewey Rd Amherst (44001) (G-582)

Butler County of Ohio..........................513 887-3728
1800 Princeton Rd Fairfield Township (45011) (G-10803)

Butler County of Ohio..........................513 887-3282
315 High St Ste 550 Hamilton (45011) (G-11561)

Butler County of Ohio..........................513 887-3154
130 High St Fl 4 Hamilton (45011) (G-11562)

Butler County of Ohio..........................513 785-6500
4631 Dixie Hwy Hamilton (45014) (G-11563)

Butler Animal Health Sup LLC (HQ)..............614 761-9095
400 Metro Pl N Ste 100 Dublin (43017) (G-10154)

Butler Animal Health Sup LLC...................614 718-2000
3820 Twin Creeks Dr Columbus (43204) (G-7100)

Butler Animal Hlth Holdg LLC (HQ)..............614 761-9095
400 Metro Pl N Ste 150 Dublin (43017) (G-10155)

Butler Animal Supply, Dublin *Also called Butler Animal Hlth Holdg LLC* (G-10155)

Butler Asphalt Co LLC..........................937 890-1141
7500 Johnson Station Rd Vandalia (45377) (G-18511)

Butler Bhavioral Hlth Svcs Inc (PA)............513 896-7887
1502 University Blvd Hamilton (45011) (G-11564)

Butler Cincione and Dicuccio...................614 221-3151
556 E Town St 100 Columbus (43215) (G-7101)

Butler Cnty Ancillary Svcs LLC (PA)............513 454-1400
3035 Hamilton Mason Rd Fairfield Township (45011) (G-10804)

Butler Cnty Cmnty Hlth Cnsrtm..................513 454-1460
300 High St 4 Hamilton (45011) (G-11565)

Butler Cnty Rgional Trnst Auth.................513 785-5237
3045 Moser Ct Hamilton (45011) (G-11566)

Butler County Bd of Mental RE..................513 785-2815
282 N Fair Ave Ste 1 Hamilton (45011) (G-11567)

Butler County Bd of Mental RE..................513 785-2870
5645 Liberty Fairfield Rd Fairfield Township (45011) (G-10805)

Butler County Board of Develop.................513 867-5913
441 Patterson Blvd Fairfield (45014) (G-10703)

Butler County Care Facility, Fairfield Township *Also called Butler County of Ohio* (G-10803)

Butler County Courts, Hamilton *Also called Butler County of Ohio* (G-11570)

Butler County Eductl Svc Ctr....................513 737-2817
23 S Front St Fl 3 Hamilton (45011) (G-11568)

Butler County Eductl Svcs Ctr, Hamilton *Also called Butler County Eductl Svc Ctr* (G-11568)

Butler County Engineers Office, Hamilton *Also called Butler County of Ohio* (G-11569)

Butler County Information Svcs, Hamilton *Also called Butler County of Ohio* (G-11571)

Butler County of Ohio..........................513 867-5744
1921 Fairgrove Ave Hamilton (45011) (G-11569)

Butler County of Ohio..........................513 887-3090
315 High St Fl 5 Hamilton (45011) (G-11570)

Butler County of Ohio..........................513 887-3418
315 High St Fl 2 Hamilton (45011) (G-11571)

Butler Institute American Art (PA)..............330 743-1711
524 Wick Ave Youngstown (44502) (G-19979)

Butler Processing...............................513 874-1400
1326 Stephanie Dr Hamilton (45013) (G-11572)

Butler Rural Electric Coop......................513 867-4400
3888 Stillwell Beckett Rd Oxford (45056) (G-15674)

Butt Construction Company Inc...................937 426-1313
3858 Germany Ln Dayton (45431) (G-9163)

Butterfield Co Inc..............................330 832-1282
401 26th St Nw Massillon (44647) (G-13666)

Butterfly Inc...................................440 892-7777
8200 E Pleasant Valley Rd Independence (44131) (G-12051)

Butts, Charles L II DDS, Lima *Also called K M Clemens DDS Inc* (G-12668)

Buxton Inn Inc..................................740 587-0001
313 Broadway E Granville (43023) (G-11335)

Buy Below Retail Inc............................216 292-7805
23600 Mercantile Rd Ste G Cleveland (44122) (G-5108)

Buyers Products Company (PA)....................440 974-8888
9049 Tyler Blvd Mentor (44060) (G-14024)

Bw Enterprises Inc..............................937 568-9660
276 Clubhouse Dr South Charleston (45368) (G-16923)

Bw Supply Co., Lyons *Also called B W Grinding Co* (G-13056)

BWC Trucking Company Inc........................740 532-5188
164 State Route 650 Ironton (45638) (G-12148)

Bwi Chassis Dynamics NA Inc.....................937 455-5230
2582 E River Rd Moraine (45439) (G-14629)

Bwi Group NA, Moraine *Also called Bwi North America Inc* (G-14630)

Bwi North America Inc...........................937 212-2892
2582 E River Rd Moraine (45439) (G-14630)

BX OHIO, Cleveland *Also called Builders Exchange Inc* (G-5102)

By-Line Transit Inc.............................937 642-2500
17075 White Stone Rd Marysville (43040) (G-13486)

Byer Steel Division, Cincinnati *Also called Byer Steel Recycling Inc* (G-3098)

Byer Steel Recycling Inc (PA)...................513 948-0300
200 W North Bend Rd Cincinnati (45216) (G-3098)

Byron Products Inc..............................513 870-9111
3781 Port Union Rd Fairfield (45014) (G-10704)

Bzak Landscaping Inc (PA).......................513 831-0907
931 Round Bottom Rd Milford (45150) (G-14375)

Bzak Ldscpg & Maintainance, Milford *Also called Bzak Landscaping Inc* (G-14375)

C & B Buck Bros Asp Maint LLC...................419 536-7325
2742 Victory Ave Toledo (43607) (G-17633)

C & C Industries, Vandalia *Also called Circuits & Cables Inc* (G-18514)

C & G Transportation Inc........................419 288-2653
11100 Wayne Rd Wayne (43466) (G-18825)

C & J Contractors Inc...........................216 391-5700
866 Addison Rd Cleveland (44103) (G-5109)

C & K Industrial Services Inc (PA)..............216 642-0055
5617 E Schaaf Rd Independence (44131) (G-12052)

C & K Industrial Services Inc...................513 829-5353
4980 Factory Dr Fairfield (45014) (G-10705)

C & L Supply, Logan *Also called Kilbarger Construction Inc* (G-12843)

C & M Express Logistics Inc.....................440 350-0802
342 Blackbrook Rd Painesville (44077) (G-15697)

C & R Inc (PA)..................................614 497-1130
5600 Clyde Moore Dr Groveport (43125) (G-11498)

C & S Associates Inc............................440 461-9661
729 Miner Rd Highland Heights (44143) (G-11732)

C & W Tank Cleaning Company.....................419 691-1995
50 N Lallendorf Rd Oregon (43616) (G-15585)

C A C Distributing, Cincinnati *Also called Habegger Corporation* (G-3669)

C A E C Inc.....................................614 337-1091
2975 Morse Rd Ste A Columbus (43231) (G-7102)

C A I Insurance Agency, Cincinnati *Also called Allan Peace & Associates Inc* (G-2923)

C and D Truck Repairs, Leipsic *Also called PGT Trucking Inc* (G-12521)

C B Mfg & Sls Co Inc (PA).......................937 866-5986
4455 Infirmary Rd Miamisburg (45342) (G-14147)

C C, Mentor *Also called Cardinalcommerce Corporation* (G-14025)

C C & S Ambulance Service Inc...................330 868-4114
207 W Lincolnway Minerva (44657) (G-14516)

C C H, Canton *Also called Canton Christian Home Inc* (G-2228)

C C I, Broadview Heights *Also called Warwick Communications Inc* (G-1850)

C C Mitchell Supply Company.....................440 526-2040
3001 E Royalton Rd Cleveland (44147) (G-5110)

C D O, Dayton *Also called Cdo Technologies Inc* (G-9164)

C E I, Canton *Also called Canton Erectors Inc* (G-2232)

C E O, Columbus *Also called Corporate Environments of Ohio* (G-7372)

C E S Credit Union Inc 561 203-5443
3030 State Route 3 Loudonville (44842) *(G-12954)*
C E S Credit Union Inc (PA) 740 397-1136
1215 Yauger Rd Mount Vernon (43050) *(G-14751)*
C E S Credit Union Inc 740 892-3323
8 N Main St Utica (43080) *(G-18454)*
C F N A, Cleveland *Also called Credit First National Assn (G-5377)*
C H Bradshaw Co 614 871-2087
2004 Hendrix Dr Grove City (43123) *(G-11417)*
C H Dean Inc (PA) 937 222-9531
3500 Pentagon Blvd # 200 Beavercreek (45431) *(G-1136)*
C H T, Cleveland *Also called Compliant Healthcare Tech LLC (G-5331)*
C I E Inc 419 986-5566
2704 County Road 13 Burgoon (43407) *(G-2011)*
C J & L Construction Inc 513 769-3600
11980 Runyan Dr Cincinnati (45241) *(G-3099)*
C K M, Coventry Township *Also called Stanley Stemer of Akron Canton (G-9043)*
C K of Cincinnati Inc 513 752-5533
7525 State Rd Ste B Cincinnati (45255) *(G-3100)*
C M Brown Nurseries Inc 440 259-5403
4906 Middle Ridge Rd Perry (44081) *(G-15820)*
C M C S, Cincinnati *Also called Comprehensive Managed Care Sys (G-3347)*
C M E F, Canton *Also called Canton Med Educatn Foundation (G-2237)*
C M I Group, Chagrin Falls *Also called Custom Materials Inc (G-2663)*
C M Limited 614 888-4567
5255 Sinclair Rd Columbus (43229) *(G-7103)*
C M S Enterprises Inc (PA) 740 653-1940
664 S Columbus St Lancaster (43130) *(G-12374)*
C Micah Rand Inc 513 605-2000
12100 Reed Hartman Hwy Cincinnati (45241) *(G-3101)*
C N G, Hilliard *Also called Cache Next Generation LLC (G-11752)*
C P R, Twinsburg *Also called Cleveland Pump Repr & Svcs LLC (G-18254)*
C P W, Brookpark *Also called Car Parts Warehouse Inc (G-1892)*
C R G, Miamisburg *Also called Cornerstone Research Group Inc (G-14155)*
C R G Health Care Systems 330 498-8107
2567 Niles Vienna Rd Ofc Niles (44446) *(G-15148)*
C R M, Clyde *Also called Chaney Roofing Maintenance (G-6741)*
C Ray Wllams Erly Chldhood Ctr, Columbus *Also called Whitehall City Schools (G-8898)*
C S I, Columbus *Also called Clinical Specialties Inc (G-7228)*
C T Columbus, Columbus *Also called C T Corporation System (G-7104)*
C T Communication, Urbana *Also called C T Wireless (G-18420)*
C T Corporation System 614 473-9749
4400 Easton Cmns Ste 300 Columbus (43219) *(G-7104)*
C T I, Akron *Also called Commercial Time Sharing Inc (G-148)*
C T Logistics, Cleveland *Also called Commercial Traffic Company (G-5319)*
C T Logistics, Cleveland *Also called Commercial Traffic Company (G-5320)*
C T Wireless 937 653-2208
731 Scioto St Urbana (43078) *(G-18420)*
C Ted Forsberg 440 992-3145
5005 State Rd Ashtabula (44004) *(G-723)*
C Tucker Cope & Assoc Inc 330 482-4472
170 Duquesne St Columbiana (44408) *(G-6782)*
C V Perry & Co (PA) 614 221-4131
370 S 5th St Columbus (43215) *(G-7105)*
C W Egg Products LLC 419 375-5800
2360 Wabash Rd Fort Recovery (45846) *(G-10987)*
C&C Clean Team Enterprises LLC 513 321-5100
2016 Madison Rd Cincinnati (45208) *(G-3102)*
C&K Trucking LLC 440 657-5249
41387 Schadden Rd Elyria (44035) *(G-10485)*
C-Auto Glass Inc 216 351-2193
2500 Brookpark Rd # 111 Cleveland (44134) *(G-5111)*
C-N-D Industries Inc 330 478-8811
359 State Ave Nw Massillon (44647) *(G-13667)*
C-Z Realtors, Cambridge *Also called The C-Z Company (G-2085)*
C-Z Trckng Co, Poland *Also called C-Z Trucking Co (G-16081)*
C-Z Trucking Co 330 758-2313
9495 Harvard Blvd Poland (44514) *(G-16081)*
C.C.i, Canton *Also called Consolidated Communications (G-2266)*
C.H. Robinson 123, Columbus *Also called CH Robinson Company Inc (G-7175)*
C.H.P., Columbus *Also called Columbus Housing Partnr Inc (G-7289)*
C2g, Dayton *Also called Legrand North America LLC (G-9561)*
CA Group 419 586-2137
4980 Mud Pike Rd Celina (45822) *(G-2586)*
CA INDUSTRIES, Celina *Also called CA Group (G-2586)*
Ca-Mj Hotel Associates Ltd 330 494-6494
4375 Metro Cir Nw Canton (44720) *(G-2223)*
Cabbage Inc (PA) 440 899-9171
4700 Liberty Ave Fl 2 Vermilion (44089) *(G-18551)*
Cabin In The Wood, Dublin *Also called Northwods Cnslting Prtners Inc (G-10292)*
Cabin Restaurant 330 562-9171
34 N Chillicothe Rd Aurora (44202) *(G-823)*
Cabinet and Granite Direct, Cleveland *Also called Direct Import Home Decor Inc (G-5424)*
Cabinet Restylers, Ashland *Also called Thiels Replacement Systems Inc (G-694)*
Cabinet Solutions By Design, Cincinnati *Also called Brower Products Inc (G-3082)*
Cable System, The, Sandusky *Also called Erie County Cablevision Inc (G-16600)*
Cable TV Services Inc 440 816-0033
6400 Kolthoff Dr Cleveland (44142) *(G-5112)*
Cache Next Generation LLC 614 850-9444
3974 Brown Park Dr Ste D Hilliard (43026) *(G-11752)*
Cadle Company II Inc 330 872-0918
100 N Center St Newton Falls (44444) *(G-15136)*
Cadna Automotive, Fairlawn *Also called Cadna Rubber Company Inc (G-10818)*
Cadna Rubber Company Inc 901 566-9090
703 S Clvland Mssillon Rd Fairlawn (44333) *(G-10818)*
Cadre Computer Resources Co (PA) 513 762-7350
201 E 5th St Ste 1800 Cincinnati (45202) *(G-3103)*
Cadre Information Security, Cincinnati *Also called Cadre Computer Resources Co (G-3103)*
Cadx Systems Inc 937 431-1464
2689 Commons Blvd Ste 100 Beavercreek (45431) *(G-1137)*
Caep-Dunlap LLC 330 456-2695
2600 6th St Sw Canton (44710) *(G-2224)*
Caesar Creek Flea Market, Dayton *Also called Ferguson Hills Inc (G-9433)*
Cafaro Co 330 652-6980
5555 Youngstown Warren Rd Niles (44446) *(G-15149)*
Cafaro Peachcreek Co Ltd 419 625-6280
1119 Sandusky Mall Blvd Sandusky (44870) *(G-16579)*
Cahall Bros Inc (PA) 937 378-4439
896 S Main St Georgetown (45121) *(G-11265)*
Cahill Corporation 330 724-1224
3951 Creek Wood Ln Uniontown (44685) *(G-18359)*
Cai/Insurance Agency Inc (PA) 513 221-1140
2035 Reading Rd Cincinnati (45202) *(G-3104)*
Cain B M W, Canton *Also called Cain Motors Inc (G-2225)*
Cain Motors Inc 330 494-5588
6527 Whipple Ave Nw Canton (44720) *(G-2225)*
Cal Crim Inc 513 563-5500
384 Deer Run Dr Trenton (45067) *(G-18187)*
Cal-Maine Foods Inc 937 337-9576
3078 Washington Rd Rossburg (45362) *(G-16457)*
Cal-Maine Foods Inc 937 968-4874
1039 Zumbrum Rd Union City (45390) *(G-18352)*
Calabresem Racek & Markos Inc 216 696-5442
1110 Euclid Ave Ste 300 Cleveland (44115) *(G-5113)*
Calafonia Dream By AAC, Cincinnati *Also called Auto Aftermarket Concepts (G-3005)*
Calfee Halter & Griswold LLP (PA) 216 831-2732
1405 E 6th St Ste 1 Cleveland (44114) *(G-5114)*
Calfee Halter & Griswold LLP 513 693-4880
255 E 5th St Cincinnati (45202) *(G-3105)*
Calfee Halter & Griswold LLP 614 621-1500
41 S High St Ste 1200 Columbus (43215) *(G-7106)*
Calfee Halgerr Griswold LLC 614 621-7003
41 S High St Ste 1200 Columbus (43215) *(G-7107)*
Caliber Home Loans Inc 937 435-5363
8534 Yankee St Dayton (45458) *(G-9272)*
Calico Court 740 455-2541
1101 Colony Dr Zanesville (43701) *(G-20286)*
Call Traditions, Cleveland *Also called Aristocrat W Nursing Hm Corp (G-5008)*
Callos Prof Employment II, Youngstown *Also called Callos Resource LLC (G-19980)*
Callos Resource LLC (PA) 330 788-3033
755 Boardman Canfield Rd N2 Youngstown (44512) *(G-19980)*
Calphalon, Bowling Green *Also called Newell Brands Inc (G-1741)*
Calvary Cemetery, Youngstown *Also called Roman Cthlic Docese Youngstown (G-20191)*
Calvary Christian Ch of Ohio 740 828-9000
338 W 3rd St Frazeysburg (43822) *(G-11048)*
Calvary Contracting Inc 937 754-0300
4125 Gibson Dr Tipp City (45371) *(G-17550)*
Calvary Industries Inc (PA) 513 874-1113
9233 Seward Rd Fairfield (45014) *(G-10706)*
Calvert Wire & Cable Corp (HQ) 216 433-7600
17909 Cleve Pkwy Ste 180 Cleveland (44142) *(G-5115)*
Calvin Electric LLC 937 670-2558
4957 Hursch Rd Arcanum (45304) *(G-624)*
Calvin Lanier 937 952-4221
4003 Foxboro Dr Dayton (45416) *(G-9273)*
Camargo Club 513 561-9292
8605 Shawnee Run Rd Cincinnati (45243) *(G-3106)*
Camargo Construction Company 513 248-1500
6801 Shawnee Run Rd Cincinnati (45243) *(G-3107)*
Camargo Manor Inc 513 605-3000
12100 Reed Hartman Hwy Cincinnati (45241) *(G-3108)*
Camargo Rental Center Inc 513 271-6510
8149 Camargo Rd Cincinnati (45243) *(G-3109)*
Cambria Green Management LLC 330 899-1263
1787 Thorn Dr Uniontown (44685) *(G-18360)*
Cambria Stes Akrn-Canton Arprt, Uniontown *Also called Cambria Green Management LLC (G-18360)*
Cambridge Associates Ltd 740 432-7313
2248 Southgate Pkwy Cambridge (43725) *(G-2051)*
Cambridge Behavioral Hospital 740 432-4906
66755 State St Cambridge (43725) *(G-2052)*
Cambridge Box & Gift Shop, Cambridge *Also called Cambridge Packaging Inc (G-2055)*
Cambridge Counseling Center 740 450-7790
326 Main St Zanesville (43701) *(G-20287)*
Cambridge Country Club Company 740 439-2744
60755 Southgate Rd Byesville (43723) *(G-2023)*

ALPHABETIC

Cambridge Country Club Corp................................740 432-2107
  60755 Southgate Rd Byesville (43723) *(G-2024)*
Cambridge Home Healthcare.............................740 432-6191
  1300 Clark St Unit 7 Cambridge (43725) *(G-2053)*
Cambridge NH LLC...740 432-7717
  66731 Old Twenty One Rd Cambridge (43725) *(G-2054)*
Cambridge Packaging Inc..................................740 432-3351
  60794 Southgate Rd Cambridge (43725) *(G-2055)*
Cambridge Property Investors...........................740 432-7313
  2248 Southgate Pkwy Cambridge (43725) *(G-2056)*
Camcar Towing, Columbus *Also called Arlington Towing Inc* *(G-6971)*
Camco Inc...740 477-3682
  24685 Us Highway 23 S Circleville (43113) *(G-4827)*
Camden FLS Rcption Cnfrnce Ctr......................419 448-7699
  2460 S State Route 231 Tiffin (44883) *(G-17511)*
Camden Health Center, Cincinnati *Also called Deaconess Long Term Care of MI* *(G-3412)*
Camden Management Inc....................................513 383-1635
  463 Ohio Pike Ste 304 Cincinnati (45255) *(G-3110)*
Camelot Realty Investments..............................740 357-5291
  10689 Us 23 Lucasville (45648) *(G-13045)*
Cameo Solutions Inc..513 645-4220
  9078 Union Centre Blvd # 200 West Chester (45069) *(G-18880)*
Cameron Mitchell Rest LLC (PA)........................614 621-3663
  390 W Nationwide Blvd # 300 Columbus (43215) *(G-7108)*
Camgen Ltd...330 204-8636
  1621 Euclid Ave Ste 220-3 Cleveland (44115) *(G-5116)*
Camgen Ltd...330 204-8636
  6693 Axtel Dr Canal Winchester (43110) *(G-2105)*
Camillus Villa Inc..440 236-5091
  10515 East River Rd Columbia Station (44028) *(G-6770)*
Camp Akita, Logan *Also called First Community Church* *(G-12835)*
Camp Paradise, Seville *Also called Sociey For Handicapped Citizen* *(G-16690)*
Camp Patmos Inc..419 746-2214
  920 Monaghan Rd Kelleys Island (43438) *(G-12209)*
Camp Pinecliff Inc...614 236-5698
  277 S Cassingham Rd Columbus (43209) *(G-7109)*
Camp Willson, Bellefontaine *Also called Young Mens Christian Assoc* *(G-1370)*
Campbell Inc (PA)...419 476-4444
  2875 Crane Way Northwood (43619) *(G-15391)*
Campbell Construction Inc (PA).........................330 262-5186
  1159 Blachleyville Rd Wooster (44691) *(G-19696)*
Campbell Family Childcare Inc...........................614 855-4780
  5351 New Albany Rd W New Albany (43054) *(G-14846)*
Campbell Sales Company..................................513 697-2900
  8805 Governors Hill Dr # 300 Cincinnati (45249) *(G-3111)*
Campeon Roofg & Waterproofing......................513 271-8972
  3535 Round Bottom Rd Cincinnati (45244) *(G-3112)*
Campolo Michael MD...740 522-7600
  1930 Tamarack Rd Newark (43055) *(G-15020)*
Campuseai Inc...216 589-9626
  1111 Superior Ave E # 310 Cleveland (44114) *(G-5117)*
Camtaylor Co Realtors, Worthington *Also called Phil Giessler* *(G-19835)*
Canaan Companies Inc......................................419 842-8373
  328 21st St Toledo (43604) *(G-17634)*
Canal Physician Group......................................330 344-4000
  1 Akron General Ave Akron (44307) *(G-116)*
Canal Road Partners...216 447-0814
  5585 Canal Rd Cleveland (44125) *(G-5118)*
Canal Square Branch, Akron *Also called Young Mens Christian Assoc* *(G-509)*
CANAL VILLAGE, Canal Winchester *Also called United Church Residences of* *(G-2123)*
Canal Winchester Dialysis, Canal Winchester *Also called Vogel Dialysis LLC* *(G-2124)*
Cancer Care Center, Youngstown *Also called Mahoning Vly Hmtlgy Onclgy Aso* *(G-20110)*
Cancer Center, Cincinnati *Also called University of Cincinnati* *(G-4720)*
CANCER NETWORK OF WEST CENTRAL, Lima *Also called Cancer Ntwk of W Cent* *(G-12611)*
Cancer Ntwk of W Cent......................................419 226-9085
  2615 Fort Amanda Rd Lima (45804) *(G-12611)*
Candlewood Carrollton, Carrollton *Also called CPX Carrollton Es LLC* *(G-2566)*
Candlewood Park Healthcare Ctr, Cleveland *Also called Belmore Leasing Co LLC* *(G-5053)*
Cando Pharmaceutical.......................................513 354-2694
  100 Commerce Dr Loveland (45140) *(G-12980)*
Canfield Healthcare Center, Youngstown *Also called Communicare Health Svcs Inc* *(G-19998)*
Caniano Bsner Pdiatrics Clinic, Columbus *Also called Nationwide Childrens Hospital* *(G-8144)*
Cannell Graphics LLC..614 781-9760
  1465 Northwest Blvd Columbus (43212) *(G-7110)*
Cannon Group Inc..614 890-0343
  5037 Pine Creek Dr Westerville (43081) *(G-19230)*
Canon Solutions America Inc.............................937 260-4495
  1 Prestige Pl Miamisburg (45342) *(G-14148)*
Canon Solutions America Inc.............................216 446-3830
  6100 Oak Tree Blvd Independence (44131) *(G-12053)*
Canon Solutions America Inc.............................216 750-2980
  6161 Oak Tree Blvd # 301 Independence (44131) *(G-12054)*
Canter Inns Inc (HQ)..740 354-7711
  711 2nd St Portsmouth (45662) *(G-16127)*
Canterbury Golf Club Inc...................................216 561-1914
  22000 S Woodland Rd Cleveland (44122) *(G-5119)*

Canterbury Villa, Centerburg *Also called Rescare Ohio Inc* *(G-2615)*
Canterbury Villa Alliance Ctr, Alliance *Also called Canterbury Vlla Oprations Corp* *(G-520)*
Canterbury Vlla Oprations Corp.........................330 821-4000
  1785 N Freshley Ave Alliance (44601) *(G-520)*
Canton Allergy Lab, Canton *Also called Ohio Head & Neck Surgeons Inc* *(G-2426)*
Canton Altman Emrgncy Physcans....................330 456-2695
  2600 6th St Sw Canton (44710) *(G-2226)*
Canton Assisted Living......................................330 492-7131
  836 34th St Nw Canton (44709) *(G-2227)*
Canton Chair Rental, Canton *Also called Maloney & Associates Inc* *(G-2384)*
Canton Christian Home Inc................................330 456-0004
  2550 Cleveland Ave Nw Canton (44709) *(G-2228)*
Canton City School District...............................330 456-3167
  2701 Coventry Blvd Ne Canton (44705) *(G-2229)*
Canton City School District...............................330 456-6710
  2030 Cleveland Ave Sw Canton (44707) *(G-2230)*
Canton Country Day School...............................330 453-8279
  3000 Demington Ave Nw Canton (44718) *(G-2231)*
Canton Erectors Inc...330 453-7363
  2009 Quimby Ave Sw Canton (44706) *(G-2232)*
Canton Floors Inc..330 492-1121
  3944 Fulton Dr Nw Canton (44718) *(G-2233)*
Canton Group Home, Canton *Also called Alternative Residences Two* *(G-2183)*
Canton Healthcare Center, Canton *Also called Communicare Health Svcs Inc* *(G-2263)*
Canton Hotel Holdings Inc.................................330 492-1331
  5345 Broadmoor Cir Nw Canton (44709) *(G-2234)*
Canton Insurance, Canton *Also called Huntington Insurance Inc* *(G-2353)*
Canton Inventory Service...................................330 453-1633
  2204 38th St Ne Canton (44705) *(G-2235)*
Canton Jewish Community Center......................330 452-6444
  432 30th St Nw Canton (44709) *(G-2236)*
CANTON JEWISH COMMUNITY FEDERA, Canton *Also called Canton Jewish Community Center* *(G-2236)*
Canton Med Educatn Foundation.......................330 363-6783
  2600 6th St Sw Canton (44710) *(G-2237)*
Canton Montessori Association..........................330 452-0148
  125 15th St Nw Canton (44703) *(G-2238)*
Canton Montessori School, Canton *Also called Canton Montessori Association* *(G-2238)*
Canton Ophthalmology Assoc............................330 994-1286
  2600 Tuscarawas St W # 200 Canton (44708) *(G-2239)*
Canton Public Works...330 489-3030
  2436 30th St Ne Canton (44705) *(G-2240)*
Canton Reg Cham of Comm Fdn........................330 456-7253
  222 Market Ave N Canton (44702) *(G-2241)*
Canton Rgnal Chmber of Cmmerce...................330 456-7253
  222 Market Ave N Ste 122 Canton (44702) *(G-2242)*
Canton S-Group Ltd...419 625-7003
  4000 Columbus Ave Sandusky (44870) *(G-16580)*
Canton School Employees Fed Cr (PA)..............330 452-9801
  1380 Market Ave N Canton (44714) *(G-2243)*
Canton School Trnsp Dept, Canton *Also called Canton City School District* *(G-2230)*
Canton Street Department, Canton *Also called Canton Public Works* *(G-2240)*
Cantrell Oil Company...937 695-8003
  18856 State Route 136 Winchester (45697) *(G-19660)*
Cantrell's Motel, Winchester *Also called 1st Stop Inc* *(G-19658)*
Canus Hospitality LLC.......................................937 323-8631
  383 E Leffel Ln Springfield (45505) *(G-17003)*
Canyon Medical Center Inc................................614 864-6010
  5969 E Broad St Ste 200 Columbus (43213) *(G-7111)*
Capa, Columbus *Also called Columbus Association For The P* *(G-7259)*
Capabilities Inc (PA)...419 394-0003
  124 S Front St Saint Marys (45885) *(G-16520)*
Capano & Associates LLC.................................513 403-6000
  8312 Alpine Aster Ct Liberty Township (45044) *(G-12578)*
Capgemini America Inc......................................678 427-6642
  10100 Innvtion Dr Ste 200 Dayton (45459) *(G-9274)*
Capital City Electric LLC....................................614 933-8700
  9798 Karmar Ct Ste B New Albany (43054) *(G-14847)*
Capital City Group Inc.......................................419 931-6757
  4314 Corduroy Rd Oregon (43616) *(G-15586)*
Capital City Indus Systems LLC.........................614 519-5047
  1494 Langram Rd Put In Bay (43456) *(G-16224)*
Capital City Medical Assoc, Columbus *Also called Central Ohio Primary Care* *(G-7165)*
Capital Drug, Columbus *Also called Capital Wholesale Drug Company* *(G-7114)*
Capital Electric, Moraine *Also called MDU Resources Group Inc* *(G-14673)*
Capital Fire Protection Co (PA)..........................614 279-9448
  3360 Valleyview Dr Columbus (43204) *(G-7112)*
Capital Health Homecare...................................740 264-8815
  201 Luray Dr 2a Steubenville (43953) *(G-17142)*
Capital Health Services Inc (PA)........................937 278-0404
  5040 Philadelphia Dr Dayton (45415) *(G-9275)*
Capital Investment Group Inc............................513 241-5090
  226 E 8th St Cincinnati (45202) *(G-3113)*
Capital Lighting Inc...614 841-1200
  901 Polaris Pkwy Columbus (43240) *(G-6802)*
Capital Partners Realty LLC..............................614 888-1000
  100 E Wilson Bridge Rd # 100 Worthington (43085) *(G-19795)*
Capital Properties MGT Ltd................................216 991-3057
  12929 Shaker Blvd Cleveland (44120) *(G-5120)*

Capital Senior Living (PA)......440 356-5444
22900 Center Ridge Rd Rocky River (44116) ***(G-16425)***
Capital Senior Living Corp......330 748-4204
9633 Valley View Rd Ofc C Macedonia (44056) ***(G-13064)***
Capital Senior Living Corp......419 874-2564
7100 S Wilkinson Way Perrysburg (43551) ***(G-15845)***
Capital Senior Living Corp......216 289-9800
261 Richmond Rd Richmond Heights (44143) ***(G-16388)***
Capital Senior Living Corp......513 829-6200
1400 Corydale Dr Fairfield (45014) ***(G-10707)***
Capital Tire Inc (PA)......419 241-5111
1001 Cherry St Toledo (43608) ***(G-17635)***
Capital Tire Inc......419 865-7151
2220 S Reynolds Rd Toledo (43614) ***(G-17636)***
Capital Transportation Inc......614 258-0400
1170 N Cassady Ave Columbus (43219) ***(G-7113)***
Capital Wholesale Drug Company......614 297-8225
873 Williams Ave Columbus (43212) ***(G-7114)***
Capitol City Cardiology Inc (PA)......614 464-0884
5825 Westbourne Ave Columbus (43213) ***(G-7115)***
Capitol City Trailers Inc......614 491-2616
3960 Groveport Rd Obetz (43207) ***(G-15523)***
Capitol Express Entps Inc (PA)......614 279-2819
3815 Twin Creeks Dr Columbus (43204) ***(G-7116)***
Capitol Tunneling Inc......614 444-0255
2216 Refugee Rd Columbus (43207) ***(G-7117)***
Capitol Varsity Sports Inc......513 523-4126
6723 Ringwood Rd Oxford (45056) ***(G-15675)***
Capri Bowling Lanes Inc......937 832-4000
2727 S Dixie Dr Dayton (45409) ***(G-9276)***
Caprice Health Care Center, North Lima *Also called Caprice Health Care Inc* ***(G-15267)***
Caprice Health Care Inc......330 965-9200
9184 Market St North Lima (44452) ***(G-15267)***
Captain D's, Circleville *Also called James Lafontaine* ***(G-4836)***
Captive-Aire Systems Inc......614 777-7378
850 Morrison Rd Gahanna (43230) ***(G-11111)***
Car Parts Warehouse Inc......440 259-2991
3382 N Ridge Rd Perry (44081) ***(G-15821)***
Car Parts Warehouse Inc (PA)......216 281-4500
5200 W 130th St Brookpark (44142) ***(G-1892)***
Car Wash......216 662-6289
5195 Northfield Rd Cleveland (44146) ***(G-5121)***
Car Wash Plus Ltd......513 683-4228
12105 Montgomery Rd Cincinnati (45249) ***(G-3114)***
Car-X Muffler & Brake, Cincinnati *Also called P & M Exhaust Systems Whse* ***(G-4195)***
Caracole Inc......513 761-1480
4138 Hamilton Ave Cincinnati (45223) ***(G-3115)***
Cararo Co Inc......330 652-6980
492 Eastwood Mall Niles (44446) ***(G-15150)***
Caraustar Industries Inc......937 298-9969
2601 E River Rd Moraine (45439) ***(G-14631)***
Caravon Golf Company Ltd......440 937-6018
4400 Nagel Rd Avon (44011) ***(G-870)***
Carbon Products, West Chester *Also called Graphel Corporation* ***(G-18934)***
Carcorp Inc......877 857-2801
2900 Morse Rd Columbus (43231) ***(G-7118)***
Cardiac Vsclar Thrcic Surgeons......513 421-3494
4030 Smith Rd Ste 300 Cincinnati (45209) ***(G-3116)***
Cardida Corporation (PA)......740 439-4359
74978 Broadhead Rd Kimbolton (43749) ***(G-12311)***
Cardinal Builders Inc......614 237-1000
4409 E Main St Columbus (43213) ***(G-7119)***
Cardinal Environmental Svc Inc......330 252-0220
180 E Miller Ave Akron (44301) ***(G-117)***
Cardinal Health Inc......614 473-0786
2215 Citygate Dr Ste D Columbus (43219) ***(G-7120)***
Cardinal Health Inc (PA)......614 757-5000
7000 Cardinal Pl Dublin (43017) ***(G-10156)***
Cardinal Health Inc......614 497-9552
2320 Mcgaw Rd Obetz (43207) ***(G-15524)***
Cardinal Health Inc......614 409-6770
5995 Commerce Center Dr Groveport (43125) ***(G-11499)***
Cardinal Health Inc......614 757-7690
2088 West Case Rd Ste 110 Columbus (43235) ***(G-7121)***
Cardinal Health 100 Inc (HQ)......614 757-5000
7000 Cardinal Pl Dublin (43017) ***(G-10157)***
Cardinal Health 200 LLC......440 349-1247
5260 Naiman Pkwy Cleveland (44139) ***(G-5122)***
Cardinal Health 200 LLC......614 491-0050
1548 Mcgaw Rd Columbus (43207) ***(G-7122)***
Cardinal Health 201 Inc (HQ)......614 757-5000
7000 Cardinal Pl Dublin (43017) ***(G-10158)***
Cardinal Health 301 LLC (HQ)......614 757-5000
7000 Cardinal Pl Dublin (43017) ***(G-10159)***
Cardinal Health 414 LLC......419 867-1077
6156 Trust Dr Ste B Holland (43528) ***(G-11877)***
Cardinal Health 414 LLC......937 438-1888
2217 Arbor Blvd Moraine (45439) ***(G-14632)***
Cardinal Health Medical, Cleveland *Also called Cardinal Health 200 LLC* ***(G-5122)***
Cardinal Healthcare......954 202-1883
P.O. Box 183005 Columbus (43218) ***(G-7123)***
Cardinal Maintenance & Svc Co......330 252-0282
180 E Miller Ave Akron (44301) ***(G-118)***
Cardinal Operating Company......740 598-4164
306 County Road 7e Brilliant (43913) ***(G-1821)***
Cardinal Orthopaedic Group Inc......614 759-1186
170 Taylor Station Rd Columbus (43213) ***(G-7124)***
Cardinal Orthopaedic Institute, Columbus *Also called Orthopedic One Inc* ***(G-8390)***
Cardinal Pacelli School......513 321-1048
927 Ellison Ave Cincinnati (45226) ***(G-3117)***
Cardinal Plant, Brilliant *Also called Buckeye Power Inc* ***(G-1820)***
Cardinal Retirement Village, Springfield *Also called Brookdale Lving Cmmunities Inc* ***(G-17002)***
Cardinal Retirement Village......330 928-7888
171 Graham Rd Cuyahoga Falls (44223) ***(G-9076)***
Cardinal Solutions Group Inc (HQ)......513 984-6700
7755 Montgomery Rd # 510 Cincinnati (45236) ***(G-3118)***
Cardinal Wds Skilled Nursing, Madison *Also called American Eagle Hlth Care Svcs* ***(G-13092)***
Cardinalcommerce Corporation......877 352-8444
8100 Tyler Blvd Ste 100 Mentor (44060) ***(G-14025)***
Cardio Thoracic Surgery......614 293-4509
410 W 10th Ave Columbus (43210) ***(G-7125)***
Cardiologist......440 882-0075
6525 Powers Blvd 301 Cleveland (44129) ***(G-5123)***
Cardiologist Clark & Champaign......937 653-8897
900 E Court St Urbana (43078) ***(G-18421)***
Cardiologist of Clark & Champ......937 323-1404
1911 E High St Springfield (45505) ***(G-17004)***
Cardiology Center Cincinnati, Cincinnati *Also called Cardiology Ctr of Cincinnati* ***(G-3119)***
Cardiology Consultants Inc......330 454-8076
2600 Tuscarawas St W # 600 Canton (44708) ***(G-2244)***
Cardiology Ctr of Cincinnati (PA)......513 745-9800
10525 Montgomery Rd A Cincinnati (45242) ***(G-3119)***
Cardiology Specialists Inc......330 297-6110
6847 N Chestnut St # 100 Ravenna (44266) ***(G-16234)***
Cardiovascular Associates Inc......330 747-6446
1001 Belmont Ave Youngstown (44504) ***(G-19981)***
Cardiovascular Clinic Inc......440 882-0075
6525 Powers Blvd Rm 301 Cleveland (44129) ***(G-5124)***
Cardiovascular Consultants Inc......330 454-8076
2600 6th St Sw Ste A2710 Canton (44710) ***(G-2245)***
Cardiovascular Medicine Assoc......440 816-2708
7255 Old Oak Blvd C208 Cleveland (44130) ***(G-5125)***
Care & Share of Erie Count......419 624-1411
241 Jackson St Sandusky (44870) ***(G-16581)***
Care Center, Cincinnati *Also called Cincinnati Anml Rfrrl* ***(G-3221)***
Care Connection of Cincinnati......513 842-1101
4420 Cooper Rd Ste 100 Cincinnati (45242) ***(G-3120)***
Care Information Systems LLC......614 496-4338
5723 Dalymount Dr Dublin (43016) ***(G-10160)***
Care of Trees Inc......800 445-8733
1500 N Mantua St Kent (44240) ***(G-12216)***
Care One LLC......937 236-6707
5440 Charlesgate Rd Dayton (45424) ***(G-9277)***
Career Cnnctions Staffing Svcs......440 471-8210
26260 Center Ridge Rd Westlake (44145) ***(G-19326)***
Career Partners Intl LLC (PA)......919 401-4260
20 S 3rd St Ste 210 Columbus (43215) ***(G-7126)***
Caregivers Health Network Inc......513 662-3400
2135 Dana Ave Ste 200 Cincinnati (45207) ***(G-3121)***
Careserve (HQ)......740 454-4000
2991 Maple Ave Zanesville (43701) ***(G-20288)***
Careserve Inc......740 962-3761
4114 N State Route 376 Nw McConnelsville (43756) ***(G-13899)***
Caresource Management Group Co......216 839-1001
5900 Landerbrook Dr # 300 Cleveland (44124) ***(G-5126)***
Caresource Management Group Co (PA)......937 224-3300
230 N Main St Dayton (45402) ***(G-9278)***
Caresource Management Group Co......614 221-3370
3455 Mill Run Dr Hilliard (43026) ***(G-11753)***
Caresource Management Group Co......937 224-3300
230 N Main St Dayton (45402) ***(G-9279)***
CARESPRING, Springboro *Also called Hillspring Health Care Center* ***(G-16970)***
CARESPRING, Cincinnati *Also called Eastgate Health Care Center* ***(G-2850)***
Carespring Health Care MGT LLC (PA)......513 943-4000
390 Wards Corner Rd Loveland (45140) ***(G-12981)***
Carestar Inc (PA)......513 618-8300
5566 Cheviot Rd Cincinnati (45247) ***(G-3122)***
Carew Realty Inc......513 241-3888
441 Vine St Ste 3900 Cincinnati (45202) ***(G-3123)***
Careworks of Ohio Inc (PA)......614 792-1085
5555 Glendon Ct Ste 300 Dublin (43016) ***(G-10161)***
Carey Electric Co......937 669-3399
3925 Vanco Ln Vandalia (45377) ***(G-18512)***
Carfagna's Cleve Meats, Columbus *Also called Carfagnas Incorporated* ***(G-7127)***
Carfagnas Incorporated......614 846-6340
1405 E Dblin Granville Rd Columbus (43229) ***(G-7127)***
Cargill Incorporated......216 651-7200
2400 Ships Channel Cleveland (44113) ***(G-5127)***
Cargill Incorporated......440 716-4664
24950 Country Club Blvd # 450 North Olmsted (44070) ***(G-15278)***
Cargill Premix and Nutrition, Brookville *Also called Provimi North America Inc* ***(G-1916)***
Carginal Retirement Village, Cuyahoga Falls *Also called Rv Properties LLC* ***(G-9123)***

ALPHABETIC

Cargotec Services USA Inc.............419 482-6000
12233 Williams Rd Perrysburg (43551) *(G-15846)*

CARILLON HISTORICAL PARK, Dayton *Also called Dayton History* *(G-9368)*
Caring Hands Inc.............330 821-6310
885 S Sawburg Ave Ste 107 Alliance (44601) *(G-521)*
Caring Hands Home Health Care.............740 532-9020
2615 S 3rd St Ironton (45638) *(G-12149)*
Caring Hearts Home Health Care (PA).............513 339-1237
6677 Summer Field Dr Mason (45040) *(G-13548)*
Carington Health Systems.............513 732-6500
4000 Golden Age Dr Batavia (45103) *(G-985)*
Carington Health Systems (PA).............513 682-2700
8200 Beckett Park Dr Hamilton (45011) *(G-11573)*
Carington Health Systems.............513 961-8881
3627 Harvey Ave Cincinnati (45229) *(G-3124)*
Carington Health Systems.............937 743-2754
421 Mission Ln Franklin (45005) *(G-11025)*
CARINGTON PARK, Ashtabula *Also called CHS-Lake Erie Inc* *(G-726)*
Carington Park, Ashtabula *Also called Salutary Providers Inc* *(G-753)*
Caritas Inc.............419 332-2589
1406 Oak Harbor Rd Fremont (43420) *(G-11060)*
Carl B Stokes Head Start Ctr, Cleveland *Also called Council For Economic Opport* *(G-5356)*
Carl E Oeder Sons Sand & Grav.............513 494-1555
1000 Mason Morrow Rd Lebanon (45036) *(G-12454)*
Carl Mills.............740 282-2382
1005 Franklin St Toronto (43964) *(G-18182)*
Carl's Body Shop & Towing, Dayton *Also called Carls Body Shop Inc* *(G-9280)*
Carles Bratwurst Inc.............419 562-7741
1210 E Mansfield St Bucyrus (44820) *(G-1981)*
Carleton Realty Inc.............740 653-5200
826 N Memorial Dr Lancaster (43130) *(G-12375)*
CARLETON SCHOOL, Syracuse *Also called Meigs Industries Inc* *(G-17469)*
Carlile Patchen & Murphy LLP (PA).............614 228-6135
366 E Broad St Columbus (43215) *(G-7128)*
Carlisle McNellie Rini Kram.............216 360-7200
24755 Chagrin Blvd Beachwood (44122) *(G-1041)*
Carlisle Fluid Tech Inc.............419 825-5186
320 Phillips Ave Toledo (43612) *(G-17637)*
Carlisle Health Care Inc.............937 746-2662
730 Hillcrest Ave Carlisle (45005) *(G-2551)*
Carlisle Hotels Inc.............614 851-5599
5625 Trabue Rd Columbus (43228) *(G-7129)*
Carls Body Shop Inc.............937 253-5166
1120 Wayne Ave Dayton (45410) *(G-9280)*
Carlson AmbInce Trnspt Svc Inc.............330 225-2400
1642 Pearl Rd Brunswick (44212) *(G-1923)*
Carlson Hotels Ltd Partnership.............740 386-5451
2091 Marion Mt Gilead Rd Marion (43302) *(G-13409)*
Carlson, L D Company, Kent *Also called Wine-Art of Ohio Inc* *(G-12269)*
Carmella's Italian Restaurant, Tiffin *Also called Camden FLS Rcption Cnfrnce Ctr* *(G-17511)*
Carmen Steering Committee.............330 756-2066
8074 Goodrich Rd Sw Navarre (44662) *(G-14822)*
Carmeuse Lime Inc.............419 638-2511
3964 County Road 41 Millersville (43435) *(G-14504)*
Carmeuse Lime Inc.............419 986-5200
1967 W County Rd 42 Bettsville (44815) *(G-1458)*
Carmeuse Lime & Stone, Millersville *Also called Carmeuse Lime Inc* *(G-14504)*
Carmeuse Natural Chemicals, Bettsville *Also called Carmeuse Lime Inc* *(G-1458)*
Carmichael Equipment Inc (PA).............740 446-2412
668 Pinecrest Dr Bidwell (45614) *(G-1467)*
Carmike Cinemas Inc.............740 264-1680
100 Mall Dr Unit C20 Steubenville (43952) *(G-17143)*
Carnation Clinic, Alliance *Also called Roger S Palutsis MD* *(G-549)*
Carnegie Capital Asset MGT LLC.............216 595-1349
30300 Chagrin Blvd Cleveland (44124) *(G-5128)*
Carnegie Companies Inc.............440 232-2300
6190 Cochran Rd Ste A Solon (44139) *(G-16831)*
Carnegie Investment Counsel, Cleveland *Also called Carnegie Capital Asset MGT LLC* *(G-5128)*
Carnegie Management & Dev Corp.............440 892-6800
27500 Detroit Rd Ste 300 Westlake (44145) *(G-19327)*
Carney McNicholas, Sheffield Village *Also called Nicholas Carney-Mc Inc* *(G-16741)*
Carol A & Ralp V H US B Fdn Tr.............513 632-4426
425 Walnut St Fl 11f Cincinnati (45202) *(G-3125)*
Carol Burton Management LLC.............419 666-5120
1800 Miami St Toledo (43605) *(G-17638)*
Carol Reese.............513 347-0252
421 Anderson Ferry Rd Cincinnati (45238) *(G-3126)*
Carol Scudere.............614 839-4357
6912 Keesee Cir New Albany (43054) *(G-14848)*
Carousel Beauty College, Dayton *Also called Yearwood Corporation* *(G-9889)*
Carpe Diem Industries LLC (PA).............419 659-5639
4599 Campbell Rd Columbus Grove (45830) *(G-8940)*
Carpe Diem Industries LLC.............419 358-0129
505 E Jefferson St Bluffton (45817) *(G-1689)*
Carpenter Lipps & Leland LLP (PA).............614 365-4100
280 N High St Ste 1300 Columbus (43215) *(G-7130)*
Carpenter Metal Solutions Inc (PA).............330 829-2771
803 S Mahoning Ave Alliance (44601) *(G-522)*
Carpet Restoration Plus, Canton *Also called Carpet Services Plus Inc* *(G-2246)*

Carpet Services Plus Inc.............330 458-2409
1807 Allen Ave Se Ste 8 Canton (44707) *(G-2246)*
Carquest Auto Parts, Columbus *Also called General Parts Inc* *(G-7653)*
Carrara Companies Inc.............330 659-2800
3774 Congress Pkwy Richfield (44286) *(G-16348)*
Carriage Court Community, Lancaster *Also called Carriage Court Company Inc* *(G-12376)*
Carriage Court Company Inc.............740 654-4422
800 Becks Knob Rd Ofc Lancaster (43130) *(G-12376)*
Carriage Court of Kenwood, Cincinnati *Also called Hackensack Meridian Health Inc* *(G-3670)*
Carriage Crt Mrysvlle Ltd Prtn.............937 642-2202
717 S Walnut St Marysville (43040) *(G-13487)*
Carriage House, Norwalk *Also called Fisher-Titus Medical Center* *(G-15437)*
Carriage House Assisted Living.............740 264-7667
63102 Saint Charles Dr Steubenville (43952) *(G-17144)*
Carriage Inn of Bowerston.............740 269-8001
102 Boyce Dr Bowerston (44695) *(G-1710)*
Carriage Inn of Cadiz Inc.............740 942-8084
308 W Warren St Cadiz (43907) *(G-2027)*
Carriage Inn of Steubenville.............740 264-7161
3102 Saint Charles Dr Steubenville (43952) *(G-17145)*
Carriage Inn of Trotwood Inc.............937 854-1180
3500 Shiloh Springs Rd Trotwood (45426) *(G-18192)*
Carriage Inn of Trotwood Inc.............937 277-0505
5020 Philadelphia Dr Dayton (45415) *(G-9281)*
Carriage Inn Retirement Cmnty.............937 278-0404
5040 Philadelphia Dr Dayton (45415) *(G-9282)*
Carriage Town Chrysler Plymuth.............740 369-9611
2815 Stratford Rd Delaware (43015) *(G-9957)*
Carrie Cerino Restaurants Inc.............440 237-3434
8922 Ridge Rd Cleveland (44133) *(G-5129)*
Carrier Industries Inc.............614 851-6363
1700 Georgesville Rd Columbus (43228) *(G-7131)*
Carroll Electric Coop Inc.............330 627-2116
250 Canton Rd Nw Carrollton (44615) *(G-2560)*
Carroll Golden Age Retreat.............330 627-4665
2202 Kensington Rd Ne Carrollton (44615) *(G-2561)*
Carroll Health Care Center.............330 627-5501
648 Longhorn St Nw Carrollton (44615) *(G-2562)*
Carroll Healthcare Center, Carrollton *Also called Carroll Health Care Center* *(G-2562)*
Carroll Hills Industries Inc.............330 627-5524
540 High St Nw Carrollton (44615) *(G-2563)*
Carroll Manufacturing & Sales.............440 937-3900
35179 Avon Commerce Pkwy Avon (44011) *(G-871)*
Carroll Properties.............513 398-8075
5589 Kings Mills Rd Mason (45040) *(G-13549)*
Carry Transport Inc.............937 236-0026
5536 Brentlinger Dr Dayton (45414) *(G-9283)*
Carstar, Blue Ash *Also called Cincinnati Collision Center* *(G-1524)*
Cartemp USA Inc (PA).............440 715-1000
29100 Aurora Rd Solon (44139) *(G-16832)*
Carter Lumber, Akron *Also called Carter-Jones Lumber Company* *(G-119)*
Carter Manufacturing Co Inc.............513 398-7303
4220 State Route 42 Mason (45040) *(G-13550)*
Carter-Jones Companies Inc (PA).............330 673-6100
601 Tallmadge Rd Kent (44240) *(G-12217)*
Carter-Jones Companies Inc.............330 674-0047
6139 State Route 39 Millersburg (44654) *(G-14462)*
Carter-Jones Lumber Company (HQ).............330 673-6100
601 Tallmadge Rd Kent (44240) *(G-12218)*
Carter-Jones Lumber Company.............330 784-5441
172 N Case Ave Akron (44305) *(G-119)*
Carter-Jones Lumber Company.............330 674-9060
6139 State Route 39 Millersburg (44654) *(G-14463)*
Carter-Jones Lumber Company.............330 673-6000
601 Tallmadge Rd Kent (44240) *(G-12219)*
Carts of America, Warren *Also called Hays Enterprises Inc* *(G-18711)*
Caruso Inc (PA).............513 860-9200
3465 Hauck Rd Cincinnati (45241) *(G-3127)*
Cas-Ker Company Inc.............513 674-7700
2550 Civic Center Dr Cincinnati (45231) *(G-3128)*
CASA, Cincinnati *Also called Addiction Services Council* *(G-2907)*
Casagrande Masonry Inc.............740 964-0781
13530 Morse Rd Sw New Albany (43054) *(G-14849)*
Casal Day Spa and Salon, Canfield *Also called Casals Hair Salon Inc* *(G-2132)*
Casals Hair Salon Inc (PA).............330 533-6766
4030 Boardman Canfield Rd Canfield (44406) *(G-2132)*
Casaro Headstart, Niles *Also called W T C S A Headstart Niles Ctr* *(G-15173)*
Cascade Audi, Cuyahoga Falls *Also called Cascade Group Inc* *(G-9077)*
Cascade Crossing, Cleveland *Also called Forest City Enterprises LP* *(G-5554)*
Cascade Group Inc.............330 929-1861
4149 State Rd Cuyahoga Falls (44223) *(G-9077)*
Cascia LLC.............440 975-8085
Classic Pk 35300 Vine St Classic Park Willoughby (44095) *(G-19509)*
Casco Mfg Solutions Inc.............513 681-0003
3107 Spring Grove Ave Cincinnati (45225) *(G-3129)*
Case Farms LLC.............330 832-0030
4001 Millennium Blvd Se Massillon (44646) *(G-13668)*
Case Western Reserve Univ.............216 368-2560
2232 Circle Dr Cleveland (44106) *(G-5130)*
Casegoods Inc.............330 825-2461
130 31st St Nw Barberton (44203) *(G-949)*

Casey Equipment Corporation........................330 750-1005
15 Union St Bldg 1 Struthers (44471) **(G-17360)**

Cash Flow Solutions Inc..............................513 524-2320
5166 College Corner Pike Oxford (45056) **(G-15676)**

Cashland Financial Svcs Inc (HQ)..................937 253-7842
100 E 3rd St Ste 200 Dayton (45402) **(G-9284)**

Caskey Cleaners, Columbus Also called Caskey Cleaning Co **(G-7132)**

Caskey Cleaning Co....................................614 443-7448
47 W Gates St Columbus (43206) **(G-7132)**

Casleo Corporation.....................................614 252-6508
2741 E 4th Ave Columbus (43219) **(G-7133)**

Casnet, Akron Also called High Line Corporation **(G-261)**

Casod Industrial Properties, Marion Also called Graham Investment Co **(G-13422)**

Cass Information Systems Inc........................614 839-4503
2644 Kirkwood Hwy Newark Columbus (43218) **(G-7134)**

Cass Information Systems Inc........................614 766-2277
2675 Corporate Exchange Columbus (43231) **(G-7135)**

Cass Logistics, Columbus Also called Cass Information Systems Inc **(G-7135)**

Cassady Alternative Elementary, Columbus Also called Columbus Public School
Dst **(G-7306)**

Cassady Schiller & Associates.......................513 483-6699
4555 Lake Forest Dr # 400 Blue Ash (45242) **(G-1519)**

Cassady Vlg Aprtments Ohio LLC...................216 520-1250
3089 Cassady Village Trl Columbus (43219) **(G-7136)**

Cassano's Pizza & Subs, Dayton Also called Cassanos Inc **(G-9285)**

Cassanos Inc (PA).....................................937 294-8400
1700 E Stroop Rd Dayton (45429) **(G-9285)**

Cassel Hills Golf Course, Vandalia Also called City of Vandalia **(G-18517)**

Cassens Transport Company.........................937 644-8886
24777 Honda Pkwy Marysville (43040) **(G-13488)**

Cassens Transport Company.........................419 727-0520
633 Matzinger Rd Toledo (43612) **(G-17639)**

Cassidy Trley Coml RE Svcs Inc....................513 771-2580
300 E Bus Way Ste 190 Cincinnati (45241) **(G-3130)**

Cassidy Turley, Norwood Also called Cushman & Wakefield Inc **(G-15461)**

Cassidy Turley, Moraine Also called Cushman & Wakefield Inc **(G-14638)**

Castaway Bay, Sandusky Also called Cedar Point Park LLC **(G-16583)**

Castilian & Co..937 836-9671
848 Union Blvd Englewood (45322) **(G-10581)**

Castilian Hair & Skin Center, Englewood Also called Castilian & Co **(G-10581)**

Castilla, Dr David DDS, Youngstown Also called Mahoning Valley Dental Service **(G-20109)**

Castle Care..440 327-3700
6043 Oakwood Cir North Ridgeville (44039) **(G-15323)**

Castle Care Landscaping, North Ridgeville Also called Castle Care **(G-15323)**

Castle Construction Co Inc...........................419 289-1122
588 Us Highway 250 E Ashland (44805) **(G-662)**

Castle Heating & Air Inc.............................216 696-3940
30355 Solon Indus Pkwy Solon (44139) **(G-16833)**

Castle Nursing Homes Inc...........................330 674-0015
6180 State Route 83 Millersburg (44654) **(G-14464)**

Casto, Columbus Also called United Management Inc **(G-8803)**

Casto Communities Cnstr Ltd........................614 228-8545
191 W Nationwide Blvd # 200 Columbus (43215) **(G-7137)**

Casto Health Care, Mansfield Also called Wedgewood Estates **(G-13262)**

Casto Health Care....................................419 884-6400
20 N Mill St Mansfield (44904) **(G-13148)**

Cat The Rental Store, Cincinnati Also called Holt Rental Services **(G-3716)**

Catalina Marketing Corporation....................513 564-8200
525 Vine St Ste 2200 Cincinnati (45202) **(G-3131)**

Catalyst Paper (usa) Inc............................937 528-3800
7777 Wash Vlg Dr Ste 210 Dayton (45459) **(G-9286)**

Catamaran Home Dlvry Ohio Inc...................440 930-5520
33381 Walker Rd Avon Lake (44012) **(G-911)**

Catawba Island Marina, Port Clinton Also called Catawba-Cleveland Dev Corp **(G-16101)**

Catawba-Cleveland Dev Corp (PA).................419 797-4424
4235 E Beachclub Rd Port Clinton (43452) **(G-16101)**

Caterpillar, Broadview Heights Also called Ohio Machinery Co **(G-1841)**

Caterpillar, Troy Also called Ohio Machinery Co **(G-18220)**

Caterpillar Authorized Dealer, Perrysburg Also called Ohio Machinery Co **(G-15897)**

Caterpillar Authorized Dealer, Broadview Heights Also called Ohio Machinery Co **(G-1840)**

Caterpillar Authorized Dealer, Canton Also called Ohio Machinery Co **(G-2427)**

Caterpillar Authorized Dealer, Girard Also called Ohio Machinery Co **(G-11295)**

Caterpillar Authorized Dealer, Zanesville Also called Ohio Machinery Co **(G-20348)**

Caterpillar Authorized Dealer, Cincinnati Also called Ohio Machinery Co **(G-4157)**

Caterpillar Authorized Dealer, Bolivar Also called Ohio Machinery Co **(G-1705)**

Catherines Care Center Inc..........................740 282-3605
717 N 6th Ave Steubenville (43952) **(G-17146)**

Catholic Association of The Di (PA).................216 641-7575
10000 Miles Ave Cleveland (44105) **(G-5131)**

Catholic Cemeteries.................................614 491-2751
6440 S High St Lockbourne (43137) **(G-12810)**

Catholic Charities Corporation.....................330 723-9615
4210 N Jefferson St Medina (44256) **(G-13915)**

Catholic Charities Corporation.....................216 939-3713
7800 Detroit Ave Cleveland (44102) **(G-5132)**

Catholic Charities Corporation.....................216 268-4006
1264 E 123rd St Cleveland (44108) **(G-5133)**

Catholic Charities Corporation.....................419 289-1903
34 W 2nd St Ste 18 Ashland (44805) **(G-663)**

Catholic Charities Corporation (PA)................216 334-2900
7911 Detroit Ave Cleveland (44102) **(G-5134)**

CATHOLIC CHARITIES DIOCESE OF, Cleveland Also called Catholic Charities
Corporation **(G-5134)**

Catholic Charities of Southwst......................937 325-8715
701 E Columbia St Springfield (45503) **(G-17005)**

Catholic Charities of SW Ohio (PA)................513 241-7745
7162 Reading Rd Ste 604 Cincinnati (45237) **(G-3132)**

Catholic Charities Services, Ashland Also called Catholic Charities Corporation **(G-663)**

Catholic Charities Svc Cuyah, Cleveland Also called Catholic Charities Corporation **(G-5132)**

Catholic Chrties Regional Agcy.....................330 744-3320
319 W Rayen Ave Youngstown (44502) **(G-19982)**

Catholic Club, Toledo Also called Diocese of Toledo **(G-17702)**

Catholic Diocese of Cleveland......................419 289-7224
501 Cottage St Ashland (44805) **(G-664)**

Catholic Diocese of Cleveland......................216 267-2850
14609 Brookpark Rd Cleveland (44142) **(G-5135)**

Catholic Diocese of Columbus......................614 276-5263
707 Salisbury Rd Columbus (43204) **(G-7138)**

Catholic Diocese of Columbus......................614 221-5891
197 E Gay St Ste 1 Columbus (43215) **(G-7139)**

Catholic Health Partners, Glandorf Also called St Ritas Medical Center **(G-11307)**

Catholic Healthcare Par, Cincinnati Also called Mercy Health **(G-4020)**

Catholic Residential Service.........................513 784-0400
100 E 8th St Ste 5 Cincinnati (45202) **(G-3133)**

Catholic Social Services Inc.........................614 221-5891
197 E Gay St Columbus (43215) **(G-7140)**

Catholic Social Svc Miami Vly (PA)................937 223-7217
922 W Riverview Ave Dayton (45402) **(G-9287)**

Catsi Inc...800 922-0468
7991 Ohio River Rd Wheelersburg (45694) **(G-19429)**

Cattrell Companies Inc..............................740 537-2481
906 Franklin St Toronto (43964) **(G-18183)**

Cavalier Distributing Company.....................513 247-9222
4650 Lake Forest Dr # 580 Blue Ash (45242) **(G-1520)**

Cavaliers Holdings LLC (PA).......................216 420-2000
1 Center Ct Cleveland (44115) **(G-5136)**

Cavaliers Operating Co LLC.........................216 420-2000
1 Center Ct Cleveland (44115) **(G-5137)**

Caveney Inc...330 497-4600
7801 Cleveland Ave Nw North Canton (44720) **(G-15192)**

Cavins Trucking & Garage LLC (PA)...............419 661-9947
100 J St C Perrysburg (43551) **(G-15847)**

Cavitch Familo & Durkin Co Lpa....................216 621-7860
1300 E 9th St Cleveland (44114) **(G-5138)**

CB Richard Ellis, Toledo Also called Ellis Richard CB Reichle Klein **(G-17711)**

CBA, Perrysburg Also called Critical Business Analysis Inc **(G-15852)**

Cbc Companies Inc...................................614 222-4343
1691 Nw Professional Plz Columbus (43220) **(G-7141)**

Cbc Companies Inc...................................614 538-6100
1651 Nw Professional Plz Columbus (43220) **(G-7142)**

Cbc Engineers & Associates Ltd (PA)..............937 428-6150
125 Westpark Rd Dayton (45459) **(G-9288)**

Cbcinnovis International Inc (HQ)...................614 222-4343
250 E Broad St Fl 21 Columbus (43215) **(G-7143)**

Cbcs, Columbus Also called Credit Bur Collectn Svcs Inc **(G-7388)**

Cbcs, Dayton Also called Credit Bur Collectn Svcs Inc **(G-9338)**

Cbf Industries, Bedford Also called Ebo Inc **(G-1279)**

Cbf Industries Inc....................................216 229-9300
23600 Aurora Rd Bedford (44146) **(G-1271)**

Cbiz Inc..330 644-2044
13680 Cleveland Ave Nw Uniontown (44685) **(G-18361)**

Cbiz Inc (PA)..216 447-9000
6050 Oak Tree Blvd # 500 Cleveland (44131) **(G-5139)**

Cbiz Accounting Tax.................................330 668-6500
4040 Embassy Pkwy Ste 100 Akron (44333) **(G-120)**

Cbiz Med MGT Professionals Inc....................614 771-2222
3455 Mill Run Dr Ste 450 Hilliard (43026) **(G-11754)**

Cbiz Operations Inc (HQ)...........................216 447-9000
6050 Oaktee Blvd Ste 500 Cleveland (44131) **(G-5140)**

Cbiz Risk & Advisory Svcs LLC......................216 447-9000
6050 Oak Tree Blvd Cleveland (44131) **(G-5141)**

Cbiz Technologies LLC..............................216 447-9000
6050 Oak Tree Blvd Independence (44131) **(G-12055)**

Cbl & Associates Prpts Inc..........................513 424-8517
3461 Towne Blvd Unit 200 Middletown (45005) **(G-14344)**

Cbord Group Inc.....................................330 498-2702
3800 Tabs Dr Uniontown (44685) **(G-18362)**

Cbre Inc..513 369-1300
201 E 5th St Ste 2200 Cincinnati (45202) **(G-3134)**

Cbre Inc..216 687-1800
950 Main Ave Ste 200 Cleveland (44113) **(G-5142)**

Cbre Inc..614 419-7429
860 Taylor Station Rd Blacklick (43004) **(G-1476)**

Cbre Inc..614 438-5488
200 Civic Center Dr Fl 14 Columbus (43215) **(G-7144)**

Cbre Heery Inc.......................................216 781-1313
1660 W 2nd St Cleveland (44113) **(G-5143)**

A
L
P
H
A
B
E
T
I
C

CBS Corporation 513 749-1035
2060 Reading Rd Fl 34 Cincinnati (45202) *(G-3135)*

CBS Radio Inc 513 699-5105
2060 Reading Rd Cincinnati (45202) *(G-3136)*

CBS Radio Inc 216 861-0100
1041 Huron Rd E Cleveland (44115) *(G-5144)*

Cbt Company, Cincinnati *Also called Belting Company of Cincinnati (G-3039)*

Cbt Company, Sidney *Also called Belting Company of Cincinnati (G-16762)*

Cbts Technology Solutions LLC (HQ) 513 841-2287
221 E 4th St Cincinnati (45202) *(G-3137)*

Ccdc, Dayton *Also called Valentour Education Inc (G-9846)*

Ccems, Coshocton *Also called Coshocton Cnty Emrgncy Med Svc (G-9005)*

Cchs Johnstown Home, Columbus *Also called Columbus Ctr For Humn Svcs Inc (G-7273)*

CCI, Mentor *Also called Cleveland Construction Inc (G-14031)*

CCI Supply Inc 440 953-0045
8620 Tyler Blvd Mentor (44060) *(G-14026)*

Ccj, Wooster *Also called Critchfeld Crtchfield Johnston (G-19720)*

CCJ Enterprises Inc 330 345-4386
3889 Friendsville Rd Wooster (44691) *(G-19697)*

Ccp Industries, Richmond Heights *Also called Tranzonic Companies (G-16395)*

CD Block K Hotel LLC 440 871-3100
2020 Crocker Rd Westlake (44145) *(G-19328)*

Cd1025 .... 614 221-9923
1036 S Front St Columbus (43206) *(G-7145)*

Cdc Capital Park Head St Ctr, Columbus *Also called Child Dvlpmnt Cncl of Frnkln (G-7186)*

Cdc Management Co 614 781-0216
4949 Freeway Dr E Columbus (43229) *(G-7146)*

Cdc of Warren, Warren *Also called Community Dialysis Center (G-18687)*

Cdd LLC 905 829-2794
6800 Cintas Blvd Mason (45040) *(G-13551)*

CDM Smith Inc 740 897-2937
3930 Us Rte 23 S Piketon (45661) *(G-15972)*

CDM SMITH INC 614 847-8340
445 Hutchinson Ave # 820 Columbus (43235) *(G-7147)*

Cdo Technologies Inc (PA) 937 258-0022
5200 Sprngfeld St Ste 320 Dayton (45431) *(G-9164)*

Cdw Technologies LLC 513 677-4100
9349 Waterstone Blvd Cincinnati (45249) *(G-3138)*

Ce Power Engineered Svcs LLC (HQ) 513 563-6150
4040 Rev Dr Cincinnati (45232) *(G-3139)*

Ce Power Holdings Inc (PA) 513 563-6150
4040 Rev Dr Cincinnati (45232) *(G-3140)*

Cec Combustion Safety LLC (HQ) 216 749-2992
2100 Apollo Dr Brookpark (44142) *(G-1893)*

Cec Entertainment Inc 937 439-1108
30 Prestige Pl Miamisburg (45342) *(G-14149)*

Cecil I Walker Machinery Co 740 286-7566
1477 Mayhew Rd Jackson (45640) *(G-12170)*

Ceco Concrete Cnstr Del LLC 513 874-6953
4535 Port Union Rd West Chester (45011) *(G-18881)*

Cecos International Inc 513 724-6114
5092 Aber Rd Williamsburg (45176) *(G-19490)*

Cedar Creek Vterinary Svcs Inc 740 467-2949
12575 Lancaster St Ne Millersport (43046) *(G-14502)*

Cedar Elec Holdings Corp 773 804-6288
5440 W Chester Rd West Chester (45069) *(G-18882)*

Cedar Fair LP (PA) 419 626-0830
1 Cedar Point Dr Sandusky (44870) *(G-16582)*

Cedar Hill Care Center, Zanesville *Also called Zandex Health Care Corporation (G-20379)*

Cedar Hill Care Center, Zanesville *Also called Zandex Inc (G-20376)*

Cedar House, Cleveland *Also called Rose Mary Johanna Grassell (G-6340)*

Cedar Point Park LLC 419 627-2500
2001 Cleveland Rd Sandusky (44870) *(G-16583)*

Cedar Springs, New Paris *Also called Foundations (G-14942)*

Cedar Springs Care Center, New Paris *Also called Heritage Park Rehabilita (G-14943)*

CEDAR VILLAGE, Mason *Also called Jewish Home of Cincinnati (G-13603)*

Cedars of Lebanon Nursing Home, Lebanon *Also called Health Care Opportunities Inc (G-12469)*

Cedarwood Construction Company 330 836-9971
1765 Merriman Rd Akron (44313) *(G-121)*

Ceder Hill, Zanesville *Also called Zandex Health Care Corporation (G-20377)*

Cefaratti Group, Cleveland *Also called Cefaratti Investigation & Prcs (G-5145)*

Cefaratti Investigation & Prcs 216 696-1161
4608 Saint Clair Ave Cleveland (44103) *(G-5145)*

Cei Physicians Inc 513 984-5133
1945 Cei Dr Blue Ash (45242) *(G-1521)*

Cei Physicians PSC Inc 513 233-2700
7794 5 Mile Rd Ste 270 Cincinnati (45230) *(G-3141)*

Cei Physicians PSC Inc 513 531-2020
4760 Red Bank Rd Ste 108 Cincinnati (45227) *(G-3142)*

Cei Physicians PSC LLC (PA) 513 984-5133
1945 Cei Dr Blue Ash (45242) *(G-1522)*

Ceiba Enterprises Incorporated 614 818-3220
159 Baranof W Westerville (43081) *(G-19231)*

Celco Ltd 330 655-7000
5600 Hudsn Indstl Pkwy Hudson (44236) *(G-11969)*

Celebrations, Plain City *Also called Made From Scratch Inc (G-16058)*

Celebrity Security Inc 216 671-6425
3408 West Blvd Cleveland (44111) *(G-5146)*

CELINA AREA VISITING NURSES AS, Van Wert *Also called Community Hlth Prfssionals Inc (G-18475)*

Celina Insurance Group, Celina *Also called Celina Mutual Insurance Co (G-2587)*

Celina Mutual Insurance Co (PA) 419 586-5181
1 Insurance Sq Celina (45822) *(G-2587)*

Celina Visting Nurses, Celina *Also called Community Hlth Prfssionals Inc (G-2589)*

Celina Waste Water Plant, Celina *Also called City of Celina (G-2588)*

Cellco Partnership 330 722-6622
2736 Medina Rd Medina (44256) *(G-13916)*

Cellco Partnership 614 560-2000
5165 Emerald Pkwy Dublin (43017) *(G-10162)*

Cellco Partnership 440 984-5200
7566 Oak Point Rd Amherst (44001) *(G-583)*

Cellco Partnership 513 923-2700
9674 Colerain Ave Cincinnati (45251) *(G-3143)*

Cellco Partnership 330 823-7758
2700 W State St Alliance (44601) *(G-523)*

Cellco Partnership 419 333-1009
2140 Enterprise St Ste C Fremont (43420) *(G-11061)*

Cellco Partnership 740 652-9540
1926 N Memorial Dr Lancaster (43130) *(G-12377)*

Cellco Partnership 740 695-3600
50641 Valley Plaza Dr Saint Clairsville (43950) *(G-16482)*

Cellco Partnership 740 432-7785
2103 Southgate Pkwy Cambridge (43725) *(G-2057)*

Cellco Partnership 330 376-8275
50 W Bowery St Akron (44308) *(G-122)*

Cellco Partnership 513 755-1666
7606 Trailside Dr West Chester (45069) *(G-18883)*

Cellco Partnership 513 697-1190
8650 Governors Hill Dr Cincinnati (45249) *(G-3144)*

Cellco Partnership 440 934-0576
36050 Detroit Rd Avon (44011) *(G-872)*

Cellco Partnership 419 381-1726
1260 S Reynolds Rd Toledo (43615) *(G-17640)*

Cellco Partnership 216 765-1444
400 Park Ave Apt 210 Beachwood (44122) *(G-1042)*

Cellco Partnership 440 998-3111
3315 N Ridge Rd E Ashtabula (44004) *(G-724)*

Cellco Partnership 513 422-3437
3663 Towne Blvd Middletown (45005) *(G-14345)*

Cellco Partnership 740 588-0018
3575 Maple Ave Zanesville (43701) *(G-20289)*

Cellco Partnership 513 688-1300
482 Ohio Pike Ste 1 Cincinnati (45255) *(G-3145)*

Cellco Partnership 419 424-2351
15073 E Us Route 224 Findlay (45840) *(G-10886)*

Cellco Partnership 419 897-9133
1378 Conant St Maumee (43537) *(G-13768)*

Cellco Partnership 440 953-1155
7685 Mentor Ave Mentor (44060) *(G-14027)*

Cellco Partnership 440 646-9625
5945 Mayfield Rd Cleveland (44124) *(G-5147)*

Cellco Partnership 440 846-8881
17290 Royalton Rd Strongsville (44136) *(G-17289)*

Cellco Partnership 740 397-6609
1002 Coshocton Ave 3 Mount Vernon (43050) *(G-14752)*

Cellco Partnership 614 459-7200
2180 Henderson Rd Columbus (43220) *(G-7148)*

Cellco Partnership 937 429-4000
2755 Fairfield Cmns Beavercreek (45431) *(G-1138)*

Cellco Partnership 513 671-2200
55 E Kemper Rd Cincinnati (45246) *(G-3146)*

Cellco Partnership 513 697-0222
9040 Union Cemetery Rd Cincinnati (45249) *(G-3147)*

Cellco Partnership 440 779-1313
24121 Lorain Rd North Olmsted (44070) *(G-15279)*

Cellco Partnership 419 843-2995
6710 W Central Ave Ste 20 Toledo (43617) *(G-17641)*

Cellco Partnership 330 493-7979
4926 Dressler Rd Nw Canton (44718) *(G-2247)*

Cellco Partnership 216 573-5880
6712 Rockside Rd Independence (44131) *(G-12056)*

Cellco Partnership 937 578-0022
1095 Delaware Ave Marysville (43040) *(G-13489)*

Cellco Partnership 440 542-9631
6440 Som Center Rd Ste C Solon (44139) *(G-16834)*

Cellco Partnership 330 626-0524
9315 State Route 14 Streetsboro (44241) *(G-17248)*

Cellco Partnership 330 308-0549
507 Mill Ave Se New Philadelphia (44663) *(G-14948)*

Cellco Partnership 614 793-8989
5520 Blazer Pkwy Dublin (43016) *(G-10163)*

Cellco Partnership 740 450-1525
2359 Maple Ave Zanesville (43701) *(G-20290)*

Cellco Partnership 440 324-9479
1621 W River Rd N Elyria (44035) *(G-10486)*

Cellco Partnership 614 793-8989
5035 Post Rd Dublin (43017) *(G-10164)*

Cellco Partnership 614 277-2900
3043 Turnberry Ct Grove City (43123) *(G-11418)*

Cellco Partnership 740 522-6446
668 Hebron Rd Newark (43056) *(G-15021)*

Cellco Partnership 330 345-6465
  4164 Burbank Rd Wooster (44691) *(G-19698)*
Cellular Sales Knoxville Inc 614 322-9975
  5976 E Main St Columbus (43213) *(G-7149)*
Cellular Technology Limited 216 791-5084
  20521 Chagrin Blvd # 200 Shaker Heights (44122) *(G-16704)*
Celtic Healthcare Ne Ohio Inc 724 742-4360
  299 Edwards St Youngstown (44502) *(G-19983)*
Cem-Base Inc 330 963-3101
  8530 N Boyle Pkwy Twinsburg (44087) *(G-18251)*
Cemp, Brooklyn *Also called Victory Capital Management Inc* *(G-1862)*
Cengage Learning Inc 513 229-1000
  5191 Natorp Blvd Lowr Mason (45040) *(G-13552)*
Centaur Associates, Maumee *Also called Centaur Mail Inc* *(G-13769)*
Centaur Mail Inc 419 887-5857
  4064 Technology Dr Ste A Maumee (43537) *(G-13769)*
Centaurus Financial Inc 419 756-9747
  58 W 3rd St Ste B Mansfield (44902) *(G-13149)*
Centene Corporation 513 469-4500
  4665 Cornell Rd Ste 300 Blue Ash (45241) *(G-1523)*
Centennial Prsrvtion Group LLC 614 238-0730
  600 N Cassady Ave Ste D Columbus (43219) *(G-7150)*
Centennial Terrace & Quarry 419 885-7106
  5773 Centennial Rd Sylvania (43560) *(G-17414)*
Center 5 .... 330 379-5900
  444 N Main St Akron (44310) *(G-123)*
Center Ed/Train Employmnt, Columbus *Also called Ohio State University* *(G-8316)*
Center For Addiction Treatment 513 381-6672
  830 Ezzard Charles Dr Cincinnati (45214) *(G-3148)*
CENTER FOR BALANCED LIVING, TH, Columbus *Also called Center For Eating Disorders (G-7153)*
Center For Child Development, Akron *Also called University of Akron* *(G-480)*
Center For Cognitive and Beh (PA) 614 459-4490
  4624 Sawmill Rd Columbus (43220) *(G-7151)*
Center For Cognitv Behav Psych 614 459-4490
  4624 Sawmill Rd Columbus (43220) *(G-7152)*
Center For Community Solutions 216 781-2944
  1501 Euclid Ave Ste 311 Cleveland (44115) *(G-5148)*
Center For Dagnstc Imaging Inc 614 841-0800
  2141 Polaris Pkwy Columbus (43240) *(G-6803)*
Center For Dialysis Care, Cleveland *Also called Community Dialysis Center* *(G-5325)*
Center For Dialysis Care, Cleveland *Also called Community Dialysis Center* *(G-5326)*
Center For Dlysis Cre of Cnfld 330 702-3040
  3695 Stutz Dr Ste 1 Canfield (44406) *(G-2133)*
Center For Eating Disorders 614 896-8222
  8001 Ravines Edge Ct # 201 Columbus (43235) *(G-7153)*
Center For Employment Resource, Cincinnati *Also called Great Oaks Inst Tech Creer Dev (G-3645)*
Center For Families & Children 440 888-0300
  5955 Ridge Rd Cleveland (44129) *(G-5149)*
Center For Families & Children (PA) 216 432-7200
  4500 Euclid Ave Cleveland (44103) *(G-5150)*
Center For Families & Children 216 932-9497
  1941 S Taylor Rd Ste 225 Cleveland Heights (44118) *(G-6715)*
Center For Families & Children 216 252-5800
  3929 Rocky River Dr Cleveland (44111) *(G-5151)*
Center For Health Affairs 800 362-2628
  1226 Huron Rd E Cleveland (44115) *(G-5152)*
Center For Human Resource RES, Columbus *Also called Ohio State University* *(G-8320)*
Center For Individual and Fmly (PA) 419 522-4357
  741 Scholl Rd Mansfield (44907) *(G-13150)*
Center For Prgressive Eye Care, Oregon *Also called Assocted Ctract Laser Surgeons (G-15583)*
Center For Spinal Disorders 419 383-4878
  3000 Arlington Ave Toledo (43614) *(G-17642)*
Center For Srgcal Drmtlogy Inc 614 847-4100
  428 County Line Rd W Westerville (43082) *(G-19150)*
Center For Urologic Health LLC (PA) 330 375-0924
  95 Arch St Ste 165 Akron (44304) *(G-124)*
Center of Hope, Union City *Also called Crotinger Nursing Home Inc* *(G-18353)*
Center of Voctnl Altrntvs Mntl (PA) 614 294-7117
  3770 N High St Columbus (43214) *(G-7154)*
Center Ridge House, Westlake *Also called Childrens Forever Haven Inc* *(G-19331)*
Center Ridge Nursing Home Inc 440 808-5500
  38600 Center Ridge Rd North Ridgeville (44039) *(G-15324)*
Center School Association 440 995-7400
  6625 Wilson Mills Rd Mayfield Village (44143) *(G-13884)*
Center Seeds, Sidney *Also called Cover Crop Shop LLC* *(G-16772)*
Center Service, Cincinnati *Also called Carol Reese* *(G-3126)*
Center Street Cmnty Clinic Inc 740 751-6380
  136 W Center St Marion (43302) *(G-13410)*
Centerburg Resp & Spclty Rehab, Centerburg *Also called Centerburg Two LLC* *(G-2614)*
Centerburg Two LLC 740 625-5774
  212 Fairview St Centerburg (43011) *(G-2614)*
Centergrid LLC 513 712-1212
  101 Knightsbridge Dr Hamilton (45011) *(G-11574)*
Centerra Co-Op (PA) 419 281-2153
  813 Clark Ave Ashland (44805) *(G-665)*
Centerra Co-Op 800 362-9598
  161 E Jefferson St Jefferson (44047) *(G-12190)*

Centers For Dialysis Care Inc (PA) 216 295-7000
  18720 Chagrin Blvd Shaker Heights (44122) *(G-16705)*
Centerville Child Development 937 434-5949
  8095 Garnet Dr Dayton (45458) *(G-9289)*
Centerville Fitness Inc 937 291-7990
  51 E Spring Valley Pike Centerville (45458) *(G-2623)*
Centerville Washington Pk Dst, Centerville *Also called Washington Township Park Dst (G-2636)*
Centimark Corporation 614 536-1960
  7077 Americana Pkwy Reynoldsburg (43068) *(G-16288)*
Centimark Corporation 937 704-9909
  319 Industrial Dr Franklin (45005) *(G-11026)*
Centimark Corporation 330 920-3560
  4665 Allen Rd Ste C Stow (44224) *(G-17194)*
Centimark Roofing Systems, Franklin *Also called Centimark Corporation* *(G-11026)*
Central 'travel, Toledo *Also called Central Travel & Ticket Inc* *(G-17644)*
Central Accounting Systems (PA) 513 605-2700
  12500 Reed Hartman Hwy Cincinnati (45241) *(G-3149)*
Central Beverage Group Ltd 614 294-3555
  8133 Highfield Dr Lewis Center (43035) *(G-12532)*
Central Billing Office, Akron *Also called Nationwide Childrens Hospital* *(G-343)*
Central Bnfits Admnstrtors Inc 614 797-5200
  5150 E Dublin Grnvlle 3 Westerville (43081) *(G-19232)*
Central Business Equipment Co (HQ) 513 891-4430
  10321 S Medallion Dr Cincinnati (45241) *(G-3150)*
Central Cadillac Limited 216 861-5800
  2801 Carnegie Ave Cleveland (44115) *(G-5153)*
Central Cadillac-Hummer, Cleveland *Also called Central Cadillac Limited* *(G-5153)*
Central Christian School, Kidron *Also called Christian Schools Inc* *(G-12305)*
Central Clinic Outpatient Svcs 513 558-9005
  311 Albert Sabin Way Cincinnati (45229) *(G-3151)*
Central Cmnty Hse of Columbus (PA) 614 253-7267
  1150 E Main St Columbus (43205) *(G-7155)*
Central Coca-Cola Btlg Co Inc 419 476-6622
  3970 Catawba St Toledo (43612) *(G-17643)*
Central Command Inc 330 723-2062
  33891 Henwell Rd Columbia Station (44028) *(G-6771)*
Central Commnty Hlth Brd of Ha 513 559-2000
  532 Maxwell Ave Cincinnati (45219) *(G-3152)*
Central Commnty Hlth Brd of Ha 513 559-2000
  536 Elliott Ave Cincinnati (45215) *(G-3153)*
Central Commnty Hlth Brd of Ha 513 559-2981
  3020 Vernon Pl Cincinnati (45219) *(G-3154)*
Central Credit Corp 614 856-5840
  2040 Brice Rd Ste 200 Reynoldsburg (43068) *(G-16289)*
Central Fire Protection Co Inc 937 322-0713
  583 Selma Rd Springfield (45505) *(G-17006)*
Central Hamilton YMCA, Hamilton *Also called Great Miami Valley YMCA* *(G-11604)*
Central Hospital Services Inc 216 696-6900
  1226 Huron Rd E Ste 2 Cleveland (44115) *(G-5154)*
Central Hummr East 216 514-2700
  25975 Central Pkwy Cleveland (44122) *(G-5155)*
Central Insulation Systems Inc 513 242-0600
  300 Murray Rd Cincinnati (45217) *(G-3155)*
CENTRAL INSURANCE COMPANIES, Van Wert *Also called Central Mutual Insurance Co (G-18474)*
CENTRAL INSURANCE COMPANIES, Van Wert *Also called All America Insurance Company (G-18472)*
Central Mutual Insurance Co (PA) 419 238-1010
  800 S Washington St Van Wert (45891) *(G-18474)*
Central OH Area Agency On Agng 614 645-7250
  3776 S High St Columbus (43207) *(G-7156)*
Central Ohio Associates Ltd 419 342-2045
  Central Oh Ind 18 Shelby (44875) *(G-16743)*
Central Ohio Bandag LP 740 454-9728
  1600 S Point Dr Zanesville (43701) *(G-20291)*
Central Ohio Building Co Inc 614 475-6392
  3756 Agler Rd Columbus (43219) *(G-7157)*
Central Ohio Contractors Inc (PA) 614 539-2579
  2879 Jackson Pike Grove City (43123) *(G-11419)*
Central Ohio Contractors Inc 740 369-7700
  888 Us Highway 42 N Delaware (43015) *(G-9958)*
Central Ohio Custom Contg LLC 614 579-4971
  10541 New Delaware Rd Mount Vernon (43050) *(G-14753)*
Central Ohio Financial Group, Columbus *Also called Northwestern Mutl Lf Insur Co* *(G-8209)*
Central Ohio Geriatrics LLC 614 530-4077
  590 Newark Granville Rd Granville (43023) *(G-11336)*
Central Ohio Home Help Agency, Columbus *Also called Ssth LLC* *(G-8679)*
Central Ohio Hospitalists 614 255-6900
  3525 Olentangy River Rd # 4330 Columbus (43214) *(G-7158)*
Central Ohio Ice Rinks Inc 614 475-7575
  7001 Dublin Park Dr Dublin (43016) *(G-10165)*
Central Ohio Medical Textiles 614 453-9274
  575 Harmon Ave Columbus (43223) *(G-7159)*
Central Ohio Mental Health Ctr (PA) 740 368-7831
  250 S Henry St Delaware (43015) *(G-9959)*
Central Ohio Nutrition Center (PA) 614 864-7225
  648 Taylor Rd Columbus (43230) *(G-7160)*
Central Ohio Poison Center 800 222-1222
  700 Childrens Dr Columbus (43205) *(G-7161)*

(PA)=Parent Co (HQ)=Headquarters (DH)=Div Headquarters

Central Ohio Poured Walls Inc 614 889-0505
7627 Fishel.Dr N Dublin (43016) (G-10166)
Central Ohio Primary Care 614 459-3687
770 Jasonway Ave Ste G2 Columbus (43214) (G-7162)
Central Ohio Primary Care 614 818-9550
285 W Schrock Rd Westerville (43081) (G-19233)
Central Ohio Primary Care 614 451-1551
4885 Olentangy River Rd # 2 Columbus (43214) (G-7163)
Central Ohio Primary Care 614 268-6555
4885 Olentangy River Rd Columbus (43214) (G-7164)
Central Ohio Primary Care 614 473-1300
2489 Stelzer Rd 101 Columbus (43219) (G-7165)
Central Ohio Primary Care 614 508-0110
615 Cpland Mill Rd Ste 2d Westerville (43081) (G-19234)
Central Ohio Primary Care 614 552-2300
6488 E Main St Ste C Reynoldsburg (43068) (G-16290)
Central Ohio Primary Care 614 891-9505
507 Executive Campus Dr # 160 Westerville (43082) (G-19151)
Central Ohio Primary Care 614 882-0708
555 W Schrock Rd Ste 110 Westerville (43081) (G-19235)
Central Ohio Primary Care 614 268-8164
3535 Olentangy River Rd Columbus (43214) (G-7166)
Central Ohio Primary Care 614 834-8042
6201 Gender Rd Canal Winchester (43110) (G-2106)
Central Ohio Primary Care 614 540-7339
760 Lakeview Plaza Blvd # 500 Worthington (43085) (G-19796)
Central Ohio Primary Care (PA) 614 326-2672
570 Polaris Pkwy Ste 250 Westerville (43082) (G-19152)
Central Ohio Primary Care 614 442-7550
4030 Henderson Rd Columbus (43220) (G-7167)
Central Ohio Pulmonary Disease, Westerville Also called Central Ohio Sleep
Medicine (G-19153)
Central Ohio Sleep Medicine 614 475-6700
484 County Line Rd W # 130 Westerville (43082) (G-19153)
Central Ohio Surgical Assoc (PA) 614 222-8000
750 Mount Carmel Mall # 380 Columbus (43222) (G-7168)
Central Ohio Transit Authority 614 275-5800
1333 Fields Ave Columbus (43201) (G-7169)
Central Ohio Transit Authority (PA) 614 275-5800
33 N High St Columbus (43215) (G-7170)
Central Ohio Youth Center, Marysville Also called Five County Joint Juvenile Det (G-13495)
Central Parking System Inc 513 381-2621
303 Broadway St Lot A Cincinnati (45202) (G-3156)
Central Pk W Rhabilitation Ctr, Toledo Also called Rehabilitation Aquatics (G-17999)
Central Power Systems, Columbus Also called Power Distributors LLC (G-8457)
Central Railroad of Indiana, Cincinnati Also called Indiana & Ohio Rail Corp (G-3756)
Central Ready Mix LLC (PA) 513 402-5001
6310 E Kemper Rd Ste 125 Cincinnati (45241) (G-3157)
Central Region, Mason Also called Dassault Systemes Simulia Corp (G-13572)
Central Repair Service Inc 513 943-0500
1606 Locust St Point Pleasant (45153) (G-16078)
Central Services Department, Cleveland Also called County of Cuyahoga (G-5366)
Central Star 419 756-9449
2003 W 4th St Ste 116 Ontario (44906) (G-15545)
Central Star Home Health Svcs, Ontario Also called Central Star (G-15545)
Central Steel and Wire Company 513 242-2233
525 Township Ave Cincinnati (45216) (G-3158)
Central Travel & Ticket Inc (PA) 419 897-2070
4540 Heatherdowns Blvd # 2 Toledo (43614) (G-17644)
Central USA Wireless LLC 513 469-1500
11210 Montgomery Rd Cincinnati (45249) (G-3159)
Centre Communications Corp 440 454-3262
70 Birch Aly Ste 240 Beavercreek (45440) (G-1209)
Centric Consulting LLC (PA) 888 781-7567
1215 Lyons Rd F Dayton (45458) (G-9290)
Centric Consulting LLC 513 791-3061
9380 Montgomery Rd # 207 Cincinnati (45242) (G-3160)
Centro Properties Group LLC 440 324-6610
3343 Midway Mall Elyria (44035) (G-10487)
Centura Inc 216 593-0226
4381 Renaissance Pkwy Cleveland (44128) (G-5156)
Centura X-Ray, Cleveland Also called Centura Inc (G-5156)
Centurion of Akron Inc 330 645-6699
1062 Jacoby Rd Copley (44321) (G-8964)
Century 21, Kent Also called Wilbur Realty Inc (G-12268)
Century 21, Mentor Also called Prudential Select Properties (G-14098)
Century 21, Lakewood Also called Prudential Lucien Realty (G-12360)
Century 21, Columbus Also called Joseph Walker Inc (G-6817)
Century 21, Marietta Also called REO Network Inc (G-13376)
Century 21, Warren Also called North Wood Realty (G-18734)
Century 21 - North Office, Columbus Also called Century 21-Joe Walker & Assoc (G-6804)
Century 21 Elite Performance 937 438-8221
2905 River Edge Cir Spring Valley (45370) (G-16957)
Century 21 Trammell Odonnell 440 888-6800
7087 Pearl Rd Cleveland (44130) (G-5157)
Century 21-Joe Walker & Assoc 614 899-1400
8800 Lyra Dr Ste 600 Columbus (43240) (G-6804)
Century Equipment Inc (PA) 419 865-7400
5959 Angola Rd Toledo (43615) (G-17645)

Century Equipment Inc 513 285-1800
8650 Bilstein Blvd Hamilton (45015) (G-11575)
Century Equipment Inc 216 292-6911
26565 Miles Rd Ste 200 Cleveland (44128) (G-5158)
Century Federal Credit Union 216 535-3600
10701 East Blvd Cleveland (44106) (G-5159)
Century Health Inc (PA) 419 425-5050
1918 N Main St Findlay (45840) (G-10887)
Century Lines Inc 216 271-0700
3184 E 79th St Cleveland (44104) (G-5160)
Century Marketing Corporation (HQ) 419 354-2591
12836 S Dixie Hwy Bowling Green (43402) (G-1727)
Century Mech Solutions Inc 513 681-5700
1554 Chase Ave Cincinnati (45223) (G-3161)
Century National Bank (HQ) 740 454-2521
14 S 5th St Zanesville (43701) (G-20292)
Century National Bank 800 548-3557
33 S 5th St Zanesville (43701) (G-20293)
Century National Bank 740 455-7330
505 Market St Zanesville (43701) (G-20294)
Century Oak Care Center, Cleveland Also called Swa Inc (G-6489)
Century Oak Care Center, Cleveland Also called Southwest Associates (G-6426)
Centurylabel, Bowling Green Also called Century Marketing Corporation (G-1727)
Centurylink Inc 614 215-4223
4650 Lakehurst Ct Dublin (43016) (G-10167)
Ceogc, Cleveland Also called Council For Economic Opport (G-5355)
CER Hotels LLC 330 422-1855
795 Mondial Pkwy Streetsboro (44241) (G-17249)
CEREBRAL PALSY SERVICES CENTER, Cincinnati Also called United Cerebral Palsy Gr
Cinc (G-4676)
Ceres Enterprises LLC 440 617-9385
835 Sharon Dr Ste 400 Westlake (44145) (G-19329)
Cerni Motor Sales Inc (PA) 330 652-9917
5751 Cerni Pl Youngstown (44515) (G-19984)
Certanteed Gyps Ciling Mfg Inc 800 233-8990
1192 S Chillicothe Rd Aurora (44202) (G-824)
Certified Angus Beef LLC (HQ) 330 345-2333
206 Riffel Rd Wooster (44691) (G-19699)
Certified Oil Inc 614 421-7500
949 King Ave Columbus (43212) (G-7171)
Certified Power Inc 419 355-1200
1110 Napoleon St Fremont (43420) (G-11062)
Certified Pressure Testing LLC (PA) 740 374-2071
2019 State Route 821 Marietta (45750) (G-13318)
Certified SEC Solutions Inc (PA) 216 785-2986
6050 Oak Tree Blvd Independence (44131) (G-12057)
Ceso Inc (PA) 937 435-8584
3601 Rigby Rd Ste 310 Miamisburg (45342) (G-14150)
Cessna Aircraft Company 419 866-6761
11591 W Airport Service R Swanton (43558) (G-17395)
Cessna Toledo Citation Svc Ctr, Swanton Also called Cessna Aircraft Company (G-17395)
Cetek, Cleveland Also called Fosbel Inc (G-5565)
Cetek Ltd 216 362-3900
6779 Engle Rd Ste A Cleveland (44130) (G-5161)
Ceva Freight LLC 614 482-5100
2727 London Groveport Rd Groveport (43125) (G-11500)
Ceva Freight LLC 216 898-6765
18601 Cleveland Pkwy Dr Cleveland (44135) (G-5162)
Ceva Logistics LLC 614 482-5000
2727 London Groveport Rd Groveport (43125) (G-11501)
Ceva Logistics US Inc 614 482-5107
2727 London Groveport Rd Columbus (43207) (G-7172)
Ceva Ocean Line, Groveport Also called Ceva Freight LLC (G-11500)
Ceva Ocean Line, Cleveland Also called Ceva Freight LLC (G-5162)
CFI Interiors, Canton Also called Canton Floors Inc (G-2233)
CFM Religion Pubg Group LLC (PA) 513 931-4050
8805 Governors Hill Dr # 400 Cincinnati (45249) (G-3162)
CFS Construction Inc 513 559-4500
2170 Gilbert Ave Ste 100 Cincinnati (45206) (G-3163)
CGB -Defiance, Defiance Also called Consolidated Grain & Barge Co (G-9907)
Cgh Global, Cincinnati Also called Cgh-Global Emerg Mngmt Strateg (G-2843)
Cgh-Global Emerg Mngmt Strateg 800 376-0655
851 Ohio Pike Ste 203 Cincinnati (45245) (G-2843)
Cgh-Global Security LLC 800 376-0655
4957 Cinnamon Cir Cincinnati (45244) (G-3164)
Cgh-Global Technologies LLC 800 376-0655
4957 Cinnamon Cir Cincinnati (45244) (G-3165)
Cgi Technologies Solutions Inc 216 687-1480
1001 Lakeside Ave E # 800 Cleveland (44114) (G-5163)
Cgi Technologies Solutions Inc 614 228-2245
88 E Broad St Ste 1425 Columbus (43215) (G-7173)
Cgi Technologies Solutions Inc 614 880-2200
2000 Polaris Pkwy Columbus (43240) (G-6805)
Ch Relty Iv/Clmbus Partners LP 614 885-3334
175 Hutchinson Ave Columbus (43235) (G-7174)
CH Robinson Company Inc 614 933-5100
800 Yard St Ste 200 Columbus (43212) (G-7175)
CH Robinson Freight Svcs Ltd 440 234-7811
7261 Engle Rd Ste 400 Cleveland (44130) (G-5164)
Ch2m Hill Inc 513 243-5070
400 E Bus Way Ste 400 Cincinnati (45241) (G-3166)

Ch2m Hill Inc..614 888-3100
  2 Easton Oval Ste 125 Columbus (43219) **(G-7176)**
Cha Consulting Inc..216 443-1700
  1501 N Marginal Rd # 200 Cleveland (44114) **(G-5165)**
Chaco Credit Union Inc (PA)................................513 785-3500
  601 Park Ave Hamilton (45013) **(G-11576)**
Chad Downing...614 532-5127
  679 Rose Way Columbus (43230) **(G-7177)**
Chagrin Falls Historical Soc................................440 247-4695
  87 E Washington St Chagrin Falls (44022) **(G-2640)**
Chagrin Valley Athletic Club...............................440 543-5141
  17260 Snyder Rd Chagrin Falls (44023) **(G-2662)**
Chagrin Valley Country Club Co...........................440 248-4310
  4700 Som Center Rd Chagrin Falls (44022) **(G-2641)**
Chagrin Valley Dispatch.......................................440 247-7321
  88 Center Rd Ste B100 Bedford (44146) **(G-1272)**
Chagrin Valley Hunt Club......................................440 423-4414
  7620 Old Mill Rd Gates Mills (44040) **(G-11234)**
Chal-Ron LLC...216 383-9050
  15751 Lake Shore Blvd Cleveland (44110) **(G-5166)**
Chalet, Strongsville Also called Cleveland Metroparks **(G-17293)**
Chalk Box Get Fit LLC...440 992-9619
  5521 Main Ave Ashtabula (44004) **(G-725)**
Chalmers P Wylie VA, Columbus Also called Veterans Health Administration **(G-8849)**
Chamber Commerce New Carlisle..........................937 845-3911
  131 S Main St New Carlisle (45344) **(G-14889)**
Chamberlain Hr..216 589-9280
  36368 Detroit Rd Ste A Avon (44011) **(G-873)**
Chambers Leasing Systems...................................937 547-9777
  5187 Chld Hm Bradford Rd Greenville (45331) **(G-11369)**
Chambers Leasing Systems Corp (PA)....................419 726-9747
  3100 N Summit St Toledo (43611) **(G-17646)**
Champagne National Bank, Urbana Also called Futura Banc Corp **(G-18434)**
Champaign Cnty Board of Dd.................................937 653-5217
  1250 E Us Highway 36 Urbana (43078) **(G-18422)**
Champaign County Board of Mrdd, Urbana Also called Champaign Cnty Board of Dd **(G-18422)**
Champaign County Engineer, Urbana Also called County of Champaign **(G-18430)**
Champaign Landmark Inc (PA)................................937 652-2135
  304 Bloomfield Ave Urbana (43078) **(G-18423)**
Champaign National Bank Urbana (HQ)....................937 653-1100
  601 Scioto St Urbana (43078) **(G-18424)**
Champaign National Bank Urbana...........................614 798-1321
  6400 Perimeter Loop Rd Dublin (43017) **(G-10168)**
Champaign Premium Grn Growers.........................937 826-3003
  24320 Woodstock Rd Milford Center (43045) **(G-14444)**
Champaign Realty, Urbana Also called Richard H Freyhof **(G-18443)**
Champaign Residential Services.............................614 481-5550
  1350 W 5th Ave Ste 230 Columbus (43212) **(G-7178)**
Champaign Residential Svcs Inc (PA)......................937 653-1320
  1150 Scioto St Ste 201 Urbana (43078) **(G-18425)**
Champaign Telephone Company (PA).......................937 653-4000
  126 Scioto St Urbana (43078) **(G-18426)**
Champion, Cincinnati Also called Enclosure Suppliers LLC **(G-3496)**
Champion Aerie 397, Springfield Also called Fraternal Order of Eagles **(G-17040)**
Champion Clg Specialists Inc................................513 871-2333
  8391 Blue Ash Rd Cincinnati (45236) **(G-3167)**
CHAMPION INDUSTRIES DIV, Troy Also called R T Industries Inc **(G-18224)**
Champion One, Beachwood Also called Champion Optical Network **(G-1043)**
Champion Opco LLC (PA).......................................513 327-7338
  12121 Champion Way Cincinnati (45241) **(G-3168)**
Champion Optical Network.....................................216 831-1800
  23645 Mercantile Rd Ste A Beachwood (44122) **(G-1043)**
Champion Spark Plug Company (HQ).........................419 535-2567
  900 Upton Ave Toledo (43607) **(G-17647)**
Champion Windows Manufacturing, Cincinnati Also called Champion Opco LLC **(G-3168)**
Championship Management Co................................740 524-4653
  1150 Wilson Rd Sunbury (43074) **(G-17385)**
Champlain Enterprises LLC (PA)............................440 779-4588
  24950 Country Club Blvd # 300 North Olmsted (44070) **(G-15280)**
Champlin Architecture, Cincinnati Also called Champlin Haupt Architects Inc **(G-3169)**
Champlin Haupt Architects Inc (PA).......................513 241-4474
  720 E Pete Rose Way # 140 Cincinnati (45202) **(G-3169)**
Champons In Making Daycare LLC.........................937 728-4886
  160 Park Dr Wilmington (45177) **(G-19607)**
Champs, Cleveland Also called Healthcomp Inc **(G-5674)**
CHAMPS MANAGEMENT SERVICES, Cleveland Also called Central Hospital Services Inc **(G-5154)**
Chander M Kohli MD Facs Inc...............................330 759-6978
  540 Parmalee Ave Ste 310 Youngstown (44510) **(G-19985)**
Chandler Products LLC...216 481-4400
  1491 Chardon Rd Cleveland (44117) **(G-5167)**
Chandler Systems Incorporated.............................888 363-9434
  710 Orange St Ashland (44805) **(G-666)**
Chaney Roofing Maintenance.................................419 639-2761
  7040 State Route 101 N Clyde (43410) **(G-6741)**
Change Healthcare Tech Enabled...........................614 566-5861
  3535 Olentangy River Rd Columbus (43214) **(G-7179)**
Change Hlth Prac MGT Solns Grp...........................937 291-7850
  3131 Newmark Dr Ste 100 Miamisburg (45342) **(G-14151)**

Change Hlthcare Operations LLC...........................330 405-0001
  300 Executive Pkwy W Hudson (44236) **(G-11970)**
Change Hlthcare Operations LLC...........................216 589-5878
  2060 E 9th St Cleveland (44115) **(G-5168)**
Changes Hair Designers Inc..................................614 846-6666
  2054 Polaris Pkwy Columbus (43240) **(G-6806)**
Changes Salon & Day Spa, Columbus Also called Changes Hair Designers Inc **(G-6806)**
CHANNEL 48, Cincinnati Also called Greater Cincinnati TV Educ Fnd **(G-3654)**
Chapel Electric Co LLC...937 222-2290
  1985 Founders Dr Dayton (45420) **(G-9291)**
Chapel Electric Co., Dayton Also called Quebe Holdings Inc **(G-9723)**
Chapel Hill Community, Marion Also called United Church Homes Inc **(G-13471)**
CHAPEL HILL COMMUNITY, Kenton Also called United Church Res of Kenton **(G-12289)**
CHAPEL HILL COMMUNITY, Marion Also called Unite Churc Resid of Oxfor Mis **(G-13469)**
Chapel Hill Management Inc..................................330 633-7100
  2000 Brittain Rd Ste 830 Akron (44310) **(G-125)**
Chapel Hill Medical Offices, Akron Also called Kaiser Foundation Hospitals **(G-296)**
Chapel Hl Chrstn Schl Endwment...........................330 929-1901
  1090 Howe Ave Cuyahoga Falls (44221) **(G-9078)**
Chapel Steel Corp...800 570-7674
  26400 Richmond Rd Bedford Heights (44146) **(G-1319)**
Chapel-Romanoff Tech LLC....................................937 222-9840
  1985 Founders Dr Dayton (45420) **(G-9292)**
Chapin Leasing, North Ridgeville Also called Chapin Logistics Inc **(G-15325)**
Chapin Logistics Inc...440 327-1360
  39111 Center Ridge Rd North Ridgeville (44039) **(G-15325)**
Chapman & Chapman Inc..440 934-4102
  36711 American Way Ste 2f Avon (44011) **(G-874)**
Chapman Industrial Cnstr Inc................................330 343-1632
  3475 Rue Depaul St Louisville (44641) **(G-12961)**
Chapter 492, Pettisville Also called Pheasants Forever Inc **(G-15944)**
Charak Ctr For Hlth & Wellness, Cleveland Also called Rakesh Ranjan MD & Assoc Inc **(G-6284)**
Chard Snyder & Associates LLC.............................513 459-9997
  6867 Cintas Blvd Mason (45040) **(G-13553)**
Chard Snyder, Mason Also called Chard Snyder & Associates LLC **(G-13553)**
Chardon Healthcare Center, Chardon Also called Water Leasing Co LLC **(G-2725)**
Chardon Laboratories Inc......................................614 860-1000
  7300 Tussing Rd Reynoldsburg (43068) **(G-16291)**
Chardon Lakes Golf Course Inc (PA).......................440 285-4653
  470 South St Chardon (44024) **(G-2689)**
Chardon Tool & Supply Co Inc...............................440 286-6440
  115 Parker Ct Chardon (44024) **(G-2690)**
Chariott Foods Inc...419 243-1101
  6163 Valley Park Dr Toledo (43623) **(G-17648)**
Charity Hospice Inc..740 264-2280
  500 Luray Dr Steubenville (43953) **(G-17147)**
Charles C Smith DDS Inc......................................937 667-2417
  110 S Tippecanoe Dr Ste A Tipp City (45371) **(G-17551)**
Charles D McIntosh Trckg Inc...............................937 378-3803
  669 E State St Georgetown (45121) **(G-11266)**
Charles F Jergens Cnstr Inc.................................937 233-1830
  1280 Brandt Pike Dayton (45404) **(G-9293)**
Charles F Kettering Mem Hosp, Kettering Also called Kettering Medical Center **(G-12295)**
CHARLES F KETTERING MEMORIAL H, Hamilton Also called Fort Hamilton Hospital **(G-11597)**
Charles H Hamilton Co...513 683-2442
  5875 S State Route 48 Maineville (45039) **(G-13113)**
Charles Jergens Contractor...................................937 233-1830
  1280 Brandt Pike Dayton (45404) **(G-9294)**
Charles L Maccallum MD Inc..................................330 655-2161
  5778 Darrow Rd Ste D Hudson (44236) **(G-11971)**
Charles Mercy Hlth-St Hospita (HQ).......................419 696-7200
  2600 Navarre Ave Oregon (43616) **(G-15587)**
Charles Rewinding Div, Canton Also called Hannon Company **(G-2339)**
Charles River Laboratories Inc.............................419 647-4196
  640 N Elizabeth St Spencerville (45887) **(G-16955)**
Charles River Labs Ashland LLC (HQ)......................419 282-8700
  1407 George Rd Ashland (44805) **(G-667)**
Charles Rver Labs Clveland Inc.............................216 332-1665
  14656 Neo Pkwy Cleveland (44128) **(G-5169)**
Charles Schwab & Co Inc......................................330 908-4478
  4150 Kinross Lakes Pkwy Richfield (44286) **(G-16349)**
Charles Schwab Corporation..................................440 617-2301
  2211 Crocker Rd Ste 100 Westlake (44145) **(G-19330)**
Charles Schwab Corporation..................................216 291-9333
  24737 Cedar Rd Cleveland (44124) **(G-5170)**
Charles V Francis Trust..513 528-5600
  19 W Vine St Cincinnati (45215) **(G-3170)**
Charles W Powers & Assoc Inc..............................513 721-5353
  1 W 4th St Ste 500 Cincinnati (45202) **(G-3171)**
Charley's Steakery, Columbus Also called Gosh Enterprises Inc **(G-7681)**
Charlie Towing Service Inc....................................440 234-5300
  55 Lou Groza Blvd Berea (44017) **(G-1417)**
Charlie's Towing Svc, Berea Also called Charlie Towing Service Inc **(G-1417)**
Charman Div, Ontario Also called Lake Erie Electric Inc **(G-15558)**
Charter Bus Service, Cincinnati Also called Queen City Transportation LLC **(G-4322)**
Charter Hotel Group Ltd Partnr (PA).......................216 772-4538
  5966 Heisley Rd Mentor (44060) **(G-14028)**

A L P H A B E T I C

Charter Vans Inc 937 898-4043
303 Corporate Center Dr # 100 Vandalia (45377) ***(G-18513)***
Charter Vans Tours, Vandalia *Also called Charter Vans Inc* ***(G-18513)***
Chartwell Group LLC (PA) 216 360-0009
1350 Euclid Ave Ste 700 Cleveland (44115) ***(G-5171)***
Chas G Buchy Packing Company 800 762-1060
10510 Evendale Dr Cincinnati (45241) ***(G-3172)***
Chase Bank and Atm, New Philadelphia *Also called Jpmorgan Chase Bank Nat Assn* ***(G-14968)***
Chase Equipment Finance Inc (HQ) 800 678-2601
1111 Polaris Pkwy Ste A3 Columbus (43240) ***(G-6807)***
Chase Equipment Finance Inc 614 213-2246
1111 Polaris Pkwy Ste A3 Columbus (43240) ***(G-6808)***
Chase HM Mrtgages Florence Off, Columbus *Also called Jpmorgan Chase Bank Nat Assn* ***(G-7873)***
Chase Manhattan Mortgage Corp 614 422-7982
200 E Campus View Blvd # 3 Columbus (43235) ***(G-7180)***
Chase Manhattan Mortgage Corp 614 422-6900
3415 Vision Dr Columbus (43219) ***(G-7181)***
Chase Phipps 330 754-0467
2993 Perry Dr Sw Canton (44706) ***(G-2248)***
Chase Suite Hotel, Dublin *Also called Hardage Hotels I LLC* ***(G-10238)***
Chase Transcriptions Inc (PA) 330 650-0539
1737 Georgetown Rd Ste G Hudson (44236) ***(G-11972)***
Chatham Steel Corporation 740 377-9310
235 Commerce Dr South Point (45680) ***(G-16929)***
Chattree and Associates Inc 216 831-1494
3355 Richmond Rd Ste 225 Cleveland (44122) ***(G-5172)***
Chavez Properties, Cincinnati *Also called J & E LLC* ***(G-3793)***
Chcc Home Health Care, East Liverpool *Also called P N P Inc* ***(G-10415)***
Chcc Home Health Care 330 759-4069
60 N Canfield Niles Rd # 50 Austintown (44515) ***(G-857)***
Check It Out 4 Me LLC 513 568-4269
7709 Greenland Pl Ste 1 Cincinnati (45237) ***(G-3173)***
Check N Go, Cincinnati *Also called CNG Financial Corporation* ***(G-3316)***
Checker Distributors, Maumee *Also called Checker Notions Company Inc* ***(G-13770)***
Checker Notions Company Inc (PA) 419 893-3636
400 W Dussel Dr Ste B Maumee (43537) ***(G-13770)***
Checkfree Services Corporation 614 564-3000
6000 Perimeter Dr Dublin (43017) ***(G-10169)***
Checksmart Financial Company (HQ) 614 798-5900
6785 Bobcat Way Ste 200 Dublin (43016) ***(G-10170)***
Cheek-O Inc 513 942-4880
639 Northland Blvd Cincinnati (45240) ***(G-3174)***
Cheers & Lakeside Chalet, Lancaster *Also called Cheers Chalet* ***(G-12378)***
Cheers Chalet 740 654-9036
1211 Coonpath Rd Nw Lancaster (43130) ***(G-12378)***
Cheeseman LLC (HQ) 419 375-4132
2200 State Route 119 Fort Recovery (45846) ***(G-10988)***
Chefs Garden Inc 419 433-4947
9009 Huron Avery Rd Huron (44839) ***(G-12022)***
Chelmsford Apartments Ltd 419 389-0800
5020 Ryan Rd Toledo (43614) ***(G-17649)***
Chelsea Court Apartments, Youngstown *Also called Giffin Management Group Inc* ***(G-20049)***
Chelsea House Fabrics, Columbus *Also called Style-Line Incorporated* ***(G-8707)***
Chemcote Inc 614 792-2683
7599 Fishel Dr N Dublin (43016) ***(G-10171)***
Chemcote Roofing Company 614 792-2683
7599 Fishel Dr N Dublin (43016) ***(G-10172)***
Chemed Corporation (PA) 513 762-6690
255 E 5th St Ste 2600 Cincinnati (45202) ***(G-3175)***
Chemgroup, Columbus *Also called Bonded Chemicals Inc* ***(G-7053)***
Chemical Bank 440 779-0807
25000 Country Club Blvd # 200 North Olmsted (44070) ***(G-15281)***
Chemical Bank 513 232-0800
7373 Beechmont Ave # 100 Cincinnati (45230) ***(G-3176)***
Chemical Bank 330 965-5806
476 Boardman Canfield Rd Youngstown (44512) ***(G-19986)***
Chemical Bank 440 926-2191
351 Main St Grafton (44044) ***(G-11316)***
Chemical Bank 330 314-1395
2 S Main St Poland (44514) ***(G-16082)***
Chemical Bank 440 323-7451
111 Antioch Dr Elyria (44035) ***(G-10488)***
Chemical Bank 330 298-0510
999 E Main St Ravenna (44266) ***(G-16235)***
Chemical Bank 330 314-1380
3900 Market St Youngstown (44512) ***(G-19987)***
Chemical Services Inc 937 898-5566
2600 Thunderhawk Ct Dayton (45414) ***(G-9295)***
Chemical Solvents Inc (PA) 216 741-9310
3751 Jennings Rd Cleveland (44109) ***(G-5173)***
Chemical Solvents Inc 216 741-9310
1010 Denison Ave Cleveland (44109) ***(G-5174)***
Chemimage Filter Tech LLC 330 686-2829
1100 Campus Dr Ste 500 Stow (44224) ***(G-17195)***
Chempower Sheetmetal, Canton *Also called Global Insulation Inc* ***(G-2327)***
Chemsteel Construction Company (PA) 440 234-3930
7850 Freeway Cir Ste 110 Middleburg Heights (44130) ***(G-14249)***
Chemstress Consultant Company (PA) 330 535-5591
39 S Main St Ste 315 Akron (44308) ***(G-126)***
Chemsultants International Inc (PA) 440 974-3080
9079 Tyler Blvd Mentor (44060) ***(G-14029)***
Chemtron Corporation 440 937-6348
35850 Schneider Ct Avon (44011) ***(G-875)***
Cherokee Hills Golf Club, Valley City *Also called Chgc Inc* ***(G-18459)***
Cherokee Hills Golf Course, Bellefontaine *Also called Vieira Inc* ***(G-1369)***
Cherry Grove Lanes, Cincinnati *Also called Cherry Grove Sports Center* ***(G-3177)***
Cherry Grove Sports Center 513 232-7199
4005 Hopper Hill Rd Cincinnati (45255) ***(G-3177)***
Cherry St Mission Ministries (PA) 419 242-5141
105 17th St Toledo (43604) ***(G-17650)***
Cherry Valley Lodge 740 788-1200
2299 Cherry Valley Rd Se Newark (43055) ***(G-15022)***
Cherry Valley Lodge and Coco, Newark *Also called Cherry Valley Lodge* ***(G-15022)***
Cheryl Ann Special Olympics, Celina *Also called County of Mercer* ***(G-2591)***
Chesapeake Research Review LLC 410 884-2900
9380 Main St Cincinnati (45242) ***(G-3178)***
Chesrown Cadillac, Granville *Also called Chesrown Oldsmobile Cadillac* ***(G-11337)***
Chesrown Oldsmobile Cadillac 740 366-7373
371 Bryn Du Dr Granville (43023) ***(G-11337)***
Chesrown Oldsmobile GMC Inc 614 846-3040
4675 Karl Rd Columbus (43229) ***(G-7182)***
Chessrown Kia Town, Columbus *Also called Chesrown Oldsmobile GMC Inc* ***(G-7182)***
Chester Township Fire Rescue, Chesterland *Also called Township of Chester* ***(G-2747)***
Chester West Dental Group Inc 513 942-8181
5900 W Chester Rd Ste A West Chester (45069) ***(G-18884)***
Chester West Dentistry 330 753-7734
1575 Vernon Odom Blvd Akron (44320) ***(G-127)***
Chester West Medical Center 513 298-3000
7700 University Dr West Chester (45069) ***(G-18885)***
Chester West YMCA 513 779-3917
6703 Yankee Rd Liberty Township (45044) ***(G-12579)***
Chesterhill Stone Co 740 849-2338
6305 Saltillo Rd East Fultonham (43735) ***(G-10388)***
Chestnut Hill Management Co 614 855-3700
5055 Thompson Rd Columbus (43230) ***(G-7183)***
Cheviot Mutual Holding Company 513 661-0457
3723 Glenmore Ave Cincinnati (45211) ***(G-3179)***
Chevrolet Buick GMC Mt Vernon, Mount Vernon *Also called Knox Auto LLC* ***(G-14771)***
Chevron Ae Resources LLC 330 654-4343
1823 State Route 14 Deerfield (44411) ***(G-9902)***
Chgc Inc 330 225-6122
5740 Center Rd Valley City (44280) ***(G-18459)***
CHI Health At Home 513 576-0262
1700 Edison Dr Ste 300 Milford (45150) ***(G-14376)***
CHI Health At Home (HQ) 513 576-0262
1700 Edison Dr Ste 300 Milford (45150) ***(G-14377)***
CHI Living Communities 567 455-0414
5942 Renaissance Pl Ste A Toledo (43623) ***(G-17651)***
CHI Omega Sorority 937 325-9323
2 Ferncliff Pl Springfield (45504) ***(G-17007)***
CHIC, Cleveland *Also called Consortium For Hlthy & Immunzd* ***(G-5336)***
Chicago Title Insurance Co 330 873-9393
799 White Pond Dr Ste A Akron (44320) ***(G-128)***
Chicago Title Insurance Co 216 241-6045
1111 Superior Ave E # 600 Cleveland (44114) ***(G-5175)***
Chick Master Incubator Company (PA) 330 722-5591
945 Lafayette Rd Medina (44256) ***(G-13917)***
Chicn Fixins Inc 614 929-8431
2041 Pine Needle Ct Columbus (43232) ***(G-7184)***
Chieftain Trucking & Excav Inc 216 485-8034
3926 Valley Rd Ste 300 Cleveland (44109) ***(G-5176)***
Child & Adolescent Speciality 937 667-7711
1483 W Main St Tipp City (45371) ***(G-17552)***
Child & Elder Care Insights 440 356-2900
18500 Lake Rd Ste 200 Rocky River (44116) ***(G-16426)***
Child Adlscent Behavioral Hlth (PA) 330 454-7917
919 2nd St Ne Canton (44704) ***(G-2249)***
Child Adlscent Behavioral Hlth 330 433-6075
4641 Fulton Dr Nw Canton (44718) ***(G-2250)***
Child Care Center, Dayton *Also called Miami Valley Hospital* ***(G-9621)***
Child Care Center, Canton *Also called Aultman Hospital* ***(G-2205)***
Child Care Resource Center (PA) 216 575-0061
4600 Euclid Ave Ste 500 Cleveland (44103) ***(G-5177)***
Child Care Resources Inc (PA) 740 454-6251
1580 Adams Ln Lbby Zanesville (43701) ***(G-20295)***
Child Dev Ctr Jackson Cnty 740 286-3995
692 Pattonsville Rd Jackson (45640) ***(G-12171)***
Child Dvlpmnt Cncl of Frnkln (PA) 614 221-1709
1077 Lexington Ave Columbus (43201) ***(G-7185)***
Child Dvlpmnt Cncl of Frnkln 614 416-5178
2150 Agler Rd Columbus (43224) ***(G-7186)***
Child Focus Inc 513 732-8800
2337 Clermont Center Dr Batavia (45103) ***(G-986)***
Child Focus Inc (PA) 513 752-1555
4629 Aicholtz Rd Ste 2 Cincinnati (45244) ***(G-3180)***
Child Focus Inc 937 444-1613
710 N High St Mount Orab (45154) ***(G-14739)***

Child Focus Learning Center 513 528-7224
4629 Aicholtz Rd Ste 2 Cincinnati (45244) ***(G-3181)***
Child Sup Dept of Job & Family, Hillsboro *Also called County of Highland* ***(G-11835)***
Child Support, New Philadelphia *Also called County of Tuscarawas* ***(G-14954)***
Child Support, Springfield *Also called County of Clark* ***(G-17025)***
Child Support Agency, Coshocton *Also called County of Coshocton* ***(G-9012)***
Child Support Enforcement Agcy, Toledo *Also called County of Lucas* ***(G-17680)***
Child Support Enforcement Agcy, Cleveland *Also called County of Cuyahoga* ***(G-5365)***
Child Support Enforcement Agcy, Columbus *Also called Franklin Cnty Bd Commissioners* ***(G-7607)***
Child Support Enforcement Agcy, Sandusky *Also called County of Erie* ***(G-16595)***
Child Support Enforcement Agcy, Millersburg *Also called County of Holmes* ***(G-14472)***
Child Support Services, Marion *Also called County of Marion* ***(G-13413)***
Childers Photography 937 256-0501
5616 Burkhardt Rd Dayton (45431) ***(G-9165)***
Children and Family Services, Cleveland *Also called Cuyahoga County* ***(G-5395)***
Children First Day Care, Columbus *Also called Children First Inc* ***(G-7187)***
Children First Inc 614 466-0945
77 S High St Fl 7 Columbus (43215) ***(G-7187)***
Children Service Unit, Norwalk *Also called County of Huron* ***(G-15432)***
Children Services, Mansfield *Also called County of Richland* ***(G-13155)***
Children Services, West Union *Also called County of Adams* ***(G-19135)***
Children Services, Dayton *Also called County of Montgomery* ***(G-9332)***
Children's Academy, Columbus *Also called Samkel Inc* ***(G-8589)***
Children's Aid Society, Cleveland *Also called Cleveland Municipal School Dst* ***(G-5278)***
Children's Aide Society Campus, Cleveland *Also called Applewood Centers Inc* ***(G-4992)***
Children's Home Healthcare, Cincinnati *Also called Childrens Hospital Medical Ctr* ***(G-3190)***
CHILDREN'S HOME HEALTHCARE, Cincinnati *Also called Chmc Cmnty Hlth Svcs Netwrk* ***(G-3196)***
CHILDREN'S HOME SCHOOL, Cincinnati *Also called Childrens HM of Cncinnati Ohio* ***(G-3182)***
Children's Hospital Northwest, Dublin *Also called Close To Home Health Care Ctr* ***(G-10176)***
Children's Medical Center, Dayton *Also called Dayton Childrens Hospital* ***(G-9358)***
Children's Outpatient North, Mason *Also called Childrens Hospital Medical Ctr* ***(G-13554)***
CHILDREN'S RESOURCE CENTER, Bowling Green *Also called Wood County Chld Svcs Assn* ***(G-1752)***
Children's Service Board, Bucyrus *Also called Crawford County Children Svcs* ***(G-1988)***
Children's World Learning Cent, Cleveland *Also called Kindercare Education LLC* ***(G-5830)***
Childrens Advocacy Center 740 432-6581
274 Highland Ave Cambridge (43725) ***(G-2058)***
Childrens Aid Society 216 521-6511
10427 Detroit Ave Cleveland (44102) ***(G-5178)***
Childrens Cmprhensive Svcs Inc 419 589-5511
1451 Lucas Rd Mansfield (44903) ***(G-13151)***
Childrens Ctr of Frst Bptst Ch, Cleveland *Also called First Baptist Day Care Center* ***(G-5530)***
Childrens Discovery Center 419 861-1060
1640 Timber Wolf Dr Holland (43528) ***(G-11878)***
Childrens Forever Haven Inc (PA) 440 652-6749
10983 Abbey Rd North Royalton (44133) ***(G-15349)***
Childrens Forever Haven Inc 440 250-9182
28700 Center Ridge Rd Westlake (44145) ***(G-19331)***
Childrens HM of Cncinnati Ohio 513 272-2800
5050 Madison Rd Cincinnati (45227) ***(G-3182)***
Childrens Home Care Dayton 937 641-4663
18 Childrens Plz Dayton (45404) ***(G-9296)***
Childrens Home Care Group 330 543-5000
185 W Cedar St Ste 203 Akron (44307) ***(G-129)***
Childrens Homecare Services 614 355-1100
455 E Mound St Columbus (43215) ***(G-7188)***
Childrens Hosp Guidance Ctrs, Columbus *Also called Nationwide Childrens Hospital* ***(G-8151)***
Childrens Hosp Med Ctr Akron 330 425-3344
8054 Darrow Rd Twinsburg (44087) ***(G-18252)***
Childrens Hosp Med Ctr Akron 330 308-5432
1045 W High Ave New Philadelphia (44663) ***(G-14949)***
Childrens Hosp Med Ctr Akron 330 629-6085
8423 Market St Ste 300 Youngstown (44512) ***(G-19988)***
Childrens Hosp Med Ctr Akron (PA) 330 543-1000
1 Perkins Sq Akron (44308) ***(G-130)***
Childrens Hosp Med Ctr Akron 330 543-8004
1 Perkins Sq Akron (44308) ***(G-131)***
Childrens Hosp Med Ctr Akron 330 676-1020
1951 State Route 59 Ste A Kent (44240) ***(G-12220)***
Childrens Hosp Med Ctr Akron 330 633-2055
143 Northwest Ave Bldg A Tallmadge (44278) ***(G-17471)***
Childrens Hospital, Columbus *Also called Central Ohio Poison Center* ***(G-7161)***
Childrens Hospital 513 636-4051
3373 Burnet Ave Cincinnati (45229) ***(G-3183)***
Childrens Hospital Foundation 614 355-0888
700 Childrens Dr Columbus (43205) ***(G-7189)***
Childrens Hospital Medical Ctr 513 541-4500
2750 Beekman St Cincinnati (45225) ***(G-3184)***
Childrens Hospital Medical Ctr 513 803-9600
7777 Yankee Rd Liberty Township (45044) ***(G-12580)***
Childrens Hospital Medical Ctr 513 636-4200
3333 Burnet Ave Cincinnati (45229) ***(G-3185)***
Childrens Hospital Medical Ctr 513 803-1751
240 Albert Sabin Way Cincinnati (45229) ***(G-3186)***
Childrens Hospital Medical Ctr 513 636-4200
2900 Vernon Pl Cincinnati (45219) ***(G-3187)***
Childrens Hospital Medical Ctr 513 636-4366
2800 Winslow Ave Fl 3 Cincinnati (45206) ***(G-3188)***
Childrens Hospital Medical Ctr 513 636-6100
7495 State Rd Ste 355 Cincinnati (45255) ***(G-3189)***
Childrens Hospital Medical Ctr (PA) 513 636-4200
3333 Burnet Ave Cincinnati (45229) ***(G-3190)***
Childrens Hospital Medical Ctr 513 636-6400
3050 Mack Rd Ste 105 Fairfield (45014) ***(G-10708)***
Childrens Hospital Medical Ctr 513 636-6036
796 Cncnnati Batavia Pike Cincinnati (45245) ***(G-2844)***
Childrens Hospital Medical Ctr 513 636-6800
9560 Children Dr Mason (45040) ***(G-13554)***
Childrens Hospital Medical Ctr 513 636-4200
3350 Elland Ave Cincinnati (45229) ***(G-3191)***
Childrens Hospital Medical Ctr 513 636-8778
3333 Burnet Ave Cincinnati (45229) ***(G-3192)***
Childrens Hospital Medical Ctr 513 636-8778
3333 Burnet Ave Cincinnati (45229) ***(G-3193)***
Childrens Hunger Alliance (PA) 614 341-7700
1105 Schrock Rd Ste 505 Columbus (43229) ***(G-7190)***
Childrens Physician Inc 330 494-5600
4575 Everhard Rd Nw Canton (44718) ***(G-2251)***
Childrens Rehabilitation Ctr 330 856-2107
885 Howland Wilson Rd Ne Warren (44484) ***(G-18683)***
Childrens Surgery Center Inc 614 722-2920
700 Childrens Dr Columbus (43205) ***(G-7191)***
Childrens World Learning Ctr, Twinsburg *Also called Kindercare Education LLC* ***(G-18289)***
Childrens World Lrng Ctr 177, Gahanna *Also called Kindercare Education LLC* ***(G-11128)***
Childs Investment Co 330 837-2100
205 Rohr Ave Nw Massillon (44646) ***(G-13669)***
Childtime Childcare Inc 330 723-8697
3550 Octagon Dr Medina (44256) ***(G-13918)***
Childvine Inc 937 748-1260
790 N Main St Springboro (45066) ***(G-16965)***
Chiller LLC (PA) 614 764-1000
7001 Dublin Park Dr Dublin (43016) ***(G-10173)***
Chiller LLC 740 549-0009
8144 Highfield Dr Lewis Center (43035) ***(G-12533)***
Chiller LLC 614 433-9600
401 E Wilson Bridge Rd Worthington (43085) ***(G-19797)***
Chiller LLC 614 475-7575
3600 Chiller Ln Columbus (43219) ***(G-7192)***
Chillicothe Bowling Lanes Inc 740 773-3300
1680 N Bridge St Chillicothe (45601) ***(G-2759)***
Chillicothe City School Dst 740 775-2936
89 Riverside St Chillicothe (45601) ***(G-2760)***
Chillicothe Country Club Co 740 775-0150
Woodbridge Ave & Arch St Chillicothe (45601) ***(G-2761)***
Chillicothe Cty Sch Trans Off, Chillicothe *Also called Chillicothe City School Dst* ***(G-2760)***
Chillicothe Family Physicians 740 779-4100
60 Capital Dr Chillicothe (45601) ***(G-2762)***
Chillicothe Long Term Care 740 773-6161
230 Cherry St Chillicothe (45601) ***(G-2763)***
Chillicothe Long Term Care (PA) 513 793-8804
7265 Kenwood Rd Ste 300 Cincinnati (45236) ***(G-3194)***
Chillicothe Motel LLC 740 773-3903
20 N Plaza Blvd Chillicothe (45601) ***(G-2764)***
Chillicothe Opco LLC 740 772-5900
60 Marietta Rd Chillicothe (45601) ***(G-2765)***
Chillicothe Racquet Club 740 773-4928
1245 Western Ave Chillicothe (45601) ***(G-2766)***
Chillicothe Telephone Company (HQ) 740 772-8200
68 E Main St Chillicothe (45601) ***(G-2767)***
Chillicothe Telephone Company 740 772-8361
861 Orange St Chillicothe (45601) ***(G-2768)***
Chillicothe VA Medical Center, Chillicothe *Also called Veterans Health Administration* ***(G-2836)***
Chima Travel Bureau Inc (PA) 330 867-4770
55 Merz Blvd Unit B Fairlawn (44333) ***(G-10819)***
Chimney Hill Apartments, Columbus *Also called Real Estate Investors Mgt Inc* ***(G-8494)***
Chimneys Inn 937 567-7850
767 Mmsburg Cnterville Rd Dayton (45459) ***(G-9297)***
Chipmatic Tool & Machine Inc 419 862-2737
212 Ottawa St Elmore (43416) ***(G-10472)***
Chippewa Golf Club, Doylestown *Also called Chippewa Golf Corp* ***(G-10109)***
Chippewa Golf Corp 330 658-2566
12147 Shank Rd Doylestown (44230) ***(G-10109)***
Chippewa Place, Brecksville *Also called Paul Dennis* ***(G-1795)***
Chippewa School District 330 658-4868
165 Brooklyn Ave Doylestown (44230) ***(G-10110)***
Chirst Hospital Surgery Center 513 272-3448
4850 Red Bank Rd Fl 1 Cincinnati (45227) ***(G-3195)***
Chmc Cmnty Hlth Svcs Netwrk 513 636-8778
3333 Burnet Ave Cincinnati (45229) ***(G-3196)***
CHN Inc - Adult Day Care 937 548-0506
5420 State Route 571 Greenville (45331) ***(G-11370)***

ALPHABETIC

(PA)=Parent Co (HQ)=Headquarters (DH)=Div Headquarters
2019 Harris Ohio Services Directory
1075

Choice Healthcare Limited 937 254-6220
1257 N Fairfield Rd Beavercreek (45432) *(G-1139)*
Choice One Engineering Corp 937 497-0200
440 E Hoewisher Rd Sidney (45365) *(G-16764)*
Choice Pharmacy Services, Columbus *Also called Pca-Corrections LLC* *(G-8430)*
Choice Recovery Inc 614 358-9900
1550 Old Henderson Rd S100 Columbus (43220) *(G-7193)*
Choices For Vctims Dom Volence 614 258-6080
770 E Main St Columbus (43205) *(G-7194)*
Choices For Vctims Dom Volence 614 224-6617
500 W Wilson Bridge Rd Worthington (43085) *(G-19798)*
Choices In Community Living (PA) 937 898-3655
1651 Needmore Rd Ste B Dayton (45414) *(G-9298)*
Chop House Restaurant, Dayton *Also called Connor Concepts Inc* *(G-9317)*
Chores Unlimited Inc 440 439-5455
26150 Richmond Rd Unit C Bedford Heights (44146) *(G-1320)*
Chp AP Shared Services 513 981-6704
P.O. Box 5203 Cincinnati (45201) *(G-3197)*
CHRC, Cincinnati *Also called Cincinnati Humn Relations Comm* *(G-3249)*
Christ Hospital 513 347-2300
5885 Harrison Ave # 2900 Cincinnati (45248) *(G-3198)*
Christ Hospital 513 721-8272
2139 Auburn Ave Cincinnati (45219) *(G-3199)*
Christ Hospital 513 564-4000
7545 Beechmont Ave Ste F Cincinnati (45255) *(G-3200)*
Christ Hospital 513 561-7809
11140 Montgomery Rd Cincinnati (45249) *(G-3201)*
Christ Hospital 513 688-1111
7545 Beechmont Ave Ste E Cincinnati (45255) *(G-3202)*
Christ Hospital 513 564-1340
4440 Red Bank Rd Ste 100 Cincinnati (45227) *(G-3203)*
Christ Hospital 513 651-0094
2123 Auburn Ave Ste 722 Cincinnati (45219) *(G-3204)*
Christ Hospital 513 272-3448
4850 Red Bank Rd Fl 1 Cincinnati (45227) *(G-3205)*
Christ Hospital 513 585-0050
2123 Auburn Ave Ste 341 Cincinnati (45219) *(G-3206)*
Christ Hospital 513 755-4700
7589 Tylers Place Blvd West Chester (45069) *(G-18886)*
Christ Hospital (PA) 513 585-2000
2139 Auburn Ave Cincinnati (45219) *(G-3207)*
Christ Hospital 513 631-3300
4803 Montgomery Rd # 114 Cincinnati (45212) *(G-3208)*
Christ Hospital 513 351-0800
2355 Norwood Ave Ste 1 Cincinnati (45212) *(G-3209)*
Christ Hospital 513 791-5200
7545 Beechmont Ave Ste J Cincinnati (45255) *(G-3210)*
CHRIST HOSPITAL HEALTH NETWORK, Cincinnati *Also called Christ Hospital* *(G-3207)*
Christ Hospital Spine Surgery 513 619-5899
4020 Smith Rd Cincinnati (45209) *(G-3211)*
Christ Hospital, The, Cincinnati *Also called Christ Hospital* *(G-3209)*
Christen & Sons Company (PA) 419 243-4161
714 George St Toledo (43608) *(G-17652)*
Christen Detroit, Toledo *Also called Christen & Sons Company* *(G-17652)*
Christian Aid Ministries (PA) 330 893-2428
4464 State Route 39 Millersburg (44654) *(G-14465)*
Christian Benevolent Assn (PA) 513 931-5000
8097 Hamilton Ave Cincinnati (45231) *(G-3212)*
CHRISTIAN BENEVOLENT ASSOCIATI, Cincinnati *Also called Mt Healthy Christian Home Inc* *(G-4081)*
Christian Chld HM Ohio Inc 330 345-7949
2685 Armstrong Rd Wooster (44691) *(G-19700)*
Christian Community Hlth Svcs 513 381-2247
5 E Liberty St Ste 4 Cincinnati (45202) *(G-3213)*
Christian Healthcare 330 848-1511
127 Hazelwood Ave Barberton (44203) *(G-950)*
Christian Heartland School 330 482-2331
28 Pittsburgh St Columbiana (44408) *(G-6783)*
Christian Missionary Alliance 614 457-4085
3750 Henderson Rd Columbus (43220) *(G-7195)*
Christian Perry Pre School 330 477-7262
139 Perry Dr Nw Canton (44708) *(G-2252)*
Christian Rivertree School 330 494-1860
7373 Portage St Nw Massillon (44646) *(G-13670)*
Christian Schools Inc 330 857-7311
3970 Kidron Rd Kidron (44636) *(G-12305)*
Christian Twigs Gymnastics CLB 937 866-8356
1900 S Alex Rd Dayton (45449) *(G-9299)*
Christian Wooster School 330 345-6436
4599 Burbank Rd Ste B Wooster (44691) *(G-19701)*
Christian Worthington Vlg Inc 614 846-6076
165 Highbluffs Blvd Columbus (43235) *(G-7196)*
Christopher C Kaeding 614 293-3600
2050 Kenny Rd Ste 3100 Columbus (43221) *(G-7197)*
Christopher D Cannell, Columbus *Also called Orthoneuro* *(G-8388)*
CHS Miami Valley Inc 330 204-1040
510 Buckeye Ave Sidney (45365) *(G-16765)*
CHS Norwood Inc 513 242-1360
1171 Towne St Cincinnati (45216) *(G-3214)*
CHS of Bowerston Oper Co Inc 937 277-0505
5020 Philadelphia Dr Dayton (45415) *(G-9300)*

CHS-Lake Erie Inc 440 964-8446
2217 West Ave Ashtabula (44004) *(G-726)*
Chs-Norwood Inc 513 351-7007
6969 Glenmeadow Ln Cincinnati (45237) *(G-3215)*
Chu Management Co Inc (PA) 330 725-4571
2875 Medina Rd Medina (44256) *(G-13919)*
Chubb, Cleveland *Also called Federal Insurance Company* *(G-5521)*
Chubb, Cincinnati *Also called Federal Insurance Company* *(G-3538)*
Chuck E. Cheese's, Miamisburg *Also called Cec Entertainment Inc* *(G-14149)*
Chuck Nicholson Pntc-GMC Trcks 330 343-7781
135 W Broadway St Dover (44622) *(G-10069)*
Church of God Retirement Cmnty 513 422-5600
4400 Vannest Ave Middletown (45042) *(G-14295)*
Church of St Mary Catholic, Chardon *Also called Saint Mary Parish* *(G-2712)*
Chute Gerdeman Inc 614 469-1001
455 S Ludlow St Columbus (43215) *(G-7198)*
Chwc, Bryan *Also called Community Hsptals Wllness Ctrs* *(G-1955)*
Ci Disposition Co 216 587-5200
1000 Valley Belt Rd Brooklyn Heights (44131) *(G-1867)*
Cicar, Dublin *Also called Chemcote Inc* *(G-10171)*
Cigna Corporation 216 642-1700
3 Summit Park Dr Ste 250 Independence (44131) *(G-12058)*
Cima Inc 513 382-8976
1010 Eaton Ave Hamilton (45013) *(G-11577)*
Cimarron Express Inc 419 855-7713
21611 State Route 51 W Genoa (43430) *(G-11252)*
Cimcool Industrial Pdts LLC (HQ) 888 246-2665
3000 Disney St Cincinnati (45209) *(G-3216)*
Cimx LLC 513 248-7700
4625 Red Bank Rd Ste 200 Cincinnati (45227) *(G-3217)*
Cimx Software, Cincinnati *Also called Cimx LLC* *(G-3217)*
Cin Legal Data Services, Dayton *Also called Credit Infonet Inc* *(G-9339)*
Cincilingua Inc 513 721-8782
322 E 4th St Cincinnati (45202) *(G-3218)*
Cincinatti Chld Hosp Med Ctr, Fairfield *Also called Childrens Hospital Medical Ctr* *(G-10708)*
Cincinnati, Cleveland *Also called Ohio Transport Inc* *(G-6125)*
Cincinnati - Vulcan Company 513 242-5300
5353 Spring Grove Ave Cincinnati (45217) *(G-3219)*
Cincinnati Air Conditioning Co 513 721-5622
2080 Northwest Dr Cincinnati (45231) *(G-3220)*
Cincinnati Anml Rfrrl 513 530-0911
6995 E Kemper Rd Cincinnati (45249) *(G-3221)*
Cincinnati Area Chapter, Cincinnati *Also called American Red Cross* *(G-2950)*
Cincinnati Area Senior Svcs (PA) 513 721-4330
2368 Victory Pkwy Ste 300 Cincinnati (45206) *(G-3222)*
CINCINNATI ART MUSEUM, Cincinnati *Also called Cincinnati Museum Association* *(G-3257)*
Cincinnati Asphalt Corporation 513 367-0250
7959 Harrison Ave Cleves (45002) *(G-6726)*
Cincinnati Assn For The Blind 513 221-8558
2045 Gilbert Ave Cincinnati (45202) *(G-3223)*
Cincinnati Ballet Company Inc 513 621-5219
1555 Central Pkwy Cincinnati (45214) *(G-3224)*
Cincinnati Bar Association 513 381-8213
225 E 6th St Fl 2 Cincinnati (45202) *(G-3225)*
Cincinnati Bell Inc (PA) 513 397-9900
221 E 4th St Ste 700 Cincinnati (45202) *(G-3226)*
Cincinnati Bell Techno 513 841-6700
4600 Montgomery Rd # 400 Cincinnati (45212) *(G-3227)*
Cincinnati Bell Tele Co LLC (HQ) 513 565-9402
209 W 7th St Fl 1 Cincinnati (45202) *(G-3228)*
Cincinnati Belt and Transm 513 621-9050
5500 Ridge Ave Cincinnati (45213) *(G-3229)*
Cincinnati Bengals Inc (PA) 513 621-3550
1 Paul Brown Stadium Cincinnati (45202) *(G-3230)*
Cincinnati Better Hearing Ctr, Cincinnati *Also called Cincinnati Head and Neck Inc* *(G-3247)*
Cincinnati Bulk Terminals LLC 513 621-4800
895 Mehring Way Cincinnati (45203) *(G-3231)*
Cincinnati Casualty Company 513 870-2000
6200 S Gilmore Rd Fairfield (45014) *(G-10709)*
Cincinnati Central Cr Un Inc (PA) 513 241-2050
1717 Western Ave Cincinnati (45214) *(G-3232)*
Cincinnati Children's Hospital, Cincinnati *Also called Childrens Hospital Medical Ctr* *(G-3191)*
Cincinnati Chld Hosp Med Ctr, Cincinnati *Also called Childrens Hospital Medical Ctr* *(G-3185)*
Cincinnati Circus Company LLC 513 921-5454
6433 Wiehe Rd Cincinnati (45237) *(G-3233)*
Cincinnati Cnslting Consortium 513 233-0011
220 Wyoming Ave Cincinnati (45215) *(G-3234)*
Cincinnati Collision Center 513 984-4445
9323 Blue Ash Rd Blue Ash (45242) *(G-1524)*
Cincinnati Coml Contg LLC 513 561-6633
4760 Red Bank Rd Ste 226 Cincinnati (45227) *(G-3235)*
Cincinnati Copiers Inc (PA) 513 769-0606
4720 Glendale Milford Rd Blue Ash (45242) *(G-1525)*
Cincinnati Country Club 513 533-5200
2348 Grandin Rd Cincinnati (45208) *(G-3236)*
Cincinnati Ctr/Psychoanalysis 513 961-8484
3001 Highland Ave Cincinnati (45219) *(G-3237)*

Cincinnati Dental Services ...513 753-6446
4360 Ferguson Dr Ste 140 Cincinnati (45245) ***(G-2845)***
Cincinnati Dental Services ...513 741-7779
8111 Cheviot Rd Ste 102 Cincinnati (45247) ***(G-3238)***
Cincinnati Dental Services (PA) ...513 721-8888
121 E Mcmillan St Cincinnati (45219) ***(G-3239)***
Cincinnati Dental Services ...513 774-8800
8944 Columbia Rd Ste 300 Loveland (45140) ***(G-12982)***
Cincinnati Division, Cincinnati *Also called The Cincinnati Cordage Ppr Co* ***(G-4590)***
Cincinnati Division, Monroe *Also called Terex Utilities Inc* ***(G-14584)***
Cincinnati Drywall Inc ...513 321-7322
659 Wilmer Ave Cincinnati (45226) ***(G-3240)***
Cincinnati Early Learning Ctr (PA) ...513 961-2690
1301 E Mcmillan St Cincinnati (45206) ***(G-3241)***
Cincinnati Early Learning Ctr ...513 367-2129
498 S State St Harrison (45030) ***(G-11663)***
Cincinnati Equitable Insur Co (HQ) ...513 621-1826
525 Vine St Ste 1925 Cincinnati (45202) ***(G-3242)***
Cincinnati Equitable Insur Co ...440 349-2210
5910 Harper Rd Ste 100 Solon (44139) ***(G-16835)***
Cincinnati Equitable Insurance, Cincinnati *Also called Alpha Investment Partnership* ***(G-2931)***
Cincinnati Eye Institute, Blue Ash *Also called Cei Physicians PSC LLC* ***(G-1522)***
Cincinnati Eye Institute, Blue Ash *Also called Cei Physicians Inc* ***(G-1521)***
Cincinnati Fifth Street Ht LLC ...513 579-1234
151 W 5th St Cincinnati (45202) ***(G-3243)***
Cincinnati Fill Inc ...513 242-7526
900 Kieley Pl Cincinnati (45217) ***(G-3244)***
Cincinnati Financial Corp (PA) ...513 870-2000
6200 S Gilmore Rd Fairfield (45014) ***(G-10710)***
Cincinnati Floor Company Inc (PA) ...513 641-4500
5162 Broerman Ave Cincinnati (45217) ***(G-3245)***
Cincinnati Group Health, Cincinnati *Also called Trihealth G LLC* ***(G-4641)***
Cincinnati Gutter Supply, West Chester *Also called Mollett Seamless Gutter Co* ***(G-18976)***
Cincinnati Gymnastics Academy ...513 860-3082
3635 Woodridge Blvd Fairfield (45014) ***(G-10711)***
Cincinnati Hand Surgery Cons (PA) ...513 961-4263
10700 Montgomery Rd # 150 Cincinnati (45242) ***(G-3246)***
Cincinnati Head and Neck Inc (PA) ...513 232-3277
2123 Auburn Ave Cincinnati (45219) ***(G-3247)***
Cincinnati Health Network Inc ...513 961-0600
2825 Burnet Ave Ste 232 Cincinnati (45219) ***(G-3248)***
Cincinnati Humn Relations Comm ...513 352-3237
801 Plum St Rm 158 Cincinnati (45202) ***(G-3249)***
Cincinnati Hyatt Regency, Cincinnati *Also called Cincinnati Fifth Street Ht LLC* ***(G-3243)***
Cincinnati Hydraulic Svc Inc ...513 874-0540
9431 Sutton Pl West Chester (45011) ***(G-18887)***
Cincinnati Indeminty Co ...513 870-2000
6200 S Gilmore Rd Fairfield (45014) ***(G-10712)***
Cincinnati Indus Actoneers Inc ...513 241-9701
2020 Dunlap St Cincinnati (45214) ***(G-3250)***
Cincinnati Institute Fine Arts (PA) ...513 871-2787
20 East Central Pkwy # 2 Cincinnati (45202) ***(G-3251)***
Cincinnati Institute Fine Arts ...513 241-0343
316 Pike St Cincinnati (45202) ***(G-3252)***
Cincinnati Life Insurance Co ...513 870-2000
6200 S Gilmore Rd Fairfield (45014) ***(G-10713)***
Cincinnati Medical Billing Svc ...513 965-8041
8160 Corp Pk Dr Ste 330 Cincinnati (45242) ***(G-3253)***
Cincinnati Metro Hsing Auth ...513 421-2642
1635 Western Ave Cincinnati (45214) ***(G-3254)***
Cincinnati Metro Hsing Auth (PA) ...513 421-8190
1635 Western Ave Cincinnati (45214) ***(G-3255)***
Cincinnati Metro Hsing Auth ...513 333-0670
1627 Western Ave Cincinnati (45214) ***(G-3256)***
Cincinnati Museum Association (PA) ...513 721-5204
953 Eden Park Dr Cincinnati (45202) ***(G-3257)***
Cincinnati Museum Center (PA) ...513 287-7000
1301 Western Ave Cincinnati (45203) ***(G-3258)***
Cincinnati Nature Center (PA) ...513 831-1711
4949 Tealtown Rd Milford (45150) ***(G-14378)***
Cincinnati Netherland Ht LLC ...513 421-9100
35 W 5th St Cincinnati (45202) ***(G-3259)***
Cincinnati Occupational Therap (PA) ...513 791-5688
4440 Carver Woods Dr # 200 Blue Ash (45242) ***(G-1526)***
Cincinnati Opera Association ...513 768-5500
1243 Elm St Cincinnati (45202) ***(G-3260)***
Cincinnati Pool Management Inc ...513 777-1444
3461 Mustafa Dr Cincinnati (45241) ***(G-3261)***
Cincinnati Public Radio Inc ...513 241-8282
1223 Central Pkwy Cincinnati (45214) ***(G-3262)***
Cincinnati Reds LLC (PA) ...513 765-7000
100 Joe Nuxhall Way Cincinnati (45202) ***(G-3263)***
Cincinnati Reds LLC ...513 765-7923
100 Main St Cincinnati (45202) ***(G-3264)***
Cincinnati Scholar House LP ...513 559-0048
1826 Race St Cincinnati (45202) ***(G-3265)***
Cincinnati Senior Care LLC ...513 272-0600
4001 Rosslyn Dr Cincinnati (45209) ***(G-3266)***
Cincinnati Shakespeare Company ...513 381-2273
217 W 12th St Cincinnati (45202) ***(G-3267)***
Cincinnati Speech Hearing Ctr (PA) ...513 221-0527
2825 Burnet Ave Ste 401 Cincinnati (45219) ***(G-3268)***
Cincinnati Sports Club, Cincinnati *Also called Cincinnati Sports Mall Inc* ***(G-3269)***
Cincinnati Sports Mall Inc ...513 527-4000
3950 Red Bank Rd Ste A Cincinnati (45227) ***(G-3269)***
Cincinnati Steel Products Co ...513 871-4444
4540 Steel Pl Cincinnati (45209) ***(G-3270)***
Cincinnati Sub-Zero Products, Cincinnati *Also called Gentherm Medical LLC* ***(G-3618)***
Cincinnati Symphony Orchestra (PA) ...513 621-1919
1241 Elm St Cincinnati (45202) ***(G-3271)***
Cincinnati Tae Kwon Do Cntr, Cincinnati *Also called Cincinnati Tae Kwon Do Inc* ***(G-3272)***
Cincinnati Tae Kwon Do Inc ...513 271-6900
4325 Red Bank Rd Ste A Cincinnati (45227) ***(G-3272)***
Cincinnati Training Trml Svcs (PA) ...513 563-4474
4000 Executive Park Dr # 402 Cincinnati (45241) ***(G-3273)***
Cincinnati USA Rgional Chamber ...513 579-3100
3 E 4th St Ste 200 Cincinnati (45202) ***(G-3274)***
Cincinnati V A Medical Center, Cincinnati *Also called Veterans Health Administration* ***(G-4759)***
Cincinnati Vending Company, Cincinnati *Also called Walter Alexander Entps Inc* ***(G-4769)***
Cincinnati Voice and Data ...513 683-4127
136 Commerce Dr Loveland (45140) ***(G-12983)***
Cincinnati Youth Collaborative ...513 475-4165
301 Oak St Cincinnati (45219) ***(G-3275)***
CINCINNATI ZOO & BOTANICAL GAR, Cincinnati *Also called Zoological Society Cincinnati* ***(G-4820)***
Cincinnati-Hmltn Cnty Comm Act (PA) ...513 569-1840
1740 Langdon Farm Rd Cincinnati (45237) ***(G-3276)***
Cincinnati-Hmltn Cnty Comm Act ...513 569-4510
1740 Langdon Farm Rd Cincinnati (45237) ***(G-3277)***
Cincinnati-Hmltn Cnty Comm Act ...513 354-3900
880 W Court St Cincinnati (45203) ***(G-3278)***
Cincinnatian Hotel ...513 381-3000
601 Vine St Cincinnati (45202) ***(G-3279)***
Cincinnatian Hotel, The, Cincinnati *Also called Cincinnatian Hotel* ***(G-3279)***
Cincinnatis Optimum RES Envir ...513 771-2673
75 Tri County Pkwy Cincinnati (45246) ***(G-3280)***
Cincinnatus Savings & Loan (PA) ...513 661-6903
3300 Harrison Ave Cincinnati (45211) ***(G-3281)***
Cincinnti Educ & RES For Vetrn ...513 861-3100
3200 Vine St Cincinnati (45220) ***(G-3282)***
Cinciti Bl Etd Trts LLC ...513 397-0963
221 E 4th St Fl 1290 Cincinnati (45202) ***(G-3283)***
Cinco Credit Union (PA) ...513 281-9988
49 William Howard Taft Rd Cincinnati (45219) ***(G-3284)***
CINCO FAMILY FINANCIAL CENTER, Cincinnati *Also called Cinco Credit Union* ***(G-3284)***
Cincom Helpdesk, Cincinnati *Also called Cincom Systems Inc* ***(G-3287)***
Cincom Intrnational Operations (HQ) ...513 612-2300
55 Merchant St Ste 100 Cincinnati (45246) ***(G-3285)***
Cincom Systems Inc (PA) ...513 612-2300
55 Merchant St Ste 100 Cincinnati (45246) ***(G-3286)***
Cincom Systems Inc ...513 459-1470
4605 Duke Dr Mason (45040) ***(G-13555)***
Cincom Systems Inc ...513 389-2344
2300 Montana Ave Ste 235 Cincinnati (45211) ***(G-3287)***
Cincysmiles Foundation Inc ...513 621-0248
635 W 7th St Ste 405 Cincinnati (45203) ***(G-3288)***
Cinemark 15, Macedonia *Also called Cinemark Usa Inc* ***(G-13065)***
Cinemark At Valley View, Cleveland *Also called Cinemark Usa Inc* ***(G-5179)***
Cinemark Carriage Pl Movies 12, Columbus *Also called Cinemark Usa Inc* ***(G-7199)***
Cinemark Movies 10, Canton *Also called Cinemark Usa Inc* ***(G-2253)***
Cinemark Movies 10, Wooster *Also called Cinemark Usa Inc* ***(G-19702)***
Cinemark Movies 10, Columbus *Also called Cinemark Usa Inc* ***(G-7200)***
Cinemark Movies 12 At Mill Run, Hilliard *Also called Cinemark Usa Inc* ***(G-11755)***
Cinemark Stnrdge Plz Movies 16, Gahanna *Also called Cinemark Usa Inc* ***(G-11112)***
Cinemark Tinseltown 7, Youngstown *Also called Cinemark Usa Inc* ***(G-19989)***
Cinemark Usa Inc ...330 965-2335
7401 Market St Rear Youngstown (44512) ***(G-19989)***
Cinemark Usa Inc ...216 447-8820
6001 Canal Rd Cleveland (44125) ***(G-5179)***
Cinemark Usa Inc ...330 908-1005
8161 Macedonia Commons Bl Macedonia (44056) ***(G-13065)***
Cinemark Usa Inc ...419 589-7300
2355 Walker Lake Rd Ontario (44903) ***(G-15546)***
Cinemark Usa Inc ...614 538-0403
2570 Bethel Rd Columbus (43220) ***(G-7199)***
Cinemark Usa Inc ...330 497-9118
6284 Dressler Rd Nw Canton (44720) ***(G-2253)***
Cinemark Usa Inc ...614 527-3773
3773 Ridge Mill Dr Hilliard (43026) ***(G-11755)***
Cinemark Usa Inc ...614 471-7620
323 Stoneridge Ln Gahanna (43230) ***(G-11112)***
Cinemark Usa Inc ...330 345-2610
4108 Burbank Rd Wooster (44691) ***(G-19702)***
Cinemark Usa Inc ...614 529-8547
5275 Westpointe Plaza Dr Columbus (43228) ***(G-7200)***
Cinergy Corp (HQ) ...513 421-9500
139 E 4th St Cincinnati (45202) ***(G-3289)***
Cinfed Credit Union, Cincinnati *Also called Cinfed Federal Credit Union* ***(G-3290)***

ALPHABETIC

Cinfed Federal Credit Union (PA) 513 333-3800
4801 Kennedy Ave Cincinnati (45209) *(G-3290)*
Cinmar LLC (HQ) 513 603-1000
5566 W Chester Rd West Chester (45069) *(G-18888)*
Cinccinnatian Hotel, The, Cincinnati Also called Brothers Properties Corp *(G-3081)*
Cintas Corporation (PA) 513 459-1200
6800 Cintas Blvd Cincinnati (45262) *(G-3291)*
Cintas Corporation 513 631-5750
5570 Ridge Ave Cincinnati (45213) *(G-3292)*
Cintas Corporation 330 821-2220
12445 Rockhill Ave Ne Alliance (44601) *(G-524)*
Cintas Corporation 513 671-7717
690 E Crscntvlle Rd Ste A Cincinnati (45246) *(G-3293)*
Cintas Corporation No 1 (HQ) 513 459-1200
6800 Cintas Blvd Mason (45040) *(G-13556)*
Cintas Corporation No 2 .... 440 746-7777
1061 Trumbull Ave Girard (44420) *(G-11284)*
Cintas Corporation No 2 .... 440 746-7777
55 Andrews Cir Ste 1a Brecksville (44141) *(G-1773)*
Cintas Corporation No 2 .... 513 459-1200
5800 Cintas Blvd Mason (45040) *(G-13557)*
Cintas Corporation No 2 .... 614 878-7313
1300 Boltonfield St Columbus (43228) *(G-7201)*
Cintas Corporation No 2 .... 440 352-4003
800 Renaissance Pkwy Painesville (44077) *(G-15698)*
Cintas Corporation No 2 .... 740 687-6230
2250 Commerce St Lancaster (43130) *(G-12379)*
Cintas Corporation No 2 .... 513 965-0800
27 Whitney Dr Milford (45150) *(G-14379)*
Cintas Corporation No 2 .... 614 860-9152
1275 Research Rd Blacklick (43004) *(G-1477)*
Cintas Corporation No 2 .... 440 838-8611
1 Andrews Cir Cleveland (44141) *(G-5180)*
Cintas Corporation No 2 .... 330 966-7800
3865 Highland Park Nw Canton (44720) *(G-2254)*
Cintas Corporation No 2 (HQ) 513 459-1200
6800 Cintas Blvd Mason (45040) *(G-13558)*
Cintas Corporation No 2 .... 513 459-1200
6800 Cintas Blvd Mason (45040) *(G-13559)*
Cintas Document Management LLC (HQ) 800 914-1960
6800 Cintas Blvd Mason (45040) *(G-13560)*
Cintas First Aid & Safety, Mason Also called Cintas Corporation No 2 *(G-13558)*
Cintas R US Inc 513 459-1200
6800 Cintas Blvd Cincinnati (45262) *(G-3294)*
Cintas Sales Corporation (HQ) 513 459-1200
6800 Cintas Blvd Cincinnati (45262) *(G-3295)*
Cintas Uniforms AP Fcilty Svcs, Cincinnati Also called Cintas Corporation *(G-3292)*
Cintas-Rus LP (HQ) 513 459-1200
6800 Cintas Blvd Mason (45040) *(G-13561)*
Cioffi & Son Construction 330 794-9448
1001 Eastwood Ave Akron (44305) *(G-132)*
CIP International Inc 513 874-9925
9575 Le Saint Dr West Chester (45014) *(G-18889)*
Cipriano Painting 440 892-1827
27387 Hollywood Dr Cleveland (44145) *(G-5181)*
Circle Building Services Inc 614 228-6090
742 Harmon Ave Columbus (43223) *(G-7202)*
Circle Health Services 216 721-4010
12201 Euclid Ave Cleveland (44106) *(G-5182)*
Circle J Home Health Care (PA) 330 482-0877
412 State Route 164 Salineville (43945) *(G-16570)*
Circle Prime Manufacturing 330 923-0019
2114 Front St Cuyahoga Falls (44221) *(G-9079)*
Circle S Farms Inc 614 878-9462
9015 London Groveport Rd Grove City (43123) *(G-11420)*
Circle S Transport Inc 614 207-2184
1008 Arcaro Dr Columbus (43230) *(G-7203)*
Circle T Logistics Inc 740 262-5096
617 W Center St Ste 26 Marion (43302) *(G-13411)*
Circleville Oil Co 740 474-7568
315 Town St Circleville (43113) *(G-4828)*
Circling Hills Golf Course 513 367-5858
10240 Carolina Trace Rd Harrison (45030) *(G-11664)*
Circlvlle Care Rhblitation Ctr, Circleville Also called Sunbridge Circleville *(G-4851)*
Circuits & Cables Inc 937 415-2070
815 S Brown School Rd Vandalia (45377) *(G-18514)*
Cisco Capitol Express, Columbus Also called Capitol Express Entps Inc *(G-7116)*
Cisco Systems Inc 937 427-4264
2661 Commons Blvd Ste 133 Beavercreek (45431) *(G-1140)*
Cisco Systems Inc 330 523-2000
4125 Highlander Pkwy Richfield (44286) *(G-16350)*
Cisco Systems Inc 614 764-4987
5400 Frantz Rd Ste 200 Dublin (43016) *(G-10174)*
Citicorp Credit Services Inc 212 559-1000
1500 Boltonfield St Columbus (43228) *(G-7204)*
Citigroup Global Markets Inc 860 291-4181
4380 Buckeye Ln Ste 200 Beavercreek (45440) *(G-1210)*
Citigroup Global Markets Inc 513 579-8300
4030 Smith Rd Ste 200 Cincinnati (45209) *(G-3296)*
Citigroup Global Markets Inc 419 842-5383
7124 W Central Ave Toledo (43617) *(G-17653)*
Citigroup Global Markets Inc 440 617-2000
2035 Crocker Rd Ste 201 Cleveland (44145) *(G-5183)*

Citigroup Inc 740 548-0594
310 Greif Pkwy Delaware (43015) *(G-9960)*
CITIZENS BANK, Martins Ferry Also called Unified Bank *(G-13479)*
Citizens Bank Company (PA) 740 984-2381
501 5th St Beverly (45715) *(G-1461)*
Citizens Bank National Assn 330 580-1913
400 Tuscarawas St W Ste 1 Canton (44702) *(G-2255)*
Citizens Bank of Ashville Ohio 740 983-2511
26 Main St E Ashville (43103) *(G-761)*
Citizens Bnk of Logan Ohio Inc (HQ) 740 380-2561
188 W Main St Logan (43138) *(G-12833)*
Citizens Capital Markets Inc 216 589-0900
200 Public Sq Ste 3750 Cleveland (44114) *(G-5184)*
Citizens Federal Sav & Ln Assn 937 593-0015
110 N Main St Bellefontaine (43311) *(G-1348)*
Citizens Financial Svcs Inc 513 385-3200
9620 Colerain Ave # 60 Cincinnati (45251) *(G-3297)*
Citizens Nat Bnk of Bluffton (HQ) 419 358-8040
102 S Main St Bluffton (45817) *(G-1690)*
Citizens Nat Bnk of Bluffton 419 224-0400
201 N Main St Lima (45801) *(G-12612)*
Citizens Nat Bnk Urbana Ohio (HQ) 937 653-1200
1 Monument Sq Urbana (43078) *(G-18427)*
Citizens National Bank (PA) 740 472-1696
143 S Main St Woodsfield (43793) *(G-19672)*
City Alliance Water Sewer Dst 330 823-5216
1015 Walnut Ave Alliance (44601) *(G-525)*
City Architecture Inc 216 881-2444
3636 Euclid Ave Fl 3 Cleveland (44115) *(G-5185)*
City Attorney, Columbus Also called City of Columbus *(G-7211)*
City Beverage Company 419 782-7065
8283 N State Route 66 Defiance (43512) *(G-9906)*
City Casters 937 224-1137
101 Pine St Ste 300 Dayton (45402) *(G-9301)*
City Dash LLC 513 562-2000
949 Laidlaw Ave Cincinnati (45237) *(G-3298)*
City Dayton Waste Collection, Dayton Also called City of Dayton *(G-9303)*
City Dayton Water Distribution, Dayton Also called City of Dayton *(G-9307)*
City Dept Streets and Sewers, Hamilton Also called City of Hamilton *(G-11578)*
City Garage, Portsmouth Also called City of Portsmouth *(G-16130)*
City Gospel Mission 513 241-5525
1805 Dalton Ave Cincinnati (45214) *(G-3299)*
CITY HALL, Montgomery Also called City of Montgomery *(G-14593)*
City Hospital Association 330 385-7200
425 W 5th St East Liverpool (43920) *(G-10399)*
City Laundry & Dry Cleaning Co, Findlay Also called Kramer Enterprises Inc *(G-10932)*
City Life Inc (PA) 216 523-5899
1382 W 9th St Ste 310 Cleveland (44113) *(G-5186)*
City Machine Technologies Inc 330 740-8186
825 Martin Luther King Jr Blvd Youngstown (44502) *(G-19990)*
City Mission (PA) 216 431-3510
5310 Carnegie Ave Cleveland (44103) *(G-5187)*
City of Akron 330 564-4075
100 W Cedar St Ste 300 Akron (44307) *(G-133)*
City of Akron 330 864-0020
530 Nome Ave Akron (44320) *(G-134)*
City of Akron 330 678-0077
1570 Ravenna Rd Kent (44240) *(G-12221)*
City of Akron 330 375-2420
1460 Triplett Blvd Akron (44306) *(G-135)*
City of Akron 330 375-2355
166 S High St Rm 701 Akron (44308) *(G-136)*
City of Akron 330 375-2666
2460 Akron Peninsula Rd Akron (44313) *(G-137)*
City of Akron 330 375-2851
1420 Triplett Blvd Akron (44306) *(G-138)*
City of Aurora 330 562-8662
158 W Pioneer Trl Aurora (44202) *(G-825)*
City of Avon 440 937-5740
36080 Chester Rd Avon (44011) *(G-876)*
City of Avon Lake 440 933-6226
201 Miller Rd Avon Lake (44012) *(G-912)*
City of Beavercreek 937 320-0742
2800 New Germany Trebein Beavercreek (45431) *(G-1141)*
City of Berea 440 826-5853
400 Barrett Rd Berea (44017) *(G-1418)*
City of Blue Ash 513 745-8534
10647 Kenwood Rd Blue Ash (45242) *(G-1527)*
City of Blue Ash 513 745-8577
4040 Cooper Rd Blue Ash (45241) *(G-1528)*
City of Brecksville 440 526-1384
9069 Brecksville Rd Brecksville (44141) *(G-1774)*
City of Brecksville 440 526-4109
1 Community Dr Brecksville (44141) *(G-1775)*
City of Brook Park 216 433-1545
17400 Holland Rd Cleveland (44142) *(G-5188)*
City of Brunswick 330 225-9144
4095 Center Rd Brunswick (44212) *(G-1924)*
City of Bucyrus 419 562-3050
200 S Spring St Bucyrus (44820) *(G-1982)*
City of Canal Winchester 614 837-8276
22 S Trine St Canal Winchester (43110) *(G-2107)*

(G-0000) Company's Geographic Section entry number

City of Canton 330 489-3080
3530 Central Ave Se Canton (44707) (G-2256)
City of Celina 419 586-2451
1125 S Elm St Celina (45822) (G-2588)
City of Centerville 937 438-3585
10000 Yankee St Dayton (45458) (G-9302)
City of Circleville 740 477-8255
108 E Franklin St Circleville (43113) (G-4829)
City of Cleveland 216 664-2555
1701 Lakeside Ave E Cleveland (44114) (G-5189)
City of Cleveland 216 664-2555
1701 Lakeside Ave E Cleveland (44114) (G-5190)
City of Cleveland 216 664-3121
955 Clague Rd Cleveland (44145) (G-5191)
City of Cleveland 216 664-2941
205 W Saint Clair Ave # 4 Cleveland (44113) (G-5192)
City of Cleveland 216 621-4231
500 Lkeside Ave Ground Fl Cleveland (44114) (G-5193)
City of Cleveland 216 664-2430
205 W Saint Clair Ave # 4 Cleveland (44113) (G-5194)
City of Cleveland 216 664-2620
601 Lakeside Ave E Rm 128 Cleveland (44114) (G-5195)
City of Cleveland 216 348-7210
21400 Chagrin Blvd Cleveland (44122) (G-5196)
City of Cleveland 216 664-6800
3765 Pearl Rd Cleveland (44109) (G-5197)
City of Cleveland 216 664-3922
1300 Lakeside Ave E Cleveland (44114) (G-5198)
City of Cleveland Heights 216 291-2323
40 Severance Cir Cleveland Heights (44118) (G-6716)
City of Cleveland Heights 216 691-7300
14200 Superior Rd Cleveland (44118) (G-5199)
City of Cleveland Heights 216 291-5995
40 Severance Cir Cleveland Heights (44118) (G-6717)
City of Columbus 614 645-7627
3500 Indianola Ave Columbus (43214) (G-7205)
City of Columbus 614 645-7490
910 Dublin Rd Ste 4050 Columbus (43215) (G-7206)
City of Columbus 614 645-1600
3433 Agler Rd Ste 2800 Columbus (43219) (G-7207)
City of Columbus 614 645-3072
1875 Morse Rd 235 Columbus (43229) (G-7208)
City of Columbus 614 645-7417
240 Parsons Ave Columbus (43215) (G-7209)
City of Columbus 614 645-8270
910 Dublin Rd Columbus (43215) (G-7210)
City of Columbus 614 645-6624
375 S High St Fl 7 Columbus (43215) (G-7211)
City of Columbus 614 645-8297
940 Dublin Rd Columbus (43215) (G-7212)
City of Columbus 614 645-3248
6977 S High St Lockbourne (43137) (G-12811)
CITY OF COMPASSION, Perrysburg Also called A Renewed Mind (G-15831)
City of Compassion 419 422-7800
1624 Tiffin Ave Findlay (45840) (G-10888)
City of Coshocton 740 622-1763
760 Chestnut St Lbby Coshocton (43812) (G-9001)
City of Cuyahoga Falls 330 971-8000
2550 Bailey Rd Cuyahoga Falls (44221) (G-9080)
City of Cuyahoga Falls 330 971-8416
1621 Bailey Rd Cuyahoga Falls (44221) (G-9081)
City of Cuyahoga Falls 330 971-8130
2310 Second St Cuyahoga Falls (44221) (G-9082)
City of Cuyahoga Falls 330 971-8030
2560 Bailey Rd Cuyahoga Falls (44221) (G-9083)
City of Dayton 937 333-4860
1010 Ottawa St Bldg 7 Dayton (45402) (G-9303)
City of Dayton 937 454-8200
3600 Terminal Rd Ste 300 Vandalia (45377) (G-18515)
City of Dayton 937 333-3725
320 W Monument Ave Dayton (45402) (G-9304)
City of Dayton 937 333-1837
2800 Guthrie Rd Ste A Dayton (45417) (G-9305)
City of Dayton 937 454-8231
3848 Wright Dr Vandalia (45377) (G-18516)
City of Dayton 937 333-6070
3210 Chuck Wagner Ln Dayton (45414) (G-9306)
City of Dayton 937 333-7138
945 Ottawa St Dayton (45402) (G-9307)
City of Delphos 419 695-4010
608 N Canal St Delphos (45833) (G-10021)
City of Dublin 614 410-4750
6555 Shier Rings Rd Dublin (43016) (G-10175)
City of Eaton 937 456-5361
391 W Lexington Rd Eaton (45320) (G-10438)
City of Elyria 440 366-2211
1194 Gulf Rd Elyria (44035) (G-10489)
City of Englewood 937 836-2434
333 W National Rd Ofc Englewood (45322) (G-10582)
City of Euclid 216 289-2800
25500 Lakeland Blvd Cleveland (44132) (G-5200)
City of Findlay 419 424-7179
1201 S River Rd Findlay (45840) (G-10889)

City of Gallipolis 740 441-6003
2501 Ohio Ave Gallipolis (45631) (G-11186)
City of Garfield Heights 216 475-1107
13600 Mccracken Rd Cleveland (44125) (G-5201)
City of Hamilton 513 785-7551
2210 S Erie Hwy Hamilton (45011) (G-11578)
City of Hamilton 513 868-5971
2451 River Rd Hamilton (45015) (G-11579)
City of Hamilton 513 785-7450
960 N 3rd St Hamilton (45011) (G-11580)
City of Hamilton Waste Water, Hamilton Also called City of Hamilton (G-11579)
City of Highland Heights 440 461-2441
5827 Highland Rd Cleveland (44143) (G-5202)
City of Hudson Village 330 650-1052
95 Owen Brown St Hudson (44236) (G-11973)
City of Huron 419 433-5000
417 Main St Huron (44839) (G-12023)
City of Independence 216 524-3262
6363 Selig Blvd Cleveland (44131) (G-5203)
City of Independence 216 524-7373
6363 Selig Blvd Cleveland (44131) (G-5204)
City of Kent 330 678-8105
930 Overholt Rd Kent (44240) (G-12222)
City of Kenton (PA) 419 674-4850
111 W Franklin St Kenton (43326) (G-12273)
City of Lakewood 216 252-4322
12920 Berea Rd Cleveland (44111) (G-5205)
City of Lakewood 216 226-0080
2019 Woodward Ave Cleveland (44107) (G-5206)
City of Lakewood 216 529-6170
12650 Detroit Ave Cleveland (44107) (G-5207)
City of Lakewood 216 941-1116
12920 Berea Rd Cleveland (44111) (G-5208)
City of Lakewood 216 521-1515
16024 Madison Ave Lakewood (44107) (G-12338)
City of Lakewood 216 521-1288
16024 Madison Ave Cleveland (44107) (G-5209)
City of Lancaster 740 687-6670
1424 Campground Rd Lancaster (43130) (G-12380)
City of Lima 419 221-5165
900 S Collett St Lima (45804) (G-12613)
City of Lima 419 221-5294
50 Town Sq Fl 3 Lima (45801) (G-12614)
City of Lima 419 221-5175
1405 Reservoir Rd Lima (45804) (G-12615)
City of Lorain 440 288-0281
100 Alabama Ave Lorain (44052) (G-12890)
City of Lorain 440 204-2500
1106 W 1st St Lorain (44052) (G-12891)
City of Louisville (PA) 330 875-3321
215 S Mill St Louisville (44641) (G-12962)
City of Marion 740 382-1479
981 W Center St Marion (43302) (G-13412)
City of Massillon 330 833-3304
100 Dig Indian Dr Sw Massillon (44646) (G-13671)
City of Miamisburg 937 866-4532
10 N 1st St Miamisburg (45342) (G-14152)
City of Miamisburg 937 866-4653
4344 Benner Rd Miamisburg (45342) (G-14153)
City of Montgomery (PA) 513 891-2424
10101 Montgomery Rd Montgomery (45242) (G-14593)
City of New Philadelphia 330 339-2121
1234 Commercial Ave Se New Philadelphia (44663) (G-14950)
City of North Olmsted 440 734-8200
26000 Lorain Rd North Olmsted (44070) (G-15282)
City of North Olmsted 440 777-0678
5873 Canterbury Rd North Olmsted (44070) (G-15283)
City of North Ridgeville 440 327-8326
35010 Bainbridge Rd North Ridgeville (44039) (G-15326)
City of North Royalton 440 582-3002
11545 Royalton Rd Cleveland (44133) (G-5210)
City of Norwalk 419 663-6715
42 Woodlawn Ave Norwalk (44857) (G-15426)
City of Oberlin (PA) 440 775-1531
85 S Main St Oberlin (44074) (G-15499)
City of Painesville 440 392-5954
325 Richmond St Painesville (44077) (G-15699)
City of Painesville 440 392-5795
7 Richmond St Painesville (44077) (G-15700)
City of Parma 440 885-8983
5680 Chevrolet Blvd Cleveland (44130) (G-5211)
City of Parma 440 885-8876
6505 Ridge Rd Cleveland (44129) (G-5212)
City of Parma 440 888-4514
7001 W Ridgewood Dr Cleveland (44129) (G-5213)
City of Perrysburg 419 872-8020
11980 Route Roached Rd Perrysburg (43551) (G-15848)
City of Pickerington 614 645-8474
1145 Clubhouse Ln Pickerington (43147) (G-15951)
City of Portsmouth 740 353-5153
605 Washington St Portsmouth (45662) (G-16128)
City of Portsmouth 740 353-5419
55 Mary Ann St Portsmouth (45662) (G-16129)

City of Portsmouth........740 353-3459
55 Mary Ann St Portsmouth (45662) *(G-16130)*
City of Rocky River........440 356-5656
21018 Hilliard Blvd Cleveland (44116) *(G-5214)*
City of Rocky River........440 356-5630
21012 Hilliard Blvd Cleveland (44116) *(G-5215)*
City of Sandusky........419 627-5829
222 Meigs St Sandusky (44870) *(G-16584)*
City of Sandusky........419 627-5907
304 Harrison St Sandusky (44870) *(G-16585)*
City of Seven Hills........216 524-6262
7777 Summitview Dr Seven Hills (44131) *(G-16673)*
City of Solon........440 248-6939
34025 Bainbridge Rd Solon (44139) *(G-16836)*
City of South Euclid........216 291-3902
1352 Victory Dr Cleveland (44121) *(G-5216)*
City of Streetsboro........330 626-2856
2094 State Route 303 Streetsboro (44241) *(G-17250)*
City of Sylvania........419 885-1167
7060 Sylvania Ave Sylvania (43560) *(G-17415)*
City of Toledo........419 245-1800
420 Madison Ave Ste 100 Toledo (43604) *(G-17654)*
City of Toledo........419 245-1001
1 Government Ctr Ste 2200 Toledo (43604) *(G-17655)*
City of Toledo........419 936-2875
2201 Ottawa Dr Toledo (43606) *(G-17656)*
City of Toledo........419 936-2924
4032 Creekside Ave Toledo (43612) *(G-17657)*
City of Toledo........419 245-1400
1 Government Ctr Ste 1800 Toledo (43604) *(G-17658)*
City of Toledo........419 936-2507
555 N Expressway Dr Toledo (43608) *(G-17659)*
City of Toledo........419 936-2275
600 Jefferson Ave Ste 300 Toledo (43604) *(G-17660)*
City of Toledo Div Wtr Dist, Toledo *Also called Toledo Cy Pub Utlity Wtr Distr (G-18082)*
City of Troy........937 335-1914
1400 Experiment Farm Rd Troy (45373) *(G-18198)*
City of Vandalia........937 890-1300
201 Clubhouse Way Vandalia (45377) *(G-18517)*
City of Wadsworth........330 334-1581
120 Maple St Wadsworth (44281) *(G-18592)*
City of Warrensville Heights........216 587-1230
19700 Miles Rd Cleveland (44128) *(G-5217)*
City of Wellston........740 384-2428
203 E Broadway St Wellston (45692) *(G-18848)*
City of Westerville........614 901-6500
350 Park Meadow Dr Westerville (43081) *(G-19236)*
City of Westerville........614 901-6700
139 E Broadway Ave Westerville (43081) *(G-19237)*
City of Westlake........440 835-6442
29800 Center Ridge Rd Westlake (44145) *(G-19332)*
City of Whitehall........614 237-5478
390 S Yearling Rd Columbus (43213) *(G-7213)*
City of Willoughby........440 942-0215
37400 N Industrial Pkwy Willoughby (44094) *(G-19510)*
City of Willoughby........440 953-4111
1 Public Sq Willoughby (44094) *(G-19511)*
City of Willoughby........440 953-4111
1 Public Sq Willoughby (44094) *(G-19512)*
City of Willoughby........440 953-4280
38890 Hodgson Rd Willoughby (44094) *(G-19513)*
City of Willoughby Hills........440 942-7207
35455 Chardon Rd Willoughby Hills (44094) *(G-19587)*
City of Wilmington........937 382-7961
260 Charles St Wilmington (45177) *(G-19608)*
City of Wooster........330 263-8636
1761 Beall Ave Wooster (44691) *(G-19703)*
City of Wooster........330 263-5266
510 N Market St Wooster (44691) *(G-19704)*
City of Wooster........330 263-8100
1761 Beall Ave Wooster (44691) *(G-19705)*
City of Xenia........937 376-7271
779 Ford Rd Xenia (45385) *(G-19893)*
City of Xenia........937 376-7260
966 Towler Rd Xenia (45385) *(G-19894)*
City of Youngstown (PA)........330 742-8700
26 S Phelps St Bsmt Youngstown (44503) *(G-19991)*
City of Youngstown........330 742-8749
26 S Phelps St Fl 3a Youngstown (44503) *(G-19992)*
City of Zanesville........740 455-0641
401 Market St Rm 1 Zanesville (43701) *(G-20296)*
City Scrap & Salvage Co........330 753-5051
760 Flora Ave Akron (44314) *(G-139)*
City Service, Loveland *Also called Dill-Elam Inc (G-12991)*
City Springsboro Public Works, Springboro *Also called Springboro Service Center (G-16984)*
City Taxicab & Transfer Co........440 992-2156
1753 W Prospect Rd Ashtabula (44004) *(G-727)*
City View Nrsing Rhabilitation, Cleveland *Also called Partners of City View LLC (G-6177)*
City View Nursing & Rehab LLC........216 361-1414
6606 Carnegie Ave Cleveland (44103) *(G-5218)*
City Yellow Cab Company........330 253-3141
650 Home Ave Akron (44310) *(G-140)*
Citynet Ohio LLC........614 364-7881
343 N Front St Ste 400 Columbus (43215) *(G-7214)*
Cityview Nrsing Rhbltation Ctr, Cleveland *Also called City View Nursing & Rehab LLC (G-5218)*
Ciulla Smith & Dale LLP (PA)........440 884-2036
6364 Pearl Rd Ste 4 Cleveland (44130) *(G-5219)*
Ciuni & Panichi Inc........216 831-7171
25201 Chagrin Blvd # 200 Cleveland (44122) *(G-5220)*
Civic Center, Cleveland *Also called City of Independence (G-5204)*
Civica CMI, Englewood *Also called Creative Microsystems Inc (G-10583)*
Civil & Environmental Cons Inc........419 724-5281
4841 Monroe St Ste 103 Toledo (43623) *(G-17661)*
Civil & Environmental Cons Inc........513 985-0226
5899 Montclair Blvd Milford (45150) *(G-14380)*
Civista Bank (HQ)........419 625-4121
100 E Water St Sandusky (44870) *(G-16586)*
Civista Bank........419 744-3100
16 Executive Dr Norwalk (44857) *(G-15427)*
CJ Mahan Construction Co LLC (PA)........614 277-4545
250 N Hartford Ave Columbus (43222) *(G-7215)*
Cj's Sports Bar, Bowling Green *Also called Al-Mar Lanes (G-1713)*
CL Zimmerman Delaware LLC........513 860-9300
5115 Excello Ct West Chester (45069) *(G-18890)*
Claire De Leigh Corp........614 459-6575
3712 Riverside Dr Columbus (43221) *(G-7216)*
Claprood Roman J Co........614 221-5515
242 N Grant Ave Columbus (43215) *(G-7217)*
Clare-Mar Camp Inc........440 647-3318
47571 New Lndon Eastrn Rd New London (44851) *(G-14931)*
Clare-Mar Lakes Rv Sales, New London *Also called Clare-Mar Camp Inc (G-14931)*
Claremont Retirement Village........614 761-2011
7041 Bent Tree Blvd Columbus (43235) *(G-7218)*
Clarion Hotel, Sandusky *Also called Cafaro Peachcreek Co Ltd (G-16579)*
Clarion Hotel Suites, Blue Ash *Also called 5901 Pfffer Rd Htels Sites LLC (G-1495)*
Claritas LLC (HQ)........513 739-6869
8044 Montgomery Rd # 455 Cincinnati (45236) *(G-3300)*
Clark Schaefer Hackett & Co........937 399-2000
14 E Main St Ste 500 Springfield (45502) *(G-17008)*
Clark Schaefer Hackett & Co (PA)........513 241-3111
1 E 4th St Ste 1200 Cincinnati (45202) *(G-3301)*
Clark Schaefer Hackett & Co........216 672-5252
600 Superior Ave E # 1300 Cleveland (44114) *(G-5221)*
Clark Schaefer Hackett & Co........419 243-0218
3166 N Republic Blvd Toledo (43615) *(G-17662)*
Clark Schaefer Hackett & Co........614 885-2208
4449 Easton Way Ste 400 Columbus (43219) *(G-7219)*
Clark Brands LLC........330 723-9886
427 N Court St Medina (44256) *(G-13920)*
Clark County Board of Developm (PA)........937 328-2675
2527 Kenton St Springfield (45505) *(G-17009)*
Clark County Board of Developm........937 328-5240
50 W Leffel Ln Springfield (45506) *(G-17010)*
Clark County Board of Developm........937 328-5200
110 W Leffel Ln Springfield (45506) *(G-17011)*
Clark County Combined Hlth Dst (PA)........937 390-5600
529 E Home Rd Springfield (45503) *(G-17012)*
Clark County Human Services, Springfield *Also called County of Clark (G-17023)*
Clark County Mrdd Trnsp, Springfield *Also called Clark County Board of Developm (G-17010)*
Clark County Office, Springfield *Also called Miami Vly Child Dev Ctrs Inc (G-17083)*
Clark Memorial Home Assn........937 399-4262
106 Kewbury Rd Springfield (45504) *(G-17013)*
Clark Royster Inc........740 335-3810
717 Robinson Rd Se Wshngtn CT Hs (43160) *(G-19864)*
Clark Shawnee Schl Transprtn........937 328-5382
725 E Leffel Ln Springfield (45505) *(G-17014)*
Clark Son Actn Liquidation Inc........330 837-9710
4500 Erie Ave Nw Canal Fulton (44614) *(G-2094)*
Clark Theders Insurance Agency........513 779-2800
9938 Crescent Park Dr West Chester (45069) *(G-18891)*
Clark Trucking Inc (HQ)........937 642-0335
11590 Township Road 157 East Liberty (43319) *(G-10390)*
Clarkdietrich Engineering Serv........513 870-1100
9100 Centre Pointe Dr West Chester (45069) *(G-18892)*
Clarke Contractors Corp........513 285-7844
4475 Muhlhauser Rd West Chester (45011) *(G-18893)*
Clarke Power Services Inc (PA)........513 771-2200
3133 E Kemper Rd Cincinnati (45241) *(G-3302)*
Clarke Power Services Inc........937 684-4402
6061 Executive Blvd Huber Heights (45424) *(G-11953)*
Clarkwood Granada Apartments, Cleveland *Also called Goldberg Companies Inc (G-5613)*
Clary Trucking Inc........740 702-4242
1177 Eastern Ave Chillicothe (45601) *(G-2769)*
Classic Accident Repair Center, Mentor *Also called Dcr Systems LLC (G-14039)*
Classic Autobody, Mentor *Also called Jim Brown Chevrolet Inc (G-14066)*
Classic Brands, Chillicothe *Also called Litter Distributing Co Inc (G-2802)*
Classic Buick Olds Cadillac........440 639-4500
1700 Mentor Ave Painesville (44077) *(G-15701)*
Classic Carriers Inc (PA)........937 604-8118
151 Industrial Pkwy Versailles (45380) *(G-18567)*

Classic Dental Labs Inc 614 443-0328
  1252 S High St Columbus (43206) (G-7220)
Classic Imports Inc (PA) 330 262-5277
  2018 Great Trails Dr Wooster (44691) (G-19706)
Classic International Inc (PA) 440 975-1222
  8470 Tyler Blvd Mentor (44060) (G-14030)
Classic Lexus, Mentor Also called Classic International Inc (G-14030)
Classic Oldsmobile, Painesville Also called Classic Buick Olds Cadillac (G-15701)
Classic Papering & Painting 614 221-0505
  1061 Goodale Blvd Columbus (43212) (G-7221)
Classic Real Estate Co 937 393-3416
  123 W Main St Hillsboro (45133) (G-11833)
Classroom Antics Inc 800 595-3776
  10143 Royalton Rd Ste G North Royalton (44133) (G-15350)
Clay Burley Products Co (PA) 740 452-3633
  455 Gordon St Roseville (43777) (G-16454)
Clay Distributing Co 419 426-3051
  15025 E Us 224 Attica (44807) (G-813)
Clay House, Zanesville Also called Assisted Living Concepts LLC (G-20277)
Claypool Electric Inc 740 653-5683
  1275 Lncstr Krkrsville Rd Lancaster (43130) (G-12381)
Claypool Electrical Contg, Lancaster Also called Claypool Electric Inc (G-12381)
Clays Heritage Carpet Inc (PA) 330 497-1280
  1440 N Main St Canton (44720) (G-2257)
Clayton Weaver Trucking Inc 513 896-6932
  3043 Lelia Ln Fairfield (45014) (G-10714)
Clayton Railroad Cnstr LLC 937 549-2952
  500 Lane Rd West Union (45693) (G-19134)
CLC, Columbus Also called Construction Labor Contrs LLC (G-7352)
Cle Transportation Company 567 805-4008
  203 Republic St Norwalk (44857) (G-15428)
Clean All Services Inc 937 498-4146
  324 Adams St Bldg 1 Sidney (45365) (G-16766)
Clean Break Inc 330 638-5648
  300 Muirwood Dr Ne Warren (44484) (G-18684)
Clean Care Inc 419 725-2100
  511 Phillips Ave Toledo (43612) (G-17663)
Clean Harbors Envmtl Svcs Inc 216 429-2402
  2900 Broadway Ave Cleveland (44115) (G-5222)
Clean Harbors Envmtl Svcs Inc 216 429-2401
  2930 Independence Rd Cleveland (44115) (G-5223)
Clean Harbors Envmtl Svcs Inc 513 681-6242
  4880 Spring Grove Ave Cincinnati (45232) (G-3303)
Clean Harbors Envmtl Svcs Inc 740 929-3532
  581 Milliken Dr Hebron (43025) (G-11711)
Clean Hrbors Es Indus Svcs Inc 937 425-0512
  6151 Executive Blvd Dayton (45424) (G-9308)
Clean Image, Circleville Also called Camco Inc (G-4827)
Clean Innovations (PA) 614 299-1187
  575 E 11th Ave Columbus (43211) (G-7222)
Clean Living Laundry LLC 513 569-0439
  2437 Gilbert Ave Cincinnati (45206) (G-3304)
Clean Water Environmental LLC (PA) 937 268-6501
  300 Cherokee Dr Dayton (45417) (G-9309)
Cleaner & Dryer Restoration, Toledo Also called J Schoen Enterprises Inc (G-17828)
Cleaner Carpet & Jantr Inc 513 469-2070
  6516 Bluebird Ct Mason (45040) (G-13562)
Cleaners Extraordinaire Inc 937 324-8488
  128 Eagle City Rd Springfield (45502) (G-17015)
Cleaning Authority, Milford Also called Premier Cleaning Services Inc (G-14426)
Clear Channel, Dayton Also called City Casters (G-9301)
Clear Channel, Lima Also called Iheartcommunications Inc (G-12664)
Clear Vision Engineering LLC 419 478-7151
  4401 Jackman Rd Toledo (43612) (G-17664)
Clearcreek Construction 740 420-3568
  11050 16th Rd Sw Stoutsville (43154) (G-17186)
Clearfield Ohio Holdings Inc 740 947-5121
  300 E 2nd St Waverly (45690) (G-18816)
Clearmont Nursing Convalecent, Milford Also called Clermont Care Inc (G-14381)
Clearmount Elementary School 330 497-5640
  150 Clearmount Ave Se Canton (44720) (G-2258)
Clearpath HM Hlth Hospice LLC 330 784-2162
  475 Wolf Ledges Pkwy Akron (44311) (G-141)
Clearview Cleaning Contractors 216 621-6688
  2140 Hamilton Ave Cleveland (44114) (G-5224)
Clearview Lantern Suites, Mineral Ridge Also called Terre Forme Enterprises Inc (G-14513)
Clearwater Services Inc 330 836-4946
  1411 Vernon Odom Blvd Akron (44320) (G-142)
Clearwater Systems, Akron Also called Clearwater Services Inc (G-142)
Cleaveland Seaman's Service, Cleveland Also called Seamans Services (G-6384)
Clem Lumber and Distrg Co 330 821-2130
  16055 Waverly St Ne Alliance (44601) (G-526)
Clemente-Mc Kay Ambulance Inc (PA) 330 755-1401
  700 5th St Ste 1 Struthers (44471) (G-17361)
Cleopatra Trucking, Columbus Also called King Tut Logistics LLC (G-7908)
Clerac LLC (HQ) 440 345-3999
  8249 Mohawk Dr Strongsville (44136) (G-17290)
Clercom Inc 513 724-6101
  3710 State Route 133 Williamsburg (45176) (G-19491)
Clerk of Courts, Hamilton Also called Butler County of Ohio (G-11561)

Clermont Care Inc 513 831-1770
  934 State Route 28 Milford (45150) (G-14381)
Clermont Cnty Wtr Rsrces Dept 513 732-7970
  4400 Haskell Ln Batavia (45103) (G-987)
Clermont Counseling Center 513 345-8555
  3730 Glenway Ave Cincinnati (45205) (G-3305)
Clermont Counseling Center (PA) 513 947-7000
  43 E Main St Amelia (45102) (G-571)
Clermont County Community, Cincinnati Also called Veterans Health Administration (G-4760)
Clermont County Community Svcs (PA) 513 732-2277
  3003 Hospital Dr Batavia (45103) (G-988)
Clermont County Gen Hlth Dst 513 732-7499
  2275 Bauer Rd Ste 300 Batavia (45103) (G-989)
Clermont County Wtr Resources, Batavia Also called Clermont Cnty Wtr Rsurces Dept (G-987)
Clermont Hills Co LLC 513 752-4400
  4501 Eastgate Blvd Cincinnati (45245) (G-2846)
Clermont North East School Dst (PA) 513 625-8283
  2792 Us Highway 50 Batavia (45103) (G-990)
Clermont Recovery Center Inc 513 735-8100
  1088 Wasserman Way Ste C Batavia (45103) (G-991)
CLERMONT SENIOR SERVICES, Batavia Also called Clermont Senior Services Inc (G-992)
Clermont Senior Services Inc (PA) 513 724-1255
  2085 James E Sauls Sr Dr Batavia (45103) (G-992)
Clevelan Clinic Hlth Sys W Reg 216 518-3444
  5555 Transportation Blvd Cleveland (44125) (G-5225)
Clevelan Clinic Hlth Sys W Reg (HQ) 216 476-7000
  18101 Lorain Ave Cleveland (44111) (G-5226)
Clevelan Clinic Hlth Sys W Reg 216 476-7606
  18200 Lorain Ave Cleveland (44111) (G-5227)
Clevelan Clinic Hlth Sys W Reg 216 476-7007
  15531 Lorain Ave Cleveland (44111) (G-5228)
Cleveland Airport Hospitality 440 871-6000
  1100 Crocker Rd Westlake (44145) (G-19333)
Cleveland All Breed Trning CLB 216 398-1118
  210 Hayes Dr Ste B Cleveland (44131) (G-5229)
Cleveland America Scores 216 881-7988
  3631 Perkins Ave Ste 2ce Cleveland (44114) (G-5230)
Cleveland Anesthesia Group 216 901-5706
  6701 Rockside Rd Ste 200 Independence (44131) (G-12059)
Cleveland Auto Livery Inc 216 421-1101
  10802 Cedar Ave Cleveland (44106) (G-5231)
Cleveland Bchwood Hsptlity LLC 216 464-5950
  3663 Park East Dr Beachwood (44122) (G-1044)
Cleveland Botanical Garden (PA) 216 721-1600
  11030 East Blvd Cleveland (44106) (G-5232)
Cleveland Browns Football LLC 440 891-5000
  76 Lou Groza Blvd Berea (44017) (G-1419)
Cleveland Business Furniture, Bedford Also called Cbf Industries Inc (G-1271)
Cleveland Cement Contractors, Brooklyn Heights Also called Cleveland Concrete Cnstr Inc (G-1868)
Cleveland Center For Etng Dsor 216 765-2535
  25550 Chagrin Blvd # 200 Beachwood (44122) (G-1045)
Cleveland Child Care Inc (PA) 216 631-3211
  3274 W 58th St Fl 1 Cleveland (44102) (G-5233)
Cleveland Christian Home, Cleveland Also called National Benevolent Associatio (G-6037)
Cleveland Christian Home Inc 216 671-0977
  4614 Prospect Ave Ste 240 Cleveland (44103) (G-5234)
Cleveland Clinic, Cleveland Also called Taussig Cancer Center (G-6500)
Cleveland Clinic, Lorain Also called Kolczun & Kolczun Orthopedics (G-12911)
Cleveland Clinic Cole Eye Inst 216 444-4508
  9500 Euclid Ave Cleveland (44195) (G-5235)
Cleveland Clinic Community Onc 216 447-9747
  6100 W Creek Rd Ste 15 Independence (44131) (G-12060)
Cleveland Clinic Coordinating, Cleveland Also called Cleveland Clinic Foundation (G-5244)
Cleveland Clinic Foundation 330 505-2280
  650 Youngstown Warren Rd Niles (44446) (G-15151)
Cleveland Clinic Foundation 330 287-4930
  1739 Cleveland Rd Wooster (44691) (G-19707)
Cleveland Clinic Foundation (PA) 216 636-8335
  9500 Euclid Ave Cleveland (44195) (G-5236)
Cleveland Clinic Foundation 440 282-6669
  1142 W 37th St Lorain (44052) (G-12892)
Cleveland Clinic Foundation 614 451-0489
  921 Jasonway Ave Columbus (43214) (G-7223)
Cleveland Clinic Foundation 216 444-2820
  9500 Euclid Ave Ste P57 Cleveland (44195) (G-5237)
Cleveland Clinic Foundation 216 445-8585
  9500 Euclid Ave P-47 Cleveland (44195) (G-5238)
Cleveland Clinic Foundation 440 988-5651
  5700 Cooper Foster Park R Lorain (44053) (G-12893)
Cleveland Clinic Foundation 216 444-5000
  9500 Euclid Ave Cleveland (44195) (G-5239)
Cleveland Clinic Foundation 800 223-2273
  2111 E 96th St Cleveland (44106) (G-5240)
Cleveland Clinic Foundation 419 609-2812
  417 Quarry Lakes Dr Sandusky (44870) (G-16587)
Cleveland Clinic Foundation 216 444-5755
  10300 Carnegie Ave Cleveland (44106) (G-5241)

A
L
P
H
A
B
E
T
I
C

Cleveland Clinic Foundation 440 327-1050
35105 Center Ridge Rd North Ridgeville (44039) *(G-15327)*

Cleveland Clinic Foundation 216 448-0116
25875 Science Park Dr Beachwood (44122) *(G-1046)*

Cleveland Clinic Foundation 216 448-4325
1950 Richmond Rd Cleveland (44124) *(G-5242)*

Cleveland Clinic Foundation 330 287-4500
1740 Cleveland Rd Wooster (44691) *(G-19708)*

Cleveland Clinic Foundation 216 444-2200
6801 Brecksville Rd # 10 Cleveland (44131) *(G-5243)*

Cleveland Clinic Foundation 440 986-4000
2001 E Royalton Rd Broadview Heights (44147) *(G-1827)*

Cleveland Clinic Foundation 440 930-6800
450 Avon Belden Rd Avon Lake (44012) *(G-913)*

Cleveland Clinic Foundation 440 366-9444
303 Chestnut Commons Dr Elyria (44035) *(G-10490)*

Cleveland Clinic Foundation 440 204-7800
5800 Coper Foster Pk Rd W Lorain (44053) *(G-12894)*

Cleveland Clinic Foundation 216 986-4000
6801 Brecksville Rd # 10 Independence (44131) *(G-12061)*

Cleveland Clinic Foundation 216 445-6439
9500 Euclid Ave Cleveland (44195) *(G-5244)*

Cleveland Clinic Foundation 216 444-5757
10000 Cedar Ave Ste 6 Cleveland (44106) *(G-5245)*

Cleveland Clinic Foundation 216 444-2200
9500 Euclid Ave Cleveland (44195) *(G-5246)*

Cleveland Clinic Guesthouse, Cleveland *Also called Clinic Care Inc (G-5306)*

CLEVELAND CLINIC HEALTH SYSTEM, Cleveland *Also called Cleveland Clinic Foundation (G-5236)*

Cleveland Clinic Health System, North Ridgeville *Also called Cleveland Clinic Foundation (G-15327)*

CLEVELAND CLINIC HEALTH SYSTEM, Cleveland *Also called Marymount Health Care Systems (G-5919)*

Cleveland Clinic Health System, Independence *Also called Cleveland Clinic Foundation (G-12061)*

Cleveland Clinic Health System 440 449-4500
6780 Mayfield Rd Cleveland (44124) *(G-5247)*

Cleveland Clinic Health System 216 692-7555
18901 Lake Shore Blvd Cleveland (44119) *(G-5248)*

Cleveland Clinic Innovations, Cleveland *Also called Cleveland Clinic Foundation (G-5245)*

Cleveland Clinic Lerner Colleg 216 445-3853
9500 Euclid Ave Cleveland (44195) *(G-5249)*

Cleveland Clinic Star Imaging, Columbus *Also called Cleveland Clinic Foundation (G-7223)*

Cleveland Clinic Wooster, Wooster *Also called Clevelnd Clnc Hlth Systm East (G-19709)*

Cleveland Clinic Wooster, Wooster *Also called Cleveland Clinic Foundation (G-19708)*

Cleveland Clnic HSP Fincl Dept, Cleveland *Also called Cleveland Clinic Foundation (G-5239)*

Cleveland Clnic Lyndhrst Cmpus, Cleveland *Also called Cleveland Clinic Foundation (G-5242)*

Cleveland Coin Mch Exch Inc (HQ) 847 842-6310
3860 Ben Hur Ave Unit 2 Willoughby (44094) *(G-19514)*

Cleveland Concrete Cnstr Inc (PA) 216 741-3954
4823 Van Epps Rd Brooklyn Heights (44131) *(G-1868)*

Cleveland Construction Inc (PA) 440 255-8000
8620 Tyler Blvd Mentor (44060) *(G-14031)*

Cleveland Construction Inc 740 927-9000
6399 Broughton Ave Columbus (43213) *(G-7224)*

Cleveland Construction Inc 440 255-8000
5390 Curseview Dr Ste 200 Mason (45040) *(G-13563)*

Cleveland Corporate Svcs Inc 216 397-1492
2929 Clarkson Rd Cleveland (44118) *(G-5250)*

CLEVELAND CRANE RENTAL, Twinsburg *Also called Forest City Erectors Inc (G-18268)*

Cleveland Crowne Plaza Airport 440 243-4040
7230 Engle Rd Cleveland (44130) *(G-5251)*

CLEVELAND DEVELOPMENT FOUNDATI, Cleveland *Also called Greater Cleveland Partnership (G-5637)*

Cleveland Division, Cleveland *Also called Millcraft Paper Company (G-5995)*

Cleveland East Hotel LLC 216 378-9191
26300 Harvard Rd Cleveland (44122) *(G-5252)*

Cleveland Elc Illuminating Co (HQ) 800 589-3101
76 S Main St Akron (44308) *(G-143)*

Cleveland Elc Illuminating Co 440 953-7650
7755 Auburn Rd Painesville (44077) *(G-15702)*

Cleveland Electric Labs, Twinsburg *Also called Cleveland Electric Labs Co (G-18253)*

Cleveland Electric Labs Co (PA) 800 447-2207
1776 Enterprise Pkwy Twinsburg (44087) *(G-18253)*

Cleveland Emergency Med Svc, Cleveland *Also called City of Cleveland (G-5190)*

Cleveland Express Trckg Co Inc 216 348-0922
3091 Rockefeller Ave Cleveland (44115) *(G-5253)*

Cleveland Eye Clinic, Cleveland *Also called Robert Wiley MD Inc (G-6335)*

Cleveland F E S Center 216 231-3257
10701 East Blvd Cleveland (44106) *(G-5254)*

Cleveland Foundation 216 861-3810
1422 Euclid Ave Ste 1300 Cleveland (44115) *(G-5255)*

Cleveland Glass Block Inc (PA) 216 531-6363
4566 E 71st St Cleveland (44105) *(G-5256)*

Cleveland Glass Block Inc 614 252-5888
3091 E 14th Ave Columbus (43219) *(G-7225)*

Cleveland Health Network (PA) 216 986-1100
6000 W Creek Rd Ste 10 Cleveland (44131) *(G-5257)*

Cleveland Heartlab Inc 866 358-9828
6701 Carnegie Ave Ste 500 Cleveland (44103) *(G-5258)*

Cleveland Heights Gospel Choir, Cleveland *Also called Cleveland Heights Highschool (G-5259)*

Cleveland Heights Highschool 216 691-5452
3638 Mount Laurel Rd Cleveland (44121) *(G-5259)*

Cleveland Heights Medical Ctr, Cleveland Heights *Also called Kaiser Foundation Hospitals (G-6721)*

Cleveland Hts Tigers Youth Spo 216 906-4168
3686 Berkeley Rd Cleveland (44118) *(G-5260)*

CLEVELAND HUNGARIAN HERITAGE M, Cleveland *Also called Cleveland Hungarian Heritg Soc (G-5261)*

Cleveland Hungarian Heritg Soc 216 523-3900
1301 E 9th St Ste 2400 Cleveland (44114) *(G-5261)*

Cleveland Indians Baseball Com (PA) 216 420-4487
2401 Ontario St Cleveland (44115) *(G-5262)*

Cleveland Jewish Federation 216 593-2900
25701 Science Park Dr Cleveland (44122) *(G-5263)*

Cleveland Job Corps Center 216 541-2500
13421 Coit Rd Cleveland (44110) *(G-5264)*

Cleveland Jsm Inc 440 876-3050
11792 Alameda Dr Strongsville (44149) *(G-17291)*

Cleveland Magazine, Cleveland *Also called Great Lakes Publishing Company (G-5630)*

Cleveland Marble Mosaic Co (PA) 216 749-2840
4595 Hinckley Indus Pkwy Cleveland (44109) *(G-5265)*

Cleveland Metal Exchange, Twinsburg *Also called Cme Acquisitions LLC (G-18255)*

Cleveland Metro Bar Assn 216 696-3525
1301 E 9th St Cleveland (44114) *(G-5266)*

Cleveland Metroparks 440 526-4285
9445 Brecksville Rd Brecksville (44141) *(G-1776)*

Cleveland Metroparks 216 661-6500
3900 Wildlife Way Cleveland (44109) *(G-5267)*

Cleveland Metroparks 440 331-5530
4600 Valley Pkwy Cleveland (44126) *(G-5268)*

Cleveland Metroparks (PA) 216 635-3200
4101 Fulton Pkwy Cleveland (44144) *(G-5269)*

Cleveland Metroparks 216 661-6500
3900 Wildlife Way Cleveland (44109) *(G-5270)*

Cleveland Metroparks 216 739-6040
9485 Eastland Rd Strongsville (44149) *(G-17292)*

Cleveland Metroparks 440 232-7184
18753 Egbert Rd Cleveland (44146) *(G-5271)*

Cleveland Metroparks 440 572-9990
16200 Valley Pkwy Strongsville (44149) *(G-17293)*

Cleveland Metroparks 440 331-1070
4811 Valley Pkwy Cleveland (44126) *(G-5272)*

Cleveland Metroparks Zoo, Cleveland *Also called Cleveland Metroparks (G-5267)*

CLEVELAND METROPOLITAN SCHOOL, Cleveland *Also called Cleveland Municipal School Dst (G-5276)*

Cleveland Municipal School Dst 216 634-7005
3832 Ridge Rd Cleveland (44144) *(G-5273)*

Cleveland Municipal School Dst 216 432-4600
870 E 79th St Cleveland (44103) *(G-5274)*

Cleveland Municipal School Dst 216 459-4200
5100 Biddulph Ave Cleveland (44144) *(G-5275)*

Cleveland Municipal School Dst (PA) 216 838-0000
1111 Superior Ave E # 1800 Cleveland (44114) *(G-5276)*

Cleveland Municipal School Dst 216 838-8700
11801 Worthington Ave Cleveland (44111) *(G-5277)*

Cleveland Municipal School Dst 216 521-6511
10427 Detroit Ave Cleveland (44102) *(G-5278)*

Cleveland Municipal School Dst 216 459-9818
3518 W 25th St Cleveland (44109) *(G-5279)*

Cleveland Mus Schl Settlement 216 421-5806
11125 Magnolia Dr Cleveland (44106) *(G-5280)*

Cleveland Orchestra, The, Cleveland *Also called Musical Arts Association (G-6028)*

Cleveland Phlhrmonic Orchestra 216 556-1800
1158 Bates Rd Rocky River (44116) *(G-16427)*

Cleveland Pick-A-Part Inc 440 236-5031
12420 Station Rd Columbia Station (44028) *(G-6772)*

Cleveland Preterm 216 991-4577
12000 Shaker Blvd Cleveland (44120) *(G-5281)*

Cleveland Pump Repr & Svcs LLC 330 963-3100
1761 Highland Rd Twinsburg (44087) *(G-18254)*

Cleveland Quarries, Vermilion *Also called Irg Operating LLC (G-18554)*

Cleveland Racquet Club Inc 216 831-2155
29825 Chagrin Blvd Cleveland (44124) *(G-5282)*

Cleveland Real Estate Partners 216 623-1600
1801 E 9th St Ste 1700 Cleveland (44114) *(G-5283)*

Cleveland Research Company LLC 216 649-7250
1375 E 9th St Ste 2700 Cleveland (44114) *(G-5284)*

Cleveland Rest Oper Ltd Partnr 216 328-1121
6000 Fredom Sq Dr Ste 280 Cleveland (44131) *(G-5285)*

Cleveland S Hospitality LLC 216 447-1300
6200 Quarry Ln Cleveland (44131) *(G-5286)*

Cleveland Scrap, Cleveland *Also called Scrap Yard LLC (G-6381)*

CLEVELAND SIGHT CENTER, Cleveland *Also called Cleveland Soc For The Blind (G-5288)*

Cleveland Skating Club...216 791-2800
2500 Kemper Rd Cleveland (44120) ***(G-5287)***
Cleveland Soc For The Blind...216 791-8118
1909 E 101st St Cleveland (44106) ***(G-5288)***
Cleveland Southeastern Trails, Chagrin Falls *Also called Garfield Hts Coach Line Inc* ***(G-2646)***
Cleveland State University...216 687-3786
1860 E 18th St Rm 344 Cleveland (44114) ***(G-5289)***
Cleveland Sysco Inc (HQ)...216 201-3000
4747 Grayton Rd Cleveland (44135) ***(G-5290)***
Cleveland Tank & Supply Inc...216 771-8265
6560 Juniata Ave Cleveland (44103) ***(G-5291)***
Cleveland Teachers Union Inc...216 861-7676
1228 Euclid Ave Ste 1100 Cleveland (44115) ***(G-5292)***
Cleveland Thermal LLC...216 241-3636
1921 Hamilton Ave Cleveland (44114) ***(G-5293)***
Cleveland Treatment Center (PA)...216 861-4246
1127 Carnegie Ave Cleveland (44115) ***(G-5294)***
Cleveland University, Cleveland *Also called University Rdlgsts of Clveland* ***(G-6602)***
Cleveland VA Medical Research...216 791-2300
10701 East Blvd Cleveland (44106) ***(G-5295)***
Cleveland Vibrator Company, Leetonia *Also called 2828 Clinton Inc* ***(G-12517)***
Cleveland Water Department...216 664-3168
5953 Deering Ave Cleveland (44130) ***(G-5296)***
Cleveland Westlake...440 892-0333
29690 Detroit Rd Westlake (44145) ***(G-19334)***
Cleveland Wheels...440 937-6211
1160 Center Rd Avon (44011) ***(G-877)***
Cleveland Works Railway Co...216 429-7267
3175 Independence Rd Cleveland (44105) ***(G-5297)***
Cleveland Yachting Club Inc...440 333-1155
200 Yacht Club Dr Cleveland (44116) ***(G-5298)***
Cleveland-Cliffs Inc (PA)...216 694-5700
200 Public Sq Ste 3300 Cleveland (44114) ***(G-5299)***
Clevelnd Clnc Chagrn Flls Fmly...440 893-9393
551 Washington St Chagrin Falls (44022) ***(G-2642)***
Clevelnd Clnc Hlth Systm East...330 287-4830
721 E Milltown Rd Wooster (44691) ***(G-19709)***
Clevelnd Clnc Hlth Systm East...330 468-0190
863 W Aurora Rd Northfield (44067) ***(G-15376)***
Clevelnd Clnc Hlth Systm East...216 761-3300
13951 Terrace Rd Cleveland (44112) ***(G-5300)***
Clevelnd Museum of Natural His...216 231-4600
1 Wade Oval Dr Cleveland (44106) ***(G-5301)***
Clgt Solutions LLC...740 920-4795
1670 Columbus Rd Ste C Granville (43023) ***(G-11338)***
CLI Incorporated...419 668-8840
306 S Norwalk Rd W Norwalk (44857) ***(G-15429)***
Click4care Inc...614 431-3700
50 S Liberty St Ste 200 Powell (43065) ***(G-16188)***
Cliff North Consultants Inc...513 251-4930
3747 Warsaw Ave Cincinnati (45205) ***(G-3306)***
Cliffs Cleveland Foundation...216 694-5700
1100 Superior Ave E # 1500 Cleveland (44114) ***(G-5302)***
Cliffs Minnesota Minerals Co...216 694-5700
1100 Superior Ave E Cleveland (44114) ***(G-5303)***
Cliffs Resources Inc (HQ)...216 694-5700
200 Public Sq Ste 200 # 200 Cleveland (44114) ***(G-5304)***
Clifton Care Center Inc...513 530-1600
625 Probasco St Cincinnati (45220) ***(G-3307)***
Clifton Steel Company (PA)...216 662-6111
16500 Rockside Rd Maple Heights (44137) ***(G-13283)***
Cliftonlarsonallen LLP...330 497-2000
4505 Stephens Cir Nw # 200 Canton (44718) ***(G-2259)***
Cliftonlarsonallen LLP...419 244-3711
1 Seagate Ste 2650 Toledo (43604) ***(G-17665)***
Cliftonlarsonallen LLP...330 376-0100
388 S Main St Ste 403 Akron (44311) ***(G-144)***
Climaco Lefkwtz Peca Wlcox & (PA)...216 621-8484
55 Public Sq Ste 1950 Cleveland (44113) ***(G-5305)***
Clime Leasing Co LLC...614 276-4400
4301 Clime Rd N Columbus (43228) ***(G-7226)***
Clinic Care Inc...216 707-4200
9601 Euclid Ave Cleveland (44106) ***(G-5306)***
Clinic5...614 598-9960
1466 Northwest Blvd Columbus (43212) ***(G-7227)***
Clinical Health Laboratories, Euclid *Also called Zak Enterprises Ltd* ***(G-10661)***
Clinical Research Center...513 636-4412
3333 Burnet Ave Rm 3641 Cincinnati (45229) ***(G-3308)***
Clinical Specialties Inc...614 659-6580
7654 Crosswoods Dr Columbus (43235) ***(G-7228)***
Clinical Technology Inc...440 526-0160
7005 S Edgerton Rd Brecksville (44141) ***(G-1777)***
Clinicl Otcms Mngmnt Syst LLC...330 650-9900
9200 S Hills Blvd Ste 200 Broadview Heights (44147) ***(G-1828)***
Clinton Aluminum Dist Inc (PA)...330 882-6743
6270 Van Buren Rd New Franklin (44216) ***(G-14907)***
Clinton County Board of Dd...937 382-7519
4425 State Route 730 Wilmington (45177) ***(G-19609)***
Clinton County Childrens Svcs, Wilmington *Also called County of Clinton* ***(G-19619)***
Clinton County Community Actn (PA)...937 382-8365
789 N Nelson Ave Wilmington (45177) ***(G-19610)***
Clinton County Community Actn...937 382-5624
789 N Nelson Ave Wilmington (45177) ***(G-19611)***
Clinton County Dept Jobs/Fmly...937 382-0963
1025 S South St Ste 200 Wilmington (45177) ***(G-19612)***
Clinton County Head Start, Wilmington *Also called Clinton County Community Actn* ***(G-19611)***
Clinton County Highway Dept, Wilmington *Also called County of Clinton* ***(G-19620)***
Clinton Memorial Fmly Hlth Ctr, Wilmington *Also called Clinton Memorial Hospital* ***(G-19614)***
Clinton Memorial Hospital, Wilmington *Also called Rchp - Wilmington LLC* ***(G-19643)***
Clinton Memorial Hospital (PA)...937 382-6611
610 W Mn St Wilmington (45177) ***(G-19613)***
Clinton Memorial Hospital...937 383-3402
825 W Locust St Wilmington (45177) ***(G-19614)***
Clinton Memorial Hospital...937 283-2273
31 Farquhar Ave Wilmington (45177) ***(G-19615)***
Clinton-Carvell Inc...614 351-8858
1131 Harrisburg Pike Columbus (43223) ***(G-7229)***
Clintonville Beechwold Communi (PA)...614 268-3539
3222 N High St Columbus (43202) ***(G-7230)***
Clintonville Community Market, Columbus *Also called Clintonville Community Mkt* ***(G-7231)***
Clintonville Community Mkt...614 261-3663
85 E Gay St Ste 1000 Columbus (43215) ***(G-7231)***
Clippard Instrument Lab Inc (PA)...513 521-4261
7390 Colerain Ave Cincinnati (45239) ***(G-3309)***
Clippard Minimatic, Cincinnati *Also called Clippard Instrument Lab Inc* ***(G-3309)***
Clipper Magazine LLC...513 794-4100
4601 Malsbary Rd 1 Blue Ash (45242) ***(G-1529)***
Clk Multi-Family MGT LLC...614 891-0011
5811 Spring Run Dr Columbus (43229) ***(G-7232)***
Clm Pallet Recycling Inc...614 272-5761
4311 Janitrol Rd Ste 150 Columbus (43228) ***(G-7233)***
Clockwork Logistics Inc...216 587-5371
4765 E 131st St Garfield Heights (44105) ***(G-11228)***
Clopay Corporation (HQ)...800 282-2260
8585 Duke Blvd Mason (45040) ***(G-13564)***
Close To Home Health Care Ctr, Westerville *Also called Nationwide Childrens Hospital* ***(G-19188)***
Close To Home Health Care Ctr, Columbus *Also called Nationwide Childrens Hospital* ***(G-8149)***
Close To Home Health Care Ctr...614 932-9013
5675 Venture Dr Dublin (43017) ***(G-10176)***
Close To Home III...740 534-1100
617 Center St Ironton (45638) ***(G-12150)***
Closeout Distribution Inc (HQ)...614 278-6800
4900 E Dblin Granville Rd Columbus (43081) ***(G-7234)***
Clossman Catering Incorporated...513 942-7744
3725 Symmes Rd Hamilton (45015) ***(G-11581)***
Cloudroute LLC...216 373-4601
59 Alpha Park Cleveland (44143) ***(G-5307)***
Cloverleaf Bowling Center Inc...216 524-4833
5619 Brecksville Rd Cleveland (44131) ***(G-5308)***
Cloverleaf Cold Storage Co...330 833-9870
950 Cloverleaf St Se Massillon (44646) ***(G-13672)***
Cloverleaf Cold Storage Co...419 599-5015
1165 Independence Dr Napoleon (43545) ***(G-14800)***
Cloverleaf Lanes, Cleveland *Also called Cloverleaf Bowling Center Inc* ***(G-5308)***
Cloverleaf Suites, Dublin *Also called Hotel 2345 LLC* ***(G-10245)***
Cloverleaf Transport Co...419 599-5015
1165 Independence Dr Napoleon (43545) ***(G-14801)***
Clovernook Inc (PA)...513 605-4000
7025 Clovernook Ave Cincinnati (45231) ***(G-3310)***
Clovernook Center For The Bli (PA)...513 522-3860
7000 Hamilton Ave Cincinnati (45231) ***(G-3311)***
Clovernook Country Club...513 521-0333
2035 W Galbraith Rd Cincinnati (45239) ***(G-3312)***
Clovernook Hlth Care Pavilion, Cincinnati *Also called Clovernook Inc* ***(G-3310)***
Clovvr LLC...740 653-2224
1566 Monmouth Dr Ste 103 Lancaster (43130) ***(G-12382)***
Cls Facilities Management Svcs, Mentor *Also called Cls Facilities MGT Svcs Inc* ***(G-14032)***
Cls Facilities MGT Svcs Inc...440 602-4600
8061 Tyler Blvd Mentor (44060) ***(G-14032)***
Club 51 Fitness, Centerville *Also called Centerville Fitness Inc* ***(G-2623)***
Club At Hillbrook Inc...440 247-4940
14800 Hillbrook Dr Chagrin Falls (44022) ***(G-2643)***
Clubcorp Usa Inc...330 724-4444
600 Swartz Rd Akron (44319) ***(G-145)***
Clubcorp Usa Inc...216 851-2582
40 Shoreby Dr Cleveland (44108) ***(G-5309)***
Clubessential LLC (PA)...800 448-1475
4600 Mcauley Pl Ste 350 Blue Ash (45242) ***(G-1530)***
Clubessential Holdings, Blue Ash *Also called Clubessential LLC* ***(G-1530)***
Clubhouse Pub N Grub...440 884-2582
6365 Pearl Rd Cleveland (44130) ***(G-5310)***
Clubhouse, The, Cleveland *Also called Clubhouse Pub N Grub* ***(G-5310)***
Clutch Interactive, Columbus *Also called Information Control Co LLC* ***(G-7817)***
Clyde-Findlay Area Cr Un Inc (PA)...419 547-7781
1455 W Mcpherson Hwy Clyde (43410) ***(G-6742)***
Clyo Internal Medicine Inc...937 435-5857
7073 Clyo Rd Centerville (45459) ***(G-2624)***

ALPHABETIC

Cm-Gc LLC 513 527-4141
  1810 Section Rd Cincinnati (45237) (G-3313)
Cmbb LLC 937 652-2151
  417 E Water St Urbana (43078) (G-18428)
CMC Daymark Corporation 419 354-2591
  12830 S Dixie Hwy Bowling Green (43402) (G-1728)
Cmdm, Powell Also called Comprehensive Med Data MGT LLC (G-16191)
Cme Acquisitions LLC 216 464-4480
  1900 Case Pkwy S Twinsburg (44087) (G-18255)
Cme Federal Credit Union (PA) 614 224-4388
  150 E Mound St Ste 100 Columbus (43215) (G-7235)
Cmha, Cincinnati Also called Cincinnati Metro Hsing Auth (G-3254)
Cmp I Blue Ash Owner LLC 513 733-4334
  4625 Lake Forest Dr Blue Ash (45242) (G-1531)
Cmp I Columbus I Owner LLC 614 764-9393
  5175 Post Rd Dublin (43017) (G-10177)
Cmp I Columbus II Owner LLC 614 436-7070
  7411 Vantage Dr Columbus (43235) (G-7236)
Cmp I Owner-T LLC 614 764-9393
  5175 Post Rd Dublin (43017) (G-10178)
Cmp I Owner-T LLC 614 436-7070
  7411 Vantage Dr Columbus (43235) (G-7237)
Cmp I Owner-T LLC 513 733-4334
  4625 Lake Forest Dr Blue Ash (45242) (G-1532)
CMS, Avon Also called Carroll Manufacturing & Sales (G-871)
CMS, Stow Also called Custom Movers Services Inc (G-17196)
CMS Business Services LLC 740 687-0577
  416 N Mount Pleasant Ave Lancaster (43130) (G-12383)
CMS Customer Solutions, Columbus Also called Continntal Mssage Solution Inc (G-7364)
Cmta Inc 502 326-3085
  222 E 14th St Cincinnati (45202) (G-3314)
CNB Bank 419 562-7040
  105 Washington Sq Bucyrus (44820) (G-1983)
Cnd Machine, Massillon Also called C-N-D Industries Inc (G-13667)
CNG Financial Corp 513 336-7735
  7755 Montgomery Rd # 400 Cincinnati (45236) (G-3315)
CNG Financial Corporation (PA) 513 336-7735
  7755 Montgomery Rd # 400 Cincinnati (45236) (G-3316)
Cni Thl Ops LLC 937 890-6112
  7087 Miller Ln Dayton (45414) (G-9310)
Cni Thl Ops LLC 614 791-8675
  5300 Parkcenter Ave Dublin (43017) (G-10179)
Cnsld Humacare- Employee MGT (PA) 513 605-3522
  9435 Waterstone Blvd # 250 Cincinnati (45249) (G-3317)
Co Open Options Inc 513 932-0724
  19 N Mechanic St Lebanon (45036) (G-12455)
Coachs Sports Corner Inc 419 609-3737
  1130 Cleveland Rd Sandusky (44870) (G-16588)
Coact Associates Ltd 866 646-4400
  2748 Centennial Rd Toledo (43617) (G-17666)
Coad, Athens Also called Corporation For OH Appalachian (G-772)
Coal Grove Long Term Care Inc 740 532-0449
  813 1/2 Marion Pike Ironton (45638) (G-12151)
Coal Services Inc 740 795-5220
  155 Highway 7 S Powhatan Point (43942) (G-16214)
Coal Services Group, Powhatan Point Also called Coal Services Inc (G-16214)
Coast To Coast Studios LLC 614 861-9800
  7522 Blacklick Ridge Blvd Blacklick (43004) (G-1478)
Coates Car Care Inc 330 652-4180
  59 Youngstown Warren Rd Niles (44446) (G-15152)
Coaxial Communications of Sout (PA) 513 797-4400
  700 Ackerman Rd Ste 280 Columbus (43202) (G-7238)
Coba/Select Sires Inc (PA) 614 878-5333
  1224 Alton Darby Creek Rd Columbus (43228) (G-7239)
Cobalt Group Inc 614 876-4013
  4635 Trueman Blvd Ste 100 Hilliard (43026) (G-11756)
Cobblestone Square 20, Elyria Also called Regal Cinemas Inc (G-10558)
Coblentz Chocolate Co, Walnut Creek Also called Walnut Creek Chocolate
Company (G-18632)
Coblentz Distributing Inc 330 852-2888
  2641 State R 39 39 R Walnut Creek (44687) (G-18631)
Cobos Insurance Centre LLC 440 324-3732
  41436 Griswold Rd Elyria (44035) (G-10491)
Coca-Cola Bottling Co Cnsld 937 878-5000
  1000 Coca Cola Blvd Dayton (45424) (G-9311)
Cocca Development Ltd 330 729-1010
  100 Debartolo Pl Ste 400 Youngstown (44512) (G-19993)
Cochin Technologies LLC 440 941-4856
  37854 Briar Lakes Dr Avon (44011) (G-878)
Cochran Electric Inc 614 847-0035
  90 Grace Dr Powell (43065) (G-16189)
Cochran W R Industrial Elc, Powell Also called Cochran Electric Inc (G-16189)
Code One Communications Inc 614 338-0321
  2785 Castlewood Rd Columbus (43209) (G-7240)
Coffee Break Corporation 513 841-1100
  1940 Losantiville Ave Cincinnati (45237) (G-3318)
Coffman Branch, Springboro Also called Young Mens Christian Assoc (G-16990)
Coffman Family Partnership 614 864-5400
  5435 Nelsonia Pl Columbus (43213) (G-7241)
Cogent-Hmg, Canton Also called Hospitalists MGT Group LLC (G-2348)

Cohen & Company Ltd 330 743-1040
  201 E Commerce St Ste 400 Youngstown (44503) (G-19994)
Cohen & Company Ltd 330 374-1040
  3500 Embassy Pkwy Akron (44333) (G-146)
COHEN & COMPANY,LTD, Youngstown Also called Cohen & Company Ltd (G-19994)
Cohen Electronics Inc 513 425-6911
  3110 S Verity Pkwy Middletown (45044) (G-14296)
Cohen Middletown, Middletown Also called Cohen Electronics Inc (G-14296)
Cohen Todd Kite Stanford LLC 513 205-7286
  250 E 5th St Ste 2350 Cincinnati (45202) (G-3319)
Cohesion Consulting LLC 513 587-7700
  5151 Pfeiffer Rd Ste 105 Blue Ash (45242) (G-1533)
Coho Creative LLC 513 751-7500
  2331 Victory Pkwy Cincinnati (45206) (G-3320)
Coilplus Inc 614 866-1338
  5677 Alshire Rd Columbus (43232) (G-7242)
Coilplus Inc 937 322-4455
  4801 Gateway Blvd Springfield (45502) (G-17016)
Coilplus Inc 937 778-8884
  100 Steelway Dr Piqua (45356) (G-16000)
Coilplus Berwick, Piqua Also called Coilplus Inc (G-16000)
Coin World, Sidney Also called Amos Media Company (G-16758)
Coit, Cleveland Also called Miles Cleaning Services Inc (G-5992)
Coit, Cincinnati Also called Velco Inc (G-4752)
Colaianni Construction Inc 740 769-2362
  2141 State Route 150 Dillonvale (43917) (G-10062)
Colas Solutions Inc 513 272-5348
  7374 Main St Cincinnati (45244) (G-3321)
Cold Fire Decor, Maumee Also called Bpf Enterprises Ltd (G-13763)
Cold Well Banker Realty, Dayton Also called David Campbell (G-9345)
Coldliner Express Inc 614 570-0836
  4921 Vulcan Ave Columbus (43228) (G-7243)
Coldstream Country Club 513 231-3900
  400 Asbury Rd Cincinnati (45255) (G-3322)
Coldstream Logistics, Independence Also called Great Lakes Cold Logistics (G-12078)
Coldwater Ems, Coldwater Also called County of Mercer (G-6757)
Coldwell Banker, Middletown Also called 1440 Corporation Inc (G-14284)
Coldwell Banker, Ashland Also called Ward Realestate Inc (G-698)
Coldwell Banker, Newark Also called Mc Mahon Realestate Co (G-15067)
Coldwell Banker, Cleveland Also called Hunter Realty Inc (G-5722)
Coldwell Banker, Dublin Also called Nrt Commercial Utah LLC (G-10293)
Coldwell Banker, Canton Also called Tom Baier & Assoc Inc (G-2513)
Coldwell Banker, Geneva Also called Hunter Realty Inc (G-11243)
Coldwell Banker 513 321-9944
  2721 Erie Ave Cincinnati (45208) (G-3323)
Coldwell Banker First Place RE 330 726-8161
  1275 Boardman Poland Rd # 1 Poland (44514) (G-16083)
Coldwell Banker King Thompson 614 759-0808
  176 Clint Dr Pickerington (43147) (G-15952)
Coldwell Banker West Shell 513 829-4000
  9106 W Chester Towne Ctr West Chester (45069) (G-18894)
Coldwell Banker West Shell 513 922-9400
  3260 Westbourne Dr Cincinnati (45248) (G-3324)
Coldwell Banker West Shell 513 385-9300
  6700 Ruwes Oak Dr Cincinnati (45248) (G-3325)
Coldwell Banker West Shell 513 777-7900
  7311 Tylers Corner Dr West Chester (45069) (G-18895)
Coldwell Banker West Shell 513 271-7200
  7203 Wooster Pike Cincinnati (45227) (G-3326)
Coldwell Bnkr Hrtg Rltors LLC 937 304-8500
  8534 Yankee St Ste 1b Dayton (45458) (G-9312)
Coldwell Bnkr Hrtg Rltors LLC 937 748-5500
  535 N Main St Springboro (45066) (G-16966)
Coldwell Bnkr Hrtg Rltors LLC (PA) 937 434-7600
  2000 Hewitt Ave Dayton (45440) (G-9313)
Coldwell Bnkr Hrtg Rltors LLC 937 426-6060
  4139 Colonel Glenn Hwy Beavercreek Township (45431) (G-1244)
Coldwell Bnkr Hrtg Rltors LLC 937 890-2200
  356 N Dixie Dr Ste 1 Vandalia (45377) (G-18518)
Cole Selby Funeral Inc 330 856-4695
  3966 Warren Sharon Rd Vienna (44473) (G-18578)
Cole + Russell Architects Inc (PA) 513 721-8080
  600 Vine St Ste 2210 Cincinnati (45202) (G-3327)
Cole-Valley Motor Co (PA) 330 372-1665
  4111 Elm Rd Ne Warren (44483) (G-18685)
Coleman Data Solutions, Kent Also called Coleman Professional Svcs Inc (G-12223)
Coleman Professional Svcs Inc (PA) 330 673-1347
  5982 Rhodes Rd Kent (44240) (G-12223)
Coleman Professional Svcs Inc 330 628-2275
  3043 Sanitarium Rd Ste 2 Akron (44312) (G-147)
Coleman Professional Svcs Inc 330 296-8313
  3920 Lovers Ln Ravenna (44266) (G-16236)
Coleman Spohn Corporation (PA) 216 431-8070
  1775 E 45th St Cleveland (44103) (G-5311)
Colerain Dry Rdge Chldcare Ltd 513 923-4300
  3998 Dry Ridge Rd Cincinnati (45252) (G-3328)
Colerain Volunteer Fire Co 740 738-0735
  72555 Colerain Rd Dillonvale (43917) (G-10063)
Colgan-Davis Inc 419 893-6116
  1682 Lance Pointe Rd Maumee (43537) (G-13771)

Colhoc Limited Partnership..614 246-4625
200 W Nationwide Blvd Columbus (43215) **(G-7244)**

Collaborative Inc..419 242-7405
1 Seagate Park Level 118 Toledo (43604) **(G-17667)**

Collaborative Pharmacy Svcs, Miamisburg Also called Kettcor Inc **(G-14178)**

Collections Acquisition Co LLC.....................................614 944-5788
2 Easton Oval Ste 350 Columbus (43219) **(G-7245)**

Collector Wells Intl Inc...614 888-6263
6360 Huntley Rd Columbus (43229) **(G-7246)**

College Engineering/Aerospace, Columbus Also called Ohio State University **(G-8305)**

College Now Grter Clveland Inc (PA)...............................216 241-5587
50 Public Sq Cleveland (44113) **(G-5312)**

College of Dentistry, Columbus Also called Ohio State University **(G-8299)**

College of Musical Arts, Bowling Green Also called Bowling Green State University **(G-1724)**

College Park HM Hlth Care Plus, Coshocton Also called College Park Inc **(G-9002)**

College Park Inc..740 623-4607
380 Browns Ln Ste 7 Coshocton (43812) **(G-9002)**

College Polymr Science & Engrg, Akron Also called University of Akron **(G-479)**

Collier Nursing Service Inc...513 791-4357
9844 Zig Zag Rd Montgomery (45242) **(G-14594)**

Colliers International, Columbus Also called Adena Commercial LLC **(G-6798)**

Colliers International, Cincinnati Also called West Shell Commercial Inc **(G-4784)**

Colliers Turley Martin Tucker, Cincinnati Also called Cassidy Trley Coml RE Svcs Inc **(G-3130)**

Collins Assoc Tchncal Svcs Inc.....................................740 574-2320
7991 Ohio River Rd Wheelersburg (45694) **(G-19430)**

Collins Career Center..740 867-6641
11627 State Route 243 Chesapeake (45619) **(G-2728)**

Collins KAO Inc...513 948-9000
8911 Rossash Rd Cincinnati (45236) **(G-3329)**

Collins Park Golf Course, Toledo Also called American Golf Corporation **(G-17589)**

Collins Salon Inc..513 683-1700
12125 N Lebanon Rd Loveland (45140) **(G-12984)**

Colloquy, Milford Also called Epsilon **(G-14387)**

Colonial Banc Corp (PA)..937 456-5544
110 W Main St Eaton (45320) **(G-10439)**

Colonial Courier Service Inc...419 891-0922
409 Osage St Maumee (43537) **(G-13772)**

Colonial Courier Service Inc (PA)...................................419 891-0922
413 Osage St Maumee (43537) **(G-13773)**

Colonial Farms, Columbus Grove Also called Tom Langhals **(G-8942)**

Colonial Heating & Cooling Co.......................................614 837-6100
671 Windmiller Dr Pickerington (43147) **(G-15953)**

Colonial Lf Accident Insur Co..614 793-8622
5600 Blazer Pkwy Ste 300 Dublin (43017) **(G-10180)**

Colonial Manor Health Care Ctr......................................419 994-4191
747 S Mount Vernon Ave Loudonville (44842) **(G-12955)**

Colonial Nursing Home, Rockford Also called Healthcare Management Cons **(G-16416)**

Colonial Senior Services Inc..513 856-8600
100 Berkley Dr Hamilton (45013) **(G-11582)**

Colonial Senior Services Inc..513 867-4006
855 Stahlheber Rd Hamilton (45013) **(G-11583)**

Colonial Senior Services Inc..513 844-8004
855 Stahlheber Rd Hamilton (45013) **(G-11584)**

Colonial Surface Solutions, Columbus Grove Also called Carpe Diem Industries LLC **(G-8940)**

Colony Healthcare Center, The, Tallmadge Also called Communicare Health Svcs Inc **(G-17472)**

Colortone Audio Visual (PA)..216 928-1530
5401 Naiman Pkwy Ste A Cleveland (44139) **(G-5313)**

Colortone Staging & Rentals, Cleveland Also called Colortone Audio Visual **(G-5313)**

Cols Boe Custodial Services, Columbus Also called Columbus Public School Dst **(G-7307)**

Cols Health & Wellness Testing......................................614 839-2781
5050 Pine Creek Dr Ste B Westerville (43081) **(G-19238)**

Colt Enterprises Inc...567 336-6062
133 E John St Maumee (43537) **(G-13774)**

Columbia, Vandalia Also called Datwyler Sling Sltions USA Inc **(G-18519)**

Columbia Energy, Columbus Also called Columbia Gas Transmission LLC **(G-7251)**

Columbia Energy, Cambridge Also called Columbia Gas Transmission LLC **(G-2059)**

Columbia Energy, Homer Also called Columbia Gas Transmission LLC **(G-11933)**

Columbia Energy, Sugar Grove Also called Columbia Gulf Transmission LLC **(G-17373)**

Columbia Energy Group..614 460-4683
200 Civic Center Dr Columbus (43215) **(G-7247)**

Columbia Gas of Ohio Inc (HQ)......................................614 460-6000
290 W Nationwide Blvd # 114 Columbus (43215) **(G-7248)**

Columbia Gas of Ohio Inc...440 891-2458
7080 Fry Rd Cleveland (44130) **(G-5314)**

Columbia Gas of Ohio Inc...419 435-7725
1800 Broad Ave Findlay (45840) **(G-10890)**

Columbia Gas of Ohio Inc...740 264-5577
300 Luray Dr Steubenville (43953) **(G-17148)**

Columbia Gas of Ohio Inc...614 481-1000
290 W Nationwide Blvd Columbus (43215) **(G-7249)**

Columbia Gas of Ohio Inc...419 539-6046
2901 E Manhattan Blvd Toledo (43611) **(G-17668)**

Columbia Gas Transmission LLC (HQ)...........................614 460-6000
200 Cizzic Ctr Dr Columbus (43216) **(G-7250)**

Columbia Gas Transmission LLC....................................740 397-8242
8484 Columbus Rd Mount Vernon (43050) **(G-14754)**

Columbia Gas Transmission LLC....................................614 460-4704
290 W Nationwide Blvd # 114 Columbus (43215) **(G-7251)**

Columbia Gas Transmission LLC....................................740 432-1612
11296 E Pike Rd Cambridge (43725) **(G-2059)**

Columbia Gas Transmission LLC....................................740 892-2552
1608 Homer Rd Nw Homer (43027) **(G-11933)**

Columbia Gulf Transmission LLC.....................................740 746-9105
6175 Old Logan Rd Sugar Grove (43155) **(G-17373)**

Columbia Hills Country CLB Inc.....................................440 236-5051
16200 East River Rd Columbia Station (44028) **(G-6773)**

Columbia Mercy Medical Center, Canton Also called Columbia-Csa/Hs Greater Canton **(G-2260)**

Columbia Properties Lima LLC......................................419 222-0004
1920 Roschman Ave Lima (45804) **(G-12616)**

Columbia Recreation Assn..740 849-2466
5960 Fourth St East Fultonham (43735) **(G-10389)**

Columbia Staffing, Cincinnati Also called Kilgore Group Inc **(G-3868)**

Columbia-Csa/Hs Greater Canton...................................330 489-1000
1320 Mercy Dr Nw 30 Canton (44708) **(G-2260)**

Columbian Corporation Mantua.......................................330 274-2576
11845 State Route 44 Mantua (44255) **(G-13265)**

Columbiana Boiler Company LLC...................................330 482-3373
200 W Railroad St Columbiana (44408) **(G-6784)**

Columbiana Service Company LLC..................................330 482-5511
338 S Main St Columbiana (44408) **(G-6785)**

Columbs/Worthington Htg AC Inc....................................614 771-5381
6363 Fiesta Dr Columbus (43235) **(G-7252)**

Columbus & Ohio River RR Co.......................................740 622-8092
47849 Papermill Rd Coshocton (43812) **(G-9003)**

Columbus AAA Corp..614 889-2840
2502 Starford Dr Dublin (43016) **(G-10181)**

Columbus Air Center, Columbus Also called Industrial Air Centers Inc **(G-7812)**

Columbus Airport Ltd Partnr..614 475-7551
1375 N Cassady Ave Columbus (43219) **(G-7253)**

Columbus Airport Marriott, Columbus Also called Columbus Airport Ltd Partnr **(G-7253)**

Columbus Alpha Bldg, Columbus Also called Equitas Health Inc **(G-7525)**

Columbus Alzheimers Care Ctr.......................................614 459-7050
700 Jasonway Ave Columbus (43214) **(G-7254)**

Columbus Area..614 251-6561
899 E Broad St Ste 100 Columbus (43205) **(G-7255)**

Columbus Area Inc..614 252-0711
1515 E Broad St Columbus (43205) **(G-7256)**

Columbus Area Community, Columbus Also called Columbus Area Integrated Healt **(G-7257)**

Columbus Area Integrated Healt (PA)...............................614 252-0711
1515 E Broad St Columbus (43205) **(G-7257)**

Columbus Arthritis Center Inc..614 486-5200
1211 Dublin Rd Columbus (43215) **(G-7258)**

Columbus Asphalt Paving Inc...614 759-9800
1196 Technology Dr Gahanna (43230) **(G-11113)**

Columbus Association For The P (PA)...............................614 469-1045
55 E State St Columbus (43215) **(G-7259)**

Columbus Association For The P.....................................614 469-0939
39 E State St Columbus (43215) **(G-7260)**

Columbus Bar Association...614 221-4112
175 S 3rd St Ste 1100 Columbus (43215) **(G-7261)**

Columbus Behavioral Health LLC (PA)..............................732 747-1800
900 E Dublin Granville Rd Columbus (43229) **(G-7262)**

Columbus Blue Jackets, Columbus Also called Colhoc Limited Partnership **(G-7244)**

Columbus Bride..614 888-4567
34 S 3rd St Columbus (43215) **(G-7263)**

Columbus Car Audio & ACC, Columbus Also called C A E C Inc **(G-7102)**

Columbus Cardiology Cons Inc.......................................614 224-2281
85 Mcnaughten Rd Ste 300 Columbus (43213) **(G-7264)**

Columbus Cardiology Cons Inc (PA).................................614 224-2281
745 W State St Ste 750 Columbus (43222) **(G-7265)**

Columbus Childrens Hospital, Columbus Also called Nationwide Childrens Hospital **(G-8147)**

Columbus Christian Center Inc (PA).................................614 416-9673
2300 N Cassady Ave Columbus (43219) **(G-7266)**

Columbus City Trnsp Div..614 645-3182
1800 E 17th Ave Columbus (43219) **(G-7267)**

Columbus Clny For Elderly Care......................................614 891-5055
1150 Colony Dr Westerville (43081) **(G-19239)**

Columbus Club Co...614 224-4131
181 E Broad St Columbus (43215) **(G-7268)**

Columbus Coal & Lime Co (PA).......................................614 224-9241
1150 Sullivant Ave Columbus (43223) **(G-7269)**

Columbus Col-Weld Corporation......................................614 276-5303
1515 Harrisburg Pike Columbus (43223) **(G-7270)**

Columbus Cold Storage, Columbus Also called D & D Investment Co **(G-7405)**

COLUMBUS COLONY ELDERLY CARE, Westerville Also called Columbus Clny For Elderly Care **(G-19239)**

Columbus Concord Ltd Partnr..614 228-3200
35 W Spring St Columbus (43215) **(G-7271)**

Columbus Country Club..614 861-0800
4831 E Broad St Columbus (43213) **(G-7272)**

Columbus Crew, The, Columbus Also called Columbus Team Soccer LLC **(G-7319)**

A
L
P
H
A
B
E
T
I
C

Columbus Ctr For Humn Svcs Inc 614 245-8180
6227 Harlem Rd New Albany (43054) *(G-14850)*
Columbus Ctr For Humn Svcs Inc (PA) 614 641-2904
540 Industrial Mile Rd Columbus (43228) *(G-7273)*
Columbus Day Care Center 614 269-8980
3389 Westerville Rd Columbus (43224) *(G-7274)*
Columbus Developmental Center, Columbus *Also called Develpmntal Dsblties Ohio Dept (G-7441)*
Columbus Dialysis, Columbus *Also called Columbus-Rna-Davita LLC (G-7322)*
Columbus Diesel Supply Co Inc 614 445-8391
3100 Delta Marine Dr Reynoldsburg (43068) *(G-16292)*
Columbus Dispatch, Lewis Center *Also called Dispatch Printing Company (G-12541)*
Columbus Dispatch, The, Columbus *Also called Dispatch Printing Company (G-7451)*
Columbus Distributing Company (PA) 614 846-1000
4949 Freeway Dr E Columbus (43229) *(G-7275)*
Columbus Distributing Company 740 726-2211
6829 Waldo Delaware Rd Waldo (43356) *(G-18629)*
Columbus Division, Etna *Also called Terex Utilities Inc (G-10620)*
Columbus Division, Columbus *Also called Millcraft Paper Company (G-8087)*
Columbus Drywall & Insulation 614 257-0257
876 N 19th St Columbus (43219) *(G-7276)*
Columbus Drywall Inc 614 257-0257
876 N 19th St Columbus (43219) *(G-7277)*
Columbus Drywall Installation, Columbus *Also called Columbus Drywall Inc (G-7277)*
Columbus Easton Hotel LLC 614 414-1000
3999 Easton Loop W Columbus (43219) *(G-7278)*
Columbus Easton Hotel LLC (PA) 614 414-5000
3900 Chagrin Dr Fl 7 Columbus (43219) *(G-7279)*
Columbus Easton Hotel LLC 614 383-2005
3900 Morse Xing Columbus (43219) *(G-7280)*
Columbus Equipment Company (PA) 614 437-0352
2323 Performance Way Columbus (43207) *(G-7281)*
Columbus Equipment Company 513 771-3922
712 Shepherd Ave Cincinnati (45215) *(G-3330)*
Columbus Equipment Company 330 659-6681
3942 Brecksville Rd Richfield (44286) *(G-16351)*
Columbus Equipment Company 614 443-6541
2323 Performance Way Columbus (43207) *(G-7282)*
Columbus Fair Auto Auction Inc 614 497-2000
4700 Groveport Rd Obetz (43207) *(G-15525)*
Columbus Financial Gr 614 785-5100
8425 Pulsar Pl Ste 450 Columbus (43240) *(G-6809)*
Columbus Foundation 614 251-4000
1234 E Broad St Columbus (43205) *(G-7283)*
Columbus Frkln Cnty Pk 614 895-6219
4265 E Dblin Granville Rd Westerville (43081) *(G-19240)*
Columbus Frkln Cnty Pk (PA) 614 891-0700
1069 W Main St Unit B Westerville (43081) *(G-19241)*
Columbus Frkln Cnty Pk 614 891-0700
1069 W Main St Westerville (43081) *(G-19242)*
Columbus Frkln Cnty Pk 614 861-3193
7309 E Livingston Ave Reynoldsburg (43068) *(G-16293)*
Columbus GF Division, Lockbourne *Also called Amerisourcebergen Drug Corp (G-12809)*
Columbus Glass Block, Columbus *Also called Cleveland Glass Block Inc (G-7225)*
Columbus Green Cabs Inc (PA) 614 444-4444
1989 Camaro Ave Columbus (43207) *(G-7284)*
Columbus Gstrntrlogy Group Inc 614 457-1213
3820 Olentangy River Rd Columbus (43214) *(G-7285)*
Columbus Healthcare Center, Columbus *Also called Clime Leasing Co LLC (G-7226)*
Columbus Heating & Vent Co 614 274-1177
182 N Yale Ave Columbus (43222) *(G-7286)*
Columbus Hospitality 614 461-2648
775 Yard St Ste 180 Columbus (43212) *(G-7287)*
Columbus Hotel Partners 513 891-1066
4243 Hunt Rd Blue Ash (45242) *(G-1534)*
Columbus Hotel Partnership LLC 614 890-8600
2700 Corporate Exch Dr Columbus (43231) *(G-7288)*
Columbus Housing Partnr Inc 614 221-8889
3443 Agler Rd Ste 200 Columbus (43219) *(G-7289)*
Columbus Infectious Disease, Westerville *Also called Central Ohio Primary Care (G-19234)*
Columbus Jan Healthnet Svcs, Columbus *Also called Clean Innovations (G-7222)*
Columbus Jewish Federation 614 237-7686
1175 College Ave Columbus (43209) *(G-7290)*
Columbus Landmarks Foundation 614 221-0227
57 Jefferson Ave Fl 1 Columbus (43215) *(G-7291)*
Columbus Leasing LLC 614 885-1885
6500 Doubletree Ave Columbus (43229) *(G-7292)*
Columbus Life Insurance Co 513 361-6700
400 E 4th St Cincinnati (45202) *(G-3331)*
Columbus Maennerchor 614 444-3531
976 S High St Columbus (43206) *(G-7293)*
Columbus Med Assn Foundation 614 240-7420
1390 Dublin Rd Columbus (43215) *(G-7294)*
Columbus Med Partners LLC 614 538-1060
758 Communications Pkwy Columbus (43214) *(G-7295)*
Columbus Medical Association 614 240-7410
1390 Dublin Rd Columbus (43215) *(G-7296)*
Columbus Metro Federal Cr Un 614 239-0210
4000 E Broad St Columbus (43213) *(G-7297)*
Columbus Metro Federal Cr Un (PA) 614 239-0210
4000 E Broad St Columbus (43213) *(G-7298)*

Columbus Montessori Education 614 231-3790
979 S James Rd Columbus (43227) *(G-7299)*
Columbus Municipal Employees (PA) 614 224-8890
365 S 4th St Columbus (43215) *(G-7300)*
Columbus Museum of Art 614 221-6801
480 E Broad St Columbus (43215) *(G-7301)*
Columbus Neighborhood Health C 614 445-0685
1905 Parsons Ave Columbus (43207) *(G-7302)*
Columbus Obgyn, Columbus *Also called Columbus Obsttrcans Gynclgists (G-7303)*
Columbus Obsttrcans Gynclgists (PA) 614 434-2400
750 Mount Carmel Mall # 100 Columbus (43222) *(G-7303)*
Columbus Oh-16 Airport Gahanna 614 501-4770
665 Taylor Rd Gahanna (43230) *(G-11114)*
Columbus Oncology Hmtlogy Assoc, Columbus *Also called Columbus Oncology Assoc Inc (G-7304)*
Columbus Oncology Assoc Inc 614 442-3130
810 Jasonway Ave Ste A Columbus (43214) *(G-7304)*
Columbus Peterbilt, Grove City *Also called Esec Corporation (G-11430)*
Columbus Prescr Phrms Inc 614 294-1600
975 Eastwind Dr Ste 155 Westerville (43081) *(G-19243)*
Columbus Pub Schl Vhcl Maint, Columbus *Also called Columbus Public School Dst (G-7305)*
Columbus Public School Dst 614 365-5263
889 E 17th Ave Columbus (43211) *(G-7305)*
Columbus Public School Dst 614 365-5456
2500 N Cassady Ave Columbus (43219) *(G-7306)*
Columbus Public School Dst 614 365-5043
889 E 17th Ave Columbus (43211) *(G-7307)*
Columbus Public School Dst 614 365-5000
450 E Fulton St Columbus (43215) *(G-7308)*
Columbus Public School Dst 614 365-6542
4001 Appian Way Columbus (43230) *(G-7309)*
Columbus Regional Airport Auth 614 239-4000
4760 E 5th Ave Ste G Columbus (43219) *(G-7310)*
Columbus Regional Airport Auth (PA) 614 239-4015
4600 Intl Gtwy Ste 2 Columbus (43219) *(G-7311)*
Columbus Regional Office, Columbus *Also called Rehabltation Corectn Ohio Dept (G-8507)*
Columbus Rhbilitation Subacute, Columbus *Also called Astoria Place Columbus LLC (G-6985)*
Columbus SAI Motors LLC 614 851-3273
1400 Auto Mall Dr Columbus (43228) *(G-7312)*
Columbus Sail and Pwr Squadron 614 384-0245
8492 Cotter St Lewis Center (43035) *(G-12534)*
Columbus Schl Dst Bus Compound, Columbus *Also called Columbus Public School Dst (G-7309)*
Columbus Serum Company (HQ) 614 444-5211
2025 S High St Columbus (43207) *(G-7313)*
Columbus Southern Power Co, Columbus *Also called American Electric Power Co Inc (G-6917)*
Columbus Southern Power Co (HQ) 614 716-1000
1 Riverside Plz Columbus (43215) *(G-7314)*
Columbus Southern Power Co 740 829-2378
47201 County Road 273 Conesville (43811) *(G-8948)*
Columbus Speech & Hearing Ctr 614 263-5151
510 E North Broadway St Columbus (43214) *(G-7315)*
Columbus Square Bowling Palace 614 895-1122
5707 Forest Hills Blvd Columbus (43231) *(G-7316)*
Columbus Steel Erectors Inc 614 876-5050
1700 Walcutt Rd Columbus (43228) *(G-7317)*
Columbus Surgical Center LLP 614 932-9503
5005 Parkcenter Ave Dublin (43017) *(G-10182)*
Columbus Symphony Orchestra 614 228-9600
55 E State St Fl 5 Columbus (43215) *(G-7318)*
Columbus Team Soccer LLC (PA) 614 447-1301
1 Black And Gold Blvd Columbus (43211) *(G-7319)*
Columbus Urban League Inc 614 257-6300
788 Mount Vernon Ave Columbus (43203) *(G-7320)*
Columbus Window Cleaning Co, Columbus *Also called E Wynn Inc (G-7487)*
Columbus Worthington Hospitali 614 885-3334
175 Hutchinson Ave Columbus (43235) *(G-7321)*
Columbus Zoo and Aquarium, Powell *Also called Columbus Zoological Park Assn (G-16190)*
Columbus Zoological Park Assn (PA) 614 645-3400
4850 Powell Rd Powell (43065) *(G-16190)*
Columbus-Gatehouse Inn, Columbus *Also called Island Hospitality MGT LLC (G-7847)*
Columbus-Marriott NW, Dublin *Also called Dublin Hotel Ltd Liability Co (G-10208)*
Columbus-Rna-Davita LLC 614 985-1732
226 Graceland Blvd Columbus (43214) *(G-7322)*
Columbus/Worthington Htg & AC, Columbus *Also called Columbs/Worthington Htg AC Inc (G-7252)*
Com Net Inc 419 739-3100
13888 County Road 25a Wapakoneta (45895) *(G-18639)*
Combined Insurance Co Amer 614 210-6209
150 E Campus View Blvd # 230 Columbus (43235) *(G-7323)*
Combs Interior Specialties Inc 937 879-2047
475 W Funderburg Rd Fairborn (45324) *(G-10665)*
Comcast Cble Cmmunications LLC 503 372-9144
100 Welday Ave Ste A Steubenville (43953) *(G-17149)*
Comcast Corporation 740 633-3437
908 National Rd Bridgeport (43912) *(G-1815)*

2019 Harris Ohio
Services Directory

(G-0000) Company's Geographic Section entry number

Comcast Spotlight..440 617-2280
  27887 Clemens Rd Ste 3 Westlake (44145) *(G-19335)*
Comcast Spotlight Inc...216 575-8016
  3300 Lakeside Ave E Cleveland (44114) *(G-5315)*
Comdoc Inc (HQ)..330 896-2346
  3458 Massillon Rd Uniontown (44685) *(G-18363)*
Comdoc Inc..330 539-4822
  6790 Belmont Ave Girard (44420) *(G-11285)*
Comenity Servicing LLC...614 729-4000
  3095 Loyalty Cir Columbus (43219) *(G-7324)*
Comex Group, Cleveland *Also called Comex North America Inc (G-5316)*
Comex North America Inc (HQ)................................303 307-2100
  101 W Prospect Ave # 1020 Cleveland (44115) *(G-5316)*
Comey & Shepherd LLC..513 489-2100
  7870 E Kemper Rd Ste 100 Cincinnati (45249) *(G-3332)*
Comey & Shepherd LLC..513 321-4343
  2716 Observatory Ave Cincinnati (45208) *(G-3333)*
Comey & Shepherd LLC..513 231-2800
  7333 Beechmont Ave Cincinnati (45230) *(G-3334)*
Comey & Shepherd LLC..513 891-4444
  9857 Montgomery Rd Cincinnati (45242) *(G-3335)*
Comey Shepherd Realtors Cy Off, Cincinnati *Also called Sweeney Team Inc (G-4559)*
Comfort Air, Cleveland *Also called Air Comfort Systems Inc (G-4915)*
Comfort Distributors, Cincinnati *Also called Schibi Heating & Cooling Corp (G-4436)*
Comfort Healthcare...216 281-9999
  8310 Detroit Ave Cleveland (44102) *(G-5317)*
Comfort Inn, Oxford *Also called Oxford Hospitality Group Inc (G-15687)*
Comfort Inn, Mentor *Also called Alliance Hospitality Inc (G-14016)*
Comfort Inn, Chillicothe *Also called Chillicothe Motel LLC (G-2764)*
Comfort Inn, Piqua *Also called M&C Hotel Interests Inc (G-16012)*
Comfort Inn, Oregon *Also called Northtown Square Ltd Partnr (G-15601)*
Comfort Inn, Seville *Also called Son-Rise Hotels Inc (G-16691)*
Comfort Inn, Cleveland *Also called Peitro Properties Ltd Partnr (G-6190)*
Comfort Inn, Bellville *Also called Valleyview Management Co Inc (G-1392)*
Comfort Inn, Canton *Also called Canton Hotel Holdings Inc (G-2234)*
Comfort Inn, Cleveland *Also called Boulevard Motel Corp (G-5070)*
Comfort Inn...740 454-4144
  500 Monroe St Zanesville (43701) *(G-20297)*
Comfort Inn Northeast..513 683-9700
  9011 Fields Ertel Rd Cincinnati (45249) *(G-3336)*
Comfort Inns...614 885-4084
  1213 E Dblin Granville Rd Columbus (43229) *(G-7325)*
Comfort Keepers, Toledo *Also called Tky Associates LLC (G-18068)*
Comfort Keepers, Cincinnati *Also called C K of Cincinnati Inc (G-3100)*
Comfort Keepers, Hilliard *Also called Quality Life Providers LLC (G-11809)*
Comfort Keepers, Hamilton *Also called Karopa Incorporate (G-11619)*
Comfort Keepers, Springfield *Also called Sdx Home Care Operations LLC (G-17109)*
Comfort Keepers..419 229-1031
  1726 Allentown Rd Lima (45805) *(G-12617)*
Comfort Keepers..440 721-0100
  368 Blackbrook Rd Painesville (44077) *(G-15703)*
Comfort Keepers Inc...937 322-6288
  101 N Fountain Ave Springfield (45502) *(G-17017)*
Comfort Systems USA Ohio Inc (HQ)...........................440 703-1600
  7401 First Pl Ste A Bedford (44146) *(G-1273)*
Command Alkon Incorporated...................................614 799-0600
  6750 Crosby Ct Dublin (43016) *(G-10183)*
Command Carpet..330 673-7404
  1976 Tallmadge Rd Kent (44240) *(G-12224)*
Command Roofing Co...937 298-1155
  2485 Arbor Blvd Moraine (45439) *(G-14633)*
Commerce Holdings Inc..513 579-1950
  312 Elm St Ste 1150 Cincinnati (45202) *(G-3337)*
Commerce Paper Company..419 241-9101
  302 S Byrne Rd Bldg 200 Toledo (43615) *(G-17669)*
Commerce Title Agcy Youngstown...............................330 743-1171
  201 E Commerce St Youngstown (44503) *(G-19995)*
Commercial Cleaning Solutions..................................937 981-4870
  10965 State Route 138 Sw Greenfield (45123) *(G-11359)*
Commercial Comfort Systems Inc................................419 481-4444
  26610 Eckel Rd Ste 3a Perrysburg (43551) *(G-15849)*
Commercial Debt Cunseling Corp...............................614 848-9800
  445 Hutchinson Ave # 500 Columbus (43235) *(G-7326)*
Commercial Drivers, North Royalton *Also called D C Transportation Service (G-15351)*
Commercial Electric Pdts Corp (PA)............................216 241-2886
  1821 E 40th St Cleveland (44103) *(G-5318)*
Commercial Electronics Inc.......................................740 281-0180
  1294 N 21st St Newark (43055) *(G-15023)*
Commercial Hvac Inc...513 396-6100
  5240 Lester Rd Ste 200 Cincinnati (45213) *(G-3338)*
Commercial Interior Products, West Chester *Also called CIP International Inc (G-18889)*
Commercial Maintenance & Repr, Akron *Also called Ohio Maint & Renovation Inc (G-360)*
Commercial Painting Inc...614 298-9963
  530 Lkview Plz Blvd Ste F Worthington (43085) *(G-19799)*
Commercial Parts & Ser..614 221-0057
  5033 Transamerica Dr Columbus (43228) *(G-7327)*
Commercial Radiator, Columbus *Also called Skinner Diesel Services Inc (G-8649)*

Commercial Svgs Bank Millersbu (HQ).........................330 674-9015
  91 N Clay St Millersburg (44654) *(G-14466)*
Commercial Time Sharing Inc....................................330 644-3059
  2740 Cory Ave Akron (44314) *(G-148)*
Commercial Traffic Company (PA)...............................216 267-2000
  12487 Plaza Dr Cleveland (44130) *(G-5319)*
Commercial Traffic Company......................................216 267-2000
  12487 Plaza Dr Cleveland (44130) *(G-5320)*
Commercial Warehouse & Cartage...............................614 409-3901
  6295 Commerce Center Dr Groveport (43125) *(G-11502)*
Committed To Care Inc..513 245-1190
  155 Tri County Pkwy # 220 Cincinnati (45246) *(G-3339)*
Commodore Denig Post No 83....................................419 625-3274
  3615 Hayes Ave Sandusky (44870) *(G-16589)*
Commodore Motel, Port Clinton *Also called Commodore Resorts Inc (G-16103)*
Commodore Prry Inns Suites LLC...............................419 732-2645
  255 W Lakeshore Dr Port Clinton (43452) *(G-16102)*
Commodore Resorts Inc..419 285-3101
  255 W Lakeshore Dr Port Clinton (43452) *(G-16103)*
Commons of Providence..419 624-1171
  5000 Providence Dr Ste 1 Sandusky (44870) *(G-16590)*
Commonwealth Financial Svcs (PA)..............................440 449-7709
  26451 Curtiss Wright Pkwy Cleveland (44143) *(G-5321)*
Commonwealth Hotels LLC.......................................216 524-5814
  5800 Rockside Woods Blvd Cleveland (44131) *(G-5322)*
Commonwealth Hotels LLC.......................................614 790-9000
  5100 Upper Metro Pl Dublin (43017) *(G-10184)*
Commquest Services Inc...330 455-0374
  625 Cleveland Ave Nw Canton (44702) *(G-2261)*
Commsys Inc..937 220-4990
  3055 Kettering Blvd # 415 Moraine (45439) *(G-14634)*
Commu Act Comm of Fayette Cnty (PA)........................740 335-7282
  1400 Us Highway 22 Nw Wshngtn CT Hs (43160) *(G-19865)*
Commun Mer OCC Healh & Medici, Springfield *Also called Mercy Health (G-17076)*
Communi Care Inc...419 382-2200
  955 Garden Lake Pkwy Toledo (43614) *(G-17670)*
Communica Inc (PA)...419 244-7766
  31 N Erie St Toledo (43604) *(G-17671)*
Communicare, Akron *Also called Pebble Creek Cnvlscnt Ctr (G-372)*
Communicare Family of Company, Blue Ash *Also called Health Care Facility MGT LLC (G-1576)*
Communicare Health Services, Deshler *Also called East Water Leasing Co LLC (G-10057)*
Communicare Health Svcs Inc....................................440 234-0454
  49 Sheldon Rd Berea (44017) *(G-1420)*
Communicare Health Svcs Inc....................................330 726-3700
  8064 South Ave Youngstown (44512) *(G-19996)*
Communicare Health Svcs Inc....................................419 485-8307
  924 Charlies Way Montpelier (43543) *(G-14610)*
Communicare Health Svcs Inc....................................330 792-7799
  650 S Meridian Rd Youngstown (44509) *(G-19997)*
Communicare Health Svcs Inc....................................419 394-7611
  1209 Indiana Ave Saint Marys (45885) *(G-16521)*
Communicare Health Svcs Inc....................................330 454-6508
  3015 17th St Nw Canton (44708) *(G-2262)*
Communicare Health Svcs Inc....................................937 399-9217
  2615 Derr Rd Springfield (45503) *(G-17018)*
Communicare Health Svcs Inc....................................330 792-5511
  2958 Canfield Rd Youngstown (44511) *(G-19998)*
Communicare Health Svcs Inc....................................877 366-5306
  135 Reichart Ave Wintersville (43953) *(G-19669)*
Communicare Health Svcs Inc....................................330 454-2152
  3015 17th St Nw Canton (44708) *(G-2263)*
Communicare Health Svcs Inc (PA)..............................513 530-1654
  4700 Ashwood Dr Ste 200 Blue Ash (45241) *(G-1535)*
Communicare Health Svcs Inc....................................740 264-1155
  135 Reichart Ave Steubenville (43953) *(G-17150)*
Communicare Health Svcs Inc....................................330 630-9780
  563 Colony Park Dr Tallmadge (44278) *(G-17472)*
Communicare of Clifton, Cincinnati *Also called Clifton Care Center Inc (G-3307)*
Communication Svc For Deaf Inc................................937 299-0917
  2448 W Dorothy Ln Moraine (45439) *(G-14635)*
Communication Svcs For Deaf, Moraine *Also called Communication Svc For Deaf Inc (G-14635)*
Communications III Inc (PA).....................................614 901-7720
  921 Eastwind Dr Ste 104 Westerville (43081) *(G-19244)*
Communiction/Journalism, Columbus *Also called Ohio State University (G-8322)*
Communities In Schools..614 268-2472
  6500 Busch Blvd Ste 105 Columbus (43229) *(G-7328)*
Community Action, Lisbon *Also called County of Columbiana (G-12798)*
Community Action Against Addic.................................216 881-0765
  5209 Euclid Ave Cleveland (44103) *(G-5323)*
COMMUNITY ACTION AKRON SUMMIT, Akron *Also called Akron Summit Cmnty Action Agcy (G-58)*
Community Action Columbiana CT (PA)..........................330 424-7221
  7880 Lincole Pl Lisbon (44432) *(G-12796)*
Community Action Columbiana CT.................................330 385-7251
  134 E 4th St East Liverpool (43920) *(G-10400)*
Community Action Comm Blmont C, Saint Clairsville *Also called Community Action Comsn Belmont (G-16483)*

Community Action Comm Pike CNT (PA)......740 289-2371
941 Market St Piketon (45661) ***(G-15973)***
Community Action Comm Pike CNT......740 961-4011
621 Broadway St Portsmouth (45662) ***(G-16131)***
Community Action Comm Pike CNT......740 286-2826
14590 State Route 93 Jackson (45640) ***(G-12172)***
Community Action Comm Pike CNT......740 947-7726
227 Valley View Dr Waverly (45690) ***(G-18817)***
Community Action Commission, Findlay *Also called Hancock Hardin Wyandot Putnam* ***(G-10918)***
Community Action Commission (PA)......419 626-6540
908 Seavers Way Sandusky (44870) ***(G-16591)***
Community Action Comsn Belmont (PA)......740 695-0293
153 1/2 W Main St Saint Clairsville (43950) ***(G-16483)***
Community Action Comsn Belmont......740 676-0800
4129 Noble St Bellaire (43906) ***(G-1332)***
Community Action Organization (PA)......740 354-7541
433 3rd St Portsmouth (45662) ***(G-16132)***
Community Action Program Comm (PA)......740 653-1711
1743 E Main St Lancaster (43130) ***(G-12384)***
Community Action Program Corp (PA)......740 373-3745
218 Putnam St Marietta (45750) ***(G-13319)***
Community Action Program Corp......740 373-6016
205 Phillips St Marietta (45750) ***(G-13320)***
Community Action Program Inc......937 382-0225
789 N Nelson Ave Wilmington (45177) ***(G-19616)***
Community Action-Wayne/Medina (PA)......330 264-8677
905 Pittsburg Ave Wooster (44691) ***(G-19710)***
Community Ambulance Service......740 454-6800
952 Linden Ave Zanesville (43701) ***(G-20298)***
Community and Rural Hlth Svcs (PA)......419 334-8943
2221 Hayes Ave Fremont (43420) ***(G-11063)***
Community Assesment and Treatm (PA)......216 441-0200
8411 Broadway Ave Cleveland (44105) ***(G-5324)***
Community Assisted Living Inc......740 653-2575
500 N Pierce Ave Lancaster (43130) ***(G-12385)***
Community Behavioral Hlth Ctr, Cleveland *Also called Chattree and Associates Inc* ***(G-5172)***
Community Behavioral Hlth Inc......513 887-8500
824 S Martin Luther King Hamilton (45011) ***(G-11585)***
Community Bus Services Inc......330 369-6060
1976 Niles Rd Se Warren (44484) ***(G-18686)***
Community Care Amblance Netwrk (PA)......440 992-1401
115 E 24th St Ashtabula (44004) ***(G-728)***
Community Care Hospice......937 382-5400
1669 Rombach Ave Wilmington (45177) ***(G-19617)***
Community Caregivers......330 725-9800
230 Quadral Dr Ste D Wadsworth (44281) ***(G-18593)***
Community Caregivers......330 533-3427
888 Boardman Canfield Rd D Youngstown (44512) ***(G-19999)***
Community Center, Athens *Also called Parks Recreation Athens* ***(G-801)***
Community Center......330 746-7721
1344 5th Ave Youngstown (44504) ***(G-20000)***
Community Choice Financial Inc......440 602-9922
34302 Euclid Ave Unit 7 Willoughby (44094) ***(G-19515)***
Community Choice Financial Inc (PA)......614 798-5900
6785 Bobcat Way Ste 200 Dublin (43016) ***(G-10185)***
Community Choice Home Care......740 574-9900
7318 Ohio River Rd Wheelersburg (45694) ***(G-19431)***
Community Concepts & Options, Mason *Also called Community Concepts Inc* ***(G-13565)***
Community Concepts Inc (PA)......513 398-8181
6699 Tri Way Dr Mason (45040) ***(G-13565)***
Community Correctional Center, Lebanon *Also called Talbert House* ***(G-12509)***
Community Corrections Assn (PA)......330 744-5143
1608 Market St Youngstown (44507) ***(G-20001)***
Community Counseling Services......419 468-8211
2458 Stetzer Rd Bucyrus (44820) ***(G-1984)***
Community Counsing Ctr Ashtabu (PA)......440 998-4210
2801 C Ct Unit 2 Ashtabula (44004) ***(G-729)***
Community Crime Patrol......614 247-1765
248 E 11th Ave Columbus (43201) ***(G-7329)***
Community Crrctions Facilities, Youngstown *Also called Community Corrections Assn* ***(G-20001)***
Community Dev For All People......614 445-7342
946 Parsons Ave Columbus (43206) ***(G-7330)***
Community Dialysis Center......216 295-7000
11717 Euclid Ave Cleveland (44106) ***(G-5325)***
Community Dialysis Center......216 229-6170
11717 Euclid Ave Cleveland (44106) ***(G-5326)***
Community Dialysis Center......330 609-0370
1950 Niles Cortland Rd Ne # 12 Warren (44484) ***(G-18687)***
Community Dialysis Center......216 295-7000
18720 Chagrin Blvd Shaker Heights (44122) ***(G-16706)***
Community Dialysis Ctr Mentor......440 255-5999
8900 Tyler Blvd Mentor (44060) ***(G-14033)***
Community Drug Board Inc (PA)......330 315-5590
725 E Market St Akron (44305) ***(G-149)***
Community Drug Board Inc......330 996-5114
380 S Portage Path Akron (44320) ***(G-150)***
Community Education Ctrs Inc......330 424-4065
8473 County Home Rd Lisbon (44432) ***(G-12797)***
Community Employment Services, Newark *Also called Licking County Board of Mrdd* ***(G-15053)***
Community Emplyment Svcs WD Ln, Bowling Green *Also called Wood County Ohio* ***(G-1758)***
Community Emrgcy Med Svcs Ohio......614 751-6651
3699 Paragon Dr Columbus (43228) ***(G-7331)***
Community Ems District......330 527-4100
10804 Forest St Garrettsville (44231) ***(G-11229)***
Community Hbilitation Svcs Inc (PA)......234 334-4288
493 Canton Rd Akron (44312) ***(G-151)***
Community Health & Wellness PA......937 599-1411
4879 Us Rt 68 S West Liberty (43357) ***(G-19118)***
Community Health Centers Ohio......216 831-1494
3355 Richmond Rd Ste 225a Beachwood (44122) ***(G-1047)***
Community Health Partners Regi (HQ)......440 960-4000
3700 Kolbe Rd Lorain (44053) ***(G-12895)***
Community Health Ptnrs Reg Fou (HQ)......440 960-4000
3700 Kolbe Rd Lorain (44053) ***(G-12896)***
Community Health Services, Fremont *Also called Community and Rural Hlth Svcs* ***(G-11063)***
Community Health Systems Inc......330 841-9011
1350 E Market St Warren (44483) ***(G-18688)***
Community Hlth Prfssionals Inc......419 634-7443
1200 S Main St Ada (45810) ***(G-3)***
Community Hlth Prfssionals Inc......419 445-5128
230 Westfield Dr Archbold (43502) ***(G-628)***
Community Hlth Prfssionals Inc (PA)......419 238-9223
1159 Westwood Dr Van Wert (45891) ***(G-18475)***
Community Hlth Prfssionals Inc......419 399-4708
250 Dooley Dr Ste A Paulding (45879) ***(G-15791)***
Community Hlth Prfssionals Inc......419 991-1822
3719 Shawnee Rd Lima (45806) ***(G-12789)***
Community Hlth Prfssionals Inc......419 586-1999
816 Pro Dr Celina (45822) ***(G-2589)***
Community Hlth Prfssionals Inc......419 586-6266
816 Pro Dr Celina (45822) ***(G-2590)***
Community Hlth Prfssionals Inc......419 695-8101
1500 E 5th St Delphos (45833) ***(G-10022)***
Community Hlth Ptnr Reg Hlth S......440 960-4000
3700 Kolbe Rd Lorain (44053) ***(G-12897)***
Community Home Care......330 971-7011
1900 23rd St Cuyahoga Falls (44223) ***(G-9084)***
Community Home Health, Austintown *Also called Chcc Home Health Care* ***(G-857)***
COMMUNITY HOSPICE, New Philadelphia *Also called Hospice Tuscarawas County Inc* ***(G-14965)***
Community Hospital of Bedford......440 735-3900
44 Blaine Ave Bedford (44146) ***(G-1274)***
Community Hospitals......419 636-1131
433 W High St Bryan (43506) ***(G-1954)***
Community Hsing Netwrk Dev Co......614 487-6700
1680 Watermark Dr Columbus (43215) ***(G-7332)***
Community Hsptals Wllness Ctrs......419 485-3154
909 E Snyder Ave Montpelier (43543) ***(G-14611)***
Community Hsptals Wllness Ctrs......419 445-2015
121 Westfield Dr Ste 1 Archbold (43502) ***(G-629)***
Community Hsptals Wllness Ctrs (PA)......419 636-1131
433 W High St Bryan (43506) ***(G-1955)***
Community Improvement Corp......440 466-4675
44 N Forest St Geneva (44041) ***(G-11238)***
Community Imprv Corp Nble Cnty......740 509-0248
44523 Marietta Rd Caldwell (43724) ***(G-2037)***
Community Insurance Company......859 282-7888
1351 Wm Howard Taft Cincinnati (45206) ***(G-3340)***
Community Invstors Bancorp Inc......419 562-7055
119 S Sandusky Ave Bucyrus (44820) ***(G-1985)***
Community Isp Inc......419 867-6060
3035 Moffat Rd Toledo (43615) ***(G-17672)***
Community Legal Aid Services......330 725-1231
120 W Washington St 2c Medina (44256) ***(G-13921)***
Community Legal Aid Services (PA)......330 535-4191
50 S Main St Ste 800 Akron (44308) ***(G-152)***
Community Living Experiences......614 588-0320
2939 Donnylane Blvd Columbus (43235) ***(G-7333)***
Community Management Corp......513 761-6339
375 W Galbraith Rd Cincinnati (45215) ***(G-3341)***
Community Medical Center, Celina *Also called Mercer Cnty Joint Townshp Hosp* ***(G-2601)***
Community Medicine, Columbus *Also called Ohiohealth Corporation* ***(G-8359)***
Community Memorial Hospital (PA)......419 542-6692
208 Columbus St Hicksville (43526) ***(G-11726)***
Community Mental Health Svc (PA)......740 695-9344
68353 Bannock Rd Saint Clairsville (43950) ***(G-16484)***
Community Mental Health Svcs, Saint Clairsville *Also called Community Mental Health Svc* ***(G-16484)***
Community Mental Healthcare (PA)......330 343-1811
201 Hospital Dr Dover (44622) ***(G-10070)***
Community Mercy Hlth Partners......937 653-5432
906 Scioto St Urbana (43078) ***(G-18429)***
Community Mercy Hlth Partners (HQ)......937 523-6670
100 Medical Center Dr Springfield (45504) ***(G-17019)***
COMMUNITY NETWORK THE, Xenia *Also called Tcn Behavioral Health Svcs Inc* ***(G-19927)***
Community Prpts Ohio III LLC......614 253-0984
42 N 17th St Columbus (43203) ***(G-7334)***
Community Prpts Ohio MGT Svcs......614 253-0984
910 E Broad St Columbus (43205) ***(G-7335)***

Community Re-Entry Inc 216 696-2717
4515 Superior Ave Cleveland (44103) (G-5327)
Community Refugee & Immigation 614 235-5747
1925 E Dublin Granville R Columbus (43229) (G-7336)
Community Services Inc 937 667-8631
3 E Main St Tipp City (45371) (G-17553)
COMMUNITY SERVICES OF STARK CO, Canton Also called Commquest Services
Inc (G-2261)
Community Shelter Board 614 221-9195
355 E Campus View Blvd # 250 Columbus (43235) (G-7337)
Community Skilled Health Care 330 373-1160
1320 Mahoning Ave Nw Warren (44483) (G-18689)
Community Solutions Assn 330 394-9090
320 High St Ne Warren (44481) (G-18690)
Community Srgl Sply Toms Rvr 614 307-2975
3823 Twin Creeks Dr Columbus (43204) (G-7338)
Community Srgl Sply Toms Rvr 216 475-8440
14500 Broadway Ave Cleveland (44125) (G-5328)
Community Support Services Inc (PA) 330 253-9388
150 Cross St Akron (44311) (G-153)
Community Support Services Inc 330 253-9675
150 Cross St Akron (44311) (G-154)
Community Support Services Inc 330 733-6203
403 Canton Rd Akron (44312) (G-155)
Community Supports Services, Fairfield Also called Butler County Board of
Develop (G-10703)
Commutair, North Olmsted Also called Champlain Enterprises LLC (G-15280)
Como Inc 614 830-2666
8670 Hill Rd S Pickerington (43147) (G-15954)
Compak Inc 330 345-5666
1130 Riffel Rd Wooster (44691) (G-19711)
Compak Inc 419 207-8888
605 Westlake Dr Ashland (44805) (G-668)
Companions of Ashland LLC (PA) 419 281-2273
1241 E Main St Ashland (44805) (G-669)
Company Inc 216 431-2334
4125 Payne Ave Cleveland (44103) (G-5329)
Compass, Toledo Also called Comprehensive Addiction Svc Sy (G-17674)
Compass Community Health 740 355-7102
1634 11th St Portsmouth (45662) (G-16133)
Compass Construction Inc 614 761-7800
7670 Fishel Dr S Dublin (43016) (G-10186)
Compass Corp For Recovery Svcs 419 241-8827
2005 Ashland Ave Toledo (43620) (G-17673)
Compass Family and Cmnty Svcs (PA) 330 743-9275
535 Marmion Ave Youngstown (44502) (G-20002)
Compass Family and Cmnty Svcs 330 743-9275
284 Broadway Ave Youngstown (44504) (G-20003)
Compass Health Brands Corp (PA) 800 947-1728
6753 Engle Rd Ste A Middleburg Heights (44130) (G-14250)
Compass Packaging LLC 330 274-2001
10585 Main St Mantua (44255) (G-13266)
Compass Professional Svcs LLC 216 705-2233
175 S 3rd St Ste 200 Columbus (43215) (G-7339)
Compass Self Storage LLC (PA) 216 458-0670
20445 Emerald Pkwy Cleveland (44135) (G-5330)
Compass Systems & Sales LLC 330 733-2111
5185 New Haven Cir Norton (44203) (G-15418)
Compassionate In Home Care 614 888-5683
7100 N High St Ste 200 Worthington (43085) (G-19800)
Compco Land Company (HQ) 330 482-0200
85 E Hylda Ave Youngstown (44507) (G-20004)
Compdrug (PA) 614 224-4506
547 E 11th Ave Columbus (43211) (G-7340)
Compel Fitness LLC 216 965-5694
10711 Princeton Pike Cincinnati (45246) (G-3342)
Compensation Programs of Ohio 330 652-9821
33 Fitch Blvd Youngstown (44515) (G-20005)
Competitive Interiors Inc 330 297-1281
625 Enterprise Pkwy Ravenna (44266) (G-16237)
Competitive Transportation 419 529-5300
7086 State Route 546 Bellville (44813) (G-1388)
Competitor Swim Products Inc 800 888-7946
5310 Career Ct Columbus (43213) (G-7341)
Complements, Cleveland Also called Amerimark Holdings LLC (G-4969)
Complete Building Maint LLC 513 235-7511
3629 Wabash Ave Cincinnati (45207) (G-3343)
Complete General Cnstr Co (PA) 614 258-9515
1221 E 5th Ave Columbus (43219) (G-7342)
Complete Home Care, Massillon Also called Health Services Inc (G-13694)
Complete Mechanical Svcs LLC 513 489-3080
11399 Grooms Rd Blue Ash (45242) (G-1536)
Complete Qlty Trnsp Sltons LLC 513 914-4882
3055 Blue Rock Rd Ste T Cincinnati (45239) (G-3344)
Complete Services Inc (PA) 513 770-5575
6345 Castle Dr Mason (45040) (G-13566)
Compliance Testing, Ravenna Also called Smithers Rapra Inc (G-16268)
Compliant Healthcare Tech LLC (PA) 216 255-9607
7123 Pearl Rd Ste 305 Cleveland (44130) (G-5331)
Compmanagement Inc (HQ) 614 376-5300
6377 Emerald Pkwy Dublin (43016) (G-10187)

Compmanagement Health Systems 614 766-5223
6377 Emerald Pkwy Dublin (43016) (G-10188)
Composite Tech Amer Inc 330 562-5201
25201 Chagrin Blvd # 360 Cleveland (44122) (G-5332)
Comprehensive Addiction Svc Sy 419 241-8827
2005 Ashland Ave Toledo (43620) (G-17674)
Comprehensive Behavioral Hlth (PA) 330 797-4050
104 Javit Ct Ste A Youngstown (44515) (G-20006)
Comprehensive Cmnty Child Care (PA) 513 221-0033
2100 Sherman Ave Ste 300 Cincinnati (45212) (G-3345)
Comprehensive Counseling Svc 513 424-0921
1659 S Breiel Blvd Ste A Middletown (45044) (G-14297)
Comprehensive Health Care (HQ) 440 329-7500
630 E River St Elyria (44035) (G-10492)
Comprehensive Health Care Inc 419 238-7777
140 Fox Rd Ste 402 Van Wert (45891) (G-18476)
Comprehensive Hr Solutions LLC 513 771-2277
1 Sheakley Way Cincinnati (45246) (G-3346)
Comprehensive Logistics Co Inc 330 233-0805
5520 Chevrolet Blvd Parma (44130) (G-15762)
Comprehensive Logistics Co Inc 440 934-0870
5401 Baumhart Rd Lorain (44053) (G-12898)
Comprehensive Logistics Co Inc 330 793-0504
365 Victoria Rd Youngstown (44515) (G-20007)
Comprehensive Logistics Co Inc 330 233-2627
1200 Chester Indus Pkwy Avon Lake (44012) (G-914)
Comprehensive Logistics Co Inc (PA) 800 734-0372
4944 Belmont Ave Ste 202 Youngstown (44505) (G-20008)
Comprehensive Managed Care Sys 513 533-0021
3380 Erie Ave Cincinnati (45208) (G-3347)
Comprehensive Med Data MGT LLC 614 717-9840
9980 Brewster Ln Ste 100 Powell (43065) (G-16191)
Comprehensive Pediatrics 440 835-8270
2001 Crocker Rd Ste 600 Westlake (44145) (G-19336)
Comprehensive Services Inc 614 442-0664
1555 Bethel Rd Columbus (43220) (G-7343)
Comprensive Health Network, Greenville Also called CHN Inc - Adult Day Care (G-11370)
Comproducts Inc (PA) 614 276-5552
1740 Harmon Ave Ste F Columbus (43223) (G-7344)
Comptech Computer Tech Inc 937 228-2667
7777 Washington Village D Dayton (45459) (G-9314)
Compton Metal Products Inc 937 382-2403
416 Steele Rd Wilmington (45177) (G-19618)
Compunet Clinical Labs, Moraine Also called Compunet Clinical Labs LLC (G-14636)
Compunet Clinical Labs LLC 937 427-2655
75 Sylvania Dr Beavercreek (45440) (G-1211)
Compunet Clinical Labs LLC 937 342-0015
2100 Emmanuel Way Ste C Springfield (45502) (G-17020)
Compunet Clinical Labs LLC (HQ) 937 296-0844
2308 Sandridge Dr Moraine (45439) (G-14636)
Compunet Clinical Labs LLC 937 208-3555
2508 Sandride Dr Dayton (45439) (G-9315)
Computer Helper Publishing 614 939-9094
450 Beecher Rd Columbus (43230) (G-7345)
Computer Sciences Corporation 937 904-5113
2435 5th St Bldg 676 Dayton (45433) (G-9166)
Computer Sciences Corporation 614 801-2343
3940 Gantz Rd Ste F Grove City (43123) (G-11421)
Computer Services, Athens Also called Ohio University (G-795)
Computer Solutions, Youngstown Also called GBS Corp (G-20046)
Comresource Inc 614 221-6348
1159 Dublin Rd Ste 200 Columbus (43215) (G-7346)
Coms Interactive, Broadview Heights Also called Clinicl Otcms Mngmnt Syst LLC (G-1828)
Comtech Global Inc 614 796-1148
355 E Campus View Blvd # 195 Columbus (43235) (G-7347)
COMTEX, Columbus Also called Central Ohio Medical Textiles (G-7159)
Comtron Professional Cons, Reynoldsburg Also called Kristi Britton (G-16315)
Comunibanc Corp (PA) 419 599-1065
122 E Washington St Napoleon (43545) (G-14802)
Con-AG, Saint Marys Also called Conag Inc (G-16522)
Conag Inc 419 394-8870
16672 County Road 66a Saint Marys (45885) (G-16522)
Concast Metal Products Co 440 965-4455
14315 State Route 113 Wakeman (44889) (G-18620)
Concentrix Cvg Corporation (HQ) 513 723-7000
201 E 4th St Cincinnati (45202) (G-3348)
Concept Freight Service Inc 330 784-1134
4386 Point Comfort Dr New Franklin (44319) (G-14908)
Concept Rehab Inc (PA) 419 843-6002
7150 Granite Cir Ste 200 Toledo (43617) (G-17675)
Concepts In Community Living (PA) 740 393-0055
700 Wooster Rd Mount Vernon (43050) (G-14755)
Conci, Columbus Also called Central Ohio Nutrition Center (G-7160)
Concord 614 882-9338
700 Brooksedge Blvd Westerville (43081) (G-19245)
Concord Biosciences LLC 440 357-3200
10845 Wellness Way Painesville (44077) (G-15704)
Concord Care Center Cortland, Cortland Also called Continent Hlth Co Cortland
LLC (G-8986)
Concord Care Center of Toledo 419 385-6616
3121 Glanzman Rd Toledo (43614) (G-17676)

ALPHABETIC

CONCORD COUNSELING SERVICES, Westerville *Also called Concord* ***(G-19245)***
Concord Dayton Hotel II LLC....937 223-1000
1414 S Patterson Blvd Dayton (45409) ***(G-9316)***
Concord Express Inc (HQ)....718 656-7821
5905 Green Pointe Dr S D Groveport (43125) ***(G-11503)***
Concord Hamiltonian Rvrfrnt Ho....513 896-6200
1 Riverfront Plz Hamilton (45011) ***(G-11586)***
Concord Health Care Inc (PA)....330 759-2357
202 Churchill Hubbard Rd Youngstown (44505) ***(G-20009)***
Concord Health Care Inc....419 626-5373
620 W Strub Rd Sandusky (44870) ***(G-16592)***
Concord Health Center Hartford, Fowler *Also called Meadowbrook Manor of Hartford* ***(G-11016)***
Concord Hlth Rhabilitation Ctr....740 574-8441
1242 Crescent Dr Wheelersburg (45694) ***(G-19432)***
Concord Testa Hotel Assoc LLC....330 252-9228
41 Furnace St Akron (44308) ***(G-156)***
Concord Therapy Group, Alliance *Also called Concorde Therapy Group Inc* ***(G-527)***
Concorde Therapy Group Inc (PA)....330 493-4210
4645 Belpar St Nw Canton (44718) ***(G-2264)***
Concorde Therapy Group Inc....330 478-1752
5156 Whipple Ave Nw Canton (44718) ***(G-2265)***
Concorde Therapy Group Inc....330 493-4210
513 E Main St Louisville (44641) ***(G-12963)***
Concorde Therapy Group Inc....330 493-4210
2484 W State St Alliance (44601) ***(G-527)***
Concordia Care....216 791-3580
2373 Euclid Heights Blvd Cleveland (44106) ***(G-5333)***
Concordia Properties LLC....513 671-0120
11700 Princeton Pike B213 Cincinnati (45246) ***(G-3349)***
Concordnce Hlthcare Sltons LLC (PA)....419 455-2153
85 Shaffer Park Dr Tiffin (44883) ***(G-17512)***
Concrete Coring Company Inc....937 864-7325
400 E Main St Enon (45323) ***(G-10607)***
Coney Island Inc....513 232-8230
6201 Kellogg Ave Cincinnati (45230) ***(G-3350)***
Conger Construction Group Inc....513 932-1206
2020 Mckinley Blvd Lebanon (45036) ***(G-12456)***
Congregate Living of America (PA)....513 899-2801
463 E Pike St Morrow (45152) ***(G-14716)***
Congregate Living of America....937 393-6700
141 Willetsville Pike Hillsboro (45133) ***(G-11834)***
Congress Lake Club Company....330 877-9318
1 East Dr Ne Hartville (44632) ***(G-11684)***
Congressional Bank....614 441-9230
4343 Easton Cmns Ste 150 Columbus (43219) ***(G-7348)***
Conie Construction Company, Columbus *Also called Jack Conie & Sons Corp* ***(G-7852)***
Connaissance Consulting LLC....614 289-5200
4071 Easton Way Columbus (43219) ***(G-7349)***
Conneaut Senior Services, Conneaut *Also called Ashtabula County Commnty Actn* ***(G-8949)***
Conneaut Telephone Company....440 593-7140
224 State St Conneaut (44030) ***(G-8953)***
Connect Call Global LLC....513 348-1800
7560 Central Parke Blvd Mason (45040) ***(G-13567)***
CONNECTIONS, Beachwood *Also called North East Ohio Health Svcs* ***(G-1086)***
Connectivity Systems Inc (PA)....740 420-5400
8120 State Route 138 Williamsport (43164) ***(G-19498)***
Connie Parks (PA)....330 759-8334
4504 Logan Way Ste B Hubbard (44425) ***(G-11943)***
Connor Concepts Inc....937 291-1661
7727 Washington Vlg Dr Dayton (45459) ***(G-9317)***
Connor Evans Hafenstein LLP....614 464-2025
2000 Henderson Rd Ste 460 Columbus (43220) ***(G-7350)***
Connor Group A RE Inv Firm LLC....937 434-3095
10510 Springboro Pike Miamisburg (45342) ***(G-14154)***
Conrad's Total Car Care, Cleveland *Also called Conrads Tire Service Inc* ***(G-5334)***
Conrads Tire Service Inc (PA)....216 941-3333
14577 Lorain Ave Cleveland (44111) ***(G-5334)***
Conserv For Cyhg Vlly Nat Prk....330 657-2909
1403 W Hines Hill Rd Peninsula (44264) ***(G-15811)***
Consoldated Graphics Group Inc....216 881-9191
1614 E 40th St Cleveland (44103) ***(G-5335)***
Consolidated Care Inc....937 465-8065
1521 N Detroit St West Liberty (43357) ***(G-19119)***
Consolidated Care Inc (PA)....937 465-8065
1521 N Detroit St West Liberty (43357) ***(G-19120)***
Consolidated Communications....330 896-3905
7015 Sunset Strip Ave Nw Canton (44720) ***(G-2266)***
Consolidated Elec Distrs Inc....614 445-8871
2101 S High St Columbus (43207) ***(G-7351)***
Consolidated Electric Coop....740 363-2641
680 Sunbury Rd Delaware (43015) ***(G-9961)***
Consolidated Electric Coop Inc....419 947-3055
5255 State Route 95 Mount Gilead (43338) ***(G-14725)***
Consolidated Grain & Barge Co....419 785-1941
11859 Krouse Rd Defiance (43512) ***(G-9907)***
Consolidated Grain & Barge Co....513 941-4805
4837 River Rd Cincinnati (45233) ***(G-3351)***
Consolidated Learning Ctrs Inc....614 791-0050
7100 Muirfield Dr Ste 200 Dublin (43017) ***(G-10189)***
Consolidated Lighting Svcs Co, Cincinnati *Also called Eco Engineering Inc* ***(G-3483)***
Consolidated Rail Corporation....440 786-3014
401 Ledge Rd Macedonia (44056) ***(G-13066)***
Consolidated Solutions, Cleveland *Also called Consoldated Graphics Group Inc* ***(G-5335)***
Consolidated Utilities, Cincinnati *Also called University of Cincinnati* ***(G-4719)***
Consortium For Hlthy & Immunzd....216 201-2001
10840 Barrington Blvd Cleveland (44130) ***(G-5336)***
Constant Aviation LLC....216 261-7119
355 Richmond Rd Cleveland (44143) ***(G-5337)***
Constant Aviation LLC (PA)....800 440-9004
18601 Cleveland Pkwy Dr 1b Cleveland (44135) ***(G-5338)***
Constellations Enterprise LLC (PA)....330 740-8208
1775 Logan Ave Youngstown (44505) ***(G-20010)***
Constructconnect, Cincinnati *Also called Isqft Inc* ***(G-3788)***
Construction Biddingcom LLC....440 716-4087
31269 Bradley Rd North Olmsted (44070) ***(G-15284)***
Construction Eqp & Sup Ltd....419 625-7192
3015 Old Railroad Rd Sandusky (44870) ***(G-16593)***
Construction First, Columbus *Also called Construction One Inc* ***(G-7353)***
Construction Labor Contrs LLC....614 932-9937
6155 Huntley Rd Ste G Columbus (43229) ***(G-7352)***
Construction One Inc....614 961-1140
101 E Town St Ste 401 Columbus (43215) ***(G-7353)***
Construction Resources Inc....440 248-9800
33900 Station St Cleveland (44139) ***(G-5339)***
Construction Systems Inc (PA)....614 252-0708
2865 E 14th Ave Columbus (43219) ***(G-7354)***
Consulate Healthcare, Wellston *Also called Edgewood Manor of Wellston* ***(G-18849)***
Consulate Healthcare Inc (PA)....419 865-1248
3231 Manley Rd Maumee (43537) ***(G-13775)***
Consulate Management Co LLC....330 837-1001
2311 Nave Rd Sw Massillon (44646) ***(G-13673)***
Consulate Management Co LLC....740 259-2351
10098 Big Bear Creek Rd Lucasville (45648) ***(G-13046)***
Consulate Management Co LLC....419 683-3436
327 W Main St Crestline (44827) ***(G-9051)***
Consulate Management Co LLC....419 886-3922
4910 Algire Rd Bellville (44813) ***(G-1389)***
Consulate Management Co LLC....440 237-7966
13900 Bennett Rd Cleveland (44133) ***(G-5340)***
Consulate Management Co LLC....419 683-3255
327 W Main St Crestline (44827) ***(G-9052)***
Consulate Management Co LLC....740 259-5536
10098 Big Bear Creek Rd Lucasville (45648) ***(G-13047)***
Consulate Management Co LLC....419 867-7926
3600 Butz Rd Maumee (43537) ***(G-13776)***
Consultants Laboratory Medici....419 535-9629
2130 W Central Ave # 300 Toledo (43606) ***(G-17677)***
Consultants To You, Cincinnati *Also called Accountants To You LLC* ***(G-2902)***
Consultnts In Gastroenterology....440 386-2250
7530 Fredle Dr Painesville (44077) ***(G-15705)***
Consumer Credit Coun (PA)....614 552-2222
690 Taylor Rd Ste 110 Gahanna (43230) ***(G-11115)***
Consumer Credit Counseling Ser (PA)....800 254-4100
1228 Euclid Ave Ste 390 Cleveland (44115) ***(G-5341)***
Consumer Foods....440 284-5972
123 Gateway Blvd N Elyria (44035) ***(G-10493)***
Consumer Support Services Inc (PA)....740 788-8257
2040 Cherry Valley Rd # 1 Newark (43055) ***(G-15024)***
Consumer Support Services Inc....330 764-4785
2575 Medina Rd Ste A Medina (44256) ***(G-13922)***
Consumer Support Services Inc....740 522-5464
640 Industrial Pkwy Newark (43056) ***(G-15025)***
Consumer Support Services Inc....330 652-8800
1254 Yngstwn Wrrn Rd B Niles (44446) ***(G-15153)***
Consumer Support Services Inc....740 344-3600
100 James St Newark (43055) ***(G-15026)***
Consumers Bancorp Inc....330 868-7701
614 E Lincolnway Minerva (44657) ***(G-14517)***
Consumers Gas Cooperative....330 682-4144
298 Tracy Bridge Rd Orrville (44667) ***(G-15627)***
Consumers Life Insurance Co, Cleveland *Also called Medical Mutual of Ohio* ***(G-5943)***
Consumers National Bank (PA)....330 868-7701
614 E Lincolnway Minerva (44657) ***(G-14518)***
Container Graphics Corp....419 531-5133
305 Ryder Rd Toledo (43607) ***(G-17678)***
CONTAINERPORT GROUP, INC., West Chester *Also called Containerport Group Inc* ***(G-18896)***
Containerport Group Inc....440 333-1330
2400 Creekway Dr Columbus (43207) ***(G-7355)***
Containerport Group Inc....513 771-0275
2700 Crescentville Rd West Chester (45069) ***(G-18896)***
Containerport Group Inc (HQ)....440 333-1330
1340 Depot St Fl 2 Cleveland (44116) ***(G-5342)***
Containerport Group Inc....216 341-4800
5155 Warner Rd Cleveland (44125) ***(G-5343)***
Containerport Group Inc....216 692-3124
24881 Rockwell Dr Euclid (44117) ***(G-10627)***
Contech Trckg & Logistics LLC....513 645-7000
9025 Centre Pointe Dr # 400 West Chester (45069) ***(G-18897)***
Contech-Gdcg....937 426-3577
4197 Research Blvd Beavercreek (45430) ***(G-1212)***

Contemporary Arts Center...513 721-0390
44 E 6th St Cincinnati (45202) ***(G-3352)***
Continent Hlth Co Cortland LLC...330 637-7906
4250 Sodom Hutchings Rd Cortland (44410) ***(G-8986)***
Continental Airlines, Vandalia *Also called United Airlines Inc* ***(G-18546)***
Continental Airlines, Cleveland *Also called United Airlines Inc* ***(G-6566)***
Continental Building Company...614 221-1800
150 E Broad St Ste 610 Columbus (43215) ***(G-7356)***
Continental Business Services...614 224-4534
41 S Grant Ave Fl 2 Columbus (43215) ***(G-7357)***
Continental Express Inc...937 497-2100
10450 State Route 47 W Sidney (45365) ***(G-16767)***
Continental GL Sls & Inv Group...614 679-1201
315 Ashmoore Ct Powell (43065) ***(G-16192)***
Continental Group, Powell *Also called Continental GL Sls & Inv Group* ***(G-16192)***
Continental Manor, Blanchester *Also called First Richmond Corp* ***(G-1486)***
Continental Mewthod Solutions, Columbus *Also called Continental Business Services* ***(G-7357)***
Continental Office Furn Corp (PA)...614 262-5010
5061 Freeway Dr E Columbus (43229) ***(G-7358)***
Continental Office Furn Corp...614 781-0080
5063 Freeway Dr E Columbus (43229) ***(G-7359)***
Continental Products Company...216 531-0710
2926 Chester Ave Cleveland (44114) ***(G-5344)***
Continental Properties...614 221-1800
150 E Broad St Ste 700 Columbus (43215) ***(G-7360)***
Continental RE Companies (PA)...614 221-1800
150 E Broad St Ste 200 Columbus (43215) ***(G-7361)***
Continental Realty Ltd...614 221-6260
180 E Broad St Ste 1708 Columbus (43215) ***(G-7362)***
Continental Transport Inc...513 360-2960
997 Platte River Blvd Monroe (45050) ***(G-14564)***
Continental/Olentangy Ht LLC...614 297-9912
1421 Olentangy River Rd Columbus (43212) ***(G-7363)***
Contining Hlthcare Sltions Inc (PA)...216 772-1105
7261 Engle Rd Ste 200 Middleburg Heights (44130) ***(G-14251)***
Contining Hlthcare Sltions Inc...440 466-1181
60 West St Geneva (44041) ***(G-11239)***
Continntal Mssage Solution Inc...614 224-4534
41 S Grant Ave Fl 2 Columbus (43215) ***(G-7364)***
Continntal Office Environments, Columbus *Also called Continental Office Furn Corp* ***(G-7358)***
Continued Care Inc...419 222-2273
920 W Market St Ste 202 Lima (45805) ***(G-12618)***
Continuum Inc...614 891-9200
142 Wetherby Ln Westerville (43081) ***(G-19246)***
Continuum Home Care Inc...440 964-3332
1100 Lake Ave Ashtabula (44004) ***(G-730)***
Contract Freighters Inc...614 577-0447
945 Mahle Dr Reynoldsburg (43068) ***(G-16294)***
Contract Lumber Inc (PA)...740 964-3147
3245 Hazelton Etna Rd Sw Pataskala (43062) ***(G-15783)***
Contract Lumber Inc...614 751-1109
200 Schofield Dr Columbus (43213) ***(G-7365)***
Contract Marketing Inc...440 639-9100
9325 Progress Pkwy Mentor (44060) ***(G-14034)***
Contract Sweepers & Eqp Co (PA)...614 221-7441
2137 Parkwood Ave Columbus (43219) ***(G-7366)***
Contract Transport Services...216 524-8435
3223 Perkins Ave Cleveland (44114) ***(G-5345)***
Contractors Materials Company...513 733-3000
10320 S Medallion Dr Cincinnati (45241) ***(G-3353)***
Contractors Steel Company...330 425-3050
8383 Boyle Pkwy Twinsburg (44087) ***(G-18256)***
Control Cleaning Solutions...330 220-3333
780 Pearl Rd Brunswick (44212) ***(G-1925)***
Controlled Credit Corporation...513 921-2600
644 Linn St Ste 1101 Cincinnati (45203) ***(G-3354)***
Controls and Sheet Metal Inc (PA)...513 721-3610
1051 Sargent St Cincinnati (45203) ***(G-3355)***
Controls Center Inc (PA)...513 772-2665
1640 E Kemper Rd Ste 2 Cincinnati (45246) ***(G-3356)***
Controls Inc...330 239-4345
5204 Portside Dr Medina (44256) ***(G-13923)***
Controlsoft Inc...440 443-3900
5387 Avion Park Dr Cleveland (44143) ***(G-5346)***
Convalarium At Indian Run, Dublin *Also called Dublin Geriatric Care Co LP* ***(G-10207)***
Convalescent Center Lucasville, Lucasville *Also called Edgewood Manor of Lucasville* ***(G-13048)***
Convenient Food Mart Inc (HQ)...800 860-4844
6078 Pinecone Dr Mentor (44060) ***(G-14035)***
Convenient Tire Service, Columbus *Also called W D Tire Warehouse Inc* ***(G-8867)***
Convention & Visitors Bureau, Cleveland *Also called Convention & Vistors Bureau of* ***(G-5347)***
Convention & Vistors Bureau of (PA)...216 875-6603
50 Public Sq Ste 3100 Cleveland (44113) ***(G-5347)***
Convergint Technologies LLC...513 771-1717
7812 Redsky Dr Cincinnati (45249) ***(G-3357)***
Convergys Cstmer MGT Group Inc (HQ)...513 723-6104
201 E 4th St Bsmt Cincinnati (45202) ***(G-3358)***
Convergys Gvrnment Sltions LLC...513 723-7006
201 E 4th St Ste Bsmt Cincinnati (45202) ***(G-3359)***
Conversa Language Center Inc...513 651-5679
817 Main St Ste 600 Cincinnati (45202) ***(G-3360)***
Converse Electric Inc...614 808-4377
3783 Gantz Rd Ste A Grove City (43123) ***(G-11422)***
Conversion Tech Intl Inc...419 924-5566
700 Oak St West Unity (43570) ***(G-19140)***
Convivo Network LLC...216 631-9000
22564 Sunnyhill Dr Rocky River (44116) ***(G-16428)***
Conwed Plas Acquisition V LLC...440 926-2607
61 N Clevlnd Msslln Rd Akron (44333) ***(G-157)***
Cook Paving and Cnstr Co...216 267-7705
4545 Spring Rd Independence (44131) ***(G-12062)***
Cooked Foods, Fairfield *Also called Koch Meat Co Inc* ***(G-10745)***
Cookie Cutters Haircutters...614 522-0220
1726 Hill Rd N Pickerington (43147) ***(G-15955)***
Coolants Plus Inc (PA)...513 892-4000
2570 Van Hook Ave Hamilton (45015) ***(G-11587)***
Coolidge Law...937 223-8177
33 W 1st St Ste 600 Dayton (45402) ***(G-9318)***
Coolidge Wall Co LPA (PA)...937 223-8177
33 W 1st St Ste 600 Dayton (45402) ***(G-9319)***
Coon Caulking & Restoration, Louisville *Also called Coon Caulking & Sealants Inc* ***(G-12964)***
Coon Caulking & Sealants Inc...330 875-2100
7349 Ravenna Ave Louisville (44641) ***(G-12964)***
Cooper Brothers Trucking LLC (PA)...330 784-1717
1355 E Archwood Ave Akron (44306) ***(G-158)***
Cooper Farms, Oakwood *Also called Cooper Hatchery Inc* ***(G-15483)***
Cooper Farms Inc (PA)...419 375-4116
2321 State Route 49 Fort Recovery (45846) ***(G-10989)***
Cooper Foods, Fort Recovery *Also called V H Cooper & Co Inc* ***(G-10994)***
Cooper Frms Spring Madow Farms...419 375-4119
13243 Cochran Rd Rossburg (45362) ***(G-16458)***
Cooper Hatchery Inc (PA)...419 594-3325
22348 Road 140 Oakwood (45873) ***(G-15483)***
Cooper-Smith Advertising LLC...419 470-5900
3500 Granite Cir Toledo (43617) ***(G-17679)***
Cooper/T Smith Corporation...419 626-0801
2705 W Monroe St Sandusky (44870) ***(G-16594)***
Cooperate Screening Services...440 816-0500
16530 Commerce Ct Ste 1 Cleveland (44130) ***(G-5348)***
Copac, Cincinnati *Also called Pac Worldwide Corporation* ***(G-4196)***
Copart Inc...614 497-1590
1680 Williams Rd Columbus (43207) ***(G-7367)***
Copc Hospitals...614 268-8164
3555 Olentangy River Rd Columbus (43214) ***(G-7368)***
Cope Farm Equipment Inc (PA)...330 821-5867
24915 State Route 62 Alliance (44601) ***(G-528)***
Copeland Access + Inc...937 498-3802
1675 Campbell Rd Sidney (45365) ***(G-16768)***
Copeland Oaks...330 938-1050
715 S Johnson Rd Sebring (44672) ***(G-16666)***
Copeland Oaks (PA)...330 938-6126
800 S 15th St Sebring (44672) ***(G-16667)***
Copley Health Center Inc...330 666-0980
155 Heritage Woods Dr Copley (44321) ***(G-8965)***
Copley Ohio Newspapers Inc...330 364-5577
629 Wabash Ave Nw New Philadelphia (44663) ***(G-14951)***
Copp Systems Inc...937 228-4188
123 S Keowee St Dayton (45402) ***(G-9320)***
Copp Systems Integrator, Dayton *Also called Copp Systems Inc* ***(G-9320)***
Copper and Brass Sales Div, Northwood *Also called Thyssenkrupp Logistics Inc* ***(G-15407)***
Cora Health Services Inc (PA)...419 221-3004
1110 Shawnee Rd Lima (45805) ***(G-12619)***
Cora Physical Therapy, Lima *Also called Cora Health Services Inc* ***(G-12619)***
Coral Company (PA)...216 932-8822
13219 Shaker Sq Cleveland (44120) ***(G-5349)***
Corbus LLC (HQ)...937 226-7724
1129 Miamisbrg Cntrvle Rd Ste Dayton (45449) ***(G-9321)***
Corcoran and Harnist Htg & AC...513 921-2227
1457 Harrison Ave Cincinnati (45214) ***(G-3361)***
Cordelia Martin Hlth Ctr, Toledo *Also called Libbey Inc* ***(G-17853)***
Core, Cincinnati *Also called Cincinnatis Optimum RES Envir* ***(G-3280)***
Core Resources Inc...513 731-1771
7795 5 Mile Rd Cincinnati (45230) ***(G-3362)***
Core-Mark Ohio...650 589-9445
30300 Emerald Valley Pkwy Solon (44139) ***(G-16837)***
Corecivic Inc...330 746-3777
2240 Hubbard Rd Youngstown (44505) ***(G-20011)***
Cori Care Inc...614 848-4357
1060 Kingsmill Pkwy Columbus (43229) ***(G-7369)***
Cork Inc...614 253-8400
2006 Kenton St Columbus (43205) ***(G-7370)***
Corna Kokosing Construction Co...614 901-8844
6235 Westerville Rd Westerville (43081) ***(G-19247)***
Cornelia C Hodgson - Architec (PA)...216 593-0057
23240 Chagrin Blvd # 300 Beachwood (44122) ***(G-1048)***
Cornell Companies Inc...419 747-3322
2775 State Route 39 Shelby (44875) ***(G-16744)***

ALPHABETIC

Corner Cafe, Delaware *Also called Authentic Food LLC (G-9954)*

Cornerstone Brands Inc (HQ)...513 603-1000
5568 W Chester Rd West Chester (45069) *(G-18898)*

Cornerstone Brands Group Inc..................................513 603-1000
5568 W Chester Rd West Chester (45069) *(G-18899)*

Cornerstone Brkrg Ins Svc Agn, Cincinnati *Also called Cornerstone Broker Ins Svcs AG (G-3363)*

Cornerstone Broker Ins Svcs AG (PA).....................513 241-7675
2101 Florence Ave Cincinnati (45206) *(G-3363)*

Cornerstone Concrete Cnstr Inc...............................937 442-2805
12577 Us Highway 62 Sardinia (45171) *(G-16658)*

Cornerstone Controls Inc...937 263-6429
1440 Nicholas Rd Dayton (45417) *(G-9322)*

Cornerstone Managed Prpts LLC...............................440 263-7708
2147 E 28th St Lorain (44055) *(G-12899)*

Cornerstone Med Svcs Midwest..................................513 554-0222
4570 Cornell Rd Blue Ash (45241) *(G-1537)*

Cornerstone Medical Associates...............................330 374-0229
453 S High St Ste 201 Akron (44311) *(G-159)*

Cornerstone Medical Services....................................513 554-0222
4570 Cornell Rd Blue Ash (45241) *(G-1538)*

CORNERSTONE OF HOPE BEREAVEMEN, Independence *Also called Bobby Tripodi Foundation Inc (G-12050)*

Cornerstone Research Group Inc...............................937 320-1877
510 Earl Blvd Miamisburg (45342) *(G-14155)*

Cornerstone Support Services (PA)...........................330 339-7850
344 W High Ave New Philadelphia (44663) *(G-14952)*

Cornucopia Inc..216 521-4600
18120 Sloane Ave Lakewood (44107) *(G-12339)*

Cornwell Quality Tools Company...............................330 628-2627
200 N Cleveland Ave Mogadore (44260) *(G-14545)*

Cornwell Quality Tools Company...............................330 335-2933
635 Seville Rd Wadsworth (44281) *(G-18594)*

Coroner, Dayton *Also called County of Montgomery (G-9334)*

Coroner's Office, Cleveland *Also called County of Cuyahoga (G-5363)*

Corporate Cleaning Inc..614 203-6051
781 Northwest Blvd # 103 Columbus (43212) *(G-7371)*

Corporate Electric Company LLC................................330 331-7517
378 S Van Buren Ave Barberton (44203) *(G-951)*

Corporate Environments of Ohio...............................614 358-3375
2899 Morse Rd Columbus (43231) *(G-7372)*

Corporate Exchange Hotel Assoc..............................614 890-8600
2700 Corporate Exch Dr Columbus (43231) *(G-7373)*

Corporate Fin Assoc of Clumbus...............................614 457-9219
671 Camden Yard Ct Columbus (43235) *(G-7374)*

Corporate Floors Inc...216 475-3232
15901 Mccracken Rd Cleveland (44128) *(G-5350)*

Corporate Health Benefits..740 348-1401
1915 Tamarack Rd Newark (43055) *(G-15027)*

Corporate Health Dimensions.....................................740 775-6119
311 Caldwell St Chillicothe (45601) *(G-2770)*

Corporate Imageworks LLC...216 292-8800
10375 State Route 43 Streetsboro (44241) *(G-17251)*

Corporate Ladder Search..330 776-4390
1549 Boettler Rd Ste D Uniontown (44685) *(G-18364)*

Corporate One Federal Cr Un (PA).............................614 825-9314
8700 Orion Pl Columbus (43240) *(G-6810)*

Corporate Plans Inc...440 542-7800
6830 Cochran Rd Solon (44139) *(G-16838)*

Corporate Screening Svcs Inc (PA)...........................440 816-0500
16530 Commerce Ct Ste 3 Cleveland (44130) *(G-5351)*

Corporate Support Inc (PA)..419 221-3838
750 Buckeye Rd Lima (45804) *(G-12620)*

Corporate United Inc..440 895-0938
24651 Center Ridge Rd # 527 Westlake (44145) *(G-19337)*

Corporate Wngs - Cleveland LLC...............................216 261-9000
355 Richmond Rd Ste A Cleveland (44143) *(G-5352)*

Corporation For OH Appalachian (PA)........................740 594-8499
1 Pinchot Pl Athens (45701) *(G-772)*

Corporation For OH Appalachian...............................330 364-8882
1260 Monroe St Nw Ste 39s New Philadelphia (44663) *(G-14953)*

Corporex Realty & Inv LLC..859 292-5500
P.O. Box 75020 Cincinnati (45275) *(G-3364)*

Correction Commission NW Ohio...............................419 428-3800
3151 County Road 2425 Stryker (43557) *(G-17369)*

Correctons Comm Sthastern Ohio.............................740 753-4060
16677 Riverside Dr Nelsonville (45764) *(G-14828)*

Corrigan Moving Systems-Ann AR.............................419 874-2900
12377 Williams Rd Perrysburg (43551) *(G-15850)*

Corrosion Fluid Products Corp (HQ)..........................248 478-0100
3000 E 14th Ave Columbus (43219) *(G-7375)*

Corrotec Inc..937 325-3585
1125 W North St Springfield (45504) *(G-17021)*

Corrpro Companies Inc (HQ)......................................330 723-5082
1055 W Smith Rd Medina (44256) *(G-13924)*

Cors & Bassett LLC (PA)...513 852-8200
537 E Pete Rose Way # 400 Cincinnati (45202) *(G-3365)*

Corso's Flower & Garden Center, Sandusky *Also called August Corso Sons Inc (G-16576)*

Cort Business Services Corp.......................................513 759-8181
7400 Squire Ct West Chester (45069) *(G-18900)*

Cort Furniture Rental, West Chester *Also called Cort Business Services Corp (G-18900)*

CORTLAND BANKS, Cortland *Also called The Cortland Sav & Bnkg Co (G-8994)*

Cortland Healthcare Center, Cortland *Also called Cortland Healthcare Group Inc (G-8987)*

Cortland Healthcare Group Inc...................................330 638-4015
369 N High St Cortland (44410) *(G-8987)*

Cos Express Inc..614 276-9000
3616 Fisher Rd Columbus (43228) *(G-7376)*

Coshocton Bhvoral Hlth Cohices, Coshocton *Also called Coshocton Drug Alcohol Council (G-9007)*

Coshocton Bowling Center..740 622-6332
775 S 2nd St Coshocton (43812) *(G-9004)*

Coshocton Cnty Emrgncy Med Svc (HQ)....................740 622-4294
513 Chestnut St Coshocton (43812) *(G-9005)*

Coshocton County Head Start....................................740 622-3667
3201 County Road 16 Coshocton (43812) *(G-9006)*

Coshocton Drug Alcohol Council................................740 622-0033
610 Walnut St Coshocton (43812) *(G-9007)*

Coshocton Healthcare and, Coshocton *Also called Coshocton Opco LLC (G-9008)*

Coshocton Opco LLC...740 622-1220
100 S Whitewoman St Coshocton (43812) *(G-9008)*

Coshocton Trucking South Inc...................................740 622-1311
2702 S 6th St Coshocton (43812) *(G-9009)*

Coshocton Village Inn & Suites, Coshocton *Also called Coshocton Village Inn Suites (G-9010)*

Coshocton Village Inn Suites.....................................740 622-9455
115 N Water St Coshocton (43812) *(G-9010)*

Cosi, Columbus *Also called Franklin County Historical Soc (G-7617)*

Cosmax USA Inc Cosmax USA Corp...........................440 600-5738
30701 Carter St Solon (44139) *(G-16839)*

Cosmic Concepts Ltd..614 228-1104
399 E Main St Ste 140 Columbus (43215) *(G-7377)*

Costello Pntg Bldg Restoration.................................513 321-3326
1113 Halpin Ave Cincinnati (45208) *(G-3366)*

Costume Specialists Inc (PA)....................................614 464-2115
211 N 5th St Ste 100 Columbus (43215) *(G-7378)*

Cota, Columbus *Also called Central Ohio Transit Authority (G-7170)*

Coti, Blue Ash *Also called Cincinnati Occupational Therap (G-1526)*

Cott Systems Inc..614 847-4405
2800 Corp Exchange Dr # 300 Columbus (43231) *(G-7379)*

Cottage Gardens Inc..440 259-2900
4992 Middle Ridge Rd Perry (44081) *(G-15822)*

Cottages of Clayton...937 280-0300
8212 N Main St Dayton (45415) *(G-9323)*

Cotter Mdse Stor of Ohio..330 773-9177
1564 Firestone Pkwy Akron (44301) *(G-160)*

Cotter Moving & Storage Co (PA)...............................330 535-5115
265 W Bowery St Akron (44308) *(G-161)*

Cottingham Party Savers, Columbus *Also called The Cottingham Paper Co (G-8742)*

Cottingham Retirement Cmnty....................................513 563-3600
3995 Cottingham Dr # 102 Cincinnati (45241) *(G-3367)*

Cottonwd Crk At Spytn-Dyvl, Sylvania *Also called Leisure Sports Inc (G-17436)*

Coughlin Automotive, Newark *Also called Coughlin Chevrolet Toyota Inc (G-15028)*

Coughlin Automotive Group, Pataskala *Also called Coughlin Chevrolet Inc (G-15784)*

Coughlin Chevrolet Inc..740 852-1122
255 Lafayette St London (43140) *(G-12862)*

Coughlin Chevrolet Inc (PA).......................................740 964-9191
9000 Broad St Sw Pataskala (43062) *(G-15784)*

Coughlin Chevrolet Toyota Inc....................................740 366-1381
1850 N 21st St Newark (43055) *(G-15028)*

Coughlin Holdings Ltd Partnr......................................614 847-1002
71 E Wilson Bridge Rd Worthington (43085) *(G-19801)*

Coughlin Realty, Worthington *Also called Coughlin Holdings Ltd Partnr (G-19801)*

Council For Economic Opport.....................................216 541-7878
14209 Euclid Ave Cleveland (44112) *(G-5353)*

Council For Economic Opport.....................................216 476-3201
14402 Puritas Ave Cleveland (44135) *(G-5354)*

Council For Economic Opport (PA).............................216 696-9077
1801 Superior Ave E Fl 4 Cleveland (44114) *(G-5355)*

Council For Economic Opport.....................................216 692-4010
1883 Torbenson Dr Cleveland (44112) *(G-5356)*

Council For Economic Opport.....................................216 736-2934
2421 Cmnty College Ave Cleveland (44115) *(G-5357)*

Council of Child & Adoles, Cleveland *Also called Cleveland Clinic Foundation (G-5237)*

Council of Ecnmc Opprtnts of G................................216 651-5154
2220 W 95th St Cleveland (44102) *(G-5358)*

Council On Aging of Southweste.................................513 721-1025
175 Tri County Pkwy # 200 Cincinnati (45246) *(G-3368)*

Council On Rur Svc Prgrams Inc.................................937 492-8787
1502 N Main Ave Sidney (45365) *(G-16769)*

Council On Rur Svc Prgrams Inc (PA).........................937 778-5220
201 Robert M Davis Pkwy B Piqua (45356) *(G-16001)*

Council On Rur Svc Prgrams Inc.................................937 773-0773
285 Robert M Davis Pkwy Piqua (45356) *(G-16002)*

Council On Rur Svc Prgrams Inc.................................937 452-1090
8263 Us Route 127 Camden (45311) *(G-2089)*

Counseling Center Huron County...............................419 663-3737
292 Benedict Ave Norwalk (44857) *(G-15430)*

COUNSELING CENTER, THE, Portsmouth *Also called Scioto County Counseling Ctr (G-16167)*

Counseling Ctr Wayne Holmes CT (PA)......................330 264-9029
2285 Benden Dr Wooster (44691) *(G-19712)*

(G-0000) Company's Geographic Section entry number

Counseling Source Inc....513 984-9838
10921 Reed Hartman Hwy # 134 Blue Ash (45242) *(G-1539)*
Countertop Alternatives Inc....937 254-3334
2325 Woodman Dr Dayton (45420) *(G-9324)*
Countrtops Cabinetry By Design, Mason *Also called Complete Services Inc (G-13566)*
Country Acres of Wayne County....330 698-2031
1240 Wildwood Dr Wooster (44691) *(G-19713)*
Country Club Inc....216 831-9200
2825 Lander Rd Cleveland (44124) *(G-5359)*
Country Club At Muirfield Vlg....614 764-1714
8715 Muirfield Dr Dublin (43017) *(G-10190)*
Country Club Center Homes Inc....330 343-6351
860 E Iron Ave Dover (44622) *(G-10071)*
Country Club Center II Ltd....740 397-2350
1350 Yauger Rd Mount Vernon (43050) *(G-14756)*
Country Club Center III, Ashtabula *Also called Country Club Retirement Center (G-731)*
Country Club of Hudson....330 650-1188
2155 Middleton Rd Hudson (44236) *(G-11974)*
Country Club of North....937 374-5000
1 Club North Dr Xenia (45385) *(G-19895)*
Country Club of Orange Park, Johnstown *Also called Opcc LLC (G-12202)*
Country Club Retirement Campus, Mount Vernon *Also called Country Club Center II Ltd (G-14756)*
COUNTRY CLUB RETIREMENT CENTER, Dover *Also called Country Club Center Homes Inc (G-10071)*
Country Club Retirement Center....440 992-0022
925 E 26th St Ashtabula (44004) *(G-731)*
Country Club Retirement Center (PA)....740 671-9330
55801 Conno Mara Dr Bellaire (43906) *(G-1333)*
COUNTRY CLUB, THE, Dublin *Also called Country Club At Muirfield Vlg (G-10190)*
Country Court Ltd....740 397-4125
1076 Coshocton Ave Mount Vernon (43050) *(G-14757)*
Country Gardens....740 522-8810
2326 Newark Granville Rd Granville (43023) *(G-11339)*
Country Living, Columbus *Also called Ohio Rural Electric Coops Inc (G-8283)*
Country Mdow Fclty Oprtons LLC....419 886-3922
4910 Algire Rd Bellville (44813) *(G-1390)*
Country Meadow Care Center, Bellville *Also called Consulate Management Co LLC (G-1389)*
Country Meadow Care Center, Bellville *Also called Country Mdow Fclty Oprtons LLC (G-1390)*
Country Meadow Care Center LLC....419 886-3922
4910 Algire Rd Bellville (44813) *(G-1391)*
Country Meadow Rehabilitation, Bellville *Also called Country Meadow Care Center LLC (G-1391)*
Country Neighbor Program Inc (PA)....440 437-6311
39 S Maple St Orwell (44076) *(G-15651)*
Country Pointe Skilled Nursing....330 264-7881
3071 N Elyria Rd Wooster (44691) *(G-19714)*
Country Saw and Knife Inc....330 332-1611
1375 W State St Salem (44460) *(G-16540)*
Country Suites By Carlson, Elyria *Also called Bindu Associates LLC (G-10483)*
Country View of Sunbury, Sunbury *Also called Morning View Delaware Inc (G-17391)*
Countryside Electric Inc....614 478-7960
2920 Switzer Ave Columbus (43219) *(G-7380)*
Countryside Rentals Inc (PA)....740 634-2666
210 S Quarry St Bainbridge (45612) *(G-930)*
Countryside Veterinary Service....330 847-7337
4680 Mahoning Ave Nw Warren (44483) *(G-18691)*
Countryside YMCA Child Dev, Lebanon *Also called Young Mens Christian (G-12516)*
Countryview Assistant Living....740 489-5351
62825 County Home Rd Lore City (43755) *(G-12952)*
Countryview Manor, Carrollton *Also called East Carroll Nursing Home (G-2567)*
Counts Container Corporation....216 433-4336
5137 W 161st St Cleveland (44142) *(G-5360)*
County Administrator's Office, Cleveland *Also called County of Cuyahoga (G-5369)*
County Animal Hospital....513 398-8000
1185 Reading Rd Mason (45040) *(G-13568)*
County Engineer, Wshngtn CT Hs *Also called County of Fayette (G-19866)*
County Engineer's Office, Coshocton *Also called County of Coshocton (G-9011)*
County Engineering Office....419 334-9731
2500 W State St Fremont (43420) *(G-11064)*
County Engineers Office, Columbus *Also called Franklin Cnty Bd Commissioners (G-7603)*
County Engineers Office, Athens *Also called County of Athens (G-773)*
County Engineers Office....740 702-3130
755 Fairgrounds Rd Chillicothe (45601) *(G-2771)*
County of Adams....937 544-5067
300 N Wilson Dr West Union (45693) *(G-19135)*
County of Allen....419 228-6065
600 S Main St Lima (45804) *(G-12621)*
County of Allen....419 221-1103
3125 Ada Rd Lima (45801) *(G-12622)*
County of Allen....419 228-2120
1501 S Dixie Hwy Lima (45804) *(G-12623)*
County of Allen....419 227-8590
123 W Spring St Lima (45801) *(G-12624)*
County of Allen....419 221-1226
2450 Ada Rd Lima (45801) *(G-12625)*
County of Allen....419 996-7050
608 W High St Lima (45801) *(G-12626)*
County of Ashtabula....440 576-2816
186 E Satin St Jefferson (44047) *(G-12191)*
County of Ashtabula....440 224-2157
2505 S Ridge Rd E Ashtabula (44004) *(G-732)*
County of Ashtabula....440 998-1811
3914 C Ct Ashtabula (44004) *(G-733)*
County of Ashtabula....440 994-1206
2924 Donahoe Dr Ashtabula (44004) *(G-734)*
County of Athens....740 593-5514
16000 Canineville Rd Athens (45701) *(G-773)*
County of Athens....740 592-3061
18 Stonybrook Dr Athens (45701) *(G-774)*
County of Auglaize....419 738-3816
13093 Infirmary Rd Wapakoneta (45895) *(G-18640)*
County of Auglaize....419 629-2419
20 E 1st St New Bremen (45869) *(G-14886)*
County of Brown....937 378-6456
25 Veterans Blvd Georgetown (45121) *(G-11267)*
County of Brown....937 378-6104
775 Mount Orab Pike Georgetown (45121) *(G-11268)*
County of Carroll....330 627-4866
P.O. Box 98 Carrollton (44615) *(G-2564)*
County of Carroll....330 627-7651
2167 Kensington Rd Ne Carrollton (44615) *(G-2565)*
County of Champaign....937 653-4848
428 Beech St Urbana (43078) *(G-18430)*
County of Clark....937 390-5600
529 E Home Rd Springfield (45503) *(G-17022)*
County of Clark....937 327-1700
1345 Lagonda Ave Springfield (45503) *(G-17023)*
County of Clark....937 327-1700
1346 Lagonda Ave Springfield (45503) *(G-17024)*
County of Clark....937 327-1700
1345 Lagonda Ave Springfield (45503) *(G-17025)*
County of Clermont....513 732-7661
2279 Clermont Center Dr Batavia (45103) *(G-993)*
County of Clermont....513 732-7970
4400 Haskell Ln Batavia (45103) *(G-994)*
County of Clinton....937 382-2449
1025 S South St Ste 300 Wilmington (45177) *(G-19619)*
County of Clinton....937 382-2078
1326 Fife Ave Wilmington (45177) *(G-19620)*
County of Columbiana....330 424-1386
7880 Lincole Pl Lisbon (44432) *(G-12798)*
County of Coshocton....740 622-2135
23194 County Road 621 Coshocton (43812) *(G-9011)*
County of Coshocton....740 622-1020
725 Pine St Coshocton (43812) *(G-9012)*
County of Crawford....419 562-0015
224 Norton Way Bucyrus (44820) *(G-1986)*
County of Crawford....419 562-7731
815 Whetstone St Bucyrus (44820) *(G-1987)*
County of Cuyahoga....419 399-8260
112 N Williams St Paulding (45879) *(G-15792)*
County of Cuyahoga....216 443-7035
310 W Lkeside Ave Ste 500 Cleveland (44113) *(G-5361)*
County of Cuyahoga....216 475-7066
14775 Broadway Ave Cleveland (44137) *(G-5362)*
County of Cuyahoga....216 721-5610
11001 Cedar Ave Ste 400 Cleveland (44106) *(G-5363)*
County of Cuyahoga....216 443-8011
2079 E 9th St Fl 6 Cleveland (44115) *(G-5364)*
County of Cuyahoga....216 443-5100
1640 Superior Ave E Cleveland (44114) *(G-5365)*
County of Cuyahoga....216 443-6954
2079 E 9th St Cleveland (44115) *(G-5366)*
County of Cuyahoga....216 241-8230
1275 Lakeside Ave E Cleveland (44114) *(G-5367)*
County of Cuyahoga....216 681-4433
13231 Euclid Ave Cleveland (44112) *(G-5368)*
County of Cuyahoga....216 443-7181
1219 Ontario St Rm 304 Cleveland (44113) *(G-5369)*
County of Cuyahoga....216 432-2621
3955 Euclid Ave Rm 344e Cleveland (44115) *(G-5370)*
County of Cuyahoga....216 443-7265
1276 W 3rd St Ste 319 Cleveland (44113) *(G-5371)*
County of Darke....937 526-4488
10242 Versailles Se Rd Versailles (45380) *(G-18568)*
County of Delaware....740 833-2240
50 Channing St Delaware (43015) *(G-9962)*
County of Delaware....740 657-3945
8647 Columbus Pike Lewis Center (43035) *(G-12535)*
County of Delaware....740 833-2400
50 Channing St Delaware (43015) *(G-9963)*
County of Delaware....740 203-2040
1 W Winter St Fl 2 Delaware (43015) *(G-9964)*
County of Erie....419 433-0617
10102 Hoover Rd Milan (44846) *(G-14360)*
County of Erie....419 627-8733
3916 Perkins Ave Huron (44839) *(G-12024)*
County of Erie....419 626-6781
221 W Parish St Sandusky (44870) *(G-16595)*

County of Erie 419 627-7710
2700 Columbus Ave Sandusky (44870) *(G-16596)*

County of Fayette 740 335-1541
1600 Robinson Rd Se Wshngtn CT Hs (43160) *(G-19866)*

County of Fulton 419 335-3816
9120 County Road 14 Wauseon (43567) *(G-18797)*

County of Gallia 740 446-3222
848 3rd Ave Gallipolis (45631) *(G-11187)*

County of Gallia 740 446-2665
1107 State Route 160 Gallipolis (45631) *(G-11188)*

County of Gallia 740 446-4009
1167 State Route 160 Gallipolis (45631) *(G-11189)*

County of Geauga 440 286-6264
8389 Mayfield Rd Ste A-2 Chesterland (44026) *(G-2738)*

County of Geauga 440 564-2246
12480 Ravenwood Dr Chardon (44024) *(G-2691)*

County of Geauga 440 285-9141
12480 Ravenwood Dr Chardon (44024) *(G-2692)*

County of Guernsey 740 439-5555
274 Highland Ave Cambridge (43725) *(G-2060)*

County of Guernsey 800 307-8422
324 Highland Ave Cambridge (43725) *(G-2061)*

County of Guernsey 740 432-2381
324 Highland Ave Cambridge (43725) *(G-2062)*

County of Guernsey 740 439-6681
1022 Carlisle Ave Cambridge (43725) *(G-2063)*

County of Hamilton 513 742-1576
2600 Civic Center Dr Cincinnati (45231) *(G-3369)*

County of Hamilton 513 552-1200
246 Bonham Rd Cincinnati (45215) *(G-3370)*

County of Hamilton 513 946-4250
138 E Court St Rm 700 Cincinnati (45202) *(G-3371)*

County of Hamilton 513 598-2965
5884 Bridgetown Rd Cincinnati (45248) *(G-3372)*

County of Hamilton 513 821-6946
7162 Reading Rd Ste 800 Cincinnati (45237) *(G-3373)*

County of Hancock 419 422-6387
318 W Main Cross St Findlay (45840) *(G-10891)*

County of Hancock 419 424-7050
7746 County Road 140 A Findlay (45840) *(G-10892)*

County of Hancock 419 422-7433
1900 Lima Ave Findlay (45840) *(G-10893)*

County of Hancock 419 425-7275
1424 E Main Cross St Findlay (45840) *(G-10894)*

County of Hardin 419 634-7729
530 N Gilbert St Ada (45810) *(G-4)*

County of Hardin 419 674-4158
705 N Ida St Kenton (43326) *(G-12274)*

County of Henry 419 592-8075
R858 County Road 15 Napoleon (43545) *(G-14803)*

County of Highland 937 393-4278
1575 N High St Ste 100 Hillsboro (45133) *(G-11835)*

County of Holmes 330 279-2801
7260 State Route 83 Holmesville (44633) *(G-11929)*

County of Holmes 330 674-1926
8478 State Route 39 Millersburg (44654) *(G-14467)*

County of Holmes 330 674-5035
85 N Grant St B Millersburg (44654) *(G-14468)*

County of Holmes 330 674-5076
7191 State Route 39 Millersburg (44654) *(G-14469)*

County of Holmes 330 674-5916
75 E Clinton St Millersburg (44654) *(G-14470)*

County of Holmes 330 674-1015
981 Wooster Rd Millersburg (44654) *(G-14471)*

County of Holmes 330 674-1111
85 N Grant St Millersburg (44654) *(G-14472)*

County of Huron 419 668-8126
185 Shady Lane Dr Norwalk (44857) *(G-15431)*

County of Huron 419 663-5437
185 Shady Lane Dr Norwalk (44857) *(G-15432)*

County of Knox 740 392-2200
11660 Upper Gilchrist Rd Mount Vernon (43050) *(G-14758)*

County of Lake 440 350-5100
8121 Deepwood Blvd Mentor (44060) *(G-14036)*

County of Lake 440 269-2193
2100 Joseph Lloyd Pkwy Willoughby (44094) *(G-19516)*

County of Licking 740 967-5951
395 W Jersey St Johnstown (43031) *(G-12199)*

County of Logan 937 599-7252
101 S Main St Rm 1 Bellefontaine (43311) *(G-1349)*

County of Logan 937 599-4221
121 S Opera St Rm 12 Bellefontaine (43311) *(G-1350)*

County of Logan 937 592-2901
2739 County Road 91 Bellefontaine (43311) *(G-1351)*

County of Logan 937 599-7290
1100 S Detroit St Bellefontaine (43311) *(G-1352)*

County of Lorain 440 329-5584
247 Hadaway St Elyria (44035) *(G-10494)*

County of Lorain 440 329-3734
1091 Infirmary Rd Elyria (44035) *(G-10495)*

County of Lorain 440 326-4700
308 2nd St Elyria (44035) *(G-10496)*

County of Lorain 440 326-5884
247 Hadaway St Elyria (44035) *(G-10497)*

County of Lorain 440 647-5803
179 E Herrick Ave Wellington (44090) *(G-18838)*

County of Lorain 440 284-1830
42495 N Ridge Rd Ste A Elyria (44035) *(G-10498)*

County of Lorain 440 989-4900
120 East Ave Elyria (44035) *(G-10499)*

County of Lorain 440 282-3074
4609 Meister Rd Lorain (44053) *(G-12900)*

County of Lorain 440 326-5880
42100 Russia Rd Elyria (44035) *(G-10500)*

County of Lorain 440 329-5340
226 Middle Ave Fl 4 Elyria (44035) *(G-10501)*

County of Lucas 419 213-3000
701 Adams St Toledo (43604) *(G-17680)*

County of Lucas 419 213-4700
700 Adams St Ste 150 Toledo (43604) *(G-17681)*

County of Lucas 419 213-8999
3210 Monroe St Toledo (43606) *(G-17682)*

County of Lucas 419 213-4018
635 N Erie St Toledo (43604) *(G-17683)*

County of Lucas 419 213-2892
1049 S Mccord Rd Bldg A Holland (43528) *(G-11879)*

County of Lucas 419 213-4500
1 Government Ctr Ste 800 Toledo (43604) *(G-17684)*

County of Lucas 419 385-6021
1154 Larc Ln Toledo (43614) *(G-17685)*

County of Madison 740 852-9404
825 Us Highway 42 Ne London (43140) *(G-12863)*

County of Marion 740 387-6688
620 Leader St Marion (43302) *(G-13413)*

County of Marion 740 389-4624
1422 Mount Vernon Ave Marion (43302) *(G-13414)*

County of Marion 740 389-2317
1680 Marion Waldo Rd Marion (43302) *(G-13415)*

County of Marion 740 387-1035
2387 Harding Hwy E Marion (43302) *(G-13416)*

County of Marion 740 382-0624
1775 Mrn Williamsprt Rd E Marion (43302) *(G-13417)*

County of Medina 330 723-9553
6144 Wedgewood Rd Medina (44256) *(G-13925)*

County of Medina 330 995-5243
4800 Ledgewood Dr Medina (44256) *(G-13926)*

County of Medina 330 723-9670
114 Bradway St Medina (44256) *(G-13927)*

County of Mercer 419 586-2369
4980 Mud Pike Rd Celina (45822) *(G-2591)*

County of Mercer 419 586-5106
220 W Livingston St # 10 Celina (45822) *(G-2592)*

County of Mercer 419 678-8071
510 W Main St Coldwater (45828) *(G-6757)*

County of Miami 937 335-1314
2100 N County Road 25a Troy (45373) *(G-18199)*

County of Monroe 740 472-0760
47026 Moore Ridge Rd Woodsfield (43793) *(G-19673)*

County of Monroe 740 472-0144
47045 Moore Ridge Rd Woodsfield (43793) *(G-19674)*

County of Montgomery 937 225-4192
345 W 2nd St Dayton (45422) *(G-9325)*

County of Montgomery 937 224-5437
3304 N Main St Dayton (45405) *(G-9326)*

County of Montgomery 937 781-3046
2550 Sandridge Dr Moraine (45439) *(G-14637)*

County of Montgomery 937 854-4576
5625 Little Richmond Rd Dayton (45426) *(G-9327)*

County of Montgomery 937 264-0460
8100 N Main St Dayton (45415) *(G-9328)*

County of Montgomery 937 225-4010
451 W 3rd St Fl 2 Dayton (45422) *(G-9329)*

County of Montgomery 937 225-4804
1111 Edwin C Moses Blvd Dayton (45422) *(G-9330)*

County of Montgomery 937 225-5623
301 W 3rd St Fl 5 Dayton (45402) *(G-9331)*

County of Montgomery 937 224-5437
3501 Merrimac Ave Dayton (45405) *(G-9332)*

County of Montgomery 937 496-3103
41 N Perry St Rm 1 Dayton (45422) *(G-9333)*

County of Montgomery 937 225-4156
361 W 3rd St Dayton (45402) *(G-9334)*

County of Morrow 419 946-2618
27 W High St Mount Gilead (43338) *(G-14726)*

County of Ottawa 419 898-7433
275 N Toussaint South Rd Oak Harbor (43449) *(G-15469)*

County of Ottawa 419 898-6459
8180 W State Route 163 Oak Harbor (43449) *(G-15470)*

County of Ottawa 419 898-2089
8444 W State Route 163 # 102 Oak Harbor (43449) *(G-15471)*

County of Paulding 419 399-3636
501 Mc Donald Pike Paulding (45879) *(G-15793)*

County of Perry 740 342-0416
445 W Broadway St Ste C New Lexington (43764) *(G-14918)*

County of Perry 740 342-2191
2645 Old Somerset Rd New Lexington (43764) *(G-14919)*

County of Pickaway 740 474-7588
110 Island Rd Ste E Circleville (43113) *(G-4830)*

2019 Harris Ohio
Services Directory

(G-0000) Company's Geographic Section entry number

County of Portage 330 296-6411
5000 Newton Falls Rd Ravenna (44266) *(G-16238)*
County of Portage 330 297-3670
449 S Meridian St Fl 3 Ravenna (44266) *(G-16239)*
County of Portage 330 297-3850
466 S Chestnut St Ravenna (44266) *(G-16240)*
County of Preble 937 839-5845
1251 State Route 503 N West Alexandria (45381) *(G-18855)*
County of Preble 937 456-2085
116 E Main St Ste B Eaton (45320) *(G-10440)*
County of Richland 419 774-4300
721 Scholl Rd Mansfield (44907) *(G-13152)*
County of Richland 419 774-5676
38 Park St S Ste B Mansfield (44902) *(G-13153)*
County of Richland 419 774-5894
3220 Olivesburg Rd Mansfield (44903) *(G-13154)*
County of Richland 419 774-4100
731 Scholl Rd Mansfield (44907) *(G-13155)*
County of Richland 419 774-5400
171 Park Ave E Mansfield (44902) *(G-13156)*
County of Richland 419 774-5578
411 S Diamond St Mansfield (44902) *(G-13157)*
County of Richland 419 774-5591
77 N Mulberry St Mansfield (44902) *(G-13158)*
County of Richland 419 774-4200
314 Cleveland Ave Mansfield (44902) *(G-13159)*
County of Ross 740 773-4169
182 Cattail Rd Chillicothe (45601) *(G-2772)*
County of Sandusky 419 637-2243
1001 Castalia St Fremont (43420) *(G-11065)*
County of Sandusky 419 334-2602
1865 Countryside Dr Fremont (43420) *(G-11066)*
County of Seneca 419 447-3863
3210 S State Route 100 Tiffin (44883) *(G-17513)*
County of Seneca 419 435-0729
602 S Corporate Dr W Fostoria (44830) *(G-10999)*
County of Seneca 419 447-5011
3362 S Township Rd Tiffin (44883) *(G-17514)*
County of Seneca 419 937-2340
P.O. Box 119 Bascom (44809) *(G-981)*
County of Shelby 937 498-7244
500 Gearhart Rd Sidney (45365) *(G-16770)*
County of Shelby 937 492-6900
2901 Fair Rd Sidney (45365) *(G-16771)*
County of Stark 330 484-4814
3041 Cleveland Ave S Canton (44707) *(G-2267)*
County of Stark 330 477-3609
798 Genoa Ave Nw Massillon (44646) *(G-13674)*
County of Stark 330 451-2303
1701 Mahoning Rd Ne Canton (44705) *(G-2268)*
County of Stark 330 477-6781
5165 Southway St Sw Canton (44706) *(G-2269)*
County of Stark 330 455-6644
121 Cleveland Ave Sw Canton (44702) *(G-2270)*
County of Summit 330 643-2300
25 N Main St Akron (44308) *(G-162)*
County of Summit 330 643-2943
650 Dan St Akron (44310) *(G-163)*
County of Summit 330 634-8193
89 E Howe Rd Tallmadge (44278) *(G-17473)*
County of Summit 330 643-2850
538 E South St Akron (44311) *(G-164)*
County of Summit 330 643-2860
601 E Crosier St Akron (44311) *(G-165)*
County of Summit 330 643-7217
47 N Main St Akron (44308) *(G-166)*
County of Summit Board of Mntl 330 634-8100
636 W Exchange St Akron (44302) *(G-167)*
County of Trumbull 330 675-2640
650 N River Rd Nw Warren (44483) *(G-18692)*
County of Tuscarawas 330 343-0099
154 2nd St Ne New Philadelphia (44663) *(G-14954)*
County of Tuscarawas 330 339-7791
389 16th St Sw New Philadelphia (44663) *(G-14955)*
County of Union 937 645-3018
128 S Main St Ste 203 Marysville (43040) *(G-13490)*
County of Union 937 645-6733
1280 Charles Ln Marysville (43040) *(G-13491)*
County of Union 937 645-4145
128 S Main St Ste 203 Marysville (43040) *(G-13492)*
County of Van Wert 419 968-2141
17872 Lincoln Hwy Middle Point (45863) *(G-14246)*
County of Warren 513 695-1420
416 S East St Unit 1 Lebanon (45036) *(G-12457)*
County of Warren 513 695-1109
300 E Silver St Ste 5 Lebanon (45036) *(G-12458)*
County of Warren 513 925-1377
406 Justice Dr Rm 323 Lebanon (45036) *(G-12459)*
County of Washington 740 376-7430
103 Westview Ave Marietta (45750) *(G-13321)*
County of Washington 740 373-2028
County House Ln Marietta (45750) *(G-13322)*
County of Washington 740 373-5513
1115 Gilman Ave Marietta (45750) *(G-13323)*

County of Wayne 330 262-1786
876 S Geyers Chapel Rd Wooster (44691) *(G-19715)*
County of Wayne 330 264-5060
356 W North St Wooster (44691) *(G-19716)*
County of Wayne 330 345-5340
2534 Burbank Rd Wooster (44691) *(G-19717)*
County of Wayne 330 287-5600
428 W Liberty St Ste 11 Wooster (44691) *(G-19718)*
County of Wayne 330 287-5500
3151 W Old Lincoln Way Wooster (44691) *(G-19719)*
County of Williams 419 485-3141
310 Lincoln Ave Ste A Montpelier (43543) *(G-14612)*
County of Williams 419 636-4508
9876 County Road 16 Bryan (43506) *(G-1956)*
County of Wood 419 686-6951
351 W Main St Portage (43451) *(G-16122)*
County of Wyandot 419 294-1714
7830 State Highway 199 Upper Sandusky (43351) *(G-18404)*
Countyside Continuing Care, Fremont Also called County of Sandusky *(G-11066)*
Couple To Couple Leag Intl Inc (PA) 513 471-2000
4290 Delhi Rd Cincinnati (45238) *(G-3374)*
Court Dialysis LLC 740 773-3733
1180 N Bridge St Chillicothe (45601) *(G-2773)*
Court House Manor, Wshngtn CT Hs Also called Hcf of Court House Inc *(G-19874)*
Court of Claims of Ohio, Columbus Also called Supreme Court of Ohio *(G-8718)*
Court Stret Center Associates 513 241-0415
250 W Court St Ste 200e Cincinnati (45202) *(G-3375)*
Courtesy Ambulance Inc 740 522-8588
1890 W Main St Newark (43055) *(G-15029)*
Courtview Justice Solutions (HQ) 330 497-0033
4825 Higbee Ave Nw # 101 Canton (44718) *(G-2271)*
Courtyard By Marriott, Stow Also called Hotel Stow LP *(G-17211)*
Courtyard By Marriott, Hamilton Also called Concord Hamiltonian Rvrfrnt Ho *(G-11586)*
Courtyard By Marriott, Akron Also called Concord Testa Hotel Assoc LLC *(G-156)*
Courtyard By Marriott, Willoughby Also called Willoughby Lodging LLC *(G-19583)*
Courtyard By Marriott, Columbus Also called Courtyard Management Corp *(G-7381)*
Courtyard By Marriott, Holland Also called Marriott International Inc *(G-11895)*
Courtyard By Marriott, North Olmsted Also called Marriott International Inc *(G-15297)*
Courtyard By Marriott, Columbus Also called Columbus Concord Ltd Partnr *(G-7271)*
Courtyard By Marriott, Willoughby Also called Moody Nat Cy Willoughby Mt LLC *(G-19551)*
Courtyard By Marriott, Mentor Also called Charter Hotel Group Ltd Partnr *(G-14028)*
Courtyard By Marriott 216 765-1900
3695 Orange Pl Cleveland (44122) *(G-5372)*
Courtyard By Marriott 513 341-4140
6250 Muhlhauser Rd West Chester (45069) *(G-18901)*
Courtyard By Marriott 440 871-3756
25050 Sperry Dr Westlake (44145) *(G-19338)*
Courtyard By Marriott 937 433-3131
100 Prestige Pl Miamisburg (45342) *(G-14156)*
Courtyard By Marriott Canton, Canton Also called Ca-Mj Hotel Associates Ltd *(G-2223)*
Courtyard By Marriott Dayton 937 220-9060
2006 S Edwin C Moses Blvd Dayton (45417) *(G-9335)*
Courtyard By Marriott Rossford 419 872-5636
9789 Clark Dr Rossford (43460) *(G-16460)*
Courtyard By Mrt Clmbs Dwntwn, Columbus Also called Moody Nat Cy Dt Clumbus Mt LLC *(G-8100)*
Courtyard Cincinnati Blue Ash, Blue Ash Also called Cmp I Blue Ash Owner LLC *(G-1531)*
Courtyard Cleveland Airport S, Middleburg Heights Also called Oh-16 Clvlnd Arprt S Prprty Su *(G-14255)*
Courtyard Columbus Downtown, Columbus Also called Hit Swn Trs LLC *(G-7755)*
Courtyard Columbus Dublin, Dublin Also called Cmp I Columbus I Owner LLC *(G-10177)*
Courtyard Columbus West, Columbus Also called Cs Hotels Limited Partnership *(G-7399)*
Courtyard Columbus Worthington, Columbus Also called Cmp I Columbus II Owner LLC *(G-7236)*
Courtyard Dayton, Dayton Also called Cni Thl Ops LLC *(G-9310)*
Courtyard Dayton Mall, Miamisburg Also called Skyline CM Portfolio LLC *(G-14222)*
Courtyard Easton, Columbus Also called Olshan Hotel Management Inc *(G-8374)*
Courtyard Ltd (PA) 513 777-5530
7373 Kingsgate Way West Chester (45069) *(G-18902)*
Courtyard Management Corp 614 475-8530
2901 Airport Dr Columbus (43219) *(G-7381)*
Courtyard Management Corp 216 901-9988
5051 W Creek Rd Cleveland (44131) *(G-5373)*
Courtyard Springfield Downtown, Springfield Also called Crefiii Waramaug *(G-17027)*
Courtyard Toledo Arprt Holland, Holland Also called Skyline CM Portfolio LLC *(G-11914)*
Cousins Waste Control LLC (PA) 419 726-1500
1701 E Matzinger Rd Toledo (43612) *(G-17686)*
Cov-Ro Inc 330 856-3176
3900 E Market St Ste 1 Warren (44484) *(G-18693)*
Cova, Columbus Also called Center of Voctnl Altrntvs Mntl *(G-7154)*
Covelli Enterprises Inc 614 889-7802
6693 Sawmill Rd Dublin (43017) *(G-10191)*
Covelli Family Ltd Partnership (PA) 330 856-3176
3900 E Market St Warren (44484) *(G-18694)*
Covenant Care Ohio Inc 419 898-5506
1330 Fulton St Port Clinton (43452) *(G-16104)*

A
L
P
H
A
B
E
T
I
C

Covenant Care Ohio Inc 419 531-4201
  4420 South Ave Toledo (43615) *(G-17687)*
Covenant Care Ohio Inc 937 378-0188
  8065 Dr Faul Rd Georgetown (45121) *(G-11269)*
Covenant Care Ohio Inc 937 878-7046
  829 Yllow Sprng Frfeld Rd Fairborn (45324) *(G-10666)*
Covenant Care Ohio Inc 937 399-5551
  701 Villa Rd Springfield (45503) *(G-17026)*
Covenant Care Ohio Inc 937 526-5570
  200 Marker Rd Versailles (45380) *(G-18569)*
Covenant Home Health Care LLC 614 465-2017
  5212 W Broad St Ste J Columbus (43228) *(G-7382)*
Covenant House, Dayton *Also called Jewish Fdrtion of Grter Dayton (G-9525)*
Covenant Transport Inc 423 821-1212
  3825 Aries Brook Dr Columbus (43207) *(G-7383)*
Cover Crop Shop LLC 937 417-3972
  739 S Vandemark Rd Sidney (45365) *(G-16772)*
Covia Holdings Corporation (HQ) 440 214-3284
  3 Summit Park Dr Ste 700 Independence (44131) *(G-12063)*
Covington Car Wash Inc 513 831-6164
  5942 Creekview Dr Milford (45150) *(G-14382)*
Covington Care Center, Covington *Also called Uvmc Nursing Care Inc (G-9049)*
COVINGTON SKILLED NURSING AND, East Palestine *Also called Covington Snf Inc (G-10419)*
Covington Snf Inc 330 426-2920
  100 Covington Dr East Palestine (44413) *(G-10419)*
Covington Square Senior APT 740 623-4603
  380 Browns Ln Coshocton (43812) *(G-9013)*
Cowan Systems LLC 513 769-4774
  10801 Evendale Dr Cincinnati (45241) *(G-3376)*
Cowan Systems LLC 513 721-6444
  2751 Crescentville Rd West Chester (45069) *(G-18903)*
Cowan Systems LLC 330 963-8483
  1882 Highland Rd Twinsburg (44087) *(G-18257)*
Cowen and Company LLC 440 331-3531
  20006 Detroit Rd Ste 100 Rocky River (44116) *(G-16429)*
Cowen Truck Line Inc 419 938-3401
  2697 State Route 39 Perrysville (44864) *(G-15940)*
Cox Automotive Inc 513 874-9310
  4969 Muhlhauser Rd West Chester (45011) *(G-18904)*
Cox Automotive Inc 614 871-2771
  3905 Jackson Pike Grove City (43123) *(G-11423)*
Cox Business, Parma *Also called Cox Ohio Telcom LLC (G-15764)*
Cox Cable Cleveland Area Inc 216 676-8300
  12221 Plaza Dr Cleveland (44130) *(G-5374)*
Cox Communications Inc 216 712-4500
  12221 Plaza Dr Parma (44130) *(G-15763)*
Cox Communications Inc 937 222-5700
  1611 S Main St Dayton (45409) *(G-9336)*
Cox Institute, Kettering *Also called Wright State University (G-12304)*
Cox Ohio Telcom LLC 216 535-3500
  12221 Plaza Dr Parma (44130) *(G-15764)*
Cox Paving Inc 937 780-3075
  2754 Us Highway 22 Nw Wshngtn CT Hs (43160) *(G-19867)*
Coy Brothers Inc 330 533-6864
  433 Fairground Blvd Canfield (44406) *(G-2134)*
Coyne Graphic Finishing Inc 740 397-6232
  1301 Newark Rd Mount Vernon (43050) *(G-14759)*
CPC Logistics Inc 513 874-5787
  8695 Seward Rd Fairfield (45011) *(G-10715)*
Cpg, Columbus *Also called Containerport Group Inc (G-7355)*
CPI, Holland *Also called Creative Products Inc (G-11880)*
CPI - Cnstr Polymers Inc (PA) 330 861-5200
  7576 Freedom Ave Nw North Canton (44720) *(G-15193)*
CPI-Hr, Solon *Also called Corporate Plans Inc (G-16838)*
Cpo Managment Services, Columbus *Also called Community Prpts Ohio MGT Svcs (G-7335)*
Cpo3, Columbus *Also called Community Prpts Ohio III LLC (G-7334)*
CPX Canton Airport LLC 330 305-0500
  7883 Freedom Ave Nw North Canton (44720) *(G-15194)*
CPX Carrollton Es LLC 330 627-1200
  1296 Canton Rd Nw Carrollton (44615) *(G-2566)*
Cr Architecture and Design, Cincinnati *Also called Cole + Russell Architects Inc (G-3327)*
Cr Brands Inc (HQ) 513 860-5039
  8790 Beckett Rd West Chester (45069) *(G-18905)*
Crabbe Brown & James LLP (PA) 614 229-4587
  500 S Front St Ste 1200 Columbus (43215) *(G-7384)*
Craft Catalog, Groveport *Also called Craft Wholesalers Inc (G-11504)*
Craft Wholesalers Inc 740 964-6210
  4600 S Hamilton Rd Groveport (43125) *(G-11504)*
Crafted Surface and Stone LLC 440 658-3799
  26050 Richmond Rd Ste D Bedford Heights (44146) *(G-1321)*
Craftsman Electric Inc 513 891-4426
  3855 Alta Ave Ste 1 Cincinnati (45236) *(G-3377)*
Craftsmen Restoration LLC (PA) 877 442-3424
  2013 N Clvland Mssllon Rd Akron (44333) *(G-168)*
Craig and Frances Lindner Cent 513 536-4673
  4075 Old Western Row Rd Mason (45040) *(G-13569)*
Craig Smith Auto Group, Galion *Also called Surfside Motors Inc (G-11183)*
Craig Transportation Co 419 874-7981
  819 Kingsbury St Ste 102 Maumee (43537) *(G-13777)*

Crain Communications Inc 330 836-9180
  1725 Merriman Rd Ste 300 Akron (44313) *(G-169)*
Crandall Medical Center Inc 330 938-6126
  800 S 15th St Apt 7318 Sebring (44672) *(G-16668)*
Crane 1 Services Inc (PA) 937 704-9900
  1027 Byers Rd Miamisburg (45342) *(G-14157)*
Crane Heating & AC Co 513 641-4700
  24 Clay St Cincinnati (45217) *(G-3378)*
Crane Pumps & Systems Inc 937 773-2442
  420 3rd St Piqua (45356) *(G-16003)*
Cranel Imaging, Columbus *Also called Cranel Incorporated (G-6811)*
Cranel Incorporated (PA) 614 431-8000
  8999 Gemini Pkwy Ste A Columbus (43240) *(G-6811)*
Cranley Surgical Associates 513 961-4335
  3747 W Fork Rd Cincinnati (45247) *(G-3379)*
Crapsey & Gillis Contractors 513 891-6333
  8887 Glendale Milford Rd Loveland (45140) *(G-12985)*
Crawford & Company 440 243-8710
  7271 Engle Rd Ste 303 Cleveland (44130) *(G-5375)*
Crawford & Company 330 652-3296
  6752 Brookhollow Dr Sw Warren (44481) *(G-18695)*
Crawford Cnty Council On Aging, Bucyrus *Also called City of Bucyrus (G-1982)*
Crawford Cnty Job & Fmly Svcs, Bucyrus *Also called County of Crawford (G-1986)*
Crawford Cnty Shared Hlth Svcs 419 468-7985
  1220 N Market St Galion (44833) *(G-11169)*
Crawford County Children Svcs (PA) 419 562-1200
  224 Norton Way Bucyrus (44820) *(G-1988)*
Crawford County Council On Agi 419 562-3050
  200 S Spring St Bucyrus (44820) *(G-1989)*
Crawford Group Inc 419 873-7360
  12611 Eckel Junction Rd Perrysburg (43551) *(G-15851)*
Crawford Group Inc 330 665-5432
  3960 Medina Rd Akron (44333) *(G-170)*
Crawford Hoying Ltd 614 335-2020
  6640 Riverside Dr Ste 500 Dublin (43017) *(G-10192)*
Crawford Manor Healthcare Ctr, Cleveland *Also called Sunset Mnor Hlthcare Group Inc (G-6481)*
Crawford Mechanical Svcs Inc 614 478-9424
  3445 Morse Rd Columbus (43231) *(G-7385)*
CRC, Columbus *Also called Clintonville Beechwold Communi (G-7230)*
Creative Center For Children 513 867-1118
  23 Court St Hamilton (45011) *(G-11588)*
Creative Childrens World LLC (PA) 513 336-7799
  7818 S Masn Montgomery Rd Mason (45040) *(G-13570)*
Creative Crafts Group LLC 303 215-5600
  10151 Carver Rd Ste 200 Blue Ash (45242) *(G-1540)*
Creative Diversified Services 937 376-7810
  335 E Market St Xenia (45385) *(G-19896)*
Creative Foundations Inc (PA) 740 362-5102
  57 N Sandusky St Delaware (43015) *(G-9965)*
Creative Foundations Inc 614 832-2121
  127 S Main St Mount Vernon (43050) *(G-14760)*
Creative Images College of B (PA) 937 478-7922
  7535 Poe Ave Dayton (45414) *(G-9337)*
Creative Imges Inst Csmetology, Dayton *Also called Creative Images College of B (G-9337)*
Creative Learning Workshop (PA) 330 393-5929
  2460 Elm Rd Ne Ste 500 Warren (44483) *(G-18696)*
Creative Learning Workshop 937 437-0146
  146 N Washington St New Paris (45347) *(G-14941)*
Creative Living Inc 614 421-1131
  150 W 10th Ave Columbus (43201) *(G-7386)*
Creative Living Housing Corp 614 421-1226
  150 W 10th Ave Ofc Columbus (43201) *(G-7387)*
Creative Marketing Enterprises 419 867-4444
  6711 Monroe St Ste 4c Sylvania (43560) *(G-17416)*
Creative Microsystems Inc 937 836-4499
  52 Hillside Ct Englewood (45322) *(G-10583)*
Creative Mold and Machine Inc 440 338-5146
  10385 Kinsman Rd Newbury (44065) *(G-15119)*
Creative Plastic Concepts LLC (HQ) 419 927-9588
  206 S Griffith St Sycamore (44882) *(G-17410)*
Creative Playroom (PA) 216 475-6464
  16574 Broadway Ave Cleveland (44137) *(G-5376)*
Creative Playroom 440 248-3100
  32750 Solon Rd Ste 3 Solon (44139) *(G-16840)*
Creative Playrooms, Westlake *Also called Westlake Mntsr Schl & Chld Dv (G-19425)*
Creative Playrooms Inc 440 572-9365
  16000 Foltz Pkwy Strongsville (44149) *(G-17294)*
Creative Playrooms Inc (PA) 440 349-9111
  32750 Solon Rd Ste 3 Solon (44139) *(G-16841)*
Creative Products Inc 419 866-5501
  1430 Kieswetter Rd Holland (43528) *(G-11880)*
Creativity For Kids, Cleveland *Also called AW Faber-Castell Usa Inc (G-5028)*
Cred-Kap Inc 330 755-1466
  400 Sexton St Struthers (44471) *(G-17362)*
Credit Adjustments Inc (PA) 419 782-3709
  330 Florence St Defiance (43512) *(G-9908)*
Credit Bur Collectn Svcs Inc (HQ) 614 223-0688
  236 E Town St Columbus (43215) *(G-7388)*
Credit Bur Collectn Svcs Inc 937 496-2577
  11 W Monument Ave Ste 200 Dayton (45402) *(G-9338)*

Credit First NA 216 362-5000
6275 Eastland Rd Brookpark (44142) **(G-1894)**
Credit First National Assn 216 362-5300
6275 Eastland Rd Cleveland (44142) **(G-5377)**
Credit Infonet Inc 866 218-1003
4540 Honeywell Ct Dayton (45424) **(G-9339)**
Credit Union of Ohio Inc (PA) 614 487-6650
5500 Britton Pkwy Hilliard (43026) **(G-11757)**
Creek At Hicksburg, Hicksville *Also called Hickory Creek Healthcare* **(G-11728)**
Creek Technologies Company 937 272-4581
2372 Lakeview Dr Ste H Beavercreek (45431) **(G-1142)**
CREEKSIDE CONDOMINIUMS, Holland *Also called Lutheran Village At Wolf Creek* **(G-11893)**
Creekside Golf Dome 330 545-5000
1300 N State St Girard (44420) **(G-11286)**
Creekside Golf Ltd 513 785-2999
6090 Golf Club Ln Fairfield Township (45011) **(G-10806)**
Creekside II LLC 614 280-4000
2 Miranova Pl Ste 100 Columbus (43215) **(G-7389)**
Creekside Ltd LLC 513 583-4977
902 Lveland Miamiville Rd Loveland (45140) **(G-12986)**
Crefiii Waramaug 937 322-3600
100 S Fountain Ave Springfield (45502) **(G-17027)**
Cremation Service Inc (PA) 216 861-2334
1612 Leonard St Cleveland (44113) **(G-5378)**
Cremation Service Inc 216 621-6222
1605 Merwin Ave Cleveland (44113) **(G-5379)**
Creme De La Creme Colorado Inc 513 459-4300
5324 Natorp Blvd Mason (45040) **(G-13571)**
Creque's Greenhouse, Sylvania *Also called Jeff Creque Farms Inc* **(G-17433)**
Crescent Park Corporation (PA) 513 759-7000
9817 Crescent Park Dr West Chester (45069) **(G-18906)**
Crest Bending Inc 419 492-2108
108 John St New Washington (44854) **(G-15001)**
Crestline Agronomy, Crestline *Also called Sunrise Cooperative Inc* **(G-9060)**
Crestline Hospital, Crestline *Also called Medcentral Health System* **(G-9057)**
Crestline Hotels & Resorts LLC 614 846-4355
7490 Vantage Dr Columbus (43235) **(G-7390)**
Crestline Hotels & Resorts LLC 513 489-3666
11435 Reed Hartman Hwy Blue Ash (45241) **(G-1541)**
Crestline Nursing Center, Crestline *Also called Consulate Management Co LLC* **(G-9052)**
Crestline Nursing Home Inc 419 683-3255
327 W Main St Crestline (44827) **(G-9053)**
Crestmont Cadillac Corporation (PA) 216 831-5300
26000 Chagrin Blvd Cleveland (44122) **(G-5380)**
Crestmont North, Lakewood *Also called Crestmont Nursing Home N Corp* **(G-12340)**
Crestmont Nursing Home N Corp (PA) 216 228-9550
13330 Detroit Ave Lakewood (44107) **(G-12340)**
Crestmont Nursing Home N Corp 216 228-9550
13330 Detroit Ave Lakewood (44107) **(G-12341)**
Cresttek LLC (PA) 248 602-2083
565 Metro Pl S Ste 420 Dublin (43017) **(G-10193)**
Crestview Health Care Center 740 695-2500
68637 Bannock Rd Saint Clairsville (43950) **(G-16485)**
CRESTVIEW MANOR I, Lancaster *Also called Crestview Manor Nursing Home* **(G-12386)**
CRESTVIEW MANOR II, Lancaster *Also called Crestview Manor Nursing Home* **(G-12387)**
Crestview Manor Nursing Home (PA) 740 654-2634
957 Becks Knob Rd Lancaster (43130) **(G-12386)**
Crestview Manor Nursing Home 740 654-2634
925 Becks Knob Rd Lancaster (43130) **(G-12387)**
Crestview Nursing Home, Saint Clairsville *Also called Crestview Health Care Center* **(G-16485)**
Crestview Partners II Gp LP 216 898-2400
4900 Tiedeman Rd Fl 4 Brooklyn (44144) **(G-1860)**
Crestview Ridge Nursing 937 393-6700
141 Willetsville Pike Hillsboro (45133) **(G-11836)**
Crestwood Mgmt LLC 440 484-2400
23550 Commerce Park # 5000 Cleveland (44122) **(G-5381)**
Crestwood RDG Skilled Nursing, Hillsboro *Also called Congregate Living of America* **(G-11834)**
Crete Carrier Corporation 614 853-4500
5400 Crosswind Dr Columbus (43228) **(G-7391)**
Crew Soccer Stadium LLC 614 447-2739
1 Black And Gold Blvd Columbus (43211) **(G-7392)**
Cricket, Xenia *Also called Diamond Company Inc* **(G-19898)**
Cridersville Health Care Ctr 419 645-4468
603 E Main St Frnt Cridersville (45806) **(G-9062)**
CRIDERSVILLE NURSING HOME, Cridersville *Also called Cridersville Health Care Ctr* **(G-9062)**
Criminal Jstice Crdnting Cncil 567 200-6850
1 Government Ctr Ste 1720 Toledo (43604) **(G-17688)**
Crisis Center, Chillicothe *Also called Sioto Paintsville Mental Hlth* **(G-2826)**
Crisis Counseling Center, Wilmington *Also called Mental Health & Recovery Ctr* **(G-19635)**
Crisis Intervention & Rcvy Ctr 330 455-9407
832 Mckinley Ave Nw Canton (44703) **(G-2272)**
Crisis Intvntn Ctr Stark Cnty 330 452-9812
2421 13th St Nw Canton (44708) **(G-2273)**
CRISIS NURSERY, Cleveland *Also called Providence House Inc* **(G-6263)**
Crisis Stablization Center, Cincinnati *Also called Central Commmty Hlth Brd of Ha* **(G-3153)**

Crispin Iron & Metal Co LLC 740 616-6213
190 Victoria Dr Granville (43023) **(G-11340)**
Criss Cross Directories, North Canton *Also called Haines & Company Inc* **(G-15210)**
Critchfeld Crtchfield Johnston (PA) 330 264-4444
225 N Market St Wooster (44691) **(G-19720)**
Critical Business Analysis Inc 419 874-0800
133 W 2nd St Ste 1 Perrysburg (43551) **(G-15852)**
Critical Care Transport Inc 614 775-0564
2936 E 14th Ave Columbus (43219) **(G-7393)**
Critical Life Inc 419 525-0502
35 Logan Rd Mansfield (44907) **(G-13160)**
Crittenton Family Services 614 251-0103
1414 E Broad St Columbus (43205) **(G-7394)**
Crock Construction Co 740 732-2306
17990 Woodsfield Rd Caldwell (43724) **(G-2038)**
Crogan Colonial Bank 419 483-2541
1 Union Sq Bellevue (44811) **(G-1375)**
Croghan Bancshares Inc 419 794-9399
6465 Wheatstone Ct Maumee (43537) **(G-13778)**
Croghan Colonial Bank (HQ) 419 332-7301
323 Croghan St Fremont (43420) **(G-11067)**
Cronins Inc 513 851-5900
9847 Kings Auto Mall Rd Cincinnati (45249) **(G-3380)**
Crooked Tree Golf Course 513 398-3933
1250 Springfield Pike # 100 Cincinnati (45215) **(G-3381)**
Cross Roads Head Start, Painesville *Also called Crossroads Lake County Adole* **(G-15706)**
Cross Truck Equipment Co Inc 330 477-8151
1801 Perry Dr Sw Canton (44706) **(G-2274)**
Crosschx Inc 800 501-3161
99 E Main St Columbus (43215) **(G-7395)**
Crossgate Bowling Lanes, Blue Ash *Also called Crossgate Lanes Inc* **(G-1542)**
Crossgate Lanes Inc 513 891-0310
4230 Hunt Rd Blue Ash (45242) **(G-1542)**
CROSSROAD HEALTH CENTER, Cincinnati *Also called Christian Community Hlth Svcs* **(G-3213)**
Crossroads Center 513 475-5300
311 Mrtin Lther King Dr E Cincinnati (45219) **(G-3382)**
Crossroads Lake County Adole (PA) 440 255-1700
8445 Munson Rd Mentor (44060) **(G-14037)**
Crossroads Lake County Adole 440 358-7370
1083 Mentor Ave Painesville (44077) **(G-15706)**
Crosswoods Ultrascreen Cinema, Columbus *Also called Marcus Theatres Corporation* **(G-8018)**
Croswell of Williamsburg LLC (PA) 513 724-2206
975 W Main St Williamsburg (45176) **(G-19492)**
Croswell of Williamsburg LLC 800 782-8747
4828 Wolf Creek Pike Dayton (45417) **(G-9340)**
Croswell VIP Motor Couch Svc, Williamsburg *Also called Croswell of Williamsburg LLC* **(G-19492)**
Crotinger Nursing Home Inc 937 968-5284
907 E Central St Union City (45390) **(G-18353)**
Crouse Implement 740 892-2086
14149 North St Utica (43080) **(G-18455)**
Crowe LLP 614 469-0001
155 W Nationwide Blvd # 500 Columbus (43215) **(G-7396)**
Crowe LLP 216 623-7500
600 Superior Ave E # 902 Cleveland (44114) **(G-5382)**
Crown Auto Top Mfg Co, Columbus *Also called Crown Dielectric Inds Inc* **(G-7397)**
CROWN CENTER, Hudson *Also called Laurel Lk Retirement Cmnty Inc* **(G-11993)**
Crown Dielectric Inds Inc 614 224-5161
830 W Broad St Columbus (43222) **(G-7397)**
Crown Equipment Corporation (PA) 419 629-2311
44 S Washington St New Bremen (45869) **(G-14887)**
Crown Equipment Corporation 419 629-2311
40 S Washington St New Bremen (45869) **(G-14888)**
Crown Heating & Cooling Inc 330 499-4988
11197 Cleveland Ave Nw Uniontown (44685) **(G-18365)**
Crown Hill Cemetery, Twinsburg *Also called Stonemor Partners LP* **(G-18325)**
Crown Lift Trucks, New Bremen *Also called Crown Equipment Corporation* **(G-14887)**
Crown Logistics, Columbus *Also called MSA Group Inc* **(G-8119)**
Crown Plaza, Cincinnati *Also called Wph Cincinnati LLC* **(G-4806)**
Crown Pointe Care Center, Columbus *Also called Franklin Shcp Inc* **(G-7619)**
Crowne Group LLC (PA) 216 589-0198
127 Public Sq Ste 5110 Cleveland (44114) **(G-5383)**
Crowne Plaza Ci, Cincinnati *Also called Sage Hospitality Resources LLC* **(G-4424)**
Crowne Plaza Cleveland, Cleveland *Also called Playhouse Square Foundation* **(G-6217)**
Crowne Plaza Cleveland Airport, Cleveland *Also called Toledo Inns Inc* **(G-6531)**
Crowne Plaza Clevenland, Independence *Also called Rockside Hospitality LLC* **(G-12115)**
Crowne Plaza Columbus Downtown, Columbus *Also called Ihg Management (maryland) LLC* **(G-7800)**
Crowne Plaza Columbus North, Columbus *Also called Columbus Leasing LLC* **(G-7292)**
Crowne Plaza Dayton, Dayton *Also called Hdi Ltd* **(G-9488)**
Crowne Plaza Dayton Hotel, Dayton *Also called Integrity Hotel Group* **(G-9517)**
Crowne Plaza Toledo 419 241-1411
444 N Summit St Toledo (43604) **(G-17689)**
Croxton Realty Company 330 492-1697
410 47th St Nw Canton (44709) **(G-2275)**

(PA)=Parent Co (HQ)=Headquarters (DH)=Div Headquarters

Croys Mowing LLC 419 523-5884
  440 N Maple St Ottawa (45875) *(G-15658)*

Crp Contracting 614 338-8501
  4477 E 5th Ave Columbus (43219) *(G-7398)*

CRST International Inc 740 599-0008
  16559 Skyline Dr Danville (43014) *(G-9149)*

Crw Inc 330 264-3785
  3716 S Elyria Rd Shreve (44676) *(G-16753)*

Crystal Arthritis Center Inc 330 668-4045
  3975 Embassy Pkwy Ste 101 Akron (44333) *(G-171)*

Crystal Care Center Portsmouth 740 354-6619
  1319 Spring St Portsmouth (45662) *(G-16134)*

Crystal Care Centers Inc 419 281-9595
  1251 E Main St Ashland (44805) *(G-670)*

Crystal Care Centers Inc 419 747-2666
  458 Vanderbilt Rd Unit 1 Mansfield (44904) *(G-13161)*

Crystal Care Centers Inc (PA) 419 747-2666
  1159 Wyandotte Ave Mansfield (44906) *(G-13162)*

Crystal Care of Mansfield, Mansfield *Also called Crystal Care Centers Inc (G-13162)*

Crystal Clean Parts Washer Svc, Toledo *Also called Heritage Envmtl Svcs LLC (G-17802)*

Crystal Clear Bldg Svcs Inc 440 439-2288
  26118 Broadway Ave Ste B Oakwood Village (44146) *(G-15488)*

Crystal Clinic Surgery Ctr Inc 330 668-4040
  3975 Embassy Pkwy Ste 202 Akron (44333) *(G-172)*

Crystal Clnic Orthpdic Ctr LLC (PA) 330 668-4040
  3925 Embassy Pkwy Ste 250 Akron (44333) *(G-173)*

Crystal Clnic Orthpdic Ctr LLC 330 535-3396
  20 Olive St Ste 200 Akron (44310) *(G-174)*

Crystal Crystal Carpet Care, Columbus *Also called Clinton-Carvell Inc (G-7229)*

Crystalwood Inc 513 605-1000
  70 Damon Rd Cincinnati (45218) *(G-3383)*

Cs Hotels Limited Partnership 614 771-8999
  2350 Westbelt Dr Columbus (43228) *(G-7399)*

Csa America Inc 216 524-4990
  8501 E Pleasant Valley Rd Cleveland (44131) *(G-5384)*

Csa Amrica Tstg Crtfcation LLC 216 524-4990
  8501 E Pleasant Valley Rd Independence (44131) *(G-12064)*

Csa Animal Nutrition LLC 866 615-8084
  6640 Poe Ave Ste 225 Dayton (45414) *(G-9341)*

Csa International Services, Cleveland *Also called Csa America Inc (G-5384)*

CSB Bancorp Inc (PA) 330 674-9015
  91 N Clay St Millersburg (44654) *(G-14473)*

CSC Distribution Inc (HQ) 614 278-6800
  4900 E Dblin Granville Rd Columbus (43081) *(G-7400)*

CSC Insurance Agency Inc 614 895-2000
  550 Polaris Pkwy Ste 300 Westerville (43082) *(G-19154)*

Csh Group 937 226-0070
  10100 Innovation Dr # 400 Miamisburg (45342) *(G-14158)*

Csi Complete Inc 800 343-0641
  8080 Corporate Blvd Plain City (43064) *(G-16048)*

Csi International, Williamsport *Also called Connectivity Systems Inc (G-19498)*

Csi International Inc 614 781-1571
  690 Lkview Plz Blvd Ste C Worthington (43085) *(G-19802)*

Csi Managed Care Inc 440 717-1700
  6955 Treeline Dr Ste A Brecksville (44141) *(G-1778)*

Csi Network Services, Brecksville *Also called Csi Managed Care Inc (G-1778)*

Csl Plasma Inc 937 331-9186
  850 N Main St Dayton (45405) *(G-9342)*

Csl Plasma Inc 614 267-4982
  2650 N High St Columbus (43202) *(G-7401)*

Csl Plasma Inc 330 535-4338
  727 Grant St Lowr Akron (44311) *(G-175)*

Csl Plasma Inc 216 398-0440
  3204 W 25th St Cleveland (44109) *(G-5385)*

CSRA LLC 937 429-9774
  3560 Pentagon Blvd Beavercreek (45431) *(G-1143)*

Csrc, Chillicothe *Also called Chillicothe Racquet Club (G-2766)*

CSS Publishing Co Inc 419 227-1818
  5450 N Dixie Hwy Lima (45807) *(G-12627)*

Csu/Career Services Center 216 687-2233
  2121 Euclid Ave Cleveland (44115) *(G-5386)*

CSX Corporation 419 225-4121
  401 E Robb Ave Lima (45801) *(G-12628)*

CSX Corporation 614 242-3932
  2600 Parsons Ave Columbus (43207) *(G-7402)*

CSX Corporation 419 933-5027
  2826 Liberty Rd Willard (44890) *(G-19479)*

CSX Transportation Inc 440 992-0871
  1709 E Prospect Rd Ashtabula (44004) *(G-735)*

CSX Transportation Inc 513 369-5514
  3601 Geringer St Cincinnati (45223) *(G-3384)*

CSX Transportation Inc 614 898-3651
  426 Landings Loop E Westerville (43082) *(G-19155)*

CSX Transportation Inc 937 642-2221
  19835 Johnson Rd Marysville (43040) *(G-13493)*

CSX Transportation Inc 419 257-1225
  17000 Deshler Rd North Baltimore (45872) *(G-15176)*

CSX Transportation Inc 513 422-2031
  1003 Forrer St Middletown (45044) *(G-14298)*

CSX Transportation Inc 419 697-2323
  600 Millard Ave Oregon (43616) *(G-15588)*

CT Communications, Urbana *Also called Champaign Telephone Company (G-18426)*

CT Consultants Inc (PA) 440 951-9000
  8150 Sterling Ct Mentor (44060) *(G-14038)*

CT Consultants Inc 513 791-1700
  11120 Kenwood Rd Blue Ash (45242) *(G-1543)*

CT Logistics Inc 216 267-1636
  12487 Plaza Dr Cleveland (44130) *(G-5387)*

CT Medical Electronics Co 440 526-3551
  1 Corporation Ctr Broadview Heights (44147) *(G-1829)*

Ctd Investments LLC (PA) 614 570-9949
  630 E Broad St Columbus (43215) *(G-7403)*

CTI, Monroe *Also called Continental Transport Inc (G-14564)*

CTI Engineers Inc 330 294-5996
  1 Cascade Plz Ste 710 Akron (44308) *(G-176)*

Ctl Analyzers, Shaker Heights *Also called Cellular Technology Limited (G-16704)*

Ctl Engineering Inc (PA) 614 276-8123
  2860 Fisher Rd Columbus (43204) *(G-7404)*

Ctm Integration Incorporated 330 332-1800
  1318 Quaker Cir Salem (44460) *(G-16541)*

Ctpartners Exec Search Inc 216 464-8710
  28601 Chagrin Blvd # 600 Beachwood (44122) *(G-1049)*

Ctrac Inc 440 572-1000
  2222 W 110th St Cleveland (44102) *(G-5388)*

CTS Construction Inc 513 489-8290
  7275 Edington Dr Cincinnati (45249) *(G-3385)*

CTS Telecommunications, Cincinnati *Also called CTS Construction Inc (G-3385)*

Ctts, Cincinnati *Also called Cincinnati Training Trml Svcs (G-3273)*

Ctv Media Inc (PA) 614 848-5800
  1490 Manning Pkwy Powell (43065) *(G-16193)*

Cuddy Farms Inc 740 599-7979
  15835 Danville Jelloway R Danville (43014) *(G-9150)*

Cui, Bedford Heights *Also called Chores Unlimited Inc (G-1320)*

Culver Art & Frame Co 740 548-6868
  7890 N Central Dr Lewis Center (43035) *(G-12536)*

Cumberford & Watts, Cleveland *Also called West Side Cardiology Assoc (G-6668)*

Cumberland Gap LLC 513 681-9300
  2285 Banning Rd Cincinnati (45239) *(G-3386)*

Cumberland Mutl Fire Insur Co 419 525-4443
  380 N Main St Ste 101 Mansfield (44902) *(G-13163)*

Cumberland Trail Golf CLB Crse 740 964-9336
  8244 Columbia Rd Sw Etna (43062) *(G-10614)*

Cummings and Davis Fnrl HM Inc 216 541-1111
  13201 Euclid Ave Cleveland (44112) *(G-5389)*

Cummins Bridgeway Columbus LLC 614 771-1000
  4000 Lyman Dr Hilliard (43026) *(G-11758)*

Cummins Building Maint Inc 740 726-9800
  5202 Marion Waldo Rd Prospect (43342) *(G-16221)*

Cummins Facility Services LLC 740 726-9800
  5202 Marion Waldo Rd Prospect (43342) *(G-16222)*

Cummins Inc 614 771-1000
  4000 Lyman Dr Hilliard (43026) *(G-11759)*

Cummins Inc 513 563-6670
  5400 Rialto Rd West Chester (45069) *(G-18907)*

Cumulus Broadcasting LLC 850 243-7676
  4805 Montgomery Rd Cincinnati (45212) *(G-3387)*

Cumulus Broadcasting LLC 330 783-1000
  4040 Simon Rd Youngstown (44512) *(G-20012)*

Cumulus Media Inc 419 725-5700
  3225 Arlington Ave Toledo (43614) *(G-17690)*

Cumulus Media Inc 513 241-9898
  4805 Montgomery Rd # 300 Cincinnati (45212) *(G-3388)*

Cumulus Media Inc 419 240-1000
  3225 Arlington Ave Toledo (43614) *(G-17691)*

Cunningham Paving Company 216 581-8600
  20814 Aurora Rd Bedford (44146) *(G-1275)*

Curiosity LLC 513 744-6000
  35 E 7th St Ste 800 Cincinnati (45202) *(G-3389)*

Curiosity Advertising, Cincinnati *Also called Curiosity LLC (G-3389)*

Current Lighting Solutions LLC (HQ) 800 435-4448
  1975 Noble Rd Ste 338e Cleveland (44112) *(G-5390)*

Curtiss-Wright Controls 937 252-5601
  2600 Paramount Pl Ste 200 Fairborn (45324) *(G-10667)*

Curtiss-Wright Flow Control 513 735-2538
  750 Kent Rd Batavia (45103) *(G-995)*

Curtiss-Wright Flow Control 513 528-7900
  4600 E Tech Dr Cincinnati (45245) *(G-2847)*

Curtiss-Wright Flow Ctrl Corp 513 528-7900
  4600 E Tech Dr Cincinnati (45245) *(G-2848)*

Cusa Li Inc 216 267-8810
  13315 Brookpark Rd Brookpark (44142) *(G-1895)*

Cushman & Wakefield Inc 513 631-1121
  4600 Montgomery Rd Norwood (45212) *(G-15461)*

Cushman & Wakefield Inc 937 222-7884
  3033 Kettering Blvd # 111 Moraine (45439) *(G-14638)*

Cuso Corporation 513 984-2876
  10485 Reading Rd Cincinnati (45241) *(G-3390)*

Custom AC & Htg Co 614 552-4822
  935 Claycraft Rd Gahanna (43230) *(G-11116)*

Custom Agri Systems Inc 419 209-0940
  1289 N Warpole St Upper Sandusky (43351) *(G-18405)*

Custom Chemical Solutions 800 291-1057
  167 Commerce Dr Loveland (45140) *(G-12987)*

Custom Cleaners, Bryan *Also called George Gardner (G-1958)*

Custom Cleaning and Maint....440 946-7028
38046 2nd St Willoughby (44094) ***(G-19517)***
Custom Cleaning Service LLC....440 774-1222
305 Artino St Unit A Oberlin (44074) ***(G-15500)***
Custom Design Benefits Inc....513 598-2929
5589 Cheviot Rd Cincinnati (45247) ***(G-3391)***
Custom Fabricators Inc (PA)....216 831-2266
1621 E 41st St Cleveland (44103) ***(G-5391)***
Custom Halthcare Proffessional....216 381-1010
5001 Mayfield Rd Ste 210 Cleveland (44124) ***(G-5392)***
Custom Lawn Care & Ldscpg LLC....740 333-1669
2411 Us Highway 22 Sw Wshngtn CT Hs (43160) ***(G-19868)***
Custom Machine Inc....419 986-5122
3315 W Township Road 158 Tiffin (44883) ***(G-17515)***
Custom Maid Cleaning Services....513 351-6571
3840 Burwood Ave Cincinnati (45212) ***(G-3392)***
Custom Mail Services, Cincinnati *Also called Ngm Inc* ***(G-4118)***
Custom Maint....330 793-2523
73 Country Green Dr Youngstown (44515) ***(G-20013)***
Custom Materials Inc....440 543-8284
16865 Park Circle Dr Chagrin Falls (44023) ***(G-2663)***
Custom Movers Services Inc....330 564-0507
3290 Kent Rd Stow (44224) ***(G-17196)***
Custom Pak, Medina *Also called Industrial Chemical Corp* ***(G-13953)***
Custom Pkg & Inspecting Inc....330 399-8961
5232 Tod Ave Sw Ste 3 Warren (44481) ***(G-18697)***
Custom Products Corporation (PA)....440 528-7100
7100 Cochran Rd Solon (44139) ***(G-16842)***
Custom Seal Inc....419 334-1020
708 Graham Dr Fremont (43420) ***(G-11068)***
Custom Seal Roofing, Fremont *Also called Custom Seal Inc* ***(G-11068)***
Custom Staffing Inc (PA)....419 221-3097
505 W Market St Lima (45801) ***(G-12629)***
Custom Trim of America, Akron *Also called Kallas Enterprises Inc* ***(G-297)***
Custom-Pak Inc....330 725-0800
885 W Smith Rd Medina (44256) ***(G-13928)***
Customized Girl, Columbus *Also called E Retailing Associates LLC* ***(G-7486)***
Custompak, Medina *Also called Custom-Pak Inc* ***(G-13928)***
Cuthbert Greenhouse Inc (PA)....614 836-3866
4900 Hendron Rd Groveport (43125) ***(G-11505)***
Cutler and Associates Inc....330 896-1680
971 E Turkeyfoot Lake Rd Akron (44312) ***(G-177)***
Cutler and Associates Inc....330 688-2100
3653 Darrow Rd Ste 1 Stow (44224) ***(G-17197)***
Cutler and Associates Inc (PA)....330 493-9323
4618 Dressler Rd Nw Canton (44718) ***(G-2276)***
Cutler G M A C Real Estate, Canton *Also called Cutler Real Estate* ***(G-2277)***
Cutler Real Estate....330 499-9922
203 Applegrove St Nw North Canton (44720) ***(G-15195)***
Cutler Real Estate (PA)....330 836-9141
2800 W Market St Fairlawn (44333) ***(G-10820)***
Cutler Real Estate....330 688-2100
3653 Darrow Rd Stow (44224) ***(G-17198)***
Cutler Real Estate....330 733-7575
525 N Scranton St Ravenna (44266) ***(G-16241)***
Cutler Real Estate (PA)....330 492-7230
4618 Dressler Rd Nw Canton (44718) ***(G-2277)***
Cutler Real Estate Inc....614 339-4664
6375 Riverside Dr Ste 210 Dublin (43017) ***(G-10194)***
Cutler Realtor, Akron *Also called Cutler and Associates Inc* ***(G-177)***
Cutler/Gmac Real Estate, Canton *Also called Cutler and Associates Inc* ***(G-2276)***
Cuttin' It Close, Mansfield *Also called Tara Flaherty* ***(G-13250)***
Cutting Edge Countertops Inc....419 873-9500
1300 Flagship Dr Perrysburg (43551) ***(G-15853)***
Cuyahoga County....216 420-6750
1701 E 12th St Ste 11 Cleveland (44114) ***(G-5393)***
Cuyahoga County....216 265-3030
12660 Plaza Dr Cleveland (44130) ***(G-5394)***
Cuyahoga County....216 431-4500
3955 Euclid Ave Cleveland (44115) ***(G-5395)***
Cuyahoga County....216 348-3800
2079 E 9th St Cleveland (44115) ***(G-5396)***
Cuyahoga County....216 443-8920
1 W Lakeside Ave Ste 146 Cleveland (44113) ***(G-5397)***
Cuyahoga County AG Soc....440 243-0090
164 Eastland Rd Berea (44017) ***(G-1421)***
Cuyahoga County Board of Menta, Cleveland *Also called County of Cuyahoga* ***(G-5367)***
Cuyahoga County Convention Fac....216 928-1600
1 Saint Clair Ave Ne Cleveland (44114) ***(G-5398)***
Cuyahoga County Dept Pub Works, Cleveland *Also called Cuyahoga County* ***(G-5396)***
Cuyahoga County Fair, Berea *Also called Cuyahoga County AG Soc* ***(G-1421)***
Cuyahoga County Sani Engrg Svc....216 443-8211
6100 W Canal Rd Cleveland (44125) ***(G-5399)***
Cuyahoga Group, The, Maple Heights *Also called Cuyahoga Vending Co Inc* ***(G-13284)***
Cuyahoga Landmark Inc (PA)....440 238-3900
21079 Westwood Dr Strongsville (44149) ***(G-17295)***
Cuyahoga Marketing Service....440 526-5350
375 Treeworth Blvd Cleveland (44147) ***(G-5400)***
Cuyahoga Vending Co Inc (PA)....216 663-1457
14250 Industrial Ave S # 104 Maple Heights (44137) ***(G-13284)***

CVNPA, Peninsula *Also called Conserv For Cyhg Vlly Nat Prk* ***(G-15811)***
Cw Financial LLC....941 907-9490
23550 Commerce Park # 5000 Beachwood (44122) ***(G-1050)***
Cwb Property Managment Inc (PA)....614 793-2244
5775 Perimeter Dr Ste 290 Dublin (43017) ***(G-10195)***
Cwm Envronmental Cleveland LLC....216 663-0808
4450 Johnston Pkwy Ste B Cleveland (44128) ***(G-5401)***
Cy Schwieterman Inc....419 753-2566
10097 Kohler Rd Wapakoneta (45895) ***(G-18641)***
Cyo & Community Services Inc (PA)....330 762-2961
795 Russell Ave Akron (44307) ***(G-178)***
Cypress Communications Inc (HQ)....404 965-7248
75 Erieview Plz Fl 4 Cleveland (44114) ***(G-5402)***
Cypress Companies Inc (PA)....330 849-6500
670 W Market St Akron (44303) ***(G-179)***
Cypress Hospice LLC....440 973-0250
2 Berea Cmns Ste 1 Berea (44017) ***(G-1422)***
D & D Advertising Enterprises....513 921-6827
801 Evans St Ste 203 Cincinnati (45204) ***(G-3393)***
D & D Investment Co....614 272-6567
3080 Valleyview Dr Columbus (43204) ***(G-7405)***
D & G Focht Construction Co....419 732-2412
2040 E State Rd Port Clinton (43452) ***(G-16105)***
D & J Master Clean Inc....614 847-1181
680 Dearborn Park Ln Columbus (43085) ***(G-7406)***
D & S Crtive Cmmunications Inc....419 524-4312
195 E 4th St Mansfield (44902) ***(G-13164)***
D & S Properties....614 224-6663
854 E Broad St Columbus (43205) ***(G-7407)***
D & V Trucking Inc....330 482-9440
12803 Clmbana Canfield Rd Columbiana (44408) ***(G-6786)***
D A Peterson Inc....330 821-1111
393 Smyth Ave Alliance (44601) ***(G-529)***
D A R Plumbing, Columbus *Also called Dar Plumbing* ***(G-7417)***
D B A Inc....513 541-6600
4239 Hamilton Ave Cincinnati (45223) ***(G-3394)***
D B Bentley Inc....440 352-8495
2649 Narrows Rd Painesville (44077) ***(G-15707)***
D C Curry Lumber Company....330 264-5223
17201 Dover Rd Dundee (44624) ***(G-10383)***
D C G, Cleveland *Also called Directconnectgroup Ltd* ***(G-5425)***
D C I, Akron *Also called Digital Color Intl LLC* ***(G-187)***
D C Minnick Contracting Ltd (PA)....937 322-1012
328 Ravenwood Dr Springfield (45504) ***(G-17028)***
D C Transportation Service....440 237-0900
5740 Royalwood Rd Ste C North Royalton (44133) ***(G-15351)***
D E Williams Electric Inc....440 543-1222
168 Solon Rd Ste B Chagrin Falls (44022) ***(G-2644)***
D G M Inc....740 226-1950
1881 Adams Rd Beaver (45613) ***(G-1120)***
D H I Cooperative Inc....614 545-0460
1224 Alton Darby Creek Rd A Columbus (43228) ***(G-7408)***
D I S A D E C C Columbus, Columbus *Also called Defense Info Systems Agcy* ***(G-7430)***
D J- Seve Group Inc....614 888-6600
10030 Columbus Pike Lewis Center (43035) ***(G-12537)***
D James Incorporated....513 574-4550
4320 Bridgetown Rd Cincinnati (45211) ***(G-3395)***
D L A Training Center....614 692-5986
3990 E Broad St Bldg 11 Columbus (43213) ***(G-7409)***
D L Belknap Trucking Inc....330 868-7766
3526 Baird Ave Se Paris (44669) ***(G-15756)***
D L Ryan Companies LLC....614 436-6558
440 Polaris Pkwy Ste 350 Westerville (43082) ***(G-19156)***
D M I, Reynoldsburg *Also called Dimensional Metals Inc* ***(G-16299)***
D M I Distribution Inc....765 584-3234
6150 Huntley Rd Ste A Columbus (43229) ***(G-7410)***
D S C, Dublin *Also called Dimension Service Corporation* ***(G-10200)***
D W Dickey, Lisbon *Also called D W Dickey and Son Inc* ***(G-12799)***
D W Dickey and Son Inc (PA)....330 424-1441
7896 Dickey Dr Lisbon (44432) ***(G-12799)***
D W F, Toledo *Also called Denver Wholesale Florists Co* ***(G-17698)***
D&D Trucking and Services Inc....419 692-3205
5191 Kill Rd Delphos (45833) ***(G-10023)***
D&M Carter LLC....513 831-8843
106 Glendale Milford Rd Miamiville (45147) ***(G-14245)***
D&M Sales & Solutions LLC....937 667-8713
9465 S State Route 202 # 1 Tipp City (45371) ***(G-17554)***
D-G Custom Chrome LLC....513 531-1881
5200 Lester Rd Cincinnati (45213) ***(G-3396)***
D-R Training Center & Workshop....419 289-0470
1256 Center St Ashland (44805) ***(G-671)***
D.C.minnick Heating and AC, Springfield *Also called D C Minnick Contracting Ltd* ***(G-17028)***
Da Vinci Group Inc....614 419-2393
7815 Pembrook Dr Reynoldsburg (43068) ***(G-16295)***
Da Vita, Marietta *Also called Davita Inc* ***(G-13325)***
Da Vita, Canton *Also called Davita Inc* ***(G-2280)***
Da Vita, Belpre *Also called Davita Inc* ***(G-1401)***
Dacas Nursing Systems Inc....330 884-2530
8747 Squires Ln Ne Warren (44484) ***(G-18698)***
DAG Construction Co Inc....513 542-8597
4924 Winton Rd Cincinnati (45232) ***(G-3397)***

ALPHABETIC

Dagger Johnston Miller (PA) 740 653-6464
144 E Main St Lancaster (43130) *(G-12388)*

Dahlberg Learning Center, Columbus *Also called Assoc Dvlpmtly Disabled (G-6982)*

Dahm Brothers Company Inc 937 461-5627
743 Valley St Dayton (45404) *(G-9343)*

Daihen Inc (HQ) 937 667-0800
1400 Blauser Dr Tipp City (45371) *(G-17555)*

Daikin Applied Americas Inc 763 553-5009
2915 Needmore Rd Dayton (45414) *(G-9344)*

Daikin Applied Parts Warehouse, Dayton *Also called Daikin Applied Americas Inc (G-9344)*

Daily Services LLC 740 326-6130
12 E Gambier St Mount Vernon (43050) *(G-14761)*

Daily Services LLC (PA) 614 431-5100
1110 Morse Rd Ste B1 Columbus (43229) *(G-7411)*

Dairy Farm, Polk *Also called Falling Star Farm Ltd (G-16092)*

Dairy Farmers America Inc 330 670-7800
1035 Medina Rd Ste 300 Medina (44256) *(G-13929)*

Dakota Girls LLC 614 801-2558
2585 London Groveport Rd Grove City (43123) *(G-11424)*

Dakota Software Corporation (PA) 216 765-7100
1375 Euclid Ave Ste 500 Cleveland (44115) *(G-5403)*

Dale Ross Trucking Inc 937 981-2168
11408 State Route 41 S Greenfield (45123) *(G-11360)*

Dale-Roy School & Training Ctr, Ashland *Also called D-R Training Center & Workshop (G-671)*

Dales Truck Parts Inc 937 766-2551
2891 Us Route 42 E Cedarville (45314) *(G-2580)*

Dalton Roofing Co 513 871-2800
4477 Eastern Ave Cincinnati (45226) *(G-3398)*

Damarc Inc 330 454-6171
4330 Kirby Ave Ne Canton (44705) *(G-2278)*

Damascus Staffing LLC 513 954-8941
2263 W Us 22 And 3 Maineville (45039) *(G-13114)*

Damon Tax Service 513 574-9087
6572 Glenway Ave Cincinnati (45211) *(G-3399)*

Damschroder Roofing Inc 419 332-5000
2228 Hayes Ave Ste D Fremont (43420) *(G-11069)*

Dan Beard Council, Cincinnati *Also called Boy Scouts of America (G-3069)*

Dan Marchetta Cnstr Co Inc 330 668-4800
525 N Cleveland Massillon Akron (44333) *(G-180)*

Dan Tobin Pontiac Buick GMC 614 889-6300
2539 Billingsley Rd Columbus (43235) *(G-7412)*

Dan-Ray Construction LLC 216 518-8484
4500 Lee Rd Ste 207 Cleveland (44128) *(G-5404)*

Dana & Pariser Attys 614 253-1010
495 E Mound St Columbus (43215) *(G-7413)*

Dana Heavy Vehicle Systems 419 866-3900
6936 Airport Hwy Holland (43528) *(G-11881)*

Dana Lauren Salon & Spa 440 262-1092
8076 Broadview Rd Broadview Heights (44147) *(G-1830)*

Dana Spicer Service Parts, Holland *Also called Dana Heavy Vehicle Systems (G-11881)*

Danbarry Dollar Svr Cinema, Dayton *Also called B and D Investment Partnership (G-9244)*

Danbarry Linemas Inc 740 779-6115
119 Pawnee Rd Chillicothe (45601) *(G-2774)*

Danberry Co 419 866-8888
3555 Briarfield Blvd Maumee (43537) *(G-13779)*

Danbury Woods of Wooster 330 264-0355
939 Portage Rd Wooster (44691) *(G-19721)*

Danby Products Inc (HQ) 419 425-8627
1800 Production Dr Findlay (45840) *(G-10895)*

Dancor Inc 614 340-2155
2155 Dublin Rd Columbus (43228) *(G-7414)*

Daniel A Terreri & Sons Inc 330 538-2950
1091 N Meridian Rd Youngstown (44509) *(G-20014)*

Daniel Logistics Inc 614 367-9442
426 Mccormick Blvd Columbus (43213) *(G-7415)*

Daniel Maury Construction Co 513 984-4096
8960 Glendale Milford Rd Loveland (45140) *(G-12988)*

Daniel's Construction, Berlin Heights *Also called Daniels Basement Waterproofing (G-1450)*

Daniels Basement Waterproofing 440 965-4332
10407 Main Rd Berlin Heights (44814) *(G-1450)*

Daniels Boarding Kennels 440 238-7179
21782 Royalton Rd Strongsville (44149) *(G-17296)*

Daniels Lumber Co Inc 330 533-2211
250 Railroad St Canfield (44406) *(G-2135)*

Danis Building Construction Co (PA) 937 228-1225
3233 Newmark Dr Miamisburg (45342) *(G-14159)*

Danis Companies 937 228-1225
3233 Newmark Dr Miamisburg (45342) *(G-14160)*

Danis Industrial Cnstr Co 937 228-1225
3233 Newmark Dr Miamisburg (45342) *(G-14161)*

Danite Holdings Ltd 614 444-3333
1640 Harmon Ave Columbus (43223) *(G-7416)*

Danite Sign Co, Columbus *Also called Danite Holdings Ltd (G-7416)*

Danny Veghs Home Entertainment, Mayfield Heights *Also called Dtv Inc (G-13873)*

Danridge Nursing Home Inc 330 746-5157
31 Maranatha Ct Youngstown (44505) *(G-20015)*

Danson Inc 513 948-0066
3033 Robertson Ave Cincinnati (45209) *(G-3400)*

Danton Eye Associates, Beavercreek *Also called Richard L Liston MD (G-1235)*

Dar Plumbing 614 445-8243
2230 Refugee Rd Columbus (43207) *(G-7417)*

Darana Hybrid Inc (PA) 513 785-7540
345 High St Fl 5 Hamilton (45011) *(G-11589)*

Darby Creek Excavating Inc 740 477-8600
19524 London Rd Circleville (43113) *(G-4831)*

Darby Creek Golf Course Inc 937 349-7491
19300 Orchard Rd Marysville (43040) *(G-13494)*

Darby Creek Nursery, Hilliard *Also called R & S Halley & Co Inc (G-11810)*

Darfus 740 380-1710
1135 W Hunter St Logan (43138) *(G-12834)*

Dari Pizza Enterprises II Inc 419 534-3000
1683 Woodlands Dr Ste A Maumee (43537) *(G-13780)*

Darice, Strongsville *Also called Lamrite West Inc (G-17321)*

Darice Inc (HQ) 440 238-9150
13000 Darice Pkwy 82 Strongsville (44149) *(G-17297)*

Darke Cnty Mental Hlth Clinic (PA) 937 548-1635
212 E Main St Greenville (45331) *(G-11371)*

Darke County Sheriffs Patrol 937 548-3399
5185 County Home Rd Greenville (45331) *(G-11372)*

Darr Farms, Newcomerstown *Also called George Darr (G-15132)*

Dart Trucking Company Inc (PA) 330 549-0994
11017 Market St North Lima (44452) *(G-15268)*

Das Dutch Kitchen Inc 330 683-0530
14278 Lincoln Way E Dalton (44618) *(G-9144)*

Das Dutch Village Inn 330 482-5050
150 E State Route 14 Columbiana (44408) *(G-6787)*

Dash Logistics Inc 937 382-9110
259 Olinger Cir Wilmington (45177) *(G-19621)*

Dash Services LLC 216 273-9133
3100 E 45th St Cleveland (44127) *(G-5405)*

Dasher Lawless Automation LLC 855 755-7275
310 Dana St Ne Warren (44483) *(G-18699)*

Dassault Systemes Simulia Corp 513 275-1430
5181 Natorp Blvd Ste 205 Mason (45040) *(G-13572)*

DAT, Akron *Also called Downtown Akron Partnership Inc (G-193)*

Data Recovery, Shaker Heights *Also called 1st All File Recovery Usa (G-16701)*

Datacomm Tech 614 755-5100
6606 Tussing Rd Ste B Reynoldsburg (43068) *(G-16296)*

Datafield Inc 614 847-9600
25 W New England Ave Worthington (43085) *(G-19803)*

Datalliance, Blue Ash *Also called Enterprise Data Management Inc (G-1554)*

Datalysys LLC 614 495-0260
5200 Upper Metro Pl # 120 Dublin (43017) *(G-10196)*

Datatech Depot (east) Inc 513 860-5651
4750 Ashley Dr West Chester (45011) *(G-18908)*

Datatrak International Inc 440 443-0082
5900 Landerbrook Dr # 170 Mayfield Heights (44124) *(G-13872)*

Datavantage Corporation (HQ) 440 498-4414
30500 Bruce Industrial Pk Cleveland (44139) *(G-5406)*

Datwyler Sling Sltions USA Inc 937 387-2800
875 Center Dr Vandalia (45377) *(G-18519)*

Datzap LLC 330 785-2100
1520 S Arlington St Akron (44306) *(G-181)*

Daugherty Construction Inc 216 731-9444
22460 Lakeland Blvd Euclid (44132) *(G-10628)*

Daugwood Inc 937 429-9465
3183 Beaver Vu Dr Ste B Beavercreek (45434) *(G-1144)*

Dav Chapter 53, Cheshire *Also called Disabled American Veterans (G-2733)*

Dave & Barb Enterprises Inc 513 553-0050
Address Unknonwn New Richmond (45157) *(G-14992)*

Dave Commercial Ground MGT 440 237-5394
9956 Akins Rd North Royalton (44133) *(G-15352)*

Dave Dennis Auto Group, Beavercreek Township *Also called Dave Dnnis Chrysler Jeep Dodge (G-1245)*

Dave Dnnis Chrysler Jeep Dodge 937 429-5566
4232 Colonel Glenn Hwy Beavercreek Township (45431) *(G-1245)*

Dave Knapp Ford Lincoln Inc (PA) 937 547-3000
500 Wagner Ave Greenville (45331) *(G-11373)*

Dave Marshall Inc (PA) 937 878-9135
1448 Kauffman Ave Fairborn (45324) *(G-10668)*

Dave Pinkerton 740 477-8888
221 Renick Ave Chillicothe (45601) *(G-2775)*

Dave Sugar Excavating LLC 330 542-1100
11640 S State Line Rd Petersburg (44454) *(G-15943)*

Dave White Chevrolet Inc 419 885-4444
5880 Monroe St Sylvania (43560) *(G-17417)*

Daves Running Shop Inc 567 525-4767
1765 Tiffin Ave Findlay (45840) *(G-10896)*

Daves Sand & Stone Inc 419 445-9256
19230 County Road F Wauseon (43567) *(G-18798)*

Davey Resource Group Inc 859 630-9879
1230 W 8th St Cincinnati (45203) *(G-3401)*

Davey Resource Group Inc (HQ) 330 673-9511
1500 N Mantua St Kent (44240) *(G-12225)*

Davey Tree & Lawn Care, Stow *Also called Davey Tree Expert Company (G-17199)*

Davey Tree & Lawn Care, Milford *Also called Davey Tree Expert Company (G-14383)*

Davey Tree & Lawn Care, Cleveland *Also called Davey Tree Expert Company (G-5407)*

Davey Tree and Lawn Care, Columbus *Also called Davey Tree Expert Company (G-7419)*

Davey Tree Expert Company 330 908-0833
837 Highland Rd E Macedonia (44056) *(G-13067)*

2019 Harris Ohio
Services Directory

(G-0000) Company's Geographic Section entry number

Davey Tree Expert Company 330 628-1499
1437 State Route 43 Ste A Mogadore (44260) ***(G-14546)***
Davey Tree Expert Company (PA) 330 673-9511
1500 N Mantua St Kent (44240) ***(G-12226)***
Davey Tree Expert Company 330 928-4911
4576 Allen Rd Stow (44224) ***(G-17199)***
Davey Tree Expert Company 330 673-9511
3567 Westerville Rd Columbus (43224) ***(G-7418)***
Davey Tree Expert Company 614 471-4144
3603 Westerville Rd Columbus (43224) ***(G-7419)***
Davey Tree Expert Company 513 575-1733
6065 Br Hill Guinea Pike Milford (45150) ***(G-14383)***
Davey Tree Expert Company 440 439-4770
7625 Bond St Cleveland (44139) ***(G-5407)***
David Barber Civic Center 740 498-4383
1066 E State St Newcomerstown (43832) ***(G-15129)***
David Campbell 937 266-7064
2000 Hewitt Ave Dayton (45440) ***(G-9345)***
David Francis Corporation (PA) 216 524-0900
250 W Huron Rd Ste 300 Cleveland (44113) ***(G-5408)***
David Hirsh, Blacklick *Also called Atrium Buying Corporation* ***(G-1474)***
David Hummel Building, Cincinnati *Also called Hummel Industries Incorporated* ***(G-3741)***
David J Joseph Company, The, Cincinnati *Also called Djj Holding Corporation* ***(G-3437)***
David L Barth Lwyr 513 852-8228
537 E Pete Rose Way Cincinnati (45202) ***(G-3402)***
David Lee Grossman MD 419 843-8150
1000 Regency Ct Ste 102 Toledo (43623) ***(G-17692)***
David M Schneider MD Inc (PA) 513 752-5700
4452 Estgate Blvd Ste 305 Cincinnati (45245) ***(G-2849)***
David R White Services Inc (PA) 740 594-8381
5315 Hebbardsville Rd Athens (45701) ***(G-775)***
David Scott Salon 440 734-7595
107a Great Northern Mall North Olmsted (44070) ***(G-15285)***
David W Milliken (PA) 740 998-5023
2 S Main St Frankfort (45628) ***(G-11018)***
David W Steinbach Inc 330 497-5959
6824 Wise Ave Nw Canton (44720) ***(G-2279)***
David White Services, Athens *Also called David R White Services Inc* ***(G-775)***
Davidson Becker Inc 330 755-2111
11 Spring St Struthers (44471) ***(G-17363)***
Davidson Trucking Inc 419 288-2318
1227 Bowling Green Rd E Bradner (43406) ***(G-1764)***
Davis 5 Star Holdings LLC (PA) 954 470-8456
14 E Main St Ste 300 Springfield (45502) ***(G-17029)***
Davis Beese Nuclear Power Stn, Oak Harbor *Also called Toledo Edison Company* ***(G-15479)***
Davis Eye Center 330 923-5676
789 Graham Rd Cuyahoga Falls (44221) ***(G-9085)***
Davis H Elliot Cnstr Co Inc 937 847-8025
1 S Gebhart Church Rd Miamisburg (45342) ***(G-14162)***
Davis Paul Restoration Dayton 937 436-3411
1960 W Dorothy Ln Ste 207 Moraine (45439) ***(G-14639)***
Davis Pickering & Company Inc 740 373-5896
165 Enterprise Dr Marietta (45750) ***(G-13324)***
Davis Tobacco Co, Cleveland *Also called The Anter Brothers Company* ***(G-6519)***
Davis Tree Farm & Nursery Inc 330 483-3324
6126 Neff Rd Valley City (44280) ***(G-18460)***
Davis Young A Legal Prof Assn (PA) 216 348-1700
600 Superior Ave E # 1200 Cleveland (44114) ***(G-5409)***
Davita 1620, Cleveland *Also called Davita Inc* ***(G-5411)***
Davita Dialysis, Dayton *Also called Davita Inc* ***(G-9346)***
Davita Healthcare Partners Inc 216 961-6498
7901 Detroit Ave Cleveland (44102) ***(G-5410)***
Davita Healthcare Partners Inc 440 353-0114
35143 Center Ridge Rd North Ridgeville (44039) ***(G-15328)***
Davita Inc 513 939-1110
1210 Hicks Blvd Fairfield (45014) ***(G-10716)***
Davita Inc 216 712-4700
19133 Hilliard Blvd Rocky River (44116) ***(G-16430)***
Davita Inc 440 891-5645
7360 Engle Rd Cleveland (44130) ***(G-5411)***
Davita Inc 740 376-2622
1019 Pike St Marietta (45750) ***(G-13325)***
Davita Inc 937 456-1174
105 E Wash Jackson Rd Eaton (45320) ***(G-10441)***
Davita Inc 330 494-2091
4685 Fulton Dr Nw Canton (44718) ***(G-2280)***
Davita Inc 216 525-0990
4801 Acorn Dr Ste 1 Independence (44131) ***(G-12065)***
Davita Inc 937 879-0433
1266 N Broad St Fairborn (45324) ***(G-10669)***
Davita Inc 937 426-6475
3070 Presidential Dr A Beavercreek (45324) ***(G-1145)***
Davita Inc 937 435-4030
5721 Bigger Rd Dayton (45440) ***(G-9346)***
Davita Inc 937 376-1453
215 S Allison Ave Ste B Xenia (45385) ***(G-19897)***
Davita Inc 440 293-6028
486 S Main St Andover (44003) ***(G-605)***
Davita Inc 513 784-1800
2109 Reading Rd Cincinnati (45202) ***(G-3403)***
Davita Inc 740 401-0607
2906 Washington Blvd Belpre (45714) ***(G-1401)***
Davita Inc 330 335-2300
195 Wadsworth Rd Wadsworth (44281) ***(G-18595)***
Davita Inc 440 251-6237
6830 N Ridge Rd Madison (44057) ***(G-13094)***
Davita Inc 615 341-6311
458 Home St Georgetown (45121) ***(G-11270)***
Davita Inc 330 733-1861
73 Massillon Rd Akron (44312) ***(G-182)***
Davita Inc 419 697-2191
3310 Dustin Rd Oregon (43616) ***(G-15589)***
Davita Inc 513 624-0400
7502 State Rd Cincinnati (45255) ***(G-3404)***
Davita Kidney Dialysis, Andover *Also called Davita Inc* ***(G-605)***
Davue Ob-Gyn Associates Inc (PA) 937 277-8988
2200 Philadelphia Dr # 101 Dayton (45406) ***(G-9347)***
Dawes Arboretum 740 323-2355
7770 Jacksontown Rd Newark (43056) ***(G-15030)***
Dawn Chemical, Willowick *Also called Dawnchem Inc* ***(G-19597)***
Dawn Incorporated 330 652-7711
2861 Sferra Ave Nw Warren (44483) ***(G-18700)***
Dawnchem Inc 440 943-3332
30510 Lakeland Blvd Frnt Willowick (44095) ***(G-19597)***
Dawson Companies 440 333-9000
3900 Kinross Lakes Pkwy Richfield (44286) ***(G-16352)***
Dawson Personnel, Columbus *Also called Dawson Resources* ***(G-7421)***
Dawson Personnel Systems, Columbus *Also called Dawson Resources* ***(G-7420)***
Dawson Resources (PA) 614 255-1400
1114 Dublin Rd Columbus (43215) ***(G-7420)***
Dawson Resources 614 274-8900
4184 W Broad St Columbus (43228) ***(G-7421)***
Day Academy, Springboro *Also called M J J B Ltd* ***(G-16973)***
Day Air Credit Union Inc (PA) 937 643-2160
3501 Wilmington Pike Dayton (45429) ***(G-9348)***
Day Ketterer Ltd (PA) 330 455-0173
200 Market Ave N Ste 300 Canton (44702) ***(G-2281)***
Day Precision Wall Inc 513 353-2999
5715 Hamilton Cleves Rd Cleves (45002) ***(G-6727)***
Day Share Ltd 513 451-1100
5915 Glenway Ave Cincinnati (45238) ***(G-3405)***
Day Spring Health Care Corp 740 984-4262
501 Pinecrest Dr Beverly (45715) ***(G-1462)***
Day-Met Credit Union Inc (PA) 937 236-2562
3199 S Dixie Dr Moraine (45439) ***(G-14640)***
Day-Mont Behavioral Hlth Care, Moraine *Also called Day-Mont Bhvoral Hlth Care Inc* ***(G-14641)***
Day-Mont Bhvoral Hlth Care Inc (PA) 937 222-8111
2710 Dryden Rd Moraine (45439) ***(G-14641)***
Daybreak Inc (PA) 937 395-4600
605 S Patterson Blvd Dayton (45402) ***(G-9349)***
Dayhuff Group LLC (PA) 614 854-9999
740 Lakeview Plaza Blvd # 300 Worthington (43085) ***(G-19804)***
Daymark Food Safety Systems 419 353-2458
12830 S Dixie Hwy Bldg B Bowling Green (43402) ***(G-1729)***
Daymark Security Systems, Bowling Green *Also called CMC Daymark Corporation* ***(G-1728)***
Daynas Homecare LLC 216 323-0323
14616 Tabor Ave Maple Heights (44137) ***(G-13285)***
Days Inn, Lewisburg *Also called Janus Hotels and Resorts Inc* ***(G-12569)***
Days Inn, Fremont *Also called Goodnight Inn Inc* ***(G-11078)***
Days Inn 740 695-0100
52601 Holiday Dr Saint Clairsville (43950) ***(G-16486)***
Days of Discovery 937 862-4465
3195 Clear Springs Rd Spring Valley (45370) ***(G-16958)***
Dayspring Health Care Center 937 864-5800
8001 Dyton Springfield Rd Fairborn (45324) ***(G-10670)***
Dayspring Healthcare Center, Beverly *Also called Appalachian Respite Care Ltd* ***(G-1460)***
Dayspring Residential Care, Mansfield *Also called County of Richland* ***(G-13154)***
Daytep Inc 937 456-5860
1816 Alexander Rd Eaton (45320) ***(G-10442)***
Dayton Aerospace Inc 937 426-4300
4141 Colonel Glenn Hwy # 252 Beavercreek Township (45431) ***(G-1246)***
Dayton Animal Hospital Assoc 937 890-4744
8015 N Main St Dayton (45415) ***(G-9350)***
Dayton Anthem 937 428-8000
1222 S Patterson Blvd # 4 Dayton (45402) ***(G-9351)***
Dayton Appliance Parts Co (PA) 937 224-0487
122 Sears St Dayton (45402) ***(G-9352)***
Dayton Area Chamber Commerce 937 226-1444
22 E 5th St Ste 200 Dayton (45402) ***(G-9353)***
Dayton Art Institute 937 223-5277
456 Belmonte Park N Dayton (45405) ***(G-9354)***
Dayton Bag & Burlap Co (PA) 937 258-8000
322 Davis Ave Dayton (45403) ***(G-9355)***
Dayton Business Journal, Dayton *Also called American City Bus Journals Inc* ***(G-9226)***
Dayton Cardiology Consultants (PA) 937 223-3053
1126 S Main St Dayton (45409) ***(G-9356)***
Dayton Childrens Hospital 937 641-3376
1 Childrens Plz Dayton (45404) ***(G-9357)***
Dayton Childrens Hospital (PA) 937 641-3000
1 Childrens Plz Dayton (45404) ***(G-9358)***
Dayton City Parks Golf Maint 937 333-3378
3383 Chuck Wagner Ln Dayton (45414) ***(G-9359)***

ALPHABETIC

Dayton City Water Department, Dayton *Also called City of Dayton (G-9306)*

Dayton Convention Visitors Bur, Dayton *Also called Dayton Cvb (G-9361)*

Dayton Country Club Company 937 294-3352
555 Kramer Rd Dayton (45419) *(G-9360)*

Dayton Crdiolgy Vascular Cons, Dayton *Also called Dayton Cardiology Consultants (G-9356)*

Dayton Cvb 937 226-8211
1 Chamber Plz Ste A Dayton (45402) *(G-9361)*

Dayton Digital Media Inc 937 223-8335
2212 Patterson Rd Dayton (45420) *(G-9362)*

Dayton Digital.com, Dayton *Also called Dayton Digital Media Inc (G-9362)*

Dayton Dmh Inc 937 436-2273
3800 Summit Glen Dr Dayton (45449) *(G-9363)*

Dayton Dog Training Club Inc 937 293-5219
3040 E River Rd Ste 5 Moraine (45439) *(G-14642)*

Dayton Door Sales Inc (PA) 937 253-9181
1112 Springfield St Dayton (45403) *(G-9364)*

Dayton Dragons Baseball, Dayton *Also called Dayton Prof Basbal CLB LLC (G-9378)*

Dayton Eye Surgery Center 937 431-9531
81 Sylvania Dr Beavercreek (45440) *(G-1213)*

Dayton Foundation Inc 937 222-0410
40 N Main St Ste 500 Dayton (45423) *(G-9365)*

Dayton Freight Lines Inc 419 589-0350
103 Cairns Rd Mansfield (44903) *(G-13165)*

Dayton Freight Lines Inc 419 661-8600
28240 Oregon Rd Perrysburg (43551) *(G-15854)*

Dayton Freight Lines Inc 614 860-1080
1406 Blatt Blvd Columbus (43230) *(G-7422)*

Dayton Freight Lines Inc 937 236-4880
6265 Executive Blvd Ste A Dayton (45424) *(G-9366)*

Dayton Freight Lines Inc 330 346-0750
280 Progress Blvd Kent (44240) *(G-12227)*

Dayton Hcri Place Denver 419 247-2800
4500 Dorr St Toledo (43615) *(G-17693)*

Dayton Heart Center Inc (PA) 937 277-4274
1530 Needmore Rd Ste 300 Dayton (45414) *(G-9367)*

Dayton Heart Hospital, Dayton *Also called Medcath Intermediate Holdings (G-9600)*

Dayton Heidelberg Distrg Co (PA) 937 222-8692
3601 Dryden Rd Moraine (45439) *(G-14643)*

Dayton Heidelberg Distrg Co 937 220-6450
3601 Dryden Rd Moraine (45439) *(G-14644)*

Dayton Heidelberg Distrg Co 419 666-9783
912 3rd St Perrysburg (43551) *(G-15855)*

Dayton Heidelberg Distrg Co 216 520-2626
9101 E Pleasant Vly Cleveland (44131) *(G-5412)*

Dayton Heidelberg Distrg Co 419 666-9783
912 3rd St Perrysburg (43551) *(G-15856)*

Dayton Heidelberg Distrg Co 937 220-6450
3601 Dryden Rd Moraine (45439) *(G-14645)*

Dayton Heidelberg Distrg Co 614 308-0400
3801 Parkwest Dr Columbus (43228) *(G-7423)*

Dayton Heidelberg Distrg Co 513 421-5000
1518 Dalton Ave Cincinnati (45214) *(G-3406)*

Dayton History 937 293-2841
1000 Carillon Blvd Dayton (45409) *(G-9368)*

Dayton Hospice Incorporated (PA) 937 256-4490
324 Wilmington Ave Dayton (45420) *(G-9369)*

Dayton Hospice Incorporated 513 422-0300
5940 Long Meadow Dr Franklin (45005) *(G-11027)*

Dayton Hotels LLC 937 832-2222
20 Rockridge Rd Englewood (45322) *(G-10584)*

Dayton Industrial Drum Inc 937 253-8933
1880 Radio Rd Dayton (45431) *(G-9167)*

Dayton Intl Peace Museum, Dayton *Also called Dayton Intl Peace Museum (G-9370)*

Dayton Intl Peace Museum 937 227-3223
208 W Monument Ave Dayton (45402) *(G-9370)*

Dayton Mailing Services Inc 937 222-5056
100 S Keowee St Dayton (45402) *(G-9371)*

Dayton Marriott, Dayton *Also called Concord Dayton Hotel II LLC (G-9316)*

Dayton Marshall Tire Sales Co 937 293-8330
3091 S Dixie Dr Moraine (45439) *(G-14646)*

Dayton Mdowbrook Cntry CLB LLC 937 836-5186
6001 Salem Ave Clayton (45315) *(G-4856)*

Dayton Medical Imaging 937 439-0390
7901 Schatz Pointe Dr Dayton (45459) *(G-9372)*

Dayton Nwborn Care Spclsts Inc 937 641-3329
1 Childrens Plz Rm 4085 Dayton (45404) *(G-9373)*

Dayton Ob Gyn 937 439-7550
330 N Main St Ste 200 Centerville (45459) *(G-2625)*

Dayton Osteopathic Hospital (HQ) 937 762-1629
405 W Grand Ave Dayton (45405) *(G-9374)*

Dayton Outpatien Practice, Dayton *Also called Pain Management Associates Inc (G-9186)*

Dayton Performing Arts Aliance 937 224-3521
126 N Main St Ste 210 Dayton (45402) *(G-9375)*

Dayton Pharmacy, Dayton *Also called Equitas Health Inc (G-9416)*

Dayton Physicians LLC (PA) 937 280-8400
6680 Poe Ave Ste 200 Dayton (45414) *(G-9376)*

Dayton Physicians LLC 937 547-0563
1111 Sweitzer St Ste C Greenville (45331) *(G-11374)*

Dayton Power and Light Company (HQ) 937 331-4063
1065 Woodman Dr Dayton (45432) *(G-9168)*

Dayton Power and Light Company 937 549-2641
745 Us Highway 52 Unit 1 Manchester (45144) *(G-13127)*

Dayton Power and Light Company 937 549-2641
14869 Us 52 Manchester (45144) *(G-13128)*

Dayton Power and Light Company 937 331-3032
1 S Gebhart Church Rd Miamisburg (45342) *(G-14163)*

Dayton Power and Light Company 937 331-4123
1900 Dryden Rd Moraine (45439) *(G-14647)*

Dayton Primary & Urgent Care 937 461-0800
301 W 1st St Ste 100 Dayton (45402) *(G-9377)*

Dayton Prof Basbal CLB LLC 937 228-2287
220 N Patterson Blvd Dayton (45402) *(G-9378)*

Dayton Public School District 937 542-3000
115 S Ludlow St Dayton (45402) *(G-9379)*

Dayton Regional Dialysis Inc (PA) 937 898-5526
8701 Old Troy Pike Ste 10 Dayton (45424) *(G-9380)*

Dayton Roof & Remodeling Co 937 224-7667
418 Merrick Dr Beavercreek (45434) *(G-1146)*

Dayton Society Natural History (PA) 937 275-7431
2600 Deweese Pkwy Dayton (45414) *(G-9381)*

Dayton Society Natural History 513 932-4421
6123 State Route 350 Oregonia (45054) *(G-15616)*

Dayton South Dialysis, Moraine *Also called Wakoni Dialysis LLC (G-14706)*

Dayton Tall Timbers Resort 937 833-3888
7796 Wellbaum Rd Brookville (45309) *(G-1913)*

Dayton Toro Motorcycle Club 937 723-9133
1536 W 3rd St Dayton (45402) *(G-9382)*

Dayton Urban League (PA) 937 226-1513
907 W 5th St Dayton (45402) *(G-9383)*

Dayton V A Medical Center, Dayton *Also called Veterans Affairs US Dept (G-9856)*

Dayton Walls & Ceilings Inc 937 277-0531
4328 Webster St Dayton (45414) *(G-9384)*

Dayton Wastewater Trtmnt Plant, Dayton *Also called City of Dayton (G-9305)*

Dayton Windustrial Co 937 461-2603
137 E Helena St Dayton (45404) *(G-9385)*

Dayton YMCA Camp Kern, Oregonia *Also called Young Mens Christian Assoc (G-15618)*

Dayton-Dixie Mufflers Inc (PA) 419 243-7281
1101 Monroe St Toledo (43604) *(G-17694)*

DB&p Logistics Inc 614 491-4035
3544 Watkins Rd Columbus (43232) *(G-7424)*

Dbi Services LLC 410 590-4181
2393 County Road 1 South Point (45680) *(G-16930)*

Dbp Enterprises LLC 740 513-2399
7301 E State Route 37 Sunbury (43074) *(G-17386)*

DCI, Columbus *Also called Digico Imaging Inc (G-7446)*

Dco LLC (HQ) 419 931-9086
900 E Boundary St Ste 8a Perrysburg (43551) *(G-15857)*

Dcp Holding Company 513 554-1100
100 Crowne Point Pl Sharonville (45241) *(G-16728)*

Dcr Systems LLC (PA) 440 205-9900
8697 Tyler Blvd Mentor (44060) *(G-14039)*

DCS Corporation 937 306-7180
4027 Colonel Glenn Hwy Beavercreek Township (45431) *(G-1247)*

DCS Sanitation Management Inc (PA) 513 891-4980
7864 Camargo Rd Cincinnati (45243) *(G-3407)*

Dct Telecom Group Inc 440 892-0300
27877 Clemens Rd Westlake (44145) *(G-19339)*

Ddhew, Columbus *Also called Division Drnking Ground Waters (G-7457)*

Ddi, Brookpark *Also called Distribution Data Incorporated (G-1896)*

Ddm Direct of Ohio, Hebron *Also called Ddm-Digital Imaging Data (G-11712)*

Ddm-Digital Imaging Data 740 928-1110
190 Milliken Dr Hebron (43025) *(G-11712)*

Ddr Corp 614 785-6445
445 Hutchinson Ave # 800 Columbus (43235) *(G-7425)*

Ddr Corp 216 755-5547
5539 Dressler Rd Nw Canton (44720) *(G-2282)*

Ddr Tucson Spectrum I LLC 216 755-5500
3300 Enterprise Pkwy Beachwood (44122) *(G-1051)*

De Bra - Kuempel, Cincinnati *Also called Debra-Kuempel Inc (G-3414)*

DE Foxx & Associates Inc (PA) 513 621-5522
324 W 9th St Fl 5 Cincinnati (45202) *(G-3408)*

DE Huddleston Inc 740 773-2130
283 S Paint St Chillicothe (45601) *(G-2776)*

De Nora Tech LLC (HQ) 440 710-5300
7590 Discovery Ln Painesville (44077) *(G-15708)*

Deacon 10 .... 216 731-4000
1353 E 260th St Ste 1 Euclid (44132) *(G-10629)*

Deaconess Associations Inc (PA) 513 559-2100
615 Elsinore Pl Bldg B Cincinnati (45202) *(G-3409)*

Deaconess Hospital of Cincinna (PA) 513 559-2100
615 Elsinore Pl Bldg B Cincinnati (45202) *(G-3410)*

Deaconess Long Term Care Inc (HQ) 513 861-0400
330 Straight St Ste 310 Cincinnati (45219) *(G-3411)*

Deaconess Long Term Care of MI (PA) 513 487-3600
330 Straight St Ste 310 Cincinnati (45219) *(G-3412)*

Deaconis Assocation Inc 419 874-9008
27062 Oakmead Dr Perrysburg (43551) *(G-15858)*

Deaconis Association, Perrysburg *Also called Deaconis Assocation Inc (G-15858)*

Dealer Supply and Eqp Ltd 419 724-8473
1549 Campbell St Toledo (43607) *(G-17695)*

Dealer Tire LLC (PA) 216 432-0088
7012 Euclid Ave Cleveland (44103) *(G-5413)*

Dealers Group Limited 440 352-4970
23240 Chagrin Blvd # 802 Beachwood (44122) *(G-1052)*

Dealers Supply North Inc (HQ) 614 274-6285
2315 Creekside Pkwy # 500 Lockbourne (43137) **(G-12812)**

Dean Financial Management, Beavercreek Also called C H Dean Inc **(G-1136)**

Deanhouston Creative Group Inc (PA) 513 421-6622
310 Culvert St Ste 300 Cincinnati (45202) **(G-3413)**

Dearman Moving & Storage Co 419 524-3456
961 N Main St Mansfield (44903) **(G-13166)**

Dearman Moving and Storage, Mansfield Also called J-Trac Inc **(G-13189)**

Dearth Management Company 419 253-0144
825 State Route 61 Marengo (43334) **(G-13302)**

Dearth Management Company 740 389-1214
677 Marion Cardington Rd Marion (43302) **(G-13418)**

Dearth Management Company (PA) 614 847-1070
134 Northwoods Blvd Ste C Columbus (43235) **(G-7426)**

Dearth Management Company 330 339-3595
2594 E High Ave New Philadelphia (44663) **(G-14956)**

Debra-Kuempel Inc (HQ) 513 271-6500
3976 Southern Ave Cincinnati (45227) **(G-3414)**

Decahealth Inc 866 908-3514
7071 W Central Ave Ste C Toledo (43617) **(G-17696)**

Decisionone Corporation 614 883-0228
3425 Urbancrest Indus Dr Urbancrest (43123) **(G-18448)**

Decker Drilling Inc 740 749-3939
11565 State Route 676 Vincent (45784) **(G-18585)**

Decker Equipment Company Inc 866 252-4395
9601 Granger Rd Cleveland (44125) **(G-5414)**

Decker Forklifts, Cleveland Also called Decker Equipment Company Inc **(G-5414)**

Deckers Nursery Inc 614 836-2130
6239 Rager Rd Groveport (43125) **(G-11506)**

Decoating Inc 419 347-9191
3955 Industrial Pkwy Shelby (44875) **(G-16745)**

Decorative Flooring Services, Maumee Also called Marble Restoration Inc **(G-13813)**

Decorative Paint Incorporated 419 485-0632
700 Randolph St Montpelier (43543) **(G-14613)**

Decorative Paving Company 513 576-1222
39 Glendale Milford Rd Loveland (45140) **(G-12989)**

Decosky GM Center, Mount Vernon Also called Decosky Motor Holdings Inc **(G-14762)**

Decosky Motor Holdings Inc 740 397-9122
510 Harcourt Rd 550 Mount Vernon (43050) **(G-14762)**

Dedicated Logistics Inc 513 275-1135
6019 Union Centre Blvd West Chester (45014) **(G-18909)**

Dedicated Nursing Assoc Inc 937 886-4559
228 Byers Rd Ste 103 Miamisburg (45342) **(G-14164)**

Dedicated Nursing Assoc Inc 888 465-6929
70 Birch Aly Ste 240 Beavercreek (45440) **(G-1214)**

Dedicated Nursing Assoc Inc 866 450-5550
11542 Springfield Pike Cincinnati (45246) **(G-3415)**

Dedicated Nursing Assoc Inc 877 411-8350
5672 W Broad St Galloway (43119) **(G-11219)**

Dedicated Nursing Assoc Inc 877 547-9144
1339a Rockside Rd Parma (44134) **(G-15765)**

Dedicated Tech Services Inc 614 309-0059
545 Metro Pl S Ste 100 Dublin (43017) **(G-10197)**

Dedicated Technologies Inc 614 460-3200
175 S 3rd St Ste 200 Columbus (43215) **(G-7427)**

Dedicated Transport LLC (HQ) 216 641-2500
700 W Resource Dr Brooklyn Heights (44131) **(G-1869)**

Dee Jay Cleaners Inc 216 731-7060
878 E 222nd St Euclid (44123) **(G-10630)**

Deed Realty Co 330 225-5220
4600 Center Rd Brunswick (44212) **(G-1926)**

Deemsys Inc (PA) 614 322-9928
800 Cross Pointe Rd Afg Gahanna (43230) **(G-11117)**

Deepwood Center, Mentor Also called County of Lake **(G-14036)**

Deepwood Industries Inc 440 350-5231
8121 Deepwood Blvd Mentor (44060) **(G-14040)**

Deer Creek State Park, Mount Sterling Also called Ohio Dept Natural Resources **(G-14746)**

Deer Park Roofing Inc (PA) 513 891-9151
7201 Blue Ash Rd Cincinnati (45236) **(G-3416)**

Deerfield Construction Co Inc (PA) 513 984-4096
8960 Glendale Milford Rd Loveland (45140) **(G-12990)**

Deerfield Estates Inc (PA) 440 838-1400
7000 S Edgerton Rd # 108 Brecksville (44141) **(G-1779)**

Deerfield Farms 330 584-4715
9041 State Route 224 Deerfield (44411) **(G-9903)**

Deerfield Farms Service Inc 330 584-4715
9041 State Route 224 Deerfield (44411) **(G-9904)**

Defense Fin & Accounting Svc 410 436-9740
3990 E Broad St Columbus (43213) **(G-7428)**

Defense Fin & Accounting Svc 614 693-6700
3990 E Broad St Columbus (43213) **(G-7429)**

Defense Info Systems Agcy 614 692-4433
3990 E Broad St Bldg 20c Columbus (43213) **(G-7430)**

Defense Research Assoc Inc 937 431-1644
3915 Germany Ln Ste 102 Dayton (45431) **(G-9169)**

Defiance Clinic, Defiance Also called Fauster-Cameron Inc **(G-9913)**

Defiance Cnty Bd Commissioners 419 782-3233
140 E Broadway St Defiance (43512) **(G-9909)**

Defiance County Senior Center, Defiance Also called Defiance Cnty Bd Commissioners **(G-9909)**

Defiance Family Physicians 419 785-3281
1250 Ralston Ave Ste 104 Defiance (43512) **(G-9910)**

Defiance Hospital Inc 419 782-6955
1200 Ralston Ave Defiance (43512) **(G-9911)**

DEFIANCE REGIONAL MEDICAL CENTER, Defiance Also called Defiance Hospital Inc **(G-9911)**

Definitions of Design Inc 419 891-0188
467 W Dussel Dr Maumee (43537) **(G-13781)**

Definitive Solutions Co Inc 513 719-9100
8180 Corp Pk Dr Ste 305 Cincinnati (45242) **(G-3417)**

Definity Partners, West Chester Also called Midwest Mfg Solutions LLC **(G-19068)**

Deform, Columbus Also called Scientific Forming Tech Corp **(G-8610)**

Degussa Construction, Beachwood Also called Master Builders LLC **(G-1076)**

Dei Fratelli, Northwood Also called Hirzel Canning Company **(G-15395)**

Dei Incorporated 513 825-5800
1550 Kemper Meadow Dr Cincinnati (45240) **(G-3418)**

Del Monde Inc 859 371-7780
2485 Belvo Rd Miamisburg (45342) **(G-14165)**

Del Monte Fresh Produce NA Inc 614 527-7398
2200 Westbelt Dr Columbus (43228) **(G-7431)**

Del-Co Water Company Inc (PA) 740 548-7746
6658 Olentangy River Rd Delaware (43015) **(G-9966)**

Delaneys Tax Accunting Svc Ltd 513 248-2829
1157b State Route 131 Milford (45150) **(G-14384)**

Delano Foods, Canton Also called Hiland Group Incorporated **(G-2344)**

Delaware City School District 740 363-5901
2462 Liberty Rd Delaware (43015) **(G-9967)**

Delaware City School Garage, Delaware Also called Delaware City School District **(G-9967)**

Delaware County Engineers, Delaware Also called County of Delaware **(G-9963)**

Delaware County Historical Soc 740 369-3831
2690 Stratford Rd Delaware (43015) **(G-9968)**

DELAWARE COURT, Mount Vernon Also called Country Court Ltd **(G-14757)**

Delaware Court Health Care Ctr, Delaware Also called Levering Management Inc **(G-9995)**

Delaware General Health Dst, Delaware Also called County of Delaware **(G-9964)**

Delaware Golf Club Inc 740 362-2582
3326 Columbus Pike Delaware (43015) **(G-9969)**

Delaware Opco LLC 502 429-8062
2270 Warrensburg Rd Delaware (43015) **(G-9970)**

Delhi Township (PA) 513 922-0060
934 Neeb Rd Cincinnati (45233) **(G-3419)**

Deliass Assets Corp 614 891-0101
780 Brooksedge Plaza Dr Westerville (43081) **(G-19248)**

Delight Connection, Avon Also called Cochin Technologies LLC **(G-878)**

Delille Oxygen Company (PA) 614 444-1177
772 Marion Rd Columbus (43207) **(G-7432)**

Delmar Distributing, Columbus Also called Columbus Distributing Company **(G-7275)**

Deloitte & Touche LLP 937 223-8821
220 E Monu Ave Ste 500 Dayton (45402) **(G-9386)**

Deloitte & Touche LLP 513 784-7100
250 E 5th St Fl 1600 Cincinnati (45202) **(G-3420)**

Deloitte & Touche LLP 614 221-1000
180 E Broad St Ste 1400 Columbus (43215) **(G-7433)**

Deloitte & Touche LLP 216 589-1300
127 Public Sq Ste 3300 Cleveland (44114) **(G-5415)**

Deloitte Consulting, Cincinnati Also called Deloitte & Touche LLP **(G-3420)**

Deloitte Consulting LLP 937 223-8821
711 E Monu Ave Ste 201 Dayton (45402) **(G-9387)**

Delphi, Warren Also called Aptiv Services Us LLC **(G-18667)**

Delphos Ambulatory Care Center 419 692-2662
1800 E 5th St Ste 1 Delphos (45833) **(G-10024)**

Delphos Plant 2, Delphos Also called Toledo Molding & Die Inc **(G-10036)**

Delta Air Lines Inc 216 265-2400
5300 Riverside Dr Ste 11 Cleveland (44135) **(G-5416)**

Delta Air Lines Inc 614 239-4440
4600 Intl Gtwy Ste 6 Columbus (43219) **(G-7434)**

Delta Airlines, Cleveland Also called Delta Air Lines Inc **(G-5416)**

Delta Airlines, Columbus Also called Delta Air Lines Inc **(G-7434)**

Delta Electrical Contrs Ltd 513 421-7744
4890 Gray Rd Cincinnati (45232) **(G-3421)**

Delta Energy LLC 614 761-3603
545 Metro Pl S Ste 400 Dublin (43017) **(G-10198)**

Delta Gamma Fraternity (PA) 614 481-8169
3250 Riverside Dr Upper Arlington (43221) **(G-18396)**

Delta Gamma Fraternity 614 487-5599
3220 Riverside Dr A2 Upper Arlington (43221) **(G-18397)**

Delta Kappa Gamma Society 419 586-6016
1030 Canterbury Dr Celina (45822) **(G-2593)**

Delta Media Group Inc 330 493-0350
4726 Hills And Dales Rd N Canton (44708) **(G-2283)**

Delta Railroad Cnstr Inc (PA) 440 992-2997
2648 W Prospect Rd Frnt Ashtabula (44004) **(G-736)**

Delta Theta Sigma Fraternity, Columbus Also called Ohio State University **(G-8336)**

Deltacraft, Cleveland Also called Millcraft Group LLC **(G-5993)**

Delth Corporation 440 255-7655
6312 Center St Ste C Mentor (44060) **(G-14041)**

Delventhal Company 419 244-5570
3796 Rockland Cir Millbury (43447) **(G-14447)**

Demarius Corporation 760 957-5500
5000 Tuttle Crossing Blvd Dublin (43016) **(G-10199)**

Dempsey Inc 330 758-2309
2803 South Ave Youngstown (44502) **(G-20016)**

A
L
P
H
A
B
E
T
I
C

(PA)=Parent Co (HQ)=Headquarters (DH)=Div Headquarters

Denier Electric Co Inc (PA) 513 738-2641
10891 State Route 128 Harrison (45030) **(G-11665)**

Denier Electric Co Inc 614 338-4664
4000 Gantz Rd Ste C Grove City (43123) **(G-11425)**

Denier Technologies Div, Harrison Also called Denier Electric Co Inc **(G-11665)**

Denmark Consultants Inc 513 530-9984
11464 Lippelman Rd # 200 Cincinnati (45246) **(G-3422)**

Dennis & Carol Liederbach 256 582-6200
8651 Wood Hollow Rd Northfield (44067) **(G-15377)**

Dennis C McCluskey MD & Assoc 330 628-2686
754 S Cleveland Ave # 300 Mogadore (44260) **(G-14547)**

Dennis Mitsubishi, Columbus Also called Carcorp Inc **(G-7118)**

Dennis Todd Painting Inc 614 879-7952
6055 Us Highway 40 West Jefferson (43162) **(G-19106)**

Dennis Top Soil & Landscaping 419 865-5656
6340 Dorr St Toledo (43615) **(G-17697)**

Denso International Amer Inc 937 393-6800
1600 N High St Hillsboro (45133) **(G-11837)**

Dent Magic, Columbus Also called Magic Industries Inc **(G-8008)**

Dent Magic 614 864-3368
4629 Poth Rd Columbus (43213) **(G-7435)**

Dental Agent, Columbus Also called Dental Facility **(G-7436)**

Dental Associates, Columbus Also called Lawrence M Shell DDS **(G-7959)**

DENTAL CARE PLUS GROUP (DCPG), Sharonville Also called Dcp Holding Company **(G-16728)**

Dental Center Northwest Ohio 419 422-7664
1800 N Blanchard St # 122 Findlay (45840) **(G-10897)**

Dental Ceramics Inc 330 523-5240
3404 Brecksville Rd Richfield (44286) **(G-16353)**

Dental Facility 614 292-1472
305 W 12th Ave Rm 1159 Columbus (43210) **(G-7436)**

Dental Health Group PA 330 630-9222
2000 Brittain Rd Ste 91 Akron (44310) **(G-183)**

Dental Health Services (PA) 330 864-9090
110 N Miller Rd Ste 200 Fairlawn (44333) **(G-10821)**

Dental One Inc 216 584-1000
6200 Oak Tree Blvd # 220 Independence (44131) **(G-12066)**

Dental Services Group, Miamisburg Also called Sentage Corporation **(G-14218)**

Dental Servics of Ohio Daniel 614 863-2222
6323 Tussing Rd Reynoldsburg (43068) **(G-16297)**

Dental Support Specialties LLC 330 639-1333
1790 Graybill Rd Ste 100 Uniontown (44685) **(G-18366)**

Dentronix Inc 330 916-7300
235 Ascot Pkwy Cuyahoga Falls (44223) **(G-9086)**

Denver Wholesale Florists Co 419 241-7241
14 N Erie St Toledo (43604) **(G-17698)**

Department Children Services, Cleveland Also called County of Cuyahoga **(G-5370)**

Department Information Tech, Cleveland Also called County of Cuyahoga **(G-5364)**

Department Jobs and Fmly Svcs, Marietta Also called County of Washington **(G-13323)**

Department of Anesthetia, Cincinnati Also called University of Cincinnati **(G-4703)**

Department of Aviation, Vandalia Also called City of Dayton **(G-18516)**

Department of Human Nutrition, Columbus Also called Ohio State University **(G-8304)**

Department of Human Services, Georgetown Also called County of Brown **(G-11268)**

Department of Internal Med Div, Columbus Also called Ohio State University **(G-8351)**

Department of Jobs & Family, Cambridge Also called County of Guernsey **(G-2062)**

Department of Neurology, Columbus Also called Neuroscience Center Inc **(G-8182)**

Department of Ob/Gyn, Cleveland Also called Metrohealth System **(G-5969)**

Department of Public Utilities, Circleville Also called City of Circleville **(G-4829)**

Department of Public Utilities, Cleveland Also called City of Cleveland **(G-5198)**

Department of Statistics, Columbus Also called William I Notz **(G-8904)**

Department of Transportation, Marion Also called County of Marion **(G-13417)**

Department Senior Adult S, Cleveland Also called Cuyahoga County **(G-5393)**

Departmental Store, Columbus Also called Northpointe Plaza **(G-8203)**

Dependable Cleaning Contrs 440 953-9191
38230 Glenn Ave Willoughby (44094) **(G-19518)**

Dependable Painting Co 216 431-4470
4403 Superior Ave Cleveland (44103) **(G-5417)**

Deporres, Martin Emrgncy Asst, Cleveland Also called Catholic Charities Corporation **(G-5133)**

Dept of Human Service, Circleville Also called County of Pickaway **(G-4830)**

Dept of Human Services, Mansfield Also called County of Richland **(G-13156)**

Dept of Neighborhoods, Toledo Also called City of Toledo **(G-17658)**

Dept of Public Utilities, Columbus Also called City of Columbus **(G-7206)**

Dept of Streets, North Ridgeville Also called City of North Ridgeville **(G-15326)**

Dept of Surgery, Columbus Also called Ohio State University **(G-8340)**

Depuy Paving Inc 614 272-0256
1850 Mckinley Ave Columbus (43222) **(G-7437)**

Der Dutchman's Restaurant, Plain City Also called Dutchman Hospitality Group Inc **(G-16050)**

Dermamed Coatings Company LLC 330 634-9449
381 Geneva Ave Tallmadge (44278) **(G-17474)**

Dermatlgists of Southwest Ohio (PA) 937 435-2094
5300 Far Hills Ave # 100 Dayton (45429) **(G-9388)**

Desalvo Construction Company 330 759-8145
1491 W Liberty St Hubbard (44425) **(G-11944)**

Desco Federal Credit Union (PA) 740 354-7791
401 Chillicothe St Portsmouth (45662) **(G-16135)**

Design Center 513 618-3133
10816 Millington Ct # 100 Blue Ash (45242) **(G-1544)**

Design Central Inc 614 890-0202
6464 Presidential Gtwy Columbus (43231) **(G-7438)**

Design Concrete Surfaces, Kent Also called Don Wartko Construction Co **(G-12229)**

Design Homes & Development Co 937 438-3667
8534 Yankee St Ste A Dayton (45458) **(G-9389)**

Design Knowledge Company 937 320-9244
3100 Presidential Dr # 103 Beavercreek (45324) **(G-1147)**

Design Rstrtion Reconstruction 330 563-0010
4305 Mount Pleasant St Nw # 103 North Canton (44720) **(G-15196)**

Design Services Cnstr Co, Holland Also called Douglas Construction Company **(G-11884)**

Deskey Associates Inc 513 721-6800
120 E 8th St Cincinnati (45202) **(G-3423)**

Desoto Dialysis LLC 419 691-1514
2702 Navarre Ave Ste 203 Oregon (43616) **(G-15590)**

Detillion Landscaping Co Inc 740 775-5305
20337 State Route 104 Chillicothe (45601) **(G-2777)**

Detmer & Sons Inc (PA) 937 879-2373
1170 Channingway Dr Fairborn (45324) **(G-10671)**

Detmer & Sons Heating & AC, Fairborn Also called Detmer & Sons Inc **(G-10671)**

Detox Health Care Corp Ohio 513 742-6310
11500 Northlake Dr # 400 Cincinnati (45249) **(G-3424)**

Detroit Diesel Corporation 330 430-4300
515 11th St Se Canton (44707) **(G-2284)**

Detroit Dover Animals Hospital 440 871-5220
27366 Detroit Rd Cleveland (44145) **(G-5418)**

Detroit Royalty Incorporated 216 771-5700
1100 Superior Ave E Fl 10 Cleveland (44114) **(G-5419)**

Detroit Westfield LLC 330 666-4131
4073 Medina Rd Akron (44333) **(G-184)**

Detwiler Park Golf Course, Toledo Also called American Golf Corporation **(G-17588)**

Deufol Worldwide Packaging LLC 440 232-1100
19800 Alexander Rd Bedford (44146) **(G-1276)**

Deufol Worldwide Packaging LLC 414 967-8000
4380 Dixie Hwy Fairfield (45014) **(G-10717)**

Deutsche Bank Securities Inc 440 237-0188
3152 Oakwood Trl Broadview Heights (44147) **(G-1831)**

Devcare Solutions Ltd 614 221-2277
131 N High St Ste 640 Columbus (43215) **(G-7439)**

Developmental Disabilities 513 732-7015
204 State Rte Hwy 50ben Owensville (45160) **(G-15671)**

Developmental Disabilities Bd, Tallmadge Also called County of Summit **(G-17473)**

Develpmntal Dsblties Ohio Dept 740 446-1642
2500 Ohio Ave Gallipolis (45631) **(G-11190)**

Develpmntal Dsblties Ohio Dept 419 385-0231
1101 S Detroit Ave Toledo (43614) **(G-17699)**

Develpmntal Dsblties Ohio Dept 330 544-2231
30 E Broad St Fl 8 Columbus (43215) **(G-7440)**

Develpmntal Dsblties Ohio Dept 614 272-0509
1601 W Broad St Columbus (43222) **(G-7441)**

Develpmntal Dsblties Ohio Dept 937 233-8108
30 E Broad St Fl 8 Columbus (43215) **(G-7442)**

Develpmntal Dsblties Ohio Dept 513 732-9200
4399 E Bauman Ln Batavia (45103) **(G-996)**

Devilbiss Auto Refinishing, Toledo Also called Carlisle Fluid Tech Inc **(G-17637)**

Devirsified Material Handling 419 865-8025
8310 Airport Hwy Holland (43528) **(G-11882)**

Devry University Inc 614 251-6969
1350 Alum Creek Dr Columbus (43209) **(G-7443)**

Dexxxon Digital Storage Inc 740 548-7179
7611 Green Meadows Dr Lewis Center (43035) **(G-12538)**

Deyor Performing Arts Center 330 744-4269
260 W Federal St Youngstown (44503) **(G-20017)**

Dfs Corporate Services LLC 614 283-2499
6500 New Albany Rd E New Albany (43054) **(G-14851)**

Dfs Corporate Services LLC 614 777-7020
3311 Mill Meadow Dr Hilliard (43026) **(G-11760)**

Dhdc, Dayton Also called Design Homes & Development Co **(G-9389)**

Dhl, Westerville Also called Exel Inc **(G-19163)**

Dhl Express (usa) Inc 614 865-8325
570 Polaris Pkwy Ste 110 Westerville (43082) **(G-19157)**

Dhl Express (usa) Inc 800 225-5345
2315 Creekside Pkwy Lockbourne (43137) **(G-12813)**

Dhl Solutions, Lockbourne Also called Exel Inc **(G-12816)**

Dhl Supply Chain (usa) 419 727-4318
1717 E Matzinger Rd Toledo (43612) **(G-17700)**

Dhl Supply Chain (usa) 513 482-6015
401 Murray Rd Cincinnati (45217) **(G-3425)**

Dhl Supply Chain (usa) 614 836-1265
6390 Commerce Ct Groveport (43125) **(G-11507)**

Dhl Supply Chain (usa) 614 895-1959
570 Polaris Pkwy Ste 110 Westerville (43082) **(G-19158)**

Dhl Supply Chain (usa) 614 492-6614
2750 Creekside Pkwy Lockbourne (43137) **(G-12814)**

Dhl Supply Chain (usa) 513 942-1575
10121 Princtn Glndle Rd B Cincinnati (45246) **(G-3426)**

Dhl Supply Chain (usa) 513 745-7445
4550 Creek Rd Blue Ash (45242) **(G-1545)**

Dhl Supply Chain USA, Lockbourne Also called Exel Inc **(G-12815)**

Dhl Transport Brokerage, Columbus Also called Exel Freight Connect Inc (G-7544)

Dhr, Strongsville Also called Massage Envy (G-17329)

Di Feo & Sons Poultry Inc..............................330 564-8172
1075 Grant St Akron (44301) (G-185)

Di Salle Real Estate Co..............................419 885-4475
4904 Holland Sylvania Rd Sylvania (43560) (G-17418)

DIA Electric Inc..............................513 281-0783
3326 Reading Rd Cincinnati (45229) (G-3427)

Dialamerica Marketing Inc..............................330 836-5293
3090 W Market St Ste 210 Fairlawn (44333) (G-10822)

Dialamerica Marketing Inc..............................440 234-4410
7271 Engle Rd Ste 400 Cleveland (44130) (G-5420)

Dialysis Center of Dayton East..............................937 252-1867
1431 Business Center Ct Dayton (45410) (G-9390)

Dialysis Clinic Inc..............................513 281-0091
499 E Mcmillan St Cincinnati (45206) (G-3428)

Dialysis Clinic Inc..............................740 351-0596
1207 17th St Portsmouth (45662) (G-16136)

Dialysis Clinic Inc..............................513 777-0855
7650 University Dr West Chester (45069) (G-18910)

Dialysis Clinic Inc..............................740 264-6687
4227 Mall Dr Steubenville (43952) (G-17151)

Dialysis Partners of NW Ohio, Toledo Also called Greenfield Health Systems Corp (G-17771)

Dialysis Specialists Fairfield..............................513 863-6331
4750 Dixie Hwy Fairfield (45014) (G-10718)

Diamond Company Inc..............................937 374-1111
823 W 2nd St Xenia (45385) (G-19898)

Diamond Heavy Haul Inc..............................330 677-8061
123 N Water St Ste A Kent (44240) (G-12228)

Diamond Hill Capital MGT Inc..............................614 255-3333
325 John H Mcconnell Blvd Columbus (43215) (G-7444)

Diamond Hill Funds..............................614 255-3333
325 John H Mcconnell Blvd # 200 Columbus (43215) (G-7445)

Diamond Machine and Mfg, Bluffton Also called Carpe Diem Industries LLC (G-1689)

Diamond Metals Dist Inc..............................216 898-7900
4635 W 160th St Cleveland (44135) (G-5421)

Diamond Plastics, Dunkirk Also called Ball Bounce and Sport Inc (G-10384)

Diamond Roofing Systems LLP..............................330 856-2500
8031 E Market St Ste 6 Warren (44484) (G-18701)

Diane Sauer Chevrolet Inc..............................330 373-1600
700 Niles Rd Se Warren (44483) (G-18702)

Diane Vishnia Rn and Assoc..............................330 929-1113
2497 State Rd Cuyahoga Falls (44223) (G-9087)

Dick Lavy Trucking Inc..............................937 448-2104
8848 State Route 121 Bradford (45308) (G-1761)

Dickerson Distributing Company..............................513 539-8483
150 Lawton Ave Monroe (45050) (G-14565)

Dickinson Fleet Services LLC..............................513 772-3629
11536 Gondola St Ste B Cincinnati (45241) (G-3429)

Dickman Supply Inc (PA)..............................937 492-6166
1991 St Marys Ave Sidney (45365) (G-16773)

Dickman Supply Inc..............................937 492-6166
1991 St Mary Ave Sidney (45365) (G-16774)

Dickman Supply Inc..............................937 492-6166
1425 Sater St Greenville (45331) (G-11375)

Dickson Industrial Park Inc..............................740 377-9162
719 County Road 1 South Point (45680) (G-16931)

Didion's Mechanical, Bellevue Also called Donald E Didion II (G-1376)

Diebold Incorporated..............................330 588-3619
217 2nd St Nw Fl 6 Canton (44702) (G-2285)

Diebold Nixdorf Incorporated..............................513 682-6216
8509 Bilstein Blvd Hamilton (45015) (G-11590)

Diebold Self Service Systems (PA)..............................330 490-5099
5995 Mayfair Rd Canton (44720) (G-2286)

Diesel-Eagle, Williamsburg Also called Clercom Inc (G-19491)

Diet Center Worldwide Inc (PA)..............................330 665-5861
395 Springside Dr Akron (44333) (G-186)

Dietary Solutions Inc..............................614 985-6567
171 Green Meadows Dr S Lewis Center (43035) (G-12539)

Diewald & Pope Inc..............................614 861-6160
245 Connell Ct Reynoldsburg (43068) (G-16298)

Digeronimo Aggregates LLC..............................216 524-2950
6220 E Schaaf Rd Independence (44131) (G-12067)

Digestive Care Inc..............................937 320-5050
75 Sylvania Dr Beavercreek (45440) (G-1215)

Digestive Disease Consultants..............................330 225-6468
1299 Industrial Pkwy N # 110 Brunswick (44212) (G-1927)

Digestive Endoscopy Center, Dayton Also called Digestive Specialists Inc (G-9391)

Digestive Health Gastrologist, Toledo Also called Promedica GI Physicians LLC (G-17991)

Digestive Specialists Inc..............................937 534-7330
999 Brubaker Dr Ste 1 Dayton (45429) (G-9391)

Digico Imaging Inc..............................614 239-5200
3487 E Fulton St Columbus (43227) (G-7446)

Digiknow Inc..............................888 482-4455
3615 Superior Ave E 4404a Cleveland (44114) (G-5422)

Digioia/Suburban Excvtg LLC..............................440 237-1978
11293 Royalton Rd North Royalton (44133) (G-15353)

Digital Color Intl LLC..............................330 762-6959
1653 Merriman Rd Ste 211 Akron (44313) (G-187)

Digital Controls Corporation (PA)..............................513 746-8118
444 Alexandersville Rd Miamisburg (45342) (G-14166)

Digital Management Inc..............................240 223-4800
4660 Duke Dr Ste 100 Mason (45040) (G-13573)

Digitek Software Inc..............................614 764-8875
650 Radio Dr Lewis Center (43035) (G-12540)

Dignity Health..............................330 493-4443
4535 Dressler Rd Nw Canton (44718) (G-2287)

Dill-Elam Inc..............................513 575-0017
1461 State Route 28 Loveland (45140) (G-12991)

Dillard Electric Inc..............................937 836-5381
106 Quinter Farm Rd Union (45322) (G-18350)

Dillin Engineered Systems Corp..............................419 666-6789
8030 Broadstone Rd Perrysburg (43551) (G-15859)

Dillon Group Homes, Fostoria Also called RES-Care Inc (G-11010)

Dillon Holdings LLC..............................513 942-5600
8050 Beckett Center Dr # 103 West Chester (45069) (G-18911)

Dillon R D, Fostoria Also called Voca of Ohio (G-11014)

Dimech Services Inc..............................419 727-0111
5505 Enterprise Blvd Toledo (43612) (G-17701)

Dimension Service Corporation..............................614 226-7455
5500 Frantz Rd Ste 100 Dublin (43017) (G-10200)

Dimensional Metals Inc (PA)..............................740 927-3633
58 Klema Dr N Reynoldsburg (43068) (G-16299)

Dimensionmark Ltd..............................513 305-3525
2909 Crescentville Rd West Chester (45069) (G-18912)

Dingledine Trucking Company..............................937 652-3454
1000 Phoenix Dr Urbana (43078) (G-18431)

Dinn Hochman and Potter LLC..............................440 446-1100
5910 Landerbrook Dr # 200 Cleveland (44124) (G-5423)

Dino Palmieri Beauty Salon (PA)..............................440 498-9411
5201 Richmond Rd Ste 1 Bedford (44146) (G-1277)

Dino Persichetti..............................330 821-9600
20040 Hrrsburg Wstvlle Rd Alliance (44601) (G-530)

Dinos Catering Inc..............................440 943-1010
30605 Ridge Rd Wickliffe (44092) (G-19455)

Dinsmore & Shohl LLP (PA)..............................513 977-8200
255 E 5th St Ste 1900 Cincinnati (45202) (G-3430)

Diocese of Toledo..............................419 243-7255
1601 Jefferson Ave Toledo (43604) (G-17702)

Diproinduca (usa) Limited LLC..............................330 722-4442
2528 Medina Rd Medina (44256) (G-13930)

Diproinduca USA, Medina Also called Diproinduca (usa) Limited LLC (G-13930)

Direct Expediting LLC..............................513 459-0100
5311 Bentley Oak Dr Mason (45040) (G-13574)

Direct Express Delivery Svc..............................513 541-0600
2841 Colerain Ave Cincinnati (45225) (G-3431)

Direct Import Home Decor Inc (PA)..............................216 898-9758
4979 W 130th St Cleveland (44135) (G-5424)

Direct Maintenance LLC..............................330 744-5211
100 E Federal St Ste 600 Youngstown (44503) (G-20018)

Direct Options Inc..............................513 779-4416
9565 Cncnnati Columbus Rd West Chester (45069) (G-18913)

Direct-X, Cincinnati Also called Direct Express Delivery Svc (G-3431)

Directconnectgroup Ltd..............................216 281-2866
5501 Cass Ave Cleveland (44102) (G-5425)

Direction Home Akron Canton AR (PA)..............................330 896-9172
1550 Corporate Woods Pkwy Uniontown (44685) (G-18367)

Directions Credit Union Inc (PA)..............................419 720-4769
5121 Whiteford Rd Sylvania (43560) (G-17419)

Directions Credit Union Inc..............................419 524-7113
777 N Main St Mansfield (44902) (G-13167)

Directions For Youth Families..............................614 258-8043
657 S Ohio Ave Columbus (43205) (G-7447)

Directions For Youth Families..............................614 694-0203
3840 Kimberly Pkwy N Columbus (43232) (G-7448)

Directions For Youth Families..............................614 294-2661
1515 Indianola Ave Columbus (43201) (G-7449)

Directions Research Inc (PA)..............................513 651-2990
401 E Court St Ste 200 Cincinnati (45202) (G-3432)

DIRTWORKS DRAINAGE, Deerfield Also called Alliance Crane & Rigging Inc (G-9901)

DISABILITY FOUNDATION THE, Dayton Also called Dayton Foundation Inc (G-9365)

DISABILLITY RIGHTS OHIO, Columbus Also called Ohio Disability Rights Law Pol (G-8249)

Disabled American Veterans..............................330 875-5795
128 Indiana Ave Louisville (44641) (G-12965)

Disabled American Veterans..............................419 526-0203
34 Park Ave W Mansfield (44902) (G-13168)

Disabled American Veterans..............................330 364-1204
824 Hardesty Ave Nw New Philadelphia (44663) (G-14957)

Disabled American Veterans..............................740 367-7973
28051 State Route 7 Cheshire (45620) (G-2733)

Disanto Companies..............................440 442-0600
1960 Caronia Dr Cleveland (44124) (G-5426)

Disaster Reconstruction Inc..............................440 918-1523
33851 Curtis Blvd Ste 202 Eastlake (44095) (G-10428)

Discount Drug Mart Inc (PA)..............................330 725-2340
211 Commerce Dr Medina (44256) (G-13931)

Discount Drug Mart Inc..............................330 343-7700
3015 N Wooster Ave Dover (44622) (G-10072)

Discover Card Services, Hilliard Also called Dfs Corporate Services LLC (G-11760)

Discover Financial Services, New Albany Also called Dfs Corporate Services LLC (G-14851)

Discover Training Inc..............................614 871-0010
4882 Rheims Way Grove City (43123) (G-11426)

Discovering The Jewish Jesus, Plain City Also called Shalom Ministries Intl Inc (G-16065)

Discovery Express Child Care, Holland *Also called Childrens Discovery Center* **(G-11878)**
Discovery School 419 756-8880
  855 Millsboro Rd Mansfield (44903) **(G-13169)**
Dish Network Corporation 614 534-2001
  3315 Mill Meadow Dr Hilliard (43026) **(G-11761)**
Diskcopy Duplication Services 440 460-0800
  107 Alpha Park Cleveland (44143) **(G-5427)**
Dispatch Color Press, Columbus *Also called Dispatch Consumer Services* **(G-7450)**
Dispatch Consumer Services 740 687-1893
  3160 W Fair Ave Lancaster (43130) **(G-12389)**
Dispatch Consumer Services (HQ) 740 548-5555
  5300 Crosswind Dr Columbus (43228) **(G-7450)**
Dispatch Printing Company (PA) 614 461-5000
  62 E Broad St Columbus (43215) **(G-7451)**
Dispatch Printing Company 740 548-5331
  7801 N Central Dr Lewis Center (43035) **(G-12541)**
Dispatch Productions Inc 614 460-3700
  770 Twin Rivers Dr Columbus (43215) **(G-7452)**
Dist-Trans Inc 614 497-1660
  1580 Williams Rd Columbus (43207) **(G-7453)**
Distillata Company (PA) 216 771-2900
  1608 E 24th St Cleveland (44114) **(G-5428)**
Distinct Advantage Cabinetry, Toledo *Also called Online Mega Sellers Corp* **(G-17964)**
Distribution and Trnsp Svc Inc (PA) 937 295-3343
  401 S Main St Fort Loramie (45845) **(G-10985)**
Distribution Center, West Chester *Also called Martin-Brower Company LLC* **(G-18971)**
Distribution Center, Wilmington *Also called PC Connection Services* **(G-19639)**
Distribution Data Incorporated (PA) 216 362-3009
  16101 Snow Rd Ste 200 Brookpark (44142) **(G-1896)**
Distribution Service Company, Wadsworth *Also called Cornwell Quality Tools Company* **(G-18594)**
District 6, Delaware *Also called Ohio Department Transportation* **(G-9999)**
District Board Health Mahoning 330 270-2855
  50 Westchester Dr Youngstown (44515) **(G-20019)**
District Office, Westerville *Also called Columbus Frkln Cnty Pk* **(G-19242)**
Distrubution Center, Columbus *Also called Ohiohealth Corporation* **(G-8363)**
Disttech LLC 800 321-3143
  8101 Union Ave Cleveland (44105) **(G-5429)**
Ditsch Usa LLC 513 782-8888
  311 Northland Blvd Cincinnati (45246) **(G-3433)**
Dittman-Adams Company 513 870-7530
  4946 Rialto Rd West Chester (45069) **(G-18914)**
Div of Refuse and Recycling, Cleveland *Also called City of Lakewood* **(G-5205)**
Dival Inc (PA) 216 831-4200
  26401 Miles Rd Warrensville Heights (44128) **(G-18777)**
Diver Steel City Auto Crushers 330 744-5083
  590 Himrod Ave Youngstown (44506) **(G-20020)**
Diverscare Healthcare Svcs Inc 513 867-4100
  1302 Millville Ave Hamilton (45013) **(G-11591)**
Diverscare Healthcare Svcs Inc 937 278-8211
  6125 N Main St Dayton (45415) **(G-9392)**
Diverscare Healthcare Svcs Inc 513 271-7010
  7010 Rowan Hill Dr Cincinnati (45227) **(G-3434)**
Diversfied Emplyee Sltions Inc 330 764-4125
  3745 Medina Rd Medina (44256) **(G-13932)**
Diversicare Leasing Corp 615 771-7575
  2159 Dogwood Ridge Rd Wheelersburg (45694) **(G-19433)**
Diversicare of Avon LLC 440 937-6201
  32900 Detroit Rd Avon (44011) **(G-879)**
Diversicare of Mansfield LLC 419 529-6447
  2124 Park Ave W Ontario (44906) **(G-15547)**
Diversicare of St. Theresa, Cincinnati *Also called Diverscare Healthcare Svcs Inc* **(G-3434)**
Diversified Air Systems Inc 330 784-3366
  1201 George Wash Blvd Akron (44312) **(G-188)**
Diversified Employment Grp II 513 428-6525
  8530 Pringle Dr Cincinnati (45231) **(G-3435)**
Diversified Fall Protection, Westlake *Also called Lorad LLC* **(G-19370)**
Diversified Health Management 614 338-8888
  3569 Refugee Rd Ste C Columbus (43232) **(G-7454)**
Diversified Labor Support LLC 440 234-3090
  7050 Engle Rd Ste 101 Cleveland (44130) **(G-5430)**
Diversified Products & Svcs 740 393-6202
  1250 Vernonview Dr Mount Vernon (43050) **(G-14763)**
Diversified Systems Inc 614 476-9939
  100 Dorchester Sq N # 103 Westerville (43081) **(G-19249)**
Diversipak Inc (PA) 513 321-7884
  838 Reedy St Cincinnati (45202) **(G-3436)**
Diversity Search Group LLC 614 352-2988
  2550 Corp Exchange Dr # 15 Columbus (43231) **(G-7455)**
Divine Healthcare Services LLC 614 899-6767
  2374 E Dublin Granvl Rd Columbus (43229) **(G-7456)**
Division 7 Inc 740 965-1970
  72 Holmes St Galena (43021) **(G-11157)**
Division 7 Roofing, Galena *Also called Division 7 Inc* **(G-11157)**
Division Drnking Ground Waters 614 644-2752
  50 W Town St Ste 700 Columbus (43215) **(G-7457)**
Division of Engineering, Columbus *Also called Natural Resources Ohio Dept* **(G-8162)**
Division of Gastroenterology, Columbus *Also called Ohio State Univ Wexner Med Ctr* **(G-8294)**

Division of Geological Survey 614 265-6576
  2045 Morse Rd Bldg C Columbus (43229) **(G-7458)**
Division of Selling Materials, Dover *Also called Smith Concrete Co* **(G-10101)**
Division of Water Resources, Batavia *Also called County of Clermont* **(G-994)**
Division Streets & Utilities, Dublin *Also called City of Dublin* **(G-10175)**
Dix & Eaton Incorporated 216 241-0405
  200 Public Sq Ste 3900 Cleveland (44114) **(G-5431)**
Dixie Management II Inc 937 832-1234
  10 Rockridge Rd Englewood (45322) **(G-10585)**
Dixon Builders & Developers 513 887-6400
  8050 Beckett Center Dr # 213 West Chester (45069) **(G-18915)**
Dixon Health Care Center, Steubenville *Also called Communicare Health Svcs Inc* **(G-17150)**
Dizer Corp (PA) 440 368-0200
  1912 Mentor Ave Painesville (44077) **(G-15709)**
Dj Neff Enterprises Inc 440 884-3100
  6405 York Rd Cleveland (44130) **(G-5432)**
Djd Express Inc 740 676-7464
  56461 Ferry Landing Rd Shadyside (43947) **(G-16694)**
Djj Holding Corporation (HQ) 513 621-8770
  300 Pike St Cincinnati (45202) **(G-3437)**
DKM Construction Inc 740 289-3006
  W Perimeter Rd Piketon (45661) **(G-15974)**
Dkmp Consulting Inc 614 733-0979
  8000 Corporate Blvd Plain City (43064) **(G-16049)**
Dlc Transport Inc 740 282-1763
  320 N 5th St Steubenville (43952) **(G-17152)**
Dlhbowles Inc (PA) 330 478-2503
  2422 Leo Ave Sw Canton (44706) **(G-2288)**
Dlr Group Inc 216 522-1350
  1422 Euclid Ave Ste 300 Cleveland (44115) **(G-5433)**
Dlz American Drilling Inc 614 888-0040
  6121 Huntley Rd Columbus (43229) **(G-7459)**
Dlz Construction Services Inc 614 888-0040
  6121 Huntley Rd Columbus (43229) **(G-7460)**
Dlz National Inc (HQ) 614 888-0040
  6121 Huntley Rd Columbus (43229) **(G-7461)**
Dlz Ohio Inc (HQ) 614 888-0040
  6121 Huntley Rd Columbus (43229) **(G-7462)**
Dlz Ohio Inc 330 923-0401
  1 Canal Square Plz # 1300 Akron (44308) **(G-189)**
DMC Consulting, Toledo *Also called DMC Technology Group* **(G-17703)**
DMC Technology Group 419 535-2900
  7657 Kings Pointe Rd Toledo (43617) **(G-17703)**
DMD Management Inc 330 405-6040
  2463 Sussex Blvd Twinsburg (44087) **(G-18258)**
DMD Management Inc 440 944-9400
  1919 Bishop Rd Wickliffe (44092) **(G-19456)**
DMD Management Inc (PA) 216 898-8399
  12380 Plaza Dr Cleveland (44130) **(G-5434)**
DMD Management Inc 216 371-3600
  12504 Cedar Rd Cleveland (44106) **(G-5435)**
Dmh Toyota Lift, Holland *Also called Toyota Industrial Eqp Dlr* **(G-11922)**
DMR Management Inc 513 771-1700
  109 Brookfield Rd Avon Lake (44012) **(G-915)**
Dna Diagnostics Center Inc (HQ) 513 881-7800
  1 Ddc Way Fairfield (45014) **(G-10719)**
Dna Technology Park, Fairfield *Also called Dna Diagnostics Center Inc* **(G-10719)**
Dno Inc 614 231-3601
  3650 E 5th Ave Columbus (43219) **(G-7463)**
Dnv GL Healthcare Usa Inc 281 396-1610
  400 Techne Center Dr # 100 Milford (45150) **(G-14385)**
Do Cut Sales & Service Inc 330 533-9878
  3375 Youngstown Rd Se Warren (44484) **(G-18703)**
Do It Best, Sidney *Also called Lochard Inc* **(G-16784)**
Do It Best, Lancaster *Also called Slaters Inc* **(G-12435)**
DO IT BEST, Kent *Also called Carter-Jones Companies Inc* **(G-12217)**
Do It Best Corp 330 725-3859
  444 Independence Dr Medina (44256) **(G-13933)**
Do-Cut True Value, Warren *Also called Do Cut Sales & Service Inc* **(G-18703)**
Doan Pyramid Electric, Cleveland *Also called Northeast Ohio Electric LLC* **(G-6093)**
Dobbins Nursing Home Inc 513 553-4139
  400 Main St New Richmond (45157) **(G-14993)**
Dobson Cellular Call Center, Youngstown *Also called AT&T Mobility LLC* **(G-19957)**
Doctor's Urgent Care Offices, Milford *Also called Ambulatory Medical Care Inc* **(G-14370)**
Doctors Consulting Service 614 793-1980
  200 Bradenton Ave Dublin (43017) **(G-10201)**
Doctors Hosp Physcn Svcs LLC 330 834-4725
  830 Amherst Rd Ne Ste 201 Massillon (44646) **(G-13675)**
Doctors Hospital Cleveland Inc 740 753-7300
  11 John Lloyd Evns Mem Dr Nelsonville (45764) **(G-14829)**
Doctors Hospital Fmly Practice, Grove City *Also called Doctors Hospital Health Center* **(G-11427)**
Doctors Hospital Health Center 614 544-0101
  2030 Stringtown Rd Fl 3 Grove City (43123) **(G-11427)**
Doctors Hospital North, Columbus *Also called Doctors Ohiohealth Corporation* **(G-7464)**
Doctors Ohiohealth Corporation (HQ) 614 544-5424
  5100 W Broad St Columbus (43228) **(G-7464)**
Doctors Urgent Care 419 586-1611
  950 S Main St Ste 10 Celina (45822) **(G-2594)**
Doctors Weaver Wallace Conley, Fairfield *Also called Affiliates In Oral & Maxlofcl* **(G-10693)**

Document Concepts Inc 330 575-5685
   607 S Main St A North Canton (44720) **(G-15197)**
Document Imging Spcialists LLC 614 868-9008
   4460 Emmas Court Hilliard Hilliard (43026) **(G-11762)**
DOCUMENT SOLUTIONS, Xenia Also called Greene Inc **(G-19907)**
Document Solutions Group, Columbus Also called Document Solutions Ohio LLC **(G-7465)**
Document Solutions Ohio LLC 614 846-2400
   100 E Campus View Blvd # 105 Columbus (43235) **(G-7465)**
Document Tech Systems Ltd 330 928-5311
   525 Portage Trail Ext W Cuyahoga Falls (44223) **(G-9088)**
Dodd Hall Inptent Rhbilitation, Columbus Also called Ohio State University **(G-8295)**
Doepker Group Inc 419 355-1409
   1303 W State St Fremont (43420) **(G-11070)**
DOGGY DAY CARE, Mantua Also called Hattie Larlham Community Svcs **(G-13269)**
Dohner Ltd 330 814-4144
   7738 Valley View Rd Hudson (44236) **(G-11975)**
Dohner Landscaping, Hudson Also called Dohner Ltd **(G-11975)**
Dolbey Systems Inc (PA) 440 392-9900
   7280 Auburn Rd Painesville (44077) **(G-15710)**
Dold Homes Inc (PA) 419 874-2535
   26610 Eckel Rd Perrysburg (43551) **(G-15860)**
Dole Fresh Vegetables Inc 937 525-4300
   600 Benjamin Dr Springfield (45502) **(G-17030)**
Dolgencorp LLC 740 588-5700
   2505 E Pointe Dr Zanesville (43701) **(G-20299)**
Dolin Supply Co 304 529-4171
   702 Solida Rd South Point (45680) **(G-16932)**
Doling & Associates Dental Lab 937 254-0075
   3318 Successful Way Dayton (45414) **(G-9393)**
Dollar General, Zanesville Also called Dolgencorp LLC **(G-20299)**
Dollar Paradise (PA) 216 432-0421
   1240 E 55th St Cleveland (44103) **(G-5436)**
Domajaparo Inc (PA) 513 742-3600
   11400 Winton Rd Cincinnati (45240) **(G-3438)**
Dome Dialysis LLC 614 882-1734
   241 W Schrock Rd Westerville (43081) **(G-19250)**
Domestic Connection, New Albany Also called Carol Scudere **(G-14848)**
Domestic Relations 937 225-4063
   301 W 3rd St Ste 500 Dayton (45402) **(G-9394)**
Domestic Violence Project Inc 330 445-2000
   720 19th St Ne Canton (44714) **(G-2289)**
Dominguez Inc 513 425-9955
   1000 Reed Dr Monroe (45050) **(G-14566)**
Dominion Energy Ohio, Cleveland Also called East Ohio Gas Company **(G-5457)**
Dominion Energy Ohio, Youngstown Also called East Ohio Gas Company **(G-20024)**
Dominion Energy Ohio, New Franklin Also called East Ohio Gas Company **(G-14909)**
Dominion Energy Ohio, Cleveland Also called East Ohio Gas Company **(G-5458)**
Dominion Energy Ohio, Ashtabula Also called East Ohio Gas Company **(G-737)**
Dominion Energy Ohio, Canton Also called East Ohio Gas Company **(G-2293)**
Dominion Energy Ohio, Wickliffe Also called East Ohio Gas Company **(G-19457)**
Dominion Energy Transm Inc 513 932-5793
   1262 W State Route 122 Lebanon (45036) **(G-12460)**
Dominion Homes Inc (HQ) 614 356-5000
   4900 Tuttle Crossing Blvd Dublin (43016) **(G-10202)**
Domino Foods Inc 216 432-3222
   2075 E 65th St Cleveland (44103) **(G-5437)**
Domino Sugar, Cleveland Also called Domino Foods Inc **(G-5437)**
Domokur Architects Inc 330 666-7878
   4651 Medina Rd Copley (44321) **(G-8966)**
Don Bosco Community Center Inc 816 421-3160
   1763 Wickford Rd Cleveland (44112) **(G-5438)**
Don Drumm Studios & Gallery 330 253-6840
   437 Crouse St Akron (44311) **(G-190)**
Don S Cisle Contractor Inc (PA) 513 867-1400
   1714 Fairgrove Ave Hamilton (45011) **(G-11592)**
Don Walter Kitchen Distrs (PA) 330 793-9338
   260 Victoria Rd Youngstown (44515) **(G-20021)**
Don Wartko Construction Co (PA) 330 673-5252
   975 Tallmadge Rd Kent (44240) **(G-12229)**
Don Wood Inc 740 593-6641
   900 E State St Athens (45701) **(G-776)**
Don Wood Buick, Oldsmobile, Athens Also called Don Wood Inc **(G-776)**
Don Wood GMC & Toyota, Athens Also called Don Wood Inc **(G-777)**
Don Wood Inc 740 593-6641
   900 E State St Athens (45701) **(G-777)**
Don's Lighthouse Inn, Cleveland Also called Strang Corporation **(G-6472)**
Donald Bowen and Assoc DDS 614 274-0454
   2575 W Broad St Unit 3 Columbus (43204) **(G-7466)**
Donald E Didion II 419 483-2226
   1027b County Road 308 Bellevue (44811) **(G-1376)**
Donald Martens Sons, Cleveland Also called Martens Donald & Sons **(G-5917)**
Donald R Kenney & Company (PA) 614 540-2404
   470 Olde Worthington Rd # 101 Westerville (43082) **(G-19159)**
Donauschwaben's Grmnamrcn Cltr, Olmsted Twp Also called Lenau Park **(G-15537)**
Done-Rite Bowling Service Co (PA) 440 232-3280
   20434 Krick Rd Bedford (44146) **(G-1278)**
Donegal Bay, Warrensville Heights Also called Trickeration Inc **(G-18782)**
Donlen Inc (HQ) 216 961-6767
   8905 Lake Ave Cleveland (44102) **(G-5439)**

Donley Concrete Cutting 614 834-0300
   151 W Borland St Pickerington (43147) **(G-15956)**
Donley Ford-Lincoln Inc (PA) 419 281-3673
   1641 Claremont Ave Ashland (44805) **(G-672)**
Donleys Inc (PA) 216 524-6800
   5430 Warner Rd Cleveland (44125) **(G-5440)**
Donnell Ford-Lincoln 330 332-0031
   152 Continental Dr Salem (44460) **(G-16542)**
Donnellon Mc Carthy Inc 937 299-3564
   2580 Lance Dr Moraine (45409) **(G-14648)**
Donnellon Mc Carthy Inc 513 681-3200
   4141 Turrill St Cincinnati (45223) **(G-3439)**
Donnellon Mc Carthy Inc 937 299-0200
   2580 Lance Dr Moraine (45409) **(G-14649)**
Dons Automotive Group LLC 419 337-3010
   720 N Shoop Ave Wauseon (43567) **(G-18799)**
Dons Brooklyn Chevrolet Inc 216 741-1500
   4941 Pearl Rd Cleveland (44109) **(G-5441)**
Donty Horton HM Care Dhhc LLC 513 463-3442
   2692 Madison Rd Ste N1192 Cincinnati (45208) **(G-3440)**
Donzell's, Akron Also called Donzells Flower & Grdn Ctr Inc **(G-191)**
Donzells Flower & Grdn Ctr Inc 330 724-0550
   937 E Waterloo Rd Akron (44306) **(G-191)**
Dooley Heating and AC LLC 614 278-9944
   2010 Zettler Rd Columbus (43232) **(G-7467)**
Door Fabrication Services Inc 937 454-9207
   3250 Old Springfield Rd # 1 Vandalia (45377) **(G-18520)**
Door Shop & Service Inc 614 423-8043
   7385 State Route 3 Ste 52 Westerville (43082) **(G-19160)**
Dorlon Golf Club 440 236-8234
   18000 Station Rd Columbia Station (44028) **(G-6774)**
Dorman, Regina MD, Tallmadge Also called Northeast Family Health Care **(G-17482)**
Dornoch Golf Club Inc 740 369-0863
   3329 Columbus Pike Delaware (43015) **(G-9971)**
Dorothy Love Retirement Cmnty, Sidney Also called Ohio Presbt Retirement Svcs **(G-16789)**
Dorsky Hodgson + Partners Inc (PA) 216 464-8600
   23240 Chagrin Blvd # 300 Cleveland (44122) **(G-5442)**
Dorsky Hodgson Parrish Yue, Cleveland Also called Dorsky Hodgson + Partners Inc **(G-5442)**
Dortronic Service Inc (PA) 216 739-3667
   201 E Granger Rd Cleveland (44131) **(G-5443)**
DOT Diamond Core Drilling Inc (PA) 440 322-6466
   780 Sugar Ln Elyria (44035) **(G-10502)**
DOT Smith LLC 740 245-5105
   3607 Garners Ford Rd Thurman (45685) **(G-17508)**
Dotloop LLC 513 257-0550
   700 W Pete Rose Way # 436 Cincinnati (45203) **(G-3441)**
Dots Market, Dayton Also called Mary C Enterprises Inc **(G-9588)**
Dotson Company 419 877-5176
   6848 Providence St Whitehouse (43571) **(G-19446)**
Double A Trailer Sales Inc (PA) 419 692-7626
   1750 E 5th St Delphos (45833) **(G-10025)**
Double Eagle Club, Galena Also called Big Red LP **(G-11156)**
Double Tree, Columbus Also called Columbus Worthington Hospitali **(G-7321)**
Double Z Construction Company 614 274-9334
   2550 Harrison Rd Columbus (43204) **(G-7468)**
Doubletree By Hilton, Cleveland Also called Tudor Arms Mstr Subtenant LLC **(G-6555)**
Doubletree By Hilton Newark, Columbus Also called Indus Newark Hotel LLC **(G-7810)**
Doubletree Columbus, Columbus Also called Hotel 50 S Front Opco L P **(G-7774)**
Doubletree Columbus Hotel, Columbus Also called Ch Relty Iv/Clmbus Partners LP **(G-7174)**
Doubletree Guest Suites Dayton 937 436-2400
   300 Prestige Pl Miamisburg (45342) **(G-14167)**
Doubletree Hotel, Cleveland Also called SM Double Tree Hotel Lake **(G-6418)**
Doubletree Hotel, Cincinnati Also called 6300 Sharonville Assoc LLC **(G-2884)**
Doubletree Hotel, Dayton Also called Renthotel Dayton LLC **(G-9731)**
Doubletree Hotel, Cleveland Also called Cleveland S Hospitality LLC **(G-5286)**
Doubletree Hotel, Miamisburg Also called Ashford Trs Lessee LLC **(G-14142)**
Doubletree Suites by Hilton, Columbus Also called 50 S Front LLC **(G-6843)**
Doug Bigelow Chevrolet Inc 330 644-7500
   894 Robinwood Hills Dr Akron (44333) **(G-192)**
Doug Chevrolet, Akron Also called Doug Bigelow Chevrolet Inc **(G-192)**
Doug Marine Motors Inc 740 335-3700
   1120 Clinton Ave Wshngtn CT Hs (43160) **(G-19869)**
Doug Walcher Farms, North Fairfield Also called Drw Packing Inc **(G-15245)**
Douglas Company (PA) 419 865-8600
   1716 Prrysburg Holland Rd Holland (43528) **(G-11883)**
Douglas Construction Company 419 865-8600
   1716 Prrysburg Holland Rd Holland (43528) **(G-11884)**
Douglas R Denny 216 236-2400
   6480 Rckside Woods Blvd S Independence (44131) **(G-12068)**
Douglass & Associates Co Lpa 216 362-7777
   4725 Grayton Rd Cleveland (44135) **(G-5444)**
Dove Building Services Inc 614 299-4700
   1691 Cleveland Ave Columbus (43211) **(G-7469)**
Dover City Schools 330 343-8880
   865 1/2 E Iron Ave Dover (44622) **(G-10073)**
Dover Cryogenics, Midvale Also called Amko Service Company **(G-14357)**
Dover Hydraulics Inc (PA) 330 364-1617
   2996 Progress St Dover (44622) **(G-10074)**

Dover Hydraulics South, Dover *Also called Dover Hydraulics Inc (G-10074)*

Dover Investments Inc 440 235-5511
7989 Columbia Rd Olmsted Falls (44138) *(G-15533)*

Dover Nursing Center 330 364-4436
1525 N Crater Ave Dover (44622) *(G-10075)*

Dover Orthopedic Center, Dover *Also called Teater Orthopedic Surgeons (G-10103)*

Dover Phila Federal Credit Un (PA) 330 364-8874
119 Filmore Ave Dover (44622) *(G-10076)*

Dover Softies, Dover *Also called L and C Soft Serve Inc (G-10086)*

Dovetail Construction Co Inc (PA) 740 592-1800
26055 Emery Rd Ste G Cleveland (44128) *(G-5445)*

Dovetail Solar and Wind, Cleveland *Also called Dovetail Construction Co Inc (G-5445)*

Dovin Dairy Farms LLC 440 653-7009
15967 State Route 58 Oberlin (44074) *(G-15501)*

Dovin Land Company, Oberlin *Also called Dovin Dairy Farms LLC (G-15501)*

Down To Earth Landscaping, Cleveland *Also called A Ressler Inc (G-4880)*

Downing Displays Inc (PA) 513 248-9800
550 Techne Center Dr Milford (45150) *(G-14386)*

Downtheroad Inc 740 452-4579
3625 Maple Ave Zanesville (43701) *(G-20300)*

Downtown Akron Partnership Inc 330 374-7676
103 S High St Fl 4 Akron (44308) *(G-193)*

Downtown Fast Park, Cincinnati *Also called Parking Company America Inc (G-4205)*

Downtown Ford Lincoln Inc 330 456-2781
1423 Tuscarawas St W Canton (44702) *(G-2290)*

Doylestown Cable, Doylestown *Also called Doylestown Telephone Company (G-10114)*

Doylestown Cable TV, Doylestown *Also called Doylestown Communications (G-10111)*

Doylestown Communications, Doylestown *Also called Doylestown Telephone Company (G-10113)*

Doylestown Communications 330 658-7000
81 N Portage St Doylestown (44230) *(G-10111)*

Doylestown Health Care Center 330 658-1533
95 Black Dr Doylestown (44230) *(G-10112)*

Doylestown Telephone Company (PA) 330 658-2121
81 N Portage St Doylestown (44230) *(G-10113)*

Doylestown Telephone Company 330 658-6666
28 E Marion St Doylestown (44230) *(G-10114)*

DPL, Manchester *Also called Dayton Power and Light Company (G-13127)*

DPL Inc (HQ) 937 331-4063
1065 Woodman Dr Dayton (45432) *(G-9170)*

Dps, Independence *Also called Canon Solutions America Inc (G-12054)*

Dr Darren Adams Dr Grge Pettit, Portsmouth *Also called George P Pettit MD Inc (G-16139)*

Dr Michael J Hulit 330 863-7173
107 N Reed Ave Malvern (44644) *(G-13122)*

Drake Center LLC 513 418-2500
151 W Galbraith Rd Cincinnati (45216) *(G-3442)*

Drake Development Inc 513 418-4370
165 W Galbraith Rd Ofc Cincinnati (45216) *(G-3443)*

Drake State Air 937 472-3740
3711 Ozias Rd Eaton (45320) *(G-10443)*

Drake State Air Systems Inc 937 472-0640
1417 E Main St Eaton (45320) *(G-10444)*

Drasc Enterprises Inc 330 852-3254
9060 Bollman Rd Sw Sugarcreek (44681) *(G-17377)*

Drb Holdings LLC (PA) 330 645-3299
3245 Pickle Rd Akron (44312) *(G-194)*

Drb Systems LLC (HQ) 330 645-3299
3245 Pickle Rd Akron (44312) *(G-195)*

Drc Holdings Inc 419 230-0188
17623 Road 4 Pandora (45877) *(G-15750)*

Drees Company 330 899-9554
3906 Kenway Blvd Uniontown (44685) *(G-18368)*

Dreier & Maller Inc (PA) 614 575-0065
6508 Taylor Rd Sw Reynoldsburg (43068) *(G-16300)*

Dresch Tolson Dental Labs 419 842-6730
8730 Resource Park Dr Sylvania (43560) *(G-17420)*

Drew Ag-Transport Inc 937 548-3200
5450 Sebring Warner Rd Greenville (45331) *(G-11376)*

Drew Medical Inc (PA) 407 363-6700
75 Milford Dr Ste 201 Hudson (44236) *(G-11976)*

Drew Shoe, Lancaster *Also called Drew Ventures Inc (G-12390)*

Drew Ventures Inc (PA) 740 653-4271
252 Quarry Rd Se Lancaster (43130) *(G-12390)*

Drivers On Call LLC 330 867-5193
1263 Norton Ave Norton (44203) *(G-15419)*

Drop In Babysitting Service, Piqua *Also called West Ohio Conference of (G-16038)*

Drs Hill & Thomas Co 440 944-8887
2785 Som Center Rd Cleveland (44194) *(G-5446)*

Drs Paul Boyles & Kennedy 614 734-3347
3545 Olentangy River Rd Columbus (43214) *(G-7470)*

Drs Signal Technologies Inc 937 429-7470
4393 Dayton Xenia Rd Beavercreek (45432) *(G-1148)*

Drt Holdings Inc (PA) 937 298-7391
618 Greenmount Blvd Dayton (45419) *(G-9395)*

Drug & Poison Information Ctr, Cincinnati *Also called Poison Information Center (G-4262)*

Drug and Alcohol, Elyria *Also called County of Lorain (G-10499)*

Drury Hotels Company LLC 614 798-8802
6170 Parkcenter Cir Dublin (43017) *(G-10203)*

Drury Hotels Company LLC 513 336-0108
9956 Escort Dr Mason (45040) *(G-13575)*

Drury Hotels Company LLC 614 221-7008
88 E Nationwide Blvd Columbus (43215) *(G-7471)*

Drury Hotels Company LLC 937 454-5200
6616 Miller Ln Dayton (45414) *(G-9396)*

Drury Hotels Company LLC 513 771-5601
2265 E Sharon Rd Cincinnati (45241) *(G-3444)*

Drury Hotels Company LLC 614 798-8802
4109 Parkway Centre Dr Grove City (43123) *(G-11428)*

Drury Inn & Suites Clmbus Conv, Columbus *Also called Drury Hotels Company LLC (G-7471)*

Drury Inn & Suites Columbus NW, Dublin *Also called Drury Hotels Company LLC (G-10203)*

Drury Inn & Suites Columbus S, Grove City *Also called Drury Hotels Company LLC (G-11428)*

Drury Inn & Suites Dayton N, Dayton *Also called Drury Hotels Company LLC (G-9396)*

Drury Inn Stes Cincinnati Masn, Mason *Also called Drury Hotels Company LLC (G-13575)*

Drury Inn Suites Cincinnati N, Cincinnati *Also called Drury Hotels Company LLC (G-3444)*

Drw Packing Inc 419 744-2427
866 State Route 162 E North Fairfield (44855) *(G-15245)*

Dry It Rite LLC 614 295-8135
4330 Groves Rd Columbus (43232) *(G-7472)*

Dry Run Limited Partnership 513 561-9119
7711 Ivy Hills Dr Cincinnati (45244) *(G-3445)*

Drywall Barn Inc 330 750-6155
408 N Meridian Rd Youngstown (44509) *(G-20022)*

Drywall Barn, The, Youngstown *Also called Drywall Barn Inc (G-20022)*

DSC Consulting, Cincinnati *Also called Definitive Solutions Co Inc (G-3417)*

DSC Logistics LLC 847 390-6800
1260 W Laskey Rd Toledo (43612) *(G-17704)*

Dsg Canusa, Loveland *Also called Shawcor Pipe Protection LLC (G-13027)*

DSI East 330 733-1861
73 Massillon Rd Akron (44312) *(G-196)*

DSI Systems Inc 614 871-1456
3650 Brookham Dr Ste K Grove City (43123) *(G-11429)*

Dsn, Lockbourne *Also called Dealers Supply North Inc (G-12812)*

Dss, Uniontown *Also called Dental Support Specialties LLC (G-18366)*

Dss Installations Ltd 513 761-7000
6717 Montgomery Rd Cincinnati (45236) *(G-3446)*

Dss/Direct TV, Cincinnati *Also called Dss Installations Ltd (G-3446)*

DSV Solutions LLC 740 989-1200
251 Arrowhead Rd Little Hocking (45742) *(G-12807)*

Dta Inc 419 529-2920
3128 Park Ave W Ontario (44906) *(G-15548)*

DTE Inc 419 522-3428
110 Baird Pkwy Mansfield (44903) *(G-13170)*

Dts, Cuyahoga Falls *Also called Document Tech Systems Ltd (G-9088)*

Dtv Inc 216 226-5465
6505 Mayfield Rd Mayfield Heights (44124) *(G-13873)*

Dualite Sales & Service Inc (PA) 513 724-7100
1 Dualite Ln Williamsburg (45176) *(G-19493)*

Duane Morris LLP 202 577-3075
1614 E 40th St Fl 3 Cleveland (44103) *(G-5447)*

Duane Morris LLP 937 424-7086
200 N High St Columbus (43215) *(G-7473)*

Dublin, Dublin *Also called Integra Cncinnati/Columbus Inc (G-10257)*

Dublin Building Systems Co 614 760-5831
6233 Avery Rd Dublin (43016) *(G-10204)*

Dublin City Schools 614 764-5926
6371 Shier Rings Rd Dublin (43016) *(G-10205)*

Dublin Cleaners Inc (PA) 614 764-9934
6845 Caine Rd Columbus (43235) *(G-7474)*

Dublin Coml Property Svcs Inc 419 732-6732
127 Madison St Port Clinton (43452) *(G-16106)*

DUBLIN COUNSELING CENTER, Dublin *Also called Syntero Inc (G-10350)*

Dublin Dance Center, Columbus *Also called Artistic Dance Enterprises (G-6974)*

Dublin Family Care Inc 614 761-2244
250 W Bridge St Ste 101 Dublin (43017) *(G-10206)*

Dublin Geriatric Care Co LP 614 761-1188
6430 Post Rd Dublin (43016) *(G-10207)*

Dublin Hotel Ltd Liability Co 513 891-1066
5605 Paul G Blazer Me Dublin (43017) *(G-10208)*

Dublin Latchkey Inc 614 793-0871
5970 Venture Dr Ste A Dublin (43017) *(G-10209)*

Dublin Learning Academy 614 761-1800
5900 Cromdale Dr Dublin (43017) *(G-10210)*

Dublin Methodist Hospital, Dublin *Also called Ohiohealth Corporation (G-10299)*

Dublin Millwork Co Inc 614 889-7776
7575 Fishel Dr S Dublin (43016) *(G-10211)*

Dubois Chemicals Inc (PA) 513 731-6350
3630 E Kemper Rd Cincinnati (45241) *(G-3447)*

Duckworth Enterprises LLC 614 575-2900
2020 Brice Rd Ste 210 Reynoldsburg (43068) *(G-16301)*

Ductbreeze, Cleveland *Also called Rwk Services Inc (G-6351)*

Ducts Inc 216 391-2400
883 Addison Rd Cleveland (44103) *(G-5448)*

Duer Construction Co Inc 330 848-9930
70 E North St Akron (44304) *(G-197)*

Dufresh Farms, West Mansfield *Also called Heartland Quality Egg Farm (G-19124)*

Dugan & Meyers Construction Co (HQ) 513 891-4300
11110 Kenwood Rd Blue Ash (45242) *(G-1546)*

ALPHABETIC SECTION
E J Robinson Glass Co

Dugan & Meyers Construction Co 614 257-7430
8740 Orion Pl Ste 220 Columbus (43240) ***(G-6812)***

Dugan & Meyers Interests Inc (PA) 513 891-4300
11110 Kenwood Rd Blue Ash (45242) ***(G-1547)***

Dugan & Meyers LLC 513 891-4300
11110 Kenwood Rd Blue Ash (45242) ***(G-1548)***

Duke Energy Beckjord LLC 513 287-2561
139 E 4th St Cincinnati (45202) ***(G-3448)***

Duke Energy Kentucky Inc 704 594-6200
139 E 4th St Cincinnati (45202) ***(G-3449)***

Duke Energy Ohio Inc (HQ) 704 382-3853
139 E 4th St Cincinnati (45202) ***(G-3450)***

Duke Energy Ohio Inc 800 544-6900
5445 Audro Dr Cincinnati (45247) ***(G-3451)***

Duke Energy Ohio Inc 513 287-1120
7600 E Kemper Rd Cincinnati (45249) ***(G-3452)***

Duke Energy Ohio Inc 513 467-5000
757 Us 52 New Richmond (45157) ***(G-14994)***

Duke Energy Ohio Inc 513 421-9500
3300 Central Pkwy Cincinnati (45225) ***(G-3453)***

Duke Enrgy Ohio Cstmer Svc Ctr, Cincinnati *Also called Duke Energy Ohio Inc* ***(G-3453)***

Duke Realty Corporation 513 651-3900
5181 Natorp Blvd Ste 600 Mason (45040) ***(G-13576)***

Duke Realty Corporation 614 932-6000
6640 Riverside Dr Ste 320 Dublin (43017) ***(G-10212)***

Duke Realty Investors, Mason *Also called Duke Realty Corporation* ***(G-13576)***

Duke-Weeks Realty, Dublin *Also called Duke Realty Corporation* ***(G-10212)***

Dummen Group (HQ) 614 850-9551
250 S High St Ste 650 Columbus (43215) ***(G-7475)***

Dummen Na Inc (PA) 614 850-9551
250 S High St Ste 650 Columbus (43215) ***(G-7476)***

Dumouchelle Art Galleries 419 255-7606
409 Jefferson Ave Toledo (43604) ***(G-17705)***

Dun Rite Home Improvement Inc 330 650-5322
8601 Freeway Dr Macedonia (44056) ***(G-13068)***

Dunbar Armored Inc 513 381-8000
1257 W 7th St Cincinnati (45203) ***(G-3454)***

Dunbar Armored Inc 614 475-1969
2300 Citygate Dr Unit B Columbus (43219) ***(G-7477)***

Dunbar Armored Inc 216 642-5700
5505 Cloverleaf Pkwy Cleveland (44125) ***(G-5449)***

Dunbar Mechanical Inc (PA) 734 856-6601
2806 N Reynolds Rd Toledo (43615) ***(G-17706)***

Duncan Aviation Inc 513 873-7523
358 Wilmer Ave 121 Cincinnati (45226) ***(G-3455)***

Duncan Falls Assoc 740 674-7105
Water St Duncan Falls (43734) ***(G-10381)***

Duncan Oil Co (PA) 937 426-5945
849 Factory Rd Dayton (45434) ***(G-9171)***

Dungan & Lefevre Co Lpa (PA) 937 339-0511
210 W Main St Troy (45373) ***(G-18200)***

Dunkin' Donuts, Girard *Also called Standard Oil Company* ***(G-11301)***

Dunlap Family Physicians Inc (PA) 330 684-2015
830 S Main St Ste Rear Orrville (44667) ***(G-15628)***

Dunlop and Johnston Inc 330 220-2700
5498 Innovation Dr Valley City (44280) ***(G-18461)***

Dunnhumby Inc 513 579-3400
3825 Edwards Rd Ste 600 Cincinnati (45209) ***(G-3456)***

Dunning Motor Sales Inc 740 439-4465
9108 Southgate Rd Cambridge (43725) ***(G-2064)***

Dunsiane Swim Club 937 433-7946
600 W Spring Valley Pike Dayton (45458) ***(G-9397)***

Dupont Inc 937 268-3411
1515 Nicholas Rd Dayton (45417) ***(G-9398)***

Dupree House, Cincinnati *Also called Episcopal Retirement Homes Inc* ***(G-3509)***

Duquesne Light Company 330 385-6103
626 Saint Clair Ave East Liverpool (43920) ***(G-10401)***

Durable Corporation 800 537-1603
75 N Pleasant St Norwalk (44857) ***(G-15433)***

Durable Slate Co (PA) 614 299-5522
3933 Groves Rd Columbus (43232) ***(G-7478)***

Durable Slate Co 216 751-0151
3530 Warrensville Ctr Rd Shaker Heights (44122) ***(G-16707)***

Durable Slate Company, The, Columbus *Also called Durable Slate Co* ***(G-7478)***

Duramax Marine LLC 440 834-5400
17990 Great Lakes Pkwy Hiram (44234) ***(G-11864)***

Durango Boot, Nelsonville *Also called Georgia-Boot Inc* ***(G-14832)***

Dure Investments LLC 419 697-7800
1761 Meijers Cir Oregon (43616) ***(G-15591)***

Durga Llc 513 771-2080
11320 Chester Rd Cincinnati (45246) ***(G-3457)***

Dusk To Dawn Protective Svcs 330 837-9992
3554 Lincoln Way E 3 Massillon (44646) ***(G-13676)***

Dutch Cntry Apple Dmplings Inc 330 683-0646
229 W Market St Orrville (44667) ***(G-15629)***

Dutch Creek Foods Inc 330 852-2631
1411 Old Route 39 Ne Sugarcreek (44681) ***(G-17378)***

Dutch Girl Cleaners, Canton *Also called Edco Cleaners Inc* ***(G-2297)***

Dutch Heritage Farms Inc 330 893-3232
Hc 39 Berlin (44610) ***(G-1446)***

Dutchess Cleaner, Youngstown *Also called Dutchess Dry Cleaners* ***(G-20023)***

Dutchess Cleaners, Youngstown *Also called Rondinelli Company Inc* ***(G-20194)***

Dutchess Dry Cleaners 330 759-9382
2710 Belmont Ave Ste D Youngstown (44505) ***(G-20023)***

Dutchman Hospitality Group Inc 614 873-3414
445 S Jefferson Ave Plain City (43064) ***(G-16050)***

Dutro Ford Lincoln-Mercury Inc (PA) 740 452-6334
132 S 5th St Zanesville (43701) ***(G-20301)***

Dutro Nissan, Zanesville *Also called Dutro Ford Lincoln-Mercury Inc* ***(G-20301)***

Duty's Towing & Auto Service, Columbus *Also called Dutys Towing* ***(G-7479)***

Dutys Towing 614 252-3336
3288 E Broad St Columbus (43213) ***(G-7479)***

Dva Healthcare - South 513 347-0444
3267 Westbourne Dr Cincinnati (45248) ***(G-3458)***

Dva Renal Healthcare Inc 740 454-2911
3120 Newark Rd Zanesville (43701) ***(G-20302)***

Dw Together LLC 330 225-8200
3698 Center Rd Brunswick (44212) ***(G-1928)***

Dwa Mrkting Prmtional Pdts LLC 216 476-0635
17000 Foltz Pkwy Strongsville (44149) ***(G-17298)***

Dwellworks LLC (PA) 216 682-4200
1317 Euclid Ave Cleveland (44115) ***(G-5450)***

Dworken & Bernstein Co Lpa (PA) 216 861-4211
1468 W 9th St Ste 135 Cleveland (44113) ***(G-5451)***

Dworken & Bernstein Co Lpa 440 352-3391
60 S Park Pl Fl 2 Painesville (44077) ***(G-15711)***

Dworken and Bernstein, Cleveland *Also called Dworken & Bernstein Co Lpa* ***(G-5451)***

Dworkin Inc (PA) 216 271-5318
5400 Harvard Ave Cleveland (44105) ***(G-5452)***

Dworkin Trucking, Cleveland *Also called Dworkin Inc* ***(G-5452)***

Dwyer Concrete Lifting Inc 614 501-0998
5650 Groveport Rd Groveport (43125) ***(G-11508)***

Dxp Enterprises Inc 513 242-2227
5177 Spring Grove Ave Cincinnati (45217) ***(G-3459)***

Dyn Marine Services Inc 937 427-2663
3040 Presidential Dr Beavercreek (45324) ***(G-1149)***

Dynalectric Company 614 529-7500
1762 Dividend Dr Columbus (43228) ***(G-7480)***

Dynamic Construction Inc 740 927-8898
172 Coors Blvd Pataskala (43062) ***(G-15785)***

Dynamic Currents Corp 419 861-2036
1761 Commerce Rd Holland (43528) ***(G-11885)***

Dynamic Mechanical Systems 513 858-6722
5623 Sigmon Way Fairfield (45014) ***(G-10720)***

Dynamic Metal Services, Bedford Heights *Also called Alloy Metal Exchange LLC* ***(G-1315)***

Dynamic Solution Associates, Independence *Also called Arysen Inc* ***(G-12047)***

Dynamic Structures Inc (PA) 330 892-0164
3790 State Route 7 Ste B New Waterford (44445) ***(G-15004)***

Dynamic Weld Corporation 419 582-2900
242 N St Osgood (45351) ***(G-15652)***

Dynamite Technologies LLC (PA) 614 538-0095
274 Marconi Blvd Ste 300 Columbus (43215) ***(G-7481)***

Dynamix Engineering Ltd 614 443-1178
855 Grandview Ave Ste 300 Columbus (43215) ***(G-7482)***

Dynatech Systems Inc 440 365-1774
161 Reaser Ct Elyria (44035) ***(G-10503)***

Dyncorp 513 942-6500
9266 Meridian Way West Chester (45069) ***(G-18916)***

Dyncorp 513 569-7415
26 W Mrtin Lther King Dr Cincinnati (45220) ***(G-3460)***

Dynegy Zimmer LLC 713 767-0483
1781 Us Rte 52 Moscow (45153) ***(G-14720)***

Dyno Nobel Transportation 740 439-5050
850 Woodlawn Ave Cambridge (43725) ***(G-2065)***

Dyno Transportation, Cambridge *Also called Dyno Nobel Transportation* ***(G-2065)***

Dynotec Inc 614 880-7320
2931 E Dublin Granv Rd Columbus (43231) ***(G-7483)***

E & A Pedco Services Inc 513 782-4920
11499 Chester Rd Ste 501 Cincinnati (45246) ***(G-3461)***

E & C Div, Cleveland *Also called Greater Cleveland* ***(G-5633)***

E & J Trailer Leasing Inc 513 563-7366
610 Wayne Park Dr Ste 5 Cincinnati (45215) ***(G-3462)***

E & J Trailer Sales & Service 513 563-2550
610 Wayne Park Dr Ste 5 Cincinnati (45215) ***(G-3463)***

E & L Premier Corporation 330 836-9901
3250 W Market St Ste 102 Fairlawn (44333) ***(G-10823)***

E & V Ventures Inc (PA) 330 794-6683
1511 E Market St Akron (44305) ***(G-198)***

E A Group, Mentor *Also called Electro-Analytical Inc* ***(G-14043)***

E A Zicka Co 513 451-1440
2714 East Tower Dr Ofc Cincinnati (45238) ***(G-3464)***

E and P Warehouse Services Ltd 330 898-4800
1666 Mcmyler St Nw Warren (44485) ***(G-18704)***

E F Bavis & Associates Inc 513 677-0500
201 Grandin Rd Maineville (45039) ***(G-13115)***

E F Boyd & Son Inc (PA) 216 791-0770
2165 E 89th St Cleveland (44106) ***(G-5453)***

E H Schmidt Executive 419 874-4331
26785 Dixie Hwy Perrysburg (43551) ***(G-15861)***

E H T Company, Euclid *Also called Euclid Heat Treating Co* ***(G-10632)***

E J Links Co The Inc 440 235-0501
26111 John Rd Olmsted Twp (44138) ***(G-15535)***

E J Robinson Glass Co 513 242-9250
5618 Center Hill Ave Cincinnati (45216) ***(G-3465)***

ALPHABETIC

E M Columbus LLC.................................614 861-3232
2740 Eastland Mall Ste B Columbus (43232) *(G-7484)*

E M H & T, New Albany *Also called Evans Mechwart Ham (G-14852)*

E M H Regional Medical Center, Amherst *Also called Amherst Hospital Association (G-580)*

E M I, Cleveland *Also called Equipment Manufacturers Intl (G-5488)*

E M I Plastic Equipment, Jackson Center *Also called EMI Corp (G-12183)*

E N T, Columbus *Also called University Otolaryngologists (G-8820)*

E N T Toledo Inc.................................419 578-7555
2865 N Reynolds Rd # 260 Toledo (43615) *(G-17707)*

E P Ferris & Associates Inc.................614 299-2999
880 King Ave Columbus (43212) *(G-7485)*

E Q M, Cincinnati *Also called Environmental Quality MGT (G-3502)*

E Retailing Associates LLC.................614 300-5785
2282 Westbrooke Dr Columbus (43228) *(G-7486)*

E S Gallon & Associates.................937 586-3100
2621 Dryden Rd Ste 105 Moraine (45439) *(G-14650)*

E S I Inc (HQ).................................513 454-3741
4696 Devitt Dr West Chester (45246) *(G-19048)*

E S Wagner Company.................................419 691-8651
840 Patchen Rd Oregon (43616) *(G-15592)*

E T B Ltd.................................740 373-6686
15 Acme St Marietta (45750) *(G-13326)*

E T Financial Service Inc.................937 716-1726
4550 Salem Ave Trotwood (45416) *(G-18193)*

E Technologies Group, West Chester *Also called E-Technologies Group LLC (G-18917)*

E Wynn Inc.................................614 444-5288
1851 S High St Columbus (43207) *(G-7487)*

E Z Cleaners, Englewood *Also called Sunset Carpet Cleaning (G-10602)*

E&I Construction LLC.................................513 421-2045
1210 Sycamore St Ste 200 Cincinnati (45202) *(G-3466)*

E&I Solutions LLC.................................937 912-0288
3610 Pentagon Blvd # 220 Beavercreek (45431) *(G-1150)*

E-Cycle LLC.................................614 832-7032
4105 Leap Rd Hilliard (43026) *(G-11763)*

E-Mek Technologies LLC.................................937 424-3163
7410 Webster St Dayton (45414) *(G-9399)*

E-Pallet, Lakewood *Also called Pallet Distributors Inc (G-12359)*

E-Tech Ohio Commision, Columbus *Also called Ohio Education Association (G-8250)*

E-Technologies Group LLC (HQ).................513 771-7271
5530 Union Centre Dr West Chester (45069) *(G-18917)*

E.M.s Rams Youth Football Team, Cleveland *Also called EMs Rams Youth Dev Group Inc (G-5478)*

E2b Teknologies Inc (PA).................................440 352-4700
521 5th Ave Chardon (44024) *(G-2693)*

Ea Vica Co.................................513 481-3500
2714 E Twr Dr Ofc Ste 007 Cincinnati (45238) *(G-3467)*

Eab Truck Service.................................216 525-0020
7951 Granger Rd Cleveland (44125) *(G-5454)*

Eagle Bridge Co.................................937 492-5654
800 S Vandemark Rd Sidney (45365) *(G-16775)*

Eagle Creek Golf Club, Norwalk *Also called Norwalk Golf Properties Inc (G-15450)*

Eagle Creek Hlthcare Group Inc.................937 544-5531
141 Spruce Ln West Union (45693) *(G-19136)*

EAGLE CREEK NURSING CENTER, West Union *Also called Eagle Creek Hlthcare Group Inc (G-19136)*

Eagle Equipment Corporation.................937 746-0510
245 Industrial Dr Franklin (45005) *(G-11028)*

Eagle Financial Bancorp Inc (PA).................513 574-0700
6415 Bridgetown Rd Cincinnati (45248) *(G-3468)*

Eagle Freight, Berea *Also called L O G Transportation Inc (G-1429)*

Eagle Hardwoods Inc.................................330 339-8838
6138 Stonecreek Rd Newcomerstown (43832) *(G-15130)*

Eagle Industrial Painting LLC.................330 866-5965
3215 Magnolia Rd Nw Magnolia (44643) *(G-13111)*

Eagle Industrial Truck Mfg LLC.................734 442-1000
1 Air Cargo Pkwy E Swanton (43558) *(G-17396)*

Eagle Industries Ohio Inc.................................513 247-2900
275 Commercial Dr Fairfield (45014) *(G-10721)*

Eagle Protective Services, Willoughby *Also called Ryno 24 Inc (G-19569)*

Eagle Realty Group LLC (HQ).................513 361-7700
421 E 4th St Cincinnati (45202) *(G-3469)*

Eagle Rock Tours, Coshocton *Also called Muskingum Coach Company (G-9023)*

Eagle Tugs, Swanton *Also called Eagle Industrial Truck Mfg LLC (G-17396)*

Eagle USA Airfreight, Columbus *Also called Ceva Logistics US Inc (G-7172)*

Eaglewood Care Center.................................937 399-7195
2000 Villa Rd Springfield (45503) *(G-17031)*

Eaglewood Villa, Springfield *Also called Wallick Construction Co (G-17132)*

Earl Twinam.................................740 820-2654
550 Field Rd Portsmouth (45662) *(G-16137)*

Earle M Jorgensen Company.................................513 771-3223
601 Redna Ter Cincinnati (45215) *(G-3470)*

Earle M Jorgensen Company.................................330 425-1500
2060 Enterprise Pkwy Twinsburg (44087) *(G-18259)*

Earley & Ross Ltd.................................740 634-3301
580 E Washington St Sabina (45169) *(G-16467)*

Early Beginnings, Tipp City *Also called Annas Child Care Lrng Ctr Inc (G-17549)*

Early Bird, The, Greenville *Also called Brothers Publishing Co LLC (G-11368)*

Early Childhood Enrichment Ctr.................216 991-9761
19824 Sussex Rd Rm 178 Cleveland (44122) *(G-5455)*

Early Childhood Learning Commu.................614 451-6418
4141 Rudy Rd Columbus (43214) *(G-7488)*

Early Construction Co.................................740 894-5150
307 County Road 120 S South Point (45680) *(G-16933)*

Early Construction Company, South Point *Also called Early Construction Co (G-16933)*

Early Express Mail Services, Dayton *Also called Early Express Services Inc (G-9400)*

Early Express Services Inc.................................937 223-5801
1333 E 2nd St Dayton (45403) *(G-9400)*

Early Learning Tree Chld Ctr (PA).................937 276-3221
2332 N Main St Dayton (45405) *(G-9401)*

Early Learning Tree Chld Ctr.................................937 293-7907
2332 N Main St Dayton (45405) *(G-9402)*

Earnest Machine Products Co (PA).................440 895-8400
1250 Linda St Ste 301 Rocky River (44116) *(G-16431)*

Earth n Wood Products Inc.................................330 644-1858
2436 S Arlington Rd Akron (44319) *(G-199)*

East Akron Neighborhood Dev.................................330 773-6838
550 S Arlington St Akron (44306) *(G-200)*

East Butler County YMCA, Fairfield Township *Also called Great Miami Valley YMCA (G-10808)*

East Carroll Nursing Home.................................330 627-6900
2193 Commerce Dr Carrollton (44615) *(G-2567)*

East Center, Toledo *Also called Unison Behavioral Health Group (G-18115)*

East Central Region, Grove City *Also called Securitas SEC Svcs USA Inc (G-11470)*

East Coast Region, Cleveland *Also called Securitas SEC Svcs USA Inc (G-6389)*

East Dayton Christian School.................................937 252-5400
999 Spinning Rd Dayton (45431) *(G-9172)*

East Elementary School, Saint Marys *Also called St Marys City Board Education (G-16533)*

EAST END COMMUNITY SERVICES CO, Dayton *Also called Westcare Ohio Inc (G-9876)*

East End Neighborhood Hse Assn.................216 791-9378
2749 Woodhill Rd Cleveland (44104) *(G-5456)*

East End Ro Burton Inc.................................440 942-2742
792 Mentor Ave Willoughby (44094) *(G-19519)*

East End Welding Company.................................330 677-6000
357 Tallmadge Rd Kent (44240) *(G-12230)*

East End YMCA Pre School, Madison *Also called Lake County YMCA (G-13099)*

East Galbraith Health Care Ctr (PA).................513 984-5220
3889 E Galbraith Rd Cincinnati (45236) *(G-3471)*

East Galbraith Nursing Home.................................513 984-5220
3889 E Galbraith Rd Cincinnati (45236) *(G-3472)*

East Lawn Manor, Marion *Also called County of Marion (G-13414)*

EAST LIVERPOOL CITY HOSPITAL, East Liverpool *Also called City Hospital Association (G-10399)*

East Liverpool Motor Lodge, East Liverpool *Also called Alsan Corporation (G-10396)*

East Liverpool Water Dept.................................330 385-8812
2220 Michigan Ave East Liverpool (43920) *(G-10402)*

East Manufacturing Corporation (PA).................330 325-9921
1871 State Rte 44 Randolph (44265) *(G-16230)*

East Mentor Recreation Inc.................................440 354-2000
65 Normandy Dr Mentor (44060) *(G-14042)*

East of Chicago Pizza Inc (PA).................................419 225-7116
121 W High St Fl 12 Lima (45801) *(G-12630)*

East Ohio Gas Company (HQ).................................800 362-7557
1201 E 55th St Cleveland (44103) *(G-5457)*

East Ohio Gas Company.................................330 742-8121
1165 W Rayen Ave Youngstown (44502) *(G-20024)*

East Ohio Gas Company.................................330 266-2169
6500 Hampsher Rd New Franklin (44216) *(G-14909)*

East Ohio Gas Company.................................330 477-9411
4725 Southway St Sw Canton (44706) *(G-2291)*

East Ohio Gas Company.................................216 736-6959
21200 Miles Rd Cleveland (44128) *(G-5458)*

East Ohio Gas Company.................................216 736-6120
7001 Center Rd Ashtabula (44004) *(G-737)*

East Ohio Gas Company.................................330 499-2501
7015 Freedom Ave Nw Canton (44720) *(G-2292)*

East Ohio Gas Company.................................330 478-1700
332 2nd St Nw Canton (44702) *(G-2293)*

East Ohio Gas Company.................................216 736-6917
29555 Clayton Ave Wickliffe (44092) *(G-19457)*

East Toledo Family Center (PA).................................419 691-1429
1020 Varland Ave Toledo (43605) *(G-17708)*

East Water Leasing Co LLC.................................419 278-6921
620 E Water St Deshler (43516) *(G-10057)*

East Way Behavioral Hlth Care.................................937 222-4900
600 Wayne Ave Dayton (45410) *(G-9403)*

Eastbury Bowling Center.................................330 452-3700
3000 Atl Blvd Ne Unit A Canton (44705) *(G-2294)*

Eastco, Dayton *Also called Eastway Corporation (G-9405)*

EASTER SEAL, Dayton *Also called Goodwill Ester Seals Miami Vly (G-9464)*

Easter Seal Northwestern Ohio, Fremont *Also called Easter Seals Metro Chicago Inc (G-11071)*

Easter Seal Society of (PA).................................330 743-1168
299 Edwards St Youngstown (44502) *(G-20025)*

EASTER SEALS, Youngstown *Also called Easter Seal Society of (G-20025)*

Easter Seals Center.................................614 228-5523
3830 Trueman Ct Hilliard (43026) *(G-11764)*

Easter Seals Metro Chicago Inc......419 332-3016
101 S Stone St Fremont (43420) ***(G-11071)***
Easter Seals Nothern Ohio Inc......440 324-6600
2173 N Ridge Rd E Ste G Lorain (44055) ***(G-12901)***
Easter Seals Tristate (HQ)......513 985-0515
4300 Rossplain Dr Blue Ash (45236) ***(G-1549)***
Easter Seals Tristate LLC (PA)......513 281-2316
2901 Gilbert Ave Cincinnati (45206) ***(G-3473)***
Easter Seals Tristate LLC......513 475-6791
447 Morgan St Cincinnati (45206) ***(G-3474)***
Eastern Community YMCA, Oregon *Also called Young Mens Christian Associat* ***(G-15615)***
Eastern Hill Internal Medicine......513 232-3500
8000 5 Mile Rd Ste 305 Cincinnati (45230) ***(G-3475)***
Eastern Hills Pediatric Assoc......513 231-3345
7502 State Rd Ste 3350 Cincinnati (45255) ***(G-3476)***
Eastern Hills Pediatrics, Cincinnati *Also called Eastern Hills Pediatric Assoc* ***(G-3476)***
Eastern Horizon Inc......614 253-7000
1640 E 5th Ave Columbus (43219) ***(G-7489)***
Eastern Mumee Bay Arts Council......419 690-5718
595 Sylvandale Ave Oregon (43616) ***(G-15593)***
Eastern Ohio P-16......330 675-7623
4314 Mahoning Ave Nw Warren (44483) ***(G-18705)***
Eastern Region Department, Dayton *Also called Acuren Inspection Inc* ***(G-9207)***
Eastern Star Hm of Cyhoga Cnty......216 761-0170
2114 Noble Rd Cleveland (44112) ***(G-5459)***
Eastgate Advntres Golf G-Karts, Loveland *Also called Recreational Golf Inc* ***(G-13024)***
Eastgate Animal Hospital Inc......513 528-0700
459 Old State Route 74 Cincinnati (45244) ***(G-3477)***
Eastgate Graphics LLC......513 228-5522
611 Norgal Dr Lebanon (45036) ***(G-12461)***
Eastgate Health Care Center......513 752-3710
4400 Glen Este Withamsvil Cincinnati (45245) ***(G-2850)***
Eastgate Professional Off Pk V......513 943-0050
4357 Ferguson Dr Ste 220 Cincinnati (45245) ***(G-2851)***
Eastgate Sod, Maineville *Also called Mike Ward Landscaping Inc* ***(G-13116)***
Eastgate Village......513 753-4400
776 Cincinnati Batavia Pi Cincinnati (45245) ***(G-2852)***
Eastgate Woods Apts, Batavia *Also called Edward Rose Associates Inc* ***(G-998)***
Eastlake Lodging LLC......440 953-8000
35000 Curtis Blvd Eastlake (44095) ***(G-10429)***
Eastland Crane & Towing, Columbus *Also called Eastland Crane Service Inc* ***(G-7490)***
Eastland Crane Service Inc......614 868-9750
2190 S Hamilton Rd Columbus (43232) ***(G-7490)***
Eastland Lanes Inc......614 868-9866
2666 Old Courtright Rd Columbus (43232) ***(G-7491)***
Eastland Mall, Columbus *Also called Glimcher Realty Trust* ***(G-7674)***
Eastland Mall, Columbus *Also called E M Columbus LLC* ***(G-7484)***
Eastman & Smith Ltd......419 241-6000
1 Seagate Ste 2400 Toledo (43604) ***(G-17709)***
Easton Town Center Guest Svcs, Columbus *Also called Easton Town Center LLC* ***(G-7493)***
Easton Town Center II LLC......614 416-7000
160 Easton Town Ctr Columbus (43219) ***(G-7492)***
Easton Town Center LLC......614 337-2560
4016 Townsfair Way # 201 Columbus (43219) ***(G-7493)***
Eastside Body Shop......513 624-1145
7636 Beechmont Ave Cincinnati (45255) ***(G-3478)***
Eastside Landscaping Inc......216 381-0070
572 Trebisky Rd Cleveland (44143) ***(G-5460)***
Eastside Mri, Cleveland *Also called Drs Hill & Thomas Co* ***(G-5446)***
Eastside Multi Care Inc......216 662-3343
19900 Clare Ave Maple Heights (44137) ***(G-13286)***
Eastside Nursery Inc......513 934-1661
2830 Greentree Rd Lebanon (45036) ***(G-12462)***
Eastside Roofg Restoration Co......513 471-0434
417 Purcell Ave Cincinnati (45205) ***(G-3479)***
EASTWAY BEHAVORIAL HEALTHCARE, Dayton *Also called Eastway Corporation* ***(G-9404)***
Eastway Corporation (PA)......937 496-2000
600 Wayne Ave Dayton (45410) ***(G-9404)***
Eastway Corporation......937 531-7000
600 Wayne Ave Dayton (45410) ***(G-9405)***
Eastway Supplies Inc......614 252-3650
1561 Alum Creek Dr Columbus (43209) ***(G-7494)***
Eastwood Mall, Niles *Also called Cararo Co Inc* ***(G-15150)***
Eastwood Mall, Niles *Also called Marion Plaza Inc* ***(G-15158)***
Eastwood Mall Kids Club, Niles *Also called Cafaro Co* ***(G-15149)***
Eastwood Residential Living......440 417-0608
6261 Chapel Rd Madison (44057) ***(G-13095)***
Eastwood Residential Living......440 428-1588
6412 N Ridge Rd Madison (44057) ***(G-13096)***
Easy 2 Technologies, Cleveland *Also called Easy2 Technologies Inc* ***(G-5461)***
EASY MONEY, Dublin *Also called Community Choice Financial Inc* ***(G-10185)***
Easy2 Technologies Inc......216 479-0482
1111 Chester Ave Cleveland (44114) ***(G-5461)***
Eaton Construction Co Inc......740 474-3414
653 Island Rd Circleville (43113) ***(G-4832)***
Eaton Corporation......440 523-5000
1000 Eaton Blvd Beachwood (44122) ***(G-1053)***
Eaton Corporation......614 839-4387
P.O. Box 182175 Columbus (43218) ***(G-7495)***
Eaton Corporation......216 523-5000
1000 Eaton Blvd Beachwood (44122) ***(G-1054)***
Eaton Corporation......216 920-2000
333 Babbitt Rd Ste 100 Cleveland (44123) ***(G-5462)***
Eaton Corporation......888 402-1915
P.O. Box 818031 Cleveland (44181) ***(G-5463)***
Eaton Fire Division, Eaton *Also called City of Eaton* ***(G-10438)***
Eaton Gardens Rehabilitation A......937 456-5537
515 S Maple St Eaton (45320) ***(G-10445)***
Eaton Group GMAC Real Estate......330 726-9999
382 Niles Cortland Rd Ne Warren (44484) ***(G-18706)***
Eaton Plumbing Inc......614 891-7005
5600 E Walnut St Westerville (43081) ***(G-19251)***
Eaton Tire & Auto Parts, Grafton *Also called Joseph Russo* ***(G-11317)***
Eaton-Aeroquip Llc......419 891-7775
1660 Indian Wood Cir Maumee (43537) ***(G-13782)***
Ebenezer Road Corp......513 941-0099
6210 Cleves Warsaw Pike Cincinnati (45233) ***(G-3480)***
Ebmc, Dublin *Also called Employee Benefit Management* ***(G-10217)***
Ebnt, Cleveland *Also called Engineering Design and Testing* ***(G-5481)***
Ebo Inc (PA)......216 229-9300
23600 Aurora Rd Bedford (44146) ***(G-1279)***
Ebony Construction Co......419 841-3455
3510 Centennial Rd Sylvania (43560) ***(G-17421)***
Ebs Asset Management, Miamisburg *Also called Eubel Brady Suttman Asset Mgt* ***(G-14169)***
Ebsco Industries Inc......330 478-0281
4150 Belden Village Mall Canton (44718) ***(G-2295)***
Ebsco Teleservice, Canton *Also called Ebsco Industries Inc* ***(G-2295)***
Ebso Inc......419 423-3823
215 Stanford Pkwy Findlay (45840) ***(G-10898)***
Ebso Inc......440 262-1133
3301 E Royalton Rd Ste 1 Cleveland (44147) ***(G-5464)***
Ebuys Inc (HQ)......858 831-0839
810 Dsw Dr Columbus (43219) ***(G-7496)***
EBY-Brown Company LLC......937 324-1036
1982 Commerce Cir Springfield (45504) ***(G-17032)***
ECDI, Columbus *Also called Economic & Cmnty Dev Inst Inc* ***(G-7500)***
Ecg Scanning & Medical Svcs (HQ)......888 346-5837
3055 Kettering Blvd 219b Moraine (45439) ***(G-14651)***
Echo 24 Inc (PA)......740 964-7081
167 Cypress St Sw Ste A Reynoldsburg (43068) ***(G-16302)***
Echo Manor Extended Care Ctr, Pickerington *Also called Home Echo Club Inc* ***(G-15958)***
ECHO Residential Support......614 210-0944
6500 Busch Blvd Ste 215 Columbus (43229) ***(G-7497)***
Echo-Tape LLC......614 892-3246
651 Dearborn Park Ln Columbus (43085) ***(G-7498)***
Echogen Power Systems Del Inc......234 542-4379
365 Water St Akron (44308) ***(G-201)***
Echoing Hills Village Inc......740 594-3541
528 1/2 Richland Ave Athens (45701) ***(G-778)***
Echoing Hills Village Inc (PA)......740 327-2311
36272 County Road 79 Warsaw (43844) ***(G-18783)***
Echoing Hills Village Inc......937 854-5151
5455 Salem Bend Dr Dayton (45426) ***(G-9406)***
Echoing Hills Village Inc......937 237-7881
7040 Union Schoolhouse Rd Dayton (45424) ***(G-9407)***
Echoing Hills Village Inc......440 989-1400
3295 Leavitt Rd Lorain (44053) ***(G-12902)***
Echoing Hills Village Inc......440 986-3085
235 W Main St South Amherst (44001) ***(G-16921)***
Echoing Lake Residential Home, Lorain *Also called Echoing Hills Village Inc* ***(G-12902)***
Echoing Lake/Renouard Home, South Amherst *Also called Echoing Hills Village Inc* ***(G-16921)***
Echoing Meadows, Athens *Also called Echoing Hills Village Inc* ***(G-778)***
ECHOING RIDGE RESIDENTIAL CENT, Warsaw *Also called Echoing Hills Village Inc* ***(G-18783)***
Echoing Valley, Dayton *Also called Echoing Hills Village Inc* ***(G-9407)***
Echoing Wood Residential Cntr, Dayton *Also called Echoing Hills Village Inc* ***(G-9406)***
Eci Macola/Max LLC (HQ)......978 539-6186
5455 Rings Rd Ste 100 Dublin (43017) ***(G-10213)***
Eci Macola/Max Holding LLC......614 410-2712
5455 Rings Rd Ste 400 Dublin (43017) ***(G-10214)***
Ecke Ranch, Columbus *Also called Dummen Na Inc* ***(G-7476)***
Eckel Logistics Inc......419 349-3118
14617 Deerwood Ct Perrysburg (43551) ***(G-15862)***
Eckert Fire Protection Systems......513 948-1030
510 W Benson St Cincinnati (45215) ***(G-3481)***
Eckinger Construction Company......330 453-2566
2340 Shepler Ch Ave Sw Canton (44706) ***(G-2296)***
Eckstein Roofing Company......513 941-1511
264 Stille Dr Cincinnati (45233) ***(G-3482)***
Eclipse Blind Systems Inc......330 296-0112
7154 State Route 88 Ravenna (44266) ***(G-16242)***
Eclipse Co LLC......440 552-9400
23209 Miles Rd Cleveland (44128) ***(G-5465)***
Eclipse Midco, Dublin *Also called Eci Macola/Max Holding LLC* ***(G-10214)***
Eclipse Real Estate Group, Columbus *Also called Multicon Construction Co* ***(G-8123)***
Eclipse Resources - Ohio LLC......740 452-4503
4900 Boggs Rd Zanesville (43701) ***(G-20303)***

ALPHABETIC

Eco Engineering Inc 513 985-8300
  11815 Highway Dr Ste 600 Cincinnati (45241) *(G-3483)*

Eco Global Corp 419 363-2681
  10803 Erastus Durbin Rd Rockford (45882) *(G-16414)*

Ecommerce LLC 800 861-9394
  1774 Dividend Dr Columbus (43228) *(G-7499)*

Econo Lodge, Toledo *Also called Carol Burton Management LLC (G-17638)*

Econo Lodge, Cincinnati *Also called Msk Hospitality Inc (G-4080)*

Econo Lodge, Elyria *Also called Lodging Industry Inc (G-10529)*

Econo Lodge 419 627-8000
  1904 Cleveland Rd Sandusky (44870) *(G-16597)*

Economic & Cmnty Dev Inst Inc 614 559-0104
  1655 Old Leonard Ave Columbus (43219) *(G-7500)*

Economy Forms, Columbus *Also called Efco Corp (G-7509)*

Economy Linen & Towel Svc Inc 740 454-6888
  508 Howard St Zanesville (43701) *(G-20304)*

Economy Prod Vegetable Co Inc (PA) 216 431-2800
  4000 Orange Ave Unit 38 Cleveland (44115) *(G-5466)*

Ecoplumbers Inc 614 299-9903
  4691 Northwest Pkwy Hilliard (43026) *(G-11765)*

Ecotage 513 782-2229
  11700 Princeton Pike # 4 Cincinnati (45246) *(G-3484)*

Ecrm, Solon *Also called Efficient Collaborative Retail (G-16843)*

Ecs Holdco Inc 614 433-0170
  705 Lkview Plz Blvd Ste A Worthington (43085) *(G-19805)*

Ed Map Inc 740 753-3439
  296 S Harper St Ste 1 Nelsonville (45764) *(G-14830)*

Ed Mullinax Ford LLC 440 984-2431
  8000 Leavitt Rd Amherst (44001) *(G-584)*

Ed Schmidt Auto Inc 419 874-4331
  26875 Dixie Hwy Perrysburg (43551) *(G-15863)*

Ed Schmidt Chevrolet, Perrysburg *Also called Schmidt Daily Rental Inc (G-15919)*

Ed Schmidt Chevrolet Inc 419 897-8600
  1425 Reynolds Rd Maumee (43537) *(G-13783)*

Ed Tomko Chryslr Jep Dge Inc 440 835-5900
  33725 Walker Rd Avon Lake (44012) *(G-916)*

Ed Wilson & Son Trucking Inc 330 549-9287
  14766 Woodworth Rd New Springfield (44443) *(G-14996)*

Edaptive Computing Inc 937 433-0477
  1245 Lyons Rd Ste G Dayton (45458) *(G-9408)*

Edco Cleaners Inc 330 477-3357
  2455 Whipple Ave Nw Canton (44708) *(G-2297)*

Eddie Lane's Diamond Showroom, Cincinnati *Also called Equity Diamond Brokers Inc (G-3511)*

Edelman Plumbing Supply Inc (PA) 216 591-0150
  26201 Richmond Rd Ste 4 Bedford Heights (44146) *(G-1322)*

Eden, Cleveland *Also called Emerald Dev Ecnomic Netwrk Inc (G-5473)*

Edendale House, Cleveland *Also called United Cerebral Palsy (G-6569)*

Edgar Trent Cnstr Co LLC 419 683-4939
  1301 Freese Works Pl Crestline (44827) *(G-9054)*

Edge Hair Design & Spa 330 477-2300
  4655 Dressler Rd Nw Canton (44718) *(G-2298)*

Edge Plastics Inc 419 522-6696
  449 Newman St Mansfield (44902) *(G-13171)*

Edgewood Manor Lucasville II, Lucasville *Also called Consulate Management Co LLC (G-13046)*

Edgewood Manor Nursing Center, Port Clinton *Also called Covenant Care Ohio Inc (G-16104)*

Edgewood Manor of Lucasville 740 259-5536
  10098 Big Bear Creek Rd Lucasville (45648) *(G-13048)*

Edgewood Manor of Wellston 740 384-5611
  405 N Park Ave Wellston (45692) *(G-18849)*

Edgewood Skate Arena 419 331-0647
  2170 Edgewood Dr Lima (45805) *(G-12631)*

Edict Systems Inc 937 429-4288
  2434 Esquire Dr Beavercreek (45431) *(G-1151)*

Edison Biotechnology Institute 740 593-4713
  101 Konneker The Rdgs Athens (45701) *(G-779)*

Edison Bus Garage, Amsterdam *Also called Edison Local School District (G-601)*

Edison Equipment (PA) 614 883-5710
  2225 Mckinley Ave Columbus (43204) *(G-7501)*

Edison Local School District 740 543-4011
  8235 Amsterdam Rd Se Amsterdam (43903) *(G-601)*

Edison Welding Institute Inc (PA) 614 688-5000
  1250 Arthur E Adams Dr Columbus (43221) *(G-7502)*

EDM Management Inc 330 726-5790
  1419 Boardman Poland Rd # 500 Youngstown (44514) *(G-20026)*

Edmond Hotel Investors LLC 614 891-2900
  24 E Lincoln St Columbus (43215) *(G-7503)*

Edrich Supply Co 440 238-9440
  22700 Royalton Rd Strongsville (44149) *(G-17299)*

Eds Tree & Turf 740 881-5800
  5801 S Section Line Rd Delaware (43015) *(G-9972)*

Education Alternatives (PA) 216 332-9360
  5445 Smith Rd Brookpark (44142) *(G-1897)*

Education Innovations Intl LLC 614 339-3676
  655 Metro Pl S Ste 750 Dublin (43017) *(G-10215)*

Education Loan Servicing Corp 216 706-8130
  1500 W 3rd St Ste 125 Cleveland (44113) *(G-5467)*

Educational and Community Rdo 513 724-3939
  Rr 276 Batavia (45103) *(G-997)*

Educational Services, Blue Ash *Also called Pcm Sales Inc (G-1628)*

Educational Solutions Co 614 989-4588
  1155 Highland St Columbus (43201) *(G-7504)*

Edw C Levy Co 419 822-8286
  6565 County Road 9 Delta (43515) *(G-10042)*

Edward C Hawkins & Co Limited, Cleveland *Also called Hawkins & Co Lpa Ltd (G-5668)*

Edward Howard & Co (PA) 216 781-2400
  1100 Superior Ave E # 1600 Cleveland (44114) *(G-5468)*

Edward Rose Associates Inc 513 752-2727
  4412 Eastwood Dr Batavia (45103) *(G-998)*

Edward W Daniel LLC 440 647-1960
  46950 State Route 18 S Wellington (44090) *(G-18839)*

Edwards Mooney & Moses 614 351-1439
  1320 Mckinley Ave Ste B Columbus (43222) *(G-7505)*

Edwards Creative Learning Ctr 614 492-8977
  3858 Alum Creek Dr Ste A Columbus (43207) *(G-7506)*

Edwards Electrical & Mech 614 485-2003
  685 Grandview Ave Columbus (43215) *(G-7507)*

Edwards Land Clearing Inc 440 988-4477
  49090 Cooper Foster Pk Rd Amherst (44001) *(G-585)*

Edwards Land Company 614 241-2070
  495 S High St Ste 150 Columbus (43215) *(G-7508)*

Edwards Mooney & Moses of Ohio, Columbus *Also called Edwards Mooney & Moses (G-7505)*

Edwards Tree Service, Amherst *Also called Edwards Land Clearing Inc (G-585)*

Edwin Shaw Rehabilitation Hosp, Akron *Also called Akron General Medical Center (G-43)*

EE, Columbus *Also called Edison Equipment (G-7501)*

Eecutive Directions, Canton *Also called R E Richards Inc (G-2448)*

Eei-Plant, Cincinnati *Also called Environmental Enterprises Inc (G-3501)*

Efco Corp 614 876-1226
  3900 Zane Trace Dr Columbus (43228) *(G-7509)*

Efficient Collaborative Retail (PA) 440 498-0500
  27070 Miles Rd Ste A Solon (44139) *(G-16843)*

Efficient Electric Corp 614 552-0200
  4800 Groves Rd Columbus (43232) *(G-7510)*

Efficient Services Ohio Inc 330 627-4440
  277 Steubenville Rd Se Carrollton (44615) *(G-2568)*

Efix Computer Repair & Svc LLC 937 985-4447
  1389 E Stroop Rd Kettering (45429) *(G-12292)*

Eger Products Inc (PA) 513 753-4200
  1132 Ferris Rd Amelia (45102) *(G-572)*

Eighth Day Sound Systems Inc 440 995-2647
  5450 Avion Park Dr Cleveland (44143) *(G-5469)*

Einstruction Corporation (HQ) 330 746-3015
  255 W Federal St Youngstown (44503) *(G-20027)*

Eis, Gahanna *Also called Estate Information Svcs LLC (G-11119)*

Eis, Willoughby *Also called Exodus Integrity Service (G-19522)*

Eitel Towing Service Inc 614 877-4139
  7111 Stahl Rd Orient (43146) *(G-15619)*

Eitels Amrcas Towing Trnsp Svc, Orient *Also called Eitel Towing Service Inc (G-15619)*

Ej Therapy, Wooster *Also called Herman Bair Enterprise (G-19727)*

EJq Home Health Care Inc 440 323-7004
  800 Middle Ave Elyria (44035) *(G-10504)*

Ekomovers USA, Cincinnati *Also called Awrs LLC (G-3009)*

Elano Div, Beavercreek *Also called Unison Industries LLC (G-1192)*

Elastizell Systems Inc 937 298-1313
  2475 Arbor Blvd Moraine (45439) *(G-14652)*

Elbe Properties (PA) 513 489-1955
  8534 E Kemper Rd Cincinnati (45249) *(G-3485)*

Elden & Strauss, Vermilion *Also called Elden Properties Ltd Partnr (G-18552)*

Elden Properties Ltd Partnr 440 967-0521
  15008 Holiday Dr Ste A Vermilion (44089) *(G-18552)*

Eldercare Services Inst LLC 216 791-8000
  11890 Fairhill Rd Cleveland (44120) *(G-5470)*

Elderly Day Care Center 419 228-2688
  225 E High St Lima (45801) *(G-12632)*

Elderly United of Springfield (PA) 937 323-4948
  125 W Main St Springfield (45502) *(G-17033)*

Eldora Enterprises Inc 937 338-3815
  13929 State Route 118 New Weston (45348) *(G-15007)*

Eldora Speedway, New Weston *Also called Eldora Enterprises Inc (G-15007)*

Elect General Contractors Inc 740 420-3437
  27634 Jackson Rd Circleville (43113) *(G-4833)*

Electra Sound Inc (PA) 216 433-9600
  5260 Commerce Pkwy W Parma (44130) *(G-15766)*

Electra Sound Inc 216 433-1050
  10779 Brookpark Rd Ste A Cleveland (44130) *(G-5471)*

Electrasound TV & Appl Svc, Parma *Also called Electra Sound Inc (G-15766)*

Electric Connection Inc 614 436-1121
  5441 Westerville Rd Westerville (43081) *(G-19252)*

Electric Division, Westerville *Also called City of Westerville (G-19237)*

Electric Motor Tech LLC (PA) 513 821-9999
  5217 Beech St Cincinnati (45217) *(G-3486)*

Electric Service Co Inc 513 271-6387
  5331 Hetzell St Cincinnati (45227) *(G-3487)*

Electric Services, Cuyahoga Falls *Also called City of Cuyahoga Falls (G-9080)*

Electric Sweeper Service Co, Twinsburg *Also called Merc Acquisitions Inc (G-18298)*

Electrical Appl Repr Svc Inc 216 459-8700
5805 Valley Belt Rd Brooklyn Heights (44131) *(G-1870)*

Electrical Construction, Barberton *Also called Corporate Electric Company LLC* *(G-951)*

Electrical Corp America Inc 440 245-3007
3807 W Erie Ave Lorain (44053) *(G-12903)*

Electrical Design & Engrg Svcs, Lewis Center *Also called Polaris Automation Inc* *(G-12560)*

Electrical Service Dept, Wadsworth *Also called City of Wadsworth* *(G-18592)*

Electro Controls, Sidney *Also called Dickman Supply Inc* *(G-16774)*

Electro Prime Group LLC (PA) 419 476-0100
4510 Lint Ave Ste B Toledo (43612) *(G-17710)*

Electro-Analytical Inc 440 951-3514
7118 Industrial Park Blvd Mentor (44060) *(G-14043)*

Electrol Systems Inc 513 942-7777
1380 Kemper Meadow Dr Cincinnati (45240) *(G-3488)*

Electromechanical North Amer, Milford *Also called Parker-Hannifin Corporation* *(G-14419)*

Electronic Merchant Systems, Cleveland *Also called David Francis Corporation* *(G-5408)*

Electronic Printing Pdts Inc 330 689-3930
4560 Darrow Rd Stow (44224) *(G-17200)*

Electronic Registry Systems 513 771-7330
155 Tri County Pkwy # 110 Cincinnati (45246) *(G-3489)*

Electrovations Inc 330 274-3558
350 Harris Dr Aurora (44202) *(G-826)*

Eleet Cryogenics Inc (PA) 330 874-4009
11132 Industrial Pkwy Nw Bolivar (44612) *(G-1702)*

Element Cincinnati 513 984-4112
3701 Port Union Rd Fairfield (45014) *(G-10722)*

Element Mtls Tech Cncnnati Inc (PA) 513 771-2536
3701 Port Union Rd Fairfield (45014) *(G-10723)*

Element Mtrls Tchnlgy Hntngtn 216 643-1208
5405 E Schaaf Rd Cleveland (44131) *(G-5472)*

Eletto Transfer, Moraine *Also called Federated Logistics* *(G-14656)*

Elevar Design Group Inc 513 721-0600
555 Carr St Cincinnati (45203) *(G-3490)*

Elford Inc 614 488-4000
1220 Dublin Rd Columbus (43215) *(G-7511)*

Elford Construction Services, Columbus *Also called Elford Inc* *(G-7511)*

Eliassen Group LLC 781 205-8100
10101 Alliance Rd Ste 195 Blue Ash (45242) *(G-1550)*

Eliokem Inc (HQ) 330 734-1100
175 Ghent Rd Fairlawn (44333) *(G-10824)*

Elite Ambulance Service LLC 888 222-1356
1451 State Route 28 Ste B Loveland (45140) *(G-12992)*

Elite Excavating Company Inc 419 683-4200
4500 Snodgrass Rd Mansfield (44903) *(G-13172)*

Elite Excavating Ohio Company, Mansfield *Also called Elite Excavating Company Inc* *(G-13172)*

Elite Expediting Corp (PA) 614 279-1181
450 W Wilson Bridge Rd # 345 Worthington (43085) *(G-19806)*

Elite Home Remodeling Inc 614 785-6700
6295a Busch Blvd Ste A Columbus (43229) *(G-7512)*

Elite Investigations SEC Group, Dayton *Also called Elite Isg* *(G-9409)*

Elite Isg 937 668-6858
7825 N Dixie Dr Ste C Dayton (45414) *(G-9409)*

Elite Logistics Worldwide, Seville *Also called Elite Transportation Svcs LLC* *(G-16684)*

Elite Proofing, Brookpark *Also called Robert Erney* *(G-1905)*

Elite Transportation Svcs LLC 330 769-5830
4940 Enterprise Pkwy Seville (44273) *(G-16684)*

Elizabeth H Farbman 330 744-5211
100 E Federal St Youngstown (44503) *(G-20028)*

Elizabeth Place Holdings LLC 323 300-3700
1 Elizabeth Pl Dayton (45417) *(G-9410)*

Elizabeth Scott Inc 419 865-3002
2720 Albon Rd Maumee (43537) *(G-13784)*

Elizabeth Scott Mem Care Ctr, Maumee *Also called Elizabeth Scott Inc* *(G-13784)*

ELIZABETH'S NEW LIFE WOMEN'S C, Dayton *Also called Elizabeths New Life Center Inc* *(G-9411)*

Elizabeths New Life Center Inc 937 226-7414
2201 N Main St Dayton (45405) *(G-9411)*

Elk & Elk Co Lpa (PA) 800 355-6446
6105 Parkland Blvd # 200 Mayfield Heights (44124) *(G-13874)*

Elks, Portsmouth *Also called Portsmouth Lodge 154 B P O E* *(G-16160)*

ELKS B P O E, Liberty Twp *Also called Hamilton Lodge 93 Benevolant P* *(G-12586)*

Elks Lodge 549, Painesville *Also called Benevolent/Protectv Order Elks* *(G-15695)*

ELKS OF THE UNITED STATES OF A, Maumee *Also called Maumee Lodge No 1850 Bnvlt* *(G-13817)*

Elks Run Golf Club, Batavia *Also called Three D Golf LLC* *(G-1011)*

Ellerbrock Heating & AC 419 782-1834
13055 Dohoney Rd Defiance (43512) *(G-9912)*

Elliott Auto Bath Inc 513 422-3700
901 Elliott Dr Middletown (45044) *(G-14299)*

Elliott Davis LLC 513 579-1717
201 E 5th St Ste 2100 Cincinnati (45202) *(G-3491)*

Elliott Heller Maas Morrow Lpa 330 792-6611
54 Westchester Dr Ste 10 Youngstown (44515) *(G-20029)*

Elliott Tool Technologies Ltd (PA) 937 253-6133
1760 Tuttle Ave Dayton (45403) *(G-9412)*

Ellipse Solutions LLC 937 312-1547
7917 Washington Woods Dr Dayton (45459) *(G-9413)*

Ellis Richard CB Reichle Klein 419 861-1100
1 Seagate Fl 26 Toledo (43604) *(G-17711)*

Ellison Technologies Inc 440 546-1920
6955 Treeline Dr Ste J Brecksville (44141) *(G-1780)*

Ellison Technologies Inc 310 323-2121
5333 Muhlhauser Rd Hamilton (45011) *(G-11593)*

Elm Springs, Green Springs *Also called Elmwood Center Inc* *(G-11350)*

Elm Valley Fishing Club Inc 937 845-0584
5118 S Dayton Brandt Rd New Carlisle (45344) *(G-14890)*

Elmco Engineering Oh Inc 419 238-1100
1171 Grill Rd Van Wert (45891) *(G-18477)*

Elmco Trucking Inc 419 983-2010
30 Railroad St Bloomville (44818) *(G-1492)*

Elmcroft of Medina, Medina *Also called Senior Care Inc* *(G-14000)*

Elms Country Club, North Lawrence *Also called Elms of Massillon Inc* *(G-15259)*

Elms Country Club Inc 330 833-2668
1608 Manchester Ave Sw North Lawrence (44666) *(G-15258)*

Elms of Massillon Inc 330 833-2668
1608 Manchester Ave Sw North Lawrence (44666) *(G-15259)*

Elms Retirement Village Inc 440 647-2414
136 S Main St Rear Wellington (44090) *(G-18840)*

Elmwood At Shawhan, Tiffin *Also called Elmwood Center Inc* *(G-17516)*

Elmwood At The Springs, Green Springs *Also called Elmwood Center Inc* *(G-11351)*

Elmwood Center Inc (PA) 419 639-2581
441 N Broadway St Green Springs (44836) *(G-11350)*

Elmwood Center Inc 419 447-6885
54 S Washington St Tiffin (44883) *(G-17516)*

Elmwood Center Inc 419 639-2626
401 N Broadway St Green Springs (44836) *(G-11351)*

Elmwood of Green Springs Ltd 419 639-2626
401 N Broadway St Green Springs (44836) *(G-11352)*

Elts Broadcasting, Elyria *Also called Elyria-Lorain Broadcasting Co* *(G-10507)*

Elyria Country Club Company 440 322-6391
41625 Oberlin Rd Elyria (44035) *(G-10505)*

Elyria Ford, Elyria *Also called Abraham Ford LLC* *(G-10477)*

Elyria Foundry Holdings LLC 440 322-4657
120 Filbert St Elyria (44035) *(G-10506)*

Elyria Waste Water Plant, Elyria *Also called City of Elyria* *(G-10489)*

Elyria-Lorain Broadcasting Co (HQ) 440 322-3761
538 Broad St 400 Elyria (44035) *(G-10507)*

Elyria-Lorain Broadcasting Co 440 322-3761
538 Broad St 400 Elyria (44035) *(G-10508)*

Em Print Group, Elyria *Also called Envelope Mart of North E Ohio* *(G-10511)*

Embassy Autumnwood MGT LLC 330 927-2060
275 E Sunset Dr Rittman (44270) *(G-16405)*

Embassy Healthcare Inc 513 868-6500
908 Symmes Rd Fairfield (45014) *(G-10724)*

Embassy Stes Akrn-Canton Arprt, North Canton *Also called CPX Canton Airport LLC* *(G-15194)*

Embassy Suites, Cleveland *Also called Commonwealth Hotels LLC* *(G-5322)*

Embassy Suites, Columbus *Also called Corporate Exchange Hotel Assoc* *(G-7373)*

Embassy Suites, Dublin *Also called Commonwealth Hotels LLC* *(G-10184)*

Embassy Suites, Beachwood *Also called IA Urban Htels Bchwood Trs LLC* *(G-1066)*

Embassy Suites, Independence *Also called Ap/Aim Indpndnce Sites Trs LLC* *(G-12045)*

Embassy Suites Columbus, Columbus *Also called Columbus Hotel Partnership LLC* *(G-7288)*

Embassy Suites Columbus, Columbus *Also called Rlj III - Em Clmbus Lessee LLC* *(G-8539)*

Embassy Suites Columbus Arprt, Columbus *Also called Airport Core Hotel LLC* *(G-6887)*

Embassy Suites Columbus Dublin, Dublin *Also called Ap/Aim Dublin Suites Trs LLC* *(G-10136)*

Ember Complete Care (PA) 740 922-6888
1800 N Water Street Ext Uhrichsville (44683) *(G-18340)*

Ember Home Care 740 922-6968
730 N Water St Uhrichsville (44683) *(G-18341)*

EMC Corporation 216 606-2000
6480 Rcksde Wds Blvd S # 330 Independence (44131) *(G-12069)*

EMC Insurance Companies, Blue Ash *Also called Employers Mutual Casualty Co* *(G-1551)*

Emcor Facilities Services Inc (HQ) 888 846-9462
9655 Reading Rd Cincinnati (45215) *(G-3492)*

Emcor Fclities Svcs N Amer Inc 614 430-5078
280 N High St Ste 1700 Columbus (43215) *(G-7513)*

EMD Millipore Corporation 513 631-0445
2909 Highland Ave Norwood (45212) *(G-15462)*

Emerald Dev Ecnomic Netwrk Inc 216 961-9690
7812 Madison Ave Cleveland (44102) *(G-5473)*

Emerald Health Network Inc (HQ) 216 479-2030
3320 W Market St 100 Fairlawn (44333) *(G-10825)*

Emerald Hilton Davis LLC 513 841-0057
2235 Langdon Farm Rd Cincinnati (45237) *(G-3493)*

Emerald Pediatrics 614 932-5050
5695 Innovation Dr Dublin (43016) *(G-10216)*

Emerald Specialties Group, Cincinnati *Also called Emerald Hilton Davis LLC* *(G-3493)*

Emerald Woods Golf Course 440 236-8940
11464 Clarke Rd Columbia Station (44028) *(G-6775)*

Emerge Counseling Service 330 865-8351
900 Mull Ave Akron (44313) *(G-202)*

Emerge Ministries Inc 330 865-8351
900 Mull Ave Akron (44313) *(G-203)*

Emergency, Cincinnati *Also called Mercy Health* (G-4019)
Emergency Medical Group Inc 419 866-6009
  5620 Southwyck Blvd 2 Toledo (43614) (G-17712)
Emergency Medical Services, Hammondsville *Also called Saline Township* (G-11657)
Emergency Medical Svcs Billing 216 664-2598
  1701 Lakeside Ave E Cleveland (44114) (G-5474)
Emergency Medical Transport 330 484-4000
  7100 Whipple Ave Nw Ste A North Canton (44720) (G-15198)
Emergency Medicine Physicians, Canton *Also called Emp Management Group Ltd* (G-2301)
Emergency Medicine Specialists 937 438-8910
  8280 Yankee St Dayton (45458) (G-9414)
Emergency Physicians Med Group, Canton *Also called Dignity Health* (G-2287)
Emergency Psychiatric Svc, Akron *Also called Portage Path Behavorial Health* (G-391)
Emergency Response & Trnng 440 349-2700
  6001 Cochran Rd Solon (44139) (G-16844)
Emergency Services Inc 614 224-6420
  2323 W 5th Ave Ste 220 Columbus (43204) (G-7514)
Emeritus Assisted Living, Canton *Also called Emeritus Corporation* (G-2299)
Emeritus At Brookside Estates, Cleveland *Also called Emeritus Corporation* (G-5475)
Emeritus At Lakeview, Groveport *Also called Emeritus Corporation* (G-11509)
Emeritus At Stow, Stow *Also called Emeritus Corporation* (G-17201)
Emeritus Corporation 330 477-5727
  4507 22nd St Nw Apt 33 Canton (44708) (G-2299)
Emeritus Corporation 440 201-9200
  15435 Bagley Rd Ste 1 Cleveland (44130) (G-5475)
Emeritus Corporation 440 269-8600
  35300 Kaiser Ct Willoughby (44094) (G-19520)
Emeritus Corporation 330 342-0934
  5511 Fishcreek Rd Stow (44224) (G-17201)
Emeritus Corporation 614 836-5990
  4000 Lakeview Xing Groveport (43125) (G-11509)
Emersion Design LLC 513 841-9100
  310 Culvert St Ste 100 Cincinnati (45202) (G-3494)
Emerson Academy, Dayton *Also called National Heritg Academies Inc* (G-9653)
Emery Leasing Co LLC 216 475-8880
  20265 Emery Rd Cleveland (44128) (G-5476)
Emh Inc (PA) 330 220-8600
  550 Crane Dr Valley City (44280) (G-18462)
Emh Regional Healthcare System, Elyria *Also called Comprehensive Health Care* (G-10492)
Emh Regional Homecare Agency 440 329-7519
  90 E Broad St Elyria (44035) (G-10509)
Emh Regional Medical Center 440 988-6800
  1997 Healthway Dr Avon (44011) (G-880)
EMI Corp (PA) 937 596-5511
  801 W Pike St Jackson Center (45334) (G-12183)
EMI Enterprises Inc 419 666-0012
  2639 Tracy Rd Northwood (43619) (G-15392)
Emil Pawuk & Associates, Richfield *Also called Empaco Equipment Corporation* (G-16354)
Emily Management Inc 440 354-6713
  10280 Pinecrest Rd Painesville (44077) (G-15712)
EMJ Cincinnati, Cincinnati *Also called Earle M Jorgensen Company* (G-3470)
EMJ Cleveland, Twinsburg *Also called Earle M Jorgensen Company* (G-18259)
Emlab P&K LLC (HQ) 330 497-9396
  4101 Shuffel St Nw # 200 North Canton (44720) (G-15199)
Emmett Dan House Ltd Partnr 740 392-6886
  150 Howard St Mount Vernon (43050) (G-14764)
Emmys Bridal Inc 419 628-7555
  336 N Main St Minster (45865) (G-14532)
Emory Rothenbuhler & Sons 740 458-1432
  47126 Sunfish Creek Rd Beallsville (43716) (G-1119)
Emp Holdings Ltd 330 493-4443
  4535 Dressler Rd Nw Canton (44718) (G-2300)
Emp Management Group Ltd 330 493-4443
  4535 Dressler Rd Nw Canton (44718) (G-2301)
Empaco Equipment Corporation (PA) 330 659-9393
  2958 Brecksville Rd Richfield (44286) (G-16354)
Empire Brass Co 216 431-6565
  5000 Superior Ave Cleveland (44103) (G-5477)
Empire Masonry Company Inc 440 230-2800
  12359 Abbey Rd Ste B North Royalton (44133) (G-15354)
Empire One LLC 330 628-9310
  1532 State Route 43 Mogadore (44260) (G-14548)
Empire Poured Walls, North Royalton *Also called Empire Masonry Company Inc* (G-15354)
Empire Refractory Services, Toledo *Also called Brand Energy & Infrastructure* (G-17623)
Employbridge Holding Company 419 874-7125
  4400 Heatherdowns Blvd 5c Toledo (43614) (G-17713)
Employee Benefit Management (PA) 614 766-5800
  4789 Rings Rd Dublin (43017) (G-10217)
Employeescreeniq Inc 216 514-2800
  6111 Oak Tree Blvd # 400 Independence (44131) (G-12070)
Employers Mutual Casualty Co 513 221-6010
  11311 Cornell Park Dr # 500 Blue Ash (45242) (G-1551)
Employment Development Inc 330 424-7711
  8330 County Home Rd Lisbon (44432) (G-12800)
Employment Network 440 324-5244
  42495 N Ridge Rd Elyria (44035) (G-10510)
Employment Relations Board 513 863-0828
  3640 Old Oxford Rd Hamilton (45013) (G-11594)
Empower Mediamarketing Inc (PA) 513 871-7779
  15 E 14th St Cincinnati (45202) (G-3495)

Empowered For Excellence 567 316-7253
  3170 W Central Ave Ste B Toledo (43606) (G-17714)
Ems, Cleveland *Also called Energy MGT Specialists Inc* (G-5479)
EMs Rams Youth Dev Group Inc 216 282-4688
  1536 E 85th St Cleveland (44106) (G-5478)
Ems Service, Milan *Also called Bellevue Four Cnty Ems N Centl* (G-14359)
Ems Station, Rittman *Also called Rittman City of Inc* (G-16408)
Emsar, Wilmington *Also called Equipment MGT Svc & Repr Inc* (G-19622)
Emsco (PA) 440 238-2100
  22350 Royalton Rd Strongsville (44149) (G-17300)
Emsco Inc (HQ) 330 830-7125
  1000 Nave Rd Se Massillon (44646) (G-13677)
Emsco Inc. 330 833-5600
  1000 Nave Rd Se Massillon (44646) (G-13678)
Emsco Distributors, Strongsville *Also called Emsco* (G-17300)
Emsi Inc (PA) 614 876-9988
  8220 Industrial Pkwy Plain City (43064) (G-16051)
Emt, Cincinnati *Also called Electric Motor Tech LLC* (G-3486)
Emt Ambulance, North Canton *Also called Emergency Medical Transport* (G-15198)
Enabling Partners LLC 440 878-9418
  13862 Basswood Cir Strongsville (44136) (G-17301)
Enclosure Suppliers LLC 513 782-3900
  12119 Champion Way Cincinnati (45241) (G-3496)
Encompass Health Corporation 513 418-5600
  151 W Galbraith Rd Cincinnati (45216) (G-3497)
Encompass Health Corporation 205 970-4869
  2685 E High St Springfield (45505) (G-17034)
Encore Healthcare LLC 330 769-2015
  83 High St Seville (44273) (G-16685)
Encore Technologies, Cincinnati *Also called Sjn Data Center LLC* (G-4488)
Endeavor Construction Ltd 513 469-1900
  6801 Long Spurling Rd Pleasant Plain (45162) (G-16073)
Endevis LLc (PA) 419 482-4848
  7643 Kings Pointe Rd # 100 Toledo (43617) (G-17715)
Endo-Surgical Center Fla LLC 440 708-0582
  8185 Washington St Chagrin Falls (44023) (G-2664)
Endocrine Lab, Cincinnati *Also called University of Cincinnati* (G-4708)
Endolite, Miamisburg *Also called Blatchford Inc* (G-14145)
Endoscopy Center 419 843-7993
  5700 Monroe St Unit 102 Sylvania (43560) (G-17422)
Endoscopy Center of Dayton (PA) 937 320-5050
  4200 Indian Ripple Rd Beavercreek (45440) (G-1216)
Enerfab Inc (PA) 513 641-0500
  4955 Spring Grove Ave Cincinnati (45232) (G-3498)
Energy Cooperative Inc (HQ) 740 348-1206
  1500 Granville Rd Newark (43055) (G-15031)
Energy MGT Specialists Inc 216 676-9045
  15800 Industrial Pkwy Cleveland (44135) (G-5479)
Energy Power Services Inc 330 343-2312
  3251 Brightwood Rd Se New Philadelphia (44663) (G-14958)
Enertech Electrical Inc 330 536-2131
  101 Yngstown Lwllville Rd Lowellville (44436) (G-13040)
Enervest Ltd 330 877-6747
  125 State Route 43 Hartville (44632) (G-11685)
Enervise Incorporated (PA) 513 761-6000
  4360 Glendale Milford Rd Blue Ash (45242) (G-1552)
Enervise Incorporated 614 885-9800
  6663 Huntley Rd Ste K Columbus (43229) (G-7515)
Enesco Properties LLC 440 473-2000
  5500 Avion Park Dr Highland Heights (44143) (G-11733)
Engaged Health Care Bus Svcs 614 457-8180
  4619 Kenny Rd Ste 100 Columbus (43220) (G-7516)
Engineer Department, Delphos *Also called City of Delphos* (G-10021)
Engineer's Office, Millersburg *Also called County of Holmes* (G-14469)
Engineer's Office, Marysville *Also called County of Union* (G-13492)
Engineered Con Structures Corp 216 520-2000
  14510 Broadway Ave Cleveland (44125) (G-5480)
Engineered Material Handling, Valley City *Also called Emh Inc* (G-18462)
Engineered Polymer Systems, Medina *Also called Prime Polymers Inc* (G-13988)
Engineering Associates Inc 330 345-6556
  1935 Eagle Pass Wooster (44691) (G-19722)
Engineering Chain Div, Sandusky *Also called US Tsubaki Power Transm LLC* (G-16653)
Engineering Department, Dayton *Also called County of Montgomery* (G-9327)
Engineering Design and Testing 440 239-0362
  P.O. Box 30160 Cleveland (44130) (G-5481)
Engineering Excellence, Blue Ash *Also called Enervise Incorporated* (G-1552)
Engineering Excellence 972 535-3756
  Blue Ash Business Park Blue Ash (45242) (G-1553)
Engisystems Inc 513 229-8860
  7588 Central Parke Blvd Mason (45040) (G-13577)
Engle Management Group 513 232-9729
  867 Yarger Dr Cincinnati (45230) (G-3499)
Englefield Inc 740 452-2707
  1400 Moxahala Ave Zanesville (43701) (G-20305)
Englefield Inc 740 323-2077
  10636 Jacksontown Rd Thornville (43076) (G-17505)
Englewood Manor, Englewood *Also called Liberty Nursing Center* (G-10593)
Englewood Square Ltd 937 836-4117
  150 Chris Dr Apt 119 Englewood (45322) (G-10586)

Englewood Square Apartments, Englewood *Also called Englewood Square Ltd* ***(G-10586)***
Englewood Trck Towing Recovery, Clayton *Also called Englewood Truck Inc* ***(G-4857)***
Englewood Truck Inc....937 836-5109
7510 Jacks Ln Clayton (45315) ***(G-4857)***
Englewood, City of, Englewood *Also called City of Englewood* ***(G-10582)***
Enhanced Home Health Care LLC....614 433-7266
700 Morse Rd Ste 206 Columbus (43214) ***(G-7517)***
Enhanced Homecare Medina Inc....330 952-2331
3745 Medina Rd Ste E Medina (44256) ***(G-13934)***
Enhanced Software Inc....877 805-8388
625 E North Broadway St Columbus (43214) ***(G-7518)***
Ennis Court, Lakewood *Also called Lakewood Health Care Center* ***(G-12355)***
Enon Firemans Association....937 864-7429
260 E Main St Enon (45323) ***(G-10608)***
Enprotech Industrial Tech LLC (HQ)....216 883-3220
4259 E 49th St Cleveland (44125) ***(G-5482)***
Enrichment Center of Wishing W (PA)....440 237-5000
14574 Ridge Rd Cleveland (44133) ***(G-5483)***
Ensafe Inc....513 621-7233
8187 Fox Knoll Dr West Chester (45069) ***(G-18918)***
ENt and Allergy Health Svcs (PA)....440 779-1112
25761 Lorain Rd Fl 3 North Olmsted (44070) ***(G-15286)***
Entec International Systems, Lakewood *Also called RAD-Con Inc* ***(G-12361)***
Entelco Corporation (PA)....419 872-4620
6528 Weatherfield Ct Maumee (43537) ***(G-13785)***
Enterprise Construction Inc....440 349-3443
30505 Bnbridge Rd Ste 200 Solon (44139) ***(G-16845)***
Enterprise Data Management Inc (HQ)....513 791-7272
4380 Malsbary Rd Ste 250 Blue Ash (45242) ***(G-1554)***
Enterprise Holdings Inc....614 866-1480
6501 Tussing Rd Reynoldsburg (43068) ***(G-16303)***
Enterprise Holdings Inc....937 879-0023
4600 Mcauley Pl Ste 150 Blue Ash (45242) ***(G-1555)***
Enterprise Rent-A-Car, Blue Ash *Also called Enterprise Holdings Inc* ***(G-1555)***
Enterprise Services LLC....740 423-9501
2505 Washington Blvd Frnt Belpre (45714) ***(G-1402)***
Enterprise Systems Sftwr LLC....419 841-3179
3351 Silica Rd Sylvania (43560) ***(G-17423)***
Enterprise Vending Inc....513 772-1373
895 Glendale Milford Rd Cincinnati (45215) ***(G-3500)***
Entertrainment Inc....513 898-8000
7379 Squire Ct West Chester (45069) ***(G-18919)***
Entertrainment Junction, West Chester *Also called Entertrainment Inc* ***(G-18919)***
Enting Water Conditioning Inc (PA)....937 294-5100
3211 Dryden Rd Frnt Frnt Moraine (45439) ***(G-14653)***
Entrust Healthcare, Columbus *Also called Entrust Solutions LLC* ***(G-7519)***
Entrust Solutions LLC....614 504-4900
20 S 3rd St Ste 210 Columbus (43215) ***(G-7519)***
Entrypoint Consulting LLC....216 674-9070
600 Superior Ave E # 1300 Cleveland (44114) ***(G-5484)***
Envelope Mart, Northwood *Also called EMI Enterprises Inc* ***(G-15392)***
Envelope Mart of North E Ohio....440 322-8862
1540 Lowell St Elyria (44035) ***(G-10511)***
Envelope Mart of Ohio Inc....440 365-8177
1540 Lowell St Elyria (44035) ***(G-10512)***
Envircare Lawn Landscacape LLC....419 874-6779
24112 Lime City Rd Perrysburg (43551) ***(G-15864)***
Envirite of Ohio Inc....330 456-6238
2050 Central Ave Se Canton (44707) ***(G-2302)***
Envirnmental Engrg Systems Inc....937 228-6492
17 Creston Ave Dayton (45404) ***(G-9415)***
Envirnmental Resources MGT Inc....216 593-5200
3333 Richmond Rd Ste 160 Beachwood (44122) ***(G-1055)***
Envirnmental Resources MGT Inc....513 830-9030
9825 Kenwood Rd Ste 100 Blue Ash (45242) ***(G-1556)***
Enviro It LLC....614 453-0709
3854 Fisher Rd Columbus (43228) ***(G-7520)***
Enviro-Flow Companies Ltd....740 453-7980
4830 Northpointe Dr Zanesville (43701) ***(G-20306)***
Envirochemical Inc....440 287-2200
29325 Aurora Rd Solon (44139) ***(G-16846)***
Environment Control of Greater....614 868-9788
2218 Dividend Dr Columbus (43228) ***(G-7521)***
Environment Ctrl Beachwood Inc....330 405-6201
1897 E Aurora Rd Twinsburg (44087) ***(G-18260)***
Environment Ctrl of Miami Cnty....937 669-9900
7939 S County Road 25a A Tipp City (45371) ***(G-17556)***
Environmental Division, Cincinnati *Also called Power Engineers Incorporated* ***(G-4266)***
Environmental Engineering Cons, Cleveland *Also called Vahalla Company Inc* ***(G-6615)***
Environmental Engineering Dept, Marysville *Also called County of Union* ***(G-13490)***
Environmental Enterprises Inc....513 541-1823
4650 Spring Grove Ave Cincinnati (45232) ***(G-3501)***
Environmental Health Dept, Springfield *Also called County of Clark* ***(G-17022)***
Environmental Quality MGT (HQ)....513 825-7500
1800 Carillion Blvd 100 Cincinnati (45240) ***(G-3502)***
Environmental Solutions (PA)....513 451-1777
4525 Este Ave Cincinnati (45232) ***(G-3503)***
Environmental Specialists Inc....740 788-8134
55 Builders Dr Newark (43055) ***(G-15032)***
Environmental Systems Research....614 933-8698
1085 Beecher Xing N Ste A Columbus (43230) ***(G-7522)***
Envirosafe Services of Ohio (HQ)....419 698-3500
876 Otter Creek Rd Oregon (43616) ***(G-15594)***
Enviroscapes....330 875-0768
7727 Paris Ave Louisville (44641) ***(G-12966)***
Enviroscience Inc (PA)....330 688-0111
5070 Stow Rd Stow (44224) ***(G-17202)***
Enviroserve Inc (HQ)....330 966-0910
7640 Whipple Ave Nw North Canton (44720) ***(G-15200)***
Envirotest Systems Corp....330 963-4464
2180 Pinnacle Pkwy Twinsburg (44087) ***(G-18261)***
Envirotest Systems Corp....330 963-4464
1291 W Bagley Rd Berea (44017) ***(G-1423)***
Envirotest Systems Corp....330 963-4464
13000 York Delta Dr Cleveland (44133) ***(G-5485)***
Envirotest Systems Corp....330 963-4464
1460t Fairchild Ave Kent (44240) ***(G-12231)***
Envirotest Systems Corp....330 963-4464
128 Reaser Ct Elyria (44035) ***(G-10513)***
Envirotest Systems Corp....330 963-4464
24770 Sperry Dr Cleveland (44145) ***(G-5486)***
Envirotest Systems Corp....330 963-4464
17202 Munn Rd Chagrin Falls (44023) ***(G-2665)***
Envirotest Systems Corp....330 963-4464
1755 N Ridge Rd Painesville (44077) ***(G-15713)***
Envirotest Systems Corp....330 963-4464
770 S Progress Dr Medina (44256) ***(G-13935)***
Envirotest Systems Corp....330 963-4464
10632 Auburn Rd Chardon (44024) ***(G-2694)***
Envirotest Systems Corp....330 963-4464
205 Sandstone Blvd Amherst (44001) ***(G-586)***
Envirotest Systems Corp....330 963-4464
408 E Main St Spencer (44275) ***(G-16953)***
Envirotest Systems Corp....330 963-4464
2180 Pinnacle Pkwy Twinsburg (44087) ***(G-18262)***
Envision Children, Cincinnati *Also called Envision Corporation* ***(G-3504)***
Envision Corporation....513 772-5437
8 Enfield St Ste 4 Cincinnati (45218) ***(G-3504)***
Envision Pharmaceutical Svcs, Twinsburg *Also called Rx Options LLC* ***(G-18314)***
Envision Phrm Svcs LLC....330 405-8080
2181 E Aurora Rd Ste 201 Twinsburg (44087) ***(G-18263)***
Envision Rx Options, Twinsburg *Also called Envision Phrm Svcs LLC* ***(G-18263)***
Envision Rx Options, North Canton *Also called Orchard Phrm Svcs LLC* ***(G-15225)***
Envision Waste Services LLC....216 831-1818
4451 Renaissance Pkwy Cleveland (44128) ***(G-5487)***
Envoy Air Inc....614 231-4391
4100 E 5th Ave Columbus (43219) ***(G-7523)***
Epcon Cmmnties Franchising Inc....614 761-1010
500 Stonehenge Pkwy Dublin (43017) ***(G-10218)***
Epcon Communities Inc....614 761-1010
500 Stonehenge Pkwy Dublin (43017) ***(G-10219)***
Epcor Foundries, Cincinnati *Also called Seilkop Industries Inc* ***(G-4448)***
Epilepsy Cncl/Grter Cincinnati (PA)....513 721-2905
895 Central Ave Ste 550 Cincinnati (45202) ***(G-3505)***
Epilepsy Cntr of Nrthwstrn OH....419 867-5950
1701 Holland Rd Maumee (43537) ***(G-13786)***
Epilepsy Council Foundation, Cincinnati *Also called Epilepsy Cncl/Grter Cincinnati* ***(G-3505)***
Epilogue Inc....440 582-5555
12333 Ridge Rd Ste E North Royalton (44133) ***(G-15355)***
Epiphany Management Group LLC....330 706-4056
283 E Waterloo Rd Akron (44319) ***(G-204)***
Epipheo Incorporated....888 687-7620
700 W Pete Rose Way 450 Cincinnati (45203) ***(G-3506)***
Epipheo Studios, Cincinnati *Also called Epipheo Incorporated* ***(G-3506)***
Epiq Systems Inc....513 794-0400
6281 Tri Ridge Blvd # 300 Loveland (45140) ***(G-12993)***
Epiqurian Inns....614 885-2600
649 High St Worthington (43085) ***(G-19807)***
Episcopal Retirement Homes....513 271-9610
3870 Virginia Ave Ste 2 Cincinnati (45227) ***(G-3507)***
Episcopal Retirement Homes Inc (PA)....513 271-9610
3870 Virginia Ave Ste 2 Cincinnati (45227) ***(G-3508)***
Episcopal Retirement Homes Inc....513 561-6363
3939 Erie Ave Cincinnati (45208) ***(G-3509)***
Episcopal Retirement Homes Inc....513 871-2090
3550 Shaw Ave Ofc Cincinnati (45208) ***(G-3510)***
Epsilon....513 248-2882
1000 Summit Dr Unit 200 Milford (45150) ***(G-14387)***
Epworth Preschool and Daycare....740 387-1062
249 E Center St Marion (43302) ***(G-13419)***
Epworth United Methodist Ch, Marion *Also called Epworth Preschool and Daycare* ***(G-13419)***
Epworth United Methodist Ch....740 387-1062
249 E Center St Marion (43302) ***(G-13420)***
Eq Ohio, Canton *Also called Envirite of Ohio Inc* ***(G-2302)***
Equip Estate Group, Columbus *Also called Schlee Malt House Condo Assn* ***(G-8600)***
Equipment Depot Ohio Inc....513 934-2121
1000 Kingsview Dr Lebanon (45036) ***(G-12463)***
Equipment Depot Ohio Inc (HQ)....513 891-0600
4331 Rossplain Dr Blue Ash (45236) ***(G-1557)***
Equipment Depot Ohio Inc....513 934-2121
1000 Kingsview Dr Lebanon (45036) ***(G-12464)***
Equipment Maintenance & Repair, Cleves *Also called Equipment Maintenance Inc* ***(G-6728)***

ALPHABETIC

Equipment Maintenance Inc (PA) 513 353-3518
 5885 Hamilton Cleves Rd Cleves (45002) *(G-6728)*
Equipment Manufacturers Intl 216 651-6700
 16151 Puritas Ave Cleveland (44135) *(G-5488)*
Equipment MGT Svc & Repr Inc 937 383-1052
 270 Davids Dr Wilmington (45177) *(G-19622)*
Equipment Yard & Maint Div, Lima *Also called Jacobs Constructors Inc (G-12667)*
Equitable Life Assurance, Solon *Also called Cincinnati Equitable Insur Co (G-16835)*
Equitable Mortgage Corporation (PA) 614 764-1232
 3530 Snouffer Rd Ste 100 Columbus (43235) *(G-7524)*
Equitas Health Inc 937 424-1440
 1222 S Patterson Blvd Dayton (45402) *(G-9416)*
Equitas Health Inc 614 926-4132
 889 E Long St Columbus (43203) *(G-7525)*
Equitas Health Inc 614 340-6700
 750 E Long St Ste 3000 Columbus (43203) *(G-7526)*
Equitas Health Inc (PA) 614 299-2437
 4400 N High St Ste 300 Columbus (43214) *(G-7527)*
Equity Central LLC 614 861-7777
 81 Mill St Ste 300 Gahanna (43230) *(G-11118)*
Equity Consultants LLC 330 659-7600
 5800 Lombardo Ctr Ste 202 Seven Hills (44131) *(G-16674)*
Equity Diamond Brokers Inc (PA) 513 793-4760
 9301 Montgomery Rd Ste 2a Cincinnati (45242) *(G-3511)*
Equity Engineering Group Inc (PA) 216 283-9519
 20600 Chagrin Blvd # 1200 Shaker Heights (44122) *(G-16708)*
Equity Inc (PA) 614 802-2900
 4653 Trueman Blvd Ste 100 Hilliard (43026) *(G-11766)*
Equity Line Mortgage Company, Columbus *Also called Trio Limited (G-8784)*
Equity Real Estate, Hilliard *Also called Equity Inc (G-11766)*
Equity Residential Properties 216 861-2700
 1701 E 12th St Ste 35 Cleveland (44114) *(G-5489)*
Equity Resources Inc 513 518-6318
 130 Tri County Pkwy # 108 Cincinnati (45246) *(G-3512)*
ERA, Findlay *Also called Noakes Rooney Rlty & Assoc Co (G-10949)*
ERA, Chillicothe *Also called J W Enterprises Inc (G-2796)*
Erb Electric Co 740 633-5055
 500 Hall St Ste 1 Bridgeport (43912) *(G-1816)*
Ergon, Delaware *Also called Alpha Group of Delaware Inc (G-9952)*
Erhal Inc 513 272-5555
 3870 Virginia Ave Cincinnati (45227) *(G-3513)*
Eric Boeppler Fmly Ltd Partnr 513 336-8108
 9331 Seward Rd Ste A Fairfield (45014) *(G-10725)*
Eric Hasemeier Do 740 594-7979
 510 W Union St Ste A Athens (45701) *(G-780)*
Eric W Warnock 419 228-2233
 230 N Eastown Rd Lima (45807) *(G-12633)*
Erie Blacktop Inc 419 625-7374
 4507 Tiffin Ave Sandusky (44870) *(G-16598)*
Erie Co Office of Ed, Huron *Also called North Point Eductl Svc Ctr (G-12028)*
Erie Construction Co, Dayton *Also called Erie Construction Mid-West Inc (G-9417)*
Erie Construction Group Inc 419 625-7374
 4507 Tiffin Ave Sandusky (44870) *(G-16599)*
Erie Construction Mid-West Inc (PA) 419 472-4200
 4271 Monroe St Toledo (43606) *(G-17716)*
Erie Construction Mid-West Inc 937 898-4688
 3520 Sudachi Dr Dayton (45414) *(G-9417)*
Erie County Cablevision Inc 419 627-0800
 409 E Market St Sandusky (44870) *(G-16600)*
Erie County Care Facility, Huron *Also called County of Erie (G-12024)*
Erie County Hwy Dept, Sandusky *Also called County of Erie (G-16596)*
Erie Huron Cac Headstart Inc 419 663-2623
 11 E League St Norwalk (44857) *(G-15434)*
Erie Indemnity Company 330 433-6300
 4690 Munson St Nw Canton (44718) *(G-2303)*
Erie Insurance Exchange 330 568-1802
 5676 Everett East Rd Hubbard (44425) *(G-11945)*
Erie Insurance Exchange 330 479-1010
 1120 Valleyview Ave Sw Canton (44710) *(G-2304)*
Erie Insurance Exchange 614 430-8530
 445 Hutchinson Ave Columbus (43235) *(G-7528)*
Erie Insurance Exchange 614 436-0224
 445 Hutchinson Ave # 350 Columbus (43235) *(G-7529)*
Erie Insurance Exchange 330 433-1925
 4690 Munson St Nw Ste A Canton (44718) *(G-2305)*
Erie Island Resort and Marina 419 734-9117
 150 E Market St Ste 300 Warren (44481) *(G-18707)*
Erie Lumber Co Division, Hartville *Also called Nilco LLC (G-11695)*
Erie Residential Living Home I, Sandusky *Also called Erie Residential Living Inc (G-16601)*
Erie Residential Living Inc 419 625-0060
 706 E Park St Sandusky (44870) *(G-16601)*
Erie Shores Credit Union Inc (PA) 419 897-8110
 1688 Woodlands Dr Maumee (43537) *(G-13787)*
Erie Shores Golf Club, Madison *Also called Lake Metroparks (G-13100)*
Erie Trucking Inc 419 625-7374
 4507 Tiffin Ave Sandusky (44870) *(G-16602)*
Erieside Medical Group 440 918-6270
 38429 Lake Shore Blvd Willoughby (44094) *(G-19521)*
Erik Balster Hlth Commissioner, Eaton *Also called Preble County General Hlth Dst (G-10460)*

Erm Midatlantic, Beachwood *Also called Envirmmental Resources MGT Inc (G-1055)*
Ermc II LP 513 424-8517
 3461 Towne Blvd Unit 250 Middletown (45005) *(G-14346)*
Ernest Fritsch 614 436-5995
 6245 Sunderland Dr Columbus (43229) *(G-7530)*
Ernest V Thomas Jr (PA) 513 961-5311
 2323 Park Ave Cincinnati (45206) *(G-3514)*
Ernst & Young LLP 216 861-5000
 950 Main Ave Ste 1800 Cleveland (44113) *(G-5490)*
Ernst & Young LLP 216 583-1823
 1660 W 2nd St Ste 200 Cleveland (44113) *(G-5491)*
Ernst & Young LLP 614 224-5678
 800 Yard St Ste 200 Columbus (43212) *(G-7531)*
Ernst & Young LLP 513 612-1400
 312 Walnut St Ste 1900 Cincinnati (45202) *(G-3515)*
Ernst & Young LLP 419 244-8000
 1 Seagate Ste 2510 Toledo (43604) *(G-17717)*
Erp Analysts Inc 614 718-9222
 425 Metro Pl N Ste 510 Dublin (43017) *(G-10220)*
Erts, Solon *Also called Emergency Response & Trnng (G-16844)*
Es3 Management Inc 440 593-6266
 22 Parrish Rd Conneaut (44030) *(G-8954)*
Esber Beverage Company 330 456-4361
 2217 Bolivar Rd Sw Canton (44706) *(G-2306)*
Esbi International Salon 330 220-3724
 4193 Center Rd Brunswick (44212) *(G-1929)*
Esc and Company Inc 614 794-0568
 2000 Toronado Blvd A Columbus (43207) *(G-7532)*
Esc of Cuyahoga County 216 524-3000
 6393 Oak Tree Blvd # 300 Independence (44131) *(G-12071)*
Escape Enterprises Inc 614 224-0300
 222 Neilston St Columbus (43215) *(G-7533)*
Esd, Sylvania *Also called Enterprise Systems Sftwr LLC (G-17423)*
Esec Corporation (PA) 330 799-1536
 44 Victoria Rd Youngstown (44515) *(G-20030)*
Esec Corporation 614 875-3732
 6240 Enterprise Pkwy Grove City (43123) *(G-11430)*
Esj Carrier Corporation 513 728-7388
 3240 Production Dr Fairfield (45014) *(G-10726)*
Esko-Graphics Inc (HQ) 937 454-1721
 8535 Gander Creek Dr Miamisburg (45342) *(G-14168)*
Eskoartwork, Miamisburg *Also called Esko-Graphics Inc (G-14168)*
Eslich Wrecking Company 330 488-8300
 3525 Broadway Ave Louisville (44641) *(G-12967)*
Eso, Carrollton *Also called Efficient Services Ohio Inc (G-2568)*
Espt Liquidation Inc 330 698-4711
 339 Mill St Apple Creek (44606) *(G-618)*
Esri, Columbus *Also called Environmental Systems Research (G-7522)*
Essendant Co 330 650-9361
 100 E Highland Rd Hudson (44236) *(G-11977)*
Essendant Co 330 425-4001
 2100 Highland Rd Twinsburg (44087) *(G-18264)*
Essendant Co 513 942-1354
 9775 International Blvd West Chester (45246) *(G-19049)*
Essendant Co 614 876-7774
 1634 Westbelt Dr Columbus (43228) *(G-7534)*
Essentialprofile1corp 614 805-4794
 735 N Wilson Rd Columbus (43204) *(G-7535)*
Essex and Associates Inc 937 432-1040
 7501 Paragon Rd Ste 100 Dayton (45459) *(G-9418)*
Essex Healthcare Corporation (PA) 614 416-0600
 2780 Airport Dr Ste 400 Columbus (43219) *(G-7536)*
Essig Research Inc 513 942-7100
 497 Circle Freeway Dr # 236 West Chester (45246) *(G-19050)*
Essilor Laboratories Amer Inc 614 274-0840
 3671 Interchange Rd Columbus (43204) *(G-7537)*
Essilor of America Inc 614 492-0888
 2400 Spiegel Dr Ste A Groveport (43125) *(G-11510)*
Estabrook Corporation (PA) 440 234-8566
 700 W Bagley Rd Berea (44017) *(G-1424)*
Estate Information Svcs LLC 614 729-1700
 670 Morrison Rd Ste 300 Gahanna (43230) *(G-11119)*
Estephenson Brenda & John, Maineville *Also called AMS Construction Inc (G-13112)*
Estes Express Lines Inc 440 327-3884
 38495 Center Ridge Rd North Ridgeville (44039) *(G-15329)*
Estes Express Lines Inc 614 275-6000
 1009 Frank Rd Columbus (43223) *(G-7538)*
Estes Express Lines Inc 419 531-1500
 5330 Angola Rd Ste B Toledo (43615) *(G-17718)*
Estes Express Lines Inc 937 237-7536
 6295 Executive Blvd Huber Heights (45424) *(G-11954)*
Estes Express Lines Inc 419 522-2641
 792 5th Ave Mansfield (44905) *(G-13173)*
Estes Express Lines Inc 513 779-9581
 6459 Allen Rd West Chester (45069) *(G-18920)*
Estes Express Lines Inc 740 401-0410
 12140 State Road 7 Belpre (45714) *(G-1403)*
Estes Express Lines 92, Toledo *Also called Estes Express Lines Inc (G-17718)*
Esther Marie Nursing Home, Geneva *Also called Contining Hlthcare Sltions Inc (G-11239)*
Estreamz Inc 513 278-7836
 1118 Groesbeck Rd Cincinnati (45224) *(G-3516)*
Esw, Oregon *Also called E S Wagner Company (G-15592)*

Etb University Properties LLC................................440 826-2212
343 W Bagley Rd Berea (44017) **(G-1425)**

Etech-Systems LLC................................216 221-6600
14600 Detroit Ave # 1500 Lakewood (44107) **(G-12342)**

Ethicon Endo-Surgery Inc (HQ)................................513 337-7000
4545 Creek Rd Blue Ash (45242) **(G-1558)**

Ethnic Voice of America................................440 845-0922
4606 Bruening Dr Cleveland (44134) **(G-5492)**

Etl, Columbus Also called Intertek Testing Svcs NA Inc **(G-7840)**

Etransmedia Technology Inc................................724 743-5960
1111 Schrock Rd Ste 200 Columbus (43229) **(G-7539)**

Eubel Brady Suttman Asset Mgt................................937 291-1223
10100 Innovation Dr # 410 Miamisburg (45342) **(G-14169)**

Euclid Adult Training Center, Euclid Also called A W S Inc **(G-10622)**

Euclid City Schools................................216 261-2900
463 Babbitt Rd Euclid (44123) **(G-10631)**

Euclid Finance Division, Euclid Also called Euclid Hospital **(G-10634)**

Euclid Fish Company................................440 951-6448
7839 Enterprise Dr Mentor (44060) **(G-14044)**

Euclid Health Care Inc (PA)................................513 561-4105
6940 Stiegler Ln Cincinnati (45243) **(G-3517)**

Euclid Heat Treating Co................................216 481-8444
1408 E 222nd St Euclid (44117) **(G-10632)**

Euclid Hospital, Cleveland Also called Cleveland Clinic Health System **(G-5248)**

Euclid Hospital (HQ)................................216 531-9000
18901 Lake Shore Blvd Euclid (44119) **(G-10633)**

Euclid Hospital................................216 445-6440
18901 Lake Shore Blvd # 4 Euclid (44119) **(G-10634)**

Euclid Indus Maint Clg Contrs................................216 361-0288
1561 E 40th St Cleveland (44103) **(G-5493)**

Euclid Medical Products, Apple Creek Also called Precision Products Group Inc **(G-620)**

Euclid SC Transportation................................216 797-7600
393 Babbitt Rd Cleveland (44123) **(G-5494)**

Eureka Midstream LLC................................740 868-1325
27710 State Route 7 Marietta (45750) **(G-13327)**

Euro Usa Inc (PA)................................216 714-0500
4481 Johnston Pkwy Cleveland (44128) **(G-5495)**

Eurolink Inc................................740 392-1549
106 W Ohio Ave Mount Vernon (43050) **(G-14765)**

Euthenics Inc (PA)................................440 260-1555
8235 Mohawk Dr Strongsville (44136) **(G-17302)**

Evangelical Lutheran................................419 365-5115
100 Powell Rd Arlington (45814) **(G-642)**

Evangelical Retirement................................937 837-5581
5790 Denlinger Rd Dayton (45426) **(G-9419)**

Evanhoe & Associates Inc................................937 235-2995
5089 Norman Blvd Dayton (45431) **(G-9173)**

Evans Mechwart Ham (PA)................................614 775-4500
5500 New Albany Rd # 100 New Albany (43054) **(G-14852)**

Evans Adhesive Corporation (HQ)................................614 451-2665
925 Old Henderson Rd Columbus (43220) **(G-7540)**

Evans Construction................................330 305-9355
4585 Aultman Ave Nw North Canton (44720) **(G-15201)**

Evans Motor Works, Dayton Also called Volvo BMW Dyton Evans Volkswag **(G-9859)**

Evanston Bulldogs Youth Footba................................513 254-9500
3060 Durrell Ave Cincinnati (45207) **(G-3518)**

Evant (PA)................................330 920-1517
1221 Commerce Dr Stow (44224) **(G-17203)**

Event Source, Cleveland Also called JBK Group Inc **(G-5784)**

Eventions Ltd................................216 952-9898
14925 Shaker Blvd Cleveland (44120) **(G-5496)**

Events On Top................................330 757-3786
143 Boardman Canfield Rd Youngstown (44512) **(G-20031)**

Ever Dry of Cincinnati, West Chester Also called Riverfront Diversified Inc **(G-18995)**

Ever Green Lawn Care Inc................................937 335-6418
625 Olympic Dr Troy (45373) **(G-18201)**

Ever-Green Turf & Landscape, Troy Also called Ever Green Lawn Care Inc **(G-18201)**

Everdry Waterproofing Toledo, Toledo Also called Rusk Industries Inc **(G-18015)**

Everest Technologies Inc................................614 436-3120
740 Lakeview Plaza Blvd # 250 Worthington (43085) **(G-19808)**

Evergreen Cooperative Ldry Inc................................216 268-3548
540 E 105th St Ste 206 Cleveland (44108) **(G-5497)**

Evergreen Healthcare Center, Montpelier Also called Communicare Health Svcs Inc **(G-14610)**

Evergreen Kindervelt Gift Shop, Cincinnati Also called Williamsburg of Cincinnati Mgt **(G-4798)**

Evergreen Pharmaceutical LLC (HQ)................................513 719-2600
201 E 4th St Ste 900 Cincinnati (45202) **(G-3519)**

Evergreen Phrm Cal Inc (HQ)................................513 719-2600
201 E 4th St Ste 900 Cincinnati (45202) **(G-3520)**

Evergreen Plastics, Clyde Also called Polychem Corporation **(G-6750)**

Everris NA Inc (HQ)................................614 726-7100
4950 Blazer Pkwy Dublin (43017) **(G-10221)**

Evers Welding Co Inc................................513 385-7352
4849 Blue Rock Rd Cincinnati (45247) **(G-3521)**

Everstaff LLC................................440 992-0238
7448 Mentor Ave Mentor (44060) **(G-14045)**

Every Child Succeeds................................513 636-2830
3333 Burnet Ave Cincinnati (45229) **(G-3522)**

Everybodys Inc................................937 293-1010
3050 Springboro Pike Moraine (45439) **(G-14654)**

Everybodys Workplace Solutions, Moraine Also called Everybodys Inc **(G-14654)**

Everyday Homecare................................937 444-1672
711 S High St Mount Orab (45154) **(G-14740)**

Everyone Counts Inc................................858 427-4673
50 Public Sq Ste 200 Cleveland (44113) **(G-5498)**

Evokes LLC................................513 947-8433
8118 Corp Way Ste 212 Mason (45040) **(G-13578)**

Evolution Ag LLC................................740 363-1341
13275 Us Highway 42 N Plain City (43064) **(G-16052)**

Evolution Crtive Solutions LLC................................513 681-4450
7107 Shona Dr Ste 110 Cincinnati (45237) **(G-3523)**

Excalibur Auto Body Inc (PA)................................440 942-5550
30520 Lakeland Blvd Willowick (44095) **(G-19598)**

Excalibur Body & Frame, Willowick Also called Excalibur Auto Body Inc **(G-19598)**

Excel Decorators Inc................................614 522-0056
3910 Groves Rd Ste A Columbus (43232) **(G-7541)**

Excel Electrical Contractor................................740 965-3795
7484 Reliance St Worthington (43085) **(G-19809)**

Excel Health Services LLC................................614 794-0006
163 N Sandusky St Ste 201 Delaware (43015) **(G-9973)**

Excel Trucking LLC................................614 826-1988
1000 Frank Rd Columbus (43223) **(G-7542)**

Excelas LLC................................440 442-7310
387 Golfview Ln Ste 200 Cleveland (44143) **(G-5499)**

Excellence Alliance Group Inc................................513 619-4800
700 Walnut St Ste 210 Cincinnati (45202) **(G-3524)**

Excellence In Motivation Inc................................763 445-3000
6 N Main St Ste 370 Dayton (45402) **(G-9420)**

Excess Share Insurance Corp................................614 764-1900
5656 Frantz Rd Dublin (43017) **(G-10222)**

Exchangebase LLC................................440 331-3600
18500 Lake Rd Rocky River (44116) **(G-16432)**

Exclusive Homecare Services................................937 236-6750
4699 Salem Ave Ste 1 Dayton (45416) **(G-9421)**

Executive Insurance Agency (PA)................................330 576-1234
130 Springside Dr Ste 300 Akron (44333) **(G-205)**

Executive Jet Management Inc (HQ)................................513 979-6600
4556 Airport Rd Cincinnati (45226) **(G-3525)**

Executive Management Services................................419 529-8800
1225 Home Rd N Ontario (44906) **(G-15549)**

Executive Properties Inc (PA)................................330 376-4037
733 W Market St Ste 102 Akron (44303) **(G-206)**

Executives Agencies................................614 466-2980
30 E Broad St Fl 26 Columbus (43215) **(G-7543)**

Exel Freight Connect Inc................................855 393-5378
226 N 5th St Ste 21 Columbus (43215) **(G-7544)**

Exel Global Logistics Inc................................440 243-5900
21500 Aerospace Pkwy Cleveland (44142) **(G-5500)**

Exel Global Logistics Inc................................614 409-4500
2144a John Glenn Ave Columbus (43217) **(G-7545)**

Exel Holdings (usa) Inc (HQ)................................614 865-8500
570 Polaris Pkwy Ste 110 Westerville (43082) **(G-19161)**

Exel Inc................................419 996-7703
635 N Cool Rd Lima (45801) **(G-12634)**

Exel Inc................................419 226-5500
3875 Reservoir Rd Lima (45801) **(G-12635)**

Exel Inc................................614 865-8294
570 Polaris Pkwy Ste 110 Westerville (43082) **(G-19162)**

Exel Inc (HQ)................................614 865-8500
570 Polaris Pkwy Westerville (43082) **(G-19163)**

Exel Inc................................740 927-1762
127 Heritage Dr Etna (43062) **(G-10615)**

Exel Inc................................614 670-6473
2450 Creekside Pkwy Lockbourne (43137) **(G-12815)**

Exel Inc................................740 929-2113
200 Arrowhead Blvd Hebron (43025) **(G-11713)**

Exel Inc................................614 662-9247
2829 Rohr Rd Groveport (43125) **(G-11511)**

Exel Inc................................800 426-8434
4900 Creekside Pkwy Lockbourne (43137) **(G-12816)**

Exel Logistics, Groveport Also called Exel Inc **(G-11511)**

Exel N Amercn Logistics Inc................................937 854-7900
5522 Little Richmond Rd Dayton (45426) **(G-9422)**

Exel N Amercn Logistics Inc (HQ)................................800 272-1052
570 Players Pkwy Westerville (43081) **(G-19253)**

Exhibitpro Inc................................614 885-9541
8900 Smiths Mill Rd New Albany (43054) **(G-14853)**

Exodus Integrity Service................................440 918-0140
37111 Euclid Ave Ste F Willoughby (44094) **(G-19522)**

Exonic Systems LLC................................330 315-3100
380 Water St Akron (44308) **(G-207)**

Expedata LLC................................937 439-6767
8073 Washington Vlg Dr Dayton (45458) **(G-9423)**

Expeditors Intl Wash Inc................................440 243-9900
18029 Cleveland Pkwy Dr Cleveland (44135) **(G-5501)**

Expeditors Intl Wash Inc................................614 492-9840
6054 Shook Rd Ste 100 Lockbourne (43137) **(G-12817)**

Expeditus Transport LLC................................419 464-9450
6600 Sylvania Ave Ste 220 Sylvania (43560) **(G-17424)**

Experis Finance Us LLC................................614 223-2300
175 S 3rd St Ste 375 Columbus (43215) **(G-7546)**

Experis Finance Us LLC 216 621-0200
  6000 Lombardo Ctr Ste 400 Seven Hills (44131) *(G-16675)*
Experis Us Inc 614 223-2300
  175 S 3rd St Ste 375 Columbus (43215) *(G-7547)*
Expert Crane Inc 216 451-9900
  5755 Grant Ave Cleveland (44105) *(G-5502)*
Explorer Rv Insurance Agcy Inc 330 659-8900
  3250 Interstate Dr Richfield (44286) *(G-16355)*
Explorys Inc 216 767-4700
  1111 Superior Ave E # 2600 Cleveland (44114) *(G-5503)*
Exponentia US Inc 614 944-5103
  424 Beecher Rd Ste A Columbus (43230) *(G-7548)*
Express Energy Svcs Oper LP 740 337-4530
  1515 Franklin St Toronto (43964) *(G-18184)*
Express Packaging Ohio Inc (PA) 740 498-4700
  301 Enterprise Dr Newcomerstown (43832) *(G-15131)*
Express Script, Dublin *Also called Medco Health Solutions Inc (G-10276)*
Express Seed Company 440 774-2259
  51051 Us Highway 20 Oberlin (44074) *(G-15502)*
Express Twing Recovery Svc Inc 513 881-1900
  9772 Prnceton Glendale Rd West Chester (45246) *(G-19051)*
Expresso Car Wash 5, Toledo *Also called Expresso Car Wash Systems Inc (G-17720)*
Expresso Car Wash Systems Inc 419 536-7540
  5440 W Central Ave Toledo (43615) *(G-17719)*
Expresso Car Wash Systems Inc 419 866-7099
  1750 S Reynolds Rd Toledo (43614) *(G-17720)*
Expressway Pk Softball Complex, Milford *Also called Max Dixons Expressway Park (G-14407)*
Extended Family Concepts Inc 330 966-2555
  913 Pittsburg Ave Nw Canton (44720) *(G-2307)*
Extreme Detail Clg Cnstr Svcs 419 392-3243
  1724 Barrows St Toledo (43613) *(G-17721)*
Exxcel Project Management LLC 614 621-4500
  328 Civic Center Dr Columbus (43215) *(G-7549)*
Ey, Cleveland *Also called Ernst & Young LLP (G-5490)*
Ey, Cleveland *Also called Ernst & Young LLP (G-5491)*
Ey, Columbus *Also called Ernst & Young LLP (G-7531)*
Ey, Cincinnati *Also called Ernst & Young LLP (G-3515)*
Ey, Toledo *Also called Ernst & Young LLP (G-17717)*
Eye Care Associates Inc (PA) 330 746-7691
  10 Dutton Dr Youngstown (44502) *(G-20032)*
Eye Centers of Ohio Inc 330 966-1111
  6407 Frank Ave Nw North Canton (44720) *(G-15202)*
Eye Centers of Ohio Inc 330 966-1111
  800 Mckinley Ave Nw Canton (44703) *(G-2308)*
Eye Inst of Northwestern OH In 419 865-3866
  5555 Airport Hwy Toledo (43615) *(G-17722)*
Eye Institute of Northwestern, Maumee *Also called Ophthalmology Associates of (G-13828)*
Eye Physicians & Surgeons, Columbus *Also called University Eye Surgeons (G-8818)*
Eye Surgery Center of Wooster, Wooster *Also called Wooster Ophthalmologists Inc (G-19787)*
Eye Surgery Center Ohio Inc (PA) 614 228-3937
  262 Neil Ave Ste 320 Columbus (43215) *(G-7550)*
EZ Grout Corporation Inc 740 962-2024
  1833 N Riverview Rd Malta (43758) *(G-13121)*
EZ Pack, Cincinnati *Also called SJS Packaging Group Inc (G-4489)*
Ezg Manufacturing, Malta *Also called EZ Grout Corporation Inc (G-13121)*
Ezra Health Care Inc 440 498-3000
  23258 Fernwood Dr Beachwood (44122) *(G-1056)*
F & M Contractors, Clayton *Also called Ideal Company Inc (G-4858)*
F & M Mafco Inc (PA) 513 367-2151
  9149 Dry Fork Rd Harrison (45030) *(G-11666)*
F A C E, Columbus *Also called Friends of Art For Cultural (G-7627)*
F B and S Masonry Inc 330 608-3442
  3021 Harriet Rd Silver Lake (44224) *(G-16807)*
F B Wright Co Cincinnati (PA) 513 874-9100
  4689 Ashley Dr West Chester (45011) *(G-18921)*
F Dohmen Co 614 757-5000
  7000 Cardinal Pl Dublin (43017) *(G-10223)*
F E E, Canal Winchester *Also called Feecorp Corporation (G-2108)*
F F A Camp Muskingum, Carrollton *Also called Ohio F F A Camps Inc (G-2574)*
F H Bonn 937 323-7024
  4300 Gateway Blvd Springfield (45502) *(G-17035)*
F H Bonn Company, Springfield *Also called F H Bonn (G-17035)*
F I L US Inc (HQ) 440 248-9500
  30403 Bruce Indus Pkwy Solon (44139) *(G-16847)*
F R S Connections 937 393-9662
  149 Chillicothe Ave Hillsboro (45133) *(G-11838)*
F S T Express Inc 614 529-7900
  1727 Georgesville Rd Columbus (43228) *(G-7551)*
F W Arnold Agency Co Inc 330 832-1556
  210 Erie St N Massillon (44646) *(G-13679)*
F+w Media Inc (HQ) 513 531-2690
  10151 Carver Rd Ste 200 Blue Ash (45242) *(G-1559)*
Fab Limousines Inc 330 792-6700
  3681 Connecticut Ave Youngstown (44515) *(G-20033)*
Fab Tours & Travel, Youngstown *Also called Fab Limousines Inc (G-20033)*
Fabco Inc 419 427-0872
  616 N Blanchard St Findlay (45840) *(G-10899)*

Fabrizi Trucking & Pav Co Inc (PA) 330 483-3291
  20389 1st Ave Cleveland (44130) *(G-5504)*
Facemyer Backhoe and Dozer Svc 740 965-1137
  72 Holmes St Sunbury (43074) *(G-17387)*
Facil North America Inc (HQ) 330 487-2500
  2242 Pinnacle Pkwy # 100 Twinsburg (44087) *(G-18265)*
Facilities Kahn Management 313 202-7607
  121 Springboro Pike Dayton (45449) *(G-9424)*
Facilities MGT Solutions LLC 513 639-2230
  250 W Court St Cincinnati (45202) *(G-3526)*
Facilities Operation and Dev, Columbus *Also called Ohio State University (G-8352)*
Facility 1, Toledo *Also called Midwest Trmnals Tledo Intl Inc (G-17917)*
Facility Connect, Twinsburg *Also called French Company LLC (G-18269)*
Facility MGT & Support Svcs, East Liberty *Also called MPW Industrial Services Inc (G-10393)*
Facility Products & Svcs LLC 330 533-8943
  330 Newton St Canfield (44406) *(G-2136)*
Facility Services, Akron *Also called Akron Public School Maint Svcs (G-51)*
Facility Svc Maint Systems Inc 513 422-7060
  3641 Commerce Dr Middletown (45005) *(G-14347)*
Facility Svcs & Maint Systems, Middletown *Also called Facility Svc Maint Systems Inc (G-14347)*
Fackler Country Gardens Inc (PA) 740 522-3128
  2326 Newark Granville Rd Granville (43023) *(G-11341)*
Facklers, Granville *Also called Country Gardens (G-11339)*
Factory Mutual Insurance Co 440 779-0651
  25050 Country Club Blvd # 400 North Olmsted (44070) *(G-15287)*
Factory Mutual Insurance Co 513 742-9516
  9 Woodcrest Dr Cincinnati (45246) *(G-3527)*
Facts Management Company 440 892-4272
  28446 W Preston Pl Westlake (44145) *(G-19340)*
Faf Inc 800 496-4696
  6800 Port Rd Groveport (43125) *(G-11512)*
Fahlgren Inc (PA) 614 383-1500
  4030 Easton Sta Ste 300 Columbus (43219) *(G-7552)*
Fahlgren Inc 614 383-1500
  4030 Easton Sta Ste 300 Columbus (43219) *(G-7553)*
Fair Haven Shelby County Home, Sidney *Also called County of Shelby (G-16771)*
Fairborn Equipment Company Inc (PA) 419 209-0760
  225 Tarhe Trl Upper Sandusky (43351) *(G-18406)*
Fairborn Fish 937 879-1313
  101 Mann Ave Fairborn (45324) *(G-10672)*
Fairborn Fish Organization, Fairborn *Also called Fairborn Fish (G-10672)*
FAIRBORN PRE SCHOOL & DAY CARE, Fairborn *Also called Fairborn St Luke Untd Mthdst (G-10673)*
Fairborn Sftball Offcials Assn 937 902-9920
  8740 Cannondale Ln Dayton (45424) *(G-9425)*
Fairborn St Luke Untd Mthdst 937 878-5042
  100 N Broad St Fairborn (45324) *(G-10673)*
Fairborn YMCA 937 754-9622
  300 S Central Ave Fairborn (45324) *(G-10674)*
Fairchild MD Leasing Co LLC 330 678-4912
  1290 Fairchild Ave Kent (44240) *(G-12232)*
Fairfax Health Care Center, Cleveland *Also called Inner City Nursing Home (G-5754)*
Fairfeld Bnquet Convention Ctr, Fairfield *Also called Toris Station (G-10791)*
Fairfeld Inn Stes Clmbus Arprt 614 237-2100
  4300 International Gtwy Columbus (43219) *(G-7554)*
Fairfield Center, Fairfield *Also called Alexson Services Inc (G-10695)*
Fairfield Cnty Chld Prtctd, Lancaster *Also called Fairfield County (G-12393)*
Fairfield Cnty Job & Fmly Svcs 800 450-8845
  239 W Main St Lancaster (43130) *(G-12391)*
Fairfield Community Health Ctr 740 277-6043
  1155 E Main St Lancaster (43130) *(G-12392)*
Fairfield County 740 653-4060
  239 W Main St Lancaster (43130) *(G-12393)*
Fairfield Diagnstc Imaging LLC 740 654-7559
  1241 River Valley Blvd Lancaster (43130) *(G-12394)*
Fairfield Federal Sav Ln Assn (PA) 740 653-3863
  111 E Main St Lancaster (43130) *(G-12395)*
Fairfield Gravel, Fairfield *Also called Martin Marietta Materials Inc (G-10750)*
Fairfield Homes Inc (PA) 740 653-3583
  603 W Wheeling St Lancaster (43130) *(G-12396)*
Fairfield Homes Inc (PA) 740 653-3583
  603 W Wheeling St Lancaster (43130) *(G-12397)*
Fairfield Homes Inc 614 873-3533
  445 Fairfield Dr Ofc Plain City (43064) *(G-16053)*
Fairfield Industries Inc 740 409-1539
  P.O. Box 160 Carroll (43112) *(G-2557)*
Fairfield Inn, Westerville *Also called Polaris Innkeepers Inc (G-19199)*
Fairfield Inn, Canton *Also called Marriott International Inc (G-2390)*
Fairfield Inn, Athens *Also called Athens OH 1013 LLC (G-769)*
Fairfield Inn, Stow *Also called Roce Group LLC (G-17227)*
Fairfield Inn, Reynoldsburg *Also called First Hospitality Company LLC (G-16304)*
Fairfield Inn, Cincinnati *Also called Tharaldson Hospitality MGT (G-2872)*
Fairfield Inn, Youngstown *Also called Alliance Hospitality (G-19950)*
Fairfield Inn, Willoughby *Also called Tramz Hotels LLC (G-19577)*
Fairfield Inn 614 267-1111
  3031 Olentangy River Rd Columbus (43202) *(G-7555)*

Fairfield Insul & Drywall LLC 740 654-8811
　1655 Election House Rd Nw Lancaster (43130) **(G-12398)**
Fairfield Medical Center, Lancaster *Also called Fairfield Diagnstc Imaging LLC* **(G-12394)**
Fairfield Medical Center (PA) 740 687-8000
　401 N Ewing St Lancaster (43130) **(G-12399)**
Fairfield National Bank (HQ) 740 653-7242
　143 W Main St Lancaster (43130) **(G-12400)**
Fairfield Tempo Club 513 863-2081
　8800 Holden Blvd Fairfield (45014) **(G-10727)**
FAIRFIELD YMCA, Hamilton *Also called Great Miami Valley YMCA* **(G-11602)**
Fairfield YMCA Pre-School, Fairfield *Also called Great Miami Valley YMCA* **(G-10732)**
Fairfld Ctr For Disablts & CER 740 653-1186
　681 E 6th Ave Lancaster (43130) **(G-12401)**
Fairhaven Community, Upper Sandusky *Also called United Church Homes Inc* **(G-18414)**
Fairhaven Sheltered Workshop 330 652-1116
　6000 Youngstown Warren Rd Niles (44446) **(G-15154)**
Fairhaven Sheltered Workshop 330 847-7275
　455 Educational Hwy Nw Warren (44483) **(G-18708)**
Fairhaven Sheltered Workshop (PA) 330 505-3644
　45 North Rd Niles (44446) **(G-15155)**
Fairhope Hospice and Palliativ 740 654-7077
　282 Sells Rd Lancaster (43130) **(G-12402)**
Fairlawn Associates Ltd 330 867-5000
　3180 W Market St Fairlawn (44333) **(G-10826)**
Fairlawn Country Club Company 330 836-5541
　200 N Wheaton Rd Akron (44313) **(G-208)**
Fairlawn Medical Offices, Fairlawn *Also called Kaiser Foundation Hospitals* **(G-10837)**
Fairlawn Opco LLC 502 429-8062
　575 S Clvland Mssillon Rd Fairlawn (44333) **(G-10827)**
Fairmont Nursing Home Inc 440 338-8220
　10190 Fairmount Rd Newbury (44065) **(G-15120)**
Fairmount Elementary School, Canton *Also called Canton City School District* **(G-2229)**
Fairmount Minerals LLC 269 926-9450
　3 Summit Park Dr Ste 700 Independence (44131) **(G-12072)**
Fairmount Montessori Assn 216 321-7571
　3380 Fairmount Blvd Cleveland (44118) **(G-5505)**
Fairmount Santrol, Independence *Also called Fairmount Minerals LLC* **(G-12072)**
Fairport Asset Management, Cleveland *Also called Roulston & Company Inc* **(G-6342)**
Fairport Enterprises Inc 330 830-9988
　2000 Sherman Cir Ne Massillon (44646) **(G-13680)**
Fairview Eye Center Inc 440 333-3060
　21375 Lorain Rd Cleveland (44126) **(G-5506)**
Fairview Hlth Sys Fderal Cr Un 216 476-7000
　18101 Lorain Ave Cleveland (44111) **(G-5507)**
FAIRVIEW HOMES, Carlisle *Also called Society For Handicapped Citzns* **(G-2554)**
Fairview Hospital, Cleveland *Also called Sabry Hospital* **(G-6359)**
Fairview Hospital (HQ) 216 476-7000
　18101 Lorain Ave Cleveland (44111) **(G-5508)**
Fairview Hospital 440 871-1063
　850 Columbia Rd Ste 100 Westlake (44145) **(G-19341)**
Fairview Skilled Nursing & Reh, Toledo *Also called Covenant Care Ohio Inc* **(G-17687)**
Fairview West Physician Center, Cleveland *Also called Fairview Hospital* **(G-5508)**
FAIRVIEW WEST PHYSICIAN CENTER, Cleveland *Also called Auxiliary Bd Fairview Gen Hosp* **(G-5026)**
Fairway Independent Mrtg Corp 513 367-6344
　1180 Stone Dr Harrison (45030) **(G-11667)**
Fairway Independent Mrtg Corp 614 930-6552
　4215 Worth Ave Ste 220 Columbus (43219) **(G-7556)**
Fairways 440 943-2050
　30630 Ridge Rd Wickliffe (44092) **(G-19458)**
Faith Christian Accademy, Columbus *Also called Columbus Christian Center Inc* **(G-7266)**
Faith Mission Inc (HQ) 614 224-6617
　245 N Grant Ave Columbus (43215) **(G-7557)**
Faith Mission Inc 614 224-6617
　245 N Grant Ave Columbus (43215) **(G-7558)**
Faithful Companions Inc 440 255-4357
　8500 Station St Ste 111 Mentor (44060) **(G-14046)**
Fak Group Inc 440 498-8465
　6750 Arnold Miller Pkwy Solon (44139) **(G-16848)**
Falcon Plaza LLC 419 352-4671
　1450 E Wooster St Ste 401 Bowling Green (43402) **(G-1730)**
Falcon Transport Co (PA) 330 793-1345
　4944 Belmont Ave Ste 201 Youngstown (44505) **(G-20034)**
Falcon Transport Co. 330 793-1345
　4944 Belmont Ave Ste 201 Youngstown (44505) **(G-20035)**
Fallen Timbers Fmly Physicians 419 893-3321
　5705 Monclova Rd Maumee (43537) **(G-13788)**
Falling Leasing Co LLC 440 238-1100
　18840 Falling Water Rd Strongsville (44136) **(G-17303)**
Falling Star Farm Ltd 419 945-2651
　626 State Route 89 Polk (44866) **(G-16092)**
Falling Water Healthcare Ctr, Strongsville *Also called Falling Leasing Co LLC* **(G-17303)**
Falls Chrysler Jeep Dodge, Cuyahoga Falls *Also called Falls Motor City Inc* **(G-9091)**
Falls Dermatology, Cuyahoga Falls *Also called Falls Family Practice Inc* **(G-9089)**
Falls Family Practice Inc (PA) 330 923-9585
　857 Graham Rd Cuyahoga Falls (44221) **(G-9089)**
Falls Heating & Cooling Inc 330 929-8777
　461 Munroe Falls Ave Cuyahoga Falls (44221) **(G-9090)**
Falls Motor City Inc 330 929-3066
　4100 State Rd Cuyahoga Falls (44223) **(G-9091)**

Falls Stamping & Welding Co (PA) 330 928-1191
　2900 Vincent St Cuyahoga Falls (44221) **(G-9092)**
Falls Supersonic Car Wash Inc 330 928-1657
　2720 2nd St Cuyahoga Falls (44221) **(G-9093)**
Falls Village Retirement Cmnty 330 945-9797
　330 Broadway St E Cuyahoga Falls (44221) **(G-9094)**
Fallsway Equipment Co Inc (PA) 330 633-6000
　1277 Devalera St Akron (44310) **(G-209)**
Fallsway Equipment Company, Akron *Also called Fallsway Equipment Co Inc* **(G-209)**
Falu Corporation 502 641-8106
　9435 Waterstone Blvd # 140 Cincinnati (45249) **(G-3528)**
Falu Security, Cincinnati *Also called Falu Corporation* **(G-3528)**
Famicos Foundation 216 791-6476
　1325 Ansel Rd Cleveland (44106) **(G-5509)**
FAMILIES THAT WORK, Ravenna *Also called Family Cmnty Svcs Portage Cnty* **(G-16243)**
Family & Child Abuse (PA) 419 244-3053
　2460 Cherry St Toledo (43608) **(G-17723)**
Family Birth Center Lima Mem 419 998-4570
　1001 Bellefontaine Ave Lima (45804) **(G-12636)**
Family Child Learning Center, Tallmadge *Also called Childrens Hosp Med Ctr Akron* **(G-17471)**
Family Cmnty Svcs Portage Cnty 330 297-0078
　705 Oakwood St Ravenna (44266) **(G-16243)**
Family Counseling Services, Newark *Also called Woodlnds Srving Centl Ohio Inc* **(G-15111)**
FAMILY COUNSELING SERVICES OF, Cuyahoga Falls *Also called Trillium Family Solutions Inc* **(G-9133)**
Family Dental Team Inc (PA) 330 733-7911
　620 Ridgewood Xing Ste K Fairlawn (44333) **(G-10828)**
Family Dentistry Inc (PA) 513 932-6991
　600 Mound Ct Lebanon (45036) **(G-12465)**
Family Entertainment Services 740 286-8587
　780 Rock Run Rd Jackson (45640) **(G-12173)**
Family Ford Lincoln Inc 740 373-9127
　909 Pike St Marietta (45750) **(G-13328)**
Family Guidance Center, Ironton *Also called Ironton and Lawrence County* **(G-12156)**
Family Health Care Center Inc 614 274-4171
　2800 W Broad St Ste B Columbus (43204) **(G-7559)**
Family Health Partners Inc 419 935-0196
　315 Crestwood Dr Willard (44890) **(G-19480)**
Family Health Plan Inc 419 241-6501
　2200 Jefferson Ave Fl 6 Toledo (43604) **(G-17724)**
Family Heritg Lf Insur Co Amer (HQ) 440 922-5200
　6001 E Royalton Rd # 200 Broadview Heights (44147) **(G-1832)**
Family Hlth Svcs Drke Cnty Inc (PA) 937 548-3806
　5735 Meeker Rd Greenville (45331) **(G-11377)**
FAMILY HOME HEALTH PLUS, Gallipolis *Also called Ohio Valley Home Health Inc* **(G-11210)**
Family Lincoln, Marietta *Also called Family Ford Lincoln Inc* **(G-13328)**
Family Lrng Ctr At Sentinel 419 448-5079
　797 E Township Road 201 Tiffin (44883) **(G-17517)**
Family Mdcine Ctr At St Thomas, Akron *Also called Summa Health System* **(G-452)**
Family Medical Group 513 389-1400
　6331 Glenway Ave Cincinnati (45211) **(G-3529)**
Family Medicine Center Minerva 330 868-4184
　200 Carolyn Ct Minerva (44657) **(G-14519)**
Family Medicine Residency, Toledo *Also called Toledo Hospital* **(G-18085)**
Family Medicine Stark County 330 499-5600
　6512 Whipple Ave Nw Canton (44720) **(G-2309)**
Family Motor Coach Assn Inc (PA) 513 474-3622
　8291 Clough Pike Cincinnati (45244) **(G-3530)**
Family Nursing Services, Chillicothe *Also called Fns Inc* **(G-2781)**
Family Physicans Associates, Cleveland *Also called Terence Isakov MD* **(G-6513)**
Family Physician Associates 614 901-2273
　291 W Schrock Rd Westerville (43081) **(G-19254)**
Family Physicians Associates (PA) 440 442-3866
　5187 Mayfield Rd Ste 102 Cleveland (44124) **(G-5510)**
Family Physicians Inc 330 494-7099
　4860 Frank Ave Nw Canton (44720) **(G-2310)**
Family Physicians of Coshocton 740 622-0332
　440 Browns Ln Coshocton (43812) **(G-9014)**
Family Physicians of Gahanna 614 471-9654
　725 Buckles Ct N Columbus (43230) **(G-7560)**
Family Planning Center 740 439-3340
　326 Highland Ave Cambridge (43725) **(G-2066)**
Family Practice & Associates 937 399-6650
　2701 Moorefield Rd Springfield (45502) **(G-17036)**
Family Practice Center Akron, Akron *Also called Summa Health System* **(G-450)**
Family Practice Center Inc 330 682-3075
　830 S Main St Ste Rear Orrville (44667) **(G-15630)**
Family Practice Ctr Salem Inc 330 332-9961
　2370 Southeast Blvd Salem (44460) **(G-16543)**
Family Recovery Center Inc (PA) 330 424-1468
　964 N Market St Lisbon (44432) **(G-12801)**
Family Resource Centers, Findlay *Also called Family Rsource Ctr NW Ohio Inc* **(G-10900)**
Family Rsource Ctr NW Ohio Inc (PA) 419 222-1168
　530 S Main St Lima (45804) **(G-12637)**
Family Rsource Ctr NW Ohio Inc 419 422-8616
　1941 Carlin St Findlay (45840) **(G-10900)**
Family Senior Care Inc 740 441-1428
　859 3rd Ave Gallipolis (45631) **(G-11191)**

Family Service (PA) 513 381-6300
　3730 Glenway Ave Cincinnati (45205) *(G-3531)*

FAMILY SERVICE AGENCY, Youngstown Also called Compass Family and Cmnty
Svcs *(G-20002)*

Family Service Agency, Youngstown Also called Rape Information & Counseling *(G-20177)*

Family Service Association 937 222-9481
　2211 Arbor Blvd Moraine (45439) *(G-14655)*

Family Service of NW Ohio (PA) 419 321-6455
　701 Jefferson Ave Ste 301 Toledo (43604) *(G-17725)*

FAMILY SERVICES AND COMMUNITY, Moraine Also called Family Service
Association *(G-14655)*

Family Stations Inc 330 783-9986
　3930 Sunset Blvd Youngstown (44512) *(G-20036)*

Family YMCA of LANcstr&fairfld 740 277-7373
　1180 E Locust St Lancaster (43130) *(G-12403)*

Family YMCA of LANcstr&fairfld (PA) 740 654-0616
　465 W 6th Ave Lancaster (43130) *(G-12404)*

Famous Distribution Inc (HQ) 330 762-9621
　2620 Ridgewood Rd Ste 200 Akron (44313) *(G-210)*

Famous Distribution Inc 330 434-5194
　166 N Union St Akron (44304) *(G-211)*

Famous Enterprises Inc 330 938-6350
　350 Courtney Rd Sebring (44672) *(G-16669)*

Famous Enterprises Inc 216 529-1010
　11200 Madison Ave Cleveland (44102) *(G-5511)*

Famous Enterprises Inc 419 478-0343
　220 Matzinger Rd Toledo (43612) *(G-17726)*

Famous Enterprises Inc (PA) 330 762-9621
　2620 Ridgewood Rd Ste 200 Akron (44313) *(G-212)*

Famous II Inc (PA) 330 762-9621
　2620 Ridgewood Rd Ste 200 Akron (44313) *(G-213)*

Famous Industries Inc (HQ) 330 535-1811
　2620 Ridgewood Rd Ste 200 Akron (44313) *(G-214)*

Famous Industries Inc 330 535-1811
　166 N Union St Akron (44304) *(G-215)*

Famous Manufacturing, Akron Also called Famous Enterprises Inc *(G-212)*

Famous Supply Companies, Akron Also called Famous Distribution Inc *(G-210)*

Fanning/Howey Associates Inc 614 764-4661
　4930 Bradenton Ave # 200 Dublin (43017) *(G-10224)*

Fanning/Howey Associates Inc 919 831-1831
　4930 Bradenton Ave Dublin (43017) *(G-10225)*

Fantastic Sams, Oak Hill Also called Legrand Services Inc *(G-15481)*

FANTON Logistics Inc (PA) 216 341-2400
　10801 Broadway Ave Cleveland (44125) *(G-5512)*

Far Oaks Orthopedists Inc 937 433-5309
　3737 Sthern Blvd Ste 2100 Dayton (45429) *(G-9426)*

Far Oaks Orthopedists Inc 937 298-0452
　55 Elva Ct Ste 100 Vandalia (45377) *(G-18521)*

Far Oaks Orthopedists Inc (PA) 937 433-5309
　6490 Centervl Bus Pkwy Dayton (45459) *(G-9427)*

Far West Center (PA) 440 835-6212
　29133 Health Campus Dr Westlake (44145) *(G-19342)*

Farber Corporation 614 294-1626
　800 E 12th Ave Columbus (43211) *(G-7561)*

Farm Inc 513 922-7020
　239 Anderson Ferry Rd Cincinnati (45238) *(G-3532)*

Farm Credit Mid-America 740 441-9312
　2368 Blizzard Ln Albany (45710) *(G-510)*

Farm House Food Distrs Inc 216 791-6948
　9000 Woodland Ave Cleveland (44104) *(G-5513)*

Farmer Smiths Market, Dover Also called Barkett Fruit Co Inc *(G-10065)*

Farmers & Merchants State Bank (HQ) 419 446-2501
　307-11 N Defiance St Archbold (43502) *(G-630)*

Farmers Bank & Savings Co Inc (PA) 740 992-0088
　211 W 2nd St Pomeroy (45769) *(G-16094)*

FARMERS CASTLE MUSEUM EDUCATIO, Belpre Also called Belpre Historical
Society *(G-1399)*

Farmers Citizens Bank (HQ) 419 562-7040
　105 Washington Sq Bucyrus (44820) *(G-1990)*

Farmers Elev Grn & Sply Assoc (PA) 419 653-4132
　16917 County Road B New Bavaria (43548) *(G-14879)*

Farmers Equipment Inc 419 339-7000
　6008 Elida Rd Lima (45807) *(G-12638)*

Farmers Equipment Inc (PA) 419 339-7000
　1749 E Us Highway 36 A Urbana (43078) *(G-18432)*

Farmers Financial Services 937 424-0643
　3888 Indian Ripple Rd Beavercreek (45440) *(G-1217)*

Farmers Group Inc 330 467-6575
　500 W Aurora Rd Ste 115 Northfield (44067) *(G-15378)*

Farmers Group Inc 614 766-6005
　7400 Safelite Way Columbus (43235) *(G-7562)*

Farmers Group Inc 614 799-3200
　2545 Farmers Dr Ste 440 Columbus (43235) *(G-7563)*

Farmers Group Inc 216 750-4010
　5990 W Creek Rd Ste 160 Independence (44131) *(G-12073)*

Farmers Insurance, Northfield Also called Farmers Group Inc *(G-15378)*

Farmers Insurance, Columbus Also called Farmers Group Inc *(G-7562)*

Farmers Insurance, Columbus Also called Farmers Group Inc *(G-7563)*

Farmers Insurance, Independence Also called Farmers Group Inc *(G-12073)*

Farmers Insurance of Columbus (HQ) 614 799-3200
　7400 Skyline Dr E Columbus (43235) *(G-7564)*

Farmers National Bank (HQ) 330 533-3341
　20 S Broad St Canfield (44406) *(G-2137)*

Farmers National Bank 330 544-7447
　51 S Main St Niles (44446) *(G-15156)*

Farmers National Bank 330 682-1010
　112 W Market St Orrville (44667) *(G-15631)*

Farmers National Bank 330 385-9200
　16924 Saint Clair Ave East Liverpool (43920) *(G-10403)*

Farmers National Bank 330 682-1030
　1444 N Main St Orrville (44667) *(G-15632)*

Farmers Produce Auction, Mount Hope Also called Mt Hope Auction Inc *(G-14737)*

Farmers Savings Bank (PA) 330 648-2441
　111 W Main St Spencer (44275) *(G-16954)*

Farmersville Fire Assn Inc 937 696-2863
　207 N Elm St Farmersville (45325) *(G-10857)*

FARMERSVILLE FIRE DEPARTMENT, Farmersville Also called Farmersville Fire Assn
Inc *(G-10857)*

Faro Services Inc (PA) 614 497-1700
　7070 Pontius Rd Groveport (43125) *(G-11513)*

Farris Enterprises Inc (PA) 614 367-9611
　7465 Worthington Galena Worthington (43085) *(G-19810)*

Farris Produce Inc 330 837-4607
　2421 Lincoln Way Nw Massillon (44647) *(G-13681)*

Farrish & Farrish Lpa, Cincinnati Also called Kelly Farrish Lpa *(G-3855)*

Farrow Cleaners Co (PA) 216 561-2355
　3788 Lee Rd Cleveland (44128) *(G-5514)*

Faruki Ireland & Cox Pllc (PA) 937 227-3700
　500 Courthouse Plz 10 Dayton (45402) *(G-9428)*

Fascor Inc 513 421-1777
　11260 Chester Rd Ste 100 Cincinnati (45246) *(G-3533)*

Fashion Architectural Designs 216 432-1600
　4005 Carnegie Ave Cleveland (44103) *(G-5515)*

Fashion Wallcoverings, Cleveland Also called Fashion Architectural Designs *(G-5515)*

Fast Switch Ltd 614 336-1122
　4900 Blazer Pkwy Dublin (43017) *(G-10226)*

Fast Track Auction Sales, Avon Lake Also called DMR Management Inc *(G-915)*

Fast Traxx Promotions LLC 740 767-3740
　17575 Jacksonville Rd Millfield (45761) *(G-14505)*

Fastball Spt Productions LLC 440 746-8000
　1333 Lakeside Ave E Cleveland (44114) *(G-5516)*

Fastems LLC 513 779-4614
　9850 Windisch Rd West Chester (45069) *(G-18922)*

Fastener Corp of America Inc 440 835-5100
　1133 Bassett Rd Westlake (44145) *(G-19343)*

Fastener Industries Inc 440 891-2031
　33 Lou Groza Blvd Berea (44017) *(G-1426)*

Faster Inc 419 868-8197
　6560 Weatherfield Ct Maumee (43537) *(G-13789)*

Fat Jacks Pizza II Inc (PA) 419 227-1813
　1806 N West St Lima (45801) *(G-12639)*

Fathom Online Marketing, Cleveland Also called Fathom Seo LLC *(G-5517)*

Fathom Seo LLC 614 291-8456
　1465 Northwest Blvd Columbus (43212) *(G-7565)*

Fathom Seo LLC (PA) 216 525-0510
　8200 Sweet Valley Dr Cleveland (44125) *(G-5517)*

Faulkner Grmhsen Keister Shenk (PA) 937 492-1271
　100 S Main Ave Sidney (45365) *(G-16776)*

Faurecia Emissions Control Sys (HQ) 812 341-2000
　543 Matzinger Rd Toledo (43612) *(G-17727)*

Fauster-Cameron Inc (PA) 419 784-1414
　1400 E 2nd St Defiance (43512) *(G-9913)*

Favret Company 614 488-5211
　1296 Dublin Rd Columbus (43215) *(G-7566)*

Favret Heating & Cooling, Columbus Also called Favret Company *(G-7566)*

Fawcett Center For Tomorrow, Columbus Also called Ohio State University *(G-8333)*

Fay Apartments, Cincinnati Also called Fay Limited Partnership *(G-3534)*

Fay Industries Inc 440 572-5030
　17200 Foltz Pkwy Strongsville (44149) *(G-17304)*

Fay Limited Partnership 513 542-8333
　3710 President Dr Cincinnati (45225) *(G-3534)*

Fay Limited Partnership (PA) 513 241-1911
　36 E 4th St 1320 Cincinnati (45202) *(G-3535)*

Fay Sharpe LLP 216 363-9000
　The Halle Bldg 1228e Cleveland (44115) *(G-5518)*

Fayette County Family YMCA, Wshngtn CT Hs Also called Fayette County Family
YMCA *(G-19870)*

Fayette County Family YMCA 740 335-0477
　100 Civic Dr Wshngtn CT Hs (43160) *(G-19870)*

Fayette County Memorial Hosp (PA) 740 335-1210
　1430 Columbus Ave Wshngtn CT Hs (43160) *(G-19871)*

Fayette County Mrdd, Wshngtn CT Hs Also called Fayette Progressive Industries *(G-19872)*

Fayette Parts Service Inc 740 282-4547
　1512 Sunset Blvd Steubenville (43952) *(G-17153)*

Fayette Parts Service Inc 724 880-3616
　618 Canton Rd Wintersville (43953) *(G-19670)*

Fayette Progressive Industries 740 335-7453
　1330 Robinson Rd Se Wshngtn CT Hs (43160) *(G-19872)*

FB Wright of Cincinnati, West Chester Also called F B Wright Co Cincinnati *(G-18921)*

Fc 1346 LLC 330 864-8170
118 Hollywood Ave Akron (44313) *(G-216)*

Fc Continental Landlord LLC 216 621-6060
50 Public Sq Ste 1360 Cleveland (44113) *(G-5519)*

FC Schwendler LLC 330 733-8715
724 Canton Rd Akron (44312) *(G-217)*

FCA US LLC 419 727-2800
4400 Chrysler Dr Toledo (43608) *(G-17728)*

FCA US LLC 419 729-5959
5925 Hagman Rd Toledo (43612) *(G-17729)*

Fchc, Lancaster *Also called Fairfield Community Health Ctr (G-12392)*

Fchs, Dayton *Also called First Community Hlth Svcs LLC (G-9434)*

Fcx Performance Inc (HQ) 614 324-6050
3000 E 14th Ave Columbus (43219) *(G-7567)*

Fdc Enterprises Inc 614 774-9182
5470 Ballentine Pike Springfield (45502) *(G-17037)*

Feazel Roofing Company 614 898-7663
5855 Chandler Ct Westerville (43082) *(G-19164)*

Fechko Excavating 330 722-2890
865 W Liberty St Ste 120 Medina (44256) *(G-13936)*

Fechko Excavating LLC 330 722-2890
865 W Liberty St Ste 120 Medina (44256) *(G-13937)*

Fed Ex Rob Carpenter 419 260-1889
4348 Beck Dr Maumee (43537) *(G-13790)*

Fed/Matrix A Joint Venture LLC 863 665-6363
249 Wayne Ave Dayton (45402) *(G-9429)*

Fedeli Group Inc 216 328-8080
5005 Rockside Rd Ste 500 Cleveland (44131) *(G-5520)*

Federal Equipment Company, Cleveland *Also called Federal Machinery & Eqp Co (G-5522)*

Federal Express Corporation 800 463-3339
2578 Corporate Pl Miamisburg (45342) *(G-14170)*

Federal Express Corporation 800 463-3339
65 Paragon Pkwy Mansfield (44903) *(G-13174)*

Federal Express Corporation 614 492-6106
7066 Cargo Rd Columbus (43217) *(G-7568)*

Federal Express Corporation 800 463-3339
5313 Majestic Pkwy Bedford (44146) *(G-1280)*

Federal Express Corporation 800 463-3339
3499 Saint Johns Rd Lima (45804) *(G-12640)*

Federal Express Corporation 800 463-3339
7600 Caple Blvd Northwood (43619) *(G-15393)*

Federal Express Corporation 800 463-3339
2424 Citygate Dr Columbus (43219) *(G-7569)*

Federal Express Corporation 800 463-3339
2850 International St Columbus (43228) *(G-7570)*

Federal Express Corporation 800 463-3339
3605 Concorde Dr Vandalia (45377) *(G-18522)*

Federal Express Corporation 800 463-3339
3301 Bruening Ave Sw Canton (44706) *(G-2311)*

Federal Express Corporation 937 898-3474
10340 Freight Dr Vandalia (45377) *(G-18523)*

Federal Home Ln Bnk Cincinnati (PA) 513 852-7500
600 Atrium Two # 2 Cincinnati (45201) *(G-3536)*

Federal Home Ln Bnk Cincinnati 513 852-5719
1000 Atrium 2 Cincinnati (45202) *(G-3537)*

Federal Hose Manufacturing, Painesville *Also called First Francis Company Inc (G-15714)*

Federal Insurance Company 216 687-1700
1375 E 9th St Ste 1960 Cleveland (44114) *(G-5521)*

Federal Insurance Company 513 721-0601
312 Walnut St Ste 2100 Cincinnati (45202) *(G-3538)*

Federal Machinery & Eqp Co (PA) 800 652-2466
8200 Bessemer Ave Cleveland (44127) *(G-5522)*

Federal Probation, Columbus *Also called Supreme Court United States (G-8717)*

Federal Rsrve Bnk of Cleveland (HQ) 216 579-2000
1455 E 6th St Cleveland (44114) *(G-5523)*

Federal Rsrve Bnk of Cleveland 513 721-4787
150 E 4th St Fl 3 Cincinnati (45202) *(G-3539)*

FEDERAL SAVINGS BANK, West Chester *Also called Guardian Savings Bank (G-18938)*

Federal-Mogul Powertrain LLC 740 432-2393
6420 Glenn Hwy Cambridge (43725) *(G-2067)*

Federated Logistics 937 294-3074
2260 Arbor Blvd Moraine (45439) *(G-14656)*

Federer Homes and Gardens RE, Dayton *Also called Big Hill Realty Corp (G-9251)*

Fedex, Miamisburg *Also called Federal Express Corporation (G-14170)*

Fedex, Mansfield *Also called Federal Express Corporation (G-13174)*

Fedex, Columbus *Also called Federal Express Corporation (G-7568)*

Fedex, Bedford *Also called Federal Express Corporation (G-1280)*

Fedex, Lima *Also called Federal Express Corporation (G-12640)*

Fedex, Northwood *Also called Federal Express Corporation (G-15393)*

Fedex, Columbus *Also called Federal Express Corporation (G-7569)*

Fedex, Columbus *Also called Federal Express Corporation (G-7570)*

Fedex, Vandalia *Also called Federal Express Corporation (G-18522)*

Fedex, Canton *Also called Federal Express Corporation (G-2311)*

Fedex, Vandalia *Also called Federal Express Corporation (G-18523)*

Fedex Corporation 440 234-0315
17831 Englewood Dr Cleveland (44130) *(G-5524)*

Fedex Corporation 614 801-0953
3423 Southpark Pl Grove City (43123) *(G-11431)*

Fedex Custom Critical Inc (HQ) 800 463-3339
1475 Boettler Rd Uniontown (44685) *(G-18369)*

Fedex Freight Inc 330 645-0879
678 Killian Rd Akron (44319) *(G-218)*

Fedex Freight Inc 937 233-4826
8101 Terminal Ln Dayton (45424) *(G-9430)*

Fedex Freight Corporation 877 661-8956
7685 Saint Clair Ave Mentor (44060) *(G-14047)*

Fedex Freight Corporation 419 729-1755
5657 Enterprise Blvd Toledo (43612) *(G-17730)*

Fedex Freight Corporation 800 390-0159
160 Industrial Pkwy Mansfield (44903) *(G-13175)*

Fedex Freight Corporation 800 521-3505
2335 Saint Johns Rd Lima (45804) *(G-12641)*

Fedex Freight Corporation 800 344-6448
10 Commerce Pkwy West Jefferson (43162) *(G-19107)*

Fedex Freight Corporation 800 728-8190
7779 Arbor Dr Northwood (43619) *(G-15394)*

Fedex Freight Corporation 800 354-9489
1705 Moxahala Ave Zanesville (43701) *(G-20307)*

Fedex Ground Package Sys Inc 800 463-3339
1415 Industrial Dr Chillicothe (45601) *(G-2778)*

Fedex Ground Package Sys Inc 800 463-3339
3245 Henry Rd Richfield (44286) *(G-16356)*

Fedex Ground Package Sys Inc 412 859-2653
103 Anart St Steubenville (43953) *(G-17154)*

Fedex Ground Package Sys Inc 800 463-3339
4600 Poth Rd Columbus (43213) *(G-7571)*

Fedex Ground Package Sys Inc 330 244-1534
8033 Pittsburg Ave Nw Canton (44720) *(G-2312)*

Fedex Ground Package Sys Inc 800 463-3339
650 S Reynolds Rd Toledo (43615) *(G-17731)*

Fedex Ground Package Sys Inc 800 463-3339
3201 Columbia Rd Richfield (44286) *(G-16357)*

Fedex Ground Package Sys Inc 513 942-4330
9667 Inter Ocean Dr West Chester (45246) *(G-19052)*

Fedex Ground Package Sys Inc 800 463-3339
6120 S Meadows Dr Grove City (43123) *(G-11432)*

Fedex Office & Print Svcs Inc 440 946-6353
34800 Euclid Ave Willoughby (44094) *(G-19523)*

Fedex Office & Print Svcs Inc 937 436-0677
1189 Mmsburg Cntrville Rd Dayton (45459) *(G-9431)*

Fedex Office & Print Svcs Inc 614 621-1100
180 N High St Columbus (43215) *(G-7572)*

Fedex Office & Print Svcs Inc 614 898-0000
604 W Schrock Rd Westerville (43081) *(G-19255)*

Fedex Office & Print Svcs Inc 216 292-2679
27450 Chagrin Blvd Beachwood (44122) *(G-1057)*

Fedex Smartpost Inc 800 463-3339
2969 Lewis Centre Way Grove City (43123) *(G-11433)*

Fedex Sup Chain Dist Sys Inc 412 820-3700
3795 Creekside Prk Way Lockbourne (43137) *(G-12818)*

Fedex Supply Chain 614 491-1518
4555 Creekside Pkwy Ste A Lockbourne (43137) *(G-12819)*

Fedex Truckload Brokerage Inc 800 463-3339
1475 Boettler Rd Uniontown (44685) *(G-18370)*

Fedvendor, Alliance *Also called QBS Inc (G-544)*

Feecorp Corporation (PA) 614 837-3010
7995 Allen Rd Nw Canal Winchester (43110) *(G-2108)*

Feecorp Industrial Services 740 533-1445
1120 Wyanoke St Ironton (45638) *(G-12152)*

Feed Lucas County Children Inc 419 260-1556
1501 Monroe St Ste 27 Toledo (43604) *(G-17732)*

Feg Consulting LLC 412 224-2263
3587 Tiffany Ridge Ln Blue Ash (45241) *(G-1560)*

Fehr Services LLC 513 829-9333
6200 Pleasant Ave Ste 3 Fairfield (45014) *(G-10728)*

Feick Contractors Inc 419 625-3241
224 E Water St Sandusky (44870) *(G-16603)*

Feinknopf Macioce Schappa ARC 614 297-1020
995 W 3rd Ave Columbus (43212) *(G-7573)*

Feintool Equipment Corporation 513 791-1118
6833 Creek Rd Blue Ash (45242) *(G-1561)*

Feldkamp Enterprises Inc 513 347-4500
3642 Muddy Creek Rd Cincinnati (45238) *(G-3540)*

Feldys 513 474-2212
8060 Beechmont Ave Cincinnati (45255) *(G-3541)*

Feller Finch & Associates Inc (PA) 419 893-3680
1683 Woodlands Dr Ste A Maumee (43537) *(G-13791)*

Fellows Riverside Gardens, Youngstown *Also called Mill Creek Metropolitan Park (G-20129)*

Fenton Bros Electric Co 330 343-0093
235 Ray Ave Ne New Philadelphia (44663) *(G-14959)*

Fenton Rigging & Contg Inc 513 631-5500
2150 Langdon Farm Rd Cincinnati (45237) *(G-3542)*

Fenton's Festival of Lights, New Philadelphia *Also called Fenton Bros Electric Co (G-14959)*

Ferfolia Funeral Homes Inc 216 663-4222
356 W Aurora Rd Northfield (44067) *(G-15379)*

Ferguson 124, Hilliard *Also called Ferguson Enterprises Inc (G-11767)*

Ferguson Construction Company (PA) 937 498-2243
400 Canal St Sidney (45365) *(G-16777)*

Ferguson Construction Company 937 274-1173
2201 Embury Park Rd Dayton (45414) *(G-9432)*

Ferguson Enterprises Inc 513 771-6566
2945 Crescentville Rd West Chester (45069) *(G-18923)*

A L P H A B E T I C

Ferguson Enterprises Inc 614 876-8555
   4363 Lyman Dr Hilliard (43026) *(G-11767)*

Ferguson Hills Inc 513 539-4497
   7812 Mcewen Rd Ste 200 Dayton (45459) *(G-9433)*

Ferguson Integrated Services, West Chester *Also called Ferguson Enterprises Inc (G-18923)*

Feridean Commons LLC 614 898-7488
   6885 Freeman Rd Westerville (43082) *(G-19165)*

Feridean Group Inc 614 898-7488
   6885 Freeman Rd Westerville (43082) *(G-19166)*

Fern Exposition Services LLC (PA) 513 621-6111
   645 Linn St Cincinnati (45203) *(G-3543)*

Ferno-Washington Inc (PA) 877 733-0911
   70 Weil Way Wilmington (45177) *(G-19623)*

Ferralloy Inc 440 250-1900
   28001 Ranney Pkwy Cleveland (44145) *(G-5525)*

Ferrante Wine Farm Inc 440 466-8466
   558 Rte 307 Geneva (44041) *(G-11240)*

Ferrous Metal Transfer 216 671-8500
   11103 Memphis Ave Brooklyn (44144) *(G-1861)*

Ferrous Processing and Trading, Cleveland *Also called Fpt Cleveland LLC (G-5569)*

Fersenius Medical Center, Columbus *Also called Mount Carmel E Dialysis Clnc (G-8109)*

Fes, Akron *Also called Firstenergy Solutions Corp (G-223)*

Festa Food Company, Cleveland *Also called Pinata Foods Inc (G-6211)*

Fetter and Son LLC 740 465-2961
   2421 Mrral Krkptrick Rd W Morral (43337) *(G-14711)*

Fetter and Son Farms, Morral *Also called Fetter and Son LLC (G-14711)*

Fetter Son Farms Ltd Lblty Co 740 465-2961
   2421 Mrral Krkptrick Rd W Morral (43337) *(G-14712)*

Fetters Construction Inc 419 542-0944
   945 E High St Hicksville (43526) *(G-11727)*

Ffd Financial Corporation (PA) 330 364-7777
   321 N Wooster Ave Dover (44622) *(G-10077)*

Fhc Enterprises LLC 614 271-3513
   5489 Blue Ash Rd Columbus (43229) *(G-7574)*

Fiber Systems, Dayton *Also called Industrial Fiberglass Spc Inc (G-9514)*

Fidelitone Inc 440 260-6523
   17851 Englewood Dr Ste I Middleburg Heights (44130) *(G-14252)*

Fidelity Charitable Gift Fund 800 952-4438
   P.O. Box 770001 Cincinnati (45277) *(G-3544)*

Fidelity Health Care 937 208-6400
   3170 Kettering Blvd Moraine (45439) *(G-14657)*

Fidelity National Fincl Inc 614 865-1562
   4111 Executive Pkwy # 304 Westerville (43081) *(G-19256)*

Fidelity Properties Inc 330 821-9700
   220 E Main St Alliance (44601) *(G-531)*

Field & Stream Bowhunters 419 423-9861
   1023 Cypress Ave Findlay (45840) *(G-10901)*

Fields Marketing Research Inc 513 821-6266
   3814 West St Ste 110 Cincinnati (45227) *(G-3545)*

Fields Research, Cincinnati *Also called Fields Marketing Research Inc (G-3545)*

Fieldstone Farm Therapeutic RI 440 708-0013
   16497 Snyder Rd Chagrin Falls (44023) *(G-2666)*

Fieldstone Limited Partnership (PA) 937 293-0900
   4000 Miller Valentine Ct Moraine (45439) *(G-14658)*

Fifth Avenue Lumber Co (HQ) 614 294-0068
   479 E 5th Ave Columbus (43201) *(G-7575)*

Fifth Third Bancorp (PA) 800 972-3030
   38 Fountain Square Plz Cincinnati (45202) *(G-3546)*

Fifth Third Bank 513 574-4457
   5830 Harrison Ave Cincinnati (45248) *(G-3547)*

Fifth Third Bank 440 984-2402
   309 N Leavitt Rd Amherst (44001) *(G-587)*

Fifth Third Bank (HQ) 513 579-5203
   38 Fountain Square Plz Cincinnati (45202) *(G-3548)*

Fifth Third Bank 419 259-7820
   606 Madison Ave Fl 8 Toledo (43604) *(G-17733)*

Fifth Third Bank 513 579-5203
   Fifth 3rd Ctr 38 Fountain Cincinnati (45263) *(G-3549)*

Fifth Third Bank 330 686-0511
   4070 Fishcreek Rd Cuyahoga Falls (44224) *(G-9095)*

Fifth Third Bank of NW Ohio 419 259-7820
   1 Seagate Ste 2200 Toledo (43604) *(G-17734)*

Fifth Third Bank of Sthrn OH (HQ) 937 840-5353
   511 N High St Hillsboro (45133) *(G-11839)*

Fifth Third Bnk of Columbus OH 614 744-7553
   21 E State St Fl 4 Columbus (43215) *(G-7576)*

Fifth Third Equipment Fin Co (HQ) 800 972-3030
   38 Fountain Square Plz Cincinnati (45202) *(G-3550)*

Figlio Wood Fired Pizza, Columbus *Also called Claire De Leigh Corp (G-7216)*

File Sharpening Company Inc 937 376-8268
   360 W Church St Xenia (45385) *(G-19899)*

Filing Scale Company Inc 330 425-3092
   1500 Enterprise Pkwy Twinsburg (44087) *(G-18266)*

Filling Memorial Home of Mercy (PA) 419 592-6451
   N160 State Route 108 Napoleon (43545) *(G-14804)*

Filltek Fulfillment Services, West Chester *Also called Fulfillment Technologies LLC (G-19055)*

Filmco, Aurora *Also called Kapstone Container Corporation (G-832)*

Filnor Inc (PA) 330 821-8731
   227 N Freedom Ave Alliance (44601) *(G-532)*

Filterfresh Coffee Service Inc 513 681-8911
   4890 Duff Dr Ste D West Chester (45246) *(G-19053)*

Filtrexx International, Akron *Also called Conwed Plas Acquisition V LLC (G-157)*

Finance Dept, Cleveland *Also called City of Cleveland (G-5194)*

Finance Dept, Cleveland *Also called City of Cleveland (G-5195)*

Finance System of Toledo Inc (PA) 419 578-4300
   2821 N Holland Sylvania R Toledo (43615) *(G-17735)*

Financial Bookkeeping Service, Cleveland *Also called Lassiter Corporation (G-5856)*

Financial Design Group Inc (PA) 419 843-4737
   3230 Central Park W # 100 Toledo (43617) *(G-17736)*

Financial Engines Inc 330 726-3100
   1449 Boardman Canfield Rd Boardman (44512) *(G-1697)*

Financial Perspective Company, Westerville *Also called Thomas Rosser (G-19301)*

Financial PInners of Cleveland 440 473-1115
   6095 Parkland Blvd # 210 Cleveland (44124) *(G-5526)*

Finastra USA Corporation 937 435-2335
   8555 Gander Creek Dr Miamisburg (45342) *(G-14171)*

Findaway World LLC 440 893-0808
   31999 Aurora Rd Solon (44139) *(G-16849)*

Findlay Country Club 419 422-9263
   1500 Country Club Dr Findlay (45840) *(G-10902)*

Findlay Implement Co (PA) 419 424-0471
   1640 Northridge Rd Findlay (45840) *(G-10903)*

Findlay Inn & Conference Ctr 419 422-5682
   200 E Main Cross St Findlay (45840) *(G-10904)*

Findlay Laboratory Services, Lima *Also called Lima Pathology Associates Labs (G-12685)*

Findlay Publishing Company 419 422-4545
   551 Lake Cascade Pkwy Findlay (45840) *(G-10905)*

FINDLAY STREET NEIGHBORHOOD, Cincinnati *Also called Seven Hlls Neighborhood Houses (G-4460)*

Findlay Truck Line Inc 419 422-1945
   106 W Front St Findlay (45840) *(G-10906)*

Findlay Waste Water Treatment, Findlay *Also called City of Findlay (G-10889)*

Findlay Womens Care LLC (PA) 419 420-0904
   1917 S Main St Findlay (45840) *(G-10907)*

Findlay Y M C A Child Dev 419 422-3174
   231 E Lincoln St Findlay (45840) *(G-10908)*

Findley Inc (PA) 419 255-1360
   1 Seagate Ste 2050 Toledo (43604) *(G-17737)*

Fine Line Graphics Corp (PA) 614 486-0276
   1481 Goodale Blvd Columbus (43212) *(G-7577)*

Finishing Touch Cleaning Svcs, Massillon *Also called Butterfield Co Inc (G-13666)*

Finishmaster Inc 614 228-4328
   212 N Grant Ave Columbus (43215) *(G-7578)*

Finit Group LLC 513 793-4648
   8050 Hosbrook Rd Ste 326 Cincinnati (45236) *(G-3551)*

Finit Solutions, Cincinnati *Also called Finit Group LLC (G-3551)*

Finlaw Construction Inc 330 889-2074
   5213 State Route 45 Bristolville (44402) *(G-1825)*

Finley Fire Equipment Co (PA) 740 962-4328
   5255 N State Route 60 Nw McConnelsville (43756) *(G-13900)*

Finneytown Contracting Corp 513 482-2700
   5151 Fishwick Dr Cincinnati (45216) *(G-3552)*

Fiorilli Construction Co Inc 216 696-5845
   1247 Medina Rd Medina (44256) *(G-13938)*

Fire Department, Blue Ash *Also called City of Blue Ash (G-1527)*

Fire Department, Antwerp *Also called Village of Antwerp (G-616)*

Fire Department, Willoughby Hills *Also called City of Willoughby Hills (G-19587)*

Fire Dept, Cincinnati *Also called Township of Colerain (G-4622)*

Fire Foe Corp 330 759-9834
   999 Trumbull Ave Girard (44420) *(G-11287)*

Fire Guard LLC 740 625-5181
   35 E Granville St Sunbury (43074) *(G-17388)*

Fire Station, Cleveland *Also called City of Cleveland (G-5197)*

Firefighters Cmnty Cr Un Inc 216 621-4644
   2300 Saint Clair Ave Ne Cleveland (44114) *(G-5527)*

Fireland Hospital, Norwalk *Also called Counseling Center Huron County (G-15430)*

Firelands Ambulance Service 419 929-1487
   25 James St New London (44851) *(G-14932)*

Firelands Counseling Recovery, Tiffin *Also called Firelands Regional Health Sys (G-17518)*

Firelands Federal Credit Union (PA) 419 483-4180
   221 E Main St Bellevue (44811) *(G-1377)*

Firelands Physicians Group, Sandusky *Also called North Coast Prof Co LLC (G-16629)*

Firelands Regional Health Sys (PA) 419 557-7400
   1111 Hayes Ave Sandusky (44870) *(G-16604)*

Firelands Regional Health Sys 419 448-9440
   76 Ashwood Dr Tiffin (44883) *(G-17518)*

Firelands Regional Health Sys 419 332-5524
   675 Bartson Rd Fremont (43420) *(G-11072)*

Firelands Regional Health Sys 419 626-7400
   1101 Decatur St Sandusky (44870) *(G-16605)*

Firelands Regional Health Sys 419 663-3737
   292 Benedict Ave Norwalk (44857) *(G-15435)*

FIRELANDS REGIONAL MEDICAL CEN, Sandusky *Also called Firelands Regional Health Sys (G-16604)*

Firelands Security Services 419 627-0562
   1210 Sycamore Line Sandusky (44870) *(G-16606)*

FireInds Cnsling Recovery Svcs, Fremont Also called Firelands Regional Health Sys (G-11072)

FireInds Cnsling Recovery Svcs, Norwalk Also called Firelands Regional Health Sys (G-15435)

Fireproof Record Center, Grove City Also called Briar-Gate Realty Inc (G-11411)

Fireproof Records Center, Grove City Also called Briar-Gate Realty Inc (G-11410)

Firestone, Cuyahoga Falls Also called Bridgestone Ret Operations LLC (G-9075)

Firestone Country Club, Akron Also called Akron Management Corp (G-48)

Firm Hahn Law 614 221-0240
65 E State St Ste 1400 Columbus (43215) (G-7579)

First 2 Market Products LLC 419 874-5444
25671 Fort Meigs Rd Ste A Perrysburg (43551) (G-15865)

First Acceptance Corporation 614 237-9700
895 S Hamilton Rd Columbus (43213) (G-7580)

First Acceptance Corporation 937 778-8888
987 E Ash St Piqua (45356) (G-16004)

First Acceptance Corporation 513 741-0811
6150 Colerain Ave Cincinnati (45239) (G-3553)

First Acceptance Corporation 614 492-1446
3497 Parsons Ave Columbus (43207) (G-7581)

First Acceptance Corporation 330 792-7181
4774 Mahoning Ave Ste 5 Youngstown (44515) (G-20037)

First Acceptance Corporation 614 853-3344
4898 W Broad St Columbus (43228) (G-7582)

First American Equity Ln Svcs (HQ) 800 221-8683
1100 Superior Ave E # 3 Cleveland (44114) (G-5528)

First American Title Insur Co 216 241-1278
1100 Superior Ave E # 200 Cleveland (44114) (G-5529)

First American Title Insur Co 419 625-8505
143 E Water St Sandusky (44870) (G-16607)

First American Title Insur Co 740 450-0006
961 Linden Ave South Zanesville (43701) (G-16951)

First Amrcn Cash Advnce SC LLC 330 644-9144
3100 Manchester Rd Akron (44319) (G-219)

First Amrcn Ttle Midland Title, Cleveland Also called Midland Title Security Inc (G-5986)

First Apostolic Church 419 885-4888
5701 W Sylvania Ave Toledo (43623) (G-17738)

First Assembly Child Care 419 529-6501
1000 Mcpherson St Mansfield (44903) (G-13176)

First Baptist Day Care Center 216 371-9394
3630 Fairmount Blvd Cleveland (44118) (G-5530)

First Call For Help Inc 419 599-1660
600 Freedom Dr Napoleon (43545) (G-14805)

First Capital Bancshares Inc 740 775-6777
33 W Main St Chillicothe (45601) (G-2779)

First Capital Enterprises Inc 740 773-2166
505 E 7th St Chillicothe (45601) (G-2780)

First Choice Cincinnati Branch, Cincinnati Also called First Choice Medical Staffing (G-3554)

First Choice Med Staff of Ohio 330 867-1409
3200 W Market St Ste 1 Fairlawn (44333) (G-10829)

First Choice Med Staff of Ohio 419 521-2700
90 W 2nd St Mansfield (44902) (G-13177)

First Choice Medical Staffing 419 861-2722
5445 Sthwyck Blvd Ste 208 Toledo (43614) (G-17739)

First Choice Medical Staffing 513 631-5656
1008 Marshall Ave Frnt Cincinnati (45225) (G-3554)

First Choice Medical Staffing 216 521-2222
1457 W 117th St Cleveland (44107) (G-5531)

First Choice Medical Staffing (PA) 216 521-2222
1457 W 117th St Cleveland (44107) (G-5532)

First Choice Medical Staffing 419 626-9740
1164 Cleveland Rd Sandusky (44870) (G-16608)

First Choice Packaging Inc (PA) 419 333-4100
1501 W State St Fremont (43420) (G-11073)

First Choice Packg Solutions, Fremont Also called First Choice Packaging Inc (G-11073)

First Christian Church 330 445-2700
6900 Market Ave N Canton (44721) (G-2313)

First Citizens Nat Bnk Inc (PA) 419 294-2351
100 N Sandusky Ave Upper Sandusky (43351) (G-18407)

First Class Limos Inc 440 248-1114
31525 Aurora Rd Ste 5 Cleveland (44139) (G-5533)

First Command Fincl Plg Inc 937 429-4490
51 Plum St Ste 260 Beavercreek (45440) (G-1218)

First Commonwealth Bank 740 548-3340
100 Delaware Xing W Delaware (43015) (G-9974)

First Commonwealth Bank 740 369-0048
100 Willow Brook Way S Delaware (43015) (G-9975)

First Commonwealth Bank 614 336-2280
10149 Brewster Ln Powell (43065) (G-16194)

First Commonwealth Bank 740 657-7000
110 Riverbend Ave Lewis Center (43035) (G-12542)

First Communications LLC 330 835-2323
3340 W Market St Fairlawn (44333) (G-10830)

First Communications LLC (PA) 330 835-2323
3340 W Market St Fairlawn (44333) (G-10831)

First Community Church (PA) 614 488-0681
1320 Cambridge Blvd Columbus (43212) (G-7583)

First Community Church 740 385-3827
29746 Logan Horns Mill Rd Logan (43138) (G-12835)

First Community Church 614 488-0681
3777 Dublin Rd Columbus (43221) (G-7584)

First Community Hlth Svcs LLC 937 247-0400
3634 Watertower Ln Ste 1 Dayton (45449) (G-9434)

First Community Mortgage Svcs, Columbus Also called Union Mortgage Services Inc (G-8799)

First Community Village 614 324-4455
1800 Riverside Dr Ofc Columbus (43212) (G-7585)

First Data Gvrnment Sltions LP 513 489-9599
11311 Cornell Park Dr Blue Ash (45242) (G-1562)

First Data Gvrnmnt Solutns Inc (HQ) 513 489-9599
11311 Cornell Park Dr Blue Ash (45242) (G-1563)

First Day Fincl Federal Cr Un (PA) 937 222-4546
1030 N Main St Dayton (45405) (G-9435)

First Defiance Financial Corp 419 353-8611
209 W Poe Rd Bowling Green (43402) (G-1731)

First Diversity MGT Group, Springfield Also called 56 Plus Management LLC (G-16991)

First Diversity Staffing Group 937 323-4114
560 E High St Springfield (45505) (G-17038)

First Energy Linde 330 384-4959
76 S Main St Bsmt Akron (44308) (G-220)

First Fdral Sav Ln Assn Galion 419 468-1518
140 N Columbus St Galion (44833) (G-11170)

First Fdral Sav Ln Assn Lkwood (PA) 216 221-7300
14806 Detroit Ave Lakewood (44107) (G-12343)

First Fdral Sav Ln Assn Lorain (PA) 440 282-6188
3721 Oberlin Ave Lorain (44053) (G-12904)

First Fdral Sav Ln Assn Newark (PA) 740 345-3494
2 N 2nd St Newark (43055) (G-15033)

First Fdral Sving Ln Assn Dlta (PA) 419 822-3131
404 Main St Delta (43515) (G-10043)

First Federal Bank of Midwest (HQ) 419 782-5015
601 Clinton St Ste 1 Defiance (43512) (G-9914)

First Federal Bank of Midwest 419 695-1055
230 E 2nd St Delphos (45833) (G-10026)

First Federal Bank of Midwest 419 855-8326
22020 Main St Genoa (43430) (G-11253)

First Federal Bank of Ohio (PA) 419 468-1518
140 N Columbus St Galion (44833) (G-11171)

First Federal Credit Control 216 360-2000
24700 Chagrin Blvd # 205 Cleveland (44122) (G-5534)

FIRST FEDERAL SAVINGS AND LOAN, Delta Also called First Fdral Sving Ln Assn Dlta (G-10043)

First Financial Bancorp 513 551-5640
225 Pictoria Dr Ste 700 Cincinnati (45246) (G-3555)

First Financial Bank 513 979-5800
255 E 5th St Ste 2900 Cincinnati (45202) (G-3556)

First Financial Bank (HQ) 877 322-9530
255 E 5th St Ste 2900 Cincinnati (45202) (G-3557)

First Fincl Title Agcy of Ohio 216 664-1920
1500 W 3rd St Ste 400 Cleveland (44113) (G-5535)

First Francis Company Inc (HQ) 440 352-8927
25 Florence Ave Painesville (44077) (G-15714)

First Fruits Child Dev Ctr I 216 862-4715
21877 Euclid Ave Euclid (44117) (G-10635)

First Group America, Cincinnati Also called First Student Inc (G-3562)

First Group Investment Partnr (HQ) 513 241-2200
600 Vine St Ste 1200 Cincinnati (45202) (G-3558)

First Group of America, Cincinnati Also called Firstgroup America Inc (G-3566)

First Hospitality Company LLC 614 864-4555
2826 Taylor Road Ext Reynoldsburg (43068) (G-16304)

First Hotel Associates LP 614 228-3800
310 S High St Columbus (43215) (G-7586)

First Interstate Properties 216 381-2900
25333 Cedar Rd Ste 300 Cleveland (44124) (G-5536)

First Louisville Arden LLC (HQ) 419 252-5500
333 N Summit St Toledo (43604) (G-17740)

First Med Urgent & Fmly Ctr 740 756-9238
1201 River Valley Blvd Lancaster (43130) (G-12405)

First Mental Retardation, Dayton Also called Second Mental Retardation (G-9756)

First Mental Retardation Corp 937 262-3077
2080 N Gettysburg Ave Dayton (45406) (G-9436)

First Merchants Bank 614 486-9000
2130 Tremont Ctr Columbus (43221) (G-7587)

First Miami Student Credit Un 513 529-1251
117 Shriver Ctr Oxford (45056) (G-15677)

First Nat Bnk of Nelsonville (PA) 740 753-1941
11 Public Sq Nelsonville (45764) (G-14831)

First National Bank Bellevue (HQ) 419 483-7340
120 North St Bellevue (44811) (G-1378)

First National Bank of Pandora (HQ) 419 384-3221
102 E Main St Pandora (45877) (G-15751)

First National Bank of Waverly (PA) 740 947-2136
107 N Market St Waverly (45690) (G-18818)

First National Bank PA 330 747-0292
1 W Federal St Youngstown (44503) (G-20038)

First National Bnk of Dennison 740 922-2532
105 Grant St Dennison (44621) (G-10049)

First Ohio Banc & Lending Inc 216 642-8900
6100 Rckside Woods Blvd N Cleveland (44131) (G-5537)

First Ohio Home Finance Inc 937 322-3396
1021 N Limestone St Springfield (45503) (G-17039)

First Page, Dayton Also called P & R Communications Svc Inc (G-9680)

First Realty Property MGT Ltd..................440 720-0100
6690 Beta Dr Ste 220 Mayfield Village (44143) *(G-13885)*

First Richmond Corp................................937 783-4949
820 E Center St Blanchester (45107) *(G-1486)*

First Scan Imaging, West Chester *Also called Proscan Imaging LLC (G-18987)*

First School Corp...................................937 433-3455
7659 Mcewen Rd Dayton (45459) *(G-9437)*

First Services Inc..................................513 241-2200
600 Vine St Ste 1200 Cincinnati (45202) *(G-3559)*

First Settlement Orthopaedics (PA)...........740 373-8756
611 2nd St Ste A Marietta (45750) *(G-13329)*

First State Bank (PA)..............................937 695-0331
19230 State Route 136 Winchester (45697) *(G-19661)*

First Student, Lorain *Also called S B S Transit Inc (G-12942)*

First Student Inc...................................513 531-6888
1801 Transpark Dr Cincinnati (45229) *(G-3560)*

First Student Inc...................................937 645-0201
4750 Sue Ann Blvd Dayton (45415) *(G-9438)*

First Student Inc...................................513 761-6100
100 Hamilton Blvd Cincinnati (45215) *(G-3561)*

First Student Inc...................................513 761-5136
100 Hamilton Blvd Cincinnati (45215) *(G-3562)*

First Student Inc...................................419 382-9915
419 N Westwood Ave Toledo (43607) *(G-17741)*

First Student Inc (HQ)............................513 241-2200
600 Vine St Ste 1400 Cincinnati (45202) *(G-3563)*

First Transit, Cincinnati *Also called Firstgroup Usa Inc (G-3569)*

First Transit Inc...................................513 732-1206
2040 Us Highway 50 Batavia (45103) *(G-999)*

First Transit Inc...................................937 652-4175
2200 S Us Highway 68 Urbana (43078) *(G-18433)*

First Transit Inc (HQ)............................513 241-2200
600 Vine St Ste 1400 Cincinnati (45202) *(G-3564)*

First Union Banc Corp............................330 896-1222
1559 Corporate Woods Pkwy Uniontown (44685) *(G-18371)*

First Vehicle Services Inc (HQ)................513 241-2200
600 Vine St Ste 1400 Cincinnati (45202) *(G-3565)*

First Virginia, Dublin *Also called Buckeye Check Cashing Inc (G-10152)*

First-Knox National Bank (HQ).................740 399-5500
1 S Main St Mount Vernon (43050) *(G-14766)*

First-Knox National Division, Mount Vernon *Also called First-Knox National Bank (G-14766)*

Firstat Nursing Services.........................216 295-1500
21825 Chagrin Blvd # 300 Cleveland (44122) *(G-5538)*

Firstenergy, Ashtabula *Also called Jersey Central Pwr & Light Co (G-744)*

Firstenergy, Sandusky *Also called Jersey Central Pwr & Light Co (G-16619)*

Firstenergy, Fairlawn *Also called Jersey Central Pwr & Light Co (G-10836)*

Firstenergy, Springfield *Also called Jersey Central Pwr & Light Co (G-17056)*

Firstenergy, Stratton *Also called Jersey Central Pwr & Light Co (G-17242)*

Firstenergy, Elyria *Also called Jersey Central Pwr & Light Co (G-10520)*

Firstenergy, Cleveland *Also called Jersey Central Pwr & Light Co (G-5791)*

Firstenergy, Brecksville *Also called Jersey Central Pwr & Light Co (G-1785)*

Firstenergy, Cleveland *Also called Jersey Central Pwr & Light Co (G-5792)*

Firstenergy, Painesville *Also called Jersey Central Pwr & Light Co (G-15716)*

Firstenergy, Oak Harbor *Also called Jersey Central Pwr & Light Co (G-15473)*

Firstenergy Corp...................................419 321-7114
5501 N State Route 2 Oak Harbor (43449) *(G-15472)*

Firstenergy Corp (PA).............................800 736-3402
76 S Main St Bsmt Akron (44308) *(G-221)*

Firstenergy Nuclear Oper Co (HQ)............800 646-0400
76 S Main St Bsmt Akron (44308) *(G-222)*

Firstenergy Nuclear Oper Co...................440 604-9836
6670 Beta Dr Cleveland (44143) *(G-5539)*

Firstenergy Solutions Corp (HQ)..............800 736-3402
341 White Pond Dr Bldg B3 Akron (44320) *(G-223)*

Firstenterprises Inc...............................740 369-5100
2000 Nutter Farms Ln Delaware (43015) *(G-9976)*

Firstgroup America Inc (HQ)....................513 241-2200
600 Vine St Ste 1400 Cincinnati (45202) *(G-3566)*

Firstgroup America Inc...........................513 419-8611
600 Vine St Ste 1400 Cincinnati (45202) *(G-3567)*

Firstgroup America Inc...........................513 241-2200
705 Central Ave Cincinnati (45202) *(G-3568)*

Firstgroup Usa Inc (HQ).........................513 241-2200
600 Vine St Ste 1400 Cincinnati (45202) *(G-3569)*

Firstlght HM Care Dblin Hliard, Dublin *Also called L JC Home Care LLC (G-10265)*

Firstmerit, Akron *Also called Huntington National Bank (G-272)*

Firstmerit Mortgage Corp........................330 478-3400
4455 Hills & Dales Rd Nw Canton (44708) *(G-2314)*

Fischer Process Industries, Loveland *Also called Fischer Pump & Valve Company (G-12994)*

Fischer Pump & Valve Company (PA)..........513 583-4800
155 Commerce Dr Loveland (45140) *(G-12994)*

Fiserv, Dublin *Also called Checkfree Services Corporation (G-10169)*

Fiserv Inc..412 577-3326
6000 Perimeter Dr Dublin (43017) *(G-10227)*

Fiserv Health, Westerville *Also called Harrington Health Services Inc (G-19259)*

Fiserv Solutions LLC..............................412 577-3000
6000 Perimeter Dr Dublin (43017) *(G-10228)*

Fish Creek Plaza Ltd..............................330 688-0450
3000 Graham Rd Unit Ofc Stow (44224) *(G-17204)*

Fishbeck Thmpson Carr Hber Inc..............513 469-2370
11353 Reed Hartman Hwy # 500 Blue Ash (45241) *(G-1564)*

Fishburn Tank Truck Service....................419 253-6031
5012 State Route 229 Marengo (43334) *(G-13303)*

Fishel Company (PA)..............................614 274-8100
1366 Dublin Rd Columbus (43215) *(G-7588)*

Fishel Company....................................614 850-9012
1600 Walcutt Rd Columbus (43228) *(G-7589)*

Fishel Company....................................937 233-2268
7651 Center Point 70 Blvd Dayton (45424) *(G-9439)*

Fishel Company....................................614 850-4400
1600 Walcutt Rd Columbus (43228) *(G-7590)*

Fishel Technologies, Columbus *Also called Fishel Company (G-7588)*

Fisher Cast Steel Products Inc (PA)...........614 879-8325
6 W Town St West Jefferson (43162) *(G-19108)*

Fisher Design Inc (PA)............................513 417-8235
4101 Spring Grove Ave B Cincinnati (45223) *(G-3570)*

Fisher Foods Marketing Inc (PA)..............330 497-3000
4855 Frank Ave Nw North Canton (44720) *(G-15203)*

Fisher-Titus Medical Center....................419 663-6464
368 Milan Ave Ste D Norwalk (44857) *(G-15436)*

Fisher-Titus Medical Center....................419 668-4228
175 Shady Lane Dr Off Norwalk (44857) *(G-15437)*

Fisher-Titus Medical Center....................440 839-2226
24 Hyde St Wakeman (44889) *(G-18621)*

Fisher-Titus Medical Center (PA)..............419 668-8101
272 Benedict Ave Norwalk (44857) *(G-15438)*

Fit Technologies LLC..............................216 583-5000
1375 Euclid Ave Ste 310 Cleveland (44115) *(G-5540)*

Fitch Inc (HQ)......................................614 885-3453
585 Suth Front St Ste 300 Columbus (43215) *(G-7591)*

Fitness Center, Avon *Also called Emh Regional Medical Center (G-880)*

Fitness International LLC........................513 298-0134
7730 Dudley Dr West Chester (45069) *(G-18924)*

Fitness International LLC........................937 427-0700
2500 N Fairfield Rd Ste F Beavercreek (45431) *(G-1152)*

Fitness International LLC........................419 482-7740
1361 Conant St Maumee (43537) *(G-13792)*

Fitton Family YMCA, Hamilton *Also called Great Miami Valley YMCA (G-11605)*

Fitworks Fitness & Spt Therapy, Cincinnati *Also called Fitworks Holding LLC (G-3572)*

Fitworks Holding LLC.............................330 688-2329
4301 Kent Rd Ste 26 Stow (44224) *(G-17205)*

Fitworks Holding LLC.............................513 923-9931
5840 Cheviot Rd Cincinnati (45247) *(G-3571)*

Fitworks Holding LLC.............................440 333-4141
20001 Center Ridge Rd Rocky River (44116) *(G-16433)*

Fitworks Holding LLC.............................513 531-1500
4600 Smith Rd Ste G Cincinnati (45212) *(G-3572)*

Fitzenrider Inc.....................................419 784-0828
827 Perry St Defiance (43512) *(G-9915)*

Five County Joint Juvenile Det.................937 642-1015
18100 State Route 4 Marysville (43040) *(G-13495)*

Five Rivers Dialysis, Dayton *Also called Lakeshore Dialysis LLC (G-9555)*

Five Rivers Health Centers (PA)................937 734-6841
2261 Philadelphia Dr # 200 Dayton (45406) *(G-9440)*

Five Seasons Landscape MGT Inc...............740 964-2915
9886 Mink St Sw Rear Etna (43068) *(G-10609)*

Five Seasons Spt Cntry CLB Inc................513 842-1188
11790 Snider Rd Cincinnati (45249) *(G-3573)*

Five Seasons Spt Cntry CLB Inc................937 848-9200
4242 Clyo Rd Dayton (45440) *(G-9441)*

Five Seasons Spt Cntry CLB Inc................440 899-4555
28105 Clemens Rd Cleveland (44145) *(G-5541)*

Five Star Power Clg & Pntg, Brewster *Also called Mike Morris (G-1811)*

Five Star Senior Living Inc......................614 451-6793
4590 Knightsbridge Blvd Columbus (43214) *(G-7592)*

Five Star Trucking Inc............................440 953-9300
4380 Glenbrook Rd Willoughby (44094) *(G-19524)*

Fixari Family Dental Inc (PA)...................614 866-7445
4241 Kimberly Pkwy Columbus (43232) *(G-7593)*

Flack Global Metals, Cleveland *Also called Flack Steel LLC (G-5542)*

Flack Steel LLC (PA)..............................216 456-0700
425 W Lkeside Ave Ste 200 Cleveland (44113) *(G-5542)*

Flag City Auto Wash, Findlay *Also called Napoleon Wash-N-Fill Inc (G-10947)*

Flag City Mack, Findlay *Also called Bulldawg Holdings LLC (G-10885)*

Flagel Huber Flagel & Co (PA)..................937 299-3400
3400 S Dixie Dr Moraine (45439) *(G-14659)*

Flagship Services of Ohio Inc..................740 533-1657
82 Township Road 1331 Ironton (45638) *(G-12153)*

Flairsoft Ltd (PA).................................614 888-0700
7720 Rivers Edge Dr Ste 2 Columbus (43235) *(G-7594)*

Flamos Enterprises Inc...........................330 478-0009
1501 Raff Rd Sw Ste 1 Canton (44710) *(G-2315)*

Flanagan Lberman Hoffman Swaim............937 223-5200
15 W 4th St Ste 100 Dayton (45402) *(G-9442)*

Flash Seats LLC (PA).............................216 420-2000
1 Center Ct Cleveland (44115) *(G-5543)*

Flat Rock Care Center............................419 483-7330
7353 County Rd 29 Flat Rock (44828) *(G-10978)*

Flavik Village Development......................216 429-1182
5620 Broadway Ave Rm 200 Cleveland (44127) *(G-5544)*

Flavorfresh Dispensers Inc 216 641-0200
4705 Van Epps Rd Brooklyn Heights (44131) ***(G-1871)***
FLCC MEALS, Toledo *Also called Feed Lucas County Children Inc* ***(G-17732)***
Fleet Management Institute, Cincinnati *Also called Nuerological & Sleep Disorders* ***(G-4138)***
Fleet Operations, Toledo *Also called City of Toledo* ***(G-17659)***
Fleet Response, Cleveland *Also called Rental Concepts Inc* ***(G-6308)***
Fleetmaster Express Inc 419 420-1835
1531 Harvard Ave Findlay (45840) ***(G-10909)***
Fleetpride West Inc 419 243-3161
200 Indiana Ave Toledo (43604) ***(G-17742)***
Fleetwood Management Inc 614 538-1277
1675 Old Henderson Rd Columbus (43220) ***(G-7595)***
Fleming Construction Co 740 494-2177
5298 Marion Marysville Rd Prospect (43342) ***(G-16223)***
Flex Fund Inc 614 766-7000
6125 Memorial Dr Dublin (43017) ***(G-10229)***
Flex Property Management, Toledo *Also called Flex Realty* ***(G-17743)***
Flex Realty 419 841-6208
5763 Talmadge Rd Ste C2 Toledo (43623) ***(G-17743)***
Flex Spas Cleveland, Cleveland *Also called Flexeco Incorporated* ***(G-5545)***
Flex Team, Akron *Also called Flex-Team Inc* ***(G-224)***
Flex Technologies Inc 330 897-6311
3430 State Route 93 Baltic (43804) ***(G-934)***
Flex Temp Employment Services 419 355-9675
524 W State St Fremont (43420) ***(G-11074)***
Flex-Team Inc (PA) 330 745-3838
753 W Waterloo Rd Akron (44314) ***(G-224)***
Flexeco Incorporated 216 812-3304
2600 Hamilton Ave Cleveland (44114) ***(G-5545)***
Flexential Corp 513 645-2900
5307 Muhlhauser Rd Hamilton (45011) ***(G-11595)***
Flexnova Inc 216 288-6961
8452 Windsor Way Broadview Heights (44147) ***(G-1833)***
Flexnova Inc 216 288-6961
6100 Oak Tree Blvd Cleveland (44131) ***(G-5546)***
Flexsys America LP (HQ) 330 666-4111
260 Springside Dr Akron (44333) ***(G-225)***
Flick Lumber Co Inc 419 468-6278
340 S Columbus St Galion (44833) ***(G-11172)***
Flick Packaging, Galion *Also called Flick Lumber Co Inc* ***(G-11172)***
Flickinger Piping Company Inc 330 364-4224
439 S Tuscarawas Ave Dover (44622) ***(G-10078)***
Flight Express Inc (HQ) 305 379-8686
7250 Star Check Dr Columbus (43217) ***(G-7596)***
Flight Options Inc (PA) 216 261-3880
26180 Curtiss Wright Pkwy Richmond Heights (44143) ***(G-16389)***
Flight Options LLC (HQ) 216 261-3500
26180 Curtiss Wright Pkwy Cleveland (44143) ***(G-5547)***
Flight Options Intl Inc (HQ) 216 261-3500
355 Richmond Rd Richmond Heights (44143) ***(G-16390)***
Flight Services & Systems Inc (PA) 216 328-0090
5005 Rockside Rd Ste 940 Cleveland (44131) ***(G-5548)***
Flint Ridge Nursing & Rehab, Newark *Also called Generation Health & Rehab Cntr* ***(G-15035)***
Flodraulic Group Incorporated 614 276-8141
765 N Hague Ave Columbus (43204) ***(G-7597)***
Flooring Specialties Div, Cleveland *Also called Frank Novak & Sons Inc* ***(G-5573)***
Floralandscape Inc 419 536-7640
130 Elmdale Rd Toledo (43607) ***(G-17744)***
Florline Group Inc 330 830-3380
800 Vista Ave Se Massillon (44646) ***(G-13682)***
Florline Midwest, Massillon *Also called Florline Group Inc* ***(G-13682)***
Flow Polymers LLC 216 249-4900
12819 Coit Rd Cleveland (44108) ***(G-5549)***
Flow-Liner Systems Ltd 800 348-0020
4830 Northpointe Dr Zanesville (43701) ***(G-20308)***
Flower Factory Inc 614 275-6220
4395 Clime Rd Columbus (43228) ***(G-7598)***
Flower Hospital 419 824-1000
5100 Harroun Rd Sylvania (43560) ***(G-17425)***
Flower Hospital (HQ) 419 824-1444
5200 Harroun Rd Sylvania (43560) ***(G-17426)***
Flowerland Garden Centers (PA) 440 439-8636
25018 Broadway Ave Oakwood Village (44146) ***(G-15489)***
Flowers Family Practice Inc 614 277-9631
3667 Marlane Dr Grove City (43123) ***(G-11434)***
Floyd Brown Group, Delaware *Also called Floyd Browne Group Inc* ***(G-9977)***
Floyd Browne Group Inc 740 363-6792
585 Sunbury Rd Delaware (43015) ***(G-9977)***
Floyd P Bucher & Son Inc 419 867-8792
5743 Larkhall Dr Toledo (43614) ***(G-17745)***
Fluid Connector Group, Waterville *Also called Parker-Hannifin Corporation* ***(G-18790)***
Fluid Line Products Inc 440 946-9470
38273 Western Pkwy Willoughby (44094) ***(G-19525)***
Fluid Mechanics LLC (PA) 216 362-7800
760 Moore Rd Avon Lake (44012) ***(G-917)***
Fluid Power Components, Franklin *Also called Eagle Equipment Corporation* ***(G-11028)***
Fluidtrols, Westlake *Also called Neff Group Distributors Inc* ***(G-19378)***
Fluor-Bwxt Portsmouth LLC 866 706-6992
3930 Us Route 23 S Piketon (45661) ***(G-15975)***
Flux A Salon By Hazelton 419 841-5100
131 W Indiana Ave Perrysburg (43551) ***(G-15866)***
Flying Colors Public Preschool 740 349-1629
119 Union St Newark (43055) ***(G-15034)***
Flypaper Studio Inc 602 801-2208
311 Elm St Ste 200 Cincinnati (45202) ***(G-3574)***
Flytz Gymnastics Inc 330 926-2900
2900 State Rd Unit A Cuyahoga Falls (44223) ***(G-9096)***
Flytz UAS Training Center, Cuyahoga Falls *Also called Flytz Gymnastics Inc* ***(G-9096)***
FM 91 Point 5, Bainbridge *Also called W K H R Radio* ***(G-932)***
FM Earth, Sunbury *Also called Facemyer Backhoe and Dozer Svc* ***(G-17387)***
FM Global, North Olmsted *Also called Factory Mutual Insurance Co* ***(G-15287)***
FM Global, Cincinnati *Also called Factory Mutual Insurance Co* ***(G-3527)***
FMC Dalysis Svcs Richland Cnty, Mansfield *Also called Bio-Mdcal Applcations Ohio Inc* ***(G-13141)***
FML Resin LLC 440 214-3200
3 Summit Park Dr Ste 700 Independence (44131) ***(G-12074)***
Fmw Rri Opco LLC (PA) 614 744-2659
605 S Front St Ste 150 Columbus (43215) ***(G-7599)***
Fnb Inc (PA) 740 922-2532
105 Grant St Dennison (44621) ***(G-10050)***
FNB Corporation 330 721-7484
3613 Medina Rd Medina (44256) ***(G-13939)***
FNB Corporation 330 425-1818
10071 Darrow Rd Twinsburg (44087) ***(G-18267)***
FNB Corporation 440 439-2200
413 Northfield Rd Cleveland (44146) ***(G-5550)***
Fns Inc 740 775-5463
24 Star Dr Chillicothe (45601) ***(G-2781)***
Foam Pac Materials Company, West Chester *Also called Storopack Inc* ***(G-19084)***
Focus Healthcare of Ohio LLC 419 891-9333
1725 Timber Line Rd Maumee (43537) ***(G-13793)***
Focus On Youth Inc 513 644-1030
8904 Brookside Ave West Chester (45069) ***(G-18925)***
Focus Solutions Inc 513 376-8349
1821 Summit Rd Ste 103 Cincinnati (45237) ***(G-3575)***
Focus Staffing, Cincinnati *Also called Focus Solutions Inc* ***(G-3575)***
Foe 2233, Bryan *Also called Fraternal Order of Eagles BR* ***(G-1957)***
Foe 2370, Canton *Also called Fraternal Order Eagles Inc* ***(G-2316)***
Foe 370, Lima *Also called Grand Aerie of The Fraternal* ***(G-12647)***
Foe 4035, Andover *Also called Fraternal Order Eagles Inc* ***(G-606)***
Foe 691, Wapakoneta *Also called Fraternal Order Eagles Inc* ***(G-18642)***
Foe 712, Fremont *Also called Fraternal Order Eagles Inc* ***(G-11075)***
Fojournerf Title Agency, Cincinnati *Also called Reisenfeld & Assoc Lpa LLC* ***(G-4354)***
Folkers Management Corporation (PA) 513 421-0230
7741 Thompson Rd Cincinnati (45247) ***(G-3576)***
Fontaine Bleu', Cleveland *Also called Mfbusiness Group* ***(G-5974)***
Food Concepts Intl Inc 513 336-7449
5010 Deerfield Blvd Mason (45040) ***(G-13579)***
Food Distributors Inc 740 439-2764
449 N 1st St Cambridge (43725) ***(G-2068)***
Food Express US, Groveport *Also called Union Supply Group Inc* ***(G-11545)***
Food For Good Thought Inc 614 447-0424
4185 N High St Columbus (43214) ***(G-7600)***
Food Safety Net Services Ltd 614 274-2070
4130 Fisher Rd Columbus (43228) ***(G-7601)***
Food Sample Express LLc 330 225-3550
2945 Carquest Dr Brunswick (44212) ***(G-1930)***
Food Service, Columbus *Also called Columbus Public School Dst* ***(G-7308)***
Foodliner Inc 937 898-0075
5560 Brentlinger Dr Dayton (45414) ***(G-9443)***
Foodliner Inc 563 451-1047
5560 Brentlinger Dr Dayton (45414) ***(G-9444)***
Foor Concrete Co Inc (PA) 740 513-4346
5361 State Route 37 E Delaware (43015) ***(G-9978)***
Foot & Ankle Care Center 937 492-1211
1000 Michigan St Sidney (45365) ***(G-16778)***
Foot & Ankle Clinic, East Liverpool *Also called Ankle and Foot Care Center* ***(G-10397)***
Foot Steps Toward Discovery, Chesterland *Also called Miss Pats Day Care Center* ***(G-2742)***
For Evers Kids LLC 330 258-9014
775 Copley Rd Akron (44320) ***(G-226)***
For Hire Carrier, Cincinnati *Also called Hc Transport Inc* ***(G-3687)***
For Kids Sake Inc 330 726-6878
1245 Boardman Canfield Rd Youngstown (44512) ***(G-20039)***
For Specialized Alternatives (PA) 419 695-8010
10100 Elida Rd Delphos (45833) ***(G-10027)***
For Women Like Me Inc 407 848-7339
8800 Woodland Ave Cleveland (44104) ***(G-5551)***
For Women Like Me Inc (PA) 407 848-7339
46 Shopping Plz Ste 155 Chagrin Falls (44022) ***(G-2645)***
Ford, Ontario *Also called Graham Chevrolet-Cadillac Co* ***(G-15551)***
Ford Development Corp 513 772-1521
11148 Woodward Ln Cincinnati (45241) ***(G-3577)***
Ford Motor Company 513 573-1101
4680 Parkway Dr Ste 420 Mason (45040) ***(G-13580)***
Foremost Insurance Company 216 674-7000
5990 W Creek Rd Ste 160 Independence (44131) ***(G-12075)***

A L P H A B E T I C

Foresight Corporation 614 791-1600
  655 Metro Pl S Ste 900 Dublin (43017) *(G-10230)*

Forest City Commercial MGT Inc (HQ) 216 621-6060
  50 Public Sq Ste 1200 Cleveland (44113) *(G-5552)*

Forest City Enterprises LP (HQ) 216 621-6060
  127 Public Sq Ste 3200 Cleveland (44114) *(G-5553)*

Forest City Enterprises LP 216 416-3756
  3454 Main St Cleveland (44113) *(G-5554)*

Forest City Enterprises LP 440 888-8664
  9233 Independence Blvd # 114 Cleveland (44130) *(G-5555)*

Forest City Enterprises LP 216 416-3780
  6880 Ridge Rd Cleveland (44129) *(G-5556)*

Forest City Enterprises LP 216 416-3766
  50 Public Sq Ste 1050 Cleveland (44113) *(G-5557)*

Forest City Enterprises LP 216 621-6060
  127 Public Sq Ste 3100 Cleveland (44114) *(G-5558)*

Forest City Erectors Inc 330 425-2345
  8200 Boyle Pkwy Ste 1 Twinsburg (44087) *(G-18268)*

Forest City Properties LLC (HQ) 216 621-6060
  127 Public Sq Ste 3100 Cleveland (44114) *(G-5559)*

Forest City Realty Trust Inc (HQ) 216 621-6060
  127 Public Sq Ste 3100 Cleveland (44114) *(G-5560)*

Forest City Residential Dev (HQ) 216 621-6060
  1170 Trml Twr 50 Pub Sq 1170 Terminal Tower Cleveland (44113) *(G-5561)*

Forest City Washington LLC (HQ) 261 621-6060
  127 Public Sq Ste 3200 Cleveland (44114) *(G-5562)*

Forest Cy Residential MGT Inc (HQ) 216 621-6060
  50 Public Sq Ste 1200 Cleveland (44113) *(G-5563)*

Forest Fair Mall, Cincinnati *Also called Mills Corporation* *(G-4056)*

Forest Hill Care Center, Saint Clairsville *Also called Zandex Inc* *(G-16513)*

Forest Hill Retirement Cmnty, Saint Clairsville *Also called Zandex Health Care Corporation* *(G-16514)*

Forest Hills Care Center, Cincinnati *Also called Beechwood Terrace Care Ctr Inc* *(G-3036)*

Forest Hills Center, Columbus *Also called Serenity Center Inc* *(G-8621)*

Forest Meadow Villas, Medina *Also called Gerspacher Companies* *(G-13943)*

Forevergreen Lawn Care 440 327-8987
  38601 Sugar Ridge Rd North Ridgeville (44039) *(G-15330)*

Forge Industries Inc (PA) 330 782-8301
  4450 Market St Youngstown (44512) *(G-20040)*

Forklift of Toledo, Toledo *Also called Towlift Inc* *(G-18106)*

Formlabs Ohio Inc 419 837-9783
  27800 Lemoyne Rd Ste J Millbury (43447) *(G-14448)*

Formu3 International Inc (PA) 330 668-1461
  395 Springside Dr Akron (44333) *(G-227)*

Formwork Services LLC 513 539-4000
  900 N Garver Rd Monroe (45050) *(G-14567)*

Forrer Development Ltd 937 431-6489
  7625 Paragon Rd Ste E Dayton (45459) *(G-9445)*

Forrest Trucking Company (PA) 614 879-7347
  7 E 1st St London (43140) *(G-12864)*

Forrest Trucking Company 614 879-8642
  540 Taylor Blair Rd West Jefferson (43162) *(G-19109)*

Forsythe Technology LLC 513 697-5100
  8845 Governors Hill Dr # 201 Cincinnati (45249) *(G-3578)*

Fort Ancient State Memorial, Oregonia *Also called Dayton Society Natural History* *(G-15616)*

Fort Austin Ltd Partnership 440 892-4200
  28550 Westlake Village Dr Cleveland (44145) *(G-5564)*

Fort Dialysis LLC 330 837-7730
  2112 Lincoln Way E Massillon (44646) *(G-13683)*

Fort Hamilton Hosp Foundation 513 867-5492
  630 Eaton Ave Hamilton (45013) *(G-11596)*

Fort Hamilton Hospital (HQ) 513 867-2000
  630 Eaton Ave Hamilton (45013) *(G-11597)*

Fort Hmltn-Hghes Hlthcare Corp (PA) 513 867-2000
  630 Eaton Ave Hamilton (45013) *(G-11598)*

Fort Jennings State Bank (PA) 419 286-2527
  120 N Water St Fort Jennings (45844) *(G-10983)*

Fort Recovery Equipment Inc 419 375-1006
  1201 Industrial Dr Fort Recovery (45846) *(G-10990)*

Fort Recovery Equity Inc (PA) 419 375-4119
  2351 Wabash Rd Fort Recovery (45846) *(G-10991)*

Fort Steuben Mall, Steubenville *Also called Goodman Properties Inc* *(G-17155)*

Fort Wash Inv Advisors Inc (HQ) 513 361-7600
  303 Broadway St Ste 1100 Cincinnati (45202) *(G-3579)*

Forte Indus Eqp Systems Inc 513 398-2800
  6037 Commerce Ct Mason (45040) *(G-13581)*

Forte Industries, Mason *Also called Forte Indus Eqp Systems Inc* *(G-13581)*

Fortec Medical Inc (PA) 330 463-1265
  6245 Hudson Crossing Pkwy Hudson (44236) *(G-11978)*

Fortec Medical Inc 513 742-9100
  2050 Northwest Dr Cincinnati (45231) *(G-3580)*

Forths Foods Inc 740 886-9769
  7604 County Road 107 Proctorville (45669) *(G-16216)*

Fortis North Canton LLC 330 682-5984
  6174 Promler St Nw North Canton (44720) *(G-15204)*

FORTNEY & WEYGANDT, North Olmsted *Also called R L Fortney Management Inc* *(G-15307)*

Fortney & Weygandt Inc 440 716-4000
  31269 Bradley Rd North Olmsted (44070) *(G-15288)*

Fortune Brands Windows Inc (HQ) 614 532-3500
  3948 Townsfair Way # 200 Columbus (43219) *(G-7602)*

Fortunefavorsthe Bold LLC 216 469-2845
  11716 Detroit Ave Lakewood (44107) *(G-12344)*

Forum At Homes, Warren *Also called Dacas Nursing Systems Inc* *(G-18698)*

Forum At Knightsbridge, Columbus *Also called Sunrise Connecticut Avenue Ass* *(G-8712)*

Forum At Knightsbridge, Columbus *Also called Five Star Senior Living Inc* *(G-7592)*

Forum Manufacturing Inc 937 349-8685
  77 Brown St Milford Center (43045) *(G-14445)*

Forwith Logistics LLC 513 386-8310
  6129 Guinea Pike Milford (45150) *(G-14388)*

Fosbel Inc (HQ) 216 362-3900
  6779 Engle Rd Ste A Cleveland (44130) *(G-5565)*

Fosbel Holding Inc (PA) 216 362-3900
  20600 Sheldon Rd Cleveland (44142) *(G-5566)*

Fosdick & Hilmer Inc 513 241-5640
  525 Vine St Ste 1100 Cincinnati (45202) *(G-3581)*

Foseco Management Inc 440 826-4548
  20200 Sheldon Rd Cleveland (44142) *(G-5567)*

FOSTER CARE TO SUCCESS, Beachwood *Also called Orphan Foundation of America* *(G-1094)*

Foster Grandparent Program, Akron *Also called Akron Summit Cmnty Action Agcy* *(G-56)*

Foster J Boyd MD Regnl Cncr CT, Wilmington *Also called Clinton Memorial Hospital* *(G-19615)*

Foster Sales & Delivery Inc 740 245-0200
  35 Corporate Dr Bidwell (45614) *(G-1468)*

FOSTORIA COMMUNITY HOSPITAL, Fostoria *Also called Fostoria Hospital Association* *(G-11000)*

Fostoria Hospital Association (HQ) 419 435-7734
  501 Van Buren St Fostoria (44830) *(G-11000)*

Fostoria Mixing Center, Fostoria *Also called Norfolk Southern Corporation* *(G-11009)*

Foti Construction Company LLP 440 347-0728
  1164 Lloyd Rd Wickliffe (44092) *(G-19459)*

Foti Contracting LLC 330 656-3454
  1164 Lloyd Rd Wickliffe (44092) *(G-19460)*

Foundation For Communit (PA) 937 461-3450
  349 S Main St Dayton (45402) *(G-9446)*

FOUNDATION FOR THE FAMILY, Cincinnati *Also called Couple To Couple Leag Intl Inc* *(G-3374)*

Foundation Park Care Center, Toledo *Also called Nursing Care MGT Amer Inc* *(G-17953)*

Foundation Pk Alzheimers Care, Toledo *Also called Tlevay Inc* *(G-18070)*

Foundation Software Inc 330 220-8383
  17999 Foltz Pkwy Strongsville (44149) *(G-17305)*

Foundation Steel LLC 419 402-4241
  12525 Airport Hwy Swanton (43558) *(G-17397)*

Foundations 937 437-2311
  7739 Us Route 40 New Paris (45347) *(G-14942)*

Foundations Hlth Solutions Inc 440 793-0200
  25000 Country Club Blvd North Olmsted (44070) *(G-15289)*

Foundtion Behavioral Hlth Svcs 419 584-1000
  4761 State Route 29 Celina (45822) *(G-2595)*

Fountain City Leasing Inc 419 785-3100
  2060 E 2nd St Ste 101 Defiance (43512) *(G-9916)*

Fountain Square MGT Group LLC 513 621-4400
  1203 Walnut St Fl 4 Cincinnati (45202) *(G-3582)*

Fountainhead Nursing Home Inc 740 354-9113
  4734 Gallia Pike Franklin Furnace (45629) *(G-11044)*

Four Bridges Country Club Ltd 513 759-4620
  8300 Four Bridges Dr Liberty Township (45044) *(G-12581)*

Four Corners Cleaning Inc 330 644-0834
  3479 E Tuscarawas Ext Barberton (44203) *(G-952)*

Four County Family Center 800 693-6000
  7320 State Route 108 A Wauseon (43567) *(G-18800)*

Four Oaks Early Intervention 937 562-6779
  245 N Valley Rd Xenia (45385) *(G-19900)*

Four Points By Sheritan, Columbus *Also called Vjp Hospitality Ltd* *(G-8858)*

Four Seasons Environmental Inc (PA) 513 539-2978
  43 New Garver Rd Monroe (45050) *(G-14568)*

Four Seasons Washington LLC 740 895-6101
  201 Courthouse Pkwy Wshngtn CT Hs (43160) *(G-19873)*

Four Towers Apts, Cincinnati *Also called Ea Vica Co* *(G-3467)*

Four Wheel Drive Hardware LLC 330 482-4733
  44488 State Route 14 Columbiana (44408) *(G-6788)*

Four Winds Nursing Facility, Jackson *Also called United Church Homes Inc* *(G-12181)*

Fowler Electric Co 440 735-2385
  26185 Broadway Ave Bedford (44146) *(G-1281)*

Fowler, Gary J DDS Ms, Lima *Also called Orthodontic Associates LLC* *(G-12713)*

Fowlers Mill Golf Course, Chesterland *Also called American Golf Corporation* *(G-2736)*

Fox 8, Cleveland *Also called Fox Television Stations Inc* *(G-5568)*

Fox Cleaners Inc (PA) 937 276-4171
  4333 N Main St Dayton (45405) *(G-9447)*

Fox Den Fairways Inc 330 678-6792
  2770 Call Rd Stow (44224) *(G-17206)*

Fox Den Golf Course, Stow *Also called Fox Den Fairways Inc* *(G-17206)*

Fox International Limited Inc (PA) 216 454-1001
  23645 Merc Rd Ste B Beachwood (44122) *(G-1058)*

Fox Run Apartments, Moraine *Also called Fieldstone Limited Partnership* *(G-14658)*

Fox Run Cntr For Chldrn & Adol, Saint Clairsville *Also called Bhc Fox Run Hospital Inc* *(G-16479)*

Fox Run Manor, Findlay *Also called Hcf of Findlay Inc* *(G-10920)*

Fox Run Manor, Findlay *Also called Hcf of Fox Run Inc* ***(G-10921)***
Fox Television Stations Inc 216 431-8888
5800 S Marginal Rd Cleveland (44103) ***(G-5568)***
Foxridge Farms Corp 740 965-1369
7273 Cheshire Rd Galena (43021) ***(G-11158)***
Foxx & Company 513 241-1616
324 W 9th St Fl 5 Cincinnati (45202) ***(G-3583)***
Foxx Construction LLC, Cincinnati *Also called Fx Facility Group LLC* ***(G-3598)***
Fpt Cleveland LLC (HQ) 216 441-3800
8550 Aetna Rd Cleveland (44105) ***(G-5569)***
Fraley & Schilling Inc 740 598-4118
708 Dandy Ln Brilliant (43913) ***(G-1822)***
Fram Group Operations LLC 419 661-6700
28399 Cedar Park Blvd Perrysburg (43551) ***(G-15867)***
Frameco, Cleveland *Also called Metal Framing Enterprises LLC* ***(G-5962)***
Frameco Inc 216 433-7080
9005 Bank St Cleveland (44125) ***(G-5570)***
Francis-Schulze Co 937 295-3941
3880 Rangeline Rd Russia (45363) ***(G-16466)***
Franciscan At St Leonard 937 433-0480
8100 Clyo Rd Dayton (45458) ***(G-9448)***
Franciscan Care Ctr Sylvania 419 882-2087
4111 N Hlland Sylvania Rd Toledo (43623) ***(G-17746)***
FRANCISCAN FRIARS, Cincinnati *Also called Friars Club Inc* ***(G-3594)***
Franciscan Sisters of Chicago 440 843-7800
6765 State Rd Cleveland (44134) ***(G-5571)***
Franck and Fric Incorporated 216 524-4451
7919 Old Rockside Rd Cleveland (44131) ***(G-5572)***
Frank Gates Service Company (HQ) 614 793-8000
5000 Bradenton Ave # 100 Dublin (43017) ***(G-10231)***
Frank Messer & Sons Cnstr Co, Cincinnati *Also called Messer Construction Co* ***(G-4040)***
Frank Novak & Sons Inc 216 475-2495
23940 Miles Rd Cleveland (44128) ***(G-5573)***
Frank Paxton Lumber Company, Cincinnati *Also called Paxton Hardwoods LLC* ***(G-4216)***
Frank Santo LLC 216 831-9374
31100 Pinetree Rd Pepper Pike (44124) ***(G-15817)***
Frank's Autobody Carstar, Fairfield *Also called Franks Auto Body Shop Inc* ***(G-10729)***
Frankes Unlimited Inc 937 642-0706
825 Collins Ave Marysville (43040) ***(G-13496)***
Frankes Wood Products LLC 937 642-0706
825 Collins Ave Marysville (43040) ***(G-13497)***
Franklin & Seidelmann Inc (PA) 216 255-5700
3700 Park East Dr Ste 300 Beachwood (44122) ***(G-1059)***
Franklin & Seidelmann LLC 216 255-5700
3700 Park East Dr Ste 300 Beachwood (44122) ***(G-1060)***
Franklin Blvd Nursing HM Inc 216 651-1600
3600 Franklin Blvd Cleveland (44113) ***(G-5574)***
Franklin Cmpt Svcs Group Inc 614 431-3327
6650 Walnut St New Albany (43054) ***(G-14854)***
Franklin Cnty Bd Commissioners 614 462-3030
970 Dublin Rd Columbus (43215) ***(G-7603)***
Franklin Cnty Bd Commissioners (PA) 614 525-3322
373 S High St Fl 26 Columbus (43215) ***(G-7604)***
Franklin Cnty Bd Commissioners 614 275-2571
855 W Mound St Columbus (43223) ***(G-7605)***
Franklin Cnty Bd Commissioners 614 462-3800
373 S High St Fl 2 Columbus (43215) ***(G-7606)***
Franklin Cnty Bd Commissioners 614 462-3275
80 E Fulton St Columbus (43215) ***(G-7607)***
Franklin Cnty Bd Commissioners 614 462-3429
399 S Front St Columbus (43215) ***(G-7608)***
Franklin Cnty Bd Commissioners 614 229-7100
4071 E Main St Columbus (43213) ***(G-7609)***
Franklin Cnty Bd Commissioners 614 462-3194
373 S High St Fl 12 Columbus (43215) ***(G-7610)***
Franklin Cnty Bd Commissioners 614 462-4360
1731 Alum Creek Dr Columbus (43207) ***(G-7611)***
Franklin Cnty Crt Common Pleas 614 525-5775
373 S High St Fl 6 Columbus (43215) ***(G-7612)***
Franklin Communications Inc 614 451-2191
4401 Carriage Hill Ln Columbus (43220) ***(G-7613)***
Franklin Communications Inc 614 459-9769
4401 Carriage Hill Ln Columbus (43220) ***(G-7614)***
Franklin Community Base Correc 614 525-4600
1745 Alum Creek Dr Columbus (43207) ***(G-7615)***
Franklin County Adamh Board 614 224-1057
447 E Broad St Columbus (43215) ***(G-7616)***
Franklin County Childrens Svcs, Columbus *Also called Franklin Cnty Bd Commissioners* ***(G-7609)***
Franklin County Historical Soc 614 228-2674
333 W Broad St Columbus (43215) ***(G-7617)***
Franklin County Pub Defender, Columbus *Also called Franklin Cnty Bd Commissioners* ***(G-7610)***
Franklin County Residential S 614 844-5847
445 E Dublin Granville Rd G Worthington (43085) ***(G-19811)***
Franklin Dental Manufacturing, Dublin *Also called Perio Inc* ***(G-10308)***
Franklin Imaging Llc (PA) 614 885-6894
500 Schrock Rd Columbus (43229) ***(G-7618)***
Franklin Iron & Metal Corp 937 253-8184
1939 E 1st St Dayton (45403) ***(G-9449)***
Franklin Plaza, Cleveland *Also called Franklin Blvd Nursing HM Inc* ***(G-5574)***
Franklin Ridge Care Facility, Hamilton *Also called Carington Health Systems* ***(G-11573)***
FRANKLIN RIDGE CARE FACILITY, Newark *Also called Arlington Care Ctr* ***(G-15011)***
FRANKLIN RIDGE CARE FACILITY, Madison *Also called Madison Care Inc* ***(G-13102)***
Franklin Ridge Care Facility, Franklin *Also called Carington Health Systems* ***(G-11025)***
Franklin Shcp Inc 440 614-0160
1850 Crown Park Ct Columbus (43235) ***(G-7619)***
Franklin Specialty Trnspt Inc (HQ) 614 529-7900
2040 Atlas St Columbus (43228) ***(G-7620)***
Franklin Township Fire and Ems 513 876-2996
718 Market St Felicity (45120) ***(G-10859)***
Franks Auto Body Shop Inc 513 829-8282
5264 Dixie Hwy Fairfield (45014) ***(G-10729)***
Frans Child Care-Mansfield 419 775-2500
750 Scholl Rd Mansfield (44907) ***(G-13178)***
Frantz Ward LLP 216 515-1660
200 Public Sq Ste 3020 Cleveland (44114) ***(G-5575)***
FRATERNAL INSURANCE, Columbus *Also called Order of Unite Commercial Tra* ***(G-8385)***
Fraternal Order Eagles Inc 330 477-8059
5024 Monticello Ave Nw Canton (44708) ***(G-2316)***
Fraternal Order Eagles Inc 419 738-2582
25 E Auglaize St Wapakoneta (45895) ***(G-18642)***
Fraternal Order Eagles Inc 419 332-3961
2570 W State St Fremont (43420) ***(G-11075)***
Fraternal Order Eagles Inc 440 293-5997
6210 State Route 85 Andover (44003) ***(G-606)***
Fraternal Order of Eagles 937 323-0671
1802 Selma Rd Springfield (45505) ***(G-17040)***
Fraternal Order of Eagles BR (PA) 419 636-7812
221 S Walnut St Bryan (43506) ***(G-1957)***
Fraternal Order of Police of O (PA) 614 224-5700
222 E Town St Fl 1e Columbus (43215) ***(G-7621)***
Frazeysburg Lions Club Inc 740 828-2313
12355 Scout Rd Frazeysburg (43822) ***(G-11049)***
Frazeysburg Restaurant & Bky, Frazeysburg *Also called Calvary Christian Ch of Ohio* ***(G-11048)***
Frch Design Worldwide - Cincin 513 241-3000
311 Elm St Ste 600 Cincinnati (45202) ***(G-3584)***
Fred A Nemann Co 513 467-9400
6480 Bender Rd Cincinnati (45233) ***(G-3585)***
Fred Christen & Sons Company (PA) 419 243-4161
714 George St Toledo (43608) ***(G-17747)***
Fred Martin Nissan LLC 330 644-8888
3388 S Arlington Rd Akron (44312) ***(G-228)***
Fred Olivieri Construction Co (PA) 330 494-1007
6315 Promway Ave Nw North Canton (44720) ***(G-15205)***
Fred W Albrecht Grocery Co 330 645-6222
3235 Manchester Rd Unit A Coventry Township (44319) ***(G-9034)***
Fred W Albrecht Grocery Co 330 666-6781
3979 Medina Rd Akron (44333) ***(G-229)***
Frederick C Smith Clinic Inc (PA) 740 383-7000
1040 Delaware Ave Marion (43302) ***(G-13421)***
Frederick C Smith Clinic Inc 740 363-9021
6 Lexington Blvd Delaware (43015) ***(G-9979)***
Frederick Steel Company LLC 513 821-6400
630 Glendale Milford Rd Cincinnati (45215) ***(G-3586)***
Fredericks Landscaping Inc 513 821-9407
301 S Cooper Ave Cincinnati (45215) ***(G-3587)***
Fredericks Wine & Dine 216 581-5299
22005 Emery Rd Cleveland (44128) ***(G-5576)***
Fredrick Ramond, Avon Lake *Also called Hinkley Lighting Inc* ***(G-920)***
Fredrics Corporation (PA) 513 874-2226
7664 Voice Of America Ctr West Chester (45069) ***(G-18926)***
Free & Accepted Masons 419 822-3736
317 Cherry Tree Ln Delta (43515) ***(G-10044)***
Free Enterprises Incorporated 330 722-2031
241 S State Rd Medina (44256) ***(G-13940)***
Free Store/Food Bank Inc (PA) 513 482-4526
1250 Tennessee Ave Cincinnati (45229) ***(G-3588)***
Free Store/Food Bank Inc 513 241-1064
1250 Tennessee Ave Cincinnati (45229) ***(G-3589)***
Freedom Center, Columbus *Also called Ohio Department Youth Services* ***(G-8244)***
Freedom Enterprises Inc 419 675-1192
11441 County Road 75 Kenton (43326) ***(G-12275)***
Freedom Harley-Davidson Inc 330 494-2453
7233 Sunset Strip Ave Nw Canton (44720) ***(G-2317)***
Freedom Rv, Akron *Also called Sirpilla Recrtl Vhcl Ctr Inc* ***(G-430)***
Freedom Specialty Insurance Co (HQ) 614 249-1545
1 W Nationwide Blvd Columbus (43215) ***(G-7622)***
Freedom Steel Inc 440 266-6800
8200 Tyler Blvd Ste G Mentor (44060) ***(G-14048)***
Freedonia Publishing LLC 440 684-9600
767 Beta Dr Cleveland (44143) ***(G-5577)***
Freeland Contracting Co 614 443-2718
2100 Integrity Dr S Columbus (43209) ***(G-7623)***
Freeman Manufacturing & Sup Co (PA) 440 934-1902
1101 Moore Rd Avon (44011) ***(G-881)***
Freestore Foodbank Inc 513 482-4500
1141 Central Pkwy Cincinnati (45202) ***(G-3590)***
Freeway Lanes Bowl Group LLC 440 946-5131
7300 Palisades Pkwy Mentor (44060) ***(G-14049)***
Freeze/Arnold A Freund Legal (PA) 937 222-2424
1 S Main St Ste 1800 Dayton (45402) ***(G-9450)***

A
L
P
H
A
B
E
T
I
C

Freiberg Spine Institute, Blue Ash *Also called Orthopaedic Offices Inc* **(G-1626)**

Freight Rite Inc (PA) 419 478-7400
4352 W Sylvania Ave Ste M Toledo (43623) **(G-17748)**

Freightliner Trcks of Cncinnati 513 772-7171
1 Freightliner Dr Cincinnati (45241) **(G-3591)**

Freisthler Paving Inc 937 498-4802
2323 Campbell Rd Sidney (45365) **(G-16779)**

Freking Betz 513 721-1975
525 Vine St Fl 6 Cincinnati (45202) **(G-3592)**

Fremont Federal Credit Union (PA) 419 334-4434
315 Croghan St Fremont (43420) **(G-11076)**

Fremont Logistics LLC 419 333-0669
1301 Heinz Rd Fremont (43420) **(G-11077)**

Fremont Plant Operations, Fremont *Also called Goodwill Industries of Erie* **(G-11079)**

Fremont Regional Dialysis, Fremont *Also called Kinswa Dialysis LLC* **(G-11083)**

Fremont TMC Head Start, Fremont *Also called W S O S Community A* **(G-11105)**

French Company LLC 330 963-4344
8289 Darrow Rd Twinsburg (44087) **(G-18269)**

Frencor Inc 330 332-1203
409 E 2nd St Ste 6 Salem (44460) **(G-16544)**

Fresch Electric Inc 419 626-2535
1414 Milan Rd Sandusky (44870) **(G-16609)**

Fresenius Kdney Care W Hmilton, Hamilton *Also called Fresenius Med Care Butler Cty* **(G-11599)**

Fresenius Kidney Care, Cuyahoga Falls *Also called Ohio Renal Care Group LLC* **(G-9116)**

Fresenius Kidney Care, Gahanna *Also called Fresenius Medical Care* **(G-11120)**

Fresenius Kidney Care Milford, Milford *Also called Fresenius Med Care Milford LLC* **(G-14389)**

Fresenius Kidney Care Olentang, Columbus *Also called Bio-Mdcal Applcations Ohio Inc* **(G-7040)**

Fresenius Med Care Butler Cty 513 737-1415
890 Nw Washington Blvd Hamilton (45013) **(G-11599)**

Fresenius Med Care Cntl Ohio E, Columbus *Also called Bio-Mdcal Applcations Ohio Inc* **(G-7041)**

Fresenius Med Care Dayton W, Trotwood *Also called Bio-Mdcal Applcations Ohio Inc* **(G-18191)**

Fresenius Med Care Grove Cy, Grove City *Also called Fresenius Medical Care Vro LLC* **(G-11435)**

Fresenius Med Care Hldings Inc 216 267-1451
14670 Snow Rd Cleveland (44142) **(G-5578)**

Fresenius Med Care Hldings Inc 800 881-5101
2355 S Hamilton Rd Columbus (43232) **(G-7624)**

Fresenius Med Care Milford LLC 513 248-1690
5890 Meadow Creek Dr Milford (45150) **(G-14389)**

Fresenius Med Care Perrysburg, Perrysburg *Also called Bio-Mdcal Applcations Ohio Inc* **(G-15839)**

Fresenius Medical Care, Marion *Also called Bio-Mdical Applications RI Inc* **(G-13405)**

Fresenius Medical Care, North Olmsted *Also called Fresenius Usa Inc* **(G-15290)**

Fresenius Medical Care 614 855-3677
991 E Johnstown Rd Gahanna (43230) **(G-11120)**

Fresenius Medical Care Vro LLC 614 875-2349
3149 Farm Bank Way Grove City (43123) **(G-11435)**

Fresenius Usa Inc 330 837-2575
2474 Lincoln Way E Massillon (44646) **(G-13684)**

Fresenius Usa Inc 419 691-2475
555 Blue Heron Dr Oregon (43616) **(G-15595)**

Fresenius Usa Inc 440 734-7474
25050 Country Club Blvd # 250 North Olmsted (44070) **(G-15290)**

Fresh and Limited, Sidney *Also called Freshway Foods Inc* **(G-16780)**

Fresh Mark Inc (PA) 330 834-3669
1888 Southway St Se Massillon (44646) **(G-13685)**

Fresh Mark Inc 330 833-9870
950 Cloverleaf St Se Massillon (44646) **(G-13686)**

Fresh Mark Inc 330 832-7491
1888 Southway St Sw Massillon (44646) **(G-13687)**

Fresh Mark Sugardale, Massillon *Also called Fresh Mark Inc* **(G-13687)**

Fresh Thyme Farmers Market, Worthington *Also called Lakes Venture LLC* **(G-19819)**

Freshealth LLC 614 231-3601
3650 E 5th Ave Columbus (43219) **(G-7625)**

Freshway Foods Inc (PA) 937 498-4664
601 Stolle Ave Sidney (45365) **(G-16780)**

Freshway Foods Inc 937 498-4664
601 Stolle Ave Sidney (45365) **(G-16781)**

Freudenberg-Nok General Partnr 419 499-2502
11617 State Re 13 Milan (44846) **(G-14361)**

Frey Electric Inc 513 385-0700
5700 Cheviot Rd Ste A Cincinnati (45247) **(G-3593)**

Friars Club Inc 513 488-8777
4300 Vine St Cincinnati (45217) **(G-3594)**

Friedberg Meyers Roman 216 831-0042
28601 Chagrin Blvd # 500 Cleveland (44122) **(G-5579)**

Friedman Domiano Smith Co Lpa 216 621-0070
55 Public Sq Ste 1055 Cleveland (44113) **(G-5580)**

Friedman Management Company 614 224-2424
50 W Broad St Ste 200 Columbus (43215) **(G-7626)**

Friedman Vlg Retirement Cmnty 419 443-1540
175 Saint Francis Ave Tiffin (44883) **(G-17519)**

Friedman-Swift Associates Inc 513 772-9200
110 Boggs Ln Ste 200 Cincinnati (45246) **(G-3595)**

Friend To Friend Program 216 861-1838
4515 Superior Ave Cleveland (44103) **(G-5581)**

Friend-Ship Child Care Ctr LLC 330 484-2051
425 45th St Sw Canton (44706) **(G-2318)**

Friendly Care Agency, Pickerington *Also called Lbs International Inc* **(G-15962)**

Friendly Inn Settlement House 216 431-7656
2386 Unwin Rd Cleveland (44104) **(G-5582)**

Friendly Nursing Home Inc 937 855-2363
4339 State Route 122 Franklin (45005) **(G-11029)**

Friends Boarding Home, Waynesville *Also called Home The Friends Inc* **(G-18832)**

Friends Business Source, Findlay *Also called Friends Service Co Inc* **(G-10910)**

FRIENDS CARE CENTER, Yellow Springs *Also called Friends Health Care Assn* **(G-19939)**

Friends Health Care Assn (PA) 937 767-7363
150 E Herman St Yellow Springs (45387) **(G-19939)**

Friends of Art For Cultural 614 888-9929
191 Melyers Ct Columbus (43235) **(G-7627)**

Friends of Good Shepherd Manor 740 289-2861
374 Good Manor Rd Lucasville (45648) **(G-13049)**

Friends of The Lib Cyahoga FLS 330 928-2117
2015 3rd St Cuyahoga Falls (44221) **(G-9097)**

Friends Service Co Inc (PA) 419 427-1704
2300 Bright Rd Findlay (45840) **(G-10910)**

Friendship Home, Ashtabula *Also called Ashtabula Community Counseling* **(G-710)**

Friendship Village of Dayton, Dayton *Also called Evangelical Retirement* **(G-9419)**

Friendship Vlg of Clumbus Ohio 614 890-8287
5757 Ponderosa Dr Columbus (43231) **(G-7628)**

Friendship Vlg of Clumbus Ohio (PA) 614 890-8282
5800 Frest Hills Blvd Ofc Columbus (43231) **(G-7629)**

Friendship Vlg of Dublin Ohio 614 764-1600
6000 Riverside Dr Ofc Ofc Dublin (43017) **(G-10232)**

Frito-Lay North America Inc 513 759-1000
7781 Service Center Dr West Chester (45069) **(G-18927)**

Frito-Lay North America Inc 513 874-0112
4696 Devitt Dr West Chester (45246) **(G-19054)**

Frito-Lay North America Inc 216 491-4000
4580 Hinckley Indus Pkwy Cleveland (44109) **(G-5583)**

Frito-Lay North America Inc 937 224-8716
49 Kelly Ave Dayton (45404) **(G-9451)**

Frito-Lay North America Inc 419 893-8171
6501 Monclova Rd Maumee (43537) **(G-13794)**

Frito-Lay North America Inc 330 786-6000
1460 E Turkeyfoot Lake Rd Akron (44312) **(G-230)**

Fritz-Rumer-Cooke Co Inc 614 444-8844
635 E Woodrow Ave Columbus (43207) **(G-7630)**

Frog & Toad Inc 419 877-1180
10835 Waterville St Whitehouse (43571) **(G-19447)**

Front Leasing Co LLC 440 243-4000
255 Front St Berea (44017) **(G-1427)**

Frontgate Catalog, West Chester *Also called Cinmar LLC* **(G-18888)**

Frontier Bassmasters Inc 740 423-9293
904 Boulevard Dr Belpre (45714) **(G-1404)**

Frontier Power Company 740 622-6755
770 S 2nd St Coshocton (43812) **(G-9015)**

Frontier Security LLC 937 247-2824
1041 Byers Rd Miamisburg (45342) **(G-14172)**

Frontier Tank Center Inc 330 659-3888
3800 Congress Pkwy Richfield (44286) **(G-16358)**

Frontier Technology Inc (PA) 937 429-3302
4141 Colonel Glenn Hwy # 140 Beavercreek Township (45431) **(G-1248)**

Frontline National LLC 513 528-7823
502 Techne Center Dr G Milford (45150) **(G-14390)**

Frontline Service, Cleveland *Also called Mental Health Services* **(G-5953)**

Frost Brown Todd LLC (PA) 513 651-6800
3300 Grt Amrcn Towe 301e Cincinnati (45202) **(G-3596)**

Frost Brown Todd LLC 614 464-1211
1 Columbus Ste 2300 10 W Columbus (43215) **(G-7631)**

Frost Roofing Inc 419 739-2701
2 Broadway St Wapakoneta (45895) **(G-18643)**

Frs Counseling Inc (PA) 937 393-0585
104 Erin Ct Hillsboro (45133) **(G-11840)**

Frs Counselling, Hillsboro *Also called F R S Connections* **(G-11838)**

Fruits of The Earth, Grove City *Also called Circle S Farms Inc* **(G-11420)**

Fruth & Co (PA) 419 435-8541
601 Parkway Dr Ste A Fostoria (44830) **(G-11001)**

Fryman-Kuck General Contrs Inc 937 274-2892
5150 Webster St Dayton (45414) **(G-9452)**

FSI Disposal, Clyde *Also called Fultz & Son Inc* **(G-6743)**

Fsmg, Cincinnati *Also called Fountain Square MGT Group LLC* **(G-3582)**

FSRc Tanks Inc 234 221-2015
11029 Industrial Pkwy Nw Bolivar (44612) **(G-1703)**

Ftech R&D North America Inc (HQ) 937 339-2777
1191 Horizon West Ct Troy (45373) **(G-18202)**

Fti, Beavercreek Township *Also called Frontier Technology Inc* **(G-1248)**

FTM Associates LLC 614 846-1834
150 E Campus View Blvd Columbus (43235) **(G-7632)**

Fts International Inc 330 754-2375
1520 Wood Ave Se East Canton (44730) **(G-10386)**

Fuchs Franklin Div, Twinsburg *Also called Fuchs Lubricants Co* **(G-18270)**

Fuchs Lubricants Co 330 963-0400
  8036 Bavaria Rd Twinsburg (44087) *(G-18270)*
Fujiyama International Inc 614 891-2224
  5755 Cleveland Ave Columbus (43231) *(G-7633)*
Fulfillment Technologies LLC 513 346-3100
  5389 E Provident Dr West Chester (45246) *(G-19055)*
Full Range Rehab LLC 513 330-5995
  4722 Interstate Dr Ste K West Chester (45246) *(G-19056)*
Fuller & Henry Ltd (PA) 419 247-2500
  1 Seagate Ste 1700 Toledo (43604) *(G-17749)*
Fullton Mill Services, Delta *Also called Edw C Levy Co (G-10042)*
Fulton County Alano Club, Wauseon *Also called Alano Club Inc (G-18796)*
Fulton County Health Center 419 335-2017
  725 S Shoop Ave Wauseon (43567) *(G-18801)*
Fulton County Health Center 419 337-8661
  725 S Shoop Ave Wauseon (43567) *(G-18802)*
Fulton County Health Center (PA) 419 335-2015
  725 S Shoop Ave Wauseon (43567) *(G-18803)*
Fulton County Health Dept 419 337-0915
  606 S Shoop Ave Wauseon (43567) *(G-18804)*
Fulton County Senior Center 419 337-9299
  240 Clinton St Wauseon (43567) *(G-18805)*
Fulton Manor Nursing Home, Wauseon *Also called Fulton County Health Center (G-18801)*
Fulton Stress Unit, Wauseon *Also called Fulton County Health Center (G-18802)*
Fultz & Son Inc 419 547-9365
  100 S Main St Clyde (43410) *(G-6743)*
Fun Day Events LLC 740 549-9000
  947 E Johnstown Rd # 163 Gahanna (43230) *(G-11121)*
Fun Makers, Tallmadge *Also called Heaven Bound Ascensions (G-17477)*
Fun n Stuff Amusements Inc 330 467-0821
  661 Highland Rd E Macedonia (44056) *(G-13069)*
Funai Service Corporation 614 409-2600
  2425 Spiegel Dr Groveport (43125) *(G-11514)*
Fund Evaluation Group LLC (PA) 513 977-4400
  201 E 5th St Ste 1600 Cincinnati (45202) *(G-3597)*
Funke & Co Hair Design, Beachwood *Also called Karen Funke Inc (G-1072)*
Funky People, Wooster *Also called Classic Imports Inc (G-19706)*
Funny Bone Comedy Club & Cafe 614 471-5653
  145 Easton Town Ctr Columbus (43219) *(G-7634)*
Funtime Parks Inc 330 562-7131
  1060 N Aurora Rd Aurora (44202) *(G-827)*
Furbay Electric Supply Co (PA) 330 454-3033
  208 Schroyer Ave Sw Canton (44702) *(G-2319)*
Furlong, Lawrence P CPA, Norwalk *Also called Payne Nickles & Co CPA (G-15452)*
Furney Group Home 419 389-0152
  4656 Glendale Ave Toledo (43614) *(G-17750)*
Furniture Bank Central Ohio 614 272-9544
  118 S Yale Ave Columbus (43222) *(G-7635)*
FURNITURE WITH A HEART, Columbus *Also called Furniture Bank Central Ohio (G-7635)*
Fusion Alliance LLC 614 852-8000
  440 Polaris Pkwy Ste 500 Westerville (43082) *(G-19167)*
Fusion Alliance LLC 513 563-8444
  4555 Lake Forest Dr # 325 Blue Ash (45242) *(G-1565)*
Fusion Ceramics Inc 330 627-5821
  237 High St Sw Carrollton (44615) *(G-2569)*
Fusion Interior Services Ltd (PA) 513 759-4100
  9823 Cincinnati Dayton Rd West Chester (45069) *(G-18928)*
Futura Banc Corp (PA) 937 653-1167
  601 Scioto St Urbana (43078) *(G-18434)*
Futura Design Service Inc 937 890-5252
  6001 N Dixie Dr Dayton (45414) *(G-9453)*
Future Advantage Inc 330 686-7707
  4923 Hudson Dr Stow (44224) *(G-17207)*
Future Poly Tech Inc (PA) 614 942-1209
  2215 Citygate Dr Ste D Columbus (43219) *(G-7636)*
Fuyao Glass America Inc (HQ) 937 496-5777
  2801 W Stroop Rd Dayton (45439) *(G-9454)*
Fwlm, Chagrin Falls *Also called For Women Like Me Inc (G-2645)*
Fx Digital Media Inc (PA) 216 241-4040
  1600 E 23rs St Rs Cleveland (44114) *(G-5584)*
Fx Facility Group LLC (HQ) 513 639-2509
  324 W 9th St Cincinnati (45202) *(G-3598)*
Fyda Freightliner Youngstown 330 797-0224
  5260 76 Dr Youngstown (44515) *(G-20041)*
Fyda Truck & Equipment, Youngstown *Also called Fyda Freightliner Youngstown (G-20041)*
G & D Alternative Living Inc 937 446-2803
  121 Charles St Sardinia (45171) *(G-16659)*
G & D Twinsburg, Twinsburg *Also called Giesecke & Devrient Amer Inc (G-18274)*
G & G Concrete Cnstr LLC 614 475-4151
  2849 Switzer Ave Columbus (43219) *(G-7637)*
G & G Investment LLC 513 984-0300
  4901 Hunt Rd Ste 300 Blue Ash (45242) *(G-1566)*
G & J Kartway, Camden *Also called Barnets Inc (G-2088)*
G & J Pepsi-Cola Bottlers Inc 740 354-9191
  4587 Gallia Pike Franklin Furnace (45629) *(G-11045)*
G & J Pepsi-Cola Bottlers Inc 740 774-2148
  400 E 7th St Chillicothe (45601) *(G-2782)*
G & J Pepsi-Cola Bottlers Inc 740 593-3366
  2001 E State St Athens (45701) *(G-781)*
G & J Pepsi-Cola Bottlers Inc 937 393-5744
  3500 Progress Way Wilmington (45177) *(G-19624)*

G & J Pepsi-Cola Bottlers Inc 740 452-2721
  335 N 6th St Zanesville (43701) *(G-20309)*
G & O Resources Ltd 330 253-2525
  96 E Crosier St Akron (44311) *(G-231)*
G & S Metal Products Co Inc 216 831-2388
  26840 Fargo Ave Cleveland (44146) *(G-5585)*
G & S Transfer Inc 330 673-3899
  4055 Highway View Dr A Kent (44240) *(G-12233)*
G Big Inc (PA) 740 867-5758
  441 Rockwood Ave Chesapeake (45619) *(G-2729)*
G E G Enterprises Inc 330 494-9160
  4080 Fulton Dr Nw Canton (44718) *(G-2320)*
G E G Enterprises Inc (PA) 330 477-3133
  4345 Tuscarawas St W Canton (44708) *(G-2321)*
G E S, Parma *Also called Ges Graphite Inc (G-15767)*
G F S Marketplace, Ontario *Also called Gordon Food Service Inc (G-15550)*
G F S Marketplace, Lima *Also called Gordon Food Service Inc (G-12646)*
G F S Marketplace, Mentor *Also called Gordon Food Service Inc (G-14052)*
G F S Marketplace, Cleveland *Also called Gordon Food Service Inc (G-5616)*
G G Marck & Associates Inc (PA) 419 478-0900
  300 Phillips Ave Toledo (43612) *(G-17751)*
G H A Inc 440 729-2130
  12670 W Geauga Plz Chesterland (44026) *(G-2739)*
G III Reitter Walls LLC 614 545-4444
  1759 Old Leonard Ave Columbus (43219) *(G-7638)*
G J Goudreau & Co (PA) 216 351-5233
  9701 Brookpark Rd Ste 200 Cleveland (44129) *(G-5586)*
G J Goudreau Operating Co 216 741-7524
  9701 Brookpark Rd Ste 200 Cleveland (44129) *(G-5587)*
G K Packaging, Wshngtn CT Hs *Also called Washington Court Hse Holdg LLC (G-19885)*
G M A C Insurance Center, Hudson *Also called Pasco Inc (G-12001)*
G M A Surgery Inc 937 429-7350
  3359 Kemp Rd Ste 120 Beavercreek (45431) *(G-1153)*
G M N Tri Cnty Community Action (PA) 740 732-2388
  615 North St Caldwell (43724) *(G-2039)*
G M Z, West Chester *Also called CL Zimmerman Delaware LLC (G-18890)*
G Mechanical Inc 614 844-6750
  6635 Singletree Dr Columbus (43229) *(G-7639)*
G P M C, Dublin *Also called Gemini Properties (G-10234)*
G P Properties, Marion *Also called Ted Graham (G-13463)*
G P S Fire Equipment, Cleveland *Also called Gene Ptacek Son Fire Eqp Inc (G-5602)*
G R B Inc (PA) 800 628-9195
  6392 Gano Rd West Chester (45069) *(G-18929)*
G R C, Mason *Also called General Revenue Corporation (G-13586)*
G Robert Toney & Assoc Inc (PA) 216 391-1900
  5401 N Marginal Rd Cleveland (44114) *(G-5588)*
G S S, Springboro *Also called Graphic Systems Services Inc (G-16967)*
G S Wiring Systems Inc (HQ) 419 423-7111
  1801 Production Dr Findlay (45840) *(G-10911)*
G Stephens Inc 614 227-0304
  1175 Dublin Rd Ste 2 Columbus (43215) *(G-7640)*
G W S, West Chester *Also called Global Workplace Solutions LLC (G-18933)*
G&A Marketing, Cincinnati *Also called Gunning & Assocaites Marketing (G-3663)*
G&K Services LLC (HQ) 952 912-5500
  6800 Cintas Blvd Mason (45040) *(G-13582)*
G&K Services LLC 937 873-4500
  1202 Dyton Yllow Sprng Rd Fairborn (45324) *(G-10675)*
G-Cor Automotive Corp (PA) 614 443-6735
  2100 Refugee Rd Columbus (43207) *(G-7641)*
G. S. I., Vienna *Also called Glowe-Smith Industrial Inc (G-18579)*
G4s Secure Solutions (usa) 513 874-0941
  625 Eden Park Dr Ste 700 Cincinnati (45202) *(G-3599)*
G4s Secure Solutions USA Inc 614 322-5100
  2211 Lake Club Dr Ste 105 Columbus (43232) *(G-7642)*
G7 Services Inc 937 256-3473
  1524 E 2nd St Dayton (45403) *(G-9455)*
GA Business Purchaser LLC 419 255-8400
  3222 W Central Ave Toledo (43606) *(G-17752)*
Gables At Green Pastures 937 642-3893
  390 Gables Dr Marysville (43040) *(G-13498)*
Gables Care Center Inc 740 937-2900
  351 Lahm Dr Hopedale (43976) *(G-11936)*
Gade Nursing Home 2, Greenville *Also called Village Green Healthcare Ctr (G-11399)*
Gahanna Animal Hospital Inc 614 471-2201
  144 W Johnstown Rd Gahanna (43230) *(G-11122)*
Gahanna Health Care Center 614 475-7222
  121 James Rd Columbus (43230) *(G-7643)*
Gahanna-Jefferson Pub Schl Dst 614 751-7581
  782 Science Blvd Columbus (43230) *(G-7644)*
Galaxie Industrial Svcs LLC 330 503-2334
  837 E Western Reserve Rd Youngstown (44514) *(G-20042)*
Galaxy Associates Inc (HQ) 513 731-6350
  3630 E Kemper Rd Cincinnati (45241) *(G-3600)*
Galaxy Balloons Incorporated 216 476-3360
  11750 Berea Rd Ste 3 Cleveland (44111) *(G-5589)*
Gale Insulation, Hamilton *Also called Truteam LLC (G-11649)*
Gale Insulation, Columbus *Also called Builder Services Group Inc (G-7095)*
Gale Insulation, Hamilton *Also called Builder Services Group Inc (G-11560)*

Galia County Council On Aging, Gallipolis *Also called Area Agency On Aging Dst 7 Inc* ***(G-11185)***
Galion Community Center YMCA......419 468-7754
500 Gill Ave Galion (44833) ***(G-11173)***
Galion Community Hospital......419 468-4841
269 Portland Way S Galion (44833) ***(G-11174)***
Galion Dialysis, Galion *Also called Steele Dialysis LLC* ***(G-11182)***
Galion East Ohio I LP......216 520-1250
1300 Harding Way E Galion (44833) ***(G-11175)***
Gallagher Bassett Services......614 764-7616
545 Metro Pl S Ste 250 Dublin (43017) ***(G-10233)***
Gallagher Benefit Services Inc......216 623-2600
1100 Superior Ave E # 1700 Cleveland (44114) ***(G-5590)***
Gallagher Gams Pryor Tallan......614 228-5151
471 E Broad St Fl 19 Columbus (43215) ***(G-7645)***
Gallagher Sharp......216 241-5310
1501 Euclid Ave Fl 7 Cleveland (44115) ***(G-5591)***
Gallagher Sks, Cincinnati *Also called Arthur J Gallagher & Co* ***(G-2991)***
Gallco Inc......740 446-3775
77 Mill Creek Rd Gallipolis (45631) ***(G-11192)***
GALLCO INDUSTRIES, Gallipolis *Also called Gallco Inc* ***(G-11192)***
Gallery Holdings LLC......773 693-6220
6111 Oak Tree Blvd Independence (44131) ***(G-12076)***
Gallia County Engineer, Gallipolis *Also called County of Gallia* ***(G-11189)***
Gallia County Human Services, Gallipolis *Also called County of Gallia* ***(G-11187)***
Gallia-Meigs Community Action (PA)......740 367-7341
8010 State Route 7 N Cheshire (45620) ***(G-2734)***
Gallipolis Auto Auction Inc......740 446-1576
286 Upper River Rd Gallipolis (45631) ***(G-11193)***
Gallipolis Care LLC......740 446-7112
170 Pinecrest Dr Gallipolis (45631) ***(G-11194)***
Gallipolis Developmental Ctr, Gallipolis *Also called Develpmntal Dsblties Ohio Dept* ***(G-11190)***
Gallipolis Hospitality Inc......740 446-0090
577 State Route 7 N Gallipolis (45631) ***(G-11195)***
Gallipolis Municipal Pool, Gallipolis *Also called City of Gallipolis* ***(G-11186)***
Gallon Takacs Boissoneault & S (PA)......419 843-2001
3516 Granite Cir Toledo (43617) ***(G-17753)***
Gallon, E S Associates, Moraine *Also called E S Gallon & Associates* ***(G-14650)***
Galt Enterprises Inc......216 464-6744
34555 Chagrin Blvd # 100 Moreland Hills (44022) ***(G-14710)***
Gamble Elzbeth Dcness HM Assn (PA)......513 751-4224
2139 Auburn Ave Cincinnati (45219) ***(G-3601)***
Gamma PHI Beta Sorority Alpha......937 324-3436
628 Woodlawn Ave Springfield (45504) ***(G-17041)***
Ganley Lincoln Middleburg Hts, Cleveland *Also called Broadvue Motors Inc* ***(G-5084)***
Gannet Fleming Engr & Archt, Westerville *Also called Gannett Fleming Inc* ***(G-19257)***
Gannett Fleming Inc......614 794-9424
4151 Executive Pkwy # 350 Westerville (43081) ***(G-19257)***
Gannett Media Tech Intl (HQ)......513 665-3777
312 Elm St Ste 2g Cincinnati (45202) ***(G-3602)***
Ganzfair Investment Inc......614 792-6630
231 Clubhouse Dr Delaware (43015) ***(G-9980)***
Ganzhorn Suites Inc......614 356-9810
10272 Sawmill Pkwy Powell (43065) ***(G-16195)***
Garage, The, Chillicothe *Also called County Engineers Office* ***(G-2771)***
Garber Ag Freight Inc......937 548-8400
4667 Us Route 127 Greenville (45331) ***(G-11378)***
Garber Connect, Englewood *Also called Garber Electrical Contrs Inc* ***(G-10587)***
Garber Electrical Contrs Inc......937 771-5202
100 Rockridge Rd Englewood (45322) ***(G-10587)***
Garbry Ridge Assisted Living......937 778-9385
1567 Garbry Rd Piqua (45356) ***(G-16005)***
Garcia Surveyors Inc (PA)......419 877-0400
6655 Providence St Whitehouse (43571) ***(G-19448)***
Garda CL Great Lakes Inc......614 863-4044
201 Schofield Dr Columbus (43213) ***(G-7646)***
Garda CL Great Lakes Inc......419 385-2411
3635 Marine Rd Toledo (43609) ***(G-17754)***
Garda CL Great Lakes Inc (HQ)......561 939-7000
201 Schofield Dr Columbus (43213) ***(G-7647)***
Garda CL Technical Svcs Inc......937 294-4099
2690 Lance Dr Moraine (45409) ***(G-14660)***
Garden II Leasing Co LLC......419 381-0037
1015 Garden Lake Pkwy Toledo (43614) ***(G-17755)***
Garden Manor Extended Care Cen......513 420-5972
6898 Hmlton Middletown Rd Middletown (45044) ***(G-14300)***
Garden Street Iron & Metal (PA)......513 853-3700
2885 Spring Grove Ave Cincinnati (45225) ***(G-3603)***
Gardeners Edge, Piqua *Also called A M Leonard Inc* ***(G-15994)***
Gardenland, Toledo *Also called Dennis Top Soil & Landscaping* ***(G-17697)***
Gardenlife Inc......800 241-7333
11335 Concord Hambden Rd Concord Twp (44077) ***(G-8945)***
Gardens At Celina The, Celina *Also called Peregrine Health Services Inc* ***(G-2606)***
Gardens At Wapakoneta......419 738-0725
505 Walnut St Wapakoneta (45895) ***(G-18644)***
Gardens Western Reserve Inc (PA)......330 342-9100
9975 Greentree Pkwy Streetsboro (44241) ***(G-17252)***
Gardens Western Reserve Inc......330 928-4500
45 Chart Rd Cuyahoga Falls (44223) ***(G-9098)***
Gardiner Service Company LLC (PA)......440 248-3400
31200 Bainbridge Rd Ste 1 Solon (44139) ***(G-16850)***
Gardner Inc (PA)......614 456-4000
3641 Interchange Rd Columbus (43204) ***(G-7648)***
Gardner Cement Contractors......419 389-0768
821 Warehouse Rd Toledo (43615) ***(G-17756)***
Gardner-Connell LLC......614 456-4000
3641 Interchange Rd Columbus (43204) ***(G-7649)***
Gareat Sports Complex, Geneva *Also called Geneva Area Recreational* ***(G-11242)***
Garfield Hts Coach Line Inc......440 232-4550
119 Manor Brook Dr Chagrin Falls (44022) ***(G-2646)***
Garick LLC......937 462-8350
11000 Huntington Rd B South Charleston (45368) ***(G-16924)***
Garland Group Inc......614 294-4411
48 E 15th Ave Frnt Columbus (43201) ***(G-7650)***
Garland/Dbs Inc......216 641-7500
3800 E 91st St Cleveland (44105) ***(G-5592)***
Garmann Miller Architects, Minster *Also called Garmann/Miller & Assoc Inc* ***(G-14533)***
Garmann/Miller & Assoc Inc......419 628-4240
38 S Lincoln Dr Minster (45865) ***(G-14533)***
Garner Transportation Group, Findlay *Also called Garner Trucking Inc* ***(G-10912)***
Garner Trucking Inc......419 422-5742
9291 County Road 313 Findlay (45840) ***(G-10912)***
Garretson Resolution Group, Loveland *Also called Epiq Systems Inc* ***(G-12993)***
Garretyson Frm Resolution Grp......513 794-0400
6281 Tri Ridge Blvd # 300 Loveland (45140) ***(G-12995)***
Gary's Place, Canton *Also called G E G Enterprises Inc* ***(G-2321)***
Gary's Place Salon & Spa, Canton *Also called G E G Enterprises Inc* ***(G-2320)***
Gary's Prescription Pharmacy, Eaton *Also called Ancillary Medical Investments* ***(G-10436)***
Garys Pharmacy Inc......937 456-5777
125 Amelia Dr Eaton (45320) ***(G-10446)***
Gas Natural Inc., Cleveland *Also called Hearthstone Utilities Inc* ***(G-5679)***
Gaslite Villa Convalescent Ctr......330 494-4500
7055 High Mill Ave Nw Canal Fulton (44614) ***(G-2095)***
Gaspar Inc......330 477-2222
1545 Whipple Ave Sw Canton (44710) ***(G-2322)***
Gastrntrlogy Assoc Clvland Inc (PA)......216 593-7700
3700 Park East Dr Ste 100 Cleveland (44122) ***(G-5593)***
Gastroenterology Associates......330 493-1480
4665 Belpar St Nw Canton (44718) ***(G-2323)***
Gatesair Inc (HQ)......513 459-3400
5300 Kings Island Dr Mason (45040) ***(G-13583)***
Gateway Concrete Forming Svcs......513 353-2000
5938 Hamilton Cleves Rd Miamitown (45041) ***(G-14241)***
Gateway Distribution Inc (PA)......513 891-4477
11755 Lebanon Rd Cincinnati (45241) ***(G-3604)***
Gateway Electric Incorporated......216 518-5500
4450 Johnston Pkwy Ste A Cleveland (44128) ***(G-5594)***
Gateway Family House......216 531-5400
1 Gateway Euclid (44119) ***(G-10636)***
Gateway Health Care Center......216 486-4949
3 Gateway Cleveland (44119) ***(G-5595)***
Gateway Hospitality Group Inc (PA)......330 405-9800
8921 Canyon Falls Blvd # 140 Twinsburg (44087) ***(G-18271)***
Gateway Products Recycling Inc (PA)......216 341-8777
4223 E 49th St Cleveland (44125) ***(G-5596)***
Gateway Recycling, Cleveland *Also called Gateway Products Recycling Inc* ***(G-5596)***
Gateways To Better Living Inc......330 480-9870
945 W Rayen Ave Youngstown (44502) ***(G-20043)***
Gateways To Better Living Inc......330 270-0952
230 Idaho Rd Youngstown (44515) ***(G-20044)***
Gateways To Better Living Inc......330 797-1764
3220 S Raccoon Rd Canfield (44406) ***(G-2138)***
Gateways To Better Living Inc (PA)......330 792-2854
6000 Mahoning Ave Ste 234 Youngstown (44515) ***(G-20045)***
Gavin AEP Plant......740 925-3166
7397 State Route 7 N Cheshire (45620) ***(G-2735)***
Gavin Scott Salon & Spa, Hudson *Also called Kristie Warner* ***(G-11992)***
Gaydosh Associates, Cleveland *Also called Royalton Financial Group* ***(G-6347)***
Gaymont Nursing Center, Norwalk *Also called Gaymont Nursing Homes Inc* ***(G-15439)***
Gaymont Nursing Homes Inc......419 668-8258
66 Norwood Ave Norwalk (44857) ***(G-15439)***
Gayston Corporation......937 743-6050
721 Richard St Miamisburg (45342) ***(G-14173)***
Gb Liquidating Company Inc......513 248-7600
22 Whitney Dr Milford (45150) ***(G-14391)***
GBA Architectural Pdts Svcs, Medina *Also called Medina Glass Block Inc* ***(G-13974)***
Gbc Design Inc......330 283-6870
565 White Pond Dr Akron (44320) ***(G-232)***
Gbq Consulting LLC......614 221-1120
230 West St Ste 700 Columbus (43215) ***(G-7651)***
Gbq Holdings LLC (PA)......614 221-1120
230 West St Ste 700 Columbus (43215) ***(G-7652)***
GBS Corp (PA)......330 494-5330
7233 Freedom Ave Nw North Canton (44720) ***(G-15206)***
GBS Corp......330 797-2700
1035 N Meridian Rd Youngstown (44509) ***(G-20046)***
GBS Printech Solutions, North Canton *Also called GBS Corp* ***(G-15206)***
Gc At Stonelick Hills......513 735-4653
3155 Sherilyn Ln Batavia (45103) ***(G-1000)***

Gc Neighborhood Ctrs Assoc Inc.....216 298-4440
1814 E 40th St Ste 4d Cleveland (44103) ***(G-5597)***
Gca Services Group Inc (HQ).....800 422-8760
1350 Euclid Ave Ste 1500 Cleveland (44115) ***(G-5598)***
Gccvb, Columbus *Also called Greatr Columbus Conventn & Vis* ***(G-7694)***
GCHA, Cleveland *Also called Greater Clvland Halthcare Assn* ***(G-5640)***
Gcha.....216 696-6900
1226 Huron Rd E Cleveland (44115) ***(G-5599)***
GCI Construction LLC (PA).....216 831-6100
25101 Chagrin Blvd Beachwood (44122) ***(G-1061)***
GE Aviation Systems LLC.....513 786-4555
7831 Ashford Glen Ct West Chester (45069) ***(G-18930)***
GE Aviation Systems LLC.....937 474-9397
111 River Park Dr Dayton (45409) ***(G-9456)***
GE Aviation Systems LLC.....937 898-5881
740 E National Rd Vandalia (45377) ***(G-18524)***
GE Engine Services LLC.....513 977-1500
201 W Crescentville Rd Cincinnati (45246) ***(G-3605)***
GE Reuter Stokes.....216 749-6332
4710 Elizabeth Ln Cleveland (44144) ***(G-5600)***
Gear's Florists & Garden Ctrs, Cincinnati *Also called Gears Garden Center Inc* ***(G-3606)***
Gearity Early Child Care Ctr.....216 371-7356
2323 Wrenford Rd Cleveland (44118) ***(G-5601)***
Gears Garden Center Inc (PA).....513 931-3800
1579 Goodman Ave Cincinnati (45224) ***(G-3606)***
Geary Family YMCA Fostria.....419 435-6608
154 W Center St Fostoria (44830) ***(G-11002)***
Geauga Cnty Visiting Nurse Svc, Chardon *Also called Visiting Nurse Service Inc* ***(G-2723)***
Geauga County General Hlth Dst, Chardon *Also called Geauga County Health District* ***(G-2695)***
Geauga County Health District.....440 279-1940
470 Center St Bldg 8 Chardon (44024) ***(G-2695)***
Geauga County Jobs & Fmly Svcs, Chardon *Also called County of Geauga* ***(G-2692)***
Geauga Mechanical Company.....440 285-2000
12585 Chardon Windsor Rd Chardon (44024) ***(G-2696)***
Geauga Savings Bank (PA).....440 564-9441
10800 Kinsman Rd Newbury (44065) ***(G-15121)***
Gecu, Cincinnati *Also called General Electric Credit Union* ***(G-3612)***
Ged Holdings Inc.....330 963-5401
9280 Dutton Dr Twinsburg (44087) ***(G-18272)***
Geddis Paving & Excavating Inc.....419 536-8501
1019 Wamba Ave Toledo (43607) ***(G-17757)***
Geeaa Park Golf Course, Cincinnati *Also called General Electric Employees* ***(G-3613)***
Geeta Hospitality Inc.....937 642-3777
16610 Square Dr Marysville (43040) ***(G-13499)***
Geico General Insurance Co.....513 794-3426
5050 Section Ave Ste 420 Cincinnati (45212) ***(G-3607)***
Geier School Company, Cincinnati *Also called Primrose School of Symmes* ***(G-4280)***
Geis Companies, Streetsboro *Also called Geis Construction Inc* ***(G-17253)***
Geis Company, Streetsboro *Also called Highland Som Development* ***(G-17256)***
Geis Construction Inc.....330 528-3500
10020 Aurora Hudson Rd Streetsboro (44241) ***(G-17253)***
Gem City Urologist Inc (PA).....937 832-8400
9000 N Main St Ste 333 Englewood (45415) ***(G-10588)***
Gem City Waterproofing.....937 220-6800
1424 Stanley Ave Dayton (45404) ***(G-9457)***
Gem Edwards Inc.....330 342-8300
5640 Hudson Indus Pkwy Hudson (44236) ***(G-11979)***
Gem Electric.....440 286-6200
12577 Gar Hwy Chardon (44024) ***(G-2697)***
Gem Industrial Inc (HQ).....419 666-6554
6842 Commodore Dr Walbridge (43465) ***(G-18622)***
Gem Interiors Inc.....513 831-6535
769 Us Route 50 Milford (45150) ***(G-14392)***
Gemco Medical, Hudson *Also called Gem Edwards Inc* ***(G-11979)***
Gemini Advertising Associates.....513 896-3541
1637 Dixie Hwy Hamilton (45011) ***(G-11600)***
Gemini Eye Care Center, Huber Heights *Also called James D Egbert Optometrist* ***(G-11955)***
Gemini Properties.....419 531-9211
3501 Executive Pkwy Ofc Toledo (43606) ***(G-17758)***
Gemini Properties.....614 764-2800
6470 Post Rd Ofc Dublin (43016) ***(G-10234)***
Genbanc.....419 855-8381
801 Main St Genoa (43430) ***(G-11254)***
Genco, Lockbourne *Also called Fedex Supply Chain* ***(G-12819)***
Genco Atc, Lockbourne *Also called Fedex Sup Chain Dist Sys Inc* ***(G-12818)***
Genco Marketing Place, Massillon *Also called Genco of Lebanon Inc* ***(G-13688)***
Genco of Lebanon Inc.....330 837-0561
4300 Sterilite St Se Massillon (44646) ***(G-13688)***
Gene Ptacek Son Fire Eqp Inc (PA).....216 651-8300
7310 Associate Ave Cleveland (44144) ***(G-5602)***
Gene Stevens Auto & Truck Ctr.....419 429-2000
1033 Bright Rd Findlay (45840) ***(G-10913)***
Gene Stevens Honda, Findlay *Also called Gene Stevens Auto & Truck Ctr* ***(G-10913)***
Gene Tolliver Corp.....440 324-7727
6222 Norwalk Rd Medina (44256) ***(G-13941)***
General Audit Corp.....419 993-2900
2348 Baton Rouge Ste A Lima (45805) ***(G-12642)***
General Building Maintenance.....330 682-2238
500 Jefferson Ave Orrville (44667) ***(G-15633)***
General Crane Rental LLC.....330 908-0001
9680 Freeway Dr Macedonia (44056) ***(G-13070)***
General Data Company Inc (PA).....513 752-7978
4354 Ferguson Dr Cincinnati (45245) ***(G-2853)***
General Electric Company.....216 883-1000
4477 E 49th St Cleveland (44125) ***(G-5603)***
General Electric Company.....513 977-1500
201 W Crescentville Rd Cincinnati (45246) ***(G-3608)***
General Electric Company.....330 256-5331
2914 Cedar Hill Rd Cuyahoga Falls (44223) ***(G-9099)***
General Electric Company.....937 587-2631
1200 Jaybird Rd Peebles (45660) ***(G-15801)***
General Electric Company.....614 527-1078
3455 Mill Run Dr Hilliard (43026) ***(G-11768)***
General Electric Company.....513 583-3626
4800 Parkway Dr Ste 100 Mason (45040) ***(G-13584)***
General Electric Company.....330 433-5163
4500 Munson St Nw Canton (44718) ***(G-2324)***
General Electric Company.....937 534-6920
950 Forrer Blvd Dayton (45420) ***(G-9458)***
General Electric Company.....513 552-2000
1 Neumann Way Cincinnati (45215) ***(G-3609)***
General Electric Company.....513 530-7107
11240 Cornell Park Dr # 114 Blue Ash (45242) ***(G-1567)***
General Electric Company.....440 255-0930
8696 Applewood Ct Mentor (44060) ***(G-14050)***
General Electric Company.....513 583-3500
8700 Governors Hill Dr Cincinnati (45249) ***(G-3610)***
General Electric Company.....937 534-2000
950 Forrer Blvd Dayton (45420) ***(G-9459)***
General Electric Company.....513 243-9404
2411 Glendale Milford Rd Cincinnati (45241) ***(G-3611)***
General Electric Credit Union (PA).....513 243-4328
10485 Reading Rd Cincinnati (45241) ***(G-3612)***
General Electric Employees.....513 243-2129
12110 Princeton Pike Cincinnati (45246) ***(G-3613)***
General Electric Intl Inc (HQ).....617 443-3000
191 Rosa Parks St Cincinnati (45202) ***(G-3614)***
General Electric Intl Inc.....330 963-2066
8941 Dutton Dr Twinsburg (44087) ***(G-18273)***
General Factory Sups Co Inc.....513 681-6300
4811 Winton Rd Cincinnati (45232) ***(G-3615)***
General Fncl Tax Cnsulting LLC.....888 496-2679
1004 Seabrook Way Cincinnati (45245) ***(G-2854)***
General Mills Inc.....513 770-0558
5181 Natorp Blvd Ste 540 Mason (45040) ***(G-13585)***
General Motors LLC.....513 874-0535
9287 Meridian Way West Chester (45069) ***(G-18931)***
General Motors LLC.....513 603-6600
8752 Jacquemin Dr West Chester (45069) ***(G-18932)***
General Parts Inc.....330 220-6500
2830 Carquest Dr Brunswick (44212) ***(G-1931)***
General Parts Inc.....614 267-5197
2825 Silver Dr Columbus (43211) ***(G-7653)***
General Pest Control Company.....216 252-7140
3561 W 105th St Cleveland (44111) ***(G-5604)***
General Plastex Inc.....330 745-7775
35 Stuver Pl Barberton (44203) ***(G-953)***
General Refrigeration, South Point *Also called Dickson Industrial Park Inc* ***(G-16931)***
General Revenue Corporation (HQ).....513 469-1472
4660 Duke Dr Ste 300 Mason (45040) ***(G-13586)***
General Services Cleaning Co.....614 840-0562
8111 Blind Brook Ct Columbus (43235) ***(G-7654)***
General Temperature Ctrl Inc.....614 837-3888
970 W Walnut St Canal Winchester (43110) ***(G-2109)***
General Theming Contrs LLC.....614 252-6342
3750 Courtright Ct Columbus (43227) ***(G-7655)***
General Tool Company (PA).....513 733-5500
101 Landy Ln Cincinnati (45215) ***(G-3616)***
General Transport Incorporated.....330 786-3400
1100 Jenkins Blvd Akron (44306) ***(G-233)***
Generation Health & Rehab Cntr.....740 344-9465
1450 W Main St Newark (43055) ***(G-15035)***
Generation Health Corp.....614 337-1066
5151 N Hamilton Rd Columbus (43230) ***(G-7656)***
Genes Refrigeration Htg & AC.....330 723-4104
6222 Norwalk Rd Medina (44256) ***(G-13942)***
Genesis 10, Akron *Also called Genesis Corp* ***(G-234)***
Genesis 10, Columbus *Also called Genesis Corp* ***(G-7657)***
Genesis Corp.....330 597-4100
1 Cascade Plz Ste 1230 Akron (44308) ***(G-234)***
Genesis Corp.....614 934-1211
4449 Easton Way Columbus (43219) ***(G-7657)***
Genesis Health & Rehab, McConnelsville *Also called Careserve Inc* ***(G-13899)***
Genesis Healthcare.....937 875-4604
2 Crescent Dr Troy (45373) ***(G-18203)***
Genesis Healthcare System (PA).....740 454-5000
2951 Maple Ave Zanesville (43701) ***(G-20310)***
Genesis Healthcare System.....740 453-4959
1238 Pfeifer Dr Zanesville (43701) ***(G-20311)***
Genesis Hspces Pallitaive Care, Zanesville *Also called Hospice of Genesis Health* ***(G-20318)***
Genesis Logistics, Westerville *Also called Exel Inc* ***(G-19162)***

Genesis Oxygen & Home Med Eqp, Portsmouth Also called Genesis Respiratory Svcs Inc (G-16138)
Genesis Rescue Systems 937 293-6240
  2780 Culver Ave Kettering (45429) **(G-12293)**
Genesis Respiratory Svcs Inc (PA) 740 354-4363
  4132 Gallia St Portsmouth (45662) **(G-16138)**
Genesis Technology Partners 513 585-5800
  3200 Burnet Ave Cincinnati (45229) **(G-3617)**
Genessa Health Marketing, Dayton Also called Hafenbrack Mktg Cmmnctions Inc (G-9482)
Genetica Dna Laboratories, Cincinnati Also called Laboratory Corporation America (G-3904)
Geneva Area City School Dst 440 466-2684
  75 North Ave E Geneva (44041) **(G-11241)**
Geneva Area Recreational 440 466-1002
  1822 S Broadway Geneva (44041) **(G-11242)**
Geneva Chervenic Realty Inc 330 686-8400
  3589 Darrow Rd Stow (44224) **(G-17208)**
Geneva Liberty Steel Ltd (PA) 330 740-0103
  947 Martin Luther King Jr Youngstown (44502) **(G-20047)**
Geneva Pipeline, Geneva Also called A2 Services LLC (G-11236)
Genicon Inc 419 491-4478
  12150 Monclova Rd Swanton (43558) **(G-17398)**
GENMAK GENEVA LIBERTY, Youngstown Also called Geneva Liberty Steel Ltd (G-20047)
Genoa Assembly 107, Elmore Also called International Ordr of Rnbow Fo (G-10473)
Genoa Banking Company (PA) 419 855-8381
  801 Main St Genoa (43430) **(G-11255)**
Genoa Care Center, Genoa Also called McClellan Management Inc (G-11258)
Genoa Legion Post 324 .... 419 855-7049
  302 West St Genoa (43430) **(G-11256)**
Genomoncology LLC 216 496-4216
  1375 E 9th St Ste 1120 Cleveland (44114) **(G-5605)**
Genox Transportation Inc 419 837-2023
  25750 Oregon Rd Perrysburg (43551) **(G-15868)**
Genric Inc 937 553-9250
  433 Allenby Dr Marysville (43040) **(G-13500)**
Gensuite LLC 513 774-1000
  4680 Parkway Dr Ste 400 Mason (45040) **(G-13587)**
Gentherm Medical LLC 513 326-5252
  12011 Mosteller Rd Cincinnati (45241) **(G-3618)**
Gentiva Health Services Inc 419 887-6700
  1745 Indian Wood Cir # 200 Maumee (43537) **(G-13795)**
Gentlebrook Inc (PA) 330 877-3694
  880 Sunnyside St Sw Hartville (44632) **(G-11686)**
Genuine Auto Parts 864, Dayton Also called Hahn Automotive Warehouse Inc (G-9483)
Geo Byers Sons Holding Inc 614 239-1084
  4185 E 5th Ave Columbus (43219) **(G-7658)**
Geo Gradel Co 419 691-7123
  3135 Front St Toledo (43605) **(G-17759)**
Geological Department, Cincinnati Also called University of Cincinnati (G-4717)
Geopfert Company, The, Akron Also called J W Geopfert Co Inc (G-285)
George Darr 740 498-5400
  21284 Township Road 257 Newcomerstown (43832) **(G-15132)**
George Fern Company, Cincinnati Also called Fern Exposition Services LLC (G-3543)
George G Ellis Jr MD 330 965-0832
  910 Boardman Canfield Rd Youngstown (44512) **(G-20048)**
George Gardner 419 636-4277
  1420 W High St Bryan (43506) **(G-1958)**
George J Igel & Co Inc 614 445-8421
  2040 Alum Creek Dr Columbus (43207) **(G-7659)**
George Knick 937 548-2832
  2637 Hllgrove Wdington Rd Greenville (45331) **(G-11379)**
George Kuhn Enterprises Inc 614 481-8838
  2200 Mckinley Ave Columbus (43204) **(G-7660)**
George P Ballas Buick GMC Trck (PA) 419 535-1000
  5715 W Central Ave Toledo (43615) **(G-17760)**
George P Pettit MD Inc 740 354-1434
  1729 27th St Bldg G Portsmouth (45662) **(G-16139)**
George Steel Fabricating Inc 513 932-2887
  1207 S Us Route 42 Lebanon (45036) **(G-12466)**
George W Arensberg Phrm Inc 740 344-2195
  1272 W Main St Newark (43055) **(G-15036)**
George W Mc Cloy 614 457-6233
  921 Chatham Ln Ste 302 Columbus (43221) **(G-7661)**
Georgesville, Columbus Also called Allied Communications Corp (G-6896)
Georgetown Life Squad 937 378-3082
  301 S Main St Unit 1 Georgetown (45121) **(G-11271)**
Georgetown Vineyards 740 435-3222
  62920 Georgetown Rd Cambridge (43725) **(G-2069)**
Georgia-Boot Inc 740 753-1951
  39 E Canal St Nelsonville (45764) **(G-14832)**
Geotex Construction Svcs Inc 614 444-5690
  1025 Stimmel Rd Columbus (43223) **(G-7662)**
Gerber Feed Service Inc 330 857-4421
  3094 Moser Rd Dalton (44618) **(G-9145)**
Gerdau Macsteel Atmosphere Ann 330 478-0314
  1501 Raff Rd Sw Canton (44710) **(G-2325)**
GERIATRICS CENTER OF MANSFIELD, Mansfield Also called Mansfield Memorial Homes LLC (G-13209)
Gerlach John J Center For Sen 614 566-5858
  180 E Broad St Fl 34 Columbus (43215) **(G-7663)**
Germain & Co Inc 937 885-5827
  10552 Success Ln Ste A Dayton (45458) **(G-9460)**

Germain Ford LLC 614 889-7777
  7250 Sawmill Rd Columbus (43235) **(G-7664)**
Germain On Scarborough LLC 614 868-0300
  5711 Scarborough Blvd Columbus (43232) **(G-7665)**
Germain Toyota, Columbus Also called Germain On Scarborough LLC (G-7665)
GERMAN AMERICAN FAMILY SOCIETY, Kent Also called German Family Society Inc (G-12234)
German Family Society Inc 330 678-8229
  3871 Ranfield Rd Kent (44240) **(G-12234)**
German Mutual Insurance Co 419 599-3993
  1000 Westmoreland Ave Napoleon (43545) **(G-14806)**
GERMAN SINGING SOCIETY, Columbus Also called Columbus Maennerchor (G-7293)
Germane Solutions, Dayton Also called Germain & Co Inc (G-9460)
Gerspacher Companies 330 725-1596
  574 Leisure Ln Medina (44256) **(G-13943)**
Ges Graphite Inc (PA) 216 658-6660
  12300 Snow Rd Parma (44130) **(G-15767)**
Get Help Home, Euclid Also called Omni Park Health Care LLC (G-10651)
Getgo Transportation Co LLC 419 666-6850
  28500 Lemoyne Rd Millbury (43447) **(G-14449)**
Gethsemane Lutheran Church 614 885-4319
  35 E Stanton Ave Columbus (43214) **(G-7666)**
Gexpro, Cleveland Also called Rexel Usa Inc (G-6318)
Gfk Custom Research LLC 513 562-1507
  11240 Cornell Park Dr Blue Ash (45242) **(G-1568)**
GFS Chemicals Inc 740 881-5501
  800 Mckinley Ave Columbus (43222) **(G-7667)**
GFS Leasing Inc (PA) 330 296-6415
  1463 Tallmadge Rd Kent (44240) **(G-12235)**
GFS Leasing Inc 330 877-2666
  1420 Smith Kramer St Ne Hartville (44632) **(G-11687)**
Gfwd Supply, Cincinnati Also called General Factory Sups Co Inc (G-3615)
Ghp II LLC 740 681-6825
  2893 W Fair Ave Lancaster (43130) **(G-12406)**
Gia USA Inc 216 831-8678
  4701 Richmond Rd Cleveland (44128) **(G-5606)**
Giambrone Masonry Inc 216 475-1200
  10000 Aurora Hudson Rd Hudson (44236) **(G-11980)**
Giammarco Properties LLC 419 885-4844
  5252 Monroe St Toledo (43623) **(G-17761)**
Giant Eagle Inc 330 364-5301
  515 Union Ave Ste 243 Dover (44622) **(G-10079)**
Giant Industries Inc 419 531-4600
  900 N Westwood Ave Toledo (43607) **(G-17762)**
Gibsonburg Health Llc 419 637-2104
  355 Windsor Ln Gibsonburg (43431) **(G-11278)**
Gideon 800 395-6014
  4122 Superior Ave Cleveland (44103) **(G-5607)**
Gideons International 513 932-2857
  8 Claridge Ct B Lebanon (45036) **(G-12467)**
Giesecke & Devrient Amer Inc 330 425-1515
  2020 Enterprise Pkwy Twinsburg (44087) **(G-18274)**
Giffin Management Group Inc 330 758-4695
  6300 South Ave Apt 1200 Youngstown (44512) **(G-20049)**
Giggles & Wiggles Inc (PA) 740 574-4536
  1207 Dogwood Ridge Rd Wheelersburg (45694) **(G-19434)**
Gilbane Building Company 614 948-4000
  145 E Rich St Fl 4 Columbus (43215) **(G-7668)**
Gilbert Heating & AC 419 625-8875
  2121 Cleveland Rd Ste A Sandusky (44870) **(G-16610)**
Gilbert Heating AC & Plumb, Sandusky Also called Gilbert Heating & AC (G-16610)
Giles Marathon Inc 440 974-8815
  8648 Tyler Blvd Mentor (44060) **(G-14051)**
Gill Podiatry Supply Co, Strongsville Also called Radebaugh-Fetzer Company (G-17340)
Gillespie Drug, Caldwell Also called Braden Med Services Inc (G-2036)
Gillette Associates LP 330 372-1960
  3310 Elm Rd Ne Warren (44483) **(G-18709)**
Gillette Nursing Home Inc 330 372-1960
  3310 Elm Rd Ne Warren (44483) **(G-18710)**
Gillmore Security Systems Inc 440 232-1000
  26165 Broadway Ave Cleveland (44146) **(G-5608)**
Gilmore Jasion Mahler Ltd (PA) 419 794-2000
  1715 Indian Wood Cir # 100 Maumee (43537) **(G-13796)**
Gingerbread Academy, Blue Ash Also called Gingerbread Inc (G-1569)
Gingerbread Inc 513 793-4122
  4215 Malsbary Rd Blue Ash (45242) **(G-1569)**
Girard Technologies Inc 330 783-2495
  1101 E Indianola Ave Youngstown (44502) **(G-20050)**
Girl Scouts Lake Erie Council 330 864-9933
  1 Girl Scout Way Macedonia (44056) **(G-13071)**
Girl Scouts North East Ohio 216 481-1313
  4019 Prospect Ave Cleveland (44103) **(G-5609)**
Girl Scouts North East Ohio (PA) 330 864-9933
  1 Girl Scout Way Macedonia (44056) **(G-13072)**
Girl Scouts of The US Amer 614 487-8101
  1700 Watermark Dr Columbus (43215) **(G-7669)**
Girl Scouts of Western Ohio (PA) 513 489-1025
  4930 Cornell Rd Blue Ash (45242) **(G-1570)**
Girl Scouts of Western Ohio 567 225-3557
  2244 Collingwood Blvd Toledo (43620) **(G-17763)**

Girl Scuts Appleseed Ridge Inc 419 225-4085
1870 W Robb Ave Lima (45805) ***(G-12643)***
Girl Scuts Ohios Heartland Inc (PA) 614 340-8820
1700 Watermark Dr Columbus (43215) ***(G-7670)***
Girl Scuts Wstn Ohio Tledo Div, Toledo *Also called Girl Scouts of Western Ohio* ***(G-17763)***
Girl Scuts Wstn Ohio Tledo Div (PA) 419 243-8216
2244 Collingwood Blvd Toledo (43620) ***(G-17764)***
Gironda Vito & Bros Inc 330 630-9399
1130 Brittain Rd Akron (44305) ***(G-235)***
GKN Freight Services Inc (HQ) 419 232-5623
700 Fox Rd Van Wert (45891) ***(G-18478)***
GL Nause Co Inc 513 722-9500
1971 Phoenix Dr Loveland (45140) ***(G-12996)***
Gladden Community House 614 221-7801
183 Hawkes Ave Columbus (43223) ***(G-7671)***
Glass City Federal Credit Un (PA) 419 887-1000
1340 Arrowhead Dr Maumee (43537) ***(G-13797)***
Glassrock Plant, Glenford *Also called Pioneer Sands LLC* ***(G-11308)***
Glaucoma Consultants, Columbus *Also called Ohio State University* ***(G-8303)***
Glavan & Accociates Architects 614 205-4060
107 S High St Ste 200 Columbus (43215) ***(G-7672)***
Glavin Industries Inc 440 349-0049
6835 Cochran Rd Ste A Solon (44139) ***(G-16851)***
Glavin Specialty Co, Solon *Also called Glavin Industries Inc* ***(G-16851)***
Glazer's of Ohio, Columbus *Also called Southern Glzers Dstrs Ohio LLC* ***(G-8664)***
Glazers Distributors Ohio Inc 440 542-7000
7800 Cochran Rd Solon (44139) ***(G-16852)***
Gleaming Systems LLC 614 348-7475
2417 Charoe St Lewis Center (43035) ***(G-12543)***
Gleason Construction Co Inc 419 865-7480
540 S Centennial Rd Holland (43528) ***(G-11886)***
Glemsure Realty Trust 740 522-6620
771 S 30th St Ste 9001 Heath (43056) ***(G-11703)***
Glen Arbors Ltd Partnership 937 293-0900
4000 Miller Valentine Ct Moraine (45439) ***(G-14661)***
Glen Meadows, Fairfield Township *Also called Glenward Inc* ***(G-10807)***
Glen Surplus Sales Inc (PA) 419 347-1212
14 E Smiley Ave Shelby (44875) ***(G-16746)***
Glen Wesley Inc 614 888-7492
5155 N High St Columbus (43214) ***(G-7673)***
Glen-Gery Corporation 419 468-4890
3785 Cardington Iberia Rd Galion (44833) ***(G-11176)***
Glenbeigh (PA) 440 563-3400
2863 State Route 45 N Rock Creek (44084) ***(G-16411)***
Glenbeigh Health Sources Inc (PA) 440 951-7000
2863 State Route 45 N Rock Creek (44084) ***(G-16412)***
Glencare Center, Cincinnati *Also called Carington Health Systems* ***(G-3124)***
Glencoe Restoration Group LLC 330 752-1244
575 Canton Rd Akron (44312) ***(G-236)***
Glendale Place Care Center LLC 513 771-1779
779 Glendale Milford Rd Cincinnati (45215) ***(G-3619)***
Glendale, The, Toledo *Also called Chelmsford Apartments Ltd* ***(G-17649)***
Glendora Health Care Center 330 264-0912
1552 N Honeytown Rd Wooster (44691) ***(G-19723)***
Glenellen, North Lima *Also called Lakeside Manor Inc* ***(G-15271)***
Glenlaurel Inc 740 385-4070
14940 Mount Olive Rd Rockbridge (43149) ***(G-16413)***
Glenlurel-A Scottish Cntry Inn, Rockbridge *Also called Glenlaurel Inc* ***(G-16413)***
Glenmont 614 876-0084
4599 Avery Rd Hilliard (43026) ***(G-11769)***
Glenmoor Country Club Inc 330 966-3600
4191 Glenmoor Rd Nw Lowr Canton (44718) ***(G-2326)***
Glenn View Manor Inc 330 652-9901
3379 Main St Star Rt 46 Mineral Ridge (44440) ***(G-14509)***
Glennco Systems Inc 740 353-4328
928 16th St Portsmouth (45662) ***(G-16140)***
Glenridge Machine Co 440 975-1055
4610 Beidler Rd Willoughby (44094) ***(G-19526)***
Glenview Cntr For Chld Cr & Lr, Cleveland *Also called Bay Village City School Dst* ***(G-5043)***
Glenward Inc 513 863-3100
3472 Hamilton Mason Rd Fairfield Township (45011) ***(G-10807)***
Glenway Automotive Service 513 921-2117
4033 Glenway Ave Cincinnati (45205) ***(G-3620)***
Glenway Family Medicine, Cincinnati *Also called Christ Hospital* ***(G-3198)***
Glenwood Assisted Living, Canton *Also called Stone Crossing Assisted Living* ***(G-2499)***
Glenwood Community Inc 740 376-9555
200 Timberline Dr Apt 206 Marietta (45750) ***(G-13330)***
Glidden House Associates Ltd 216 231-8900
1901 Ford Dr Cleveland (44106) ***(G-5610)***
Glidden House Inn, Cleveland *Also called Glidden House Associates Ltd* ***(G-5610)***
Glimcher Properties Ltd Partnr, Columbus *Also called Washington PRI* ***(G-8875)***
Glimcher Realty Trust (PA) 614 861-3232
2740 Eastland Mall Ste B Columbus (43232) ***(G-7674)***
Glm Transport Inc (PA) 419 363-2041
12806 State Route 118 Rockford (45882) ***(G-16415)***
Glo-Tone Cleaners, Saint Clairsville *Also called St Clair 60 Minute Clrs Inc* ***(G-16506)***
Global Cnsld Holdings Inc (PA) 513 703-0965
3965 Marble Ridge Ln Mason (45040) ***(G-13588)***
Global Exec Slutions Group LLC 330 666-3354
3505 Embassy Pkwy Ste 200 Akron (44333) ***(G-237)***
Global Graphene Group Inc 937 331-9884
1240 Mccook Ave Dayton (45404) ***(G-9461)***
Global Ground, Cleveland *Also called Servisair LLC* ***(G-6400)***
Global Gvrnment Edcatn Sltions 937 368-2308
6450 Poe Ave Ste 200 Dayton (45414) ***(G-9462)***
Global Insulation Inc (PA) 330 479-3100
4450 Belden Village St Nw # 306 Canton (44718) ***(G-2327)***
Global Mall Unlimited 740 533-7203
1423 Missouri Ave Delaware (43015) ***(G-9981)***
Global Meals, Columbus *Also called Casleo Corporation* ***(G-7133)***
Global Military Expert Co 800 738-9795
2670e Indian Ripple Rd Beavercreek (45440) ***(G-1219)***
Global Risk Consultants Corp 440 746-8861
7000 S Edgerton Rd # 100 Brecksville (44141) ***(G-1781)***
Global Tchnical Recruiters Inc (PA) 216 251-9560
27887 Clemens Rd Ste 1 Westlake (44145) ***(G-19344)***
Global Tchnical Recruiters Inc 440 365-1670
27887 Clemens Rd Ste 1 Westlake (44145) ***(G-19345)***
Global Technology Center, Holland *Also called Tekni-Plex Inc* ***(G-11918)***
Global Telehealth Services, Hudson *Also called Integrated Telehealth Inc* ***(G-11985)***
Global Transportation Services 614 409-0770
7139 Americana Pkwy Reynoldsburg (43068) ***(G-16305)***
Global Workplace Solutions LLC (PA) 513 759-6000
9823 Cincinnati Dayton Rd West Chester (45069) ***(G-18933)***
Global-Pak Inc (PA) 330 482-1993
9636 Elkton Rd Lisbon (44432) ***(G-12802)***
Globaltranz Enterprises Inc 513 745-0138
10945 Reed Hartman Hwy Blue Ash (45242) ***(G-1571)***
Globe Food Equipment Company 937 299-5493
2153 Dryden Rd Moraine (45439) ***(G-14662)***
Globe Trucking Inc 419 727-8307
5261 Stickney Ave Toledo (43612) ***(G-17765)***
Gloria Gadmack Do 216 363-2353
17800 Shaker Blvd Cleveland (44120) ***(G-5611)***
Glow Industries Inc (PA) 419 872-4772
12962 Eckel Junction Rd Perrysburg (43551) ***(G-15869)***
Glowe-Smith Industrial Inc 330 638-5088
812 Youngstwn Kgsvl Rd Se Vienna (44473) ***(G-18579)***
Glt Inc 937 395-0508
2691 Lance Dr Moraine (45409) ***(G-14663)***
Glt Products, Solon *Also called Great Lakes Textiles Inc* ***(G-16854)***
GMAC, Canfield *Also called Ally Financial Inc* ***(G-2130)***
GMAC Insurance, Akron *Also called Sbm Business Services Inc* ***(G-419)***
GMAC Insurance, Richfield *Also called Explorer Rv Insurance Agcy Inc* ***(G-16355)***
GMAC Realestate, Warren *Also called Eaton Group GMAC Real Estate* ***(G-18706)***
GMC Excavation & Trucking 419 468-0121
1859 Biddle Rd Galion (44833) ***(G-11177)***
GMI Holdings Inc 330 794-0846
2850 Gilchrist Rd Akron (44305) ***(G-238)***
Gms Inc 937 222-4444
1509 Stanley Ave Dayton (45404) ***(G-9463)***
Gms Management Co Inc (PA) 216 766-6000
4645 Richmond Rd Ste 101 Cleveland (44128) ***(G-5612)***
Gms Realty, Cleveland *Also called Gms Management Co Inc* ***(G-5612)***
Gmti, Cincinnati *Also called Gannett Media Tech Intl* ***(G-3602)***
Gng Music Instruction, New Albany *Also called Qwaide Enterprises LLC* ***(G-14868)***
Gnw Aluminum Inc 330 821-7955
1356 Beeson St Ne Alliance (44601) ***(G-533)***
Go 2 It Group, Westlake *Also called Career Cnnctions Staffing Svcs* ***(G-19326)***
Goddard School, Columbus *Also called Bailey & Long Inc* ***(G-7011)***
Goddard School, Grove City *Also called Dakota Girls LLC* ***(G-11424)***
Goddard School, Strongsville *Also called Hewlettco Inc* ***(G-17309)***
Goddard School 513 697-9663
782 Lveland Miamiville Rd Loveland (45140) ***(G-12997)***
Goddard School 614 920-9810
6405 Canal St Canal Winchester (43110) ***(G-2110)***
Goddard School 513 271-6311
4430 Red Bank Rd Cincinnati (45227) ***(G-3621)***
Goddard School of Avon 440 934-3300
2555 Hale St Avon (44011) ***(G-882)***
Goddard School of Landon, The, Mason *Also called Krieger Enterprises Inc* ***(G-13607)***
Goddard School of New Albany, New Albany *Also called Campbell Family Childcare Inc* ***(G-14846)***
Goddard School of Twinsburg 330 487-0394
2608 Glenwood Dr Twinsburg (44087) ***(G-18275)***
Goddard School, The, Westerville *Also called Powell Enterprises Inc* ***(G-19200)***
Goddard School, The, Cincinnati *Also called Goddard School* ***(G-3621)***
Goddard School, The, Mason *Also called P J & R J Connection Inc* ***(G-13624)***
Goddard Schools, Hudson *Also called J Nan Enterprises LLC* ***(G-11986)***
Godfrey & Wing Inc (PA) 330 562-1440
220 Campus Dr Aurora (44202) ***(G-828)***
Godman Guild (PA) 614 294-5476
303 E 6th Ave Columbus (43201) ***(G-7675)***
Goettle Co 513 825-8100
12071 Hamilton Ave Cincinnati (45231) ***(G-3622)***
Goettle Construction, Cincinnati *Also called Goettle Holding Company Inc* ***(G-3623)***
Goettle Holding Company Inc (PA) 513 825-8100
12071 Hamilton Ave Cincinnati (45231) ***(G-3623)***

ALPHABETIC

Goettsch International Inc 513 563-6500
  9852 Redhill Dr Blue Ash (45242) *(G-1572)*

Going Home Medical Holding Co 305 340-1034
  15830 Foltz Pkwy Strongsville (44149) *(G-17306)*

Gokeyless, Miamisburg *Also called 21st Century Solutions Ltd (G-14134)*

Gold Cross, Youngstown *Also called Rural/Metro Corporation (G-20200)*

Gold Cross Ambulance Svcs Inc 330 744-4161
  1122 E Midlothian Blvd Youngstown (44502) *(G-20051)*

Gold Cross Limousine Service 330 757-3053
  26 Sexton St Struthers (44471) *(G-17364)*

Gold Key Homes, Miamisburg *Also called Oberer Residential Cnstr (G-14200)*

Gold Star Chili Inc (PA) 513 231-4541
  650 Lunken Park Dr Cincinnati (45226) *(G-3624)*

Gold Star Insulation L P 614 221-3241
  495 S High St Columbus (43215) *(G-7676)*

Goldberg Companies Inc 216 475-2600
  4440 Granada Blvd Apt 1 Cleveland (44128) *(G-5613)*

Golden Buckeye Program, Portsmouth *Also called Ussa Inc (G-16179)*

Golden Endings Golden Ret Resc 614 486-0773
  1043 Elmwood Ave Columbus (43212) *(G-7677)*

Golden Hawk Inc 419 683-3304
  4594 Lincoln Hwy 30 Crestline (44827) *(G-9055)*

Golden Hawk Transportation Co (PA) 419 683-3304
  4594 Lincoln Hwy Crestline (44827) *(G-9056)*

Golden Jersey Inn, Yellow Springs *Also called Youngs Jersey Dairy Inc (G-19941)*

Golden Key Ctr For Excptnl Chl 330 493-4400
  1431 30th St Nw Canton (44709) *(G-2328)*

Golden Lamb 513 932-5065
  27 S Broadway St Lebanon (45036) *(G-12468)*

Golden Lamb Rest Ht & Gift Sp, Lebanon *Also called Golden Lamb (G-12468)*

Golden Leaf, Solon *Also called Snf Wadsworth LLC (G-16898)*

Golden Living LLC 419 599-4070
  240 Northcrest Dr Napoleon (43545) *(G-14807)*

Golden Living LLC 419 227-2154
  599 S Shawnee St Lima (45804) *(G-12644)*

Golden Living LLC 440 247-4200
  150 Cleveland St Chagrin Falls (44022) *(G-2647)*

Golden Living LLC 614 861-6666
  1425 Yorkland Rd Columbus (43232) *(G-7678)*

Golden Living LLC 440 256-8100
  9679 Chillicothe Rd Willoughby (44094) *(G-19527)*

Golden Living LLC 330 297-5781
  565 Bryn Mawr St Ravenna (44266) *(G-16244)*

Golden Living LLC 330 762-6486
  721 Hickory St Akron (44303) *(G-239)*

Golden Living LLC 330 335-1558
  365 Johnson Rd Wadsworth (44281) *(G-18596)*

Golden Living LLC 330 725-3393
  555 Springbrook Dr Medina (44256) *(G-13944)*

Golden String Inc 330 503-3894
  16 S Phelps St Youngstown (44503) *(G-20052)*

Golden Years Health Care, Hamilton *Also called Golden Years Nursing Home Inc (G-11601)*

Golden Years Nursing Home Inc 513 893-0471
  2436 Old Oxford Rd Hamilton (45013) *(G-11601)*

Goldfish Swim School 216 364-9090
  4670 Richmond Rd Ste 100 Warrensville Heights (44128) *(G-18778)*

Goldwood Primary School Pta 440 356-6720
  21600 Center Ridge Rd Rocky River (44116) *(G-16434)*

Goldwood Pta, Rocky River *Also called Goldwood Primary School Pta (G-16434)*

Golf and Swim Club, Canton *Also called Meadowlake Corporation (G-2397)*

Golf Center At Kings Island, Mason *Also called Grizzly Golf Center Inc (G-13590)*

Golf Club Co 614 855-7326
  4522 Kitzmiller Rd New Albany (43054) *(G-14855)*

Golf Club of Dublin LLC 614 792-3825
  5805 Eiterman Rd Dublin (43016) *(G-10235)*

Golf Course At Yankee Trace, Dayton *Also called City of Centerville (G-9302)*

Golf Course Maintenance 330 262-9141
  1599 Mechanicsburg Rd Wooster (44691) *(G-19724)*

Golf Galaxy Golfworks Inc 740 328-4193
  4820 Jacksontown Rd Newark (43056) *(G-15037)*

Golfworks, The, Newark *Also called Golf Galaxy Golfworks Inc (G-15037)*

Goliath Contracting Ltd 614 568-7878
  405 Waggoner Rd Reynoldsburg (43068) *(G-16306)*

Gonda Lawn Care LLC 330 701-7232
  7822 2nd St Masury (44438) *(G-13740)*

Good Night Medical Ohio LLC 614 384-7433
  8999 Gemini Pkwy Ste A Columbus (43240) *(G-6813)*

Good Park Golf Course, Akron *Also called City of Akron (G-134)*

Good Samaritan Hosp Cincinnati (HQ) 513 569-6251
  375 Dixmyth Ave Cincinnati (45220) *(G-3625)*

Good Samaritan Hospital Med, Cincinnati *Also called Kidney & Hypertension Center (G-3867)*

Good Samaritan Soc - Arlington, Arlington *Also called Evangelical Lutheran (G-642)*

GOOD SAMARITAN, THE, Millersburg *Also called Christian Aid Ministries (G-14465)*

Good Shepard Village LLC 937 322-1911
  422 N Burnett Rd Springfield (45503) *(G-17042)*

Good Shepard, The, Ashland *Also called Lutheran Scial Svcs Centl Ohio (G-678)*

Good Shepherd Home 419 937-1801
  725 Columbus Ave Fostoria (44830) *(G-11003)*

Good Shepherd Home For Aged 614 228-5200
  622 Center St Ashland (44805) *(G-673)*

Good Smaritan Netwrk Ross Cnty 740 774-6303
  133 E 7th St Chillicothe (45601) *(G-2783)*

Goodall Complex, Cincinnati *Also called Goodall Properties Ltd (G-3626)*

Goodall Properties Ltd 513 621-5522
  324 W 9th St Ste 500 Cincinnati (45202) *(G-3626)*

Goodin Electric Inc 740 522-3113
  605 Garfield Ave Ste A Newark (43055) *(G-15038)*

Goodman Beverage Co Inc 440 787-2255
  5901 Baumhart Rd Lorain (44053) *(G-12905)*

Goodman Properties Inc 740 264-7781
  100 Mall Dr Ofc Ofc Steubenville (43952) *(G-17155)*

Goodnight Inn Inc 419 334-9551
  3701 N State Route 53 Fremont (43420) *(G-11078)*

Goodremonts 419 476-1492
  1017 W Sylvania Ave Toledo (43612) *(G-17766)*

Goodrich Avionics, Columbus *Also called L3 Aviation Products Inc (G-7938)*

Goodrich Gannett Headstart, Cleveland *Also called Goodrich Gnnett Nghborhood Ctr (G-5614)*

Goodrich Gnnett Nghborhood Ctr 216 432-1717
  1400 E 55th St Cleveland (44103) *(G-5614)*

Goodw Indus of Erie, Huron, Ot, Sandusky *Also called Goodwill Industries of Erie (G-16611)*

GOODWILL COLUMBUS, Columbus *Also called Goodwill Inds Centl Ohio Inc (G-7679)*

Goodwill Ester Seals Miami Vly 937 461-4800
  660 S Main St Dayton (45402) *(G-9464)*

Goodwill Ester Seals Miami Vly 937 461-4800
  660 S Main St Dayton (45402) *(G-9465)*

Goodwill Idstrs Grtr Clvlnd L 440 783-1168
  16160 Pearl Rd Strongsville (44136) *(G-17307)*

Goodwill Idstrs Grtr Clvlnd L 216 581-6320
  12650 Rockside Rd Cleveland (44125) *(G-5615)*

Goodwill Idstrs Grtr Clvlnd L (PA) 330 454-9461
  408 9th St Sw Canton (44707) *(G-2329)*

Goodwill Inds Centl Ohio Inc (PA) 614 294-5181
  1331 Edgehill Rd Columbus (43212) *(G-7679)*

Goodwill Inds Centl Ohio Inc 740 439-7000
  1712 Southgate Pkwy Cambridge (43725) *(G-2070)*

Goodwill Inds Centl Ohio Inc 740 373-1304
  1303 Colegate Dr Marietta (45750) *(G-13331)*

Goodwill Inds Centl Ohio Inc 614 274-5296
  890 N Hague Ave Columbus (43204) *(G-7680)*

Goodwill Inds NW Ohio Inc (PA) 419 255-0070
  1120 Madison Ave Toledo (43604) *(G-17767)*

Goodwill Inds of Ashtabula (PA) 440 964-3565
  621 Goodwill Dr Ashtabula (44004) *(G-738)*

Goodwill Inds Rhbilitation Ctr (PA) 330 454-9461
  408 9th St Sw Canton (44707) *(G-2330)*

Goodwill Industries (PA) 330 264-1300
  1034 Nold Ave Wooster (44691) *(G-19725)*

Goodwill Industries Inc 330 724-6995
  570 E Waterloo Rd Akron (44319) *(G-240)*

Goodwill Industries of Akron (PA) 330 724-6995
  570 E Waterloo Rd Akron (44319) *(G-241)*

Goodwill Industries of Erie (PA) 419 625-4744
  419 W Market St Sandusky (44870) *(G-16611)*

Goodwill Industries of Erie 419 334-7566
  1597 Pontiac Ave Fremont (43420) *(G-11079)*

Goodwill Industries of Lima (PA) 419 228-4821
  940 N Cable Rd Ste 1 Lima (45805) *(G-12645)*

Goodwill Industry, Ashtabula *Also called Goodwill Inds of Ashtabula (G-738)*

Goodwill Retail Store, Zanesville *Also called Zanesvlle Welfre Orgnztn/Goodw (G-20387)*

Goodyear Tire & Rubber Company (PA) 330 796-2121
  200 E Innovation Way Akron (44316) *(G-242)*

Goodyear Tire & Rubber Company 440 735-9910
  7230 Northfield Rd Walton Hills (44146) *(G-18636)*

Goofy Golf II Inc 419 732-6671
  1530 S Danbury Rd Port Clinton (43452) *(G-16107)*

Goofy Golf Inc 419 625-1308
  3020 Milan Rd Sandusky (44870) *(G-16612)*

Gooseberry Patch, Columbus *Also called H & M Patch Company (G-7706)*

Gorant Chocolatier LLC (PA) 330 726-8821
  8301 Market St Boardman (44512) *(G-1698)*

Gorant's Yum Yum Tree, Boardman *Also called Gorant Chocolatier LLC (G-1698)*

Gorbett Enterprises of Solon (PA) 440 248-3950
  6531 Cochran Rd Solon (44139) *(G-16853)*

Gordon Bernard Company LLC 513 248-7600
  22 Whitney Dr Milford (45150) *(G-14393)*

Gordon Bros Water, Salem *Also called Gordon Brothers Inc (G-16545)*

Gordon Brothers Inc (PA) 800 331-7611
  776 N Ellsworth Ave Salem (44460) *(G-16545)*

Gordon Flesch Company Inc 419 884-2031
  2756 Lexington Ave Mansfield (44904) *(G-13179)*

Gordon Food Service Inc 419 747-1212
  1310 N Lexngtn Sprngmill Ontario (44906) *(G-15550)*

Gordon Food Service Inc 419 225-8983
  3447 Elida Rd Lima (45807) *(G-12646)*

Gordon Food Service Inc 440 953-1785
  7220 Mentor Ave Mentor (44060) *(G-14052)*

Gordon Food Service Inc 216 573-4900
  7575 Granger Rd Cleveland (44125) *(G-5616)*

Gordon Milk Transport, Sugarcreek Also called Drasc Enterprises Inc (G-17377)

Gorell Enterprises Inc (PA) 724 465-1800
10250 Philipp Pkwy Streetsboro (44241) (G-17254)

Gorell Windows & Doors, Streetsboro Also called Gorell Enterprises Inc (G-17254)

Gorilla Glue Company (PA) 513 271-3300
2101 E Kemper Rd Cincinnati (45241) (G-3627)

Gorjanc Comfort Services Inc 440 449-4411
42 Alpha Park Cleveland (44143) (G-5617)

Gorjanc Mechanical, Cleveland Also called Gorjanc Comfort Services Inc (G-5617)

Gorsuch Management, Lancaster Also called Fairfield Homes Inc (G-12396)

Gorsuch Management, Lancaster Also called Fairfield Homes Inc (G-12397)

Gosh Enterprises Inc (PA) 614 923-4700
2500 Farmers Dr 140 Columbus (43235) (G-7681)

Gosiger Inc (PA) 937 228-5174
108 Mcdonough St Dayton (45402) (G-9466)

Gosiger Inc 937 228-5174
108 Mcdonough St Dayton (45402) (G-9467)

Goss Supply Company (PA) 740 454-2571
620 Marietta St Zanesville (43701) (G-20312)

Gottlieb Johnson Beam Dal P 740 452-7555
320 Main St Zanesville (43701) (G-20313)

Goudreau Management, Cleveland Also called G J Goudreau & Co (G-5586)

Goudy Internal Medicine Inc 419 468-8323
270 Portland Way S Rear Galion (44833) (G-11178)

Goudy, James A II MD, Galion Also called Goudy Internal Medicine Inc (G-11178)

Govana Hospital, Newark Also called Yeater Alene K MD (G-15112)

Government Acquisitions Inc 513 721-8700
720 E Pete Rose Way # 330 Cincinnati (45202) (G-3628)

Government Resource Partners, Columbus Also called Fhc Enterprises LLC (G-7574)

Governor's Room, Oxford Also called Alexander House Inc (G-15672)

Governor's Village Assisted Ll, Cleveland Also called Governors Village LLC (G-5618)

Governors Pointe LLC 440 205-1570
8506 Hendricks Rd Ofc Mentor (44060) (G-14053)

Governors Village LLC 440 449-8788
280 N Cmmons Blvd Apt 101 Cleveland (44143) (G-5618)

Gowdy Partners LLC 614 488-4424
1533 Lake Shore Dr Ste 50 Columbus (43204) (G-7682)

Goza Dialysis LLC 513 738-0276
3825 Kraus Ln Ste S Fairfield (45014) (G-10730)

GP Strategies Corporation 513 583-8810
3794 E Galbraith Rd Cincinnati (45236) (G-3629)

GPA, Cincinnati Also called Gus Perdikakis Associates (G-3665)

Gpax Ltd 614 501-7622
555 Lancaster Ave Reynoldsburg (43068) (G-16307)

Gpc Contracting Company 740 264-6060
500 E Church St Ste 3 Steubenville (43953) (G-17156)

Gpd Associates, Akron Also called Gpd Services Company Inc (G-243)

Gpd Group, Columbus Also called Schomer Glaus Pyle (G-8604)

Gpd Group, Cleveland Also called Schomer Glaus Pyle (G-6376)

Gpd Group, Akron Also called Schomer Glaus Pyle (G-420)

Gpd Group, Coventry Township Also called Schomer Glaus Pyle (G-9042)

Gpd Services Company Inc (PA) 330 572-2100
520 S Main St Ste 2531 Akron (44311) (G-243)

Gprs, Toledo Also called Penetrating R Ground (G-17975)

Graber Metal Works Inc 440 237-8422
9664 Akins Rd Ste 1 North Royalton (44133) (G-15356)

Grabill Plumbing & Heating 330 756-2075
10235 Manchester Ave Sw Beach City (44608) (G-1024)

Grace Baptist Church (PA) 937 652-1133
960 Childrens Home Rd Urbana (43078) (G-18435)

Grace Baptist Preschool, Urbana Also called Grace Baptist Church (G-18435)

Grace Brethren Village Inc 937 836-4011
1010 Taywood Rd Ofc Englewood (45322) (G-10589)

Grace Brthren Ch Columbus Ohio (PA) 614 888-7733
8724 Olde Worthington Rd Westerville (43082) (G-19168)

Grace Consulting Inc (PA) 440 647-6672
510 Dickson St Lowr Wellington (44090) (G-18841)

Grace Hospice LLC 513 458-5545
4850 Smith Rd Ste 100 Cincinnati (45212) (G-3630)

Grace Hospice LLC 937 293-1381
3033 Kettering Blvd # 220 Moraine (45439) (G-14664)

Grace Hospice LLC 216 288-7413
7314 Industrial Park Blvd Mentor (44060) (G-14054)

Grace Hospice LLC 440 826-0350
16600 W Sprague Rd Ste 35 Cleveland (44130) (G-5619)

Grace Hospice of Middleburg, Cleveland Also called Grace Hospice LLC (G-5619)

Grace Hospital 216 476-2704
18101 Lorain Ave Cleveland (44111) (G-5620)

Grace Hospital 216 687-1500
44 Blaine Ave Bedford (44146) (G-1282)

Grace Hospital 216 687-1500
20000 Harvard Ave Warrensville Heights (44122) (G-18779)

Grace Hospital 216 687-4013
254 Cleveland Ave Amherst (44001) (G-588)

Grace Polaris Church, Westerville Also called Grace Brthren Ch Columbus Ohio (G-19168)

Grace Resurrection Association 937 548-2595
Grace Rsrrction Cmnty Ctr Greenville (45331) (G-11380)

Grace Resurrection Cmnty Ctr, Greenville Also called Grace Resurrection Association (G-11380)

Graceworks Lutheran Services 937 436-6850
6443 Bethany Village Dr Dayton (45459) (G-9468)

Graceworks Lutheran Services (PA) 937 433-2140
6430 Inner Mission Way Dayton (45459) (G-9469)

Graceworks Lutheran Services 937 433-2110
6430 Inner Mission Way Dayton (45459) (G-9470)

Gracie Plum Investments Inc 740 355-9029
609 2nd St Unit 2 Portsmouth (45662) (G-16141)

Graco Ohio Inc 330 494-1313
8400 Port Jackson Ave Nw Canton (44720) (G-2331)

Gracor Language Services, Westerville Also called Ceiba Enterprises Incorporated (G-19231)

Gradient Corporation 513 779-0000
9900 Princtn Glndl Rd 1 Cincinnati (45246) (G-3631)

Grady Memorial Hospital (PA) 740 615-1000
561 W Central Ave Delaware (43015) (G-9982)

Grady Rentals LLC 330 627-2022
4094 Canton Rd Nw Carrollton (44615) (G-2570)

Grady Veterinary Hospital Inc 513 931-8675
9255 Winton Rd Cincinnati (45231) (G-3632)

Grae-Con Construction Inc (PA) 740 282-6830
880 Kingsdale Rd Steubenville (43952) (G-17157)

Grae-Con Contructions, Steubenville Also called Grae-Con Construction Inc (G-17157)

Graf and Sons Inc 614 481-2020
2300 International St Columbus (43228) (G-7683)

Graf Growers, Akron Also called White Pond Gardens Inc (G-500)

Graffiti Co, Cleveland Also called Barbs Graffiti Inc (G-5036)

Graffiti Inc 216 881-5550
3200 Carnegie Ave Cleveland (44115) (G-5621)

Graftech Holdings Inc 216 676-2000
6100 Oak Tree Blvd # 300 Independence (44131) (G-12077)

Graham Chevrolet-Cadillac Co (PA) 419 989-4012
1515 W 4th St Ontario (44906) (G-15551)

Graham Investment Co (PA) 740 382-0902
3007 Harding Hwy E # 203 Marion (43302) (G-13422)

Graham Packaging Holdings Co 419 628-1070
255 Southgate Minster (45865) (G-14534)

Graham Packg Plastic Pdts Inc 419 423-3271
170 Stanford Pkwy Findlay (45840) (G-10914)

Grainger 152, Blue Ash Also called WW Grainger Inc (G-1683)

Grainger 165, Macedonia Also called WW Grainger Inc (G-13090)

Grainger 176, Columbus Also called WW Grainger Inc (G-8921)

Granary Gift & Furniture Barn, Mount Cory Also called S&D Farms Inc (G-14722)

Grand Aerie of The Fraternal (PA) 614 883-2200
1623 Gateway Cir Grove City (43123) (G-11436)

Grand Aerie of The Fraternal 419 227-1566
800 W Robb Ave Lima (45801) (G-12647)

Grand Central Auto Recycling, Massillon Also called Greenleaf Ohio LLC (G-13690)

Grand Court, The, Findlay Also called Brookdale Senior Living Inc (G-10883)

Grand Heritage Hotel Portland 440 734-4477
25105 Country Club Blvd North Olmsted (44070) (G-15291)

GRAND LAKE HEALTH SYSTEM, Saint Marys Also called Joint Township Dst Mem Hosp (G-16524)

Grand Lake Primary Care, Saint Marys Also called Joint Township Dst Mem Hosp (G-16523)

Grand Rapids Care Center, Grand Rapids Also called Rapids Nursing Homes Inc (G-11329)

Grand Rapids Care Center, Grand Rapids Also called Saber Healthcare Group LLC (G-11330)

Grand River Seafood Supply, Grand River Also called 101 River Inc (G-11331)

Grand Valley Country Manor, Windsor Also called Lynnhaven V LLC (G-19665)

Grand View Inn Inc 740 377-4388
154 County Road 450 South Point (45680) (G-16934)

Grande Oaks & Grande Pavillion, Cleveland Also called Oakwood Health Care Svcs Inc (G-6109)

Grande Pointe Healthcare Cmnty, Cleveland Also called Merit Leasing Co LLC (G-5955)

Grandmas Gardens Inc 937 885-2973
8107 State Route 48 Waynesville (45068) (G-18831)

Grandview Avenue Home, Waverly Also called Buckeye Community Services Inc (G-18815)

Grandview Family Practice 740 258-9267
1550 W 5th Ave Lowr Columbus (43212) (G-7684)

Grandview Hospital & Med Ctr, Dayton Also called Dayton Osteopathic Hospital (G-9374)

Grandview Ht Ltd Partnr Ohio 937 766-5519
383 E Leffel Ln Springfield (45505) (G-17043)

Grandview Inn, South Point Also called Grand View Inn Inc (G-16934)

Grange Indemnity Insurance Co 614 445-2900
671 S High St Columbus (43206) (G-7685)

Grange Insurance Companies, Columbus Also called Grange Mutual Casualty Company (G-7687)

Grange Life Insurance Company 800 445-3030
671 S High St Columbus (43206) (G-7686)

Grange Mutual Casualty Co 601, Cleveland Also called Grange Mutual Casualty Company (G-5622)

Grange Mutual Casualty Co 721, Cincinnati Also called Grange Mutual Casualty Company (G-3633)

Grange Mutual Casualty Company, Columbus Also called Grange Indemnity Insurance Co (G-7685)

Grange Mutual Casualty Company (PA) 614 445-2900
671 S High St Columbus (43206) ***(G-7687)***

Grange Mutual Casualty Company 614 337-4400
7271 Engle Rd Ste 400 Cleveland (44130) ***(G-5622)***

Grange Mutual Casualty Company 513 671-3722
12021 Sheraton Ln Cincinnati (45246) ***(G-3633)***

Granger Township 330 239-2111
3737 Ridge Rd Medina (44256) ***(G-13945)***

Granger Township Fire & Rescue, Medina *Also called Granger Township* ***(G-13945)***

Granite Transformations, Dayton *Also called Countertop Alternatives Inc* ***(G-9324)***

Grant Hospital, Columbus *Also called Ohiohealth Corporation* ***(G-8364)***

Grant Thornton LLP 216 771-1400
1375 E 9th St Ste 1500 Cleveland (44114) ***(G-5623)***

Grant Thornton LLP 513 762-5000
4000 Smith Rd Ste 500 Cincinnati (45209) ***(G-3634)***

Granville Builders Supply, Columbus *Also called Columbus Coal & Lime Co* ***(G-7269)***

Granville Hospitality Llc 740 587-3333
314 Broadway E Granville (43023) ***(G-11342)***

Granville Milling Co (PA) 740 587-0221
400 S Main St Granville (43023) ***(G-11343)***

Graphel Corporation 513 779-6166
6115 Centre Park Dr West Chester (45069) ***(G-18934)***

Graphic Enterprises Inc 800 553-6616
3874 Highland Park Nw North Canton (44720) ***(G-15207)***

Graphic Entps Off Slutions Inc 800 553-6616
3874 Highland Park Nw North Canton (44720) ***(G-15208)***

Graphic Publications Inc 330 674-2300
7368 County Road 623 Millersburg (44654) ***(G-14474)***

Graphic Systems Services Inc 937 746-0708
400 S Pioneer Blvd Springboro (45066) ***(G-16967)***

Grasan Equipment Company Inc 419 526-4440
440 S Illinois Ave Mansfield (44907) ***(G-13180)***

Gray & Pape Inc (PA) 513 287-7700
1318 Main St Fl 1 Cincinnati (45202) ***(G-3635)***

Gray Media Group Inc 216 367-7300
1717 E 12th St Cleveland (44114) ***(G-5624)***

Gray Media Group Inc 513 421-1919
635 W 7th St Ste 200 Cincinnati (45203) ***(G-3636)***

Gray Television Group Inc 419 531-1313
4247 Dorr St Toledo (43607) ***(G-17768)***

Graybar Electric Company Inc 216 573-6144
6161 Halle Dr Cleveland (44125) ***(G-5625)***

Graybar Electric Company Inc 513 719-7400
1022 W 8th St Cincinnati (45203) ***(G-3637)***

Graybar Electric Company Inc 614 486-4391
1200 Kinnear Rd Columbus (43212) ***(G-7688)***

Graybar Electric Company Inc 330 799-3220
1100 Ohio Works Dr Youngstown (44510) ***(G-20053)***

Graybar Youngstown Nat Zone, Youngstown *Also called Graybar Electric Company Inc* ***(G-20053)***

Graybill Gallery Kitchens Bath, Beach City *Also called Grabill Plumbing & Heating* ***(G-1024)***

Great American Advisors Inc (HQ) 513 357-3300
301 E 4th St Fl 8 Cincinnati (45202) ***(G-3638)***

Great American Insurance Co (HQ) 513 369-5000
301 E 4th St Fl 8 Cincinnati (45202) ***(G-3639)***

Great American Insurance Co 513 603-2570
9450 Seward Rd Fairfield (45014) ***(G-10731)***

Great American Life Insur Co (HQ) 513 357-3300
250 E 5th St Ste 1000 Cincinnati (45202) ***(G-3640)***

Great American Woodies, Columbus *Also called Competitor Swim Products Inc* ***(G-7341)***

Great Amrcn Fncl Resources Inc (HQ) 513 333-5300
250 E 5th St Ste 1000 Cincinnati (45202) ***(G-3641)***

Great Amrcn Plan Admin Inc 513 412-2316
525 Vine St Fl 7 Cincinnati (45202) ***(G-3642)***

Great Bear Lodge Sandusky LLC 419 609-6000
4600 Milan Rd Sandusky (44870) ***(G-16613)***

Great Clips, Cincinnati *Also called Image Engineering Inc* ***(G-3752)***

Great Clips, Dayton *Also called R L O Inc* ***(G-9724)***

Great Dane Columbus Inc 614 876-0666
4080 Lyman Dr Hilliard (43026) ***(G-11770)***

Great Day Tours Chrtr Bus Svc, Cleveland *Also called Cuyahoga Marketing Service* ***(G-5400)***

Great Eastern Theatre Company 419 691-9668
4500 Navarre Ave Oregon (43616) ***(G-15596)***

Great Expectations, Cleveland *Also called Great Southern Video Inc* ***(G-5632)***

Great Expectations D CA Center 330 782-9500
755 Boardman Canfield Rd F8 Youngstown (44512) ***(G-20054)***

Great Expressions, Akron *Also called Dental Health Group PA* ***(G-183)***

Great Lakes Cheese Co Inc (PA) 440 834-2500
17825 Great Lakes Pkwy Hiram (44234) ***(G-11865)***

Great Lakes Cold Logistics 216 520-0930
6548 Brecksville Rd Independence (44131) ***(G-12078)***

Great Lakes Cold Storage, Solon *Also called Gorbett Enterprises of Solon* ***(G-16853)***

Great Lakes Companies Inc 513 554-0720
925 Laidlaw Ave Cincinnati (45237) ***(G-3643)***

Great Lakes Computer Corp 440 937-1100
33675 Lear Indus Pkwy Avon (44011) ***(G-883)***

Great Lakes Contractors LLC 216 631-7777
1234 West Blvd Cleveland (44102) ***(G-5626)***

Great Lakes Crushing Ltd 440 944-5500
30831 Euclid Ave Wickliffe (44092) ***(G-19461)***

Great Lakes Energy 440 582-4662
332 Clearview Ct Broadview Heights (44147) ***(G-1834)***

Great Lakes Fasteners Inc 330 425-4488
1962 Case Pkwy Twinsburg (44087) ***(G-18276)***

Great Lakes Group 216 621-4854
4500 Division Ave Cleveland (44102) ***(G-5627)***

Great Lakes Home Hlth Svcs Inc 888 260-9835
3425 Executive Pkwy # 206 Toledo (43606) ***(G-17769)***

Great Lakes Home Hlth Svcs Inc 888 260-9835
1530 W Market St Akron (44313) ***(G-244)***

Great Lakes Home Hlth Svcs Inc 888 260-9835
5966 Heisley Rd Ste 100 Mentor (44060) ***(G-14055)***

Great Lakes Management Inc (PA) 216 883-6500
2700 E 40th St Ste 1 Cleveland (44115) ***(G-5628)***

Great Lakes Medical Staffing, Perrysburg *Also called Prueter Enterprises Ltd* ***(G-15907)***

Great Lakes Mktg Assoc Inc 419 534-4700
3361 Executive Pkwy # 201 Toledo (43606) ***(G-17770)***

Great Lakes Museum of Science 216 694-2000
601 Erieside Ave Cleveland (44114) ***(G-5629)***

Great Lakes Packers Inc 419 483-2956
400 Great Lakes Pkwy Bellevue (44811) ***(G-1379)***

Great Lakes Power Products Inc (PA) 440 951-5111
7455 Tyler Blvd Mentor (44060) ***(G-14056)***

Great Lakes Publishing Company (PA) 216 771-2833
1422 Euclid Ave Ste 730 Cleveland (44115) ***(G-5630)***

Great Lakes Record Center, Mentor *Also called Moving Solutions Inc* ***(G-14090)***

Great Lakes Science Center, Cleveland *Also called Great Lakes Museum of Science* ***(G-5629)***

Great Lakes Telcom Ltd 330 629-8848
590 E Western Reserve Rd Youngstown (44514) ***(G-20055)***

Great Lakes Textiles Inc (PA) 440 914-1122
6810 Cochran Rd Solon (44139) ***(G-16854)***

Great Lakes Towing, Cleveland *Also called Great Lakes Group* ***(G-5627)***

Great Lakes Water Treatment 216 464-8292
4949 Galaxy Pkwy Ste Q Cleveland (44128) ***(G-5631)***

Great Lakes Western Star, Toledo *Also called Mizar Motors Inc* ***(G-17919)***

Great Lkes Cmnty Action Partnr, Fremont *Also called W S O S Community A* ***(G-11104)***

Great Miami Valley YMCA 513 217-5501
5750 Innovation Dr Middletown (45005) ***(G-14348)***

Great Miami Valley YMCA (PA) 513 887-0001
105 N 2nd St Hamilton (45011) ***(G-11602)***

Great Miami Valley YMCA 513 892-9622
6645 Morris Rd Fairfield Township (45011) ***(G-10808)***

Great Miami Valley YMCA 513 867-0600
4803 Augspurger Rd Hamilton (45011) ***(G-11603)***

Great Miami Valley YMCA 513 887-0014
105 N 2nd St Hamilton (45011) ***(G-11604)***

Great Miami Valley YMCA 513 868-9622
1307 Nw Washington Blvd Hamilton (45013) ***(G-11605)***

Great Miami Valley YMCA 513 829-3091
5220 Bibury Rd Fairfield (45014) ***(G-10732)***

Great Nthrn Cnsulting Svcs Inc (PA) 614 890-9999
200 E Campus View Blvd # 200 Columbus (43235) ***(G-7689)***

Great Oaks Inst Tech Creer Dev (PA) 513 613-3657
110 Great Oaks Dr Cincinnati (45241) ***(G-3644)***

Great Oaks Inst Tech Creer Dev 513 771-8840
3254 E Kemper Rd Cincinnati (45241) ***(G-3645)***

Great Rivers, Cleveland *Also called American Heart Assn Ohio Vly* ***(G-4953)***

Great Southern Video Inc 216 642-8855
4511 Rockside Rd Ste 210 Cleveland (44131) ***(G-5632)***

Great Traditions Dev Group Inc (PA) 513 563-4070
4000 Executive Park Dr # 250 Cincinnati (45241) ***(G-3646)***

Great Traditions Homes 513 759-7444
7267 Hamilton Mason Rd West Chester (45069) ***(G-18935)***

Great Value Storage 614 848-8420
5301 Tamarack Cir E Columbus (43229) ***(G-7690)***

Great Wolf Lodge, Sandusky *Also called Great Bear Lodge Sandusky LLC* ***(G-16613)***

Great Wolf Lodge, Mason *Also called Mason Family Resorts LLC* ***(G-13615)***

Greater Akron Dialysis Center, Akron *Also called Bio-Mdcal Applcations Ohio Inc* ***(G-98)***

Greater Andrson Premotes Peace 513 588-8391
7642 Athenia Dr Cincinnati (45244) ***(G-3647)***

Greater Arms Holistic Health 513 970-2767
260 Northland Blvd 131b Cincinnati (45246) ***(G-3648)***

Greater Cin Cardi Consults In 513 751-4222
2123 Auburn Ave Cincinnati (45219) ***(G-3649)***

Greater Cincinnati Behavioral (PA) 513 354-7000
1501 Madison Rd Walnut Hills (45206) ***(G-18634)***

Greater Cincinnati Behavioral 513 755-2203
1501 Madison Rd Fl 1 Walnut Hills (45206) ***(G-18635)***

Greater Cincinnati Cnvntn/Vstr 513 621-2142
525 Vine St Ste 1500 Cincinnati (45202) ***(G-3650)***

Greater Cincinnati Credit Un 513 559-1234
7948 S Masn Montgomery Rd Mason (45040) ***(G-13589)***

Greater Cincinnati Dental Labs 513 385-4222
3719 Struble Rd Cincinnati (45251) ***(G-3651)***

Greater Cincinnati Gastro Assc (PA) 513 336-8636
2925 Vernon Pl Ste 100 Cincinnati (45219) ***(G-3652)***

Greater Cincinnati Ob/Gyn Inc (PA) 513 245-3103
2830 Victory Pkwy Ste 140 Cincinnati (45206) ***(G-3653)***

GREATER CINCINNATI ORAL HEALTH, Cincinnati *Also called Cincysmiles Foundation Inc* ***(G-3288)***

ALPHABETIC SECTION
Greg Ford Sweet Inc

Greater Cincinnati Redevelopme, Cincinnati *Also called Port Grter Cincinnati Dev Auth* ***(G-4263)***
Greater Cincinnati TV Educ Fnd 513 381-4033
1223 Central Pkwy Cincinnati (45214) ***(G-3654)***
Greater Cleveland 216 566-5107
1240 W 6th St Fl 6 Cleveland (44113) ***(G-5633)***
Greater Cleveland Auto Auction 216 433-7777
5801 Engle Rd Cleveland (44142) ***(G-5634)***
Greater Cleveland Food Bnk Inc 216 738-2265
15500 S Waterloo Rd Cleveland (44110) ***(G-5635)***
Greater Cleveland Hosp Assn, Cleveland *Also called Center For Health Affairs* ***(G-5152)***
Greater Cleveland Hosp Assn 216 696-6900
1226 Huron Rd E Ste 2 Cleveland (44115) ***(G-5636)***
Greater Cleveland Partnership (PA) 216 621-3300
1240 Huron Rd E Ste 300 Cleveland (44115) ***(G-5637)***
Greater Cleveland Regional 216 575-3932
1240 W 6th St Cleveland (44113) ***(G-5638)***
Greater Cleveland Regional 216 781-1110
4601 Euclid Ave Cleveland (44103) ***(G-5639)***
Greater Clmbus Chmber Commerce, Columbus *Also called Greater Columbus Chmbr Commrce* ***(G-7692)***
Greater Clmbus Convention Ctr, Columbus *Also called Smg Holdings Inc* ***(G-8654)***
Greater Clmbus Convention Ctr 614 827-2500
400 N High St Fl 4 Columbus (43215) ***(G-7691)***
Greater Clvland Halthcare Assn 216 696-6900
1226 Huron Rd E Cleveland (44115) ***(G-5640)***
Greater Cnncnati Crime Stopper 859 468-1310
P.O. Box 14330 Cincinnati (45250) ***(G-3655)***
Greater Cnti Crdovascular Cons, Cincinnati *Also called Greater Cin Cardi Consults In* ***(G-3649)***
Greater Columbus Chmbr Commrce 614 221-1321
150 S Front St Ste 220 Columbus (43215) ***(G-7692)***
Greater Columbus Regional 614 228-9114
285 E State St Ste 170 Columbus (43215) ***(G-7693)***
Greater Dayton Cnstr Ltd 937 426-3577
4197 Research Blvd Beavercreek (45430) ***(G-1220)***
Greater Dayton Mvg & Stor Co 937 235-0011
3516 Wright Way Rd Ste 2 Dayton (45424) ***(G-9471)***
Greater Dayton Public TV (PA) 937 220-1600
110 S Jefferson St Dayton (45402) ***(G-9472)***
Greater Dayton Surgery Ctr LLC 937 535-2200
1625 Delco Park Dr Dayton (45420) ***(G-9473)***
Greater Dyton Rgnal Trnst Auth (PA) 937 425-8310
4 S Main St Ste C Dayton (45402) ***(G-9474)***
Greater Dyton Rgnal Trnst Auth 937 425-8400
600 Cmpus 600 Lngworth St 600 Longworth Dayton (45401) ***(G-9475)***
Greater Dyton Rgnal Trnst Auth 937 425-8400
600 Cmpus 600 Lngworth St 600 Longworth Dayton (45401) ***(G-9476)***
Greatr Columbus Conventn & Vis (PA) 614 221-6623
277 W Nationwide Blvd Columbus (43215) ***(G-7694)***
Green Haines Sgambati Lpa 330 743-5101
100 E Federal St Ste 800 Youngstown (44503) ***(G-20056)***
Green Circle Growers Inc (PA) 440 775-1411
51051 Us Highway 20 Oberlin (44074) ***(G-15503)***
Green Circle Growers Inc 440 775-1411
15650 State Route 511 Oberlin (44074) ***(G-15504)***
Green County Engineer, Xenia *Also called Greene County* ***(G-19903)***
Green County Housing Program, Xenia *Also called American National Red Cross* ***(G-19889)***
Green Gate, Cortland *Also called J Gilmore Design Limited* ***(G-8988)***
Green Haven Memorial Gardens 330 533-6811
3495 S Canfield Niles Rd Canfield (44406) ***(G-2139)***
GREEN HILLS, West Liberty *Also called West Liberty Care Center Inc* ***(G-19122)***
Green Impressions LLC 440 240-8508
842 Abbe Rd Sheffield Village (44054) ***(G-16734)***
Green King Company Inc 614 861-4132
9562 Taylor Rd Sw Reynoldsburg (43068) ***(G-16308)***
Green Lawn Cemetery Assn 614 444-1123
1000 Greenlawn Ave Columbus (43223) ***(G-7695)***
Green Leaf Motor Express, Ashtabula *Also called Ashtabula Chemical Corp* ***(G-707)***
Green Lines Transportation Inc (PA) 330 863-2111
7089 Alliance Rd Nw Malvern (44644) ***(G-13123)***
Green Madows Hlth Wellness Ctr, Louisville *Also called Progressive Green Meadows LLC* ***(G-12971)***
Green Springs Residential Ltd 419 639-2581
430 N Broadway St Green Springs (44836) ***(G-11353)***
Green Township Hospitality LLC (PA) 513 574-6000
5505 Rybolt Rd Cincinnati (45248) ***(G-3656)***
Greenbriar CONference& Pty Ctr, Wooster *Also called Black Tie Affair Inc* ***(G-19691)***
Greenbriar Healthcare Center, Youngstown *Also called Communicare Health Svcs Inc* ***(G-19996)***
Greenbriar Nursing Center, The, Eaton *Also called October Enterprises Inc* ***(G-10456)***
Greenbriar Retirement Center, Cleveland *Also called Greenbrier Senior Living Cmnty* ***(G-5641)***
Greenbrier Retirement Cmnty, Cleveland *Also called Greenbrier Senior Living Cmnty* ***(G-5642)***
Greenbrier Senior Living Cmnty 440 888-5900
6455 Pearl Rd Cleveland (44130) ***(G-5641)***
Greenbrier Senior Living Cmnty 440 888-0400
6457 Pearl Rd Cleveland (44130) ***(G-5642)***
Greene Cnty Chld Svc Brd Frbrn 937 878-1415
601 Ledbetter Rd Ste A Xenia (45385) ***(G-19901)***
Greene Cnty Combined Hlth Dst 937 374-5600
360 Wilson Dr Xenia (45385) ***(G-19902)***
Greene County 937 562-7500
615 Dayton Xenia Rd Xenia (45385) ***(G-19903)***
Greene County 937 562-6000
541 Ledbetter Rd Xenia (45385) ***(G-19904)***
Greene County 937 562-7800
641 Dayton Xenia Rd Xenia (45385) ***(G-19905)***
Greene County Career Center 937 372-6941
2960 W Enon Rd Xenia (45385) ***(G-19906)***
Greene County Public Health, Xenia *Also called Greene Cnty Combined Hlth Dst* ***(G-19902)***
Greene County Services, Xenia *Also called Greene County* ***(G-19905)***
Greene Inc 937 562-4200
121 Fairground Rd Xenia (45385) ***(G-19907)***
Greene Memorial Hosp Svcs Inc 937 352-2000
1 Prestige Pl Ste 910 Miamisburg (45342) ***(G-14174)***
Greene Memorial Hospital Inc (HQ) 937 352-2000
1141 N Monroe Dr Xenia (45385) ***(G-19908)***
Greene Memorial Hospital Inc 937 458-4500
3359 Kemp Rd Beavercreek (45431) ***(G-1154)***
Greene Oaks 937 352-2800
164 Office Park Dr Xenia (45385) ***(G-19909)***
Greene Oaks Health Center, Xenia *Also called Greene Oaks* ***(G-19909)***
Greene Town Center LLC 937 490-4990
4452 Buckeye Ln Beavercreek (45440) ***(G-1221)***
Greene, The, Beavercreek *Also called Greene Town Center LLC* ***(G-1221)***
Greeneview Foods LLC 937 675-4161
96 W Washington St Jamestown (45335) ***(G-12187)***
GREENFIELD AREA MEDICAL CENTER, Chillicothe *Also called Adena Health System* ***(G-2751)***
Greenfield Area Medical Ctr 937 981-9400
550 Mirabeau St Greenfield (45123) ***(G-11361)***
Greenfield Family Health Ctr, Greenfield *Also called Healthsource of Ohio Inc* ***(G-11363)***
Greenfield Health Systems Corp (PA) 419 389-9681
3401 Glendale Ave Ste 110 Toledo (43614) ***(G-17771)***
Greenfield Hts Oper Group LLC 312 877-1153
1318 Chestnut St Lima (45804) ***(G-12648)***
Greenfield Products Inc 937 981-2696
1230 N Washington St Greenfield (45123) ***(G-11362)***
Greenleaf Auto Recyclers LLC 330 832-6001
12192 Lincoln Way Nw Massillon (44647) ***(G-13689)***
Greenleaf Family Center (PA) 330 376-9494
580 Grant St Akron (44311) ***(G-245)***
Greenleaf Landscapes Inc 740 373-1639
414 Muskingum Dr Marietta (45750) ***(G-13332)***
Greenleaf Ohio LLC 330 832-6001
12192 Lincoln Way Nw Massillon (44647) ***(G-13690)***
Greenline Foods Inc (HQ) 419 354-1149
12700 S Dixie Hwy Bowling Green (43402) ***(G-1732)***
Greenpro Services Inc 937 748-1559
2969 Beal Rd Franklin (45005) ***(G-11030)***
Greens of Lyndhurst The Inc 440 460-1000
1555 Brainard Rd Apt 305 Cleveland (44124) ***(G-5643)***
Greenscapes Landscape Arch, Columbus *Also called Greenscapes Landscape Company* ***(G-7696)***
Greenscapes Landscape Company 614 837-1869
4220 Winchester Pike Columbus (43232) ***(G-7696)***
Greenspace Enterprise Tech Inc 888 309-8517
8401 Claude Thomas Rd # 28 Franklin (45005) ***(G-11031)***
Greenstar Mid-America LLC 330 784-1167
1535 Exeter Rd Akron (44306) ***(G-246)***
Greentech Corporation 937 339-4758
1405 S County Road 25a Troy (45373) ***(G-18204)***
Greentech Lawn and Irrigation, Troy *Also called Greentech Corporation* ***(G-18204)***
Greentown Volunteer Fire Dept 330 494-3002
10100 Cleveland Ave Nw Uniontown (44685) ***(G-18372)***
Greentree Group Inc (PA) 937 490-5500
1360 Tech Ct Ste 100 Dayton (45430) ***(G-9477)***
Greentree Inn, Sandusky *Also called Sortino Management & Dev Co* ***(G-16643)***
Greenville Federal 937 548-4158
690 Wagner Ave Greenville (45331) ***(G-11381)***
Greenville National Bancorp (PA) 937 548-1114
446 S Bwy St Greenville (45331) ***(G-11382)***
Greenville National Bank 937 548-1114
446 S Broadway St Greenville (45331) ***(G-11383)***
Greenville Noland, Moraine *Also called Noland Company* ***(G-14684)***
Greenville Township Rescue 937 548-9339
1401 Sater St Greenville (45331) ***(G-11384)***
Greenwood Chevrolet Inc 330 270-1299
4695 Mahoning Ave Youngstown (44515) ***(G-20057)***
Greenwood's Oldsmobile, Hubbard *Also called Greenwoods Hubbard Chevy-Olds* ***(G-11946)***
Greenwoods Hubbard Chevy-Olds 330 568-4335
2635 N Main St Hubbard (44425) ***(G-11946)***
Greer & Whitehead Cnstr Inc 513 202-1757
510 S State St Ste D Harrison (45030) ***(G-11668)***
Greer Steel Company 330 343-8811
1 Boat St Dover (44622) ***(G-10080)***
Greg Ford Sweet Inc 440 593-7714
4011 E Center St North Kingsville (44068) ***(G-15257)***

ALPHABETIC

Greg Sweet Ford, North Kingsville Also called Greg Ford Sweet Inc (G-15257)
Greiner Dental & Associates, Mentor Also called Raymond A Greiner DDS Inc (G-14100)
Greiner Dental Association..440 255-2600
  7553 Center St Mentor (44060) (G-14057)
Greiser Transportation, Wauseon Also called Daves Sand & Stone Inc (G-18798)
Grenada Stamping Assembly Inc (HQ)..................................419 842-3600
  3810 Herr Rd Sylvania (43560) (G-17427)
GREY STONE, Canton Also called Stone Products Inc (G-2500)
Greyhound Lines Inc...513 421-7442
  1005 Gilbert Ave Cincinnati (45202) (G-3657)
Greyhound Lines Inc...614 221-0577
  111 E Town St Ste 100 Columbus (43215) (G-7697)
Greystone Health and, Cambridge Also called Cambridge NH LLC (G-2054)
Grgstormpro, Akron Also called Glencoe Restoration Group LLC (G-236)
Gribble Foods, Loudonville Also called Jo Lynn Inc (G-12958)
Griffin Wheel, Groveport Also called Amsted Industries Incorporated (G-11493)
Grimes Aerospace Company..937 484-2001
  550 State Route 55 Urbana (43078) (G-18436)
Grimes Seeds, Concord Twp Also called Gardenlife Inc (G-8945)
Grippo Foods Inc...513 923-1900
  6750 Colerain Ave Cincinnati (45239) (G-3658)
Grismer Tire Company (PA)..937 643-2526
  1099 S Main St Centerville (45458) (G-2626)
Grizzly Golf Center Inc...513 398-5200
  6042 Fairway Dr Mason (45040) (G-13590)
Grl Engineers Inc (PA)..216 831-6131
  30725 Aurora Rd Solon (44139) (G-16855)
Grob Systems Inc...419 358-9015
  1070 Navajo Dr Bluffton (45817) (G-1691)
Grocery Outlet Supermarket, Hartville Also called Sommers Market LLC (G-11699)
Grogans Towne Chrysler Inc (PA)..419 476-0761
  6100 Telegraph Rd Toledo (43612) (G-17772)
Grogg, Terry W MD, Grove City Also called Southwestern Obstetricians & G (G-11473)
Grooveryde Cle...323 595-1701
  1120 Chester Ave Cleveland (44114) (G-5644)
Gross Builders, Cleveland Also called I & M J Gross Company (G-5731)
Gross Electric Inc (PA)...419 537-1818
  2807 N Reynolds Rd Toledo (43615) (G-17773)
Gross Lumber Inc...330 683-2055
  8848 Ely Rd Apple Creek (44606) (G-619)
Gross Plumbing Incorporated..440 324-9999
  6843 Lake Ave Elyria (44035) (G-10514)
Gross Supply, Elyria Also called Gross Plumbing Incorporated (G-10514)
Grote Enterprises LLC (PA)...513 731-5700
  5240 Lester Rd Cincinnati (45213) (G-3659)
Ground Effects LLC..440 565-5925
  31000 Viking Pkwy Westlake (44145) (G-19346)
Ground Tech Inc...330 270-0700
  240 Sinter Ct Youngstown (44510) (G-20058)
Groundspro LLC...513 242-1700
  9405 Sutton Pl West Chester (45011) (G-18936)
Groundsystems Inc (PA)..800 570-0213
  11315 Williamson Rd Blue Ash (45241) (G-1573)
Groundsystems Inc...937 903-5325
  2929 Northlawn Ave Moraine (45439) (G-14665)
Group Health Associates, Cincinnati Also called Trihealth G LLC (G-4644)
Group Management Services Inc (PA)....................................330 659-0100
  3750 Timberlake Dr Richfield (44286) (G-16359)
Group Midwest, North Canton Also called Midwest Communications Inc (G-15221)
Group Transportation Svcs Inc, Hudson Also called Ascent Global Logistics Holdin (G-11967)
Groupcle LLC...216 251-9641
  12500 Berea Rd Cleveland (44111) (G-5645)
Grove City Community Club...614 875-6074
  3397 Civic Pl Grove City (43123) (G-11437)
Grove City-Doh, Grove City Also called Synnex Corporation (G-11475)
Grove Cy Chrstn Child Care Ctr...614 875-2551
  4770 Hoover Rd Grove City (43123) (G-11438)
Grove Walnut Country Club Inc..937 253-3109
  5050 Linden Ave Dayton (45432) (G-9174)
Groveport Warehouse, Groveport Also called Nifco America Corporation (G-11528)
Growthplay, Dayton Also called Silver Spruce Holding LLC (G-9770)
Grubb Construction Inc...419 293-2316
  896 State Route 613 Mc Comb (45858) (G-13894)
Grunwell-Cashero Co..419 476-2426
  5212 Tractor Rd Toledo (43612) (G-17774)
Gs Ohio Inc..614 885-5350
  8573 Owenfield Dr Powell (43065) (G-16196)
Gs1 Us Inc...609 620-0200
  7887 Wash Vlg Dr Ste 300 Dayton (45459) (G-9478)
Gsf North American Jantr Svc..513 733-1451
  9850 Prnceton Glendale Rd West Chester (45246) (G-19057)
GTC Artist With Machines, Columbus Also called General Theming Contrs LLC (G-7655)
GTE Internet...614 508-6000
  6816 Lauffer Rd Columbus (43231) (G-7698)
GTM Service Inc (PA)...440 944-5099
  1366 Rockefeller Rd Wickliffe (44092) (G-19462)
Guaranteed Truck Service, Cleveland Also called W W Williams Company LLC (G-6646)
Guardian Alarm, Toledo Also called GA Business Purchaser LLC (G-17752)

Guardian Angels Senior HM Svc, Sylvania Also called Guardian Angls Home Hlth Svcs (G-17428)
Guardian Angls Home Hlth Svcs...419 517-7797
  8553 Sylvania Metamora Rd Sylvania (43560) (G-17428)
Guardian Business Services...614 416-6090
  3948 Townsfair Way # 220 Columbus (43219) (G-7699)
Guardian Care Services..614 436-8500
  665 E Dublin Granville Rd # 330 Columbus (43229) (G-7700)
Guardian Elde..419 225-9040
  804 S Mumaugh Rd Lima (45804) (G-12649)
Guardian Elder Care LLC..330 549-0898
  9625 Market St North Lima (44452) (G-15269)
Guardian Elder Care Columbus...614 868-9306
  2425 Kimberly Pkwy E Columbus (43232) (G-7701)
Guardian Enterprise Group Inc..614 416-6080
  3948 Townsfair Way # 220 Columbus (43219) (G-7702)
Guardian Home Technology, Youngstown Also called Guardian Protection Svcs Inc (G-20059)
Guardian Life Insur Co of Amer..513 579-1114
  419 Plum St Cincinnati (45202) (G-3660)
Guardian Protection Svcs Inc...513 422-5319
  9852 Windisch Rd West Chester (45069) (G-18937)
Guardian Protection Svcs Inc...330 797-1570
  5401 Ashley Cir Ste A Youngstown (44515) (G-20059)
Guardian Savings Bank (PA)...513 942-3535
  6100 W Chester Rd West Chester (45069) (G-18938)
Guardian Savings Bank...513 528-8787
  560 Ohio Pike Cincinnati (45255) (G-3661)
Guardian Water & Power Inc (PA)..614 291-3141
  1160 Goodale Blvd Columbus (43212) (G-7703)
Guardsmark LLC..513 851-5523
  4050 Executive Park Dr # 350 Cincinnati (45241) (G-3662)
Guardsmark LLC..419 229-9300
  209 N Main St Ste 4a Lima (45801) (G-12650)
Gudenkauf Corporation (PA)...614 488-1776
  2679 Mckinley Ave Columbus (43204) (G-7704)
Guenther & Sons Inc..513 738-1448
  2578 Long St Ross (45061) (G-16456)
Guenther Mechanical Inc..419 289-6900
  1248 Middle Rowsburg Rd Ashland (44805) (G-674)
Guerbet, Cincinnati Also called Liebel-Flarsheim Company LLC (G-3926)
Guernsey Cnty Children Svcs Bd, Cambridge Also called County of Guernsey (G-2060)
Guernsey Co Public Info Agency, Cambridge Also called County of Guernsey (G-2061)
GUERNSEY COUNTY CDC, Cambridge Also called Guernsey County Cmnty Dev Corp (G-2071)
Guernsey County Cmnty Dev Corp..740 439-0020
  905 Wheeling Ave Cambridge (43725) (G-2071)
Guernsey County Senior Center, Cambridge Also called County of Guernsey (G-2063)
Guernsey Health Enterprises..740 439-3561
  1341 Clark St Cambridge (43725) (G-2072)
Guernsey Health Systems (HQ)...740 439-3561
  1341 Clark St Cambridge (43725) (G-2073)
GUERNSEY INDUSTRIES, Byesville Also called Ken Harper (G-2025)
Guernsey-Muskingum Elc Coop, New Concord Also called Guernsy-Muskingum Elc Coop Inc (G-14900)
Guernsy Counseling Center, Cambridge Also called Allwell Behavioral Health Svcs (G-2049)
Guernsy-Muskingum Elc Coop Inc (PA)...................................740 826-7661
  17 S Liberty St New Concord (43762) (G-14900)
Guess Motors Inc (PA)..866 890-0522
  457 Steubenville Rd Se Carrollton (44615) (G-2571)
Guild Associates Inc (PA)..614 798-8215
  5750 Shier Rings Rd Dublin (43016) (G-10236)
Guild Biosciences, Dublin Also called Guild Associates Inc (G-10236)
Guild Custom Drapery, Cleveland Also called Farrow Cleaners Co (G-5514)
Gulf South Medical Supply Inc...614 501-9080
  915 Taylor Rd Unit A Gahanna (43230) (G-11123)
Gulfport Energy Corporation..740 251-0407
  67185 Executive Dr Saint Clairsville (43950) (G-16487)
Gummer Wholesale Inc (PA)...740 928-0415
  1945 James Pkwy Heath (43056) (G-11704)
Gund Sports Marketing Llc..216 420-2000
  100 Gateway Plz Cleveland (44115) (G-5646)
Gundlach Sheet Metal Works Inc (PA)....................................419 626-4525
  910 Columbus Ave Sandusky (44870) (G-16614)
Gundlach Sheet Metal Works Inc..419 734-7351
  2439 E Gill Rd Port Clinton (43452) (G-16108)
Gunning & Assocaites Marketing..513 688-1370
  6355 E Kemper Rd Ste 250 Cincinnati (45241) (G-3663)
Gunton Corporation (PA)...216 831-2420
  26150 Richmond Rd Cleveland (44146) (G-5647)
Gus Holthaus Signs Inc..513 861-0060
  817 Ridgeway Ave Cincinnati (45229) (G-3664)
Gus Perdikakis Associates...513 583-0900
  9155 Governors Way Unit A Cincinnati (45249) (G-3665)
Gust Gallucci Co...216 881-0045
  6610 Euclid Ave Cleveland (44103) (G-5648)
Gutknecht Construction Company..614 532-5410
  2280 Citygate Dr Columbus (43219) (G-7705)
Guy's Party Ctr, Akron Also called Guys Party Center (G-247)
Guyler Automotive, Middletown Also called I-75 Pierson Automotive Inc (G-14350)

Guys Party Center 330 724-6373
  500 E Waterloo Rd Akron (44319) (G-247)
Gw Business Solutions LLC 740 645-9861
  65 S 5th St Newark (43055) (G-15039)
Gw Sutherland MD 419 578-7200
  2865 N Reynolds Rd # 160 Toledo (43615) (G-17775)
Gws FF&e LLC 513 759-6000
  9823 Cincinnati Dayton Rd West Chester (45069) (G-18939)
Gymnastic World Inc 440 526-2970
  6630 Harris Rd Cleveland (44147) (G-5649)
Gymnastics Center, Canton Also called Y M C A Central Stark County (G-2540)
Gyneclgic Onclgists of Ne Ohio (PA) 330 384-6041
  224 W Exchange St Ste 140 Akron (44302) (G-248)
Gypc Inc 309 677-0405
  475 Stonehaven Rd Dayton (45429) (G-9479)
H & B Window Cleaning Inc 440 934-6158
  753 Avon Belden Rd Ste D Avon Lake (44012) (G-918)
H & C Building Supplies, Huron Also called Huron Cement Products Company (G-12026)
H & D Steel Service Inc 440 237-3390
  9960 York Alpha Dr North Royalton (44133) (G-15357)
H & D Steel Service Center, North Royalton Also called H & D Steel Service Inc (G-15357)
H & H Auto Parts Inc (PA) 330 456-4778
  300 15th St Sw Canton (44707) (G-2332)
H & H Auto Parts Inc 330 494-2975
  6434 Wise Ave Nw Canton (44720) (G-2333)
H & H Retreading Inc 740 682-7721
  5400 State Route 93 Oak Hill (45656) (G-15480)
H & M Harley Davidson, Dover Also called Adventure Harley Davidson (G-10064)
H & M Patch Company 614 339-8950
  2500 Farmers Dr 110 Columbus (43235) (G-7706)
H & M Plumbing Co 614 491-4880
  4015 Alum Creek Dr Columbus (43207) (G-7707)
H & M Precision Concrete LLC 937 547-0012
  7805 Arcanum Bearsmill Rd Greenville (45331) (G-11385)
H & R Block, Nevada Also called Phillip Mc Guire (G-14838)
H & R Block, Cleveland Also called H&R Block Inc (G-5653)
H & R Block 419 352-9467
  241 S Main St Bowling Green (43402) (G-1733)
H & R Block Inc 330 345-1040
  2831 Cleveland Rd Wooster (44691) (G-19726)
H & R Block Inc 513 868-1818
  2304a Dixie Hwy Hamilton (45015) (G-11606)
H & R Block Brunswick, Brunswick Also called Dw Together LLC (G-1928)
H & R Concrete Inc 937 885-2910
  9120 State Route 48 Dayton (45458) (G-9480)
H & W Contractors Inc 330 833-0982
  1722 1st St Ne Massillon (44646) (G-13691)
H & W Holdings LLC 800 826-3560
  341 County Road 120 S South Point (45680) (G-16935)
H A Dorsten Inc 419 628-2327
  146 N Main St Minster (45865) (G-14535)
H A M Landscaping Inc 216 663-6666
  4667 Northfield Rd Cleveland (44128) (G-5650)
H B Magruder Memorial Hospital 419 734-4539
  611 Fulton St Port Clinton (43452) (G-16109)
H C F Inc 740 289-2528
  7143 Us Rte 23 Piketon (45661) (G-15976)
H C R Corp 419 472-0076
  4293 Monroe St Toledo (43606) (G-17776)
H Dennert Distributing Corp 513 871-7272
  351 Wilmer Ave Cincinnati (45226) (G-3666)
H E R, Westerville Also called Her Inc (G-19172)
H E R Realtors, Worthington Also called Her Inc (G-19814)
H E R Realtors, Columbus Also called Her Inc (G-7742)
H E R Realtors, Columbus Also called Her Inc (G-7743)
H E R Realtors, Dublin Also called Her Inc (G-10240)
H E R Realtors, Hilliard Also called Her Inc (G-11772)
H F A, Akron Also called Hitchcock Fleming & Assoc Inc (G-263)
H G C, Cincinnati Also called Hgc Construction Co (G-370)
H G R, Euclid Also called Hgr Industrial Surplus Inc (G-10639)
H Hansen Industries, Toledo Also called Riverside Marine Inds Inc (G-18008)
H K M, Cleveland Also called Hkm Drect Mkt Cmmnications Inc (G-5696)
H L C Trucking Inc 740 676-6181
  57245 Ferry Landing Rd Shadyside (43947) (G-16695)
H Leff Electric Company (PA) 216 325-0941
  4700 Spring Rd Cleveland (44131) (G-5651)
H M Miller Construction Co 330 628-4811
  1225 Waterloo Rd Mogadore (44260) (G-14549)
H M T Dermatology Inc 330 725-0569
  5783 Wooster Pike Medina (44256) (G-13946)
H O C J Inc 614 539-4601
  2135 Hardy Parkway St Grove City (43123) (G-11439)
H P Products Corporation 513 683-8553
  7135 E Kemper Rd Cincinnati (45249) (G-3667)
H R Chally Group, Dayton Also called SSS Consulting Inc (G-9788)
H T I Express 419 423-9555
  110 Bentley Ct Findlay (45840) (G-10915)
H T V Industries Inc 216 514-0060
  30195 Chagrin Blvd 310n Cleveland (44124) (G-5652)

H&H Custom Homes LLC 419 994-4070
  16573 State Route 3 Loudonville (44842) (G-12956)
H&R Block Inc 440 282-4288
  1980 G Coper Foster Pk Rd Amherst (44001) (G-589)
H&R Block Inc 216 861-1185
  2068 W 25th St Cleveland (44113) (G-5653)
H. Meyer Dairy, Cincinnati Also called Borden Dairy Co Cincinnati LLC (G-3068)
Haag-Streit USA Inc 513 336-7255
  5500 Courseview Dr Mason (45040) (G-13591)
Haag-Streit USA Inc (HQ) 513 336-7255
  3535 Kings Mills Rd Mason (45040) (G-13592)
Haas Doors, Wauseon Also called Nofziger Door Sales Inc (G-18808)
Haasz Automall LLC 330 296-2866
  4886 State Route 59 Ravenna (44266) (G-16245)
Hab Computer Services, Solon Also called Hab Inc (G-16856)
Hab Inc 608 785-7650
  28925 Fountain Pkwy Solon (44139) (G-16856)
Habco Tool and Dev Co Inc 440 946-5546
  7725 Metric Dr Mentor (44060) (G-14058)
Habegger Corporation (PA) 513 853-6644
  4995 Winton Rd Cincinnati (45232) (G-3668)
Habegger Corporation 330 499-4328
  7580 Whipple Ave Nw North Canton (44720) (G-15209)
Habegger Corporation 513 612-4700
  11413 Enterprise Park Dr Cincinnati (45241) (G-3669)
Habitat For Humanity 216 429-1299
  2110 W 110th St Cleveland (44102) (G-5654)
Habitat For Humanity-Midohio (PA) 614 422-4828
  6665 Busch Blvd Columbus (43229) (G-7708)
Habitec Security Inc (PA) 419 537-6768
  1545 Timber Wolf Dr Holland (43528) (G-11887)
Hackensack Meridian Health Inc 513 792-9697
  4650 E Galbraith Rd Cincinnati (45236) (G-3670)
Hadassah Dayton Chapter 937 275-0227
  880 Fernshire Dr Dayton (45459) (G-9481)
Hadler Company, Columbus Also called Hadler Realty Company (G-7709)
Hadler Realty Company 614 457-6650
  2000 Henderson Rd Ste 500 Columbus (43220) (G-7709)
Hadler-Zimmerman Inc 614 457-6650
  2000 Henderson Rd Ste 500 Columbus (43220) (G-7710)
Hafenbrack Mktg Cmmnctions Inc 937 424-8950
  116 E 3rd St Dayton (45402) (G-9482)
Haggerty Logistics Inc 734 713-9800
  95 W Crescentville Rd Cincinnati (45246) (G-3671)
Hague Water Conditioning Inc (PA) 614 482-8121
  4581 Homer Ohio Ln Groveport (43125) (G-11515)
Hahmooeser & Parks 330 864-5550
  200 Public Sq Ste 2000 Cleveland (44114) (G-5655)
Hahn Automotive Warehouse Inc 937 223-1068
  32 Franklin St Dayton (45402) (G-9483)
Hahn Loeser & Parks, Columbus Also called Firm Hahn Law (G-7579)
Hahn Loeser & Parks LLP (PA) 216 621-0150
  200 Public Sq Ste 2800 Cleveland (44114) (G-5656)
Hahs Factory Outlet 330 405-4227
  1993 Case Pkwy Twinsburg (44087) (G-18277)
Haid Acquisitions LLC 513 941-8700
  1053 Ebenezer Rd Cincinnati (45233) (G-3672)
Haines & Company Inc (PA) 330 494-9111
  8050 Freedom Ave Nw A North Canton (44720) (G-15210)
Hair Forum 513 245-0800
  5801 Cheviot Rd Unit 1 Cincinnati (45247) (G-3673)
Hair Removal Center of So, Dayton Also called Laser Hair Removal Center (G-9559)
Hair Shoppe Inc 330 497-1651
  6460 Wise Ave Nw Canton (44720) (G-2334)
Hairitage, The, Zanesville Also called Brenwood Inc (G-20283)
Hairy Cactus Salon Inc 513 771-9335
  9437 Civic Centre Blvd B West Chester (45069) (G-18940)
Hajoca Corporation 216 447-0050
  6606 Granger Rd Cleveland (44131) (G-5657)
Hal Homes Inc (PA) 513 984-5360
  9545 Kenwood Rd Ste 401 Blue Ash (45242) (G-1574)
Halcomb Concrete Construction 513 829-3576
  1409 Veterans Dr Fairfield (45014) (G-10733)
Hale Farm & Village, Bath Also called Western Reserve Historical Soc (G-1019)
HALE FARM & VILLAGE, Cleveland Also called Western Reserve Historical Soc (G-6675)
Halker Drywall & Plastering, Columbus Grove Also called Halker Drywall Inc (G-8941)
Halker Drywall Inc 419 646-3679
  21457 Road 15u Columbus Grove (45830) (G-8941)
Hall Contracting Services Inc 440 930-0050
  33540 Pin Oak Pkwy Avon Lake (44012) (G-919)
Hall Nazareth Inc 419 832-2900
  21211 W State Route 65 Grand Rapids (43522) (G-11325)
Halleen Kia, North Olmsted Also called Affordable Cars & Finance Inc (G-15277)
Halley Consulting Group LLC 614 899-7325
  1224 Oak Bluff Ct Westerville (43081) (G-19258)
Halliburton Energy Svcs Inc 740 617-2917
  4999 E Pointe Dr Zanesville (43701) (G-20314)
Hallmark Home Mortgage LLC 614 568-1960
  7965 N High St Ste 100 Columbus (43235) (G-7711)
Hallmark Management Associates (PA) 216 681-0080
  1821 Noble Rd Ofc C Cleveland (44112) (G-5658)

A
L
P
H
A
B
E
T
I
C

Haly Chapter 136, Napoleon *Also called Royal Arch Masons of Ohio* ***(G-14816)***
Hamilton Automotive Warehouse (PA)....513 896-4100
630 Maple Ave Hamilton (45011) ***(G-11607)***
Hamilton Cnty Auditor Office....513 946-4000
138 E Court St Rm 501 Cincinnati (45202) ***(G-3674)***
Hamilton Counseling Center T/S, Hamilton *Also called Butler Bhavioral Hlth Svcs Inc* ***(G-11564)***
Hamilton County Eductl Svc Ctr....513 674-4200
924 Waycross Rd Cincinnati (45240) ***(G-3675)***
Hamilton County Parks District....513 825-3701
10999 Mill Rd Cincinnati (45240) ***(G-3676)***
Hamilton County Society (PA)....513 541-6100
3949 Colerain Ave Cincinnati (45223) ***(G-3677)***
Hamilton Healthcare, Columbus *Also called Hamilton Homecare Inc* ***(G-7712)***
Hamilton Homecare Inc....614 221-0022
309 S 4th St Columbus (43215) ***(G-7712)***
Hamilton Ice Arena, Cleveland *Also called City of Rocky River* ***(G-5214)***
Hamilton Lodge 93 Benevolant P....513 887-4384
4444 Hmlton Middletown Rd Liberty Twp (45011) ***(G-12586)***
Hamilton Manufacturing Corp....419 867-4858
1026 Hamilton Dr Holland (43528) ***(G-11888)***
Hamilton Parks Conservancy....513 785-7055
106 N 2nd St Hamilton (45011) ***(G-11608)***
Hamilton Safe Products Co Inc....614 268-5530
4770 Northwest Pkwy Hilliard (43026) ***(G-11771)***
Hamilton Scrap Processors....513 863-3474
134 Hensel Pl Hamilton (45011) ***(G-11609)***
Hamilton-Parker Company (PA)....614 358-7800
1865 Leonard Ave Columbus (43219) ***(G-7713)***
Hamlet Manor, Chagrin Falls *Also called Golden Living LLC* ***(G-2647)***
Hamlet Nursing Home, Chagrin Falls *Also called Hamlet Village In Chagrin FLS* ***(G-2648)***
Hamlet Village In Chagrin FLS....440 247-4200
150 Cleveland St Chagrin Falls (44022) ***(G-2648)***
Hamlet Village In Chagrin FLS (PA)....216 263-6033
200 Hamlet Hills Dr Ofc Chagrin Falls (44022) ***(G-2649)***
Hammacher Schlemmer & Co Inc....513 860-4570
9180 La Saint Dr West Chester (45069) ***(G-18941)***
Hammer Smith Agency, Massillon *Also called F W Arnold Agency Co Inc* ***(G-13679)***
Hammond Construction Inc....330 455-7039
1278 Park Ave Sw Canton (44706) ***(G-2335)***
Hammond Law Group LLC....513 381-2011
441 Vine St Ste 3200 Cincinnati (45202) ***(G-3678)***
Hammontree & Associates Ltd (PA)....330 499-8817
5233 Stoneham Rd Canton (44720) ***(G-2336)***
Hampson Insurance Agency, Lancaster *Also called Nl of Ky Inc* ***(G-12423)***
Hampton Inn, Fremont *Also called Sunrise Hospitality Inc* ***(G-11102)***
Hampton Inn, Rossford *Also called Rossford Hospitality Group Inc* ***(G-16464)***
Hampton Inn, Columbus *Also called Carlisle Hotels Inc* ***(G-7129)***
Hampton Inn, Columbus *Also called Riverview Hotel LLC* ***(G-8538)***
Hampton Inn, Cincinnati *Also called Sree Hotels LLC* ***(G-4525)***
Hampton Inn, Columbus *Also called Indus Airport Hotel II LLC* ***(G-7808)***
Hampton Inn, Marietta *Also called March Investors Ltd* ***(G-13346)***
Hampton Inn, Marysville *Also called Geeta Hospitality Inc* ***(G-13499)***
Hampton Inn, Lima *Also called Roschmans Restaurant ADM* ***(G-12734)***
Hampton Inn, Streetsboro *Also called Meander Hsptality Group II LLC* ***(G-17260)***
Hampton Inn, Maumee *Also called Bennett Enterprises Inc* ***(G-13762)***
Hampton Inn, Bowling Green *Also called R & Y Holding* ***(G-1747)***
Hampton Inn, Saint Clairsville *Also called Somnus Corporation* ***(G-16505)***
Hampton Inn, Columbus *Also called Ntk Hotel Group II LLC* ***(G-8212)***
Hampton Inn, Troy *Also called S P S Inc* ***(G-18228)***
Hampton Inn, Hilliard *Also called Parkins Incorporated* ***(G-11805)***
Hampton Inn & Suite Inc....440 234-0206
7074 Engle Rd Middleburg Heights (44130) ***(G-14253)***
Hampton Inn and Suites, Beachwood *Also called Buffalo-Gtb Associates LLC* ***(G-1040)***
Hampton Inn Cinc Nw/Fairfield, Fairfield *Also called Middletown Innkeepers Inc* ***(G-10758)***
Hampton Inn Cleveland, North Olmsted *Also called Grand Heritage Hotel Portland* ***(G-15291)***
Hampton Inn Columbus Airport, Dublin *Also called Hit Portfolio I Hil Trs LLC* ***(G-10243)***
Hampton Inn Stes Clmbus Hllard, Hilliard *Also called Indus Hilliard Hotel LLC* ***(G-11777)***
Hampton Inn Youngstown West, Youngstown *Also called Meander Inn Incorporated* ***(G-20121)***
Hampton Inn-Newark/Heath, Newark *Also called Kribha LLC* ***(G-15046)***
Hampton Inns LLC....330 492-0151
5335 Broadmoor Cir Nw Canton (44709) ***(G-2337)***
Hampton Inns LLC....330 422-0500
800 Mondial Pkwy Streetsboro (44241) ***(G-17255)***
Hampton Woods Nursing Ctr Inc....330 707-1400
1525 E Western Reserve Rd Poland (44514) ***(G-16084)***
Hanby Farms Inc....740 763-3554
10790 Newark Rd Nashport (43830) ***(G-14819)***
Hanco Ambulance Inc....419 423-2912
417 6th St Findlay (45840) ***(G-10916)***
Hanco International....330 456-9407
1605 Waynesburg Dr Se Canton (44707) ***(G-2338)***
Hancock County Engineer, Findlay *Also called County of Hancock* ***(G-10893)***
Hancock County Home, Findlay *Also called County of Hancock* ***(G-10892)***
Hancock Federal Credit Union....419 420-0338
1701 E Melrose Ave Findlay (45840) ***(G-10917)***
Hancock Hardin Wyandot Putnam (PA)....419 423-3755
122 Jefferson St Findlay (45840) ***(G-10918)***
Hancock Hotel, Findlay *Also called 631 South Main Street Dev LLC* ***(G-10861)***
Hancock Job & Family Services....419 424-7022
7814 County Road 140 Findlay (45840) ***(G-10919)***
Hancock Park District, Findlay *Also called County of Hancock* ***(G-10894)***
Hancock-Wood Electric Coop Inc (PA)....419 257-3241
1399 Business Park Dr S North Baltimore (45872) ***(G-15177)***
Hand Ctr At Orthopaedic Inst....937 298-4417
3205 Woodman Dr Dayton (45420) ***(G-9484)***
Hand Rehabilitation Associates....330 668-4055
3925 Embassy Pkwy Ste 200 Akron (44333) ***(G-249)***
Handl-It Inc....440 439-9400
7120 Krick Rd Ste 1a Bedford (44146) ***(G-1283)***
Handl-It Inc (PA)....330 468-0734
360 Highland Rd E 2 Macedonia (44056) ***(G-13073)***
Handson Central Ohio Inc....614 221-2255
1105 Schrock Rd Ste 107 Columbus (43229) ***(G-7714)***
Handy Hubby....419 754-1150
2010 N Reynolds Rd Toledo (43615) ***(G-17777)***
Haney Inc....513 561-1441
5657 Wooster Pike Cincinnati (45227) ***(G-3679)***
Haney PRC, Cincinnati *Also called Haney Inc* ***(G-3679)***
Hanger Prosthetics & (HQ)....330 633-9807
33 North Ave Ste 101 Tallmadge (44278) ***(G-17475)***
Hankook Tire Akron Office, Uniontown *Also called Hankook Tire America Corp* ***(G-18373)***
Hankook Tire America Corp....330 896-6199
3535 Forest Lake Dr Uniontown (44685) ***(G-18373)***
Hanlin-Rainaldi Construction....614 436-4204
6610 Singletree Dr Columbus (43229) ***(G-7715)***
Hanna Cambell & Powell....330 670-7300
3737 Embassy Pkwy Ste 100 Akron (44333) ***(G-250)***
Hanna Chevrolet Cadillac, Steubenville *Also called Transmerica Svcs Technical Sup* ***(G-17175)***
Hanna Commercial LLC....216 861-7200
1350 Euclid Ave Ste 700 Cleveland (44115) ***(G-5659)***
Hanna Commercial Real Estate, Cleveland *Also called Hanna Commercial LLC* ***(G-5659)***
Hanna Holdings Inc....440 971-5600
9485 W Sprague Rd North Royalton (44133) ***(G-15358)***
Hanna Holdings Inc....440 933-6195
2100 Center Rd Ste L Avon (44011) ***(G-884)***
Hanna Holdings Inc....330 707-1000
100 W Mckinley Way Poland (44514) ***(G-16085)***
HANNA PERKIN CENTER, Shaker Heights *Also called Hanna Perkins School* ***(G-16709)***
Hanna Perkins School....216 991-4472
19910 Malvern Rd Shaker Heights (44122) ***(G-16709)***
Hannon Co, The, Canton *Also called Hanco International* ***(G-2338)***
Hannon Company (PA)....330 456-4728
1605 Waynesburg Dr Se Canton (44707) ***(G-2339)***
Hanover House Inc....330 837-1741
435 Avis Ave Nw Massillon (44646) ***(G-13692)***
Hanover Insurance Company....614 408-9000
545 Metro Pl S Ste 380 Dublin (43017) ***(G-10237)***
Hanover Insurance Company....513 829-4555
6061 Winton Rd Fairfield (45014) ***(G-10734)***
Hans Rothenbuhler & Son Inc....440 632-6000
15815 Nauvoo Rd Middlefield (44062) ***(G-14270)***
Hans Truck and Trlr Repr Inc....216 581-0046
14520 Broadway Ave Cleveland (44125) ***(G-5660)***
Hans Zwart MD & Associates (PA)....937 433-4183
1520 S Main St Ste 3 Dayton (45409) ***(G-9485)***
Hans' Freightliner Cleveland, Cleveland *Also called Hans Truck and Trlr Repr Inc* ***(G-5660)***
Hansen-Mueller Co....419 729-5535
1800 N Water St Toledo (43611) ***(G-17778)***
Hanser Music Group Inc (PA)....859 817-7100
9615 Inter Ocean Dr West Chester (45246) ***(G-19058)***
Hanson Aggregates, Sandusky *Also called Wagner Quarries Company* ***(G-16655)***
Hanson Aggregates East LLC....740 773-2172
33 Renick Ave Chillicothe (45601) ***(G-2784)***
Hanson Aggregates East LLC....937 587-2671
848 Plum Run Rd Peebles (45660) ***(G-15802)***
Hanson Aggregates East LLC....419 483-4390
9220 Portland Rd Castalia (44824) ***(G-2578)***
Hanson Aggregates East LLC....937 442-6009
13526 Overstake Rd Winchester (45697) ***(G-19662)***
Hanson Concrete Products Ohio....614 443-4846
1500 Haul Rd Columbus (43207) ***(G-7716)***
Hanson Distributing Co Inc....419 435-3214
22116 Township Road 218 Fostoria (44830) ***(G-11004)***
Hanson McClain Inc....513 469-7500
7890 E Kemper Rd Ste 200 Cincinnati (45249) ***(G-3680)***
Hanson McClain Advisors, Cincinnati *Also called Hanson McClain Inc* ***(G-3680)***
Hanson Pipe & Products, Columbus *Also called Hanson Concrete Products Ohio* ***(G-7716)***
Hanson Productions Inc....419 327-6100
1695 Indian Wood Cir # 200 Maumee (43537) ***(G-13798)***
Hanson Services Inc (PA)....216 226-5425
17017 Madison Ave Lakewood (44107) ***(G-12345)***
Happy Day School, Ravenna *Also called Portage County Board* ***(G-16255)***

Harbor (PA) 419 479-3233
   6629 W Central Ave Ste 1 Toledo (43617) *(G-17779)*
Harbor 419 241-6191
   123 22nd St Ste 1 Toledo (43604) *(G-17780)*
Harbor 800 444-3353
   5331 Bennett Rd Toledo (43612) *(G-17781)*
Harbor Court, Rocky River *Also called Capital Senior Living (G-16425)*
Harbor House Inc 740 498-7213
   349 E High Ave New Philadelphia (44663) *(G-14960)*
Harbor Light Hospice, Cleveland *Also called Hospice of Ohio LLC (G-5710)*
Harbor Services, Bellaire *Also called Bellaire Harbor Service LLC (G-1329)*
Harborside Clveland Ltd Partnr 440 871-5900
   27601 Westchester Pkwy Westlake (44145) *(G-19347)*
Harborside Clveland Ltd Partnr 440 526-4770
   2801 E Royalton Rd Broadview Heights (44147) *(G-1835)*
Harborside Healthcare Corp 937 436-6155
   3797 Summit Glen Dr Frnt Dayton (45449) *(G-9486)*
Harborside Healthcare Corp 419 825-1111
   401 W Airport Hwy Swanton (43558) *(G-17399)*
Harborside Healthcare NW Ohio 419 636-5071
   1104 Wesley Ave Bryan (43506) *(G-1959)*
Harborside Healthcarebroadview, Broadview Heights *Also called Harborside Clveland Ltd Partnr (G-1835)*
Harborside Pointe Place LLC 419 727-7870
   6101 N Summit St Toledo (43611) *(G-17782)*
Harborside Sylvania LLC 419 882-1875
   5757 Whiteford Rd Sylvania (43560) *(G-17429)*
Harborside Troy LLC 937 335-7161
   512 Crescent Dr Troy (45373) *(G-18205)*
Harcacus Tri-County Cmty Actn, New Philadelphia *Also called Harcatus Tri-County Community (G-14961)*
Harcatus Tri-County Community (PA) 740 922-0933
   225 Fair Ave Ne New Philadelphia (44663) *(G-14961)*
Harcatus Tri-County Community 330 602-5442
   504 Bowers Ave Nw New Philadelphia (44663) *(G-14962)*
Harco Industries Inc 419 674-4159
   707 N Ida St Kenton (43326) *(G-12276)*
Hardage Hotels I LLC 614 766-7762
   4130 Tuller Rd Dublin (43017) *(G-10238)*
Hardin Cnty Cncil On Aging Inc 419 673-1102
   100 Memorial Dr Kenton (43326) *(G-12277)*
Hardin Cnty Dept Mntl Hlth Ret, Kenton *Also called County of Hardin (G-12274)*
Hardin County Engineer 419 673-2232
   1040 W Franklin St Kenton (43326) *(G-12278)*
Hardin County Family YMCA 419 673-6131
   918 W Franklin St Kenton (43326) *(G-12279)*
Hardin County Home 419 673-0961
   1211 W Lima St Kenton (43326) *(G-12280)*
Hardin Hills Health Center, Kenton *Also called Hardin County Home (G-12280)*
Hardin Memorial Hospital (HQ) 419 673-0761
   921 E Franklin St Kenton (43326) *(G-12281)*
Harding Park Cycle, Canton *Also called Damarc Inc (G-2278)*
Hardlines Design Company (PA) 614 784-8733
   4608 Indianola Ave Ste D Columbus (43214) *(G-7717)*
Hardrock Excavating LLC 330 792-9524
   2761 Salt Springs Rd Youngstown (44509) *(G-20060)*
Hardwood Lumber Co, Burton *Also called Stephen M Trudick (G-2019)*
Hardwood Wholesalers Exporters, Lima *Also called T J Ellis Enterprises Inc (G-12761)*
Hardy Diagnostics 937 550-2768
   429 S Pioneer Blvd Springboro (45066) *(G-16968)*
Haribol Haribol Inc (PA) 330 339-7731
   145 Bluebell Dr Sw New Philadelphia (44663) *(G-14963)*
Harley-Dvidson Dlr Systems Inc 216 573-1393
   9885 Rockside Rd Ste 100 Cleveland (44125) *(G-5661)*
Harmer Place, Marietta *Also called United Church Homes Inc (G-13392)*
Harmon Inc 513 645-1550
   4290 Port Union Rd West Chester (45011) *(G-18942)*
Harmon Media Group 330 478-5325
   4650 Hills And Dales Rd N Canton (44708) *(G-2340)*
Harmony Court, Cincinnati *Also called Chs-Norwood Inc (G-3215)*
Harmony Home Care Inc 440 877-1977
   12608 State Rd Ste 1a North Royalton (44133) *(G-15359)*
Harnett Vision Transportation, Ashtabula *Also called Lt Trucking Inc (G-747)*
Harold J Becker Company Inc 614 279-1414
   3946 Indian Ripple Rd Beavercreek (45440) *(G-1222)*
Harold Tatman & Sons Entps Inc 740 655-2880
   9171 State Route 180 Kingston (45644) *(G-12315)*
Harrington Electric Company 216 361-5101
   3800 Perkins Ave Cleveland (44114) *(G-5662)*
Harrington Health Services Inc (HQ) 614 212-7000
   780 Brooksedge Plaza Dr Westerville (43081) *(G-19259)*
Harrington Hoppe Mitchell Ltd 330 744-1111
   26 Market St Ste 1200 Youngstown (44503) *(G-20061)*
Harris Mackessy & Brennan 614 221-6831
   570 Polaris Pkwy Ste 125 Westerville (43082) *(G-19169)*
Harris & Burgin 513 891-3270
   9545 Kenwood Rd Ste 301 Blue Ash (45242) *(G-1575)*
Harris & Heavener Excavating 740 927-1423
   149 Humphries Dr Etna (43068) *(G-10610)*

Harris Distributing Co 513 541-4222
   4261 Crawford Ave Cincinnati (45223) *(G-3681)*
Harrison Building and Ln Assn (PA) 513 367-2015
   10490 New Haven Rd Harrison (45030) *(G-11669)*
Harrison Co County Home 740 942-3573
   41500 Cadiz Dennison Rd Cadiz (43907) *(G-2028)*
Harrison Community Hospital, Cadiz *Also called Wheeling Hospital Inc (G-2034)*
Harrison Community Hospital, Cadiz *Also called Wheeling Hospital Inc (G-2035)*
Harrison Construction Inc 740 373-7000
   1408 Colegate Dr Marietta (45750) *(G-13333)*
Harrison Contruction, Marietta *Also called Harrison Construction Inc (G-13333)*
Harrison County Coal Company (PA) 740 338-3100
   46226 National Rd Saint Clairsville (43950) *(G-16488)*
Harrison Hub, Scio *Also called M3 Midstream LLC (G-16663)*
Harrison Industries Inc 740 942-2988
   82460 Cadiz Jewett Rd Cadiz (43907) *(G-2029)*
Harrison Pavilion 513 662-5800
   2171 Harrison Ave Cincinnati (45211) *(G-3682)*
Harry C Lobalzo & Sons Inc (PA) 330 666-6758
   61 N Cleveland Ave Akron (44333) *(G-251)*
Harry Rock & Company 330 644-3748
   8550 Aetna Rd Cleveland (44105) *(G-5663)*
Hart Associates Inc 419 893-9600
   811 Madison Ave Toledo (43604) *(G-17783)*
Hart Industrial Products Div, Middletown *Also called Hart Industries Inc (G-14301)*
Hart Industries Inc (PA) 513 541-4278
   931 Jeanette St Middletown (45044) *(G-14301)*
Hart Roofing Inc 330 452-4055
   437 Mcgregor Ave Nw Canton (44703) *(G-2341)*
Hart-Greer, Bellevue *Also called Amrstrong Distributors Inc (G-1371)*
Harter Ventures Inc 419 224-4075
   3623 S Buckskin Trl Lima (45807) *(G-12651)*
Hartford Fire Insurance Co 216 447-1000
   7100 E Pleasant Valley Rd # 200 Cleveland (44131) *(G-5664)*
Hartland Petroleum LLC 740 452-3115
   4560 West Pike Zanesville (43701) *(G-20315)*
Hartsfield Atlanta Intl Arprt, Cincinnati *Also called Parking Company America Inc (G-4204)*
Hartung Brothers Inc 419 352-3000
   815 S Dunbridge Rd Bowling Green (43402) *(G-1734)*
Hartville Group Inc (PA) 330 484-8166
   1210 Massillon Rd Akron (44306) *(G-252)*
Hartville Hardware Inc 330 877-4690
   1315 Edison St Nw Hartville (44632) *(G-11688)*
Hartwig Transit Inc 513 563-1765
   11971 Reading Rd Cincinnati (45241) *(G-3683)*
Hartzell Hardwoods Inc (PA) 937 773-7054
   1025 S Roosevelt Ave Piqua (45356) *(G-16006)*
Hartzell Industries Inc (PA) 937 773-6295
   1025 S Roosevelt Ave Piqua (45356) *(G-16007)*
Harvest Facility Holdings LP 419 472-7115
   4560 W Alexis Rd Apt 9 Toledo (43623) *(G-17784)*
Harvest Facility Holdings LP 440 268-9555
   19205 Pearl Rd Ofc Cleveland (44136) *(G-5665)*
Harwick Standard Dist Corp (PA) 330 798-9300
   60 S Seiberling St Akron (44305) *(G-253)*
Hasenstab Architects Inc (PA) 330 434-4464
   190 N Union St Ste 400 Akron (44304) *(G-254)*
Haslett Heating & Cooling Inc 614 299-2133
   7686 Fishel Dr N A Dublin (43016) *(G-10239)*
Hassler Medical Center, Cleveland *Also called Clevelan Clinic Hlth Sys W Reg (G-5227)*
Hastings Home Health Ctr Inc 216 898-3300
   211 Commerce Dr Medina (44256) *(G-13947)*
Hastings Water Works Inc (PA) 440 832-7700
   10331 Brecksville Rd Brecksville (44141) *(G-1782)*
Hat White Management LLC (PA) 800 525-7967
   121 S Main St Ste 107 Akron (44308) *(G-255)*
Hatfield Lincoln Mercury, Columbus *Also called Sonic Automotive-1495 Automall (G-8659)*
Hatifield Hyundai, Columbus *Also called Columbus SAI Motors LLC (G-7312)*
Hattenbach Company (PA) 216 881-5200
   5309 Hamilton Ave Cleveland (44114) *(G-5666)*
Hattie Larlham Center For (PA) 330 274-2272
   9772 Diagonal Rd Mantua (44255) *(G-13267)*
Hattie Larlham Center For 330 274-2272
   9772 Diagonal Rd Mantua (44255) *(G-13268)*
Hattie Larlham Community Svcs 330 274-2272
   9772 Diagonal Rd Mantua (44255) *(G-13269)*
Hattie Larlham Community Svcs 330 274-2272
   9772 Diagonal Rd Mantua (44255) *(G-13270)*
Hatzel & Buehler Inc 740 420-3088
   3381 Congo Dr Circleville (43113) *(G-4834)*
Hauck Hospitality LLC 513 563-8330
   3855 Hauck Rd Cincinnati (45241) *(G-3684)*
Hauser Group, The, Cincinnati *Also called Art Hauser Insurance Inc (G-2990)*
Havar Inc (PA) 740 594-3533
   396 Richland Ave Athens (45701) *(G-782)*
Havar Inc 740 373-7175
   416 3rd St Marietta (45750) *(G-13334)*
Haven Bhavioral Healthcare Inc 937 234-0100
   1 Elizabeth Pl Ste A Dayton (45417) *(G-9487)*
Haven Financial Enterprise 800 265-2401
   675 Alpha Dr Ste E Cleveland (44143) *(G-5667)*

Haven Hill Home, North Royalton *Also called Childrens Forever Haven Inc* (G-15349)
Haven Rest Ministries Inc (PA) 330 535-1563
175 E Market St Akron (44308) (G-256)
Haverhill Coke Company LLC 740 355-9819
2446 Gallia Pike Franklin Furnace (45629) (G-11046)
Havsco Inc 440 439-8900
5018 Richmond Rd Bedford (44146) (G-1284)
Hawa Incorporated (PA) 614 451-1711
980 Old Henderson Rd C Columbus (43220) (G-7718)
Hawkeye Hotels Inc 614 782-8292
1668 Buckeye Pl Grove City (43123) (G-11440)
Hawkins & Co Lpa Ltd 216 861-1365
1267 W 9th St Ste 500 Cleveland (44113) (G-5668)
Hawkins Markets Inc 330 435-4611
2800 E Pleasant Home Rd Creston (44217) (G-9061)
Hawks Nest Golf Club, Creston *Also called Hawkins Markets Inc* (G-9061)
Hawthorn Glenn Nursing Center, Middletown *Also called Semma Enterprises Inc* (G-14328)
Hawthorne Hydrophonics/Botanic, Marysville *Also called Hawthorne Hydroponics LLC* (G-13501)
Hawthorne Hydroponics LLC 480 777-2000
14111 Scottslawn Rd Marysville (43040) (G-13501)
Hawthorne Valley Country Club 440 232-1400
25250 Rockside Rd Ste 1 Bedford (44146) (G-1285)
Haydocy Automotive Inc 614 279-8880
3895 W Broad St Columbus (43228) (G-7719)
Haydocy Automotors, Columbus *Also called Haydocy Automotive Inc* (G-7719)
Hayes Concrete Construction 513 648-9400
2120 Waycross Rd Cincinnati (45240) (G-3685)
Haynes Manufacturing Company, Westlake *Also called R and J Corporation* (G-19394)
Hays & Sons Construction Inc 513 671-9110
190 Container Pl Cincinnati (45246) (G-3686)
Hays Enterprises Inc 330 392-2278
1901 Ellsworth Bailey Rd Warren (44481) (G-18711)
Hayward Distributing Co (PA) 614 272-5953
4061 Perimeter Dr Columbus (43228) (G-7720)
Hbi Payments Ltd 614 944-5788
3 Easton Oval Ste 210 Columbus (43219) (G-7721)
Hbk, Canfield *Also called Hill Barth & King LLC* (G-2141)
Hbk CPA & Consultants, Columbus *Also called Hill Barth & King LLC* (G-7749)
Hbl Automotive, Columbus *Also called Lindsey Accura Inc* (G-7981)
Hc Transport Inc 513 574-1800
6045 Bridgetown Rd Cincinnati (45248) (G-3687)
HCA Holdings Inc 440 826-3240
19250 Bagley Rd Ste 100 Cleveland (44130) (G-5669)
Hccao, Hillsboro *Also called HighInd Cnty Commnty Action or* (G-11845)
Hcf Management Inc 740 289-2394
7143 Us Highway 23 Piketon (45661) (G-15977)
Hcf Management Inc 419 435-8112
25 Christopher Dr Fostoria (44830) (G-11005)
Hcf Management Inc (PA) 419 999-2010
1100 Shawnee Rd Lima (45805) (G-12652)
Hcf Management Inc 419 999-2055
2535 Fort Amanda Rd Lima (45804) (G-12653)
Hcf of Bowl Green Care Ctr Inc 419 352-7558
850 W Poe Rd Bowling Green (43402) (G-1735)
Hcf of Bowling Green Inc 419 352-4694
1021 W Poe Rd Bowling Green (43402) (G-1736)
Hcf of Briarwood Inc 419 678-2311
100 Don Desch Dr D Coldwater (45828) (G-6758)
Hcf of Court House Inc 740 335-9290
555 N Glenn Ave Wshngtn CT Hs (43160) (G-19874)
Hcf of Crestview Inc 937 426-5033
4381 Tonawanda Trl Beavercreek (45430) (G-1223)
Hcf of Findlay Inc 419 999-2010
11745 Township Road 145 Findlay (45840) (G-10920)
Hcf of Fox Run Inc 419 424-0832
11745 Township Road 145 Findlay (45840) (G-10921)
Hcf of Lima Inc 419 999-2010
1100 Shawnee Rd Lima (45805) (G-12654)
Hcf of Perrysburg Inc 419 874-0306
250 Manor Dr Perrysburg (43551) (G-15870)
Hcf of Piqua Inc 937 773-0040
1840 W High St Piqua (45356) (G-16008)
Hcf of Roselawn Inc 419 647-4115
420 E 4th St Spencerville (45887) (G-16956)
Hcf of Shawnee Inc 419 999-2055
2535 Fort Amanda Rd Lima (45804) (G-12655)
Hcf of Van Wert Inc 419 999-2010
160 Fox Rd Van Wert (45891) (G-18479)
Hcf of Wapakoneta Inc 419 738-3711
1010 Lincoln Hwy Wapakoneta (45895) (G-18645)
Hcf of Washington Inc 419 999-2010
555 N Glenn Ave Wshngtn CT Hs (43160) (G-19875)
HCFW, Cleveland *Also called Hitchcock Center For Women Inc* (G-5695)
Hcg Inc 513 539-9269
203 N Garver Rd Monroe (45050) (G-14569)
Hcl of Dayton Inc 937 384-8300
4000 Mmsbrg Ctrvle Rd 4 Ste Miamisburg (45342) (G-14175)
Hcr Manor Care, Toledo *Also called Leader Nuring & Rehabilitation* (G-17850)
Hcr Manor Care Svc Fla III Inc (HQ) 419 252-5500
333 N Summit St Toledo (43604) (G-17785)

Hcr Manorcare Med Svcs Fla LLC 513 745-9600
4580 E Galbraith Rd Cincinnati (45236) (G-3688)
Hcr Manorcare Med Svcs Fla LLC 513 233-0831
6870 Clough Pike Cincinnati (45244) (G-3689)
Hcr Manorcare Med Svcs Fla LLC 419 252-5500
35 Bierly Rd Ste 2 Portsmouth (45662) (G-16142)
Hcr Manorcare Med Svcs Fla LLC 419 531-2127
3450 W Central Ave # 230 Toledo (43606) (G-17786)
Hcr Manorcare Med Svcs Fla LLC 330 753-5005
85 3rd St Se Barberton (44203) (G-954)
Hcr Manorcare Med Svcs Fla LLC 513 561-4111
4900 Cooper Rd Cincinnati (45242) (G-3690)
Hcr Manorcare Med Svcs Fla LLC 614 882-1511
140 Old County Line Rd Westerville (43081) (G-19260)
Hcr Manorcare Med Svcs Fla LLC 330 668-6889
171 N Clvland Mssillon Rd Akron (44333) (G-257)
Hcr Manorcare Med Svcs Fla LLC (HQ) 419 252-5500
333 N Summit St Ste 100 Toledo (43604) (G-17787)
Hcr Manorcare Med Svcs Fla LLC 216 251-3300
4102 Rocky River Dr Cleveland (44135) (G-5670)
Hcr Manorcare Med Svcs Fla LLC 440 473-0090
6757 Mayfield Rd Cleveland (44124) (G-5671)
Hcr Manorcare Med Svcs Fla LLC 216 486-2300
16101 Euclid Beach Blvd Cleveland (44110) (G-5672)
Hcr Manorcare Med Svcs Fla LLC 937 436-9700
1001 E Alex Bell Rd Centerville (45459) (G-2627)
Hcr Manorcare Med Svcs Fla LLC 419 691-3088
3953 Navarre Ave Oregon (43616) (G-15597)
Hcr Manorcare Med Svcs Fla LLC 440 808-9275
28400 Center Ridge Rd Westlake (44145) (G-19348)
Hcr Manorcare Med Svcs Fla LLC 513 591-0400
2250 Banning Rd Cincinnati (45239) (G-3691)
Hcr Manorcare Med Svcs Fla LLC 440 887-1442
9205 W Sprague Rd North Royalton (44133) (G-15360)
Hd Supply Inc 614 771-4849
6200 Commerce Center Dr Groveport (43125) (G-11516)
Hd Supply Facilities Maint Ltd 440 542-9188
30311 Emerald Valley Pkwy Solon (44139) (G-16857)
Hdi Ltd 937 224-0800
33 E 5th St Dayton (45402) (G-9488)
HDR Engineering Inc 614 839-5770
2800 Corp Exchange Dr # 100 Columbus (43231) (G-7722)
Hdt Engineered Technologies, Solon *Also called Hunter Defense Tech Inc* (G-16859)
He Hari Inc 614 436-0700
7007 N High St Worthington (43085) (G-19812)
He Hari Inc (PA) 614 846-6600
600 Enterprise Dr Lewis Center (43035) (G-12544)
Head Inc 614 338-8501
4477 E 5th Ave Columbus (43219) (G-7723)
Head Mercantile Co Inc 440 847-2700
29065 Clemens Rd Ste 200 Westlake (44145) (G-19349)
Head Qaurters Salon & Spa, Lorain *Also called Head Quarters Inc* (G-12906)
Head Quarters Inc 440 233-8508
6071 Middle Ridge Rd Lorain (44053) (G-12906)
Head Start, Cincinnati *Also called Child Focus Learning Center* (G-3181)
HEAD START, Lima *Also called West Ohio Cmnty Action Partnr* (G-12782)
Head Start Program, Lorain *Also called Lorain County Community Action* (G-12918)
Headstart Program, Circleville *Also called Pickaway County Community Acti* (G-4840)
Healing Hands Home Health Ltd 740 385-0710
30605 Stage Coach Rd Logan (43138) (G-12836)
Healing Hrts Cunseling Ctr Inc 419 528-5993
680 Park Ave W Mansfield (44906) (G-13181)
Healing Touch Healthcare 937 610-5555
627 S Edwin C Moses Blvd 3I Dayton (45417) (G-9489)
Health & HM Care Concepts Inc 740 383-4968
353 S State St Marion (43302) (G-13423)
Health & Homecare Concepts, Marion *Also called Health & HM Care Concepts Inc* (G-13423)
Health and Safety Sciences LLC 513 488-1952
3189 Princeton Rd Fairfield Township (45011) (G-10809)
Health Care Dataworks Inc 614 255-5400
4215 Worth Ave Ste 320 Columbus (43219) (G-7724)
Health Care Facilities, Lima *Also called Hcf Management Inc* (G-12652)
Health Care Facility MGT LLC (HQ) 513 489-7100
4700 Ashwood Dr Ste 200 Blue Ash (45241) (G-1576)
Health Care Logistics Inc 800 848-1633
6106 Bausch Rd Galloway (43119) (G-11220)
Health Care Management Group, Cincinnati *Also called Central Accounting Systems* (G-3149)
Health Care Opportunities Inc (PA) 513 932-0300
102 E Silver St Lebanon (45036) (G-12469)
Health Care Opportunities Inc 513 932-4861
220 S Mechanic St Lebanon (45036) (G-12470)
Health Care Personnel, Columbus *Also called Prn Nurse Inc* (G-8464)
Health Care Plus (HQ) 614 340-7587
470 Olde Worthington Rd # 200 Westerville (43082) (G-19170)
Health Care Retirement Corp 419 252-5500
333 N Summit St Ste 100 Toledo (43604) (G-17788)
Health Care Rtrement Corp Amer (HQ) 419 252-5500
333 N Summit St Ste 103 Toledo (43604) (G-17789)
Health Care Rtrement Corp Amer 419 474-6021
4293 Monroe St Toledo (43606) (G-17790)

Health Care Rtrement Corp Amer 740 286-5026
  8668 State Route 93 Jackson (45640) *(G-12174)*
Health Care Rtrement Corp Amer 419 562-9907
  1170 W Mansfield St Bucyrus (44820) *(G-1991)*
Health Care Rtrement Corp Amer 937 298-8084
  3313 Wilmington Pike Dayton (45429) *(G-9490)*
Health Care Rtrement Corp Amer 740 373-8920
  5001 State Route 60 Marietta (45750) *(G-13335)*
Health Care Rtrement Corp Amer 937 429-1106
  1974 N Fairfield Rd Dayton (45432) *(G-9175)*
Health Care Rtrement Corp Amer 937 456-5537
  515 S Maple St Eaton (45320) *(G-10447)*
Health Care Rtrement Corp Amer 740 773-5000
  1058 Columbus St Chillicothe (45601) *(G-2785)*
Health Care Rtrement Corp Amer 740 354-4505
  20 Easter Dr Portsmouth (45662) *(G-16143)*
Health Care Rtrement Corp Amer 614 882-3782
  215 Huber Village Blvd Westerville (43081) *(G-19261)*
Health Care Rtrement Corp Amer 937 599-5123
  221 School St Bellefontaine (43311) *(G-1353)*
Health Care Rtrement Corp Amer 614 464-2273
  920 Thurber Dr W Columbus (43215) *(G-7725)*
Health Care Rtrement Corp Amer 937 390-0005
  2615 Derr Rd Springfield (45503) *(G-17044)*
Health Care Rtrement Corp Amer 740 894-3287
  7743 County Road 1 South Point (45680) *(G-16936)*
Health Care Rtrement Corp Amer 937 393-5766
  1141 Northview Dr Hillsboro (45133) *(G-11841)*
Health Care Rtrement Corp Amer 440 946-1912
  8200 Mentor Hills Dr Mentor (44060) *(G-14059)*
Health Care Rtrement Corp Amer 740 635-4600
  300 Commercial Dr Bridgeport (43912) *(G-1817)*
Health Care Rtrement Corp Amer 937 773-9346
  275 Kienle Dr Piqua (45356) *(G-16009)*
Health Care Rtrement Corp Amer 419 874-3578
  10540 Fremont Pike Perrysburg (43551) *(G-15871)*
Health Care Rtrement Corp Amer 937 866-8885
  450 Oak Ridge Blvd Miamisburg (45342) *(G-14176)*
Health Care Rtrement Corp Amer 937 548-3141
  243 Marion Dr Greenville (45331) *(G-11386)*
Health Care Rtrement Corp Amer 419 337-3050
  303 W Leggett St Wauseon (43567) *(G-18806)*
Health Care Rtrement Corp Amer 419 878-8523
  8885 Browning Dr Waterville (43566) *(G-18789)*
Health Care Rtrement Corp Amer 513 751-0880
  510 Oak St Cincinnati (45219) *(G-3692)*
Health Care Specialists 740 454-4530
  945 Bethesda Dr Ste 300 Zanesville (43701) *(G-20316)*
Health Carousel LLC (PA) 866 665-4544
  3805 Edwards Rd Ste 700 Cincinnati (45209) *(G-3693)*
Health Collaborative 513 618-3600
  615 Elsinore Pl Ste 500 Cincinnati (45202) *(G-3694)*
Health Data MGT Solutions Inc 216 595-1232
  3201 Enterprise Pkwy Beachwood (44122) *(G-1062)*
Health Dept, Columbus Also called City of Columbus *(G-7207)*
Health Dept, Columbus Also called City of Columbus *(G-7208)*
Health Dept, Cincinnati Also called County of Hamilton *(G-3373)*
Health Design Plus Inc 330 656-1072
  1755 Georgetown Rd Hudson (44236) *(G-11981)*
Health Force, Eaton Also called Personal Touch HM Care IPA Inc *(G-10458)*
HEALTH FOUNDATION OF GREATER C, Cincinnati Also called Interact For Health *(G-3774)*
Health Partners Health Clinic 937 645-8488
  19900 State Route 739 Marysville (43040) *(G-13502)*
Health Partners Western Ohio 419 679-5994
  111 W Espy St Kenton (43326) *(G-12282)*
Health Partners Western Ohio (PA) 419 221-3072
  441 E 8th St Lima (45804) *(G-12656)*
Health Plan of Ohio Inc 330 837-6880
  100 Lillian Gish Blvd Sw # 301 Massillon (44647) *(G-13693)*
Health Recovery Services Inc (PA) 740 592-6720
  224 Columbus Rd Ste 102 Athens (45701) *(G-783)*
Health Right, Springboro Also called Right At Home *(G-16983)*
Health Science Campus, Toledo Also called University of Toledo *(G-18128)*
Health Science Campus, Toledo Also called University of Toledo *(G-18130)*
Health Service Preferred, Cincinnati Also called Integra Group Inc *(G-3767)*
Health Services Coshocton Cnty 740 622-7311
  230 S 4th St Coshocton (43812) *(G-9016)*
Health Services Inc. 330 837-7678
  2520 Wales Ave Nw Ste 120 Massillon (44646) *(G-13694)*
Health Smile Center 440 992-2700
  2010 W 19th St Ashtabula (44004) *(G-739)*
Health Works Mso Inc (PA) 740 368-5366
  561 W Central Ave Delaware (43015) *(G-9983)*
Health, Dept Of- Admin, Columbus Also called City of Columbus *(G-7209)*
Healthcare and Social 614 461-1199
  1395 Dublin Rd Columbus (43215) *(G-7726)*
Healthcare Circle Inc 440 331-7347
  18149 Williamsburg Oval Strongsville (44136) *(G-17308)*
Healthcare Facility MGT LLC 419 382-2200
  955 Garden Lake Pkwy Toledo (43614) *(G-17791)*
Healthcare Facility MGT LLC 330 836-7953
  200 Wyant Rd Akron (44313) *(G-258)*

Healthcare Holdings Inc 513 530-1600
  4700 Ashwood Dr Ste 200 Blue Ash (45241) *(G-1577)*
Healthcare Management Cons 419 363-2193
  201 Buckeye St Rockford (45882) *(G-16416)*
Healthcare Walton Group LLC 440 439-4433
  19859 Alexander Rd Cleveland (44146) *(G-5673)*
Healthcomp Inc 216 696-6900
  1226 Huron Rd E Ste 2 Cleveland (44115) *(G-5674)*
Healthlinx Inc 513 402-2018
  602 Main St Ste 300 Cincinnati (45202) *(G-3695)*
Healthpro Medical Billing Inc 419 223-2717
  4132 Elida Rd Lima (45807) *(G-12657)*
Healthquest Blanchester Inc 937 783-4535
  661 W Main St Blanchester (45107) *(G-1487)*
Healthscope Benefits Inc 614 797-5200
  5150 E Dublin Granvll 3 Westerville (43081) *(G-19262)*
Healthsource of Ohio Inc 513 707-1997
  2055 Hospital Dr Ste 320 Batavia (45103) *(G-1001)*
Healthsource of Ohio Inc 937 392-4381
  631 E State St Georgetown (45121) *(G-11272)*
Healthsource of Ohio Inc 937 981-7707
  1075 N Washington St Greenfield (45123) *(G-11363)*
HealthSouth, Cincinnati Also called Encompass Health Corporation *(G-3497)*
HealthSouth, Springfield Also called Encompass Health Corporation *(G-17034)*
HealthSouth 937 424-8200
  1 Elizabeth Pl Dayton (45417) *(G-9491)*
Healthspan Integrated Care 440 937-2350
  36711 American Way Fl 1 Avon (44011) *(G-885)*
Healthspan Integrated Care 216 362-2000
  12301 Snow Rd Cleveland (44130) *(G-5675)*
Healthspan Integrated Care 216 524-7377
  3733 Park East Dr Cleveland (44122) *(G-5676)*
Healthspan Integrated Care (HQ) 216 621-5600
  1001 Lakeside Ave E # 1200 Cleveland (44114) *(G-5677)*
Healthspan Integrated Care 440 572-1000
  17406 Royalton Rd Cleveland (44136) *(G-5678)*
Healthspan Integrated Care 330 767-3436
  360 Wabash Ave N Brewster (44613) *(G-1810)*
Healthspan Integrated Care 330 486-2800
  8920 Canyon Falls Blvd Twinsburg (44087) *(G-18278)*
Healthspan Integrated Care 330 877-4018
  900 W Maple St Hartville (44632) *(G-11689)*
Healthspan Integrated Care 330 334-1549
  120 High St Wadsworth (44281) *(G-18597)*
Healthspan Integrated Care 216 362-2277
  14600 Detroit Ave Apt 700 Lakewood (44107) *(G-12346)*
Healthspan-Concord Med Offs, Concord Township Also called Kaiser Foundation Hospitals *(G-8943)*
Healthy Advice Networks, Cincinnati Also called Patientpint Ntwrk Slutions LLC *(G-4210)*
Healthy Life HM Healthcare LLC 614 865-3368
  5454 Cleveland Ave # 201 Columbus (43231) *(G-7727)*
Healthy Smile Center The, Ashtabula Also called Health Smile Center *(G-739)*
Heap Home Energy Assistance 419 626-6540
  908 Seavers Way Sandusky (44870) *(G-16615)*
Hearing Spch Deaf Ctr Grtr Cnc 513 221-0527
  2825 Burnet Ave Ste 330 Cincinnati (45219) *(G-3696)*
Heart & HM Assistant Friedman, Tiffin Also called Friedman Vlg Retirement Cmnty *(G-17519)*
Heart Care 614 533-5000
  765 N Hamilton Rd Ste 120 Gahanna (43230) *(G-11124)*
Heart Center Northeastern Ohio, Youngstown Also called Heart Center of N Eastrn Ohio *(G-20062)*
Heart Center of N Eastrn Ohio (PA) 330 758-7703
  250 Debartolo Pl Ste 2750 Youngstown (44512) *(G-20062)*
Heart of Marion Dialysis, Marion Also called Tonka Bay Dialysis LLC *(G-13464)*
Heart of OH Cncl Bsa 740 389-4615
  1310 Mount Vernon Ave Marion (43302) *(G-13424)*
Heart of OH Cncl Bsa (PA) 419 522-8300
  3 N Main St Ste 303 Mansfield (44902) *(G-13182)*
Heart Ohio Family Health Ctrs 614 235-5555
  882 S Hamilton Rd Columbus (43213) *(G-7728)*
Heart Specialists of Ohio 614 538-0527
  3650 Olentangy River Rd # 300 Columbus (43214) *(G-7729)*
Heart To Heart Home Health 330 335-9999
  250 Smokerise Dr Apt 302 Wadsworth (44281) *(G-18598)*
Heartbeat International Inc 614 885-7577
  5000 Arlington Centre Blv Columbus (43220) *(G-7730)*
Heartbeats To City Inc 330 452-4524
  1352 Market Ave S Canton (44707) *(G-2342)*
Hearthstone Utilities Inc (HQ) 440 974-3770
  1375 E 9th St Ste 3100 Cleveland (44114) *(G-5679)*
Heartland - Beavercreek, Dayton Also called Health Care Rtrement Corp Amer *(G-9175)*
Heartland - Holly Glen, Toledo Also called Health Care Rtrement Corp Amer *(G-17790)*
Heartland - Lansing, Bridgeport Also called Health Care Rtrement Corp Amer *(G-1817)*
Heartland - Victorian Village, Columbus Also called Health Care Rtrement Corp Amer *(G-7725)*
Heartland Bank (HQ) 614 337-4600
  850 N Hamilton Rd Gahanna (43230) *(G-11125)*
Heartland Bhavioral Healthcare 330 833-3135
  3000 Erie St S Massillon (44646) *(G-13695)*

A
L
P
H
A
B
E
T
I
C

Heartland Care Partners 3555, Toledo *Also called Hcr Manorcare Med Svcs Fla LLC* ***(G-17786)***
Heartland Employment Svcs LLC 419 252-5500
333 N Summit St Ste 103 Toledo (43604) ***(G-17792)***
Heartland Fort Myers Fl LLC (HQ) 419 252-5500
333 N Summit St Toledo (43604) ***(G-17793)***
Heartland Healthcare Svcs LLC (PA) 419 535-8435
4755 South Ave Toledo (43615) ***(G-17794)***
Heartland HM Hlth Care Hospice, Columbus *Also called Heartland Hospice Services LLC* ***(G-7732)***
Heartland HM Hlth Care Hospice, Lucasville *Also called Heartland Hospice Services LLC* ***(G-13050)***
Heartland HM Hlth Care Hospice, Perrysburg *Also called Heartland Hospice Services LLC* ***(G-15872)***
Heartland HM Hlth Care Hospice, Toledo *Also called In Home Health LLC* ***(G-17819)***
Heartland HM Hlth Care Hospice, Dayton *Also called Heartland Hospice Services LLC* ***(G-9492)***
Heartland HM Hlth Care Hospice, Independence *Also called Heartland Hospice Services LLC* ***(G-12079)***
Heartland HM Hlth Care Hospice, Fremont *Also called In Home Health LLC* ***(G-11081)***
Heartland Holly Glen Care Ctr, Toledo *Also called H C R Corp* ***(G-17776)***
Heartland Home Care LLC (HQ) 419 252-5500
333 N Summit St Ste 100 Toledo (43604) ***(G-17795)***
Heartland Home Care LLC 614 433-0423
6500 Busch Blvd Ste 210 Columbus (43229) ***(G-7731)***
Heartland Home Health Care, Columbus *Also called Heartland Home Care LLC* ***(G-7731)***
Heartland Hospice Services, Cincinnati *Also called In Home Health LLC* ***(G-3754)***
Heartland Hospice Services, Toledo *Also called Hcr Manor Care Svc Fla III Inc* ***(G-17785)***
Heartland Hospice Services LLC 614 433-0423
6500 Busch Blvd Ste 210 Columbus (43229) ***(G-7732)***
Heartland Hospice Services LLC 740 351-0575
35 Bierly Rd Ste 2 Portsmouth (45662) ***(G-16144)***
Heartland Hospice Services LLC 740 259-0281
205 North St Lucasville (45648) ***(G-13050)***
Heartland Hospice Services LLC 419 531-0440
28555 Starbright Blvd E Perrysburg (43551) ***(G-15872)***
Heartland Hospice Services LLC 937 299-6980
580 Lincoln Park Blvd # 320 Dayton (45429) ***(G-9492)***
Heartland Hospice Services LLC 216 901-1464
4807 Rockside Rd Ste 110 Independence (44131) ***(G-12079)***
Heartland of Bellefontaine, Bellefontaine *Also called Health Care Rtrement Corp Amer* ***(G-1353)***
Heartland of Bucyrus, Bucyrus *Also called Health Care Rtrement Corp Amer* ***(G-1991)***
Heartland of Chillicothe, Chillicothe *Also called Health Care Rtrement Corp Amer* ***(G-2785)***
Heartland of Eaton, Eaton *Also called Health Care Rtrement Corp Amer* ***(G-10447)***
Heartland of Greenville, Greenville *Also called Health Care Rtrement Corp Amer* ***(G-11386)***
Heartland of Hillsboro, Hillsboro *Also called Health Care Rtrement Corp Amer* ***(G-11841)***
Heartland of Jackson, Jackson *Also called Health Care Rtrement Corp Amer* ***(G-12174)***
Heartland of Kettering, Dayton *Also called Health Care Rtrement Corp Amer* ***(G-9490)***
Heartland of Marietta, Marietta *Also called Health Care Rtrement Corp Amer* ***(G-13335)***
Heartland of Mentor, Mentor *Also called Health Care Rtrement Corp Amer* ***(G-14059)***
Heartland of Oak Ridge, Miamisburg *Also called Health Care Rtrement Corp Amer* ***(G-14176)***
Heartland of Oregon, Oregon *Also called Hcr Manorcare Med Svcs Fla LLC* ***(G-15597)***
Heartland of Piqua, Piqua *Also called Health Care Rtrement Corp Amer* ***(G-16009)***
Heartland of Portsmouth, Portsmouth *Also called Health Care Rtrement Corp Amer* ***(G-16143)***
Heartland of Riverview, South Point *Also called Health Care Rtrement Corp Amer* ***(G-16936)***
HEARTLAND OF RIVERVIEW #4148, South Point *Also called Heartlnd-Riverview S Pt OH LLC* ***(G-16937)***
Heartland of Springfield, Springfield *Also called Health Care Rtrement Corp Amer* ***(G-17044)***
Heartland of Waterville, Waterville *Also called Health Care Rtrement Corp Amer* ***(G-18789)***
Heartland of Wauseon, Wauseon *Also called Health Care Rtrement Corp Amer* ***(G-18806)***
Heartland Payment Systems LLC 513 518-6125
3455 Steeplechase Ln Loveland (45140) ***(G-12998)***
Heartland Petroleum LLC (PA) 614 441-4001
4001 E 5th Ave Columbus (43219) ***(G-7733)***
Heartland Quality Egg Farm 937 355-5103
9800 County Road 26 West Mansfield (43358) ***(G-19124)***
Heartland Rhblitation Svcs Inc (HQ) 419 537-0764
3425 Executive Pkwy # 128 Toledo (43606) ***(G-17796)***
Heartlight Pharmacy Services, Lima *Also called Schaaf Drugs LLC* ***(G-12736)***
Heartlnd-Riverview S Pt OH LLC 740 894-3287
7743 County Road 1 South Point (45680) ***(G-16937)***
Heartsong Presents, Uhrichsville *Also called Barbour Publishing Inc* ***(G-18339)***
Heartspring Home Hlth Care LLC 937 531-6920
1251 E Dorothy Ln Dayton (45419) ***(G-9493)***
Heat and Frost Insulators Jatc, Toledo *Also called Toledo Area Insulator Wkrs Jac* ***(G-18073)***
HEat Ttal Fclty Slutions Inc 740 965-3005
5064 Red Bank Rd Galena (43021) ***(G-11159)***
Heatermeals, Cincinnati *Also called Luxfer Magtech Inc* ***(G-3952)***
Heath Nursing Care Center 740 522-1171
717 S 30th St Newark (43056) ***(G-15040)***
Heather Hl Rehabilitation Hosp, Chardon *Also called University Hospitals Health* ***(G-2722)***
Heather Knoll Nursing Center, Tallmadge *Also called Heather Knoll Retirement Vlg* ***(G-17476)***
Heather Knoll Retirement Vlg 330 688-8600
1134 North Ave Tallmadge (44278) ***(G-17476)***
Heather Ridge Commons, Canton *Also called Extended Family Concepts Inc* ***(G-2307)***
Heatherdowns Nursing Center, Columbus *Also called Rossford Grtric Care Ltd Prtnr* ***(G-8554)***
Heathergreene Nursing Homes, Xenia *Also called Liberty Nursing Home Inc* ***(G-19917)***
Heatherhill Care Communities 440 285-4040
12340 Bass Lake Rd Chardon (44024) ***(G-2698)***
Heatherwoode Golf Course 937 748-3222
88 Heatherwoode Blvd Springboro (45066) ***(G-16969)***
Heaven Bound Ascensions 330 633-3288
66 N Village View Rd Tallmadge (44278) ***(G-17477)***
Heavenly Home Health 740 859-4735
1800 Old State Route 7 Rayland (43943) ***(G-16272)***
Hebco Products Inc 419 562-7987
1232 Whetstone St Bucyrus (44820) ***(G-1992)***
Heck's Diamond Printing, Toledo *Also called Hecks Direct Mail & Prtg Svc* ***(G-17798)***
Hecks Direct Mail & Prtg Svc (PA) 419 697-3505
417 Main St Toledo (43605) ***(G-17797)***
Hecks Direct Mail & Prtg Svc 419 661-6028
202 W Florence Ave Toledo (43605) ***(G-17798)***
Hecla Water Association (PA) 740 533-0526
3190 State Route 141 Ironton (45638) ***(G-12154)***
Heco Operations Inc 614 888-5700
7440 Pingue Dr Worthington (43085) ***(G-19813)***
Hector A Buch Jr MD 419 227-7399
750 W High St Ste 250 Lima (45801) ***(G-12658)***
Hedstrom Fitness, Ashland *Also called Ball Bounce and Sport Inc* ***(G-654)***
Hedstrom Plastics, Ashland *Also called Ball Bounce and Sport Inc* ***(G-655)***
Heery International Inc 216 510-4701
5445 West Blvd Cleveland (44137) ***(G-5680)***
Heidelberg Distributing Co 614 308-0400
3801 Parkwest Dr Columbus (43228) ***(G-7734)***
Heidelberg Distributing Div, Moraine *Also called Dayton Heidelberg Distrg Co* ***(G-14643)***
Heidelberg Distributing Lorain, Lorain *Also called Goodman Beverage Co Inc* ***(G-12905)***
Heidelberg USA Inc 937 492-1281
1660 Campbell Rd Sidney (45365) ***(G-16782)***
Heider Cleaners Inc 937 298-6631
3720 Wilmington Pike Dayton (45429) ***(G-9494)***
Heidtman Steel Products 419 691-4646
2401 Front St Toledo (43605) ***(G-17799)***
Heidtman Steel Products Inc 216 641-6995
4600 Heidtman Pkwy Cleveland (44105) ***(G-5681)***
Heidtman Steel Products Inc 419 385-0636
135 N Flearing Blvd Toledo (43609) ***(G-17800)***
Heidtman Toledo Blank, Toledo *Also called Heidtman Steel Products Inc* ***(G-17800)***
Heights Emergency Food Center 216 381-0707
3663 Mayfield Rd Cleveland (44121) ***(G-5682)***
Heights Laundry & Dry Cleaning (PA) 216 932-9666
1863 Coventry Rd Cleveland Heights (44118) ***(G-6718)***
Heimerl Farms Ltd 740 967-0063
3891 Mink St Johnstown (43031) ***(G-12200)***
Heinzerling Developmental Ctr, Columbus *Also called Heinzerling Foundation* ***(G-7736)***
Heinzerling Foundation (PA) 614 272-8888
1800 Heinzerling Dr Columbus (43223) ***(G-7735)***
Heinzerling Foundation 614 272-2000
1755 Heinzerling Dr Columbus (43223) ***(G-7736)***
Heinzerling Mem Foundation, Columbus *Also called Heinzerling Foundation* ***(G-7735)***
Heiser Staffing Services LLC 614 800-4188
330 W Spring St Ste 205 Columbus (43215) ***(G-7737)***
Heitmeyer Group LLC 614 573-5571
140 Commerce Park Dr C Westerville (43082) ***(G-19171)***
Heits Building Services Cincin, Cincinnati *Also called Heits Building Svcs Cnkd LLC* ***(G-3697)***
Heits Building Svcs Cnkd LLC 855 464-3487
52 E Crescentville Rd Cincinnati (45246) ***(G-3697)***
Helen Purcell Home 740 453-1745
1854 Norwood Blvd Zanesville (43701) ***(G-20317)***
Hellandale Community, Fairfield Township *Also called Burchwood Care Center* ***(G-10802)***
Heller Maas Moro & Magill 330 393-6602
54 Westchester Dr Ste 10 Youngstown (44515) ***(G-20063)***
Heller Mass Morrow and Migue, Youngstown *Also called Elliott Heller Maas Morrow Lpa* ***(G-20029)***
Helm and Associates Inc 419 893-1480
501 W Sophia St Unit 8 Maumee (43537) ***(G-13799)***
Helmsman Management Svcs LLC 614 478-8282
700 Taylor Rd Ste 220 Columbus (43230) ***(G-7738)***
Help Foundation Inc 216 289-7710
27348 Oak Ct Euclid (44132) ***(G-10637)***
Help Foundation Inc 216 486-5258
17702 Nottingham Rd Cleveland (44119) ***(G-5683)***
Help Foundation Inc (PA) 216 432-4810
26900 Euclid Ave Euclid (44132) ***(G-10638)***
Help Hotline Crisis Center, Youngstown *Also called Community Center* ***(G-20000)***
Help Hotline Crisis Center 330 747-5111
261 E Wood St Youngstown (44503) ***(G-20064)***

1144 2019 Harris Ohio Services Directory (G-0000) Company's Geographic Section entry number

Help Line of Dlware Mrrow Cnty 740 369-3316
  11 N Franklin St Delaware (43015) (G-9984)
Help ME Grow 419 738-4773
  214 S Wagner Ave Wapakoneta (45895) (G-18646)
Help Network of Northeast Ohio, Youngstown Also called Help Hotline Crisis
Center (G-20064)
Helping Hands, Lima Also called Community Hlth Prfssionals Inc (G-12789)
Helping Hands Health Care Inc 513 755-4181
  9692 Cncnnati Columbus Rd West Chester (45241) (G-19059)
HELPLINE, Delaware Also called Help Line of Dlware Mrrow Cnty (G-9984)
Helton Enterprises (PA) 419 423-4180
  151 Stanford Pkwy Findlay (45840) (G-10922)
Hemlock Landscapes Inc 440 247-3631
  7209 Chagrin Rd Ste A Chagrin Falls (44023) (G-2667)
Hemodialysis Services Inc 216 378-2691
  25550 Chagrin Blvd # 404 Beachwood (44122) (G-1063)
Hempstead Manor 740 354-8150
  727 8th St Portsmouth (45662) (G-16145)
Henderson Road Rest Systems (PA) 614 442-3310
  1615 Old Henderson Rd Columbus (43220) (G-7739)
Henderson Trucking, Delaware Also called Rjw Trucking Company Ltd (G-10004)
Henderson Trucking Inc 740 369-6100
  124 Henderson Ct Delaware (43015) (G-9985)
Henderson Turf Farm Inc 937 748-1559
  2969 Beal Rd Franklin (45005) (G-11032)
Hendrickson Auxiliary Axles, Hebron Also called Hendrickson International Corp (G-11714)
Hendrickson International Corp 740 929-5600
  277 N High St Hebron (43025) (G-11714)
Henkle Schueler Realtors, Lebanon Also called Henkle-Schueler & Associates (G-12471)
Henkle-Schueler & Associates (PA) 513 932-6070
  3000 Henkle Dr G Lebanon (45036) (G-12471)
Henley & Assoc SEC Group LLC 614 378-3727
  967 Jefferson Chase Way Blacklick (43004) (G-1479)
Henningson Drham Richardson PC 513 984-7500
  9987 Carver Rd Ste 200 Blue Ash (45242) (G-1578)
HENNIS CARE CENTER OF BOLIVAR, Bolivar Also called Megco Management Inc (G-1704)
HENNIS CARE CENTRE AT DOVER, Dover Also called Hennis Nursing Home (G-10081)
Hennis Nursing Home 330 364-8849
  1720 N Cross St Dover (44622) (G-10081)
Henry Call Inc 216 433-5609
  308 Pines St Ste 100 Cleveland (44135) (G-5684)
Henry County Bank (HQ) 419 599-1065
  122 E Washington St Napoleon (43545) (G-14808)
Henry County Hospital Inc 419 592-4015
  1600 E Riverview Ave Frnt Napoleon (43545) (G-14809)
Henry Gurtzweiler Inc 419 729-3955
  921 Galena St Toledo (43611) (G-17801)
Henry P Thompson Company (PA) 513 248-3200
  101 Main St Ste 300 Milford (45150) (G-14394)
Henry Schein Inc 440 349-0891
  30600 Aurora Rd Ste 110 Cleveland (44139) (G-5685)
Henry Schein Animal Health, Dublin Also called Butler Animal Health Sup LLC (G-10154)
Henry Schein Animal Health, Columbus Also called Butler Animal Health Sup LLC (G-7100)
Henrys King Touring Company 330 628-1886
  1369 Burbridge Dr Mogadore (44260) (G-14550)
Hensley Industries Inc (PA) 513 769-6666
  2150 Langdon Farm Rd Cincinnati (45237) (G-3698)
Her Inc 614 240-7400
  583 1/2 S 3rd St Columbus (43215) (G-7740)
Her Inc (PA) 614 221-7400
  4261 Morse Rd Columbus (43230) (G-7741)
Her Inc 614 888-7400
  681 High St Worthington (43085) (G-19814)
Her Inc 614 239-7400
  2815 E Main St Columbus (43209) (G-7742)
Her Inc 614 878-4734
  4680 W Broad St Columbus (43228) (G-7743)
Her Inc 614 864-7400
  1450 Tussing Rd Pickerington (43147) (G-15957)
Her Inc 614 889-7400
  5725 Perimeter Dr Dublin (43017) (G-10240)
Her Inc 614 771-7400
  3499 Main St Hilliard (43026) (G-11772)
Her Inc 614 890-7400
  413 N State St Westerville (43082) (G-19172)
Her Real Living, Columbus Also called Her Inc (G-7740)
Heraeus Precious Metals North 937 264-1000
  970 Industrial Park Dr Vandalia (45377) (G-18525)
Herb Thyme Farms Inc 866 386-0854
  8600 S Wilkinson Way G Perrysburg (43551) (G-15873)
Herbert E Orr Company 419 399-4866
  335 W Wall St Paulding (45879) (G-15794)
Herbst Electric Company, Cleveland Also called Benevento Enterprises Inc (G-5054)
Hercules Tire & Rubber Company 419 425-6400
  14801 Township Rd 212 Findlay (45840) (G-10923)
Heritage Administration Svcs, Dublin Also called Heritage Wrrnty Insur Rrg Inc (G-10241)
Heritage Beverage Company LLC 440 255-5550
  7333 Corporate Blvd Mentor (44060) (G-14060)
Heritage Carpet & HM Dctg Ctrs, Canton Also called Clays Heritage Carpet Inc (G-2257)

Heritage Club 513 459-7711
  6690 Heritage Club Dr Mason (45040) (G-13593)
Heritage Cooperative Inc (PA) 419 294-2371
  11177 Township Road 133 West Mansfield (43358) (G-19125)
Heritage Day Health Centers (HQ) 614 451-2151
  2335 N Bank Dr Columbus (43220) (G-7744)
Heritage Development, Solon Also called Breezy Point Ltd Partnership (G-16828)
Heritage Elemtary School, Medina Also called Heritage Pto (G-13948)
Heritage Envmtl Svcs LLC 419 729-1321
  5451 Enterprise Blvd Toledo (43612) (G-17802)
Heritage Equipment Company 614 873-3941
  9000 Heritage Dr Plain City (43064) (G-16054)
Heritage Golf Club Ltd Partnr 614 777-1690
  3525 Heritage Club Dr Hilliard (43026) (G-11773)
Heritage Health Care Services 419 222-2404
  3748 Allentown Rd Lima (45807) (G-12659)
Heritage Health Care Services (PA) 419 867-2002
  1745 Indian Wood Cir # 252 Maumee (43537) (G-13800)
Heritage Home Health Care 440 333-1925
  20800 Center Ridge Rd # 401 Rocky River (44116) (G-16435)
HERITAGE HOUSE NURSING HOME, Columbus Also called Wexner Heritage
Village (G-8894)
HERITAGE HOUSE NURSING HOME, Columbus Also called Shalom House Inc (G-8629)
Heritage Manor, Youngstown Also called Youngstown Area Jwish Fdration (G-20257)
HERITAGE MANOR JEWISH HOME FOR, Youngstown Also called Youngstown Area Jwish
Fdration (G-20256)
Heritage Manor Skilled Nursing, Columbus Also called I Vrable Inc (G-7795)
Heritage Marble of Ohio Inc 614 436-1464
  7086 Huntley Rd Columbus (43229) (G-7745)
Heritage Marbles, Columbus Also called Heritage Marble of Ohio Inc (G-7745)
Heritage Park Rehabilita 937 437-2311
  7739 Us Route 40 New Paris (45347) (G-14943)
Heritage Professional Services 740 456-8245
  3304 Rhodes Ave New Boston (45662) (G-14880)
Heritage Pto 330 636-4400
  833 Guilford Blvd Medina (44256) (G-13948)
Heritage Sportswear Inc (PA) 740 928-7771
  102 Reliance Dr Hebron (43025) (G-11715)
Heritage Square New Boston, New Boston Also called Heritage Professional
Services (G-14880)
HERITAGE VILLAGE OF CLYDE, Clyde Also called Astoria Place of Clyde LLC (G-6739)
Heritage Wrrnty Insur Rrg Inc 800 753-5236
  400 Metro Pl N Ste 300 Dublin (43017) (G-10241)
Heritage, The, Findlay Also called Manleys Manor Nursing Home Inc (G-10937)
Herman Bair Enterprise 330 262-4449
  210 E Milltown Rd Ste A Wooster (44691) (G-19727)
Hernandez Cnstr Svcs Inc 330 796-0500
  1160 Gorge Blvd Ste D Akron (44310) (G-259)
Hernando Zegarra 216 831-5700
  3401 Entp Pkwy Ste 300 Cleveland (44122) (G-5686)
Herrnstein Auto Group, Chillicothe Also called Herrnstein Chrysler Inc (G-2786)
Herrnstein Chrysler Inc (PA) 740 773-2203
  133 Marietta Rd Chillicothe (45601) (G-2786)
Herschman Architects, Cleveland Also called Onyx Creative Inc (G-6137)
Hersh Construction Inc 330 877-1515
  650 S Prospect Ave # 200 Hartville (44632) (G-11690)
Hertz, Columbus Also called Geo Byers Sons Holding Inc (G-7658)
Hertz Clvland 600 Superior LLC 310 584-8108
  600 Superior Ave E # 100 Cleveland (44114) (G-5687)
Hertz Corporation 216 267-8900
  19025 Maplewood Ave Cleveland (44135) (G-5688)
Hertz Corporation 513 533-3161
  Cincinnati N Kentucky A P Cincinnati (45275) (G-3699)
Hertz Corporation 937 890-2721
  James Cox Intrl Arpt Vandalia (45377) (G-18526)
Hertz Corporation 937 898-5806
  3350 S Valet Cir Vandalia (45377) (G-18527)
Hertzfeld Poultry Farms Inc 419 832-2070
  15799 Milton Rd Grand Rapids (43522) (G-11326)
Herzig-Krall Medical Group 513 896-9595
  5150 Sandy Ln Fairfield (45014) (G-10735)
Hester Masonry Co Inc 937 890-2283
  10867 Engle Rd Vandalia (45377) (G-18528)
Hewlettco Inc 440 238-4600
  13590 Falling Water Rd Strongsville (44136) (G-17309)
Hexpol Compounding LLC 440 834-4644
  14330 Kinsman Rd Burton (44021) (G-2016)
Heyburn Dialysis LLC 614 876-3610
  2447 Hilliard Rome Rd Hilliard (43026) (G-11774)
Heyman Ralph E Attorney At Law 937 449-2820
  10 N Ludlow St Dayton (45402) (G-9495)
Hgc Construction Co (PA) 513 861-8866
  2814 Stanton Ave Cincinnati (45206) (G-3700)
Hgcc of Allentown Inc 419 252-5500
  333 N Summit St Toledo (43604) (G-17803)
Hgr Industrial Surplus Inc (PA) 216 486-4567
  20001 Euclid Ave Euclid (44117) (G-10639)
HI Tecmetal Group Inc 440 373-5101
  28910 Lakeland Blvd Wickliffe (44092) (G-19463)

A
L
P
H
A
B
E
T
I
C

HI Tecmetal Group Inc...440 946-2280
　34800 Lakeland Blvd Willoughby (44095) *(G-19528)*
Hi-Five Development Svcs Inc.......................................513 336-9280
　202 W Main St Ste C Mason (45040) *(G-13594)*
Hi-Tek Manufacturing Inc...513 459-1094
　6050 Hi Tek Ct Mason (45040) *(G-13595)*
Hi-Way Distributing Corp Amer.....................................330 645-6633
　3716 E State St Coventry Township (44203) *(G-9035)*
Hi-Way Paving Inc..614 876-1700
　4343 Weaver Ct N Hilliard (43026) *(G-11775)*
Hiab USA Inc (HQ)...419 482-6000
　12233 Williams Rd Perrysburg (43551) *(G-15874)*
Hickey Metal Fabrication Roofg.....................................330 337-9329
　873 Georgetown Rd Salem (44460) *(G-16546)*
Hickman Cancer Center...419 824-1952
　5200 Harroun Rd Sylvania (43560) *(G-17430)*
Hickory Creek Healthcare..419 542-7795
　401 Fountain St Hicksville (43526) *(G-11728)*
Hickory Harvest Foods, Coventry Township *Also called Ohio Hickory Harvest Brand*
Pro (G-9040)
Hickory Health Care Inc..330 762-6486
　721 Hickory St Akron (44303) *(G-260)*
Hickory Woods Golf Course Inc.....................................513 575-3900
　1240 Hickory Woods Dr Loveland (45140) *(G-12999)*
Hicks Industrial Roofing, New Philadelphia *Also called Hicks Roofing Inc (G-14964)*
Hicks Roofing Inc...330 364-7737
　2162 Pleasant Vly Rd Ne New Philadelphia (44663) *(G-14964)*
Hicksville Bank Inc (HQ)...419 542-7726
　144 E High St Hicksville (43526) *(G-11729)*
Hicon Inc..513 242-3612
　93 Caldwell Dr A Cincinnati (45216) *(G-3701)*
Hidden Lake Condominiums..614 488-1131
　1363 Lake Shore Dr Columbus (43204) *(G-7746)*
Hide-A-Way Hills Club..740 746-9589
　29042 Hide Away Hills Rd Sugar Grove (43155) *(G-17374)*
Hidy Honda, Dayton *Also called Hidy Motors Inc (G-9176)*
Hidy Motors Inc (PA)...937 426-9564
　2300 Hller Drv Bevr Crk Beaver Creek Dayton (45434) *(G-9176)*
Higgins Building Company Inc.......................................740 439-5553
　11342 E Pike Rd Cambridge (43725) *(G-2074)*
Higgins Sheltered Workshop, Canton *Also called County of Stark (G-2267)*
High Banks Care Centre, Columbus *Also called Provider Services Inc (G-8476)*
High Line Corporation...330 848-8800
　2420 Wedgewood Dr Ste 20 Akron (44312) *(G-261)*
High Point Animal Hospital...419 865-3611
　6020 Manley Rd Maumee (43537) *(G-13801)*
High Power Inc..937 667-1772
　15 Industry Park Ct Tipp City (45371) *(G-17557)*
High TEC Industrial Services, Tipp City *Also called Saftek Industrial Service Inc (G-17566)*
High Voltage Maintenance Corp (HQ)..............................937 278-0811
　5100 Energy Dr Dayton (45414) *(G-9496)*
High-TEC Industrial Services..937 667-1772
　15 Industry Park Ct Tipp City (45371) *(G-17558)*
High-Tech Pools Inc..440 979-5070
　31330 Industrial Pkwy North Olmsted (44070) *(G-15292)*
Highbanks Care Center LLC..614 888-2021
　111 Lazelle Rd Columbus (43235) *(G-7747)*
Highland County Family YMCA.......................................937 840-9622
　201 Diamond Dr Hillsboro (45133) *(G-11842)*
Highland County Joint...937 393-6100
　1275 N High St Hillsboro (45133) *(G-11843)*
Highland County Water Co Inc (PA)................................937 393-4281
　6686 Us Highway 50 Hillsboro (45133) *(G-11844)*
Highland Ctr Early Head Start, Portsmouth *Also called Scioto County C A O*
Headstart (G-16166)
HIGHLAND DISTRICT HOSPITAL, Hillsboro *Also called Highland County Joint (G-11843)*
Highland Relief Organization..614 843-5152
　2761 Regaldo Dr Columbus (43219) *(G-7748)*
Highland Som Development (PA).....................................330 528-3500
　10020 Aurora Hudson Rd Streetsboro (44241) *(G-17256)*
Highland Village Ltd Partnr..614 863-4640
　160 W Main St New Albany (43054) *(G-14856)*
Highlnd Cnty Commnty Action or (PA).............................937 393-3060
　1487 N High St Ste 500 Hillsboro (45133) *(G-11845)*
Highpoint Home Healthcare Agcy...................................330 491-1805
　4767 Higbee Ave Nw Canton (44718) *(G-2343)*
Hightowers Petroleum Company....................................513 423-4272
　3577 Commerce Dr Middletown (45005) *(G-14349)*
Highway Department, Millersburg *Also called County of Holmes (G-14470)*
Highway Maintenance, Akron *Also called County of Summit (G-165)*
Highway Patrol..740 354-2888
　7611 Us Highway 23 Lucasville (45648) *(G-13051)*
Hiland Group Incorporated (PA).....................................330 499-8404
　7600 Supreme St Nw Canton (44720) *(G-2344)*
Hill Barth & King LLC (PA)..330 758-8613
　6603 Summit Dr Canfield (44406) *(G-2140)*
Hill Barth & King LLC..614 228-4000
　226 N 5th St Ste 500 Columbus (43215) *(G-7749)*
Hill Barth & King LLC..330 747-1903
　6603 Summit Dr Canfield (44406) *(G-2141)*

Hill Distributing Company...614 276-6533
　5080 Tuttle Crossing Blvd # 325 Dublin (43016) *(G-10242)*
Hill Intl Trcks NA LLC (PA)...330 386-6440
　47866 Y And O Rd East Liverpool (43920) *(G-10404)*
Hill Manor 1 Inc...740 972-3227
　3244 Southfield Dr E Columbus (43207) *(G-7750)*
Hill Manor Enterprises (PA)..614 567-7134
　5585 Morgan Ct Groveport (43125) *(G-11517)*
Hill Side Plaza...216 486-6300
　18220 Euclid Ave Cleveland (44112) *(G-5689)*
Hill View Retirement Center...740 354-3135
　1610 28th St Portsmouth (45662) *(G-16146)*
Hillandale Farms Inc...740 968-3597
　72165 Mrrstown Flshing Rd Flushing (43977) *(G-10979)*
Hillandale Farms Corporation (PA).................................330 724-3199
　1330 Austin Ave Akron (44306) *(G-262)*
Hillandale Farms Trnsp...740 893-2232
　10513 Croton Rd Johnstown (43031) *(G-12201)*
Hillandale Healthcare Inc..513 813-5595
　8073 Tylersville Rd West Chester (45069) *(G-18943)*
Hillbrook Club Inc...440 247-4940
　17200 S Woodland Rd Cleveland (44120) *(G-5690)*
Hillcrest Ambulance Svc Inc...216 797-4000
　26420 Lakeland Blvd Euclid (44132) *(G-10640)*
Hillcrest Egg & Cheese Co (PA).....................................216 361-4625
　2735 E 40th St Cleveland (44115) *(G-5691)*
Hillcrest Foodservice, Cleveland *Also called Hillcrest Egg & Cheese Co (G-5691)*
Hillcrest Hospital, Cleveland *Also called Cleveland Clinic Health System (G-5247)*
Hillcrest Hospital Auxiliary..440 449-4500
　6780 Mayfield Rd Cleveland (44124) *(G-5692)*
Hillcrest Training School, Cincinnati *Also called County of Hamilton (G-3370)*
Hillcrest Ymca-Adrian, Cleveland *Also called Young MNS Chrstn Assn Clveland (G-6704)*
Hillebrand Home Health Inc...513 598-6648
　4343 Bridgetown Rd Cincinnati (45211) *(G-3702)*
Hillebrand Nursing & Rehab, Cincinnati *Also called D James Incorporated (G-3395)*
Hilliard Electric, Cleveland *Also called JZE Electric Inc (G-5810)*
Hilliard Station Dialysis, Hilliard *Also called Heyburn Dialysis LLC (G-11774)*
Hillman Companies Inc..513 851-4900
　10590 Hamilton Ave Cincinnati (45231) *(G-3703)*
Hillman Companies Inc..513 851-4900
　1700 Carillion Blvd Cincinnati (45240) *(G-3704)*
Hillman Companies Inc (HQ)..513 851-4900
　10590 Hamilton Ave Cincinnati (45231) *(G-3705)*
Hillman Group Inc..513 874-5905
　9950 Prnceton Glendale Rd West Chester (45246) *(G-19060)*
Hillman Group Inc (HQ)...513 851-4900
　10590 Hamilton Ave Cincinnati (45231) *(G-3706)*
Hillman Group Anchor Wire, Cincinnati *Also called Hillman Companies Inc (G-3703)*
Hills Communities Inc..513 984-0300
　4901 Hunt Rd Ste 300 Blue Ash (45242) *(G-1579)*
Hills Developers Inc..513 984-0300
　4901 Hunt Rd Ste 300 Blue Ash (45242) *(G-1580)*
Hills Property Management Inc (PA)................................513 984-0300
　4901 Hunt Rd Ste 300 Blue Ash (45242) *(G-1581)*
Hills Real Estate Group, Blue Ash *Also called Hills Property Management Inc (G-1581)*
Hills Supply Inc...740 477-8994
　8476 Us Highway 22 E Circleville (43113) *(G-4835)*
Hillsboro Health Center Inc..937 393-5781
　1108 Northview Dr Ste 1 Hillsboro (45133) *(G-11846)*
Hillsboro Transportation Co...513 772-9223
　2889 E Crescentville Rd Cincinnati (45246) *(G-3707)*
Hillside Acres Nursing Home, Willard *Also called Liberty Nursing of Willard (G-19483)*
Hillside Maint Sup Co Inc..513 751-4100
　3300 Spring Grove Ave Cincinnati (45225) *(G-3708)*
Hillside Plaza, Cleveland *Also called Hill Side Plaza (G-5689)*
Hillspring Health Care Center.......................................937 748-1100
　325 E Central Ave Springboro (45066) *(G-16970)*
Hilltop, Columbus *Also called Young Mens Christian Assoc (G-8928)*
Hilltop Basic Resources Inc...513 621-1500
　511 W Water St Cincinnati (45202) *(G-3709)*
Hilltop Concrete, Cincinnati *Also called Hilltop Basic Resources Inc (G-3709)*
Hilltop Village..216 261-8383
　25900 Euclid Ave Ofc Cleveland (44132) *(G-5693)*
Hilltrux Tank Lines Inc...330 965-1103
　6331 Southern Blvd Youngstown (44512) *(G-20065)*
Hilltrux Tank Lines Inc...330 538-3700
　200 Rosemont Rd North Jackson (44451) *(G-15246)*
Hilscher-Clarke Electric Co (PA).....................................330 452-9806
　519 4th St Nw Canton (44703) *(G-2345)*
Hilscher-Clarke Electric Co..740 622-5557
　572 S 3rd St Coshocton (43812) *(G-9017)*
Hilton, Cleveland *Also called Park Hotels & Resorts Inc (G-6165)*
Hilton, Cleveland *Also called Park Hotels & Resorts Inc (G-6166)*
Hilton, Westlake *Also called Ceres Enterprises LLC (G-19329)*
Hilton Akron Fairlawn, Fairlawn *Also called Fairlawn Associates Ltd (G-10826)*
Hilton Cleveland/Beachwood, Beachwood *Also called Cleveland Bchwood Hsptlity*
LLC (G-1044)
Hilton Cncnnati Netherland Plz, Cincinnati *Also called Park Hotels & Resorts Inc (G-4202)*

Hilton Cncnnati Netherland Plz, Cincinnati *Also called Cincinnati Netherland Ht LLC (G-3259)*

Hilton Columbus At Easton, Columbus *Also called Columbus Easton Hotel LLC (G-7279)*

Hilton Columbus Polaris, Columbus *Also called Hilton Polaris (G-6815)*

Hilton Garden Blue Ash, Blue Ash *Also called Blue-Kenwood LLC (G-1515)*

Hilton Garden Inn 614 263-7200
3232 Olentangy River Rd Columbus (43202) *(G-7751)*

Hilton Garden Inn Akron 330 966-4907
5251 Landmark Blvd Canton (44720) *(G-2346)*

Hilton Garden Inn Beavercreek 937 458-2650
3498 Pentagon Park Blvd Dayton (45431) *(G-9177)*

Hilton Garden Inn Perrysburg, Perrysburg *Also called Levis Commons Hotel LLC (G-15889)*

Hilton Garden Inn Twinsburg, Twinsburg *Also called Apple Gate Operating Co Inc (G-18245)*

Hilton Grdn Inn Clmbus Polaris 614 846-8884
8535 Lyra Dr Columbus (43240) *(G-6814)*

Hilton Grdn Inn Clvland Dwntwn, Cleveland *Also called Hotel 1100 Carnegie Opco L P (G-5715)*

Hilton Grdn Inn Columbus Arprt, Columbus *Also called Indus Airport Hotels I LLC (G-7809)*

Hilton Grdn Inn Columbus Arprt 614 231-2869
4265 Sawyer Rd Columbus (43219) *(G-7752)*

Hilton Homewood Suites, Columbus *Also called Rose Gracias (G-8550)*

Hilton Polaris 614 885-1600
8700 Lyra Dr Columbus (43240) *(G-6815)*

Hilty Child Care Center 419 384-3220
304 Hilty Dr Pandora (45877) *(G-15752)*

Hilty Memorial Home Inc 419 384-3218
304 Hilty Dr Pandora (45877) *(G-15753)*

Hinckley Roofing Inc 330 722-7663
3587 Ridge Rd Medina (44256) *(G-13949)*

Hinkley Lighting Inc (PA) 440 653-5500
33000 Pin Oak Pkwy Avon Lake (44012) *(G-920)*

Hiram Maintenance Bldg, Windham *Also called Turnpike and Infrastructure Co (G-19664)*

Hirsch Division, Chagrin Falls *Also called Lake Horry Electric (G-2651)*

Hirsch International Holdings 513 733-4111
4 Kovach Dr Ste 470a Cincinnati (45215) *(G-3710)*

Hirts Greenhouse and Flowers, Strongsville *Also called Hirts Greenhouse Inc (G-17310)*

Hirts Greenhouse Inc 440 238-8200
14407 Pearl Rd Strongsville (44136) *(G-17310)*

Hirzel Canning Company (PA) 419 693-0531
411 Lemoyne Rd Northwood (43619) *(G-15395)*

Hirzel Farms Inc 419 837-2710
20790 Bradner Rd Luckey (43443) *(G-13054)*

Hirzel Transfer Co 419 287-3288
115 Columbus St Pemberville (43450) *(G-15804)*

Hit Portfolio I Hil Trs LLC 614 235-0717
3920 Tuller Rd Dublin (43017) *(G-10243)*

Hit Portfolio I Misc Trs LLC 216 575-1234
420 Superior Ave E Cleveland (44114) *(G-5694)*

Hit Portfolio I Misc Trs LLC 513 241-3575
151 W 5th St Cincinnati (45202) *(G-3711)*

Hit Portfolio I Misc Trs LLC 614 228-1234
75 E State St Columbus (43215) *(G-7753)*

Hit Portfolio I Trs LLC 614 846-4355
7490 Vantage Dr Columbus (43235) *(G-7754)*

Hit Swn Trs LLC 614 228-3200
35 W Spring St Columbus (43215) *(G-7755)*

Hitachi Hlthcare Americas Corp 330 425-1313
1959 Summit Commerce Park Twinsburg (44087) *(G-18279)*

Hitachi Medical Systems Amer, Twinsburg *Also called Hitachi Hlthcare Americas Corp (G-18279)*

Hitchcock Center For Women Inc 216 421-0662
1227 Ansel Rd Cleveland (44108) *(G-5695)*

Hitchcock Fleming & Assoc Inc 330 376-2111
500 Wolf Ledges Pkwy Akron (44311) *(G-263)*

Hite Parts Exchange Inc 614 272-5115
2235 Mckinley Ave Columbus (43204) *(G-7756)*

Hixson Archtcts/Ngnrs/Nteriors, Cincinnati *Also called Hixson Incorporated (G-3712)*

Hixson Incorporated 513 241-1230
659 Van Meter St Ste 300 Cincinnati (45202) *(G-3712)*

HJ Benken Flor & Greenhouses 513 891-1040
6000 Plainfield Rd Cincinnati (45213) *(G-3713)*

HJ Ford Associates Inc 937 429-9711
2940 Presidential Dr # 150 Beavercreek (45324) *(G-1155)*

Hkm Drect Mkt Cmmnications Inc (PA) 216 651-9500
5501 Cass Ave Cleveland (44102) *(G-5696)*

Hkt Teleservices Inc (PA) 614 652-6300
3400 Southpark Pl Ste F Grove City (43123) *(G-11441)*

Hmb Information Sys Developers, Westerville *Also called Harris Mackessy & Brennan (G-19169)*

HMC Group Inc 440 847-2720
29065 Clemens Rd Ste 200 Westlake (44145) *(G-19350)*

HMS Construction & Rental Co 330 628-4811
1225 Waterloo Rd Mogadore (44260) *(G-14551)*

Hmshost Corporation 419 547-8667
888 N County Road 260 Clyde (43410) *(G-6744)*

Hmt Associates Inc 216 369-0109
335 Treeworth Blvd Broadview Heights (44147) *(G-1836)*

Hmt Dermatology Associates Inc (PA) 330 725-0569
5783 Wooster Pike Medina (44256) *(G-13950)*

Hntb Corporation 216 522-1140
1100 Superior Ave E # 1701 Cleveland (44114) *(G-5697)*

Hobart, Troy *Also called ITW Food Equipment Group LLC (G-18208)*

Hobart Bros Stick Electrode 937 332-5375
101 Trade Sq E Troy (45373) *(G-18206)*

Hobart Sales & Service, Akron *Also called Harry C Lobalzo & Sons Inc (G-251)*

Hobby Lobby Stores Inc 330 686-1508
4332 Kent Rd Ste 3 Stow (44224) *(G-17209)*

Hobby Smile Center, Ashtabula *Also called Shelley Elizabeth Blum (G-755)*

Hobe Lcas Crtif Pub Accntants 216 524-7167
4807 Rockside Rd Ste 510 Cleveland (44131) *(G-5698)*

Hobsons Inc (HQ) 513 891-5444
50 E-Business Way Ste 300 Cincinnati (45241) *(G-3714)*

Hoc Transport Company 330 630-0100
1569 Industrial Pkwy Akron (44310) *(G-264)*

Hochstedler Construction Ltd 740 427-4880
24761 Dennis Church Rd Gambier (43022) *(G-11224)*

Hockaden & Associates Inc 614 252-0993
883 N Cassady Ave Columbus (43219) *(G-7757)*

Hocking College Addc 740 541-2221
19234 Taylor Ridge Rd Glouster (45732) *(G-11309)*

Hocking Valley Community Ho (PA) 740 380-8336
601 State Route 664 N Logan (43138) *(G-12837)*

Hocking Valley Industries Inc 740 385-2118
1369 E Front St Logan (43138) *(G-12838)*

Hocking Vly Bnk of Athens Co (PA) 740 592-4441
7 W Stimson Ave Athens (45701) *(G-784)*

Hocking Vly Cmnty Rsdntial Ctr 740 753-4400
111 W 29 Dr Nelsonville (45764) *(G-14833)*

Hockingthensperry Cmnty Action 740 385-6813
1005 C I C Dr Logan (43138) *(G-12839)*

Hockingthensperry Cmnty Action 740 767-4500
3 Cardaras Dr Glouster (45732) *(G-11310)*

Hodell-Natco Industries Inc (PA) 773 472-2305
7825 Hub Pkwy Cleveland (44125) *(G-5699)*

Hoeting Inc (PA) 513 451-4800
6048 Bridgetown Rd Cincinnati (45248) *(G-3715)*

Hoeting Realtors, Cincinnati *Also called Hoeting Inc (G-3715)*

Hoffman Group The, Medina *Also called James B Oswald Company (G-13959)*

Hoffman Products, Macedonia *Also called TPC Wire & Cable Corp (G-13085)*

Hofstetter Orran Inc (PA) 330 683-8070
12024 Lincoln Way E Orrville (44667) *(G-15634)*

Hogan Services Inc 614 491-8402
1500 Obetz Rd Columbus (43207) *(G-7758)*

Hogan Truck Leasing Inc 513 454-3500
2001 Ddc Way Fairfield (45014) *(G-10736)*

Hoge Brush, New Knoxville *Also called Hoge Lumber Company (G-14917)*

Hoge Lumber Company (PA) 419 753-2263
701 S Main St State New Knoxville (45871) *(G-14917)*

Hoglund Chwlkowski Mrozik Pllc 330 252-8009
520 S Main St Akron (44311) *(G-265)*

Hoglund Law, Akron *Also called Hoglund Chwlkowski Mrozik Pllc (G-265)*

Hokuto USA Inc 614 782-6200
2200 Southwest Blvd Ste F Grove City (43123) *(G-11442)*

Holand Management, Sharon Center *Also called Holland Professional Group (G-16723)*

Holbrook & Manter (PA) 740 387-8620
181 E Center St Marion (43302) *(G-13425)*

Holden Arboretum 440 946-4400
9500 Sperry Rd Willoughby (44094) *(G-19529)*

Holiday Inn, Wilmington *Also called S & S Management Inc (G-19647)*

Holiday Inn, Cambridge *Also called Cambridge Property Investors (G-2056)*

Holiday Inn, Dayton *Also called S & S Management Inc (G-9745)*

Holiday Inn, Cincinnati *Also called Green Township Hospitality LLC (G-3656)*

Holiday Inn, Sunbury *Also called Dbp Enterprises LLC (G-17386)*

Holiday Inn, Gahanna *Also called Star Group Ltd (G-11146)*

Holiday Inn, Lancaster *Also called Lancaster Host LLC (G-12412)*

Holiday Inn, Worthington *Also called He Hari Inc (G-19812)*

Holiday Inn, Blue Ash *Also called W & H Realty Inc (G-1677)*

Holiday Inn, Springfield *Also called Grandview Ht Ltd Partnr Ohio (G-17043)*

Holiday Inn, Perrysburg *Also called Bennett Enterprises Inc (G-15838)*

Holiday Inn, Gallipolis *Also called Gallipolis Hospitality Inc (G-11195)*

Holiday Inn, Newton Falls *Also called Liberty Ashtabula Holdings (G-15140)*

Holiday Inn, Obetz *Also called Synergy Hotels LLC (G-15530)*

Holiday Inn, Cleveland *Also called Summit Associates Inc (G-6475)*

Holiday Inn, Cleveland *Also called Integrated CC LLC (G-5757)*

Holiday Inn, Beavercreek *Also called PH Fairborn Ht Owner 2800 LLC (G-1176)*

Holiday Inn, Cincinnati *Also called Six Continents Hotels Inc (G-4487)*

Holiday Inn, Cleveland *Also called Seagate Hospitality Group LLC (G-6383)*

Holiday Inn, Cleveland *Also called Jagi Clveland Independence LLC (G-5778)*

Holiday Inn, Cambridge *Also called Cambridge Associates Ltd (G-2051)*

Holiday Inn, Cincinnati *Also called Jagi Juno LLC (G-3804)*

Holiday Inn, Cleveland *Also called Mrm-Newgar Hotel Ltd (G-6020)*

Holiday Inn, Cincinnati *Also called Clermont Hills Co LLC (G-2846)*

Holiday Inn, Youngstown *Also called Rukh Boardman Properties LLC (G-20198)*

Holiday Inn, Akron *Also called Detroit Westfield LLC (G-184)*

Holiday Inn, Marietta *Also called Valley Hospitality Inc* ***(G-13395)***
Holiday Inn, Lima *Also called Columbia Properties Lima LLC* ***(G-12616)***
Holiday Inn, Cincinnati *Also called Hauck Hospitality LLC* ***(G-3684)***
Holiday Inn, Columbus *Also called Town Inn Co LLC* ***(G-8766)***
Holiday Inn, Beavercreek *Also called Wright Executive Ht Ltd Partnr* ***(G-1196)***
Holiday Inn, Lima *Also called Sterling Lodging LLC* ***(G-12755)***
Holiday Inn, Englewood *Also called Dixie Management II Inc* ***(G-10585)***
Holiday Inn, Wickliffe *Also called Ridgehills Hotel Ltd Partnr* ***(G-19475)***
Holiday Inn, Wapakoneta *Also called S & S Management Inc* ***(G-18653)***
Holiday Inn, Strongsville *Also called Strongsville Lodging Assoc 1* ***(G-17348)***
Holiday Inn, New Philadelphia *Also called N P Motel System Inc* ***(G-14975)***
Holiday Inn, Cleveland *Also called A C Management Inc* ***(G-4876)***
Holiday Inn, Bedford *Also called Oakwood Hospitality Corp* ***(G-1296)***
Holiday Inn, New Philadelphia *Also called Haribol Haribol Inc* ***(G-14963)***
Holiday Inn 419 691-8800
3154 Navarre Ave Oregon (43616) ***(G-15598)***
Holiday Inn Canton, Canton *Also called Rukh-Jagi Holdings LLC* ***(G-2465)***
Holiday Inn Express 419 332-7700
1501 Hospitality Ct Fremont (43420) ***(G-11080)***
Holiday Inn Express 937 424-5757
5655 Wilmington Pike Dayton (45459) ***(G-9497)***
Holiday Inn Express 614 447-1212
3045 Olentangy River Rd Columbus (43202) ***(G-7759)***
Holiday Lanes Inc 614 861-1600
4589 E Broad St Columbus (43213) ***(G-7760)***
Holland Management Inc (PA) 330 239-4474
1383 Sharon Copley Rd Sharon Center (44274) ***(G-16722)***
Holland Oil Company (PA) 330 835-1815
1485 Marion Ave Akron (44313) ***(G-266)***
Holland Operations Center, Holland *Also called Toledo Edison Company* ***(G-11920)***
Holland Professional Group 330 239-4474
1343 Sharon Copley Sharon Center (44274) ***(G-16723)***
Holland Roofing Inc 330 963-0237
9221 Ravenna Rd Twinsburg (44087) ***(G-18280)***
Holland Roofing Inc 614 430-3724
3494 E 7th Ave Columbus (43219) ***(G-7761)***
Holland Roofing of Columbus, Columbus *Also called Holland Roofing Inc* ***(G-7761)***
Holly Hill Nursing Home, Newbury *Also called Fairmont Nursing Home Inc* ***(G-15120)***
Hollywood 20, Beavercreek *Also called Regal Cinemas Inc* ***(G-1181)***
Hollywood Casino Toledo 419 661-5200
1968 Miami St Toledo (43605) ***(G-17804)***
Holmes County Board of Dd 330 674-8045
8001 Township Road 574 Holmesville (44633) ***(G-11930)***
Holmes County Fire Department, Millersburg *Also called County of Holmes* ***(G-14467)***
Holmes County Health Dept, Millersburg *Also called County of Holmes* ***(G-14468)***
Holmes County Home, Holmesville *Also called County of Holmes* ***(G-11929)***
HOLMES COUNTY TRAINING CENTER, Holmesville *Also called Lynn Hope Industries Inc* ***(G-11931)***
Holmes Crane, Berlin *Also called Berlin Contractors* ***(G-1445)***
Holmes Lumber & Bldg Ctr Inc 330 674-9060
6139 Hc 39 Millersburg (44654) ***(G-14475)***
Holmes Lumber & Supply, Millersburg *Also called Holmes Lumber & Bldg Ctr Inc* ***(G-14475)***
Holmes Siding Contractors 330 674-2867
6767 County Road 624 Millersburg (44654) ***(G-14476)***
Holmes-Wayne Electric Coop 330 674-1055
6060 State Route 83 Millersburg (44654) ***(G-14477)***
Holo Pundits Inc 614 707-5225
425 Metro Pl N Ste 440 Dublin (43017) ***(G-10244)***
Holt Rental Services (PA) 513 771-0515
11330 Mosteller Rd Cincinnati (45241) ***(G-3716)***
Holthaus Lackner Signs, Cincinnati *Also called Gus Holthaus Signs Inc* ***(G-3664)***
Holthouse Farms of Michigan, Willard *Also called Holthouse Farms of Ohio Inc* ***(G-19481)***
Holthouse Farms of Ohio Inc (PA) 419 935-1041
4373 State Route 103 S Willard (44890) ***(G-19481)***
Holub Iron & Steel Company 330 252-5655
470 N Arlington St Akron (44305) ***(G-267)***
Holy Cross Cemetary, Cleveland *Also called Catholic Diocese of Cleveland* ***(G-5135)***
Holy Family, Lakewood *Also called Lakewood Catholic Academy* ***(G-12351)***
Holy Family Home and Hospice, Parma *Also called St Augustine Manor* ***(G-15777)***
Holzer Clinic Lawrence County, Proctorville *Also called Holzer Clinic LLC* ***(G-16217)***
Holzer Clinic LLC 304 746-3701
100 Jackson Pike Gallipolis (45631) ***(G-11196)***
Holzer Clinic LLC (HQ) 740 446-5411
90 Jackson Pike Gallipolis (45631) ***(G-11197)***
Holzer Clinic LLC 304 744-2300
100 Jackson Pike Gallipolis (45631) ***(G-11198)***
Holzer Clinic LLC 740 886-9403
98 State St Proctorville (45669) ***(G-16217)***
Holzer Clinic LLC 740 446-5412
90 Jackson Pike Gallipolis (45631) ***(G-11199)***
Holzer Clinic LLC 740 589-3100
2131 E State St Athens (45701) ***(G-785)***
Holzer Cnsld Hlth Systems, Gallipolis *Also called Holzer Health System* ***(G-11200)***
Holzer Health Center, Gallipolis *Also called Holzer Clinic LLC* ***(G-11197)***
Holzer Health System (PA) 740 446-5060
100 Jackson Pike Gallipolis (45631) ***(G-11200)***
Holzer Hospital, Gallipolis *Also called Holzer Clinic LLC* ***(G-11199)***
Holzer Hospital Foundation (HQ) 740 446-5000
100 Jackson Pike Gallipolis (45631) ***(G-11201)***
Holzer Hospital Foundation 740 446-5000
90 Jackson Pike Gallipolis (45631) ***(G-11202)***
Holzer Medical Center, Gallipolis *Also called Holzer Hospital Foundation* ***(G-11201)***
Holzer Medical Ctr - Jackson 740 288-4625
500 Burlington Rd Jackson (45640) ***(G-12175)***
Holzer Senior Care Center 740 446-5001
380 Colonial Dr Bidwell (45614) ***(G-1469)***
Homan Inc 419 925-4349
6915 Olding Rd Maria Stein (45860) ***(G-13307)***
Homan Transportation Inc 419 465-2626
22 Fort Monroe Pkwy Monroeville (44847) ***(G-14588)***
Home and Farm Insurance Co 937 778-5000
1 Heritage Pl Piqua (45356) ***(G-16010)***
Home Bldrs Assn Grter Cncnnati 513 851-6300
11260 Chester Rd Ste 800 Cincinnati (45246) ***(G-3717)***
Home Care Advantage 330 337-4663
718 E 3rd St Ste C Salem (44460) ***(G-16547)***
Home Care By Black Stone, Piqua *Also called Black Stone Cincinnati LLC* ***(G-15997)***
Home Care By Blackstone, Columbus *Also called Almost Family Inc* ***(G-6900)***
Home Care Network Inc (PA) 937 435-1142
190 E Spring Valley Pike A Dayton (45458) ***(G-9498)***
Home Care Relief Inc 216 692-2270
753 E 200th St Euclid (44119) ***(G-10641)***
Home City Ice Company (PA) 513 574-1800
6045 Bridgetown Rd Ste 1 Cincinnati (45248) ***(G-3718)***
Home City Ice Company 614 836-2877
4505 S Hamilton Rd Groveport (43125) ***(G-11518)***
Home Depot USA Inc 614 523-0600
6333 Cleveland Ave Columbus (43231) ***(G-7762)***
Home Depot USA Inc 330 965-4790
7001 Southern Blvd Boardman (44512) ***(G-1699)***
Home Depot USA Inc 330 497-1810
4873 Portage St Nw Canton (44720) ***(G-2347)***
Home Depot USA Inc 513 688-1654
520 Ohio Pike Cincinnati (45255) ***(G-3719)***
Home Depot USA Inc 330 922-3448
325 Howe Ave Cuyahoga Falls (44221) ***(G-9100)***
Home Depot USA Inc 937 312-9053
345 N Springboro Pike Dayton (45449) ***(G-9499)***
Home Depot USA Inc 937 312-9076
5860 Wilmington Pike Dayton (45459) ***(G-9500)***
Home Depot USA Inc 216 692-2780
877 E 200th St Euclid (44119) ***(G-10642)***
Home Depot USA Inc 216 676-9969
10800 Brookpark Rd Cleveland (44130) ***(G-5700)***
Home Depot USA Inc 216 581-6611
21000 Libby Rd Maple Heights (44137) ***(G-13287)***
Home Depot USA Inc 937 431-7346
3775 Presidential Dr Beavercreek (45324) ***(G-1156)***
Home Depot USA Inc 330 245-0280
2811 S Arlington Rd Akron (44312) ***(G-268)***
Home Depot USA Inc 937 837-1551
5200 Salem Ave Unit A Dayton (45426) ***(G-9501)***
Home Depot USA Inc 216 297-1303
3460 Mayfield Rd Cleveland Heights (44118) ***(G-6719)***
Home Depot USA Inc 513 661-2413
6300 Glenway Ave Cincinnati (45211) ***(G-3720)***
Home Depot USA Inc 513 887-1450
6562 Winford Ave Fairfield Township (45011) ***(G-10810)***
Home Depot USA Inc 419 476-4573
1035 W Alexis Rd Toledo (43612) ***(G-17805)***
Home Depot USA Inc 440 357-0428
9615 Diamond Centre Dr Mentor (44060) ***(G-14061)***
Home Depot USA Inc 513 631-1705
3400 Highland Ave Cincinnati (45213) ***(G-3721)***
Home Depot USA Inc 440 684-1343
6199 Wilson Mills Rd Highland Heights (44143) ***(G-11734)***
Home Depot USA Inc 419 537-1920
3200 Secor Rd Toledo (43606) ***(G-17806)***
Home Depot USA Inc 614 878-9150
100 S Grener Ave Columbus (43228) ***(G-7763)***
Home Depot USA Inc 440 826-9092
8199 Pearl Rd Strongsville (44136) ***(G-17311)***
Home Depot USA Inc 614 939-5036
5200 N Hamilton Rd Columbus (43230) ***(G-7764)***
Home Depot USA Inc 440 937-2240
35930 Detroit Rd Avon (44011) ***(G-886)***
Home Depot USA Inc 614 577-1601
2480 Brice Rd Reynoldsburg (43068) ***(G-16309)***
Home Depot USA Inc 330 220-2654
3330 Center Rd Brunswick (44212) ***(G-1932)***
Home Depot USA Inc 419 626-6493
715 Crossings Rd Sandusky (44870) ***(G-16616)***
Home Depot USA Inc 614 876-5558
4101 Trueman Blvd Hilliard (43026) ***(G-11776)***
Home Depot USA Inc 440 324-7222
150 Market Dr Elyria (44035) ***(G-10515)***
Home Depot USA Inc 419 529-0015
2000 August Dr Ontario (44906) ***(G-15552)***

Home Depot USA Inc...216 251-3091
  11901 Berea Rd Cleveland (44111) *(G-5701)*
Home Depot, The, Columbus *Also called Home Depot USA Inc (G-7762)*
Home Depot, The, Boardman *Also called Home Depot USA Inc (G-1699)*
Home Depot, The, Canton *Also called Home Depot USA Inc (G-2347)*
Home Depot, The, Cincinnati *Also called Home Depot USA Inc (G-3719)*
Home Depot, The, Cuyahoga Falls *Also called Home Depot USA Inc (G-9100)*
Home Depot, The, Dayton *Also called Home Depot USA Inc (G-9499)*
Home Depot, The, Dayton *Also called Home Depot USA Inc (G-9500)*
Home Depot, The, Euclid *Also called Home Depot USA Inc (G-10642)*
Home Depot, The, Cleveland *Also called Home Depot USA Inc (G-5700)*
Home Depot, The, Maple Heights *Also called Home Depot USA Inc (G-13287)*
Home Depot, The, Beavercreek *Also called Home Depot USA Inc (G-1156)*
Home Depot, The, Akron *Also called Home Depot USA Inc (G-268)*
Home Depot, The, Dayton *Also called Home Depot USA Inc (G-9501)*
Home Depot, The, Cleveland Heights *Also called Home Depot USA Inc (G-6719)*
Home Depot, The, Cincinnati *Also called Home Depot USA Inc (G-3720)*
Home Depot, The, Fairfield Township *Also called Home Depot USA Inc (G-10810)*
Home Depot, The, Toledo *Also called Home Depot USA Inc (G-17805)*
Home Depot, The, Mentor *Also called Home Depot USA Inc (G-14061)*
Home Depot, The, Cincinnati *Also called Home Depot USA Inc (G-3721)*
Home Depot, The, Highland Heights *Also called Home Depot USA Inc (G-11734)*
Home Depot, The, Toledo *Also called Home Depot USA Inc (G-17806)*
Home Depot, The, Columbus *Also called Home Depot USA Inc (G-7763)*
Home Depot, The, Strongsville *Also called Home Depot USA Inc (G-17311)*
Home Depot, The, Columbus *Also called Home Depot USA Inc (G-7764)*
Home Depot, The, Avon *Also called Home Depot USA Inc (G-886)*
Home Depot, The, Reynoldsburg *Also called Home Depot USA Inc (G-16309)*
Home Depot, The, Brunswick *Also called Home Depot USA Inc (G-1932)*
Home Depot, The, Sandusky *Also called Home Depot USA Inc (G-16616)*
Home Depot, The, Hilliard *Also called Home Depot USA Inc (G-11776)*
Home Depot, The, Elyria *Also called Home Depot USA Inc (G-10515)*
Home Depot, The, Ontario *Also called Home Depot USA Inc (G-15552)*
Home Depot, The, Cleveland *Also called Home Depot USA Inc (G-5701)*
Home Dialysis of Dayton South, Kettering *Also called Total Renal Care Inc (G-12301)*
Home Echo Club Inc...614 864-1718
  10270 Blacklick Rd Pickerington (43147) *(G-15958)*
Home Health Agency, Marietta *Also called Amedisys Inc (G-13309)*
Home Health Care, Ashtabula *Also called Continuum Home Care Inc (G-730)*
Home Health Connection Inc.....................................614 839-4545
  6797 N High St Ste 113 Worthington (43085) *(G-19815)*
Home Helper Direct Link...330 865-5730
  1720 Merriman Rd Unit B Akron (44313) *(G-269)*
Home Helpers...937 393-8600
  503 E Main St Hillsboro (45133) *(G-11847)*
Home Helpers and Direct Link, Hillsboro *Also called Home Helpers (G-11847)*
Home Hlth Svcs Southwest Hosp, Cleveland *Also called Southwest General Health Ctr (G-6433)*
Home Instead Senior Care, Toledo *Also called Sar Enterprises LLC (G-18019)*
Home Instead Senior Care..330 334-4664
  1 Park Centre Dr Ste 15 Wadsworth (44281) *(G-18599)*
Home Instead Senior Care..740 393-2500
  400 W High St Mount Vernon (43050) *(G-14767)*
Home Instead Senior Care..330 729-1233
  5437 Mahoning Ave Ste 22 Youngstown (44515) *(G-20066)*
Home Instead Senior Care..614 432-8524
  3220 Riverside Dr Ste C4 Upper Arlington (43221) *(G-18398)*
Home Mortgage, Chillicothe *Also called Huntington National Bank (G-2792)*
Home Mortgage, Lima *Also called Huntington National Bank (G-12662)*
Home Mortgage, Cleveland *Also called Huntington National Bank (G-5725)*
Home Nursing Service & Hospice, Marietta *Also called Marietta Memorial Hospital (G-13355)*
Home Run Inc (PA)..800 543-9198
  1299 Lavelle Dr Xenia (45385) *(G-19910)*
Home Savings Bank...330 499-1900
  600 S Main St North Canton (44720) *(G-15211)*
Home State Protective Svcs LLC...............................513 253-3095
  1821 Summit Rd Ste 0-11 Cincinnati (45237) *(G-3722)*
Home The Friends Inc...513 897-6050
  514 High St Waynesville (45068) *(G-18832)*
Home Town Realtors LLC...937 890-9111
  9201 N Dixie Dr Dayton (45414) *(G-9502)*
Home2 By Hilton..513 422-3454
  7145 Liberty Centre Dr West Chester (45069) *(G-18944)*
Home2 Suites, The, Perrysburg *Also called Hoster Hotels LLC (G-15876)*
Homecare Mtters HM Hlth Hspice...............................419 562-2001
  133 S Sandusky Ave Bucyrus (44820) *(G-1993)*
Homecare Service Inc..513 655-5022
  10979 Reed Hartman Hwy # 320 Blue Ash (45242) *(G-1582)*
Homefull...937 293-1945
  33 W 1st St Ste 100 Dayton (45402) *(G-9503)*
Homeland Credit Union Inc (PA)................................740 775-3024
  310 Caldwell St Chillicothe (45601) *(G-2787)*

Homeland Credit Union Inc..740 775-3331
  25 Consumer Center Dr Chillicothe (45601) *(G-2788)*
Homeland Defense Solutions......................................513 333-7800
  128 E 6th St Cincinnati (45202) *(G-3723)*
Homeless Center, Cleveland *Also called Lutheran Metropolitan Ministry (G-5890)*
Homeless Families Foundation...................................614 461-9427
  33 N Grubb St Columbus (43215) *(G-7765)*
Homelife Companies Inc (PA).....................................740 369-1297
  13 E Winter St Delaware (43015) *(G-9986)*
Homereach Inc..614 566-0850
  7708 Green Meadows Dr D Lewis Center (43035) *(G-12545)*
Homereach Inc (HQ)...614 566-0850
  404 E Wilson Bridge Rd Worthington (43085) *(G-19816)*
Homereach Healthcare, Lewis Center *Also called Homereach Inc (G-12545)*
Homes America Inc...614 848-8551
  83 E Stanton Ave Columbus (43214) *(G-7766)*
Homes By John Hershberger, Hartville *Also called Hersh Construction Inc (G-11690)*
Homes For Kids of Ohio Inc.......................................330 544-8005
  165 E Park Ave Niles (44446) *(G-15157)*
Homestead, Geneva *Also called 599 W Main Corporation (G-11235)*
Homestead Care Rhblitation Ctr, Lancaster *Also called Sunbridge Care Enterprises Inc (G-12439)*
Homestead Golf Course Inc.......................................937 698-4876
  5327 Worley Rd Tipp City (45371) *(G-17559)*
Homestead Healthcare Center, Springfield *Also called Communicare Health Svcs Inc (G-17018)*
Homestead II, Painesville *Also called Multi-Care Inc (G-15728)*
Homestead II Healthcare Group..................................440 352-0788
  60 Wood St Painesville (44077) *(G-15715)*
Hometown Bank (PA)...330 673-9827
  142 N Water St Kent (44240) *(G-12236)*
Hometown Improvement Co..614 846-1060
  1430 Halfhill Way Columbus (43207) *(G-7767)*
Hometown Urgent Care..937 372-6012
  101 S Orange St Xenia (45385) *(G-19911)*
Hometown Urgent Care..614 263-4400
  4400 N High St Ste 101 Columbus (43214) *(G-7768)*
Hometown Urgent Care..330 505-9400
  1997 Niles Cortland Rd Se Warren (44484) *(G-18712)*
Hometown Urgent Care..330 629-2300
  1305 Boardman Poland Rd Youngstown (44514) *(G-20067)*
Hometown Urgent Care..937 342-9520
  1200 Vester Ave Springfield (45503) *(G-17045)*
Hometown Urgent Care..740 363-3133
  1100 Sunbury Rd Ste 706 Delaware (43015) *(G-9987)*
Hometown Urgent Care..937 252-2000
  4164 Burbank Rd Wooster (44691) *(G-19728)*
Hometown Urgent Care..614 472-2880
  2880 Stelzer Rd Columbus (43219) *(G-7769)*
Hometown Urgent Care..614 272-1100
  4300 Clime Rd Ste 110 Columbus (43228) *(G-7770)*
Hometown Urgent Care..937 236-8630
  6210 Brandt Pike Dayton (45424) *(G-9504)*
Hometown Urgent Care..937 322-6222
  1301 W 1st St Springfield (45504) *(G-17046)*
Hometown Urgent Care..614 835-0400
  3813 S Hamilton Rd Groveport (43125) *(G-11519)*
Hometown Urgent Care..513 831-5900
  1068 State Route 28 Ste C Milford (45150) *(G-14395)*
Homewood Corporation (PA).......................................614 898-7200
  2700 E Dublin Granville R Columbus (43231) *(G-7771)*
Homewood Residence At Rockefel, Cleveland *Also called American Retirement Corp (G-4966)*
Homewood Rsdnce At Rchmond Hts, Cleveland *Also called American Retirement Corp (G-4965)*
Homewood Suites, Miamisburg *Also called Req/Jqh Holdings Inc (G-14211)*
Homewood Suites, Columbus *Also called Arvind Sagar Inc (G-6975)*
Homewood Suites, Beavercreek *Also called Wright Executive Ht Ltd Partnr (G-1197)*
Homewood Suites Dublin, Dublin *Also called Cni Thl Ops LLC (G-10179)*
Homier & Sons Inc (PA)...419 596-3965
  21133 State Route 613 Continental (45831) *(G-8961)*
Homier Implement Company, Continental *Also called Homier & Sons Inc (G-8961)*
Honda East, Maumee *Also called Randy L Fork Inc (G-13841)*
Honda Federal Credit Union.......................................937 642-6000
  24000 Honda Pkwy Marysville (43040) *(G-13503)*
Honda Logistics North Amer Inc (HQ)..........................937 642-0335
  11590 Township Road 298 East Liberty (43319) *(G-10391)*
Honda Marysville Location, Raymond *Also called Honda R&D Americas Inc (G-16275)*
Honda North America Inc..937 642-5000
  24000 Honda Pkwy Marysville (43040) *(G-13504)*
Honda of America Mfg Inc...937 644-0724
  19900 State Route 739 Marysville (43040) *(G-13505)*
Honda R&D Americas Inc...937 644-0439
  21001 State Route 739 Raymond (43067) *(G-16275)*
Honda Research Center, Marysville *Also called Sumitomo Elc Wirg Systems Inc (G-13532)*
Honda Support Office, Marysville *Also called Honda of America Mfg Inc (G-13505)*
Honda Trading America Corp......................................937 644-8004
  19900 State Route 739 Marysville (43040) *(G-13506)*

Honey Run Retreats LLC (PA) 330 674-0011
  6920 County Road 203 Millersburg (44654) *(G-14478)*
Honeywell, Urbana *Also called Grimes Aerospace Company (G-18436)*
Honeywell, Perrysburg *Also called Fram Group Operations LLC (G-15867)*
Honeywell Authorized Dealer, Batavia *Also called Bachmans Inc (G-983)*
Honeywell Authorized Dealer, Cincinnati *Also called Century Mech Solutions Inc (G-3161)*
Honeywell Authorized Dealer, Lima *Also called Timmerman John P Heating AC Co (G-12764)*
Honeywell Authorized Dealer, Cincinnati *Also called Crane Heating & AC Co (G-3378)*
Honeywell Authorized Dealer, Sandusky *Also called Gundlach Sheet Metal Works Inc (G-16614)*
Honeywell Authorized Dealer, Hilliard *Also called Bruner Corporation (G-11749)*
Honeywell Authorized Dealer, Marietta *Also called Morrison Inc (G-13361)*
Honeywell Authorized Dealer, Cincinnati *Also called Cincinnati Air Conditioning Co (G-3220)*
Honeywell Authorized Dealer, Cleveland *Also called Mc Phillips Plbg Htg & AC Co (G-5929)*
Honeywell Authorized Dealer, Columbus *Also called Farber Corporation (G-7561)*
Honeywell Authorized Dealer, Canton *Also called Miracle Plumbing & Heating Co (G-2406)*
Honeywell Authorized Dealer, Cleveland *Also called Gillmore Security Systems Inc (G-5608)*
Honeywell Authorized Dealer, Cincinnati *Also called Feldkamp Enterprises Inc (G-3540)*
Honeywell Authorized Dealer, Coventry Township *Also called Lakes Heating and AC (G-9038)*
Honeywell Authorized Dealer, Dayton *Also called Envirnmental Engrg Systems Inc (G-9415)*
Honeywell Authorized Dealer, Coventry Township *Also called K Company Incorporated (G-9037)*
Honeywell Authorized Dealer, Gahanna *Also called Custom AC & Htg Co (G-11116)*
Honeywell Authorized Dealer, Columbus *Also called Wenger Temperature Control (G-8887)*
Honeywell Authorized Dealer, Cincinnati *Also called Commercial Hvac Inc (G-3338)*
Honeywell Authorized Dealer, Dayton *Also called Trame Mechanical Inc (G-9820)*
Honeywell Authorized Dealer, West Chester *Also called Guardian Protection Svcs Inc (G-18937)*
Honeywell Authorized Dealer, Cincinnati *Also called Corcoran and Harnist Htg & AC (G-3361)*
Honeywell Authorized Dealer, Ashland *Also called Ashland Comfort Control Inc (G-650)*
Honeywell Authorized Dealer, Dayton *Also called Superior Mechanical Svcs Inc (G-9187)*
Honeywell Authorized Dealer, Sidney *Also called Area Energy & Electric Inc (G-16759)*
Honeywell Authorized Dealer, Cincinnati *Also called Mechancal/Industrial Contg Inc (G-3991)*
Honeywell Authorized Dealer, Uniontown *Also called Crown Heating & Cooling Inc (G-18365)*
Honeywell Authorized Dealer, Cincinnati *Also called Perfection Group Inc (G-4230)*
Honeywell Authorized Dealer, Bedford *Also called Smylie One Heating & Cooling (G-1307)*
Honeywell Authorized Dealer, Toledo *Also called Noron Inc (G-17947)*
Honeywell Authorized Dealer, Pickerington *Also called Colonial Heating & Cooling Co (G-15953)*
Honeywell Authorized Dealer, Cuyahoga Falls *Also called Falls Heating & Cooling Inc (G-9090)*
Honeywell Authorized Dealer, Anna *Also called Wells Brothers Inc (G-611)*
Honeywell Authorized Dealer, Dublin *Also called Haslett Heating & Cooling Inc (G-10239)*
Honeywell Authorized Dealer, Columbus *Also called American Mechanical Group Inc (G-6930)*
Honeywell Authorized Dealer, Fairborn *Also called Advanced Mechanical Svcs Inc (G-10662)*
Honeywell Authorized Dealer, Canal Winchester *Also called Kessler Heating & Cooling (G-2113)*
Honeywell Authorized Dealer, Cincinnati *Also called TP Mechanical Contractors Inc (G-4623)*
Honeywell International Inc 216 459-6053
  925 Keynote Cir Ste 100 Cleveland (44131) *(G-5702)*
Honeywell International Inc 513 745-7200
  1280 Kemper Meadow Dr Cincinnati (45240) *(G-3724)*
Honeywell International Inc 614 717-2270
  2080 Arlingate Ln Columbus (43228) *(G-7772)*
Hooberry Associates Inc 330 872-1991
  2200 Milton Blvd Newton Falls (44444) *(G-15137)*
Hoosier Express Inc (PA) 419 436-9590
  1827 Sandusky St Fostoria (44830) *(G-11006)*
Hoover & Wells Inc 419 691-9220
  2011 Seaman St Toledo (43605) *(G-17807)*
Hope Ctr For Cncer Care Warren 330 856-8600
  1745 Niles Crtlnd Rd Ne Warren (44484) *(G-18713)*
Hope Homes Inc 330 688-4935
  2044 Bryn Mawr Dr Stow (44224) *(G-17210)*
Hope Hotel & Conference Center, Fairborn *Also called Visicon Inc (G-10687)*
Hopedale Mining LLC 740 937-2225
  86900 Sinfield Rd Hopedale (43976) *(G-11937)*
Hopes Drams Childcare Lrng Ctr 330 793-8260
  33 N Wickliffe Cir Youngstown (44515) *(G-20068)*
Hopewell (PA) 440 693-4074
  9637 State Route 534 Mesopotamia (44439) *(G-14130)*
Hopewell Day Treatment Center, Cleveland *Also called Positive Education Program (G-6223)*
Hopewell Dental Care 740 522-5000
  572 Industrial Pkwy Ste B Newark (43056) *(G-15041)*
Hopewell Health Centers Inc 740 385-8468
  460 E 2nd St Logan (43138) *(G-12840)*

Hopewell Health Centers Inc 740 596-5249
  31891 State Route 93 Mc Arthur (45651) *(G-13890)*
Hopewell Health Centers Inc 740 773-1006
  1049 Western Ave Chillicothe (45601) *(G-2789)*
Hopewell Health Centers Inc 740 385-6594
  541 State Route 664 N C Logan (43138) *(G-12841)*
Hopewell Industries Inc (PA) 740 622-3563
  637 Chestnut St Coshocton (43812) *(G-9018)*
Hopewell Therapeutic Farm, Mesopotamia *Also called Hopewell (G-14130)*
Hopkin Arprt Lmsine Shttle Svc 216 267-8282
  1315 Brookpark Rd Cleveland (44109) *(G-5703)*
Hopkin S Airport Limosine Svc, Cleveland *Also called Hopkin Arprt Lmsine Shttle Svc (G-5703)*
Hopkins Airport Limousine Svc (PA) 216 267-8810
  13315 Brookpark Rd Cleveland (44142) *(G-5704)*
Hopkins Partners 216 267-1500
  5300 Riverside Dr Ste 30 Cleveland (44135) *(G-5705)*
Hopkins Transportation Svcs, Cleveland *Also called Hopkins Airport Limousine Svc (G-5704)*
Hoppes Construction LLC 580 310-0090
  4036 Coral Rd Nw Malvern (44644) *(G-13124)*
Hord Livestock Company Inc 419 562-0277
  887 State Route 98 Bucyrus (44820) *(G-1994)*
Horenstein Nicho & Blume A L 937 224-7200
  124 E 3rd St Fl 5 Dayton (45402) *(G-9505)*
Horizon Education Centers 440 322-0288
  233 Bond St Elyria (44035) *(G-10516)*
Horizon Education Centers 440 458-5115
  10347 Dewhurst Rd Elyria (44035) *(G-10517)*
Horizon Freight, Cleveland *Also called Horizon South Inc (G-5708)*
Horizon Freight System Inc (PA) 216 341-7410
  8777 Rockside Rd Cleveland (44125) *(G-5706)*
Horizon Health Management LLC 513 793-5220
  3889 E Galbraith Rd Cincinnati (45236) *(G-3725)*
Horizon HM Hlth Care Agcy LLC 614 279-2933
  3035 W Broad St Ste 102 Columbus (43204) *(G-7773)*
Horizon Home Health Care 937 264-3155
  410 Corporate Center Dr Vandalia (45377) *(G-18529)*
Horizon House Apartments LLC 740 354-6393
  700 2nd St Portsmouth (45662) *(G-16147)*
Horizon Mechanical and Elec 419 529-2738
  323 N Trimble Rd Mansfield (44906) *(G-13183)*
Horizon Mid Atlantic Inc 800 480-6829
  8777 Rockside Rd Cleveland (44125) *(G-5707)*
Horizon Payroll Services Inc 937 434-8244
  2700 Miamisburg Centervil Dayton (45459) *(G-9506)*
Horizon Pcs Inc (HQ) 740 772-8200
  68 E Main St Chillicothe (45601) *(G-2790)*
Horizon Personnel Resources (PA) 440 585-0031
  1516 Lincoln Rd Wickliffe (44092) *(G-19464)*
Horizon South Inc 800 480-6829
  8777 Rockside Rd Cleveland (44125) *(G-5708)*
Horizon Telcom Inc (PA) 740 772-8200
  68 E Main St Chillicothe (45601) *(G-2791)*
Horizons Employment Svcs LLC 419 254-9644
  2024 W Terrace View St Toledo (43607) *(G-17808)*
Horizons Imaging & Therapy Ctr, Columbus *Also called Mount Carmel Imaging & Therapy (G-8114)*
Horizons Tuscarawas/Carroll 330 262-4183
  527 N Market St Wooster (44691) *(G-19729)*
Hormel Foods Corp Svcs LLC 513 563-0211
  4055 Executive Park Dr # 300 Cincinnati (45241) *(G-3726)*
Horn Electric Company 330 364-7784
  608 S Tuscarawas Ave Dover (44622) *(G-10082)*
Horn Engineering, Dover *Also called Horn Electric Company (G-10082)*
Horn Nursing and Rehab Center (HQ) 330 262-2951
  230 N Market St Wooster (44691) *(G-19730)*
Horn Nursing Rehabilation Ctr, Wooster *Also called Horn Nursing and Rehab Center (G-19730)*
Horner Industrial Services Inc 937 390-6667
  5330 Prosperity Dr Springfield (45502) *(G-17047)*
Horseshoe Cleveland MGT LLC 216 297-4777
  100 Public Sq Ste 100 # 100 Cleveland (44113) *(G-5709)*
Horter Investment MGT LLC 513 984-9933
  11726 7 Gables Rd Cincinnati (45249) *(G-3727)*
Horticultural Management Inc 937 427-8835
  1350 Shaw Ln Beavercrck Twp (45385) *(G-1265)*
Hoskins International LLC 419 628-6015
  5116 State Route 119 Minster (45865) *(G-14536)*
Hoskins Intl SEC Invstigations, Minster *Also called Hoskins International LLC (G-14536)*
Hospice Butler and Warren Cnty, Dayton *Also called Dayton Hospice Incorporated (G-9369)*
Hospice Care Ohio (PA) 330 665-1455
  3358 Ridgewood Rd Fairlawn (44333) *(G-10832)*
Hospice Caring Way 419 238-9223
  1159 Westwood Dr Van Wert (45891) *(G-18480)*
Hospice Cincinnati Inc 513 862-1100
  2800 Winslow Ave Cincinnati (45206) *(G-3728)*
Hospice Cincinnati Inc (HQ) 513 891-7700
  4360 Cooper Rd Ste 300 Cincinnati (45242) *(G-3729)*
Hospice of Care, Chardon *Also called Parkside Care Corporation (G-2707)*
Hospice of Central Ohio (PA) 740 344-0311
  2269 Cherry Valley Rd Se Newark (43055) *(G-15042)*

Hospice of Darke County Inc......419 678-4808
230 W Main St Coldwater (45828) ***(G-6759)***
Hospice of Darke County Inc (PA)......937 548-2999
1350 N Broadway St Greenville (45331) ***(G-11387)***
Hospice of Genesis Health......740 454-5381
713 Forest Ave Zanesville (43701) ***(G-20318)***
Hospice of Hamilton......513 895-1270
1010 Eaton Ave Hamilton (45013) ***(G-11610)***
Hospice of Hope Inc......937 444-4900
215 Hughes Blvd Mount Orab (45154) ***(G-14741)***
Hospice of Knox County......740 397-5188
17700 Coshocton Rd Mount Vernon (43050) ***(G-14768)***
Hospice of Memorial Hospita L......419 334-6626
430 S Main St Clyde (43410) ***(G-6745)***
Hospice of Miami County Inc......937 335-5191
550 Summit Ave Ste 101 Troy (45373) ***(G-18207)***
Hospice of Miami Valley LLC (PA)......937 458-6028
46 N Detroit St Ste B Xenia (45385) ***(G-19912)***
Hospice of Miami Valley LLC......937 521-1444
1948 N Limestone St Springfield (45503) ***(G-17048)***
Hospice of Middletown......513 424-2273
3909 Central Ave Middletown (45044) ***(G-14302)***
Hospice of North Central Ohio......419 524-9200
2131 Park Ave W Ontario (44906) ***(G-15553)***
Hospice of North Central Ohio (PA)......419 281-7107
1050 Dauch Dr Ashland (44805) ***(G-675)***
Hospice of Northwest Ohio (PA)......419 661-4001
30000 E River Rd Perrysburg (43551) ***(G-15875)***
Hospice of Ohio LLC (PA)......440 286-2500
677 Alpha Dr Ste H Cleveland (44143) ***(G-5710)***
Hospice of Southern Ohio......740 356-2567
2201 25th St Portsmouth (45662) ***(G-16148)***
Hospice of The Valley Inc (PA)......330 788-1992
5190 Market St Youngstown (44512) ***(G-20069)***
Hospice of The Western Reserve......440 951-8692
34900 Chardon Rd Ste 105 Willoughby Hills (44094) ***(G-19588)***
Hospice of The Western Reserve......440 357-5833
34900 Chardon Rd Ste 105 Willoughby Hills (44094) ***(G-19589)***
Hospice of The Western Reserve......330 800-2240
5075 Windfall Rd Medina (44256) ***(G-13951)***
Hospice of The Western Reserve......800 707-8921
4670 Richmond Rd Ste 200 Cleveland (44128) ***(G-5711)***
Hospice of The Western Reserve......440 414-7349
30080 Hospice Way Westlake (44145) ***(G-19351)***
Hospice of The Western Reserve......440 787-2080
2173 N Ridge Rd E Ste H Lorain (44055) ***(G-12907)***
Hospice of The Western Reserve (PA)......216 383-2222
17876 Saint Clair Ave Cleveland (44110) ***(G-5712)***
Hospice of The Western Reserve......440 997-6619
1166 Lake Ave Ashtabula (44004) ***(G-740)***
Hospice of The Western Reserve......800 707-8922
17876 Saint Clair Ave Cleveland (44110) ***(G-5713)***
Hospice of The Western Reserve......216 227-9048
22730 Fairview Center Dr # 100 Cleveland (44126) ***(G-5714)***
Hospice Southwest Ohio Inc......513 770-0820
7625 Camargo Rd Cincinnati (45243) ***(G-3730)***
Hospice Tuscarawas County Inc (PA)......330 343-7605
716 Commercial Ave Sw New Philadelphia (44663) ***(G-14965)***
Hospice Visiting Nurse Service, Fairlawn *Also called Hospice Care Ohio* ***(G-10832)***
Hospitalists MGT Group LLC (HQ)......866 464-7497
4535 Dressler Rd Nw Canton (44718) ***(G-2348)***
Hospitality Home East, Xenia *Also called Xenia East Management Systems* ***(G-19936)***
Hospitality Home West, Xenia *Also called Xenia West Management Systems* ***(G-19937)***
Hospitality House, Massillon *Also called Childs Investment Co* ***(G-13669)***
Hoss, Dayton *Also called Voss Auto Network Inc* ***(G-9860)***
Hoss II Inc......937 669-4300
155 S Garber Dr Tipp City (45371) ***(G-17560)***
Hoss Value Cars & Trucks Inc (PA)......937 428-2400
766 Mmsburg Cnterville Rd Dayton (45459) ***(G-9507)***
Hosser Assisted Living......740 286-8785
101 Markham Dr Jackson (45640) ***(G-12176)***
Host Cincinnati Hotel LLC......513 621-7700
21 E 5th St Ste A Cincinnati (45202) ***(G-3731)***
Hoster Hotels LLC......419 931-8900
5995 Levis Commons Blvd Perrysburg (43551) ***(G-15876)***
Hotel 1100 Carnegie Opco L P......216 658-6400
1100 Carnegie Ave Cleveland (44115) ***(G-5715)***
Hotel 2345 LLC......614 766-7762
4130 Tuller Rd Dublin (43017) ***(G-10245)***
Hotel 50 S Front Opco L P......614 885-3334
50 S Front St Columbus (43215) ***(G-7774)***
Hotel 50 S Front Opco LP......614 228-4600
50 S Front St Columbus (43215) ***(G-7775)***
Hotel 75 E State Opco L P......614 365-4500
75 E State St Columbus (43215) ***(G-7776)***
Hotel Stow LP......330 945-9722
4047 Bridgewater Pkwy Stow (44224) ***(G-17211)***
Hoty Enterprises Inc (PA)......419 609-7000
5003 Milan Rd Sandusky (44870) ***(G-16617)***
Hough Health Center, Cleveland *Also called Northeast OH Neighborhood Heal* ***(G-6089)***
House Calls LLC......513 841-9800
1936 Elm Ave Cincinnati (45212) ***(G-3732)***
House of La Rose Cleveland......440 746-7500
6745 Southpointe Pkwy Brecksville (44141) ***(G-1783)***
House of Loreto......330 453-8137
2812 Harvard Ave Nw Canton (44709) ***(G-2349)***
House of New Hope......740 345-5437
8135 Mount Vernon Rd Saint Louisville (43071) ***(G-16518)***
House of Plastics, Cleveland *Also called HP Manufacturing Company Inc* ***(G-5721)***
Household Centralized Svc Inc......419 474-5754
2052 W Sylvania Ave Toledo (43613) ***(G-17809)***
Houston Dick Plbg & Htg Inc......740 763-3961
724 Montgomery Rd Ne Newark (43055) ***(G-15043)***
Houston Plumbing & Heating, Newark *Also called Houston Dick Plbg & Htg Inc* ***(G-15043)***
Hovest Construction......419 456-3426
4997 Old State Route 224 Ottawa (45875) ***(G-15659)***
Howard Hanna RE & Mrtg Svcs, North Royalton *Also called Hanna Holdings Inc* ***(G-15358)***
Howard Hanna Real Estate, Avon *Also called Hanna Holdings Inc* ***(G-884)***
Howard Hanna Real Estate Svcs, Pepper Pike *Also called Howard Hanna Smythe Cramer* ***(G-15818)***
Howard Hanna Smythe Cramer......440 237-8888
5730 Wallings Rd North Royalton (44133) ***(G-15361)***
Howard Hanna Smythe Cramer......330 345-2244
177 W Milltown Rd Unit A Wooster (44691) ***(G-19731)***
Howard Hanna Smythe Cramer......440 248-3000
6240 Som Center Rd # 100 Solon (44139) ***(G-16858)***
Howard Hanna Smythe Cramer......800 656-7356
4374 Boardman Canfield Rd Canfield (44406) ***(G-2142)***
Howard Hanna Smythe Cramer......216 831-0210
28879 Chagrin Blvd Beachwood (44122) ***(G-1064)***
Howard Hanna Smythe Cramer (HQ)......216 447-4477
6000 Parkland Blvd Cleveland (44124) ***(G-5716)***
Howard Hanna Smythe Cramer......440 333-6500
19204 Detroit Rd Rocky River (44116) ***(G-16436)***
Howard Hanna Smythe Cramer......216 447-4477
2603 W Market St Ste 100a Akron (44313) ***(G-270)***
Howard Hanna Smythe Cramer......330 468-6833
907 E Aurora Rd Macedonia (44056) ***(G-13074)***
Howard Hanna Smythe Cramer......330 725-4137
3565 Medina Rd Medina (44256) ***(G-13952)***
Howard Hanna Smythe Cramer......440 835-2800
27115 Knickerbocker Rd Cleveland (44140) ***(G-5717)***
Howard Hanna Smythe Cramer......440 282-8002
1711 Cooper Foster Pk Rd Amherst (44001) ***(G-590)***
Howard Hanna Smythe Cramer......330 686-1166
3925 Darrow Rd Ste 101 Stow (44224) ***(G-17212)***
Howard Hanna Smythe Cramer......440 516-4444
34601 Ridge Rd Ste 3 Willoughby (44094) ***(G-19530)***
Howard Hanna Smythe Cramer......440 248-3380
6240 Som Center Rd # 100 Cleveland (44139) ***(G-5718)***
Howard Hanna Smythe Cramer......216 751-8550
24465 Greenwich Ln Beachwood (44122) ***(G-1065)***
Howard Hanna Smythe Cramer......216 831-9310
3550 Lander Rd Ste 300 Pepper Pike (44124) ***(G-15818)***
Howard Hanna Smythe Cramer......330 562-6188
195 Barrington Town Sq Dr Aurora (44202) ***(G-829)***
Howard Hanna Smythe Cramer......440 428-1818
2757 Hubbard Rd Madison (44057) ***(G-13097)***
Howard Hanna Smythe Cramer......330 493-6555
4758 Dressler Rd Nw Canton (44718) ***(G-2350)***
Howard Hanna Smythe Cramer......440 526-1800
8949 Brecksville Rd Cleveland (44141) ***(G-5719)***
Howard Hanna Smythe Cramer......330 896-3333
3700 Massillon Rd Ste 300 Uniontown (44685) ***(G-18374)***
Howard Hannah Smythe Cramer, Cleveland *Also called Howard Hanna Smythe Cramer* ***(G-5717)***
Howard Johnson, Cincinnati *Also called Johnson Howard International* ***(G-3829)***
Howard Johnson, Girard *Also called Universal Development MGT Inc* ***(G-11303)***
Howard Johnson, Brookpark *Also called 16644 Snow Rd LLC* ***(G-1889)***
Howard Johnson......513 825-3129
400 Glensprin Dr L 275 Sr Cincinnati (45246) ***(G-3733)***
Howard Johnson Lima, Lima *Also called R & K Gorby LLC* ***(G-12728)***
Howard Wershbale & Co (PA)......216 831-1200
23240 Chagrin Blvd # 700 Cleveland (44122) ***(G-5720)***
Howland Corners Twn & Ctry Vet......330 856-1862
8000 E Market St Warren (44484) ***(G-18714)***
Howland Logistics LLC......513 469-5263
930 Tennessee Ave Cincinnati (45229) ***(G-3734)***
Howley Bread Group Ltd (PA)......440 808-1600
159 Crocker Park Blvd # 290 Westlake (44145) ***(G-19352)***
Howmet Corporation (HQ)......757 825-7086
1616 Harvard Ave Newburgh Heights (44105) ***(G-15114)***
Hoyer Poured Walls Inc......937 642-6148
18205 Poling Rd Marysville (43040) ***(G-13507)***
HP Manufacturing Company Inc (PA)......216 361-6500
3705 Carnegie Ave Cleveland (44115) ***(G-5721)***
Hpj Industries Inc......419 278-1000
299 S Chestnut St Deshler (43516) ***(G-10058)***
Hpj Industries Inc (PA)......419 278-1000
510 W Broadway St North Baltimore (45872) ***(G-15178)***
Hr Associates Personnel Svc, Piqua *Also called S & H Risner Inc* ***(G-16027)***
Hr Butler LLC......614 923-2900
63 Corbins Mill Dr Ste A Dublin (43017) ***(G-10246)***

Hr Plus, Independence Also called Gallery Holdings LLC (G-12076)
Hr Profile, Cincinnati Also called Human Resource Profile Inc (G-3738)
Hr Services Inc..419 224-2462
675 W Market St Ste 200 Lima (45801) *(G-12660)*
Hrm Enterprises Inc (PA).................................330 877-9353
1015 Edison St Nw Ste 3 Hartville (44632) *(G-11691)*
Hrm Leasing, Findlay Also called Bob Miller Rigging Inc (G-10880)
Hrnchar's Fairway Ford, Canfield Also called Paul Hrnchar Ford-Mercury Inc (G-2155)
HRP Capital Inc..419 865-3111
6855 Spring Valley Dr # 120 Holland (43528) *(G-11889)*
Hs Express LLC..419 729-2400
6003 Benore Rd Toledo (43612) *(G-17810)*
Hs Financial Group LLC...................................440 871-8484
25651 Detroit Rd Ste 203 Westlake (44145) *(G-19353)*
Hsc Dept of Psychiatry, Toledo Also called University of Toledo (G-18125)
Hsi Hemodialysis Services, Beachwood Also called Hemodialysis Services Inc (G-1063)
Hsps Special Operations, Cincinnati Also called Home State Protective Svcs LLC (G-3722)
Hsr Business To Business, Cincinnati Also called Hsr Marketing Communications (G-3735)
Hsr Marketing Communications..........................513 671-3811
300 E Bus Way Ste 500 Cincinnati (45241) *(G-3735)*
Hst Lessee Cincinnati LLC................................513 852-2702
21 E 5th St Cincinnati (45202) *(G-3736)*
HTI - Hall Trucking Inc.....................................419 423-9555
110 Bentley Ct Findlay (45840) *(G-10924)*
Htp Inc...614 885-1272
8720 Orion Pl Ste 300 Columbus (43240) *(G-6816)*
Hub City Terminals Inc.....................................440 779-2226
27476 Detroit Rd Ste 102 Westlake (44145) *(G-19354)*
Hub City Terminals Inc.....................................419 217-5200
811 Madison Ave Ste 601 Toledo (43604) *(G-17811)*
Hubbard Company...419 784-4455
612 Clinton St Defiance (43512) *(G-9917)*
Hubbard Radio Cincinnati LLC...........................513 699-5102
2060 Reading Rd Ste 400 Cincinnati (45202) *(G-3737)*
Hubbell Power Systems Inc...............................330 335-2361
8711 Wadsworth Rd Wadsworth (44281) *(G-18600)*
Huber Heights Dialysis, Huber Heights Also called Pendster Dialysis LLC (G-11956)
Huber Heights YMCA.......................................937 236-9622
7251 Shull Rd Dayton (45424) *(G-9508)*
Huber Investment Corporation (PA).....................937 233-1122
5550 Huber Rd Dayton (45424) *(G-9509)*
Hubert Company LLC (HQ)................................513 367-8600
9555 Dry Fork Rd Harrison (45030) *(G-11670)*
Huckleberry House..614 294-5553
1421 Hamlet St Columbus (43201) *(G-7777)*
Hudec Dental Associates Inc (PA)......................216 485-5788
6700 W Snowville Rd Brecksville (44141) *(G-1784)*
Hudson City Engineering Dept...........................330 342-1770
115 Executive Pkwy # 400 Hudson (44236) *(G-11982)*
Hudson Montessori Association..........................330 650-0424
7545 Darrow Rd Hudson (44236) *(G-11983)*
HUDSON MONTESSORI SCHOOL, Hudson Also called Hudson Montessori
Association (G-11983)
Hueston Woods Lodge,, College Corner Also called Ohio State Parks Inc (G-6768)
Huffman Health Care Inc...................................937 476-1000
20 Livingston Ave Dayton (45403) *(G-9510)*
Hugh White Buick, Lancaster Also called Tbn Acquisition LLC (G-12441)
Hughes & Knollman Construction........................614 237-6167
4601 E 5th Ave Columbus (43219) *(G-7778)*
Hughes Corporation (PA)..................................440 238-2550
16900 Foltz Pkwy Strongsville (44149) *(G-17312)*
Hughes Corporation...440 238-2550
16900 Foltz Pkwy Strongsville (44149) *(G-17313)*
Hughes Kitchens and Bath LLC..........................330 455-5269
1258 Cleveland Ave Nw Canton (44703) *(G-2351)*
Hull & Associates Inc (PA)................................614 793-8777
6397 Emerald Pkwy Ste 200 Dublin (43016) *(G-10247)*
Hull & Associates Inc.......................................419 385-2018
219 S Erie St Toledo (43604) *(G-17812)*
Hull Bros Inc..419 375-2827
520 E Boundary St Fort Recovery (45846) *(G-10992)*
Hull Builders Supply Inc...................................440 967-3159
685 Main St Vermilion (44089) *(G-18553)*
Human Resource Profile Inc..............................513 388-4300
8506 Beechmont Ave Cincinnati (45255) *(G-3738)*
Human Resources Services...............................740 587-3484
465 Buckstone Pl Westerville (43082) *(G-19173)*
Human Services, Xenia Also called Greene County (G-19904)
Humana Health Plan Ohio Inc............................513 784-5200
111 Merchant St Cincinnati (45246) *(G-3739)*
Humana Inc..330 877-5464
1289 Edison St Nw Hartville (44632) *(G-11692)*
Humana Inc..216 328-2047
6100 Oak Tree Blvd Independence (44131) *(G-12080)*
Humana Inc..614 210-1038
485 Metro Pl S Ste 410 Dublin (43017) *(G-10248)*
Humana Inc..330 498-0537
4690 Munson St Nw Ste C Canton (44718) *(G-2352)*
Humantics Innovative Solutions.........................567 265-5200
900 Denton Dr Huron (44839) *(G-12025)*

Humaserve Hr LLC..513 605-3522
9435 Waterstone Blvd Cincinnati (45249) *(G-3740)*
Hume Supply Inc...419 991-5751
1359 E Hanthorn Rd Lima (45804) *(G-12661)*
Humility House..330 505-0144
755 Ohltown Rd Youngstown (44515) *(G-20070)*
Humility of Mary Info Systems...........................330 884-6600
250 E Federal St Ste 200 Youngstown (44503) *(G-20071)*
Hummel Construction Company..........................330 274-8584
127 E Main St Ravenna (44266) *(G-16246)*
Hummel Group Inc...330 683-1050
461 Wadsworth Rd Orrville (44667) *(G-15635)*
Hummel Industries Incorporated.........................513 242-1321
93 Caldwell Dr B Cincinnati (45216) *(G-3741)*
Hunt Club LLC..419 885-4647
5600 Alexis Rd Sylvania (43560) *(G-17431)*
Hunt Products Inc..440 667-2457
3982 E 42nd St Newburgh Heights (44105) *(G-15115)*
Hunter Defense Tech Inc (PA)...........................216 438-6111
30500 Aurora Rd Ste 100 Solon (44139) *(G-16859)*
Hunter Realty Inc..216 831-2911
25101 Chagrin Blvd # 170 Cleveland (44122) *(G-5722)*
Hunter Realty Inc..440 466-9177
385 S Broadway Geneva (44041) *(G-11243)*
Huntington Auto Trust 2015-1............................302 636-5401
Huntington Ctr 41 S High Columbus (43287) *(G-7779)*
Huntington Auto Trust 2016-1............................302 636-5401
41 S High St Columbus (43215) *(G-7780)*
Huntington Bancshares Inc (PA).........................614 480-8300
41 S High St Columbus (43215) *(G-7781)*
Huntington Bank, Findlay Also called Huntington Insurance Inc (G-10925)
Huntington Capital I...614 480-4038
41 S High St Columbus (43215) *(G-7782)*
Huntington Hlls Recreation CLB.........................614 837-0293
6600 Springbrook Dr Pickerington (43147) *(G-15959)*
Huntington Insurance Inc (HQ)...........................419 720-7900
519 Madison Ave Toledo (43604) *(G-17813)*
Huntington Insurance Inc..................................614 480-3800
7 Easton Oval Columbus (43219) *(G-7783)*
Huntington Insurance Inc..................................419 429-4627
236 S Main St Findlay (45840) *(G-10925)*
Huntington Insurance Inc..................................216 206-1787
925 Euclid Ave Ste 550 Cleveland (44115) *(G-5723)*
Huntington Insurance Inc..................................330 262-6611
121 N Market St Ste 600 Wooster (44691) *(G-19732)*
Huntington Insurance Inc..................................614 899-8500
37 W Broad St Ste 1100 Columbus (43215) *(G-7784)*
Huntington Insurance Inc..................................330 337-9933
193 S Lincoln Ave Salem (44460) *(G-16548)*
Huntington Insurance Inc..................................330 674-2931
212 N Washington St Millersburg (44654) *(G-14479)*
Huntington Insurance Inc..................................330 430-1300
220 Market Ave S Ste 40 Canton (44702) *(G-2353)*
Huntington National Bank..................................513 762-1860
525 Vine St Ste 14 Cincinnati (45202) *(G-3742)*
Huntington National Bank..................................330 742-7013
23 Federal Plaza Central Youngstown (44503) *(G-20072)*
Huntington National Bank..................................330 343-6611
232 W 3rd St Ste 207 Dover (44622) *(G-10083)*
Huntington National Bank..................................740 773-2681
445 Western Ave Chillicothe (45601) *(G-2792)*
Huntington National Bank..................................614 480-0067
4078 Powell Ave Columbus (43213) *(G-7785)*
Huntington National Bank..................................614 336-4620
4300 Tuller Rd Dublin (43017) *(G-10249)*
Huntington National Bank..................................740 335-3771
134 E Court St Wshngtn CT Hs (43160) *(G-19876)*
Huntington National Bank..................................330 996-6300
Iii Cascade Plz Fl 7 Flr 7 Akron (44308) *(G-271)*
Huntington National Bank (PA)...........................614 480-4293
17 S High St Fl 1 Columbus (43215) *(G-7786)*
Huntington National Bank..................................330 384-7201
106 S Main St Fl 5 Akron (44308) *(G-272)*
Huntington National Bank..................................740 452-8444
422 Main St Zanesville (43701) *(G-20319)*
Huntington National Bank (HQ)...........................614 480-4293
17 S High St Fl 1 Columbus (43215) *(G-7787)*
Huntington National Bank..................................740 695-3323
154 W Main St Saint Clairsville (43950) *(G-16489)*
Huntington National Bank..................................330 384-7092
121 S Main St Ste 200 Akron (44308) *(G-273)*
Huntington National Bank..................................419 226-8200
631 W Market St Lima (45801) *(G-12662)*
Huntington National Bank..................................216 621-1717
101 W Prospect Ave Cleveland (44115) *(G-5724)*
Huntington National Bank..................................614 480-8300
2361 Morse Rd Columbus (43229) *(G-7788)*
Huntington National Bank..................................216 515-6401
905 Euclid Ave Cleveland (44115) *(G-5725)*
Huntington National Bank..................................419 782-5050
405 W 3rd St Defiance (43512) *(G-9918)*
Huntington Street 16, Medina Also called Regal Cinemas Inc (G-13996)

Huntington Technology Finance 614 480-5169
37 W Broad St Columbus (43215) (G-7789)

Huntington Wealth Advisors, Cincinnati Also called The Huntington Investment Co (G-4593)

Huntleigh USA Corporation 216 265-3707
11147 Barrington Blvd Cleveland (44130) (G-5726)

Huntley Trucking Co 740 385-7615
23525 Pumpkin Ridge Rd New Plymouth (45654) (G-14991)

Huntsey Corporation 614 568-5030
470 Olde Worthington Rd Westerville (43082) (G-19174)

Huron Cement Products Company (PA) 419 433-4161
617 Main St Huron (44839) (G-12026)

Huron Health Care Center Inc 419 433-4990
1920 Cleveland Rd W Huron (44839) (G-12027)

Huron School of Nursing, Cleveland Also called Clevelnd Clnc Hlth Systm East (G-5300)

Husky Energy, Dublin Also called Husky Marketing and Supply Co (G-10250)

Husky Marketing and Supply Co 614 210-2300
5550 Blazer Pkwy Ste 200 Dublin (43017) (G-10250)

Hustead Emergency Medical Svc 937 324-3031
6215 Springfield Xenia Rd Springfield (45502) (G-17049)

Huston Nursing Home 740 384-3485
38500 State Route 160 Hamden (45634) (G-11552)

Huttig Building Products Inc 614 492-8248
2160 Mcgaw Rd Obetz (43207) (G-15526)

Huttig Sash & Door Co, Obetz Also called Huttig Building Products Inc (G-15526)

Hvac, Mentor Also called Burrier Service Company Inc (G-14023)

HWH Archtcts-Ngnrs-Plnners Inc 216 875-4000
600 Superior Ave E # 1100 Cleveland (44114) (G-5727)

Hwy Garage, Wapakoneta Also called Ohio Department Transportation (G-18651)

Hwy. Department, Greenville Also called Ohio Department Transportation (G-11391)

Hwz Contracting, Fairfield Also called Bradcorp Ohio II LLC (G-10700)

Hwz Contracting LLC 513 671-3300
4730 Ashley Dr West Chester (45011) (G-18945)

Hy-Grade Corporation (PA) 216 341-7711
3993 E 93rd St Cleveland (44105) (G-5728)

Hy-Tek Material Handling Inc (PA) 614 497-2500
2222 Rickenbacker Pkwy W Columbus (43217) (G-7790)

Hyatt Corporation 614 463-1234
350 N High St Columbus (43215) (G-7791)

Hyatt Hotel, Cleveland Also called Hit Portfolio I Misc Trs LLC (G-5694)

Hyatt Hotel, Columbus Also called Hyatt Corporation (G-7791)

Hyatt Hotel, Cincinnati Also called Hit Portfolio I Misc Trs LLC (G-3711)

Hyatt Legal Plans Inc 216 241-0022
1111 Superior Ave E # 800 Cleveland (44114) (G-5729)

Hyatt On Capitol Square, Columbus Also called Hit Portfolio I Misc Trs LLC (G-7753)

Hyatt Pl Cincinnati-Northeast, Mason Also called Select Hotels Group LLC (G-13638)

Hyatt Pl Clveland/Independence, Cleveland Also called Select Hotels Group LLC (G-6393)

Hyatt Pl Columbus Worthington, Columbus Also called Hit Portfolio J Trs LLC (G-7754)

Hyatt Place, Westlake Also called CD Block K Hotel LLC (G-19328)

Hyatt Place Cleveland/, Cleveland Also called Legacy Village Hospitality LLC (G-5861)

Hyatt Place Columbus/Dublin, Dublin Also called Select Hotels Group LLC (G-10332)

Hyatt Regency Columbus 614 463-1234
350 N High St Columbus (43215) (G-7792)

Hyde Park Golf & Country Club 513 321-3721
3740 Erie Ave Cincinnati (45208) (G-3743)

Hyde Park Grille, Columbus Also called Henderson Road Rest Systems (G-7739)

Hyde Park Health Center 513 272-0600
3763 Hopper Hill Rd Cincinnati (45255) (G-3744)

Hyde Park Landscaping, Cincinnati Also called Hyde Park Ldscp & Tree Svc Inc (G-3745)

Hyde Park Ldscp & Tree Svc Inc 513 731-1334
5055 Wooster Rd Cincinnati (45226) (G-3745)

Hyde Park Play School 513 631-2095
3846 Drake Ave Cincinnati (45209) (G-3746)

Hydraulic Parts Store Inc 330 364-6667
145 1st Dr Ne New Philadelphia (44663) (G-14966)

Hydraulic Specialists Inc 740 922-3343
5655 Gundy Dr Midvale (44653) (G-14358)

Hydro-Dyne Inc 330 832-5076
225 Wetmore Ave Se Massillon (44646) (G-13696)

Hydrogeologic Inc 330 463-3303
581 Boston Mills Rd # 600 Hudson (44236) (G-11984)

Hyland Software Inc (HQ) 440 788-5000
28500 Clemens Rd Westlake (44145) (G-19355)

Hylant Administrative Services (PA) 419 255-1020
811 Madison Ave Fl 11 Toledo (43604) (G-17814)

Hylant Group, Dublin Also called Hylant-Maclean Inc (G-10252)

Hylant Group Inc 513 985-2400
50 E-Business Way Ste 420 Cincinnati (45241) (G-3747)

Hylant Group Inc 614 932-1200
565 Metro Pl S Ste 450 Dublin (43017) (G-10251)

Hylant Group Inc (PA) 419 255-1020
811 Madison Ave Fl 11 Toledo (43604) (G-17815)

Hylant Group Inc 216 447-1050
6000 Fredom Sq Dr Ste 400 Cleveland (44131) (G-5730)

Hylant Group of Cincinnati, Cincinnati Also called Hylant Group Inc (G-3747)

Hylant Group of Cleveland, Cleveland Also called Hylant Group Inc (G-5730)

Hylant Group of Columbus, Dublin Also called Hylant Group Inc (G-10251)

Hylant-Maclean Inc 614 932-1200
565 Metro Pl S Ste 450 Dublin (43017) (G-10252)

Hynes Industries Inc (PA) 330 799-3221
3805 Hendricks Rd Ste A Youngstown (44515) (G-20073)

Hyperlogistics Group Inc (PA) 614 497-0800
9301 Intermodal Ct N Columbus (43217) (G-7793)

Hyperquake LLC 513 563-6555
205 W 4th St Ste 1010 Cincinnati (45202) (G-3748)

Hyway Trucking Company 419 423-7145
10060 W Us Route 224 Findlay (45840) (G-10926)

Hzw Environmental Cons LLC (PA) 800 804-8484
6105 Heisley Rd Mentor (44060) (G-14062)

I & M J Gross Company (PA) 440 237-1681
14300 Ridge Rd Ste 100 Cleveland (44133) (G-5731)

I C S, Cincinnati Also called Industrial Comm & Sound Inc (G-3759)

I C S, Groveport Also called Innovtive Crtive Solutions LLC (G-11520)

I H S Services Inc 419 224-8811
3225 W Elm St Ste D Lima (45805) (G-12663)

I H Schlezinger Inc 614 252-1188
1041 Joyce Ave Columbus (43219) (G-7794)

I L S, Cleveland Also called Supply Technologies LLC (G-6485)

I L S, Hamilton Also called Innovtive Lbling Solutions Inc (G-11614)

I P S, Cincinnati Also called Integrated Protection Svcs Inc (G-3770)

I P S, Rossford Also called Industrial Power Systems Inc (G-16461)

I P S Interior Landscaping, Canal Winchester Also called Rentokil North America Inc (G-2117)

I Supply Co 937 878-5240
1255 Spangler Rd Fairborn (45324) (G-10676)

I T E LLC 513 576-6200
424 Wards Corner Rd # 300 Loveland (45140) (G-13000)

I V C, Lebanon Also called Industrial Vibrations Cons (G-12472)

I Vrable Inc 614 545-5500
3248 Henderson Rd Columbus (43220) (G-7795)

I-75 Pierson Automotive Inc 513 424-1881
3456 S Dixie Hwy Middletown (45005) (G-14350)

I-Force LLC 614 431-5100
1110 Morse Rd Ste 200 Columbus (43229) (G-7796)

I-Tran Inc 330 659-0801
4100 Congress Pkwy W Richfield (44286) (G-16360)

I-X Center Corporation 216 265-2675
6200 Riverside Dr Cleveland (44135) (G-5732)

IA Urban Htels Bchwood Trs LLC 216 765-8066
3775 Park East Dr Beachwood (44122) (G-1066)

Iacominis Papa Joes Inc 330 923-7999
1561 Akron Peninsula Rd Akron (44313) (G-274)

Iacovetta Builders Inc 614 272-6464
2525 Fisher Rd Columbus (43204) (G-7797)

Iaitam, Canton Also called International Association of (G-2357)

IAMS Company 937 962-7782
6571 State Route 503 N Lewisburg (45338) (G-12568)

Iap Government Services Group, Columbus Also called Innovative Architectural (G-7820)

Iarc, Ontario Also called Intercity Amateur Rdo CLB Inc (G-15554)

IBH, Coventry Township Also called Interval Brotherhood Homes (G-9036)

Ibi, Chillicothe Also called Ingle-Barr Inc (G-2793)

Ibi Group Engrg Svcs USA Inc (HQ) 614 818-4900
635 Brooksedge Blvd Westerville (43081) (G-19263)

Ibi Group Engrg Svcs USA Inc 513 942-3141
23 Triangle Park Dr # 2300 Cincinnati (45246) (G-3749)

IBM, Beavercreek Also called International Bus Mchs Corp (G-1158)

IBP, Columbus Also called Installed Building Pdts Inc (G-7828)

IBP Columbus, Columbus Also called Installed Building Pdts LLC (G-7829)

Ic Roofing, Mason Also called Interstate Contractors LLC (G-13601)

Ice Land USA Lakewood 216 529-1200
14740 Lakewood Hts Blvd Lakewood (44107) (G-12347)

Ice Land USA Ltd 440 268-2800
15381 Royalton Rd Strongsville (44136) (G-17314)

Ice Miller LLP 614 462-2700
250 West St Ste 700 Columbus (43215) (G-7798)

Ice Zone Ltd 330 965-1423
2445 Belmont Ave Youngstown (44505) (G-20074)

ICM, Bedford Heights Also called Intergrated Consulting (G-1323)

ICM Distributing Company Inc 234 212-3030
1755 Entp Pkwy Ste 200 Twinsburg (44087) (G-18281)

Icon Environmental Group LLC 513 426-6767
24 Whitney Dr Ste D Milford (45150) (G-14396)

Icon Government (HQ) 330 278-2343
1265 Ridge Rd Ste A Hinckley (44233) (G-11859)

Icon Property Rescue, Milford Also called Icon Environmental Group LLC (G-14396)

Icr Engineering, Mason Also called Icr Inc (G-13596)

Icr Inc 513 900-7007
4770 Duke Dr Ste 370 Mason (45040) (G-13596)

Ics Electrical Services, Cincinnati Also called Instrmntation Ctrl Systems Inc (G-3765)

Icx Corporation (HQ) 330 656-3611
2 Summit Park Dr Ste 105 Cleveland (44131) (G-5733)

ID Networks Inc 440 992-0062
7720 Jefferson Rd Ashtabula (44004) (G-741)

Ideal Company Inc (PA) 937 836-8683
8313 Kimmel Rd Ste A Clayton (45315) (G-4858)

Ideal Image Inc 937 832-1660
115 Haas Dr Englewood (45322) (G-10590)

Ideal Setech LLC 419 782-5522
24862 Elliott Rd Defiance (43512) *(G-9919)*
Idealease Miami Valley Intl, Cincinnati *Also called Miami Valley Intl Trcks Inc (G-4045)*
Ideastream (PA) 216 916-6100
1375 Euclid Ave Cleveland (44115) *(G-5734)*
Identitek Systems Inc 330 832-9844
1100 Industrial Ave Sw Massillon (44647) *(G-13697)*
Idexx Laboratories Inc 330 629-6076
945 Boardman Canfield Rd Youngstown (44512) *(G-20075)*
Ieh Auto Parts LLC 740 373-8327
123 Tennis Center Dr Marietta (45750) *(G-13336)*
Ieh Auto Parts LLC 740 732-2395
218 West St Caldwell (43724) *(G-2040)*
Ieh Auto Parts LLC 216 351-2560
4565 Hinckley Indus Pkwy Cleveland (44109) *(G-5735)*
Ieh Auto Parts LLC 740 373-8151
121 Tennis Center Dr Marietta (45750) *(G-13337)*
Ies Infrstrcture Solutions LLC (HQ) 330 830-3500
800 Nave Rd Se Massillon (44646) *(G-13698)*
Ies Systems Inc 330 533-6683
464 Lisbon St Canfield (44406) *(G-2143)*
Iet Inc 419 385-1233
3539 Glendale Ave Ste C Toledo (43614) *(G-17816)*
Iewc Corp 440 835-5601
1991 Crocker Rd Ste 110 Westlake (44145) *(G-19356)*
Iforce, Columbus *Also called I-Force LLC (G-7796)*
Ifs Financial Services Inc (HQ) 513 362-8000
370 S Cleveland Ave Westerville (43081) *(G-19264)*
Igh II Inc 419 874-3575
110 Industrial Dr Mansfield (44904) *(G-13184)*
Igs Solar LLC 844 447-7652
6100 Emerald Pkwy Dublin (43016) *(G-10253)*
Iheartcommunications Inc 419 625-1010
1640 Cleveland Rd Sandusky (44870) *(G-16618)*
Iheartcommunications Inc 937 224-1137
101 Pine St Dayton (45402) *(G-9511)*
Iheartcommunications Inc 614 486-6101
2323 W 5th Ave Ste 200 Columbus (43204) *(G-7799)*
Iheartcommunications Inc 937 224-1137
101 Pine St Ste 300 Dayton (45402) *(G-9512)*
Iheartcommunications Inc 513 241-1550
8044 Montgomery Rd # 650 Cincinnati (45236) *(G-3750)*
Iheartcommunications Inc 440 992-9700
3226 Jefferson Rd Ashtabula (44004) *(G-742)*
Iheartcommunications Inc 216 520-2600
6200 Oak Tree Blvd Fl 4 Cleveland (44131) *(G-5736)*
Iheartcommunications Inc 419 289-2605
1197 Us Highway 42 Ashland (44805) *(G-676)*
Iheartcommunications Inc 419 529-2211
1400 Radio Ln Mansfield (44906) *(G-13185)*
Iheartcommunications Inc 330 965-0057
7461 South Ave Youngstown (44512) *(G-20076)*
Iheartcommunications Inc 216 409-9673
310 W Lakeside Ave Fl 6 Cleveland (44113) *(G-5737)*
Iheartcommunications Inc 513 763-5500
1906 Highland Ave Cincinnati (45219) *(G-3751)*
Iheartcommunications Inc 419 782-9336
2110 Radio Dr Defiance (43512) *(G-9920)*
Iheartcommunications Inc 419 223-2060
667 W Market St Lima (45801) *(G-12664)*
Ihg Management (maryland) LLC 614 461-4100
33 E Nationwide Blvd Columbus (43215) *(G-7800)*
IHNWC, Lebanon *Also called Interfaith Hosptlty Ntwrk of W (G-12473)*
IHS Enterprise Inc (PA) 216 588-9078
5755 Granger Rd Ste 905 Independence (44131) *(G-12081)*
Ijus LLC (PA) 614 470-9882
690 Taylor Rd Ste 100 Gahanna (43230) *(G-11126)*
Ikps, Fredericktown *Also called Integrity Kokosing Pipeline Sv (G-11054)*
Ilead LLC 440 846-2346
20376 Kelsey Ln Strongsville (44149) *(G-17315)*
Ilead Marketing, Strongsville *Also called Ilead LLC (G-17315)*
Illinois & Midland RR Inc (HQ) 217 670-1242
4349 Easton Way Ste 110 Columbus (43219) *(G-7801)*
Illinois Central Railroad Co 419 726-6028
4820 Schwartz Rd Toledo (43611) *(G-17817)*
Illinois Tool Works Inc 513 891-7485
10125 Carver Rd Blue Ash (45242) *(G-1583)*
Illumetek Corp 330 342-7582
121 E Ascot Ln Cuyahoga Falls (44223) *(G-9101)*
Illumination Research Inc 513 774-9531
5947 Drfield Blvd Ste 203 Mason (45040) *(G-13597)*
Illumination Works LLC 937 938-1321
2689 Commons Blvd Ste 120 Beavercreek (45431) *(G-1157)*
Illusion Unlimited, Cleveland *Also called Merle-Holden Enterprises Inc (G-5957)*
Ilpea Industries Inc 330 562-2916
1300 Danner Dr Aurora (44202) *(G-830)*
Ils Technology LLC 800 695-8650
6065 Parkland Blvd Cleveland (44124) *(G-5738)*
Image By J & K LLC 888 667-6929
1575 Henthorne Dr Maumee (43537) *(G-13802)*
Image Consulting Services Inc (PA) 440 951-9919
1775 Donwell Dr Cleveland (44121) *(G-5739)*
Image Engineering Inc 513 541-8544
7038 Golfway Dr Cincinnati (45239) *(G-3752)*
Image Pavement Maintenance 937 833-9200
425 Carr Dr Brookville (45309) *(G-1914)*
Imagepace LLC 513 579-9911
5375 Medpace Way Cincinnati (45227) *(G-3753)*
IMAGINATION STATION, Toledo *Also called Toledo Science Center (G-18096)*
Imagistics International, Dayton *Also called Mike Rennie (G-9634)*
Imam WD Mohammed Comm Devt, Springfield *Also called Lateef Elmin Mhammad Inv Group (G-17060)*
Imcd Us LLC (HQ) 216 228-8900
14725 Detroit Ave Ste 300 Lakewood (44107) *(G-12348)*
Imco Carbide Tool Inc 419 661-6313
28170 Cedar Park Blvd Perrysburg (43551) *(G-15877)*
Imco Recycling of Ohio LLC 740 922-2373
7335 Newport Rd Se Uhrichsville (44683) *(G-18342)*
Imflux Inc 513 488-1017
3550 Symmes Rd Ste 100 Hamilton (45015) *(G-11611)*
Imhoff Construction, Orrville *Also called Ben D Imhoff Inc (G-15625)*
Immaculate Interiors 440 324-9300
123 Brace Ave Elyria (44035) *(G-10518)*
Immediate Health Associates 614 794-0481
575 Cpland Mill Rd Ste 1d Westerville (43081) *(G-19265)*
Immediate Medical Service Inc 330 823-0400
2461 W State St Ste E Alliance (44601) *(G-534)*
Impact Ceramics LLC 440 554-3624
17000 Saint Clair Ave # 3 Cleveland (44110) *(G-5740)*
Impact Community Action 614 252-2799
700 Bryden Rd Fl 2 Columbus (43215) *(G-7802)*
Impact Fulfillment Svcs LLC 614 262-8911
2035 Innis Rd Columbus (43224) *(G-7803)*
Impact Medical Mgt Group 440 365-7014
1120 E Broad St Elyria (44035) *(G-10519)*
Impact Products LLC (HQ) 419 841-2891
2840 Centennial Rd Toledo (43617) *(G-17818)*
Impact Sales Inc 937 274-1905
2501 Neff Rd Dayton (45414) *(G-9513)*
Imperial Alum - Minerva LLC 330 868-7765
217 Roosevelt St Minerva (44657) *(G-14520)*
Imperial Express Inc 937 399-9400
202 N Limestone St # 300 Springfield (45503) *(G-17050)*
Imperial Foods, Cleveland *Also called Gust Gallucci Co (G-5648)*
Imperial Heating and Coolg Inc (PA) 440 498-1788
30685 Solon Industrial Pk Solon (44139) *(G-16860)*
Imperial Lumber, Eaton *Also called Maronda Homes Inc Florida (G-10451)*
Impressive Packaging Inc 419 368-6808
627 County Rd 30 A Hayesville (44838) *(G-11701)*
Improve It Home Remodeling (PA) 614 297-5121
4580 Bridgeway Ave B Columbus (43219) *(G-7804)*
Improvedge LLC 614 793-1738
9878 Brewster Ln 210 Powell (43065) *(G-16197)*
Impullitti Landscaping Inc 440 834-1866
14659 Ravenna Rd Burton (44021) *(G-2017)*
IMS Company 440 543-1615
10373 Stafford Rd Chagrin Falls (44023) *(G-2668)*
IMT, Brunswick *Also called Integrated Marketing Tech Inc (G-1933)*
In His Prsence Ministries Intl 614 516-1812
5757 Karl Rd Columbus (43229) *(G-7805)*
In Home Health LLC 419 531-0440
3450 W Central Ave # 132 Toledo (43606) *(G-17819)*
In Home Health LLC 513 831-5800
3960 Red Bank Rd Ste 140 Cincinnati (45227) *(G-3754)*
In Home Health LLC 419 355-9209
907 W State St Ste A Fremont (43420) *(G-11081)*
In Terminal Services Corp 216 518-8407
5300 Greenhurst Ext Maple Heights (44137) *(G-13288)*
In-Plas Recycling Inc 513 541-9800
4211 Crawford Ave Cincinnati (45223) *(G-3755)*
Inacomp Computer Centers, Lewis Center *Also called Pcm Sales Inc (G-12558)*
Inc/Ballew A Head Joint Ventr 614 338-5801
4477 E 5th Ave Columbus (43219) *(G-7806)*
Incentisoft Solutions LLC 877 562-4461
20445 Emerald Pkwy # 400 Cleveland (44135) *(G-5741)*
Incept Corporation 330 649-8000
4150 Belden Village St Nw # 205 Canton (44718) *(G-2354)*
Incubit LLC 740 362-1401
40 N Sandusky St Ste 200 Delaware (43015) *(G-9988)*
Indecon Solutions LLC 614 799-1850
655 Metro Pl S Ste 740 Dublin (43017) *(G-10254)*
Independence 10, Akron *Also called Regal Cinemas Inc (G-399)*
Independence Bank 216 447-1444
4401 Rockside Rd Cleveland (44131) *(G-5742)*
Independence Business Supply, Cleveland *Also called Indepndence Office Bus Sup Inc (G-5746)*
Independence Care Community 419 435-8505
1000 Independence Ave Fostoria (44830) *(G-11007)*
Independence Excavating Inc (PA) 216 524-1700
5720 E Schaaf Rd Independence (44131) *(G-12082)*
Independence Foundation Inc 330 296-2851
161 E Main St Ravenna (44266) *(G-16247)*
Independence House, Fostoria *Also called Independence Care Community (G-11007)*

Independence Local Schools 216 642-5865
6111 Archwood Rd Independence (44131) *(G-12083)*
Independence Oncology 216 524-7979
6100 W Creek Rd Ste 16 Cleveland (44131) *(G-5743)*
Independence Place II, Cleveland Also called Forest City Enterprises LP *(G-5555)*
Independence Travel 216 447-9950
5000 Rockside Rd Ste 240 Cleveland (44131) *(G-5744)*
Independent Evaluators Inc 419 872-5650
27457 Holiday Ln Ste B Perrysburg (43551) *(G-15878)*
Independent Hotel Partners LLC 216 524-0700
5300 Rockside Rd Cleveland (44131) *(G-5745)*
Independent Living of Ohio 937 323-8400
530 S Burnett Rd Springfield (45505) *(G-17051)*
Independent Order Odd Fellows 740 548-5038
5230 Cypress Dr Lewis Center (43035) *(G-12546)*
Independent Order-Odd Fellows, Conneaut Also called Odd Fellows Hall *(G-8957)*
Independent Radio Taxi Inc 330 746-8844
308 And One Half W Youngstown (44503) *(G-20077)*
Independent Steel Company LLC 330 225-7741
615 Liverpool Dr Valley City (44280) *(G-18463)*
Indepndence Office Bus Sup Inc 216 398-8880
4550 Hinckley Indus Pkwy Cleveland (44109) *(G-5746)*
Indian Hills Senior Community 216 486-7700
1541 E 191st St Euclid (44117) *(G-10643)*
Indian HIls HIthcare Group Inc 216 486-8880
1500 E 191st St Euclid (44117) *(G-10644)*
Indian Learning Head Start, Bellaire Also called Community Action Comsn Belmont *(G-1332)*
Indian Mound Mall, Heath Also called Glemsure Realty Trust *(G-11703)*
Indian Nation Inc 740 532-6143
1051 Skyline Cir Se North Canton (44709) *(G-15212)*
Indian Ridge Golf Club L L C 513 524-4653
2600 Oxford Millville Rd Oxford (45056) *(G-15678)*
Indiana & Ohio Central RR 740 385-3127
665 E Front St Logan (43138) *(G-12842)*
Indiana & Ohio Rail, Logan Also called Indiana & Ohio Central RR *(G-12842)*
Indiana & Ohio Rail Corp (HQ) 513 860-1000
2856 Cypress Way Cincinnati (45212) *(G-3756)*
Indiana & Ohio Rail Corp 419 229-1010
1750 N Sugar St Lima (45801) *(G-12665)*
Indiana & Ohio Railway Company 513 860-1000
2856 Cypress Way Cincinnati (45212) *(G-3757)*
Indiana Michigan Power Company (HQ) 614 716-1000
1 Riverside Plz Columbus (43215) *(G-7807)*
Indico LLC (HQ) 440 775-7777
528 E Lorain St Oberlin (44074) *(G-15505)*
Indigo Group 513 557-8794
4645 Stonehaven Dr Liberty Twp (45011) *(G-12587)*
Indrolect Co 513 821-4788
630 W Wyoming Ave Cincinnati (45215) *(G-3758)*
Indus Airport Hotel II LLC 614 235-0717
4280 International Gtwy Columbus (43219) *(G-7808)*
Indus Airport Hotels I LLC 614 231-2869
4265 Sawyer Rd Columbus (43219) *(G-7809)*
Indus Hilliard Hotel LLC 614 334-1800
3950 Lyman Dr Hilliard (43026) *(G-11777)*
Indus Newark Hotel LLC 740 322-6455
4265 Sawyer Rd Columbus (43219) *(G-7810)*
Indus Trade & Technology LLC (PA) 614 527-0257
2249 Westbrooke Dr Bldg H Columbus (43228) *(G-7811)*
Industrial Air Centers Inc 614 274-9171
2840 Fisher Rd Ste E Columbus (43204) *(G-7812)*
Industrial Air Control Inc 330 772-6422
1276 Brookfield Rd Hubbard (44425) *(G-11947)*
Industrial Chemical Corp (PA) 330 725-0800
885 W Smith Rd Medina (44256) *(G-13953)*
Industrial Cleaning, Canton Also called MPW Industrial Services Inc *(G-2410)*
Industrial Cleaning, Lorain Also called MPW Industrial Services Inc *(G-12928)*
Industrial Comm & Sound Inc 614 276-8123
2105 Schappelle Ln Cincinnati (45240) *(G-3759)*
Industrial Controls Distrs LLC 513 733-5200
9407 Meridian Way West Chester (45069) *(G-18946)*
Industrial Energy Systems Inc 216 267-9590
15828 Industrial Pkwy # 3 Cleveland (44135) *(G-5747)*
Industrial Fiberglass Spc Inc 937 222-9000
521 Kiser St Dayton (45404) *(G-9514)*
Industrial Financial Svcs Inc 614 777-0000
3001 Bethel Rd Ste 108 Columbus (43220) *(G-7813)*
Industrial First Inc (PA) 216 991-8605
25840 Miles Rd Ste 2 Bedford (44146) *(G-1286)*
Industrial Fluid Management, Mc Clure Also called Poggemeyer Design Group Inc *(G-13893)*
Industrial Insul Coatings LLC 800 506-1399
142 E 2nd St Girard (44420) *(G-11288)*
Industrial Maint Svcs Inc 440 729-2068
9824 Washington St Ste A Chagrin Falls (44023) *(G-2669)*
Industrial Mill Maintenance 330 746-1155
1609 Wilson Ave Ste 2 Youngstown (44506) *(G-20078)*
Industrial Origami Inc 440 260-0000
6755 Engle Rd Ste A Cleveland (44130) *(G-5748)*
Industrial Parts & Service Co 330 966-5025
6440 Promler St Nw Canton (44720) *(G-2355)*
Industrial Parts and Service, Canton Also called Industrial Parts & Service Co *(G-2355)*

Industrial Power Systems Inc 419 531-3121
146 Dixie Hwy Rossford (43460) *(G-16461)*
Industrial Repair & Mfg Inc (PA) 419 822-4232
1140 E Main St Ste A Delta (43515) *(G-10045)*
Industrial Sorting Services 513 772-6501
2599 Commerce Blvd Cincinnati (45241) *(G-3760)*
Industrial Tube and Steel Corp (PA) 330 474-5530
4658 Crystal Pkwy Kent (44240) *(G-12237)*
Industrial Vibrations Cons (PA) 513 932-4678
210 S West St Lebanon (45036) *(G-12472)*
Industrial Waste Control Inc 330 270-9900
240 Sinter Ct Youngstown (44510) *(G-20079)*
Industry Insights Inc 614 389-2100
6235 Emerald Pkwy Columbus (43235) *(G-7814)*
Industry Products Co (PA) 937 778-0585
500 W Statler Rd Piqua (45356) *(G-16011)*
Inertial Aerospace Services, Cleveland Also called Inertial Airline Services Inc *(G-5749)*
Inertial Airline Services Inc 440 995-6555
375 Alpha Park Cleveland (44143) *(G-5749)*
Inet Interactive LLC 513 322-5600
9100 W Chester Towne Ctr West Chester (45069) *(G-18947)*
Infectious Diseases Department, Columbus Also called Ohio State University *(G-8321)*
Infinite SEC Solutions LLC 419 720-5678
663 Gawil Ave Toledo (43609) *(G-17820)*
Infinite Shares LLC 216 317-1601
9401 Mentor Ave 167 Mentor (44060) *(G-14063)*
Infinity, Cleveland Also called Aleph Home & Senior Care Inc *(G-4927)*
Infinity Health Services Inc (PA) 440 614-0145
975 Crocker Rd A Westlake (44145) *(G-19357)*
Info Line Inc 330 252-8064
703 S Main St Ste 200 Akron (44311) *(G-275)*
Info Trak &, Mansfield Also called Info Trak Incorporated *(G-13186)*
Info Trak Incorporated 419 747-9296
165 Marion Ave Mansfield (44903) *(G-13186)*
Infoaccessnet LLC 216 328-0100
8801 E Pleasant Valley Rd Cleveland (44131) *(G-5750)*
Infocision Management Corp (PA) 330 668-1411
325 Springside Dr Akron (44333) *(G-276)*
Infocision Management Corp 330 726-0872
6951 Southern Blvd Ste E Youngstown (44512) *(G-20080)*
Infocision Management Corp 419 529-8685
1404 Park Ave E Mansfield (44905) *(G-13187)*
Infocision Management Corp 330 668-6615
250 N Clvland Mssillon Rd Akron (44333) *(G-277)*
Infocision Management Corp 937 259-2400
101 Woodman Dr Dayton (45431) *(G-9178)*
Infocision Management Corp 330 544-1400
5740 Interstate Blvd Youngstown (44515) *(G-20081)*
Infoquest Information Services 614 761-3003
2000 Henderson Rd Ste 300 Columbus (43220) *(G-7815)*
Infor (us) Inc 678 319-8000
2800 Corp Exchange Dr # 350 Columbus (43231) *(G-7816)*
Informa Business Media Inc 216 696-7000
1100 Superior Ave E # 800 Cleveland (44114) *(G-5751)*
Information & Referral Center, Lima Also called County of Allen *(G-12623)*
Information Builders Inc 513 891-2338
1 Financial Way Ste 307 Montgomery (45242) *(G-14595)*
Information Control Co LLC 614 523-3070
2500 Corporate Exch Dr Columbus (43231) *(G-7817)*
Information Management Svcs, Hilliard Also called Document Imging Spcialists LLC *(G-11762)*
Information Systems Dept, Batavia Also called County of Clermont *(G-993)*
Infoscitex Corporation 937 429-9008
4027 Colonel Glenn Hwy # 210 Beavercreek Township (45431) *(G-1249)*
Infostore LLC 216 749-4636
1200 E Granger Rd Cleveland (44131) *(G-5752)*
Infotelecom Holdings LLC (PA) 216 373-4811
75 Erieview Plz Fl 4 Cleveland (44114) *(G-5753)*
Infoverity Inc 614 310-1709
5131 Post Rd Ste 220 Dublin (43017) *(G-10255)*
Infovision 21 Inc 614 761-8844
6077 Frantz Rd Ste 105 Dublin (43017) *(G-10256)*
Infra-Metals Co 740 353-1350
1 Sturgill Way Portsmouth (45662) *(G-16149)*
Infusion Partners Inc (HQ) 513 396-6060
4623 Wesley Ave Ste H Cincinnati (45212) *(G-3761)*
Ingersoll-Rand Company 419 633-6800
209 N Main St Bryan (43506) *(G-1960)*
Ingle-Barr Inc (PA) 740 702-6117
20 Plyleys Ln Chillicothe (45601) *(G-2793)*
Ingleside Investments Inc 614 221-1025
1036 S Front St Columbus (43206) *(G-7818)*
Ingram Entrmt Holdings Inc 419 662-3132
668 1st St Perrysburg (43551) *(G-15879)*
Initial Tropical Plant Svcs, Groveport Also called Rentokil North America Inc *(G-11534)*
Injection Molders Supply, Chagrin Falls Also called IMS Company *(G-2668)*
Inland Products Inc (PA) 614 443-3425
599 Frank Rd Columbus (43223) *(G-7819)*
Inliner American Inc 614 529-6440
4143 Weaver Ct S Hilliard (43026) *(G-11778)*
Inloes Heating and Cooling, Hamilton Also called Inloes Mechanical Inc *(G-11612)*

A L P H A B E T I C

Inloes Mechanical Inc...513 896-9499
　157 N B St Hamilton (45013) *(G-11612)*

Inman Nationwide Shipping, Cleveland *Also called Cremation Service Inc (G-5379)*

Inn At Chestnut Hill, The, Columbus *Also called Chestnut Hill Management Co (G-7183)*

Inn At Christine Valley...330 270-3347
　3150 S Schenley Ave Youngstown (44511) *(G-20082)*

Inn At Hillenvale Ltd..740 392-8245
　1615 Yauger Rd Ste B26 Mount Vernon (43050) *(G-14769)*

Inn At Honey Run, Millersburg *Also called Honey Run Retreats LLC (G-14478)*

Inn At Marietta Ltd..740 373-9600
　150 Browns Rd Ofc Marietta (45750) *(G-13338)*

Inn At Medina Limited LLC..330 723-0110
　100 High Point Dr Ofc Medina (44256) *(G-13954)*

Inn At Medina The, Medina *Also called Inn At Medina Limited LLC (G-13954)*

Inn At North Hills, Zanesville *Also called North Hills Management Company (G-20346)*

Inn At Univ Vlg MGT Co LLC......................................330 837-3000
　2650 Ohio State Dr Se Massillon (44646) *(G-13699)*

Inn At Wickliffe LLC...440 585-0600
　28600 Ridgehills Dr Wickliffe (44092) *(G-19465)*

Inner City Nursing Home...216 795-1363
　9014 Cedar Ave Cleveland (44106) *(G-5754)*

Inner-Space Cleaning Corp.......................................440 646-0701
　6151 Wilson Mills Rd # 240 Cleveland (44143) *(G-5755)*

Innerworkings Inc..513 984-9500
　7141 E Kemper Rd Cincinnati (45249) *(G-3762)*

Inno-Pak LLC (PA)..740 363-0090
　1932 Pittsburgh Dr Delaware (43015) *(G-9989)*

Innmark Communications, Fairfield *Also called Pakmark LLC (G-10768)*

Innmark Communications LLC....................................937 425-6152
　12080 Mosteller Rd Sharonville (45241) *(G-16729)*

Innosource, West Chester *Also called Vallen Distribution Inc (G-19028)*

Innovairre Communications LLC.................................330 869-8500
　3200 W Market St Ste 302 Fairlawn (44333) *(G-10833)*

Innovative Architectural..614 416-0614
　2740 Airport Dr Ste 300 Columbus (43219) *(G-7820)*

Innovative Concept, Girard *Also called Boardman Medical Supply Co (G-11283)*

Innovative Controls Corp..419 691-6684
　1354 E Broadway St Toledo (43605) *(G-17821)*

Innovative Dialysis...419 473-9900
　3829 Woodley Rd Ste 12 Toledo (43606) *(G-17822)*

Innovative Enrgy Solutions LLC.................................937 228-3044
　3680 Symmes Rd Hamilton (45015) *(G-11613)*

Innovative Joint Utility Svcs, Gahanna *Also called Ijus LLC (G-11126)*

Innovative Logistics Group Inc...................................937 832-9350
　30 Lau Pkwy Englewood (45315) *(G-10591)*

Innovative Logistics Svcs Inc....................................330 468-6422
　201 E Twinsburg Rd Northfield (44067) *(G-15380)*

Innovative Studnt Ln Solutions, Cincinnati *Also called Student Loan Strategies LLC (G-4550)*

Innovative Technologies Corp (PA)..............................937 252-2145
　1020 Woodman Dr Ste 100 Dayton (45432) *(G-9179)*

Innovel Solutions Inc..614 878-2092
　5330 Crosswind Dr Columbus (43228) *(G-7821)*

Innovel Solutions Inc..614 492-5304
　4100 Lockbourne Industria Columbus (43207) *(G-7822)*

Innovis Data Solutions Inc..614 222-4343
　250 E Broad St Columbus (43215) *(G-7823)*

Innovtive Cllectn Concepts Inc...................................513 489-5500
　11353 Reed Hartman Hwy # 100 Blue Ash (45241) *(G-1584)*

Innovtive Crtive Solutions LLC...................................614 491-9638
　5835 Green Pointe Dr S B Groveport (43125) *(G-11520)*

Innovtive Lbling Solutions Inc....................................513 860-2457
　4000 Hmlton Middletown Rd Hamilton (45011) *(G-11614)*

Innovtive Sltons Unlimited LLC (PA)............................740 289-3282
　1862 Shyville Rd Piketon (45661) *(G-15978)*

Innovtive Sltons Unlimited LLC...................................740 289-3282
　1862 Shyville Rd Piketon (45661) *(G-15979)*

Inovative Facility Svcs LLC.......................................419 861-1710
　1573 Henthorne Dr Maumee (43537) *(G-13803)*

INPREM HOLISTIC COMMUNITY RESO, Columbus *Also called In His Prsence Ministries Intl (G-7805)*

Inquiry Systems Inc...614 464-3800
　1195 Goodale Blvd Columbus (43212) *(G-7824)*

Inreality LLC...513 218-9603
　403 Vine St Ste 200 Cincinnati (45202) *(G-3763)*

Inside Foodland, Gallipolis *Also called Ohio Valley Bank Company (G-11206)*

Inside Out (PA)..937 525-7880
　501 S Wittenberg Ave Springfield (45506) *(G-17052)*

INSIDE OUT CHILD CARE, Springfield *Also called Inside Out (G-17052)*

Inside Outfitters, Lewis Center *Also called Lumenomics Inc (G-12550)*

Insight Communications, Columbus *Also called Time Warner Cable Inc (G-8756)*

Insight Communications of Co....................................614 236-1200
　3770 E Livingston Ave Columbus (43227) *(G-7825)*

Insight Direct Usa Inc..614 456-0423
　375 N Front St Columbus (43215) *(G-7826)*

Insight Ohio, Columbus *Also called Insight Communications of Co (G-7825)*

INSIGHT TECHNICAL SERVICES, Sandusky *Also called All Phase Power and Ltg Inc (G-16574)*

Inspection Group Incorporated...................................614 891-3606
　440 Polaris Pkwy Ste 170 Westerville (43082) *(G-19175)*

Installed Building Pdts II LLC.....................................626 812-6070
　495 S High St Ste 50 Columbus (43215) *(G-7827)*

Installed Building Pdts Inc (PA)..................................614 221-3399
　495 S High St Ste 50 Columbus (43215) *(G-7828)*

Installed Building Pdts LLC.......................................614 308-9900
　1320 Mckinley Ave Ste A Columbus (43222) *(G-7829)*

Installed Building Pdts LLC.......................................330 798-9640
　2783 Gilchrist Rd Unit B Akron (44305) *(G-278)*

Installed Building Pdts LLC.......................................419 662-4524
　6412 Fairfield Dr Ste A Northwood (43619) *(G-15396)*

Installed Products & Services, West Chester *Also called Reading Rock Residential LLC (G-19075)*

Instanceworkplace, Columbus *Also called M J S Holding (G-8003)*

Instant Tax Service, Beavercreek *Also called Its Financial LLC (G-1224)*

Instantwhip Foods Inc...330 688-8825
　4870 Hudson Dr Stow (44224) *(G-17213)*

Instantwhip-Akron Inc...614 488-2536
　4870 Hudson Dr Stow (44224) *(G-17214)*

Instantwhip-Columbus Inc (HQ).................................614 871-9447
　3855 Marlane Dr Grove City (43123) *(G-11443)*

Institute Environmental Health, Cincinnati *Also called University of Cincinnati (G-4713)*

Institute For Human Services (PA)...............................614 251-6000
　1706 E Broad St Columbus (43203) *(G-7830)*

Institute For Orthpdic Surgery, Lima *Also called West Central Ohio Group Ltd (G-12778)*

Institute/Reproductive Health.....................................513 585-2355
　2123 Auburn Ave Ste A44 Cincinnati (45219) *(G-3764)*

Institutional Care Pharmacy (PA)................................419 447-6216
　1815 W County Road 54 Tiffin (44883) *(G-17520)*

Institutional Foods, Warren *Also called J V Hansel Inc (G-18716)*

Instrmntation Ctrl Systems Inc...................................513 662-2600
　11355 Sebring Dr Cincinnati (45240) *(G-3765)*

Insulating Sales Co Inc..513 742-2600
　11430 Sebring Dr Cincinnati (45240) *(G-3766)*

Insulation Northwest, Columbus *Also called Installed Building Pdts II LLC (G-7827)*

Insurance Claims MGT Inc...937 328-4300
　14 E Main St Fl 4 Springfield (45502) *(G-17053)*

Insurance Intermediaries Inc.....................................614 846-1111
　280 N High St Ste 300 Columbus (43215) *(G-7831)*

Integer Holdings Corporation.....................................216 937-2800
　1771 E 30th St Cleveland (44114) *(G-5756)*

Integra Cncinnati/Columbus Inc.................................614 764-8040
　6241 Riverside Dr Dublin (43017) *(G-10257)*

Integra Group Inc...513 326-5600
　16 Triangle Park Dr # 1600 Cincinnati (45246) *(G-3767)*

Integra Ohio Inc..513 378-5214
　4900 Charlemar Dr Bldg A Cincinnati (45227) *(G-3768)*

Integra Realty Resources - Cin...................................513 561-2305
　8241 Cornell Rd Ste 210 Cincinnati (45249) *(G-3769)*

Integrated AG Services, Milford Center *Also called Champaign Premium Grn Growers (G-14444)*

Integrated CC LLC..216 707-4132
　8650 Euclid Ave Cleveland (44106) *(G-5757)*

Integrated Data Services Inc......................................937 656-5496
　111 Harries St Apt 202 Dayton (45402) *(G-9515)*

Integrated Marketing Tech Inc....................................330 225-3550
　2945 Carquest Dr Brunswick (44212) *(G-1933)*

Integrated Power Services LLC...................................216 433-7808
　5325 W 130th St Cleveland (44130) *(G-5758)*

Integrated Power Services LLC...................................513 863-8816
　2175a Schlichter Dr Hamilton (45015) *(G-11615)*

Integrated Prj Resources LLC.....................................330 272-0998
　600 E 2nd St Salem (44460) *(G-16549)*

Integrated Protection Svcs Inc (PA).............................513 631-5505
　5303 Lester Rd Cincinnati (45213) *(G-3770)*

Integrated Services of Appala.....................................740 594-6807
　11 Graham Dr Athens (45701) *(G-786)*

Integrated Solutions and..513 826-1932
　1430 Yankee Park Pl Dayton (45458) *(G-9516)*

Integrated Telehealth Inc..216 373-2221
　75 Milford Dr Ste 201 Hudson (44236) *(G-11985)*

Integrated Youth Services Inc....................................937 427-3837
　1055 E High St Springfield (45505) *(G-17054)*

Integres Fast Forward Shipping, Medina *Also called Integres Global Logistics Inc (G-13955)*

Integres Global Logistics Inc (HQ)..............................866 347-2101
　84 Medina Rd Medina (44256) *(G-13955)*

Integrity Enterprizes (PA)...216 289-8801
　27801 Euclid Ave Ste 440 Euclid (44132) *(G-10645)*

Integrity Ex Logistics LLC (PA)...................................888 374-5138
　4420 Cooper Rd Ste 400 Cincinnati (45242) *(G-3771)*

Integrity Global Marketing LLC...................................330 492-9989
　4735 Belpar St Nw Canton (44718) *(G-2356)*

Integrity Gymnstics Chrleading...................................614 733-0818
　8185 Business Way Plain City (43064) *(G-16055)*

Integrity Hotel Group...937 224-0800
　33 E 5th St Dayton (45402) *(G-9517)*

Integrity Information Tech Inc.....................................937 846-1769
　2742 N Dayton Lakeview Rd New Carlisle (45344) *(G-14891)*

Integrity It, New Carlisle *Also called Integrity Information Tech Inc (G-14891)*

Integrity Kokosing Pipeline Sv....740 694-6315
17531 Waterford Rd Fredericktown (43019) ***(G-11054)***
Integrity Processing LLC....330 285-6937
1055 Wooster Rd N Barberton (44203) ***(G-955)***
Integrity Stainless, Streetsboro *Also called Olympic Steel Inc* ***(G-17263)***
Integrity Stainless, Streetsboro *Also called Is Acquisition Inc* ***(G-17257)***
Integrity Wall & Ceiling Inc....419 381-1855
5242 Angola Rd Ste 180 Toledo (43615) ***(G-17823)***
Integrted Prcision Systems Inc....330 963-0064
9321 Ravenna Rd Ste C Twinsburg (44087) ***(G-18282)***
Intelisol Inc....614 409-0052
4555 Creekside Pkwy Lockbourne (43137) ***(G-12820)***
Intellicorp Records Inc....216 450-5200
3000 Auburn Dr Ste 410 Beachwood (44122) ***(G-1067)***
Intelligent Information Inc....513 860-4233
4838 Duff Dr Ste C West Chester (45246) ***(G-19061)***
Intelligrated Systems Inc (HQ)....866 936-7300
7901 Innovation Way Mason (45040) ***(G-13598)***
Intelligrated Systems LLC....513 701-7300
7901 Innovation Way Mason (45040) ***(G-13599)***
Intelligrated Systems Ohio LLC (HQ)....513 701-7300
7901 Innovation Way Mason (45040) ***(G-13600)***
Intellinet Corporation (PA)....216 289-4100
1111 Chester Ave Ste 200 Cleveland (44114) ***(G-5759)***
Intelliq Health....513 489-8838
5050 Section Ave Ste 320 Cincinnati (45212) ***(G-3772)***
Intellitarget Marketing Svcs, Coshocton *Also called ITM Marketing Inc* ***(G-9019)***
Inter Distr Svcs of Cleve....330 468-4949
8055 Highland Pointe Pkwy Macedonia (44056) ***(G-13075)***
Inter Healt Care of Cambr Zane (PA)....614 436-9404
960 Checkrein Ave Ste A Columbus (43229) ***(G-7832)***
Inter Healt Care of Cambr Zane....513 984-1110
8050 Hosbrook Rd Ste 406 Cincinnati (45236) ***(G-3773)***
Inter Healt Care of North OH I....740 453-5130
2809 Bell St Ste D Zanesville (43701) ***(G-20320)***
Inter Healt Care of North OH I....419 422-5328
2129 Stephen Ave Ste 3 Findlay (45840) ***(G-10927)***
Inter Tel, West Chester *Also called Mitel (delaware) Inc* ***(G-18974)***
Interact For Health....513 458-6600
3805 Edwards Rd Ste 500 Cincinnati (45209) ***(G-3774)***
Interact One Inc....513 469-7042
4665 Cornell Rd Ste 255 Blue Ash (45241) ***(G-1585)***
Interactive Bus Systems Inc....513 984-2205
130 Tri County Pkwy # 208 Cincinnati (45246) ***(G-3775)***
Interactive Engineering Corp....330 239-6888
884 Medina Rd Medina (44256) ***(G-13956)***
Interactive Solutions Intl LLC....513 619-5100
155 Tri County Pkwy 111 Cincinnati (45246) ***(G-3776)***
Interbake Foods LLC....614 294-4931
1740 Joyce Ave Columbus (43219) ***(G-7833)***
Interbake Foods LLC....614 294-4931
1700 E 17th Ave Columbus (43219) ***(G-7834)***
Interbrand Design Forum LLC....513 421-2210
700 W Pete Rose Way # 460 Cincinnati (45203) ***(G-3777)***
Interbrand Hulefeld Inc....513 421-2210
700 W Pete Rose Way Cincinnati (45203) ***(G-3778)***
Intercity Amateur Rdo CLB Inc....419 989-3429
120 Homewood Rd Ontario (44906) ***(G-15554)***
Intercnnect Cbling Netwrk Svcs....440 891-0465
125 Pelret Indus Pkwy Berea (44017) ***(G-1428)***
Intercntnntal Ht Group Rsurces....216 707-4300
8800 Euclid Ave Cleveland (44106) ***(G-5760)***
Intercoastal Trnsp Systems....513 829-1287
5284 Winton Rd Fairfield (45014) ***(G-10737)***
Intercontinental Hotels Group....216 707-4100
9801 Carnegie Ave Cleveland (44106) ***(G-5761)***
Interdesign Inc....440 248-0136
30725 Solon Indus Pkwy Solon (44139) ***(G-16861)***
Interdyne Corporation....419 229-8192
931 N Jefferson St Lima (45801) ***(G-12666)***
Interfaith Hosptlty Ntwrk of W....513 934-5250
203 E Warren St Lebanon (45036) ***(G-12473)***
Intergrated Consulting....216 214-7547
5311 Northfield Rd Bedford Heights (44146) ***(G-1323)***
Interim Halthcare Columbus Inc (HQ)....614 888-3130
784 Morrison Rd Gahanna (43230) ***(G-11127)***
Interim Halthcare Columbus Inc....330 836-5571
3040 W Market St Ste 1 Fairlawn (44333) ***(G-10834)***
Interim Halthcare Columbus Inc....740 349-8700
900 Sharon Valley Rd Newark (43055) ***(G-15044)***
INTERIM HEALTHCARE, Columbus *Also called Salo Inc* ***(G-8585)***
Interim Healthcare, Zanesville *Also called Inter Healt Care of North OH I* ***(G-20320)***
Interim Healthcare (PA)....740 354-5550
4130 Gallia St Portsmouth (45662) ***(G-16150)***
Interim Healthcare of Dayton....937 291-5330
30 W Rahn Rd Ste 2 Dayton (45429) ***(G-9518)***
Interim Healthcare SE Ohio Inc....740 373-3800
1017 Pike St Marietta (45750) ***(G-13339)***
Interim Services, Dayton *Also called Interim Healthcare of Dayton* ***(G-9518)***
Interim Services, Gahanna *Also called Interim Halthcare Columbus Inc* ***(G-11127)***
Interim Services, Fairlawn *Also called Interim Halthcare Columbus Inc* ***(G-10834)***
Interim Services, Findlay *Also called Inter Healt Care of North OH I* ***(G-10927)***
Interim Services, Newark *Also called Interim Halthcare Columbus Inc* ***(G-15044)***
INTERIM SERVICES, Columbus *Also called Inter Healt Care of Cambr Zane* ***(G-7832)***
Interim Services, Cincinnati *Also called Inter Healt Care of Cambr Zane* ***(G-3773)***
Interior Supply Cincinnati LLC....614 424-6611
481 E 11th Ave Columbus (43211) ***(G-7835)***
Internal Mdcine Cons of Clmbus....614 878-6413
104 N Murray Hill Rd Columbus (43228) ***(G-7836)***
Internal Medical Center, Akron *Also called Summa Health System* ***(G-451)***
Internal Medicine, Columbus *Also called Ohio State University* ***(G-8297)***
Internal Medicine of Akron....330 376-2728
150 Springside Dr 320c Akron (44333) ***(G-279)***
Internash Global Svc Group LLC....513 772-0430
4621 Interstate Dr West Chester (45246) ***(G-19062)***
International Assn Lions....740 986-6502
24920 Locust Grove Rd Williamsport (43164) ***(G-19499)***
International Assn Lions Clubs, Newark *Also called Licking Valley Lions Club* ***(G-15060)***
International Association of (PA)....330 628-3012
4848 Munson St Nw Canton (44718) ***(G-2357)***
International Bus Mchs Corp....917 406-7400
3000 Presidential Dr # 300 Beavercreek (45324) ***(G-1158)***
International Chem Wkrs Cr Un (PA)....330 926-1444
1655 W Market St Fl 6 Akron (44313) ***(G-280)***
International Data MGT Inc (PA)....330 869-8500
3200 W Market St Ste 302 Fairlawn (44333) ***(G-10835)***
International Exposition Ctr, Cleveland *Also called I-X Center Corporation* ***(G-5732)***
International Frat of Del....330 922-5959
2735 Elmwood St Cuyahoga Falls (44221) ***(G-9102)***
International Healthcare Corp....513 731-3338
2837 Burnet Ave Cincinnati (45219) ***(G-3779)***
International Management Group (HQ)....216 522-1200
1360 E 9th St Ste 100 Cleveland (44114) ***(G-5762)***
International Masonry Inc....614 469-8338
135 Spruce St Columbus (43215) ***(G-7837)***
International Mdsg Corp (HQ)....216 522-1200
1360 E 9th St Ste 100 Cleveland (44114) ***(G-5763)***
International Merchants, Blue Ash *Also called Req/Jqh Holdings Inc* ***(G-1645)***
International MGT Counsel, Sandusky *Also called YMCA of Sandusky Ohio Inc* ***(G-16657)***
International Ordr of Rnbow Fo....419 862-3009
18706 W State Route 105 Elmore (43416) ***(G-10473)***
International Paper, Fairfield *Also called Veritiv Operating Company* ***(G-10798)***
International Paper, Toledo *Also called Veritiv Operating Company* ***(G-18137)***
International Paper, Fairfield *Also called Veritiv Operating Company* ***(G-10799)***
International Paper Compa....513 248-6000
6283 Tri Ridge Blvd Loveland (45140) ***(G-13001)***
International Steel Group....330 841-2800
2234 Main Street Ext Sw Warren (44481) ***(G-18715)***
International Technegroup Inc (PA)....513 576-3900
5303 Dupont Cir Milford (45150) ***(G-14397)***
International Truck & Eng Corp....937 390-4045
6125 Urbana Rd Springfield (45502) ***(G-17055)***
International Un Elev Constrs....614 291-5859
23 W 2nd Ave Ste C Columbus (43201) ***(G-7838)***
International Union United Au....216 447-6080
5000 Rockside Rd Ste 300 Cleveland (44131) ***(G-5764)***
International Union United Au....513 897-4939
8137 Lytle Trails Rd Waynesville (45068) ***(G-18833)***
International Union United Au....513 563-1252
10708 Reading Rd Cincinnati (45241) ***(G-3780)***
International Union United Au....419 893-4677
1691 Woodlands Dr Maumee (43537) ***(G-13804)***
International Union Elvtor Cns, Columbus *Also called International Un Elev Constrs* ***(G-7838)***
Interntional Assn Firefighters....330 823-5222
63 E Broadway St Alliance (44601) ***(G-535)***
Interntional Molasses Corp Ltd....937 276-7980
4744 Wolf Creek Pike Dayton (45417) ***(G-9519)***
Interntional Towers I Ohio Ltd....216 520-1250
25 Market St Youngstown (44503) ***(G-20083)***
Interntnal Pckg Pallets Crates, Sidney *Also called Wappoo Wood Products Inc* ***(G-16805)***
Interntnal Spcial Adit Systems, Cleveland *Also called First Federal Credit Control* ***(G-5534)***
Interntonal Aliance Thea Stage....440 734-4883
4689 Georgette Ave North Olmsted (44070) ***(G-15293)***
Interphace Phtgrphy Cmmnctions....254 289-6270
1365 Meadowlark Ln Amelia (45102) ***(G-573)***
Interscope Manufacturing Inc....513 423-8866
2901 Carmody Blvd Middletown (45042) ***(G-14303)***
Interstate Coml GL & Door, Northwood *Also called A E D Inc* ***(G-15388)***
Interstate Construction Inc....614 539-1188
3511 Farm Bank Way Grove City (43123) ***(G-11444)***
Interstate Contractors LLC....513 372-5393
762 Reading Rd G Mason (45040) ***(G-13601)***
Interstate Diesel Service Inc (PA)....216 881-0015
5300 Lakeside Ave E Cleveland (44114) ***(G-5765)***
Interstate Gas Supply Inc (PA)....614 659-5000
6100 Emerald Pkwy Dublin (43016) ***(G-10258)***
Interstate Lanes of Ohio Ltd....419 666-2695
819 Lime City Rd Rossford (43460) ***(G-16462)***
Interstate Lift Truck, Holland *Also called Devirsified Material Handling* ***(G-11882)***
Interstate Optical Co (HQ)....419 529-6800
680 Lindaire Ln E Ontario (44906) ***(G-15555)***

ALPHABETIC

Interstate Shredding LLC..................................330 545-5477
  27 Furnace Ln Girard (44420) *(G-11289)*
Interstate Truckway Inc...................................614 771-1220
  5440 Renner Rd Columbus (43228) *(G-7839)*
Interstate Truckway Inc (PA).............................513 542-5500
  1755 Dreman Ave Cincinnati (45223) *(G-3781)*
Interstate Warehousing VA LLC...........................513 874-6500
  110 Distribution Dr Fairfield (45014) *(G-10738)*
Interstate-Mcbee, Cleveland *Also called McBee Supply Corporation (G-5930)*
Intertec Corporation......................................419 537-9711
  3400 Executive Pkwy Toledo (43606) *(G-17824)*
Intertek Testing Svcs NA Inc.............................614 279-8090
  1717 Arlingate Ln Columbus (43228) *(G-7840)*
Interval Brotherhood Homes..............................330 644-4095
  3445 S Main St Coventry Township (44319) *(G-9036)*
Intervention For Peace Inc................................330 725-1298
  689 W Liberty St Ste 7 Medina (44256) *(G-13957)*
Intex Supply Company.....................................216 535-4300
  26301 Curtiss Wright Pkwy Richmond Heights (44143) *(G-16391)*
Intgrted Bridge Communications..........................513 381-1380
  302 W 3rd St Ste 900 Cincinnati (45202) *(G-3782)*
Intitle Agency Inc...513 241-8780
  120 E 4th St Ste 400 Cincinnati (45202) *(G-3783)*
Intl Europa Salon & Spa...................................216 292-6969
  24700 Chagrin Blvd # 101 Cleveland (44122) *(G-5766)*
Intown Suites Management Inc.............................937 433-9038
  8981 Kingsridge Dr Dayton (45458) *(G-9520)*
Intralot Inc...440 268-2900
  13500 Darice Pkwy Ste C Strongsville (44149) *(G-17316)*
Intren Inc..815 482-0651
  1267 Tennessee Ave Cincinnati (45229) *(G-3784)*
Intrepid USA Healthcare Svcs, Elyria *Also called NC Hha Inc (G-10542)*
Intrigue Salon & Day Spa..................................330 493-7003
  4762 Dressler Rd Nw Canton (44718) *(G-2358)*
Intrust It, Blue Ash *Also called Lan Solutions Inc (G-1594)*
Inventory Controlled Mdsg, Twinsburg *Also called ICM Distributing Company Inc (G-18281)*
Inverness Club...419 578-9000
  4601 Dorr St Ste 1 Toledo (43615) *(G-17825)*
Invest, Tiffin *Also called Old Fort Banking Company (G-17530)*
Investek Management Svcs F/C............................419 873-1236
  1090 W South Boundary St # 100 Perrysburg (43551) *(G-15880)*
Investek Realty LLC.......................................419 873-1236
  1090 W South Boundary St # 100 Perrysburg (43551) *(G-15881)*
Investmerica limited.......................................216 618-3296
  547 Washington St Ste 10 Chagrin Falls (44022) *(G-2650)*
Invotec Engineering Inc (PA).............................937 886-3232
  10909 Industry Ln Miamisburg (45342) *(G-14177)*
Ionno Properties s Corp...................................330 479-9267
  4412 Pleasant Vly Rd Se Dennison (44621) *(G-10051)*
Ioof Home of Ohio Inc.....................................419 352-3014
  139 Eberly Ave Bowling Green (43402) *(G-1737)*
Iowa 80 Group, Hebron *Also called Truckomat Corporation (G-11725)*
Ipi, Hayesville *Also called Impressive Packaging Inc (G-11701)*
Ips, Avon Lake *Also called Catamaran Home Dlvry Ohio Inc (G-911)*
Ipsos-Asi LLC..513 872-4300
  3505 Columbia Pkwy # 300 Cincinnati (45226) *(G-3785)*
Ipsos-Asi, Inc., Cincinnati *Also called Ipsos-Asi LLC (G-3785)*
Ipsos-Insight LLC...513 552-1100
  11499 Chester Rd Ste 401 Cincinnati (45246) *(G-3786)*
Iq Innovations LLC..614 222-0882
  580 N 4th St Ste 560 Columbus (43215) *(G-7841)*
Irace Inc...330 836-7247
  2265 W Market St Akron (44313) *(G-281)*
Irace Automotive, Akron *Also called Irace Inc (G-281)*
Ireland Cancer Center, Cleveland *Also called University Hospitals (G-6590)*
Irg Operating LLC..440 963-4008
  850 W River Rd Vermilion (44089) *(G-18554)*
Irg Realty Advisors LLC (PA).............................330 659-4060
  4020 Kinross Lakes Pkwy Richfield (44286) *(G-16361)*
Irish Envy LLC...440 808-8000
  30307 Detroit Rd Westlake (44145) *(G-19358)*
Iron City Distributing, Mingo Junction *Also called Bellas Co (G-14527)*
Iron Mountain Incorporated...............................513 874-3535
  9247 Meridian Way West Chester (45069) *(G-18948)*
Iron Mountain Incorporated...............................614 801-0151
  3250 Urbancrest Indus Dr Urbancrest (43123) *(G-18449)*
Iron Mountain Info MGT LLC..............................513 297-3268
  5845 Highland Ridge Dr Cincinnati (45232) *(G-3787)*
Iron Mountain Info MGT LLC..............................513 942-7300
  3790 Symmes Rd Hamilton (45015) *(G-11616)*
Iron Mountain Info MGT LLC..............................513 297-1906
  9247 Meridian Way West Chester (45069) *(G-18949)*
Iron Mountain Info MGT LLC..............................614 840-9321
  4848 Evanswood Dr Columbus (43229) *(G-7842)*
Iron Mountain Info MGT LLC..............................440 248-0999
  5101 Naiman Pkwy Ste B Solon (44139) *(G-16862)*
Iron Mountain Info MGT LLC..............................513 247-2183
  11350 Deerfield Rd Blue Ash (45242) *(G-1586)*
Irongate Inc (PA)...937 433-3300
  122 N Main St Centerville (45459) *(G-2628)*

Irongate Inc..937 298-6000
  4461 Far Hills Ave Dayton (45429) *(G-9521)*
Irongate Inc..937 432-3432
  1353 Lyons Rd Dayton (45458) *(G-9522)*
Irongate Inc Realtors, Dayton *Also called Irongate Inc (G-9521)*
Irongate Realtors, Centerville *Also called Irongate Inc (G-2628)*
Ironton and Lawrence County (PA).......................740 532-3534
  305 N 5th St Ironton (45638) *(G-12155)*
Ironton and Lawrence County.............................740 532-7855
  1518 S 3rd St Ironton (45638) *(G-12156)*
Irth Solutions Inc (PA)....................................614 459-2328
  5009 Horizons Dr Ste 100 Columbus (43220) *(G-7843)*
Is Acquisition Inc (HQ)....................................440 287-0150
  3000 Crane Centre Dr Streetsboro (44241) *(G-17257)*
Isaac Brant Ledman Teetor LLP..........................614 221-2121
  2 Miranova Pl Ste 700 Columbus (43215) *(G-7844)*
Isaac Wiles Burkholder & Teeto..........................614 221-5216
  2 Miranova Pl Ste 700 Columbus (43215) *(G-7845)*
Isabelle Ridgway Care Ctr Inc............................614 252-4931
  1520 Hawthorne Ave Columbus (43203) *(G-7846)*
Isd Renal Inc...330 375-6848
  525 E Market St Bldg 50 Akron (44304) *(G-282)*
Ishikawa Gasket America Inc.............................419 353-7300
  828 Van Camp Rd Bowling Green (43402) *(G-1738)*
ISI Systems Inc (PA).......................................740 942-0050
  43029 Industrial Park Rd Cadiz (43907) *(G-2030)*
Island Bike Rental Inc......................................419 285-2016
  2071 Langram Rd Put In Bay (43456) *(G-16225)*
Island Hospitality MGT LLC................................614 864-8844
  2084 S Hamilton Rd Columbus (43232) *(G-7847)*
Island House Inc..419 734-0100
  102 Madison St Port Clinton (43452) *(G-16110)*
Island House Inn, Port Clinton *Also called Island House Inc (G-16110)*
Island Service Company...................................419 285-3695
  341 Bayview Ave Put In Bay (43456) *(G-16226)*
ISLAND VIEW GIFTS, Put In Bay *Also called Miller Boat Line Inc (G-16227)*
Islander Apartments, Cleveland *Also called Islander Company (G-5767)*
Islander Company..440 243-0593
  7711 Normandie Blvd Cleveland (44130) *(G-5767)*
Isomedix Operations Inc...................................614 836-5757
  4405 Marketing Pl Groveport (43125) *(G-11521)*
Isomedix Operations Inc (HQ).............................440 354-2600
  5960 Heisley Rd Mentor (44060) *(G-14064)*
Isqft Inc (HQ)...513 645-8004
  3825 Edwards Rd Ste 800 Cincinnati (45209) *(G-3788)*
Israel Adath (PA)...513 793-1800
  3201 E Galbraith Rd Cincinnati (45236) *(G-3789)*
It Services, Kettering *Also called Efix Computer Repair & Svc LLC (G-12292)*
Itc, Dayton *Also called Innovative Technologies Corp (G-9179)*
Itcube LLC...513 891-7300
  10999 Reed Hartman Hwy Blue Ash (45242) *(G-1587)*
Itelligence Inc (HQ).......................................513 956-2000
  10856 Reed Hartman Hwy Cincinnati (45242) *(G-3790)*
Itelligence Outsourcing Inc (HQ).........................513 956-2000
  10856 Reed Hartman Hwy Cincinnati (45242) *(G-3791)*
Iticketscom...614 410-4140
  700 Taylor Rd Ste 210 Columbus (43230) *(G-7848)*
ITM Marketing Inc..740 295-3575
  470 Downtowner Plz Coshocton (43812) *(G-9019)*
Its Financial LLC..937 425-6889
  51 Plum St Ste 260 Beavercreek (45440) *(G-1224)*
Its Technologies Inc (PA).................................419 842-2100
  7060 Spring Meadows Dr W D Holland (43528) *(G-11890)*
Its Traffic Systems Inc....................................440 892-4500
  28915 Clemens Rd Ste 200 Westlake (44145) *(G-19359)*
ITW Food Equipment Group LLC (HQ)....................937 332-2396
  701 S Ridge Ave Troy (45374) *(G-18208)*
Ivan Law Inc..330 533-5000
  2200 Hubbard Rd Youngstown (44505) *(G-20084)*
Ivan Weaver Construction Co (PA)........................330 695-3461
  124 N Mill St Fredericksburg (44627) *(G-11051)*
Ivory Services Inc...216 344-3094
  2122 Saint Clair Ave Ne Cleveland (44114) *(G-5768)*
Ivy Health Care Inc (PA)..................................513 251-2557
  2025 Wyoming Ave Cincinnati (45205) *(G-3792)*
Ivy Hills Country Club, Cincinnati *Also called Dry Run Limited Partnership (G-3445)*
Ivy House Care Center, Painesville *Also called United Rest Homes Inc (G-15745)*
Ivy Woods Care Center, Cincinnati *Also called Ivy Health Care Inc (G-3792)*
Iwi Incorporated (PA)......................................440 585-5900
  1399 Rockefeller Rd Wickliffe (44092) *(G-19466)*
Izaak Walton League America.............................740 532-2342
  1738 County Road 6 Ironton (45638) *(G-12157)*
J & B Classical Glass & Mirror, Mansfield *Also called J & B Equipment & Supply Inc (G-13188)*
J & B Equipment & Supply Inc............................419 884-1155
  2750 Lexington Ave Mansfield (44904) *(G-13188)*
J & B Interests Inc (PA)...................................513 874-1722
  9430 Sutton Pl West Chester (45011) *(G-18950)*
J & B Leasing Inc of Ohio.................................419 269-1440
  435 Dura Ave Toledo (43612) *(G-17826)*

J & B Systems Company Inc 513 732-2000
5055 State Route 276 Batavia (45103) *(G-1002)*
J & C Ambulance Services Inc (PA) 330 899-0022
7100 Whipple Ave Nw Ste G North Canton (44720) *(G-15213)*
J & D Basement Sytems, Reynoldsburg *Also called J & D Home Improvement Inc (G-16310)*
J & D Home Improvement Inc (PA) 740 927-0722
13659 E Main St Reynoldsburg (43068) *(G-16310)*
J & D Mining Inc 330 339-4935
3497 University Dr Ne New Philadelphia (44663) *(G-14967)*
J & E LLC 513 241-0429
250 W Court St Ste 200e Cincinnati (45202) *(G-3793)*
J & F Construction and Dev Inc 419 562-6662
2141 State Route 19 Bucyrus (44820) *(G-1995)*
J & H Erectors, Portsmouth *Also called J&H Rnfrcing Strl Erectors Inc (G-16151)*
J & J, Dayton *Also called Joe and Jill Lewis Inc (G-9526)*
J & J Carriers LLC 614 447-2615
2572 Cleveland Ave Ste 5 Columbus (43211) *(G-7849)*
J & J Entps Westerville Inc 614 898-5997
660 Kintner Pkwy Sunbury (43074) *(G-17389)*
J & J General Maintenance Inc 740 533-9729
2430 S 3rd St Ironton (45638) *(G-12158)*
J & J Schlaegel Inc 937 652-2045
1250 E Us Highway 36 Urbana (43078) *(G-18437)*
J & N, Cincinnati *Also called Building 8 Inc (G-3088)*
J & R Associates 440 250-4080
14803 Holland Rd Brookpark (44142) *(G-1898)*
J & S Industrial Mch Pdts Inc 419 691-1380
123 Oakdale Ave Toledo (43605) *(G-17827)*
J A A Interior & Coml Cnstr 216 431-7633
3615 Superior Ave E 3103h Cleveland (44114) *(G-5769)*
J A Donadee Corporation (PA) 330 533-3305
535 N Broad St Ste 5 Canfield (44406) *(G-2144)*
J A G Black Gold Management Co 614 565-3246
6301 S High St Lockbourne (43137) *(G-12821)*
J A Guy Inc 937 642-3415
13116 Weaver Rd Marysville (43040) *(G-13508)*
J and J Environmental Inc 513 398-4521
7611 Easy St Mason (45040) *(G-13602)*
J and J Sales, Delaware *Also called Aci Industries Converting Ltd (G-9949)*
J and S Tool Incorporated 216 676-8330
15330 Brookpark Rd Cleveland (44135) *(G-5770)*
J B Express Inc 740 702-9830
27311 Old Route 35 Chillicothe (45601) *(G-2794)*
J B Hunt Transport Inc 419 547-2777
600 N Woodland Ave Clyde (43410) *(G-6746)*
J B M Cleaning & Supply Co 330 837-8805
3106 Sheila St Nw Massillon (44646) *(G-13700)*
J C Direct Mail Inc 614 836-4848
4241 Williams Rd Groveport (43125) *(G-11522)*
J D Byrider, Youngstown *Also called Midwest Motors Inc (G-20128)*
J D Drilling Co 740 949-2512
107 S 3rd St Racine (45771) *(G-16229)*
J D S Leasing Inc 440 236-6575
27230 Royalton Rd Columbia Station (44028) *(G-6776)*
J D Williamson Cnstr Co Inc 330 633-1258
441 Geneva Ave Tallmadge (44278) *(G-17478)*
J Daniel & Company Inc 513 575-3100
1975 Phoenix Dr Loveland (45140) *(G-13002)*
J E Davis Corporation 440 377-4700
5187 Smith Ct Ste 100 Sheffield Village (44054) *(G-16735)*
J E F Inc 513 921-4130
1857 Grand Ave Cincinnati (45214) *(G-3794)*
J F Bernard Inc 330 785-3830
359 Stanton Ave Akron (44301) *(G-283)*
J F Good Co, Akron *Also called Famous Industries Inc (G-215)*
J F Painting Co, Columbus *Also called Johnson & Fischer Inc (G-7862)*
J Feldkamp Design Build Ltd 513 870-0601
10036 Springfield Pike Cincinnati (45215) *(G-3795)*
J G Martin Inc 216 491-1584
4159 Lee Rd Cleveland (44128) *(G-5771)*
J Gilmore Design Limited 330 638-8224
3172 Niles Cortland Rd Ne Cortland (44410) *(G-8988)*
J I T, Lebanon *Also called Jlt Packaging Cincinnati Inc (G-12474)*
J K Enterprises Inc 614 481-8838
2200 Mckinley Ave Columbus (43204) *(G-7850)*
J K Meurer Corp 513 831-7500
33 Glendale Milford Rd Loveland (45140) *(G-13003)*
J L Swaney Inc 740 884-4450
975 Vigo Rd Chillicothe (45601) *(G-2795)*
J M T Cartage Inc 330 478-2430
4925 Southway St Sw Canton (44706) *(G-2359)*
J M T Freight Specialists, Seville *Also called Jarrells Moving & Transport Co (G-16686)*
J M Towning Inc 614 876-7335
3690 Lacon Rd Hilliard (43026) *(G-11779)*
J McCoy Lumber Co Ltd (PA) 937 587-3423
6 N Main St Peebles (45660) *(G-15803)*
J Nan Enterprises LLC 330 653-3766
5601 Darrow Rd Hudson (44236) *(G-11986)*
J P Farley Corporation (PA) 440 250-4300
29055 Clemens Rd Westlake (44145) *(G-19360)*
J P Jenks Inc 440 428-4500
4493 S Madison Rd Madison (44057) *(G-13098)*
J P Sand & Gravel Company 614 497-0083
5911 Lockbourne Rd Lockbourne (43137) *(G-12822)*
J P Transportation Company 513 424-6978
2518 Oxford State Rd Middletown (45044) *(G-14304)*
J Peterman Company LLC 888 647-2555
5345 Creek Rd Blue Ash (45242) *(G-1588)*
J R Johnson Engineering Inc 440 234-9972
6673 Eastland Rd Cleveland (44130) *(G-5772)*
J R Mead Industrial Contrs 614 891-4466
6606 Lake Of The Woods Pt Galena (43021) *(G-11160)*
J Rayl Transport Inc 330 940-1668
24881 Rockwell Dr Euclid (44117) *(G-10646)*
J Russell Construction 330 633-6462
180 Southwest Ave Tallmadge (44278) *(G-17479)*
J Rutledge Enterprises Inc 502 241-4100
3512 Spring Grove Ave Cincinnati (45223) *(G-3796)*
J S P A Inc 407 957-6664
2717 Burnaby Dr Columbus (43209) *(G-7851)*
J Schoen Enterprises Inc (PA) 419 536-0970
5056 Angola Rd Toledo (43615) *(G-17828)*
J T Adams Co 216 641-3290
4520 Willow Pkwy Cleveland (44125) *(G-5773)*
J T Eaton & Co Inc 330 425-7801
1393 Highland Rd Twinsburg (44087) *(G-18283)*
J T Express Inc 513 727-8185
1200 N Main St Monroe (45050) *(G-14570)*
J V Hansel Inc 330 716-0806
6055 Louise Ct Nw Warren (44481) *(G-18716)*
J V Janitorial Services Inc 216 749-1150
1230 E Schaaf Rd Ste 1 Cleveland (44131) *(G-5774)*
J W Didado Electric Inc 330 374-0070
1033 Kelly Ave Akron (44306) *(G-284)*
J W Enterprises Inc (PA) 740 774-4500
159 E Main St Chillicothe (45601) *(G-2796)*
J W Geopfert Co Inc 330 762-2293
1024 Home Ave Akron (44310) *(G-285)*
J W J Investments Inc 419 643-3161
800 Ambrose Dr Delphos (45833) *(G-10028)*
J Way Leasing Ltd 440 934-1020
1284 Miller Rd Avon (44011) *(G-887)*
J&B Sprafka Enterprises Inc (PA) 330 733-4212
1430 Goodyear Blvd Akron (44305) *(G-286)*
J&B Steel Contractors, West Chester *Also called J&B Steel Erectors Inc (G-18951)*
J&B Steel Erectors Inc 513 874-1722
9430 Sutton Pl West Chester (45011) *(G-18951)*
J&H Rnfrcing Strl Erectors Inc 740 355-0141
55 River Ave Portsmouth (45662) *(G-16151)*
J&J Precision Machine Ltd 330 923-5783
1474 Main St Cuyahoga Falls (44221) *(G-9103)*
J-C-R Tech Inc 937 783-2296
936 Cherry St Blanchester (45107) *(G-1488)*
J-Mak Industries, Columbus *Also called Panacea Products Corporation (G-8418)*
J-Trac Inc 419 524-3456
961 N Main St Mansfield (44903) *(G-13189)*
J-Vac Industries Inc 740 384-2155
202 S Pennsylvania Ave Wellston (45692) *(G-18850)*
J. Peterman, Blue Ash *Also called J Peterman Company LLC (G-1588)*
J.L.L., Brecksville *Also called Jones Lang Lsalle Americas Inc (G-1787)*
Jac-Lin Manor 419 994-5700
695 S Mount Vernon Ave Loudonville (44842) *(G-12957)*
Jack & Jill Babysitter Serv, Cincinnati *Also called Jack & Jill Babysitting Svc (G-3797)*
Jack & Jill Babysitting Svc 513 731-5261
6252 Beechmont Ave Apt 11 Cincinnati (45230) *(G-3797)*
Jack A Hamilton & Assoc Inc 740 968-4947
342 High St Flushing (43977) *(G-10980)*
Jack Cincinnati Casino LLC 513 252-0777
1000 Broadway St Cincinnati (45202) *(G-3798)*
Jack Conie & Sons Corp 614 291-5931
1340 Windsor Ave Columbus (43211) *(G-7852)*
Jack Cooper Transport Co Inc 440 949-2044
5211 Oster Rd Sheffield Village (44054) *(G-16736)*
Jack Entertainment, Cleveland *Also called Horseshoe Cleveland MGT LLC (G-5709)*
Jack Gibson Construction Co 330 394-5280
2460 Parkman Rd Nw Warren (44485) *(G-18717)*
Jack Gray 216 688-0466
8044 Montgomery Rd Cincinnati (45236) *(G-3799)*
Jack Matia Honda, Elyria *Also called Matia Motors Inc (G-10534)*
Jack Thistledown Racino LLC (PA) 216 662-8600
21501 Emery Rd Cleveland (44128) *(G-5775)*
Jack, The, Cincinnati *Also called Jack Gray (G-3799)*
Jackson Comfort Htg Coolg Sys, Northfield *Also called Jackson Comfort Systems Inc (G-15381)*
Jackson Comfort Systems Inc 330 468-3111
499 E Twinsburg Rd Northfield (44067) *(G-15381)*
Jackson Community YMCA, Massillon *Also called Y M C A Central Stark County (G-13736)*
Jackson County Board On Aging (PA) 740 286-2909
25 E Mound St Jackson (45640) *(G-12177)*
Jackson County Hlth Facilities 740 384-0722
142 Jenkins Memorial Rd Wellston (45692) *(G-18851)*
JACKSON COUNTY SENIOR CITIZENS, Jackson *Also called Jackson County Board On Aging (G-12177)*

ALPHABETIC

Jackson Hewitt Tax Service, Trotwood *Also called E T Financial Service Inc* **(G-18193)**
Jackson I-94 Ltd Partnership 614 793-2244
  6059 Frantz Rd Ste 205 Dublin (43017) **(G-10259)**
Jackson Kelly Pllc 330 252-9060
  17 S Main St 1 Akron (44308) **(G-287)**
Jackson Kohrman & Pll Krantz 216 696-8700
  1375 E 9th St Fl 29 Cleveland (44114) **(G-5776)**
JACKSON VINTON COMMUNITY ACTIO, Wellston *Also called Jackson-Vinton Cmnty Action* **(G-18852)**
Jackson-Vinton Cmnty Action (PA) 740 384-3722
  118 S New York Ave Wellston (45692) **(G-18852)**
Jaco Waterproofing LLC 513 738-0084
  4350 Wade Mill Rd Fairfield (45014) **(G-10739)**
Jacob Neal Salon, Columbus *Also called Salon Communication Services* **(G-8586)**
Jacob Real Estate Services 216 687-0500
  127 Public Sq Ste 2828 Cleveland (44114) **(G-5777)**
Jacobs Constructors Inc 419 226-1344
  1840 Buckeye Rd Gatew Lima (45804) **(G-12667)**
Jacobs Constructors Inc 513 595-7900
  1880 Waycross Rd Cincinnati (45240) **(G-3800)**
Jacobs Dwelling Nursing Home 740 824-3635
  25680 Bethlehem Township Coshocton (43812) **(G-9020)**
Jacobs Engineering Group Inc 513 595-7500
  1880 Waycross Rd Cincinnati (45240) **(G-3801)**
Jacobs Engineering Group Inc 513 595-7500
  1880 Waycross Rd Cincinnati (45240) **(G-3802)**
Jacobs Mechanical Co 513 681-6800
  4500 W Mitchell Ave Cincinnati (45232) **(G-3803)**
Jacobs Real Estate Services 216 514-9830
  1000 Eaton Blvd Beachwood (44122) **(G-1068)**
Jacobs Technology Inc 937 429-5056
  4027 Colonel Glenn Hwy Beavercreek Township (45431) **(G-1250)**
Jacobs Telephone Contrs Inc 614 527-8977
  3660 Parkway Ln Ste E Hilliard (43026) **(G-11780)**
Jacobson Warehouse Company Inc 614 314-1091
  3880 Groveport Rd Obetz (43207) **(G-15527)**
Jacobson Warehouse Company Inc 614 409-0003
  2450 Spiegel Dr Ste H Groveport (43125) **(G-11523)**
Jacobson Warehouse Company Inc 614 497-6300
  6600 Port Rd Ste 200 Groveport (43125) **(G-11524)**
Jacor LLC 330 441-4182
  1011 Lake Rd Medina (44256) **(G-13958)**
Jade Investments 330 425-3141
  2300 E Aurora Rd Twinsburg (44087) **(G-18284)**
Jade-Sterling Steel Co Inc (PA) 330 425-3141
  2300 E Aurora Rd Twinsburg (44087) **(G-18285)**
Jae Co 2, Westerville *Also called Mark Humrichouser* **(G-19184)**
Jaekle Group Inc 330 405-9353
  1410 Highland Rd E Macedonia (44056) **(G-13076)**
Jag Healthcare Inc 440 385-4370
  220 Buckingham Rd Rocky River (44116) **(G-16437)**
Jagi Clveland Independence LLC 216 524-8050
  6001 Rockside Rd Cleveland (44131) **(G-5778)**
Jagi Juno LLC (PA) 513 489-1955
  8534 E Kemper Rd Cincinnati (45249) **(G-3804)**
Jagi Springhill LLC 216 264-4190
  6060 Rockside Pl Independence (44131) **(G-12084)**
Jaguar Volvo, Canton *Also called Kempthorn Motors Inc* **(G-2365)**
Jainco International Inc 440 519-0100
  30405 Solon Rd Ste 9 Solon (44139) **(G-16863)**
Jaincotech, Solon *Also called Jainco International Inc* **(G-16863)**
Jake Sweeney Automotive Inc 513 782-2800
  33 W Kemper Rd Cincinnati (45246) **(G-3805)**
Jake Sweeney Body Shop 513 782-1100
  169 Northland Blvd Ste 1 Cincinnati (45246) **(G-3806)**
Jake Sweeney Chevrolet Imports, Cincinnati *Also called Jake Sweeney Body Shop* **(G-3806)**
James Advantage Funds 937 426-7640
  1349 Fairground Rd Xenia (45385) **(G-19913)**
James Air Cargo Inc 440 243-9095
  6519 Eastland Rd Ste 6 Cleveland (44142) **(G-5779)**
James B Oswald Company 330 723-3637
  5000 Foote Rd Medina (44256) **(G-13959)**
James C Sass Atty 419 843-3545
  226 N Main St Swanton (43558) **(G-17400)**
James Cancer Center, Columbus *Also called Ohio State University* **(G-8342)**
James D Egbert Optometrist (PA) 937 236-1770
  6557 Brandt Pike Huber Heights (45424) **(G-11955)**
James H Alvis Trucking Inc 513 623-8121
  9570 State Route 128 Harrison (45030) **(G-11671)**
James Hunt Construction Co Inc 513 721-0559
  1865 Summit Rd Cincinnati (45237) **(G-3807)**
James L Jacobson 937 223-1130
  40 N Main St Ste 2700 Dayton (45423) **(G-9523)**
James Lafontaine 740 474-5052
  25050 Us Highway 23 S Circleville (43113) **(G-4836)**
James Powers 614 566-9397
  340 E Town St Ste 8700 Columbus (43215) **(G-7853)**
James Ray Lozier 419 884-2656
  84 Foxcroft Rd Mansfield (44904) **(G-13190)**
James Recker 419 837-5378
  1446 Ottawa Rd Genoa (43430) **(G-11257)**
Janat Clemmons Center, Hamilton *Also called Butler County Bd of Mental RE* **(G-11567)**

Jancoa Janitorial Services Inc 513 351-7200
  5235 Montgomery Rd Cincinnati (45212) **(G-3808)**
Janell Inc (PA) 513 489-9111
  6130 Cornell Rd Blue Ash (45242) **(G-1589)**
Janell Concrete & Masonry Eqp, Blue Ash *Also called Janell Inc* **(G-1589)**
Jani-Source LLC 740 374-6298
  478 Bramblewood Hts Rd Marietta (45750) **(G-13340)**
Janik LLP (PA) 440 838-7600
  9200 S Hills Blvd Ste 300 Cleveland (44147) **(G-5780)**
Janiking, Cincinnati *Also called Jenkins Enterprises LLC* **(G-2857)**
Janitec Building Service, New Richmond *Also called Dave & Barb Enterprises Inc* **(G-14992)**
Janitorial Management Services, Greenville *Also called Ktm Enterprises Inc* **(G-11388)**
Janitorial Services Inc 216 341-8601
  4830 E 49th St Cleveland (44125) **(G-5781)**
Janitorial Support Services, Columbus *Also called Academic Support Services LLC* **(G-6857)**
Janotta & Herner, Monroeville *Also called Jhi Group Inc* **(G-14589)**
Janson Industries 330 455-7029
  1200 Garfield Ave Sw Canton (44706) **(G-2360)**
Jantech Building Services Inc 216 661-6102
  4963 Schaaf Ln Brooklyn Heights (44131) **(G-1872)**
Janus Hotel and Resort, Cincinnati *Also called Elbe Properties.* **(G-3485)**
Janus Hotels and Resorts Inc 513 631-8500
  6840 State Route 503 N Lewisburg (45338) **(G-12569)**
Jaro Transportation Svcs Inc (PA) 330 393-5659
  975 Post Rd Nw Warren (44483) **(G-18718)**
Jarrells Moving & Transport Co 330 952-1240
  1155 Industrial Pkwy Medina (44256) **(G-13960)**
Jarrells Moving & Transport Co (PA) 330 764-4333
  5076 Park Ave W Seville (44273) **(G-16686)**
Jarrett Logistics Systems Inc 330 682-0099
  1347 N Main St Orrville (44667) **(G-15636)**
Jarvis Mechanical Constrs Inc (PA) 513 831-0055
  803 Us Route 50 Milford (45150) **(G-14398)**
Jasar Recycling Inc 864 233-5421
  183 Edgeworth Ave East Palestine (44413) **(G-10420)**
Jason Wilson 937 604-8209
  5575 Ross Rd Tipp City (45371) **(G-17561)**
Javitch Block LLC 513 381-3051
  700 Walnut St Ste 300 Cincinnati (45202) **(G-3809)**
Javitch Block LLC (PA) 216 623-0000
  1100 Superior Ave E Fl 19 Cleveland (44114) **(G-5782)**
Javitch Block LLC 216 623-0000
  140 E Town St Ste 1250 Columbus (43215) **(G-7854)**
Jay Blue Communications 216 661-2828
  7500 Associate Ave Cleveland (44144) **(G-5783)**
Jay-Mac, Canton *Also called Young Truck Sales Inc* **(G-2541)**
JB Hunt Transport Svcs Inc 614 335-6681
  5435 Crosswind Dr Columbus (43228) **(G-7855)**
JB Management Inc 419 841-2596
  6540 W Central Ave Ste A Toledo (43617) **(G-17829)**
JB Roofing, Tiffin *Also called Tecta America Corp* **(G-17541)**
JB Steel, West Chester *Also called J & B Interests Inc* **(G-18950)**
Jbentley Studio & Spa LLC 614 790-8828
  8882 Moreland St Powell (43065) **(G-16198)**
Jbj Enterprises Inc 440 992-6051
  2450 W Prospect Rd Ashtabula (44004) **(G-743)**
Jbjs Acquisitions LLC 513 769-0393
  11939 Tramway Dr Cincinnati (45241) **(G-3810)**
JBK Group Inc (PA) 216 901-0000
  6001 Towpath Dr Cleveland (44125) **(G-5784)**
Jbm Cleaning, Massillon *Also called J B M Cleaning & Supply Co* **(G-13700)**
Jbo Holding Company 216 367-8787
  1100 Superior Ave E # 1500 Cleveland (44114) **(G-5785)**
JC Penney, Akron *Also called JC Penney Corporation Inc* **(G-288)**
JC Penney Corporation Inc 330 633-7700
  2000 Brittain Rd Ste 600 Akron (44310) **(G-288)**
Jc's 5 Star Outlet, Columbus *Also called Sb Capital Acquisitions LLC* **(G-8596)**
Jcc, Sylvania *Also called Jewish Cmnty Ctr of Toledo* **(G-17434)**
JD Music Tile Co 740 420-9611
  105 E Ohio St Circleville (43113) **(G-4837)**
Jdd Inc (PA) 216 464-8855
  3615 Superior Ave E 3104a Cleveland (44114) **(G-5786)**
Jdel Inc 614 436-2418
  200 W Nationwide Blvd # 1 Columbus (43215) **(G-7856)**
Jdi Group Inc 419 725-7161
  360 W Dussel Dr Maumee (43537) **(G-13805)**
Jdrm Engineering Inc 419 824-2400
  5604 Main St Ste 200 Sylvania (43560) **(G-17432)**
JE Carsten Company (PA) 330 794-4440
  7481 Herrick Park Dr Hudson (44236) **(G-11987)**
Jeanne B McCoy Comm (PA) 614 245-4701
  100 E Dublin Granville Rd New Albany (43054) **(G-14857)**
Jed Industries Inc 440 639-9973
  320 River St Grand River (44045) **(G-11332)**
Jedson Engineering Inc (PA) 513 965-5999
  705 Central Ave Cincinnati (45202) **(G-3811)**
Jee Foods 513 917-1712
  3371 Hamilton Cleves Rd Hamilton (45013) **(G-11617)**

(G-0000) Company's Geographic Section entry number

Jeff Creque Farms Inc 419 829-2941
9700 Sylvania Ave Sylvania (43560) *(G-17433)*
Jeff Plumber Inc (PA) 330 940-2600
1100 Tower Dr Akron (44305) *(G-289)*
Jeff Wyler Automotive Fmly Inc (PA) 513 752-7450
829 Eastgate South Dr Cincinnati (45245) *(G-2855)*
Jeff Wyler Ft Thomas Inc 513 752-7450
829 Eastgate South Dr Cincinnati (45245) *(G-2856)*
Jefferey Anderson Real Estate, Cincinnati *Also called Pfh Partners LLC (G-4239)*
Jeffers Crane Service Inc (HQ) 419 693-0421
5421 Navarre Ave Oregon (43616) *(G-15599)*
Jefferson Behavioral Hlth Sys (PA) 740 264-7751
1 Ross Park Blvd Ste 201 Steubenville (43952) *(G-17158)*
Jefferson Cnty Cmmnty Action (PA) 740 282-0971
114 N 4th St Steubenville (43952) *(G-17159)*
Jefferson Golf & Country Club 614 759-7500
7271 Jefferson Meadows Dr Blacklick (43004) *(G-1480)*
Jefferson Invstgtors Scurities 740 283-3681
1439 Sunset Blvd Steubenville (43952) *(G-17160)*
Jefferson Medical Co 216 443-9000
950 Main Ave Ste 500 Cleveland (44113) *(G-5787)*
Jeffrey Carr Construction Inc 330 879-5210
4164 Erie Ave Sw Massillon (44646) *(G-13701)*
Jeffrey W Smith 740 532-9000
411 Center St Ironton (45638) *(G-12159)*
Jeg's High-Performance Center, Delaware *Also called Jegs Automotive Inc (G-9990)*
Jegs Automotive Inc (PA) 614 294-5050
101 Jegs Pl Delaware (43015) *(G-9990)*
Jelly Bean Junction Lrng Ctr, Dublin *Also called Consolidated Learning Ctrs Inc (G-10189)*
Jenkins Enterprises LLC 513 752-7896
849 Locust Corner Rd Cincinnati (45245) *(G-2857)*
Jenkins Memorial Health Fcilty, Wellston *Also called Jackson County Hlth Facilities (G-18851)*
Jenne Inc 440 835-0040
33665 Chester Rd Avon (44011) *(G-888)*
Jennings Eliza Home Inc (HQ) 216 226-0282
10603 Detroit Ave Cleveland (44102) *(G-5788)*
Jennings Eliza Senior Care (PA) 216 226-5000
26376 John Rd Ofc C Olmsted Twp (44138) *(G-15536)*
Jennings & Associates 740 369-4426
26 Northwood Dr Delaware (43015) *(G-9991)*
Jennings Ctr For Older Adults 216 581-2900
10204 Granger Rd 232 Cleveland (44125) *(G-5789)*
Jennings Hall Nursing Facility, Cleveland *Also called Jennings Ctr For Older Adults (G-5789)*
Jennings Heating & Cooling, Akron *Also called Jennings Heating Company Inc (G-290)*
Jennings Heating Company Inc 330 784-1286
1671 E Market St Akron (44305) *(G-290)*
Jennite Co 419 531-1791
4694 W Bancroft St Toledo (43615) *(G-17830)*
Jergens Inc (PA) 216 486-5540
15700 S Waterloo Rd Cleveland (44110) *(G-5790)*
Jericho Investments Company, Etna *Also called William D Taylor Sr Inc (G-10621)*
Jerl Machine Inc 419 873-0270
11140 Avenue Rd Perrysburg (43551) *(G-15882)*
Jerry Haag Motors Inc 937 402-2090
1475 N High St Hillsboro (45133) *(G-11848)*
Jerry L Garver Branch, Canal Winchester *Also called Young Mens Christian Assoc (G-2129)*
Jersey Central Pwr & Light Co (HQ) 800 736-3402
76 S Main St Akron (44308) *(G-291)*
Jersey Central Pwr & Light Co 440 994-8271
2210 S Ridge W Ashtabula (44004) *(G-744)*
Jersey Central Pwr & Light Co 419 366-2915
2508 W Perkins Ave Sandusky (44870) *(G-16619)*
Jersey Central Pwr & Light Co 330 315-6713
395 Ghent Rd Rm 407 Fairlawn (44333) *(G-10836)*
Jersey Central Pwr & Light Co 937 327-1218
420 York St Springfield (45505) *(G-17056)*
Jersey Central Pwr & Light Co 740 537-6308
29503 State Route 7 Stratton (43961) *(G-17242)*
Jersey Central Pwr & Light Co 440 326-3222
6326 Lake Ave Elyria (44035) *(G-10520)*
Jersey Central Pwr & Light Co 216 432-6330
6800 S Marginal Rd Cleveland (44103) *(G-5791)*
Jersey Central Pwr & Light Co 440 546-8609
6896 Miller Rd Brecksville (44141) *(G-1785)*
Jersey Central Pwr & Light Co 330 336-9884
9681 Silvercreek Rd Wadsworth (44281) *(G-18601)*
Jersey Central Pwr & Light Co 216 479-1132
2423 Payne Ave Cleveland (44114) *(G-5792)*
Jersey Central Pwr & Light Co 440 953-7651
7755 Auburn Rd Painesville (44077) *(G-15716)*
Jersey Central Pwr & Light Co 419 321-7207
5501 N State Route 2 Oak Harbor (43449) *(G-15473)*
JES Foods Inc (PA) 216 883-8987
4733 Broadway Ave Cleveland (44127) *(G-5793)*
Jess Hauer Masonry Inc 513 521-2178
2400 W Kemper Rd Cincinnati (45231) *(G-3812)*
Jess Howard Electric Company 614 864-2167
6630 Taylor Rd Blacklick (43004) *(G-1481)*
Jet Express Inc (PA) 937 274-7033
4518 Webster St Dayton (45414) *(G-9524)*
Jet Machine & Manufacturing, Cincinnati *Also called Wulco Inc (G-4808)*

Jet Mintenance Consulting Corp 937 205-2406
1113 Airport Rd Ste Jmcc Wilmington (45177) *(G-19625)*
Jet Rubber Company 330 325-1821
4457 Tallmadge Rd Rootstown (44272) *(G-16450)*
Jetro Cash and Carry Entps LLC 216 525-0101
6150 Halle Dr Cleveland (44125) *(G-5794)*
Jetselect LLC (PA) 614 338-4380
4130 E 5th Ave Columbus (43219) *(G-7857)*
Jetson Engineering 513 965-5999
705 Central Ave Cincinnati (45202) *(G-3813)*
Jewish Cmnty Ctr of Toledo 419 885-4485
6465 Sylvania Ave Sylvania (43560) *(G-17434)*
JEWISH COMMUNITY CARE AT HOME, Cleveland *Also called Jewish Family Services Associa (G-5795)*
Jewish Community Center Inc 513 761-7500
8485 Ridge Rd Cincinnati (45236) *(G-3814)*
Jewish Community Ctr Cleveland 216 831-0700
26001 S Woodland Rd Beachwood (44122) *(G-1069)*
Jewish Day Schl Assoc Grtr Clv (PA) 216 763-1400
27601 Fairmount Blvd Pepper Pike (44124) *(G-15819)*
Jewish Edcatn Ctr of Cleveland 216 371-0446
2030 S Taylor Rd Cleveland Heights (44118) *(G-6720)*
Jewish Family Service of 513 469-1188
8487 Ridge Rd Cincinnati (45236) *(G-3815)*
Jewish Family Services 614 231-1890
1070 College Ave Ste A Columbus (43209) *(G-7858)*
Jewish Family Services Associa 216 292-3999
3659 Green Rd Ste 322 Cleveland (44122) *(G-5795)*
Jewish Family Services Associa 216 292-3999
24075 Commerce Park # 105 Cleveland (44122) *(G-5796)*
Jewish Fderation of Cincinnati 513 985-1500
8499 Ridge Rd Cincinnati (45236) *(G-3816)*
Jewish Fdrtion of Grter Dayton 937 837-2651
4911 Covenant House Dr Dayton (45426) *(G-9525)*
Jewish Home of Cincinnati 513 754-3100
5467 Cedar Village Dr Mason (45040) *(G-13603)*
Jewish Hospital LLC 513 686-3000
4777 E Galbraith Rd Cincinnati (45236) *(G-3817)*
Jewish Hospital Cincinnati Inc 513 686-3303
4777 E Galbraith Rd Cincinnati (45236) *(G-3818)*
Jh Instruments, Columbus *Also called Fcx Performance Inc (G-7567)*
Jhi Group Inc (PA) 419 465-4611
309 Monroe St Monroeville (44847) *(G-14589)*
Jiffy Products America Inc 440 282-2818
5401 Baumhart Rd Ste B Lorain (44053) *(G-12908)*
Jilco Industries Inc (PA) 330 698-0280
11234 Hackett Rd Kidron (44636) *(G-12306)*
Jim Brown Chevrolet Inc (PA) 440 255-5511
6877 Center St Mentor (44060) *(G-14065)*
Jim Brown Chevrolet Inc 440 255-5511
8490 Tyler Blvd Mentor (44060) *(G-14066)*
Jim Hayden Inc 513 563-8828
3154 Exon Ave Cincinnati (45241) *(G-3819)*
Jim Keim Ford 614 888-3333
5575 Keim Cir Columbus (43228) *(G-7859)*
Jim May Auto Sales & Svc Ctr, Findlay *Also called May Jim Auto Sales LLC (G-10940)*
Jimmy's Limousine Service, West Chester *Also called Jls Enterprises Inc (G-18952)*
Jims Electric Inc 440 327-8800
39221 Center Ridge Rd North Ridgeville (44039) *(G-15331)*
Jit Milrob, Aurora *Also called JIT Packaging Inc (G-831)*
JIT Packaging Inc (PA) 330 562-8080
250 Page Rd Aurora (44202) *(G-831)*
Jlt Packaging Cincinnati Inc (PA) 513 933-0250
1550 Kingsview Dr Lebanon (45036) *(G-12474)*
JJO Construction Inc 440 255-1515
9045 Osborne Dr Mentor (44060) *(G-14067)*
Jjr Solutions LLC 937 912-0288
3610 Pentagon Blvd # 220 Beavercreek (45431) *(G-1159)*
Jk-Co LLC 419 422-5240
16960 E State Route 12 Findlay (45840) *(G-10928)*
Jke, Westlake *Also called Jordan Kyli Enterprises Inc (G-19361)*
JKL Construction Inc 513 553-3333
620 Hamilton St New Richmond (45157) *(G-14995)*
JKL Development Company (PA) 937 390-0358
2101 E Home Rd Springfield (45503) *(G-17057)*
Jls Enterprises Inc 513 769-1888
7879 Cincinnati Dayton Rd West Chester (45069) *(G-18952)*
JLW Marketing LLC 513 260-8418
4240 Airport Rd Ste 106 Cincinnati (45226) *(G-3820)*
Jma Healthcare LLC 440 439-7976
24579 Broadway Ave Cleveland (44146) *(G-5797)*
Jmax Enterprises, Brecksville *Also called A Sainato Enterprises Inc (G-1765)*
Jmt, Columbus *Also called Johnson Mirmiran Thompson Inc (G-7864)*
JMw Welding and Mfg 330 484-2428
512 45th St Sw Canton (44706) *(G-2361)*
Jo Lin Health Center Inc 740 532-0860
1050 Clinton St Ironton (45638) *(G-12160)*
Jo Lynn Inc 419 994-3204
430 N Jefferson St Loudonville (44842) *(G-12958)*
Jo-Ann Fabrics & Crafts, Hudson *Also called Jo-Ann Stores Holdings Inc (G-11988)*
Jo-Ann Stores Holdings Inc (PA) 888 739-4120
5555 Darrow Rd Hudson (44236) *(G-11988)*

Job & Family Svcs Clinton Cnty, Wilmington *Also called Clinton County Dept Jobs/Fmly* (G-19612)

Job and Family Service, Chardon *Also called County of Geauga* (G-2691)

Job and Family Services, Norwalk *Also called County of Huron* (G-15431)

Job and Family Services Dept, Toledo *Also called County of Lucas* (G-17682)

Job Center LLC 440 499-1000
2100 N Ridge Rd Elyria (44035) (G-10521)

Job Service of Ohio, Akron *Also called Ohio Dept of Job & Fmly Svcs* (G-357)

Job1usa, Toledo *Also called Rumpf Corporation* (G-18014)

Job1usa Inc (HQ) 419 255-5005
701 Jefferson Ave Ste 202 Toledo (43604) (G-17831)

Jobar Enterprise Inc 216 561-5184
3361 E 147th St Cleveland (44120) (G-5798)

Jobes Henderson & Assoc Inc 740 344-5451
59 Grant St Newark (43055) (G-15045)

Jobs On Site, Mansfield *Also called Edge Plastics Inc* (G-13171)

Jobsohio 614 224-6446
41 S High St Columbus (43215) (G-7860)

Joe and Jill Lewis Inc 937 718-8829
716 N Broadway St Dayton (45402) (G-9526)

Joe Dickey Electric Inc 330 549-3976
180 W South Range Rd North Lima (44452) (G-15270)

Joe Dodge Kidd Inc 513 752-1804
1065 Ohio Pike Cincinnati (45245) (G-2858)

Joe Lasita & Sons Inc 513 241-5288
940 W 5th St Cincinnati (45203) (G-3821)

Joe McClelland Inc (PA) 740 452-3036
98 E La Salle St Zanesville (43701) (G-20321)

Joel Pomerene Memorial Hosp, Millersburg *Also called County of Holmes* (G-14471)

Joel Pomerene Memorial Hosp (PA) 330 674-1015
981 Wooster Rd Millersburg (44654) (G-14480)

Joes Ldscpg Beavercreek Inc 937 427-1133
2500 National Rd Beavercreek Township (45324) (G-1251)

Joey Boyle 216 273-8317
11 Garfield Ave Athens (45701) (G-787)

John A Becker Co (PA) 937 226-1341
1341 E 4th St Dayton (45402) (G-9527)

John A Becker Co 513 771-2550
11310 Mosteller Rd Cincinnati (45241) (G-3822)

John A Becker Co 614 272-8800
3825 Business Park Dr Columbus (43204) (G-7861)

John Atwood Inc 440 777-4147
28800 Lorain Rd North Olmsted (44070) (G-15294)

John Brown Trucking Inc 330 758-0841
8063 Southern Blvd Youngstown (44512) (G-20085)

John Deere Authorized Dealer, Alliance *Also called Cope Farm Equipment Inc* (G-528)

John Deere Authorized Dealer, Coldwater *Also called Lefeld Implement Inc* (G-6761)

John Deere Authorized Dealer, Georgetown *Also called Cahall Bros Inc* (G-11265)

John Deere Authorized Dealer, Bloomingdale *Also called Kuester Implement Company Inc* (G-1490)

John Deere Authorized Dealer, North Royalton *Also called Shearer Farm Inc* (G-15367)

John Deere Authorized Dealer, Wooster *Also called Shearer Farm Inc* (G-19768)

John Deere Authorized Dealer, Monroeville *Also called Shearer Farm Inc* (G-14590)

John Deere Authorized Dealer, Upper Sandusky *Also called Wyandot Tractor & Implement Co* (G-18417)

John Deere Authorized Dealer, Findlay *Also called Findlay Implement Co* (G-10903)

John Deere Authorized Dealer, Mentor *Also called Great Lakes Power Products Inc* (G-14056)

John Deere Authorized Dealer, Copley *Also called Shetlers Sales & Service Inc* (G-8975)

John Deere Authorized Dealer, Zanesville *Also called Ag-Pro Ohio LLC* (G-20273)

John Deere Authorized Dealer, Canton *Also called Western Branch Diesel Inc* (G-2534)

John Deere Authorized Dealer, Hartville *Also called Hartville Hardware Inc* (G-11688)

John Deere Authorized Dealer, Ontario *Also called Shearer Farm Inc* (G-15571)

John Deere Authorized Dealer, Cincinnati *Also called Murphy Tractor & Eqp Co Inc* (G-4086)

John Deere Authorized Dealer, Marietta *Also called E T B Ltd* (G-13326)

John Dellagnese & Assoc Inc 330 668-4000
4000 Embassy Pkwy Ste 400 Akron (44333) (G-292)

John Eramo & Sons Inc 614 777-0020
3670 Lacon Rd Hilliard (43026) (G-11781)

John F Gallagher Plumbing Co 440 946-4256
36360 Lakeland Blvd Eastlake (44095) (G-10430)

John F Stambaugh & Co 419 687-6833
5063 Bevier Rd Plymouth (44865) (G-16077)

John Glenn Columbus Intl Arprt, Columbus *Also called Columbus Regional Airport Auth* (G-7311)

John H Cooper Elec Contg Co 513 471-9900
1769 Elmore St Cincinnati (45223) (G-3823)

John H Kappus Co (PA) 216 367-6677
4755 W 150th St Cleveland (44135) (G-5799)

John O Bostock Jr 937 263-8540
5107 Midway Ave Dayton (45417) (G-9528)

John P Novatny Electric Co 330 630-8900
955 Evans Ave Akron (44305) (G-293)

John Rbrts Hair Studio Spa Inc (PA) 216 839-1430
673 Alpha Dr Ste F Cleveland (44143) (G-5800)

John S Knight Center, Akron *Also called Akron-Summit Convention* (G-62)

John Stewart Company 513 703-5412
6819 Montgomery Rd Cincinnati (45236) (G-3824)

John W. Schaeffer, M.d, Lorain *Also called North Ohio Heart Center* (G-12936)

John Zidian Co Inc (PA) 330 743-6050
574 Mcclurg Rd Youngstown (44512) (G-20086)

Johnny Appleseed Broadcasting 419 529-5900
2900 Park Ave W Ontario (44906) (G-15556)

Johnnys Carwash 513 474-6603
7901 Beechmont Ave Cincinnati (45255) (G-3825)

Johns Manville Corporation 419 784-7000
600 Jackson Ave Defiance (43512) (G-9921)

Johnson Adams & Protrouski 419 238-6251
1178 Professional Dr Van Wert (45891) (G-18481)

Johnson & Fischer Inc 614 276-8868
5303 Trabue Rd Columbus (43228) (G-7862)

Johnson Bros Greenwich, Greenwich *Also called Johnson Bros Rubber Co Inc* (G-11402)

Johnson Bros Rubber Co Inc (PA) 419 853-4122
42 W Buckeye St West Salem (44287) (G-19128)

Johnson Bros Rubber Co Inc 419 752-4814
41 Center St Greenwich (44837) (G-11402)

Johnson Cntrls SEC Sltions LLC 330 497-0850
5590 Lauby Rd Ste 6 Canton (44720) (G-2362)

Johnson Cntrls SEC Sltions LLC 440 262-1084
6650 W Snowville Rd Ste K Brecksville (44141) (G-1786)

Johnson Cntrls SEC Sltions LLC 561 988-3600
6175 Shamrock Ct Ste S Dublin (43016) (G-10260)

Johnson Cntrls SEC Sltions LLC 513 277-4966
4750 Wesley Ave Ste Q Cincinnati (45212) (G-3826)

Johnson Cntrls SEC Sltions LLC 419 243-8400
1722 Indian Wood Cir F Maumee (43537) (G-13806)

Johnson Contrls Authorized Dlr, Dayton *Also called Allied Supply Company Inc* (G-9216)

Johnson Contrls Authorized Dlr, Canton *Also called Morrow Control and Supply Inc* (G-2408)

Johnson Contrls Authorized Dlr, Akron *Also called Famous Industries Inc* (G-214)

Johnson Contrls Authorized Dlr, Cincinnati *Also called Habegger Corporation* (G-3668)

Johnson Contrls Authorized Dlr, Cincinnati *Also called Controls Center Inc* (G-3356)

Johnson Contrls Authorized Dlr, Northwood *Also called Yanfeng US Automotive* (G-15416)

Johnson Contrls Authorized Dlr, Toledo *Also called Famous Enterprises Inc* (G-17726)

Johnson Contrls Authorized Dlr, Akron *Also called Famous Distribution Inc* (G-211)

Johnson Controls 513 874-1227
9685 Cincinnati Dayton Rd West Chester (45069) (G-18953)

Johnson Controls 614 717-9079
6175 Shamrock Ct Ste S Dublin (43016) (G-10261)

Johnson Controls Inc 440 268-1160
17295 Foltz Pkwy Ste G Strongsville (44149) (G-17317)

Johnson Controls Inc 614 895-6600
835 Green Crest Dr Westerville (43081) (G-19266)

Johnson Controls Inc 330 270-4385
1044 N Meridian Rd Ste A Youngstown (44509) (G-20087)

Johnson Controls Inc 513 489-0950
7863 Palace Dr Cincinnati (45249) (G-3827)

Johnson Electric Supply Co (PA) 513 421-3700
1841 Riverside Dr Cincinnati (45202) (G-3828)

Johnson Howard International 513 401-8683
400 Glensprings Dr Cincinnati (45246) (G-3829)

Johnson Institutional MGT, Cincinnati *Also called Johnson Trust Co* (G-3830)

Johnson Mirmiran Thompson Inc 614 714-0270
2800 Corp Exchange Dr # 250 Columbus (43231) (G-7863)

Johnson Mirmiran Thompson Inc 614 714-0270
4600 Mcauley Pl Ste 150 Blue Ash (45242) (G-1590)

Johnson Mirmiran Thompson Inc 614 714-0270
2800 Corp Exchange Dr Columbus (43231) (G-7864)

Johnson Mirmiran Thompson Inc 614 714-0270
959 W Saint Clair Ave # 300 Cleveland (44113) (G-5801)

Johnson Trust Co 513 598-8859
3777 W Fork Rd Fl 2 Cincinnati (45247) (G-3830)

Joint Emergency Med Svc Inc 937 746-3471
201 E 6th St Franklin (45005) (G-11033)

Joint Implant Surgeons Inc 614 221-6331
7727 Smiths Mill Rd 200 New Albany (43054) (G-14858)

Joint Township Dst Mem Hosp 419 394-9959
1040 Hager St Saint Marys (45885) (G-16523)

Joint Township Dst Mem Hosp (PA) 419 394-3335
200 Saint Clair Ave Saint Marys (45885) (G-16524)

Joint Township Home Health 419 394-3335
1122 E Spring St Saint Marys (45885) (G-16525)

Jolly Tots Too Inc 614 471-0688
5511 N Hamilton Rd Columbus (43230) (G-7865)

Jon R Dvorak MD 419 872-7700
1090 W South Boundary St # 5 Perrysburg (43551) (G-15883)

Jonathon R Johnson & Assoc 216 932-6529
1489 Rydalmount Rd Cleveland (44118) (G-5802)

Jones & Henry Engineers Ltd (PA) 419 473-9611
3103 Executive Pkwy # 300 Toledo (43606) (G-17832)

Jones Cochenour & Co Inc (PA) 740 653-9581
125 W Mulberry St Lancaster (43130) (G-12407)

Jones Day Limited Partnership 614 469-3939
325 John H Mcconnell Blvd # 600 Columbus (43215) (G-7866)

Jones Day Limited Partnership (PA) 216 586-3939
901 Lakeside Ave E Ste 2 Cleveland (44114) (G-5803)

Jones Group Interiors Inc 330 253-9180
701 S Broadway St Ste 200 Akron (44311) (G-294)

ALPHABETIC SECTION Jtd Health Systems Inc

Jones Home, The, Cleveland *Also called Cleveland Municipal School Dst* ***(G-5279)***
Jones Lang Lsalle Americas Inc...216 447-5276
9921 Brecksville Rd Brecksville (44141) ***(G-1787)***
Jones Law Group LLC...614 545-9998
513 E Rich St Ste 100 Columbus (43215) ***(G-7867)***
Jones Metal Products Company...740 545-6341
305 N Center St West Lafayette (43845) ***(G-19114)***
Jones Potato Chip Co (PA)...419 529-9424
823 Bowman St Mansfield (44903) ***(G-13191)***
Jones Truck & Spring Repr Inc...614 443-4619
350 Frank Rd Columbus (43207) ***(G-7868)***
Jonle Co Inc...513 662-2282
4117 Bridgetown Rd Cincinnati (45211) ***(G-3831)***
Jonle Heating & Cooling, Cincinnati *Also called Jonle Co Inc* ***(G-3831)***
Jordan Kyli Enterprises Inc...216 256-3773
24650 Center Ridge Rd Westlake (44145) ***(G-19361)***
Jordan Realtors Inc...513 791-0281
7658 Montgomery Rd Cincinnati (45236) ***(G-3832)***
Joseph A Girgis MD Inc (PA)...440 930-6095
5334 Meadow Lane Ct Sheffield Village (44035) ***(G-16737)***
Joseph and Florence Mandel...216 464-4055
26500 Shaker Blvd Beachwood (44122) ***(G-1070)***
Joseph Chevrolet Oldsmobile Co...513 741-6700
8733 Colerain Ave Cincinnati (45251) ***(G-3833)***
Joseph Industries Inc...330 528-0091
10039 Aurora Hudson Rd Streetsboro (44241) ***(G-17258)***
Joseph Northland Porsche Audi, Cincinnati *Also called Cronins Inc* ***(G-3380)***
Joseph R Harrison Company Lpa...330 666-6900
36 37th St Sw Barberton (44203) ***(G-956)***
Joseph Russo...440 748-2690
12044 Island Rd Grafton (44044) ***(G-11317)***
Joseph S Mischell...513 542-9800
5109 Winton Rd Cincinnati (45232) ***(G-3834)***
Joseph Schmidt Realty Inc...330 225-6688
47 Pearl Rd Brunswick (44212) ***(G-1934)***
Joseph T Ryerson & Son Inc...513 896-4600
1108 Central Ave Hamilton (45011) ***(G-11618)***
Joseph Walker Inc...614 895-3840
8800 Lyra Dr Ste 600 Columbus (43240) ***(G-6817)***
Joseph, Mann & Creed, Twinsburg *Also called Media Collections Inc* ***(G-18297)***
Joshen Paper & Packaging Co (PA)...216 441-5600
5800 Grant Ave Cleveland (44105) ***(G-5804)***
Joshua Homes, Columbus *Also called Joshua Investment Company Inc* ***(G-7869)***
Joshua Investment Company Inc...614 428-5555
3065 Mcctcheon Crssing Dr Columbus (43219) ***(G-7869)***
Josina Lott Foundation...419 866-9013
120 S Holland Sylvania Rd Toledo (43615) ***(G-17833)***
Josina Lott Residential Home, Toledo *Also called Josina Lott Foundation* ***(G-17833)***
Joslin Diabetes Center Inc...937 401-7575
1989 Miambrg Ctrvl Rd 2 Ste Dayton (45459) ***(G-9529)***
Jostin Construction Inc...513 559-9390
2335 Florence Ave Cincinnati (45206) ***(G-3835)***
Joyce Buick Inc...419 529-3211
1400 Park Ave W Ontario (44906) ***(G-15557)***
Joyce Buick GMC of Mansfield, Ontario *Also called Joyce Buick Inc* ***(G-15557)***
JP Flooring Systems Inc...513 346-4300
9097 Union Centre Blvd West Chester (45069) ***(G-18954)***
JP Recovery Services Inc...440 331-2200
20220 Center Ridge Rd # 200 Rocky River (44116) ***(G-16438)***
Jpmorgan Chase Bank Nat Assn...614 759-8955
8445 E Main St Reynoldsburg (43068) ***(G-16311)***
Jpmorgan Chase Bank Nat Assn...614 248-2410
2025 Brice Rd Reynoldsburg (43068) ***(G-16312)***
Jpmorgan Chase Bank Nat Assn (HQ)...614 436-3055
1111 Polaris Pkwy Columbus (43240) ***(G-6818)***
Jpmorgan Chase Bank Nat Assn...614 476-1910
4000 Morse Xing Columbus (43219) ***(G-7870)***
Jpmorgan Chase Bank Nat Assn...513 221-1040
4805 Montgomery Rd Cincinnati (45212) ***(G-3836)***
Jpmorgan Chase Bank Nat Assn...513 826-2317
9019 Plainfield Rd Blue Ash (45236) ***(G-1591)***
Jpmorgan Chase Bank Nat Assn...419 358-4055
135 S Main St Bluffton (45817) ***(G-1692)***
Jpmorgan Chase Bank Nat Assn...216 781-2127
3415 Vision Dr Columbus (43219) ***(G-7871)***
Jpmorgan Chase Bank Nat Assn...740 423-4111
321 Main St Belpre (45714) ***(G-1405)***
Jpmorgan Chase Bank Nat Assn...614 248-5391
100 E Broad St Ste 2460 Columbus (43215) ***(G-7872)***
Jpmorgan Chase Bank Nat Assn...513 985-5120
822 Delta Ave Cincinnati (45226) ***(G-3837)***
Jpmorgan Chase Bank Nat Assn...513 784-0770
45 E 4th St Cincinnati (45202) ***(G-3838)***
Jpmorgan Chase Bank Nat Assn...740 363-8032
61 N Sandusky St Delaware (43015) ***(G-9992)***
Jpmorgan Chase Bank Nat Assn...330 364-7242
141 E High Ave New Philadelphia (44663) ***(G-14968)***
Jpmorgan Chase Bank Nat Assn...740 382-7362
165 W Center St Marion (43302) ***(G-13426)***
Jpmorgan Chase Bank Nat Assn...419 394-2358
125 W Spring St Saint Marys (45885) ***(G-16526)***
Jpmorgan Chase Bank Nat Assn...419 294-4944
335 N Sandusky Ave Upper Sandusky (43351) ***(G-18408)***
Jpmorgan Chase Bank Nat Assn...740 676-2671
3201 Belmont St Ste 100 Bellaire (43906) ***(G-1334)***
Jpmorgan Chase Bank Nat Assn...330 972-1905
2647 Bailey Rd Cuyahoga Falls (44221) ***(G-9104)***
Jpmorgan Chase Bank Nat Assn...513 985-5350
967 Lila Ave Milford (45150) ***(G-14399)***
Jpmorgan Chase Bank Nat Assn...513 595-6450
11745 Princeton Pike Cincinnati (45246) ***(G-3839)***
Jpmorgan Chase Bank Nat Assn...440 442-7800
5332 Mayfield Rd Cleveland (44124) ***(G-5805)***
Jpmorgan Chase Bank Nat Assn...330 972-1735
5638 Manchester Rd New Franklin (44319) ***(G-14910)***
Jpmorgan Chase Bank Nat Assn...330 287-5101
601 Portage Rd Wooster (44691) ***(G-19733)***
Jpmorgan Chase Bank Nat Assn...330 650-0476
136 W Streetsboro St Hudson (44236) ***(G-11989)***
Jpmorgan Chase Bank Nat Assn...440 352-5491
2772 N Ridge Rd Perry (44081) ***(G-15823)***
Jpmorgan Chase Bank Nat Assn...419 424-7570
1971 Broad Ave Findlay (45840) ***(G-10929)***
Jpmorgan Chase Bank Nat Assn...937 534-8218
950 Forrer Blvd Dayton (45420) ***(G-9530)***
Jpmorgan Chase Bank Nat Assn...843 679-3653
3415 Vision Dr Columbus (43219) ***(G-7873)***
Jpmorgan Chase Bank Nat Assn...330 325-7855
4000 Waterloo Rd Randolph (44265) ***(G-16231)***
Jpmorgan Chase Bank Nat Assn...330 287-5101
601 Portage Rd Wooster (44691) ***(G-19734)***
Jpmorgan Chase Bank Nat Assn...419 946-3015
16 N Main St Mount Gilead (43338) ***(G-14727)***
Jpmorgan Chase Bank Nat Assn...419 586-6668
205 W Market St Celina (45822) ***(G-2596)***
Jpmorgan Chase Bank Nat Assn...440 352-5969
30 S Park Pl Ste 100 Painesville (44077) ***(G-15717)***
Jpmorgan Chase Bank Nat Assn...330 545-2551
43 W Liberty St Girard (44420) ***(G-11290)***
Jpmorgan Chase Bank Nat Assn...440 286-6111
100 Center St Ste 100 # 100 Chardon (44024) ***(G-2699)***
Jpmorgan Chase Bank Nat Assn...330 972-1915
1805 Brittain Rd Akron (44310) ***(G-295)***
Jpmorgan Chase Bank Nat Assn...330 759-1750
3999 Belmont Ave Youngstown (44505) ***(G-20088)***
Jpmorgan Chase Bank Nat Assn...419 424-7512
500 S Main St Findlay (45840) ***(G-10930)***
Jpmorgan Chase Bank Nat Assn...614 248-5800
275 W Schrock Rd Westerville (43081) ***(G-19267)***
Jpmorgan Chase Bank Nat Assn...614 920-4182
6314 Gender Rd Canal Winchester (43110) ***(G-2111)***
Jpmorgan Chase Bank Nat Assn...614 834-3120
7915 Refugee Rd Pickerington (43147) ***(G-15960)***
Jpmorgan Chase Bank Nat Assn...614 853-2999
5684 W Broad St Galloway (43119) ***(G-11221)***
Jpmorgan Chase Bank Nat Assn...614 248-3315
4066 Powell Rd Powell (43065) ***(G-16199)***
Jpmorgan Chase Bank Nat Assn...740 657-8906
8681 Columbus Pike Lewis Center (43035) ***(G-12547)***
Jpmorgan Chase Bank Nat Assn...216 524-0600
7703 Broadview Rd Seven Hills (44131) ***(G-16676)***
Jpmorgan Chase Bank Nat Assn...740 374-2263
125 Putnam St Marietta (45750) ***(G-13341)***
Jpmorgan Chase Bank Nat Assn...614 248-7505
713 Brooksedge Plaza Dr Westerville (43081) ***(G-19268)***
Jpmorgan Chase Bank Nat Assn...614 248-5800
800 Brooksedge Blvd Westerville (43081) ***(G-19269)***
Jpmorgan Chase Bank Nat Assn...440 277-1038
1882 E 29th St Lorain (44055) ***(G-12909)***
Jpmorgan Chase Bank Nat Assn...419 739-3600
801 Defiance St Wapakoneta (45895) ***(G-18647)***
Jpmorgan Chase Bank Nat Assn...330 722-6626
3626 Medina Rd Medina (44256) ***(G-13961)***
Jpmorgan Chase Bank Nat Assn...614 248-2083
1199 Corrugated Way Columbus (43201) ***(G-7874)***
Jpmorgan Chase Bank Nat Assn...216 781-4437
1300 E 9th St Fl 13 Cleveland (44114) ***(G-5806)***
Jpmorgan High Yield Fund...614 248-7017
1111 Polaris Pkwy Columbus (43240) ***(G-6819)***
Jpmorgan Inv Advisors Inc (HQ)...614 248-5800
1111 Polaris Pkwy Columbus (43240) ***(G-6820)***
Jr Engineering Inc...330 848-0960
123 9th St Nw Barberton (44203) ***(G-957)***
JS Bova Excavating LLC...234 254-4040
235 State St Struthers (44471) ***(G-17365)***
JS Paris Excavating Inc...330 538-3048
12240 Commissioner Dr North Jackson (44451) ***(G-15247)***
Jsw Steel USA Ohio Inc...740 535-8172
1500 Commercial St Mingo Junction (43938) ***(G-14528)***
Jtc Contracting Inc...216 635-0745
7635 Hub Pkwy Ste C Cleveland (44125) ***(G-5807)***
Jtc Office Services, Cleveland *Also called Jtc Contracting Inc* ***(G-5807)***
Jtd Health Systems Inc...419 394-3335
200 Saint Clair Ave Saint Marys (45885) ***(G-16527)***

ALPHABETIC

Jtekt Auto Tenn Morristown 440 835-1000
29570 Clemens Rd Westlake (44145) ***(G-19362)***
Jtf Construction Inc 513 860-9835
4235 Muhlhauser Rd Fairfield (45014) ***(G-10740)***
Jti Transportation Inc 419 661-9360
5601 Cherry St Stony Ridge (43463) ***(G-17184)***
Jto Club Corp 440 352-1900
6011 Heisley Rd Mentor (44060) ***(G-14068)***
Jubilee Academy, Cleveland *Also called Chal-Ron LLC* ***(G-5166)***
Judson (PA) 216 791-2004
2181 Ambleside Dr Apt 411 Cleveland (44106) ***(G-5808)***
Judson 216 791-2555
1890 E 107th St Cleveland (44106) ***(G-5809)***
Judson Care Center Inc 513 662-5880
2373 Harrison Ave Cincinnati (45211) ***(G-3840)***
Judson Manor, Cleveland *Also called Judson* ***(G-5809)***
Judson Palmer Home Corp 419 422-9656
2911 N Main St Findlay (45840) ***(G-10931)***
JUDSON UNIVERSITY CIRCLE, Cleveland *Also called Judson* ***(G-5808)***
JUDSON VILLAGE, Cincinnati *Also called Baptist Home and Center* ***(G-3018)***
Judy Mills Company Inc (PA) 513 271-4241
3360 Red Bank Rd Cincinnati (45227) ***(G-3841)***
Juice Technologies Inc 800 518-5576
350 E 1st Ave Ste 210 Columbus (43201) ***(G-7875)***
Julian & Grube Inc 614 846-1899
333 County Line Rd W A Westerville (43082) ***(G-19176)***
Julian Speer Co 614 261-6331
5255 Sinclair Rd Columbus (43229) ***(G-7876)***
Julius Zorn Inc 330 923-4999
3690 Zorn Dr Cuyahoga Falls (44223) ***(G-9105)***
Jumplinecom Inc 614 859-1170
5000 Arlngton Centre Blvd Columbus (43220) ***(G-7877)***
Junior Achvment Mhning Vly Inc 330 539-5268
1601 Motor Inn Dr Ste 305 Girard (44420) ***(G-11291)***
Juniper Networks Inc 614 932-1432
545 Metro Pl S Ste 164 Dublin (43017) ***(G-10262)***
Jurus Stanley R Atty At Law 614 486-0297
1375 Dublin Rd Columbus (43215) ***(G-7878)***
Jurus Law Office, Columbus *Also called Jurus Stanley R Atty At Law* ***(G-7878)***
Just 4 Kidz Childcare 440 285-2221
13896 Gar Hwy Chardon (44024) ***(G-2700)***
Just Cheking Cash, Fairfield *Also called Southern Glazers Wine and Sp* ***(G-10786)***
Just In Time Care Inc 614 985-3555
5320 E Main St Ste 200 Columbus (43213) ***(G-7879)***
Just In Time Care Services, Columbus *Also called Just In Time Care Inc* ***(G-7879)***
Justice & Business Svcs LLC 740 423-5005
210 Florence St Belpre (45714) ***(G-1406)***
Justice & Co Inc 330 225-6000
2462 Pearl Rd Medina (44256) ***(G-13962)***
Juvenile Court Cnty Muskingum 740 453-0351
1860 East Pike Zanesville (43701) ***(G-20322)***
Juvenile Detention Center, Columbus *Also called Franklin Cnty Bd Commissioners* ***(G-7608)***
Juzo, Cuyahoga Falls *Also called Julius Zorn Inc* ***(G-9105)***
Jvc Sports Corp 330 726-1757
8249 South Ave Youngstown (44512) ***(G-20089)***
JWF Technologies Llc (PA) 513 769-9611
6820 Fairfield Bus Ctr Fairfield (45014) ***(G-10741)***
Jyg Innovations LLC 937 630-3858
6450 Poe Ave Ste 103 Dayton (45414) ***(G-9531)***
JZE Electric Inc (PA) 440 243-7600
6800 Eastland Rd Cleveland (44130) ***(G-5810)***
K & D Enterprises Inc 440 946-3600
4420 Sherwin Rd Ste 1 Willoughby (44094) ***(G-19531)***
K & K Interiors Inc 419 627-0039
2230 Superior St Sandusky (44870) ***(G-16620)***
K & L Floormasters LLC 330 493-0869
1518 Cadney St Ne Canton (44714) ***(G-2363)***
K & L Trucking Inc 419 822-3836
490 W Main St Delta (43515) ***(G-10046)***
K & M Construction Company 330 723-3681
230 E Smith Rd Medina (44256) ***(G-13963)***
K & M Contracting Ohio Inc 330 759-1090
5635 Sampson Dr Girard (44420) ***(G-11292)***
K & M International Inc (PA) 330 425-2550
1955 Midway Dr Ste A Twinsburg (44087) ***(G-18286)***
K & M Kleening Service Inc 614 737-3750
4429 Professional Pkwy Groveport (43125) ***(G-11525)***
K & M Tire Inc (PA) 419 695-1061
965 Spencerville Rd Delphos (45833) ***(G-10029)***
K & M Tire Inc 419 695-1060
502 N Main St Delphos (45833) ***(G-10030)***
K & P Trucking LLC 419 935-8646
3862 State Route 103 S Willard (44890) ***(G-19482)***
K & R Distributors Inc 937 864-5495
7606 Dayton Rd Fairborn (45324) ***(G-10677)***
K & W Roofing Inc 740 927-3122
8356 National Rd Sw Etna (43062) ***(G-10616)***
K - O - I Warehouse Inc 937 323-5585
622 W Main St Springfield (45504) ***(G-17058)***
K - O - I Warehouse Inc (HQ) 513 357-2400
2701 Spring Grove Ave Cincinnati (45225) ***(G-3842)***
K 100 Radio Station, Toledo *Also called Cumulus Media Inc* ***(G-17691)***
K A P C O, Kent *Also called Kent Adhesive Products Co* ***(G-12239)***
K Amalia Enterprises Inc 614 733-3800
8025 Corporate Blvd Plain City (43064) ***(G-16056)***
K and R, Fairlawn *Also called Kenneth Zerrusen* ***(G-10838)***
K and W Roofing, Etna *Also called K & W Roofing Inc* ***(G-10616)***
K C M Consulting, Toledo *Also called Knight Crockett Miller Ins* ***(G-17841)***
K Company Incorporated 330 773-5125
2234 S Arlington Rd Coventry Township (44319) ***(G-9037)***
K F T Inc 513 241-5910
726 Mehring Way Cincinnati (45203) ***(G-3843)***
K H F Inc 330 928-0694
3884 State Rd Cuyahoga Falls (44223) ***(G-9106)***
K Hovnanian Summit Homes LLC (HQ) 330 454-4048
2000 10th St Ne Canton (44705) ***(G-2364)***
K M & M 216 651-3333
9715 Clinton Rd Cleveland (44144) ***(G-5811)***
K M B Inc 330 889-3451
1306 State Route 88 Bristolville (44402) ***(G-1826)***
K M Clemens DDS Inc 419 228-4036
2115 Allentown Rd Ste C Lima (45805) ***(G-12668)***
K M I, Columbus *Also called Knowledge MGT Interactive Inc* ***(G-7919)***
K M T Service 614 777-7770
3786 Fishinger Blvd Hilliard (43026) ***(G-11782)***
K O I, Cincinnati *Also called KOI Enterprises Inc* ***(G-3886)***
K O I Auto Parts, Cincinnati *Also called K - O - I Warehouse Inc* ***(G-3842)***
K R Drenth Trucking Inc 708 983-6340
119 E Court St Cincinnati (45202) ***(G-3844)***
K S Bandag Inc 330 264-9237
737 Industrial Blvd Wooster (44691) ***(G-19735)***
K W Zellers & Son Inc 330 877-9371
13494 Duquette Ave Ne Hartville (44632) ***(G-11693)***
K West Group LLC 972 722-3874
8305 Fremont Pike Perrysburg (43551) ***(G-15884)***
K&D Group Inc (PA) 440 946-3600
4420 Sherwin Rd Ste 1 Willoughby (44094) ***(G-19532)***
K&K Technical Group Inc 513 202-1300
10053 Simonson Rd Ste 2 Harrison (45030) ***(G-11672)***
K-Limited Carrier Ltd (PA) 419 269-0002
131 Matzinger Rd Toledo (43612) ***(G-17834)***
K-M-S Industries Inc 440 243-6680
6519 Eastland Rd Ste 1 Brookpark (44142) ***(G-1899)***
K-Y Residential Coml Indus Dev 330 448-4055
505 Bedford Rd Se Brookfield (44403) ***(G-1852)***
K.M.S., Brookpark *Also called K-M-S Industries Inc* ***(G-1899)***
K4 Architecture LLC 513 455-5005
555 Gest St Cincinnati (45203) ***(G-3845)***
Ka Architecture, Seven Hills *Also called Nelson* ***(G-16677)***
KA Bergquist Inc (PA) 419 865-4196
1100 King Rd Toledo (43617) ***(G-17835)***
Kace Logistics LLC 419 273-3388
1515 Matzinger Rd Toledo (43612) ***(G-17836)***
Kademenos Wisehart Hines (PA) 419 524-6011
6 W 3rd St Ste 200 Mansfield (44902) ***(G-13192)***
Kaffenbarger Truck Eqp Co (PA) 937 845-3804
10100 Ballentine Pike New Carlisle (45344) ***(G-14892)***
Kaffenbarger Truck Eqp Co 513 772-6800
3260 E Kemper Rd Cincinnati (45241) ***(G-3846)***
Kahan & Kahan, Cleveland *Also called Shapiro Shapiro & Shapiro* ***(G-6404)***
Kaiser Consulting LLC 614 378-5361
818 Riverbend Ave Powell (43065) ***(G-16200)***
Kaiser Foundation Health Plan, Avon *Also called Healthspan Integrated Care* ***(G-885)***
Kaiser Foundation Health Plan, Cleveland *Also called Healthspan Integrated Care* ***(G-5675)***
Kaiser Foundation Health Plan, Cleveland *Also called Healthspan Integrated Care* ***(G-5676)***
Kaiser Foundation Health Plan, Cleveland *Also called Healthspan Integrated Care* ***(G-5678)***
Kaiser Foundation Health Plan, Brewster *Also called Healthspan Integrated Care* ***(G-1810)***
Kaiser Foundation Health Plan, Twinsburg *Also called Healthspan Integrated Care* ***(G-18278)***
Kaiser Foundation Health Plan, Hartville *Also called Healthspan Integrated Care* ***(G-11689)***
Kaiser Foundation Health Plan, Wadsworth *Also called Healthspan Integrated Care* ***(G-18597)***
Kaiser Foundation Health Plan, Lakewood *Also called Healthspan Integrated Care* ***(G-12346)***
Kaiser Foundation Hospitals 440 350-3614
7536 Fredle Dr Concord Township (44077) ***(G-8943)***
Kaiser Foundation Hospitals 330 633-8400
1260 Independence Ave Akron (44310) ***(G-296)***
Kaiser Foundation Hospitals 216 524-7377
36711 American Way Avon (44011) ***(G-889)***
Kaiser Foundation Hospitals 800 524-7377
10 Severance Cir Cleveland Heights (44118) ***(G-6721)***
Kaiser Foundation Hospitals 216 524-7377
5400 Lancaster Dr Brooklyn Heights (44131) ***(G-1873)***
Kaiser Foundation Hospitals 800 524-7377
4914 Portage Rd North Canton (44720) ***(G-15214)***
Kaiser Foundation Hospitals 800 524-7377
3443 Medina Rd Medina (44256) ***(G-13964)***
Kaiser Foundation Hospitals 800 524-7377
4055 Embassy Pkwy Ste 110 Fairlawn (44333) ***(G-10837)***

Kaiser Foundation Hospitals 800 524-7377
  7695 Mentor Ave Mentor (44060) *(G-14069)*
Kaiser Foundation Hospitals 800 524-7377
  2500 State Route 59 Kent (44240) *(G-12238)*
Kaiser Foundation Hospitals 216 524-7377
  20575 Ctr Ridgerd Ste 500 Rocky River (44116) *(G-16439)*
Kaiser Foundation Hospitals 800 524-7377
  5400 Lancaster Dr Brooklyn Heights (44131) *(G-1874)*
Kaiser Foundation Hospitals 216 524-7377
  17406 Royalton Rd Strongsville (44136) *(G-17318)*
Kaiser Foundation Hospitals 330 486-2800
  8920 Canyon Falls Blvd Twinsburg (44087) *(G-18287)*
Kaiser Foundation Hospitals 216 524-7377
  5105 S O M Center Rd Willoughby (44094) *(G-19533)*
Kaiser Logistics LLC 937 534-0213
  201 Lawton Ave Monroe (45050) *(G-14571)*
Kaiser Wells Pharmacy, Norwalk *Also called Kaiser-Wells Inc (G-15440)*
Kaiser-Wells Inc 419 668-7651
  251 Benedict Ave Norwalk (44857) *(G-15440)*
Kal Electric Inc 740 593-8720
  5265 Hebbardsville Rd Athens (45701) *(G-788)*
Kalahari Resort, Sandusky *Also called Lmn Development LLC (G-16623)*
Kallas Enterprises Inc 330 253-6893
  916 E Buchtel Ave Akron (44305) *(G-297)*
Kalmbach Pork Finishing LLC 419 294-3838
  7148 State Highway 199 Upper Sandusky (43351) *(G-18409)*
Kalypso LP (PA) 216 378-4290
  3659 Green Rd Ste 100 Beachwood (44122) *(G-1071)*
Kaman Corporation 330 468-1811
  7900 Empire Pkwy Macedonia (44056) *(G-13077)*
Kandy Kane Childrens Lrng Ctr (PA) 330 864-6642
  1010 S Hawkins Ave Akron (44320) *(G-298)*
Kandy Kane Chrstn Day Care Ctr, Akron *Also called Kandy Kane Childrens Lrng Ctr (G-298)*
Kangaroo Pouch Daycare Inc 440 473-4725
  488 Leverett Ln Cleveland (44143) *(G-5812)*
Kansas City Hardwood Corp 913 621-1975
  17717 Hilliard Rd Lakewood (44107) *(G-12349)*
KAO Collins Inc (PA) 513 948-9000
  1201 Edison Dr Cincinnati (45216) *(G-3847)*
Kaplan Trucking Company (PA) 216 341-3322
  8777 Rockside Rd Cleveland (44125) *(G-5813)*
Kapp Construction Inc 937 324-0134
  329 Mount Vernon Ave Springfield (45503) *(G-17059)*
Kappa House Corp of Delta 614 487-9461
  3220 Riverside Dr Ste A2 Upper Arlington (43221) *(G-18399)*
Kappa Kappa Gamma Foundation (PA) 614 228-6515
  6640 Riverside Dr Ste 200 Dublin (43017) *(G-10263)*
Kappa Kappa Gamma Fraternity, Dublin *Also called Kappa Kappa Gamma Foundation (G-10263)*
Kappus Company, Cleveland *Also called John H Kappus Co (G-5799)*
Kapstone Container Corporation 330 562-6111
  1450 S Chillicothe Rd Aurora (44202) *(G-832)*
Kapton Caulking & Building 440 526-0670
  6500 Harris Rd Cleveland (44147) *(G-5814)*
Karam & Simon Realty Inc 330 929-0707
  207 Portage Trail Ext W # 101 Cuyahoga Falls (44223) *(G-9107)*
Karamu House Inc (PA) 216 795-7070
  2355 E 89th St Cleveland (44106) *(G-5815)*
KARAMU THEATRE, Cleveland *Also called Karamu House Inc (G-5815)*
Karcher Group Inc 330 493-6141
  5590 Lauby Rd Ste 8 North Canton (44720) *(G-15215)*
Kare A Lot 614 298-8933
  1030 King Ave Columbus (43212) *(G-7880)*
Kare A Lot Child Care Center, Columbus *Also called Kare A Lot Infnt Tddlr Dev Ctr (G-7881)*
Kare A Lot Infnt Tddlr Dev Ctr 614 481-7532
  3164 Riverside Dr Columbus (43221) *(G-7881)*
Kare Medical Trnspt Svcs LLP 937 578-0263
  1002 Columbus Ave Marysville (43040) *(G-13509)*
Karen Funke Inc 216 464-4311
  27730 Chagrin Blvd Beachwood (44122) *(G-1072)*
Karl Hc LLC 614 846-5420
  5700 Karl Rd Columbus (43229) *(G-7882)*
Karlsberger Companies (PA) 614 461-9500
  99 E Main St Columbus (43215) *(G-7883)*
Karopa Incorporate 513 860-1616
  3987 Hmiltn Mddltwn Rd Hamilton (45011) *(G-11619)*
Karpinski Engineering Inc 614 430-9820
  8800 Lyra Dr Ste 530 Columbus (43240) *(G-6821)*
Karpinski Engineering Inc (PA) 216 391-3700
  3135 Euclid Ave Ste 200 Cleveland (44115) *(G-5816)*
Karrington Operating Co Inc (HQ) 614 324-5951
  919 Old Henderson Rd Columbus (43220) *(G-7884)*
Karst & Sons Inc 614 501-9530
  6496 Taylor Rd Sw Reynoldsburg (43068) *(G-16313)*
Kastle Electric Co LLC 937 254-2681
  4501 Kettering Blvd Moraine (45439) *(G-14666)*
Kastle Electric Company 937 254-2681
  4501 Kettering Blvd Moraine (45439) *(G-14667)*
Kastle Electric Company 513 360-2901
  100 Cart Path Dr Monroe (45050) *(G-14572)*
Kastle Technologies, Monroe *Also called Kastle Electric Company (G-14572)*

Kastle Technologies Co LLC (HQ) 513 360-2901
  100 Cart Path Dr Monroe (45050) *(G-14573)*
Kastle Technologies Co LLC 614 433-9860
  185-H Huntley Rd Columbus (43229) *(G-7885)*
Kathleen K Karol MD 419 878-7992
  2865 N Reynolds Rd # 170 Toledo (43615) *(G-17837)*
Kathman Electric Co Inc 513 353-3365
  8969 Harrison Pike Cleves (45002) *(G-6729)*
Katz Teller, Cincinnati *Also called Katz Teller Brant Hild Co Lpa (G-3848)*
Katz Teller Brant Hild Co Lpa 513 721-4532
  255 E 5th St Fl 24 Cincinnati (45202) *(G-3848)*
Kaufman Container Company (PA) 216 898-2000
  1000 Keystone Pkwy # 100 Cleveland (44135) *(G-5817)*
Kaval-Levine Management Co 440 944-5402
  34500 Chardon Rd Ste 5 Willoughby Hills (44094) *(G-19590)*
Kbec Sugarcreek Health Center, Dayton *Also called Kettering Medical Center (G-9540)*
Kcbs LLC 513 421-9422
  7800 E Kemper Rd Ste 160 Cincinnati (45249) *(G-3849)*
Keaney Investment, Dayton *Also called Kig Enterprises LLC (G-9544)*
Keating Muething & Klekamp Pll (PA) 513 579-6400
  1 E 4th St Ste 1400 Cincinnati (45202) *(G-3850)*
Keebler Hall, Akron *Also called Community Support Services Inc (G-155)*
Keen & Cross Envmtl Svcs Inc 513 674-1700
  504 Northland Blvd Cincinnati (45240) *(G-3851)*
Kegler Brown Hl Ritter Co Lpa (PA) 614 462-5400
  65 E State St Ste 1800 Columbus (43215) *(G-7886)*
Kegler Brown Hl Ritter Co Lpa 216 586-6650
  600 Superior Ave E # 2500 Cleveland (44114) *(G-5818)*
Keidel Supply Company Inc (PA) 513 351-1600
  1150 Tennessee Ave Cincinnati (45229) *(G-3852)*
Keihin Thermal Tech Amer Inc 740 869-3000
  10500 Oday Harrison Rd Mount Sterling (43143) *(G-14745)*
Keim Concrete LLC 330 264-5313
  4175 W Old Lincoln Way Wooster (44691) *(G-19736)*
Keim Lumber Company 330 893-2251
  State Rte 557 Baltic (43804) *(G-935)*
Keim, Jim Ford Sales, Columbus *Also called Jim Keim Ford (G-7859)*
Keith D Weiner & Assoc Lpa, Cleveland *Also called Weiner Keith D Co L P A Inc (G-6659)*
Keithley Instruments LLC (HQ) 440 248-0400
  28775 Aurora Rd Solon (44139) *(G-16864)*
Keithley Instruments Intl Corp 440 248-0400
  28775 Aurora Rd Cleveland (44139) *(G-5819)*
Kelchner Inc (HQ) 937 704-9890
  50 Advanced Dr Springboro (45066) *(G-16971)*
Keller Farms Landscape & Nurs, Columbus *Also called Keller Group Limited (G-7887)*
Keller Group Limited 614 866-9551
  3909 Groves Rd Columbus (43232) *(G-7887)*
Keller Logistics Group Inc 419 784-4805
  24862 Elliott Rd Ste 101 Defiance (43512) *(G-9922)*
Keller Logistics Group Inc (PA) 866 276-9486
  24862 Elliott Rd Ste 101 Defiance (43512) *(G-9923)*
Keller Ochs Koch Inc 419 332-8288
  416 S Arch St Fremont (43420) *(G-11082)*
Keller Warehousing & Dist LLC 419 784-4805
  1160 Carpenter Rd Defiance (43512) *(G-9924)*
Keller Williams Advisors LLC 513 766-9200
  3505 Columbia Pkwy # 125 Cincinnati (45226) *(G-3853)*
Keller Williams Advisory Rlty 513 372-6500
  8276 Beechmont Ave Cincinnati (45255) *(G-3854)*
Keller Williams Classic Pro 614 451-8500
  1510 W Lane Ave Columbus (43221) *(G-7888)*
Keller Williams Realtors, Beachwood *Also called Murwood Real Estate Group LLC (G-1085)*
Keller Williams Rlty M Walker 330 571-2020
  3589 Darrow Rd Stow (44224) *(G-17215)*
Kellermyer Bergensons Svcs LLC (PA) 419 867-4300
  1575 Henthorne Dr Maumee (43537) *(G-13807)*
Kelley & Ferraro LLP 216 575-0777
  950 Main Ave Ste 1300 Cleveland (44113) *(G-5820)*
Kelley Brothers Roofing Inc 513 829-7717
  4905 Factory Dr Fairfield (45014) *(G-10742)*
Kelley Companies 330 668-6100
  190 Montrose West Ave # 200 Copley (44321) *(G-8967)*
Kelley Steel Erectors Inc (PA) 440 232-1573
  7220 Division St Cleveland (44146) *(G-5821)*
Kelleys Isle Ferry Boat Lines 419 798-9763
  510 W Main St Marblehead (43440) *(G-13301)*
Kelli Woods Management Inc 419 478-1200
  4708 Angola Rd Toledo (43615) *(G-17838)*
Kellison & Co (PA) 216 464-5160
  4925 Galaxy Pkwy Ste U Cleveland (44128) *(G-5822)*
Kelly Farrish Lpa 513 621-8700
  810 Sycamore St Fl 6 Cincinnati (45202) *(G-3855)*
KElly Youth Services Inc 513 761-0700
  800 Compton Rd Unit 11 Cincinnati (45231) *(G-3856)*
Kemba Credit Union Inc (PA) 513 762-5070
  8763 Union Centre Blvd # 101 West Chester (45069) *(G-18955)*
Kemba Financial Credit Un Inc 614 235-2395
  4311 N High St Columbus (43214) *(G-7889)*
Kemba Financial Credit Union 614 235-2395
  4220 E Broad St Columbus (43213) *(G-7890)*
Kemper Company 440 846-1100
  10890 Prospect Rd Strongsville (44149) *(G-17319)*

A L P H A B E T I C

Kemper House of Strongsville, Strongsville Also called Kemper Company (G-17319)

Kemper Insurance, Canton Also called Sirak-Moore Insurance Agcy Inc (G-2478)

Kemper Shuttle Services, Cincinnati Also called Universal Work and Power LLC (G-4696)

Kempthorn Motors Inc (PA) 800 451-3877
1449 Cleveland Ave Nw Canton (44703) (G-2365)

Kempthorn Motors Inc 330 452-6511
1449 Cleveland Ave Nw Canton (44703) (G-2366)

Kemron Environmental Svcs Inc 740 373-4071
2343 State Route 821 Marietta (45750) (G-13342)

Ken Harper 740 439-4452
60772 Southgate Rd Byesville (43723) (G-2025)

Ken Heiberger Paving Inc 614 837-0290
458 W Waterloo St Canal Winchester (43110) (G-2112)

Ken Miller Supply Inc 330 264-9146
1537 Blachleyville Rd Wooster (44691) (G-19737)

Ken Neyer Plumbing Inc 513 353-3311
4895 Hamilton Cleves Rd Cleves (45002) (G-6730)

Kenakore Solutions, Perrysburg Also called TRT Management Corporation (G-15927)

Kenan Advantage Group Inc (PA) 800 969-5419
4366 Mount Pleasant St Nw North Canton (44720) (G-15216)

Kencor Properties Inc 513 984-3870
7565 Kenwood Rd Ste 100 Cincinnati (45236) (G-3857)

Kenda USA, Reynoldsburg Also called American Kenda Rbr Indus Ltd (G-16283)

Kendal At Granville 740 321-0400
2158 Columbus Rd Granville (43023) (G-11344)

Kendal At Oberlin 440 775-0094
600 Kendal Dr Oberlin (44074) (G-15506)

Kendal Home Care, Chillicothe Also called Khc Inc (G-2797)

Kendall Holdings Ltd (PA) 614 486-4750
2111 Builders Pl Columbus (43204) (G-7891)

Kendis & Associates Co Lpa 216 579-1818
614 W Superior Ave # 1500 Cleveland (44113) (G-5823)

Kendle International Inc 513 763-1414
441 Vine St Ste 500 Cincinnati (45202) (G-3858)

Kendrick-Mollenauer Pntg Co 614 443-7037
1099 Stimmel Rd Columbus (43223) (G-7892)

Kenexis Consulting Corporation 614 451-7031
3366 Riverside Dr Ste 200 Upper Arlington (43221) (G-18400)

Kenmar Landscaping Company, Medina Also called Kenmar Lawn & Grdn Care Co
LLC (G-13965)

Kenmar Lawn & Grdn Care Co LLC 330 239-2924
3665 Ridge Rd Medina (44256) (G-13965)

Kenmarc Electrical Contractors, Cincinnati Also called Kenmarc Inc (G-3859)

Kenmarc Inc 513 541-2791
1055 Heywood St Cincinnati (45225) (G-3859)

Kenmore Construction Co Inc (PA) 330 762-8936
700 Home Ave Akron (44310) (G-299)

Kenmore Construction Co Inc 330 832-8888
9500 Forty Corners Rd Nw Massillon (44647) (G-13702)

Kenmore Research Company 330 297-1407
935 N Freedom St Ravenna (44266) (G-16248)

Kenn-Feld Group LLC (PA) 419 678-2375
5228 State Route 118 Coldwater (45828) (G-6760)

Kennedy Graphics, Cleveland Also called Kennedy Mint Inc (G-5824)

Kennedy Group Enterprises Inc 440 879-0078
13370 Prospect Rd 2c Strongsville (44149) (G-17320)

Kennedy Mint Inc 440 572-3222
12102 Pearl Rd Rear Cleveland (44136) (G-5824)

Kenneth G Myers Cnstr Co Inc 419 639-2051
201 Smith St Green Springs (44836) (G-11354)

Kenneth Zerrusen 330 869-9007
3412 W Market St Fairlawn (44333) (G-10838)

Kenneth's Design Group, Columbus Also called Kenneths Hair Salons & Day Sp (G-7893)

Kenneths Hair Salons & Day Sp (PA) 614 457-7712
5151 Reed Rd Ste 250b Columbus (43220) (G-7893)

Kenny Obayashi Joint Venture V 703 969-0611
144 Cuyahoga St Akron (44304) (G-300)

Kenoil Inc 330 262-1144
1537 Blachleyville Rd Wooster (44691) (G-19738)

Kenosha Beef International Ltd 614 771-1330
1821 Dividend Dr Columbus (43228) (G-7894)

Kens Beverage Inc 513 874-8200
3219 Homeward Way Fairfield (45014) (G-10743)

Kens Flower Shop Inc 419 841-9590
140 W South Boundary St Perrysburg (43551) (G-15885)

Kensington Care Center, Aurora Also called Anna Maria of Aurora Inc (G-815)

Kensington Place Inc 614 252-5276
1001 Parkview Blvd Columbus (43219) (G-7895)

Kensington Plant, Kensington Also called M3 Midstream LLC (G-12210)

Kent Adhesive Products Co 330 678-1626
1000 Cherry St Kent (44240) (G-12239)

Kent Automotive Inc 330 678-5520
1080 W Main St Kent (44240) (G-12240)

Kent Healthcare Center, Kent Also called Fairchild MD Leasing Co LLC (G-12232)

Kent Lincoln-Mercury Sales, Kent Also called Kent Automotive Inc (G-12240)

Kent Medical Offices, Kent Also called Kaiser Foundation Hospitals (G-12238)

Kent Place Housing 614 942-2020
1414 Gault St Columbus (43205) (G-7896)

Kent Ridge At Golden Pond Ltd 330 677-4040
5241 Sunnybrook Rd Kent (44240) (G-12241)

Kent State University 330 672-2607
237 Schwartz Ste 237 Kent (44242) (G-12242)

Kent State University 330 672-3114
1613 E Summit St Kent (44240) (G-12243)

Kenthworth of Dayton, Dayton Also called Palmer Trucks Inc (G-9683)

Kenton Auto and Truck Wrecking 419 673-8234
13188 Us Highway 68 Kenton (43326) (G-12283)

Kenton Community Health Center, Kenton Also called Health Partners Western
Ohio (G-12282)

Kenton Motor Sales, Kenton Also called Kenton Auto and Truck Wrecking (G-12283)

Kentucky Heart Institute Inc 740 353-8100
2001 Scioto Trl Ste 200 Portsmouth (45662) (G-16152)

Kentucky Window Cleaning, Tipp City Also called Ohio Window Cleaning Inc (G-17563)

Kenwood Country Club Inc 513 527-3590
6501 Kenwood Rd Cincinnati (45243) (G-3860)

Kenwood Management, Cincinnati Also called Urban Retail Properties LLC (G-4736)

Kenwood Office, Cincinnati Also called Sibcy Cline Inc (G-4474)

Kenwood Ter Hlth Care Ctr Inc 513 793-2255
7450 Keller Rd Cincinnati (45243) (G-3861)

Kenwood Terrace Care Center, Cincinnati Also called Kenwood Ter Hlth Care Ctr
Inc (G-3861)

Kenworth of Cincinnati Inc 513 771-5831
65 Partnership Way Cincinnati (45241) (G-3862)

Kenworth Truck Co, Chillicothe Also called Rumpke/Kenworth Contract (G-2824)

Kenyon Co, Coshocton Also called Novelty Advertising Co Inc (G-9024)

Kenyon College 740 427-2202
100 W Wegan St Gambier (43022) (G-11225)

Kenyon Inn, Gambier Also called Kenyon College (G-11225)

Kerkan Roofing Inc 513 821-0556
721 W Wyoming Ave Cincinnati (45215) (G-3863)

Kerns Chevrolet Buick GMC, Celina Also called Kerns Chevrolet-Buick-Gmc Inc (G-2597)

Kerns Chevrolet-Buick-Gmc Inc 419 586-5131
218 S Walnut St Celina (45822) (G-2597)

Kerr House Inc 419 832-1733
17777 Beaver St Grand Rapids (43522) (G-11327)

Kerrington Health Systems Inc 513 863-0360
2923 Hamilton Mason Rd Fairfield Township (45011) (G-10811)

Kerry Ford Inc (PA) 513 671-6400
155 W Kemper Rd Cincinnati (45246) (G-3864)

Kerry Mitsubishi, Cincinnati Also called Kerry Ford Inc (G-3864)

Kessler Heating & Cooling 614 837-9961
9793 Basil Western Rd Nw Canal Winchester (43110) (G-2113)

Kessler Outdoor Advertising, Zanesville Also called Kessler Sign Company (G-20323)

Kessler Sign Company (PA) 740 453-0668
2669 National Rd Zanesville (43701) (G-20323)

Kettcor Inc 937 458-4949
4301 Lyons Rd Miamisburg (45342) (G-14178)

Kettering Adventist Healthcare 937 426-0049
2510 Commons Blvd Ste 100 Beavercreek (45431) (G-1160)

Kettering Adventist Healthcare 937 534-4651
5350 Lamme Rd Moraine (45439) (G-14668)

Kettering Adventist Healthcare 937 298-3399
3533 Southern Blvd Kettering (45429) (G-12294)

Kettering Adventist Healthcare 937 878-8644
1045 Channingway Dr Fairborn (45324) (G-10678)

Kettering Adventist Healthcare 937 401-6306
1989 Miamisbg Cntrvll Rd Centerville (45459) (G-2629)

Kettering Adventist Healthcare 937 294-1658
1079 W Stroop Rd Dayton (45429) (G-9532)

Kettering Adventist Healthcare 937 298-4331
3965 Southern Blvd Dayton (45429) (G-9533)

Kettering Adventist Healthcare 937 762-1361
1 Prestige Pl Miamisburg (45342) (G-14179)

Kettering Adventist Healthcare (PA) 937 298-4331
3535 Southern Blvd Dayton (45429) (G-9534)

Kettering Adventist Healthcare 937 395-8816
2110 Leiter Rd Miamisburg (45342) (G-14180)

Kettering Anesthesia Assoc Inc 937 298-4331
3533 Sthern Blvd Ste 5200 Dayton (45429) (G-9535)

Kettering Animal Hospital Inc 937 294-5211
1600 Delco Park Dr Dayton (45420) (G-9536)

Kettering City School District 937 297-1990
2636 Wilmington Pike Dayton (45419) (G-9537)

Kettering City School District 937 499-1770
2640 Wilmington Pike Dayton (45419) (G-9538)

Kettering College Medical Art, Dayton Also called Kettering Medical Center (G-9539)

Kettering Health Network, Kettering Also called Kettering Adventist Healthcare (G-12294)

KETTERING HEALTH NETWORK, Miamisburg Also called Greene Memorial Hosp Svcs
Inc (G-14174)

Kettering Health Network, Miamisburg Also called Kettering Adventist Healthcare (G-14179)

KETTERING HEALTH NETWORK, Dayton Also called Kettering Adventist
Healthcare (G-9534)

Kettering Health Network, Dayton Also called Kettering Medical Center (G-9541)

Kettering Health Network Khn, Miamisburg Also called Kettering Adventist
Healthcare (G-14180)

Kettering Hospital Youth Svcs, Moraine Also called Kettering Adventist Healthcare (G-14668)

Kettering Medical Center 937 702-4000
3535 Pentagon Park Blvd Beavercreek (45431) (G-1161)

Kettering Medical Center (HQ)......937 298-4331
3535 Southern Blvd Kettering (45429) ***(G-12295)***
Kettering Medical Center......937 866-0551
4000 Mmsburg Cntrville Rd Miamisburg (45342) ***(G-14181)***
Kettering Medical Center......937 298-4331
3535 Southern Blvd Dayton (45429) ***(G-9539)***
Kettering Medical Center......937 866-2984
317 Sycamore Glen Dr Ofc Miamisburg (45342) ***(G-14182)***
Kettering Medical Center......937 299-0099
580 Lincoln Park Blvd # 200 Dayton (45429) ***(G-9540)***
Kettering Medical Center......937 384-8750
1251 E Dorothy Ln Dayton (45419) ***(G-9541)***
Kettering Monogramming, Dayton *Also called Zimmer Enterprises Inc* ***(G-9899)***
Kettering Recreation Center......937 296-2587
2900 Glengarry Dr Dayton (45420) ***(G-9542)***
Kettering School Maintainence, Dayton *Also called Kettering City School District* ***(G-9537)***
Kettering Tennis Center......937 434-6602
4565 Gateway Cir Dayton (45440) ***(G-9543)***
Keuchel & Associates Inc......330 945-9455
175 Muffin Ln Cuyahoga Falls (44223) ***(G-9108)***
Kevin C McDonnell MD......330 344-6401
224 W Exchange St Ste 220 Akron (44302) ***(G-301)***
Kevin D Arnold, Columbus *Also called Center For Cognitive and Beh* ***(G-7151)***
Kevin Kennedy Associates Inc......317 536-7000
275 Outerbelt St Columbus (43213) ***(G-7897)***
Key Blue Prints Inc (PA)......614 228-3285
195 E Livingston Ave Columbus (43215) ***(G-7898)***
Key Career Place......216 987-3029
2415 Woodland Ave Cleveland (44115) ***(G-5825)***
Key Color, Columbus *Also called Key Blue Prints Inc* ***(G-7898)***
Key II Security Inc......937 339-8530
110 W Main St Troy (45373) ***(G-18209)***
Key Office Services......419 747-9749
1999 Leppo Rd Mansfield (44903) ***(G-13193)***
Key Realty Ltd......419 270-7445
130 Fountain Dr Holland (43528) ***(G-11891)***
Keybanc Capital Markets Inc (HQ)......800 553-2240
127 Public Sq Cleveland (44114) ***(G-5826)***
Keybank National Association (HQ)......800 539-2968
127 Public Sq Ste 5600 Cleveland (44114) ***(G-5827)***
Keybank National Association......216 689-8481
100 Public Sq Ste 600 Cleveland (44113) ***(G-5828)***
Keybank National Association......216 813-0000
4910 Tiedeman Rd Cleveland (44144) ***(G-5829)***
Keybridge Medical Revenue MGT, Lima *Also called General Audit Corp* ***(G-12642)***
Keysource Acquisition LLC......513 469-7881
7820 Palace Dr Cincinnati (45249) ***(G-3865)***
Keysource Medical, Cincinnati *Also called Keysource Acquisition LLC* ***(G-3865)***
Keystone Automotive Inds Inc......513 961-5500
2831 Stanton Ave Cincinnati (45206) ***(G-3866)***
Keystone Automotive Inds Inc......330 759-8019
1282 Trumbull Ave Ste C Girard (44420) ***(G-11293)***
Keystone Business Solutions, Akron *Also called Keystone Technology Cons* ***(G-302)***
Keystone Foods LLC......419 843-3009
4763 High Oaks Blvd Toledo (43623) ***(G-17839)***
Keystone Freight Corp......614 542-0320
2545 Parsons Ave Columbus (43207) ***(G-7899)***
Keystone Technology Cons......330 666-6200
787 Wye Rd Akron (44333) ***(G-302)***
Keyw Corporation......937 702-9512
1415 Research Park Dr Beavercreek (45432) ***(G-1162)***
Kf Construction and Excvtg LLC......419 547-7555
220 Norwest St Clyde (43410) ***(G-6747)***
KF Express LLC......614 258-8858
10440 Delwood Pl Powell (43065) ***(G-16201)***
Kforce Inc......614 436-4027
200 E Campus View Blvd # 225 Columbus (43235) ***(G-7900)***
Kforce Inc......216 643-8141
3 Summit Park Dr Ste 550 Independence (44131) ***(G-12085)***
Kgbo Holdings Inc (PA)......513 831-2600
4289 Ivy Pointe Blvd Cincinnati (45245) ***(G-2859)***
Kgk Gardening Design Corp......330 656-1709
1975 Norton Rd Hudson (44236) ***(G-11990)***
Khc Inc......740 775-5463
24 Star Dr Chillicothe (45601) ***(G-2797)***
Khempco Bldg Sup Co Ltd Partnr (PA)......740 549-0465
130 Johnson Dr Delaware (43015) ***(G-9993)***
Khm Consulting Inc......330 460-5635
1152 Pearl Rd Brunswick (44212) ***(G-1935)***
Khm Travel Group, Brunswick *Also called Khm Consulting Inc* ***(G-1935)***
Kiddie Academy, Delaware *Also called Znm Wecare Corporation* ***(G-10018)***
Kiddie Kollege & Academy, Zanesville *Also called Genesis Healthcare System* ***(G-20311)***
Kiddie Kollege Inc......440 327-5435
33169 Center Ridge Rd North Ridgeville (44039) ***(G-15332)***
Kiddie Korral, Sandusky *Also called Kiddle Korral* ***(G-16621)***
Kiddie Party Company LLC......440 273-7680
1690 Lander Rd Mayfield Heights (44124) ***(G-13875)***
Kiddie West Pediatric Center......614 276-7733
4766 W Broad St Columbus (43228) ***(G-7901)***
Kiddle Korral......419 626-9082
315 W Follett St Sandusky (44870) ***(G-16621)***
Kidney & Hypertension Center (PA)......513 861-0800
2123 Auburn Ave 404 Cincinnati (45219) ***(G-3867)***
Kidney & Hypertension Cons......330 649-9400
4689 Fulton Dr Nw Canton (44718) ***(G-2367)***
Kidney Center of Bexley LLC......614 231-2200
1151 College Ave Columbus (43209) ***(G-7902)***
Kidney Center Partnership......330 799-1150
139 Javit Ct Youngstown (44515) ***(G-20090)***
Kidney Group Inc......330 746-1488
1340 Belmont Ave Ste 2300 Youngstown (44504) ***(G-20091)***
Kidney Services W Centl Ohio......419 227-0918
750 W High St Ste 100 Lima (45801) ***(G-12669)***
Kidron Auction Inc......330 857-2641
4885 Kidron Rd Kidron (44636) ***(G-12307)***
Kidron Electric Inc......330 857-2871
5358 Kidron Rd Kidron (44636) ***(G-12308)***
Kidron Electric & Mech Contrs, Kidron *Also called Kidron Electric Inc* ***(G-12308)***
Kids 'r' Kids 3 OH, Springboro *Also called Childvine Inc* ***(G-16965)***
Kids Ahead Inc......330 628-7404
726 S Cleveland Ave Mogadore (44260) ***(G-14552)***
Kids Country, Medina *Also called Medina Advantage Inc* ***(G-13970)***
Kids Country, Stow *Also called Future Advantage Inc* ***(G-17207)***
Kids Country......330 899-0909
1801 Town Park Blvd Uniontown (44685) ***(G-18375)***
Kids First Learning Centers......440 235-2500
26184 Bagley Rd Olmsted Falls (44138) ***(G-15534)***
Kids In Need Foundation......937 296-1230
3055 Kettering Blvd # 119 Moraine (45439) ***(G-14669)***
Kids Kastle Day Care......419 586-0903
6783 Staeger Rd Celina (45822) ***(G-2598)***
Kids Play Green, Uniontown *Also called Kids-Play Inc* ***(G-18376)***
Kids R Kids 1 Ohio Inc......513 398-9944
7439 S Masn Montgomery Rd Mason (45040) ***(G-13604)***
Kids R Kids 2 Ohio......513 860-3197
9077 Union Centre Blvd West Chester (45069) ***(G-18956)***
Kids R Kids Schools Qulty Lrng......937 748-1260
790 N Main St Springboro (45066) ***(G-16972)***
Kids World......614 473-9229
2812 Morse Rd Columbus (43231) ***(G-7903)***
Kids-Play Inc......330 896-2400
1651 Boettler Rd Uniontown (44685) ***(G-18376)***
Kids-Play Inc......330 896-2400
1651 Boettler Rd Canton (44721) ***(G-2368)***
Kidstown LLC......330 502-4484
55 Stadium Dr Youngstown (44512) ***(G-20092)***
Kidz By Riverside Inc......330 392-0700
421 Main Ave Sw Warren (44481) ***(G-18719)***
Kidz Watch, Centerville *Also called Agj Kidz LLC* ***(G-2618)***
Kiemle-Hankins Company (PA)......419 661-2430
94 H St Perrysburg (43551) ***(G-15886)***
Kig Enterprises LLC......937 263-6429
1440 Nicholas Rd Dayton (45417) ***(G-9544)***
Kil Kare Inc......937 429-2961
1166 Dayton Xenia Rd Xenia (45385) ***(G-19914)***
Kil-Kare Speedway & Drag Strip, Xenia *Also called Kil Kare Inc* ***(G-19914)***
Kilbarger Construction Inc......740 385-6019
450 Gallagher Ave Logan (43138) ***(G-12843)***
Kilgore Group Inc......513 684-3721
201 E 4th St Ste 800 Cincinnati (45202) ***(G-3868)***
Killbuck Savings Bank Co Inc (HQ)......330 276-4881
165 N Main St Killbuck (44637) ***(G-12310)***
Killer Creative Media, Cincinnati *Also called Killer Spotscom Inc* ***(G-3869)***
Killer Spotscom Inc......513 201-1380
463 Ohio Pike Ste 301 Cincinnati (45255) ***(G-3869)***
Kimball Midwest, Columbus *Also called Midwest Motor Supply Co* ***(G-8082)***
Kimble Companies Inc......330 963-5493
8500 Chamberlin Rd Twinsburg (44087) ***(G-18288)***
Kimble Recycl & Disposal Inc (PA)......330 343-1226
3596 State Route 39 Nw Dover (44622) ***(G-10084)***
Kimes Convalescent Center......740 593-3391
75 Kimes Ln Athens (45701) ***(G-789)***
Kimmel Cleaners Inc (PA)......419 294-1959
225 N Sandusky Ave Upper Sandusky (43351) ***(G-18410)***
Kin Care, Lima *Also called Comfort Keepers* ***(G-12617)***
Kinane Inc......513 459-0177
7440 S Masn Montgomery Rd Mason (45040) ***(G-13605)***
Kinder Care Learning Center, Fairfield Township *Also called Kindercare Education LLC* ***(G-10812)***
Kinder Garden School......513 791-4300
10969 Reed Hartman Hwy Blue Ash (45242) ***(G-1592)***
Kinder Kare Day Nursery......740 886-6905
627 County Road 411 Proctorville (45669) ***(G-16218)***
Kinder Mrgan Lqds Trminals LLC......513 841-0500
5297 River Rd Cincinnati (45233) ***(G-3870)***
Kindercare Center 1480, Dayton *Also called Kindercare Learning Ctrs Inc* ***(G-9545)***
Kindercare Child Care Network, Solon *Also called Kindercare Learning Ctrs LLC* ***(G-16865)***
Kindercare Child Care Network, Cincinnati *Also called Kindercare Learning Ctrs LLC* ***(G-3871)***
Kindercare Child Care Network, Worthington *Also called Kindercare Learning Ctrs Inc* ***(G-19817)***

Kindercare Child Care Network, Cleveland *Also called Kindercare Learning Ctrs LLC (G-5831)*

Kindercare Child Care Network, Cincinnati *Also called Kindercare Learning Ctrs LLC (G-3872)*

Kindercare Child Care Network, Cincinnati *Also called Kindercare Learning Ctrs LLC (G-3873)*

Kindercare Education LLC 513 896-4769
7939 Morris Rd Fairfield Township (45011) *(G-10812)*

Kindercare Education LLC 330 405-5556
2572 Glenwood Dr Twinsburg (44087) *(G-18289)*

Kindercare Education LLC 614 337-2035
4885 Cherry Bottom Rd Gahanna (43230) *(G-11128)*

Kindercare Education LLC 440 442-3360
679 Alpha Dr Cleveland (44143) *(G-5830)*

Kindercare Learning Ctrs Inc 937 435-2353
951 E Rahn Rd Dayton (45429) *(G-9545)*

Kindercare Learning Ctrs Inc 614 888-9696
77 Caren Ave Worthington (43085) *(G-19817)*

Kindercare Learning Ctrs LLC 440 248-5437
6140 Kruse Dr Solon (44139) *(G-16865)*

Kindercare Learning Ctrs LLC 513 771-8787
1459 E Kemper Rd Cincinnati (45246) *(G-3871)*

Kindercare Learning Ctrs LLC 740 549-0264
96 Neverland Dr Lewis Center (43035) *(G-12548)*

Kindercare Learning Ctrs LLC 440 442-8067
5684 Mayfield Rd Cleveland (44124) *(G-5831)*

Kindercare Learning Ctrs LLC 614 866-4446
6601 Bartlett Rd Reynoldsburg (43068) *(G-16314)*

Kindercare Learning Ctrs LLC 513 961-3164
2850 Winslow Ave Cincinnati (45206) *(G-3872)*

Kindercare Learning Ctrs LLC 614 759-6622
5959 E Broad St Columbus (43213) *(G-7904)*

Kindercare Learning Ctrs LLC 513 791-4712
10580 Montgomery Rd Cincinnati (45242) *(G-3873)*

Kindertown Educational Centers (PA) 859 344-8802
8720 Bridgetown Rd Cleves (45002) *(G-6731)*

Kindred Healthcare Inc 937 222-5963
707 S Edwin C Moses Blvd Dayton (45417) *(G-9546)*

Kindred Healthcare Inc 513 336-0178
411 Western Row Rd Mason (45040) *(G-13606)*

Kindred Healthcare Inc 937 222-5963
601 S Edwin C Moses Blvd Dayton (45417) *(G-9547)*

Kindred Healthcare Oper Inc 740 545-6355
620 E Main St West Lafayette (43845) *(G-19115)*

Kindred Healthcare Oper Inc 740 439-4437
1471 Wills Creek Vly Dr Cambridge (43725) *(G-2075)*

Kindred Healthcare Operating 330 762-0901
145 Olive St Akron (44310) *(G-303)*

Kindred Healthcare Operating 419 877-5338
11239 Waterville St Whitehouse (43571) *(G-19449)*

Kindred Hosp - Clveland - Gtwy, Cleveland *Also called Specialty Hosp Cleveland Inc (G-6443)*

Kindred Hospital, Dayton *Also called Kindred Healthcare Inc (G-9546)*

Kindred Hospital Central Ohio 419 526-0777
730 W Market St Lima (45801) *(G-12670)*

Kindred Hospital-Dayton, Dayton *Also called Kindred Healthcare Inc (G-9547)*

Kindred Nrsing Rhbltton- Lbnon, Lebanon *Also called Kindred Nursing Centers E LLC (G-12475)*

Kindred Nursing, Cambridge *Also called Kindred Healthcare Oper Inc (G-2075)*

Kindred Nursing Centers E LLC 740 772-5900
60 Marietta Rd Chillicothe (45601) *(G-2798)*

Kindred Nursing Centers E LLC 513 932-0105
700 Monroe Rd Lebanon (45036) *(G-12475)*

Kindred Nursing Centers E LLC 614 276-8222
2770 Clime Rd Columbus (43223) *(G-7905)*

Kindred Nursing Centers E LLC 614 837-9666
36 Lehman Dr Canal Winchester (43110) *(G-2114)*

Kindred Nursing Centers E LLC 314 631-3000
1300 Hill Rd N Pickerington (43147) *(G-15961)*

Kindred Nursing Centers E LLC 502 596-7300
300 Arlington Ave Logan (43138) *(G-12844)*

Kindred Transitional, Chillicothe *Also called Kindred Nursing Centers E LLC (G-2798)*

Kindred Transitional Care, Columbus *Also called Kindred Nursing Centers E LLC (G-7905)*

Kindred Transitional Care, Pickerington *Also called Kindred Nursing Centers E LLC (G-15961)*

Kindred Transitional Care, Logan *Also called Kindred Nursing Centers E LLC (G-12844)*

Kindred Transitional Care and, Painesville *Also called Personacare of Ohio Inc (G-15733)*

Kinetic Renovations LLC 937 321-1576
2299 Jasper Rd Xenia (45385) *(G-19915)*

King Bros Feed & Supply, Bristolville *Also called K M B Inc (G-1826)*

King Business Interiors Inc 614 430-0020
1400 Goodale Blvd Ste 102 Columbus (43212) *(G-7906)*

King Collision (PA) 330 729-0525
8020 Market St Youngstown (44512) *(G-20093)*

King Collision Inc 330 372-3242
2000 N River Rd Ne Warren (44483) *(G-18720)*

King Group Inc 216 831-9330
25550 Chagrin Blvd # 300 Beachwood (44122) *(G-1073)*

King James Group, Westlake *Also called King James Park Ltd (G-19364)*

King James Group IV Ltd 440 250-1851
24700 Center Ridge Rd G50 Westlake (44145) *(G-19363)*

King James Park Ltd 440 835-1100
24700 Center Ridge Rd G50 Westlake (44145) *(G-19364)*

King Kold Inc 937 836-2731
331 N Main St Englewood (45322) *(G-10592)*

King Memory LLC 614 418-6044
380 Morrison Rd Ste A Columbus (43213) *(G-7907)*

King Saver, Marion *Also called Sack n Save Inc (G-13458)*

King Tree Leasing Co LLC 937 278-0723
1390 King Tree Dr Dayton (45405) *(G-9548)*

King Tut Logistics LLC 614 538-0509
3600 Enterprise Ave Columbus (43228) *(G-7908)*

KING'S DAUGHTERS' MEDICAL CENT, Portsmouth *Also called Portsmouth Hospital Corp (G-16159)*

King's Electric Services, Lebanon *Also called Kween Industries Inc (G-12477)*

King-Lincoln Medical Center, Columbus *Also called Equitas Health Inc (G-7526)*

Kingdom Kids Inc 513 851-6400
6106 Havenwood Ct Hamilton (45011) *(G-11620)*

Kings Cove Automotive LLC 513 677-0177
5726 Dixie Hwy Fairfield (45014) *(G-10744)*

Kings Island Company 513 754-5700
6300 Kings Island Dr Kings Mills (45034) *(G-12313)*

Kings Island Park LLC 513 754-5901
6300 Kings Island Dr Kings Mills (45034) *(G-12314)*

Kings Mazda Kia, Cincinnati *Also called Auto Center USA Inc (G-3006)*

Kings Medical Company 330 653-3968
1920 Georgetown Rd A Hudson (44236) *(G-11991)*

Kings Toyota Inc 513 583-4333
4700 Fields Ertel Rd Cincinnati (45249) *(G-3874)*

Kings Toyota Scion, Cincinnati *Also called Kings Toyota Inc (G-3874)*

Kings Welding and Fabg Inc 330 738-3592
5259 Bane Rd Ne Mechanicstown (44651) *(G-13905)*

Kings-Mason Properties,, Lebanon *Also called Kingsmason Properties Ltd (G-12476)*

Kingsbury Tower I Ltd 216 795-3950
8925 Hough Ave Cleveland (44106) *(G-5832)*

Kingsley Gate Partners LLC 216 400-9880
6155 Rockside Rd Ste 203 Independence (44131) *(G-12086)*

Kingsmason Properties Ltd 513 932-6010
3000 Henkle Dr Ste G Lebanon (45036) *(G-12476)*

Kingston Healthcare Company 937 866-9089
1120 Dunaway St Miamisburg (45342) *(G-14183)*

Kingston Healthcare Company 419 824-4200
4125 King Rd Sylvania (43560) *(G-17435)*

Kingston Healthcare Company 440 967-1800
4210 Telegraph Ln Vermilion (44089) *(G-18555)*

Kingston Healthcare Company 740 389-2311
464 James Way Ofc Marion (43302) *(G-13427)*

Kingston Healthcare Company 419 289-3859
20 Amberwood Pkwy Ashland (44805) *(G-677)*

Kingston Healthcare Company (PA) 419 247-2880
1 Seagate Ste 1960 Toledo (43604) *(G-17840)*

Kingston National Bank Inc (PA) 740 642-2191
2 N Main St Kingston (45644) *(G-12316)*

Kingston of Ashland, Ashland *Also called Kingston Healthcare Company (G-677)*

Kingston of Miamisburg, Miamisburg *Also called Kingston Healthcare Company (G-14183)*

Kingston of Vermilion, Vermilion *Also called Kingston Healthcare Company (G-18555)*

Kingston Residence, Toledo *Also called Kingston Healthcare Company (G-17840)*

Kingston Residence of Marion, Marion *Also called Kingston Healthcare Company (G-13427)*

Kingston Rsdnce Perrysburg LLC 419 872-6200
333 E Boundary St Perrysburg (43551) *(G-15887)*

Kingwood Center 419 522-0211
900 Park Ave W Mansfield (44906) *(G-13194)*

Kinker Eveleigh Insurance, Loveland *Also called Wilmared Inc (G-13035)*

Kinnect 216 692-1161
1427 E 36th St Ste 4203f Cleveland (44114) *(G-5833)*

Kinsale Golf & Fitnes CLB LLC 740 881-6500
3737 Village Club Dr Powell (43065) *(G-16202)*

Kinswa Dialysis LLC 419 332-0310
100 Pinnacle Dr Fremont (43420) *(G-11083)*

Kirby Vacuum Cleaner, Westlake *Also called Scott Fetzer Company (G-19403)*

Kirila Contractors Inc 330 448-4055
505 Bedford Rd Se Brookfield (44403) *(G-1853)*

Kirila Fire Trning Fclties Inc 724 854-5207
509 Bedford Rd Se Brookfield (44403) *(G-1854)*

Kirila Realty, Brookfield *Also called K-Y Residential Coml Indus Dev (G-1852)*

Kirk & Blum Manufacturing Co (HQ) 513 458-2600
4625 Red Bank Rd Ste 200 Cincinnati (45227) *(G-3875)*

Kirk Bros Co Inc 419 595-4020
11942 Us Highway 224 Alvada (44802) *(G-561)*

Kirk Key Interlock Company LLC 330 833-8223
9048 Meridian Cir Nw North Canton (44720) *(G-15217)*

Kirk NationaLease Co (PA) 937 498-1151
3885 Michigan St Sidney (45365) *(G-16783)*

Kirk Williams Company Inc 614 875-9023
2734 Home Rd Grove City (43123) *(G-11445)*

Kirtland Country Club Company 440 942-4400
39438 Kirtland Rd Willoughby (44094) *(G-19534)*

Kissel Bros Shows Inc 513 741-1080
6104 Rose Petal Dr Cincinnati (45247) *(G-3876)*

Kissel Entertainment LLC 513 266-4505
3748 State Line Rd Okeana (45053) ***(G-15532)***
Kissel Rides & Shows, Okeana *Also called Kissel Entertainment LLC* ***(G-15532)***
Kitchen Collection LLC 740 773-9150
133 Redd St Chillicothe (45601) ***(G-2799)***
Kitchen Katering Inc 216 481-8080
24111 Rockwell Dr Euclid (44117) ***(G-10647)***
Kittyhawk Golf Course, Dayton *Also called Dayton City Parks Golf Maint* ***(G-9359)***
Kiwanis International Inc 740 385-5887
13519 Lakefront Dr Logan (43138) ***(G-12845)***
Kiwi Hospitality - Cincinnati 513 241-8660
800 W 8th St Cincinnati (45203) ***(G-3877)***
Kiwiplan Inc 513 554-1500
7870 E Kemper Rd Ste 200 Cincinnati (45249) ***(G-3878)***
Klaben Auto Group, Kent *Also called Klaben Lincoln Ford Inc* ***(G-12246)***
Klaben Auto Group, Kent *Also called 1106 West Main Inc* ***(G-12212)***
Klaben Family Dodge Inc 330 673-9971
1338 W Main St Kent (44240) ***(G-12244)***
Klaben Leasing and Sales Inc 330 673-9971
1338 W Main St Kent (44240) ***(G-12245)***
Klaben Lincoln Ford Inc (PA) 330 673-3139
1089 W Main St Kent (44240) ***(G-12246)***
Klais and Company Inc (PA) 330 867-8443
3320 W Market St 100 Fairlawn (44333) ***(G-10839)***
Klarna Inc 614 615-4705
629 N High St Ste 300 Columbus (43215) ***(G-7909)***
Klase Enterprises Inc (PA) 330 452-6300
713 12th St Ne Canton (44704) ***(G-2369)***
Klassic Hardwood Flooring, Cuyahoga Falls *Also called K H F Inc* ***(G-9106)***
Klean A Kar Inc (PA) 614 221-3145
3383 S High St Columbus (43207) ***(G-7910)***
Klein Associates Inc 937 873-8166
1750 Commerce Center Blvd Fairborn (45324) ***(G-10679)***
Kleingers Group Inc 614 882-4311
350 Worthington Rd Ste B Westerville (43082) ***(G-19177)***
Kleingers Group Inc (PA) 513 779-7851
6305 Centre Park Dr West Chester (45069) ***(G-18957)***
Kleman Services LLC 419 339-0871
2150 Baty Rd Lima (45807) ***(G-12671)***
Klingbeil Capital MGT LLC (PA) 614 396-4919
500 W Wilson Bridge Rd Worthington (43085) ***(G-19818)***
Klingbeil Management Group Co (PA) 614 220-8900
21 W Broad St Fl 10 Columbus (43215) ***(G-7911)***
Klingbeil Multifamilty Fund IV 415 398-0106
21 W Broad St Fl 11 Columbus (43215) ***(G-7912)***
Klingshirn & Sons Trucking 937 338-5000
14884 St Rt 118 S Burkettsville (45310) ***(G-2012)***
Klingshirn, Tom & Sons Trckng, Burkettsville *Also called Klingshirn & Sons Trucking* ***(G-2012)***
Kllee Trucking Inc 740 867-6454
1714 Township Road 278 Chesapeake (45619) ***(G-2730)***
Kloeckner Metals Corporation 513 769-4000
11501 Reading Rd Cincinnati (45241) ***(G-3879)***
Klosterman Baking Co 513 242-1004
1000 E Ross Ave Cincinnati (45217) ***(G-3880)***
Km2 Solutions LLC 610 213-1408
2400 Corp Exchange Dr # 120 Columbus (43231) ***(G-7913)***
Kmh Systems Inc 513 469-9400
675 Redna Ter Cincinnati (45215) ***(G-3881)***
Kmi Inc 614 326-6304
5025 Arlington Centre Blv Columbus (43220) ***(G-7914)***
Kmj Leasing Ltd 614 871-3883
7001 Harrisburg Pike Orient (43146) ***(G-15620)***
Kmk, Cincinnati *Also called Keating Muething & Klekamp Pll* ***(G-3850)***
KMu Trucking & Excvtg Inc 440 934-1008
4436 Center Rd Avon (44011) ***(G-890)***
Knall Beverage Inc 216 252-2500
4550 Tiedeman Rd Ste 1 Cleveland (44144) ***(G-5834)***
Knapp Veterinary Hospital Inc 614 267-3124
596 Oakland Park Ave Columbus (43214) ***(G-7915)***
Kneisel Contracting Corp 513 615-8816
3461 Mustafa Dr Cincinnati (45241) ***(G-3882)***
Knight Crockett Miller Ins 419 254-2400
22 N Erie St Ste A Toledo (43604) ***(G-17841)***
Knight Transportation Inc 614 308-4900
4275 Westward Ave Columbus (43228) ***(G-7916)***
Knight-Swift Trnsp Hldings Inc 614 274-5204
4141 Parkwest Dr Columbus (43228) ***(G-7917)***
Knights Inn, Mansfield *Also called Mansfield Hotel Partnership* ***(G-13206)***
Knights Inn, Maumee *Also called Maumee Lodging Enterprises* ***(G-13818)***
Knights of Columbus 937 890-2971
6050 Dog Leg Rd Dayton (45415) ***(G-9549)***
Knights of Columbus 419 628-2089
40 N Main St Minster (45865) ***(G-14537)***
Knights of Columbus 740 382-3671
1242 E Center St Marion (43302) ***(G-13428)***
KNIGHTS OF COLUMBUS #3766, Mantua *Also called Columbian Corporation Mantua* ***(G-13265)***
Knisely Inc 330 343-5812
5885 Crown Rd Nw Dover (44622) ***(G-10085)***
Kno-Ho-Co- Ashland Community A (PA) 740 622-9801
120 N 4th St Coshocton (43812) ***(G-9021)***
Knoch Corporation 330 244-1440
1015 Schneider St Se 1a Canton (44720) ***(G-2370)***
Knollman Construction LLC 614 841-0130
4601 E 5th Ave Columbus (43219) ***(G-7918)***
Knollwood Florists Inc 937 426-0861
3766 Dayton Xenia Rd Beavercreek (45432) ***(G-1163)***
Knollwood Garden Center, Beavercreek *Also called Knollwood Florists Inc* ***(G-1163)***
Knotice LLC 800 801-4194
526 S Main St Ste 705 Akron (44311) ***(G-304)***
Know Theatre of Cincinnati 513 300-5669
1120 Jackson St Cincinnati (45202) ***(G-3883)***
Knowledge MGT Interactive Inc 614 224-0664
330 W Spring St Ste 320 Columbus (43215) ***(G-7919)***
Knowledgeworks Foundation (PA) 513 241-1422
1 W 4th St Ste 200 Cincinnati (45202) ***(G-3884)***
Knox Area Transit 740 392-7433
25 Columbus Rd Mount Vernon (43050) ***(G-14770)***
Knox Area Transit Kat, Mount Vernon *Also called Knox Area Transit* ***(G-14770)***
Knox Auto LLC 330 701-5266
510 Harcourt Rd Mount Vernon (43050) ***(G-14771)***
Knox Community Hosp Foundation 740 393-9814
1330 Coshocton Ave Mount Vernon (43050) ***(G-14772)***
Knox Community Hospital 740 393-9000
1330 Coshocton Ave Mount Vernon (43050) ***(G-14773)***
Knox County Engineer 740 397-1590
422 Columbus Rd Mount Vernon (43050) ***(G-14774)***
Knox County Head Start Inc (PA) 740 397-1344
11700 Upper Gilchrist Rd B Mount Vernon (43050) ***(G-14775)***
Knox County Health Department, Mount Vernon *Also called County of Knox* ***(G-14758)***
Knox New Hope Industries Inc 740 397-4601
1375 Newark Rd Mount Vernon (43050) ***(G-14776)***
Knoxbi Company LLC 440 892-6800
27500 Detroit Rd Westlake (44145) ***(G-19365)***
Kns Financial Inc 800 215-1136
2034 Austin Bluffs Ct Toledo (43615) ***(G-17842)***
KOA Dayton Tall Timbers Resort, Brookville *Also called Dayton Tall Timbers Resort* ***(G-1913)***
Koch Aluminum Mfg Inc 419 625-5956
1615 E Perkins Ave Sandusky (44870) ***(G-16622)***
Koch Knight LLC (HQ) 330 488-1651
5385 Orchardview Dr Se East Canton (44730) ***(G-10387)***
Koch Meat Co Inc 513 874-3500
4100 Port Union Rd Fairfield (45014) ***(G-10745)***
Koehlke Components Inc 937 435-5435
1201 Commerce Center Dr Franklin (45005) ***(G-11034)***
Koester Pavilion Nursing Home, Troy *Also called Uvmc Nursing Care Inc* ***(G-18238)***
Kohler Catering, Dayton *Also called Kohler Foods Inc* ***(G-9550)***
Kohler Day Care, Cleveland *Also called Phillis Wheatley* ***(G-6204)***
Kohler Foods Inc (PA) 937 291-3600
4572 Presidential Way Dayton (45429) ***(G-9550)***
Kohlmyer Sporting Goods Inc 440 277-8296
5000 Grove Ave Lorain (44055) ***(G-12910)***
Kohlmyer Sports, Lorain *Also called Kohlmyer Sporting Goods Inc* ***(G-12910)***
Kohnen & Patton 513 381-0656
201 E 5th St Ste 800 Cincinnati (45202) ***(G-3885)***
Kohr Royer Griffith Dev Co LLC 614 228-2471
1480 Dublin Rd Columbus (43215) ***(G-7920)***
KOI Enterprises Inc (HQ) 513 357-2400
2701 Spring Grove Ave Cincinnati (45225) ***(G-3886)***
Koinonia Homes Inc 216 588-8777
6161 Oak Tree Blvd # 400 Cleveland (44131) ***(G-5835)***
Koinonia Homes Inc 216 351-5361
4248 W 35th St Cleveland (44109) ***(G-5836)***
Kokosing Construction Inc 330 263-4168
1516 Timken Rd Wooster (44691) ***(G-19739)***
Kokosing Construction Co Inc (HQ) 614 228-1029
6235 Westerville Rd Westerville (43081) ***(G-19270)***
Kokosing Construction Co Inc 440 323-9346
1539 Lowell St Elyria (44035) ***(G-10522)***
Kokosing Construction Co Inc 614 228-1029
6235 Westerville Rd Westerville (43081) ***(G-19271)***
Kokosing Inc (PA) 614 212-5700
6235 Wstrville Rd Ste 200 Westerville (43081) ***(G-19272)***
Kokosing Industrial Inc (HQ) 614 212-5700
6235 Westerville Rd Westerville (43081) ***(G-19273)***
Kolbus America Inc (HQ) 216 931-5100
812 Huron Rd E Ste 750 Cleveland (44115) ***(G-5837)***
Kolczun & Kolczun Orthopedics 440 985-3113
5800 Coper Foster Pk Rd W Lorain (44053) ***(G-12911)***
Kollander World Travel Inc 216 692-1000
761 E 200th St Cleveland (44119) ***(G-5838)***
Koltcz Concrete Block Co 440 232-3630
7660 Oak Leaf Rd Bedford (44146) ***(G-1287)***
Komar Plumbing Co 330 758-5073
49 Roche Way Youngstown (44512) ***(G-20094)***
Kone Inc 330 762-8886
6670 W Snowville Rd Ste 7 Cleveland (44141) ***(G-5839)***
Kone Inc 614 866-1751
735 Cross Pointe Rd Ste G Gahanna (43230) ***(G-11129)***
Konica Minolta Business Soluti 614 766-7800
4700 Lakehurst Ct Ste 225 Dublin (43016) ***(G-10264)***

ALPHABETIC

Konica Minolta Business Soluti 910 990-5837
2 Summit Park Dr Ste 450 Cleveland (44131) *(G-5840)*
Konica Minolta Business Soluti 440 546-5795
9150 S Hills Blvd Ste 100 Broadview Heights (44147) *(G-1837)*
Konica Minolta Business Soluti 419 536-7720
3131 Executive Pkwy # 101 Toledo (43606) *(G-17843)*
Konkus Marble & Granite Inc 614 876-4000
3737 Zane Trace Dr Columbus (43228) *(G-7921)*
Koorsen Fire & Security Inc 614 878-2228
727 Manor Park Dr Columbus (43228) *(G-7922)*
Koorsen Fire & Security Inc 614 878-2228
727 Manor Park Dr Columbus (43228) *(G-7923)*
Koorsen Fire & Security Inc 419 526-2212
100 Swarn Pkwy Mansfield (44903) *(G-13195)*
Koorsen Fire & Security Inc 937 324-9405
3577 Concorde Dr Vandalia (45377) *(G-18530)*
Kopf Construction Corporation (PA) 440 933-6908
420 Avon Belden Rd Ste A Avon Lake (44012) *(G-921)*
Kopf Construction Corporation 440 933-0250
750 Aqua Marine Blvd Avon Lake (44012) *(G-922)*
Korman Construction Corp 614 274-2170
3695 Interchange Rd Columbus (43204) *(G-7924)*
Koroseal Interior Products LLC 855 753-5474
700 Bf Goodrich Rd Marietta (45750) *(G-13343)*
Kottler Metal Products Co Inc 440 946-7473
1595 Lost Nation Rd Willoughby (44094) *(G-19535)*
Kovachy Auto Parts, Cleveland Also called Ieh Auto Parts LLC *(G-5735)*
Kozmic Korner 330 494-4148
8282 Port Jackson Ave Nw Canton (44720) *(G-2371)*
Kpmg Llp 513 421-6430
312 Walnut Strste 3400 Cincinnati (45202) *(G-3887)*
Kpmg Llp 614 249-2300
191 W Nationwide Blvd # 500 Columbus (43215) *(G-7925)*
Kpmg Llp 216 696-9100
1375 E 9th St Ste 2600 Cleveland (44114) *(G-5841)*
Kraft Electrical & Telecom Svs, Cincinnati Also called Kraft Electrical Contg Inc *(G-3888)*
Kraft Electrical Contg Inc (PA) 513 467-0500
5710 Hillside Ave Cincinnati (45233) *(G-3888)*
Kraft Electrical Contg Inc 614 836-9300
4407 Professional Pkwy Groveport (43125) *(G-11526)*
Kraftmaid Trucking Inc (PA) 440 632-2531
16052 Industrial Pkwy Middlefield (44062) *(G-14271)*
Krakowski Trucking Inc 330 722-7935
1100 W Smith Rd Medina (44256) *(G-13966)*
Kramer & Feldman Inc 513 821-7444
7636 Production Dr Cincinnati (45237) *(G-3889)*
Kramer & Kramer Inc 937 456-1101
420 N Barron St Eaton (45320) *(G-10448)*
Kramer & Kramer Realtors, Eaton Also called Kramer & Kramer Inc *(G-10448)*
Kramer Enterprises Inc (PA) 419 422-7924
116 E Main Cross St Findlay (45840) *(G-10932)*
Kraton Polymers US LLC 740 423-7571
2419 State Rd 618 Belpre (45714) *(G-1407)*
Kreber Graphics Inc (PA) 614 529-5701
2580 Westbelt Dr Columbus (43228) *(G-7926)*
Krebs Steve BP Oil Co 513 641-0150
930 Tennessee Ave Cincinnati (45229) *(G-3890)*
Kreller Bus Info Group Inc 513 723-8900
817 Main St Ste 300 Cincinnati (45202) *(G-3891)*
Kreller Group, Cincinnati Also called Kreller Bus Info Group Inc *(G-3891)*
Kribha LLC 740 788-8991
1008 Hebron Rd Newark (43056) *(G-15046)*
Krieger Enterprises Inc 513 573-9132
3613 Scialville Foster Rd Mason (45040) *(G-13607)*
Krieger Ford Inc (PA) 614 888-3320
1800 Morse Rd Columbus (43229) *(G-7927)*
Kristi Britton 614 868-7612
6400 E Main St Ste 203 Reynoldsburg (43068) *(G-16315)*
Kristie Warner 330 650-4450
4960 Darrow Rd Hudson (44224) *(G-11992)*
Kroger Co 513 782-3300
150 Tri County Pkwy Cincinnati (45246) *(G-3892)*
Kroger Co 740 335-4030
548 Clinton Ave Wshngtn CT Hs (43160) *(G-19877)*
Kroger Co 937 294-7210
2917 W Alex Bell Rd Dayton (45459) *(G-9551)*
Kroger Co 614 898-3200
4111 Executive Pkwy # 100 Westerville (43081) *(G-19274)*
Kroger Co 740 363-4398
1840 Columbus Pike Delaware (43015) *(G-9994)*
Kroger Co 614 759-2745
850 S Hamilton Rd Columbus (43213) *(G-7928)*
Kroger Co 937 376-7962
1700 W Park Sq Xenia (45385) *(G-19916)*
Kroger Co 937 848-5990
6480 Wilmington Pike Dayton (45459) *(G-9552)*
Kroger Co Foundation 513 762-4000
1014 Vine St Ste 1000 Cincinnati (45202) *(G-3893)*
Kroger Refill Center 614 333-5017
2270 Rickenbacker Pkwy W Columbus (43217) *(G-7929)*
Krohn Conservatory Gift Shop, Cincinnati Also called Park Cincinnati Board *(G-4201)*
Kronis Coatings, Mansfield Also called Systems Jay LLC Nanogate *(G-13249)*

Kross Acquisition Company LLC 513 554-0555
10690 Loveland Madeira Rd Loveland (45140) *(G-13004)*
Krugliak Wilkins Grifiyhd & 330 364-3472
158 N Broadway St New Philadelphia (44663) *(G-14969)*
Krugliak Wilkins Grifiyhd & (PA) 330 497-0700
4775 Munson St Nw Canton (44718) *(G-2372)*
Krumroy-Cozad Cnstr Corp 330 376-4136
376 W Exchange St Akron (44302) *(G-305)*
Krush Technology, Kettering Also called Oovoo LLC *(G-12298)*
Krystowski Ford Tractor Sales, Wellington Also called Krystowski Tractor Sales
Inc *(G-18842)*
Krystowski Tractor Sales Inc 440 647-2015
47117 State Route 18 Wellington (44090) *(G-18842)*
KS Associates Inc 440 365-4730
260 Burns Rd Ste 100 Elyria (44035) *(G-10523)*
Kst Security Inc 614 878-2228
727 Manor Park Dr Columbus (43228) *(G-7930)*
Ktc Quell, Dayton Also called Kettering Tennis Center *(G-9543)*
Ktib Inc 330 722-7935
1100 W Smith Rd Medina (44256) *(G-13967)*
Ktm Enterprises Inc 937 548-8357
120 W 3rd St Greenville (45331) *(G-11388)*
Ktm North America Inc (PA) 855 215-6360
1119 Milan Ave Amherst (44001) *(G-591)*
Kubota Authorized Dealer, Columbus Also called Columbus Equipment Company *(G-7281)*
Kubota Authorized Dealer, Fort Recovery Also called Hull Bros Inc *(G-10992)*
Kubota Authorized Dealer, Plain City Also called Evolution Ag LLC *(G-16052)*
Kubota Authorized Dealer, Granville Also called Fackler Country Gardens Inc *(G-11341)*
Kubota Authorized Dealer, Urbana Also called Farmers Equipment Inc *(G-18432)*
Kubota Authorized Dealer, Findlay Also called Streacker Tractor Sales Inc *(G-10965)*
Kucera International Inc (PA) 440 975-4230
38133 Western Pkwy Willoughby (44094) *(G-19536)*
Kuehne + Nagel Inc 419 635-4051
Erie Industrial Park # 2 Port Clinton (43452) *(G-16111)*
Kuempel Service Inc 513 271-6500
3976 Southern Ave Cincinnati (45227) *(G-3894)*
Kuester Implement Company Inc 740 944-1502
1436 State Route 152 Bloomingdale (43910) *(G-1490)*
Kuhlman Construction Products, Maumee Also called Kuhlman Corporation *(G-13808)*
Kuhlman Corporation (PA) 419 897-6000
1845 Indian Wood Cir Maumee (43537) *(G-13808)*
Kuhnle Bros Trucking, Newbury Also called Kuhnle Brothers Inc *(G-15122)*
Kuhnle Brothers Inc 440 564-7168
14905 Cross Creek Pkwy Newbury (44065) *(G-15122)*
Kumler Automotive, Lancaster Also called Kumler Collision Inc *(G-12408)*
Kumler Collision Inc 740 653-4301
2313 E Main St Lancaster (43130) *(G-12408)*
Kunesh Eye Center Inc 937 298-1703
2601 Far Hills Ave Ste 2 Oakwood (45419) *(G-15482)*
Kunkel Apothecary, Cincinnati Also called Kunkel Pharmaceuticals Inc *(G-3895)*
Kunkel Pharmaceuticals Inc 513 231-1943
7717 Beechmont Ave Cincinnati (45255) *(G-3895)*
Kunkle Farm Limited 419 237-2748
20674 Us Highway 20 Alvordton (43501) *(G-562)*
Kuno Creative Group LLC 440 225-4144
36901 American Way Ste 2a Avon (44011) *(G-891)*
Kuntzman Trucking Inc (PA) 330 821-9160
13515 Oyster Rd Alliance (44601) *(G-536)*
Kurtz Bros Compost Services 330 864-2621
2677 Riverview Rd Akron (44313) *(G-306)*
Kurzhals Inc 513 941-4624
6847 Menz Ln Cincinnati (45233) *(G-3896)*
Kusan Co 614 262-1818
4060 Indianola Ave Columbus (43214) *(G-7931)*
Kween Industries Inc 513 932-2293
2964 S State Route 42 Lebanon (45036) *(G-12477)*
Kwik Parking 419 246-0454
709 Madison Ave Ste 205 Toledo (43604) *(G-17844)*
Kyocera SGS Precision Tools (PA) 330 688-6667
55 S Main St Munroe Falls (44262) *(G-14797)*
KZF Bwsc Joint Venture 513 621-6211
700 Broadway St Cincinnati (45202) *(G-3897)*
KZF Design Inc 513 621-6211
700 Broadway St Cincinnati (45202) *(G-3898)*
L & H Wholesale & Supply, Sheffield Village Also called Luxury Heating Co *(G-16738)*
L & I Custom Walls Inc 513 683-2045
10369 Cones Rd Loveland (45140) *(G-13005)*
L & M Products Inc 937 456-7141
1407 N Barron St Eaton (45320) *(G-10449)*
L & W Supply Corporation 614 276-6391
1150 Mckinley Ave Columbus (43222) *(G-7932)*
L & W Supply Corporation 513 723-1150
3274 Spring Grove Ave Cincinnati (45225) *(G-3899)*
L A Fitness Intl LLC 937 439-2795
45 W Alex Bell Rd Washington Township (45459) *(G-18785)*
L A Hair Force 419 756-3101
1509 Lexington Ave Mansfield (44907) *(G-13196)*
L A King Trucking Inc 419 727-9398
434 Matzinger Rd Toledo (43612) *(G-17845)*

L and C Soft Serve Inc 330 364-3823
  717 N Wooster Ave Dover (44622) *(G-10086)*
L and M Investment Co 740 653-3583
  603 W Wheeling St Lancaster (43130) *(G-12409)*
L B & B Associates Inc 216 451-2672
  555 E 88th St Cleveland (44108) *(G-5842)*
L B Brunk & Sons Inc 330 332-0359
  10460 Salem Warren Rd Salem (44460) *(G-16550)*
L B Foster Company 330 652-1461
  1193 Salt Springs Rd Mineral Ridge (44440) *(G-14510)*
L B Industries Inc 330 750-1002
  534 Lowellville Rd Struthers (44471) *(G-17366)*
L Brands, Columbus *Also called Mast Industries Inc (G-8034)*
L Brands Service Company LLC 614 415-7000
  3 Limited Pkwy Columbus (43230) *(G-7933)*
L Brands Store Dsign Cnstr Inc 614 415-7000
  3 Ltd Pkwy Columbus (43230) *(G-7934)*
L C A D A, Lorain *Also called Lorain County Alcohol and Drug (G-12917)*
L Calvin Jones & Company 330 533-1195
  3744 Starrs Centre Dr Canfield (44406) *(G-2145)*
L J F Management Inc 513 688-0104
  4719 Alma Ave Ofc 200 Blue Ash (45242) *(G-1593)*
L J Navy Trucking Company 614 754-8929
  2365 Performance Way Columbus (43207) *(G-7935)*
L Jack Ruscilli 614 876-9484
  2041 Arlingate Ln Columbus (43228) *(G-7936)*
L JC Home Care LLC 614 495-0276
  6543 Commerce Pkwy Ste D Dublin (43017) *(G-10265)*
L M Berry and Company (PA) 937 296-2121
  3170 Kettering Blvd Moraine (45439) *(G-14670)*
L M Berry and Company 513 768-7700
  312 Plum St Ste 600 Cincinnati (45202) *(G-3900)*
L O G Transportation Inc 440 891-0850
  120 Blaze Industrial Pkwy Berea (44017) *(G-1429)*
L O M Inc 216 363-6009
  1370 Ontario St Ste 2000 Cleveland (44113) *(G-5843)*
L P K, Cincinnati *Also called Libby Prszyk Kthman Hldngs Inc (G-3923)*
L R G Inc 937 890-0510
  3795 Wyse Rd Dayton (45414) *(G-9553)*
L S C Service Corp 216 521-7260
  14306 Detroit Ave Apt 237 Lakewood (44107) *(G-12350)*
L S R, Cincinnati *Also called Lerner Sampson & Rothfuss (G-3918)*
L S R, Hebron *Also called Legend Smelting and Recycl Inc (G-11716)*
L T O B, Grove City *Also called Little Theater Off Broadway (G-11450)*
L V I, Dayton *Also called Lion-Vallen Ltd Partnership (G-9571)*
L V Trckng, Columbus *Also called L V Trucking Inc (G-7937)*
L V Trucking Inc 614 275-4994
  2440 Harrison Rd Columbus (43204) *(G-7937)*
L Van & Associates Corporation 419 208-9145
  4151 Emmajean Rd Toledo (43607) *(G-17846)*
L W Limited (PA) 513 721-2744
  212 E 3rd St Ste 300 Cincinnati (45202) *(G-3901)*
L&T Technology Services Ltd 732 688-4402
  5550 Blazer Pkwy Ste 125 Dublin (43017) *(G-10266)*
L'U Vabella, Lowellville *Also called M & M Wine Cellar Inc (G-13041)*
L-3 Cmmncations Nova Engrg Inc 877 282-1168
  4393 Digital Way Mason (45040) *(G-13608)*
L3 Aviation Products Inc 614 825-2001
  1105 Schrock Rd Ste 800 Columbus (43229) *(G-7938)*
La Fitness West Chester, West Chester *Also called Fitness International LLC (G-18924)*
La Force Inc 614 875-2545
  3940 Gantz Rs Unit E Grove City (43123) *(G-11446)*
La Force Inc 513 772-0783
  2851 E Kemper Rd Cincinnati (45241) *(G-3902)*
La France Crystal Dry Cleaners, Youngstown *Also called La France South Inc (G-20095)*
La France South Inc (PA) 330 782-1400
  2607 Glenwood Ave Youngstown (44511) *(G-20095)*
La King Trucking Inc 419 225-9039
  1516 Findlay Rd Lima (45801) *(G-12672)*
La Piazza Pasta & Grill, Troy *Also called Leos La Piazza Inc (G-18210)*
La Quinta Inn, Richfield *Also called Shree Shankar LLC (G-16379)*
La Quinta Inn, Reynoldsburg *Also called Lq Management LLC (G-16318)*
La Quinta Inn, Cincinnati *Also called Lq Management LLC (G-3951)*
La Quinta Inn, Cleveland *Also called Lq Management LLC (G-5883)*
La Quinta Inn, Cleveland *Also called Lq Management LLC (G-5884)*
La Villa Cnference Banquet Ctr 216 265-9305
  11500 Brookpark Rd Cleveland (44130) *(G-5844)*
La-Z-Boy Incorporated 614 478-0898
  4228 Easton Gateway Dr Columbus (43219) *(G-7939)*
Lab Care, Barberton *Also called Summa Health (G-967)*
Lab Care, Stow *Also called Summa Health (G-17234)*
Labcare 330 753-3649
  165 5th St Se Ste A Barberton (44203) *(G-958)*
Labelle Hmhealth Care Svcs LLC 440 842-3005
  5500 Ridge Rd Ste 138 Cleveland (44129) *(G-5845)*
Labelle Hmhealth Care Svcs LLC 740 392-1405
  314 S Main St Ste B Mount Vernon (43050) *(G-14777)*
Labelle News Agency Inc 740 282-9731
  814 University Blvd Steubenville (43952) *(G-17161)*

Labone Inc 513 585-9000
  3200 Burnet Ave Cincinnati (45229) *(G-3903)*
Labor Ready, Steubenville *Also called Trueblue Inc (G-17182)*
Laboratory Corporation America 614 475-7852
  941 E Johnstown Rd Columbus (43230) *(G-7940)*
Laboratory Corporation America 937 383-6964
  630 W Main St Wilmington (45177) *(G-19626)*
Laboratory Corporation America 330 865-3624
  1 Park West Blvd Ste 290 Akron (44320) *(G-307)*
Laboratory Corporation America 440 951-6841
  38429 Lake Shore Blvd Willoughby (44094) *(G-19537)*
Laboratory Corporation America 614 882-6278
  5888 Cleveland Ave Columbus (43231) *(G-7941)*
Laboratory Corporation America 513 242-6800
  1737 Tennessee Ave Cincinnati (45229) *(G-3904)*
Laboratory Corporation America 937 866-8188
  415 Byers Rd Ste 100 Miamisburg (45342) *(G-14184)*
Laboratory Corporation America 614 336-3993
  5920 Wilcox Pl Ste F Dublin (43016) *(G-10267)*
Laboratory Corporation America 440 328-3275
  418 E Broad St Mansfield (44907) *(G-13197)*
Laboratory Corporation America 440 884-1591
  6789 Ridge Rd Ste 210 Cleveland (44129) *(G-5846)*
Laboratory Corporation America 740 522-2034
  95 S Terrace Ave Newark (43055) *(G-15047)*
Laboratory Corporation America 330 686-0194
  4482 Darrow Rd Stow (44224) *(G-17216)*
Laboratory Corporation America 440 205-8299
  8300 Tyler Blvd Mentor (44060) *(G-14070)*
Laboratory Corporation America 440 838-0404
  2525 E Royalton Rd Ste 3 Cleveland (44147) *(G-5847)*
Laboratory of Dermatopathology 937 434-2351
  7835 Paragon Rd Dayton (45459) *(G-9554)*
Lacaisse Inc 513 621-6211
  700 Broadway St Cincinnati (45202) *(G-3905)*
Lacca, Lima *Also called West Ohio Cmnty Action Partnr (G-12781)*
Lacp St Ritas Medical Ctr LLC 419 324-4075
  708 W Spring St Lima (45801) *(G-12673)*
Ladan Learning Center 614 426-4306
  6028 Cleveland Ave Columbus (43231) *(G-7942)*
Ladd Inc 513 861-4089
  3603 Victory Pkwy Cincinnati (45229) *(G-3906)*
Ladd Distribution LLC (HQ) 937 438-2646
  4849 Hempstead Station Dr Kettering (45429) *(G-12296)*
Ladder Man Inc 614 784-1120
  1505 E Bowman St Wooster (44691) *(G-19740)*
Ladera Healthcare Company 614 459-1313
  1661 Old Henderson Rd Columbus (43220) *(G-7943)*
Lads and Lasses, Warren *Also called Wee Care Daycare (G-18771)*
Lafayette Life Insurance Co (HQ) 800 443-8793
  400 Broadway St Cincinnati (45202) *(G-3907)*
Laibe Electric Co 419 724-8200
  404 N Byrne Rd Toledo (43607) *(G-17847)*
Laibe Electric/Technology, Toledo *Also called Laibe Electric Co (G-17847)*
Laidlaw Education Services, Cincinnati *Also called First Student Inc (G-3561)*
Laidlaw Educational Services, Cincinnati *Also called Firstgroup America Inc (G-3567)*
Laidlaw Transit Services Inc (HQ) 513 241-2200
  600 Vine St Ste 1400 Cincinnati (45202) *(G-3908)*
Lairson Trucking LLC 513 894-0452
  99 N Riverside Dr Hamilton (45011) *(G-11621)*
Lake Center Depot, Cleveland *Also called Cleveland Municipal School Dst (G-5274)*
Lake Club 330 549-3996
  1140 Paulin Rd Poland (44514) *(G-16086)*
Lake Cnty Captains Prof Basbal, Willoughby *Also called Cascia LLC (G-19509)*
Lake Cnty Deptmntl Retrdtn/Dvl, Willoughby *Also called County of Lake (G-19516)*
Lake County Council On Aging (PA) 440 205-8111
  8520 East Ave Mentor (44060) *(G-14071)*
Lake County Family Practice 440 352-4880
  9500 Mentor Ave Ste 100 Mentor (44060) *(G-14072)*
Lake County Local Hazmat 440 350-5499
  8505 Garfield Rd Mentor (44060) *(G-14073)*
Lake County Nursery, Madison *Also called Lcn Holdings Inc (G-13101)*
Lake County YMCA (PA) 440 352-3303
  933 Mentor Ave Fl 2 Painesville (44077) *(G-15718)*
Lake County YMCA 440 946-1160
  37100 Euclid Ave Willoughby (44094) *(G-19538)*
Lake County YMCA 440 259-2724
  4540 River Rd Perry (44081) *(G-15824)*
Lake County YMCA 440 428-5125
  730 N Lake St Madison (44057) *(G-13099)*
Lake Data Center Inc 440 944-2020
  800 Lloyd Rd Wickliffe (44092) *(G-19467)*
Lake Erie Construction Co 419 668-3302
  25 S Norwalk Rd E Norwalk (44857) *(G-15441)*
Lake Erie Correctional Fcilty, Conneaut *Also called Management & Training Corp (G-8955)*
Lake Erie Electric Inc (PA) 440 835-5565
  25730 1st St Westlake (44145) *(G-19366)*
Lake Erie Electric Inc 330 724-1241
  1888 Brown St Akron (44301) *(G-308)*
Lake Erie Electric Inc 419 529-4611
  539 Home Rd N Ontario (44906) *(G-15558)*

A
L
P
H
A
B
E
T
I
C

Lake Erie Home Repair 419 871-0687
257 Milan Ave Norwalk (44857) ***(G-15442)***
Lake Erie Med Surgical Sup Inc 734 847-3847
6920 Hall St Holland (43528) ***(G-11892)***
Lake Erie Nature & Science Ctr 440 871-2900
28728 Wolf Rd Bay Village (44140) ***(G-1022)***
Lake Farm Park, Kirtland *Also called Lake Metroparks* ***(G-12322)***
Lake Front II Inc 330 337-8033
12688 Salem Warren Rd Salem (44460) ***(G-16551)***
Lake Health, Painesville *Also called Tripoint Medical Center* ***(G-15744)***
Lake Horry Electric (PA) 440 808-8791
255 Bramley Ct Chagrin Falls (44022) ***(G-2651)***
Lake Hospital System Inc 440 953-9600
36000 Euclid Ave Willoughby (44094) ***(G-19539)***
Lake Hospital System Inc 440 632-3024
15050 S Springdale Ave Middlefield (44062) ***(G-14272)***
Lake Hospital System Inc (PA) 440 375-8100
7590 Auburn Rd Painesville (44077) ***(G-15719)***
Lake Hospital Systems, Madison *Also called Madison Medical Campus* ***(G-13104)***
Lake Isabella Recreation Assn, East Fultonham *Also called Columbia Recreation Assn* ***(G-10389)***
Lake Local Board of Education 330 877-9383
13188 Kent Ave Ne Hartville (44632) ***(G-11694)***
Lake Metroparks (PA) 440 639-7275
11211 Spear Rd Painesville (44077) ***(G-15720)***
Lake Metroparks 440 428-3164
7298 Lake Rd Madison (44057) ***(G-13100)***
Lake Metroparks 440 256-2122
8800 Chardon Rd Kirtland (44094) ***(G-12322)***
Lake Metroparks 440 256-1404
8668 Kirtland Chardon Rd Willoughby (44094) ***(G-19540)***
Lake Mhawk Prperty Owners Assn 330 863-0000
1 N Mohawk Dr Malvern (44644) ***(G-13125)***
Lake Park At Flower Hospital, Sylvania *Also called Flower Hospital* ***(G-17425)***
Lake Pnte Rhblttion Nrsing Ctr, Conneaut *Also called Es3 Management Inc* ***(G-8954)***
Lake Side Building Maintenance 216 589-9900
200 Public Sq Cleveland (44114) ***(G-5848)***
Lake Univ Ireland Cancer Ctr, Mentor *Also called University Hospitals Cleveland* ***(G-14119)***
Lake Urgent & Family Med Ctr (PA) 440 255-6400
8655 Market St Mentor (44060) ***(G-14074)***
Lake Urgent Care Centers, Mentor *Also called Lake Urgent & Family Med Ctr* ***(G-14074)***
Lake Wynoka Prprty Owners Assn 937 446-3774
1 Waynoka Dr Lake Waynoka (45171) ***(G-12328)***
Lake-West Hospital, Willoughby *Also called Lake Hospital System Inc* ***(G-19539)***
Lakefront Lines Inc (HQ) 216 267-8810
13315 Brookpark Rd Brookpark (44142) ***(G-1900)***
Lakefront Lines Inc 419 537-0677
3152 Hill Ave Toledo (43607) ***(G-17848)***
Lakefront Lines Inc 614 476-1113
3152 E 17th Ave Columbus (43219) ***(G-7944)***
Lakefront Lines Inc 513 829-8290
4991 Factory Dr Fairfield (45014) ***(G-10746)***
Lakefront Trailways, Toledo *Also called Lakefront Lines Inc* ***(G-17848)***
Lakefront Trailways, Columbus *Also called Lakefront Lines Inc* ***(G-7944)***
Lakefront Trailways, Fairfield *Also called Lakefront Lines Inc* ***(G-10746)***
Lakeland Foundation 440 525-7094
7700 Clocktower Dr C2089 Willoughby (44094) ***(G-19541)***
Lakeland Glass Co (PA) 440 277-4527
4994 Grove Ave Lorain (44055) ***(G-12912)***
Lakes Country Club Inc 614 882-4167
7129 Africa Rd Galena (43021) ***(G-11161)***
Lakes Golf & Country Club Inc 614 882-2582
6740 Worthington Rd Westerville (43082) ***(G-19178)***
Lakes Golf and Country Club, Galena *Also called Lakes Country Club Inc* ***(G-11161)***
Lakes Heating and AC 330 644-7811
2476 N Turkeyfoot Rd Coventry Township (44319) ***(G-9038)***
Lakes Venture LLC 614 681-7050
933 High St Worthington (43085) ***(G-19819)***
Lakeshore Dialysis LLC 937 278-0516
4750 N Main St Dayton (45405) ***(G-9555)***
Lakeside Association 419 798-4461
236 Walnut Ave Lakeside (43440) ***(G-12329)***
Lakeside Manor Inc 330 549-2545
9661 Market St North Lima (44452) ***(G-15271)***
Lakeside Realty LLC 330 793-4200
1749 S Raccoon Rd Youngstown (44515) ***(G-20096)***
Lakeside Sand & Gravel Inc 330 274-2569
3498 Frost Rd Mantua (44255) ***(G-13271)***
Lakeside Supply Co 216 941-6800
3000 W 117th St Cleveland (44111) ***(G-5849)***
Lakeside Title Escrow Agcy Inc 216 503-5600
29550 Detroit Rd Ste 301 Westlake (44145) ***(G-19367)***
Laketec Communications Inc 440 892-2001
27881 Lorain Rd North Olmsted (44070) ***(G-15295)***
Laketran 440 350-1000
555 Lakeshore Blvd Painesville (44077) ***(G-15721)***
Lakewood Acceptance Corp 216 658-1234
15200 Lorain Ave Cleveland (44111) ***(G-5850)***
Lakewood Catholic Academy 216 521-4352
14808 Lake Ave Lakewood (44107) ***(G-12351)***
Lakewood Chrysler-Plymouth 216 521-1000
13001 Brookpark Rd Brookpark (44142) ***(G-1901)***
Lakewood City School District 216 529-4400
14740 Lakewood Hts Blvd Lakewood (44107) ***(G-12352)***
Lakewood Clveland Fmly Med Ctr 216 227-2162
16215 Madison Ave Lakewood (44107) ***(G-12353)***
Lakewood Community Care Center, Cleveland *Also called City of Lakewood* ***(G-5206)***
Lakewood Community Care Center 216 226-0080
2019 Woodward Ave Lakewood (44107) ***(G-12354)***
Lakewood Country Club Company 440 871-0400
2613 Bradley Rd Cleveland (44145) ***(G-5851)***
Lakewood Greenhouse Inc 419 691-3541
909 Lemoyne Rd Northwood (43619) ***(G-15397)***
Lakewood Health Care Center 216 226-3103
13315 Detroit Ave Lakewood (44107) ***(G-12355)***
Lakewood Hospital Association (HQ) 216 529-7160
14519 Detroit Ave Lakewood (44107) ***(G-12356)***
Lakewood Hospital Association 216 228-5437
1450 Belle Ave Cleveland (44107) ***(G-5852)***
Lakewood Police Dept, Cleveland *Also called City of Lakewood* ***(G-5207)***
Lakewood Y, Lakewood *Also called Young MNS Chrstn Assn Clveland* ***(G-12364)***
Lakewoods II Ltd 937 254-6141
980 Wilmington Ave Dayton (45420) ***(G-9556)***
Lakota Bus Garage 419 986-5558
5186 Sandusky Cty Rd 13 Kansas (44841) ***(G-12208)***
Lakota Local School District 513 777-2150
6947 Yankee Rd Liberty Township (45044) ***(G-12582)***
Lally Pipe & Tube, Struthers *Also called L B Industries Inc* ***(G-17366)***
Lamalfa Party Center, Mentor *Also called Michaels Inc* ***(G-14085)***
Lamar Advertising Company 216 676-4321
12222 Plaza Dr Cleveland (44130) ***(G-5853)***
Lamar Advertising Company 740 699-0000
52610 Holiday Dr Saint Clairsville (43950) ***(G-16490)***
Lamrite West Inc (HQ) 440 238-9150
13000 Darice Pkwy Strongsville (44149) ***(G-17321)***
Lamrite West Inc 440 572-9946
17647 Foltz Pkwy Strongsville (44149) ***(G-17322)***
Lamrite West Inc 440 268-0634
14225 Pearl Rd Strongsville (44136) ***(G-17323)***
Lan Solutions Inc 513 469-6500
9850 Redhill Dr Blue Ash (45242) ***(G-1594)***
Lancaster Bingo Company, Lancaster *Also called Lancaster Bingo Company Inc* ***(G-12410)***
Lancaster Bingo Company Inc (PA) 740 681-4759
200 Quarry Rd Se Lancaster (43130) ***(G-12410)***
Lancaster Commercial Pdts LLC 740 286-5081
2353 Westbrooke Dr Columbus (43228) ***(G-7945)***
Lancaster Country Club 740 654-3535
3100 Country Club Rd Sw Lancaster (43130) ***(G-12411)***
Lancaster Host LLC 740 654-4445
1861 Riverway Dr Lancaster (43130) ***(G-12412)***
Lancaster Municipal Gas, Lancaster *Also called City of Lancaster* ***(G-12380)***
Lancaster Pollard & Co LLC (HQ) 614 224-8800
65 E State St Ste 1600 Columbus (43215) ***(G-7946)***
Lancaster Pollard Mrtg Co LLC (PA) 614 224-8800
65 E State St Ste 1600 Columbus (43215) ***(G-7947)***
Lancaster Transportation, Cincinnati *Also called Mv Transportation Inc* ***(G-4088)***
LANCASTER-FAIRFIELD COMMUNITY, Lancaster *Also called Community Action Program Comm* ***(G-12384)***
Lance A1 Cleaning Services LLC 614 370-0550
342 Hanton Way Columbus (43213) ***(G-7948)***
Lancer Insurance Company 440 473-1634
6095 Parkland Blvd # 310 Cleveland (44124) ***(G-5854)***
Lancia Nursing Home Inc 740 695-4404
51999 Guirino Dr Saint Clairsville (43950) ***(G-16491)***
Lancia Nursing Home Inc (PA) 740 264-7101
1852 Sinclair Ave Steubenville (43953) ***(G-17162)***
Lancia Villa Royal, Steubenville *Also called Lancia Nursing Home Inc* ***(G-17162)***
Lanco Global Systems Inc 937 660-8090
1430c Yankee Park Pl Dayton (45458) ***(G-9557)***
Land Art Inc (PA) 419 666-5296
7728 Ponderosa Rd Perrysburg (43551) ***(G-15888)***
Land Design Consultants 440 255-8463
9025 Osborne Dr Mentor (44060) ***(G-14075)***
Land OLakes Inc 330 879-2158
8485 Navarre Rd Sw Massillon (44646) ***(G-13703)***
Landes Fresh Meats Inc 937 836-3613
9476 Haber Rd Clayton (45315) ***(G-4859)***
Landing Gear Test Facility 937 255-5740
1981 5th St Dayton (45433) ***(G-9180)***
Landmark America Inc (PA) 330 372-6800
1268 N River Rd Ne Ste 1 Warren (44483) ***(G-18721)***
Landrum & Brown Incorporated (PA) 513 530-5333
4445 Lake Forest Dr # 400 Blue Ash (45242) ***(G-1595)***
Landscape & Christmas Tree, Akron *Also called Acro Tool & Die Company* ***(G-17)***
Landscape Dsgn-Bld-Maintenance, Plain City *Also called MJ Design Associates Inc* ***(G-16061)***
Landscping Rclmtion Spcialists 330 339-4900
3497 University Dr Ne New Philadelphia (44663) ***(G-14970)***
Landsel Title Agency Inc (PA) 614 337-1928
961 N Hamilton Rd Ste 100 Gahanna (43230) ***(G-11130)***

Lane Alton & Horst LLC 614 228-6885
  2 Miranova Pl Ste 220 Columbus (43215) *(G-7949)*
Lane Aviation Corporation 614 237-3747
  4389 International Gtwy # 228 Columbus (43219) *(G-7950)*
Lane Chevrolet 937 426-2313
  635 S Orchard Ln Beavercreek Township (45434) *(G-1252)*
Lane Life Corp (PA) 330 799-1002
  5801 Mahoning Ave Youngstown (44515) *(G-20097)*
Lane Life Trans, Youngstown *Also called Lane Life Corp (G-20097)*
Lane Wood Industries 419 352-5059
  991 S Main St Bowling Green (43402) *(G-1739)*
Lane's Moving & Storage, Lima *Also called Lanes Transfer Inc (G-12674)*
Lanes Transfer Inc 419 222-8692
  245 E Murphy St Lima (45801) *(G-12674)*
Lang Chevrolet Co 937 426-2313
  635 Orchard Ln Beavercreek Township (45434) *(G-1253)*
Lang Chevrolet Geo, Beavercreek Township *Also called Lang Chevrolet Co (G-1253)*
Lang Financial Group Inc 513 699-2966
  4225 Malsbary Rd Ste 100 Blue Ash (45242) *(G-1596)*
Lang Masonry Contractors Inc 740 749-3512
  405 Watertown Rd Waterford (45786) *(G-18786)*
Lang Stone Company Inc (PA) 614 235-4099
  4099 E 5th Ave Columbus (43219) *(G-7951)*
Langdon Inc 513 733-5955
  9865 Wayne Ave Cincinnati (45215) *(G-3909)*
Language Logic 513 241-9112
  600 Vine St Ste 2020 Cincinnati (45202) *(G-3910)*
Lanhan Contractors Inc 440 918-1099
  2220 Lost Nation Rd Willoughby (44094) *(G-19542)*
Lannings Foods, Mount Vernon *Also called S and S Gilardi Inc (G-14788)*
Lanxess Corporation 440 279-2367
  145 Parker Ct Chardon (44024) *(G-2701)*
Lap Technology LLC 937 415-5794
  6101 Webster St Dayton (45414) *(G-9558)*
Lapham-Hickey Steel Corp 614 443-4881
  753 Marion Rd Columbus (43207) *(G-7952)*
Larchwood Health Group LLC 216 941-6100
  4110 Rcky Rver Dr Ste 251 Cleveland (44135) *(G-5855)*
Larchwood Village Independent, Cleveland *Also called Larchwood Health Group LLC (G-5855)*
Laria Chevrolet-Buick Inc 330 925-2015
  112 E Ohio Ave Rittman (44270) *(G-16406)*
Lariche Chevrolet-Cadillac, Findlay *Also called Lariche Subaru Inc (G-10933)*
Lariche Subaru Inc 419 422-1855
  215 E Main Cross St Findlay (45840) *(G-10933)*
Larlham Care Hattie Group 330 274-2272
  9772 Diagonal Rd Mantua (44255) *(G-13272)*
Larosas Inc (PA) 513 347-5660
  2334 Boudinot Ave Cincinnati (45238) *(G-3911)*
Larrimer & Larrimer LLC 419 222-6266
  165 N High St Columbus (43215) *(G-7953)*
Larrimer & Larrimer LLC (PA) 614 221-7548
  165 N High St Fl 3 Columbus (43215) *(G-7954)*
Larrimer & Larrimer LLC 740 366-0184
  2000 Newark Granville Rd # 200 Granville (43023) *(G-11345)*
Larry L Minges 513 738-4901
  4396 Wade Mill Rd Hamilton (45014) *(G-11622)*
Larry Lang Excavating Inc 740 984-4750
  19371 State Route 60 Beverly (45715) *(G-1463)*
Larry Smith Contractors Inc 513 367-0218
  5737 Dry Fork Rd Cleves (45002) *(G-6732)*
Larry Smith Plumbing, Cleves *Also called Larry Smith Contractors Inc (G-6732)*
Larue Enterprises Inc 937 438-5711
  3331 Seajay Dr Beavercreek (45430) *(G-1225)*
Laser Craft Inc 440 327-4300
  38900 Taylor Pkwy North Ridgeville (44035) *(G-15333)*
Laser Hair Removal Center 937 433-7536
  5300 Far Hills Ave # 250 Dayton (45429) *(G-9559)*
Laser Label Technologies, Stow *Also called Electronic Printing Pdts Inc (G-17200)*
Laser Reproductions, Columbus *Also called Bordner and Associates Inc (G-7054)*
Laserflex Corporation (HQ) 614 850-9600
  3649 Parkway Ln Hilliard (43026) *(G-11783)*
Lash Paving Inc 740 635-4335
  70700 Swingle Rd Bridgeport (43912) *(G-1818)*
Lasik Plus Vision Center 513 794-9964
  7840 Montgomery Rd Cincinnati (45236) *(G-3912)*
Lassiter Corporation 216 391-4800
  3700 Kelley Ave Cleveland (44114) *(G-5856)*
Lasting Impressions Event 614 252-5400
  5080 Sinclair Rd Ste 200 Columbus (43229) *(G-7955)*
Lasting Imprssions Event Rentl, Columbus *Also called Lasting Impressions Event (G-7955)*
Lata, Westerville *Also called Los Alamos Technical Assoc Inc (G-19275)*
Lateef Elmin Mhammad Inv Group 937 450-3388
  524 W Liberty St Springfield (45506) *(G-17060)*
Lathrop Company Inc (HQ) 419 893-7000
  28 N Saint Clair St Toledo (43604) *(G-17849)*
Latorre Concrete Cnstr Inc 614 257-1401
  850 N Cassady Ave Columbus (43219) *(G-7956)*
Latrobe Spcialty Mtls Dist Inc (HQ) 330 609-5137
  1551 Vienna Pkwy Vienna (44473) *(G-18580)*

Laudan Properties LLC 234 212-3225
  2204 E Enterprise Pkwy Twinsburg (44087) *(G-18290)*
Laughlin Music & Vending Svc 740 593-7778
  148 W Union St Athens (45701) *(G-790)*
Laughlin Music and Vending Svc, Athens *Also called Laughlin Music & Vending Svc (G-790)*
Laukhuf, Gary DDS, Ashtabula *Also called Ashtabula Dental Associates (G-717)*
Laurel Development Corporation 614 794-8800
  8181 Worthington Rd Westerville (43082) *(G-19179)*
Laurel Health Care Company 740 264-5042
  500 Stanton Blvd Steubenville (43952) *(G-17163)*
Laurel Health Care Company (HQ) 614 794-8800
  8181 Worthington Rd Uppr Westerville (43082) *(G-19180)*
Laurel Health Care Company 614 888-4553
  6830 N High St Worthington (43085) *(G-19820)*
Laurel Health Care Company 614 885-0408
  1030 High St Worthington (43085) *(G-19821)*
Laurel Healthcare 419 782-7879
  1701 Jefferson Ave Defiance (43512) *(G-9925)*
Laurel Hlth Care Battle Creek (HQ) 614 794-8800
  8181 Worthington Rd Westerville (43082) *(G-19181)*
Laurel Hlth Care of Mt Plasant (HQ) 614 794-8800
  8181 Worthington Rd # 2 Westerville (43082) *(G-19182)*
Laurel Lk Retirement Cmnty Inc 330 650-0681
  200 Laurel Lake Dr Rear Hudson (44236) *(G-11993)*
Laurel School (PA) 216 464-1441
  1 Lyman Cir Cleveland (44122) *(G-5857)*
Laurels of Bedford, The, Westerville *Also called Laurel Hlth Care Battle Creek (G-19181)*
Laurels of Defiance, The, Westerville *Also called Oak Health Care Investors (G-19193)*
Laurels of Hillsboro 937 393-1925
  175 Chillicothe Ave Hillsboro (45133) *(G-11849)*
LAURELS OF MASSILLON, THE, Massillon *Also called Fairport Enterprises Inc (G-13680)*
Laurels of Mt Pleasant, Westerville *Also called Laurel Hlth Care of Mt Plasant (G-19182)*
Laurels of Mt Vernon, Mount Vernon *Also called Oak Health Care Investors (G-14784)*
Laurels of Norworth, Worthington *Also called Laurel Health Care Company (G-19820)*
Laurels of Steubenville, The, Steubenville *Also called Laurel Health Care Company (G-17163)*
LAURELWOOD CENTER FOR BEHAVIOU, Willoughby *Also called Laurelwood Hospital (G-19543)*
Laurelwood Hospital (PA) 440 953-3000
  35900 Euclid Ave Willoughby (44094) *(G-19543)*
Laurelwood, The, Dayton *Also called Harborside Healthcare Corp (G-9486)*
Laurie Ann Home Health Care 330 872-7512
  2200 Milton Blvd Newton Falls (44444) *(G-15138)*
LAURIE ANN NURSING HOME, Newton Falls *Also called Hooberry Associates Inc (G-15137)*
Laurito & Laurito LLC 937 743-4878
  7550 Paragon Rd Dayton (45459) *(G-9560)*
LAURRELS OF DEFIANCE, Defiance *Also called Laurel Healthcare (G-9925)*
Lavery Buick, Alliance *Also called Lavery Chevrolet-Buick Inc (G-537)*
Lavery Chevrolet-Buick Inc (PA) 330 823-1100
  1096 W State St Alliance (44601) *(G-537)*
Lavy Concrete Construction 937 606-4754
  7277 W Piqua Clayton Rd Covington (45318) *(G-9047)*
Law Excavating Inc 740 745-3420
  9128 Mount Vernon Rd Saint Louisville (43071) *(G-16519)*
Law Offces Rbert A Schrger Lpa 614 824-5731
  81 S 5th St Ste 400 Columbus (43215) *(G-7957)*
Law Offices of John D Clunk C 330 436-0300
  4500 Courthouse Blvd # 400 Stow (44224) *(G-17217)*
Lawhon and Associates Inc (PA) 614 481-8600
  1441 King Ave Columbus (43212) *(G-7958)*
Lawn & Garden Equipment, Moraine *Also called Buckeye Power Sales Co Inc (G-14628)*
Lawn Management Sprinkler Co 513 272-3808
  3828 Round Bottom Rd F Cincinnati (45244) *(G-3913)*
Lawnfield Properties LLC 440 974-3572
  8434 Mentor Ave Mentor (44060) *(G-14076)*
Lawnmark, Stow *Also called Prusa Inc (G-17225)*
Lawnview Industries Inc 937 653-5217
  1250 E Us Highway 36 Urbana (43078) *(G-18438)*
Lawo, Toledo *Also called Legal Aid Western Ohio Inc (G-17851)*
Lawrence A Cervino MD 330 668-4065
  3975 Embassy Pkwy Ste 203 Akron (44333) *(G-309)*
Lawrence Cnty Bd Dev Dsblties 740 377-2356
  1749 County Road 1 South Point (45680) *(G-16938)*
Lawrence Cnty Early Chldhd Ctr, South Point *Also called Lawrence Cnty Bd Dev Dsblties (G-16938)*
Lawrence Cnty Hstorical Museum 740 532-1222
  506 S 6th St Ironton (45638) *(G-12161)*
Lawrence Industries Inc (PA) 216 518-7000
  4500 Lee Rd Ste 120 Cleveland (44128) *(G-5858)*
Lawrence M Shell DDS 614 235-3444
  2862 E Main St Ste A Columbus (43209) *(G-7959)*
Lawrence Saltis Plaza, Stow *Also called Fish Creek Plaza Ltd (G-17204)*
Lawyers Title Cincinnati Inc (HQ) 513 421-1313
  3500 Red Bank Rd Cincinnati (45227) *(G-3914)*
Layh & Associates 937 767-9171
  416 Xenia Ave Yellow Springs (45387) *(G-19940)*
Layton Inc (PA) 740 349-7101
  169 Dayton Rd Ne Newark (43055) *(G-15048)*

A
L
P
H
A
B
E
T
I
C

Lazar Brothers Inc 440 585-9333
30030 Lakeland Blvd Wickliffe (44092) ***(G-19468)***
Lazer Kraze 513 339-1030
6075 Braymoore Dr Galena (43021) ***(G-11162)***
Lbi Starbucks DC 3 614 415-6363
3 Limited Pkwy Columbus (43230) ***(G-7960)***
Lbk Health Care Inc (PA) 937 296-1550
4336 W Franklin St Ste A Bellbrook (45305) ***(G-1339)***
Lbs International Inc 614 866-3688
12920 Sheffield Dr Pickerington (43147) ***(G-15962)***
Lc, Cleveland *Also called Logan Clutch Corporation* ***(G-5879)***
Lca-Vision Inc (HQ) 513 792-9292
7840 Montgomery Rd Cincinnati (45236) ***(G-3915)***
Lccaa-Hopkins Locke-Head Start, Lorain *Also called Lorain County Community Action* ***(G-12919)***
Lcd Home Health Agency LLC 513 497-0441
6 S 2nd St Ste 409 Hamilton (45011) ***(G-11623)***
Lcd Nurse Aide Academy, Hamilton *Also called Lcd Home Health Agency LLC* ***(G-11623)***
Lcn Holdings Inc 440 259-5571
5052 S Ridge Rd Madison (44057) ***(G-13101)***
Lcnb National Bank (HQ) 513 932-1414
2 N Broadway St Lowr Lebanon (45036) ***(G-12478)***
Lcnb National Bank 740 775-6777
33 W Main St Frnt Chillicothe (45601) ***(G-2800)***
Lcnb National Bank 937 456-5544
110 W Main St Eaton (45320) ***(G-10450)***
Lcs, Cincinnati *Also called London Computer Systems Inc* ***(G-3942)***
Lcs Inc 419 678-8600
411 Stachler Dr Saint Henry (45883) ***(G-16516)***
Le Chaperon Rouge (PA) 440 934-0296
1504 Travelers Pt Avon (44011) ***(G-892)***
Le Chaperon Rouge Company 440 899-9477
27390 Center Ridge Rd Westlake (44145) ***(G-19368)***
Le Nails (PA) 440 846-1866
1144 Southpark Ctr Cleveland (44136) ***(G-5859)***
LE Smith Company (PA) 419 636-4555
1030 E Wilson St Bryan (43506) ***(G-1961)***
Leadec Corp (HQ) 513 731-3590
9395 Kenwood Rd Ste 200 Blue Ash (45242) ***(G-1597)***
Leader Nuring & Rehabilitation (HQ) 419 252-5718
333 N Summit St Toledo (43604) ***(G-17850)***
Leader Promotions Inc (PA) 614 416-6565
790 E Johnstown Rd Columbus (43230) ***(G-7961)***
Leader Technologies Inc (PA) 614 890-1986
674 Enterprise Dr Lewis Center (43035) ***(G-12549)***
Leaderpromos.com, Columbus *Also called Leader Promotions Inc* ***(G-7961)***
Leaders Family Farms 419 599-1570
0064 County Rd 16 Napoleon (43545) ***(G-14810)***
Leaders Moving & Storage Co, Worthington *Also called Leaders Moving Company* ***(G-19822)***
Leaders Moving Company 614 785-9595
7455 Alta View Blvd Worthington (43085) ***(G-19822)***
Leadership Circle LLC 801 518-2980
10918 Springbrook Ct Whitehouse (43571) ***(G-19450)***
Leading Edje LLC 614 636-3353
5555 Perimeter Dr Ste 101 Dublin (43017) ***(G-10268)***
LEADS COMMUNITY ACTION AGENCY, Newark *Also called Leads Inc* ***(G-15049)***
Leads Inc (PA) 740 349-8606
159 Wilson St Newark (43055) ***(G-15049)***
Leaffilter North LLC (PA) 330 655-7950
1595 Georgetown Rd Ste G Hudson (44236) ***(G-11994)***
LEAP, Cleveland *Also called Linking Employment Abilities* ***(G-5872)***
Learning Tree Childcare Ctr 419 229-5484
775 S Thayer Rd Lima (45806) ***(G-12790)***
Leather Gallery Inc 513 312-1722
50 Farnese Ct Lebanon (45036) ***(G-12479)***
Leatherman Nursing Ctrs Corp (PA) 330 336-6684
200 Smokerise Dr Ste 300 Wadsworth (44281) ***(G-18602)***
Lebanon Chrysler - Plymuth Inc 513 932-2717
518 W Main St Lebanon (45036) ***(G-12480)***
Lebanon Nursing & Rehab Ctr 513 932-1121
115 Oregonia Rd Lebanon (45036) ***(G-12481)***
Lebanon Nursing Home, Lebanon *Also called Health Care Opportunities Inc* ***(G-12470)***
Lebanon Presbyterian Church 513 932-0369
123 N East St Lebanon (45036) ***(G-12482)***
Led Transportation 330 484-2772
4645 Monica Ave Sw Canton (44706) ***(G-2373)***
Ledger 6031, Columbus *Also called Eaton Corporation* ***(G-7495)***
Lee & Associates - Columbus, Dublin *Also called Lee & Associates Inc* ***(G-10269)***
Lee & Associates Inc 614 923-3300
5100 Prkcnter Ave Ste 100 Dublin (43017) ***(G-10269)***
Lee Personnel Inc 513 744-6780
621 E Mehring Way # 807 Cincinnati (45202) ***(G-3916)***
Leeda Services Inc (PA) 330 392-6006
1441 Parkman Rd Nw Warren (44485) ***(G-18722)***
Leeda Services Inc 330 325-1560
4123 Tallmadge Rd Rootstown (44272) ***(G-16451)***
Leef Bros Inc 952 912-5500
6800 Cintas Blvd Mason (45040) ***(G-13609)***
Leef Services, Mason *Also called Leef Bros Inc* ***(G-13609)***
Lees Roby Inc 330 872-0983
425 Ridge Rd Newton Falls (44444) ***(G-15139)***
Leesville Plant, Dennison *Also called M3 Midstream LLC* ***(G-10052)***
Lefco Worthington LLC 216 432-4422
18451 Euclid Ave Cleveland (44112) ***(G-5860)***
Lefeld Implement Inc (PA) 419 678-2375
5228 State Route 118 Coldwater (45828) ***(G-6761)***
Lefeld Supplies Rental, Coldwater *Also called Lefeld Welding & Stl Sups Inc* ***(G-6762)***
Lefeld Welding & Stl Sups Inc (PA) 419 678-2397
600 N 2nd St Coldwater (45828) ***(G-6762)***
Legacy Commercial Finishes, Columbus *Also called Legacy Commercial Flooring Ltd* ***(G-7962)***
Legacy Commercial Flooring Ltd (PA) 614 476-1043
800 Morrison Rd Columbus (43230) ***(G-7962)***
Legacy Consultant Pharmacy 336 760-1670
26691 Richmond Rd Bedford (44146) ***(G-1288)***
Legacy Freedom Treatment Ctr 614 741-2100
751 Northwest Blvd # 200 Columbus (43212) ***(G-7963)***
Legacy Health Services, Wickliffe *Also called DMD Management Inc* ***(G-19456)***
Legacy Health Services, Cleveland *Also called DMD Management Inc* ***(G-5434)***
Legacy Industrial Services LLC 606 584-8953
9272 Scoffield Rd Ripley (45167) ***(G-16400)***
Legacy Marble and Granite, Findlay *Also called Legacy Ntral Stone Srfaces LLC* ***(G-10934)***
Legacy Ntral Stone Srfaces LLC 419 420-7440
229 Stanford Pkwy Findlay (45840) ***(G-10934)***
Legacy Place, Twinsburg *Also called DMD Management Inc* ***(G-18258)***
Legacy Village Hospitality LLC 216 382-3350
24665 Cedar Rd Cleveland (44124) ***(G-5861)***
Legacy Village Management Off 216 382-3871
25333 Cedar Rd Ste 303 Cleveland (44124) ***(G-5862)***
Legal Aid Society Cincinnati (PA) 513 241-9400
215 E 9th St Ste 200 Cincinnati (45202) ***(G-3917)***
Legal Aid Society of Cleveland (PA) 216 861-5500
1223 W 6th St Fl 4 Cleveland (44113) ***(G-5863)***
Legal Aid Society of Columbus (PA) 614 737-0139
1108 City Park Ave # 100 Columbus (43206) ***(G-7964)***
LEGAL AID SOCIETY OF GREATER C, Cincinnati *Also called Legal Aid Society Cincinnati* ***(G-3917)***
Legal Aid Western Ohio Inc 419 724-0030
525 Jefferson Ave 400 Toledo (43604) ***(G-17851)***
Legal Hair and Day Spa, Steubenville *Also called Philip Icuss Jr* ***(G-17169)***
Legend Equities Corporation 216 741-3113
5755 Granger Rd Ste 910 Independence (44131) ***(G-12087)***
Legend Lake Golf Club Inc 440 285-3110
11135 Auburn Rd Chardon (44024) ***(G-2702)***
Legend Smelting and Recycl Inc (PA) 740 928-0139
717 Oneill Dr Hebron (43025) ***(G-11716)***
Legends Care Center, Massillon *Also called Consulate Management Co LLC* ***(G-13673)***
Legndary Cleaners LLC 216 374-1205
1215 W 10th St Apt 1003 Cleveland (44113) ***(G-5864)***
Legrand North America LLC 937 224-0639
6500 Poe Ave Dayton (45414) ***(G-9561)***
Legrand North America LLC 937 224-0639
1501 Webster St Dayton (45404) ***(G-9562)***
Legrand Services Inc 740 682-6046
230 W Hill St Oak Hill (45656) ***(G-15481)***
Lehigh Outfitters LLC (HQ) 740 753-1951
39 E Canal St Nelsonville (45764) ***(G-14834)***
Lehn Painting Inc (PA) 513 732-1515
4175 Taylor Rd Batavia (45103) ***(G-1003)***
Lei Cbus LLC 614 302-8830
7492 Sancus Blvd Worthington (43085) ***(G-19823)***
Leidos Inc 330 405-9810
8866 Commons Blvd Ste 201 Twinsburg (44087) ***(G-18291)***
Leidos Inc 937 431-2270
3745 Pentagon Blvd Beavercreek (45431) ***(G-1164)***
Leidos Inc 858 826-6000
4449 Easton Way Ste 150 Columbus (43219) ***(G-7965)***
Leidos Inc 937 431-2220
3745 Pentagon Blvd Beavercreek (45431) ***(G-1165)***
Leidos Engineering LLC 330 405-9810
8866 Commons Blvd Ste 201 Twinsburg (44087) ***(G-18292)***
Leidos Technical Services Inc 513 672-8400
497 Circle Freeway Dr # 236 West Chester (45246) ***(G-19063)***
Leikin Motor Companies Inc 440 946-6900
38750 Mentor Ave Willoughby (44094) ***(G-19544)***
Leisure Sports Inc 419 829-2891
9501 Central Ave Sylvania (43560) ***(G-17436)***
Lemmon & Lemmon Inc 330 497-8686
1201 S Main St Ste 200 North Canton (44720) ***(G-15218)***
Lenau Park 440 235-2646
7370 Columbia Rd Olmsted Twp (44138) ***(G-15537)***
Lencyk Masonry Co Inc 330 729-9780
7671 South Ave Youngstown (44512) ***(G-20098)***
Lennox Industries Inc 614 871-3017
3750 Brookham Dr Ste A Grove City (43123) ***(G-11447)***
Lenny's Collision Center, Barberton *Also called Lennys Auto Sales Inc* ***(G-959)***
Lennys Auto Sales Inc 330 848-2993
893 Wooster Rd N Barberton (44203) ***(G-959)***
Lenz Inc 937 277-9364
3301 Klepinger Rd Dayton (45406) ***(G-9563)***

Lenz Company, Dayton *Also called Lenz Inc* ***(G-9563)***
Leo A Dick & Sons Co (PA)....330 452-5010
935 Mckinley Ave Nw Canton (44703) ***(G-2374)***
Leo Yannenoff Jewish Community (PA)....614 231-2731
1125 College Ave Columbus (43209) ***(G-7966)***
Leonard Insur Svcs Agcy Inc (HQ)....330 266-1904
4244 Mount Pleasant St Nw Canton (44720) ***(G-2375)***
Leos La Piazza Inc....937 339-5553
2 N Market St Troy (45373) ***(G-18210)***
Lepi Enterprises Inc....740 453-2980
630 Gw Morse St Zanesville (43701) ***(G-20324)***
Leppo Inc (PA)....330 633-3999
176 West Ave Tallmadge (44278) ***(G-17480)***
Leppo Inc....330 456-2930
1534 Shepler Ch Ave Sw Canton (44706) ***(G-2376)***
LEPPO EQUIPMENT, Tallmadge *Also called Leppo Inc* ***(G-17480)***
Leppo Equipment, Canton *Also called Leppo Inc* ***(G-2376)***
Lerner Sampson & Rothfuss (PA)....513 241-3100
120 E 4th St Cincinnati (45202) ***(G-3918)***
Leroy Twp Fire Dept....440 254-4124
13028 Leroy Center Rd Painesville (44077) ***(G-15722)***
Lesaint Logistics Inc....513 874-3900
4487 Le Saint Ct West Chester (45014) ***(G-18958)***
Lesaint Logistics LLC....513 988-0101
5564 Alan B Shepherd St Trenton (45067) ***(G-18188)***
Lesaint Logistics LLC....513 874-3900
4487 Le Saint Ct West Chester (45014) ***(G-18959)***
Lesco Inc (HQ)....216 706-9250
1385 E 36th St Cleveland (44114) ***(G-5865)***
Level 3 Communications Inc....330 256-8999
520 S Main St Ste 2435 Akron (44311) ***(G-310)***
Level 3 Telecom LLC....234 542-6279
1019 E Turkeyfoot Lake Rd Akron (44312) ***(G-311)***
Level 3 Telecom LLC....513 841-0000
3268 Highland Ave Cincinnati (45213) ***(G-3919)***
Level 3 Telecom LLC....513 841-0000
3268 Highland Ave Cincinnati (45213) ***(G-3920)***
Level 3 Telecom LLC....513 682-7806
9490 Meridian Way West Chester (45069) ***(G-18960)***
Level 3 Telecom LLC....513 682-7806
9490 Meridian Way West Chester (45069) ***(G-18961)***
Level 3 Telecom LLC....513 682-7806
9490 Meridian Way West Chester (45069) ***(G-18962)***
Level 3 Telecom LLC....513 841-0000
3268 Highland Ave Cincinnati (45213) ***(G-3921)***
Level Seven....216 524-9055
4807 Rockside Rd Ste 700 Independence (44131) ***(G-12088)***
Levering Management Inc (PA)....740 397-3897
201 N Main St Mount Vernon (43050) ***(G-14778)***
Levering Management Inc....419 768-2401
115 N Portland St Chesterville (43317) ***(G-2748)***
Levering Management Inc....740 369-6400
4 New Market Dr Delaware (43015) ***(G-9995)***
Levering Management Inc....740 387-9545
195 Executive Dr Marion (43302) ***(G-13429)***
Levering Management Inc....419 756-4747
70 Winchester Rd Mansfield (44907) ***(G-13198)***
Levine Arnold S Law Offices....513 241-6748
324 Reading Rd Cincinnati (45202) ***(G-3922)***
Levis Commons Hotel LLC....419 873-3573
6165 Levis Commons Blvd Perrysburg (43551) ***(G-15889)***
Levy & Associates LLC....614 898-5200
4645 Executive Dr Columbus (43220) ***(G-7967)***
Lewis & Michael Inc (PA)....937 252-6683
1827 Woodman Dr Dayton (45420) ***(G-9564)***
Lewis & Michael Mvg & Stor Co....614 275-2997
845 Harrisburg Pike Columbus (43223) ***(G-7968)***
Lewis and Michael SEC Stor, Cincinnati *Also called Security Storage Co Inc* ***(G-4445)***
Lewis Landscaping Inc....330 666-2655
3606 Minor Rd Copley (44321) ***(G-8968)***
Lewis P C Jackson....216 750-0404
6100 Oak Tree Blvd # 400 Independence (44131) ***(G-12089)***
Lewis P C Jackson....937 306-6304
70 Birch Aly Beavercreek (45440) ***(G-1226)***
Lewis Price Realty Co....330 856-1911
8031 E Market St Warren (44484) ***(G-18723)***
Lexamed....419 693-5307
705 Front St Toledo (43605) ***(G-17852)***
Lexington Court Care Center, Mansfield *Also called Casto Health Care* ***(G-13148)***
Lexington Court Care Center....419 884-2000
250 Delaware Ave Mansfield (44904) ***(G-13199)***
Lexis Nexis, Miamisburg *Also called PNC Bank-Atm* ***(G-14206)***
Lexis Nexis, Miamisburg *Also called Relx Inc* ***(G-14210)***
Lexisnexis Group (HQ)....937 865-6800
9443 Springboro Pike Miamisburg (45342) ***(G-14185)***
Lextant Corporation....614 228-9711
250 S High St Ste 600 Columbus (43215) ***(G-7969)***
Lexus of Dayton, Dayton *Also called Team Rahal of Dayton Inc* ***(G-9807)***
Lgstx Services Inc (HQ)....866 931-2337
145 Hunter Dr Wilmington (45177) ***(G-19627)***
Lha Developments....330 785-3219
910 Eller Ave Akron (44306) ***(G-312)***

Libbey Inc....419 671-6000
1250 Western Ave Toledo (43609) ***(G-17853)***
Libby Prszyk Kthman Hldngs Inc (PA)....513 241-6401
19 Garfield Pl Cincinnati (45202) ***(G-3923)***
Liberty Ashtabula Holdings....330 872-6000
4185 State Route 5 Newton Falls (44444) ***(G-15140)***
Liberty Bible Academy Assn....513 754-1234
4900 Old Irwin Simpson Rd Mason (45040) ***(G-13610)***
Liberty Capital Inc (PA)....937 382-1000
3435 Airborne Rd Ste B Wilmington (45177) ***(G-19628)***
Liberty Capital Services LLC....614 505-0620
438 E Wilson Bridge Rd Worthington (43085) ***(G-19824)***
Liberty Casting Company LLC....740 363-1941
407 Curtis St Delaware (43015) ***(G-9996)***
Liberty Center AC By Marriott, Liberty Township *Also called Liberty Ctr Lodging Assoc LLC* ***(G-12583)***
Liberty Comm Sftwr Sltions Inc....614 318-5000
1050 Kingsmill Pkwy Columbus (43229) ***(G-7970)***
Liberty Ctr Lodging Assoc LLC....608 833-4100
7505 Gibson St Liberty Township (45069) ***(G-12583)***
Liberty Dlysis Md-Mrica Dlysis, Columbus *Also called Fresenius Med Care Hldings Inc* ***(G-7624)***
Liberty Ems Services LLC....216 630-6626
1294 W 70th St Cleveland (44102) ***(G-5866)***
Liberty Ford Southwest Inc....440 888-2600
6600 Pearl Rd Cleveland (44130) ***(G-5867)***
Liberty Health Care Center, Youngstown *Also called Windsor House Inc* ***(G-20247)***
Liberty Health Care Center Inc....937 296-1550
4336 W Franklin St 100 Bellbrook (45305) ***(G-1340)***
Liberty Healthshare Inc....855 585-4237
4845 Fulton Dr Nw Ste 1 Canton (44718) ***(G-2377)***
Liberty Insulation Co Inc (PA)....513 621-0108
2903 Kant Pl Beavercreek (45431) ***(G-1166)***
Liberty Insulation Co Inc....513 621-0108
5782 Deerfield Rd Milford (45150) ***(G-14400)***
Liberty Maintenance Inc....330 755-7711
777 N Meridian Rd Youngstown (44509) ***(G-20099)***
Liberty Mortgage Company Inc....614 224-4000
473 E Rich St Columbus (43215) ***(G-7971)***
Liberty Mutual, Fairfield *Also called Ohio Casualty Insurance Co* ***(G-10763)***
Liberty Mutual Insurance Co....614 864-4100
630 Morrison Rd Ste 300 Gahanna (43230) ***(G-11131)***
Liberty Mutual Insurance Co....614 855-6193
440 Polaris Pkwy Ste 150 Westerville (43082) ***(G-19183)***
Liberty Mutual Insurance Co....513 984-0550
9450 Seward Rd Fairfield (45014) ***(G-10747)***
Liberty Nrsing Ctr of Jmestown....937 675-3311
4960 Old Us Route 35 E Jamestown (45335) ***(G-12188)***
Liberty Nrsing Ctr Rvrside LLC....513 557-3621
315 Lilienthal St Cincinnati (45204) ***(G-3924)***
Liberty Nursing Center....937 836-5143
425 Lauricella Ct Englewood (45322) ***(G-10593)***
Liberty Nursing Center of Thre....513 941-0787
7800 Jandaracres Dr Cincinnati (45248) ***(G-3925)***
Liberty Nursing Home Inc....937 376-2121
126 Wilson Dr Xenia (45385) ***(G-19917)***
Liberty Nursing of Willard....419 935-0148
370 E Howard St Willard (44890) ***(G-19483)***
Liberty Residence II....330 334-3262
1054 Freedom Dr Apt 115 Wadsworth (44281) ***(G-18603)***
Liberty Savings Bank FSB (HQ)....937 382-1000
2251 Rombach Ave Wilmington (45177) ***(G-19629)***
Liberty Steel Industries Inc....330 372-6363
2207 Larchmont Ave Ne Warren (44483) ***(G-18724)***
Liberty Steel Products Inc (PA)....330 538-2236
11650 Mahoning Ave North Jackson (44451) ***(G-15248)***
Liberty Steel Products Inc....330 534-7998
7193 Masury Rd Hubbard (44425) ***(G-11948)***
Liberty Tire Recycling LLC....614 871-8097
3041 Jackson Pike Grove City (43123) ***(G-11448)***
Liberty Township, Liberty Township *Also called Four Bridges Country Club Ltd* ***(G-12581)***
Liberty Village Manor, Dublin *Also called Liberty Vlg Senior Communities* ***(G-10270)***
Liberty Vlg Senior Communities....614 889-5002
4248 Tuller Rd Ste 201 Dublin (43017) ***(G-10270)***
Liberty West Nursing Center, Toledo *Also called Parkview Manor Inc* ***(G-17972)***
Liberty-Alpha III JV....330 755-7711
24 Madison St Campbell (44405) ***(G-2091)***
Licco Inc....740 522-8345
600 Industrial Pkwy Newark (43056) ***(G-15050)***
Licensing Section, Columbus *Also called Public Safety Ohio Department* ***(G-8478)***
Licking Cnty Alcoholism Prvntn....740 281-3639
62 E Stevens St Newark (43055) ***(G-15051)***
Licking County Aging Program....740 345-0821
1058 E Main St Newark (43055) ***(G-15052)***
Licking County Board of Mrdd....740 349-6588
116 N 22nd St Newark (43055) ***(G-15053)***
Licking County Players Inc....740 349-2287
131 W Main St Newark (43055) ***(G-15054)***
Licking Knox Labor Council....740 345-1765
34 N 4th St Newark (43055) ***(G-15055)***

ALPHABETIC

LICKING MEMORIAL HEALTH SYSTEMS, Newark *Also called Licking Memorial Hospital* ***(G-15057)***

Licking Memorial Hlth Systems (PA) ... 220 564-4000
1320 W Main St Newark (43055) ***(G-15056)***

Licking Memorial Hospital (HQ) ... 740 348-4137
1320 W Main St Newark (43055) ***(G-15057)***

Licking Muskingum Cmnty Correc ... 740 349-6980
20 S 2nd St Newark (43055) ***(G-15058)***

Licking Rhabilitation Svcs Inc ... 740 345-2837
11177 Lambs Ln Newark (43055) ***(G-15059)***

Licking Rural Electrification (PA) ... 740 892-2071
11339 Mount Vernon Rd Utica (43080) ***(G-18456)***

Licking Valley Lions Club ... 740 763-3733
3187 Licking Valley Rd Newark (43055) ***(G-15060)***

Licking-Knox Goodwill Inds Inc (PA) ... 740 345-9861
65 S 5th St Newark (43055) ***(G-15061)***

Liebel-Flarsheim Company LLC ... 513 761-2700
2111 E Galbraith Rd Cincinnati (45237) ***(G-3926)***

Lieben Wooster LP ... 330 390-5722
6834 County Road 672 # 102 Millersburg (44654) ***(G-14481)***

Liechty Inc (HQ) ... 419 445-1565
1701 S Defiance St Archbold (43502) ***(G-631)***

Life Care Center of Cleveland, Westlake *Also called Life Care Centers America Inc* ***(G-19369)***

Life Care Center of Medina, Medina *Also called Medina Medical Investors Ltd* ***(G-13978)***

Life Care Centers America Inc ... 440 365-5200
1212 Abbe Rd S Elyria (44035) ***(G-10524)***

Life Care Centers America Inc ... 440 871-3030
26520 Center Ridge Rd Westlake (44145) ***(G-19369)***

Life Care Centers America Inc ... 614 889-6320
3000 Bethel Rd Columbus (43220) ***(G-7972)***

Life Care Centers America Inc ... 330 483-3131
2400 Columbia Rd Valley City (44280) ***(G-18464)***

Life Care Centers of Medina, Valley City *Also called Life Care Centers America Inc* ***(G-18464)***

Life Care Medical Services, North Canton *Also called J & C Ambulance Services Inc* ***(G-15213)***

Life Center Adult Day Care ... 614 866-7212
2225 State Route 256 Reynoldsburg (43068) ***(G-16316)***

LIFE CENTER AT WESLEY RIDGE, Reynoldsburg *Also called Life Center Adult Day Care* ***(G-16316)***

Life Connection of Ohio ... 419 893-4891
3661 Brrfeld Blvd Ste 105 Maumee (43537) ***(G-13809)***

Life Connection of Ohio Inc ... 937 223-8223
40 Wyoming St Dayton (45409) ***(G-9565)***

Life Enriching Communities (PA) ... 513 719-3510
6279 Tri Ridge Blvd # 320 Loveland (45140) ***(G-13006)***

Life Insurance Mktg Co Inc ... 330 867-1707
91 Mayfield Ave Akron (44313) ***(G-313)***

Life Line Screening ... 216 581-6556
6150 Oak Tree Blvd # 200 Independence (44131) ***(G-12090)***

Life Line Screening Amer Ltd ... 216 581-6556
6150 Oak Tree Blvd # 200 Independence (44131) ***(G-12091)***

Life Line Screening Amer Ltd (PA) ... 216 581-6556
6150 Oak Tree Blvd Independence (44131) ***(G-12092)***

Life Skills Center, Akron *Also called Hat White Management LLC* ***(G-255)***

Life Star Rescue Inc ... 419 238-2507
1171 Production Dr Van Wert (45891) ***(G-18482)***

Life Time Inc ... 614 428-6000
3900 Easton Sta Columbus (43219) ***(G-7973)***

Life Time Fitness Inc ... 513 234-0660
8310 Wilkens Blvd Mason (45040) ***(G-13611)***

Life Time Fitness Inc ... 952 229-7158
3825 Hard Rd Dublin (43016) ***(G-10271)***

Lifebanc ... 216 752-5433
4775 Richmond Rd Cleveland (44128) ***(G-5868)***

Lifecare Alliance ... 614 278-3130
1699 W Mound St Columbus (43223) ***(G-7974)***

Lifecare Ambulance Inc ... 440 323-2527
598 Cleveland St Elyria (44035) ***(G-10525)***

Lifecare Ambulance Inc (PA) ... 440 323-6111
640 Cleveland St Elyria (44035) ***(G-10526)***

Lifecare Fmly Hlth & Dntl Ctr ... 330 454-2000
2725 Lincoln St E Canton (44707) ***(G-2378)***

Lifecare Hospice (PA) ... 330 264-4899
1900 Akron Rd Wooster (44691) ***(G-19741)***

Lifecare Hospice ... 330 336-6595
102 Main St Wadsworth (44281) ***(G-18604)***

Lifecare Medical Services ... 614 258-2545
3065 E 14th Ave Columbus (43219) ***(G-7975)***

LIFECARE PALLIVATIVE MEDICINE, Wooster *Also called Lifecare Hospice* ***(G-19741)***

Lifecare Pallivative Medicine, Wadsworth *Also called Lifecare Hospice* ***(G-18604)***

Lifecenter Organ Donor Network (PA) ... 513 558-5555
615 Elsinore Pl Ste 400 Cincinnati (45202) ***(G-3927)***

Lifecycle Solutions Jv LLC ... 937 938-1321
2689 Cmmons Blvd Ste 120 Beavercreek (45431) ***(G-1167)***

Lifeline Systems Company ... 330 762-5627
703 S Main St Ste 211 Akron (44311) ***(G-314)***

Lifepoint Solutions, Amelia *Also called Clermont Counseling Center* ***(G-571)***

Lifeservices Development Corp ... 440 257-3866
7685 Lake Shore Blvd Mentor (44060) ***(G-14077)***

Lifeshare Cmnty Blood Svcs Inc (PA) ... 440 322-6159
105 Cleveland St Ste 101 Elyria (44035) ***(G-10527)***

Lifeshare Community Blood Svcs ... 440 322-6573
105 Cliffland St Elyria (44035) ***(G-10528)***

Lifespan Incorporated (PA) ... 513 868-3210
1900 Fairgrove Ave Hamilton (45011) ***(G-11624)***

Lifestar Ambulance Inc ... 419 245-6210
1402 Lagrange St Toledo (43608) ***(G-17854)***

Lifestges Smrtan Ctr For Women ... 937 277-8988
2200 Philadelphia Dr # 101 Dayton (45406) ***(G-9566)***

Lifestgs-Smrtan Ctrs For Women, Dayton *Also called Lifestges Smrtan Ctr For Women* ***(G-9566)***

Lifestyle Communities Ltd (PA) ... 614 918-2000
230 West St Ste 200 Columbus (43215) ***(G-7976)***

Lifestyle Landscaping Inc ... 440 353-0333
34613 Center Ridge Rd North Ridgeville (44039) ***(G-15334)***

Lifeteam Ambulance Service, East Liverpool *Also called Lifeteam Ems Inc* ***(G-10405)***

Lifeteam Ems Inc ... 330 386-9284
740 Dresden Ave Ste A East Liverpool (43920) ***(G-10405)***

Lifetime, Mason *Also called Life Time Fitness Inc* ***(G-13611)***

Lifetime Fitness, Columbus *Also called Life Time Inc* ***(G-7973)***

Lifetouch Inc ... 419 435-2646
922 Springville Ave Ste B Fostoria (44830) ***(G-11008)***

Lifetouch Inc ... 937 298-6275
3701 Wilmington Pike Dayton (45429) ***(G-9567)***

Lifetouch Nat Schl Studios Inc ... 419 483-8200
102 Commerce Park Dr Bellevue (44811) ***(G-1380)***

Lifetouch Nat Schl Studios Inc ... 330 497-1291
1300 S Main St Ste 300 Canton (44720) ***(G-2379)***

Lifetouch Nat Schl Studios Inc ... 513 772-2110
11815 Highway Dr Ste 100 Cincinnati (45241) ***(G-3928)***

Lifeworks At Southwest General, Cleveland *Also called Southwest General Health Ctr* ***(G-6430)***

Light of Hearts Villa ... 440 232-1991
283 Union St Ofc Cleveland (44146) ***(G-5869)***

Lighthouse Insurance Group LLC (PA) ... 216 503-2439
6100 Rockside Woods Blvd # 300 Independence (44131) ***(G-12093)***

Lighthouse Medical Staffing ... 614 937-6259
3970 Brown Park Dr Ste B Hilliard (43026) ***(G-11784)***

Lighthouse Youth Services Inc ... 513 221-1017
3603 Washington Ave Cincinnati (45229) ***(G-3929)***

Lighthouse Youth Services Inc ... 513 861-1111
2522 Highland Ave Cincinnati (45219) ***(G-3930)***

Lighthouse Youth Services Inc (PA) ... 513 221-3350
401 E Mcmillan St Cincinnati (45206) ***(G-3931)***

Lighthouse Youth Services Inc ... 740 634-3094
1071 Tong Hollow Rd Bainbridge (45612) ***(G-931)***

Lighting Maint Harmon Sign ... 419 841-6658
7844 W Central Ave Toledo (43617) ***(G-17855)***

Lighting Services Inc ... 330 405-4879
9001 Dutton Dr Twinsburg (44087) ***(G-18293)***

Lightwell Inc (PA) ... 614 310-2700
565 Metro Pl S Ste 220 Dublin (43017) ***(G-10272)***

Lillian and Betty Ratner Schl ... 216 464-0033
27575 Shaker Blvd Cleveland (44124) ***(G-5870)***

Lima Auto Mall Inc ... 419 993-6000
2200 N Cable Rd Lima (45807) ***(G-12675)***

Lima Cdllac Pntiac Olds Nissan, Lima *Also called Lima Auto Mall Inc* ***(G-12675)***

Lima City School Central Svcs, Lima *Also called Lima City School District* ***(G-12676)***

Lima City School District ... 419 996-3450
600 E Wayne St Lima (45801) ***(G-12676)***

Lima Cnvlscent HM Fndation Inc (PA) ... 419 227-5450
1650 Allentown Rd Lima (45805) ***(G-12677)***

Lima Communications Corp ... 419 228-8835
1424 Rice Ave Lima (45805) ***(G-12678)***

Lima Community Health Center, Lima *Also called Health Partners Western Ohio* ***(G-12656)***

Lima Dental Assoc Risolvato Lt ... 419 228-4036
2115 Allentown Rd Ste C Lima (45805) ***(G-12679)***

Lima Distribution Center, Lima *Also called Spartannash Company* ***(G-12744)***

Lima Division, Lima *Also called Benjamin Steel Company Inc* ***(G-12605)***

Lima Family YMCA (PA) ... 419 223-6045
345 S Elizabeth St Lima (45801) ***(G-12680)***

Lima Mall Inc ... 419 331-6255
2400 Elida Rd Ste 166 Lima (45805) ***(G-12681)***

Lima Manor, Lima *Also called Hcf of Lima Inc* ***(G-12654)***

Lima Medical Supplies Inc ... 419 226-9581
770 W North St Lima (45801) ***(G-12682)***

Lima Memorial Health System, Lima *Also called Lima Memorial Hospital* ***(G-12683)***

Lima Memorial Hospital (HQ) ... 419 228-3335
1001 Bellefontaine Ave Lima (45804) ***(G-12683)***

Lima Memorial Hospital La ... 419 738-5151
1251 Lincoln Hwy Wapakoneta (45895) ***(G-18648)***

Lima Memorial Joint Oper Co (PA) ... 419 228-5165
1001 Belelfontaine Ave Lima (45804) ***(G-12684)***

Lima Pathology Associates Labs (PA) ... 419 226-9595
415 W Market St Ste B Lima (45801) ***(G-12685)***

Lima Radio Hospital Inc (PA) ... 419 229-6010
608 N Main St Lima (45801) ***(G-12686)***

Lima Sheet Metal Machine & Mfg ... 419 229-1161
1001 Bowman Rd Lima (45804) ***(G-12687)***

Lima Superior Federal Cr Un (PA) ... 419 223-9746
4230 Elida Rd Lima (45807) ***(G-12688)***

Lima-Allen County Paramedics, Lima *Also called Harter Ventures Inc* ***(G-12651)***
Limbach Company LLC 614 299-2175
851 Williams Ave Columbus (43212) ***(G-7977)***
Limbach Company LLC 614 299-2175
822 Cleveland Ave Columbus (43201) ***(G-7978)***
Limited, Columbus *Also called L Brands Store Dsign Cnstr Inc* ***(G-7934)***
Limited Services Corporation, Columbus *Also called L Brands Service Company LLC* ***(G-7933)***
Limited Technology Svcs Inc, Columbus *Also called Mast Technology Services Inc* ***(G-8036)***
Limitless Solutions Inc 614 577-1550
600 Claycraft Rd Columbus (43230) ***(G-7979)***
Lin R Rogers Elec Contrs Inc 614 876-9336
5050 Nike Dr Ste C Hilliard (43026) ***(G-11785)***
Lincare Inc 330 928-0884
1566 Akron Peninsula Rd # 2 Akron (44313) ***(G-315)***
Lincoln Crawford Nrsg/Rehab CT 513 861-2044
1346 Lincoln Ave Cincinnati (45206) ***(G-3932)***
Lincoln Fincl Advisors Corp 216 765-7400
28601 Chagrin Blvd # 300 Beachwood (44122) ***(G-1074)***
Lincoln Fincl Advisors Corp 614 888-6516
7650 Rivers Edge Dr # 200 Columbus (43235) ***(G-7980)***
Lincoln Hts Hlth Connection, Cincinnati *Also called The Healthcare Connection Inc* ***(G-4592)***
Lincoln Moving & Storage Co 216 741-5500
8686 Brookpark Rd Cleveland (44129) ***(G-5871)***
Lincoln Mrcury Kings Auto Mall (PA) 513 683-3800
9600 Kings Auto Mall Rd Cincinnati (45249) ***(G-3933)***
Lincoln Park Associates II LP 937 297-4300
694 Isaac Prugh Way Dayton (45429) ***(G-9568)***
Lincoln Park Manor, Dayton *Also called Lincoln Park Associates II LP* ***(G-9568)***
Lincolnview Local Schools (PA) 419 968-2226
15945 Middle Point Rd Van Wert (45891) ***(G-18483)***
Lincolnway Home, Middle Point *Also called County of Van Wert* ***(G-14246)***
Linde Gas, Cincinnati *Also called Airgas Usa LLC* ***(G-2916)***
Linden Home Dialysis, Dayton *Also called Total Renal Care Inc* ***(G-9817)***
Linden Industries Inc 330 928-4064
137 Ascot Pkwy Cuyahoga Falls (44223) ***(G-9109)***
Linden Medical Center, Columbus *Also called Family Health Care Center Inc* ***(G-7559)***
LINDER CENTER OF HOPE, Mason *Also called Craig and Frances Lindner Cent* ***(G-13569)***
Lindhorst & Dreidame Co Lpa 513 421-6630
312 Walnut St Ste 3100 Cincinnati (45202) ***(G-3934)***
Lindley Inn 740 797-9701
9000 Hocking Hills Dr The Plains (45780) ***(G-17503)***
Lindner Clinical Trial Center 513 585-1777
2123 Auburn Ave Ste 424 Cincinnati (45219) ***(G-3935)***
Lindsey Accura Inc 800 980-8199
5880 Scarborough Blvd Columbus (43232) ***(G-7981)***
Lindsey Cnstr & Design Inc 330 785-9931
2151 S Arlington Rd Akron (44306) ***(G-316)***
Lineage Logistics LLC 937 328-3349
1985 Airpark Dr Springfield (45502) ***(G-17061)***
Linemaster Services LLC 614 507-9945
5736 Buckeye Pkwy Grove City (43123) ***(G-11449)***
Liniform Service, Barberton *Also called Barberton Laundry & Cleaning* ***(G-947)***
Link & Reneissance Inc 440 235-0501
26111 John Rd Olmsted Twp (44138) ***(G-15538)***
Link Construction Group Inc 937 292-7774
895 County Road 32 N Bellefontaine (43311) ***(G-1354)***
Link Iq LLC (PA) 859 983-6080
125 Westpark Rd Dayton (45459) ***(G-9569)***
Linking Employment Abilities (PA) 216 696-2716
2545 Lorain Ave Cleveland (44113) ***(G-5872)***
Linkmedia 360, Independence *Also called National Yllow Pages Media LLC* ***(G-12101)***
Links 937 644-9988
200 Gallery Dr Marysville (43040) ***(G-13510)***
Links At The Renaissance, Olmsted Twp *Also called E J Links Co The Inc* ***(G-15535)***
Links At Windy Knoll LLC 937 631-3744
500 Roscommon Dr Springfield (45503) ***(G-17062)***
Links Golf Course, Olmsted Twp *Also called Link & Reneissance Inc* ***(G-15538)***
Linn Street Holdings LLC 513 699-8825
2135 Dana Ave Ste 200 Cincinnati (45207) ***(G-3936)***
Linsalata Capital Partners Fun 440 684-1400
5900 Landerbrook Dr # 280 Cleveland (44124) ***(G-5873)***
Linwood Park Company 440 963-0481
4920 Liberty Ave Vermilion (44089) ***(G-18556)***
Lion Group Inc (HQ) 937 898-1949
7200 Poe Ave Ste 400 Dayton (45414) ***(G-9570)***
Lion Uniform Group, Fairborn *Also called G&K Services LLC* ***(G-10675)***
Lion's Den, Worthington *Also called Mile Inc* ***(G-19829)***
Lion's Gate Trning SEC Sltions, Euclid *Also called Lions Gate SEC Solutions Inc* ***(G-10648)***
Lion-Vallen Ltd Partnership (PA) 937 898-1949
7200 Poe Ave Ste 400 Dayton (45414) ***(G-9571)***
Lions Club International Inc 330 424-3490
38240 Industrial Park Rd Lisbon (44432) ***(G-12803)***
Lions Den, Columbus *Also called Mile Inc* ***(G-8085)***
Lions Gate SEC Solutions Inc 440 539-8382
2073 E 221st St Euclid (44117) ***(G-10648)***
Lippincott Plumbing-Heating AC 419 222-0856
872 Saint Johns Ave Lima (45804) ***(G-12689)***

Liqui-Box Corporation 614 888-9280
480 Schrock Rd Ste G Columbus (43229) ***(G-7982)***
Liqui-Box International Inc 614 888-9280
480 Schrock Rd Ste G Columbus (43229) ***(G-7983)***
Liquid Transport Corp 513 769-4777
10711 Evendale Dr Cincinnati (45241) ***(G-3937)***
Liquid Wste Solidification LLC (PA) 440 285-4648
12488 Gar Hwy Chardon (44024) ***(G-2703)***
Lisbon Lions Club, Lisbon *Also called Lions Club International Inc* ***(G-12803)***
Lisnr Inc 513 322-8400
920 Race St Ste 4 Cincinnati (45202) ***(G-3938)***
Litco International Inc (PA) 330 539-5433
1 Litco Dr Vienna (44473) ***(G-18581)***
Literature Fulfillment Svcs 513 774-8600
11400 Grooms Rd Ste 112 Blue Ash (45242) ***(G-1598)***
Lithko Contracting LLC 614 733-0300
8065 Corporate Blvd Plain City (43064) ***(G-16057)***
Lithko Contracting LLC (PA) 513 564-2000
2958 Crescentville Rd West Chester (45069) ***(G-18963)***
Lithko Contracting LLC 513 863-5100
900 N Garver Rd Monroe (45050) ***(G-14574)***
Lithko Restoration Tech LLC (PA) 513 863-5500
990 N Main St Monroe (45050) ***(G-14575)***
Lithko Restoration Tech LLC 614 221-0711
1059 Cable Ave Columbus (43222) ***(G-7984)***
Lithuanian World Community 513 542-0076
5927 Monticello Ave Cincinnati (45224) ***(G-3939)***
Litigation Management Inc 440 484-2000
6000 Parkland Blvd # 100 Mayfield Heights (44124) ***(G-13876)***
Litigation Support Svcs Inc 513 241-5605
817 Main St Ste 400 Cincinnati (45202) ***(G-3940)***
Litter Bob Fuel & Heating Co (HQ) 740 773-2196
524 Eastern Ave Chillicothe (45601) ***(G-2801)***
Litter Distributing Co Inc 740 774-2831
656 Hospital Rd Chillicothe (45601) ***(G-2802)***
Litter Quality Propane, Chillicothe *Also called Litter Bob Fuel & Heating Co* ***(G-2801)***
Little Bark View Limited (PA) 216 520-1250
8111 Rockside Rd Ste 200 Cleveland (44125) ***(G-5874)***
Little Drmers Big Blievers LLC 614 824-4666
870 Michigan Ave Columbus (43215) ***(G-7985)***
Little Lambs Childrens Center 614 471-9269
425 S Hamilton Rd Gahanna (43230) ***(G-11132)***
Little Miami Home Care Inc 513 248-8988
5371 S Milford Rd Apt 16 Milford (45150) ***(G-14401)***
Little Miami River Catering Co 937 848-2464
80 E Franklin St Bellbrook (45305) ***(G-1341)***
Little Mountain Country Club, Painesville *Also called Madison Route 20 LLC* ***(G-15723)***
Little Squirt Sports Park 419 227-6200
1996 W Robb Ave Lima (45805) ***(G-12690)***
Little Theater Off Broadway 614 875-3919
3981 Broadway Grove City (43123) ***(G-11450)***
Little Turtle Golf Club, Westerville *Also called Turtle Golf Management Ltd* ***(G-19303)***
Littler Mendelson PC 216 696-7600
1100 Superior Ave E Fl 20 Cleveland (44114) ***(G-5875)***
Live Technologies LLC 614 278-7777
3445 Millennium Ct Columbus (43219) ***(G-7986)***
Liverpool Coil Processing Inc 330 558-2600
880 Steel Dr Valley City (44280) ***(G-18465)***
Liverpool-Coil-Processing, Valley City *Also called Liverpool Coil Processing Inc* ***(G-18465)***
Livin Care Alter of Kirke Inc 740 927-3209
205 E Main St Kirkersville (43033) ***(G-12320)***
Living Assistance Services 330 733-1532
22 Northwest Ave Tallmadge (44278) ***(G-17481)***
Living Care Alternatives 740 927-3209
205 E Main St Kirkersville (43033) ***(G-12321)***
Living Care Altrntves of Utica 740 892-3414
233 N Main St Utica (43080) ***(G-18457)***
Living In Family Environment 614 475-5305
142 N High St Gahanna (43230) ***(G-11133)***
Living Matters LLC 866 587-8074
13613 Caine Ave Cleveland (44105) ***(G-5876)***
Livinginston Court Flea Market, Columbus *Also called Rainbow Flea Market Inc* ***(G-8486)***
Livingston Care Center, Dayton *Also called Huffman Health Care Inc* ***(G-9510)***
Livingston Painting, Union City *Also called Rl Painting and Mfg Inc* ***(G-18354)***
Lkq Triplettasap Inc (HQ) 330 733-6333
1435 Triplett Blvd Akron (44306) ***(G-317)***
Llanfair Retirement Community, Cincinnati *Also called Ohio Living* ***(G-4156)***
LLP Ziegler Metzger 216 781-5470
1111 Superior Ave E # 1000 Cleveland (44114) ***(G-5877)***
Lm Constrction Trry Lvrini Inc 740 695-9604
67682 Clark Rd Saint Clairsville (43950) ***(G-16492)***
Lmn Development LLC (PA) 419 433-7200
7000 Kalahari Dr Sandusky (44870) ***(G-16623)***
Lmt Enterprises Maumee Inc 419 891-7325
1772 Indian Wood Cir Maumee (43537) ***(G-13810)***
LNS America Inc (HQ) 513 528-5674
4621 E Tech Dr Cincinnati (45245) ***(G-2860)***
Loan Protector Insurance Svcs, Solon *Also called LP Insurance Services LLC* ***(G-16866)***
Lobby Shoppes Inc (PA) 937 324-0002
200 N Murray St Springfield (45503) ***(G-17063)***
Lobby Shoppes Inc-Springfield, Springfield *Also called Lobby Shoppes Inc* ***(G-17063)***

ALPHABETIC

LOCAL 17A, Canton *Also called United Food & Commercial Wkr* *(G-2517)*
Local 18 IUOE (PA) 216 432-3131
　3515 Prospect Ave E Fl 1　Cleveland　(44115)　*(G-5878)*
Local 268, Cleveland *Also called Amalgamated Transit Union* *(G-4945)*
Local 5-689, Piketon *Also called Pace International Union* *(G-15983)*
Local 883, North Olmsted *Also called Interntonal Aliance Thea Stage* *(G-15293)*
Local 911 United Mine Workers 740 256-6083
　5102 State Route 218　Gallipolis　(45631)　*(G-11203)*
Local Union 856 Uaw Bldg Corp 330 733-6231
　501 Kelly Ave　Akron　(44306)　*(G-318)*
Lochard Inc 937 492-8811
　903 Wapakoneta Ave　Sidney　(45365)　*(G-16784)*
Locker Moving & Storage Inc (PA) 330 784-0477
　131 Perry Dr Nw　Canton　(44708)　*(G-2380)*
Lockes Garden Center Inc 440 774-6981
　461 E Lorain St　Oberlin　(44074)　*(G-15507)*
Lockhart Concrete Co (PA) 330 745-6520
　800 W Waterloo Rd　Akron　(44314)　*(G-319)*
Lockheed Martin, West Chester *Also called Leidos Technical Services Inc* *(G-19063)*
Locktooth Division, Cleveland *Also called Hodell-Natco Industries Inc* *(G-5699)*
Locum Medical Group LLC 216 464-2125
　6100 Oak Tree Blvd　Independence　(44131)　*(G-12094)*
Locust Dental Center 330 535-7876
　300 Locust St Ste 430　Akron　(44302)　*(G-320)*
Locust Hills Golf Course, Springfield *Also called Locust Hills Golf Inc* *(G-17064)*
Locust Hills Golf Inc 937 265-5152
　5575 N River Rd　Springfield　(45502)　*(G-17064)*
Locust Ridge Nursing Home Inc (PA) 937 444-2920
　12745 Elm Corner Rd　Williamsburg　(45176)　*(G-19494)*
Lodge At Saw Mill Creek, The, Huron *Also called Saw Mill Creek Ltd* *(G-12030)*
Lodge Care Center Inc 513 683-9966
　9370 Union Cemetery Rd　Loveland　(45140)　*(G-13007)*
Lodge Nursing & Rehab Center, Loveland *Also called Boy-Ko Management Inc* *(G-12979)*
Lodge Stone Wood 513 769-4325
　11350 Swing Rd　Blue Ash　(45241)　*(G-1599)*
Lodging First LLC 614 792-2770
　94 N High St Ste 250　Dublin　(43017)　*(G-10273)*
Lodging Industry Inc 440 323-7488
　7704 Milan Rd　Sandusky　(44870)　*(G-16624)*
Lodging Industry Inc 419 732-2929
　1723 E Perry St　Port Clinton　(43452)　*(G-16112)*
Lodging Industry Inc 440 324-3911
　523 Griswold Rd　Elyria　(44035)　*(G-10529)*
Lodi Community Hospital (PA) 330 948-1222
　225 Elyria St　Lodi　(44254)　*(G-12827)*
Loeb Electric Company (PA) 614 294-6351
　1800 E 5th Ave Ste A　Columbus　(43219)　*(G-7987)*
Lofino's Investment, Dayton *Also called Lofinos Inc* *(G-9572)*
Lofinos Inc 937 431-1662
　6018 Wilmington Pike　Dayton　(45459)　*(G-9572)*
Logan Acres, Bellefontaine *Also called County of Logan* *(G-1351)*
Logan Clutch Corporation 440 808-4258
　28855 Ranney Pkwy　Cleveland　(44145)　*(G-5879)*
Logan Cnty Prbate Juvenile Crt, Bellefontaine *Also called County of Logan* *(G-1349)*
Logan County Board of Mrdd, Bellefontaine *Also called Logan Housing Corp Inc* *(G-1356)*
Logan County Childrens Svcs, Bellefontaine *Also called County of Logan* *(G-1352)*
Logan County Engineering Off 937 592-2791
　1991 County Road 13　Bellefontaine　(43311)　*(G-1355)*
Logan Health Care Center 740 385-2155
　300 Arlington Ave　Logan　(43138)　*(G-12846)*
Logan Healthcare Leasing LLC 216 367-1214
　300 Arlington Ave　Logan　(43138)　*(G-12847)*
Logan Housing Corp Inc 937 592-2009
　1973 State Route 47 W　Bellefontaine　(43311)　*(G-1356)*
Logan Logistics, Canton *Also called W L Logan Trucking Company* *(G-2529)*
Logan-Hocking School District 740 385-7844
　13483 Mysville William Rd　Logan　(43138)　*(G-12848)*
Logic Soft Inc 614 884-5544
　5900 Sawmill Rd Ste 200　Dublin　(43017)　*(G-10274)*
Logikor LLC 513 762-7678
　463 Ohio Pike Ste 105　Cincinnati　(45255)　*(G-3941)*
Logistics Department, Dayton *Also called Wright Brothers Aero Inc* *(G-9887)*
Logistics Inc 419 478-1514
　6010 Skyview Dr　Toledo　(43612)　*(G-17856)*
Logos Logistics Inc 734 304-1777
　5657 Enterprise Blvd　Toledo　(43612)　*(G-17857)*
Lolly The Trolley, Cleveland *Also called Trolley Tours of Cleveland* *(G-6550)*
London Computer Systems Inc 513 583-0840
　9140 Waterstone Blvd　Cincinnati　(45249)　*(G-3942)*
London Health & Rehab Ctr LLC 740 852-3100
　218 Elm St　London　(43140)　*(G-12865)*
Long-Stanton Mfg Company 513 874-8020
　9388 Sutton Pl　West Chester　(45011)　*(G-18964)*
Longbow Research LLC (PA) 216 986-0700
　6050 Oak Tree Blvd # 350　Independence　(44131)　*(G-12095)*
Longmeadow Care Center Inc 330 297-5781
　565 Bryn Mawr St　Ravenna　(44266)　*(G-16249)*
Longterm Lodging Inc 614 224-0614
　721 S Souder Ave　Columbus　(43223)　*(G-7988)*
Longwood Family YMCA, Macedonia *Also called Young Mens Christian Assoc* *(G-13091)*

Longwood Phase One Assoc LP 561 998-0700
　3750 Fleming Ave　Cleveland　(44115)　*(G-5880)*
Longworth Enterprises Inc 513 738-4663
　8050 Beckett Center Dr　West Chester　(45069)　*(G-18965)*
Longyear Company 740 373-2190
　1010 Greene St　Marietta　(45750)　*(G-13344)*
Lorad LLC 216 265-2862
　24400 Sperry Dr　Westlake　(44145)　*(G-19370)*
Lorain City School District 440 233-2239
　1930 W 19th St　Lorain　(44052)　*(G-12913)*
Lorain Cnty Brd Mntl Rtrdtn, Elyria *Also called County of Lorain* *(G-10495)*
Lorain Cnty Bys Girls CLB Inc (PA) 440 775-2582
　4111 Pearl Ave　Lorain　(44055)　*(G-12914)*
Lorain Cnty Elderly Hsing Corp 440 288-1600
　1600 Kansas Ave　Lorain　(44052)　*(G-12915)*
Lorain Cnty Sty Off Eqp Co Inc 440 960-7070
　1953 Cooper Foster Pk Rd　Amherst　(44001)　*(G-592)*
Lorain Country Job & Fmly Svcs, Elyria *Also called County of Lorain* *(G-10498)*
Lorain County Alcohol and Drug 440 246-0109
　305 W 20th St　Lorain　(44052)　*(G-12916)*
Lorain County Alcohol and Drug (PA) 440 989-4900
　2115 W Park Dr　Lorain　(44053)　*(G-12917)*
Lorain County Board 440 329-3734
　1091 Infirmary Rd　Elyria　(44035)　*(G-10530)*
Lorain County Childrens Svcs, Elyria *Also called County of Lorain* *(G-10501)*
Lorain County Community Action (PA) 440 245-2009
　936 Broadway　Lorain　(44052)　*(G-12918)*
Lorain County Community Action 440 246-0480
　1050 Reid Ave　Lorain　(44052)　*(G-12919)*
Lorain County Engineers, Elyria *Also called County of Lorain* *(G-10497)*
Lorain County Garage, Elyria *Also called County of Lorain* *(G-10500)*
Lorain County Landfill, Oberlin *Also called Republic Services Inc* *(G-15518)*
Lorain County Sani Engineers, Elyria *Also called County of Lorain* *(G-10494)*
Lorain Family Hlth & RES Ctrs, Lorain *Also called Cleveland Clinic Foundation* *(G-12893)*
Lorain Glass Co Inc 440 277-6004
　1865 N Ridge Rd E Ste E　Lorain　(44055)　*(G-12920)*
Lorain Life Care Ambulance Svc 440 244-6467
　109 W 23rd St　Lorain　(44052)　*(G-12921)*
Lorain Lifecare Ambulance, Elyria *Also called Lifecare Ambulance Inc* *(G-10526)*
Lorain National Bank (HQ) 440 244-6000
　457 Broadway　Lorain　(44052)　*(G-12922)*
Lorain Party Center 440 282-5599
　5900 S Mayflower Dr　Lorain　(44053)　*(G-12923)*
Loraine Cnty Bd Mntal Rtrdtion, Lorain *Also called County of Lorain* *(G-12900)*
Lorantffy Care Center Inc 330 666-2631
　2631 Copley Rd　Copley　(44321)　*(G-8969)*
Lorenz Corporation (PA) 937 228-6118
　501 E 3rd St　Dayton　(45402)　*(G-9573)*
Lori Holding Co (PA) 740 342-3230
　1400 Commerce Dr　New Lexington　(43764)　*(G-14920)*
Lorraine Elyria Broadcasting, Elyria *Also called Weol* *(G-10571)*
Lory Dialysis LLC 740 522-2955
　65 S Terrace Ave　Newark　(43055)　*(G-15062)*
Los Alamos Technical Assoc Inc 614 508-1200
　756 Park Meadow Rd　Westerville　(43081)　*(G-19275)*
Losantiville Country Club 513 631-4133
　3097 Losantiville Ave　Cincinnati　(45213)　*(G-3943)*
Lost Creek Care Center, Lima *Also called Volunters Amer Care Facilities* *(G-12774)*
Lost Creek Country Club Inc 419 229-2026
　2409 Lost Creek Blvd　Lima　(45804)　*(G-12691)*
Lost Creek Health C, Lima *Also called Guardian Elde* *(G-12649)*
Lost Creek Health Care 419 225-9040
　804 S Mumaugh Rd　Lima　(45804)　*(G-12692)*
Lost Nation Golf Course, Willoughby *Also called City of Willoughby* *(G-19513)*
Lost Nation Sports Park 440 602-4000
　38630 Jet Center Pl　Willoughby　(44094)　*(G-19545)*
Loth Inc (PA) 513 554-4900
　3574 E Kemper Rd　Cincinnati　(45241)　*(G-3944)*
Loth Inc 614 487-4000
　855 Grandview Ave Ste 2　Columbus　(43215)　*(G-7989)*
Lott Industries Incorporated 419 476-2516
　5500 Telegraph Rd　Toledo　(43612)　*(G-17858)*
Lott Industries Incorporated 419 891-5215
　1645 Holland Rd　Maumee　(43537)　*(G-13811)*
Lott Industries Incorporated (PA) 419 534-4980
　3350 Hill Ave　Toledo　(43607)　*(G-17859)*
Lott Industries Incorporated 419 534-4980
　3350 Hill Ave　Toledo　(43607)　*(G-17860)*
Lou Ritenour Decorators Inc 330 425-3232
　2066 Case Pkwy S　Twinsburg　(44087)　*(G-18294)*
Lou-Ray Associates Inc 330 220-1999
　1378 Pearl Rd Ste 201　Brunswick　(44212)　*(G-1936)*
Louderback Fmly Invstments Inc 937 845-1762
　3545 S Dayton Lakeview Rd　New Carlisle　(45344)　*(G-14893)*
Louieville Title Agncy For Nrt 419 248-4611
　626 Madison Ave Ste 100　Toledo　(43604)　*(G-17861)*
Louis Perry & Associates Inc 330 334-1585
　165 Smokerise Dr　Wadsworth　(44281)　*(G-18605)*
Louis Stokes Cleveland Vamc, Cleveland *Also called Veterans Health Administration* *(G-6625)*

Louis Stokes Head Start 216 295-0854
4075 E 173rd St Cleveland (44128) *(G-5881)*

Louis Trauth Dairy LLC (HQ) 859 431-7553
9991 Commerce Park Dr West Chester (45246) *(G-19064)*

Louisville Child Care Center 330 875-4303
3477 Elmhurst Cir Uniontown (44685) *(G-18377)*

Louisville Frternal Order of E 330 875-2113
306 W Main St Louisville (44641) *(G-12968)*

Louisville YMCA, Louisville *Also called Y M C A Central Stark County* *(G-12975)*

Louisvlle Title Agcy For NW OH (PA) 419 248-4611
626 Madison Ave Ste 100 Toledo (43604) *(G-17862)*

LOURIES OF HILLSBORO, Hillsboro *Also called Laurels of Hillsboro* *(G-11849)*

Love N Comfort Home Care 740 450-7658
2814 Maple Ave Zanesville (43701) *(G-20325)*

Loveland Excavating Inc 513 965-6600
260 Osborne Dr Fairfield (45014) *(G-10748)*

Loveland Excavating and Paving, Fairfield *Also called Loveland Excavating Inc* *(G-10748)*

Loveland Health Care Center 513 605-6000
501 N 2nd St Loveland (45140) *(G-13008)*

Loveman Steel Corporation 440 232-6200
5455 Perkins Rd Bedford (44146) *(G-1289)*

Loving Care Hospice Inc (PA) 740 852-7755
56 S Oak St London (43140) *(G-12866)*

Loving Family Home Care Inc 888 469-2178
2600 N Reynolds Rd 101a Toledo (43615) *(G-17863)*

Loving Hands Home Care Inc. 330 792-7032
4179 Nottingham Ave Youngstown (44511) *(G-20100)*

Low Country Metal, Richfield *Also called I-Tran Inc* *(G-16360)*

Lowe's Greenhouses & Gift Shop, Chagrin Falls *Also called Lowes Grnhse & Gift Sp Inc (G-2670)*

Lower Great Lakes Kenworth Inc 419 874-3511
12650 Eckel Junction Rd Perrysburg (43551) *(G-15890)*

Lowes Grnhse & Gift Sp Inc 440 543-5123
16540 Chillicothe Rd Chagrin Falls (44023) *(G-2670)*

Lowes Home Centers LLC 216 351-4723
7327 Northcliff Ave Cleveland (44144) *(G-5882)*

Lowes Home Centers LLC 419 739-1300
1340 Bellefontaine St Wapakoneta (45895) *(G-18649)*

Lowes Home Centers LLC 937 235-2920
8421 Old Troy Pike Dayton (45424) *(G-9574)*

Lowes Home Centers LLC 740 574-6200
7915 Ohio River Rd Wheelersburg (45694) *(G-19435)*

Lowes Home Centers LLC 330 665-9356
186 N Clvland Mssilon Rd Akron (44333) *(G-321)*

Lowes Home Centers LLC 330 829-2700
2595 W State St Alliance (44601) *(G-538)*

Lowes Home Centers LLC 937 599-4000
2168 Us Highway 68 S Bellefontaine (43311) *(G-1357)*

Lowes Home Centers LLC 419 420-7531
1077 Bright Rd Findlay (45840) *(G-10935)*

Lowes Home Centers LLC 330 832-1901
101 Massillon Marketplace Massillon (44646) *(G-13704)*

Lowes Home Centers LLC 513 741-0585
10235 Colerain Ave Cincinnati (45251) *(G-3945)*

Lowes Home Centers LLC 614 433-9957
1465 Polaris Pkwy Columbus (43240) *(G-6822)*

Lowes Home Centers LLC 740 389-9737
1840 Marion Mt Gilead Rd Marion (43302) *(G-13430)*

Lowes Home Centers LLC 740 450-5500
3755 Frazeysburg Rd Zanesville (43701) *(G-20326)*

Lowes Home Centers LLC 513 598-7050
6150 Harrison Ave Cincinnati (45247) *(G-3946)*

Lowes Home Centers LLC 614 769-9940
8231 E Broad St Reynoldsburg (43068) *(G-16317)*

Lowes Home Centers LLC 614 853-6200
1675 Georgesville Sq Dr Columbus (43228) *(G-7990)*

Lowes Home Centers LLC 440 937-3500
1445 Center Rd Avon (44011) *(G-893)*

Lowes Home Centers LLC 513 445-1000
575 Corwin Nixon Blvd South Lebanon (45065) *(G-16926)*

Lowes Home Centers LLC 216 831-2860
24500 Miles Rd Bedford (44146) *(G-1290)*

Lowes Home Centers LLC 937 327-6000
1601 N Bechtle Ave Springfield (45504) *(G-17065)*

Lowes Home Centers LLC 419 331-3598
2411 N Eastown Rd Lima (45807) *(G-12693)*

Lowes Home Centers LLC 740 681-3464
2240 Lowes Dr Lancaster (43130) *(G-12413)*

Lowes Home Centers LLC 614 659-0530
6555 Dublin Center Dr Dublin (43017) *(G-10275)*

Lowes Home Centers LLC 614 238-2601
3616 E Broad St Columbus (43213) *(G-7991)*

Lowes Home Centers LLC 740 522-0003
888 Hebron Rd Newark (43056) *(G-15063)*

Lowes Home Centers LLC 740 773-7777
867 N Bridge St Chillicothe (45601) *(G-2803)*

Lowes Home Centers LLC 440 998-6555
2416 Dillon Dr Ashtabula (44004) *(G-745)*

Lowes Home Centers LLC 513 753-5094
618 Mount Moriah Dr Cincinnati (45245) *(G-2861)*

Lowes Home Centers LLC 614 497-6170
3899 S High St Columbus (43207) *(G-7992)*

Lowes Home Centers LLC 513 731-6127
5385 Ridge Ave Cincinnati (45213) *(G-3947)*

Lowes Home Centers LLC 330 287-2261
3788 Burbank Rd Wooster (44691) *(G-19742)*

Lowes Home Centers LLC 937 339-2544
2000 W Main St Troy (45373) *(G-18211)*

Lowes Home Centers LLC 440 392-0027
9600 Mentor Ave Mentor (44060) *(G-14078)*

Lowes Home Centers LLC 440 942-2759
36300 Euclid Ave Willoughby (44094) *(G-19546)*

Lowes Home Centers LLC 740 374-2151
842 Pike St Marietta (45750) *(G-13345)*

Lowes Home Centers LLC 419 874-6758
10295 Fremont Pike Perrysburg (43551) *(G-15891)*

Lowes Home Centers LLC 330 626-2980
1210 State Route 303 Streetsboro (44241) *(G-17259)*

Lowes Home Centers LLC 419 389-9464
5501 Airport Hwy Toledo (43615) *(G-17864)*

Lowes Home Centers LLC 419 843-9758
7000 W Central Ave Toledo (43617) *(G-17865)*

Lowes Home Centers LLC 614 447-2851
2345 Silver Dr Columbus (43211) *(G-7993)*

Lowes Home Centers LLC 330 245-4300
940 Interstate Pkwy Akron (44312) *(G-322)*

Lowes Home Centers LLC 513 965-3280
5694 Romar Dr Milford (45150) *(G-14402)*

Lowes Home Centers LLC 330 908-2750
8224 Golden Link Blvd Northfield (44067) *(G-15382)*

Lowes Home Centers LLC 419 470-2491
1136 W Alexis Rd Toledo (43612) *(G-17866)*

Lowes Home Centers LLC 513 336-9741
9380 S Masn Montgomery Rd Mason (45040) *(G-13612)*

Lowes Home Centers LLC 937 498-8400
2700 W Michigan St Sidney (45365) *(G-16785)*

Lowes Home Centers LLC 740 699-3000
50421 Valley Plaza Dr Saint Clairsville (43950) *(G-16493)*

Lowes Home Centers LLC 330 920-9280
3570 Hudson Dr Stow (44224) *(G-17218)*

Lowes Home Centers LLC 740 589-3750
983 E State St Athens (45701) *(G-791)*

Lowes Home Centers LLC 740 393-5350
1010 Coshocton Ave Mount Vernon (43050) *(G-14779)*

Lowes Home Centers LLC 937 547-2400
1550 Wagner Ave Greenville (45331) *(G-11389)*

Lowes Home Centers LLC 330 335-1900
1065 Wlliams Reserve Blvd Wadsworth (44281) *(G-18606)*

Lowes Home Centers LLC 937 347-4000
126 Hospitality Dr Xenia (45385) *(G-19918)*

Lowes Home Centers LLC 440 239-2630
9149 Pearl Rd Strongsville (44136) *(G-17324)*

Lowes Home Centers LLC 513 755-4300
7975 Tylersville Sq Rd West Chester (45069) *(G-18966)*

Lowes Home Centers LLC 513 671-2093
505 E Kemper Rd Cincinnati (45246) *(G-3948)*

Lowes Home Centers LLC 440 331-1027
20639 Center Ridge Rd Rocky River (44116) *(G-16440)*

Lowes Home Centers LLC 330 677-3040
218 Nicholas Way Kent (44240) *(G-12247)*

Lowes Home Centers LLC 419 747-1920
940 N Lexington Spring Rd Ontario (44906) *(G-15559)*

Lowes Home Centers LLC 330 339-1936
495 Mill Rd New Philadelphia (44663) *(G-14971)*

Lowes Home Centers LLC 440 985-5700
7500 Oak Point Rd Lorain (44053) *(G-12924)*

Lowes Home Centers LLC 419 447-4101
1025 W Market St Tiffin (44883) *(G-17521)*

Lowes Home Centers LLC 937 578-4440
15775 Us Highway 36 Marysville (43040) *(G-13511)*

Lowes Home Centers LLC 440 324-5004
646 Midway Blvd Elyria (44035) *(G-10531)*

Lowes Home Centers LLC 937 438-4900
2900 Martins Dr Dayton (45449) *(G-9575)*

Lowes Home Centers LLC 937 427-1110
2850 Centre Dr Ste I Beavercreek (45324) *(G-1168)*

Lowes Home Centers LLC 937 848-5600
6300 Wilmington Pike Dayton (45459) *(G-9576)*

Lowes Home Centers LLC 614 529-5900
3600 Park Mill Run Dr Hilliard (43026) *(G-11786)*

Lowes Home Centers LLC 513 737-3700
1495 Main St Hamilton (45013) *(G-11625)*

Lowes Home Centers LLC 419 355-0221
1952 N State Route 53 Fremont (43420) *(G-11084)*

Lowes Home Centers LLC 419 624-6000
5500 Milan Rd Ste 304 Sandusky (44870) *(G-16625)*

Lowes Home Centers LLC 419 782-9000
1831 N Clinton St Defiance (43512) *(G-9926)*

Lowes Home Centers LLC 330 609-8000
940 Niles Cortland Rd Se Warren (44484) *(G-18725)*

Lowes Home Centers LLC 740 894-7120
294 County Road 120 S South Point (45680) *(G-16939)*

Lowes Home Centers LLC 513 727-3900
3125 Towne Blvd Middletown (45044) *(G-14305)*

Lowes Home Centers LLC 330 497-2720
6375 Strip Ave Nw Canton (44720) *(G-2381)*

Lowes Home Centers LLC 740 266-3500
4115 Mall Dr Steubenville (43952) *(G-17164)*
Lowes Home Centers LLC 330 965-4500
1100 Doral Dr Youngstown (44514) *(G-20101)*
Lowes Home Centers LLC 937 383-7000
1175 Rombach Ave Wilmington (45177) *(G-19630)*
Lowes Home Centers LLC 937 854-8200
5252 Salem Ave Dayton (45426) *(G-9577)*
Lowes Home Centers LLC 614 476-7100
4141 Morse Xing Columbus (43219) *(G-7994)*
Lowry Controls Inc 513 583-0182
273 E Kemper Rd Loveland (45140) *(G-13009)*
Loyal American Life Insur Co (HQ) 800 633-6752
250 E 5th St Fl 8 Cincinnati (45202) *(G-3949)*
Loyal Oak Golf Course Inc 330 825-2904
2909 Clvland Massillon Rd Barberton (44203) *(G-960)*
LP Insurance Services LLC 877 369-5121
6000 Cochran Rd Solon (44139) *(G-16866)*
Lpl Financial Holdings Inc 513 772-2592
11260 Chester Rd Ste 250 Cincinnati (45246) *(G-3950)*
Lq Management LLC 614 866-6456
2447 Brice Rd. Reynoldsburg (43068) *(G-16318)*
Lq Management LLC 513 771-0300
11029 Dowlin Dr Cincinnati (45241) *(G-3951)*
Lq Management LLC 216 447-1133
6161 Quarry Ln Cleveland (44131) *(G-5883)*
Lq Management LLC 216 251-8500
4222 W 150th St Cleveland (44135) *(G-5884)*
LSI Adl Techonology LLC 614 345-9040
2727 Scioto Pkwy Columbus (43221) *(G-7995)*
LSI Industries Inc 913 281-1100
10000 Alliance Rd Blue Ash (45242) *(G-1600)*
LT Harnett Trucking Inc 440 997-5528
2440 State Rd Ashtabula (44004) *(G-746)*
Lt Land Development LLC 937 382-0072
94 N South St Ste A Wilmington (45177) *(G-19631)*
Lt Trucking Inc 440 997-5528
2440 State Rd Ashtabula (44004) *(G-747)*
Ltc Nursing, North Royalton Also called Epilogue Inc *(G-15355)*
Ltc Pharmacy, Twinsburg Also called Pharmerica Long-Term Care Inc *(G-18305)*
Ltd Productions LLC 440 688-1905
9904 S Highland Ave Cleveland (44125) *(G-5885)*
Lti Inc 614 278-7777
3445 Millennium Ct Columbus (43219) *(G-7996)*
Lu-Jean Feng Clinic LLC 216 831-7007
31200 Pinetree Rd Cleveland (44124) *(G-5886)*
LUBRIZOL ADVANCED MATERIALS, INC., Avon Lake Also called Lubrizol Advanced Mtls Inc *(G-923)*
Lubrizol Advanced Mtls Inc 440 933-0400
550 Moore Rd Avon Lake (44012) *(G-923)*
Luburgh Inc (PA) 740 452-3668
4174 East Pike Zanesville (43701) *(G-20327)*
Lucas & Clark Family Dentistry 937 393-3494
624 S High St Hillsboro (45133) *(G-11850)*
Lucas Building Mainenance LLC 740 479-1800
323 Mastin Ave Ironton (45638) *(G-12162)*
Lucas County Asphalt Inc. 419 476-0705
7540 Hollow Creek Dr Toledo (43617) *(G-17867)*
Lucas County Board of Developm 419 380-4000
1154 Larc Ln Toledo (43614) *(G-17868)*
Lucas County Engineer, Holland Also called County of Lucas *(G-11879)*
Lucas County Home Training, Oregon Also called Desoto Dialysis LLC *(G-15590)*
Lucas County Prosecution, Toledo Also called County of Lucas *(G-17681)*
Lucas County Regional Hlth Dst, Toledo Also called County of Lucas *(G-17683)*
LUCAS COUNTY TASC, Toledo Also called Tasc of Northwest Ohio Inc *(G-18060)*
Lucas Funeral Homes Inc (PA) 419 294-1985
476 S Sandusky Ave Upper Sandusky (43351) *(G-18411)*
Lucas Metropolitan Hsing Auth. 419 259-9457
435 Nebraska Ave Toledo (43604) *(G-17869)*
Lucas Plumbing & Heating Inc 440 282-4567
2125 W Park Dr Lorain (44053) *(G-12925)*
Lucas Precision LLC 216 451-5588
13020 Saint Clair Ave Cleveland (44108) *(G-5887)*
Lucas-Batton Funeral Homes, Upper Sandusky Also called Lucas Funeral Homes Inc *(G-18411)*
Luce Smith & Scott Inc 440 746-1700
6860 W Snwvlle Rd Ste 110 Brecksville (44141) *(G-1788)*
Lucien Realty 440 331-8500
18630 Detroit Ave Cleveland (44107) *(G-5888)*
Luckey Transfer LLC 800 435-4371
401 E Robb Ave Lima (45801) *(G-12694)*
Ludy Greenhouse Mfg Corp (PA) 800 255-5839
122 Railroad St New Madison (45346) *(G-14937)*
Luis F Soto MD 330 649-9400
4689 Fulton Dr Nw Canton (44718) *(G-2382)*
Luk-Aftermarket Service Inc 330 273-4383
5370 Wegman Dr Valley City (44280) *(G-18466)*
Luke Immediate Care Center 419 227-2245
825 W Market St Ste 205 Lima (45805) *(G-12695)*
Luke Medical Center, Lima Also called Luke Immediate Care Center *(G-12695)*
Luke Theis Contractors, Findlay Also called Luke Theis Enterprises Inc *(G-10936)*

Luke Theis Enterprises Inc 419 422-2040
14120 State Route 568 Findlay (45840) *(G-10936)*
Lumber Craft, Columbus Also called Fifth Avenue Lumber Co *(G-7575)*
Lumberjack's Creative Bldg Ctr, Akron Also called Lumberjacks Inc *(G-323)*
Lumberjacks Inc (PA) 330 762-2401
723 E Tallmadge Ave Ste 1 Akron (44310) *(G-323)*
Lumenance LLC (PA) 319 541-6811
4449 Easton Way Fl 2 Columbus (43219) *(G-7997)*
Lumenomics Inc 614 798-3500
8333 Green Meadows Dr N Lewis Center (43035) *(G-12550)*
Luminex HD&f Company, Blue Ash Also called Luminex Home Decor *(G-1601)*
Luminex Home Decor (PA) 513 563-1113
10521 Millington Ct Blue Ash (45242) *(G-1601)*
Luper Neidental & Logan A Leg 614 221-7663
1160 Dublin Rd Ste 400 Columbus (43215) *(G-7998)*
Lusk & Harkin Ltd 614 221-3707
35 N 4th St Fl 5 Columbus (43215) *(G-7999)*
Lusk Hrkin Architects Planners, Columbus Also called Lusk & Harkin Ltd *(G-7999)*
Lute Supply Inc (PA) 740 353-1447
3920 Us Highway 23 Portsmouth (45662) *(G-16153)*
Luther Home of Mercy 419 836-3918
5810 N Main St Williston (43468) *(G-19500)*
Lutheran Home 419 724-1414
131 N Wheeling St Ofc Toledo (43605) *(G-17870)*
Lutheran Home 440 871-0090
2116 Dover Center Rd Cleveland (44145) *(G-5889)*
Lutheran Homes Society Inc 419 724-1525
2411 Seaman St Toledo (43605) *(G-17871)*
Lutheran Hospital, Solon Also called Lutheran Medical Center *(G-16867)*
Lutheran Housing Services Inc 419 861-4990
2021 N Mccord Rd Ste B Toledo (43615) *(G-17872)*
Lutheran Medical Center (HQ) 216 696-4300
33001 Solon Rd Ste 112 Solon (44139) *(G-16867)*
Lutheran Memorial Home Inc 419 502-5700
2021 N Mccord Rd Toledo (43615) *(G-17873)*
Lutheran Metropolitan Ministry 216 658-4638
2100 Lakeside Ave E Cleveland (44114) *(G-5890)*
Lutheran Outdr Ministries OH (PA) 614 890-2267
863 Eastwind Dr Westerville (43081) *(G-19276)*
Lutheran Scial Svcs Centl Ohio (PA) 419 289-3523
500 W Wilson Bridge Rd Worthington (43085) *(G-19825)*
Lutheran Scial Svcs Centl Ohio 419 289-3523
622 Center St Ashland (44805) *(G-678)*
Lutheran Senior City Inc (HQ) 614 228-5200
935 N Cassady Ave Columbus (43219) *(G-8000)*
Lutheran Social 419 229-2222
205 W Market St Ste 500 Lima (45801) *(G-12696)*
Lutheran Social Services of 614 228-5200
500 W Wilson Bridge Rd # 245 Worthington (43085) *(G-19826)*
Lutheran Village At Wolf Creek 419 861-2233
2001 Prrysbrg Hllnd Ofc Holland (43528) *(G-11893)*
Lutheran Village Courtyard, Columbus Also called Lutheran Senior City Inc *(G-8000)*
Luxfer Magtech Inc (HQ) 513 772-3066
2940 Highland Ave Ste 210 Cincinnati (45212) *(G-3952)*
Luxury Heating Co 440 366-0971
5327 Ford Rd Sheffield Village (44035) *(G-16738)*
Lws, Chardon Also called Liquid Wste Solidification LLC *(G-2703)*
Lyden Company 419 868-6800
310 S Reynolds Rd Ste A Toledo (43615) *(G-17874)*
Lyden Oil Company 330 832-7800
3249 Wales Ave Nw Massillon (44646) *(G-13705)*
Lyden Oil Company 330 792-1100
3711 Leharps Dr Ste A Youngstown (44515) *(G-20102)*
Lykins Companies Inc (PA) 513 831-8820
5163 Wlfpn Plsnt Hl Rd Milford (45150) *(G-14403)*
Lykins Energy Solutions, Milford Also called Lykins Companies Inc *(G-14403)*
Lykins Oil Company (HQ) 513 831-8820
5163 Wlfpn Plsnt Hl Rd Milford (45150) *(G-14404)*
Lykins Transportation Inc 513 831-8820
5163 Wlfpn Plsnt Hl Rd Milford (45150) *(G-14405)*
Lyman W Liggins Urban Affairs 419 385-2532
2155 Arlington Ave Toledo (43609) *(G-17875)*
Lyndco Inc 740 671-9098
56805 Ferry Landing Rd 8a Shadyside (43947) *(G-16696)*
Lynk Packaging Inc 330 562-8080
1250 Page Rd Aurora (44202) *(G-833)*
Lynn Hope Industries Inc 330 674-8045
8001 Township Rd Ste 574 Holmesville (44633) *(G-11931)*
Lynnhaven V LLC 440 272-5600
5165 State Route 322 Windsor (44099) *(G-19665)*
Lynnhaven Xii LLC 419 756-7111
535 Lexington Ave Mansfield (44907) *(G-13200)*
Lyondell Chemical Company 513 530-4000
11530 Northlake Dr Cincinnati (45249) *(G-3953)*
Lyons Doughty & Veldhuis PC 614 229-3888
471 E Broad St Fl 12 Columbus (43215) *(G-8001)*
M & A Distributing Co Inc (PA) 440 703-4580
31031 Diamond Pkwy Solon (44139) *(G-16868)*
M & A Distributing Co Inc 614 294-3555
871 Michigan Ave Columbus (43215) *(G-8002)*
M & A Distribution, Solon Also called M & A Distributing Co Inc *(G-16868)*

M & B Trucking Express Corp 440 236-8820
27457 Royalton Rd Columbia Station (44028) *(G-6777)*

M & D Blacktop Sealing, Grove City *Also called Pavement Protectors Inc* *(G-11464)*

M & L Electric Inc 937 833-5154
4439a New Market Banta Rd Lewisburg (45338) *(G-12570)*

M & L Leasing Co 330 343-8910
8999 Bay Dr Ne Mineral City (44656) *(G-14506)*

M & M Heating & Cooling, Toledo *Also called M&M Heating & Cooling Inc* *(G-17876)*

M & M Metals International Inc 513 221-4411
840 Dellway St Cincinnati (45229) *(G-3954)*

M & M Wine Cellar Inc 330 536-6450
259 Bedford Rd Lowellville (44436) *(G-13041)*

M & M Wintergreens Inc 216 398-1288
3728 Fulton Rd Cleveland (44109) *(G-5891)*

M & R Electric Motor Svc Inc 937 222-6282
1516 E 5th St Dayton (45403) *(G-9578)*

M & R Fredericktown Ltd Inc 440 801-1563
895 Home Ave Akron (44310) *(G-324)*

M & S Drywall Inc 513 738-1510
10999 State Route 128 Harrison (45030) *(G-11673)*

M A Folkes Company Inc 513 785-4200
3095 Mcbride Ct Hamilton (45011) *(G-11626)*

M C Hair Consultants Inc 234 678-3987
833 Portage Trl Cuyahoga Falls (44221) *(G-9110)*

M C M & One Com, Dayton *Also called McM Electronics Inc* *(G-9596)*

M C Trucking Company LLC 937 584-2486
228 Melvin Rd Wilmington (45177) *(G-19632)*

M Conley Company (PA) 330 456-8243
1312 4th St Se Canton (44707) *(G-2383)*

M Consultants LLC 614 839-4639
750 Brooksedge Blvd Westerville (43081) *(G-19277)*

M E Theaters Inc 937 596-6424
106 W Pike St Jackson Center (45334) *(G-12184)*

M G Management, Blue Ash *Also called Murray Guttman* *(G-1617)*

M G Q Inc 419 992-4236
1525 W County Road 42 Tiffin (44883) *(G-17522)*

M H EBY Inc 614 879-6901
4435 State Route 29 West Jefferson (43162) *(G-19110)*

M H Equipment, Hudson *Also called MH Logistics Corp* *(G-11997)*

M H Equipment - Ohio, Dayton *Also called Mh Equipment Company* *(G-9613)*

M J Baumann, Columbus *Also called Mj Baumann Co Inc* *(G-8092)*

M J J B Ltd 937 748-4414
505 N Main St Springboro (45066) *(G-16973)*

M J Lanese Landscaping Inc 440 942-3444
37115 Code Ave Willoughby (44094) *(G-19547)*

M J S Holding 614 410-2512
226 N 5th St Columbus (43215) *(G-8003)*

M K Moore & Sons Inc 937 236-1812
5150 Wagner Ford Rd Dayton (45414) *(G-9579)*

M L S, Columbus *Also called Microwave Leasing Services LLC* *(G-8072)*

M M Construction 513 553-0106
1924 St Routee 222 Bethel (45106) *(G-1453)*

M P & A Fibers Inc 440 926-1074
1024 Commerce Dr Grafton (44044) *(G-11318)*

M P Dory Co 614 444-2138
2001 Integrity Dr S Columbus (43209) *(G-8004)*

M R C, West Chester *Also called MRC Global (us) Inc* *(G-18977)*

M R I Center, Toledo *Also called Associated Imaging Corporation* *(G-17602)*

M R S I, Cincinnati *Also called Marketing Research Svcs Inc* *(G-3971)*

M Retail Engineering Inc 614 818-2323
750 Brooksedge Blvd Westerville (43081) *(G-19278)*

M S, Twinsburg *Also called The Mau-Sherwood Supply Co* *(G-18326)*

M S G, Maumee *Also called Mannik & Smith Group Inc* *(G-13812)*

M S I Design, Columbus *Also called Myers/Schmalenberger Inc* *(G-8125)*

M T Business Technologies, Holland *Also called Office Products Toledo Inc* *(G-11904)*

M T Business Technologies 440 933-7682
33588 Pin Oak Pkwy Avon Lake (44012) *(G-924)*

M T Golf Course Managment Inc (PA) 513 923-1188
9799 Prechtel Rd Cincinnati (45252) *(G-3955)*

M W Recycling LLC (HQ) 440 753-5400
5875 Landerbrook Dr # 200 Mayfield Heights (44124) *(G-13877)*

M&C Hotel Interests Inc 440 543-1331
17021 Chillicothe Rd Chagrin Falls (44023) *(G-2671)*

M&C Hotel Interests Inc 937 778-8100
987 E Ash St Ste 171 Piqua (45356) *(G-16012)*

M&J Fox Investments, Cleveland *Also called Wtb Inc* *(G-6692)*

M&M Heating & Cooling Inc 419 243-3005
1515 Washington St Toledo (43604) *(G-17876)*

M&W Construction Entps LLC 419 227-2000
1201 Crestwood Dr Lima (45805) *(G-12697)*

M-A Building and Maint Co 216 391-5577
5515 Old Brecksville Rd Independence (44131) *(G-12096)*

M-E Companies, Inc., Westerville *Also called Ibi Group Engrg Svcs USA Inc* *(G-19263)*

M-Engineering, Westerville *Also called M Consultants LLC* *(G-19277)*

M-V Rlty Mller Valentine Group, Cincinnati *Also called Miller-Valentine Partners Ltd* *(G-4054)*

M.O.M., Blue Ash *Also called Modern Office Methods Inc* *(G-1613)*

M/I Financial LLC (HQ) 614 418-8650
3 Easton Oval Ste 340 Columbus (43219) *(G-8005)*

M/I Homes Inc (PA) 614 418-8000
3 Easton Oval Ste 500 Columbus (43219) *(G-8006)*

M/I Homes of Austin LLC 614 418-8000
3 Easton Oval Ste 500 Columbus (43219) *(G-8007)*

M3 Midstream LLC 740 945-1170
37950 Crimm Rd Scio (43988) *(G-16663)*

M3 Midstream LLC 330 679-5580
10 E Main St Salineville (43945) *(G-16571)*

M3 Midstream LLC 330 223-2220
11543 Sr 644 Kensington (44427) *(G-12210)*

M3 Midstream LLC 740 431-4168
8349 Azalea Rd Sw Dennison (44621) *(G-10052)*

MA Architects, Columbus *Also called Meacham & Apel Architects Inc* *(G-8048)*

Maag Automatik Inc 330 677-2225
235 Progress Blvd Kent (44240) *(G-12248)*

Maag Reduction Engineering, Kent *Also called Maag Automatik Inc* *(G-12248)*

Mac Group, The, Strongsville *Also called Hughes Corporation* *(G-17313)*

Mac Kenzie Nursery Supply Inc 440 259-3517
3891 Shepard Rd Perry (44081) *(G-15825)*

Mac Manufacturing Inc (PA) 330 823-9900
14599 Commerce St Ne Alliance (44601) *(G-539)*

Mac Manufacturing Inc 330 829-1680
1453 Allen Rd Salem (44460) *(G-16552)*

Mac Queen Orchards Inc 419 865-2916
7605 Garden Rd Holland (43528) *(G-11894)*

Mac Trailer Manufacturing Inc (PA) 330 823-9900
14599 Commerce St Ne Alliance (44601) *(G-540)*

Macair Aviation LLC 937 347-1302
140 N Valley Rd Xenia (45385) *(G-19919)*

Macalogic, Beavercreek *Also called Tm Capture Services LLC* *(G-1238)*

Macaulay-Brown Inc (PA) 937 426-3421
4021 Executive Dr Beavercreek (45430) *(G-1227)*

Macb, Beavercreek *Also called Macaulay-Brown Inc* *(G-1227)*

Macdonald Mott LLC 216 535-3640
18013 Cleveland Pkwy Dr # 200 Cleveland (44135) *(G-5892)*

Mace Personal Def & SEC Inc (HQ) 440 424-5321
4400 Carnegie Ave Cleveland (44103) *(G-5893)*

Machine Tool Division, Bluffton *Also called Grob Systems Inc* *(G-1691)*

Mack Communications LLC 330 347-4020
2994 Roosevelt Dr Ste B Youngstown (44504) *(G-20103)*

Mack Industries 419 353-7081
507 Derby Ave Bowling Green (43402) *(G-1740)*

Macke Brothers Inc 513 771-7500
10355 Spartan Dr Cincinnati (45215) *(G-3956)*

Mackil Inc 937 833-3310
705 Arlington Rd Brookville (45309) *(G-1915)*

Mackin Book Company 330 854-0099
9326 Paulding St Nw Massillon (44646) *(G-13706)*

Macmillan Sobanski & Todd LLC (PA) 419 255-5900
1 Maritime Plz Fl 5 Toledo (43604) *(G-17877)*

Maco Construction Services 330 482-4472
170 Duquesne St Columbiana (44408) *(G-6789)*

Maco Inc 740 472-5445
47013 State Route 26 Woodsfield (43793) *(G-19675)*

Macomb Group Inc 419 666-6899
2830 Crane Way Northwood (43619) *(G-15398)*

Macomb Group Toledo Division, Northwood *Also called Macomb Group Inc* *(G-15398)*

Macys Cr & Customer Svcs Inc 513 881-9950
9249 Meridian Way West Chester (45069) *(G-18967)*

Macys Cr & Customer Svcs Inc (HQ) 513 398-5221
9111 Duke Blvd Mason (45040) *(G-13613)*

Mad River Mountain Resort 937 303-3646
1000 Snow Valley Rd Zanesfield (43360) *(G-20272)*

Made From Scratch Inc (PA) 614 873-3344
7500 Montgomery Rd Plain City (43064) *(G-16058)*

Madeira Health Care Center, Cincinnati *Also called Euclid Health Care Inc* *(G-3517)*

Madeira Health Care Center 513 561-4105
6940 Stiegler Ln Cincinnati (45243) *(G-3957)*

Madison Avenue Mktg Group Inc 419 473-9000
1600 Madison Ave Toledo (43604) *(G-17878)*

Madison Bowl Inc 513 271-2700
4761 Madison Rd Cincinnati (45227) *(G-3958)*

Madison Care Inc 440 428-1492
7600 S Ridge Rd Madison (44057) *(G-13102)*

Madison Cnty Lndon Cy Hlth Dst 740 852-3065
306 Lafayette St Ste B London (43140) *(G-12867)*

Madison County Engineer, London *Also called County of Madison* *(G-12863)*

Madison Family Health Corp 740 845-7000
210 N Main St London (43140) *(G-12868)*

Madison House Inc 740 845-0145
351 Keny Blvd London (43140) *(G-12869)*

Madison Local School, Mansfield *Also called SC Madison Bus Garage* *(G-13241)*

Madison Local School District (PA) 419 589-2600
1379 Grace St Mansfield (44905) *(G-13201)*

Madison Local School District 440 428-5111
92 E Main St Madison (44057) *(G-13103)*

Madison Medical Campus 440 428-6800
6270 N Ridge Rd Madison (44057) *(G-13104)*

Madison Motor Service Inc 419 332-0727
2921 W State St Fremont (43420) *(G-11085)*

Madison Route 20 LLC 440 358-7888
7667 Hermitage Rd Painesville (44077) *(G-15723)*

Madison Square Apartments, Plain City *Also called Fairfield Homes Inc* ***(G-16053)***
Madison Tree & Landscape Co 614 207-5422
3180 Glade Run Rd West Jefferson (43162) ***(G-19111)***
Madison Tree Care & Ldscpg Inc 513 576-6391
636 Round Bottom Rd Milford (45150) ***(G-14406)***
Mae Holding Company (PA) 513 751-2424
7290 Deaconsbench Ct Cincinnati (45244) ***(G-3959)***
Magic Castle Inc 937 434-4911
4990 Wilmington Pike Dayton (45440) ***(G-9580)***
Magic Industries Inc 614 759-8422
4651 Poth Rd Columbus (43213) ***(G-8008)***
Magnetech, Massillon *Also called 3-D Service Ltd* ***(G-13656)***
Magnetech Industrial Svcs Inc (HQ) 330 830-3500
800 Nave Rd Se Massillon (44646) ***(G-13707)***
Magnetech Industrial Svcs Inc 330 830-3500
800 Nave Rd Se Massillon (44646) ***(G-13708)***
Magnetic Springs Water Company (PA) 614 421-1780
1917 Joyce Ave Columbus (43219) ***(G-8009)***
Magnum Management Corporation 419 627-2334
1 Cedar Point Dr Sandusky (44870) ***(G-16626)***
Magnum Medical Overseas JV LLC 979 848-8169
2936 Vernon Pl 3 Cincinnati (45219) ***(G-3960)***
Magolius Margolius & Assoc Lpa 216 621-2034
55 Public Sq Ste 1100 Cleveland (44113) ***(G-5894)***
Maguire & Schneider LLP 614 224-1222
1650 Lake Shore Dr # 150 Columbus (43204) ***(G-8010)***
Mahajan Tita & Katra, Toledo *Also called R I D Inc* ***(G-17996)***
Mahalls 20 Lanes 216 521-3280
13200 Madison Ave Cleveland (44107) ***(G-5895)***
Mahoney Dialysis LLC 937 642-0676
491 Colemans Xing Marysville (43040) ***(G-13512)***
Mahoning Clmbana Training Assn 330 747-5639
20 W Federal St Ste 604 Youngstown (44503) ***(G-20104)***
Mahoning Country Club Inc 330 545-2517
710 E Liberty St Girard (44420) ***(G-11294)***
Mahoning County 330 793-5514
761 Industrial Rd Youngstown (44509) ***(G-20105)***
Mahoning County 330 799-1581
940 Bears Den Rd Youngstown (44511) ***(G-20106)***
Mahoning County 330 797-2837
4795 Woodridge Dr Youngstown (44515) ***(G-20107)***
Mahoning County Childrens Svcs 330 941-8888
222 W Federal St Fl 4 Youngstown (44503) ***(G-20108)***
Mahoning County Engineers, Youngstown *Also called Mahoning County* ***(G-20106)***
Mahoning Valley Dental Service (PA) 330 759-1771
5100 Belmont Ave Ste 1 Youngstown (44505) ***(G-20109)***
Mahoning Valley Hospital, Youngstown *Also called Vibra Hosp Mahoning Vly LLC* ***(G-20237)***
Mahoning Valley Scrappers, Niles *Also called Palisdes Bsbal A Cal Ltd Prtnr* ***(G-15166)***
Mahoning Vly Hmtlgy Onclgy Aso 330 318-1100
500 Gypsy Ln Youngstown (44504) ***(G-20110)***
Mahoning Vly Hmtology Oncology, Warren *Also called Trumbull Mem Hosp Foundation* ***(G-18760)***
Mahoning Vly Infusioncare Inc (PA) 330 759-9487
4891 Belmont Ave Youngstown (44505) ***(G-20111)***
Mahoning Youngstown Community (PA) 330 747-7921
1325 5th Ave Youngstown (44504) ***(G-20112)***
MAI Capital Management LLC 216 920-4800
1360 E 9th St Ste 1100 Cleveland (44114) ***(G-5896)***
MAI Capital Management LLC 216 920-4913
1360 E 9th St Ste 1100 Cleveland (44114) ***(G-5897)***
MAI Manufacturing, Marysville *Also called Straight 72 Inc* ***(G-13530)***
Maids Home Service of Cincy 513 396-6900
1830 Sherman Ave Cincinnati (45212) ***(G-3961)***
Mail Contractors America Inc 513 769-5967
3065 Cresecentville Rd Cincinnati (45262) ***(G-3962)***
Mail It Corp 419 249-4848
380 S Erie St Toledo (43604) ***(G-17879)***
Mailender Inc 513 942-5453
9500 Glades Dr West Chester (45011) ***(G-18968)***
Main Line Supply Co Inc (PA) 937 254-6910
300 N Findlay St Dayton (45403) ***(G-9581)***
Main Lite Electric Co Inc 330 369-8333
3000 Sferra Ave Nw Warren (44483) ***(G-18726)***
Main Place Inc (PA) 740 345-6246
112 S 3rd St Newark (43055) ***(G-15064)***
Main Sail LLC 216 472-5100
20820 Chagrin Blvd # 102 Cleveland (44122) ***(G-5898)***
Main Sequence Technology Inc (PA) 440 946-5214
5370 Pinehill Dr Mentor On The Lake (44060) ***(G-14129)***
Main Street Terrace Care Ctr 740 653-8767
1318 E Main St Lancaster (43130) ***(G-12414)***
Maines Collision Repr & Bdy Sp 937 322-4618
1717 E Pleasant St Springfield (45505) ***(G-17066)***
Maines Paper & Food Svc Inc 216 643-7500
199 Oak Leaf Oval Bedford (44146) ***(G-1291)***
Maines Towing & Recovery Svc, Springfield *Also called Maines Collision Repr & Bdy Sp* ***(G-17066)***
Maintenance Department, Logan *Also called Logan-Hocking School District* ***(G-12848)***
Maintenance Systems Nthrn Ohio, Elyria *Also called Purple Marlin Inc* ***(G-10557)***
Maintenance Systerms of N Ohio 440 323-1291
42208 Albrecht Rd Ste 1 Elyria (44035) ***(G-10532)***
Maintenance Unlimited Inc 440 238-1162
12351 Prospect Rd Strongsville (44149) ***(G-17325)***
Mainthia Technologies Inc 216 433-2198
21000 Brookpark Rd Cleveland (44135) ***(G-5899)***
Majaac Inc 419 636-5678
820 E Edgerton St Bryan (43506) ***(G-1962)***
Majastan Group LLC 216 231-6400
12200 Fairhill Rd B201 Cleveland (44120) ***(G-5900)***
Majestic Manufacturing Inc 330 457-2447
4536 State Route 7 New Waterford (44445) ***(G-15005)***
Majestic Steel Properties Inc 440 786-2666
31099 Chagrin Blvd # 150 Cleveland (44124) ***(G-5901)***
Majestic Steel Service, Cleveland *Also called Majestic Steel Usa Inc* ***(G-5902)***
Majestic Steel Usa Inc (PA) 440 786-2666
31099 Chagrin Blvd # 150 Cleveland (44124) ***(G-5902)***
Majestic Tool and Machine Inc 440 248-5058
30700 Carter St Ste C Solon (44139) ***(G-16869)***
Majidzadeh Enterprises Inc (PA) 614 823-4949
6350 Presidential Gtwy Columbus (43231) ***(G-8011)***
Major Electronix Corp 440 942-0054
33801 Curtis Blvd Ste 110 Eastlake (44095) ***(G-10431)***
Major Legal Services, Independence *Also called Alliance Legal Solutions LLC* ***(G-12043)***
Major Metals Company 419 886-4600
844 Kochheiser Rd Mansfield (44904) ***(G-13202)***
Make Believe, Parma *Also called Y & E Entertainment Group LLC* ***(G-15781)***
Maketewah Country Club Company 513 242-9333
5401 Reading Rd Cincinnati (45237) ***(G-3963)***
Making Evrlasting Memories LLC 513 864-0100
11475 Northlake Dr Cincinnati (45249) ***(G-3964)***
Makoy Center Inc 614 777-1211
5462 Center St Hilliard (43026) ***(G-11787)***
Malavite Excavating Inc 330 484-1274
5508 Ridge Ave Se East Sparta (44626) ***(G-10423)***
Malik Punam 513 636-1333
3333 Burnet Ave Cincinnati (45229) ***(G-3965)***
Mall Park Southern 330 758-4511
7401 Market St Rm 267 Youngstown (44512) ***(G-20113)***
Mall Realty Inc 937 866-3700
862 Watertower Ln Dayton (45449) ***(G-9582)***
Mallard Cove Senior Dev LLC 513 772-6655
1410 Mallard Cove Dr Ofc Cincinnati (45246) ***(G-3966)***
Mallard Cove Senior Living, Cincinnati *Also called Mallard Cove Senior Dev LLC* ***(G-3966)***
Malley's Chocolates, Cleveland *Also called Malleys Candies Inc* ***(G-5903)***
Malleys Candies Inc 216 529-6262
13400 Brookpark Rd Cleveland (44135) ***(G-5903)***
Maloney & Associates Inc 330 479-7084
4850 Southway St Sw Canton (44706) ***(G-2384)***
Maloney + Novotny LLC (PA) 216 363-0100
1111 Superior Ave E # 700 Cleveland (44114) ***(G-5904)***
Mammana Custom Woodworking Inc 216 581-9059
14400 Industrial Ave N Maple Heights (44137) ***(G-13289)***
Mammoth Restoration and Clg, Worthington *Also called Farris Enterprises Inc* ***(G-19810)***
Mammovan Inc 330 726-2064
61 Midgewood Dr Youngstown (44512) ***(G-20114)***
Man Golf Ohio LLC 440 635-5178
14107 Mayfield Rd Huntsburg (44046) ***(G-12018)***
Man-Tansky Inc 740 454-2512
3260 Maple Ave Zanesville (43701) ***(G-20328)***
Managed Technology Svcs LLC 937 247-8915
3366 S Tech Blvd Miamisburg (45342) ***(G-14186)***
Management & Training Corp 801 693-2600
501 Thompson Rd Conneaut (44030) ***(G-8955)***
Management Information Svcs, Dayton *Also called County of Montgomery* ***(G-9333)***
Management Recruiters Intl, Columbus *Also called Management Recruiters Intl Inc* ***(G-8012)***
Management Recruiters Intl, Chagrin Falls *Also called Management Recruiters Intl Inc* ***(G-2672)***
Management Recruiters Intl Inc 614 252-6200
800 E Broad St Columbus (43205) ***(G-8012)***
Management Recruiters Intl Inc 440 543-1284
17632 Walnut Trl Chagrin Falls (44023) ***(G-2672)***
Manatron Inc (HQ) 937 431-4000
4105 Executive Dr Beavercreek (45430) ***(G-1228)***
Manatron Sabre Systems and Svc (HQ) 937 431-4000
4105 Executive Dr Beavercreek (45430) ***(G-1229)***
Mancan Inc 440 884-9675
13500 Pearl Rd Ste 109 Strongsville (44136) ***(G-17326)***
Manchester Bennett Towers & Ul 330 743-1171
201 E Commerce St Ste 200 Youngstown (44503) ***(G-20115)***
Mandalay Inc 937 294-6600
2700 E River Rd Moraine (45439) ***(G-14671)***
Mandalay Banquet Center, Moraine *Also called Mandalay Inc* ***(G-14671)***
MANDEL JEWISH COMMUNITY OF CLE, Beachwood *Also called Jewish Community Ctr Cleveland* ***(G-1069)***
Manfield Living Center Ltd 419 512-1711
73 Madison Rd Mansfield (44905) ***(G-13203)***
Manhattan Associates Inc 440 878-0771
10153 S Bexley Cir Strongsville (44136) ***(G-17327)***
Manhattan Mortgage Group Ltd 614 933-8955
6833 Clark State Rd Blacklick (43004) ***(G-1482)***
Manifest Software, Upper Arlington *Also called Manifest Solutions Corp* ***(G-18401)***

1182 2019 Harris Ohio Services Directory (G-0000) Company's Geographic Section entry number

Manifest Solutions Corp 614 930-2800
　2035 Riverside Dr Upper Arlington (43221) *(G-18401)*
Manley Deas & Kochalski LLC (PA) 614 220-5611
　1555 Lake Shore Dr Columbus (43204) *(G-8013)*
Manleys Manor Nursing Home Inc 419 424-0402
　2820 Greenacre Dr Findlay (45840) *(G-10937)*
Mannik & Smith Group Inc (PA) 419 891-2222
　1800 Indian Wood Cir Maumee (43537) *(G-13812)*
Mannik & Smith Group Inc 740 942-4222
　104 S Main St Cadiz (43907) *(G-2031)*
Mannik Smith Group, The, Cadiz *Also called Mannik & Smith Group Inc (G-2031)*
Mannion & Gray Co LpA 216 344-9422
　1375 E 9th St Ste 1600 Cleveland (44114) *(G-5905)*
Mannon Pipeline LLC 740 643-1534
　9160 State Route 378 Willow Wood (45696) *(G-19595)*
Mano Logistics LLC 330 454-1307
　1934 Navarre Rd Sw Canton (44706) *(G-2385)*
Manor 1, Orrville *Also called Orrvilla Retirement Community (G-15638)*
Manor At Autumn Hills, Niles *Also called Niles Residential Care LLC (G-15164)*
Manor At Perrysburg, The, Perrysburg *Also called Hcf of Perrysburg Inc (G-15870)*
Manor At Whitehall, The, Columbus *Also called Shg Whitehall Holdings LLC (G-8633)*
Manor Care, Cincinnati *Also called Hcr Manorcare Med Svcs Fla LLC (G-3688)*
Manor Care, Barberton *Also called Hcr Manorcare Med Svcs Fla LLC (G-954)*
Manor Care, Cincinnati *Also called Hcr Manorcare Med Svcs Fla LLC (G-3690)*
Manor Care, Toledo *Also called Hcr Manorcare Med Svcs Fla LLC (G-17787)*
Manor Care Inc (HQ) 419 252-5500
　333 N Summit St Ste 103 Toledo (43604) *(G-17880)*
Manor Care Hlth Svcs Cntrville, Centerville *Also called Hcr Manorcare Med Svcs Fla LLC (G-2627)*
Manor Care Nursing Center (HQ) 419 252-5500
　333 N Summit St Ste 100 Toledo (43604) *(G-17881)*
Manor Care of America Inc 440 543-6766
　8100 Washington St Chagrin Falls (44023) *(G-2673)*
Manor Care of America Inc 330 867-8530
　1211 W Market St Akron (44313) *(G-325)*
Manor Care of America Inc 330 492-7835
　5005 Higbee Ave Nw Canton (44718) *(G-2386)*
Manor Care of America Inc 440 779-6900
　23225 Lorain Rd North Olmsted (44070) *(G-15296)*
Manor Care of America Inc 440 951-5551
　37603 Euclid Ave Willoughby (44094) *(G-19548)*
Manor Care of America Inc 440 345-9300
　9055 W Sprague Rd North Royalton (44133) *(G-15362)*
Manor Care of Boynton Beach (HQ) 419 252-5500
　333 N Summit St Ste 103 Toledo (43604) *(G-17882)*
Manor Care of Kansas Inc (HQ) 419 252-5500
　333 N Summit St Ste 100 Toledo (43604) *(G-17883)*
Manor Care of North Olmsted 419 252-5500
　333 N Summit St Ste 100 Toledo (43604) *(G-17884)*
Manor Care of Plantation Inc 419 252-5500
　333 N Summit St Ste 100 Toledo (43604) *(G-17885)*
Manor Care of York North Inc 419 252-5500
　333 N Summit St Ste 100 Toledo (43604) *(G-17886)*
Manor Care Wilmington Inc (HQ) 419 252-5500
　333 N Summit St Ste 100 Toledo (43604) *(G-17887)*
Manor Care York (south) Inc 419 252-5500
　333 N Summit St Ste 100 Toledo (43604) *(G-17888)*
Manor Care-North, Toledo *Also called Manor Care of York North Inc (G-17886)*
Manor Cr-Mprial Rchmond VA LLC (HQ) 419 252-5000
　333 N Summit St Toledo (43604) *(G-17889)*
Manor Hse Bnquet Cnference Ctr, Mason *Also called Kinane Inc (G-13605)*
Manor, The, Niles *Also called C R G Health Care Systems (G-15148)*
Manor, The, Euclid *Also called Kitchen Katering Inc (G-10647)*
Manorcare Health Services LLC (HQ) 419 252-5500
　333 N Summit St Ste 100 Toledo (43604) *(G-17890)*
Manorcare Health Svcs VA Inc (HQ) 419 252-5500
　333 N Summit St Ste 100 Toledo (43604) *(G-17891)*
Manorcare Hlth Svcs Lakeshore, Cleveland *Also called Hcr Manorcare Med Svcs Fla LLC (G-5672)*
Manorcare Hlth Svcs Rcky River, Cleveland *Also called Hcr Manorcare Med Svcs Fla LLC (G-5670)*
Manorcare Hlth Svcs Wsterville, Westerville *Also called Hcr Manorcare Med Svcs Fla LLC (G-19260)*
Manorcare Hlth Svcs-Mayfield H, Cleveland *Also called Hcr Manorcare Med Svcs Fla LLC (G-5671)*
Manorcare of Kingston Court 419 252-5500
　333 N Summit St Ste 100 Toledo (43604) *(G-17892)*
Manorcare of Willoughby Inc 419 252-5500
　333 N Summit St Ste 100 Toledo (43604) *(G-17893)*
Mansfield Ambulance Inc 419 525-3311
　369 Marion Ave Mansfield (44903) *(G-13204)*
Mansfield City Building Maint 419 755-9698
　30 N Diamond St Mansfield (44902) *(G-13205)*
Mansfield Distributing Co Div, Mansfield *Also called The Maple City Ice Company (G-13252)*
Mansfield Express, Ontario *Also called Mansfield Whsng & Dist Inc (G-15560)*
Mansfield Fabricated Products, Mansfield *Also called The Mansfield Strl & Erct Co (G-13251)*

Mansfield Family Practice, Mansfield *Also called American Hlth Ntwrk & Fmly PRC (G-13135)*
Mansfield Hotel Partnership 419 529-2100
　555 N Trimble Rd Mansfield (44906) *(G-13206)*
Mansfield Hotel Partnership (PA) 419 529-1000
　500 N Trimble Rd Mansfield (44906) *(G-13207)*
Mansfield Memorial Homes 419 774-5100
　55 Wood St Mansfield (44903) *(G-13208)*
Mansfield Memorial Homes LLC (PA) 419 774-5100
　50 Blymyer Ave Mansfield (44903) *(G-13209)*
Mansfield Opco LLC 502 429-8062
　1600 Crider Rd Mansfield (44903) *(G-13210)*
Mansfield Plumbing Pdts LLC (HQ) 419 938-5211
　150 E 1st St Perrysville (44864) *(G-15941)*
Mansfield Plumbing Pdts LLC 330 496-2301
　13211 State Route 226 Big Prairie (44611) *(G-1472)*
Mansfield Truck Sls & Svc Inc 419 522-9811
　85 Longview Ave E Mansfield (44903) *(G-13211)*
Mansfield Warehouse & Distrg, Shelby *Also called Mwd Logistics Inc (G-16748)*
Mansfield Whsng & Dist Inc (HQ) 419 522-3510
　222 Tappan Dr N Ontario (44906) *(G-15560)*
MANSION HOMES, Bryan *Also called Manufactured Housing Entps Inc (G-1963)*
Mansuetto Roofing Company, Martins Ferry *Also called N F Mansuetto & Sons Inc (G-13477)*
Manta Media Inc 888 875-5833
　8760 Orion Pl Ste 200 Columbus (43240) *(G-6823)*
Mantaline Corporation 330 274-2264
　4754 E High St Mantua (44255) *(G-13273)*
Mantua Bed Frames, Solon *Also called Mantua Manufacturing Co (G-16870)*
Mantua Manufacturing Co (PA) 800 333-8333
　31050 Diamond Pkwy Solon (44139) *(G-16870)*
Manufactured Comfort, Athens *Also called White & Chambers Partnership (G-811)*
Manufactured Housing Entps Inc 419 636-4511
　9302 Us Highway 6 Bryan (43506) *(G-1963)*
Manufacturing Services Intl 937 299-9922
　15 W Dorothy Ln Dayton (45429) *(G-9583)*
Manzano Dialysis LLC 937 879-0433
　1266 N Broad St Fairborn (45324) *(G-10680)*
MAP SYSTEMS AND SOLUTIONS, Columbus *Also called Mapsys Inc (G-8014)*
Maple Crest, Bluffton *Also called Mennonite Memorial Home (G-1694)*
Maple Crest Assisted Living, Bucyrus *Also called Maplecrst Asistd Lvg Intl Ordr (G-1996)*
Maple Crest Builders, Delaware *Also called Eds Tree & Turf (G-9972)*
Maple Crest Nrsing HM For Aged, Struthers *Also called Cred-Kap Inc (G-17362)*
Maple Crest Senior Living Vlg, Bluffton *Also called Mennonite Memorial Home (G-1693)*
Maple Gardens Rehab, Eaton *Also called Eaton Gardens Rehabilitation A (G-10445)*
Maple Grove Companies, Tiffin *Also called M G Q Inc (G-17522)*
Maple Heights Atc, Cleveland *Also called County of Cuyahoga (G-5362)*
Maple Knoll Communities Inc 513 524-7990
　6727 Contreras Rd Oxford (45056) *(G-15679)*
Maple Knoll Communities Inc (PA) 513 782-2400
　11100 Springfield Pike Cincinnati (45246) *(G-3967)*
MAPLE KNOLL VILLAGE, Cincinnati *Also called Maple Knoll Communities Inc (G-3967)*
Maple Lee Greenhouse, Powell *Also called Gs Ohio Inc (G-16196)*
Maple Mountain Industries Inc 330 948-2510
　312 Bank St Lodi (44254) *(G-12828)*
Maplecrst Asistd Lvg Intl Ordr 419 562-4988
　717 Rogers St Bucyrus (44820) *(G-1996)*
Mapleside Bakery, Brunswick *Also called Mapleside Valley LLC (G-1937)*
Mapleside Valley LLC (PA) 330 225-5576
　294 Pearl Rd Brunswick (44212) *(G-1937)*
Mapleview Farms Inc (PA) 419 826-3671
　2425 S Fulton Lucas Rd Swanton (43558) *(G-17401)*
Maplewood At Bath Creek LLC 234 208-9872
　190 W Bath Rd Cuyahoga Falls (44223) *(G-9111)*
Maplewood At Cuyahoga Falls, Cuyahoga Falls *Also called Maplewood At Bath Creek LLC (G-9111)*
Maplewood Nursing Center Inc 740 383-2126
　409 Bellefontaine Ave Marion (43302) *(G-13431)*
Mapother & Mapother Attorneys, Cincinnati *Also called Javitch Block LLC (G-3809)*
Mapp Building Service LLC 513 253-3990
　11367 Deerfield Rd 200 Blue Ash (45242) *(G-1602)*
Mapsys Inc (PA) 614 255-7258
　920 Michigan Ave Columbus (43215) *(G-8014)*
Marathon Canton Refinery, Canton *Also called Mplx Terminals LLC (G-2409)*
Marathon Manufacturing, New Philadelphia *Also called S S T Enterprises Inc (G-14979)*
Marathon Mfg & Sup Co 330 343-2656
　5165 Main St Ne New Philadelphia (44663) *(G-14972)*
Marathon Petroleum Company LP 330 479-5688
　3500 21st St Sw Canton (44706) *(G-2387)*
Marathon Petroleum Company LP 614 274-1125
　Lincoln Village Sta Columbus (43228) *(G-8015)*
Marathon Petroleum Company LP 513 932-6007
　999 W State Route 122 Lebanon (45036) *(G-12483)*
Marathon Petroleum Corporation (PA) 419 422-2121
　539 S Main St Findlay (45840) *(G-10938)*
Marathon Pipe Line LLC (HQ) 419 422-2121
　539 S Main St Ste 7614 Findlay (45840) *(G-10939)*
Marble Cliff Block & Bldrs Sup, Lockbourne *Also called J P S Sand & Gravel Company (G-12822)*

A L P H A B E T I C

Marble Restoration Inc...................................419 865-9000
  6539 Weatherfield Ct Maumee (43537) *(G-13813)*
Marc Glassman Inc..216 265-7700
  19101 Snow Rd Cleveland (44142) *(G-5906)*
Marc Glassman Inc..330 995-9246
  300 Aurora Commons Cir Aurora (44202) *(G-834)*
Marc's 45, Aurora Also called Marc Glassman Inc *(G-834)*
Marc's Distribution Center, Cleveland Also called Marc Glassman Inc *(G-5906)*
Marca Industries Inc......................................740 387-1035
  2387 Harding Hwy E Marion (43302) *(G-13432)*
Marca Terrace Widows....................................937 252-1661
  50 S Findlay St Dayton (45403) *(G-9584)*
March Investors Ltd.......................................740 373-5353
  508 Pike St Marietta (45750) *(G-13346)*
Marco Photo Service Inc.................................419 529-9010
  1655 Nussbaum Pkwy Ontario (44906) *(G-15561)*
Marco's Pizza, Toledo Also called Marcos Inc *(G-17894)*
Marcos Inc...419 885-4844
  5252 Monroe St Toledo (43623) *(G-17894)*
Marcum Conference Center, Oxford Also called Miami University *(G-15681)*
Marcums Don Pool Care Inc.............................513 561-7050
  6841 Main St Ste 1 Cincinnati (45244) *(G-3968)*
Marcus Hotels Inc...614 228-3800
  310 S High St Columbus (43215) *(G-8016)*
Marcus Mllchap RE Inv Svcs Inc.......................614 360-9800
  230 West St Ste 100 Columbus (43215) *(G-8017)*
Marcus Theatres Corporation..........................614 759-6500
  1776 Hill Rd N Pickerington (43147) *(G-15963)*
Marcus Theatres Corporation..........................614 436-9818
  200 Hutchinson Ave Columbus (43235) *(G-8018)*
Marcus Thomas Llc (PA)..................................216 292-4700
  4781 Richmond Rd Cleveland (44128) *(G-5907)*
Marcus Thomas Llc.......................................330 793-3000
  5212 Mahoning Ave Ste 311 Youngstown (44515) *(G-20116)*
Marcy Industries Company LLC.........................740 943-2343
  1836 Likens Rd Marion (43302) *(G-13433)*
Marfo Company (PA).......................................614 276-3352
  799 N Hague Ave Columbus (43204) *(G-8019)*
Marfre Inc..513 321-3377
  4785 Morse St Cincinnati (45226) *(G-3969)*
Margaret B Shipley Child Hlth (PA)....................330 478-6333
  919 2nd St Ne Canton (44704) *(G-2388)*
Margret Wagner House, Cleveland Also called Benjamin Rose Institute *(G-5056)*
Maria Child Care, Toledo Also called Sisters of Notre D *(G-18035)*
Maria Gardens LLC (PA)..................................440 238-7637
  20465 Royalton Rd Strongsville (44149) *(G-17328)*
Marian Living Center, North Lima Also called Assumption Village *(G-15264)*
Marietta Aquatic Center.................................740 373-2445
  233 Pennsylvania Ave Marietta (45750) *(G-13347)*
Marietta Bantam Baseball Leag........................740 350-9844
  103 Chalet Ln Marietta (45750) *(G-13348)*
Marietta Center For Health &...........................740 373-1867
  117 Bartlett St Marietta (45750) *(G-13349)*
Marietta Coal Co (PA).....................................740 695-2197
  67705 Friends Church Rd Saint Clairsville (43950) *(G-16494)*
Marietta College..740 376-4790
  213 4th St Marietta (45750) *(G-13350)*
Marietta Community Based, Marietta Also called Veterans Health Administration *(G-13396)*
Marietta Country Club Inc...............................740 373-7722
  705 Pike St Marietta (45750) *(G-13351)*
MARIETTA FAMILY YMCA, Marietta Also called Young Mens Christian Assn *(G-13402)*
Marietta Gynecologic Assoc............................740 374-3622
  410 2nd St Marietta (45750) *(G-13352)*
Marietta Industrial Entps Inc (PA).....................740 373-2252
  17943 State Route 7 Marietta (45750) *(G-13353)*
Marietta Memorial Hospital.............................740 401-0362
  809 Farson St Belpre (45714) *(G-1408)*
Marietta Memorial Hospital (PA).......................740 374-1400
  401 Matthew St Marietta (45750) *(G-13354)*
Marietta Memorial Hospital.............................740 373-8549
  210 N 7th St Ste 300 Marietta (45750) *(G-13355)*
Marietta Nursing and Rehab Ctr, Marietta Also called Marietta Center For Health & *(G-13349)*
Marietta Silos LLC..740 373-2822
  2417 Waterford Rd Marietta (45750) *(G-13356)*
Marietta Transfer Company.............................740 896-3565
  11569 State Route 60 Lowell (45744) *(G-13038)*
Marilyn Wagner, Uniontown Also called Louisville Child Care Center *(G-18377)*
Marimor Industries, Lima Also called County of Allen *(G-12625)*
Marimor Industries Inc..................................419 221-1226
  2450 Ada Rd Lima (45801) *(G-12698)*
Mario's Beauty Salon, Aurora Also called Marios International Spa & Ht *(G-835)*
Marion Area Counseling Ctr (PA).......................740 387-5210
  320 Executive Dr Marion (43302) *(G-13434)*
Marion Area Health Center, Marion Also called Frederick C Smith Clinic Inc *(G-13421)*
Marion Cnty Bd Dev Dsabilities.........................740 387-1035
  2387 Harding Hwy E Marion (43302) *(G-13435)*
Marion Country Club Company..........................740 387-0974
  2415 Crissinger Rd Marion (43302) *(G-13436)*
Marion Country Club, The, Marion Also called Marion Country Club Company *(G-13436)*
Marion Country Inn & Suites, Marion Also called Carlson Hotels Ltd Partnership *(G-13409)*

Marion County Board of Mr Dd, Marion Also called Marion Cnty Bd Dev Dsabilities *(G-13435)*
Marion District, Marion Also called Ohio-American Water Co Inc *(G-13451)*
Marion Family YMCA......................................740 725-9622
  645 Barks Rd E Marion (43302) *(G-13437)*
Marion Gen Social Work Dept...........................740 383-8788
  1000 Mckinley Park Dr Marion (43302) *(G-13438)*
Marion General Hosp HM Hlth...........................740 383-8770
  278 Barks Rd W Marion (43302) *(G-13439)*
Marion General Hospital, Marion Also called Marion Gen Social Work Dept *(G-13438)*
Marion General Hospital Inc (HQ).....................740 383-8400
  1000 Mckinley Park Dr Marion (43302) *(G-13440)*
Marion Goodwill Industries (PA)........................740 387-7023
  340 W Fairground St Marion (43302) *(G-13441)*
Marion Head Start Center...............................740 382-6858
  2387 Harding Hwy E Marion (43302) *(G-13442)*
Marion Manor, Mount Vernon Also called Levering Management Inc *(G-14778)*
Marion Manor...740 387-9545
  195 Executive Dr Marion (43302) *(G-13443)*
Marion Manor Nursing Home, Marion Also called Levering Management Inc *(G-13429)*
Marion Plaza Inc...330 747-2661
  5577 Youngstown Warren Rd Niles (44446) *(G-15158)*
Marion Road Enterprises.................................614 228-6525
  477 S Front St Columbus (43215) *(G-8020)*
Marios International Spa & Ht (PA).....................330 562-5141
  34 N Chillicothe Rd Aurora (44202) *(G-835)*
Marios International Spa & Ht...........................440 845-7373
  7155 W Pleasant Valley Rd Cleveland (44129) *(G-5908)*
Maritz Travel Company...................................660 626-1501
  1740 Indian Wood Cir Maumee (43537) *(G-13814)*
Maritzcx Research LLC...................................419 725-4000
  1740 Indian Wood Cir Maumee (43537) *(G-13815)*
Marjorie P Lee Rtirement Cmnty, Cincinnati Also called Episcopal Retirement Homes Inc *(G-3510)*
Mark Dura Inc...330 995-0883
  11384 Chamberlain Rd Aurora (44202) *(G-836)*
Mark E Grosinger (PA)....................................937 382-2000
  1150 W Locust St Ste 500 Wilmington (45177) *(G-19633)*
Mark Feldstein & Assoc Inc.............................419 867-9500
  6703 Monroe St Sylvania (43560) *(G-17437)*
Mark Humrichouser..614 324-5231
  6295 Maxtown Rd Ste 100 Westerville (43082) *(G-19184)*
Mark Luikart Inc..330 339-9141
  715 Cookson Ave Se New Philadelphia (44663) *(G-14973)*
Mark Schaffer Excvtg Trckg Inc........................419 668-5990
  1623 Old State Rd N Norwalk (44857) *(G-15443)*
Mark Thomas Ford Inc....................................330 638-1010
  3098 State Route 5 Cortland (44410) *(G-8989)*
Mark-L Inc...614 863-8832
  1180 Claycraft Rd Gahanna (43230) *(G-11134)*
Mark-L Construction, Gahanna Also called Mark-L Inc *(G-11134)*
Market Inquiry Llc...513 794-1088
  5825 Creek Rd Blue Ash (45242) *(G-1603)*
Market Ready Services, Columbus Also called Mrap LLC *(G-8117)*
Marketing Comm Resource Inc..........................440 484-3010
  4800 E 345th St Willoughby (44094) *(G-19549)*
Marketing Indus Solutions Corp (HQ)..................513 703-0965
  3965 Marble Ridge Ln Mason (45040) *(G-13614)*
Marketing Research Svcs Inc............................513 772-7580
  110 Boggs Ln Ste 380 Cincinnati (45246) *(G-3970)*
Marketing Research Svcs Inc (HQ).....................513 579-1555
  310 Culvert St Fl 2 Cincinnati (45202) *(G-3971)*
Marketing Results Ltd....................................614 575-9300
  3985 Groves Rd Columbus (43232) *(G-8021)*
Marketing Support Services Inc (PA)...................513 752-1200
  4921 Para Dr Cincinnati (45237) *(G-3972)*
Marketvision Research Inc..............................513 603-6340
  5426 W Chester Rd West Chester (45069) *(G-18969)*
Marketvision Research Inc (PA).........................513 791-3100
  5151 Pfeiffer Rd Ste 300 Blue Ash (45242) *(G-1604)*
Markfrank Hair Salons, Cleveland Also called Z A F Inc *(G-6707)*
Markowitz Rosenberg Assoc Drs........................440 646-2200
  5850 Landerbrook Dr # 100 Cleveland (44124) *(G-5909)*
Marks Cleaning Service Inc.............................330 725-5702
  325 S Elmwood Ave Medina (44256) *(G-13968)*
Marlin Mechanical LLC...................................800 669-2645
  6600 Grant Ave Cleveland (44105) *(G-5910)*
Marmon Highway Tech LLC...............................330 878-5595
  6332 Columbia Rd Nw Dover (44622) *(G-10087)*
Maronda Homes Inc Florida..............................937 472-3907
  1050 S Barron St Eaton (45320) *(G-10451)*
Marous Brothers Cnstr Inc..............................440 951-3904
  1702 Joseph Lloyd Pkwy Willoughby (44094) *(G-19550)*
Marquardt, Richard F Od, Mansfield Also called Ohio Eye Associates Inc *(G-13229)*
Marquette Group, Dayton Also called Gypc Inc *(G-9479)*
Marquis Mobility Inc......................................330 497-5373
  4051 Whipple Ave Nw Ste E Canton (44718) *(G-2389)*
Marriage License Bureau, Cleveland Also called Cuyahoga County *(G-5397)*
Marrik Dish Company LLC.................................419 475-6538
  4102 Monroe St Toledo (43606) *(G-17895)*
Marriott, Columbus Also called Columbus Easton Hotel LLC *(G-7278)*
Marriott, Clyde Also called Hmshost Corporation *(G-6744)*

Marriott, Dublin *Also called Winegardner & Hammons Inc* ***(G-10376)***
Marriott, Cleveland *Also called Cleveland East Hotel LLC* ***(G-5252)***
Marriott, West Chester *Also called Union Centre Hotel LLC* ***(G-19026)***
Marriott 440 542-2375
31225 Bainbridge Rd Ste A Solon (44139) ***(G-16871)***
Marriott Columbus Univ Area, Columbus *Also called Uph Holdings LLC* ***(G-8823)***
Marriott Hotel Services Inc 216 252-5333
4277 W 150th St Cleveland (44135) ***(G-5911)***
Marriott International Inc 614 861-1400
695 Taylor Rd Columbus (43230) ***(G-8022)***
Marriott International Inc 330 484-0300
4025 Greentree Ave Sw Canton (44706) ***(G-2390)***
Marriott International Inc 513 487-3800
151 Goodman St Cincinnati (45219) ***(G-3973)***
Marriott International Inc 513 487-3800
151 Goodman St Cincinnati (45219) ***(G-3974)***
Marriott International Inc 216 696-9200
127 Public Sq Fl 1 Cleveland (44114) ***(G-5912)***
Marriott International Inc 614 228-5050
50 N 3rd St Columbus (43215) ***(G-8023)***
Marriott International Inc 614 436-7070
7411 Vantage Dr Columbus (43235) ***(G-8024)***
Marriott International Inc 614 475-8530
2901 Airport Dr Columbus (43219) ***(G-8025)***
Marriott International Inc 614 864-8844
2084 S Hamilton Rd Columbus (43232) ***(G-8026)***
Marriott International Inc 614 222-2610
36 E Gay St Columbus (43215) ***(G-8027)***
Marriott International Inc 614 885-0799
7300 Huntington Park Dr Columbus (43235) ***(G-8028)***
Marriott International Inc 330 666-4811
120 Montrose West Ave Copley (44321) ***(G-8970)***
Marriott International Inc 419 866-1001
1435 E Mall Dr Holland (43528) ***(G-11895)***
Marriott International Inc 440 716-9977
24901 Country Club Blvd North Olmsted (44070) ***(G-15297)***
Marriott International Inc 513 530-5060
11401 Reed Hartman Hwy Blue Ash (45241) ***(G-1605)***
Marriott McKinley Grande Hotel, Canton *Also called American Prprty-Mnagement Corp* ***(G-2187)***
Mars Electric Company (PA) 440 946-2250
6655 Beta Dr Ste 200 Cleveland (44143) ***(G-5913)***
Marsam Metalfab Inc 330 405-1520
1870 Enterprise Pkwy Twinsburg (44087) ***(G-18295)***
Marsden Holding LLC 440 973-7774
6751 Engle Rd Ste H Middleburg Heights (44130) ***(G-14254)***
Marsh Berry & Company Inc (PA) 440 354-3230
28601 Chagrin Blvd # 400 Beachwood (44122) ***(G-1075)***
Marsh Inc (PA) 513 421-1234
333 E 8th St Cincinnati (45202) ***(G-3975)***
Marsh & McLennan Agency LLC 513 248-4888
6279 Tri Ridge Blvd # 400 Loveland (45140) ***(G-13010)***
Marsh & McLennan Agency LLC 937 228-4135
409 E Monu Ave Ste 400 Dayton (45402) ***(G-9585)***
Marsh Building Products Inc (PA) 937 222-3321
2030 Winners Cir Dayton (45404) ***(G-9586)***
Marsh Foundation 419 238-1695
1229 Lincoln Hwy Van Wert (45891) ***(G-18484)***
Marsh USA Inc 216 937-1700
200 Public Sq Ste 3760 Cleveland (44114) ***(G-5914)***
Marsh USA Inc 513 287-1600
525 Vine St Ste 1600 Cincinnati (45202) ***(G-3976)***
Marsh USA Inc 614 227-6200
325 John H Mcconnell Blvd # 350 Columbus (43215) ***(G-8029)***
Marsh USA Inc 216 830-8000
200 Public Sq Ste 900 Cleveland (44114) ***(G-5915)***
Marshall & Associates Inc 513 683-6396
1537 Durango Dr Loveland (45140) ***(G-13011)***
Marshall & Melhorn LLC 419 249-7100
4 Seagate Ste 800 Toledo (43604) ***(G-17896)***
Marshall Ford Leasing, Cleveland *Also called Sorbir Inc* ***(G-6421)***
Marshall Information Svcs LLC 614 430-0355
6665 Busch Blvd Columbus (43229) ***(G-8030)***
Marshallville Packing Co Inc 330 855-2871
50 E Market St Marshallville (44645) ***(G-13474)***
Marsol Apartments 440 449-5800
6503 1/2 Marsol Rd Cleveland (44124) ***(G-5916)***
Martens Donald & Sons (PA) 216 265-4211
10830 Brookpark Rd Cleveland (44130) ***(G-5917)***
Martguild, Chagrin Falls *Also called Wirefree Home Automation* ***(G-2661)***
Martin + WD Apprisal Group Ltd 419 241-4998
43 S Saint Clair St Toledo (43604) ***(G-17897)***
Martin Altmeyer Funeral Home 330 385-3650
15872 Saint Clair Ave East Liverpool (43920) ***(G-10406)***
Martin Carpet Cleaning Company 614 443-4655
795 S Wall St Columbus (43206) ***(G-8031)***
Martin Chevrolet Inc 937 849-1381
8560 Troy Pike Dayton (45424) ***(G-9587)***
Martin Greg Excavating Inc 513 727-9300
1501 S University Blvd Middletown (45044) ***(G-14306)***
Martin Healthcare Group, The, Cleveland *Also called Physician Staffing Inc* ***(G-6209)***
Martin Logistics Inc 330 456-8000
4526 Louisville St Ne Canton (44705) ***(G-2391)***
Martin Ls DDS Ms (PA) 513 829-8999
1211 Nilles Rd Fairfield (45014) ***(G-10749)***
Martin Marietta Aggragate, West Chester *Also called Martin Marietta Materials Inc* ***(G-18970)***
Martin Marietta Aggregates, Grove City *Also called Martin Marietta Materials Inc* ***(G-11451)***
Martin Marietta Materials Inc 513 701-1140
9277 Centre Pointe Dr # 250 West Chester (45069) ***(G-18970)***
Martin Marietta Materials Inc 513 353-1400
10905 Us 50 North Bend (45052) ***(G-15182)***
Martin Marietta Materials Inc 513 829-6446
107 River Cir Bldg 1 Fairfield (45014) ***(G-10750)***
Martin Marietta Materials Inc 614 871-6708
3300 Jackson Pike Grove City (43123) ***(G-11451)***
Martin Periodontics, Fairfield *Also called Martin Ls DDS Ms* ***(G-10749)***
Martin Trnsp Systems Inc 419 726-1348
320 Matzinger Rd Toledo (43612) ***(G-17898)***
Martin-Brower Company LLC 513 773-2301
4260 Port Union Rd West Chester (45011) ***(G-18971)***
Marucci and Gaffney Excvtg Co (PA) 330 743-8170
18 Hogue St Youngstown (44502) ***(G-20117)***
Marvel Consultants (PA) 216 292-2855
28601 Chagrin Blvd # 210 Cleveland (44122) ***(G-5918)***
Marvin W Mielke Inc 330 725-8845
1040 Industrial Pkwy Medina (44256) ***(G-13969)***
Marxent Labs LLC 937 999-5005
3100 Res Blvd Ste 360 Kettering (45420) ***(G-12297)***
Mary C Enterprises Inc (PA) 937 253-6169
2274 Patterson Rd Dayton (45420) ***(G-9588)***
Mary Evans Childcare Center, Columbus *Also called First Community Church* ***(G-7584)***
Mary Hammond Center, McConnelsville *Also called Mary Hmmond Adult Actvties Ctr* ***(G-13901)***
Mary Hmmond Adult Actvties Ctr 740 962-4200
900 S Riverside Dr Ne McConnelsville (43756) ***(G-13901)***
Mary Rtan Hlth Assn Logan Cnty (PA) 937 592-4015
205 E Palmer Rd Bellefontaine (43311) ***(G-1358)***
Mary Rutan Hospital, Bellefontaine *Also called Mary Rtan Hlth Assn Logan Cnty* ***(G-1358)***
Mary Rutan Hospital (HQ) 937 592-4015
205 E Palmer Rd Bellefontaine (43311) ***(G-1359)***
Mary Scott Nursing Home Inc 937 278-0761
3109 Campus Dr Dayton (45406) ***(G-9589)***
Maryann McEowen 330 638-6385
272 Wae Trl Cortland (44410) ***(G-8990)***
Maryhaven Inc (PA) 614 449-1530
1791 Alum Creek Dr Columbus (43207) ***(G-8032)***
Maryhaven Inc 937 644-9192
715 S Plum St Marysville (43040) ***(G-13513)***
Marymount Health Care Systems 216 332-1100
13900 Mccracken Rd Cleveland (44125) ***(G-5919)***
Marymount Hospital Inc (HQ) 216 581-0500
9500 Euclid Ave Cleveland (44195) ***(G-5920)***
Marysville Food Pantry 937 644-3248
333 Ash St Marysville (43040) ***(G-13514)***
Marysville Steel Inc 937 642-5971
323 E 8th St Marysville (43040) ***(G-13515)***
Marysvlle Ohio Srgical Ctr LLC (PA) 937 642-6622
122 Professional Pkwy Marysville (43040) ***(G-13516)***
Marysvlle Ohio Srgical Ctr LLC 937 578-4200
17853 State Route 31 Marysville (43040) ***(G-13517)***
Marzetti Distribution Center, Grove City *Also called Tmarzetti Company* ***(G-11477)***
Mas Inc (PA) 330 659-3333
2718 Brecksville Rd Richfield (44286) ***(G-16362)***
Mas International Mktg LLC 614 446-2003
3498 Derbyshire Dr Apt C Columbus (43224) ***(G-8033)***
Masco Inc 330 797-2904
160 Marwood Cir Youngstown (44512) ***(G-20118)***
Maslyk Landscaping Inc 440 748-3635
12289 Eaton Commerce Pkwy # 2 Columbia Station (44028) ***(G-6778)***
Mason Family Resorts LLC 513 339-0141
2501 Great Wolf Dr Mason (45040) ***(G-13615)***
Mason Health Care Center 513 398-2881
5640 Cox Smith Rd Mason (45040) ***(G-13616)***
Mason Steel, Walton Hills *Also called Mason Structural Steel Inc* ***(G-18637)***
Mason Steel Erecting Inc 440 439-1040
7500 Northfield Rd Cleveland (44146) ***(G-5921)***
Mason Structural Steel Inc 440 439-1040
7500 Northfield Rd Walton Hills (44146) ***(G-18637)***
Masonic Healthcare Inc 937 525-3001
3 Masonic Dr Springfield (45504) ***(G-17067)***
Massachusetts Mutl Lf Insur Co 513 579-8555
1 W 4th St Ste 1000 Cincinnati (45202) ***(G-3977)***
Massachusetts Mutl Lf Insur Co 216 592-7359
1660 W 2nd St Ste 850 Cleveland (44113) ***(G-5922)***
Massage Envy, Westlake *Also called Irish Envy LLC* ***(G-19358)***
Massage Envy 440 878-0500
6 Southpark Ctr Strongsville (44136) ***(G-17329)***
Massey's Pizza, Columbus *Also called Premier Broadcasting Co Inc* ***(G-8458)***
Massillon Automobile Club 330 833-1084
1972 Wales Rd Ne Ste 1 Massillon (44646) ***(G-13709)***
Massillon Cable TV Inc (PA) 330 833-4134
814 Cable Ct Nw Massillon (44647) ***(G-13710)***

ALPHABETIC

Massillon City School Bus Gar 330 830-1849
1 George Red Bird Dr Se Massillon (44646) *(G-13711)*
Massillon Cmnty Hosp Hlth Plan, Massillon *Also called Health Plan of Ohio Inc (G-13693)*
Massillon Community Dialysis, Massillon *Also called Fort Dialysis LLC (G-13683)*
Massillon Feed Mill, Massillon *Also called Case Farms LLC (G-13668)*
Massillon Health System LLC 330 837-7200
400 Austin Ave Nw Massillon (44646) *(G-13712)*
Mast Global Fashions, Reynoldsburg *Also called Mast Industries Inc (G-16319)*
Mast Industries Inc (HQ) 614 415-7000
2 Limited Pkwy Columbus (43230) *(G-8034)*
Mast Industries Inc 614 856-6000
8655 E Broad St Reynoldsburg (43068) *(G-16319)*
Mast Logistics Services Inc 614 415-7500
2 Limited Pkwy Columbus (43230) *(G-8035)*
Mast Technology Services Inc 614 415-7000
3 Limited Pkwy Columbus (43230) *(G-8036)*
Mast Trucking Inc 330 674-8913
6471 County Road 625 Millersburg (44654) *(G-14482)*
Master Builders LLC (HQ) 216 831-5500
23700 Chagrin Blvd Beachwood (44122) *(G-1076)*
Master Clean Carpet & Uphlstry, Columbus *Also called D & J Master Clean Inc (G-7406)*
Master Maintenance Co, Lima *Also called Nicholas D Starr Inc (G-12706)*
Master-Halco Inc 513 869-7600
620 Commerce Center Dr Fairfield (45011) *(G-10751)*
Masterpiece Painting Company 330 395-9900
546 Washington St Ne Warren (44483) *(G-18727)*
Masterplan, Cincinnati *Also called Genesis Technology Partners (G-3617)*
Masters Agency Inc 330 805-5985
1108 Ledgestone Dr Wadsworth (44281) *(G-18607)*
Masters Drug Company Inc 800 982-7922
3600 Pharma Way Lebanon (45036) *(G-12484)*
Masters of Disasters, Cleveland *Also called A-Team LLC (G-4885)*
Masters Pharmaceutical, Lebanon *Also called Masters Drug Company Inc (G-12484)*
Masur Trucking Inc 513 860-9600
11825 Reading Rd Ste 1 Cincinnati (45241) *(G-3978)*
Mat, Lima *Also called Allen Metro Hsing MGT Dev Corp (G-12597)*
Matandy Steel & Metal Pdts LLC 513 844-2277
1200 Central Ave Hamilton (45011) *(G-11627)*
Matandy Steel Sales, Hamilton *Also called Matandy Steel & Metal Pdts LLC (G-11627)*
Matco Industries Inc 740 852-7054
204 Maple St London (43140) *(G-12870)*
Matco Properties Inc 440 366-5501
823 Leona St Elyria (44035) *(G-10533)*
MATCO SERVICES, London *Also called Matco Industries Inc (G-12870)*
Matco Tools Corporation (HQ) 330 929-4949
4403 Allen Rd Stow (44224) *(G-17219)*
Material Management, Columbus *Also called Ohio Department Transportation (G-8242)*
Material Suppliers Inc 419 298-2440
2444 State Route 49 Edgerton (43517) *(G-10468)*
Matern Ohio Management Inc 614 457-7660
1241 Dublin Rd Ste 200 Columbus (43215) *(G-8037)*
Maternohio Clinical Assoicates 614 457-7660
1241 Dublin Rd Ste 102 Columbus (43215) *(G-8038)*
Maternohio Management Services, Columbus *Also called Matern Ohio Management Inc (G-8037)*
Matesich Distributing Co 740 349-8686
1190 E Main St Newark (43055) *(G-15065)*
Matheson Tri-Gas Inc 614 771-1311
4579 Sutphen Ct Hilliard (43026) *(G-11788)*
Mathews Josiah 567 204-8818
602 E 5th St Lima (45804) *(G-12699)*
Mathews Auto Group, Marion *Also called Mathews Kennedy Ford L-M Inc (G-13445)*
Mathews Dodge Chrysler Jeep 740 389-2341
1866 Marion Waldo Rd Marion (43302) *(G-13444)*
Mathews Ford Inc 740 522-2181
500 Hebron Rd Newark (43056) *(G-15066)*
Mathews Ford-Oregon, Oregon *Also called Oregon Ford Inc (G-15605)*
Mathews Kennedy Ford L-M Inc (PA) 740 387-3673
1155 Delaware Ave Marion (43302) *(G-13445)*
Matia Motors Inc 440 365-7311
823 Leona St Elyria (44035) *(G-10534)*
Matlock Electric Co Inc (PA) 513 731-9600
2780 Highland Ave Cincinnati (45212) *(G-3979)*
Mato Inc 440 729-9008
8027 Mayfield Rd Chesterland (44026) *(G-2740)*
Matrix Claims Management Inc 513 351-1222
644 Linn St Ste 900 Cincinnati (45203) *(G-3980)*
Matrix Invstgations Consulting, Cincinnati *Also called Matrix Claims Management Inc (G-3980)*
Matrix Management Solutions 330 470-3700
5200 Stoneham Rd Canton (44720) *(G-2392)*
Matrix Media Services Inc 614 228-2200
463 E Town St Ste 200 Columbus (43215) *(G-8039)*
Matrix Pointe Software LLC 216 333-1263
30400 Detroit Rd Ste 400 Westlake (44145) *(G-19371)*
Matrix Research Inc 937 427-8433
3844 Research Blvd Beavercreek (45430) *(G-1230)*
Matrix Sys Auto Finishes LLC 248 668-8135
600 Nova Dr Se Massillon (44646) *(G-13713)*
Matrix Technologies Inc (PA) 419 897-7200
1760 Indian Wood Cir Maumee (43537) *(G-13816)*
Matt Construction Services 216 641-0030
6600 Grant Ave Cleveland (44105) *(G-5923)*
Mattingly Foods Inc (PA) 740 454-0136
302 State St Zanesville (43701) *(G-20329)*
Mattlin Construction Inc 513 598-5402
5835 Hamilton Cleves Rd Cleves (45002) *(G-6733)*
Matvest Inc 614 487-8720
1380 Dublin Rd Ste 200 Columbus (43215) *(G-8040)*
Maumee Bay Golf Course, Oregon *Also called TW Recreational Services (G-15613)*
Maumee Lodge No 1850 Bnvlt 419 893-7272
137 W Wayne St Maumee (43537) *(G-13817)*
Maumee Lodging Enterprises 419 865-1380
1520 S Hlland Sylvania Rd Maumee (43537) *(G-13818)*
Maumee Ob Gyn Assoc 419 891-6201
660 Beaver Creek Cir # 200 Maumee (43537) *(G-13819)*
Maumee Plumbing & Htg Sup Inc (PA) 419 874-7991
12860 Eckel Junction Rd Perrysburg (43551) *(G-15892)*
Maumee Valley Guidance Center (PA) 419 782-8856
211 Biede Ave Defiance (43512) *(G-9927)*
Maumee Youth Center, Liberty Center *Also called Youth Services Ohio Department (G-12576)*
Mauser Usa LLC 740 397-1762
219 Commerce Dr Mount Vernon (43050) *(G-14780)*
Mauser Usa LLC 740 397-1762
219 Commerce Dr Mount Vernon (43050) *(G-14781)*
Maval Industries LLC 330 405-1600
1555 Enterprise Pkwy Twinsburg (44087) *(G-18296)*
Maval Manufacturing, Twinsburg *Also called Maval Industries LLC (G-18296)*
Maverick Media (PA) 419 331-1600
57 Town Sq Lima (45801) *(G-12700)*
Max Dixons Expressway Park 513 831-2273
689 Us Route 50 Milford (45150) *(G-14407)*
Maxim Healthcare Services Inc 740 772-4100
83 E Water St Chillicothe (45601) *(G-2804)*
Maxim Healthcare Services Inc 216 606-3000
6155 Rockside Rd Independence (44131) *(G-12097)*
Maxim Healthcare Services Inc 614 986-3001
735 Taylor Rd Gahanna (43230) *(G-11135)*
Maxim Technologies Inc 614 457-6325
3960 Brown Park Dr Ste D Hilliard (43026) *(G-11789)*
Maximum Call Center, Cincinnati *Also called Maximum Communications Inc (G-3981)*
Maximum Communications Inc 513 489-3414
117 Williams St Cincinnati (45215) *(G-3981)*
Maxwell Lightning Protection 937 228-7250
621 Pond St Dayton (45402) *(G-9590)*
May Jim Auto Sales LLC 419 422-9797
3690 Speedway Dr Findlay (45840) *(G-10940)*
Mayer Laminates MA, Hudson *Also called Meyer Decorative Surfaces USA (G-11996)*
Mayers Electric Co Inc 513 272-2900
4004 Erie Ct Ste B Cincinnati (45227) *(G-3982)*
Mayfair Country Club Inc 330 699-2209
2229 Raber Rd Uniontown (44685) *(G-18378)*
Mayfair Nursing Care Centers 614 889-6320
3000 Bethel Rd Columbus (43220) *(G-8041)*
Mayfair School, Toledo *Also called Harbor (G-17781)*
MAYFAIR VILLAGE, Columbus *Also called Mayfair Nursing Care Centers (G-8041)*
Mayfare Village, Columbus *Also called Life Care Centers America Inc (G-7972)*
Mayfield Clinic Inc (PA) 513 221-1100
3825 Edwards Rd Ste 300 Cincinnati (45209) *(G-3983)*
Mayfield Sand Ridge Club 216 381-0826
1545 Sheridan Rd Cleveland (44121) *(G-5924)*
Mayfield Village, Cleveland *Also called Skoda Minotti Holdings LLC (G-6411)*
Mayflower Nursing Home Inc 330 492-7131
836 34th St Nw Canton (44709) *(G-2393)*
Maza Inc 614 760-0003
7635 Commerce Pl Plain City (43064) *(G-16059)*
Mazanec Raskin & Ryder, Cleveland *Also called Mazanec Raskin & Ryder Co Lpa (G-5925)*
Mazanec Raskin & Ryder Co Lpa (PA) 440 248-7906
34305 Solon Rd Ste 100 Cleveland (44139) *(G-5925)*
Mazda Saab of Bedford, Bedford *Also called Partners Auto Group Bdford Inc (G-1299)*
Mazel Company, The, Solon *Also called Aurora Wholesalers LLC (G-16825)*
Mazella Companies, Cleveland *Also called Mazzella Holding Company Inc (G-5926)*
Mazzella Holding Company Inc (PA) 513 772-4466
21000 Aerospace Pkwy Cleveland (44142) *(G-5926)*
MB Financial Inc 937 283-2027
2251 Rombach Ave Wilmington (45177) *(G-19634)*
MBC Cardiologist Inc 937 223-4461
122 Wyoming St Dayton (45409) *(G-9591)*
MBC Holdings Inc (PA) 419 445-1015
1613 S Defiance St Archbold (43502) *(G-632)*
MBI Solutions Inc 937 619-4000
332 Congress Park Dr Dayton (45459) *(G-9592)*
MBI Tree Service LLC 513 926-9857
9447 Cold Springs Ln Waynesville (45068) *(G-18834)*
Mbs Acquisition, Mason *Also called Remtec Engineering (G-13635)*
Mc Alarney Pool Spas and Billd 740 373-6698
908 Pike St Marietta (45750) *(G-13357)*

Mc Auley Center 937 653-5432
906 Scioto St Urbana (43078) *(G-18439)*

Mc Cloy Financial Services 614 457-6233
921 Chatham Ln Ste 300 Columbus (43221) *(G-8042)*

Mc Clurg & Creamer Inc 419 866-7080
7450 Hill Ave Holland (43528) *(G-11896)*

Mc Cormack Advisors Intl 216 522-1200
1360 E 9th St Ste 100 Cleveland (44114) *(G-5927)*

Mc Daniel Motor Co (Inc) 740 389-2355
1111 Mount Vernon Ave Marion (43302) *(G-13446)*

Mc Fadden Construction Inc 419 668-4165
4426 Old State Rd N Norwalk (44857) *(G-15444)*

Mc Graw-Hill Educational Pubg, Ashland *Also called McGraw-Hill School Education
H (G-679)*

Mc Gregor Family Enterprises (PA) 513 583-0040
9990 Kings Auto Mall Rd Cincinnati (45249) *(G-3984)*

Mc Group, Mentor *Also called Mc Sign LLC (G-14079)*

Mc Mahon Realestate Co (PA) 740 344-2250
591 Country Club Dr Newark (43055) *(G-15067)*

Mc Meechan Construction Co 216 581-9373
17633 S Miles Rd Cleveland (44128) *(G-5928)*

Mc Neal Industries Inc 440 721-0400
835 Richmond Rd Painesville (44077) *(G-15724)*

Mc Phillips Plbg Htg & AC Co 216 481-1400
16115 Waterloo Rd Cleveland (44110) *(G-5929)*

Mc Sign LLC (PA) 440 209-6200
8959 Tyler Blvd Mentor (44060) *(G-14079)*

McAfee Air Duct Cleaning, Dayton *Also called McAfee Heating & AC Co Inc (G-9593)*

McAfee Heating & AC Co Inc 937 438-1976
4750 Hempstead Station Dr Dayton (45429) *(G-9593)*

McAlarney Pols Spas Billd More, Marietta *Also called Mc Alarney Pool Spas and
Billd (G-13357)*

McArthur Lumber and Post, Mc Arthur *Also called Appalachia Wood Inc (G-13889)*

McBee Supply Corporation 216 881-0015
5300 Lakeside Ave E Cleveland (44114) *(G-5930)*

McCad, Mount Gilead *Also called Morrow County Council On Drugs (G-14729)*

McCafferty Community Based, Cleveland *Also called Veterans Health
Administration (G-6626)*

McCallisters Landscaping & Sup 440 259-3348
2519 N Ridge Rd Painesville (44077) *(G-15725)*

McCarthy Burgess & Wolff Inc (PA) 440 735-5100
26000 Cannon Rd Bedford (44146) *(G-1292)*

McCaslin Imbus & Mccaslin Lpa (PA) 513 421-4646
600 Vine St Ste 400 Cincinnati (45202) *(G-3985)*

McCc Sportswear Inc 513 583-9210
9944 Prnceton Glendale Rd West Chester (45246) *(G-19065)*

McCdp, Youngstown *Also called Meridian Healthcare (G-20127)*

McClellan Management Inc 419 855-7755
300 Cherry St Genoa (43430) *(G-11258)*

McClintock Electric Inc 330 264-6380
402 E Henry St Wooster (44691) *(G-19743)*

McCloy Engineering LLC 513 984-4112
3701 Port Union Rd Fairfield (45014) *(G-10752)*

McCluskey Automotive, Cincinnati *Also called McCluskey Chevrolet Inc (G-3986)*

McCluskey Chevrolet Inc (PA) 513 761-1111
8525 Reading Rd Cincinnati (45215) *(G-3986)*

McCo, Portsmouth *Also called Mechanical Construction Co (G-16154)*

McCo, Cleveland *Also called Medical Center Co (inc) (G-5942)*

McConnell Excavating Ltd 440 774-4578
15804 State Route 58 Oberlin (44074) *(G-15508)*

McCormick Equipment Co Inc (PA) 513 677-8888
112 Northeast Dr Loveland (45140) *(G-13012)*

McCoy Center For The Arts, New Albany *Also called Jeanne B McCoy Comm (G-14857)*

McCoy Landscape Services Inc 740 375-2730
2391 Likens Rd Marion (43302) *(G-13447)*

McCrate Delaet & Co 937 492-3161
100 S Main Ave Ste 203 Sidney (45365) *(G-16786)*

McCrate Delaet & Co Cpa's, Sidney *Also called McCrate Delaet & Co (G-16786)*

McCrea Manor Nursing, Alliance *Also called Peregrine Health Services Inc (G-543)*

McCullough-Hyde Mem Hosp Inc (PA) 513 523-2111
110 N Poplar St Oxford (45056) *(G-15680)*

McCullough-Hyde Mem Hosp Inc 513 863-2215
1390 Eaton Ave Hamilton (45013) *(G-11628)*

McDaniels Cnstr Corp Inc 614 252-5852
1069 Woodland Ave Columbus (43219) *(G-8043)*

McDermott International Inc 740 687-4292
2600 E Main St Lancaster (43130) *(G-12415)*

McDonald Finanacial Group, Cleveland *Also called Keybanc Capital Markets Inc (G-5826)*

MCDONALD HOPKINS LLC (PA) 216 348-5400
600 Superior Ave E # 2100 Cleveland (44114) *(G-5931)*

McDonald's, Mount Gilead *Also called Pam Johnsonident (G-14733)*

McDonald's, Lewis Center *Also called D J- Seve Group Inc (G-12537)*

McDonalds 3490 .... 330 762-7747
578 E Market St Akron (44304) *(G-326)*

McDonalds Corporation 614 682-1128
2600 Corporate Exch Dr Columbus (43231) *(G-8044)*

McDonalds Design & Build Inc 419 782-4191
101 Clinton St Ste 2200 Defiance (43512) *(G-9928)*

McElvain Group Home 419 589-6697
634 Mcbride Rd Mansfield (44905) *(G-13212)*

McEp, Dayton *Also called Medical Center At Elizabeth Pl (G-9601)*

McFarland Truck Lines Inc 937 854-2200
1844 Invention Dr Dayton (45426) *(G-9594)*

McGill Airclean LLC 614 829-1200
1777 Refugee Rd Columbus (43207) *(G-8045)*

McGill Smith Punshon Inc 513 759-0004
3700 Park 42 Dr Ste 190b Cincinnati (45241) *(G-3987)*

McGinnis Inc (HQ) 740 377-4391
502 2nd St E South Point (45680) *(G-16940)*

McGinnis Inc 513 941-8070
5525 River Rd Cincinnati (45233) *(G-3988)*

McGohan Brabender, Moraine *Also called McGohan/Brabender Agency Inc (G-14672)*

McGohan/Brabender Agency Inc (PA) 937 293-1600
3931 S Dixie Dr Moraine (45439) *(G-14672)*

McGowan & Company Inc (PA) 800 545-1538
20595 Lorain Rd Ste 300 Cleveland (44126) *(G-5932)*

McGowan Program Administrators, Cleveland *Also called McGowan & Company
Inc (G-5932)*

McGraw-Hill School Education H 419 207-7400
1250 George Rd Ashland (44805) *(G-679)*

McGraw/Kokosing Inc 614 212-5700
101 Clark Blvd Monroe (45044) *(G-14576)*

McGregor Senior Ind Hsing 216 851-8200
14900 Private Dr Cleveland (44112) *(G-5933)*

Mch Services Inc 260 432-9699
190 E Spring Valley Pike Dayton (45458) *(G-9595)*

MCI Communications Svcs Inc 216 265-9953
21000 Brookpark Rd Cleveland (44135) *(G-5934)*

MCI Communications Svcs Inc 440 635-0418
12956 Taylor Wells Rd Chardon (44024) *(G-2704)*

McKeen Security Inc 740 699-1301
69100 Bayberry Dr Ste 200 Saint Clairsville (43950) *(G-16495)*

McKeever & Niekamp Elc Inc 937 431-9363
1834 Woods Dr Beavercreek (45432) *(G-1169)*

McKesson Corporation 740 636-3500
3000 Kenskill Ave Wshngtn CT Hs (43160) *(G-19878)*

McKesson Medical-Surgical Inc 614 539-2600
3500 Centerpoint Dr Urbancrest (43123) *(G-18450)*

McKesson Medical-Surgical Top 513 985-0525
12074 Champion Way Cincinnati (45241) *(G-3989)*

McKinley Air Transport Inc 330 497-6956
5430 Lauby Rd Bldg 4 Canton (44720) *(G-2394)*

McKinley Early Childhood Ctr (PA) 330 454-4800
1350 Cherry Ave Ne Canton (44714) *(G-2395)*

McKinley Early Childhood Ctr 330 252-2552
440 Vernon Odom Blvd Akron (44307) *(G-327)*

McKinley Hall Inc 937 328-5300
2624 Lexington Ave Springfield (45505) *(G-17068)*

McKinley Life Care Center LLC 330 456-1014
800 Market Ave N Ste 1560 Canton (44702) *(G-2396)*

MCKINLEY NATIONAL MEMORIAL, Canton *Also called Stark Cnty Historical Soc
Inc (G-2489)*

McKinsey & Company Inc 216 274-4000
950 Main Ave Ste 1200 Cleveland (44113) *(G-5935)*

McKinsey & Company Inc 216 274-4000
950 Main Ave Ste 1200 Cleveland (44113) *(G-5936)*

McM Capital Partners 216 514-1840
25201 Chagrin Blvd # 360 Beachwood (44122) *(G-1077)*

McM Electronics Inc 937 434-0031
650 Congress Park Dr Dayton (45459) *(G-9596)*

McM Electronics Inc (HQ) 888 235-4692
650 Congress Park Dr Centerville (45459) *(G-2630)*

McM General Properties Ltd 216 851-8000
13829 Euclid Ave Cleveland (44112) *(G-5937)*

McMaster Farms 330 482-2913
345 Old Fourteen Rd Columbiana (44408) *(G-6790)*

McMicken College of Asa, Cincinnati *Also called University of Cincinnati (G-4711)*

McMullen Transportation LLC 937 981-4455
11350 State Route 41 Greenfield (45123) *(G-11364)*

McNational Inc (PA) 740 377-4391
502 2nd St E South Point (45680) *(G-16941)*

McNaughton-Mckay Elc Ohio Inc (HQ) 614 476-2800
2255 Citygate Dr Columbus (43219) *(G-8046)*

McNaughton-Mckay Elc Ohio Inc 419 422-2984
1950 Industrial Dr Findlay (45840) *(G-10941)*

McNaughton-Mckay Elc Ohio Inc 419 891-0262
355 Tomahawk Dr Unit 1 Maumee (43537) *(G-13820)*

McNaughton-Mckay Electric Ohio, Columbus *Also called McNaughton-Mckay Elc Ohio
Inc (G-8046)*

McNeil Industries Inc 440 951-7756
835 Richmond Rd Ste 2 Painesville (44077) *(G-15726)*

McNerney & Associates LLC (PA) 513 241-9951
440 Northland Blvd Cincinnati (45240) *(G-3990)*

McNerney & Son Inc 419 666-0200
1 Maritime Plz Fl 7 Toledo (43604) *(G-17899)*

McPaul Corp 419 447-6313
981 S Morgan St Tiffin (44883) *(G-17523)*

McPc Inc (PA) 440 238-0102
21500 Aerospace Pkwy Brookpark (44142) *(G-1902)*

McPc Tech Pdts & Solutions, Brookpark *Also called McPc Inc (G-1902)*

**A
L
P
H
A
B
E
T
I
C**

McR LLC 937 879-5055
  2601 Missi Point Blvd Ste Beavercreek (45431) *(G-1170)*
MCR Services Inc 614 421-0860
  638 E 5th Ave Columbus (43201) *(G-8047)*
McSteen & Associates Inc 440 585-9800
  1415 E 286th St Wickliffe (44092) *(G-19469)*
McTech Corp (PA) 216 391-7700
  8100 Grand Ave Ste 100 Cleveland (44104) *(G-5938)*
McV Health Care Facilities 513 398-1486
  411 Western Row Rd Mason (45040) *(G-13617)*
McWane Inc 740 622-6651
  2266 S 6th St Coshocton (43812) *(G-9022)*
MD Business Solutions Inc 513 872-4500
  9825 Kenwood Rd Ste 108 Blue Ash (45242) *(G-1606)*
Mds Foods Inc (PA) 330 879-9780
  4676 Erie Ave Sw Ste A Navarre (44662) *(G-14823)*
MDU Resources Group Inc 937 424-2550
  3150 Encrete Ln Moraine (45439) *(G-14673)*
Meacham & Apel Architects Inc 614 764-0407
  775 Yard St Ste 325 Columbus (43212) *(G-8048)*

Mead Family Medical Ctr, Chillicothe *Also called Corporate Health Dimensions (G-2770)*
Meadbrook Care Center, Cincinnati *Also called Trinity Healthcare Corporation (G-4648)*
Meade Construction Inc (PA) 740 694-5525
  13 N Mill St Lexington (44904) *(G-12574)*
Meade Construction Company, Lexington *Also called Meade Construction Inc (G-12574)*
Meaden & Moore LLP (PA) 216 241-3272
  1375 E 9th St Ste 1800 Cleveland (44114) *(G-5939)*
Meadow Wind Hlth Care Ctr Inc 330 833-2026
  300 23rd St Ne Massillon (44646) *(G-13714)*
Meadowbrook Mall Company (PA) 330 747-2661
  2445 Belmont Ave Youngstown (44505) *(G-20119)*
Meadowbrook Manor of Hartford 330 772-5253
  3090 Five Pnts Hrtford Rd Fowler (44418) *(G-11016)*
Meadowbrook Meat Company Inc 614 771-9660
  4300 Diplomacy Dr Columbus (43228) *(G-8049)*
Meadowhawk Dialysis, Marysville *Also called Mahoney Dialysis LLC (G-13512)*
Meadowlake Corporation 330 492-2010
  1211 39th St Ne Ste A Canton (44714) *(G-2397)*
Meadowood Golf Course, Westlake *Also called City of Westlake (G-19332)*
Meadows Healthcare, West Chester *Also called Mkjb Inc (G-18975)*
Meadowview Care Center, Seville *Also called Encore Healthcare LLC (G-16685)*
Meals On Wheels, Columbus *Also called Lifecare Alliance (G-7974)*
MEALS ON WHEELS, Dayton *Also called Senior Resource Connection (G-9759)*
Meals On Wheels-Older Adult Al 740 681-5050
  253 Boving Rd Lancaster (43130) *(G-12416)*
Meander Hospitality Group Inc 330 702-0226
  6599 Seville Dr Ste 100 Canfield (44406) *(G-2146)*
Meander Hsptality Group II LLC 330 422-0500
  800 Mondial Pkwy Streetsboro (44241) *(G-17260)*
Meander Inn Inc 330 544-2378
  870 N Canfield Niles Rd Youngstown (44515) *(G-20120)*
Meander Inn Incorporated 330 544-0660
  880 N Canfield Niles Rd Youngstown (44515) *(G-20121)*
Mecco Inc 513 422-3651
  2100 S Main St Middletown (45044) *(G-14307)*
Mechancal/Industrial Contg Inc 513 489-8282
  11863 Solzman Rd Cincinnati (45249) *(G-3991)*
Mechanical Cnstr Managers LLC (PA) 937 274-1987
  5245 Wadsworth Rd Dayton (45414) *(G-9597)*
Mechanical Construction Co 740 353-5668
  2302 8th St Portsmouth (45662) *(G-16154)*
Mechanical Contractors, Marysville *Also called J A Guy Inc (G-13508)*
Mechanical Support Svcs Inc 614 777-8808
  4641 Northwest Pkwy Hilliard (43026) *(G-11790)*
Mechanical Systems Dayton Inc 937 254-3235
  4401 Springfield St Dayton (45431) *(G-9181)*
Mechanics Bank (PA) 419 524-0831
  2 S Main St Mansfield (44902) *(G-13213)*
Med -Center/Med Partners 440 349-6400
  34055 Solon Rd Ste 106 Cleveland (44139) *(G-5940)*
Med America Hlth Systems Corp (PA) 937 223-6192
  1 Wyoming St Dayton (45409) *(G-9598)*
Med Assist Prgram of Info Line 330 762-0609
  703 S Main St Ste 211 Akron (44311) *(G-328)*
Med Center, Cleveland *Also called Med -Center/Med Partners (G-5940)*
Med Center One Streetsboro 330 626-3455
  9318 State Route 14 Streetsboro (44241) *(G-17261)*
Med Central HM Hlth & Hospice, Mansfield *Also called Medcentral Health System (G-13214)*
Med Clean 614 207-3317
  5725 Westbourne Ave Columbus (43213) *(G-8050)*
Med Cntral Hlth Sys Child Care, Mansfield *Also called Medcentral Health System (G-13217)*
Med Ride Ems 614 747-9744
  2741 E 4th Ave Columbus (43219) *(G-8051)*
Med Star Emgncy Mdcl Srv (PA) 330 394-6611
  1600 Youngstown Rd Se Warren (44484) *(G-18728)*
Med Star Ems, Warren *Also called Med Star Emgncy Mdcl Srv (G-18728)*
Med Vet Associates, Worthington *Also called Medvet Associates Inc (G-19827)*
Med-Pass Incorporated 937 438-8884
  1 Reynolds Way Dayton (45430) *(G-9599)*

Med-Trans Inc (PA) 937 325-4926
  714 W Columbia St Springfield (45504) *(G-17069)*
Med-Trans Inc 937 293-9771
  3510 Encrete Ln Moraine (45439) *(G-14674)*
Meda-Care Transportation Inc 513 521-4799
  270 Northland Blvd # 227 Cincinnati (45246) *(G-3992)*
Medallion Club (PA) 614 794-6999
  5000 Club Dr Westerville (43082) *(G-19185)*
Medben Companies, Newark *Also called Medical Benefits Mutl Lf Insur (G-15069)*
MEDBEN COMPANIES, Newark *Also called Medical Bnfits Admnstrtors Inc (G-15070)*
Medcare Ambulance, Columbus *Also called Community Emrgcy Med Svcs Ohio (G-7331)*
Medcath Intermediate Holdings 937 221-8016
  707 S Edwin Moses Blvd Dayton (45408) *(G-9600)*
Medcentral Health System 419 526-8900
  1750 W 4th St Ste 1 Ontario (44906) *(G-15562)*
Medcentral Health System 419 526-8442
  335 Glessner Ave Mansfield (44903) *(G-13214)*
Medcentral Health System (HQ) 419 526-8000
  335 Glessner Ave Mansfield (44903) *(G-13215)*
Medcentral Health System 419 526-8970
  770 Balgreen Dr Ste 105 Mansfield (44906) *(G-13216)*
Medcentral Health System 419 683-1040
  291 Heiser Ct Crestline (44827) *(G-9057)*
Medcentral Health System 419 342-5015
  199 W Main St Shelby (44875) *(G-16747)*
Medcentral Health System 419 526-8043
  160 S Linden Rd Mansfield (44906) *(G-13217)*
Medcentral Hlth Sys Spt Mdcine, Ontario *Also called Medcentral Health System (G-15562)*
Medcentral Workable 419 526-8444
  1750 W 4th St Ste 5 Ontario (44906) *(G-15563)*
Medco Health Solutions Inc 614 822-2000
  5151 Blazer Pkwy Ste B Dublin (43017) *(G-10276)*
Medcorp Inc 419 425-9700
  330 N Cory St Findlay (45840) *(G-10942)*
Medcorp Inc (PA) 419 727-7000
  745 Medcorp Dr Toledo (43608) *(G-17900)*
Medflight of Ohio, Columbus *Also called Ohio Medical Trnsp Inc (G-8274)*
Medhurst Mason Contractors Inc 440 543-8885
  17111 Munn Rd Ste 1 Chagrin Falls (44023) *(G-2674)*
Medi Home Care, Gallipolis *Also called Medi Home Health Agency Inc (G-11204)*
Medi Home Health Agency Inc (HQ) 740 266-3977
  105 Main St Steubenville (43953) *(G-17165)*
Medi Home Health Agency Inc 740 441-1779
  412 2nd Ave Gallipolis (45631) *(G-11204)*
Medi-Home Care, Steubenville *Also called Medi Home Health Agency Inc (G-17165)*
Media Advertising Cons LLC 614 615-1398
  1629 Anchor Dr W Columbus (43207) *(G-8052)*
Media Collections Inc 216 831-5626
  8948 Canyon Falls Blvd # 200 Twinsburg (44087) *(G-18297)*
Media Group At Michael's, The, Dayton *Also called Mfh Inc (G-9611)*
Media Source Inc (PA) 614 873-7635
  7858 Industrial Pkwy Plain City (43064) *(G-16060)*
Media-Com Inc 330 673-2323
  2449 State Route 59 Kent (44240) *(G-12249)*
Mediadvertiser Company 513 651-0265
  337 Lorelei Dr Fayetteville (45118) *(G-10858)*
Medic Management Group LLC (PA) 330 670-5316
  275 Springside Dr Akron (44333) *(G-329)*
Medic Response Service Inc (PA) 419 522-1998
  98 S Diamond St Mansfield (44902) *(G-13218)*
Medical & Home Health, Westlake *Also called Applied Marketing Services (G-19317)*
Medical Account Services Inc 937 297-6072
  3131 S Dixie Dr Ste 535 Moraine (45439) *(G-14675)*
Medical Administrators Inc 440 899-2229
  28301 Ranney Pkwy Westlake (44145) *(G-19372)*
Medical and Surgical Assoc 740 522-7600
  1930 Tamarack Rd Newark (43055) *(G-15068)*
Medical Arts Physician Center 216 431-1500
  2475 E 22nd St Ste 120 Cleveland (44115) *(G-5941)*
Medical Assoc Cambridge Inc 740 439-3515
  1515 Maple Dr Ste 1 Cambridge (43725) *(G-2076)*
Medical Associates of Mid-Ohio 419 289-1331
  2109 Claremont Ave Ashland (44805) *(G-680)*
Medical Benefits Mutl Lf Insur (PA) 740 522-8425
  1975 Tamarack Rd Newark (43055) *(G-15069)*
Medical Bnfits Admnstrtors Inc 740 522-8425
  1975 Tamarack Rd Newark (43055) *(G-15070)*
Medical Care PSC Inc 513 281-4400
  2950 Robertson Ave Fl 2 Cincinnati (45209) *(G-3993)*
Medical Care Reimbursement 513 281-4400
  2950 Robertson Ave Fl 2 Cincinnati (45209) *(G-3994)*
Medical Center, Columbus *Also called Ohio State University (G-8302)*
Medical Center, Columbus *Also called Ohio State University (G-8309)*
Medical Center, Columbus *Also called Ohio State University (G-8328)*
Medical Center At Elizabeth Pl 937 223-6237
  1 Elizabeth Pl Dayton (45417) *(G-9601)*
Medical Center Co (inc) 216 368-4256
  2250 Circle Dr Cleveland (44106) *(G-5942)*
Medical Center Security, Columbus *Also called Ohio State University (G-8346)*
Medical College of Ohio, Toledo *Also called Stephen R Saddemi MD (G-18047)*

Medical College of Ohio................................419 383-7100
　3355 Glendale Ave Fl 3 Toledo (43614) *(G-17901)*
Medical Diagnostic Lab Inc (PA)....................440 333-1375
　36711 American Way Ste 2a Avon (44011) *(G-894)*
Medical Flight 2, Marysville *Also called Ohio Medical Trnsp Inc (G-13521)*
Medical Group Associates Inc.......................740 283-4773
　114 Brady Cir E Steubenville (43952) *(G-17166)*
Medical Imaging Equipment, Cleveland *Also called Philips Medical Systems Clevel (G-6203)*
Medical Mutual of Ohio (PA).........................216 687-7000
　2060 E 9th St Frnt Ste Cleveland (44115) *(G-5943)*
Medical Mutual of Ohio................................440 878-4800
　15885 W Sprague Rd Strongsville (44136) *(G-17330)*
Medical Mutual of Ohio................................419 473-7100
　3737 W Sylvania Ave Toledo (43623) *(G-17902)*
Medical Mutual of Ohio................................216 292-0400
　23700 Commerce Park Beachwood (44122) *(G-1078)*
Medical Mutual of Ohio................................614 621-4585
　10 W Broad St Ste 1400 Columbus (43215) *(G-8053)*
Medical Mutual Services LLC (HQ)................440 878-4800
　17800 Royalton Rd Strongsville (44136) *(G-17331)*
Medical Office, Athens *Also called Ohio University (G-798)*
Medical Onclgy-Hematology Assn...................937 223-2183
　3737 Sthern Blvd Ste 4200 Dayton (45429) *(G-9602)*
Medical Radiation Physics, Milford *Also called Mrp Inc (G-14412)*
Medical Records, Steubenville *Also called Trinity Health System (G-17178)*
Medical Records Department, Columbus *Also called Ohio State University (G-8343)*
Medical Recovery Systems Inc.......................513 872-7000
　3372 Central Pkwy Cincinnati (45225) *(G-3995)*
Medical Reimbursement, Cincinnati *Also called Medical Care Reimbursement (G-3994)*
Medical Reimbursment, Cincinnati *Also called Medical Care PSC Inc (G-3993)*
Medical Service Company (PA)......................440 232-3000
　24000 Broadway Ave Bedford (44146) *(G-1293)*
Medical Solutions LLC................................513 936-3468
　9987 Carver Rd Ste 510 Blue Ash (45242) *(G-1607)*
Medical Specialties Distrs LLC.....................440 232-0320
　26350 Broadway Ave Oakwood Village (44146) *(G-15490)*
Medical Transport Systems Inc......................330 837-9818
　909 Las Olas Blvd Nw North Canton (44720) *(G-15219)*
Medicine Midwest LLC (PA)..........................513 533-1199
　4700 Smith Rd Ste A Cincinnati (45212) *(G-3996)*
Medicine Midwest LLC................................937 435-8786
　979 Congress Park Dr Dayton (45459) *(G-9603)*
Medicount Management Inc.........................513 772-4465
　10361 Spartan Dr Cincinnati (45215) *(G-3997)*
Medigistics Inc (PA).................................614 430-5700
　1111 Schrock Rd Ste 200 Columbus (43229) *(G-8054)*
Medill Elemntary Sch of Volntr.....................740 687-7352
　1160 Sheridan Dr Lancaster (43130) *(G-12417)*
Medina Advantage Inc...............................330 723-8697
　3550 Octagon Dr Medina (44256) *(G-13970)*
Medina Automall, Medina *Also called Medina Management Company LLC (G-13976)*
Medina Cnty Jvnile Dtntion Ctr......................330 764-8408
　655 Independence Dr Medina (44256) *(G-13971)*
Medina Community Recrtl Ctr, Medina *Also called Rec Center (G-13993)*
Medina County Health Dept, Medina *Also called County of Medina (G-13926)*
Medina County Home, Medina *Also called County of Medina (G-13925)*
Medina County Sanitary..............................330 273-3610
　791 W Smith Rd Medina (44256) *(G-13972)*
Medina County Sheltered Inds......................330 334-4491
　150 Quadral Dr Ste D Wadsworth (44281) *(G-18608)*
Medina Creative Accessibility.......................330 591-4434
　232 N Court St Medina (44256) *(G-13973)*
Medina Glass Block Inc.............................330 239-0239
　1213 Medina Rd Ste A Medina (44256) *(G-13974)*
Medina Hospital.....................................330 723-3117
　1000 E Washington St Medina (44256) *(G-13975)*
Medina Management Company LLC................330 723-3291
　3205 Medina Rd Medina (44256) *(G-13976)*
Medina Meadows.....................................330 725-1550
　550 Miner Dr Medina (44256) *(G-13977)*
Medina Medical Investors Ltd.......................330 483-3131
　2400 Columbia Rd Medina (44256) *(G-13978)*
Medina Medical Offices, Medina *Also called Kaiser Foundation Hospitals (G-13964)*
Medina World Cars Inc..............................330 725-4901
　11800 Pearl Rd Strongsville (44136) *(G-17332)*
Mediquant Inc (PA)..................................440 746-2300
　6900 S Edgerton Rd # 100 Brecksville (44141) *(G-1789)*
Medisync Midwest Ltd Lblty Co.....................513 533-1199
　25 Merchant St Ste 220 Cincinnati (45246) *(G-3998)*
Medline Diamed LLC (HQ).........................330 484-1450
　3800 Commerce St Sw Canton (44706) *(G-2398)*
Medlink of Ohio Inc (HQ)............................216 751-5900
　20600 Chagrin Blvd # 290 Cleveland (44122) *(G-5944)*
Medlink of Ohio Inc................................330 773-9434
　1225 E Waterloo Rd Akron (44306) *(G-330)*
Medohio Family Care Center, Columbus *Also called Ohio State University (G-8301)*
Medone Hospital Physicians........................314 255-6900
　3525 Olentangy River Rd Columbus (43214) *(G-8055)*
Medpace Inc......................................513 366-3220
　5355 Medpace Way Cincinnati (45227) *(G-3999)*

Medpace Inc (HQ)..................................513 579-9911
　5375 Medpace Way Cincinnati (45227) *(G-4000)*
Medpace Bioanalytical Labs LLC....................513 366-3260
　5365 Medpace Way Cincinnati (45227) *(G-4001)*
Medport Inc..216 244-6832
　8104 Madison Ave Cleveland (44102) *(G-5945)*
Medpro LLC...937 336-5586
　251 W Lexington Rd Eaton (45320) *(G-10452)*
Medsearch Staffing Svcs Inc (PA)..................440 243-6363
　16600 W Sprague Rd # 190 Cleveland (44130) *(G-5946)*
Medvet Associates Inc.............................937 293-2714
　2714 Springboro W Moraine (45439) *(G-14676)*
Medvet Associates Inc (PA)........................614 846-5800
　300 E Wilson Bridge Rd # 100 Worthington (43085) *(G-19827)*
Medwork LLC.......................................937 449-0800
　7187 Tarryton Rd Dayton (45459) *(G-9604)*
Medwork Occupational Hlth Care, Dayton *Also called Medwork LLC (G-9604)*
Meeder Asset Management Inc......................614 760-2112
　6125 Memor Dr Dublin (43017) *(G-10277)*
Mees Distributors Inc (PA).........................513 541-2311
　1541 W Fork Rd Cincinnati (45223) *(G-4002)*
Mega Techway Inc..................................440 605-0700
　760 Beta Dr Ste F Cleveland (44143) *(G-5947)*
Megacity Fire Protection Inc (PA)..................937 335-0775
　8210 Expansion Way Dayton (45424) *(G-9605)*
Megco Management Inc.............................330 874-9999
　300 Yant St Bolivar (44612) *(G-1704)*
Megen Construction Company Inc (PA)..............513 742-9191
　11130 Ashburn Rd Cincinnati (45240) *(G-4003)*
Mehler & Hagestrom, Cleveland *Also called Mehler and Hagestrom Inc (G-5948)*
Mehler and Hagestrom Inc (PA)....................216 621-4984
　1660 W 2nd St Ste 780 Cleveland (44113) *(G-5948)*
MEI Hotels Incorporated............................216 589-0441
　1375 E 9th St Ste 2800 Cleveland (44114) *(G-5949)*
Meigs Center Ltd...................................740 992-6472
　333 Page St Middleport (45760) *(G-14281)*
Meigs Cnty Dept Jobs Fmly Svcs, Middleport *Also called Bedford Township (G-14280)*
Meigs County Council On Aging.....................740 992-2161
　112 E Memorial Dr Fl 1 Pomeroy (45769) *(G-16095)*
Meigs County Emrgncy Med Svcs, Pomeroy *Also called Bedford Township (G-16093)*
Meigs Industries Inc...............................740 992-6681
　1310 Carleton St Syracuse (45779) *(G-17469)*
Meigs Local School District.........................740 742-2990
　36895 State Route 124 Middleport (45760) *(G-14282)*
Mel Lanzer Co......................................419 592-2801
　2266 Scott St Napoleon (43545) *(G-14811)*
Melamed Riley Advertising LLC.....................216 241-2141
　1375 Euclid Ave Ste 410 Cleveland (44115) *(G-5950)*
Mellott & Mellott PII................................513 241-2940
　12 Walnut St Ste 2500 Cincinnati (45216) *(G-4004)*
Melo International Inc..............................440 519-0526
　3700 Kelley Ave Cleveland (44114) *(G-5951)*
Melrose Rehab LLC.................................419 424-9625
　2201 Jennifer Ln Findlay (45840) *(G-10943)*
Mels Auto Glass Inc................................513 563-7771
　11775 Reading Rd Cincinnati (45241) *(G-4005)*
Melvin Stone, Wilmington *Also called M C Trucking Company LLC (G-19632)*
Melzers Fuel Service Inc...........................800 367-0203
　755 E Erie St Painesville (44077) *(G-15727)*
Memorial Complex, Madison *Also called Madison Local School District (G-13103)*
Memorial Health System, Marietta *Also called Marietta Memorial Hospital (G-13354)*
Memorial Hospital (PA).............................419 334-6657
　715 S Taft Ave Fremont (43420) *(G-11086)*
Memorial Hospital..................................419 547-6419
　430 S Main St Clyde (43410) *(G-6748)*
MEMORIAL HOSPITAL HEALTHLINK, Fremont *Also called Memorial Hospital (G-11086)*
Memorial Hospital Union County....................937 644-1001
　660 London Ave Marysville (43040) *(G-13518)*
Memorial Hospital Union County (PA)...............937 644-6115
　500 London Ave Marysville (43040) *(G-13519)*
Memorial Tournament, The, Dublin *Also called Muirfield Village Golf Club (G-10284)*
Menard Inc...419 726-4029
　1415 E Alexis Rd Toledo (43612) *(G-17903)*
Menard Inc..937 630-3550
　8480 Springboro Pike Miamisburg (45342) *(G-14187)*
Menard Inc..513 737-2204
　2865 Princeton Rd Fairfield Township (45011) *(G-10813)*
Menard Inc..614 501-1654
　6800 E Broad St Columbus (43213) *(G-8056)*
Mended Reeds Home................................740 533-1883
　803 Vernon St Ironton (45638) *(G-12163)*
Mendelson Electronics Co Inc......................937 461-3525
　340 E 1st St Dayton (45402) *(G-9606)*
Mendelson Liquidation Outlet, Dayton *Also called Mendelson Electronics Co Inc (G-9606)*
Mendelson Realty Ltd..............................937 461-3525
　340 E 1st St Dayton (45402) *(G-9607)*
Menke Bros Construction Co........................419 286-2086
　24266 Road T Delphos (45833) *(G-10031)*
Menlo Logistics Inc................................740 963-1154
　107 Heritage Dr Etna (43062) *(G-10617)*
Mennel Milling Company.............................740 385-6824
　1 W Front St Logan (43138) *(G-12849)*

Mennel Milling Company..........740 385-6824
1 W Front St Logan (43138) *(G-12850)*
Mennel Milling Logan, Logan *Also called Mennel Milling Company (G-12849)*
Mennel Milling Logan, Logan *Also called Mennel Milling Company (G-12850)*
Mennonite Memorial Home (PA)..........419 358-1015
410 W Elm St Bluffton (45817) *(G-1693)*
Mennonite Memorial Home..........419 358-7654
700 Maple Crest Ct Bluffton (45817) *(G-1694)*
Menorah Park Center For Senio (PA)..........216 831-6500
27100 Cedar Rd Cleveland (44122) *(G-5952)*
Menorah Park Center For Senio..........216 831-6515
27200 Cedar Rd Beachwood (44122) *(G-1079)*
Menorah Park Center For Senio..........330 867-2143
405 Tallmadge Rd Ste 1 Cuyahoga Falls (44221) *(G-9112)*
Mental Health & Recovery Ctr (PA)..........937 383-3031
953 S South St Wilmington (45177) *(G-19635)*
Mental Health and Addi Serv..........419 381-1881
930 S Detroit Ave Toledo (43614) *(G-17904)*
Mental Health and Addi Serv..........513 948-3600
1101 Summit Rd Cincinnati (45237) *(G-4006)*
Mental Health and Addi Serv..........614 752-0333
2200 W Broad St Columbus (43223) *(G-8057)*
Mental Health and Addi Serv..........330 467-7131
1756 Sagamore Rd Northfield (44067) *(G-15383)*
Mental Health and Addi Serv..........614 752-0333
2200 W Broad St Columbus (43223) *(G-8058)*
Mental Health and Addi Serv..........740 594-5000
100 Hospital Dr Athens (45701) *(G-792)*
Mental Health Service..........937 399-9500
474 N Yellow Springs St Springfield (45504) *(G-17070)*
Mental Health Services (PA)..........216 623-6555
1744 Payne Ave Cleveland (44114) *(G-5953)*
Mental Hlth Serv For CL & Mad..........937 390-7980
1086 Mound St Springfield (45505) *(G-17071)*
Mental Hlth Serv For CL & Mad (PA)..........937 399-9500
474 N Yellow Springs St Springfield (45504) *(G-17072)*
Mental Hlth Serv For CL & Mad..........740 852-6256
210 N Main St London (43140) *(G-12871)*
Mental Memorial Golf Course..........614 645-8453
6005 Alkire Rd Galloway (43119) *(G-11222)*
Mental Retardation & Dev, Cincinnati *Also called County of Hamilton (G-3369)*
Mental Retardation & Dev, Cincinnati *Also called County of Hamilton (G-3372)*
Mental Rtrdtion Preble Cnty Bd (PA)..........937 456-5891
201 E Lexington Rd Ste A Eaton (45320) *(G-10453)*
Mentor Exempted Vlg Schl Dst..........440 974-5260
7060 Hopkins Rd Mentor (44060) *(G-14080)*
Mentor Hsley Rcquet Fitnes CLB, Mentor *Also called Jto Club Corp (G-14068)*
Mentor Lagoons Yacht Club Inc..........440 205-3625
8365 Harbor Dr Mentor (44060) *(G-14081)*
Mentor Lumber and Supply Co (PA)..........440 255-8814
7180 Center St Mentor (44060) *(G-14082)*
Mentor Medical Offices, Mentor *Also called Kaiser Foundation Hospitals (G-14069)*
Mentor School Service Trnsp, Mentor *Also called Mentor Exempted Vlg Schl Dst (G-14080)*
Mentor Surgery Center Ltd..........440 205-5725
9485 Mentor Ave Ste 1 Mentor (44060) *(G-14083)*
Mentor Way Nursing & Rehab Cen..........440 255-9309
8881 Schaeffer St Mentor (44060) *(G-14084)*
Mentor Wholesale Lumber, Mentor *Also called Mentor Lumber and Supply Co (G-14082)*
MENTORING CENTER FOR CENTRAL O, Columbus *Also called Big Broth and Big Siste of Cen (G-7034)*
Menzies Aviation (texas) Inc..........216 362-6565
5921 Cargo Rd Cleveland (44135) *(G-5954)*
Merc Acquisitions Inc..........216 925-5918
1933 Highland Rd Twinsburg (44087) *(G-18298)*
Mercelina Mobile Home Park..........419 586-5407
424 Elmgrove Dr Celina (45822) *(G-2599)*
Mercer (us) Inc..........513 632-2600
525 Vine St Ste 1600 Cincinnati (45202) *(G-4007)*
Mercer Cnty Joint Townshp Hosp..........419 584-0143
909 E Wayne St Ste 126 Celina (45822) *(G-2600)*
Mercer Cnty Joint Townshp Hosp..........419 678-2341
800 W Main St Coldwater (45828) *(G-6763)*
Mercer Cnty Joint Townshp Hosp..........419 586-1611
950 S Main St Celina (45822) *(G-2601)*
Mercer County Community Hosp, Coldwater *Also called Mercer Cnty Joint Townshp Hosp (G-6763)*
Mercer Landmark Inc..........419 586-7443
417 W Market St Celina (45822) *(G-2602)*
Mercer Residential Services..........419 586-4709
334 Godfrey Ave Celina (45822) *(G-2603)*
Mercer Residential Svcs Inc..........419 586-4709
420 S Sugar St Celina (45822) *(G-2604)*
Merchandise Inc..........513 353-2200
5929 State Rte 128 Miamitown (45041) *(G-14242)*
Merchandising Services Co..........866 479-8246
10999 Reed Hartman Hwy Blue Ash (45242) *(G-1608)*
Merchant Data Service Inc..........937 847-6585
2275 E Central Ave Miamisburg (45342) *(G-14188)*
Merchants 5 Star Ltd..........740 373-0313
18192 State Route 7 Marietta (45750) *(G-13358)*
Merchants National Bank (HQ)..........937 393-1134
100 N High St Hillsboro (45133) *(G-11851)*
Merchants Scrty Srvc of Dayton..........937 256-9373
2015 Wayne Ave Dayton (45410) *(G-9608)*
Mercier's Tree Experts, South Point *Also called Merciers Incorporated (G-16942)*
Merciers Incorporated..........410 590-4181
2393 County Road 1 South Point (45680) *(G-16942)*
Mercy Allen Hospital, Oberlin *Also called Mercy Health (G-15511)*
Mercy Anderson Ambulatory Ctr, Cincinnati *Also called Mercy Health Anderson Hospital (G-4025)*
Mercy Anderson Cancer Center, Cincinnati *Also called Mercy Health Anderson Hospital (G-4026)*
Mercy Clinic, Toledo *Also called Mercy Hlth St Vincent Med LLC (G-17910)*
Mercy Ctr For Hlth Promtn St, Oregon *Also called Sisters of Mercy Amer Reg Comm (G-15609)*
Mercy Franciscan Hosp Mt Airy, Cincinnati *Also called Mercy Health Partners (G-4030)*
Mercy Franciscan Hosp Mt Airy (PA)..........513 853-5101
2446 Kipling Ave Cincinnati (45239) *(G-4008)*
Mercy Franciscan Hospital, Cincinnati *Also called Mercy Health Partners (G-4029)*
Mercy Franciscan Senior Netwrk, Cincinnati *Also called Mercy Health Partners (G-4031)*
Mercy Frncscan Hosp Wstn Hills..........513 389-5000
3131 Queen City Ave Cincinnati (45238) *(G-4009)*
Mercy Hamilton Hospital..........513 603-8600
3000 Mack Rd Fairfield (45014) *(G-10753)*
Mercy Health..........937 323-4585
160 Tuttle Rd Springfield (45503) *(G-17073)*
Mercy Health..........330 729-1372
250 Debartolo Pl Youngstown (44512) *(G-20122)*
Mercy Health..........419 935-0187
218 S Myrtle Ave Willard (44890) *(G-19484)*
Mercy Health..........330 792-7418
6252 Mahoning Ave Youngstown (44515) *(G-20123)*
Mercy Health..........513 829-1700
2960 Mack Rd Ste 201 Fairfield (45014) *(G-10754)*
Mercy Health..........513 686-5392
4750 E Galbraith Rd # 207 Cincinnati (45236) *(G-4010)*
Mercy Health..........330 841-4406
8600 E Market St Ste 5 Warren (44484) *(G-18729)*
Mercy Health..........513 981-4700
154 Health Partners Cir Mount Orab (45154) *(G-14742)*
Mercy Health..........513 639-0250
P.O. Box 5203 Cincinnati (45201) *(G-4011)*
Mercy Health..........419 492-1300
202 W Mansfield St New Washington (44854) *(G-15002)*
Mercy Health..........513 981-5750
3301 Mercy Health Blvd Cincinnati (45211) *(G-4012)*
Mercy Health..........440 355-4206
105 Opportunity Way Lagrange (44050) *(G-12325)*
Mercy Health..........937 390-1700
211 Northparke Dr Ste 101 Springfield (45503) *(G-17074)*
Mercy Health..........937 390-9665
100 W Mccreight Ave # 400 Springfield (45504) *(G-17075)*
Mercy Health..........513 248-0100
201 Old Bank Rd Ste 103 Milford (45150) *(G-14408)*
Mercy Health (PA)..........513 639-2800
1701 Mercy Health Pl Cincinnati (45237) *(G-4013)*
Mercy Health..........513 232-7100
8094 Beechmont Ave Cincinnati (45255) *(G-4014)*
Mercy Health..........440 988-1009
578 N Leavitt Rd Amherst (44001) *(G-593)*
Mercy Health..........937 653-3445
1300 S Us Highway 68 Urbana (43078) *(G-18440)*
Mercy Health..........513 686-8100
9403 Kenwood Rd Ste D203 Blue Ash (45242) *(G-1609)*
Mercy Health..........561 358-1619
3200 Vine St Cincinnati (45220) *(G-4015)*
Mercy Health..........513 981-5463
5525 Marie Ave Cincinnati (45248) *(G-4016)*
Mercy Health..........513 985-0741
4750 E Galbraith Rd # 207 Cincinnati (45236) *(G-4017)*
Mercy Health..........440 937-4600
1480 Center Rd Ste A Avon (44011) *(G-895)*
Mercy Health..........440 336-2239
1120 E Broad St Fl 2 Elyria (44035) *(G-10535)*
Mercy Health..........440 327-7372
6115 Emerald St North Ridgeville (44039) *(G-15335)*
Mercy Health..........440 775-1881
319 W Lorain St Oberlin (44074) *(G-15509)*
Mercy Health..........440 934-8344
5054 Waterford Dr Sheffield Village (44035) *(G-16739)*
Mercy Health..........440 967-8713
1607 State Route 50 Ste 6 Vermilion (44089) *(G-18557)*
Mercy Health..........513 639-2800
1701 Mercy Health Pl Cincinnati (45237) *(G-4018)*
Mercy Health..........513 979-2999
4101 Edwards Rd Fl 2 Cincinnati (45209) *(G-4019)*
Mercy Health..........513 233-6736
7500 State Rd Cincinnati (45255) *(G-4020)*
Mercy Health..........419 251-2659
2213 Cherry St Toledo (43608) *(G-17905)*

Mercy Health 513 924-8200
11550 Winton Rd Cincinnati (45240) *(G-4021)*

Mercy Health 419 264-5800
106 N Wilhelm St Holgate (43527) *(G-11866)*

Mercy Health 513 339-0800
5232 Scialville Foster Rd Mason (45040) *(G-13618)*

Mercy Health 513 870-7008
3000 Mack Rd Fairfield (45014) *(G-10755)*

Mercy Health 440 324-0400
41201 Schadden Rd Elyria (44035) *(G-10536)*

Mercy Health 440 366-5577
39263 Center Ridge Rd North Ridgeville (44039) *(G-15336)*

Mercy Health 419 407-3990
3930 Sunforest Ct Ste 100 Toledo (43623) *(G-17906)*

Mercy Health 440 775-1211
200 W Lorain St Oberlin (44074) *(G-15510)*

Mercy Health 330 746-7211
1044 Belmont Ave Youngstown (44504) *(G-20124)*

Mercy Health 513 585-9600
10475 Reading Rd Ste 209 Cincinnati (45241) *(G-4022)*

Mercy Health 419 475-4666
3425 Executive Pkwy 200nw Toledo (43606) *(G-17907)*

Mercy Health 419 226-9064
959 W North St Lima (45805) *(G-12701)*

Mercy Health 937 328-8700
2501 E High St Springfield (45505) *(G-17076)*

Mercy Health 440 233-1000
3700 Kolbe Rd Lorain (44053) *(G-12926)*

Mercy Health 937 390-5075
2600 N Limestone St Springfield (45503) *(G-17077)*

Mercy Health 440 774-6800
200 W Lorain St Oberlin (44074) *(G-15511)*

Mercy Health 513 741-8200
5819 Cheviot Rd Cincinnati (45247) *(G-4023)*

Mercy Health - Cincinnati, Cincinnati *Also called Mercy Health Cincinnati LLC (G-4027)*

Mercy Health - Deerfield, Mason *Also called Mercy Health (G-13618)*

Mercy Health - Heart Institute, Cincinnati *Also called Mercy Health (G-4017)*

Mercy Health - Mt Orab Med Ctr, Mount Orab *Also called Mercy Med Ctr (G-14742)*

Mercy Health - Springfield C 937 323-5001
148 W North St Springfield (45504) *(G-17078)*

Mercy Health - St 419 696-7465
2600 Navarre Ave Oregon (43616) *(G-15600)*

Mercy Health - St R (HQ) 419 227-3361
730 W Market St Lima (45801) *(G-12702)*

Mercy Health - Tiffin Hosp LLC (HQ) 419 455-7000
45 St Lawrence Dr Tiffin (44883) *(G-17524)*

Mercy Health - Westside, Cincinnati *Also called Mercy Health (G-4016)*

Mercy Health Anderson Hospital (HQ) 513 624-4500
7500 State Rd Cincinnati (45255) *(G-4024)*

Mercy Health Anderson Hospital 513 624-1950
7520 State Rd Cincinnati (45255) *(G-4025)*

Mercy Health Anderson Hospital 513 624-4025
8000 5 Mile Rd Ste 105 Cincinnati (45230) *(G-4026)*

Mercy Health Cincinnati LLC (HQ) 513 952-5000
1701 Mercy Health Pl Cincinnati (45237) *(G-4027)*

Mercy Health Foundation 937 523-6670
100 W Mccreight Ave # 200 Springfield (45504) *(G-17079)*

MERCY HEALTH FOUNDATION, SPRIN, Springfield *Also called Community Mercy Hlth Partners (G-17019)*

Mercy Health Partners 513 233-2444
8000 5 Mile Rd Ste 350 Cincinnati (45230) *(G-4028)*

Mercy Health Partners 513 389-5000
3301 Mercy Health Blvd # 100 Cincinnati (45211) *(G-4029)*

Mercy Health Partners 513 853-5101
2446 Kipling Ave Cincinnati (45239) *(G-4030)*

Mercy Health Partners 513 451-8900
2950 West Park Dr Ofc Cincinnati (45238) *(G-4031)*

Mercy Health Partners 513 981-5056
4600 Mcauley Pl Ste A Blue Ash (45242) *(G-1610)*

Mercy Health Partners 513 686-4800
4750 E Galbraith Rd # 207 Cincinnati (45236) *(G-4032)*

MERCY HEALTH PARTNERS OF SOUTHWEST OHIO, Cincinnati *Also called Mercy Health Partners (G-4028)*

Mercy Health Sys - Nthrn Reg (HQ) 419 251-1359
2200 Jefferson Ave Toledo (43604) *(G-17908)*

Mercy Health West Park 513 451-8900
2950 West Park Dr Cincinnati (45238) *(G-4033)*

Mercy Health Youngstown LLC 330 729-1420
8401 Market St Youngstown (44512) *(G-20125)*

Mercy Health Youngstown LLC (HQ) 330 746-7211
1044 Belmont Ave Youngstown (44504) *(G-20126)*

Mercy Health Youngstown LLC 330 841-4000
667 Eastland Ave Se Warren (44484) *(G-18730)*

Mercy Healthplexm LLC 513 870-7101
3050 Mack Rd Ste 210 Fairfield (45014) *(G-10756)*

Mercy Hlth - Clermont Hosp LLC (HQ) 513 732-8200
3000 Hospital Dr Batavia (45103) *(G-1004)*

Mercy Hlth - White Oak Imaging, Cincinnati *Also called Mercy Health (G-4023)*

Mercy Hlth St Vincent Med LLC (PA) 419 251-3232
2213 Cherry St Toledo (43608) *(G-17909)*

Mercy Hlth St Vincent Med LLC 419 251-0580
2200 Jefferson Ave Toledo (43604) *(G-17910)*

MERCY HOSPITAL ANDERSON, Cincinnati *Also called Mercy Health Anderson Hospital (G-4024)*

Mercy Hospital of Defiance 419 782-8444
1400 E 2nd St Defiance (43512) *(G-9929)*

Mercy Hospital of Willard, Willard *Also called Sisters of Mrcy of Wllard Ohio (G-19488)*

Mercy House Partners, Cincinnati *Also called West Park Retirement Community (G-4783)*

Mercy McAuley Center, Urbana *Also called Community Mercy Hlth Partners (G-18429)*

Mercy Medical Associates 513 686-4840
4750 E Galbraith Rd # 207 Cincinnati (45236) *(G-4034)*

Mercy Medical Center 937 390-5000
1343 N Fountain Blvd Springfield (45504) *(G-17080)*

Mercy Medical Center Inc 330 649-4380
4369 Whipple Ave Nw Canton (44718) *(G-2399)*

Mercy Medical Center Inc (HQ) 330 489-1000
1320 Mercy Dr Nw Canton (44708) *(G-2400)*

Mercy Medical Center Inc 330 627-7641
125 Canton Rd Nw Carrollton (44615) *(G-2572)*

Mercy Medical Center Hospice, Canton *Also called Mercy Medical Center Inc (G-2399)*

Mercy Professional Care 330 832-2280
2859 Aaronwood Ave Ne Massillon (44646) *(G-13715)*

Mercy St Theresa Center Inc 513 271-7010
7010 Rowan Hill Dr # 200 Cincinnati (45227) *(G-4035)*

Mergis Group, The, Maumee *Also called Randstad Professionals Us LLC (G-13840)*

Mergis Group, The, Blue Ash *Also called Randstad Professionals Us LP (G-1639)*

Meridian Healthcare (PA) 330 797-0070
527 N Meridian Rd Youngstown (44509) *(G-20127)*

Meriprise Financial, Canton *Also called Aeea LLC (G-2176)*

Merit House LLC 419 478-5131
4645 Lewis Ave Toledo (43612) *(G-17911)*

Merit Leasing Co LLC 216 261-9592
3 Merit Dr Cleveland (44143) *(G-5955)*

Meritech Inc 216 459-8333
4577 Hinckley Indus Pkwy Cleveland (44109) *(G-5956)*

Merle-Holden Enterprises Inc (PA) 216 661-6887
5715 Broadview Rd Cleveland (44134) *(G-5957)*

Merlene Enterprises Inc 440 593-6771
734 Harbor St Conneaut (44030) *(G-8956)*

Merrick Body Shop 440 243-6700
520 Front St Berea (44017) *(G-1430)*

Merrick Chevrolet Co 440 878-6700
15303 Royalton Rd Strongsville (44136) *(G-17333)*

Merrick House (PA) 216 771-5077
1050 Starkweather Ave Cleveland (44113) *(G-5958)*

MERRICK HOUSE CLARK/FULTON, Cleveland *Also called Merrick House (G-5958)*

Merrill Lynch Pierce Fenner 614 225-3152
65 E State St Ste 2600 Columbus (43215) *(G-8059)*

Merrill Lynch Pierce Fenner 419 891-2091
3292 Levis Commons Blvd Perrysburg (43551) *(G-15893)*

Merrill Lynch Pierce Fenner 740 335-2930
209 E Court St Wshngtn CT Hs (43160) *(G-19879)*

Merrill Lynch Pierce Fenner 614 475-2798
2 Easton Oval Ste 100 Columbus (43219) *(G-8060)*

Merrill Lynch Pierce Fenner 740 452-3681
905 Zane St Ste 3 Zanesville (43701) *(G-20330)*

Merrill Lynch Pierce Fenner 614 225-3197
1155 Scanlon Ln Springfield (45503) *(G-17081)*

Merrill Lynch Pierce Fenner 937 847-4000
10100 Innovation Dr # 300 Miamisburg (45342) *(G-14189)*

Merrill Lynch Pierce Fenner 614 225-3000
4661 Sawmill Rd Ste 200 Columbus (43220) *(G-8061)*

Merrill Lynch Pierce Fenner 330 670-2400
4000 Embassy Pkwy Ste 300 Akron (44333) *(G-331)*

Merrill Lynch Pierce Fenner 216 363-6500
1375 E 9th St Ste 1400 Cleveland (44114) *(G-5959)*

Merrill Lynch Pierce Fenner 330 670-2400
4000 Embassy Pkwy Ste 300 Akron (44333) *(G-332)*

Merrill Lynch Pierce Fenner 614 825-0350
8425 Pulsar Pl Ste 200 Columbus (43240) *(G-6824)*

Merrill Lynch Pierce Fenner 513 579-3600
425 Walnut St Ste 2500 Cincinnati (45202) *(G-4036)*

Merrill Lynch Pierce Fenner 216 292-8000
30195 Chagrin Blvd # 120 Cleveland (44124) *(G-5960)*

Merrill Lynch Pierce Fenner 513 562-2100
312 Walnut St Ste 2400 Cincinnati (45202) *(G-4037)*

Merrill Lynch Pierce Fenner 614 798-4354
555 Metro Pl N Ste 550 Dublin (43017) *(G-10278)*

Merrill Lynch Pierce Fenner 330 497-6600
4300 Munson St Nw Ste 300 Canton (44718) *(G-2401)*

Merrill Lynch Pierce Fenner 330 702-7300
4137 Boardman Canfield Rd Canfield (44406) *(G-2147)*

Merrill Lynch Pierce Fenner 330 702-0535
4137 Boardman Canfield Rd # 201 Canfield (44406) *(G-2148)*

Merrill Lynch Pierce Fenner 330 655-2312
10 W Streetsboro St # 305 Hudson (44236) *(G-11995)*

Merrill Lynch Pierce Fenner 330 670-2400
4000 Embassy Pkwy Ste 210 Bath (44210) *(G-1017)*

Merrill Lynch Business 513 791-5700
5151 Pfeiffer Rd Ste 100 Blue Ash (45242) *(G-1611)*

Merry Maids, Beavercreek *Also called Larue Enterprises Inc (G-1225)*

Merry Moppets Early Learning 614 529-1730
5075 Britton Pkwy Hilliard (43026) *(G-11791)*

Mershon Center For Education, Columbus Also called Ohio State University (G-8308)

Mes, Sunbury Also called Mine Equipment Services LLC (G-17390)

Mesa Industries Inc (PA) 513 321-2950
4027 Eastern Ave Cincinnati (45226) (G-4038)

Mesi, South Point Also called Mike Enyart & Sons Inc (G-16943)

Mesilla Dialysis LLC 937 484-4600
1430 E Us Highway 36 Urbana (43078) (G-18441)

Messer Construction Co 513 672-5000
2495 Langdon Farm Rd Cincinnati (45237) (G-4039)

Messer Construction Co (PA) 513 242-1541
643 W Court St Cincinnati (45203) (G-4040)

Messer Construction Co 937 291-1300
4801 Hempstead Station Dr A Dayton (45429) (G-9609)

Messer Construction Co 614 275-0141
3705 Business Park Dr Columbus (43204) (G-8062)

Met Group 330 864-1916
2640 W Market St Fairlawn (44333) (G-10840)

Met-Chem Inc 216 881-7900
837 E 79th St Cleveland (44103) (G-5961)

Met-Ed, Akron Also called Metropolitan Edison Company (G-336)

Meta Manufacturing Corporation 513 793-6382
8901 Blue Ash Rd Ste 1 Blue Ash (45242) (G-1612)

Metal Conversions Ltd (PA) 419 525-0011
849 Crawford Ave N Mansfield (44905) (G-13219)

Metal Framing Enterprises LLC 216 433-7080
9005 Bank St Cleveland (44125) (G-5962)

Metal Management Ohio Inc 419 782-7791
27063 State Route 281 Defiance (43512) (G-9930)

Metal Masters Inc 330 343-3515
125 Williams Dr Nw Dover (44622) (G-10088)

Metal Shredders Inc 937 866-0777
5101 Farmersville W Miamisburg (45342) (G-14190)

Metalico Akron Inc (HQ) 330 376-1400
943 Hazel St Akron (44305) (G-333)

Metalico Annaco, Akron Also called Metalico Akron Inc (G-333)

Metals USA Crbn Flat Rlled Inc 937 882-6354
5750 Lower Valley Pike Springfield (45502) (G-17082)

Metals USA Flat Rlled Cntl Inc 618 451-4700
1070 W Liberty St Wooster (44691) (G-19744)

Metamateria Partners LLC 614 340-1690
1275 Kinnear Rd Columbus (43212) (G-8063)

Metcalf & Eddy Inc 216 910-2000
1375 E 9th St Ste 2801 Cleveland (44114) (G-5963)

Metcon Ltd (PA) 937 447-9200
6730 Greentree Rd Bradford (45308) (G-1762)

Metcut Research Associates Inc (PA) 513 271-5100
3980 Rosslyn Dr Cincinnati (45209) (G-4041)

METHODIST ELDER CARE SERVICES, Reynoldsburg Also called Wesley Ridge
Inc (G-16337)

MetLife, Dublin Also called Metropolitan Life Insur Co (G-10279)

MetLife Auto HM Insur Agcy Inc (HQ) 815 266-5301
9797 Springboro Pike Dayton (45448) (G-9610)

Metro Air, Hilliard Also called Metro Heating and AC Co (G-11792)

Metro Health Dental Associates 216 778-4982
2500 Metrohealth Dr Cleveland (44109) (G-5964)

Metro Health System 330 669-2249
6022 N Honeytown Rd Smithville (44677) (G-16811)

Metro Heating and AC Co 614 777-1237
4731 Northwest Pkwy Hilliard (43026) (G-11792)

Metro Parks, Westerville Also called Columbus Frkln Cnty Pk (G-19241)

Metro Recycling, Cincinnati Also called Charles V Francis Trust (G-3170)

Metro Regional Transit Auth 330 762-0341
631 S Broadway St Akron (44311) (G-334)

Metro Regional Transit Auth (PA) 330 762-0341
416 Kenmore Blvd Akron (44301) (G-335)

Metro Safety and Security LLC 614 792-2770
5785 Emporium Sq Columbus (43231) (G-8064)

Metrohealth Beachwood Hlth Ctr, Beachwood Also called Metrohealth System (G-1080)

Metrohealth Broadway Hlth Ctr, Cleveland Also called Metrohealth System (G-5970)

Metrohealth Buckeye Health Ctr, Cleveland Also called Metrohealth System (G-5968)

Metrohealth Dept of Dentistry 216 778-4739
2500 Metrohealth Dr Cleveland (44109) (G-5965)

Metrohealth Premier Health Ctr, Westlake Also called Metrohealth System (G-19373)

Metrohealth System 216 957-5000
3838 W 150th St Cleveland (44111) (G-5966)

Metrohealth System (PA) 216 398-6000
2500 Metrohealth Dr Cleveland (44109) (G-5967)

Metrohealth System 216 957-4000
2816 E 116th St Cleveland (44120) (G-5968)

Metrohealth System 216 778-8446
2500 Metrohealth Dr Cleveland (44109) (G-5969)

Metrohealth System 216 957-1500
6835 Broadway Ave Cleveland (44105) (G-5970)

Metrohealth System 216 778-3867
2500 Metrohealth Dr Cleveland (44109) (G-5971)

Metrohealth System 216 765-0733
3609 Park East Dr Ste 300 Beachwood (44122) (G-1080)

Metrohealth System 216 957-2100
4229 Pearl Rd Cleveland (44109) (G-5972)

Metrohealth System 216 957-3200
25200 Center Ridge Rd Westlake (44145) (G-19373)

Metrohealth System 216 591-0523
3609 Park East Dr Ste 206 Beachwood (44122) (G-1081)

Metrohealth West Park Hlth Ctr, Cleveland Also called Metrohealth System (G-5966)

Metrohlth Pepper Pike Hlth Ctr, Beachwood Also called Metrohealth System (G-1081)

Metropltan Vterinary Med Group 330 253-2544
1053 S Clvland Mssllon Rd Copley (44321) (G-8971)

Metropolitan Armored Car, Toledo Also called Garda CL Great Lakes Inc (G-17754)

Metropolitan Cleaners, Dayton Also called Rentz Corp (G-9732)

Metropolitan Edison Company (HQ) 800 736-3402
76 S Main St Akron (44308) (G-336)

Metropolitan Envmtl Svcs Inc 614 771-1881
5055 Nike Dr Hilliard (43026) (G-11793)

Metropolitan Family Care, Reynoldsburg Also called Metropolitian Family Care
Inc (G-16320)

Metropolitan Life Insur Co 614 792-1463
5600 Blazer Pkwy Ste 100 Dublin (43017) (G-10279)

Metropolitan Pool Service Co 216 741-9451
3427 Brookpark Rd Parma (44134) (G-15768)

Metropolitan Pools, Parma Also called Metropolitan Pool Service Co (G-15768)

Metropolitan Security Svcs Inc 216 298-4076
801 W Superior Ave Cleveland (44113) (G-5973)

Metropolitan Security Svcs Inc 330 253-6459
2 S Main St Akron (44308) (G-337)

Metropolitan Sewer District 513 244-1300
1600 Gest St Cincinnati (45204) (G-4042)

Metropolitan Veterinary Hosp, Copley Also called Metropltan Vterinary Med Group (G-8971)

Metropolitan YMCA, Englewood Also called Young Mens Christian Assoc (G-10606)

Metropolitian Family Care Inc 614 237-1067
7094 E Main St Reynoldsburg (43068) (G-16320)

Metzenbaum Sheltered Inds Inc 440 729-1919
8090 Cedar Rd Chesterland (44026) (G-2741)

Meyer Decorative Surfaces USA (HQ) 800 776-3900
300 Executive Pkwy W # 100 Hudson (44236) (G-11996)

Meyer Hill Lynch Corporation 419 897-9797
1771 Indian Wood Cir Maumee (43537) (G-13821)

Meyerpt, Hudson Also called Wbc Group LLC (G-12012)

Meyers + Associates Arch LLC 614 221-9433
232 N 3rd St Ste 300 Columbus (43215) (G-8065)

Meyers Ldscp Svcs & Nurs Inc 614 210-1194
6081 Columbus Pike Lewis Center (43035) (G-12551)

Mfbusiness Group 216 510-0717
14037 Puritas Ave Cleveland (44135) (G-5974)

Mff Somerset LLC 216 752-5600
3550 Northfield Rd Shaker Heights (44122) (G-16710)

Mfh Inc (PA) 937 435-4701
241 E Alex Bell Rd Dayton (45459) (G-9611)

Mfh Inc 937 435-4701
241 E Alex Bell Rd Dayton (45459) (G-9612)

MGF Sourcing Us LLC (HQ) 614 904-3300
4200 Regent St Ste 205 Columbus (43219) (G-8066)

MGM Health Care Winchstr, Canal Winchester Also called Kindred Nursing Centers E
LLC (G-2114)

Mh Equipment, West Chester Also called MH Logistics Corp (G-19066)

Mh Equipment Company 937 890-6800
3000 Production Ct Dayton (45414) (G-9613)

Mh Equipment Company 614 871-1571
2055 Hardy Parkway St Grove City (43123) (G-11452)

Mh Equipment Company 513 681-2200
2650 Spring Grove Ave Cincinnati (45214) (G-4043)

MH Logistics Corp 513 681-2200
106 Circle Freeway Dr West Chester (45246) (G-19066)

MH Logistics Corp 330 425-2476
1892 Georgetown Rd Hudson (44236) (G-11997)

Mhc Medical Products LLC (PA) 877 358-4342
8695 Seward Rd Fairfield (45011) (G-10757)

Mhrs Board of Stark County, Canton Also called County of Stark (G-2270)

MHS, Cleveland Also called Montessori High School Assn (G-6008)

MI, Miamitown Also called Merchandise Inc (G-14242)

MI - De - Con Inc 740 532-2277
3331 S 3rd St Ironton (45638) (G-12164)

Miami Cnty Cmnty Action Cuncil 937 335-7921
1695 Troy Sidney Rd Troy (45373) (G-18212)

Miami Co Highway Dept, Troy Also called County of Miami (G-18199)

Miami Co YMCA Child Care 937 778-5241
325 W Ash St Piqua (45356) (G-16013)

Miami Conservancy District (PA) 937 223-1271
38 E Monument Ave Dayton (45402) (G-9614)

Miami Corporation (PA) 800 543-0448
720 Anderson Ferry Rd Cincinnati (45238) (G-4044)

Miami County Childrens Svcs Bd 937 335-4103
510 W Water St Ste 210 Troy (45373) (G-18213)

MIAMI COUNTY JOB TRAINING PART, Troy Also called Miami Cnty Cmnty Action
Cuncil (G-18212)

Miami County Park District 937 335-6273
2645 E State Route 41 Troy (45373) (G-18214)

Miami Fort Power Station, North Bend Also called Vistra Energy Corp (G-15183)

Miami Industrial Trucks Inc (PA) 937 293-4194
2830 E River Rd Moraine (45439) (G-14677)

(G-0000) Company's Geographic Section entry number

Miami Industrial Trucks Inc ... 419 424-0042
130 Stanford Pkwy Findlay (45840) *(G-10944)*
Miami Rifle Pistol Club ... 513 732-9943
P.O. Box 235 Milford (45150) *(G-14409)*
Miami University ... 513 727-3200
4200 E University Blvd Middletown (45042) *(G-14308)*
Miami University ... 513 529-6911
Fisher Dr Oxford (45056) *(G-15681)*
Miami University ... 513 529-1251
701 E Spring St Ste 117 Oxford (45056) *(G-15682)*
Miami University ... 513 529-1230
725 E Chestnut St Oxford (45056) *(G-15683)*
Miami University-Middletown, Middletown *Also called Miami University (G-14308)*
MIAMI VALLEY, Dayton *Also called Premier Health Partners (G-9704)*
Miami Valley Bekins Inc ... 937 278-4296
5941 Milo Rd Dayton (45414) *(G-9615)*
Miami Valley Broadcasting Corp ... 937 259-2111
1611 S Main St Dayton (45409) *(G-9616)*
Miami Valley Community Action (PA) ... 937 222-1009
719 S Main St Dayton (45402) *(G-9617)*
Miami Valley Community Action ... 937 456-2800
308 Eaton Lewisburg Rd Eaton (45320) *(G-10454)*
Miami Valley Community Action ... 937 548-8143
1469 Sweitzer St Greenville (45331) *(G-11390)*
Miami Valley Family Care Ctr, Dayton *Also called Catholic Social Svc Miami Vly (G-9287)*
Miami Valley Gaming & Racg LLC ... 513 934-7070
6000 W State Route 63 Lebanon (45036) *(G-12485)*
Miami Valley Golf Club (PA) ... 937 278-7381
3311 Salem Ave Dayton (45406) *(G-9618)*
Miami Valley Hospital ... 937 436-5200
2400 Miami Valley Dr Dayton (45459) *(G-9619)*
Miami Valley Hospital ... 937 208-7065
211 Kenbrook Dr Vandalia (45377) *(G-18531)*
Miami Valley Hospital (HQ) ... 937 208-8000
1 Wyoming St Dayton (45409) *(G-9620)*
Miami Valley Hospital ... 937 224-3916
28 Hill St Dayton (45409) *(G-9621)*
Miami Valley Hospitalist Group ... 937 208-8394
30 E Apple St Ste 3300 Dayton (45409) *(G-9622)*
Miami Valley Hsing Assn I Inc ... 937 263-4449
907 W 5th St Dayton (45402) *(G-9623)*
Miami Valley Insurance Assoc, Dayton *Also called Norman-Spencer Agency Inc (G-9659)*
Miami Valley Intl Trcks Inc ... 513 733-8500
11775 Highway Dr Ste D Cincinnati (45241) *(G-4045)*
Miami Valley Memory Grdns Assn (HQ) ... 937 885-7779
1639 E Lytle 5 Points Rd Dayton (45458) *(G-9624)*
Miami Valley Moving & Storage, Dayton *Also called Miami Valley Bekins Inc (G-9615)*
Miami Valley Regional Plg Comm ... 937 223-6323
10 N Ludlow St Ste 700 Dayton (45402) *(G-9625)*
Miami Valley School ... 937 434-4444
5151 Denise Dr Dayton (45429) *(G-9626)*
Miami Valley South Campus, Dayton *Also called Miami Valley Hospital (G-9619)*
Miami Valley Steel Service Inc ... 937 773-7127
201 Fox Dr Piqua (45356) *(G-16014)*
Miami Valley Urgent Care ... 937 252-2000
6229 Troy Pike Dayton (45424) *(G-9627)*
Miami View Head Start, Dayton *Also called Miami Vly Child Dev Ctrs Inc (G-9629)*
Miami Vly Child Dev Ctrs Inc (PA) ... 937 226-5664
215 Horace St Dayton (45402) *(G-9628)*
Miami Vly Child Dev Ctrs Inc ... 937 325-2559
1450 S Yellow Springs St Springfield (45506) *(G-17083)*
Miami Vly Child Dev Ctrs Inc ... 937 228-1644
215 Horace St Dayton (45402) *(G-9629)*
Miami Vly Fandom For Literacy ... 513 933-0452
222 S Mechanic St Lebanon (45036) *(G-12486)*
Miami Vly Hsing Oprtunties Inc (PA) ... 937 263-4449
907 W 5th St Dayton (45402) *(G-9630)*
Miami Vly Jvnile Rhbltion Ctr ... 937 562-4000
2100 Greene Way Blvd Xenia (45385) *(G-19920)*
Miami-Luken Inc (PA) ... 937 743-7775
265 S Pioneer Blvd Springboro (45066) *(G-16974)*
Miamisburg City School Dst ... 937 866-1283
200 N 12th St Miamisburg (45342) *(G-14191)*
Miamisburg Dialysis, Miamisburg *Also called Morro Dialysis LLC (G-14195)*
Miamisburg Family Practice ... 937 866-2494
415 Byers Rd Ste 300 Miamisburg (45342) *(G-14192)*
Miamisburg Pk Recreation Dept, Miamisburg *Also called City of Miamisburg (G-14152)*
Miamisburg Transportation Dept, Miamisburg *Also called Miamisburg City School Dst (G-14191)*
Miba Bearings US LLC ... 740 962-4242
5037 N State Route 60 Nw McConnelsville (43756) *(G-13902)*
Miceli Dairy Products Co (PA) ... 216 791-6222
2721 E 90th St Cleveland (44104) *(G-5975)*
Micha Ltd ... 740 653-6464
144 E Main St Lancaster (43130) *(G-12418)*
Michael A Garcia Salon ... 614 235-1605
2440 E Main St Columbus (43209) *(G-8067)*
Michael Baker Intl Inc ... 330 453-3110
101 Cleveland Ave Nw # 106 Canton (44702) *(G-2402)*
Michael Baker Intl Inc ... 412 269-6300
1111 Superior Ave E # 2300 Cleveland (44114) *(G-5976)*
Michael Baker Intl Inc ... 614 418-1773
250 West St Ste 420 Columbus (43215) *(G-8068)*
Michael Benza and Assoc Inc ... 440 526-4206
6860 W Snowville Rd # 100 Brecksville (44141) *(G-1790)*
Michael Brothers Inc ... 419 332-5716
3728 Hayes Ave Fremont (43420) *(G-11087)*
Michael Christopher Salon Inc ... 440 449-0999
6255 Wilson Mills Rd Cleveland (44143) *(G-5977)*
Michael G Lawley ... 513 793-3933
8099 Cornell Rd Cincinnati (45249) *(G-4046)*
Michael Schuster Associates ... 513 241-5666
316 W 4th St Ste 600 Cincinnati (45202) *(G-4047)*
Michael T Lee Dvm ... 330 722-5076
1060 S Court St Medina (44256) *(G-13979)*
Michael's Bakery & Deli, Cleveland *Also called Michaels Bakery Inc (G-5978)*
Michael's Cafe & Bakery, Toledo *Also called Michaels Gourmet Catering (G-17912)*
Michaels Inc ... 440 357-0384
5783 Heisley Rd Mentor (44060) *(G-14085)*
Michaels Bakery Inc ... 216 351-7530
4478 Broadview Rd Cleveland (44109) *(G-5978)*
Michaels For Hair, Dayton *Also called Mfh Inc (G-9612)*
Michaels Gourmet Catering ... 419 698-2988
101 Main St Ste 7 Toledo (43605) *(G-17912)*
Michel Tires Plus 227571, Celina *Also called Bridgestone Ret Operations LLC (G-2585)*
Michel Tires Plus 227925, Harrison *Also called Bridgestone Ret Operations LLC (G-11662)*
Mickis Creative Options Inc ... 419 526-4254
1841 S Main St Mansfield (44907) *(G-13220)*
Micnan Inc (PA) ... 330 920-6200
3365 Cavalier Trl Cuyahoga Falls (44224) *(G-9113)*
Micro Center, Hilliard *Also called Micro Electronics Inc (G-11795)*
Micro Center, Cincinnati *Also called Micro Electronics Inc (G-4048)*
Micro Center Inc ... 614 850-3000
4119 Leap Rd Hilliard (43026) *(G-11794)*
Micro Center Computer Educatn, Columbus *Also called Micro Electronics Inc (G-8070)*
Micro Center Online Inc ... 614 326-8500
747 Bethel Rd Columbus (43214) *(G-8069)*
Micro Construction LLC ... 740 862-0751
8675 Lncster Newark Rd Ne Baltimore (43105) *(G-937)*
Micro Electronics Inc ... 614 326-8500
747 Bethel Rd Columbus (43214) *(G-8070)*
Micro Electronics Inc ... 614 334-1430
2701 Charter St Ste B Columbus (43228) *(G-8071)*
Micro Electronics Inc (PA) ... 614 850-3000
4119 Leap Rd Hilliard (43026) *(G-11795)*
Micro Electronics Inc ... 614 850-3500
4055 Leap Rd Hilliard (43026) *(G-11796)*
Micro Electronics Inc ... 440 449-7000
1349 Som Center Rd Cleveland (44124) *(G-5979)*
Micro Electronics Inc ... 513 782-8500
11755 Mosteller Rd Rear Cincinnati (45241) *(G-4048)*
Micro Industries Corporation (PA) ... 740 548-7878
8399 Green Meadows Dr N Westerville (43081) *(G-19279)*
Micro Products Co Inc ... 440 943-0258
26653 Curtiss Wright Pkwy Willoughby Hills (44092) *(G-19591)*
Micro Roll Off Containers, Baltimore *Also called Micro Construction LLC (G-937)*
Micro Thinner, Hilliard *Also called Micro Electronics Inc (G-11796)*
Microanalysis Society Inc ... 614 256-8063
3405 Scioto Run Blvd Hilliard (43026) *(G-11797)*
Microcenter DC, Columbus *Also called Micro Electronics Inc (G-8071)*
Microman Inc (PA) ... 614 923-8000
4393 Tuller Rd Ste A Dublin (43017) *(G-10280)*
Microplex Inc ... 330 498-0600
7568 Whipple Ave Nw North Canton (44720) *(G-15220)*
Micros Retail, Cleveland *Also called Datavantage Corporation (G-5406)*
Microsoft Corporation ... 614 719-5900
8800 Lyra Dr Ste 400 Columbus (43240) *(G-6825)*
Microsoft Corporation ... 216 986-1440
6050 Oak Tree Blvd # 300 Cleveland (44131) *(G-5980)*
Microsoft Corporation ... 513 339-2800
4605 Duke Dr Ste 800 Mason (45040) *(G-13619)*
Microwave Leasing Services LLC ... 614 308-5433
2860 Fisher Rd Columbus (43204) *(G-8072)*
Mid America Glass Block, Cleveland *Also called Cleveland Glass Block Inc (G-5256)*
Mid America Trucking Company ... 216 447-0814
5585 Canal Rd Cleveland (44125) *(G-5981)*
Mid Atlantic Stor Systems Inc ... 740 335-2019
1551 Robinson Rd Se Wshngtn CT Hs (43160) *(G-19880)*
Mid County Ems ... 419 898-9366
222 W Washington St Oak Harbor (43449) *(G-15474)*
Mid Ohio Dialysis, Ontario *Also called Wallowa Dialysis LLC (G-15578)*
Mid Ohio Emergency Svcs LLC ... 614 566-5070
3525 Olentangy Blvd # 4330 Columbus (43214) *(G-8073)*
Mid Ohio Employment Services (PA) ... 419 747-5466
2282 Village Mall Dr # 2 Ontario (44906) *(G-15564)*
Mid Ohio Home Health Ltd ... 419 529-3883
1332 W 4th St Ontario (44906) *(G-15565)*
Mid Ohio Vly Bulk Trnspt Inc ... 740 373-2481
16380 State Route 7 Marietta (45750) *(G-13359)*
Mid State Systems Inc ... 740 928-1115
9455 Lancaster Rd Hebron (43025) *(G-11717)*

ALPHABETIC

Mid-America Gutters Inc (PA) 513 671-4000
  862 E Crescentville Rd West Chester (45246) *(G-19067)*

Mid-America Stainless, Cleveland *Also called Mid-America Steel Corp (G-5982)*

Mid-America Steel Corp 800 282-3466
  20900 Saint Clair Ave Cleveland (44117) *(G-5982)*

Mid-American Clg Contrs Inc 937 859-6222
  360 Gargrave Rd Ste E Dayton (45449) *(G-9631)*

Mid-American Clg Contrs Inc 419 429-6222
  1648 Tiffin Ave Findlay (45840) *(G-10945)*

Mid-American Clg Contrs Inc (PA) 419 229-3899
  447 N Elizabeth St Lima (45801) *(G-12703)*

Mid-American Clg Contrs Inc 614 291-7170
  1046 King Ave Columbus (43212) *(G-8074)*

Mid-Continent Construction Co 440 439-6100
  7235 Free Ave Ste A Oakwood Village (44146) *(G-15491)*

Mid-Ohio Air Conditioning 614 291-4664
  456 E 5th Ave Columbus (43201) *(G-8075)*

Mid-Ohio Contracting Inc 330 343-2925
  1817 Horns Ln Nw Dover (44622) *(G-10089)*

Mid-Ohio Electric Co 614 274-8000
  1170 Mckinley Ave Columbus (43222) *(G-8076)*

Mid-Ohio Energy Cooperative 419 568-5321
  1210 W Lima St Kenton (43326) *(G-12284)*

Mid-Ohio Foodbank 614 317-9400
  3960 Brookham Dr Grove City (43123) *(G-11453)*

Mid-Ohio Forklifts Inc 330 633-1230
  1336 Home Ave Akron (44310) *(G-338)*

Mid-Ohio Harley-Davidson 937 322-3590
  2100 Quality Ln Springfield (45505) *(G-17084)*

Mid-Ohio Heart Clinic Inc 419 524-8151
  335 Glessner Ave Mansfield (44903) *(G-13221)*

Mid-Ohio Mechanical Inc 740 587-3362
  1844 Lancaster Rd Granville (43023) *(G-11346)*

Mid-Ohio Pdiatrics Adolescents 614 899-0000
  595 Cpland Mill Rd Ste 2a Westerville (43081) *(G-19280)*

Mid-Ohio Pipeline Company Inc 419 884-3772
  4244 State Route 546 Mansfield (44904) *(G-13222)*

Mid-Ohio Pipeline Services, Mansfield *Also called Mid-Ohio Pipeline Company Inc (G-13222)*

Mid-Ohio Psychological Svcs Inc (PA) 740 687-0042
  624 E Main St Lancaster (43130) *(G-12419)*

Mid-Ohio Regional Plg Comm (PA) 614 228-2663
  111 Liberty St Ste 100 Columbus (43215) *(G-8077)*

Mid-Ohio Valley Lime Inc (PA) 740 373-1006
  State Rt 7 S Marietta (45750) *(G-13360)*

Mid-Ohio Wines Inc 440 989-1011
  5901 Baumhart Rd Lorain (44053) *(G-12927)*

Mid-State Bolt and Nut Co Inc (PA) 614 253-8631
  1575 Alum Creek Dr Columbus (43209) *(G-8078)*

Mid-States Packaging Inc 937 843-3243
  12163 State Route 274 Lewistown (43333) *(G-12572)*

Mid-West Materials Inc 440 259-5200
  3687 Shepard Rd Perry (44081) *(G-15826)*

Mid-Western Childrens Home 513 877-2141
  4585 Long Spurling Rd Pleasant Plain (45162) *(G-16074)*

Midas Auto Systems Experts (PA) 419 243-7281
  1101 Monroe St Toledo (43604) *(G-17913)*

Midas Muffler, Toledo *Also called Dayton-Dixie Mufflers Inc (G-17694)*

Midas Muffler, Toledo *Also called Midas Auto Systems Experts (G-17913)*

Middle Bass Ferry Company, The, Put In Bay *Also called Island Service Company (G-16226)*

Middletown City Divison Fire 513 425-7996
  2300 Roosevelt Blvd Middletown (45044) *(G-14309)*

Middletown Innkeepers Inc. 513 942-3440
  430 Kolb Dr Fairfield (45014) *(G-10758)*

Middletown School Vhcl Svc Ctr 513 420-4568
  2951 Cincinnati Dayton Rd Middletown (45044) *(G-14310)*

Middltown Area Senior Citizens 513 423-1734
  3907 Central Ave Middletown (45044) *(G-14311)*

Middltown Crdvscular Assoc Inc 513 217-6400
  103 Mcknight Dr Ste A Middletown (45044) *(G-14312)*

Middough Inc (PA) 216 367-6000
  1901 E 13th St Ste 400 Cleveland (44114) *(G-5983)*

Mideast Baptist Conference 440 834-8984
  14282 Butternut Rd Burton (44021) *(G-2018)*

Midfitz Inc 216 663-8816
  23800 Corbin Dr Cleveland (44128) *(G-5984)*

Midland Atlantic Prpts LLC (PA) 513 792-5000
  8044 Montgomery Rd # 710 Cincinnati (45236) *(G-4049)*

Midland Company 513 947-5503
  7000 Midland Blvd Amelia (45102) *(G-574)*

Midland Contracting Inc. 440 439-4571
  7239 Free Ave Cleveland (44146) *(G-5985)*

Midland Council Governments 330 264-6047
  2125 Eagle Pass Wooster (44691) *(G-19745)*

Midland Title Security Inc (HQ) 216 241-6045
  1111 Superior Ave E # 700 Cleveland (44114) *(G-5986)*

Midland-Guardian Co (HQ) 513 943-7100
  7000 Midland Blvd Amelia (45102) *(G-575)*

Midlands Millroom Supply Inc 330 453-9100
  1911 36th St Ne Canton (44705) *(G-2403)*

Midohio Crdiolgy Vascular Cons (PA) 614 262-6772
  3705 Olentangy River Rd # 100 Columbus (43214) *(G-8079)*

Midohio Energy Cooperative, Kenton *Also called Mid-Ohio Energy Cooperative (G-12284)*

Midpark Animal Hospital 216 362-6622
  6611 Smith Rd Cleveland (44130) *(G-5987)*

Midusa Credit Union (PA) 513 420-8640
  1201 Crawford St Middletown (45044) *(G-14313)*

Midusa Credit Union 513 420-8640
  3600 Towne Blvd Ste A Middletown (45005) *(G-14351)*

Midway Bowling Lanes Inc 330 762-7477
  1925 20th St Cuyahoga Falls (44223) *(G-9114)*

Midway Delivery Service 216 391-0700
  4699 Commerce Ave Cleveland (44103) *(G-5988)*

Midway Garage Inc 740 345-0699
  140 Everett Ave Newark (43055) *(G-15071)*

Midway Mall Merchants Assoc 440 244-1245
  3343 Midway Mall Elyria (44035) *(G-10537)*

Midway Realty Company 440 324-2404
  1800 Lorain Blvd Elyria (44035) *(G-10538)*

Midwest Allergy Associates (PA) 614 846-5944
  8080 Ravines Edge Ct # 100 Columbus (43235) *(G-8080)*

Midwest Behavioral Care Ltd 937 454-0092
  3821 Little York Rd Dayton (45414) *(G-9632)*

Midwest Church Cnstr Ltd 419 874-0838
  634 Eckel Rd Ste A Perrysburg (43551) *(G-15894)*

Midwest Cmnty Federal Cr Un 419 782-9856
  1481 Deerwood Dr Defiance (43512) *(G-9931)*

Midwest Cmnty Hlth Assoc Inc (HQ) 419 633-4034
  442 W High St Ste 3 Bryan (43506) *(G-1964)*

Midwest Communications Inc 800 229-4756
  4721 Eagle St Nw North Canton (44720) *(G-15221)*

Midwest Contracting Inc 419 866-4560
  1428 Albon Rd Holland (43528) *(G-11897)*

Midwest Curtainwalls Inc 216 641-7900
  5171 Grant Ave Cleveland (44125) *(G-5989)*

Midwest Digital Inc 330 966-4744
  4721 Eagle St Nw North Canton (44720) *(G-15222)*

Midwest Division - Brunswick, Brunswick *Also called W W Williams Company LLC (G-1945)*

Midwest East Division, Cincinnati *Also called Intren Inc (G-3784)*

Midwest Emergency Services LLC 586 294-2700
  3585 Ridge Park Dr Fairlawn (44333) *(G-10841)*

Midwest Environmental Inc 419 382-9200
  28757 Glenwood Rd Perrysburg (43551) *(G-15895)*

Midwest Equipment Co 216 441-1400
  9800 Broadway Ave Cleveland (44125) *(G-5990)*

Midwest Express Inc (HQ) 937 642-0335
  11590 Township Road 298 East Liberty (43319) *(G-10392)*

Midwest Eye Center, Cincinnati *Also called David M Schneider MD Inc (G-2849)*

Midwest Fairborn Dialysis, Fairborn *Also called Manzano Dialysis LLC (G-10680)*

Midwest Fasteners Inc 937 866-0463
  450 Richard St Miamisburg (45342) *(G-14193)*

Midwest Fitness LLC 216 965-5694
  25935 Detroit Rd Ste 336 Westlake (44145) *(G-19374)*

Midwest Fresh Foods Inc 614 469-1492
  38 N Glenwood Ave Columbus (43222) *(G-8081)*

Midwest Health Services Inc 330 828-0779
  107 Tommy Henrich Dr Nw Massillon (44647) *(G-13716)*

Midwest Heating & Cooling, Columbus *Also called Midwest Roofing & Furnace Co (G-8084)*

Midwest Industrial Supply Inc 800 321-0699
  1929 E Manhattan Blvd Toledo (43608) *(G-17914)*

Midwest Industrial Supply Inc (PA) 330 456-3121
  1101 3rd St Se Canton (44707) *(G-2404)*

Midwest Iron and Metal Co 937 222-5992
  461 Homestead Ave Dayton (45417) *(G-9633)*

Midwest Laundry Inc 513 563-5560
  10110 Cncnnati Dyton Pike Cincinnati (45241) *(G-4050)*

Midwest Liquidators Inc. 614 433-7355
  6827 N High St Ste 109 Worthington (43085) *(G-19828)*

Midwest Logistics Systems 419 584-1414
  8779 State Route 703 Celina (45822) *(G-2605)*

Midwest Mfg Solutions LLC 513 381-7200
  5474 Spellmire Dr West Chester (45246) *(G-19068)*

Midwest Mosaic Inc 419 377-3894
  2268 Robinwood Ave Toledo (43620) *(G-17915)*

Midwest Motor Supply Co (PA) 800 233-1294
  4800 Roberts Rd Columbus (43228) *(G-8082)*

Midwest Motors Inc 330 758-5800
  7871 Market St Youngstown (44512) *(G-20128)*

Midwest Optoelectronics LLC 419 724-0565
  2801 W Bancroft St 230 Toledo (43606) *(G-17916)*

Midwest Painting, Dayton *Also called Muha Construction Inc (G-9647)*

Midwest Physcans Ansthsia Svcs 614 884-0641
  5151 Reed Rd Ste 225c Columbus (43220) *(G-8083)*

Midwest Physicians, Columbus *Also called Change Healthcare Tech Enabled (G-7179)*

Midwest Poultry Services Lp 419 375-4417
  374 New Wston Ft Lrmie Rd Fort Recovery (45846) *(G-10993)*

Midwest Rehab Inc 419 692-3405
  118 E Highland Ave Ada (45810) *(G-5)*

Midwest Reinforcing Contrs 937 390-8998
  1839 N Fountain Blvd Springfield (45504) *(G-17085)*

Midwest Retina Inc 614 233-9500
  2935 Maple Ave Zanesville (43701) *(G-20331)*

Midwest Roofing & Furnace Co 614 252-5241
  646 S Nelson Rd Columbus (43205) *(G-8084)*

Midwest Seafood Inc (PA) 937 746-8856
475 Victory Ln Springboro (45066) *(G-16975)*

Midwest Service Center, Grove City *Also called Safety Today Inc (G-11468)*

Midwest Tape LLC 419 868-9370
1417 Timber Wolf Dr Holland (43528) *(G-11898)*

Midwest Trailer Sales & Svc 513 772-2818
3000 Crescentville Rd West Chester (45069) *(G-18972)*

Midwest Trmnals Tldeo Intl Inc 419 897-6868
3518 Saint Lawrence Dr Toledo (43605) *(G-17917)*

Midwest Trmnals Tldeo Intl Inc 419 698-8171
3518 Saint Lawrence Dr Toledo (43605) *(G-17918)*

Midwest Urbana Dialysis, Urbana *Also called Mesilla Dialysis LLC (G-18441)*

Midwestern Auto Group, Dublin *Also called Brentlinger Enterprises (G-10150)*

Midwestern Plumbing Service 513 753-0050
3984 Bach Buxton Rd Cincinnati (45202) *(G-4051)*

Mie, Marietta *Also called Marietta Industrial Entps Inc (G-13353)*

Miencorp Inc 330 978-8511
706 Robbins Ave Niles (44446) *(G-15159)*

Mighty Mac Investments Inc (PA) 937 335-2928
1494 Lytle Rd Troy (45373) *(G-18215)*

Migrant Head Start 937 846-0699
476 N Dayton Lakeview Rd New Carlisle (45344) *(G-14894)*

Mike Castrucci Ford 513 831-7010
1020 State Route 28 Milford (45150) *(G-14410)*

Mike Coates Cnstr Co Inc 330 652-0190
800 Summit Ave Niles (44446) *(G-15160)*

Mike Enyart & Sons Inc 740 523-0235
77 Private Drive 615 South Point (45680) *(G-16943)*

Mike George Excavating 419 855-4147
24366 W Hellwig Rd Genoa (43430) *(G-11259)*

Mike Morris 330 767-4122
505 Wabash Ave N Brewster (44613) *(G-1811)*

Mike Pusateri Excavating Inc 330 385-5221
16363 Saint Clair Ave East Liverpool (43920) *(G-10407)*

Mike Rennie 513 830-0020
300 E Bus Way Ste 270 Dayton (45401) *(G-9634)*

Mike Ward Landscaping Inc 513 683-6436
424 E Us Highway 22 And 3 Maineville (45039) *(G-13116)*

Mike's Truck & Trailer, West Chester *Also called Midwest Trailer Sales & Svc (G-18972)*

Mike-Sells Potato Chip Co (HQ) 937 228-9400
333 Leo St Dayton (45404) *(G-9635)*

Mikes Carwash Inc (PA) 513 677-4700
100 Northeast Dr Loveland (45140) *(G-13013)*

Mikes Trucking Ltd 614 879-8808
570 Plain City Grgsvlle Galloway (43119) *(G-11223)*

Mikesell Transportation Broker 937 996-5731
1476 State Route 503 Arcanum (45304) *(G-625)*

Mikouis Enterprise Inc 330 424-1418
38655 Saltwell Rd Lisbon (44432) *(G-12804)*

Milan Skilled Nursing LLC 216 727-3996
185 S Main St Milan (44846) *(G-14362)*

Milcon Concrete Inc 937 339-6274
1360 S County Road 25a 25 A Troy (45373) *(G-18216)*

Mildred Byer Clnic For Hmeless, Toledo *Also called Toledo Family Health Center (G-18083)*

Mile Inc 614 252-6724
1144 Alum Creek Dr Columbus (43209) *(G-8085)*

Mile Inc (PA) 614 794-2203
110 E Wilson Bridge Rd # 100 Worthington (43085) *(G-19829)*

Miles Alloy Inc 216 245-8893
13800 Miles Ave Cleveland (44105) *(G-5991)*

Miles Cleaning Services Inc 330 633-8562
23580 Miles Rd Cleveland (44128) *(G-5992)*

Miles Farmers Market Inc 440 248-5222
28560 Miles Rd Solon (44139) *(G-16872)*

Miles-Mcclellan Cnstr Co Inc (PA) 614 487-7744
2100 Builders Pl Columbus (43204) *(G-8086)*

Milestone, Cleveland *Also called Clean Harbors Envmtl Svcs Inc (G-5222)*

Milestone Ventures LLC 317 908-2093
1776 Tamarack Rd Newark (43055) *(G-15072)*

Milford Coml Clg Svcs Inc 513 575-5678
701 Us Highway 50 Ste A Milford (45150) *(G-14411)*

Military Resources LLC 330 263-1040
1036 Burbank Rd Wooster (44691) *(G-19746)*

Military Resources LLC (PA) 330 309-9970
1834 Cleveland Rd Ste 301 Wooster (44691) *(G-19747)*

Mill Creek Golf Club, Ostrander *Also called Mill Creek Golf Course Corp (G-15654)*

Mill Creek Golf Course, Youngstown *Also called Mill Creek Metropolitan Park (G-20130)*

Mill Creek Golf Course Corp 740 666-7711
7259 Penn Rd Ostrander (43061) *(G-15654)*

Mill Creek Metro Parks, Canfield *Also called Mill Creek Metropolitan Park (G-2149)*

Mill Creek Metropolitan Park (PA) 330 702-3000
7574 Clmbiana Canfield Rd Canfield (44406) *(G-2149)*

Mill Creek Metropolitan Park 330 740-7116
123 Mckinley Ave Youngstown (44509) *(G-20129)*

Mill Creek Metropolitan Park 330 740-7112
Boardman Canfield Rd Youngstown (44502) *(G-20130)*

Mill Creek Nursing 419 468-4046
900 Wedgewood Cir Galion (44833) *(G-11179)*

Mill Distributors Inc 330 995-9200
45 Aurora Industrial Pkwy Aurora (44202) *(G-837)*

Mill Manor Nursing Home Inc 440 967-6614
983 Exchange St Vermilion (44089) *(G-18558)*

Mill Pond Family Physicians 330 928-3111
265 Portage Trail Ext W Cuyahoga Falls (44223) *(G-9115)*

Mill Rose Laboratories Inc 440 974-6730
7310 Corp Blvd Mentor (44060) *(G-14086)*

Mill Run Care Center LLC 614 527-3000
3399 Mill Run Dr Hilliard (43026) *(G-11798)*

Mill Run Gardens & Care Center, Hilliard *Also called Mill Run Care Center LLC (G-11798)*

Mill-Rose Company (PA) 440 255-9171
7995 Tyler Blvd Mentor (44060) *(G-14087)*

Millar Elevator Service, Cleveland *Also called Schindler Elevator Corporation (G-6374)*

Millcraft Group LLC (PA) 216 441-5500
6800 Grant Ave Cleveland (44105) *(G-5993)*

Millcraft Paper Company (HQ) 216 441-5505
6800 Grant Ave Cleveland (44105) *(G-5994)*

Millcraft Paper Company 937 222-7829
1200 Leo St Dayton (45404) *(G-9636)*

Millcraft Paper Company 614 675-4800
4311 Janitrol Rd Ste 600 Columbus (43228) *(G-8087)*

Millcraft Paper Company 216 441-5500
6800 Grant Ave Cleveland (44105) *(G-5995)*

Millenium Control Systems LLC 440 510-0050
34525 Melinz Pkwy Ste 205 Eastlake (44095) *(G-10432)*

Millennia Housing MGT Ltd (PA) 216 520-1250
127 Public Sq Ste 1300 Cleveland (44114) *(G-5996)*

Millennium Cpitl Recovery Corp 330 528-1450
95 Executive Pkwy Ste 100 Hudson (44236) *(G-11998)*

Millennium Leather LLC 201 541-7121
4680 Parkway Dr Ste 200 Mason (45040) *(G-13620)*

Miller & Co Portable Toil Svcs 330 453-9472
2400 Shepler Ch Ave Sw Canton (44706) *(G-2405)*

Miller Boat Line Inc (PA) 419 285-2421
535 Bayview Ave Put In Bay (43456) *(G-16227)*

Miller Bros Const Inc 419 445-1015
1613 S Defiance St Archbold (43502) *(G-633)*

Miller Bros Paint & Decorating, Cincinnati *Also called Miller Bros Wallpaper Company (G-4052)*

Miller Bros Wallpaper Company 513 231-4470
8460 Beechmont Ave Ste A Cincinnati (45255) *(G-4052)*

Miller Brothers Cnstr Dem LLC 513 257-1082
3685 Oxford Millville Rd Oxford (45056) *(G-15684)*

Miller Cable Company 419 639-2091
210 S Broadway St Green Springs (44836) *(G-11355)*

Miller Cnfeld Pddock Stone PLC 513 394-5252
511 Walnut St Cincinnati (45202) *(G-4053)*

Miller Consolidated Industries (PA) 937 294-2681
2221 Arbor Blvd Moraine (45439) *(G-14678)*

Miller Contracting Group Inc 419 453-3825
17359 S Rt E 66 Ottoville (45876) *(G-15670)*

Miller Engineering, Marietta *Also called Thomas L Miller (G-13385)*

Miller Fireworks Company Inc (PA) 419 865-7329
501 Glengary Rd Holland (43528) *(G-11899)*

Miller Fireworks Novelty, Holland *Also called Miller Fireworks Company Inc (G-11899)*

Miller Homes of Kidron LLC 330 857-0161
6397 Kidron Rd Kidron (44636) *(G-12309)*

Miller House, Celina *Also called Assisted Living Concepts LLC (G-2584)*

Miller Industrial Svc Team Inc 513 877-2708
8485 State Route 132 Pleasant Plain (45162) *(G-16075)*

Miller Logging Inc 330 279-4721
8373 State Route 83 Holmesville (44633) *(G-11932)*

Miller Pipeline LLC 937 506-8837
11990 Peters Pike Tipp City (45371) *(G-17562)*

Miller Pipeline LLC 614 777-8377
5000 Scioto Darby Rd Hilliard (43026) *(G-11799)*

Miller Products Inc 330 238-4200
1421 W Main St Alliance (44601) *(G-541)*

Miller Supply of WvA Inc (PA) 330 264-9146
1537 Blachleyville Rd Wooster (44691) *(G-19748)*

Miller Transfer and Rigging Co (HQ) 330 325-2521
3833 State Route 183 Rootstown (44272) *(G-16452)*

Miller Valentine Group, Dayton *Also called Miller-Valentine Operations Inc (G-9638)*

Miller Valentine Group, Dayton *Also called Miller-Valentine Operations Inc (G-9639)*

Miller Yount Paving Inc 330 372-4408
2295 Hagland Blackstub Rd Cortland (44410) *(G-8991)*

Miller's Textiles, Springfield *Also called Springfeld Unfrm-Linen Sup Inc (G-17116)*

Miller-Valentine Construction 937 293-0900
137 N Main St Ste 900 Dayton (45402) *(G-9637)*

Miller-Valentine Partners 937 293-0900
4000 Miller Valentine Ct Moraine (45439) *(G-14679)*

Miller-Valentine Partners Ltd 513 588-1000
9349 Waterstone Blvd # 200 Cincinnati (45249) *(G-4054)*

Miller-Vlentine Operations Inc (PA) 937 293-0900
137 N Main St Ste 900 Dayton (45402) *(G-9638)*

Miller-Vlentine Operations Inc 513 771-0900
9435 Waterstone Blvd Dayton (45409) *(G-9639)*

Miller-Vlntine Partners Ltd Lc 513 588-1000
9349 Waterstone Blvd # 200 Cincinnati (45249) *(G-4055)*

Millers Rental and Sls Co Inc (PA) 330 753-8600
2023 Romig Rd Akron (44320) *(G-339)*

Millers Rental and Sls Co Inc 216 642-1447
5410 Warner Rd Cleveland (44125) *(G-5997)*

Millers Textile Services Inc 419 738-3552
1002 Bellefontaine St Wapakoneta (45895) *(G-18650)*

Millers Textile Services Inc......614 262-1206
540 E Columbia St Springfield (45503) *(G-17086)*
Millersburg Hotel, Millersburg *Also called Bird Enterprises LLC (G-14460)*
Millersburg Tire Service Inc......330 674-1085
7375 State Route 39 Millersburg (44654) *(G-14483)*
Milliken Millwork Inc......513 874-6771
400 Circle Freeway Dr West Chester (45246) *(G-19069)*
Milliken's Dairy Cone, Frankfort *Also called David W Milliken (G-11018)*
Millikin & Fitton, Hamilton *Also called Millikin and Fitton Law Firm (G-11629)*
Millikin and Fitton Law Firm (PA)......513 829-6700
232 High St Hamilton (45011) *(G-11629)*
Milliron Iron & Metal, Mansfield *Also called Milliron Recycling Inc (G-13223)*
Milliron Recycling Inc......419 747-6522
2384 Springmill Rd Mansfield (44903) *(G-13223)*
Millis Transfer Inc......513 863-0222
1982 Jackson Rd Hamilton (45011) *(G-11630)*
Mills Corporation......513 671-2882
600 Cincinnati Mills Dr Cincinnati (45240) *(G-4056)*
Mills Creek Association......440 327-5336
5175 Mills Creek Ln North Ridgeville (44039) *(G-15337)*
Mills Fence Co Inc (PA)......513 631-0333
6315 Wiehe Rd Cincinnati (45237) *(G-4057)*
Mills James Productions, Hilliard *Also called Mills/James Inc (G-11800)*
Mills Security Alarm Systems......513 921-4600
490 Mount Hope Ave Cincinnati (45204) *(G-4058)*
Mills Transfer, Lowell *Also called Marietta Transfer Company (G-13038)*
Mills/James Inc......614 777-9933
3545 Fishinger Blvd Hilliard (43026) *(G-11800)*
Millwood Inc (PA)......330 393-4400
3708 International Blvd Vienna (44473) *(G-18582)*
Millwood Natural LLC......330 393-4400
3708 International Blvd Vienna (44473) *(G-18583)*
Millwood Plant, Howard *Also called Pioneer Sands LLC (G-11940)*
Mim Software Inc (PA)......216 896-9798
25800 Science Park Dr # 180 Beachwood (44122) *(G-1082)*
Mimrx Co Inc......614 850-6672
2787 Charter St Columbus (43228) *(G-8088)*
Minamyer Residential Mr/Dd Svc......614 802-0190
967 Worthington Woods Loo Columbus (43085) *(G-8089)*
Minature Society Cincinnati......513 931-9708
6718 Siebern Ave Cincinnati (45236) *(G-4059)*
Mine Equipment Services LLC (PA)......740 936-5427
3958 State Route 3 Sunbury (43074) *(G-17390)*
Minerva Elder Care Inc......330 868-4147
1035 E Lincolnway Minerva (44657) *(G-14521)*
Minerva Elderly Care, Minerva *Also called Minerva Elder Care Inc (G-14521)*
Minerva Medical Center, Minerva *Also called Family Medicine Center Minerva (G-14519)*
Minerva Welding and Fabg Inc......330 868-7731
22133 Us Route 30 Minerva (44657) *(G-14522)*
Minford Retirement Center LLC......740 820-2821
9641 State Route 335 Minford (45653) *(G-14526)*
Minges Drywall, Hamilton *Also called Larry L Minges (G-11622)*
Mini University, Dayton *Also called Wright State University (G-9192)*
Mini University Inc......513 275-5184
401 Western College Dr Oxford (45056) *(G-15685)*
Mini University Inc (PA)......937 426-1414
115 Harbert Dr Ste A Beavercreek (45440) *(G-1231)*
Ministerial Dare Care, Cleveland *Also called Ministerial Day Care-Headstart (G-5998)*
Ministerial Day Care-Headstart (PA)......216 881-6924
7020 Superior Ave Cleveland (44103) *(G-5998)*
Minster Bank (PA)......419 628-2351
95 W 4th St Minster (45865) *(G-14538)*
Mintek Resources Inc......937 431-0218
3725 Pentagon Blvd # 100 Beavercreek (45431) *(G-1171)*
Minute Men Inc (PA)......216 426-2225
3740 Carnegie Ave Ste 201 Cleveland (44115) *(G-5999)*
Minute Men of FL, Cleveland *Also called Minute Men Inc (G-5999)*
Mlp Interent Enterprises LLC......614 917-8705
720c 5th Ave Mansfield (44905) *(G-13224)*
Miracle Health Care, Columbus *Also called Svh Holdings LLC (G-8722)*
Miracle Method of Columbus, Columbus *Also called Sayles Company LLC (G-8595)*
Miracle Plumbing & Heating Co......330 477-2402
2121 Whipple Ave Nw Canton (44708) *(G-2406)*
Miracle Renovations......513 371-0750
2786 Shaffer Ave Cincinnati (45211) *(G-4060)*
Miracle Spirtl Retrst Orgnsizn......216 324-4287
11609 Wade Park Ave Cleveland (44106) *(G-6000)*
Miraclecorp Products (PA)......937 293-9994
2425 W Dorothy Ln Moraine (45439) *(G-14680)*
Mircale Health Care......614 237-7702
3245 E Livingston Ave # 108 Columbus (43227) *(G-8090)*
Mirifex Systems LLC (PA)......440 891-1210
4577 Hinckley Indus Pkwy Cleveland (44109) *(G-6001)*
Mirka USA Inc......330 963-6421
2375 Edison Blvd Twinsburg (44087) *(G-18299)*
Mispace Inc......614 626-2602
5954 Rockland Ct Columbus (43221) *(G-8091)*
Miss Pats Day Care Center (PA)......440 729-8255
8553 Herrick Dr Chesterland (44026) *(G-2742)*
Mission Essntial Personnel LLC (PA)......614 416-2345
6525 W Campus Oval # 101 New Albany (43054) *(G-14859)*
Mission Support, Beavercreek *Also called Leidos Inc (G-1164)*
Mistras Group Inc......419 836-5904
3094 Moline Martin Rd Millbury (43447) *(G-14450)*
Mistras Group Inc......740 788-9188
1480 James Pkwy Heath (43056) *(G-11705)*
Mistras Group Inc......330 244-1541
1415 Raff Rd Sw Canton (44710) *(G-2407)*
Mistras Group Inc......419 227-4100
3157 Harding Hwy Bldg Lima (45804) *(G-12704)*
Mitchell & Sons Moving & Stor......419 289-3311
1217 Township Road 1153 Ashland (44805) *(G-681)*
Mitchells Salon & Day Spa (PA)......513 793-0900
5901 E Galbraith Rd # 230 Cincinnati (45236) *(G-4061)*
Mitchells Salon & Day Spa......513 793-0900
7795 University Ct Ste A West Chester (45069) *(G-18973)*
Mitchells Salon & Day Spa......513 772-3200
11330 Princeton Pike Cincinnati (45246) *(G-4062)*
Mitchells Salon & Day Spa......513 731-0600
2692 Madison Rd Cincinnati (45208) *(G-4063)*
Mitel (delaware) Inc......513 733-8000
9100 W Chester Towne Ctr West Chester (45069) *(G-18974)*
Miter Masonry Contractors......513 821-3334
421 Maple Ave Arlington Heights (45215) *(G-643)*
Mitosis LLC......937 557-3440
116 N Jefferson St # 300 Dayton (45402) *(G-9640)*
Mitsubshi Intl Fd Ingrdnts Inc (HQ)......614 652-1111
5080 Tuttle Crossing Blvd Dublin (43016) *(G-10281)*
Mizar Motors Inc (HQ)......419 729-2400
6003 Benore Rd Toledo (43612) *(G-17919)*
MJ Auto Parts Inc (PA)......440 205-6272
7900 Tyler Blvd Mentor (44060) *(G-14088)*
Mj Baumann Co Inc......614 759-7100
6400 Broughton Ave Columbus (43213) *(G-8092)*
MJ Design Associates Inc......614 873-7333
8463 Estates Ct Plain City (43064) *(G-16061)*
Mj-6 LLC......419 517-7725
2621 Liverpool Ct Toledo (43617) *(G-17920)*
Mjr Sales, Plain City *Also called K Amalia Enterprises Inc (G-16056)*
Mjr-Construction Co......216 523-8050
3101 W 25th St Ste 100 Cleveland (44109) *(G-6002)*
Mjs Snow & Landscape LLC......419 656-6724
6660 W Fritchie Rd Port Clinton (43452) *(G-16113)*
Mk Childcare Warsaw Ave LLC......513 922-6279
3711 Warsaw Ave Cincinnati (45205) *(G-4064)*
Mkc Associates Inc......740 657-3202
90 Hidden Ravines Dr Powell (43065) *(G-16203)*
Mkjb Inc......513 851-8400
4515 Guildford Dr West Chester (45069) *(G-18975)*
Mkm Distribution Services Inc......330 549-9670
100 Eastgate Dr North Lima (44452) *(G-15272)*
Mksk Inc......614 621-2796
462 S Ludlow St Columbus (43215) *(G-8093)*
Mlm Childcare LLC......513 623-8243
16 Beaufort Hunt Ln Cincinnati (45242) *(G-4065)*
Mmi II, West Chester *Also called Milliken Millwork Inc (G-19069)*
Mmi of Kentucky, Cincinnati *Also called Contractors Materials Company (G-3353)*
Mmi-Cpr LLC......216 674-0645
7100 E Pleasant Valley Rd Independence (44131) *(G-12098)*
Mmic Inc......513 697-0445
6867 Obannon Blf Loveland (45140) *(G-13014)*
Mobilcomm Inc......513 742-5555
1211 W Sharon Rd Cincinnati (45240) *(G-4066)*
Mobile Cardiac Imaging LLC......419 251-3711
2409 Cherry St Ste 100 Toledo (43608) *(G-17921)*
Mobile Instr Svc & Repr Inc (PA)......937 592-5025
333 Water Ave Bellefontaine (43311) *(G-1360)*
Mobile Meals (PA)......330 376-7717
1357 Home Ave Ste 1 Akron (44310) *(G-340)*
Mobile Meals of Salem Inc......330 332-2160
1995 E State St Salem (44460) *(G-16553)*
Mobilex USA, Columbus *Also called Trident USA Health Svcs LLC (G-8779)*
Mobility Revolution LLC......909 980-2259
6753 Engle Rd Ste A Cleveland (44130) *(G-6003)*
MOBILITY WORKS FOUNDATION, THE, Richfield *Also called Wmk Inc (G-16384)*
Mobilityworks, Mentor *Also called Wmk LLC (G-14125)*
Moca Cleveland, Cleveland *Also called Museum Cntmprary Art Cleveland (G-6027)*
Mocha House Inc (PA)......330 392-3020
467 High St Ne Warren (44481) *(G-18731)*
Modal Shop Inc......513 351-9919
3149 E Kemper Rd Cincinnati (45241) *(G-4067)*
Model Group Inc......513 559-0048
2170 Gilbert Ave Ste 100 Cincinnati (45206) *(G-4068)*
Modern Builders Supply Inc......216 273-3605
4549 Industrial Pkwy Cleveland (44135) *(G-6004)*
Modern Builders Supply Inc......330 726-7000
500 Victoria Rd Youngstown (44515) *(G-20131)*
Modern Builders Supply Inc (PA)......419 241-3961
3500 Phillips Ave Toledo (43608) *(G-17922)*
Modern Builders Supply Inc......937 222-2627
2627 Stanley Ave Dayton (45404) *(G-9641)*

Modern Builders Supply Inc 513 531-1000
  6225 Wiehe Rd Cincinnati (45237) **(G-4069)**
Modern Day Concrete Cnstr 513 738-1026
  9773 Crosby Rd Harrison (45030) **(G-11674)**
Modern Glass Pnt & Tile Co Inc 740 454-1253
  933 Linden Ave Zanesville (43701) **(G-20332)**
Modern Medical Inc 800 547-3330
  250 Progressive Way Westerville (43082) **(G-19186)**
Modern Office Methods Inc (PA) 513 791-0909
  4747 Lake Forest Dr # 200 Blue Ash (45242) **(G-1613)**
Modern Office Methods Inc 614 891-3693
  929 Eastwind Dr Ste 220 Westerville (43081) **(G-19281)**
Modern Poured Walls Inc 440 647-6661
  41807 State Route 18 Wellington (44090) **(G-18843)**
Modern Tech Solutions Inc 937 426-9025
  4141 Colonel Glenn Hwy # 115 Beavercreek Township (45431) **(G-1254)**
Modern Welding Co Ohio Inc 740 344-9425
  1 Modern Way Newark (43055) **(G-15073)**
Modlich Stone Works, Columbus Also called Modlich Stoneworks Inc **(G-8094)**
Modlich Stoneworks Inc 614 276-2848
  2255 Harper Rd Columbus (43204) **(G-8094)**
Modular Systems Technicians 216 459-2630
  15708 Industrial Pkwy Cleveland (44135) **(G-6005)**
Moeller Trucking Inc 419 925-4799
  8100 Industrial Dr Maria Stein (45860) **(G-13308)**
Mohawk Golf Club 419 447-5876
  4399 S State Route 231 Tiffin (44883) **(G-17525)**
Mohawk RE-Bar Services Inc 440 268-0780
  15110 Foltz Pkwy Ste 106 Strongsville (44149) **(G-17334)**
Mohican Hills Golf Club Inc 419 368-4700
  25 County Road 1950 Jeromesville (44840) **(G-12193)**
Mohican State Park Lodge & Con, Perrysville Also called Natural Resources Ohio Dept **(G-15942)**
Mohun Health Care Center 614 416-6132
  2320 Airport Dr Columbus (43219) **(G-8095)**
MOHUN HEALTH CARE CENTER GIFT, Columbus Also called Mohun Health Care Center **(G-8095)**
Moisture Guard Corporation 330 928-7200
  4370 Allen Rd Stow (44224) **(G-17220)**
Molina Healthcare Inc 800 642-4168
  3000 Corp Exchange Dr # 100 Columbus (43231) **(G-8096)**
Molina Healthcare Inc 216 606-1400
  6161 Oak Tree Blvd Independence (44131) **(G-12099)**
Molina Healthcare of Ohio, Columbus Also called Molina Healthcare Inc **(G-8096)**
Molina Healthcare of Ohio, Independence Also called Molina Healthcare Inc **(G-12099)**
Mollett Seamless Gutter Co 513 825-0500
  9345 Prnceton Glendale Rd West Chester (45011) **(G-18976)**
Molloy Roofing Company 513 791-7400
  11099 Deerfield Rd Blue Ash (45242) **(G-1614)**
Molly Maid of Lorain County 440 327-0000
  753 Leona St Elyria (44035) **(G-10539)**
Molyet Crop Production Inc 419 992-4288
  546 E County Road 51 Tiffin (44883) **(G-17526)**
Monarch, Cleveland Also called Integrated Power Services LLC **(G-5758)**
Monarch Construction Company 513 351-6900
  1654 Sherman Ave Cincinnati (45212) **(G-4070)**
Monarch Electric Service Co (HQ) 216 433-7800
  5325 W 130th St Cleveland (44130) **(G-6006)**
Monarch Steel Company Inc 216 587-8000
  4650 Johnston Pkwy Cleveland (44128) **(G-6007)**
Monco Enterprises Inc (PA) 937 461-0034
  700 Liberty Ln Dayton (45449) **(G-9642)**
Mondelez Global LLC 330 626-6500
  545 Mondial Pkwy Streetsboro (44241) **(G-17262)**
Mondo Polymer Technologies Inc 740 376-9396
  27620 State Rte 7 Reno (45773) **(G-16277)**
Monesi Trucking & Eqp Repr Inc 614 921-9183
  1715 Atlas St Columbus (43228) **(G-8097)**
Monode Marking Products Inc (PA) 440 975-8802
  9200 Tyler Blvd Mentor (44060) **(G-14089)**
Monro Inc 440 835-2393
  29778 Detroit Rd Westlake (44145) **(G-19375)**
Monro Inc 937 999-3202
  4 Remick Blvd Springboro (45066) **(G-16976)**
Monro Inc 614 235-3684
  2869 E Main St Columbus (43209) **(G-8098)**
Monro Inc 614 360-3883
  4570 W Broad St Columbus (43228) **(G-8099)**
Monro Muffler Brake, Westlake Also called Monro Inc **(G-19375)**
Monro Muffler Brake, Springboro Also called Monro Inc **(G-16976)**
Monro Muffler Brake, Columbus Also called Monro Inc **(G-8099)**
Monroe Achievement Center, Woodsfield Also called Board Mental Retardation Dvlpm **(G-19671)**
MONROE ADULT CRAFTS ORGANIZATI, Woodsfield Also called Maco Inc **(G-19675)**
Monroe County Association For 740 472-1712
  47011 State Route 26 Woodsfield (43793) **(G-19676)**
Monroe County Care Center, Woodsfield Also called County of Monroe **(G-19674)**
Monroe County Engineers Dept, Woodsfield Also called County of Monroe **(G-19673)**
Monroe Family Health Center 740 472-0757
  37984 Airport Rd Woodsfield (43793) **(G-19677)**

Monroe Heating and AC, Monroe Also called Monroe Mechanical Incorporated **(G-14577)**
Monroe Mechanical Incorporated 513 539-7555
  150 Breaden Dr B Monroe (45050) **(G-14577)**
Monsoon Lagoon Water Park, Port Clinton Also called Goofy Golf II Inc **(G-16107)**
Monster Worldwide Inc 513 719-3331
  10296 Springfield Pike # 500 Cincinnati (45215) **(G-4071)**
Montefiore Home 216 360-9080
  1 David N Myers Pkwy Beachwood (44122) **(G-1083)**
Monterey Care Center, Grove City Also called Whetstone Care Center LLC **(G-11487)**
MONTESSORI CHILDREN SCHOOL, Westlake Also called Bay Village Montessori Inc **(G-19321)**
Montessori Community School 740 344-9411
  621 Country Club Dr Newark (43055) **(G-15074)**
Montessori High School Assn 216 421-3033
  2254 Tudor Dr Cleveland (44106) **(G-6008)**
Montford Heights, Cincinnati Also called Duke Energy Ohio Inc **(G-3451)**
Montgmery Cnty Prosecutors Off, Dayton Also called County of Montgomery **(G-9331)**
Montgomery Care Center, Cincinnati Also called Nursing Care MGT Amer Inc **(G-4142)**
Montgomery Cnty Children Svcs, Dayton Also called County of Montgomery **(G-9326)**
Montgomery County Dept of Job, Dayton Also called County of Montgomery **(G-9330)**
Montgomery County N Incertr, Moraine Also called County of Montgomery **(G-14637)**
Montgomery Developmental Ctr, Columbus Also called Develpmntal Dsblties Ohio Dept **(G-7442)**
Montgomery Ear Nose/Throat CL, Wilmington Also called Mark E Grosinger **(G-19633)**
Montgomery Iron & Paper Co Inc 937 222-4059
  400 E 4th St Dayton (45402) **(G-9643)**
Montgomery Jeep Eagle, Cincinnati Also called Lincoln Mrcury Kings Auto Mall **(G-3933)**
Montgomery Paper Co Div, Dayton Also called Montgomery Iron & Paper Co Inc **(G-9643)**
Montgomery Swim & Tennis Club 513 793-6433
  9941 Orchard Club Dr Montgomery (45242) **(G-14596)**
Montgomery Trucking Company 740 384-2138
  103 E 13th St Wellston (45692) **(G-18853)**
Montpelier Auto Auction Ohio 419 485-1691
  14125 County Road M50 Montpelier (43543) **(G-14614)**
Montpelier Exempted Vlg Schl (PA) 419 485-3676
  1015 E Brown Rd Montpelier (43543) **(G-14615)**
Montpelier Gardens, Columbus Also called Buckeye Cmnty Twenty Six LP **(G-7088)**
Montpelier Hospital, Montpelier Also called Community Hsptals Wllness Ctrs **(G-14611)**
Montpelier Senior Center 419 485-3218
  325 N Jonesville St Montpelier (43543) **(G-14616)**
Montrose Cinema 12, Akron Also called Regal Cinemas Inc **(G-398)**
Montrose Ford Inc (PA) 330 666-0711
  3960 Medina Rd Fairlawn (44333) **(G-10842)**
Montrose Sheffield LLC 440 934-6699
  5033 Detroit Rd Sheffield Village (44054) **(G-16740)**
Moo Moo Carwash, Etna Also called Moo Moo North Hamilton LLC **(G-10611)**
Moo Moo North Hamilton LLC (PA) 614 751-9274
  13375 National Rd Sw D Etna (43068) **(G-10611)**
Moody Nat Cy Dt Clumbus Mt LLC 614 228-3200
  35 W Spring St Columbus (43215) **(G-8100)**
Moody Nat Cy Willoughby Mt LLC 440 530-1100
  35103 Maplegrove Rd Willoughby (44094) **(G-19551)**
Moody-Nolan Inc (PA) 614 461-4664
  300 Spruce St Ste 300 # 300 Columbus (43215) **(G-8101)**
Moodys of Dayton Inc (PA) 614 443-3898
  4359 Infirmary Rd Miamisburg (45342) **(G-14194)**
Moonlight Security Inc 937 252-1600
  2710 Dryden Rd Moraine (45439) **(G-14681)**
Moore Self Storage, Cleveland Also called Compass Self Storage LLC **(G-5330)**
Moore Transport of Tulsa LLC 419 726-4499
  4015 Stickney Ave Toledo (43612) **(G-17923)**
Moose Fmly Ctr 501 Middletown, Middletown Also called Moose International Inc **(G-14314)**
Moose International Inc 513 422-6776
  3009 S Main St Middletown (45044) **(G-14314)**
Moraine Country Club 937 294-6200
  4075 Southern Blvd Unit 1 Dayton (45429) **(G-9644)**
Morelia Consultants LLC 513 469-1500
  11210 Montgomery Rd Cincinnati (45249) **(G-4072)**
Morelia Group LLC 513 469-1500
  8600 Governors Hill Dr # 160 Cincinnati (45249) **(G-4073)**
Morgan & Sons Moving & Storage, Dayton Also called Van Howards Lines Inc **(G-9848)**
Morgan County Public Transit 740 962-1322
  37 S 5th St McConnelsville (43756) **(G-13903)**
Morgan Services Inc 419 243-2214
  34 10th St Toledo (43604) **(G-17924)**
Morgan Services Inc 216 241-3107
  2013 Columbus Rd Cleveland (44113) **(G-6009)**
Morgan Services Inc 937 223-5241
  817 Webster St Dayton (45404) **(G-9645)**
Morgan Stanley 513 721-2000
  221 E 4th St Ste 2200 Cincinnati (45202) **(G-4074)**
Morgan Stanley 440 835-6750
  159 Crocker Park Blvd # 460 Westlake (44145) **(G-19376)**
Morgan Stanley 216 523-3000
  1301 E 9th St Ste 3100 Cleveland (44114) **(G-6010)**
Morgan Stanley 330 670-4600
  3700 Embassy Pkwy Ste 340 Akron (44333) **(G-341)**
Morgan Stanley 614 473-2086
  4449 Easton Way Ste 300 Columbus (43219) **(G-8102)**

Morgan Stanley & Co LLC 614 798-3100
545 Metro Pl S Ste 300 Dublin (43017) *(G-10282)*
Morgan Stanley & Co LLC 614 228-0600
41 S High St Ste 2700 Columbus (43215) *(G-8103)*
Morgan Stnley Smith Barney LLC 216 360-4900
31099 Chagrin Blvd Fl 3 Cleveland (44124) *(G-6011)*
Morgan Uniforms & Linen Rental, Cleveland *Also called Morgan Services Inc (G-6009)*
Moring View Care Center, New Philadelphia *Also called Dearth Management Company (G-14956)*
Morning View Care Center, Marion *Also called Dearth Management Company (G-13418)*
Morning View Care Center, Columbus *Also called Dearth Management Company (G-7426)*
Morning View Delaware Inc 740 965-3984
14961 N Old 3c Rd Sunbury (43074) *(G-17391)*
Morphick Inc 844 506-6774
4555 Lake Forest Dr # 150 Blue Ash (45242) *(G-1615)*
Morral Companies LLC (HQ) 740 465-3251
132 Postle Ave Morral (43337) *(G-14713)*
Morris Cadillac Buick GMC (PA) 440 327-4181
26100 Lorain Rd North Olmsted (44070) *(G-15298)*
Morris Schneider Wittstadt LLC 440 942-5168
35110 Euclid Ave Ste 2 Willoughby (44094) *(G-19552)*
Morris Technologies Inc 513 733-1611
11988 Tramway Dr Cincinnati (45241) *(G-4075)*
Morrison Inc 740 373-5869
410 Colegate Dr Marietta (45750) *(G-13361)*
Morro Dialysis LLC 937 865-0633
290 Alexandersville Rd Miamisburg (45342) *(G-14195)*
Morrow Co Ed Service Center, Mount Gilead *Also called County of Morrow (G-14726)*
Morrow Control and Supply Inc (PA) 330 452-9791
810 Marion Motley Ave Ne Canton (44705) *(G-2408)*
Morrow County Child Care Ctr 419 946-5007
406 Bank St Mount Gilead (43338) *(G-14728)*
Morrow County Council On Drugs 419 947-4055
950 Meadow Dr Mount Gilead (43338) *(G-14729)*
Morrow County Emergency Squad, Mount Gilead *Also called Morrow County Fire Fighter (G-14730)*
Morrow County Fire Fighter 419 946-7976
140 S Main St Mount Gilead (43338) *(G-14730)*
Morrow County Hospital 419 949-3085
651 W Marion Rd Mount Gilead (43338) *(G-14731)*
Morrow County Hospital (PA) 419 946-5015
651 W Marion Rd Mount Gilead (43338) *(G-14732)*
Morrow County Hospital HM Hlth, Mount Gilead *Also called Morrow County Hospital (G-14732)*
Morrow County Hospital MCH At, Mount Gilead *Also called Morrow County Hospital (G-14731)*
Morrow Manor Nursing Home, Chesterville *Also called Levering Management Inc (G-2748)*
Morse Van Line, Painesville *Also called William R Morse (G-15748)*
Mortgage Information Services (PA) 216 514-7480
4877 Galaxy Pkwy Ste I Cleveland (44128) *(G-6012)*
Mortgage Now Inc (PA) 800 245-1050
9700 Rockside Rd Ste 295 Cleveland (44125) *(G-6013)*
Mortgage Service Center, Canton *Also called Security Savings Mortgage Corp (G-2472)*
Morton Buildings Inc 419 675-2311
14483 State Route 31 Kenton (43326) *(G-12285)*
Morton Buildings Plant, Kenton *Also called Morton Buildings Inc (G-12285)*
Morton Landscape Dev Co, Columbia Station *Also called Mortons Lawn Service Inc (G-6779)*
Morton Salt Inc 330 925-3015
151 Industrial Ave Rittman (44270) *(G-16407)*
Mortons Lawn Service Inc 440 236-3550
11564 Station Rd Columbia Station (44028) *(G-6779)*
Mosier Industrial Services 419 683-4000
900 S Wiley St Crestline (44827) *(G-9058)*
Moskowitz Family Ltd 513 729-2300
7220 Pippin Rd Cincinnati (45239) *(G-4076)*
Moskowitz Family Trust, Cincinnati *Also called Moskowitz Family Ltd (G-4076)*
Mosley Pfundt & Glick Inc 419 861-1120
6455 Wheatstone Ct Maumee (43537) *(G-13822)*
Moss Affiliate Marketing, Solon *Also called Paul Moss LLC (G-16881)*
Mosser Glass Incorporated 740 439-1827
9279 Cadiz Rd Cambridge (43725) *(G-2077)*
Motel 6, Troy *Also called R P L Corporation (G-18223)*
Motel 6 Operating LP 614 431-2525
7474 N High St Columbus (43235) *(G-8104)*
Motel Investments Marietta Inc 740 374-8190
700 Pike St Marietta (45750) *(G-13362)*
Moti Corporation 440 734-4500
22115 Brookpark Rd Cleveland (44126) *(G-6014)*
Motion Controls Robotics Inc 419 334-5886
1500 Walter Ave Fremont (43420) *(G-11088)*
Motion Industries Inc 513 860-8400
9965 Farr Ct West Chester (45246) *(G-19070)*
Moto Franchise Corporation (PA) 937 291-1900
7086 Corporate Way Ste 2 Dayton (45459) *(G-9646)*
Motophoto, Dayton *Also called Moto Franchise Corporation (G-9646)*
Motor Carrier Service Inc 419 693-6207
815 Lemoyne Rd Northwood (43619) *(G-15399)*
Motorists Coml Mutl Insur Co (PA) 614 225-8211
471 E Broad St Bsmt Columbus (43215) *(G-8105)*
MOTORISTS INSURANCE GROUP, Columbus *Also called Motorists Mutual Insurance Co (G-8107)*
MOTORISTS INSURANCE GROUP, Columbus *Also called Motorists Life Insurance Co (G-8106)*
MOTORISTS INSURANCE GROUP, Columbus *Also called Motorists Coml Mutl Insur Co (G-8105)*
Motorists Life Ins Co, Columbus *Also called Motorists Mutual Insurance Co (G-8108)*
Motorists Life Insurance Co 614 225-8211
471 E Broad St Ste 200 Columbus (43215) *(G-8106)*
Motorists Mutual Insurance Co (PA) 614 225-8211
471 E Broad St Ste 200 Columbus (43215) *(G-8107)*
Motorists Mutual Insurance Co 440 779-8900
28111 Lorain Rd North Olmsted (44070) *(G-15299)*
Motorists Mutual Insurance Co 330 896-9311
3532 Massillon Rd Uniontown (44685) *(G-18379)*
Motorists Mutual Insurance Co 937 435-5540
471 E Broad St Bsmt Columbus (43215) *(G-8108)*
Motz Group Inc (PA) 513 533-6452
3607 Church St Ste 300 Cincinnati (45244) *(G-4077)*
Mougianis Industries Inc 740 264-6372
1626 Cadiz Rd Steubenville (43953) *(G-17167)*
Mound Builders Guidance Center 740 522-2828
65 Messimer Dr Unit 2 Newark (43055) *(G-15075)*
Mound Technologies Inc 937 748-2937
25 Mound Park Dr Springboro (45066) *(G-16977)*
Moundbuilders Country Club Co 740 344-4500
125 N 33rd St Newark (43055) *(G-15076)*
Moundbuilders Guidance Ctr Inc 740 397-0442
8402 Blackjack Rd Mount Vernon (43050) *(G-14782)*
Mount Aloysius Corp 740 342-3343
5375 Tile Plant Rd Se New Lexington (43764) *(G-14921)*
Mount Alverna Home, Cleveland *Also called Franciscan Sisters of Chicago (G-5571)*
Mount Auburn Obstetrics & Gyne (PA) 513 241-4774
2123 Auburn Ave Ste 724 Cincinnati (45219) *(G-4078)*
Mount Carmel Central Ohio 614 268-9561
955 Eastwind Dr Ste B Westerville (43081) *(G-19282)*
Mount Carmel E Dialysis Clnc 614 322-0433
85 Mcnaughten Rd Columbus (43213) *(G-8109)*
Mount Carmel East Hospital 614 234-6000
6001 E Broad St Columbus (43213) *(G-8110)*
Mount Carmel Health (HQ) 614 234-5000
793 W State St Columbus (43222) *(G-8111)*
Mount Carmel Health 614 234-8170
730 W Rich St Columbus (43222) *(G-8112)*
Mount Carmel Health 614 855-4878
55 N High St Ste A New Albany (43054) *(G-14860)*
Mount Carmel Health 614 234-0100
501 W Schrock Rd Ste 350 Westerville (43081) *(G-19283)*
Mount Carmel Health System (HQ) 614 234-6000
6150 E Broad St Columbus (43213) *(G-8113)*
Mount Carmel Health System 614 775-6600
7333 Smiths Mill Rd New Albany (43054) *(G-14861)*
Mount Carmel Home Care, Westerville *Also called Mount Carmel Health (G-19283)*
Mount Carmel Imaging & Therapy 614 234-8080
5969 E Broad St Ste 100 Columbus (43213) *(G-8114)*
Mount Carmel Kindercare, Columbus *Also called Kindercare Learning Ctrs LLC (G-7904)*
Mount Carmel/Walnut Hills, Columbus *Also called Walnut Hills Physical Therapy (G-8872)*
Mount Crmel Hospice Evrgrn Ctr 614 234-0200
1144 Dublin Rd Columbus (43215) *(G-8115)*
Mount Orab Ems, Mount Orab *Also called Mt Orab Fire Department Inc (G-14743)*
MOUNT ST JOSEPH NURSING HOME, Euclid *Also called Sisters Od Saint Joseph of SAI (G-10656)*
Mount Vernon NH LLC 740 392-1099
1135 Gambier Rd Mount Vernon (43050) *(G-14783)*
Mount Vrnon Hlth Rhbltion Ctr, Mount Vernon *Also called Mount Vernon NH LLC (G-14783)*
Mountain Foods Inc 440 286-7177
9761 Ravenna Rd Chardon (44024) *(G-2705)*
Mountain Laurel Assurance Co 440 461-5000
6300 Wilson Mills Rd Cleveland (44143) *(G-6015)*
Moving Solutions Inc 440 946-9300
8001 Moving Way Mentor (44060) *(G-14090)*
Mowerys Collision Inc 614 274-6072
155 Phillipi Rd Columbus (43228) *(G-8116)*
Mowry Construction & Engrg Inc 419 289-2262
2105 Claremont Ave Ashland (44805) *(G-682)*
Moyal and Petroff MD 440 461-6477
730 Som Center Rd Ste 230 Cleveland (44143) *(G-6016)*
Moyer Industries Inc 937 832-7283
7555 Jacks Ln Clayton (45315) *(G-4860)*
Mp Biomedicals LLC 440 337-1200
29525 Fountain Pkwy Solon (44139) *(G-16873)*
Mpf Sales and Mktg Group LLC 513 793-6241
11243 Cornell Park Dr Blue Ash (45242) *(G-1616)*
Mpg Transport, Toledo *Also called United Road Services Inc (G-18120)*
Mpi Label Systems Eqp Rfid Div, Alliance *Also called Miller Products Inc (G-541)*
Mplx LP (PA) 419 421-2414
200 E Hardin St Findlay (45840) *(G-10946)*

Mplx Terminals LLC..........440 526-4653
10439 Brecksville Rd Cleveland (44141) ***(G-6017)***
Mplx Terminals LLC..........330 479-5539
2408 Gambrinus Ave Sw Canton (44706) ***(G-2409)***
Mplx Terminals LLC..........504 252-8064
840 Heath Rd Heath (43056) ***(G-11706)***
Mplx Terminals LLC..........513 451-0485
4015 River Rd Cincinnati (45204) ***(G-4079)***
Mpower Inc..........614 783-0478
4643 Winery Way Gahanna (43230) ***(G-11136)***
MPS Group Inc..........937 746-2117
512 Linden Ave Carlisle (45005) ***(G-2552)***
MPW Construction Services..........440 647-6661
41807 State Route 18 Wellington (44090) ***(G-18844)***
MPW Container Management Corp..........216 362-8400
4848 W 130th St Cleveland (44135) ***(G-6018)***
MPW Industrial Services Inc..........330 454-1898
907 Belden Ave Se Canton (44707) ***(G-2410)***
MPW Industrial Services Inc (HQ)..........800 827-8790
9711 Lancaster Rd Hebron (43025) ***(G-11718)***
MPW Industrial Services Inc..........740 774-5251
65 Kenworth Dr Chillicothe (45601) ***(G-2805)***
MPW Industrial Services Inc..........740 345-2431
150 S 29th St Newark (43055) ***(G-15077)***
MPW Industrial Services Inc..........937 644-0200
11000 State Route 347 East Liberty (43319) ***(G-10393)***
MPW Industrial Services Inc..........440 277-9072
1930 E 28th St Lorain (44055) ***(G-12928)***
MPW Industrial Svcs Group Inc (PA)..........740 927-8790
9711 Lancaster Rd Hebron (43025) ***(G-11719)***
MPW Industrial Water Svcs Inc..........800 827-8790
9711 Lancaster Rd Hebron (43025) ***(G-11720)***
Mr Box, Mansfield *Also called Skybox Packaging LLC* ***(G-13243)***
Mr Excavator Inc..........440 256-2008
8616 Euclid Chardon Rd Kirtland (44094) ***(G-12323)***
Mr Magic Car Wash & Detail Ctr, Beachwood *Also called Mr Magic Carnegie Inc* ***(G-1084)***
Mr Magic Carnegie Inc..........440 461-7572
23511 Chagrin Blvd # 306 Beachwood (44122) ***(G-1084)***
Mr Rooter Plumbing Corporation..........419 625-4444
8200 E Pleasant Valley Rd Independence (44131) ***(G-12100)***
Mr. Beams, Mayfield Village *Also called Wireless Environment LLC* ***(G-13888)***
Mrap LLC..........614 545-3190
1721 Westbelt Dr Columbus (43228) ***(G-8117)***
MRC Global (us) Inc..........419 324-0039
3110 Frenchmens Rd Toledo (43607) ***(G-17925)***
MRC Global (us) Inc..........513 489-6922
9085 Le Saint Dr West Chester (45014) ***(G-18977)***
MRDD, Sandusky *Also called Ability Works Inc* ***(G-16572)***
Mreto, Cincinnati *Also called Southwest OH Trans Auth* ***(G-4507)***
Mri Network, Akron *Also called Global Exec Slutions Group LLC* ***(G-237)***
Mri Software LLC (PA)..........800 321-8770
28925 Fountain Pkwy Solon (44139) ***(G-16874)***
Mrivera Construction, Cleveland *Also called Mjr-Construction Co* ***(G-6002)***
MRM Construction Inc..........740 388-0079
110 Bellomy Dr Gallipolis (45631) ***(G-11205)***
Mrn Limited Partnership..........216 589-5631
629 Euclid Ave Fl 2 Cleveland (44114) ***(G-6019)***
Mrn-Newgar Hotel Ltd..........216 443-1000
629 Euclid Ave Lbby 1 Cleveland (44114) ***(G-6020)***
Mrp Inc..........513 965-9700
5632 Sugar Camp Rd Milford (45150) ***(G-14412)***
Mrs Dennis Potato Farm Inc..........419 335-2778
15370 County Road K Wauseon (43567) ***(G-18807)***
Mrsi, Cincinnati *Also called Medical Recovery Systems Inc* ***(G-3995)***
Ms Consultants Inc (PA)..........330 744-5321
333 E Federal St Youngstown (44503) ***(G-20132)***
Ms Consultants Inc..........614 898-7100
2221 Schrock Rd Columbus (43229) ***(G-8118)***
Ms Consultants Inc..........216 522-1926
600 Superior Ave E # 1300 Cleveland (44114) ***(G-6021)***
MSA Architects, Cincinnati *Also called Michael Schuster Associates* ***(G-4047)***
MSA Family Medicine, Newark *Also called Medical and Surgical Assoc* ***(G-15068)***
MSA Group Inc..........614 334-0400
2839 Charter St Columbus (43228) ***(G-8119)***
Msab Park Creek LLC..........440 842-5100
20375 Center Ridge Rd # 204 Rocky River (44116) ***(G-16441)***
Msd, Dayton *Also called Mechanical Systems Dayton Inc* ***(G-9181)***
Msdgc, Cincinnati *Also called Metropolitan Sewer District* ***(G-4042)***
MSI, Chesterland *Also called Metzenbaum Sheltered Inds Inc* ***(G-2741)***
MSI International LLC..........330 869-6459
6100 Oak Tree Blvd # 200 Cleveland (44131) ***(G-6022)***
Msk Hospitality Inc..........513 771-0370
11620 Chester Rd Cincinnati (45246) ***(G-4080)***
Mssl Consolidated Inc..........330 766-5510
8640 E Market St Warren (44484) ***(G-18732)***
Msstaff LLC..........419 868-8536
5950 Airport Hwy Ste 12 Toledo (43615) ***(G-17926)***
Mt Auburn Women's Center, Cincinnati *Also called Mount Auburn Obstetrics & Gyne* ***(G-4078)***
Mt Business Technologies, Avon Lake *Also called M T Business Technologies* ***(G-924)***
Mt Business Technologies Inc (HQ)..........419 529-6100
1150 National Pkwy Mansfield (44906) ***(G-13225)***
Mt Carmel Medical Group..........614 277-9631
3667 Marlane Dr Grove City (43123) ***(G-11454)***
Mt Healthy Christian Home Inc..........513 931-5000
8097 Hamilton Ave Cincinnati (45231) ***(G-4081)***
Mt Hope Auction Inc (PA)..........330 674-6188
8076 State Rte 241 Mount Hope (44660) ***(G-14737)***
Mt Orab Fire Department Inc..........937 444-3945
113 Spice St Mount Orab (45154) ***(G-14743)***
Mt Royal Villa Care Center, Cleveland *Also called Consulate Management Co LLC* ***(G-5340)***
Mt Texas LLC..........513 853-4400
3055 Colerain Ave Cincinnati (45225) ***(G-4082)***
Mt View Terrace, Blue Ash *Also called Sycamore Senior Center* ***(G-1654)***
Mt Washington Care Center Inc..........513 231-4561
6900 Beechmont Ave Cincinnati (45230) ***(G-4083)***
MTA Leasing, Fairlawn *Also called Montrose Ford Inc* ***(G-10842)***
Mtd Holdings Inc (PA)..........330 225-2600
5965 Grafton Rd Valley City (44280) ***(G-18467)***
MTI, Cleveland *Also called Mainthia Technologies Inc* ***(G-5899)***
Mtm Technologies (texas) Inc..........513 786-6600
8044 Montgomery Rd # 700 Cincinnati (45236) ***(G-4084)***
Mto Suncoke, Middletown *Also called Suncoke Energy Nc* ***(G-14333)***
Mtsi, Beavercreek Township *Also called Modern Tech Solutions Inc* ***(G-1254)***
Mud Pike Group Home The, Celina *Also called Mercer Residential Services* ***(G-2603)***
Mueller Art Cover & Binding Co..........440 238-3303
12005 Alameda Dr Strongsville (44149) ***(G-17335)***
Muetzel Plumbing & Heating Co..........614 299-7700
1661 Kenny Rd Columbus (43212) ***(G-8120)***
Muha Construction Inc..........937 435-0678
855 Congress Park Dr # 101 Dayton (45459) ***(G-9647)***
Muirfield Association Inc..........614 889-0922
8372 Muirfield Dr Dublin (43017) ***(G-10283)***
Muirfield Village Golf Club..........614 889-6700
5750 Memorial Dr Dublin (43017) ***(G-10284)***
Mulberry Garden A L S..........330 630-3980
395 S Main St Apt 210 Munroe Falls (44262) ***(G-14798)***
Mulch Masters of Ohio, Miamisburg *Also called Gayston Corporation* ***(G-14173)***
Mull Iron, Rittman *Also called Rittman Inc* ***(G-16409)***
Mullett Company..........440 564-9000
14980 Cross Creek Pkwy Newbury (44065) ***(G-15123)***
Mullinax East LLC..........440 296-3020
28825 Euclid Ave Wickliffe (44092) ***(G-19470)***
Mullinax Ford North Canton Inc..........330 238-3206
5900 Whipple Ave Nw Canton (44720) ***(G-2411)***
Mullins International Sls Corp..........937 233-4213
2949 Valley Pike Dayton (45404) ***(G-9648)***
Multi Cntry SEC Slutions Group..........216 973-0291
3459 W 117th St Cleveland (44111) ***(G-6023)***
Multi County Juvenile Det Ctr..........740 652-1525
923 Liberty Dr Lancaster (43130) ***(G-12420)***
Multi Flow Transport Inc..........216 641-0200
4705 Van Epps Rd Brooklyn Heights (44131) ***(G-1875)***
Multi Products Company..........330 674-5981
7188 State Route 39 Millersburg (44654) ***(G-14484)***
Multi-Care Inc..........440 352-0788
60 Wood St Painesville (44077) ***(G-15728)***
Multi-Cnty Jvnile Attntion Sys (PA)..........330 484-6471
815 Faircrest St Sw Canton (44706) ***(G-2412)***
Multi-Flow Dispensers Ohio Inc (PA)..........216 641-0200
4705 Van Epps Rd Brooklyn Heights (44131) ***(G-1876)***
Multi-Fund Inc (PA)..........216 750-2331
9700 Rockside Rd Ste 100 Cleveland (44125) ***(G-6024)***
Multi-Plastics Inc (PA)..........740 548-4894
7770 N Central Dr Lewis Center (43035) ***(G-12552)***
Multicare Home Health Services..........216 731-8900
27691 Euclid Ave Ste B-1 Euclid (44132) ***(G-10649)***
Multicare Management Group..........513 868-6500
908 Symmes Rd Fairfield (45014) ***(G-10759)***
Multicon Builders Inc (PA)..........614 241-2070
495 S High St Ste 150 Columbus (43215) ***(G-8121)***
Multicon Builders Inc..........614 463-1142
503 S High St Columbus (43215) ***(G-8122)***
Multicon Construction, Columbus *Also called Multicon Builders Inc* ***(G-8122)***
Multicon Construction Co..........614 351-2683
1320 Mckinley Ave Ste C Columbus (43222) ***(G-8123)***
Multifab, Elyria *Also called Multilink Inc* ***(G-10540)***
Multilink Inc..........440 366-6966
580 Ternes Ln Elyria (44035) ***(G-10540)***
Munich Reinsurance America Inc..........614 221-7123
471 E Broad St Fl 17 Columbus (43215) ***(G-8124)***
Municipal Garage, Cleveland *Also called City of Lakewood* ***(G-5208)***
Municipal Golf Course, Pickerington *Also called City of Pickerington* ***(G-15951)***
Municipal Government, Toledo *Also called City of Toledo* ***(G-17655)***
Municipal Power Plant, Hamilton *Also called City of Hamilton* ***(G-11580)***
Municipal Water Supply, Kent *Also called City of Akron* ***(G-12221)***
Municpal Cntrs Saling Pdts Inc..........513 482-3300
7740 Reinhold Dr Cincinnati (45237) ***(G-4085)***
Mural & Son Inc..........216 267-3322
11340 Brookpark Rd Cleveland (44130) ***(G-6025)***

ALPHABETIC

Murphy Contracting Co 330 743-8915
  285 Andrews Ave Youngstown (44505) *(G-20133)*
Murphy Tractor & Eqp Co Inc 513 772-3232
  11441 Mosteller Rd Cincinnati (45241) *(G-4086)*
Murray & Murray Co Lpa (PA) 419 624-3000
  111 E Shoreline Dr Ste 2 Sandusky (44870) *(G-16627)*
Murray American Energy Inc 740 338-3100
  46226 National Rd Saint Clairsville (43950) *(G-16496)*
Murray Guttman 513 984-0300
  4901 Hunt Rd Ste 300 Blue Ash (45242) *(G-1617)*
Murray Leasing Inc 330 386-4757
  14778 E Liverpool Rd East Liverpool (43920) *(G-10408)*
Murray Ridge Production Center 440 329-3734
  1091 Infirmary Rd Elyria (44035) *(G-10541)*
Murray Wells Wendeln & Robinsn, Piqua *Also called Murray Wlls Wndeln Rbnson*
Cpas *(G-16015)*
Murray Wlls Wndeln Rbnson Cpas (PA) 937 773-6373
  326 N Wayne St Piqua (45356) *(G-16015)*
Murtech Consulting LLC 216 328-8580
  4700 Rockside Rd Ste 310 Cleveland (44131) *(G-6026)*
Murwood Real Estate Group LLC 216 839-5500
  29225 Chagrin Blvd Beachwood (44122) *(G-1085)*
Museum Cntmprary Art Cleveland 216 421-8671
  11400 Euclid Ave Cleveland (44106) *(G-6027)*
Musical Arts Association (PA) 216 231-7300
  11001 Euclid Ave Cleveland (44106) *(G-6028)*
Muskingum Cnty Ctr For Seniors 740 454-9761
  160 Nth St Zanesville (44701) *(G-20333)*
Muskingum Coach Company (PA) 740 622-2545
  1662 S 2nd St Coshocton (43812) *(G-9023)*
Muskingum County Adult and CHI 740 849-2344
  4155 Roseville Rd Zanesville (43701) *(G-20334)*
Muskingum County Engineers Off, Zanesville *Also called Muskingum County*
Ohio (G-20337)
MUSKINGUM COUNTY HEADSTART, Zanesville *Also called Child Care Resources*
Inc (G-20295)
Muskingum County Home, Zanesville *Also called Muskingum County Ohio (G-20336)*
Muskingum County Ohio 740 452-0678
  160 N 4th St Zanesville (43701) *(G-20335)*
Muskingum County Ohio 740 454-1911
  401 Main St Zanesville (43701) *(G-20336)*
Muskingum County Ohio 740 453-0381
  155 Rehl Rd Zanesville (43701) *(G-20337)*
Muskingum Iron & Metal Co 740 452-9351
  345 Arthur St Zanesville (43701) *(G-20338)*
Muskingum Livestock Auction, Zanesville *Also called Muskingum Livestock Sales*
Inc (G-20339)
Muskingum Livestock Sales Inc 740 452-9984
  944 Malinda St Zanesville (43701) *(G-20339)*
Muskingum Residentials Inc 740 453-5350
  1900 Montgomery Ave Zanesville (43701) *(G-20340)*
Muskingum Starlight Industries (PA) 740 453-4622
  1304 Newark Rd Zanesville (43701) *(G-20341)*
Muskingum Starlight Industries 740 453-4622
  1330 Newark Rd Zanesville (43701) *(G-20342)*
Muskingum Vly Bancshares Inc 740 984-2381
  Ullman & Fifth Sts # 5 Beverly (45715) *(G-1464)*
Muskingum Vly Nrsing Rhblttion 740 984-4262
  501 Pinecrest Dr Beverly (45715) *(G-1465)*
Muskingum Vly Symphonic Winds 740 826-8095
  163 Stormont St New Concord (43762) *(G-14901)*
Muskingum Wtrshed Cnsrvncy Dst 330 343-6647
  1319 3rd St Nw New Philadelphia (44663) *(G-14974)*
Muskingum Wtrshed Cnsrvncy Dst 740 685-6013
  22172 Park Rd Senecaville (43780) *(G-16670)*
Muskingum Wtrshed Cnsrvncy Dst 330 343-6780
  4956 Shop Rd Ne Mineral City (44656) *(G-14507)*
Mussun Sales Inc (PA) 216 431-5088
  3419 Carnegie Ave Cleveland (44115) *(G-6029)*
Mustard Seed Health Fd Mkt Inc 440 519-3663
  6025 Kruse Dr Ste 100 Solon (44139) *(G-16875)*
Mutual Health Services Company 216 687-7000
  2060 E 9th St Cleveland (44115) *(G-6030)*
Mutual Holding Company, Cleveland *Also called Mutual Health Services Company (G-6030)*
Mutual Shareholder Svcs LLC 440 922-0067
  8000 Town Centre Dr # 400 Broadview Heights (44147) *(G-1838)*
Mv Communities, Cincinnati *Also called Miller-Vlntine Partners Ltd Lc (G-4055)*
Mv Land Development Company 937 293-0900
  137 N Main St Ste 900 Dayton (45402) *(G-9649)*
Mv Residential Cnstr Inc 513 588-1000
  9349 Waterstone Blvd # 200 Cincinnati (45249) *(G-4087)*
Mv Residential Development LLC 937 293-0900
  4000 Miller Valentine Ct Moraine (45439) *(G-14682)*
Mv Transportation Inc 419 627-0740
  1230 N Depot St Sandusky (44870) *(G-16628)*
Mv Transportation Inc 740 681-5086
  1801 Transpark Dr Cincinnati (45229) *(G-4088)*
Mvcap, Dayton *Also called Miami Valley Community Action (G-9617)*
Mvcdc, Dayton *Also called Miami Vly Child Dev Ctrs Inc (G-9628)*
Mvd Communications LLC (PA) 513 683-4711
  5188 Cox Smith Rd Mason (45040) *(G-13621)*

Mvd Connect, Mason *Also called Mvd Communications LLC (G-13621)*
Mvfl, Lebanon *Also called Miami Vly Fandom For Literacy (G-12486)*
Mvhe Inc (HQ) 937 499-8211
  110 N Main St Ste 370 Dayton (45402) *(G-9650)*
MVHO, Dayton *Also called Miami Vly Hsing Oprtunties Inc (G-9630)*
Mvi Home Care, Youngstown *Also called Mahoning Vly Infusioncare Inc (G-20111)*
Mw Mielke, Medina *Also called Marvin W Mielke Inc (G-13969)*
Mw Mosaic, Toledo *Also called Midwest Mosaic Inc (G-17915)*
Mwa Enterprises Ltd 419 599-3835
  900 American Rd Napoleon (43545) *(G-14812)*
Mwd Logistics Inc 419 342-6253
  151 S Martin Dr Shelby (44875) *(G-16748)*
Mwd Logistics Inc 440 266-2500
  7236 Justin Way Mentor (44060) *(G-14091)*
Mxd Group, New Albany *Also called Ryder Last Mile Inc (G-14873)*
Mxr Sourceone, Mentor *Also called Sourceone Healthcare Tech Inc (G-14111)*
My Community Health Center 330 363-6242
  2600 7th St Sw Canton (44710) *(G-2413)*
My First Days Daycare LLC 419 466-3354
  580 N Byrne Rd Toledo (43607) *(G-17927)*
My Lawn Ldscp & Irrigation Co, Spring Valley *Also called Tim Mundy (G-16959)*
My Place Child Care 740 349-3505
  1335 E Main St Newark (43055) *(G-15078)*
Myca Mltmdia Trning Sltons LLC 513 544-2379
  4555 Lake Forest Dr # 650 Blue Ash (45242) *(G-1618)*
MYCAP, Youngstown *Also called Mahoning Youngstown Community (G-20112)*
Mycity Transportation Co 216 591-1900
  16781 Shgrin Blvd Ste 283 Shaker Heights (44120) *(G-16711)*
Myers Bus Parts and Sups Co 330 533-2275
  8860 Akron Canfield Rd Canfield (44406) *(G-2150)*
Myers Equipment, Canfield *Also called Myers Bus Parts and Sups Co (G-2150)*
Myers Equipment Corporation 330 533-5556
  8860 Akron Canfield Rd Canfield (44406) *(G-2151)*
Myers Industries Inc (PA) 330 253-5592
  1293 S Main St Akron (44301) *(G-342)*
Myers Machinery Movers Inc 614 871-5052
  2210 Hardy Parkway St Grove City (43123) *(G-11455)*
Myers/Schmalenberger Inc (PA) 614 621-2796
  462 S Ludlow St Columbus (43215) *(G-8125)*
Myocare Nursing Home Inc 216 252-7555
  24340 Sperry Dr Cleveland (44145) *(G-6031)*
Mzf Inc 216 464-3910
  27629 Chagrin Blvd 101b Cleveland (44122) *(G-6032)*
N & C Active Learning LLC 937 545-1342
  1380 N Fairfield Rd Beavercreek (45432) *(G-1172)*
N A A C P, Youngstown *Also called Natio Assoc For The Advan of (G-20136)*
N A L C, Northwood *Also called National Assn Ltr Carriers (G-15400)*
N A S, Cleveland *Also called Nas Rcrtment Cmmunications LLC (G-6036)*
N C B International Department 216 488-7990
  23000 Millcreek Blvd # 7350 Cleveland (44122) *(G-6033)*
N C B-F S B, Hillsboro *Also called National Cooperative Bank NA (G-11853)*
N C R Employee Benefit Assn 937 299-3571
  4435 Dogwood Trl Dayton (45429) *(G-9651)*
N Cook Inc 513 275-9872
  5762 Argus Rd Cincinnati (45224) *(G-4089)*
N E C Columbus, Columbus *Also called National Electric Coil Inc (G-8131)*
N F Mansuetto & Sons Inc 740 633-7320
  116 Wood St Martins Ferry (43935) *(G-13477)*
N L C, Independence *Also called Nations Lending Corporation (G-12102)*
N P I, Cleveland *Also called Neighborhood Progress Inc (G-6054)*
N P I Audio Video Solutions, Cleveland *Also called Northeast Projections Inc (G-6094)*
N P Motel System Inc 330 339-7731
  145 Bluebell Dr Sw New Philadelphia (44663) *(G-14975)*
N R I, Columbus *Also called Nationwide Rlty Investors Ltd (G-8161)*
N Safe Sound Security Inc 888 317-7233
  5555 County Road 203 Millersburg (44654) *(G-14485)*
N Services Inc 513 793-2000
  10901 Reed Hartman Hwy Blue Ash (45242) *(G-1619)*
N W O, Northwood *Also called Nwo Beverage Inc (G-15403)*
N Wasserstrom & Sons Inc (HQ) 614 228-5550
  2300 Lockbourne Rd Columbus (43207) *(G-8126)*
N-T Steel, Cleveland *Also called Associated Steel Company Inc (G-5015)*
N. S. Farrington & Co., Fairfield *Also called Norm Sharlotte Inc (G-10760)*
Nabisco, Streetsboro *Also called Mondelez Global LLC (G-17262)*
Nacco Industries Inc (PA) 440 229-5151
  5875 Landerbrook Dr # 220 Cleveland (44124) *(G-6034)*
Nadler Nadler & Burdman Co Lpa 330 533-6195
  6550 Seville Dr Ste B Canfield (44406) *(G-2152)*
Naf Wright Patterson Afb, Dayton *Also called Air Force US Dept of (G-9157)*
Nahhas, Ahed T MD, Toledo *Also called Toledo Cardiology Inc (G-18077)*
Nai Ohio Equities, Realtors, Columbus *Also called Ohio Equities LLC (G-8253)*
Nam Showcase Cinemas Milford, Milford *Also called National Amusements Inc (G-14413)*
Nami of Preble County Ohio 937 456-4947
  800 E Saint Clair St Eaton (45320) *(G-10455)*
Namru-Dayton, Dayton *Also called United States Dept of Navy (G-9189)*
Namsa, Northwood *Also called North Amercn Science Assoc Inc (G-15401)*

(G-0000) Company's Geographic Section entry number

Namsa Sterilzation Products, Northwood *Also called North Amercn Science Assoc Inc* **(G-15402)**
Nanaeles Day Care Inc 216 991-6139
3685 Lee Rd Cleveland (44120) **(G-6035)**
Nannicola Wholesale Co 330 799-0888
2750 Salt Springs Rd Youngstown (44509) **(G-20134)**
NAPA Auto Parts, Mentor *Also called MJ Auto Parts Inc* **(G-14088)**
Napoleon Machine LLC 419 591-7010
476 E Riverview Ave Napoleon (43545) **(G-14813)**
Napoleon Wash-N-Fill Inc (PA) 419 422-7216
339 E Main Cross St Findlay (45840) **(G-10947)**
Napoleon Wash-N-Fill Inc (PA) 419 592-0851
485 N Perry St Napoleon (43545) **(G-14814)**
Naragon Companies Inc 330 745-7700
2197 Wadsworth Rd Norton (44203) **(G-15420)**
Narrow Way Custom Technology 937 743-1611
100 Industry Dr Carlisle (45005) **(G-2553)**
Nas Rcrtment Cmmunications LLC (HQ) 216 478-0300
9700 Rockside Rd Ste 170 Cleveland (44125) **(G-6036)**
Nas Ventures 614 338-8501
4477 E 5th Ave Columbus (43219) **(G-8127)**
NASA-Trmi Group Inc 937 387-6517
7918 N Main St Dayton (45415) **(G-9652)**
Nasco Roofing and Cnstr Inc 330 746-3566
1900 Mccartney Rd Youngstown (44505) **(G-20135)**
Nassief Automotive Inc 440 997-5151
2920 Gh Dr Austinburg (44010) **(G-853)**
Nassief Honda, Austinburg *Also called Nassief Automotive Inc* **(G-853)**
Nat'l Rglartory RES Institutue, Columbus *Also called Ohio State University* **(G-8341)**
Nate, Cincinnati *Also called August Food & Wine LLC* **(G-3003)**
Natio Assoc For The Advan of 330 782-9777
1350 5th Ave Youngstown (44504) **(G-20136)**
National Administative Svc LLC 614 358-3607
400 Metro Pl N Ste 360 Dublin (43017) **(G-10285)**
National Affrdbl Hsing Tr Inc (PA) 614 451-9929
2245 N Bank Dr Ste 200 Columbus (43220) **(G-8128)**
National All-Jersey Inc (PA) 614 861-3636
6486 E Main St Reynoldsburg (43068) **(G-16321)**
National Amusements Inc 513 699-1500
500 Rivers Edge Milford (45150) **(G-14413)**
National Amusements Inc 513 699-1500
760 Cincinnati Mills Dr Cincinnati (45240) **(G-4090)**
National Amusements Inc 419 215-3095
2300 Village Dr W # 1700 Maumee (43537) **(G-13823)**
National Assn Ltr Carriers 419 289-8359
530 Claremont Ave Ashland (44805) **(G-683)**
National Assn Ltr Carriers 419 693-8392
4437 Woodville Rd Northwood (43619) **(G-15400)**
National Auto Care Corporation 800 548-1875
440 Polaris Pkwy Ste 250 Westerville (43082) **(G-19187)**
National Auto Experts LLC 440 274-5114
8370 Dow Cir Ste 100 Strongsville (44136) **(G-17336)**
National Benevolent Associatio 216 476-0333
4614 Prospect Ave Ste 240 Cleveland (44103) **(G-6037)**
National Blanking LLC 419 385-0636
135 N Fearing Blvd Toledo (43607) **(G-17928)**
National Board of Boiler (PA) 614 888-8320
1055 Crupper Ave Columbus (43229) **(G-8129)**
National Bronze Mtls Ohio Inc 440 277-1226
5311 W River Rd Lorain (44055) **(G-12929)**
National Car Mart III Inc 216 398-2228
9255 Brookpark Rd Cleveland (44129) **(G-6038)**
National Car Rental, Strongsville *Also called Clerac LLC* **(G-17290)**
National Center For Space Expl, Cleveland *Also called Universities Space Res Assn* **(G-6584)**
National Ch Rsdnces Brstol Vlg, Waverly *Also called Waverly Care Center Inc* **(G-18824)**
National Ch Rsdnces Stygler Rd, Columbus *Also called Traditions At Stygler Road* **(G-8772)**
National Ch Rsidences Mill Run, Hilliard *Also called Traditions At Mill Run* **(G-11823)**
National Child Support Center, Blue Ash *Also called Innovtive Cllectn Concepts Inc* **(G-1584)**
National Church, Cuyahoga Falls *Also called Traditions At Bath Rd Inc* **(G-9132)**
National Church Residences (PA) 614 451-2151
2335 N Bank Dr Columbus (43220) **(G-8130)**
NATIONAL CHURCH RESIDENCES CENTER FOR SENIOR HEALTH, Columbus *Also called Heritage Day Health Centers* **(G-7744)**
NATIONAL CHURCH RESIDENCES FIRST COMMUNITY VILLAGE, Columbus *Also called First Community Village* **(G-7585)**
National City Bank, Akron *Also called PNC Bank National Association* **(G-387)**
National City Bank, Newark *Also called PNC Bank National Association* **(G-15092)**
National City Bank, Sandusky *Also called PNC Bank National Association* **(G-16632)**
National City Bank, Toledo *Also called PNC Bank National Association* **(G-17981)**
National City Cmnty Dev Corp 216 575-2000
1900 E 9th St Cleveland (44114) **(G-6039)**
National City Mortgage 614 401-5030
545 Metro Pl S Ste 100 Dublin (43017) **(G-10286)**
National City Mortgage Inc (HQ) 937 910-1200
3232 Newmark Dr Miamisburg (45342) **(G-14196)**
National Colloid Company 740 282-1171
906 Adams St Steubenville (43952) **(G-17168)**
National Compressor Svcs LLC (PA) 419 868-4980
10349 Industrial St Holland (43528) **(G-11900)**
National Concession Company 216 881-9911
4582 Willow Pkwy Cleveland (44125) **(G-6040)**
National Conference of Veteran, Cincinnati *Also called Mercy Health* **(G-4015)**
National Consumer Coop Bnk 937 393-4246
139 S High St Hillsboro (45133) **(G-11852)**
National Continental Insur Co 631 320-2405
6300 Wilson Mills Rd Cleveland (44143) **(G-6041)**
National Cooperative Bank NA (HQ) 937 393-4246
139 S High St Ste 1 Hillsboro (45133) **(G-11853)**
National Dentex LLC 216 671-0577
3873 Rocky River Dr Cleveland (44111) **(G-6042)**
National Electric Coil Inc (PA) 614 488-1151
800 King Ave Columbus (43212) **(G-8131)**
National Electro-Coatings Inc 216 898-0080
15655 Brookpark Rd Cleveland (44142) **(G-6043)**
National Engrg & Contg Co 440 238-3331
50 Public Sq Ste 2175 Cleveland (44113) **(G-6044)**
National Engrg Archtctral Svcs, Columbus *Also called Barr Engineering Incorporated* **(G-7019)**
National Entp Systems Inc (PA) 440 542-1360
29125 Solon Rd Solon (44139) **(G-16876)**
National Exchange Club 419 535-3232
3050 W Central Ave Toledo (43606) **(G-17929)**
National Exchange Club Foundat 419 535-3232
3050 W Central Ave Toledo (43606) **(G-17930)**
National Express Transit Corp 513 322-6214
8041 Hosbrook Rd Ste 330 Cincinnati (45236) **(G-4091)**
National Flight Services Inc (HQ) 419 865-2311
10971 E Airport Svc Rd Swanton (43558) **(G-17402)**
National Football Museum Inc 330 456-8207
2121 George Halas Dr Nw Canton (44708) **(G-2414)**
National Gas & Oil Corporation (HQ) 740 344-2102
1500 Granville Rd Newark (43055) **(G-15079)**
National Gas & Oil Corporation 740 454-7252
1423 Lake Dr Zanesville (43701) **(G-20343)**
National Gas Oil Corp 740 348-1243
120 O Neill Dr Hebron (43025) **(G-11721)**
National General Insurance 212 380-9462
800 Superior Ave E Cleveland (44114) **(G-6045)**
National Golf Links, South Charleston *Also called Bw Enterprises Inc* **(G-16923)**
National Ground Water Assn Inc 614 898-7791
601 Dempsey Rd Westerville (43081) **(G-19284)**
National Guard Ohio 614 492-3166
7370 Minuteman Way Columbus (43217) **(G-8132)**
National Heat Exch Clg Corp 330 482-0893
8397 Southern Blvd Youngstown (44512) **(G-20137)**
National Heritg Academies Inc 937 223-2889
501 Hickory St Dayton (45410) **(G-9653)**
National Heritg Academies Inc 513 251-6000
1798 Queen City Ave Cincinnati (45214) **(G-4092)**
National Heritg Academies Inc 419 269-2247
5130 Bennett Rd Toledo (43612) **(G-17931)**
National Heritg Academies Inc 513 751-5555
1712 Duck Creek Rd Cincinnati (45207) **(G-4093)**
National Heritg Academies Inc 419 531-3285
305 Wenz Rd Toledo (43615) **(G-17932)**
National Heritg Academies Inc 937 235-5498
173 Avondale Dr Dayton (45404) **(G-9654)**
National Heritg Academies Inc 937 278-6671
3901 Turner Rd Dayton (45415) **(G-9655)**
National Heritg Academies Inc 216 731-0127
860 E 222nd St Euclid (44123) **(G-10650)**
National Heritg Academies Inc 216 451-1725
16005 Terrace Rd Cleveland (44112) **(G-6046)**
National Heritg Academies Inc 330 792-4806
2420 Donald Ave Youngstown (44509) **(G-20138)**
National Highway Equipment Co 614 459-4900
971 Old Henderson Rd Columbus (43220) **(G-8133)**
National Hot Rod Association 740 928-5706
2650 National Rd Sw Ste B Hebron (43025) **(G-11722)**
National Housing Corporation (PA) 614 481-8106
45 N 4th St Ste 200 Columbus (43215) **(G-8134)**
National Housing Tr Ltd Partnr 614 451-9929
2335 N Bank Dr Columbus (43220) **(G-8135)**
National Interstate Corp (HQ) 330 659-8900
3250 Interstate Dr Richfield (44286) **(G-16363)**
National Interstate Insur Co (HQ) 330 659-8900
3250 Interstate Dr Richfield (44286) **(G-16364)**
National Labor Relations Board 216 522-3716
1240 E 9th St Ste 1695 Cleveland (44199) **(G-6047)**
National Lien Digest, Highland Heights *Also called C & S Associates Inc* **(G-11732)**
National Lime and Stone Co 419 396-7671
370 N Patterson St Carey (43316) **(G-2545)**
National Lime and Stone Co 740 548-4206
2406 S Section Line Rd Delaware (43015) **(G-9997)**
National Lime and Stone Co 419 562-0771
4580 Bethel Rd Bucyrus (44820) **(G-1997)**
National Lime and Stone Co 419 423-3400
9860 County Road 313 Findlay (45840) **(G-10948)**
National Lime and Stone Co 614 497-0083
5911 Lockbourne Rd Lockbourne (43137) **(G-12823)**

ALPHABETIC

National Lime Stone Clmbus Reg, Delaware *Also called National Lime and Stone Co* ***(G-9997)***
National Liquidators, Cleveland *Also called G Robert Toney & Assoc Inc* ***(G-5588)***
National Marketshare Group (PA)....513 921-0800
2155 W 8th St Cincinnati (45204) ***(G-4094)***
National Mentor Inc....216 525-1885
9800 Rockside Rd Ste 800 Cleveland (44125) ***(G-6048)***
National Metal Trading LLC....440 487-9771
3950 Ben Hur Ave Willoughby (44094) ***(G-19553)***
National Multiple Sclerosis....330 759-9066
4300 Belmont Ave Youngstown (44505) ***(G-20139)***
National Office, Cleveland *Also called National Electro-Coatings Inc* ***(G-6043)***
National Railroad Pass Corp....419 246-0159
415 Emerald Ave Toledo (43604) ***(G-17933)***
National Realty Services Inc (HQ)....614 798-0971
2261 Sandover Rd Columbus (43220) ***(G-8136)***
National Registry-Emergency, Columbus *Also called National Rgstry Emrgncy Mdcl* ***(G-8138)***
National Rent A Car, Vandalia *Also called National Rental (us) Inc* ***(G-18532)***
National Rent A Car, Columbus *Also called National Rental (us) Inc* ***(G-8137)***
National Rental (us) Inc....937 890-0100
3600 Terminal Rd Vandalia (45377) ***(G-18532)***
National Rental (us) Inc....614 239-3270
4600 International Gtwy Columbus (43219) ***(G-8137)***
National Rgstry Emrgncy Mdcl....614 888-4484
6610 Busch Blvd Columbus (43229) ***(G-8138)***
National Service Club, Toledo *Also called National Exchange Club Foundat* ***(G-17930)***
National Service Information....740 387-6806
145 Baker St Marion (43302) ***(G-13448)***
National Smallwares, Columbus *Also called Wasserstrom Company* ***(G-8878)***
National Staffing Alternative, Lima *Also called Rkpl Inc* ***(G-12732)***
National Staffing Group Ltd....440 546-0800
8221 Brecksville Rd # 202 Brecksville (44141) ***(G-1791)***
National Testing Laboratories (PA)....440 449-2525
6571 Wilson Mills Rd # 3 Cleveland (44143) ***(G-6049)***
National Trail Raceway, Hebron *Also called National Hot Rod Association* ***(G-11722)***
National Trnsp Solutions Inc....330 405-2660
1831 Highland Rd Twinsburg (44087) ***(G-18300)***
National Underground Railroad....513 333-7500
1301 Western Ave Cincinnati (45203) ***(G-4095)***
National Valuation Consultants....513 929-4100
441 Vine St Cincinnati (45202) ***(G-4096)***
National Veterinary Assoc Inc....330 652-0055
1007 Youngstown Warren Rd Niles (44446) ***(G-15161)***
National Weather Service....937 383-0031
1901 S State Route 134 Wilmington (45177) ***(G-19636)***
National Weather Service....216 265-2370
5301 W Hngr Fdral Fclties Cleveland (44135) ***(G-6050)***
National Weather Service....419 522-1375
2101 Harrington Mem Rd Mansfield (44903) ***(G-13226)***
National Yllow Pages Media LLC....216 447-9400
2 Summit Park Dr Ste 630 Independence (44131) ***(G-12101)***
National Youth Advocate Progra....740 349-7511
15 N 3rd St Fl 3 Newark (43055) ***(G-15080)***
National Youth Advocate Progra (PA)....614 487-8758
1801 Watermark Dr Ste 200 Columbus (43215) ***(G-8139)***
National Youth Advocate Progra....614 252-6927
1303 E Main St Columbus (43205) ***(G-8140)***
NationaLease, Girard *Also called Aim Leasing Company* ***(G-11282)***
NationaLease, Girard *Also called Aim Integrated Logistics Inc* ***(G-11281)***
Nations Lending Corporation....440 842-4817
30700 Center Ridge Rd # 3 Westlake (44145) ***(G-19377)***
Nations Lending Corporation (PA)....440 842-4817
4 Summit Park Dr Ste 200 Independence (44131) ***(G-12102)***
Nations Roof of Ohio LLC....937 439-4160
275 S Pioneer Blvd Springboro (45066) ***(G-16978)***
Nations Title Agency of Ohio (HQ)....614 839-3848
3700 Corporate Dr Ste 200 Columbus (43231) ***(G-8141)***
Nationstar Mortgage LLC....614 985-9500
150 E Campus View Blvd Columbus (43235) ***(G-8142)***
Nationwide, Cincinnati *Also called Rick Blazing Insurance Agency* ***(G-4371)***
Nationwide Biweekly ADM Inc....937 376-5800
855 Lower Bellbrook Rd Xenia (45385) ***(G-19921)***
Nationwide Childrens Hospital....614 722-2700
700 Childrens Dr Columbus (43205) ***(G-8143)***
Nationwide Childrens Hospital....614 722-5750
555 S 18th St Ste 6g Columbus (43205) ***(G-8144)***
Nationwide Childrens Hospital (PA)....614 722-2000
700 Childrens Dr Columbus (43205) ***(G-8145)***
Nationwide Childrens Hospital....513 636-6000
796 Old State Route 74 # 200 Cincinnati (45245) ***(G-2862)***
Nationwide Childrens Hospital....330 253-5200
1 Canal Square Plz # 110 Akron (44308) ***(G-343)***
Nationwide Childrens Hospital....614 722-2000
700 Childrens Dr Columbus (43205) ***(G-8146)***
Nationwide Childrens Hospital....614 355-8300
433 N Cleveland Ave Westerville (43082) ***(G-19188)***
Nationwide Childrens Hospital....614 722-8200
655 E Livingston Ave Columbus (43205) ***(G-8147)***
Nationwide Childrens Hospital....614 864-9216
1310 Hill Rd N Pickerington (43147) ***(G-15964)***
Nationwide Childrens Hospital....614 355-0802
3433 Agler Rd Ste 1400 Columbus (43219) ***(G-8148)***
Nationwide Childrens Hospital....614 355-8100
6435 E Broad St Columbus (43213) ***(G-8149)***
Nationwide Childrens Hospital....614 355-9200
1125 E Main St Columbus (43205) ***(G-8150)***
Nationwide Childrens Hospital....614 355-8000
495 E Main St Columbus (43215) ***(G-8151)***
Nationwide Corporation (HQ)....614 249-7111
1 Nationwide Plz Columbus (43215) ***(G-8152)***
Nationwide Corporation....330 452-8705
1000 Market Ave N Canton (44702) ***(G-2415)***
Nationwide Corporation....614 277-5103
3400 Southpark Pl Ste A Grove City (43123) ***(G-11456)***
NATIONWIDE E&S/SPECIALTY, Columbus *Also called Freedom Specialty Insurance Co* ***(G-7622)***
Nationwide Energy Partners LLC....614 918-2031
230 West St Ste 150 Columbus (43215) ***(G-8153)***
Nationwide Fin Inst Dis Agency....614 249-6825
1 Nationwide Plz 2-0501 Columbus (43215) ***(G-8154)***
Nationwide Financial Svcs Inc (HQ)....614 249-7111
1 Nationwide Plz Columbus (43215) ***(G-8155)***
Nationwide General Insur Co....614 249-7111
1 W Nationwide Blvd # 100 Columbus (43215) ***(G-8156)***
Nationwide Health MGT LLC....440 888-8888
5700 Chevrolet Blvd Parma (44130) ***(G-15769)***
Nationwide Inv Svcs Corp....614 249-7111
2 Nationwide Plz Columbus (43215) ***(G-8157)***
Nationwide Life Insur Co Amer....800 688-5177
P.O. Box 182928 Columbus (43218) ***(G-8158)***
Nationwide Mutl Fire Insur Co (HQ)....614 249-7111
1 W Nationwide Blvd # 100 Columbus (43215) ***(G-8159)***
Nationwide Mutual Insurance Co (PA)....614 249-7111
1 Nationwide Plz Columbus (43215) ***(G-8160)***
Nationwide Mutual Insurance Co....402 420-6153
3400 Southpark Pl Ste A Grove City (43123) ***(G-11457)***
Nationwide Mutual Insurance Co....330 489-5000
1000 Market Ave N Canton (44702) ***(G-2416)***
Nationwide Mutual Insurance Co....614 948-4153
955 County Line Rd W Westerville (43082) ***(G-19189)***
Nationwide Mutual Insurance Co....614 430-3047
9243 Columbus Pike Lewis Center (43035) ***(G-12553)***
Nationwide Rlty Investors Ltd (HQ)....614 857-2330
375 N Front St Ste 200 Columbus (43215) ***(G-8161)***
Nationwide Rtrment Sltions Inc (HQ)....614 854-8300
5900 Parkwood Pl Dublin (43016) ***(G-10287)***
Nationwide Transport Llc....513 554-0203
4445 Lk Frest Dr Ste 475 Cincinnati (45242) ***(G-4097)***
Nationwide Truck Brokers Inc....937 335-9229
3355 S County Road 25a Troy (45373) ***(G-18217)***
Natl City Coml Capitol LLC....513 455-9746
995 Dalton Ave Cincinnati (45203) ***(G-4098)***
Natrop Inc....513 242-1375
4400 Reading Rd Cincinnati (45229) ***(G-4099)***
Natural Foods Inc (PA)....419 537-1713
3040 Hill Ave Toledo (43607) ***(G-17934)***
Natural Resources Ohio Dept....419 394-3611
834 Edgewater Dr Saint Marys (45885) ***(G-16528)***
Natural Resources Ohio Dept....419 938-5411
1098 Ashlnd Cnty Rd 300 Perrysville (44864) ***(G-15942)***
Natural Resources Ohio Dept....614 265-6948
2045 Morse Rd Bldg C Columbus (43229) ***(G-8162)***
Natural Resources Ohio Dept....614 265-6852
1894 Fountain Square Ct Columbus (43224) ***(G-8163)***
Nature Fresh Farms Usa Inc....419 330-5080
9250 Us Highway 20a Delta (43515) ***(G-10047)***
Nature Stone, Bedford *Also called Ohio Concrete Resurfacing Inc* ***(G-1297)***
Natures Bin, Lakewood *Also called Cornucopia Inc* ***(G-12339)***
Nautica Queen, Cleveland *Also called Paul A Ertel* ***(G-6183)***
Navigtor MGT Prtners Ltd Lblty....614 796-0090
1400 Goodale Blvd Ste 100 Columbus (43212) ***(G-8164)***
Navistar Intl Trnsp Corp....937 390-4242
5975 Urbana Rd Springfield (45502) ***(G-17087)***
Nayak, Naresh K MD, Marietta *Also called First Settlement Orthopaedics* ***(G-13329)***
Nb Trucking Inc....740 335-9331
1659 Rte 22 E Washington Court Hou (43160) ***(G-18784)***
Nba, Xenia *Also called Nationwide Biweekly ADM Inc* ***(G-19921)***
NBBJ Construction Services, Columbus *Also called NBBJ LLC* ***(G-8165)***
NBBJ LLC (PA)....206 223-5026
250 S High St Ste 300 Columbus (43215) ***(G-8165)***
Nbw Inc....216 377-1700
4556 Industrial Pkwy Cleveland (44135) ***(G-6051)***
NC Hha Inc....216 593-7750
1170 E Broad St Ste 101 Elyria (44035) ***(G-10542)***
Nca Financial Planners, Cleveland *Also called Financial Plnners of Cleveland* ***(G-5526)***
NCC ASSOCIATES, Columbus *Also called North Cntl Mntal Hlth Svcs Inc* ***(G-8198)***
NCMF, Canton *Also called Aultman North Canton Med Group* ***(G-2206)***
Ncop LLC....419 599-4070
240 Northcrest Dr Napoleon (43545) ***(G-14815)***
NCR At Home Health & Wellness....614 451-2151
2335 N Bank Dr Columbus (43220) ***(G-8166)***

NCR Corporation 330 497-7300
5590 Lauby Rd Ste J Canton (44720) ***(G-2417)***
NCR Country Club, Dayton *Also called N C R Employee Benefit Assn* ***(G-9651)***
Ncs Healthcare of Ohio LLC 330 364-5011
1360 Reimer Rd Wadsworth (44281) ***(G-18609)***
Ncs Healthcare of Ohio LLC (HQ) 513 719-2600
201 E 4th St Ste 900 Cincinnati (45202) ***(G-4100)***
Ncs Healthcare of Ohio LLC 614 534-0400
2305 Westbrooke Dr Bldg C Columbus (43228) ***(G-8167)***
Ncs Incorporated 440 684-9455
729 Miner Rd Cleveland (44143) ***(G-6052)***
Nds, Ravenna *Also called Neighborhood Development Svcs* ***(G-16250)***
Neace Assoc Insur Agcy of Ohio 614 224-0772
285 Cozzins St Columbus (43215) ***(G-8168)***
Neace Lukens, Rocky River *Also called Nl of Ky Inc* ***(G-16442)***
Neace Lukens, Columbus *Also called Nl of Ky Inc* ***(G-8192)***
Neals Construction Company 513 489-7700
7770 E Kemper Rd Cincinnati (45249) ***(G-4101)***
Neals Design Remodel, Cincinnati *Also called Neals Construction Company* ***(G-4101)***
Nearly New Shop, Findlay *Also called Blanchard Valley Hospital* ***(G-10873)***
Necco Center 740 534-1386
115 Private Road 977 Pedro (45659) ***(G-15800)***
Needmore Road Primary Care, Dayton *Also called Primary Cr Ntwrk Prmr Hlth Prt* ***(G-9707)***
Neff & Associates, Cleveland *Also called T J Neff Holdings Inc* ***(G-6494)***
Neff and Associates, Cleveland *Also called Dj Neff Enterprises Inc* ***(G-5432)***
Neff Group Distributors Inc 440 835-7010
909 Canterbury Rd Ste G Westlake (44145) ***(G-19378)***
Neff Machinery and Supplies 740 454-0128
112 S Shawnee Ave Zanesville (43701) ***(G-20344)***
Neff Parts, Zanesville *Also called Neff Machinery and Supplies* ***(G-20344)***
Neff Paving Ltd (PA) 740 453-3063
6575 West Pike Zanesville (43701) ***(G-20345)***
Nehemiah Manufacturing Co LLC 513 351-5700
1907 South St Cincinnati (45204) ***(G-4102)***
Neighborcare Inc (HQ) 513 719-2600
201 E 4th St Ste 900 Cincinnati (45202) ***(G-4103)***
Neighborhood Centers, Cleveland *Also called Gc Neighborhood Ctrs Assoc Inc* ***(G-5597)***
Neighborhood Development Svcs 330 296-2003
120 E Main St Ravenna (44266) ***(G-16250)***
Neighborhood Family Practice, Cleveland *Also called Neighborhood Health Care Inc* ***(G-6053)***
Neighborhood Health Asso (PA) 419 720-7883
313 Jefferson Ave Toledo (43604) ***(G-17935)***
Neighborhood Health Care Inc (PA) 216 281-8945
4115 Bridge Ave 300 Cleveland (44113) ***(G-6053)***
Neighborhood Health Care Inc (PA) 513 221-4949
2415 Auburn Ave Cincinnati (45219) ***(G-4104)***
Neighborhood House (PA) 614 252-4941
1000 Atcheson St Columbus (43203) ***(G-8169)***
Neighborhood Hsg Servs Toledo 419 691-2900
704 2nd St Toledo (43605) ***(G-17936)***
Neighborhood Logistics Co Inc 440 466-0020
5449 Bishop Rd Geneva (44041) ***(G-11244)***
Neighborhood Progress Inc (PA) 216 830-2770
11327 Shaker Blvd Ste 500 Cleveland (44104) ***(G-6054)***
Neighborhood Properties Inc 419 473-2604
2753 W Central Ave Toledo (43606) ***(G-17937)***
NEIL KENNEDY RECOVERY CLINIC, Youngstown *Also called Youngstown Committee On Alchol* ***(G-20260)***
Neil Kravitz Group Sales Inc 513 961-8697
412 S Cooper Ave Cincinnati (45215) ***(G-4105)***
Nelsen Corporation (PA) 330 745-6000
3250 Barber Rd Norton (44203) ***(G-15421)***
Nelson 216 781-9144
6000 Lombardo Ctr Ste 500 Seven Hills (44131) ***(G-16677)***
Nelson & Bold Inc 440 975-1422
36060 Euclid Ave Ste 201 Willoughby (44094) ***(G-19554)***
Nelson Financial Group 513 686-7800
3195 Dayton Xenia Rd # 900 Dayton (45434) ***(G-9182)***
Nelson Manufacturing Company 419 523-5321
6448 State Route 224 Ottawa (45875) ***(G-15660)***
Nelson Packaging Company Inc 419 229-3471
1801 Reservoir Rd Lima (45804) ***(G-12705)***
Nelson Park Apartments, Beachwood *Also called Npa Associates* ***(G-1088)***
Nelson Stark Company 513 489-0866
7685 Fields Ertel Rd D2 Cincinnati (45241) ***(G-4106)***
Nelson Stud Welding Inc 440 250-9242
101 Liberty Ct Elyria (44035) ***(G-10543)***
Nelson Tree Service Inc (HQ) 937 294-1313
3300 Office Park Dr # 205 Dayton (45439) ***(G-9656)***
Nemco Inc 419 542-7751
301 Meuse Argonne St Hicksville (43526) ***(G-11730)***
Nemco Food Equipment, Hicksville *Also called Nemco Inc* ***(G-11730)***
Nentwick Convalescent Home 330 385-5001
500 Selfridge St East Liverpool (43920) ***(G-10409)***
Neo-Pet LLC 440 893-9949
1894 E 123rd St Apt 1 Cleveland (44106) ***(G-6055)***
Neocap/Cbcf 330 675-2669
411 Pine Ave Se Warren (44483) ***(G-18733)***
Neocom, Warren *Also called Northeast Ohio Communic* ***(G-18735)***
Neopost USA Inc 440 526-3196
6670 W Snowville Rd Ste 2 Brecksville (44141) ***(G-1792)***
Nephrology Department, Cincinnati *Also called University of Cincinnati* ***(G-4721)***
Neptune Plumbing & Heating Co 216 475-9100
23860 Miles Rd Ste G Cleveland (44128) ***(G-6056)***
Nerone & Sons Inc 216 662-2235
19501 S Miles Rd Ste 1 Cleveland (44128) ***(G-6057)***
Nes, Solon *Also called National Entp Systems Inc* ***(G-16876)***
Nest Tenders Limited 614 901-1570
5083 Westerville Rd Columbus (43231) ***(G-8170)***
Nestle Product Technology Ctr, Marysville *Also called R & D Nestle Center Inc* ***(G-13524)***
Nestle Quality Assurance Ctr, Dublin *Also called Nestle Usa Inc* ***(G-10288)***
Nestle Usa Inc 513 576-4930
6279 Tri Ridge Blvd # 100 Loveland (45140) ***(G-13015)***
Nestle Usa Inc 614 526-5300
6625 Eiterman Rd Dublin (43016) ***(G-10288)***
NETCARE ACCESS, Columbus *Also called Netcare Corporation* ***(G-8171)***
Netcare Corporation (PA) 614 274-9500
199 S Cent Ave Columbus (43223) ***(G-8171)***
Netcare Corporation 614 274-9500
199 S Central Ave Columbus (43223) ***(G-8172)***
Netco, Cleveland *Also called National Engrg & Contg Co* ***(G-6044)***
Neteam Systems LLC 330 523-5100
1111 Superior Ave E # 1111 Cleveland (44114) ***(G-6058)***
Netjets Assn Shred Arcft Plots 614 532-0555
2740 Airport Dr Ste 330 Columbus (43219) ***(G-8173)***
Netjets Aviation Inc 614 239-5501
760 Morrison Rd Ste 250 Gahanna (43230) ***(G-11137)***
Netjets Inc (HQ) 614 239-5500
4111 Bridgeway Ave Columbus (43219) ***(G-8174)***
Netjets International Inc (HQ) 614 239-5500
4111 Bridgeway Ave Columbus (43219) ***(G-8175)***
Netjets Large Aircraft Inc 614 239-4853
4111 Bridgeway Ave Columbus (43219) ***(G-8176)***
Netjets Sales Inc 614 239-5500
4111 Bridgeway Ave Columbus (43219) ***(G-8177)***
Netmap Analytics, Worthington *Also called Verisk Crime Analytics Inc* ***(G-19857)***
Netsmart Technologies Inc 440 942-4040
30775 Bnbridge Rd Ste 200 Solon (44139) ***(G-16877)***
Nettleton Steel Treating Div, Cleveland *Also called Thermal Treatment Center Inc* ***(G-6521)***
Netwave Corporation 614 850-6300
5910 Wilcox Pl Ste F Dublin (43016) ***(G-10289)***
Network, Canton *Also called M Conley Company* ***(G-2383)***
Network Housing 2005 Inc 614 487-6700
1680 Watermark Dr Columbus (43215) ***(G-8178)***
Network Restorations II 614 253-0984
129 E 7th Ave Columbus (43201) ***(G-8179)***
Network Restorations III LLC 614 253-0984
910 E Broad St Columbus (43205) ***(G-8180)***
Neumeric Technologies Corp 248 204-0652
470 Olde Worthington Rd # 325 Westerville (43082) ***(G-19190)***
Neundorfer Inc 440 942-8990
4590 Hamann Pkwy Willoughby (44094) ***(G-19555)***
Neundorfer Engineering Service, Willoughby *Also called Neundorfer Inc* ***(G-19555)***
Neurological Associates Inc 614 544-4455
931 Chatham Ln Ste 200 Columbus (43221) ***(G-8181)***
Neurology Nroscience Assoc Inc (PA) 330 572-1011
701 White Pond Dr Akron (44320) ***(G-344)***
Neuroscience Center Inc 614 293-8930
1654 Upham Dr Fl 4 Columbus (43210) ***(G-8182)***
Neurosurgical Network Inc 419 251-1155
3909 Woodley Rd Ste 600 Toledo (43606) ***(G-17938)***
Neutral Telecom Corporation 440 377-4700
6472 Monroe Ln Ste 200 North Ridgeville (44039) ***(G-15338)***
New Age Communications Cnstr, Cincinnati *Also called Davey Resource Group Inc* ***(G-3401)***
New Age Container, Cleveland *Also called New Age Logistics LLC* ***(G-6059)***
New Age Logistics LLC 440 439-0846
7120 Krick Rd Ste 1b Cleveland (44146) ***(G-6059)***
New Albany Athc Booster CLB 614 413-8325
7600 Fodor Rd New Albany (43054) ***(G-14862)***
New Albany Care Center LLC 614 855-8866
5691 Thompson Rd Columbus (43230) ***(G-8183)***
New Albany Cleaning Services 614 855-9990
108 N High St Ste B New Albany (43054) ***(G-14863)***
New Albany Country Club Comm A 614 939-8500
1 Club Ln New Albany (43054) ***(G-14864)***
New Albany Links Dev Co Ltd 614 939-5914
7100 New Albany Links Dr New Albany (43054) ***(G-14865)***
New Albany Plain Loc SC Transp 614 855-2033
55 N High St Ste A New Albany (43054) ***(G-14866)***
New Albany Surgery Center LLC 614 775-1616
5040 Forest Dr Ste 100 New Albany (43054) ***(G-14867)***
New Avenues To Independence (PA) 216 481-1907
17608 Euclid Ave Cleveland (44112) ***(G-6060)***
New Avenues To Independence 216 671-8224
12131 Bennington Ave Cleveland (44135) ***(G-6061)***
New Avenues To Independence 888 853-8905
4230 Lake Ave Ashtabula (44004) ***(G-748)***
New Beginnings Pediatrics Inc 419 483-4122
1400 W Main St Ste G Bellevue (44811) ***(G-1381)***

ALPHABETIC

New Bgnnngs Assembly of God Ch 614 497-2658
492 Williams Rd Columbus (43207) ***(G-8184)***
New Birch Manor I Assoc LLC 330 723-3404
23875 Miner Dr Medina (44256) ***(G-13980)***
New Boston Aerie 2271 FOE 740 456-0171
3200 Rhodes Ave New Boston (45662) ***(G-14881)***
New Boston Eagles, New Boston *Also called New Boston Aerie 2271 FOE* ***(G-14881)***
New Carlisle Spt & Fitnes Ctr 937 846-1000
524 N Dayton Lakeview Rd New Carlisle (45344) ***(G-14895)***
New Channel Direct, Cleveland *Also called Angstrom Graphics Inc Midwest* ***(G-4981)***
NEW CONCEPTS, Toledo *Also called Philio Inc* ***(G-17976)***
New Concord Health Center 740 826-4135
1280 Friendship Dr New Concord (43762) ***(G-14902)***
New Dawn Child Care Center, Dover *Also called Dover City Schools* ***(G-10073)***
New Dawn Health Care Inc 330 343-5521
865 E Iron Ave Dover (44622) ***(G-10090)***
New Dawn Retirement Community, Dover *Also called New Dawn Health Care Inc* ***(G-10090)***
New Diamond Line Cont Corp 330 644-9993
760 Killian Rd Ste B Coventry Township (44319) ***(G-9039)***
New Directions Inc 216 591-0324
30800 Chagrin Blvd Cleveland (44124) ***(G-6062)***
New England Life Insurance Co 614 457-6233
921 Chatham Ln Ste 300 Columbus (43221) ***(G-8185)***
New England Rms Inc 401 384-6759
402 E Wilson Bridge Rd A Worthington (43085) ***(G-19830)***
New England Securities, Columbus *Also called New England Life Insurance Co* ***(G-8185)***
New Enland Life Ins Co, Columbus *Also called Mc Cloy Financial Services* ***(G-8042)***
New Haven Estates Inc (PA) 419 933-2181
2744 E State Highway 224 New Haven (44850) ***(G-14916)***
New Holland Lions Club, Williamsport *Also called International Assn Lions* ***(G-19499)***
New Hope & Horizons 513 761-7999
4055 Executive Park Dr # 100 Cincinnati (45241) ***(G-4107)***
New Hope Center, Mansfield *Also called County of Richland* ***(G-13159)***
New Hope Christian Academy 740 477-6427
2264 Walnut Creek Pike Circleville (43113) ***(G-4838)***
New Hope Vocational Services, Mentor *Also called Richcreek Bailey Rehabilitatio* ***(G-14104)***
New Horizon Youth Center Co 740 782-0092
40060 National Rd Bethesda (43719) ***(G-1456)***
New Horizon Youth Family Ctr (PA) 740 687-0835
1592 Granville Pike Lancaster (43130) ***(G-12421)***
New Horizons Surgery Center 740 375-5854
1167 Independence Ave Marion (43302) ***(G-13449)***
New Innovations Inc 330 899-9954
3540 Forest Lake Dr Uniontown (44685) ***(G-18380)***
New Jersey Aquarium LLC 614 414-7300
4016 Townsfair Way # 201 Columbus (43219) ***(G-8186)***
New Lexington City of 740 342-1633
215 S Main St New Lexington (43764) ***(G-14922)***
New Lexington Mncpl Water Plnt, New Lexington *Also called New Lexington City of* ***(G-14922)***
New Lfcare Hspitals Dayton LLC 937 384-8300
4000 Mmsburg Cntrville Rd Miamisburg (45342) ***(G-14197)***
New Life Christian Center 740 687-1572
2642 Clumbus Lancaster Rd Lancaster (43130) ***(G-12422)***
New Life Hospice Ctr St Joseph, Lorain *Also called New Life Hospice Inc* ***(G-12930)***
New Life Hospice Inc 440 934-1458
3500 Kolbe Rd Lorain (44053) ***(G-12930)***
New Life Hospice Inc (HQ) 440 934-1458
3500 Kolbe Rd Lorain (44053) ***(G-12931)***
New London Area Historical Soc 419 929-3674
210 E Main St New London (44851) ***(G-14933)***
New Lxngton Care Rhblttion Ctr, New Lexington *Also called Sunbridge Healthcare LLC* ***(G-14929)***
New Nghbors Rsdential Svcs Inc 937 717-5731
4230 E National Rd Springfield (45505) ***(G-17088)***
New NV Co LLC 330 896-7611
3777 Boettler Oaks Dr Uniontown (44685) ***(G-18381)***
New Path International LLC 614 410-3974
1476 Manning Pkwy Ste A Powell (43065) ***(G-16204)***
New Philadelphia General Svcs, New Philadelphia *Also called City of New Philadelphia* ***(G-14950)***
New Pittsburgh Fire & Rescue F 330 264-1230
3311 N Elyria Rd Wooster (44691) ***(G-19749)***
New River Electrical Corp 614 891-1142
6005 Westerville Rd Westerville (43081) ***(G-19285)***
New School Inc 513 281-7999
3 Burton Woods Ln Cincinnati (45229) ***(G-4108)***
NEW SCHOOL MONTESSORI, THE, Cincinnati *Also called New School Inc* ***(G-4108)***
New Tech West High School, Cleveland *Also called Cleveland Municipal School Dst* ***(G-5277)***
New Technology Steel LLC 419 385-0636
135 N Fearing Blvd Toledo (43607) ***(G-17939)***
New Technology Steel LLC (PA) 419 385-0636
2401 Front St Toledo (43605) ***(G-17940)***
New Vision Medical Labs, Lima *Also called St Ritas Medical Center* ***(G-12750)***
New Vulco Mfg & Sales Co LLC 513 242-2672
5353 Spring Grove Ave Cincinnati (45217) ***(G-4109)***
New Waterford Fireman 330 457-2363
3766 E Main St New Waterford (44445) ***(G-15006)***
New Wembley LLC 440 543-8171
8345 Woodberry Blvd Chagrin Falls (44023) ***(G-2675)***
New World Energy Resources (PA) 740 344-4087
1500 Granville Rd Newark (43055) ***(G-15081)***
New World Van Lines Ohio Inc 614 836-5720
4633 Homer Ohio Ln Groveport (43125) ***(G-11527)***
New York Community Bank 440 734-7040
4800 Great Northern Blvd North Olmsted (44070) ***(G-15300)***
New York Community Bank 216 741-7333
5767 Broadview Rd Cleveland (44134) ***(G-6063)***
New York Community Bank 216 736-3480
1801 E 9th St Cleveland (44114) ***(G-6064)***
New York Life Insurance Co 216 520-1345
6100 Oak Tree Blvd # 300 Independence (44131) ***(G-12103)***
New York Life Insurance Co 513 621-9999
5905 E Galbraith Rd # 4000 Cincinnati (45236) ***(G-4110)***
New York Life Insurance Co 216 221-1100
14600 Detroit Ave Apt 900 Lakewood (44107) ***(G-12357)***
Newark Care and Rehabilitation, Newark *Also called Newark Leasing LLC* ***(G-15083)***
Newark Care Center LLC 740 366-2321
151 Price Rd Newark (43055) ***(G-15082)***
Newark Corporation 330 523-4457
4180 Highlander Pkwy Richfield (44286) ***(G-16365)***
Newark Drywall Inc 740 763-3572
18122 Nashport Rd Nashport (43830) ***(G-14820)***
Newark Electronics Corporation 330 523-4912
4180 Highlander Pkwy Richfield (44286) ***(G-16366)***
NEWARK HILLS HEALTH AND REHABI, Newark *Also called Newark NH LLC* ***(G-15085)***
Newark Leasing LLC 740 344-0357
75 Mcmillen Dr Newark (43055) ***(G-15083)***
Newark Management Partners LLC 740 322-6455
50 N 2nd St Newark (43055) ***(G-15084)***
Newark Metropolitan Hotel, Newark *Also called Newark Management Partners LLC* ***(G-15084)***
Newark NH LLC 740 345-9197
17 Forry St Newark (43055) ***(G-15085)***
Newark Parcel Service Company 614 253-3777
640 N Cassady Ave Columbus (43219) ***(G-8187)***
Newark Resident Homes Inc 740 345-7231
15 W Saint Clair St Apt C Newark (43055) ***(G-15086)***
Newark Sleep Diagnostic Center 740 522-9499
1900 Tamarack Rd Ste 1908 Newark (43055) ***(G-15087)***
Newbold Technologies, East Liverpool *Also called Soaring Eagle Inc* ***(G-10418)***
Newcome Corp 614 848-5688
9005 Antares Ave Columbus (43240) ***(G-6826)***
Newcome Electronic Systems, Columbus *Also called Newcome Corp* ***(G-6826)***
Newcomer Concrete Services Inc (PA) 419 668-2789
646 Townline Road 151 Norwalk (44857) ***(G-15445)***
Newcomer Funeral Svc Group Inc 513 521-1971
7830 Hamilton Ave Cincinnati (45231) ***(G-4111)***
Newcomerstown Development Inc 740 498-5165
1100 E State Rd Newcomerstown (43832) ***(G-15133)***
Newcomerstown Progress Corp 740 498-5165
1100 E State Rd Newcomerstown (43832) ***(G-15134)***
Newell Brands Inc 419 662-2225
20750 Midstar Dr Bowling Green (43402) ***(G-1741)***
Newfound Technologies, Columbus *Also called Liberty Comm Sftwr Sltions Inc* ***(G-7970)***
Newlex Classic Riders Inc 740 342-3885
810 N Main St New Lexington (43764) ***(G-14923)***
Newmark & Company RE Inc 216 453-3000
1350 Euclid Ave Ste 300 Cleveland (44115) ***(G-6065)***
Newmark Grubb Knight Frank, Cleveland *Also called Newmark & Company RE Inc* ***(G-6065)***
Newport Walking Tours LLC 859 951-8560
6292 Eagles Lake Dr Cincinnati (45248) ***(G-4112)***
Newstart Loan , The, Cincinnati *Also called 722 Redemption Funding Inc* ***(G-2885)***
Newtown Nine Inc (PA) 440 781-0623
8155 Roll And Hold Pkwy Macedonia (44056) ***(G-13078)***
Newtown Nine Inc 330 376-7741
568 E Crosier St Akron (44311) ***(G-345)***
Nex Transport Inc 937 645-3761
13900 State Route 287 East Liberty (43319) ***(G-10394)***
Nexeo Solutions LLC 330 405-0461
1842 Enterprise Pkwy Twinsburg (44087) ***(G-18301)***
Nexeo Solutions LLC 330 405-0461
7577 State Route 821 Whipple (45788) ***(G-19442)***
Nexgen Building Supply, Cincinnati *Also called L & W Supply Corporation* ***(G-3899)***
Nexstar Broadcasting Inc 614 263-4444
3165 Olentangy River Rd Columbus (43202) ***(G-8188)***
Nexstar Broadcasting Inc 937 293-2101
4595 S Dixie Dr Moraine (45439) ***(G-14683)***
Nexstep Healthcare LLC 216 797-4040
673 Alpha Dr Ste G Cleveland (44143) ***(G-6066)***
Next Generation, Columbus *Also called Rcs Enterprises Inc* ***(G-8492)***
Nextel Communications Inc 513 891-9200
7878 Montgomery Rd Cincinnati (45236) ***(G-4113)***
Nextel Communications Inc 614 801-9267
1727 Stringtown Rd Grove City (43123) ***(G-11458)***
Nextel Partners Operating Corp 330 305-1365
6791 Strip Ave Nw North Canton (44720) ***(G-15223)***
Nextel Partners Operating Corp 419 380-2000
5350 Airport Hwy Ste 110 Toledo (43615) ***(G-17941)***

Nextmed Systems Inc (PA)....................216 674-0511
 16 Triangle Park Dr Cincinnati (45246) *(G-4114)*
Nextrx LLC..317 532-6000
 8990 Duke Blvd Mason (45040) *(G-13622)*
Nextt Corp..513 813-6398
 106 Koehler Ave Apt 4 Cincinnati (45215) *(G-4115)*
Nexus Engineering Group LLC (PA)............216 404-7867
 1422 Euclid Ave Ste 1400 Cleveland (44115) *(G-6067)*
Nexxtshow Exposition Svcs LLC...............877 836-3131
 645 Linn St Cincinnati (45203) *(G-4116)*
Neyer Management, Cincinnati *Also called Neyer Real Estate MGT LLC (G-4117)*
Neyer Real Estate MGT LLC....................513 618-6000
 3927 Brotherton Rd # 200 Cincinnati (45209) *(G-4117)*
Nf II Cleveland Op Co LLC.......................216 443-9043
 527 Prospect Ave E Cleveland (44115) *(G-6068)*
Nfgm Inc..800 236-2600
 6465 Reflections Dr # 240 Dublin (43017) *(G-10290)*
Nfm/Welding Engineers Inc.....................330 837-3868
 1339 Duncan St Sw Massillon (44647) *(G-13717)*
Ngic, Cleveland *Also called National General Insurance (G-6045)*
Ngm Inc..513 821-7363
 7676 Reinhold Dr Cincinnati (45237) *(G-4118)*
Ngn Electric Corp..................................330 923-2777
 10310 Brecksville Rd Brecksville (44141) *(G-1793)*
Ngts, Beavercreek Township *Also called Northrop Grumman Technical (G-1255)*
Ngwa, Westerville *Also called National Ground Water Assn Inc (G-19284)*
Nhs - Totco Inc.....................................419 691-2900
 704 2nd St Toledo (43605) *(G-17942)*
NHS WEATHERIZATION PROGRAM, Toledo *Also called Neighborhood Hsg Servs Toledo (G-17936)*
Nht, Columbus *Also called National Housing Tr Ltd Partnr (G-8135)*
Niagara Health Corporation (HQ)...............614 898-4000
 6150 E Broad St Columbus (43213) *(G-8189)*
Nichalex Inc...330 726-1422
 801 Kentwood Dr Youngstown (44512) *(G-20140)*
Nicholas Carney-Mc Inc.........................440 243-8560
 2931 Abbe Rd Sheffield Village (44054) *(G-16741)*
Nicholas D Starr Inc (PA).......................419 229-3192
 301 W Elm St Lima (45801) *(G-12706)*
Nicholas E Davis...................................937 228-2838
 40 N Main St Ste 1700 Dayton (45423) *(G-9657)*
Nick Amster Inc (PA).............................330 264-9667
 1700b Old Mansfield Rd Wooster (44691) *(G-19750)*
Nick Amster Inc....................................330 264-9667
 326 N Hillcrest Dr Ste C Wooster (44691) *(G-19751)*
Nick Mayer Lincoln-Mercury Inc...............440 835-3700
 24400 Center Ridge Rd Westlake (44145) *(G-19379)*
Nick Strimbu Inc (PA)............................330 448-4046
 3500 Parkway Dr Brookfield (44403) *(G-1855)*
Nick Strimbu Inc...................................330 448-4046
 303 Oxford St Dover (44622) *(G-10091)*
Nickle Bakery, Washington Court Hou *Also called Nb Trucking Inc (G-18784)*
Nickolas Rsidential Trtmnt Ctr.................937 496-7100
 5581 Dayton Liberty Rd Dayton (45417) *(G-9658)*
Nicola Gudbranson & Cooper LLC.............216 621-7227
 25 W Prospect Ave # 1400 Cleveland (44115) *(G-6069)*
Nicolozakes Trckg & Cnstr Inc..................740 432-5648
 8555 Georgetown Rd Cambridge (43725) *(G-2078)*
Niederst Management Ltd (PA)..................440 331-8800
 21400 Lorain Rd Cleveland (44126) *(G-6070)*
Nielsen Consumer Insights Inc.................513 489-9000
 4665 Cornell Rd Ste 160 Blue Ash (45241) *(G-1620)*
Nieman Plumbing Inc..............................513 851-5588
 2030 Stapleton Ct Cincinnati (45240) *(G-4119)*
Niese Leasing, Ottawa *Also called Niese Transport Inc (G-15661)*
Niese Transport Inc...............................419 523-4400
 418 N Agner St Ottawa (45875) *(G-15661)*
Nifco America Corporation.......................614 836-8733
 2435 Spiegel Dr Groveport (43125) *(G-11528)*
Nightingale Holdings LLC (PA)..................330 645-0200
 670 Jarvis Rd Akron (44319) *(G-346)*
Nightingale Home Healthcare....................614 408-0104
 5945 Wilcox Pl Ste C Dublin (43016) *(G-10291)*
Nightingale Montessori Inc......................937 324-0336
 1106 E High St Springfield (45505) *(G-17089)*
Nightingale Montessori School, Springfield *Also called Nightingale Montessori Inc (G-17089)*
Nightngl-Alan Med Eqp Svcs LLC...............513 247-8200
 11418 Deerfield Rd Bldg 1 Blue Ash (45242) *(G-1621)*
Nightrider Overnite Copy Svc, Cleveland *Also called Ricoh Usa Inc (G-6324)*
Nightrider Overnite Copy Svc, Akron *Also called Ricoh Usa Inc (G-408)*
Nilco LLC (HQ).......................................888 248-5151
 1221 W Maple St Ste 100 Hartville (44632) *(G-11695)*
Nilco LLC...330 538-3386
 489 Rosemont Rd North Jackson (44451) *(G-15249)*
Niles Generating Station, Niles *Also called NRG Power Midwest LP (G-15165)*
Niles Historical Society...........................330 544-2143
 503 Brown St Niles (44446) *(G-15162)*
Niles Iron & Metal Company LLC (PA)..........330 652-2262
 700 S Main St Niles (44446) *(G-15163)*

Niles Residential Care LLC.......................216 727-3996
 2567 Niles Vienna Rd Niles (44446) *(G-15164)*
Niles Scrap Iron & Metal Co, Niles *Also called Niles Iron & Metal Company LLC (G-15163)*
Nimers & Woody II Inc.............................937 898-2060
 7482 Webster St Vandalia (45377) *(G-18533)*
Nimishillen & Tuscarawas LLC..................330 438-5821
 2633 8th St Ne Canton (44704) *(G-2418)*
Nippon Express USA Inc..........................614 801-5695
 3705 Urbancrest Indus Dr Grove City (43123) *(G-11459)*
Nisbet Corporation.................................513 563-1111
 11575 Reading Rd Cincinnati (45241) *(G-4120)*
Nisource Inc...614 460-4878
 290 W Nationwide Blvd Columbus (43215) *(G-8190)*
Nissin Intl Trnspt USA Inc.......................937 644-2644
 16940 Square Dr Marysville (43040) *(G-13520)*
NJ Executive Services Inc........................614 239-2996
 4111 Bridgeway Ave Columbus (43219) *(G-8191)*
Njasap, Columbus *Also called Netjets Assn Shred Arcft Plots (G-8173)*
Nk Parts Industries Inc...........................937 493-4651
 2640 Campbell Rd Sidney (45365) *(G-16787)*
Nkp West, Sidney *Also called Nk Parts Industries Inc (G-16787)*
NI of Ky Inc..740 689-9876
 2680 Kull Rd Lancaster (43130) *(G-12423)*
NI of Ky Inc..216 643-7100
 1340 Depot St Ste 300 Rocky River (44116) *(G-16442)*
NI of Ky Inc..614 224-0772
 285 Cozzins St Columbus (43215) *(G-8192)*
NM Residential, Cleveland *Also called Niederst Management Ltd (G-6070)*
Nmoble Hardwoods, Beverly *Also called Adkins Timber Products Inc (G-1459)*
Nms Inc Certif Pub Accountants (PA)..........440 286-5222
 121 South St Chardon (44024) *(G-2706)*
Nmtc, Inc., Stow *Also called Matco Tools Corporation (G-17219)*
No Cages Harley-Davidson.......................614 764-2453
 7610 Commerce Pl Plain City (43064) *(G-16062)*
Noaca, Cleveland *Also called Northeast Ohio Areawide (G-6091)*
Noahs Ark Child Dev Ctr..........................513 988-0921
 3259 Wayne Madison Rd Trenton (45067) *(G-18189)*
Noahs Ark Creative Care..........................740 323-3664
 1255 Nadine Dr Newark (43056) *(G-15088)*
Noahs Ark Learning Center.......................740 965-1668
 100 Tippett Ct Ste 103 Sunbury (43074) *(G-17392)*
Noakes Rooney Rlty & Assoc Co..................419 423-4861
 2113 Tiffin Ave Ste 103 Findlay (45840) *(G-10949)*
Nobel County Engineers Office...................740 732-4400
 Courthouse Rm 220 St Rm 2 Caldwell (43724) *(G-2041)*
Nobel Learning Center.............................740 732-4722
 44135 Marietta Rd Caldwell (43724) *(G-2042)*
Noble Cnty Nble Cnty Cmmsoners...............740 732-4958
 44069 Marietta Rd Caldwell (43724) *(G-2043)*
Noble County Health Department, Caldwell *Also called Noble Cnty Nble Cnty Cmmsoners (G-2043)*
Noble Technologies Corp (PA)...................330 287-1530
 2020 Noble Dr Wooster (44691) *(G-19752)*
Noble-Davis Consulting Inc......................440 519-0850
 6190 Cochran Rd Ste D Solon (44139) *(G-16878)*
Nobletek, Wooster *Also called Noble Technologies Corp (G-19752)*
Noco Company......................................216 464-8131
 30339 Diamond Pkwy # 102 Solon (44139) *(G-16879)*
Nofziger Door Sales Inc (PA)....................419 337-9900
 320 Sycamore St Wauseon (43567) *(G-18808)*
Noggins Hair Design Inc..........................513 474-4405
 8556 Beechmont Ave # 450 Cincinnati (45255) *(G-4121)*
Noic, Sylvania *Also called Northern Ohio Investment Co (G-17438)*
Noland Company (HQ).............................937 396-7980
 3110 Kettering Blvd Moraine (45439) *(G-14684)*
Nollenberger Truck Center (PA).................419 837-5996
 5320 Fremont Pike Stony Ridge (43463) *(G-17185)*
Non Emergency Ambulance Svc..................330 296-4541
 4830 Harding Ave Ravenna (44266) *(G-16251)*
Noneman Real Estate Company...................419 531-4020
 3519 Secor Rd Toledo (43606) *(G-17943)*
Nooney & Moses, Akron *Also called Installed Building Pdts LLC (G-278)*
NOR Corp..440 366-0099
 10247 Dewhurst Rd Ste 101 Elyria (44035) *(G-10544)*
Noramco, Carrollton *Also called North American Plas Chem Inc (G-2573)*
Noramco Transport Corp (PA)....................513 245-9050
 9252 Colerain Ave Ste 4 Cincinnati (45251) *(G-4122)*
Norandex Bldg Mtls Dist Inc.....................330 656-8924
 300 Executive Park Hudson (44236) *(G-11999)*
Norandex Building Mtls Dist, Hudson *Also called Norandex Bldg Mtls Dist Inc (G-11999)*
Norcare Enterprises Inc (PA)....................440 233-7232
 6140 S Broadway Lorain (44053) *(G-12932)*
Norcia Bakery.......................................330 454-1077
 624 Belden Ave Ne Canton (44704) *(G-2419)*
Nord Center..440 233-7232
 6140 S Broadway Lorain (44053) *(G-12933)*
Nord Center Associates Inc (HQ)...............440 233-7232
 6140 S Broadway Lorain (44053) *(G-12934)*
Nord Center Associates Inc......................440 233-7232
 3150 Clifton Ave Lorain (44055) *(G-12935)*

Nord Rehabilitation Center, Lorain *Also called Nord Center Associates Inc* ***(G-12935)***
Nordmann Roofing Co Inc...419 691-5737
1722 Starr Ave Toledo (43605) ***(G-17944)***
Nordson Corporation...440 985-4496
300 Nordson Dr Amherst (44001) ***(G-594)***
Norfab, Elyria *Also called Northern Ohio Roofg Shtmtl Inc* ***(G-10549)***
Norfolk Southern Corporation...419 436-2408
3101 N Township Road 47 Fostoria (44830) ***(G-11009)***
Norfolk Southern Corporation...614 251-2684
3329 Thoroughbred Dr Columbus (43217) ***(G-8193)***
Norfolk Southern Corporation...419 381-5505
2101 Hill Ave Toledo (43607) ***(G-17945)***
Norfolk Southern Corporation...419 254-1562
341 Emerald Ave Toledo (43604) ***(G-17946)***
Norfolk Southern Corporation...440 992-2274
645 E 6th St Ashtabula (44004) ***(G-749)***
Norfolk Southern Corporation...440 992-2215
2886 Harbor Sta Ashtabula (44004) ***(G-750)***
Norfolk Southern Corporation...216 362-6087
6409 Clark Ave Cleveland (44102) ***(G-6071)***
Norfolk Southern Corporation...419 529-4574
2586 Park Ave W Ontario (44906) ***(G-15566)***
Norfolk Southern Corporation...419 483-1423
24424 N Prairie Rd Bellevue (44811) ***(G-1382)***
Norfolk Southern Corporation...419 485-3510
701 Linden St Montpelier (43543) ***(G-14617)***
Norfolk Southern Corporation...216 518-8407
5300 Greenhurst Ext Maple Heights (44137) ***(G-13290)***
Norfolk Southern Corporation...216 362-6087
4860 W 150th St Cleveland (44135) ***(G-6072)***
Norfolk Southern Corporation...740 353-4529
2435 8th St Portsmouth (45662) ***(G-16155)***
Norfolk Southern Corporation...937 297-5420
3101 Springboro Pike Moraine (45439) ***(G-14685)***
Norfolk Southern Corporation...513 977-3246
1410 Gest St Fl 2 Cincinnati (45203) ***(G-4123)***
Norfolk Southern Corporation...740 574-8491
914 Hayport Rd Wheelersburg (45694) ***(G-19436)***
Norfolk Southern Railway Co...440 439-1827
7847 Northfield Rd Bedford (44146) ***(G-1294)***
Norfolk Sthern Ashtbula Cltock, Ashtabula *Also called Norfolk Southern Corporation* ***(G-750)***
Norhteast Ohio Museum...330 336-7657
6807 Boneta Rd Medina (44256) ***(G-13981)***
Norm Sharlotte Inc...336 788-7705
300 Distribution Cir A Fairfield (45014) ***(G-10760)***
Norman Jones Enlow & Co (PA)...614 228-4000
226 N 5th St Ste 500 Columbus (43215) ***(G-8194)***
Norman Noble Inc...216 761-2133
6120 Parkland Blvd # 306 Cleveland (44124) ***(G-6073)***
Norman-Spencer Agency Inc (PA)...800 543-3248
8075 Washington Vlg Dr Dayton (45458) ***(G-9659)***
Normandy Group LLC...513 745-0990
5151 Pfeiffer Rd Ste 210 Blue Ash (45242) ***(G-1622)***
Normandy Manor of Rocky River...440 333-5401
22709 Lake Rd Rocky River (44116) ***(G-16443)***
Normandy Office Associates...513 381-8696
1055 Saint Paul Pl Cincinnati (45202) ***(G-4124)***
Normanity Town, Cincinnati *Also called Normandy Office Associates* ***(G-4124)***
Noron Inc...419 726-2677
5465 Enterprise Blvd Toledo (43612) ***(G-17947)***
Norris Brothers Co Inc...216 771-2233
2138 Davenport Ave Cleveland (44114) ***(G-6074)***
Norse Dairy Systems Inc...614 294-4931
1700 E 17th Ave Columbus (43219) ***(G-8195)***
Norstar Aluminum Molds Inc...440 632-0853
15986 Valplast St Middlefield (44062) ***(G-14273)***
North Amercn Science Assoc Inc (PA)...419 666-9455
6750 Wales Rd Northwood (43619) ***(G-15401)***
North Amercn Science Assoc Inc...419 666-9455
2261 Tracy Rd Northwood (43619) ***(G-15402)***
North American Broadcasting...614 481-7800
1458 Dublin Rd Columbus (43215) ***(G-8196)***
North American Plas Chem Inc...330 627-2210
750 Garfield Ave Nw Carrollton (44615) ***(G-2573)***
North American Properties Inc...513 721-2744
212 E 3rd St Ste 300 Cincinnati (45202) ***(G-4125)***
North American Van Lines, West Chester *Also called University Moving & Storage Co* ***(G-19027)***
North Bay Construction Inc...440 835-1898
25800 1st St Ste 1 Westlake (44145) ***(G-19380)***
North Branch Nursery Inc...419 287-4679
3359 Kesson Rd Pemberville (43450) ***(G-15805)***
North Broadway Childrens Ctr...614 262-6222
48 E North Broadway St Columbus (43214) ***(G-8197)***
North Canton City School Dst...330 497-5615
387 Pershing Ave Ne Canton (44720) ***(G-2420)***
North Canton Medical Offices, North Canton *Also called Kaiser Foundation Hospitals* ***(G-15214)***
North Canton Schl Transprtatn, Canton *Also called North Canton City School Dst* ***(G-2420)***
North Cape Manufacturing, Streetsboro *Also called Technology House Ltd* ***(G-17274)***
NORTH CENTER, THE, Lorain *Also called Norcare Enterprises Inc* ***(G-12932)***
North Central Elc Coop Inc...800 426-3072
350 Stump Pike Rd Attica (44807) ***(G-814)***
North Central Ems, Milan *Also called Norwalk Area Health Services* ***(G-14363)***
North Central Sales Inc...216 481-2418
528 E 200th St Cleveland (44119) ***(G-6075)***
North Cntl Mntal Hlth Svcs Inc (PA)...614 227-6865
1301 N High St Columbus (43201) ***(G-8198)***
North Coast Bearings LLC...440 930-7600
1050 Jaycox Rd Avon (44011) ***(G-896)***
North Coast Cancer Campus, Sandusky *Also called Cleveland Clinic Foundation* ***(G-16587)***
NORTH COAST CENTER, Willoughby *Also called Signature Health Inc* ***(G-19571)***
North Coast Coml Roofg Systems, Twinsburg *Also called Beacon Sales Acquisition Inc* ***(G-18250)***
North Coast Concrete Inc...216 642-1114
6061 Carey Dr Cleveland (44125) ***(G-6076)***
North Coast Lift Trck Ohio LLC...419 836-2100
300 W Mill St Curtice (43412) ***(G-9066)***
North Coast Logistics Inc (PA)...216 362-7159
18901 Snow Rd Frnt Brookpark (44142) ***(G-1903)***
North Coast Perennials Inc...440 428-1277
3754 Dayton Rd Madison (44057) ***(G-13105)***
North Coast Prof Co LLC...419 557-5541
1031 Pierce St Sandusky (44870) ***(G-16629)***
North Coast Sales...440 632-0793
15200 Madison Rd 101c Middlefield (44062) ***(G-14274)***
North Community Counseling Ctr (PA)...614 846-2588
4897 Karl Rd Columbus (43229) ***(G-8199)***
North Dayton School Discovery, Dayton *Also called National Heritg Academies Inc* ***(G-9655)***
North East Family Healthcare, Tallmadge *Also called Pioneer Physicians Networking* ***(G-17484)***
North East Mechanical Inc...440 871-7525
26200 1st St Westlake (44145) ***(G-19381)***
North East Ohio Health Svcs (PA)...216 831-6466
24200 Chagrin Blvd # 126 Beachwood (44122) ***(G-1086)***
North Electric Inc...216 331-4141
12117 Bennington Ave # 200 Cleveland (44135) ***(G-6077)***
North Gateway Tire Co Inc...330 725-8473
4001 Pearl Rd Medina (44256) ***(G-13982)***
North Hills Management Company...740 450-9999
1575 Bowers Ln Apt C13 Zanesville (43701) ***(G-20346)***
North Lima Dairy Queen Inc (PA)...330 549-3220
10067 Market St North Lima (44452) ***(G-15273)***
North Main Animal Clinic, Dayton *Also called Dayton Animal Hospital Assoc* ***(G-9350)***
North Ohio Heart Center...440 204-4000
3600 Kolbe Rd Ste 127 Lorain (44053) ***(G-12936)***
North Ohio Heart Center Inc...440 414-9500
7255 Old Oak Blvd C408 Cleveland (44130) ***(G-6078)***
North Ohio Heart Center Inc...440 366-3600
10325 Dewhurst Rd Elyria (44035) ***(G-10545)***
North Ohio Heart Center Inc...440 204-4000
1220 Moore Rd Ste B Avon (44011) ***(G-897)***
North Ohio Heart Center Inc (PA)...440 204-4000
3600 Kolbe Rd Ste 127 Lorain (44053) ***(G-12937)***
North Ohio Heart Center Inc...440 326-4120
125 E Broad St Ste 305 Elyria (44035) ***(G-10546)***
North Park Care Center LLC...440 250-4080
14803 Holland Rd Brookpark (44142) ***(G-1904)***
North Park Retirement Cmnty (PA)...216 267-0555
14801 Holland Rd Lbby Cleveland (44142) ***(G-6079)***
North Point Eductl Svc Ctr...440 967-0904
710 Cleveland Rd W Huron (44839) ***(G-12028)***
North Randall Village (PA)...216 663-1112
21937 Miles Rd Side Cleveland (44128) ***(G-6080)***
North Ridge Veterinary Hosp...440 428-5166
6336 N Ridge Rd Madison (44057) ***(G-13106)***
North Shore Door Co Inc...800 783-6112
162 Edgewood St Elyria (44035) ***(G-10547)***
North Shore Gastroenterology &, Westlake *Also called North Shore Gstrenterology Inc* ***(G-19382)***
North Shore Gstrenterology Inc...440 808-1212
850 Columbia Rd Ste 200 Westlake (44145) ***(G-19382)***
North Shore Retirement Cmnty...419 798-8203
9400 E Northshore Blvd Lakeside (43440) ***(G-12330)***
North Side Bank and Trust Co (PA)...513 542-7800
4125 Hamilton Ave Cincinnati (45223) ***(G-4126)***
North Side Bank and Trust Co...513 533-8000
2739 Madison Rd Cincinnati (45209) ***(G-4127)***
North Star Asphalt, Dalton *Also called Wenger Asphalt Inc* ***(G-9147)***
North Star Critical Care LLC...330 386-9110
16356 State Route 267 East Liverpool (43920) ***(G-10410)***
North Star Golf Club, Sunbury *Also called Championship Management Co* ***(G-17385)***
North Star Painting Co Inc...330 743-2333
3526 Mccartney Rd Youngstown (44505) ***(G-20141)***
North Star Realty Incorporated...513 737-1700
3501 Tylersville Rd Ste G Fairfield (45011) ***(G-10761)***
North Valley Bank (PA)...740 452-7920
2775 Maysville Pike Zanesville (43701) ***(G-20347)***
North Wood Realty (PA)...330 423-0837
1315 Boardman Poland Rd # 7 Youngstown (44514) ***(G-20142)***
North Wood Realty...330 856-3915
1985 Niles Cortland Rd Se Warren (44484) ***(G-18734)***

1206 2019 Harris Ohio Services Directory (G-0000) Company's Geographic Section entry number

Northast Ohio Eye Surgeons Inc (PA) 330 678-0201
  2013 State Route 59 Kent (44240) *(G-12250)*
Northast Ohio Eye Surgeons Inc 330 836-8545
  4099 Embassy Pkwy Akron (44333) *(G-347)*
Northast Ohio Med Rserve Corps 216 789-6653
  3612 Ridge Park Dr Broadview Heights (44147) *(G-1839)*
Northast Ohio Orthpedics Assoc 330 344-1980
  224 W Exchange St Ste 440 Akron (44302) *(G-348)*
Northast Ohio Rgonal Sewer Dst (PA) 216 881-6600
  3900 Euclid Ave Cleveland (44115) *(G-6081)*
Northast Ohio Rgonal Sewer Dst 216 641-3200
  6000 Canal Rd Cleveland (44125) *(G-6082)*
Northast Ohio Rgonal Sewer Dst 216 961-2187
  5800 Cleveland Mem Shr Cleveland (44102) *(G-6083)*
Northast Ohio Rgonal Sewer Dst 216 641-6000
  4747 E 49th St Cleveland (44125) *(G-6084)*
Northast Ohio Rgonal Sewer Dst 216 531-4892
  14021 Lake Shore Blvd Cleveland (44110) *(G-6085)*
Northast Ohio Sstnble Cmmnties 216 410-7698
  146 S High St Ste 800 Akron (44308) *(G-349)*
Northast Ohio Trnching Svc Inc 216 663-6006
  17900 Miles Rd Cleveland (44128) *(G-6086)*
Northast Srgical Assoc of Ohio (PA) 216 643-2780
  6100 Rckside Woods Blvd N Independence (44131) *(G-12104)*
Northastern Eductl TV Ohio Inc 330 677-4549
  1750 W Campus Center Dr Kent (44240) *(G-12251)*
Northastern Ohio Alzheimer Ctr, Columbiana Also called Windsor House Inc *(G-6796)*
Northbend Archtctural Pdts Inc 513 577-7988
  2080 Waycross Rd Cincinnati (45240) *(G-4128)*
Northcast Bhvral Halthcare Sys, Northfield Also called Mental Health and Addi
Serv *(G-15383)*
Northcoast Behavior Healthcare, Toledo Also called Mental Health and Addi Serv *(G-17904)*
Northcoast Duplicating Inc 216 573-6681
  7850 Hub Pkwy Cleveland (44125) *(G-6087)*
Northcoast Healthcare MGT 216 591-2000
  23611 Chagrin Blvd # 380 Beachwood (44122) *(G-1087)*
Northcoast Moving Enterprising 440 943-3900
  1420 Lloyd Rd Wickliffe (44092) *(G-19471)*
Northcutt Trucking Inc 440 458-5139
  40259 Butternut Ridge Rd Elyria (44035) *(G-10548)*
Northeast Cincinnati Hotel LLC 513 459-9800
  9664 S Masn Montgomery Rd Mason (45040) *(G-13623)*
Northeast Concrete & Cnstr 614 898-5728
  7243 Saddlewood Dr Westerville (43082) *(G-19191)*
Northeast Family Health Care 330 630-2332
  65 Community Rd Ste C Tallmadge (44278) *(G-17482)*
Northeast Furniture Rental, Akron Also called Beacon Company *(G-92)*
Northeast Lubricants Ltd (PA) 216 478-0507
  4500 Renaissance Pkwy Cleveland (44128) *(G-6088)*
Northeast OH Neighborhood Heal 216 231-7700
  8300 Hough Ave Cleveland (44103) *(G-6089)*
Northeast OH Neighborhood Heal (PA) 216 231-7700
  4800 Payne Ave Cleveland (44103) *(G-6090)*
Northeast Ohio Areawide 216 621-3055
  1299 Superior Ave E Cleveland (44114) *(G-6091)*
Northeast Ohio Cardiology Svcs 330 253-8195
  95 Arch St Ste 300350 Akron (44304) *(G-350)*
Northeast Ohio Chapter Natnl (PA) 216 696-8220
  6155 Rockside Rd Ste 202 Cleveland (44131) *(G-6092)*
Northeast Ohio Communic 330 399-2700
  2910 Youngstown Rd Se Warren (44484) *(G-18735)*
Northeast Ohio Community Alter, Warren Also called Neocap/Cbcf *(G-18733)*
Northeast Ohio Corrections, Youngstown Also called Corecivic Inc *(G-20011)*
Northeast Ohio Dukes 330 360-0968
  4289 N Park Ave Warren (44483) *(G-18736)*
Northeast Ohio Electric LLC (PA) 216 587-9510
  5069 Corbin Dr Cleveland (44128) *(G-6093)*
Northeast Professional Hm Care (PA) 330 966-2311
  1177 S Main St Ste 11 Canton (44720) *(G-2421)*
Northeast Projections Inc 216 514-5023
  8600 Sweet Valley Dr Cleveland (44125) *(G-6094)*
Northeast Scene Inc 216 241-7550
  737 Bolivar Rd Cleveland (44115) *(G-6095)*
Northern Automotive Inc (PA) 614 436-2001
  8600 N High St Columbus (43235) *(G-8200)*
Northern Bckeye Edcatn Council, Archbold Also called Northwest Ohio Computer
Assn *(G-634)*
Northern Datacomm Corp 330 665-0344
  3700 Embassy Pkwy Ste 141 Akron (44333) *(G-351)*
Northern Frozen Foods Inc 440 439-0600
  21500 Alexander Rd Cleveland (44146) *(G-6096)*
Northern Haserot, Cleveland Also called Northern Frozen Foods Inc *(G-6096)*
Northern Indus Enrgy Dev Inc 330 498-9130
  4100 Holiday St Nw # 201 Canton (44718) *(G-2422)*
Northern Management & Leasing 216 676-4600
  5231 Engle Rd Cleveland (44142) *(G-6097)*
Northern Ohio Explosives, Forest Also called Wampum Hardware Co *(G-10982)*
Northern Ohio Investment Co 419 885-8300
  6444 Monroe St Ste 6 Sylvania (43560) *(G-17438)*
Northern Ohio Med Spclists LLC 419 625-2841
  2500 W Strub Rd Ste 210 Sandusky (44870) *(G-16630)*

Northern Ohio Plumbing Co 440 951-3370
  35601 Curtis Blvd Unit 1 Eastlake (44095) *(G-10433)*
Northern Ohio Realty, Elyria Also called NOR Corp *(G-10544)*
Northern Ohio Roofg Shtmtl Inc 440 322-8262
  880 Infirmary Rd Elyria (44035) *(G-10549)*
Northern Ohio Rural Water 419 668-7213
  2205 Us Highway 20 E Norwalk (44857) *(G-15446)*
Northern Plumbing Systems 513 831-5111
  1708 State Route 28 Goshen (45122) *(G-11313)*
Northern Style Cnstr LLC 330 412-9594
  344 Lease St Ste 104 Akron (44306) *(G-352)*
Northern Tier Hospitality LLC 570 888-7711
  1100 Crocker Rd Westlake (44145) *(G-19383)*
Northfield Presbt Day Care Ctr 330 467-4411
  7755 S Boyden Rd Northfield (44067) *(G-15384)*
Northgate Chrysler Jeep Inc 513 385-3900
  8536 Colerain Ave Cincinnati (45251) *(G-4129)*
Northgate Pk Retirement Cmnty, Cincinnati Also called Atria Senior Living Inc *(G-3001)*
Northgate Pk Retirement Cmnty 513 923-3711
  9191 Round Top Rd Ofc Cincinnati (45251) *(G-4130)*
Northgate Sears, Cincinnati Also called Sears Roebuck and Co *(G-4442)*
Northland Brdg Franklin Cnty 614 846-2588
  4897 Karl Rd Columbus (43229) *(G-8201)*
Northland Hotel Inc 614 885-1601
  1078 E Dblin Granville Rd Columbus (43229) *(G-8202)*
Northland Lanes Inc 419 224-1961
  721 N Cable Rd Lima (45805) *(G-12707)*
Northmont Service Center 937 832-5050
  7277 Hoke Rd Englewood (45315) *(G-10594)*
Northpoint Senior Services LLC 740 369-9614
  2270 Warrensburg Rd Delaware (43015) *(G-9998)*
Northpoint Senior Services LLC 740 373-3597
  400 N 7th St Marietta (45750) *(G-13363)*
Northpoint Senior Services LLC 513 248-1655
  5900 Meadow Creek Dr Milford (45150) *(G-14414)*
Northpointe Plaza 614 744-2229
  191 W Nationwide Blvd # 200 Columbus (43215) *(G-8203)*
Northpointe Property MGT LLC 614 579-9712
  3250 Henderson Rd Ste 103 Columbus (43220) *(G-8204)*
Northridge Health Center, North Ridgeville Also called Altercare Inc *(G-15320)*
Northrop Grumman Systems Corp 937 429-6450
  4020 Executive Dr Beavercreek (45430) *(G-1232)*
Northrop Grumman Technical 937 320-3100
  4065 Colonel Glenn Hwy Beavercreek Township (45431) *(G-1255)*
Northside Baptist Church, Lebanon Also called Northside Baptst Child Dev Ctr *(G-12487)*
Northside Baptst Child Dev Ctr 513 932-5642
  161 Miller Rd Lebanon (45036) *(G-12487)*
Northside Internal Medicine, Westerville Also called Central Ohio Primary Care *(G-19235)*
Northstar Alloys & Machine Co 440 234-3069
  631 Wyleswood Dr Berea (44017) *(G-1431)*
Northstar Asphalt Inc 330 497-0936
  7345 Sunset Strip Ave Nw North Canton (44720) *(G-15224)*
Northtown Square Ltd Partnr 419 691-8911
  2930 Navarre Ave Oregon (43616) *(G-15601)*
Northview Senior Living Center, Johnstown Also called Zandex Inc *(G-12205)*
Northview Senior Living Center, Johnstown Also called Zandex Health Care
Corporation *(G-12206)*
Northwest Bank 330 342-4018
  178 W Streetsboro St # 1 Hudson (44236) *(G-12000)*
Northwest Bldg Resources Inc (PA) 419 286-5400
  23734 State Route 189 Fort Jennings (45844) *(G-10984)*
Northwest Child Development An 937 559-9565
  2823 Campus Dr Dayton (45406) *(G-9660)*
Northwest Cmmuntiy Action Comm, Bryan Also called Pulaski Head Start *(G-1972)*
Northwest Columbus Urology 937 342-9260
  1164 E Home Rd Ste J Springfield (45503) *(G-17090)*
Northwest Counseling Services, Columbus Also called Northwest Mental Health
Svcs *(G-8207)*
Northwest Country Place Inc 440 488-2700
  9223 Amber Wood Dr Willoughby (44094) *(G-19556)*
Northwest Electrical Contg Inc 419 865-4757
  1617 Shanrock Dr Holland (43528) *(G-11901)*
Northwest Eye Surgeons Inc (PA) 614 451-7550
  2250 N Bank Dr Columbus (43220) *(G-8205)*
NORTHWEST FAMILY SERVICES DDA, Lima Also called Family Rsource Ctr NW Ohio
Inc *(G-12637)*
Northwest Fire Ambulance 937 437-8354
  135 N Washington St New Paris (45347) *(G-14944)*
Northwest Firestop Inc 419 517-4777
  328 21st St Toledo (43604) *(G-17948)*
Northwest Hts Title Agcy LLC 614 451-6313
  4200 Regent St Ste 210 Columbus (43219) *(G-8206)*
Northwest Limousine Inc 440 322-5804
  642 Sugar Ln Ste 207 Elyria (44035) *(G-10550)*
Northwest Local School Dst 513 923-1000
  3308 Compton Rd Cincinnati (45251) *(G-4131)*
Northwest Mental Health Svcs 614 457-7876
  1560 Fishinger Rd Ste 100 Columbus (43221) *(G-8207)*
Northwest Ohio Cardiology Cons (PA) 419 842-3000
  2121 Hughes Dr Ste 850 Toledo (43606) *(G-17949)*

Northwest Ohio Chapter Cfma.....419 891-1040
145 Chesterfield Ln Maumee (43537) *(G-13824)*
Northwest Ohio Computer Assn (PA).....419 267-5565
209 Nolan Pkwy Archbold (43502) *(G-634)*
Northwest Ohio Dvlopmental Ctr, Toledo *Also called Develpmntal Dsblties Ohio Dept (G-17699)*
Northwest Ohio Orthopedic & Sp.....419 427-1984
7595 County Road 236 Findlay (45840) *(G-10950)*
Northwest Ohio Orthopedics.....419 885-2553
6444 Monroe St Ste 1 Sylvania (43560) *(G-17439)*
Northwest Ohio Practice, Maumee *Also called William Vaughan Company (G-13869)*
Northwest Ohio Urgent Care Inc.....419 720-7363
1421 S Reynolds Rd Toledo (43615) *(G-17950)*
Northwest Products, Stryker *Also called Quadco Rehabilitation Ctr Inc (G-17370)*
Northwest Products Div, Archbold *Also called Quadco Rehabilitation Center (G-636)*
Northwest Swim Club Inc.....614 442-8716
1064 Bethel Rd Columbus (43220) *(G-8208)*
Northwest Ttl Agy of OH MI In (PA).....419 241-8195
328 N Erie St Toledo (43604) *(G-17951)*
Northwesterly Assisted Living, Cleveland *Also called Northwesterly Ltd (G-6098)*
Northwesterly Ltd.....216 228-2266
1341 Marlowe Ave Cleveland (44107) *(G-6098)*
Northwestern Healthcare Center, Berea *Also called Rocky River Leasing Co LLC (G-1436)*
Northwestern Mutl Fincl Netwrk, Cleveland *Also called Brown WD General Agency Inc (G-5094)*
Northwestern Mutl Lf Insur Co.....513 366-3600
3805 Edwards Rd Ste 200 Cincinnati (45209) *(G-4132)*
Northwestern Mutl Lf Insur Co.....614 221-5287
800 Yard St Ste 300 Columbus (43212) *(G-8209)*
Northwestern Mutual Inv Svcs, Toledo *Also called Bruce Klinger (G-17630)*
Northwestern Mutual Life, Copley *Also called Kelley Companies (G-8967)*
NORTHWESTERN OHIO ADMINISTRATO, Holland *Also called Union Cnstr Wkrs Hlth Plan (G-11923)*
Northwestern Ohio SEC Systems (PA).....419 227-1655
121 E High St Lima (45801) *(G-12708)*
Northwestern Water & Sewer Dst.....419 354-9090
12560 Middleton Pike Bowling Green (43402) *(G-1742)*
Northwestrn OH Communty Action (PA).....419 784-2150
1933 E 2nd St Defiance (43512) *(G-9932)*
Northwind Industries Inc.....216 433-0666
15500 Commerce Park Dr Cleveland (44142) *(G-6099)*
Northwods Cnslting Prtners Inc.....614 781-7800
5815 Wall St Dublin (43017) *(G-10292)*
Northwstern Ohio Admnistrators.....419 248-2401
7142 Nightingale Dr 1 Holland (43528) *(G-11902)*
Nortone Service Inc.....740 527-2057
164 Slocum Ave Buckeye Lake (43008) *(G-1975)*
Norwalk Area Health Services.....419 499-2515
12513 State Route 250 Milan (44846) *(G-14363)*
Norwalk Area Health Services (HQ).....419 668-8101
272 Benedict Ave Norwalk (44857) *(G-15447)*
Norwalk Area Hlth Systems Inc (PA).....419 668-8101
272 Benedict Ave Norwalk (44857) *(G-15448)*
Norwalk Clinic Inc.....419 668-4851
257 Benedict Ave Ste C1 Norwalk (44857) *(G-15449)*
Norwalk Golf Properties Inc.....419 668-8535
2406 New State Rd Norwalk (44857) *(G-15450)*
Norwich Elementary Pto.....614 921-6000
4454 Davidson Rd Hilliard (43026) *(G-11801)*
Norwood Endoscopy Center.....513 731-5600
4746 Montgomery Rd # 100 Cincinnati (45212) *(G-4133)*
Norwood Hardware & Supply Co (PA).....513 733-1175
2906 Glendale Milford Rd Cincinnati (45241) *(G-4134)*
Norwood Health Care Center LLC.....513 351-0153
1578 Sherman Ave Cincinnati (45212) *(G-4135)*
Norwood School, Marietta *Also called Community Action Program Corp (G-13320)*
Notoweega Nation Inc.....740 777-1480
38494 Mysvlle Grendale Rd Logan (43138) *(G-12851)*
Notre Dame Academy Apartments.....216 707-1590
1325 Ansel Rd Cleveland (44106) *(G-6100)*
Notre Dame Pre-School, Chardon *Also called Sisters of Notre Dame of Chard (G-2714)*
Nottingham Home, Cleveland *Also called Help Foundation Inc (G-5683)*
Nottingham-Spirk Des.....216 800-5782
2200 Overlook Rd Cleveland (44106) *(G-6101)*
Nova Technology Solutions LLC.....937 426-2596
3100 Presidential Dr # 310 Beavercreek (45324) *(G-1173)*
Novco, Ashville *Also called Noxious Vegetation Control Inc (G-762)*
Novel Writing Workshop, Blue Ash *Also called F+w Media Inc (G-1559)*
Novelart Manufacturing Company (PA).....513 351-7700
2121 Section Rd Cincinnati (45237) *(G-4136)*
Novelty Advertising Co Inc.....740 622-3113
1148 Walnut St Coshocton (43812) *(G-9024)*
Novotec Recycling LLC (PA).....614 231-8326
3960 Groves Rd Columbus (43232) *(G-8210)*
Novus Clinic.....330 630-9699
518 West Ave Tallmadge (44278) *(G-17483)*
Now Security Group, Cincinnati *Also called US Protection Service LLC (G-4742)*
Noxious Vegetation Control Inc.....614 486-8994
14923 State Route 104 Ashville (43103) *(G-762)*

Npa Associates.....614 258-4053
23875 Commerce Park # 120 Beachwood (44122) *(G-1088)*
Npc Group Inc.....312 627-6000
8500 Governors Hill Dr Symmes Twp (45249) *(G-17466)*
Npk Construction Equipment Inc (HQ).....440 232-7900
7550 Independence Dr Bedford (44146) *(G-1295)*
Nr2, Columbus *Also called Network Restorations II (G-8179)*
Nr3, Columbus *Also called Network Restorations III LLC (G-8180)*
NRG Power Midwest LP.....440 930-6401
33570 Lake Rd Avon Lake (44012) *(G-925)*
NRG Power Midwest LP.....330 505-4327
1047 Belmont Ave Niles (44446) *(G-15165)*
Nri Global Inc.....905 790-2828
3401 Rodgers Rd Delta (43515) *(G-10048)*
Nrp Contractors LLC (HQ).....216 475-8900
1228 Euclid Ave Fl 4 Cleveland (44115) *(G-6102)*
Nrp Group LLC (PA).....216 475-8900
1228 Euclid Ave Ste 400 Cleveland (44115) *(G-6103)*
Nrp Holdings LLC.....216 475-8900
5309 Transportation Blvd Cleveland (44125) *(G-6104)*
Nrt Commercial Utah LLC.....614 239-0808
2288 E Main St Columbus (43209) *(G-8211)*
Nrt Commercial Utah LLC.....614 889-0808
4535 W Dblin Granville Rd Dublin (43017) *(G-10293)*
Nsa Technologies LLC.....330 576-4600
3867 Medina Rd Ste 256 Akron (44333) *(G-353)*
Nsb Retail Systems Inc.....614 840-1421
400 Venture Dr Lewis Center (43035) *(G-12554)*
Nsd, Elyria *Also called North Shore Door Co Inc (G-10547)*
Nsl Analytical Services Inc (PA).....216 438-5200
4450 Cranwood Pkwy Cleveland (44128) *(G-6105)*
Ntk Hotel Group II LLC.....614 559-2000
501 N High St Columbus (43215) *(G-8212)*
Ntt Data Inc.....513 794-1400
3284 North Bend Rd # 107 Cincinnati (45239) *(G-4137)*
Nu Waves Ltd.....513 360-0800
132 Edison Dr Middletown (45044) *(G-14315)*
Nu-Di Corporation, Cleveland *Also called Nu-Di Products Co Inc (G-6106)*
Nu-Di Products Co Inc.....216 251-9070
12730 Triskett Rd Cleveland (44111) *(G-6106)*
Nucentury Textile Services LLC (PA).....419 241-2267
1 Southard Ave Toledo (43604) *(G-17952)*
Nuclear Reactor Laboratory, Columbus *Also called Ohio State University (G-8331)*
Nucon International Inc.....614 846-5710
6800 Huntley Rd Columbus (43229) *(G-8213)*
Nuerocare Center Inc.....330 494-2917
4105 Holiday St Nw Canton (44718) *(G-2423)*
Nuerological & Sleep Disorders.....513 721-7533
8250 Kenwood Crossing Way Cincinnati (45236) *(G-4138)*
Nueterra Holdings LLC.....614 451-0500
930 Bethel Rd Columbus (43214) *(G-8214)*
Nugrowth Solutions LLC (PA).....800 747-9273
4181 Arlingate Plz Columbus (43228) *(G-8215)*
Number 1 Landscaping, Medina *Also called South Star Corp (G-14004)*
Numotion, Maumee *Also called United Seating & Mobility LLC (G-13866)*
Nunn Productions LLC.....614 695-5350
341 S 3rd St 100-291 Columbus (43215) *(G-8216)*
Nuray Radiologists Inc.....513 965-8059
8160 Corp Pk Dr Ste 330 Cincinnati (45242) *(G-4139)*
Nurenberg Plevin Heller.....440 423-0750
600 Superior Ave E # 1200 Cleveland (44114) *(G-6107)*
Nurotoco Massachusetts Inc.....513 762-6690
255 E 5th St Cincinnati (45202) *(G-4140)*
Nurse Medicial Healthcare Svcs.....614 801-1300
3421 Farm Bank Way Grove City (43123) *(G-11460)*
Nursefinders, Akron *Also called Medlink of Ohio Inc (G-330)*
Nurses Care Inc (PA).....513 424-1141
9009 Springboro Pike Miamisburg (45342) *(G-14198)*
Nurses Care Inc.....513 791-0233
9200 Montgomery Rd 13b Cincinnati (45242) *(G-4141)*
Nurses Heart Med Staffing LLC.....614 648-5111
1100 Morse Rd Ste 104 Columbus (43229) *(G-8217)*
Nursing Care MGT Amer Inc.....740 927-9888
144 E Broad St Pataskala (43062) *(G-15786)*
Nursing Care MGT Amer Inc.....513 793-5092
7777 Cooper Rd Cincinnati (45242) *(G-4142)*
Nursing Care MGT Amer Inc.....419 385-3958
1621 S Byrne Rd Toledo (43614) *(G-17953)*
Nursing Resources Corp.....419 333-3000
3600 Brrfeld Blvd Ste 100 Maumee (43537) *(G-13825)*
Nurtur Holdings LLC (PA).....614 487-3033
6279 Tri Ridge Blvd # 250 Loveland (45140) *(G-13016)*
Nurtury.....330 723-1800
250 N Spring Grove St Medina (44256) *(G-13983)*
Nutis Press Inc (PA).....614 237-8626
3540 E Fulton St Columbus (43227) *(G-8218)*
Nutrition Program, Toledo *Also called Lyman W Liggins Urban Affairs (G-17875)*
Nutrition Trnsp Svcs LLC.....937 962-2661
6531 State Route 503 N Lewisburg (45338) *(G-12571)*
Nutur Holdings LLC.....513 576-9333
6281 Try Rdge Blvd Ste 14 Loveland (45140) *(G-13017)*
Nuwaves Engineering, Middletown *Also called Nu Waves Ltd (G-14315)*

Nuway Incorporated 740 587-2452
  996 Thornwood Dr Heath (43056) *(G-11707)*

Nvr Inc 440 933-7734
  2553 Palmer Ln Avon (44011) *(G-898)*

Nvr Inc 440 584-4200
  4034 Willow Way Kent (44240) *(G-12252)*

Nvr Inc 440 639-0525
  408 Greenfield Ln Painesville (44077) *(G-15729)*

Nvr Inc 513 494-0167
  5153 Riverview Dr South Lebanon (45065) *(G-16927)*

Nvr Inc 513 202-0323
  9439 Tebbs Ct Harrison (45030) *(G-11675)*

Nvr Inc 937 529-7000
  2094 Northwest Pkwy Dayton (45426) *(G-9661)*

Nvr Inc 440 584-4250
  6770 W Snowville Rd 100 Brecksville (44141) *(G-1794)*

Nwd Arena District II LLC 614 857-2330
  375 N Front St Ste 200 Columbus (43215) *(G-8219)*

Nwo Beverage Inc 419 725-2162
  6700 Wales Rd Northwood (43619) *(G-15403)*

Nwo Gastroenterology Assoc Inc 419 471-1317
  4841 Monroe St Ste 110 Toledo (43623) *(G-17954)*

Nwo Resources Inc (PA) 419 636-1117
  200 W High St Bryan (43506) *(G-1965)*

Nyap - Care Management, Columbus *Also called National Youth Advocate Progra (G-8140)*

Nyap - Newark, Newark *Also called National Youth Advocate Progra (G-15080)*

Nye F A & Sons Enterprises 419 986-5400
  7443 N Township Road 70 Tiffin (44883) *(G-17527)*

Nyman Construction Co 216 475-7800
  23209 Miles Rd Fl 2 Cleveland (44128) *(G-6108)*

Nzr Retail of Toledo Inc 419 724-0005
  4820 Monroe St Toledo (43623) *(G-17955)*

O A I, Cleveland *Also called Ohio Aerospace Institute (G-6114)*

O A R D C, Wooster *Also called Ohio State University (G-19754)*

O B M, Cleveland *Also called Ohio Business Machines LLC (G-6117)*

O C I, Cincinnati *Also called Oncolgy/Hmatology Care Inc PSC (G-4174)*

O C I Construction Co Inc 440 338-3166
  8560 Pekin Rd Novelty (44072) *(G-15465)*

O C P, Holland *Also called OCP Contractors Inc (G-11903)*

O D Miller Electric Co Inc 330 875-1651
  1115 W Main St Louisville (44641) *(G-12969)*

O D W, Columbus *Also called Odw Logistics Inc (G-8225)*

O E Meyer Co (PA) 419 625-1256
  3303 Tiffin Ave Sandusky (44870) *(G-16631)*

O K Coal & Concrete, Zanesville *Also called Joe McClelland Inc (G-20321)*

O N Equity Sales Company 513 794-6794
  1 Financial Way Ste 100 Montgomery (45242) *(G-14597)*

O S U Faculty Club 614 292-2262
  181 S Oval Mall Columbus (43210) *(G-8220)*

O S U Telephone Service, Columbus *Also called Ohio State University (G-8319)*

O'Neil Healthcare - N Olmstead, North Olmsted *Also called Wellington Place LLC (G-15316)*

O-Heil Irrigation, Dayton *Also called Ohio Irrigation Lawn Sprinkler (G-9670)*

O.C.S.E.a, Westerville *Also called Ohio Civil Service Employees A (G-19195)*

O/B Leasing Company, Cincinnati *Also called Budco Group Inc (G-3086)*

Oad, Grove City *Also called Ohio Auto Delivery Inc (G-11461)*

Oak Associates Ltd 330 666-5263
  3875 Embassy Pkwy Ste 250 Akron (44333) *(G-354)*

Oak Brook Garden Apartments, North Royalton *Also called Oak Brook Gardens (G-15363)*

Oak Brook Gardens 440 237-3613
  13911 Oakbrook Dr Apt 205 North Royalton (44133) *(G-15363)*

Oak Creek Terrace Inc 937 439-1454
  2316 Springmill Rd Dayton (45440) *(G-9662)*

Oak Creek United Church 937 434-3941
  5280 Bigger Rd Dayton (45440) *(G-9663)*

Oak Grove Manor Inc 419 589-6222
  1670 Crider Rd Mansfield (44903) *(G-13227)*

Oak Harbor Lions Club 419 898-3828
  101 S Brookside Dr Oak Harbor (43449) *(G-15475)*

Oak Health Care Investor (HQ) 614 794-8800
  8181 Worthington Rd Westerville (43082) *(G-19192)*

Oak Health Care Investors 740 397-3200
  13 Avalon Rd Mount Vernon (43050) *(G-14784)*

Oak Health Care Investors (HQ) 614 794-8800
  8181 Worthington Rd Westerville (43082) *(G-19193)*

Oak Hills Swim & Racquet 513 922-1827
  5850 Muddy Creek Rd Cincinnati (45233) *(G-4143)*

Oak Hlls Nrsing Rehabilitation, Cincinnati *Also called Oaktree LLC (G-4145)*

Oak Park Health Care Center, Cleveland *Also called Jma Healthcare LLC (G-5797)*

Oak Pavilion Nursing & Rehabil, Cincinnati *Also called Health Care Rtrement Corp Amer (G-3692)*

Oakdale Elementary Pta 513 574-1100
  3850 Virginia Ct Cincinnati (45248) *(G-4144)*

Oakdale Estates II Inv LLC 216 520-1250
  310 Rice Dr West Union (45693) *(G-19137)*

Oakhill Manor Care Center 330 875-5060
  4466 Lynnhaven Ave Louisville (44641) *(G-12970)*

Oakhill Medical Associates 937 599-1411
  4879 Us Highway 68 S West Liberty (43357) *(G-19121)*

Oakhurst Country Club, Grove City *Also called American Golf Corporation (G-11405)*

Oakland Nursery Inc (PA) 614 268-3834
  1156 Oakland Park Ave Columbus (43224) *(G-8221)*

Oakland Pk Cnservation CLB Inc 614 989-8739
  3138 Strathaven Ct Dublin (43017) *(G-10294)*

Oakleaf Toledo Ltd Partnership 419 885-3934
  4220 N Hllnd Sylvnia Ofc Toledo (43623) *(G-17956)*

Oakleaf Village, Toledo *Also called Oakleaf Toledo Ltd Partnership (G-17956)*

Oakleaf Village Ltd 614 431-1739
  5500 Karl Rd Apt 113 Columbus (43229) *(G-8222)*

Oakponte Nrsing Rehabilitation, Baltic *Also called Baltic Health Care Corp (G-933)*

Oaks of Brecksville, The, Brecksville *Also called Saber Healthcare Group LLC (G-1803)*

Oaks of Brecksville, The, Brecksville *Also called Brecksvlle Halthcare Group Inc (G-1772)*

Oaks of West Kettering Inc 937 293-1152
  1150 W Dorothy Ln Dayton (45409) *(G-9664)*

Oaktree LLC 513 598-8000
  4307 Bridgetown Rd Cincinnati (45211) *(G-4145)*

Oakwood Health Care Svcs Inc 440 439-7976
  24579 Broadway Ave Cleveland (44146) *(G-6109)*

Oakwood Hospitality Corp 440 786-1998
  23303 Oakwood Commons Dr Bedford (44146) *(G-1296)*

Oakwood Management Company 740 774-3570
  402 W Main St Chillicothe (45601) *(G-2806)*

Oakwood Management Company (PA) 614 866-8702
  6950 Americana Pkwy Ste A Reynoldsburg (43068) *(G-16322)*

Oakwood Optical, Oakwood *Also called Kunesh Eye Center Inc (G-15482)*

Oapse, Dayton *Also called Ohio Assn Pub Schl Employees (G-9183)*

Oapse-Local 4, Columbus *Also called Ohio Assn Pub Schl Employees (G-8228)*

Oarnet, Columbus *Also called Ohio State University (G-8338)*

Oasis Golf Club, Loveland *Also called Creekside Ltd LLC (G-12986)*

Oasis Systems Inc 937 426-1295
  4141 Colonel Glenn Hwy Beavercreek Township (45431) *(G-1256)*

Oasis Thrptic Fster Care Ntwrk 740 698-0340
  34265 State Route 681 S Albany (45710) *(G-511)*

Oasis Turf & Tree Inc 513 697-9090
  8900 Glendl Milford Rd A4 Loveland (45140) *(G-13018)*

Oatey Company, Cleveland *Also called Oatey Supply Chain Svcs Inc (G-6110)*

Oatey Distribution Center, Cleveland *Also called Oatey Supply Chain Svcs Inc (G-6111)*

Oatey Supply Chain Svcs Inc (HQ) 216 267-7100
  20600 Emerald Pkwy Cleveland (44135) *(G-6110)*

Oatey Supply Chain Svcs Inc 216 267-7100
  4565 Industrial Pkwy Cleveland (44135) *(G-6111)*

Ob Gyn Associates of Lancaster 740 653-5088
  1532 Wesley Way Lancaster (43130) *(G-12424)*

Ob-Gyn Specialists Lima Inc 419 227-0610
  830 W High St Ste 101 Lima (45801) *(G-12709)*

Obaco, Bowling Green *Also called Ohio Biliffs Crt Officers Assn (G-1743)*

OBannon Creek Golf Club 513 683-5657
  6842 Oakland Rd Loveland (45140) *(G-13019)*

Oberer Companies, Miamisburg *Also called Oberer Development Co (G-14199)*

Oberer Development Co (PA) 937 910-0851
  3445 Newmark Dr Miamisburg (45342) *(G-14199)*

Oberer Residential Cnstr 937 278-0851
  3475 Newmark Dr Miamisburg (45342) *(G-14200)*

OBERER THOMPSON CO, Beavercreek *Also called Greater Dayton Cnstr Ltd (G-1220)*

Oberers Flowers Inc (PA) 937 223-1253
  1448 Troy St Dayton (45404) *(G-9665)*

Oberlanders Tree & Ldscp Ltd 419 562-8733
  1874 E Mansfield St Bucyrus (44820) *(G-1998)*

Oberlin Clinic Inc 440 774-7337
  224 W Lorain St Ste P Oberlin (44074) *(G-15512)*

Oberlin College 440 775-8519
  200 Woodland St Oberlin (44074) *(G-15513)*

Oberlin College 440 775-8500
  200 Woodland St Oberlin (44074) *(G-15514)*

Oberlin College 440 935-1475
  10 E College St Oberlin (44074) *(G-15515)*

Oberlin College Recreation Ctr, Oberlin *Also called Oberlin College (G-15513)*

Oberlin Early Childhood Center 440 774-8193
  317 E College St Oberlin (44074) *(G-15516)*

Oberlin Inn, Oberlin *Also called Oberlin College (G-15515)*

OBERLIN MUNICIPAL LIGHT & POWE, Oberlin *Also called City of Oberlin (G-15499)*

Obetz Animal Hospital 614 491-5676
  3999 Alum Creek Dr Columbus (43207) *(G-8223)*

Obr Cooling Towers Inc 419 243-3443
  9665 S Compass Dr Rossford (43460) *(G-16463)*

OBrien Law Firm Company Lpa 216 685-7500
  29550 Detroit Rd Westlake (44145) *(G-19384)*

Obstetrics & Gynecology Assoc (PA) 513 221-3800
  3050 Mack Rd Ste 375 Fairfield (45014) *(G-10762)*

Obstetrics & Gynecology S Inc (PA) 937 296-0167
  3533 Sthern Blvd Ste 4600 Dayton (45429) *(G-9666)*

Obstetrics Gynclogy of Reserve 330 666-1166
  799 Wye Rd Akron (44333) *(G-355)*

Occasions Party Centre 330 882-5113
  6800 Manchester Rd New Franklin (44216) *(G-14911)*

Occupational Health Center, Lorain *Also called Barb Linden (G-12884)*

Occupational Health Link (PA) 614 885-0039
  445 Hutchinson Ave # 205 Columbus (43235) *(G-8224)*

Occupational Health Services 937 492-7296
  915 Michigan St Sidney (45365) *(G-16788)*

Occupational Hlth Safety Dept, Independence *Also called Sterling Infosystems Inc* **(G-12125)**
Ocean Prime, Columbus *Also called Cameron Mitchell Rest LLC* **(G-7108)**
Ocean Wide Seafood Company 937 610-5740
2601 W 8th St Apt 10 Cincinnati (45204) **(G-4146)**
Oclc Inc (PA) 614 764-6000
6565 Kilgour Pl Dublin (43017) **(G-10295)**
OConnor Acciani & Levy LLC (PA) 513 241-7111
600 Vine St Ste 1600 Cincinnati (45202) **(G-4147)**
OCP Contractors Inc (PA) 419 865-7168
1740 Commerce Rd Holland (43528) **(G-11903)**
Ocr Services Corporation 513 719-2600
201 E 4th St Ste 900 Cincinnati (45202) **(G-4148)**
October Enterprises Inc 937 456-9535
501 W Lexington Rd Eaton (45320) **(G-10456)**
Odd Fellows Hall 440 599-7973
253 Liberty St Conneaut (44030) **(G-8957)**
Odnr Computer Communication, Columbus *Also called Natural Resources Ohio Dept* **(G-8163)**
Odot District 4, Canfield *Also called Ohio Department Transportation* **(G-2153)**
Odw Logistics Inc (PA) 614 549-5000
400 W Nationwide Blvd # 200 Columbus (43215) **(G-8225)**
Odyssey Consulting Services 614 523-4248
2531 Oakstone Dr Columbus (43231) **(G-8226)**
Odyssey Healthcare Inc 614 414-0500
540 Officenter Pl Ste 295 Gahanna (43230) **(G-11138)**
Odyssey Healthcare Inc 937 298-2800
3085 Woodman Dr Ste 200 Dayton (45420) **(G-9667)**
Odyssey Healthcare of Columbus, Gahanna *Also called Odyssey Healthcare Inc* **(G-11138)**
Oeconnection LLC (PA) 888 776-5792
4205 Highlander Pkwy Richfield (44286) **(G-16367)**
Oeder Carl E Sons Sand & Grav 513 494-1238
1000 Mason Mrrow Mlgrv Rd Lebanon (45036) **(G-12488)**
OEM Parts Outlet 419 472-2237
1815 W Sylvania Ave Toledo (43613) **(G-17957)**
Oesterlen-Services For Youth 937 399-6101
1918 Mechanicsburg Rd Springfield (45503) **(G-17091)**
Ofeq Institute Inc 440 943-1497
28772 Johnson Dr Wickliffe (44092) **(G-19472)**
Office Concepts Inc 419 221-2679
1064 W Market St Lima (45805) **(G-12710)**
Office Concepts of Ohio, Lima *Also called Office Concepts Inc* **(G-12710)**
Office Depot Inc 800 463-3768
9880 Sweet Valley Dr # 2 Cleveland (44125) **(G-6112)**
Office For Children Fmly Svcs, Columbus *Also called Ohio Dept of Job & Fmly Svcs* **(G-8247)**
Office Furniture Resources Inc 216 781-8200
1213 Prospect Ave E Cleveland (44115) **(G-6113)**
Office Furniture Solution, North Canton *Also called Document Concepts Inc* **(G-15197)**
Office Furniture USA, Columbus *Also called Thomas W Ruff and Company* **(G-8747)**
Office of Divisional Support, Oxford *Also called Miami University* **(G-15683)**
Office of Procurement Services, Columbus *Also called Administrative Svcs Ohio Dept* **(G-6872)**
Office Products Toledo Inc 419 865-7001
1205 Corporate Dr Holland (43528) **(G-11904)**
Office World Inc (PA) 419 991-4694
3820 S Dixie Hwy Lima (45806) **(G-12791)**
OfficeMax North America Inc 614 899-6186
87 Huber Village Blvd Westerville (43081) **(G-19286)**
Officeteam, Dublin *Also called Robert Half International Inc* **(G-10324)**
Official Investigations Inc 844 263-3424
3284 North Bend Rd # 302 Cincinnati (45239) **(G-4149)**
Ofori, Jason MD, Toledo *Also called Vision Associates Inc* **(G-18139)**
OFSWCD, Reynoldsburg *Also called Ohio Federation of Soil and WA* **(G-16323)**
OGara Group Inc (PA) 513 338-0660
9113 Le Street Dr Cincinnati (45249) **(G-4150)**
Oglethorpe Middlepoint LLC 419 968-2950
17872 Lincoln Hwy Middle Point (45863) **(G-14247)**
Ogs Industries, Akron *Also called Ohio Gasket and Shim Co Inc* **(G-359)**
OH St Trans Dist 02 Outpost 419 693-8870
200 Lemoyne Rd Northwood (43619) **(G-15404)**
Oh-16 Cleveland Westlake 440 892-4275
25052 Sperry Dr Westlake (44145) **(G-19385)**
Oh-16 Clvlnd Arprt S Prprty Su 440 243-8785
7345 Engle Rd Middleburg Heights (44130) **(G-14255)**
Ohashi Technica USA Inc (HQ) 740 965-5115
111 Burrer Dr Sunbury (43074) **(G-17393)**
Oherbein Kpsic Rtirement Cmnty, Leipsic *Also called Otterbein Snior Lfstyle Chices* **(G-12520)**
Ohfa, Columbus *Also called Ohio Housing Finance Agency* **(G-8268)**
Ohi-Rail Corp (PA) 740 765-5083
992 State Route 43 Richmond (43944) **(G-16386)**
Ohic Insurance Company (HQ) 614 221-7777
300 E Broad St Ste 450 Columbus (43215) **(G-8227)**
Ohigro Inc (PA) 740 726-2429
6720 Gillette Rd Waldo (43356) **(G-18630)**
Ohio & Indiana Roofing 937 339-8768
17 S Market St Troy (45373) **(G-18218)**
Ohio & Michigan Paper Company 419 666-1500
350 4th St Perrysburg (43551) **(G-15896)**
Ohio Academy of Science 614 488-2228
5930 Wilcox Pl Ste F Dublin (43016) **(G-10296)**
Ohio Aerospace Institute (PA) 440 962-3000
22800 Cedar Point Rd Cleveland (44142) **(G-6114)**
Ohio Agriculture RES & Dev Ctr, Wooster *Also called Ohio State University* **(G-19755)**
Ohio Alarm Inc 216 692-1204
750 W Resource Dr Ste 200 Independence (44131) **(G-12105)**
Ohio and Indiana Roofing Co, Saint Henry *Also called Bruns Building & Dev Corp Inc* **(G-16515)**
Ohio Anestisia, Canton *Also called Russell D Ens Do* **(G-2467)**
Ohio Assn Pub Schl Employees (PA) 614 890-4770
6805 Oak Creek Dr Ste 1 Columbus (43229) **(G-8228)**
Ohio Assn Pub Schl Employees 937 253-5100
1675 Woodman Dr Dayton (45432) **(G-9183)**
Ohio Assn Pub Schl Employees 330 659-7335
3380 Brecksville Rd # 101 Richfield (44286) **(G-16368)**
Ohio Assn Pub Treasurers 937 415-2237
333 James Bohanan Dr Vandalia (45377) **(G-18534)**
Ohio Association of Foodbanks 614 221-4336
101 E Town St Ste 540 Columbus (43215) **(G-8229)**
Ohio Association Realtors Inc 614 228-6675
200 E Town St Columbus (43215) **(G-8230)**
Ohio Auto Auction, Grove City *Also called Cox Automotive Inc* **(G-11423)**
Ohio Auto Delivery Inc 614 277-1445
1700 Feddern Ave Grove City (43123) **(G-11461)**
Ohio Auto Supply Company 330 454-5105
1128 Tuscarawas St W Canton (44702) **(G-2424)**
Ohio Automobile Club (PA) 614 431-7901
90 E Wilson Bridge Rd # 1 Worthington (43085) **(G-19831)**
Ohio Automobile Club 614 559-0000
2400 Sobeck Rd Columbus (43232) **(G-8231)**
Ohio Automobile Club 614 277-1310
4750 Big Run South Rd B Grove City (43123) **(G-11462)**
Ohio Automobile Club 513 870-0951
8210 Highland Pointe Dr West Chester (45069) **(G-18978)**
Ohio Automotive Supply Co 419 422-1655
525 W Main Cross St Findlay (45840) **(G-10951)**
Ohio Ballet, Akron *Also called Ohio Chamber Ballet* **(G-356)**
Ohio Bar Title Insurance Co 614 310-8098
8740 Orion Pl Ste 310 Columbus (43240) **(G-6827)**
Ohio Bell Telephone Company (HQ) 216 822-3439
45 Erieview Plz Cleveland (44114) **(G-6115)**
Ohio Biliffs Crt Officers Assn 419 354-9302
1 Court House Sq Bowling Green (43402) **(G-1743)**
Ohio Blow Pipe Company (PA) 216 681-7379
446 E 131st St Cleveland (44108) **(G-6116)**
Ohio Board of Cosmetology, Grove City *Also called State of Ohio* **(G-11474)**
Ohio Bridge Corporation 740 432-6334
201 Wheeling Ave Cambridge (43725) **(G-2079)**
Ohio Broach & Machine Company 440 946-1040
35264 Topps Indus Pkwy Willoughby (44094) **(G-19557)**
Ohio Builders Resources LLC 614 865-0306
5901 Chandler Ct Ste D Westerville (43082) **(G-19194)**
Ohio Building Service Inc 513 761-0268
2212 Losantiville Ave Cincinnati (45237) **(G-4151)**
Ohio Business Machines LLC (PA) 216 485-2000
1111 Superior Ave E # 105 Cleveland (44114) **(G-6117)**
Ohio Camp Cherith Inc 330 725-4202
3854 Remsen Rd Medina (44256) **(G-13984)**
Ohio Cancer Specialists (PA) 419 756-2122
1125 Aspira Ct Mansfield (44906) **(G-13228)**
Ohio Carts, Mentor *Also called Omni Cart Services Inc* **(G-14093)**
Ohio Casualty Insurance, Montgomery *Also called Ohio National Life Insur Co* **(G-14601)**
Ohio Casualty Insurance Co (HQ) 800 843-6446
9450 Seward Rd Fairfield (45014) **(G-10763)**
Ohio Casualty Insurance Co 513 867-3000
136 N 3rd St Hamilton (45011) **(G-11631)**
Ohio Cat, Cadiz *Also called Ohio Machinery Co* **(G-2032)**
Ohio Catholic Federal Cr Un (PA) 216 663-6800
13623 Rockside Rd Cleveland (44125) **(G-6118)**
Ohio Chamber Ballet 330 972-7900
354 E Market St Akron (44325) **(G-356)**
Ohio Chamber of Commerce 614 228-4201
34 S 3rd St Ste 100 Columbus (43215) **(G-8232)**
Ohio Citizen Action (PA) 216 861-5200
614 W Superior Ave # 1200 Cleveland (44113) **(G-6119)**
Ohio Citrus Juices Inc 614 539-0030
2201 Hardy Parkway St Grove City (43123) **(G-11463)**
Ohio Civil Service Employees A 614 865-4700
390 Worthington Rd Ste A Westerville (43082) **(G-19195)**
Ohio Cle Institute, Columbus *Also called Ohio State Bar Association* **(G-8288)**
Ohio Cllbrtive Lrng Sltons Inc (PA) 216 595-5289
24700 Chagrin Blvd # 104 Beachwood (44122) **(G-1089)**
Ohio Con Sawing & Drlg Inc (PA) 419 841-1330
8534 Central Ave Sylvania (43560) **(G-17440)**
Ohio Con Sawing & Drlg Inc 614 252-1122
2935 E 14th Ave Ste 200 Columbus (43219) **(G-8233)**
Ohio Concrete Resurfacing Inc (PA) 440 786-9100
15 N Park St Bedford (44146) **(G-1297)**

1210 2019 Harris Ohio Services Directory (G-0000) Company's Geographic Section entry number

Ohio Consumers Counsel 614 466-8574
65 E State St Ste 700 Columbus (43215) *(G-8234)*

Ohio Custodial Maintenance 614 443-1232
1291 S High St Columbus (43206) *(G-8235)*

Ohio Custodial Management, Columbus *Also called Ohio Custodial Maintenance* *(G-8235)*

Ohio Department of Aging 614 466-5500
246 N High St Fl 1 Columbus (43215) *(G-8236)*

Ohio Department of Commerce 614 644-7381
77 S High St Fl 22 Columbus (43215) *(G-8237)*

Ohio Department of Commerce 614 728-8400
77 S High St Fl 21 Columbus (43215) *(G-8238)*

Ohio Department of Education 740 289-2908
175 Beaver Creek Rd Piketon (45661) *(G-15980)*

Ohio Department of Health 330 792-2397
50 Westchester Dr Ste 202 Austintown (44515) *(G-858)*

Ohio Department of Health 614 645-3621
3850 Sullivant Ave # 102 Columbus (43228) *(G-8239)*

Ohio Department of Health 614 466-1521
246 N High St Columbus (43215) *(G-8240)*

Ohio Department of Health 937 285-6250
1323 W 3rd St Dayton (45402) *(G-9668)*

Ohio Department of Health 419 447-1450
600 N River Rd Tiffin (44883) *(G-17528)*

Ohio Department of Health 614 438-1255
400 E Campus View Blvd Columbus (43235) *(G-8241)*

Ohio Department Transportation 740 363-1251
400 E William St Delaware (43015) *(G-9999)*

Ohio Department Transportation 937 548-3015
1144 Martin St Greenville (45331) *(G-11391)*

Ohio Department Transportation 419 738-4214
511 Converse Dr Wapakoneta (45895) *(G-18651)*

Ohio Department Transportation 614 275-1324
1600 W Broad St Columbus (43223) *(G-8242)*

Ohio Department Transportation 330 533-4351
501 W Main St Canfield (44406) *(G-2153)*

Ohio Department Transportation 330 637-5951
310 2nd St Cortland (44410) *(G-8992)*

Ohio Department Veterans Svcs 614 644-0898
77 S High St Fl 7 Columbus (43215) *(G-8243)*

Ohio Department Youth Services 740 881-3337
51 N High St Fl 5 Columbus (43215) *(G-8244)*

Ohio Dept Amvet Svc Foundation (PA) 614 431-6990
1395 E Dublin Granville R Columbus (43229) *(G-8245)*

Ohio Dept Natural Resources 740 869-3124
20635 State Park Road 20 Mount Sterling (43143) *(G-14746)*

Ohio Dept of Job & Fmly Svcs 614 752-9494
4300 Kimberly Pkwy N Columbus (43232) *(G-8246)*

Ohio Dept of Job & Fmly Svcs 330 484-5402
161 S High St Ste 300 Akron (44308) *(G-357)*

Ohio Dept of Job & Fmly Svcs 419 334-3891
2511 Countryside Dr Fremont (43420) *(G-11089)*

Ohio Dept of Job & Fmly Svcs 614 466-1213
255 E Main St Fl 3 Columbus (43215) *(G-8247)*

Ohio Dept Rhbilitation Corectn 614 274-9000
770 W Broad St Columbus (43222) *(G-8248)*

Ohio Design Centre 216 831-1245
23533 Mercantile Rd Beachwood (44122) *(G-1090)*

Ohio Desk Co 216 623-0600
4851 Van Epps Rd Ste B Brooklyn Heights (44131) *(G-1877)*

Ohio Disability Rights Law Pol 614 466-7264
200 Civic Center Dr Columbus (43215) *(G-8249)*

Ohio District 5 Area 419 522-5612
2131 Park Ave W Ontario (44906) *(G-15567)*

Ohio Drilling Company (PA) 330 832-1521
2405 Bostic Blvd Sw Massillon (44647) *(G-13718)*

Ohio E Check, Painesville *Also called Envirotest Systems Corp* *(G-15713)*

Ohio E-Check, Cleveland *Also called Envirotest Systems Corp* *(G-5486)*

Ohio Eastern Star Home 740 397-1706
1451 Gambier Rd Ofc Mount Vernon (43050) *(G-14785)*

Ohio Edison Company (HQ) 800 736-3402
76 S Main St Bsmt Akron (44308) *(G-358)*

Ohio Edison Company 740 671-2900
57246 Ferry Landing Rd Shadyside (43947) *(G-16697)*

Ohio Edison Company 330 740-7754
730 South Ave Youngstown (44502) *(G-20143)*

Ohio Edison Company 330 336-9880
9681 Silvercreek Rd Wadsworth (44281) *(G-18610)*

Ohio Education Association 614 485-6000
2470 North Star Rd Columbus (43221) *(G-8250)*

Ohio Education Association (PA) 614 228-4526
225 E Broad St Fl 2 Columbus (43215) *(G-8251)*

Ohio Educational Credit Union (PA) 216 621-6296
4141 Rockside Rd Ste 400 Seven Hills (44131) *(G-16678)*

Ohio Entertainment Security 937 325-7216
3749 Mahar Rd South Vienna (45369) *(G-16948)*

Ohio Equities LLC 614 207-1805
6210 Busch Blvd Columbus (43229) *(G-8252)*

Ohio Equities LLC 614 469-0058
17 S High St Ste 799 Columbus (43215) *(G-8253)*

Ohio Equity Fund Inc 614 469-1797
88 E Broad St Ste 1800 Columbus (43215) *(G-8254)*

Ohio Exposition Center 614 644-4000
717 E 17th Ave Columbus (43211) *(G-8255)*

Ohio Exterminating Co Inc 614 294-6311
1347 N High St Columbus (43201) *(G-8256)*

Ohio Eye Alliance (PA) 330 823-1680
985 S Sawburg Ave Alliance (44601) *(G-542)*

Ohio Eye Associates Inc 800 423-0694
466 S Trimble Rd Mansfield (44906) *(G-13229)*

Ohio Eye Specialists Inc 800 948-3937
50 N Plaza Blvd Chillicothe (45601) *(G-2807)*

Ohio F F A Camps Inc 330 627-2208
3266 Dyewood Rd Sw Carrollton (44615) *(G-2574)*

Ohio Fair Plan Undwrt Assn 614 839-6446
2500 Corp Exchange Dr # 250 Columbus (43231) *(G-8257)*

Ohio Farm Bur Federation Inc (PA) 614 249-2400
280 N High St Fl 6 Columbus (43215) *(G-8258)*

Ohio Farmers Insurance Company (PA) 800 243-0210
1 Park Cir Westfield Center (44251) *(G-19308)*

Ohio Farmers Insurance Company 330 484-5660
1801 Faircrest St Se Canton (44707) *(G-2425)*

Ohio Farmers Insurance Company 614 848-6174
2000 Polaris Pkwy Ste 202 Columbus (43240) *(G-6828)*

Ohio Federation of Soil and WA 614 784-1900
8995 E Main St Reynoldsburg (43068) *(G-16323)*

Ohio Field Office, Dublin *Also called The Nature Conservancy* *(G-10356)*

Ohio Fresh Eggs LLC (PA) 740 893-7200
11212 Croton Rd Croton (43013) *(G-9065)*

Ohio Fresh Eggs LLC 937 354-2233
20449 County Road 245 Mount Victory (43340) *(G-14796)*

Ohio Gas Company (HQ) 419 636-1117
200 W High St Bryan (43506) *(G-1966)*

Ohio Gas Company 419 636-3642
715 E Wilson St Bryan (43506) *(G-1967)*

Ohio Gasket and Shim Co Inc (PA) 330 630-0626
976 Evans Ave Akron (44305) *(G-359)*

Ohio Gstroenterology Group Inc 614 221-8355
815 W Broad St Ste 220 Columbus (43222) *(G-8259)*

Ohio Gstroenterology Group Inc 614 754-5500
85 Mcnaughten Rd Ste 320 Columbus (43213) *(G-8260)*

Ohio Gstroenterology Group Inc (PA) 614 754-5500
3400 Olentangy River Rd Columbus (43202) *(G-8261)*

Ohio Gypsum Supply, Springfield *Also called Robinson Insulation Co Inc* *(G-17102)*

Ohio Head & Neck Surgeons Inc (PA) 330 492-2844
4912 Higbee Ave Nw # 200 Canton (44718) *(G-2426)*

Ohio Health, Columbus *Also called Gerlach John J Center For Sen* *(G-7663)*

Ohio Health, Nelsonville *Also called Doctors Hospital Cleveland Inc* *(G-14829)*

Ohio Health Care Employees, Columbus *Also called Healthcare and Social* *(G-7726)*

Ohio Health Choice Inc (HQ) 800 554-0027
6000 Parkland Blvd # 100 Cleveland (44124) *(G-6120)*

Ohio Health Council 614 221-7614
155 E Broad St Ste 301 Columbus (43215) *(G-8262)*

Ohio Health Group LLC 614 566-0010
155 E Broad St Ste 1700 Columbus (43215) *(G-8263)*

Ohio Health Physician Group 740 594-8819
75 Hospital Dr Ste 216 Athens (45701) *(G-793)*

Ohio Healthcare Federal Cr Un (PA) 614 737-6034
3955 W Dblin Granville Rd Dublin (43017) *(G-10297)*

Ohio Heart 513 206-1320
7545 Beechmont Ave Ste E Cincinnati (45255) *(G-4152)*

Ohio Heart and Vascular 513 206-1800
5885 Harrison Ave # 1900 Cincinnati (45248) *(G-4153)*

Ohio Heart Health Center Inc (PA) 513 351-9900
237 Wlliam Howard Taft Rd Cincinnati (45219) *(G-4154)*

Ohio Heart Instit, Youngstown *Also called Cardiovascular Associates Inc* *(G-19981)*

Ohio Heart Institute Inc (PA) 330 747-6446
1001 Belmont Ave Youngstown (44504) *(G-20144)*

Ohio Heating & AC Inc 614 863-6666
1465 Clara St Columbus (43211) *(G-8264)*

Ohio Heavy Equipment Lsg LLC (PA) 513 965-6600
9520 Le Saint Dr Fairfield (45014) *(G-10764)*

Ohio HI Point Career Center 937 599-3010
412 N Main St Urbana (43078) *(G-18442)*

Ohio Hickory Harvest Brand Pro 330 644-6266
90 Logan Pkwy Coventry Township (44319) *(G-9040)*

Ohio High School Football Coac 419 673-1286
138 Purple Finch Loop Etna (43062) *(G-10618)*

Ohio Hills Health Service, Woodsfield *Also called Monroe Family Health Center* *(G-19677)*

Ohio Hills Health Services (PA) 740 425-5165
101 E Main St Barnesville (43713) *(G-978)*

Ohio Historical Society (PA) 614 297-2300
800 E 17th Ave Columbus (43211) *(G-8265)*

OHIO HISTORY CONNECTION, Columbus *Also called Ohio Historical Society* *(G-8265)*

Ohio Home Health Care Inc 937 853-0271
5050 Nebraska Ave Ste 5 Dayton (45424) *(G-9669)*

Ohio Hospital Association 614 221-7614
155 E Broad St Ste 301 Columbus (43215) *(G-8266)*

Ohio Hospital For Psychiatry 877 762-9026
880 Greenlawn Ave Columbus (43223) *(G-8267)*

Ohio Housing Finance Agency 614 466-7970
57 E Main St Fl 3 Columbus (43215) *(G-8268)*

Ohio Hrtland Cmnty Action Comm (PA) 740 387-1039
372 E Center St Marion (43302) *(G-13450)*

Ohio Hrtland Cmnty Action Comm 419 468-5121
124 Buehler St Galion (44833) *(G-11180)*

Ohio Hydraulics Inc 513 771-2590
2510 E Sharon Rd Ste 1 Cincinnati (45241) *(G-4155)*

Ohio Indemnity Company 614 228-1601
250 E Broad St Fl 7 Columbus (43215) *(G-8269)*

Ohio Inns Inc 937 440-9303
87 Troy Town Dr Troy (45373) *(G-18219)*

Ohio Institute of Cardiac Care (PA) 937 322-1700
2451 Patrick Blvd Dayton (45431) *(G-9184)*

Ohio Irrigation Lawn Sprinkler (PA) 937 432-9911
2109 E Social Row Rd Dayton (45458) *(G-9670)*

Ohio Kepro Inc 216 447-9604
5700 Lombardo Ctr Ste 100 Seven Hills (44131) *(G-16679)*

Ohio Laminating & Binding Inc 614 771-4868
4364 Reynolds Dr Hilliard (43026) *(G-11802)*

Ohio Laundry, Columbus *Also called Super Laundry Inc (G-8713)*

Ohio Lbrers Frnge Bneft Prgram 614 898-9006
800 Hillsdowne Rd Westerville (43081) *(G-19287)*

Ohio Legal Rights Service 614 466-7264
50 W Broad St Ste 1400 Columbus (43215) *(G-8270)*

Ohio Light Opera 330 263-2345
1189 Beall Ave Wooster (44691) *(G-19753)*

Ohio Living 330 638-2420
303 N Mecca St Cortland (44410) *(G-8993)*

Ohio Living 614 224-1651
645 Neil Ave Ofc Columbus (43215) *(G-8271)*

Ohio Living 513 681-4230
1701 Llanfair Ave Cincinnati (45224) *(G-4156)*

Ohio Living 440 942-4342
36855 Ridge Rd Willoughby (44094) *(G-19558)*

Ohio Living (PA) 614 888-7800
1001 Kingsmill Pkwy Columbus (43229) *(G-8272)*

Ohio Machinery Co 419 874-7975
25970 Dixie Hwy Perrysburg (43551) *(G-15897)*

Ohio Machinery Co 740 942-4626
1016 E Market St Cadiz (43907) *(G-2032)*

Ohio Machinery Co (PA) 440 526-6200
3993 E Royalton Rd Broadview Heights (44147) *(G-1840)*

Ohio Machinery Co 330 478-6525
4731 Corporate St Sw Canton (44706) *(G-2427)*

Ohio Machinery Co 330 530-9010
1 Ohio Machinery Blvd Girard (44420) *(G-11295)*

Ohio Machinery Co 740 453-0563
3415 East Pike Zanesville (43701) *(G-20348)*

Ohio Machinery Co 513 771-0515
11330 Mosteller Rd Cincinnati (45241) *(G-4157)*

Ohio Machinery Co 614 878-2287
5252 Walcutt Ct Columbus (43228) *(G-8273)*

Ohio Machinery Co 330 874-1003
10955 Industrial Pkwy Nw Bolivar (44612) *(G-1705)*

Ohio Machinery Co 440 526-0520
900 Ken Mar Indus Pkwy Broadview Heights (44147) *(G-1841)*

Ohio Machinery Co 937 335-7660
1281 Brukner Dr Troy (45373) *(G-18220)*

Ohio Maint & Renovation Inc (PA) 330 315-3101
124 Darrow Rd Akron (44305) *(G-360)*

Ohio Masonic Retirement Vlg 937 525-1743
4 Masonic Dr Springfield (45504) *(G-17092)*

Ohio Materials Handling, Macedonia *Also called Newtown Nine Inc (G-13078)*

Ohio Medical Group, Cleveland *Also called North Ohio Heart Center Inc (G-6078)*

Ohio Medical Group, Avon *Also called North Ohio Heart Center Inc (G-897)*

Ohio Medical Group (PA) 440 414-9400
29325 Health Campus Dr # 3 Westlake (44145) *(G-19386)*

Ohio Medical Trnsp Inc 937 747-3540
22758 Wilbur Rd Marysville (43040) *(G-13521)*

Ohio Medical Trnsp Inc 740 962-2055
975 E Airport Rd Ne McConnelsville (43756) *(G-13904)*

Ohio Medical Trnsp Inc (PA) 614 791-4400
2827 W Dblin Granville Rd Columbus (43235) *(G-8274)*

Ohio Metal Processing Inc 740 286-6457
16064 Beaver Pike Jackson (45640) *(G-12178)*

Ohio Minority Medical 513 400-5011
517 Broadway St Ste 500 East Liverpool (43920) *(G-10411)*

Ohio Mutual Insurance Company (PA) 419 562-3011
1725 Hopley Ave Bucyrus (44820) *(G-1999)*

Ohio Nat Mutl Holdings Inc (PA) 513 794-6100
1 Financial Way Ste 100 Montgomery (45242) *(G-14598)*

Ohio National Fincl Svcs Inc (HQ) 513 794-6100
1 Financial Way Ste 100 Montgomery (45242) *(G-14599)*

Ohio National Life Assurance 513 794-6100
1 Financial Way Ste 100 Montgomery (45242) *(G-14600)*

Ohio National Life Insur Co (HQ) 513 794-6100
1 Financial Way Ste 100 Montgomery (45242) *(G-14601)*

Ohio News Network 614 460-3700
770 Twin Rivers Dr Columbus (43215) *(G-8275)*

Ohio News Network 216 367-7493
3001 Euclid Ave Cleveland (44115) *(G-6121)*

Ohio News Network, The, Columbus *Also called Ohio News Network (G-8275)*

Ohio North E Hlth Systems Inc 330 747-9551
726 Wick Ave Youngstown (44505) *(G-20145)*

Ohio North E Hlth Systems Inc (PA) 330 747-9551
726 Wick Ave Youngstown (44505) *(G-20146)*

Ohio Nut & Bolt Company Div, Berea *Also called Fastener Industries Inc (G-1426)*

Ohio Oil Gathering Corporation (HQ) 740 828-2892
9320 Blackrun Rd Nashport (43830) *(G-14821)*

Ohio Operating Engineers Apprn 614 487-6531
1184 Dublin Rd Columbus (43215) *(G-8276)*

Ohio Orthopedic Center, Lancaster *Also called River Vly Orthpdics Spt Mdcine (G-12431)*

Ohio Orthpd Surgery Inst LLC 614 827-8777
4605 Sawmill Rd Columbus (43220) *(G-8277)*

Ohio Osteopathic Hospital Assn 614 299-2107
52 W 3rd Ave Columbus (43201) *(G-8278)*

Ohio Paving & Cnstr Co Inc 440 975-8929
38220 Willoughby Pkwy Willoughby (44094) *(G-19559)*

Ohio Paving Group LLC 216 475-1700
4873 Osborn Rd Cleveland (44128) *(G-6122)*

Ohio Pediatrics Inc 937 299-2339
7200 Poe Ave Ste 201 Dayton (45414) *(G-9671)*

Ohio Pediatrics Inc (PA) 937 299-2743
1775 Delco Park Dr Dayton (45420) *(G-9672)*

Ohio Pia Service Corporation 614 552-8000
600 Cross Pointe Rd Gahanna (43230) *(G-11139)*

Ohio Pizza Products Inc (HQ) 937 294-6969
201 Lawton Ave Monroe (45050) *(G-14578)*

Ohio Pools & Spas Inc (PA) 330 494-7755
6815 Whipple Ave Nw Canton (44720) *(G-2428)*

Ohio Power Company (HQ) 614 716-1000
1 Riverside Plz Columbus (43215) *(G-8279)*

Ohio Power Company 888 216-3523
1 Riverside Plz Canton (44701) *(G-2429)*

Ohio Power Company 419 443-4634
2622 S State Route 100 Tiffin (44883) *(G-17529)*

Ohio Power Company 740 695-7800
47687 National Rd Saint Clairsville (43950) *(G-16497)*

Ohio Presbt Retirement Svcs 330 746-2944
1216 5th Ave Youngstown (44504) *(G-20147)*

Ohio Presbt Retirement Svcs 330 867-2150
1150 W Market St Akron (44313) *(G-361)*

Ohio Presbt Retirement Svcs 937 498-2391
3003 Cisco Rd Sidney (45365) *(G-16789)*

Ohio Presbt Retirement Svcs 513 539-7391
225 Britton Ln Monroe (45050) *(G-14579)*

Ohio Presbt Retirement Svcs 937 415-5666
6520 Poe Ave Dayton (45414) *(G-9673)*

Ohio Presbt Retirement Svcs 614 228-8888
717 Neil Ave Columbus (43215) *(G-8280)*

Ohio Presbt Retirement Vlg, Monroe *Also called Ohio Presbt Retirement Svcs (G-14579)*

Ohio Presbyterian Rtr Svcs 614 888-7800
1001 Kingsmill Pkwy Columbus (43229) *(G-8281)*

Ohio Pressure Grouting, Cuyahoga Falls *Also called Technical Construction Spc (G-9129)*

Ohio Pub Emplyees Rtrement Sys 614 228-8471
277 E Town St Columbus (43215) *(G-8282)*

Ohio Real Title Agency LLC (PA) 216 373-9900
1213 Prospect Ave E # 200 Cleveland (44115) *(G-6123)*

Ohio Rehabilitation Svcs Comm 330 643-3080
161 S High St Ste 103 Akron (44308) *(G-362)*

Ohio Renal Care Group LLC 440 974-3459
8840 Tyler Blvd Mentor (44060) *(G-14092)*

Ohio Renal Care Group LLC 330 928-4511
320 Broadway St E Cuyahoga Falls (44221) *(G-9116)*

Ohio Renal Care Grp Mentor Dia, Mentor *Also called Ohio Renal Care Group LLC (G-14092)*

Ohio Republican Party, Columbus *Also called Republican State Central Execu (G-8517)*

Ohio Resources, Westerville *Also called Ohio Builders Resources LLC (G-19194)*

Ohio Retina Associates Inc (PA) 330 966-9800
4690 Munson St Nw Ste D Canton (44718) *(G-2430)*

Ohio River Forecast, Wilmington *Also called National Weather Service (G-19636)*

Ohio Rural Electric Coops, Columbus *Also called Buckeye Power Inc (G-7089)*

Ohio Rural Electric Coops Inc 614 846-5757
6677 Busch Blvd Columbus (43229) *(G-8283)*

Ohio Rver Vly Wtr Snttion Comm 513 231-7719
5735 Kellogg Ave Cincinnati (45230) *(G-4158)*

Ohio Savings Bank, Cleveland *Also called New York Community Bank (G-6064)*

Ohio School Boards Association 614 540-4000
8050 N High St Ste 100 Columbus (43235) *(G-8284)*

Ohio School Pictures, Bellevue *Also called Royal Color Inc (G-1385)*

Ohio School Psychologists Assn 614 414-5980
4449 Easton Way Fl 2offi Columbus (43219) *(G-8285)*

Ohio Senior Home Hlth Care LLC 614 470-6070
6004 Cleveland Ave Columbus (43231) *(G-8286)*

Ohio Skate Inc (PA) 419 476-2808
5735 Opportunity Dr Toledo (43612) *(G-17958)*

Ohio Soc of Crtif Pub Accntnts 614 764-2727
4249 Easton Way Ste 150 Columbus (43219) *(G-8287)*

OHIO SOCEITY OF CPAS, Columbus *Also called Ohio Soc of Crtif Pub Accntnts (G-8287)*

Ohio State Bar Association 614 487-2050
1700 Lake Shore Dr Columbus (43204) *(G-8288)*

Ohio State Bar Association 614 487-2050
1700 Lake Shore Dr Columbus (43204) *(G-8289)*

Ohio State Home Services Inc (PA) 330 467-1055
365 Highland Rd E Macedonia (44056) *(G-13079)*

Ohio State Home Services Inc. 614 850-5600
4271 Weaver Ct N Hilliard (43026) *(G-11803)*

Ohio State Medical Association (PA) 614 527-6762
5115 Prkcnter Ave Ste 200 Dublin (43017) *(G-10298)*

Ohio State Parks Inc...513 664-3504
5201 Lodge Rd College Corner (45003) ***(G-6768)***
Ohio State Univ Alumni Assn...614 292-2200
2200 Olentangy River Rd Columbus (43210) ***(G-8290)***
Ohio State Univ Child Care, Columbus *Also called Ohio State University* ***(G-8311)***
Ohio State Univ Spt Mdcine Ctr, Columbus *Also called Ohio State University* ***(G-8339)***
Ohio State Univ Vtrnarian Hosp, Columbus *Also called Ohio State University* ***(G-8334)***
Ohio State Univ Wexner Med Ctr...614 293-2663
369 Grenadine Way Columbus (43235) ***(G-8291)***
Ohio State Univ Wexner Med Ctr (HQ)...614 293-8000
410 W 10th Ave Columbus (43210) ***(G-8292)***
Ohio State Univ Wexner Med Ctr...614 366-3687
1492 E Broad St Columbus (43205) ***(G-8293)***
Ohio State Univ Wexner Med Ctr...614 293-6255
410 W 10th Ave Columbus (43210) ***(G-8294)***
Ohio State University...614 366-3692
480 Medical Center Dr Columbus (43210) ***(G-8295)***
Ohio State University...614 688-3939
555 Borror Dr Columbus (43210) ***(G-8296)***
Ohio State University...614 293-8045
410 W 10th Ave Rm 205 Columbus (43210) ***(G-8297)***
Ohio State University...614 293-2800
2050 Kenny Rd Ste 1010 Columbus (43221) ***(G-8298)***
Ohio State University...614 292-5578
305 W 12th Ave Columbus (43210) ***(G-8299)***
Ohio State University...614 257-3000
300 W 10th Ave Columbus (43210) ***(G-8300)***
Ohio State University...614 293-7417
1615 Fishinger Rd Columbus (43221) ***(G-8301)***
Ohio State University...614 293-8750
480 W 9th Ave Columbus (43210) ***(G-8302)***
Ohio State University...614 293-8116
915 Olentangy River Rd Columbus (43212) ***(G-8303)***
Ohio State University...330 263-3700
1680 Madison Ave Wooster (44691) ***(G-19754)***
Ohio State University...614 292-5504
350 Campbell Hl Columbus (43210) ***(G-8304)***
Ohio State University...740 376-7431
202 Davis Ave Marietta (45750) ***(G-13364)***
Ohio State University...614 292-5491
2300 West Case Rd Columbus (43235) ***(G-8305)***
Ohio State University...614 292-4139
1248 Arthur E Adams Dr Columbus (43221) ***(G-8306)***
Ohio State University...614 292-2624
555 Borror Dr Ste 1030 Columbus (43210) ***(G-8307)***
Ohio State University...614 292-1681
1501 Neil Ave Columbus (43201) ***(G-8308)***
Ohio State University...740 593-2657
1 Park Pl Athens (45701) ***(G-794)***
Ohio State University...614 293-3860
1375 Perry St Columbus (43201) ***(G-8309)***
Ohio State University...614 247-4000
2110 Tuttle Park Pl Columbus (43210) ***(G-8310)***
Ohio State University...614 292-4453
725 Ackerman Rd Columbus (43202) ***(G-8311)***
Ohio State University...614 292-4510
2400 Olentangy River Rd Columbus (43210) ***(G-8312)***
Ohio State University...330 263-3701
1680 Madison Ave Wooster (44691) ***(G-19755)***
Ohio State University...614 292-4843
1121 Kinnear Rd Bldg E Columbus (43212) ***(G-8313)***
Ohio State University...614 257-5200
420 N James Rd Columbus (43219) ***(G-8314)***
Ohio State University...614 292-6831
901 Woody Hayes Dr Columbus (43210) ***(G-8315)***
Ohio State University...614 292-4353
1900 Kenny Rd Columbus (43210) ***(G-8316)***
Ohio State University...614 293-4997
395 W 12th Ave Columbus (43210) ***(G-8317)***
Ohio State University...614 293-2494
2130 Neil Ave Columbus (43210) ***(G-8318)***
Ohio State University...614 292-7788
320 W 8th Ave Columbus (43201) ***(G-8319)***
Ohio State University...614 442-7300
921 Chatham Ln Ste 100 Columbus (43221) ***(G-8320)***
Ohio State University...614 293-8732
N.1135 Doan Hl Columbus (43210) ***(G-8321)***
Ohio State University...614 292-6291
3007 Derby Rd Columbus (43221) ***(G-8322)***
Ohio State University...614 293-8158
410 W 10th Ave Rm 130 Columbus (43210) ***(G-8323)***
Ohio State University...614 292-0110
1875 Millikin Rd Fl 3 Columbus (43210) ***(G-8324)***
Ohio State University...614 292-6741
Ps Pschology Rm 225 St Rm 2 Columbus (43210) ***(G-8325)***
Ohio State University...614 292-5144
305 W 12th Ave Ste 2131 Columbus (43210) ***(G-8326)***
Ohio State University...330 263-3725
5119 Lauby Rd Canton (44720) ***(G-2431)***
Ohio State University...614 293-8732
456 W 10th Ave Rm 4725 Columbus (43210) ***(G-8327)***
Ohio State University...614 293-8588
410 W 10th Ave Columbus (43210) ***(G-8328)***
Ohio State University...614 688-5721
29 W Woodruff Ave Ofc 121 Columbus (43210) ***(G-8329)***
Ohio State University...614 293-3737
650 Ackerman Rd Ste 135 Columbus (43202) ***(G-8330)***
Ohio State University...614 688-8220
1298 Kinnear Rd Columbus (43212) ***(G-8331)***
Ohio State University...614 292-6122
2578 Kenny Rd Columbus (43210) ***(G-8332)***
Ohio State University...614 292-3238
2400 Olentangy River Rd Columbus (43210) ***(G-8333)***
Ohio State University...614 292-6661
601 Vernon Tharp St Columbus (43210) ***(G-8334)***
Ohio State University...614 292-5990
930 Kinnear Rd Columbus (43212) ***(G-8335)***
Ohio State University...614 294-2635
80 E 13th Ave Columbus (43201) ***(G-8336)***
Ohio State University...614 292-6251
1070 Carmack Rd Columbus (43210) ***(G-8337)***
Ohio State University...614 728-8100
1224 Kinnear Rd Columbus (43212) ***(G-8338)***
Ohio State University...614 293-2222
2050 Kenny Rd Fl 3 Columbus (43221) ***(G-8339)***
Ohio State University...614 293-8133
410 W 10th Ave Fl 7 Columbus (43210) ***(G-8340)***
Ohio State University...614 292-9404
1080 Carmack Rd Columbus (43210) ***(G-8341)***
Ohio State University...614 293-5066
300 W 10th Ave 924 Columbus (43210) ***(G-8342)***
Ohio State University...614 293-8419
410 W 10th Ave Rm 140 Columbus (43210) ***(G-8343)***
Ohio State University...614 292-1472
305 W 12th Ave Columbus (43210) ***(G-8344)***
Ohio State University...614 293-8196
N924 Doan Hall 410 W 10 Columbus (43210) ***(G-8345)***
Ohio State University...614 293-8333
450 W 10th Ave Columbus (43210) ***(G-8346)***
Ohio State University...614 293-8000
450 W 10th Ave Columbus (43210) ***(G-8347)***
Ohio State University...614 293-4925
2050 Kenny Rd Ste 2200 Columbus (43221) ***(G-8348)***
Ohio State University...614 293-8074
915 Olentangy River Rd Columbus (43212) ***(G-8349)***
Ohio State University...614 292-2751
305 W 12th Ave Columbus (43210) ***(G-8350)***
Ohio State University...614 293-4967
473 W 12th Ave Columbus (43210) ***(G-8351)***
Ohio State University...614 292-6158
2003 Millikin Rd Rm 150 Columbus (43210) ***(G-8352)***
Ohio State University EXT, Marietta *Also called Ohio State University* ***(G-13364)***
OHIO STATE UNIVERSITY FACULTY, Columbus *Also called O S U Faculty Club* ***(G-8220)***
Ohio State Waterproofing, Macedonia *Also called Ohio State Home Services Inc* ***(G-13079)***
Ohio Steel Sheet & Plate Inc...800 827-2401
7845 Chestnut Ridge Rd Hubbard (44425) ***(G-11949)***
Ohio Steel Slitters Inc...330 477-6741
1401 Raff Rd Sw Canton (44710) ***(G-2432)***
Ohio Structures Inc (HQ)...330 533-0084
535 N Broad St Ste 5 Canfield (44406) ***(G-2154)***
Ohio Support Services Corp (PA)...614 443-0291
1291 S High St Columbus (43206) ***(G-8353)***
Ohio Surgery Center, Columbus *Also called Nueterra Holdings LLC* ***(G-8214)***
Ohio Surgery Center Ltd...614 451-0500
930 Bethel Rd Columbus (43214) ***(G-8354)***
Ohio Tctcal Enfrcment Svcs LLC...614 989-9485
6100 Channingway Blvd Columbus (43232) ***(G-8355)***
Ohio Technical College Inc...216 881-1700
1374 E 51st St Cleveland (44103) ***(G-6124)***
Ohio Technical Services Inc...614 372-0829
1949 Camaro Ave Columbus (43207) ***(G-8356)***
Ohio Textile Service Inc...740 450-4900
2270 Fairview Rd Zanesville (43701) ***(G-20349)***
Ohio Tpk & Infrastructure Comm (HQ)...440 234-2081
682 Prospect St Berea (44017) ***(G-1432)***
Ohio Tpk & Infrastructure Comm...419 826-4831
8891 County Road 1 Swanton (43558) ***(G-17403)***
Ohio Tpk & Infrastructure Comm...440 234-2081
682 Prospect St Berea (44017) ***(G-1433)***
Ohio Tpk & Infrastructure Comm...440 234-2081
3245 Boston Mills Rd Richfield (44286) ***(G-16369)***
Ohio Transmission Corporation (HQ)...614 342-6247
1900 Jetway Blvd Columbus (43219) ***(G-8357)***
Ohio Transmission Corporation...419 468-7866
1311 Freese Works Pl Galion (44833) ***(G-11181)***
Ohio Transmission Corporation...614 342-6247
1900 Jetway Blvd Columbus (43219) ***(G-8358)***
Ohio Transport Corporation (PA)...513 539-0576
5593 Hmlton Middletown Rd Middletown (45044) ***(G-14316)***
Ohio Transport Inc...216 741-8000
3750 Valley Rd Ste A Cleveland (44109) ***(G-6125)***
Ohio University...740 593-1000
3 Station St Apt D Athens (45701) ***(G-795)***
Ohio University...740 593-1771
Woub 35 S Cllg St 395 Athens (45701) ***(G-796)***

ALPHABETIC

Ohio University..740 593-1771
  35 S College St Athens (45701) *(G-797)*
Ohio University..740 593-2195
  227 W Washington St Apt 1 Athens (45701) *(G-798)*
Ohio University..740 593-1660
  2 Health Center Dr Rm 110 Athens (45701) *(G-799)*
Ohio Utilities Protection Svc...............................800 311-3692
  12467 Mahoning Ave North Jackson (44451) *(G-15250)*
Ohio Valley Acquisition Inc.................................513 553-0768
  250 E 5th St Ste 1200 Cincinnati (45202) *(G-4159)*
Ohio Valley Ambulatory Surgery...........................740 423-4684
  608 Washington Blvd Belpre (45714) *(G-1409)*
Ohio Valley Bank Company....................................740 446-2168
  236 2nd Ave Gallipolis (45631) *(G-11206)*
Ohio Valley Bank Company (HQ)...........................740 446-2631
  420 3rd Ave Gallipolis (45631) *(G-11207)*
Ohio Valley Bank Company....................................740 446-1646
  100 Jackson Pike Gallipolis (45631) *(G-11208)*
Ohio Valley Bank Company....................................740 446-2631
  143 3rd Ave Gallipolis (45631) *(G-11209)*
Ohio Valley Coal, Saint Clairsville Also called Ohio Valley Resources Inc *(G-16499)*
Ohio Valley Coal Company (HQ)............................740 926-1351
  46226 National Rd Saint Clairsville (43950) *(G-16498)*
Ohio Valley Elec Svcs LLC...................................513 771-2410
  4585 Cornell Rd Blue Ash (45241) *(G-1623)*
Ohio Valley Electric Corp (HQ)............................740 289-7200
  3932 Us Rte 23 Piketon (45661) *(G-15981)*
Ohio Valley Electric Corp....................................740 289-7225
  3932 Us Rt 23 Piketon (45661) *(G-15982)*
Ohio Valley Flooring Inc (PA)............................513 271-3434
  5555 Murray Ave Cincinnati (45227) *(G-4160)*
Ohio Valley Group Inc.......................................440 543-0500
  16965 Park Circle Dr Chagrin Falls (44023) *(G-2676)*
Ohio Valley Home Care LLC................................330 385-2333
  425 W 5th St East Liverpool (43920) *(G-10412)*
Ohio Valley Home Health Inc................................740 249-4219
  2097 E State St Ste B1 Athens (45701) *(G-800)*
Ohio Valley Home Health Inc (PA).........................740 441-1393
  1480 Jackson Pike Gallipolis (45631) *(G-11210)*
Ohio Valley Home Hlth Svcs Inc (PA)....................330 385-2333
  425 W 5th St East Liverpool (43920) *(G-10413)*
Ohio Valley Integration Svcs...............................937 492-0008
  2005 Commerce Dr Sidney (45365) *(G-16790)*
Ohio Valley Manor Inc..937 392-4318
  5280 Us Highway 62 And 68 Ripley (45167) *(G-16401)*
Ohio Valley Medical Center LLC............................937 521-3900
  100 E Main St Springfield (45502) *(G-17093)*
Ohio Valley Resources Inc.................................740 795-5220
  46226 National Rd Saint Clairsville (43950) *(G-16499)*
Ohio Valley Sports, Inc., Cincinnati Also called Cincinnati Bengals Inc *(G-3230)*
Ohio Valley Technical Services, Cincinnati Also called Clean Harbors Envmtl Svcs Inc *(G-3303)*
Ohio Valley Transloading Co...............................740 795-4967
  46226 National Rd Saint Clairsville (43950) *(G-16500)*
Ohio Valley Wine & Beer, Cincinnati Also called Ohio Valley Wine Company *(G-4161)*
Ohio Valley Wine Company (PA)...........................513 771-9370
  10975 Medallion Dr Cincinnati (45241) *(G-4161)*
Ohio Vision of Toledo Inc Opt, Oregon Also called Optivue Inc *(G-15602)*
Ohio Window Cleaning Inc...................................937 877-0832
  4582 Us Route 40 Tipp City (45371) *(G-17563)*
Ohio's Country Journal, Columbus Also called Agri Communicators Inc *(G-6885)*
Ohio-American Water Co Inc (HQ)..........................740 382-3993
  365 E Center St Marion (43302) *(G-13451)*
Ohio-Kentucky Steel Corp...................................937 743-4600
  2001 Commerce Center Dr Franklin (45005) *(G-11035)*
Ohio-Kentucky-Indiana Regional...........................513 621-6300
  720 E Pete Rose Way # 420 Cincinnati (45202) *(G-4162)*
Ohio/Oklahoma Hearst TV Inc..............................513 412-5000
  1700 Young St Cincinnati (45202) *(G-4163)*
Ohioans Home Health Care Inc.............................419 843-4422
  28315 Kensington Ln Perrysburg (43551) *(G-15898)*
Ohiocare Ambulatory Surgery...............................419 897-5501
  5959 Monclova Rd Maumee (43537) *(G-13826)*
Ohioguidestone (PA)...440 234-2006
  434 Eastland Rd Berea (44017) *(G-1434)*
Ohioguidestone...440 260-8900
  3500 Carnegie Ave Cleveland (44115) *(G-6126)*
Ohiohealth, Kenton Also called Hardin Memorial Hospital *(G-12281)*
Ohiohealth Corporation.......................................614 566-5456
  3595 Olentangy River Rd Columbus (43214) *(G-8359)*
Ohiohealth Corporation.......................................614 544-8000
  7500 Hospital Dr Dublin (43016) *(G-10299)*
Ohiohealth Corporation.......................................614 566-2124
  180 E Broad St Columbus (43215) *(G-8360)*
Ohiohealth Corporation.......................................614 566-3500
  3333 Chippewa St Columbus (43204) *(G-8361)*
Ohiohealth Corporation (PA).................................614 788-8860
  180 E Broad St Columbus (43215) *(G-8362)*
Ohiohealth Corporation.......................................614 566-5977
  2601 Silver Dr Columbus (43211) *(G-8363)*
Ohiohealth Corporation.......................................614 566-9000
  111 S Grant Ave Columbus (43215) *(G-8364)*

Ohiohealth Corporation.......................................614 566-4800
  755 Thomas Ln Columbus (43214) *(G-8365)*
Ohiohealth Corporation.......................................614 566-5414
  697 Thomas Ln Columbus (43214) *(G-8366)*
Ohiohealth Mansfield Hospital, Mansfield Also called Medcentral Health System *(G-13215)*
Ohiohealth O'Bleness Hospital, Athens Also called Sheltering Arms Hospital Found *(G-802)*
Ohiohealth Research Institute..............................614 566-4297
  3545 Olentangy River Rd # 328 Columbus (43214) *(G-8367)*
Ohiohlth Rverside Methdst Hosp...........................614 566-5000
  3535 Olentangy River Rd Columbus (43214) *(G-8368)*
Ohiosolutions.org, Beachwood Also called A+ Solutions LLC *(G-1025)*
Ohs LLC...513 252-2249
  11427 Reed Hartman Hwy Blue Ash (45241) *(G-1624)*
Ohs Media Group, Blue Ash Also called Ohs LLC *(G-1624)*
Oicc, Dayton Also called Ohio Institute of Cardiac Care *(G-9184)*
Oid Associates..330 666-3161
  215 Springside Dr Akron (44333) *(G-363)*
OK Interiors Corp...513 742-3278
  11100 Ashburn Rd Cincinnati (45240) *(G-4164)*
Oki Auction LLC..513 679-7910
  120 Citycentre Dr Cincinnati (45216) *(G-4165)*
Oki Auto Auction, Cincinnati Also called Oki Auction LLC *(G-4165)*
Oki Rgonal Council Governments, Cincinnati Also called Ride Share Information *(G-4373)*
OKL Can Line Inc...513 825-1655
  11235 Sebring Dr Cincinnati (45240) *(G-4166)*
Ol' Smokehaus, Clayton Also called Landes Fresh Meats Inc *(G-4859)*
Old Barn Out Back Inc.......................................419 999-3989
  3175 W Elm St Lima (45805) *(G-12711)*
Old Barn Out Back Restaurant, Lima Also called Old Barn Out Back Inc *(G-12711)*
Old Dominion Freight Line Inc.............................330 545-8628
  1730 N State St Girard (44420) *(G-11296)*
Old Dominion Freight Line Inc.............................937 235-1596
  3100 Transportation Rd Dayton (45404) *(G-9674)*
Old Dominion Freight Line Inc.............................513 771-1486
  6431 Centre Park Dr West Chester (45069) *(G-18979)*
Old Dominion Freight Line Inc.............................419 726-4032
  5950 Stickney Ave Toledo (43612) *(G-17959)*
Old Dominion Freight Line Inc.............................614 491-3903
  2885 Alum Creek Dr Columbus (43207) *(G-8369)*
Old Dominion Freight Line Inc.............................216 641-5566
  8055 Old Granger Rd Cleveland (44125) *(G-6127)*
Old Fort Banking Company..................................419 447-4790
  33 E Market St Tiffin (44883) *(G-17530)*
Old Montgomery, Cincinnati Also called L W Limited *(G-3901)*
Old Rpblic Ttle Nthrn Ohio LLC............................216 524-5700
  6480 Rckside Woods Blvd S Independence (44131) *(G-12106)*
Old Time Pottery Inc...513 825-5211
  1191 Smiley Ave Cincinnati (45240) *(G-4167)*
Old Time Pottery Inc...440 842-1244
  7011 W 130th St Ste 1 Cleveland (44130) *(G-6128)*
Old Time Pottery Inc...614 337-1258
  2200 Morse Rd Columbus (43229) *(G-8370)*
Old Towne Windows & Doors, Milan Also called Olde Towne Windows Inc *(G-14364)*
Old Trail School..330 666-1118
  2315 Ira Rd Bath (44210) *(G-1018)*
Olde Towne Windows Inc....................................419 626-9613
  9501 Us Highway 250 N # 1 Milan (44846) *(G-14364)*
Older Wiser Life Services LLC.............................330 659-2111
  4028 Broadview Rd Ste 1 Richfield (44286) *(G-16370)*
Oldies 95, Dayton Also called Miami Valley Broadcasting Corp *(G-9616)*
Olentangy Village Apartments, Columbus Also called Olentangy Village Associates *(G-8371)*
Olentangy Village Associates...............................614 515-4680
  2907 N High St Columbus (43202) *(G-8371)*
Oliver House Rest Complex..................................419 243-1302
  27 Broadway St Ste A Toledo (43604) *(G-17960)*
Oliver Steel Plate, Bedford Also called AM Castle & Co *(G-1269)*
Olmsted Lanes Inc..440 777-6363
  24488 Lorain Rd North Olmsted (44070) *(G-15301)*
Olmsted Manor Nursing Home...............................440 250-4080
  27500 Mill Rd North Olmsted (44070) *(G-15302)*
Olmsted Manor Retirement Prpts..........................440 250-4080
  26612 Center Ridge Rd Westlake (44145) *(G-19387)*
Olmsted Mnor Rtrment Cmnty Ltd.........................440 779-8886
  27420 Mill Rd North Olmsted (44070) *(G-15303)*
Olmsted Parks and Recreation, North Olmsted Also called City of North Olmsted *(G-15282)*
Olmsted Residence Corporation...........................440 235-7100
  26376 John Rd Ofc Olmsted Twp (44138) *(G-15539)*
Olmstedfalls Intermediate Schl, Olmsted Twp Also called Pta Olms Falls Int Sch *(G-15540)*
Ologie LLC...614 221-1107
  447 E Main St Ste 122 Columbus (43215) *(G-8372)*
Olon Ricerca Bioscience LLC...............................440 357-3300
  7528 Auburn Rd Painesville (44077) *(G-15730)*
Olshan Hotel Management Inc.............................614 414-1000
  3999 Easton Loop W Columbus (43219) *(G-8373)*
Olshan Hotel Management Inc.............................614 416-8000
  3900 Morse Xing Columbus (43219) *(G-8374)*
Olympia Candies, Strongsville Also called Robert E McGrath Inc *(G-17341)*
Olympic Steel Inc (PA)......................................216 292-3800
  22901 Millcreek Blvd # 650 Cleveland (44122) *(G-6129)*

Olympic Steel Inc...216 292-3800
5092 Richmond Rd Cleveland (44146) ***(G-6130)***
Olympic Steel Inc...440 287-0150
3000 Crane Centre Dr Streetsboro (44241) ***(G-17263)***
Olympic Steel Inc...216 292-3800
5080 Richmond Rd Bedford (44146) ***(G-1298)***
Om Group, Westlake *Also called Borchers Americas Inc* ***(G-19323)***
Omega Laboratories Inc...330 628-5748
400 N Cleveland Ave Mogadore (44260) ***(G-14553)***
Omega Sea LLC...440 639-2372
1000 Bacon Rd Painesville (44077) ***(G-15731)***
Omega Title Agency LLC...330 436-0600
4500 Courthouse Blvd # 100 Stow (44224) ***(G-17221)***
Omicron Investment Company LLC...419 891-1040
145 Chesterfield Ln Maumee (43537) ***(G-13827)***
Omni Cart Services Inc...440 205-8363
7370 Production Dr Mentor (44060) ***(G-14093)***
Omni Construction Company Inc...216 514-6664
25825 Science Park Dr # 100 Beachwood (44122) ***(G-1091)***
Omni Fasteners Inc...440 838-1800
909 Towpath Trl Broadview Heights (44147) ***(G-1842)***
Omni Fireproofing Co LLC...513 870-9115
9305 Le Saint Dr West Chester (45014) ***(G-18980)***
Omni Interglobal Inc...216 239-3833
600 Superior Ave E # 1300 Cleveland (44114) ***(G-6131)***
Omni Manor Inc (PA)...330 545-1550
101 W Liberty St Girard (44420) ***(G-11297)***
Omni Manor Inc...330 793-5648
3245 Vestal Rd Youngstown (44509) ***(G-20148)***
Omni Nursing Home, Youngstown *Also called Omni Manor Inc* ***(G-20148)***
Omni Park Health Care LLC...216 289-8963
27801 Euclid Ave Ste 600 Euclid (44132) ***(G-10651)***
Omnicare Inc (HQ)...513 719-2600
900 Omnicare Ctr 201e4t Cincinnati (45202) ***(G-4168)***
Omnicare Distribution Ctr LLC...419 720-8200
201 E 4th St Ste 1 Cincinnati (45202) ***(G-4169)***
Omnicare Management Company...513 719-1535
201 E 4th St Ste 900 Cincinnati (45202) ***(G-4170)***
Omnicare of Central Ohio, Columbus *Also called Ncs Healthcare of Ohio LLC* ***(G-8167)***
Omnicare of Dover, Wadsworth *Also called Ncs Healthcare of Ohio LLC* ***(G-18609)***
Omnicare of Northwest Ohio, Perrysburg *Also called Westhaven Services Co LLC* ***(G-15935)***
Omnicare of St. George, Cincinnati *Also called Superior Care Pharmacy Inc* ***(G-4556)***
Omnicare Phrm of Midwest LLC (HQ)...513 719-2600
201 E 4th St Ste 900 Cincinnati (45202) ***(G-4171)***
Omnicare Purch Ltd Partner Inc...800 990-6664
201 E 4th St Ste 900 Cincinnati (45202) ***(G-4172)***
Omnisource LLC...419 537-1631
2453 Hill Ave Toledo (43607) ***(G-17961)***
Omnisource LLC...419 784-5669
880 Linden St Defiance (43512) ***(G-9933)***
Omnisource LLC...419 227-3411
1610 E 4th St Lima (45804) ***(G-12712)***
Omnisource LLC...419 394-3351
04575 County Road 33a Saint Marys (45885) ***(G-16529)***
Omnisource LLC...419 537-9400
5130 N Detroit Ave Toledo (43612) ***(G-17962)***
Omnova Solutions Inc...330 794-6300
2990 Gilchrist Rd Akron (44305) ***(G-364)***
Omya Industries Inc (HQ)...513 387-4600
9987 Carver Rd Ste 300 Blue Ash (45242) ***(G-1625)***
On Call Medical, Athens *Also called Eric Hasemeier Do* ***(G-780)***
On Site Instruments LLC...614 846-1900
403 Venture Dr Lewis Center (43035) ***(G-12555)***
On-Call Nursing Inc...216 577-8890
15644 Madison Ave Lakewood (44107) ***(G-12358)***
On-Power Inc...513 228-2100
3525 Grant Ave Ste A Lebanon (45036) ***(G-12489)***
Oncall LLC...513 381-4320
8044 Montgomery Rd # 700 Cincinnati (45236) ***(G-4173)***
Oncodiagnostic Laboratory Inc...216 861-5846
812 Huron Rd E Ste 520 Cleveland (44115) ***(G-6132)***
Oncolgy/Hmatology Care Inc PSC (PA)...513 751-2145
5053 Wooster Rd Cincinnati (45226) ***(G-4174)***
Oncology Partners Network, Cincinnati *Also called Trihealth Oncology Inst LLC* ***(G-4645)***
One Call Now, Dayton *Also called Swn Communications Inc* ***(G-9803)***
One Lincoln Park...937 298-0594
590 Isaac Prugh Way Dayton (45429) ***(G-9675)***
One Main Financial Services...419 841-0785
2232 Centennial Rd Toledo (43617) ***(G-17963)***
One Sky Flight LLC...877 703-2348
26180 Curtiss Wright Pkwy Cleveland (44143) ***(G-6133)***
One Source Technology LLC...216 420-1700
1111 Superior Ave E # 2000 Cleveland (44114) ***(G-6134)***
One Stop Remodeling, Columbus *Also called Wingler Construction Corp* ***(G-8910)***
One Way Express Incorporated...440 439-9182
380 Solon Rd Ste 5 Cleveland (44146) ***(G-6135)***
One Way Farm Children's Home, Fairfield *Also called One Way Farm of Fairfield Inc* ***(G-10765)***
One Way Farm of Fairfield Inc...513 829-3276
6131 E River Rd Fairfield (45014) ***(G-10765)***
One10 LLC...763 445-3000
130 W 2nd St Ste 500 Dayton (45402) ***(G-9676)***
Oneeighty Inc...330 263-6021
104 Spink St Wooster (44691) ***(G-19756)***
ONeil & Associates Inc (PA)...937 865-0800
495 Byers Rd Miamisburg (45342) ***(G-14201)***
ONeil Awning and Tent Inc...614 837-6352
895 W Walnut St Canal Winchester (43110) ***(G-2115)***
Oneill Hlthcare - N Ridgeville, North Ridgeville *Also called Center Ridge Nursing Home Inc* ***(G-15324)***
ONeill Senior Center Inc (PA)...740 373-3914
333 4th St Marietta (45750) ***(G-13365)***
Onesco, Montgomery *Also called O N Equity Sales Company* ***(G-14597)***
Onestaff Inc...859 815-1345
2358 Harrison Ave Apt 20 Cincinnati (45211) ***(G-4175)***
Onex Construction Inc...330 995-9015
1430 Miller Pkwy Streetsboro (44241) ***(G-17264)***
Online Imaging Solutions, Cleveland *Also called American Copy Equipment Inc* ***(G-4952)***
Online Mega Sellers Corp (PA)...888 384-6468
4236 W Alexis Rd Toledo (43623) ***(G-17964)***
Ontario Commons, Ontario *Also called Diversicare of Mansfield LLC* ***(G-15547)***
Ontario Local School District...419 529-3814
3644 Pearl St Ontario (44906) ***(G-15568)***
Ontario Mechanical LLC...419 529-2578
2880 Park Ave W Ontario (44906) ***(G-15569)***
Onx Entrprise Solutions US Inc...440 569-2300
5910 Landerbrook Dr 2 Mayfield Heights (44124) ***(G-13878)***
Onx USA LLC (HQ)...440 569-2300
5910 Landerbrook Dr # 250 Cleveland (44124) ***(G-6136)***
Onyx Creative Inc (PA)...216 223-3200
25001 Emery Rd Ste 400 Cleveland (44128) ***(G-6137)***
Oovoo LLC...917 515-2074
1700 S Patterson Blvd Kettering (45409) ***(G-12298)***
Opcc LLC...904 276-7660
243 Sunset Dr S Johnstown (43031) ***(G-12202)***
Open Arms Health Systems Llc...614 385-8354
868 Freeway Dr N Columbus (43229) ***(G-8375)***
Open Door Christian School...440 322-6386
8287 W Ridge Rd Elyria (44035) ***(G-10551)***
Open Online LLC (PA)...614 481-6999
1650 Lake Shore Dr # 350 Columbus (43204) ***(G-8376)***
Open Text Inc...614 658-3588
3671 Ridge Mill Dr Hilliard (43026) ***(G-11804)***
Openonline, Columbus *Also called Open Online LLC* ***(G-8376)***
Opers Legal Dept...614 227-0550
277 E Town St Columbus (43215) ***(G-8377)***
Ophthalmology Associates of...419 865-3866
3509 Briarfield Blvd Maumee (43537) ***(G-13828)***
Ophthlmic Srgeons Cons of Ohio...614 221-7464
262 Neil Ave Ste 430 Columbus (43215) ***(G-8378)***
Opinions Ltd (PA)...440 893-0300
33 River St Chagrin Falls (44022) ***(G-2652)***
Oppenheimer & Co Inc...513 723-9200
5905 E Galbraith Rd # 6200 Cincinnati (45236) ***(G-4176)***
Opportunities For Ohioans (HQ)...614 438-1200
150 E Campus View Blvd Columbus (43235) ***(G-8379)***
Opportunities For Ohioans...513 852-3260
895 Central Ave Fl 7 Cincinnati (45202) ***(G-4177)***
Opportunity Homes Inc...330 424-1411
7891 State Route 45 Lisbon (44432) ***(G-12805)***
OPRS FOUNDATION, Columbus *Also called Ohio Presbyterian Rtr Svcs* ***(G-8281)***
Optima 777 LLC...216 771-7700
777 Saint Clair Ave Ne Cleveland (44114) ***(G-6138)***
Optimist International...419 238-5086
1008 Woodland Ave Van Wert (45891) ***(G-18485)***
Optimum Graphics, Westerville *Also called Optimum System Products Inc* ***(G-19288)***
Optimum System Products Inc (PA)...614 885-4464
921 Eastwind Dr Ste 133 Westerville (43081) ***(G-19288)***
Optimum Technology Inc (PA)...614 785-1110
100 E Campus View Blvd # 380 Columbus (43235) ***(G-8380)***
Optio-Vision By Kahn & Diehl, Oregon *Also called Ottivue* ***(G-15606)***
Option Care Enterprises Inc...513 576-8400
50 W Techne Center Dr J Milford (45150) ***(G-14415)***
Option Care Infusion Svcs Inc...614 431-6453
7654 Crosswoods Dr Columbus (43235) ***(G-8381)***
Option Care Infusion Svcs Inc...513 576-8400
25 Whitney Dr Ste 114 Milford (45150) ***(G-14416)***
Option Line...614 586-1380
665 E Dublin Granville Rd # 290 Columbus (43229) ***(G-8382)***
Options Flight Support Inc...216 261-3500
26180 Curtiss Wright Pkwy Cleveland (44143) ***(G-6139)***
Options For Family & Youth...216 267-7070
11351 Pearl Rd Ste 103 Strongsville (44136) ***(G-17337)***
Optis Solutions...513 948-2070
6705 Steger Dr Cincinnati (45237) ***(G-4178)***
Optivue Inc...419 891-1391
2740 Navarre Ave Oregon (43616) ***(G-15602)***
Optumrx Inc...614 794-3300
250 Progressive Way Westerville (43082) ***(G-19196)***
OR Colan Associates LLC...440 827-6116
22710 Fairview Center Dr # 150 Cleveland (44126) ***(G-6140)***

Oracle Corporation..513 826-5632
3610 Pentagon Blvd # 205 Beavercreek (45431) *(G-1174)*
Oracle Systems Corporation..................................513 826-6000
3333 Richmond Rd Ste 420 Beachwood (44122) *(G-1092)*
Oracle Systems Corporation..................................216 328-9100
3333 Richmond Rd Ste 420 Beachwood (44122) *(G-1093)*
Oral & Maxillofacial Surgeons (PA)........................419 385-5743
1850 Eastgate Rd Ste A Toledo (43614) *(G-17965)*
Oral & Maxillofacial Surgeons................................419 471-0300
4646 Nantuckett Dr Ste A Toledo (43623) *(G-17966)*
Orange Barrel Media LLC.....................................614 294-4898
250 N Hartford Ave Columbus (43222) *(G-8383)*
Orbit Industries Inc (PA).......................................440 243-3311
6840 Lake Abrams Dr Cleveland (44130) *(G-6141)*
Orbit Movers & Erectors Inc.................................937 277-8080
1101 Negley Pl Dayton (45402) *(G-9677)*
Orbit Systems Inc...614 504-8011
615 Carle Ave Lewis Center (43035) *(G-12556)*
Orc International Inc...419 893-0029
1900 Indian Wood Cir # 200 Maumee (43537) *(G-13829)*
Orca House..216 231-3772
1905 E 89th St Cleveland (44106) *(G-6142)*
Orcha of North Livin & Rehab C, Napoleon *Also called Ncop LLC (G-14815)*
Orchard Hill Swim Club..513 385-0211
8601 Cheviot Rd Cincinnati (45251) *(G-4179)*
Orchard Hills Country Club, Bryan *Also called Buckeye Golf Club Co Inc (G-1953)*
Orchard Hiltz & McCliment Inc..............................614 418-0600
580 N 4th St Ste 610 Columbus (43215) *(G-8384)*
Orchard Phrm Svcs LLC.......................................330 491-4200
7835 Freedom Ave Nw North Canton (44720) *(G-15225)*
Orchard Villa Inc..419 697-4100
2841 Munding Dr Oregon (43616) *(G-15603)*
Orchards of Ridgewood Livin, Fairlawn *Also called Rwdop LLC (G-10845)*
Order of Symposiarchs America.............................740 387-9713
704 Vernon Heights Blvd Marion (43302) *(G-13452)*
Order of Unite Commercial Tra (PA).......................614 487-9680
1801 Watermark Dr Ste 100 Columbus (43215) *(G-8385)*
Oregon Clean Energy Center.................................419 566-9466
816 N Lallendorf Rd Oregon (43616) *(G-15604)*
Oregon Ford Inc...419 698-4444
2811 Navarre Ave Oregon (43616) *(G-15605)*
OReilly Automotive Inc..330 494-0042
1233 N Main St North Canton (44720) *(G-15226)*
OReilly Automotive Inc..419 630-0811
1116 S Main St Bryan (43506) *(G-1968)*
OReilly Automotive Inc..330 318-3136
8308 Market St Boardman (44512) *(G-1700)*
OReilly Automotive Inc..513 783-1343
1835 Central Ave Middletown (45044) *(G-14317)*
OReilly Automotive Inc..330 267-4383
1196 W Maple St Hartville (44632) *(G-11696)*
OReilly Automotive Inc..513 800-1169
1198 W Galbraith Rd Cincinnati (45231) *(G-4180)*
OReilly Automotive Inc..513 818-4166
3480 Spring Grove Ave Cincinnati (45223) *(G-4181)*
Organizational Horizons Inc..................................614 268-6013
5721 N High St Ste Lla Worthington (43085) *(G-19832)*
Organized Living Ltd...513 674-5484
3100 E Kemper Rd Ste A Cincinnati (45241) *(G-4182)*
Oriana House Inc..330 374-9610
941 Sherman St Akron (44311) *(G-365)*
Oriana House Inc (PA)...330 535-8116
885 E Buchtel Ave Akron (44305) *(G-366)*
Oriana House Inc..419 447-1444
3055 S State Route 100 Tiffin (44883) *(G-17531)*
Oriana House Inc..330 996-7730
15 Frederick Ave Akron (44310) *(G-367)*
Oriana House Inc..216 361-9655
3540 Croton Ave Cleveland (44115) *(G-6143)*
Oriana House Inc..330 643-2171
205 E Crosier St Akron (44311) *(G-368)*
Original Hartstone Pottery Inc...............................740 452-9999
1719 Dearborn St Zanesville (43701) *(G-20350)*
Original Partners Ltd Partnr (PA)...........................513 381-8696
1055 Saint Paul Pl Cincinnati (45202) *(G-4183)*
Orin Group LLC..330 630-3937
537 N Clvland Mssillon Rd Akron (44333) *(G-369)*
Orion Academy, Cincinnati *Also called National Heritg Academies Inc (G-4092)*
Orion Care Services LLC......................................216 752-3600
18810 Harvard Ave Cleveland (44122) *(G-6144)*
Orkin, Columbus *Also called Steve Shaffer (G-8698)*
Orkin LLC...614 888-5811
6230 Huntley Rd Columbus (43229) *(G-8386)*
Orkin Pest Control 561, Columbus *Also called Orkin LLC (G-8386)*
ORourke Wrecking Company..................................513 871-1400
660 Lunken Park Dr Cincinnati (45226) *(G-4184)*
Orphan Foundation of America...............................571 203-0270
23811 Chagrin Blvd # 210 Beachwood (44122) *(G-1094)*
Orrvilla Inc...330 683-4455
333 E Sassafras St Orrville (44667) *(G-15637)*
Orrvilla Retirement Community..............................330 683-4455
333 E Sassafras St Orrville (44667) *(G-15638)*

Orrville Boys and Girls Club..................................330 683-4888
820 N Ella St Orrville (44667) *(G-15639)*
Orrville Hospital Foundation..................................330 684-4700
832 S Main St Orrville (44667) *(G-15640)*
Orrville Trucking & Grading Co (PA)......................330 682-4010
475 Orr St Orrville (44667) *(G-15641)*
Ors Nasco Inc..918 781-5300
9901 Princeton Glendale West Chester (45246) *(G-19071)*
Orsanco, Cincinnati *Also called Ohio Rver Vly Wtr Snttion Comm (G-4158)*
Ortho Neuro, Westerville *Also called Orthoneuro (G-19289)*
Orthodontic Associates LLC (PA)...........................419 229-8771
260 S Eastown Rd Lima (45807) *(G-12713)*
Orthodontic Association..419 523-4014
1020 N Perry St Ottawa (45875) *(G-15662)*
Ortholink Physicians, New Albany *Also called Joint Implant Surgeons Inc (G-14858)*
Orthoneuro (PA)...614 890-6555
70 S Cleveland Ave Westerville (43081) *(G-19289)*
Orthoneuro..614 890-6555
4420 Refugee Rd Columbus (43232) *(G-8387)*
Orthoneuro..614 890-6555
1313 Olentangy River Rd Columbus (43212) *(G-8388)*
Orthopaedic & Spine Center At..............................614 468-0300
6810 Perimeter Dr 200a Dublin (43016) *(G-10300)*
Orthopaedic Institute Ohio Inc (PA).......................419 222-6622
801 Medical Dr Ste A Lima (45804) *(G-12714)*
Orthopaedic Offices Inc.......................................513 221-5500
9825 Kenwood Rd Ste 200 Blue Ash (45242) *(G-1626)*
Orthopdic Spt Mdicine Cons Inc............................513 777-7714
275 N Breiel Blvd Middletown (45042) *(G-14318)*
Orthopedic Assoc of Zanesville.............................740 454-3273
2854 Bell St Zanesville (43701) *(G-20351)*
Orthopedic Associates...800 824-9861
7117 Dutchland Pkwy Liberty Township (45044) *(G-12584)*
Orthopedic Associates (PA)..................................937 415-9100
7677 Yankee St Ste 110 Centerville (45459) *(G-2631)*
Orthopedic Associates Dayton...............................937 280-4988
7980 N Main St Dayton (45415) *(G-9678)*
Orthopedic Associates Inc....................................440 892-1440
24723 Detroit Rd Westlake (44145) *(G-19388)*
Orthopedic Cons Cincinnati (PA)...........................513 733-8894
4701 Creek Rd Ste 110 Blue Ash (45242) *(G-1627)*
Orthopedic Cons Cincinnati..................................513 753-7488
4440 Glnste Wthmsville Rd Cincinnati (45245) *(G-2863)*
Orthopedic Cons Cincinnati..................................513 232-6677
7575 5 Mile Rd Cincinnati (45230) *(G-4185)*
Orthopedic Cons Cincinnati..................................513 245-2500
7663 5 Mile Rd Cincinnati (45230) *(G-4186)*
Orthopedic Cons Cincinnati..................................513 347-9999
6909 Good Samaritan Dr Cincinnati (45247) *(G-4187)*
Orthopedic Diagnstc Trtmnt Ctr.............................513 791-6611
10547 Montgomery Rd 400a Montgomery (45242) *(G-14602)*
Orthopedic Diagnstc Trtmnt Ctr.............................513 221-4848
4600 Smith Rd Ste B Cincinnati (45212) *(G-4188)*
Orthopedic One Inc...614 827-8700
4605 Sawmill Rd Columbus (43220) *(G-8389)*
Orthopedic One Inc (PA).....................................614 545-7900
170 Taylor Station Rd Columbus (43213) *(G-8390)*
Orthorpdics Mltspcialty Netwrk (PA)......................330 493-1630
4760 Belpar St Nw Canton (44718) *(G-2433)*
Orton Edward Jr Crmic Fndation.............................614 895-2663
6991 S Old 3c Hwy Westerville (43082) *(G-19197)*
Orville Pet Spa & Resort......................................330 683-3335
1669 N Main St Orrville (44667) *(G-15642)*
Os Hill Leasing Inc...330 386-6440
47866 Y And O Rd East Liverpool (43920) *(G-10414)*
Osborn Engineering Company (PA)........................216 861-2020
1100 Superior Ave E # 300 Cleveland (44114) *(G-6145)*
Osborn Marketing Research Corp..........................440 871-1047
1818 Century Oaks Dr Westlake (44145) *(G-19389)*
Osborne Co...440 942-7000
7954 Reynolds Rd Mentor (44060) *(G-14094)*
Osborne Materials Company (PA)..........................440 357-7026
1 Williams St Grand River (44045) *(G-11333)*
Osborne Trucking Company (PA)...........................513 874-2090
325 Osborne Dr Fairfield (45014) *(G-10766)*
Osburn Associates Inc (PA)..................................740 385-5732
9383 Vanatta Rd Logan (43138) *(G-12852)*
Osf International Inc..513 942-6620
6320 S Gilmore Rd Fairfield (45014) *(G-10767)*
Osgood State Bank (inc) (PA)...............................419 582-2681
275 W Main St Osgood (45351) *(G-15653)*
OSMA, Dublin *Also called Ohio State Medical Association (G-10298)*
Osmans Pies Inc..330 607-9083
3678 Elm Rd Stow (44224) *(G-17222)*
Ostendorf-Morris Properties..................................216 861-7200
1100 Superior Ave E # 800 Cleveland (44114) *(G-6146)*
Osterfeld Champion Service..................................937 254-8437
121 Commerce Park Dr Dayton (45404) *(G-9679)*
Osterwisch Company Inc......................................513 791-3282
6755 Highland Ave Cincinnati (45236) *(G-4189)*
Osu Cnter For Wllness Prvntion, Columbus *Also called Ohio State University (G-8298)*
Osu Dept Psychology, Columbus *Also called Ohio State University (G-8325)*

Osu Division of Pulmonary, Columbus *Also called Ohio State University (G-8348)*
Osu Emergency Medicine LLC................................614 947-3700
  700 Ackerman Rd Ste 270 Columbus (43202) *(G-8391)*
Osu Faculty Practice, Columbus *Also called Ohio State University (G-8344)*
Osu Hospitals, Columbus *Also called Ohio State University (G-8347)*
Osu Industrial Welding Sy, Columbus *Also called Ohio State University (G-8306)*
Osu Internal Medicine LLC (PA)................................614 293-0080
  3900 Stoneridge Ln Ste B Dublin (43017) *(G-10301)*
Osu Medical Staff ADM, Columbus *Also called Ohio State University (G-8323)*
Osu Nephrology Medical Ctr................................614 293-8300
  410 W 10th Ave Columbus (43210) *(G-8392)*
Osu Obgyn, Columbus *Also called Ohio State University (G-8317)*
Osu Orthodontic Clinic................................614 292-1058
  2010 901 Woody Hayes Dr Columbus (43210) *(G-8393)*
Osu Pathology Services LLC................................614 247-6461
  1645 Neil Ave Columbus (43210) *(G-8394)*
Osu Personnel, Columbus *Also called Ohio State University (G-8318)*
Osu Physical Medicine LLC................................614 366-6398
  480 Medical Center Dr # 1036 Columbus (43210) *(G-8395)*
Osu Psychiatry LLC................................614 794-1818
  700 Ackerman Rd Ste 600 Columbus (43202) *(G-8396)*
Osu Radiology LLC................................614 293-8315
  395 W 12th Ave Columbus (43210) *(G-8397)*
OSu Spt Mdcine Physcians Inc................................614 293-3600
  2835 Fred Taylor Dr Columbus (43202) *(G-8398)*
Osu Surgery LLC................................614 293-8116
  915 Olentangy River Rd # 2100 Columbus (43212) *(G-8399)*
Osu Surgery LLC (PA)................................614 261-1141
  700 Ackerman Rd Ste 350 Columbus (43202) *(G-8400)*
Osu Value City Arena, Columbus *Also called Ohio State University (G-8307)*
Osu-Infectious Diseases, Columbus *Also called Ohio State University (G-8327)*
Osup Community Outreach LLC................................614 685-1542
  700 Ackerman Rd Ste 600 Columbus (43202) *(G-8401)*
Oswald Companies, Cleveland *Also called Jbo Holding Company (G-5785)*
Oti, Columbus *Also called Optimum Technology Inc (G-8380)*
Otis Elevator Company................................513 531-7888
  2463 Crowne Point Dr Cincinnati (45241) *(G-4190)*
Otis Elevator Company................................614 777-6500
  777 Dearborn Park Ln L Columbus (43085) *(G-8402)*
Otis Elevator Company................................216 573-2333
  9800 Rockside Rd Ste 1200 Cleveland (44125) *(G-6147)*
Otis Wright & Sons Inc................................419 227-4400
  1601 E 4th St Lima (45804) *(G-12715)*
Otolaryngology Department, Columbus *Also called Ohio State Univ Wexner Med Ctr (G-8293)*
Otp Holding LLC................................614 342-6123
  1900 Jetway Blvd Columbus (43219) *(G-8403)*
Otp Industrial Solutions, Columbus *Also called Ohio Transmission Corporation (G-8357)*
Ots-NJ LLC................................732 833-0600
  21 Traxler St Butler (44822) *(G-2021)*
Ottawa Cnty Sr Healthcare, Oak Harbor *Also called County of Ottawa (G-15470)*
Ottawa County Board M R D D................................419 734-6650
  235 N Toussaint St Oak Harbor (43449) *(G-15476)*
Ottawa County Dept Human Svcs, Oak Harbor *Also called County of Ottawa (G-15471)*
Ottawa County Transit Board................................419 898-7433
  275 N Toussaint South Rd Oak Harbor (43449) *(G-15477)*
Ottawa Hills Memorial Park................................419 539-0218
  4210 W Central Ave Ste 1 Ottawa Hills (43606) *(G-15668)*
Ottawa House, Toledo *Also called Zepf Housing Corp One Inc (G-18180)*
Otterbein Cridersville, Cridersville *Also called Otterbein Snior Lfstyle Chices (G-9063)*
Otterbein Homes................................513 933-5439
  580 N State Route 741 Lebanon (45036) *(G-12490)*
Otterbein Lebanon................................513 933-5465
  585 N State Route 741 Lebanon (45036) *(G-12491)*
Otterbein North Shore, Lakeside *Also called North Shore Retirement Cmnty (G-12330)*
Otterbein Portage Valley Inc................................888 749-4950
  20311 Pemberville Rd Ofc Pemberville (43450) *(G-15806)*
Otterbein Portage Vly Rtrmnt, Pemberville *Also called Otterbein Portage Valley Inc (G-15806)*
Otterbein Snior Lfstyle Chices, Lebanon *Also called Otterbein Homes (G-12490)*
Otterbein Snior Lfstyle Chices................................513 260-7690
  105 Atrium Dr Middletown (45005) *(G-14352)*
Otterbein Snior Lfstyle Chices (PA)................................513 933-5400
  585 N State Route 741 Lebanon (45036) *(G-12492)*
Otterbein Snior Lfstyle Chices................................419 943-4376
  901 E Main St Leipsic (45856) *(G-12520)*
Otterbein Snior Lfstyle Chices................................419 645-5114
  100 Red Oak Dr Cridersville (45806) *(G-9063)*
Otterbein Snior Lfstyle Chices................................419 394-2366
  11230 State Route 364 Saint Marys (45885) *(G-16530)*
OTTERBEIN ST MARY'S, Lebanon *Also called Otterbein Snior Lfstyle Chices (G-12492)*
Otterbein St Marys Retrmnt, Saint Marys *Also called Otterbein Snior Lfstyle Chices (G-16530)*
Ottivue (PA)................................419 693-4444
  2740 Navarre Ave Oregon (43616) *(G-15606)*
Otto Falkenberg Excavating................................330 626-4215
  9350 Coit Rd Mantua (44255) *(G-13274)*

Our House Inc................................440 835-2110
  27633 Bassett Rd Westlake (44145) *(G-19390)*
Our Lady of Bethlehem Schools................................614 459-8285
  4567 Olentangy River Rd Columbus (43214) *(G-8404)*
Our Lady Prptul Hlp Cnmty Bngo................................513 742-3200
  9908 Shellbark Ln Cincinnati (45231) *(G-4191)*
Our Ohio Communications, Columbus *Also called Ohio Farm Bur Federation Inc (G-8258)*
Ourday At Messiah Preschool................................614 882-4416
  51 N State St Westerville (43081) *(G-19290)*
Out Patient, Sandusky *Also called Firelands Regional Health Sys (G-16605)*
Outdoor Family Center, Perry *Also called Lake County YMCA (G-15824)*
Outlook Point At Xenia, Xenia *Also called Balanced Care Corporation (G-19892)*
Outlook Pointe, Northfield *Also called Balanced Care Corporation (G-15373)*
Outpatient Anderson, Cincinnati *Also called Childrens Hospital Medical Ctr (G-3189)*
Outreach Community Living Svcs................................330 263-0862
  337 W North St Wooster (44691) *(G-19757)*
Outreach Professional Svcs Inc................................216 472-4094
  2351 E 22nd St Cleveland (44115) *(G-6148)*
Ovations................................216 687-9292
  2000 Prospect Ave E Cleveland (44115) *(G-6149)*
Ovations Food Services LP................................513 419-7254
  525 Elm St Cincinnati (45202) *(G-4192)*
Overbrook Center, Middleport *Also called Meigs Center Ltd (G-14281)*
Overbrook Park, Chillicothe *Also called Overbrook Park Ltd (G-2808)*
Overbrook Park Ltd................................740 773-1159
  2179 Anderson Station Rd Chillicothe (45601) *(G-2808)*
Overcashier and Horst Htg & AC................................419 841-3333
  3745 Centennial Rd Sylvania (43560) *(G-17441)*
Overhead Door Co of Dayton, Dayton *Also called Dayton Door Sales Inc (G-9364)*
Overhead Door Co of Toledo, Toledo *Also called Overhead Inc (G-17967)*
Overhead Door Co- Cincinnati................................513 346-4000
  9345 Prnceton Glendale Rd West Chester (45011) *(G-18981)*
Overhead Door Company, Columbus *Also called Graf and Sons Inc (G-7683)*
Overhead Door Corporation................................330 674-7015
  1 Door Dr Mount Hope (44660) *(G-14738)*
Overhead Inc (PA)................................419 476-7811
  340 New Towne Square Dr Toledo (43612) *(G-17967)*
Overland Xpress LLC (PA)................................513 528-1158
  431 Ohio Pike Ste 311 Cincinnati (45255) *(G-4193)*
Overlook House................................216 795-3550
  2187 Overlook Rd Cleveland (44106) *(G-6150)*
Ovm Investment Group LLC................................937 392-0145
  5280 Us Hwy 62 & 88 Ripley (45167) *(G-16402)*
Owens Corning Basement Finishi, Columbus *Also called US Home Center LLC (G-8834)*
Owens Corning Sales LLC (HQ)................................419 248-8000
  1 Owens Corning Pkwy Toledo (43659) *(G-17968)*
Owens Corning Sales LLC................................740 587-3562
  2790 Columbus Rd Granville (43023) *(G-11347)*
Owners Management................................440 439-3800
  25250 Rockside Rd Ste 1 Cleveland (44146) *(G-6151)*
Owners Management Company................................440 439-3800
  5555 Powers Blvd Parma (44129) *(G-15770)*
Owv Exc, Shadyside *Also called Virginia Ohio-West Excvtg Co (G-16698)*
Oxcyon Inc................................440 239-3345
  17520 Engle Lake Dr Ste 1 Cleveland (44130) *(G-6152)*
Oxford Blazer Company Inc................................614 792-2220
  5700 Blazer Pkwy Ste B Dublin (43017) *(G-10302)*
Oxford Country Club Inc................................513 524-0801
  6200 Contreras Rd Oxford (45056) *(G-15686)*
Oxford Hospitality Group Inc................................513 524-0114
  5056 College Corner Pike Oxford (45056) *(G-15687)*
Oxford Mining Company Inc................................740 342-7666
  2500 Township Rd 205 New Lexington (43764) *(G-14924)*
Oxford Square, Blue Ash *Also called L J F Management Inc (G-1593)*
Oyer Electric Inc................................740 773-2828
  14650 Pleasant Valley Rd Chillicothe (45601) *(G-2809)*
Ozanne Construction Co Inc................................216 696-2876
  1635 E 25th St Cleveland (44114) *(G-6153)*
P & D Removal Service................................513 226-7687
  400 N Wayne Ave Cincinnati (45215) *(G-4194)*
P & D Transportation Inc................................614 577-1130
  4274 Groves Rd Columbus (43232) *(G-8405)*
P & D Transportation Inc (PA)................................740 454-1221
  1705 Moxahala Ave Zanesville (43701) *(G-20352)*
P & M Exhaust Systems Whse................................513 825-2660
  11843 Kemper Springs Dr Cincinnati (45240) *(G-4195)*
P & R Communications Svc Inc (PA)................................937 222-0861
  700 E 1st St Dayton (45402) *(G-9680)*
P & W Painting Contractors Inc................................419 698-2209
  3031 Front St Toledo (43605) *(G-17969)*
P B S Animal Health, Massillon *Also called Robert J Matthews Company (G-13724)*
P C B, New Albany *Also called Rossman (G-14872)*
P C C Refrigerated Ex Inc................................614 754-8929
  2365 Performance Way Columbus (43207) *(G-8406)*
P C S, Akron *Also called Pastoral Counseling Svc Summit (G-371)*
P C Vpa................................937 293-2133
  3033 Kettering Blvd # 100 Moraine (45439) *(G-14686)*
P C Vpa................................440 826-0500
  16600 W Sprague Rd Ste 80 Cleveland (44130) *(G-6154)*

A
L
P
H
A
B
E
T
I
C

P C Workshop Inc.................................419 399-4805
900 W Caroline St Paulding (45879) *(G-15795)*

P D I, Springboro *Also called Pdi Communication Systems Inc (G-16979)*

P E I, Akron *Also called Power Engineers Incorporated (G-392)*

P E Miller & Assoc.................................614 231-4743
1341 S Hamilton Rd Columbus (43227) *(G-8407)*

P E Miller & Associates Inc.....................614 231-4743
1341 S Hamilton Rd Columbus (43227) *(G-8408)*

P E Systems Inc...................................937 258-0141
5100 Sprngfeld St Ste 510 Dayton (45431) *(G-9185)*

P I & I Motor Express Inc (PA)................330 448-4035
908 Broadway St Masury (44438) *(G-13741)*

P I C C A, Circleville *Also called Pickaway County Community Acti (G-4839)*

P J & R J Connection Inc.........................513 398-2777
754 Reading Rd Mason (45040) *(G-13624)*

P J McNerney & Associates, Cincinnati *Also called McNerney & Associates LLC (G-3990)*

P JS Hair Styling Shoppe........................440 333-1244
20400 Lorain Rd Cleveland (44126) *(G-6155)*

P K Wadsworth Heating & Coolg.................440 248-4821
34280 Solon Rd Frnt Solon (44139) *(G-16880)*

P N P Inc...330 386-1231
48444 Bell School Rd East Liverpool (43920) *(G-10415)*

P P I, Cleveland *Also called Project Packaging Inc (G-6260)*

P R Machine Works Inc............................419 529-5748
1825 Nussbaum Pkwy Ontario (44906) *(G-15570)*

P S G, Youngstown *Also called Phoenix Systems Group Inc (G-20156)*

P T I, Walbridge *Also called Professional Transportation (G-18623)*

P-Americas LLC....................................419 227-3541
1750 Greely Chapel Rd Lima (45804) *(G-12716)*

P-Americas LLC....................................330 746-7652
500 Pepsi Pl Youngstown (44502) *(G-20149)*

P-Americas LLC....................................216 252-7377
4561 Industrial Pkwy Cleveland (44135) *(G-6156)*

P-N-D Communications Inc......................419 683-1922
7900 Middletown Rd Crestline (44827) *(G-9059)*

P3 Infrastructure Inc............................330 686-1129
3105 Preakness Dr Stow (44224) *(G-17223)*

Pac Manufacturing, Middletown *Also called Pac Worldwide Corporation (G-14319)*

Pac Worldwide Corporation......................800 535-0039
12110 Champion Way Cincinnati (45241) *(G-4196)*

Pac Worldwide Corporation......................800 610-9367
3131 Cincinnati Dayton Rd Middletown (45044) *(G-14319)*

Paccar Leasing Corporation.....................937 235-2589
7740 Center Point 70 Blvd Dayton (45424) *(G-9681)*

Pace Analytical Services Inc...................614 486-5421
4860 Blazer Pkwy Dublin (43017) *(G-10303)*

Pace International Union.........................419 929-1335
100 New London Ave New London (44851) *(G-14934)*

Pace International Union.........................740 772-2038
170 S Hickory St Chillicothe (45601) *(G-2810)*

Pace International Union.........................740 289-2368
2288 Wakefield Mound Rd Piketon (45661) *(G-15983)*

Pace Sankar Landscaping Inc..................330 343-0858
4005 Johnstown Rd Ne Dover (44622) *(G-10092)*

Pace-Sankar Landscaping, Dover *Also called Pace Sankar Landscaping Inc (G-10092)*

Pacer, Dublin *Also called Xpo Intermodal Solutions Inc (G-10378)*

Pacer Stacktrain, Dublin *Also called Xpo Stacktrain LLC (G-10379)*

Pache Management Company Inc...............614 451-5919
5026 Dierker Rd Ofc Columbus (43220) *(G-8409)*

Pacific Heritg Inn Polaris LLC................614 880-9080
9090 Lyra Dr Columbus (43240) *(G-6829)*

Pacific MGT Holdings LLC.......................440 324-3339
250 Warden Ave Elyria (44035) *(G-10552)*

Pacific Valve, Piqua *Also called Crane Pumps & Systems Inc (G-16003)*

Packaging & Pads R Us LLC (PA)...............419 499-2905
12406 Us Highway 250 N C Milan (44846) *(G-14365)*

Packship Usa Inc (PA)...........................330 682-7225
1347 N Main St Orrville (44667) *(G-15643)*

PacLease, Cincinnati *Also called Kenworth of Cincinnati (G-3862)*

PacLease, Dayton *Also called Paccar Leasing Corporation (G-9681)*

Pactiv LLC..614 771-5400
2120 Westbelt Dr Columbus (43228) *(G-8410)*

Pactiv LLC..614 777-4019
1999 Dividend Dr Columbus (43228) *(G-8411)*

Padgett-Young & Associates, Ashland *Also called Buren Insurance Group Inc (G-661)*

Pae & Associates Inc............................937 833-0013
7925 Paragon Rd Dayton (45459) *(G-9682)*

Pagan, Fremont *Also called Flex Temp Employment Services (G-11074)*

Pager Plus One Inc...............................513 748-3788
927 Old State Rt 28 Ste G Milford (45150) *(G-14417)*

Pagetech Ltd.......................................614 238-0518
951 Robinwood Ave Ste F Columbus (43213) *(G-8412)*

Pain Control Consultants Inc...................614 430-5727
1680 Watermark Dr 100 Columbus (43215) *(G-8413)*

Pain Management Associates Inc...............937 252-2000
1010 Woodman Dr Ste 100 Dayton (45432) *(G-9186)*

Pain Net Inc..614 481-5960
99 N Brice Rd Ste 270 Columbus (43213) *(G-8414)*

Painesville Dental Group Inc (PA)............440 354-2183
128 Mentor Ave Painesville (44077) *(G-15732)*

Painesville Municipal Electric, Painesville *Also called City of Painesville (G-15699)*

Paint Creek Youth Center, Bainbridge *Also called Lighthouse Youth Services Inc (G-931)*

Painters District Council 6......................440 239-4575
8257 Dow Cir Cleveland (44136) *(G-6157)*

Painters Local Union 555........................740 353-1431
2101 7th St Portsmouth (45662) *(G-16156)*

Painting Company.................................614 873-1334
6969 Industrial Pkwy Plain City (43064) *(G-16063)*

Paisley House For Aged Women.................330 799-9431
1408 Mahoning Ave Youngstown (44509) *(G-20150)*

Pajka Eye Center Inc.............................419 228-7432
855 W Market St Ste A Lima (45805) *(G-12717)*

Pak Lab...513 735-4777
5069 State Route 276 Batavia (45103) *(G-1005)*

Paklab, Batavia *Also called Universal Packg Systems Inc (G-1013)*

Paklab, Cincinnati *Also called Universal Packg Systems Inc (G-4695)*

Pakmark LLC.......................................513 285-1040
420 Distribution Cir Fairfield (45014) *(G-10768)*

Pakteem Technical Services.....................513 772-1515
1201 Glendale Milford Rd Cincinnati (45215) *(G-4197)*

Paladin Professional Sound, Cleveland *Also called Paladin Protective Systems Inc (G-6158)*

Paladin Protective Systems Inc................216 441-6500
7680 Hub Pkwy Cleveland (44125) *(G-6158)*

Palazzo Brothers Electric Inc..................419 668-1100
2811 State Route 18 Norwalk (44857) *(G-15451)*

Palestine Chld Relief Fund......................330 678-2645
1340 Morris Rd Kent (44240) *(G-12253)*

Palisdes Bsbal A Cal Ltd Prtnr................330 505-0000
111 Eastwood Mall Blvd Niles (44446) *(G-15166)*

Palladium Healthcare LLC.......................216 644-4383
16910 Harvard Ave Cleveland (44128) *(G-6159)*

Pallet Distributors Inc (PA)....................888 805-9670
14701 Detroit Ave Ste 610 Lakewood (44107) *(G-12359)*

Palliative Care of Ohio, Newark *Also called Hospice of Central Ohio (G-15042)*

Palm Crest East Inc..............................440 322-0726
1251 East Ave Elyria (44035) *(G-10553)*

Palm Crest Nursing Homes, Elyria *Also called Palm Crest East Inc (G-10553)*

Palmer Associates, Toledo *Also called Clear Vision Engineering LLC (G-17664)*

Palmer Express Incorporated...................440 942-3333
34799 Curtis Blvd Ste A Willoughby (44095) *(G-19560)*

Palmer Holland Inc...............................440 686-2300
25000 Country Club Blvd # 444 North Olmsted (44070) *(G-15304)*

Palmer Trucks Inc.................................937 235-3318
7740 Center Point 70 Blvd Dayton (45424) *(G-9683)*

Palmer Volkema Thomas Inc....................614 221-4400
140 E Town St Ste 1100 Columbus (43215) *(G-8415)*

Palmer-Donavin Mfg Co (PA)...................800 652-1234
3210 Centerpoint Dr Columbus (43212) *(G-8416)*

Palmer-Donavin Mfg Co..........................419 692-5000
911 Spencerville Rd Delphos (45833) *(G-10032)*

Palmer-Donavin Mfg Co..........................614 277-2777
3210 Centerpoint Dr Urbancrest (43123) *(G-18451)*

Palmetto Construction Svcs LLC...............614 503-7150
892 Scott St Columbus (43222) *(G-8417)*

Palmieri Enterprises, Bedford *Also called Dino Palmieri Beauty Salon (G-1277)*

Pam Johnsonident................................419 946-4551
535 W Marion Rd Mount Gilead (43338) *(G-14733)*

PAm Transportation Svcs Inc...................330 270-7900
12274 Mahoning Ave North Jackson (44451) *(G-15251)*

PAm Transportation Svcs Inc...................419 935-9501
2501 Miller Rd Willard (44890) *(G-19485)*

Pan-Glo of St Louis, Urbana *Also called Russell T Bundy Associates Inc (G-18444)*

Panacea Products Corporation (PA)...........614 850-7000
2711 International St Columbus (43228) *(G-8418)*

Panache Hair Salon, Youngstown *Also called Vip Inc (G-20238)*

Panasonic Corp North America.................513 770-9294
6402 Thornberry Ct Mason (45040) *(G-13625)*

Panasonic Corp North America.................201 392-6872
1400 W Market St Troy (45373) *(G-18221)*

Pandora Bancshares Inc (HQ)..................419 384-3221
102 E Main St Pandora (45877) *(G-15754)*

Pandora Manufacturing Llc (PA)...............419 384-3241
157 W Main St Ottawa (45875) *(G-15663)*

Panelmatic Inc.....................................330 782-8007
1125 Meadowbrook Ave Youngstown (44512) *(G-20151)*

Panelmatic Youngstown, Youngstown *Also called Panelmatic Inc (G-20151)*

Panera Bread, Westlake *Also called Howley Bread Group Ltd (G-19352)*

Panera Bread, Warren *Also called Covelli Family Ltd Partnership (G-18694)*

Panini North America Inc........................937 291-2195
577 Congress Park Dr Dayton (45459) *(G-9684)*

Panther II Transportation Inc (HQ)...........800 685-0657
84 Medina Rd Medina (44256) *(G-13985)*

Panther Premium Logistics Inc (HQ)..........800 685-0657
84 Medina Rd Medina (44256) *(G-13986)*

Paper Alied Indus Chem & Enrgy, Chillicothe *Also called Pace International Union (G-2810)*

Pappas Leah......................................614 621-7007
41 S High St Fl 12 Columbus (43215) *(G-8419)*

Par International Inc.............................614 529-1300
2160 Mcgaw Rd Obetz (43207) *(G-15528)*

Paradigm Industrial LLC.........................937 224-4415
1345 Stanley Ave Dayton (45404) *(G-9685)*

Paragon Consulting Inc...440 684-3101
5900 Landerbrook Dr # 205 Cleveland (44124) *(G-6160)*
Paragon Machine Company, Bedford *Also called Done-Rite Bowling Service Co (G-1278)*
Paragon Salons Inc (PA)...513 574-7610
6775 Harrison Ave Cincinnati (45247) *(G-4198)*
Paragon Salons Inc...513 651-4600
441 Race St Cincinnati (45202) *(G-4199)*
Paragon Salons Inc...513 683-6700
12064 Montgomery Rd Cincinnati (45249) *(G-4200)*
Paragon Tec Inc...216 361-5555
3740 Carnegie Ave Ste 302 Cleveland (44115) *(G-6161)*
Parallel Technologies Inc...614 798-9700
4868 Blazer Pkwy Dublin (43017) *(G-10304)*
Paramount Care Inc (HQ)...419 887-2500
1901 Indian Wood Cir Maumee (43537) *(G-13830)*
Paramount Confection Co, Springboro *Also called Miami-Luken Inc (G-16974)*
Paramount Health Care, Maumee *Also called Paramount Care Inc (G-13830)*
Paramount Lawn Service Inc...513 984-5200
8900 Glendale Milford Rd A1 Loveland (45140) *(G-13020)*
Paramount Support Service...740 526-0540
252 W Main St Ste H Saint Clairsville (43950) *(G-16501)*
Paran Management Company Ltd...216 921-5663
2720 Van Aken Blvd # 200 Cleveland (44120) *(G-6162)*
Paris Cleaners Inc...330 296-3300
650 Enterprise Pkwy Ravenna (44266) *(G-16252)*
Paris Healthcare Linen, Ravenna *Also called Paris Cleaners Inc (G-16252)*
Park Arrowhead Golf Club Inc...419 628-2444
2211 Dirksen Rd Minster (45865) *(G-14539)*
Park Centre Lanes Inc...330 499-0555
7313 Whipple Ave Nw Canton (44720) *(G-2434)*
Park Cincinnati Board...513 421-4086
1501 Eden Park Dr Cincinnati (45202) *(G-4201)*
Park Corporation (PA)...216 267-4870
6200 Riverside Dr Cleveland (44135) *(G-6163)*
Park Creek Center, Rocky River *Also called Msab Park Creek LLC (G-16441)*
Park Creek Rtirement Cmnty Inc...440 842-5100
10064 N Church Dr Cleveland (44130) *(G-6164)*
Park Dist Maintenance, Massillon *Also called County of Stark (G-13674)*
Park Group Co of America Inc...440 238-9440
22700 Royalton Rd Strongsville (44149) *(G-17338)*
Park Haven Home, Ashtabula *Also called Park Haven Inc (G-751)*
Park Haven Inc...440 992-9441
6434 Lee Road Ext Ashtabula (44004) *(G-751)*
Park Health Center, Saint Clairsville *Also called Belmont County Home (G-16472)*
Park Hotels & Resorts Inc...216 447-0020
6200 Quarry Ln Cleveland (44131) *(G-6165)*
Park Hotels & Resorts Inc...513 421-9100
35 W 5th St Cincinnati (45202) *(G-4202)*
Park Hotels & Resorts Inc...216 464-5950
3663 Park East Dr Cleveland (44122) *(G-6166)*
Park Hotels & Resorts Inc...937 436-2400
300 Prestige Pl Miamisburg (45342) *(G-14202)*
Park Inn...419 241-3000
101 N Summit St Toledo (43604) *(G-17970)*
Park International Theme Svcs...513 381-6131
2195 Victory Pkwy Cincinnati (45206) *(G-4203)*
Park Management Specialist (PA)...419 893-4879
216 W Wayne St Maumee (43537) *(G-13831)*
Park n Fly Inc...404 264-1000
19000 Snow Rd Cleveland (44142) *(G-6167)*
Park National Bank (HQ)...740 349-8451
50 N 3rd St Newark (43055) *(G-15089)*
Park National Bank...614 228-0063
140 E Town St Ste 1400 Columbus (43215) *(G-8420)*
Park National Bank...740 349-8451
21 S 1st St Ste Front Newark (43055) *(G-15090)*
Park National Bank...937 324-6800
40 S Limestone St Springfield (45502) *(G-17094)*
Park Place Airport Parking, Cleveland *Also called Park Place Management Inc (G-6168)*
Park Place International LLC...877 991-1991
8401 Chagrin Rd Ste 15a Chagrin Falls (44023) *(G-2677)*
Park Place Management Inc...216 362-1080
18975 Snow Rd Cleveland (44142) *(G-6168)*
Park Place Nursery, Cleveland *Also called T L C Landscaping Inc (G-6495)*
Park Place Technologies LLC...603 617-7123
5910 Landerbrook Dr # 300 Cleveland (44124) *(G-6169)*
Park Place Technologies LLC...610 544-0571
5910 Landerbrook Dr # 300 Mayfield Heights (44124) *(G-13879)*
Park Place Technologies LLC (PA)...877 778-8707
5910 Landerbrook Dr # 300 Mayfield Heights (44124) *(G-13880)*
Park Side Dialysis, Westerville *Also called Dome Dialysis LLC (G-19250)*
Park View Nursing Center, Edgerton *Also called Peregrine Health Services Inc (G-10469)*
Park Village Health Care Ctr, Dover *Also called Dover Nursing Center (G-10075)*
Park Vista Retirement Cmnty, Youngstown *Also called Ohio Presbt Retirement Svcs (G-20147)*
Park-N-Go Inc...937 890-7275
2700 W National Rd Dayton (45414) *(G-9686)*
Park-N-Go Airport Parking, Dayton *Also called Park-N-Go Inc (G-9686)*
Parkcliffe Development...419 381-9447
4226 Parkcliff Ln Toledo (43615) *(G-17971)*

Parker Marketing Research LLC...513 248-8100
5405 Dupont Cir Ste B Milford (45150) *(G-14418)*
Parker Steel Company, Maumee *Also called Parker Steel International Inc (G-13832)*
Parker Steel International Inc (PA)...419 473-2481
1625 Indian Wood Cir Maumee (43537) *(G-13832)*
Parker, Michael G MD, Akron *Also called Akron Plastic Surgeons Inc (G-50)*
Parker-Hannifin Corporation...937 456-5571
725 N Beech St Eaton (45320) *(G-10457)*
Parker-Hannifin Corporation...513 831-2340
50 W Techne Center Dr H Milford (45150) *(G-14419)*
Parker-Hannifin Corporation...614 279-7070
3885 Gateway Blvd Columbus (43228) *(G-8421)*
Parker-Hannifin Corporation...216 896-3000
6035 Parkland Blvd Cleveland (44124) *(G-6170)*
Parker-Hannifin Corporation...419 878-7000
1290 Wtrville Monclova Rd Waterville (43566) *(G-18790)*
Parker-Hannifin Corporation...216 531-3000
6035 Parkland Blvd Cleveland (44124) *(G-6171)*
Parker-Hannifin Intl Corp (HQ)...216 896-3000
6035 Parkland Blvd Cleveland (44124) *(G-6172)*
Parking Company America Inc...513 241-0415
250 W Court St Ste 200e Cincinnati (45202) *(G-4204)*
Parking Company America Inc...216 265-0500
18899 Snow Rd Cleveland (44142) *(G-6173)*
Parking Company America Inc...513 381-2179
250 W Court St Ste 100e Cincinnati (45202) *(G-4205)*
Parking Company of America, Cincinnati *Also called Court Stret Center Associates (G-3375)*
Parking Sltions For Healthcare, Columbus *Also called Parking Solutions Inc (G-8422)*
Parking Solutions Inc (HQ)...614 469-7000
353 W Nationwide Blvd Columbus (43215) *(G-8422)*
Parkins Incorporated...614 334-1800
3950 Lyman Dr Hilliard (43026) *(G-11805)*
Parklane Manor of Akron Inc...330 724-3315
744 Colette Dr Akron (44306) *(G-370)*
Parkmead Apartments, Grove City *Also called Wallick Properties Midwest LLC (G-11482)*
Parkops Columbus LLC...877 499-9155
56 E Long St Columbus (43215) *(G-8423)*
Parks Drilling Company (PA)...614 761-7707
5745 Avery Rd Dublin (43016) *(G-10305)*
Parks Ob Gyn Assoc, Chillicothe *Also called Adena Health System (G-2750)*
Parks Recreation & Prpts Dept, Cleveland *Also called City of Cleveland (G-5196)*
Parks Recreation Athens...740 592-0046
701 E State St Athens (45701) *(G-801)*
Parks Recreation Division...937 496-7135
455 Infirmary Rd Dayton (45417) *(G-9687)*
Parkside Behavioral Healthcare...614 471-2552
349 Olde Ridenour Rd Gahanna (43230) *(G-11140)*
Parkside Care Corporation...440 286-2273
831 South St Chardon (44024) *(G-2707)*
Parkside Health Care Center, Columbiana *Also called Windsor House Inc (G-6795)*
PARKSIDE MANOR, Maumee *Also called Consulate Healthcare Inc (G-13775)*
Parkside Nrsing Rehabilitation, Fairfield *Also called Embassy Healthcare Inc (G-10724)*
Parkside Nrsing Rhbltation Ctr, Fairfield *Also called Multicare Management Group (G-10759)*
PARKVIEW CARE CENTER, Fremont *Also called Caritas Inc (G-11060)*
Parkview Health Care, Sandusky *Also called United Church Homes Inc (G-16651)*
Parkview Manor Inc (PA)...937 296-1550
425 Lauricella Ct Englewood (45322) *(G-10595)*
Parkview Manor Inc...419 243-5191
2051 Collingwood Blvd Toledo (43620) *(G-17972)*
Parkview Physicians Group, Bryan *Also called Midwest Cmnty Hlth Assoc Inc (G-1964)*
Parkwood Apartments, Toledo *Also called Lucas Metropolitan Hsing Auth (G-17869)*
Parkwood Corporation (PA)...216 875-6500
1000 Lakeside Ave E Cleveland (44114) *(G-6174)*
Parma Adult Training Center, Cleveland *Also called Cuyahoga County (G-5394)*
Parma Care Center Inc...216 661-6800
5553 Broadview Rd Cleveland (44134) *(G-6175)*
PARMA CARE NURSING AND REHABIL, Cleveland *Also called Parma Care Center Inc (G-6175)*
Parma Clinic Cancer Center...440 743-4747
6525 Parma Blvd Fl 2 Flr 2 Cleveland (44129) *(G-6176)*
Parma Communirty Hospital, Cleveland *Also called Parma Clinic Cancer Center (G-6176)*
Parma Community General Hosp (PA)...440 743-3000
7007 Powers Blvd Parma (44129) *(G-15771)*
Parma Community General Hosp...440 743-4280
7007 Powers Blvd Parma (44129) *(G-15772)*
Parma Medical Center, Brooklyn Heights *Also called Kaiser Foundation Hospitals (G-1874)*
Parma Service Garage, Cleveland *Also called City of Parma (G-5211)*
Parman Group Inc (PA)...513 673-0077
4501 Hilton Corporate Dr Columbus (43232) *(G-8424)*
Parmatown South, Cleveland *Also called Forest City Enterprises LP (G-5556)*
PARMAUTO FEDERAL CREDIT UNION, Cleveland *Also called Best Reward Credit Union (G-5059)*
Parole & Community Services, Columbus *Also called Ohio Dept Rhbilitation Corectn (G-8248)*
Parrish McIntyre Tire, Mogadore *Also called Parrish Tire Company of Akron (G-14554)*
Parrish Tire Company of Akron...330 628-6800
3833 Mogadore Indus Pkwy Mogadore (44260) *(G-14554)*

ALPHABETIC

Parsec Inc (PA) 513 621-6111
 1100 Gest St Cincinnati (45203) **(G-4206)**
Parsec Intermodal Cannada, Cincinnati Also called Parsec Inc **(G-4206)**
Parta, Kent Also called Portage Area Rgonal Trnsp Auth **(G-12254)**
Partners Auto Group Bdford Inc 440 439-2323
 11 Broadway Ave Bedford (44146) **(G-1299)**
Partners of City View LLC 216 361-1414
 6606 Carnegie Ave Cleveland (44103) **(G-6177)**
Partners of Marion Care, Marion Also called Sunbrdge Marion Hlth Care Corp **(G-13461)**
Partnership LLC 440 471-8310
 29077 Clemens Rd Cleveland (44145) **(G-6178)**
Parts Plus, West Chester Also called Smyth Automotive Inc **(G-19010)**
Parts Plus, Bethel Also called Smyth Automotive Inc **(G-1454)**
Parts Pro Automotive Warehouse, Wickliffe Also called GTM Service Inc **(G-19462)**
Partssource Inc 330 562-9900
 777 Lena Dr Aurora (44202) **(G-838)**
Pas Technologies Inc 937 840-1000
 214 Hobart Dr Hillsboro (45133) **(G-11854)**
Pasco Inc 330 650-0613
 5600 Hudsn Indstl Pkwy Hudson (44236) **(G-12001)**
Passion To Heal Healthcare 216 849-0180
 4228 W 58th St Cleveland (44144) **(G-6179)**
Passport, Columbus Also called Central OH Area Agency On Agng **(G-7156)**
Passport, Cleveland Also called Western Reserve Area Agency **(G-6674)**
Passprt Accept Fclty Mansfld P 419 755-4621
 200 N Diamond St Mansfield (44901) **(G-13230)**
Pastoral Care Management Svcs 513 205-1398
 1240 Rosemont Ave Cincinnati (45205) **(G-4207)**
Pastoral Counseling Svc Summit 330 996-4600
 611 W Market St Akron (44303) **(G-371)**
Pat Catan's, Strongsville Also called Lamrite West Inc **(G-17323)**
Pat Catan's Craft Centers, Strongsville Also called Darice Inc **(G-17297)**
Pat Henry Group LLC (PA) 216 447-0831
 6046 Bridgehaven Dr Milford (45150) **(G-14420)**
Pat Young Service Co Inc (PA) 216 447-8550
 6100 Hillcrest Dr Cleveland (44125) **(G-6180)**
Pat Young Service Co Inc 440 891-1550
 1260 Moore Rd Ste K Avon (44011) **(G-899)**
Pataskala Oaks Care Center, Pataskala Also called Nursing Care MGT Amer Inc **(G-15786)**
Patella Carpet & Tile, Youngstown Also called Patellas Floor Center Inc **(G-20152)**
Patellas Floor Center Inc 330 758-4099
 6620 Market St Youngstown (44512) **(G-20152)**
Patented Acquisition Corp (PA) 937 353-2299
 2490 Cross Pointe Dr Miamisburg (45342) **(G-14203)**
Path Forward It, Cincinnati Also called Recker Consulting LLC **(G-4345)**
Path Robotics Inc 330 808-2788
 1768 E 25th St Cleveland (44114) **(G-6181)**
Pathlabs, Toledo Also called Pathology Laboratories Inc **(G-17973)**
Pathology Laboratories Inc (HQ) 419 255-4600
 1946 N 13th St Ste 301 Toledo (43604) **(G-17973)**
Pathway Inc 419 242-7304
 505 Hamilton St Toledo (43604) **(G-17974)**
Pathway 2 Hope Inc 866 491-3040
 3036 Gilbert Ave Cincinnati (45206) **(G-4208)**
Pathway Caring For Children (PA) 330 493-0083
 4895 Dressler Rd Nw Ste A Canton (44718) **(G-2435)**
Pathway House LLC 872 223-9797
 15539 Saranac Rd Cleveland (44110) **(G-6182)**
Pathway School of Discovery, Dayton Also called National Heritg Academies Inc **(G-9654)**
Pathways Center, Columbus Also called Columbus Area Inc **(G-7256)**
Pathways Inc (PA) 440 918-1000
 7350 Palisades Pkwy Mentor (44060) **(G-14095)**
Pathways of Central Ohio 740 345-6166
 1627 Bryn Mawr Dr Newark (43055) **(G-15091)**
Patient Account MGT Svcs LLC 614 575-0044
 950 Taylor Station Rd I Columbus (43230) **(G-8425)**
Patient Financial Services, Rocky River Also called JP Recovery Services Inc **(G-16438)**
Patientpint Hosp Solutions LLC 513 936-6800
 8230 Montgomery Rd # 300 Cincinnati (45236) **(G-4209)**
Patientpint Ntwrk Slutions LLC (HQ) 513 936-6800
 5901 E Galbraith Rd Cincinnati (45236) **(G-4210)**
Patientpoint LLC (PA) 513 936-6800
 5901 E Galbraith Rd Cincinnati (45236) **(G-4211)**
Patricia A Dickerson MD 937 436-1117
 1299 E Alex Bell Rd Dayton (45459) **(G-9688)**
Patrick J Burke & Co 513 455-8200
 901 Adams Crossing Fl 1 Cincinnati (45202) **(G-4212)**
Patrick Mahoney 614 292-5766
 1223 Neil Ave Columbus (43201) **(G-8426)**
Patrick Staffing Inc (PA) 937 743-5585
 1200 E 2nd St Ste B Franklin (45005) **(G-11036)**
Patriot Emergency Med Svcs Inc 740 532-2222
 2914 S 4th St Ironton (45638) **(G-12165)**
Patriot Indus Contg Svcs LLC 513 248-8222
 200 Olympic Dr Milford (45150) **(G-14421)**
Patriot Ridge Community, Fairborn Also called United Church Homes Inc **(G-10684)**
Patriot Software LLC 877 968-7147
 4883 Dressler Rd Nw # 301 Canton (44718) **(G-2436)**
Patrol Urban Services LLC 614 620-4672
 4563 E Walnut St Westerville (43081) **(G-19291)**

Patterson Pope, Cincinnati Also called Central Business Equipment Co **(G-3150)**
Patterson Pope Inc 513 891-4430
 10321 S Medallion Dr Cincinnati (45241) **(G-4213)**
Pattie Group Inc (PA) 440 338-1288
 15533 Chillicothe Rd Novelty (44072) **(G-15466)**
Pattie's Landscaping, Novelty Also called Pattie Group Inc **(G-15466)**
Paul A Ertel 216 696-8888
 1153 Main Ave Cleveland (44113) **(G-6183)**
Paul Davis Restoration, Moraine Also called Davis Paul Restoration Dayton **(G-14639)**
Paul Dennis 440 746-8600
 7005 Stadium Dr Ofc Brecksville (44141) **(G-1795)**
Paul Hrnchar Ford-Mercury Inc 330 533-3673
 366 W Main St Canfield (44406) **(G-2155)**
Paul Mitchell School Columbus, Columbus Also called Skyland Columbus LLC **(G-8651)**
Paul Moss LLC 216 765-1580
 5895 Harper Rd Solon (44139) **(G-16881)**
Paul Paratto, Willoughby Also called Howard Hanna Smythe Cramer **(G-19530)**
Paul Peterson Company (PA) 614 486-4375
 950 Dublin Rd Columbus (43215) **(G-8427)**
Paul Peterson Safety Div Inc 614 486-4375
 950 Dublin Rd Columbus (43215) **(G-8428)**
Paul R Young Funeral Homes (PA) 513 521-9303
 7345 Hamilton Ave Cincinnati (45231) **(G-4214)**
Paul Werth Associates Inc (PA) 614 224-8114
 10 N High St Ste 300 Columbus (43215) **(G-8429)**
Paul, Elaine MD, Columbus Also called Drs Paul Boyles & Kennedy **(G-7470)**
Paula Jo Moore 330 894-2910
 10990 Myers Rd Kensington (44427) **(G-12211)**
Paulding Area Visiting Nurses, Paulding Also called Community Hlth Prfssionals Inc **(G-15791)**
Paulding County Hospital 419 399-4080
 1035 W Wayne St Paulding (45879) **(G-15796)**
Paulding Exempted Vlg Schl Dst (PA) 419 594-3309
 405 N Water St Paulding (45879) **(G-15797)**
PAULDING PUTNAM ELECTRIC COOPE, Paulding Also called Paulding-Putnam Electric Coop **(G-15798)**
Paulding-Putnam Electric Coop (PA) 419 399-5015
 401 Mc Donald Pike Paulding (45879) **(G-15798)**
Paulo Products Company 440 942-0153
 4428 Hamann Pkwy Willoughby (44094) **(G-19561)**
Pauls Bus Service Inc 513 851-5089
 3561 W Kemper Rd Cincinnati (45251) **(G-4215)**
Pavement Protectors Inc 614 875-9989
 2020 Longwood Ave Grove City (43123) **(G-11464)**
Pavilion At Piketon For Nursin 740 289-2394
 7143 Us Highway 23 Piketon (45661) **(G-15984)**
Pavilion At Piketon, The, Piketon Also called Pavilion At Piketon For Nursin **(G-15984)**
Pavillion At Camargo, The, Cincinnati Also called Camargo Manor Inc **(G-3108)**
Pawnee Maintenance Inc 740 373-6861
 101 Rathbone Rd Marietta (45750) **(G-13366)**
Paws Inn Inc 937 435-1500
 8926 Kingsridge Dr Dayton (45458) **(G-9689)**
Pax Steel Products Inc 419 678-1481
 104 E Vine St Coldwater (45828) **(G-6764)**
Paxton Hardwoods LLC 513 984-8200
 7455 Dawson Rd Cincinnati (45243) **(G-4216)**
Paychex Inc 614 781-6143
 600 Lkview Plz Blvd Ste G Worthington (43085) **(G-19833)**
Paychex Inc 330 342-0530
 100 E Hines Hill Rd Hudson (44236) **(G-12002)**
Paychex Inc 513 727-9182
 3420 Atrium Blvd Ste 200 Middletown (45005) **(G-14353)**
Paychex Inc 800 939-2462
 675 W Market St Lima (45801) **(G-12718)**
Paychex Inc 614 210-0400
 5080 Tuttle Crossing Blvd # 450 Dublin (43016) **(G-10306)**
Paycom Software Inc 888 678-0796
 255 E 5th St Ste 1420 Cincinnati (45202) **(G-4217)**
Paycor Inc 614 985-6140
 250 E Wilson Bridge Rd # 110 Worthington (43085) **(G-19834)**
Paycor Inc 216 447-7913
 4500 Rockside Rd Ste 320 Cleveland (44131) **(G-6184)**
Paycor Inc (PA) 513 381-0505
 4811 Montgomery Rd Cincinnati (45212) **(G-4218)**
Paygro, South Charleston Also called Garick LLC **(G-16924)**
Payne Nickles & Co CPA (PA) 419 668-2552
 257 Benedict Ave Ste D Norwalk (44857) **(G-15452)**
Payroll Services Unlimited 740 653-9581
 125 W Mulberry St Lancaster (43130) **(G-12425)**
Pbsi, Cincinnati Also called Positive Bus Solutions Inc **(G-4265)**
PC Connection Inc 937 382-4800
 3336 Progress Way Bldg 11 Wilmington (45177) **(G-19637)**
PC Connection Sales Corp 937 382-4800
 2870 Old State 1 Wilmington (45177) **(G-19638)**
PC Connection Services 937 382-4800
 2870 Old State Route 73 # 1 Wilmington (45177) **(G-19639)**
Pca-Corrections LLC 614 297-8244
 4014 Venture Ct Columbus (43228) **(G-8430)**
PCC Transportation, Columbus Also called P C C Refrigerated Ex Inc **(G-8406)**
Pcm Inc 614 854-1399
 8337 Green Meadows Dr N Lewis Center (43035) **(G-12557)**

(G-0000) Company's Geographic Section entry number

Pcm Logistics, Lewis Center *Also called Pcm Inc (G-12557)*
Pcm Sales Inc 501 342-1000
  8200 Sweet Valley Dr # 108 Cleveland (44125) *(G-6185)*
Pcm Sales Inc 513 842-3500
  4600 Mcauley Pl Ste 200 Blue Ash (45242) *(G-1628)*
Pcm Sales Inc 740 548-2222
  8337 Green Meadows Dr N Lewis Center (43035) *(G-12558)*
Pcm Sales Inc 937 885-6444
  3020 S Tech Blvd Miamisburg (45342) *(G-14204)*
Pcms Datafit Inc 513 587-3100
  4270 Glendale Milford Rd Blue Ash (45242) *(G-1629)*
Pcrf, The, Kent *Also called Palestine Chld Relief Fund (G-12253)*
Pcs Cost 216 771-1090
  1360 E 9th St Ste 910 Cleveland (44114) *(G-6186)*
Pcy Enterprises Inc 513 241-5566
  3111 Spring Grove Ave Cincinnati (45225) *(G-4219)*
PDG, Bowling Green *Also called Poggemeyer Design Group Inc (G-1746)*
Pdi Communication Systems Inc (PA) 937 743-6010
  40 Greenwood Ln Springboro (45066) *(G-16979)*
Pdi Plastics, Westerville *Also called Cannon Group Inc (G-19230)*
Pdk Construction Inc 740 992-6451
  34070 Crew Rd Pomeroy (45769) *(G-16096)*
Pds, Fairfield *Also called CPC Logistics Inc (G-10715)*
Pdsi Technical Services, Dayton *Also called Production Design Services Inc (G-9716)*
Pe, Westlake *Also called North Bay Construction Inc (G-19380)*
Peabody Coal Company 740 450-2420
  2810 East Pike Apt 3 Zanesville (43701) *(G-20353)*
Peabody Landscape Cnstr Inc 614 488-2877
  2253 Dublin Rd Columbus (43228) *(G-8431)*
Peabody Landscape Group, Columbus *Also called Peabody Landscape Cnstr Inc (G-8431)*
Peace Foundation, Medina *Also called Intervention For Peace Inc (G-13957)*
Peak Performance Center Inc 440 838-5600
  1 Eagle Valley Ct Broadview Heights (44147) *(G-1843)*
Peak Transportation Inc 419 874-5201
  26624 Glenwood Rd Perrysburg (43551) *(G-15899)*
Pearl Crossing, Cleveland *Also called Harvest Facility Holdings LP (G-5665)*
Pearl Interactive Network Inc 614 258-2943
  1103 Schrock Rd Ste 109 Columbus (43229) *(G-8432)*
Pearne & Gordon LLP 216 579-1700
  1801 E 9th St Ste 1200 Cleveland (44114) *(G-6187)*
Pearne Gordon McCoy & Granger, Cleveland *Also called Pearne & Gordon LLP (G-6187)*
Pease & Associates LLC (PA) 216 348-9600
  1422 Euclid Ave Ste 801 Cleveland (44115) *(G-6188)*
Pebble Creek, Akron *Also called Nightingale Holdings LLC (G-346)*
Pebble Creek Cnvlscnt Ctr 330 645-0200
  670 Jarvis Rd Akron (44319) *(G-372)*
Pebble Creek Golf Club, Mansfield *Also called Bramarjac Inc (G-13144)*
Pebble Creek Golf Course, Cincinnati *Also called M T Golf Course Managment Inc (G-3955)*
Peck Distributors Inc 216 587-6814
  17000 Rockside Rd Maple Heights (44137) *(G-13291)*
Peck Food Service, Maple Heights *Also called Peck Distributors Inc (G-13291)*
Peck Hannaford Briggs Service, Cincinnati *Also called Peck-Hannaford Briggs Svc Corp (G-4220)*
Peck-Hannaford Briggs Svc Corp 513 681-1200
  4673 Spring Grove Ave Cincinnati (45232) *(G-4220)*
Peco II Inc 614 431-0694
  7060 Huntley Rd Columbus (43229) *(G-8433)*
Pedersen Insulation Company 614 471-3788
  2901 Johnstown Rd Columbus (43219) *(G-8434)*
Pediatric Assoc Cincinnati 513 791-1222
  4360 Cooper Rd Ste 201 Cincinnati (45242) *(G-4221)*
Pediatric Assoc of Fairfield 513 874-9460
  5502 Dixie Hwy Ste A Fairfield (45014) *(G-10769)*
Pediatric Assoc of Springfield 937 328-2320
  1640 N Limestone St Springfield (45503) *(G-17095)*
Pediatric Associates Inc (PA) 614 501-7337
  1021 Country Club Rd A Columbus (43213) *(G-8435)*
Pediatric Associates of Dayton (PA) 937 832-7337
  9000 N Main St Ste 332 Englewood (45415) *(G-10596)*
Pediatric Care Inc (PA) 513 931-6357
  800 Compton Rd Unit 25 Cincinnati (45231) *(G-4222)*
Pediatric Services Inc (PA) 440 845-1500
  6707 Powers Blvd Ste 203 Cleveland (44129) *(G-6189)*
Pediatrics Assoc of Mt Carmel 513 752-3650
  4371 Ferguson Dr Cincinnati (45245) *(G-2864)*
Pediatrics of Akron Inc 330 253-7753
  300 Locust St Ste 200 Akron (44302) *(G-373)*
Pediatrics of Lima Inc 419 222-4045
  830 W High St Ste 102 Lima (45801) *(G-12719)*
Peerless Technologies Corp 937 490-5000
  2300 National Rd Beavercreek Township (45324) *(G-1257)*
Pegasus Technical Services Inc 513 793-0094
  46 E Hollister St Cincinnati (45219) *(G-4223)*
Peitro Properties Ltd Partnr 216 328-7777
  6191 Quarry Ln Cleveland (44131) *(G-6190)*
Pel LLC 216 267-5775
  4666 Manufacturing Ave Cleveland (44135) *(G-6191)*
Pella Corporation 513 948-8480
  145 B Colwell Dr Cincinnati (45216) *(G-4224)*
Pella Window & Door, Cleveland *Also called Gunton Corporation (G-5647)*

Pembrooke Place Skilled, Columbus *Also called Vrable IV Inc (G-8866)*
Pemco North Canton Division, Canton *Also called Powell Electrical Systems Inc (G-2438)*
Pen Brands LLC (HQ) 216 447-1199
  220 Eastview Dr Ste 102 Brooklyn Heights (44131) *(G-1878)*
Pendster Dialysis LLC 937 237-0769
  7769 Old Country Ct Huber Heights (45424) *(G-11956)*
Penetrating R Ground (PA) 419 843-9804
  5217 Monroe St Toledo (43623) *(G-17975)*
Penn Mutual Life Insurance Co 330 668-9065
  130 Springside Dr Ste 100 Akron (44333) *(G-374)*
Penn Ohio Electrical Contrs, Masury *Also called Penn-Ohio Electrical Company (G-13742)*
PENN POWER, Akron *Also called Pennsylvania Power Company (G-376)*
Penn Tool, Youngstown *Also called Pennsylvania TI Sls & Svc Inc (G-20153)*
Penn-Ohio Electrical Company 330 448-1234
  1370 Sharon Hogue Rd Masury (44438) *(G-13742)*
Pennington International Inc 513 631-2130
  1977 Section Rd Ste 1 Cincinnati (45237) *(G-4225)*
Pennington Seed Inc 513 642-8980
  9530 Le Saint Dr Fairfield (45014) *(G-10770)*
Pennsylvania Electric Company (HQ) 800 545-7741
  76 S Main St Bsmt Akron (44308) *(G-375)*
Pennsylvania Power Company (HQ) 800 720-3600
  76 S Main St Bsmt Akron (44308) *(G-376)*
Pennsylvania TI Sls & Svc Inc (PA) 330 758-0845
  625 Bev Rd Youngstown (44512) *(G-20153)*
Pension Corporation America 513 281-3366
  2133 Luray Ave Cincinnati (45206) *(G-4226)*
Penske Logistics LLC 216 765-5475
  3000 Auburn Dr Ste 100 Beachwood (44122) *(G-1095)*
Penske Logistics LLC 330 626-7623
  9777 Mopar Dr Streetsboro (44241) *(G-17265)*
Penske Logistics LLC 419 547-2615
  600 N Woodland Ave Clyde (43410) *(G-6749)*
Penske Logistics LLC 440 232-5811
  7600 First Pl Cleveland (44146) *(G-6192)*
Penske Truck Leasing Co LP 419 873-8611
  12222 Williams Rd Perrysburg (43551) *(G-15900)*
Penske Truck Leasing Co LP 614 658-0000
  2470 Westbelt Dr Columbus (43228) *(G-8436)*
Penske Truck Leasing Co LP 513 771-7701
  2528 Commodity Cir Cincinnati (45241) *(G-4227)*
Penske Truck Leasing Co LP 330 645-3100
  3000 Fortuna Dr Akron (44312) *(G-377)*
Penske Truck Leasing Co LP 440 232-5811
  7600 First Pl Bedford (44146) *(G-1300)*
Pentaflex Inc 937 325-5551
  4981 Gateway Blvd Springfield (45502) *(G-17096)*
Pentair Rsdntial Fltration LLC 440 286-4116
  220 Park Dr Chardon (44024) *(G-2708)*
People To My Site LLC 614 452-8179
  580 N 4th St Ste 500 Columbus (43215) *(G-8437)*
People To Site, Columbus *Also called People To My Site LLC (G-8437)*
Peoples Bancorp Inc (PA) 740 373-3155
  138 Putnam St Marietta (45750) *(G-13367)*
Peoples Bancorp Inc 740 947-4372
  951 W Emmitt Ave Waverly (45690) *(G-18819)*
Peoples Bancorp Inc 740 574-9100
  7920 Ohio River Rd Wheelersburg (45694) *(G-19437)*
Peoples Bancorp Inc 513 793-2422
  9813 Montgomery Rd Cincinnati (45242) *(G-4228)*
Peoples Bancorp Inc 513 271-9100
  7114 Miami Ave Cincinnati (45243) *(G-4229)*
Peoples Bank 937 748-0067
  95 Edgebrooke Dr Springboro (45066) *(G-16980)*
Peoples Bank (HQ) 740 373-3155
  138 Putnam St Marietta (45750) *(G-13368)*
Peoples Bank 740 286-6773
  101 E A St Wellston (45692) *(G-18854)*
Peoples Bank 937 382-1441
  48 N South St Wilmington (45177) *(G-19640)*
Peoples Bank 740 354-3177
  503 Chillicothe St Portsmouth (45662) *(G-16157)*
Peoples Bank 740 439-2767
  845 Wheeling Ave Cambridge (43725) *(G-2080)*
Peoples Bank National Assn 937 746-5733
  1400 E 2nd St Franklin (45005) *(G-11037)*
Peoples Cartage Inc 330 833-8571
  8045 Navarre Rd Sw Massillon (44648) *(G-13719)*
Peoples Federal Sav & Ln Assn (HQ) 937 492-6129
  101 E Court St Sidney (45365) *(G-16791)*
Peoples Hospital, Ashland *Also called Samaritan Regional Health Sys (G-690)*
Peoples Nat Bnk of New Lxngton (PA) 740 342-5111
  110 N Main St New Lexington (43764) *(G-14925)*
Peoples Savings and Loan Co (PA) 419 562-6896
  300 S Walnut St Bucyrus (44820) *(G-2000)*
Peoples Services Inc (PA) 330 453-3709
  2207 Kimball Rd Se Canton (44707) *(G-2437)*
Peoples-Sidney Financial Corp (PA) 937 492-6129
  101 E Court St Sidney (45365) *(G-16792)*
Peopleworks Dev of Hr LLC 419 636-4637
  3440 County Road 9 Bryan (43506) *(G-1969)*

A
L
P
H
A
B
E
T
I
C

Pep Boys - Manny Moe & Jack..........614 864-2092
2830 S Hamilton Rd Columbus (43232) ***(G-8438)***
Pepco, Toledo *Also called Professional Electric Pdts Co* ***(G-17989)***
Pepper Cnstr Co Ohio LLC..........614 793-4477
495 Metro Pl S Ste 350 Dublin (43017) ***(G-10307)***
Pepper Pike Club Company Inc..........216 831-9400
2800 Som Center Rd Cleveland (44124) ***(G-6193)***
PEPPER PIKE GOLF CLUB, Cleveland *Also called Pepper Pike Club Company Inc* ***(G-6193)***
Pepperl + Fuchs Inc (HQ)..........330 425-3555
1600 Enterprise Pkwy Twinsburg (44087) ***(G-18302)***
Pepperl + Fuchs Americas Inc..........330 425-3555
1600 Enterprise Pkwy Twinsburg (44087) ***(G-18303)***
Pepsi-Cola Metro Btlg Co Inc..........330 336-3553
904 Seville Rd Wadsworth (44281) ***(G-18611)***
Pepsi-Cola Metro Btlg Co Inc..........937 461-4664
526 Milburn Ave Dayton (45404) ***(G-9690)***
Pepsi-Cola Metro Btlg Co Inc..........440 323-5524
925 Lorain Blvd Elyria (44035) ***(G-10554)***
Pepsi-Cola Metro Btlg Co Inc..........937 328-6750
233 Dayton Ave Springfield (45506) ***(G-17097)***
Pepsi-Cola Metro Btlg Co Inc..........330 963-0426
1999 Enterprise Pkwy Twinsburg (44087) ***(G-18304)***
Pepsico, Franklin Furnace *Also called G & J Pepsi-Cola Bottlers Inc* ***(G-11045)***
Pepsico, Chillicothe *Also called G & J Pepsi-Cola Bottlers Inc* ***(G-2782)***
Pepsico, Zanesville *Also called G & J Pepsi-Cola Bottlers Inc* ***(G-20309)***
Pepsico, Youngstown *Also called P-Americas LLC* ***(G-20149)***
Per Diem Nurse Staffing LLT..........419 878-8880
18 N 3rd St Lowr Waterville (43566) ***(G-18791)***
Perceptionist Inc..........614 384-7500
178 W Schrock Rd Ste C Westerville (43081) ***(G-19292)***
Perceptis LLC..........216 458-4122
1250 Old River Rd Ste 300 Cleveland (44113) ***(G-6194)***
Perco Inc..........740 342-5156
2235 State Route 13 Ne New Lexington (43764) ***(G-14926)***
Perduco Group Inc..........937 401-0271
2647 Commons Blvd Beavercreek (45431) ***(G-1175)***
Peregrine Health Services Inc..........419 586-4135
1301 Myers Rd Celina (45822) ***(G-2606)***
Peregrine Health Services Inc..........330 823-9005
2040 Mccrea St Alliance (44601) ***(G-543)***
Peregrine Health Services Inc..........419 298-2321
328 W Vine St Edgerton (43517) ***(G-10469)***
Perfect Cut-Off Inc..........440 943-0000
29201 Anderson Rd Wickliffe (44092) ***(G-19473)***
Perfection Bakeries Inc..........937 492-2220
1900 Progress Way Sidney (45365) ***(G-16793)***
Perfection Group Inc (PA)..........513 772-7545
2649 Commerce Blvd Cincinnati (45241) ***(G-4230)***
Perfection Services Inc..........513 772-7545
2649 Commerce Blvd Cincinnati (45241) ***(G-4231)***
Performance Lexus, Fairfield *Also called Kings Cove Automotive LLC* ***(G-10744)***
Performance Painting LLC..........440 735-3340
7603 First Pl Oakwood Village (44146) ***(G-15492)***
Performnce Fodservice - Presto, Monroe *Also called Ohio Pizza Products Inc* ***(G-14578)***
Perinatal Partners, Dayton *Also called Primary Cr Ntwrk Prmr Hlth Prt* ***(G-9710)***
Perio Inc (PA)..........614 791-1207
6156 Wilcox Rd Dublin (43016) ***(G-10308)***
Perk Company Inc (PA)..........216 391-1444
8100 Grand Ave Ste 300 Cleveland (44104) ***(G-6195)***
Perkfect Design Solutions..........614 778-3560
308 E 9th Ave Columbus (43201) ***(G-8439)***
Perkinelmer Hlth Sciences Inc..........330 825-4525
520 S Main St Ste 2423 Akron (44311) ***(G-378)***
Perkins Family Restaurant, Alliance *Also called Dino Persichetti* ***(G-530)***
Perkins Motor Service Ltd (PA)..........440 277-1256
1864 E 28th St Lorain (44055) ***(G-12938)***
Permanent Family Solutions, Columbus *Also called Buckeye Ranch Inc* ***(G-7090)***
Permanent Gen Asrn Corp Ohio..........216 986-3000
9700 Rockside Rd Cleveland (44125) ***(G-6196)***
Permatex Inc..........440 914-3100
6875 Parkland Blvd Solon (44139) ***(G-16882)***
Permedion Inc..........614 895-9900
350 Worthington Rd Ste H Westerville (43082) ***(G-19198)***
Permian Oil & Gas Division, Newark *Also called National Gas & Oil Corporation* ***(G-15079)***
Perram Electric Inc..........330 239-2661
6882 Ridge Rd Wadsworth (44281) ***(G-18612)***
Perrin Asphalt Co Inc..........330 253-1020
525 Dan St Akron (44310) ***(G-379)***
Perry Contract Services Inc..........614 274-4350
2319 Scioto Harper Dr Columbus (43204) ***(G-8440)***
Perry County Engineer, New Lexington *Also called County of Perry* ***(G-14919)***
Perry Interiors Inc..........513 761-9333
4054 Clough Woods Dr Batavia (45103) ***(G-1006)***
Perry Kelly Plumbing Inc..........513 528-6554
4498 Mt Carmel Tobasco Rd Cincinnati (45244) ***(G-4232)***
Perry Pro Tech Inc (PA)..........419 228-1360
545 W Market St Lowr Lowr Lima (45801) ***(G-12720)***
Perry Pro Tech Inc..........419 475-9030
1270 Flagship Dr Perrysburg (43551) ***(G-15901)***
Perry Transportation Dept..........440 259-3005
3829 Main St Perry (44081) ***(G-15827)***
Perrysburg Board of Education..........419 874-3127
25715 Fort Meigs Rd Perrysburg (43551) ***(G-15902)***
Perrysburg Bus Garage, Perrysburg *Also called Perrysburg Board of Education* ***(G-15902)***
Perrysburg Pediatrics..........419 872-7700
1601 Brigham Dr Ste 200 Perrysburg (43551) ***(G-15903)***
Perrysburg Rsdntial Seal Cting..........419 872-7325
26651 Eckel Rd Perrysburg (43551) ***(G-15904)***
Personacare of Ohio Inc..........440 357-1311
70 Normandy Dr Painesville (44077) ***(G-15733)***
Personal & Fmly Counseling Svc..........330 343-8171
1433 5th St Nw New Philadelphia (44663) ***(G-14976)***
Personal Lawn Care Inc..........440 934-5296
3910 Long Rd Avon (44011) ***(G-900)***
Personal Service Insurance Co..........800 282-9416
2760 Airport Dr Ste 130 Columbus (43219) ***(G-8441)***
Personal Touch HM Care IPA Inc..........216 986-0885
4500 Rockside Rd Ste 460 Cleveland (44131) ***(G-6197)***
Personal Touch HM Care IPA Inc..........937 456-4447
302 Eaton Lewisburg Rd Eaton (45320) ***(G-10458)***
Personal Touch HM Care IPA Inc..........513 868-2272
7924 Jessies Way Ste C Hamilton (45011) ***(G-11632)***
Personal Touch HM Care IPA Inc..........513 984-9600
8260 Northcreek Dr # 140 Cincinnati (45236) ***(G-4233)***
Personal Touch HM Care IPA Inc..........614 227-6952
454 E Main St Ste 227 Columbus (43215) ***(G-8442)***
Personal Touch HM Care IPA Inc..........330 263-1112
543 Riffel Rd Ste F Wooster (44691) ***(G-19758)***
Personalized Data Corporation..........216 289-2200
26155 Euclid Ave Uppr Cleveland (44132) ***(G-6198)***
Personalized Data Entry & Word, Cleveland *Also called Personalized Data Corporation* ***(G-6198)***
Perspectus Architecture LLC (PA)..........216 752-1800
13212 Shaker Sq Ste 204 Cleveland (44120) ***(G-6199)***
Pet Central Lodge & Grooming..........440 282-1811
1425 C Foster Pk Rd C Amherst (44001) ***(G-595)***
Pet Food Holdings Inc..........419 394-3374
1601 Mckinley Rd Saint Marys (45885) ***(G-16531)***
Pete Baur Buick Gmc Inc (PA)..........440 238-5600
14000 Pearl Rd Cleveland (44136) ***(G-6200)***
Peter A Wimberg Company Inc..........513 271-2332
5401 Hetzell St Cincinnati (45227) ***(G-4234)***
Peter Graham Dunn Inc..........330 816-0035
1417 Zuercher Rd Dalton (44618) ***(G-9146)***
Peter M Kostoff..........330 849-6681
222 S Main St Fl 4 Akron (44308) ***(G-380)***
Peterbilt of Cincinnati..........513 772-1740
2550 Annuity Dr Cincinnati (45241) ***(G-4235)***
Peterbilt of Northwest Ohio..........419 423-3441
1330 Trenton Ave Findlay (45840) ***(G-10952)***
Peterj Brodhead..........216 696-3232
1001 Lakeside Ave E Cleveland (44114) ***(G-6201)***
Peterman..........513 722-2229
6757 Linton Rd Goshen (45122) ***(G-11314)***
Peterman Associates Inc..........419 722-9566
3480 N Main St Findlay (45840) ***(G-10953)***
Peterman Plumbing and Htg Inc..........330 364-4497
525 W 15th St Dover (44622) ***(G-10093)***
Petermann..........513 539-0324
505 Yankee Rd Monroe (45050) ***(G-14580)***
Petermann Ltd..........330 653-3323
91 Owen Brown St Hudson (44236) ***(G-12003)***
Petermann Northeast LLC..........513 351-7383
8041 Hosbrook Rd Ste 330 Cincinnati (45236) ***(G-4236)***
Peters Main Street Photography (PA)..........740 852-2731
314 N Main St London (43140) ***(G-12872)***
Peters Tschantz & Assoc Inc..........330 666-3702
275 Springside Dr Ste 300 Akron (44333) ***(G-381)***
Peterson Construction Company..........419 941-2233
18817 State Route 501 Wapakoneta (45895) ***(G-18652)***
Petitti Garden Centers, Oakwood Village *Also called Flowerland Garden Centers* ***(G-15489)***
Petland Inc (PA)..........740 775-2464
250 Riverside St Chillicothe (45601) ***(G-2811)***
Petro Cells, Cincinnati *Also called Petro Environmental Tech* ***(G-4237)***
Petro Environmental Tech (PA)..........513 489-6789
8160 Corp Pk Dr Ste 300 Cincinnati (45242) ***(G-4237)***
Petro Stopping Center, Westlake *Also called Ta Operating LLC* ***(G-19411)***
Petro-Com Corp (PA)..........440 327-6900
32523 Lorain Rd North Ridgeville (44039) ***(G-15339)***
Petrolube, Napoleon *Also called Trep Ltd* ***(G-14818)***
Petros Homes Inc..........440 546-9000
10474 Broadview Rd Cleveland (44147) ***(G-6202)***
Petsmart Inc..........513 336-0365
8175 Arbor Square Dr Mason (45040) ***(G-13626)***
Petsmart Inc..........513 248-4954
245 Rivers Edge Milford (45150) ***(G-14422)***
Petsmart Inc..........513 752-8463
650 Eastgate South Dr B Cincinnati (45245) ***(G-2865)***
Petsmart Inc..........937 236-1335
8281 Old Troy Pike Huber Heights (45424) ***(G-11957)***
Petsmart Inc..........614 418-9389
3713 Easton Market Columbus (43219) ***(G-8443)***

Petsmart Inc 330 922-4114
  355 Howe Ave Cuyahoga Falls (44221) *(G-9117)*
Petsmart Inc 330 629-2479
  1101 Doral Dr Youngstown (44514) *(G-20154)*
Petsmart Inc 330 544-1499
  5812 Youngstown Warren Rd Niles (44446) *(G-15167)*
Petsmart Inc 614 497-3001
  6499 Adelaide Ct Groveport (43125) *(G-11529)*
Petsmart Inc 440 974-1100
  9122 Mentor Ave Mentor (44060) *(G-14096)*
Petsuites of America Inc 513 554-4408
  3701 Hauck Rd Cincinnati (45241) *(G-4238)*
Pf Holdings LLC 740 549-3558
  8522 Cotter St Lewis Center (43035) *(G-12559)*
Pfg Ventures LP (PA) 216 520-8400
  8800 E Pleasant Valley Rd # 1 Independence (44131) *(G-12107)*
Pfh Partners LLC 513 241-5800
  3805 Edwards Rd Ste 700 Cincinnati (45209) *(G-4239)*
Pfpc Enterprises Inc 513 941-6200
  5750 Hillside Ave Cincinnati (45233) *(G-4240)*
Pgim Inc 419 331-6604
  2100 Harding Hwy Ste 4 Lima (45804) *(G-12721)*
PGT Trucking Inc 419 943-3437
  6302 Road 5 Leipsic (45856) *(G-12521)*
PH B, Cincinnati *Also called The Peck-Hannaford Briggs Co (G-4595)*
PH Fairborn Ht Owner 2800 LLC 937 426-7800
  2800 Presidential Dr Beavercreek (45324) *(G-1176)*
Phantom Technical Services Inc 614 868-9920
  111 Outerbelt St Columbus (43213) *(G-8444)*
Pharmacy Benefit Direct, Youngstown *Also called Pharmacy Data Management
Inc (G-20155)*
Pharmacy Data Management Inc (PA) 330 757-1500
  1170 E Western Reserve Rd Youngstown (44514) *(G-20155)*
Pharmacy-Lite Packaging, Elyria *Also called Pacific MGT Holdings LLC (G-10552)*
Pharmed Corporation 440 250-5400
  24340 Sperry Dr Westlake (44145) *(G-19391)*
Pharmed Institutional Pharmacy, Westlake *Also called Pharmed Corporation (G-19391)*
Pharmerica Long-Term Care Inc 330 425-4450
  1750 Highland Rd Ste F Twinsburg (44087) *(G-18305)*
PHC Foundation, Cincinnati *Also called Private HM Care Foundation Inc (G-4285)*
Pheasants Forever Inc 567 454-6319
  173 Main St Pettisville (43553) *(G-15944)*
Phelan Insurance Agency Inc (PA) 800 843-3069
  863 E Main St Versailles (45380) *(G-18570)*
Phg Retail Services, Milford *Also called Pat Henry Group LLC (G-14420)*
Phil Giessler 614 888-0307
  882 High St Ste A Worthington (43085) *(G-19835)*
Phil Wagler Construction Inc 330 899-0316
  3710 Tabs Dr Uniontown (44685) *(G-18382)*
Philio Inc 419 531-5544
  5301 Reynolds Rd Toledo (43615) *(G-17976)*
Philip Icuss Jr 740 264-4647
  2311 Sunset Blvd Steubenville (43952) *(G-17169)*
Philips Medical Systems Clevel (HQ) 440 247-2652
  595 Miner Rd Cleveland (44143) *(G-6203)*
Phillip Mc Guire 740 482-2701
  1585 County Highway 62 Nevada (44849) *(G-14838)*
Phillips Companies 937 426-5461
  620 Phillips Dr Beavercreek Township (45434) *(G-1258)*
Phillips Edison & Company LLC (HQ) 513 554-1110
  11501 Northlake Dr Fl 1 Cincinnati (45249) *(G-4241)*
Phillips Mfg and Tower Co (PA) 419 347-1720
  5578 State Route 61 N Shelby (44875) *(G-16749)*
Phillips Ready Mix Co 937 426-5151
  620 Phillips Dr Beavercreek Township (45434) *(G-1259)*
Phillips Sand & Gravel Co, Beavercreek Township *Also called Phillips Companies (G-1258)*
Phillips Supply Company (PA) 513 579-1762
  1230 Findlay St Cincinnati (45214) *(G-4242)*
Phillis Wheatley 216 391-4443
  4450 Cedar Ave Ste 1 Cleveland (44103) *(G-6204)*
Phillis Wheatley Association, Cleveland *Also called Phyllis Wheatley Assn Dev (G-6208)*
Philo Band Boosters 740 221-3023
  1359 Wheeling Ave Zanesville (43701) *(G-20354)*
Phinney Industrial Roofing 614 308-9000
  700 Hadley Dr Columbus (43228) *(G-8445)*
Phisical Plant, Marietta *Also called Marietta College (G-13350)*
Phoenix 513 721-8901
  812 Race St Cincinnati (45202) *(G-4243)*
Phoenix Corporation 513 727-4763
  1211 Hook Dr Middletown (45042) *(G-14320)*
Phoenix Cosmopolitan Group LLC 814 746-4863
  36550 Chester Rd Apt 1505 Avon (44011) *(G-901)*
Phoenix Group Holding Co 937 704-9850
  4 Sycamore Creek Dr Ste A Springboro (45066) *(G-16981)*
Phoenix Homes Inc (PA) 419 692-2421
  238 N Main St Delphos (45833) *(G-10033)*
Phoenix International Frt Svcs, Cleveland *Also called CH Robinson Freight Svcs
Ltd (G-5164)*
Phoenix Metals, Middletown *Also called Phoenix Corporation (G-14320)*
Phoenix Residential Centers 440 887-6097
  6465 Pearl Rd Ste 1 Cleveland (44130) *(G-6205)*

Phoenix Residential Ctrs Inc (PA) 440 428-9082
  1954 Hubbard Rd Ste 1 Madison (44057) *(G-13107)*
Phoenix Resource Network LLC 800 990-4948
  602 Main St Ste 202 Cincinnati (45202) *(G-4244)*
Phoenix School Program, Akron *Also called Young Mens Christian Assoc (G-507)*
Phoenix Steel Service Inc 216 332-0600
  4679 Johnston Pkwy Cleveland (44128) *(G-6206)*
Phoenix Systems Group Inc 330 726-6500
  755 Brdmn Cnfeld Rd Ste G Youngstown (44512) *(G-20156)*
Phoenix Technologies Intl LLC (PA) 419 353-7738
  1098 Fairview Ave Bowling Green (43402) *(G-1744)*
Phpk Technologies, Columbus *Also called Kendall Holdings Ltd (G-7891)*
Phycal Inc 440 460-2477
  51 Alpha Park Cleveland (44143) *(G-6207)*
PhyCor, Holland *Also called HRP Capital Inc (G-11889)*
Phyllis At Madison 513 321-1300
  2324 Madison Rd Ste 1 Cincinnati (45208) *(G-4245)*
Phyllis Wheatley Assn Dev 216 391-4443
  4450 Cedar Ave Ste 1 Cleveland (44103) *(G-6208)*
Physical Thrapy Consulting Svc, Columbus *Also called Patrick Mahoney (G-8426)*
Physician Hospital Alliance 937 558-3456
  10050 Innovation Dr # 240 Miamisburg (45342) *(G-14205)*
Physician Providers North, Columbus *Also called Provider Physicians Inc (G-8475)*
Physician Sales & Service, Cincinnati *Also called McKesson Medical-Surgical Top (G-3989)*
Physician Staffing Inc 440 542-5000
  30575 Bnbridge Rd Ste 200 Cleveland (44139) *(G-6209)*
Physicians Ambulance Svc Inc (PA) 216 332-1667
  4495 Cranwood Pkwy Cleveland (44128) *(G-6210)*
Physicians Care of Marietta (PA) 740 373-2519
  800 Pike St Ste 2 Marietta (45750) *(G-13369)*
Physicians Care of Marrita, Marietta *Also called Physicians Care of Marietta (G-13369)*
Physicians Choice Inc 513 844-1608
  5130 Prnceton Glendale Rd Liberty Twp (45011) *(G-12588)*
Physicians In Family Practice 440 775-1881
  319 W Lorain St Oberlin (44074) *(G-15517)*
Physicians Medical Trnspt Team, Cleveland *Also called Physicians Ambulance Svc
Inc (G-6210)*
Physicians Surgeons For Women 937 323-7340
  1821 E High St Springfield (45505) *(G-17098)*
Physicians Urology Centre, Akron *Also called Center For Urologic Health LLC (G-124)*
Physicians Weight Ls Ctr Amer (PA) 330 666-7952
  395 Springside Dr Akron (44333) *(G-382)*
Piasans Mill Inc 419 448-0100
  255 Riverside Dr Tiffin (44883) *(G-17532)*
Piatt Park Ltd Partnership 513 381-8696
  1055 Saint Paul Pl # 300 Cincinnati (45202) *(G-4246)*
Pic, Akron *Also called Goodwill Industries Inc (G-240)*
Pica, Columbus *Also called Professional Investigating (G-8468)*
Picasso For Nail LLC 440 308-4470
  35494 Spatterdock Ln Solon (44139) *(G-16883)*
Pickaway County Community Acti (PA) 740 477-1655
  469 E Ohio St Circleville (43113) *(G-4839)*
Pickaway County Community Acti 740 474-7411
  145 E Corwin St Circleville (43113) *(G-4840)*
Pickaway County Community Acti 740 477-1655
  590 E Ohio St Circleville (43113) *(G-4841)*
Pickaway Diversfied Industries 740 474-1522
  548 Lancaster Pike Circleville (43113) *(G-4842)*
Pickaway Diversified 740 474-1522
  548 Lancaster Pike Circleville (43113) *(G-4843)*
Pickaway Manor Care Center, Circleville *Also called Whetstone Care Center LLC (G-4853)*
Pickaway Manor Inc 740 474-5400
  391 Clark Dr Circleville (43113) *(G-4844)*
Pickaway Plains Ambulance Svc (PA) 740 474-4180
  1950 Stoneridge Dr Circleville (43113) *(G-4845)*
Pickaway Senior Citizen Center, Circleville *Also called Pickaway County Community
Acti (G-4841)*
Pickerington Marcus Cinemas, Pickerington *Also called Marcus Theatres
Corporation (G-15963)*
Pickerngton Area Cunseling Ctr, Lancaster *Also called New Horizon Youth Family
Ctr (G-12421)*
Pickett Concrete, Chesapeake *Also called G Big Inc (G-2729)*
Picklesimer Trucking Inc 937 642-1091
  360 Palm Dr Marysville (43040) *(G-13522)*
Pickrel Brothers Inc 937 461-5960
  901 S Perry St Dayton (45402) *(G-9691)*
Pickrel Schaeffer Ebeling Lpa 937 223-1130
  40 N Main St Ste 2700 Dayton (45423) *(G-9692)*
Pier n Port Travel Inc 513 841-9900
  2692 Madison Rd Ste H1 Cincinnati (45208) *(G-4247)*
Pierce Cleaners Inc 614 888-4225
  5205 N High St Columbus (43214) *(G-8446)*
Pierceton Trucking Co Inc 740 446-0114
  4311 State Route 160 Gallipolis (45631) *(G-11211)*
Pike Cnty Adult Activities Ctr 740 947-7503
  301 Clough St Waverly (45690) *(G-18820)*
Pike Cnty Recovery Council Inc (PA) 740 835-8437
  218 E North St Waverly (45690) *(G-18821)*
Pike County Dialysis, Waverly *Also called Alomie Dialysis LLC (G-18813)*

Pike County Head Start Inc 740 289-2371
941 Market St Piketon (45661) *(G-15985)*
Pike County YMCA 740 947-8862
400 Pride Dr Waverly (45690) *(G-18822)*
Pike Run Golf Club Inc 419 538-7000
10807 Road H Ottawa (45875) *(G-15664)*
Piketon Nursing Center Inc 740 289-4074
300 Overlook Dr Piketon (45661) *(G-15986)*
Pilgrim United Church Christ 513 574-4208
4418 Bridgetown Rd Cincinnati (45211) *(G-4248)*
Piling & Shoring Services, Columbus *Also called Righter Construction Svcs Inc (G-8532)*
Pillar of Fire 513 542-1212
6275 Collegevue Pl Cincinnati (45224) *(G-4249)*
Pilot Dogs Incorporated 614 221-6367
625 W Town St Columbus (43215) *(G-8447)*
Pinata Foods Inc 216 281-8811
3590 W 58th St Cleveland (44102) *(G-6211)*
Pine Brook Golf Club Inc 440 748-2939
11043 Durkee Rd Grafton (44044) *(G-11319)*
Pine Hills Continuing Care Ctr 740 753-1931
1950 Mount Saint Marys Dr # 2 Nelsonville (45764) *(G-14835)*
Pine Hills Golf Club Inc 330 225-4477
433 W 130th St Hinckley (44233) *(G-11860)*
Pine Kirk Nursing Home, Kirkersville *Also called Livin Care Alter of Kirke Inc (G-12320)*
Pine Lake Trout Club, Chagrin Falls *Also called M&C Hotel Interests Inc (G-2671)*
Pine Ridge Pine Vllg Resdntl H 513 724-3460
146 N 3rd St Williamsburg (45176) *(G-19495)*
Pine Valley Care Center, Richfield *Also called Brecksville Leasing Co LLC (G-16347)*
Pinecraft Land Holdings LLC 330 390-5722
6834 County Road 672 # 102 Millersburg (44654) *(G-14486)*
Pines At Glenwood, Marietta *Also called Glenwood Community Inc (G-13330)*
Pines Golf Club 330 684-1414
1319 N Millborne Rd Orrville (44667) *(G-15644)*
Pines Healthcare Center, The, Canton *Also called Communicare Health Svcs Inc (G-2262)*
Pines Manufacturing Inc (PA) 440 835-5553
29100 Lakeland Blvd Westlake (44145) *(G-19392)*
Pines Technology, Westlake *Also called Pines Manufacturing Inc (G-19392)*
Pinewood Home, Sardinia *Also called G & D Alternative Living Inc (G-16659)*
Pinewood Place Apartments 419 243-1413
1210 Collingwood Blvd Toledo (43604) *(G-17977)*
Pinnacle Academy, Euclid *Also called National Heritg Academies Inc (G-10650)*
Pinnacle Environmental Cons (PA) 513 533-1823
486 Old State Route 74 Cincinnati (45244) *(G-4250)*
Pinnacle Paving & Sealing Inc 513 474-4900
787 Round Bottom Rd Milford (45150) *(G-14423)*
Pinnacle Recycling LLC 330 745-3700
2330 Romig Rd Akron (44320) *(G-383)*
Pinney Doc Co, Ashtabula *Also called Ashtabula Stevedore Company (G-720)*
Pinney Dock & Transport LLC 440 964-7186
1149 E 5th St Ashtabula (44004) *(G-752)*
Pins & Needles Inc (PA) 440 243-6400
7300 Pearl Rd Cleveland (44130) *(G-6212)*
Pioneer Automotive Tech Inc (HQ) 937 746-2293
100 S Pioneer Blvd Springboro (45066) *(G-16982)*
Pioneer Cldding Glzing Systems 216 816-4242
2550 Brookpark Rd Cleveland (44134) *(G-6213)*
Pioneer Cldding Glzing Systems (PA) 513 583-5925
4074 Bethany Rd Mason (45040) *(G-13627)*
Pioneer Communications America, Columbus *Also called Pioneer North America Inc (G-8448)*
Pioneer Group, Marietta *Also called Pioneer Pipe Inc (G-13370)*
Pioneer Hi-Bred Intl Inc 740 657-6120
59 Greif Pkwy Ste 200 Delaware (43015) *(G-10000)*
Pioneer Hi-Bred Intl Inc 419 748-8051
15180 Henry Wood Rd Grand Rapids (43522) *(G-11328)*
Pioneer North America Inc 614 771-1050
2161 Dividend Dr Columbus (43228) *(G-8448)*
Pioneer Packing Co 419 352-5283
510 Napoleon Rd Bowling Green (43402) *(G-1745)*
Pioneer Physicians Networking 330 633-6601
65 Community Rd Ste C Tallmadge (44278) *(G-17484)*
Pioneer Pipe Inc 740 376-2400
2021 Hanna Rd Marietta (45750) *(G-13370)*
Pioneer Rural Electric Coop (PA) 800 762-0997
344 W Us Route 36 Piqua (45356) *(G-16016)*
Pioneer Sands LLC 740 659-2241
2446 State Route 204 Glenford (43739) *(G-11308)*
Pioneer Sands LLC 740 599-7773
26900 Coshocton Rd Howard (43028) *(G-11940)*
Pioneer Solutions LLC 216 383-3400
24800 Rockwell Dr Euclid (44117) *(G-10652)*
Pioneer Trails Inc 330 674-1234
7572 State Route 241 Millersburg (44654) *(G-14487)*
Pipeline Packaging Corporation (HQ) 440 349-3200
30310 Emerald Valley Pkwy Solon (44139) *(G-16884)*
Piper Plumbing Inc 330 274-0160
2480 Bartlett Rd Mantua (44255) *(G-13275)*
Pipestone Golf Course, Miamisburg *Also called City of Miamisburg (G-14153)*
Piqua Country Club Holding Co 937 773-7744
9812 Country Club Rd Piqua (45356) *(G-16017)*

PIQUA COUNTRY CLUB POOL, Piqua *Also called Piqua Country Club Holding Co (G-16017)*
Piqua Industrial Cut & Sew 937 773-7397
727 E Ash St Piqua (45356) *(G-16018)*
Piqua Manor, Piqua *Also called Hcf of Piqua Inc (G-16008)*
Piqua Materials Inc 937 773-4824
1750 W Statler Rd Piqua (45356) *(G-16019)*
Piqua Materials Inc (PA) 513 771-0820
11641 Mosteller Rd Ste 1 Cincinnati (45241) *(G-4251)*
Piqua Mineral Division, Piqua *Also called Piqua Materials Inc (G-16019)*
Piqua Steel Co 937 773-3632
4243 W Us Route 36 Piqua (45356) *(G-16020)*
Piqua Transfer & Storage Co 937 773-3743
9782 Looney Rd Piqua (45356) *(G-16021)*
Piqua Village Rehab LLC 937 773-9537
1345 Covington Ave Piqua (45356) *(G-16022)*
Pirhl Contractors LLC 216 378-9690
800 W Saint Clair Ave 4 Cleveland (44113) *(G-6214)*
Pitmark Services Inc 330 876-2217
7925 State Route 5 Kinsman (44428) *(G-12319)*
Pitney Bowes Inc 203 426-7025
6910 Treeline Dr Ste C Brecksville (44141) *(G-1796)*
Pitney Bowes Inc 740 374-5535
111 Marshall Rd Marietta (45750) *(G-13371)*
Pitney Bowes Presort Svcs Inc 513 860-3607
10085 International Blvd West Chester (45246) *(G-19072)*
Pitt-Ohio Express LLC 614 801-1064
2101 Hardy Parkway St Grove City (43123) *(G-11465)*
Pitt-Ohio Express LLC 419 726-6523
5200 Stickney Ave Toledo (43612) *(G-17978)*
Pitt-Ohio Express LLC 513 860-3424
5000 Duff Dr West Chester (45246) *(G-19073)*
Pitt-Ohio Express LLC 419 729-8173
5200 Stickney Ave Toledo (43612) *(G-17979)*
Pitt-Ohio Express LLC 216 433-9000
15225 Industrial Pkwy Cleveland (44135) *(G-6215)*
Pittsburgh & Conneaut Dock, Conneaut *Also called Bessemer and Lake Erie RR Co (G-8951)*
Pittsburgh Plumbing & Htg Sup, Akron *Also called Famous II Inc (G-213)*
Pivotek LLC 513 372-6205
910 Lila Ave Rear Milford (45150) *(G-14424)*
Pizzuti, Columbus *Also called Creekside II LLC (G-7389)*
Pizzuti Builders LLC 614 280-4000
2 Miranova Pl Ste 800 Columbus (43215) *(G-8449)*
Pizzuti Inc (PA) 614 280-4000
629 N High St 500 Columbus (43215) *(G-8450)*
Pk Management LLC (PA) 216 472-1870
26301 Curtiss Wright Pkwy Richmond Heights (44143) *(G-16392)*
Places Inc 937 461-4300
11 W Monument Ave Ste 700 Dayton (45402) *(G-9693)*
Plane Detail LLC 614 734-1201
2720 S 3 Bs And K Rd Galena (43021) *(G-11163)*
Planes Companies, West Chester *Also called Planes Moving & Storage Inc (G-18982)*
Planes Moving & Storage Inc (PA) 513 759-6000
9823 Cincinnati Dayton Rd West Chester (45069) *(G-18982)*
Planes Mvg & Stor Co Columbus 614 777-9090
2000 Dividend Dr Columbus (43228) *(G-8451)*
Planned Parenthood Association (PA) 937 226-0780
224 N Wilkinson St Dayton (45402) *(G-9694)*
Planned Parenthood NW Ohio Inc 419 255-1115
1301 Jefferson Ave Toledo (43604) *(G-17980)*
Planned Parenthood of SW OH (PA) 513 721-7635
2314 Auburn Ave Cincinnati (45219) *(G-4252)*
Planned Prenthood Greater Ohio (PA) 614 224-2235
206 E State St Columbus (43215) *(G-8452)*
Planned Prenthood Greater Ohio 330 535-2671
444 W Exchange St Akron (44302) *(G-384)*
Planned Prenthood Greater Ohio 216 961-8804
25350 Rockside Rd Bedford Heights (44146) *(G-1324)*
Planned Prenthood Greater Ohio 330 788-2487
77 E Midlothian Blvd Youngstown (44507) *(G-20157)*
Planned Prnthood of Grter Mami, Dayton *Also called Planned Parenthood Association (G-9694)*
Planned Prnthood of Mhning Vly 330 788-6506
77 E Midlothian Blvd Youngstown (44507) *(G-20158)*
Plantscaping Inc 216 367-1200
1865 E 40th St Cleveland (44103) *(G-6216)*
Plastic Recycling Tech Inc (PA) 937 615-9286
9054 N County Road 25a Piqua (45356) *(G-16023)*
Plastic Recycling Tech Inc 419 238-9395
7600 Us Route 127 Van Wert (45891) *(G-18486)*
Plastic Surgery Group Inc (PA) 513 791-4440
4050 Red Bank Rd Ste 42 Cincinnati (45227) *(G-4253)*
Plastic Technologies Inc (PA) 419 867-5400
1440 Timber Wolf Dr Holland (43528) *(G-11905)*
Plastics R Unique Inc 330 334-4820
330 Grandview Ave Wadsworth (44281) *(G-18613)*
Plastipak Packaging Inc 330 725-0205
850 W Smith Rd Medina (44256) *(G-13987)*
Platform Cement Inc 440 602-9750
7503 Tyler Blvd Mentor (44060) *(G-14097)*
Platform Contracting, Mentor *Also called Platform Cement Inc (G-14097)*

2019 Harris Ohio
Services Directory

(G-0000) Company's Geographic Section entry number

Platform Lab, Columbus *Also called Rev1 Ventures (G-8529)*
Platinum Express Inc 937 235-9540
  2549 Stanley Ave Dayton (45404) *(G-9695)*
Platinum Prestige Property 614 705-2251
  4120 Beechbank Rd Columbus (43213) *(G-8453)*
Platinum RE Professionals LLC 440 942-2100
  10 Public Sq Willoughby (44094) *(G-19562)*
Platinum Restoration Contrs 440 327-0699
  104 Reaser Ct Elyria (44035) *(G-10555)*
Platinum Restoration Inc 440 327-0699
  104 Reaser Ct Elyria (44035) *(G-10556)*
Platinum Technologies 216 926-1080
  121 S Main St Ste 200 Akron (44308) *(G-385)*
Play It Again Sports, Cincinnati *Also called Mc Gregor Family Enterprises (G-3984)*
Play Time Day Nursery Inc 513 385-8281
  9550 Colerain Ave Cincinnati (45251) *(G-4254)*
Playhouse Square Foundation 216 615-7500
  1260 Euclid Ave Cleveland (44115) *(G-6217)*
Playhouse Square Foundation (PA) 216 771-4444
  1501 Euclid Ave Ste 200 Cleveland (44115) *(G-6218)*
Playhouse Square Holdg Co LLC (PA) 216 771-4444
  1501 Euclid Ave Ste 200 Cleveland (44115) *(G-6219)*
Playtime Preschool LLC 614 975-1005
  1030 Alum Creek Dr Columbus (43209) *(G-8454)*
Plaz-Way Inc 330 264-9025
  1983 E Lincoln Way Wooster (44691) *(G-19759)*
Plaza Properties Inc (PA) 614 237-3726
  3016 Maryland Ave Columbus (43209) *(G-8455)*
Pleasant Hill Golf Club, Middletown *Also called Amix Inc (G-14288)*
Pleasant Hill Leasing LLC 740 289-2394
  7143 Us Rte 23 S Piketon (45661) *(G-15987)*
Pleasant Hill Manor, Piketon *Also called Pleasant Hill Leasing LLC (G-15987)*
Pleasant Hl Otptent Thrapy Ctr, Piketon *Also called H C F Inc (G-15976)*
Pleasant Lake Apartments Ltd 440 845-2694
  10129 S Lake Blvd Cleveland (44130) *(G-6220)*
Pleasant Lake Nursing Home 440 842-2273
  7260 Ridge Rd Cleveland (44129) *(G-6221)*
Pleasant Lake Villa, Cleveland *Also called Pleasant Lake Nursing Home (G-6221)*
Pleasant Ridge Care Center Inc (PA) 513 631-1310
  5501 Verulam Ave Cincinnati (45213) *(G-4255)*
Pleasant View Health Care Ctr, Barberton *Also called Pleasant View Nursing Home (G-961)*
Pleasant View Nursing Home (PA) 330 745-6028
  401 Snyder Ave Barberton (44203) *(G-961)*
Pleasant View Nursing Home 330 848-5028
  220 3rd St Se Barberton (44203) *(G-962)*
Pleasantview Nursing Home, Cleveland *Also called Ridge Pleasant Valley Inc (G-6325)*
Plevniak Construction Inc 330 718-1600
  1235 Townsend Ave Youngstown (44505) *(G-20159)*
Ploger Transportation LLC (PA) 419 465-2100
  15581 County Road 46 Bellevue (44811) *(G-1383)*
Pls Protective Services 513 521-3581
  8263 Clara Ave Cincinnati (45239) *(G-4256)*
Plug Smart, Columbus *Also called Juice Technologies Inc (G-7875)*
Plumbing Contractor, Westerville *Also called Eaton Plumbing Inc (G-19251)*
Plumbline Solutions Inc 419 581-2963
  1219 W Main Cross St # 101 Findlay (45840) *(G-10954)*
Plus Management Services Inc (PA) 419 225-9018
  2440 Baton Rouge Ofc C Lima (45805) *(G-12722)*
Plus One Communications LLC 330 255-4500
  1115 S Main St Akron (44301) *(G-386)*
Plus Realty Cincinnati Inc 513 575-4500
  1160 State Route 28 Milford (45150) *(G-14425)*
Ply-Trim Enterprises Inc 330 799-7876
  550 N Meridian Rd Youngstown (44509) *(G-20160)*
Ply-Trim South Inc 330 799-7876
  550 N Meridian Rd Youngstown (44509) *(G-20161)*
PMC Acquisitions Inc 419 429-0042
  2040 Industrial Dr Findlay (45840) *(G-10955)*
PMC Systems Limited 330 538-2268
  12155 Commissioner Dr North Jackson (44451) *(G-15252)*
Pmwi LLC 614 975-5004
  3177 Overbridge Dr Hilliard (43026) *(G-11806)*
PNC Bank National Association 330 375-8342
  1 Cascade Plz Ste 200 Akron (44308) *(G-387)*
PNC Bank National Association 740 349-8431
  68 W Church St Fl 1 Newark (43055) *(G-15092)*
PNC Bank National Association 513 721-2500
  5 Main Dr Cincinnati (45231) *(G-4257)*
PNC Bank National Association 330 742-4426
  100 E Federal St Ste 100 # 100 Youngstown (44503) *(G-20162)*
PNC Bank National Association 330 562-9700
  7044 N Aurora Rd Aurora (44202) *(G-839)*
PNC Bank National Association 513 455-9522
  995 Dalton Ave Cincinnati (45203) *(G-4258)*
PNC Bank National Association 419 621-2930
  129 W Perkins Ave Sandusky (44870) *(G-16632)*
PNC Bank National Association 330 854-0974
  420 Beverly Ave Canal Fulton (44614) *(G-2096)*
PNC Bank National Association 440 546-6760
  6750 Miller Rd Brecksville (44141) *(G-1797)*
PNC Bank National Association 419 259-5466
  405 Madison Ave Ste 4 Toledo (43604) *(G-17981)*

PNC Bank-Atm 937 865-6800
  9333 Springboro Pike Miamisburg (45342) *(G-14206)*
PNC Equipment Finance LLC 513 421-9191
  995 Dalton Ave Cincinnati (45203) *(G-4259)*
PNC Mortgage Company (HQ) 412 762-2000
  3232 Newmark Dr Bldg 2 Miamisburg (45342) *(G-14207)*
Png Telecommunications Inc (PA) 513 942-7900
  8805 Governors Hill Dr # 250 Cincinnati (45249) *(G-4260)*
Pnk (ohio) LLC 513 232-8000
  6301 Kellogg Rd Cincinnati (45230) *(G-4261)*
Poelking Bowling Centers 937 435-3855
  8871 Kingsridge Dr Dayton (45458) *(G-9696)*
Poelking Lanes Inc (PA) 937 299-5573
  1403 Wilmington Ave Dayton (45420) *(G-9697)*
Poggemeyer Design Group Inc (PA) 419 244-8074
  1168 N Main St Bowling Green (43402) *(G-1746)*
Poggemeyer Design Group Inc 419 748-7438
  2926 Us Highway 6 Mc Clure (43534) *(G-13893)*
Point Place, Toledo *Also called Harborside Pointe Place LLC (G-17782)*
Point Plus Personnel, Columbus *Also called Chad Downing (G-7177)*
Pointclickcare, Milford *Also called Wescom Solutions Inc (G-14443)*
Poison & Toxic Control Center, Lorain *Also called Mercy Health (G-12926)*
Poison Information Center 513 636-5111
  3333 Burnet Ave Fl 3 Cincinnati (45229) *(G-4262)*
Poland Middle School Pto 330 757-7003
  47 College St Youngstown (44514) *(G-20163)*
Polaris Automation Inc 614 431-0170
  8333 Green Meadows Dr N A Lewis Center (43035) *(G-12560)*
Polaris Innkeepers Inc 614 568-0770
  9000 Worthington Rd Westerville (43082) *(G-19199)*
Polaris Kindercare, Lewis Center *Also called Kindercare Learning Ctrs LLC (G-12548)*
Polaris Technologies, Toledo *Also called Modern Builders Supply Inc (G-17922)*
Polaris Towne Center LLC 614 456-0123
  1500 Polaris Pkwy # 3000 Columbus (43240) *(G-6830)*
Polish American Citizens Club 330 253-0496
  472 E Glenwood Ave Akron (44310) *(G-388)*
Polish-American Club, Akron *Also called Polish American Citizens Club (G-388)*
Pollak Distributing Co Inc 216 851-9911
  1200 Babbitt Rd Euclid (44132) *(G-10653)*
Pollak Foods, Euclid *Also called Pollak Distributing Co Inc (G-10653)*
Pollock Research & Design Inc 330 332-3300
  1134 Salem Pkwy Salem (44460) *(G-16554)*
Poly Flex, Baltic *Also called Flex Technologies Inc (G-934)*
Polychem Corporation 419 547-1400
  202 Watertower Dr Clyde (43410) *(G-6750)*
Polycom Inc 937 245-1853
  35 Rockridge Rd Ste A Englewood (45322) *(G-10597)*
Polymer Additives Holdings Inc (HQ) 216 875-7200
  7500 E Pleasant Valley Rd Independence (44131) *(G-12108)*
Polymer Packaging Inc (PA) 330 832-2000
  8333 Navarre Rd Se Massillon (44646) *(G-13720)*
Polymer Protective Packaging, Massillon *Also called Polymer Packaging Inc (G-13720)*
Polymershapes LLC 937 877-1903
  1480 Blauser Dr Tipp City (45371) *(G-17564)*
Polyone Corporation 440 930-1000
  733 E Water St North Baltimore (45872) *(G-15179)*
Polyone Corporation (PA) 440 930-1000
  33587 Walker Rd Avon Lake (44012) *(G-926)*
Pomerene Hospital, Millersburg *Also called Joel Pomerene Memorial Hosp (G-14480)*
Pomeroy It Solutions Sls Inc 440 717-1364
  6670 W Snowville Rd Ste 3 Brecksville (44141) *(G-1798)*
Pomeroy It Solutions Sls Inc 937 439-9682
  478 Windsor Park Dr Dayton (45459) *(G-9698)*
Pond-Woolpert LLC 937 461-5660
  4454 Idea Center Blvd Beavercreek (45430) *(G-1233)*
Pontiac Bill Delord Autocenter, Lebanon *Also called Bill Delord Autocenter Inc (G-12452)*
Pontoon Solutions Inc 855 881-1533
  1695 Indian Wood Cir # 200 Maumee (43537) *(G-13833)*
Pope & Associates Inc 513 671-1277
  9277 Centre Pointe Dr # 150 West Chester (45069) *(G-18983)*
Pope Consulting, West Chester *Also called Pope & Associates Inc (G-18983)*
Popper & Associates Msrp LLC 614 798-8991
  7153 Timberview Dr Dublin (43017) *(G-10309)*
Pork Champ LLC 740 493-2164
  1136 Coldicott Hill Rd Lucasville (45648) *(G-13052)*
Port Clnton Bpo Elks Ldge 1718 .... 419 734-1900
  231 Buckeye Blvd Port Clinton (43452) *(G-16114)*
Port Grter Cincinnati Dev Auth 513 621-3000
  3 E 4th St Ste 300 Cincinnati (45202) *(G-4263)*
Port Lawrence Title and Tr Co (HQ) 419 244-4605
  4 Seagate Ste 101 Toledo (43604) *(G-17982)*
Porta-Kleen, Lancaster *Also called Pro-Kleen Industrial Svcs Inc (G-12427)*
Portage Animal Clinic, Kent *Also called Stow-Kent Animal Hospital Inc (G-12260)*
Portage Area Rgonal Trnsp Auth 330 678-1287
  2000 Summit Rd Kent (44240) *(G-12254)*
Portage Bancshares Inc (PA) 330 296-8090
  1311 E Main St Ravenna (44266) *(G-16253)*
Portage Community Bank, Ravenna *Also called Portage Bancshares Inc (G-16253)*
Portage Community Bank Inc (HQ) 330 296-8090
  1311 E Main St Ravenna (44266) *(G-16254)*

A
L
P
H
A
B
E
T
I
C

Portage Country Club Company 330 836-8565
240 N Portage Path Akron (44303) *(G-389)*

Portage County Board 330 678-2400
2500 Brady Lake Rd Ravenna (44266) *(G-16255)*

Portage County Board (PA) 330 297-6209
2606 Brady Lake Rd Ravenna (44266) *(G-16256)*

Portage County Engineer Office, Ravenna *Also called County of Portage (G-16238)*

Portage Family Medicine 330 626-5566
9480 Rosemont Dr Streetsboro (44241) *(G-17266)*

Portage Group Werner Home, Portage *Also called County of Wood (G-16122)*

Portage Industries Inc 330 296-3996
7008 State Route 88 Ravenna (44266) *(G-16257)*

PORTAGE LEARNING CENTERS, Ravenna *Also called Portage Private Industry (G-16259)*

Portage Path Behavorial Health (PA) 330 253-3100
340 S Broadway St Akron (44308) *(G-390)*

Portage Path Behavorial Health 330 762-6110
10 Penfield Ave Akron (44310) *(G-391)*

Portage Pediatrics 330 297-8824
6847 N Chestnut St # 200 Ravenna (44266) *(G-16258)*

Portage Private Industry 330 297-7795
145 N Chestnut St Lowr Ravenna (44266) *(G-16259)*

Porter Drywall Inc 614 890-2111
297 Old County Line Rd Westerville (43081) *(G-19293)*

Porter Wrght Morris Arthur LLP 513 381-4700
250 E 5th St Ste 2200 Cincinnati (45202) *(G-4264)*

Porter Wrght Morris Arthur LLP 216 443-2506
950 Main Ave Ste 500 Cleveland (44113) *(G-6222)*

Porter Wrght Morris Arthur LLP 937 449-6810
1 S Main St Ste 1600 Dayton (45402) *(G-9699)*

Portsmouth Ambulance 740 289-2932
2796 Gallia St Portsmouth (45662) *(G-16158)*

Portsmouth Health Department, Portsmouth *Also called City of Portsmouth (G-16128)*

Portsmouth Hospital Corp 740 991-4000
1901 Argonne Rd Portsmouth (45662) *(G-16159)*

Portsmouth Lodge 154 B P O E (PA) 740 353-1013
544 4th St Portsmouth (45662) *(G-16160)*

Portsmouth Metro Housing Auth (PA) 740 354-4547
410 Court St Portsmouth (45662) *(G-16161)*

Portsmuth Emrgncy Amblance Svc 740 354-3122
2796 Gallia St Portsmouth (45662) *(G-16162)*

Positions, Lima *Also called Hector A Buch Jr MD (G-12658)*

Positive Bus Solutions Inc 513 772-2255
200 Northland Blvd 100 Cincinnati (45246) *(G-4265)*

Positive Education Program 216 227-2730
11500 Franklin Blvd Cleveland (44102) *(G-6223)*

Positive Education Program 440 471-8200
4320 W 220th St Cleveland (44126) *(G-6224)*

Positive Electric Inc 937 428-0606
4738 Gateway Cir Ste C Dayton (45440) *(G-9700)*

Post Browning, Cincinnati *Also called Convergint Technologies LLC (G-3357)*

Post-Up Stand, Maple Heights *Also called Suntwist Corp (G-13300)*

Postal Mail Sort Inc 330 747-1515
1024 Mahoning Ave Ste 8 Youngstown (44502) *(G-20164)*

Postema Insurance & Investment 419 782-2500
2014 Baltimore St Defiance (43512) *(G-9934)*

Potter Inc (PA) 419 636-5624
630 Commerce Dr Bryan (43506) *(G-1970)*

Potter Technologies LLC 419 380-8404
843 Warehouse Rd Toledo (43615) *(G-17983)*

Pottery Barn Inc 614 478-3154
3945 Easton Square Pl W H-1 Columbus (43219) *(G-8456)*

Pottery Making Illustrate, Westerville *Also called American Ceramic Society (G-19144)*

Poultry Service Associates 937 968-3339
9317 Young Rd Dayton (45390) *(G-9152)*

Powel Crosley Jr Branch, Cincinnati *Also called Young Mens Christian Associat (G-4812)*

Powell Company Ltd (PA) 419 228-3552
3255 Saint Johns Rd Lima (45804) *(G-12723)*

Powell Electrical Systems Inc 330 966-1750
8967 Pleasantwood Ave Nw Canton (44720) *(G-2438)*

Powell Enterprises Inc 614 882-0111
8750 Olde Worthington Rd Westerville (43082) *(G-19200)*

Power Direct, Cleveland *Also called R D D Inc (G-6273)*

Power Distributors LLC (PA) 614 876-3533
3700 Paragon Dr Columbus (43228) *(G-8457)*

Power Engineers Incorporated 513 326-1500
11733 Chesterdale Rd Cincinnati (45246) *(G-4266)*

Power Engineers Incorporated 234 678-9875
1 S Main St Ste 501 Akron (44308) *(G-392)*

Power Management Inc (PA) 937 222-2909
420 Davis Ave Dayton (45403) *(G-9701)*

Power Scheduling Group, Piketon *Also called Ohio Valley Electric Corp (G-15982)*

Power System Engineering Inc 740 568-9220
2349a State Route 821 Marietta (45750) *(G-13372)*

Power Train Components Inc 419 636-4430
509 E Edgerton St Bryan (43506) *(G-1971)*

Power-Pack Conveyor Company 440 975-9955
38363 Airport Pkwy Willoughby (44094) *(G-19563)*

Powernet Global Communications, Cincinnati *Also called Png Telecommunications Inc (G-4260)*

Powers Agency, Cincinnati *Also called Charles W Powers & Assoc Inc (G-3171)*

Powers Equipment 740 746-8220
7265 Sugar Grove Rd Sugar Grove (43155) *(G-17375)*

PPG Architectural Finishes Inc 440 826-5100
16651 W Sprague Rd Strongsville (44136) *(G-17339)*

Ppmc, Columbus *Also called Engaged Health Care Bus Svcs (G-7516)*

Pps Holding LLC 513 985-6400
4605 E Galbraith Rd # 200 Cincinnati (45236) *(G-4267)*

PQ Systems, Dayton *Also called Productivity Qulty Systems Inc (G-9717)*

Practical Solution, Dayton *Also called Centric Consulting LLC (G-9290)*

Prairie Farms Dairy Inc 937 235-5930
5820 Executive Blvd Huber Heights (45424) *(G-11958)*

Praxair Distribution Inc 330 376-2242
1760 E Market St Akron (44305) *(G-393)*

PRC Medical LLC (PA) 330 493-9004
111 Stow Ave Ste 200 Cuyahoga Falls (44221) *(G-9118)*

Pre-Clinical Services, Spencerville *Also called Charles River Laboratories Inc (G-16955)*

Pre-Fore Inc 740 467-2206
410 Blacklick Rd Millersport (43046) *(G-14503)*

Preble County Council On Aging 937 456-4947
800 E Saint Clair St Eaton (45320) *(G-10459)*

Preble County General Hlth Dst 937 472-0087
615 Hillcrest Dr Eaton (45320) *(G-10460)*

Precesion Finning Bending Inc 330 382-9351
1250 Saint George St # 6 East Liverpool (43920) *(G-10416)*

Precious Angels Child Care I, Cleveland *Also called Precious Angels Lrng Ctr Inc (G-6225)*

Precious Angels Lrng Ctr Inc 440 886-1919
5574 Pearl Rd Cleveland (44129) *(G-6225)*

Precious Cargo Transportation 440 564-8039
15050 Cross Creek Pkwy Newbury (44065) *(G-15124)*

Precision Broadbnd Installatns 614 523-2917
7642 Red Bank Rd Westerville (43082) *(G-19201)*

Precision Coatings Systems 937 642-4727
948 Columbus Ave Marysville (43040) *(G-13523)*

Precision Electrical Services 740 474-4490
201 W Main St Circleville (43113) *(G-4846)*

Precision Endoscopy Amer Inc (PA) 410 527-9598
4575 Hudson Dr Stow (44224) *(G-17224)*

Precision Environmental Co (HQ) 216 642-6040
5500 Old Brecksvlle Rd Independence (44131) *(G-12109)*

Precision Funding Corp 330 405-1313
2132 Case Pkwy Ste A Twinsburg (44087) *(G-18306)*

Precision Geophysical Inc (PA) 330 674-2198
2695 State Route 83 Millersburg (44654) *(G-14488)*

Precision Metalforming Assn (PA) 216 241-1482
6363 Oak Tree Blvd Independence (44131) *(G-12110)*

Precision Mtal Fabrication Inc (PA) 937 235-9261
191 Heid Ave Dayton (45404) *(G-9702)*

Precision Paving Inc 419 499-7283
3414 State Route 113 E Milan (44846) *(G-14366)*

Precision Pipeline Svcs LLC 740 652-1679
10 Whiley Rd Lancaster (43130) *(G-12426)*

Precision Products Group Inc 330 698-4711
339 Mill St Apple Creek (44606) *(G-620)*

Precision Steel Services Inc (PA) 419 476-5702
31 E Sylvania Ave Toledo (43612) *(G-17984)*

Precision Strip Inc 937 667-6255
315 Park Ave Tipp City (45371) *(G-17565)*

Precision Strip Inc (HQ) 419 628-2343
86 S Ohio St Minster (45865) *(G-14540)*

Precision Strip Inc 419 674-4186
190 Bales Rd Kenton (43326) *(G-12286)*

Precision Strip Inc 419 661-1100
7401 Ponderosa Rd Perrysburg (43551) *(G-15905)*

Precision Strip Inc 513 423-4166
4400 Oxford State Rd Middletown (45044) *(G-14321)*

Precision Supply Company Inc 330 225-5530
2845 Interstate Pkwy Brunswick (44212) *(G-1938)*

Precision Vhcl Solutions LLC 513 651-9444
559 Liberty Hl Cincinnati (45202) *(G-4268)*

Precision Welding Corporation 216 524-6110
7900 Exchange St Cleveland (44125) *(G-6226)*

Predator Trucking Company 419 849-2601
1121 State Route 105 Woodville (43469) *(G-19682)*

Predator Trucking Company (PA) 330 530-0712
3181 Trumbull Ave Mc Donald (44437) *(G-13897)*

Predict Technologies Div, Cleveland *Also called Reid Asset Management Company (G-6298)*

Predictive Service LLC (PA) 866 772-6770
25200 Chagrin Blvd # 300 Cleveland (44122) *(G-6227)*

Preemptive Solutions LLC 440 443-7200
767 Beta Dr Cleveland (44143) *(G-6228)*

Preferred Acquisition Co LLC (PA) 216 587-0957
4871 Neo Pkwy Cleveland (44128) *(G-6229)*

Preferred Airparts, Kidron *Also called Jilco Industries Inc (G-12306)*

Preferred Capital Lending Inc 216 472-1391
200 Public Sq Ste 160 Cleveland (44114) *(G-6230)*

Preferred Living, Westerville *Also called Preferred RE Investments LLC (G-19202)*

Preferred Medical Group Inc 404 403-8310
23600 Commerce Park Beachwood (44122) *(G-1096)*

Preferred RE Investments LLC 614 901-2400
470 Olde Worthington Rd # 470 Westerville (43082) *(G-19202)*

Preferred Real Estate Group (PA) 513 533-4111
3522 Erie Ave Cincinnati (45208) *(G-4269)*

2019 Harris Ohio
Services Directory

(G-0000) Company's Geographic Section entry number

Preferred Roofing Ohio Inc.....216 587-0957
4871 Neo Pkwy Cleveland (44128) ***(G-6231)***
Preferred Roofing Services LLC.....216 587-0957
4871 Neo Pkwy Cleveland (44128) ***(G-6232)***
Preferred Temporary Services.....330 494-5502
4791 Munson St Nw Canton (44718) ***(G-2439)***
Pregnancy Care of Cincinnati.....513 487-7777
2415 Auburn Ave Cincinnati (45219) ***(G-4270)***
Premier Asphalt Paving Co Inc.....440 237-6600
10519 Royalton Rd North Royalton (44133) ***(G-15364)***
Premier Broadcasting Co Inc.....614 866-0700
5310 E Main St Ste 101 Columbus (43213) ***(G-8458)***
Premier Care.....614 431-0599
500 W Wilson Bridge Rd # 235 Worthington (43085) ***(G-19836)***
Premier Cleaning Services Inc.....513 831-2492
5866 Wlfpen Plasant Hl Rd Milford (45150) ***(G-14426)***
Premier Construction Company.....513 874-2611
9361 Seward Rd Fairfield (45014) ***(G-10771)***
Premier Estate of Three Rivers, Cincinnati *Also called Premier Estates 521 LLC* ***(G-4271)***
Premier Estates 521 LLC.....765 288-2488
7800 Jandacres Dr Cincinnati (45248) ***(G-4271)***
Premier Estates 525 LLC.....513 631-6800
1578 Sherman Ave Cincinnati (45212) ***(G-4272)***
Premier Estates 526 LLC.....513 922-1440
5999 Bender Rd Cincinnati (45233) ***(G-4273)***
Premier Esttes Cncnnt-Rverside, Cincinnati *Also called Pristine Senior Living* ***(G-4284)***
Premier Esttes Cncnnt-Rverview, Cincinnati *Also called Premier Estates 526 LLC* ***(G-4273)***
Premier Feeds LLC.....937 584-2411
238 Melvin Rd Wilmington (45177) ***(G-19641)***
Premier Health Care MGT Inc.....248 644-5522
4750 Ashwood Dr Ste 300 Blue Ash (45241) ***(G-1630)***
Premier Health Group LLC.....937 535-4100
110 N Main St Ste 350 Dayton (45402) ***(G-9703)***
Premier Health Partners (PA).....937 499-9596
110 N Main St Ste 450 Dayton (45402) ***(G-9704)***
Premier Health Partners.....937 526-3235
471 Marker Rd Versailles (45380) ***(G-18571)***
Premier Health Specialists Inc (HQ).....937 223-4518
110 N Main St Ste 350 Dayton (45402) ***(G-9705)***
Premier Heart Associates Inc.....937 832-2425
6251 Good Samaritan Way # 220 Dayton (45424) ***(G-9706)***
Premier Heart Inc.....937 832-2425
9000 N Main St Ste 101 Englewood (45415) ***(G-10598)***
Premier Integrated Med Assoc (PA).....937 291-6813
6520 Acro Ct Centerville (45459) ***(G-2632)***
Premier Integration, Girard *Also called Prisma Integration Corp* ***(G-11298)***
Premier Management Co Inc.....740 867-2144
805 3rd Ave Chesapeake (45619) ***(G-2731)***
Premier Physican Centers, Avon *Also called Medical Diagnostic Lab Inc* ***(G-894)***
Premier Physicians, Cleveland *Also called Gloria Gadmack Do* ***(G-5611)***
Premier Physicians Centers Inc (PA).....440 895-5085
24651 Center Ridge Rd # 350 Westlake (44145) ***(G-19393)***
Premier Radiology Group Inc.....937 431-9729
2145 N Fairfield Rd Ste A Beavercreek (45431) ***(G-1177)***
Premier Rstrtion Mech Svcs LLC.....513 420-1600
2890 S Main St Middletown (45044) ***(G-14322)***
Premier System Integrators Inc.....513 217-7294
2660 Towne Blvd Middletown (45044) ***(G-14323)***
Premier Transcription Service.....513 741-1800
7 Hetherington Ct Cincinnati (45246) ***(G-4274)***
Premier Transcription Services, Cincinnati *Also called Premier Transcription Service* ***(G-4274)***
Premier Truck Parts Inc.....216 642-5000
5800 W Canal Rd Cleveland (44125) ***(G-6233)***
Premier Truck Sls & Rentl Inc.....800 825-1255
7700 Wall St Cleveland (44125) ***(G-6234)***
Premiere Kidney Center Newark, Newark *Also called Lory Dialysis LLC* ***(G-15062)***
Premiere Produce, Cleveland *Also called Anselmo Rssis Premier Prod Ltd* ***(G-4983)***
Premiere Service Mortgage Corp (PA).....513 546-9895
6266 Centre Park Dr West Chester (45069) ***(G-18984)***
Premierfirst Home Health Care.....614 443-3110
3033 Sullivant Ave Columbus (43204) ***(G-8459)***
Premium Beverage Supply Ltd.....614 777-1007
3701 Lacon Rd Hilliard (43026) ***(G-11807)***
Premium Trnsp Logistics LLC (PA).....419 861-3430
5445 Sthwyck Blvd Ste 210 Toledo (43614) ***(G-17985)***
Premix Holding Company.....330 666-3751
3637 Ridgewood Rd Fairlawn (44333) ***(G-10843)***
Prengers, Oregonia *Also called Roger Shawn Houck* ***(G-15617)***
Presbyterian Child Center.....740 852-3190
211 Garfield Ave London (43140) ***(G-12873)***
Prescription Hope Inc.....877 296-4673
253 N State St Ste 250 Westerville (43081) ***(G-19294)***
Prescription Supply Inc.....419 661-6600
2233 Tracy Rd Northwood (43619) ***(G-15405)***
Presidio Infrastructure.....419 241-8303
20 N Saint Clair St Toledo (43604) ***(G-17986)***
Presidio Infrastructure.....614 381-1400
5025 Bradenton Ave Ste B Dublin (43017) ***(G-10310)***
Presort America Ltd.....614 836-5120
4227 Williams Rd Groveport (43125) ***(G-11530)***
Press Wood Management, Beachwood *Also called Cw Financial LLC* ***(G-1050)***
Pressley Ridge Foundation.....513 752-4548
4355 Ferguson Dr Ste 125 Cincinnati (45245) ***(G-2866)***
Pressley Ridge Foundation.....513 737-0400
734 Dayton St Hamilton (45011) ***(G-11633)***
Pressley Ridge Pryde.....513 559-1402
7162 Reading Rd Ste 300 Cincinnati (45237) ***(G-4275)***
Prestige Audio Visual Inc.....513 641-1600
4835 Para Dr Cincinnati (45237) ***(G-4276)***
Prestige AV & Creative Svcs, Cincinnati *Also called Prestige Audio Visual Inc* ***(G-4276)***
Prestige Delivery Systems LLC.....614 836-8980
4279 Directors Blvd Groveport (43125) ***(G-11531)***
PRESTIGE HEALTHCARE, Gallipolis *Also called Gallipolis Care LLC* ***(G-11194)***
Prestige Interiors Inc.....330 425-1690
2239 E Enterprise Pkwy Twinsburg (44087) ***(G-18307)***
Prestige Technical Svcs Inc (PA).....513 779-6800
7908 Cincinnati Dayton Rd T West Chester (45069) ***(G-18985)***
Prestige Valet Inc.....513 871-4220
4220 Appleton St Cincinnati (45209) ***(G-4277)***
Prevent Blindness - Ohio.....614 464-2020
1500 W 3rd Ave Ste 200 Columbus (43212) ***(G-8460)***
Price Rd Hlth Rhbilitation Ctr, Newark *Also called Newark Care Center LLC* ***(G-15082)***
Price Thrice Supply, Columbus *Also called Valley Interior Systems Inc* ***(G-8840)***
Price Woods Products Inc.....513 722-1200
6507 Snider Rd Loveland (45140) ***(G-13021)***
Pricewaterhousecoopers LLP.....216 875-3000
200 Public Sq Fl 18 Cleveland (44114) ***(G-6235)***
Pricewaterhousecoopers LLP.....419 254-2500
406 Washington St Ste 200 Toledo (43604) ***(G-17987)***
Pricewaterhousecoopers LLP.....513 723-4700
201 E 5th St Ste 2300 Cincinnati (45202) ***(G-4278)***
Pricewaterhousecoopers LLP.....614 225-8700
41 S High St Ste 25 Columbus (43215) ***(G-8461)***
Pride -N- Joy Preschool Inc.....740 522-3338
1319 W Main St Newark (43055) ***(G-15093)***
Pride Transportation Inc.....419 424-2145
611 Howard St Findlay (45840) ***(G-10956)***
Pridecraft Enterprises, Cincinnati *Also called Standard Textile Co Inc* ***(G-4533)***
Primary Care Nursing Services.....614 764-0960
3140 Lilly Mar Ct Dublin (43017) ***(G-10311)***
Primary Care Physicians Assn.....330 499-9944
4575 Stephens Cir Nw Canton (44718) ***(G-2440)***
Primary Cr Ntwrk Prmr Hlth Prt.....513 492-5940
4859 Nixon Park Dr Ste A Mason (45040) ***(G-13628)***
Primary Cr Ntwrk Prmr Hlth Prt.....937 890-6644
900 S Dixie Dr Ste 40 Vandalia (45377) ***(G-18535)***
Primary Cr Ntwrk Prmr Hlth Prt.....937 278-5854
1530 Needmore Rd Ste 200 Dayton (45414) ***(G-9707)***
Primary Cr Ntwrk Prmr Hlth Prt.....937 208-9090
1222 S Patterson Blvd # 120 Dayton (45402) ***(G-9708)***
Primary Cr Ntwrk Prmr Hlth Prt.....937 208-7000
722 N Fairfield Rd Beavercreek (45434) ***(G-1178)***
Primary Cr Ntwrk Prmr Hlth Prt.....937 743-5965
8401 Claude Thomas Rd Franklin (45005) ***(G-11038)***
Primary Cr Ntwrk Prmr Hlth Prt.....513 420-5233
1 Medical Center Dr Middletown (45005) ***(G-14354)***
Primary Cr Ntwrk Prmr Hlth Prt.....513 204-5785
7450 S Masn Montgomery Rd Mason (45040) ***(G-13629)***
Primary Cr Ntwrk Prmr Hlth Prt (PA).....937 226-7085
110 N Main St Ste 350 Dayton (45402) ***(G-9709)***
Primary Cr Ntwrk Prmr Hlth Prt.....937 424-9800
2350 Miami Valley Dr # 410 Dayton (45459) ***(G-9710)***
Primary Dayton Innkeepers LLC.....937 938-9550
7701 Washington Vlg Dr Dayton (45459) ***(G-9711)***
Primary Eyecare Associates (PA).....937 492-2351
1086 Fairington Dr Sidney (45365) ***(G-16794)***
Primary Solutions, Columbus *Also called Marshall Information Svcs LLC* ***(G-8030)***
Primatech Inc (PA).....614 841-9800
50 Northwoods Blvd Ste A Columbus (43235) ***(G-8462)***
Primavista, Cincinnati *Also called Queens Tower Restaurant Inc* ***(G-4324)***
Primax Marketing Group.....513 443-2797
2300 Montana Ave Ste 102 Cincinnati (45211) ***(G-4279)***
Prime Ae Group Inc.....614 839-0250
8415 Pulsar Pl Ste 300 Columbus (43240) ***(G-6831)***
Prime Home Care LLC (PA).....513 340-4183
2775 W Us Hwy 22 3 Ste 1 Maineville (45039) ***(G-13117)***
Prime Home Care LLC.....419 535-1414
3454 Oak Alley Ct Ste 304 Toledo (43606) ***(G-17988)***
Prime Polymers Inc.....330 662-4200
2600 Medina Rd Medina (44256) ***(G-13988)***
Prime Prodata Inc.....330 497-2578
800 N Main St North Canton (44720) ***(G-15227)***
Prime Time Delivery & Whse, Cleveland *Also called Prime Time Enterprises Inc* ***(G-6236)***
Prime Time Enterprises Inc.....440 891-8855
6410 Eastland Rd Ste A Cleveland (44142) ***(G-6236)***
Prime Time Party Rental Inc.....937 296-9262
5225 Springboro Pike Moraine (45439) ***(G-14687)***
Primecare Sutheastern Ohio Inc.....740 454-8551
1210 Ashland Ave Zanesville (43701) ***(G-20355)***
Primed.....937 435-9013
979 Congress Park Dr Dayton (45459) ***(G-9712)***
Primed At Congress Park, Dayton *Also called Medicine Midwest LLC* ***(G-9603)***

ALPHABETIC

Primed Physicians, Dayton *Also called Primed Premier Integrated Med (G-9714)*
Primed Physicians, Centerville *Also called Premier Integrated Med Assoc (G-2632)*
Primed Physicians 937 298-8058
  540 Lincoln Park Blvd # 390 Dayton (45429) *(G-9713)*
Primed Premier Integrated Med (PA) 937 291-6893
  6520 Acro Ct Dayton (45459) *(G-9714)*
Primehalth Wns Hlth Specialist 440 918-4630
  35040 Chardon Rd Ste 205 Willoughby Hills (44094) *(G-19592)*
Primerica, Canton *Also called Rick Allman (G-2461)*
Primero Home Loans LLC 877 959-2921
  4725 Lakehurst Ct Ste 400 Dublin (43016) *(G-10312)*
Primetals Technologies USA LLC 419 929-1554
  81 E Washburn St New London (44851) *(G-14935)*
Primetech Communications Inc 513 942-6000
  4505 Muhlhauser Rd West Chester (45011) *(G-18986)*
Primetime, Canton *Also called Aultman Hospital (G-2204)*
Primo Properties LLC 330 606-6746
  5555 Cerni Pl Austintown (44515) *(G-859)*
Primrose Rtrment Cmmnities LLC 419 224-1200
  3500 W Elm St Lima (45807) *(G-12724)*
Primrose School At Golf Vlg 740 881-5830
  8771 Moreland St Powell (43065) *(G-16205)*
Primrose School At Polaris 614 899-2588
  561 Westar Blvd Westerville (43082) *(G-19203)*
Primrose School of Symmes 513 697-6970
  9175 Governors Way Cincinnati (45249) *(G-4280)*
Primrose School of Worthington, Worthington *Also called Ajm Worthington Inc (G-19791)*
Printed Resources, Columbus *Also called Nutis Press Inc (G-8218)*
Printing Concepts, Stow *Also called Traxium LLC (G-17236)*
Printing Services 440 708-1999
  16750 Park Circle Dr Chagrin Falls (44023) *(G-2678)*
Printpack Inc 513 891-7886
  8044 Montgomery Rd # 600 Cincinnati (45236) *(G-4281)*
Priority 1 Construction Svcs 513 922-0203
  5178 Crookshank Rd Cincinnati (45238) *(G-4282)*
Priority Building Services Inc 937 233-7030
  2370 National Rd Beavercreek Township (45324) *(G-1260)*
Priority Designs Inc 614 337-9979
  100 S Hamilton Rd Columbus (43213) *(G-8463)*
Priority Dispatch Inc (PA) 513 791-3900
  4665 Malsbary Rd Blue Ash (45242) *(G-1631)*
Priority Dispatch Inc. 216 332-9852
  5385 Naiman Pkwy Solon (44139) *(G-16885)*
Priority III Contracting Inc 513 922-0203
  5178 Crookshank Rd Cincinnati (45238) *(G-4283)*
Priority Mortgage Corp 614 431-1141
  150 E Wilson Bridge Rd # 350 Worthington (43085) *(G-19837)*
Prisma Integration Corp 330 545-8690
  50 Harry St Girard (44420) *(G-11298)*
Pristine Senior Living, Cincinnati *Also called Premier Estates 525 LLC (G-4272)*
Pristine Senior Living 513 471-8667
  315 Lilienthal St Cincinnati (45204) *(G-4284)*
Pristine Senior Living and, Willard *Also called Pristine Senior Living of (G-19486)*
Pristine Senior Living of 419 935-0148
  370 E Howard St Willard (44890) *(G-19486)*
Pristine Snior Lving Englewood 937 836-5143
  425 Lauricella Ct Englewood (45322) *(G-10599)*
Private Duty & Visiting Nurses, Celina *Also called Community Hlth Prfssionals Inc (G-2590)*
Private Duty Services Inc 419 238-3714
  1157 Westwood Dr Van Wert (45891) *(G-18487)*
Private HM Care Foundation Inc 513 662-8999
  3808 Applegate Ave Cincinnati (45211) *(G-4285)*
Private Practice Nurses Inc 216 481-1305
  403 Cary Jay Blvd Cleveland (44143) *(G-6237)*
Private School Aid Service, Westlake *Also called Facts Management Company (G-19340)*
Prn Health Services Inc 513 792-2217
  8044 Montgomery Rd # 700 Cincinnati (45236) *(G-4286)*
Prn Nurse Inc 614 864-9292
  6161 Radekin Rd Columbus (43232) *(G-8464)*
Pro Care Janitor Supply 937 778-2275
  317 N Main St Piqua (45356) *(G-16024)*
Pro Care Medical Trnsp Svc, Circleville *Also called Pickaway Plains Ambulance Svc (G-4845)*
Pro Century, Westerville *Also called CSC Insurance Agency Inc (G-19154)*
Pro Ed Communications Inc 216 595-7919
  25101 Chagrin Blvd # 230 Cleveland (44122) *(G-6238)*
Pro Health Care Services Ltd 614 856-9111
  270 Main St Ste A Groveport (43125) *(G-11532)*
Pro Kids & Families Program, Cleveland *Also called Ohioguidestone (G-6126)*
Pro Oncall Technologies LLC (PA) 513 489-7660
  6902 E Kemper Rd Cincinnati (45249) *(G-4287)*
Pro Seniors Inc 513 345-4160
  7162 Reading Rd Ste 1150 Cincinnati (45237) *(G-4288)*
Pro-Kleen Industrial Svcs Inc 740 689-1886
  1030 Mill Park Dr Lancaster (43130) *(G-12427)*
Pro-Lam, Milford *Also called Professonal Laminate Mllwk Inc (G-14427)*
Pro-Touch, Columbus *Also called T&L Global Management LLC (G-8727)*
Pro-Touch Inc. 614 586-0303
  721 N Rose Ave Columbus (43219) *(G-8465)*

Pro-Tow Inc 614 444-8697
  1669 Harmon Ave Columbus (43223) *(G-8466)*
Proactive Occpational Medicine, Wheelersburg *Also called Proactive Occpational Medicine (G-19438)*
Proactive Occpational Medicine 740 574-8728
  1661 State Route 522 # 3 Wheelersburg (45694) *(G-19438)*
Proactive Occptnal Mdicine Inc 740 574-8728
  1661 State Route 522 Wheelersburg (45694) *(G-19439)*
Proampac, Cincinnati *Also called Ampac Holdings LLC (G-2955)*
Procamps Inc 513 745-5855
  4600 Mcauley Pl Fl 4 Blue Ash (45242) *(G-1632)*
Process Construction Inc 513 251-2211
  2128 State Ave Cincinnati (45214) *(G-4289)*
Process Plus LLC (PA) 513 742-7590
  135 Merchant St Ste 300 Cincinnati (45246) *(G-4290)*
Process Pump & Seal Inc 513 988-7000
  2993 Woodsdale Rd Trenton (45067) *(G-18190)*
Procter & Gamble Distrg LLC 513 945-7960
  2 P&G Plz Tn8 235 Cincinnati (45202) *(G-4291)*
Procter & Gamble Distrg LLC 937 387-5189
  1800 Union Park Blvd Union (45377) *(G-18351)*
Procterville Food Fair, Proctorville *Also called Forths Foods Inc (G-16216)*
Procurement Payments, Kent *Also called Kent State University (G-12242)*
Prodrivers, Columbus *Also called Professional Drivers GA Inc (G-8467)*
Produce One Inc 931 253-4749
  904 Woodley Rd Dayton (45403) *(G-9715)*
Producer Group LLC (PA) 440 871-7700
  19111 Detroit Rd Ste 304 Rocky River (44116) *(G-16444)*
Production Design Services Inc (PA) 937 866-3377
  313 Mound St Dayton (45402) *(G-9716)*
Production Services Unlimited 513 695-1658
  575 Columbus Ave Lebanon (45036) *(G-12493)*
Productivity Qulty Systems Inc (PA) 937 885-2255
  210b E Spring Valley Pike Dayton (45458) *(G-9717)*
Professional Building Maint, Dayton *Also called Space Management Inc (G-9781)*
Professional Contract Systems 513 469-8800
  11804 Conrey Rd Ste 100 Cincinnati (45249) *(G-4292)*
Professional Detailing Pdts, Canton *Also called Ohio Auto Supply Company (G-2424)*
Professional Drivers GA Inc 614 529-8282
  4251 Diplomacy Dr Columbus (43228) *(G-8467)*
Professional Electric Pdts Co 419 269-3790
  501 Phillips Ave Toledo (43612) *(G-17989)*
Professional Fleet Management, Loveland *Also called Professional Transit Mgt (G-13022)*
Professional Hse Clg Svcs Inc 440 729-7866
  8228 Mayfield Rd Ste 1b Chesterland (44026) *(G-2743)*
Professional Investigating (PA) 614 228-7422
  551 S 3rd St Columbus (43215) *(G-8468)*
Professional Maint Dayton 937 461-5259
  223 E Helena St Dayton (45404) *(G-9718)*
Professional Maint of Columbus 614 443-6528
  541 Stimmel Rd Columbus (43223) *(G-8469)*
Professional Maint of Columbus 513 579-1762
  1 Crosley Field Ln Cincinnati (45214) *(G-4293)*
Professional Nursing Service, Cuyahoga Falls *Also called Diane Vishnia Rn and Assoc (G-9087)*
Professional Nursing Service, Cuyahoga Falls *Also called Vishnia & Associates Inc (G-9137)*
Professional Plumbing Services 740 454-1066
  3570 Old Wheeling Rd Zanesville (43701) *(G-20356)*
Professional Property Maint, New Carlisle *Also called Louderback Fmly Invstments Inc (G-14893)*
Professional Restoration Svc 330 825-1803
  1170 Industrial Pkwy Medina (44256) *(G-13989)*
Professional Rfrgn & AC, Millersport *Also called Pre-Fore Inc (G-14503)*
Professional Sales Associates 330 299-7343
  5045 Park Ave W Ste 1b Seville (44273) *(G-16687)*
Professional Service Inds, Columbus *Also called Professional Service Inds Inc (G-8470)*
Professional Service Inds Inc. 614 876-8000
  4960 Vulcan Ave Ste C Columbus (43228) *(G-8470)*
Professional Service Inds Inc. 216 447-1335
  5555 Canal Rd Cleveland (44125) *(G-6239)*
Professional Services, Cleveland *Also called Jewish Family Services Associa (G-5796)*
Professional Telecom Svcs 513 232-7700
  2119 Beechmont Ave Cincinnati (45230) *(G-4294)*
Professional Transit Mgt (PA) 513 677-6000
  6405 Brch Hll Gna Pg 20 Loveland (45140) *(G-13022)*
Professional Transportation 419 661-0576
  30801 Drouillard Rd Walbridge (43465) *(G-18623)*
Professional Travel Inc (PA) 440 734-8800
  25000 Country Club Blvd # 170 North Olmsted (44070) *(G-15305)*
Professionals For Womens Hlth (PA) 614 268-8800
  921 Jasonway Ave Ste B Columbus (43214) *(G-8471)*
Professnal Glfers Assn of Amer 419 882-3197
  5201 Corey Rd Sylvania (43560) *(G-17442)*
Professnal Mint Cincinnati Inc 513 579-1161
  1230 Findlay St Cincinnati (45214) *(G-4295)*
Professnal Mint Lttle Ohio Div, Cincinnati *Also called Professional Maint of Columbus (G-4293)*
Professonal Data Resources Inc (PA) 513 792-5100
  4555 Lake Forest Dr # 220 Blue Ash (45242) *(G-1633)*

Professional Football Hall Fame, Canton Also called National Football Museum Inc (G-2414)

Professonal Laminate Mllwk Inc 513 891-7858
1003 Tech Dr Milford (45150) (G-14427)

Profile Digital Printing LLC 937 866-4241
5449 Marina Dr Dayton (45449) (G-9719)

Profiol, Canton Also called Graco Ohio Inc (G-2331)

Profit Recovery of Ohio 440 243-1743
16510 Webster Rd Cleveland (44130) (G-6240)

Proforma, Independence Also called Pfg Ventures LP (G-12107)

Progresive Spclty Ins Agcy Inc 440 461-5000
6300 Wilson Mills Rd Cleveland (44143) (G-6241)

Progressive Advanced Insur Co 440 461-5000
6300 Wilson Mills Rd Cleveland (44143) (G-6242)

Progressive Casualty Insur Co (HQ) 440 461-5000
6300 Wilson Mills Rd Mayfield Village (44143) (G-13886)

Progressive Casualty Insur Co 440 683-8164
651 Beta Dr 150 Cleveland (44143) (G-6243)

Progressive Casualty Insur Co 440 603-4033
747 Alpha Dr Ste A21 Cleveland (44143) (G-6244)

Progressive Choice Insur Co 440 461-5000
6300 Wilson Mills Rd Cleveland (44143) (G-6245)

Progressive Corporation 800 925-2886
600 Mills Rd Cleveland (44101) (G-6246)

Progressive Corporation 440 461-5000
300 N Commons Blvd Cleveland (44143) (G-6247)

Progressive Dodge, Massillon Also called Progrssive Oldsmobile Cadillac (G-13721)

Progressive Entps Holdings Inc 614 794-3300
250 Progressive Way Westerville (43082) (G-19204)

Progressive Express Insur Co 440 461-5000
6300 Wilson Mills Rd Cleveland (44143) (G-6248)

Progressive Fishing Assn 419 877-9909
8050 Schadel Rd Whitehouse (43571) (G-19451)

Progressive Flooring Svcs Inc 614 868-9005
100 Heritage Dr Etna (43062) (G-10619)

Progressive Freedom Insur Co 440 461-5000
6300 Wilson Mills Rd Cleveland (44143) (G-6249)

Progressive Furniture Inc (HQ) 419 446-4500
502 Middle St Archbold (43502) (G-635)

Progressive Grdn State Insur 440 461-5000
6300 Wilson Mills Rd Cleveland (44143) (G-6250)

Progressive Green Meadows LLC 330 875-1456
7770 Columbus Rd Louisville (44641) (G-12971)

Progressive Insurance, Cleveland Also called Progressive Corporation (G-6246)

PROGRESSIVE INSURANCE, Mayfield Village Also called Progressive Casualty Insur Co (G-13886)

PROGRESSIVE INSURANCE, Cleveland Also called Progressive Grdn State Insur (G-6250)

Progressive Insurance, Youngstown Also called Progressive Max Insurance Co (G-20165)

PROGRESSIVE INSURANCE, Cleveland Also called Progressive Advanced Insur Co (G-6242)

PROGRESSIVE INSURANCE, Cleveland Also called Progressive Freedom Insur Co (G-6249)

Progressive Insurance, Cleveland Also called Progresive Spclty Ins Agcy Inc (G-6241)

Progressive Insurance, Cleveland Also called Progressive Rsc Inc (G-6255)

Progressive Insurance, Cleveland Also called Progressive Vehicle Service Co (G-6258)

Progressive Insurance, Cleveland Also called Progressive Casualty Insur Co (G-6243)

PROGRESSIVE INSURANCE, Cleveland Also called Progressive West Insurance Co (G-6259)

PROGRESSIVE INSURANCE, Cleveland Also called Progressive Northwestern Insur (G-6251)

Progressive Insurance, Cleveland Also called Progressive Universal Insur Co (G-6257)

PROGRESSIVE INSURANCE, Cleveland Also called Progressive Premier Insurance (G-6254)

PROGRESSIVE INSURANCE, Cleveland Also called Progressive Corporation (G-6247)

PROGRESSIVE INSURANCE, Cleveland Also called Progressive Select Insur Co (G-6256)

PROGRESSIVE INSURANCE, Cleveland Also called Progressive Choice Insur Co (G-6245)

Progressive Insurance, Cleveland Also called Progressive Paloverde Insur Co (G-6252)

PROGRESSIVE INSURANCE, Cleveland Also called Progressive Express Insur Co (G-6248)

Progressive International, Archbold Also called Progressive Furniture Inc (G-635)

Progressive Macedonia LLC 330 908-1260
9730 Valley View Rd Macedonia (44056) (G-13080)

Progressive Max Insurance Co 330 533-8733
120 Westchester Dr Ste 1 Youngstown (44515) (G-20165)

Progressive Medical Intl, Dublin Also called Demarius Corporation (G-10199)

Progressive Northwestern Insur 440 461-5000
6300 Wilson Mills Rd Cleveland (44143) (G-6251)

Progressive Paloverde Insur Co 440 461-5000
6300 Wilson Mills Rd Cleveland (44143) (G-6252)

Progressive Park LLC 330 434-4514
5553 Broadview Rd Cleveland (44134) (G-6253)

Progressive Premier Insurance 440 461-5000
6300 Wilson Mills Rd W33 Cleveland (44143) (G-6254)

Progressive Quality Care Inc 330 875-7866
7770 Columbus Rd Louisville (44641) (G-12972)

Progressive Quality Care Inc (PA) 216 661-6800
5553 Broadview Rd Parma (44134) (G-15773)

Progressive Rsc Inc 440 461-5000
6300 Wilson Mills Rd Cleveland (44143) (G-6255)

Progressive Select Insur Co 440 461-5000
6300 Wilson Mills Rd Cleveland (44143) (G-6256)

Progressive Universal Insur Co 440 461-5000
6300 Wilson Mills Rd Cleveland (44143) (G-6257)

Progressive Vehicle Service Co 440 461-5000
6300 Wilson Mills Rd Cleveland (44143) (G-6258)

Progressive West Insurance Co 440 446-5100
6300 Wilson Mills Rd Cleveland (44143) (G-6259)

Progressive Womens Care 330 629-8466
6505 Market St Ste C112 Youngstown (44512) (G-20166)

Progrssive Oldsmobile Cadillac 330 833-8585
7966 Hills & Dales Rd Ne Massillon (44646) (G-13721)

Progrssive Sweeping Contrs Inc (PA) 419 464-0130
5202 Enterprise Blvd Toledo (43612) (G-17990)

Prohealth Partners Inc 419 491-7150
12661 Eckel Junction Rd Perrysburg (43551) (G-15906)

Project C U R E Inc 937 262-3500
200 Daruma Pkwy Dayton (45439) (G-9720)

Project Packaging Inc 216 451-7878
17877 Saint Clair Ave # 6 Cleveland (44110) (G-6260)

Project Rebuild Inc 330 639-1559
406 Shorb Ave Nw Canton (44703) (G-2441)

Projetech Inc 513 481-4900
3815 Harrison Ave Cincinnati (45211) (G-4296)

Prokids Inc 513 281-2000
2605 Burnet Ave Cincinnati (45219) (G-4297)

Prolift Industrial Equipment, West Chester Also called Toyota Industries N Amer Inc (G-19018)

Prolift Industrial Equipment, Dayton Also called Toyota Industries N Amer Inc (G-9819)

Proline Electric Inc 740 687-4571
301 Cedar Hill Rd Lancaster (43130) (G-12428)

Proline Xpress Inc 440 777-8120
24371 Lorain Rd Ste 206 North Olmsted (44070) (G-15306)

Prologue Research Intl Inc 614 324-1500
580 N 4th St Ste 270 Columbus (43215) (G-8472)

Promanco Inc 740 374-2120
27823 State Route 7 Marietta (45750) (G-13373)

Prome Conti Care Serv Corpo 419 885-1715
5855 Monroe St Ste 200 Sylvania (43560) (G-17443)

Promedica, Toledo Also called Bay Park Community Hospital (G-17606)

PROMEDICA, Maumee Also called St Lukes Hospital (G-13855)

Promedica, Toledo Also called Toledo Hospital (G-18087)

Promedica 419 291-3450
1695 Indian Wood Cir # 100 Maumee (43537) (G-13834)

Promedica Defiance Regional 419 783-6802
1200 Ralston Ave Defiance (43512) (G-9935)

Promedica GI Physicians LLC 419 843-7996
3439 Granite Cir Toledo (43617) (G-17991)

Promedica Gnt-Urinary Surgeons (PA) 419 531-8558
2100 W Central Ave Toledo (43606) (G-17992)

Promedica Health Systems Inc (PA) 567 585-7454
100 Madison Ave Toledo (43604) (G-17993)

Promedica Health Systems Inc 419 891-6201
660 Beaver Creek Cir # 200 Maumee (43537) (G-13835)

PROMEDICA HOME HEALTH CARE, Sylvania Also called Prome Conti Care Serv Corpo (G-17443)

Promedica Physcn Cntinuum Svcs 419 824-7200
5855 Monroe St Fl 1 Sylvania (43560) (G-17444)

Promedica Physician, Toledo Also called Sunforest Ob Gyn Associates (G-18053)

Promedica Physician Group, Sylvania Also called Promedica Physcn Cntinuum Svcs (G-17444)

PROMEDICA TOLEDO HOSPITAL, Toledo Also called Toledo Hospital (G-18086)

Promedidcal Heath Syytem, Maumee Also called Promedica Health Systems Inc (G-13835)

Promerus LLC 440 922-0300
9921 Brecksville Rd Brecksville (44141) (G-1799)

Prop Shop, Cleveland Also called Playhouse Square Holdg Co LLC (G-6219)

Property 3, Cleveland Also called Weston Inc (G-6679)

Property Estate Management LLC 513 684-0418
1526 Elm St Ste 1 Cincinnati (45202) (G-4298)

Pros Freight Corporation 440 543-7555
16687 Hilltop Park Pl Chagrin Falls (44023) (G-2679)

Proscan Imaging LLC (PA) 513 281-3400
5400 Kennedy Ave Ste 1 Cincinnati (45213) (G-4299)

Proscan Imaging LLC 513 759-7350
7307 Tylers Corner Dr West Chester (45069) (G-18987)

Prosource, Blue Ash Also called Cincinnati Copiers Inc (G-1525)

Prospect Mold & Die Company 330 929-3311
1100 Main St Cuyahoga Falls (44221) (G-9119)

Prosperity Care Service 614 430-8626
2021 Dublin Rd Columbus (43228) (G-8473)

Protech Alarm Systems, Canton Also called Protech Security Inc (G-2442)

Protech Security Inc 330 499-3555
7026 Sunset Strip Ave Nw Canton (44720) (G-2442)

Protective Coatings Inc 937 275-7711
4321 Webster St Dayton (45414) (G-9721)

Protem Homecare LLC 216 663-8188
3535 Lee Rd Cleveland (44120) (G-6261)

Proterra Inc (PA) 216 383-8449
29103 Euclid Ave Wickliffe (44092) (G-19474)

Protiviti Inc 216 696-6010
1001 Lakeside Ave E Cleveland (44114) (G-6262)

Prout Boiler Htg & Wldg Inc 330 744-0293
3124 Temple St Youngstown (44510) *(G-20167)*
Provantage LLC 330 494-3781
7576 Freedom Ave Nw North Canton (44720) *(G-15228)*
Provato LLC 440 546-0768
8748 Brecksville Rd # 125 Brecksville (44141) *(G-1800)*
Provenitfinance LLC 888 958-1060
195 Fox Glen Dr W Pickerington (43147) *(G-15965)*
Provia - Heritage Stone, Sugarcreek *Also called Provia Holdings Inc (G-17379)*
Provia Holdings Inc (PA) 330 852-4711
2150 State Route 39 Sugarcreek (44681) *(G-17379)*
Providence Care Center 419 627-2273
2025 Hayes Ave Sandusky (44870) *(G-16633)*
Providence Care Centers, Sandusky *Also called Commons of Providence (G-16590)*
Providence Health Partners LLC 937 297-8999
2912 Springboro W Ste 201 Moraine (45439) *(G-14688)*
Providence House Inc 216 651-5982
2050 W 32nd St Cleveland (44113) *(G-6263)*
Providence Medical Group Inc 937 297-8999
2912 Springboro W Ste 201 Moraine (45439) *(G-14689)*
Providence Rees Inc 614 833-6231
2111 Builders Pl Columbus (43204) *(G-8474)*
Provident Travel Corporation 513 247-1100
11309 Montgomery Rd Ste B Cincinnati (45249) *(G-4300)*
Provider Physicians Inc 614 755-3000
6096 E Main St Ste 112 Columbus (43213) *(G-8475)*
Provider Services, North Olmsted *Also called Foundations Hlth Solutions Inc (G-15289)*
Provider Services Inc 614 888-2021
111 Lazelle Rd Columbus (43235) *(G-8476)*
Providian Med Field Svc LLC 440 833-0460
5335 Avion Park Dr Unit A Highland Heights (44143) *(G-11735)*
Provimi North America Inc (HQ) 937 770-2400
10 Collective Way Brookville (45309) *(G-1916)*
Province Kent OH LLC 330 673-3808
609 S Lincoln St Ste F Kent (44240) *(G-12255)*
Province of St John The Baptis 513 241-5615
28 W Liberty St Cincinnati (45202) *(G-4301)*
Proware, Cincinnati *Also called Sadler-Necamp Financial Svcs (G-4421)*
Prt, Piqua *Also called Plastic Recycling Tech Inc (G-16023)*
Prudential, Columbus *Also called Residential One Realty Inc (G-8521)*
Prudential, Lima *Also called Pgim Inc (G-12721)*
Prudential Calhoon Co Realtors 614 777-1000
3535 Fishinger Blvd # 100 Hilliard (43026) *(G-11808)*
Prudential Insur Co of Amer 513 612-6400
3 Crowne Point Ct Ste 100 Cincinnati (45241) *(G-4302)*
Prudential Insur Co of Amer 330 896-7200
3515 Massillon Rd Ste 200 Uniontown (44685) *(G-18383)*
Prudential Insur Co of Amer 440 684-4409
5875 Landerbrook Dr # 110 Cleveland (44124) *(G-6264)*
Prudential Insur Co of Amer 419 893-6227
1705 Indian Wood Cir # 115 Maumee (43537) *(G-13836)*
Prudential Lucien Realty 216 226-4673
18630 Detroit Ave Lakewood (44107) *(G-12360)*
Prudential Select Properties (PA) 440 255-1111
7395 Center St Mentor (44060) *(G-14098)*
Prudential Welsh Realty 440 974-3100
7400 Center St Mentor (44060) *(G-14099)*
Prueter Enterprises Ltd 419 872-5343
25660 Dixie Hwy Ste 2 Perrysburg (43551) *(G-15907)*
Prus Construction Company 513 321-7774
5325 Wooster Pike Cincinnati (45226) *(G-4303)*
Prusa Inc 330 688-8500
1049 Mccauley Rd Stow (44224) *(G-17225)*
PS Lifestyle LLC 440 600-1595
55 Public Sq Ste 1180 Cleveland (44113) *(G-6265)*
Psa Airlines Inc 937 454-9338
3634 Cargo Rd Vandalia (45377) *(G-18536)*
Psa Airlines Inc (HQ) 937 454-1116
3400 Terminal Rd Vandalia (45377) *(G-18537)*
PSC Crane & Rigging, Piqua *Also called Piqua Steel Co (G-16020)*
PSC Metals Inc 330 455-0212
237 Tuscarawas St E Canton (44702) *(G-2443)*
PSC Metals Inc 614 299-4175
1283 Joyce Ave Columbus (43219) *(G-8477)*
PSC Metals Inc 234 208-2331
284 7th St Nw Barberton (44203) *(G-963)*
PSC Metals Inc 330 745-4437
701 W Hopocan Ave Barberton (44203) *(G-964)*
PSC Metals Inc 330 484-7610
3101 Varley Ave Sw Canton (44706) *(G-2444)*
PSC Metals Inc 216 341-3400
4250 E 68th Berdelle Cleveland (44105) *(G-6266)*
PSC Metals - Wooster LLC 330 264-8956
972 Columbus Rd Wooster (44691) *(G-19760)*
PSC Metals Inc 330 879-5001
780 Warmington St Sw Navarre (44662) *(G-14824)*
Pse, Marietta *Also called Power System Engineering Inc (G-13372)*
PSI Associates Inc 330 425-8474
2112 Case Pkwy Ste 10 Twinsburg (44087) *(G-18308)*
PSI Supply Chain Solutions LLC 614 389-4717
5050 Bradenton Ave Dublin (43017) *(G-10313)*
PSI Testing and Engineering, Cleveland *Also called Professional Service Inds Inc (G-6239)*
Psp Operations Inc 614 888-5700
7440 Pingue Dr Worthington (43085) *(G-19838)*
Psy-Care Inc 330 856-6663
8577 E Market St Warren (44484) *(G-18737)*
Psycare Inc (PA) 330 759-2310
2980 Belmont Ave Youngstown (44505) *(G-20168)*
Psychiatric Psychological Svcs, Elyria *Also called Santantonio Diana and Assoc (G-10560)*
Psychiatric Solutions Inc 440 953-3000
35900 Euclid Ave Willoughby (44094) *(G-19564)*
Psychiatric Solutions Inc 330 759-2700
615 Churchill Hubbard Rd Youngstown (44505) *(G-20169)*
Psychiatric Solutions Inc 419 891-9333
1725 Timber Line Rd Maumee (43537) *(G-13837)*
Psychiatric Solutions Inc 740 695-2131
67670 Traco Dr Saint Clairsville (43950) *(G-16502)*
Psychlgcal Behavioral Cons LLC (PA) 216 456-8123
25101 Chagrin Blvd # 100 Beachwood (44122) *(G-1097)*
Psychology Consultants Inc 330 764-7916
3591 Reserve Commons Dr # 301 Medina (44256) *(G-13990)*
Psychpros Inc 513 651-9500
2404 Auburn Ave Cincinnati (45219) *(G-4304)*
Pta OH Cong McVay Elem Pta 614 797-7230
270 S Hempstead Rd Westerville (43081) *(G-19295)*
Pta Ohio Cngrss - Msn Elem Pta 330 588-2156
316 30th St Nw Canton (44709) *(G-2445)*
Pta Olms Falls Int Sch 440 427-6500
27043 Bagley Rd Olmsted Twp (44138) *(G-15540)*
Ptc Holdings Inc 216 771-6960
1422 Euclid Ave Ste 1130 Cleveland (44115) *(G-6267)*
Pti, Holland *Also called Plastic Technologies Inc (G-11905)*
Pti, Bowling Green *Also called Phoenix Technologies Intl LLC (G-1744)*
Pti Qlity Cntnment Sltions LLC 313 304-8677
5655 Opportunity Dr Ste 4 Toledo (43612) *(G-17994)*
Ptmj Enterprises 440 543-8000
32000 Aurora Rd Solon (44139) *(G-16886)*
Pubco Corporation (PA) 216 881-5300
3830 Kelley Ave Cleveland (44114) *(G-6268)*
Public Broadcasting Found NW (PA) 419 380-4600
1270 S Detroit Ave Toledo (43614) *(G-17995)*
Public Safety, Cleveland *Also called City of Cleveland (G-5189)*
Public Safety Ohio Department 937 335-6209
1275 Experiment Farm Rd Troy (45373) *(G-18222)*
Public Safety Ohio Department 419 768-3955
3980 County Road 172 Mount Gilead (43338) *(G-14734)*
Public Safety Ohio Department 614 752-7600
1970 W Broad St Columbus (43223) *(G-8478)*
Public Service Company Okla (HQ) 614 716-1000
1 Riverside Plz Columbus (43215) *(G-8479)*
Public Service Dept, Portsmouth *Also called City of Portsmouth (G-16129)*
Public Services Department, Westerville *Also called City of Westerville (G-19236)*
Public Storage 216 220-7978
22800 Miles Rd Bedford Heights (44128) *(G-1325)*
Public Utilities- Water Div, Columbus *Also called City of Columbus (G-7212)*
Public Utilities- Water Div, Lockbourne *Also called City of Columbus (G-12811)*
Public Utlties-Electricity Div, Columbus *Also called City of Columbus (G-7205)*
Pucher Paint Co Inc (PA) 440 234-0991
50 Park St Berea (44017) *(G-1435)*
Pucher's Decorating Center, Berea *Also called Pucher Paint Co Inc (G-1435)*
Pulaski Head Start 419 636-8862
6678 Us Highway 127 Bryan (43506) *(G-1972)*
Pulmonary & Medicine Dayton (PA) 937 439-3600
4000 Miamisburg Centervil Miamisburg (45342) *(G-14208)*
Pulmonary Crtcal Care Spcalist 419 843-7800
1661 Holland Rd Ste 200 Maumee (43537) *(G-13838)*
Pulmonary Division, Cincinnati *Also called University of Cincinnati (G-4724)*
Pulte Homes Inc 330 239-1587
387 Medina Rd Ste 1700 Medina (44256) *(G-13991)*
Pump House Ministries 419 207-3900
1661 Cleveland Rd Ashland (44805) *(G-684)*
Punderson Manor Resort, Newbury *Also called TW Recreational Services Inc (G-15126)*
Pups Paradise 419 873-6115
12615 Roachton Rd Perrysburg (43551) *(G-15908)*
Pure Concept Ecosalon & Spa, Mason *Also called Pure Concept Salon Inc (G-13630)*
Pure Concept Salon Inc 513 770-2120
5625 Deerfield Cir Mason (45040) *(G-13630)*
Pure Concept Salon Inc (PA) 513 794-0202
8740 Montgomery Rd Ste 7 Cincinnati (45236) *(G-4305)*
Pure Led Solutions, Cleveland *Also called C-Auto Glass Inc (G-5111)*
Pure Romance LLC (PA) 513 248-8656
655 Plum St Ste 3 Cincinnati (45202) *(G-4306)*
Purepay, Columbus *Also called Hbi Payments Ltd (G-7721)*
Purple Marlin Inc 440 323-1291
42208 Albrecht Rd Ste 1 Elyria (44035) *(G-10557)*
Put In Bay Transportation 419 285-4855
2009 Langram Rd Put In Bay (43456) *(G-16228)*
Putman Janitorial Service Inc 513 942-1900
4836 Duff Dr Ste D West Chester (45246) *(G-19074)*
Putnam Cnty Amblatory Care Ctr, Lima *Also called Mercy Health - St R (G-12702)*
Putnam Cnty Amblatory Care Ctr, Lima *Also called St Ritas Medical Center (G-12752)*

Putnam Cnty Homecare & Hospice 419 523-4449
 575 Ottawa Ottawa (45875) **(G-15665)**
Putnam County Y M C A, Ottawa Also called Young Mens Christian Assoc **(G-15667)**
Putnam Logistics, Columbus Also called P & D Transportation Inc **(G-8405)**
Putnam Truck Load Direct, Zanesville Also called P & D Transportation Inc **(G-20352)**
PWC International, Independence Also called IHS Enterprise Inc **(G-12081)**
Pxp Ohio 614 575-4242
 6800 Tussing Rd Reynoldsburg (43068) **(G-16324)**
Pymatuning Ambulance Service 440 293-7991
 153 Station St Andover (44003) **(G-607)**
Pyramid Control Systems Inc 513 679-7400
 5546 Fair Ln Cincinnati (45227) **(G-4307)**
Pyramid Controls, Cincinnati Also called Pyramid Control Systems Inc **(G-4307)**
Pyramyd Air Ltd (PA) 216 896-0893
 5135 Naiman Pkwy Solon (44139) **(G-16887)**
Pyxis Data Systems, Dublin Also called Cardinal Health 301 LLC **(G-10159)**
Q Fact Marketing Research Inc (PA) 513 891-2271
 11767 Thayer Ln Cincinnati (45249) **(G-4308)**
Q Laboratories, Cincinnati Also called Q Labs LLC **(G-4309)**
Q Labs LLC (PA) 513 471-1300
 1911 Radcliff Dr Cincinnati (45204) **(G-4309)**
Q, The, Cleveland Also called Cavaliers Operating Co LLC **(G-5137)**
Qbase LLC (PA) 888 458-0345
 3725 Pentagon Blvd # 100 Beavercreek (45431) **(G-1179)**
QBS Inc 330 821-8801
 1548 S Linden Ave Alliance (44601) **(G-544)**
Qes Pressure Control LLC 740 489-5721
 64201 Wintergreen Rd Lore City (43755) **(G-12953)**
Qh Management Company LLC 440 497-1100
 11080 Concord Hambden Rd Concord Twp (44077) **(G-8946)**
Qsr Parent Co 330 425-8472
 1700 Highland Rd Twinsburg (44087) **(G-18309)**
QT Equipment Company (PA) 330 724-3055
 151 W Dartmore Ave Akron (44301) **(G-394)**
Quad Ambulance District 330 866-9847
 6930 Minerva Rd Se Waynesburg (44688) **(G-18829)**
Quadax Inc 330 759-4600
 17 Colonial Dr Ste 101 Youngstown (44505) **(G-20170)**
Quadax Inc (PA) 440 777-6300
 7500 Old Oak Blvd Middleburg Heights (44130) **(G-14256)**
Quadax Inc 614 882-1200
 4151 Executive Pkwy # 360 Westerville (43081) **(G-19296)**
Quadco Rehabilitation Center 419 445-1950
 600 Oak St Archbold (43502) **(G-636)**
Quadco Rehabilitation Ctr Inc (PA) 419 682-1011
 427 N Defiance St Stryker (43557) **(G-17370)**
Quail Hollow Management Inc. 440 639-4000
 11295 Quail Hollow Dr Painesville (44077) **(G-15734)**
Quail Hollow Resort, Concord Twp Also called Qh Management Company LLC **(G-8946)**
Quail Hollow Resort Cntry CLB, Painesville Also called Quail Hollow Management Inc **(G-15734)**
Quaker Heights Care Community, Waynesville Also called Quaker Heights Nursing HM Inc **(G-18835)**
Quaker Heights Nursing HM Inc 513 897-6050
 514 High St Waynesville (45068) **(G-18835)**
Quaker Steak & Lube, Westlake Also called Travelcenters of America LLC **(G-19415)**
Quaker Steak and Lube, Westlake Also called Travelcenters of America LLC **(G-19414)**
Qualchoice Inc 330 656-1231
 3605 Warrensville Ctr Rd Beachwood (44122) **(G-1098)**
Quality Aero Inc (PA) 614 436-1609
 6797 N High St Ste 324 Worthington (43085) **(G-19839)**
Quality Air Heating and AC, Columbus Also called Kusan Inc **(G-7931)**
Quality Assured Cleaning Inc 614 798-1505
 6407 Nicholas Dr Columbus (43235) **(G-8480)**
Quality Block & Supply Inc (HQ) 330 364-4411
 Rr 250 Mount Eaton (44659) **(G-14723)**
Quality Care Nursing Svcs LLC 740 377-9095
 501 Washington St Ste 13 South Point (45680) **(G-16944)**
Quality Carriers Inc 419 222-6800
 1586 Findlay Rd Lima (45801) **(G-12725)**
Quality Cleaners of Ohio Inc 330 688-5616
 3773 Darrow Rd Stow (44224) **(G-17226)**
Quality Cleaning Systems LLC 330 567-2050
 7945 Shreve Rd Shreve (44676) **(G-16754)**
Quality Clg Svc of NW Ohio 419 335-9105
 861 N Fulton St Wauseon (43567) **(G-18809)**
Quality Control Inspection (PA) 440 359-1900
 40 Tarbell Ave Cleveland (44146) **(G-6269)**
Quality Electrical & Mech Inc 419 294-3591
 1190 E Kibby St Lima (45804) **(G-12726)**
Quality Fabricated Metals Inc 330 332-7008
 14000 W Middletown Rd Salem (44460) **(G-16555)**
Quality Inn, Bellville Also called Bellville Hotel Company **(G-1387)**
Quality Inn, Montpelier Also called Bob Mor Inc **(G-14607)**
Quality Inn, Port Clinton Also called Lodging Industry Inc **(G-16112)**
Quality Inn, Tiffin Also called McPaul Corp **(G-17523)**
Quality Inn, Richfield Also called Richfield Banquet & Confer **(G-16375)**
Quality Inn, Mansfield Also called Mansfield Hotel Partnership **(G-13207)**

Quality Inn, Marietta Also called Motel Investments Marietta Inc **(G-13362)**
Quality Life Providers LLC 614 527-9999
 3974 Brown Park Dr Ste E Hilliard (43026) **(G-11809)**
Quality Lines Inc 740 815-1165
 2440 Bright Rd Findlay (45840) **(G-10957)**
Quality Maintenance Company, Marion Also called Quality Masonry Company Inc **(G-13453)**
Quality Masonry Company Inc 740 387-6720
 1001 S Prospect St # 101 Marion (43302) **(G-13453)**
Quality Mechanical Services, Lima Also called Quality Electrical & Mech Inc **(G-12726)**
Quality Plant Productions Inc 440 526-8711
 4586 Newton Rd Richfield (44286) **(G-16371)**
Quality Plus, Painesville Also called Emily Management Inc **(G-15712)**
Quality Restaurant Supply, Cincinnati Also called Quality Supply Co **(G-4310)**
Quality Steels Corp (HQ) 937 294-4133
 2221 Arbor Blvd Moraine (45439) **(G-14690)**
Quality Supply Chain Co-Op Inc 614 764-3124
 1 Dave Thomas Blvd Dublin (43017) **(G-10314)**
Quality Supply Co (PA) 937 890-6114
 4020 Rev Dr Cincinnati (45232) **(G-4310)**
Quality Towing, West Chester Also called Sprandel Enterprises Inc **(G-19011)**
Quality Welding Inc 419 483-6067
 104 Ronald Ln Bellevue (44811) **(G-1384)**
Quality Wldg & Fabrication LLC 419 225-6208
 4330 East Rd Lima (45807) **(G-12727)**
Qualtech NP, Batavia Also called Curtiss-Wright Flow Control **(G-995)**
Qualtech NP, Cincinnati Also called Curtiss-Wright Flow Ctrl Corp **(G-2848)**
Qualtech NP, Cincinnati Also called Curtiss-Wright Flow Control **(G-2847)**
Quandel Construction Group Inc 717 657-0909
 774 Park Meadow Rd Westerville (43081) **(G-19297)**
Quandel Group Main Office, Westerville Also called Quandel Construction Group Inc **(G-19297)**
Quanexus Inc 937 885-7272
 571 Congress Park Dr Dayton (45459) **(G-9722)**
Quantech Services Inc 937 490-8461
 4141 Colonel Glenn Hwy # 273 Beavercreek Township (45431) **(G-1261)**
Quantum Construction Company 513 351-6903
 1654 Sherman Ave Cincinnati (45212) **(G-4311)**
Quantum Health, Blanchester Also called Healthquest Blanchester Inc **(G-1487)**
Quantum Health Inc 614 846-4318
 7450 Huntington Park Dr Columbus (43235) **(G-8481)**
Quantum Metals Inc 513 573-0144
 3675 Taft Rd Lebanon (45036) **(G-12494)**
Quantum Services, Columbus Also called Accurate Inventory and C **(G-6863)**
Quarry Pines, Poland Also called Reserve Run Golf Club LLC **(G-16087)**
Quasonix Inc (PA) 513 942-1287
 6025 Schumacher Park Dr West Chester (45069) **(G-18988)**
Quebe Holdings Inc (PA) 937 222-2290
 1985 Founders Dr Dayton (45420) **(G-9723)**
Queen City Blacktop Company 513 251-8400
 2130 Osterfeld St Cincinnati (45214) **(G-4312)**
Queen City Electric Inc 513 591-2600
 4015 Cherry St Ste 2 Cincinnati (45223) **(G-4313)**
Queen City General & Vascular (PA) 513 232-8181
 10506 Montgomery Rd # 101 Cincinnati (45242) **(G-4314)**
Queen City Generl Consultants, Cincinnati Also called Queen City General & Vascular **(G-4314)**
Queen City Hospice LLC 513 510-4406
 8250 Kenwood Crossing Way # 200 Cincinnati (45236) **(G-4315)**
QUEEN CITY HOSPICE AND PALLIAT, Cincinnati Also called Queen City Hospice LLC **(G-4315)**
Queen City Jobs, Cincinnati Also called Hubbard Radio Cincinnati LLC **(G-3737)**
Queen City Mechanicals Inc 513 353-1430
 1950 Waycross Rd Cincinnati (45240) **(G-4316)**
Queen City Medical Group 513 528-5600
 7991 Beechmont Ave Cincinnati (45255) **(G-4317)**
Queen City of Physicians, Cincinnati Also called Queen City Physicians **(G-4318)**
Queen City Physicians 513 872-2061
 2475 W Galbraith Rd Ste 3 Cincinnati (45239) **(G-4318)**
Queen City Physicians Ltd 513 791-6992
 7825 Laurel Ave Cincinnati (45243) **(G-4319)**
Queen City Polymers Inc (PA) 513 779-0990
 6101 Schumacher Park Dr West Chester (45069) **(G-18989)**
Queen City Racquet Club LLC 513 771-2835
 11275 Chester Rd Cincinnati (45246) **(G-4320)**
Queen City Reprographics 513 326-2300
 2863 E Sharon Rd Cincinnati (45241) **(G-4321)**
Queen City Transportation LLC 513 941-8700
 211 Township Ave Ste 2 Cincinnati (45216) **(G-4322)**
Queen Cy Spt Mdcine Rhbltation 513 561-1111
 3950 Red Bank Rd Cincinnati (45227) **(G-4323)**
Queens Tower Restaurant Inc 513 251-6467
 810 Matson Pl Ph 3 Cincinnati (45204) **(G-4324)**
Queensgate Food Group LLC 513 721-5503
 619 Linn St Cincinnati (45203) **(G-4325)**
Queensgate Food Service, Cincinnati Also called Queensgate Food Group LLC **(G-4325)**
Quest Ase, Cincinnati Also called Quest Global Services-Na Inc **(G-4328)**
Quest Def Systems Slutions Inc 860 573-5950
 11499 Chester Rd Ste 600 Cincinnati (45246) **(G-4326)**
Quest Diagnostics, Beavercreek Also called Wright State University **(G-1199)**

A L P H A B E T I C

Quest Global Services-Na Inc..........................513 563-8855
11499 Chester Rd Ste 600 Cincinnati (45246) *(G-4327)*

Quest Global Services-Na Inc (HQ)....................860 787-1600
11499 Chester Rd Fl 7 Cincinnati (45246) *(G-4328)*

Quest Quality Services LLC..............................419 704-7407
8036 Joshua Ln Maumee (43537) *(G-13839)*

Quest Recovery Prevention Svcs (PA)................330 453-8252
1341 Market Ave N Canton (44714) *(G-2446)*

Quest Software Inc...614 336-9223
6500 Emerald Pkwy Ste 400 Dublin (43016) *(G-10315)*

Questar Solutions LLC....................................330 966-2070
7948 Freedom Ave Nw North Canton (44720) *(G-15229)*

Questar, Inc., North Canton *Also called Questar Solutions LLC (G-15229)*

Questmark, Cincinnati *Also called Diversipak Inc (G-3436)*

Questmark, Stow *Also called Centimark Corporation (G-17194)*

Quick Delivery Service Inc (HQ)......................330 453-3709
2207 Kimball Rd Se Canton (44707) *(G-2447)*

Quick Solutions Inc..614 825-8000
440 Polaris Pkwy Ste 500 Westerville (43082) *(G-19205)*

Quick Tab II Inc (PA)..419 448-6622
241 Heritage Dr Tiffin (44883) *(G-17533)*

Quicken Loans Arena, Cleveland *Also called Cavaliers Holdings LLC (G-5136)*

Quicken Loans Inc..216 586-8900
100 Public Sq Ste 400 Cleveland (44113) *(G-6270)*

Quickslide, Springboro *Also called Hardy Diagnostics (G-16968)*

Quilalea Corporation..330 487-0777
3861 Sawbridge Dr Richfield (44286) *(G-16372)*

Quilter Cvlian Cnsrvation Camp, Green Springs *Also called W S O S Community A (G-11356)*

Quincy Amusements Inc...................................419 874-2154
2005 Hollenbeck Dr Perrysburg (43551) *(G-15909)*

Quincy Mall Inc (PA)...614 228-5331
191 W Nationwide Blvd # 200 Columbus (43215) *(G-8482)*

Quintus Technologies LLC...............................614 891-2732
8270 Green Meadows Dr N Lewis Center (43035) *(G-12561)*

Quotient Technology Inc...................................513 229-8659
5191 Natorp Blvd Ste 420 Mason (45040) *(G-13631)*

Qvidian Corporation...513 631-1155
10260 Alliance Rd Ste 210 Blue Ash (45242) *(G-1634)*

Qwaide Enterprises LLC...................................614 209-0551
6044 Phar Lap Dr New Albany (43054) *(G-14868)*

Qwest Corporation...614 793-9258
4650 Lakehurst Ct Ste 100 Dublin (43016) *(G-10316)*

R & A Sports Inc..216 289-2254
23780 Lakeland Blvd Euclid (44132) *(G-10654)*

R & B Contractors LLC.....................................513 738-0954
3730 Schloss Ln Shandon (45063) *(G-16721)*

R & D Nestle Center Inc (HQ)...........................937 642-7015
809 Collins Ave Marysville (43040) *(G-13524)*

R & D Nestle Center Inc...................................440 349-5757
5750 Harper Rd Solon (44139) *(G-16888)*

R & E Joint Venture Inc....................................614 891-9404
6843 Regency Dr Westerville (43082) *(G-19206)*

R & F Inc..419 868-2909
6228 Merger Dr Holland (43528) *(G-11906)*

R & H Service Inc...330 626-2888
9420 State Route 14 Streetsboro (44241) *(G-17267)*

R & J Investment Co Inc...................................440 934-5204
37800 French Creek Rd Avon (44011) *(G-902)*

R & J Trucking, Youngstown *Also called American Bulk Commodities Inc (G-19953)*

R & J Trucking Inc (HQ)....................................800 262-9365
8063 Southern Blvd Youngstown (44512) *(G-20171)*

R & J Trucking Inc..330 758-0841
147 Curtis Dr Shelby (44875) *(G-16750)*

R & J Trucking Inc..740 374-3050
14530 Sr 7 Marietta (45750) *(G-13374)*

R & J Trucking Inc..440 960-1508
5250 Baumhart Rd Lorain (44053) *(G-12939)*

R & J Trucking Inc..419 837-9937
3423 Genoa Rd Perrysburg (43551) *(G-15910)*

R & K Gorby LLC...419 222-0004
1920 Roschman Ave Lima (45804) *(G-12728)*

R & L Carriers, Norwalk *Also called R & L Transfer Inc (G-15453)*

R & L Carriers Inc...419 874-5976
134 W South Boundary St Perrysburg (43551) *(G-15911)*

R & L Transfer Inc..216 531-3324
1403 State Route 18 Norwalk (44857) *(G-15453)*

R & L Transfer Inc..330 743-3609
5550 Dunlap Rd Youngstown (44515) *(G-20172)*

R & L Transfer Inc..330 482-5800
1320 Springfield Rd Columbiana (44408) *(G-6791)*

R & M, Springfield *Also called R&M Materials Handling Inc (G-17099)*

R & M Delivery...740 574-2113
8375 Gallia Pike Franklin Furnace (45629) *(G-11047)*

R & M Fluid Power Inc......................................330 758-2766
7953 Southern Blvd Youngstown (44512) *(G-20173)*

R & R Inc (PA)..330 799-1536
44 Victoria Rd Youngstown (44515) *(G-20174)*

R & R Cleveland Mack Sales, Youngstown *Also called R & R Inc (G-20174)*

R & R Hvac Systems...419 861-0266
1650 Eber Rd Ste E Holland (43528) *(G-11907)*

R & R Pipeline Inc (PA).....................................740 345-3692
155 Dayton Rd Ne Newark (43055) *(G-15094)*

R & R Sanitation Inc...330 325-2311
1447 Martin Rd Mogadore (44260) *(G-14555)*

R & R Truck Sales Inc......................................330 784-5881
1650 E Waterloo Rd Akron (44306) *(G-395)*

R & R Wiring Contractors Inc...........................513 752-6304
1269 Clough Pike Batavia (45103) *(G-1007)*

R & S Halley & Co Inc......................................614 771-0388
6368 Scioto Darby Rd Hilliard (43026) *(G-11810)*

R & S Lines Inc..419 682-7807
102 Ellis St Stryker (43557) *(G-17371)*

R & Y Holding...419 353-3464
142 Campbell Hill Rd Bowling Green (43402) *(G-1747)*

R A Hermes Inc..513 251-5200
4015 Cherry St Ste 27 Cincinnati (45223) *(G-4329)*

R A I, Cleveland *Also called Research Associates Inc (G-6312)*

R and G Enterprises of Ohio............................440 845-6870
9213 Harrow Dr Cleveland (44129) *(G-6271)*

R and J Corporation...440 871-6009
24142 Detroit Rd Westlake (44145) *(G-19394)*

R B C Apollo Equity Partners (HQ)....................216 875-2626
600 Superior Ave E # 2300 Cleveland (44114) *(G-6272)*

R B Development Company Inc.........................513 829-8100
5200 Camelot Dr Fairfield (45014) *(G-10772)*

R B Jergens Contractors Inc...........................937 669-9799
11418 N Dixie Dr Vandalia (45377) *(G-18538)*

R B Stout Inc..330 666-8811
1285 N Clvland Mssllon Rd Akron (44333) *(G-396)*

R C Enterprises Inc..330 782-2111
5234 Southern Blvd Ste C Youngstown (44512) *(G-20175)*

R C Hemm Glass Shops Inc (PA)......................937 773-5591
514 S Main St Piqua (45356) *(G-16025)*

R C M, Akron *Also called Rubber City Machinery Corp (G-411)*

R D D Inc (PA)..216 781-5858
4719 Blythin Rd Cleveland (44125) *(G-6273)*

R D Jergens Contractors Inc (PA).....................937 669-9799
11418 N Dixie Dr. Vandalia (45377) *(G-18539)*

R D Jones Excavating Inc................................419 648-5870
10225 Alger Rd Harrod (45850) *(G-11681)*

R Dorsey & Company Inc.................................614 486-8900
400 W Wilson Bridge Rd # 105 Worthington (43085) *(G-19840)*

R E Kramig & Co Inc..513 761-4010
323 S Wayne Ave Cincinnati (45215) *(G-4330)*

R E Richards Inc...330 499-1001
9701 Cleveland Ave Nw # 100 Canton (44720) *(G-2448)*

R E Warner & Associates Inc...........................440 835-9400
25777 Detroit Rd Ste 200 Westlake (44145) *(G-19395)*

R E Watson Inc...513 863-0070
2728 Hamilton Cleves Rd Hamilton (45013) *(G-11634)*

R G Barry Corporation (HQ).............................614 864-6400
13405 Yarmouth Rd Nw Pickerington (43147) *(G-15966)*

R G Seller Co, Moraine *Also called R G Sellers Company (G-14691)*

R G Sellers Company (PA)................................937 299-1545
3185 Elbee Rd Moraine (45439) *(G-14691)*

R G Smith Company...419 524-4778
166 W 6th St Mansfield (44902) *(G-13231)*

R I D Inc...419 251-4790
2222 Cherry St Ste 1400 Toledo (43608) *(G-17996)*

R J Martin Elec Svcs Inc.................................216 662-7100
22841 Aurora Rd Bedford Heights (44146) *(G-1326)*

R J W, Cleveland *Also called Total Transportation Trckg Inc (G-6534)*

R K Campf Corp...330 332-7089
465 Newgarden Ave Salem (44460) *(G-16556)*

R K Hydro-Vac Inc (PA)....................................937 773-8600
322 Wyndham Way Piqua (45356) *(G-16026)*

R K Industries Inc..419 523-5001
725 N Locust St Ottawa (45875) *(G-15666)*

R Kelly Inc...513 631-8488
7645 Production Dr Cincinnati (45237) *(G-4331)*

R L Baugher, Dvm, Warren *Also called Countryside Veterinary Service (G-18691)*

R L Fortney Management Inc (PA).....................440 716-4000
31269 Bradley Rd North Olmsted (44070) *(G-15307)*

R L King Insurance Agency..............................419 255-9947
7723 Airport Hwy Ste F Holland (43528) *(G-11908)*

R L Lipton Distributing LLC..............................800 321-6553
425 Victoria Rd Ste B Austintown (44515) *(G-860)*

R L Lipton Distributing Co................................216 475-4150
5900 Pennsylvania Ave Maple Heights (44137) *(G-13292)*

R L Morrissey & Assoc Inc (PA).......................440 498-3730
30450 Bruce Indus Pkwy Solon (44139) *(G-16889)*

R L O Inc (PA)..937 620-9998
466 Windsor Park Dr Dayton (45459) *(G-9724)*

R L S Corporation...740 773-1440
990 Eastern Ave Chillicothe (45601) *(G-2812)*

R L S Recycling, Chillicothe *Also called R L S Corporation (G-2812)*

R M X, Roseville *Also called Rmx Freight Systems Inc (G-16455)*

R N R Consulting, Cleveland *Also called Rahim Inc (G-6283)*

R P Cunningham DDS Inc.................................614 885-2022
7227 N High St Ste 1 Worthington (43085) *(G-19841)*

R P L Corporation...937 335-0021
1375 W Market St Troy (45373) *(G-18223)*

R P Marketing Public Relations....419 241-2221
1500 Timber Wolf Dr Holland (43528) *(G-11909)*
R S Sewing Inc....330 478-3360
1387 Clarendon Ave Sw # 10 Canton (44710) *(G-2449)*
R Square Inc....216 328-2077
6100 Oak Tree Blvd # 200 Cleveland (44131) *(G-6274)*
R T A, Lima *Also called Allen Cnty Regional Trnst Auth (G-12594)*
R T A, Dayton *Also called Greater Dyton Rgnal Trnst Auth (G-9474)*
R T Industries Inc (PA)....937 335-5784
110 Foss Way Troy (45373) *(G-18224)*
R T Industries Inc....937 339-8313
1625 Troy Sidney Rd Troy (45373) *(G-18225)*
R T Vernal Paving Inc....330 549-3189
11299 South Ave North Lima (44452) *(G-15274)*
R W Godbey Railroad Services....513 651-3800
2815 Spring Grove Ave Cincinnati (45225) *(G-4332)*
R W Sauder Inc....330 359-5440
2648 Us Rt 62 Winesburg (44690) *(G-19666)*
R W Sidley Incorporated (PA)....440 352-9343
436 Casement Ave Painesville (44077) *(G-15735)*
R W Sidley Incorporated....440 352-9343
436 Casement Ave Painesville (44077) *(G-15736)*
R W Sidley Incorporated....330 793-7374
3424 Oregon Ave Youngstown (44509) *(G-20176)*
R&F Erectors Inc....513 574-8273
5763 Snyder Rd Cincinnati (45247) *(G-4333)*
R&M Materials Handling Inc....937 328-5100
4501 Gateway Blvd Springfield (45502) *(G-17099)*
R+l Pramount Trnsp Systems Inc....937 382-1494
600 Gilliam Rd Wilmington (45177) *(G-19642)*
R-Cap Security LLC....216 761-6355
7800 Superior Ave Cleveland (44103) *(G-6275)*
R-K-Campf Transport, Salem *Also called R K Campf Corp (G-16556)*
R.dorsey & Company, Worthington *Also called R Dorsey & Company Inc (G-19840)*
Ra Consultants LLC....513 469-6600
10856 Kenwood Rd Blue Ash (45242) *(G-1635)*
RA Staff Company Inc....440 891-9900
16500 W Sprague Rd Cleveland (44130) *(G-6276)*
Racaza International LLC....614 973-9266
555 N Metro Pls Ste 245 Dublin (43017) *(G-10317)*
Raceway Foods Inc....513 932-2457
665 N Brdway Lbnon Rceway Lebanon (45036) *(G-12495)*
Rack & Ballauer Excvtg Co Inc....513 738-7000
11321 Paddys Run Rd Hamilton (45013) *(G-11635)*
Rack Seven Paving Co Inc....513 271-4863
7208 Main St Cincinnati (45244) *(G-4334)*
Racksquared LLC....614 737-8812
325 E Spring St Columbus (43215) *(G-8483)*
Raco Industries LLC (HQ)....513 984-2101
5481 Creek Rd Blue Ash (45242) *(G-1636)*
Raco Wireless LLC (HQ)....513 870-6480
4460 Carver Woods Dr # 100 Blue Ash (45242) *(G-1637)*
Racquet Club At Harper's Point, Cincinnati *Also called Towne Properties Assoc Inc (G-4618)*
RAD-Con Inc (PA)....440 871-5720
13001 Athens Ave Ste 300 Lakewood (44107) *(G-12361)*
Radebaugh-Fetzer Company....440 878-4700
22400 Ascoa Ct Strongsville (44149) *(G-17340)*
Radial South LP....678 584-4047
6360-6440 Port Rd Groveport (43125) *(G-11533)*
Radio Page Leasing, Cleveland *Also called Answering Service Inc (G-4984)*
Radio Promotions....513 381-5000
2518 Spring Grove Ave Cincinnati (45214) *(G-4335)*
Radio Seaway Inc....216 916-6100
1375 Euclid Ave Ste 450 Cleveland (44115) *(G-6277)*
Radio Station Wclv, Cleveland *Also called Radio Seaway Inc (G-6277)*
Radiohio Incorporated....614 460-3850
605 S Front St Fl 3 Columbus (43215) *(G-8484)*
Radiology Assoc Canton Inc....330 363-2842
2600 6th St Sw Canton (44710) *(G-2450)*
Radiology Department, Steubenville *Also called Trinity Health System (G-17176)*
Radiology Physicians Inc....614 717-9840
3769 Columbus Pike # 220 Delaware (43015) *(G-10001)*
Radiometer America Inc....440 871-8900
810 Sharon Dr Westlake (44145) *(G-19396)*
Radisson Eastlake, Eastlake *Also called Eastlake Lodging LLC (G-10429)*
Radisson Hotel Cleve....440 734-5060
25070 Country Club Blvd North Olmsted (44070) *(G-15308)*
Radisson Hotel Cleveland Gtwy....216 377-9000
651 Huron Rd E Cleveland (44115) *(G-6278)*
Radisson Inn, Cleveland *Also called Radisson Hotel Cleveland Gtwy (G-6278)*
Radix Wire Co (PA)....216 731-9191
26000 Lakeland Blvd Cleveland (44132) *(G-6279)*
Radix Wire Company, The, Cleveland *Also called Radix Wire Co (G-6279)*
Rae Ann West Lake, Westlake *Also called Rae-Ann Holdings Inc (G-19397)*
Rae-Ann Center, Cleveland *Also called Raeann Inc (G-6282)*
Rae-Ann Enterprises Inc....440 249-5092
27310 W Oviatt Rd Cleveland (44140) *(G-6280)*
Rae-Ann Geneva Skld Nrsng/Rehb, Geneva *Also called Raeann Inc (G-11245)*
Rae-Ann Holdings Inc....440 871-0500
28303 Detroit Rd Westlake (44145) *(G-19397)*
Rae-Ann Holdings Inc....440 871-5181
29505 Detroit Rd Cleveland (44145) *(G-6281)*
Rae-Ann Suburban, Cleveland *Also called Rae-Ann Enterprises Inc (G-6280)*
Rae-Ann Suburban Inc....440 871-5181
29505 Detroit Rd Westlake (44145) *(G-19398)*
Rae-Suburban, Cleveland *Also called Rae-Ann Holdings Inc (G-6281)*
Raeann Inc....440 466-5733
839 W Main St Geneva (44041) *(G-11245)*
Raeann Inc (PA)....440 871-5181
P.O. Box 40175 Bay Village (44140) *(G-6282)*
Raf Automation, Solon *Also called Fak Group Inc (G-16848)*
Raf Celina LLC....216 464-6626
1915-1955 Haveman Rd Celina (45822) *(G-2607)*
Rahal Land and Racing, Hilliard *Also called Team Rahal Inc (G-11820)*
Rahf IV Kent LLC....216 621-6060
1546 S Water St Kent (44240) *(G-12256)*
Rahim Inc....216 621-8977
1111 Superior Ave E # 1330 Cleveland (44114) *(G-6283)*
Rahn Dental Group Inc....937 435-0324
5660 Far Hills Ave Dayton (45429) *(G-9725)*
Railway Equipment Lsg & Maint, Solon *Also called RELAM Inc (G-16891)*
Railworks Track Services Inc....330 538-2261
1550 N Bailey Rd North Jackson (44451) *(G-15253)*
Rain Tree, The, Mansfield *Also called County of Richland (G-13152)*
Rainbow Bowling Lanes, Columbus *Also called Rainbow Lanes Inc (G-8487)*
Rainbow Connection Day Care, Mentor *Also called Delth Corporation (G-14041)*
Rainbow Data Systems Inc....937 431-8000
2358 Lakeview Dr Ste A Beavercreek (45431) *(G-1180)*
Rainbow Express Inc (PA)....614 444-5600
2000 S High St Fl 2 Columbus (43207) *(G-8485)*
Rainbow Flea Market Inc (PA)....614 291-3133
865 King Ave Columbus (43212) *(G-8486)*
Rainbow Lanes Inc....614 491-7155
3224 S High St Columbus (43207) *(G-8487)*
Rainbow Residentials LLC....330 819-4202
193 East Ave Ste 103 Tallmadge (44278) *(G-17485)*
Rainbow Station Day Care Inc (PA)....614 759-8667
226 Durand St Pickerington (43147) *(G-15967)*
Rainforest At Zoo, Cleveland *Also called Cleveland Metroparks (G-5270)*
Raintree Country Club Inc....330 699-3232
4350 Mayfair Rd Uniontown (44685) *(G-18384)*
Raise, Chesterland *Also called RES-Care Inc (G-2744)*
Raisin Rack Inc (PA)....614 882-5886
2545 W Schrock Rd Westerville (43081) *(G-19298)*
Raisin Rack Natural Food Mkt, Westerville *Also called Raisin Rack Inc (G-19298)*
Raitz Inc....513 769-1200
11402 Reading Rd Cincinnati (45241) *(G-4336)*
Rak Corrosion Control Inc....440 985-2171
7455 S Dewey Rd Amherst (44001) *(G-596)*
Rakesh Ranjan MD & Assoc Inc (PA)....216 375-9897
12395 Mccracken Rd Ste A Cleveland (44125) *(G-6284)*
Ram Construction Services....440 740-0100
100 Corporation Ctr # 4 Broadview Heights (44147) *(G-1844)*
Ram Construction Services of....513 297-1857
4710 Ashley Dr West Chester (45011) *(G-18990)*
Ram Resources, Dayton *Also called Ram Restoration LLC (G-9726)*
Ram Restoration LLC....937 347-7418
11125 Yankee St Ste A Dayton (45458) *(G-9726)*
Rama Inc....614 473-9888
2890 Airport Dr Columbus (43219) *(G-8488)*
Rama Tika Developers LLC....419 806-6446
719 Earick Rd Mansfield (44903) *(G-13232)*
Ramada Hotel & Conference Ctr, Toledo *Also called Westgate Limited Partnership (G-18155)*
Ramada Inn, Dublin *Also called Sb Hotel LLC (G-10329)*
Ramada Inn, Portsmouth *Also called Canter Inns Inc (G-16127)*
Ramada Inn, Sandusky *Also called Americas Best Value Inn (G-16575)*
Ramada Inn, Cleveland *Also called Moti Corporation (G-6014)*
Ramada Inn, Wadsworth *Also called Akron Inn Limited Partnership (G-18587)*
Ramada Inn, Wickliffe *Also called Inn At Wickliffe LLC (G-19465)*
Ramada Inn Cumberland Hotel, Cincinnati *Also called Cumberland Gap LLC (G-3386)*
Ramada Inn East - Airport, Columbus *Also called Broad Street Hotel Assoc LP (G-7076)*
Ramada Xenia, Xenia *Also called AK Group Hotels Inc (G-19888)*
Ramar-Genesis, Akron *Also called Community Drug Board Inc (G-150)*
Ramos Trucking Corporation....216 781-0770
2890 W 3rd St Cleveland (44113) *(G-6285)*
Ranac Computer Corporation....317 844-0141
3460 S Dixie Dr Moraine (45439) *(G-14692)*
Randall Mortgage Services (PA)....614 336-7948
655 Metro Pl S Ste 600 Dublin (43017) *(G-10318)*
Randall R Leab....330 689-6263
1895 Township Road 1215 Ashland (44805) *(G-685)*
Randolph & Assoc Real Estate, Columbus *Also called Randolph and Associates RE (G-8489)*
Randolph and Associates RE....614 269-8418
239 Buttonwood Ct Columbus (43230) *(G-8489)*
Randstad Engineering, Blue Ash *Also called Randstad Professional Us LP (G-1638)*
Randstad Professional Us LP....513 792-6658
4555 Lake Forest Dr # 300 Blue Ash (45242) *(G-1638)*

ALPHABETIC

Randstad Professionals Us LLC.................419 893-2400
1745 Indian Wood Cir # 150 Maumee (43537) *(G-13840)*
Randstad Professionals Us LP.................513 791-8600
5151 Pfeiffer Rd Ste 120 Blue Ash (45242) *(G-1639)*
Randstad Technologies LLC.................614 436-0961
8415 Pulsar Pl Ste 110 Columbus (43240) *(G-6832)*
Randstad Technologies LLC.................216 520-0206
6100 Oak Tree Blvd # 110 Independence (44131) *(G-12111)*
Randy L Fork Inc.................419 891-1230
1230 Conant St Maumee (43537) *(G-13841)*
Range Rsurces - Appalachia LLC.................330 866-3301
1748 Saltwell Rd Nw Dover (44622) *(G-10094)*
Rankin & Rankin Inc.................740 452-7575
806 Market St Zanesville (43701) *(G-20357)*
Ranpak Corp (PA).................440 354-4445
7990 Auburn Rd Concord Township (44077) *(G-8944)*
Rape Information & Counseling.................330 782-3936
535 Marmion Ave Youngstown (44502) *(G-20177)*
Rapid Aerial Imaging, Cincinnati *Also called Rapid Mortgage Company (G-4338)*
Rapid Delivery Service Co Inc.................513 733-0500
529 N Wayne Ave Cincinnati (45215) *(G-4337)*
Rapid Mortgage Company.................937 748-8888
7870 E Kemper Rd Ste 280 Cincinnati (45249) *(G-4338)*
Rapid Plumbing Inc.................513 575-1509
1407 State Route 28 Loveland (45140) *(G-13023)*
Rapids Nursing Homes Inc.................216 292-5706
24201 W 3rd St Grand Rapids (43522) *(G-11329)*
Rapier Electric Inc.................513 868-9087
4845 Augspurger Rd Hamilton (45011) *(G-11636)*
Rapistan Systems, Brecksville *Also called Siemens Industry Inc (G-1805)*
Raritan National, New Springfield *Also called Ruritan (G-14997)*
Rascal House Pizza, Cleveland *Also called S R Restaurant Corp (G-6356)*
Rassak LLC.................513 791-9453
7680 Demar Rd Cincinnati (45243) *(G-4339)*
Rathbone Group LLC.................800 870-5521
1100 Superior Ave E # 1850 Cleveland (44114) *(G-6286)*
Rave - Rlable Audio Video Elec, Dayton *Also called Reliable Contractors Inc (G-9730)*
Ravenna Assembly of God Inc.................330 297-1493
6401 State Route 14 Ravenna (44266) *(G-16260)*
RAVENWOOD HEALTH, Chardon *Also called Ravenwood Mental Hlth Ctr Inc (G-2709)*
Ravenwood Mental Health Center.................440 632-5355
16030 E High St Middlefield (44062) *(G-14275)*
Ravenwood Mental Hlth Ctr Inc (PA).................440 285-3568
12557 Ravenwood Dr Chardon (44024) *(G-2709)*
Rawiga Country Club Inc.................330 336-2220
10353 Rawiga Rd Seville (44273) *(G-16688)*
Ray Bertolini Trucking Co.................330 867-0666
2070 Wright Rd Akron (44320) *(G-397)*
Ray Fogg Building Methods Inc.................216 351-7976
981 Keynote Cir Ste 15 Cleveland (44131) *(G-6287)*
Ray Hamilton Companies.................513 641-5400
11083 Kenwood Rd Blue Ash (45242) *(G-1640)*
Ray Hamilton Company, Cincinnati *Also called Wnb Group LLC (G-4801)*
Ray Hamilton Company, Blue Ash *Also called Ray Hamilton Companies (G-1640)*
Ray St Clair Roofing Inc.................513 874-1234
3810 Port Union Rd Fairfield (45014) *(G-10773)*
Raymond A Greiner DDS Inc.................440 951-6688
7553 Center St Mentor (44060) *(G-14100)*
Raymond James Fincl Svcs Inc.................513 287-6777
255 E 5th St Ste 2210 Cincinnati (45202) *(G-4340)*
Raymond James Fincl Svcs Inc.................419 586-5121
225 N Main St Celina (45822) *(G-2608)*
Raymond Recepton House.................614 276-6127
3860 Trabue Rd Columbus (43228) *(G-8490)*
Raymond Storage Concepts Inc (PA).................513 891-7290
5480 Creek Rd Unit 1 Blue Ash (45242) *(G-1641)*
Rbm Environmental and Cnstr.................419 693-5840
4526 Bayshore Rd Oregon (43616) *(G-15607)*
Rbp Atlanta LLC.................614 246-2522
4100 Regent St Ste G Columbus (43219) *(G-8491)*
Rcf Group, West Chester *Also called River City Furniture LLC (G-18994)*
Rchp - Wilmington LLC (PA).................937 382-6611
610 W Main St Wilmington (45177) *(G-19643)*
Rcr East Inc (PA).................513 793-2090
6922 Ohio Ave Cincinnati (45236) *(G-4341)*
Rcr East Inc.................513 231-8292
6164 Salem Rd Cincinnati (45230) *(G-4342)*
Rcs Enterprises Inc.................614 337-8520
139 W Johnstown Rd Columbus (43230) *(G-8492)*
RCT Engineering Inc (PA).................561 684-7534
24880 Shaker Blvd Beachwood (44122) *(G-1099)*
Rcwc Col Inc.................614 564-9344
955 W 5th Ave Ste 7 Columbus (43212) *(G-8493)*
Rde System Corp.................513 933-8000
986 Winzig Ln Lebanon (45036) *(G-12496)*
Rde System Corporation.................513 933-8000
986 Windsor Ave Dayton (45402) *(G-9727)*
RDF Logistics, Lorain *Also called RDF Trucking Corporation (G-12940)*
RDF Trucking Corporation.................440 282-9060
7425 Industrial Pkwy Dr Lorain (44053) *(G-12940)*
Rdi Corporation.................513 524-3320
110 S Locust St Ste A Oxford (45056) *(G-15688)*

Rdl Architects Inc.................216 752-4300
16102 Chagrin Blvd # 200 Cleveland (44120) *(G-6288)*
Rdp Foodservice Ltd.................614 261-5661
4200 Parkway Ct Hilliard (43026) *(G-11811)*
Rdsi Banking Systems, Defiance *Also called Rurbanc Data Services Inc (G-9938)*
RE Middleton Cnstr LLC.................513 398-9255
503 W Main St Mason (45040) *(G-13632)*
Re/Max, Cincinnati *Also called Preferred Real Estate Group (G-4269)*
Re/Max.................937 477-4997
51 Plum St Ste 220 Beavercreek (45440) *(G-1234)*
Re/Max Consultant Group.................614 855-2822
6650 Walnut St New Albany (43054) *(G-14869)*
RE/Max Experts Realty.................330 364-7355
720 N Wooster Ave Dover (44622) *(G-10095)*
RE/Max Real Estate Experts.................440 255-6505
8444 Mentor Ave Mentor (44060) *(G-14101)*
REA & Associates Inc.................330 722-8222
694 E Washington St Medina (44256) *(G-13992)*
REA & Associates Inc (PA).................330 339-6651
419 W High Ave New Philadelphia (44663) *(G-14977)*
REA & Associates Inc.................419 331-1040
2579 Shawnee Rd Lima (45806) *(G-12792)*
REA & Associates Inc.................330 674-6055
212 N Washington St # 100 Millersburg (44654) *(G-14489)*
REA & Associates Inc.................440 266-0077
122 4th St Nw New Philadelphia (44663) *(G-14978)*
REA & Associates Inc.................614 889-8725
5775 Perimeter Dr Ste 200 Dublin (43017) *(G-10319)*
Reading Family Practice.................513 563-6934
9400 Reading Rd Ste 2 Cincinnati (45215) *(G-4343)*
Reading Rock Residential LLC.................513 874-4770
4677 Devitt Dr West Chester (45246) *(G-19075)*
Ready Set Grow.................614 855-5100
5200 New Albany Rd New Albany (43054) *(G-14870)*
Reagan Elementary School, Ashland *Also called Ashland City School District (G-646)*
Real America Inc.................216 261-1177
24555 Lake Shore Blvd Cleveland (44123) *(G-6289)*
Real Art Design Group Inc (PA).................937 223-9955
520 E 1st St Dayton (45402) *(G-9728)*
Real Estate, Cincinnati *Also called Camden Management Inc (G-3110)*
Real Estate Capital Fund LLC.................216 491-3990
20820 Chagrin Blvd # 300 Cleveland (44122) *(G-6290)*
Real Estate II Inc.................937 390-3119
1140 E Home Rd Springfield (45503) *(G-17100)*
Real Estate Investors Mgt Inc (PA).................614 777-2444
4041 Roberts Rd Columbus (43228) *(G-8494)*
Real Estate Mortgage Corp.................440 356-5373
200 Jackson Dr Chagrin Falls (44022) *(G-2653)*
Real Estate Showcase.................740 389-2000
731 E Center St Marion (43302) *(G-13454)*
Real Living Title Agency Ltd.................440 974-7810
7470b Auburn Rd Painesville (44077) *(G-15737)*
Real Living Title Agency Ltd (PA).................614 459-7400
77 E Nationwide Blvd Columbus (43215) *(G-8495)*
Real Property Management, Columbus *Also called Hidden Lake Condominiums (G-7746)*
Real Property Management Inc (PA).................614 766-6500
5550 Blazer Pkwy Ste 175 Dublin (43017) *(G-10320)*
Real Time Systems, Cincinnati *Also called Tyco International MGT Co LLC (G-4658)*
Realm Technologies LLC.................513 297-3095
954 Greengate Dr Lebanon (45036) *(G-12497)*
Realty Corporation of America.................216 522-0020
3048 Meadowbrook Blvd Cleveland Heights (44118) *(G-6722)*
Rebiz LLC.................844 467-3249
1925 Saint Clair Ave Ne Cleveland (44114) *(G-6291)*
Rebman Recreation Inc.................440 282-6761
5300 Oberlin Ave Lorain (44053) *(G-12941)*
Rebman Truck Service Inc.................419 589-8161
1004 Vanderbilt Rd Mansfield (44904) *(G-13233)*
Rec Center.................330 721-6900
855 Weymouth Rd Medina (44256) *(G-13993)*
Recaro Child Safety LLC.................248 904-1570
4921 Para Dr Cincinnati (45237) *(G-4344)*
Receivable MGT Svcs Corp.................330 659-1000
4836 Brecksville Rd Richfield (44286) *(G-16373)*
Recker & Boerger Appliances, West Chester *Also called Recker and Boerger Inc (G-19076)*
Recker and Boerger Inc.................513 942-9663
10115 Transportation Way West Chester (45246) *(G-19076)*
Recker Brothers, Genoa *Also called James Recker (G-11257)*
Recker Consulting LLC.................513 924-5500
6871 Steger Dr Cincinnati (45237) *(G-4345)*
Reco Equipment Inc (PA).................740 619-8071
41245 Reco Rd Belmont (43718) *(G-1395)*
Reconstructive Ortho Sports, Cincinnati *Also called Reconstructive Orthopedics (G-4346)*
Reconstructive Orthopedics (PA).................513 793-3933
10615 Montgomery Rd # 200 Cincinnati (45242) *(G-4346)*
Record Express LLC.................513 685-7329
4295 Armstrong Blvd Batavia (45103) *(G-1008)*
Recording Workshop.................740 663-1000
455 Massieville Rd Chillicothe (45601) *(G-2813)*
Recording Workshop, The, Chillicothe *Also called Recording Workshop (G-2813)*
Recovery & Prevention Resource.................740 369-6811
118 Stover Dr Delaware (43015) *(G-10002)*

Recovery Center 740 687-4500
  201 S Columbus St Lancaster (43130) *(G-12429)*
Recovery One LLC 614 336-4207
  3240 Henderson Rd Ste A Columbus (43220) *(G-8496)*
Recovery Resources (PA) 216 431-4131
  3950 Chester Ave Cleveland (44114) *(G-6292)*
Recovery Resources 216 431-4131
  4269 Pearl Rd Ste 300 Cleveland (44109) *(G-6293)*
Recovery Works Healing Ctr LLC 937 384-0580
  100 Elmwood Park Dr West Carrollton (45449) *(G-18856)*
Recreation Dept, Cleveland *Also called City of Independence (G-5203)*
Recreational Golf Inc 513 677-0347
  203 Glen Lake Rd Loveland (45140) *(G-13024)*
Recreational Sports & Svc, Berea *Also called Baldwin Wallace University (G-1413)*
Recruiting Department, Dayton *Also called Greater Dyton Rgnal Trnst Auth (G-9475)*
Recruiting Department, Dayton *Also called Greater Dyton Rgnal Trnst Auth (G-9476)*
Recruitmilitary, Loveland *Also called Rvet Operating LLC (G-13025)*
Recycled Systems Furniture Inc 614 880-9110
  401 E Wilson Bridge Rd Worthington (43085) *(G-19842)*
Recycling Services Inc (PA) 419 381-7762
  3940 Technology Dr Maumee (43537) *(G-13842)*
Red Barn, Willoughby *Also called Red Oak Camp (G-19565)*
Red Brick Property MGT LLC 513 524-9340
  21 N Poplar St Oxford (45056) *(G-15689)*
Red Capital Advisors, Columbus *Also called Red Capital Partners LLC (G-8498)*
Red Capital Markets LLC 614 857-1400
  10 W Broad St Ste 1800 Columbus (43215) *(G-8497)*
Red Capital Partners LLC (HQ) 614 857-1400
  10 W Broad St Fl 8 Columbus (43215) *(G-8498)*
Red Carpet Car Wash Inc 330 477-5772
  4546 Tuscarawas St W Canton (44708) *(G-2451)*
Red Carpet Health Care Center 740 439-4401
  8420 Georgetown Rd Cambridge (43725) *(G-2081)*
Red Carpet Janitorial Service (PA) 513 242-7575
  3478 Hauck Rd Ste D Cincinnati (45241) *(G-4347)*
Red Dog Pet Resort & Spa 513 733-3647
  4975 Babson Pl Cincinnati (45227) *(G-4348)*
Red Mortgage Capital LLC (HQ) 614 857-1400
  10 W Broad St Ste 1800 Columbus (43215) *(G-8499)*
Red Oak Camp 440 256-0716
  9057 Kirtland Chardon Rd Willoughby (44094) *(G-19565)*
Red Robin Gourmet Burgers Inc 330 305-1080
  6522 Strip Ave Nw Canton (44720) *(G-2452)*
Red Roof Inn, Columbus *Also called Fmw Rri Opco LLC (G-7599)*
Red Roof Inns Inc (HQ) 614 744-2600
  7815 Walton Pkwy New Albany (43054) *(G-14871)*
Red Roof Inns Inc 614 224-6539
  111 Nationwide Plz Columbus (43215) *(G-8500)*
Red Roof Inns Inc 440 892-7920
  29595 Clemens Rd Cleveland (44145) *(G-6294)*
Red Roof Inns Inc 740 695-4057
  68301 Red Roof Ln Saint Clairsville (43950) *(G-16503)*
Red Roof Inns Inc 440 243-5166
  17555 Bagley Rd Cleveland (44130) *(G-6295)*
Red Squirrel, Fairfield Township *Also called Robiden Inc (G-10814)*
Red Tail Golf Club, Avon *Also called Caravon Golf Company Ltd (G-870)*
Reddy Electric Co 937 372-8205
  1145 Bellbrook Ave Xenia (45385) *(G-19922)*
Redefine Enterprises LLC 330 952-2024
  3839 Pearl Rd Medina (44256) *(G-13994)*
Redwood Living Inc 216 360-9441
  7510 E Pleasant Valley Rd Independence (44131) *(G-12112)*
Reece-Campbell Inc 513 542-4600
  10839 Chester Rd Cincinnati (45246) *(G-4349)*
Reed Hartman Corporate Center 513 984-3030
  10925 Reed Hartman Hwy # 200 Blue Ash (45242) *(G-1642)*
Reese Pyle Drake & Meyer (PA) 740 345-3431
  36 N 2nd St Newark (43055) *(G-15095)*
Refectory Restaurant Inc 614 451-9774
  1092 Bethel Rd Columbus (43220) *(G-8501)*
Reflections Hair Studio Inc 330 725-5782
  3605 Medina Rd Medina (44256) *(G-13995)*
Reflektions Ltd 614 560-6994
  560 Sunbury Rd Ste 1 Delaware (43015) *(G-10003)*
Refrigeration Systems Company (HQ) 614 263-0913
  1770 Genessee Ave Columbus (43211) *(G-8502)*
Refuse / Recycling, Athens *Also called Athens-Hcking Cnty Recycl Ctrs (G-770)*
Regal Carpet Center Inc 216 475-1844
  5411 Northfield Rd Cleveland (44146) *(G-6296)*
Regal Carpet Co, Cleveland *Also called Regal Carpet Center Inc (G-6296)*
Regal Cinema South 10, Youngstown *Also called Regal Cinemas Inc (G-20178)*
Regal Cinemas Inc 614 853-0850
  1800 Georgesville Sq Columbus (43228) *(G-8503)*
Regal Cinemas Inc 330 723-4416
  200 W Reagan Pkwy Medina (44256) *(G-13996)*
Regal Cinemas Inc 440 975-8820
  36655 Euclid Ave Willoughby (44094) *(G-19566)*
Regal Cinemas Inc 937 431-9418
  2651 Fairfield Cmns Beavercreek (45431) *(G-1181)*
Regal Cinemas Inc 440 934-3356
  5500 Abbe Rd Elyria (44035) *(G-10558)*

Regal Cinemas Inc 330 666-9373
  4020 Medina Rd Ste 100 Akron (44333) *(G-398)*
Regal Cinemas Inc 440 871-4546
  30147 Detroit Rd Westlake (44145) *(G-19399)*
Regal Cinemas Inc 330 758-0503
  7420 South Ave Youngstown (44512) *(G-20178)*
Regal Cinemas Inc 330 633-7668
  1210 Independence Ave Akron (44310) *(G-399)*
Regal Cinemas Corporation 513 770-0713
  5500 Deerfield Blvd Mason (45040) *(G-13633)*
Regal Cinemas Corporation 440 720-0500
  631 Richmond Rd Richmond Heights (44143) *(G-16393)*
Regal Cinemas Inc 440 891-9845
  18348 Bagley Rd Cleveland (44130) *(G-6297)*
Regal Entertainment Group, Columbus *Also called Regal Cinemas Inc (G-8503)*
Regal Entertainment Group, Westlake *Also called Regal Cinemas Inc (G-19399)*
Regal Hospitality LLC 614 436-0004
  201 Hutchinson Ave Columbus (43235) *(G-8504)*
Regal Plumbing & Heating Co 937 492-2894
  9303 State Route 29 W Sidney (45365) *(G-16795)*
Regency Hospital Cincinnati 513 862-4700
  10500 Montgomery Rd Cincinnati (45242) *(G-4350)*
Regency Hospital Toledo LLC 419 318-5700
  5220 Alexis Rd Sylvania (43560) *(G-17445)*
Regency Leasing Co LLC 614 542-3100
  2000 Regency Manor Cir Columbus (43207) *(G-8505)*
Regency Manor Rehab, Columbus *Also called Regency Leasing Co LLC (G-8505)*
Regency Office Furniture, Akron *Also called Regency Seating Inc (G-400)*
Regency Park 330 682-2273
  230 S Crown Hill Rd Orrville (44667) *(G-15645)*
Regency Park Eye Associates (PA) 419 882-0588
  1000 Regency Ct Ste 100 Toledo (43623) *(G-17997)*
Regency Park Nursing & Rehab 330 682-2273
  230 S Crown Hill Rd Orrville (44667) *(G-15646)*
Regency Roofing Companies Inc (PA) 330 468-1021
  576 Highland Rd E Ste A Macedonia (44056) *(G-13081)*
Regency Seating Inc 330 848-3700
  2375 Romig Rd Akron (44320) *(G-400)*
Regency Technologies LLC, Solon *Also called RSR Partners LLC (G-16894)*
Regency Windows Corporation 330 963-4077
  2288 E Aurora Rd Twinsburg (44087) *(G-18310)*
Regency, The, Cincinnati *Also called 2444 Mdson Rd Cndo Owners Assn (G-2880)*
Regensis Stna Training Program 614 849-0115
  415 E Mound St Columbus (43215) *(G-8506)*
Regent Electric Inc 419 476-8333
  5235 Tractor Rd Toledo (43612) *(G-17998)*
Regent Systems Inc 937 640-8010
  7590 Paragon Rd Dayton (45459) *(G-9729)*
Region 2b, Maumee *Also called International Union United Au (G-13804)*
Region 8, Cleveland *Also called National Labor Relations Board (G-6047)*
Regional Express Inc 516 458-3514
  4615 W Streetsboro Rd Richfield (44286) *(G-16374)*
Regional Food Program, Logan *Also called Tri-County Community Act (G-12857)*
Regional Imaging Cons Corp 330 726-9006
  819 Mckay Ct Ste B103 Youngstown (44512) *(G-20179)*
Regional Income Tax Agency (PA) 800 860-7482
  10107 Brecksville Rd Brecksville (44141) *(G-1801)*
Registered Contractors Inc 440 205-0873
  8425 Station St Mentor (44060) *(G-14102)*
Rehab & Nursing Ctr Sprng Crk, Dayton *Also called 5440 Charlesgate Rd Oper LLC (G-9195)*
Rehab Center 330 297-2770
  6847 N Chestnut St Ravenna (44266) *(G-16261)*
Rehab Continuum Inc 513 984-8070
  10921 Reed Hartman Hwy # 133 Blue Ash (45242) *(G-1643)*
Rehab Continuum, The, Blue Ash *Also called Rehab Continuum Inc (G-1643)*
Rehab Continuum, The, Blue Ash *Also called Counseling Source Inc (G-1539)*
Rehab Medical Inc 513 381-3740
  1150 W 8th St Ste 110 Cincinnati (45203) *(G-4351)*
Rehab Nursing Ctr At Firelands, New London *Also called 204 W Main Street Oper Co LLC (G-14930)*
Rehab Resources 513 474-4123
  8595 Beechmont Ave # 204 Cincinnati (45255) *(G-4352)*
Rehabcare Group MGT Svcs Inc 740 779-6732
  230 Cherry St Chillicothe (45601) *(G-2814)*
Rehabcare Group MGT Svcs Inc 740 356-6160
  1202 18th St Portsmouth (45662) *(G-16163)*
Rehabcenter, Ravenna *Also called Rehab Center (G-16261)*
Rehabilitation Aquatics 419 843-2500
  3130 Central Park W Ste A Toledo (43617) *(G-17999)*
Rehabilitation Services, Columbus *Also called Ohio Department of Health (G-8241)*
REHABILITATION SERVICES OF NOR, Mansfield *Also called Center For Individual and Fmly (G-13150)*
Rehabltation Corectn Ohio Dept 614 752-0800
  1030 Alum Creek Dr Columbus (43209) *(G-8507)*
Rehablttion Ctr At Mrietta Mem 740 374-1407
  401 Matthew St Marietta (45750) *(G-13375)*
Rehablttion Ctr At Mrtta Mmori, Marietta *Also called Rehablttion Ctr At Mrietta Mem (G-13375)*

A
L
P
H
A
B
E
T
I
C

Rehmann LLC 419 865-8118
7124 W Central Ave Toledo (43617) *(G-18000)*

Rei Telecom Inc (PA) 614 255-3100
7890 Robinett Way Canal Winchester (43110) *(G-2116)*

Reichard Industries, LLC, Columbiana *Also called Columbiana Service Company LLC (G-6785)*

Reid Asset Management Company 216 642-3223
9555 Rockside Rd Ste 350 Cleveland (44125) *(G-6298)*

Reid Physician Associates Inc 937 456-4400
109b Wash Jackson Rd Eaton (45320) *(G-10461)*

Reid Physicians Associates, Eaton *Also called Reid Physician Associates Inc (G-10461)*

Reilly Painting Co 216 371-8160
1899 S Taylor Rd Cleveland Heights (44118) *(G-6723)*

Reilly Sweeping Inc 440 786-8400
120350 Hannan Pkwy Cleveland (44146) *(G-6299)*

Reimer Law Co 440 600-5500
30455 Solon Rd Ste 1 Solon (44139) *(G-16890)*

Reinhart Foodservice LLC 513 421-9184
535 Shepherd Ave Cincinnati (45215) *(G-4353)*

Reinnovations Contracting Inc 330 505-9035
3711 Main St Mineral Ridge (44440) *(G-14511)*

Reis Trucking Inc 513 353-1960
10080 Valley Junction Rd Cleves (45002) *(G-6734)*

Reisenfeld & Assoc Lpa LLC (PA) 513 322-7000
3962 Red Bank Rd Cincinnati (45227) *(G-4354)*

Reitter Stucco Inc 614 291-2212
1100 King Ave Columbus (43212) *(G-8508)*

Reitter Wall Systems Inc 614 545-4444
1178 Joyce Ave Columbus (43219) *(G-8509)*

Reladyne LLC (HQ) 513 489-6000
8280 Montgomery Rd # 101 Cincinnati (45236) *(G-4355)*

RELAM Inc 440 232-3354
7695 Bond St Solon (44139) *(G-16891)*

Relay Gear Ltd 888 735-2943
3738 Paragon Dr Columbus (43228) *(G-8510)*

Relay Rail Div., Mineral Ridge *Also called L B Foster Company (G-14510)*

Relentless Recovery Inc 216 621-8333
1898 Scranton Rd Uppr Cleveland (44113) *(G-6300)*

Reliability First Corporation 216 503-0600
3 Summit Park Dr Ste 600 Cleveland (44131) *(G-6301)*

Reliable Appl Installation Inc 614 817-1801
3755 Interchange Rd Columbus (43204) *(G-8511)*

Reliable Appl Installation Inc 614 246-6840
3736 Paragon Dr Columbus (43228) *(G-8512)*

Reliable Appl Installation Inc 330 784-7474
2850 Gilchrist Rd Ste 1b Akron (44305) *(G-401)*

Reliable Contractors Inc 937 433-0262
94 Compark Rd Ste 200 Dayton (45459) *(G-9730)*

Reliable Polymer Services LP 800 321-0954
300 1st St Wadsworth (44281) *(G-18614)*

Reliable Rnners Curier Svc Inc 440 578-1011
8624 Station St Mentor (44060) *(G-14103)*

Reliable Trnsp Solutions LLC 937 378-2700
642 E State St Georgetown (45121) *(G-11273)*

Reliance Financial Services NA 419 783-8007
401 Clinton St Defiance (43512) *(G-9936)*

Reliant Capital Solutions LLC 614 452-6100
670 Cross Pointe Rd Gahanna (43230) *(G-11141)*

Reliant Recovery Solutions, Gahanna *Also called Reliant Capital Solutions LLC (G-11141)*

Relmec Mechanical LLC 216 391-1030
4975 Hamilton Ave Cleveland (44114) *(G-6302)*

Relx Inc 937 865-6800
9443 Springboro Pike Miamisburg (45342) *(G-14209)*

Relx Inc 937 865-6800
9443 Springboro Pike Miamisburg (45342) *(G-14210)*

REM Corp 740 828-2601
26 E 3rd St Frazeysburg (43822) *(G-11050)*

REM Electronics Supply Co Inc (PA) 330 373-1300
525 S Park Ave Warren (44483) *(G-18738)*

REM Ohio Waivered Services, Reynoldsburg *Also called REM-Ohio Inc (G-16325)*

REM-Ohio Inc 937 335-8267
721 Lincoln Ave Troy (45373) *(G-18226)*

REM-Ohio Inc 440 986-3337
214 W Main St South Amherst (44001) *(G-16922)*

REM-Ohio Inc 330 644-9730
470 Portage Lakes Dr # 207 Coventry Township (44319) *(G-9041)*

REM-Ohio Inc 614 367-1370
6402 E Main St Ste 103 Reynoldsburg (43068) *(G-16325)*

Remax Homesource 440 951-2500
3500 Kaiser Ct Ste 300 Willoughby (44095) *(G-19567)*

Remax Results Plus, Milford *Also called Plus Realty Cincinnati Inc (G-14425)*

Remax Traditions, Chagrin Falls *Also called Western Reserve Realty LLC (G-2659)*

Remco Security, Youngstown *Also called R C Enterprises Inc (G-20175)*

Remedi Seniorcare of Ohio LLC (HQ) 800 232-4239
962 S Dorset Rd Troy (45373) *(G-18227)*

Remedy Intelligent Staffing, West Chester *Also called Select Staffing (G-19001)*

Remel Products, Oakwood Village *Also called Thermo Fisher Scientific Inc (G-15495)*

Remelt Sources Incorporated (PA) 216 289-4555
27151 Tungsten Rd Cleveland (44132) *(G-6303)*

Reminger Co LPA (PA) 216 687-1311
101 W Prospect Ave # 1400 Cleveland (44115) *(G-6304)*

Reminger Co LPA 419 254-1311
405 Madison Ave Ste 2300 Toledo (43604) *(G-18001)*

Reminger Co LPA 614 228-1311
65 E State St Ste 400 Columbus (43215) *(G-8513)*

Reminger Co LPA 513 721-1311
525 Vine St Ste 1700 Cincinnati (45202) *(G-4356)*

Remington Steel, Springfield *Also called Westfield Steel Inc (G-17136)*

Remote Support Services, Green Springs *Also called Wynn-Reeth Inc (G-11357)*

Remtec Automation LLC 877 759-8151
6049 Hi Tek Ct Mason (45040) *(G-13634)*

Remtec Engineering 513 860-4299
6049 Hi Tek Ct Mason (45040) *(G-13635)*

Renaissance Cleveland Hotel, Cleveland *Also called Skyline Clvland Rnaissance LLC (G-6414)*

Renaissance Home Health Care 216 662-8702
5311 Northfield Rd Bedford (44146) *(G-1301)*

Renaissance Hotel Operating Co 216 696-5600
24 Public Sq Fl 1 Cleveland (44113) *(G-6305)*

Renaissance House Inc 419 663-1316
48 Executive Dr Ste 1 Norwalk (44857) *(G-15454)*

Renaissance House Inc 419 626-1110
158 E Market St Ste 805 Sandusky (44870) *(G-16634)*

RENAISSANCE, THE, Olmsted Twp *Also called Olmsted Residence Corporation (G-15539)*

Renal Life Link Inc 937 383-3338
1675 Alex Dr Wilmington (45177) *(G-19644)*

Rendigs Fry Kiely & Dennis LLP (PA) 513 381-9200
600 Vine St Ste 2602 Cincinnati (45202) *(G-4357)*

Renhill Stffing Srvces-America (HQ) 419 254-2800
28315 Kensington Ln Ste B Perrysburg (43551) *(G-15912)*

Renier Construction Corp 614 866-4580
2164 Citygate Dr Columbus (43219) *(G-8514)*

Renner Kenner Grieve Bobak (PA) 330 376-1242
106 S Main St Akron (44308) *(G-402)*

Renner Otto Boiselle & Sklar 216 621-1113
1621 Euclid Ave Ste 1900 Cleveland (44115) *(G-6306)*

Rennie & Jonson Montgomery 513 241-4722
36 E 7th St Ste 2100 Cincinnati (45202) *(G-4358)*

Renovo Neural Inc 216 445-4202
10000 Cedar Ave Cleveland (44106) *(G-6307)*

Rent To Own, Bainbridge *Also called Countryside Rentals Inc (G-930)*

Rent-A-Center Inc 330 337-1107
2870 E State St Ste 500 Salem (44460) *(G-16557)*

Rent-A-Center Inc 419 382-8585
3418 Glendale Ave Toledo (43614) *(G-18002)*

Rent-N-Roll 513 528-6929
7841 Laurel Ave Cincinnati (45243) *(G-4359)*

Rental Concepts Inc (PA) 216 525-3870
6450 Rockside Woods Blvd Cleveland (44131) *(G-6308)*

Rentech Solutions Inc 216 398-1111
4934 Campbell Rd Ste C Willoughby (44094) *(G-19568)*

Renthotel Dayton LLC 937 461-4700
11 S Ludlow St Dayton (45402) *(G-9731)*

Rentokil Initial PLC, Youngstown *Also called Rentokil North America Inc (G-20180)*

Rentokil North America Inc 330 797-9090
5560 W Webb Rd Youngstown (44515) *(G-20180)*

Rentokil North America Inc 216 328-0700
1240 Valley Belt Rd Brooklyn Heights (44131) *(G-1879)*

Rentokil North America Inc 216 328-0700
1240 Valley Belt Rd Brooklyn Heights (44131) *(G-1880)*

Rentokil North America Inc 614 837-0099
6300 Commerce Center Dr G Groveport (43125) *(G-11534)*

Rentokil North America Inc 614 837-0099
6300 Cmmerce Ctr Dr Ste G Canal Winchester (43110) *(G-2117)*

Rentwear Inc 330 535-2301
7944 Whipple Ave Nw Canton (44720) *(G-2453)*

Rentz Corp (PA) 937 434-2774
759 Grants Trl Dayton (45459) *(G-9732)*

REO Network Inc 740 374-8900
203 Pike St Marietta (45750) *(G-13376)*

Repro Acquisition Company LLC 216 738-3800
25001 Rockwell Dr Cleveland (44117) *(G-6309)*

Reprocenter, The, Cleveland *Also called Repro Acquisition Company LLC (G-6309)*

Reproductive Gynecology Inc 330 375-7722
95 Arch St Ste 250 Akron (44304) *(G-403)*

Reproductive Gynecology Inc 330 452-6010
2600 Tuscarawas St W # 560 Canton (44708) *(G-2454)*

Reps Resource LLC 513 874-0500
9120 Union Centre Blvd # 300 West Chester (45069) *(G-18991)*

Reptiles By Mack LLC 937 372-9570
1332 Burnett Dr Xenia (45385) *(G-19923)*

Republic Bank 513 793-7666
9683 Kenwood Rd Blue Ash (45242) *(G-1644)*

Republic N&T Railroad Inc 330 438-5826
2633 8th St Ne Canton (44704) *(G-2455)*

Republic Parking System Inc 937 415-0016
3600 Terminal Rd Vandalia (45377) *(G-18540)*

Republic Services, Solon *Also called Browning-Ferris Industries LLC (G-16830)*

Republic Services Inc 937 593-3566
2946 Us Rt 68 N Bellefontaine (43311) *(G-1361)*

Republic Services Inc 330 536-8013
8100 S State Line Rd Lowellville (44436) *(G-13042)*

Republic Services Inc 419 925-4592
6141 Depweg Rd Celina (45822) *(G-2609)*

Republic Services Inc 419 626-2454
4005 Tiffin Ave Sandusky (44870) *(G-16635)*

Republic Services Inc 216 741-4013
8123 Jones Rd Cleveland (44105) *(G-6310)*

Republic Services Inc 216 741-4013
8123 Jones Rd Cleveland (44105) *(G-6311)*

Republic Services Inc 440 458-5191
40195 Butternut Ridge Rd Elyria (44035) *(G-10559)*

Republic Services Inc 330 830-9050
2800 Erie St S Massillon (44646) *(G-13722)*

Republic Services Inc 330 793-7676
450 Thacher Ln Youngstown (44515) *(G-20181)*

Republic Services Inc 330 793-7676
3870 Hendricks Rd Youngstown (44515) *(G-20182)*

Republic Services Inc 330 793-7676
3870 Henricks Rd Youngstown (44515) *(G-20183)*

Republic Services Inc 419 636-5109
12359 County Road G Bryan (43506) *(G-1973)*

Republic Services Inc 440 774-4060
43502 Oberlin Elyria Rd Oberlin (44074) *(G-15518)*

Republic Services Inc 513 554-0237
10751 Evendale Dr Cincinnati (45241) *(G-4360)*

Republic Services Inc 937 268-8110
1577 W River Rd Dayton (45417) *(G-9733)*

Republic Services Inc 567 712-6634
956 S Broadway St Lima (45804) *(G-12729)*

Republic Services Inc 614 308-3000
933 Frank Rd Columbus (43223) *(G-8515)*

Republic Services Inc 740 969-4487
933 Frank Rd Columbus (43223) *(G-8516)*

Republic Services Inc 800 247-3644
2800 Erie St S Massillon (44646) *(G-13723)*

Republic Services Inc 330 434-9183
964 Hazel St Akron (44305) *(G-404)*

Republic Services Inc 800 331-0988
97 Hubbard Ave Gallipolis (45631) *(G-11212)*

Republic Services Inc 419 396-3581
11164 Co Rd 4 Carey (43316) *(G-2546)*

Republic Services Inc 419 635-2367
530 N Camp Rd Port Clinton (43452) *(G-16115)*

Republic Services Inc 419 726-9465
6196 Hagman Rd Toledo (43612) *(G-18003)*

Republic Services Inc 937 492-3470
1600 Riverside Dr Sidney (45365) *(G-16796)*

Republic Telcom Worldwide LLC 330 244-8285
8000 Freedom Ave Nw North Canton (44720) *(G-15230)*

Republic Telcom Worldwide LLC (HQ) 330 966-4586
3939 Everhard Rd Nw Canton (44709) *(G-2456)*

Republican Headquarters 330 343-6131
203 S Wooster Ave Dover (44622) *(G-10096)*

Republican State Central Execu 614 228-2481
211 S 5th St Columbus (43215) *(G-8517)*

Req/Jqh Holdings Inc (PA) 513 891-1066
4243 Hunt Rd Ste 2 Blue Ash (45242) *(G-1645)*

Req/Jqh Holdings Inc 937 432-0000
3100 Contemporary Ln Miamisburg (45342) *(G-14211)*

RES Care, Waverly Also called RES-Care Inc *(G-18823)*

RES Care OH, Carrollton Also called RES-Care Inc *(G-2575)*

RES-Care Inc 740 782-1476
39555 National Rd Bethesda (43719) *(G-1457)*

RES-Care Inc 740 526-0285
66387 Airport Rd Saint Clairsville (43950) *(G-16504)*

RES-Care Inc 440 729-2432
8228 Mayfield Rd Ste 5b Chesterland (44026) *(G-2744)*

RES-Care Inc 513 858-4550
7908 Cincinnati Dayton Rd West Chester (45069) *(G-18992)*

RES-Care Inc 740 968-0181
41743 Mount Hope Rd Flushing (43977) *(G-10981)*

RES-Care Inc 330 627-7552
520 S Lisbon St Carrollton (44615) *(G-2575)*

RES-Care Inc 740 941-1178
212 Saint Anns Ln Waverly (45690) *(G-18823)*

RES-Care Inc 419 435-6620
1016 Dillon Cir Fostoria (44830) *(G-11010)*

RES-Care Inc 740 446-7549
240 3rd Ave Gallipolis (45631) *(G-11213)*

RES-Care Inc 330 453-4144
2915 33rd St Ne Canton (44705) *(G-2457)*

Rescare Ohio Inc 330 479-9841
2821 Whipple Ave Nw # 100 Canton (44708) *(G-2458)*

Rescare Ohio Inc 740 625-6873
80 Miller St Centerburg (43011) *(G-2615)*

Rescare Ohio Inc 740 867-4568
1107 Us Hwy 52 Chesapeake (45619) *(G-2732)*

Rescare Ohio Inc (HQ) 513 724-1177
348 W Main St Williamsburg (45176) *(G-19496)*

Rescare Ohio Inc 513 829-8992
5099 Camelot Dr Hamilton (45014) *(G-11637)*

Rescue Incorporated 419 255-9585
3350 Collingwood Blvd # 2 Toledo (43610) *(G-18004)*

Rescue Mental HLTh&addctn Svcs, Toledo Also called Rescue Incorporated *(G-18004)*

Rescue Mission of Mahoning Val (PA) 330 744-5485
962 Martin L King Jr Blvd Youngstown (44510) *(G-20184)*

Rescue Mission of Mahoning Val 330 744-5485
2246 Glenwood Ave Youngstown (44511) *(G-20185)*

Rescue Rooter of Columbus, Columbus Also called American Residential Svcs
LLC *(G-6937)*

Rescue Squad, Greenville Also called Greenville Township Rescue *(G-11384)*

Research & Development, Maumee Also called Bprex Closures LLC *(G-13764)*

Research & Investigation Assoc 419 526-1299
186 Sturges Ave Mansfield (44903) *(G-13234)*

Research and Education The, Cincinnati Also called Lindner Clinical Trial Center *(G-3935)*

Research Associates Inc (PA) 440 892-1000
27999 Clemens Rd Frnt Cleveland (44145) *(G-6312)*

Research Institute, Dayton Also called University of Dayton *(G-9841)*

Research Institute At Nation 614 722-2700
700 Childrens Dr Columbus (43205) *(G-8518)*

Research Institute Univ Hosp, Cleveland Also called University Hospitals Cleveland *(G-6592)*

Resers Fine Foods Inc 216 231-7112
1921 E 119th St Cleveland (44106) *(G-6313)*

Reserve 330 666-1166
3636 Yellow Creek Rd Akron (44333) *(G-405)*

Reserve Ftl LLC 440 519-1768
1831 Highland Rd Twinsburg (44087) *(G-18311)*

Reserve Ftl LLC 773 721-8740
1451 Trump Ave Ne Canton (44730) *(G-2459)*

Reserve Iron Ohio, Canton Also called Reserve Ftl LLC *(G-2459)*

Reserve Management Group, Twinsburg Also called Reserve Ftl LLC *(G-18311)*

Reserve Run Golf Club LLC 330 758-1017
625 E Western Reserve Rd Poland (44514) *(G-16087)*

Reserve Square Apts, Cleveland Also called Equity Residential Properties *(G-5489)*

Reserves Network Inc (PA) 440 779-1400
22021 Brookpark Rd # 220 Cleveland (44126) *(G-6314)*

Residence Artists Inc 440 286-8822
220 5th Ave Chardon (44024) *(G-2710)*

Residence At Garden Gate, Cincinnati Also called Rcr East Inc *(G-4341)*

Residence At Huntington Court, Hamilton Also called Residence At Kensington
Place *(G-11638)*

Residence At Kensington Place 513 863-4218
350 Hancock Ave Hamilton (45011) *(G-11638)*

Residence At Salem Woods, Cincinnati Also called Rcr East Inc *(G-4342)*

Residence Inn 614 222-2610
36 E Gay St Columbus (43215) *(G-8519)*

Residence Inn By Marriott, Cleveland Also called Amitel Beachwood Ltd Partnr *(G-4970)*

Residence Inn By Marriott, Troy Also called Ohio Inns Inc *(G-18219)*

Residence Inn By Marriott, Cleveland Also called Summit Hotel Trs 144 LLC *(G-6476)*

Residence Inn By Marriott, Columbus Also called Olshan Hotel Management Inc *(G-8373)*

Residence Inn By Marriott, Columbus Also called Marriott International Inc *(G-8026)*

Residence Inn By Marriott, Columbus Also called Marriott International Inc *(G-8027)*

Residence Inn By Marriott, Columbus Also called Marriott International Inc *(G-8028)*

Residence Inn By Marriott, Copley Also called Marriott International Inc *(G-8970)*

Residence Inn By Marriott, Blue Ash Also called Marriott International Inc *(G-1605)*

Residence Inn By Marriott, Columbus Also called 5 Star Hotel Management IV LP *(G-6842)*

Residence Inn By Marriott, Columbus Also called Residence Inn *(G-8519)*

Residence Inn By Marriott, Cleveland Also called Amitel Beachwood Ltd Partnr *(G-4971)*

Residence Inn By Marriott, Cleveland Also called Amitel Rockside Ltd Partnr *(G-4972)*

Residence Inn By Marriott Beav 937 427-3914
2779 Frfield Commons Blvd Beavercreek (45431) *(G-1182)*

Residence Inn Cleveland Dwntwn, Cleveland Also called Nf II Cleveland Op Co
LLC *(G-6068)*

Residence of Chardon 440 286-2277
501 Chardon Windsor Rd Chardon (44024) *(G-2711)*

Resident Home Association 937 278-0791
3661 Salem Ave Dayton (45406) *(G-9734)*

RESIDENT HOME, THE, Cincinnati Also called Rhc Inc *(G-4367)*

Residential Concepts Inc 513 724-6067
117 Kermit Ave Williamsburg (45176) *(G-19497)*

Residential Finance Corp (PA) 614 324-4700
1 Easton Oval Ste 400 Columbus (43219) *(G-8520)*

Residential Hm Assn of Marion (PA) 740 387-9999
205 W Center St Ste 100 Marion (43302) *(G-13455)*

Residential Home For The Devlp (PA) 740 622-9778
925 Chestnut St Coshocton (43812) *(G-9025)*

Residential Home For The Devlp 740 452-5133
3484 Old Wheeling Rd Zanesville (43701) *(G-20358)*

Residential Inc 740 342-4158
226 S Main St New Lexington (43764) *(G-14927)*

Residential Management Systems 419 222-8806
1555 Allentown Rd Lima (45805) *(G-12730)*

Residential Management Systems (PA) 614 880-6014
402 E Wilson Bridge Rd Worthington (43085) *(G-19843)*

Residential Management Systems 419 255-6060
1446 Reynolds Rd Ste 100 Maumee (43537) *(G-13843)*

Residential One Realty Inc (PA) 614 436-9830
8351 N High St Ste 150 Columbus (43235) *(G-8521)*

Residents of Chardon, Chardon Also called Residence of Chardon *(G-2711)*

Residnce Inn Cincinnati Dwntwn, Cincinnati Also called 506 Phelps Holdings LLC *(G-2883)*

A
L
P
H
A
B
E
T
I
C

Residntial Coml Rnovations Inc 330 815-1476
  7686 S Clvland Mssllon Rd Clinton (44216) *(G-6737)*
Resolute Bank 419 868-1750
  3425 Brrfeld Blvd Ste 100 Maumee (43537) *(G-13844)*
Resolvit Resources LLC (PA) 703 734-3330
  895 Central Ave Ste 1050 Cincinnati (45202) *(G-4361)*
Resolvit Resources LLC 513 619-5900
  895 Central Ave Ste 350 Cincinnati (45202) *(G-4362)*
Resolvit Resources LLC 703 564-2100
  895 Central Ave Ste 1050 Cincinnati (45202) *(G-4363)*
Resource Interactive, Columbus Also called Resource Ventures Ltd *(G-8524)*
Resource Interactive 614 621-2888
  250 S High St Ste 400 Columbus (43215) *(G-8522)*
Resource International, Columbus Also called Majidzadeh Enterprises Inc *(G-8011)*
Resource International 513 769-6998
  4480 Lake Forest Dr # 308 Blue Ash (45242) *(G-1646)*
Resource International Inc (HQ) 614 823-4949
  6350 Presidential Gtwy Columbus (43231) *(G-8523)*
Resource One Cmpt Systems Inc 614 485-4800
  651 Lkview Plz Blvd Ste E Worthington (43085) *(G-19844)*
Resource Title Agency Inc (PA) 216 520-0050
  7100 E Pleasant Vly # 100 Cleveland (44131) *(G-6315)*
Resource Title Nat Agcy Inc 216 520-0050
  7100 E Pleasant Valley Rd # 100 Independence (44131) *(G-12113)*
Resource Ventures Ltd (HQ) 614 621-2888
  250 S High St Ste 400 Columbus (43215) *(G-8524)*
Rest Haven Nursing Home, Mc Dermott Also called Voiers Enterprises Inc *(G-13896)*
Rest Haven Nursing Home Inc 937 548-1138
  1096 N Ohio St Greenville (45331) *(G-11392)*
Restaurant Depot, Cleveland Also called Jetro Cash and Carry Entps LLC *(G-5794)*
Restaurant Depot LLC 513 542-3000
  4501 W Mitchell Ave Cincinnati (45232) *(G-4364)*
Restaurant Depot LLC 614 272-6670
  270 N Wilson Rd Columbus (43204) *(G-8525)*
Restaurant Depot LLC 216 525-0101
  6150 Halle Dr Cleveland (44125) *(G-6316)*
Restaurant Equippers Inc 614 358-6622
  635 W Broad St Columbus (43215) *(G-8526)*
Restaurant Finance Corporation 614 764-3100
  4288 W Dblin Granville Rd Dublin (43017) *(G-10321)*
Restaurant On The Dam, Stockport Also called Stockport Mill Country Inn Inc *(G-17183)*
Restaurant Refreshment Service, Cincinnati Also called Coffee Break Corporation *(G-3318)*
Restaurant Specialties Inc 614 885-9707
  801 W Cherry St Ste 200 Sunbury (43074) *(G-17394)*
Restoration Resources Inc 330 650-4486
  1546 Georgetown Rd Hudson (44236) *(G-12004)*
Retail 4 Less, Columbus Also called Sb Capital Group LLC *(G-8597)*
Retail Distribution Center, Maumee Also called Andersons Inc *(G-13752)*
Retail Forward Inc 614 355-4000
  2 Easton Oval Ste 500 Columbus (43219) *(G-8527)*
Retail Renovations Inc (PA) 330 334-4501
  7530 State Rd Wadsworth (44281) *(G-18615)*
Retalix Inc 937 384-2277
  2490 Technical Dr Miamisburg (45342) *(G-14212)*
Retalix Usa Inc 937 384-2277
  2490 Technical Dr Miamisburg (45342) *(G-14213)*
Retina Associate of Cleveland (PA) 216 831-5700
  3401 Entp Pkwy Ste 300 Beachwood (44122) *(G-1100)*
Retina Associate of Cleveland 216 221-2878
  4350 Crocker Rd Ste 200 Westlake (44145) *(G-19400)*
Retina Group Inc (PA) 614 464-3937
  262 Neil Ave Ste 220 Columbus (43215) *(G-8528)*
Retrobox.com, Gahanna Also called Arrow Globl Asset Dspstion Inc *(G-11110)*
Return Polymers Inc 419 289-1998
  400 Westlake Dr Ashland (44805) *(G-686)*
Reuben Co (PA) 419 241-3400
  24 S Huron St Toledo (43604) *(G-18005)*
Reupert Heating and AC Co Inc 513 922-5050
  5137 Crookshank Rd Cincinnati (45238) *(G-4365)*
Rev1 Ventures 614 487-3700
  1275 Kinnear Rd Columbus (43212) *(G-8529)*
Revenue Assistance Corporation 216 763-2100
  3711 Chester Ave Cleveland (44114) *(G-6317)*
Revenue Group, Cleveland Also called Revenue Assistance Corporation *(G-6317)*
Reverse Center Clinic 419 885-8800
  5465 Main St Sylvania (43560) *(G-17446)*
Reves Salon & Spa 419 885-1140
  5633 Main St Sylvania (43560) *(G-17447)*
Reville Tire Co (PA) 330 468-1900
  8044 Olde 8 Rd Northfield (44067) *(G-15385)*
Reville Wholesale Distributing, Northfield Also called Reville Tire Co *(G-15385)*
Revlocal Inc 740 392-9246
  895 Harcourt Rd Ste C Mount Vernon (43050) *(G-14786)*
Revolution Group Inc 614 212-1111
  600 N Cleveland Ave # 110 Westerville (43082) *(G-19207)*
Rex Reliable, Canton Also called Rexs Air Conditioning Company *(G-2460)*
Rexel Usa Inc 216 778-6400
  5605 Granger Rd Cleveland (44131) *(G-6318)*
Rexel Usa Inc 440 248-3800
  2699 Solon Sales 30310 Solon (44139) *(G-16892)*

Rexel Usa Inc 419 625-6761
  140 Lane St Sandusky (44870) *(G-16636)*
Rexel Usa Inc 614 771-7373
  3670 Parkway Ln Ste A Hilliard (43026) *(G-11812)*
Rexs Air Conditioning Company 330 499-8733
  7801 Freedom Ave Nw Canton (44720) *(G-2460)*
Reynolds & Co Inc 740 353-1040
  839 Gallia St Portsmouth (45662) *(G-16164)*
Reynolds & Company Cpa's, Portsmouth Also called Reynolds & Co Inc *(G-16164)*
Reynolds and Reynolds Company (HQ) 937 485-2000
  1 Reynolds Way Kettering (45430) *(G-12299)*
Reynolds Electric Company Inc 419 228-5448
  413 Flanders Ave Lima (45801) *(G-12731)*
Reynolds Industries Inc 330 889-9466
  380 W Main St West Farmington (44491) *(G-19102)*
Reynolds Road Surgical Ctr LLC 419 578-7500
  2865 N Reynolds Rd # 190 Toledo (43615) *(G-18006)*
Reynolds, De Witt Securities, Cincinnati Also called Sena Weller Rohs Williams *(G-4451)*
Reynoldsburg City Schools 614 501-1041
  7932 E Main St Reynoldsburg (43068) *(G-16326)*
Reynoldsburg Kindercare, Reynoldsburg Also called Kindercare Learning Ctrs
LLC *(G-16314)*
Reynoldsburg Swim Club Inc 614 866-3211
  7215 E Main St Reynoldsburg (43068) *(G-16327)*
REZ STONE, Toledo Also called Hoover & Wells Inc *(G-17807)*
Rezod, Columbus Also called Trubuilt Construction Svcs LLC *(G-8785)*
Rgis LLC 216 447-1744
  4500 Rockside Rd Ste 340 Independence (44131) *(G-12114)*
Rgis LLC 330 799-1566
  5423 Mahoning Ave Ste C Youngstown (44515) *(G-20186)*
Rgis LLC 248 651-2511
  6488 E Main St Ste B Reynoldsburg (43068) *(G-16328)*
Rgis LLC 330 896-9802
  767 E Turkey Foot Lake Rd Akron (44319) *(G-406)*
Rgis LLC 513 772-5990
  4000 Executive Park Dr # 105 Cincinnati (45241) *(G-4366)*
Rh Meyers Apartments, Beachwood Also called Menorah Park Center For Senio *(G-1079)*
Rham, Marion Also called Residential Hm Assn of Marion *(G-13455)*
Rhc Inc (PA) 513 389-7501
  3030 W Fork Rd Cincinnati (45211) *(G-4367)*
Rhdd, Zanesville Also called Residential Home For The Devlp *(G-20358)*
Rhenium Alloys Inc (PA) 440 365-7388
  38683 Taylor Pkwy North Ridgeville (44035) *(G-15340)*
Rhiel Supply Co Inc (PA) 330 799-7777
  3735 Oakwood Ave Austintown (44515) *(G-861)*
Rhiel Supply Co, The, Austintown Also called Rhiel Supply Co Inc *(G-861)*
Rhinegeist LLC 513 381-1367
  1910 Elm St Cincinnati (45202) *(G-4368)*
Rhinegeist Brewery, Cincinnati Also called Rhinegeist LLC *(G-4368)*
Rhodes Hs-Sch of Leadership, Cleveland Also called Cleveland Municipal School
Dst *(G-5275)*
Ricart Automotive, Groveport Also called Ricart Ford Inc *(G-11535)*
Ricart Ford Inc 614 836-5321
  4255 S Hamilton Rd Groveport (43125) *(G-11535)*
Ricco Enterprises Incorporated 216 883-7775
  6010 Fleet Ave Frnt Ste Cleveland (44105) *(G-6319)*
Rich Crites & Dittmer LLC 614 228-5822
  6400 Rverside Dr Ste D100 Dublin (43017) *(G-10322)*
Richard A Broock 937 449-2840
  10 N Ludlow St Dayton (45402) *(G-9735)*
Richard Allen Group LLC (PA) 614 623-2654
  391 Glenside Ln Powell (43065) *(G-16206)*
Richard E Jacobs Group LLC 440 871-4800
  25425 Center Ridge Rd Cleveland (44145) *(G-6320)*
Richard Goettle Inc 513 825-8100
  12071 Hamilton Ave Cincinnati (45231) *(G-4369)*
Richard H Freyhof (PA) 937 653-5837
  1071 S Main St Urbana (43078) *(G-18443)*
Richard Health Systems LLC 419 534-2371
  5237 Renwyck Dr Ste A Toledo (43615) *(G-18007)*
Richard J Nelson MD 419 578-7555
  6005 Monclova Rd Ste 320 Maumee (43537) *(G-13845)*
Richard L Bowen & Assoc Inc (PA) 216 491-9300
  13000 Shaker Blvd Ste 1 Cleveland (44120) *(G-6321)*
Richard L Liston MD 937 320-2020
  89 Sylvania Dr Beavercreek (45440) *(G-1235)*
Richard R Jencen & Associates 216 781-0131
  2850 Euclid Ave Cleveland (44115) *(G-6322)*
Richard Tomm MD 216 297-3060
  1611 S Green Rd Ste 213 Cleveland (44121) *(G-6323)*
Richard Wolfe Trucking Inc 740 392-2445
  7299 Newark Rd Mount Vernon (43050) *(G-14787)*
Richard's Fence Company, Akron Also called Richards Whl Fence Co Inc *(G-407)*
Richards Electric Sup Co Inc (PA) 513 242-8800
  4620 Reading Rd Cincinnati (45229) *(G-4370)*
Richards Whl Fence Co Inc 330 773-0423
  1600 Firestone Pkwy Akron (44301) *(G-407)*
Richardson Glass Service Inc (PA) 740 366-5090
  1165 Mount Vernon Rd Newark (43055) *(G-15096)*

(G-0000) Company's Geographic Section entry number

RICHARDSON GLASS SERVICE INC DBA LEE'S GLASS SERVICE, Newark *Also called Richardson Glass Service Inc (G-15096)*
Richardson Printing Corp (PA).....740 373-5362
201 Acme St Marietta (45750) *(G-13377)*
Richcreek Bailey Rehabilitatio.....440 527-8610
7600 Tyler Blvd Mentor (44060) *(G-14104)*
Richfield Banquet & Confer.....330 659-6151
4742 Brecksville Rd Richfield (44286) *(G-16375)*
Richfield Financial Group Inc.....440 546-4288
8223 Brecksville Rd # 201 Brecksville (44141) *(G-1802)*
Richfield Labs, Blue Ash *Also called Ameripath Cincinnati Inc (G-1505)*
Richland Co & Associates Inc (PA).....419 782-0141
101 Clinton St Ste 2200 Defiance (43512) *(G-9937)*
Richland County Child Support.....419 774-5700
161 Park Ave E Mansfield (44902) *(G-13235)*
Richland County Engineers, Mansfield *Also called County of Richland (G-13158)*
Richland County Prosectors Off, Mansfield *Also called County of Richland (G-13153)*
Richland Mall Shopping Ctr.....419 529-4003
2209 Lexington Ave Mansfield (44907) *(G-13236)*
Richland Manor, Delphos *Also called J W J Investments Inc (G-10028)*
Richland Newhope Industries (PA).....419 774-4400
150 E 4th St Mansfield (44902) *(G-13237)*
Richland Newhope Industries.....419 774-4200
314 Cleveland Ave Mansfield (44902) *(G-13238)*
Richland Newhope Industries.....419 774-4496
985 W Longview Ave Mansfield (44906) *(G-13239)*
Richland Township Fire Dept.....740 536-7313
3150 Market St Rushville (43150) *(G-16465)*
Richland Trust Company (HQ).....419 525-8700
3 N Main St Ste 1 Mansfield (44902) *(G-13240)*
Richmond Medical Center (PA).....440 585-6500
27100 Chardon Rd Richmond Heights (44143) *(G-16394)*
Richs Towing & Service Inc (PA).....440 234-3435
20531 1st Ave Middleburg Heights (44130) *(G-14257)*
Richter Landscaping.....513 539-0300
240 Senate Dr Monroe (45050) *(G-14581)*
Richwood Banking Company (HQ).....740 943-2317
28 N Franklin St Richwood (43344) *(G-16397)*
Richwood Banking Company.....937 390-0470
2454 N Limestone St Springfield (45503) *(G-17101)*
Rick Allman.....330 699-1660
4450 Belden Village St Nw Nw800 Canton (44718) *(G-2461)*
Rick Blazing Insurance Agency.....513 677-8300
300 E Bus Way Ste 200 Cincinnati (45241) *(G-4371)*
Rick Eplion Paving.....740 446-3000
7159 State Route 7 S Gallipolis (45631) *(G-11214)*
Rick Kuntz Trucking Inc.....330 296-9311
9056 State Route 88 Windham (44288) *(G-19663)*
Rickerier and Eckler.....513 870-6565
9277 Centre Pointe Dr # 100 West Chester (45069) *(G-18993)*
Ricketts Excavating Inc.....740 687-0338
230 Hamburg Rd Sw Lancaster (43130) *(G-12430)*
Ricking Paper and Specialty Co.....513 825-3551
525 Northland Blvd Cincinnati (45240) *(G-4372)*
Ricks Hair Center.....330 545-5120
27 Churchill Rd Girard (44420) *(G-11299)*
Ricoh Usa Inc.....513 984-9898
400 E Business Way # 125 Sharonville (45241) *(G-16730)*
Ricoh Usa Inc.....614 310-6500
300 W Wilson Bridge Rd # 110 Worthington (43085) *(G-19845)*
Ricoh Usa Inc.....216 574-9111
1360 E 9th St Bsmt 1 Cleveland (44114) *(G-6324)*
Ricoh Usa Inc.....330 523-3900
4125 Highlander Pkwy # 175 Richfield (44286) *(G-16376)*
Ricoh Usa Inc.....330 384-9111
80 W Center St Akron (44308) *(G-408)*
Riddell Inc.....440 366-8225
7501 Performance Ln North Ridgeville (44039) *(G-15341)*
Riddell All American Sport, North Ridgeville *Also called All American Sports Corp (G-15319)*
Riddle, Kevin L MD, Miamisburg *Also called Miamisburg Family Practice (G-14192)*
Ride Share Information.....513 621-6300
720 E Pete Rose Way # 420 Cincinnati (45202) *(G-4373)*
Riders 1812 Inn.....440 354-0922
792 Mentor Ave Painesville (44077) *(G-15738)*
Riders Inn, Willoughby *Also called East End Ro Burton Inc (G-19519)*
Ridge Manor Nuseries Inc.....440 466-5781
7925 N Ridge Rd Madison (44057) *(G-13108)*
Ridge Murray Prod Ctr Oberlin.....440 774-7400
285 Artino St Oberlin (44074) *(G-15519)*
Ridge Pleasant Valley Inc (PA).....440 845-0200
7377 Ridge Rd Cleveland (44129) *(G-6325)*
Ridge Road Depot, Cleveland *Also called Cleveland Municipal School Dst (G-5273)*
Ridgehills Hotel Ltd Partnr.....440 585-0600
28600 Ridgehills Dr Wickliffe (44092) *(G-19475)*
Ridgepark Center, Akron *Also called Kindred Healthcare Operating (G-303)*
Ridgepark Medical Associates.....216 749-8256
7575 Northcliff Ave # 307 Cleveland (44144) *(G-6326)*
Ridgeview Hospital, Middle Point *Also called Oglethorpe Middlepoint LLC (G-14247)*
Ridgeville Community Choir.....419 267-3820
633 First St Ridgeville Corners (43555) *(G-16398)*
Ridgewood At Friendship Vlg.....614 890-8285
5675 Ponderosa Dr Ofc Columbus (43231) *(G-8530)*
Ridgewood Golf Course, Cleveland *Also called City of Parma (G-5212)*
RIECK SERVICES, Dayton *Also called Mechanical Cnstr Managers LLC (G-9597)*
Rieman Arszman Cstm Distrs Inc.....513 874-5444
9190 Seward Rd Fairfield (45014) *(G-10774)*
Riepenhoff Landscape Ltd.....614 876-4683
3872 Scoto Darby Creek Rd Hilliard (43026) *(G-11813)*
Riggs School Buses, Cincinnati *Also called Marfre Inc (G-3969)*
Right At Home, Maumee *Also called Colt Enterprises Inc (G-13774)*
Right At Home, Beavercreek *Also called Daugwood Inc (G-1144)*
Right At Home.....937 291-2244
15 Dinsley Pl Springboro (45066) *(G-16983)*
Right At Home LLC.....614 734-1110
8828 Commerce Loop Dr Columbus (43240) *(G-6833)*
Righter Co Inc.....614 272-9700
2424 Harrison Rd Columbus (43204) *(G-8531)*
Righter Construction Svcs Inc.....614 272-9700
2424 Harrison Rd Columbus (43204) *(G-8532)*
Rightthing LLC (HQ).....419 420-1830
3401 Technology Dr Findlay (45840) *(G-10958)*
Rightthing, The, Findlay *Also called Rightthing LLC (G-10958)*
Rightway Food Service, Lima *Also called Powell Company Ltd (G-12723)*
Rightway Investments LLC.....216 854-7697
1959 Edgewood Dr Twinsburg (44087) *(G-18312)*
Rii, Columbus *Also called Resource International Inc (G-8523)*
Rilco Industrial Controls Inc (HQ).....513 530-0055
649 Dorgene Ln Cincinnati (45244) *(G-4374)*
Ringler Feedlots LLC.....419 253-5300
461 State Route 61 Marengo (43334) *(G-13304)*
Ringler Inc.....419 253-5300
461 State Route 61 Marengo (43334) *(G-13305)*
Ripcho Studio.....216 631-0664
7630 Lorain Ave Cleveland (44102) *(G-6327)*
Rippe & Kingston Systems Inc (PA).....513 977-4578
1077 Celestial St Ste 124 Cincinnati (45202) *(G-4375)*
Rise Fitness, Medina *Also called Redefine Enterprises LLC (G-13994)*
Riser Foods Company (HQ).....216 292-7000
5300 Richmond Rd Bedford Heights (44146) *(G-1327)*
Rising Sun Express, Jackson Center *Also called Rse Group Inc (G-12186)*
Rising Sun Express LLC.....937 596-6167
1003 S Main St Jackson Center (45334) *(G-12185)*
Risk International Svcs Inc (HQ).....216 255-3400
4055 Embassy Pkwy Ste 100 Fairlawn (44333) *(G-10844)*
Ritchies Food Distributors Inc.....740 443-6303
527 S West St Piketon (45661) *(G-15988)*
Rite Rug Co.....614 478-3365
5465 N Hamilton Rd Columbus (43230) *(G-8533)*
Rite Rug Co.....937 318-9197
2015 Commerce Center Blvd Fairborn (45324) *(G-10681)*
Rite Way Restoration, Columbus *Also called Dry It Rite LLC (G-7472)*
Riten Industries.....740 335-5353
1110 Lakeview Ave Wshngtn CT Hs (43160) *(G-19881)*
Ritenour Industrial, Twinsburg *Also called Lou Ritenour Decorators Inc (G-18294)*
Rittenhouse.....513 423-2322
3000 Mcgee Ave Middletown (45044) *(G-14324)*
Ritter & Associates Inc.....419 535-5757
1690 Woodlands Dr Ste 103 Maumee (43537) *(G-13846)*
Ritter & Randolph LLC.....513 381-5700
1 E 4th St Ste 700 Cincinnati (45202) *(G-4376)*
Rittman City of Inc.....330 925-2065
25 N State St Rittman (44270) *(G-16408)*
Rittman Inc.....330 927-6855
10 Mull Dr Rittman (44270) *(G-16409)*
Rivals Sports Grille LLC.....216 267-0005
6710 Smith Rd Middleburg Heights (44130) *(G-14258)*
River City Furniture LLC (PA).....513 612-7303
6454 Centre Park Dr West Chester (45069) *(G-18994)*
River City Pharma.....513 870-1680
8695 Seward Rd Fairfield (45011) *(G-10775)*
River Consulting LLC (HQ).....614 797-2480
445 Hutchinson Ave # 740 Columbus (43235) *(G-8534)*
River Downs, Cincinnati *Also called Pnk (ohio) LLC (G-4261)*
River Downs Race Course, Cincinnati *Also called River Downs Turf Club Inc (G-4377)*
River Downs Turf Club Inc.....513 232-8000
6301 Kellogg Rd Cincinnati (45230) *(G-4377)*
River Greens Golf Course Inc.....740 545-7817
22749 State Route 751 West Lafayette (43845) *(G-19116)*
River Plumbing & Supply, Avon *Also called River Plumbing Inc (G-903)*
River Plumbing Inc.....440 934-3720
1756 Moore Rd Avon (44011) *(G-903)*
River Recycling Entps Ltd (PA).....216 459-2100
4195 Bradley Rd Cleveland (44109) *(G-6328)*
River Road Family Physicians.....419 872-7745
1601 Brigham Dr Ste 250 Perrysburg (43551) *(G-15913)*
River Road Hotel Corp.....614 267-7461
3110 Olentangy River Rd Columbus (43202) *(G-8535)*
River Rock Rehabilitation.....740 382-4035
990 S Prospect St Ste 4 Marion (43302) *(G-13456)*
River Rose Obstetrics & Gyneco, Athens *Also called Ohio Health Physician Group (G-793)*

ALPHABETIC

River Valley Credit Union Inc (PA) 937 859-1970
505 Earl Blvd Miamisburg (45342) ***(G-14214)***
River View Surgery Center, Lancaster *Also called Riverview Surgery Center* ***(G-12432)***
River Vly Orthpdics Spt Mdcine (PA) 740 687-3346
2405 N Columbus St # 120 Lancaster (43130) ***(G-12431)***
Rivera, Mary, Cincinnati *Also called Reading Family Practice* ***(G-4343)***
Riverain Technologies LLC 937 425-6811
3020 S Tech Blvd Miamisburg (45342) ***(G-14215)***
Riverbend Music Center, Cincinnati *Also called Cincinnati Symphony Orchestra* ***(G-3271)***
Riverfront Diversified Inc 513 874-7200
9814 Harwood Ct West Chester (45014) ***(G-18995)***
Riverhills Healthcare Inc (PA) 513 241-2370
111 Wellington Pl Lowr Cincinnati (45219) ***(G-4378)***
Riverhills Healthcare Inc 513 791-6400
4805 Montgomery Rd # 150 Cincinnati (45212) ***(G-4379)***
Rivers Bend Health Care LLC 740 894-3476
335 Township Road 1026 South Point (45680) ***(G-16945)***
Riverside Care Center LLC 740 962-5303
856 Riverside Dr S Mc Connelsville (43756) ***(G-13895)***
Riverside Cmnty Urban Redev 330 929-3000
1989 Front St Cuyahoga Falls (44221) ***(G-9120)***
Riverside Cnstr Svcs Inc 513 723-0900
218 W Mcmicken Ave Cincinnati (45214) ***(G-4380)***
Riverside Commons Ltd Partnr 614 863-4640
6880 Tussing Rd Reynoldsburg (43068) ***(G-16329)***
Riverside Company, The, Cleveland *Also called Riversidecompanycom* ***(G-6330)***
Riverside Drives Inc 216 362-1211
4509 W 160th St Cleveland (44135) ***(G-6329)***
Riverside Drives Disc, Cleveland *Also called Riverside Drives Inc* ***(G-6329)***
Riverside Drv Animal Care Ctr 614 414-2668
6924 Riverside Dr Dublin (43017) ***(G-10323)***
Riverside Electric Inc (PA) 513 936-0100
680 Redna Ter Cincinnati (45215) ***(G-4381)***
Riverside Manor, Newcomerstown *Also called Newcomerstown Progress Corp* ***(G-15134)***
Riverside Marine Inds Inc 419 729-1621
2824 N Summit St Toledo (43611) ***(G-18008)***
Riverside Mnor Nrsing Rhab Ctr, Newcomerstown *Also called Newcomerstown Development Inc* ***(G-15133)***
Riverside Nephrology Assoc Inc 614 538-2250
929 Jasonway Ave Ste A Columbus (43214) ***(G-8536)***
Riverside Nrsing Rhabilitation, Dayton *Also called King Tree Leasing Co LLC* ***(G-9548)***
Riverside of Miami County, Troy *Also called R T Industries Inc* ***(G-18225)***
Riverside Radiology and (PA) 614 340-7747
100 E Campus View Blvd # 100 Columbus (43235) ***(G-8537)***
Riverside Research Institute 937 431-3810
2640 Hibiscus Way Beavercreek (45431) ***(G-1183)***
Riverside Veterinary Hospital, Dublin *Also called Beechwold Veterinary Hospital* ***(G-10143)***
Riversidecompanycom 216 344-1040
50 Public Sq Ste 2900 Cleveland (44113) ***(G-6330)***
Rivertreechristian.com, Massillon *Also called Christian Rivertree School* ***(G-13670)***
Riverview Community, Cincinnati *Also called United Church Homes Inc* ***(G-4677)***
Riverview Health Institute 937 222-5390
1 Elizabeth Pl Dayton (45417) ***(G-9736)***
Riverview Hotel LLC 614 268-8700
3160 Olentangy River Rd Columbus (43202) ***(G-8538)***
Riverview Industries Inc 419 898-5250
8380 W State Route 163 Oak Harbor (43449) ***(G-15478)***
Riverview Surgery Center 740 681-2700
2401 N Columbus St Lancaster (43130) ***(G-12432)***
RJ Runge Company Inc 419 740-5781
3539 Ne Catawba Rd Port Clinton (43452) ***(G-16116)***
Rjb Acquisitions LLC 513 314-2711
2915 Highland Ave Cincinnati (45219) ***(G-4382)***
Rjw Trucking Company Ltd 740 363-5343
124 Henderson Ct Delaware (43015) ***(G-10004)***
Rk Express International LLC 513 574-2400
5474 Sanrio Ct Cincinnati (45247) ***(G-4383)***
Rk Family Inc 740 389-2674
233 America Blvd Marion (43302) ***(G-13457)***
Rk Family Inc 513 737-0436
1416 Main St Hamilton (45013) ***(G-11639)***
Rk Family Inc 419 443-1663
2300 W Market St Tiffin (44883) ***(G-17534)***
Rk Family Inc 419 355-8230
1800 E State St Fremont (43420) ***(G-11090)***
Rk Family Inc 330 264-5475
3541 E Lincoln Way Wooster (44691) ***(G-19761)***
Rk Family Inc 513 934-0015
1879 Deerfield Rd Lebanon (45036) ***(G-12498)***
Rkpl Inc 419 224-2121
216 N Elizabeth St Lima (45801) ***(G-12732)***
RL Best Company 330 758-8601
723 Bev Rd Boardman (44512) ***(G-1701)***
Rl Global Services, Wilmington *Also called R+l Pramount Trnsp Systems Inc* ***(G-19642)***
Rl Painting and Mfg Inc 937 968-5526
10001 Oh In State Line Union City (45390) ***(G-18354)***
Rla Investments Inc 513 554-1470
389 Wade St Cincinnati (45214) ***(G-4384)***
Rlj III - Em Clmbus Lessee LLC 614 890-8600
2700 Corporate Exch Dr Columbus (43231) ***(G-8539)***
Rlj Management Co Inc (PA) 614 942-2020
3021 E Dblin Granville Rd Columbus (43231) ***(G-8540)***
RLR Investments LLC 937 382-1494
600 Gilliam Rd Wilmington (45177) ***(G-19645)***
Rls Disposal Company Inc 740 773-1440
990 Eastern Ave Chillicothe (45601) ***(G-2815)***
Rm Advisory Group Inc 513 242-2100
5300 Vine St Cincinnati (45217) ***(G-4385)***
Rmb Enterprises Inc 513 539-3431
2742 Oxford State Rd Middletown (45044) ***(G-14325)***
Rmf Nooter Inc 419 727-1970
915 Matzinger Rd Toledo (43612) ***(G-18009)***
Rmi International Inc 937 642-5032
24500 Honda Pwky Marysville (43040) ***(G-13525)***
RMS Aquaculture Inc (PA) 216 433-1340
6629 Engle Rd Ste 108 Cleveland (44130) ***(G-6331)***
RMS Management, Westlake *Also called RMS of Ohio Inc* ***(G-19401)***
RMS of Ohio Inc 440 617-6605
24651 Center Ridge Rd # 300 Westlake (44145) ***(G-19401)***
RMS of Ohio Inc 513 841-0990
2824 E Kemper Rd Cincinnati (45241) ***(G-4386)***
RMS of Ohio Inc 937 291-3622
5335 Far Hills Ave # 306 Dayton (45429) ***(G-9737)***
Rmx Freight Systems Inc (PA) 740 849-2374
4550 Roseville Rd Roseville (43777) ***(G-16455)***
Rnw Holdings Inc 330 792-0600
200 Division Street Ext Youngstown (44510) ***(G-20187)***
Roadrunner Trnsp Systems Inc 330 920-4101
89 Cuyhoga Fls Indus Pkwy Peninsula (44264) ***(G-15812)***
Roadtrippers Inc 917 688-9887
131 E Mcmicken Ave Cincinnati (45202) ***(G-4387)***
Roadway Express, Toledo *Also called Yrc Inc* ***(G-18174)***
Rob's Restaurant & Catering, Brookville *Also called Mackil Inc* ***(G-1915)***
Robbins Kelly Patterson Tucker 513 721-3330
7 W 7th St Ste 1400 Cincinnati (45202) ***(G-4388)***
Robeck Fluid Power Co 330 562-1140
350 Lena Dr Aurora (44202) ***(G-840)***
Robert A Kaufmann Inc 216 663-1150
5210 Northfield Rd Maple Heights (44137) ***(G-13293)***
Robert E Kose 419 843-7800
1661 Holland Rd Ste 200 Maumee (43537) ***(G-13847)***
Robert E Lubow MD 513 961-8861
3001 Highland Ave Cincinnati (45219) ***(G-4389)***
Robert E McGrath Inc 440 572-7747
11606 Pearl Rd Strongsville (44136) ***(G-17341)***
Robert Ellis 513 821-0275
175 W Galbraith Rd Cincinnati (45216) ***(G-4390)***
Robert Erney 312 788-9005
14830 Larkfield Dr Brookpark (44142) ***(G-1905)***
Robert F Arrom Md Inc 513 893-4107
1020 Symmes Rd Fairfield (45014) ***(G-10776)***
Robert F Lindsay Co (PA) 419 476-6221
4268 Rose Garden Dr Toledo (43623) ***(G-18010)***
Robert G Owen Trucking Inc (PA) 330 756-1013
9260 Erie Ave Sw Navarre (44662) ***(G-14825)***
Robert Half International Inc 937 224-7376
1 S Main St Ste 300 Dayton (45402) ***(G-9738)***
Robert Half International Inc 330 629-9494
970 Windham Ct Ste 1a Youngstown (44512) ***(G-20188)***
Robert Half International Inc 513 563-0770
10300 Alliance Rd Ste 220 Blue Ash (45242) ***(G-1647)***
Robert Half International Inc 614 221-8326
277 W Nationwide Blvd Columbus (43215) ***(G-8541)***
Robert Half International Inc 614 602-0505
5550 Blazer Pkwy Ste 250 Dublin (43017) ***(G-10324)***
Robert Half International Inc 513 621-8367
201 E 5th St Ste 2000a Cincinnati (45202) ***(G-4391)***
Robert Half International Inc 216 621-4253
1001 Lakeside Ave E 1320a Cleveland (44114) ***(G-6332)***
Robert Half International Inc 614 221-1544
277 W Nationwide Blvd # 200 Columbus (43215) ***(G-8542)***
Robert J Matthews Company (PA) 330 834-3000
2780 Richville Dr Se Massillon (44646) ***(G-13724)***
ROBERT K FOX FAMILY WIDE, Lancaster *Also called Family YMCA of LANcstr&fairfld* ***(G-12404)***
Robert L Dawson M.D., James, Galion *Also called Avita Health System* ***(G-11166)***
Robert L Stark Enterprises Inc 216 292-0242
1350 W 3rd St Cleveland (44113) ***(G-6333)***
Robert Lucke Homes Inc 513 683-3300
8825 Chapelsquare Ln B Cincinnati (45249) ***(G-4392)***
Robert M Neff Inc 614 444-1562
711 Stimmel Rd Columbus (43223) ***(G-8543)***
Robert McConnell, Shandon *Also called R & B Contractors LLC* ***(G-16721)***
Robert Neff & Son Inc 740 454-0128
132 S Shawnee Ave Zanesville (43701) ***(G-20359)***
Robert Stough Ventures Corp 419 882-4073
5409 Monroe St Toledo (43623) ***(G-18011)***
Robert Sturges Memorial Homes, Mansfield *Also called Mansfield Memorial Homes* ***(G-13208)***
Robert W Baird & Co Inc 216 737-7330
200 Public Sq Ste 1650 Cleveland (44114) ***(G-6334)***

Robert Wiley MD Inc 216 621-3211
2740 Carnegie Ave Cleveland (44115) *(G-6335)*
Robert Winner Sons Inc (PA) 419 582-4321
8544 State Route 705 Yorkshire (45388) *(G-19942)*
ROBERTSON BEREAVEMENT CENTER, Medina *Also called Bridgeshome Health Care (G-13913)*
Robertson Cnstr Svcs Inc 740 929-1000
1801 Thornwood Dr Heath (43056) *(G-11708)*
Robertson Heating Sup Co Ohio (PA) 800 433-9532
2155 W Main St Alliance (44601) *(G-545)*
Robertson Htg Sup Aliance Ohio (PA) 330 821-9180
2155 W Main St Alliance (44601) *(G-546)*
Robertson Htg Sup Canton Ohio (PA) 330 821-9180
2155 W Main St Alliance (44601) *(G-547)*
Robertson Htg Sup Clumbus Ohio (PA) 330 821-9180
2155 W Main St Alliance (44601) *(G-548)*
Robex LLC 419 270-0770
8600 S Wilkinson Way A Perrysburg (43551) *(G-15914)*
Robiden Inc 513 421-0000
6059 Creekside Way Fairfield Township (45011) *(G-10814)*
Robinson Health System Inc 330 678-4100
6847 N Chestnut St Ravenna (44266) *(G-16262)*
Robinson Health System Inc (HQ) 330 297-0811
6847 N Chestnut St Ravenna (44266) *(G-16263)*
Robinson Health System Inc 330 297-0811
1993 State Route 59 Kent (44240) *(G-12257)*
Robinson Hlth Affl Med Ctr One, Streetsboro *Also called Robinson Memorial Hospital (G-17268)*
Robinson Htg Air-Conditioning 513 422-6812
1208 2nd Ave Middletown (45044) *(G-14326)*
Robinson Insulation Co Inc 937 323-9599
4715 Urbana Rd Springfield (45502) *(G-17102)*
Robinson Investments Ltd 937 593-1849
811 N Main St Bellefontaine (43311) *(G-1362)*
Robinson Memorial Hospital 330 626-3455
9424 State Route 14 Streetsboro (44241) *(G-17268)*
Robinson Surgery Center, Ravenna *Also called Robinson Health System Inc (G-16262)*
Robinson Visitn Nrs Asoc/Hospc 330 297-8899
6847 N Chestnut St Ravenna (44266) *(G-16264)*
Robots and Pencils LP 587 350-4095
24245 Mercantile Rd Beachwood (44122) *(G-1101)*
Roby Lees Restaurant & Catrg, Newton Falls *Also called Lees Roby Inc (G-15139)*
Roce Group LLC 330 969-2627
4170 Steels Pointe Stow (44224) *(G-17227)*
Rock and Roll of Fame and Muse 216 781-7625
1100 Rock And Roll Blvd Cleveland (44114) *(G-6336)*
Rock Creek Medical Center, Rock Creek *Also called Glenbeigh (G-16411)*
Rock House Entrmt Group Inc 440 232-7625
7809 First Pl Oakwood Village (44146) *(G-15493)*
Rockbridge Capital LLC (PA) 614 246-2400
4100 Regent St Ste G Columbus (43219) *(G-8544)*
Rockfish Interactive Corp 513 381-1583
659 Van Meter St Ste 520 Cincinnati (45202) *(G-4393)*
Rockford Homes Inc (PA) 614 785-0015
999 Polaris Pkwy Ste 200 Columbus (43240) *(G-6834)*
Rocking Horse Chld Hlth Ctr (PA) 937 328-7266
651 S Limestone St Springfield (45505) *(G-17103)*
Rocknstarr Holdings LLC 330 509-9086
112 S Meridian Rd Youngstown (44509) *(G-20189)*
Rockside Hospitality LLC 216 524-0700
5300 Rockside Rd Independence (44131) *(G-12115)*
Rockwell Automation Ohio Inc (HQ) 513 576-6151
1700 Edison Dr Milford (45150) *(G-14428)*
Rockwell Springs Trout Club (PA) 419 684-7971
1581 County Road 310 Clyde (43410) *(G-6751)*
Rockwood Dry Cleaners Corp 614 471-3700
171 Granville St Gahanna (43230) *(G-11142)*
Rockwood Equity Partners LLC (PA) 216 342-1760
3201 Entp Pkwy Ste 370 Cleveland (44122) *(G-6337)*
Rocky Creek Hlth Rhabilitation, Columbus *Also called Gahanna Health Care Center (G-7643)*
Rocky River Leasing Co LLC 440 243-5688
570 N Rocky River Dr Berea (44017) *(G-1436)*
Rocky River Medical Offices, Rocky River *Also called Kaiser Foundation Hospitals (G-16439)*
ROCKY RIVER RIDING, Cleveland *Also called Valley Riding (G-6618)*
Rockynol, Fairlawn *Also called Senior Independence (G-10850)*
Rockynol Retirment Community, Akron *Also called Ohio Presbt Retirement Svcs (G-361)*
Rod Lightning Mutual Insur Co (PA) 330 262-9060
1685 Cleveland Rd Wooster (44691) *(G-19762)*
Rodbat Security Services, Marysville *Also called Rmi International Inc (G-13525)*
Roddy Group Inc 216 763-0088
24500 Chagrin Blvd # 200 Beachwood (44122) *(G-1102)*
Rodem Inc (PA) 513 922-6140
5095 Crookshank Rd Cincinnati (45238) *(G-4394)*
Rodem Process Equipment, Cincinnati *Also called Rodem Inc (G-4394)*
Roderick Linton Belfance LLP 330 434-3000
50 S Main St Fl 10 Akron (44308) *(G-409)*
Rodeway Inn, Dublin *Also called Jackson I-94 Ltd Partnership (G-10259)*
Roe Dental Laboratory Inc 216 663-2233
7165 E Pleasant Valley Rd Independence (44131) *(G-12116)*
Roeder Cartage Company Inc (PA) 419 221-1600
1979 N Dixie Hwy Lima (45801) *(G-12733)*
Roediger Realty Inc 937 322-0352
331 Mount Vernon Ave Springfield (45503) *(G-17104)*
Roehrenbeck Electric Inc 614 443-9709
2525 English Rd Columbus (43207) *(G-8545)*
Roemer Land Investment Co 419 475-5151
3912 Sunforest Ct Ste A Toledo (43623) *(G-18012)*
Roetzel and Andress A Legal P (PA) 330 376-2700
222 S Main St Ste 400 Akron (44308) *(G-410)*
Roetzel and Andress A Legal P 614 463-9489
41 S High St Fl 21 Columbus (43215) *(G-8546)*
Roetzel and Andress A Legal P 216 623-0150
1375 E 9th St Fl 10 Cleveland (44114) *(G-6338)*
Roger Bettis Trucking Inc 330 863-2111
7089 Alliance Rd Nw Malvern (44644) *(G-13126)*
Roger Kreps Drywall & Plst Inc 330 726-6090
939 Augusta Dr Youngstown (44512) *(G-20190)*
Roger S Palutsis MD 330 821-0201
1401 S Arch Ave Alliance (44601) *(G-549)*
Roger Shawn Houck 513 933-0563
7887 Wilmington Rd Oregonia (45054) *(G-15617)*
Roger Zatkoff Company 248 478-2400
2475 Edison Blvd Twinsburg (44087) *(G-18313)*
Rogosin Institute Inc 937 374-3116
740 Birch Rd Xenia (45385) *(G-19924)*
Roholt Vision Institute Inc 330 702-8755
25 Manor Hill Dr Canfield (44406) *(G-2156)*
Rohrs Farms 419 757-0110
810 Courtright St Mc Guffey (45859) *(G-13898)*
Roll Formed Products Co Div, Youngstown *Also called Hynes Industries Inc (G-20073)*
Rollandia Golf & Magic Castle, Dayton *Also called A To Z Golf Managment Co (G-9200)*
Rolling Acres Care Center, North Lima *Also called Guardian Elder Care LLC (G-15269)*
Rolling Hills Health Care Ctr, Blue Ash *Also called St Joseph Leasing Co LLC (G-1652)*
Rolling Hlls Rhab Wellness Ctr 330 225-9121
4426 Homestead Dr Brunswick (44212) *(G-1939)*
Rollins Moving and Storage Inc 937 525-4013
1050 Wheel St Springfield (45503) *(G-17105)*
Rolls Realty 614 792-5662
6706 Harriott Rd Powell (43065) *(G-16207)*
Rolta Advizex Technologies LLC (HQ) 216 901-1818
6480 S Rockside Woods Independence (44131) *(G-12117)*
Roman Cthlic Docese Youngstown 330 875-5562
2308 Reno Dr Louisville (44641) *(G-12973)*
Roman Cthlic Docese Youngstown 330 792-4721
248 S Belle Vista Ave Youngstown (44509) *(G-20191)*
Roman Plumbing Company 330 455-5155
2411 Shepler Ch Ave Sw Canton (44706) *(G-2462)*
Romanelli & Hughes Building Co 614 891-2042
148 W Schrock Rd Westerville (43081) *(G-19299)*
Romanelli & Hughes Contractors, Westerville *Also called Romanelli & Hughes Building Co (G-19299)*
Romanoff Electric Inc (PA) 614 755-4500
1288 Research Rd Gahanna (43230) *(G-11143)*
Romanoff Electric Co LLC 937 640-7925
5570 Enterprise Blvd Toledo (43612) *(G-18013)*
Romaster Corp 330 825-1945
3013 Wadsworth Rd Norton (44203) *(G-15422)*
Rometrics Too Hair Nail Gllery 440 808-1391
26155 Detroit Rd Westlake (44145) *(G-19402)*
Romitech Inc (PA) 937 297-9529
2000 Composite Dr Dayton (45420) *(G-9739)*
Ron Burge Trucking Inc 330 624-5373
1876 W Britton Rd Burbank (44214) *(G-2009)*
Ron Carrocce Trucking Company 330 758-0841
8063 Southern Blvd Youngstown (44512) *(G-20192)*
Ron Foth Advertising, Columbus *Also called Ron Foth Retail Inc (G-8547)*
Ron Foth Retail Inc 614 888-7771
8100 N High St Columbus (43235) *(G-8547)*
Ron Johnson Plumbing and Htg 419 433-5365
14805 Shawmill Rd Norwalk (44857) *(G-15455)*
Ron Kreps Drywall Plst Compang 330 726-8252
6042 Market St Youngstown (44512) *(G-20193)*
Ron Marhofer Automall Inc 330 835-6707
1260 Main St Cuyahoga Falls (44221) *(G-9121)*
Ron Marhofer Automall Inc (PA) 330 923-5059
1350 Main St Cuyahoga Falls (44221) *(G-9122)*
Ron Marhofer Collision Center 330 686-2262
1585 Commerce Dr Stow (44224) *(G-17228)*
Ron Marhofer Lincoln Mercury, Cuyahoga Falls *Also called Ron Marhofer Automall Inc (G-9122)*
Ron Neff Her Realtors, Chillicothe *Also called Ron Neff Real Estate (G-2816)*
Ron Neff Real Estate (PA) 740 773-4670
153 S Paint St Chillicothe (45601) *(G-2816)*
Ronald McDonald Hse Grtr Cinci 513 636-7642
341 Erkenbrecher Ave Cincinnati (45229) *(G-4395)*
Rondinelli Company Inc (PA) 330 726-7643
207 Boardman Canfield Rd Youngstown (44512) *(G-20194)*
Rondinellis Tuxedo 330 726-7768
207 Boardman Canfield Rd Youngstown (44512) *(G-20195)*

A L P H A B E T I C

Rondy & Co., Barberton *Also called Tahoma Rubber & Plastics Inc* ***(G-970)***
Rondy Fleet Services Inc......330 745-9016
255 Wooster Rd N Barberton (44203) ***(G-965)***
Rood Trucking Company Inc (PA)......330 652-3519
3505 Union St Mineral Ridge (44440) ***(G-14512)***
Roofing By Insulation Inc......937 315-5024
1727 Dalton Dr New Carlisle (45344) ***(G-14896)***
Roofing Supply Group LLC......614 239-1111
1288 Essex Ave Columbus (43201) ***(G-8548)***
Root Inc (PA)......419 874-0077
5470 Main St Ste 100 Sylvania (43560) ***(G-17448)***
Root Insurance Company......866 980-9431
80 E Rich St Fl 5 Columbus (43215) ***(G-8549)***
Root Map Module, Sylvania *Also called Root Inc* ***(G-17448)***
Rootstown Township......330 296-8240
4268 Sandy Lake Rd Ravenna (44266) ***(G-16265)***
Roppe Distribution, Fostoria *Also called Roppe Holding Company* ***(G-11011)***
Roppe Holding Company......419 435-9335
1500 Sandusky St Fostoria (44830) ***(G-11011)***
Roricks Inc......330 497-6888
4701 Eagle St Nw Canton (44720) ***(G-2463)***
Roricks Ceiling Center, Canton *Also called Roricks Inc* ***(G-2463)***
Rosary Care Center......419 824-3600
6832 Convent Blvd Sylvania (43560) ***(G-17449)***
Rosby Brothers Grnhse & Grnhse, Cleveland *Also called Rosby Brothers Inc* ***(G-6339)***
Rosby Brothers Inc......216 351-0850
42 E Schaaf Rd Cleveland (44131) ***(G-6339)***
Roschmans Restaurant ADM......419 225-8300
1933 Roschman Ave Lima (45804) ***(G-12734)***
Roscoe Medical, Middleburg Heights *Also called Compass Health Brands Corp* ***(G-14250)***
Roscoe Village Foundation......740 622-2222
200 N Whitewoman St Coshocton (43812) ***(G-9026)***
Rose & Dobyns An Ohio Partnr......740 335-4700
298 N Fayette St Wshngtn CT Hs (43160) ***(G-19882)***
Rose & Dobyns An Ohio Partnr (PA)......937 382-2838
97 N South St Wilmington (45177) ***(G-19646)***
Rose City Manufacturing Inc......937 325-5561
900 W Leffel Ln Springfield (45506) ***(G-17106)***
Rose Community Management LLC (PA)......917 542-3600
6000 Fredom Sq Dr Ste 500 Independence (44131) ***(G-12118)***
Rose Gracias......614 785-0001
115 Hutchinson Ave 101-136 Columbus (43235) ***(G-8550)***
Rose Lane Health Center, Massillon *Also called Rose Ln Hlth Rhabilitation Inc* ***(G-13725)***
Rose Ln Hlth Rhabilitation Inc......330 833-3174
5425 High Mill Ave Nw Massillon (44646) ***(G-13725)***
Rose Mary Johanna Grassell (PA)......216 481-4823
2346 W 14th St Cleveland (44113) ***(G-6340)***
Rose Metal Industries, Cleveland *Also called Rose Properties Inc* ***(G-6341)***
Rose Products and Services Inc......614 443-7647
545 Stimmel Rd Columbus (43223) ***(G-8551)***
Rose Properties Inc......216 881-6000
1536 E 43rd St Cleveland (44103) ***(G-6341)***
Rose Transport Inc......614 864-4004
6747 Taylor Rd Sw Reynoldsburg (43068) ***(G-16330)***
Rosebud Mining Company......740 658-4217
28490 Birmingham Rd Freeport (43973) ***(G-11055)***
Rosebud Mining Company......740 768-2097
9076 County Road 53 Bergholz (43908) ***(G-1444)***
Rosebud Mining Company......740 922-9122
5600 Pleasant Vly Rd Se Uhrichsville (44683) ***(G-18343)***
Roseland Lanes Inc......440 439-0097
26383 Broadway Ave Bedford (44146) ***(G-1302)***
Roselawn Health Services Corp......330 823-0618
11999 Klinger Ave Ne Alliance (44601) ***(G-550)***
Roselawn Terrace, Alliance *Also called Roselawn Health Services Corp* ***(G-550)***
Rosemark Paper Inc (PA)......614 443-0303
1845 Progress Ave Columbus (43207) ***(G-8552)***
Roseville Motor Express Inc......614 921-2121
2720 Westbelt Dr Columbus (43228) ***(G-8553)***
Ross Sinclaire & Assoc LLC (PA)......513 381-3939
700 Walnut St Ste 600 Cincinnati (45202) ***(G-4396)***
Ross Brittain Schonberg Lpa......216 447-1551
6480 Rckside Woods Blvd S Independence (44131) ***(G-12119)***
Ross Cnty Cmmittee For Elderly......740 773-3544
1824 Western Ave Chillicothe (45601) ***(G-2817)***
Ross Cnty Job & Family Svcs, Chillicothe *Also called Ross County Children Svcs Ctr* ***(G-2818)***
Ross Consolidated Corp (PA)......440 748-5800
36790 Giles Rd Grafton (44044) ***(G-11320)***
Ross County Children Svcs Ctr (PA)......740 773-2651
150 E 2nd St Chillicothe (45601) ***(G-2818)***
Ross County Community (PA)......740 702-7222
250 N Woodbridge Ave Chillicothe (45601) ***(G-2819)***
Ross County Health District......740 775-1114
150 E 2nd St Chillicothe (45601) ***(G-2820)***
Ross County Sportsmen and Wild......740 649-9614
550 Musselman Mill Rd Chillicothe (45601) ***(G-2821)***
Ross County Water Company Inc......740 774-4117
663 Fairgrounds Rd Chillicothe (45601) ***(G-2822)***
Ross County YMCA......740 772-4340
100 Mill St Chillicothe (45601) ***(G-2823)***
Ross Dialysis, Fairfield *Also called Goza Dialysis LLC* ***(G-10730)***
Ross Incineration Services Inc......440 366-2000
36790 Giles Rd Grafton (44044) ***(G-11321)***
Ross Training Center Inc......937 592-0025
334 E Columbus Ave Bellefontaine (43311) ***(G-1363)***
Ross Transportation Svcs Inc......440 748-5900
36790 Giles Rd Grafton (44044) ***(G-11322)***
Rossford Grtric Care Ltd Prtnr......614 459-0445
1661 Old Henderson Rd Columbus (43220) ***(G-8554)***
Rossford Hospitality Group Inc......419 874-2345
9753 Clark Dr Rossford (43460) ***(G-16464)***
Rossman......614 523-4150
7795 Walton Pkwy Ste 360 New Albany (43054) ***(G-14872)***
Roth Blair Roberts (PA)......330 744-5211
100 E Federal St Ste 600 Youngstown (44503) ***(G-20196)***
Roth Blair, Youngstown *Also called Roth Blair Roberts* ***(G-20196)***
Roth Bros Inc (HQ)......330 793-5571
3847 Crum Rd Youngstown (44515) ***(G-20197)***
Rothert Farm Inc......419 467-0095
1084 S Opfer Lentz Rd Elmore (43416) ***(G-10474)***
Roto Group LLC (PA)......614 760-8690
7001 Discovery Blvd Fl 2 Dublin (43017) ***(G-10325)***
Roto Rt Inc (HQ)......513 762-6690
255 E 5th St Ste 2500 Cincinnati (45202) ***(G-4397)***
Roto-Rooter, Cincinnati *Also called Nurotoco Massachusetts Inc* ***(G-4140)***
Roto-Rooter, Cincinnati *Also called Roto Rt Inc* ***(G-4397)***
Roto-Rooter Development Co (HQ)......513 762-6690
255 E 5th St Ste 2500 Cincinnati (45202) ***(G-4398)***
Roto-Rooter Group Inc (HQ)......513 762-6690
2500 Chemed Ctr Cincinnati (45202) ***(G-4399)***
Roto-Rooter Services Company......614 238-8006
4480 Bridgeway Ave Ste B Columbus (43219) ***(G-8555)***
Roto-Rooter Services Company (HQ)......513 762-6690
255 E 5th St Ste 2500 Cincinnati (45202) ***(G-4400)***
Roto-Rooter Services Company......513 541-3840
2125 Montana Ave Cincinnati (45211) ***(G-4401)***
Roto-Rooter Services Company......216 429-1928
5375 Naiman Pkwy Solon (44139) ***(G-16893)***
Rouen Chrysler Plymouth Dodge......419 837-6228
1091 Fremont Pike Woodville (43469) ***(G-19683)***
Rouen Dodge, Woodville *Also called Rouen Chrysler Plymouth Dodge* ***(G-19683)***
Rough Brothers Mfg Inc......513 242-0310
5513 Vine St Ste 1 Cincinnati (45217) ***(G-4402)***
Roulston & Company Inc (PA)......216 431-3000
1350 Euclid Ave Ste 400 Cleveland (44115) ***(G-6342)***
Roulston Research Corp......216 431-3000
1350 Euclid Ave Ste 400 Cleveland (44115) ***(G-6343)***
Round Room LLC......330 880-0660
3 Massillon Mrktplc Dr Sw Massillon (44646) ***(G-13726)***
Round Room LLC......937 429-2230
3301 Dayton Xenia Rd Beavercreek (45432) ***(G-1184)***
Roundstone Management Ltd......440 617-0333
15422 Detroit Ave Lakewood (44107) ***(G-12362)***
Roundtable Online Learning LLC......440 220-5252
8401 Chagrin Rd Ste 6 Chagrin Falls (44023) ***(G-2680)***
Roundtower Technologies LLC (PA)......513 247-7900
5905 E Galbraith Rd # 3000 Cincinnati (45236) ***(G-4403)***
Roush Equipment Inc (PA)......614 882-1535
100 W Schrock Rd Westerville (43081) ***(G-19300)***
Roush Honda, Westerville *Also called Roush Equipment Inc* ***(G-19300)***
Rovisys Building Tech LLC (PA)......330 954-7600
260 Campus Dr Aurora (44202) ***(G-841)***
Rovisys Building Tech Rbt, Aurora *Also called Rovisys Building Tech LLC* ***(G-841)***
Rovisys Company (PA)......330 562-8600
1455 Danner Dr Aurora (44202) ***(G-842)***
Roy J Miller......330 674-2405
6739 State Route 241 Millersburg (44654) ***(G-14490)***
Royal American Links Golf Club, Galena *Also called American Golf Corporation* ***(G-11154)***
Royal Appliance Manufacturing, Solon *Also called TTI Floor Care North Amer Inc* ***(G-16909)***
Royal Appliance Mfg Co (HQ)......440 996-2000
7005 Cochran Rd Cleveland (44139) ***(G-6344)***
Royal Arch Masons of Ohio......419 762-5565
109 E School St Napoleon (43545) ***(G-14816)***
Royal Building Cleaning Svcs, Toledo *Also called W David Maupin Inc* ***(G-18141)***
Royal Car Wash, Canton *Also called Royal Sheen Service Center* ***(G-2464)***
Royal Car Wash Inc......513 385-2777
6925 Colerain Ave Cincinnati (45239) ***(G-4404)***
Royal Color Inc......440 234-1337
550 Goodrich Rd Bellevue (44811) ***(G-1385)***
Royal Electric Cnstr Corp......614 253-6600
1250 Memory Ln N Columbus (43209) ***(G-8556)***
Royal Manor Health Care Inc (PA)......216 752-3600
18810 Harvard Ave Cleveland (44122) ***(G-6345)***
Royal Manor Homes, Cleveland *Also called Royal Oak Nrsing Rhbltion Ctr* ***(G-6346)***
Royal Oak Nrsing Rhbltion Ctr......440 884-9191
6973 Pearl Rd Cleveland (44130) ***(G-6346)***
Royal Paper Stock Company Inc (PA)......614 851-4714
1300 Norton Rd Columbus (43228) ***(G-8557)***
Royal Paper Stock Company Inc......513 870-5780
339 Circle Freeway Dr West Chester (45246) ***(G-19077)***

1242 2019 Harris Ohio Services Directory (G-0000) Company's Geographic Section entry number

Royal Rdeemer Lutheran Ch Schl, North Royalton *Also called Royal Redeemer Lutheran Church (G-15365)*
Royal Redeemer Lutheran Church..........440 237-7958
11680 Royalton Rd North Royalton (44133) ***(G-15365)***
Royal Sheen Service Center..........330 966-7200
6720 Bridgestone Cir Ne Canton (44721) ***(G-2464)***
Royalton Financial Group..........440 582-3020
13374 Ridge Rd Ste 1 Cleveland (44133) ***(G-6347)***
Royalton Senior Living Inc..........440 582-4111
14277 State Rd North Royalton (44133) ***(G-15366)***
Royalton Woods, North Royalton *Also called Royalton Senior Living Inc (G-15366)*
Royalty Mooney & Moses, Northwood *Also called Installed Building Pdts LLC (G-15396)*
Royce Leasing Co LLC..........740 354-1240
2125 Royce St Portsmouth (45662) ***(G-16165)***
Royce Security Services, Cleveland *Also called Sam-Tom Inc (G-6369)*
RPC Electronics Inc (PA)..........440 461-4700
749 Miner Rd Highland Heights (44143) ***(G-11736)***
RPC Electronics Inc..........877 522-7927
749 Miner Rd Ste 4 Cleveland (44143) ***(G-6348)***
RPC Mechanical Services (HQ)..........513 733-1641
5301 Lester Rd Cincinnati (45213) ***(G-4405)***
Rpf Consulting LLC..........678 494-8030
7870 E Kemper Rd Ste 300 Cincinnati (45249) ***(G-4406)***
Rpg Inc..........419 289-2757
400 Westlake Dr Ashland (44805) ***(G-687)***
RPM Midwest LLC..........513 762-9000
352 Gest St Cincinnati (45203) ***(G-4407)***
RR Donnelley & Sons Company..........614 539-5527
3801 Gantz Rd Ste A Grove City (43123) ***(G-11466)***
Rrp Packaging..........419 666-6119
327 5th St Perrysburg (43551) ***(G-15915)***
Rrr Express LLC..........800 723-3424
6432 Centre Park Dr West Chester (45069) ***(G-18996)***
Rrr Logistics, West Chester *Also called Rrr Express LLC (G-18996)*
Rse Group Inc..........937 596-6167
1003 S Main St Jackson Center (45334) ***(G-12186)***
Rsfi Office Furniture, Worthington *Also called Recycled Systems Furniture Inc (G-19842)*
RSI, Dayton *Also called Regent Systems Inc (G-9729)*
RSI Construction, Sunbury *Also called Restaurant Specialties Inc (G-17394)*
RSM US LLP..........937 298-0201
2000 W Dorothy Ln Moraine (45439) ***(G-14693)***
RSM US LLP..........614 224-7722
250 West St Ste 200 Columbus (43215) ***(G-8558)***
RSM US LLP..........216 523-1900
1001 Lakeside Ave E # 200 Cleveland (44114) ***(G-6349)***
RSR Partners LLC..........440 248-3991
6111 Cochran Rd Solon (44139) ***(G-16894)***
Rss, Cleveland *Also called Dwellworks LLC (G-5450)*
Rt80 Express Inc..........330 706-0900
4409 Clvland Massillon Rd Barberton (44203) ***(G-966)***
RTC Employment Services, Bellefontaine *Also called RTC Industries Inc (G-1364)*
RTC Industries Inc..........937 592-0534
36 County Road 32 S Bellefontaine (43311) ***(G-1364)***
Rthrford B Hayes Prsdntial Ctr..........419 332-2081
Spiegel Grv Fremont (43420) ***(G-11091)***
Rti, Akron *Also called Parklane Manor of Akron Inc (G-370)*
RTS, Georgetown *Also called Reliable Trnsp Solutions LLC (G-11273)*
Rtw Inc..........614 594-9217
544 W Walnut St Columbus (43215) ***(G-8559)***
Rtw Inc (HQ)..........952 893-0403
15245 Lincoln St Se Minerva (44657) ***(G-14523)***
Rubber & Plastics News, Akron *Also called Crain Communications Inc (G-169)*
Rubber City Machinery Corp..........330 434-3500
1 Thousand Sweitzer Ave Akron (44311) ***(G-411)***
Rubber City Radio Group (PA)..........330 869-9800
1795 W Market St Akron (44313) ***(G-412)***
Rubber City Realty Inc..........330 745-9034
942 Kenmore Blvd Akron (44314) ***(G-413)***
Rubber Seal Products, Dayton *Also called Teknol Inc (G-9808)*
Rubin Erb..........330 852-4423
2149 Dutch Valley Dr Nw Sugarcreek (44681) ***(G-17380)***
Rudolph Brothers & Co..........614 833-0707
6550 Oley Speaks Way Canal Winchester (43110) ***(G-2118)***
Rudolph Libbe Inc (HQ)..........419 241-5000
6494 Latcha Rd Walbridge (43465) ***(G-18624)***
RUDOLPH/LIBBE, Walbridge *Also called Rudolph Libbe Inc (G-18624)*
Rudolph/Libbe Companies Inc (PA)..........419 241-5000
6494 Latcha Rd Walbridge (43465) ***(G-18625)***
Rudzik Excavating Inc..........330 755-1540
401 Lowellville Rd Struthers (44471) ***(G-17367)***
RUFFING MONTESSORI SCHOOL, Cleveland *Also called Fairmount Montessori Assn (G-5505)*
Ruffing Montessori School..........440 333-2250
1285 Orchard Park Dr Rocky River (44116) ***(G-16445)***
Ruhl Electric Co..........330 823-7230
6428 Union Ave Ne Alliance (44601) ***(G-551)***
Ruhlin Company (PA)..........330 239-2800
6931 Ridge Rd Sharon Center (44274) ***(G-16724)***
Rukh Boardman Properties LLC..........330 726-5472
7410 South Ave Youngstown (44512) ***(G-20198)***
Rukh-Jagi Holdings LLC..........330 494-2770
4520 Everhard Rd Nw Canton (44718) ***(G-2465)***
Rumpf Ambulance, Toledo *Also called Brookeside Ambulance Services (G-17628)*
Rumpf Corporation (PA)..........419 255-5005
701 Jefferson Ave Ste 201 Toledo (43604) ***(G-18014)***
Rumpke Amusements Inc..........513 738-2646
10795 Hughes Rd Cincinnati (45251) ***(G-4408)***
Rumpke Cnsld Companies Inc (PA)..........513 738-0800
3963 Kraus Ln Hamilton (45014) ***(G-11640)***
Rumpke Container Service, Dayton *Also called Rumpke Transportation Co LLC (G-9740)*
Rumpke Container Service, Cincinnati *Also called Rumpke Transportation Co LLC (G-4410)*
Rumpke Recycling, Cincinnati *Also called Rumpke Waste Inc (G-4412)*
Rumpke Recycling, Circleville *Also called Rumpke Waste Inc (G-4847)*
Rumpke Sanitary Landfill Inc..........513 851-0122
10795 Hughes Rd Cincinnati (45251) ***(G-4409)***
Rumpke Softball Park, Cincinnati *Also called Rumpke Amusements Inc (G-4408)*
Rumpke Transportation Co LLC..........937 461-0004
1932 E Monument Ave Dayton (45402) ***(G-9740)***
Rumpke Transportation Co LLC..........513 242-4600
553 Vine St Cincinnati (45202) ***(G-4410)***
Rumpke Waste Inc (HQ)..........513 851-0122
10795 Hughes Rd Cincinnati (45251) ***(G-4411)***
Rumpke Waste Inc..........937 548-1939
5474 Jaysville St John Rd Greenville (45331) ***(G-11393)***
Rumpke Waste Inc..........937 378-4126
9427 Beyers Rd Georgetown (45121) ***(G-11274)***
Rumpke Waste Inc..........513 242-4401
5535 Vine St Cincinnati (45217) ***(G-4412)***
Rumpke Waste Inc..........740 474-9790
819 Island Rd Circleville (43113) ***(G-4847)***
Rumpke Waste and Recycl Svcs, Hamilton *Also called Rumpke Cnsld Companies Inc (G-11640)*
Rumpke/Kenworth Contract..........740 774-5111
65 Kenworth Dr Chillicothe (45601) ***(G-2824)***
Run Jump-N-Play..........513 701-7529
5897 Pfeiffer Rd Blue Ash (45242) ***(G-1648)***
Runt Ware & Sanitary Service..........330 494-5776
7944 Whipple Ave Nw Canton (44720) ***(G-2466)***
Runyon & Sons Roofing Inc..........440 974-6810
8745 Munson Rd Mentor (44060) ***(G-14105)***
Rupp/Rosebrock Inc..........419 533-7999
7464 County Road 424 Liberty Center (43532) ***(G-12575)***
Rural Lorain County Water Auth..........440 355-5121
42401 State Route 303 Lagrange (44050) ***(G-12326)***
RURAL WATER UTILITY, Chillicothe *Also called Ross County Water Company Inc (G-2822)*
Rural/Metro Corporation..........216 749-2211
1122 E Midlothian Blvd Youngstown (44502) ***(G-20199)***
Rural/Metro Corporation..........330 744-4161
1122 E Midlothian Blvd Youngstown (44502) ***(G-20200)***
Rural/Metro Corporation..........440 543-3313
8401 Chagrin Rd Ste 15a Chagrin Falls (44023) ***(G-2681)***
Ruralogic Inc..........419 630-0500
24500 Chagrin Blvd # 300 Beachwood (44122) ***(G-1103)***
Rurbanc Data Services Inc..........419 782-2530
7622 N State Route 66 Defiance (43512) ***(G-9938)***
Ruritan..........330 542-2308
3814 Columbiana Rd New Springfield (44443) ***(G-14997)***
Ruscilli Construction Co Inc (PA)..........614 876-9484
5000 Arlngtn Ctr Blvd # 300 Columbus (43220) ***(G-8560)***
Ruscilli Investment Co, Columbus *Also called L Jack Ruscilli (G-7936)*
Rush Expediting Inc..........937 885-0894
2619 Needmore Rd Dayton (45414) ***(G-9741)***
Rush Lincoln Mercury, Columbus *Also called Rush Motor Sales Inc (G-8561)*
Rush Motor Sales Inc..........614 471-9980
2350 Morse Rd Columbus (43229) ***(G-8561)***
Rush Package Delivery Inc (PA)..........937 224-7874
2619 Needmore Rd Dayton (45414) ***(G-9742)***
Rush Package Delivery Inc..........937 297-6182
2619 Needmore Rd Dayton (45414) ***(G-9743)***
Rush Package Delivery Inc..........513 771-7874
10091 Moteller Ln Cincinnati (45201) ***(G-4413)***
Rush Trans, Cincinnati *Also called Rush Package Delivery Inc (G-4413)*
Rush Trnsp & Logistics, Dayton *Also called Rush Package Delivery Inc (G-9742)*
Rush Trnsp & Logistics, Dayton *Also called Rush Package Delivery Inc (G-9743)*
Rush Truck Center, Cincinnati, Cincinnati *Also called Rush Truck Centers Ohio Inc (G-4414)*
Rush Truck Center, Lima, Lima *Also called Rush Truck Centers Ohio Inc (G-12735)*
Rush Truck Centers Ohio Inc (HQ)..........513 733-8500
11775 Highway Dr Cincinnati (45241) ***(G-4414)***
Rush Truck Centers Ohio Inc..........419 224-6045
2655 Saint Johns Rd Lima (45804) ***(G-12735)***
Rushcard, Blue Ash *Also called Unifund Corporation (G-1672)*
Rusk Industries Inc..........419 841-6055
2930 Centennial Rd Toledo (43617) ***(G-18015)***
Russell D Ens Do..........330 499-5700
4665 Douglas Cir Nw # 101 Canton (44718) ***(G-2467)***
Russell Hawk Enterprises Inc..........330 343-4612
2198 Donald Dr Dover (44622) ***(G-10097)***
Russell T Bundy Associates Inc (PA)..........937 652-2151
417 E Water St Ste 1 Urbana (43078) ***(G-18444)***

ALPHABETIC

Russell Weisman Jr MD 216 844-3127
  11100 Euclid Ave Cleveland (44106) *(G-6350)*

Rusty Oak Nursery Ltd 330 225-7704
  1547 Marks Rd Valley City (44280) *(G-18468)*

Rustys Towing Service Inc 614 491-6288
  4845 Obetz Reese Rd Columbus (43207) *(G-8562)*

Ruth McMillan Cancer Center, Xenia *Also called US Oncology Inc (G-19932)*

Rutherford Funeral Home Inc (PA) 614 451-0593
  2383 N High St Columbus (43202) *(G-8563)*

Rutherford Museums, Fremont *Also called Rthrford B Hayes Prsdntial Ctr (G-11091)*

Ruthman Pump and Engineering 937 783-2411
  459 E Fancy St Blanchester (45107) *(G-1489)*

Rutland Bus Garage, Middleport *Also called Meigs Local School District (G-14282)*

Rutledge Environmental Svcs, Cincinnati *Also called J Rutledge Enterprises Inc (G-3796)*

Rv Properties LLC 330 928-7888
  171 Graham Rd Cuyahoga Falls (44223) *(G-9123)*

Rvet Operating LLC 513 683-5020
  422 W Loveland Ave Loveland (45140) *(G-13025)*

Rwb Properties and Cnstr LLC 513 541-0900
  611 Shepherd Dr Unit 6 Cincinnati (45215) *(G-4415)*

Rwc Inc 614 890-0600
  6210 Frost Rd Westerville (43082) *(G-19208)*

Rwdop LLC 330 666-3776
  3558 Ridgewood Rd Fairlawn (44333) *(G-10845)*

Rwk Services Inc (PA) 440 526-2144
  4700 Rockside Rd Ste 330 Cleveland (44131) *(G-6351)*

RWS Enterprises LLC 513 598-6770
  9019 Colerain Ave Cincinnati (45251) *(G-4416)*

Rx Home Health Care Inc (PA) 216 295-0056
  2020 Carnegie Ave Ste 2 Cleveland (44115) *(G-6352)*

Rx Options LLC (HQ) 330 405-8080
  2181 E Aurora Rd Ste 101 Twinsburg (44087) *(G-18314)*

Rxp Ohio LLC 614 937-2844
  630 E Broad St Columbus (43215) *(G-8564)*

Rxp Wireless, Columbus *Also called Rxp Ohio LLC (G-8564)*

Rxp Wireless LLC 330 264-1500
  3417 Cleveland Rd Wooster (44691) *(G-19763)*

Ryan Logistics Inc 937 642-4158
  711 Clymer Rd Marysville (43040) *(G-13526)*

Ryan Partnership, Westerville *Also called D L Ryan Companies LLC (G-19156)*

Ryan Sheridan 330 270-2380
  45 N Canfield Niles Rd Youngstown (44515) *(G-20201)*

Ryan, Charles R MD Facog, Lima *Also called Ob-Gyn Specialists Lima Inc (G-12709)*

Ryans All-Glass Incorporated (PA) 513 771-4440
  9884 Springfield Pike Cincinnati (45215) *(G-4417)*

Rybac Inc 614 228-3578
  407 E Livingston Ave Columbus (43215) *(G-8565)*

Rycon Construction Inc 440 481-3770
  7661 W Ridgewood Dr Parma (44129) *(G-15774)*

Ryder Last Mile Inc 614 801-0621
  1650 Watermark Dr Ste 100 Columbus (43215) *(G-8566)*

Ryder Last Mile Inc (HQ) 866 711-3129
  7795 Walton Pkwy New Albany (43054) *(G-14873)*

Ryder Truck Rental Inc 614 846-6780
  775 Schrock Rd Columbus (43229) *(G-8567)*

Ryder Truck Rental Inc 513 241-7736
  1190 Gest St Cincinnati (45203) *(G-4418)*

Ryder Truck Rental Inc 419 666-9833
  1380 4th St Perrysburg (43551) *(G-15916)*

Ryder Truck Rental Inc 614 876-0405
  2600 Westbelt Dr Columbus (43228) *(G-8568)*

Ryder Truck Rental Inc 937 236-1650
  3580 Needmore Rd Dayton (45414) *(G-9744)*

Ryder Truck Rental Inc 513 772-0223
  2575 Commodity Cir Cincinnati (45241) *(G-4419)*

Ryder Truck Rental Inc 216 433-4700
  11250 Brookpark Rd Cleveland (44130) *(G-6353)*

Ryerson Coil Processing, Hamilton *Also called Joseph T Ryerson & Son Inc (G-11618)*

Ryno 24 Inc 440 946-7700
  4429 Hamann Pkwy Frnt Willoughby (44094) *(G-19569)*

S & B Enterprises LLC 740 753-2646
  668 Poplar St Nelsonville (45764) *(G-14836)*

S & B Trucking Inc (PA) 614 554-4090
  3045 Gale Dr Hubbard (44425) *(G-11950)*

S & D Application LLC (PA) 419 288-3660
  158 Church St Wayne (43466) *(G-18826)*

S & E Electric Inc 330 425-7866
  1521 Highland Rd Twinsburg (44087) *(G-18315)*

S & H Risner Inc 937 778-8563
  314 N Wayne St Piqua (45356) *(G-16027)*

S & K Asphalt & Concrete 330 848-6284
  2275 Manchester Rd Akron (44314) *(G-414)*

S & P Solutions Inc 440 918-9111
  35000 Chardon Rd Ste 110 Willoughby Hills (44094) *(G-19593)*

S & S Inc 216 383-1880
  21300 Saint Clair Ave Cleveland (44117) *(G-6354)*

S & S Halthcare Strategies Ltd 513 772-8866
  1385 Kemper Meadow Dr Cincinnati (45240) *(G-4420)*

S & S Management Inc 937 382-5858
  155 Holiday Dr Wilmington (45177) *(G-19647)*

S & S Management Inc 937 235-2000
  5612 Merily Way Dayton (45424) *(G-9745)*

S & S Management Inc 567 356-4151
  1510 Saturn Dr Wapakoneta (45895) *(G-18653)*

S & T Truck and Auto Svc Inc 614 272-8163
  3150 Valleyview Dr Rm 8 Columbus (43204) *(G-8569)*

S & W Properties, Columbus *Also called D & S Properties (G-7407)*

S A, Columbus *Also called Safe Auto Insurance Company (G-8571)*

S A F Y, Delphos *Also called For Specialized Alternatives (G-10027)*

S A I, New Albany *Also called Shremshock Architects Inc (G-14874)*

S A Storer and Sons Company 419 843-3133
  3135 Centennial Rd Sylvania (43560) *(G-17450)*

S A T Landscaping, Columbus *Also called Spray A Tree Inc (G-8674)*

S A W - Rocky River Adult Trai, Rocky River *Also called A W S Inc (G-16420)*

S A W Adult Training Center, Cleveland *Also called A W S Inc (G-4881)*

S and R Leasing 330 276-3061
  9705 Township Rd Millersburg (44654) *(G-14491)*

S and S Gilardi Inc 740 397-2751
  1033 Newark Rd Mount Vernon (43050) *(G-14788)*

S B Morabito Trucking Inc 216 441-3070
  3560 E 55th St Cleveland (44105) *(G-6355)*

S B S Transit Inc 440 288-2222
  1800 Colorado Ave Lorain (44052) *(G-12942)*

S C A T, Tiffin *Also called Seneca-Crawford Area Trnsp (G-17540)*

S C E, Brookpark *Also called Standard Contg & Engrg Inc (G-1906)*

S C O R E, Cleveland *Also called Service Corps Retired Execs (G-6398)*

S C O R E, Toledo *Also called Service Corps Retired Execs (G-18026)*

S C O R E 81, Akron *Also called Service Corps Retired Execs (G-424)*

S D Myers Inc 330 630-7000
  180 South Ave Tallmadge (44278) *(G-17486)*

S E S, West Chester *Also called Superior Envmtl Sltons SES Inc (G-19086)*

S E S, West Chester *Also called Superior Envmtl Solutions LLC (G-19087)*

S E T Inc 330 536-6724
  235 E Water St Ste C Lowellville (44436) *(G-13043)*

S F S, Clyde *Also called Spader Freight Services Inc (G-6754)*

S G I, Cincinnati *Also called The Sheakley Group Inc (G-4596)*

S G Loewendick and Sons Inc 614 539-2582
  2877 Jackson Pike Grove City (43123) *(G-11467)*

S L Klabunde Corp (PA) 614 508-6012
  893 N 4th St Columbus (43201) *(G-8570)*

S M C, Upper Sandusky *Also called Schmidt Machine Company (G-18412)*

S M E, Columbus *Also called Settle Muter Electric Ltd (G-8625)*

S O R T A, Cincinnati *Also called Southwest OH Trans Auth (G-4506)*

S P C A Cincinnati, Cincinnati *Also called Hamilton County Society (G-3677)*

S P Richards Company 614 497-2270
  2410 Mcgaw Rd Obetz (43207) *(G-15529)*

S P S & Associates Inc 330 283-4267
  2926 Ivanhoe Rd Silver Lake (44224) *(G-16808)*

S P S Inc 937 339-7801
  45 Troy Town Dr Troy (45373) *(G-18228)*

S R Door Inc (PA) 740 927-3558
  1120 O Neill Dr Hebron (43025) *(G-11723)*

S R Restaurant Corp 216 781-6784
  1836 Euclid Ave Ste 800 Cleveland (44115) *(G-6356)*

S S Kemp & Company (HQ) 216 271-7062
  4567 Willow Pkwy Cleveland (44125) *(G-6357)*

S S T Enterprises Inc 330 343-2656
  5165 Main St Ne New Philadelphia (44663) *(G-14979)*

S W S, Akron *Also called Sws Equipment Services Inc (G-462)*

S&D Farms Inc (PA) 419 859-3785
  13466 Township Road 53 Mount Cory (45868) *(G-14722)*

S&D/Osterfeld Mech Contrs Inc 937 277-1700
  1101 Negley Pl Dayton (45402) *(G-9746)*

S&Me Inc 614 793-2226
  6190 Enterprise Ct Dublin (43016) *(G-10326)*

S&P Data Ohio LLC 216 965-0018
  1500 W 3rd St Ste 130 Cleveland (44113) *(G-6358)*

S&P Global Inc 614 835-2444
  6405 Commerce Ct Groveport (43125) *(G-11536)*

S&P Global Inc 330 482-9544
  41438 Kings Ct Leetonia (44431) *(G-12519)*

S&S Car Care Inc 330 494-9535
  5340 Mayfair Rd Canton (44720) *(G-2468)*

S&V Industries Inc (PA) 330 666-1986
  5054 Paramount Dr Medina (44256) *(G-13997)*

S-L Distribution Company LLC 740 676-6932
  3157 Guernsey St Bellaire (43906) *(G-1335)*

S. B. Stone & Company, Independence *Also called Level Seven (G-12088)*

S. Rose Company, Cleveland *Also called Office Furniture Resources Inc (G-6113)*

S.E.I., New Philadelphia *Also called Starlight Enterprises Inc (G-14983)*

S.E.S., Alliance *Also called Steel Eqp Specialists Inc (G-555)*

S.O.S., Cleveland *Also called Senior Outreach Services (G-6397)*

S.O.S. Electric, Chillicothe *Also called Oyer Electric Inc (G-2809)*

Sabco Industries Inc 419 531-5347
  5242 Angola Rd Ste 150 Toledo (43615) *(G-18016)*

Saber Healthcare Group LLC 440 546-0643
  8757 Brecksville Rd Brecksville (44141) *(G-1803)*

Saber Healthcare Group LLC 440 352-0788
  60 Wood St Painesville (44077) *(G-15739)*

Saber Healthcare Group LLC 216 486-5736
  1500 E 191st St Euclid (44117) (G-10655)
Saber Healthcare Group LLC 216 662-3343
  19900 Clare Ave Maple Heights (44137) (G-13294)
Saber Healthcare Group LLC 937 826-3351
  1649 Park Rd Woodstock (43084) (G-19680)
Saber Healthcare Group LLC 937 779-4150
  141 Spruce Ln West Union (45693) (G-19138)
Saber Healthcare Group LLC 419 484-1111
  24201 W 3rd St Grand Rapids (43522) (G-11330)
Saber Healthcare Group LLC (PA) 216 292-5706
  26691 Richmond Rd Frnt Bedford (44146) (G-1303)
Saber Healthcare Group LLC 740 852-3100
  218 Elm St London (43140) (G-12874)
SABER SKILLED NURSING UNIT AT, Wadsworth Also called Barberton Healthcare Group
LLC (G-18591)
Sable Creek Golf Course Inc 330 877-9606
  5942 Edison St Ne Hartville (44632) (G-11697)
Sabroske Electric Inc 419 332-6444
  115 Lincoln St Fremont (43420) (G-11092)
Sabry Hospital 216 476-7052
  18101 Lorain Ave Cleveland (44111) (G-6359)
Sack n Save Inc 740 382-2464
  725 Richmond Ave Marion (43302) (G-13458)
Sacs Cnsltng Invstigative Svc, Akron Also called Sacs Cnsltng Training Ctr Inc (G-415)
Sacs Cnsltng Training Ctr Inc 330 255-1101
  520 S Main St Ste 2516 Akron (44311) (G-415)
Sadguru Krupa LLC 330 644-2111
  897 Arlington Rdg E Akron (44312) (G-416)
Sadler-Necamp Financial Svcs 513 489-5477
  7621 E Kemper Rd Cincinnati (45249) (G-4421)
Saec/Kinetic Vision Inc 513 793-4959
  10255 Evendale Commons Dr Cincinnati (45241) (G-4422)
Safari Club International 440 247-8614
  5084 Garrett Dr North Ridgeville (44039) (G-15342)
Safe Auto Insurance Company 740 472-1900
  47060 Black Walnut Pkwy Woodsfield (43793) (G-19678)
Safe Auto Insurance Company (HQ) 614 231-0200
  4 Easton Oval Columbus (43219) (G-8571)
Safe Auto Insurance Group Inc (PA) 614 231-0200
  4 Easton Oval Columbus (43219) (G-8572)
Safe-N-Sound Security Inc 330 491-1148
  5555 County Road 203 Millersburg (44654) (G-14492)
Safegard Bckgrund Screening LLC 216 370-7345
  3711 Chester Ave Cleveland (44114) (G-6360)
Safeguard Properties LLC (HQ) 216 739-2900
  7887 Safeguard Cir Cleveland (44125) (G-6361)
Safeguard Properties MGT LLC (PA) 216 739-2900
  7887 Hub Pkwy Cleveland (44125) (G-6362)
Safelite Autoglass, Columbus Also called Safelite Fulfillment Inc (G-8573)
Safelite Autoglass, Cleveland Also called Safelite Fulfillment Inc (G-6363)
Safelite Autoglass, Columbus Also called Safelite Group Inc (G-8576)
Safelite Autoglass, Columbus Also called Safelite Glass Corp (G-8575)
Safelite Fulfillment Inc 614 781-5449
  760 Dearborn Park Ln Columbus (43085) (G-8573)
Safelite Fulfillment Inc 216 475-7781
  6050 Towpath Dr Ste A Cleveland (44125) (G-6363)
Safelite Fulfillment Inc 614 210-9050
  7400 Safelite Way Columbus (43235) (G-8574)
Safelite Glass Corp (HQ) 614 210-9000
  7400 Safelite Way Columbus (43235) (G-8575)
Safelite Glass Corp. 614 431-4936
  600 Lkview Plz Blvd Ste A Worthington (43085) (G-19846)
Safelite Group Inc (HQ) 614 210-9000
  7400 Safelite Way Columbus (43235) (G-8576)
Safelite Solutions LLC 614 210-9000
  7400 Safelite Way Columbus (43235) (G-8577)
Safely Home Inc 440 232-9310
  121 Center Rd Ofc Bedford (44146) (G-1304)
Safety and Hygiene, Pickerington Also called Bureau Workers Compensation (G-15950)
Safety and Sustainment Branch, Dayton Also called Landing Gear Test Facility (G-9180)
Safety Grooving & Grinding LP 419 592-8666
  13226 County Road R Napoleon (43545) (G-14817)
Safety Resources Company Ohio 330 477-1100
  4650 Southway St Sw Canton (44706) (G-2469)
Safety Solutions Inc (HQ) 614 799-9900
  6999 Huntley Rd Ste L Columbus (43229) (G-8578)
Safety Today Inc (HQ) 614 409-7200
  3287 Southwest Blvd Grove City (43123) (G-11468)
Safety-Kleen Systems Inc 513 563-0931
  4120 Thunderbird Ln Fairfield (45014) (G-10777)
Safety-Kleen Systems Inc 740 929-3532
  581 Milliken Dr Hebron (43025) (G-11724)
Safeway Electric Company Inc 614 443-7672
  1973 Lockbourne Rd Columbus (43207) (G-8579)
Safran Humn Rsrces Support Inc (HQ) 513 552-3230
  111 Merchant St Cincinnati (45246) (G-4423)
Safran Power Usa LLC 330 487-2000
  8380 Darrow Rd Twinsburg (44087) (G-18316)
Saftek Industrial Service Inc 937 667-1772
  15 Industry Park Ct Tipp City (45371) (G-17566)
SAFY, Delphos Also called Specialized Alternatives For F (G-10035)

Safy Behavioral Health of Lima, Lima Also called Specialized Alternatives For F (G-12746)
Safy of Cleveland, Shaker Heights Also called Specialized Alternatives For F (G-16714)
Saga Communications Neng Inc 614 451-2191
  4401 Carriage Hill Ln Columbus (43220) (G-8580)
Sagamore Hills Medical Center, Northfield Also called Clevelnd Clnc Hlth Systm
East (G-15376)
Sagar Satyavolu MD 937 323-1404
  1911 E High St Springfield (45505) (G-17107)
Sage Hospitality Resources LLC 513 771-2080
  11320 Chester Rd Cincinnati (45246) (G-4424)
Sage Sustainable Elec LLC (HQ) 844 472-4373
  2801 Charter St Columbus (43228) (G-8581)
Saia Motor Freight Line LLC 419 726-9761
  1919 E Manhattan Blvd Toledo (43608) (G-18017)
Saia Motor Freight Line LLC 330 659-4277
  2920 Brecksville Rd Ste B Richfield (44286) (G-16377)
Saia Motor Freight Line LLC 614 870-8778
  1717 Krieger St Columbus (43228) (G-8582)
Saini, Hari MD, Miamisburg Also called Schuster Cardiology (G-14216)
Saint Cecilia Church 614 878-5353
  440 Norton Rd Columbus (43228) (G-8583)
Saint Edward Housing Corp 330 668-2828
  3125 Smith Rd Ofc Fairlawn (44333) (G-10846)
Saint Edward's Church, Ashland Also called Catholic Diocese of Cleveland (G-664)
Saint Francis De Sales Church 440 884-2319
  3434 George Ave Cleveland (44134) (G-6364)
Saint James Day Care Center 513 662-2287
  3929 Boudinot Ave Cincinnati (45211) (G-4425)
Saint Johns Villa 330 627-4662
  701 Crest St Nw Carrollton (44615) (G-2576)
Saint Joseph Orphanage 513 231-5010
  274 Sutton Rd Cincinnati (45230) (G-4426)
Saint Joseph Orphanage (PA) 513 741-3100
  5400 Edalbert Dr Cincinnati (45239) (G-4427)
Saint Mary Parish 440 285-7051
  401 North St Chardon (44024) (G-2712)
Saint Marys Cy Schools-Bus Gar, Saint Marys Also called St Marys City Board
Education (G-16532)
Saint Marys Living Center, Saint Marys Also called Communicare Health Svcs Inc (G-16521)
Saint Moritz Security Services, Youngstown Also called St Moritz Security Svcs
Inc (G-20216)
Saint Rtas Bhavioral Hlth Svcs, Lima Also called St Ritas Medical Center (G-12749)
Saleh, Hady DMD, Tipp City Also called Charles C Smith DDS Inc (G-17551)
Salem Area Visiting Nurse Assoc 330 332-9986
  718 E 3rd St Ste A Salem (44460) (G-16558)
Salem Church of God Inc 937 836-6500
  6500 Southway Rd Unit 2 Clayton (45315) (G-4861)
Salem Community Center Inc 330 332-5885
  1098 N Ellsworth Ave Salem (44460) (G-16559)
Salem Community Hospital (PA) 330 332-1551
  1995 E State St Salem (44460) (G-16560)
Salem Dental Laboratory, Cleveland Also called National Dentex LLC (G-6042)
Salem Healthcare MGT LLC 330 332-1588
  1985 E Pershing St Salem (44460) (G-16561)
Salem Hills Golf and Cntry CLB, Salem Also called Lake Front II Inc (G-16551)
Salem Historical Soc Museum 330 337-6733
  208 S Broadway Ave Salem (44460) (G-16562)
SALEM HOME MEDICAL, Salem Also called Salem Community Hospital (G-16560)
Salem Internal Medicine Assoc 330 332-5232
  564 E 2nd St Salem (44460) (G-16563)
Salem Media Group Inc 216 901-0921
  4 Summit Park Dr Ste 150 Cleveland (44131) (G-6365)
Salem West Healthcare Center, Salem Also called Bentley Leasing Co LLC (G-16536)
Salem West Healthcare Center, Wintersville Also called Communicare Health Svcs
Inc (G-19669)
Sales Building Systems, Mentor Also called Contract Marketing Inc (G-14034)
Salidawoods, Mentor Also called Lifeservices Development Corp (G-14077)
Saline Township 330 532-2195
  164 Main St Hammondsville (43930) (G-11657)
Salineville Office, Salineville Also called M3 Midstream LLC (G-16571)
Sally Beauty Supply 9927, Columbus Also called Sally Beauty Supply LLC (G-8584)
Sally Beauty Supply LLC 937 548-7684
  5805 Jaysville St John Rd Greenville (45331) (G-11394)
Sally Beauty Supply LLC 614 278-1691
  4309 Janitrol Rd Columbus (43228) (G-8584)
Salo Inc 740 623-2331
  232 Chestnut St Coshocton (43812) (G-9027)
Salo Inc (PA) 614 436-9404
  960 Checkrein Ave Ste A Columbus (43229) (G-8585)
Salo Inc 740 964-2904
  350 S Main St B Pataskala (43062) (G-15787)
Saloma Intl Co Since 1978 .... 440 941-1527
  430 Grant St Akron (44311) (G-417)
Salomanetics, Akron Also called Saloma Intl Co Since 1978 (G-417)
Salon Alexandre Inc 513 207-8406
  9755 Cncnnati Columbus Rd West Chester (45241) (G-19078)
Salon Communication Services 614 233-8500
  650 N High St Columbus (43215) (G-8586)

A
L
P
H
A
B
E
T
I
C

Salon Hazelton 419 874-9404
  131 W Indiana Ave Perrysburg (43551) *(G-15917)*
Salon La 513 784-1700
  2711 Edmondson Rd Cincinnati (45209) *(G-4428)*
Salon PS, Cleveland *Also called PS Lifestyle LLC (G-6265)*
Salon Spa & Wellness Center, West Chester *Also called Hairy Cactus Salon Inc (G-18940)*
Salon Ware Inc 330 665-2244
  1298 Centerview Cir Copley (44321) *(G-8972)*
Sals Heating and Cooling Inc 216 676-4949
  11701 Royalton Rd Cleveland (44133) *(G-6366)*
Salt Fork Resort Club Inc 740 498-8116
  74978 Broadhead Rd Kimbolton (43749) *(G-12312)*
Salutary Providers Inc 440 964-8446
  2217 West Ave Ashtabula (44004) *(G-753)*
Salvagedata Recovery LLC (PA) 914 600-2434
  43 Alpha Park Cleveland (44143) *(G-6367)*
Salvagnini America Inc (HQ) 513 874-8284
  27 Bicentennial Ct Hamilton (45015) *(G-11641)*
Salvation Army, Galion *Also called Ohio Hrtland Cmnty Action Comm (G-11180)*
Salvation Army 614 252-7171
  966 E Main St Columbus (43205) *(G-8587)*
Salvation Army 937 528-5100
  1000 N Keowee St Dayton (45404) *(G-9747)*
Salvation Army 419 447-2252
  505 E Market St Tiffin (44883) *(G-17535)*
Salvation Army 859 255-5791
  2250 Park Ave Cincinnati (45212) *(G-4429)*
Salvation Army 800 728-7825
  1675 S High St Columbus (43207) *(G-8588)*
Salvation Army 513 762-5600
  114 East Central Pkwy Cincinnati (45202) *(G-4430)*
Salvation Army 216 861-8185
  2507 E 22nd St Cleveland (44115) *(G-6368)*
Salvation Army 330 773-3331
  1006 Grant St Akron (44311) *(G-418)*
Salvation Army 330 735-2671
  5037 Edgewood Rd Sw Carrollton (44615) *(G-2577)*
Sam BS Restaurant 419 353-2277
  163 S Main St Bowling Green (43402) *(G-1748)*
Sam's Distribution Center, Westerville *Also called Dhl Supply Chain (usa) (G-19158)*
Sam-Tom Inc 216 426-7752
  3740 Euclid Ave Ste 102 Cleveland (44115) *(G-6369)*
Samanritan Family Care, Dayton *Also called Primary Cr Ntwrk Prmr Hlth Prt (G-9709)*
Samaritan Behavioral Health (HQ) 937 276-8333
  601 Enid Ave Dayton (45429) *(G-9748)*
Samaritan Care Center & Villa, Medina *Also called Ahf Ohio Inc (G-13907)*
Samaritan Care Center & Villa 330 725-4123
  806 E Washington St Medina (44256) *(G-13998)*
Samaritan Health & Rehab Ctr, Ashland *Also called Samaritan Regional Health Sys (G-689)*
Samaritan Health Partners (HQ) 937 208-8400
  2222 Philadelphia Dr Dayton (45406) *(G-9749)*
Samaritan N Surgery Ctr Ltd 937 567-6100
  9000 N Main St Englewood (45415) *(G-10600)*
Samaritan Professional Corp 419 289-0491
  1025 Center St Ashland (44805) *(G-688)*
Samaritan Regional Health Sys 419 281-1330
  2163 Claremont Ave Ashland (44805) *(G-689)*
Samaritan Regional Health Sys (PA) 419 289-0491
  1025 Center St Ashland (44805) *(G-690)*
Sami S Rafidi 330 799-9508
  2000 Canfield Rd Youngstown (44511) *(G-20202)*
Samkel Inc 614 491-3270
  100 Obetz Rd Columbus (43207) *(G-8589)*
Sammy's, Cleveland *Also called City Life Inc (G-5186)*
Sample Machining Inc 937 258-3338
  220 N Jersey St Dayton (45403) *(G-9750)*
Samples Chuck-General Contr 419 586-1434
  1460 E Wayne St Celina (45822) *(G-2610)*
Samron Inc 330 782-6539
  674 Bev Rd Youngstown (44512) *(G-20203)*
Samsel Rope & Marine Supply Co (PA) 216 241-0333
  1285 Old River Rd Uppr Cleveland (44113) *(G-6370)*
Samsel Supply Company, Cleveland *Also called Samsel Rope & Marine Supply Co (G-6370)*
Samuel Son & Co (usa) Inc 419 470-7070
  1500 Coining Dr Toledo (43612) *(G-18018)*
Samuel Steel Pickling Company (PA) 330 963-3777
  1400 Enterprise Pkwy Twinsburg (44087) *(G-18317)*
Samuel Strapping Systems Inc 740 522-2500
  1455 James Pkwy Heath (43056) *(G-11709)*
Samuels Products Inc 513 891-4456
  9851 Redhill Dr Blue Ash (45242) *(G-1649)*
Sanborn Vending, Nelsonville *Also called S & B Enterprises LLC (G-14836)*
Sanctuary At The Ohio Valley, Ironton *Also called Ahf Ohio Inc (G-12144)*
Sanctuary At Tuttle Crossing 614 408-0182
  4880 Tuttle Rd Dublin (43017) *(G-10327)*
Sanctuary At Wilmington Place 937 256-4663
  264 Wilmington Ave Dayton (45420) *(G-9751)*
Sanctuary of The Ohio Valley, Ironton *Also called Bryant Health Center Inc (G-12147)*
Sanctuary Software Studio Inc 330 666-9690
  3560 W Market St Ste 100 Fairlawn (44333) *(G-10847)*

Sand Ridge Golf Club 440 285-8088
  12150 Mayfield Rd Chardon (44024) *(G-2713)*
Sand Run Supports LLC 330 256-2127
  2695 Sand Run Pkwy Fairlawn (44333) *(G-10848)*
SAND T NURSING HOME, Brunswick *Also called Willowood Care Center (G-1947)*
Sandco Industries 419 334-9090
  567 Premier Dr Clyde (43410) *(G-6752)*
Sandel Corp 614 475-5898
  152 N High St Gahanna (43230) *(G-11144)*
Sander Woody Ford (PA) 513 541-5586
  235 W Mitchell Ave Cincinnati (45232) *(G-4431)*
Sandridge Food Corporation 330 725-8883
  133 Commerce Dr Medina (44256) *(G-13999)*
Sandridge Gourmet Salads, Medina *Also called Sandridge Food Corporation (G-13999)*
Sands Decker Cps Llc (PA) 614 459-6992
  1495 Old Henderson Rd Columbus (43220) *(G-8590)*
Sands Hill Coal Hauling Co Inc (PA) 740 384-4211
  38701 State Route 160 Hamden (45634) *(G-11553)*
Sandusky Area YMCA Foundation 419 621-9622
  224 E Water St 2 Sandusky (44870) *(G-16637)*
Sandusky Cnty Job & Fmly Svcs, Fremont *Also called Ohio Dept of Job & Fmly Svcs (G-11089)*
Sandusky County Engr & Hwy Gar 419 334-9731
  2500 W State St Fremont (43420) *(G-11093)*
Sandusky Harbor Marina Inc 419 627-1201
  1 Huron St Sandusky (44870) *(G-16638)*
Sandusky Harbour Marina, Sandusky *Also called Sandusky Harbor Marina Inc (G-16638)*
Sandusky Newspaper Group, Sandusky *Also called Sandusky Newspapers Inc (G-16639)*
Sandusky Newspapers Inc (PA) 419 625-5500
  314 W Market St Sandusky (44870) *(G-16639)*
Sandusky Register 419 625-5500
  314 W Market St Sandusky (44870) *(G-16640)*
Sandusky Rotary Club Charitabl 419 625-1707
  1722 Sandpiper Ct Huron (44839) *(G-12029)*
Sandusky Yacht Club Inc 419 625-6567
  529 E Water St Sandusky (44870) *(G-16641)*
Sandusky YMCA, Sandusky *Also called Sandusky Area YMCA Foundation (G-16637)*
Sandy Creek Joint Fire Dst 330 868-5193
  505 E Lincolnway Minerva (44657) *(G-14524)*
Sandys Auto & Truck Svc Inc 937 461-4980
  3053 Springboro W Moraine (45439) *(G-14694)*
Sandys Towing (PA) 937 461-4980
  3053 Springboro W Moraine (45439) *(G-14695)*
Sanese Services Inc (PA) 614 436-1234
  2590 Elm Rd Ne Warren (44483) *(G-18739)*
Sanfillipo Produce Co Inc 614 237-3300
  4561 E 5th Ave Ste 1 Columbus (43219) *(G-8591)*
Sanfillipo Produce Company, Columbus *Also called Sanfillipo Produce Co Inc (G-8591)*
Sanfillipos Automotive Service, Cincinnati *Also called Glenway Automotive Service (G-3620)*
Sanfrey Freight Services Inc 330 372-1883
  695 Summit St Nw Ste 1 Warren (44485) *(G-18740)*
Sanico Inc 440 439-5686
  7601 First Pl Ste 12 Cleveland (44146) *(G-6371)*
Sanitation & Garage Services, Marion *Also called City of Marion (G-13412)*
Sanoh America Inc 740 392-9200
  7905 Industrial Park Dr Mount Vernon (43050) *(G-14789)*
Santa Maria Community Svcs Inc (PA) 513 557-2720
  617 Steiner St Cincinnati (45204) *(G-4432)*
Santantonio Diana and Assoc 440 323-5121
  750 Abbe Rd S Elyria (44035) *(G-10560)*
Santas Hide Away Hollow Inc 440 632-5000
  15400 Bundysburg Rd Middlefield (44062) *(G-14276)*
Santmyer Oil Co Inc (PA) 330 262-6501
  3000 Old Airport Rd Wooster (44691) *(G-19764)*
Santo Salon & Spa, Pepper Pike *Also called Frank Santo LLC (G-15817)*
Sap America Inc 513 762-7630
  312 Walnut St Ste 1600 Cincinnati (45202) *(G-4433)*
Sar Biren 419 865-0407
  6425 Kit Ln Maumee (43537) *(G-13848)*
Sar Enterprises LLC 419 472-8181
  2631 W Central Ave Toledo (43606) *(G-18019)*
Sarah Jane Living Center Ltd 419 692-6618
  328 W 2nd St Delphos (45833) *(G-10034)*
SARAH MOORE COMMUNITY, Delaware *Also called Sarah Moore Hlth Care Ctr Inc (G-10005)*
Sarah Moore Hlth Care Ctr Inc 740 362-9641
  26 N Union St Delaware (43015) *(G-10005)*
Saras Garden 419 335-7272
  620 W Leggett St Wauseon (43567) *(G-18810)*
Sardinia Life Squad 937 446-2178
  159 Winchester St Sardinia (45171) *(G-16660)*
Sargus Juvenille Center, Saint Clairsville *Also called Bellmont County (G-16471)*
Sarnova Inc (PA) 614 760-5000
  5000 Tuttle Crossing Blvd Dublin (43016) *(G-10328)*
Saro Truck Dispatch Inc 419 873-1358
  26180 Glenwood Rd Perrysburg (43551) *(G-15918)*
Sarta, Canton *Also called Stark Area Regional Trnst Auth (G-2487)*
Sasi, Toledo *Also called Compass Corp For Recovery Svcs (G-17673)*
Satcom Service LLC 614 863-6470
  7052 Americana Pkwy Reynoldsburg (43068) *(G-16331)*

Sateri Home Inc (PA) 330 758-8106
  7246 Ronjoy Pl Youngstown (44512) *(G-20204)*
Sattlerpearson Inc 419 698-3822
  3055 E Plaza Blvd Northwood (43619) *(G-15406)*
Saturn Electric Inc 937 278-2580
  2628 Nordic Rd Dayton (45414) *(G-9752)*
Saturn of Toledo Inc 419 841-9070
  6141 W Central Ave Toledo (43615) *(G-18020)*
Saturn-West, Columbus Also called Northern Automotive Inc *(G-8200)*
Sauder Haritage Inn 419 445-6408
  22611 State Route 2 Archbold (43502) *(G-637)*
Sauder Village 419 446-2541
  22611 State Route 2 Archbold (43502) *(G-638)*
Sauder Woodworking Co (PA) 419 446-2711
  502 Middle St Archbold (43502) *(G-639)*
Sauder's Quality Eggs, Winesburg Also called R W Sauder Inc *(G-19666)*
Sauer Group Inc 614 853-2500
  1801 Lone Eagle St Columbus (43228) *(G-8592)*
Sauer Incorporated 614 853-2500
  1801 Lone Eagle St Columbus (43228) *(G-8593)*
Savage and Associates Inc (PA) 419 475-8665
  655 Beaver Creek Cir Maumee (43537) *(G-13849)*
Savage Auto Supply Div, Hamilton Also called Hamilton Automotive Warehouse *(G-11607)*
Save Edge USA, Xenia Also called File Sharpening Company Inc *(G-19899)*
Savings Bank (PA) 740 474-3191
  118 N Court St 120 Circleville (43113) *(G-4848)*
Saw Mill Creek Ltd 419 433-3800
  400 Sawmill Creek Dr W Huron (44839) *(G-12030)*
Saw Service and Supply Company 216 252-5600
  11925 Zelis Rd Cleveland (44135) *(G-6372)*
Saw Systems Inc (PA) 330 963-2992
  1579 Enterprise Pkwy Twinsburg (44087) *(G-18318)*
Sawdey Solution Services Inc (PA) 937 490-4060
  1430 Oak Ct Ste 304 Beavercreek (45430) *(G-1236)*
Sawmill Creek Golf Racquet CLB, Huron Also called Sawmill Greek Golf Racquet
CLB *(G-12032)*
Sawmill Creek Resort Ltd 419 433-3800
  400 Sawmill Creek Dr W Huron (44839) *(G-12031)*
Sawmill Greek Golf Racquet CLB 419 433-3789
  300 Sawmill Creek Dr W Huron (44839) *(G-12032)*
Sawmill Road Management Co LLC (PA) 937 342-9071
  1990 Kingsgate Rd Ste A Springfield (45502) *(G-17108)*
Sawyer Realtors 513 423-6521
  1505 S Breiel Blvd Middletown (45044) *(G-14327)*
Sawyer Steel Erectors Inc 419 867-8050
  1761 Commerce Rd Holland (43528) *(G-11910)*
Sax 5th Ave Car Wash Inc (PA) 614 486-9093
  1319 W 5th Ave Columbus (43212) *(G-8594)*
Sax Car Wash, Columbus Also called Sax 5th Ave Car Wash Inc *(G-8594)*
Saxon House Condo 440 333-8675
  3167 Linden Rd Cleveland (44116) *(G-6373)*
Saxton Real Estate Co (PA) 614 875-2327
  3703 Broadway Grove City (43123) *(G-11469)*
Sayles Company LLC 614 801-0432
  1575 Integrity Dr E Columbus (43209) *(G-8595)*
Sb Capital Acquisitions LLC 614 443-4080
  4010 E 5th Ave Columbus (43219) *(G-8596)*
Sb Capital Group LLC (PA) 516 829-2400
  4300 E 5th Ave Columbus (43219) *(G-8597)*
Sb Financial Group Inc (PA) 419 783-8950
  401 Clinton St Defiance (43512) *(G-9939)*
Sb Hotel LLC (PA) 614 793-2244
  5775 Perimeter Dr Ste 290 Dublin (43017) *(G-10329)*
SBC Recycling, Centerburg Also called Shredded Bedding Corporation *(G-2616)*
Sbh I & II, Columbus Also called Spruce Bough Homes LLC *(G-8678)*
Sbm Business Services Inc (HQ) 330 396-7000
  333 S Main St Ste 200 Akron (44308) *(G-419)*
SBS of Canton Jv LLC 330 966-6620
  3879 Everhard Rd Nw Canton (44709) *(G-2470)*
SC Chippewa Preschool, Doylestown Also called Chippewa School District *(G-10110)*
SC Madison Bus Garage 419 589-3373
  600 Esley Ln Mansfield (44905) *(G-13241)*
Sca Acquisitions Inc (HQ) 216 777-2750
  4141 Rockside Rd Ste 210 Seven Hills (44131) *(G-16680)*
Scanner Applications LLC 513 248-5588
  400 Milford Pkwy Milford (45150) *(G-14429)*
Scanner Applications, Inc., Milford Also called Scanner Applications LLC *(G-14429)*
Scarbrough E Tennis Fitnes CLB, Columbus Also called Scarbrough E Tennis Fitnes
Ctr *(G-8598)*
Scarbrough E Tennis Fitnes Ctr 614 751-2597
  5641 Alshire Rd Columbus (43232) *(G-8598)*
Scared Heart Nursing Home, Oregon Also called Sisters of Little *(G-15608)*
Scarffs Nursery Inc 937 845-3130
  411 N Dayton Lakeview Rd New Carlisle (45344) *(G-14897)*
Scarlet & Gray Cleaning Svc 513 661-4483
  3247 Glenmore Ave Apt 1 Cincinnati (45211) *(G-4434)*
SCCAA, Canton Also called Stark County Cmnty Action Agcy *(G-2491)*
Scene Magazine, Cleveland Also called Northeast Scene Inc *(G-6095)*
Scenic Ridge Fruit Farms 419 368-3353
  2031 State Route 89 Jeromesville (44840) *(G-12194)*

Scg Fields LLC 440 546-1200
  10303 Brecksville Rd Brecksville (44141) *(G-1804)*
Schaaf Drugs LLC (PA) 419 879-4327
  1331 N Cole St Lima (45801) *(G-12736)*
Schauer Group Incorporated 330 453-7721
  200 Market Ave N Ste 100 Canton (44702) *(G-2471)*
Schauer Indpendence Insur Agcy, Canton Also called Steele W W Jr Agency Inc *(G-2497)*
Schawk, Cincinnati Also called Sgk LLC *(G-4461)*
SCHECHTER, GROSS DAY SCHOOL, Pepper Pike Also called Jewish Day Schl Assoc Grtr
Clv *(G-15819)*
Scheeser Buckley Mayfield LLC 330 896-4664
  1540 Corporate Woods Pkwy Uniontown (44685) *(G-18385)*
Scheiderer Transport Inc 614 873-5103
  8520 State Route 161 E Plain City (43064) *(G-16064)*
Schenker Inc 614 662-7217
  2842 Spiegel Dr Groveport (43125) *(G-11537)*
Schenker Inc 614 257-8365
  2525 Rohr Rd Ste C Lockbourne (43137) *(G-12824)*
Schenker Inc 419 491-1055
  2 Air Cargo Pkwy E Swanton (43558) *(G-17404)*
Schenker Inc 419 866-6390
  1 Air Cargo Pkwy E Swanton (43558) *(G-17405)*
Scher Group, Beachwood Also called Dealers Group Limited *(G-1052)*
Scherer Industrial Group, Springfield Also called Horner Industrial Services Inc *(G-17047)*
Scherzinger Corp 513 531-7848
  10557 Medallion Dr Cincinnati (45241) *(G-4435)*
Scherzinger Drilling Inc 513 738-2000
  9629 State Route 128 Harrison (45030) *(G-11676)*
Scherzinger Trmt & Pest Ctrl, Cincinnati Also called Scherzinger Corp *(G-4435)*
Schibi Heating & Cooling Corp 513 385-3344
  5025 Hubble Rd Cincinnati (45247) *(G-4436)*
Schiff Agency, Fairfield Also called Schiff John J & Thomas R & Co *(G-10778)*
Schiff John J & Thomas R & Co 513 870-2580
  6200 S Gilmore Rd Fairfield (45014) *(G-10778)*
Schill Grounds Management, North Ridgeville Also called Schill Landscaping and Lawn
CA *(G-15343)*
Schill Landscaping and Lawn CA (PA) 440 327-3030
  5000 Mills Indus Pkwy North Ridgeville (44039) *(G-15343)*
Schimpf Ginocchio Mullins Lpa 513 977-5570
  36 E 7th St Ste 2600 Cincinnati (45202) *(G-4437)*
Schindewolf Express Inc 937 585-5919
  200 S Boggs St De Graff (43318) *(G-9900)*
Schindler Elevator Corporation 216 391-8600
  1100 E 55th St Cleveland (44103) *(G-6374)*
Schindler Elevator Corporation 513 341-2600
  5426 Duff Dr West Chester (45246) *(G-19079)*
Schindler Elevator Corporation 419 867-5100
  1530 Timber Wolf Dr Holland (43528) *(G-11911)*
Schindler Elevator Corporation 419 861-5900
  1530 Timber Wolf Dr Holland (43528) *(G-11912)*
Schindler Elevator Corporation 614 573-2777
  3607 Interchange Rd Columbus (43204) *(G-8599)*
Schindler Elevator Corporation 216 370-9524
  18013 Clvlnd Pkw Dr 140 Cleveland (44135) *(G-6375)*
Schirmer Construction Co 440 716-4900
  31350 Industrial Pkwy North Olmsted (44070) *(G-15309)*
Schlabach Wood Design Inc 330 897-2600
  52567 State Route 651 Baltic (43804) *(G-936)*
Schlee Malt House Condo Assn 614 463-1999
  495 S High St Ste 10 Columbus (43215) *(G-8600)*
Schlessman Seed Co (PA) 419 499-2572
  11513 Us Highway 250 N Milan (44846) *(G-14367)*
Schlezinger Metals, Columbus Also called I H Schlezinger Inc *(G-7794)*
Schlosser, David W DDS, Stow Also called Stow Dental Group Inc *(G-17231)*
Schmid Mechanical Inc 330 264-3633
  207 N Hillcrest Dr Wooster (44691) *(G-19765)*
Schmid Mechanical Co 614 261-6331
  5255 Sinclair Rd Columbus (43229) *(G-8601)*
Schmids Service Now Inc 330 264-2040
  258 S Columbus Ave Wooster (44691) *(G-19766)*
Schmidt Bros Inc 419 826-3671
  420 N Hallett Ave Swanton (43558) *(G-17406)*
Schmidt Daily Rental Inc 419 874-4331
  26875 Dixie Hwy Perrysburg (43551) *(G-15919)*
Schmidt Machine Company 419 294-3814
  7013 State Highway 199 Upper Sandusky (43351) *(G-18412)*
Schmidt-Vogel Consulting, Cincinnati Also called Itelligence Outsourcing Inc *(G-3791)*
Schneder Elc Bldngs Amrcas Inc 513 398-9800
  1770 Masn Mrrw Millgrv Rd Lebanon (45036) *(G-12499)*
Schneider Downs & Co Inc 614 621-4060
  65 E State St Ste 2000 Columbus (43215) *(G-8602)*
Schneider Electric 324, Richfield Also called Schneider Electric Usa Inc *(G-16378)*
Schneider Electric Usa Inc 440 526-9070
  3623 Brecksville Rd Ste A Richfield (44286) *(G-16378)*
Schneider Electric Usa Inc 513 755-5000
  9870 Crescent Park Dr West Chester (45069) *(G-18997)*
Schneider Home Equipment Co (PA) 513 522-1200
  7948 Pippin Rd Cincinnati (45239) *(G-4438)*
Schneider Nat Carriers Inc 740 362-6910
  600 London Rd Delaware (43015) *(G-10006)*

Schneider National Inc 419 673-0254
  808 Fontaine St Kenton (43326) *(G-12287)*
Schneider Saddlery LLC 440 543-2700
  8255 Washington St Chagrin Falls (44023) *(G-2682)*
Schneller Heating and AC Co 859 341-1200
  1079 Ohio Pike Cincinnati (45245) *(G-2867)*
Schneller LLC 330 673-1299
  6019 Powdermill Rd Kent (44240) *(G-12258)*
Schnippel Construction Inc 937 693-3831
  302 N Main St Botkins (45306) *(G-1709)*
Schoch Tile & Carpet Inc 513 922-3466
  5282 Crookshank Rd Cincinnati (45238) *(G-4439)*
Schodorf Truck Body & Eqp Co 614 228-6793
  885 Harmon Ave Columbus (43223) *(G-8603)*
Schoenbrunn Healthcare 330 339-3595
  2594 E High Ave New Philadelphia (44663) *(G-14980)*
Schoenbrunn Landscaping Inc 330 364-3688
  1505 State Route 39 Nw Dover (44622) *(G-10098)*
Schoenbrunn Ldscp & Lawn Svc, Dover Also called Schoenbrunn Landscaping
Inc *(G-10098)*
Scholastic Book Fairs Inc 513 714-1000
  5459 W Chester Rd Ste C West Chester (45069) *(G-18998)*
Schomer Glaus Pyle 614 210-0751
  1801 Watermark Dr Ste 210 Columbus (43215) *(G-8604)*
Schomer Glaus Pyle 216 518-5544
  5595 Transportation Blvd Cleveland (44125) *(G-6376)*
Schomer Glaus Pyle (PA) 330 572-2100
  520 S Main St Ste 2531 Akron (44311) *(G-420)*
Schomer Glaus Pyle 330 645-2131
  470 Portage Lakes Dr Coventry Township (44319) *(G-9042)*
Schoner Chevrolet Inc 330 877-6731
  720 W Maple St Hartville (44632) *(G-11698)*
School Age Child Care, Columbus Also called Upper Arlington City Schl Dst *(G-8824)*
School Bus Garage, Reynoldsburg Also called Reynoldsburg City Schools *(G-16326)*
School Bus Garage, Goshen Also called Peterman *(G-11314)*
School Choice Ohio Inc 614 223-1555
  88 E Broad St Ste 640 Columbus (43215) *(G-8605)*
School Edctl Policy Leadership, Columbus Also called Ohio State University *(G-8329)*
School Employees Lorain County 440 324-3400
  340 Griswold Rd Elyria (44035) *(G-10561)*
School Employees Retirement 614 222-5853
  300 E Broad St Ste 100 Columbus (43215) *(G-8606)*
School Transportation 937 855-3897
  59 Peffley St Germantown (45327) *(G-11277)*
Schooley Caldwell Associates 614 628-0300
  300 Marconi Blvd Ste 100 Columbus (43215) *(G-8607)*
Schottenstein Center, The, Columbus Also called Ohio State University *(G-8296)*
Schottenstein Property Group, Columbus Also called Schottenstein Realty LLC *(G-8609)*
Schottenstein RE Group LLC 614 418-8900
  2 Easton Oval Ste 510 Columbus (43219) *(G-8608)*
Schottenstein Realty LLC 614 445-8461
  4300 E 5th Ave Columbus (43219) *(G-8609)*
Schroedel Scullin & Bestic LLC 330 533-1131
  196 N Broad St Ste A Canfield (44406) *(G-2157)*
Schroeder Associates Inc (PA) 419 258-5075
  5554 County Road 424 Antwerp (45813) *(G-614)*
Schroeder Company (PA) 419 473-3139
  4668 Talmadge Rd Toledo (43623) *(G-18021)*
Schroer Properties Inc 740 687-5100
  1590 Chartwell St Ofc Lancaster (43130) *(G-12433)*
Schroer Properties Inc (PA) 330 498-8200
  339 E Maple St North Canton (44720) *(G-15231)*
Schroer Properties Inc 440 357-7900
  9901 Johnnycake Ridge Rd Mentor (44060) *(G-14106)*
Schroer Properties of Lanfair, Lancaster Also called Schroer Properties Inc *(G-12433)*
Schrudder Prfmce Group LLC 513 652-7675
  7723 Tylers Place Blvd West Chester (45069) *(G-18999)*
Schumacher & Co Inc 859 655-9000
  920 Lila Ave Milford (45150) *(G-14430)*
Schumacher Homes, Belmont Also called 50 X 20 Holding Company Inc *(G-1394)*
Schumacher Homes, Canton Also called 50 X 20 Holding Company Inc *(G-2168)*
Schumm Plumbing & Heating, Van Wert Also called Schumm Richard A Plbg &
Htg *(G-18488)*
Schumm Richard A Plbg & Htg 419 238-4994
  9883 Liberty Union Rd Van Wert (45891) *(G-18488)*
Schuster Cardiology 937 866-0637
  4000 Miamisburg Ctr Ste Miamisburg (45342) *(G-14216)*
Schuster Electronics Inc 330 425-8134
  2057d E Aurora Rd Twinsburg (44087) *(G-18319)*
Schuster/Cleveland, Twinsburg Also called Schuster Electronics Inc *(G-18319)*
Schusters Greenhouse Ltd 440 235-2440
  9165 Columbia Rd Cleveland (44138) *(G-6377)*
Schwebel Baking Co-Solon Bky, Solon Also called Schwebel Baking Company *(G-16895)*
Schwebel Baking Company 440 248-1500
  6250 Camp Industrial Rd Solon (44139) *(G-16895)*
Schweizer Dipple Inc 440 786-8090
  7227 Division St Cleveland (44146) *(G-6378)*
Schwendeman Agency Inc (PA) 740 373-6793
  109 Putnam St Marietta (45750) *(G-13378)*

Schwendeman Sigafoos Agcy, Marietta Also called Schwendeman Agency Inc *(G-13378)*
SCI, Fremont Also called Keller Ochs Koch Inc *(G-11082)*
SCI, Miamisburg Also called Shawntech Communications Inc *(G-14220)*
SCI Direct LLC 330 494-5504
  7800 Whipple Ave Nw North Canton (44720) *(G-15232)*
SCI Ohio, North Ridgeville Also called Safari Club International *(G-15342)*
Scientific Forming Tech Corp (PA) 614 451-8330
  2545 Farmers Dr Ste 200 Columbus (43235) *(G-8610)*
Scioto County C A O Headstart 740 354-3333
  1511 Hutchins St Portsmouth (45662) *(G-16166)*
Scioto County Child Services, New Boston Also called Scioto County Ohio *(G-14882)*
Scioto County Counseling Ctr 740 354-6685
  1634 11th St Portsmouth (45662) *(G-16167)*
Scioto County Ohio 740 456-4164
  3940 Gallia St New Boston (45662) *(G-14882)*
Scioto County Region Wtr Dst 1 ....740 259-2301
  326 Robert Lucas Rd Lucasville (45648) *(G-13053)*
Scioto Downs Inc 614 295-4700
  6000 S High St Columbus (43207) *(G-8611)*
SCIOTO MEMORIAL HOSPITAL CAMPU, Portsmouth Also called Southern Ohio Medical
Center *(G-16171)*
Scioto Packaging Inc 614 491-1500
  6969 Alum Creek Dr Columbus (43217) *(G-8612)*
Scioto Pnt Vly Mental Hlth Ctr, Wshngtn CT Hs Also called Scioto Pnt Vly Mental Hlth
Ctr *(G-19883)*
Scioto Pnt Vly Mental Hlth Ctr (PA) 740 775-1260
  4449 State Route 159 Chillicothe (45601) *(G-2825)*
Scioto Pnt Vly Mental Hlth Ctr 740 335-6935
  1300 E Paint St Wshngtn CT Hs (43160) *(G-19883)*
Scioto Reserve Inc (PA) 740 881-9082
  7383 Scioto Pkwy Powell (43065) *(G-16208)*
Scioto Reserve Inc 740 881-6500
  3982 Powell Rd Ste 332 Powell (43065) *(G-16209)*
Scioto Reserve Country Club, Powell Also called Scioto Reserve Inc *(G-16209)*
Scioto Reserve Golf & Athc CLB, Powell Also called Scioto Reserve Inc *(G-16208)*
Scioto Residential Services 740 353-0288
  2333 Vinton Ave Portsmouth (45662) *(G-16168)*
Scioto Sand & Gravel, Prospect Also called Fleming Construction Co *(G-16223)*
Scioto Services LLc (HQ) 937 644-0888
  405 S Oak St Marysville (43040) *(G-13527)*
Scioto-Darby Concrete Inc 614 876-3114
  4540 Edgewyn Ave Hilliard (43026) *(G-11814)*
Scores Fun Center, Mentor Also called East Mentor Recreation Inc *(G-14042)*
Scot Burton Contractors LLC 440 564-1011
  11330 Kinsman Rd Newbury (44065) *(G-15125)*
Scot Industries Inc 330 262-7585
  6578 Ashland Rd Wooster (44691) *(G-19767)*
Scott D Phillips 513 870-8200
  9277 Centre Pointe Dr West Chester (45069) *(G-19000)*
Scott Fetzer Co, Cleveland Also called Scott Fetzer Financial Group *(G-6380)*
Scott Fetzer Company (HQ) 440 892-3000
  28800 Clemens Rd Westlake (44145) *(G-19403)*
Scott Fetzer Company 216 267-9000
  4801 W 150th St Cleveland (44135) *(G-6379)*
Scott Fetzer Financial Group 440 892-3000
  28800 Clemens Rd Cleveland (44145) *(G-6380)*
Scott Industrial Systems Inc (PA) 937 233-8146
  4433 Interpoint Blvd Dayton (45424) *(G-9753)*
Scott Scriven & Wahoff LLP 614 222-8686
  250 E Broad St Ste 900 Columbus (43215) *(G-8613)*
Scott Steel LLC 937 552-9670
  125 Clark Ave Piqua (45356) *(G-16028)*
Scotts Commercial Truck Svcs, Toledo Also called Scotts Towing Co *(G-18022)*
Scotts Company LLC (HQ) 937 644-0011
  14111 Scottslawn Rd Marysville (43040) *(G-13528)*
Scotts Miracle-Gro Company (PA) 937 644-0011
  14111 Scottslawn Rd Marysville (43040) *(G-13529)*
Scotts Miracle-Gro Products, Marysville Also called Scotts Company LLC *(G-13528)*
Scotts Towing Co 419 729-7888
  5930 Benore Rd Toledo (43612) *(G-18022)*
Scrap Yard LLC 216 271-5825
  15000 Miles Ave Cleveland (44128) *(G-6381)*
Screen Works Inc (PA) 937 264-9111
  3970 Image Dr Dayton (45414) *(G-9754)*
Scribes & Scrbblr Chld Dev Ctr 440 884-5437
  14101 Uhlin Dr Cleveland (44130) *(G-6382)*
Scrip Pharmacy, Columbus Also called Mimrx Co Inc *(G-8088)*
Scrogginsgrear Inc 513 672-4281
  200 Northland Blvd Cincinnati (45246) *(G-4440)*
Scs Construction Services Inc 513 929-0260
  2130 Western Ave Cincinnati (45214) *(G-4441)*
Scwashtan, Reynoldsburg Also called Duckworth Enterprises LLC *(G-16301)*
SD Myers LLC 330 630-7000
  180 South Ave Tallmadge (44278) *(G-17487)*
SDA, Dublin Also called Sunny Day Academy LLC *(G-10344)*
Sdr Services LLC 513 625-0695
  2109 State Route 28 B Goshen (45122) *(G-11315)*
SDS Earth Moving Inc 330 358-2132
  3966 Wayland Rd Diamond (44412) *(G-10061)*

(G-0000) Company's Geographic Section entry number

Sdx Home Care Operations LLC 937 322-6288
  101 N Fountain Ave Springfield (45502) *(G-17109)*
Sea Ltd (PA) 614 888-4160
  7001 Buffalo Pkwy Columbus (43229) *(G-8614)*
Sea-Land Chemical Co (PA) 440 871-7887
  821 Westpoint Pkwy Westlake (44145) *(G-19404)*
Seacrist Landscaping and Cnstr 440 946-2731
  9442 Mercantile Dr Mentor (44060) *(G-14107)*
Seagate Hospitality Group LLC 216 252-7700
  4181 W 150th St Cleveland (44135) *(G-6383)*
Seagate Office Products Inc 419 861-6161
  1044 Hamilton Dr Holland (43528) *(G-11913)*
Seagate Roofg & Waterproofing, Toledo Also called Burbank Inc *(G-17632)*
Seal Aftermarket Products LLC 419 355-1200
  1110 Napoleon St Fremont (43420) *(G-11094)*
Seal Mayfield LLC 440 684-4100
  6103 Landerhaven Dr Mayfield Heights (44124) *(G-13881)*
Seal-Rite Door, Hebron Also called S R Door Inc *(G-11723)*
Seals Construction Inc 614 836-7200
  10283 Busey Rd Nw Canal Winchester (43110) *(G-2119)*
Seamans Services 216 621-4107
  1050 W 3rd St Cleveland (44114) *(G-6384)*
Seapine Software Inc (HQ) 513 754-1655
  6960 Cintas Blvd Mason (45040) *(G-13636)*
Seaport Division, Toledo Also called Toledo-Lucas County Port Auth *(G-18103)*
Search 2 Close Columbus Ltd (PA) 614 389-5353
  10254 Sawmill Pkwy Powell (43065) *(G-16210)*
Searidge, Madison Also called Eastwood Residential Living *(G-13096)*
Sears, Columbus Also called Innovel Solutions Inc *(G-7821)*
Sears, Columbus Also called Innovel Solutions Inc *(G-7822)*
Sears Roebuck and Co 513 741-6422
  9405 Colerain Ave Cincinnati (45251) *(G-4442)*
Sears Roebuck and Co 614 797-2095
  1280 Polaris Pkwy Columbus (43240) *(G-6835)*
Sears Roebuck and Co 937 427-8528
  2727 Fairfield Cmns Beavercreek (45431) *(G-1185)*
Sears Roebuck and Co 419 226-4172
  2400 Elida Rd Ste 100 Lima (45805) *(G-12737)*
Sears Roebuck and Co 614 760-7195
  4975 Tuttle Crossing Blvd Dublin (43016) *(G-10330)*
Sears Roebuck and Co 330 629-7700
  7401 Market St Rm 7 Youngstown (44512) *(G-20205)*
Sears Roebuck and Co 440 845-0120
  13200 Smith Rd Cleveland (44130) *(G-6385)*
Sears Roebuck and Co 330 652-5128
  5555 Youngstown Warren Rd # 120 Niles (44446) *(G-15168)*
Sears Roebuck and Co 440 846-3595
  17271 Southpark Ctr Cleveland (44136) *(G-6386)*
Sears Auto Center, Beavercreek Also called Sears Roebuck and Co *(G-1185)*
Sears Auto Center, Niles Also called Sears Roebuck and Co *(G-15168)*
Sears Auto Center, Cleveland Also called Sears Roebuck and Co *(G-6386)*
Sears Credit Central, Cleveland Also called Sears Roebuck and Co *(G-6385)*
Sears Product Service 1474, Youngstown Also called Sears Roebuck and Co *(G-20205)*
Season Contractors Inc 440 717-0188
  55 Eagle Valley Ct Broadview Heights (44147) *(G-1845)*
Seaway Building Services, Toledo Also called Seaway Sponge & Chamois Co *(G-18023)*
Seaway Cash N Carry, Cleveland Also called Total Wholesale Inc *(G-6535)*
Seaway Sponge & Chamois Co (PA) 419 691-4694
  458 2nd St Toledo (43605) *(G-18023)*
Seaworld Entertainment Inc 330 562-8101
  1100 Squires Rd Aurora (44202) *(G-843)*
Sebaly Shillito & Dyer Lpa (PA) 937 222-2500
  1900 Kettering Tower 40n Dayton (45423) *(G-9755)*
Sebastiani Trucking Inc 330 286-0059
  61 Railroad St Canfield (44406) *(G-2158)*
Sebesta Inc 216 351-7621
  2802 Tuxedo Ave Parma (44134) *(G-15775)*
Sechkar Company 740 385-8900
  4831 2nd St Nelsonville (45764) *(G-14837)*
Second Harvest Food Bank, Springfield Also called Archdiocese of Cincinnati *(G-16996)*
Second Mental Retardation 937 262-3077
  2080 N Gettysburg Ave Dayton (45406) *(G-9756)*
Second National Bank (HQ) 937 548-2122
  499 S Broadway St Greenville (45331) *(G-11395)*
Second Phase Inc 330 797-9930
  191 S Four Mile Run Rd Youngstown (44515) *(G-20206)*
Section 8, Cincinnati Also called Cincinnati Metro Hsing Auth *(G-3256)*
Section 8 Housing Assistance, Portsmouth Also called Portsmouth Metro Housing Auth *(G-16161)*
Secure Trnsp Co Ohio LLC 800 856-9994
  777 Dearborn Park Ln S Worthington (43085) *(G-19847)*
Securestate LLC 216 927-0115
  23340 Miles Rd Cleveland (44128) *(G-6387)*
Securitas Electronic SEC Inc (HQ) 855 331-0359
  3800 Tabs Dr Uniontown (44685) *(G-18386)*
Securitas SEC Svcs USA Inc 216 431-3139
  3747 Euclid Ave Cleveland (44115) *(G-6388)*
Securitas SEC Svcs USA Inc 513 639-7615
  655 Plum St 150 Cincinnati (45202) *(G-4443)*

Securitas SEC Svcs USA Inc 937 224-7432
  118 W 1st St Dayton (45402) *(G-9757)*
Securitas SEC Svcs USA Inc 614 871-6051
  2180 Southwest Blvd Grove City (43123) *(G-11470)*
Securitas SEC Svcs USA Inc 440 887-6800
  12000 Snow Rd Ste 5 Cleveland (44130) *(G-6389)*
Securitas SEC Svcs USA Inc 216 503-2021
  9885 Rockside Rd Ste 155 Cleveland (44125) *(G-6390)*
Security Check LLC (PA) 614 944-5788
  2 Easton Oval Ste 350 Columbus (43219) *(G-8615)*
Security Fence Group Inc (PA) 513 681-3700
  4260 Dane Ave Cincinnati (45223) *(G-4444)*
Security Investments LLC 614 441-4601
  3681 Corporate Dr Columbus (43231) *(G-8616)*
Security Nat Auto Accptnce LLC 513 459-8118
  6951 Cintas Blvd Mason (45040) *(G-13637)*
Security National Bank & Tr Co (HQ) 740 426-6384
  50 N 3rd St Newark (43055) *(G-15097)*
Security National Bank & Tr Co. 937 324-6800
  40 S Limestone St Springfield (45502) *(G-17110)*
Security Savings Mortgage Corp 330 455-2833
  300 Tuscarawas St W Fl 8 Canton (44702) *(G-2472)*
Security Storage Co Inc 513 961-2700
  706 Oak St Cincinnati (45206) *(G-4445)*
Security Title Guarantee Agcy 513 651-3393
  150 E 4th St Fl 4 Cincinnati (45202) *(G-4446)*
Sedgwick CMS Holdings Inc 614 658-0900
  3455 Mill Run Dr Hilliard (43026) *(G-11815)*
Sedgwick CMS Holdings Inc 800 825-6755
  6377 Emerald Pkwy Dublin (43016) *(G-10331)*
Sedlak Management Consultants 216 206-4700
  22901 Millcreek Blvd # 600 Cleveland (44122) *(G-6391)*
Seed Consultants Inc (HQ) 740 333-8644
  648 Miami Trace Rd Sw Wshngtn CT Hs (43160) *(G-19884)*
Seeley Enterprises Company (PA) 440 293-6600
  104 Parker Dr Andover (44003) *(G-608)*
Seeley Medical, Andover Also called Seeley Enterprises Company *(G-608)*
Seeley Medical Oxygen Co (HQ) 440 255-7163
  104 Parker Dr Andover (44003) *(G-609)*
Seeley Svdge Ebert Gourash Lpa 216 566-8200
  26600 Detroit Rd Fl 3 Cleveland (44145) *(G-6392)*
Seg of Ohio Inc (PA) 614 414-7300
  4016 Townsfair Way # 201 Columbus (43219) *(G-8617)*
Segmint Inc 330 594-5379
  365 Water St Akron (44308) *(G-421)*
Sehlhorst Equipment Svcs Inc 513 353-9300
  4450 Monroe Ave Hooven (45033) *(G-11935)*
SEI - Cincinnati LLC 513 459-1992
  7870 E Kemper Rd Ste 400 Cincinnati (45249) *(G-4447)*
SEI Cincinnati, Cincinnati Also called Systems Evolution Inc *(G-4563)*
Seibert-Keck Insurance Agency (PA) 330 867-3140
  2950 W Market St Ste A Fairlawn (44333) *(G-10849)*
Seifert & Group Inc 330 833-2700
  2323 Nave Rd Se Massillon (44646) *(G-13727)*
Seifert Technologies Inc (PA) 330 833-2700
  2323 Nave Rd Se Massillon (44646) *(G-13728)*
Seilkop Industries Inc (PA) 513 761-1035
  425 W North Bend Rd Cincinnati (45216) *(G-4448)*
Selby General Hospital 740 568-2037
  1338 Colegate Dr Marietta (45750) *(G-13379)*
Selby General Hospital (PA) 740 568-2000
  1106 Colegate Dr Marietta (45750) *(G-13380)*
Select Genetics LLC 740 599-7979
  15835 Dnville Jelloway Rd Danville (43014) *(G-9151)*
Select Hotels Group LLC 513 754-0003
  5070 Natorp Blvd Mason (45040) *(G-13638)*
Select Hotels Group LLC 216 328-1060
  6025 Jefferson Dr Cleveland (44131) *(G-6393)*
Select Hotels Group LLC 614 799-1913
  6161 Parkcenter Cir Dublin (43017) *(G-10332)*
Select Industries Corp 937 233-9191
  60 Heid Ave Dayton (45404) *(G-9758)*
Select Medical Corporation 216 983-8030
  11900 Fairhill Rd Ste 100 Cleveland (44120) *(G-6394)*
Select Medical Corporation 330 761-7500
  200 E Market St Akron (44308) *(G-422)*
Select Spclty Hsptal-Akron LLC 330 761-7500
  200 E Market St Akron (44308) *(G-423)*
Select Specialty Hosp Columbus 614 291-8467
  1087 Dennison Ave Columbus (43201) *(G-8618)*
Select Specialty Hospital, Cleveland Also called Select Medical Corporation *(G-6394)*
Select Specialty Hospital 513 862-4700
  375 Dixmyth Ave Fl 15 Cincinnati (45220) *(G-4449)*
Select Spclty Hospi- Colmbus 614 293-6931
  410 W 10th Ave Columbus (43210) *(G-8619)*
Select Staffing 513 247-9772
  7682 Overglen Dr West Chester (45069) *(G-19001)*
Select Steel Inc 330 652-1756
  1825 Hunter Ave Niles (44446) *(G-15169)*
Selection MGT Systems Inc 513 522-8764
  155 Tri County Pkwy # 150 Cincinnati (45246) *(G-4450)*
Selection.com, Cincinnati Also called Selection MGT Systems Inc *(G-4450)*

A
L
P
H
A
B
E
T
I
C

Selective Networking Inc 740 574-2682
8407 Hayport Rd Wheelersburg (45694) *(G-19440)*

Selecttech Services Corp 937 438-9905
8045 Washington Vlg Dr Centerville (45458) *(G-2633)*

Self Reliance Inc 937 525-0809
3674 E National Rd Ste 3 Springfield (45505) *(G-17111)*

Self-Funded Plans Inc (PA) 216 566-1455
1432 Hamilton Ave Cleveland (44114) *(G-6395)*

Selinsky Force LLC 330 477-4527
4015 23rd St Sw Canton (44706) *(G-2473)*

Selman & Company (PA) 440 646-9336
6110 Parkland Blvd Cleveland (44124) *(G-6396)*

SEM Villa Inc 513 831-3262
6409 Small House Cir Loveland (45140) *(G-13026)*

SEM VILLA RETIREMENT COMMUNITY, Loveland Also called SEM Villa Inc *(G-13026)*

Seminole 8 Theaters, Avon Lake Also called Seminole Theater Co LLC *(G-927)*

Seminole Theater Co LLC 440 934-6998
32818 Walker Rd Avon Lake (44012) *(G-927)*

Semma Enterprises Inc 513 863-7775
5414 Hankins Rd Middletown (45044) *(G-14328)*

Sena Weller Rohs Williams 513 241-6443
300 Main St Fl 4 Cincinnati (45202) *(G-4451)*

Seneca County Dialysis, Tiffin Also called Seneca Dialysis LLC *(G-17538)*

Seneca County Ems 419 447-0266
126 Hopewell Ave Tiffin (44883) *(G-17536)*

Seneca County Firemens Assn 419 447-7909
1070 S County Road 17 Tiffin (44883) *(G-17537)*

Seneca County Highway Dept, Tiffin Also called County of Seneca *(G-17513)*

Seneca County Human Services, Tiffin Also called County of Seneca *(G-17514)*

Seneca Dialysis LLC 419 443-1051
10 St Lawrence Dr Tiffin (44883) *(G-17538)*

Seneca Lake Park, Senecaville Also called Muskingum Wtrshed Cnsrvncy Dst *(G-16670)*

Seneca Medical, Tiffin Also called Concordnce Hlthcare Sltons LLC *(G-17512)*

Seneca Medical LLC (HQ) 419 447-0236
85 Shaffer Park Dr Tiffin (44883) *(G-17539)*

Seneca RE ADS Ind Fostoria Div 419 435-0729
602 S Corporate Dr W Fostoria (44830) *(G-11012)*

Seneca Steel Erectors Inc (PA) 740 385-0517
975 E Main St Logan (43138) *(G-12853)*

Seneca-Crawford Area Trnsp (PA) 419 937-2428
3446 S Township Road 151 Tiffin (44883) *(G-17540)*

Senior Behaviroal Health, Cincinnati Also called Trihealth Inc *(G-4637)*

Senior Care Inc 937 372-1530
60 Paceline Cir Xenia (45385) *(G-19925)*

Senior Care Inc 330 721-2000
1046 N Jefferson St Medina (44256) *(G-14000)*

Senior Care Inc 937 291-3211
8630 Washington Church Rd Miamisburg (45342) *(G-14217)*

Senior Care Inc 419 516-4788
2075 N Eastown Rd Lima (45807) *(G-12738)*

Senior Care Management Inc 419 578-7000
3501 Executive Pkwy # 219 Toledo (43606) *(G-18024)*

Senior Center, Chillicothe Also called Ross Cnty Cmmittee For Elderly *(G-2817)*

Senior Center West, Lakewood Also called City of Lakewood *(G-12338)*

SENIOR CITIZENS CENTER, Portsmouth Also called United Scoto Senior Activities *(G-16176)*

Senior Help Solutions, Mount Vernon Also called Home Instead Senior Care *(G-14767)*

Senior Independence 330 873-3468
83 N Miller Rd Ste 101 Fairlawn (44333) *(G-10850)*

Senior Independence 330 744-5071
1110 5th Ave Youngstown (44504) *(G-20207)*

Senior Independence Adult 440 954-8372
36855 Ridge Rd Willoughby (44094) *(G-19570)*

Senior Independence Adult 513 681-8174
25 Indiana Ave Monroe (45050) *(G-14582)*

Senior Independence Adult 513 539-2697
27 Indiana Ave Monroe (45050) *(G-14583)*

Senior Lifestyle Corporation 513 777-4457
7222 Heritagespring Dr West Chester (45069) *(G-19002)*

Senior Lifestyle Evergreen Ltd 513 948-2308
230 W Galbraith Rd Cincinnati (45215) *(G-4452)*

Senior Nutrition, Zanesville Also called Muskingum County Ohio *(G-20335)*

Senior Outreach Services 216 421-6900
2390 E 79th St Cleveland (44104) *(G-6397)*

Senior Resource Connection (PA) 937 223-8246
222 Salem Ave Dayton (45406) *(G-9759)*

Senior Select Home Health Care 330 665-4663
2830 Copley Rd 2 Copley (44321) *(G-8973)*

Senior Star Management Company 513 271-1747
5435 Kenwood Rd Cincinnati (45227) *(G-4453)*

Sensation Research 513 602-1611
1159 Chaucer Pl Maineville (45039) *(G-13118)*

Sensi Care 3 .... 440 323-6310
1243 East Ave Elyria (44035) *(G-10562)*

Sensor Technology Systems, Miamisburg Also called Steiner Eoptics Inc *(G-14226)*

Sentage Corporation 937 865-5900
1037 Byers Rd Miamisburg (45342) *(G-14218)*

Sentinel Fluid Controls LLC (HQ) 419 478-9086
5702 Opportunity Dr Toledo (43612) *(G-18025)*

Sequent Inc (PA) 614 436-5880
8415 Pulsar Pl Ste 200 Columbus (43240) *(G-6836)*

SEQUENT INFORMATION SOLUTIONS, Columbus Also called Sequent Inc *(G-6836)*

Sequoia Pro Bowl 614 885-7043
5501 Sandalwood Blvd Columbus (43229) *(G-8620)*

Serco Inc 937 331-4180
2210 Arbor Blvd Ste 200 Moraine (45439) *(G-14696)*

Serenity Center Inc 614 891-1111
2841 E Dblin Granville Rd Columbus (43231) *(G-8621)*

Serenity HM Halthcare Svcs LLC 937 222-0002
33 White Allen Ave Dayton (45405) *(G-9760)*

Serex Corporation (PA) 330 726-6062
55 Victoria Rd Youngstown (44515) *(G-20208)*

Serv Pro of Barberton/Norton, Medina Also called Professional Restoration Svc *(G-13989)*

Serv-A-Lite Products Inc (HQ) 309 762-7741
10590 Hamilton Ave Cincinnati (45231) *(G-4454)*

Servall Electric Company Inc 513 771-5584
11697 Lebanon Rd Cincinnati (45241) *(G-4455)*

Servatii Inc (PA) 513 271-5040
3888 Virginia Ave Cincinnati (45227) *(G-4456)*

Servatii Pastry and Dealey, Cincinnati Also called Servatii Inc *(G-4456)*

Service Building, Dayton Also called Dayton Public School District *(G-9379)*

Service Center Title Agency 937 312-3080
6718 Loop Rd Dayton (45459) *(G-9761)*

Service Center Warehouse, Euclid Also called Euclid City Schools *(G-10631)*

Service Corporation Intl, Cleveland Also called Cummings and Davis Fnrl HM Inc *(G-5389)*

Service Corps Retired Execs 216 522-4194
1350 Euclid Ave Ste 216 Cleveland (44115) *(G-6398)*

Service Corps Retired Execs 330 379-3163
1 Cascade Plz Fl 18 Akron (44308) *(G-424)*

Service Corps Retired Execs 419 259-7598
2200 Jefferson Ave Fl 1 Toledo (43604) *(G-18026)*

Service Department, Hudson Also called City of Hudson Village *(G-11973)*

Service Dept, Cleveland Also called City of Warrensville Heights *(G-5217)*

Service Dept, Streetsboro Also called City of Streetsboro *(G-17250)*

Service Experts Htg & AC LLC 937 426-3444
2600 S Limestone St Springfield (45505) *(G-17112)*

Service Experts Htg & AC LLC 513 489-3361
4610 Carlynn Dr Blue Ash (45241) *(G-1650)*

Service Experts Htg & AC LLC 614 859-6993
1751 Dividend Dr Columbus (43228) *(G-8622)*

Service Experts LLC 330 577-3918
847 Home Ave Akron (44310) *(G-425)*

Service Experts of Columbus, Columbus Also called Service Experts Htg & AC LLC *(G-8622)*

Service Garage, Cleveland Also called City of Garfield Heights *(G-5201)*

Service King Cllision Repr Ctr, Cleveland Also called Service King Holdings LLC *(G-6399)*

Service King Cllision Repr Ctr, Stow Also called Service King Holdings LLC *(G-17229)*

Service King Holdings LLC 216 362-1600
15703 Puritas Ave Cleveland (44135) *(G-6399)*

Service King Holdings LLC 330 926-0100
26 E Steels Corners Rd Stow (44224) *(G-17229)*

Service Master By Allen Keith, Canton Also called Allen-Keith Construction Co *(G-2178)*

Service Master Co 330 864-7300
33851 Curtis Blvd Ste 202 Eastlake (44095) *(G-10434)*

Service Mstr By Disaster Recon, Eastlake Also called Service Master Co *(G-10434)*

Service Pronet Inc 614 874-4300
1535 Georgesville Rd Columbus (43228) *(G-8623)*

Service Steel Div, Cincinnati Also called Van Pelt Corporation *(G-4750)*

Service-Tech, Cleveland Also called A Bee C Service Inc *(G-4875)*

Servicelink Field Services LLC 440 424-0058
30825 Aurora Rd Ste 140 Solon (44139) *(G-16896)*

ServiceMaster, Lima Also called Kleman Services LLC *(G-12671)*

ServiceMaster, Youngstown Also called Dempsey Inc *(G-20016)*

ServiceMaster, Lebanon Also called A 1 Janitorial Cleaning Svc *(G-12446)*

ServiceMaster, Lancaster Also called C M S Enterprises Inc *(G-12374)*

ServiceMaster, Berea Also called T & L Enterprises Inc *(G-1439)*

ServiceMaster By Angler, Dayton Also called G7 Services Inc *(G-9455)*

ServiceMaster By Sidwell Inc 740 687-1077
430 E Mulberry St Lancaster (43130) *(G-12434)*

ServiceMaster By Steinbach 330 497-5959
6824 Wise Ave Nw Canton (44720) *(G-2474)*

ServiceMaster of Defiance Inc 419 784-5570
1255 Carpenter Rd Defiance (43512) *(G-9940)*

Services & Support ADM, Oak Harbor Also called Ottawa County Board M R D D *(G-15476)*

Services On Deck Inc (PA) 513 759-2854
8263 Kyles Station Rd # 1 Liberty Township (45044) *(G-12585)*

Services On Mark Inc 614 846-5400
705 Lkview Plz Blvd Ste L Worthington (43085) *(G-19848)*

Servicmaster By Disaster Recon, Eastlake Also called Disaster Reconstruction Inc *(G-10428)*

Servicmster Coml Clg Advantage, Lancaster Also called CMS Business Services LLC *(G-12383)*

Servisair LLC (HQ) 216 267-9910
5851 Cargo Rd Cleveland (44135) *(G-6400)*

SERVPRO, Worthington Also called Heco Operations Inc *(G-19813)*

ALPHABETIC SECTION | Sheedy Paving Inc

SERVPRO, Hudson *Also called Restoration Resources Inc* ***(G-12004)***
SERVPRO, North Canton *Also called Caveney Inc* ***(G-15192)***
Sesco, Brooklyn Heights *Also called Specialty Equipment Sales Co* ***(G-1882)***
Setco Sales Company (HQ) 513 941-5110
5880 Hillside Ave Cincinnati (45233) ***(G-4457)***
Setiawan Associates LLC 614 285-5815
50 W Broad St Ste 1800 Columbus (43215) ***(G-8624)***
Seton Catholic School Hudson 330 342-4200
6923 Stow Rd Hudson (44236) ***(G-12005)***
Settle Muter Electric Ltd (PA) 614 866-7554
711 Claycraft Rd Columbus (43230) ***(G-8625)***
Seven Hills Fireman Assn 216 524-3321
7195 Broadview Rd Seven Hills (44131) ***(G-16681)***
Seven Hills Obgyn Associates 513 922-6666
6350 Glenway Ave Ste 205 Cincinnati (45211) ***(G-4458)***
Seven Hills Womens Health Ctrs (PA) 513 721-3200
2060 Reading Rd Ste 150 Cincinnati (45202) ***(G-4459)***
Seven Hlls Neighborhood Houses (PA) 513 407-5362
901 Findlay St Cincinnati (45214) ***(G-4460)***
Seven Secured Inc 281 362-2887
15830 Foltz Pkwy Strongsville (44149) ***(G-17342)***
Seven Seventeen Credit Un Inc (PA) 330 372-8100
3181 Larchmont Ave Ne Warren (44483) ***(G-18741)***
Seven Seventeen Credit Un Inc 330 372-8100
100 Brewster Dr Se Warren (44484) ***(G-18742)***
Sewell Leasing Corporation 937 382-3847
370 Davids Dr Wilmington (45177) ***(G-19648)***
Sewell Motor Express, Wilmington *Also called Sewell Leasing Corporation* ***(G-19648)***
Sewer & Drainage Services, Toledo *Also called City of Toledo* ***(G-17657)***
Sewer Department, Sandusky *Also called City of Sandusky* ***(G-16585)***
Sewer Rodding Equipment Co 419 991-2065
3434 S Dixie Hwy Lima (45804) ***(G-12739)***
Sewer Savors, Cincinnati *Also called Municpal Cntrs Saling Pdts Inc* ***(G-4085)***
Sexton Industrial Inc 513 530-5555
366 Circle Freeway Dr West Chester (45246) ***(G-19080)***
Seymour & Associates 419 517-7079
1760 Manley Rd Maumee (43537) ***(G-13850)***
Sfa Architects, Cincinnati *Also called Elevar Design Group Inc* ***(G-3490)***
Sfa Architects Inc 937 281-0600
120 W 2nd St Ste 1800 Dayton (45402) ***(G-9762)***
Sfc Graphics Inc 419 255-1283
110 E Woodruff Ave Toledo (43604) ***(G-18027)***
Sfn Group Inc 419 727-4104
1212 E Alexis Rd Toledo (43612) ***(G-18028)***
Sfr Group, Youngstown *Also called Sami S Rafidi* ***(G-20202)***
Sgi Matrix LLC (PA) 937 438-9033
1041 Byers Rd Miamisburg (45342) ***(G-14219)***
Sgk LLC 513 569-9900
537 E Pete Rose Way # 100 Cincinnati (45202) ***(G-4461)***
Sgl Carbon Technic LLC 440 572-3600
21945 Drake Rd Strongsville (44149) ***(G-17343)***
SGS North America Inc 513 674-7048
650 Northland Blvd # 600 Cincinnati (45240) ***(G-4462)***
SH Bell Company 412 963-9910
2217 Michigan Ave East Liverpool (43920) ***(G-10417)***
Sh-91 Limited Partnership 330 535-1581
1221 Everton Dr Akron (44307) ***(G-426)***
Shadco Inc 310 217-8777
100 Titanium Way Toronto (43964) ***(G-18185)***
Shade Tree Cool Living LLC 614 844-5990
6317 Busch Blvd Columbus (43229) ***(G-8626)***
Shadoart Productions Inc 614 416-7625
503 S Front St Ste 260 Columbus (43215) ***(G-8627)***
Shadow Valley Tennis & Fitness 419 861-3986
1661 N Hlland Sylvania Rd Toledo (43615) ***(G-18029)***
Shadow Valley Tennis Club 419 865-1141
1661 S Hlland Sylvania Rd Maumee (43537) ***(G-13851)***
SHADOWBOX, Columbus *Also called Shadoart Productions Inc* ***(G-8627)***
Shady Hollow Cntry CLB Co Inc 330 832-1581
4865 Wales Ave Nw Massillon (44646) ***(G-13729)***
SHADY LANE CHILDREN'S HOME, Groveport *Also called Hill Manor Enterprises* ***(G-11517)***
SHADY LAWN NURSING HOME, Dalton *Also called A Provide Care Inc* ***(G-9143)***
Shadyside Care Center, Shadyside *Also called Zandex Inc* ***(G-16700)***
Shadyside Health Center, Shadyside *Also called Wheeling Hospital Inc* ***(G-16699)***
Shafer Confession 419 399-4662
411 E Jackson St Paulding (45879) ***(G-15799)***
Shaffer Distributing Company (PA) 614 421-6800
1100 W 3rd Ave Columbus (43212) ***(G-8628)***
Shaffer Pomeroy Ltd 419 756-7302
909 S Main St Mansfield (44907) ***(G-13242)***
Shaias Parking Inc 216 621-0328
812 Huron Rd E Ste 701 Cleveland (44115) ***(G-6401)***
Shakemasters, Macedonia *Also called Regency Roofing Companies Inc* ***(G-13081)***
SHAKER GARDENS NURSING & REHAB, Shaker Heights *Also called Mff Somerset LLC* ***(G-16710)***
Shaker Heights Country Club Co 216 991-3324
3300 Courtland Blvd Shaker Heights (44122) ***(G-16712)***
Shaker House 216 991-6000
3700 Northfield Rd Ste 3 Cleveland (44122) ***(G-6402)***
Shaker Run Golf Club 513 727-0007
1320 Golf Club Dr Lebanon (45036) ***(G-12500)***
Shaker Valley Foods Inc 216 961-8600
3304 W 67th Pl Cleveland (44102) ***(G-6403)***
Shalom House Inc (HQ) 614 239-1999
1135 College Ave Columbus (43209) ***(G-8629)***
Shalom Ministries Intl Inc 614 504-6052
9018 Heritage Dr Plain City (43064) ***(G-16065)***
Shamas Ltd 419 872-9908
102 W Indiana Ave Perrysburg (43551) ***(G-15920)***
Shamrock Acquisition Company, Westlake *Also called Shamrock Companies Inc* ***(G-19405)***
Shamrock Companies Inc (PA) 440 899-9510
24090 Detroit Rd Westlake (44145) ***(G-19405)***
Shamrock Golf Club, Delaware *Also called Ganzfair Investment Inc* ***(G-9980)***
Shamrock Moving & Storage Co, Strongsville *Also called Tersher Corporation* ***(G-17352)***
Shamrock Taxi Ltd 614 263-8294
P.O. Box 360363 Columbus (43236) ***(G-8630)***
Shamrock Towing Inc (PA) 614 882-3555
6333 Frost Rd Westerville (43082) ***(G-19209)***
Shan-Rod Inc 419 588-2066
7308 Driver Rd Berlin Heights (44814) ***(G-1451)***
Shancliff Investments Ltd 330 883-5560
9463 Chardon Cir Apt 301 West Chester (45069) ***(G-19003)***
Shane Security Services Inc 330 757-4001
7217 Pennsylvania Ave Poland (44514) ***(G-16088)***
Shapiro Shapiro & Shapiro 216 927-2030
4469 Renaissance Pkwy Cleveland (44128) ***(G-6404)***
Shared PET Imaging Llc 330 491-0480
4825 Higbee Ave Nw # 201 Canton (44718) ***(G-2475)***
Shared Services, Cleveland *Also called Securitas SEC Svcs USA Inc* ***(G-6390)***
Shared Services LLC 513 821-4278
5905 E Galbraith Rd # 8000 Cincinnati (45236) ***(G-4463)***
Sharon Twnship Frfighters Assn 330 239-4992
1274 Sharon Copley Rd Sharon Center (44274) ***(G-16725)***
Sharonview Nursing Home, South Vienna *Also called Vienna Enterprises Inc* ***(G-16949)***
Sharonville Car Wash 513 769-4219
11727 Lebanon Rd Cincinnati (45241) ***(G-4464)***
Sharonville Mthdist Wkdays Nrs 513 563-8278
3751 Creek Rd Cincinnati (45241) ***(G-4465)***
Sharp Edge LLC 440 255-5917
8855 Twinbrook Rd Mentor (44060) ***(G-14108)***
Sharp's Valet Parkg, Fairfield *Also called Sharps Valet Parking* ***(G-10779)***
Sharpnack Chvrlet Bick Cdillac 419 935-0194
1330 S Conwell Ave Willard (44890) ***(G-19487)***
Sharps Valet Parking 513 863-1777
843 Southwind Dr Fairfield (45014) ***(G-10779)***
Sharron Group Inc (PA) 614 873-5856
7605 Commerce Pl Plain City (43064) ***(G-16066)***
Shaw Group Inc 937 593-2022
2946 Us Highway 68 N Bellefontaine (43311) ***(G-1365)***
Shaw Jewish Community Center 330 867-7850
750 White Pond Dr Akron (44320) ***(G-427)***
Shawcor Pipe Protection LLC 513 683-7800
173 Commerce Dr Loveland (45140) ***(G-13027)***
Shawnee Animal Clinic Inc 740 353-5758
101 Bierly Rd Portsmouth (45662) ***(G-16169)***
Shawnee Country Club 419 227-7177
1700 Shawnee Rd Lima (45805) ***(G-12740)***
Shawnee Hills Golf Course, Cleveland *Also called Cleveland Metroparks* ***(G-5271)***
Shawnee Manor, Lima *Also called Hcf of Shawnee Inc* ***(G-12655)***
Shawnee Manor Nursing Home, Lima *Also called Hcf Management Inc* ***(G-12653)***
Shawnee Optical Inc 440 997-2020
3705 State Rd Ashtabula (44004) ***(G-754)***
Shawnee Trophies & Sptg Gds, Chillicothe *Also called Chillicothe Bowling Lanes Inc* ***(G-2759)***
Shawnee Weekday Early Lrng Ctr 419 991-4806
2600 Zurmehly Rd Lima (45806) ***(G-12793)***
Shawneespring Hlth Cre Cntr Rl 513 943-4000
390 Wards Corner Rd Loveland (45140) ***(G-13028)***
Shawntech Communications Inc (PA) 937 898-4900
8521 Gander Creek Dr Miamisburg (45342) ***(G-14220)***
Sheakley, Cincinnati *Also called Comprehensive Hr Solutions LLC* ***(G-3346)***
Sheakley Cente 513 487-7106
401 E Mcmillan St Cincinnati (45206) ***(G-4466)***
Sheakley Unicomp Inc 513 771-2277
1 Sheakley Way Ste 100 Cincinnati (45246) ***(G-4467)***
Sheakley-Uniservice Inc 513 771-2277
1 Sheakley Way Ste 100 Cincinnati (45246) ***(G-4468)***
Shearer Farm Inc 440 237-4806
11204 Royalton Rd North Royalton (44133) ***(G-15367)***
Shearer Farm Inc (PA) 330 345-9023
7762 Cleveland Rd Wooster (44691) ***(G-19768)***
Shearer Farm Inc 419 465-4622
13 Fort Monroe Pkwy Monroeville (44847) ***(G-14590)***
Shearer Farm Inc 419 529-6160
2715 W 4th St Ontario (44906) ***(G-15571)***
Shearer's Snacks, Massillon *Also called Shearers Foods LLC* ***(G-13730)***
Shearers Foods LLC (PA) 330 834-4030
100 Lincoln Way E Massillon (44646) ***(G-13730)***
Sheedy Paving Inc 614 252-2111
730 N Rose Ave Columbus (43219) ***(G-8631)***

ALPHABETIC

Sheer Professionals Inc 330 345-8666
2912 Cleveland Rd Wooster (44691) *(G-19769)*

Sheet Metal Workers Local No (PA) 216 267-1645
12515 Corporate Dr Parma (44130) *(G-15776)*

Shelby County Child Care, Sidney *Also called Council On Rur Svc Prgrams Inc* *(G-16769)*

Shelby County Highway Dept, Sidney *Also called County of Shelby* *(G-16770)*

Shelby County Mem Hosp Assn (PA) 937 498-2311
915 Michigan St Sidney (45365) *(G-16797)*

Shelby County Mem Hosp Assn 937 492-9591
705 Fulton St Sidney (45365) *(G-16798)*

Shelby Welded Tube Div, Shelby *Also called Phillips Mfg and Tower Co* *(G-16749)*

Sheldon Harry E Calvary Camp 440 593-4381
4411 Lake Rd Conneaut (44030) *(G-8958)*

Shelley Elizabeth Blum 440 964-0542
2614 W 13th St Ashtabula (44004) *(G-755)*

Shells Inc (PA) 330 808-5558
1245 S Cleveland Massillo Copley (44321) *(G-8974)*

Shelly and Sands Inc 740 859-2104
1731 Old State Route 7 Rayland (43943) *(G-16273)*

Shelly and Sands Inc 614 444-5100
1515 Harmon Ave Columbus (43223) *(G-8632)*

Shelly and Sands Inc 419 529-8455
1300 W 4th St Rear Ontario (44906) *(G-15572)*

Shelly and Sands Inc 740 453-0721
3570 S River Rd Zanesville (43701) *(G-20360)*

Shelly Company 419 396-7641
1794 County Highway 99 Carey (43316) *(G-2547)*

Shelly Company 740 441-1714
24537 Canal Rd Circleville (43113) *(G-4849)*

Shelly Company 330 425-7861
8920 Canyon Falls Blvd # 3 Twinsburg (44087) *(G-18320)*

Shelly Company, The, Thornville *Also called Shelly Materials Inc* *(G-17506)*

Shelly Materials, East Fultonham *Also called Chesterhill Stone Co* *(G-10388)*

Shelly Materials Inc 740 666-5841
8328 Watkins Rd Ostrander (43061) *(G-15655)*

Shelly Materials Inc (HQ) 740 246-6315
80 Park Dr Thornville (43076) *(G-17506)*

Shelter House Volunteer Group (PA) 513 721-0643
411 Gest St Cincinnati (45203) *(G-4469)*

Shelter Moving & Storage, West Chester *Also called Shetler Moving & Stor of Ohio* *(G-19004)*

Sheltering Arms Hospital Found 740 592-9300
55 Hospital Dr Athens (45701) *(G-802)*

Shepards Meadows, Poland *Also called Shepherd of The Valley Luthera* *(G-16089)*

Shepards Wood Nursing, Youngstown *Also called Shepherd of The Valley Luthera* *(G-20210)*

Shepherd Excavating Inc 614 889-1115
6295 Cosgray Rd Dublin (43016) *(G-10333)*

Shepherd of The Valley Luthera (PA) 330 530-4038
5525 Silica Rd Youngstown (44515) *(G-20209)*

Shepherd of The Valley Luthera 330 726-9061
7148 West Blvd Youngstown (44512) *(G-20210)*

Shepherd of The Valley Luthera 330 726-7110
301 W Western Reserve Rd Poland (44514) *(G-16089)*

SHEPHERDS WOODS, Youngstown *Also called Shepherd of The Valley Luthera* *(G-20209)*

Sheraton Airport Hotel, Cleveland *Also called Hopkins Partners* *(G-5705)*

Sheraton Columbus, Columbus *Also called Hotel 75 E State Opco L P* *(G-7776)*

Sheraton Suites Akron, Cuyahoga Falls *Also called Riverside Cmnty Urban Redev* *(G-9120)*

Sheraton Suites Columbus, Columbus *Also called Regal Hospitality* *(G-8504)*

Shereton Hotel Independance, Cleveland *Also called Independent Hotel Partners LLC* *(G-5745)*

Sheriff's Office, Dayton *Also called County of Montgomery* *(G-9325)*

Sherman Financial Group LLC 513 707-3000
8600 Governors Hill Dr # 201 Cincinnati (45249) *(G-4470)*

Sherman Thompson Oh Tc LP 216 520-1250
275 N 3rd St Ironton (45638) *(G-12166)*

Sherwood Fd Dstrs Clveland Div, Maple Heights *Also called Sherwood Food Distributors LLC* *(G-13295)*

Sherwood Food Distributors LLC 216 662-8000
16625 Granite Rd Maple Heights (44137) *(G-13295)*

Sherwood Food Distributors LLC 216 662-6794
16625 Granite Rd Maple Heights (44137) *(G-13296)*

Shetler Moving & Stor of Ohio 513 755-0700
9917 Charter Park Dr West Chester (45069) *(G-19004)*

Shetlers Sales & Service Inc 330 760-3358
3500 Copley Rd Copley (44321) *(G-8975)*

Shg Whitehall Holdings LLC 614 501-8271
4805 Langley Ave Columbus (43213) *(G-8633)*

Shield Security Service 330 650-2001
P.O. Box 1001 Hudson (44236) *(G-12006)*

Shields Capital Corporation 216 767-1340
20600 Chagrin Blvd # 800 Beachwood (44122) *(G-1104)*

Shilling AC Heating & Plumbing, Port Clinton *Also called Gundlach Sheet Metal Works Inc* *(G-16108)*

Shiloh Group 937 833-2219
14336 Amity Rd Brookville (45309) *(G-1917)*

Shiloh Manufacturing LLC (HQ) 330 558-2693
880 Steel Dr Valley City (44280) *(G-18469)*

SHILOH SPRINGS CARE CENTER, Trotwood *Also called Carriage Inn of Trotwood Inc* *(G-18192)*

Shiloh Springs Care Center, Dayton *Also called Carriage Inn of Trotwood Inc* *(G-9281)*

Shiloh Springs Care Center, Brookville *Also called Shiloh Group* *(G-1917)*

Shima Limousine Services Inc 440 918-6400
7555 Tyler Blvd Ste 12 Mentor (44060) *(G-14109)*

Shindler Neff Holmes Schlag 419 243-6281
300 Madison Ave Ste 1200 Toledo (43604) *(G-18030)*

Shining Company LLC 614 588-4115
3739 Wynds Dr Columbus (43232) *(G-8634)*

Ship Shape Marine Inc 419 734-1554
410 W Perry St Port Clinton (43452) *(G-16117)*

Ship-Paq Inc 513 860-0700
3845 Port Union Rd Fairfield (45014) *(G-10780)*

Shippers Cartage & Dist, Cleveland *Also called Shippers Consolidated Dist* *(G-6405)*

Shippers Consolidated Dist 216 579-9303
1840 Carter Rd Cleveland (44113) *(G-6405)*

Shipping & Receiving Dept, Cleveland *Also called Case Western Reserve Univ* *(G-5130)*

Shipyard, The, Columbus *Also called Smart Harbor LLC* *(G-8653)*

Shirleys Gourmet Popcorn Co, Pandora *Also called Drc Holdings Inc* *(G-15750)*

Shiv Hotels LLC 740 374-8190
700 Pike St Marietta (45750) *(G-13381)*

Shiver Security Systems Inc 513 719-4000
6404 Thornberry Ct # 410 Mason (45040) *(G-13639)*

Shoemaker Electric Company 614 294-5626
831 Bonham Ave Columbus (43211) *(G-8635)*

Shoemaker Industrial Solutions, Columbus *Also called Shoemaker Electric Company* *(G-8635)*

Shoemetro, Columbus *Also called Ebuys Inc* *(G-7496)*

Shook Construction Co 440 838-5400
4977 Northcutt Pl Ste 200 Dayton (45414) *(G-9763)*

Shoptech Industrial Sftwr 513 985-9900
400 E Bus Way Ste 300 Cincinnati (45241) *(G-4471)*

Shoreby Club, Cleveland *Also called Clubcorp Usa Inc* *(G-5309)*

Shoreby Club Inc 216 851-2587
40 Shoreby Dr Cleveland (44108) *(G-6406)*

Shoreline Company, Strongsville *Also called Shoreline Transportation Inc* *(G-17345)*

Shoreline Express Inc 440 878-3750
20137 Progress Dr Strongsville (44149) *(G-17344)*

Shoreline Transportation Inc 440 878-2000
20137 Progress Dr Strongsville (44149) *(G-17345)*

Short and Sweet, Columbus *Also called Nationwide Childrens Hospital* *(G-8143)*

Short Freight Lines Inc 419 729-1691
6180 Benore Rd Toledo (43612) *(G-18031)*

Shotstop Ballistics LLC 330 686-0020
4319 Lorwood Dr Ste 102 Stow (44224) *(G-17230)*

Shoupes Constuction 937 352-6457
1410 Ludlow Rd Xenia (45385) *(G-19926)*

Show What You Know, Dayton *Also called Lorenz Corporation* *(G-9573)*

Showcase Cinemas, Maumee *Also called National Amusements Inc* *(G-13823)*

Showe Builders Inc (HQ) 614 481-8106
45 N 4th St Columbus (43215) *(G-8636)*

Shp Leading Design (PA) 513 381-2112
312 Plum St Ste 700 Cincinnati (45202) *(G-4472)*

Shr Management Resources Corp 937 274-1546
2222 Philadelphia Dr Dayton (45406) *(G-9764)*

Shrader Tire & Oil Inc (PA) 419 472-2128
2045 W Sylvania Ave # 51 Toledo (43613) *(G-18032)*

Shrader Tire & Oil Inc 614 445-6601
2021 Harmon Ave Columbus (43223) *(G-8637)*

Shred It, Columbus *Also called TDS Document Management Ltd* *(G-8734)*

Shred-It USA LLC 847 288-0377
6838 Firfield Bus Ctr Dr Fairfield (45014) *(G-10781)*

Shred-It USA LLC (HQ) 800 697-4733
6838 Firfield Bus Ctr Dr Fairfield (45014) *(G-10782)*

Shredded Bedding Corporation (PA) 740 893-3567
6589 Bennington Chapel Rd Centerburg (43011) *(G-2616)*

Shree Shankar LLC 440 734-4477
3971 Evergreen Ln Richfield (44286) *(G-16379)*

Shremshock Architects Inc (PA) 614 545-4550
7400 W Campus Rd Ste 150 New Albany (43054) *(G-14874)*

Shriners Hspitals For Children 513 872-6000
3229 Burnet Ave Cincinnati (45229) *(G-4473)*

Shumaker Loop & Kendrick LLP (PA) 419 241-9000
1000 Jackson St Toledo (43604) *(G-18033)*

Shumsky Enterprises Inc (PA) 937 223-2203
811 E 4th St Dayton (45402) *(G-9765)*

Shumsky Promotional, Dayton *Also called Boost Technologies LLC* *(G-9259)*

Shurmer Place At Altenheim 440 238-9001
18821 Shurmer Rd Strongsville (44136) *(G-17346)*

Sibcy Cline Inc 937 610-3404
8353 Yankee St Dayton (45458) *(G-9766)*

Sibcy Cline Inc 513 752-4000
792 Eastgate South Dr # 800 Cincinnati (45245) *(G-2868)*

Sibcy Cline Inc 513 793-2121
8040 Montgomery Rd Cincinnati (45236) *(G-4474)*

Sibcy Cline Inc 513 385-3330
600 Wessel Dr Fairfield (45014) *(G-10783)*

Sibcy Cline Inc (PA) 513 984-4100
8044 Montgomery Rd # 300 Cincinnati (45236) *(G-4475)*

(G-0000) Company's Geographic Section entry number

Sibcy Cline Inc..513 829-0044
  600 Wessel Dr Fairfield (45014) *(G-10784)*

Sibcy Cline Inc..513 777-8100
  7677 Voice Of Amer Ctr Dr West Chester (45069) *(G-19005)*

Sibcy Cline Inc..513 793-2700
  9979 Montgomery Rd Cincinnati (45242) *(G-4476)*

Sibcy Cline Inc..513 931-7700
  9250 Winton Rd Cincinnati (45231) *(G-4477)*

Sibcy Cline Inc..513 677-1830
  7395 Mason Montgomery Rd Mason (45040) *(G-13640)*

Sibcy Cline Inc..937 429-2101
  2476 Commons Blvd Ste E Beavercreek (45431) *(G-1186)*

Sibcy Cline Inc..513 932-6334
  103 Oregonia Rd Lebanon (45036) *(G-12501)*

Sibcy Cline Mortgage Services.........................513 984-6776
  8044 Montgomery Rd # 301 Cincinnati (45236) *(G-4478)*

Sibcy Cline Realtors, Cincinnati *Also called Sibcy Cline Inc (G-4475)*

Sibcy Cline Realtors, West Chester *Also called Sibcy Cline Inc (G-19005)*

Sibcy Cline Realtors, Cincinnati *Also called Sibcy Cline Inc (G-4477)*

Sibcy Cline Realtors, Mason *Also called Sibcy Cline Inc (G-13640)*

Sibcy, Cline Realtors, Lebanon *Also called Sibcy Cline Inc (G-12501)*

Sickle Cell Awaremess Grp................................513 281-4450
  3458 Reading Rd Cincinnati (45229) *(G-4479)*

Sidaris Italian Foods, Cleveland *Also called Resers Fine Foods Inc (G-6313)*

Side Effects Inc..937 704-9696
  259 Industrial Dr Franklin (45005) *(G-11039)*

Sidle Transit Service Inc...................................330 683-2807
  5454 N Crown Hill Rd Orrville (44667) *(G-15647)*

Sidney Care Center, Sidney *Also called CHS Miami Valley Inc (G-16765)*

Sidney Electric Company (PA)...........................419 222-1109
  840 S Vandemark Rd Sidney (45365) *(G-16799)*

Sidney-Shelby County YMCA (PA)....................937 492-9134
  300 E Parkwood St Sidney (45365) *(G-16800)*

Sidwell Materials Inc...740 849-2394
  4200 Maysville Pike Zanesville (43701) *(G-20361)*

Siebenthaler Company (PA).............................937 427-4110
  3001 Catalpa Dr Dayton (45405) *(G-9767)*

Siebenthaler's Garden Center, Dayton *Also called Siebenthaler Company (G-9767)*

Siegel Siegel J & Jennings Co (PA)................216 763-1004
  23425 Commerce Park # 103 Beachwood (44122) *(G-1105)*

Siegfried Group LLP...216 522-1910
  600 Superior Ave E Cleveland (44114) *(G-6407)*

Siemens Energy Inc..740 393-8897
  105 N Sandusky St Mount Vernon (43050) *(G-14790)*

Siemens Industry Inc..614 846-9540
  530 Lkview Plz Blvd Ste D Worthington (43085) *(G-19849)*

Siemens Industry Inc..440 526-2770
  6930 Treeline Dr Ste A Brecksville (44141) *(G-1805)*

Siemens Industry Inc..513 742-5590
  1310 Kemper Meadow Dr # 500 Cincinnati (45240) *(G-4480)*

Siemens Industry Inc..800 879-8079
  4170 Columbia Rd Lebanon (45036) *(G-12502)*

Siemens Product Life Mgmt Sftw......................513 576-2400
  2000 Eastman Dr Milford (45150) *(G-14431)*

Siemer Distributing, New Lexington *Also called Lori Holding Co (G-14920)*

Siemer Distributing Company...........................740 342-3230
  1400 Commerce Dr New Lexington (43764) *(G-14928)*

Siena Springs II...513 639-2800
  6217 N Main St Dayton (45415) *(G-9768)*

Sienna Hills Nursing & Rehab...........................740 546-3013
  73841 Pleasant Grove Rd Adena (43901) *(G-8)*

Sierra Lobo Inc (PA)..419 332-7101
  102 Pinnacle Dr Fremont (43420) *(G-11095)*

Sievers Security Systems Inc (PA)....................216 383-1234
  18210 Saint Clair Ave Cleveland (44110) *(G-6408)*

Siffrin Residential Assn.....................................330 799-8932
  136 Westchester Dr Ste 1 Youngstown (44515) *(G-20211)*

Sight Resource Corporation (PA)......................513 942-4423
  8100 Beckett Center Dr West Chester (45069) *(G-19006)*

Sigma CHI Frat...614 297-8783
  260 E 15th Ave Columbus (43201) *(G-8638)*

Sigma T E K, Cincinnati *Also called Sigmatek Systems LLC (G-4481)*

Sigma Technologies Ltd.....................................419 874-9262
  27096 Oakmead Dr Perrysburg (43551) *(G-15921)*

Sigma-Aldrich, Miamisburg *Also called Aldrich Chemical (G-14138)*

Sigmatek Systems LLC (PA).............................513 674-0005
  1445 Kemper Meadow Dr Cincinnati (45240) *(G-4481)*

Sign America Incorporated................................740 765-5555
  3887 State Route 43 Richmond (43944) *(G-16387)*

Sign Source USA Inc..419 224-1130
  1700 S Dixie Hwy Lima (45804) *(G-12741)*

Signal Office Supply Inc...................................513 821-2280
  415 W Benson St Cincinnati (45215) *(G-4482)*

Signal Productions Inc.......................................323 382-0000
  1267 W 9th St Cleveland (44113) *(G-6409)*

Signature Inc..614 734-0010
  5115 Prkcnter Ave Ste 200 Dublin (43017) *(G-10334)*

Signature Assoc-A Cushman, Toledo *Also called Signature Associates Inc (G-18034)*

Signature Associates Inc...................................419 244-7505
  4 Seagate Ste 608 Toledo (43604) *(G-18034)*

Signature Boutique Hotel LP.............................216 595-0900
  1010 Eaton Blvd Beachwood (44122) *(G-1106)*

Signature Concrete Inc......................................937 723-8435
  517 Windsor Park Dr Dayton (45459) *(G-9769)*

Signature Control Systems LLC.........................614 864-2222
  2228 Citygate Dr Columbus (43219) *(G-8639)*

Signature Controls, Columbus *Also called Signature Control Systems LLC (G-8639)*

Signature Health Inc..440 953-9999
  38882 Mentor Ave Willoughby (44094) *(G-19571)*

Signature Healthcare LLC.................................330 372-1977
  2473 North Rd Ne Warren (44483) *(G-18743)*

Signature Healthcare LLC.................................440 232-1800
  5386 Majestic Pkwy Bedford (44146) *(G-1305)*

Signature Salon, Cleveland *Also called Best Cuts Inc (G-5058)*

Signature Solon Golf Course, Solon *Also called Weymouth Valley Inc (G-16915)*

Signet Management Co Ltd................................330 762-9102
  19 N High St Akron (44308) *(G-428)*

Signum LLC..440 248-2233
  32000 Aurora Rd Ste C Solon (44139) *(G-16897)*

Sika Corporation..740 387-9224
  1682 Mrn Williamsprt Rd E Marion (43302) *(G-13459)*

Silco Fire Protection Company..........................330 535-4343
  451 Kennedy Rd Akron (44305) *(G-429)*

Siler Excavation Services..................................513 400-8628
  6025 Catherine Dr Milford (45150) *(G-14432)*

Silliker Laboratories Ohio Inc...........................614 486-0150
  2057 Builders Pl Columbus (43204) *(G-8640)*

Silvan Trucking Company Ohio, Columbus *Also called S & T Truck and Auto Svc Inc (G-8569)*

Silver Lake Country Club...................................330 688-6066
  1325 Graham Rd Silver Lake (44224) *(G-16809)*

Silver Lake Management Corp...........................330 688-6066
  1325 Graham Rd Silver Lake (44224) *(G-16810)*

Silver Spruce Holding LLC................................937 259-1200
  3123 Res Blvd Ste 250 Dayton (45420) *(G-9770)*

Sima Marine Sales Inc (PA).............................440 269-3200
  200 Forest Dr Willoughby (44095) *(G-19572)*

Simco Controls, Columbus *Also called Simco Supply Co (G-8641)*

Simco Supply Co...614 253-1999
  3000 E 14th Ave Columbus (43219) *(G-8641)*

Simmons Brothers Corporation.........................330 722-1415
  780 W Smith Rd Ste A Medina (44256) *(G-14001)*

Simms Metal Management Ohio, Defiance *Also called Metal Management Ohio Inc (G-9930)*

Simon Knton Cncil Byscuts Amer (PA)..............614 436-7200
  807 Kinnear Rd Columbus (43212) *(G-8642)*

Simon Property Group..614 717-9300
  5043 Tuttle Crossing Blvd Dublin (43016) *(G-10335)*

Simon Roofing and Shtmtl Corp (PA)................330 629-7392
  70 Karago Ave Youngstown (44512) *(G-20212)*

Simone Health Management Inc........................614 224-1347
  750 E Broad St Ste 300 Columbus (43205) *(G-8643)*

Simonson Construction Svcs Inc.......................419 281-8299
  2112 Troy Rd Ashland (44805) *(G-691)*

Simonton Windows, Columbus *Also called Fortune Brands Windows Inc (G-7602)*

Simplex Time Recorder 514, West Chester *Also called Simplex Time Recorder LLC (G-19081)*

Simplex Time Recorder LLC................................800 746-7539
  8910 Beckett Rd West Chester (45069) *(G-19007)*

Simplex Time Recorder LLC................................937 291-0355
  8899 Gander Creek Dr Miamisburg (45342) *(G-14221)*

Simplex Time Recorder LLC................................513 874-1227
  10182 International Blvd West Chester (45246) *(G-19081)*

Simplifi Eso LLC..614 635-8679
  2 Miranova Pl Ste 500 Columbus (43215) *(G-8644)*

Simplified Logistics LLC...................................440 250-8912
  28915 Clemens Rd Ste 220 Westlake (44145) *(G-19406)*

Simply Youth LLC..330 284-2537
  123 Cleveland Ave Nw Canton (44702) *(G-2476)*

Simpson Strong-Tie Company Inc.....................614 876-8060
  2600 International St Columbus (43228) *(G-8645)*

Sims Buick-G M C Truck Inc..............................330 372-3500
  3100 Elm Rd Ne Warren (44483) *(G-18744)*

Sims GMC Trucks, Warren *Also called Sims Buick-G M C Truck Inc (G-18744)*

Sims-Lohman Inc (PA)..513 651-3510
  6325 Este Ave Cincinnati (45232) *(G-4483)*

Sims-Lohman Fine Kitchens Gran, Cincinnati *Also called Sims-Lohman Inc (G-4483)*

Sinclair Broadcast Group Inc............................513 641-4400
  1906 Highland Ave Cincinnati (45219) *(G-4484)*

Sinclair Broadcast Group Inc............................513 641-4400
  1906 Highland Ave Cincinnati (45219) *(G-4485)*

Sinclair Media II Inc..614 481-6666
  1261 Dublin Rd Columbus (43215) *(G-8646)*

Sinclair Media II Inc..614 481-6666
  1261 Dublin Rd Columbus (43215) *(G-8647)*

Sinclair Media II Inc..614 481-6666
  1261 Dublin Rd Columbus (43215) *(G-8648)*

Sines Inc...440 352-6572
  1744 N Ridge Rd Painesville (44077) *(G-15740)*

Singer Steel Company..330 562-7200
  1 Singer Dr Streetsboro (44241) *(G-17269)*

A
L
P
H
A
B
E
T
I
C

Singleton Health Care Center.............................216 231-0076
  1867 E 82nd St Cleveland (44103) *(G-6410)*

Sioto Paintsville Mental Hlth.............................740 775-1260
  4449 State Route 159 Chillicothe (45601) *(G-2826)*

Sirak Financial Companies, Canton *Also called Sirak Financial Services Inc* *(G-2477)*

Sirak Financial Services Inc (PA).........................330 493-0642
  4700 Dressler Rd Nw Canton (44718) *(G-2477)*

Sirak-Moore Insurance Agcy Inc...........................330 493-3211
  4700 Dressler Rd Nw Canton (44718) *(G-2478)*

Sirna & Sons Inc (PA)....................................330 298-2222
  7176 State Route 88 Ravenna (44266) *(G-16266)*

Sirna's Market & Deli, Ravenna *Also called Sirna & Sons Inc* *(G-16266)*

Sirpilla Recrtl Vhcl Ctr Inc.............................330 494-2525
  1005 Interstate Pkwy Akron (44312) *(G-430)*

Sirva Inc..216 606-4000
  6200 Oak Tree Blvd # 300 Independence (44131) *(G-12120)*

Sirva Mortgage Inc.......................................800 531-3837
  6200 Oak Tree Blvd # 300 Independence (44131) *(G-12121)*

Sirva Relocation LLC (HQ)................................216 606-4000
  6200 Oak Tree Blvd # 300 Independence (44131) *(G-12122)*

Sirva Worldwide Relocation Mvg, Independence *Also called Sirva Relocation LLC* *(G-12122)*

Sisler Heating & Cooling Inc.............................330 722-7101
  249 S State Rd Medina (44256) *(G-14002)*

Sisters Od Saint Joseph of SAI...........................216 531-7426
  21800 Chardon Rd Euclid (44117) *(G-10656)*

Sisters of Charity of Cinc (HQ)..........................513 347-5200
  5900 Delhi Rd Mount Saint Joseph (45051) *(G-14744)*

Sisters of Little..216 464-1222
  4291 Richmond Rd Warrensville Heights (44122) *(G-18780)*

Sisters of Little..419 698-4331
  930 S Wynn Rd Oregon (43616) *(G-15608)*

Sisters of Little..513 281-8001
  476 Riddle Rd Cincinnati (45220) *(G-4486)*

Sisters of Mercy...419 332-8208
  1220 Tiffin St Fremont (43420) *(G-11096)*

Sisters of Mercy Amer Reg Comm..........................419 696-7203
  1001 Isaac Streets Dr Oregon (43616) *(G-15609)*

Sisters of Mercy Fremont, Ohio, Fremont *Also called Sisters of Mercy* *(G-11096)*

Sisters of Mrcy of Wllard Ohio (HQ)......................419 964-5000
  1100 Neal Zick Rd Willard (44890) *(G-19488)*

Sisters of Notre D.......................................419 471-0170
  3912 Sunforest Ct Ste B Toledo (43623) *(G-18035)*

Sisters of Notre Dame of Chard...........................440 279-0575
  13000 Auburn Rd Chardon (44024) *(G-2714)*

Sisters of The Transfiguration, Cincinnati *Also called Society of The Transfiguration* *(G-4501)*

Site 046, Bellefontaine *Also called Allied Waste Systems Inc* *(G-1344)*

Site 091b, Bryan *Also called Allied Waste Systems Inc* *(G-1951)*

Site Centers Corp (PA)...................................216 755-5500
  3300 Enterprise Pkwy Beachwood (44122) *(G-1107)*

Site K62, Williamsburg *Also called Cecos International Inc* *(G-19490)*

Site L10, Morrow *Also called Browning-Ferris Industries Inc* *(G-14715)*

Site R24, Oberlin *Also called Allied Waste Industries LLC* *(G-15498)*

Site Worx LLC..513 229-0295
  3980 Turtlecreek Rd Lebanon (45036) *(G-12503)*

Siteworx, Lebanon *Also called Site Worx LLC* *(G-12503)*

Six C Fabrication Inc....................................330 296-5594
  5245 S Prospect St Ravenna (44266) *(G-16267)*

Six Continents Hotels Inc................................513 563-8330
  3855 Hauck Rd Cincinnati (45241) *(G-4487)*

Six Disciplines LLC (PA).................................419 424-6647
  1219 W Main Cross St # 205 Findlay (45840) *(G-10959)*

Six Flags Ohio, Aurora *Also called Funtime Parks Inc* *(G-827)*

Six Sigma Logistics Inc..................................440 666-6026
  6745 Ciffside Dr Vermilion (44089) *(G-18559)*

Sjn Data Center LLC (PA).................................513 386-7871
  4620 Wesley Ave Cincinnati (45212) *(G-4488)*

SJS Packaging Group Inc..................................513 841-1351
  6545 Wiehe Rd Cincinnati (45237) *(G-4489)*

Sk Rigging Co Inc..513 771-7766
  11515 Rockfield Ct Cincinnati (45241) *(G-4490)*

Skally's Restaurant, Cincinnati *Also called Skallys Old World Bakery Inc* *(G-4491)*

Skallys Old World Bakery Inc.............................513 931-1411
  1933 W Galbraith Rd Cincinnati (45239) *(G-4491)*

Skanska USA Building Inc.................................513 421-0082
  201 E 5th St Ste 2020 Cincinnati (45202) *(G-4492)*

Skate Town U S A...513 874-9855
  8730 N Pavillion West Chester (45069) *(G-19008)*

Skateworld Inc (PA)......................................937 294-4032
  1601 E David Rd Dayton (45429) *(G-9771)*

Skateworld of Kettering, Dayton *Also called Skateworld Inc* *(G-9771)*

Skidmore Sales & Distrg Co Inc (PA)......................513 755-4200
  9889 Cincinnati Dayton Rd West Chester (45069) *(G-19009)*

Skillsoft Corporation....................................216 524-5200
  6645 Acres Dr Independence (44131) *(G-12123)*

Skinner Diesel Services Inc..............................614 491-8785
  2440 Lockbourne Rd Columbus (43207) *(G-8649)*

Skipco Financial Adjusters (PA)..........................330 854-4800
  2306 Locust St S Canal Fulton (44614) *(G-2097)*

Skoda Minotti Holdings LLC (PA)..........................440 449-6800
  6685 Beta Dr Cleveland (44143) *(G-6411)*

Skoda Mntti Crtif Pub Accntnts (HQ)......................440 449-6800
  6685 Beta Dr Mayfield Village (44143) *(G-13887)*

SKW Management LLC.......................................937 382-7938
  3841 Panhandle Rd Lynchburg (45142) *(G-13055)*

Sky Climber Twr Solutions LLC............................740 203-3900
  1800 Pittsburgh Dr Delaware (43015) *(G-10007)*

Sky Financial Capital Tr III.............................614 480-3278
  41 S High St Columbus (43215) *(G-8650)*

Sky Lane Drive-Thru, Garrettsville *Also called Skylane LLC* *(G-11230)*

Sky Zone Boston Heights, Hudson *Also called Wonderworker Inc* *(G-12015)*

Sky Zone Indoor Trampoline Pk, Cincinnati *Also called Sky Zone Indoor Trampoline Pk* *(G-4493)*

Sky Zone Indoor Trampoline Pk............................614 302-6093
  11745 Commons Dr Cincinnati (45246) *(G-4493)*

Skybox Packaging LLC.....................................419 525-7209
  1275 Pollock Pkwy Mansfield (44905) *(G-13243)*

Skycasters LLC...330 785-2100
  1520 S Arlington St # 100 Akron (44306) *(G-431)*

Skye Development Company LLC.............................216 223-0160
  25001 Emery Rd Ste 420 Cleveland (44128) *(G-6412)*

Skyland Columbus LLC.....................................614 478-0922
  3000 Morse Rd Columbus (43231) *(G-8651)*

Skylane LLC..330 527-9999
  8311 Windham St Garrettsville (44231) *(G-11230)*

Skylight Financial Group LLC (PA)........................216 621-5680
  2012 W 25th St Ste 900 Cleveland (44113) *(G-6413)*

Skyline Chili Inc (PA)...................................513 874-1188
  4180 Thunderbird Ln Fairfield (45014) *(G-10785)*

Skyline Clvland Rnaissance LLC...........................216 696-5600
  24 Public Sq Cleveland (44113) *(G-6414)*

Skyline CM Portfolio LLC.................................937 433-3131
  100 Prestige Pl Miamisburg (45342) *(G-14222)*

Skyline CM Portfolio LLC.................................419 866-1001
  1435 E Mall Dr Holland (43528) *(G-11914)*

Skyview Baptist Ranch Inc................................330 674-7511
  7241 Township Road 319 Millersburg (44654) *(G-14493)*

SL Wellspring LLC..513 948-2339
  8000 Evergreen Ridge Dr Cincinnati (45215) *(G-4494)*

Slagle Mechanical Contractors............................937 492-4151
  877 W Russell Rd Sidney (45365) *(G-16801)*

Slaters Inc..740 654-2204
  1141 N Memorial Dr Lancaster (43130) *(G-12435)*

Slavic Village Development...............................216 429-1182
  5620 Broadway Ave Uppr Cleveland (44127) *(G-6415)*

Slawson Equipment Co Inc.................................216 391-7263
  7851 Freeway Cir Cleveland (44130) *(G-6416)*

Slay Transportation Inc..................................740 865-2910
  Rr 7 Box 34684 Sardis (43946) *(G-16661)*

SLC Custom Packaging, Macedonia *Also called Specialty Lubricants Corp* *(G-13082)*

Sleep Care Inc...614 901-8989
  985 Schrock Rd Ste 204 Columbus (43229) *(G-8652)*

Sleep Inn, Oregon *Also called Dure Investments LLC* *(G-15591)*

Sleep Network Inc (PA)...................................419 535-9282
  3450 W Central Ave # 346 Toledo (43606) *(G-18036)*

Sleepy Hollow Golf Course, Brecksville *Also called Cleveland Metroparks* *(G-1776)*

Slesnick Iron & Metal Co.................................330 453-8475
  927 Warner Rd Se Canton (44707) *(G-2479)*

Slick Automated Solutions Inc............................567 247-1080
  1825 Nussbaum Pkwy Ontario (44906) *(G-15573)*

Sliddy Ent LLC...419 376-1797
  417 Bronson Ave Toledo (43608) *(G-18037)*

Sliddy Entertainment, Toledo *Also called Sliddy Ent LLC* *(G-18037)*

Slimans Chrysler Plymouth Dodge, Amherst *Also called Slimans Sales & Service Inc* *(G-597)*

Slimans Sales & Service Inc..............................440 988-4484
  7498 Leavitt Rd Amherst (44001) *(G-597)*

Slipgrips, Nelsonville *Also called Lehigh Outfitters LLC* *(G-14834)*

Sliver Lake Country Club, Silver Lake *Also called Silver Lake Management Corp* *(G-16810)*

Slovene Home For The Aged................................216 486-0268
  18621 Neff Rd Cleveland (44119) *(G-6417)*

Slush Puppie..513 771-0940
  44 Carnegie Way West Chester (45246) *(G-19082)*

SM Double Tree Hotel Lake................................216 241-5100
  1111 Lakeside Ave E Cleveland (44114) *(G-6418)*

Small Sand & Gravel Inc..................................740 427-3130
  10229 Killduff Rd Gambier (43022) *(G-11226)*

Smalls Asphalt Paving Inc................................740 427-4096
  10229 Killduff Rd Gambier (43022) *(G-11227)*

Smart (PA)...216 228-9400
  24950 Country Club Blvd # 340 North Olmsted (44070) *(G-15310)*

Smart - Transportation Div, North Olmsted *Also called Smart* *(G-15310)*

Smart Harbor LLC (PA)....................................800 295-4519
  580 N 4th St Ste 500 Columbus (43215) *(G-8653)*

Smart Solutions, Beachwood *Also called Ohio Cllbrtive Lrng Sltons Inc* *(G-1089)*

Smb Construction Co Inc (PA).............................419 269-1473
  5120 Jackman Rd Toledo (43613) *(G-18038)*

SMG AGENT FOR CLEVELAND CONVEN, Cleveland *Also called Cuyahoga County Convention Fac* *(G-5398)*

(G-0000) Company's Geographic Section entry number

Smg Holdings Inc 614 827-2500
  400 N High St Fl 2 Columbus (43215) (G-8654)
Smgoa, Columbus Also called Sports Medicine Grant Inc (G-8673)
Smile Brands Inc 419 627-1255
  1313 W Bogart Rd Ste D Sandusky (44870) (G-16642)
Smile Development Inc 419 882-7187
  5860 Alexis Rd Ste 1 Sylvania (43560) (G-17451)
Smink Electric Inc 440 322-5518
  215 Winckles St Elyria (44035) (G-10563)
Smith & Associates Excavating 740 362-3355
  2765 Drake Rd Columbus (43219) (G-8655)
Smith & English II Inc 513 697-9300
  12191 State Route 22 3 Loveland (45140) (G-13029)
Smith & Oby Company 440 735-5333
  7676 Northfield Rd Walton Hills (44146) (G-18638)
Smith & Oby Service Co 440 735-5322
  7676 Northfield Rd Bedford (44146) (G-1306)
Smith Ambulance Service Inc 330 825-0205
  214 W 3rd St Dover (44622) (G-10099)
Smith Ambulance Service Inc (PA) 330 602-0050
  214 W 3rd St Dover (44622) (G-10100)
Smith Barney, Beavercreek Also called Citigroup Global Markets Inc (G-1210)
Smith Barney, Toledo Also called Citigroup Global Markets Inc (G-17653)
Smith Barney, Cleveland Also called Citigroup Global Markets Inc (G-5183)
Smith Brothers Erection Inc 740 373-3575
  101 Industry Rd Marietta (45750) (G-13382)
Smith Clinic, Delaware Also called Women Health Partners (G-10017)
Smith Concrete Co (PA) 740 373-7441
  2301 Progress St Dover (44622) (G-10101)
Smith Construction Group Inc 937 426-0500
  731 Orchard Ln Beavercreek Township (45434) (G-1262)
Smith Peter Kalail Co Lpa 216 503-5055
  6480 Rcksde Wds Blvd S # 300 Independence (44131) (G-12124)
Smith Rolfes & Skazdahl Lpa (PA) 513 579-0080
  600 Vine St Ste 2600 Cincinnati (45202) (G-4495)
Smith Tandy Company 614 224-9255
  555 City Park Ave Columbus (43215) (G-8656)
Smith Trucking Inc 419 841-8676
  3775 Centennial Rd Sylvania (43560) (G-17452)
Smith, Matthew J Co Lpa, Cincinnati Also called Smith Rolfes & Skazdahl Lpa (G-4495)
Smith, R G of Mansfield, Mansfield Also called R G Smith Company (G-13231)
Smithbarney, Cincinnati Also called Citigroup Global Markets Inc (G-3296)
Smithers Group Inc (PA) 330 762-7441
  121 S Main St Ste 300 Akron (44308) (G-432)
Smithers Quality Assessments 330 762-4231
  121 S Main St Ste 300 Akron (44308) (G-433)
Smithers Rapra Inc 330 297-1495
  1150 N Freedom St Ravenna (44266) (G-16268)
Smithers Rapra Inc (HQ) 330 762-7441
  425 W Market St Akron (44303) (G-434)
Smithers Tire & Auto Testng TX 330 762-7441
  425 W Market St Akron (44303) (G-435)
Smithers Trnsp Test Ctrs, Akron Also called Smithers Tire & Auto Testng TX (G-435)
Smithfoods Orrville Inc 330 683-8710
  1381 Dairy Ln Orrville (44667) (G-15648)
Smithpearlman & Co 513 248-9210
  100 Techne Center Dr # 200 Milford (45150) (G-14433)
Smithville Western Commons, Wooster Also called Bluesky Healthcare Inc (G-19692)
Smoky Row Childrens Center 614 766-2122
  8615 Smoky Row Rd Powell (43065) (G-16211)
Smoot Construction Co Ohio (HQ) 614 253-9000
  1907 Leonard Ave Ste 200 Columbus (43219) (G-8657)
SMS, Alliance Also called Stark Metal Sales Inc (G-554)
SMS Group Inc 330 426-4126
  49560 State Route 14 East Palestine (44413) (G-10421)
SMS Technical Services, East Palestine Also called SMS Group Inc (G-10421)
SMS Transport LLC 937 813-8897
  8235 Old Troy Pike 272 Dayton (45424) (G-9772)
Smylie One Heating & Cooling 440 449-4328
  5108 Richmond Rd Bedford (44146) (G-1307)
Smyth Automotive Inc (PA) 513 528-2800
  4275 Mt Carmel Tobasco Rd Cincinnati (45244) (G-4496)
Smyth Automotive Inc 513 528-0061
  4271 Mt Carmel Tobasco Rd Cincinnati (45244) (G-4497)
Smyth Automotive Inc 513 575-2000
  1900 State Route 131 Milford (45150) (G-14434)
Smyth Automotive Inc 513 777-6400
  8868 Cincinnati Columbus West Chester (45069) (G-19010)
Smyth Automotive Inc 513 734-7800
  685 W Plane St Bethel (45106) (G-1454)
Smyth Automotive Parts Plus, Milford Also called Smyth Automotive Inc (G-14434)
Smythe Cramer Co, Uniontown Also called Howard Hanna Smythe Cramer (G-18374)
Smythe Cramer Reltrs, Cleveland Also called Howard Hanna Smythe Cramer (G-5718)
Smythe-Cramer Co Madison, Madison Also called Howard Hanna Smythe Cramer (G-13097)
Snapblox Hosted Solutions LLC 866 524-7707
  131 Eight Mile Rd Cincinnati (45255) (G-4498)
Snavely Building Company (PA) 440 585-9091
  7139 Pine St Ste 110 Chagrin Falls (44022) (G-2654)
Snavely Development Company (PA) 440 585-9091
  7139 Pine St Chagrin Falls (44022) (G-2655)

Snelling, Fairlawn Also called E & L Premier Corporation (G-10823)
Snf Wadsworth LLC 330 336-3472
  5625 Emerald Ridge Pkwy Solon (44139) (G-16898)
Snl Designs Ltd 440 247-2344
  13 N Franklin St Chagrin Falls (44022) (G-2656)
Snow Hill Country Club Inc 937 987-2491
  11093 State Route 73 New Vienna (45159) (G-14999)
Snows Lakeside Tavern 513 954-5626
  4344 Dry Ridge Rd Cincinnati (45252) (G-4499)
Snpj Recreation Farm 440 256-3423
  10946 Heath Rd Willoughby (44094) (G-19573)
Snyder Brick and Block, Moraine Also called Snyder Concrete Products Inc (G-14697)
Snyder Concrete Products Inc (PA) 937 885-5176
  2301 W Dorothy Ln Moraine (45439) (G-14697)
Snyder's Potato Chips, Bellaire Also called S-L Distribution Company LLC (G-1335)
Snyder's Service Now, Wooster Also called Schmids Service Now Inc (G-19766)
Snyders Antique Auto Parts Inc 330 549-5313
  12925 Woodworth Rd New Springfield (44443) (G-14998)
Snyders-Lance Inc 419 289-0787
  2041 Claremont Ave Ashland (44805) (G-692)
Soaring Eagle Inc 330 385-5579
  114 W 5th St East Liverpool (43920) (G-10418)
Soccer Centre Inc 419 893-5419
  1620 Market Place Dr # 1 Maumee (43537) (G-13852)
Soccer Centre Owners Ltd 419 893-5425
  1620 Market Place Dr Maumee (43537) (G-13853)
SOCIAL MINISTRY ORGANIZATION, Springfield Also called Oesterlen-Services For Youth (G-17091)
Social Services of Allen, Augl, Lima Also called Lutheran Social (G-12696)
Society For Handicapped Citzns 937 746-4201
  624 Fairview Dr Carlisle (45005) (G-2554)
Society For Rehabilitation 440 209-0135
  9290 Lake Shore Blvd Mentor (44060) (G-14110)
Society Handicapped Citz Medin (PA) 330 722-1900
  4283 Paradise Rd Seville (44273) (G-16689)
Society Handicapped Citz Medin 330 722-1710
  5810 Deerview Ln Medina (44256) (G-14003)
Society of St Vincent De Paul 513 421-2273
  1125 Bank St Cincinnati (45214) (G-4500)
Society of The Transfiguration (PA) 513 771-7462
  555 Albion Ave Cincinnati (45246) (G-4501)
Society Plastics Engineers Inc 419 287-4898
  15520 S River Rd Pemberville (43450) (G-15807)
Society Rehabilitation, Mentor Also called Society For Rehabilitation (G-14110)
Sociey For Handicapped Citizen 330 725-7041
  4283 Paradise Rd Seville (44273) (G-16690)
Sodexo Inc 330 425-0709
  2333 Sandalwood Dr Twinsburg (44087) (G-18321)
Sofco Erectors Inc (PA) 513 771-1600
  10360 Wayne Ave Cincinnati (45215) (G-4502)
Sofo Importing Company, Toledo Also called Antonio Sofo Son Importing Co (G-17596)
Soft Touch Wood LLC 330 545-4204
  1560 S State St Girard (44420) (G-11300)
Soft Tuch Furn Repr Rfinishing, Girard Also called Soft Touch Wood LLC (G-11300)
Software Answers Inc 440 526-0095
  6770 W Snowville Rd 200 Brecksville (44141) (G-1806)
Software Info Systems LLC 513 791-7777
  8805 Governors Hill Dr Cincinnati (45249) (G-4503)
Software Management Group 513 618-2165
  1128 Main St Fl 6 Cincinnati (45202) (G-4504)
Software Solutions Inc (PA) 513 932-6667
  420 E Main St Lebanon (45036) (G-12504)
Software Support Group Inc 216 566-0555
  22211 Westchester Rd Shaker Heights (44122) (G-16713)
Sogeti, Dayton Also called Capgemini America Inc (G-9274)
Sogeti USA LLC 614 847-4477
  579 Executive Campus Dr # 300 Westerville (43082) (G-19210)
Sogeti USA LLC 937 433-3334
  6494 Centervl Bus Pkwy Dayton (45459) (G-9773)
Sogeti USA LLC (HQ) 937 291-8100
  10100 Innovation Dr # 200 Miamisburg (45342) (G-14223)
Sogeti USA LLC 216 654-2230
  6055 Rockside Woods # 170 Cleveland (44131) (G-6419)
Sogeti USA LLC 513 824-3000
  4445 Lake Forest Dr # 550 Blue Ash (45242) (G-1651)
Soho Development Company 614 207-3261
  501 Cole Dr Johnstown (43031) (G-12203)
Soin Medical Center, Beavercreek Also called Kettering Medical Center (G-1161)
Sojourn Lodging Inc 330 422-1855
  795 Mondial Pkwy Streetsboro (44241) (G-17270)
Sojourner Home, Hamilton Also called Sojourner Recovery Services (G-11642)
Sojourner Recovery Services (PA) 513 868-7654
  294 N Fair Ave Hamilton (45011) (G-11642)
Solar Imaging LLC 614 626-8536
  825 Taylor Rd Gahanna (43230) (G-11145)
Solar Testing Laboratories Inc (PA) 216 741-7007
  1125 Valley Belt Rd Brooklyn Heights (44131) (G-1881)
Solenis LLC 614 336-1101
  5200 Blazer Pkwy Dublin (43017) (G-10336)
Solid Waste Auth Centl Ohio 614 871-5100
  4239 London Groveport Rd Grove City (43123) (G-11471)

A
L
P
H
A
B
E
T
I
C

Solidarity Health Network Inc...................216 831-1220
  4853 Galaxy Pkwy Ste K Cleveland (44128) (G-6420)
Solomon Cloud Solutions, Findlay Also called Plumbline Solutions Inc (G-10954)
Solomon Lei & Associates Inc...................419 246-6931
  947 Belmont Ave Toledo (43607) (G-18039)
Solomon, Lei & Associates, Toledo Also called Solomon Lei & Associates Inc (G-18039)
Solon Branch, Solon Also called Agilysys Inc (G-16816)
Solon Creative Playroom Center, Solon Also called Creative Playroom (G-16840)
Solon Crtive Plyroom Mntessori, Cleveland Also called Creative Playroom (G-5376)
Solon Fire Department, Solon Also called City of Solon (G-16836)
Solon Lodging Associates LLC...................440 248-9600
  30100 Aurora Rd Solon (44139) (G-16899)
Solon Pnte At Emrald Ridge LLC...................440 498-3000
  5625 Emerald Ridge Pkwy Solon (44139) (G-16900)
Solupay Consulting Inc...................216 535-9016
  1900 Entp Pkwy Ste A Twinsburg (44087) (G-18322)
Solutions Through Innovative T...................937 320-9994
  3152 Presidential Dr Beavercreek (45324) (G-1187)
Somc, Portsmouth Also called Southern Ohio Medical Center (G-16173)
Somc Foundation Inc...................740 356-5000
  1805 27th St Portsmouth (45662) (G-16170)
Somc Hospice, Portsmouth Also called Hospice of Southern Ohio (G-16148)
Somc Speech and Hearing Svcs, Portsmouth Also called Rehabcare Group MGT Svcs Inc (G-16163)
Somc Urgent Care Ctr Prtsmouth, Portsmouth Also called Southern Ohio Medical Center (G-16172)
SOMERSET HEALTH AND REHABILITA, Somerset Also called Somerset NH LLC (G-16918)
Somerset NH LLC...................740 743-2924
  411 S Columbus St Somerset (43783) (G-16918)
Something Special Lrng Ctr Inc...................419 422-1400
  655 Fox Run Rd Ste J Findlay (45840) (G-10960)
Something Special Lrng Ctr Inc (PA)...................419 878-4190
  8251 Wterville Swanton Rd Waterville (43566) (G-18792)
Sommers Market LLC (PA)...................330 352-7470
  214 Market Ave Sw Hartville (44632) (G-11699)
Sommers Mobil Leasing, Elyria Also called Midway Realty Company (G-10538)
Sommerset Development Ltd...................440 286-6194
  10585 Somerset Dr Chardon (44024) (G-2715)
Somnus Corporation...................740 695-3961
  51130 National Rd Saint Clairsville (43950) (G-16505)
Son-Rise Hotels Inc...................330 769-4949
  4949 Park Ave W Seville (44273) (G-16691)
Sonesta Intl Hotels Corp...................614 791-8554
  435 Metro Pl S Dublin (43017) (G-10337)
Sonic Automotive...................614 870-8200
  1500 Auto Mall Dr Columbus (43228) (G-8658)
Sonic Automotive-1495 Automall...................614 317-4326
  1495 Auto Mall Dr Columbus (43228) (G-8659)
Sonit Systems LLC...................419 446-2151
  130 Westfield Dr Archbold (43502) (G-640)
Sonitrol of South West Ohio, Mason Also called Shiver Security Systems Inc (G-13639)
Sonitrol Security Systems, Mansfield Also called Research & Investigation Assoc (G-13234)
Sonoco Products Company...................937 429-0040
  761 Space Dr Beavercreek Township (45434) (G-1263)
Sonoco Prtective Solutions Inc...................937 890-7628
  6061 Milo Rd Dayton (45414) (G-9774)
Sons of Un Vtrans of Civil War...................740 992-6144
  600 Grant St Middleport (45760) (G-14283)
Sonshine Commercial Cleaning, Dayton Also called Rde System Corporation (G-9727)
Sophisticated Systems Inc (PA)...................614 418-4600
  2191 Citygate Dr Columbus (43219) (G-8660)
Sorbir Inc (PA)...................440 449-1000
  6200 Mayfield Rd Cleveland (44124) (G-6421)
Sordyl & Associates Inc...................419 866-6811
  2962 W Course Rd Maumee (43537) (G-13854)
Sortino Management & Dev Co...................419 626-6761
  1935 Cleveland Rd Sandusky (44870) (G-16643)
Sos2000, Cincinnati Also called Signal Office Supply Inc (G-4482)
Sotera Health LLC (PA)...................440 262-1410
  9100 S Hills Blvd Ste 300 Broadview Heights (44147) (G-1846)
Soto Salon & Spa...................419 872-5555
  580 Craig Dr Ste 6 Perrysburg (43551) (G-15922)
Sottile & Barile LLC...................513 345-0592
  394 Wards Corner Rd # 180 Loveland (45140) (G-13030)
Sound Com Corporation...................440 234-2604
  227 Depot St Berea (44017) (G-1437)
Sound Com System, Berea Also called Sound Com Corporation (G-1437)
Soundtrack Printing...................330 606-7117
  1400 Sackett Ave Cuyahoga Falls* (44223) (G-9124)
Source Diagnostics LLC (PA)...................440 542-9481
  5275 Naiman Pkwy Ste E Solon (44139) (G-16901)
Sourcelink Ohio LLC...................937 885-8000
  3303 W Tech Blvd Miamisburg (45342) (G-14224)
Sourceone Healthcare Tech Inc (HQ)...................440 701-1200
  8020 Tyler Blvd Mentor (44060) (G-14111)
Sourcepoint...................740 363-6677
  800 Cheshire Rd Delaware (43015) (G-10008)
South Beach Grille, Cincinnati Also called Waterfront & Associates Inc (G-4770)

South Beach Resort...................419 798-4900
  8620 E Bayshore Rd Lakeside Marblehead (43440) (G-12331)
South Broadway...................330 339-2151
  245 S Broadway St 251 New Philadelphia (44663) (G-14981)
South Central Ohio Cmpt Assn, Piketon Also called Ohio Department of Education (G-15980)
South Central Ohio Eductl Ctr...................740 456-0517
  522 Glenwood Ave New Boston (45662) (G-14883)
South Central Power Company...................740 474-6045
  2100 Chickasaw Dr Circleville (43113) (G-4850)
South Central Power Company (PA)...................740 653-4422
  2780 Coonpath Rd Ne Lancaster (43130) (G-12436)
South Central Power Company...................614 837-4351
  10229 Busey Rd Nw Canal Winchester (43110) (G-2120)
South Central Power Company...................740 425-4018
  37801 Brnsvlle Bthesda Rd Barnesville (43713) (G-979)
South Cmty Family YMCA Cdc, Dayton Also called Young Mens Christian Assoc (G-9893)
South Cntrl OH Rgnl Juv Dtn CT, Chillicothe Also called County of Ross (G-2772)
South Community Inc (PA)...................937 293-8300
  3095 Kettering Blvd Ste 1 Moraine (45439) (G-14698)
South Community Inc...................937 252-0100
  2745 S Smthvlle Rd Ste 14 Dayton (45420) (G-9775)
South Dayton Acute Care Cons...................937 433-8990
  33 W Rahn Rd Dayton (45429) (G-9776)
South Dyton Urlgcal Asscations (PA)...................937 294-1489
  10 Southmoor Cir Nw Ste 1 Dayton (45429) (G-9777)
South E Harley Davidson Sls Co (PA)...................440 439-5300
  23105 Aurora Rd Cleveland (44146) (G-6422)
South E Harley Davidson Sls Co...................440 439-3013
  23165 Aurora Rd Cleveland (44146) (G-6423)
South East Chevrolet Co...................440 585-9300
  2810 Bishop Rd Willoughby Hills (44092) (G-19594)
South Eastern Erectors, Cincinnati Also called R&F Erectors Inc (G-4333)
South Franklin Circle...................440 247-1300
  16575 S Franklin St Chagrin Falls (44023) (G-2683)
South Lrrain Cnty Amblance Dst, Wellington Also called County of Lorain (G-18838)
South Mill Pet Care Center...................330 758-6479
  8105 South Ave Youngstown (44512) (G-20213)
South Shore Cable Cnstr Inc...................440 816-0033
  6400 Kolthoff Dr Cleveland (44142) (G-6424)
South Shore Controls Inc...................440 259-2500
  4485 N Ridge Rd Perry (44081) (G-15828)
South Shore Electric Inc...................440 366-6289
  589 Ternes Ln Elyria (44035) (G-10564)
South Shore Marine Services...................419 433-5798
  1611 Sawmill Pkwy Huron (44839) (G-12033)
South Star Corp...................330 239-5466
  3775 Ridge Rd Medina (44256) (G-14004)
South Town Painting Inc...................937 847-1600
  320 E Linden Ave Miamisburg (45342) (G-14225)
South Transportation...................216 691-2040
  5044 Mayfield Rd Cleveland (44124) (G-6425)
South Western Head Start, Grove City Also called South- Western City School Dst (G-11472)
South- Western City School Dst...................614 801-8438
  4308 Haughn Rd Grove City (43123) (G-11472)
Southast Cmnty Mental Hlth Ctr (PA)...................614 225-0980
  16 W Long St Columbus (43215) (G-8661)
Southast Cmnty Mental Hlth Ctr...................614 444-0800
  1455 S 4th St Columbus (43207) (G-8662)
Southast Cmnty Mental Hlth Ctr...................614 445-6832
  1705 S High St Columbus (43207) (G-8663)
Southast Cmnty Mental Hlth Ctr...................614 293-9613
  445 E Granville Rd Worthington (43085) (G-19850)
Southbrook Care Center, Springfield Also called Southbrook Health Care Ctr Inc (G-17113)
Southbrook Health Care Ctr Inc...................937 322-3436
  2299 S Yellow Springs St Springfield (45506) (G-17113)
Southeast, New Philadelphia Also called Cornerstone Support Services (G-14952)
Southeast Area Law Enforcement...................216 475-1234
  165 Center Rd Bedford (44146) (G-1308)
Southeast Area Transit (PA)...................740 454-8574
  375 Fairbanks St Zanesville (43701) (G-20362)
Southeast Asia Collection, Athens Also called Ohio State University (G-794)
Southeast Counseling, Worthington Also called Southast Cmnty Mental Hlth Ctr (G-19850)
Southeast Diversified Inds...................740 432-4241
  1401 Burgess Ave Cambridge (43725) (G-2082)
Southeast Golf Cars, Cleveland Also called South E Harley Davidson Sls Co (G-6422)
Southeast Golf Cars, Cleveland Also called South E Harley Davidson Sls Co (G-6423)
Southeast Security Corporation...................330 239-4600
  1385 Wolf Creek Trl Sharon Center (44274) (G-16726)
Southeastern Equipment Co Inc...................614 889-1073
  6390 Shier Rings Rd Dublin (43016) (G-10338)
Southeastern Med, Cambridge Also called Southstern Ohio Rgonal Med Ctr (G-2083)
Southeastern Ohio Brdcstg Sys...................740 452-5431
  629 Downard Rd Zanesville (43701) (G-20363)
Southeastern Ohio Symphony Orc...................740 826-8197
  163 Stormont St New Concord (43762) (G-14903)
Southeastern Ohio TV Sys (PA)...................740 452-5431
  629 Downard Rd Zanesville (43701) (G-20364)
Southeastern Rehabilitation...................740 679-2111
  62222 Frankfort Rd Salesville (43778) (G-16568)

Southerly Waste Water Plant, Cleveland *Also called Northast Ohio Rgonal Sewer Dst (G-6085)*

Southern Care Inc 419 774-0555
41 Briggs Dr Ontario (44906) *(G-15574)*

Southern Express Lubes Inc 937 278-5807
3781 Salem Ave Dayton (45406) *(G-9778)*

Southern Glazers Wine and Sp 330 422-9463
9450 Rosemont Dr Streetsboro (44241) *(G-17271)*

Southern Glazers Wine and Sp 513 755-7082
4305 Muhlhauser Rd Ste 4 Fairfield (45014) *(G-10786)*

Southern Glzers Dstrs Ohio LLC (HQ) 614 552-7900
4800 Poth Rd Columbus (43213) *(G-8664)*

Southern Graphic Systems Inc 419 662-9873
9648 Grassy Creek Dr Perrysburg (43551) *(G-15923)*

Southern Hills Skilled, Columbus *Also called Vrable II Inc (G-8865)*

Southern Mill Creek Pdts Ohio, Eastlake *Also called Univar Inc (G-10435)*

Southern Ohio Door Contrls Inc (PA) 513 353-4793
8080 Furlong Dr Miamitown (45041) *(G-14243)*

Southern Ohio Eye Assoc LLC (PA) 740 773-6347
159 E 2nd St Chillicothe (45601) *(G-2827)*

Southern Ohio Gun Distrs Inc 513 932-8148
240 Harmon Ave Lebanon (45036) *(G-12505)*

Southern Ohio Health, Georgetown *Also called Healthsource of Ohio Inc (G-11272)*

Southern Ohio Medical Center (PA) 740 354-5000
1805 27th St Portsmouth (45662) *(G-16171)*

Southern Ohio Medical Center 740 356-5000
1248 Kinneys Ln Portsmouth (45662) *(G-16172)*

Southern Ohio Medical Center 740 354-5000
1805 27th St Portsmouth (45662) *(G-16173)*

Southern Ohio Wns Cancer Prj 740 775-7332
150 E 2nd St Chillicothe (45601) *(G-2828)*

Southern Park Limo Service, Youngstown *Also called Sutton Motor Coach Tours Inc (G-20219)*

Southern Title of Ohio Ltd (PA) 419 525-4600
58 W 3rd St Ste D Mansfield (44902) *(G-13244)*

Southerntier Telecom (PA) 614 505-6365
651 Lkview Plz Blvd Ste E Worthington (43085) *(G-19851)*

Southgate Corp 740 522-2151
1499 W Main St Newark (43055) *(G-15098)*

Southrly Wstwater Trtmnt Plant, Cleveland *Also called Northast Ohio Rgonal Sewer Dst (G-6082)*

Southside Envmtl Group LLC 330 299-0027
1806 Warren Ave Niles (44446) *(G-15170)*

Southside Learning & Dev Ctr 614 444-1529
280 Reeb Ave Columbus (43207) *(G-8665)*

Southstern Ohio Rgional Fd Ctr 740 385-6813
1005 C I C Dr Logan (43138) *(G-12854)*

Southstern Ohio Rgonal Med Ctr (PA) 740 439-3561
1341 Clark St Cambridge (43725) *(G-2083)*

Southtown Heating & Cooling 937 320-9900
3024 Springboro W Moraine (45439) *(G-14699)*

Southway Fence Company 330 477-5251
5156 Southway St Sw Canton (44706) *(G-2480)*

Southwest Associates 440 243-7888
7250 Old Oak Blvd Cleveland (44130) *(G-6426)*

Southwest Cleveland Sleep Ctr (PA) 440 239-7533
18100 Jefferson Park Rd # 103 Cleveland (44130) *(G-6427)*

Southwest Cmnty Hlth Systems 440 816-8000
18697 Bagley Rd Cleveland (44130) *(G-6428)*

Southwest Community Center, Urbancrest *Also called Young Mens Christian Assoc (G-18453)*

Southwest Family Physicians 440 816-2750
7225 Old Oak Blvd A210 Cleveland (44130) *(G-6429)*

Southwest Financial Svcs Ltd 513 621-6699
537 E Pete Rose Way Ste 3 Cincinnati (45202) *(G-4505)*

Southwest General Health Ctr, Cleveland *Also called Southwest General Health Ctr (G-6431)*

Southwest General Health Ctr 440 816-4202
7390 Old Oak Blvd Cleveland (44130) *(G-6430)*

Southwest General Health Ctr 440 816-4900
18181 Pearl Rd Ste B104 Strongsville (44136) *(G-17347)*

Southwest General Health Ctr 440 816-8200
18697 Oak Vw Cleveland (44130) *(G-6431)*

Southwest General Health Ctr (PA) 440 816-8000
18697 Bagley Rd Cleveland (44130) *(G-6432)*

Southwest General Health Ctr 440 816-8005
17951 Jefferson Park Rd Cleveland (44130) *(G-6433)*

Southwest General Hospital, Cleveland *Also called Southwest Cmnty Hlth Systems (G-6428)*

Southwest General Med Group 440 816-8000
18697 Bagley Rd Middleburg Heights (44130) *(G-14259)*

Southwest Healthcare of Brown 937 378-7800
425 Home St Georgetown (45121) *(G-11275)*

Southwest Internal Medicine 440 816-2777
7255 Old Oak Blvd C209 Cleveland (44130) *(G-6434)*

Southwest OH Trans Auth (PA) 513 621-4455
602 Main St Ste 1100 Cincinnati (45202) *(G-4506)*

Southwest OH Trans Auth 513 632-7511
1401 Bank St Cincinnati (45214) *(G-4507)*

Southwest Ohio Amblatry Srgery 513 425-0930
295 N Breiel Blvd Middletown (45042) *(G-14329)*

Southwest Ohio Dvlopmental Ctr, Batavia *Also called Develpmntal Dsblties Ohio Dept (G-996)*

Southwest Ohio Ent Spclsts Inc (PA) 937 496-2600
1222 S Patterson Blvd # 400 Dayton (45402) *(G-9779)*

Southwest Regional Medical Ctr, Georgetown *Also called Southwest Healthcare of Brown (G-11275)*

Southwest Urology Wmen Cnnctons, Cleveland *Also called Southwest Urology LLC (G-6435)*

Southwest Urology LLC (PA) 440 845-0900
6900 Pearl Rd Ste 200 Cleveland (44130) *(G-6435)*

Southwestern Electric Power Co (HQ) 614 716-1000
1 Riverside Plz Columbus (43215) *(G-8666)*

Southwestern Obstetrians & G 614 875-0444
4461 Broadway 200 Grove City (43123) *(G-11473)*

Southwestern Tile and MBL Co 614 464-1257
1030 Cable Ave Columbus (43222) *(G-8667)*

Southwood Auto Sales 330 788-8822
5334 South Ave Youngstown (44512) *(G-20214)*

Southwstern PCF Spclty Fin Inc (HQ) 513 336-7735
7755 Montgomery Rd # 400 Cincinnati (45236) *(G-4508)*

Sovereign Healthcare, Cleveland *Also called North Park Retirement Cmnty (G-6079)*

Sowder Concrete Contractors, Dayton *Also called Sowder Concrete Corporation (G-9780)*

Sowder Concrete Corporation 937 890-1633
8510 N Dixie Dr Dayton (45414) *(G-9780)*

Sp Medical, Cleveland *Also called Superior Products Llc (G-6483)*

Sp Plus Corporation 216 444-2255
9500 Euclid Ave Wb1 Cleveland (44195) *(G-6436)*

Sp Plus Corporation 216 687-0141
1301 E 9th St Ste 1050 Cleveland (44114) *(G-6437)*

Sp Plus Corporation 216 267-7275
5300 Riverside Dr Cleveland (44135) *(G-6438)*

Sp Plus Corporation 216 267-5030
5300 Riverside Dr Cleveland (44135) *(G-6439)*

Spa At River Ridge Salon, The, Dublin *Also called Urban Oassis Inc (G-10361)*

Spa Fitness Centers Inc (PA) 419 476-6018
343 New Towne Square Dr Toledo (43612) *(G-18040)*

Space Management Inc 937 254-6622
2109 S Smithville Rd Dayton (45420) *(G-9781)*

Spader Freight Carriers Inc 419 547-1117
1134 E Mcpherson Hwy Clyde (43410) *(G-6753)*

Spader Freight Services Inc (PA) 419 547-1117
1134 E Mcpherson Hwy Clyde (43410) *(G-6754)*

Spagnas 740 376-9245
301 Gilman Ave Marietta (45750) *(G-13383)*

Spall Autoc Syste / US Millwr, Lima *Also called Spallinger Millwright Svc Co (G-12742)*

Spallinger Millwright Svc Co 419 225-5830
1155 E Hanthorn Rd Lima (45804) *(G-12742)*

Spangenberg Law Firm, Cleveland *Also called Spangenberg Shibley Liber LLP (G-6440)*

Spangenberg Shibley Liber LLP 216 215-7445
1001 Lakeside Ave E # 1700 Cleveland (44114) *(G-6440)*

Spanish American Committee (PA) 216 961-2100
4407 Lorain Ave Fl 1 Cleveland (44113) *(G-6441)*

Spanish Portugese Translation, Westlake *Also called Advanced Translation/Cnsltng (G-19311)*

Spano Brothers Cnstr Co 330 645-1544
2595 Pressler Rd Akron (44312) *(G-436)*

Sparkbase Inc 216 867-0877
3615 Superior Ave E 4403d Cleveland (44114) *(G-6442)*

Sparkle Wash of Lima 419 224-9274
301 W Elm St Lima (45801) *(G-12743)*

Spartan Asset Rcvery Group Inc 786 930-0188
8483 Fields Ertel Rd Cincinnati (45249) *(G-4509)*

Spartan Construction Co Inc 419 389-1854
2021 Mescher Dr Monclova (43542) *(G-14559)*

Spartan Logistics, Columbus *Also called Spartan Whse & Dist Co Inc (G-8668)*

Spartan Supply Co Inc 513 932-6954
942 Old 122 Rd Lebanon (45036) *(G-12506)*

Spartan Whse & Dist Co Inc (PA) 614 497-1777
4140 Lockbourne Rd Columbus (43207) *(G-8668)*

Spartannash Company 937 599-1110
4067 County Road 130 Bellefontaine (43311) *(G-1366)*

Spartannash Company 419 228-3141
1100 Prosperity Rd Lima (45801) *(G-12744)*

Spartannash Company 419 998-2562
1257 Neubrecht Rd Lima (45801) *(G-12745)*

Spartannash Company 937 599-1110
4067 County Road 130 Bellefontaine (43311) *(G-1367)*

Spartannash Company 513 793-6300
1 Sheakley Way Ste 160 Cincinnati (45246) *(G-4510)*

Spaulding Construction Co Inc 330 494-1776
7640 Whipple Ave Nw Canton (44720) *(G-2481)*

Speacialty Care Vision, Newark *Also called Surgicenter Ltd (G-15102)*

Spears Transf & Expediting Inc 937 275-2443
2637 Nordic Rd Dayton (45414) *(G-9782)*

Special Metals Corporation (HQ) 216 755-3030
4832 Richmond Rd Ste 100 Warrensville Heights (44128) *(G-18781)*

Special Touch Homecare LLC 937 549-1843
207 Pike St Manchester (45144) *(G-13129)*

Specialized Alternatives For F. 216 295-7239
20600 Chagrin Blvd # 320 Shaker Heights (44122) *(G-16714)*

Specialized Alternatives For F. 419 222-1527
658 W Market St Ste 101 Lima (45801) *(G-12746)*

Specialized Alternatives For F (PA) 419 695-8010
10100 Elida Rd Delphos (45833) *(G-10035)*

Specialized Pharmacy Svcs - N, Cincinnati *Also called Specialized Pharmacy Svcs LLC* ***(G-4511)***
Specialized Pharmacy Svcs LLC (HQ)........513 719-2600
201 E 4th St Ste 900 Cincinnati (45202) ***(G-4511)***
Specialty Equipment Engrg Div, Solon *Also called Belcan LLC* ***(G-16827)***
Specialty Equipment Sales Co........216 351-2559
5705 Valley Belt Rd Brooklyn Heights (44131) ***(G-1882)***
Specialty Hosp Cleveland Inc........216 592-2830
2351 E 22nd St Fl 7 Cleveland (44115) ***(G-6443)***
Specialty Logistics Inc (PA)........513 421-2041
1440 W 8th St Cincinnati (45203) ***(G-4512)***
Specialty Lubricants Corp........330 425-2567
8300 Corporate Park Dr Macedonia (44056) ***(G-13082)***
Specialty Medical Services........440 245-8010
221 W 8th St Lorain (44052) ***(G-12943)***
Specialty Steel Co Inc........800 321-8500
18250 Miles Rd Cleveland (44128) ***(G-6444)***
Speck Sales Incorporated........419 353-8312
17746 N Dixie Hwy Bowling Green (43402) ***(G-1749)***
Spectra Medical Distribution, Akron *Also called M & R Fredericktown Ltd Inc* ***(G-324)***
Spectra Photopolymers Inc., Millbury *Also called Formlabs Ohio Inc* ***(G-14448)***
Spectrum Eye Care Inc........419 423-8665
15840 Medical Dr S Ste A Findlay (45840) ***(G-10961)***
Spectrum MGT Holdg Co LLC........614 481-5408
3760 Interchange Rd Columbus (43204) ***(G-8669)***
Spectrum MGT Holdg Co LLC........740 455-9705
737 Howard St Zanesville (43701) ***(G-20365)***
Spectrum MGT Holdg Co LLC........330 856-2343
8600 E Market St Ste 4 Warren (44484) ***(G-18745)***
Spectrum MGT Holdg Co LLC........419 386-0040
2853 East Harbor Rd Ste A Port Clinton (43452) ***(G-16118)***
Spectrum MGT Holdg Co LLC........740 762-0291
32 Enterprise Pl Chillicothe (45601) ***(G-2829)***
Spectrum MGT Holdg Co LLC........513 469-1112
3290 Westbourne Dr Cincinnati (45248) ***(G-4513)***
Spectrum MGT Holdg Co LLC........614 344-4159
1015 Olentangy River Rd Columbus (43212) ***(G-8670)***
Spectrum MGT Holdg Co LLC........937 552-5760
75 W Main St Springfield (45502) ***(G-17114)***
Spectrum MGT Holdg Co LLC........740 200-3385
28 Station St Athens (45701) ***(G-803)***
Spectrum MGT Holdg Co LLC........614 503-4153
3652 Main St Hilliard (43026) ***(G-11816)***
Spectrum MGT Holdg Co LLC........440 319-3271
2904 State Rd Ashtabula (44004) ***(G-756)***
Spectrum MGT Holdg Co LLC........419 775-9292
1280 Park Ave W Mansfield (44906) ***(G-13245)***
Spectrum MGT Holdg Co LLC........330 208-9028
530 Suth Main St Ste 1751 Akron (44311) ***(G-437)***
Spectrum MGT Holdg Co LLC........937 684-8891
275 Leo St Dayton (45404) ***(G-9783)***
Spectrum MGT Holdg Co LLC........740 772-7809
1315 Granville Pike Ne Lancaster (43130) ***(G-12437)***
Spectrum MGT Holdg Co LLC........937 294-6800
3691 Turner Rd Dayton (45415) ***(G-9784)***
Spectrum MGT Holdg Co LLC........937 306-6082
614 N Main St Piqua (45356) ***(G-16029)***
Spectrum Networks Inc........513 697-2000
9145 Governors Way Cincinnati (45249) ***(G-4514)***
Spectrum Orthpedics Inc Canton (PA)........330 455-5367
7442 Frank Ave Nw North Canton (44720) ***(G-15233)***
Spectrum Rehabilitation, Cincinnati *Also called Christ Hospital* ***(G-3202)***
Spectrum Supportive Services, Cleveland *Also called Spectrum Supportive Services* ***(G-6445)***
Spectrum Supportive Services........216 875-0460
4269 Pearl Rd Ste 300 Cleveland (44109) ***(G-6445)***
Speech Center, Saint Marys *Also called Jtd Health Systems Inc* ***(G-16527)***
Speech Language Hearing Clinic, Columbus *Also called Ohio State University* ***(G-8337)***
Speedeon Data LLC........440 264-2100
5875 Landerbrook Dr # 130 Cleveland (44124) ***(G-6446)***
Speedie Auto Salvage Ltd........330 878-9961
6995 Eberhart Rd Nw Dover (44622) ***(G-10102)***
Speelman Electric Inc........330 633-1410
358 Commerce St Tallmadge (44278) ***(G-17488)***
Speer Industries Incorporated (PA)........614 261-6331
5255 Sinclair Rd Columbus (43229) ***(G-8671)***
Speer Mechanical, Columbus *Also called Julian Speer Co* ***(G-7876)***
Speer Mechanical, Columbus *Also called Speer Industries Incorporated* ***(G-8671)***
Spengler Nathanson PLL........419 241-2201
4 Seagate Ste 400 Toledo (43604) ***(G-18041)***
Sphere, The, Fairfield *Also called AB Marketing LLC* ***(G-10691)***
Spherion of Lima Inc (PA)........419 224-8367
216 N Elizabeth St Lima (45801) ***(G-12747)***
Spherion Outsourcing Group, Toledo *Also called Sfn Group Inc* ***(G-18028)***
Spieker Company........419 872-7000
8350 Fremont Pike Perrysburg (43551) ***(G-15924)***
Spillman Company........614 444-2184
1701 Moler Rd Columbus (43207) ***(G-8672)***
Spires Motors Inc........614 771-2345
3820 Parkway Ln Hilliard (43026) ***(G-11817)***
Spirit Health, Cincinnati *Also called Spirit Women Health Netwrk LLC* ***(G-2869)***
Spirit Medical Transport LLC........937 548-2800
5484 S State Route 49 Greenville (45331) ***(G-11396)***
Spirit Services, Solon *Also called Van Dyne-Crotty Co* ***(G-16911)***
Spirit Services Company, Columbus *Also called Van Dyne-Crotty Co* ***(G-8842)***
Spirit Services Company, Columbus *Also called Van Dyne-Crotty Co* ***(G-8843)***
Spirit Women Health Netwrk LLC........561 544-2004
4270 Ivy Pointe Blvd # 220 Cincinnati (45245) ***(G-2869)***
Spitzer Auto World Amherst........440 988-4444
200 N Leavitt Rd Amherst (44001) ***(G-598)***
Spitzer Chevrolet Company........330 966-9524
7111 Sunset Strip Ave Nw Canton (44720) ***(G-2482)***
Spitzer Chevrolet Inc........330 467-4141
333 E Aurora Rd Northfield (44067) ***(G-15386)***
Spitzer Lakewood, Brookpark *Also called Lakewood Chrysler-Plymouth* ***(G-1901)***
Spitzer Motor City Inc........567 307-7119
1777 W 4th St Ontario (44906) ***(G-15575)***
Spitzer Motors of Mansfield, Ontario *Also called Spitzer Motor City Inc* ***(G-15575)***
Splish Splash Auto Bath, Springfield *Also called JKL Development Company* ***(G-17057)***
Split Rock Golf Club Inc........614 877-9755
10210 Scioto Darby Rd Orient (43146) ***(G-15621)***
Sponseller Group Inc (PA)........419 861-3000
1600 Timber Wolf Dr Holland (43528) ***(G-11915)***
Sports Care Rehabilitation........419 578-7530
2865 N Reynolds Rd # 110 Toledo (43615) ***(G-18042)***
Sports Construction Group, Brecksville *Also called Sports Surfaces Cnstr LLC* ***(G-1807)***
Sports Facility Acoustics Inc........440 323-1400
801 Bond St Elyria (44035) ***(G-10565)***
Sports Medicine and Spine Ctr, Middletown *Also called Atrium Medical Center* ***(G-14289)***
Sports Medicine Grant Inc........614 461-8199
417 Hill Rd N Ste 401 Pickerington (43147) ***(G-15968)***
Sports Medicine Grant Inc (PA)........614 461-8174
323 E Town St Ste 100 Columbus (43215) ***(G-8673)***
Sports Surfaces Cnstr LLC........440 546-1200
10303 Brecksville Rd Brecksville (44141) ***(G-1807)***
Sports Therapy Inc........513 671-5841
11729 Springfield Pike Cincinnati (45246) ***(G-4515)***
Sports Therapy Inc........513 531-1698
4600 Smith Rd Ste B Cincinnati (45212) ***(G-4516)***
Sportsman Gun & Reel Club Inc........440 233-8287
44165 Middle Ridge Rd Lorain (44053) ***(G-12944)***
Sportsmans Market Inc........513 735-9100
2001 Sportys Dr Batavia (45103) ***(G-1009)***
Sportstime Ohio, Cleveland *Also called Fastball Spt Productions LLC* ***(G-5516)***
Sportsworld, Youngstown *Also called Jvc Sports Corp* ***(G-20089)***
Sporty Events........440 342-5046
8430 Mayfield Rd Chesterland (44026) ***(G-2745)***
Sportys Pilot Shop, Batavia *Also called Sportsmans Market Inc* ***(G-1009)***
Spotlight Labs, Beavercreek *Also called Global Military Expert Co* ***(G-1219)***
Sprandel Enterprises Inc........513 777-6622
6467 Gano Rd West Chester (45069) ***(G-19011)***
Spray A Tree Inc........614 457-8257
1585 Pemberton Dr Columbus (43221) ***(G-8674)***
Sprayworks Equipment Group LLC........330 587-4141
945 Mckinley Ave Sw Canton (44707) ***(G-2483)***
Spread Eagle Tavern Inc........330 223-1583
10150 Plymouth St Hanoverton (44423) ***(G-11658)***
Sprenger Enterprises Inc........440 244-2019
3756 W Erie Ave Apt 201 Lorain (44053) ***(G-12945)***
SPRENGER HEALTH CARE SYSTEMS, Lorain *Also called Anchor Lodge Nursing Home Inc* ***(G-12880)***
Spring Creek Apts, Columbus *Also called Clk Multi-Family MGT LLC* ***(G-7232)***
Spring Creek Nursing Center, Dayton *Also called Care One LLC* ***(G-9277)***
Spring Grove Center, Cincinnati *Also called Talbert House* ***(G-4570)***
Spring Grove Cmtry & Arboretum (PA)........513 681-7526
4521 Spring Grove Ave Cincinnati (45232) ***(G-4517)***
Spring Grove Funeral Homes Inc........513 681-7526
4389 Spring Grove Ave Cincinnati (45223) ***(G-4518)***
Spring Grove Rsrce Rcovery Inc........513 681-6242
4879 Spring Grove Ave Cincinnati (45232) ***(G-4519)***
Spring Hill Apartments, Akron *Also called Sh-91 Limited Partnership* ***(G-426)***
Spring Hill Suites........513 381-8300
610 Eden Park Dr Cincinnati (45202) ***(G-4520)***
Spring Hills At Middletown, Middletown *Also called Springhills LLC* ***(G-14355)***
Spring Hills At Singing Woods, Dayton *Also called Springhills LLC* ***(G-9786)***
Spring Hills Golf Club........740 543-3270
99 Corder Dr East Springfield (43925) ***(G-10426)***
Spring Hills Golf Club........330 825-2439
6571 Clvland Massillon Rd New Franklin (44216) ***(G-14912)***
Spring Meadow Extended Care Ce (PA)........419 866-6124
1125 Clarion Ave Holland (43528) ***(G-11916)***
Spring Meadow Extended Care Ce........419 866-6124
105 S Main St Mansfield (44902) ***(G-13246)***
Spring Meadows Care Center, Woodstock *Also called Woodstock Healthcare Group Inc* ***(G-19681)***
Spring Meadows Care Center, Woodstock *Also called Saber Healthcare Group LLC* ***(G-19680)***
Spring Valley Golf & Athc CLB........440 365-1411
257 Crocker Park Blvd Westlake (44145) ***(G-19407)***

ALPHABETIC SECTION St Ritas Medical Center

Springboro Service Center...937 748-0020
220 E Mill St Springboro (45066) ***(G-16984)***
Springcar Company LLC...440 892-6800
27500 Detroit Rd Ste 300 Westlake (44145) ***(G-19408)***
Springdale Family Medicine PC...513 771-7213
212 W Sharon Rd Cincinnati (45246) ***(G-4521)***
Springdale Ice Cream Beverage...513 699-4984
11801 Chesterdale Rd Cincinnati (45246) ***(G-4522)***
Springdot Inc...513 542-4000
2611 Colerain Ave Cincinnati (45214) ***(G-4523)***
Springfeld Rgnal Otpatient Ctr...937 390-8310
2610 N Limestone St Springfield (45503) ***(G-17115)***
Springfeld Unfrm-Linen Sup Inc...937 323-5544
141 N Murray St Springfield (45503) ***(G-17116)***
Springfield Business Eqp Co (PA)...937 322-3828
3783 W National Rd Springfield (45504) ***(G-17117)***
Springfield Cartage LLC...937 222-2120
1546 Stanley Ave Dayton (45404) ***(G-9785)***
Springfield Country Club Co...937 399-4215
2315 Signal Hill Rd Springfield (45504) ***(G-17118)***
Springfield Family Y M C A...937 323-3781
300 S Limestone St Springfield (45505) ***(G-17119)***
Springfield Little Tigers Foot...330 549-2359
49 Philrose Ln Youngstown (44514) ***(G-20215)***
Springfield Urology, Springfield *Also called Northwest Columbus Urology* ***(G-17090)***
Springhill Suites, Cincinnati *Also called Spring Hill Suites* ***(G-4520)***
Springhill Suites, Columbus *Also called Black Sapphire C Columbus Univ* ***(G-7045)***
Springhill Suites, Gahanna *Also called Columbus Oh-16 Airport Gahanna* ***(G-11114)***
Springhill Suites, Solon *Also called Solon Lodging Associates LLC* ***(G-16899)***
Springhill Suites Independence, Independence *Also called Jagi Springhill LLC* ***(G-12084)***
Springhills LLC...937 274-1400
140 E Woodbury Dr Dayton (45415) ***(G-9786)***
Springhills LLC...513 424-9999
3851 Towne Blvd Middletown (45005) ***(G-14355)***
Springleaf Financial Svc., Toledo *Also called One Main Financial Services* ***(G-17963)***
Springleaf Fincl Holdings LLC...419 334-9748
2200 Sean Dr Ste J Fremont (43420) ***(G-11097)***
Springmeade, Tipp City *Also called Uvmc Nursing Care Inc* ***(G-17572)***
Springs Window Fashions LLC...614 492-6770
6295 Commerce Center Dr Groveport (43125) ***(G-11538)***
Springside Racquet Fitnes CLB, Akron *Also called Oid Associates* ***(G-363)***
Springvale Golf Crse Ballroom, North Olmsted *Also called City of North Olmsted* ***(G-15283)***
Springview Manor Nursing Home...419 227-3661
883 W Spring St Lima (45805) ***(G-12748)***
Sprint, North Canton *Also called Nextel Partners Operating Corp* ***(G-15223)***
Sprint, Toledo *Also called Nextel Partners Operating Corp* ***(G-17941)***
Sprint Communications Co LP...419 725-2444
1708 W Alexis Rd Toledo (43613) ***(G-18043)***
Sprint Spectrum LP...440 686-2600
25363 Lorain Rd North Olmsted (44070) ***(G-15311)***
Sprint Spectrum LP...614 575-5500
2367 S Hamilton Rd Columbus (43232) ***(G-8675)***
Sprint Spectrum LP...614 793-2500
6614 Sawmill Rd Columbus (43235) ***(G-8676)***
Sprint Spectrum LP...614 428-2300
3918 Townsfair Way Columbus (43219) ***(G-8677)***
Sprint Spectrum LP...330 470-4614
4470 Belden Village St Nw Canton (44718) ***(G-2484)***
Spruce Bough Homes LLC...614 253-0984
18 E 3rd Ave Columbus (43201) ***(G-8678)***
Spryance Inc...678 808-0600
3101 Executive Pkwy # 600 Toledo (43606) ***(G-18044)***
Spunfab, Cuyahoga Falls *Also called Keuchel & Associates Inc* ***(G-9108)***
Spurlock Truck Service...937 268-6100
129 Lincoln Park Blvd Dayton (45429) ***(G-9787)***
Sqa, Akron *Also called Smithers Quality Assessments* ***(G-433)***
Squire Patton Boggs (us) LLP...513 361-1200
201 E 4th St Ste 324 Cincinnati (45202) ***(G-4524)***
Sr Improvements Services LLC...567 207-6488
1485 County Road 268 Vickery (43464) ***(G-18575)***
Sreco Flexible, Lima *Also called Sewer Rodding Equipment Co* ***(G-12739)***
Sree Hotels LLC...513 354-2430
617 Vine St Ste A Cincinnati (45202) ***(G-4525)***
Srinsoft Inc...614 893-6535
7243 Sawmill Rd Ste 205 Dublin (43016) ***(G-10339)***
Ssg, Shaker Heights *Also called Software Support Group Inc* ***(G-16713)***
Ssi Fabricated Inc...513 217-3535
2860 Cincinnati Dayton Rd Middletown (45044) ***(G-14330)***
Ssoe Inc...330 821-7198
885 S Sawburg Ave Ste 106 Alliance (44601) ***(G-552)***
SSP Fittings Corp (PA)...330 425-4250
8250 Boyle Pkwy Twinsburg (44087) ***(G-18323)***
SSS Consulting Inc...937 259-1200
3123 Res Blvd Ste 250 Dayton (45420) ***(G-9788)***
Ssth LLC...614 884-0793
739 S James Rd Ste 100 Columbus (43227) ***(G-8679)***
St Aloysius Services Inc...513 482-1745
4721 Reading Rd Cincinnati (45237) ***(G-4526)***
St Anne Mercy Hospital...419 407-2663
3404 W Sylvania Ave Toledo (43623) ***(G-18045)***
St Anthony Messenger Press, Cincinnati *Also called Province of St John The Baptis* ***(G-4301)***
St Augustine Corporation...216 939-7600
1341 Nicholson Ave Lakewood (44107) ***(G-12363)***
St Augustine Manor...440 888-7722
6707 State Rd Parma (44134) ***(G-15777)***
St Augustine Towers...216 634-7444
7821 Lake Ave Apt 304 Cleveland (44102) ***(G-6447)***
St Bartholomew Cons School, Cincinnati *Also called Archdiocese of Cincinnati* ***(G-2980)***
St Catherine's Manor, Fostoria *Also called St Catherines Care Centers O* ***(G-11013)***
St Catherines Care Centers O...419 435-8112
25 Christopher Dr Fostoria (44830) ***(G-11013)***
St Catherines Care Ctr Findlay...419 422-3978
8455 County Road 140 Findlay (45840) ***(G-10962)***
St Cecilia School, Columbus *Also called Saint Cecilia Church* ***(G-8583)***
St Charles Child Dev Center, Oregon *Also called Mercy Health - St* ***(G-15600)***
St Clair 60 Minute Clrs Inc (PA)...740 695-3100
116 N Sugar St Saint Clairsville (43950) ***(G-16506)***
St Clair Auto Body...216 531-7300
13608 Saint Clair Ave Cleveland (44110) ***(G-6448)***
St Clair Auto Body Shop, Cleveland *Also called St Clair Auto Body* ***(G-6448)***
St Clairsville V A Primary, Saint Clairsville *Also called Veterans Health Administration* ***(G-16509)***
St Clare Commons, Toledo *Also called CHI Living Communities* ***(G-17651)***
St Edward Home...330 668-2828
3131 Smith Rd Fairlawn (44333) ***(G-10851)***
St Elizabeth Boardman Hospital, Youngstown *Also called Mercy Health Youngstown LLC* ***(G-20125)***
St Elizabeth Health Center, Youngstown *Also called Mercy Health Youngstown LLC* ***(G-20126)***
St Francis De Sales Church (PA)...740 345-9874
40 Granville St Newark (43055) ***(G-15099)***
St George & Co Inc...330 733-7528
2586 Robindale Ave Akron (44312) ***(G-438)***
St George Company, Akron *Also called St George & Co Inc* ***(G-438)***
St Joseph Care Center, Louisville *Also called Roman Cthlic Docese Youngstown* ***(G-12973)***
St Joseph Infant Maternity Hm...513 563-2520
10722 Wyscarver Rd Cincinnati (45241) ***(G-4527)***
St Joseph Leasing Co LLC...513 530-1654
4700 Ashwood Dr Blue Ash (45241) ***(G-1652)***
ST JOSEPH`S HOME, Cincinnati *Also called St Joseph Infant Maternity Hm* ***(G-4527)***
St Jude Social Concern Hot...440 365-7971
636 Sycamore St Elyria (44035) ***(G-10566)***
St Lawrence Holdings LLC...330 562-9000
16500 Rockside Rd Maple Heights (44137) ***(G-13297)***
St Luke Lutheran Community...330 868-5600
4301 Woodale Ave Se Minerva (44657) ***(G-14525)***
St Luke Lutheran Community...330 644-3914
615 Latham Ln New Franklin (44319) ***(G-14913)***
St Luke Lutheran Community...330 644-3914
615 Latham Ln New Franklin (44319) ***(G-14914)***
St Lukes Gift Shop, Maumee *Also called Auxiliary St Lukes Hospital* ***(G-13759)***
St Lukes Hospital...419 441-1002
900 Wterville Monclova Rd Waterville (43566) ***(G-18793)***
St Lukes Hospital (PA)...419 893-5911
5901 Monclova Rd Maumee (43537) ***(G-13855)***
St Lukes Wtrvlle Physcl Thrapy, Waterville *Also called St Lukes Hospital* ***(G-18793)***
St Mary & Joseph Home, Warrensville Heights *Also called Sisters of Little* ***(G-18780)***
St Marys City Board Education...419 394-1116
1445 Celina Rd Saint Marys (45885) ***(G-16532)***
St Marys City Board Education...419 394-2616
650 Armstrong St Saint Marys (45885) ***(G-16533)***
St Moritz Security Svcs Inc...330 270-5922
32 N Four Mile Run Rd Youngstown (44515) ***(G-20216)***
St Moritz Security Svcs Inc...614 351-8798
705 Lkview Plz Blvd Ste G Worthington (43085) ***(G-19852)***
St Patrick Church Inc (PA)...937 335-2833
409 E Main St Troy (45373) ***(G-18229)***
St Patrick School, Troy *Also called St Patrick Church Inc* ***(G-18229)***
St Pauls Catholic Church (PA)...330 724-1263
433 Mission Dr Akron (44301) ***(G-439)***
St Pauls Community Center...419 255-5520
230 13th St Toledo (43604) ***(G-18046)***
St Regis Investment LLC...216 520-1250
8111 Rockside Rd Cleveland (44125) ***(G-6449)***
St Rita's Homecare, Lima *Also called St Ritas Medical Center* ***(G-12751)***
St Ritas Medical Center...419 226-9067
730 W Market St Lima (45801) ***(G-12749)***
St Ritas Medical Center...419 538-6288
601 Us 224 Glandorf (45848) ***(G-11307)***
St Ritas Medical Center...419 226-9229
750 W High St Ste 400 Lima (45801) ***(G-12750)***
St Ritas Medical Center...419 538-7025
959 W North St Lima (45805) ***(G-12751)***
St Ritas Medical Center...419 227-3361
4357 Ottawa Rd Lima (45801) ***(G-12752)***
St Ritas Medical Center...419 996-5895
967 Bellefontaine Ave # 201 Lima (45804) ***(G-12753)***

ALPHABETIC

St Stephen United Church Chrst.................................419 624-1814
  905 E Perkins Ave Sandusky (44870) *(G-16644)*

St Stephens Community House.................................614 294-6347
  1500 E 17th Ave Columbus (43219) *(G-8680)*

ST STEPHENS COMMUNITY SERVICE, Columbus Also called St Stephens Community
House *(G-8680)*

St Thomas Episcopal Church.................................513 831-6908
  100 Miami Ave Terrace Park (45174) *(G-17500)*

St Thomas Nursery School, Terrace Park Also called St Thomas Episcopal
Church *(G-17500)*

St Vincent Charity Med Ctr (PA).................................216 861-6200
  2351 E 22nd St Cleveland (44115) *(G-6450)*

St Vincent De Paul Scl Svs.................................937 222-7349
  1133 S Edwin C Moses Blvd Dayton (45417) *(G-9789)*

St Vincent Family Centers (PA).................................614 252-0731
  1490 E Main St Columbus (43205) *(G-8681)*

St Vincent Medical Group, Cleveland Also called Medical Arts Physician Center *(G-5941)*

St. Cthrnes Manor Wash Crt Hse, Wshngtn CT Hs Also called Hcf of Washington
Inc *(G-19875)*

St. Elizabeth Youngstown Hosp, Youngstown Also called Mercy Health *(G-20124)*

St. Joseph Warren Hospital, Warren Also called Mercy Health Youngstown LLC *(G-18730)*

St. Rita's Home Care, Lima Also called Mercy Health *(G-12701)*

St. Vincent Hospit, Toledo Also called Mercy Hlth St Vincent Med LLC *(G-17909)*

St. Vincent Medical Group, Cleveland Also called Outreach Professional Svcs Inc *(G-6148)*

Staarmann Concrete Inc.................................513 756-9191
  4316 Stahlheber Rd Hamilton (45013) *(G-11643)*

Stachler Concrete Inc.................................419 678-3867
  431 Stachler Dr Saint Henry (45883) *(G-16517)*

Stack Container Service Inc.................................216 531-7555
  24881 Rockwell Dr Euclid (44117) *(G-10657)*

Stafast Products Inc (PA).................................440 357-5546
  505 Lakeshore Blvd Painesville (44077) *(G-15741)*

Stafast West, Painesville Also called Stafast Products Inc *(G-15741)*

Staffco-Campisano, Cleveland Also called RA Staff Company Inc *(G-6276)*

Staffmark Holdings Inc (HQ).................................513 651-1111
  201 E 4th St Ste 800 Cincinnati (45202) *(G-4528)*

Staffmark Investment LLC (HQ).................................513 651-3600
  201 E 4th St Ste 800 Cincinnati (45202) *(G-4529)*

Stage Works.................................513 522-3118
  7800 Perry St Cincinnati (45231) *(G-4530)*

Stagnaro Saba Patterson Co Lpa.................................513 533-2700
  7373 Beechmont Ave Cincinnati (45230) *(G-4531)*

Stahlheber & Sons Inc.................................513 726-4446
  4205 Hamilton Eaton Rd Hamilton (45011) *(G-11644)*

Stahlheber Excavating, Hamilton Also called Stahlheber & Sons Inc *(G-11644)*

Staid Logic LLC (PA).................................309 807-0575
  595 E Broad St Ste 206 Columbus (43215) *(G-8682)*

Staley Inc.................................614 552-2333
  8040 Corporate Blvd Plain City (43064) *(G-16067)*

Staley Technologies Inc (PA).................................330 339-2898
  1035 Front Ave Sw New Philadelphia (44663) *(G-14982)*

Stallion Oilfield Cnstr LLC.................................330 868-2083
  3361 Baird Ave Se Paris (44669) *(G-15757)*

Stambaugh Charter Academy, Youngstown Also called National Heritg Academies
Inc *(G-20138)*

Stamm Contracting Co Inc.................................330 274-8230
  4566 Orchard St Mantua (44255) *(G-13276)*

Stammen Insurance Agency LLC.................................419 586-7500
  115-117 S Main St Celina (45822) *(G-2611)*

Stamper Staffing LLC.................................937 938-7010
  2812 Purdue Dr Kettering (45420) *(G-12300)*

Stan Hywet Hall and Grdns Inc.................................330 836-5533
  714 N Portage Path Akron (44303) *(G-440)*

Stand Energy Corporation.................................513 621-1113
  1077 Celestial St Ste 110 Cincinnati (45202) *(G-4532)*

Standard Contg & Engrg Inc.................................440 243-1001
  6356 Eastland Rd Brookpark (44142) *(G-1906)*

Standard Laboratories Inc.................................513 422-1088
  2601 S Verity Pkwy Middletown (45044) *(G-14331)*

Standard Oil Company.................................330 530-8049
  2720 Salt Springs Rd Girard (44420) *(G-11301)*

Standard Parking, Cleveland Also called Sp Plus Corporation *(G-6436)*

Standard Plumbing & Heating Co (PA).................................330 453-5150
  435 Walnut Ave Se Canton (44702) *(G-2485)*

Standard Retirement Svcs Inc.................................440 808-2724
  24610 Detroit Rd Ste 2000 Westlake (44145) *(G-19409)*

Standard Textile Co Inc (PA).................................513 761-9256
  1 Knollcrest Dr Cincinnati (45237) *(G-4533)*

Standard Welding & Lift Truck, Lorain Also called Perkins Motor Service Ltd *(G-12938)*

Standards Testing Labs Inc (PA).................................330 833-8548
  1845 Harsh Ave Se Massillon (44646) *(G-13731)*

Standex Electronics Inc (HQ).................................513 871-3777
  4538 Camberwell Rd Cincinnati (45209) *(G-4534)*

Standing Stone National Bank (PA).................................740 653-5115
  137 W Wheeling St Lancaster (43130) *(G-12438)*

Standley Law Group LLP.................................614 792-5555
  6300 Riverside Dr Dublin (43017) *(G-10340)*

Standrdaero Component Svcs Inc (HQ).................................513 618-9588
  11550 Mosteller Rd Cincinnati (45241) *(G-4535)*

Stanley Miller Construction Co.................................330 484-2229
  2250 Howenstine Dr Se East Sparta (44626) *(G-10424)*

Stanley Steamer, Youngstown Also called Samron Inc *(G-20203)*

Stanley Steemer, Wickliffe Also called Lazar Brothers Inc *(G-19468)*

Stanley Steemer, Conneaut Also called Merlene Enterprises Inc *(G-8956)*

Stanley Steemer Carpet Cleaner, Dublin Also called Stanley Steemer Intl Inc *(G-10341)*

Stanley Steemer Carpet Clr 05, Dublin Also called Stanley Steemer Intl Inc *(G-10342)*

Stanley Steemer Carpet Clr 07, Cincinnati Also called Stanley Steemer Intl Inc *(G-4536)*

Stanley Steemer Intl Inc (PA).................................614 764-2007
  5800 Innovation Dr Dublin (43016) *(G-10341)*

Stanley Steemer Intl Inc.................................419 227-1212
  1253 N Cole St Lima (45801) *(G-12754)*

Stanley Steemer Intl Inc.................................513 771-0213
  637 Redna Ter Cincinnati (45215) *(G-4536)*

Stanley Steemer Intl Inc.................................614 652-2241
  5500 Stanley Steemer Pkwy Dublin (43016) *(G-10342)*

Stanley Stemer of Akron Canton.................................330 785-5005
  76 Hanna Pkwy Coventry Township (44319) *(G-9043)*

Stansley Mineral Resources Inc (PA).................................419 843-2813
  3793 Silica Rd B Sylvania (43560) *(G-17453)*

Stantec Arch & Engrg PC.................................216 454-2150
  3700 Park East Dr Ste 200 Cleveland (44122) *(G-6451)*

Stantec Arch & Engrg PC.................................614 486-4383
  1500 Lake Shore Dr # 100 Columbus (43204) *(G-8683)*

Stantec Architecture Inc.................................216 621-2407
  1300 E 9th St Ste 1100 Cleveland (44114) *(G-6452)*

Stantec Architecture Inc.................................216 454-2150
  1001 Lakeside Ave E # 1600 Cleveland (44114) *(G-6453)*

Stantec Consulting Svcs Inc.................................216 454-2150
  3700 Park East Dr Ste 200 Cleveland (44122) *(G-6454)*

Stantec Consulting Svcs Inc.................................513 842-8200
  11687 Lebanon Rd Cincinnati (45241) *(G-4537)*

Stantec Consulting Svcs Inc.................................614 486-4383
  1500 Lake Shore Dr # 100 Columbus (43204) *(G-8684)*

Stantec Consulting Svcs Inc.................................216 621-2407
  1001 Lakeside Ave E # 1600 Cleveland (44114) *(G-6455)*

Staples Inc.................................740 845-5600
  500 E High St London (43140) *(G-12875)*

Staples Inc.................................614 472-2014
  700 Taylor Rd Ste 100 Columbus (43230) *(G-8685)*

Star 64, Cincinnati Also called Sinclair Broadcast Group Inc *(G-4485)*

Star 93.3 FM, Cincinnati Also called Pillar of Fire *(G-4249)*

Star Beauty Plus LLC (PA).................................216 662-9750
  20900 Libby Rd Maple Heights (44137) *(G-13298)*

Star Builders Inc.................................440 986-5951
  46405 Telegraph Rd Amherst (44001) *(G-599)*

Star County Home Consortium.................................330 451-7395
  201 3rd St Ne Fl 2201 Canton (44702) *(G-2486)*

Star Dist & Manufacturring LLC.................................513 860-3573
  9818 Prnceton Glendale Rd West Chester (45246) *(G-19083)*

Star Group Ltd.................................614 428-8678
  460 Waterbury Ct Gahanna (43230) *(G-11146)*

Star House Foundation.................................614 826-5868
  1220 Corrugated Way Columbus (43201) *(G-8686)*

Star Inc.................................740 354-1517
  2625 Gallia St Portsmouth (45662) *(G-16174)*

Star Leasing Co (PA).................................614 278-9999
  4080 Business Park Dr Columbus (43204) *(G-8687)*

Star Manufacturring, West Chester Also called Star Dist & Manufacturring LLC *(G-19083)*

Star One Holdings Inc.................................513 474-9100
  8118 Beechmont Ave Cincinnati (45255) *(G-4538)*

Star One Holdings Inc.................................513 779-9500
  6875 Fountains Blvd Ste A West Chester (45069) *(G-19012)*

Star One Holdings Inc.................................513 300-6663
  9722 Montgomery Rd Cincinnati (45242) *(G-4539)*

Star Packaging Inc.................................614 564-9936
  1796 Frebis Ave Columbus (43206) *(G-8688)*

Star-Ex Inc.................................937 473-2397
  1600 Mote Dr Covington (45318) *(G-9048)*

Starfire, Hamilton Also called Coolants Plus Inc *(G-11587)*

Starforce National Corporation.................................513 979-3600
  455 Delta Ave Ste 410 Cincinnati (45226) *(G-4540)*

Stark and Summit Regional EXT, Canton Also called Ohio State University *(G-2431)*

Stark Area Regional Trnst Auth (PA).................................330 477-2782
  1600 Gateway Blvd Se Canton (44707) *(G-2487)*

Stark Cnty Dept Job Fmly Svcs.................................330 451-8400
  221 3rd St Se Canton (44702) *(G-2488)*

Stark Cnty Historical Soc Inc.................................330 455-7043
  800 Mckinley Monu Dr Nw Canton (44708) *(G-2489)*

Stark County Board of Developm.................................330 477-5200
  4065 Bradley Cir Nw Canton (44718) *(G-2490)*

Stark County Cmnty Action Agcy (PA).................................330 454-1676
  1366 Market Ave N Canton (44714) *(G-2491)*

Stark County Cmnty Action Agcy.................................330 821-5977
  321 Franklin Ave Alliance (44601) *(G-553)*

Stark County Engineer, Canton Also called County of Stark *(G-2269)*

Stark County Federation of Con.................................330 268-1652
  6323 Richville Dr Sw Canton (44706) *(G-2492)*

Stark County Neurologists Inc.................................330 494-2097
  4105 Holiday St Nw Canton (44718) *(G-2493)*

Stark County Park District 330 477-3552
  5300 Tyner Ave Nw Canton (44708) *(G-2494)*

Stark County Sewer Dept, Canton *Also called County of Stark (G-2268)*

Stark County Womens Clinic Inc 330 493-0313
  5000 Higbee Ave Nw Canton (44718) *(G-2495)*

Stark Industrial LLC 330 493-9773
  5103 Stoneham Rd North Canton (44720) *(G-15234)*

Stark Knoll 330 376-3300
  3475 Richwood Rd Akron (44333) *(G-441)*

Stark Medical Specialties Inc (PA) 330 837-1111
  323 Marion Ave Nw Ste 200 Massillon (44646) *(G-13732)*

Stark Metal Sales Inc 330 823-7383
  432 Keystone St Alliance (44601) *(G-554)*

Stark Sandblasting & Pntg Co, Canton *Also called Flamos Enterprises Inc (G-2315)*

Stark Summit Ambulance, North Canton *Also called Medical Transport Systems Inc (G-15219)*

Starlight Enterprises Inc 330 339-2020
  400 E High Ave New Philadelphia (44663) *(G-14983)*

Starlight Special School, Zanesville *Also called Muskingum Starlight Industries (G-20342)*

Start, Cleveland *Also called Support To At Risk Teens (G-6486)*

Start-Black Servicesjv LLC 740 598-4891
  797 Cool Spring Rd Mingo Junction (43938) *(G-14529)*

Startek Inc 419 528-7801
  850 W 4th St Ontario (44906) *(G-15576)*

Starting Point, Cleveland *Also called Child Care Resource Center (G-5177)*

Starwin Industries LLC 937 293-8568
  3387 Woodman Dr Dayton (45429) *(G-9790)*

Starwin Industries, Inc., Dayton *Also called Starwin Industries LLC (G-9790)*

Starwood, Middlefield *Also called Norstar Aluminum Molds Inc (G-14273)*

Starwood Hotels & Resorts, Cincinnati *Also called Host Cincinnati Hotel LLC (G-3731)*

Starwood Hotels & Resorts 614 345-9291
  3030 Plaza Prpts Blvd Columbus (43219) *(G-8689)*

Starwood Hotels & Resorts 614 888-8230
  888 E Dublin Granville Rd Columbus (43229) *(G-8690)*

Stat Communications, Columbus *Also called Universal Recovery Systems (G-8817)*

Stat Express Delivery LLC (PA) 614 880-7828
  705 Lkview Plz Blvd Ste M Worthington (43085) *(G-19853)*

Stat Integrated Tech Inc (PA) 440 286-7663
  10779 Mayfield Rd Chardon (44024) *(G-2716)*

State 8 Motorcycle & Atv, Peninsula *Also called Wholecycle Inc (G-15815)*

State Alarm Inc (PA) 888 726-8111
  5956 Market St Youngstown (44512) *(G-20217)*

State Alarm Systems, Youngstown *Also called State Alarm Inc (G-20217)*

State Auto Financial Corp (HQ) 614 464-5000
  518 E Broad St Columbus (43215) *(G-8691)*

State Auto Insurance Companies, Columbus *Also called State Automobile Mutl Insur Co (G-8692)*

STATE AUTO INSURANCE COMPANIES, Columbus *Also called State Auto Financial Corp (G-8691)*

State Automobile Mutl Insur Co (PA) 833 724-3577
  518 E Broad St Columbus (43215) *(G-8692)*

State Bank and Trust Company (HQ) 419 783-8950
  401 Clinton St Defiance (43512) *(G-9941)*

State Bank and Trust Company 419 485-5521
  1201 E Main St Montpelier (43543) *(G-14618)*

State Chemical, Cleveland *Also called Zucker Building Company (G-6714)*

State Chemical Manufacturing, Cleveland *Also called State Industrial Products Corp (G-6458)*

State Crest Carpet & Flooring (PA) 440 232-3980
  5400 Perkins Rd Bedford (44146) *(G-1309)*

State Farm General Insur Co 740 364-5000
  1440 Granville Rd Newark (43055) *(G-15100)*

State Farm Insurance, Newark *Also called State Farm General Insur Co (G-15100)*

State Farm Insurance, Perrysburg *Also called State Farm Mutl Auto Insur Co (G-15925)*

State Farm Insurance, Cleveland *Also called State Farm Mutl Auto Insur Co (G-6456)*

State Farm Insurance, Dayton *Also called State Farm Life Insurance Co (G-9791)*

State Farm Insurance, New Albany *Also called State Farm Mutl Auto Insur Co (G-14875)*

State Farm Insurance, Newark *Also called State Farm Mutl Auto Insur Co (G-15101)*

State Farm Insurance, Cleveland *Also called State Farm Mutl Auto Insur Co (G-6457)*

State Farm Life Insurance Co 937 276-1900
  1436 Needmore Rd Dayton (45414) *(G-9791)*

State Farm Mutl Auto Insur Co 419 873-0100
  13001 Roachton Rd Perrysburg (43551) *(G-15925)*

State Farm Mutl Auto Insur Co 216 621-3723
  2700 W 25th St Cleveland (44113) *(G-6456)*

State Farm Mutl Auto Insur Co 614 775-2001
  5400 New Albany Rd New Albany (43054) *(G-14875)*

State Farm Mutl Auto Insur Co 740 364-5000
  1440 Granville Rd Newark (43055) *(G-15101)*

State Farm Mutl Auto Insur Co 216 321-1422
  2245 Warrensville Ctr Rd Cleveland (44118) *(G-6457)*

State Highway Dept Gallia, Gallipolis *Also called County of Gallia (G-11188)*

State Highway Garage, Chillicothe *Also called Transportation Ohio Department (G-2832)*

State Industrial Products Corp (PA) 877 747-6986
  5915 Landerbrook Dr # 300 Cleveland (44124) *(G-6458)*

State Industrial Products Corp 216 861-6363
  12420 Plaza Dr Cleveland (44130) *(G-6459)*

State of Heart HM Hlth Hospice, Coldwater *Also called Hospice of Darke County Inc (G-6759)*

State of Ohio 614 466-3455
  4200 Surface Rd Columbus (43228) *(G-8693)*

State of Ohio 614 466-3834
  1929 Gateway Cir Grove City (43123) *(G-11474)*

State of The Heart Hospice, Greenville *Also called Hospice of Darke County Inc (G-11387)*

State Park Motors Inc 740 264-3113
  766 Canton Rd Steubenville (43953) *(G-17170)*

State Tchers Rtrement Sys Ohio (HQ) 614 227-4090
  275 E Broad St Columbus (43215) *(G-8694)*

State Valley Dental Center 330 920-8060
  63 Graham Rd Ste 3 Cuyahoga Falls (44223) *(G-9125)*

State-Wide Express Inc 216 676-4600
  5231 Engle Rd Cleveland (44142) *(G-6460)*

Stateco Financial Services 614 464-5000
  518 E Broad St Columbus (43215) *(G-8695)*

Status Solutions LLC 866 846-7272
  999 County Line Rd W A Westerville (43082) *(G-19211)*

Staufs Coffee Roasters II Inc (PA) 614 487-6050
  705 Hadley Dr Columbus (43228) *(G-8696)*

Stautberg Family LLC 513 941-5070
  3871 Deerpath Ln Cincinnati (45248) *(G-4541)*

Staybrdge Sites Columbus Arprt, Columbus *Also called Rama Inc (G-8488)*

Staybridge Suites, Canfield *Also called Meander Hospitality Group Inc (G-2146)*

Staybridge Suites, Mayfield Heights *Also called Seal Mayfield LLC (G-13881)*

Staybridge Suites Canton, Canton *Also called SBS of Canton Jv LLC (G-2470)*

Stb Enterprises 330 478-0044
  4417 17th St Nw Canton (44708) *(G-2496)*

Steak Escape, Columbus *Also called Escape Enterprises Inc (G-7533)*

Stearns Companies LLC 419 422-0241
  4404 Township Road 142 Findlay (45840) *(G-10963)*

Stedman Floor Co Inc 614 836-3190
  420 Lowery Ct Groveport (43125) *(G-11539)*

Steel Eqp Specialists Inc (PA) 330 823-8260
  1507 Beeson St Ne Alliance (44601) *(G-555)*

Steel Plate LLC 888 894-8818
  8333 Boyle Pkwy Twinsburg (44087) *(G-18324)*

Steel Valley Construction Co. 330 392-8391
  135 Pine Ave Se Ste 203 Warren (44481) *(G-18746)*

Steel Warehouse Cleveland LLC (HQ) 888 225-3760
  3193 Independence Rd Cleveland (44105) *(G-6461)*

Steel Warehouse Company LLC 216 206-2800
  4700 Heidtman Pkwy Cleveland (44105) *(G-6462)*

Steel Warehouse of Ohio LLC 888 225-3760
  4700 Heidtman Pkwy Cleveland (44105) *(G-6463)*

Steel Warehouse Ohio, Cleveland *Also called Steel Warehouse Company LLC (G-6462)*

Steele Dialysis LLC 419 462-1028
  865 Harding Way W Galion (44833) *(G-11182)*

Steele W W Jr Agency Inc 330 453-7721
  200 Market Ave N Ste 100 Canton (44702) *(G-2497)*

Steelial Cnstr Met Fabrication, Vinton *Also called Steelial Wldg Met Fbrction Inc (G-18586)*

Steelial Wldg Met Fbrction Inc 740 669-5300
  70764 State Route 124 Vinton (45686) *(G-18586)*

Steelsummit Holdings Inc 513 825-8550
  11150 Southland Rd Cincinnati (45240) *(G-4542)*

Steelsummit Ohio, Jackson *Also called Ohio Metal Processing Inc (G-12178)*

Stein Inc 216 883-4277
  1034 Holmden Ave Cleveland (44109) *(G-6464)*

Stein Hospice Services Inc 419 447-0475
  1200 Sycamore Line Sandusky (44870) *(G-16645)*

Stein Hospice Services Inc 419 502-0019
  126 Columbus Ave Sandusky (44870) *(G-16646)*

Stein Hospice Services Inc (PA) 800 625-5269
  1200 Sycamore Line Sandusky (44870) *(G-16647)*

Stein Hospice Services Inc 419 663-3222
  150 Milan Ave Norwalk (44857) *(G-15456)*

Steinbach Painiting, Canton *Also called David W Steinbach Inc (G-2279)*

Steiner Associates, Columbus *Also called Easton Town Center II LLC (G-7492)*

Steiner Associates, Columbus *Also called Seg of Ohio Inc (G-8617)*

Steiner Eoptics Inc (PA) 937 426-2341
  3475 Newmark Dr Miamisburg (45342) *(G-14226)*

Steingass Mechanical Contg 330 725-6090
  754 S Progress Dr Medina (44256) *(G-14005)*

Stella Maris Inc 216 781-0550
  1320 Washington Ave Cleveland (44113) *(G-6465)*

Stella Mris Detoxification Ctr, Cleveland *Also called Stella Maris Inc (G-6465)*

Stellar Automotive Group, Seville *Also called Stellar Srkg Acquisition LLC (G-16692)*

Stellar Srkg Acquisition LLC 330 769-8484
  4935 Enterprise Pkwy Seville (44273) *(G-16692)*

Stembanc Inc 440 332-4279
  100 7th Ave Ste 200 Chardon (44024) *(G-2717)*

Step By Step Emplyment Trining 440 967-9042
  664 Exchange St Vermilion (44089) *(G-18560)*

Stephen A Rudolph Inc 216 381-1367
  1611 S Green Rd Ste 260 Cleveland (44121) *(G-6466)*

Stephen M Trudick 440 834-1891
  13813 Station Rd Burton (44021) *(G-2019)*

Stephen R Saddemi MD 419 578-7200
  2865 N Reynolds Rd # 160 Toledo (43615) *(G-18047)*

A L P H A B E T I C

Stephens-Matthews Mktg Inc 740 984-8011
605 Center St Beverly (45715) ***(G-1466)***
Stepping Stones Child Care, Cleveland *Also called Gearity Early Child Care Ctr* ***(G-5601)***
STEPS AT LIBERTY CENTER, Wooster *Also called Oneeighty Inc* ***(G-19756)***
Stepstone Group Real Estate LP 216 522-0330
127 Public Sq Ste 5050 Cleveland (44114) ***(G-6467)***
Stericycle Inc 330 393-0370
1901 Pine Ave Se Warren (44483) ***(G-18747)***
Stericycle Inc 419 729-1934
1301 E Alexis Rd Toledo (43612) ***(G-18048)***
Steriltek Inc (PA) 615 627-0241
11910 Briarwyck Woods Dr Painesville (44077) ***(G-15742)***
Steris Isomedix, Groveport *Also called Isomedix Operations Inc* ***(G-11521)***
Sterling Buying Group LLC 513 564-9000
3802 Ford Cir Cincinnati (45227) ***(G-4543)***
Sterling Heights Gsa Prpts Ltd 419 609-7000
5003 Milan Rd Sandusky (44870) ***(G-16648)***
Sterling House Bowling Green, Bowling Green *Also called Brookdale Snior Lving Cmmnties* ***(G-1726)***
Sterling House of Alliance, Alliance *Also called Brookdale Senior Living Commun* ***(G-519)***
Sterling House of Findlay, Findlay *Also called Brookdale Snior Lving Cmmnties* ***(G-10884)***
Sterling House of Greenville, Greenville *Also called Brookdale Senior Living Commun* ***(G-11367)***
Sterling House of Lancaster, Lancaster *Also called Brookdale Snior Lving Cmmnties* ***(G-12373)***
Sterling House of Mansfield, Mansfield *Also called Brookdale Senior Living Inc* ***(G-13146)***
Sterling House of Mansfield, Mansfield *Also called Brookdale Snior Lving Cmmnties* ***(G-13147)***
Sterling House of Newark, Newark *Also called Brookdale Snior Lving Cmmnties* ***(G-15015)***
Sterling House of Piqua, Piqua *Also called Brookdale Snior Lving Cmmnties* ***(G-15998)***
Sterling House of Youngstown, Youngstown *Also called Brookdale Snior Lving Cmmnties* ***(G-19976)***
Sterling Infosystems Inc 216 685-7600
4511 Rockside Rd Independence (44131) ***(G-12125)***
Sterling Joint Ambulance Dst 740 869-3006
24 S London St Mount Sterling (43143) ***(G-14747)***
Sterling Land Title Agency 937 438-2000
7016 Corporate Way Ste B Dayton (45459) ***(G-9792)***
Sterling Land Title Agency 513 755-3700
7594 Cox Ln West Chester (45069) ***(G-19013)***
Sterling Lodging LLC 419 879-4000
803 S Leonard Ave Lima (45804) ***(G-12755)***
Sterling Med Staffing Group, Cincinnati *Also called Sterling Medical Corporation* ***(G-4546)***
Sterling Medical Associates 513 984-1800
411 Oak St Cincinnati (45219) ***(G-4544)***
Sterling Medical Corporation 513 984-1800
411 Oak St Cincinnati (45219) ***(G-4545)***
Sterling Medical Corporation (PA) 513 984-1800
411 Oak St Cincinnati (45219) ***(G-4546)***
Sterling Paper Co (HQ) 614 443-0303
1845 Progress Ave Columbus (43207) ***(G-8697)***
Stern Advertising Inc (PA) 216 331-5827
950 Main Ave Ste 700 Cleveland (44113) ***(G-6468)***
Steubenville Country CLB Manor 740 266-6118
575 Lovers Ln Steubenville (43953) ***(G-17171)***
Steubenville Country Club Inc 740 264-0521
413 Lovers Ln Steubenville (43953) ***(G-17172)***
STEUBENVILLE HOME TRAINING, Steubenville *Also called Barrington Dialysis LLC* ***(G-17140)***
Steubenville Truck Center Inc 740 282-2711
620 South St Steubenville (43952) ***(G-17173)***
Steve Austin Auto Group 937 592-3015
2500 S Main St Bellefontaine (43311) ***(G-1368)***
Steve Austins of Hardin County, Bellefontaine *Also called Steve Austin Auto Group* ***(G-1368)***
Steve Brown 937 436-2700
1353 Lyons Rd Dayton (45458) ***(G-9793)***
Steve Byerly Masonry, Columbus *Also called Steven H Byerly Inc* ***(G-8699)***
Steve S Towing and Recovery 513 422-0254
6475 Trenton Franklin Rd Middletown (45042) ***(G-14332)***
Steve Shaffer 614 276-6355
3905 Sullivant Ave Columbus (43228) ***(G-8698)***
Steven H Byerly Inc 614 882-0092
4890 Cleveland Ave Columbus (43231) ***(G-8699)***
Steven L Sawdai 513 829-3830
6120 Pleasant Ave Fairfield (45014) ***(G-10787)***
Steven Schaefer Associates Inc (PA) 513 542-3300
537 E Pete Rose Way # 400 Cincinnati (45202) ***(G-4547)***
Stevens Aviation Inc 937 890-0189
3500 Hangar Dr Vandalia (45377) ***(G-18541)***
Stevenson Service Experts, Blue Ash *Also called Service Experts Htg & AC LLC* ***(G-1650)***
Steward Trumbull Mem Hosp Inc 330 841-9011
1350 E Market St Warren (44483) ***(G-18748)***
Stewart Advnced Land Title Ltd (PA) 513 753-2800
792 Eastgate South Dr Cincinnati (45245) ***(G-2870)***
Stewart Lodge Inc 440 417-1898
7774 Warner Rd Madison (44057) ***(G-13109)***
Stewart Title Company 440 520-7130
4212 State Route 306 Willoughby (44094) ***(G-19574)***
Stg Communication Services Inc 330 482-0500
1401 Wardingsley Ave Columbiana (44408) ***(G-6792)***
Stg Communication Services Inc 330 482-0500
1401 Wardingsley Ave Columbiana (44408) ***(G-6793)***
STI Technologies, Beavercreek *Also called Solutions Through Innovative T* ***(G-1187)***
Stickelman Schneider Assoc LLC (HQ) 513 475-6000
1130 Channingway Dr Fairborn (45324) ***(G-10682)***
Still Water Family Care, Versailles *Also called Premier Health Partners* ***(G-18571)***
Stillwater Center, Dayton *Also called County of Montgomery* ***(G-9328)***
Stilson & Associates Inc 614 847-0300
6121 Huntley Rd Columbus (43229) ***(G-8700)***
Stingray Pressure Pumping LLC (PA) 405 648-4177
42739 National Rd Belmont (43718) ***(G-1396)***
Stock Equipment Company, Chagrin Falls *Also called Stock Fairfield Corporation* ***(G-2684)***
Stock Fairfield Corporation 440 543-6000
16490 Chillicothe Rd Chagrin Falls (44023) ***(G-2684)***
Stocker Sand & Gravel Co (PA) 740 254-4635
Rr 36 Gnadenhutten (44629) ***(G-11312)***
Stockmeister Enterprises Inc 740 286-1619
700 E Main St Jackson (45640) ***(G-12179)***
Stockport Mill Country Inn Inc 740 559-2822
1995 Broadway St Stockport (43787) ***(G-17183)***
Stoddard Imported Cars Inc 440 951-1040
8599 Market St Mentor (44060) ***(G-14112)***
Stofcheck Ambulance Inc 740 383-2787
314 W Center St Marion (43302) ***(G-13460)***
Stofcheck Ambulance Service, Marion *Also called Stofcheck Ambulance Inc* ***(G-13460)***
Stofcheck Ambulance Svc Inc (PA) 740 499-2200
220 S High St La Rue (43332) ***(G-12324)***
Stokes Fruit Farm 937 382-4004
3182 Center Rd Wilmington (45177) ***(G-19649)***
Stoll Farms Inc 330 682-5786
15040 Fox Lake Rd Marshallville (44645) ***(G-13475)***
Stolle Machinery Company LLC 330 493-0444
4150 Belden Village St Nw Canton (44718) ***(G-2498)***
Stolle Machinery Company LLC 330 453-2015
4337 Excel St North Canton (44720) ***(G-15235)***
Stolly Financial Planning, Lima *Also called Stolly Insurance Agency Inc* ***(G-12756)***
Stolly Insurance Agency Inc 419 227-2570
1730 Allentown Rd Lima (45805) ***(G-12756)***
Stone Coffman Company LLC 614 861-4668
6015 Taylor Rd Gahanna (43230) ***(G-11147)***
Stone Crossing Assisted Living 330 492-7131
820 34th St Nw Canton (44709) ***(G-2499)***
Stone Gardens 216 292-0070
27090 Cedar Rd Cleveland (44122) ***(G-6469)***
Stone Mart, Columbus *Also called Indus Trade & Technology LLC* ***(G-7811)***
Stone Oak Country Club 419 867-0969
100 Stone Oak Blvd Holland (43528) ***(G-11917)***
Stone Products Inc (HQ) 800 235-6088
3105 Varley Ave Sw Canton (44706) ***(G-2500)***
Stone Ridge Golf Club, Bowling Green *Also called Wryneck Development LLC* ***(G-1760)***
Stoneco Inc (HQ) 419 422-8854
1700 Fostoria Ave Ste 200 Findlay (45840) ***(G-10964)***
Stoneco Inc 419 393-2555
13762 Road 179 Oakwood (45873) ***(G-15484)***
Stonegate Construction Inc 740 423-9170
1378 Way Rd Belpre (45714) ***(G-1410)***
Stonehedge Enterprises Inc 330 928-2161
580 E Cuyahoga Falls Ave Akron (44310) ***(G-442)***
Stonehedge Place, Akron *Also called Stonehedge Enterprises Inc* ***(G-442)***
Stonehenge Capital Company LLC 614 246-2456
191 W Nationwide Blvd Columbus (43215) ***(G-8701)***
Stonehenge Fincl Holdings Inc (PA) 614 246-2500
191 W Nationwide Blvd # 600 Columbus (43215) ***(G-8702)***
Stonemor Partners LP 330 491-8001
4450 Belden Village St Nw # 802 Canton (44718) ***(G-2501)***
Stonemor Partners LP 937 866-4135
6722 Hemple Rd Dayton (45439) ***(G-9794)***
Stonemor Partners LP 330 425-8128
8592 Darrow Rd Twinsburg (44087) ***(G-18325)***
Stonewood Residential Inc (PA) 216 267-9777
6320 Smith Rd Cleveland (44142) ***(G-6470)***
Stoney Hollow Tire Inc 740 635-5200
1st & Hanover Sts Martins Ferry (43935) ***(G-13478)***
Stoney Lodge Inc 419 837-6409
3491 Latcha Rd Millbury (43447) ***(G-14451)***
Stoops Freightliner of Dayton, Dayton *Also called Stoops Frghtlnr-Qlity Trlr Inc* ***(G-9795)***
Stoops Frghtlnr-Qlity Trlr Inc 937 236-4092
7800 Center Point 70 Blvd Dayton (45424) ***(G-9795)***
Stoops of Lima Inc 419 228-4334
598 E Hanthorn Rd Lima (45804) ***(G-12757)***
Store & Haul Inc 419 238-4284
1165 Grill Rd Van Wert (45891) ***(G-18489)***
Store & Haul Trucking, Van Wert *Also called Store & Haul Inc* ***(G-18489)***
Stork Herron Cleveland, Cleveland *Also called Element Mtrls Tchnlgy Hntngtn* ***(G-5472)***
Stork Studios Inc 419 841-7766
3830 Woodley Rd Ste A Toledo (43606) ***(G-18049)***
Storopack Inc (HQ) 513 874-0314
4758 Devitt Dr West Chester (45246) ***(G-19084)***

Stouffer Realty Inc (PA)..330 835-4900
  130 N Miller Rd Ste A Fairlawn (44333) *(G-10852)*
Stout Lori Cleaning & Such.......................................419 637-7644
  503 N Main St Gibsonburg (43431) *(G-11279)*
Stout Risius Ross LLC..216 685-5000˝
  600 Superior Ave E # 1700 Cleveland (44114) *(G-6471)*
Stover Excavating Inc..614 873-5865
  7500 Industrial Pkwy Plain City (43064) *(G-16068)*
Stover Transportation Inc...614 777-4184
  3710 Lacon Rd Hilliard (43026) *(G-11818)*
Stow Dental Group Inc...330 688-6456
  3506 Darrow Rd Stow (44224) *(G-17231)*
Stow Montessori Center, Stow Also called All Around Children Montessori *(G-17190)*
Stow Opco LLC..502 429-8062
  2910 Lermitage Pl Stow (44224) *(G-17232)*
Stow-Kent Animal Hospital Inc (PA)..........................330 673-0049
  4559 Kent Rd Kent (44240) *(G-12259)*
Stow-Kent Animal Hospital Inc..................................330 673-1002
  4148 State Route 43 Kent (44240) *(G-12260)*
Strader's Green House, Columbus Also called Straders Garden Centers Inc *(G-8703)*
Straders Garden Centers Inc (PA).............................614 889-1314
  5350 Riverside Dr Columbus (43220) *(G-8703)*
Straight 72 Inc..740 943-5730
  20078 State Route 4 Marysville (43040) *(G-13530)*
Stranahan Theatre & Great Hall, Toledo Also called Stranahan Theatre Trust *(G-18050)*
Stranahan Theatre Trust..419 381-8851
  4645 Heatherdowns Blvd # 2 Toledo (43614) *(G-18050)*
Strand Associates Inc...513 861-5600
  615 Elsinore Pl Ste 320 Cincinnati (45202) *(G-4548)*
Strand Associates Inc...614 835-0460
  4433 Professional Pkwy Groveport (43125) *(G-11540)*
Strang Corporation (PA)...216 961-6767
  8905 Lake Ave Fl 1 Cleveland (44102) *(G-6472)*
Stratacache Inc (PA)...937 224-0485
  2 Emmet St Ste 200 Dayton (45405) *(G-9796)*
Stratacache Products, Dayton Also called Stratacache Inc *(G-9796)*
Stratagraph Ne Inc...740 373-3091
  116 Ellsworth Ave Marietta (45750) *(G-13384)*
Strategic Data Systems Inc....................................513 772-7374
  11260 Chester Rd Ste 425 Cincinnati (45246) *(G-4549)*
Strategic Insurance Software, Columbus Also called Nugrowth Solutions LLC *(G-8215)*
Strategic Research Group Inc..................................614 220-8860
  995 Goodale Blvd Ste 1 Columbus (43212) *(G-8704)*
Strategic Systems Inc..614 717-4774
  485 Metro Pl S Ste 270 Dublin (43017) *(G-10343)*
Stratford Commons Inc...440 914-0900
  7000 Cochran Rd Solon (44139) *(G-16902)*
Stratos Wealth Partners Ltd....................................440 519-2500
  3750 Park East Dr Ste 200 Beachwood (44122) *(G-1108)*
Stratton Chevrolet Co...330 537-3151
  16050 State Route 14a Beloit (44609) *(G-1398)*
Strawser Construction Inc (HQ)................................614 276-5501
  1392 Dublin Rd Columbus (43215) *(G-8705)*
Strawser Equipment & Lsg Inc.................................614 444-2521
  1235 Stimmel Rd Columbus (43223) *(G-8706)*
Streacker Tractor Sales Inc....................................419 422-6973
  1218 Trenton Ave Findlay (45840) *(G-10965)*
Streamline Technical Svcs LLC................................614 441-7448
  4555 Creekside Pkwy Lockbourne (43137) *(G-12825)*
Streamlink Software Inc (PA)...................................216 377-5500
  812 Huron Rd E Ste 550 Cleveland (44115) *(G-6473)*
Street and Service Department, Cleveland Also called City of North Royalton *(G-5210)*
Street Deparment, Norwalk Also called City of Norwalk *(G-15426)*
Street Department, Cuyahoga Falls Also called City of Cuyahoga Falls *(G-9083)*
Streets & Sewer Departments, Cleveland Also called City of Euclid *(G-5200)*
Streetsboro Board Education....................................330 626-4909
  1901 Annalane Dr Streetsboro (44241) *(G-17272)*
Streetsboro Bus Garage, Streetsboro Also called Streetsboro Board Education *(G-17272)*
Streetsboro Opco LLC..502 429-8062
  1645 Maplewood Dr Streetsboro (44241) *(G-17273)*
Streetsboro Operations, Twinsburg Also called Facil North America Inc *(G-18265)*
Stress Engineering Svcs Inc....................................513 336-6701
  7030 Stress Engrg Way Mason (45040) *(G-13641)*
Stricker Auto Sales, Batavia Also called Stricker Bros Inc *(G-1010)*
Stricker Bros Inc...513 732-1152
  4955 Benton Rd Batavia (45103) *(G-1010)*
Strike Logistics, Toledo Also called Bolt Express LLC *(G-17619)*
Strike Zone Inc...440 235-4420
  8501 Stearns Rd Olmsted Twp (44138) *(G-15541)*
Strollo Architects Inc...330 743-1177
  201 W Federal St Youngstown (44503) *(G-20218)*
Strongsville Lodging Assoc 1....................................440 238-8800
  15471 Royalton Rd Strongsville (44136) *(G-17348)*
Strongsville Medical Offices, Strongsville Also called Kaiser Foundation Hospitals *(G-17318)*
Strongsville Recreation Complex..............................440 580-3230
  18688 Royalton Rd Strongsville (44136) *(G-17349)*
Strs Ohio, Columbus Also called State Tchers Rtrement Sys Ohio *(G-8694)*
Structural Building Systems.....................................330 656-9353
  5802 Akron Cleveland Rd Hudson (44236) *(G-12007)*

Struktol Company America LLC (HQ)........................330 928-5188
  201 E Steels Corners Rd Stow (44224) *(G-17233)*
STS Logistics Inc...419 294-1498
  13863 County Highway 119 Upper Sandusky (43351) *(G-18413)*
STS Management, Toledo Also called STS Restaurant Management Inc *(G-18051)*
STS Restaurant Management Inc..............................419 246-0730
  420 Madison Ave Ste 103 Toledo (43604) *(G-18051)*
Studebaker Electric Company...................................937 890-9510
  8459 N Main St Ste 114 Dayton (45415) *(G-9797)*
Studebaker Nurseries Inc..800 845-0584
  11140 Milton Carlisle Rd New Carlisle (45344) *(G-14898)*
Studebaker Wholesale Nurseries, New Carlisle Also called Studebaker Nurseries Inc *(G-14898)*
Student Loan Strategies LLC...................................513 645-5400
  151 W 4th St Frnt Cincinnati (45202) *(G-4550)*
Student Wilce Health Center, Columbus Also called Ohio State University *(G-8324)*
Studer-Obringer Inc..419 492-2121
  525 S Kibler St New Washington (44854) *(G-15003)*
Studio Mz Hair Design, Cleveland Also called Mzf Inc *(G-6032)*
Studio of Prime Ae Group, Akron Also called Braun & Steidl Architects Inc *(G-104)*
Stykemain Pntiac-Buick-Gmc Ltd (PA).......................419 784-5252
  25124 Elliott Rd Defiance (43512) *(G-9942)*
Style Crest Inc..419 332-7369
  605 Hagerty Dr Fremont (43420) *(G-11098)*
Style Crest Inc (HQ)...419 332-7369
  2450 Enterprise St Fremont (43420) *(G-11099)*
Style Crest Enterprises Inc (PA)...............................419 355-8586
  2450 Enterprise St Fremont (43420) *(G-11100)*
Style Crest Transport Inc.......................................419 332-7369
  2450 Enterprise St Fremont (43420) *(G-11101)*
Style-Line Incorporated (PA)....................................614 291-0600
  901 W 3rd Ave Ste A Columbus (43212) *(G-8707)*
Styx Acquisition LLC...330 264-9900
  3540 Burbank Rd Wooster (44691) *(G-19770)*
Su-Jon Enterprises...330 372-1100
  2448 Weir Rd Ne Warren (44483) *(G-18749)*
Suarez Corporation Industries..................................330 494-4282
  7800 Whipple Ave Nw Canton (44767) *(G-2502)*
Suburban Collision Centers......................................440 243-5533
  1151 W Bagley Rd Berea (44017) *(G-1438)*
Suburban Gala Lanes Inc (PA)..................................419 468-7488
  975 Hopley Ave Bucyrus (44820) *(G-2001)*
Suburban Maint & Cnstr Inc.....................................440 237-7765
  16330 York Rd Ste 2 North Royalton (44133) *(G-15368)*
Suburban Maintenance & Contrs...............................440 237-7765
  16330 York Rd North Royalton (44133) *(G-15369)*
Suburban Medical Laboratory....................................330 929-7992
  26300 Euclid Ave Ste 810 Euclid (44132) *(G-10658)*
SUBURBAN PAVILION NURSING AND, Cleveland Also called Emery Leasing Co
LLC *(G-5476)*
Suburban Pediatrics Inc (PA)...................................440 498-0065
  20220 Farnsleigh Rd Shaker Heights (44122) *(G-16715)*
Suburban Pediatrics Inc (PA)...................................513 336-6700
  12061 Sheraton Ln Cincinnati (45246) *(G-4551)*
Suburban School, Brunswick Also called Suburban Transportation Co Inc *(G-1940)*
Suburban Transportation Co Inc................................440 846-9291
  1289 Pearl Rd Brunswick (44212) *(G-1940)*
Suburban Veterinarian Clinic.....................................937 433-2160
  102 E Spring Valley Pike Dayton (45458) *(G-9798)*
Success Kidz 24-Hr Enrchmt Ctr...............................614 419-2276
  1800 Parsons Ave Columbus (43207) *(G-8708)*
Successful Eductl Seminars, Dayton Also called Nelson Financial Group *(G-9182)*
Sudhi Infomatics Inc...614 882-7309
  470 Olde Worthington Rd Westerville (43082) *(G-19212)*
Sue Smedley...937 399-5155
  417 Wildwood Dr Springfield (45504) *(G-17120)*
Sugar Creek Packing Co...513 551-5255
  4360 Creek Rd Blue Ash (45241) *(G-1653)*
Sugar Valley Meats, Sugarcreek Also called Rubin Erb *(G-17380)*
Sugarbush Golf Club, Garrettsville Also called Sugarbush Golf Inc *(G-11231)*
Sugarbush Golf Inc..330 527-4202
  11186 State Route 88 Garrettsville (44231) *(G-11231)*
Suite 224 Internet..440 593-7113
  224 State St Conneaut (44030) *(G-8959)*
Suite Solutions Technologies, Toledo Also called Marrik Dish Company LLC *(G-17895)*
Suite224 and Cablesuite541, Conneaut Also called Conneaut Telephone Company *(G-8953)*
Suma Health Sys St Thomas Hosp, Akron Also called Center 5 *(G-123)*
Sumaria Systems Inc...937 429-6070
  3164 Presidential Dr Beavercreek (45324) *(G-1188)*
Sumitomo Demag Plstc Machinery.............................440 876-8960
  11792 Alameda Dr Strongsville (44149) *(G-17350)*
Sumitomo Elc Wirg Systems Inc................................937 642-7579
  14800 Industrial Pkwy Marysville (43040) *(G-13531)*
Sumitomo Elc Wirg Systems Inc................................937 642-7579
  16960 Square Dr Marysville (43040) *(G-13532)*
Summa Akron City Hospital, Akron Also called Summa Health System *(G-449)*
Summa Barberton Hospital, Barberton Also called Summa Health System *(G-968)*
Summa Care, Akron Also called Summa Health System *(G-448)*
Summa Health..330 873-1518
  1 Park West Blvd Ste 130 Akron (44320) *(G-443)*

A
L
P
H
A
B
E
T
I
C

Summa Health..330 836-9023
750 White Pond Dr Ste 500 Akron (44320) (G-444)
Summa Health..330 252-0095
1077 Gorge Blvd Akron (44310) (G-445)
Summa Health..330 926-0384
2345 4th St Cuyahoga Falls (44221) (G-9126)
Summa Health..330 630-9726
182 East Ave Tallmadge (44278) (G-17489)
Summa Health..330 753-3649
165 5th St Se Ste A Barberton (44203) (G-967)
Summa Health..330 375-3315
55 Arch St Ste 1b Akron (44304) (G-446)
Summa Health..330 688-4531
3869 Darrow Rd Ste 208 Stow (44224) (G-17234)
Summa Health..330 864-8060
1 Park West Blvd Ste 130 Akron (44320) (G-447)
Summa Health Center Lk Medina.....................330 952-0014
3780 Medina Rd Ste 220 Medina (44256) (G-14006)
Summa Health System.....................................330 535-7319
168 E Market St Ste 208 Akron (44308) (G-448)
Summa Health System.....................................330 375-3000
525 E Market St Akron (44304) (G-449)
Summa Health System.....................................330 334-1504
195 Wadsworth Rd Wadsworth (44281) (G-18616)
Summa Health System.....................................330 375-3584
75 Arch St Ste 303 Akron (44304) (G-450)
Summa Health System.....................................330 375-3315
75 Arch St Ste 302 Akron (44304) (G-451)
Summa Health System.....................................330 375-3000
444 N Main St Akron (44310) (G-452)
Summa Health System.....................................330 615-3000
155 5th St Ne Barberton (44203) (G-968)
Summa Insurance Company Inc (HQ)...............800 996-8411
10 N Main St Akron (44308) (G-453)
Summa Park West, Akron Also called Summa Health (G-447)
Summa Physicians, Tallmadge Also called Summa Health (G-17489)
Summa Rehab Hospital LLC.............................330 572-7300
29 N Adams St Akron (44304) (G-454)
Summa Rehabilitation Services, Akron Also called Summa Health (G-444)
Summacare, Akron Also called Summa Insurance Company Inc (G-453)
Summacare Inc...330 996-8410
10 N Main St Unit 1 Akron (44308) (G-455)
Summerfield Homes LLC..................................614 253-0984
27 Linwood Ave Columbus (43205) (G-8709)
Summers Acquisition Corp (HQ)......................216 941-7700
12555 Berea Rd Cleveland (44111) (G-6474)
Summers Rubber Company, Cleveland Also called Summers Acquisition Corp (G-6474)
Summerville At Mentor, Mentor Also called Summerville Senior Living Inc (G-14113)
Summerville Senior Living Inc.........................440 354-5499
5700 Emerald Ct Mentor (44060) (G-14113)
Summit Acres Inc (PA).....................................740 732-2364
44565 Sunset Rd Caldwell (43724) (G-2044)
SUMMIT ACRES NURSING HOME, Caldwell Also called Summit Acres Inc (G-2044)
Summit Advantage LLC....................................330 835-2453
3340 W Market St Ste 100 Fairlawn (44333) (G-10853)
Summit Associates Inc.....................................216 831-3300
3750 Orange Pl Cleveland (44122) (G-6475)
Summit At Park Hills LLC.................................317 462-8048
2270 Park Hills Dr Ofc Fairborn (45324) (G-10683)
Summit Bhvioral Healthcare Ctr, Cincinnati Also called Mental Health and Addi
Serv (G-4006)
Summit Claim Services LLC..............................330 706-9898
5511 Manchester Rd Ste C New Franklin (44319) (G-14915)
Summit Cnty Dept Job Fmly Svcs.....................330 643-8200
1180 S Main St Ste 102 Akron (44301) (G-456)
Summit Cnty Internists & Assoc (PA)...............330 375-3690
55 Arch St Ste 1a Akron (44304) (G-457)
Summit Cnty Juvenile CT, Akron Also called County of Summit (G-163)
Summit County Jail, Akron Also called Oriana House Inc (G-368)
Summit County Probation Offs, Akron Also called County of Summit (G-162)
Summit Enterprises Contg Corp.......................513 426-1623
726 E Main St Ste F166 Lebanon (45036) (G-12507)
Summit Environmental Tech Inc (PA)...............330 253-8211
3310 Win St Cuyahoga Falls (44223) (G-9127)
Summit Facility Operations LLC.......................330 633-0555
330 Southwest Ave Tallmadge (44278) (G-17490)
Summit Financial Strategies...........................614 885-1115
7965 N High St Ste 350 Columbus (43235) (G-8710)
Summit Funding Group Inc (PA).......................513 489-1222
4680 Parkway Dr Ste 300 Mason (45040) (G-13642)
Summit Hand Center Inc..................................330 668-4055
3975 Embassy Pkwy Ste 201 Akron (44333) (G-458)
Summit Home Health Care Svcs, Cuyahoga Falls Also called Menorah Park Center For
Senio (G-9112)
Summit Hotel..513 527-9900
5345 Medpace Way Cincinnati (45227) (G-4552)
Summit Hotel Trs 144 LLC...............................216 443-9043
527 Prospect Ave E Cleveland (44115) (G-6476)
Summit Management Services Inc....................330 723-0864
201 Northland Dr Ofc Medina (44256) (G-14007)

Summit Opthomology Optical..........................330 864-8060
1 Park West Blvd Ste 150 Akron (44320) (G-459)
Summit Psychological Assoc Inc (PA)..............330 535-8181
37 N Broadway St Akron (44308) (G-460)
Summit Quest, Dayton Also called Summit Solutions Inc (G-9799)
Summit Quest Academy, Dublin Also called Viaquest Behavioral Health LLC (G-10363)
Summit Solutions Inc.......................................937 291-4333
446 Windsor Park Dr Dayton (45459) (G-9799)
Summit Towing, Dayton Also called Spurlock Truck Service (G-9787)
Summit Villa Care Center, Tallmadge Also called Summit Facility Operations LLC (G-17490)
Summitt Ohio Leasing Co LLC..........................937 436-2273
3800 Summit Glen Dr Dayton (45449) (G-9800)
Sumner Home For The Aged Inc (PA)...............330 666-2952
4327 Cobblestone Dr Copley (44321) (G-8976)
Sumner On Merriman, Copley Also called Sumner Home For The Aged Inc (G-8976)
Sumner On Ridgewood.....................................330 664-1360
970 Sumner Pkwy Copley (44321) (G-8977)
Sumner Solutions Inc......................................513 531-6382
3610 Sherbrooke Dr Cincinnati (45241) (G-4553)
Sumser Health Care Center, Canton Also called Mayflower Nursing Home Inc (G-2393)
Sumtotal Systems LLC......................................352 264-2800
100 E Campus View Blvd # 250 Columbus (43235) (G-8711)
Sun Behavioral Columbus, Columbus Also called Columbus Behavioral Health LLC (G-7262)
Sun Coke Energy, Franklin Furnace Also called Haverhill Coke Company LLC (G-11046)
Sun Federal Credit Union.................................419 537-0200
3341 Executive Pkwy Toledo (43606) (G-18052)
Sun Federal Credit Union (PA)..........................800 786-0945
1625 Holland Rd Maumee (43537) (G-13856)
Sun Healthcare Group Inc................................419 784-1450
395 Harding St Defiance (43512) (G-9943)
Sun Valley Infosys LLC....................................937 267-6435
1750 N Fountain Blvd Springfield (45504) (G-17121)
Sunbelt Rentals Inc...216 362-0300
13800 Brookpark Rd Cleveland (44135) (G-6477)
Sunbrdge Marion Hlth Care Corp....................740 389-6306
524 James Way Marion (43302) (G-13461)
Sunbridge Care Enterprises Inc.......................740 653-8630
1900 E Main St Lancaster (43130) (G-12439)
Sunbridge Circleville.......................................740 477-1695
1155 Atwater Ave Circleville (43113) (G-4851)
Sunbridge Healthcare LLC...............................740 342-5161
920 S Main St New Lexington (43764) (G-14929)
Suncoke Energy Nc..513 727-5571
3353 Yankee Rd Middletown (45044) (G-14333)
Suncrest Gardens Inc......................................330 650-4969
5157 Akron Cleveland Rd Peninsula (44264) (G-15813)
Sunesis Construction Company........................513 326-6000
2610 Crescentville Rd West Chester (45069) (G-19014)
Sunesis Environmental LLC.............................513 326-6000
325 Commercial Dr Fairfield (45014) (G-10788)
Sunforest Ob Gyn Associates..........................419 473-6622
3740 W Sylvania Ave # 103 Toledo (43623) (G-18053)
Sunny Border Ohio Inc.....................................440 858-9660
3637 State Route 167 Jefferson (44047) (G-12192)
Sunny Day Academy LLC (PA)..........................614 718-1717
255 Bradenton Ave Dublin (43017) (G-10344)
Sunny Side Farms, Fort Recovery Also called Midwest Poultry Services Lp (G-10993)
Sunny Slope Nursing Home, Dayton Also called CHS of Bowerston Oper Co Inc (G-9300)
Sunny Slope Nursing Home, Bowerston Also called Carriage Inn of Bowerston Inc (G-1710)
Sunny View Nursing Home, Zanesville Also called Careserve (G-20288)
Sunnyside Toyota Inc.......................................440 777-9911
27000 Lorain Rd North Olmsted (44070) (G-15312)
Sunplus HM Care - Circleville, Circleville Also called Accentcare Home Health Cal
Inc (G-4823)
Sunplus Home Health - Marion, Circleville Also called Accentcare Home Health Cal
Inc (G-4822)
Sunpoint Senior Living Hamlet.........................440 247-4200
150 Cleveland St Chagrin Falls (44022) (G-2657)
Sunpower Inc...740 594-2221
2005 E State St Ste 104 Athens (45701) (G-804)
Sunrise At Finneytown, Cincinnati Also called Sunrise Senior Living LLC (G-4554)
Sunrise At Parma, Cleveland Also called Sunrise Senior Living LLC (G-6480)
Sunrise At Shaker Heights, Cleveland Also called Sunrise Senior Living Inc (G-6479)
Sunrise Connecticut Avenue Ass......................614 451-6766
4590 Knightsbridge Blvd Columbus (43214) (G-8712)
Sunrise Cooperative Inc..................................937 462-8341
149 N Chillicothe St South Charleston (45368) (G-16925)
Sunrise Cooperative Inc..................................419 683-7340
3000 W Bucyrus St Crestline (44827) (G-9060)
Sunrise Cooperative Inc..................................937 575-6780
215 Looney Rd Piqua (45356) (G-16030)
Sunrise Cooperative Inc..................................937 382-1633
1425 Rombach Ave Wilmington (45177) (G-19650)
Sunrise Cooperative Inc..................................937 323-7536
821 N Belmont Ave Springfield (45503) (G-17122)
Sunrise Healthcare Group LLC.........................216 662-3343
19900 Clare Ave Maple Heights (44137) (G-13299)
Sunrise Homes, Lisbon Also called Mikouis Enterprise Inc (G-12804)

2019 Harris Ohio
Services Directory

(G-0000) Company's Geographic Section entry number

Sunrise Hospitality Inc..419 332-7650
540 E County Road 89 Fremont (43420) *(G-11102)*

Sunrise Industries Harps Jantr, Warren *Also called Turn Around Group Inc* *(G-18762)*

Sunrise Land Co (HQ)...216 621-6060
1250 Trml Twr 50 Pub Sq 1250 Terminal Tower Cleveland (44113) *(G-6478)*

Sunrise Manor Convalescent Ctr.................................513 797-5144
3434 State Route 132 Amelia (45102) *(G-576)*

Sunrise Mortgage Services Inc...................................614 989-5412
3596 Ringling Ln Gahanna (43230) *(G-11148)*

Sunrise of Cuyahoga Falls, Cuyahoga Falls *Also called Sunrise Senior Living LLC* *(G-9128)*

Sunrise of Dublin, Dublin *Also called Sunrise Senior Living LLC* *(G-10345)*

Sunrise of Findlay, Findlay *Also called Sunrise Senior Living LLC* *(G-10966)*

Sunrise of Gahanna, Gahanna *Also called Sunrise Senior Living Inc* *(G-11149)*

Sunrise of Hamilton, Hamilton *Also called Sunrise Senior Living LLC* *(G-11645)*

Sunrise of Poland, Poland *Also called Sunrise Senior Living LLC* *(G-16090)*

Sunrise of Rocky River, Rocky River *Also called Sunrise Senior Living Inc* *(G-16446)*

Sunrise of Wooster, Wooster *Also called Sunrise Senior Living LLC* *(G-19771)*

Sunrise On The Scioto, Upper Arlington *Also called Sunrise Senior Living Inc* *(G-18402)*

Sunrise PI For Memory Impaired, Worthington *Also called Sunrise Senior Living Inc* *(G-19854)*

Sunrise Pointe, Maple Heights *Also called Eastside Multi Care Inc* *(G-13286)*

Sunrise Pointe, Maple Heights *Also called Saber Healthcare Group LLC* *(G-13294)*

SUNRISE POINTE CARE AND REHABILITATION CENTER, Maple Heights *Also called Sunrise Healthcare Group LLC* *(G-13299)*

Sunrise Senior Living Inc..614 846-6500
6525 N High St Worthington (43085) *(G-19854)*

Sunrise Senior Living Inc..937 438-0054
6800 Paragon Rd Ofc Dayton (45459) *(G-9801)*

Sunrise Senior Living Inc..614 418-9775
775 E Johnstown Rd Gahanna (43230) *(G-11149)*

Sunrise Senior Living Inc..440 895-2383
21600 Detroit Rd Rocky River (44116) *(G-16446)*

Sunrise Senior Living Inc..440 808-0074
27819 Center Ridge Rd Ofc Westlake (44145) *(G-19410)*

Sunrise Senior Living Inc..614 457-3500
3500 Riverside Dr Upper Arlington (43221) *(G-18402)*

Sunrise Senior Living Inc..216 751-0930
16333 Chagrin Blvd Cleveland (44120) *(G-6479)*

Sunrise Senior Living LLC...937 836-9617
95 W Wenger Rd Englewood (45322) *(G-10601)*

Sunrise Senior Living LLC...330 262-1615
1615 Cleveland Rd Wooster (44691) *(G-19771)*

Sunrise Senior Living LLC...419 425-3440
401 Lake Cascade Pkwy Findlay (45840) *(G-10966)*

Sunrise Senior Living LLC...330 707-1313
335 W Mckinley Way Poland (44514) *(G-16090)*

Sunrise Senior Living LLC...513 729-5233
9101 Winton Rd Cincinnati (45231) *(G-4554)*

Sunrise Senior Living LLC...330 929-8500
1500 State Rd Cuyahoga Falls (44223) *(G-9128)*

Sunrise Senior Living LLC...216 447-8909
7766 Broadview Rd Cleveland (44134) *(G-6480)*

Sunrise Senior Living LLC...614 718-2062
4175 Stoneridge Ln Dublin (43017) *(G-10345)*

Sunrise Senior Living LLC...513 893-9000
896 Nw Washington Blvd Hamilton (45013) *(G-11645)*

Sunrise Television Corp...937 293-2101
4595 S Dixie Dr Moraine (45439) *(G-14700)*

Sunrise Television Corp...740 282-9999
9 Red Donely Plz Mingo Junction (43938) *(G-14530)*

Sunrise Television Corp...419 244-2197
4 Seagate Ste 101 Toledo (43604) *(G-18054)*

Sunrush Construction Co Inc (PA)..............................740 775-1300
1988 Western Ave Chillicothe (45601) *(G-2830)*

Sunset Carpet Cleaning...937 836-5531
9 Beckenham Rd Englewood (45322) *(G-10602)*

Sunset Hills Cemetery Corp..330 494-2051
5001 Everhard Rd Nw Canton (44718) *(G-2503)*

Sunset House Inc..419 536-4645
4020 Indian Rd Toledo (43606) *(G-18055)*

Sunset Memorial Park Assn...440 777-0450
6265 Columbia Rd North Olmsted (44070) *(G-15313)*

Sunset Mnor Hlthcare Group Inc.................................216 795-5710
1802 Crawford Rd Cleveland (44106) *(G-6481)*

Sunset Nursing Center, Ironton *Also called Coal Grove Long Term Care Inc* *(G-12151)*

Sunset Rtrment Communities Inc (PA).........................419 724-1200
4040 Indian Rd Ottawa Hills (43606) *(G-15669)*

Sunshine Communities (PA).......................................419 865-0251
7223 Maumee Western Rd Maumee (43537) *(G-13857)*

Sunshine Homecare..419 207-9900
320 Pleasant St Ashland (44805) *(G-693)*

Sunshine Housekeeping, Lebanon *Also called Rde System Corp* *(G-12496)*

Sunshine Inc. Northwest Ohio, Maumee *Also called Sunshine Communities* *(G-13857)*

Sunshine Nursery School, Columbus *Also called Christian Missionary Alliance* *(G-7195)*

Sunstorm Games LLC..216 403-4820
23245 Mercantile Rd Ste A Beachwood (44122) *(G-1109)*

Suntwist Corp..800 935-3534
5461 Dunham Rd Maple Heights (44137) *(G-13300)*

Super 8 Motel, Millbury *Also called Stoney Lodge Inc* *(G-14451)*

Super 8 Motel, Sandusky *Also called Lodging Industry Inc* *(G-16624)*

Super 8 Motel Columbus North, Columbus *Also called Northland Hotel Inc* *(G-8202)*

Super Laundry, Cincinnati *Also called Clean Living Laundry LLC* *(G-3304)*

Super Laundry Inc..614 258-5147
2268 Westbrooke Dr Columbus (43228) *(G-8713)*

Super Shine Inc...513 423-8999
1549 S Breiel Blvd Ste A Middletown (45044) *(G-14334)*

Super Systems Inc (PA)..513 772-0060
7205 Edington Dr Cincinnati (45249) *(G-4555)*

Super Tan..330 722-2799
1110 N Court St Medina (44256) *(G-14008)*

Superior Abrasives LLC...937 278-9123
1620 Fieldstone Way Vandalia (45377) *(G-18542)*

Superior Apartments..216 861-6405
1850 Superior Ave E 102a Cleveland (44114) *(G-6482)*

Superior Bev Group Centl Ohio, Lewis Center *Also called Central Beverage Group Ltd* *(G-12532)*

Superior Beverage Company Inc..................................440 703-4580
31031 Diamond Pkwy Solon (44139) *(G-16903)*

Superior Beverage Group Ltd.....................................614 294-3555
8133 Highfield Dr Lewis Center (43035) *(G-12562)*

Superior Beverage Group Ltd (PA)..............................440 703-4580
31031 Diamond Pkwy Solon (44139) *(G-16904)*

Superior Bulk Logistics Inc..513 874-3440
4963 Provident Dr West Chester (45246) *(G-19085)*

Superior Care Pharmacy Inc.......................................513 719-2600
201 E 4th St Ste 900 Cincinnati (45202) *(G-4556)*

Superior Carriers, West Chester *Also called Superior Bulk Logistics Inc* *(G-19085)*

Superior Clay Corp...740 922-4122
6566 Superior Rd Se Uhrichsville (44683) *(G-18344)*

Superior Credit Union Inc..419 738-4512
202 Willipie St Wapakoneta (45895) *(G-18654)*

Superior Dental Care Inc..937 438-0283
6683 Centervl Bus Pkwy Dayton (45459) *(G-9802)*

Superior Envmtl Sltons SES Inc...................................513 874-6910
9976 Joseph James Dr West Chester (45246) *(G-19086)*

Superior Envmtl Solutions LLC (PA).............................513 874-8355
9996 Joseph James Dr West Chester (45246) *(G-19087)*

Superior Group...614 488-8035
740 Waterman Ave Columbus (43215) *(G-8714)*

Superior Kraft Homes LLC..740 947-7710
3404 Rhodes Ave New Boston (45662) *(G-14884)*

Superior Linen & AP Svcs Inc.....................................513 751-1345
481 Wayne St Cincinnati (45206) *(G-4557)*

Superior Linen & Apparel Svcs, Cincinnati *Also called Superior Linen & AP Svcs Inc* *(G-4557)*

Superior Marine Ways Inc...740 894-6224
5852 County Rd 1 Suoth Pt Proctorville (45669) *(G-16219)*

Superior Mechanical Svcs Inc.....................................937 259-0082
3100 Plainfield Rd Ste C Dayton (45432) *(G-9187)*

Superior Med LLC (PA)..740 439-8839
1251 Clark St Cambridge (43725) *(G-2084)*

Superior Medical Care, Sheffield Village *Also called Joseph A Girgis MD Inc* *(G-16737)*

Superior Medical Care Inc..440 282-7420
5172 Leavitt Rd Ste B Lorain (44053) *(G-12946)*

Superior Packaging Toledo LLC...................................419 380-3335
2970 Airport Hwy Toledo (43609) *(G-18056)*

Superior Paving & Materials..330 499-5849
5947 Whipple Ave Nw Canton (44720) *(G-2504)*

Superior Products Llc..216 651-9400
3786 Ridge Rd Cleveland (44144) *(G-6483)*

Superior Products LLC...216 651-9400
3786 Ridge Rd Cleveland (44144) *(G-6484)*

Superior Street Partners LLC.......................................216 862-0058
19010 Shaker Blvd Shaker Heights (44122) *(G-16716)*

Superior Water Conditioning Co, Moraine *Also called Enting Water Conditioning Inc* *(G-14653)*

SUPERIOR WHOLESALE DISTRIBUTOR, Lima *Also called Swd Corporation* *(G-12759)*

Superior's Brand Meats, Massillon *Also called Fresh Mark Inc* *(G-13685)*

Superkids Reading Program, Columbus *Also called Zaner-Bloser Inc* *(G-8935)*

Supermedia LLC..740 369-2391
19 E Central Ave Fl 1 Flr 1 Marion (43302) *(G-13462)*

Superr-Spdie Portable Svcs Inc...................................330 733-9000
1050 Killian Rd Akron (44312) *(G-461)*

Supers Landscaping Inc...440 775-0027
48211 State Route 511 Oberlin (44074) *(G-15520)*

Supply Network Inc..614 527-5800
2353 International St Columbus (43228) *(G-8715)*

Supply Tech of Columbus LLC.....................................614 299-0184
5197 Trabue Rd Columbus (43228) *(G-8716)*

Supply Technologies LLC (HQ)....................................440 947-2100
6065 Parkland Blvd Ste 2 Cleveland (44124) *(G-6485)*

Support Fincl Resources Inc..800 444-5465
830 E Franklin St Ste A Centerville (45459) *(G-2634)*

Support To At Risk Teens...216 696-5507
4515 Superior Ave Cleveland (44103) *(G-6486)*

Supportcare Inc..216 446-2650
4700 Rockside Rd Ste 100 Independence (44131) *(G-12126)*

Supportcare Inc (PA)..614 889-5837
525 Metro PI N Ste 350 Dublin (43017) *(G-10346)*

Supportcare Ohio, Dublin *Also called Supportcare Inc* *(G-10346)*

A
L
P
H
A
B
E
T
I
C

Supreme Court United States.............................419 213-5800
  1946 N 13th St Ste 292 Toledo (43604) *(G-18057)*
Supreme Court United States.............................614 719-3107
  85 Marconi Blvd Rm 546 Columbus (43215) *(G-8717)*
Supreme Court United States.............................513 564-7575
  100 E 5th St Rm 110 Cincinnati (45202) *(G-4558)*
Supreme Court United States.............................216 357-7300
  801 W Superior Ave 20-100 Cleveland (44113) *(G-6487)*
Supreme Court of Ohio.....................................937 898-3996
  245 James Bohanan Dr Vandalia (45377) *(G-18543)*
Supreme Court of Ohio.....................................614 387-9800
  65 S Front St Fl 1 Columbus (43215) *(G-8718)*
Supreme Touch Home Health Svcs........................614 783-1115
  2547 W Broad St Columbus (43204) *(G-8719)*
Surburan Collision Ctr, Berea *Also called Suburban Collision Centers (G-1438)*
Sure Home Improvments LLC..............................614 586-0610
  6031 E Main St Ste 222 Columbus (43213) *(G-8720)*
Suresite Consulting Group LLC (PA).....................216 593-0400
  3659 Green Rd Ste 214 Beachwood (44122) *(G-1110)*
Surface Combustion Inc....................................419 878-8444
  1270 Wtrville Monclova Rd Waterville (43566) *(G-18794)*
Surfside Motors Inc (PA)...................................419 462-1746
  7459 State Route 309 Galion (44833) *(G-11183)*
Surgere Inc...330 526-7971
  5399 Lauby Rd Ste 200 North Canton (44720) *(G-15236)*
Surgery and Gynecology Inc (PA).........................614 294-1603
  114r W 3rd Ave Columbus (43201) *(G-8721)*
Surgery Center, Cincinnati *Also called Christ Hospital (G-3205)*
Surgery Center Cincinnati LLC............................513 947-1130
  4415 Aicholtz Rd Cincinnati (45245) *(G-2871)*
Surgery Center Howland Ltd...............................330 609-7874
  1934 Niles Cortland Rd Ne Warren (44484) *(G-18750)*
Surgery Center, The, Cleveland *Also called Surgery Ctr An Ohio Ltd Partnr (G-6488)*
Surgery Ctr An Ohio Ltd Partnr...........................440 826-3240
  19250 Bagley Rd Cleveland (44130) *(G-6488)*
Surgi Care Ambulatory, Maumee *Also called Ohiocare Ambulatory Surgery (G-13826)*
Surgical Oncology Division, Columbus *Also called Ohio State University (G-8345)*
Surgicenter Ltd...740 522-3937
  1651 W Main St Newark (43055) *(G-15102)*
Surgicenter of Mansfield...................................419 774-9410
  1030 Cricket Ln Mansfield (44906) *(G-13247)*
Surreal Entertainment LLC.................................330 262-5277
  2018 Great Trails Dr Wooster (44691) *(G-19772)*
Susan A Smith Crystal Care...............................419 747-2666
  5375 Teeter Rd Butler (44822) *(G-2022)*
Suter Produce Inc...419 384-3665
  12200 Pandora Rd Pandora (45877) *(G-15755)*
Sutphen Corporation (PA).................................800 726-7030
  6450 Eiterman Rd Dublin (43016) *(G-10347)*
Sutton Motor Coach Tours Inc............................330 726-2800
  7338 Southern Blvd Youngstown (44512) *(G-20219)*
Suzie Roselius Real Estate, Beavercreek *Also called Big Hill Realty Corp (G-1206)*
Svh Holdings LLC..844 560-7775
  4322 N Hamilton Rd Columbus (43230) *(G-8722)*
Swa Inc..440 243-7888
  7250 Old Oak Blvd Cleveland (44130) *(G-6489)*
Swaco, Grove City *Also called Solid Waste Auth Centl Ohio (G-11471)*
Swagelok Company..440 349-5934
  31400 Aurora Rd Solon (44139) *(G-16905)*
Swagelok Company..440 542-1250
  32550 Old South Miles Rd Solon (44139) *(G-16906)*
Swan Pnte Fclty Operations LLC.........................419 867-7926
  3600 Butz Rd Maumee (43537) *(G-13858)*
Swan Point Care Center, Maumee *Also called Consulate Management Co LLC (G-13776)*
Swanton Hlth Care Rtrement Ctr.........................419 825-1145
  214 S Munson Rd Swanton (43558) *(G-17407)*
Swanton Maintenance Building, Swanton *Also called Ohio Tpk & Infrastructure Comm (G-17403)*
Swanton Vly Care Rhblttion Ctr, Swanton *Also called Harborside Healthcare Corp (G-17399)*
Swartz Contracting, Lima *Also called Swartz Enterprises Inc (G-12758)*
Swartz Enterprises Inc.....................................419 331-1024
  2622 Baty Rd Lima (45807) *(G-12758)*
Swd Corporation...419 227-2436
  435 N Main St Lima (45801) *(G-12759)*
Sweeney Chrysler Dodge Jeep, Lebanon *Also called Lebanon Chrysler - Plymouth Inc (G-12480)*
Sweeney Robert E Co Lpa...................................216 696-0606
  55 Public Sq Ste 1500 Cleveland (44113) *(G-6490)*
Sweeney Team Inc..513 934-0700
  576 Mound Ct Ste A Lebanon (45036) *(G-12508)*
Sweeney Team Inc (PA).....................................513 241-3400
  1440 Main St Cincinnati (45202) *(G-4559)*
Swift Filters Inc (PA).......................................440 735-0995
  24040 Forbes Rd Oakwood Village (44146) *(G-15494)*
Swim Incorporated..614 885-1619
  400 W Dublin Granville Rd Worthington (43085) *(G-19855)*
Swings N Things Family Fun Pk, Olmsted Twp *Also called Strike Zone Inc (G-15541)*
Swiss Tech Products, Solon *Also called Interdesign Inc (G-16861)*
Swn Communications Inc....................................877 698-3262
  6450 Poe Ave Ste 500 Dayton (45414) *(G-9803)*

Sws Environmental Services................................254 629-1718
  3820 Ventura Dr Findlay (45840) *(G-10967)*
Sws Equipment Services Inc...............................330 806-2767
  712 Palisades Dr Akron (44303) *(G-462)*
Swx Enterprises Inc...216 676-4600
  5231 Engle Rd Brookpark (44142) *(G-1907)*
Sycamore Board of Education..............................513 489-3937
  9609 Montgomery Rd Cincinnati (45242) *(G-4560)*
Sycamore Creek Country Club.............................937 748-0791
  8300 Country Club Ln Springboro (45066) *(G-16985)*
Sycamore Glen Retirement Cmnty, Miamisburg *Also called Kettering Medical Center (G-14182)*
Sycamore Hills Golf Club, Fremont *Also called Michael Brothers Inc (G-11087)*
Sycamore Lake Inc...440 729-9775
  10620 Mayfield Rd Chesterland (44026) *(G-2746)*
Sycamore Medical Center, Miamisburg *Also called Kettering Medical Center (G-14181)*
Sycamore Run Nursing, Millersburg *Also called Castle Nursing Homes Inc (G-14464)*
Sycamore Senior Center (PA)..............................513 984-1234
  4455 Carver Woods Dr Blue Ash (45242) *(G-1654)*
Sydney ASC, Piqua *Also called Valley Regional Surgery Center (G-16037)*
Sygma Network Inc..614 734-2500
  5550 Blazer Pkwy Ste 300 Dublin (43017) *(G-10348)*
Sygma Network Inc (HQ)....................................614 734-2500
  5550 Blazer Pkwy Ste 300 Dublin (43017) *(G-10349)*
Sygma Network Inc..614 771-3801
  2400 Harrison Rd Columbus (43204) *(G-8723)*
Sylvania Center, Sylvania *Also called Harborside Sylvania LLC (G-17429)*
Sylvania Community Svcs Ctr.............................419 885-2451
  4747 N Hlland Sylvania Rd Sylvania (43560) *(G-17454)*
Sylvania Country Club......................................419 392-0530
  5201 Corey Rd Sylvania (43560) *(G-17455)*
Sylvania Franciscan Health (HQ).........................419 882-8373
  1715 Indian Wood Cir # 200 Maumee (43537) *(G-13859)*
Sylvania Lighting Svcs Corp...............................440 742-8208
  35405 Spatterdock Ln Solon (44139) *(G-16907)*
Sylvania Ultrasound Institute, Toledo *Also called Stork Studios Inc (G-18049)*
Sylvania Veterinary Hospital (PA)........................419 885-4421
  4801 N Hlland Sylvania Rd Sylvania (43560) *(G-17456)*
Sylvester Materials Co......................................419 841-3874
  7901 Sylvania Ave Sylvania (43560) *(G-17457)*
Symantec Corporation......................................216 643-6700
  6100 Oak Tree Blvd Independence (44131) *(G-12127)*
Symatic Inc...330 225-1510
  2831 Center Rd Brunswick (44212) *(G-1941)*
Symcox Grinding & Steele Co..............................330 678-1080
  825 Tallmadge Rd Kent (44240) *(G-12261)*
Syneos Health LLC..513 381-5550
  441 Vine St Ste 1200 Cincinnati (45202) *(G-4561)*
Synergy Consulting Group Inc............................330 899-9301
  3700 Massillon Rd Ste 300 Uniontown (44685) *(G-18387)*
Synergy Health North Amer Inc...........................513 398-6406
  7086 Industrial Row W Mason (45040) *(G-13643)*
Synergy Healthcare Systems, Cleveland *Also called A-1 Healthcare Staffing LLC (G-4884)*
Synergy Healthcare Systems, Lakewood *Also called A-1 Healthcare Staffing LLC (G-12334)*
Synergy Homecare, Westerville *Also called Huntsey Corporation (G-19174)*
Synergy Homecare...937 610-0555
  501 Windsor Park Dr Dayton (45459) *(G-9804)*
Synergy Homecare South Dayton, Dayton *Also called Synergy Homecare (G-9804)*
Synergy Hotels LLC...614 492-9000
  4870 Old Rathmell Ct Obetz (43207) *(G-15530)*
Synnex Corporation...614 539-6995
  4001 Gantz Rd Ste A Grove City (43123) *(G-11475)*
Synoran..614 236-4014
  2389 Bryden Rd Columbus (43209) *(G-8724)*
Syntero Inc (PA)...614 889-5722
  299 Cramer Creek Ct Dublin (43017) *(G-10350)*
Synthetic Stucco Corporation............................513 897-9227
  4571 Isaac Ct Waynesville (45068) *(G-18836)*
Syracuse Water Dept..740 992-7777
  2581 3rd St Pomeroy (45769) *(G-16097)*
Sysco Central Ohio Inc......................................614 272-0658
  2400 Harrison Rd Columbus (43204) *(G-8725)*
Sysco Cincinnati LLC..513 563-6300
  10510 Evendale Dr Cincinnati (45241) *(G-4562)*
System EDM of Ohio, Mason *Also called Hi-Tek Manufacturing Inc (G-13595)*
System Optics Csmt Srgcal Arts..........................330 630-9699
  518 West Ave Tallmadge (44278) *(G-17491)*
System Optics Laser Vision Ctr..........................330 630-2451
  518 West Ave Tallmadge (44278) *(G-17492)*
System Seals Inc (HQ)......................................440 735-0200
  9505 Midwest Ave Cleveland (44125) *(G-6491)*
Systemax Manufacturing Inc..............................937 368-2300
  6450 Poe Ave Ste 200 Dayton (45414) *(G-9805)*
Systems Alternatives Intl..................................419 891-1100
  1705 Indian Wood Cir # 100 Maumee (43537) *(G-13860)*
Systems Evolution Inc......................................513 459-1992
  7870 E Kemper Rd Ste 400 Cincinnati (45249) *(G-4563)*
Systems Evolution Inc (PA)................................513 459-1992
  7870 E Kemper Rd Ste 400 Cincinnati (45249) *(G-4564)*
Systems Jay LLC Nanogate (HQ)..........................419 524-3778
  150 Longview Ave E Mansfield (44903) *(G-13248)*

2019 Harris Ohio
Services Directory

(G-0000) Company's Geographic Section entry number

Systems Jay LLC Nanogate 419 747-6639
1575 W Longview Ave Mansfield (44906) ***(G-13249)***
Systems Pack Inc 330 467-5729
649 Highland Rd E Macedonia (44056) ***(G-13083)***
Sytronics Inc 937 431-6100
4433 Dayton Xenia Rd # 1 Beavercreek (45432) ***(G-1189)***
Syvania Pediatric Dental Care, Sylvania *Also called Smile Development Inc* ***(G-17451)***
T & B Electric Ltd 740 881-5696
7464 Watkins Rd Ostrander (43061) ***(G-15656)***
T & B Transportation Inc 330 495-0316
4938 Southway St Sw Canton (44706) ***(G-2505)***
T & F Systems Inc 216 881-3525
1599 E 40th St Cleveland (44103) ***(G-6492)***
T & L Enterprises Inc 440 234-5900
1060 W Bagley Rd Ste 101 Berea (44017) ***(G-1439)***
T & L Transport Inc 330 674-0655
4395 County Road 58 Millersburg (44654) ***(G-14494)***
T & R Properties (PA) 614 923-4000
3895 Stoneridge Ln Dublin (43017) ***(G-10351)***
T & R Property Management, Dublin *Also called T & R Properties* ***(G-10351)***
T Allen Inc 440 234-2366
200 Depot St Berea (44017) ***(G-1440)***
T and D Interiors Incorporated 419 331-4372
3626 Allentown Rd Lima (45807) ***(G-12760)***
T and J Trnstnal HM For Dsbled 216 703-4673
17635 Parkmount Ave Cleveland (44135) ***(G-6493)***
T C P, Aurora *Also called Technical Consumer Pdts Inc* ***(G-844)***
T C Rumpke Waste Collection 513 385-7627
5665 Dunlap Rd Cincinnati (45252) ***(G-4565)***
T E S - East, Versailles *Also called Bnsf Logistics LLC* ***(G-18566)***
T H Winston Company 513 271-2123
4817 Glenshade Ave Cincinnati (45227) ***(G-4566)***
T J Automation Inc 419 267-5687
U075 State Route 66 Archbold (43502) ***(G-641)***
T J D Industrial Clg & Maint 419 425-5025
12340 Township Road 109 Findlay (45840) ***(G-10968)***
T J Ellis Enterprises Inc (PA) 419 999-5026
1505 Neubrecht Rd Lima (45801) ***(G-12761)***
T J Neff Holdings Inc 440 884-3100
6405 York Rd Cleveland (44130) ***(G-6494)***
T J Williams Electric Co 513 738-5366
7925 New Haven Rd Harrison (45030) ***(G-11677)***
T K Edwards LLC 614 406-8064
782 N High St Columbus (43215) ***(G-8726)***
T K Holdings, Piqua *Also called Tk Holdings Inc* ***(G-16031)***
T L C Child Development Center 330 655-2797
187 Ravenna St Hudson (44236) ***(G-12008)***
T L C Landscaping Inc 440 248-4852
38000 Aurora Rd Cleveland (44139) ***(G-6495)***
T L Express, Mantua *Also called Triple Ladys Agency Inc* ***(G-13277)***
T M C Systems LLC 440 740-1234
7655 Town Centre Dr Broadview Heights (44147) ***(G-1847)***
T M I, Columbus *Also called Team Management Inc* ***(G-8735)***
T M R, Brunswick *Also called Total Marketing Resources LLC* ***(G-1943)***
T M S, Cincinnati *Also called Modal Shop Inc* ***(G-4067)***
T N C Construction Inc 614 554-5330
6058 Winnebago St Grove City (43123) ***(G-11476)***
T N C Recovery and Maintenance, Grove City *Also called T N C Construction Inc* ***(G-11476)***
T O J Inc (PA) 440 352-1900
6011 Heisley Rd Mentor (44060) ***(G-14114)***
T P McHncal Cntrs Svc Fbrction, Columbus *Also called TP Mechanical Contractors Inc* ***(G-8768)***
T R L Inc 330 448-4071
3500 Parkway Dr Brookfield (44403) ***(G-1856)***
T W I International Inc (HQ) 440 439-1830
24460 Aurora Rd Cleveland (44146) ***(G-6496)***
T W Ruff, Columbus *Also called Loth Inc* ***(G-7989)***
T X I, Greenville *Also called Telecom Expertise Inds Inc* ***(G-11397)***
T&B Manufacturing, Miamiville *Also called Aim Mro Holdings Inc* ***(G-14244)***
T&L Global Management LLC 614 586-0303
1572 Lafayette Dr Columbus (43220) ***(G-8727)***
T&T Enterprises of Ohio Inc 513 942-1141
5100 Duff Dr West Chester (45246) ***(G-19088)***
T-Cetra LLC 877 956-2359
7240 Muirfield Dr Ste 200 Dublin (43017) ***(G-10352)***
T-Shirt City, Cincinnati *Also called TSC Apparel LLC* ***(G-4651)***
T/R Rsdntial Care Fclities Inc 740 754-2600
507 Main St Dresden (43821) ***(G-10116)***
Ta Operating LLC (HQ) 440 808-9100
24601 Center Ridge Rd # 200 Westlake (44145) ***(G-19411)***
Tab Construction Company Inc 330 454-5228
530 Walnut Ave Ne Canton (44702) ***(G-2506)***
Table Rock Golf Club Inc 740 625-6859
3005 Wilson Rd Centerburg (43011) ***(G-2617)***
TAC Enterprises, Springfield *Also called TAC Industries Inc* ***(G-17123)***
TAC Industries Inc (PA) 937 328-5200
2160 Old Selma Rd Springfield (45505) ***(G-17123)***
TAC Industries Inc 937 328-5200
2160 Old Selma Rd Springfield (45505) ***(G-17124)***
Tacg LLC (PA) 937 203-8201
1430 Oak Ct Ste 100 Beavercreek (45430) ***(G-1237)***
Tack-Anew Inc 419 734-4212
451 W Lakeshore Dr Port Clinton (43452) ***(G-16119)***
Tafaro John 513 381-0656
1 W 4th St Ste 800 Cincinnati (45202) ***(G-4567)***
Taft Law, Dayton *Also called Nicholas E Davis* ***(G-9657)***
Taft Museum, Cincinnati *Also called Cincinnati Institute Fine Arts* ***(G-3252)***
Taft Museum of Art 513 241-0343
316 Pike St Cincinnati (45202) ***(G-4568)***
Taft Stettinius Hollister LLP (PA) 513 381-2838
425 Walnut St Ste 1800 Cincinnati (45202) ***(G-4569)***
Taft Stettinius Hollister LLP 614 221-4000
65 E State St Ste 1000 Columbus (43215) ***(G-8728)***
Taft Stettinius Hollister LLP 216 241-3141
200 Public Sq Ste 3500 Cleveland (44114) ***(G-6497)***
Tahoma Enterprises Inc (PA) 330 745-9016
255 Wooster Rd N Barberton (44203) ***(G-969)***
Tahoma Rubber & Plastics Inc (HQ) 330 745-9016
255 Wooster Rd N Barberton (44203) ***(G-970)***
Tailored Healthcare Staffing, Cincinnati *Also called Health Carousel LLC* ***(G-3693)***
Tailored Management Services (PA) 614 859-1500
1165 Dublin Rd Columbus (43215) ***(G-8729)***
Takkt America Holding Inc (PA) 513 367-8600
9555 Dry Fork Rd Harrison (45030) ***(G-11678)***
Talbert House 513 541-0127
3129 Spring Grove Ave Cincinnati (45225) ***(G-4570)***
Talbert House 513 751-7747
5837 Hamilton Ave Cincinnati (45224) ***(G-4571)***
Talbert House 513 541-1184
1611 Emerson Ave Cincinnati (45239) ***(G-4572)***
Talbert House (PA) 513 872-5863
2600 Victory Pkwy Cincinnati (45206) ***(G-4573)***
Talbert House 513 684-7968
328 Mcgregor Ave Ste 106 Cincinnati (45219) ***(G-4574)***
Talbert House 513 933-9304
5234 W State Route 63 Lebanon (45036) ***(G-12509)***
Talbert House Health (HQ) 513 541-7577
4868 Glenway Ave Cincinnati (45238) ***(G-4575)***
Talemed LLC 513 774-7300
6279 Tri Ridge Blvd # 110 Loveland (45140) ***(G-13031)***
Talentlaunch, Independence *Also called Alliance Solutions Group LLC* ***(G-12044)***
Taleris Credit Union Inc 216 739-2300
6111 Oak Tree Blvd # 110 Independence (44131) ***(G-12128)***
Tallmadge Asphalt & Pav Co Inc 330 677-0000
741 Tallmadge Rd Kent (44240) ***(G-12262)***
Tallmadge Board of Education 330 633-2215
89 W Overdale Dr Tallmadge (44278) ***(G-17493)***
Tallmadge Collision Center (PA) 330 630-2188
195 Northeast Ave Tallmadge (44278) ***(G-17494)***
Tallmadge Schools Bus Garage, Tallmadge *Also called Tallmadge Board of Education* ***(G-17493)***
Talmage N Porter MD 937 435-9013
979 Congress Park Dr Dayton (45459) ***(G-9806)***
Talmer Bank and Trust 330 726-3396
2 S Broad St Canfield (44406) ***(G-2159)***
Talon Title Agency LLC (PA) 614 818-0500
570 Polaris Pkwy Ste 140 Westerville (43082) ***(G-19213)***
Talx Corporation 614 527-9404
3455 Mill Run Dr Hilliard (43026) ***(G-11819)***
Tam-O-Shanter Sports Complex, Sylvania *Also called City of Sylvania* ***(G-17415)***
Tamaron Country Club, Toledo *Also called Tamaron Golf LLC* ***(G-18058)***
Tamaron Golf LLC 419 474-5067
2162 W Alexis Rd Toledo (43613) ***(G-18058)***
Tamer Win Golf & Country Club, Cortland *Also called Win Tamer Corporation* ***(G-8996)***
Tameran Graphic Systems Inc 440 349-7100
30300 Solon Ind Pkwy F Solon (44139) ***(G-16908)***
Tan Products 513 288-9264
406 Dexter Ave Cincinnati (45215) ***(G-4576)***
Tangoe Us Inc 614 842-9918
200 E Campus View Blvd Columbus (43235) ***(G-8730)***
Tank Leasing Corp 330 339-3333
2743 Brightwood Rd Se New Philadelphia (44663) ***(G-14984)***
Tank Services Company, Dennison *Also called Ionno Properties s Corp* ***(G-10051)***
Tanner Heating & AC Inc 937 299-2500
2238 E River Rd Moraine (45439) ***(G-14701)***
Tanos Salon 216 831-7880
24225 Chagrin Blvd Cleveland (44122) ***(G-6498)***
Tansky Honda, Zanesville *Also called Man-Tansky Inc* ***(G-20328)***
Tansky Motors Inc (PA) 650 322-7069
297 E Main St Logan (43138) ***(G-12855)***
Tape Products Company (PA) 513 489-8840
11630 Deerfield Rd Cincinnati (45242) ***(G-4577)***
Tappan Lake Marina Inc 740 269-2031
33315 Cadiz Dennison Rd Scio (43988) ***(G-16664)***
Tappan Marina, Scio *Also called Tappan Lake Marina Inc* ***(G-16664)***
Tara Flaherty 419 565-1334
1872 White Pine Dr Mansfield (44904) ***(G-13250)***
Taragon Advisors, Cleveland *Also called Real Estate Capital Fund LLC* ***(G-6290)***
Target Auto Body Inc 216 391-1942
5005 Carnegie Ave Cleveland (44103) ***(G-6499)***

ALPHABETIC

Target Corporation 614 801-6700
  1 Walker Way West Jefferson (43162) *(G-19112)*
Target Stores Inc 614 279-4224
  3720 Soldano Blvd Columbus (43228) *(G-8731)*
Target Trans-Logic, Austintown *Also called 44444 LLC (G-855)*
Tarrier Foods Corp 614 876-8594
  2700 International St # 100 Columbus (43228) *(G-8732)*
Tarry House Inc 330 253-6689
  564 Diagonal Rd Akron (44320) *(G-463)*
Tarsec, Columbus *Also called Norfolk Southern Corporation (G-8193)*
Tarta, Toledo *Also called Toledo Area Rgional Trnst Auth (G-18074)*
Tartan Fields Golf Club Ltd 614 792-0900
  8070 Tartan Fields Dr Dublin (43017) *(G-10353)*
Tasc New Town LLC 419 242-9955
  701 Jefferson Ave Ste 101 Toledo (43604) *(G-18059)*
Tasc of Northwest Ohio Inc (PA) 419 242-9955
  701 Jefferson Ave Ste 101 Toledo (43604) *(G-18060)*
Tasc of Southeast Ohio 740 594-2276
  86 Columbus Rd Athens (45701) *(G-805)*
Tasco Inc Ohio, Cleveland *Also called Telemessaging Services Inc (G-6509)*
Tasty Pure Food Company (PA) 330 434-8141
  1557 Industrial Pkwy Akron (44310) *(G-464)*
Tata America Intl Corp 513 677-6500
  1000 Summit Dr Unit 1 Milford (45150) *(G-14435)*
Tata Consultancy Services, Milford *Also called Tata America Intl Corp (G-14435)*
Tata Steel Plating, Warren *Also called Thomas Steel Strip Corporation (G-18751)*
Tatman, Harold & Sons, Kingston *Also called Harold Tatman & Sons Entps Inc (G-12315)*
Taussig Cancer Center 866 223-8100
  10201 Carnegie Ave Cleveland (44106) *(G-6500)*
Tax Department, Coldwater *Also called Village of Coldwater (G-6767)*
Taylor - Winfield Corporation 330 797-0300
  3200 Innovation Pl Youngstown (44509) *(G-20220)*
Taylor Chevrolet Inc 740 653-2091
  2510 N Memorial Dr Lancaster (43130) *(G-12440)*
Taylor Construction Company 330 628-9310
  1532 State Route 43 Mogadore (44260) *(G-14556)*
Taylor Corporation 419 420-0790
  1920 Breckenridge Rd # 110 Findlay (45840) *(G-10969)*
Taylor Dealership, Lancaster *Also called Taylor Chevrolet Inc (G-12440)*
Taylor Distributing Company 513 771-1850
  9756 International Blvd West Chester (45246) *(G-19089)*
Taylor House, Findlay *Also called Taylor Corporation (G-10969)*
Taylor Logistics Inc (PA) 513 771-1850
  9756 International Blvd West Chester (45246) *(G-19090)*
Taylor Made Graphics 440 882-6318
  7921 Hollenbeck Cir Cleveland (44129) *(G-6501)*
Taylor Murtis Human Svcs Sys 216 283-4400
  12395 Mccracken Rd Cleveland (44125) *(G-6502)*
Taylor Murtis Human Svcs Sys (PA) 216 283-4400
  13422 Kinsman Rd Cleveland (44120) *(G-6503)*
Taylor Murtis Human Svcs Sys 216 281-7192
  3167 Fulton Rd Cleveland (44109) *(G-6504)*
Taylor Murtis Human Svcs Sys 216 283-4400
  16005 Terrace Rd Cleveland (44112) *(G-6505)*
Taylor Stn Surgical Ctr Ltd 614 751-4466
  275 Taylor Station Rd Ab Columbus (43213) *(G-8733)*
Taylor Telecommunications Inc 330 628-5501
  3470 Gilchrist Rd Mogadore (44260) *(G-14557)*
Taylor Warehouse Corporation 513 771-2956
  9756 International Blvd West Chester (45246) *(G-19091)*
Taylors Staffing LLC 740 446-3305
  37817 State Route 124 Pomeroy (45769) *(G-16098)*
Tazmanian Freight Fwdg Inc (PA) 216 265-7881
  6640 Engle Rd Ste A Middleburg Heights (44130) *(G-14260)*
Tazmanian Freight Systems, Middleburg Heights *Also called Tazmanian Freight Fwdg Inc (G-14260)*
Tbn Acquisition LLC 740 653-2091
  2480 N Memorial Dr Lancaster (43130) *(G-12441)*
TCI, Cincinnati *Also called Technical Consultants Inc (G-4579)*
Tcn Behavioral Health Svcs Inc (PA) 937 376-8700
  452 W Market St Xenia (45385) *(G-19927)*
TCS, Cincinnati *Also called Trans-Continental Systems Inc (G-4626)*
Tdg Facilities LLC 513 834-6105
  6819 Ashfield Dr Blue Ash (45242) *(G-1655)*
Tdk Refrigeration Leasing, Delphos *Also called All Temp Refrigeration Inc (G-10019)*
TDS Document Management Ltd 614 367-9633
  161 Jackson St Columbus (43206) *(G-8734)*
Teac, Columbus *Also called Turtles Envmtl Abatement Co (G-8790)*
Team Green Lawn LLC 937 673-4315
  1070 Union Rd Xenia (45385) *(G-19928)*
Team Industrial Services Inc 440 498-9494
  5901 Harper Rd Cleveland (44139) *(G-6506)*
Team Management Inc 614 486-0864
  2018 N 4th St Columbus (43201) *(G-8735)*
Team NEO 216 363-5400
  1111 Superior Ave E # 1600 Cleveland (44114) *(G-6507)*
Team Rahal Inc 614 529-7000
  4601 Lyman Dr Hilliard (43026) *(G-11820)*
Team Rahal of Dayton Inc (PA) 937 438-3800
  8111 Yankee St Dayton (45458) *(G-9807)*

Teasdale Fenton Carpet Cleanin 513 797-0900
  12145 Centron Pl Cincinnati (45246) *(G-4578)*
Teater Orthopedic Surgeons 330 343-3335
  515 Union Ave Ste 167 Dover (44622) *(G-10103)*
Tebo Financial Services Inc 234 207-2500
  4740 Belpar St Nw Ste A Canton (44718) *(G-2507)*
TEC Engineering Inc (PA) 513 771-8828
  7288 Central Parke Blvd Mason (45040) *(G-13644)*
Tech Center Inc 330 762-6212
  265 S Main St Ste 200 Akron (44308) *(G-465)*
Tech International, Johnstown *Also called Technical Rubber Company Inc (G-12204)*
Tech Mahindra (americas) Inc 216 912-2002
  200 W Prospect Ave Cleveland (44113) *(G-6508)*
Tech Pro Inc 330 923-3546
  3030 Gilchrist Rd Akron (44305) *(G-466)*
Tech Products Corporation (HQ) 937 438-1100
  2215 Lyons Rd Miamisburg (45342) *(G-14227)*
Techdisposal, Reynoldsburg *Also called Datacomm Tech (G-16296)*
Techncal Sltons Specialists Inc 513 792-8930
  4250 Creek Rd Blue Ash (45241) *(G-1656)*
Technical Assurance Inc 440 953-3147
  38112 2nd St Willoughby (44094) *(G-19575)*
Technical Construction Spc 330 929-1088
  3341 Cavalier Trl Cuyahoga Falls (44224) *(G-9129)*
Technical Consultants Inc 513 521-2696
  8228 Winton Rd Ste 200a Cincinnati (45231) *(G-4579)*
Technical Consumer Pdts Inc 800 324-1496
  325 Campus Dr Aurora (44202) *(G-844)*
Technical Rubber Company Inc (PA) 740 967-9015
  200 E Coshocton St Johnstown (43031) *(G-12204)*
Technicolor Entertainment Svcs, Wilmington *Also called Technicolor Thomson Group (G-19651)*
Technicolor Thomson Group 937 383-6000
  3418 Progress Way Wilmington (45177) *(G-19651)*
Technology House Ltd (PA) 440 248-3025
  10036 Aurora Hudson Rd Streetsboro (44241) *(G-17274)*
Technology Hub, Columbus *Also called Km2 Solutions LLC (G-7913)*
Technology Recovery Group Ltd (PA) 440 250-9970
  31390 Viking Pkwy Westlake (44145) *(G-19412)*
Techsoft Systems Inc 513 772-5010
  10296 Springfield Pike Cincinnati (45215) *(G-4580)*
Techsolve Inc 513 948-2000
  6705 Steger Dr Cincinnati (45237) *(G-4581)*
Tecta America Corp 419 447-1716
  1480 S County Road 594 Tiffin (44883) *(G-17541)*
Tecta America Zero Company LLC (HQ) 513 541-1848
  6225 Wiehe Rd Cincinnati (45237) *(G-4582)*
Ted Graham 740 223-3509
  3007 Harding Hwy E Marion (43302) *(G-13463)*
Ted Ruck Co Inc 419 738-2613
  101 N Wood St Wapakoneta (45895) *(G-18655)*
Tegam Inc (PA) 440 466-6100
  10 Tegam Way Geneva (44041) *(G-11246)*
Tegna Inc 419 248-1111
  730 N Summit St Toledo (43604) *(G-18061)*
Tek Systems 614 789-6200
  5115 Prkcnter Ave Ste 170 Dublin (43017) *(G-10354)*
Tek-Collect Incorporated 614 299-2766
  871 Park St Columbus (43215) *(G-8736)*
Tekmar-Dohrmann, Mason *Also called Teledyne Tekmar Company (G-13646)*
Tekni-Plex Inc 419 491-2399
  1445 Timber Wolf Dr Holland (43528) *(G-11918)*
Teknobility LLC 216 255-9433
  3013 Gary Kyle Ct Medina (44256) *(G-14009)*
Teknol Inc (PA) 937 264-0190
  5751 Webster St Dayton (45414) *(G-9808)*
Teksystems Inc 216 606-3600
  5990 W Creek Rd Ste 175 Independence (44131) *(G-12129)*
Teksystems Inc 513 719-3950
  3825 Edwards Rd Ste 500 Cincinnati (45209) *(G-4583)*
Teksystems 611, Cincinnati *Also called Teksystems Inc (G-4583)*
Telamon Corporation 937 254-2004
  600 N Irwin St Dayton (45403) *(G-9809)*
Telarc International Corp (PA) 216 464-2313
  23412 Commerce Park Beachwood (44122) *(G-1111)*
Telcom Construction Svcs Inc 330 239-6900
  5067 Paramount Dr Medina (44256) *(G-14010)*
Tele-Solutions Inc (PA) 330 782-2888
  6001 Suthern Blvd Ste 102 Youngstown (44512) *(G-20221)*
Tele-Vac Environmental, Mason *Also called J and J Environmental Inc (G-13602)*
Telecmmnctons Stffing Slutions 614 799-9300
  8191 Glencree Pl Dublin (43016) *(G-10355)*
Telecom Expertise Inds Inc (PA) 937 548-5254
  5879 Jysville St Johns Rd Greenville (45331) *(G-11397)*
Teledyne Instruments Inc 513 229-7000
  4736 Scialville Foster Rd Mason (45040) *(G-13645)*
Teledyne Tekmar, Mason *Also called Teledyne Instruments Inc (G-13645)*
Teledyne Tekmar Company (HQ) 513 229-7000
  4736 Scialville Foster Rd Mason (45040) *(G-13646)*
Telemessaging Services Inc 440 845-5400
  7441 W Ridgewood Dr # 130 Cleveland (44129) *(G-6509)*
Telepage Communication Systems, Marietta *Also called Twin Comm Inc (G-13390)*

Teleperformance USA, Akron *Also called Tpusa Inc* ***(G-472)***
Teleperformance USA, Columbus *Also called Tpusa Inc* ***(G-8769)***
Telephone & Cmpt Contrs Inc....419 726-8142
5560 308th St Toledo (43611) ***(G-18062)***
Telephone Service Company, Wapakoneta *Also called TSC Communications Inc* ***(G-18657)***
Telephony & Data Solutions, Dublin *Also called Microman Inc* ***(G-10280)***
Teletronic Services Inc (PA)....216 778-6500
22550 Ascoa Ct Strongsville (44149) ***(G-17351)***
Teletronics Communications, Strongsville *Also called Teletronic Services Inc* ***(G-17351)***
Telhio Credit Union Inc (PA)....614 221-3233
96 N 4th St Columbus (43215) ***(G-8737)***
Telhio Credit Union Inc....614 221-3233
201 Outerbelt St Columbus (43213) ***(G-8738)***
Telinx Solutions LLC....330 819-0657
961 Mallet Hill Ct Medina (44256) ***(G-14011)***
Telligen Tech Inc....614 934-1554
2740 Airport Dr Ste 190 Columbus (43219) ***(G-8739)***
Tembec Btlsr Inc....419 244-5856
2112 Sylvan Ave Toledo (43606) ***(G-18063)***
Tems, Toronto *Also called Toronto Emergency Medical Svc* ***(G-18186)***
Ten Thousand Villages Cleveland....216 575-1058
12425 Cedar Rd Cleveland (44106) ***(G-6510)***
Tenable Protective Svcs Inc (PA)....216 361-0002
2423 Payne Ave Cleveland (44114) ***(G-6511)***
Tenable Protective Svcs Inc....513 741-3560
5643 Cheviot Rd Ste 5 Cincinnati (45247) ***(G-4584)***
Tender Mercies Inc (PA)....513 721-8666
27 W 12th St Cincinnati (45202) ***(G-4585)***
Tender Nursing Care....614 856-3508
7668 Slate Ridge Blvd Reynoldsburg (43068) ***(G-16332)***
Tendon Manufacturing Inc....216 663-3200
20805 Aurora Rd Cleveland (44146) ***(G-6512)***
Tenk Machine, Strongsville *Also called Cleveland Jsm Inc* ***(G-17291)***
Tennis Unlimited Inc....330 928-8763
2108 Akron Peninsula Rd Akron (44313) ***(G-467)***
Tensile Tsting Mtllurgical Lab, Cleveland *Also called J T Adams Co* ***(G-5773)***
Teradata Operations Inc (HQ)....937 242-4030
10000 Innovation Dr Miamisburg (45342) ***(G-14228)***
Terence Isakov MD....440 449-1014
5187 Mayfield Rd Ste 102 Cleveland (44124) ***(G-6513)***
Terex Utilities Inc....614 444-7373
110 Venture Dr Etna (43062) ***(G-10620)***
Terex Utilities Inc....937 293-6526
4401 Gateway Blvd Springfield (45502) ***(G-17125)***
Terex Utilities Inc....513 539-9770
920 Deneen Ave Monroe (45050) ***(G-14584)***
Terik Roofing Inc....330 785-0060
72 Hanna Pkwy Coventry Township (44319) ***(G-9044)***
Terminal Ready-Mix Inc....440 288-0181
524 Colorado Ave Lorain (44052) ***(G-12947)***
Terminal Warehouse Inc (HQ)....330 773-2056
2207 Kimball Rd Se Canton (44707) ***(G-2508)***
Terminix Intl Co Ltd Partnr....513 942-6670
4305 Muhlhauser Rd Ste 2 Fairfield (45014) ***(G-10789)***
Terminix Intl Co Ltd Partnr....216 518-1091
5350 Transportation Blvd Cleveland (44125) ***(G-6514)***
Terminix Intl Co Ltd Partnr....419 868-8290
6541 Weatherfield Ct Maumee (43537) ***(G-13861)***
Terminix Intl Co Ltd Partnr....513 539-7846
4455 Salman Rd Middletown (45044) ***(G-14335)***
Terminix Intl Co Ltd Partnr....978 744-2402
2680 Roberts Ave Nw Ste A Canton (44709) ***(G-2509)***
Terminix Intl Coml Xenia....513 539-7846
4455 Salzman Rd Middletown (45044) ***(G-14336)***
Terra Star Inc....405 200-1336
111 N Main St Waynesburg (44688) ***(G-18830)***
Terrace Construction Co Inc....216 739-3170
3965 Pearl Rd Cleveland (44109) ***(G-6515)***
Terrace Park Country Club Inc....513 965-4061
5341 S Milford Rd Milford (45150) ***(G-14436)***
Terracon Consultants Inc....513 321-5816
611 Lunken Park Dr Cincinnati (45226) ***(G-4586)***
Terracon Consultants Inc....614 863-3113
800 Morrison Rd Gahanna (43230) ***(G-11150)***
Terracon Consultants N1, Cincinnati *Also called Terracon Consultants Inc* ***(G-4586)***
Terracon Consultants N4, Gahanna *Also called Terracon Consultants Inc* ***(G-11150)***
Terrafirm Construction LLC....913 433-2998
250 N Hartford Ave Columbus (43222) ***(G-8740)***
Terre Forme Enterprises Inc....330 847-6800
3000 Austintown Warren Rd Mineral Ridge (44440) ***(G-14513)***
Terry Asphalt Materials Inc (HQ)....513 874-6192
8600 Bilstein Blvd Hamilton (45015) ***(G-11646)***
Terry J Reppa & Associates....440 888-8533
7029 Pearl Rd Ste 350 Cleveland (44130) ***(G-6516)***
Tersher Corporation....440 439-8383
17000 Foltz Pkwy Strongsville (44149) ***(G-17352)***
Tersigni Cargill Entps LLC....330 351-0942
4315 Hudson Dr Stow (44224) ***(G-17235)***
Tesar Industrial Contrs Inc (PA)....216 741-8008
3920 Jennings Rd Cleveland (44109) ***(G-6517)***
Tesco-Transportion Eqp Sls....419 836-2835
6401 Seaman Rd Oregon (43616) ***(G-15610)***
Test America, North Canton *Also called Emlab P&K LLC* ***(G-15199)***
Testa Enterprises Inc....330 926-9060
2335 2nd St Ste A Cuyahoga Falls (44221) ***(G-9130)***
Testamerica Laboratories Inc (HQ)....800 456-9396
4101 Shuffel St Nw # 100 North Canton (44720) ***(G-15237)***
Testamerica Laboratories Inc....513 733-5700
11416 Reading Rd Cincinnati (45241) ***(G-4587)***
Testamerica Laboratories Inc....937 294-6856
2017 Springboro W Moraine (45439) ***(G-14702)***
Testing and Inspection Fcilty, Troy *Also called Public Safety Ohio Department* ***(G-18222)***
Tetra Tech Inc....513 251-2730
250 W Court St Ste 200w Cincinnati (45202) ***(G-4588)***
Teva Womens Health Inc (HQ)....513 731-9900
5040 Duramed Rd Cincinnati (45213) ***(G-4589)***
Texas Eastern Transmission LP....513 932-1816
1157 W State Route 122 Lebanon (45036) ***(G-12510)***
Texas Infusion Partners, Cincinnati *Also called Infusion Partners Inc* ***(G-3761)***
Texo International Inc....513 731-6350
2828 Highland Ave Norwood (45212) ***(G-15463)***
Tfh-Eb Inc....614 253-7246
550 Schrock Rd Columbus (43229) ***(G-8741)***
Tfi Transportation Inc....330 332-4655
10370 W South Range Rd Salem (44460) ***(G-16564)***
Tgs International Inc....330 893-4828
4464 State Route 39 Millersburg (44654) ***(G-14495)***
TH Martin Inc....216 741-2020
8500 Brookpark Rd Cleveland (44129) ***(G-6518)***
Tharaldson Hospitality MGT....513 947-9402
4521 Eastgate Blvd Cincinnati (45245) ***(G-2872)***
Thayer Power & Comm Line, Pataskala *Also called Thayer Pwr Comm Line Cnstr LLC* ***(G-15788)***
Thayer Pwr Comm Line Cnstr LLC....330 922-4950
3432 State Rd Cuyahoga Falls (44223) ***(G-9131)***
Thayer Pwr Comm Line Cnstr LLC (PA)....740 927-0021
12345 Worthington Rd Nw Pataskala (43062) ***(G-15788)***
The Abbewood, Elyria *Also called Abbewood Limited Partnership* ***(G-10476)***
The Anter Brothers Company (PA)....216 252-4555
12501 Elmwood Ave Cleveland (44111) ***(G-6519)***
The Boys and Girls Club of (PA)....330 773-3375
889 Jonathan Ave Akron (44306) ***(G-468)***
The C-Z Company (PA)....740 432-6334
201 Wheeling Ave Cambridge (43725) ***(G-2085)***
The Cadle Company (PA)....330 872-0918
100 N Center St Newton Falls (44444) ***(G-15141)***
The Cincinnati Cordage Ppr Co....513 242-3600
800 E Ross Ave Cincinnati (45217) ***(G-4590)***
The Cleveland-Cliffs Iron Co....216 694-5700
1100 Superior Ave E # 1500 Cleveland (44114) ***(G-6520)***
The Columbia Oil Co....513 868-8700
4951 Hmlton Middletown Rd Liberty Twp (45011) ***(G-12589)***
The Cortland Sav & Bnkg Co (HQ)....330 637-8040
194 W Main St Cortland (44410) ***(G-8994)***
The Cottingham Paper Co....614 294-6444
324 E 2nd Ave Columbus (43201) ***(G-8742)***
The Daimler Group Inc....614 488-4424
1533 Lake Shore Dr Columbus (43204) ***(G-8743)***
The Famous Manufacturing Co....330 762-9621
2620 Ridgewood Rd Ste 200 Akron (44313) ***(G-469)***
The First Central National Bnk (PA)....937 663-4186
103 S Springfield St Saint Paris (43072) ***(G-16534)***
The Foodbank Inc....937 461-0265
56 Armor Pl Dayton (45417) ***(G-9810)***
The For Cincinnati Association (PA)....513 744-3344
650 Walnut St Cincinnati (45202) ***(G-4591)***
The For National Association....937 470-1059
4215 Breezewood Ave Dayton (45406) ***(G-9811)***
The Fountain On The Greens, Cleveland *Also called Greens of Lyndhurst The Inc* ***(G-5643)***
The Good Shepherd, Ashland *Also called Good Shepherd Home For Aged* ***(G-673)***
The Healthcare Connection Inc (PA)....513 588-3623
1401 Steffen Ave Cincinnati (45215) ***(G-4592)***
The Huntington Investment Co (HQ)....614 480-3600
41 S High St Fl 7 Columbus (43215) ***(G-8744)***
The Huntington Investment Co....513 351-2555
525 Vine St Ste 2100 Cincinnati (45202) ***(G-4593)***
The In Cincinnati Playhouse....513 421-3888
962 Mount Adams Cir Cincinnati (45202) ***(G-4594)***
The Interlake Steamship Co....440 260-6900
7300 Engle Rd Middleburg Heights (44130) ***(G-14261)***
The Liberty Nat Bankof Ada....419 673-1217
100 E Franklin St Kenton (43326) ***(G-12288)***
The Mahoning Valley Sani Dst....330 799-6315
1181 Ohltown Mcdonald Rd Mineral Ridge (44440) ***(G-14514)***
The Maids....440 735-6243
23480 Aurora Rd Ste 1 Bedford Heights (44146) ***(G-1328)***
The Mansfield Strl & Erct Co (PA)....419 522-5911
429 Park Ave E Mansfield (44905) ***(G-13251)***
The Maple City Ice Company (PA)....419 668-2531
371 Cleveland Rd Norwalk (44857) ***(G-15457)***
The Maple City Ice Company....419 747-4777
1245 W Longview Ave Mansfield (44906) ***(G-13252)***
The Maria-Joseph Center....937 278-2692
4830 Salem Ave Dayton (45416) ***(G-9812)***

ALPHABETIC

The Mau-Sherwood Supply Co (PA) 330 405-1200
  8400 Darrow Rd Ste 1 Twinsburg (44087) *(G-18326)*
The Middlefield Banking Co (HQ) 440 632-1666
  15985 E High St Middlefield (44062) *(G-14277)*
The Nature Conservancy 614 717-2770
  6375 Riverside Dr Ste 100 Dublin (43017) *(G-10356)*
The Oaks Lodge 330 769-2601
  5878 Longacre Ln Chippewa Lake (44215) *(G-2838)*
The Pavilion, Sidney Also called Shelby County Mem Hosp Assn *(G-16798)*
The Peck-Hannaford Briggs Co (PA) 513 681-4600
  4670 Chester Ave Cincinnati (45232) *(G-4595)*
The Peoples Bank Co Inc (PA) 419 678-2385
  112 W Main St 114 Coldwater (45828) *(G-6765)*
The Peoples Bank Co Inc 419 678-2385
  112 W Main St Coldwater (45828) *(G-6766)*
The Peoples Savings and Ln Co (PA) 937 653-1600
  10 Monument Sq Urbana (43078) *(G-18445)*
The Sheakley Group Inc (PA) 513 771-2277
  1 Sheakley Way Ste 100 Cincinnati (45246) *(G-4596)*
The Surgery Center, Cleveland Also called HCA Holdings Inc *(G-5669)*
The Villa At Lake MGT Co 440 599-1999
  48 Parrish Rd Ofc Conneaut (44030) *(G-8960)*
Theatre Management Corporation 513 723-1180
  125 E Court St Ste 1000 Cincinnati (45202) *(G-4597)*
Thelen Associates Inc 513 825-4350
  1780 Carillion Blvd Cincinnati (45240) *(G-4598)*
Theodore C Rumpke, Cincinnati Also called T C Rumpke Waste Collection *(G-4565)*
Therapy In Motion LLC 216 459-2846
  5000 Rockside Rd Ste 500 Independence (44131) *(G-12130)*
Therapy Support Inc 513 469-6999
  4351 Creek Rd Blue Ash (45241) *(G-1657)*
Theratrust 740 345-7688
  23 Forry St Newark (43055) *(G-15103)*
Thermal Solutions Inc 513 742-2836
  9491 Seward Rd Fairfield (45014) *(G-10790)*
Thermal Solutions Inc 740 886-2861
  9329 County Road 107 Proctorville (45669) *(G-16220)*
Thermal Treatment Center Inc (HQ) 216 881-8100
  1101 E 55th St Cleveland (44103) *(G-6521)*
Thermaltech Engineering Inc (PA) 513 561-2271
  3960 Red Bank Rd Ste 250 Cincinnati (45227) *(G-4599)*
Thermo Fisher Scientific Inc 800 871-8909
  1 Thermo Fisher Way Oakwood Village (44146) *(G-15495)*
Thermo King, Cincinnati Also called Transport Specialists Inc *(G-4628)*
Thermo-TEC Insulation Inc 216 663-3842
  1415 E 222nd St Euclid (44117) *(G-10659)*
Thiels Replacement Systems Inc 419 289-6139
  419 E 8th St Ashland (44805) *(G-694)*
Things Remembered, Highland Heights Also called Enesco Properties LLC *(G-11733)*
Think Patented, Miamisburg Also called Patented Acquisition Corp *(G-14203)*
THINK TV, Dayton Also called Greater Dayton Public TV *(G-9472)*
Think-Ability LLC 419 589-2238
  1256 Warner Ave Mansfield (44905) *(G-13253)*
Thinkpath Engineering Svcs LLC (PA) 937 291-8374
  9080 Springboro Pike # 300 Miamisburg (45342) *(G-14229)*
Thinktv Network 937 220-1600
  110 S Jefferson St Dayton (45402) *(G-9813)*
Thinkware Incorporated 513 598-3300
  7611 Cheviot Rd Ste 2 Cincinnati (45247) *(G-4600)*
Third Dimension Inc (PA) 877 926-3223
  633 Pleasant Ave Geneva (44041) *(G-11247)*
Third Federal Savings (HQ) 800 844-7333
  7007 Broadway Ave Cleveland (44105) *(G-6522)*
Third Federal Savings 440 885-4900
  5950 Ridge Rd Cleveland (44129) *(G-6523)*
Third Federal Savings 440 716-1865
  26949 Lorain Rd North Olmsted (44070) *(G-15314)*
Third Federal Savings 440 843-6300
  6849 Pearl Rd Cleveland (44130) *(G-6524)*
Third Federal Savings & Loan, Cleveland Also called Third Federal Savings *(G-6524)*
Third Savings, Piqua Also called Unity National Bank *(G-16033)*
Thirty-One Gifts LLC (PA) 614 414-4300
  3425 Morse Xing Columbus (43219) *(G-8745)*
Thistledown Inc 216 662-8600
  21501 Emery Rd Cleveland (44128) *(G-6525)*
Thistledown Racetrack, Cleveland Also called Thistledown Inc *(G-6525)*
Thoman Weil Moving & Stor Co 513 251-5000
  5151 Fischer Ave Cincinnati (45217) *(G-4601)*
Thomas & Thomas, Cincinnati Also called Ernest V Thomas Jr *(G-3514)*
Thomas A Wildey School, Owensville Also called Developmental Disabilities *(G-15671)*
Thomas and Associates 330 494-2111
  1421 Portage St Nw Ste C Canton (44720) *(G-2510)*
Thomas and King Inc 614 527-0571
  5561 Wstchster Woods Blvd Hilliard (43026) *(G-11821)*
Thomas Do-It Center Inc (PA) 740 446-2002
  176 Mccormick Rd Gallipolis (45631) *(G-11215)*
Thomas Door Controls Inc 614 263-1756
  4196 Indianola Ave Columbus (43214) *(G-8746)*
Thomas E Anderson DDS Inc 330 467-6466
  147 E Aurora Rd Northfield (44067) *(G-15387)*

Thomas E Keller Trucking Inc 419 784-4805
  24862 Elliott Rd Defiance (43512) *(G-9944)*
Thomas E Rojewski MD Inc 740 454-0158
  2945 Maple Ave Zanesville (43701) *(G-20366)*
Thomas Glass Company Inc (PA) 614 268-8611
  400 E Wilson Bridge Rd A Worthington (43085) *(G-19856)*
Thomas J Dyer Company (PA) 513 321-8100
  5240 Lester Rd Cincinnati (45213) *(G-4602)*
Thomas L Miller 740 374-3041
  111 Strecker Hl Marietta (45750) *(G-13385)*
Thomas L Stover Inc 330 665-8060
  754 S Cleveland Ave # 300 Mogadore (44260) *(G-14558)*
Thomas Packer & Co (PA) 330 533-9777
  6601 Westford Pl Ste 101 Canfield (44406) *(G-2160)*
Thomas R Truitt Od 937 644-8637
  1001 W 5th St Marysville (43040) *(G-13533)*
Thomas Rental, Gallipolis Also called Thomas Do-It Center Inc *(G-11215)*
Thomas Rosser 614 890-2900
  855 S Sunbury Rd Westerville (43081) *(G-19301)*
Thomas Steel Strip Corporation 330 841-6429
  2518 W Market St Warren (44485) *(G-18751)*
Thomas Transport Delivery Inc 330 908-3100
  9055 Freeway Dr Unit 1 Macedonia (44056) *(G-13084)*
Thomas Trucking Inc 513 731-8411
  2558 Apple Ridge Ln Cincinnati (45236) *(G-4603)*
Thomas W Ruff and Company 800 828-0234
  855 Grandview Ave Ste 2 Columbus (43215) *(G-8747)*
Tompkins Child Adlescent Svcs 740 622-4470
  1199 S 2nd St Coshocton (43812) *(G-9028)*
Thompson Capri Lanes Inc 614 888-3159
  5860 Roche Dr Columbus (43229) *(G-8748)*
Thompson Concrete Ltd 740 756-7256
  6182 Winchester Rd Carroll (43112) *(G-2558)*
Thompson Electric Inc 330 686-2300
  49 Northmoreland Ave Munroe Falls (44262) *(G-14799)*
Thompson Hall & Jordan Fnrl HM, Cincinnati Also called Domajaparo Inc *(G-3438)*
Thompson Hall & Jordan Fnrl HM 513 761-8881
  400 N Wayne Ave Cincinnati (45215) *(G-4604)*
Thompson Heating & Cooling 513 242-4450
  800 E Ross Ave Cincinnati (45217) *(G-4605)*
Thompson Heating Corporation 513 769-7696
  6 N Commerce Park Dr Cincinnati (45215) *(G-4606)*
Thompson Hine LLP 614 469-3200
  10 W Broad St Ste 700 Columbus (43215) *(G-8749)*
Thompson Hine LLP 614 469-3200
  41 S High St Ste 1700 Columbus (43215) *(G-8750)*
Thompson Hine LLP 937 443-6859
  10050 Innovation Dr # 400 Miamisburg (45342) *(G-14230)*
Thompson Hine LLP (PA) 216 566-5500
  127 Public Sq Cleveland (44114) *(G-6526)*
Thompson Metals and Tubing, Hamilton Also called Butler Processing Inc *(G-11572)*
Thompson Plumbing Htg Coolg, Cincinnati Also called Thompson Heating
Corporation *(G-4606)*
Thomsons Landscaping 740 374-9353
  26130 State Route 7 Marietta (45750) *(G-13386)*
Thor Construction, Columbus Also called Central Ohio Building Co Inc *(G-7157)*
Thornton Landscape Inc 513 683-8100
  424 E Us Highway 22 And 3 Maineville (45039) *(G-13119)*
THORNVILLE HEALTH AND REHABILI, Thornville Also called Thornville NH LLC *(G-17507)*
Thornville NH LLC 740 246-5253
  14100 Zion Rd Thornville (43076) *(G-17507)*
Thorsens Greenhouse LLC 740 363-5069
  2069 Hyatts Rd Delaware (43015) *(G-10009)*
Thorson Baker & Assoc Inc (PA) 330 659-6688
  3030 W Streetsboro Rd Richfield (44286) *(G-16380)*
Thos A Lupica 419 252-6298
  608 Madison Ave Ste 1000 Toledo (43604) *(G-18064)*
Thp Limited Inc 513 241-3222
  100 E 8th St Ste 3 Cincinnati (45202) *(G-4607)*
Thrasher Dinsmore & Dolan (PA) 440 285-2242
  100 7th Ave Ste 150 Chardon (44024) *(G-2718)*
Thrasher Disnmore & Doland, Chardon Also called Thrasher Dinsmore & Dolan *(G-2718)*
Thread Information Design Inc 419 887-6801
  4635 W Alexis Rd Toledo (43623) *(G-18065)*
Thread Marketing Group, Toledo Also called Thread Information Design Inc *(G-18065)*
Three C Body Shop Inc (PA) 614 274-9700
  2300 Briggs Rd Columbus (43223) *(G-8751)*
Three C Body Shop Inc 614 885-0900
  8321 N High St Columbus (43235) *(G-8752)*
Three D Golf LLC 513 732-0295
  2000 Elklick Rd Batavia (45103) *(G-1011)*
Three D Metals Inc (PA) 330 220-0451
  5462 Innovation Dr Valley City (44280) *(G-18470)*
Three M Associates 330 674-9646
  7488 State Route 241 Millersburg (44654) *(G-14496)*
Three Rivers Energy LLC 740 623-3035
  18137 County Road 271 Coshocton (43812) *(G-9029)*
Three Rivers Heating & Air, Cincinnati Also called Apollo Heating and AC Inc *(G-2975)*
Three Village Condominium 440 461-1483
  5150 Three Village Dr Cleveland (44124) *(G-6527)*
Three-D Transport Inc 419 924-5368
  14237 Us Highway 127 West Unity (43570) *(G-19141)*

2019 Harris Ohio
Services Directory
(G-0000) Company's Geographic Section entry number

Threshold Residential Svcs Inc (PA) 330 426-4553
50 N Sumner St East Palestine (44413) *(G-10422)*

Thrifty Car Rental, Cleveland *Also called Thrifty Rent-A-Car System Inc* *(G-6528)*

Thrifty Rent-A-Car System Inc 440 842-1660
7701 Day Dr Cleveland (44129) *(G-6528)*

Thriverx, Cincinnati *Also called Biorx LLC* *(G-3051)*

Thurns Bakery & Deli 614 221-9246
541 S 3rd St Columbus (43215) *(G-8753)*

Thyssen Krupp Logistics, Northwood *Also called Tkx Logistics* *(G-15409)*

Thyssenkrupp Bilstein Amer Inc (HQ) 513 881-7600
8685 Bilstein Blvd Hamilton (45015) *(G-11647)*

Thyssenkrupp Bilstein Amer Inc 513 881-7600
4440 Muhlhauser Rd West Chester (45011) *(G-19015)*

Thyssenkrupp Bilstein Amer Inc 513 881-7600
3033 Symmes Rd Hamilton (45015) *(G-11648)*

Thyssenkrupp Elevator Corp 440 717-0080
9200 Market Pl Broadview Heights (44147) *(G-1848)*

Thyssenkrupp Elevator Corp 513 241-0222
934 Dalton Ave Cincinnati (45203) *(G-4608)*

Thyssenkrupp Elevator Corp 513 241-6000
934 Dalton Ave Cincinnati (45203) *(G-4609)*

Thyssenkrupp Elevator Corp 614 895-8930
929 Eastwind Dr Ste 218 Westerville (43081) *(G-19302)*

Thyssenkrupp Logistics Inc (HQ) 419 662-1800
8001 Thyssenkrupp Pkwy Northwood (43619) *(G-15407)*

Thyssenkrupp Materials NA Inc 216 883-8100
6050 Oak Tree Blvd # 110 Independence (44131) *(G-12131)*

Thyssenkrupp Materials NA Inc 937 898-7400
10100 Innovation Dr # 210 Miamisburg (45342) *(G-14231)*

Thyssenkrupp Materials NA Inc 440 234-7500
17901 Englewood Dr Cleveland (44130) *(G-6529)*

Thyssenkrupp Onlinemetals LLC 206 285-8603
8001 Thyssenkrupp Pkwy Northwood (43619) *(G-15408)*

Tidewater River Rail Oper LLC 817 659-0091
440 S 3rd St Steubenville (43952) *(G-17174)*

Tier One Distribution LLC 937 323-6325
2105 Sheridan Ave Springfield (45505) *(G-17126)*

Tiffany's Banquet Center, Brookfield *Also called A Tara Tiffanys Property* *(G-1851)*

Tiffin Cmnty YMCA Rcration Ctr (PA) 419 447-8711
180 Summit St Tiffin (44883) *(G-17542)*

Tiffin Developmental Center, Tiffin *Also called Ohio Department of Health* *(G-17528)*

Tiffin Loader Crane Company 419 448-8156
4151 W State Route 18 Tiffin (44883) *(G-17543)*

Tiffin Paper Company (PA) 419 447-2121
265 6th Ave Tiffin (44883) *(G-17544)*

Tiffin Womens Care, Findlay *Also called Findlay Womens Care LLC* *(G-10907)*

Tiger 2010 LLC (PA) 330 236-5100
6929 Portage St Nw North Canton (44720) *(G-15238)*

Tiki Bowling Lanes Inc 740 654-4513
1521 Tiki Ln Lancaster (43130) *(G-12442)*

Tiki Lounge & Restaurant, Lancaster *Also called Tiki Bowling Lanes Inc* *(G-12442)*

Tilden Mining Company LC (HQ) 216 694-5700
200 Public Sq Ste 3300 Cleveland (44114) *(G-6530)*

Tilton Corporation 419 227-6421
330 S Pine St Lima (45804) *(G-12762)*

Tim Mundy 937 862-8686
3159 State Route 42 Spring Valley (45370) *(G-16959)*

Timbertop Apartments, Akron *Also called Bernard Busson Builder* *(G-95)*

Time Staffing, Fremont *Also called Doepker Group Inc* *(G-11070)*

Time Warner, Columbus *Also called Spectrum MGT Holdg Co LLC* *(G-8669)*

Time Warner, Zanesville *Also called Spectrum MGT Holdg Co LLC* *(G-20365)*

Time Warner, Warren *Also called Spectrum MGT Holdg Co LLC* *(G-18745)*

Time Warner, Port Clinton *Also called Spectrum MGT Holdg Co LLC* *(G-16118)*

Time Warner, Chillicothe *Also called Spectrum MGT Holdg Co LLC* *(G-2829)*

Time Warner, Columbus *Also called Spectrum MGT Holdg Co LLC* *(G-8670)*

Time Warner, Springfield *Also called Spectrum MGT Holdg Co LLC* *(G-17114)*

Time Warner, Lancaster *Also called Spectrum MGT Holdg Co LLC* *(G-12437)*

Time Warner, Dayton *Also called Spectrum MGT Holdg Co LLC* *(G-9784)*

Time Warner Cable, Akron *Also called Level 3 Telecom LLC* *(G-311)*

Time Warner Cable, Cincinnati *Also called Level 3 Telecom LLC* *(G-3919)*

Time Warner Cable, Cincinnati *Also called Level 3 Telecom LLC* *(G-3920)*

Time Warner Cable, Akron *Also called TW Telecom Inc* *(G-474)*

Time Warner Cable, Cincinnati *Also called Level 3 Telecom LLC* *(G-3921)*

Time Warner Cable Entps LLC 614 255-6289
1600 Dublin Rd Fl 2 Columbus (43215) *(G-8754)*

Time Warner Cable Entps LLC 513 489-5000
11325 Reed Hartman Hwy # 110 Blue Ash (45241) *(G-1658)*

Time Warner Cable Entps LLC 614 481-5072
1125 Chambers Rd Columbus (43212) *(G-8755)*

Time Warner Cable Inc 513 354-1100
9825 Kenwood Rd Ste 102 Blue Ash (45242) *(G-1659)*

Time Warner Cable Inc 614 236-1200
3770 E Livingston Ave Columbus (43227) *(G-8756)*

Time Warner Cable Inc 440 366-0416
578 Ternes Ln Elyria (44035) *(G-10567)*

Time Warner Cable Inc 419 331-1111
3100 Elida Rd Lima (45805) *(G-12763)*

Time Warner Cable Inc 614 481-5050
1980 Alum Creek Dr Columbus (43207) *(G-8757)*

Time Warner Cable Inc 330 800-3874
1919 Brittain Rd Akron (44310) *(G-470)*

Time Warner Cable Inc 614 481-5000
1266 Dublin Rd Columbus (43215) *(G-8758)*

Time Warner Cable Inc 330 494-9200
5520 Whipple Ave Nw Canton (44720) *(G-2511)*

Time Warner Cable Inc 330 633-9203
755 Wick Ave Youngstown (44505) *(G-20222)*

Time Warner Cable Inc 513 489-5000
11252 Cornell Park Dr Blue Ash (45242) *(G-1660)*

Time Warner Cable Inc 937 471-1572
419 S Barron St Eaton (45320) *(G-10462)*

Time Warner Cable Inc 513 523-6333
114 S Locust St Oxford (45056) *(G-15690)*

Time Warner Cable Inc 937 483-5152
1450 Experiment Farm Rd Troy (45373) *(G-18230)*

Time Warner Cable Inc 937 667-8302
1440 Commerce Park Dr Tipp City (45371) *(G-17567)*

Time Warner Cable Inc 937 492-4145
1602 Wapakoneta Ave Sidney (45365) *(G-16802)*

Time Warner Telecom, West Chester *Also called Level 3 Telecom LLC* *(G-18960)*

Time Warner Telecom, West Chester *Also called Level 3 Telecom LLC* *(G-18961)*

Time Warner Telecom, West Chester *Also called Level 3 Telecom LLC* *(G-18962)*

Times Reporter/Midwest Offset, New Philadelphia *Also called Copley Ohio Newspapers Inc (G-14951)*

Timeware Inc 330 963-2700
9329 Ravenna Rd Ste D Twinsburg (44087) *(G-18327)*

Timken Company 330 471-2121
4500 Mount Pleasant St Nw Canton (44720) *(G-2512)*

Timken Company 234 262-3000
1819 N Main St Niles (44446) *(G-15171)*

Timken Corporation (HQ) 330 471-3378
4500 Mount Pleasant St Nw North Canton (44720) *(G-15239)*

Timken Mercy Health Center, Carrollton *Also called Mercy Medical Center Inc* *(G-2572)*

Timmerman John P Heating AC Co (PA) 419 229-4015
4563 Elida Rd Lima (45807) *(G-12764)*

Timothy Sinfield 740 685-3684
54962 Marietta Rd Pleasant City (43772) *(G-16072)*

Tiny Tots Day Nursery 330 755-6473
310 Argonne St Struthers (44471) *(G-17368)*

Tipharah Designs, Dayton *Also called Tipharah Group Corp (G-9814)*

Tipharah Group Corp (PA) 937 430-6266
252 Burgess Ave Dayton (45415) *(G-9814)*

Tipharah Group Corp 937 430-6266
252 Burgess Ave Dayton (45415) *(G-9815)*

Tipharah Hospitality, Dayton *Also called Tipharah Group Corp (G-9815)*

Tipp City Veterinary Hosp Inc 937 667-8489
4900 S County Road 25a Tipp City (45371) *(G-17568)*

Tipp-Monroe Community Svcs Inc 937 667-8631
3 E Main St Tipp City (45371) *(G-17569)*

Tippecanoe Country Club Inc 330 758-7518
5870 Tippecanoe Rd Canfield (44406) *(G-2161)*

TIPPECANOE PRO SHOP, Canfield *Also called Tippecanoe Country Club Inc (G-2161)*

Tire Waste Transport Inc 419 363-2681
10803 Erastus Durbin Rd Rockford (45882) *(G-16417)*

Titan Transfer Inc 513 458-4233
6432 Centre Park Dr West Chester (45069) *(G-19016)*

Title Division, Lewis Center *Also called County of Delaware (G-12535)*

Title First Agency Inc (PA) 614 224-9207
3650 Olentangy River Rd # 400 Columbus (43214) *(G-8759)*

Tj Metzgers Inc 419 861-8611
207 Arco Dr Toledo (43607) *(G-18066)*

Tjm Clmbus LLC Tjm Clumbus LLC 614 885-1885
6500 Doubletree Ave Columbus (43229) *(G-8760)*

Tjm Express Inc 216 385-4164
212 Sandstone Ridge Way Berea (44017) *(G-1441)*

Tk Gas Services Inc 740 826-0303
2303 John Glenn Hwy New Concord (43762) *(G-14904)*

Tk Holdings Inc 937 778-9713
1401 Innovation Pkwy Piqua (45356) *(G-16031)*

Tk Homecare Llc 419 517-7000
7110 W Central Ave Ste A Toledo (43617) *(G-18067)*

Tkx Logistics 419 662-1800
8001 Thyssenkrupp Pkwy Northwood (43619) *(G-15409)*

Tky Associates LLC 419 535-7777
2451 N Reynolds Rd Toledo (43615) *(G-18068)*

TL Industries Inc (PA) 419 666-8144
2541 Tracy Rd Northwood (43619) *(G-15410)*

TLC Eyecare 419 882-2020
3000 Regency Ct Ste 100 Toledo (43623) *(G-18069)*

TLC Health Wellness & Fitness 330 527-4852
1 Memory Ln Garrettsville (44231) *(G-11232)*

TLC Home Health Care Inc 740 732-5211
43 Kennedy Dr Caldwell (43724) *(G-2045)*

Tlevay Inc 419 385-3958
1621 S Byrne Rd Toledo (43614) *(G-18070)*

Tm Capture Services LLC 937 728-1781
4380 Buckeye Ln Ste 222 Beavercreek (45440) *(G-1238)*

Tm Wallick Rsdntl Prpts I Ltd 614 863-4640
6880 Tussing Rd Reynoldsburg (43068) *(G-16333)*

Tmarzetti Company 614 277-3577
5800 N Meadows Dr Grove City (43123) *(G-11477)*

TMR Inc 330 220-8564
2945 Carquest Dr Brunswick (44212) *(G-1942)*

Tms International LLC 419 747-5500
1344 Bowman St Mansfield (44903) *(G-13254)*

Tmt Inc 419 592-1041
655 D St Perrysburg (43551) *(G-15926)*

Tmt Logistics, Perrysburg *Also called Tmt Inc* *(G-15926)*

Tmw Systems Inc (HQ) 216 831-6606
6085 Parkland Blvd Mayfield Heights (44124) *(G-13882)*

Tnr Properties, Delaware *Also called Delaware Golf Club Inc* *(G-9969)*

Tns Global, Cincinnati *Also called Tns North America Inc* *(G-4610)*

Tns North America Inc 513 621-7887
600 Vine St Ste 300 Cincinnati (45202) *(G-4610)*

Tns Retail Forward, Columbus *Also called Retail Forward Inc* *(G-8527)*

TNT Equipment Company (PA) 614 882-1549
6677 Broughton Ave Columbus (43213) *(G-8761)*

TNT Mobile Powerwash Inc 614 402-7474
260 Pfeifer Dr Canal Winchester (43110) *(G-2121)*

TNT Power Wash Inc 614 662-3110
3220 Toy Rd Groveport (43125) *(G-11541)*

TNT Power Wash Inc (PA) 614 662-3110
3220 Toy Rd Groveport (43125) *(G-11542)*

TNT Services, Groveport *Also called TNT Power Wash Inc* *(G-11541)*

TNT Services, Groveport *Also called TNT Power Wash Inc* *(G-11542)*

TOA Technologies Inc (PA) 216 360-8106
3333 Richmond Rd Ste 420 Beachwood (44122) *(G-1112)*

Tobh, Cleveland *Also called Tours of Black Heritage Inc* *(G-6536)*

Tobin, Dan Pontiac, Columbus *Also called Dan Tobin Pontiac Buick GMC* *(G-7412)*

Todd A Ruck Inc 614 527-9927
5100 Harvest Meadow Ct Hilliard (43026) *(G-11822)*

Todd Alspaugh & Associates 419 476-8126
415 E State Line Rd Toledo (43612) *(G-18071)*

Todd Associates Inc (PA) 440 461-1101
23825 Commerce Park Ste A Beachwood (44122) *(G-1113)*

Todd Organization, The, Rocky River *Also called Producer Group LLC* *(G-16444)*

Toddler's School, Toledo *Also called Young Services Inc* *(G-18171)*

Todds Enviroscapes Inc 330 875-0768
7727 Paris Ave Louisville (44641) *(G-12974)*

Tolco Corporation 419 241-1113
1920 Linwood Ave Toledo (43604) *(G-18072)*

Toledo Area Insulator Wkrs Jac 419 531-5911
4535 Hill Ave Toledo (43615) *(G-18073)*

Toledo Area Rgional Trnst Auth (PA) 419 243-7433
1127 W Central Ave Toledo (43610) *(G-18074)*

Toledo Assembly Complex, Toledo *Also called FCA US LLC* *(G-17728)*

Toledo Building Services Co 419 241-3101
2121 Adams St Toledo (43604) *(G-18075)*

Toledo Cardiology Cons Inc (PA) 419 251-6183
2409 Cherry St Ste 100 Toledo (43608) *(G-18076)*

Toledo Cardiology Inc 419 479-5690
4235 Secor Rd Toledo (43623) *(G-18077)*

Toledo City Parks, Toledo *Also called City of Toledo* *(G-17656)*

Toledo Clinic Inc 419 865-3111
6135 Trust Dr Ste 230 Holland (43528) *(G-11919)*

Toledo Clinic Inc (PA) 419 473-3561
4235 Secor Rd Toledo (43623) *(G-18078)*

Toledo Clinic Inc 419 381-9977
1414 S Byrne Rd Toledo (43614) *(G-18079)*

Toledo Clinic Inc 419 841-1600
3909 Woodley Rd Ste 800 Toledo (43606) *(G-18080)*

Toledo Club 419 243-2200
235 14th St Toledo (43604) *(G-18081)*

Toledo Ctr For Eting Disorders, Sylvania *Also called Reverse Center Clinic* *(G-17446)*

Toledo Cutting Tools, Perrysburg *Also called Imco Carbide Tool Inc* *(G-15877)*

Toledo Cy Pub Utlity Wtr Distr 419 936-2506
401 S Erie St Toledo (43604) *(G-18082)*

Toledo District Nurses Assn 419 255-0983
5520 Monroe St Sylvania (43560) *(G-17458)*

Toledo Driveline, Fremont *Also called Certified Power Inc* *(G-11062)*

Toledo Ear Nose and Throat, Maumee *Also called Richard J Nelson MD* *(G-13845)*

Toledo Edison Company (HQ) 800 447-3333
76 S Main St Bsmt Akron (44308) *(G-471)*

Toledo Edison Company 419 321-8488
5501 N State Route 2 Oak Harbor (43449) *(G-15479)*

Toledo Edison Company 419 249-5364
6099 Angola Rd Holland (43528) *(G-11920)*

Toledo Express Airport, Swanton *Also called Toledo-Lucas County Port Auth* *(G-17408)*

Toledo Family Health Center, Toledo *Also called Neighborhood Health Asso* *(G-17935)*

Toledo Family Health Center 419 241-1554
313 Jefferson Ave Toledo (43604) *(G-18083)*

Toledo Glass LLC (PA) 419 241-3151
103 Avondale Ave Toledo (43604) *(G-18084)*

Toledo Hospital 419 291-2051
2051 W Central Ave Toledo (43606) *(G-18085)*

Toledo Hospital (HQ) 419 291-4000
2142 N Cove Blvd Toledo (43606) *(G-18086)*

Toledo Hospital 419 291-2273
5520 Monroe St Sylvania (43560) *(G-17459)*

Toledo Hospital 419 291-8701
2150 W Central Ave Ste A Toledo (43606) *(G-18087)*

Toledo Inns Inc 440 243-4040
7230 Engle Rd Cleveland (44130) *(G-6531)*

Toledo Jewelers Supply Co 419 241-4181
245 23rd St Toledo (43604) *(G-18088)*

Toledo Legal Aid Society 419 720-3048
520 Madison Ave Ste 640 Toledo (43604) *(G-18089)*

Toledo Maintance Center, Toledo *Also called Toledo Public Schools* *(G-18095)*

Toledo Medical Equipment Co (PA) 419 866-7120
4060 Technology Dr Maumee (43537) *(G-13862)*

Toledo Memorial Pk & Mausoleum 419 882-7151
6382 Monroe St Sylvania (43560) *(G-17460)*

Toledo Metro Area Cncl Gvrnmnt 419 241-9155
300 M Luther King Jr Dr Toledo (43604) *(G-18090)*

Toledo Mirror & Glass, Toledo *Also called Toledo Glass LLC* *(G-18084)*

Toledo Molding & Die Inc 419 692-6022
24086 State Route 697 Delphos (45833) *(G-10036)*

Toledo Mud Hens Basbal CLB Inc 419 725-4367
406 Washington St Fl 5 Toledo (43604) *(G-18091)*

Toledo Museum of Art 419 255-8000
2445 Monroe St Toledo (43620) *(G-18092)*

Toledo Opco LLC 502 429-8062
7120 Port Sylvania Dr Toledo (43617) *(G-18093)*

Toledo Optical Laboratory Inc 419 248-3384
1201 Jefferson Ave Toledo (43604) *(G-18094)*

Toledo Public Schools 419 243-6422
130 S Hawley St Toledo (43609) *(G-18095)*

Toledo Railways and Light Co, Akron *Also called Toledo Edison Company* *(G-471)*

Toledo Refining Company LLC (HQ) 419 698-6600
1819 Woodville Rd Oregon (43616) *(G-15611)*

Toledo Science Center 419 244-2674
1 Discovery Way Toledo (43604) *(G-18096)*

Toledo Shredding LLC 419 698-1153
275 Millard Ave Bldg 3 Toledo (43605) *(G-18097)*

Toledo Sign Company Inc (PA) 419 244-4444
2021 Adams St Toledo (43604) *(G-18098)*

Toledo Sports Center Inc 419 693-0687
1516 Starr Ave Toledo (43605) *(G-18099)*

Toledo Swiss Singers 419 693-4110
3860 Starr Ave Oregon (43616) *(G-15612)*

Toledo Television Investors LP 419 535-0024
300 S Byrne Rd Toledo (43615) *(G-18100)*

Toledo V A Outpatient Clinic, Toledo *Also called Veterans Health Administration* *(G-18138)*

Toledo Zoo 419 385-5721
2700 Broadway St Toledo (43609) *(G-18101)*

Toledo Zoological Society (PA) 419 385-4040
2 Hippo Way Toledo (43609) *(G-18102)*

Toledo-Lucas County Port Auth (PA) 419 243-8251
1 Maritime Plz Ste 701 Toledo (43604) *(G-18103)*

Toledo-Lucas County Port Auth 419 865-2351
11013 Airport Hwy Ste 11 Swanton (43558) *(G-17408)*

Tolson Enterprises Inc 419 843-6465
6591 W Central Ave # 100 Toledo (43617) *(G-18104)*

Tolson Investment Property, Toledo *Also called Tolson Enterprises Inc* *(G-18104)*

Tom Ahl Chryslr-Plymouth-Dodge 419 227-0202
617 King Ave Lima (45805) *(G-12765)*

Tom Baier & Assoc Inc 330 497-3115
4686 Douglas Cir Nw Canton (44718) *(G-2513)*

Tom Langhals 419 659-5629
4599 Campbell Rd Columbus Grove (45830) *(G-8942)*

Tom Paige Catering Company 216 431-4236
2275 E 55th St Cleveland (44103) *(G-6532)*

Tom Properties LLC 614 781-0055
777 Dearborn Park Ln A Columbus (43085) *(G-8762)*

Tom Schaefer Plumbing Inc 440 602-7300
4350 Glenbrook Rd Willoughby (44094) *(G-19576)*

Tom Tise Golf Professional 937 836-5186
6001 Salem Ave Clayton (45315) *(G-4862)*

Tomita USA Inc (HQ) 614 873-6509
7801 Corp Blvd Unit G Plain City (43064) *(G-16069)*

Tomm, Richard MD, Cleveland *Also called Richard Tomm MD* *(G-6323)*

Tommy Bahama Group Inc 614 750-9668
4185 The Strand Columbus (43219) *(G-8763)*

Toms Installation Co Inc 419 584-1218
5349 State Route 29 Celina (45822) *(G-2612)*

Tomson Steel Company 513 420-8600
1400 Made Industrial Dr Middletown (45044) *(G-14337)*

Toni & Marie Bader 937 339-3621
831 E Main St Troy (45373) *(G-18231)*

Tonka Bay Dialysis LLC 740 375-0849
1221 Delaware Ave Marion (43302) *(G-13464)*

Tony Packo's Food Company, Toledo *Also called Tony Packos Toledo LLC* *(G-18105)*

Tony Packos Toledo LLC (PA) 419 691-6054
1902 Front St Toledo (43605) *(G-18105)*

Tool Testing Lab Inc 937 898-5696
11601 N Dixie Dr Tipp City (45371) *(G-17570)*

Tool Testing Lab Inc (PA) 937 898-5696
11601 N Dixie Dr Tipp City (45371) *(G-17571)*

Tooling Components Division, Cleveland *Also called Jergens Inc* *(G-5790)*

Top Dawg Group LLC 216 398-1066
220 Eastview Dr Ste 103 Brooklyn Heights (44131) *(G-1883)*

(G-0000) Company's Geographic Section entry number

Top Echelon Contracting Inc 330 454-3508
 4883 Dressler Rd Nw # 200 Canton (44718) *(G-2514)*
Top Gun Sales Performance Inc 513 770-0870
 5155 Financial Way Ste 1 Mason (45040) *(G-13647)*
Top Network, Columbus Also called Essilor Laboratories Amer Inc *(G-7537)*
Top Performance, Ashtabula Also called Jbj Enterprises Inc *(G-743)*
Top Tier Soccer LLC 937 903-6114
 1268 Walnut Valley Ln Dayton (45458) *(G-9816)*
Topicz, Cincinnati Also called Novelart Manufacturing Company *(G-4136)*
Topmind/Planex Construction 248 719-0474
 831 Elliott Dr Middletown (45044) *(G-14338)*
Toris Station 513 829-7815
 8657 N Gilmore Rd Fairfield (45014) *(G-10791)*
Toronto Emergency Medical Svc 740 537-3891
 201 S 4th St Toronto (43964) *(G-18186)*
Toshiba Amer Bus Solutions Inc 216 642-7555
 7850 Hub Pkwy Cleveland (44125) *(G-6533)*
Tosoh America Inc (HQ) 614 539-8622
 3600 Gantz Rd Grove City (43123) *(G-11478)*
Total Carpet & Cleaning Svc, Dayton Also called John O Bostock Jr *(G-9528)*
Total Fleet Solutions LLC 419 868-8853
 7050 Spring Meadows Dr W A Holland (43528) *(G-11921)*
Total Loop Inc 888 614-5667
 1790 Town Park Blvd Ste A Uniontown (44685) *(G-18388)*
Total Marketing Resources LLC 330 220-1275
 2811 Carquest Dr Brunswick (44212) *(G-1943)*
Total Package Express Inc (PA) 513 741-5500
 5871 Cheviot Rd Ste 1 Cincinnati (45247) *(G-4611)*
Total Quality Logistics LLC 800 580-3101
 6525 Centervl Bus Pkwy Centerville (45459) *(G-2635)*
Total Quality Logistics LLC 800 580-3101
 8488 Shepherd Farm Dr West Chester (45069) *(G-19017)*
Total Quality Logistics LLC 513 831-2600
 1701 Edison Dr Milford (45150) *(G-14437)*
Total Quality Logistics LLC 513 831-2600
 5130 Glncrssing Way Ste 3 Cincinnati (45238) *(G-4612)*
Total Quality Logistics LLC 513 831-2600
 1701 Edison Dr Milford (45150) *(G-14438)*
Total Quality Logistics LLC (HQ) 513 831-2600
 4289 Ivy Pointe Blvd Cincinnati (45245) *(G-2873)*
Total Renal Care Inc 937 294-6711
 3030 S Dixie Dr Kettering (45409) *(G-12301)*
Total Renal Care Inc 937 252-1867
 1431 Business Center Ct Dayton (45410) *(G-9817)*
Total Rhabilitation Specialist 440 236-8527
 23050 Louise Ln Columbia Station (44028) *(G-6780)*
Total Solutions, Northwood Also called Campbell Inc *(G-15391)*
Total Transportation Trckg Inc 216 398-6090
 5755 Granger Rd Ste 400 Cleveland (44131) *(G-6534)*
Total Warehousing Services 419 562-2878
 115 Crossroads Blvd Bucyrus (44820) *(G-2002)*
Total Wholesale Inc 216 361-5757
 3900 Woodland Ave Cleveland (44115) *(G-6535)*
Toth Renovation LLC 614 542-9683
 444 Siebert St Columbus (43206) *(G-8764)*
Touchmark, Dublin Also called Advanced Prgrm Resources Inc *(G-10119)*
Touchstone Group Assoc LLC 513 791-1717
 9675 Montgomery Rd # 201 Cincinnati (45242) *(G-4613)*
Touchstone Mdse Group LLC (HQ) 513 741-0400
 7200 Industrial Row Dr Mason (45040) *(G-13648)*
Toula Industries Ltd LLC 937 689-1818
 1019 Valley Vista Way Dayton (45429) *(G-9818)*
Tour De Force Inc 419 425-4800
 14601 County Road 212 # 1 Findlay (45840) *(G-10970)*
Tours of Black Heritage Inc 440 247-2737
 8800 Woodland Ave Cleveland (44104) *(G-6536)*
Toward Independence Inc (PA) 937 376-3996
 81 E Main St Xenia (45385) *(G-19929)*
Towards Employment Inc 216 696-5750
 1255 Euclid Ave Ste 300 Cleveland (44115) *(G-6537)*
Towe & Associates Inc 937 275-0900
 415 S Miami St Ste 415 # 415 West Milton (45383) *(G-19127)*
Towe and Associates, West Milton Also called Towe & Associates Inc *(G-19127)*
Towlift Inc (PA) 216 749-6800
 1395 Valley Belt Rd Brooklyn Heights (44131) *(G-1884)*
Towlift Inc 419 666-1333
 2860 Crane Way Northwood (43619) *(G-15411)*
Towlift Inc 614 851-1001
 1200 Milepost Dr Columbus (43228) *(G-8765)*
Towlift Inc 419 531-6110
 140 N Byrne Rd Toledo (43607) *(G-18106)*
Town & Country Adult Services, Springfield Also called TAC Industries Inc *(G-17124)*
Town & Country School, Springfield Also called Clark County Board of Developm *(G-17009)*
Town House Motor Lodge Corp 740 452-4511
 135 N 7th St Zanesville (43701) *(G-20367)*
Town Inn Co LLC 614 221-3281
 175 E Town St Columbus (43215) *(G-8766)*
Town of Canal Fulton (PA) 330 854-9448
 155 Market St E Ste A Canal Fulton (44614) *(G-2098)*
Towne & Country Vet Clinic, Warren Also called Howland Corners Twn & Ctry Vet *(G-18714)*
Towne Building Group Inc (PA) 513 381-8696
 1055 Saint Paul Pl Cincinnati (45202) *(G-4614)*

Towne Construction Svcs LLC 513 561-3700
 500 Kent Rd Ste A Batavia (45103) *(G-1012)*
Towne Development Group Ltd 513 381-8696
 1055 Saint Paul Pl # 300 Cincinnati (45202) *(G-4615)*
Towne Investment Company LP 513 381-8696
 1055 Saint Paul Pl Cincinnati (45202) *(G-4616)*
Towne Mall, Middletown Also called Ermc II LP *(G-14346)*
Towne Mall, Middletown Also called Cbl & Associates Prpts Inc *(G-14344)*
Towne Management Realty, Cincinnati Also called Towne Properties Assoc Inc *(G-4619)*
Towne Properties, Cincinnati Also called Original Partners Ltd Partnr *(G-4183)*
Towne Properties Asset MGT, Cincinnati Also called Towne Properties Asset MGT *(G-4617)*
Towne Properties Asset MGT (PA) 513 381-8696
 1055 Saint Paul Pl # 100 Cincinnati (45202) *(G-4617)*
Towne Properties Assoc Inc 513 489-9700
 8675 E Kemper Rd Cincinnati (45249) *(G-4618)*
Towne Properties Assoc Inc 513 489-4059
 11340 Montgomery Rd # 202 Cincinnati (45249) *(G-4619)*
Towne Properties Assoc Inc 513 874-3737
 11840 Kemper Springs Dr C Cincinnati (45240) *(G-4620)*
Towne Properties Machine Group, Batavia Also called Towne Construction Svcs
LLC *(G-1012)*
TownePlace Suites, Westlake Also called Oh-16 Cleveland Westlake *(G-19385)*
TownePlace Suites By Marriott, Streetsboro Also called CER Hotels LLC *(G-17249)*
TownePlace Suites By Marriott, Streetsboro Also called Sojourn Lodging Inc *(G-17270)*
TownePlace Suites By Marriott 513 774-0610
 9369 Waterstone Blvd Cincinnati (45249) *(G-4621)*
Townhall 2 .... 330 678-3006
 155 N Water St Kent (44240) *(G-12263)*
TOWNHALL 2 24 HOUR HELPLINE, Kent Also called Townhall 2 *(G-12263)*
Townhomes Management Inc 614 228-3578
 407 E Livingston Ave Columbus (43215) *(G-8767)*
Township Administration Office, Fowler Also called Township of Fowler *(G-11017)*
Township of Chester 440 729-9951
 8552 Parkside Dr Chesterland (44026) *(G-2747)*
Township of Colerain 513 741-7551
 3360 W Galbraith Rd Cincinnati (45239) *(G-4622)*
Township of Copley 330 666-1853
 1540 S Clvlnd Mssillon Rd Copley (44321) *(G-8978)*
Township of Fowler (PA) 330 637-2653
 4562 State Route 305 Fowler (44418) *(G-11017)*
TOWPATH RACQUET CLUB, Akron Also called Tennis Unlimited Inc *(G-467)*
Toyota Industrial Eqp Dlr 419 865-8025
 8310 Airport Hwy Holland (43528) *(G-11922)*
Toyota Industries N Amer Inc 513 779-7500
 9890 Charter Park Dr West Chester (45069) *(G-19018)*
Toyota Industries N Amer Inc 937 237-0976
 6254 Executive Blvd Dayton (45424) *(G-9819)*
Toyota Material Hdlg Ohio Inc (PA) 216 328-0970
 5667 E Schaaf Rd Independence (44131) *(G-12132)*
Toyota of Bedford 440 439-8600
 18151 Rockside Rd Bedford (44146) *(G-1310)*
Toyota of Logan, Logan Also called Tansky Motors Inc *(G-12855)*
Toyota West, Columbus Also called Sonic Automotive *(G-8658)*
TP Mechanical Contractors Inc (PA) 513 851-8881
 1500 Kemper Meadow Dr Cincinnati (45240) *(G-4623)*
TP Mechanical Contractors Inc 614 253-8556
 2130 Franklin Rd Columbus (43209) *(G-8768)*
TPC Food Service, Tiffin Also called Tiffin Paper Company *(G-17544)*
TPC Wire & Cable Corp (HQ) 800 521-7935
 9600 Valley View Rd Macedonia (44056) *(G-13085)*
Tpg Noramco LLC 513 245-9050
 9252 Colerain Ave Ste 4 Cincinnati (45251) *(G-4624)*
Tpusa Inc 330 374-1232
 150 E Market St Akron (44308) *(G-472)*
Tpusa Inc 614 621-5512
 4335 Equity Dr Columbus (43228) *(G-8769)*
Tql, Milford Also called Total Quality Logistics LLC *(G-14437)*
Tql, Cincinnati Also called Total Quality Logistics LLC *(G-2873)*
TRAC, Athens Also called Tri County Mental Health Svcs *(G-806)*
Tracy Appliance, Lima Also called Tracy Refrigeration Inc *(G-12766)*
Tracy Refrigeration Inc 419 223-4786
 4064 Elida Rd Lima (45807) *(G-12766)*
Tradeglobal LLC 866 345-5835
 5389 E Provident Dr West Chester (45246) *(G-19092)*
Trademark Games, Lorain Also called Trademark Global LLC *(G-12948)*
Trademark Global LLC (HQ) 440 960-6200
 7951 W Erie Ave Lorain (44053) *(G-12948)*
Trader Buds Westside Dodge 614 272-0000
 4000 W Broad St Columbus (43228) *(G-8770)*
Tradesmen Group Inc 614 799-0889
 8465 Rausch Dr Plain City (43064) *(G-16070)*
Tradesmen International LLC 419 502-9140
 2419 E Perkins Ave Sandusky (44870) *(G-16649)*
Tradesmen International LLC 513 771-1115
 4398 Glendale Milford Rd Blue Ash (45242) *(G-1661)*
Tradesmen International LLC (PA) 440 349-3432
 9760 Shepard Rd Macedonia (44056) *(G-13086)*
Tradesmen Services LLC 440 349-3432
 9760 Shepard Rd Macedonia (44056) *(G-13087)*

A
L
P
H
A
B
E
T
I
C

Tradesmen Services, Inc., Macedonia *Also called Tradesmen Services LLC* **(G-13087)**
Tradesource Inc 216 801-4944
  5504 State Rd Parma (44134) **(G-15778)**
Tradesource Inc 614 824-3883
  1550 Old Henderson Rd Columbus (43220) **(G-8771)**
Trading Corp of America, Columbus *Also called Marfo Company* **(G-8019)**
Traditions At Bath Rd Inc 330 929-6272
  300 E Bath Rd Cuyahoga Falls (44223) **(G-9132)**
Traditions At Mill Run 614 771-0100
  3550 Fishinger Blvd Hilliard (43026) **(G-11823)**
Traditions At Stygler Road 614 475-8778
  167 N Stygler Rd Columbus (43230) **(G-8772)**
Traditions of Chillicothe 740 773-8107
  142 University Dr Ofc Chillicothe (45601) **(G-2831)**
Traffic Ctrl Safety Svcs LLC 330 904-2732
  8970 Allen Dr Ne Alliance (44601) **(G-556)**
Traffic Engineering, Akron *Also called City of Akron* **(G-138)**
Trafftech Inc 216 361-8808
  7000 Hubbard Ave Cleveland (44127) **(G-6538)**
Trafzer Excavating Inc 740 383-2616
  1560 Likens Rd Marion (43302) **(G-13465)**
Traichal Construction Company (PA) 800 255-3667
  332 Plant St Niles (44446) **(G-15172)**
Training Center, The, Columbus *Also called Vertical Adventures Inc* **(G-8846)**
Trak Staffing Services Inc (PA) 513 333-4199
  625 Eden Park Dr Ste 300 Cincinnati (45202) **(G-4625)**
Trame Mechanical Inc 937 258-1000
  2721 Timber Ln Dayton (45414) **(G-9820)**
Tramz Hotels LLC 440 975-9922
  35110 Maplegrove Rd Willoughby (44094) **(G-19577)**
Trane Cleveland, Cleveland *Also called Trane Inc* **(G-6539)**
Trane Inc 440 946-7823
  9555 Rockside Rd Ste 350 Cleveland (44125) **(G-6539)**
Trans Con Buildings, Cleveland *Also called Owners Management* **(G-6151)**
Trans Core, Cleveland *Also called Transcore Its LLC* **(G-6541)**
Trans Healthcare, Wapakoneta *Also called Gardens At Wapakoneta* **(G-18644)**
Trans Vac Inc 419 229-8192
  931 N Jefferson St Lima (45801) **(G-12767)**
Trans World Alloys, Toronto *Also called Shadco Inc* **(G-18185)**
Trans-Continental Systems Inc (PA) 513 769-4774
  10801 Evendale Dr Ste 105 Cincinnati (45241) **(G-4626)**
Trans-States Express Inc 513 679-7100
  7750 Reinhold Dr Cincinnati (45237) **(G-4627)**
Transamerica Premier Lf Insur 614 488-5983
  1335 Dublin Rd Ste 200c Columbus (43215) **(G-8773)**
Transamerica Premier Lf Insur 216 524-1436
  6480 Rockside Woods S 1 Independence (44131) **(G-12133)**
Transco Railway Products Inc 419 726-3383
  4800 Schwartz Rd Toledo (43611) **(G-18107)**
Transcon Builders Inc (PA) 440 439-3400
  25250 Rockside Rd Ste 2 Cleveland (44146) **(G-6540)**
Transcore Its LLC 440 243-2222
  6930 Engle Rd Ste Y Cleveland (44130) **(G-6541)**
Transcriptiongear Inc 888 834-2392
  7280 Auburn Rd Painesville (44077) **(G-15743)**
Transcriptiongear.com, Painesville *Also called Transcriptiongear Inc* **(G-15743)**
Transdigm Group Incorporated (PA) 216 706-2960
  1301 E 9th St Ste 3000 Cleveland (44114) **(G-6542)**
Transforce Inc 513 860-4402
  8080 Beckett Center Dr # 202 West Chester (45069) **(G-19019)**
Transformation Network (PA) 419 207-1188
  1310 Claremont Ave Unit A Ashland (44805) **(G-695)**
Transfreight Inc 937 332-0366
  3355 S County Road 25a B Troy (45373) **(G-18232)**
Transit Service Company 330 782-3343
  1130 Prfmce Pl Unit A Youngstown (44502) **(G-20223)**
Transitional Living Inc (HQ) 513 863-6383
  2052 Princeton Rd Fairfield Township (45011) **(G-10815)**
Transitworks LLC (HQ) 330 861-1118
  4199 Kinross Lakes Pkwy Richfield (44286) **(G-16381)**
Transmerica Svcs Technical Sup 740 282-3695
  4404 Scioto Dr Steubenville (43953) **(G-17175)**
Transport Corp America Inc 330 538-3328
  1951 N Bailey Rd North Jackson (44451) **(G-15254)**
Transport Service Co., North Canton *Also called Kenan Advantage Group Inc* **(G-15216)**
Transport Services Inc (PA) 440 582-4900
  10499 Royalton Rd Cleveland (44133) **(G-6543)**
Transport Specialists Inc (PA) 513 771-2220
  12130 Best Pl Cincinnati (45241) **(G-4628)**
Transportatin Office, Youngstown *Also called Mahoning County* **(G-20107)**
Transportation Center, Warren *Also called Warren City Board Education* **(G-18768)**
Transportation Department, Ontario *Also called Ontario Local School District* **(G-15568)**
Transportation Department, Ashtabula *Also called Ashtabula Area City School Dst* **(G-705)**
Transportation Department, Columbus *Also called Ohio State University* **(G-8332)**
Transportation Dept, Dayton *Also called Kettering City School District* **(G-9538)**
Transportation Group, Mantua *Also called Mantaline Corporation* **(G-13273)**
Transportation Ohio Department 614 275-1300
  1600 W Broad St Columbus (43223) **(G-8774)**
Transportation Ohio Department 740 773-3191
  255 Larrick Ln Chillicothe (45601) **(G-2832)**

Transportation Unlimited Inc (PA) 216 426-0088
  3740 Carnegie Ave Ste 101 Cleveland (44115) **(G-6544)**
Transtar Electric Inc 419 385-7573
  767 Warehouse Rd Ste B Toledo (43615) **(G-18108)**
Transworld News, Cleveland *Also called Windy Hill Ltd Inc* **(G-6684)**
Transystems Corporation 614 433-7800
  400 W Nationwide Blvd # 225 Columbus (43215) **(G-8775)**
Transystems Corporation 216 861-1780
  1100 Superior Ave E # 1000 Cleveland (44114) **(G-6545)**
Tranzonic Companies (PA) 216 535-4300
  26301 Curtiss Wright Pkwy # 200 Richmond Heights (44143) **(G-16395)**
Travel Authority (PA) 513 272-2887
  6800 Wooster Pike Cincinnati (45227) **(G-4629)**
Travelcenters America Inc (HQ) 440 808-9100
  24601 Center Ridge Rd # 200 Westlake (44145) **(G-19413)**
Travelcenters of America LLC 330 769-2053
  Junction Of I 71 And I 76 Lodi (44254) **(G-12829)**
Travelcenters of America LLC 724 981-9464
  24601 Center Ridge Rd # 200 Westlake (44145) **(G-19414)**
Travelcenters of America LLC (PA) 440 808-9100
  24601 Center Ridge Rd # 200 Westlake (44145) **(G-19415)**
Travelcenters of America LLC 330 793-4426
  I 80 Rte 46 Exit 223 A Rt 46 Youngstown (44515) **(G-20224)**
Travelers Insurance, Cincinnati *Also called Travelers Property Cslty Corp* **(G-4630)**
Travelers Insurance, Cleveland *Also called Travelers Property Cslty Corp* **(G-6546)**
Travelers Property Cslty Corp 513 639-5300
  615 Elsinore Pl Bldg B Cincinnati (45202) **(G-4630)**
Travelers Property Cslty Corp 216 643-2100
  6150 Oak Tree Blvd # 400 Cleveland (44131) **(G-6546)**
Traxium LLC 330 572-8200
  4246 Hudson Dr Stow (44224) **(G-17236)**
Treasurers Office, Dayton *Also called County of Montgomery* **(G-9329)**
Tremco Incorporated (HQ) 216 292-5000
  3735 Green Rd Beachwood (44122) **(G-1114)**
Tremor LLC 513 983-1100
  9545 Kenwood Rd Ste 303 Blue Ash (45242) **(G-1662)**
Trend Construction, Cincinnati *Also called Ford Development Corp* **(G-3577)**
Trend Consulting Services, Solon *Also called Netsmart Technologies Inc* **(G-16877)**
Trep Ltd 419 717-5624
  900 American Rd Napoleon (43545) **(G-14818)**
Trepanier Daniels & Trepanier 740 286-1288
  80 Dixon Run Rd Ste 80 # 80 Jackson (45640) **(G-12180)**
Treu House of Munch Inc 419 666-7770
  8000 Arbor Dr Northwood (43619) **(G-15412)**
Trg Maintenance LLC 614 891-4850
  514 N State St Ste B Westerville (43082) **(G-19214)**
Trg Repair, Westlake *Also called Technology Recovery Group Ltd* **(G-19412)**
Tri Area Electric Co Inc 330 744-0151
  37 Wayne Ave Youngstown (44502) **(G-20225)**
Tri County Assembly of God 513 874-8575
  7350 Dixie Hwy Fairfield (45014) **(G-10792)**
Tri County Concrete Inc (PA) 330 425-4464
  9423 Darrow Rd Twinsburg (44087) **(G-18328)**
Tri County Eggs, Versailles *Also called Weaver Bros Inc* **(G-18573)**
Tri County Extended Care Ctr 513 829-3555
  5200 Camelot Dr Fairfield (45014) **(G-10793)**
Tri County Family Physicians 614 837-6363
  11925 Lithopolis Rd Nw Canal Winchester (43110) **(G-2122)**
Tri County Help Center Inc (PA) 740 695-5441
  104 1/2 N Marietta St Saint Clairsville (43950) **(G-16507)**
Tri County Mall Promotion Fund, Cincinnati *Also called Concordia Properties LLC* **(G-3349)**
Tri County Mental Health Svcs (PA) 740 592-3091
  90 Hospital Dr Athens (45701) **(G-806)**
Tri County Mental Health Svcs 740 594-5045
  90 Hospital Dr Athens (45701) **(G-807)**
Tri County Nite Hunter Assn Ci 740 385-7341
  2940 Laurel Run Rd Logan (43138) **(G-12856)**
Tri County Tower Service 330 538-9874
  8900 Mahoning Ave North Jackson (44451) **(G-15255)**
Tri County Visitng Nrs Prvt 419 738-7430
  803 Brewfield Dr Wapakoneta (45895) **(G-18656)**
Tri Green Interstate Equipment 614 879-7731
  1499 Us Highway 42 Ne London (43140) **(G-12876)**
Tri Modal Service Inc 614 876-6325
  2015 Walcutt Rd Columbus (43228) **(G-8776)**
Tri State Corporation 513 763-0215
  923 Glenwood Ave Cincinnati (45229) **(G-4631)**
Tri State Forest Products, Springfield *Also called Tier One Distribution LLC* **(G-17126)**
Tri State Urlogic Svcs PSC Inc (PA) 513 841-7400
  2000 Joseph E Sanker Blvd Cincinnati (45212) **(G-4632)**
Tri Tech Service Systems Inc 937 787-4664
  9501 Pleasant Valley Rd Somerville (45064) **(G-16919)**
Tri Village Joint Ambulance, New Madison *Also called Tri Village Rescue Service* **(G-14938)**
Tri Village Rescue Service 937 996-3155
  320 N Main St New Madison (45346) **(G-14938)**
Tri Zob Inc 216 252-4500
  4117 Rocky River Dr Cleveland (44135) **(G-6547)**
Tri-America Contractors Inc (PA) 740 574-0148
  1664 State Route 522 Wheelersburg (45694) **(G-19441)**
Tri-Anim Health Services Inc (HQ) 614 760-5000
  5000 Tuttle Crossing Blvd Dublin (43016) **(G-10357)**

Tri-Con Incorporated 513 530-9844
11160 Kenwood Rd Ste 200 Blue Ash (45242) *(G-1663)*
Tri-County Community Act 740 385-6812
1005 C I C Dr Logan (43138) *(G-12857)*
Tri-County Computer Svcs Assn, Wooster *Also called Midland Council Governments (G-19745)*
Tri-County Heating & Cooling, Barberton *Also called Blind & Son LLC (G-948)*
Tri-County Mulch, Akron *Also called Tri-County Pallet Recycl Inc (G-473)*
Tri-County Pallet Recycl Inc 330 848-0313
900 Flora Ave Akron (44314) *(G-473)*
Tri-Mor Corp 330 963-3101
8530 N Boyle Pkwy Twinsburg (44087) *(G-18329)*
Tri-State Aluminium Inc (HQ) 419 666-0100
1663 Tracy St Toledo (43605) *(G-18109)*
Tri-State Amblnce Pramedic Svc 304 233-2331
7100 Whipple Ave Nw Ste C North Canton (44720) *(G-15240)*
Tri-State Asphalt Co, Rayland *Also called Shelly and Sands Inc (G-16273)*
Tri-State Beef Co Inc 513 579-1722
2124 Baymiller St Cincinnati (45214) *(G-4633)*
Tri-State Forest Products Inc (PA) 937 323-6325
2105 Sheridan Ave Springfield (45505) *(G-17127)*
Tri-State Industries Inc 740 532-0406
606 Carlton Davidson Ln Coal Grove (45638) *(G-6756)*
Tri-State Mobile Notaries, Cincinnati *Also called Official Investigations Inc (G-4149)*
Tri-State Trailer Sales Inc 412 747-7777
5230 Duff Dr West Chester (45246) *(G-19093)*
Tri-Tech Associates Inc 937 306-1630
1785 S Metro Pkwy Dayton (45459) *(G-9821)*
Tri-Tech Engineering, Dayton *Also called Tri-Tech Associates Inc (G-9821)*
Triad Energy Corporation 740 374-2940
125 Putnam St Marietta (45750) *(G-13387)*
Triad Engineering & Contg Co (PA) 440 786-1000
9715 Clinton Rd Cleveland (44144) *(G-6548)*
Triad Governmental Systems 937 376-5446
358 S Monroe St Xenia (45385) *(G-19930)*
Triad Group Inc (PA) 419 228-8800
855 W Market St Lowr Lima (45805) *(G-12768)*
Triad Oil & Gas Engineering 740 374-2940
27724 State Route 7 Marietta (45750) *(G-13388)*
Triad Pll 740 374-2940
27724 State Route 7 Marietta (45750) *(G-13389)*
Triad Residential (PA) 419 482-0711
1605 Holland Rd Ste A4 Maumee (43537) *(G-13863)*
Triad Technologies LLC (PA) 937 832-2861
985 Falls Creek Dr Vandalia (45377) *(G-18544)*
Triad Transport Inc 614 491-9497
1484 Williams Rd Columbus (43207) *(G-8777)*
Triangle Commercial Properties, Westerville *Also called Donald R Kenney & Company (G-19159)*
Triangle Label, West Chester *Also called G R B Inc (G-18929)*
Triangle Office Park LLC 513 563-7555
2135 Dana Ave Ste 200 Cincinnati (45207) *(G-4634)*
Triangle Precision Industries 937 299-6776
1650 Delco Park Dr Dayton (45420) *(G-9822)*
Tribute Contracting & Cons LLC 740 451-1010
2125 County Road 1 South Point (45680) *(G-16946)*
Trickeration Inc 216 360-9966
26055 Emery Rd Ste E Warrensville Heights (44128) *(G-18782)*
Tricont Trucking Company 614 527-7398
2200 Westbelt Dr Columbus (43228) *(G-8778)*
Tricor Emplyment Screening Ltd 800 818-5116
110 Blaze Industrial Pkwy Berea (44017) *(G-1442)*
Tricor Industrial, Wooster *Also called Tricor Metals (G-19774)*
Tricor Industrial Inc (PA) 330 264-3299
3225 W Old Lincoln Way Wooster (44691) *(G-19773)*
Tricor Metals, Wooster *Also called Tricor Industrial Inc (G-19773)*
Tricor Metals 330 264-3299
3225 W Old Lincoln Way Wooster (44691) *(G-19774)*
Tricor Pacific Capital Partner, Burton *Also called Bfg Supply Co Llc (G-2015)*
Tricounty Ambulance Service 440 951-4600
7000 Spinach Dr Mentor (44060) *(G-14115)*
Tridec Technologies LLC 937 938-8160
4764 Fishburg Rd Ste D Huber Heights (45424) *(G-11959)*
Trident USA Health Svcs LLC 614 888-2226
6185 Huntley Rd Ste Q Columbus (43229) *(G-8779)*
Triec Electrical Services Inc 937 323-3721
1630 Progress Rd Springfield (45505) *(G-17128)*
TRIHEALTH, Cincinnati *Also called Hospice Cincinnati Inc (G-3729)*
Trihealth Inc 513 929-0020
415 W Court St Ste 100 Cincinnati (45203) *(G-4635)*
Trihealth Inc 513 865-1111
10506 Montgomery Rd Cincinnati (45242) *(G-4636)*
Trihealth Inc 513 569-6777
375 Dixmyth Ave Cincinnati (45220) *(G-4637)*
Trihealth Inc 513 891-1627
4665 Cornell Rd Ste 350 Blue Ash (45241) *(G-1664)*
Trihealth Inc (HQ) 513 569-6111
619 Oak St Cincinnati (45206) *(G-4638)*
Trihealth Inc 513 871-2340
2753 Erie Ave Cincinnati (45208) *(G-4639)*
Trihealth Evendale Hospital (HQ) 513 454-2222
3155 Glendale Milford Rd Cincinnati (45241) *(G-4640)*
Trihealth Fitnes Hlth Pavilion, Montgomery *Also called Trihealth Inc (G-14603)*
Trihealth G LLC (HQ) 513 732-0700
4600 Wesley Ave Ste N Cincinnati (45212) *(G-4641)*
Trihealth G LLC 513 346-5000
55 Progress Pl Cincinnati (45246) *(G-4642)*
Trihealth G LLC 513 624-5535
7691 5 Mile Rd Ste 214 Cincinnati (45230) *(G-4643)*
Trihealth G LLC 513 922-1200
2001 Anderson Ferry Rd Cincinnati (45238) *(G-4644)*
Trihealth Hf LLC 513 398-3445
7423 S Mason Mntgomery Mason (45040) *(G-13649)*
Trihealth Inc 513 985-0900
6200 Pfeiffer Rd Ste 330 Montgomery (45242) *(G-14603)*
Trihealth Oncology Inst LLC 513 451-4033
5520 Cheviot Rd Cincinnati (45247) *(G-4645)*
Trihealth Orthpd & Spine Inst, Montgomery *Also called Trihealth Os LLC (G-14604)*
Trihealth Os LLC 513 791-6611
10547 Montgomery Rd 400a Montgomery (45242) *(G-14604)*
Trihealth Rehabilitation Hosp 513 601-0600
2155 Dana Ave Cincinnati (45207) *(G-4646)*
Trihealth Work Capacity Center, Cincinnati *Also called Hospice Cincinnati Inc (G-3728)*
Trillium Creek Dermatology, Medina *Also called H M T Dermatology Inc (G-13946)*
Trillium Creek Drmtlogy Srgery, Medina *Also called Hmt Dermatology Associates Inc (G-13950)*
Trillium Family Solutions Inc 330 454-7066
111 Stow Ave Ste 100 Cuyahoga Falls (44221) *(G-9133)*
Trilogy Fulfillment LLC 614 491-0553
6600 Alum Creek Dr Groveport (43125) *(G-11543)*
Trilogy Health Services LLC 419 935-6511
1050 Neal Zick Rd Willard (44890) *(G-19489)*
Trilogy Healthcare Allen LLC 419 643-3161
800 Ambrose Dr Delphos (45833) *(G-10037)*
Trilogy Healthcare Putnam LLC 419 532-2961
755 Ottawa St Kalida (45853) *(G-12207)*
Trilogy Rehab Services LLC 740 452-3000
2991 Maple Ave Zanesville (43701) *(G-20368)*
Trimark Ss Kemp, Cleveland *Also called S S Kemp & Company (G-6357)*
Trimark Usa LLC 216 271-7700
4567 Willow Pkwy Cleveland (44125) *(G-6549)*
Trimat Construction Inc 740 388-9515
13621 State Route 554 Bidwell (45614) *(G-1470)*
Trimble & Julian, Westerville *Also called Julian & Grube Inc (G-19176)*
Trimble Engineering & Cnstr 937 233-8921
5475 Kellenburger Rd Dayton (45424) *(G-9823)*
Trimor, Twinsburg *Also called Tri-Mor Corp (G-18329)*
Trimor, Twinsburg *Also called Cem-Base Inc (G-18251)*
Trinity Action Partnership 937 456-2800
308 Eaton Lewisburg Rd Eaton (45320) *(G-10463)*
Trinity Community, Beavercreek *Also called United Church Homes Inc (G-1239)*
Trinity Contracting Inc 614 905-4410
4878 Mgnolia Blossom Blvd Columbus (43230) *(G-8780)*
Trinity Credit Counseling Inc 513 769-0621
11229 Reading Rd Ste 1 Cincinnati (45241) *(G-4647)*
TRINITY DEBT MANAGEMENT, Cincinnati *Also called Trinity Credit Counseling Inc (G-4647)*
Trinity Health Corporation 614 846-5420
5700 Karl Rd Columbus (43229) *(G-8781)*
Trinity Health Corporation 419 448-3124
485 W Market St Tiffin (44883) *(G-17545)*
Trinity Health Group Ltd 614 899-4830
827 Yard St Columbus (43212) *(G-8782)*
Trinity Health System 740 283-7848
380 Summit Ave Steubenville (43952) *(G-17176)*
Trinity Health System 740 264-8000
4000 Johnson Rd Fl 1 Steubenville (43952) *(G-17177)*
Trinity Health System 740 264-8101
4000 Johnson Rd Fl 1 Steubenville (43952) *(G-17178)*
Trinity Health System (HQ) 740 283-7000
380 Summit Ave Steubenville (43952) *(G-17179)*
Trinity Health West, Steubenville *Also called Trinity Health System (G-17177)*
Trinity Healthcare Corporation 513 489-2444
8211 Weller Rd Cincinnati (45242) *(G-4648)*
Trinity Home Builders Inc 614 889-7830
2700 E Dublin Granville Columbus (43231) *(G-8783)*
Trinity Hospital Holding Co (HQ) 740 264-8000
380 Summit Ave Steubenville (43952) *(G-17180)*
Trinity Hospital Twin City 740 922-2800
819 N 1st St Dennison (44621) *(G-10053)*
Trinity Medical Center East, Steubenville *Also called Trinity Hospital Holding Co (G-17180)*
Trinity Medical Center East, Steubenville *Also called Trinity Health System (G-17179)*
Trinity West 740 264-8000
4000 Johnson Rd Fl 1 Steubenville (43952) *(G-17181)*
Trio Limited (PA) 614 898-5463
2400 Corporate Exch Dr Columbus (43231) *(G-8784)*
Trio Trucking Inc 513 679-7100
7750 Reinhold Dr Cincinnati (45237) *(G-4649)*
Tripack LLC 513 248-1255
401 Milford Pkwy Ste C Milford (45150) *(G-14439)*

ALPHABETIC

Triple Ladys Agency Inc (PA)...330 274-1100
  4626 State Route 82 Mantua (44255) *(G-13277)*
Triple Q Foundations Co Inc...513 932-3121
  139 Harmon Ave Lebanon (45036) *(G-12511)*
Triple T Transport Inc (PA)...740 657-3244
  433 Lewis Center Rd Lewis Center (43035) *(G-12563)*
Triplefin LLC (PA)...855 877-5346
  11333 Cornell Park Dr Blue Ash (45242) *(G-1665)*
Triplefin LLC...513 794-9870
  11333 Cornell Park Dr Blue Ash (45242) *(G-1666)*
Triplett ASAP, Akron *Also called Lkq Triplettasap Inc (G-317)*
Tripoint Medical Center, Painesville *Also called Lake Hospital System Inc (G-15719)*
Tripoint Medical Center...440 375-8100
  7590 Auburn Rd Painesville (44077) *(G-15744)*
Trippe, Glen MD, Bellevue *Also called New Beginnings Pediatrics Inc (G-1381)*
Trisco Systems Incorporated...419 339-9912
  2000 Baty Rd Lima (45807) *(G-12769)*
Tristate Concrete, Metamora *Also called Tscs Inc (G-14133)*
Triton Services Inc...513 679-6800
  8162 Duke Blvd Mason (45040) *(G-13650)*
Triumph Energy Corporation...513 367-9900
  9171 Dry Fork Rd Harrison (45030) *(G-11679)*
Triumph Hospital Mansfield...419 526-0777
  335 Glessner Ave Mansfield (44903) *(G-13255)*
Triversity Construction Co LLC...513 733-0046
  5050 Section Ave Ste 330 Cincinnati (45212) *(G-4650)*
Troilo & Associates, New Albany *Also called Allstars Travel Group Inc (G-14842)*
Trolley Tours of Cleveland...216 771-4484
  1790 Columbus Rd Cleveland (44113) *(G-6550)*
Troy Bowl, Troy *Also called Bigelow Corporation (G-18196)*
Troy Built Building LLC...419 425-1093
  1001 Fishlock Ave Findlay (45840) *(G-10971)*
TROY CENTER, Troy *Also called Genesis Healthcare (G-18203)*
Troy Center, Troy *Also called Harborside Troy LLC (G-18205)*
Troy Christian School...937 339-5692
  1586 Mckaig Rd Troy (45373) *(G-18233)*
Troy City Water Distribution, Troy *Also called City of Troy (G-18198)*
Troy Country Club Inc...937 335-5691
  1830 Peters Rd Troy (45373) *(G-18234)*
Troyer Cheese Inc...330 893-2479
  6597 County Road 625 Millersburg (44654) *(G-14497)*
Troyers Home Pantry (PA)...330 698-4182
  668 W Main St Apple Creek (44606) *(G-621)*
TRT Management Corporation (PA)...419 661-1233
  487 J St Perrysburg (43551) *(G-15927)*
Tru Green-Chemlawn, Hilliard *Also called Trugreen Limited Partnership (G-11824)*
Tru Green-Chemlawn, Springboro *Also called Trugreen Limited Partnership (G-16986)*
Tru Green-Chemlawn, Mansfield *Also called Trugreen Limited Partnership (G-13256)*
Tru Green-Chemlawn, Bedford *Also called Trugreen Limited Partnership (G-1311)*
Tru Green-Chemlawn, Fairfield *Also called Trugreen Limited Partnership (G-10794)*
Tru Green-Chemlawn, Mentor *Also called Trugreen Limited Partnership (G-14116)*
Tru Green-Chemlawn, Lewis Center *Also called Trugreen Limited Partnership (G-12564)*
Tru Green-Chemlawn, Lima *Also called Trugreen Limited Partnership (G-12771)*
Tru Green-Chemlawn, Elyria *Also called Trugreen Limited Partnership (G-10568)*
Tru Green-Chemlawn, Groveport *Also called Trugreen Limited Partnership (G-11544)*
Tru Green-Chemlawn, Canton *Also called Trugreen Limited Partnership (G-2515)*
Tru Green-Chemlawn, Brilliant *Also called Trugreen Limited Partnership (G-1823)*
Tru Green-Chemlawn, Dayton *Also called Trugreen Limited Partnership (G-9824)*
Tru Green-Chemlawn, Vandalia *Also called Trugreen Limited Partnership (G-18545)*
Tru-Gro Landscaping, Dayton *Also called Woody Tree Medics (G-9886)*
Trubuilt Construction Svcs LLC...614 279-4800
  777 Harrison Dr Columbus (43204) *(G-8785)*
Trucco Construction Co Inc...740 417-9010
  3531 Airport Rd Delaware (43015) *(G-10010)*
Truck Country Indiana Inc...419 228-4334
  598 E Hanthorn Rd Lima (45804) *(G-12770)*
Trucking and Logistics, South Point *Also called H & W Holdings LLC (G-16935)*
Trucking Division, Toledo *Also called FCA US LLC (G-17729)*
Truckmen, Geneva *Also called Neighborhood Logistics Co Inc (G-11244)*
Truckomat Corporation...740 467-2818
  10707 Lancaster Rd Ste 37 Hebron (43025) *(G-11725)*
Truckstops of America, Lodi *Also called Travelcenters of America LLC (G-12829)*
Truckway Leasing, Cincinnati *Also called Interstate Truckway Inc (G-3781)*
True Core Federal Credit Union...740 345-6608
  215 Deo Dr Newark (43055) *(G-15104)*
True North Energy LLC...440 442-0060
  6411 Mayfield Rd Mayfield Heights (44124) *(G-13883)*
True North Energy LLC (PA)...877 245-9336
  10346 Brecksville Rd Brecksville (44141) *(G-1808)*
True North Trucking, Toledo *Also called Lyden Company (G-17874)*
True Value, Hartville *Also called Hrm Enterprises Inc (G-11691)*
True2form Collision Repair Ctr (PA)...330 399-6659
  3924 Youngstown Rd Se Warren (44484) *(G-18752)*
Trueblue Inc...740 282-1079
  2125 Sunset Blvd Steubenville (43952) *(G-17182)*

Truechoicepack Corp...937 630-3832
  5155 Financial Way Ste 6 Mason (45040) *(G-13651)*
Truenorth Cultural Arts...440 949-5200
  739 Moore Rd Ste 1 Avon Lake (44012) *(G-928)*
Truenorth Energy, Mayfield Heights *Also called True North Energy LLC (G-13883)*
Truepoint Inc...513 792-6648
  4901 Hunt Rd Ste 200 Blue Ash (45242) *(G-1667)*
Trugreen Chemlawn, Mansfield *Also called Igh II Inc (G-13184)*
Trugreen Limited Partnership...614 527-7070
  5150 Nike Dr Hilliard (43026) *(G-11824)*
Trugreen Limited Partnership...937 557-0060
  760 Pleasant Valley Dr Springboro (45066) *(G-16986)*
Trugreen Limited Partnership...419 884-3636
  110 Industrial Dr Mansfield (44904) *(G-13256)*
Trugreen Limited Partnership...440 786-7200
  20375 Hannan Pkwy Bedford (44146) *(G-1311)*
Trugreen Limited Partnership...513 223-3707
  4041 Thunderbird Ln Fairfield (45014) *(G-10794)*
Trugreen Limited Partnership...440 290-3340
  7460 Clover Ave Mentor (44060) *(G-14116)*
Trugreen Limited Partnership...614 285-3721
  461 Enterprise Dr Lewis Center (43035) *(G-12564)*
Trugreen Limited Partnership...419 516-4200
  2083 N Dixie Hwy Lima (45801) *(G-12771)*
Trugreen Limited Partnership...440 540-4209
  151 Keep Ct Elyria (44035) *(G-10568)*
Trugreen Limited Partnership...614 610-4142
  4045 Lakeview Xing Groveport (43125) *(G-11544)*
Trugreen Limited Partnership...330 409-2861
  6302 Promway Ave Nw Canton (44720) *(G-2515)*
Trugreen Limited Partnership...740 598-4724
  198 Penn St Brilliant (43913) *(G-1823)*
Trugreen Limited Partnership...937 866-8399
  767 Liberty Ln Dayton (45449) *(G-9824)*
Trugreen Limited Partnership...937 410-4055
  800 Center Dr Vandalia (45377) *(G-18545)*
Trugreen-Chem Lawn...330 533-2839
  8529 South Ave Poland (44514) *(G-16091)*
Truitt Thos R & Truitt Susan M, Marysville *Also called Thomas R Truitt Od (G-13533)*
Trumball Cnty Fire Chiefs Assn...330 675-6602
  640 N River Rd Nw Warren (44483) *(G-18753)*
Trumball Cnty Hzardous Mtl Bur, Warren *Also called Trumball Cnty Fire Chiefs Assn (G-18753)*
Trumbll-Mhoning Med Group Phrm, Cortland *Also called Trumbull-Mahoning Med Group (G-8995)*
Trumbull Cmnty Action Program (PA)...330 393-2507
  1230 Palmyra Rd Sw Warren (44485) *(G-18754)*
Trumbull County Engineering (PA)...330 675-2640
  650 N River Rd Nw Warren (44483) *(G-18755)*
Trumbull County Engineers, Warren *Also called County of Trumbull (G-18692)*
Trumbull County One Stop...330 675-2000
  280 N Park Ave Warren (44481) *(G-18756)*
Trumbull Housing Dev Corp...330 369-1533
  4076 Youngstown Rd Se # 101 Warren (44484) *(G-18757)*
Trumbull Industries Inc...330 393-6624
  850 Bronze Rd Ne Warren (44483) *(G-18758)*
Trumbull Industries Inc...330 270-7800
  1040 N Meridian Rd Youngstown (44509) *(G-20226)*
Trumbull Manufacturing Inc...330 393-6624
  400 Dietz Rd Ne Warren (44483) *(G-18759)*
Trumbull Mem Hosp Foundation...330 841-9376
  1350 E Market St Warren (44483) *(G-18760)*
Trumbull Special Courier Inc...330 841-0074
  346 Willard Ave Se Warren (44483) *(G-18761)*
Trumbull-Mahoning Med Group...330 372-8800
  2600 State Route 5 Cortland (44410) *(G-8995)*
Trustaff Management Inc...513 272-3999
  4675 Cornell Rd Ste 100 Blue Ash (45241) *(G-1668)*
Trustaff Travel Nurses, Blue Ash *Also called Trustaff Management Inc (G-1668)*
Trusted Homecare Solutions...937 506-7063
  2324 Stanley Ave Ste 115 Dayton (45404) *(G-9825)*
Truteam LLC...513 942-2204
  28 Kiesland Ct Hamilton (45015) *(G-11649)*
Trx Great Plains Inc...855 259-9259
  6600 Bessemer Ave Cleveland (44127) *(G-6551)*
Trx Great Plains, Inc., Cleveland *Also called Horizon Mid Atlantic Inc (G-5707)*
TS Tech Americas Inc...740 593-5958
  10 Kenny Dr Athens (45701) *(G-808)*
TS Tech Americas Inc (HQ)...614 575-4100
  8458 E Broad St Reynoldsburg (43068) *(G-16334)*
TSA Inspections, Mansfield *Also called James Ray Lozier (G-13190)*
TSC Apparel LLC (PA)...513 771-1138
  Centennial Plaza Iii 895 Cincinnati (45202) *(G-4651)*
TSC Communications Inc...419 739-2200
  2 Willipie St Wapakoneta (45895) *(G-18657)*
TSC Television Inc...419 941-6001
  2 Willipie St Wapakoneta (45895) *(G-18658)*
Tscs Inc...419 644-3921
  14293 State Route 64 Metamora (43540) *(G-14133)*
Tsg Resources Inc...330 498-8200
  339 E Maple St Ste 110 North Canton (44720) *(G-15241)*

Tsg-Cincinnati LLC..........513 793-6241
11243 Cornell Park Dr Blue Ash (45242) *(G-1669)*

Tsi Inc..........419 468-1855
1263 State Route 598 Galion (44833) *(G-11184)*

Tsk Assisted Living Services..........330 297-2000
240 W Riddle Ave Ravenna (44266) *(G-16269)*

Tsl Ltd (PA)..........419 843-3200
5217 Monroe St Ste A1 Toledo (43623) *(G-18110)*

Tsm Logistics LLC..........419 234-6074
4567 Old Town Run Rd Rockford (45882) *(G-16418)*

TSS Acquisition Company (HQ)..........513 772-7000
25101 Chagrin Blvd D Cleveland (44122) *(G-6552)*

TSS Resources, Dublin *Also called Telecmmnctons Stffing Slutions* *(G-10355)*

TSS Technologies, Cleveland *Also called TSS Acquisition Company* *(G-6552)*

TTI Floor Care North Amer Inc (HQ)..........440 996-2000
7005 Cochran Rd Solon (44139) *(G-16909)*

TTI Floor Care North America, Cleveland *Also called Royal Appliance Mfg Co* *(G-6344)*

Ttl Associates Inc (PA)..........419 241-4556
1915 N 12th St Toledo (43604) *(G-18111)*

Tube Fittings Division, Columbus *Also called Parker-Hannifin Corporation* *(G-8421)*

Tucker Ellis LLP..........720 897-4400
950 Main Ave Ste 1100 Cleveland (44113) *(G-6553)*

Tucker Ellis LLP (PA)..........216 592-5000
950 Main Ave Ste 1100 Cleveland (44113) *(G-6554)*

Tucker Ellis LLP..........614 358-9717
175 S 3rd St Ste 520 Columbus (43215) *(G-8786)*

Tucker Landscaping Inc..........440 786-9840
1000 Broadway Ave Bedford (44146) *(G-1312)*

Tucker Landscaping Company, Bedford *Also called Tucker Landscaping Inc* *(G-1312)*

Tucson Inc..........330 339-4935
3497 University Dr Ne New Philadelphia (44663) *(G-14985)*

Tudor Arms Mstr Subtenant LLC..........216 696-6611
10660 Carnegie Ave Cleveland (44106) *(G-6555)*

Tuffy Associates Corp (PA)..........419 865-6900
7150 Granite Cir Ste 100 Toledo (43617) *(G-18112)*

Tuffy Auto Service Centers, Toledo *Also called Tuffy Associates Corp* *(G-18112)*

Tunnell Hill Reclamation, New Lexington *Also called Oxford Mining Company Inc* *(G-14924)*

Turbo Parts LLC..........740 223-1695
1676 Cascade Dr Marion (43302) *(G-13466)*

Turfscape Inc..........330 405-0741
8490 Tower Dr Twinsburg (44087) *(G-18330)*

Turn Around Group Inc..........330 372-0064
1512 Phoenix Rd Ne Warren (44483) *(G-18762)*

Turn-Key Industrial Svcs LLC..........614 274-1128
820 Distribution Dr Columbus (43228) *(G-8787)*

Turner Construction Company..........513 721-4224
250 W Court St Ste 300w Cincinnati (45202) *(G-4652)*

Turner Construction Company..........216 522-1180
1422 Euclid Ave Ste 1400 Cleveland (44115) *(G-6556)*

Turner Construction Company..........513 363-0883
2315 Iowa Ave Cincinnati (45206) *(G-4653)*

Turner Construction Company..........614 984-3000
262 Hanover St Columbus (43215) *(G-8788)*

Turney's, Chesterland *Also called G H A Inc* *(G-2739)*

Turning Pt Counseling Svcs Inc (PA)..........330 744-2991
611 Belmont Ave Youngstown (44502) *(G-20227)*

Turning Technologies LLC (PA)..........330 746-3015
255 W Federal St Youngstown (44503) *(G-20228)*

Turnkey Network Solutions LLC..........614 876-9944
3450 Millikin Ct Ste A Columbus (43228) *(G-8789)*

Turnpike and Infrastructure Co..........330 527-2169
9196 State Route 700 Windham (44288) *(G-19664)*

Turpin Hills Swim Racquet CLB..........513 231-3242
3814 West St Ste 311 Cincinnati (45227) *(G-4654)*

Turtle Golf Management Ltd (HQ)..........614 882-5920
5400 Little Turtle Way W Westerville (43081) *(G-19303)*

Turtles Envmtl Abatement Co..........614 603-9439
5601 Little Ben Cir Apt B Columbus (43231) *(G-8790)*

Tuscan Villa, Cleveland *Also called Aristocrat W Nursing Hm Corp* *(G-5007)*

Tuscany Spa Salon..........513 489-8872
11355 Montgomery Rd Cincinnati (45249) *(G-4655)*

Tuscarawas Cnty Job Fmly Svcs, New Philadelphia *Also called County of Tuscarawas* *(G-14955)*

Tuscarawas County Commitee..........330 364-6611
425 Prospect St Dover (44622) *(G-10104)*

Tuscarawas County Help ME Grow..........330 339-3493
1433 5th St Nw New Philadelphia (44663) *(G-14986)*

TUSCARAWAS COUNTY SENIOR CENTE, Dover *Also called Tuscarawas County Commitee* *(G-10104)*

Tusco Grocers Inc..........740 922-8721
30 S 4th St Dennison (44621) *(G-10054)*

Tusco Imaa Chapter No 602..........330 878-7369
6607 Cherry Run Rd Nw Strasburg (44680) *(G-17240)*

Tusco RC Club, Strasburg *Also called Tusco Imaa Chapter No 602* *(G-17240)*

Tusing Builders Ltd..........419 465-3100
2596 Us Route 20 E Monroeville (44847) *(G-14591)*

Tuttle Crossing Associates, Dublin *Also called Simon Property Group* *(G-10335)*

Tuttle Landscaping & Grdn Ctr..........419 756-7555
1295 S Trimble Rd Mansfield (44907) *(G-13257)*

TV Minority Company Inc..........937 832-9350
30 Lau Pkwy Englewood (45315) *(G-10603)*

TV Minority Company Inc..........937 226-1559
1700 E Monument Ave Dayton (45402) *(G-9826)*

TVC Home Health Care..........330 755-1110
70 W Mckinley Way Ste 8 Youngstown (44514) *(G-20229)*

TW Recreational Services..........419 836-1466
1750 State Park Rd 2 Oregon (43616) *(G-15613)*

TW Recreational Services Inc..........440 564-9144
11755 Kinsman Rd Newbury (44065) *(G-15126)*

TW Telecom Inc..........234 542-6279
1019 E Turkeyfoot Lake Rd Akron (44312) *(G-474)*

TWC Concrete Services LLC..........513 771-8192
10737 Medallion Dr Cincinnati (45241) *(G-4656)*

Twelve Inc (PA)..........330 837-3555
619 Tremont Ave Sw Massillon (44647) *(G-13733)*

TWELVE OF OHIO, THE, Massillon *Also called Twelve Inc* *(G-13733)*

Twh, Hicksville *Also called Wholesale House Inc* *(G-11731)*

Twigs Kids, Dayton *Also called Christian Twigs Gymnastics CLB* *(G-9299)*

Twilight Gardens Healthcare..........419 668-2086
196 W Main St Norwalk (44857) *(G-15458)*

TWILIGHT GARDENS HOME, Norwalk *Also called Twilight Gardens Healthcare* *(G-15458)*

Twin Cedars Services Inc..........513 932-0399
935 Old Ralph 122 Lebanon (45036) *(G-12512)*

Twin City Water and Sewer Dst..........740 922-1460
308 Grant St Dennison (44621) *(G-10055)*

Twin Comm Inc..........740 774-4701
2349 State Route 821 Marietta (45750) *(G-13390)*

Twin Haven Reception Hall..........330 425-1616
10439 Ravenna Rd Twinsburg (44087) *(G-18331)*

Twin Maples Nursing Home..........740 596-5955
31054 State Route 93 Mc Arthur (45651) *(G-13891)*

Twin Med LLC..........440 973-4555
6950 Engle Rd Middleburg Heights (44130) *(G-14262)*

Twin Oaks Care Center Inc..........419 524-1205
73 Madison Rd Mansfield (44905) *(G-13258)*

Twin Pines Retreat Care Center..........330 688-5553
456 Seasons Rd Stow (44224) *(G-17237)*

Twin Rvers Care Rhbltation Ctr, Defiance *Also called Sun Healthcare Group Inc* *(G-9943)*

Twin Vly Behavioral Healthcare, Columbus *Also called Mental Health and Addi Serv* *(G-8057)*

Twin Vly Behavioral Hlth Care, Columbus *Also called Mental Health and Addi Serv* *(G-8058)*

Twinbrook Hills Baptist Church..........513 863-3107
40 Wrenwood Dr Hamilton (45013) *(G-11650)*

Twinoaks Living and Lrng Ctr, Mansfield *Also called Manfield Living Center Ltd* *(G-13203)*

Twinsburg Medical Offices, Twinsburg *Also called Kaiser Foundation Hospitals* *(G-18287)*

Twism Enterprises LLC..........513 800-1098
12110 Regency Run Ct # 9 Cincinnati (45240) *(G-4657)*

Twist Inc..........937 675-9581
1380 Lavelle Dr Xenia (45385) *(G-19931)*

Two Happy Frogs Incorporated..........330 633-1666
165 Northeast Ave Tallmadge (44278) *(G-17495)*

Two K General Company, Delaware *Also called Twok General Co* *(G-10011)*

Two M Precision Co Inc..........440 946-2120
1747 Joseph Lloyd Pkwy # 3 Willoughby (44094) *(G-19578)*

Two Men & A Truck, Columbus *Also called Nest Tenders Limited* *(G-8170)*

Two Men & A Vacuum LLC..........614 300-7970
81 S 4th St Ste 100 Columbus (43215) *(G-8791)*

Two Men & Truck Inc..........419 882-1002
2800 Tremainsville Rd A Toledo (43613) *(G-18113)*

Two Men and A Truck, Toledo *Also called Two Men & Truck Inc* *(G-18113)*

Two Men and A Truck, Akron *Also called E & V Ventures Inc* *(G-198)*

TWO MEN AND A TRUCK/CLEVELAND, Wickliffe *Also called Northcoast Moving Enterprising* *(G-19471)*

Two-X Engners Constructers LLC..........330 995-0592
570 Club Dr Aurora (44202) *(G-845)*

Twok General Co..........740 417-9195
19 Gruber St Ste B Delaware (43015) *(G-10011)*

Tyco International MGT Co LLC..........888 787-8324
2884 E Kemper Rd Cincinnati (45241) *(G-4658)*

Tycor Roofing Inc..........330 452-8150
1704 Warner Rd Se Canton (44707) *(G-2516)*

Tyler Technologies Inc..........937 276-5261
4100 Miller Valentine Ct Moraine (45439) *(G-14703)*

Tylinter Inc (HQ)..........800 321-6188
8570 Tyler Blvd Mentor (44060) *(G-14117)*

U A W Region 2 Headquarters, Cleveland *Also called International Union United Au* *(G-5764)*

U C Child Care Center Inc..........513 961-2825
3310 Ruther Ave Cincinnati (45220) *(G-4659)*

U C Health Dermatology, West Chester *Also called Uc Health Llc* *(G-19021)*

U C M Residential Services..........937 643-3757
400 Gade Ave Union City (45390) *(G-18355)*

U D F, Cincinnati *Also called United Dairy Farmers Inc* *(G-4678)*

U H Ahuja Medical Center, Cleveland *Also called University Hospitals* *(G-6587)*

U Haul Co of Northwestern Ohio (HQ)..........419 478-1101
50 W Alexis Rd Toledo (43612) *(G-18114)*

U S A Concrete Specialists..........330 482-9150
145 Nulf Dr Columbiana (44408) *(G-6794)*

U S A Plumbing Company 614 882-6402
1425 Community Park Dr Columbus (43229) ***(G-8792)***
U S A Waterproofing Inc 330 425-2440
1632 Enterprise Pkwy Twinsburg (44087) ***(G-18332)***
U S Army Corps of Engineers 740 269-2681
86801 Eslick Rd Uhrichsville (44683) ***(G-18345)***
U S Army Corps of Engineers 740 767-3527
23560 Jenkins Dam Rd Glouster (45732) ***(G-11311)***
U S Army Corps of Engineers 513 684-3048
550 Main St Ste 10022 Cincinnati (45202) ***(G-4660)***
U S Associates Realty Inc 216 663-3400
4700 Rockside Rd Ste 150 Cleveland (44131) ***(G-6557)***
U S Bank Arena, Cincinnati *Also called Arena Management Holdings LLC* ***(G-2984)***
U S C, Miamisburg *Also called Ulliman Schutte Cnstr LLC* ***(G-14233)***
U S Cargo, Cleveland *Also called United States Cargo & Courier* ***(G-6579)***
U S Dental Care, Columbus *Also called US Dental Care/M D Gelender* ***(G-8833)***
U S Development Corp (PA) 330 673-6900
900 W Main St Kent (44240) ***(G-12264)***
U S Diagnostics, Dayton *Also called Dayton Medical Imaging* ***(G-9372)***
U S Laboratories Inc 440 248-1223
33095 Bainbridge Rd Cleveland (44139) ***(G-6558)***
U S Protective Services, Independence *Also called United States Protective* ***(G-12135)***
U S Title Agency Inc 216 621-1424
1213 Prospect Ave E # 400 Cleveland (44115) ***(G-6559)***
U S Weatherford L P 330 746-2502
1100 Performance Pl Youngstown (44502) ***(G-20230)***
U S Xpress Inc 937 328-4100
825 W Leffel Ln Springfield (45506) ***(G-17129)***
U S Xpress Inc 740 363-0700
2000 Nutter Farms Ln Delaware (43015) ***(G-10012)***
U S Xpress Inc 740 452-4153
2705 E Pointe Dr Zanesville (43701) ***(G-20369)***
U Save Auto Rental 330 925-2015
112 E Ohio Ave Rittman (44270) ***(G-16410)***
U T C, Beavercreek *Also called Universal Technology Corp* ***(G-1193)***
U Z Engineered Products Co, Cleveland *Also called State Industrial Products Corp* ***(G-6459)***
U-Co Industries Inc 937 644-3021
16900 Square Dr Ste 110 Marysville (43040) ***(G-13534)***
U-Haul, Toledo *Also called U Haul Co of Northwestern Ohio* ***(G-18114)***
U-Haul Neighborhood Dealer -Ce 419 929-3724
1005 Us Highway 250 S New London (44851) ***(G-14936)***
U-Save Auto Rental, Rittman *Also called U Save Auto Rental* ***(G-16410)***
U.S. Bridge, Cambridge *Also called Ohio Bridge Corporation* ***(G-2079)***
U.S. Rnal Care NW Ohio Dalysis, Toledo *Also called Innovative Dialysis* ***(G-17822)***
U.S.t Environmental Contractor, Logan *Also called Alco Inc* ***(G-12830)***
Uahs Heather Hill Home Health 440 285-5098
12340 Bass Lake Rd Chardon (44024) ***(G-2719)***
Uasi, Cincinnati *Also called United Audit Systems Inc* ***(G-4675)***
Uaw Local 863, Cincinnati *Also called International Union United Au* ***(G-3780)***
UBS Financial Services Inc 330 655-8319
43 Village Way Ste 201 Hudson (44236) ***(G-12009)***
UBS Financial Services Inc 440 414-2740
2055 Crocker Rd Ste 201 Westlake (44145) ***(G-19416)***
UBS Financial Services Inc 419 624-6800
111 E Shoreline Dr Ste 3 Sandusky (44870) ***(G-16650)***
UBS Financial Services Inc 740 336-7823
324 3rd St Marietta (45750) ***(G-13391)***
UBS Financial Services Inc 513 576-5000
312 Walnut St Ste 3300 Cincinnati (45202) ***(G-4661)***
UBS Financial Services Inc 419 318-5525
5757 Monroe St Sylvania (43560) ***(G-17461)***
UBS Financial Services Inc 937 428-1300
7887 Wash Vlg Dr Ste 100 Dayton (45459) ***(G-9827)***
UBS Financial Services Inc 513 792-2146
8044 Montgomery Rd # 200 Cincinnati (45236) ***(G-4662)***
UBS Financial Services Inc 216 831-3400
2000 Auburn Dr Ste 100 Cleveland (44122) ***(G-6560)***
UBS Financial Services Inc 614 460-6559
41 S High St Ste 3300 Columbus (43215) ***(G-8793)***
UBS Financial Services Inc 614 442-6240
5025 Arlngtn Ctr Blvd # 120 Columbus (43220) ***(G-8794)***
UBS Financial Services Inc 937 223-3141
3601 Rigby Rd Ste 500 Miamisburg (45342) ***(G-14232)***
UBS Financial Services Inc 513 792-2100
8044 Montgomery Rd # 200 Cincinnati (45236) ***(G-4663)***
Uc Health, Cincinnati *Also called University Radiology Assoc* ***(G-4729)***
Uc Health Llc 513 584-6999
9313 S Mason Montgomery R Mason (45040) ***(G-13652)***
Uc Health Llc 513 475-7458
7700 University Ct # 1800 West Chester (45069) ***(G-19020)***
Uc Health Llc 513 475-7630
7690 Discovery Dr # 1700 West Chester (45069) ***(G-19021)***
Uc Health Llc 513 475-7880
222 Piedmont Ave Ste 6000 Cincinnati (45219) ***(G-4664)***
Uc Health Llc 513 475-8881
7700 University Ct West Chester (45069) ***(G-19022)***
Uc Health Llc 513 585-7600
3200 Burnet Ave Cincinnati (45229) ***(G-4665)***
Uc Health Llc 513 298-3000
7798 Discovery Dr Ste F West Chester (45069) ***(G-19023)***
Uc Health Llc 513 475-7777
7710 University Ct West Chester (45069) ***(G-19024)***
Uc Health Llc 513 648-9077
11590 Century Blvd # 102 Cincinnati (45246) ***(G-4666)***
Uc Health Llc 513 584-8600
3120 Burnet Ave Ste 203 Cincinnati (45229) ***(G-4667)***
Uc Health Llc 513 475-7500
7798 Discovery Dr Ste E West Chester (45069) ***(G-19025)***
Uc Health Llc (PA) 513 585-6000
3200 Burnet Ave Cincinnati (45229) ***(G-4668)***
Uc Health Dermatology, Cincinnati *Also called Univ Dermatology* ***(G-4692)***
Uc Health Primary Care Mason, Mason *Also called Uc Health Llc* ***(G-13652)***
Uc Physician, Cincinnati *Also called Bruce R Bracken* ***(G-3084)***
Ucb, Toledo *Also called United Collection Bureau Inc* ***(G-18117)***
Ucc Childrens Center 513 217-5501
5750 Innovation Dr Middletown (45005) ***(G-14356)***
UCI, Cleveland *Also called University Circle Incorporated* ***(G-6586)***
Uct Property Inc 614 228-3276
1801 Watermark Dr Ste 100 Columbus (43215) ***(G-8795)***
Ucvp For Research, Cincinnati *Also called University of Cincinnati* ***(G-4712)***
Ues Inc (PA) 937 426-6900
4401 Dayton Xenia Rd Beavercreek (45432) ***(G-1190)***
Ues Metals Group 937 255-9340
4401 Dayton Xenia Rd Beavercreek (45432) ***(G-1191)***
Ufcw 75 Real Estate Corp 937 677-0075
7250 Poe Ave Ste 400 Dayton (45414) ***(G-9828)***
Ufcw Local 1059, Columbus *Also called United Food Comml Wrkrs Un* ***(G-8800)***
Ufcw Local No. 75, Dayton *Also called United Food and Coml Wkrs* ***(G-9831)***
Uhhs Westlake Medical Center 440 250-2070
960 Clague Rd Ste 3201 Westlake (44145) ***(G-19417)***
Uhhs-Geauga Regional Hospital, Chardon *Also called University Hospitals* ***(G-2721)***
Uhhs-Memorial Hosp of Geneva 440 466-1141
870 W Main St Geneva (44041) ***(G-11248)***
Uhhs/Csahs - Cuyahoga Inc 440 746-3401
6935 Treeline Dr Ste J Cleveland (44141) ***(G-6561)***
Uhl's Jamestown Market, Jamestown *Also called Greeneview Foods LLC* ***(G-12187)***
Uhmg Department of Urologist (PA) 216 844-3009
11100 Euclid Ave Cleveland (44106) ***(G-6562)***
Uhrichsville Health Care Ctr 740 922-2208
5166 Spanson Dr Se Uhrichsville (44683) ***(G-18346)***
UIC General Contractors, Ashtabula *Also called Union Industrial Contractors* ***(G-757)***
Uima, Cincinnati *Also called University of Cincinnati* ***(G-4715)***
Ull Inc (PA) 440 543-5195
9812 Washington St Chagrin Falls (44023) ***(G-2685)***
Ulliman Schutte Cnstr LLC (PA) 937 247-0375
9111 Springboro Pike Miamisburg (45342) ***(G-14233)***
Ulmer & Berne Illinois, Cleveland *Also called Ulmer & Berne LLP* ***(G-6563)***
Ulmer & Berne LLP 513 698-5000
600 Vine St Ste 2800 Cincinnati (45202) ***(G-4669)***
Ulmer & Berne LLP (PA) 216 583-7000
1660 W 2nd St Ste 1100 Cleveland (44113) ***(G-6563)***
Ulmer & Berne LLP 513 698-5000
600 Vine St Ste 2800 Cincinnati (45202) ***(G-4670)***
Ulmer & Berne LLP 513 698-5058
600 Vine St Ste 2800 Cincinnati (45202) ***(G-4671)***
Ulmer & Berne LLP 614 229-0000
65 E State St Ste 1100 Columbus (43215) ***(G-8796)***
Ulrich Professional Group 330 673-9501
401 Devon Pl Ste 215 Kent (44240) ***(G-12265)***
Ultimate Air Shuttle, North Canton *Also called Ultimate Jetcharters LLC* ***(G-15242)***
Ultimate Building Maintenance 330 369-9771
3229 Youngstown Rd Se Warren (44484) ***(G-18763)***
Ultimate Health Care, South Point *Also called Quality Care Nursing Svcs LLC* ***(G-16944)***
Ultimate Jetcharters LLC 330 497-3344
6061 W Airport Dr North Canton (44720) ***(G-15242)***
Ultimate Rehab Ltd 513 563-8777
11305 Reed Hartman Hwy # 226 Blue Ash (45241) ***(G-1670)***
Ultimus Fund Solutions LLC (PA) 513 587-3400
225 Pictoria Dr Ste 450 Cincinnati (45246) ***(G-4672)***
Ultra Tech Machinery Inc 330 929-5544
297 Ascot Pkwy Cuyahoga Falls (44223) ***(G-9134)***
Ulysses Caremark Holding Corp 440 542-4214
29100 Aurora Rd Solon (44139) ***(G-16910)***
Underground Utilities Inc 419 465-2587
416 Monroe St Monroeville (44847) ***(G-14592)***
UNI-Facs, Columbus *Also called Universal Fabg Cnstr Svcs Inc* ***(G-8815)***
Unico Alloys & Metals Inc 614 299-0545
1177 Joyce Ave Ste B Columbus (43219) ***(G-8797)***
Unicon International Inc (PA) 614 861-7070
241 Outerbelt St Columbus (43213) ***(G-8798)***
Unicustom Inc 513 874-9806
3263 Homeward Way Fairfield (45014) ***(G-10795)***
Unified Bank (HQ) 740 633-0445
201 S 4th St Martins Ferry (43935) ***(G-13479)***
Unified Cnstr Systems Ltd (PA) 330 773-2511
1920 S Main St Akron (44301) ***(G-475)***
Unifirst Corporation 614 575-9999
211 Reynoldsburg New Albn Blacklick (43004) ***(G-1483)***
Unifirst Corporation 216 658-6900
1450 E Granger Rd Independence (44131) ***(G-12134)***

Unifirst Corporation 937 746-0531
265 Industrial Dr Franklin (45005) *(G-11040)*

Unifund Ccr LLC 513 489-8877
10625 Techwoods Cir Blue Ash (45242) *(G-1671)*

Unifund Corporation 513 489-8877
10625 Techwoods Cir Blue Ash (45242) *(G-1672)*

Uniglobe Travel Designers, Columbus *Also called West Enterprises Inc (G-8889)*

Union Bank Company 740 387-2265
111 S Main St Marion (43302) *(G-13467)*

Union Central Life Insur Co (HQ) 866 696-7478
1876 Waycross Rd Cincinnati (45240) *(G-4673)*

Union Centre Hotel LLC 513 874-7335
6189 Muhlhauser Rd West Chester (45069) *(G-19026)*

Union Christel Manor Inc 937 968-6265
400 S Melvin Eley Ave Union City (45390) *(G-18356)*

Union City Crystal Manor, Union City *Also called Union Christel Manor Inc (G-18356)*

Union Club Company 216 621-4230
1211 Euclid Ave Cleveland (44115) *(G-6564)*

Union Cnstr Wkrs Hlth Plan 419 248-2401
7142 Nightingale Dr Ste 1 Holland (43528) *(G-11923)*

Union Cnty Board of Devlpmt, Marysville *Also called County of Union (G-13491)*

Union Country Club 330 343-5544
1000 N Bellevue Ave Dover (44622) *(G-10105)*

Union Home Mortgage Corp (PA) 440 234-4300
8241 Dow Cir Strongsville (44136) *(G-17353)*

Union Hospital Association (HQ) 330 343-3311
659 Boulevard St Dover (44622) *(G-10106)*

Union Hospital Home Hlth Care 330 343-6909
659 Boulevard St Dover (44622) *(G-10107)*

Union Industrial Contractors 440 998-7871
1800 E 21st St Ashtabula (44004) *(G-757)*

Union Mortgage Services Inc (PA) 614 457-4815
1080 Fishinger Rd Columbus (43221) *(G-8799)*

Union Rural Electric Coop Inc (PA) 937 642-1826
15461 Us Highway 36 Marysville (43040) *(G-13535)*

Union Savings Bank 937 434-1254
5651 Far Hills Ave Dayton (45429) *(G-9829)*

Union Security Insurance Co 513 621-1924
312 Elm St Ste 1500 Cincinnati (45202) *(G-4674)*

Union Supply Group Inc 614 409-1444
3321 Toy Rd Groveport (43125) *(G-11545)*

Union Tank Car Company 419 864-7216
939 Holland Rd W Marion (43302) *(G-13468)*

Unique Construction Svcs Inc 513 608-1363
10999 Reed Hartman Hwy # 313 Blue Ash (45242) *(G-1673)*

Unique Home Solutions Inc 800 800-1971
1545 W 130th St Ste A2 Hinckley (44233) *(G-11861)*

Unirush LLC (HQ) 866 766-2229
4701 Creek Rd Ste 200 Blue Ash (45242) *(G-1674)*

Uniserv, Brookfield *Also called United Steel Service LLC (G-1857)*

Unison Behavioral Health Group 419 693-0631
1425 Starr Ave Toledo (43605) *(G-18115)*

Unison Bhvioral Hlth Group Inc (PA) 419 214-4673
1425 Starr Ave Toledo (43605) *(G-18116)*

Unison Industries LLC 904 667-9904
2455 Dayton Xenia Rd Dayton (45434) *(G-9188)*

Unison Industries LLC 937 427-0550
2070 Heller Dr Beavercreek (45434) *(G-1192)*

Unistrut-Columbus, Columbus *Also called Loeb Electric Company (G-7987)*

Unite Churc Resid of Oxfor Mis (HQ) 740 382-4885
170 E Center St Marion (43302) *(G-13469)*

United Agencies Inc 216 696-8044
1422 Euclid Ave Ste 510 Cleveland (44115) *(G-6565)*

United Airlines Inc 937 454-2009
3600 Terminal Rd Ste 213 Vandalia (45377) *(G-18546)*

United Airlines Inc 216 501-4700
5970 Cargo Rd Cleveland (44135) *(G-6566)*

United Alloys and Metals, Columbus *Also called Unico Alloys & Metals Inc (G-8797)*

United Amblnce Svc of Cmbridge (HQ) 740 439-7787
1331 Campbell Ave Cambridge (43725) *(G-2086)*

United Ambulance Service 740 732-5653
523 Main St Caldwell (43724) *(G-2046)*

United American Insurance Co 440 265-9200
10749 Pearl Rd Ste D Strongsville (44136) *(G-17354)*

United Architectural Mtls Inc 330 433-9220
7830 Cleveland Ave Nw North Canton (44720) *(G-15243)*

United Armored Services, Columbus *Also called Garda CL Great Lakes Inc (G-7647)*

United Art and Education 800 322-3247
799 Lyons Rd Dayton (45459) *(G-9830)*

United Atmtc Htng Spply of Clv (PA) 216 621-5571
2125 Superior Ave E Cleveland (44114) *(G-6567)*

United Audit Systems Inc 513 723-1122
1924 Dana Ave Cincinnati (45207) *(G-4675)*

United Bank N A, Bucyrus *Also called United Bank National Assn (G-2003)*

United Bank National Assn (HQ) 419 562-3040
401 S Sandusky Ave Bucyrus (44820) *(G-2003)*

United Building Materials, Dayton *Also called Gms Inc (G-9463)*

United Cerebral Palsy (PA) 216 791-8363
10011 Euclid Ave Cleveland (44106) *(G-6568)*

United Cerebral Palsy 216 381-9993
1374 Edendale St Cleveland (44121) *(G-6569)*

United Cerebral Palsy Gr Cinc 513 221-4606
2300 Drex Ave Cincinnati (45212) *(G-4676)*

United Church Homes 740 382-4885
170 E Center St Marion (43302) *(G-13470)*

United Church Homes Inc 513 922-1440
5999 Bender Rd Cincinnati (45233) *(G-4677)*

United Church Homes Inc 937 878-0262
789 Stoneybrook Trl Fairborn (45324) *(G-10684)*

United Church Homes Inc 330 854-4177
12200 Strausser St Nw Canal Fulton (44614) *(G-2099)*

United Church Homes Inc 937 426-8481
3218 Indian Ripple Rd Beavercreek (45440) *(G-1239)*

United Church Homes Inc (PA) 740 382-4885
170 E Center St Marion (43302) *(G-13471)*

United Church Homes Inc 740 376-5600
401 Harmar St Marietta (45750) *(G-13392)*

United Church Homes Inc 740 286-7551
215 Seth Ave Jackson (45640) *(G-12181)*

United Church Homes Inc 419 294-4973
850 Marseilles Ave Upper Sandusky (43351) *(G-18414)*

United Church Homes Inc 419 621-1900
3800 Boardwalk Blvd Sandusky (44870) *(G-16651)*

United Church Res of Kenton 740 382-4885
900 E Columbus St Kenton (43326) *(G-12289)*

United Church Residences of 614 837-2008
85 Covenant Way Canal Winchester (43110) *(G-2123)*

United Collection Bureau Inc (PA) 419 866-6227
5620 Southwyck Blvd Toledo (43614) *(G-18117)*

United Collection Bureau Inc 419 866-6227
1345 Ford St Maumee (43537) *(G-13864)*

United Community Fincl Corp (PA) 330 742-0500
275 W Federal St Youngstown (44503) *(G-20231)*

United Consumer Fincl Svcs Co 440 835-3230
865 Bassett Rd Cleveland (44145) *(G-6570)*

United Dairy Farmers Inc (PA) 513 396-8700
3955 Montgomery Rd Cincinnati (45212) *(G-4678)*

United Dental Laboratories (PA) 330 253-1810
261 South Ave Tallmadge (44278) *(G-17496)*

United Disability Services Inc (PA) 330 374-1169
701 S Main St Akron (44311) *(G-476)*

United Discount, Cleveland *Also called Dollar Paradise (G-5436)*

United Electric Company Inc 502 459-5242
1309 Ethan Ave Cincinnati (45225) *(G-4679)*

United Electric Motor Repair, Cleveland *Also called United Atmtc Htng Spply of Clv (G-6567)*

United Engraving, Cincinnati *Also called Wood Graphics Inc (G-4804)*

United Fd & Coml Wkrs Intl Un 216 241-2828
9199 Market Pl Broadview Heights (44147) *(G-1849)*

United Fd Coml Wkrs Local 880 (PA) 216 241-5930
2828 Euclid Ave Cleveland (44115) *(G-6571)*

United Food & Commercial Wkr 330 452-4850
1800 Cleveland Ave Nw Canton (44709) *(G-2517)*

United Food and Coml Wkrs 937 665-0075
7250 Poe Ave Ste 400 Dayton (45414) *(G-9831)*

United Food Comml Wrkrs Un 614 235-3635
4150 E Main St Fl 2 Columbus (43213) *(G-8800)*

United Garage & Service Corp (PA) 216 623-1550
2069 W 3rd St Cleveland (44113) *(G-6572)*

United GL & Panl Systems Inc 330 244-9745
4250 Strausser St Nw Canton (44720) *(G-2518)*

United Group Services Inc (PA) 800 633-9690
9740 Near Dr West Chester (45246) *(G-19094)*

United Health Network Ltd 330 492-2102
4455 Dressler Rd Nw Canton (44718) *(G-2519)*

United Healthcare, Cincinnati *Also called Unitedhealth Group Inc (G-4691)*

United Healthcare Ohio Inc 216 694-4080
1001 Lkeside Ave Ste 1000 Cleveland (44114) *(G-6573)*

United Healthcare Ohio Inc (HQ) 614 410-7000
9200 Worthington Rd Columbus (43085) *(G-8801)*

United Healthcare Ohio Inc 513 603-6200
400 E Bus Way Ste 100 Cincinnati (45241) *(G-4680)*

United Home Health Services 614 880-8686
297 Woodland Ave Columbus (43203) *(G-8802)*

United Hsptality Solutions LLC 800 238-0487
11998 Clay Pike Rd Buffalo (43722) *(G-2007)*

United Hydraulics, Willoughby *Also called Two M Precision Co Inc (G-19578)*

United Insurance Company Amer 513 771-6771
135 Merchant St Ste 120 Cincinnati (45246) *(G-4681)*

United Insurance Company Amer 419 531-4289
1650 N Reynolds Rd Toledo (43615) *(G-18118)*

United Insurance Company Amer 216 514-1904
23215 Commerce Park # 310 Beachwood (44122) *(G-1115)*

United Labor Agency Inc 216 664-3446
737 Bolivar Rd Ste 3000 Cleveland (44115) *(G-6574)*

United Management Inc (PA) 614 228-5331
250 Civic Center Dr Columbus (43215) *(G-8803)*

United Management Inc 513 936-8568
8280 Montgomery Rd # 303 Cincinnati (45236) *(G-4682)*

United McGill Corporation (HQ) 614 829-1200
1 Mission Park Groveport (43125) *(G-11546)*

United Mercantile Corporation 513 831-1300
575 Chamber Dr Milford (45150) *(G-14440)*

United Methodist Camps, Worthington *Also called West Ohio Conference of (G-19859)*

A
L
P
H
A
B
E
T
I
C

United Methodist Childrens (PA) 614 885-5020
431 E Broad St Columbus (43215) *(G-8804)*

United Methodist Childrens HM, Columbus *Also called United Methodist Childrens* *(G-8804)*

United Methodist Community Ctr 330 743-5149
4580 Canfield Rd Canfield (44406) *(G-2162)*

United Ohio Insurance Company 419 562-3011
1725 Hopley Ave Bucyrus (44820) *(G-2004)*

United Omaha Life Insurance Co 216 573-6900
6060 Rockside Woods # 330 Cleveland (44131) *(G-6575)*

United Parcel Service Inc 614 385-9100
1711 Georgesville Rd Columbus (43228) *(G-8805)*

United Parcel Service Inc 440 826-2591
17940 Englewood Dr Cleveland (44130) *(G-6576)*

United Parcel Service Inc 937 859-2314
225 S Alex Rd West Carrollton (45449) *(G-18857)*

United Parcel Service Inc 800 742-5877
1536 N Bridge St Chillicothe (45601) *(G-2833)*

United Parcel Service Inc 440 243-3344
6940 Engle Rd Ste C Middleburg Heights (44130) *(G-14263)*

United Parcel Service Inc 614 431-0600
118 Graceland Blvd Columbus (43214) *(G-8806)*

United Parcel Service Inc 440 846-6000
13500 Pearl Rd Ste 139 Strongsville (44136) *(G-17355)*

United Parcel Service Inc OH 419 747-3080
875 W Longview Ave Mansfield (44906) *(G-13259)*

United Parcel Service Inc OH 513 852-6135
500 Gest St Cincinnati (45203) *(G-4683)*

United Parcel Service Inc OH 800 742-5877
4300 E 68th St Cleveland (44105) *(G-6577)*

United Parcel Service Inc OH 740 373-0772
105 Industry Rd Marietta (45750) *(G-13393)*

United Parcel Service Inc OH 419 222-7399
801 Industry Ave Lima (45804) *(G-12772)*

United Parcel Service Inc OH 216 676-4560
18685 Sheldon Rd Cleveland (44130) *(G-6578)*

United Parcel Service Inc OH 740 363-0636
1675 Us Highway 42 S Delaware (43015) *(G-10013)*

United Parcel Service Inc OH 440 826-3320
3250 Old Airport Rd Wooster (44691) *(G-19775)*

United Parcel Service Inc OH 419 891-6776
1550 Holland Rd Maumee (43537) *(G-13865)*

United Parcel Service Inc OH 419 424-9494
1301 Commerce Pkwy Findlay (45840) *(G-10972)*

United Parcel Service Inc OH 330 545-0177
800 Trumbull Ave Girard (44420) *(G-11302)*

United Parcel Service Inc OH 440 275-3301
1553 State Route 45 Austinburg (44010) *(G-854)*

United Parcel Service Inc OH 330 339-6281
241 8th Street Ext Sw New Philadelphia (44663) *(G-14987)*

United Parcel Service Inc OH 740 598-4293
500 Labelle St Brilliant (43913) *(G-1824)*

United Parcel Service Inc OH 740 592-4570
1 Kenny Dr Athens (45701) *(G-809)*

United Parcel Service Inc OH 614 277-3300
3500 Centerpoint Dr Urbancrest (43123) *(G-18452)*

United Parcel Service Inc OH 740 968-3508
44191 Lafferty Rd Saint Clairsville (43950) *(G-16508)*

United Parcel Service Inc OH 614 841-7159
100 E Campus View Blvd # 300 Columbus (43235) *(G-8807)*

United Parcel Service Inc OH 800 742-5877
1507 Augusta St Zanesville (43701) *(G-20370)*

United Parcel Service Inc OH 419 891-6841
1212 E Alexis Rd Toledo (43612) *(G-18119)*

United Parcel Service Inc OH 330 478-1007
4850 Navarre Rd Sw Canton (44706) *(G-2520)*

United Parcel Service Inc OH 419 586-8556
1851 Industrial Dr Celina (45822) *(G-2613)*

United Parcel Service Inc OH 513 241-5289
640 W 3rd St Cincinnati (45202) *(G-4684)*

United Parcel Service Inc OH 614 383-4580
1476 Likens Rd Marion (43302) *(G-13472)*

United Parcel Service Inc OH 513 782-4000
11141 Canal Rd Cincinnati (45241) *(G-4685)*

United Parcel Service Inc OH 513 241-5316
644 Linn St Ste 325 Cincinnati (45203) *(G-4686)*

United Parcel Service Inc OH 419 872-0211
12171 Eckel Rd Perrysburg (43551) *(G-15928)*

United Parcel Service Inc OH 614 272-8500
2450 Rathmell Rd Obetz (43207) *(G-15531)*

United Parcel Service Inc OH 614 870-4111
5101 Trabue Rd Columbus (43228) *(G-8808)*

United Parcel Service Inc OH 513 863-1681
1951 Logan Ave Hamilton (45015) *(G-11651)*

United Parcel Service Inc OH 937 773-4762
8460 Industry Park Dr Piqua (45356) *(G-16032)*

United Parcel Service Inc OH 419 782-3552
820 Carpenter Rd Defiance (43512) *(G-9945)*

United Parcel Service Inc OH 937 382-0658
2500 S Us Highway 68 Wilmington (45177) *(G-19652)*

United Parcel Service Inc OH 740 962-7971
21 Gingersnap Rd Portsmouth (45662) *(G-16175)*

United Parcel Service Inc OH 800 742-5877
95 Karago Ave Ste 4 Youngstown (44512) *(G-20232)*

United Performance Metals Inc (HQ) 513 860-6500
3475 Symmes Rd Hamilton (45015) *(G-11652)*

United Producers Inc 937 456-4161
617 S Franklin St Eaton (45320) *(G-10464)*

United Producers Inc (PA) 614 433-2150
8351 N High St Ste 250 Columbus (43235) *(G-8809)*

United Rehabilitation Services 937 233-1230
4710 Troy Pike Dayton (45424) *(G-9832)*

United Rentals North Amer Inc 800 877-3687
620 Eckel Rd Perrysburg (43551) *(G-15929)*

United Rest Homes Inc 440 354-2131
308 S State St Painesville (44077) *(G-15745)*

United Retail Logistics Svcs 937 332-1500
1501 Experiment Farm Rd Troy (45373) *(G-18235)*

United Road Services Inc 419 837-2703
27400 Luckey Rd Toledo (43605) *(G-18120)*

United Sales Co, Canton *Also called Klase Enterprises Inc (G-2369)*

United Scoto Senior Activities (PA) 740 354-6672
117 Market St 119 Portsmouth (45662) *(G-16176)*

United Seating & Mobility LLC 567 302-4000
412 W Dussel Dr Maumee (43537) *(G-13866)*

UNITED SENIOR SERVICES, Springfield *Also called Elderly United of Springfield (G-17033)*

United Skates America Inc 440 944-5300
30325 Palisades Pkwy Wickliffe (44092) *(G-19476)*

United Software Group Inc (PA) 614 791-3223
565 Metro Pl S Ste 110 Dublin (43017) *(G-10358)*

United Srgcal Prtners Intl Inc 330 702-1489
4147 Westford Dr Canfield (44406) *(G-2163)*

United States Cargo & Courier 216 325-0483
4735 W 150th St Ste D Cleveland (44135) *(G-6579)*

United States Cargo & Courier 614 449-2854
2036 Williams Rd Columbus (43207) *(G-8810)*

United States Commemrtv Art GA 330 494-5504
7800 Whipple Ave Nw Canton (44767) *(G-2521)*

United States Dept Agriculture 419 626-8439
2900 Columbus Ave Sandusky (44870) *(G-16652)*

United States Dept of Navy 937 938-3926
2624 Q St Bldg 851 Area B Dayton (45433) *(G-9189)*

United States Endoscopy (HQ) 440 639-4494
5976 Heisley Rd Mentor (44060) *(G-14118)*

United States Enrichment Corp 740 897-2331
3930 Us Highway 23 Anx Piketon (45661) *(G-15989)*

United States Enrichment Corp 740 897-2457
3930 Us Rte 23 S Piketon (45661) *(G-15990)*

United States Protective (PA) 216 475-8550
750 W Resource Dr Ste 200 Independence (44131) *(G-12135)*

United States Trotting Assn (PA) 614 224-2291
6130 S Sunbury Rd Westerville (43081) *(G-19304)*

United States Trotting Assn 614 224-2291
800 Michigan Ave Columbus (43215) *(G-8811)*

United Steel Service LLC (PA) 330 448-4057
4500 Parkway Dr Brookfield (44403) *(G-1857)*

United Steelworkers 740 772-5988
196 Burbridge Ave Chillicothe (45601) *(G-2834)*

United Steelworkers 740 928-0157
2100 James Pkwy Newark (43056) *(G-15105)*

United Steelworkers 440 979-1050
24371 Lorain Rd Ste 207 North Olmsted (44070) *(G-15315)*

United Steelworkers 419 238-7980
351 Pleasant St Ste 1 Van Wert (45891) *(G-18490)*

United Steelworkers 740 633-0899
705 Main St Martins Ferry (43935) *(G-13480)*

United Steelworkers 440 244-1358
2501 Broadway Lorain (44052) *(G-12949)*

United Steelworkers 440 354-2328
50 Branch Ave Painesville (44077) *(G-15746)*

United Steelworkers 614 272-8609
4467 Village Park Dr Columbus (43228) *(G-8812)*

United Steelworkers 740 622-8860
1048 S 6th St Coshocton (43812) *(G-9030)*

United Steelworkers 513 793-0272
8968 Blue Ash Rd Cincinnati (45242) *(G-4687)*

United Steelworkers of America 330 493-7721
4069 Bradley Cir Nw Canton (44718) *(G-2522)*

United Sttes Bowl Congress Inc 740 922-3120
710 Gorley St Uhrichsville (44683) *(G-18347)*

United Sttes Bowl Congress Inc 513 761-3338
520 W Wyoming Ave Cincinnati (45215) *(G-4688)*

United Sttes Bowl Congress Inc 419 531-4058
5062 Dorr St Toledo (43615) *(G-18121)*

United Sttes Bowl Congress Inc 440 327-0102
38931 Center Ridge Rd North Ridgeville (44039) *(G-15344)*

United Sttes Bowl Congress Inc 614 237-3716
643 S Hamilton Rd Columbus (43213) *(G-8813)*

United Studios of America, Canton *Also called Usam Inc (G-2525)*

United Technical Support Svcs 330 562-3330
10325 State Route 43 F Streetsboro (44241) *(G-17275)*

United Technical Support Svcs 330 562-3330
206 E Garfield Rd Aurora (44202) *(G-846)*

United Telemanagement Corp 937 454-1888
6450 Poe Ave Ste 401 Dayton (45414) *(G-9833)*

United Telephone Company Ohio 419 227-1660
122 S Elizabeth St Lima (45801) *(G-12773)*

2019 Harris Ohio
Services Directory
(G-0000) Company's Geographic Section entry number

UNITED WAY, Cincinnati *Also called Family Service* *(G-3531)*
United Way Central Ohio Inc 614 227-2700
  360 S 3rd St Columbus (43215) *(G-8814)*
United Way Greater Cincinnati (PA) 513 762-7100
  2400 Reading Rd Cincinnati (45202) *(G-4689)*
United Way Greater Cleveland (PA) 216 436-2100
  1331 Euclid Ave Cleveland (44115) *(G-6580)*
United Way Greater Stark Cnty 330 491-0445
  401 Market Ave N Ste 300 Canton (44702) *(G-2523)*
United Way of Greater Toledo (PA) 419 254-4742
  424 Jackson St Toledo (43604) *(G-18122)*
United Way of Summit County 330 762-7601
  37 N High St Ste A Akron (44308) *(G-477)*
United Way of The Greater Dayt (PA) 937 225-3060
  33 W 1st St Ste 500 Dayton (45402) *(G-9834)*
United-Maier Signs Inc 513 681-6600
  1030 Straight St Cincinnati (45214) *(G-4690)*
Unitedhealth Group Inc 513 603-6200
  400 E Bus Way Ste 100 Cincinnati (45241) *(G-4691)*
Unity Health Network LLC 330 655-3820
  5655 Hudson Dr Ste 110 Hudson (44236) *(G-12010)*
Unity Health Network LLC (PA) 330 923-5899
  3033 State Rd Cuyahoga Falls (44223) *(G-9135)*
Unity Health Network LLC 330 626-0549
  9150 Market Square Dr Streetsboro (44241) *(G-17276)*
Unity Health Network LLC 330 678-7782
  307 W Main St Kent (44240) *(G-12266)*
Unity Health Network LLC 330 633-7782
  116 East Ave Tallmadge (44278) *(G-17497)*
Unity I Home Healthcare LLC 740 351-0500
  221 Market St Portsmouth (45662) *(G-16177)*
Unity National Bank (HQ) 937 773-0752
  215 N Wayne St Piqua (45356) *(G-16033)*
Univ Dermatology 513 475-7630
  5575 Cheviot Rd Ste 1 Cincinnati (45247) *(G-4692)*
Univ Hospital, The, Cincinnati *Also called University of Cincinnati* *(G-4723)*
Univar Inc 440 510-1259
  33851 Curtis Blvd Ste 208 Eastlake (44095) *(G-10435)*
Univar USA Inc 513 714-5264
  4600 Dues Dr West Chester (45246) *(G-19095)*
Univar USA Inc 419 666-7880
  30450 Tracy Rd Walbridge (43465) *(G-18626)*
Univar USA Inc 330 425-4330
  1686 Highland Rd Twinsburg (44087) *(G-18333)*
Univar USA Inc 513 870-4050
  12 Standen Dr Hamilton (45015) *(G-11653)*
Univar USA Inc 440 238-8550
  21600 Drake Rd Strongsville (44149) *(G-17356)*
Univenture Inc (PA) 937 645-4600
  4266 Tuller Rd Ste 101 Dublin (43017) *(G-10359)*
Univenture Inc 937 645-4600
  4266 Tuller Rd Ste 101 Dublin (43017) *(G-10360)*
Univenture CD Packg & Systems, Dublin *Also called Univenture Inc* *(G-10359)*
Universal 1 Credit Union Inc (PA) 800 762-9555
  1 River Park Dr Dayton (45409) *(G-9835)*
Universal Advertising Assoc 513 522-5000
  2530 Civic Center Dr Cincinnati (45231) *(G-4693)*
Universal Contracting, Cincinnati *Also called Finneytown Contracting Corp* *(G-3552)*
Universal Contracting Corp 513 482-2700
  5151 Fishwick Dr Cincinnati (45216) *(G-4694)*
Universal Development MGT Inc (PA) 330 759-7017
  1607 Motor Inn Dr Ste 1 Girard (44420) *(G-11303)*
Universal Disposal Inc 440 286-3153
  9954 Old State Rd Chardon (44024) *(G-2720)*
Universal Enterprises Inc (PA) 419 529-3500
  545 Beer Rd Ontario (44906) *(G-15577)*
Universal Fabg Cnstr Svcs Inc 614 274-1128
  1241 Mckinley Ave Columbus (43222) *(G-8815)*
Universal Green Energy Solutio 844 723-7768
  2086 Belltree Dr Reynoldsburg (43068) *(G-16335)*
Universal Grinding Corporation 216 631-9410
  1234 W 78th St Cleveland (44102) *(G-6581)*
Universal Health Care Svcs Inc 614 547-0282
  2873 Suwanee Rd Columbus (43224) *(G-8816)*
Universal Marketing Group LLC 419 720-9696
  5454 Airport Hwy Toledo (43615) *(G-18123)*
Universal Nursing Services (PA) 330 434-7318
  483 Augusta Dr Akron (44333) *(G-478)*
Universal Oil Inc 216 771-4300
  265 Jefferson Ave Cleveland (44113) *(G-6582)*
Universal Packg Systems Inc 513 732-2000
  5055 State Route 276 Batavia (45103) *(G-1013)*
Universal Packg Systems Inc 513 674-9400
  470 Northland Blvd Cincinnati (45240) *(G-4695)*
Universal Packg Systems Inc 513 735-4777
  5069 State Route 276 Batavia (45103) *(G-1014)*
Universal Recovery Systems 614 299-0184
  5197 Trabue Rd Columbus (43228) *(G-8817)*
Universal Refrigeration Div, Ontario *Also called Universal Enterprises Inc* *(G-15577)*
Universal Steel Company 216 883-4972
  6600 Grant Ave Cleveland (44105) *(G-6583)*
Universal Technology Corp (PA) 937 426-2808
  1270 N Fairfield Rd Beavercreek (45432) *(G-1193)*

Universal Transportation Syste 513 539-9491
  220 Senate Dr Monroe (45050) *(G-14585)*
Universal Transportation Syste (PA) 513 829-1287
  5284 Winton Rd Fairfield (45014) *(G-10796)*
Universal Veneer Mill Corp 740 522-1147
  1776 Tamarack Rd Newark (43055) *(G-15106)*
Universal Veneer Sales Corp 740 522-2000
  2825 Hallie Ln Granville (43023) *(G-11348)*
Universal Work and Power LLC 513 981-1111
  6320 E Kemper Rd Ste 150 Cincinnati (45241) *(G-4696)*
Universial Transportation, Fairfield *Also called Intercoastal Trnsp Systems* *(G-10737)*
Universities Space Res Assn 216 368-0750
  10900 Euclid Ave Cleveland (44106) *(G-6584)*
University Anesthesiologists 216 844-3777
  11100 Euclid Ave Ste 2517 Cleveland (44106) *(G-6585)*
University Cincinnati Book Str, Cincinnati *Also called University of Cincinnati* *(G-4714)*
University Circle Incorporated (PA) 216 791-3900
  10831 Magnolia Dr Cleveland (44106) *(G-6586)*
University Club Inc 513 721-2600
  401 E 4th St Cincinnati (45202) *(G-4697)*
University Dayton RES Inst, Dayton *Also called University of Dayton* *(G-9840)*
University Dermatology Cons 513 584-4775
  234 Goodman St A3 Cincinnati (45219) *(G-4698)*
University Dermatology Cons 513 475-7630
  222 Piedmont Ave Ste 5300 Cincinnati (45219) *(G-4699)*
University Eye Surgeons 614 293-5635
  456 W 10th Ave Ste 5241 Columbus (43210) *(G-8818)*
University Family Physicians 513 929-0104
  2123 Auburn Ave Cincinnati (45219) *(G-4700)*
University Family Physicians 513 475-7505
  175 W Galbraith Rd Cincinnati (45216) *(G-4701)*
University GYN&ob Cnsltnts Inc (PA) 614 293-8697
  1654 Upham Dr Rm N500 Columbus (43210) *(G-8819)*
University Hosp A & MBL Care, Cincinnati *Also called University of Cincinnati* *(G-4704)*
University Hosp Hlth Sys Shake, Willoughby *Also called University Prmry Care Prctices* *(G-19579)*
University Hosp Prtage Med Ctr, Ravenna *Also called Robinson Health System Inc* *(G-16263)*
University Hosp Rdilology Dept, Cincinnati *Also called University of Cincinnati* *(G-4710)*
University Hospital, Cleveland *Also called University Orthpedic Assoc Inc* *(G-6601)*
University Hospital, Cincinnati *Also called University of Cincinnati* *(G-4725)*
University Hospitals 440 250-2001
  960 Clague Rd Ste 2410 Westlake (44145) *(G-19418)*
University Hospitals 216 593-5500
  3999 Richmond Rd Cleveland (44122) *(G-6587)*
University Hospitals 216 536-3020
  2915 Ludlow Rd Cleveland (44120) *(G-6588)*
University Hospitals 440 285-6000
  13207 Ravenna Rd Chardon (44024) *(G-2721)*
University Hospitals (PA) 216 767-8900
  3605 Warrensville Ctr Rd Shaker Heights (44122) *(G-16717)*
University Hospitals 440 743-3000
  7007 Powers Blvd Parma (44129) *(G-15779)*
University Hospitals 216 844-6400
  12200 Fairhill Rd Frnt Cleveland (44120) *(G-6589)*
University Hospitals 216 844-8797
  11100 Euclid Ave Wrn5065 Cleveland (44106) *(G-6590)*
University Hospitals 216 767-8500
  11001 Euclid Ave Cleveland (44106) *(G-6591)*
University Hospitals Cleveland 216 844-1000
  11100 Euclid Ave Cleveland (44106) *(G-6592)*
University Hospitals Cleveland 440 205-5755
  9485 Mentor Ave Ste 102 Mentor (44060) *(G-14119)*
University Hospitals Cleveland (HQ) 216 844-1000
  11100 Euclid Ave Cleveland (44106) *(G-6593)*
University Hospitals Cleveland 216 844-4663
  4510 Richmond Rd Cleveland (44128) *(G-6594)*
University Hospitals Cleveland 216 844-3323
  3605 Warrensville Ctr Rd Shaker Heights (44122) *(G-16718)*
University Hospitals Cleveland 216 342-5556
  23215 Commerce Park # 300 Beachwood (44122) *(G-1116)*
University Hospitals Cleveland 216 844-3528
  11100 Euclid Ave Cleveland (44106) *(G-6595)*
University Hospitals He 216 844-4663
  4510 Richmond Rd Cleveland (44128) *(G-6596)*
University Hospitals Health (PA) 440 285-4040
  12340 Bass Lake Rd Chardon (44024) *(G-2722)*
University Hospitals Health Sy 216 844-4663
  11100 Euclid Ave Cleveland (44106) *(G-6597)*
University Hospitals Hlth Sys, Bedford *Also called Community Hospital of Bedford* *(G-1274)*
University Hospitals Hlth Sys, Beachwood *Also called Qualchoice Inc* *(G-1098)*
University Hospitals Parma, Parma *Also called University Hospitals* *(G-15779)*
University Hospitals St John 440 835-8000
  29000 Center Ridge Rd Westlake (44145) *(G-19419)*
University Hsptl-Uc Physicians, Cincinnati *Also called University of Cincinnati* *(G-4705)*
UNIVERSITY MANOR HEALTH CARE CENTER, Cleveland *Also called University Manor Healthcare* *(G-6598)*
University Manor Healthcare 216 721-1400
  2186 Ambleside Dr Cleveland (44106) *(G-6598)*

University Manor Hlth Care Ctr.....216 721-1400
2186 Ambleside Dr Cleveland (44106) **(G-6599)**
University Marketing, Dayton *Also called University of Dayton* **(G-9838)**
University Medical Assoc Inc.....740 593-0753
350 Parks Hall Athens (45701) **(G-810)**
University Mednet (PA).....216 383-0100
18599 Lake Shore Blvd Euclid (44119) **(G-10660)**
University Mednet.....440 255-0800
9000 Mentor Ave Ste 101 Mentor (44060) **(G-14120)**
University Mednet.....440 285-9079
22750 Rockside Rd Ste 210 Bedford (44146) **(G-1313)**
University Moving & Storage Co.....248 615-7000
8735 Rite Track Way West Chester (45069) **(G-19027)**
University Neurology Inc.....513 475-8730
222 Piedmont Ave Ste 3200 Cincinnati (45219) **(G-4702)**
University of Akron.....330 972-6008
170 University Ave Akron (44325) **(G-479)**
University of Akron.....330 972-8210
108 Fir Hl Akron (44325) **(G-480)**
University of Cincinnati.....513 558-4194
231 Albert Sabin Way Cincinnati (45267) **(G-4703)**
University of Cincinnati.....513 584-7522
3200 Burnet Ave Cincinnati (45229) **(G-4704)**
University of Cincinnati.....513 475-8771
222 Piedmont Ave Ste 7000 Cincinnati (45219) **(G-4705)**
University of Cincinnati.....513 558-1200
3130 Highland Ave Fl 3 Cincinnati (45219) **(G-4706)**
University of Cincinnati.....513 556-6381
51 Goodman St Cincinnati (45219) **(G-4707)**
University of Cincinnati.....513 558-4444
3125 Eden Ave Cincinnati (45219) **(G-4708)**
University of Cincinnati.....513 556-5511
260 Stetson St Ste 5300 Cincinnati (45219) **(G-4709)**
University of Cincinnati.....513 584-4396
234 Goodman St 761 Cincinnati (45219) **(G-4710)**
University of Cincinnati.....513 556-5087
146 Mcmicken Hall Cincinnati (45221) **(G-4711)**
University of Cincinnati.....513 556-4054
2614 Mecken Cir Cincinnati (45221) **(G-4712)**
University of Cincinnati.....513 558-5439
3223 Eden Avenue Cincinnati (45267) **(G-4713)**
University of Cincinnati.....513 556-4200
51 W Goodman Dr Cincinnati (45221) **(G-4714)**
University of Cincinnati.....513 558-4231
231 Albert Sabin Way Cincinnati (45267) **(G-4715)**
University of Cincinnati.....513 584-5331
234 Goodman St Cincinnati (45219) **(G-4716)**
University of Cincinnati.....513 556-3732
500 Geo Physics Bldg 5f Cincinnati (45221) **(G-4717)**
University of Cincinnati.....513 556-4603
2751 O'vrsity Way Ste 880 Cincinnati (45221) **(G-4718)**
University of Cincinnati.....513 558-1799
3001 Short Vine St Cincinnati (45219) **(G-4719)**
University of Cincinnati.....513 584-3200
234 Goodman St Cincinnati (45219) **(G-4720)**
University of Cincinnati.....513 558-5471
231 Albert Sabin Way G258 Cincinnati (45267) **(G-4721)**
University of Cincinnati.....513 475-8524
222 Piedmont Ave Ste 6000 Cincinnati (45219) **(G-4722)**
University of Cincinnati.....513 584-1000
331 Albert Sabin Way Cincinnati (45229) **(G-4723)**
University of Cincinnati.....513 558-4831
231 Albert Sabin Way Cincinnati (45267) **(G-4724)**
University of Cincinnati.....513 584-1000
234 Goodman St Cincinnati (45219) **(G-4725)**
University of Cincinnati.....513 556-3803
Edwards 1 Bldg Cincinnati (45221) **(G-4726)**
University of Cncnnati Srgeons (PA).....513 245-3300
2830 Victory Pkwy Ste 320 Cincinnati (45206) **(G-4727)**
University of Dayton.....937 255-3141
300 College Park Ave Dayton (45469) **(G-9836)**
University of Dayton (PA).....937 229-2919
300 College Park Ave Dayton (45469) **(G-9837)**
University of Dayton.....937 229-5432
300 College Park Ave Dayton (45469) **(G-9838)**
University of Dayton.....937 229-2113
300 College St Dayton (45402) **(G-9839)**
University of Dayton.....937 229-3822
711 E Monu Ave Ste 101 Dayton (45469) **(G-9840)**
University of Dayton.....937 229-3913
1529 Brown St Dayton (45469) **(G-9841)**
University of Dyton Schl Engrg, Dayton *Also called University of Dayton* **(G-9839)**
University of Individuality, Akron *Also called Community Hbilitation Svcs Inc* **(G-151)**
University of Tledo Foundation.....419 530-7730
2801 W Bancroft St 1002 Toledo (43606) **(G-18124)**
University of Toledo.....419 534-3770
3120 Glendale Ave Ste 79 Toledo (43614) **(G-18125)**
University of Toledo.....419 383-3556
4430 N Hllnd Sylvnia Rd Toledo (43623) **(G-18126)**
University of Toledo.....419 383-4000
3000 Arlington Ave Toledo (43614) **(G-18127)**
University of Toledo.....419 383-5322
3000 Arlington Ave Toledo (43614) **(G-18128)**
University of Toledo.....419 383-3759
3000 Arlington Ave Toledo (43614) **(G-18129)**
University of Toledo.....419 383-4229
3000 Arlington Ave Toledo (43614) **(G-18130)**
University of Toledo Med Ctr, Toledo *Also called University of Toledo* **(G-18127)**
University Ophthalmology Assoc.....216 382-8022
1611 S Green Rd Ste 306c Cleveland (44121) **(G-6600)**
University Orthopaedic Cnsltnt.....513 475-8690
222 Piedmont Ave Ste 2200 Cincinnati (45219) **(G-4728)**
University Orthpedic Assoc Inc (PA).....216 844-1000
11100 Euclid Ave Ste 3001 Cleveland (44106) **(G-6601)**
University Otolaryngologists (PA).....614 273-2241
810 Mackenzie Dr Columbus (43220) **(G-8820)**
University Park Nursing Home, Cleveland *Also called Progressive Park LLC* **(G-6253)**
University Plz Ht Cnfrence Ctr, Columbus *Also called River Road Hotel Corp* **(G-8535)**
University Prmry Care Physcans, Shaker Heights *Also called Suburban Pediatrics Inc* **(G-16715)**
University Prmry Care Prctices (HQ).....440 946-7391
4212 State Route 306 # 304 Willoughby (44094) **(G-19579)**
University Radiology Assoc.....513 475-8760
222 Piedmont Ave Ste 2100 Cincinnati (45219) **(G-4729)**
University Rdlgsts of Clveland.....216 844-1700
2485 Euclid Ave Cleveland (44115) **(G-6602)**
University Settlement Inc (PA).....216 641-8948
4800 Broadway Ave Cleveland (44127) **(G-6603)**
University Suburban Health Ctr (PA).....216 382-8920
1611 S Green Rd Ste A61 Cleveland (44121) **(G-6604)**
University Surgeons Inc.....216 844-3021
11100 Euclid Ave 7002 Cleveland (44106) **(G-6605)**
University Tech Service, Columbus *Also called Ohio State University* **(G-8313)**
University Toledo Medical Ctr, Toledo *Also called University of Toledo* **(G-18126)**
University Toledo Physicians, Toledo *Also called Medical College of Ohio* **(G-17901)**
University Womens Healthcare.....937 208-2948
627 S Edwin C Moses Blvd Dayton (45417) **(G-9842)**
Universty of Cincinnti Medcl C (HQ).....513 584-1000
234 Goodman St Cincinnati (45219) **(G-4730)**
Unknown, Massillon *Also called Round Room LLC* **(G-13726)**
Unknown, Beavercreek *Also called Round Room LLC* **(G-1184)**
UNUM Life Insurance Co Amer.....614 807-2500
445 Hutchinson Ave # 300 Columbus (43235) **(G-8821)**
Upgrade Homes.....614 975-8532
586 Blenheim Rd Columbus (43214) **(G-8822)**
Uph Holdings LLC.....614 447-9777
3100 Olentangy River Rd Columbus (43202) **(G-8823)**
Upper Arlington City Schl Dst.....614 487-5133
4770 Burbank Dr Columbus (43220) **(G-8824)**
Upper Arlington Lutheran Ch (PA).....614 451-3736
2300 Lytham Rd Columbus (43220) **(G-8825)**
Upper Arlington Surgery Center.....614 442-6515
2240 N Bank Dr Columbus (43220) **(G-8826)**
Upper Valley Family Care.....937 339-5355
200 Kienle Dr Piqua (45356) **(G-16034)**
Upper Valley Financial Inc.....937 381-0054
1262 E Ash St Piqua (45356) **(G-16035)**
Upreach LLC.....614 442-7702
4488 Mobile Dr Columbus (43220) **(G-8827)**
UPS, Mansfield *Also called United Parcel Service Inc OH* **(G-13259)**
UPS, Cincinnati *Also called United Parcel Service Inc OH* **(G-4683)**
UPS, Cleveland *Also called United Parcel Service Inc OH* **(G-6577)**
UPS, Marietta *Also called United Parcel Service Inc OH* **(G-13393)**
UPS, Lima *Also called United Parcel Service Inc OH* **(G-12772)**
UPS, Cleveland *Also called United Parcel Service Inc OH* **(G-6578)**
UPS, Delaware *Also called United Parcel Service Inc OH* **(G-10013)**
UPS, Wooster *Also called United Parcel Service Inc OH* **(G-19775)**
UPS, Maumee *Also called United Parcel Service Inc OH* **(G-13865)**
UPS, Findlay *Also called United Parcel Service Inc OH* **(G-10972)**
UPS, Girard *Also called United Parcel Service Inc OH* **(G-11302)**
UPS, Columbus *Also called United Parcel Service Inc* **(G-8805)**
UPS, Austinburg *Also called United Parcel Service Inc OH* **(G-854)**
UPS, New Philadelphia *Also called United Parcel Service Inc OH* **(G-14987)**
UPS, Brilliant *Also called United Parcel Service Inc OH* **(G-1824)**
UPS, Cleveland *Also called United Parcel Service Inc* **(G-6576)**
UPS, Athens *Also called United Parcel Service Inc OH* **(G-809)**
UPS, West Carrollton *Also called United Parcel Service Inc* **(G-18857)**
UPS, Urbancrest *Also called United Parcel Service Inc OH* **(G-18452)**
UPS, Saint Clairsville *Also called United Parcel Service Inc OH* **(G-16508)**
UPS, Chillicothe *Also called United Parcel Service Inc* **(G-2833)**
UPS, Columbus *Also called United Parcel Service Inc OH* **(G-8807)**
UPS, Zanesville *Also called United Parcel Service Inc OH* **(G-20370)**
UPS, Toledo *Also called United Parcel Service Inc OH* **(G-18119)**
UPS, Canton *Also called United Parcel Service Inc OH* **(G-2520)**
UPS, Celina *Also called United Parcel Service Inc OH* **(G-2613)**
UPS, Cincinnati *Also called United Parcel Service Inc OH* **(G-4684)**
UPS, Middleburg Heights *Also called United Parcel Service Inc* **(G-14263)**
UPS, Marion *Also called United Parcel Service Inc OH* **(G-13472)**

UPS, Cincinnati *Also called United Parcel Service Inc OH* ***(G-4685)***
UPS, Cincinnati *Also called United Parcel Service Inc OH* ***(G-4686)***
UPS, Perrysburg *Also called United Parcel Service Inc OH* ***(G-15928)***
UPS, Obetz *Also called United Parcel Service Inc OH* ***(G-15531)***
UPS, Columbus *Also called United Parcel Service Inc OH* ***(G-8808)***
UPS, Hamilton *Also called United Parcel Service Inc OH* ***(G-11651)***
UPS, Piqua *Also called United Parcel Service Inc OH* ***(G-16032)***
UPS, Defiance *Also called United Parcel Service Inc OH* ***(G-9945)***
UPS, Wilmington *Also called United Parcel Service Inc OH* ***(G-19652)***
UPS, Columbus *Also called United Parcel Service Inc* ***(G-8806)***
UPS, Portsmouth *Also called United Parcel Service Inc OH* ***(G-16175)***
UPS, Youngstown *Also called United Parcel Service Inc OH* ***(G-20232)***
UPS, Strongsville *Also called United Parcel Service Inc* ***(G-17355)***
UPS Ground Freight Inc..........330 659-6693
3495 Brecksville Rd Richfield (44286) ***(G-16382)***
UPS Ground Freight Inc..........937 236-4700
3730 Valley St Dayton (45424) ***(G-9843)***
UPS Ground Freight Inc..........330 448-0440
7945 3rd St Masury (44438) ***(G-13743)***
Upscale Lawn Care, Cincinnati *Also called Upscale Lawncre & Prprty Maint* ***(G-4731)***
Upscale Lawncre & Prprty Maint..........513 266-1165
4200 N Bend Rd Cincinnati (45211) ***(G-4731)***
Uptime Corporation..........216 661-1655
4820 Van Epps Rd Brooklyn Heights (44131) ***(G-1885)***
Uptown Hair & Day Spa, Englewood *Also called Uptown Hair Studio Inc* ***(G-10604)***
Uptown Hair Studio Inc..........937 832-2111
390 W National Rd Englewood (45322) ***(G-10604)***
Uptown Rental Properties LLC..........513 861-9394
2718 Short Vine St Cincinnati (45219) ***(G-4732)***
Uranium Disposition Svcs LLC..........740 289-3620
3930 Us Highway 23 Anx Piketon (45661) ***(G-15991)***
Urban Craft, Grove City *Also called Young Mens Christian Assoc* ***(G-11491)***
Urban Express Transportation, Columbus *Also called Eastern Horizon Inc* ***(G-7489)***
Urban Leagu of Greater Clevlnd..........216 622-0999
2930 Prospect Ave E Cleveland (44115) ***(G-6606)***
Urban League of Greater Southw..........513 281-9955
3458 Reading Rd Cincinnati (45229) ***(G-4733)***
Urban Oassis Inc..........614 766-9946
5555 Wall St Dublin (43017) ***(G-10361)***
Urban One Inc..........216 579-1111
6555 Carnegie Ave Cleveland (44103) ***(G-6607)***
Urban One Inc..........513 749-1009
1821 Summit Rd Ste 400 Cincinnati (45237) ***(G-4734)***
Urban One Inc..........614 487-1444
350 E 1st Ave Ste 100 Columbus (43201) ***(G-8828)***
Urban One Inc..........216 861-0100
1041 Huron Rd E Cleveland (44115) ***(G-6608)***
Urban One Inc..........513 679-6000
705 Central Ave Ste 200 Cincinnati (45202) ***(G-4735)***
Urban Retail Properties LLC..........513 346-4482
7875 Montgomery Rd Cincinnati (45236) ***(G-4736)***
Urbancrest Affrdbl Hsing LLC..........614 228-3578
3443 Agler Rd Ste 200 Columbus (43219) ***(G-8829)***
Urological Associates Inc..........614 221-5189
750 Mount Carmel Mall # 350 Columbus (43222) ***(G-8830)***
Urology Group, Cincinnati *Also called Tri State Urlogic Svcs PSC Inc* ***(G-4632)***
URS, Cleveland *Also called Aecom Energy & Cnstr Inc* ***(G-4907)***
URS, Cleveland *Also called Aecom Energy & Cnstr Inc* ***(G-4908)***
URS, Cleveland *Also called Aecom Energy & Cnstr Inc* ***(G-4909)***
URS Group Inc..........330 836-9111
564 White Pond Dr Akron (44320) ***(G-481)***
URS Group Inc..........216 622-2300
1300 E 9th St Ste 500 Cleveland (44114) ***(G-6609)***
URS Group Inc..........614 464-4500
277 W Nationwide Blvd Columbus (43215) ***(G-8831)***
URS Group Inc..........513 651-3440
525 Vine St Ste 1900 Cincinnati (45202) ***(G-4737)***
URS-Smith Group VA Idiq Joint..........614 464-4500
277 W Nationwide Blvd Columbus (43215) ***(G-8832)***
Ursuline Center, Toledo *Also called Ursuline Convent Sacred Heart* ***(G-18131)***
Ursuline Convent Sacred Heart..........419 531-8990
4035 Indian Rd Toledo (43606) ***(G-18131)***
US Airways, Cleveland *Also called American Airlines Inc* ***(G-4947)***
US Airways, Vandalia *Also called American Airlines Inc* ***(G-18501)***
US Airways Express, Vandalia *Also called Psa Airlines Inc* ***(G-18537)***
US Bank, Cincinnati *Also called US Bank National Association* ***(G-4738)***
US Bank, Portsmouth *Also called US Bank National Association* ***(G-16178)***
US Bank, Cincinnati *Also called US Bank National Association* ***(G-4739)***
US Bank, Cincinnati *Also called US Bank National Association* ***(G-4740)***
US Bank, Fairborn *Also called US Bank National Association* ***(G-10685)***
US Bank, Troy *Also called US Bank National Association* ***(G-18236)***
US Bank, Sidney *Also called US Bank National Association* ***(G-16803)***
US Bank National Association (HQ)..........513 632-4234
425 Walnut St Fl 14 Cincinnati (45202) ***(G-4738)***
US Bank National Association..........740 353-4151
602 Chillicothe St Frnt Portsmouth (45662) ***(G-16178)***
US Bank National Association..........513 979-1000
5065 Wooster Rd Cincinnati (45226) ***(G-4739)***
US Bank National Association..........513 458-2844
2300 Wall St Ste A Cincinnati (45212) ***(G-4740)***
US Bank National Association..........937 873-7845
1 W Main St Fairborn (45324) ***(G-10685)***
US Bank National Association..........937 335-8351
910 W Main St Troy (45373) ***(G-18236)***
US Bank National Association..........937 498-1131
115 E Court St Sidney (45365) ***(G-16803)***
US Bronco Services Inc..........513 829-9880
280 Donald Dr Fairfield (45014) ***(G-10797)***
US Communications and Elc Inc..........440 519-0880
4933 Neo Pkwy Cleveland (44128) ***(G-6610)***
US Dental Care/M D Gelender..........614 252-3181
949 E Livingston Ave Columbus (43205) ***(G-8833)***
US Dept of the Air Force..........937 257-0837
4881 Sug Mple Dr Bldg 830 Dayton (45433) ***(G-9190)***
US Dept of the Air Force..........937 255-5150
2856 G St Dayton (45433) ***(G-9191)***
US Endoscopy, Mentor *Also called United States Endoscopy* ***(G-14118)***
US Expediting Logistics LLC..........937 235-1014
4311 Old Springfield Rd Vandalia (45377) ***(G-18547)***
US Federal District Court, Dayton *Also called 6th Circuit Court* ***(G-9196)***
US Foods Inc..........330 963-6789
8000 Bavaria Rd Twinsburg (44087) ***(G-18334)***
US Foods Inc..........614 539-7993
5445 Spellmire Dr West Chester (45246) ***(G-19096)***
US Home Center LLC (PA)..........614 737-9000
2050 Integrity Dr S Columbus (43209) ***(G-8834)***
US Inspection Services Inc (HQ)..........937 660-9879
7333 Paragon Rd Ste 240 Dayton (45459) ***(G-9844)***
US Inspection Services Inc..........513 671-7073
502 W Crescentville Rd Cincinnati (45246) ***(G-4741)***
US Molding Machinery Co Inc..........440 918-1701
38294 Pelton Rd Willoughby (44094) ***(G-19580)***
US Oncology Inc..........937 352-2140
1141 N Monroe Dr Xenia (45385) ***(G-19932)***
US Probation, Toledo *Also called Supreme Court United States* ***(G-18057)***
US Probation & Parole Svc., Cincinnati *Also called Supreme Court United States* ***(G-4558)***
US Probation Office, Cleveland *Also called Supreme Court United States* ***(G-6487)***
US Probation Office, Columbus *Also called 6th Circuit Court* ***(G-6844)***
US Protection Service LLC..........513 422-7910
1850 W Galbraith Rd Cincinnati (45239) ***(G-4742)***
US Safetygear Inc (PA)..........330 898-1344
5001 Enterprise Dr Nw Warren (44481) ***(G-18764)***
US Security Associates Inc..........513 381-7033
230 Northland Blvd # 307 Cincinnati (45246) ***(G-4743)***
US Security Associates Inc..........937 454-9035
69 N Dixie Dr Ste F Vandalia (45377) ***(G-18548)***
US Security Holdings Inc..........614 488-6110
1350 W 5th Ave Ste 300 Columbus (43212) ***(G-8835)***
US Swimming Lake Erie Swimming..........330 423-0485
301 Rockledge Dr Bay Village (44140) ***(G-1023)***
US Tech Arospc Engrg Corp (PA)..........330 455-1181
4200 Munson St Nw Canton (44718) ***(G-2524)***
US Technology Aerospace, Canton *Also called US Tech Arospc Engrg Corp* ***(G-2524)***
US Tsubaki Power Transm LLC..........419 626-4560
1010 Edgewater Ave Sandusky (44870) ***(G-16653)***
US Tubular Products Inc..........330 832-1734
14852 Lincoln Way W North Lawrence (44666) ***(G-15260)***
US Utility Electrical Svcs..........419 837-9753
3592 Genoa Rd Perrysburg (43551) ***(G-15930)***
USA Parking Systems Inc..........216 621-9255
1325 Carnegie Ave Frnt Cleveland (44115) ***(G-6611)***
Usaf-Medical Center, Dayton *Also called US Dept of the Air Force* ***(G-9190)***
Usam Inc..........330 244-8782
4450 Belden Village St Nw # 305 Canton (44718) ***(G-2525)***
Usavinyl LLC..........614 771-4805
5795 Green Pointe Dr S Groveport (43125) ***(G-11547)***
Usec, Piketon *Also called United States Enrichment Corp* ***(G-15989)***
USF Holland Inc..........740 441-1200
95 Holland Dr Gallipolis (45631) ***(G-11216)***
USF Holland LLC..........513 874-8960
10074 Prncton Glendale Rd West Chester (45246) ***(G-19097)***
USF Holland LLC..........419 354-6633
20820 Midstar Dr Bowling Green (43402) ***(G-1750)***
USF Holland LLC..........614 529-9300
4800 Journal St Columbus (43228) ***(G-8836)***
USF Holland LLC..........937 233-7600
2700 Valley Pike Dayton (45404) ***(G-9845)***
USF Holland LLC..........216 941-4340
10720 Memphis Ave Cleveland (44144) ***(G-6612)***
USF Holland LLC..........330 549-2917
10855 Market St North Lima (44452) ***(G-15275)***
USFreightways, West Chester *Also called USF Holland LLC* ***(G-19097)***
USFreightways, Columbus *Also called USF Holland LLC* ***(G-8836)***
USFreightways, Dayton *Also called USF Holland LLC* ***(G-9845)***
USFreightways, Cleveland *Also called USF Holland LLC* ***(G-6612)***
USFreightways, North Lima *Also called USF Holland LLC* ***(G-15275)***

USFreightways, Gallipolis *Also called USF Holland Inc (G-11216)*
Ushc Physicians Inc 216 382-2036
  1611 S Green Rd Ste 260 Cleveland (44121) *(G-6613)*
Usi Inc 419 243-1191
  1120 Madison Ave Toledo (43604) *(G-18132)*
USI Cable Corp 937 606-2636
  102 Fox Dr Piqua (45356) *(G-16036)*
USI Inc 513 954-4561
  9585 Cilley Rd Cleves (45002) *(G-6735)*
USI Insurance Services Nat Inc 614 228-5565
  580 N 4th St Ste 400 Columbus (43215) *(G-8837)*
USI Midwest LLC (HQ) 513 852-6300
  312 Elm St Ste 24 Cincinnati (45202) *(G-4744)*
Usic Locating Services LLC 330 733-9393
  441 Munroe Falls Rd Akron (44312) *(G-482)*
Usic Locating Services LLC 419 874-9988
  12769 Eagleville Rd B North Baltimore (45872) *(G-15180)*
Usic Locating Services LLC 513 554-0456
  3478 Hauck Rd Ste D Cincinnati (45241) *(G-4745)*
Ussa Inc 740 354-6672
  117 119 Market St Portsmouth (45662) *(G-16179)*
Uswa, Chillicothe *Also called United Steelworkers (G-2834)*
Uswa, Newark *Also called United Steelworkers (G-15105)*
Uswa, North Olmsted *Also called United Steelworkers (G-15315)*
Uswa, Van Wert *Also called United Steelworkers (G-18490)*
Uswa, Martins Ferry *Also called United Steelworkers (G-13480)*
Uswa, Lorain *Also called United Steelworkers (G-12949)*
Uswa, Painesville *Also called United Steelworkers (G-15746)*
Uswa, Columbus *Also called United Steelworkers (G-8812)*
Uswa, Coshocton *Also called United Steelworkers (G-9030)*
Uswa, Cincinnati *Also called United Steelworkers (G-4687)*
Uswa, Canton *Also called United Steelworkers of America (G-2522)*
Utah Spas, Toledo *Also called Spa Fitness Centers Inc (G-18040)*
Utica East Ohio Midstream LLC 740 431-4168
  8349 Azalea Rd Sw Dennison (44621) *(G-10056)*
Utica National Insurance Group 614 823-5300
  2600 Corp Exchange Dr # 200 Columbus (43231) *(G-8838)*
Utica Nursing Home, Utica *Also called Living Care Altrntves of Utica (G-18457)*
Utica Volunteer Emrgncy Squad 740 892-2369
  39 Spring St Utica (43080) *(G-18458)*
Utilicon Corporation 216 391-8500
  6140 Parkland Blvd Cleveland (44124) *(G-6614)*
Utilities Department, Toledo *Also called City of Toledo (G-17654)*
Utilities Dept, Painesville *Also called City of Painesville (G-15700)*
Utility Field Services, Lima *Also called City of Lima (G-12615)*
Utility Technologies Intl Corp 614 879-7624
  4700 Homer Ohio Ln Groveport (43125) *(G-11548)*
Utility Trailer Mfg Co 513 436-2600
  4225 Curliss Ln Batavia (45103) *(G-1015)*
Uts, Fairfield *Also called Universal Transportation Syste (G-10796)*
Uts Inc 513 332-9000
  P.O. Box 36342 Cincinnati (45236) *(G-4746)*
Utter Construction Inc 513 876-2246
  1302 State Route 133 Bethel (45106) *(G-1455)*
Uvmc Management Corporation (HQ) 937 440-4000
  3130 N County Road 25a Troy (45373) *(G-18237)*
Uvmc Nursing Care Inc 937 440-7663
  3232 N County Road 25a Troy (45373) *(G-18238)*
Uvmc Nursing Care Inc 937 473-2075
  75 Mote Dr Covington (45318) *(G-9049)*
Uvmc Nursing Care Inc 937 667-7500
  4375 S County Road 25a Tipp City (45371) *(G-17572)*
Uww, Hudson *Also called Veritiv Pubg & Print MGT Inc (G-12011)*
V & P Hydraulic Products LLC 740 203-3600
  1700 Pittsburgh Dr Delaware (43015) *(G-10014)*
V and V Appliance Parts Inc (PA) 330 743-5144
  27 W Myrtle Ave Youngstown (44507) *(G-20233)*
V Clew LLC 740 687-2273
  1201 River Valley Blvd Lancaster (43130) *(G-12443)*
V F, Portsmouth *Also called Valley Wholesale Foods Inc (G-16180)*
V H Cooper & Co Inc (HQ) 419 375-4116
  2321 State Route 49 Fort Recovery (45846) *(G-10994)*
V M Systems Inc 419 535-1044
  3125 Hill Ave Toledo (43607) *(G-18133)*
V Vrable Inc 614 545-5500
  3248 Henderson Rd Ste 104 Columbus (43220) *(G-8839)*
V Westaar Inc 740 803-2803
  6249 Westwick Pl Lewis Center (43035) *(G-12565)*
VA Medical Center Automated RE 740 772-7118
  17273 State Route 104 Chillicothe (45601) *(G-2835)*
Vacationland Federal Credit Un 440 967-5155
  2911 Hayes Ave Sandusky (44870) *(G-16654)*
Vadakin Inc 740 373-7518
  110 Industry Rd Marietta (45750) *(G-13394)*
Vahalla Company Inc 216 326-2245
  3257 E 139th St Cleveland (44120) *(G-6615)*
Valentine Buick Gmc Inc 937 878-7371
  1105 N Central Ave Fairborn (45324) *(G-10686)*
Valentine Group, Dayton *Also called Mv Land Development Company (G-9649)*

Valentour Education Inc .... ● 937 434-5949
  8095 Garnet Dr Dayton (45458) *(G-9846)*
Valicor Environmental Svcs LLC (HQ) 513 733-4666
  1045 Reed Dr Ste A Monroe (45050) *(G-14586)*
Validex, Cincinnati *Also called DE Foxx & Associates Inc (G-3408)*
Valleaire Golf Club Inc 440 237-9191
  6969 Boston Rd Hinckley (44233) *(G-11862)*
Vallejo Company 216 741-3933
  1340 E 38th St Cleveland (44114) *(G-6616)*
Vallen Distribution Inc 513 942-9100
  9407 Meridian Way West Chester (45069) *(G-19028)*
Valley Acoustics Inc 330 799-1894
  1203 N Meridian Rd Youngstown (44509) *(G-20234)*
Valley Care Health System, Warren *Also called Community Health Systems Inc (G-18688)*
Valley Electrical Cnsld Inc 330 539-4044
  977 Tibbetts Wick Rd Girard (44420) *(G-11304)*
Valley Fleet, Ashland *Also called Valley Transportation Inc (G-696)*
Valley Ford Truck Inc (PA) 216 524-2400
  5715 Canal Rd Cleveland (44125) *(G-6617)*
Valley Gstrnterology Endoscopy, Martins Ferry *Also called Wheeling Hospital Inc (G-13481)*
Valley Harley Davidson Co (PA) 740 695-9591
  41255 Reco Rd Belmont (43718) *(G-1397)*
Valley Harley Davidson-Buell, Belmont *Also called Valley Harley Davidson Co (G-1397)*
Valley Hospice Inc (PA) 740 859-5041
  10686 State Route 150 Rayland (43943) *(G-16274)*
Valley Hospitality Inc 740 374-9660
  701 Pike St Marietta (45750) *(G-13395)*
Valley Industrial Trucks Inc (PA) 330 788-4081
  1152 Meadowbrook Ave Youngstown (44512) *(G-20235)*
Valley Interior Systems Inc 937 890-7319
  2760 Thunderhawk Ct Dayton (45414) *(G-9847)*
Valley Interior Systems Inc (PA) 513 961-0400
  2203 Fowler St Cincinnati (45206) *(G-4747)*
Valley Interior Systems Inc 614 351-8440
  3840 Fisher Rd Columbus (43228) *(G-8840)*
Valley Machine Tool Co Inc 513 899-2737
  9773 Morrow Cozaddale Rd Morrow (45152) *(G-14717)*
Valley Regional Surgery Center 877 858-5029
  283 Looney Rd Piqua (45356) *(G-16037)*
Valley Riding 216 267-2525
  19901 Puritas Ave Cleveland (44135) *(G-6618)*
Valley Roofing LLC 513 831-9444
  5293 Tech Valley Dr Milford (45150) *(G-14441)*
Valley Sterling of Cleveland, Cleveland *Also called Valley Ford Truck Inc (G-6617)*
Valley Title & Escro Agency 330 392-6171
  2833 Elm Rd Ne Warren (44483) *(G-18765)*
Valley Title & Escrow Agency 440 632-9833
  15985 E High St Ste 203 Middlefield (44062) *(G-14278)*
Valley Transportation Inc 419 289-6200
  1 Valley Dr Ashland (44805) *(G-696)*
Valley View Alzhimers Care Ctr 740 998-2948
  3363 Ragged Ridge Rd Frankfort (45628) *(G-11019)*
Valley View Fire Dept 216 524-7200
  6899 Hathaway Rd Cleveland (44125) *(G-6619)*
Valley View Health Center, Portsmouth *Also called Community Action Comm Pike CNT (G-16131)*
Valley View Health Center, Jackson *Also called Community Action Comm Pike CNT (G-12172)*
Valley View Place 740 454-7720
  3200 Shale Dr Zanesville (43701) *(G-20371)*
Valley Wholesale Foods Inc (PA) 740 354-5216
  415 Market St Portsmouth (45662) *(G-16180)*
Valleyview Management Co Inc 419 886-4000
  855 Comfort Plaza Dr Bellville (44813) *(G-1392)*
Valleywood Golf Club Inc 419 826-3991
  13501 Airport Hwy Swanton (43558) *(G-17409)*
Valmark Financial Group LLC 330 576-1234
  130 Springside Dr Ste 300 Akron (44333) *(G-483)*
Valmark Securities Inc (HQ) 330 576-1234
  130 Springside Dr Ste 300 Akron (44333) *(G-484)*
Valmer Land Title Agency (PA) 614 860-0005
  2227 State Route 256 B Reynoldsburg (43068) *(G-16336)*
Valmer Land Title Agency 614 875-7001
  3383 Farm Bank Way Grove City (43123) *(G-11479)*
Valtris, Independence *Also called Polymer Additives Holdings Inc (G-12108)*
Valucadd Solutions, Cincinnati *Also called Twism Enterprises LLC (G-4657)*
Value Auto Auction LLC 740 982-3030
  3776 Hc 93 Crooksville (43731) *(G-9064)*
Value Recovery Group Inc (PA) 614 324-5959
  919 Old Henderson Rd Columbus (43220) *(G-8841)*
Valvoline Inc 513 451-1753
  4050 River Rd Cincinnati (45204) *(G-4748)*
Valvoline Instant Oil Change 937 548-0123
  661 Wagner Ave Greenville (45331) *(G-11398)*
Valvoline LLC 513 557-3100
  3901 River Rd Cincinnati (45204) *(G-4749)*
Van Buren Dental Associates 937 253-9115
  1950 S Smithville Rd Kettering (45420) *(G-12302)*
Van Devere Inc (PA) 330 253-6137
  300 W Market St Akron (44303) *(G-485)*
Van Devere Buick, Akron *Also called Van Devere Inc (G-485)*

Van Dyk Mortgage Corporation....513 429-2122
4680 Parkway Dr Ste 100 Mason (45040) ***(G-13653)***
Van Dyne-Crotty Co (PA)....614 684-0048
2150 Fairwood Ave Columbus (43207) ***(G-8842)***
Van Dyne-Crotty Co....614 491-3903
2150 Fairwood Ave Columbus (43207) ***(G-8843)***
Van Dyne-Crotty Co....440 248-6935
30400 Bruce Indus Pkwy Solon (44139) ***(G-16911)***
Van Howards Lines Inc....937 235-0007
3516 Wright Way Rd Ste 2 Dayton (45424) ***(G-9848)***
Van Mayberrys & Storage Inc....937 298-8800
1850 Cardington Rd Moraine (45409) ***(G-14704)***
Van Mills Lines Inc....440 846-0200
14675 Foltz Pkwy Strongsville (44149) ***(G-17357)***
Van Ness Stone Inc....440 564-1111
10500 Kinsman Rd Newbury (44065) ***(G-15127)***
Van Pelt Corporation....513 242-6000
5170 Broerman Ave Cincinnati (45217) ***(G-4750)***
Van Rue Incorporated....419 238-0715
10357 Van Wert Decatur Rd Van Wert (45891) ***(G-18491)***
Van Stevens Lines Inc....419 729-8871
64 N Fearing Blvd Toledo (43607) ***(G-18134)***
Van Tassel Construction Corp....419 873-0188
25591 Fort Meigs Rd Ste A Perrysburg (43551) ***(G-15931)***
Van Wert County Day Care Inc....419 238-9918
10485 Van Wert Decatur Rd Van Wert (45891) ***(G-18492)***
Van Wert County Engineers....419 238-0210
1192 Grill Rd Van Wert (45891) ***(G-18493)***
Van Wert County Hospital Assn (PA)....419 238-2390
1250 S Washington St Van Wert (45891) ***(G-18494)***
Van Wert County Hospital Assn....419 232-2077
140 Fox Rd Ste 201 Van Wert (45891) ***(G-18495)***
Van Wert Manor, Van Wert *Also called Hcf of Van Wert Inc* ***(G-18479)***
Van Wert Medical Services Ltd....419 238-7727
140 Fox Rd Ste 105 Van Wert (45891) ***(G-18496)***
Vana Solutions LLC....937 242-6399
4027 Col Glenn Hwy 110 Beavercreek (45431) ***(G-1194)***
Vancare Inc....937 898-4202
208 N Cassel Rd Vandalia (45377) ***(G-18549)***
Vance Property Management LLC....419 467-9548
4200 South Ave Toledo (43615) ***(G-18135)***
Vance Property Management LLC (PA)....419 887-1878
4200 South Ave Toledo (43615) ***(G-18136)***
Vance Road Enterprises Inc....937 268-6953
1431 N Gettysburg Ave Dayton (45417) ***(G-9849)***
Vancrest Ltd....419 695-2871
1425 E 5th St Delphos (45833) ***(G-10038)***
Vancrest Ltd....419 749-2194
510 E Tully St Convoy (45832) ***(G-8962)***
Vancrest Ltd....937 456-3010
1600 Park Ave Eaton (45320) ***(G-10465)***
Vancrest Apts....419 695-7335
310 Elida Rd Delphos (45833) ***(G-10039)***
Vancrest Health Care Center, Van Wert *Also called Van Rue Incorporated* ***(G-18491)***
Vancrest Health Care Center....419 264-0700
600 Joe E Brown Ave Holgate (43527) ***(G-11867)***
Vancrest Healthcare Cntr, Delphos *Also called Vancrest Ltd* ***(G-10038)***
Vancrest Healthcare Cntr Eaton, Eaton *Also called Vancrest Ltd* ***(G-10465)***
Vancrest of Convoy, Convoy *Also called Vancrest Ltd* ***(G-8962)***
Vand Corp....216 481-3788
1301 E 9th St Ste 1900 Cleveland (44114) ***(G-6620)***
Vandalia Blacktop Seal Coating....937 454-0571
6740 Webster St Dayton (45414) ***(G-9850)***
Vandalia Municipal Court, Vandalia *Also called Supreme Court of Ohio* ***(G-18543)***
Vandalia Park, Vandalia *Also called Vancare Inc* ***(G-18549)***
Vandalia Rental, Vandalia *Also called Bnd Rentals Inc* ***(G-18508)***
Vandra Bros Construction Inc....440 232-3030
24629 Broadway Ave Cleveland (44146) ***(G-6621)***
Vanguard Imaging Partners....937 236-4780
6251 Good Samaritan Way # 140 Dayton (45424) ***(G-9851)***
Vanguard Wines LLC (PA)....614 291-3493
1020 W 5th Ave Columbus (43212) ***(G-8844)***
Vans Express Inc....216 224-5388
222 Concord Ln Hinckley (44233) ***(G-11863)***
Vantage Aging....440 324-3588
42495 N Ridge Rd Elyria (44035) ***(G-10569)***
Vantage Aging (PA)....330 253-4597
2279 Romig Rd Akron (44320) ***(G-486)***
Vantage Aging....330 785-9770
1155 E Tallmadge Ave Akron (44310) ***(G-487)***
Vantage Financial Group, Cleveland *Also called 6200 Rockside LLC* ***(G-4872)***
Vantage Land Title, Dayton *Also called Service Center Title Agency* ***(G-9761)***
Vantage Partners LLC....216 925-1302
3000 Aerospace Pkwy Brookpark (44142) ***(G-1908)***
Vantiv, LLC, Symmes Twp *Also called Worldpay LLC* ***(G-17468)***
Varco LP....440 277-8696
1807 E 28th St Lorain (44055) ***(G-12950)***
Vargo Inc....614 876-1163
3709 Parkway Ln Hilliard (43026) ***(G-11825)***
Various Views Research Inc....513 489-9000
11353 Reed Hartman Hwy # 200 Blue Ash (45241) ***(G-1675)***
Varney Dispatch Inc....513 682-4200
4 Triangle Park Dr # 404 Cincinnati (45246) ***(G-4751)***
Varo Engineers Inc....513 729-9313
6039 Schumacher Park Dr West Chester (45069) ***(G-19029)***
Varo Engineers Inc....740 587-2228
2790 Columbus Rd Granville (43023) ***(G-11349)***
Vartek Services Inc....937 438-3550
4770 Hempstead Station Dr A Dayton (45429) ***(G-9852)***
Vasconcellos Inc....513 576-1250
400 Techne Center Dr # 406 Milford (45150) ***(G-14442)***
Vaughn Industries LLC (PA)....419 396-3900
1201 E Findlay St Carey (43316) ***(G-2548)***
Vaughn Industries LLC....740 548-7100
7749 Green Meadows Dr Lewis Center (43035) ***(G-12566)***
VCA Animal Hospitals Inc....419 423-7232
2141 Bright Rd Findlay (45840) ***(G-10973)***
VCA Findlay Animal Hospital, Findlay *Also called VCA Animal Hospitals Inc* ***(G-10973)***
VCA Green Animal Hospital, Uniontown *Also called VCA Green Animal Medical Ctr* ***(G-18389)***
VCA Green Animal Medical Ctr....330 896-4040
1620 Corporate Woods Cir Uniontown (44685) ***(G-18389)***
Vds, Columbus *Also called Video Duplication Services Inc* ***(G-8850)***
Vec, Girard *Also called Valley Electrical Cnsld Inc* ***(G-11304)***
Vec Inc....330 539-4044
977 Tibbetts Wick Rd Girard (44420) ***(G-11305)***
Vecmar Computer Solutions, Mentor *Also called Vecmar Corporation* ***(G-14121)***
Vecmar Corporation....440 953-1119
7595 Jenther Dr Mentor (44060) ***(G-14121)***
Vector Security Inc....440 466-7233
50 E Main St Geneva (44041) ***(G-11249)***
Vector Security Inc....330 726-9841
4259 Boardman Canfield Rd # 5 Canfield (44406) ***(G-2164)***
Vector Technical Inc....440 946-8800
38033 Euclid Ave Ste T9 Willoughby (44094) ***(G-19581)***
Vediscovery LLC....216 241-3443
1382 W 9th St Ste 400 Cleveland (44113) ***(G-6622)***
Velco Inc....513 772-4226
10280 Chester Rd Cincinnati (45215) ***(G-4752)***
Velocity Grtest Phone Ever Inc....419 868-9983
7130 Spring Meadows Dr W Holland (43528) ***(G-11924)***
Velocys Inc....614 733-3300
7950 Corporate Blvd Plain City (43064) ***(G-16071)***
Velotta Company....330 239-1211
6740 Ridge Rd Sharon Center (44274) ***(G-16727)***
Venco Venturo Industries LLC (PA)....513 772-8448
12110 Best Pl Cincinnati (45241) ***(G-4753)***
Venco/Venturo Div, Cincinnati *Also called Venco Venturo Industries LLC* ***(G-4753)***
Vendor Supply of Ohio, West Chester *Also called Vendors Supply Inc* ***(G-19030)***
Vendors Supply Inc....513 755-2111
6448 Gano Rd West Chester (45069) ***(G-19030)***
Venezia Hauling, New Middletown *Also called Venezia Transport Service Inc* ***(G-14939)***
Venezia Transport Service Inc....330 542-9735
6017 E Calla Rd New Middletown (44442) ***(G-14939)***
Ventech Solutions Inc (PA)....614 757-1167
8425 Pulsar Pl Ste 300 Columbus (43240) ***(G-6837)***
Ventra Salem LLC....330 337-3240
383 Mullins St Salem (44460) ***(G-16565)***
Ventra Salem LLC (HQ)....330 337-8002
800 Pennsylvania Ave Salem (44460) ***(G-16566)***
Venture Lighting Intl Inc (HQ)....800 451-2606
2451 E Enterprise Pkwy Twinsburg (44087) ***(G-18335)***
Venture Productions Inc....937 544-2823
11516 State Route 41 West Union (45693) ***(G-19139)***
Venturo Manufacturing Inc....513 772-8448
12110 Best Pl Cincinnati (45241) ***(G-4754)***
Veolia Es Tchncal Slutions LLC....937 859-6101
4301 Infirmary Rd Miamisburg (45342) ***(G-14234)***
Ver-A-Fast Corp....440 331-0250
20545 Center Ridge Rd # 300 Rocky River (44116) ***(G-16447)***
Verantis Corporation (HQ)....440 243-0700
7251 Engle Rd Ste 300 Middleburg Heights (44130) ***(G-14264)***
Verified Person Inc....901 767-6121
4511 Rockside Rd Ste 400 Independence (44131) ***(G-12136)***
Verisk Crime Analytics Inc....614 865-6000
250 Old Wilson Brg Worthington (43085) ***(G-19857)***
Veritas Enterprises Inc....513 578-2748
918 Tall Trees Dr Cincinnati (45245) ***(G-2874)***
Veritiv Operating Company....513 242-0800
375 Distribution Cir Fairfield (45014) ***(G-10798)***
Veritiv Operating Company....614 251-7100
3265 Southpark Pl Grove City (43123) ***(G-11480)***
Veritiv Operating Company....216 573-7400
7575 E Pleasant Valley Rd # 200 Independence (44131) ***(G-12137)***
Veritiv Operating Company....419 243-6100
1320 Locust St Toledo (43608) ***(G-18137)***
Veritiv Operating Company....513 285-0999
6120 S Gilmore Rd Fairfield (45014) ***(G-10799)***
Veritiv Operating Company....216 901-5700
9797 Sweet Valley Dr Cleveland (44125) ***(G-6623)***
Veritiv Pubg & Print MGT Inc (HQ)....330 650-5522
5700 Darrow Rd Ste 110 Hudson (44236) ***(G-12011)***
Verizon, Dublin *Also called Cellco Partnership* ***(G-10162)***

ALPHABETIC

Verizon, Cincinnati *Also called Cellco Partnership (G-3143)*
Verizon, Alliance *Also called Cellco Partnership (G-523)*
Verizon, Fremont *Also called Cellco Partnership (G-11061)*
Verizon, Marion *Also called Supermedia LLC (G-13462)*
Verizon, Sheffield Village *Also called ABC Phones North Carolina Inc (G-16731)*
Verizon, Cincinnati *Also called Cellco Partnership (G-3145)*
Verizon, Findlay *Also called Cellco Partnership (G-10886)*
Verizon, Maumee *Also called Cellco Partnership (G-13768)*
Verizon, Mentor *Also called Cellco Partnership (G-14027)*
Verizon, Cleveland *Also called Cellco Partnership (G-5147)*
Verizon, Strongsville *Also called Cellco Partnership (G-17289)*
Verizon, Mount Vernon *Also called Cellco Partnership (G-14752)*
Verizon, Columbus *Also called Cellco Partnership (G-7148)*
Verizon, Beavercreek *Also called Cellco Partnership (G-1138)*
Verizon, Cincinnati *Also called Cellco Partnership (G-3146)*
Verizon, Cincinnati *Also called Cellco Partnership (G-3147)*
Verizon, Toledo *Also called Cellco Partnership (G-17641)*
Verizon, Canton *Also called Cellco Partnership (G-2247)*
Verizon, Elyria *Also called Cellco Partnership (G-10486)*
Verizon, Dublin *Also called Cellco Partnership (G-10164)*
Verizon, Newark *Also called Cellco Partnership (G-15021)*
Verizon, Wooster *Also called Cellco Partnership (G-19698)*
Verizon Bus Netwrk Svcs Inc 513 897-1501
  9073 Lytle Ferry Rd Waynesville (45068) *(G-18837)*
Verizon Business, Cleveland *Also called MCI Communications Svcs Inc (G-5934)*
Verizon Business, Chardon *Also called MCI Communications Svcs Inc (G-2704)*
Verizon Business Global LLC 614 219-2317
  5000 Britton Pkwy Hilliard (43026) *(G-11826)*
Verizon Communications Inc 330 334-1268
  1114 Williams Reserve Wadsworth (44281) *(G-18617)*
Verizon Communications Inc 440 892-4504
  30171 Detroit Rd Westlake (44145) *(G-19420)*
Verizon New York Inc 614 301-2498
  5000 Britton Pkwy Hilliard (43026) *(G-11827)*
Verizon North Inc 740 942-2566
  994 E Market St Cadiz (43907) *(G-2033)*
Verizon Select Services Inc 908 559-2054
  12300 Ridge Rd North Royalton (44133) *(G-15370)*
Verizon Wireless, Wooster *Also called Rxp Wireless LLC (G-19763)*
Verizon Wireless, Amherst *Also called Cellco Partnership (G-583)*
Verizon Wireless, Lancaster *Also called Cellco Partnership (G-12377)*
Verizon Wireless, Saint Clairsville *Also called Cellco Partnership (G-16482)*
Verizon Wireless, Cambridge *Also called Cellco Partnership (G-2057)*
Verizon Wireless, Akron *Also called Cellco Partnership (G-122)*
Verizon Wireless, West Chester *Also called Cellco Partnership (G-18883)*
Verizon Wireless, Avon *Also called Cellco Partnership (G-872)*
Verizon Wireless, Toledo *Also called Cellco Partnership (G-17640)*
Verizon Wireless, Beachwood *Also called Cellco Partnership (G-1042)*
Verizon Wireless, Ashtabula *Also called Cellco Partnership (G-724)*
Verizon Wireless, Middletown *Also called Cellco Partnership (G-14345)*
Verizon Wireless, Zanesville *Also called Cellco Partnership (G-20289)*
Verizon Wireless, North Olmsted *Also called Cellco Partnership (G-15279)*
Verizon Wireless, Independence *Also called Cellco Partnership (G-12056)*
Verizon Wireless, Marysville *Also called Cellco Partnership (G-13489)*
Verizon Wireless, Solon *Also called Cellco Partnership (G-16834)*
Verizon Wireless, Streetsboro *Also called Cellco Partnership (G-17248)*
Verizon Wireless, New Philadelphia *Also called Cellco Partnership (G-14948)*
Verizon Wireless, Dublin *Also called Cellco Partnership (G-10163)*
Verizon Wireless, Zanesville *Also called Cellco Partnership (G-20290)*
Verizon Wireless, Grove City *Also called Cellco Partnership (G-11418)*
Verizon Wireless 330 963-1300
  2000 Highland Rd Twinsburg (44087) *(G-18336)*
Verizon Wireless Inc 937 434-2355
  2799 Mmsburg Cntrville Rd Dayton (45459) *(G-9853)*
Verizon Wreless Authorized Ret, Strongsville *Also called Aka Wireless Inc (G-17282)*
Verizon Wreless Authorized Ret, Columbus *Also called Cellular Sales Knoxville Inc (G-7149)*
Vermeer Sales & Service Inc (PA) 330 723-8383
  2389 Medina Rd Medina (44256) *(G-14012)*
Vermilion Board of Education 440 204-1700
  1065 Decatur St Vermilion (44089) *(G-18561)*
Vermilion Boat Club Inc 440 967-6634
  5416 Liberty Ave Vermilion (44089) *(G-18562)*
Vermilion Family YMCA 440 967-4208
  320 Aldrich Rd Vermilion (44089) *(G-18563)*
Vermilion Farm Market 440 967-9666
  2901 Liberty Ave Vermilion (44089) *(G-18564)*
Vermilion School Bus Garage, Vermilion *Also called Vermilion Board of Education (G-18561)*
Vernon F Glaser & Associates 937 298-5536
  3085 Woodman Dr Ste 250 Dayton (45420) *(G-9854)*
Versailles Gardens Apts, Canton *Also called Brookwood Management Company (G-2219)*
Versailles Health Care Center, Versailles *Also called Covenant Care Ohio Inc (G-18569)*

Versailles Util Dept, Versailles *Also called Village of Versailles (G-18572)*
Versatex LLC 513 639-3119
  324 W 9th St Cincinnati (45202) *(G-4755)*
Verst Group Logistics Inc 513 782-1725
  98 Glendale Milford Rd Cincinnati (45215) *(G-4756)*
Verst Group Logistics Inc 513 772-2494
  11880 Enterprise Dr Cincinnati (45241) *(G-4757)*
Verti Insurance Company 844 448-3784
  3590 Twin Creeks Dr Columbus (43204) *(G-8845)*
Vertical Adventures Inc 614 888-8393
  6295 Busch Blvd Ste B Columbus (43229) *(G-8846)*
Vertical Knowledge LLC (PA) 216 920-7790
  8 E Washington St Ste 200 Chagrin Falls (44022) *(G-2658)*
Vertiv, Dayton *Also called High Voltage Maintenance Corp (G-9496)*
Vertiv Corporation (HQ) 614 888-0246
  1050 Dearborn Dr Columbus (43085) *(G-8847)*
Vertiv Corporation 614 841-6400
  610 Executive Campus Dr Westerville (43082) *(G-19215)*
Vertiv Corporation 614 841-6104
  6700 Huntley Rd Ste A Columbus (43229) *(G-8848)*
Vertiv Energy Systems Inc 440 288-1122
  1510 Kansas Ave Lorain (44052) *(G-12951)*
Vesco Oil Corporation 614 367-1412
  254 Business Center Dr Blacklick (43004) *(G-1484)*
Vet Path Services Inc 513 469-0777
  6450 Castle Dr Mason (45040) *(G-13654)*
Veteran Security Patrol Co 937 222-7333
  601 S E C Moses Blvd # 170 Dayton (45417) *(G-9855)*
Veteran Security Patrol Co 513 381-4482
  36 E 7th St Ste 2201 Cincinnati (45202) *(G-4758)*
Veterans ADM Out Ptient Clinic, Columbus *Also called Ohio State University (G-8314)*
Veterans Affairs US Dept 937 268-6511
  4100 W 3rd St Dayton (45428) *(G-9856)*
Veterans Clinic, Canton *Also called Veterans Health Administration (G-2526)*
Veterans Fgn Wars Post 2850 ....216 631-2585
  3296 W 61st St Cleveland (44102) *(G-6624)*
Veterans Health Administration 740 568-0412
  418 Colegate Dr Marietta (45750) *(G-13396)*
Veterans Health Administration 740 773-1141
  17273 State Route 104 Chillicothe (45601) *(G-2836)*
Veterans Health Administration 513 861-3100
  3200 Vine St Cincinnati (45220) *(G-4759)*
Veterans Health Administration 513 943-3680
  4600 Beechwood Rd Cincinnati (45244) *(G-4760)*
Veterans Health Administration 216 791-3800
  10701 East Blvd Cleveland (44106) *(G-6625)*
Veterans Health Administration 614 257-5524
  420 N James Rd Columbus (43219) *(G-8849)*
Veterans Health Administration 866 463-0912
  4314 Main Ave Frnt Ashtabula (44004) *(G-758)*
Veterans Health Administration 740 695-9321
  103 Plaza Dr Ste A Saint Clairsville (43950) *(G-16509)*
Veterans Health Administration 419 259-2000
  3333 Glendale Ave Toledo (43614) *(G-18138)*
Veterans Health Administration 330 740-9200
  2031 Belmont Ave Youngstown (44505) *(G-20236)*
Veterans Health Administration 216 939-0699
  4242 Lorain Ave Cleveland (44113) *(G-6626)*
Veterans Health Administration 330 489-4600
  733 Market Ave S Canton (44702) *(G-2526)*
Veterinary RFRrl&emer Ctr of 330 665-4996
  1321 Centerview Cir Copley (44321) *(G-8979)*
Vexor Technology Inc (PA) 330 721-9773
  955 W Smith Rd Medina (44256) *(G-14013)*
Veyance Industrial Svcs Inc (PA) 307 682-7855
  703 S Clvland Mssillon Rd Fairlawn (44333) *(G-10854)*
Vgs Inc 216 431-7800
  2239 E 55th St Cleveland (44103) *(G-6627)*
Via Quest, Dublin *Also called Alexson Services Inc (G-10125)*
Viaquest Inc (PA) 614 889-5837
  525 Metro Pl N Ste 300 Dublin (43017) *(G-10362)*
Viaquest Behavioral Health LLC (PA) 614 339-0868
  525 Metro Pl N Ste 450 Dublin (43017) *(G-10363)*
Viaquest Home Health LLC (HQ) 800 645-3267
  525 Metro Pl N Dublin (43017) *(G-10364)*
Vibo Construction Inc 614 210-6780
  4140 Tuller Rd Ste 112 Dublin (43017) *(G-10365)*
Vibra Healthcare LLC 330 675-5555
  1350 E Market St Warren (44483) *(G-18766)*
Vibra Hosp Mahoning Vly LLC 330 726-5000
  8049 South Ave Youngstown (44512) *(G-20237)*
Viconsi Company, Cleveland *Also called Visconsi Management Inc (G-6635)*
Victor McKenzie Drilling Co 740 453-0834
  3596 Maple Ave Ste A Zanesville (43701) *(G-20372)*
Victory Capital Management Inc (HQ) 216 898-2400
  4900 Tiedeman Rd Fl 4 Brooklyn (44144) *(G-1862)*
Victory Lanes Inc 937 323-8684
  1906 Commerce Cir Springfield (45504) *(G-17130)*
Victory Machine and Fab 937 693-3171
  920 S Vandemark Rd Sidney (45365) *(G-16804)*
Victory Pool, Cleveland *Also called City of South Euclid (G-5216)*

Victory Sq Aprtmnts Ltd Partnr.................................330 455-8035
  1206 Lppert Rd Ne Apt 211 Canton (44705) *(G-2527)*
Victory White Metal Company (PA).........................216 271-1400
  6100 Roland Ave Cleveland (44127) *(G-6628)*
Victory White Metal Company................................216 271-1400
  3027 E 55th St Cleveland (44127) *(G-6629)*
Victory Wholesale Grocery, Springboro *Also called Brothers Trading Co Inc (G-16964)*
Video Duplication Services Inc (PA).......................614 871-3827
  3777 Busineoh Pk Dr Ste A Columbus (43204) *(G-8850)*
Vieira Inc...937 599-3221
  4622 County Road 49 Bellefontaine (43311) *(G-1369)*
Vienna Enterprises Inc..937 568-4524
  125 E National Rd South Vienna (45369) *(G-16949)*
Vietnam Veterans America Inc...............................330 877-6017
  874 Marigold St Nw Hartville (44632) *(G-11700)*
Vewray Technologies Inc......................................440 703-3210
  2 Thermo Fisher Way Oakwood Village (44146) *(G-15496)*
Vigilant Defense..513 309-0672
  8366 Princeton Glendale West Chester (45069) *(G-19031)*
Vigilant Global Trade Svcs LLC (PA)......................260 417-1825
  3140 Courtland Blvd # 3400 Shaker Heights (44122) *(G-16719)*
Vigilant Technology Solutions, West Chester *Also called Vigilant Defense (G-19031)*
Viking Explosives LLC..218 263-8845
  25800 Science Park Dr Cleveland (44122) *(G-6630)*
Viking Fabricators Inc...740 374-5246
  2021 Hanna Rd Marietta (45750) *(G-13397)*
Viking Office Products Inc.....................................513 881-7200
  4700 Muhlhauser Rd West Chester (45011) *(G-19032)*
Villa Angela Care Center, Columbus *Also called Karl Hc LLC (G-7882)*
Villa Georgetown, Georgetown *Also called Covenant Care Ohio Inc (G-11269)*
Villa Milano Inc..614 882-2058
  1630 Schrock Rd Columbus (43229) *(G-8851)*
Villa Mlano Bnquet Cnfrnce Ctr, Columbus *Also called Villa Milano Inc (G-8851)*
Villa Restaurant, Carrollton *Also called Saint Johns Villa (G-2576)*
Villa Springfield, Springfield *Also called Covenant Care Ohio Inc (G-17026)*
VILLAGE AT SAINT EDWARD, Fairlawn *Also called St Edward Home (G-10851)*
Village At St Edward Ind Lving, Fairlawn *Also called Saint Edward Housing Corp (G-10846)*
Village At The Greene, Beavercreek *Also called Hcf of Crestview Inc (G-1223)*
Village At Wstrvlle Retiremnt, Westerville *Also called Health Care Rtrement Corp Amer (G-19261)*
VILLAGE CHRISTIAN SCHOOLS, Pleasant Plain *Also called Mid-Western Childrens Home (G-16074)*
Village Chrysler-Dodge, Millersburg *Also called Village Motors Inc (G-14498)*
Village Communities LLC..614 540-2400
  470 Olde Worthington Rd # 100 Westerville (43082) *(G-19216)*
Village Green Healthcare Ctr..................................937 548-1993
  405 Chestnut St Greenville (45331) *(G-11399)*
Village Handyman, The, Akron *Also called Craftsmen Restoration LLC (G-168)*
Village Inn Restaurant, Coshocton *Also called Roscoe Village Foundation (G-9026)*
Village Motors Inc..330 674-2055
  784 Wooster Rd Millersburg (44654) *(G-14498)*
Village Network (PA)...330 264-0650
  2000 Noble Dr Wooster (44691) *(G-19776)*
Village of Antwerp (PA)...419 258-7422
  118 N Main St Antwerp (45813) *(G-615)*
Village of Antwerp..419 258-6631
  203 S Cleveland St Antwerp (45813) *(G-616)*
Village of Byesville...740 685-5901
  221 Main St Byesville (43723) *(G-2026)*
Village of Coldwater..419 678-2685
  610 W Sycamore St Coldwater (45828) *(G-6767)*
Village of Cuyahoga Heights (PA)...........................216 641-7020
  4863 E 71st St Frnt Cleveland (44125) *(G-6631)*
Village of Groveport..614 830-2060
  655 Blacklick St Groveport (43125) *(G-11549)*
Village of Strasburg..330 878-7115
  358 5th St Sw Strasburg (44680) *(G-17241)*
Village of Valley View..216 524-6511
  6848 Hathaway Rd Cleveland (44125) *(G-6632)*
Village of Versailles..937 526-4191
  177 N Center St Versailles (45380) *(G-18572)*
Village Transport Corp..440 461-5000
  6300 Wilson Mills Rd Cleveland (44143) *(G-6633)*
Vimas Painting Company Inc.................................330 536-2222
  4328 Mccartney Rd Lowellville (44436) *(G-13044)*
Vin Devers (PA)..888 847-9535
  5570 Monroe St Sylvania (43560) *(G-17462)*
Vincent Ltg Systems Co Inc (PA)............................216 475-7600
  6161 Cochran Rd Ste D Solon (44139) *(G-16912)*
Vinifera Imports Ltd...440 942-9463
  7551 Plaza Blvd Mentor (44060) *(G-14122)*
Vintage Wine Distributor Inc................................614 876-2580
  2277 Westbrooke Dr Columbus (43228) *(G-8852)*
VINTON CO NATIONAL BANK, Mc Arthur *Also called Vinton County Nat Bnk McArthur (G-13892)*
Vinton County Nat Bnk McArthur (HQ)....................740 596-2525
  112 W Main St Mc Arthur (45651) *(G-13892)*
Vinyl Design Corporation.......................................419 283-4009
  7856 Hill Ave Holland (43528) *(G-11925)*

Viox Services, Cincinnati *Also called Emcor Facilities Services Inc (G-3492)*
VIP Building Exteriors Contrs, Cuyahoga Falls *Also called VIP Restoration Inc (G-9136)*
VIP Electric Company..440 255-0180
  8358 Mentor Ave Mentor (44060) *(G-14123)*
VIP Home Care, Akron *Also called VIP Homecare Inc (G-488)*
VIP Homecare Inc...330 929-2838
  545 E Cuyahoga Falls Ave Akron (44310) *(G-488)*
VIP Restoration Inc (PA).......................................216 426-9500
  650 Graham Rd Ste 106 Cuyahoga Falls (44221) *(G-9136)*
Virginia Ohio-West Excvtg Co.................................740 676-7464
  56461 Ferry Landing Rd Shadyside (43947) *(G-16698)*
Virginia T'S, Hebron *Also called Heritage Sportswear Inc (G-11715)*
Virginia Tile Company...216 741-8400
  4749 Spring Rd Brooklyn Heights (44131) *(G-1886)*
Virtual Hold Technology LLC (PA)...........................330 670-2200
  3875 Embassy Pkwy Ste 350 Akron (44333) *(G-489)*
Virtual Pc's, Lima *Also called Office World Inc (G-12791)*
Virtual Technologies Group (PA).............................419 991-4694
  3820 S Dixie Hwy Lima (45806) *(G-12794)*
Virtuoso, Cincinnati *Also called Pier n Port Travel Inc (G-4247)*
Visconsi Companies Ltd..216 464-5550
  30050 Chagrin Blvd # 360 Cleveland (44124) *(G-6634)*
Visconsi Management Inc.......................................216 464-5550
  30050 Chagrin Blvd # 360 Cleveland (44124) *(G-6635)*
Vishnia & Associates Inc.......................................330 929-5512
  2497 State Rd Cuyahoga Falls (44223) *(G-9137)*
Visicon Inc...937 879-2696
  Area A Bldg 823 Fairborn (45324) *(G-10687)*
Vision & Vocational Services (PA)...........................614 294-5571
  1393 N High St Columbus (43201) *(G-8853)*
Vision America of Ohio, Chillicothe *Also called Ohio Eye Specialists Inc (G-2807)*
Vision Associates Inc (PA).....................................419 578-7598
  2865 N Reynolds Rd # 170 Toledo (43615) *(G-18139)*
Vision Express Inc...740 922-8848
  801 W 1st St Uhrichsville (44683) *(G-18348)*
Vision Service Plan...614 471-7511
  3400 Morris Xing Columbus (43219) *(G-8854)*
Visions Matter LLC...513 934-1934
  838 W State Route 122 Lebanon (45036) *(G-12513)*
Visiting Angels, Cincinnati *Also called RWS Enterprises LLC (G-4416)*
Visiting Angels, Toledo *Also called Tk Homecare Llc (G-18067)*
Visiting Angels, Ravenna *Also called Tsk Assisted Living Services (G-16269)*
Visiting Angels, Tallmadge *Also called Living Assistance Services (G-17481)*
Visiting Angels, Salem *Also called Frencor Inc (G-16544)*
Visiting Angels, Cleveland *Also called Majastan Group LLC (G-5900)*
Visiting Angels Lvng Asst, West Chester *Also called Dillon Holdings LLC (G-18911)*
Visiting Nrse Assn of Clveland................................419 281-2480
  1165 E Main St Ashland (44805) *(G-697)*
Visiting Nrse Assn of Clveland................................419 522-4969
  40 W 4th St Mansfield (44902) *(G-13260)*
Visiting Nrse Assn of Mid-Ohio...............................216 931-1300
  2500 E 22nd St Cleveland (44115) *(G-6636)*
Visiting Nurse Assn Ashland, Ashland *Also called Visiting Nrse Assn of Clveland (G-697)*
Visiting Nurse Associat (PA)...................................513 345-8000
  2400 Reading Rd Ste 207 Cincinnati (45202) *(G-4761)*
Visiting Nurse Association.....................................216 931-1300
  925 Keynote Cir Ste 300 Independence (44131) *(G-12138)*
Visiting Nurse Service Inc (PA).............................330 745-1601
  1 Home Care Pl Akron (44320) *(G-490)*
Visiting Nurse Service Inc....................................440 286-9461
  13221 Ravenna Rd Ste 1 Chardon (44024) *(G-2723)*
VISITING NURSES ASSOCIATION, Sylvania *Also called Toledo District Nurses Assn (G-17458)*
VISON SUPPORT SERVICES, Akron *Also called Akron Blind Center & Workshop (G-29)*
Vista Centre...330 424-5852
  100 Vista Dr Lisbon (44432) *(G-12806)*
Vista Color Imaging Inc...216 651-2830
  4770 Van Epps Rd Ste 1 Brooklyn Heights (44131) *(G-1887)*
Vista Industrial Packaging LLC...............................800 454-6117
  4700 Fisher Rd Columbus (43228) *(G-8855)*
Vista Packaging & Logistics, Columbus *Also called Vista Industrial Packaging LLC (G-8855)*
Vistacare USA Inc...614 975-3230
  540 Officenter Pl Ste 100 Columbus (43230) *(G-8856)*
Vistra Energy Corp...513 467-5289
  1781 Us 52 Moscow (45153) *(G-14721)*
Vistra Energy Corp...513 467-4900
  11021 Brower Rd North Bend (45052) *(G-15183)*
Visual Art Graphic Services....................................330 274-2775
  5244 Goodell Rd Mantua (44255) *(G-13278)*
Visual Edge Technology Inc (PA)...........................330 494-9694
  3874 Highland Park Nw Canton (44720) *(G-2528)*
Visual Evidence/E-Discovery, Cleveland *Also called Vediscovery LLC (G-6622)*
Vita Pup, Hudson *Also called JE Carsten Company (G-11987)*
Vital Resources Inc..440 614-5150
  1119 Sheltered Brook Dr Huron (44839) *(G-12034)*
Vitalyst..216 201-9070
  3615 Superior Ave E 4406a Cleveland (44114) *(G-6637)*
Vitas Healthcare Corp of Ohio, Cincinnati *Also called Detox Health Care Corp Ohio (G-3424)*

A
L
P
H
A
B
E
T
I
C

Vitas Healthcare Corporation 513 742-6310
  11500 Northlake Dr # 400 Cincinnati (45249) *(G-4762)*

Vitran Express Inc 614 870-2255
  5075 Krieger Ct Columbus (43228) *(G-8857)*

Vitran Express Inc 216 426-8584
  5300 Crayton Ave Cleveland (44104) *(G-6638)*

Vitran Express Inc 513 771-4894
  2789 Crescentville Rd West Chester (45069) *(G-19033)*

Vivial Media LLC 513 768-7800
  720 E Pete Rose Way # 350 Cincinnati (45202) *(G-4763)*

Vivial Media LLC 937 610-4100
  3100 Res Blvd Ste 250 Dayton (45420) *(G-9857)*

Vizmeg Landscape Inc 330 686-0901
  778 Mccauley Rd Unit 100 Stow (44224) *(G-17238)*

Vjp Hospitality Ltd 614 475-8383
  3030 Plaza Prpts Blvd Columbus (43219) *(G-8858)*

Vloan, Strongsville Also called Union Home Mortgage Corp *(G-17353)*

Vlp Inc 330 758-8811
  7301 West Blvd Ste A3 Youngstown (44512) *(G-20238)*

Vmi Group Inc 330 405-4146
  8854 Valley View Rd Macedonia (44056) *(G-13088)*

VNA, Cleveland Also called Visiting Nrse Assn of Mid-Ohio *(G-6636)*

Vna of Mid Ohio, Mansfield Also called Visiting Nrse Assn of Clveland *(G-13260)*

Voc Works Ltd 614 760-3515
  5555 Glendon Ct Ste 300 Dublin (43016) *(G-10366)*

Voca of Ohio 419 435-5836
  1021 Dillon Rd Fostoria (44830) *(G-11014)*

Vocalink Inc 937 223-1415
  405 W 1st St Ste A Dayton (45402) *(G-9858)*

Vocational Guidance Services (PA) 216 431-7800
  2239 E 55th St Cleveland (44103) *(G-6639)*

Vocational Guidance Services 440 322-1123
  359 Lowell St Elyria (44035) *(G-10570)*

Vocational Rehabilitation, Cincinnati Also called Opportunities For Ohioans *(G-4177)*

Vocational Services, Elyria Also called Vocational Guidance Services *(G-10570)*

Vocational Services Inc 216 431-8085
  2239 E 55th St Cleveland (44103) *(G-6640)*

Vocon Design Inc (PA) 216 588-0800
  3142 Prospect Ave E Cleveland (44115) *(G-6641)*

Vocworks, Dublin Also called Careworks of Ohio Inc *(G-10161)*

Voestlpine Precision Strip LLC (HQ) 330 220-7800
  3052 Interstate Pkwy Brunswick (44212) *(G-1944)*

Vogel Dialysis LLC 614 834-3564
  3568 Gender Rd Canal Winchester (43110) *(G-2124)*

Vogt Warehouse, Cincinnati Also called Specialty Logistics Inc *(G-4512)*

Voiers Enterprises Inc 740 259-2838
  2274 Mc Dermott Pond Crk Mc Dermott (45652) *(G-13896)*

Volk Optical Inc 440 942-6161
  7893 Enterprise Dr Mentor (44060) *(G-14124)*

Volpone Enterprises Inc 440 969-1141
  5223 N Ridge Rd W Ste 2 Ashtabula (44004) *(G-759)*

Volt Management Corp 513 791-2600
  8044 Montgomery Rd # 630 Cincinnati (45236) *(G-4764)*

Volt Workforce Solutions, Cincinnati Also called Volt Management Corp *(G-4764)*

Volunteer Energy Services Inc (PA) 614 856-3128
  790 Windmiller Dr Ste A Pickerington (43147) *(G-15969)*

Volunteer of Amer Autemwood CA, Tiffin Also called Volunteers Amer Care Facilities *(G-17546)*

Volunteers America Ohio & Ind (PA) 614 253-6100
  1776 E Broad St Frnt Columbus (43203) *(G-8859)*

Volunteers of America NW Ohio 419 248-3733
  701 Jefferson Ave Ste 203 Toledo (43604) *(G-18140)*

Volunters Amer Care Facilities 419 447-7151
  670 E State Route 18 Tiffin (44883) *(G-17546)*

Volunters Amer Care Facilities 419 225-9040
  804 S Mumaugh Rd Lima (45804) *(G-12774)*

Volunters Amer Care Facilities 419 334-9521
  600 N Brush St Fremont (43420) *(G-11103)*

Volunters of Amer Greater Ohio 614 861-8551
  4280 Macsway Ave Columbus (43232) *(G-8860)*

Volunters of Amer Greater Ohio 216 541-9000
  775 E 152nd St Cleveland (44110) *(G-6642)*

Volunters of Amer Greater Ohio 614 372-3120
  2335 N Bank Dr Columbus (43220) *(G-8861)*

Volunters of Amer Greater Ohio 419 524-5013
  921 N Main St Mansfield (44903) *(G-13261)*

Volunters of Amer Greater Ohio 614 263-9134
  3620 Indianola Ave Columbus (43214) *(G-8862)*

Volunters of America Cntl Ohio 614 801-1655
  4026 Mcdowell Rd Grove City (43123) *(G-11481)*

Volvo BMW Dyton Evans Volkswag 937 890-6200
  7124 Poe Ave Dayton (45414) *(G-9859)*

Vora Ventures LLC 513 792-5100
  10290 Alliance Rd Blue Ash (45242) *(G-1676)*

Vorys Sater Seymour Pease LLP 216 479-6100
  200 Public Sq Ste 1400 Cleveland (44114) *(G-6643)*

Vorys Sater Seymour Pease LLP 513 723-4000
  301 E 4th St Ste 3410 Cincinnati (45202) *(G-4765)*

Voss Auto Network Inc (PA) 937 428-2447
  766 Mmsburg Cnterville Rd Dayton (45459) *(G-9860)*

Voss Auto Network Inc 937 433-1444
  100 Loop Rd Dayton (45459) *(G-9861)*

Voss Chevrolet Inc 937 428-2500
  100 Loop Rd Dayton (45459) *(G-9862)*

Voss Dodge (PA) 937 435-7800
  90 Loop Rd Dayton (45459) *(G-9863)*

Voss Honda, Tipp City Also called Hoss II Inc *(G-17560)*

Voss Hyundai, Dayton Also called Hoss Value Cars & Trucks Inc *(G-9507)*

Voss Toyota Inc 937 431-2100
  2110 Heller Dr Beavercreek (45434) *(G-1195)*

Vox Mobile 800 536-9030
  6100 Rockside Woods # 100 Independence (44131) *(G-12139)*

Voya Financial Inc 614 431-5000
  7965 N High St Columbus (43235) *(G-8863)*

Vps, Inc., Mason Also called Vet Path Services Inc *(G-13654)*

Vrable Healthcare Inc (PA) 614 545-5500
  3248 Henderson Rd Columbus (43220) *(G-8864)*

Vrable II Inc 614 545-5502
  3248 Henderson Rd Columbus (43220) *(G-8865)*

Vrable III Inc 740 446-7150
  311 Buck Ridge Rd Bidwell (45614) *(G-1471)*

Vrable IV Inc (HQ) 614 545-5502
  3248 Henderson Rd Columbus (43220) *(G-8866)*

Vsync, Columbus Also called Enhanced Software Inc *(G-7518)*

Vulcan Enterprises Inc 419 396-3535
  2600 State Highway 568 A Carey (43316) *(G-2549)*

Vulcan Feg 937 332-2763
  750 Lincoln Ave Troy (45373) *(G-18239)*

Vulcan Fire Protection, Carey Also called Vulcan Enterprises Inc *(G-2549)*

Vulcan Machinery Corporation 330 376-6025
  20 N Case Ave Akron (44305) *(G-491)*

Vulcan Oil Company, Cincinnati Also called New Vulco Mfg & Sales Co LLC *(G-4109)*

Vwc Liquidation Company LLC 330 372-6776
  1701 Henn Pkwy Sw Warren (44481) *(G-18767)*

VWR Chemicals LLC 330 425-2522
  220 Lena Dr Aurora (44202) *(G-847)*

VWR International, Aurora Also called VWR Chemicals LLC *(G-847)*

W & H Realty Inc (PA) 513 891-1066
  4243 Hunt Rd Blue Ash (45242) *(G-1677)*

W B Mason Co Inc 216 267-5000
  12985 Snow Rd Cleveland (44130) *(G-6644)*

W B N X T V 55 .... 330 922-5500
  2690 State Rd Cuyahoga Falls (44223) *(G-9138)*

W C National Mailing Corp 614 836-5703
  4241 Williams Rd Groveport (43125) *(G-11550)*

W C P O - T V, Cincinnati Also called Wfts *(G-4794)*

W D Tire Warehouse Inc (PA) 614 461-8944
  3805 E Livingston Ave Columbus (43227) *(G-8867)*

W David Maupin Inc 419 389-0458
  3564 Marine Rd Toledo (43609) *(G-18141)*

W E Quicksall and Assoc Inc (PA) 330 339-6676
  554 W High Ave New Philadelphia (44663) *(G-14988)*

W F Bolin Company Inc 614 276-6397
  4100 Fisher Rd Columbus (43228) *(G-8868)*

W F H M - F M 95.5, Cleveland Also called Salem Media Group Inc *(G-6365)*

W G Lockhart Construction Co 330 745-6520
  800 W Waterloo Rd Akron (44314) *(G-492)*

W G U C-FM RADIO, Cincinnati Also called Cincinnati Public Radio Inc *(G-3262)*

W H O T Inc (PA) 330 783-1000
  4040 Simon Rd Ste 1 Youngstown (44512) *(G-20239)*

W J Alarm Service, Warren Also called Wj Service Co Inc *(G-18773)*

W K H R Radio 440 708-0915
  17425 Snyder Rd Bainbridge (45612) *(G-932)*

W K S, Cleves Also called Wm Kramer and Sons Inc *(G-6736)*

W K Y C Channel 3, Cleveland Also called Wkyc-Tv Inc *(G-6687)*

W L Logan Trucking Company 330 478-1404
  3224 Navarre Rd Sw Canton (44706) *(G-2529)*

W L W TT V 5 .... 513 412-5000
  1700 Young St Cincinnati (45202) *(G-4766)*

W M V O 1300 AM 740 397-1000
  17421 Coshocton Rd Mount Vernon (43050) *(G-14791)*

W N W O, Toledo Also called Barrington Toledo LLC *(G-17605)*

W O I O, Cleveland Also called Gray Media Group Inc *(G-5624)*

W P Dolle LLC 513 421-6515
  201 E 5th St Ste 1000 Cincinnati (45202) *(G-4767)*

W Pol Contracting Inc 330 325-7177
  4188 Ohio 14 Ravenna (44266) *(G-16270)*

W R G Inc 216 351-8494
  3961 Pearl Rd Cleveland (44109) *(G-6645)*

W R Shepherd Inc (PA) 614 889-2896
  390 W Olentangy St Powell (43065) *(G-16212)*

W S E M, Cleveland Also called West Side Ecumenical Ministry *(G-6671)*

W S N Y F M Sunny 95, Columbus Also called Franklin Communications Inc *(G-7613)*

W S O S Community A 419 729-8035
  1500 N Superior St # 303 Toledo (43604) *(G-18142)*

W S O S Community A (PA) 419 333-6068
  127 S Front St Fremont (43420) *(G-11104)*

W S O S Community A 419 639-2802
  1518 E County Road 113 Green Springs (44836) *(G-11356)*

W S O S Community A 419 334-8511
  765 S Buchanan St Fremont (43420) *(G-11105)*

W S T R, Cincinnati Also called Sinclair Broadcast Group Inc *(G-4484)*

W T C S A Headstart Niles Ctr 330 652-0338
309 N Rhodes Ave Niles (44446) *(G-15173)*
W T Sports Inc 740 654-0035
5288 Aryshire Dr Dublin (43017) *(G-10367)*
W U P W, Toledo *Also called Sunrise Television Corp (G-18054)*
W W Schaub Electric Co 330 494-3560
501 Applegrove St Nw Canton (44720) *(G-2530)*
W W W M 419 240-1055
3225 Arlington Ave Toledo (43614) *(G-18143)*
W W Williams Company LLC 419 837-5067
3325 Libbey Rd Perrysburg (43551) *(G-15932)*
W W Williams Company LLC 330 534-1161
7125 Masury Rd Hubbard (44425) *(G-11951)*
W W Williams Company LLC 419 837-5067
3325 Libbey Rd Perrysburg (43551) *(G-15933)*
W W Williams Company LLC 216 252-9977
4545 Industrial Pkwy Cleveland (44135) *(G-6646)*
W W Williams Company LLC 800 336-6651
4806 Interstate Dr West Chester (45246) *(G-19098)*
W W Williams Company LLC (HQ) 614 228-5000
5025 Bradenton Ave # 130 Dublin (43017) *(G-10368)*
W W Williams Company LLC 330 225-7751
1176 Industrial Pkwy N Brunswick (44212) *(G-1945)*
W W Williams Company LLC 614 527-9400
3535 Parkway Ln Hilliard (43026) *(G-11828)*
W W Williams Company LLC 614 527-9400
3535 Parkway Ln Hilliard (43026) *(G-11829)*
W W Wllams Company-Midwest Div, Hilliard *Also called W W Williams Company LLC (G-11829)*
W X I X, Cincinnati *Also called Gray Media Group Inc (G-3636)*
W.F. Hann & Sons, Warrensville Heights *Also called Dival Inc (G-18777)*
W.G. Nord Cmnty Mntal Hlth Ctr, Lorain *Also called Nord Center Associates Inc (G-12934)*
Wabe Maquaw Holdings Inc 419 243-1191
17 Corey Creek Rd Toledo (43623) *(G-18144)*
Wabush Mines Cliffs Mining Co 216 694-5700
200 Public Sq Ste 3300 Cleveland (44114) *(G-6647)*
Wachter Inc 513 777-0701
10186 International Blvd West Chester (45246) *(G-19099)*
Wackenhut, Columbus *Also called G4s Secure Solutions USA Inc (G-7642)*
Wade & Gatton Nurseries 419 883-3191
1288 Gatton Rock Rd Bellville (44813) *(G-1393)*
Wade Trim 216 363-0300
1100 Superior Ave E # 1710 Cleveland (44114) *(G-6648)*
Wadell Village Children Svcs, Marion *Also called County of Marion (G-13415)*
Wadsworth Galaxy Rest Inc 330 334-3663
201 Park Centre Dr Wadsworth (44281) *(G-18618)*
Wadsworth Service Inc 419 861-8181
7851 Freeway Cir Middleburg Heights (44130) *(G-14265)*
Wadsworth Solutions Northeast, Perrysburg *Also called Wadsworth-Slawson Inc (G-15934)*
Wadsworth-Slawson Inc 216 391-7263
1500 Michael Owens Way Perrysburg (43551) *(G-15934)*
Waelzholz North America LLC 216 267-5500
5221 W 164th St Cleveland (44142) *(G-6649)*
Wagler Homes, Uniontown *Also called Phil Wagler Construction Inc (G-18382)*
Wagner Industrial Electric Inc (HQ) 937 298-7481
3178 Encrete Ln Moraine (45439) *(G-14705)*
Wagner Lincoln-Mercury Inc 419 435-8131
1200 S Vance St Carey (43316) *(G-2550)*
Wagner Quarries Company 419 625-8141
4203 Milan Rd Sandusky (44870) *(G-16655)*
Wagner Smith Company, Moraine *Also called Wagner Industrial Electric Inc (G-14705)*
Waids Rainbow Rental Inc 216 524-3736
1050 Killian Rd Akron (44312) *(G-493)*
Wakoni Dialysis LLC 937 294-7188
4700 Springboro Pike A Moraine (45439) *(G-14706)*
Walden Club 330 995-7162
1119 Aurora Hudson Rd Aurora (44202) *(G-848)*
Walden Company Ltd 330 562-7145
1119 Aurora Hudson Rd Aurora (44202) *(G-849)*
Walden Country Club, Aurora *Also called Walden Company Ltd (G-849)*
Walden Ponds Golf Club, Fairfield Township *Also called Creekside Golf Ltd (G-10806)*
Walden Security, Cleveland *Also called Metropolitan Security Svcs Inc (G-5973)*
Walden Security, Akron *Also called Metropolitan Security Svcs Inc (G-337)*
Walden Turf Center 330 995-0023
375 Deer Island Dr Aurora (44202) *(G-850)*
Waldon Management Corp (PA) 330 792-7688
111 Westchester Dr Youngstown (44515) *(G-20240)*
Waldorf Marking Devices Div, Mentor *Also called Monode Marking Products Inc (G-14089)*
Walgreen Co 937 433-5314
6485 Wilmington Pike Dayton (45459) *(G-9864)*
Walgreen Co 614 236-8622
3015 E Livingston Ave Columbus (43209) *(G-8869)*
Walgreen Co 330 677-5650
320 S Water St Kent (44240) *(G-12267)*
Walgreen Co 330 745-2674
900 Wooster Rd N Barberton (44203) *(G-971)*
Walgreen Co 937 396-1358
4497 Far Hills Ave Kettering (45429) *(G-12303)*
Walgreen Co 937 781-9561
2600 S Smithville Rd Dayton (45420) *(G-9865)*
Walgreen Co 330 733-4237
302 Canton Rd Akron (44312) *(G-494)*
Walgreen Co 937 277-6022
2710 Salem Ave Dayton (45406) *(G-9866)*
Walgreen Co 740 368-9380
19 London Rd Delaware (43015) *(G-10015)*
Walgreen Co 614 336-0431
6805 Hospital Dr Dublin (43016) *(G-10369)*
Walgreen Co 937 859-3879
1260 E Central Ave Miamisburg (45342) *(G-14235)*
Walgreen Co 330 928-5444
2645 State Rd Cuyahoga Falls (44223) *(G-9139)*
Walgreens, Dayton *Also called Walgreen Co (G-9864)*
Walgreens, Columbus *Also called Walgreen Co (G-8869)*
Walgreens, Kent *Also called Walgreen Co (G-12267)*
Walgreens, Barberton *Also called Walgreen Co (G-971)*
Walgreens, Kettering *Also called Walgreen Co (G-12303)*
Walgreens, Dayton *Also called Walgreen Co (G-9865)*
Walgreens, Akron *Also called Walgreen Co (G-494)*
Walgreens, Dayton *Also called Walgreen Co (G-9866)*
Walgreens, Delaware *Also called Walgreen Co (G-10015)*
Walgreens, Dublin *Also called Walgreen Co (G-10369)*
Walgreens, Miamisburg *Also called Walgreen Co (G-14235)*
Walgreens, Cuyahoga Falls *Also called Walgreen Co (G-9139)*
Walker Auto Group Inc 937 433-4950
8457 Springboro Pike Miamisburg (45342) *(G-14236)*
Walker Machinery and Lift, Jackson *Also called Cecil I Walker Machinery Co (G-12170)*
Walker Mitsubishi, Miamisburg *Also called Walker Auto Group Inc (G-14236)*
Walker National Inc 614 492-1614
2195 Wright Brothers Ave Columbus (43217) *(G-8870)*
Wall2wall Soccer LLC 513 573-9898
846 Reading Rd Mason (45040) *(G-13655)*
Wallace, Grove City *Also called RR Donnelley & Sons Company (G-11466)*
Wallace & Turner Insurance Inc 937 324-8492
30 Warder St Ste 200 Springfield (45504) *(G-17131)*
Wallace F Ackley Co (PA) 614 231-3661
695 Kenwick Rd Columbus (43209) *(G-8871)*
Walleye Power LLC 567 298-7400
4701 Bay Shore Rd Oregon (43616) *(G-15614)*
Wallick Co., New Albany *Also called Highland Village Ltd Partnr (G-14856)*
Wallick Companies Cnstr Prpts, New Albany *Also called Wallick Enterprises Inc (G-14877)*
Wallick Company, The, New Albany *Also called Brodhead Village Ltd (G-14845)*
Wallick Construction Co 937 399-7009
3001 Middle Urbana Rd Springfield (45502) *(G-17132)*
Wallick Construction LLC 614 863-4640
160 W Main St Ste 200 New Albany (43054) *(G-14876)*
Wallick Enterprises Inc 614 863-4640
160 W Main St New Albany (43054) *(G-14877)*
Wallick Properties Midwest LLC 614 539-9041
4243 Farr Ct Grove City (43123) *(G-11482)*
Wallick Properties Midwest LLC (PA) 419 381-7477
160 W Main St Ste 200 New Albany (43054) *(G-14878)*
Wallover Enterprises Inc (HQ) 440 238-9250
21845 Drake Rd Strongsville (44149) *(G-17358)*
Wallowa Dialysis LLC 419 747-4039
2148 W 4th St Ontario (44906) *(G-15578)*
Walman Optical Company 419 248-3384
1201 Jefferson Ave Toledo (43604) *(G-18145)*
Walmart Inc 937 843-3681
11040 Pear Ln Belle Center (43310) *(G-1342)*
Walmart Inc 937 399-0370
2100 N Bechtle Ave Springfield (45504) *(G-17133)*
Walmart Inc 740 286-8203
100 Walmart Dr Jackson (45640) *(G-12182)*
Walnut Creek Chocolate Company 330 893-2995
4917 State Rte 515 Walnut Creek (44687) *(G-18632)*
Walnut Creek Foods, Walnut Creek *Also called Coblentz Distributing Inc (G-18631)*
Walnut Creek Nursing Facility, Moraine *Also called April Enterprises Inc (G-14623)*
Walnut Hills Apartments, Cincinnati *Also called Walnut Hills Preservation LP (G-4768)*
Walnut Hills Center Location, Cincinnati *Also called Easter Seals Tristate LLC (G-3474)*
Walnut Hills Inc 330 852-2457
4748 Olde Pump St Walnut Creek (44687) *(G-18633)*
Walnut Hills Physical Therapy 614 234-8000
5965 E Broad St Ste 390 Columbus (43213) *(G-8872)*
Walnut Hills Preservation LP 513 281-1288
861 Beecher St Ofc Ofc Cincinnati (45206) *(G-4768)*
Walnut Ridge Management 234 678-3900
520 S Main St Ste 2457 Akron (44311) *(G-495)*
Waltek Inc 614 469-0156
399 W State St Columbus (43215) *(G-8873)*
Walter Alexander Entps Inc 513 841-1100
1940 Losantiville Ave Cincinnati (45237) *(G-4769)*
Walter F Stephens Jr Inc 937 746-0521
415 South Ave Franklin (45005) *(G-11041)*
Walter Haverfield LLP (PA) 216 781-1212
1301 E 9th St Ste 3500 Cleveland (44114) *(G-6650)*
Walthall LLP (PA) 216 573-2330
6300 Rockside Rd Ste 100 Cleveland (44131) *(G-6651)*

ALPHABETIC

Walton Manor Health Care Ctr, Cleveland Also called Healthcare Walton Group LLC *(G-5673)*
Walton Manor Health Care Ctr.................................440 439-4433
19859 Alexander Rd Cleveland (44146) *(G-6652)*
Wampum Hardware Co.....................................740 685-2585
60711 Dynamite Rd Salesville (43778) *(G-16569)*
Wampum Hardware Co.....................................419 273-2542
17507 Township Road 50 Forest (45843) *(G-10982)*
Wannemacher Enterprises Inc (PA).................419 225-9060
400 E Hanthorn Rd Lima (45804) *(G-12775)*
Wannemacher Truck Lines, Lima Also called Wannemacher Enterprises Inc *(G-12775)*
Wapakoneta Manor, Wapakoneta Also called Hcf of Wapakoneta Inc *(G-18645)*
Wapakoneta YMCA..419 739-9622
1100 Defiance St Wapakoneta (45895) *(G-18659)*
Wappoo Wood Products Inc.............................937 492-1166
12877 Kirkwood Rd Sidney (45365) *(G-16805)*
Ward & Werner Co...614 885-0741
6620 Plesenton Dr W Worthington (43085) *(G-19858)*
Ward Realestate Inc...419 281-2000
600 E Main St Ashland (44805) *(G-698)*
Ward Trucking LLC..330 659-6658
2800 Brecksville Rd Richfield (44286) *(G-16383)*
Ward Trucking LLC..614 275-3800
1601 Mckinley Ave Columbus (43222) *(G-8874)*
Wardjet LLC..330 677-9100
180 South Ave Tallmadge (44278) *(G-17498)*
Warehouse, Findlay Also called Hercules Tire & Rubber Company *(G-10923)*
Warehouse, Columbus Also called Restaurant Equippers Inc *(G-8526)*
Warehouse, Cleveland Also called Basista Furniture Inc *(G-5040)*
Warehouse Services Group Llc........................419 868-6400
6145 Merger Dr Holland (43528) *(G-11926)*
Warm 98, Cincinnati Also called Cumulus Media Inc *(G-3388)*
Warner Buick-Nissan Inc.................................419 423-7161
1060 County Road 95 Findlay (45840) *(G-10974)*
Warner Dennehey Marshall..............................216 912-3787
127 Public Sq Ste 3510 Cleveland (44114) *(G-6653)*
Warner Mechanical Corporation.......................419 332-7116
1609 Dickinson St Fremont (43420) *(G-11106)*
Warner Nissan, Findlay Also called Warner Buick-Nissan Inc *(G-10974)*
Warnock Tanner & Assoc Inc...........................419 897-6999
959 Illinois Ave Ste C Maumee (43537) *(G-13867)*
Warren Bros & Sons Inc (PA)..........................740 373-1430
108b S 7th St Marietta (45750) *(G-13398)*
Warren City Board Education...........................330 841-2265
600 Roanoke Ave Sw Warren (44483) *(G-18768)*
Warren Co Human Services Dept, Lebanon Also called County of Warren *(G-12457)*
Warren County Board Devlpmntal.....................513 925-1813
42 Kings Way Lebanon (45036) *(G-12514)*
Warren County Community Svcs (PA)...............513 695-2100
570 N State Route 741 Lebanon (45036) *(G-12515)*
WARREN COUNTY OF PRODUCTION SE, Lebanon Also called Production Services
Unlimited *(G-12493)*
Warren County Park District, Lebanon Also called County of Warren *(G-12458)*
Warren County Wtr & Sewer Dept, Lebanon Also called County of Warren *(G-12459)*
Warren Dermatology and Allergy, Warren Also called Warren Drmatology Allergies
PC *(G-18769)*
Warren Door, Niles Also called Traichal Construction Company *(G-15172)*
Warren Drilling Co Inc.....................................740 783-2775
305 Smithson St Dexter City (45727) *(G-10060)*
Warren Drmatology Allergies PC......................330 856-6365
735 Niles Cortland Rd Se Warren (44484) *(G-18769)*
Warren Guillard Brick Layers, Tallmadge Also called Warren Guillard Bricklayers *(G-17499)*
Warren Guillard Bricklayers............................330 633-3855
107 Potomac Ave Tallmadge (44278) *(G-17499)*
Warren Housing Development...........................330 369-1533
4076 Youngstown Rd Se # 101 Warren (44484) *(G-18770)*
Warren Plant 11, Warren Also called Aptiv Services Us LLC *(G-18666)*
Warren Trucking, Dexter City Also called Warren Drilling Co Inc *(G-10060)*
Warren Twnship Vlntr Fire Dept.......................740 373-2424
17305 State Route 550 Marietta (45750) *(G-13399)*
Warrens IGA, Marietta Also called Warren Bros & Sons Inc *(G-13398)*
Warrenton Copper LLC....................................636 456-3488
1240 Marquette St Cleveland (44114) *(G-6654)*
Warsteiner Importers Agency...........................513 942-9872
9359 Allen Rd West Chester (45069) *(G-19034)*
Warsteiner USA, West Chester Also called Warsteiner Importers Agency *(G-19034)*
Warstler Brothers Landscaping........................330 492-9500
4125 Salway Ave Nw Canton (44718) *(G-2531)*
Warwick Communications Inc (PA)...................216 787-0300
405 Ken Mar Indus Pkwy Broadview Heights (44147) *(G-1850)*
Wasco Inc (PA)...740 373-3418
340 Muskingum Dr Marietta (45750) *(G-13400)*
Washing Systems LLC (HQ).............................800 272-1974
167 Commerce Dr Loveland (45140) *(G-13032)*
Washington Cnty Engineers Off, Marietta Also called County of Washington *(G-13321)*
Washington County Home, Marietta Also called County of Washington *(G-13322)*
Washington Court Hse Holdg LLC.....................614 873-7733
1850 Lowes Blvd Wshngtn CT Hs (43160) *(G-19885)*
Washington Group, Cleveland Also called Aecom Energy & Cnstr Inc *(G-4906)*

Washington Group, Oregon Also called Aecom Energy & Cnstr Inc *(G-15582)*
Washington Local Schools...............................419 473-8356
5201 Douglas Rd Toledo (43613) *(G-18146)*
Washington Manor Inc (PA).............................937 433-3441
7300 Mcewen Rd Dayton (45459) *(G-9867)*
Washington Manor Nursing Ctr, Dayton Also called Washington Manor Inc *(G-9867)*
Washington PRI (HQ)......................................614 621-9000
180 E Broad St Fl 22 Columbus (43215) *(G-8875)*
Washington Prime Group LP (HQ).....................614 621-9000
180 E Broad St Columbus (43215) *(G-8876)*
Washington Prime Group Inc (PA)....................614 621-9000
180 E Broad St Fl 21 Columbus (43215) *(G-8877)*
Washington Square Apartments.......................740 349-8353
340 Eastern Ave Ofc Newark (43055) *(G-15107)*
Washington Township Park Dst (PA).................937 433-5155
221 N Main St Centerville (45459) *(G-2636)*
Washington Twnship Mntgomery......................937 433-0130
895 Mmsburg Cnterville Rd Dayton (45459) *(G-9868)*
Washington Twnship Rcrtion Ctr, Dayton Also called Washington Twnship
Mntgomery *(G-9868)*
Wasiniak Construction Inc...............................419 668-8624
2519 State Route 61 Norwalk (44857) *(G-15459)*
Wassarstrom Rest Sup Super Str, Columbus Also called Wasserstrom Company *(G-8879)*
Wasserstom Disrtributing Ofc, Columbus Also called Marion Road Enterprises *(G-8020)*
Wasserstrom Company (PA).............................614 228-6525
4500 E Broad St Columbus (43213) *(G-8878)*
Wasserstrom Company....................................614 228-6525
2777 Silver Dr Columbus (43211) *(G-8879)*
Wasserstrom Holdings Inc...............................614 228-6525
477 S Front St Columbus (43215) *(G-8880)*
Wasserstrom Marketing Division, Columbus Also called N Wasserstrom & Sons
Inc *(G-8126)*
Waste Management, Waynesburg Also called American Landfill Inc *(G-18828)*
Waste Management of Lima, Lima Also called Waste Management Ohio Inc *(G-12776)*
Waste Management Ohio Inc.............................440 201-1235
6705 Richmond Rd Solon (44139) *(G-16913)*
Waste Management Ohio Inc.............................800 910-2831
116 N Bauer Rd Wooster (44691) *(G-19777)*
Waste Management Ohio Inc.............................330 452-9000
1800 9th St Ne Canton (44705) *(G-2532)*
Waste Management Ohio Inc.............................614 382-6342
1006 W Walnut St Canal Winchester (43110) *(G-2125)*
Waste Management Ohio Inc.............................419 547-7791
3956 State Route 412 Vickery (43464) *(G-18576)*
Waste Management Ohio Inc.............................866 797-9018
12201 Council Dr North Jackson (44451) *(G-15256)*
Waste Management Ohio Inc.............................800 343-6047
1700 N Broad St Fairborn (45324) *(G-10688)*
Waste Management Ohio Inc.............................866 409-4671
6525 Wales Rd Northwood (43619) *(G-15413)*
Waste Management Ohio Inc.............................440 286-7116
9954 Old State Rd Chardon (44024) *(G-2724)*
Waste Management Ohio Inc.............................740 345-1212
100 Ecology Row Newark (43055) *(G-15108)*
Waste Management Ohio Inc.............................419 221-3644
1550 E 4th St Lima (45804) *(G-12776)*
Waste Management Ohio Inc.............................614 833-5290
1046 W Walnut St Canal Winchester (43110) *(G-2126)*
Waste Management Ohio Inc (HQ).....................800 343-6047
1700 N Broad St Fairborn (45324) *(G-10689)*
Waste Management Ohio Inc.............................440 285-6767
4339 Tuttle Rd Geneva (44041) *(G-11250)*
Waste Management Ohio Inc.............................419 221-2029
1550 E 4th St Lima (45804) *(G-12777)*
Waste Management Ohio NW, Northwood Also called Waste Management Ohio
Inc *(G-15413)*
Waste Parchment Inc......................................330 674-6868
4510 Township Road 307 Millersburg (44654) *(G-14499)*
Waste Water Treatment Plant, Massillon Also called City of Massillon *(G-13671)*
Waste Water Treatment Plant, Zanesville Also called City of Zanesville *(G-20296)*
Wastren - Energx Mission................................740 897-3724
1571 Shyville Rd Piketon (45661) *(G-15992)*
Wastren Advantage Inc (PA)............................970 254-1277
1571 Shyville Rd Piketon (45661) *(G-15993)*
Water & Sewer Department, Johnstown Also called County of Licking *(G-12199)*
Water & Sewer Department, Avon Lake Also called City of Avon Lake *(G-912)*
WATER 1, Lucasville Also called Scioto County Region Wtr Dst 1 *(G-13053)*
Water Department, Dayton Also called City of Dayton *(G-9304)*
Water Department, Cuyahoga Falls Also called City of Cuyahoga Falls *(G-9082)*
Water Leasing Co LLC.....................................440 285-9400
620 Water St Chardon (44024) *(G-2725)*
Water Pollution Control, Lorain Also called City of Lorain *(G-12890)*
Water Pollution Control Ctrl, Canton Also called City of Canton *(G-2256)*
Water Transport LLC.......................................740 937-2199
100 Sammi Dr Hopedale (43976) *(G-11938)*
Waterbeds n Stuff Inc (PA).............................614 871-1171
3933 Brookham Dr Grove City (43123) *(G-11483)*
Waterford Bank National Assn (HQ).................419 720-3900
3900 N Mccord Rd Toledo (43617) *(G-18147)*

Waterfront & Associates Inc 859 581-1414
700 Walnut St Ste 200 Cincinnati (45202) *(G-4770)*
Waterhouse Bath and Kit Studio, Perrysburg *Also called Maumee Plumbing & Htg Sup Inc (G-15892)*
Watertown Steel Company LLC 740 749-3512
405 Watertown Rd Waterford (45786) *(G-18787)*
Waterville Care LLC 419 878-3901
555 Anthony Wayne Trl Waterville (43566) *(G-18795)*
Waterway Gas & Wash Company 330 995-2900
7010 N Aurora Rd Aurora (44202) *(G-851)*
Waterworks America Inc 440 526-4815
5005 Rcksde Rd Crwn Cn 6f Crown Centre Cleveland (44131) *(G-6655)*
Waterworks Crystals, Cleveland *Also called Waterworks America Inc (G-6655)*
Waterworks, The, Columbus *Also called Tfh-Eb Inc (G-8741)*
Watkins Mechanical Inc (PA) 937 748-0220
10 Parker Dr Springboro (45066) *(G-16987)*
Watkins Mechanical Services, Springboro *Also called Watkins Mechanical Inc (G-16987)*
Watson Gravel Inc (PA) 513 863-0070
2728 Hamilton Cleves Rd Hamilton (45013) *(G-11654)*
Watteredge LLC (HQ) 440 933-6110
567 Miller Rd Avon Lake (44012) *(G-929)*
Wauseon Dialysis LLC 419 335-0695
721 S Shoop Ave Wauseon (43567) *(G-18811)*
Wauseon Machine & Mfg Inc (PA) 419 337-0940
995 Enterprise Ave Wauseon (43567) *(G-18812)*
Waverly Care Center Inc 740 947-2113
444 Cherry St Frnt Waverly (45690) *(G-18824)*
Waxman Consumer Pdts Group Inc 614 491-0500
5920 Green Pointe Dr S A Groveport (43125) *(G-11551)*
Waxman Consumer Pdts Group Inc (HQ) 440 439-1830
24455 Aurora Rd Cleveland (44146) *(G-6656)*
Waxman Industries Inc (PA) 440 439-1830
24460 Aurora Rd Cleveland (44146) *(G-6657)*
Waycraft Inc (PA) 419 563-0550
118 River St Bucyrus (44820) *(G-2005)*
Waycraft Inc 419 562-3321
118 River St Bucyrus (44820) *(G-2006)*
Wayne County Care Center, Wooster *Also called County of Wayne (G-19715)*
Wayne County Child Support, Wooster *Also called County of Wayne (G-19718)*
Wayne County Childrens Svcs, Wooster *Also called County of Wayne (G-19717)*
Wayne County Engineers Wooster, Wooster *Also called County of Wayne (G-19719)*
Wayne Employment Training Ctr, Wooster *Also called County of Wayne (G-19716)*
Wayne Healthcare (PA) 937 548-1141
835 Sweitzer St Greenville (45331) *(G-11400)*
Wayne Homes, Uniontown *Also called Wh Midwest LLC (G-18390)*
Wayne Industries Inc 937 548-6025
5844 Jysville St Johns Rd Greenville (45331) *(G-11401)*
Wayne Lanes, Wooster *Also called Plaz-Way Inc (G-19759)*
Wayne Mutual Insurance Co 330 345-8100
3873 Cleveland Rd Wooster (44691) *(G-19778)*
Wayne Savings Bancshares Inc (PA) 330 264-5767
151 N Market St Wooster (44691) *(G-19779)*
Wayne Savings Community Bank (HQ) 330 264-5767
151 N Market St Wooster (44691) *(G-19780)*
Wayne Trail Technologies Inc 937 295-2120
407 S Main St Fort Loramie (45845) *(G-10986)*
Wayne Water Systems, Harrison *Also called Wayne/Scott Fetzer Company (G-11680)*
Wayne/Scott Fetzer Company 800 237-0987
101 Production Dr Harrison (45030) *(G-11680)*
Waypoint Aviation LLC 800 769-4765
4765 Airport Rd Cincinnati (45226) *(G-4771)*
Wayside Body Shop Inc (PA) 937 233-3182
6000 Executive Blvd Ste A Dayton (45424) *(G-9869)*
Wayside Collision Center, Dayton *Also called Wayside Body Shop Inc (G-9869)*
Wayside Farms Inc 330 666-7716
4557 Quick Rd Peninsula (44264) *(G-15814)*
Wayside Farms Nursing, Peninsula *Also called Wayside Farms Inc (G-15814)*
Wb Services Inc 330 390-5722
6834 County Road 672 # 102 Millersburg (44654) *(G-14500)*
Wbc Group LLC (PA) 866 528-2144
6333 Hudson Crossing Pkwy Hudson (44236) *(G-12012)*
Wbgu FM 88 1, Bowling Green *Also called Bowling Green State University (G-1723)*
Wbns Tv Inc 614 460-3700
770 Twin Rivers Dr Columbus (43215) *(G-8881)*
Wbns-AM Sports Radio 1460 Fan, Columbus *Also called Radiohio Incorporated (G-8484)*
Wbnx TV 55, Cuyahoga Falls *Also called Winston Brdcstg Netwrk Inc (G-9140)*
WCCS, Lebanon *Also called Warren County Community Svcs (G-12515)*
Wcdp, Fremont *Also called Wsos Child Development Program (G-11107)*
WCH, Bowling Green *Also called Wood County Hospital Assoc (G-1754)*
Wckx-FM, Columbus *Also called Urban One Inc (G-8828)*
Wcmh, Columbus *Also called Nexstar Broadcasting Inc (G-8188)*
Wcoil, Lima *Also called West Central Ohio Internet (G-12779)*
WD Partners Inc 614 634-7000
7007 Discovery Blvd Dublin (43017) *(G-10370)*
Wdpn, Alliance *Also called D A Peterson Inc (G-529)*
Wdtn, Moraine *Also called Sunrise Television Corp (G-14700)*
Wdtn, Moraine *Also called Nexstar Broadcasting Inc (G-14683)*

Weastec, Hillsboro *Also called Denso International Amer Inc (G-11837)*
Weastec Incorporated 614 734-9645
6195 Enterprise Ct Dublin (43016) *(G-10371)*
Weatherables, Groveport *Also called Usavinyl LLC (G-11547)*
Weatherproofing Tech Inc (HQ) 216 292-5000
3735 Green Rd Beachwood (44122) *(G-1117)*
Weatherwax, Middletown *Also called Wmvh LLC (G-14340)*
Weaver Bros Inc (PA) 937 526-3907
895 E Main St Versailles (45380) *(G-18573)*
Weaver Bros Inc 937 526-4777
10638 State Route 47 Versailles (45380) *(G-18574)*
Weaver Brothers Farm, Versailles *Also called Weaver Bros Inc (G-18574)*
Weaver Custom Homes Inc 330 264-5444
124 E Liberty St Ste A Wooster (44691) *(G-19781)*
Weaver Fab & Finishing, Akron *Also called Bogie Industries Inc Ltd (G-102)*
Weaver Industries Inc 330 379-3606
636 W Exchange St Akron (44302) *(G-496)*
Weaver Industries Inc (PA) 330 379-3660
520 S Main St Ste 2441 Akron (44311) *(G-497)*
Weaver Industries Inc 330 666-5114
340 N Clvland Mssillon Rd Akron (44333) *(G-498)*
Weaver Industries Inc 330 745-2400
2337 Romig Rd Ste 2 Akron (44320) *(G-499)*
Weaver Secure Shred, Akron *Also called Weaver Industries Inc (G-499)*
Web Yoga Inc 937 428-0000
938 Senate Dr Dayton (45459) *(G-9870)*
WEBa Outreach Food Pantry 740 543-3227
346 N Main St Amsterdam (43903) *(G-602)*
Webb, Barry W, Cincinnati *Also called Springdale Family Medicine PC (G-4521)*
Weber Associates, Columbus *Also called Weber Partners Ltd (G-8882)*
Weber Health Care Center Inc 440 647-2088
214 E Herrick Ave Wellington (44090) *(G-18845)*
Weber Obrien Ltd 419 885-8338
5580 Monroe St Ste 210 Sylvania (43560) *(G-17463)*
Weber Partners Ltd (PA) 614 222-6806
775 Yard St Ste 350 Columbus (43212) *(G-8882)*
Webert & Co, Sylvania *Also called Weber Obrien Ltd (G-17463)*
Webmd Health Corp 330 425-3241
2045 Midway Dr Twinsburg (44087) *(G-18337)*
Wedgewood Estates 419 756-7400
600 S Trimble Rd Mansfield (44906) *(G-13262)*
Wedgewood Golf & Country Club 614 793-9600
9600 Wedgewood Blvd Powell (43065) *(G-16213)*
Wedgewood Lanes Inc 330 792-1949
1741 S Raccoon Rd Youngstown (44515) *(G-20241)*
Wedgewood Urgent Care, Westerville *Also called Immediate Health Associates (G-19265)*
Wednesday Auto Auction, Obetz *Also called Columbus Fair Auto Auction Inc (G-15525)*
Wee Care Day Care Lrng Centre, Youngstown *Also called Nichalex Inc (G-20140)*
Wee Care Daycare 330 856-1313
1145 Niles Cortland Rd Se Warren (44484) *(G-18771)*
WEE CARE LEARNING CENTER, Van Wert *Also called Van Wert County Day Care Inc (G-18492)*
Wee Care Learning Center 937 454-9363
9675 N Dixie Dr Dayton (45414) *(G-9871)*
Weeber-Morse, Carmen MD, Perrysburg *Also called Jon R Dvorak MD (G-15883)*
Weed Man Lawncare LLC 513 683-6310
12100 Phanpion Way Cincinnati (45241) *(G-4772)*
Weekleys Mailing Service Inc 440 234-4325
1420 W Bagley Rd Berea (44017) *(G-1443)*
Wege, Lima *Also called Maverick Media (G-12700)*
Wegman Hessler Vanderburg 216 642-3342
6055 Rockside Woods Blvd # 200 Cleveland (44131) *(G-6658)*
Wegman Company, Cincinnati *Also called Wegman Construction Company (G-4773)*
Wegman Construction Company 513 381-1111
1101 York St Ste 500 Cincinnati (45214) *(G-4773)*
Weiffenbach Marble & Tile Co 937 832-7055
150 Lau Pkwy Englewood (45315) *(G-10605)*
Weiland's Gourmet Market, Columbus *Also called Weilands Fine Meats Inc (G-8883)*
Weilands Fine Meats Inc 614 267-9910
3600 Indianola Ave Columbus (43214) *(G-8883)*
Weiner Keith D Co L P A Inc 216 771-6500
75 Public Sq Ste 600 Cleveland (44113) *(G-6659)*
Weinstein and Associates, Painesville *Also called Weinstein Donald Jay PHD (G-15747)*
Weinstein Donald Jay PHD 216 831-1040
54 S State St Painesville (44077) *(G-15747)*
Welch Holdings Inc 513 353-3220
8953 E Miami River Rd Cincinnati (45247) *(G-4774)*
Welch Packaging LLC 937 223-3958
321 Hopeland St Dayton (45417) *(G-9872)*
Welch Packaging Columbus, Columbus *Also called Welch Packaging Group Inc (G-8884)*
Welch Packaging Group Inc 419 726-3491
1240 Matzinger Rd Toledo (43612) *(G-18148)*
Welch Packaging Group Inc 216 447-9800
6090 Hillcres Dr Cleveland (44125) *(G-6660)*
Welch Packaging Group Inc 614 870-2000
4700 Alkire Rd Columbus (43228) *(G-8884)*
Welcome Nursing Home, Oberlin *Also called Wessell Generations Inc (G-15521)*
Weld Plus Inc 513 941-4411
4790 River Rd Cincinnati (45233) *(G-4775)*

ALPHABETIC

Welker-Mckee Div, Cleveland *Also called Hajoca Corporation* (G-5657)

Well Point Anthem, Dayton *Also called Dayton Anthem* (G-9351)

Welles Bowen Realty Inc 419 535-0011
2460 N Reynolds Rd Toledo (43615) (G-18149)

Wellington Group LLC 216 525-2200
6133 Rockside Rd Ste 205 Independence (44131) (G-12140)

Wellington Implement Co Inc (PA) 440 647-3725
625 S Main St Wellington (44090) (G-18846)

Wellington Manor, Fairfield Township *Also called Kerrington Health Systems Inc* (G-10811)

Wellington Orthopedics, Cincinnati *Also called Orthopedic Cons Cincinnati* (G-4185)

Wellington Orthpd Spt Medicine, Blue Ash *Also called Orthopedic Cons Cincinnati* (G-1627)

Wellington Orthpd Spt Medicine, Cincinnati *Also called Orthopedic Cons Cincinnati* (G-4186)

Wellington Orthpd Spt Medicine, Cincinnati *Also called Orthopedic Cons Cincinnati* (G-4187)

Wellington Place LLC 440 734-9933
4800 Clague Rd Apt 108 North Olmsted (44070) (G-15316)

Wellington Technologies Inc 440 238-4377
802 Sharon Dr Westlake (44145) (G-19421)

Wellpoint Health Networks, Mason *Also called Nextrx LLC* (G-13622)

Wells & Sons Janitorial Svc 937 878-4375
1877 S Maple Ave Ste 250 Fairborn (45324) (G-10690)

Wells Brothers Inc 937 394-7559
105 Shue Dr Anna (45302) (G-611)

Wells Fargo Advisors, Dublin *Also called Wells Fargo Clearing Svcs LLC* (G-10372)

Wells Fargo Advisors, Cleveland *Also called Wells Fargo Clearing Svcs LLC* (G-6661)

Wells Fargo Advisors, Columbus *Also called Wells Fargo Clearing Svcs LLC* (G-8885)

Wells Fargo Advisors, Toledo *Also called Wells Fargo Clearing Svcs LLC* (G-18150)

Wells Fargo Advisors, Westlake *Also called Wells Fargo Clearing Svcs LLC* (G-19422)

Wells Fargo Advisors, Toledo *Also called Wells Fargo Clearing Svcs LLC* (G-18151)

Wells Fargo Advisors, Cincinnati *Also called Wells Fargo Clearing Svcs LLC* (G-4776)

Wells Fargo Advisors, Cleveland *Also called Wells Fargo Clearing Svcs LLC* (G-6662)

Wells Fargo Bank National Assn 513 424-6640
1076 Summitt Dr Middletown (45042) (G-14339)

Wells Fargo Clearing Svcs LLC 614 764-2040
485 Metro Pl S Ste 300 Dublin (43017) (G-10372)

Wells Fargo Clearing Svcs LLC 216 378-2722
30100 Chagrin Blvd # 200 Cleveland (44124) (G-6661)

Wells Fargo Clearing Svcs LLC 614 221-8371
1 Easton Oval Ste 520 Columbus (43219) (G-8885)

Wells Fargo Clearing Svcs LLC 419 356-3272
3450 W Central Ave # 130 Toledo (43606) (G-18150)

Wells Fargo Clearing Svcs LLC 440 835-9250
25 Main St Fl 2 Westlake (44145) (G-19422)

Wells Fargo Clearing Svcs LLC 419 720-9700
7335 Crossleigh Ct # 100 Toledo (43617) (G-18151)

Wells Fargo Clearing Svcs LLC 513 241-9900
255 E 5th St Ste 1400 Cincinnati (45202) (G-4776)

Wells Fargo Clearing Svcs LLC 216 574-7300
950 Main Ave Ste 300 Cleveland (44113) (G-6662)

Wells Fargo Home Mortgage Inc 614 781-8847
485 Metro Pl S Ste 300 Dublin (43017) (G-10373)

Wells, Mark D MD, Akron *Also called Lawrence A Cervino MD* (G-309)

Wellspring Health Care, Cincinnati *Also called SL Wellspring LLC* (G-4494)

Wellston Auditor's Office, Wellston *Also called City of Wellston* (G-18848)

Welltower Inc (PA) 419 247-2800
4500 Dorr St Toledo (43615) (G-18152)

Welsh Home For The Aged, Rocky River *Also called Womens Welsh Clubs of America* (G-16449)

Welspun Usa Inc 614 945-5100
3901 Gantz Rd Ste A Grove City (43123) (G-11484)

Weltman Weinberg & Reis Co Lpa 216 739-5100
965 Keynote Cir Brooklyn Heights (44131) (G-1888)

Weltman Weinberg & Reis Co Lpa (PA) 216 685-1000
323 W Lkeside Ave Ste 200 Cleveland (44113) (G-6663)

Weltman Weinberg & Reis Co Lpa 614 801-2600
3705 Marlane Dr Grove City (43123) (G-11485)

Weltman Weinberg & Reis Co Lpa 513 723-2200
525 Vine St Ste 800 Cincinnati (45202) (G-4777)

Weltman Weinberg & Reis Co Lpa 216 459-8633
981 Keynote Cir Cleveland (44131) (G-6664)

Welty Building Company Ltd (PA) 330 867-2400
3421 Ridgewood Rd Ste 200 Fairlawn (44333) (G-10855)

Wembley Club, The, Chagrin Falls *Also called New Wembley LLC* (G-2675)

Wems, Piketon *Also called Wastren - Energx Mission* (G-15992)

Wenco Inc 937 849-6002
1807 Dalton Dr New Carlisle (45344) (G-14899)

Wendel Poultry Service Inc 419 375-2439
1860 Union City Rd Fort Recovery (45846) (G-10995)

Wendt-Bristol Health Services (PA) 614 403-9966
921 Jasonway Ave Ste B Columbus (43214) (G-8886)

Wendys Company (PA) 614 764-3100
1 Dave Thomas Blvd Dublin (43017) (G-10374)

Wendys Restaurants LLC (HQ) 614 764-3100
1 Dave Thomas Blvd Dublin (43017) (G-10375)

Wenger Asphalt Inc 330 837-4767
26 N Cochran St Dalton (44618) (G-9147)

Wenger Excavating Inc 330 837-4767
26 N Cochran St Dalton (44618) (G-9148)

Wenger Temperature Control 614 586-4016
2005 Progress Ave Columbus (43207) (G-8887)

Wenzler Daycare & Learning Ctr, Dayton *Also called Wenzler Daycare Learning Ctr* (G-9873)

Wenzler Daycare Learning Ctr 937 435-8200
4535 Presidential Way Dayton (45429) (G-9873)

Weol 440 236-9283
538 Broad St Elyria (44035) (G-10571)

Weol/Wnwv Radio, Elyria *Also called Elyria-Lorain Broadcasting Co* (G-10508)

Were-AM, Cleveland *Also called Urban One Inc* (G-6608)

Werlor Inc 419 784-4285
1420 Ralston Ave Defiance (43512) (G-9946)

Werlor Waste Control, Defiance *Also called Werlor Inc* (G-9946)

Wern-Rausch Locke Advertising 330 493-8866
4470 Dressler Rd Nw Canton (44718) (G-2533)

Werner Enterprises Inc 937 325-5403
4395 Laybourne Rd Springfield (45505) (G-17134)

Wernli Realty Inc 937 258-7878
1300 Grange Hall Rd Beavercreek (45430) (G-1240)

Wesbanco Inc 614 208-7298
2000 Henderson Rd Ste 100 Columbus (43220) (G-8888)

Wesbanco Inc 740 532-0263
311 S 5th St Ironton (45638) (G-12167)

Wesbanco Bank Inc 740 425-1927
230 E Main St Barnesville (43713) (G-980)

Wesbanco Bank Inc 513 741-5766
5511 Cheviot Rd Cincinnati (45247) (G-4778)

Weschler Instruments, Strongsville *Also called Hughes Corporation* (G-17312)

Wesco Distribution Inc 216 741-0441
4741 Hinckley Indus Pkwy Cleveland (44109) (G-6665)

Wesco Distribution Inc 937 228-9668
2080 Winners Cir Dayton (45404) (G-9874)

Wesco Distribution Inc 419 666-1670
6519 Fairfield Dr Northwood (43619) (G-15414)

Wescom Solutions Inc 513 831-1207
300 Techne Center Dr A Milford (45150) (G-14443)

Wesley Community Center Inc 937 263-3556
3730 Delphos Ave Dayton (45417) (G-9875)

Wesley Community Services LLC 513 661-2777
2091 Radcliff Dr Cincinnati (45204) (G-4779)

Wesley Educ Cntr For Chldrn 513 569-1840
525 Hale Ave Cincinnati (45229) (G-4780)

WESLEY RIDGE, Columbus *Also called Glen Wesley Inc* (G-7673)

Wesley Ridge Inc 614 759-0023
2225 Taylor Park Dr Reynoldsburg (43068) (G-16337)

Wesleyan Senior Living (PA) 440 284-9000
807 West Ave Elyria (44035) (G-10572)

WESLEYAN VILLAGE, Elyria *Also called Wesleyan Senior Living* (G-10572)

Wesleyan Village 440 284-9000
807 West Ave Elyria (44035) (G-10573)

Wessell Generations Inc 440 775-1491
417 S Main St Oberlin (44074) (G-15521)

West Bay Care Rhbilitation Ctr, Westlake *Also called Harborside Clveland Ltd Partnr* (G-19347)

West Central Ohio Group Ltd 419 224-7586
801 Medical Dr Ste B Lima (45804) (G-12778)

West Central Ohio Internet 419 229-2645
215 N Elizabeth St Lima (45801) (G-12779)

West Central Ohio Surgery & En 419 226-8700
770 W High St Ste 100 Lima (45801) (G-12780)

West Chester Chrstn Chld 513 777-6300
7951 Tylersville Rd West Chester (45069) (G-19035)

West Chester Holdings LLC 800 647-1900
11500 Canal Rd Cincinnati (45241) (G-4781)

West Chester Hospital, West Chester *Also called Chester West Medical Center* (G-18885)

West Chester Protective Gear, Cincinnati *Also called West Chester Holdings LLC* (G-4781)

West Chester, Barrington of, West Chester *Also called Senior Lifestyle Corporation* (G-19002)

West Corporation 330 574-0510
5185 Youngstown Warren Rd Niles (44446) (G-15174)

West Denison Baseball League 216 251-5790
3556 W 105th St Cleveland (44111) (G-6666)

West End Branch, Willoughby *Also called Lake County YMCA* (G-19538)

West End Health Center Inc 513 621-2726
1413 Linn St Cincinnati (45214) (G-4782)

West End YMCA, Cincinnati *Also called Young Mens Christian Associat* (G-4815)

West Enterprises Inc 614 237-4488
480 S 3rd St Columbus (43215) (G-8889)

West Entitlement Operations, Columbus *Also called Defense Fin & Accounting Svc* (G-7429)

West Jefferson Plbg Htg Coolin, West Jefferson *Also called West Jefferson Plumbing Htg* (G-19113)

West Jefferson Plumbing Htg 614 879-9606
174 E Main St West Jefferson (43162) (G-19113)

West Lafytt Rehabltion, West Lafayette *Also called Kindred Healthcare Oper Inc* (G-19115)

West Liberty Care Center Inc 937 465-5065
6557 Us Highway 68 S West Liberty (43357) (G-19122)

West Market Optical Service, Akron *Also called Summit Opthomology Optical* (G-459)

West Memory Gardens, Dayton *Also called Stonemor Partners LP* (G-9794)

West Montrose Properties (PA) 330 867-4013
2841 Riviera Dr Ste 300 Fairlawn (44333) (G-10856)

West Ohio Cmnty Action Partnr 419 227-2586
540 S Central Ave Lima (45804) (G-12781)

West Ohio Cmnty Action Partnr (PA) 419 227-2586
  540 S Central Ave Lima (45804) *(G-12782)*
West Ohio Conference of (PA) 614 844-6200
  32 Wesley Blvd Worthington (43085) *(G-19859)*
West Ohio Conference of 937 773-5313
  415 W Greene St Piqua (45356) *(G-16038)*
West Park Animal Hospital, Cleveland *Also called Tri Zob Inc (G-6547)*
West Park Family Physician 419 472-1124
  3425 Executive Pkwy # 100 Toledo (43606) *(G-18153)*
West Park Health Partners, Toledo *Also called West Park Family Physician (G-18153)*
West Park Healthcare, Cleveland *Also called Myocare Nursing Home Inc (G-6031)*
West Park Place, Toledo *Also called Gemini Properties (G-17758)*
West Park Retirement Community, Cincinnati *Also called Mercy Health West Park (G-4033)*
West Park Retirement Community 513 451-8900
  2950 West Park Dr Ofc Cincinnati (45238) *(G-4783)*
West Roofing Systems Inc (PA) 800 356-5748
  121 Commerce Dr Lagrange (44050) *(G-12327)*
West Shell Coml Encore Intl, Cincinnati *Also called Nisbet Corporation (G-4120)*
West Shell Commercial Inc 513 721-4200
  425 Walnut St Ste 1200 Cincinnati (45202) *(G-4784)*
West Shell Gale Schnetzer 513 683-3833
  748 Wards Corner Rd Loveland (45140) *(G-13033)*
West Shore Child Care Center 440 333-2040
  20401 Hilliard Blvd Cleveland (44116) *(G-6667)*
West Shore Day Treatment Ctr, Cleveland *Also called Positive Education Program (G-6224)*
West Side Cardiology Assoc 440 333-8600
  20455 Lorain Rd Fl 2 Cleveland (44126) *(G-6668)*
West Side Cardiology Assoc 440 333-8600
  20455 Lorain Rd Fl 2 Cleveland (44126) *(G-6669)*
West Side Community House 216 771-7297
  9300 Lorain Ave Cleveland (44102) *(G-6670)*
West Side Dtscher Fruen Verein 440 238-3361
  18627 Shurmer Rd Strongsville (44136) *(G-17359)*
West Side Ecumenical Ministry (PA) 216 325-9369
  5209 Detroit Ave Cleveland (44102) *(G-6671)*
West Side Montessori 419 866-1931
  7115 W Bancroft St Toledo (43615) *(G-18154)*
West Side Pediatrics Inc (PA) 513 922-8200
  663 Anderson Ferry Rd # 1 Cincinnati (45238) *(G-4785)*
West Union Elementary School, West Union *Also called Adams Cnty /Ohio Vly Schl Dst (G-19129)*
West View Manor Inc 330 264-8640
  1715 Mechanicsburg Rd Wooster (44691) *(G-19782)*
WEST VIEW MANOR RETIREMENT CEN, Wooster *Also called West View Manor Inc (G-19782)*
West-Way Management Company 440 250-1851
  24700 Center Ridge Rd G50 Westlake (44145) *(G-19423)*
Westainer Lines, Middleburg Heights *Also called World Ex Shipg Tmsp Fwdg Svcs (G-14266)*
Westark Family Services Inc 330 832-5043
  42 1st St Ne Massillon (44646) *(G-13734)*
Westcare Ohio Inc 937 259-1898
  624 Xenia Ave Dayton (45410) *(G-9876)*
Westerly Wstwater Trtmnt Plant, Cleveland *Also called Northast Ohio Rgonal Sewer Dst (G-6083)*
Western & Southern Lf Insur Co (HQ) 513 629-1800
  400 Broadway St Cincinnati (45202) *(G-4786)*
Western & Southern Lf Insur Co 614 277-4800
  1931 Ohio Dr Grove City (43123) *(G-11486)*
Western & Southern Lf Insur Co 234 380-4525
  85 Executive Pkwy Ste 200 Hudson (44236) *(G-12013)*
Western & Southern Lf Insur Co 440 324-2626
  347 Midway Blvd Ste 101 Elyria (44035) *(G-10574)*
Western & Southern Lf Insur Co 330 792-6818
  320 S Canfield Niles Rd Youngstown (44515) *(G-20242)*
Western & Southern Lf Insur Co 330 825-9935
  4172 Clvland Massillon Rd Barberton (44203) *(G-972)*
Western & Southern Lf Insur Co 937 435-1964
  2 Prestige Pl Ste 310 Miamisburg (45342) *(G-14237)*
Western & Southern Lf Insur Co 740 653-3210
  1583 Victor Rd Nw Lancaster (43130) *(G-12444)*
Western & Southern Lf Insur Co 513 891-0777
  6281 Tri Ridge Blvd # 310 Loveland (45140) *(G-13034)*
Western & Southern Lf Insur Co 614 898-1066
  8425 Pulsar Pl Ste 310 Columbus (43240) *(G-6838)*
Western & Southern Lf Insur Co 937 773-5303
  1255 E Ash St Ste 2 Piqua (45356) *(G-16039)*
Western & Southern Lf Insur Co 937 399-7696
  30 Warder St Ste 130 Springfield (45504) *(G-17135)*
Western & Southern Lf Insur Co 740 354-2848
  35 Bierly Rd Ste 1 Portsmouth (45662) *(G-16181)*
Western & Southern Lf Insur Co 937 393-1969
  902 N High St Ste B Hillsboro (45133) *(G-11855)*
Western & Southern Lf Insur Co 419 524-1800
  1989 W 4th St Ontario (44906) *(G-15579)*
Western Branch Diesel Inc 330 454-8800
  1616 Metric Ave Sw Canton (44706) *(G-2534)*
Western Family Physicians 513 853-4900
  3425 North Bend Rd Ste A Cincinnati (45239) *(G-4787)*

Western Hills Care Center 513 941-0099
  6210 Cleves Warsaw Pike Cincinnati (45233) *(G-4788)*
Western Hills Country Club 513 922-0011
  5780 Cleves Warsaw Pike Cincinnati (45233) *(G-4789)*
Western Hills Dialysis, Cincinnati *Also called Dva Healthcare - South (G-3458)*
Western Hills Retirement Vlg, Cincinnati *Also called Ebenezer Road Corp (G-3480)*
Western Hills Sportsplex Inc (PA) 513 451-4900
  2323 Ferguson Rd Ste 1 Cincinnati (45238) *(G-4790)*
Western KY Coal Resources LLC 740 338-3100
  46226 National Rd Saint Clairsville (43950) *(G-16510)*
Western Management Inc (PA) 216 941-3333
  14577 Lorain Ave Cleveland (44111) *(G-6672)*
Western Reserve Area Agency (PA) 216 621-0303
  1700 E 13th St Ste 114 Cleveland (44114) *(G-6673)*
Western Reserve Area Agency 216 621-0303
  1700 E 13th St Ste 114 Cleveland (44114) *(G-6674)*
Western Reserve Group (PA) 330 262-9060
  1685 Cleveland Rd Wooster (44691) *(G-19783)*
Western Reserve Historical Soc 330 666-3711
  2686 Oak Hill Dr Bath (44210) *(G-1019)*
Western Reserve Historical Soc (PA) 216 721-5722
  10825 East Blvd Cleveland (44106) *(G-6675)*
Western Reserve Interiors Inc 216 447-1081
  7777 Exchange St Ste 7 Cleveland (44125) *(G-6676)*
WESTERN RESERVE LEGAL SERVICES, Akron *Also called Community Legal Aid Services (G-152)*
Western Reserve Mechanical Inc 330 652-3888
  3041 S Main St Niles (44446) *(G-15175)*
Western Reserve Public Media, Kent *Also called Northastern Eductl TV Ohio Inc (G-12251)*
Western Reserve Racquet Club 330 653-3103
  11013 Aurora Hudson Rd Streetsboro (44241) *(G-17277)*
Western Reserve Realty LLC 440 247-3707
  26 S Main St Ste 100 Chagrin Falls (44022) *(G-2659)*
Western Reserve Transit Auth (PA) 330 744-8431
  604 Mahoning Ave Youngstown (44502) *(G-20243)*
Western Rserve Wtr Systems Inc 216 341-9797
  4133 E 49th St Newburgh Heights (44105) *(G-15116)*
Western Rsrve Girl Scout Cncil 330 864-9933
  1 Girl Scout Way Macedonia (44056) *(G-13089)*
Western Rsrve Land Conservancy (PA) 440 729-9621
  3850 Chagrin River Rd Chagrin Falls (44022) *(G-2660)*
Western Rsrve Msonic Cmnty Inc 330 721-3000
  4931 Nettleton Rd # 4318 Medina (44256) *(G-14014)*
Western Southern Life Insur, Ontario *Also called Western & Southern Lf Insur Co (G-15579)*
Western Southern Mutl Holdg Co (PA) 866 832-7719
  400 Broadway St Cincinnati (45202) *(G-4791)*
Western Sports Mall, Cincinnati *Also called Western Hills Sportsplex Inc (G-4790)*
Western States Envelope Co 419 666-7480
  6859 Commodore Dr Walbridge (43465) *(G-18627)*
Western States Envelope Label, Walbridge *Also called Western States Envelope Co (G-18627)*
Western Sthern Fincl Group Inc (HQ) 866 832-7719
  400 Broadway St Cincinnati (45202) *(G-4792)*
Western Tradewinds Inc (PA) 937 859-4300
  521 Byers Rd Miamisburg (45342) *(G-14238)*
Western-Southern Life, Cincinnati *Also called Western & Southern Lf Insur Co (G-4786)*
Western-Southern Life Insur, Grove City *Also called Western & Southern Lf Insur Co (G-11486)*
Westerville Dermatology Inc 614 895-0400
  235 W Schrock Rd Westerville (43081) *(G-19305)*
Westerville-Worthington Learni 614 891-4105
  149 Charring Cross Dr S Westerville (43081) *(G-19306)*
Westfall Aggregate & Mtls Inc 740 420-9090
  19522 London Rd Circleville (43113) *(G-4852)*
Westfall Towing LLC 740 371-5185
  1200 Pike St Marietta (45750) *(G-13401)*
Westfield Bank Fsb (HQ) 800 368-8930
  2 Park Cir Westfield Center (44251) *(G-19309)*
Westfield Belden Village 330 494-5490
  4230 Belden Village Mall Canton (44718) *(G-2535)*
Westfield Electric Inc 419 862-0078
  2995 State Route 51 Gibsonburg (43431) *(G-11280)*
Westfield Group, Westfield Center *Also called Ohio Farmers Insurance Company (G-19308)*
Westfield Group, Columbus *Also called Ohio Farmers Insurance Company (G-6828)*
Westfield Services Inc (PA) 614 796-7700
  2000 Polaris Pkwy Ste 202 Columbus (43240) *(G-6839)*
Westfield Steel Inc 937 322-2414
  1120 S Burnett Rd Springfield (45505) *(G-17136)*
Westgate Lanes Incorporated 419 229-3845
  721 N Cable Rd Lima (45805) *(G-12783)*
Westgate Limited Partnership 419 535-7070
  457 S Reynolds Rd Toledo (43615) *(G-18155)*
Westhafer Trucking Inc 330 698-3030
  6333 E Messner Rd Apple Creek (44606) *(G-622)*
Westhaven Services Co LLC 419 661-2200
  7643 Ponderosa Rd Perrysburg (43551) *(G-15935)*
Westin Cincinnati, The, Cincinnati *Also called Hst Lessee Cincinnati LLC (G-3736)*
Westin Cleveland, Cleveland *Also called Optima 777 LLC (G-6138)*
Westin Columbus, Columbus *Also called Wm Columbus Hotel LLC (G-8911)*
Westin Columbus, Columbus *Also called Marcus Hotels Inc (G-8016)*

Westin Hotel, Columbus *Also called First Hotel Associates LP* ***(G-7586)***
Westlake Cab Service 440 331-5000
2069 W 3rd St Cleveland (44113) ***(G-6677)***
Westlake Marriott....440 892-6887
30100 Clemens Rd Westlake (44145) ***(G-19424)***
Westlake Mntsr Schl & Chld Dv 440 835-5858
26830 Detroit Rd Westlake (44145) ***(G-19425)***
Westlake Reed Leskosky, Cleveland *Also called Dlr Group Inc* ***(G-5433)***
Westlake Village, Cleveland *Also called Fort Austin Ltd Partnership* ***(G-5564)***
Westlake Village Inc 440 892-4200
28550 Westlake Village Dr Cleveland (44145) ***(G-6678)***
Westland Heating & AC, Westlake *Also called North East Mechanical Inc* ***(G-19381)***
Westminster Financial Company 937 898-5010
125 N Wilkinson St Dayton (45402) ***(G-9877)***
Westminster Fincl Companies, Dayton *Also called Westmnster Fncl Securities Inc* ***(G-9878)***
Westminster Management Company....614 274-5154
2731 Clime Rd Columbus (43223) ***(G-8890)***
Westminster Thurber, Columbus *Also called Ohio Living* ***(G-8271)***
Westminster Thurber Community, Columbus *Also called Ohio Presbt Retirement Svcs* ***(G-8280)***
Westmnster Fncl Securities Inc 937 898-5010
40 N Main St Ste 2400 Dayton (45423) ***(G-9878)***
Westmoreland Place, Chillicothe *Also called Chillicothe Long Term Care* ***(G-2763)***
Westmoreland Place, Cincinnati *Also called Chillicothe Long Term Care* ***(G-3194)***
Weston Inc (PA) 440 349-9000
4760 Richmond Rd Ste 200 Cleveland (44128) ***(G-6679)***
Weston Inc 440 349-9001
32000 Aurora Rd Solon (44139) ***(G-16914)***
Westover Preparatory School, Hamilton *Also called Colonial Senior Services Inc* ***(G-11583)***
Westover Retirement Communitry, Hamilton *Also called Colonial Senior Services Inc* ***(G-11584)***
Westpatrick Corp....614 875-8200
250 N Hartford Ave 300 Columbus (43222) ***(G-8891)***
Westpost Columbus LLC 614 885-1885
6500 Doubletree Ave Columbus (43229) ***(G-8892)***
Westrock Cp LLC....770 448-2193
1010 Mead St Wshngtn CT Hs (43160) ***(G-19886)***
Westshore Prmry Care Assoc Inc 440 934-0276
5323 Meadow Lane Ct Sheffield Village (44035) ***(G-16742)***
Westshore Ymca/Westlake Chrn, Westlake *Also called Young MNS Chrstn Assn Clveland* ***(G-19426)***
Westside Family Practice Inc 614 878-4541
5206 Chaps Ct Columbus (43221) ***(G-8893)***
Westside Health Care, Cincinnati *Also called J E F Inc* ***(G-3794)***
Westview Apartments Ohio LLC 216 520-1250
3111 Leo Ave Youngstown (44509) ***(G-20244)***
Westview-Youngstown Ltd....330 799-2787
3111 Leo Ave Youngstown (44509) ***(G-20245)***
Westwat Management, Westlake *Also called King James Group IV Ltd* ***(G-19363)***
Westway Trml Cincinnati LLC 513 921-8441
3500 Southside Ave Cincinnati (45204) ***(G-4793)***
Westwood Behavioral Health Ctr....419 238-3434
1158 Westwood Dr Van Wert (45891) ***(G-18497)***
Westwood Bhvioural Hlth Centre, Paulding *Also called County of Paulding* ***(G-15793)***
Westwood Country Club Company 440 331-3016
22625 Detroit Rd Rocky River (44116) ***(G-16448)***
Wetherngton Golf Cntry CLB Inc (PA) 513 755-2582
7337 Country Club Ln West Chester (45069) ***(G-19036)***
Wexner Heritage Village (PA)....614 231-4900
1151 College Ave Columbus (43209) ***(G-8894)***
Wexner Research Institute, Columbus *Also called Nationwide Childrens Hospital* ***(G-8146)***
Weymouth Valley Inc....440 498-8888
39000 Signature Dr Solon (44139) ***(G-16915)***
Wf Services, Canton *Also called Workforce Services Inc* ***(G-2538)***
Wfin AM, Findlay *Also called Findlay Publishing Company* ***(G-10905)***
Wfmj Television Inc 330 744-8611
101 W Boardman St Youngstown (44503) ***(G-20246)***
Wfts....216 431-5555
3001 Euclid Ave Cleveland (44115) ***(G-6680)***
Wfts....513 721-9900
1720 Gilbert Ave Cincinnati (45202) ***(G-4794)***
Wgte-Tv-Fm, Toledo *Also called Public Broadcasting Found NW* ***(G-17995)***
Wh Midwest LLC (PA)....330 896-7611
3777 Boettler Oaks Dr Uniontown (44685) ***(G-18390)***
Whalen & Co CPA, Worthington *Also called Whalen and Company Inc* ***(G-19860)***
Whalen and Company Inc....614 396-4200
250 W Old Wlsn Brg Rd # 300 Worthington (43085) ***(G-19860)***
Wheatland Tube Company, Cambridge *Also called Zekelman Industries Inc* ***(G-2087)***
Wheaton & Sprague Engineering (PA) 330 923-5560
1151 Campus Dr Ste 100 Stow (44224) ***(G-17239)***
Wheaton Sprague Bldg Envelope, Stow *Also called Wheaton & Sprague Engineering* ***(G-17239)***
Wheeling & Lake Erie Rlwy Co (HQ)....330 767-3401
100 1st St Se Brewster (44613) ***(G-1812)***
Wheeling Hospital Inc 740 695-2090
107 Plaza Dr Ste D Saint Clairsville (43950) ***(G-16511)***
Wheeling Hospital Inc 740 671-0850
4000 Central Ave Shadyside (43947) ***(G-16699)***
Wheeling Hospital Inc 740 633-4765
90 N 4th St Martins Ferry (43935) ***(G-13481)***
Wheeling Hospital Inc 740 676-4623
3000 Guernsey St Bellaire (43906) ***(G-1336)***
Wheeling Hospital Inc 740 942-4631
951 E Market St Cadiz (43907) ***(G-2034)***
Wheeling Hospital Inc 740 942-4116
943 E Market St Cadiz (43907) ***(G-2035)***
Whelco Industrial Ltd 419 873-6134
28210 Cedar Park Blvd Perrysburg (43551) ***(G-15936)***
Whetstone Care Center LLC 614 875-7700
3929 Hoover Rd Grove City (43123) ***(G-11487)***
Whetstone Care Center LLC 614 457-1100
3710 Olentangy River Rd Columbus (43214) ***(G-8895)***
Whetstone Care Center LLC 740 474-6036
391 Clark Dr Circleville (43113) ***(G-4853)***
Whetstone Center, Columbus *Also called Whetstone Care Center LLC* ***(G-8895)***
Whetstone Industries Inc....419 947-9222
440 Douglas St Mount Gilead (43338) ***(G-14735)***
WHETSTONE SCHOOL, Mount Gilead *Also called Whetstone Industries Inc* ***(G-14735)***
Whirlpool Corporation 740 383-7122
1300 Marion Agosta Rd Marion (43302) ***(G-13473)***
Whirlpool Corporation 419 423-6097
4325 County Road 86 Findlay (45840) ***(G-10975)***
Whirlpool Corporation 419 547-2610
1081 W Mcpherson Hwy Clyde (43410) ***(G-6755)***
Whisler Plumbing & Heating Inc 330 833-2875
2521 Lincoln Way E Massillon (44646) ***(G-13735)***
Whispering Hills Care Center....740 392-3982
416 Wooster Rd Mount Vernon (43050) ***(G-14792)***
Whitaker Masonry Inc....330 225-7970
4910 Grafton Rd Brunswick (44212) ***(G-1946)***
Whitcomb & Hess Inc....419 289-7007
1020 Cleveland Ave Ashland (44805) ***(G-699)***
White & Chambers Partnership....740 594-8381
5315 Hebbardsville Rd Athens (45701) ***(G-811)***
White Allen Chevrolet, Dayton *Also called White Family Companies Inc* ***(G-9879)***
White Barn Candle Co....614 856-6000
7 Limited Pkwy E Reynoldsburg (43068) ***(G-16338)***
White Cars, Sylvania *Also called Dave White Chevrolet Inc* ***(G-17417)***
White Castle System Inc (PA) 614 228-5781
555 W Goodale St Columbus (43215) ***(G-8896)***
White Family Collision Center....419 885-8885
5328 Alexis Rd Sylvania (43560) ***(G-17464)***
White Family Companies Inc....937 222-3701
442 N Main St Dayton (45405) ***(G-9879)***
White Glove Executive Services 614 226-2553
2647 Bryan Cir Grove City (43123) ***(G-11488)***
White Gorilla Corporation....202 384-6486
6218 Lampton Pond Dr Hilliard (43026) ***(G-11830)***
White Oak Investments Inc....614 491-1000
3730 Lockbourne Rd Columbus (43207) ***(G-8897)***
White Pond Gardens Inc....330 836-2727
1015 White Pond Dr Akron (44320) ***(G-500)***
White Rock Quarry L P....419 855-8388
3800 Bolander Rd Clay Center (43408) ***(G-4855)***
White' S Ford, Urbana *Also called Whites Service Center Inc* ***(G-18446)***
Whited Seigneur Sams & Rahe 740 702-2600
213 S Paint St Chillicothe (45601) ***(G-2837)***
Whiteford Greenhouse....419 882-4110
4554 Whiteford Rd Toledo (43623) ***(G-18156)***
Whiteford Kenworth, Perrysburg *Also called Lower Great Lakes Kenworth Inc* ***(G-15890)***
Whitehall City Schools....614 417-5680
4738 Kae Ave Columbus (43213) ***(G-8898)***
Whitehall Division of Fire, Columbus *Also called City of Whitehall* ***(G-7213)***
Whitehall Frmens Bnvlence Fund....614 237-5478
390 S Yearling Rd Columbus (43213) ***(G-8899)***
Whitehouse Country Manor, Whitehouse *Also called Whitehouse Operator LLC* ***(G-19452)***
Whitehouse Inn, Whitehouse *Also called Frog & Toad Inc* ***(G-19447)***
Whitehouse Operator LLC....419 877-5338
11239 Waterville St Whitehouse (43571) ***(G-19452)***
Whitehurst Company (PA) 419 865-0799
6325 Garden Rd Maumee (43537) ***(G-13868)***
Whites Service Center Inc 937 653-5279
1246 N Main St Urbana (43078) ***(G-18446)***
Whitespace Creative, Akron *Also called Whitespace Design Group Inc* ***(G-501)***
Whitespace Design Group Inc....330 762-9320
243 Furnace St Akron (44304) ***(G-501)***
Whitestone Group Inc 614 501-7007
6422 E Main St Ste 101 Reynoldsburg (43068) ***(G-16339)***
Whitewater Car & Van Wash Co, Toledo *Also called Robert Stough Ventures Corp* ***(G-18011)***
Whitford Woods Co Inc....440 693-4344
16192 Bundysburg Rd Middlefield (44062) ***(G-14279)***
Whiting-Turner Contracting Co....614 459-6515
250 W Old Wilson Bridge R Worthington (43085) ***(G-19861)***
Whiting-Turner Contracting Co 440 449-9200
5875 Landerbrook Dr # 100 Cleveland (44124) ***(G-6681)***
Whitt Inc 513 753-7707
1152 Ferris Rd Amelia (45102) ***(G-577)***
Whitt Plumbing, Amelia *Also called Whitt Inc* ***(G-577)***

1294 2019 Harris Ohio Services Directory (G-0000) Company's Geographic Section entry number

Whittguard Security Services........................440 288-7233
  37435 Colorado Ave Avon (44011) *(G-904)*
Whiz Am-FM, Zanesville *Also called Southeastern Ohio Brdcstg Sys (G-20363)*
Whiz-TV, Zanesville *Also called Southeastern Ohio TV Sys (G-20364)*
Whole Health Dentistry, Lima *Also called Eric W Warnock (G-12633)*
Whole Health Management Inc (HQ)............216 921-8601
  1375 E 9th St Ste 2500 Cleveland (44114) *(G-6682)*
Wholecycle Inc...330 929-8123
  100 Cyhoga Fls Indus Pkwy Peninsula (44264) *(G-15815)*
Wholesale House Inc (PA)...........................419 542-1315
  503 W High St Hicksville (43526) *(G-11731)*
Wholesale Tire Division, Toledo *Also called Capital Tire Inc (G-17635)*
Wholesale Tire Division, Toledo *Also called Capital Tire Inc (G-17636)*
Wic, Columbus *Also called Ohio Department of Health (G-8239)*
Wic Program, Austintown *Also called Ohio Department of Health (G-858)*
Wicked Woods Golf Club, Newbury *Also called Wicked Woods Gulf Club Inc (G-15128)*
Wicked Woods Gulf Club Inc.......................440 564-7960
  14085 Ravenna Rd Newbury (44065) *(G-15128)*
Wickens Hrzer Pnza Cook Btista...................440 695-8000
  35765 Chester Rd Avon (44011) *(G-905)*
Wickertree Tnnis Ftnes CLB LLC..................614 882-5724
  5760 Maple Canyon Ave Columbus (43229) *(G-8900)*
Wickliffe Associates Partnr.........................440 585-3505
  30315 Euclid Ave Wickliffe (44092) *(G-19477)*
Wickliffe Country Place, Parma *Also called 3g Operating Company LLC (G-15758)*
Wickliffe Country Place Ltd.........................440 944-9400
  1919 Bishop Rd Wickliffe (44092) *(G-19478)*
Wickliffe Lanes, Wickliffe *Also called Wickliffe Associates Partnr (G-19477)*
Wickline Floral & Garden Ctr, Xenia *Also called Wickline Landscaping Inc (G-19933)*
Wickline Landscaping Inc (PA).....................937 372-0521
  1625 N Detroit St Xenia (45385) *(G-19933)*
Widepint Intgrted Sltions Corp.....................614 410-1587
  8351 N High St Ste 200 Columbus (43235) *(G-8901)*
Widmer's, Cincinnati *Also called C&C Clean Team Enterprises LLC (G-3102)*
Widmer's Drycleaners, Cincinnati *Also called Widmers LLC (G-4795)*
Widmers LLC (HQ)....................................513 321-5100
  2016 Madison Rd Cincinnati (45208) *(G-4795)*
Widows Home of Dayton Ohio.......................937 252-1661
  50 S Findlay St Dayton (45403) *(G-9880)*
Wiechart Enterprises Inc.............................419 227-0027
  4511 Elida Rd Lima (45807) *(G-12784)*
Wiegands Lake Park Inc..............................440 338-5795
  9390 Kinsman Rd Novelty (44072) *(G-15467)*
Wiggins Clg & Crpt Svc Inc (PA)...................937 279-9080
  4699 Salem Ave Ste 2 Dayton (45416) *(G-9881)*
Wilbur Realty Inc (PA)................................330 673-5883
  548 S Water St Kent (44240) *(G-12268)*
Wild Republic, Twinsburg *Also called K & M International Inc (G-18286)*
WILDWOOD SURGICAL CENTER, Toledo *Also called Reynolds Road Surgical Ctr LLC (G-18006)*
Wildwood Yacht Club Inc.............................216 531-9052
  P.O. Box 19001 Cleveland (44119) *(G-6683)*
Wiles Boyle Burkholder &...........................614 221-5216
  2 Miranova Pl Ste 700 Columbus (43215) *(G-8902)*
Wiles Doucher, Columbus *Also called Wiles Boyle Burkholder & (G-8902)*
WILEY AVENUE GROUP HOME, Saint Clairsville *Also called Alternative Residences Two (G-16468)*
Wiley Homes Inc.......................................419 535-3988
  4011 Angola Rd Toledo (43615) *(G-18157)*
Wilkes & Company Inc................................419 433-2325
  205 Sprowl Rd Huron (44839) *(G-12035)*
Wilkris Company.......................................513 271-9344
  411 Terrace Pl Terrace Park (45174) *(G-17501)*
Will-Burt Company (PA)..............................330 682-7015
  169 S Main St Orrville (44667) *(G-15649)*
Will-Burt Company.....................................330 682-7015
  312 Collins Blvd Orrville (44667) *(G-15650)*
Willard Head Start Day Care, Cleveland *Also called Council of Ecnmc Opprtnts of G (G-5358)*
Willcare, Euclid *Also called Bracor Inc (G-10626)*
Willglo Services Inc..................................614 443-3020
  995 Thurman Ave Columbus (43206) *(G-8903)*
William & Clippard YMCA, Cincinnati *Also called Young Mens Christian Associat (G-4816)*
William D Taylor Sr Inc (PA).........................614 653-6683
  263 Trail E Etna (43062) *(G-10621)*
William H Zimmer Power Station, Moscow *Also called Vistra Energy Corp (G-14721)*
William Hafer Drayage Inc...........................513 771-5000
  11320 Mosteller Rd Ste 1 Cincinnati (45241) *(G-4796)*
William I Notz...614 292-3154
  1958 Neil Ave Rm 319 Columbus (43210) *(G-8904)*
William Kerfoot Masonry Inc........................330 772-6460
  4948 State Route 7 Burghill (44404) *(G-2010)*
William Patrick Day, Cleveland *Also called Council For Economic Opport (G-5357)*
William R Morse.......................................440 352-2600
  83 S State St Painesville (44077) *(G-15748)*
William Sydney Druen................................614 444-7655
  85 E Deshler Ave Columbus (43206) *(G-8905)*
William Thomas Group Inc..........................800 582-3107
  10795 Hughes Rd Cincinnati (45251) *(G-4797)*

William Vaughan Company..........................419 891-1040
  145 Chesterfield Ln Maumee (43537) *(G-13869)*
William Wood...740 543-4052
  8392 County Road 39 Bloomingdale (43910) *(G-1491)*
William X Greene Bus Advisor, Cincinnati *Also called Scrogginsgrear Inc (G-4440)*
William Zamarelli Realtors..........................330 856-2299
  8700 E Market St Ste 6 Warren (44484) *(G-18772)*
Williams Bros Builders Inc...........................440 365-3261
  686 Sugar Ln Elyria (44035) *(G-10575)*
Williams Concrete Cnstr Co Inc.....................330 745-6388
  2959 Barber Rd Ste 100 Norton (44203) *(G-15423)*
Williams Conty Hllsd Cntry Lvg, Bryan *Also called County of Williams (G-1956)*
Williams County Health Dept, Montpelier *Also called County of Williams (G-14612)*
Williams County Landfill, Bryan *Also called Republic Services Inc (G-1973)*
Williams Dtroit Diesel-Allison, Hilliard *Also called W W Williams Company LLC (G-11828)*
Williams Freight Logistics...........................614 333-9173
  1893 Fiesta Ct Apt D Columbus (43229) *(G-8906)*
Williams Homes LLC..................................419 472-1005
  1841 Eastgate Rd Toledo (43614) *(G-18158)*
Williams Partners LP.................................330 966-3674
  7235 Whipple Ave Nw North Canton (44720) *(G-15244)*
Williams Street Apartments, Columbus *Also called Buckeye Cmnty Eighty One LP (G-7086)*
Williams Super Service Inc..........................330 733-7750
  9462 Main Ave Se East Sparta (44626) *(G-10425)*
Williams Toyota Lift, East Sparta *Also called Williams Super Service Inc (G-10425)*
Williamsburg of Cincinnati Mgt.....................513 948-2308
  230 W Galbraith Rd Cincinnati (45215) *(G-4798)*
Willimsburg Rsdntial Altrntves, Williamsburg *Also called Rescare Ohio Inc (G-19496)*
Willis Day Management Inc (PA)...................419 476-8000
  4100 Bennett Rd Ste 1 Toledo (43612) *(G-18159)*
Willis of Ohio Inc (HQ)...............................614 457-7000
  775 Yard St Ste 200 Columbus (43212) *(G-8907)*
Willis One Hour Heating & AC.......................513 752-2512
  756 Cncnnati Batavia Pike Cincinnati (45245) *(G-2875)*
Willis Towers Watson, Cleveland *Also called Wtw Delaware Holdings LLC (G-6693)*
WILLISTON LUTHER HOME OF MERCY, Williston *Also called Luther Home of Mercy (G-19500)*
Willo Maintenance, Willoughby *Also called Dependable Cleaning Contrs (G-19518)*
Willo Security Inc.....................................614 481-9456
  1989 W 5th Ave Ste 3 Columbus (43212) *(G-8908)*
Willo Security Inc (PA)...............................440 953-9191
  38230 Glenn Ave Willoughby (44094) *(G-19582)*
Willo Transportation, Willoughby *Also called Palmer Express Incorporated (G-19560)*
Willory LLC...330 576-5486
  1970 N Cleveland Mssiln Bath (44210) *(G-1020)*
Willoughby City Garage, Willoughby *Also called City of Willoughby (G-19510)*
Willoughby Commons 16, Willoughby *Also called Regal Cinemas Inc (G-19566)*
Willoughby Lodging LLC.............................440 530-1100
  35103 Maplegrove Rd Fl 3 Willoughby (44094) *(G-19583)*
Willoughby Medical Offices, Willoughby *Also called Kaiser Foundation Hospitals (G-19533)*
Willoughby Montessori Day Schl....................440 942-5602
  5543 Som Center Rd Willoughby (44094) *(G-19584)*
Willow & Cane, Springboro *Also called Willow and Cane LLC (G-16988)*
Willow and Cane LLC.................................609 280-1150
  1110 Lakemont Dr Springboro (45066) *(G-16988)*
Willow Brook Christian Home, Columbus *Also called Brook Willow Chrstn Cmmunities (G-7079)*
WILLOW BROOK CHRISTIAN VILLAGE, Delaware *Also called Willow Brook Chrstn Cmmunities (G-10016)*
Willow Brook Chrstn Cmmunities (PA).............740 369-0048
  100 Delaware Xing W Delaware (43015) *(G-10016)*
Willow Dialysis Cntr, Wilmington *Also called Renal Life Link Inc (G-19644)*
Willow Haven Nursing Home, Zanesville *Also called Zandex Health Care Corporation (G-20380)*
Willow Knoll Nursing Center, Middletown *Also called Church of God Retirement Cmnty (G-14295)*
Willow Ridge Nursery, Madison *Also called Ridge Manor Nuseries Inc (G-13108)*
Willoway Nurseries Inc (PA).........................440 934-4435
  4534 Center Rd Avon (44011) *(G-906)*
Willowbend Nurseries LLC...........................440 259-3121
  4654 Davis Rd Perry (44081) *(G-15829)*
Willowood Care Center...............................330 225-3156
  1186 Hadcock Rd Brunswick (44212) *(G-1947)*
Willows At Willard, The, Willard *Also called Trilogy Health Services LLC (G-19489)*
WILLOWS HEALTH & REHAB CENTER, THE, Euclid *Also called Indian Hlls Hlthcare Group Inc (G-10644)*
Willows Health and Rehab Ctr, Euclid *Also called Saber Healthcare Group LLC (G-10655)*
Wilmared Inc...513 891-6615
  6279 Tri Ridge Blvd Loveland (45140) *(G-13035)*
Wilmer Cutler Pick Hale Dorr.......................937 395-2100
  3139 Research Blvd Dayton (45420) *(G-9882)*
Wilmerhale, Dayton *Also called Wilmer Cutler Pick Hale Dorr (G-9882)*
Wilmington City Cab Service, Wilmington *Also called City of Wilmington (G-19608)*
Wilmington Halthcare Group Inc....................937 382-1621
  75 Hale St Wilmington (45177) *(G-19653)*

ALPHABETIC

Wilmington Iron and Met Co Inc......................937 382-3867
2149 S Us Highway 68 Wilmington (45177) *(G-19654)*

Wilmington Medical Associates......................937 382-1616
1184 W Locust St Wilmington (45177) *(G-19655)*

Wilmington Nrsng & Rehab Cntr, Wilmington *Also called Wilmington Halthcare Group Inc (G-19653)*

Wilson Shannon & Snow Inc......................740 345-6611
10 W Locust St Newark (43055) *(G-15109)*

Wilson Enterprises Inc......................614 444-8873
1600 Universal Rd Columbus (43207) *(G-8909)*

Wilson Health, Sidney *Also called Shelby County Mem Hosp Assn (G-16797)*

Wilson Mem Hosp Occptnal Clnic, Sidney *Also called Occupational Health Services (G-16788)*

Wilson Sporting Goods Co......................419 634-9901
217 Liberty St Ada (45810) *(G-6)*

Wilson's Garden Center, Newark *Also called Wilsons Hillview Farm Inc (G-15110)*

Wilson's Turf, Columbus *Also called Wilson Enterprises Inc (G-8909)*

Wilsons Hillview Farm Inc......................740 763-2873
10923 Lambs Ln Newark (43055) *(G-15110)*

Wimberg Lansdscaping, Cincinnati *Also called Peter A Wimberg Company Inc (G-4234)*

Win Tamer Corporation......................330 637-2881
2940 Niles Cortland Rd Ne Cortland (44410) *(G-8996)*

WINCHESTER CARE & REHABILITATION, Canal Winchester *Also called Winchester Place Leasing LLC (G-2127)*

Winchester Place Leasing LLC......................614 834-2273
36 Lehman Dr Canal Winchester (43110) *(G-2127)*

Winchester Terrace, Mansfield *Also called Levering Management Inc (G-13198)*

Winchester Wholesale, Winchester *Also called Cantrell Oil Company (G-19660)*

WINDFALL INDUSTRIES, Wadsworth *Also called Medina County Sheltered Inds (G-18608)*

Window Factory of America (PA)......................440 439-3050
21600 Alexander Rd Bedford (44146) *(G-1314)*

Windsong Care Center, Akron *Also called Windsong Healthcare Group LLC (G-502)*

Windsong Healthcare Group LLC......................216 292-5706
120 Brookmont Rd Akron (44333) *(G-502)*

Windsor Companies (PA)......................740 653-8822
1430 Collins Rd Nw Lancaster (43130) *(G-12445)*

Windsor Construction, Brookpark *Also called J & R Associates (G-1898)*

Windsor Health Care, Youngstown *Also called Windsor House Inc (G-20248)*

Windsor House Inc......................330 759-7858
1355 Churchill Hubbard Rd Youngstown (44505) *(G-20247)*

Windsor House Inc......................330 743-1393
1735 Belmont Ave Youngstown (44504) *(G-20248)*

Windsor House Inc......................330 482-1375
930 E Park Ave Columbiana (44408) *(G-6795)*

Windsor House Inc......................330 549-9259
1899 W Garfield Rd Columbiana (44408) *(G-6796)*

Windsor House Inc......................440 834-0544
14095 E Center St Burton (44021) *(G-2020)*

Windsor Lane Health Care, Gibsonburg *Also called Gibsonburg Health Llc (G-11278)*

Windsor Medical Center Inc......................330 499-8300
1454 E Maple St Canton (44720) *(G-2536)*

Windsorwood Place Inc......................740 623-4600
255 Browns Ln Coshocton (43812) *(G-9031)*

Windwood Swim & Tennis Club......................513 777-2552
6649 N Windwood Dr West Chester (45069) *(G-19037)*

Windy Hill Ltd Inc (PA)......................216 391-4800
3700 Kelley Ave Cleveland (44114) *(G-6684)*

Windy Knoll Golf Club, Springfield *Also called Links At Windy Knoll LLC (G-17062)*

Wine Trends Inc......................216 520-2626
9101 E Pleasant Valley Rd Independence (44131) *(G-12141)*

Wine-Art of Ohio Inc......................330 678-7733
463 Portage Blvd Kent (44240) *(G-12269)*

Winegardner & Hammons Inc......................614 791-1000
5605 Paul G Blzr Mmrl Pkw Dublin (43017) *(G-10376)*

Winegrdner Hmmons Ht Group LLC (PA)......................513 891-1066
4243 Hunt Rd Blue Ash (45242) *(G-1678)*

Winelco Inc......................513 755-8050
6141 Centre Park Dr West Chester (45069) *(G-19038)*

Wing-FM, Dayton *Also called Alpha Media LLC (G-9220)*

Wingler Construction Corp......................614 626-8546
771 S Hamilton Rd Columbus (43213) *(G-8910)*

Wings Investors Company Ltd......................513 241-5800
3805 Edwards Rd Ste 200 Cincinnati (45209) *(G-4799)*

Wingspan Care Group (PA)......................216 932-2800
22001 Fairmount Blvd Shaker Heights (44118) *(G-16720)*

Winking Lizard Inc......................330 220-9944
3634 Center Rd Brunswick (44212) *(G-1948)*

Winking Lizard Inc......................330 467-1002
1615 Main St Peninsula (44264) *(G-15816)*

Winkle Electric Company Inc (PA)......................330 744-5303
1900 Hubbard Rd Youngstown (44505) *(G-20249)*

Winkle Industries Inc......................330 823-9730
2080 W Main St Alliance (44601) *(G-557)*

Winn-Scapes Inc......................614 866-9466
6079 Taylor Rd Gahanna (43230) *(G-11151)*

Winncom Technologies Corp......................440 498-9510
28900 Ftn Pkwy Unit B Solon (44139) *(G-16916)*

Winner Aviation Corporation......................330 856-5000
1453 Youngstown Kingsvill Vienna (44473) *(G-18584)*

Winner's Meat Service, Yorkshire *Also called Robert Winner Sons Inc (G-19942)*

Winnscapes Inc/Schmidt Nurs Co, Gahanna *Also called Winn-Scapes Inc (G-11151)*

Winston Brdcstg Netwrk Inc (PA)......................330 928-5711
2690 State Rd Cuyahoga Falls (44223) *(G-9140)*

Winston Products LLC......................440 478-1418
30339 Diamond Pkwy # 105 Cleveland (44139) *(G-6685)*

Winsupply Inc (PA)......................937 294-5331
3110 Kettering Blvd Moraine (45439) *(G-14707)*

Winsupply Inc......................937 865-0796
9300 Byers Rd Miamisburg (45342) *(G-14239)*

Winter Drive In Theater, Toledo *Also called A and S Ventures Inc (G-17575)*

Winterfield Venture Academy, Toledo *Also called National Heritg Academies Inc (G-17932)*

Winterhurst Ice Rink, Lakewood *Also called Lakewood City School District (G-12352)*

Wintersong Village of Delaware, Delaware *Also called A L K Inc (G-9947)*

Wirefree Home Automation......................440 247-8978
576 Industrial Pkwy Chagrin Falls (44022) *(G-2661)*

Wireless Center Inc (PA)......................216 503-3777
1925 Saint Clair Ave Ne Cleveland (44114) *(G-6686)*

Wireless Connections, Norwalk *Also called Advanced Cmpt Connections LLC (G-15424)*

Wireless Environment LLC......................216 455-0192
600 Beta Dr Ste 100 Mayfield Village (44143) *(G-13888)*

Wireless Source Entps LLC......................419 266-5556
16545 Euler Rd Bowling Green (43402) *(G-1751)*

Wirtzberger Enterprises Corp......................440 428-1901
136 W Main St Madison (44057) *(G-13110)*

Wise Choices In Learning Ltd......................440 324-6056
352 Griswold Rd Elyria (44035) *(G-10576)*

Wise Services Inc......................937 854-0281
1705 Guenther Rd Dayton (45417) *(G-9883)*

Witmers Inc......................330 427-2147
39821 Salem Unity Rd Salem (44460) *(G-16567)*

Witt Glvnzing - Cincinnati Inc......................513 871-5700
4454 Steel Pl Cincinnati (45209) *(G-4800)*

Wittenberg University, Springfield *Also called Board of Dir of Wittenbe (G-17000)*

Wize-AM, Dayton *Also called Iheartcommunications Inc (G-9511)*

Wizf-FM, Cincinnati *Also called Urban One Inc (G-4734)*

Wj Service Co Inc (PA)......................330 372-5040
2592 Elm Rd Ne Warren (44483) *(G-18773)*

Wkrc-Tv/Cbs, Cincinnati *Also called Iheartcommunications Inc (G-3751)*

Wksu FM Natl Public Radio, Kent *Also called Kent State University (G-12243)*

Wkyc-Tv Inc......................216 344-3300
1333 Lakeside Ave E Cleveland (44114) *(G-6687)*

Wlio Television-Channel 35, Lima *Also called Lima Communications Corp (G-12678)*

Wm Columbus Hotel LLC......................614 228-3800
310 S High St Columbus (43215) *(G-8911)*

Wm Kramer and Sons Inc......................513 353-1142
9171 Harrison Pike # 12 Cleves (45002) *(G-6736)*

Wman, Mansfield *Also called Iheartcommunications Inc (G-13185)*

Wmji-FM, Cleveland *Also called Iheartcommunications Inc (G-5737)*

Wmjk FM, Sandusky *Also called Iheartcommunications Inc (G-16618)*

Wmk Inc......................630 782-1900
4199 Kinross Lakes Pkwy Richfield (44286) *(G-16384)*

Wmk LLC......................440 951-4335
7588 Tyler Blvd Mentor (44060) *(G-14125)*

Wmvh LLC......................513 425-7886
4616 Manchester Rd Middletown (45042) *(G-14340)*

Wmvx Radio, Cleveland *Also called Iheartcommunications Inc (G-5736)*

Wnb Group LLC......................513 641-5400
4817 Section Ave Cincinnati (45212) *(G-4801)*

Wnbs Channel 10 Weatherline, Columbus *Also called Wbns Tv Inc (G-8881)*

Wnir/FM, Kent *Also called Media-Com Inc (G-12249)*

Wnwo-TV, Toledo *Also called Toledo Television Investors LP (G-18100)*

Woda Construction Inc......................614 396-3200
500 S Front St Fl 10 Columbus (43215) *(G-8912)*

Wojos Heating & AC Inc......................419 693-3220
5523 Woodville Rd Northwood (43619) *(G-15415)*

Wolcott Group......................330 666-5900
1684 Medina Rd Ste 204 Medina (44256) *(G-14015)*

Wolf Creek Company Inc (PA)......................937 854-2694
6051 Wolf Creek Pike Dayton (45426) *(G-9884)*

Wolf Group, The, Blue Ash *Also called Wolf Sensory Inc (G-1680)*

Wolf Machine Company (PA)......................513 791-5194
5570 Creek Rd Blue Ash (45242) *(G-1679)*

Wolf Sensory Inc......................513 891-9100
10860 Kenwood Rd Blue Ash (45242) *(G-1680)*

Wolfes Roofing Inc......................419 666-6233
6568 State Route 795 Walbridge (43465) *(G-18628)*

Wolff Bros Supply Inc......................419 425-8511
6000 Fostoria Ave Findlay (45840) *(G-10976)*

Wolff Bros Supply Inc......................330 400-5990
2800 W Strub Rd Sandusky (44870) *(G-16656)*

Wolff Bros Supply Inc......................330 264-5900
565 N Applecreek Rd Wooster (44691) *(G-19784)*

Wolff Bros Supply Inc......................330 786-4140
1200 Kelly Ave Akron (44306) *(G-503)*

Wolters Kluwer Clinical Drug......................330 650-6506
1100 Terex Rd Hudson (44236) *(G-12014)*

Wolverton Inc......................330 220-3320
3048 Nationwide Pkwy Brunswick (44212) *(G-1949)*

(G-0000) Company's Geographic Section entry number

Wolves Club Inc 419 476-4418
  5930 Dalton Rd Toledo (43612) *(G-18160)*

Womans Health Center, Wooster *Also called Cleveland Clinic Foundation (G-19707)*

Women Health Partners 740 363-9021
  6 Lexington Blvd Delaware (43015) *(G-10017)*

Women Physicans of Ob/Gyn Inc (PA) 614 734-3340
  3525 Olentangy River Rd # 6350 Columbus (43214) *(G-8913)*

Womens Care Inc 419 756-6000
  500 S Trimble Rd Mansfield (44906) *(G-13263)*

Womens Centers-Dayton 937 228-2222
  359 Forest Ave Ste 106 Dayton (45405) *(G-9885)*

Womens Civic Club Grove City 614 871-0145
  3881 Tamara Dr Grove City (43123) *(G-11489)*

Womens Recovery Center 937 562-2400
  515 Martin Dr Xenia (45385) *(G-19934)*

Womens Welsh Clubs of America 440 331-0420
  22199 Center Ridge Rd Rocky River (44116) *(G-16449)*

Wonderworker Inc 234 249-3030
  6217 Chittenden Rd Hudson (44236) *(G-12015)*

Wong Margaret W Assoc Co Lpa (PA) 313 527-9989
  3150 Chester Ave Cleveland (44114) *(G-6688)*

Wood Herron & Evans LLP (PA) 513 241-2324
  441 Vine St Ste 2700 Cincinnati (45202) *(G-4802)*

Wood & Lamping LLP 513 852-6000
  600 Vine St Ste 2500 Cincinnati (45202) *(G-4803)*

Wood County Chld Svcs Assn 419 352-7588
  1045 Klotz Rd Bowling Green (43402) *(G-1752)*

Wood County Committee On Aging (PA) 419 353-5661
  305 N Main St Bowling Green (43402) *(G-1753)*

Wood County Health Department, Bowling Green *Also called Wood County Ohio (G-1757)*

Wood County Hospital Assoc (PA) 419 354-8900
  960 W Wooster St Bowling Green (43402) *(G-1754)*

Wood County Ohio 419 354-9201
  1 Court House Sq Bowling Green (43402) *(G-1755)*

Wood County Ohio 419 353-8411
  1965 E Gypsy Lane Rd Bowling Green (43402) *(G-1756)*

Wood County Ohio 419 353-6914
  1840 E Gypsy Lane Rd Bowling Green (43402) *(G-1757)*

Wood County Ohio 419 352-5059
  705 W Newton Rd Bowling Green (43402) *(G-1758)*

Wood Electric Inc 330 339-7002
  210 11th St Nw New Philadelphia (44663) *(G-14989)*

Wood Environment & 513 489-6611
  4460 Lake Forest Dr # 200 Blue Ash (45242) *(G-1681)*

Wood Glen Alzheimers Community, Dayton *Also called Summitt Ohio Leasing Co LLC (G-9800)*

Wood Glenn Nursing Center, Dayton *Also called Dayton Dmh Inc (G-9363)*

Wood Graphics Inc (HQ) 513 771-6300
  8075 Reading Rd Ste 301 Cincinnati (45237) *(G-4804)*

Wood Haven Health Care, Bowling Green *Also called Wood County Ohio (G-1756)*

Wood Health Company LLC 419 353-7069
  745 Haskins Rd Ste B Bowling Green (43402) *(G-1759)*

Woodard Photographic Inc (HQ) 419 483-3364
  550 Goodrich Rd Bellevue (44811) *(G-1386)*

Woodcraft Supply LLC 513 407-8371
  11711 Princeton Pike # 251 Cincinnati (45246) *(G-4805)*

Woodhill Supply Inc (PA) 440 269-1100
  4665 Beidler Rd Willoughby (44094) *(G-19585)*

Woodhull LLC (PA) 937 294-5311
  125 Commercial Way Springboro (45066) *(G-16989)*

Woodland Assisted Living Resi 614 755-7591
  5380 E Broad St Ofc Columbus (43213) *(G-8914)*

Woodland Centers Inc (PA) 740 446-5500
  3086 State Route 160 Gallipolis (45631) *(G-11217)*

Woodland Country Manor Inc 513 523-4449
  4166 Somerville Rd Somerville (45064) *(G-16920)*

Woodland Run Equin Vet Facilty 614 871-4919
  1474 Borror Rd Grove City (43123) *(G-11490)*

WOODLANDS AT HAMPTON, Poland *Also called Hampton Woods Nursing Ctr Inc (G-16084)*

WOODLANDS AT SUNSET HOUSE, Toledo *Also called Sunset House Inc (G-18055)*

Woodlands Healthcare Group LLC 330 297-4564
  6831 N Chestnut St Ravenna (44266) *(G-16271)*

Woodlands of Columbus, Columbus *Also called Woodland Assisted Living Resi (G-8914)*

Woodlawn Nursing Home, Mansfield *Also called Lynnhaven Xii LLC (G-13200)*

WoodInds Hlth Rhbilitation Ctr, Ravenna *Also called Woodlands Healthcare Group LLC (G-16271)*

WoodInds Srving Centl Ohio Inc 740 349-7051
  68 W Church St Ste 318 Newark (43055) *(G-15111)*

Woodrow Manufacturing Co 937 399-9333
  4300 River Rd Springfield (45502) *(G-17137)*

Woodruff Enterprises Inc 937 399-9300
  4951 Gateway Blvd Springfield (45502) *(G-17138)*

Woods Edge Point, Cincinnati *Also called CHS Norwood Inc (G-3214)*

Woods Hardware, Cincinnati *Also called AWH Holdings Inc (G-3008)*

Woodsfield Opco LLC 502 429-8062
  37930 Airport Rd Woodsfield (43793) *(G-19679)*

Woodside Village Care Center 419 947-2015
  841 W Marion Rd Mount Gilead (43338) *(G-14736)*

Woodstock Healthcare Group Inc 937 826-3351
  1649 Park Rd Woodstock (43084) *(G-19681)*

Woodward Construction Inc 513 247-9241
  11425 Deerfield Rd Blue Ash (45242) *(G-1682)*

Woodward Excavating Co 614 866-4384
  7340 Tussing Rd Reynoldsburg (43068) *(G-16340)*

Woody Tree Medics 937 298-5316
  4350 Delco Dell Rd Dayton (45429) *(G-9886)*

Woolace Electric Corp 419 428-3161
  1978 County Road 22a Stryker (43557) *(G-17372)*

Woolpert Inc 614 476-6000
  1 Easton Oval Ste 400 Columbus (43219) *(G-8915)*

Woolprt-Mrrick Joint Ventr LLP 937 461-5660
  4454 Idea Center Blvd Beavercreek (45430) *(G-1241)*

Wooster Community Hospital, Wooster *Also called City of Wooster (G-19705)*

Wooster Country Club Inc 330 263-1890
  1251 Oak Hill Rd Wooster (44691) *(G-19785)*

Wooster Division Fire, Wooster *Also called City of Wooster (G-19704)*

Wooster Motor Ways Inc (PA) 330 264-9557
  3501 W Old Lincoln Way Wooster (44691) *(G-19786)*

Wooster Ophthalmologists Inc 330 345-7800
  3519 Friendsville Rd Wooster (44691) *(G-19787)*

Work Connections Intl LLC 419 448-4655
  525 Wall St Ste A Tiffin (44883) *(G-17547)*

Work Leads To Independence, Bowling Green *Also called Lane Wood Industries (G-1739)*

Work Solutions Group LLC 440 205-8297
  8324 Tyler Blvd Mentor (44060) *(G-14126)*

Work Tech, Akron *Also called Community Support Services Inc (G-154)*

Workers Compensation Ohio Bur 800 644-6292
  30 W Spring St Columbus (43215) *(G-8916)*

Workers Compensation Ohio Bur (HQ) 800 644-6292
  30 W Spring St Fl 2-29 Columbus (43215) *(G-8917)*

Workforce Initiative Assn (PA) 330 433-9675
  822 30th St Nw Canton (44709) *(G-2537)*

Workforce One, Hamilton *Also called Butler County of Ohio (G-11563)*

Workforce Services Inc (PA) 330 484-2566
  6245 Sherman Ch Ave Sw Canton (44706) *(G-2538)*

Working Community Services, Columbus *Also called Goodwill Inds Centl Ohio Inc (G-7680)*

Workshops of David T Smith 513 932-2472
  3600 Shawhan Rd Morrow (45152) *(G-14718)*

Workshops, The, Canton *Also called Stark County Board of Developm (G-2490)*

Workspeed Management LLC 917 369-9025
  28925 Fountain Pkwy Solon (44139) *(G-16917)*

World Auto Parts Inc 216 781-8418
  1240 Carnegie Ave Cleveland (44115) *(G-6689)*

World Ex Shipg Trnsp Fwdg Svcs (PA) 440 826-5055
  17851 Jefferson Park Rd Middleburg Heights (44130) *(G-14266)*

World Harvest Church (PA) 614 837-1990
  4595 Gender Rd Canal Winchester (43110) *(G-2128)*

World Shipping Inc (PA) 440 356-7676
  1340 Depot St Ste 200 Cleveland (44116) *(G-6690)*

World Tableware Inc (HQ) 419 325-2608
  300 Madison Ave Fl 4 Toledo (43604) *(G-18161)*

World Trck Towing Recovery Inc 330 723-1116
  4970 Park Ave W Seville (44273) *(G-16693)*

World Wide Travel Service, Cincinnati *Also called AAA Allied Group Inc (G-2894)*

World Wide Travel Service, Sidney *Also called AAA Shelby County Motor Club (G-16756)*

Worldpay Inc (PA) 513 900-5250
  8500 Governors Hill Dr Symmes Twp (45249) *(G-17467)*

Worldpay LLC (HQ) 877 713-5964
  8500 Governors Hill Dr Symmes Twp (45249) *(G-17468)*

Worlds of Worthington, Worthington *Also called Laurel Health Care Company (G-19821)*

Worly Plumbing Supply Inc (PA) 614 445-1000
  400 Greenlawn Ave Columbus (43223) *(G-8918)*

Worthington Industries Inc 513 539-9291
  350 Lawton Ave Monroe (45050) *(G-14587)*

Worthington Inn, The, Worthington *Also called Epiqurian Inns (G-19807)*

Worthington Public Library 614 807-2626
  820 High St Worthington (43085) *(G-19862)*

WORTHINGTON SWIMMING POOL, Worthington *Also called Swim Incorporated (G-19855)*

Worthlington Dental Group, Worthington *Also called Association of Prosthodontics (G-19794)*

Worthngton Stelpac Systems LLC (HQ) 614 438-3205
  1205 Dearborn Dr Columbus (43085) *(G-8919)*

Wosu Am-FM TV, Columbus *Also called Ohio State University (G-8312)*

Woub Channel 20 & 44, Athens *Also called Ohio University (G-797)*

Woub Public Media, Athens *Also called Ohio University (G-796)*

Wph Cincinnati LLC 513 771-2080
  11320 Chester Rd Cincinnati (45246) *(G-4806)*

Wpmi Inc 440 392-2171
  9325 Progress Pkwy Mentor (44060) *(G-14127)*

Wqio 93q Request 740 392-9370
  17421 Coshocton Rd Mount Vernon (43050) *(G-14793)*

Wqkt/Wkvx, Wooster *Also called Wwst Corporation LLC (G-19788)*

Wqmx 94.9 FM, Akron *Also called Rubber City Radio Group (G-412)*

Wqmx Love Fund 330 869-9800
  1795 W Market St Akron (44313) *(G-504)*

WRAAA, Cleveland *Also called Western Reserve Area Agency (G-6673)*

Wrench Ltd Company (PA) 740 654-5304
  4805 Scooby Ln Carroll (43112) *(G-2559)*

A
L
P
H
A
B
E
T
I
C

Wright Brothers Inc (PA) 513 731-2222
  1930 Losantiville Ave Cincinnati (45237) *(G-4807)*
Wright Brothers Aero Inc 937 454-8475
  3700 Mccall St Dayton (45417) *(G-9887)*
Wright Brothers Aero Inc (PA) 937 890-8900
  3700 Mccauley Dr Ste C Vandalia (45377) *(G-18550)*
Wright Center 216 382-1868
  1611 S Green Rd Ste 124 Cleveland (44121) *(G-6691)*
Wright Distribution Ctrs Inc 419 227-7621
  1000 E Hanthorn Rd Lima (45804) *(G-12785)*
Wright Executive Ht Ltd Partnr 937 283-3200
  123 Gano Rd Wilmington (45177) *(G-19656)*
Wright Executive Ht Ltd Partnr (PA) 937 426-7800
  2800 Presidential Dr Beavercreek (45324) *(G-1196)*
Wright Executive Ht Ltd Partnr 937 429-0600
  2750 Presidential Dr Beavercreek (45324) *(G-1197)*
Wright Harvey House, The, Northwood *Also called Sattlerpearson Inc (G-15406)*
Wright Material Solutions Ltd 614 530-6999
  55 N Green St Columbus (43222) *(G-8920)*
Wright Patterson Afb Lodging, Dayton *Also called Army & Air Force Exchange Svc (G-9160)*
Wright State Physcans Drmtlogy (PA) 937 224-7546
  725 University Blvd Beavercreek (45324) *(G-1198)*
Wright State University 937 775-4070
  3640 Colonel Glenn Hwy Dayton (45435) *(G-9192)*
Wright State University 937 298-4331
  3525 Southern Blvd Kettering (45429) *(G-12304)*
Wright State University 937 775-3333
  3640 Colonel Glenn Hwy Beavercreek (45324) *(G-1199)*
Wright Surgery Center, Cleveland *Also called Wright Center (G-6691)*
Wright-Patt Credit Union Inc (PA) 937 912-7000
  3560 Pentagon Blvd Beavercreek (45431) *(G-1200)*
Wrightway Fd Svc Rest Sup Inc 419 222-7911
  3255 Saint Johns Rd Lima (45804) *(G-12786)*
Wrkz, Columbus *Also called North American Broadcasting (G-8196)*
Wrl Advertising, Canton *Also called Wern-Rausch Locke Advertising (G-2533)*
Wrwk 1065 .... 419 725-5700
  3225 Arlington Ave Toledo (43614) *(G-18162)*
Wryneck Development LLC 419 354-2535
  1553 Muirfield Dr Bowling Green (43402) *(G-1760)*
Ws One Investment Usa LLC (PA) 855 895-3728
  1263 S Chillicothe Rd Aurora (44202) *(G-852)*
Ws1, Aurora *Also called Ws One Investment Usa LLC (G-852)*
Wsb Rehabilitation Svcs Inc 330 847-7819
  4329 Mahoning Ave Nw B Warren (44483) *(G-18774)*
Wsb Rehabilitation Svcs Inc (PA) 330 533-1338
  510 W Main St Ste B Canfield (44406) *(G-2165)*
Wsny FM, Columbus *Also called Franklin Communications Inc (G-7614)*
Wsny Radio Station, Columbus *Also called Saga Communications Neng Inc (G-8580)*
Wsos Child Development Program 419 334-8511
  765 S Buchanan St Fremont (43420) *(G-11107)*
Wss- Dayton, Moraine *Also called Winsupply Inc (G-14707)*
Wssr Cpas, Chillicothe *Also called Whited Seigneur Sams & Rahe (G-2837)*
Wsyx and ABC 6, Columbus *Also called Sinclair Media II Inc (G-8647)*
Wta Consulting, Maumee *Also called Warnock Tanner & Assoc Inc (G-13867)*
Wtb Inc 216 298-1895
  815 Superior Ave E Cleveland (44114) *(G-6692)*
Wtol, Toledo *Also called Tegna Inc (G-18061)*
Wtov TV 9, Mingo Junction *Also called Sunrise Television Corp (G-14530)*
Wtvg-TV, Toledo *Also called Gray Television Group Inc (G-17768)*
Wtw Delaware Holdings LLC 216 937-4000
  1001 Lakeside Ave E Cleveland (44114) *(G-6693)*
Wulco Inc (PA) 513 679-2600
  6899 Steger Dr Ste A Cincinnati (45237) *(G-4808)*
Wulff & Associates CPA LLC (PA) 513 245-1010
  5554 Cheviot Rd G Cincinnati (45247) *(G-4809)*
Wunderlich Securities Inc 440 646-1400
  5885 Landerbrook Dr # 304 Cleveland (44124) *(G-6694)*
Wupw LLC 419 244-3600
  730 N Summit St Toledo (43604) *(G-18163)*
Wurtec Incorporated (PA) 419 726-1066
  6200 Brent Dr Toledo (43611) *(G-18164)*
Wviz/Pbs Hd, Cleveland *Also called Ideastream (G-5734)*
Wvno-FM, Ontario *Also called Johnny Appleseed Broadcasting (G-15556)*
Wvxu Radio, Cincinnati *Also called Xavier University (G-4810)*
Ww CD Radio, Columbus *Also called Ingleside Investments Inc (G-7818)*
WW Grainger Inc 513 563-7100
  4420 Glendale Milford Rd Blue Ash (45242) *(G-1683)*
WW Grainger Inc 614 276-5231
  3640 Interchange Rd Columbus (43204) *(G-8921)*
WW Grainger Inc 330 425-8387
  8211 Bavaria Rd Macedonia (44056) *(G-13090)*
WW&r, Cleveland *Also called Weltman Weinberg & Reis Co Lpa (G-6663)*
Wwcd, Columbus *Also called Cd1025 (G-7145)*
Wwho TV, Columbus *Also called Sinclair Media II Inc (G-8646)*
Wwst Corporation LLC 330 264-5122
  186 S Hillcrest Dr Wooster (44691) *(G-19788)*
Www.logicsoftusa.com, Dublin *Also called Logic Soft Inc (G-10274)*
Wxeg-FM, Dayton *Also called Iheartcommunications Inc (G-9512)*

Wxkr, Toledo *Also called Cumulus Media Inc (G-17690)*
Wyandot County AG Soc 419 294-4320
  10171 State Highway 53 N Upper Sandusky (43351) *(G-18415)*
Wyandot County Fair, Upper Sandusky *Also called Wyandot County AG Soc (G-18415)*
Wyandot County Home, Upper Sandusky *Also called County of Wyandot (G-18404)*
Wyandot Memorial Hospital 419 294-4991
  885 N Sandusky Ave Upper Sandusky (43351) *(G-18416)*
Wyandot Tractor & Implement Co 419 294-2349
  10264 County Highway 121 Upper Sandusky (43351) *(G-18417)*
Wyandotte Athletic Club 614 861-6303
  5198 Riding Club Ln Columbus (43213) *(G-8922)*
Wyant Leasing Co LLC 330 836-7953
  200 Wyant Rd Akron (44313) *(G-505)*
Wyant Woods Care Center, Akron *Also called Healthcare Facility MGT LLC (G-258)*
Wyant Woods Care Center, Akron *Also called Wyant Leasing Co LLC (G-505)*
Wyfm FM, Youngstown *Also called Cumulus Broadcasting LLC (G-20012)*
Wyle Laboratories Inc 937 912-3470
  2601 Mission Point Blvd # 300 Beavercreek (45431) *(G-1201)*
Wyle Laboratories Inc 937 320-2712
  2700 Indian Ripple Rd Beavercreek (45440) *(G-1242)*
Wyler, Jeff, Dealer Group, Cincinnati *Also called Jeff Wyler Automotive Fmly Inc (G-2855)*
Wyndham International Inc 330 666-9300
  200 Montrose West Ave Copley (44321) *(G-8980)*
Wynn-Reeth Inc 419 639-2094
  137 S Broadway St Green Springs (44836) *(G-11357)*
Wyoming Family Practice Center, Cincinnati *Also called University Family Physicians (G-4701)*
Wyse Advertising Inc (PA) 216 696-2424
  668 Euclid Ave Ste 100 Cleveland (44114) *(G-6695)*
Wz Management Inc 330 628-4881
  3417 E Waterloo Rd Akron (44312) *(G-506)*
Wzak, Cleveland *Also called Urban One Inc (G-6607)*
Wzoo-FM, Ashtabula *Also called Ashtabula Broadcasting Station (G-706)*
Wzrx 419 223-2060
  667 W Market St Lima (45801) *(G-12787)*
X F Construction Svcs Inc 614 575-2700
  1120 Claycraft Rd Columbus (43230) *(G-8923)*
X F Petroleum Equipment, Columbus *Also called X F Construction Svcs Inc (G-8923)*
X-Ray Industries Inc 216 642-0100
  5403 E Schaaf Rd Cleveland (44131) *(G-6696)*
X-S Merchandise Inc (PA) 216 524-5620
  7000 Granger Rd Ste 2 Independence (44131) *(G-12142)*
XA Technologies LLC 330 787-7846
  22 Early Rd Youngstown (44505) *(G-20250)*
Xact, Xenia *Also called Xenia Area Cmnty Theater Inc (G-19935)*
Xavier University 513 745-3335
  3800 Victory Pkwy Unit 1 Cincinnati (45207) *(G-4810)*
Xenia Area Cmnty Theater Inc 937 372-0516
  45 E 2nd St Xenia (45385) *(G-19935)*
Xenia East Management Systems 937 372-4495
  1301 N Monroe Dr Xenia (45385) *(G-19936)*
Xenia Waster Water, Xenia *Also called City of Xenia (G-19893)*
Xenia West Management Systems 937 372-8081
  1384 N Monroe Dr Xenia (45385) *(G-19937)*
Xerox Corporation 740 592-5609
  35 Elliott St Athens (45701) *(G-812)*
Xerox Corporation 419 418-6500
  600 Jefferson Ave Ste 200 Toledo (43604) *(G-18165)*
Xerox Corporation 216 642-7806
  6000 Fredom Sq Dr Ste 100 Cleveland (44131) *(G-6697)*
Xerox Corporation 513 554-3200
  10560 Ashview Pl Blue Ash (45242) *(G-1684)*
Xigent Automation Systems Inc 740 548-3700
  8303 Green Meadows Dr N Lewis Center (43035) *(G-12567)*
Xo Communications LLC 216 619-3200
  3 Summit Park Dr Ste 250 Cleveland (44131) *(G-6698)*
Xpedx, Cleveland *Also called Veritiv Operating Company (G-6623)*
Xpo Cnw Inc 440 716-8971
  5498 Dorothy Dr North Olmsted (44070) *(G-15317)*
Xpo Intermodal Inc (HQ) 614 923-1400
  5165 Emerald Pkwy 300 Dublin (43017) *(G-10377)*
Xpo Intermodal Solutions Inc (HQ) 614 923-1400
  5165 Emerald Pkwy Dublin (43017) *(G-10378)*
Xpo Logistics, Obetz *Also called Jacobson Warehouse Company Inc (G-15527)*
Xpo Logistics, Groveport *Also called Jacobson Warehouse Company Inc (G-11523)*
Xpo Logistics, Groveport *Also called Jacobson Warehouse Company Inc (G-11524)*
Xpo Logistics Freight Inc 513 870-0044
  5289 Duff Dr West Chester (45246) *(G-19100)*
Xpo Logistics Freight Inc 614 876-7100
  2625 Westbelt Dr Columbus (43228) *(G-8924)*
Xpo Logistics Freight Inc 937 898-9808
  3410 Stop 8 Rd Dayton (45414) *(G-9888)*
Xpo Logistics Freight Inc 419 499-8888
  12518 State Route 250 Milan (44846) *(G-14368)*
Xpo Logistics Freight Inc 216 433-1000
  12901 Snow Rd Parma (44130) *(G-15780)*
Xpo Logistics Freight Inc 740 894-3859
  96 Private Drive 339 South Point (45680) *(G-16947)*
Xpo Logistics Freight Inc 330 824-2242
  6700 Muth Rd Sw Warren (44481) *(G-18775)*

Xpo Logistics Freight Inc......................................419 294-5728
1850 E Wyandot Ave Upper Sandusky (43351) *(G-18418)*

Xpo Logistics Freight Inc......................................419 666-3022
28291 Glenwood Rd Perrysburg (43551) *(G-15937)*

Xpo Logistics Freight Inc......................................937 364-2361
5215 Us Route 50 Hillsboro (45133) *(G-11856)*

Xpo Logistics Freight Inc......................................740 922-5614
2401 N Water Street Ext Uhrichsville (44683) *(G-18349)*

Xpo Logistics Freight Inc......................................330 896-7300
3733 Massillon Rd Uniontown (44685) *(G-18391)*

Xpo Logistics Freight Inc......................................937 492-3899
2021 Campbell Rd Sidney (45365) *(G-16806)*

Xpo Stacktrain LLC..614 923-1400
5165 Emerald Pkwy Dublin (43017) *(G-10379)*

Xpress Loan Servicing, Cleveland *Also called Education Loan Servicing Corp* *(G-5467)*

Xri Testing, Cleveland *Also called X-Ray Industries Inc* *(G-6696)*

Xto Energy Inc...740 671-9901
2358 W 23rd St Bellaire (43906) *(G-1337)*

Xtreme Contracting Ltd.......................................614 568-7030
7600 Asden Ct Reynoldsburg (43068) *(G-16341)*

Xzamcorp..330 629-2218
4119 Logans Way Perry (44081) *(G-15830)*

Y & E Entertainment Group LLC...............................440 385-5500
8303 Day Dr Parma (44129) *(G-15781)*

Y M C A, Cincinnati *Also called Young Mens Christian Associat* *(G-4813)*

Y M C A, Circleville *Also called Young Mens Christian Assoc* *(G-4854)*

Y M C A, Middletown *Also called Ucc Childrens Center* *(G-14356)*

Y M C A, Versailles *Also called County of Darke* *(G-18568)*

Y M C A, Shelby *Also called Young Mens Christn Assn Shelby* *(G-16751)*

Y M C A, Toledo *Also called Young Mens Christian Associat* *(G-18170)*

Y M C A Central Stark County................................330 305-5437
200 Charlotte St Nw Canton (44720) *(G-2539)*

Y M C A Central Stark County................................330 875-1611
1421 S Nickelplate St Louisville (44641) *(G-12975)*

Y M C A Central Stark County................................330 877-8933
11928 King Church Ave Nw Uniontown (44685) *(G-18392)*

Y M C A Central Stark County................................330 830-6275
7389 Caritas Cir Nw Massillon (44646) *(G-13736)*

Y M C A Central Stark County................................330 498-4082
7241 Whipple Ave Nw Canton (44720) *(G-2540)*

Y M C A of Ashland Ohio Inc.................................419 289-0626
207 Miller St Ashland (44805) *(G-700)*

Y M C A-Head Start, East Liverpool *Also called Community Action Columbiana CT* *(G-10400)*

Y Town Realty Inc...330 743-8844
1641 5th Ave Youngstown (44504) *(G-20251)*

Y W C A, Hamilton *Also called YWCA of Hamilton* *(G-11655)*

Yanfeng US Automotive.......................................419 662-4905
7560 Arbor Dr Northwood (43619) *(G-15416)*

Yankee Run Golf Course......................................330 448-8096
7610 Warren Sharon Rd Brookfield (44403) *(G-1858)*

Yardmaster Inc (PA)...440 357-8400
1447 N Ridge Rd Painesville (44077) *(G-15749)*

Yardmaster of Columbus Inc..................................614 863-4510
570 Rynldsburg New Albany Blacklick (43004) *(G-1485)*

Yark Automotive Group Inc (PA)..............................419 841-7771
6019 W Central Ave Toledo (43615) *(G-18166)*

Yark Subaru, Toledo *Also called Yark Automotive Group Inc* *(G-18166)*

Yashco Systems Inc..614 467-4600
3974 Brown Park Dr Hilliard (43026) *(G-11831)*

Yearwood Corporation (PA)...................................937 223-3572
125 E 2nd St Dayton (45402) *(G-9889)*

Yeater Alene K MD...740 348-4694
15 Messimer Dr Newark (43055) *(G-15112)*

Yeck Brothers Company.......................................937 294-4000
2222 Arbor Blvd Moraine (45439) *(G-14708)*

Yellow Cabs, Columbus *Also called Columbus Green Cabs Inc* *(G-7284)*

Yellow Transportation, West Chester *Also called Yrc Inc* *(G-19101)*

Yellow Transportation, Richfield *Also called Yrc Inc* *(G-16385)*

Yellow Transportation, Columbus *Also called Yrc Inc* *(G-8933)*

Yerman & Young Painting Inc.................................330 861-0022
811 Brady Ave Barberton (44203) *(G-973)*

YMCA, Lockbourne *Also called Young Mens Christian Assoc* *(G-12826)*

YMCA, Mansfield *Also called Frans Child Care-Mansfield* *(G-13178)*

YMCA, Fremont *Also called Young Mens Christian Assn* *(G-11108)*

YMCA, Columbus *Also called Young Mens Christian Assoc* *(G-8927)*

YMCA, Akron *Also called Young Mens Christian Assoc* *(G-508)*

YMCA, Ashland *Also called Y M C A of Ashland Ohio Inc* *(G-700)*

YMCA, Gahanna *Also called Young Mens Christian Assoc* *(G-11152)*

YMCA, Hilliard *Also called Young Mens Christian Assoc* *(G-11832)*

YMCA, Van Wert *Also called Young Mens Christian Assn* *(G-18498)*

YMCA, Columbus *Also called Young Mens Christian Assoc* *(G-8929)*

YMCA, Uniontown *Also called Y M C A Central Stark County* *(G-18392)*

YMCA, Chardon *Also called Young Mns Christian Assn Clveland* *(G-2726)*

YMCA, Mount Vernon *Also called Young Mens Christian Mt Vernon* *(G-14794)*

YMCA, Columbus *Also called Young Mens Christian Assoc* *(G-8930)*

YMCA..330 823-1930
205 S Union Ave Alliance (44601) *(G-558)*

YMCA..937 653-9622
191 Community Dr Urbana (43078) *(G-18447)*

YMCA Camp Campbell Gard, Hamilton *Also called Great Miami Valley YMCA* *(G-11603)*

YMCA Child Care, Canton *Also called Y M C A Central Stark County* *(G-2539)*

YMCA Crayon Club Chld Care, Dayton *Also called Young Mens Christian Assoc* *(G-9895)*

YMCA Cuyahoga Falls Branch, Cuyahoga Falls *Also called Young Mens Christian Assoc* *(G-9141)*

YMCA of Ashtabula County Inc................................440 997-5321
263 W Prospect Rd Ashtabula (44004) *(G-760)*

YMCA of Clermont County Inc.................................513 724-9622
2075 James E Sauls Sr Dr Batavia (45103) *(G-1016)*

YMCA of Findlay, Findlay *Also called Young MNS Christn Assn Findlay* *(G-10977)*

YMCA of Greater Dayton, Dayton *Also called Young Mens Christian Assoc* *(G-9892)*

YMCA of Greater Toledo, Toledo *Also called Young Mens Christian Assoc* *(G-18167)*

YMCA of Greater Toledo, Perrysburg *Also called Young Mens Christian Associat* *(G-15938)*

YMCA of Massillon (PA)......................................330 837-5116
131 Tremont Ave Se Massillon (44646) *(G-13737)*

YMCA of Massillon...330 879-0800
1226 Market St Ne Navarre (44662) *(G-14826)*

YMCA of Sandusky Ohio Inc...................................419 621-9622
2101 W Perkins Ave Sandusky (44870) *(G-16657)*

YMCA OF THE USA, Wooster *Also called Young Mens Christian Assoc* *(G-19789)*

YMCA OF WESTERN STARK COUNTY, Massillon *Also called YMCA of Massillon* *(G-13737)*

YMCA of Youngstown, Youngstown *Also called Young Mens Christian Assn* *(G-20253)*

YMCA West Park, Cleveland *Also called Young MNS Chrstn Assn Clveland* *(G-6702)*

Ymca/M.e.lions, Cincinnati *Also called Young Mens Christian Associat* *(G-4814)*

YNDC, Youngstown *Also called Youngstown Neighborhood Dev* *(G-20263)*

Yockey Group Inc..513 899-2188
6344 E Us Hwy 22 And 3 Morrow (45152) *(G-14719)*

Yocum Realty Company..419 222-3040
421 S Cable Rd Lima (45805) *(G-12788)*

Yoder Drilling and Geothermal...............................330 852-4342
997 State Route 93 Nw Sugarcreek (44681) *(G-17381)*

Yoder Industries Inc (PA)...................................937 278-5769
2520 Needmore Rd Dayton (45414) *(G-9890)*

Yoder Machinery Sales Company...............................419 865-5555
1500 Holloway Rd Holland (43528) *(G-11927)*

Yoder Trading Company, Barberton *Also called Aris Horticulture Inc* *(G-942)*

York Building Maintenance Inc...............................216 398-8100
4748 Broadview Rd Cleveland (44109) *(G-6699)*

York Golf Club, Columbus *Also called York Temple Country Club Inc* *(G-8925)*

York Risk Services Group Inc................................866 391-9675
5555 Glendon Ct Dublin (43016) *(G-10380)*

York Risk Services Group Inc................................440 863-2500
16560 Commerce Ct Ste 100 Cleveland (44130) *(G-6700)*

York Rite...216 751-1417
13512 Kinsman Rd Cleveland (44120) *(G-6701)*

York Temple Country Club Inc................................614 885-5459
7459 N High St Columbus (43235) *(G-8925)*

York-Mahoning Mech Contrs Inc...............................330 788-7011
724 Canfield Rd Youngstown (44511) *(G-20252)*

Yorkland Health Care Inc....................................614 751-2525
1425 Yorkland Rd Columbus (43232) *(G-8926)*

Yorkland Park Care Center, Columbus *Also called Yorkland Health Care Inc* *(G-8926)*

Young & Alexander Co Lpa (PA)...............................937 224-9291
130 W 2nd St Ste 1500 Dayton (45402) *(G-9891)*

Young & Bertke Air Systems, Cincinnati *Also called Pcy Enterprises Inc* *(G-4219)*

Young & Rubicam Inc...513 419-2300
110 Shillito Pl Cincinnati (45202) *(G-4811)*

Young and Associates Inc....................................330 678-0524
121 E Main St Kent (44240) *(G-12270)*

Young Chemical Co LLC (HQ)..................................330 486-4210
1755 Entp Pkwy Ste 400 Twinsburg (44087) *(G-18338)*

Young Medical, Maumee *Also called Apria Healthcare LLC* *(G-13758)*

Young Medical Services, Maumee *Also called Toledo Medical Equipment Co* *(G-13862)*

Young Mens Christian..513 932-1424
1699 Deerfield Rd Lebanon (45036) *(G-12516)*

Young Mens Christian Assn, Mount Vernon *Also called Young MNS Chrstn Assn Grter NY* *(G-14795)*

Young Mens Christian Assn...................................419 332-9622
1000 North St Fremont (43420) *(G-11108)*

Young Mens Christian Assn (PA)..............................330 744-8411
17 N Champion St Youngstown (44503) *(G-20253)*

Young Mens Christian Assn...................................740 373-2250
300 N 7th St Marietta (45750) *(G-13402)*

Young Mens Christian Assn...................................419 238-0443
241 W Main St Van Wert (45891) *(G-18498)*

Young Mens Christian Assoc..................................614 491-0980
1570 Rohr Rd Lockbourne (43137) *(G-12826)*

Young Mens Christian Assoc (PA).............................419 729-8135
1500 N Superior St Fl 2 Toledo (43604) *(G-18167)*

Young Mens Christian Assoc..................................614 871-9622
3600 Discovery Dr Grove City (43123) *(G-11491)*

Young Mens Christian Assoc (PA).............................937 223-5201
118 W 1st St Ste 300 Dayton (45402) *(G-9892)*

Young Mens Christian Assoc..................................330 923-5223
544 Broad Blvd Cuyahoga Falls (44221) *(G-9141)*

Young Mens Christian Assoc 330 467-8366
8761 Shepard Rd Macedonia (44056) *(G-13091)*

Young Mens Christian Assoc 330 264-3131
680 Woodland Ave Wooster (44691) *(G-19789)*

Young Mens Christian Assoc 330 784-0408
888 Jonathan Ave Akron (44306) *(G-507)*

Young Mens Christian Assoc 740 477-1661
440 Nicholas Dr Circleville (43113) *(G-4854)*

Young Mens Christian Assoc 614 885-4252
1640 Sandalwood Pl Columbus (43229) *(G-8927)*

Young Mens Christian Assoc 330 724-1255
350 E Wilbeth Rd Akron (44301) *(G-508)*

Young Mens Christian Assoc 330 376-1335
80 W Center St Akron (44308) *(G-509)*

Young Mens Christian Assoc 614 416-9622
555 Ymca Pl Gahanna (43230) *(G-11152)*

Young Mens Christian Assoc 614 334-9622
4515 Cosgray Rd Hilliard (43026) *(G-11832)*

Young Mens Christian Assoc 937 312-1810
4545 Marshall Rd Dayton (45429) *(G-9893)*

Young Mens Christian Assoc 614 539-1770
3500 1st Ave Urbancrest (43123) *(G-18453)*

Young Mens Christian Assoc 614 276-8224
2879 Valleyview Dr Columbus (43204) *(G-8928)*

Young Mens Christian Assoc 513 932-3756
5291 State Route 350 Oregonia (45054) *(G-15618)*

Young Mens Christian Assoc 614 252-3166
130 Woodland Ave Columbus (43203) *(G-8929)*

Young Mens Christian Assoc 937 426-9622
111 W 1st St Ste 207 Dayton (45402) *(G-9894)*

Young Mens Christian Assoc 937 836-9622
1200 W National Rd Englewood (45315) *(G-10606)*

Young Mens Christian Assoc 419 523-5233
101 Putnam Pkwy Ottawa (45875) *(G-15667)*

Young Mens Christian Assoc 937 228-9622
316 N Wilkinson St Dayton (45402) *(G-9895)*

Young Mens Christian Assoc 937 223-5201
88 Remick Blvd Springboro (45066) *(G-16990)*

Young Mens Christian Assoc 614 878-7269
600 Fox Ridge St Columbus (43228) *(G-8930)*

Young Mens Christian Assoc 937 593-9001
2732 County Road 11 Bellefontaine (43311) *(G-1370)*

Young Mens Christian Assoc 614 834-9622
6767 Refugee Rd Canal Winchester (43110) *(G-2129)*

Young Mens Christian Associat 419 475-3496
2110 Tremainsville Rd Toledo (43613) *(G-18168)*

Young Mens Christian Associat 419 794-7304
716 Askin St Maumee (43537) *(G-13870)*

Young Mens Christian Associat 513 521-7112
9601 Winton Rd Cincinnati (45231) *(G-4812)*

Young Mens Christian Associat 419 251-9622
13415 Eckel Junction Rd Perrysburg (43551) *(G-15938)*

Young Mens Christian Associat 513 731-0115
2039 Sherman Ave Cincinnati (45212) *(G-4813)*

Young Mens Christian Associat 513 791-5000
5000 Ymca Dr Blue Ash (45242) *(G-1685)*

Young Mens Christian Associat 513 474-1400
8108 Clough Pike Fl 1 Cincinnati (45244) *(G-4814)*

Young Mens Christian Associat 513 241-9622
1425b Linn St Cincinnati (45214) *(G-4815)*

Young Mens Christian Associat 513 923-4466
8920 Cheviot Rd Cincinnati (45251) *(G-4816)*

Young Mens Christian Associat 419 474-3995
1500 N Superior St Fl 2 Toledo (43604) *(G-18169)*

Young Mens Christian Associat 419 866-9622
2100 S Hlland Sylvania Rd Maumee (43537) *(G-13871)*

Young Mens Christian Associat 419 475-3496
2020 Tremainsville Rd Toledo (43613) *(G-18170)*

Young Mens Christian Associat 419 691-3523
2960 Pickle Rd Oregon (43616) *(G-15615)*

Young Mens Christian Mt Vernon 740 392-9622
103 N Main St Mount Vernon (43050) *(G-14794)*

Young Mens Christn Assn Shelby 419 347-1312
111 W Smiley Ave Shelby (44875) *(G-16751)*

Young Mens Christn Assosiation, Fairborn Also called Fairborn YMCA *(G-10674)*

Young MNS Christn Assn Findlay (PA) 419 422-4424
300 E Lincoln St Findlay (45840) *(G-10977)*

Young MNS Chrstn Assn Clveland 216 521-8400
16915 Detroit Ave Lakewood (44107) *(G-12364)*

Young MNS Chrstn Assn Clveland 216 941-4654
15501 Lorain Ave Cleveland (44111) *(G-6702)*

Young MNS Chrstn Assn Clveland 216 731-7454
631 Babbitt Rd Cleveland (44123) *(G-6703)*

Young MNS Chrstn Assn Clveland 216 382-4300
5000 Mayfield Rd Cleveland (44124) *(G-6704)*

Young MNS Chrstn Assn Clveland 440 285-7543
12460 Bass Lake Rd Chardon (44024) *(G-2726)*

Young MNS Chrstn Assn Clveland 440 808-8150
1575 Columbia Rd Westlake (44145) *(G-19426)*

Young MNS Chrstn Assn Grter NY 740 392-9622
103 N Main St Mount Vernon (43050) *(G-14795)*

Young Services Inc (PA) 419 704-2009
806 Starr Ave Toledo (43605) *(G-18171)*

Young Truck Sales Inc (PA) 330 477-6271
4970 Southway St Sw Canton (44706) *(G-2541)*

Young Wns Christn Assn Canton (PA) 330 453-7644
231 6th St Ne Canton (44702) *(G-2542)*

Young Womens Christian 419 241-3235
1018 Jefferson Ave Toledo (43604) *(G-18172)*

Young Womens Christian 419 238-6639
408 E Main St Van Wert (45891) *(G-18499)*

Young Womens Christian Assn (PA) 614 224-9121
65 S 4th St Columbus (43215) *(G-8931)*

Young Womens Christian Associ (PA) 216 881-6878
4019 Prospect Ave Cleveland (44103) *(G-6705)*

Young Womns Chrstn Assc Canton 330 453-0789
1700 Gateway Blvd Se Canton (44707) *(G-2543)*

Young Womns Chrstn Assc Lima 419 241-3230
1018 Jefferson Ave Toledo (43604) *(G-18173)*

Youngs Jersey Dairy Inc 937 325-0629
6880 Springfield Xenia Rd Yellow Springs (45387) *(G-19941)*

Youngstown ARC Engraving Co 330 793-2471
380 Victoria Rd Youngstown (44515) *(G-20254)*

Youngstown Area Goodwill Inds (PA) 330 759-7921
2747 Belmont Ave Youngstown (44505) *(G-20255)*

Youngstown Area Jwish Fdration (PA) 330 746-3251
505 Gypsy Ln Youngstown (44504) *(G-20256)*

Youngstown Area Jwish Fdration 330 746-1076
517 Gypsy Ln Youngstown (44504) *(G-20257)*

Youngstown Automatic Door Co 330 747-3135
1223 Gibson St Youngstown (44502) *(G-20258)*

Youngstown Club 330 744-3111
201 E Commerce St Ste 400 Youngstown (44503) *(G-20259)*

Youngstown Committee On Alchol 330 744-1181
2151 Rush Blvd Youngstown (44507) *(G-20260)*

Youngstown Community Hlth Ctr, Youngstown Also called Ohio North E Hlth Systems Inc *(G-20146)*

Youngstown Country Club 330 759-1040
1402 Country Club Dr Youngstown (44505) *(G-20261)*

Youngstown Developmental Ctr, Columbus Also called Develpmntal Dsblties Ohio Dept *(G-7440)*

Youngstown Health Center, Youngstown Also called Planned Prenthood Greater Ohio *(G-20157)*

Youngstown Hearing Speech Ctr (PA) 330 726-8391
299 Edwards St Youngstown (44502) *(G-20262)*

Youngstown Lithographing Co, Youngstown Also called Youngstown ARC Engraving Co *(G-20254)*

Youngstown Neighborhood Dev 330 480-0423
820 Canfield Rd Youngstown (44511) *(G-20263)*

Youngstown Ohio Otpatient Svcs 330 884-2020
6426 Market St Youngstown (44512) *(G-20264)*

Youngstown Orthopaedic Assoc 330 726-1466
6470 Tippecanoe Rd Ste A Canfield (44406) *(G-2166)*

Youngstown Plastic Tooling (PA) 330 782-7222
1209 Velma Ct Youngstown (44512) *(G-20265)*

Youngstown Propane Inc (PA) 330 792-6571
810 N Meridian Rd Youngstown (44509) *(G-20266)*

Youngstown V A Otptient Clinic, Youngstown Also called Veterans Health Administration *(G-20236)*

Youngstown Water Dept, Youngstown Also called City of Youngstown *(G-19992)*

Youngstown Window Cleaning Co 330 743-3880
1057 Trumbull Ave Ste G Girard (44420) *(G-11306)*

Youngstown-Kenworth Inc (PA) 330 534-9761
7255 Hubbard Masury Rd Hubbard (44425) *(G-11952)*

Youngstown-Warren Reg Chamber (PA) 330 744-2131
11 Central Sq Ste 1600 Youngstown (44503) *(G-20267)*

Your Home Court Advantage LLC 330 364-6602
1243 Monroe St Nw New Philadelphia (44663) *(G-14990)*

Youth Advocate Services 614 258-9927
825 Grandview Ave Columbus (43215) *(G-8932)*

Youth Development Center, Cincinnati Also called Lighthouse Youth Services Inc *(G-3929)*

Youth Mntrng & At Rsk Intrvntn 216 324-2451
2092 Washington Dr Richmond Heights (44143) *(G-16396)*

Youth Opportunities Unlimited 216 566-5445
1361 Euclid Ave Cleveland (44115) *(G-6706)*

Youth Partial Hospitalization, Dayton Also called South Community Inc *(G-9775)*

Youth Services, Cleveland Also called County of Cuyahoga *(G-5371)*

Youth Services Ohio Department 419 875-6965
Township Rd 1 D U 469 Liberty Center (43532) *(G-12576)*

YOUTH TO YOUTH, Columbus Also called Compdrug *(G-7340)*

Yowell Transportation Svc Inc 937 294-5933
1840 Cardington Rd Moraine (45409) *(G-14709)*

Yp, Youngstown Also called Youngstown Propane Inc *(G-20266)*

Yrc Inc 513 874-9320
10074 Prncton Glendale Rd West Chester (45246) *(G-19101)*

Yrc Inc 330 659-4151
5250 Brecksville Rd Richfield (44286) *(G-16385)*

Yrc Inc 419 729-0631
4431 South Ave Toledo (43615) *(G-18174)*

Yrc Inc 330 665-0274
1275 Oh Ave Copley (44321) *(G-8981)*

Yrc Inc 614 878-9281
5400 Fisher Rd Columbus (43228) *(G-8933)*

Yrc Inc.....913 344-5174
1275 Oh Ave Copley (44321) *(G-8982)*
Yrc Ubc Cargo Claim Dept, Copley *Also called Yrc Inc (G-8982)*
Ysd Industries Inc.....330 792-6521
3710 Henricks Rd Youngstown (44515) *(G-20268)*
Yund Car Care Center, Massillon *Also called Yund Inc (G-13738)*
Yund Inc.....330 837-9358
205 1st St Nw Massillon (44647) *(G-13738)*
YWCA, Columbus *Also called Young Womens Christian Assn (G-8931)*
YWCA, Toledo *Also called Young Womns Chrstn Assc Lima (G-18173)*
YWCA, Van Wert *Also called Young Womens Christian (G-18499)*
YWCA Dayton.....937 461-5550
141 W 3rd St Dayton (45402) *(G-9896)*
YWCA Mahoning Valley.....330 746-6361
25 W Rayen Ave Youngstown (44503) *(G-20269)*
YWCA of Canton, Canton *Also called Young Wns Christn Assn Canton (G-2542)*
YWCA of Cleveland, Cleveland *Also called Young Womens Christian Associ (G-6705)*
YWCA of Greater Cincinnati (PA).....513 241-7090
898 Walnut St Fl 1 Cincinnati (45202) *(G-4817)*
YWCA of Hamilton.....513 856-9800
244 Dayton St Hamilton (45011) *(G-11655)*
YWCA Shelter & Housing Network.....937 222-6333
141 W 3rd St Dayton (45402) *(G-9897)*
Z A F Inc.....216 291-1234
2165 S Green Rd Cleveland (44121) *(G-6707)*
Z L B, Cleveland *Also called Csl Plasma Inc (G-5385)*
Z Produce Co Inc.....614 224-4373
720 Harmon Ave Columbus (43223) *(G-8934)*
Z Snow Removal Inc.....513 683-7719
8177 S State Route 48 Maineville (45039) *(G-13120)*
Z Wireless, Hartville *Also called Aka Wireless Inc (G-11682)*
Z-Bus, Zanesville *Also called Southeast Area Transit (G-20362)*
Zack Pack, Monroe *Also called Hcg Inc (G-14569)*
Zak Enterprises Ltd (PA).....216 261-9700
26250 Euclid Ave Ste 810 Euclid (44132) *(G-10661)*
Zamarelli William Relators, Warren *Also called William Zamarelli Realtors (G-18772)*
Zandex Inc.....740 695-3281
100 Reservoir Rd Ofc 2 Saint Clairsville (43950) *(G-16512)*
Zandex Inc.....740 676-8381
60583 State Route 7 Shadyside (43947) *(G-16700)*
Zandex Inc (PA).....740 454-1400
1122 Taylor St Zanesville (43701) *(G-20373)*
Zandex Inc.....740 452-2087
1126 Adair Ave Zanesville (43701) *(G-20374)*
Zandex Inc.....740 872-0809
1280 Friendship Dr New Concord (43762) *(G-14905)*
Zandex Inc.....740 454-9769
1856 Adams Ln Zanesville (43701) *(G-20375)*
Zandex Inc.....740 695-7233
100 Reservoir Rd Ofc 1 Saint Clairsville (43950) *(G-16513)*
Zandex Inc.....740 967-1111
267 N Main St Johnstown (43031) *(G-12205)*
Zandex Inc.....740 454-6823
1136 Adair Ave Zanesville (43701) *(G-20376)*
Zandex Health Care, Zanesville *Also called Zandex Inc (G-20373)*
Zandex Health Care Corporation.....740 452-4636
1136 Adair Ave Zanesville (43701) *(G-20377)*
Zandex Health Care Corporation.....740 454-9769
1856 Adams Ln Zanesville (43701) *(G-20378)*
Zandex Health Care Corporation.....740 695-7233
100 Reservoir Rd Saint Clairsville (43950) *(G-16514)*
Zandex Health Care Corporation (HQ).....740 454-1400
1122 Taylor St Zanesville (43701) *(G-20379)*
Zandex Health Care Corporation.....740 454-9747
1020 Taylor St Zanesville (43701) *(G-20380)*
Zandex Health Care Corporation.....740 454-1400
267 N Main St Johnstown (43031) *(G-12206)*
Zandex Health Care Corporation.....740 454-1400
1280 Friendship Dr New Concord (43762) *(G-14906)*
Zaner-Bloser Inc (HQ).....614 486-0221
1400 Goodale Blvd Ste 200 Columbus (43212) *(G-8935)*
Zanesville, Zanesville *Also called Cambridge Counseling Center (G-20287)*
Zanesville Bulk, Zanesville *Also called Englefield Inc (G-20305)*
Zanesville Chevrolet Cadillac.....740 452-3611
3657 Maple Ave Zanesville (43701) *(G-20381)*
Zanesville Country Club.....740 452-2726
1300 Country Club Dr Zanesville (43701) *(G-20382)*
Zanesville Dialysis, Zanesville *Also called Dva Renal Healthcare Inc (G-20302)*
ZANESVILLE HEALTH AND REHABILI, Zanesville *Also called Zanesville NH LLC (G-20384)*
Zanesville Metro Hsing Auth (PA).....740 454-9714
407 Pershing Rd Zanesville (43701) *(G-20383)*
Zanesville NH LLC.....740 452-4351
4200 Harrington Dr Zanesville (43701) *(G-20384)*
Zanesville Surgery Center LLC.....740 453-5713
2907 Bell St Zanesville (43701) *(G-20385)*
Zanesville Welfare Organizatio.....740 450-6060
3610 West Pike Zanesville (43701) *(G-20386)*
Zanesvlle Welfre Orgnztn/Goodw (PA).....740 450-6060
3610 West Pike Zanesville (43701) *(G-20387)*
Zarcal Zanesville LLC.....216 226-2132
14600 Detroit Ave # 1500 Lakewood (44107) *(G-12365)*
Zaremba Group Incorporated.....216 221-6600
14600 Detroit Ave # 1500 Cleveland (44107) *(G-6708)*
Zaremba Group LLC.....216 221-6600
14600 Detroit Ave Lakewood (44107) *(G-12366)*
Zaremba LLC.....216 221-6600
14600 Detroit Ave # 1500 Cleveland (44107) *(G-6709)*
Zaremba Zanesville LLC.....216 221-6600
14600 Detroit Ave # 1500 Lakewood (44107) *(G-12367)*
Zartran LLC.....513 870-4800
3035 Symmes Rd Hamilton (45015) *(G-11656)*
Zashin & Rich Co LPA (PA).....216 696-4441
950 Main Ave Fl 4 Cleveland (44113) *(G-6710)*
Zatkoff Seals & Packings, Twinsburg *Also called Roger Zatkoff Company (G-18313)*
Zavarella Brothers Cnstr Co.....440 232-2243
5381 Erie St Ste B Cleveland (44146) *(G-6711)*
Zebec of North America Inc.....513 829-5533
210 Donald Dr Fairfield (45014) *(G-10800)*
Zebo Productions.....937 339-0397
1875 Barnhart Rd Troy (45373) *(G-18240)*
Zebu Compliance Solutions LLC.....740 355-9029
609 2nd St Unit 2 Portsmouth (45662) *(G-16182)*
Zeiger Tigges & Little LLP.....614 365-9900
41 S High St Ste 3500 Columbus (43215) *(G-8936)*
Zeiter Leasing, Norwalk *Also called Zeiter Trucking Inc (G-15460)*
Zeiter Trucking Inc.....419 668-2229
2590 State Route 18 Norwalk (44857) *(G-15460)*
Zekelman Industries Inc.....740 432-2146
9208 Jeffrey Dr Cambridge (43725) *(G-2087)*
Zemba Bros Inc.....740 452-1880
3401 East Pike Zanesville (43701) *(G-20388)*
Zender Electric.....419 436-1538
966 Springville Ave Fostoria (44830) *(G-11015)*
Zenith Systems LLC (PA).....216 587-9510
5055 Corbin Dr Cleveland (44128) *(G-6712)*
Zep Inc.....440 239-1580
6777 Engle Rd Ste A Cleveland (44130) *(G-6713)*
Zepf Center.....419 255-4050
905 Nebraska Ave Toledo (43607) *(G-18175)*
Zepf Center (PA).....419 841-7701
6605 W Central Ave # 100 Toledo (43617) *(G-18176)*
Zepf Center.....419 213-5627
6605 W Central Ave # 100 Toledo (43617) *(G-18177)*
Zepf Center.....419 255-4050
525 Hamilton St Ste 101a Toledo (43604) *(G-18178)*
Zepf Center.....419 213-5627
1301 Monroe St Toledo (43604) *(G-18179)*
Zepf Housing Corp One Inc.....419 531-0019
5310 Hill Ave Toledo (43615) *(G-18180)*
Zicka Development, Cincinnati *Also called Zicka Walker Builders Ltd (G-4818)*
Zicka Walker Builders Ltd.....513 247-3500
7861 E Kemper Rd Cincinnati (45249) *(G-4818)*
Zide Screen Printing, Marietta *Also called Zide Sport Shop of Ohio Inc (G-13403)*
Zide Sport Shop of Ohio Inc (PA).....740 373-6446
253 2nd St Marietta (45750) *(G-13403)*
Ziebart, Fairborn *Also called Dave Marshall Inc (G-10668)*
Ziegler Bolt & Nut House, Canton *Also called Ziegler Bolt & Parts Co (G-2544)*
Ziegler Bolt & Parts Co (PA).....330 478-2542
4848 Corporate St Sw Canton (44706) *(G-2544)*
Ziegler Tire and Supply Co (PA).....330 353-1499
4150 Millennium Blvd Se Massillon (44646) *(G-13739)*
Ziggler Heating, Ashtabula *Also called Volpone Enterprises Inc (G-759)*
Ziks Family Pharmacy 100.....937 225-9350
1130 W 3rd St Dayton (45402) *(G-9898)*
Zimmer Enterprises Inc (PA).....937 428-1057
911 Senate Dr Dayton (45459) *(G-9899)*
Zimmer Ohio, Columbus *Also called S L Klabunde Corp (G-8570)*
Zin Technologies Inc (PA).....440 625-2200
6745 Engle Rd Ste 105 Middleburg Heights (44130) *(G-14267)*
Zincks In Berlin Inc (PA).....330 893-2071
4799 E Main St Berlin (44610) *(G-1447)*
Zincks Inn (PA).....330 893-6600
4703 State Rt 39 Berlin (44610) *(G-1448)*
Zink Calls.....419 732-6171
30 Park Dr Port Clinton (43452) *(G-16120)*
Zink Commercial, Columbus *Also called Zink Foodservice Group (G-8937)*
Zink Foodservice Group.....800 492-7400
655 Dearborn Park Ln C Columbus (43085) *(G-8937)*
Zinner & Co.....216 831-0733
3201 Entp Pkwy Ste 410 Beachwood (44122) *(G-1118)*
Zinz Cnstr & Restoration.....330 332-7939
6487 Mahoning Ave Youngstown (44515) *(G-20270)*
Zion Christian School.....330 792-4066
3300 Canfield Rd Youngstown (44511) *(G-20271)*
Zip Center, The-Division, Marietta *Also called Richardson Printing Corp (G-13377)*
Zipline Logistics LLC.....888 469-4754
2300 W 5th Ave Columbus (43215) *(G-8938)*
Zipscene LLC.....513 201-5174
615 Main St Fl 5 Cincinnati (45202) *(G-4819)*
Znm Wecare Corporation.....740 548-2022
7166 Gooding Blvd Delaware (43015) *(G-10018)*

ALPHABETIC

Zoff Heating & Plumbing, Akron *Also called A To Zoff Co Inc* *(G-12)*

Zone Transportation Co 440 324-3544
  41670 Schadden Rd Elyria (44035) *(G-10577)*

Zoological Society Cincinnati 513 281-4700
  3400 Vine St Cincinnati (45220) *(G-4820)*

Zucker Building Company 216 861-7114
  5915 Landerbrook Dr # 300 Cleveland (44124) *(G-6714)*

Zurich American Insurance Co 216 328-9400
  5005 Rockside Rd Ste 200 Independence (44131) *(G-12143)*

Zusman Community Hospice 614 559-0350
  1151 College Ave Columbus (43209) *(G-8939)*

Zvn Properties Inc 330 854-5890
  957 Cherry St E Canal Fulton (44614) *(G-2100)*

SERVICES INDEX

• Service categories are listed in alphabetical order.

A

ABORTION CLINIC
ABRASIVES
ACADEMIC TUTORING SVCS
ACADEMY
ACCELERATORS: Linear
ACCIDENT & HEALTH INSURANCE CARRIERS
ACCIDENT INSURANCE CARRIERS
ACCOUNTING SVCS, NEC
ACCOUNTING SVCS: Certified Public
ACUPUNCTURISTS' OFFICES
ADDRESSING SVCS
ADHESIVES
ADHESIVES & SEALANTS
ADJUSTMENT BUREAU, EXC INSURANCE
ADOPTION SVCS
ADULT DAYCARE CENTERS
ADULT EDUCATION SCHOOLS, PUBLIC
ADVERTISING AGENCIES
ADVERTISING AGENCIES: Consultants
ADVERTISING COPY WRITING SVCS
ADVERTISING MATERIAL DISTRIBUTION
ADVERTISING REPRESENTATIVES: Electronic Media
ADVERTISING REPRESENTATIVES: Media
ADVERTISING REPRESENTATIVES: Newspaper
ADVERTISING REPRESENTATIVES: Printed Media
ADVERTISING REPRESENTATIVES: Radio
ADVERTISING REPRESENTATIVES: Television & Radio
  Time Sales
ADVERTISING SPECIALTIES, WHOLESALE
ADVERTISING SVCS, NEC
ADVERTISING SVCS: Billboards
ADVERTISING SVCS: Direct Mail
ADVERTISING SVCS: Display
ADVERTISING SVCS: Outdoor
ADVERTISING SVCS: Sample Distribution
ADVERTISING SVCS: Transit
ADVERTISING: Aerial
ADVOCACY GROUP
AGENTS, BROKERS & BUREAUS: Personal Service
AGRICULTURAL EQPT: BARN, SILO, POULTRY,
  DAIRY/LIVESTOCK MACH
AGRICULTURAL EQPT: Fertilizing Machinery
AGRICULTURAL MACHINERY & EQPT: Wholesalers
AGRICULTURAL PROG REG OFFICES, GOVT: Agriculture
  Fair Board
AID TO FAMILIES WITH DEPENDENT CHILDREN OR AFDC
AIR CONDITIONING & VENTILATION EQPT & SPLYS:
  Wholesales
AIR CONDITIONING EQPT
AIR CONDITIONING EQPT, WHOLE HOUSE: Wholesalers
AIR CONDITIONING REPAIR SVCS
AIR DUCT CLEANING SVCS
AIR POLLUTION CONTROL EQPT & SPLYS WHOLE-
  SALERS
AIR POLLUTION MEASURING SVCS
AIR PURIFICATION EQPT
AIR TRAFFIC CONTROL SVCS
AIR, WATER & SOLID WASTE PROGRAMS ADMINISTRA-
  TION SVCS
AIR-CONDITIONING SPLY SVCS
AIRCRAFT & HEAVY EQPT REPAIR SVCS
AIRCRAFT CLEANING & JANITORIAL SVCS
AIRCRAFT DEALERS
AIRCRAFT ELECTRICAL EQPT REPAIR SVCS
AIRCRAFT ENGINES & ENGINE PARTS: Pumps
AIRCRAFT ENGINES & PARTS
AIRCRAFT EQPT & SPLYS WHOLESALERS
AIRCRAFT FLIGHT INSTRUMENTS
AIRCRAFT FUELING SVCS
AIRCRAFT HANGAR OPERATION SVCS
AIRCRAFT MAINTENANCE & REPAIR SVCS
AIRCRAFT PARTS & EQPT, NEC
AIRCRAFT PARTS WHOLESALERS
AIRCRAFT SERVICING & REPAIRING
AIRLINE TRAINING
AIRPORT
AIRPORT TERMINAL SVCS

AIRPORTS & FLYING FIELDS
AIRPORTS, FLYING FIELDS & SVCS
ALARM SYSTEMS WHOLESALERS
ALCOHOL TREATMENT CLINIC, OUTPATIENT
ALCOHOLISM COUNSELING, NONTREATMENT
ALKALIES & CHLORINE
ALL-TERRAIN VEHICLE DEALERS
ALLOYS: Additive, Exc Copper Or Made In Blast Furnaces
ALUMINUM
ALUMINUM: Coil & Sheet
ALUMINUM: Slabs, Primary
AMBULANCE SVCS
AMBULANCE SVCS: Air
AMBULATORY SURGICAL CENTERS
AMUSEMENT & REC SVCS: Attractions, Concessions &
  Rides
AMUSEMENT & REC SVCS: Baseball Club, Exc Pro & Semi-
  Pro
AMUSEMENT & REC SVCS: Flying Field, Maintained By Av
  Clubs
AMUSEMENT & RECREATION SVCS, NEC
AMUSEMENT & RECREATION SVCS: Agricultural Fair
AMUSEMENT & RECREATION SVCS: Amusement Arcades
AMUSEMENT & RECREATION SVCS: Amusement Mach
  Rental, Coin-Op
AMUSEMENT & RECREATION SVCS: Amusement Ride
AMUSEMENT & RECREATION SVCS: Arcades
AMUSEMENT & RECREATION SVCS: Boating Club, Mem-
  bership
AMUSEMENT & RECREATION SVCS: Bowling Instruction
AMUSEMENT & RECREATION SVCS: Carnival Operation
AMUSEMENT & RECREATION SVCS: Concession Operator
AMUSEMENT & RECREATION SVCS: Exhibition Operation
AMUSEMENT & RECREATION SVCS: Exposition Operation
AMUSEMENT & RECREATION SVCS: Festival Operation
AMUSEMENT & RECREATION SVCS: Fishing Lakes & Piers,
  Op
AMUSEMENT & RECREATION SVCS: Gambling & Lottery
  Svcs
AMUSEMENT & RECREATION SVCS: Gambling, Coin Ma-
  chines
AMUSEMENT & RECREATION SVCS: Golf Club, Member-
  ship
AMUSEMENT & RECREATION SVCS: Golf Professionals
AMUSEMENT & RECREATION SVCS: Golf Svcs & Profes-
  sionals
AMUSEMENT & RECREATION SVCS: Gun & Hunting Clubs
AMUSEMENT & RECREATION SVCS: Gun Club, Member-
  ship
AMUSEMENT & RECREATION SVCS: Hunting Club, Mem-
  bership
AMUSEMENT & RECREATION SVCS: Ice Skating Rink
AMUSEMENT & RECREATION SVCS: Indoor Court Clubs
AMUSEMENT & RECREATION SVCS: Instruction Schools,
  Camps
AMUSEMENT & RECREATION SVCS: Kiddie Park
AMUSEMENT & RECREATION SVCS: Lottery Tickets, Sales
AMUSEMENT & RECREATION SVCS: Outdoor Field Clubs
AMUSEMENT & RECREATION SVCS: Picnic Ground Opera-
  tion
AMUSEMENT & RECREATION SVCS: Pool Parlor
AMUSEMENT & RECREATION SVCS: Racquetball Club,
  Membership
AMUSEMENT & RECREATION SVCS: Recreation Center
AMUSEMENT & RECREATION SVCS: Recreation SVCS
AMUSEMENT & RECREATION SVCS: Soccer Club, Exc
  Pro/Semi-Pro
AMUSEMENT & RECREATION SVCS: Swimming Club, Mem-
  bership
AMUSEMENT & RECREATION SVCS: Swimming Pool, Non-
  Membership
AMUSEMENT & RECREATION SVCS: Tennis & Profession-
  als
AMUSEMENT & RECREATION SVCS: Tennis Club, Member-
  ship
AMUSEMENT & RECREATION SVCS: Theme Park
AMUSEMENT & RECREATION SVCS: Tourist Attraction,
  Commercial

AMUSEMENT & RECREATION SVCS: Trampoline Operation
AMUSEMENT & RECREATION SVCS: Video Game Arcades
AMUSEMENT ARCADES
AMUSEMENT PARK DEVICES & RIDES: Carnival Mach &
  Eqpt, NEC
AMUSEMENT PARKS
AMUSEMENT/REC SVCS: Ticket Sales, Sporting Events,
  Contract
ANATOMICAL SPECIMENS & RESEARCH MATERIAL,
  WHOLESALE
ANIMAL & REPTILE EXHIBIT
ANIMAL FEED & SUPPLEMENTS: Livestock & Poultry
ANIMAL FEED: Wholesalers
ANIMAL FOOD & SUPPLEMENTS: Bird Food, Prepared
ANIMAL FOOD & SUPPLEMENTS: Dog
ANIMAL FOOD & SUPPLEMENTS: Dog & Cat
ANIMAL FOOD & SUPPLEMENTS: Livestock
ANIMAL FOOD & SUPPLEMENTS: Poultry
ANTENNA REPAIR & INSTALLATION SVCS
ANTENNAS: Radar Or Communications
ANTIPOVERTY BOARD
ANTIQUE & CLASSIC AUTOMOBILE RESTORATION
APARTMENT LOCATING SVCS
APPAREL DESIGNERS: Commercial
APPLIANCES, HOUSEHOLD OR COIN OPERATED: Laundry
  Dryers
APPLIANCES, HOUSEHOLD: Kitchen, Major, Exc Refrigs &
  Stoves
APPLIANCES: Household, Refrigerators & Freezers
APPLIANCES: Major, Cooking
APPLIANCES: Small, Electric
APPLICATIONS SOFTWARE PROGRAMMING
APPRAISAL SVCS, EXC REAL ESTATE
ARBORETUM
ARCHEOLOGICAL EXPEDITIONS
ARCHITECTURAL SVCS
ARCHITECTURAL SVCS: Engineering
ARCHITECTURAL SVCS: Engineering
ARCHITECTURAL SVCS: House Designer
ARMATURE REPAIRING & REWINDING SVC
ARMORED CAR SVCS
ART & ORNAMENTAL WARE: Pottery
ART DESIGN SVCS
ART GALLERIES
ART GOODS & SPLYS WHOLESALERS
ART GOODS, WHOLESALE
ART RELATED SVCS
ART SCHOOL, EXC COMMERCIAL
ART SPLY STORES
ARTS & CRAFTS SCHOOL
ARTS OR SCIENCES CENTER
ASPHALT & ASPHALT PRDTS
ASPHALT COATINGS & SEALERS
ASPHALT MIXTURES WHOLESALERS
ASSOCIATION FOR THE HANDICAPPED
ASSOCIATIONS: Alumni
ASSOCIATIONS: Bar
ASSOCIATIONS: Business
ASSOCIATIONS: Dentists'
ASSOCIATIONS: Engineering
ASSOCIATIONS: Fraternal
ASSOCIATIONS: Homeowners
ASSOCIATIONS: Parent Teacher
ASSOCIATIONS: Real Estate Management
ASSOCIATIONS: Trade
ATHLETIC CLUB & GYMNASIUMS, MEMBERSHIP
ATHLETIC EQPT INSPECTION SVCS
ATHLETIC ORGANIZATION
ATOMIZERS
AUCTION SVCS: Livestock
AUCTION SVCS: Motor Vehicle
AUCTIONEERS: Fee Basis
AUDIO & VIDEO EQPT, EXC COMMERCIAL
AUDIO & VIDEO TAPES WHOLESALERS
AUDIO-VISUAL PROGRAM PRODUCTION SVCS
AUDITING SVCS
AUTO & HOME SUPPLY STORES: Auto & Truck Eqpt & Parts
AUTO & HOME SUPPLY STORES: Automotive Access

AUTO & HOME SUPPLY STORES: Automotive parts
AUTO & HOME SUPPLY STORES: Batteries, Automotive & Truck
AUTO & HOME SUPPLY STORES: Truck Eqpt & Parts
AUTO SPLYS & PARTS, NEW, WHSLE: Exhaust Sys, Mufflers, Etc
AUTOMATED TELLER MACHINE NETWORK
AUTOMATED TELLER MACHINE OR ATM REPAIR SVCS
AUTOMATIC REGULATING CONTROL: Building Svcs Monitoring, Auto
AUTOMATIC TELLER MACHINES: Wholesalers
AUTOMOBILE FINANCE LEASING
AUTOMOBILE RECOVERY SVCS
AUTOMOBILE STORAGE GARAGE
AUTOMOBILES & OTHER MOTOR VEHICLES WHOLESALERS
AUTOMOBILES: Wholesalers
AUTOMOTIVE & TRUCK GENERAL REPAIR SVC
AUTOMOTIVE BATTERIES WHOLESALERS
AUTOMOTIVE BODY SHOP
AUTOMOTIVE BODY, PAINT & INTERIOR REPAIR & MAINTENANCE SVC
AUTOMOTIVE BRAKE REPAIR SHOPS
AUTOMOTIVE COLLISION SHOPS
AUTOMOTIVE CUSTOMIZING SVCS, NONFACTORY BASIS
AUTOMOTIVE DEALERS, NEC
AUTOMOTIVE EMISSIONS TESTING SVCS
AUTOMOTIVE GLASS REPLACEMENT SHOPS
AUTOMOTIVE LETTERING & PAINTING SVCS
AUTOMOTIVE PAINT SHOP
AUTOMOTIVE PARTS, ACCESS & SPLYS
AUTOMOTIVE PRDTS: Rubber
AUTOMOTIVE RADIATOR REPAIR SHOPS
AUTOMOTIVE REPAIR SHOPS: Brake Repair
AUTOMOTIVE REPAIR SHOPS: Diesel Engine Repair
AUTOMOTIVE REPAIR SHOPS: Engine Repair, Exc Diesel
AUTOMOTIVE REPAIR SHOPS: Frame & Front End Repair Svcs
AUTOMOTIVE REPAIR SHOPS: Frame Repair Shops
AUTOMOTIVE REPAIR SHOPS: Machine Shop
AUTOMOTIVE REPAIR SHOPS: Muffler Shop, Sale/Rpr/Installation
AUTOMOTIVE REPAIR SHOPS: Rebuilding & Retreading Tires
AUTOMOTIVE REPAIR SHOPS: Tire Recapping
AUTOMOTIVE REPAIR SHOPS: Trailer Repair
AUTOMOTIVE REPAIR SHOPS: Truck Engine Repair, Exc Indl
AUTOMOTIVE REPAIR SHOPS: Turbocharger & Blower Repair
AUTOMOTIVE REPAIR SHOPS: Wheel Alignment
AUTOMOTIVE REPAIR SVC
AUTOMOTIVE REPAIR SVCS, MISCELLANEOUS
AUTOMOTIVE RUSTPROOFING & UNDERCOATING SHOPS
AUTOMOTIVE SPLYS & PARTS, NEW, WHOL: Auto Servicing Eqpt
AUTOMOTIVE SPLYS & PARTS, NEW, WHOL: Testing Eqpt, Electric
AUTOMOTIVE SPLYS & PARTS, NEW, WHOLESALE: Bumpers
AUTOMOTIVE SPLYS & PARTS, NEW, WHOLESALE: Engines/Eng Parts
AUTOMOTIVE SPLYS & PARTS, NEW, WHOLESALE: Seat Covers
AUTOMOTIVE SPLYS & PARTS, NEW, WHOLESALE: Splys
AUTOMOTIVE SPLYS & PARTS, NEW, WHOLESALE: Tools & Eqpt
AUTOMOTIVE SPLYS & PARTS, NEW, WHOLESALE: Trailer Parts
AUTOMOTIVE SPLYS & PARTS, NEW, WHOLESALE: Wheels
AUTOMOTIVE SPLYS & PARTS, USED, WHOLESALE
AUTOMOTIVE SPLYS & PARTS, USED, WHOLESALE: Dry Cell Batt
AUTOMOTIVE SPLYS & PARTS, WHOLESALE, NEC
AUTOMOTIVE SPLYS, USED, WHOLESALE & RETAIL
AUTOMOTIVE SPLYS/PART, NEW, WHOL: Spring, Shock Absorb/Strut
AUTOMOTIVE SPLYS/PARTS, NEW, WHOL: Body Rpr/Paint Shop Splys
AUTOMOTIVE SVCS, EXC REPAIR & CARWASHES: Customizing
AUTOMOTIVE SVCS, EXC REPAIR & CARWASHES: Insp & Diagnostic

AUTOMOTIVE SVCS, EXC REPAIR & CARWASHES: Lubrication
AUTOMOTIVE SVCS, EXC REPAIR & CARWASHES: Maintenance
AUTOMOTIVE SVCS, EXC REPAIR & CARWASHES: Road Svc
AUTOMOTIVE SVCS, EXC REPAIR: Carwash, Automatic
AUTOMOTIVE SVCS, EXC REPAIR: Carwash, Self-Service
AUTOMOTIVE SVCS, EXC REPAIR: Truck Wash
AUTOMOTIVE SVCS, EXC REPAIR: Washing & Polishing
AUTOMOTIVE SVCS, EXC RPR/CARWASHES: High Perf Auto Rpr/Svc
AUTOMOTIVE TOWING & WRECKING SVC
AUTOMOTIVE TOWING SVCS
AUTOMOTIVE TRANSMISSION REPAIR SVC
AUTOMOTIVE UPHOLSTERY SHOPS
AUTOMOTIVE WELDING SVCS
AUTOMOTIVE: Seat Frames, Metal
AVIATION PROPELLER & BLADE REPAIR SVCS
AVIATION SCHOOL

B

BABYSITTING BUREAU
BADGES, WHOLESALE
BAGS: Plastic
BAGS: Plastic, Made From Purchased Materials
BAGS: Shopping, Made From Purchased Materials
BAIL BONDING SVCS
BAKERIES, COMMERCIAL: On Premises Baking Only
BAKERIES: On Premises Baking & Consumption
BAKERY PRDTS: Cookies & crackers
BAKERY PRDTS: Pretzels
BAKERY PRDTS: Wholesalers
BAKERY: Wholesale Or Wholesale & Retail Combined
BAKING PAN GLAZING & CLEANING SVCS
BALLET PRODUCTION SVCS
BANKS: Commercial, NEC
BANKS: Federal Reserve
BANKS: Federal Reserve Branches
BANKS: Mortgage & Loan
BANKS: National Commercial
BANKS: State Commercial
BANQUET HALL FACILITIES
BAR
BARBER SHOPS
BARGES BUILDING & REPAIR
BARS: Concrete Reinforcing, Fabricated Steel
BASKETS, WHOLESALE
BATTERY CHARGERS
BEADS, WHOLESALE
BEARINGS & PARTS Ball
BEAUTY & BARBER SHOP EQPT
BEAUTY CULTURE SCHOOL
BEAUTY SALONS
BED & BREAKFAST INNS
BEDDING & BEDSPRINGS STORES
BEDDING, BEDSPREADS, BLANKETS & SHEETS: Comforters & Quilts
BEER & ALE WHOLESALERS
BEER & ALE, WHOLESALE: Beer & Other Fermented Malt Liquors
BEER, WINE & LIQUOR STORES: Beer, Packaged
BEER, WINE & LIQUOR STORES: Wine
BELTING: Plastic
BELTS: Seat, Automotive & Aircraft
BEVERAGE STORES
BEVERAGES, ALCOHOLIC: Near Beer
BEVERAGES, ALCOHOLIC: Wines
BEVERAGES, BEER & ALE, WHOLESALE: Ale
BEVERAGES, NONALCOHOLIC: Bottled & canned soft drinks
BEVERAGES, NONALCOHOLIC: Carbonated
BEVERAGES, NONALCOHOLIC: Carbonated, Canned & Bottled, Etc
BEVERAGES, NONALCOHOLIC: Flavoring extracts & syrups, nec
BEVERAGES, NONALCOHOLIC: Soft Drinks, Canned & Bottled, Etc
BEVERAGES, WINE & DISTILLED ALCOHOLIC, WHOLESALE: Wine
BEVERAGES, WINE/DISTILLED ALCOH, WHOL: Brandy/Brandy Spirits
BIBLE CAMPS
BICYCLE SHOPS
BILLIARD & POOL PARLORS

BILLIARD EQPT & SPLYS WHOLESALERS
BILLIARD TABLE REPAIR SVCS
BILLING & BOOKKEEPING SVCS
BINDING SVC: Books & Manuals
BINDING SVC: Pamphlets
BINGO HALL
BIOFEEDBACK CENTERS
BIOLOGICAL PRDTS: Exc Diagnostic
BIRTH CONTROL CLINIC
BLASTING SVC: Sand, Metal Parts
BLOCK & BRICK: Sand Lime
BLOCKS: Standard, Concrete Or Cinder
BLOOD BANK
BLOOD DONOR STATIONS
BLOOD RELATED HEALTH SVCS
BLOWERS & FANS
BLUEPRINTING SVCS
BOARDING SCHOOL
BOAT BUILDING & REPAIR
BOAT DEALERS
BOAT DEALERS: Motor
BOAT REPAIR SVCS
BOAT YARD: Boat yards, storage & incidental repair
BODIES: Truck & Bus
BOILER & HEATING REPAIR SVCS
BOILER REPAIR SHOP
BOND & MORTGAGE COMPANIES
BOOK STORES
BOOK STORES: Religious
BOOKS, WHOLESALE
BOTANICAL GARDENS
BOTTLED GAS DEALERS: Propane
BOTTLED WATER DELIVERY
BOTTLES: Plastic
BOUTIQUE STORES
BOWLING CENTERS
BOWLING EQPT & SPLY STORES
BOWLING EQPT & SPLYS
BOXES & CRATES: Rectangular, Wood
BOXES & SHOOK: Nailed Wood
BOXES: Corrugated
BOXES: Wooden
BOYS' CAMPS
BOYS' TOWNS
BRAKES & BRAKE PARTS
BRASS FOUNDRY, NEC
BRASS GOODS, WHOLESALE
BRAZING SVCS
BRAZING: Metal
BRICK, STONE & RELATED PRDTS WHOLESALERS
BRIDAL SHOPS
BROACHING MACHINES
BROADCASTING & COMMS EQPT: Antennas, Transmitting/Comms
BROADCASTING STATIONS, RADIO: Educational
BROADCASTING STATIONS, RADIO: Exc Music Format
BROADCASTING STATIONS, RADIO: Music Format
BROADCASTING STATIONS, RADIO: Rock Music
BROADCASTING STATIONS, RADIO: Sports
BROADCASTING STATIONS, TELEVISION: Translator Station
BROKERS & DEALERS: Mortgages, Buying & Selling
BROKERS & DEALERS: Securities
BROKERS & DEALERS: Security
BROKERS & DEALERS: Stock
BROKERS' SVCS
BROKERS, MARINE TRANSPORTATION
BROKERS: Business
BROKERS: Food
BROKERS: Loan
BROKERS: Mortgage, Arranging For Loans
BROKERS: Printing
BROKERS: Security
BROOMS & BRUSHES
BROOMS & BRUSHES: Household Or Indl
BUCKETS: Plastic
BUILDING & OFFICE CLEANING SVCS
BUILDING & STRUCTURAL WOOD MEMBERS
BUILDING CLEANING & MAINTENANCE SVCS
BUILDING CLEANING SVCS
BUILDING COMPONENT CLEANING SVCS
BUILDING COMPONENTS: Structural Steel
BUILDING INSPECTION SVCS
BUILDING MAINTENANCE SVCS, EXC REPAIRS
BUILDING PRDTS & MATERIALS DEALERS

BUILDING SCALES MODELS
BUILDINGS & COMPONENTS: Prefabricated Metal
BUILDINGS, PREFABRICATED: Wholesalers
BUILDINGS: Farm & Utility
BUILDINGS: Prefabricated, Metal
BUILDINGS: Prefabricated, Wood
BURGLAR ALARM MAINTENANCE & MONITORING SVCS
BURIAL VAULTS: Concrete Or Precast Terrazzo
BURLAP WHOLESALERS
BUS BARS: Electrical
BUS CHARTER SVC: Local
BUS CHARTER SVC: Long-Distance
BUS TERMINALS & SVC FACILITIES
BUSES: Wholesalers
BUSHINGS & BEARINGS
BUSINESS ACTIVITIES: Non-Commercial Site
BUSINESS FORMS WHOLESALERS
BUSINESS FORMS: Printed, Manifold
BUSINESS MACHINE REPAIR, ELECTRIC
BUSINESS SUPPORT SVCS
BUSINESS TRAINING SVCS
BUTTER WHOLESALERS

C

CABINETS: Entertainment
CABINETS: Entertainment Units, Household, Wood
CABINETS: Kitchen, Wood
CABINETS: Office, Wood
CABINETS: Show, Display, Etc, Wood, Exc Refrigerated
CABLE & OTHER PAY TELEVISION DISTRIBUTION
CABLE & PAY TELEVISION SVCS: Closed Circuit
CABLE & PAY TELEVISION SVCS: Direct Broadcast Satellite
CABLE & PAY TELEVISION SVCS: Multipoint Distribution Sys/MDS
CABLE TELEVISION
CABLE WIRING SETS: Battery, Internal Combustion Engines
CABLE: Noninsulated
CABS, FOR HIRE: Horse Drawn
CAFES
CAFETERIAS
CALENDARS, WHOLESALE
CALIBRATING SVCS, NEC
CAMERA & PHOTOGRAPHIC SPLYS STORES
CAMPGROUNDS
CAMPSITES
CANDLES
CANDLES: Wholesalers
CANDY & CONFECTIONS: Chocolate Covered Dates
CANDY & CONFECTIONS: Cough Drops, Exc Pharmaceutical Preps
CANDY, NUT & CONFECTIONERY STORE: Popcorn, Incl Caramel Corn
CANDY, NUT & CONFECTIONERY STORES: Candy
CANDY, NUT & CONFECTIONERY STORES: Produced For Direct Sale
CANDY: Chocolate From Cacao Beans
CANNED SPECIALTIES
CANS: Fiber
CANVAS PRDTS
CANVAS PRDTS: Convertible Tops, Car/Boat, Fm Purchased Mtrl
CANVAS PRDTS: Shades, Made From Purchased Materials
CAR LOADING SVCS
CAR WASH EQPT
CAR WASHES
CARBON & GRAPHITE PRDTS, NEC
CARBON PAPER & INKED RIBBONS
CARDS: Beveled
CARNIVAL & AMUSEMENT PARK EQPT WHOLESALERS
CARPET & RUG CLEANING PLANTS
CARPET & UPHOLSTERY CLEANING SVCS
CARPET & UPHOLSTERY CLEANING SVCS: Carpet/Furniture, On Loc
CARPET & UPHOLSTERY CLEANING SVCS: On Customer Premises
CARTONS: Egg, Molded Pulp, Made From Purchased Materials
CASH REGISTERS WHOLESALERS
CASINO HOTELS & MOTELS
CASTINGS: Commercial Investment, Ferrous
CASTINGS: Die, Aluminum
CASTINGS: Die, Nonferrous
CASTINGS: Machinery, Aluminum
CASTINGS: Precision
CATALOG & MAIL-ORDER HOUSES

CATALOG SALES
CATALYSTS: Chemical
CATAPULTS
CATERERS
CEMENT & CONCRETE RELATED PRDTS & EQPT: Bituminous
CEMENT ROCK: Crushed & Broken
CEMENT: Hydraulic
CEMETERIES
CEMETERIES: Real Estate Operation
CEMETERY ASSOCIATION
CEMETERY MEMORIAL DEALERS
CERAMIC FLOOR & WALL TILE WHOLESALERS
CHAINS: Power Transmission
CHAMBERS OF COMMERCE
CHARGE ACCOUNT SVCS
CHARTER FLYING SVC
CHASSIS: Motor Vehicle
CHECK CASHING SVCS
CHECK CLEARING SVCS
CHECK VALIDATION SVCS
CHEESE WHOLESALERS
CHEMICAL CLEANING SVCS
CHEMICAL PROCESSING MACHINERY & EQPT
CHEMICAL SPLYS FOR FOUNDRIES
CHEMICALS & ALLIED PRDTS WHOLESALERS, NEC
CHEMICALS & ALLIED PRDTS, WHOL: Chemicals, Swimming Pool/Spa
CHEMICALS & ALLIED PRDTS, WHOL: Food Additives/Preservatives
CHEMICALS & ALLIED PRDTS, WHOL: Gases, Compressed/Liquefied
CHEMICALS & ALLIED PRDTS, WHOLESALE: Adhesives
CHEMICALS & ALLIED PRDTS, WHOLESALE: Alkalines & Chlorine
CHEMICALS & ALLIED PRDTS, WHOLESALE: Anti-Corrosion Prdts
CHEMICALS & ALLIED PRDTS, WHOLESALE: Caustic Soda
CHEMICALS & ALLIED PRDTS, WHOLESALE: Chemicals, Indl
CHEMICALS & ALLIED PRDTS, WHOLESALE: Chemicals, Indl & Heavy
CHEMICALS & ALLIED PRDTS, WHOLESALE: Compressed Gas
CHEMICALS & ALLIED PRDTS, WHOLESALE: Concrete Additives
CHEMICALS & ALLIED PRDTS, WHOLESALE: Detergent/Soap
CHEMICALS & ALLIED PRDTS, WHOLESALE: Detergents
CHEMICALS & ALLIED PRDTS, WHOLESALE: Dry Ice
CHEMICALS & ALLIED PRDTS, WHOLESALE: Essential Oils
CHEMICALS & ALLIED PRDTS, WHOLESALE: Glue
CHEMICALS & ALLIED PRDTS, WHOLESALE: Oxygen
CHEMICALS & ALLIED PRDTS, WHOLESALE: Plastics Film
CHEMICALS & ALLIED PRDTS, WHOLESALE: Plastics Materials, NEC
CHEMICALS & ALLIED PRDTS, WHOLESALE: Plastics Prdts, NEC
CHEMICALS & ALLIED PRDTS, WHOLESALE: Plastics Sheets & Rods
CHEMICALS & ALLIED PRDTS, WHOLESALE: Plastics, Basic Shapes
CHEMICALS & ALLIED PRDTS, WHOLESALE: Resins
CHEMICALS & ALLIED PRDTS, WHOLESALE: Resins, Plastics
CHEMICALS & ALLIED PRDTS, WHOLESALE: Rubber, Synthetic
CHEMICALS & ALLIED PRDTS, WHOLESALE: Salts & Polishes, Indl
CHEMICALS & ALLIED PRDTS, WHOLESALE: Sanitation Preparations
CHEMICALS & ALLIED PRDTS, WHOLESALE: Sealants
CHEMICALS & ALLIED PRDTS, WHOLESALE: Spec Clean/Sanitation
CHEMICALS & ALLIED PRDTS, WHOLESALE: Syn Resin, Rub/Plastic
CHEMICALS, AGRICULTURE: Wholesalers
CHEMICALS: Agricultural
CHEMICALS: Aluminum Compounds
CHEMICALS: Bleaching Powder, Lime Bleaching Compounds
CHEMICALS: High Purity, Refined From Technical Grade
CHEMICALS: Inorganic, NEC
CHEMICALS: Isotopes, Radioactive
CHEMICALS: NEC
CHEMICALS: Organic, NEC

CHICKEN SLAUGHTERING & PROCESSING
CHILD & YOUTH SVCS, NEC
CHILD DAY CARE SVCS
CHILD GUIDANCE SVCS
CHILD RESTRAINT SEATS, AUTOMOTIVE, WHOLESALE
CHILDBIRTH PREPARATION CLINIC
CHILDREN'S & INFANTS' CLOTHING STORES
CHILDREN'S AID SOCIETY
CHILDREN'S BOARDING HOME
CHILDREN'S DANCING SCHOOL
CHILDREN'S HOME
CHINAWARE WHOLESALERS
CHIROPRACTORS' OFFICES
CHOCOLATE, EXC CANDY FROM BEANS: Chips, Powder, Block, Syrup
CHURCHES
CIRCUIT BOARD REPAIR SVCS
CLAIMS ADJUSTING SVCS
CLEANING & DESCALING SVC: Metal Prdts
CLEANING & DYEING PLANTS, EXC RUGS
CLEANING EQPT: Commercial
CLEANING EQPT: Floor Washing & Polishing, Commercial
CLEANING OR POLISHING PREPARATIONS, NEC
CLEANING PRDTS: Sanitation Preps, Disinfectants/Deodorants
CLEANING PRDTS: Specialty
CLEANING SVCS
CLEANING SVCS: Industrial Or Commercial
CLEARINGHOUSE ASSOCIATIONS: Bank Or Check
CLOTHING & ACCESS, WOMEN, CHILD & INFANT, WHSLE: Sportswear
CLOTHING & ACCESS, WOMEN, CHILDREN & INFANT, WHOL: Handbags
CLOTHING & ACCESS, WOMEN, CHILDREN & INFANT, WHOL: Uniforms
CLOTHING & ACCESS: Costumes, Theatrical
CLOTHING & ACCESS: Hospital Gowns
CLOTHING & FURNISHINGS, MEN'S & BOYS', WHOLESALE: Gloves
CLOTHING & FURNISHINGS, MEN'S & BOYS', WHOLESALE: Uniforms
CLOTHING & FURNISHINGS, MENS & BOYS, WHOL: Sportswear/Work
CLOTHING & FURNISHINGS, MENS & BOYS, WHOLESALE: Apprl Belts
CLOTHING STORES, NEC
CLOTHING STORES: Dancewear
CLOTHING STORES: Designer Apparel
CLOTHING STORES: Formal Wear
CLOTHING STORES: Lingerie & Corsets, Underwear
CLOTHING STORES: T-Shirts, Printed, Custom
CLOTHING/ACCESS, WOMEN, CHILDREN/INFANT, WHOL: Hosp Gowns
CLOTHING/FURNISHINGS, MEN/BOY, WHOL: Furnishings, Exc Shoes
CLOTHING: Caps, Baseball
CLOTHING: Hospital, Men's
CLOTHING: T-Shirts & Tops, Knit
CLOTHING: Uniforms & Vestments
CLOTHING: Uniforms, Ex Athletic, Women's, Misses' & Juniors'
CLOTHING: Uniforms, Military, Men/Youth, Purchased Materials
CLOTHING: Uniforms, Work
CLUTCHES, EXC VEHICULAR
COAL & OTHER MINERALS & ORES WHOLESALERS
COAL MINING SERVICES
COAL MINING SVCS: Bituminous, Contract Basis
COAL MINING: Anthracite
COAL MINING: Bituminous & Lignite Surface
COAL MINING: Bituminous Coal & Lignite-Surface Mining
COAL MINING: Bituminous Underground
COAL MINING: Bituminous, Strip
COAL MINING: Bituminous, Surface, NEC
COAL MINING: Lignite, Surface, NEC
COATING SVC: Aluminum, Metal Prdts
COATING SVC: Metals & Formed Prdts
COATING SVC: Metals, With Plastic Or Resins
COATINGS: Epoxy
COCKTAIL LOUNGE
COFFEE SVCS
COIN COUNTERS
COIN OPERATED LAUNDRIES & DRYCLEANERS
COIN-OPERATED LAUNDRY
COIN-OPERATED LAUNDRY MACHINE ROUTES

SVCS INDEX

COINS, WHOLESALE
COLLECTION AGENCIES
COLLECTION AGENCY, EXC REAL ESTATE
COLLEGE, EXC JUNIOR
COLLEGES, UNIVERSITIES & PROFESSIONAL SCHOOLS
COLOR SEPARATION: Photographic & Movie Film
COMBINATION UTILITIES, NEC
COMBINED ELEMENTARY & SECONDARY SCHOOLS, PRIVATE
COMMERCIAL & INDL SHELVING WHOLESALERS
COMMERCIAL & OFFICE BUILDINGS RENOVATION & REPAIR
COMMERCIAL ART & GRAPHIC DESIGN SVCS
COMMERCIAL ART & ILLUSTRATION SVCS
COMMERCIAL CONTAINERS WHOLESALERS
COMMERCIAL EQPT & SPLYS, WHOLESALE: Price Marking
COMMERCIAL EQPT WHOLESALERS, NEC
COMMERCIAL EQPT, WHOLESALE: Bakery Eqpt & Splys
COMMERCIAL EQPT, WHOLESALE: Coffee Brewing Eqpt & Splys
COMMERCIAL EQPT, WHOLESALE: Comm Cooking & Food Svc Eqpt
COMMERCIAL EQPT, WHOLESALE: Restaurant, NEC
COMMERCIAL EQPT, WHOLESALE: Scales, Exc Laboratory
COMMERCIAL EQPT, WHOLESALE: Teaching Machines, Electronic
COMMERCIAL EQPT, WHOLESALE: Vending Machines, Coin-Operated
COMMERCIAL PHOTOGRAPHIC STUDIO
COMMERCIAL PRINTING & NEWSPAPER PUBLISHING COMBINED
COMMODITIES SAMPLING SVC
COMMODITY CONTRACT POOL OPERATORS
COMMODITY CONTRACTS BROKERS, DEALERS
COMMODITY INVESTORS
COMMON SAND MINING
COMMUNICATIONS CARRIER: Wired
COMMUNICATIONS EQPT REPAIR & MAINTENANCE
COMMUNICATIONS EQPT WHOLESALERS
COMMUNICATIONS SVCS
COMMUNICATIONS SVCS: Cellular
COMMUNICATIONS SVCS: Data
COMMUNICATIONS SVCS: Electronic Mail
COMMUNICATIONS SVCS: Internet Connectivity Svcs
COMMUNICATIONS SVCS: Internet Host Svcs
COMMUNICATIONS SVCS: Nonvocal Message
COMMUNICATIONS SVCS: Online Svc Providers
COMMUNICATIONS SVCS: Radio Pager Or Beeper
COMMUNICATIONS SVCS: Signal Enhancement Network Svcs
COMMUNICATIONS SVCS: Telegram
COMMUNICATIONS SVCS: Telephone Or Video
COMMUNICATIONS SVCS: Telephone, Broker
COMMUNICATIONS SVCS: Telephone, Data
COMMUNICATIONS SVCS: Telephone, Local
COMMUNICATIONS SVCS: Telephone, Local & Long Distance
COMMUNICATIONS SVCS: Telephone, Long Distance
COMMUNICATIONS SVCS: Telephone, Voice
COMMUNICATIONS SVCS: Television Antenna Construction & Rent
COMMUNITY ACTION AGENCY
COMMUNITY CENTER
COMMUNITY CENTERS: Adult
COMMUNITY CENTERS: Youth
COMMUNITY COLLEGE
COMMUNITY DEVELOPMENT GROUPS
COMMUNITY SVCS EMPLOYMENT TRAINING PROGRAM
COMMUNITY THEATER PRODUCTION SVCS
COMMUTATORS: Electronic
COMPACT DISCS OR CD'S, WHOLESALE
COMPOST
COMPRESSORS, AIR CONDITIONING: Wholesalers
COMPRESSORS: Air & Gas, Including Vacuum Pumps
COMPRESSORS: Repairing
COMPRESSORS: Wholesalers
COMPUTER & COMPUTER SOFTWARE STORES
COMPUTER & COMPUTER SOFTWARE STORES: Peripheral Eqpt
COMPUTER & COMPUTER SOFTWARE STORES: Personal Computers
COMPUTER & COMPUTER SOFTWARE STORES: Software & Access
COMPUTER & COMPUTER SOFTWARE STORES: Software, Bus/Non-Game

COMPUTER & DATA PROCESSING EQPT REPAIR & MAINTENANCE
COMPUTER & OFFICE MACHINE MAINTENANCE & REPAIR
COMPUTER DATA ESCROW SVCS
COMPUTER FACILITIES MANAGEMENT SVCS
COMPUTER GRAPHICS SVCS
COMPUTER INTERFACE EQPT: Indl Process
COMPUTER PERIPHERAL EQPT REPAIR & MAINTENANCE
COMPUTER PERIPHERAL EQPT, NEC
COMPUTER PERIPHERAL EQPT, WHOLESALE
COMPUTER PERIPHERAL EQPT: Decoders
COMPUTER PROGRAMMING SVCS
COMPUTER PROGRAMMING SVCS: Custom
COMPUTER RELATED MAINTENANCE SVCS
COMPUTER RELATED SVCS, NEC
COMPUTER SOFTWARE DEVELOPMENT
COMPUTER SOFTWARE DEVELOPMENT & APPLICATIONS
COMPUTER SOFTWARE SYSTEMS ANALYSIS & DESIGN: Custom
COMPUTER SOFTWARE WRITERS
COMPUTER SOFTWARE WRITERS: Freelance
COMPUTER STORAGE DEVICES, NEC
COMPUTER SYSTEM SELLING SVCS
COMPUTER SYSTEMS ANALYSIS & DESIGN
COMPUTER TERMINALS
COMPUTER TRAINING SCHOOLS
COMPUTER-AIDED DESIGN SYSTEMS SVCS
COMPUTER-AIDED ENGINEERING SYSTEMS SVCS
COMPUTERS, NEC
COMPUTERS, NEC, WHOLESALE
COMPUTERS, PERIPHERAL & SOFTWARE, WHOLESALE: Word Processing
COMPUTERS, PERIPHERALS & SOFTWARE, WHOLESALE: Printers
COMPUTERS, PERIPHERALS & SOFTWARE, WHOLESALE: Software
COMPUTERS, PERIPHERALS & SOFTWARE, WHOLESALE: Terminals
CONCERT MANAGEMENT SVCS
CONCRETE BUILDING PRDTS WHOLESALERS
CONCRETE CURING & HARDENING COMPOUNDS
CONCRETE PRDTS
CONCRETE: Asphaltic, Not From Refineries
CONCRETE: Dry Mixture
CONCRETE: Ready-Mixed
CONDENSERS: Heat Transfer Eqpt, Evaporative
CONES, PYROMETRIC: Earthenware
CONFECTIONERY PRDTS WHOLESALERS
CONFECTIONS & CANDY
CONFINEMENT SURVEILLANCE SYS MAINTENANCE & MONITORING SVCS
CONNECTORS: Electronic
CONSERVATION PROGRAMS ADMINISTRATION SVCS
CONSTRUCTION & MINING MACHINERY WHOLESALERS
CONSTRUCTION EQPT REPAIR SVCS
CONSTRUCTION EQPT: Cranes
CONSTRUCTION EQPT: Roofing Eqpt
CONSTRUCTION MATERIALS, WHOLESALE: Aggregate
CONSTRUCTION MATERIALS, WHOLESALE: Air Ducts, Sheet Metal
CONSTRUCTION MATERIALS, WHOLESALE: Awnings
CONSTRUCTION MATERIALS, WHOLESALE: Block, Concrete & Cinder
CONSTRUCTION MATERIALS, WHOLESALE: Brick, Exc Refractory
CONSTRUCTION MATERIALS, WHOLESALE: Building Stone
CONSTRUCTION MATERIALS, WHOLESALE: Building Stone, Granite
CONSTRUCTION MATERIALS, WHOLESALE: Building Stone, Marble
CONSTRUCTION MATERIALS, WHOLESALE: Building, Exterior
CONSTRUCTION MATERIALS, WHOLESALE: Building, Interior
CONSTRUCTION MATERIALS, WHOLESALE: Ceiling Systems & Prdts
CONSTRUCTION MATERIALS, WHOLESALE: Cement
CONSTRUCTION MATERIALS, WHOLESALE: Ceramic, Exc Refractory
CONSTRUCTION MATERIALS, WHOLESALE: Door Frames

CONSTRUCTION MATERIALS, WHOLESALE: Doors, Garage
CONSTRUCTION MATERIALS, WHOLESALE: Drywall Materials
CONSTRUCTION MATERIALS, WHOLESALE: Eavestroughing, Part/Sply
CONSTRUCTION MATERIALS, WHOLESALE: Glass
CONSTRUCTION MATERIALS, WHOLESALE: Gravel
CONSTRUCTION MATERIALS, WHOLESALE: Hardboard
CONSTRUCTION MATERIALS, WHOLESALE: Joists
CONSTRUCTION MATERIALS, WHOLESALE: Lime Building Prdts
CONSTRUCTION MATERIALS, WHOLESALE: Lime, Exc Agricultural
CONSTRUCTION MATERIALS, WHOLESALE: Limestone
CONSTRUCTION MATERIALS, WHOLESALE: Masons' Materials
CONSTRUCTION MATERIALS, WHOLESALE: Metal Buildings
CONSTRUCTION MATERIALS, WHOLESALE: Millwork
CONSTRUCTION MATERIALS, WHOLESALE: Molding, All Materials
CONSTRUCTION MATERIALS, WHOLESALE: Pallets, Wood
CONSTRUCTION MATERIALS, WHOLESALE: Particleboard
CONSTRUCTION MATERIALS, WHOLESALE: Prefabricated Structures
CONSTRUCTION MATERIALS, WHOLESALE: Roof, Asphalt/Sheet Metal
CONSTRUCTION MATERIALS, WHOLESALE: Roofing & Siding Material
CONSTRUCTION MATERIALS, WHOLESALE: Sand
CONSTRUCTION MATERIALS, WHOLESALE: Septic Tanks
CONSTRUCTION MATERIALS, WHOLESALE: Sewer Pipe, Clay
CONSTRUCTION MATERIALS, WHOLESALE: Siding, Exc Wood
CONSTRUCTION MATERIALS, WHOLESALE: Stone, Crushed Or Broken
CONSTRUCTION MATERIALS, WHOLESALE: Trim, Sheet Metal
CONSTRUCTION MATERIALS, WHOLESALE: Veneer
CONSTRUCTION MATERIALS, WHOLESALE: Windows
CONSTRUCTION MATLS, WHOL: Lumber, Rough, Dressed/Finished
CONSTRUCTION MATLS, WHOLESALE: Soil Erosion Cntrl Fabrics
CONSTRUCTION MTRLS, WHOL: Exterior Flat Glass, Plate/Window
CONSTRUCTION SAND MINING
CONSTRUCTION SITE PREPARATION SVCS
CONSTRUCTION: Agricultural Building
CONSTRUCTION: Airport Runway
CONSTRUCTION: Apartment Building
CONSTRUCTION: Athletic Field
CONSTRUCTION: Bridge
CONSTRUCTION: Commercial & Institutional Building
CONSTRUCTION: Commercial & Office Building, New
CONSTRUCTION: Commercial & Office Buildings, Prefabricated
CONSTRUCTION: Concrete Patio
CONSTRUCTION: Condominium
CONSTRUCTION: Curb
CONSTRUCTION: Dams, Waterways, Docks & Other Marine
CONSTRUCTION: Drainage System
CONSTRUCTION: Electric Power Line
CONSTRUCTION: Elevated Highway
CONSTRUCTION: Fire Station
CONSTRUCTION: Food Prdts Manufacturing or Packing Plant
CONSTRUCTION: Garage
CONSTRUCTION: Gas Main
CONSTRUCTION: Golf Course
CONSTRUCTION: Grain Elevator
CONSTRUCTION: Greenhouse
CONSTRUCTION: Guardrails, Highway
CONSTRUCTION: Heavy
CONSTRUCTION: Heavy Highway & Street
CONSTRUCTION: Hospital
CONSTRUCTION: Hotel & Motel, New
CONSTRUCTION: Indl Building & Warehouse
CONSTRUCTION: Indl Building, Prefabricated
CONSTRUCTION: Indl Buildings, New, NEC
CONSTRUCTION: Indl Plant
CONSTRUCTION: Institutional Building
CONSTRUCTION: Irrigation System
CONSTRUCTION: Land Preparation

CONSTRUCTION: Marine
CONSTRUCTION: Multi-Family Housing
CONSTRUCTION: Multi-family Dwellings, New
CONSTRUCTION: Nonresidential Buildings, Custom
CONSTRUCTION: Oil & Gas Line & Compressor Station
CONSTRUCTION: Oil & Gas Pipeline Construction
CONSTRUCTION: Pharmaceutical Manufacturing Plant
CONSTRUCTION: Pipeline, NEC
CONSTRUCTION: Power & Communication Transmission Tower
CONSTRUCTION: Power Plant
CONSTRUCTION: Railroad & Subway
CONSTRUCTION: Railway Roadbed
CONSTRUCTION: Refineries
CONSTRUCTION: Religious Building
CONSTRUCTION: Residential, Nec
CONSTRUCTION: Restaurant
CONSTRUCTION: School Building
CONSTRUCTION: Sewer Line
CONSTRUCTION: Shopping Center & Mall
CONSTRUCTION: Silo, Agricultural
CONSTRUCTION: Single-Family Housing
CONSTRUCTION: Single-family Housing, New
CONSTRUCTION: Steel Buildings
CONSTRUCTION: Street Sign Installation & Mntnce
CONSTRUCTION: Street Surfacing & Paving
CONSTRUCTION: Svc Station
CONSTRUCTION: Swimming Pools
CONSTRUCTION: Telephone & Communication Line
CONSTRUCTION: Tennis Court
CONSTRUCTION: Transmitting Tower, Telecommunication
CONSTRUCTION: Tunnel
CONSTRUCTION: Utility Line
CONSTRUCTION: Warehouse
CONSTRUCTION: Waste Disposal Plant
CONSTRUCTION: Waste Water & Sewage Treatment Plant
CONSTRUCTION: Water & Sewer Line
CONSTRUCTION: Water Main
CONSULTING SVC: Actuarial
CONSULTING SVC: Business, NEC
CONSULTING SVC: Computer
CONSULTING SVC: Data Processing
CONSULTING SVC: Educational
CONSULTING SVC: Engineering
CONSULTING SVC: Executive Placement & Search
CONSULTING SVC: Financial Management
CONSULTING SVC: Human Resource
CONSULTING SVC: Management
CONSULTING SVC: Marketing Management
CONSULTING SVC: New Business Start Up
CONSULTING SVC: Online Technology
CONSULTING SVC: Personnel Management
CONSULTING SVC: Productivity Improvement
CONSULTING SVC: Sales Management
CONSULTING SVC: Telecommunications
CONSULTING SVCS, BUSINESS: Agricultural
CONSULTING SVCS, BUSINESS: City Planning
CONSULTING SVCS, BUSINESS: Communications
CONSULTING SVCS, BUSINESS: Economic
CONSULTING SVCS, BUSINESS: Employee Programs Administration
CONSULTING SVCS, BUSINESS: Energy Conservation
CONSULTING SVCS, BUSINESS: Environmental
CONSULTING SVCS, BUSINESS: Indl Development Planning
CONSULTING SVCS, BUSINESS: Lighting
CONSULTING SVCS, BUSINESS: Safety Training Svcs
CONSULTING SVCS, BUSINESS: Sys Engnrg, Exc Computer/Prof
CONSULTING SVCS, BUSINESS: Systems Analysis & Engineering
CONSULTING SVCS, BUSINESS: Test Development & Evaluation
CONSULTING SVCS, BUSINESS: Testing, Educational Or Personnel
CONSULTING SVCS, BUSINESS: Traffic
CONSULTING SVCS, BUSINESS: Urban Planning & Consulting
CONSULTING SVCS: Nuclear
CONSULTING SVCS: Physics
CONSULTING SVCS: Psychological
CONSULTING SVCS: Scientific
CONSUMER BUYING SVCS
CONSUMER CREDIT REPORTING BUREAU
CONSUMER PURCHASING SVCS
CONTAINERS: Cargo, Wood

CONTAINERS: Corrugated
CONTAINERS: Metal
CONTAINERS: Plastic
CONTAINERS: Shipping, Bombs, Metal Plate
CONTAINERS: Shipping, Wood
CONTAINMENT VESSELS: Reactor, Metal Plate
CONTRACTOR: Dredging
CONTRACTOR: Framing
CONTRACTOR: Rigging & Scaffolding
CONTRACTORS: Access Control System Eqpt
CONTRACTORS: Access Flooring System Installation
CONTRACTORS: Acoustical & Ceiling Work
CONTRACTORS: Acoustical & Insulation Work
CONTRACTORS: Artificial Turf Installation
CONTRACTORS: Asbestos Removal & Encapsulation
CONTRACTORS: Asphalt
CONTRACTORS: Awning Installation
CONTRACTORS: Banking Machine Installation & Svc
CONTRACTORS: Bathtub Refinishing
CONTRACTORS: Boiler Maintenance Contractor
CONTRACTORS: Boiler Setting
CONTRACTORS: Bricklaying
CONTRACTORS: Bridge Painting
CONTRACTORS: Building Eqpt & Machinery Installation
CONTRACTORS: Building Fireproofing
CONTRACTORS: Building Sign Installation & Mntnce
CONTRACTORS: Building Site Preparation
CONTRACTORS: Cable Laying
CONTRACTORS: Cable Splicing Svcs
CONTRACTORS: Cable TV Installation
CONTRACTORS: Caisson Drilling
CONTRACTORS: Carpentry Work
CONTRACTORS: Carpentry, Cabinet & Finish Work
CONTRACTORS: Carpentry, Cabinet Building & Installation
CONTRACTORS: Carpet Laying
CONTRACTORS: Ceramic Floor Tile Installation
CONTRACTORS: Chimney Construction & Maintenance
CONTRACTORS: Closet Organizers, Installation & Design
CONTRACTORS: Coating, Caulking & Weather, Water & Fire
CONTRACTORS: Commercial & Office Building
CONTRACTORS: Communications Svcs
CONTRACTORS: Computer Installation
CONTRACTORS: Concrete
CONTRACTORS: Concrete Pumping
CONTRACTORS: Concrete Reinforcement Placing
CONTRACTORS: Concrete Repair
CONTRACTORS: Concrete Structure Coating, Plastic
CONTRACTORS: Construction Caulking
CONTRACTORS: Construction Site Cleanup
CONTRACTORS: Construction Site Metal Structure Coating
CONTRACTORS: Core Drilling & Cutting
CONTRACTORS: Countertop Installation
CONTRACTORS: Demolition, Building & Other Structures
CONTRACTORS: Diamond Drilling & Sawing
CONTRACTORS: Directional Oil & Gas Well Drilling Svc
CONTRACTORS: Drapery Track Installation
CONTRACTORS: Driveway
CONTRACTORS: Drywall
CONTRACTORS: Earthmoving
CONTRACTORS: Electric Power Systems
CONTRACTORS: Electrical
CONTRACTORS: Electronic Controls Installation
CONTRACTORS: Energy Management Control
CONTRACTORS: Epoxy Application
CONTRACTORS: Erection & Dismantling, Poured Concrete Forms
CONTRACTORS: Excavating
CONTRACTORS: Exterior Concrete Stucco
CONTRACTORS: Exterior Painting
CONTRACTORS: Fence Construction
CONTRACTORS: Fiber Optic Cable Installation
CONTRACTORS: Fire Detection & Burglar Alarm Systems
CONTRACTORS: Fire Sprinkler System Installation Svcs
CONTRACTORS: Floor Laying & Other Floor Work
CONTRACTORS: Flooring
CONTRACTORS: Food Concessions
CONTRACTORS: Food Svcs Eqpt Installation
CONTRACTORS: Foundation & Footing
CONTRACTORS: Foundation Building
CONTRACTORS: Fountain Installation
CONTRACTORS: Garage Doors
CONTRACTORS: Gas Field Svcs, NEC
CONTRACTORS: General Electric
CONTRACTORS: Glass Tinting, Architectural & Automotive
CONTRACTORS: Glass, Glazing & Tinting

CONTRACTORS: Gutters & Downspouts
CONTRACTORS: Heating & Air Conditioning
CONTRACTORS: Heating Systems Repair & Maintenance Svc
CONTRACTORS: Highway & Street Construction, General
CONTRACTORS: Highway & Street Paving
CONTRACTORS: Highway & Street Resurfacing
CONTRACTORS: Home & Office Intrs Finish, Furnish/Remodel
CONTRACTORS: Hotel, Motel/Multi-Famly Home Renovtn/Remodel
CONTRACTORS: Hydraulic Eqpt Installation & Svcs
CONTRACTORS: Hydronics Heating
CONTRACTORS: Indl Building Renovation, Remodeling & Repair
CONTRACTORS: Insulation Installation, Building
CONTRACTORS: Kitchen & Bathroom Remodeling
CONTRACTORS: Lighting Conductor Erection
CONTRACTORS: Lighting Syst
CONTRACTORS: Lightweight Steel Framing Installation
CONTRACTORS: Machine Rigging & Moving
CONTRACTORS: Machinery Dismantling
CONTRACTORS: Machinery Installation
CONTRACTORS: Maintenance, Parking Facility Eqpt
CONTRACTORS: Marble Installation, Interior
CONTRACTORS: Marble Masonry, Exterior
CONTRACTORS: Masonry & Stonework
CONTRACTORS: Mechanical
CONTRACTORS: Millwrights
CONTRACTORS: Mosaic Work
CONTRACTORS: Multi-Family Home Remodeling
CONTRACTORS: Nonresidential Building Design & Construction
CONTRACTORS: Office Furniture Installation
CONTRACTORS: Oil & Gas Field Fire Fighting Svcs
CONTRACTORS: Oil & Gas Field Geological Exploration Svcs
CONTRACTORS: Oil & Gas Field Geophysical Exploration Svcs
CONTRACTORS: Oil & Gas Well Casing Cement Svcs
CONTRACTORS: Oil & Gas Well Drilling Svc
CONTRACTORS: Oil & Gas Well Flow Rate Measurement Svcs
CONTRACTORS: Oil & Gas Well On-Site Foundation Building Svcs
CONTRACTORS: Oil & Gas Well Redrilling
CONTRACTORS: Oil Field Haulage Svcs
CONTRACTORS: Oil Field Mud Drilling Svcs
CONTRACTORS: Oil Sampling Svcs
CONTRACTORS: Oil/Gas Field Casing,Tube/Rod Running,Cut/Pull
CONTRACTORS: Oil/Gas Well Construction, Rpr/Dismantling Svcs
CONTRACTORS: On-Site Welding
CONTRACTORS: Ornamental Metal Work
CONTRACTORS: Paint & Wallpaper Stripping
CONTRACTORS: Painting & Wall Covering
CONTRACTORS: Painting, Commercial
CONTRACTORS: Painting, Commercial, Exterior
CONTRACTORS: Painting, Commercial, Interior
CONTRACTORS: Painting, Indl
CONTRACTORS: Painting, Residential
CONTRACTORS: Parking Facility Eqpt Installation
CONTRACTORS: Parking Lot Maintenance
CONTRACTORS: Patio & Deck Construction & Repair
CONTRACTORS: Pavement Marking
CONTRACTORS: Pile Driving
CONTRACTORS: Pipe & Boiler Insulating
CONTRACTORS: Pipe Laying
CONTRACTORS: Plastering, Plain or Ornamental
CONTRACTORS: Plumbing
CONTRACTORS: Pollution Control Eqpt Installation
CONTRACTORS: Post Disaster Renovations
CONTRACTORS: Power Generating Eqpt Installation
CONTRACTORS: Precast Concrete Struct Framing & Panel Placing
CONTRACTORS: Prefabricated Window & Door Installation
CONTRACTORS: Process Piping
CONTRACTORS: Refractory or Acid Brick Masonry
CONTRACTORS: Refrigeration
CONTRACTORS: Resilient Floor Laying
CONTRACTORS: Roof Repair
CONTRACTORS: Roofing
CONTRACTORS: Safety & Security Eqpt
CONTRACTORS: Sandblasting Svc, Building Exteriors

CONTRACTORS: Septic System
CONTRACTORS: Sheet Metal Work, NEC
CONTRACTORS: Sheet metal Work, Architectural
CONTRACTORS: Shoring & Underpinning
CONTRACTORS: Sidewalk
CONTRACTORS: Siding
CONTRACTORS: Single-Family Home Fire Damage Repair
CONTRACTORS: Single-family Home General Remodeling
CONTRACTORS: Skylight Installation
CONTRACTORS: Solar Energy Eqpt
CONTRACTORS: Sound Eqpt Installation
CONTRACTORS: Special Trades, NEC
CONTRACTORS: Specialized Public Building
CONTRACTORS: Spraying, Nonagricultural
CONTRACTORS: Sprinkler System
CONTRACTORS: Steam Cleaning, Building Exterior
CONTRACTORS: Stone Masonry
CONTRACTORS: Storage Tank Erection, Metal
CONTRACTORS: Store Fixture Installation
CONTRACTORS: Structural Iron Work, Structural
CONTRACTORS: Structural Steel Erection
CONTRACTORS: Svc Station Eqpt
CONTRACTORS: Svc Station Eqpt Installation, Maint & Repair
CONTRACTORS: Tile Installation, Ceramic
CONTRACTORS: Trenching
CONTRACTORS: Tuck Pointing & Restoration
CONTRACTORS: Underground Utilities
CONTRACTORS: Ventilation & Duct Work
CONTRACTORS: Wall Covering
CONTRACTORS: Wall Covering, Commercial
CONTRACTORS: Warm Air Heating & Air Conditioning
CONTRACTORS: Water Well Drilling
CONTRACTORS: Water Well Servicing
CONTRACTORS: Waterproofing
CONTRACTORS: Window Treatment Installation
CONTRACTORS: Windows & Doors
CONTRACTORS: Wood Floor Installation & Refinishing
CONTRACTORS: Wrecking & Demolition
CONTROL EQPT: Electric
CONTROL EQPT: Noise
CONTROL PANELS: Electrical
CONTROLS & ACCESS: Indl, Electric
CONTROLS: Environmental
CONTROLS: Relay & Ind
CONVALESCENT HOME
CONVALESCENT HOMES
CONVENIENCE STORES
CONVENTION & TRADE SHOW SVCS
CONVERTERS: Data
CONVERTERS: Phase Or Rotary, Electrical
CONVEYOR SYSTEMS
CONVEYOR SYSTEMS: Belt, General Indl Use
CONVEYOR SYSTEMS: Robotic
CONVEYORS & CONVEYING EQPT
CONVEYORS: Overhead
COOKING & FOOD WARMING EQPT: Commercial
COPPER ORE MINING
COPY MACHINES WHOLESALERS
CORRECTIONAL FACILITY OPERATIONS
CORRECTIONAL INSTITUTIONS
CORRECTIONAL INSTITUTIONS, GOVERNMENT: Detention Center
CORRECTIONAL INSTITUTIONS, GOVERNMENT: Prison, government
CORRECTIONAL INSTITUTIONS, GOVERNMENT: State
CORRESPONDENCE SCHOOLS
CORRUGATED PRDTS: Boxes, Partition, Display Items, Sheet/Pad
COSMETIC PREPARATIONS
COSMETICS & TOILETRIES
COSMETICS WHOLESALERS
COSMETOLOGIST
COSMETOLOGY & PERSONAL HYGIENE SALONS
COSMETOLOGY SCHOOL
COUNCIL FOR SOCIAL AGENCY
COUNTER & SINK TOPS
COUNTERS & COUNTING DEVICES
COUNTRY CLUBS
COURIER OR MESSENGER SVCS
COURIER SVCS, AIR: Letter Delivery, Private
COURIER SVCS, AIR: Package Delivery, Private
COURIER SVCS, AIR: Parcel Delivery, Private
COURIER SVCS: Air
COURIER SVCS: Ground

COURIER SVCS: Package By Vehicle
COURIER SVCS: Parcel By Vehicle
COURT REPORTING SVCS
COURTS
COURTS OF LAW: County Government
COURTS OF LAW: Federal
COURTS OF LAW: Local
COURTS OF LAW: State
COVERS: Automobile Seat
CRANE & AERIAL LIFT SVCS
CRANES & MONORAIL SYSTEMS
CRANES: Indl Plant
CRANES: Indl Truck
CRANES: Overhead
CRANKSHAFTS & CAMSHAFTS: Machining
CREATIVE SVCS: Advertisers, Exc Writers
CREDIT & OTHER FINANCIAL RESPONSIBILITY INSURANCE
CREDIT AGENCIES: Federal & Federally Sponsored
CREDIT AGENCIES: Federal Home Loan Mortgage Corporation
CREDIT AGENCIES: National Consumer Cooperative Bank
CREDIT BUREAUS
CREDIT CARD PROCESSING SVCS
CREDIT CARD SVCS
CREDIT INST, SHORT-TERM BUSINESS: Financing Dealers
CREDIT INSTITUTIONS, SHORT-TERM BUS: Buying Install Notes
CREDIT INSTITUTIONS, SHORT-TERM BUS: Wrkg Capital Finance
CREDIT INSTITUTIONS: Personal
CREDIT INSTITUTIONS: Short-Term Business
CREDIT UNIONS: Federally Chartered
CREDIT UNIONS: State Chartered
CREMATORIES
CRISIS CENTER
CRISIS INTERVENTION CENTERS
CRUDE PETROLEUM & NATURAL GAS PRODUCTION
CRUDE PETROLEUM & NATURAL GAS PRODUCTION
CRUDE PETROLEUM PRODUCTION
CRYSTAL GOODS, WHOLESALE
CUPS: Paper, Made From Purchased Materials
CURTAIN & DRAPERY FIXTURES: Poles, Rods & Rollers
CURTAIN WALLS: Building, Steel
CURTAINS: Window, From Purchased Materials
CUSTODIAL SVCS: School, Contract Basis
CUSTOMIZING SVCS
CUSTOMS CLEARANCE OF FREIGHT
CUT STONE & STONE PRODUCTS
CUTLERY
CYLINDER & ACTUATORS: Fluid Power
CYLINDERS: Pressure
Convents

D

DAIRY PRDTS STORE: Ice Cream, Packaged
DAIRY PRDTS STORES
DAIRY PRDTS WHOLESALERS: Fresh
DAIRY PRDTS: Butter
DAIRY PRDTS: Cheese
DAIRY PRDTS: Dietary Supplements, Dairy & Non-Dairy Based
DAIRY PRDTS: Frozen Desserts & Novelties
DAIRY PRDTS: Ice Cream & Ice Milk
DAIRY PRDTS: Milk, Condensed & Evaporated
DAIRY PRDTS: Milk, Fluid
DAIRY PRDTS: Milk, Processed, Pasteurized, Homogenized/Btld
DAIRY PRDTS: Natural Cheese
DAIRY PRDTS: Whipped Topping, Exc Frozen Or Dry Mix
DANCE HALL OR BALLROOM OPERATION
DANCE HALL SVCS
DANCE INSTRUCTOR & SCHOOL
DATA ENTRY SVCS
DATA PROCESSING & PREPARATION SVCS
DATA PROCESSING SVCS
DATABASE INFORMATION RETRIEVAL SVCS
DATING SVCS
DEBT COUNSELING OR ADJUSTMENT SVCS: Individuals
DECORATIVE WOOD & WOODWORK
DEGREASING MACHINES
DELIVERY SVCS, BY VEHICLE
DENTAL EQPT & SPLYS
DENTAL EQPT & SPLYS WHOLESALERS
DENTAL EQPT & SPLYS: Orthodontic Appliances

DENTISTS' OFFICES & CLINICS
DEPARTMENT STORES
DEPARTMENT STORES: Non-Discount
DEPARTMENT STORES: Surplus & Salvage
DEPOSIT INSURANCE
DESALTER KITS: Sea Water
DESIGN SVCS, NEC
DESIGN SVCS: Commercial & Indl
DESIGN SVCS: Computer Integrated Systems
DETECTIVE & ARMORED CAR SERVICES
DETECTIVE AGENCY
DETECTIVE SVCS
DETOXIFICATION CENTERS, OUTPATIENT
DIAGNOSTIC SUBSTANCES
DICE & DICE CUPS
DIES & TOOLS: Special
DIET & WEIGHT REDUCING CENTERS
DIETICIANS' OFFICES
DIODES: Light Emitting
DIRECT SELLING ESTABLISHMENTS: Appliances, House-To-House
DIRECT SELLING ESTABLISHMENTS: Telemarketing
DISASTER SVCS
DISC JOCKEYS
DISCOUNT DEPARTMENT STORES
DISINFECTING SVCS
DISKETTE DUPLICATING SVCS
DISPLAY FIXTURES: Wood
DISPLAY ITEMS: Solid Fiber, Made From Purchased Materials
DOCK EQPT & SPLYS, INDL
DOCUMENT DESTRUCTION SVC
DOCUMENT STORAGE SVCS
DOLOMITE: Crushed & Broken
DOMESTIC HELP SVCS
DOMICILIARY CARE FACILITY
DOOR & WINDOW REPAIR SVCS
DOORS & WINDOWS WHOLESALERS: All Materials
DOORS & WINDOWS: Storm, Metal
DOORS: Garage, Overhead, Metal
DOORS: Garage, Overhead, Wood
DOORS: Glass
DOORS: Wooden
DRAFTING SPLYS WHOLESALERS
DRAFTING SVCS
DRAGSTRIP OPERATION
DRAPERIES & CURTAINS
DRAPERIES & DRAPERY FABRICS, COTTON
DRAPERIES: Plastic & Textile, From Purchased Materials
DRAPERY & UPHOLSTERY STORES: Draperies
DRAPES & DRAPERY FABRICS, FROM MANMADE FIBER
DRIED FRUITS WHOLESALERS
DRINKING PLACES: Alcoholic Beverages
DRINKING PLACES: Bars & Lounges
DRINKING PLACES: Tavern
DRIVE-A-WAY AUTOMOBILE SVCS
DRUG ABUSE COUNSELOR, NONTREATMENT
DRUG CLINIC, OUTPATIENT
DRUG STORES
DRUGS & DRUG PROPRIETARIES, WHOL: Biologicals/Allied Prdts
DRUGS & DRUG PROPRIETARIES, WHOLESALE
DRUGS & DRUG PROPRIETARIES, WHOLESALE: Antiseptics
DRUGS & DRUG PROPRIETARIES, WHOLESALE: Biotherapeutics
DRUGS & DRUG PROPRIETARIES, WHOLESALE: Blood Plasma
DRUGS & DRUG PROPRIETARIES, WHOLESALE: Druggists' Sundries
DRUGS & DRUG PROPRIETARIES, WHOLESALE: Medicinals/Botanicals
DRUGS & DRUG PROPRIETARIES, WHOLESALE: Patent Medicines
DRUGS & DRUG PROPRIETARIES, WHOLESALE: Pharmaceuticals
DRUGS & DRUG PROPRIETARIES, WHOLESALE: Vitamins & Minerals
DRYCLEANING & LAUNDRY SVCS: Commercial & Family
DRYCLEANING PLANTS
DRYCLEANING SVC: Collecting & Distributing Agency
DRYCLEANING SVC: Drapery & Curtain
DRYERS & REDRYERS: Indl
DUCTS: Sheet Metal
DURABLE GOODS WHOLESALERS, NEC

DYES & PIGMENTS: Organic

E

EARTH SCIENCE SVCS
EATING PLACES
ECONOMIC PROGRAMS ADMINISTRATION SVCS, NEC
EDUCATIONAL PROGRAM ADMINISTRATION, GOVERNMENT: County
EDUCATIONAL PROGRAM ADMINISTRATION, GOVERNMENT: State
EDUCATIONAL PROGRAMS ADMINISTRATION SVCS
EDUCATIONAL SVCS
EDUCATIONAL SVCS, NONDEGREE GRANTING: Continuing Education
EGG WHOLESALERS
ELECTRIC & OTHER SERVICES COMBINED
ELECTRIC FENCE CHARGERS
ELECTRIC MOTOR REPAIR SVCS
ELECTRIC POWER DISTRIBUTION TO CONSUMERS
ELECTRIC POWER GENERATION: Fossil Fuel
ELECTRIC POWER, COGENERATED
ELECTRIC SERVICES
ELECTRIC SVCS, NEC Power Broker
ELECTRIC SVCS, NEC Power Transmission
ELECTRIC SVCS, NEC: Power Generation
ELECTRICAL APPARATUS & EQPT WHOLESALERS
ELECTRICAL APPLIANCES, TELEVISIONS & RADIOS WHOLESALERS
ELECTRICAL CONSTRUCTION MATERIALS WHOLESALERS
ELECTRICAL CURRENT CARRYING WIRING DEVICES
ELECTRICAL DISCHARGE MACHINING, EDM
ELECTRICAL EQPT & SPLYS
ELECTRICAL EQPT FOR ENGINES
ELECTRICAL EQPT REPAIR & MAINTENANCE
ELECTRICAL EQPT REPAIR SVCS
ELECTRICAL EQPT: Automotive, NEC
ELECTRICAL GOODS, WHOLESALE: Alarms & Signaling Eqpt
ELECTRICAL GOODS, WHOLESALE: Boxes & Fittings
ELECTRICAL GOODS, WHOLESALE: Burglar Alarm Systems
ELECTRICAL GOODS, WHOLESALE: Cable Conduit
ELECTRICAL GOODS, WHOLESALE: Closed Circuit Television Or TV
ELECTRICAL GOODS, WHOLESALE: Connectors
ELECTRICAL GOODS, WHOLESALE: Electrical Appliances, Major
ELECTRICAL GOODS, WHOLESALE: Electrical Entertainment Eqpt
ELECTRICAL GOODS, WHOLESALE: Electronic Parts
ELECTRICAL GOODS, WHOLESALE: Facsimile Or Fax Eqpt
ELECTRICAL GOODS, WHOLESALE: Fire Alarm Systems
ELECTRICAL GOODS, WHOLESALE: Generators
ELECTRICAL GOODS, WHOLESALE: Intercommunication Eqpt
ELECTRICAL GOODS, WHOLESALE: Light Bulbs & Related Splys
ELECTRICAL GOODS, WHOLESALE: Lighting Fittings & Access
ELECTRICAL GOODS, WHOLESALE: Lighting Fixtures, Comm & Indl
ELECTRICAL GOODS, WHOLESALE: Mobile telephone Eqpt
ELECTRICAL GOODS, WHOLESALE: Modems, Computer
ELECTRICAL GOODS, WHOLESALE: Motor Ctrls, Starters & Relays
ELECTRICAL GOODS, WHOLESALE: Motors
ELECTRICAL GOODS, WHOLESALE: Paging & Signaling Eqpt
ELECTRICAL GOODS, WHOLESALE: Radio Parts & Access, NEC
ELECTRICAL GOODS, WHOLESALE: Security Control Eqpt & Systems
ELECTRICAL GOODS, WHOLESALE: Semiconductor Devices
ELECTRICAL GOODS, WHOLESALE: Sound Eqpt
ELECTRICAL GOODS, WHOLESALE: Telephone & Telegraphic Eqpt
ELECTRICAL GOODS, WHOLESALE: Telephone Eqpt
ELECTRICAL GOODS, WHOLESALE: Vacuum Cleaners, Household
ELECTRICAL GOODS, WHOLESALE: Washing Machines
ELECTRICAL GOODS, WHOLESALE: Wire & Cable
ELECTRICAL GOODS, WHOLESALE: Wire & Cable, Ctrl & Sig

ELECTRICAL GOODS, WHOLESALE: Wire & Cable, Electronic
ELECTRICAL HOUSEHOLD APPLIANCE REPAIR
ELECTRICAL MEASURING INSTRUMENT REPAIR & CALIBRATION SVCS
ELECTRICAL SPLYS
ELECTRODES: Thermal & Electrolytic
ELECTROMEDICAL EQPT
ELECTROMETALLURGICAL PRDTS
ELECTRONIC EQPT REPAIR SVCS
ELECTRONIC PARTS & EQPT WHOLESALERS
ELECTRONIC SHOPPING
ELEMENTARY & SECONDARY PRIVATE DENOMINATIONAL SCHOOLS
ELEMENTARY & SECONDARY SCHOOLS, COMBINED CATHOLIC
ELEMENTARY & SECONDARY SCHOOLS, PRIVATE NEC
ELEMENTARY & SECONDARY SCHOOLS, PUBLIC
ELEMENTARY & SECONDARY SCHOOLS, SPECIAL EDUCATION
ELEMENTARY SCHOOLS, CATHOLIC
ELEMENTARY SCHOOLS, PRIVATE
ELEMENTARY SCHOOLS, PUBLIC
ELEVATOR: Grain, Storage Only
ELEVATORS & EQPT
ELEVATORS WHOLESALERS
ELEVATORS: Automobile
ELEVATORS: Installation & Conversion
EMBROIDERING & ART NEEDLEWORK FOR THE TRADE
EMBROIDERING SVC
EMBROIDERY ADVERTISING SVCS
EMERGENCY & RELIEF SVCS
EMERGENCY SHELTERS
EMPLOYEE LEASING SVCS
EMPLOYMENT AGENCY SVCS
EMPLOYMENT SVCS: Labor Contractors
EMPLOYMENT SVCS: Nurses' Registry
ENGINEERING HELP SVCS
ENGINEERING SVCS
ENGINEERING SVCS: Acoustical
ENGINEERING SVCS: Aviation Or Aeronautical
ENGINEERING SVCS: Civil
ENGINEERING SVCS: Construction & Civil
ENGINEERING SVCS: Electrical Or Electronic
ENGINEERING SVCS: Energy conservation
ENGINEERING SVCS: Fire Protection
ENGINEERING SVCS: Heating & Ventilation
ENGINEERING SVCS: Industrial
ENGINEERING SVCS: Machine Tool Design
ENGINEERING SVCS: Mechanical
ENGINEERING SVCS: Mining
ENGINEERING SVCS: Pollution Control
ENGINEERING SVCS: Professional
ENGINEERING SVCS: Sanitary
ENGINEERING SVCS: Structural
ENGINES: Internal Combustion, NEC
ENGRAVING SVCS
ENTERTAINERS & ENTERTAINMENT GROUPS
ENTERTAINMENT PROMOTION SVCS
ENTERTAINMENT SVCS
ENVELOPES
ENVELOPES WHOLESALERS
ENVIR QLTY PROG ADMN, GOV: Land, Minl & Wildlif Consv, State
ENVIRON QUALITY PROGS ADMIN, GOVT: Sanitary Engineering
ENVIRON QUALITY PROGS ADMIN, GOVT: Water Control & Quality
ENVIRONMENTAL QUALITY PROGS ADMIN, GOVT: Recreational
ENVIRONMENTAL QUALITY PROGS ADMIN, GOVT: Waste Mgmt
ENZYMES
EQUIPMENT & VEHICLE FINANCE LEASING COMPANIES
EQUIPMENT: Rental & Leasing, NEC
ETCHING SVC: Metal
EXCAVATING MACHINERY & EQPT WHOLESALERS
EXECUTIVE OFFICES: Federal, State & Local
EXHIBITORS, ITINERANT, MOTION PICTURE
EXPLOSIVES
EXPLOSIVES, EXC AMMO & FIREWORKS WHOLESALERS
EXTENDED CARE FACILITY
EXTERMINATING & FUMIGATING SVCS
EYEGLASSES

F

FABRIC STORES
FABRICS: Broadwoven, Synthetic Manmade Fiber & Silk
FABRICS: Metallized
FABRICS: Trimmings
FABRICS: Woven, Narrow Cotton, Wool, Silk
FACIAL SALONS
FACILITIES SUPPORT SVCS
FACILITY RENTAL & PARTY PLANNING SVCS
FAMILY COUNSELING SVCS
FAMILY OR MARRIAGE COUNSELING
FAMILY PLANNING CENTERS
FAMILY PLANNING CLINIC
FAMILY SVCS AGENCY
FARM & GARDEN MACHINERY WHOLESALERS
FARM MACHINERY REPAIR SVCS
FARM PRDTS, RAW MATERIAL, WHOLESALE: Tobacco & Tobacco Prdts
FARM PRDTS, RAW MATERIALS, WHOLESALE: Farm Animals
FARM PRDTS, RAW MATERIALS, WHOLESALE: Hides
FARM SPLY STORES
FARM SPLYS WHOLESALERS
FARM SPLYS, WHOLESALE: Feed
FARM SPLYS, WHOLESALE: Flower & Field Bulbs
FARM SPLYS, WHOLESALE: Garden Splys
FARM SPLYS, WHOLESALE: Greenhouse Eqpt & Splys
FARM SPLYS, WHOLESALE: Herbicides
FARM SPLYS, WHOLESALE: Seed, Grass
FASTENERS WHOLESALERS
FASTENERS: Metal
FASTENERS: Notions, NEC
FEDERAL SAVINGS & LOAN ASSOCIATIONS
FEDERAL SAVINGS BANKS
FENCING DEALERS
FENCING: Chain Link
FERRALLOY ORES, EXC VANADIUM
FERTILIZER MINERAL MINING
FERTILIZER, AGRICULTURAL: Wholesalers
FERTILIZERS: NEC
FERTILIZERS: Phosphatic
FIBER & FIBER PRDTS: Synthetic Cellulosic
FIBER OPTICS
FIELD WAREHOUSING SVCS
FILE FOLDERS
FILM & SHEET: Unsuppported Plastic
FILM: Rubber
FILTER ELEMENTS: Fluid & Hydraulic Line
FILTERS
FILTERS & SOFTENERS: Water, Household
FINANCIAL INVESTMENT ACTIVITIES, NEC: Security Transfer
FINANCIAL INVESTMENT ADVICE
FINANCIAL SVCS
FINGERPRINTING SVCS
FINISHING SVCS
FIRE ALARM MAINTENANCE & MONITORING SVCS
FIRE CONTROL EQPT REPAIR SVCS, MILITARY
FIRE EXTINGUISHER SVC
FIRE EXTINGUISHERS, WHOLESALE
FIRE LOSS APPRAISAL
FIRE OR BURGLARY RESISTIVE PRDTS
FIRE PROTECTION EQPT
FIRE PROTECTION SVCS: Contracted
FIRE PROTECTION, EXC CONTRACT
FIRE PROTECTION, GOVERNMENT: County
FIRE PROTECTION, GOVERNMENT: Fire Department, Volunteer
FIRE PROTECTION, GOVERNMENT: Local
FIREARMS & AMMUNITION, EXC SPORTING, WHOLESALE
FIREARMS, EXC SPORTING, WHOLESALE
FIREWOOD, WHOLESALE
FIREWORKS SHOPS
FIREWORKS: Wholesalers
FISH & SEAFOOD WHOLESALERS
FISH, PACKAGED FROZEN: Wholesalers
FISHING CAMPS
FITTINGS & ASSEMBLIES: Hose & Tube, Hydraulic Or Pneumatic
FITTINGS: Pipe
FLAT GLASS: Construction
FLEA MARKET
FLIGHT TRAINING SCHOOLS
FLOATING DRY DOCKS

FLOOR COVERING STORES
FLOOR COVERING STORES: Carpets
FLOOR COVERING STORES: Floor Tile
FLOOR COVERING: Plastic
FLOOR COVERINGS WHOLESALERS
FLOOR WAXING SVCS
FLORIST: Flowers, Fresh
FLORIST: Plants, Potted
FLORISTS
FLORISTS' SPLYS, WHOLESALE
FLOTATION COMPANIES: Securities
FLOWERS & FLORISTS' SPLYS WHOLESALERS
FLOWERS & NURSERY STOCK, WHOLESALE
FLOWERS, ARTIFICIAL, WHOLESALE
FLOWERS, FRESH, WHOLESALE
FLUID POWER PUMPS & MOTORS
FLUID POWER VALVES & HOSE FITTINGS
FLUXES
FOAMS & RUBBER, WHOLESALE
FOIL & LEAF: Metal
FOOD PRDTS, CANNED: Chili
FOOD PRDTS, CANNED: Ethnic
FOOD PRDTS, CANNED: Fruits
FOOD PRDTS, CANNED: Tomatoes
FOOD PRDTS, CONFECTIONERY, WHOLESALE: Candy
FOOD PRDTS, CONFECTIONERY, WHOLESALE: Nuts, Salted/Roasted
FOOD PRDTS, CONFECTIONERY, WHOLESALE: Potato Chips
FOOD PRDTS, CONFECTIONERY, WHOLESALE: Snack Foods
FOOD PRDTS, CONFECTIONERY, WHOLESALE: Syrups, Fountain
FOOD PRDTS, DAIRY, WHOLESALE: Milk & Cream, Fluid
FOOD PRDTS, FISH & SEAFOOD, WHOLESALE: Fresh
FOOD PRDTS, FISH & SEAFOOD, WHOLESALE: Frozen, Unpackaged
FOOD PRDTS, FISH & SEAFOOD, WHOLESALE: Seafood
FOOD PRDTS, FROZEN: NEC
FOOD PRDTS, FRUITS & VEG, FRESH, WHOL: Banana Ripening Svc
FOOD PRDTS, FRUITS & VEGETABLES, FRESH, WHOLESALE
FOOD PRDTS, FRUITS & VEGETABLES, FRESH, WHOLESALE: Potatoes
FOOD PRDTS, FRUITS & VEGETABLES, FRESH, WHOLESALE: Vegetable
FOOD PRDTS, FRUITS & VEGETABLES, FRESH, WHOLESALE: Vegetable
FOOD PRDTS, MEAT & MEAT PRDTS, WHOLESALE: Brokers
FOOD PRDTS, MEAT & MEAT PRDTS, WHOLESALE: Cured Or Smoked
FOOD PRDTS, MEAT & MEAT PRDTS, WHOLESALE: Fresh
FOOD PRDTS, MEAT & MEAT PRDTS, WHOLESALE: Lard
FOOD PRDTS, POULTRY, WHOLESALE: Live/Dressed/Frozen, Unpkgd
FOOD PRDTS, WHOL: Canned Goods, Fruit, Veg, Seafood/Meats
FOOD PRDTS, WHOLESALE: Baking Splys
FOOD PRDTS, WHOLESALE: Beverage Concentrates
FOOD PRDTS, WHOLESALE: Beverages, Exc Coffee & Tea
FOOD PRDTS, WHOLESALE: Chocolate
FOOD PRDTS, WHOLESALE: Coffee & Tea
FOOD PRDTS, WHOLESALE: Coffee, Green Or Roasted
FOOD PRDTS, WHOLESALE: Corn
FOOD PRDTS, WHOLESALE: Dried or Canned Foods
FOOD PRDTS, WHOLESALE: Grain Elevators
FOOD PRDTS, WHOLESALE: Grains
FOOD PRDTS, WHOLESALE: Health
FOOD PRDTS, WHOLESALE: Juices
FOOD PRDTS, WHOLESALE: Molasses, Indl
FOOD PRDTS, WHOLESALE: Natural & Organic
FOOD PRDTS, WHOLESALE: Pizza Splys
FOOD PRDTS, WHOLESALE: Salt, Edible
FOOD PRDTS, WHOLESALE: Sandwiches
FOOD PRDTS, WHOLESALE: Spaghetti
FOOD PRDTS, WHOLESALE: Specialty
FOOD PRDTS, WHOLESALE: Starch
FOOD PRDTS, WHOLESALE: Water, Mineral Or Spring, Bottled
FOOD PRDTS, WHOLESALE: Wine Makers' Eqpt & Splys
FOOD PRDTS, Dried & Dehydrated Fruits, Vegetables & Soup Mix
FOOD PRDTS: Eggs, Processed

FOOD PRDTS: Eggs, Processed, Frozen
FOOD PRDTS: Flour & Other Grain Mill Products
FOOD PRDTS: Mixes, Flour
FOOD PRDTS: Potato & Corn Chips & Similar Prdts
FOOD PRDTS: Potato Chips & Other Potato-Based Snacks
FOOD PRDTS: Poultry, Processed, Frozen
FOOD PRDTS: Preparations
FOOD PRDTS: Salads
FOOD PRDTS: Sugar
FOOD PRDTS: Turkey, Processed, NEC
FOOD PRODUCTS MACHINERY
FOOD STORES: Convenience, Chain
FOOD STORES: Convenience, Independent
FOOD STORES: Delicatessen
FOOD STORES: Grocery, Chain
FOOD STORES: Grocery, Independent
FOOD STORES: Supermarket, More Than 100K Sq Ft, Hypermrkt
FOOD STORES: Supermarkets
FOOD STORES: Supermarkets, Chain
FOOD STORES: Supermarkets, Independent
FOOTWEAR, WHOLESALE: Athletic
FOOTWEAR, WHOLESALE: Shoes
FOOTWEAR, WHOLESALE: Slippers, House
FOREIGN CURRENCY EXCHANGE
FORGINGS
FORGINGS: Iron & Steel
FORGINGS: Nonferrous
FORGINGS: Plumbing Fixture, Nonferrous
FORMS: Concrete, Sheet Metal
FOUNDRIES: Aluminum
FOUNDRIES: Brass, Bronze & Copper
FOUNDRIES: Nonferrous
FOUNDRIES: Steel
FOUNDRY MACHINERY & EQPT
FRAMES & FRAMING WHOLESALE
FRANCHISES, SELLING OR LICENSING
FREIGHT CAR LOADING & UNLOADING SVCS
FREIGHT CONSOLIDATION SVCS
FREIGHT FORWARDING ARRANGEMENTS
FREIGHT FORWARDING ARRANGEMENTS: Domestic
FREIGHT FORWARDING ARRANGEMENTS: Foreign
FREIGHT HANDLING SVCS: Air
FREIGHT TRANSPORTATION ARRANGEMENTS
FROZEN FRUITS WHOLESALERS
FRUIT & VEGETABLE MARKETS
FRUIT STANDS OR MARKETS
FRUITS & VEGETABLES WHOLESALERS: Fresh
FUEL OIL DEALERS
FUND RAISING ORGANIZATION, NON-FEE BASIS
FUNDRAISING SVCS
FUNERAL HOME
FUNERAL HOMES & SVCS
FUNGICIDES OR HERBICIDES
FURNACES & OVENS: Indl
FURNACES: Indl, Electric
FURNACES: Warm Air, Electric
FURNITURE & CABINET STORES: Custom
FURNITURE REFINISHING SVCS
FURNITURE REPAIR & MAINTENANCE SVCS
FURNITURE STORES
FURNITURE STORES: Office
FURNITURE STORES: Outdoor & Garden
FURNITURE WHOLESALERS
FURNITURE, OFFICE: Wholesalers
FURNITURE, PUBLIC BUILDING: Wholesalers
FURNITURE, WHOLESALE: Bedsprings
FURNITURE, WHOLESALE: Filing Units
FURNITURE, WHOLESALE: Tables, Occasional
FURNITURE: Bed Frames & Headboards, Wood
FURNITURE: Frames, Box Springs Or Bedsprings, Metal
FURNITURE: Household, Upholstered, Exc Wood Or Metal
FURNITURE: Household, Wood
FURNITURE: Institutional, Exc Wood
FURNITURE: Mattresses & Foundations
FURNITURE: Office, Exc Wood
FURNITURE: Office, Wood
FURNITURE: Play Pens, Children's, Wood
FURNITURE: Upholstered
FUTURES ADVISORY SVCS

G

GAMES & TOYS: Child Restraint Seats, Automotive
GARAGE DOOR REPAIR SVCS
GARMENT: Pressing & cleaners' agents

GAS & OIL FIELD EXPLORATION SVCS
GAS & OIL FIELD SVCS, NEC
GAS & OTHER COMBINED SVCS
GAS FIELD MACHINERY & EQPT
GAS PRODUCTION & DISTRIBUTION: Liq Petroleum, Distrib-Mains
GAS STATIONS
GAS STATIONS WITH CONVENIENCE STORES
GAS SYSTEM CONVERSION SVCS
GASES: Acetylene
GASES: Indl
GASKETS
GASKETS & SEALING DEVICES
GASOLINE FILLING STATIONS
GASOLINE WHOLESALERS
GATES: Ornamental Metal
GEARS: Power Transmission, Exc Auto
GENERAL COUNSELING SVCS
GENERAL ECONOMIC PROGRAM ADMINISTRATION, GOVERNMENT: State
GENERAL MERCHANDISE, NONDURABLE, WHOLESALE
GERIATRIC RESIDENTIAL CARE FACILITY
GERIATRIC SOCIAL SVCS
GIFT SHOP
GIFT, NOVELTY & SOUVENIR STORES: Party Favors
GIFTS & NOVELTIES: Wholesalers
GIRLS CAMPS
GLASS FABRICATORS
GLASS PRDTS, FROM PURCHASED GLASS: Windshields
GLASS PRDTS, PRESSED OR BLOWN: Glass Fibers, Textile
GLASS PRDTS, PRESSED OR BLOWN: Glassware, Novelty
GLASS STORES
GLASS, AUTOMOTIVE: Wholesalers
GLASS: Fiber
GLASS: Flat
GLASS: Pressed & Blown, NEC
GLASS: Structural
GLASSWARE STORES
GLASSWARE, NOVELTY, WHOLESALE
GLOVES: Work
GO-CART DEALERS
GOLF CARTS: Powered
GOLF CARTS: Wholesalers
GOLF COURSES: Public
GOLF DRIVING RANGES
GOLF EQPT
GOLF GOODS & EQPT
GOURMET FOOD STORES
GOVERNMENT, EXECUTIVE OFFICES: City & Town Managers' Offices
GOVERNMENT, EXECUTIVE OFFICES: County Supervisor/Exec Office
GOVERNMENT, EXECUTIVE OFFICES: Local
GOVERNMENT, EXECUTIVE OFFICES: Mayors'
GOVERNMENT, GENERAL: Administration
GOVERNMENT, GENERAL: Administration, County
GOVERNMENT, GENERAL: Administration, State
GOVERNMENT, GENERAL: Supply Agency
GOVERNMENT, LEGISLATIVE BODIES: County
GOVERNMENT, LEGISLATIVE BODIES: County Commissioner
GOVERNMENT, LEGISLATIVE BODIES: Legislative Assembly
GOVERNMENT, LEGISLATIVE BODIES: Town Council
GRADING SVCS
GRAIN & FIELD BEANS WHOLESALERS
GRANITE: Crushed & Broken
GRANITE: Cut & Shaped
GRANTMAKING FOUNDATIONS
GRAPHIC ARTS & RELATED DESIGN SVCS
GRAPHITE MINING SVCS
GRAVEL MINING
GREASES & INEDIBLE FATS, RENDERED
GREENHOUSES: Prefabricated Metal
GREETING CARD SHOPS
GRINDING SVC: Precision, Commercial Or Indl
GROCERIES WHOLESALERS, NEC
GROCERIES, GENERAL LINE WHOLESALERS
GROUP DAY CARE CENTER
GROUP FOSTER HOME
GROUP HOSPITALIZATION PLANS
GUARD PROTECTIVE SVCS
GUARD SVCS
GYMNASTICS INSTRUCTION

H

HAIRDRESSERS
HALFWAY GROUP HOME, PERSONS WITH SOCIAL OR PERSONAL PROBLEMS
HALFWAY HOME FOR DELINQUENTS & OFFENDERS
HAND TOOLS, NEC: Wholesalers
HANDYMAN SVCS
HANGARS & OTHER AIRCRAFT STORAGE FACILITIES
HARDWARE
HARDWARE & BUILDING PRDTS: Plastic
HARDWARE & EQPT: Stage, Exc Lighting
HARDWARE STORES
HARDWARE STORES: Door Locks & Lock Sets
HARDWARE STORES: Pumps & Pumping Eqpt
HARDWARE STORES: Tools
HARDWARE WHOLESALERS
HARDWARE, WHOLESALE: Bolts
HARDWARE, WHOLESALE: Builders', NEC
HARDWARE, WHOLESALE: Casters & Glides
HARDWARE, WHOLESALE: Garden Tools, Hand
HARDWARE, WHOLESALE: Nuts
HARDWARE, WHOLESALE: Power Tools & Access
HARDWARE, WHOLESALE: Saw Blades
HARDWARE, WHOLESALE: Screws
HARDWARE: Rubber
HARNESS ASSEMBLIES: Cable & Wire
HEAD START CENTER, EXC IN CONJUNCTION WITH SCHOOL
HEALTH & ALLIED SERVICES, NEC
HEALTH & WELFARE COUNCIL
HEALTH CLUBS
HEALTH FOOD & SUPPLEMENT STORES
HEALTH INSURANCE CARRIERS
HEALTH MAINTENANCE ORGANIZATION: Insurance Only
HEALTH PRACTITIONERS' OFFICES, NEC
HEALTH SCREENING SVCS
HEALTH SYSTEMS AGENCY
HEARING TESTING SVCS
HEAT TREATING: Metal
HEATERS: Room & Wall, Including Radiators
HEATING & AIR CONDITIONING EQPT & SPLYS WHOLESALERS
HEATING EQPT & SPLYS
HELP SUPPLY SERVICES
HELPING HAND SVCS, INCLUDING BIG BROTHER, ETC
HIGHWAY & STREET MAINTENANCE SVCS
HIGHWAY BRIDGE OPERATION
HISTORICAL SOCIETY
HOBBY & CRAFT SPLY STORES
HOBBY, TOY & GAME STORES: Arts & Crafts & Splys
HOBBY, TOY & GAME STORES: Toys & Games
HOGS WHOLESALERS
HOLDING COMPANIES, NEC
HOLDING COMPANIES: Banks
HOLDING COMPANIES: Investment, Exc Banks
HOLDING COMPANIES: Personal, Exc Banks
HOLDING COMPANIES: Public Utility
HOME CENTER STORES
HOME FOR THE DESTITUTE
HOME FOR THE EMOTIONALLY DISTURBED
HOME FOR THE MENTALLY HANDICAPPED
HOME FOR THE MENTALLY RETARDED
HOME FOR THE MENTALLY RETARDED, EXC SKILLED OR INTERMEDIATE
HOME FOR THE PHYSICALLY HANDICAPPED
HOME FURNISHINGS WHOLESALERS
HOME HEALTH CARE SVCS
HOME IMPROVEMENT & RENOVATION CONTRACTOR AGENCY
HOMEBUILDERS & OTHER OPERATIVE BUILDERS
HOMEFURNISHING STORES: Fireplaces & Wood Burning Stoves
HOMEFURNISHING STORES: Lighting Fixtures
HOMEFURNISHING STORES: Metalware
HOMEFURNISHING STORES: Pottery
HOMEFURNISHINGS & SPLYS, WHOLESALE: Decorative
HOMEFURNISHINGS, WHOLESALE: Blankets
HOMEFURNISHINGS, WHOLESALE: Blinds, Venetian
HOMEFURNISHINGS, WHOLESALE: Carpets
HOMEFURNISHINGS, WHOLESALE: Draperies
HOMEFURNISHINGS, WHOLESALE: Grills, Barbecue
HOMEFURNISHINGS, WHOLESALE: Kitchenware
HOMEFURNISHINGS, WHOLESALE: Pottery
HOMEFURNISHINGS, WHOLESALE: Rugs

HOMEFURNISHINGS, WHOLESALE: Wood Flooring
HOMES FOR THE ELDERLY
HOSE: Automobile, Rubber
HOSE: Flexible Metal
HOSES & BELTING: Rubber & Plastic
HOSPITAL EQPT REPAIR SVCS
HOSPITALS: AMA Approved Residency
HOSPITALS: Cancer
HOSPITALS: Children's
HOSPITALS: Chronic Disease
HOSPITALS: Hospital, Professional Nursing School
HOSPITALS: Medical & Surgical
HOSPITALS: Medical School Affiliated With Nursing
HOSPITALS: Medical School Affiliated with Residency
HOSPITALS: Medical School Affiliation
HOSPITALS: Mental Retardation
HOSPITALS: Mental, Exc For The Mentally Retarded
HOSPITALS: Orthopedic
HOSPITALS: Professional Nursing School With AMA Residency
HOSPITALS: Psychiatric
HOSPITALS: Rehabilitation, Alcoholism
HOSPITALS: Rehabilitation, Drug Addiction
HOSPITALS: Specialty, NEC
HOSPITALS: Substance Abuse
HOTEL: Franchised
HOTELS & MOTELS
HOTLINE
HOUSEHOLD APPLIANCE PARTS: Wholesalers
HOUSEHOLD APPLIANCE REPAIR SVCS
HOUSEHOLD APPLIANCE STORES
HOUSEHOLD APPLIANCE STORES: Air Cond Rm Units, Self-Contnd
HOUSEHOLD APPLIANCE STORES: Appliance Parts
HOUSEHOLD APPLIANCE STORES: Electric
HOUSEHOLD APPLIANCE STORES: Electric Household, Major
HOUSEHOLD APPLIANCE STORES: Gas Appliances
HOUSEHOLD FURNISHINGS, NEC
HOUSEKEEPING & MAID SVCS
HOUSES: Fraternity & Sorority
HOUSES: Lodging, Organization
HOUSES: Rooming & Boarding
HOUSEWARE STORES
HOUSEWARES, ELECTRIC: Cooking Appliances
HOUSING AUTHORITY OPERATOR
HOUSING PROGRAM ADMIN, GOVT: Housing Authority, Nonoperating
HOUSING PROGRAM ADMINISTRATION, GOVT: Planning & Development
HOUSING PROGRAMS ADMINISTRATION SVCS
HUMAN RESOURCE, SOCIAL WORK & WELFARE ADMINISTRATION SVCS
HUMANE SOCIETIES
HYDRAULIC EQPT REPAIR SVC

I

ICE
ICE CREAM & ICES WHOLESALERS
ICE WHOLESALERS
IGNEOUS ROCK: Crushed & Broken
INCUBATORS & BROODERS: Farm
INDL & PERSONAL SVC PAPER WHOLESALERS
INDL & PERSONAL SVC PAPER, WHOL: Bags, Paper/Disp Plastic
INDL & PERSONAL SVC PAPER, WHOL: Boxes, Corrugtd/Solid Fiber
INDL & PERSONAL SVC PAPER, WHOL: Paper, Wrap/Coarse/Prdts
INDL & PERSONAL SVC PAPER, WHOLESALE: Disposable
INDL & PERSONAL SVC PAPER, WHOLESALE: Paper Tubes & Cores
INDL & PERSONAL SVC PAPER, WHOLESALE: Patterns, Paper
INDL & PERSONAL SVC PAPER, WHOLESALE: Press Sensitive Tape
INDL & PERSONAL SVC PAPER, WHOLESALE: Shipping Splys
INDL & PERSONAL SVC PAPER, WHOLESALE: Towels, Paper
INDL CONTRACTORS: Exhibit Construction
INDL DIAMONDS WHOLESALERS
INDL EQPT CLEANING SVCS
INDL EQPT SVCS
INDL GASES WHOLESALERS

INDL HELP SVCS
INDL MACHINERY & EQPT WHOLESALERS
INDL MACHINERY REPAIR & MAINTENANCE
INDL PROCESS INSTRUMENTS: Controllers, Process Variables
INDL SPLYS WHOLESALERS
INDL SPLYS, WHOL: Fasteners, Incl Nuts, Bolts, Screws, Etc
INDL SPLYS, WHOLESALE: Abrasives
INDL SPLYS, WHOLESALE: Abrasives & Adhesives
INDL SPLYS, WHOLESALE: Adhesives, Tape & Plasters
INDL SPLYS, WHOLESALE: Barrels, New Or Reconditioned
INDL SPLYS, WHOLESALE: Bearings
INDL SPLYS, WHOLESALE: Bins & Containers, Storage
INDL SPLYS, WHOLESALE: Bottler Splys
INDL SPLYS, WHOLESALE: Drums, New Or Reconditioned
INDL SPLYS, WHOLESALE: Electric Tools
INDL SPLYS, WHOLESALE: Fasteners & Fastening Eqpt
INDL SPLYS, WHOLESALE: Filters, Indl
INDL SPLYS, WHOLESALE: Fittings
INDL SPLYS, WHOLESALE: Gaskets
INDL SPLYS, WHOLESALE: Gaskets & Seals
INDL SPLYS, WHOLESALE: Hydraulic & Pneumatic Pistons/Valves
INDL SPLYS, WHOLESALE: Knives, Indl
INDL SPLYS, WHOLESALE: Mill Splys
INDL SPLYS, WHOLESALE: Plastic, Pallets
INDL SPLYS, WHOLESALE: Power Transmission, Eqpt & Apparatus
INDL SPLYS, WHOLESALE: Rubber Goods, Mechanical
INDL SPLYS, WHOLESALE: Seals
INDL SPLYS, WHOLESALE: Signmaker Eqpt & Splys
INDL SPLYS, WHOLESALE: Tools
INDL SPLYS, WHOLESALE: Tools, NEC
INDL SPLYS, WHOLESALE: Valves & Fittings
INDL TOOL GRINDING SVCS
INDL TRUCK REPAIR SVCS
INDOOR PARKING SVCS
INDUSTRIAL & COMMERCIAL EQPT INSPECTION SVCS
INFORMATION BUREAU SVCS
INFORMATION RETRIEVAL SERVICES
INFORMATION SVCS: Consumer
INNS
INSECTICIDES & PESTICIDES
INSPECTION & TESTING SVCS
INSPECTION SVCS, TRANSPORTATION
INSTRUMENTS, MEASURING & CNTRL: Testing, Abrasion, Etc
INSTRUMENTS, MEASURING & CONTROLLING: Cable Testing
INSTRUMENTS: Analytical
INSTRUMENTS: Eye Examination
INSTRUMENTS: Indl Process Control
INSTRUMENTS: Measurement, Indl Process
INSTRUMENTS: Measuring & Controlling
INSTRUMENTS: Measuring Electricity
INSTRUMENTS: Measuring, Electrical Energy
INSTRUMENTS: Medical & Surgical
INSTRUMENTS: Power Measuring, Electrical
INSTRUMENTS: Test, Electrical, Engine
INSTRUMENTS: Test, Electronic & Electric Measurement
INSTRUMENTS: Test, Electronic & Electrical Circuits
INSULATION & CUSHIONING FOAM: Polystyrene
INSULATION MATERIALS WHOLESALERS
INSULATION: Fiberglass
INSULATORS & INSULATION MATERIALS: Electrical
INSURANCE AGENCIES & BROKERS
INSURANCE AGENTS, NEC
INSURANCE BROKERS, NEC
INSURANCE CARRIERS: Automobile
INSURANCE CARRIERS: Bank Deposit
INSURANCE CARRIERS: Dental
INSURANCE CARRIERS: Direct Accident & Health
INSURANCE CARRIERS: Hospital & Medical
INSURANCE CARRIERS: Life
INSURANCE CARRIERS: Pet, Health
INSURANCE CARRIERS: Property & Casualty
INSURANCE CARRIERS: Title
INSURANCE CARRIERS: Worker's Compensation
INSURANCE CLAIM ADJUSTERS, NOT EMPLOYED BY INSURANCE COMPANY
INSURANCE CLAIM PROCESSING, EXC MEDICAL
INSURANCE EDUCATION SVCS
INSURANCE INFORMATION & CONSULTING SVCS
INSURANCE RESEARCH SVCS
INSURANCE: Agents, Brokers & Service

MACHINERY & EQPT, AGRICULTURAL, WHOLESALE: Agricultural, NEC
MACHINERY & EQPT, AGRICULTURAL, WHOLESALE: Dairy
MACHINERY & EQPT, AGRICULTURAL, WHOLESALE: Farm Implements
MACHINERY & EQPT, AGRICULTURAL, WHOLESALE: Hydroponic
MACHINERY & EQPT, AGRICULTURAL, WHOLESALE: Landscaping Eqpt
MACHINERY & EQPT, AGRICULTURAL, WHOLESALE: Lawn
MACHINERY & EQPT, AGRICULTURAL, WHOLESALE: Lawn & Garden
MACHINERY & EQPT, AGRICULTURAL, WHOLESALE: Livestock Eqpt
MACHINERY & EQPT, AGRICULTURAL, WHOLESALE: Tractors
MACHINERY & EQPT, INDL, WHOL: Brewery Prdts Mfrg, Commercial
MACHINERY & EQPT, INDL, WHOL: Controlling Instruments/Access
MACHINERY & EQPT, INDL, WHOL: Environ Pollution Cntrl, Air
MACHINERY & EQPT, INDL, WHOLESALE: Cement Making
MACHINERY & EQPT, INDL, WHOLESALE: Chemical Process
MACHINERY & EQPT, INDL, WHOLESALE: Conveyor Systems
MACHINERY & EQPT, INDL, WHOLESALE: Cranes
MACHINERY & EQPT, INDL, WHOLESALE: Dairy Prdts Manufacturing
MACHINERY & EQPT, INDL, WHOLESALE: Drilling Bits
MACHINERY & EQPT, INDL, WHOLESALE: Engines & Parts, Diesel
MACHINERY & EQPT, INDL, WHOLESALE: Engines, Gasoline
MACHINERY & EQPT, INDL, WHOLESALE: Engs & Parts, Air-Cooled
MACHINERY & EQPT, INDL, WHOLESALE: Fans
MACHINERY & EQPT, INDL, WHOLESALE: Food Manufacturing
MACHINERY & EQPT, INDL, WHOLESALE: Food Product Manufacturng
MACHINERY & EQPT, INDL, WHOLESALE: Heat Exchange
MACHINERY & EQPT, INDL, WHOLESALE: Hoists
MACHINERY & EQPT, INDL, WHOLESALE: Hydraulic Systems
MACHINERY & EQPT, INDL, WHOLESALE: Indl Machine Parts
MACHINERY & EQPT, INDL, WHOLESALE: Instruments & Cntrl Eqpt
MACHINERY & EQPT, INDL, WHOLESALE: Lift Trucks & Parts
MACHINERY & EQPT, INDL, WHOLESALE: Machine Tools & Access
MACHINERY & EQPT, INDL, WHOLESALE: Machine Tools & Metalwork
MACHINERY & EQPT, INDL, WHOLESALE: Measure/Test, Electric
MACHINERY & EQPT, INDL, WHOLESALE: Noise Control
MACHINERY & EQPT, INDL, WHOLESALE: Packaging
MACHINERY & EQPT, INDL, WHOLESALE: Paper Manufacturing
MACHINERY & EQPT, INDL, WHOLESALE: Petroleum Industry
MACHINERY & EQPT, INDL, WHOLESALE: Plastic Prdts Machinery
MACHINERY & EQPT, INDL, WHOLESALE: Pneumatic Tools
MACHINERY & EQPT, INDL, WHOLESALE: Processing & Packaging
MACHINERY & EQPT, INDL, WHOLESALE: Propane Conversion
MACHINERY & EQPT, INDL, WHOLESALE: Pulverizing
MACHINERY & EQPT, INDL, WHOLESALE: Recycling
MACHINERY & EQPT, INDL, WHOLESALE: Robots
MACHINERY & EQPT, INDL, WHOLESALE: Safety Eqpt
MACHINERY & EQPT, INDL, WHOLESALE: Tanks, Storage
MACHINERY & EQPT, INDL, WHOLESALE: Woodworking
MACHINERY & EQPT, WHOLESALE: Construction & Mining, Ladders
MACHINERY & EQPT, WHOLESALE: Construction, Cranes
MACHINERY & EQPT, WHOLESALE: Construction, General
MACHINERY & EQPT, WHOLESALE: Contractors Materials
MACHINERY & EQPT, WHOLESALE: Drilling, Wellpoints
MACHINERY & EQPT, WHOLESALE: Logging
MACHINERY & EQPT, WHOLESALE: Masonry

MACHINERY & EQPT, WHOLESALE: Oil Field Eqpt
MACHINERY & EQPT, WHOLESALE: Road Construction & Maintenance
MACHINERY & EQPT: Electroplating
MACHINERY & EQPT: Farm
MACHINERY & EQPT: Gas Producers, Generators/Other Rltd Eqpt
MACHINERY CLEANING SVCS
MACHINERY, MAILING: Postage Meters
MACHINERY, METALWORKING: Assembly, Including Robotic
MACHINERY, METALWORKING: Cutting & Slitting
MACHINERY, OFFICE: Paper Handling
MACHINERY, PACKAGING: Wrapping
MACHINERY, WOODWORKING: Pattern Makers'
MACHINERY/EQPT, INDL, WHOL: Cleaning, High Press, Sand/Steam
MACHINERY: Ammunition & Explosives Loading
MACHINERY: Assembly, Exc Metalworking
MACHINERY: Automotive Related
MACHINERY: Binding
MACHINERY: Bottling & Canning
MACHINERY: Construction
MACHINERY: Custom
MACHINERY: Folding
MACHINERY: Glassmaking
MACHINERY: Logging Eqpt
MACHINERY: Metalworking
MACHINERY: Mining
MACHINERY: Packaging
MACHINERY: Plastic Working
MACHINERY: Printing Presses
MACHINERY: Recycling
MACHINERY: Road Construction & Maintenance
MACHINERY: Rubber Working
MACHINERY: Textile
MACHINERY: Wire Drawing
MAGAZINES, WHOLESALE
MAGNETS: Permanent
MAIL PRESORTING SVCS
MAIL-ORDER HOUSE, NEC
MAIL-ORDER HOUSES: Arts & Crafts Eqpt & Splys
MAIL-ORDER HOUSES: Automotive Splys & Eqpt
MAIL-ORDER HOUSES: Books, Exc Book Clubs
MAIL-ORDER HOUSES: Cheese
MAIL-ORDER HOUSES: Computer Software
MAIL-ORDER HOUSES: Computers & Peripheral Eqpt
MAIL-ORDER HOUSES: Educational Splys & Eqpt
MAIL-ORDER HOUSES: Food
MAIL-ORDER HOUSES: Gift Items
MAILBOX RENTAL & RELATED SVCS
MAILING & MESSENGER SVCS
MAILING LIST: Compilers
MAILING SVCS, NEC
MANAGEMENT CONSULTING SVCS: Administrative
MANAGEMENT CONSULTING SVCS: Automation & Robotics
MANAGEMENT CONSULTING SVCS: Banking & Finance
MANAGEMENT CONSULTING SVCS: Business
MANAGEMENT CONSULTING SVCS: Business Planning & Organizing
MANAGEMENT CONSULTING SVCS: Compensation & Benefits Planning
MANAGEMENT CONSULTING SVCS: Construction Project
MANAGEMENT CONSULTING SVCS: Corporation Organizing
MANAGEMENT CONSULTING SVCS: Distribution Channels
MANAGEMENT CONSULTING SVCS: Food & Beverage
MANAGEMENT CONSULTING SVCS: Foreign Trade
MANAGEMENT CONSULTING SVCS: Franchising
MANAGEMENT CONSULTING SVCS: General
MANAGEMENT CONSULTING SVCS: Hospital & Health
MANAGEMENT CONSULTING SVCS: Industrial & Labor
MANAGEMENT CONSULTING SVCS: Industry Specialist
MANAGEMENT CONSULTING SVCS: Information Systems
MANAGEMENT CONSULTING SVCS: Maintenance
MANAGEMENT CONSULTING SVCS: Management Engineering
MANAGEMENT CONSULTING SVCS: Manufacturing
MANAGEMENT CONSULTING SVCS: Merchandising
MANAGEMENT CONSULTING SVCS: New Products & Svcs
MANAGEMENT CONSULTING SVCS: Planning
MANAGEMENT CONSULTING SVCS: Public Utilities
MANAGEMENT CONSULTING SVCS: Quality Assurance
MANAGEMENT CONSULTING SVCS: Real Estate
MANAGEMENT CONSULTING SVCS: Restaurant & Food

MANAGEMENT CONSULTING SVCS: Retail Trade Consultant
MANAGEMENT CONSULTING SVCS: Training & Development
MANAGEMENT CONSULTING SVCS: Transportation
MANAGEMENT SERVICES
MANAGEMENT SVCS, FACILITIES SUPPORT: Environ Remediation
MANAGEMENT SVCS, FACILITIES SUPPORT: Jails, Privately Ops
MANAGEMENT SVCS: Administrative
MANAGEMENT SVCS: Business
MANAGEMENT SVCS: Circuit, Motion Picture Theaters
MANAGEMENT SVCS: Construction
MANAGEMENT SVCS: Financial, Business
MANAGEMENT SVCS: Hospital
MANAGEMENT SVCS: Hotel Or Motel
MANAGEMENT SVCS: Nursing & Personal Care Facility
MANAGEMENT SVCS: Restaurant
MANAGERS: Athletes
MANPOWER POOLS
MANPOWER TRAINING
MANUFACTURING INDUSTRIES, NEC
MARBLE, BUILDING: Cut & Shaped
MARINAS
MARINE CARGO HANDLING SVCS
MARINE CARGO HANDLING SVCS: Loading
MARINE CARGO HANDLING SVCS: Loading & Unloading
MARINE CARGO HANDLING SVCS: Marine Terminal
MARINE SPLYS WHOLESALERS
MARINE SVC STATIONS
MARKETS: Meat & fish
MARKING DEVICES: Embossing Seals & Hand Stamps
MARKING DEVICES: Screens, Textile Printing
MARRIAGE BUREAU
MARTIAL ARTS INSTRUCTION
MASSAGE PARLOR & STEAM BATH SVCS
MASSAGE PARLORS
MATERIALS HANDLING EQPT WHOLESALERS
MATS OR MATTING, NEC: Rubber
MATS, MATTING & PADS: Auto, Floor, Exc Rubber Or Plastic
MATS, MATTING & PADS: Nonwoven
MEAL DELIVERY PROGRAMS
MEAT & MEAT PRDTS WHOLESALERS
MEAT CUTTING & PACKING
MEAT MARKETS
MEAT PRDTS: Cooked Meats, From Purchased Meat
MEAT PRDTS: Frozen
MEAT PRDTS: Pork, From Slaughtered Meat
MEAT PRDTS: Prepared Beef Prdts From Purchased Beef
MEAT PROCESSED FROM PURCHASED CARCASSES
MEATS, PACKAGED FROZEN: Wholesalers
MEDIA BUYING AGENCIES
MEDICAL & HOSPITAL EQPT WHOLESALERS
MEDICAL & SURGICAL SPLYS: Bandages & Dressings
MEDICAL & SURGICAL SPLYS: Clothing, Fire Resistant & Protect
MEDICAL & SURGICAL SPLYS: Hosiery, Support
MEDICAL CENTERS
MEDICAL EQPT REPAIR SVCS, NON-ELECTRIC
MEDICAL FIELD ASSOCIATION
MEDICAL HELP SVCS
MEDICAL INSURANCE CLAIM PROCESSING: Contract Or Fee Basis
MEDICAL RESCUE SQUAD
MEDICAL SVCS ORGANIZATION
MEDICAL TRAINING SERVICES
MEDICAL X-RAY MACHINES & TUBES WHOLESALERS
MEDICAL, DENTAL & HOSP EQPT, WHOLESALE: X-ray Film & Splys
MEDICAL, DENTAL & HOSPITAL EQPT, WHOL: Dentists' Prof Splys
MEDICAL, DENTAL & HOSPITAL EQPT, WHOL: Hospital Eqpt & Splys
MEDICAL, DENTAL & HOSPITAL EQPT, WHOL: Hosptl Eqpt/Furniture
MEDICAL, DENTAL & HOSPITAL EQPT, WHOL: Physician Eqpt/Splys
MEDICAL, DENTAL & HOSPITAL EQPT, WHOL: Surgical Eqpt & Splys
MEDICAL, DENTAL & HOSPITAL EQPT, WHOLESALE: Artificial Limbs
MEDICAL, DENTAL & HOSPITAL EQPT, WHOLESALE: Diagnostic, Med

SVCS INDEX

MEDICAL, DENTAL & HOSPITAL EQPT, WHOLESALE: Med Eqpt & Splys
MEDICAL, DENTAL & HOSPITAL EQPT, WHOLESALE: Medical Lab
MEDICAL, DENTAL & HOSPITAL EQPT, WHOLESALE: Orthopedic
MEDICAL, DENTAL & HOSPITAL EQPT, WHOLESALE: Safety
MEDICAL, DENTAL & HOSPITAL EQPT, WHOLESALE: Therapy
MEDICAL, DENTAL/HOSPITAL EQPT, WHOL: Tech Aids, Handicapped
MEDICAL, DENTAL/HOSPITAL EQPT, WHOL: Veterinarian Eqpt/Sply
MEMBER ORGS, CIVIC, SOCIAL & FRATERNAL: Bars & Restaurants
MEMBERSHIP HOTELS
MEMBERSHIP ORGANIZATIONS, BUSINESS: Community Affairs & Svcs
MEMBERSHIP ORGANIZATIONS, BUSINESS: Contractors' Association
MEMBERSHIP ORGANIZATIONS, BUSINESS: Merchants' Association
MEMBERSHIP ORGANIZATIONS, BUSINESS: Public Utility Assoc
MEMBERSHIP ORGANIZATIONS, CIVIC, SOCIAL/FRAT: Boy Scout Org
MEMBERSHIP ORGANIZATIONS, CIVIC, SOCIAL/FRAT: Rec Assoc
MEMBERSHIP ORGANIZATIONS, CIVIC, SOCIAL/FRAT: Social Assoc
MEMBERSHIP ORGANIZATIONS, CIVIC, SOCIAL/FRAT: Youth Orgs
MEMBERSHIP ORGANIZATIONS, LABOR UNIONS & SIMILAR: Trade
MEMBERSHIP ORGANIZATIONS, NEC: Amateur Sports Promotion
MEMBERSHIP ORGANIZATIONS, NEC: Art Council
MEMBERSHIP ORGANIZATIONS, NEC: Automobile Owner Association
MEMBERSHIP ORGANIZATIONS, NEC: Charitable
MEMBERSHIP ORGANIZATIONS, NEC: Food Co-Operative
MEMBERSHIP ORGANIZATIONS, NEC: Historical Club
MEMBERSHIP ORGANIZATIONS, NEC: Personal Interest
MEMBERSHIP ORGANIZATIONS, PROF: Education/Teacher Assoc
MEMBERSHIP ORGANIZATIONS, PROFESSIONAL: Accounting Assoc
MEMBERSHIP ORGANIZATIONS, PROFESSIONAL: Health Association
MEMBERSHIP ORGANIZATIONS, REL: Christian & Reformed Church
MEMBERSHIP ORGANIZATIONS, RELIGIOUS: Apostolic Church
MEMBERSHIP ORGANIZATIONS, RELIGIOUS: Assembly Of God Church
MEMBERSHIP ORGANIZATIONS, RELIGIOUS: Baptist Church
MEMBERSHIP ORGANIZATIONS, RELIGIOUS: Brethren Church
MEMBERSHIP ORGANIZATIONS, RELIGIOUS: Catholic Church
MEMBERSHIP ORGANIZATIONS, RELIGIOUS: Church Of Christ
MEMBERSHIP ORGANIZATIONS, RELIGIOUS: Church Of God
MEMBERSHIP ORGANIZATIONS, RELIGIOUS: Community Church
MEMBERSHIP ORGANIZATIONS, RELIGIOUS: Lutheran Church
MEMBERSHIP ORGANIZATIONS, RELIGIOUS: Methodist Church
MEMBERSHIP ORGANIZATIONS, RELIGIOUS: Nonchurch
MEMBERSHIP ORGANIZATIONS, RELIGIOUS: Pentecostal Church
MEMBERSHIP ORGANIZATIONS, RELIGIOUS: Presbyterian Church
MEMBERSHIP ORGS, CIVIC, SOCIAL & FRAT: Comm Member Club
MEMBERSHIP ORGS, CIVIC, SOCIAL & FRAT: Dwelling-Related
MEMBERSHIP ORGS, CIVIC, SOCIAL & FRAT: Girl Scout
MEMBERSHIP ORGS, CIVIC, SOCIAL & FRATERNAL: Civic Assoc

MEMBERSHIP ORGS, CIVIC, SOCIAL & FRATERNAL: Condo Assoc
MEMBERSHIP ORGS, CIVIC, SOCIAL & FRATERNAL: Protection
MEMBERSHIP ORGS, CIVIC, SOCIAL & FRATERNAL: Singing Society
MEMBERSHIP ORGS, CIVIC, SOCIAL & FRATERNAL: University Club
MEMBERSHIP ORGS, CIVIC, SOCIAL/FRAT: Educator's Assoc
MEMBERSHIP ORGS, LABOR UNIONS/SIMILAR: Employees' Assoc
MEMBERSHIP ORGS, RELIGIOUS: Non-Denominational Church
MEMBERSHIP SPORTS & RECREATION CLUBS
MEN'S & BOYS' CLOTHING STORES
MEN'S & BOYS' CLOTHING WHOLESALERS, NEC
MEN'S & BOYS' SPORTSWEAR WHOLESALERS
MENTAL HEALTH CLINIC, OUTPATIENT
MENTAL HEALTH PRACTITIONERS' OFFICES
MERCHANDISING MACHINE OPERATORS: Vending
METAL & STEEL PRDTS: Abrasive
METAL COMPONENTS: Prefabricated
METAL CUTTING SVCS
METAL FABRICATORS: Architechtural
METAL FABRICATORS: Plate
METAL FABRICATORS: Sheet
METAL MINING SVCS
METAL SERVICE CENTERS & OFFICES
METAL SLITTING & SHEARING
METAL STAMPING, FOR THE TRADE
METAL STAMPINGS: Patterned
METALS SVC CENTERS & WHOL: Semifinished Prdts, Iron/Steel
METALS SVC CENTERS & WHOL: Structural Shapes, Iron Or Steel
METALS SVC CENTERS & WHOLESALERS: Cable, Wire
METALS SVC CENTERS & WHOLESALERS: Casting, Rough,Iron/Steel
METALS SVC CENTERS & WHOLESALERS: Concrete Reinforcing Bars
METALS SVC CENTERS & WHOLESALERS: Copper
METALS SVC CENTERS & WHOLESALERS: Ferroalloys
METALS SVC CENTERS & WHOLESALERS: Ferrous Metals
METALS SVC CENTERS & WHOLESALERS: Flat Prdts, Iron Or Steel
METALS SVC CENTERS & WHOLESALERS: Foundry Prdts
METALS SVC CENTERS & WHOLESALERS: Iron & Steel Prdt, Ferrous
METALS SVC CENTERS & WHOLESALERS: Nonferrous Sheets, Etc
METALS SVC CENTERS & WHOLESALERS: Pipe & Tubing, Steel
METALS SVC CENTERS & WHOLESALERS: Plates, Metal
METALS SVC CENTERS & WHOLESALERS: Rope, Wire, Exc Insulated
METALS SVC CENTERS & WHOLESALERS: Sheets, Galvanized/Coated
METALS SVC CENTERS & WHOLESALERS: Sheets, Metal
METALS SVC CENTERS & WHOLESALERS: Stampings, Metal
METALS SVC CENTERS & WHOLESALERS: Steel
METALS SVC CENTERS & WHOLESALERS: Strip, Metal
METALS SVC CENTERS & WHOLESALERS: Tubing, Metal
METALS SVC CNTRS & WHOL: Metal Wires, Ties, Cables/Screening
METALS SVC CTRS & WHOLESALERS: Aluminum Bars, Rods, Etc
METALS: Primary Nonferrous, NEC
METALWORK: Miscellaneous
METER READERS: Remote
MGMT CONSULTING SVCS: Matls, Incl Purch, Handle & Invntry
MGT SVCS, FACIL SUPPT: Base Maint Or Provide Personnel
MICROFILM EQPT WHOLESALERS
MICROFILM SVCS
MILITARY INSIGNIA
MILK, FLUID: Wholesalers
MILLING: Cereal Flour, Exc Rice
MILLWORK
MINE & QUARRY SVCS: Nonmetallic Minerals
MINERALS: Ground or Treated
MINIATURE GOLF COURSES
MINING MACHINES & EQPT: Crushers, Stationary

MISC FINAN INVEST ACTIVITY: Mutual Fund, Ind Salesperson
MIXTURES & BLOCKS: Asphalt Paving
MOBILE HOME REPAIR SVCS
MOBILE HOMES, EXC RECREATIONAL
MODELS
MODELS: General, Exc Toy
MOLDED RUBBER PRDTS
MOLDING COMPOUNDS
MOLDS: Indl
MOLDS: Plastic Working & Foundry
MONEY ORDER ISSUANCE SVCS
MONTESSORI CHILD DEVELOPMENT CENTER
MOPS: Floor & Dust
MORTGAGE BANKERS
MORTGAGE COMPANIES: Urban
MOTEL
MOTION PICTURE & VIDEO DISTRIBUTION
MOTION PICTURE & VIDEO PRODUCTION SVCS
MOTION PICTURE DISTRIBUTION SVCS
MOTION PICTURE PRODUCTION & DISTRIBUTION
MOTION PICTURE PRODUCTION & DISTRIBUTION: Television
MOTION PICTURE PRODUCTION ALLIED SVCS
MOTOR INN
MOTOR SCOOTERS & PARTS
MOTOR VEHICLE ASSEMBLY, COMPLETE: Autos, Incl Specialty
MOTOR VEHICLE ASSEMBLY, COMPLETE: Fire Department Vehicles
MOTOR VEHICLE DEALERS: Automobiles, New & Used
MOTOR VEHICLE DEALERS: Cars, Used Only
MOTOR VEHICLE DEALERS: Pickups & Vans, Used
MOTOR VEHICLE DEALERS: Pickups, New & Used
MOTOR VEHICLE DEALERS: Trucks, Tractors/Trailers, New & Used
MOTOR VEHICLE PARTS & ACCESS: Body Components & Frames
MOTOR VEHICLE PARTS & ACCESS: Booster Cables, Jump-Start
MOTOR VEHICLE PARTS & ACCESS: Clutches
MOTOR VEHICLE PARTS & ACCESS: Engines & Parts
MOTOR VEHICLE PARTS & ACCESS: Fuel Systems & Parts
MOTOR VEHICLE PARTS & ACCESS: Mufflers, Exhaust
MOTOR VEHICLE PARTS & ACCESS: Power Steering Eqpt
MOTOR VEHICLE PARTS & ACCESS: Pumps, Hydraulic Fluid Power
MOTOR VEHICLE PARTS & ACCESS: Wiring Harness Sets
MOTOR VEHICLE RACING & DRIVER SVCS
MOTOR VEHICLE SPLYS & PARTS WHOLESALERS: New
MOTOR VEHICLE SPLYS & PARTS WHOLESALERS: Used
MOTOR VEHICLE: Shock Absorbers
MOTOR VEHICLES & CAR BODIES
MOTOR VEHICLES, WHOLESALE: Ambulances
MOTOR VEHICLES, WHOLESALE: Commercial
MOTOR VEHICLES, WHOLESALE: Trailers, Truck, New & Used
MOTOR VEHICLES, WHOLESALE: Truck bodies
MOTOR VEHICLES, WHOLESALE: Truck tractors
MOTOR VEHICLES, WHOLESALE: Trucks, commercial
MOTOR VEHICLES, WHOLESALE: Vans, commercial
MOTORCYCLE DEALERS
MOTORCYCLE DEALERS
MOTORCYCLE PARTS & ACCESS DEALERS
MOTORCYCLE REPAIR SHOPS
MOTORCYCLES: Wholesalers
MOTORS: Electric
MOTORS: Generators
MOVIE THEATERS, EXC DRIVE-IN
MOVING SVC & STORAGE: Local
MOVING SVC: Local
MOVING SVC: Long-Distance
MULTI-SVCS CENTER
MUSEUMS
MUSEUMS & ART GALLERIES
MUSIC BROADCASTING SVCS
MUSIC RECORDING PRODUCER
MUSIC SCHOOLS
MUSICAL INSTRUMENTS & ACCESS: NEC
MUSICAL INSTRUMENTS WHOLESALERS
MUSICIAN
MUTUAL ACCIDENT & HEALTH ASSOCIATIONS
MUTUAL FUND MANAGEMENT

N

NAIL SALONS
NATIONAL SECURITY FORCES
NATIONAL SECURITY, GOVERNMENT: Air Force
NATIONAL SECURITY, GOVERNMENT: Army
NATIONAL SECURITY, GOVERNMENT: National Guard
NATIONAL SECURITY, GOVERNMENT: Navy
NATURAL GAS DISTRIBUTION TO CONSUMERS
NATURAL GAS PRODUCTION
NATURAL GAS TRANSMISSION
NATURAL GAS TRANSMISSION & DISTRIBUTION
NATURAL GASOLINE PRODUCTION
NATURAL RESOURCE PRESERVATION SVCS
NAUTICAL & NAVIGATIONAL INSTRUMENT REPAIR SVCS
NAUTICAL REPAIR SVCS
NAVIGATIONAL SYSTEMS & INSTRUMENTS
NEIGHBORHOOD CENTER
NEIGHBORHOOD DEVELOPMENT GROUP
NEPHELINE SYENITE MINING
NETS: Launderers & Dyers
NEW & USED CAR DEALERS
NEWS SYNDICATES
NEWSPAPERS & PERIODICALS NEWS REPORTING SVCS
NEWSSTAND
NONCURRENT CARRYING WIRING DEVICES
NONMETALLIC MINERALS DEVELOPMENT & TEST BORING SVC
NOTARIES PUBLIC
NOVELTIES, PAPER, WHOLESALE
NOVELTY SHOPS
NURSERIES & LAWN & GARDEN SPLY STORE, RET: Lawn/Garden Splys
NURSERIES & LAWN & GARDEN SPLY STORES, RETAIL
NURSERIES & LAWN & GARDEN SPLY STORES, RETAIL: Fertilizer
NURSERIES & LAWN & GARDEN SPLY STORES, RETAIL: Top Soil
NURSERIES & LAWN/GARDEN SPLY STORE, RET: Lawnmowers/Tractors
NURSERIES & LAWN/GARDEN SPLY STORE, RET: Garden Splys/Tools
NURSERIES/LAWN/GARDEN SPLY STORES, RET: Hydroponic Eqpt/Sply
NURSERIES/LAWN/GRDN SPLY STORE, RET: Nursery Stck, Seed/Bulb
NURSERY & GARDEN CENTERS
NURSERY SCHOOLS
NURSERY STOCK, WHOLESALE
NURSING & PERSONAL CARE FACILITIES, NEC
NURSING CARE FACILITIES: Skilled
NURSING HOME, EXC SKILLED & INTERMEDIATE CARE FACILITY
NUTRITION SVCS
NUTS: Metal

O

OFC/CLINIC OF MED DRS: Special, Phys Or Surgeon, Eye Or ENT
OFC/CLINIC OF MED DRS: Specl, Phys Or Surgeon, Occup & Indl
OFC/CLINIC, MED DRS: Specl, Phys Or Surgeon, Infect Disease
OFCS & CLINICS,MEDICAL DRS: Specl, Physician Or Surgn, ENT
OFFICE CLEANING OR CHARRING SVCS
OFFICE EQPT & ACCESSORY CUSTOMIZING SVCS
OFFICE EQPT WHOLESALERS
OFFICE EQPT, WHOLESALE: Blueprinting
OFFICE EQPT, WHOLESALE: Duplicating Machines
OFFICE EQPT, WHOLESALE: Photocopy Machines
OFFICE FURNITURE REPAIR & MAINTENANCE SVCS
OFFICE MANAGEMENT SVCS
OFFICE SPLY & STATIONERY STORES
OFFICE SPLY & STATIONERY STORES: Office Forms & Splys
OFFICE SPLY & STATIONERY STORES: School Splys
OFFICE SPLYS, NEC, WHOLESALE
OFFICES & CLINICS DOCTORS OF MED: Intrnl Med Practitioners
OFFICES & CLINICS DRS OF MED: Psychiatrists/Psychoanalysts
OFFICES & CLINICS HLTH PRACTITNRS: Psychiatric Social Wrkr
OFFICES & CLINICS OF DENTISTS: Dental Clinic

OFFICES & CLINICS OF DENTISTS: Dental Surgeon
OFFICES & CLINICS OF DENTISTS: Dentists' Office
OFFICES & CLINICS OF DENTISTS: Periodontist
OFFICES & CLINICS OF DENTISTS: Prosthodontist
OFFICES & CLINICS OF DENTISTS: Specialist, Practitioners
OFFICES & CLINICS OF DOCTORS OF MEDICINE: Allergist
OFFICES & CLINICS OF DOCTORS OF MEDICINE: Anesthesiologist
OFFICES & CLINICS OF DOCTORS OF MEDICINE: Dermatologist
OFFICES & CLINICS OF DOCTORS OF MEDICINE: Dispensary
OFFICES & CLINICS OF DOCTORS OF MEDICINE: Endocrinologist
OFFICES & CLINICS OF DOCTORS OF MEDICINE: Gastronomist
OFFICES & CLINICS OF DOCTORS OF MEDICINE: Group Health Assoc
OFFICES & CLINICS OF DOCTORS OF MEDICINE: Gynecologist
OFFICES & CLINICS OF DOCTORS OF MEDICINE: Hematologist
OFFICES & CLINICS OF DOCTORS OF MEDICINE: Med Insurance Plan
OFFICES & CLINICS OF DOCTORS OF MEDICINE: Nephrologist
OFFICES & CLINICS OF DOCTORS OF MEDICINE: Neurologist
OFFICES & CLINICS OF DOCTORS OF MEDICINE: Neurosurgeon
OFFICES & CLINICS OF DOCTORS OF MEDICINE: Obstetrician
OFFICES & CLINICS OF DOCTORS OF MEDICINE: Oncologist
OFFICES & CLINICS OF DOCTORS OF MEDICINE: Ophthalmologist
OFFICES & CLINICS OF DOCTORS OF MEDICINE: Pathologist
OFFICES & CLINICS OF DOCTORS OF MEDICINE: Pediatrician
OFFICES & CLINICS OF DOCTORS OF MEDICINE: Psychiatric Clinic
OFFICES & CLINICS OF DOCTORS OF MEDICINE: Psychiatrist
OFFICES & CLINICS OF DOCTORS OF MEDICINE: Radiologist
OFFICES & CLINICS OF DOCTORS OF MEDICINE: Surgeon
OFFICES & CLINICS OF DOCTORS OF MEDICINE: Surgeon, Plastic
OFFICES & CLINICS OF DOCTORS OF MEDICINE: Urologist
OFFICES & CLINICS OF DOCTORS, MEDICINE: Gen & Fam Practice
OFFICES & CLINICS OF DRS OF MED: Cardiologist & Vascular
OFFICES & CLINICS OF DRS OF MED: Clinic, Op by Physicians
OFFICES & CLINICS OF DRS OF MED: Em Med Ctr, Freestanding
OFFICES & CLINICS OF DRS OF MED: Health Maint Org Or HMO
OFFICES & CLINICS OF DRS OF MED: Physician/Surgeon, Int Med
OFFICES & CLINICS OF DRS OF MED: Physician/Surgeon, Phy Med
OFFICES & CLINICS OF DRS OF MED: Specialist/Phy, Fertility
OFFICES & CLINICS OF DRS OF MEDICINE: Geriatric
OFFICES & CLINICS OF DRS OF MEDICINE: Med Clinic, Pri Care
OFFICES & CLINICS OF DRS OF MEDICINE: Med Insurance Assoc
OFFICES & CLINICS OF DRS OF MEDICINE: Physician, Orthopedic
OFFICES & CLINICS OF DRS OF MEDICINE: Pulmonary
OFFICES & CLINICS OF DRS OF MEDICINE: Rheumatology
OFFICES & CLINICS OF DRS OF MEDICINE: Sports Med
OFFICES & CLINICS OF DRS, MED: Specialized Practitioners
OFFICES & CLINICS OF HEALTH PRACTITIONERS: Coroner
OFFICES & CLINICS OF HEALTH PRACTITIONERS: Nurse & Med Asst
OFFICES & CLINICS OF HEALTH PRACTITIONERS: Nutrition

OFFICES & CLINICS OF HEALTH PRACTITIONERS: Nutritionist
OFFICES & CLINICS OF HEALTH PRACTITIONERS: Occu Therapist
OFFICES & CLINICS OF HEALTH PRACTITIONERS: Paramedic
OFFICES & CLINICS OF HEALTH PRACTITIONERS: Physical Therapy
OFFICES & CLINICS OF HEALTH PRACTITIONERS: Physiotherapist
OFFICES & CLINICS OF HEALTH PRACTITIONERS: Speech Pathology
OFFICES & CLINICS OF HEALTH PRACTITIONERS: Speech Therapist
OFFICES & CLINICS OF HLTH PRACTRS: Clinical Psychologist
OFFICES & CLINICS OF HLTH PRACTITIONERS: Reg/Practical Nurse
OFFICES & CLINICS OF OPTOMETRISTS: Group & Corporate
OFFICES & CLINICS OF OPTOMETRISTS: Specialist, Contact Lens
OFFICES & CLINICS OF OPTOMETRISTS: Specialist, Optometrists
OIL & GAS FIELD EQPT: Drill Rigs
OIL FIELD MACHINERY & EQPT
OIL FIELD SVCS, NEC
OIL ROYALTY TRADERS
OILS & GREASES: Blended & Compounded
OILS & GREASES: Lubricating
OILS: Lubricating
OLD AGE ASSISTANCE
OLEFINS
ON-LINE DATABASE INFORMATION RETRIEVAL SVCS
OPERATIVE BUILDERS: Condominiums
OPERATIVE BUILDERS: Townhouse
OPERATOR TRAINING, COMPUTER
OPERATOR: Apartment Buildings
OPERATOR: Nonresidential Buildings
OPHTHALMIC GOODS
OPHTHALMIC GOODS WHOLESALERS
OPHTHALMIC GOODS, NEC, WHOLESALE: Lenses
OPHTHALMIC GOODS: Lenses, Ophthalmic
OPTICAL GOODS STORES
OPTICAL GOODS STORES: Contact Lenses, Prescription
OPTICAL INSTRUMENTS & LENSES
OPTICAL SCANNING SVCS
OPTOMETRIC EQPT & SPLYS WHOLESALERS
OPTOMETRISTS' OFFICES
ORCHESTRAS & BANDS
ORGAN BANK
ORGANIZATIONS & UNIONS: Labor
ORGANIZATIONS, NEC
ORGANIZATIONS: Civic & Social
ORGANIZATIONS: Educational Research Agency
ORGANIZATIONS: Medical Research
ORGANIZATIONS: Noncommercial Social Research
ORGANIZATIONS: Physical Research, Noncommercial
ORGANIZATIONS: Political
ORGANIZATIONS: Political Campaign
ORGANIZATIONS: Professional
ORGANIZATIONS: Religious
ORGANIZATIONS: Research Institute
ORGANIZATIONS: Scientific Research Agency
ORGANIZATIONS: Veterans' Membership
ORPHANAGE
ORTHODONTIST
OUTDOOR PARKING SVCS
OUTREACH PROGRAM
OXYGEN TENT SVCS

P

PACKAGE DESIGN SVCS
PACKAGED FROZEN FOODS WHOLESALERS, NEC
PACKAGING & LABELING SVCS
PACKAGING MATERIALS, INDL: Wholesalers
PACKAGING MATERIALS, WHOLESALE
PACKAGING MATERIALS: Paper
PACKAGING MATERIALS: Plastic Film, Coated Or Laminated
PACKAGING MATERIALS: Polystyrene Foam
PACKAGING: Blister Or Bubble Formed, Plastic
PACKING & CRATING SVC
PACKING & CRATING SVCS: Containerized Goods For Shipping
PACKING SVCS: Shipping

SVCS INDEX

PADS: Athletic, Protective
PAGING SVCS
PAINT STORE
PAINTING SVC: Metal Prdts
PAINTS & ADDITIVES
PAINTS & ALLIED PRODUCTS
PAINTS, VARNISHES & SPLYS WHOLESALERS
PAINTS, VARNISHES & SPLYS, WHOLESALE: Paints
PALLET REPAIR SVCS
PALLETIZERS & DEPALLETIZERS
PALLETS & SKIDS: Wood
PALLETS: Plastic
PALLETS: Wooden
PANELS: Building, Wood
PAPER & BOARD: Die-cut
PAPER CONVERTING
PAPER PRDTS: Napkins, Sanitary, Made From Purchased Material
PAPER PRDTS: Sanitary
PAPER PRDTS: Towels, Napkins/Tissue Paper, From Purchd Mtrls
PAPER, WHOLESALE: Fine
PAPER, WHOLESALE: Printing
PAPER: Adhesive
PAPER: Cloth, Lined, Made From Purchased Materials
PAPER: Coated & Laminated, NEC
PAPER: Wrapping & Packaging
PAPERBOARD
PARKING GARAGE
PARKING LOTS
PARKING LOTS & GARAGES
PAROLE OFFICE
PARTITIONS & FIXTURES: Except Wood
PARTITIONS WHOLESALERS
PARTITIONS: Wood & Fixtures
PARTS: Metal
PARTY & SPECIAL EVENT PLANNING SVCS
PASSENGER AIRLINE SVCS
PATENT OWNERS & LESSORS
PATIENT MONITORING EQPT WHOLESALERS
PATROL SVCS: Electric Transmission Or Gas Lines
PATTERNS: Indl
PAYROLL SVCS
PENSION & RETIREMENT PLAN CONSULTANTS
PENSION FUNDS
PERFORMING ARTS CENTER PRODUCTION SVCS
PERIODICALS, WHOLESALE
PERSONAL APPEARANCE SVCS
PERSONAL CARE FACILITY
PERSONAL CREDIT INSTITUTIONS: Auto Loans, Incl Insurance
PERSONAL CREDIT INSTITUTIONS: Consumer Finance Companies
PERSONAL CREDIT INSTITUTIONS: Finance Licensed Loan Co's, Sm
PERSONAL CREDIT INSTITUTIONS: Financing, Autos, Furniture
PERSONAL CREDIT INSTITUTIONS: Install Sales Finance
PERSONAL DOCUMENT & INFORMATION SVCS
PERSONAL FINANCIAL SVCS
PERSONAL INVESTIGATION SVCS
PERSONAL SHOPPING SVCS
PERSONAL SVCS
PERSONAL SVCS, NEC
PEST CONTROL IN STRUCTURES SVCS
PEST CONTROL SVCS
PET & PET SPLYS STORES
PET FOOD WHOLESALERS
PET SPLYS
PET SPLYS WHOLESALERS
PETROLEUM & PETROLEUM PRDTS, WHOL Svc Station Splys, Petro
PETROLEUM & PETROLEUM PRDTS, WHOLESALE Crude Oil
PETROLEUM & PETROLEUM PRDTS, WHOLESALE Diesel Fuel
PETROLEUM & PETROLEUM PRDTS, WHOLESALE Fuel Oil
PETROLEUM & PETROLEUM PRDTS, WHOLESALE: Bulk Stations
PETROLEUM PRDTS WHOLESALERS
PHARMACEUTICALS
PHARMACEUTICALS: Mail-Order Svc
PHARMACIES & DRUG STORES
PHOSPHATES

PHOTOCOPY MACHINE REPAIR SVCS
PHOTOCOPY MACHINES
PHOTOCOPY SPLYS WHOLESALERS
PHOTOCOPYING & DUPLICATING SVCS
PHOTOENGRAVING SVC
PHOTOFINISHING LABORATORIES
PHOTOFINISHING LABORATORIES
PHOTOGRAMMATIC MAPPING SVCS
PHOTOGRAPH DEVELOPING & RETOUCHING SVCS
PHOTOGRAPHIC EQPT & SPLYS WHOLESALERS
PHOTOGRAPHY SVCS: Commercial
PHOTOGRAPHY SVCS: Portrait Studios
PHOTOGRAPHY SVCS: School
PHOTOGRAPHY SVCS: Still Or Video
PHOTOGRAPHY: Aerial
PHOTOTYPESETTING SVC
PHYSICAL EXAMINATION & TESTING SVCS
PHYSICAL EXAMINATION SVCS, INSURANCE
PHYSICAL FITNESS CENTERS
PHYSICAL FITNESS CLUBS WITH TRAINING EQPT
PHYSICIANS' OFFICES & CLINICS: Medical
PHYSICIANS' OFFICES & CLINICS: Medical doctors
PHYSICIANS' OFFICES & CLINICS: Osteopathic
PICTURE FRAMING SVCS, CUSTOM
PIECE GOODS, NOTIONS & DRY GOODS, WHOL: Textiles, Woven
PIECE GOODS, NOTIONS & DRY GOODS, WHOL: Yard Goods, Woven
PIECE GOODS, NOTIONS & DRY GOODS, WHOLESALE: Fabrics
PIECE GOODS, NOTIONS & DRY GOODS, WHOLESALE: Tape, Textile
PIECE GOODS, NOTIONS/DRY GOODS, WHOL: Drapery Mtrl, Woven
PIECE GOODS, NOTIONS/DRY GOODS, WHOL: Sewing Splys/Notions
PILOT SVCS: Aviation
PIPE & FITTING: Fabrication
PIPE & FITTINGS: Cast Iron
PIPE FITTINGS: Plastic
PIPE SECTIONS, FABRICATED FROM PURCHASED PIPE
PIPE: Seamless Steel
PIPELINE & POWER LINE INSPECTION SVCS
PIPELINE TERMINAL FACILITIES: Independent
PIPELINES, EXC NATURAL GAS: Gasoline, Common Carriers
PIPELINES: Crude Petroleum
PIPELINES: Natural Gas
PIPELINES: Refined Petroleum
PIPES & TUBES: Steel
PIPES OR FITTINGS: Sewer, Clay
PISTONS & PISTON RINGS
PLANETARIUMS
PLANNING & DEVELOPMENT ADMIN, GOVT: Urban & Community, Local
PLANNING & DEVELOPMENT ADMIN, GOVT: Urban/Community, County
PLANNING & DEVELOPMENT ADMINISTRATION, GOVT: County Agency
PLANTING MACHINERY & EQPT WHOLESALERS
PLANTS, POTTED, WHOLESALE
PLAQUES: Picture, Laminated
PLASMAPHEROUS CENTER
PLASTIC COLORING & FINISHING
PLASTIC PRDTS REPAIR SVCS
PLASTICS FILM & SHEET
PLASTICS MATERIAL & RESINS
PLASTICS MATERIALS, BASIC FORMS & SHAPES WHOLESALERS
PLASTICS PROCESSING
PLASTICS SHEET: Packing Materials
PLASTICS: Cast
PLASTICS: Extruded
PLASTICS: Injection Molded
PLASTICS: Molded
PLASTICS: Polystyrene Foam
PLASTICS: Thermoformed
PLATE WORK: For Nuclear Industry
PLATES
PLATES: Sheet & Strip, Exc Coated Prdts
PLATING & POLISHING SVC
PLEATING & STITCHING SVC
PLUMBING & HEATING EQPT & SPLY, WHOLESALE: Hydronic Htg Eqpt
PLUMBING & HEATING EQPT & SPLYS WHOLESALERS

PLUMBING & HEATING EQPT & SPLYS, WHOL: Fireplaces, Prefab
PLUMBING & HEATING EQPT & SPLYS, WHOL: Pipe/Fitting, Plastic
PLUMBING & HEATING EQPT & SPLYS, WHOL: Plumbing Fitting/Sply
PLUMBING & HEATING EQPT & SPLYS, WHOL: Plumbng/Heatng Valves
PLUMBING & HEATING EQPT & SPLYS, WHOL: Water Purif Eqpt
PLUMBING FIXTURES
PLUMBING FIXTURES: Plastic
PLUMBING FIXTURES: Vitreous
PODIATRISTS' OFFICES
POLICE PROTECTION
POLICE PROTECTION: Local Government
POLICE PROTECTION: Sheriffs' Office
POLICE PROTECTION: State Highway Patrol
POLICYHOLDERS' CONSULTING SVCS
POLITICAL ACTION COMMITTEES
POLYETHYLENE CHLOROSULFONATED RUBBER
POLYVINYLIDENE CHLORIDE RESINS
POSTERS, WHOLESALE
POULTRY & POULTRY PRDTS WHOLESALERS
POULTRY & SMALL GAME SLAUGHTERING & PROCESSING
POWDER: Metal
POWER MOWERS WHOLESALERS
POWER SUPPLIES: Transformer, Electronic Type
POWER TOOL REPAIR SVCS
POWER TRANSMISSION EQPT WHOLESALERS
POWER TRANSMISSION EQPT: Mechanical
POWER TRANSMISSION EQPT: Vehicle
PRACTICAL NURSING SCHOOL
PRECIPITATORS: Electrostatic
PRESCHOOL CENTERS
PRESSED FIBER & MOLDED PULP PRDTS, EXC FOOD PRDTS
PRINTED CIRCUIT BOARDS
PRINTERS' SVCS: Folding, Collating, Etc
PRINTING & WRITING PAPER WHOLESALERS
PRINTING MACHINERY
PRINTING MACHINERY, EQPT & SPLYS: Wholesalers
PRINTING TRADES MACHINERY & EQPT REPAIR SVCS
PRINTING, COMMERCIAL: Labels & Seals, NEC
PRINTING, COMMERCIAL: Literature, Advertising, NEC
PRINTING, COMMERCIAL: Music, Sheet, NEC
PRINTING, COMMERCIAL: Screen
PRINTING, LITHOGRAPHIC: Calendars
PRINTING, LITHOGRAPHIC: Calendars & Cards
PRINTING, LITHOGRAPHIC: Forms & Cards, Business
PRINTING, LITHOGRAPHIC: Forms, Business
PRINTING, LITHOGRAPHIC: Offset & photolithographic printing
PRINTING, LITHOGRAPHIC: On Metal
PRINTING: Books
PRINTING: Commercial, NEC
PRINTING: Flexographic
PRINTING: Gravure, Color
PRINTING: Gravure, Rotogravure
PRINTING: Laser
PRINTING: Letterpress
PRINTING: Lithographic
PRINTING: Offset
PRINTING: Photolithographic
PRINTING: Screen, Fabric
PRINTING: Screen, Manmade Fiber & Silk, Broadwoven Fabric
PRIVATE INVESTIGATOR SVCS
PROBATION OFFICE
PRODUCT STERILIZATION SVCS
PROFESSIONAL DANCE SCHOOLS
PROFESSIONAL EQPT & SPLYS, WHOLESALE: Bank
PROFESSIONAL EQPT & SPLYS, WHOLESALE: Engineers', NEC
PROFESSIONAL EQPT & SPLYS, WHOLESALE: Optical Goods
PROFESSIONAL EQPT & SPLYS, WHOLESALE: Precision Tools
PROFESSIONAL INSTRUMENT REPAIR SVCS
PROFESSIONAL SCHOOLS
PROFESSIONAL STANDARDS REVIEW BOARDS
PROFILE SHAPES: Unsupported Plastics
PROGRAM ADMINISTRATION, GOVERNMENT: Social & Human Resources

PROGRAM ADMINISTRATION, GOVERNMENT: Social & Manpower, State
PROGRAM ADMINISTRATION, GOVT: Social & Manpower, County
PROMOTION SVCS
PROOFREADING SVCS
PROPERTY & CASUALTY INSURANCE AGENTS
PROPERTY DAMAGE INSURANCE
PUBLIC FINANCE, TAX & MONETARY POLICY OFFICES, GOVT: State
PUBLIC FINANCE, TAXATION & MONETARY POLICY OFFICES
PUBLIC HEALTH PROGRAM ADMIN, GOVT: Health Statistics Ctr
PUBLIC HEALTH PROGRAM ADMIN, GOVT: Mental Health Agency
PUBLIC HEALTH PROGRAM ADMINISTRATION, GOVERNMENT: County
PUBLIC HEALTH PROGRAM ADMINISTRATION, GOVERNMENT: Local
PUBLIC HEALTH PROGRAM ADMINISTRATION, GOVERNMENT: State
PUBLIC HEALTH PROGRAM ADMINISTRATION, GOVT: Child Health
PUBLIC HEALTH PROGRAMS ADMINISTRATION SVCS
PUBLIC LIBRARY
PUBLIC ORDER & SAFETY ACTIVITIES, NEC
PUBLIC ORDER & SAFETY OFFICES, GOVERNMENT: County
PUBLIC ORDER & SAFETY OFFICES, GOVT: Emergency Mgmt Office
PUBLIC RELATIONS & PUBLICITY SVCS
PUBLIC RELATIONS SVCS
PUBLIC WELFARE CENTER
PUBLISHERS: Book
PUBLISHERS: Books, No Printing
PUBLISHERS: Magazines, No Printing
PUBLISHERS: Miscellaneous
PUBLISHERS: Music, Sheet
PUBLISHERS: Newspaper
PUBLISHERS: Newspapers, No Printing
PUBLISHERS: Periodical, With Printing
PUBLISHERS: Periodicals, Magazines
PUBLISHERS: Periodicals, No Printing
PUBLISHERS: Technical Manuals
PUBLISHERS: Telephone & Other Directory
PUBLISHERS: Trade journals, No Printing
PUBLISHING & BROADCASTING: Internet Only
PUBLISHING & PRINTING: Books
PUBLISHING & PRINTING: Directories, NEC
PUBLISHING & PRINTING: Magazines: publishing & printing
PUBLISHING & PRINTING: Newspapers
PUBLISHING & PRINTING: Trade Journals
PULP MILLS
PUMPS
PUMPS & PARTS: Indl
PUMPS & PUMPING EQPT REPAIR SVCS
PUMPS & PUMPING EQPT WHOLESALERS
PUMPS: Domestic, Water Or Sump
PUMPS: Measuring & Dispensing
PUMPS: Oil Well & Field
PURCHASING SVCS

Q

QUARTZ CRYSTAL MINING SVCS

R

RACE TRACK OPERATION
RACETRACKS: Auto
RACETRACKS: Horse
RACKS: Display
RADIO & TELEVISION COMMUNICATIONS EQUIPMENT
RADIO & TELEVISION OR TV ANNOUNCING SVCS
RADIO & TELEVISION REPAIR
RADIO BROADCASTING & COMMUNICATIONS EQPT
RADIO BROADCASTING STATIONS
RADIO COMMUNICATIONS: Airborne Eqpt
RADIO COMMUNICATIONS: Carrier Eqpt
RADIO REPAIR & INSTALLATION SVCS
RADIO REPAIR SHOP, NEC
RADIO, TELEVISION & CONSUMER ELECTRONICS STORES: Eqpt, NEC
RADIO, TV & CONSUMER ELEC STORES: Automotive Sound Eqpt

RADIO, TV & CONSUMER ELEC STORES: High Fidelity Stereo Eqpt
RADIO, TV/CONSUMER ELEC STORES: Antennas, Satellite Dish
RADIOS WHOLESALERS
RAILROAD CAR CUSTOMIZING SVCS
RAILROAD CAR RENTING & LEASING SVCS
RAILROAD CAR REPAIR SVCS
RAILROAD CARGO LOADING & UNLOADING SVCS
RAILROAD EQPT
RAILROAD EQPT & SPLYS WHOLESALERS
RAILROAD EQPT: Cars, Rebuilt
RAILROAD MAINTENANCE & REPAIR SVCS
RAILROAD SWITCHING & TERMINAL SVCS
RAILROADS: Long Haul
REAL ESTATE AGENCIES & BROKERS
REAL ESTATE AGENCIES: Buying
REAL ESTATE AGENCIES: Commercial
REAL ESTATE AGENCIES: Leasing & Rentals
REAL ESTATE AGENCIES: Multiple Listing Svc
REAL ESTATE AGENCIES: Rental
REAL ESTATE AGENCIES: Residential
REAL ESTATE AGENCIES: Selling
REAL ESTATE AGENTS & MANAGERS
REAL ESTATE APPRAISERS
REAL ESTATE AUCTION
REAL ESTATE ESCROW AGENCIES
REAL ESTATE INVESTMENT TRUSTS
REAL ESTATE MANAGERS: Cemetery
REAL ESTATE MANAGERS: Condominium
REAL ESTATE MANAGERS: Cooperative Apartment
REAL ESTATE OPERATORS, EXC DEVEL: Prprty, Auditorium/Theater
REAL ESTATE OPERATORS, EXC DEVELOPERS: Apartment Hotel
REAL ESTATE OPERATORS, EXC DEVELOPERS: Auditorium & Hall
REAL ESTATE OPERATORS, EXC DEVELOPERS: Commercial/Indl Bldg
REAL ESTATE OPERATORS, EXC DEVELOPERS: Property, Retail
REAL ESTATE OPERATORS, EXC DEVELOPERS: Residential Hotel
REAL ESTATE OPERATORS, EXC DEVELOPERS: Retirement Hotel
REAL ESTATE OPERATORS, EXC DEVELOPERS: Shopping Ctr
REAL ESTATE OPERATORS, EXC DEVELOPERS: Shopping Ctr, Commnty
REAL ESTATE OPS, EXC DEVELOPER: Residential Bldg, 4 Or Less
REALTY INVESTMENT TRUSTS
RECLAIMED RUBBER: Reworked By Manufacturing Process
RECOVERY SVCS: Solvents
RECREATIONAL & SPORTING CAMPS
RECREATIONAL CAMPS
RECREATIONAL DAY CAMPS
RECREATIONAL SPORTING EQPT REPAIR SVCS
RECREATIONAL VEHICLE DEALERS
RECREATIONAL VEHICLE PARKS
RECREATIONAL VEHICLE PARKS & CAMPGROUNDS
RECYCLABLE SCRAP & WASTE MATERIALS WHOLESALERS
REFERRAL SVCS, PERSONAL & SOCIAL PROBLEMS
REFINERS & SMELTERS: Aluminum
REFINERS & SMELTERS: Lead, Secondary
REFINERS & SMELTERS: Nonferrous Metal
REFINING: Petroleum
REFRACTORIES: Nonclay
REFRACTORY MATERIALS WHOLESALERS
REFRIGERATION & HEATING EQUIPMENT
REFRIGERATION EQPT & SPLYS WHOLESALERS
REFRIGERATION EQPT & SPLYS, WHOL: Refrig Units, Motor Veh
REFRIGERATION EQPT & SPLYS, WHOLESALE: Commercial Eqpt
REFRIGERATION REPAIR SVCS
REFRIGERATION SVC & REPAIR
REFUGEE SVCS
REFUSE SYSTEMS
REGULATION & ADMIN, GOVT: Public Svc Commission, Exc Transp
REGULATION & ADMINISTRATION, GOVT: Transp Dept, Nonoperating
REGULATORS: Power

REHABILITATION CENTER, OUTPATIENT TREATMENT
REHABILITATION CTR, RESIDENTIAL WITH HEALTH CARE INCIDENTAL
REHABILITATION SVCS
REINSURANCE CARRIERS: Accident & Health
REINSURANCE CARRIERS: Surety
RELOCATION SVCS
REMOTE DATABASE INFORMATION RETRIEVAL SVCS
RENT-A-CAR SVCS
RENTAL CENTERS: Furniture
RENTAL CENTERS: Party & Banquet Eqpt & Splys
RENTAL CENTERS: Tools
RENTAL SVCS: Aircraft
RENTAL SVCS: Appliance
RENTAL SVCS: Audio-Visual Eqpt & Sply
RENTAL SVCS: Beach & Water Sports Eqpt
RENTAL SVCS: Bicycle
RENTAL SVCS: Business Machine & Electronic Eqpt
RENTAL SVCS: Clothing
RENTAL SVCS: Costume
RENTAL SVCS: Dress Suit
RENTAL SVCS: Electronic Eqpt, Exc Computers
RENTAL SVCS: Golf Cart, Power
RENTAL SVCS: Home Cleaning & Maintenance Eqpt
RENTAL SVCS: Invalid Splys
RENTAL SVCS: Mobile Communication Eqpt
RENTAL SVCS: Office Facilities & Secretarial Svcs
RENTAL SVCS: Oil Eqpt
RENTAL SVCS: Sound & Lighting Eqpt
RENTAL SVCS: Sporting Goods, NEC
RENTAL SVCS: Stores & Yards Eqpt
RENTAL SVCS: Television
RENTAL SVCS: Tent & Tarpaulin
RENTAL SVCS: Trailer
RENTAL SVCS: Tuxedo
RENTAL SVCS: Vending Machine
RENTAL SVCS: Video Disk/Tape, To The General Public
RENTAL SVCS: Work Zone Traffic Eqpt, Flags, Cones, Etc
RENTAL: Passenger Car
RENTAL: Portable Toilet
RENTAL: Trucks, With Drivers
RENTAL: Video Tape & Disc
REPOSSESSION SVCS
REPRODUCTION SVCS: Video Tape Or Disk
RESEARCH & DEVELOPMENT SVCS, COMMERCIAL: Engineering Lab
RESEARCH, DEV & TESTING SVCS, COMM: Chem Lab, Exc Testing
RESEARCH, DEVELOPMENT & TEST SVCS, COMM: Business Analysis
RESEARCH, DEVELOPMENT & TEST SVCS, COMM: Cmptr Hardware Dev
RESEARCH, DEVELOPMENT & TEST SVCS, COMM: Research, Exc Lab
RESEARCH, DEVELOPMENT & TESTING SVCS, COMM: Agricultural
RESEARCH, DEVELOPMENT & TESTING SVCS, COMM: Bus Economic Sve
RESEARCH, DEVELOPMENT & TESTING SVCS, COMM: Natural Resource
RESEARCH, DEVELOPMENT & TESTING SVCS, COMM: Research Lab
RESEARCH, DEVELOPMENT & TESTING SVCS, COMM: Sociological
RESEARCH, DEVELOPMENT & TESTING SVCS, COMMERCIAL: Business
RESEARCH, DEVELOPMENT & TESTING SVCS, COMMERCIAL: Economic
RESEARCH, DEVELOPMENT & TESTING SVCS, COMMERCIAL: Education
RESEARCH, DEVELOPMENT & TESTING SVCS, COMMERCIAL: Energy
RESEARCH, DEVELOPMENT & TESTING SVCS, COMMERCIAL: Food
RESEARCH, DEVELOPMENT & TESTING SVCS, COMMERCIAL: Medical
RESEARCH, DEVELOPMENT & TESTING SVCS, COMMERCIAL: Physical
RESEARCH, DVLPT & TEST SVCS, COMM: Mkt Analysis or Research
RESEARCH, DVLPT & TESTING SVCS, COMM: Mkt, Bus & Economic
RESEARCH, DVLPT & TESTING SVCS, COMM: Survey, Mktg
RESIDENTIAL CARE FOR CHILDREN

RESIDENTIAL CARE FOR THE HANDICAPPED
RESIDENTIAL MENTAL HEALTH & SUBSTANCE ABUSE FA-
CILITIES
RESIDENTIAL MENTALLY HANDICAPPED FACILITIES
RESIDENTIAL REMODELERS
RESINS: Custom Compound Purchased
RESORT HOTEL: Franchised
RESORT HOTELS
RESPIRATORY THERAPY CLINIC
REST HOME, WITH HEALTH CARE INCIDENTAL
RESTAURANT EQPT REPAIR SVCS
RESTAURANTS: Fast Food
RESTAURANTS:Full Svc, American
RESTAURANTS:Full Svc, Diner
RESTAURANTS:Full Svc, Ethnic Food
RESTAURANTS:Full Svc, Family
RESTAURANTS:Full Svc, Family, Chain
RESTAURANTS:Full Svc, Family, Independent
RESTAURANTS:Full Svc, French
RESTAURANTS:Full Svc, Italian
RESTAURANTS:Full Svc, Mexican
RESTAURANTS:Full Svc, Seafood
RESTAURANTS:Full Svc, Steak
RESTAURANTS:Full Svc, Steak & Barbecue
RESTAURANTS:Limited Svc, Box Lunch Stand
RESTAURANTS:Limited Svc, Carry-Out Only, Exc Pizza
RESTAURANTS:Limited Svc, Chicken
RESTAURANTS:Limited Svc, Coffee Shop
RESTAURANTS:Limited Svc, Fast-Food, Chain
RESTAURANTS:Limited Svc, Fast-Food, Independent
RESTAURANTS:Limited Svc, Grill
RESTAURANTS:Limited Svc, Ice Cream Stands Or Dairy
Bars
RESTAURANTS:Limited Svc, Lunch Counter
RESTAURANTS:Limited Svc, Pizza
RESTAURANTS:Limited Svc, Pizzeria, Chain
RESTAURANTS:Limited Svc, Pizzeria, Independent
RESTAURANTS:Ltd Svc, Ice Cream, Soft Drink/Fountain
Stands
RESTROOM CLEANING SVCS
RETAIL BAKERY: Bagels
RETAIL BAKERY: Bread
RETAIL FIREPLACE STORES
RETAIL LUMBER YARDS
RETAIL STORES: Alarm Signal Systems
RETAIL STORES: Alcoholic Beverage Making Eqpt & Splys
RETAIL STORES: Audio-Visual Eqpt & Splys
RETAIL STORES: Business Machines & Eqpt
RETAIL STORES: Christmas Lights & Decorations
RETAIL STORES: Cleaning Eqpt & Splys
RETAIL STORES: Communication Eqpt
RETAIL STORES: Concrete Prdts, Precast
RETAIL STORES: Educational Aids & Electronic Training Mat
RETAIL STORES: Electronic Parts & Eqpt
RETAIL STORES: Farm Eqpt & Splys
RETAIL STORES: Farm Machinery, NEC
RETAIL STORES: Fiberglass Materials, Exc Insulation
RETAIL STORES: Fire Extinguishers
RETAIL STORES: Hair Care Prdts
RETAIL STORES: Hearing Aids
RETAIL STORES: Hospital Eqpt & Splys
RETAIL STORES: Ice
RETAIL STORES: Medical Apparatus & Splys
RETAIL STORES: Mobile Telephones & Eqpt
RETAIL STORES: Orthopedic & Prosthesis Applications
RETAIL STORES: Pet Food
RETAIL STORES: Pet Splys
RETAIL STORES: Photocopy Machines
RETAIL STORES: Picture Frames, Ready Made
RETAIL STORES: Plumbing & Heating Splys
RETAIL STORES: Police Splys
RETAIL STORES: Religious Goods
RETAIL STORES: Safety Splys & Eqpt
RETAIL STORES: Technical Aids For The Handicapped
RETAIL STORES: Telephone & Communication Eqpt
RETAIL STORES: Telephone Eqpt & Systems
RETAIL STORES: Theatrical Eqpt & Splys
RETAIL STORES: Tropical Fish
RETAIL STORES: Typewriters & Business Machines
RETAIL STORES: Water Purification Eqpt
RETAIL STORES: Welding Splys
RETIREMENT COMMUNITIES WITH NURSING
REUPHOLSTERY & FURNITURE REPAIR
RIDING APPAREL STORES
RIDING STABLES

ROBOTS: Assembly Line
RODS: Steel & Iron, Made In Steel Mills
ROLL FORMED SHAPES: Custom
ROLLING MILL MACHINERY
ROOFING MATERIALS: Asphalt
ROOFING MATERIALS: Sheet Metal
ROOMING & BOARDING HOUSES: Dormitory, Commercially
Operated
RUBBER
RUBBER PRDTS: Mechanical
RUBBER PRDTS: Reclaimed
RUBBER, CRUDE, WHOLESALE

S

SADDLERY STORES
SAFETY EQPT & SPLYS WHOLESALERS
SAFETY INSPECTION SVCS
SALES PROMOTION SVCS
SALT MINING: Common
SAND & GRAVEL
SAND MINING
SAND: Hygrade
SANDBLASTING SVC: Building Exterior
SANDSTONE: Dimension
SANITARY SVC, NEC
SANITARY SVCS: Disease Control
SANITARY SVCS: Environmental Cleanup
SANITARY SVCS: Hazardous Waste, Collection & Disposal
SANITARY SVCS: Incinerator, Operation Of
SANITARY SVCS: Medical Waste Disposal
SANITARY SVCS: Oil Spill Cleanup
SANITARY SVCS: Refuse Collection & Disposal Svcs
SANITARY SVCS: Rubbish Collection & Disposal
SANITARY SVCS: Sanitary Landfill, Operation Of
SANITARY SVCS: Sewage Treatment Facility
SANITARY SVCS: Toxic Or Hazardous Waste Cleanup
SANITARY SVCS: Waste Materials, Disposal At Sea
SANITARY SVCS: Waste Materials, Recycling
SANITATION CHEMICALS & CLEANING AGENTS
SATELLITES: Communications
SAVINGS & LOAN ASSOCIATIONS, NOT FEDERALLY
CHARTERED
SAVINGS INSTITUTIONS: Federally Chartered
SAVINGS INSTITUTIONS: Not Federally Chartered
SAW BLADES
SAWING & PLANING MILLS
SCAFFOLDING WHOLESALERS
SCALE REPAIR SVCS
SCHOOL BUS SVC
SCHOOL FOR PHYSICALLY HANDICAPPED, NEC
SCHOOL FOR RETARDED, NEC
SCHOOL SPLYS, EXC BOOKS: Wholesalers
SCHOOLS & EDUCATIONAL SVCS, NEC
SCHOOLS: Elementary & Secondary
SCHOOLS: Vocational, NEC
SCRAP & WASTE MATERIALS, WHOLESALE: Auto Wreck-
ing For Scrap
SCRAP & WASTE MATERIALS, WHOLESALE: Ferrous Metal
SCRAP & WASTE MATERIALS, WHOLESALE: Junk & Scrap
SCRAP & WASTE MATERIALS, WHOLESALE: Metal
SCRAP & WASTE MATERIALS, WHOLESALE: Nonferrous
Metals Scrap
SCRAP & WASTE MATERIALS, WHOLESALE: Paper
SCRAP & WASTE MATERIALS, WHOLESALE: Rags
SCRAP & WASTE MATERIALS, WHOLESALE: Rubber Scrap
SCRAP STEEL CUTTING
SCREW MACHINE PRDTS
SCREWS: Metal
SEALANTS
SEALING COMPOUNDS: Sealing, synthetic rubber or plastic
SEARCH & NAVIGATION SYSTEMS
SEARCH & RESCUE SVCS
SEAT BELTS: Automobile & Aircraft
SECRETARIAL SVCS
SECURE STORAGE SVC: Document
SECURE STORAGE SVC: Household & Furniture
SECURITY DEVICES
SECURITY EQPT STORES
SECURITY GUARD SVCS
SECURITY PROTECTIVE DEVICES MAINTENANCE &
MONITORING SVCS
SECURITY SYSTEMS SERVICES
SECURITY UNDERWRITERS
SELF-HELP GROUP HOME
SELF-HELP ORGANIZATION, NEC

SELF-PROPELLED AIRCRAFT DEALER
SEMICONDUCTOR CIRCUIT NETWORKS
SEMICONDUCTORS & RELATED DEVICES
SENIOR HIGH SCHOOLS, PUBLIC
SEPTIC TANK CLEANING SVCS
SERVICE STATION EQPT REPAIR SVCS
SERVICES, NEC
SETTLEMENT HOUSE
SEWAGE & WATER TREATMENT EQPT
SEWAGE FACILITIES
SEWER CLEANING & RODDING SVC
SEWING CONTRACTORS
SEWING MACHINE STORES
SEWING, NEEDLEWORK & PIECE GOODS STORE: Quilting
Matls/Splys
SEWING, NEEDLEWORK & PIECE GOODS STORES: Knit-
ting Splys
SHAPES & PILINGS, STRUCTURAL: Steel
SHEET METAL SPECIALTIES, EXC STAMPED
SHEETING: Laminated Plastic
SHELTERED WORKSHOPS
SHIMS: Metal
SHIPBUILDING & REPAIR
SHIPPING AGENTS
SHOE STORES: Men's
SHOES & BOOTS WHOLESALERS
SHOES: Men's
SHOES: Plastic Or Rubber
SHOES: Women's
SHOPPING CART REPAIR SVCS
SHOPPING CENTERS & MALLS
SIDING: Plastic
SIGN PAINTING & LETTERING SHOP
SIGNALS: Traffic Control, Electric
SIGNS & ADVERTISING SPECIALTIES
SIGNS & ADVERTISING SPECIALTIES: Signs
SIGNS & ADVERTSG SPECIALTIES: Displays/Cutouts Win-
dow/Lobby
SIGNS, ELECTRICAL: Wholesalers
SIGNS, EXC ELECTRIC, WHOLESALE
SIGNS: Electrical
SILICA MINING
SILK SCREEN DESIGN SVCS
SKATING RINKS: Roller
SKI LODGE
SKILL TRAINING CENTER
SNACK & NONALCOHOLIC BEVERAGE BARS
SNOW PLOWING SVCS
SOAPS & DETERGENTS
SOCIAL CHANGE ASSOCIATION
SOCIAL CLUBS
SOCIAL SERVICES INFORMATION EXCHANGE
SOCIAL SERVICES, NEC
SOCIAL SVCS CENTER
SOCIAL SVCS, HANDICAPPED
SOCIAL SVCS: Individual & Family
SOCIAL WORKER
SOFT DRINKS WHOLESALERS
SOFTWARE PUBLISHERS: Application
SOFTWARE PUBLISHERS: Business & Professional
SOFTWARE PUBLISHERS: Education
SOFTWARE PUBLISHERS: Home Entertainment
SOFTWARE PUBLISHERS: NEC
SOFTWARE PUBLISHERS: Operating Systems
SOFTWARE PUBLISHERS: Publisher's
SOFTWARE TRAINING, COMPUTER
SOLDERS
SORORITY HOUSES
SOUND EFFECTS & MUSIC PRODUCTION: Motion Picture
SOUND RECORDING STUDIOS
SOYBEAN PRDTS
SPACE VEHICLE EQPT
SPARK PLUGS: Internal Combustion Engines
SPAS
SPECIAL EDUCATION SCHOOLS, PRIVATE
SPECIAL EDUCATION SCHOOLS, PUBLIC
SPECIAL EVENTS DECORATION SVCS
SPECIALIZED LIBRARIES
SPECIALTY FOOD STORES: Eggs & Poultry
SPECIALTY FOOD STORES: Health & Dietetic Food
SPECIALTY FOOD STORES: Juices, Fruit Or Vegetable
SPECIALTY OUTPATIENT CLINICS, NEC
SPECULATIVE BUILDERS: Multi-Family Housing
SPECULATIVE BUILDERS: Single-Family Housing
SPEECH DEFECT CLINIC

SPEED CHANGERS
SPICE & HERB STORES
SPONGES, ANIMAL, WHOLESALE
SPORTING & RECREATIONAL GOODS & SPLYS WHOLE-SALERS
SPORTING & RECREATIONAL GOODS, WHOL: Water Slides, Rec Park
SPORTING & RECREATIONAL GOODS, WHOLESALE: Athletic Goods
SPORTING & RECREATIONAL GOODS, WHOLESALE: Boat Access & Part
SPORTING & RECREATIONAL GOODS, WHOLESALE: Bowling
SPORTING & RECREATIONAL GOODS, WHOLESALE: Fitness
SPORTING & RECREATIONAL GOODS, WHOLESALE: Golf
SPORTING & RECREATIONAL GOODS, WHOLESALE: Gymnasium
SPORTING FIREARMS WHOLESALERS
SPORTING GOODS
SPORTING GOODS STORES, NEC
SPORTING GOODS STORES: Firearms
SPORTING GOODS STORES: Gymnasium Eqpt, NEC
SPORTING GOODS STORES: Pool & Billiard Tables
SPORTING GOODS STORES: Skating Eqpt
SPORTING GOODS STORES: Specialty Sport Splys, NEC
SPORTING GOODS STORES: Tennis Goods & Eqpt
SPORTS APPAREL STORES
SPORTS CLUBS, MANAGERS & PROMOTERS
SPORTS TEAMS & CLUBS: Baseball
SPORTS TEAMS & CLUBS: Basketball
SPORTS TEAMS & CLUBS: Football
SPORTS TEAMS & CLUBS: Ice Hockey
SPORTS TEAMS & CLUBS: Soccer
SPRAYS: Self-Defense
SPRINGS: Steel
SPRINGS: Wire
SPRINKLING SYSTEMS: Fire Control
STADIUM EVENT OPERATOR SERVICES
STAFFING, EMPLOYMENT PLACEMENT
STAINLESS STEEL
STAMPINGS: Automotive
STAMPINGS: Metal
STATE CREDIT UNIONS, NOT FEDERALLY CHARTERED
STATE SAVINGS BANKS, NOT FEDERALLY CHARTERED
STATIONARY & OFFICE SPLYS, WHOL: Computer/Photocopying Splys
STATIONARY & OFFICE SPLYS, WHOLESALE: Laser Printer Splys
STATIONARY & OFFICE SPLYS, WHOLESALE: Stationery
STATIONARY & OFFICE SPLYS WHOLESALERS
STEAM HEATING SYSTEMS SPLY SVCS
STEAM SPLY SYSTEMS SVCS INCLUDING GEOTHERMAL
STEAM, HEAT & AIR CONDITIONING DISTRIBUTION SVC
STEEL FABRICATORS
STEEL MILLS
STEEL, COLD-ROLLED: Flat Bright, From Purchased Hot-Rolled
STEEL, COLD-ROLLED: Sheet Or Strip, From Own Hot-Rolled
STEEL, HOT-ROLLED: Sheet Or Strip
STEEL: Cold-Rolled
STEVEDORING SVCS
STITCHING SVCS: Custom
STONE: Dimension, NEC
STONEWARE PRDTS: Pottery
STORE FIXTURES, EXC REFRIGERATED: Wholesalers
STORE FIXTURES: Wood
STORES: Auto & Home Supply
STUDIOS: Artists & Artists' Studios
STUDIOS: Sculptor's
STUDS & JOISTS: Sheet Metal
SUB-LESSORS: Real Estate
SUBSCRIPTION FULFILLMENT SVCS: Magazine, Newspaper, Etc
SUBSTANCE ABUSE CLINICS, OUTPATIENT
SUBSTANCE ABUSE COUNSELING
SUMMER CAMPS, EXC DAY & SPORTS INSTRUCTIONAL
SUPERMARKETS & OTHER GROCERY STORES
SURGICAL APPLIANCES & SPLYS
SURGICAL EQPT: See Also Instruments
SURGICAL INSTRUMENT REPAIR SVCS
SURVEYING & MAPPING: Land Parcels
SVC ESTABLISHMENT EQPT & SPLYS WHOLESALERS

SVC ESTABLISHMENT EQPT, WHOL: Cleaning & Maint Eqpt & Splys
SVC ESTABLISHMENT EQPT, WHOL: Concrete Burial Vaults & Boxes
SVC ESTABLISHMENT EQPT, WHOL: Laundry/Dry Cleaning Eqpt/Sply
SVC ESTABLISHMENT EQPT, WHOLESALE : Barber Shop Eqpt & Splys
SVC ESTABLISHMENT EQPT, WHOLESALE: Beauty Parlor Eqpt & Sply
SVC ESTABLISHMENT EQPT, WHOLESALE: Firefighting Eqpt
SVC ESTABLISHMENT EQPT, WHOLESALE: Laundry Eqpt & Splys
SVC ESTABLISHMENT EQPT, WHOLESALE: Restaurant Splys
SVC ESTABLISHMENT EQPT, WHOLESALE: Vending Machines & Splys
SWIMMING INSTRUCTION
SWIMMING POOL & HOT TUB CLEANING & MAINTE-NANCE SVCS
SWIMMING POOL SPLY STORES
SWIMMING POOLS, EQPT & SPLYS: Wholesalers
SWITCHES: Thermostatic
SWITCHGEAR & SWITCHBOARD APPARATUS
SYMPHONY ORCHESTRA
SYNAGOGUES
SYRUPS, DRINK
SYSTEMS ENGINEERING: Computer Related
SYSTEMS INTEGRATION SVCS
SYSTEMS INTEGRATION SVCS: Local Area Network
SYSTEMS INTEGRATION SVCS: Office Computer Automation
SYSTEMS SOFTWARE DEVELOPMENT SVCS

T

TABULATING SVCS
TAGS & LABELS: Paper
TANK & BOILER CLEANING SVCS
TANK REPAIR & CLEANING SVCS
TANK REPAIR SVCS
TANKS: Cryogenic, Metal
TANKS: Lined, Metal
TANKS: Standard Or Custom Fabricated, Metal Plate
TANNING SALONS
TAPES: Pressure Sensitive
TAX RETURN PREPARATION SVCS
TAXI CABS
TECHNICAL & TRADE SCHOOLS, NEC
TECHNICAL INSTITUTE
TECHNICAL MANUAL PREPARATION SVCS
TECHNICAL WRITING SVCS
TELECOMMUNICATION EQPT REPAIR SVCS, EXC TELE-PHONES
TELECOMMUNICATION SYSTEMS & EQPT
TELECOMMUNICATIONS CARRIERS & SVCS: Wired
TELECOMMUNICATIONS CARRIERS & SVCS: Wireless
TELEMARKETING BUREAUS
TELEPHONE ANSWERING SVCS
TELEPHONE COUNSELING SVCS
TELEPHONE EQPT INSTALLATION
TELEPHONE EQPT: NEC
TELEPHONE SET REPAIR SVCS
TELEPHONE SVCS
TELEVISION BROADCASTING STATIONS
TELEVISION FILM PRODUCTION SVCS
TELEVISION REPAIR SHOP
TEMPORARY HELP SVCS
TEN PIN CENTERS
TENANT SCREENING SVCS
TERMITE CONTROL SVCS
TEST BORING SVCS: Nonmetallic Minerals
TEST BORING, METAL MINING
TESTERS: Gas, Exc Indl Process
TESTING SVCS
TEXTILE & APPAREL SVCS
THEATER COMPANIES
THEATRICAL PRODUCERS & SVCS
THERMOCOUPLES: Indl Process
THERMOPLASTIC MATERIALS
TICKET OFFICES & AGENCIES: Theatrical
TICKET OFFICES & AGENCIES: Travel
TIRE & TUBE REPAIR MATERIALS, WHOLESALE
TIRE CORD & FABRIC
TIRE DEALERS

TIRE INNER-TUBES
TIRE RECAPPING & RETREADING
TIRE SUNDRIES OR REPAIR MATERIALS: Rubber
TIRES & TUBES WHOLESALERS
TIRES & TUBES, WHOLESALE: Automotive
TIRES & TUBES, WHOLESALE: Truck
TITLE & TRUST COMPANIES
TITLE ABSTRACT & SETTLEMENT OFFICES
TITLE INSURANCE AGENTS
TITLE INSURANCE: Real Estate
TITLE SEARCH COMPANIES
TOBACCO & PRDTS, WHOLESALE: Cigarettes
TOBACCO & TOBACCO PRDTS WHOLESALERS
TOILETRIES, COSMETICS & PERFUME STORES
TOILETRIES, WHOLESALE: Hair Preparations
TOILETRIES, WHOLESALE: Razor Blades
TOILETRIES, WHOLESALE: Toiletries
TOILETS, PORTABLE, WHOLESALE
TOLL BRIDGE OPERATIONS
TOLL ROAD OPERATIONS
TOOL REPAIR SVCS
TOOLS: Hand
TOOLS: Hand, Plumbers'
TOOLS: Hand, Power
TOUR OPERATORS
TOURIST INFORMATION BUREAU
TOURIST LODGINGS
TOWELS: Fabric & Nonwoven, Made From Purchased Materials
TOWERS: Cooling, Sheet Metal
TOWING & TUGBOAT SVC
TOWING SVCS: Marine
TOYS
TOYS & HOBBY GOODS & SPLYS, WHOLESALE: Arts/Crafts Eqpt/Sply
TOYS & HOBBY GOODS & SPLYS, WHOLESALE: Balloons, Novelty
TOYS & HOBBY GOODS & SPLYS, WHOLESALE: Bingo Games & Splys
TOYS & HOBBY GOODS & SPLYS, WHOLESALE: Educational Toys
TOYS & HOBBY GOODS & SPLYS, WHOLESALE: Toys & Games
TOYS & HOBBY GOODS & SPLYS, WHOLESALE: Toys, NEC
TOYS & HOBBY GOODS & SPLYS, WHOLESALE: Video Games
TOYS, HOBBY GOODS & SPLYS WHOLESALERS
TRADE SHOW ARRANGEMENT SVCS
TRAFFIC CONTROL FLAGGING SVCS
TRAILERS & PARTS: Truck & Semi's
TRAILERS & TRAILER EQPT
TRAILERS: Bodies
TRAILERS: Semitrailers, Truck Tractors
TRAINING SCHOOL FOR DELINQUENTS
TRANS PROG REG & ADMIN, GOVT: Motor Vehicle Licensing & Insp
TRANSFORMERS: Electric
TRANSFORMERS: Furnace, Electric
TRANSFORMERS: Power Related
TRANSLATION & INTERPRETATION SVCS
TRANSPORTATION AGENTS & BROKERS
TRANSPORTATION ARRANGEMENT SVCS, PASSENGER: Carpool/Vanpool
TRANSPORTATION ARRANGEMENT SVCS, PASSENGER: Tours, Conducted
TRANSPORTATION BROKERS: Truck
TRANSPORTATION EPQT & SPLYS, WHOL: Aircraft Engs/Eng Parts
TRANSPORTATION EPQT & SPLYS, WHOLESALE: Tanks & Tank Compnts
TRANSPORTATION EQPT & SPLYS WHOLESALERS, NEC
TRANSPORTATION EQUIPMENT, NEC
TRANSPORTATION INSPECTION SVCS
TRANSPORTATION PROG REG & ADMIN, GOVT: Bureau, Public Roads
TRANSPORTATION PROGRAM REGULATION & ADMIN GOVT: Local
TRANSPORTATION PROGRAM REGULATION & ADMIN, GOVT: Federal
TRANSPORTATION PROGRAM REGULATION & ADMIN, GOVT: State
TRANSPORTATION PROGRAMS REGULATION & ADMINIS-TRATION SVCS

TRANSPORTATION SVCS, AIR, NONSCHEDULED: Air Cargo Carriers
TRANSPORTATION SVCS, NEC
TRANSPORTATION SVCS, WATER: Boat Cleaning
TRANSPORTATION SVCS, WATER: Canal Barge Operations
TRANSPORTATION SVCS, WATER: Cleaning
TRANSPORTATION SVCS, WATER: Intracoastal, Freight
TRANSPORTATION SVCS: Airport
TRANSPORTATION SVCS: Airport, Regular Route
TRANSPORTATION SVCS: Bus Line Operations
TRANSPORTATION SVCS: Bus Line, Interstate
TRANSPORTATION SVCS: Maint Facilities, Vehicle Passenger
TRANSPORTATION SVCS: Maintenance Facilities, Buses
TRANSPORTATION SVCS: Railroad Terminals
TRANSPORTATION SVCS: Railroad, Passenger
TRANSPORTATION SVCS: Railroads, Interurban
TRANSPORTATION SVCS: Railroads, Steam
TRANSPORTATION SVCS: Rental, Local
TRANSPORTATION SVCS: Subway Operation
TRANSPORTATION SVCS: Vanpool Operation
TRANSPORTATION: Air, Nonscheduled Passenger
TRANSPORTATION: Air, Nonscheduled, NEC
TRANSPORTATION: Air, Scheduled Freight
TRANSPORTATION: Air, Scheduled Passenger
TRANSPORTATION: Bus Transit Systems
TRANSPORTATION: Bus Transit Systems
TRANSPORTATION: Deep Sea Foreign Freight
TRANSPORTATION: Deep Sea Passenger
TRANSPORTATION: Great Lakes Domestic Freight
TRANSPORTATION: Local Passenger, NEC
TRANSPORTATION: Passenger Ferries
TRANSPORTATION: Transit Systems, NEC
TRAVEL AGENCIES
TRAVEL TRAILER DEALERS
TRAVEL TRAILERS & CAMPERS
TRAVELER ACCOMMODATIONS, NEC
TRAVELERS' CHECK ISSUANCE SVCS
TROPHIES, NEC
TROPHY & PLAQUE STORES
TRUCK & BUS BODIES: Ambulance
TRUCK & BUS BODIES: Truck, Motor Vehicle
TRUCK & BUS BODIES: Utility Truck
TRUCK & FREIGHT TERMINALS & SUPPORT ACTIVITIES
TRUCK BODIES: Body Parts
TRUCK BODY SHOP
TRUCK DRIVER SVCS
TRUCK GENERAL REPAIR SVC
TRUCK PAINTING & LETTERING SVCS
TRUCK PARTS & ACCESSORIES: Wholesalers
TRUCK STOPS
TRUCKING & HAULING SVCS: Baggage Transfer Svcs
TRUCKING & HAULING SVCS: Building Materials
TRUCKING & HAULING SVCS: Coal, Local
TRUCKING & HAULING SVCS: Contract Basis
TRUCKING & HAULING SVCS: Draying, Local, Without Storage
TRUCKING & HAULING SVCS: Furniture Moving & Storage, Local
TRUCKING & HAULING SVCS: Furniture, Local W/out Storage
TRUCKING & HAULING SVCS: Garbage, Collect/Transport Only
TRUCKING & HAULING SVCS: Haulage & Cartage, Light, Local
TRUCKING & HAULING SVCS: Hazardous Waste
TRUCKING & HAULING SVCS: Heavy Machinery, Local
TRUCKING & HAULING SVCS: Heavy, NEC
TRUCKING & HAULING SVCS: Liquid Petroleum, Exc Local
TRUCKING & HAULING SVCS: Liquid, Local
TRUCKING & HAULING SVCS: Live Poultry
TRUCKING & HAULING SVCS: Lumber & Timber
TRUCKING & HAULING SVCS: Machinery, Heavy
TRUCKING & HAULING SVCS: Mail Carriers, Contract
TRUCKING & HAULING SVCS: Petroleum, Local
TRUCKING & HAULING SVCS: Safe Moving, Local
TRUCKING & HAULING SVCS: Trailer/Container On Flat Car
TRUCKING, AUTOMOBILE CARRIER
TRUCKING, DUMP
TRUCKING, REFRIGERATED: Long-Distance
TRUCKING: Except Local
TRUCKING: Local, With Storage
TRUCKING: Local, Without Storage

TRUCKING: Long-Distance, Less Than Truckload
TRUCKS & TRACTORS: Industrial
TRUCKS, INDL: Wholesalers
TRUSSES: Wood, Floor
TRUSSES: Wood, Roof
TRUST COMPANIES: National With Deposits, Commercial
TRUST COMPANIES: State Accepting Deposits, Commercial
TRUST MANAGEMENT SVCS: Charitable
TRUST MANAGEMENT SVCS: Personal Investment
TUBE & TUBING FABRICATORS
TUBES: Steel & Iron
TUBING: Flexible, Metallic
TUBING: Plastic
TUGBOAT SVCS
TUNGSTEN MILL PRDTS
TURBINES & TURBINE GENERATOR SETS
TURBINES: Gas, Mechanical Drive
TURNKEY VENDORS: Computer Systems
TYPESETTING SVC
TYPESETTING SVC: Computer

U

UNIFORM SPLY SVCS: Indl
UNIFORM STORES
UNISEX HAIR SALONS
UNITED FUND COUNCILS
UNIVERSITY
UPHOLSTERY WORK SVCS
USED CAR DEALERS
USED CLOTHING STORES
USED MERCHANDISE STORES
USED MERCHANDISE STORES: Clothing & Shoes
USED MERCHANDISE STORES: Furniture
USHER SVC
UTILITY PROGRAM ADMINISTRATION & REGULATION, GOVT: Local

V

VACATION LODGES
VACUUM CLEANER STORES
VACUUM CLEANERS: Household
VALET PARKING SVCS
VALUE-ADDED RESELLERS: Computer Systems
VALVE REPAIR SVCS, INDL
VALVES & PIPE FITTINGS
VALVES: Aerosol, Metal
VALVES: Aircraft, Hydraulic
VALVES: Indl
VALVES: Nuclear Power Plant, Ferrous
VAN CONVERSIONS
VARIETY STORE MERCHANDISE, WHOLESALE
VARIETY STORES
VEGETABLE STANDS OR MARKETS
VEHICLES: All Terrain
VENDING MACHINE OPERATORS: Beverage
VENDING MACHINE OPERATORS: Food
VENDING MACHINE OPERATORS: Sandwich & Hot Food
VENDING MACHINE REPAIR SVCS
VENDING MACHINES & PARTS
VENTILATING EQPT: Metal
VENTURE CAPITAL COMPANIES
VESSELS: Process, Indl, Metal Plate
VETERANS AFFAIRS ADMINISTRATION SVCS
VETERANS' AFFAIRS ADMINISTRATION, GOVERNMENT: Federal
VETERINARY PRDTS: Instruments & Apparatus
VIDEO & AUDIO EQPT, WHOLESALE
VIDEO PRODUCTION SVCS
VIDEO REPAIR SVCS
VIDEO TAPE PRODUCTION SVCS
VIDEO TAPE WHOLESALERS, RECORDED
VINYL RESINS, NEC
VISITING NURSE
VISUAL COMMUNICATIONS SYSTEMS
VOCATIONAL OR TECHNICAL SCHOOLS, PUBLIC
VOCATIONAL REHABILITATION AGENCY
VOCATIONAL TRAINING AGENCY

W

WALL COVERINGS WHOLESALERS
WALLPAPER STORE
WALLS: Curtain, Metal

WAREHOUSING & STORAGE FACILITIES, NEC
WAREHOUSING & STORAGE, REFRIGERATED: Cold Storage Or Refrig
WAREHOUSING & STORAGE, REFRIGERATED: Frozen Or Refrig Goods
WAREHOUSING & STORAGE: Automobile, Dead Storage
WAREHOUSING & STORAGE: General
WAREHOUSING & STORAGE: General
WAREHOUSING & STORAGE: Liquid
WAREHOUSING & STORAGE: Miniwarehouse
WAREHOUSING & STORAGE: Refrigerated
WAREHOUSING & STORAGE: Self Storage
WAREHOUSING & STORAGE: Textile
WARM AIR HEATING & AC EQPT & SPLYS, WHOLESALE Air Filters
WARM AIR HEATING & AC EQPT & SPLYS, WHOLESALE Furnaces
WARM AIR HEATING & AC EQPT & SPLYS, WHOLESALE Furnaces, Elec
WARM AIR HEATING/AC EQPT/SPLYS, WHOL Warm Air Htg Eqpt/Splys
WARM AIR HEATING/AC EQPT/SPLYS, WHOL: Ventilating Eqpt/Sply
WARRANTY INSURANCE: Automobile
WASHERS: Metal
WASTE CLEANING SVCS
WATCH REPAIR SVCS
WATCHES & PARTS, WHOLESALE
WATER SOFTENER SVCS
WATER SOFTENING WHOLESALERS
WATER SPLY: Irrigation
WATER SUPPLY
WATER: Distilled
WATERBEDS & ACCESS STORES
WEATHER FORECASTING SVCS
WEDDING CHAPEL: Privately Operated
WELDING EQPT & SPLYS WHOLESALERS
WELDING REPAIR SVC
WELDING SPLYS, EXC GASES: Wholesalers
WELDMENTS
WELFARE PENSIONS
WHEELS
WHEELS & BRAKE SHOES: Railroad, Cast Iron
WINDOW & DOOR FRAMES
WINDOW CLEANING SVCS
WINDOW FRAMES & SASHES: Plastic
WINDOW FRAMES, MOLDING & TRIM: Vinyl
WINE & DISTILLED ALCOHOLIC BEVERAGES WHOLESALERS
WINE CELLARS, BONDED: Wine, Blended
WIRE & WIRE PRDTS
WIRE FENCING & ACCESS WHOLESALERS
WIRE MATERIALS: Steel
WIRE WINDING OF PURCHASED WIRE
WIRE, FLAT: Strip, Cold-Rolled, Exc From Hot-Rolled Mills
WIRE: Nonferrous
WOMEN'S & CHILDREN'S CLOTHING WHOLESALERS, NEC
WOMEN'S & GIRLS' SPORTSWEAR WHOLESALERS
WOMEN'S CLOTHING STORES
WOOD & WOOD BY-PRDTS, WHOLESALE
WOOD CHIPS, PRODUCED AT THE MILL
WOOD PRDTS: Moldings, Unfinished & Prefinished
WOOD PRDTS: Mulch, Wood & Bark
WOOD PRDTS: Survey Stakes
WOODWORK & TRIM: Interior & Ornamental
WORK EXPERIENCE CENTER

X

X-RAY EQPT & TUBES
X-RAY EQPT REPAIR SVCS

Y

YACHT CLUBS
YOUTH CAMPS
YOUTH SELF-HELP AGENCY

Z

ZOOLOGICAL GARDEN, NONCOMMERCIAL
ZOOS & BOTANICAL GARDENS

SERVICES SECTION

Service category → **BOXES: Folding**

Edgar & Son Paperboard ....G...... 999 999-9999
Yourtown *(G-11480)*

Ready Box Co. ....E 999 999-9999
City → Anytown *(G-7097)*

Indicates approximate employment figure
A = Over 500 employees, B = 251-500
C = 101-250, D = 51-100, E = 25-50

Business phone

Geographic Section entry number where full
company information appears.

See footnotes for symbols and codes identification.

• Refer to the Services Index preceding this section to locate service headings.

ABORTION CLINIC

Cleveland Preterm ....E 216 991-4577
Cleveland *(G-5281)*

ABRASIVES

ARC Abrasives Inc ....D 800 888-4885
Troy *(G-18194)*

Lawrence Industries Inc ....C 216 518-7000
Cleveland *(G-5858)*

Mill-Rose Company ....C 440 255-9171
Mentor *(G-14087)*

National Lime and Stone Co ....C 419 396-7671
Carey *(G-2545)*

ACADEMIC TUTORING SVCS

Academic Support Services LLC ....E 740 274-6138
Columbus *(G-6857)*

ACADEMY

Ohio Academy of Science ....E 614 488-2228
Dublin *(G-10296)*

ACCELERATORS: Linear

Ci Disposition Co ....E 216 587-5200
Brooklyn Heights *(G-1867)*

ACCIDENT & HEALTH INSURANCE CARRIERS

American Modrn Insur Group Inc ....C 800 543-2644
Amelia *(G-568)*

Medical Mutual of Ohio ....B 216 292-0400
Beachwood *(G-1078)*

ACCIDENT INSURANCE CARRIERS

Liberty Mutual Insurance Co ....E 614 855-6193
Westerville *(G-19183)*

Nationwide Corporation ....E 614 249-7111
Columbus *(G-8152)*

Nationwide Mutual Insurance Co ....A 614 249-7111
Columbus *(G-8160)*

Paramount Care Inc ....B 419 887-2500
Maumee *(G-13830)*

Progressive Casualty Insur Co ....D 440 603-4033
Cleveland *(G-6244)*

ACCOUNTING SVCS, NEC

American Electric Pwr Svc Corp ....B 614 716-1000
Columbus *(G-6919)*

Brott Mardis & Co ....E 330 762-5022
Akron *(G-111)*

C H Dean Inc ....D 937 222-9531
Beavercreek *(G-1136)*

Cliftonlarsonallen LLP ....E 330 376-0100
Akron *(G-144)*

Defense Fin & Accounting Svc ....A 614 693-6700
Columbus *(G-7429)*

Deloitte & Touche LLP ....C 614 221-1000
Columbus *(G-7433)*

Elliott Davis LLC ....E 513 579-1717
Cincinnati *(G-3491)*

Fehr Services LLC ....E 513 829-9333
Fairfield *(G-10728)*

Flex Fund Inc ....E 614 766-7000
Dublin *(G-10229)*

Grant Thornton LLP ....D 513 762-5000
Cincinnati *(G-3634)*

Klingbeil Management Group Co ....E 614 220-8900
Columbus *(G-7911)*

Kpmg Llp ....C 614 249-2300
Columbus *(G-7925)*

Mutual Shareholder Svcs LLC ....E 440 922-0067
Broadview Heights *(G-1838)*

Ohio State University ....E 614 292-6831
Columbus *(G-8315)*

Pease & Associates LLC ....E 216 348-9600
Cleveland *(G-6188)*

Rlj Management Co Inc ....E 614 942-2020
Columbus *(G-8540)*

ACCOUNTING SVCS: Certified Public

415 Group Inc ....E 330 492-0094
Canton *(G-2167)*

Apple Growth Partners Inc ....D 330 867-7350
Akron *(G-76)*

Barnes Dennig & Co Ltd ....D 513 241-8313
Cincinnati *(G-3021)*

Barnes Wendling Cpas Inc ....E 216 566-9000
Cleveland *(G-5037)*

Bdo Usa LLP ....D 614 488-3126
Columbus *(G-7023)*

Bdo Usa LLP ....D 513 592-2400
Cincinnati *(G-3027)*

Bdo Usa LLP ....D 216 325-1700
Cleveland *(G-5046)*

Bdo Usa LLP ....D 330 668-9696
Akron *(G-91)*

Bkd LLP ....D 513 621-8300
Cincinnati *(G-3053)*

Blue & Co LLC ....C 513 241-4507
Cincinnati *(G-3057)*

Bober Markey Fedorovich ....D 330 762-9785
Fairlawn *(G-10817)*

Bodine Perry LLC ....E 330 702-8100
Canfield *(G-2131)*

Brady Ware & Schoenfeld Inc ....D 614 885-7407
Columbus *(G-7059)*

Brady Ware & Schoenfeld Inc ....D 937 223-5247
Miamisburg *(G-14146)*

Brady Ware & Schoenfeld Inc ....D 614 825-6277
Columbus *(G-7060)*

Burke & Schindler Pllc ....E 859 344-8887
Cincinnati *(G-3091)*

Cassady Schiller & Associates ....E 513 483-6699
Blue Ash *(G-1519)*

Ciulla Smith & Dale LLP ....D 440 884-2036
Cleveland *(G-5219)*

Ciuni & Panichi Inc ....D 216 831-7171
Cleveland *(G-5220)*

Clark Schaefer Hackett & Co ....E 937 399-2000
Springfield *(G-17008)*

Clark Schaefer Hackett & Co ....D 513 241-3111
Cincinnati *(G-3301)*

Clark Schaefer Hackett & Co ....D 216 672-5252
Cleveland *(G-5221)*

Clark Schaefer Hackett & Co ....D 419 243-0218
Toledo *(G-17662)*

Clark Schaefer Hackett & Co ....D 614 885-2208
Columbus *(G-7060)*

Cliftonlarsonallen LLP ....D 330 497-2000
Canton *(G-2259)*

Cliftonlarsonallen LLP ....D 419 244-3711
Toledo *(G-17665)*

Cohen & Company Ltd ....E 330 743-1040
Youngstown *(G-19994)*

Cohen & Company Ltd ....D 330 374-1040
Akron *(G-146)*

Crowe LLP ....C 614 469-0001
Columbus *(G-7396)*

Crowe LLP ....E 216 623-7500
Cleveland *(G-5382)*

Csh Group ....E 937 226-0070
Miamisburg *(G-14158)*

Deloitte & Touche LLP ....D 937 223-8821
Dayton *(G-9386)*

Deloitte & Touche LLP ....B 513 784-7100
Cincinnati *(G-3420)*

Deloitte & Touche LLP ....C 216 589-1300
Cleveland *(G-5415)*

Ernst & Young LLP ....D 216 861-5000
Cleveland *(G-5490)*

Ernst & Young LLP ....C 216 583-1823
Cleveland *(G-5491)*

Ernst & Young LLP ....D 614 224-5678
Columbus *(G-7531)*

Ernst & Young LLP ....C 513 612-1400
Cincinnati *(G-3515)*

Ernst & Young LLP ....C 419 244-8000
Toledo *(G-17717)*

Essex and Associates Inc ....E 937 432-1040
Dayton *(G-9418)*

Flagel Huber Flagel & Co ....E 937 299-3400
Moraine *(G-14659)*

Foundations Hlth Solutions Inc ....D 440 793-0200
North Olmsted *(G-15289)*

Foxx & Company ....E 513 241-1616
Cincinnati *(G-3583)*

Fruth & Co ....E 419 435-8541
Fostoria *(G-11001)*

Gbq Holdings LLC ....E 614 221-1120
Columbus *(G-7652)*

Gilmore Jasion Mahler Ltd ....D 419 794-2000
Maumee *(G-13796)*

Grant Thornton LLP ....C 216 771-1400
Cleveland *(G-5623)*

Hill Barth & King LLC ....E 330 758-8613
Canfield *(G-2140)*

Hill Barth & King LLC ....D 614 228-4000
Columbus *(G-7749)*

Hill Barth & King LLC ....D 330 747-1903
Canfield *(G-2141)*

Hobe Lcas Crtif Pub Accntants ....E 216 524-7167
Cleveland *(G-5698)*

Holbrook & Manter ....E 740 387-8620
Marion *(G-13425)*

Howard Wershbale & Co ....D 216 831-1200
Cleveland *(G-5720)*

Jones Cochenour & Co Inc ....E 740 653-9581
Lancaster *(G-12407)*

Julian & Grube Inc ....E 614 846-1899
Westerville *(G-19176)*

Kpmg LLP ....C 513 421-6430
Cincinnati *(G-3887)*

Kpmg LLP ....C 216 696-9100
Cleveland *(G-5841)*

Maloney + Novotny LLC ....D 216 363-0100
Cleveland *(G-5904)*

McCrate Delaet & Co ....E 937 492-3161
Sidney *(G-16786)*

Meaden & Moore LLP ....D 216 241-3272
Cleveland *(G-5939)*

Mellott & Mellott Pll ....E 513 241-2940
Cincinnati *(G-4004)*

Mosley Pfundt & Glick Inc ....E 419 861-1120
Maumee *(G-13822)*

Murray Wlls Wndeln Rbnson Cpas ......E 937 773-6373
Piqua *(G-16015)*

Nms Inc Certif Pub Accountants ....E 440 286-5222
Chardon *(G-2706)*

Norman Jones Enlow & Co ....E 614 228-4000
Columbus *(G-8194)*

Employee Codes: A=Over 500 employees, B=251-500
C=101-250, D=51-100, E=25-50

2019 Harris Ohio
Services Directory

1321

SERVICES

Omicron Investment Company LLC ......D 419 891-1040
   Maumee *(G-13827)*
Patrick J Burke & Co ....E 513 455-8200
   Cincinnati *(G-4212)*
Payne Nickles & Co CPA ....E 419 668-2552
   Norwalk *(G-15452)*
Pricewaterhousecoopers LLP ....B 216 875-3000
   Cleveland *(G-6235)*
Pricewaterhousecoopers LLP ....E 419 254-2500
   Toledo *(G-17987)*
Pricewaterhousecoopers LLP ....D 513 723-4700
   Cincinnati *(G-4278)*
Pricewaterhousecoopers LLP ....C 614 225-8700
   Columbus *(G-8461)*
REA & Associates Inc ....E 330 722-8222
   Medina *(G-13992)*
REA & Associates Inc ....D 330 339-6651
   New Philadelphia *(G-14977)*
REA & Associates Inc ....E 419 331-1040
   Lima *(G-12792)*
REA & Associates Inc ....E 330 674-6055
   Millersburg *(G-14489)*
REA & Associates Inc ....D 440 266-0077
   New Philadelphia *(G-14978)*
REA & Associates Inc ....E 614 889-8725
   Dublin *(G-10319)*
Rehmann LLC ....D 419 865-8118
   Toledo *(G-18000)*
Reynolds & Co Inc ....E 740 353-1040
   Portsmouth *(G-16164)*
RSM US LLP ....C 937 298-0201
   Moraine *(G-14693)*
RSM US LLP ....E 614 224-7722
   Columbus *(G-8558)*
RSM US LLP ....C 216 523-1900
   Cleveland *(G-6349)*
Schneider Downs & Co Inc ....D 614 621-4060
   Columbus *(G-8602)*
Schroedel Scullin & Bestic LLC ....E 330 533-1131
   Canfield *(G-2157)*
Siegfried Group LLP ....E 216 522-1910
   Cleveland *(G-6407)*
Skoda Mntti Crtif Pub Accntnts ....D 440 449-6800
   Mayfield Village *(G-13887)*
Smithpearlman & Co ....E 513 248-9210
   Milford *(G-14433)*
Thomas Packer & Co ....E 330 533-9777
   Canfield *(G-2160)*
Walthall LLP ....E 216 573-2330
   Cleveland *(G-6651)*
Weber Obrien Ltd ....E 419 885-8338
   Sylvania *(G-17463)*
Whalen and Company Inc ....E 614 396-4200
   Worthington *(G-19860)*
Whitcomb & Hess Inc ....E 419 289-7007
   Ashland *(G-699)*
Whited Seigneur Sams & Rahe ....E 740 702-2600
   Chillicothe *(G-2837)*
William Vaughan Company ....D 419 891-1040
   Maumee *(G-13869)*
Wilson Shannon & Snow Inc ....E 740 345-6611
   Newark *(G-15109)*
Wulff & Associates CPA LLC ....E 513 245-1010
   Cincinnati *(G-4809)*
Zinner & Co ....E 216 831-0733
   Beachwood *(G-1118)*

ACUPUNCTURISTS' OFFICES

Central Ohio Primary Care ....D 614 818-9550
   Westerville *(G-19233)*
Central Ohio Primary Care ....E 614 268-6555
   Columbus *(G-7164)*
Central Ohio Primary Care ....E 614 442-7550
   Columbus *(G-7167)*
Ohio Presbt Retirement Svcs ....C 614 228-8888
   Columbus *(G-8280)*

ADDRESSING SVCS

Hecks Direct Mail & Prtg Svc ....E 419 697-3505
   Toledo *(G-17797)*

ADHESIVES

Conversion Tech Intl Inc ....E 419 924-5566
   West Unity *(G-19140)*
Evans Adhesive Corporation ....E 614 451-2665
   Columbus *(G-7540)*

ADHESIVES & SEALANTS

Cincinnati Assn For The Blind ....C 513 221-8558
   Cincinnati *(G-3223)*
Continental Products Company ....E 216 531-0710
   Cleveland *(G-5344)*
Hexpol Compounding LLC ....C 440 834-4644
   Burton *(G-2016)*
Hoover & Wells Inc ....E 419 691-9220
   Toledo *(G-17807)*
Sonoco Products Company ....D 937 429-0040
   Beavercreek Township *(G-1263)*
United McGill Corporation ....E 614 829-1200
   Groveport *(G-11546)*

ADJUSTMENT BUREAU, EXC INSURANCE

Roddy Group Inc ....E 216 763-0088
   Beachwood *(G-1102)*

ADOPTION SVCS

Beech Acres Parenting Center ....D 513 231-6630
   Cincinnati *(G-3030)*
County of Lorain ....C 440 329-5340
   Elyria *(G-10501)*
Heartbeat International Inc ....E 614 885-7577
   Columbus *(G-7730)*
Mahoning County Childrens Svcs ....C 330 941-8888
   Youngstown *(G-20108)*
Options For Family & Youth ....E 216 267-7070
   Strongsville *(G-17337)*
United Methodist Childrens ....E 614 885-5020
   Columbus *(G-8804)*

ADULT DAYCARE CENTERS

2100 Lakeside Shelter For Men ....E 216 566-0047
   Cleveland *(G-4869)*
CA Group ....E 419 586-2137
   Celina *(G-2586)*
CHN Inc - Adult Day Care ....E 937 548-0506
   Greenville *(G-11370)*
Consumer Support Services Inc ....D 740 344-3600
   Newark *(G-15026)*
DMD Management Inc ....A 216 371-3600
   Cleveland *(G-5435)*
Gardens Western Reserve Inc ....D 330 342-9100
   Streetsboro *(G-17252)*
Inn At Christine Valley ....D 330 270-3347
   Youngstown *(G-20082)*
Life Center Adult Day Care ....E 614 866-7212
   Reynoldsburg *(G-16316)*
ONeill Senior Center Inc ....E 740 373-3914
   Marietta *(G-13365)*
Senior Independence Adult ....E 440 954-8372
   Willoughby *(G-19570)*
Senior Independence Adult ....E 513 681-8174
   Monroe *(G-14582)*
Senior Independence Adult ....E 513 539-2697
   Monroe *(G-14583)*

ADULT EDUCATION SCHOOLS, PUBLIC

Cleveland Municipal School Dst ....D 216 459-4200
   Cleveland *(G-5275)*
Great Oaks Inst Tech Creer Dev ....E 513 771-8840
   Cincinnati *(G-3645)*

ADVERTISING AGENCIES

Albrecht Inc ....E 513 576-9900
   Milford *(G-14369)*
AMP Advertising Inc ....E 513 333-4100
   Cincinnati *(G-2954)*
Barefoot LLC ....E 513 861-3668
   Cincinnati *(G-3020)*
BBDO Worldwide Inc ....E 513 861-3668
   Cincinnati *(G-3026)*
Bbs & Associates Inc ....D 330 665-5227
   Akron *(G-89)*
Black River Group Inc ....D 419 524-6699
   Mansfield *(G-13142)*
Commerce Holdings Inc ....E 513 579-1950
   Cincinnati *(G-3337)*
Detroit Royalty Incorporated ....D 216 771-5700
   Cleveland *(G-5419)*
Dix & Eaton Incorporated ....D 216 241-0405
   Cleveland *(G-5431)*
Epipheo Incorporated ....E 888 687-7620
   Cincinnati *(G-3506)*
Hsr Marketing Communications ....D 513 671-3811
   Cincinnati *(G-3735)*

Inquiry Systems Inc ....E 614 464-3800
   Columbus *(G-7824)*
Kuno Creative Group LLC ....E 440 225-4144
   Avon *(G-891)*
L M Berry and Company ....A 937 296-2121
   Moraine *(G-14670)*
Madison Avenue Mktg Group Inc ....E 419 473-9000
   Toledo *(G-17878)*
Marketing Support Services Inc ....D 513 752-1200
   Cincinnati *(G-3972)*
Monster Worldwide Inc ....D 513 719-3331
   Cincinnati *(G-4071)*
National Yllow Pages Media LLC ....E 216 447-9400
   Independence *(G-12101)*
People To My Site LLC ....E 614 452-8179
   Columbus *(G-8437)*
Rockfish Interactive Corp ....D 513 381-1583
   Cincinnati *(G-4393)*
Sgk LLC ....D 513 569-9900
   Cincinnati *(G-4461)*
Thread Information Design Inc ....E 419 887-6801
   Toledo *(G-18065)*
Touchstone Mdse Group LLC ....D 513 741-0400
   Mason *(G-13648)*
Vivial Media LLC ....E 937 610-4100
   Dayton *(G-9857)*
Wern-Rausch Locke Advertising ....E 330 493-8866
   Canton *(G-2533)*
Young & Rubicam Inc ....C 513 419-2300
   Cincinnati *(G-4811)*

ADVERTISING AGENCIES: Consultants

Airmate Company ....D 419 636-3184
   Bryan *(G-1950)*
AMG Marketing Resources Inc ....E 216 621-1835
   Solon *(G-16820)*
Brokaw Inc ....E 216 241-8003
   Cleveland *(G-5085)*
Charles W Powers & Assoc Inc ....E 513 721-5353
   Cincinnati *(G-3171)*
Cooper-Smith Advertising LLC ....E 419 470-5900
   Toledo *(G-17679)*
Curiosity LLC ....D 513 744-6000
   Cincinnati *(G-3389)*
Deanhouston Creative Group Inc ....E 513 421-6622
   Cincinnati *(G-3413)*
Fahlgren Inc ....E 614 383-1500
   Columbus *(G-7552)*
Fahlgren Inc ....D 614 383-1500
   Columbus *(G-7553)*
Guardian Enterprise Group Inc ....E 614 416-6080
   Columbus *(G-7702)*
Gypc Inc ....C 309 677-0405
   Dayton *(G-9479)*
Hart Associates Inc ....D 419 893-9600
   Toledo *(G-17783)*
Hitchcock Fleming & Assoc Inc ....D 330 376-2111
   Akron *(G-263)*
Kreber Graphics Inc ....E 614 529-5701
   Columbus *(G-7926)*
Marcus Thomas Llc ....D 216 292-4700
   Cleveland *(G-5907)*
Marcus Thomas Llc ....D 330 793-3000
   Youngstown *(G-20116)*
Matrix Media Services Inc ....E 614 228-2200
   Columbus *(G-8039)*
Melamed Riley Advertising LLC ....E 216 241-2141
   Cleveland *(G-5950)*
Nas Rcrtment Cmmunications LLC .....C 216 478-0300
   Cleveland *(G-6036)*
Real Art Design Group Inc ....E 937 223-9955
   Dayton *(G-9728)*
Ron Foth Retail Inc ....D 614 888-7771
   Columbus *(G-8547)*
Stern Advertising Inc ....E 216 331-5827
   Cleveland *(G-6468)*
Universal Advertising Assoc ....E 513 522-5000
   Cincinnati *(G-4693)*
Whitespace Design Group Inc ....E 330 762-9320
   Akron *(G-501)*
Wyse Advertising Inc ....D 216 696-2424
   Cleveland *(G-6695)*

ADVERTISING COPY WRITING SVCS

Madison Avenue Mktg Group Inc ....E 419 473-9000
   Toledo *(G-17878)*

ADVERTISING MATERIAL DISTRIBUTION

Berry Network LLC ....C...... 800 366-1264
  Moraine (G-14625)
Dispatch Consumer Services ....D...... 740 687-1893
  Lancaster (G-12389)
Dispatch Consumer Services ....E...... 740 548-5555
  Columbus (G-7450)

ADVERTISING REPRESENTATIVES: Electronic Media

Ctv Media Inc ....E...... 614 848-5800
  Powell (G-16193)
Madison Avenue Mktg Group Inc ....E...... 419 473-9000
  Toledo (G-17878)
Segmint Inc ....E...... 330 594-5379
  Akron (G-421)

ADVERTISING REPRESENTATIVES: Media

Agri Communicators Inc ....E...... 614 273-0465
  Columbus (G-6885)
Creative Crafts Group LLC....................D...... 303 215-5600
  Blue Ash (G-1540)
Maverick Media ....E...... 419 331-1600
  Lima (G-12700)

ADVERTISING REPRESENTATIVES: Newspaper

American City Bus Journals Inc............E...... 937 528-4400
  Dayton (G-9226)
B G News ....E...... 419 372-2601
  Bowling Green (G-1715)
Copley Ohio Newspapers Inc ....C...... 330 364-5577
  New Philadelphia (G-14951)
Sandusky Register ....E...... 419 625-5500
  Sandusky (G-16640)

ADVERTISING REPRESENTATIVES: Printed Media

Manta Media Inc ....E...... 888 875-5833
  Columbus (G-6823)

ADVERTISING REPRESENTATIVES: Radio

Iheartcommunications Inc ....C...... 937 224-1137
  Dayton (G-9512)
Killer Spotscom Inc ....D...... 513 201-1380
  Cincinnati (G-3869)

ADVERTISING REPRESENTATIVES: Television & Radio Time Sales

Thinktv Network ....E...... 937 220-1600
  Dayton (G-9813)

ADVERTISING SPECIALTIES, WHOLESALE

Boost Technologies LLC ....D...... 800 223-2203
  Dayton (G-9259)
Bottomline Ink Corporation ....E...... 419 897-8000
  Perrysburg (G-15840)
Corporate Imageworks LLC....................E...... 216 292-8800
  Streetsboro (G-17251)
D & D Advertising Enterprises...............E...... 513 921-6827
  Cincinnati (G-3393)
Dayton Heidelberg Distrg Co ....D...... 937 220-6450
  Moraine (G-14644)
Evolution Crtive Solutions LLC ....E...... 513 681-4450
  Cincinnati (G-3523)
Galaxy Balloons Incorporated ....C...... 216 476-3360
  Cleveland (G-5589)
L M Berry and Company..........................D...... 513 768-7700
  Cincinnati (G-3900)
Leader Promotions Inc ....D...... 614 416-6565
  Columbus (G-7961)
Marathon Mfg & Sup Co ....D...... 330 343-2656
  New Philadelphia (G-14972)
Media Advertising Cons LLC ....E...... 614 615-1398
  Columbus (G-8052)
Novelty Advertising Co Inc ....E...... 740 622-3113
  Coshocton (G-9024)
Nutis Press Inc ....C...... 614 237-8626
  Columbus (G-8218)
Peter Graham Dunn Inc ....E...... 330 816-0035
  Dalton (G-9146)
Relay Gear Ltd..E...... 888 735-2943
  Columbus (G-8510)

S S T Enterprises Inc ....D...... 330 343-2656
  New Philadelphia (G-14979)
Screen Works Inc ....E...... 937 264-9111
  Dayton (G-9754)
Shamrock Companies Inc ....D...... 440 899-9510
  Westlake (G-19405)
Shumsky Enterprises Inc ....E...... 937 223-2203
  Dayton (G-9765)
Traichal Construction Company............E...... 800 255-3667
  Niles (G-15172)

ADVERTISING SVCS, NEC

Ohs LLC ....D...... 513 252-2249
  Blue Ash (G-1624)

ADVERTISING SVCS: Billboards

Lamar Advertising Company ....E...... 740 699-0000
  Saint Clairsville (G-16490)

ADVERTISING SVCS: Direct Mail

A W S Inc ....C...... 440 333-1791
  Rocky River (G-16420)
A W S Inc ....B...... 216 749-0356
  Cleveland (G-4881)
Amerimark Holdings LLC ....B...... 440 325-2000
  Cleveland (G-4969)
Angstrom Graphics Inc Midwest ....B...... 216 271-5300
  Cleveland (G-4980)
Atco Inc ....C...... 740 592-6659
  Athens (G-765)
Clipper Magazine LLC ....D...... 513 794-4100
  Blue Ash (G-1529)
Consolidated Graphics Group Inc...........C...... 216 881-9191
  Cleveland (G-5335)
Ddm-Digital Imaging Data ....D...... 740 928-1110
  Hebron (G-11712)
Deepwood Industries Inc ....E...... 440 350-5231
  Mentor (G-14040)
Digital Color Intl LLC ....E...... 330 762-6959
  Akron (G-187)
Hecks Direct Mail & Prtg Svc ....E...... 419 661-6028
  Toledo (G-17798)
Pickaway Diversfied Industries ....D...... 740 474-1522
  Circleville (G-4842)
Popper & Associates Msrp LLC ....E...... 614 798-8991
  Dublin (G-10309)
Resource Interactive ....E...... 614 621-2888
  Columbus (G-8522)
Sourcelink Ohio LLC ....C...... 937 885-8000
  Miamisburg (G-14224)
TMR Inc ....C...... 330 220-8564
  Brunswick (G-1942)
Traxium LLC ....E...... 330 572-8200
  Stow (G-17236)

ADVERTISING SVCS: Display

Digital Color Intl LLC ....E...... 330 762-6959
  Akron (G-187)
Downing Displays Inc ....D...... 513 248-9800
  Milford (G-14386)
Groupcle LLC ....E...... 216 251-9641
  Cleveland (G-5645)
Innomark Communications LLC ....E...... 937 425-6152
  Sharonville (G-16729)
Team Management Inc ....C...... 614 486-0864
  Columbus (G-8735)

ADVERTISING SVCS: Outdoor

Kessler Sign Company ....E...... 740 453-0668
  Zanesville (G-20323)
Lamar Advertising Company ....E...... 216 676-4321
  Cleveland (G-5853)
Matrix Media Services Inc ....E...... 614 228-2200
  Columbus (G-8039)
Orange Barrel Media LLC ....E...... 614 294-4898
  Columbus (G-8383)

ADVERTISING SVCS: Sample Distribution

Signum LLC ....D...... 440 248-2233
  Solon (G-16897)

ADVERTISING SVCS: Transit

Paul Werth Associates Inc ....E...... 614 224-8114
  Columbus (G-8429)

ADVERTISING: Aerial

Hillman Group Inc ....E...... 513 874-5905
  West Chester (G-19060)

ADVOCACY GROUP

Center For Community Solutions............E...... 216 781-2944
  Cleveland (G-5148)
Childrens Hunger Alliance ....E...... 614 341-7700
  Columbus (G-7190)
Choices For Vctims Dom Volence...........E...... 614 224-6617
  Worthington (G-19798)
Cleveland Municipal School Dst ....B...... 216 838-0000
  Cleveland (G-5276)
Cleveland Municipal School Dst ....B...... 216 838-8700
  Cleveland (G-5277)
Columbus Landmarks Foundation..........E...... 614 221-0227
  Columbus (G-7291)
Lincare Inc ....E...... 330 928-0884
  Akron (G-315)
Mahoning Youngstown Community ....D...... 330 747-7921
  Youngstown (G-20112)
Miami Vly Fandom For Literacy ....E...... 513 933-0452
  Lebanon (G-12486)
National Youth Advocate Progra ....E...... 614 487-8758
  Columbus (G-8139)
Nationwide Childrens Hospital ....B...... 614 722-8200
  Columbus (G-8147)
Ohio Legal Rights Service ....E...... 614 466-7264
  Columbus (G-8270)
Pavilion At Piketon For Nursin ....D...... 740 289-2394
  Piketon (G-15984)
Phyllis Wheatley Assn Dev ....E...... 216 391-4443
  Cleveland (G-6208)
Prescription Hope Inc ....E...... 877 296-4673
  Westerville (G-19294)
Salvation Army ....E...... 513 762-5600
  Cincinnati (G-4430)
Salvation Army ....D...... 614 252-7171
  Columbus (G-8587)
T and J Trnstnal HM For Dsbled ....E...... 216 703-4673
  Cleveland (G-6493)
United Methodist Community Ctr............E...... 330 743-5149
  Canfield (G-2162)

AGENTS, BROKERS & BUREAUS: Personal Service

A Sainato Enterprises Inc ....E...... 216 795-5167
  Brecksville (G-1765)
Abraham Ford LLC ....E...... 440 233-7402
  Elyria (G-10477)
Aecom Energy & Cnstr Inc......................A...... 216 523-5600
  Cleveland (G-4907)
Aecom Energy & Cnstr Inc......................A...... 216 523-5600
  Cleveland (G-4908)
Another Chance Inc ....E...... 614 868-3541
  Pickerington (G-15946)
Canton S-Group Ltd................................B...... 419 625-7003
  Sandusky (G-16580)
Cass Information Systems Inc.................C...... 614 766-2277
  Columbus (G-7135)
Coast To Coast Studios LLC....................E...... 614 861-9800
  Blacklick (G-1478)
Corporate United Inc ....E...... 440 895-0938
  Westlake (G-19337)
Covelli Enterprises Inc ....D...... 614 889-7802
  Dublin (G-10191)
Douglas R Denny ....E...... 216 236-2400
  Independence (G-12068)
Essilor of America Inc ....C...... 614 492-0888
  Groveport (G-11510)
Etransmedia Technology Inc ....E...... 724 743-5960
  Columbus (G-7539)
Finastra USA Corporation ....E...... 937 435-2335
  Miamisburg (G-14171)
Hamilton Cnty Auditor Office ....C...... 513 946-4000
  Cincinnati (G-3674)
Legend Equities Corporation ....D...... 216 741-3113
  Independence (G-12087)
Limitless Solutions Inc ....E...... 614 577-1550
  Columbus (G-7979)
Progressive Quality Care Inc ....A...... 330 875-7866
  Louisville (G-12972)
Progressive Quality Care Inc ....E...... 216 661-6800
  Parma (G-15773)
Return Polymers Inc ....D...... 419 289-1998
  Ashland (G-686)
Sander Woody Ford ....D...... 513 541-5586
  Cincinnati (G-4431)

SERVICES

Southern Graphic Systems Inc...........B.......419 662-9873
　Perrysburg (G-15923)
United Parcel Service Inc OH................B.......740 962-7971
　Portsmouth (G-16175)

AGRICULTURAL EQPT: BARN, SILO, POULTRY, DAIRY/LIVESTOCK MACH

Fort Recovery Equipment Inc................E.......419 375-1006
　Fort Recovery (G-10990)

AGRICULTURAL EQPT: Fertilizing Machinery

Shearer Farm Inc...............................E.......330 345-9023
　Wooster (G-19768)

AGRICULTURAL MACHINERY & EQPT: Wholesalers

Ag-Pro Ohio LLC.................................C.......614 879-6620
　London (G-12858)
Baker & Sons Equipment Co.................E.......740 567-3317
　Lewisville (G-12573)
Buckeye Companies..............................E.......740 452-3641
　Zanesville (G-20284)
Deerfield Farms Service Inc.................D.......330 584-4715
　Deerfield (G-9904)
Liechty Inc..E.......419 445-1565
　Archbold (G-631)
Wyandot Tractor & Implement Co..........E.......419 294-2349
　Upper Sandusky (G-18417)

AGRICULTURAL PROG REG OFFICES, GOVT: Agriculture Fair Board

United States Dept Agriculture.............D.......419 626-8439
　Sandusky (G-16652)

AID TO FAMILIES WITH DEPENDENT CHILDREN OR AFDC

Shelter House Volunteer Group..............E.......513 721-0643
　Cincinnati (G-4469)

AIR CONDITIONING & VENTILATION EQPT & SPLYS: Wholesales

Gardiner Service Company LLC..............C.......440 248-3400
　Solon (G-16850)
Lute Supply Inc..................................E.......740 353-1447
　Portsmouth (G-16153)
Thompson Heating Corporation.............D.......513 769-7696
　Cincinnati (G-4606)
Wolff Bros Supply Inc..........................E.......419 425-8511
　Findlay (G-10976)

AIR CONDITIONING EQPT

Vertiv Corporation..............................A.......614 888-0246
　Columbus (G-8847)

AIR CONDITIONING EQPT, WHOLE HOUSE: Wholesalers

Controls Center Inc.............................D.......513 772-2665
　Cincinnati (G-3356)
Habegger Corporation..........................D.......513 612-4700
　Cincinnati (G-3669)
Industrial Controls Distrs LLC...............E.......513 733-5200
　West Chester (G-18946)
Noland Company.................................C.......937 396-7980
　Moraine (G-14684)
United Atmtc Htng Spply of Clv.............E.......216 621-5571
　Cleveland (G-6567)

AIR CONDITIONING REPAIR SVCS

Columbs/Worthington Htg AC Inc..........E.......614 771-5381
　Columbus (G-7252)
Cov-Ro Inc..E.......330 856-3176
　Warren (G-18693)
Mid-Ohio Air Conditioning...................E.......614 291-4664
　Columbus (G-8075)
Osterfeld Champion Service..................E.......937 254-8437
　Dayton (G-9679)
Smith & Oby Service Co.......................E.......440 735-5322
　Bedford (G-1306)

AIR DUCT CLEANING SVCS

A Bee C Service Inc............................E.......440 735-1505
　Cleveland (G-4875)

Southtown Heating & Cooling...............E.......937 320-9900
　Moraine (G-14699)

AIR POLLUTION CONTROL EQPT & SPLYS WHOLESALERS

Verantis Corporation...........................E.......440 243-0700
　Middleburg Heights (G-14264)

AIR POLLUTION MEASURING SVCS

Terminix Intl Co Ltd Partnr...................E.......513 539-7846
　Middletown (G-14335)

AIR PURIFICATION EQPT

Verantis Corporation...........................E.......440 243-0700
　Middleburg Heights (G-14264)

AIR TRAFFIC CONTROL SVCS

Corporate Wngs - Cleveland LLC...........E.......216 261-9000
　Cleveland (G-5352)

AIR, WATER & SOLID WASTE PROGRAMS ADMINISTRATION SVCS

City of Cleveland...............................E.......216 664-3121
　Cleveland (G-5191)
City of Columbus...............................E.......614 645-8297
　Columbus (G-7212)
City of Columbus...............................D.......614 645-3248
　Lockbourne (G-12811)
County of Hamilton............................E.......513 946-4250
　Cincinnati (G-3371)

AIR-CONDITIONING SPLY SVCS

Marketing Comm Resource Inc..............D.......440 484-3010
　Willoughby (G-19549)

AIRCRAFT & HEAVY EQPT REPAIR SVCS

Airborne Maint Engrg Svcs Inc..............A.......937 366-2559
　Wilmington (G-19604)
Airborne Maint Engrg Svcs Inc..............D.......937 382-5591
　Wilmington (G-19605)
Constant Aviation LLC.........................E.......216 261-7119
　Cleveland (G-5337)
Equipment Maintenance Inc..................E.......513 353-3518
　Cleves (G-6728)
Grimes Aerospace Company..................B.......937 484-2001
　Urbana (G-18436)
McNational Inc...................................E.......740 377-4391
　South Point (G-16941)
Mt Texas LLC....................................E.......513 853-4400
　Cincinnati (G-4082)
Ohio Machinery Co.............................C.......440 526-6200
　Broadview Heights (G-1840)
Pas Technologies Inc...........................D.......937 840-1000
　Hillsboro (G-11854)
Terex Utilities Inc..............................C.......937 293-6526
　Springfield (G-17125)

AIRCRAFT CLEANING & JANITORIAL SVCS

Legndary Cleaners LLC.........................E.......216 374-1205
　Cleveland (G-5864)
McKinley Air Transport Inc...................E.......330 497-6956
　Canton (G-2394)
Plane Detail LLC................................E.......614 734-1201
　Galena (G-11163)

AIRCRAFT DEALERS

Options Flight Support Inc....................C.......216 261-3500
　Cleveland (G-6139)

AIRCRAFT ELECTRICAL EQPT REPAIR SVCS

General Electric Company......................B.......513 977-1500
　Cincinnati (G-3608)

AIRCRAFT ENGINES & ENGINE PARTS: Pumps

At Holdings Corporation........................A.......216 692-6000
　Cleveland (G-5016)

AIRCRAFT ENGINES & PARTS

General Electric Company......................A.......513 552-2000
　Cincinnati (G-3609)
Hi-Tek Manufacturing Inc......................C.......513 459-1094
　Mason (G-13595)
Pas Technologies Inc............................D.......937 840-1000
　Hillsboro (G-11854)

AIRCRAFT EQPT & SPLYS WHOLESALERS

Cleveland Wheels................................E.......440 937-6211
　Avon (G-877)
GE Engine Services LLC........................B.......513 977-1500
　Cincinnati (G-3605)
NJ Executive Services Inc......................E.......614 239-2996
　Columbus (G-8191)
Sportsmans Market Inc.........................C.......513 735-9100
　Batavia (G-1009)
Transdigm Group Incorporated..............C.......216 706-2960
　Cleveland (G-6542)

AIRCRAFT FLIGHT INSTRUMENTS

L3 Aviation Products Inc.......................D.......614 825-2001
　Columbus (G-7938)

AIRCRAFT FUELING SVCS

McKinley Air Transport Inc....................E.......330 497-6956
　Canton (G-2394)
Winner Aviation Corporation..................D.......330 856-5000
　Vienna (G-18584)

AIRCRAFT HANGAR OPERATION SVCS

General Electric Company......................A.......513 552-2000
　Cincinnati (G-3609)

AIRCRAFT MAINTENANCE & REPAIR SVCS

Aitheras Aviation Group LLC..................E.......216 298-9060
　Cleveland (G-4923)
ATI Aviation Services LLC......................E.......216 268-4888
　Cleveland (G-5019)
Constant Aviation LLC..........................C.......800 440-9004
　Cleveland (G-5338)
Duncan Aviation Inc............................D.......513 873-7523
　Cincinnati (G-3455)
Netjets Large Aircraft Inc......................D.......614 239-4853
　Columbus (G-8176)

AIRCRAFT PARTS & EQPT, NEC

At Holdings Corporation........................A.......216 692-6000
　Cleveland (G-5016)
Drt Holdings Inc.................................D.......937 298-7391
　Dayton (G-9395)
General Electric Company......................B.......513 977-1500
　Cincinnati (G-3608)
Schneller LLC....................................D.......330 673-1299
　Kent (G-12258)
Transdigm Group Incorporated..............C.......216 706-2960
　Cleveland (G-6542)
Unison Industries LLC..........................B.......904 667-9904
　Dayton (G-9188)
Unison Industries LLC..........................B.......937 427-0550
　Beavercreek (G-1192)
Wayne Trail Technologies Inc.................D.......937 295-2120
　Fort Loramie (G-10986)

AIRCRAFT PARTS WHOLESALERS

Abx Air Inc.......................................B.......937 382-5591
　Wilmington (G-19600)
Airborne Maint Engrg Svcs Inc..............A.......937 366-2559
　Wilmington (G-19604)
Airborne Maint Engrg Svcs Inc..............D.......937 382-5591
　Wilmington (G-19605)
Grimes Aerospace Company..................B.......937 484-2001
　Urbana (G-18436)
Jilco Industries Inc.............................E.......330 698-0280
　Kidron (G-12306)
Netjets Inc..E.......614 239-5500
　Columbus (G-8174)
Netjets Sales Inc................................C.......614 239-5500
　Columbus (G-8177)

AIRCRAFT SERVICING & REPAIRING

Abx Air Inc.......................................B.......937 382-5591
　Wilmington (G-19600)
Cessna Aircraft Company......................D.......419 866-6761
　Swanton (G-17395)

Huntleigh USA Corporation ....B 216 265-3707
Cleveland (G-5726)

Lane Aviation Corporation ....C 614 237-3747
Columbus (G-7950)

National Flight Services Inc ....D 419 865-2311
Swanton (G-17402)

Unison Industries LLC ....B 904 667-9904
Dayton (G-9188)

Unison Industries LLC ....B 937 427-0550
Beavercreek (G-1192)

AIRLINE TRAINING

Macair Aviation LLC ....E 937 347-1302
Xenia (G-19919)

AIRPORT

ABM Aviation Inc ....B 859 767-7507
Cincinnati (G-2897)

Akron-Canton Regional Airport ....E 330 499-4059
North Canton (G-15186)

City of Dayton ....C 937 454-8200
Vandalia (G-18515)

City of Dayton ....E 937 454-8231
Vandalia (G-18516)

Columbus Regional Airport Auth ....E 614 239-4000
Columbus (G-7310)

Columbus Regional Airport Auth ....B 614 239-4015
Columbus (G-7311)

Park-N-Go Inc ....E 937 890-7275
Dayton (G-9686)

Toledo-Lucas County Port Auth ....E 419 865-2351
Swanton (G-17408)

AIRPORT TERMINAL SVCS

American Airlines Inc ....E 216 898-1347
Cleveland (G-4948)

Servisair LLC ....C 216 267-9910
Cleveland (G-6400)

Stevens Aviation Inc ....D 937 890-0189
Vandalia (G-18541)

Wright Brothers Aero Inc ....D 937 890-8900
Vandalia (G-18550)

AIRPORTS & FLYING FIELDS

Macair Aviation LLC ....E 937 347-1302
Xenia (G-19919)

AIRPORTS, FLYING FIELDS & SVCS

Aviation Manufacturing Co Inc ....D 419 435-7448
Fostoria (G-10996)

Executive Jet Management Inc ....B 513 979-6600
Cincinnati (G-3525)

GE Aviation Systems LLC ....B 513 786-4555
West Chester (G-18930)

Menzies Aviation (texas) Inc ....E 216 362-6565
Cleveland (G-5954)

Ultimate Jetcharters LLC ....D 330 497-3344
North Canton (G-15242)

ALARM SYSTEMS WHOLESALERS

Asset Protection Corporation ....E 419 531-3400
Toledo (G-17601)

Ohio Alarm Inc ....E 216 692-1204
Independence (G-12105)

ALCOHOL TREATMENT CLINIC, OUTPATIENT

Behavral Cnnctions WD Cnty Inc ....C 419 352-5387
Bowling Green (G-1716)

Behavral Cnnctions WD Cnty Inc ....E 419 872-2419
Perrysburg (G-15836)

Behavral Cnnctions WD Cnty Inc ....E 419 352-5387
Bowling Green (G-1717)

Century Health Inc ....D 419 425-5050
Findlay (G-10887)

County of Lorain ....E 440 989-4900
Elyria (G-10499)

Firelands Regional Health Sys ....E 419 663-3737
Norwalk (G-15435)

Hitchcock Center For Women Inc ....E 216 421-0662
Cleveland (G-5695)

Mental Health & Recovery Ctr ....E 937 383-3031
Wilmington (G-19635)

Orca House ....E 216 231-3772
Cleveland (G-6142)

Recovery & Prevention Resource ....E 740 369-6811
Delaware (G-10002)

ALCOHOLISM COUNSELING, NONTREATMENT

Addiction Services Council ....E 513 281-7880
Cincinnati (G-2907)

Amethyst Inc ....D 614 242-1284
Columbus (G-6943)

Licking Cnty Alcoholism Prvntn ....D 740 281-3639
Newark (G-15051)

Oriana House Inc ....D 330 535-8116
Akron (G-366)

Scioto County Counseling Ctr ....D 740 354-6685
Portsmouth (G-16167)

Sojourner Recovery Services ....D 513 868-7654
Hamilton (G-11642)

Turning Pt Counseling Svcs Inc ....D 330 744-2991
Youngstown (G-20227)

ALKALIES & CHLORINE

National Colloid Company ....E 740 282-1171
Steubenville (G-17168)

National Lime and Stone Co ....C 419 396-7671
Carey (G-2545)

ALL-TERRAIN VEHICLE DEALERS

Randy L Fork Inc ....E 419 891-1230
Maumee (G-13841)

ALLOYS: Additive, Exc Copper Or Made In Blast Furnaces

Morris Technologies Inc ....C 513 733-1611
Cincinnati (G-4075)

ALUMINUM

Benjamin Steel Company Inc ....E 937 233-1212
Springfield (G-16998)

ALUMINUM: Coil & Sheet

Monarch Steel Company Inc ....E 216 587-8000
Cleveland (G-6007)

ALUMINUM: Slabs, Primary

Imperial Alum - Minerva LLC ....D 330 868-7765
Minerva (G-14520)

AMBULANCE SVCS

1st Advanced Ems LLC ....D 614 348-9991
Columbus (G-6841)

American Med ....B 330 762-8999
Akron (G-69)

American Medical Response Inc ....E 330 455-3579
Canton (G-2186)

Anna Rescue Squad ....E 937 394-7377
Anna (G-610)

Athens County Emrgncy Med Svcs ......D 740 797-9560
The Plains (G-17502)

Bedford Township ....E 740 992-6617
Pomeroy (G-16093)

Bellevue Four Cnty Ems N Centl ....C 419 483-3322
Milan (G-14359)

Bkp Ambulance District ....E 419 674-4574
Kenton (G-12271)

Brookeside Ambulance Services ....E 419 476-7442
Toledo (G-17628)

Buckeye Ambulance LLC ....D 937 435-1584
Dayton (G-9263)

C C & S Ambulance Service Inc ....D 330 868-4114
Minerva (G-14516)

Carlson Ambince Trnspt Svc Inc ....E 330 225-2400
Brunswick (G-1923)

City of Cleveland ....B 216 664-2555
Cleveland (G-5189)

City of Cleveland ....B 216 664-2555
Cleveland (G-5190)

City of Eaton ....E 937 456-5361
Eaton (G-10438)

Clemente-Mc Kay Ambulance Inc ....E 330 755-1401
Struthers (G-17361)

Community Ambulance Service ....D 740 454-6800
Zanesville (G-20298)

Community Care Amblance Netwrk ......D 440 992-1401
Ashtabula (G-728)

Community Emrgcy Med Svcs Ohio .....C 614 751-6651
Columbus (G-7331)

Coshocton Cnty Emrgncy Med Svc ......E 740 622-4294
Coshocton (G-9005)

County of Hardin ....E 419 634-7729
Ada (G-4)

County of Lorain ....E 440 647-5803
Wellington (G-18838)

County of Seneca ....E 419 937-2340
Bascom (G-981)

Courtesy Ambulance Inc ....E 740 522-8588
Newark (G-15029)

Critical Care Transport Inc ....E 614 775-0564
Columbus (G-7393)

Elite Ambulance Service LLC ....E 888 222-1356
Loveland (G-12992)

Emergency Medical Transport ....D 330 484-4000
North Canton (G-15198)

Firelands Ambulance Service ....E 419 929-1487
New London (G-14932)

Franklin Township Fire and Ems ....E 513 876-2996
Felicity (G-10859)

Georgetown Life Squad ....E 937 378-3082
Georgetown (G-11271)

Gold Cross Ambulance Svcs Inc ....C 330 744-4161
Youngstown (G-20051)

Greenville Township Rescue ....E 937 548-9339
Greenville (G-11384)

Guernsey Health Enterprises ....A 740 439-3561
Cambridge (G-2072)

Hanco Ambulance Inc ....E 419 423-2912
Findlay (G-10916)

Harter Ventures Inc ....D 419 224-4075
Lima (G-12651)

Hillcrest Ambulance Svc Inc ....C 216 797-4000
Euclid (G-10640)

Homecare Service Inc ....E 513 655-5022
Blue Ash (G-1582)

Hustead Emergency Medical Svc ....E 937 324-3031
Springfield (G-17049)

J & C Ambulance Services Inc ....C 330 899-0022
North Canton (G-15213)

Kare Medical Trnspt Svcs LLP ....E 937 578-0263
Marysville (G-13509)

Lacp St Ritas Medical Ctr LLC ....D 419 324-4075
Lima (G-12673)

Lane Life Corp ....E 330 799-1002
Youngstown (G-20097)

Liberty Ems Services LLC ....E 216 630-6626
Cleveland (G-5866)

Lifecare Ambulance Inc ....D 440 323-2527
Elyria (G-10525)

Lifecare Ambulance Inc ....E 440 323-6111
Elyria (G-10526)

Lifecare Medical Services ....E 614 258-2545
Columbus (G-7975)

Lifestar Ambulance Inc ....C 419 245-6210
Toledo (G-17854)

Lifeteam Ems Inc ....E 330 386-9284
East Liverpool (G-10405)

Lorain Life Care Ambulance Svc ....D 440 244-6467
Lorain (G-12921)

Mansfield Ambulance Inc ....E 419 525-3311
Mansfield (G-13204)

Martens Donald & Sons ....D 216 265-4211
Cleveland (G-5917)

Med Ride Ems ....E 614 747-9744
Columbus (G-8051)

Med Star Emgncy Mdcl Srv ....E 330 394-6611
Warren (G-18728)

Med-Trans Inc ....D 937 325-4926
Springfield (G-17069)

Med-Trans Inc ....E 937 293-9771
Moraine (G-14674)

Meda-Care Transportation Inc ....E 513 521-4799
Cincinnati (G-3992)

Medcorp Inc ....C 419 425-9700
Findlay (G-10942)

Medcorp Inc ....E 419 727-7000
Toledo (G-17900)

Medic Response Service Inc ....E 419 522-1998
Mansfield (G-13218)

Medical Transport Systems Inc ....D 330 837-9818
North Canton (G-15219)

Medpro LLC ....D 937 336-5586
Eaton (G-10452)

Mercy Health ....E 440 775-1211
Oberlin (G-15510)

Metrohealth System ....E 216 778-3867
Cleveland (G-5971)

Metrohealth System...............................C....... 216 957-4000
  Cleveland (G-5968)
Mid County Ems.....................................E....... 419 898-9366
  Oak Harbor (G-15474)
Morgan County Public Transit..............E....... 740 962-1322
  McConnelsville (G-13903)
Morrow County Fire Fighter..................D....... 419 946-7976
  Mount Gilead (G-14730)
Mt Orab Fire Department Inc.................E....... 937 444-3945
  Mount Orab (G-14743)
Non Emergency Ambulance Svc............E....... 330 296-4541
  Ravenna (G-16251)
North Star Critical Care LLC.................E....... 330 386-9110
  East Liverpool (G-10410)
Northwest Fire Ambulance.....................E....... 937 437-8354
  New Paris (G-14944)
Norwalk Area Health Services..............C....... 419 499-2515
  Milan (G-14363)
Norwalk Area Health Services..............C....... 419 668-8101
  Norwalk (G-15447)
Ohio Medical Trnsp Inc.........................E....... 937 747-3540
  Marysville (G-13521)
Ohio Medical Trnsp Inc.........................D....... 740 962-2055
  McConnelsville (G-13904)
Ohio Medical Trnsp Inc.........................D....... 614 791-4400
  Columbus (G-8274)
Patriot Emergency Med Svcs Inc..........E....... 740 532-2222
  Ironton (G-12165)
Physicians Ambulance Svc Inc..............E....... 216 332-1667
  Cleveland (G-6210)
Pickaway Plains Ambulance Svc...........C....... 740 474-4180
  Circleville (G-4845)
Portage Path Behavorial Health...........D....... 330 762-6110
  Akron (G-391)
Portsmouth Ambulance..........................C....... 740 289-2932
  Portsmouth (G-16158)
Portsmouth Emrgncy Amblance Svc.....B....... 740 354-3122
  Portsmouth (G-16162)
Pymatuning Ambulance Service............E....... 440 293-7991
  Andover (G-607)
Quad Ambulance District........................E....... 330 866-9847
  Waynesburg (G-18829)
Rittman City of Inc.................................E....... 330 925-2065
  Rittman (G-16408)
Rural/Metro Corporation.........................C....... 216 749-2211
  Youngstown (G-20199)
Rural/Metro Corporation.........................C....... 330 744-4161
  Youngstown (G-20200)
Rural/Metro Corporation.........................C....... 440 543-3313
  Chagrin Falls (G-2681)
Sardinia Life Squad...............................E....... 937 446-2178
  Sardinia (G-16660)
Smith Ambulance Service Inc................E....... 330 825-0205
  Dover (G-10099)
Smith Ambulance Service Inc................E....... 330 602-0050
  Dover (G-10100)
Spirit Medical Transport LLC.................D....... 937 548-2800
  Greenville (G-11396)
Sterling Joint Ambulance Dst................E....... 740 869-3006
  Mount Sterling (G-14747)
Stofcheck Ambulance Inc.......................C....... 740 383-2787
  Marion (G-13460)
Stofcheck Ambulance Svc Inc................E....... 740 499-2200
  La Rue (G-12324)
Toronto Emergency Medical Svc............E....... 740 537-3891
  Toronto (G-18186)
Tri Village Rescue Service.....................E....... 937 996-3155
  New Madison (G-14938)
Tri-State Amblnce Pramedic Svc...........E....... 304 233-2331
  North Canton (G-15240)
Tricounty Ambulance Service................D....... 440 951-4600
  Mentor (G-14115)
United Amblnce Svc of Cmbridge..........E....... 740 439-7787
  Cambridge (G-2086)
United Ambulance Service......................E....... 740 732-5653
  Caldwell (G-2046)
Utica Volunteer Emrgncy Squad............E....... 740 892-2369
  Utica (G-18458)
Village of Antwerp.................................E....... 419 258-6631
  Antwerp (G-616)

AMBULANCE SVCS: Air

Ohio Medical Trnsp Inc.........................D....... 614 791-4400
  Columbus (G-8274)

AMBULATORY SURGICAL CENTERS

Childrens Surgery Center Inc................D....... 614 722-2920
  Columbus (G-7191)
Columbus Surgical Center LLP..............E....... 614 932-9503
  Dublin (G-10182)

Endoscopy Center...................................E....... 419 843-7993
  Sylvania (G-17422)
Med Center One Streetsboro..................E....... 330 626-3455
  Streetsboro (G-17261)
Mentor Surgery Center Ltd.....................E....... 440 205-5725
  Mentor (G-14083)
Ohio Surgery Center Ltd.........................D....... 614 451-0500
  Columbus (G-8354)
Ohio Valley Ambulatory Surgery...........E....... 740 423-4684
  Belpre (G-1409)
Ohiocare Ambulatory Surgery................E....... 419 897-5501
  Maumee (G-13826)
Riverview Surgery Center.......................E....... 740 681-2700
  Lancaster (G-12432)
Southwest Ohio Amblatry Srgery...........E....... 513 425-0930
  Middletown (G-14329)
Surgery Center Howland Ltd..................E....... 330 609-7874
  Warren (G-18750)
The Healthcare Connection Inc..............E....... 513 588-3623
  Cincinnati (G-4592)
United Srgcal Prtners Intl Inc................E....... 330 702-1489
  Canfield (G-2163)
Valley Regional Surgery Center.............E....... 877 858-5029
  Piqua (G-16037)
West Central Ohio Surgery & En............E....... 419 226-8700
  Lima (G-12780)
Zanesville Surgery Center LLC...............D....... 740 453-5713
  Zanesville (G-20385)

AMUSEMENT & REC SVCS: Attractions, Concessions & Rides

Coney Island Inc...................................E....... 513 232-8230
  Cincinnati (G-3350)
Dayton History.......................................C....... 937 293-2841
  Dayton (G-9368)
Mill Creek Metropolitan Park..................D....... 330 702-3000
  Canfield (G-2149)

AMUSEMENT & REC SVCS: Baseball Club, Exc Pro & Semi-Pro

Cascia LLC..E....... 440 975-8085
  Willoughby (G-19509)

AMUSEMENT & REC SVCS: Flying Field, Maintained By Av Clubs

Macair Aviation LLC..............................E....... 937 347-1302
  Xenia (G-19919)

AMUSEMENT & RECREATION SVCS, NEC

Kettering Recreation Center...................E....... 937 296-2587
  Dayton (G-9542)
Leaders Family Farms............................E....... 419 599-1570
  Napoleon (G-14810)

AMUSEMENT & RECREATION SVCS: Agricultural Fair

Cuyahoga County AG Soc......................E....... 440 243-0090
  Berea (G-1421)
Wyandot County AG Soc.........................E....... 419 294-4320
  Upper Sandusky (G-18415)

AMUSEMENT & RECREATION SVCS: Amusement Arcades

Entertrainment Inc.................................E....... 513 898-8000
  West Chester (G-18919)

AMUSEMENT & RECREATION SVCS: Amusement Mach Rental, Coin-Op

S & B Enterprises LLC...........................E....... 740 753-2646
  Nelsonville (G-14836)

AMUSEMENT & RECREATION SVCS: Amusement Ride

Bates Bros Amusement Co......................D....... 740 266-2950
  Wintersville (G-19668)
Kissel Bros Shows Inc............................E....... 513 741-1080
  Cincinnati (G-3876)

AMUSEMENT & RECREATION SVCS: Arcades

16 Bit Bar...E....... 513 381-1616
  Cincinnati (G-2876)

AMUSEMENT & RECREATION SVCS: Boating Club, Membership

Columbus Sail and Pwr Squadron.........C....... 614 384-0245
  Lewis Center (G-12534)
Island Service Company..........................C....... 419 285-3695
  Put In Bay (G-16226)
Sandusky Yacht Club Inc........................D....... 419 625-6567
  Sandusky (G-16641)
Vermilion Boat Club Inc.........................E....... 440 967-6634
  Vermilion (G-18562)

AMUSEMENT & RECREATION SVCS: Bowling Instruction

Beaver-Vu Bowl.....................................E....... 937 426-6771
  Beavercreek (G-1130)

AMUSEMENT & RECREATION SVCS: Carnival Operation

Amusements of America Inc....................C....... 614 297-8863
  Columbus (G-6945)
Kissel Entertainment LLC.......................E....... 513 266-4505
  Okeana (G-15532)

AMUSEMENT & RECREATION SVCS: Concession Operator

Flash Seats LLC....................................E....... 216 420-2000
  Cleveland (G-5543)
National Concession Company.................E....... 216 881-9911
  Cleveland (G-6040)

AMUSEMENT & RECREATION SVCS: Exhibition Operation

Asm International...................................D....... 440 338-5151
  Novelty (G-15464)
Roto Group LLC....................................D....... 614 760-8690
  Dublin (G-10325)

AMUSEMENT & RECREATION SVCS: Exposition Operation

Ohio Exposition Center..........................D....... 614 644-4000
  Columbus (G-8255)
Park Corporation...................................B....... 216 267-4870
  Cleveland (G-6163)
Relx Inc..E....... 937 865-6800
  Miamisburg (G-14210)

AMUSEMENT & RECREATION SVCS: Festival Operation

Circle S Farms Inc.................................E....... 614 878-9462
  Grove City (G-11420)

AMUSEMENT & RECREATION SVCS: Fishing Lakes & Piers, Op

Snows Lakeside Tavern...........................E....... 513 954-5626
  Cincinnati (G-4499)

AMUSEMENT & RECREATION SVCS: Gambling & Lottery Svcs

Miami Valley Gaming & Racg LLC...........D....... 513 934-7070
  Lebanon (G-12485)

AMUSEMENT & RECREATION SVCS: Gambling, Coin Machines

Jack Thistledown Racino LLC..................E....... 216 662-8600
  Cleveland (G-5775)

AMUSEMENT & RECREATION SVCS: Golf Club, Membership

797 Elks Golf Club Inc..........................E....... 937 382-2666
  Wilmington (G-19599)
Akron Management Corp.........................B....... 330 644-8441
  Akron (G-48)
American Golf Corporation.....................D....... 440 286-9544
  Chesterland (G-2736)
American Golf Corporation.....................E....... 740 965-5122
  Galena (G-11154)
American Golf Corporation.....................E....... 310 664-4278
  Grove City (G-11405)

(G-0000) Company's Geographic Section entry number

Avalon Golf and Cntry CLB Inc ....D....... 330 856-8898
Warren (G-18672)
Barrington Golf Club Inc ....D....... 330 995-0600
Aurora (G-820)
Barrington Golf Club Inc ....D....... 330 995-0821
Aurora (G-821)
Big Red LP ....D....... 740 548-7799
Galena (G-11156)
Brass Ring Golf Club Ltd ....E....... 740 385-8966
Logan (G-12832)
Breezy Point Ltd Partnership................D....... 330 995-0600
Aurora (G-822)
Breezy Point Ltd Partnership................C....... 440 247-3363
Solon (G-16828)
Canterbury Golf Club Inc ....D....... 216 561-1914
Cleveland (G-5119)
City of Parma ....E....... 440 885-8876
Cleveland (G-5212)
Congress Lake Club Company ....E....... 330 877-9318
Hartville (G-11684)
Dornoch Golf Club Inc ....E....... 740 369-0863
Delaware (G-9971)
Golf Club Co ....E....... 614 855-7326
New Albany (G-14855)
Heritage Club.......................................D....... 513 459-7711
Mason (G-13593)
Jefferson Golf & Country Club ....E....... 614 759-7500
Blacklick (G-1480)
Lake Club...C....... 330 549-3996
Poland (G-16086)
Lakes Country Club Inc ....C....... 614 882-4167
Galena (G-11161)
Legend Lake Golf Club Inc...................E....... 440 285-3110
Chardon (G-2702)
Leisure Sports Inc...............................E....... 419 829-2891
Sylvania (G-17436)
Lost Creek Country Club Inc ....E....... 419 229-2026
Lima (G-12691)
Madison Route 20 LLC ....E....... 440 358-7888
Painesville (G-15723)
Mill Creek Golf Course Corp ....E....... 740 666-7711
Ostrander (G-15654)
Mohawk Golf Club.................................E....... 419 447-5876
Tiffin (G-17525)
Muirfield Village Golf Club ....E....... 614 889-6700
Dublin (G-10284)
New Albany Links Dev Co Ltd ....D....... 614 939-5914
New Albany (G-14865)
OBannon Creek Golf Club.....................E....... 513 683-5657
Loveland (G-13019)
Pepper Pike Club Company Inc............D....... 216 831-9400
Cleveland (G-6193)
Pike Run Golf Club Inc ....E....... 419 538-7000
Ottawa (G-15664)
Quail Hollow Management Inc...............D....... 440 639-4000
Painesville (G-15734)
Sand Ridge Golf Club ....D....... 440 285-8088
Chardon (G-2713)
Sawmill Creek Golf Racquet CLB..........D....... 419 433-3789
Huron (G-12032)
Spring Valley Golf & Athc CLB ....D....... 440 365-1411
Westlake (G-19407)
Stone Oak Country Club ....D....... 419 867-0969
Holland (G-11917)
Tartan Fields Golf Club Ltd ....D....... 614 792-0900
Dublin (G-10353)
Valleaire Golf Club Inc ....E....... 440 237-9191
Hinckley (G-11862)
Walden Club ....D....... 330 995-7162
Aurora (G-848)

AMUSEMENT & RECREATION SVCS: Golf Professionals

Tom Tise Golf Professional...................D....... 937 836-5186
Clayton (G-4862)

AMUSEMENT & RECREATION SVCS: Golf Svcs & Professionals

Avalon Holdings Corporation ....D....... 330 856-8800
Warren (G-18673)
Delaware Golf Club Inc.........................E....... 740 362-2582
Delaware (G-9969)
Magic Castle Inc..................................E....... 937 434-4911
Dayton (G-9580)
Man Golf Ohio LLC ....E....... 440 635-5178
Huntsburg (G-12018)
Spring Hills Golf Club...........................E....... 740 543-3270
East Springfield (G-10426)

AMUSEMENT & RECREATION SVCS: Gun & Hunting Clubs

Field & Stream Bowhunters...................D....... 419 423-9861
Findlay (G-10901)

AMUSEMENT & RECREATION SVCS: Gun Club, Membership

Sportsman Gun & Reel Club Inc............C....... 440 233-8287
Lorain (G-12944)

AMUSEMENT & RECREATION SVCS: Hunting Club, Membership

Columbia Recreation Assn ....E....... 740 849-2466
East Fultonham (G-10389)
Elm Valley Fishing Club Inc ....D....... 937 845-0584
New Carlisle (G-14890)
Tri County Nite Hunter Assn Ci ....E....... 740 385-7341
Logan (G-12856)

AMUSEMENT & RECREATION SVCS: Ice Skating Rink

Alice Noble Ice Arena ....E....... 330 345-8686
Wooster (G-19686)
Central Ohio Ice Rinks Inc ....E....... 614 475-7575
Dublin (G-10165)
Chiller LLC...D....... 614 764-1000
Dublin (G-10173)
Chiller LLC...E....... 740 549-0009
Lewis Center (G-12533)
Chiller LLC...E....... 614 433-9600
Worthington (G-19797)
Chiller LLC...E....... 614 475-7575
Columbus (G-7192)
City of Sylvania ....E....... 419 885-1167
Sylvania (G-17415)
Ice Land USA Lakewood ....E....... 216 529-1200
Lakewood (G-12347)
Ice Land USA Ltd ....D....... 440 268-2800
Strongsville (G-17314)
Ice Zone Ltd ....E....... 330 965-1423
Youngstown (G-20074)
Lakewood City School District ....E....... 216 529-4400
Lakewood (G-12352)

AMUSEMENT & RECREATION SVCS: Indoor Court Clubs

Soccer Centre Owners Ltd....................E....... 419 893-5425
Maumee (G-13853)
Western Hills Sportsplex Inc ....D....... 513 451-4900
Cincinnati (G-4790)

AMUSEMENT & RECREATION SVCS: Instruction Schools, Camps

Vertical Adventures Inc ....D....... 614 888-8393
Columbus (G-8846)

AMUSEMENT & RECREATION SVCS: Kiddie Park

Little Squirt Sports Park.......................E....... 419 227-6200
Lima (G-12690)

AMUSEMENT & RECREATION SVCS: Lottery Tickets, Sales

Fat Jacks Pizza II Inc ....E....... 419 227-1813
Lima (G-12639)

AMUSEMENT & RECREATION SVCS: Outdoor Field Clubs

Frontier Bassmasters Inc......................E....... 740 423-9293
Belpre (G-1404)
West Denison Baseball League.............E....... 216 251-5790
Cleveland (G-6666)

AMUSEMENT & RECREATION SVCS: Picnic Ground Operation

Wiegands Lake Park Inc ....E....... 440 338-5795
Novelty (G-15467)

AMUSEMENT & RECREATION SVCS: Pool Parlor

S & S Management Inc ....E....... 567 356-4151
Wapakoneta (G-18653)

AMUSEMENT & RECREATION SVCS: Racquetball Club, Membership

Beechmont Racquet Club Inc ....E....... 513 528-5700
Cincinnati (G-3033)
Courtyard Ltd ....E....... 513 777-5530
West Chester (G-18902)
Western Reserve Racquet Club............E....... 330 653-3103
Streetsboro (G-17277)

AMUSEMENT & RECREATION SVCS: Recreation Center

Baldwin Wallace University ....E....... 440 826-2285
Berea (G-1413)
City of Brook Park.................................E....... 216 433-1545
Cleveland (G-5188)
City of Miamisburg ....E....... 937 866-4532
Miamisburg (G-14152)
City of North Olmsted...........................D....... 440 734-8200
North Olmsted (G-15282)
City of Rocky River...............................E....... 440 356-5656
Cleveland (G-5214)
City of Seven Hills................................C....... 216 524-6262
Seven Hills (G-16673)
Community Action Columbiana CT........E....... 330 385-7251
East Liverpool (G-10400)
Goofy Golf Inc ....E....... 419 625-1308
Sandusky (G-16612)
Makoy Center Inc ....E....... 614 777-1211
Hilliard (G-11787)
Max Dixons Expressway Park ....E....... 513 831-2273
Milford (G-14407)
Oberlin College ....C....... 440 775-8519
Oberlin (G-15513)
Rec Center ....E....... 330 721-6900
Medina (G-13993)
Society of The Transfiguration ....E....... 513 771-7462
Cincinnati (G-4501)
Washington Twnship Mntgomery..........C....... 937 433-0130
Dayton (G-9868)
YMCA ....D....... 937 653-9622
Urbana (G-18447)
Young Mens Christian Assoc.................D....... 330 264-3131
Wooster (G-19789)
Young Mens Christian Assoc.................D....... 614 276-8224
Columbus (G-8928)
Young Mens Christian Assoc.................D....... 740 477-1661
Circleville (G-4854)
Young Mens Christian Assoc.................C....... 614 885-4252
Columbus (G-8927)
Young Mens Christian Assoc.................E....... 937 228-9622
Dayton (G-9895)
YWCA of Hamilton ....E....... 513 856-9800
Hamilton (G-11655)

AMUSEMENT & RECREATION SVCS: Recreation SVCS

Anderson Township Park Dst ....E....... 513 474-0003
Cincinnati (G-2963)
Army & Air Force Exchange Svc ....A....... 937 257-7736
Dayton (G-9161)
City of Independence.............................E....... 216 524-3262
Cleveland (G-5203)
Cleveland Metroparks...........................D....... 440 331-5530
Cleveland (G-5268)
Cleveland Metroparks...........................B....... 216 635-3200
Cleveland (G-5269)
Cleveland Metroparks...........................B....... 216 739-6040
Strongsville (G-17292)
Cleveland Metroparks...........................E....... 440 572-9990
Strongsville (G-17293)
Columbus Frkln Cnty Pk ....E....... 614 891-0700
Westerville (G-19241)
County of Hancock................................E....... 419 425-7275
Findlay (G-10894)
Goodrich Gnnett Nghborhood Ctr.........E....... 216 432-1717
Cleveland (G-5614)
Lake Metroparks...................................B....... 440 639-7275
Painesville (G-15720)
Lake Metroparks ....E....... 440 428-3164
Madison (G-13100)

SERVICES

Lake Metroparks ....D 440 256-2122
Kirtland *(G-12322)*
Lake Metroparks ....E 440 256-1404
Willoughby *(G-19540)*
Mill Creek Metropolitan Park ....E 330 740-7116
Youngstown *(G-20129)*
Stark County Park District ....D 330 477-3552
Canton *(G-2494)*
Strike Zone Inc ....D 440 235-4420
Olmsted Twp *(G-15541)*
Washington Township Park Dst ......E 937 433-5155
Centerville *(G-2636)*

AMUSEMENT & RECREATION SVCS: Soccer Club, Exc Pro/Semi-Pro

Soccer Centre Inc ....E 419 893-5419
Maumee *(G-13852)*

AMUSEMENT & RECREATION SVCS: Swimming Club, Membership

Dunsiane Swim Club ....E 937 433-7946
Dayton *(G-9397)*
Lancaster Country Club ....D 740 654-3535
Lancaster *(G-12411)*
Northwest Swim Club Inc ....E 614 442-8716
Columbus *(G-8208)*
Oak Hills Swim & Racquet ....E 513 922-1827
Cincinnati *(G-4143)*
Orchard Hill Swim Club ....D 513 385-0211
Cincinnati *(G-4179)*
Reynoldsburg Swim Club Inc ....E 614 866-3211
Reynoldsburg *(G-16327)*
Swim Incorporated ....E 614 885-1619
Worthington *(G-19855)*
Turpin Hills Swim Racquet CLB ......E 513 231-3242
Cincinnati *(G-4654)*
US Swimming Lake Erie Swimming ...E 330 423-0485
Bay Village *(G-1023)*
Young Mens Christian Assoc ....E 614 878-7269
Columbus *(G-8930)*

AMUSEMENT & RECREATION SVCS: Swimming Pool, Non-Membership

Alliance Hospitality Inc ....E 440 951-7333
Mentor *(G-14016)*
Centennial Terrace & Quarry ....E 419 885-7106
Sylvania *(G-17414)*
City of Gallipolis ....E 740 441-6003
Gallipolis *(G-11186)*
City of South Euclid ....E 216 291-3902
Cleveland *(G-5216)*
Huntington Hlls Recreation CLB .....E 614 837-0293
Pickerington *(G-15959)*
Marietta Aquatic Center ....E 740 373-2445
Marietta *(G-13347)*

AMUSEMENT & RECREATION SVCS: Tennis & Professionals

Heaven Bound Ascensions ....E 330 633-3288
Tallmadge *(G-17477)*

AMUSEMENT & RECREATION SVCS: Tennis Club, Membership

Chillicothe Racquet Club ....E 740 773-4928
Chillicothe *(G-2766)*
Cleveland Racquet Club Inc ....D 216 831-2155
Cleveland *(G-5282)*
Kettering Tennis Center ....E 937 434-6602
Dayton *(G-9543)*
Scarbrough E Tennis Fitnes Ctr .....E 614 751-2597
Columbus *(G-8598)*
Shadow Valley Tennis & Fitness .....E 419 861-3986
Toledo *(G-18029)*
Shadow Valley Tennis Club ....E 419 865-1141
Maumee *(G-13851)*
Tennis Unlimited Inc ....E 330 928-8763
Akron *(G-467)*
Western Hills Sportsplex Inc ....D 513 451-4900
Cincinnati *(G-4790)*
Wickertree Tnnis Ftnes CLB LLC .....E 614 882-5724
Columbus *(G-8900)*

AMUSEMENT & RECREATION SVCS: Theme Park

Cedar Fair LP ....A 419 626-0830
Sandusky *(G-16582)*
Cedar Point Park LLC ....D 419 627-2500
Sandusky *(G-16583)*
Fun n Stuff Amusements Inc ....C 330 467-0821
Macedonia *(G-13069)*
Funtime Parks Inc ....C 330 562-7131
Aurora *(G-827)*
Kings Island Park LLC ....C 513 754-5901
Kings Mills *(G-12314)*
Linwood Park Company ....E 440 963-0481
Vermilion *(G-18556)*
Lodge Stone Wood ....E 513 769-4325
Blue Ash *(G-1599)*
Seaworld Entertainment Inc ....E 330 562-8101
Aurora *(G-843)*
Strongville Recreation Complex .....C 440 580-3230
Strongsville *(G-17349)*

AMUSEMENT & RECREATION SVCS: Tourist Attraction, Commercial

Dutch Heritage Farms Inc ....E 330 893-3232
Berlin *(G-1446)*

AMUSEMENT & RECREATION SVCS: Trampoline Operation

Sky Zone Indoor Trampoline Pk ......D 614 302-6093
Cincinnati *(G-4493)*
Wonderworker Inc ....D 234 249-3030
Hudson *(G-12015)*

AMUSEMENT & RECREATION SVCS: Video Game Arcades

Strike Zone Inc ....D 440 235-4420
Olmsted Twp *(G-15541)*

AMUSEMENT ARCADES

Bell Music Company ....E 330 376-6337
Akron *(G-93)*
Magic Castle Inc ....E 937 434-4911
Dayton *(G-9580)*
Pnk (ohio) LLC ....A 513 232-8000
Cincinnati *(G-4261)*
Stonehedge Enterprises Inc ....E 330 928-2161
Akron *(G-442)*

AMUSEMENT PARK DEVICES & RIDES: Carnival Mach & Eqpt, NEC

Majestic Manufacturing Inc ....E 330 457-2447
New Waterford *(G-15005)*

AMUSEMENT PARKS

CCJ Enterprises Inc ....E 330 345-4386
Wooster *(G-19697)*
Columbus Frkln Cnty Pk ....E 614 895-6219
Westerville *(G-19240)*
Kings Island Company ....C 513 754-5700
Kings Mills *(G-12313)*
Lazer Kraze ....E 513 339-1030
Galena *(G-11162)*
Lmn Development LLC ....D 419 433-7200
Sandusky *(G-16623)*
Lost Nation Sports Park ....E 440 602-4000
Willoughby *(G-19545)*
Magnum Management Corporation .....A 419 627-2334
Sandusky *(G-16626)*
Muskingum Wtrshed Cnsrvncy Dst ....E 740 685-6013
Senecaville *(G-16670)*
Muskingum Wtrshed Cnsrvncy Dst ....E 330 343-6780
Mineral City *(G-14507)*
Rumpke Amusements Inc ....E 513 738-2646
Cincinnati *(G-4408)*
Y & E Entertainment Group LLC ......E 440 385-5500
Parma *(G-15781)*

AMUSEMENT/REC SVCS: Ticket Sales, Sporting Events, Contract

Iticketscom ....E 614 410-4140
Columbus *(G-7848)*

ANATOMICAL SPECIMENS & RESEARCH MATERIAL, WHOLESALE

Labelle News Agency Inc ....E 740 282-9731
Steubenville *(G-17161)*

ANIMAL & REPTILE EXHIBIT

Toledo Zoo ....E 419 385-5721
Toledo *(G-18101)*

ANIMAL FEED & SUPPLEMENTS: Livestock & Poultry

Cooper Hatchery Inc ....C 419 594-3325
Oakwood *(G-15483)*
Provimi North America Inc ....B 937 770-2400
Brookville *(G-1916)*

ANIMAL FEED: Wholesalers

Land OLakes Inc ....E 330 879-2158
Massillon *(G-13703)*
Provimi North America Inc ....B 937 770-2400
Brookville *(G-1916)*

ANIMAL FOOD & SUPPLEMENTS: Bird Food, Prepared

Centerra Co-Op ....E 800 362-9598
Jefferson *(G-12190)*
Centerra Co-Op ....E 419 281-2153
Ashland *(G-665)*

ANIMAL FOOD & SUPPLEMENTS: Dog

IAMS Company ....D 937 962-7782
Lewisburg *(G-12568)*

ANIMAL FOOD & SUPPLEMENTS: Dog & Cat

Land OLakes Inc ....E 330 879-2158
Massillon *(G-13703)*

ANIMAL FOOD & SUPPLEMENTS: Livestock

Hanby Farms Inc ....E 740 763-3554
Nashport *(G-14819)*
Land OLakes Inc ....E 330 879-2158
Massillon *(G-13703)*

ANIMAL FOOD & SUPPLEMENTS: Poultry

Cooper Farms Inc ....D 419 375-4116
Fort Recovery *(G-10989)*

ANTENNA REPAIR & INSTALLATION SVCS

Central USA Wireless LLC ....E 513 469-1500
Cincinnati *(G-3159)*
Dss Installations Ltd ....E 513 761-7000
Cincinnati *(G-3446)*

ANTENNAS: Radar Or Communications

Circle Prime Manufacturing ....E 330 923-0019
Cuyahoga Falls *(G-9079)*
Quasonix Inc ....E 513 942-1287
West Chester *(G-18988)*

ANTIPOVERTY BOARD

Akron Summit Cmnty Action Agcy .....C 330 572-8532
Akron *(G-56)*
Akron Summit Cmnty Action Agcy .....D 330 733-2290
Akron *(G-57)*
Ashtabula County Commnty Actn ......C 440 997-1721
Ashtabula *(G-711)*
Ashtabula County Commnty Actn ......D 440 593-6441
Conneaut *(G-8949)*
Ashtabula County Commnty Actn ......D 440 576-6911
Jefferson *(G-12189)*
Ashtabula County Commnty Actn ......D 440 993-7716
Ashtabula *(G-712)*
Council For Economic Opport ....D 216 541-7878
Cleveland *(G-5353)*
Council For Economic Opport ....D 216 696-9077
Cleveland *(G-5355)*
Council For Economic Opport ....E 216 692-4010
Cleveland *(G-5356)*
Warren County Community Svcs ....C 513 695-2100
Lebanon *(G-12515)*

ANTIQUE & CLASSIC AUTOMOBILE RESTORATION

Service King Holdings LLC ....E 330 926-0100
Stow *(G-17229)*

APARTMENT LOCATING SVCS

Akron Metropolitan Hsing Auth ....C 330 920-1652
Stow *(G-17189)*
Alpha PHI Alpha Homes Inc ....D 330 376-2115
Akron *(G-68)*

APPAREL DESIGNERS: Commercial

Atrium Apparel Corporation ....D 740 966-8200
Johnstown *(G-12195)*
Tommy Bahama Group Inc ....C 614 750-9668
Columbus *(G-8763)*

APPLIANCES, HOUSEHOLD OR COIN OPERATED: Laundry Dryers

Whirlpool Corporation ....C 740 383-7122
Marion *(G-13473)*

APPLIANCES, HOUSEHOLD: Kitchen, Major, Exc Refrigs & Stoves

ABC Appliance Inc ....E 419 693-4414
Oregon *(G-15581)*
New Path International LLC ....E 614 410-3974
Powell *(G-16204)*

APPLIANCES: Household, Refrigerators & Freezers

Whirlpool Corporation ....C 740 383-7122
Marion *(G-13473)*

APPLIANCES: Major, Cooking

Nacco Industries Inc ....E 440 229-5151
Cleveland *(G-6034)*

APPLIANCES: Small, Electric

Johnson Bros Rubber Co Inc ....E 419 752-4814
Greenwich *(G-11402)*

APPLICATIONS SOFTWARE PROGRAMMING

1 Edi Source Inc ....C 440 519-7800
Solon *(G-16812)*
B-Tek Scales LLC ....E 330 471-8900
Canton *(G-2208)*
Campuseai Inc ....C 216 589-9626
Cleveland *(G-5117)*
Foundation Software Inc ....D 330 220-8383
Strongsville *(G-17305)*
Icr Inc ....D 513 900-7007
Mason *(G-13596)*
Jenne Inc ....C 440 835-0040
Avon *(G-888)*
Managed Technology Svcs LLC ....D 937 247-8915
Miamisburg *(G-14186)*
Manhattan Associates Inc ....D 440 878-0771
Strongsville *(G-17327)*
Synoran ....E 614 236-4014
Columbus *(G-8724)*

APPRAISAL SVCS, EXC REAL ESTATE

Amos Media Company ....C 937 498-2111
Sidney *(G-16758)*

ARBORETUM

Dawes Arboretum ....E 740 323-2355
Newark *(G-15030)*
Holden Arboretum ....D 440 946-4400
Willoughby *(G-19529)*

ARCHEOLOGICAL EXPEDITIONS

ASC Group Inc ....E 614 268-2514
Columbus *(G-6976)*

ARCHITECTURAL SVCS

Aptiv Services Us LLC ....E 330 373-3568
Warren *(G-18666)*
Arcadis US Inc ....E 216 781-6177
Cleveland *(G-5005)*

ASC Group Inc ....E 614 268-2514
Columbus *(G-6976)*
Behal Sampson Dietz Inc ....E 614 464-1933
Columbus *(G-7025)*
Big Red Rooster ....E 614 255-0200
Columbus *(G-7036)*
Burgess & Niple Inc ....D 440 354-9700
Painesville *(G-15696)*
Burgess & Niple-Heapy LLC ....D 614 459-2050
Columbus *(G-7099)*
Cbre Heery Inc ....E 216 781-1313
Cleveland *(G-5143)*
Ceso Inc ....C 937 435-8584
Miamisburg *(G-14150)*
Cha Consulting Inc ....C 216 443-1700
Cleveland *(G-5165)*
Chemstress Consultant Company ....C 330 535-5591
Akron *(G-126)*
Chute Gerdeman Inc ....D 614 469-1001
Columbus *(G-7198)*
City Architecture Inc ....E 216 881-2444
Cleveland *(G-5185)*
CT Consultants Inc ....E 440 951-9000
Mentor *(G-14038)*
Design Center ....E 513 618-3133
Blue Ash *(G-1544)*
Dlr Group Inc ....E 216 522-1350
Cleveland *(G-5433)*
Dlz Ohio Inc ....E 614 888-0040
Columbus *(G-7462)*
Emersion Design LLC ....E 513 841-9100
Cincinnati *(G-3494)*
Fanning/Howey Associates Inc ....D 919 831-1831
Dublin *(G-10225)*
Garland/Dbs Inc ....C 216 641-7500
Cleveland *(G-5592)*
Gbc Design Inc ....E 330 283-6870
Akron *(G-232)*
Glavan & Accociates Architects ....E 614 205-4060
Columbus *(G-7672)*
Gpd Services Company Inc ....D 330 572-2100
Akron *(G-243)*
Heery International Inc ....E 216 510-4701
Cleveland *(G-5680)*
Holland Professional Group ....D 330 239-4474
Sharon Center *(G-16723)*
HWH Archtcts-Ngnrs-Plnners Inc ....E 216 875-4000
Cleveland *(G-5727)*
Karlsberger Companies ....C 614 461-9500
Columbus *(G-7883)*
KZF Bwsc Joint Venture ....E 513 621-6211
Cincinnati *(G-3897)*
Loth Inc ....C 513 554-4900
Cincinnati *(G-3944)*
Louis Perry & Associates Inc ....C 330 334-1585
Wadsworth *(G-18605)*
Meyers + Associates Arch LLC ....E 614 221-9433
Columbus *(G-8065)*
Ms Consultants Inc ....C 330 744-5321
Youngstown *(G-20132)*
Nelson ....C 216 781-9144
Seven Hills *(G-16677)*
Perkfect Design Solutions ....E 614 778-3560
Columbus *(G-8439)*
Poggemeyer Design Group Inc ....C 419 244-8074
Bowling Green *(G-1746)*
Rdl Architects Inc ....E 216 752-4300
Cleveland *(G-6288)*
Richard R Jencen & Associates ....E 216 781-0131
Cleveland *(G-6322)*
Schomer Glaus Pyle ....D 614 210-0751
Columbus *(G-8604)*
Schomer Glaus Pyle ....E 216 518-5544
Cleveland *(G-6376)*
Schomer Glaus Pyle ....B 330 572-2100
Akron *(G-420)*
Shp Leading Design ....D 513 381-2112
Cincinnati *(G-4472)*
Shremshock Architects Inc ....D 614 545-4550
New Albany *(G-14874)*
Simonson Construction Svcs Inc ....D 419 281-8299
Ashland *(G-691)*
Stantec Arch & Engrg PC ....E 216 454-2150
Cleveland *(G-6451)*
Stantec Arch & Engrg PC ....E 614 486-4383
Columbus *(G-8683)*
Stantec Architecture Inc ....D 216 621-2407
Cleveland *(G-6452)*
Stantec Architecture Inc ....E 216 454-2150
Cleveland *(G-6453)*

Stantec Consulting Svcs Inc ....E 216 454-2150
Cleveland *(G-6454)*
Stantec Consulting Svcs Inc ....D 513 842-8200
Cincinnati *(G-4537)*
Stantec Consulting Svcs Inc ....C 614 486-4383
Columbus *(G-8684)*
Stilson & Associates Inc ....E 614 847-0300
Columbus *(G-8700)*
Trinity Health Group Ltd ....E 614 899-4830
Columbus *(G-8782)*
United Architectural Mtls Inc ....C 330 433-9220
North Canton *(G-15243)*
URS Group Inc ....C 614 464-4500
Columbus *(G-8831)*
WD Partners Inc ....E 614 634-7000
Dublin *(G-10370)*

ARCHITECTURAL SVCS: Engineering

Aecom Global II LLC ....B 614 726-3500
Dublin *(G-10120)*
Dei Incorporated ....D 513 825-5800
Cincinnati *(G-3418)*
E & A Pedco Services Inc ....E 513 782-4920
Cincinnati *(G-3461)*
Fed/Matrix A Joint Venture LLC ....E 863 665-6363
Dayton *(G-9429)*
Johnson Mirmiran Thompson Inc ....D 614 714-0270
Columbus *(G-7863)*
Orchard Hiltz & McCliment Inc ....D 614 418-0600
Columbus *(G-8384)*
Prime Ae Group Inc ....E 614 839-0250
Columbus *(G-6831)*
Technical Assurance Inc ....E 440 953-3147
Willoughby *(G-19575)*
Twism Enterprises LLC ....E 513 800-1098
Cincinnati *(G-4657)*

ARCHITECTURAL SVCS: Engineering

A D A Architects Inc ....E 216 521-5134
Cleveland *(G-4877)*
Acock Assoc Architects LLC ....E 614 228-1586
Columbus *(G-6866)*
Aecom Global II LLC ....D 216 523-5600
Cleveland *(G-4910)*
Austin Building and Design Inc ....C 440 544-2600
Cleveland *(G-5023)*
Balog Steines Hendricks & Manc ....E 330 744-4401
Youngstown *(G-19961)*
Baxter Hodell Donnelly Preston ....C 513 271-1634
Cincinnati *(G-3025)*
Berardi + Partners ....E 614 221-1110
Columbus *(G-7028)*
Bostwick Design Partnr Inc ....E 216 621-7900
Cleveland *(G-5069)*
Braun & Steidl Architects Inc ....E 330 864-7755
Akron *(G-104)*
Burgess & Niple Inc ....C 513 579-0042
Cincinnati *(G-3089)*
Burgess & Niple Inc ....B 502 254-2344
Columbus *(G-7098)*
Champlin Haupt Architects Inc ....D 513 241-4474
Cincinnati *(G-3169)*
Cole + Russell Architects Inc ....E 513 721-8080
Cincinnati *(G-3327)*
Collaborative Inc ....E 419 242-7405
Toledo *(G-17667)*
Cornelia C Hodgson - Architec ....E 216 593-0057
Beachwood *(G-1048)*
CT Consultants Inc ....E 513 791-1700
Blue Ash *(G-1543)*
Domokur Architects Inc ....E 330 666-7878
Copley *(G-8966)*
Dorsky Hodgson + Partners Inc ....D 216 464-8600
Cleveland *(G-5442)*
Elevar Design Group Inc ....E 513 721-0600
Cincinnati *(G-3490)*
Fanning/Howey Associates Inc ....E 614 764-4661
Dublin *(G-10224)*
Feinknopf Macioce Schappa ARC ....E 614 297-1020
Columbus *(G-7573)*
Garmann/Miller & Assoc Inc ....E 419 628-4240
Minster *(G-14533)*
Hardlines Design Company ....E 614 784-8733
Columbus *(G-7717)*
Hasenstab Architects Inc ....E 330 434-4464
Akron *(G-254)*
Hixson Incorporated ....C 513 241-1230
Cincinnati *(G-3712)*
Jdi Group Inc ....D 419 725-7161
Maumee *(G-13805)*

K4 Architecture LLC .... D 513 455-5005
Cincinnati (G-3845)

KZF Design Inc .... D 513 621-6211
Cincinnati (G-3898)

Lacaisse Inc .... D 513 621-6211
Cincinnati (G-3905)

Lusk & Harkin Ltd .... E 614 221-3707
Columbus (G-7999)

McGill Smith Punshon Inc .... E 513 759-0004
Cincinnati (G-3987)

Meacham & Apel Architects Inc .... D 614 764-0407
Columbus (G-8048)

Michael Schuster Associates .... E 513 241-5666
Cincinnati (G-4047)

Middough Inc .... B 216 367-6000
Cleveland (G-5983)

Mkc Associates Inc .... E 740 657-3202
Powell (G-16203)

Moody-Nolan Inc .... C 614 461-4664
Columbus (G-8101)

NBBJ LLC .... A 206 223-5026
Columbus (G-8165)

Onyx Creative Inc .... D 216 223-3200
Cleveland (G-6137)

Osborn Engineering Company .... D 216 861-2020
Cleveland (G-6145)

Perspectus Architecture LLC .... E 216 752-1800
Cleveland (G-6199)

Pond-Woolpert LLC .... D 937 461-5660
Beavercreek (G-1233)

R E Warner & Associates Inc .... E 440 835-9400
Westlake (G-19395)

Richard L Bowen & Assoc Inc .... D 216 491-9300
Cleveland (G-6321)

Schooley Caldwell Associates .... D 614 628-0300
Columbus (G-8607)

Sfa Architects Inc .... E 937 281-0600
Dayton (G-9762)

Ssoe Inc .... E 330 821-7198
Alliance (G-552)

Strollo Architects Inc .... E 330 743-1177
Youngstown (G-20218)

URS Group Inc .... D 330 836-9111
Akron (G-481)

Woolprt-Mrrick Joint Ventr LLP ...... E 937 461-5660
Beavercreek (G-1241)

ARCHITECTURAL SVCS: House Designer

Frch Design Worldwide - Cincin ...... B 513 241-3000
Cincinnati (G-3584)

ARMATURE REPAIRING & REWINDING SVC

City Machine Technologies Inc .... E 330 740-8186
Youngstown (G-19990)

Dolin Supply Co .... E 304 529-4171
South Point (G-16932)

Integrated Power Services LLC .... E 216 433-7808
Cleveland (G-5758)

Setco Sales Company .... D 513 941-5110
Cincinnati (G-4457)

ARMORED CAR SVCS

Brinks Incorporated .... E 419 729-5389
Toledo (G-17625)

Brinks Incorporated .... E 614 291-1268
Columbus (G-7073)

Brinks Incorporated .... E 614 291-0624
Columbus (G-7074)

Brinks Incorporated .... D 216 621-7493
Cleveland (G-5080)

Brinks Incorporated .... E 330 633-5351
Akron (G-108)

Brinks Incorporated .... D 513 621-9310
Cincinnati (G-3075)

Brinks Incorporated .... E 937 253-9777
Dayton (G-9162)

Brinks Incorporated .... E 330 832-6130
Massillon (G-13665)

Brinks Incorporated .... E 330 758-7379
Youngstown (G-19974)

Dunbar Armored Inc .... E 513 381-8000
Cincinnati (G-3454)

Dunbar Armored Inc .... E 614 475-1969
Columbus (G-7477)

Dunbar Armored Inc .... E 216 642-5700
Cleveland (G-5449)

Garda CL Great Lakes Inc .... E 614 863-4044
Columbus (G-7646)

Garda CL Great Lakes Inc .... E 419 385-2411
Toledo (G-17754)

Garda CL Great Lakes Inc .... B 561 939-7000
Columbus (G-7647)

Garda CL Technical Svcs Inc .... E 937 294-4099
Moraine (G-14660)

ART & ORNAMENTAL WARE: Pottery

J-Vac Industries Inc .... D 740 384-2155
Wellston (G-18850)

ART DESIGN SVCS

Shamrock Companies Inc .... D 440 899-9510
Westlake (G-19405)

ART GALLERIES

Columbus Museum of Art .... D 614 221-6801
Columbus (G-7301)

Dumouchelle Art Galleries .... E 419 255-7606
Toledo (G-17705)

Fairfield Industries Inc .... E 740 409-1539
Carroll (G-2557)

ART GOODS & SPLYS WHOLESALERS

Checker Notions Company Inc .... D 419 893-3636
Maumee (G-13770)

Distribution Data Incorporated ...... E 216 362-3009
Brookpark (G-1896)

Lamrite West Inc .... E 440 572-9946
Strongsville (G-17322)

Lamrite West Inc .... C 440 238-9150
Strongsville (G-17321)

ART GOODS, WHOLESALE

Cannell Graphics LLC .... E 614 781-9760
Columbus (G-7110)

Don Drumm Studios & Gallery .... E 330 253-6840
Akron (G-190)

ART RELATED SVCS

Grenada Stamping Assembly Inc .... E 419 842-3600
Sylvania (G-17427)

ART SCHOOL, EXC COMMERCIAL

Cincinnati Museum Association .... C 513 721-5204
Cincinnati (G-3257)

Cleveland Mus Schl Settlement .... C 216 421-5806
Cleveland (G-5280)

ART SPLY STORES

Don Drumm Studios & Gallery .... E 330 253-6840
Akron (G-190)

Lamrite West Inc .... C 440 238-9150
Strongsville (G-17321)

United Art and Education Inc 800 322-3247
Dayton (G-9830)

ARTS & CRAFTS SCHOOL

South Central Ohio Eductl Ctr .... C 740 456-0517
New Boston (G-14883)

ARTS OR SCIENCES CENTER

Cincinnati Nature Center .... E 513 831-1711
Milford (G-14378)

Contemporary Arts Center .... E 513 721-0390
Cincinnati (G-3352)

Deyor Performing Arts Center .... E 330 744-4269
Youngstown (G-20017)

ASPHALT & ASPHALT PRDTS

Lucas County Asphalt Inc .... E 419 476-0705
Toledo (G-17867)

Shelly and Sands Inc .... E 740 453-0721
Zanesville (G-20360)

Shelly Materials Inc .... E 740 666-5841
Ostrander (G-15655)

Stoneco Inc .... D 419 422-8854
Findlay (G-10964)

ASPHALT COATINGS & SEALERS

Hy-Grade Corporation .... E 216 341-7711
Cleveland (G-5728)

Owens Corning Sales LLC .... A 419 248-8000
Toledo (G-17968)

Simon Roofing and Shtmtl Corp ...... C 330 629-7392
Youngstown (G-20212)

State Industrial Products Corp ...... B 877 747-6986
Cleveland (G-6458)

Terry Asphalt Materials Inc .... E 513 874-6192
Hamilton (G-11646)

ASPHALT MIXTURES WHOLESALERS

Barrett Paving Materials Inc .... C 513 271-6200
Middletown (G-14343)

Hy-Grade Corporation .... E 216 341-7711
Cleveland (G-5728)

ASSOCIATION FOR THE HANDICAPPED

Cincinnati Assn For The Blind .... C 513 221-8558
Cincinnati (G-3223)

Cleveland Soc For The Blind .... C 216 791-8118
Cleveland (G-5288)

County of Mercer .... D 419 586-2369
Celina (G-2591)

Hattie Larlham Community Svcs .... E 330 274-2272
Mantua (G-13269)

Medina Creative Accessibility .... D 330 591-4434
Medina (G-13973)

Northeast Ohio Chapter Natnl .... E 216 696-8220
Cleveland (G-6092)

Southeast Diversified Inds .... D 740 432-4241
Cambridge (G-2082)

Spectrum Supportive Services .... E 216 875-0460
Cleveland (G-6445)

ASSOCIATIONS: Alumni

Ohio State Univ Alumni Assn .... D 614 292-2200
Columbus (G-8290)

ASSOCIATIONS: Bar

Cincinnati Bar Association .... E 513 381-8213
Cincinnati (G-3225)

Columbus Bar Association .... E 614 221-4112
Columbus (G-7261)

Ohio State Bar Association .... D 614 487-2050
Columbus (G-8289)

ASSOCIATIONS: Business

A Fox Construction .... E 614 506-1685
Canal Winchester (G-2101)

American Legion Post .... E 330 872-5475
Newton Falls (G-15135)

Blue Ash Business Association .... D 513 253-1006
Cincinnati (G-3058)

Certified Angus Beef LLC .... D 330 345-2333
Wooster (G-19699)

City of Kenton .... E 419 674-4850
Kenton (G-12273)

City of Louisville .... E 330 875-3321
Louisville (G-12962)

City of Montgomery .... D 513 891-2424
Montgomery (G-14593)

City of Oberlin .... E 440 775-1531
Oberlin (G-15499)

City of Toledo .... A 419 245-1001
Toledo (G-17655)

City of Toledo .... E 419 245-1400
Toledo (G-17658)

Consolidated Electric Coop Inc ...... D 419 947-3055
Mount Gilead (G-14725)

County of Montgomery .... E 937 225-4010
Dayton (G-9329)

Enon Firemans Association .... E 937 864-7429
Enon (G-10608)

Hirzel Canning Company .... D 419 693-0531
Northwood (G-15395)

Interstate Contractors LLC .... E 513 372-5393
Mason (G-13601)

Mahoning Clmbana Training Assn ...... E 330 747-5639
Youngstown (G-20104)

Mid-Ohio Regional Plg Comm .... D 614 228-2663
Columbus (G-8077)

National Hot Rod Association .... C 740 928-5706
Hebron (G-11722)

Odd Fellows Hall .... E 440 599-7973
Conneaut (G-8957)

Ohio Assn Pub Treasurers .... C 937 415-2237
Vandalia (G-18534)

Ohio Bliffs Crt Officers Assn .... D 419 354-9302
Bowling Green (G-1743)

Ohio Civil Service Employees A ....D 614 865-4700
  Westerville (G-19195)
Ohio Department of Commerce ....C 614 728-8400
  Columbus (G-8238)
Ohio Farm Bur Federation Inc ....D 614 249-2400
  Columbus (G-8258)
Ross County YMCA ....D 740 772-4340
  Chillicothe (G-2823)
Service Corps Retired Execs ....E 216 522-4194
  Cleveland (G-6398)
Service Corps Retired Execs ....E 419 259-7598
  Toledo (G-18026)
Southeast Area Law Enforcement ....E 216 475-1234
  Bedford (G-1308)
Superior Clay Corp ....D 740 922-4122
  Uhrichsville (G-18344)
Town of Canal Fulton ....E 330 854-9448
  Canal Fulton (G-2098)
Union Rural Electric Coop Inc ....E 937 642-1826
  Marysville (G-13535)
Universal Advertising Assoc ....E 513 522-5000
  Cincinnati (G-4693)
Village of Antwerp ....E 419 258-7422
  Antwerp (G-615)

ASSOCIATIONS: Dentists'

Dental Support Specialties LLC ....E 330 639-1333
  Uniontown (G-18366)

ASSOCIATIONS: Engineering

Society Plastics Engineers Inc ....C 419 287-4898
  Pemberville (G-15807)

ASSOCIATIONS: Fraternal

Beta RHO House Assoc Kappa ....D 513 221-1280
  Cincinnati (G-3045)
Bpo Elks of USA ....E 740 622-0794
  Coshocton (G-9000)
Delta Gamma Fraternity ....E 614 481-8169
  Upper Arlington (G-18396)
Enon Firemans Association ....E 937 864-7429
  Enon (G-10608)
Fraternal Order Eagles Inc ....E 330 477-8059
  Canton (G-2316)
Fraternal Order Eagles Inc ....E 419 738-2582
  Wapakoneta (G-18642)
Fraternal Order Eagles Inc ....E 419 332-3961
  Fremont (G-11075)
Fraternal Order Eagles Inc ....E 440 293-5997
  Andover (G-606)
Fraternal Order of Eagles ....E 937 323-0671
  Springfield (G-17040)
Fraternal Order of Eagles BR ....E 419 636-7812
  Bryan (G-1957)
Fraternal Order of Police of O ....E 614 224-5700
  Columbus (G-7621)
Grand Aerie of The Fraternal ....E 419 227-1566
  Lima (G-12647)
Hamilton Lodge 93 Benevolant P ....E 513 887-4384
  Liberty Twp (G-12586)
Ioof Home of Ohio Inc ....C 419 352-3014
  Bowling Green (G-1737)
Knights of Columbus ....E 937 890-2971
  Dayton (G-9549)
Knights of Columbus ....E 419 628-2089
  Minster (G-14537)
Knights of Columbus ....D 740 382-3671
  Marion (G-13428)
Louisville Frternal Order of E ....E 330 875-2113
  Louisville (G-12968)
Maumee Lodge No 1850 Bnvlt ....E 419 893-7272
  Maumee (G-13817)
New Boston Aerie 2271 FOE ....E 740 456-0171
  New Boston (G-14881)
Order of Unite Commercial Tra ....D 614 487-9680
  Columbus (G-8385)
Polish American Citizens Club ....E 330 253-0496
  Akron (G-388)
Portsmouth Lodge 154 B P O E ....E 740 353-1013
  Portsmouth (G-16160)
Schlee Malt House Condo Assn ....E 614 463-1999
  Columbus (G-8600)

ASSOCIATIONS: Homeowners

Apple Vly Property Owners Assn ....E 740 397-3311
  Howard (G-11939)
Lake Mhawk Prperty Owners Assn ....E 330 863-0000
  Malvern (G-13125)

Lake Wynoka Prprty Owners Assn ....E 937 446-3774
  Lake Waynoka (G-12328)
Mills Creek Association ....E 440 327-5336
  North Ridgeville (G-15337)
Muirfield Association Inc ....E 614 889-0922
  Dublin (G-10283)

ASSOCIATIONS: Parent Teacher

Barrington Elem School Pto ....D 614 487-5180
  Upper Arlington (G-18395)
Bridgetown Middle School Pta ....D 513 574-3511
  Cincinnati (G-3074)
Buckeye Vly E Elementary Pto ....D 740 747-2266
  Ashley (G-701)
Clearmount Elementary School ....E 330 497-5640
  Canton (G-2258)
Goldwood Primary School Pta ....E 440 356-6720
  Rocky River (G-16434)
Heritage Pto ....E 330 636-4400
  Medina (G-13948)
Norwich Elementary Pto ....E 614 921-6000
  Hilliard (G-11801)
Oakdale Elementary Pta ....D 513 574-1100
  Cincinnati (G-4144)
Poland Middle School Pto ....E 330 757-7003
  Youngstown (G-20163)
Pta OH Cong McVay Elem Pta ....E 614 797-7230
  Westerville (G-19295)
Pta Ohio Cngrss - Msn Elem Pta ....E 330 588-2156
  Canton (G-2445)
Pta Olms Falls Int Sch ....E 440 427-6500
  Olmsted Twp (G-15540)

ASSOCIATIONS: Real Estate Management

Al Neyer LLC ....E 513 271-6400
  Cincinnati (G-2917)
American Bulk Commodities Inc ....C 330 758-0841
  Youngstown (G-19953)
Capital Properties MGT Ltd ....E 216 991-3057
  Cleveland (G-5120)
Cleveland Real Estate Partners ....E 216 623-1600
  Cleveland (G-5283)
E M Columbus LLC ....E 614 861-3232
  Columbus (G-7484)
Eagle Realty Group LLC ....E 513 361-7700
  Cincinnati (G-3469)
Executive Properties Inc ....E 330 376-4037
  Akron (G-206)
Fairfield Homes Inc ....E 740 653-3583
  Lancaster (G-12396)
First Realty Property MGT Ltd ....E 440 720-0100
  Mayfield Village (G-13885)
Fleetwood Management Inc ....E 614 538-1277
  Columbus (G-7595)
Forest City Commercial MGT Inc ....C 216 621-6060
  Cleveland (G-5552)
Forest Cy Residential MGT Inc ....C 216 621-6060
  Cleveland (G-5563)
G H A Inc ....E 440 729-2130
  Chesterland (G-2739)
G J Goudreau & Co ....E 216 351-5233
  Cleveland (G-5586)
Hallmark Management Associates ....E 216 681-0080
  Cleveland (G-5658)
I H S Services Inc ....E 419 224-8811
  Lima (G-12663)
Investek Realty LLC ....E 419 873-1236
  Perrysburg (G-15881)
Irg Realty Advisors LLC ....E 330 659-4060
  Richfield (G-16361)
John Dellagnese & Assoc Inc ....E 330 668-4000
  Akron (G-292)
John Stewart Company ....D 513 703-5412
  Cincinnati (G-3824)
Kaval-Levine Management Co ....E 440 944-5402
  Willoughby Hills (G-19590)
Kencor Properties Inc ....E 513 984-3870
  Cincinnati (G-3857)
Kettering Medical Center ....D 937 866-2984
  Miamisburg (G-14182)
Klingbeil Management Group Co ....E 614 220-8900
  Columbus (G-7911)
L J F Management Inc ....E 513 688-0104
  Blue Ash (G-1593)
L O M Inc ....E 216 363-6009
  Cleveland (G-5843)
Marion Plaza Inc ....D 330 747-2661
  Niles (G-15158)
Miller-Vlentine Operations Inc ....E 937 293-0900
  Dayton (G-9638)

Miller-Vlentine Operations Inc ....A 513 771-0900
  Dayton (G-9639)
Model Group Inc ....E 513 559-0048
  Cincinnati (G-4068)
Morelia Consultants LLC ....D 513 469-1500
  Cincinnati (G-4072)
North American Properties Inc ....E 513 721-2744
  Cincinnati (G-4125)
Oakwood Management Company ....E 614 866-8702
  Reynoldsburg (G-16322)
Olmsted Residence Corporation ....C 440 235-7100
  Olmsted Twp (G-15539)
Pache Management Company Inc ....E 614 451-5919
  Columbus (G-8409)
Paran Management Company Ltd ....E 216 921-5663
  Cleveland (G-6162)
Pizzuti Inc ....E 614 280-4000
  Columbus (G-8450)
Plaza Properties Inc ....E 614 237-3726
  Columbus (G-8455)
Preferred RE Investments LLC ....E 614 901-2400
  Westerville (G-19202)
Real Property Management Inc ....E 614 766-6500
  Dublin (G-10320)
Red Brick Property MGT LLC ....E 513 524-9340
  Oxford (G-15689)
Reuben Co ....E 419 241-3400
  Toledo (G-18005)
Rlj Management Co Inc ....C 614 942-2020
  Columbus (G-8540)
Rose Community Management LLC ....C 917 542-3600
  Independence (G-12118)
RPM Midwest LLC ....E 513 762-9000
  Cincinnati (G-4407)
Schottenstein RE Group LLC ....E 614 418-8900
  Columbus (G-8608)
Schroeder Company ....E 419 473-3139
  Toledo (G-18021)
STS Restaurant Management Inc ....D 419 246-0730
  Toledo (G-18051)
T & R Properties ....E 614 923-4000
  Dublin (G-10351)
Tolson Enterprises Inc ....E 419 843-6465
  Toledo (G-18104)
Towne Properties Assoc Inc ....E 513 489-4059
  Cincinnati (G-4619)
United Management Inc ....E 513 936-8568
  Cincinnati (G-4682)
Wallick Properties Midwest LLC ....C 614 539-9041
  Grove City (G-11482)
Wallick Properties Midwest LLC ....A 419 381-7477
  New Albany (G-14878)
West-Way Management Company ....E 440 250-1851
  Westlake (G-19423)
Weston Inc ....E 440 349-9001
  Solon (G-16914)
Whitehurst Company ....E 419 865-0799
  Maumee (G-13868)
Zaremba Group Incorporated ....E 216 221-6600
  Cleveland (G-6708)
Zaremba Group LLC ....C 216 221-6600
  Lakewood (G-12366)

ASSOCIATIONS: Trade

American Jersey Cattle Assn ....E 614 861-3636
  Reynoldsburg (G-16282)
Buckeye Power Inc ....E 614 781-0573
  Columbus (G-7089)
Greater Clvland Halthcare Assn ....D 216 696-6900
  Cleveland (G-5640)
Gs1 Us Inc ....D 609 620-0200
  Dayton (G-9478)
National All-Jersey Inc ....E 614 861-3636
  Reynoldsburg (G-16321)
National Ground Water Assn Inc ....E 614 898-7791
  Westerville (G-19284)
New Waterford Fireman ....E 330 457-2363
  New Waterford (G-15006)
Ohio Association Realtors Inc ....E 614 228-6675
  Columbus (G-8230)
Ohio Rural Electric Coops Inc ....E 614 846-5757
  Columbus (G-8283)
Precision Metalforming Assn ....E 216 241-1482
  Independence (G-12110)
United States Trotting Assn ....D 614 224-2291
  Westerville (G-19304)
Vigilant Global Trade Svcs LLC ....E 260 417-1825
  Shaker Heights (G-16719)

ATHLETIC CLUB & GYMNASIUMS, MEMBERSHIP

Cincinnati Sports Mall Inc ....D...... 513 527-4000
Cincinnati (G-3269)
Friars Club Inc.......................................D...... 513 488-8777
Cincinnati (G-3594)
Life Time Fitness Inc ....E...... 513 234-0660
Mason (G-13611)
Young Mens Christian Associat ....E 513 731-0115
Cincinnati (G-4813)

ATHLETIC EQPT INSPECTION SVCS

Side Effects Inc ....E 937 704-9696
Franklin (G-11039)

ATHLETIC ORGANIZATION

Center For Health Affairs ....D...... 800 362-2628
Cleveland (G-5152)
Oberlin College ....E...... 440 775-8500
Oberlin (G-15514)
Professnal Glfers Assn of Amer ....E......419 882-3197
Sylvania (G-17442)
United Sttes Bowl Congress Inc ....D...... 740 922-3120
Uhrichsville (G-18347)
United Sttes Bowl Congress Inc ....D...... 513 761-3338
Cincinnati (G-4688)
United Sttes Bowl Congress Inc ....D...... 419 531-4058
Toledo (G-18121)
United Sttes Bowl Congress Inc ....D...... 614 237-3716
Columbus (G-8813)
University of Cincinnati...........................C...... 513 556-4603
Cincinnati (G-4718)

ATOMIZERS

Cr Brands Inc ....D...... 513 860-5039
West Chester (G-18905)

AUCTION SVCS: Livestock

Barnesville Livestock Sales Co ....E 740 425-3611
Barnesville (G-976)
Mt Hope Auction Inc ....E 330 674-6188
Mount Hope (G-14737)
Muskingum Livestock Sales Inc ....E 740 452-9984
Zanesville (G-20339)
United Producers Inc ....E 937 456-4161
Eaton (G-10464)
United Producers Inc ....C...... 614 433-2150
Columbus (G-8809)

AUCTION SVCS: Motor Vehicle

ABC Detroit/Toledo Auto Auctn ....E 419 872-0872
Perrysburg (G-15832)
Adesa Corporation LLC..........................C...... 937 746-5361
Franklin (G-11021)
Adesa-Ohio Llc ....C...... 330 467-8280
Northfield (G-15372)
Auction Broadcasting Co LLC.................C...... 419 872-0872
Perrysburg (G-15833)
Columbus Fair Auto Auction Inc ....A...... 614 497-2000
Obetz (G-15525)
Copart Inc ....E...... 614 497-1590
Columbus (G-7367)
Cox Automotive Inc ....C...... 513 874-9310
West Chester (G-18904)
Cox Automotive Inc ....B...... 614 871-2771
Grove City (G-11423)
Gallipolis Auto Auction Inc ....E...... 740 446-1576
Gallipolis (G-11193)
Greater Cleveland Auto Auction ....D...... 216 433-7777
Cleveland (G-5634)
Montpelier Auto Auction Ohio ....C...... 419 485-1691
Montpelier (G-14614)
Value Auto Auction LLC..........................D...... 740 982-3030
Crooksville (G-9064)

AUCTIONEERS: Fee Basis

Auction Services Inc ....A...... 614 497-2000
Obetz (G-15522)
Baker Bnngson Rlty Auctioneers ....E......419 547-7777
Clyde (G-6740)
Kidron Auction Inc ....E...... 330 857-2641
Kidron (G-12307)
Kramer & Kramer Inc ....E...... 937 456-1101
Eaton (G-10448)
Mt Hope Auction Inc ....E...... 330 674-6188
Mount Hope (G-14737)

Oki Auction LLC......................................D...... 513 679-7910
Cincinnati (G-4165)
Skipco Financial Adjusters ....D...... 330 854-4800
Canal Fulton (G-2097)
Tri Green Interstate Equipment ....E...... 614 879-7731
London (G-12876)

AUDIO & VIDEO EQPT, EXC COMMERCIAL

Pioneer Automotive Tech Inc.................C...... 937 746-2293
Springboro (G-16982)
Tech Products Corporation.....................E...... 937 438-1100
Miamisburg (G-14227)

AUDIO & VIDEO TAPES WHOLESALERS

Killer Spotscom Inc ....D...... 513 201-1380
Cincinnati (G-3869)

AUDIO-VISUAL PROGRAM PRODUCTION SVCS

Bkg Holdings LLC....................................E...... 614 252-7455
Columbus (G-7042)
Intgrted Bridge Communications ....E 513 381-1380
Cincinnati (G-3782)
Pagetech Ltd ....E...... 614 238-0518
Columbus (G-8412)
Ron Foth Retail Inc ....E...... 614 888-7771
Columbus (G-8547)
Universal Technology Corp ....D...... 937 426-2808
Beavercreek (G-1193)

AUDITING SVCS

City of Wellston......................................D...... 740 384-2428
Wellston (G-18848)
Protiviti Inc ....E...... 216 696-6010
Cleveland (G-6262)

AUTO & HOME SUPPLY STORES: Auto & Truck Eqpt & Parts

Allstate Trk Sls of Estrn OH ....E...... 330 339-5555
New Philadelphia (G-14945)
Dutro Ford Lincoln-Mercury Inc ....D...... 740 452-6334
Zanesville (G-20301)
MJ Auto Parts Inc...................................E...... 440 205-6272
Mentor (G-14088)
Pete Baur Buick Gmc Inc ....E...... 440 238-5600
Cleveland (G-6200)
Stricker Bros Inc ....E...... 513 732-1152
Batavia (G-1010)

AUTO & HOME SUPPLY STORES: Automotive Access

Cox Automotive Inc ....B...... 614 871-2771
Grove City (G-11423)
H & H Auto Parts Inc ....E...... 330 494-2975
Canton (G-2333)
Jim Hayden Inc.......................................D...... 513 563-8828
Cincinnati (G-3819)

AUTO & HOME SUPPLY STORES: Automotive parts

Bridgeport Auto Parts Inc ....E...... 740 635-0441
Bridgeport (G-1814)
Car Parts Warehouse Inc ....E...... 216 281-4500
Brookpark (G-1892)
Cole-Valley Motor Co ....D...... 330 372-1665
Warren (G-18685)
Crown Dielectric Inds Inc ....C...... 614 224-5161
Columbus (G-7397)
Dave Dnnis Chrysler Jeep Dodge ....E...... 937 429-5566
Beavercreek Township (G-1245)
Four Wheel Drive Hardware LLC ....D...... 330 482-4733
Columbiana (G-6788)
General Parts Inc ....E...... 614 267-5197
Columbus (G-7653)
Greenleaf Ohio LLC ....E...... 330 832-6001
Massillon (G-13690)
H & H Auto Parts Inc ....D...... 330 456-4778
Canton (G-2332)
Haasz Automall LLC ....D...... 330 296-2866
Ravenna (G-16245)
Hahn Automotive Warehouse Inc ....E...... 937 223-1068
Dayton (G-9483)
Hamilton Automotive Warehouse..........D...... 513 896-4100
Hamilton (G-11607)

Jegs Automotive Inc ....C...... 614 294-5050
Delaware (G-9990)
Joseph Russo ....E...... 440 748-2690
Grafton (G-11317)
K - O - I Warehouse Inc ....E...... 937 323-5585
Springfield (G-17058)
K-M-S Industries Inc ....E...... 440 243-6680
Brookpark (G-1899)
Man-Tansky Inc ....E...... 740 454-2512
Zanesville (G-20328)
Ohio Auto Supply Company ....D...... 330 454-5105
Canton (G-2424)
Pat Young Service Co Inc.......................E...... 216 447-8550
Cleveland (G-6180)
Pep Boys - Manny Moe & Jack ....E...... 614 864-2092
Columbus (G-8438)
Santmyer Oil Co Inc................................D...... 330 262-6501
Wooster (G-19764)
Smyth Automotive Inc ....D...... 513 528-2800
Cincinnati (G-4496)
Smyth Automotive Inc ....D...... 513 528-0061
Cincinnati (G-4497)
Snyders Antique Auto Parts Inc ....E...... 330 549-5313
New Springfield (G-14998)
Stoops Frghtlnr-Qlity Trlr Inc ....E...... 937 236-4092
Dayton (G-9795)
Voss Toyota Inc ....E...... 937 431-2100
Beavercreek (G-1195)

AUTO & HOME SUPPLY STORES: Batteries, Automotive & Truck

OReilly Automotive Inc...........................D...... 330 494-0042
North Canton (G-15226)
OReilly Automotive Inc...........................E...... 419 630-0811
Bryan (G-1968)
OReilly Automotive Inc...........................E...... 330 318-3136
Boardman (G-1700)

AUTO & HOME SUPPLY STORES: Truck Eqpt & Parts

Bulldawg Holdings LLC............................E...... 419 423-3131
Findlay (G-10885)
Dales Truck Parts Inc ....E...... 937 766-2551
Cedarville (G-2580)
Esec Corporation ....E...... 614 875-3732
Grove City (G-11430)
Helton Enterprises Inc ....E...... 419 423-4180
Findlay (G-10922)
Hill Intl Trcks NA LLC ....D...... 330 386-6440
East Liverpool (G-10404)
Kaffenbarger Truck Eqp Co ....E...... 513 772-6800
Cincinnati (G-3846)
Palmer Trucks Inc ....E...... 937 235-3318
Dayton (G-9683)
Perkins Motor Service Ltd.......................E...... 440 277-1256
Lorain (G-12938)
Premier Truck Parts Inc ....E...... 216 642-5000
Cleveland (G-6233)
Transport Specialists Inc ....E...... 513 771-2220
Cincinnati (G-4628)
Valley Ford Truck Inc ....D...... 216 524-2400
Cleveland (G-6617)
Western Branch Diesel Inc......................E...... 330 454-8800
Canton (G-2534)
Wz Management Inc.................................E...... 330 628-4881
Akron (G-506)

AUTO SPLYS & PARTS, NEW, WHSLE: Exhaust Sys, Mufflers, Etc

P & M Exhaust Systems Whse.................E...... 513 825-2660
Cincinnati (G-4195)

AUTOMATED TELLER MACHINE NETWORK

PNC Bank-Atm ....E...... 937 865-6800
Miamisburg (G-14206)

AUTOMATED TELLER MACHINE OR ATM REPAIR SVCS

Atm Solutions Inc ....D...... 513 742-4900
Cincinnati (G-3000)
Cbord Group Inc ....C...... 330 498-2702
Uniontown (G-18362)

AUTOMATIC REGULATING CONTROL:
Building Svcs Monitoring, Auto

Evokes LLC ....E 513 947-8433
  Mason *(G-13578)*

AUTOMATIC TELLER MACHINES:
Wholesalers

Continuum Inc ....E 614 891-9200
  Westerville *(G-19246)*

AUTOMOBILE FINANCE LEASING

BMW Financial Services Na LLC ....E 614 718-6900
  Hilliard *(G-11747)*
BMW Financial Services Na LLC ....C 614 718-6900
  Dublin *(G-10148)*
Ford Motor Company ....E 513 573-1101
  Mason *(G-13580)*
Kempthorn Motors Inc ....D 330 452-6511
  Canton *(G-2366)*
Keybank National Association ....B 800 539-2968
  Cleveland *(G-5827)*
Kings Cove Automotive LLC ....E 513 677-0177
  Fairfield *(G-10744)*
Klaben Leasing and Sales Inc ....D 330 673-9971
  Kent *(G-12245)*
Security Nat Auto Accptnce LLC ....C 513 459-8118
  Mason *(G-13637)*

AUTOMOBILE RECOVERY SVCS

Almost Family Inc ....E 513 662-3400
  Cincinnati *(G-2930)*
Quadax Inc ....E 330 759-4600
  Youngstown *(G-20170)*
Tbn Acquisition LLC ....D 740 653-2091
  Lancaster *(G-12441)*
West Corporation ....B 330 574-0510
  Niles *(G-15174)*

AUTOMOBILE STORAGE GARAGE

Chillicothe City School Dst ....E 740 775-2936
  Chillicothe *(G-2760)*
City of New Philadelphia ....E 330 339-2121
  New Philadelphia *(G-14950)*
Dasher Lawless Automation LLC ....E 855 755-7275
  Warren *(G-18699)*
United Parcel Service Inc OH ....C 419 424-9494
  Findlay *(G-10972)*

AUTOMOBILES & OTHER MOTOR VEHICLES WHOLESALERS

1106 West Main Inc ....E 330 673-2122
  Kent *(G-12212)*
Abers Garage Inc ....E 419 281-5500
  Ashland *(G-644)*
Akron Auto Auction Inc ....C 330 724-7708
  Coventry Township *(G-9032)*
Baker Vehicle Systems Inc ....E 330 467-2250
  Macedonia *(G-13061)*
Bobb Automotive Inc ....E 614 853-3000
  Columbus *(G-7052)*
Chuck Nicholson Pntc-GMC Trcks ....E 330 343-7781
  Dover *(G-10069)*
Coughlin Chevrolet Inc ....D 740 964-9191
  Pataskala *(G-15784)*
Dave Knapp Ford Lincoln Inc ....E 937 547-3000
  Greenville *(G-11373)*
Donley Ford-Lincoln Inc ....E 419 281-3673
  Ashland *(G-672)*
Dons Automotive Group LLC ....E 419 337-3010
  Wauseon *(G-18799)*
Dons Brooklyn Chevrolet Inc ....E 216 741-1500
  Cleveland *(G-5441)*
Doug Bigelow Chevrolet Inc ....D 330 644-7500
  Akron *(G-192)*
Doug Marine Motors Inc ....E 740 335-3700
  Wshngtn CT Hs *(G-19869)*
Downtown Ford Lincoln Inc ....D 330 456-2781
  Canton *(G-2290)*
Dutro Ford Lincoln-Mercury Inc ....D 740 452-6334
  Zanesville *(G-20301)*
Ed Schmidt Auto Inc ....C 419 874-4331
  Perrysburg *(G-15863)*
Ed Tomko Chryslr Jep Dge Inc ....E 440 835-5900
  Avon Lake *(G-916)*
Gene Stevens Auto & Truck Ctr ....E 419 429-2000
  Findlay *(G-10913)*

George P Ballas Buick GMC Trck ....D 419 535-1000
  Toledo *(G-17760)*
Graham Chevrolet-Cadillac Co ....D 419 989-4012
  Ontario *(G-15551)*
Haydocy Automotive Inc ....D 614 279-8880
  Columbus *(G-7719)*
Hidy Motors Inc ....D 937 426-9564
  Dayton *(G-9176)*
Interstate Truckway Inc ....E 614 771-1220
  Columbus *(G-7839)*
Klaben Lincoln Ford Inc ....D 330 673-3139
  Kent *(G-12246)*
Laria Chevrolet-Buick Inc ....E 330 925-2015
  Rittman *(G-16406)*
McCluskey Chevrolet Inc ....C 513 761-1111
  Cincinnati *(G-3986)*
Mullinax East LLC ....D 440 296-3020
  Wickliffe *(G-19470)*
National Car Mart III Inc ....E 216 398-2228
  Cleveland *(G-6038)*
Rush Truck Centers Ohio Inc ....D 513 733-8500
  Cincinnati *(G-4414)*
Rush Truck Centers Ohio Inc ....E 419 224-6045
  Lima *(G-12735)*
Sims Buick-G M C Truck Inc ....D 330 372-3500
  Warren *(G-18744)*
Slimans Sales & Service Inc ....E 440 988-4484
  Amherst *(G-597)*
South East Chevrolet Co ....E 440 585-9300
  Willoughby Hills *(G-19594)*
Stoops Frghtlnr-Qlity Trlr Inc ....E 937 236-4092
  Dayton *(G-9795)*
Stratton Chevrolet Co ....D 330 537-3151
  Beloit *(G-1398)*
Valley Ford Truck Inc ....D 216 524-2400
  Valley View *(G-6617)*
Village Motors Inc ....D 330 674-2055
  Millersburg *(G-14498)*
Voss Auto Network Inc ....E 937 428-2447
  Dayton *(G-9860)*
Voss Chevrolet Inc ....C 937 428-2500
  Dayton *(G-9862)*
Voss Dodge ....E 937 435-7800
  Dayton *(G-9863)*
Warner Buick-Nissan Inc ....E 419 423-7161
  Findlay *(G-10974)*
White Family Companies Inc ....C 937 222-3701
  Dayton *(G-9879)*

AUTOMOBILES: Wholesalers

Albert Mike Leasing Inc ....C 513 563-1400
  Cincinnati *(G-2919)*
Beechmont Motors Inc ....E 513 388-3883
  Cincinnati *(G-3031)*
Beechmont Toyota Inc ....D 513 388-3800
  Cincinnati *(G-3034)*
Broadvue Motors Inc ....D 440 845-6000
  Cleveland *(G-5084)*
Central Hummr East ....E 216 514-2700
  Cleveland *(G-5155)*
Honda North America Inc ....D 937 642-5000
  Marysville *(G-13504)*
Medina Management Company LLC ....D 330 723-3291
  Medina *(G-13976)*
Midwest Motors Inc ....E 330 758-5800
  Youngstown *(G-20128)*
Stykemain Pntiac-Buick-Gmc Ltd ....D 419 784-5252
  Defiance *(G-9942)*

AUTOMOTIVE & TRUCK GENERAL REPAIR SVC

Abraham Ford LLC ....E 440 233-7402
  Elyria *(G-10477)*
Advantage Ford Lincoln Mercury ....D 419 334-9751
  Fremont *(G-11056)*
Ashtabula Area City School Dst ....D 440 992-1221
  Ashtabula *(G-705)*
Auto Center USA Inc ....E 513 683-4900
  Cincinnati *(G-3006)*
Beechmont Ford Inc ....C 513 752-6611
  Cincinnati *(G-2842)*
Bill Delord Autocenter Inc ....D 513 932-3000
  Lebanon *(G-12452)*
Bob-Boyd Ford Inc ....D 614 860-0606
  Lancaster *(G-12372)*
Bowling Green Lncln-Mrcury Inc ....D 419 352-2553
  Bowling Green *(G-1722)*
Brentlinger Enterprises ....C 614 889-2571
  Dublin *(G-10150)*

Brondes Ford ....D 419 473-1411
  Toledo *(G-17627)*
Brown Motor Sales Co ....E 419 531-0151
  Toledo *(G-17629)*
Burtons Collision ....E 513 984-3396
  Cincinnati *(G-3094)*
Cain Motors Inc ....E 330 494-5588
  Canton *(G-2225)*
Cascade Group Inc ....E 330 929-1861
  Cuyahoga Falls *(G-9077)*
Central Cadillac Limited ....E 216 861-5800
  Cleveland *(G-5153)*
Chillicothe City School Dst ....E 740 775-2936
  Chillicothe *(G-2760)*
City of Berea ....E 440 826-5853
  Berea *(G-1418)*
Classic International Inc ....D 440 975-1222
  Mentor *(G-14030)*
Cole-Valley Motor Co ....D 330 372-1665
  Warren *(G-18685)*
Columbus SAI Motors LLC ....E 614 851-3273
  Columbus *(G-7312)*
Conrads Tire Service Inc ....E 216 941-3333
  Cleveland *(G-5334)*
Coughlin Chevrolet Inc ....D 740 964-9191
  Pataskala *(G-15784)*
County Engineering Office ....E 419 334-9731
  Fremont *(G-11064)*
County Engineers Office ....E 740 702-3130
  Chillicothe *(G-2771)*
County of Lorain ....D 440 326-5880
  Elyria *(G-10500)*
Crestmont Cadillac Corporation ....E 216 831-5300
  Cleveland *(G-5380)*
Dan Tobin Pontiac Buick GMC ....D 614 889-6300
  Columbus *(G-7412)*
Dave Dnnis Chrysler Jeep Dodge ....E 937 429-5566
  Beavercreek Township *(G-1245)*
Dave White Chevrolet Inc ....E 419 885-4444
  Sylvania *(G-17417)*
Dcr Systems LLC ....E 440 205-9900
  Mentor *(G-14039)*
Decosky Motor Holdings Inc ....E 740 397-9122
  Mount Vernon *(G-14762)*
Delaware City School District ....E 740 363-5901
  Delaware *(G-9967)*
Don Wood Inc ....D 740 593-6641
  Athens *(G-776)*
Don Wood Inc ....E 740 593-6641
  Athens *(G-777)*
Donnell Ford-Lincoln ....E 330 332-0031
  Salem *(G-16542)*
Doug Bigelow Chevrolet Inc ....D 330 644-7500
  Akron *(G-192)*
Doug Marine Motors Inc ....E 740 335-3700
  Wshngtn CT Hs *(G-19869)*
Downtheroad Inc ....E 740 452-4579
  Zanesville *(G-20300)*
Downtown Ford Lincoln Inc ....D 330 456-2781
  Canton *(G-2290)*
Dunning Motor Sales Inc ....E 740 439-4465
  Cambridge *(G-2064)*
Dutro Ford Lincoln-Mercury Inc ....D 740 452-6334
  Zanesville *(G-20301)*
Ed Mullinax Ford LLC ....C 440 984-2431
  Amherst *(G-584)*
Ed Schmidt Auto Inc ....C 419 874-4331
  Perrysburg *(G-15863)*
Ed Tomko Chryslr Jep Dge Inc ....E 440 835-5900
  Avon Lake *(G-916)*
Family Ford Lincoln Inc ....D 740 373-9127
  Marietta *(G-13328)*
FCA US LLC ....E 419 727-2800
  Toledo *(G-17728)*
Flagship Services of Ohio Inc ....D 740 533-1657
  Ironton *(G-12153)*
Germain On Scarborough LLC ....C 614 868-0300
  Columbus *(G-7665)*
Giles Marathon Inc ....E 440 974-8815
  Mentor *(G-14051)*
Glenway Automotive Service ....E 513 921-2117
  Cincinnati *(G-3620)*
Goodyear Tire & Rubber Company ....A 330 796-2121
  Akron *(G-242)*
Greenwood Chevrolet Inc ....C 330 270-1299
  Youngstown *(G-20057)*
Greenwoods Hubbard Chevy-Olds ....E 330 568-4335
  Hubbard *(G-11946)*
Greg Ford Sweet Inc ....E 440 593-7714
  North Kingsville *(G-15257)*

SERVICES

Grismer Tire Company ....E...... 937 643-2526	Matia Motors Inc ....E 440 365-7311	Valentine Buick Gmc Inc ....D...... 937 878-7371
Centerville *(G-2626)*	Elyria *(G-10534)*	Fairborn *(G-10686)*
Grogans Towne Chrysler Inc ......D...... 419 476-0761	May Jim Auto Sales LLC ....E...... 419 422-9797	Vin Devers ....C 888 847-9535
Toledo *(G-17772)*	Findlay *(G-10940)*	Sylvania *(G-17462)*
Guess Motors Inc ....E...... 866 890-0522	Medina World Cars Inc ....E...... 330 725-4901	Volvo BMW Dyton Evans Volkswag ......E...... 937 890-6200
Carrollton *(G-2571)*	Strongsville *(G-17332)*	Dayton *(G-9859)*
Haydocy Automotive Inc ....D...... 614 279-8880	Mike Castrucci Ford ....C...... 513 831-7010	Voss Auto Network Inc ....E...... 937 428-2447
Columbus *(G-7719)*	Milford *(G-14410)*	Dayton *(G-9860)*
Hill Intl Trcks NA LLC ....D...... 330 386-6440	Monro Inc ....D...... 440 835-2393	Voss Toyota Inc ....E...... 937 431-2100
East Liverpool *(G-10404)*	Westlake *(G-19375)*	Beavercreek *(G-1195)*
Hoss Value Cars & Trucks Inc ......E...... 937 428-2400	Montrose Ford Inc ....D...... 330 666-0711	Wagner Lincoln-Mercury Inc ....E...... 419 435-8131
Dayton *(G-9507)*	Fairlawn *(G-10842)*	Carey *(G-2550)*
I-75 Pierson Automotive Inc ....E...... 513 424-1881	Morris Cadillac Buick GMC ....E...... 440 327-4181	Walker Auto Group Inc ....D...... 937 433-4950
Middletown *(G-14350)*	North Olmsted *(G-15298)*	Miamisburg *(G-14236)*
Irace Inc ....E...... 330 836-7247	Mullinax East LLC ....D...... 440 296-3020	Warner Buick-Nissan Inc ....E...... 419 423-7161
Akron *(G-281)*	Wickliffe *(G-19470)*	Findlay *(G-10974)*
Jake Sweeney Automotive Inc ......C...... 513 782-2800	Nassief Automotive Inc ....E...... 440 997-5151	Young Truck Sales Inc ....E...... 330 477-6271
Cincinnati *(G-3805)*	Austinburg *(G-853)*	Canton *(G-2541)*
Jerry Haag Motors Inc ....E...... 937 402-2090	National Auto Experts LLC ....E...... 440 274-5114	Youngstown-Kenworth Inc ....E...... 330 534-9761
Hillsboro *(G-11848)*	Strongsville *(G-17336)*	Hubbard *(G-11952)*
Jim Brown Chevrolet Inc ....E...... 440 255-5511	Nick Mayer Lincoln-Mercury Inc ......E...... 440 835-3700	Zanesville Chevrolet Cadillac ....E...... 740 452-3611
Mentor *(G-14066)*	Westlake *(G-19379)*	Zanesville *(G-20381)*
Jim Keim Ford ....D...... 614 888-3333	Northern Automotive Inc ....E...... 614 436-2001	Zender Electric ....E...... 419 436-1538
Columbus *(G-7859)*	Columbus *(G-8200)*	Fostoria *(G-11015)*
Joe Dodge Kidd Inc ....E...... 513 752-1804	Northgate Chrysler Jeep Inc ....D...... 513 385-3900	
Cincinnati *(G-2858)*	Cincinnati *(G-4129)*	## AUTOMOTIVE BATTERIES WHOLESALERS
Joseph Chevrolet Oldsmobile Co ......C...... 513 741-6700	Ohio Automobile Club ....E...... 614 559-0000	
Cincinnati *(G-3833)*	Columbus *(G-8231)*	Bills Battery Company Inc ....E...... 513 922-0100
Joseph Russo ....E...... 440 748-2690	Oregon Ford Inc ....C...... 419 698-4444	Cincinnati *(G-3050)*
Grafton *(G-11317)*	Oregon *(G-15605)*	Hankook Tire America Corp ....E...... 330 896-6199
Jtekt Auto Tenn Morristown ....C...... 440 835-1000	OReilly Automotive Inc ....E...... 513 783-1343	Uniontown *(G-18373)*
Westlake *(G-19362)*	Middletown *(G-14317)*	
Kempthorn Motors Inc ....C...... 800 451-3877	OReilly Automotive Inc ....E...... 330 267-4383	## AUTOMOTIVE BODY SHOP
Canton *(G-2365)*	Hartville *(G-11696)*	
Kennedy Mint Inc ....D...... 440 572-3222	OReilly Automotive Inc ....E...... 513 800-1169	American Nat Fleet Svc Inc ....D...... 216 447-6060
Cleveland *(G-5824)*	Cincinnati *(G-4180)*	Cleveland *(G-4961)*
Kent Automotive Inc ....E...... 330 678-5520	OReilly Automotive Inc ....E...... 513 818-4166	Bakers Cllsion Repr Specialist ....E...... 419 524-1350
Kent *(G-12240)*	Cincinnati *(G-4181)*	Mansfield *(G-13138)*
Kenworth of Cincinnati Inc ....D...... 513 771-5831	Palmer Trucks Inc ....E...... 937 235-3318	Bauman Chrysler Jeep Dodge ....E...... 419 332-8291
Cincinnati *(G-3862)*	Dayton *(G-9683)*	Fremont *(G-11059)*
Kerns Chevrolet-Buick-Gmc Inc ......E...... 419 586-5131	Parrish Tire Company of Akron ......E...... 330 628-6800	Buddies Inc ....E...... 216 642-3362
Celina *(G-2597)*	Mogadore *(G-14554)*	Cleveland *(G-5100)*
Kerry Ford Inc ....D...... 513 671-6400	Pep Boys - Manny Moe & Jack ......E...... 614 864-2092	Burtons Collision ....E...... 513 984-3396
Cincinnati *(G-3864)*	Columbus *(G-8438)*	Cincinnati *(G-3094)*
Kings Toyota Inc ....D...... 513 583-4333	Progrssive Oldsmobile Cadillac ......E...... 330 833-8585	Busam Fairfield LLC ....E...... 513 771-8100
Cincinnati *(G-3874)*	Massillon *(G-13721)*	Fairfield *(G-10702)*
Klaben Family Dodge Inc ....E...... 330 673-9971	Ricart Ford Inc ....B...... 614 836-5321	Carls Body Shop Inc ....E...... 937 253-5166
Kent *(G-12244)*	Groveport *(G-11535)*	Dayton *(G-9280)*
Knox Auto LLC ....E...... 330 701-5266	Ron Marhofer Automall Inc ....E...... 330 923-5059	Cincinnati Collision Center ....E...... 513 984-4445
Mount Vernon *(G-14771)*	Cuyahoga Falls *(G-9122)*	Blue Ash *(G-1524)*
Krieger Ford Inc ....C...... 614 888-3320	Rondy Fleet Services Inc ....C...... 330 745-9016	Coughlin Chevrolet Inc ....E...... 740 852-1122
Columbus *(G-7927)*	Barberton *(G-965)*	London *(G-12862)*
Lakewood Chrysler-Plymouth ....E...... 216 521-1000	Roush Equipment Inc ....E...... 614 882-1535	Dave Dnnis Chrysler Jeep Dodge ......D...... 937 429-5566
Brookpark *(G-1901)*	Westerville *(G-19300)*	Beavercreek Township *(G-1245)*
Lakota Bus Garage ....E...... 419 986-5558	Rush Motor Sales Inc ....E...... 614 471-9980	Dent Magic ....E...... 614 864-3368
Kansas *(G-12208)*	Columbus *(G-8561)*	Columbus *(G-7435)*
Lane Chevrolet ....D...... 937 426-2313	Rush Truck Centers Ohio Inc ....D...... 513 733-8500	Eastside Body Shop ....E...... 513 624-1145
Beavercreek Township *(G-1252)*	Cincinnati *(G-4414)*	Cincinnati *(G-3478)*
Lang Chevrolet Co ....D...... 937 426-2313	Rush Truck Centers Ohio Inc ....E...... 419 224-6045	Excalibur Auto Body Inc ....E...... 440 942-5550
Beavercreek Township *(G-1253)*	Lima *(G-12735)*	Willowick *(G-19598)*
Lariche Subaru Inc ....D...... 419 422-1855	Schoner Chevrolet Inc ....E...... 330 877-6731	Franks Auto Body Shop Inc ....E...... 513 829-8282
Findlay *(G-10933)*	Hartville *(G-11698)*	Fairfield *(G-10729)*
Lavery Chevrolet-Buick Inc ....E...... 330 823-1100	Sonic Automotive ....E...... 614 870-8200	Jake Sweeney Body Shop ....E...... 513 782-1100
Alliance *(G-537)*	Columbus *(G-8658)*	Cincinnati *(G-3806)*
Lebanon Chrysler - Plymouth Inc ......E...... 513 932-2717	Spires Motors Inc ....E...... 614 771-2345	Jeff Wyler Ft Thomas Inc ....D...... 513 752-7450
Lebanon *(G-12480)*	Hilliard *(G-11817)*	Cincinnati *(G-2856)*
Lima Auto Mall Inc ....D...... 419 993-6000	Spitzer Chevrolet Inc ....D...... 330 467-4141	Joyce Buick Inc ....E...... 419 529-3211
Lima *(G-12675)*	Northfield *(G-15386)*	Ontario *(G-15557)*
Lima City School District ....E...... 419 996-3450	Spitzer Motor City Inc ....E...... 567 307-7119	King Collision Inc ....E...... 330 372-3242
Lima *(G-12676)*	Ontario *(G-15575)*	Warren *(G-18720)*
Lincoln Mrcury Kings Auto Mall ......C...... 513 683-3800	Stratton Chevrolet Co ....E...... 330 537-3151	Kumler Collision Inc ....E...... 740 653-4301
Cincinnati *(G-3933)*	Beloit *(G-1398)*	Lancaster *(G-12408)*
Lindsey Accura Inc ....E...... 800 980-8199	Sunnyside Toyota Inc ....E...... 440 777-9911	Magic Industries Inc ....E...... 614 759-8422
Columbus *(G-7981)*	North Olmsted *(G-15312)*	Columbus *(G-8008)*
Lower Great Lakes Kenworth Inc ......E...... 419 874-3511	Surfside Motors Inc ....E...... 419 462-1746	Maines Collision Repr & Bdy Sp ......D...... 937 322-4618
Perrysburg *(G-15890)*	Galion *(G-11183)*	Springfield *(G-17066)*
Madison Motor Service Inc ....E...... 419 332-0727	Tallmadge Board of Education ....E...... 330 633-2215	Medina World Cars Inc ....E...... 330 725-4901
Fremont *(G-11085)*	Tallmadge *(G-17493)*	Strongsville *(G-17332)*
Man-Tansky Inc ....E...... 740 454-2512	Tansky Motors Inc ....E...... 650 322-7069	Mowerys Collision Inc ....E...... 614 274-6072
Zanesville *(G-20328)*	Logan *(G-12855)*	Columbus *(G-8116)*
Mark Thomas Ford Inc ....E...... 330 638-1010	Taylor Chevrolet Inc ....E...... 740 653-2091	Northgate Chrysler Jeep Inc ....D...... 513 385-3900
Cortland *(G-8989)*	Lancaster *(G-12440)*	Cincinnati *(G-4129)*
Martin Chevrolet Inc ....E...... 937 849-1381	Trader Buds Westside Dodge ....E...... 614 272-0000	Paul Hrnchar Ford-Mercury Inc ......E...... 330 533-3673
Dayton *(G-9587)*	Columbus *(G-8770)*	Canfield *(G-2155)*
Mathews Dodge Chrysler Jeep ......E...... 740 389-2341	Travelcenters of America LLC ....D...... 330 769-2053	Ron Marhofer Automall Inc ....B...... 330 835-6707
Marion *(G-13444)*	Lodi *(G-12829)*	Cuyahoga Falls *(G-9121)*
Mathews Ford Inc ....D...... 740 522-2181	Trepanier Daniels & Trepanier ....D...... 740 286-1288	Ron Marhofer Collision Center ....E...... 330 686-2262
Newark *(G-15066)*	Jackson *(G-12180)*	Stow *(G-17228)*
Mathews Kennedy Ford L-M Inc ......D...... 740 387-3673	United Parcel Service Inc OH ....C...... 419 872-0211	Service King Holdings LLC ....D...... 216 362-1600
Marion *(G-13445)*	Perrysburg *(G-15928)*	Cleveland *(G-6399)*
		St Clair Auto Body ....E...... 216 531-7300
		Cleveland *(G-6448)*

(G-0000) Company's Geographic Section entry number

Suburban Collision Centers ....E 440 243-5533
Berea *(G-1438)*

Target Auto Body Inc ....E 216 391-1942
Cleveland *(G-6499)*

Three C Body Shop Inc ....D 614 274-9700
Columbus *(G-8751)*

Three C Body Shop Inc ....E 614 885-0900
Columbus *(G-8752)*

Voss Auto Network Inc ....B 937 433-1444
Dayton *(G-9861)*

Wayside Body Shop Inc ....E 937 233-3182
Dayton *(G-9869)*

White Family Collision Center ....E 419 885-8885
Sylvania *(G-17464)*

AUTOMOTIVE BODY, PAINT & INTERIOR REPAIR & MAINTENANCE SVC

Advantage Ford Lincoln Mercury ....E 419 334-9751
Fremont *(G-11056)*

Arch Abraham Susuki Ltd ....E 440 934-6001
Elyria *(G-10479)*

Bobbart Industries Inc ....E 419 350-5477
Sylvania *(G-17412)*

Brondes Ford ....D 419 473-1411
Toledo *(G-17627)*

Brown Motor Sales Co ....E 419 531-0151
Toledo *(G-17629)*

Chesrown Oldsmobile GMC Inc ....E 614 846-3040
Columbus *(G-7182)*

Coughlin Chevrolet Inc ....D 740 964-9191
Pataskala *(G-15784)*

Coughlin Chevrolet Toyota Inc ....D 740 366-1381
Newark *(G-15028)*

Dan Tobin Pontiac Buick GMC ....D 614 889-6300
Columbus *(G-7412)*

Dave White Chevrolet Inc ....C 419 885-4444
Sylvania *(G-17417)*

Donnell Ford-Lincoln ....E 330 332-0031
Salem *(G-16542)*

Doug Bigelow Chevrolet Inc ....D 330 644-7500
Akron *(G-192)*

Dutro Ford Lincoln-Mercury Inc ....D 740 452-6334
Zanesville *(G-20301)*

Ed Mullinax Ford LLC ....C 440 984-2431
Amherst *(G-584)*

Ed Schmidt Auto Inc ....C 419 874-4331
Perrysburg *(G-15863)*

Family Ford Lincoln Inc ....D 740 373-9127
Marietta *(G-13328)*

George P Ballas Buick GMC Trck ......D 419 535-1000
Toledo *(G-17760)*

Grogans Towne Chrysler Inc ....D 419 476-0761
Toledo *(G-17772)*

Haydocy Automotive Inc ....D 614 279-8880
Columbus *(G-7719)*

I-75 Pierson Automotive Inc ....E 513 424-1881
Middletown *(G-14350)*

Jake Sweeney Automotive Inc ....C 513 782-2800
Cincinnati *(G-3805)*

Joe Dodge Kidd Inc ....E 513 752-1804
Cincinnati *(G-2858)*

Joseph Chevrolet Oldsmobile Co ....C 513 741-6700
Cincinnati *(G-3833)*

Kerry Ford Inc ....D 513 671-6400
Cincinnati *(G-3864)*

Lang Chevrolet Co ....D 937 426-2313
Beavercreek Township *(G-1253)*

Lavery Chevrolet-Buick Inc ....E 330 823-1100
Alliance *(G-537)*

Leikin Motor Companies Inc ....D 440 946-6900
Willoughby *(G-19544)*

Lima Auto Mall Inc ....D 419 993-6000
Lima *(G-12675)*

Mark Thomas Ford Inc ....E 330 638-1010
Cortland *(G-8989)*

Mathews Ford Inc ....D 740 522-2181
Newark *(G-15066)*

Mathews Kennedy Ford L-M Inc ....D 740 387-3673
Marion *(G-13445)*

Matia Motors Inc ....E 440 365-7311
Elyria *(G-10534)*

Mike Castrucci Ford ....C 513 831-7010
Milford *(G-14410)*

Montrose Ford Inc ....D 330 666-0711
Fairlawn *(G-10842)*

Mullinax East LLC ....D 440 296-3020
Wickliffe *(G-19470)*

Oregon Ford Inc ....C 419 698-4444
Oregon *(G-15605)*

Ron Marhofer Automall Inc ....E 330 923-5059
Cuyahoga Falls *(G-9122)*

Roush Equipment Inc ....C 614 882-1535
Westerville *(G-19300)*

Sonic Automotive-1495 Automall ....E 614 317-4326
Columbus *(G-8659)*

Sunnyside Toyota Inc ....D 440 777-9911
North Olmsted *(G-15312)*

Surfside Motors Inc ....E 419 462-1746
Galion *(G-11183)*

Tansky Motors Inc ....E 650 322-7069
Logan *(G-12855)*

Walker Auto Group Inc ....D 937 433-4950
Miamisburg *(G-14236)*

Warner Buick-Nissan Inc ....E 419 423-7161
Findlay *(G-10974)*

AUTOMOTIVE BRAKE REPAIR SHOPS

Bridgestone Ret Operations LLC ....E 330 929-3391
Cuyahoga Falls *(G-9075)*

AUTOMOTIVE COLLISION SHOPS

Auto Body North Inc ....D 614 436-3700
Columbus *(G-7004)*

Downtown Ford Lincoln Inc ....D 330 456-2781
Canton *(G-2290)*

King Collision ....E 330 729-0525
Youngstown *(G-20093)*

Lennys Auto Sales Inc ....E 330 848-2993
Barberton *(G-959)*

Sharpnack Chvrlet Bick Cdillac ....D 419 935-0194
Willard *(G-19487)*

Tallmadge Collision Center ....E 330 630-2188
Tallmadge *(G-17494)*

True2form Collision Repair Ctr ....E 330 399-6659
Warren *(G-18752)*

AUTOMOTIVE CUSTOMIZING SVCS, NONFACTORY BASIS

Transitworks LLC ....D 330 861-1118
Richfield *(G-16381)*

AUTOMOTIVE DEALERS, NEC

Lindsey Accura Inc ....E 800 980-8199
Columbus *(G-7981)*

AUTOMOTIVE EMISSIONS TESTING SVCS

Envirotest Systems Corp ....E 330 963-4464
Twinsburg *(G-18261)*

Envirotest Systems Corp ....E 330 963-4464
Berea *(G-1423)*

Envirotest Systems Corp ....E 330 963-4464
Cleveland *(G-5485)*

Envirotest Systems Corp ....E 330 963-4464
Kent *(G-12231)*

Envirotest Systems Corp ....E 330 963-4464
Elyria *(G-10513)*

Envirotest Systems Corp ....E 330 963-4464
Cleveland *(G-5486)*

Envirotest Systems Corp ....E 330 963-4464
Chagrin Falls *(G-2665)*

Envirotest Systems Corp ....E 330 963-4464
Painesville *(G-15713)*

Envirotest Systems Corp ....E 330 963-4464
Medina *(G-13935)*

Envirotest Systems Corp ....E 330 963-4464
Chardon *(G-2694)*

Envirotest Systems Corp ....E 330 963-4464
Amherst *(G-586)*

Envirotest Systems Corp ....E 330 963-4464
Spencer *(G-16953)*

Envirotest Systems Corp ....E 330 963-4464
Twinsburg *(G-18262)*

AUTOMOTIVE GLASS REPLACEMENT SHOPS

Advanced Auto Glass Inc ....E 412 373-6675
Akron *(G-19)*

Belletech Corp ....D 937 599-3774
Bellefontaine *(G-1347)*

C-Auto Glass Inc ....E 216 351-2193
Cleveland *(G-5111)*

Mels Auto Glass Inc ....E 513 563-7771
Cincinnati *(G-4005)*

Ryans All-Glass Incorporated ....E 513 771-4440
Cincinnati *(G-4417)*

Safelite Fulfillment Inc ....E 614 781-5449
Columbus *(G-8573)*

Safelite Fulfillment Inc ....E 216 475-7781
Cleveland *(G-6363)*

Safelite Fulfillment Inc ....E 614 210-9050
Columbus *(G-8574)*

Safelite Glass Corp ....A 614 210-9000
Columbus *(G-8575)*

Safelite Glass Corp ....E 614 431-4936
Worthington *(G-19846)*

Safelite Group Inc ....A 614 210-9000
Columbus *(G-8576)*

Wiechart Enterprises Inc ....E 419 227-0027
Lima *(G-12784)*

AUTOMOTIVE LETTERING & PAINTING SVCS

Sharonville Car Wash ....E 513 769-4219
Cincinnati *(G-4464)*

AUTOMOTIVE PAINT SHOP

American Bulk Commodities Inc ....C 330 758-0841
Youngstown *(G-19953)*

Decorative Paint Incorporated ....D 419 485-0632
Montpelier *(G-14613)*

Jim Brown Chevrolet Inc ....E 440 255-5511
Mentor *(G-14066)*

Merrick Body Shop ....E 440 243-6700
Berea *(G-1430)*

Precision Coatings Systems ....E 937 642-4727
Marysville *(G-13523)*

AUTOMOTIVE PARTS, ACCESS & SPLYS

Accel Performance Group LLC ....C 216 658-6413
Independence *(G-12036)*

Alex Products Inc ....C 419 399-4500
Paulding *(G-15790)*

Amsted Industries Incorporated ....C 614 836-2323
Groveport *(G-11493)*

Atlas Industries Inc ....B 419 637-2117
Tiffin *(G-17509)*

Bobbart Industries Inc ....E 419 350-5477
Sylvania *(G-17412)*

Buyers Products Company ....C 440 974-8888
Mentor *(G-14024)*

Certified Power Inc ....D 419 355-1200
Fremont *(G-11062)*

Comprehensive Logistics Co Inc ....E 330 793-0504
Youngstown *(G-20007)*

Doug Marine Motors Inc ....E 740 335-3700
Wshngtn CT Hs *(G-19869)*

Falls Stamping & Welding Co ....C 330 928-1191
Cuyahoga Falls *(G-9092)*

Federal-Mogul Powertrain LLC ....C 740 432-2393
Cambridge *(G-2067)*

Ftech R&D North America Inc ....D 937 339-2777
Troy *(G-18202)*

Hendrickson International Corp ....D 740 929-5600
Hebron *(G-11714)*

Hi-Tek Manufacturing Inc ....C 513 459-1094
Mason *(G-13595)*

Honda of America Mfg Inc ....C 937 644-0724
Marysville *(G-13505)*

Industry Products Co ....B 937 778-0585
Piqua *(G-16011)*

Ishikawa Gasket America Inc ....C 419 353-7300
Bowling Green *(G-1738)*

Joseph Industries Inc ....D 330 528-0091
Streetsboro *(G-17258)*

Leadec Corp ....E 513 731-3590
Blue Ash *(G-1597)*

Marmon Highway Tech LLC ....E 330 878-5595
Dover *(G-10087)*

Ohio Auto Supply Company ....E 330 454-5105
Canton *(G-2424)*

Parker-Hannifin Corporation ....A 216 531-3000
Cleveland *(G-6171)*

Pioneer Automotive Tech Inc ....C 937 746-2293
Springboro *(G-16982)*

Sanoh America Inc ....C 740 392-9200
Mount Vernon *(G-14789)*

Thyssenkrupp Bilstein Amer Inc ....E 513 881-7600
West Chester *(G-19015)*

Toledo Molding & Die Inc ....D 419 692-6022
Delphos *(G-10036)*

Unison Industries LLC ....B 904 667-9904
Dayton *(G-9188)*

US Tsubaki Power Transm LLC ....C 419 626-4560
Sandusky *(G-16653)*

S E R V I C E S

Venco Venturo Industries LLC ....E 513 772-8448
Cincinnati (G-4753)
Western Branch Diesel Inc ....E 330 454-8800
Canton (G-2534)

AUTOMOTIVE PRDTS: Rubber

Myers Industries Inc ....E 330 253-5592
Akron (G-342)

AUTOMOTIVE RADIATOR REPAIR SHOPS

Perkins Motor Service Ltd ....E 440 277-1256
Lorain (G-12938)

AUTOMOTIVE REPAIR SHOPS: Brake Repair

Monro Inc ....E 614 235-3684
Columbus (G-8098)
Tuffy Associates Corp ....E 419 865-6900
Toledo (G-18112)

AUTOMOTIVE REPAIR SHOPS: Diesel Engine Repair

Columbus Diesel Supply Co Inc ....E 614 445-8391
Reynoldsburg (G-16292)
Cummins Inc ....E 614 771-1000
Hilliard (G-11759)
Skinner Diesel Services Inc ....E 614 491-8785
Columbus (G-8649)
W W Williams Company LLC ....E 419 837-5067
Perrysburg (G-15932)
W W Williams Company LLC ....D 614 228-5000
Dublin (G-10368)
W W Williams Company LLC ....E 330 225-7751
Brunswick (G-1945)

AUTOMOTIVE REPAIR SHOPS: Engine Repair, Exc Diesel

Columbus Col-Weld Corporation ....E 614 276-5303
Columbus (G-7270)

AUTOMOTIVE REPAIR SHOPS: Frame & Front End Repair Svcs

Burtons Collision ....E 513 984-3396
Cincinnati (G-3094)

AUTOMOTIVE REPAIR SHOPS: Frame Repair Shops

Three C Body Shop Inc ....D 614 274-9700
Columbus (G-8751)

AUTOMOTIVE REPAIR SHOPS: Machine Shop

RL Best Company ....E 330 758-8601
Boardman (G-1701)

AUTOMOTIVE REPAIR SHOPS: Muffler Shop, Sale/Rpr/Installation

Dayton-Dixie Mufflers Inc ....E 419 243-7281
Toledo (G-17694)
Midas Auto Systems Experts ....E 419 243-7281
Toledo (G-17913)
Monro Inc ....D 937 999-3202
Springboro (G-16976)
Monro Inc ....D 614 360-3883
Columbus (G-8099)
Monro Inc ....D 440 835-2393
Westlake (G-19375)
Tuffy Associates Corp ....E 419 865-6900
Toledo (G-18112)

AUTOMOTIVE REPAIR SHOPS: Rebuilding & Retreading Tires

Grismer Tire Company ....E 937 643-2526
Centerville (G-2626)
K S Bandag Inc ....E 330 264-9237
Wooster (G-19735)

AUTOMOTIVE REPAIR SHOPS: Tire Recapping

Best One Tire & Svc Lima Inc ....E 419 229-2380
Lima (G-12606)

Central Ohio Bandag LP ....E 740 454-9728
Zanesville (G-20291)
H & H Retreading Inc ....D 740 682-7721
Oak Hill (G-15480)

AUTOMOTIVE REPAIR SHOPS: Trailer Repair

Bbt Fleet Services LLC ....E 419 462-7722
Mansfield (G-13139)
Capitol City Trailers Inc ....D 614 491-2616
Obetz (G-15523)
Double A Trailer Sales Inc ....E 419 692-7626
Delphos (G-10025)
Hans Truck and Trlr Repr Inc ....E 216 581-0046
Cleveland (G-5660)
Jones Truck & Spring Repr Inc ....D 614 443-4619
Columbus (G-7868)
Mac Trailer Manufacturing Inc ....C 330 823-9900
Alliance (G-540)
Marmon Highway Tech LLC ....E 330 878-5595
Dover (G-10087)
Nelson Manufacturing Company ....D 419 523-5321
Ottawa (G-15660)
Stoops Frghtlnr-Qlity Trlr Inc ....E 937 236-4092
Dayton (G-9795)
Transport Services Inc ....D 440 582-4900
Cleveland (G-6543)

AUTOMOTIVE REPAIR SHOPS: Truck Engine Repair, Exc Indl

Allied Truck Parts Co ....E 330 477-8127
Canton (G-2181)
Carl E Oeder Sons Sand & Grav ....E 513 494-1555
Lebanon (G-12454)
Hartwig Transit Inc ....E 513 563-1765
Cincinnati (G-3683)
Hy-Tek Material Handling Inc ....D 614 497-2500
Columbus (G-7790)
J D S Leasing Inc ....E 440 236-6575
Columbia Station (G-6776)
Kaffenbarger Truck Eqp Co ....E 513 772-6800
Cincinnati (G-3846)
Kirk NationaLease Co ....E 937 498-1151
Sidney (G-16783)
Maines Collision Repr & Bdy Sp ....D 937 322-4618
Springfield (G-17066)
Midway Garage Inc ....E 740 345-0699
Newark (G-15071)
Mizar Motors Inc ....D 419 729-2400
Toledo (G-17919)
Newtown Nine Inc ....E 330 376-7741
Akron (G-345)
Scotts Towing Co ....E 419 729-7888
Toledo (G-18022)
Steubenville Truck Center Inc ....E 740 282-2711
Steubenville (G-17173)

AUTOMOTIVE REPAIR SHOPS: Turbocharger & Blower Repair

Star Leasing Co ....D 614 278-9999
Columbus (G-8687)

AUTOMOTIVE REPAIR SHOPS: Wheel Alignment

Speck Sales Incorporated ....E 419 353-8312
Bowling Green (G-1749)

AUTOMOTIVE REPAIR SVC

Beechmont Motors Inc ....E 513 388-3883
Cincinnati (G-3031)
Beechmont Toyota Inc ....D 513 388-3800
Cincinnati (G-3034)
Bobby Layman Cadillac GMC Inc ....E 740 654-9590
Carroll (G-2556)
Broad & James Inc ....E 614 231-8697
Columbus (G-7075)
Certified Power Inc ....D 419 355-1200
Fremont (G-11062)
Coates Car Care Inc ....E 330 652-4180
Niles (G-15152)
East Manufacturing Corporation ....B 330 325-9921
Randolph (G-16230)
First Services Inc ....A 513 241-2200
Cincinnati (G-3559)
First Transit Inc ....B 513 241-2200
Cincinnati (G-3564)

Fleetpride West Inc ....E 419 243-3161
Toledo (G-17742)
Fred Martin Nissan LLC ....E 330 644-8888
Akron (G-228)
Germain Ford LLC ....C 614 889-7777
Columbus (G-7664)
Goodyear Tire & Rubber Company ....A 330 796-2121
Akron (G-242)
Haasz Automall LLC ....E 330 296-2866
Ravenna (G-16245)
Hoss II Inc ....E 937 669-4300
Tipp City (G-17560)
Irace Inc ....E 330 836-7247
Akron (G-281)
Kings Cove Automotive LLC ....D 513 677-0177
Fairfield (G-10744)
Montrose Sheffield LLC ....E 440 934-6699
Sheffield Village (G-16740)
Paul Hrnchar Ford-Mercury Inc ....E 330 533-3673
Canfield (G-2155)
Professional Transit Mgt ....E 513 677-6000
Loveland (G-13022)
S&S Car Care Inc ....E 330 494-9535
Canton (G-2468)
Sanoh America Inc ....C 740 392-9200
Mount Vernon (G-14789)
Spitzer Chevrolet Inc ....E 330 467-4141
Northfield (G-15386)
United Garage & Service Corp ....D 216 623-1550
Cleveland (G-6572)

AUTOMOTIVE REPAIR SVCS, MISCELLANEOUS

County of Stark ....E 330 477-3609
Massillon (G-13674)
St Marys City Board Education ....E 419 394-1116
Saint Marys (G-16532)

AUTOMOTIVE RUSTPROOFING & UNDERCOATING SHOPS

Buddies Inc ....E 216 642-3362
Cleveland (G-5100)
Dave Marshall Inc ....D 937 878-9135
Fairborn (G-10668)

AUTOMOTIVE SPLYS & PARTS, NEW, WHOL: Auto Servicing Eqpt

Columbus Public School Dst ....C 614 365-5263
Columbus (G-7305)

AUTOMOTIVE SPLYS & PARTS, NEW, WHOL: Testing Eqpt, Electric

Nu-Di Products Co Inc ....D 216 251-9070
Cleveland (G-6106)

AUTOMOTIVE SPLYS & PARTS, NEW, WHOLESALE: Bumpers

Durable Corporation ....D 800 537-1603
Norwalk (G-15433)

AUTOMOTIVE SPLYS & PARTS, NEW, WHOLESALE: Engines/Eng Parts

Auto Aftermarket Concepts ....E 513 942-2535
Cincinnati (G-3005)
Cadna Rubber Company Inc ....E 901 566-9090
Fairlawn (G-10818)
Interstate Diesel Service Inc ....B 216 881-0015
Cleveland (G-5765)
Keihin Thermal Tech Amer Inc ....B 740 869-3000
Mount Sterling (G-14745)

AUTOMOTIVE SPLYS & PARTS, NEW, WHOLESALE: Seat Covers

Jim Hayden Inc ....D 513 563-8828
Cincinnati (G-3819)

AUTOMOTIVE SPLYS & PARTS, NEW, WHOLESALE: Splys

Advance Stores Company Inc ....C 740 369-4491
Delaware (G-9950)
Automotive Distributors Co Inc ....E 330 785-7290
Akron (G-82)

Car Parts Warehouse Inc ....E ... 216 281-4500
Brookpark (G-1892)

Finishmaster Inc ....D ... 614 228-4328
Columbus (G-7578)

General Parts Inc ....E ... 614 267-5197
Columbus (G-7653)

Winston Products LLC ....D ... 440 478-1418
Cleveland (G-6685)

AUTOMOTIVE SPLYS & PARTS, NEW, WHOLESALE: Tools & Eqpt

Cedar Elec Holdings Corp ....D ... 773 804-6288
West Chester (G-18882)

Cornwell Quality Tools Company ....E ... 330 335-2933
Wadsworth (G-18594)

Matco Tools Corporation ....B ... 330 929-4949
Stow (G-17219)

Myers Industries Inc ....E ... 330 253-5592
Akron (G-342)

AUTOMOTIVE SPLYS & PARTS, NEW, WHOLESALE: Trailer Parts

Frontier Tank Center Inc ....E ... 330 659-3888
Richfield (G-16358)

Knox Auto LLC ....E ... 330 701-5266
Mount Vernon (G-14771)

Transport Services Inc ....D ... 440 582-4900
Cleveland (G-6543)

AUTOMOTIVE SPLYS & PARTS, NEW, WHOLESALE: Wheels

Herbert E Orr Company ....C ... 419 399-4866
Paulding (G-15794)

Rocknstarr Holdings LLC ....E ... 330 509-9086
Youngstown (G-20189)

AUTOMOTIVE SPLYS & PARTS, USED, WHOLESALE

G-Cor Automotive Corp ....E ... 614 443-6735
Columbus (G-7641)

Greenleaf Ohio LLC ....E ... 330 832-6001
Massillon (G-13690)

Myers Bus Parts and Sups Co ....E ... 330 533-2275
Canfield (G-2150)

AUTOMOTIVE SPLYS & PARTS, USED, WHOLESALE: Dry Cell Batt

Bob Sumerel Tire Co Inc ....E ... 614 527-9700
Columbus (G-7051)

AUTOMOTIVE SPLYS & PARTS, WHOLESALE, NEC

Accel Performance Group LLC ....C ... 216 658-6413
Independence (G-12036)

Alex Products Inc ....C ... 419 399-4500
Paulding (G-15790)

Atlas Industries Inc ....B ... 419 637-2117
Tiffin (G-17509)

Automotive Distributors Co Inc ....D ... 614 476-1315
Columbus (G-7005)

Automotive Distributors Co Inc ....E ... 216 398-2014
Cleveland (G-5025)

Bendix Coml Vhcl Systems LLC ....B ... 440 329-9000
Elyria (G-10482)

Bridgeport Auto Parts Inc ....E ... 740 635-0441
Bridgeport (G-1814)

Brookville Roadster Inc ....E ... 937 833-4605
Brookville (G-1912)

Building 8 Inc ....E ... 513 771-8000
Cincinnati (G-3088)

Car Parts Warehouse Inc ....E ... 440 259-2991
Perry (G-15821)

Certified Power Inc ....D ... 419 355-1200
Fremont (G-11062)

Columbus Diesel Supply Co Inc ....E ... 614 445-8391
Reynoldsburg (G-16292)

Crown Dielectric Inds Inc ....C ... 614 224-5161
Columbus (G-7397)

D-G Custom Chrome LLC ....D ... 513 531-1881
Cincinnati (G-3396)

Dana Heavy Vehicle Systems ....D ... 419 866-3900
Holland (G-11881)

Fayette Parts Service Inc ....C ... 740 282-4547
Steubenville (G-17153)

Four Wheel Drive Hardware LLC ....C ... 330 482-4733
Columbiana (G-6788)

Freudenberg-Nok General Partnr ....B ... 419 499-2502
Milan (G-14361)

G-Cor Automotive Corp ....E ... 614 443-6735
Columbus (G-7641)

General Parts Inc ....D ... 330 220-6500
Brunswick (G-1931)

Greenleaf Auto Recyclers LLC ....E ... 330 832-6001
Massillon (G-13689)

H & H Auto Parts Inc ....D ... 330 456-4778
Canton (G-2332)

H & H Auto Parts Inc ....E ... 330 494-2975
Canton (G-2333)

Hahn Automotive Warehouse Inc ....E ... 937 223-1068
Dayton (G-9483)

Hamilton Automotive Warehouse ....D ... 513 896-4100
Hamilton (G-11607)

Hebco Products Inc ....A ... 419 562-7987
Bucyrus (G-1992)

Hite Parts Exchange Inc ....E ... 614 272-5115
Columbus (G-7756)

Honda Trading America Corp ....C ... 937 644-8004
Marysville (G-13506)

Ieh Auto Parts LLC ....E ... 740 373-8327
Marietta (G-13336)

Ieh Auto Parts LLC ....E ... 740 732-2395
Caldwell (G-2040)

Ieh Auto Parts LLC ....E ... 740 373-8151
Marietta (G-13337)

Jegs Automotive Inc ....C ... 614 294-5050
Delaware (G-9990)

Joseph Russo ....E ... 440 748-2690
Grafton (G-11317)

K - O - I Warehouse Inc ....E ... 937 323-5585
Springfield (G-17058)

K - O - I Warehouse Inc ....E ... 513 357-2400
Cincinnati (G-3842)

Kenton Auto and Truck Wrecking ....E ... 419 673-8234
Kenton (G-12283)

Keystone Automotive Inds Inc ....D ... 513 961-5500
Cincinnati (G-3866)

Keystone Automotive Inds Inc ....E ... 330 759-8019
Girard (G-11293)

KOI Enterprises Inc ....D ... 513 357-2400
Cincinnati (G-3886)

McBee Supply Corporation ....D ... 216 881-0015
Cleveland (G-5930)

MJ Auto Parts Inc ....E ... 440 205-6272
Mentor (G-14088)

National Marketshare Group ....E ... 513 921-0800
Cincinnati (G-4094)

Ohashi Technica USA Inc ....E ... 740 965-5115
Sunbury (G-17393)

Ohio Auto Supply Company ....E ... 330 454-5105
Canton (G-2424)

OReilly Automotive Inc ....D ... 330 494-0042
North Canton (G-15226)

OReilly Automotive Inc ....E ... 419 630-0811
Bryan (G-1968)

OReilly Automotive Inc ....E ... 330 318-3136
Boardman (G-1700)

Par International Inc ....E ... 614 529-1300
Obetz (G-15528)

Pat Young Service Co Inc ....E ... 216 447-8550
Cleveland (G-6180)

R L Morrissey & Assoc Inc ....E ... 440 498-3730
Solon (G-16889)

Shiloh Manufacturing LLC ....E ... 330 558-2693
Valley City (G-18469)

Smyth Automotive Inc ....D ... 513 528-2800
Cincinnati (G-4496)

Smyth Automotive Inc ....E ... 513 528-0061
Cincinnati (G-4497)

Smyth Automotive Inc ....E ... 513 575-2000
Milford (G-14434)

Smyth Automotive Inc ....E ... 513 777-6400
West Chester (G-19010)

Smyth Automotive Inc ....E ... 513 734-7800
Bethel (G-1454)

Snyders Antique Auto Parts Inc ....E ... 330 549-5313
New Springfield (G-14998)

Stellar Srkg Acquisition LLC ....E ... 330 769-8484
Seville (G-16692)

Stoddard Imported Cars Inc ....D ... 440 951-1040
Mentor (G-14112)

Thyssenkrupp Bilstein Amer Inc ....E ... 513 881-7600
West Chester (G-19015)

Turbo Parts LLC ....E ... 740 223-1695
Marion (G-13466)

Ventra Salem LLC ....A ... 330 337-8002
Salem (G-16566)

Voss Toyota Inc ....E ... 937 431-2100
Beavercreek (G-1195)

W W Williams Company LLC ....E ... 419 837-5067
Perrysburg (G-15932)

Whites Service Center Inc ....E ... 937 653-5279
Urbana (G-18446)

World Auto Parts Inc ....E ... 216 781-8418
Cleveland (G-6689)

AUTOMOTIVE SPLYS, USED, WHOLESALE & RETAIL

Cedar Elec Holdings Corp ....D ... 773 804-6288
West Chester (G-18882)

Lkq Triplettasap Inc ....C ... 330 733-6333
Akron (G-317)

Speedie Auto Salvage Ltd ....E ... 330 878-9961
Dover (G-10102)

Stricker Bros Inc ....E ... 513 732-1152
Batavia (G-1010)

AUTOMOTIVE SPLYS/PART, NEW, WHOL: Spring, Shock Absorb/Strut

Thyssenkrupp Bilstein Amer Inc ....C ... 513 881-7600
Hamilton (G-11647)

AUTOMOTIVE SPLYS/PARTS, NEW, WHOL: Body Rpr/Paint Shop Splys

Klase Enterprises Inc ....E ... 330 452-6300
Canton (G-2369)

AUTOMOTIVE SVCS, EXC REPAIR & CARWASHES: Customizing

AGC Automotive Americas ....D ... 937 599-3131
Bellefontaine (G-1343)

Auto Concepts Cincinnatti LLC ....E ... 513 769-4540
Cincinnati (G-3007)

Cresttek LLC ....E ... 248 602-2083
Dublin (G-10193)

Ground Effects LLC ....E ... 440 565-5925
Westlake (G-19346)

TSS Acquisition Company ....D ... 513 772-7000
Cleveland (G-6552)

AUTOMOTIVE SVCS, EXC REPAIR & CARWASHES: Insp & Diagnostic

SGS North America Inc ....E ... 513 674-7048
Cincinnati (G-4462)

AUTOMOTIVE SVCS, EXC REPAIR & CARWASHES: Lubrication

Coates Car Care Inc ....E ... 330 652-4180
Niles (G-15152)

Reladyne LLC ....E ... 513 489-6000
Cincinnati (G-4355)

Southern Express Lubes Inc ....E ... 937 278-5807
Dayton (G-9778)

Valvoline Inc ....D ... 513 451-1753
Cincinnati (G-4748)

Yund Inc ....E ... 330 837-9358
Massillon (G-13738)

AUTOMOTIVE SVCS, EXC REPAIR & CARWASHES: Maintenance

AAA Ohio Auto Club ....D ... 614 431-7800
Worthington (G-19790)

Aptiv Services Us LLC ....E ... 330 373-3568
Warren (G-18666)

Auto Warehousing Co Inc ....E ... 330 824-5149
Warren (G-18670)

Cintas Corporation No 1 ....A ... 513 459-1200
Mason (G-13556)

Cleveland Pick-A-Part Inc ....E ... 440 236-5031
Columbia Station (G-6772)

Dealer Supply and Eqp Ltd ....E ... 419 724-8473
Toledo (G-17695)

Eaton Corporation ....B ... 440 523-5000
Beachwood (G-1053)

Fayette Parts Service Inc ....C ... 724 880-3616
Wintersville (G-19670)

First Vehicle Services Inc ....C ... 513 241-2200
Cincinnati (G-3565)

Herrnstein Chrysler Inc ....D 740 773-2203
  Chillicothe (G-2786)
Industrial Sorting Services ....E 513 772-6501
  Cincinnati (G-3760)
Mathews Ford Inc...........................D 740 522-2181
  Newark (G-15066)
Pete Baur Buick Gmc Inc ....E 440 238-5600
  Cleveland (G-6200)
Quest Quality Services LLC ....D 419 704-7407
  Maumee (G-13839)
Sears Roebuck and Co ....C 614 797-2095
  Columbus (G-6835)
Sears Roebuck and Co ....E 937 427-8528
  Beavercreek (G-1185)
Sears Roebuck and Co ....D 419 226-4172
  Lima (G-12737)
Sears Roebuck and Co ....D 614 760-7195
  Dublin (G-10330)
Sears Roebuck and Co ....C 330 652-5128
  Niles (G-15168)
Sears Roebuck and Co ....C 440 846-3595
  Cleveland (G-6386)
Valvoline Instant Oil Change ....C 937 548-0123
  Greenville (G-11398)
Valvoline LLC ....D 513 557-3100
  Cincinnati (G-4749)

AUTOMOTIVE SVCS, EXC REPAIR & CARWASHES: Road Svc

Van Wert County Engineers..............E 419 238-0210
  Van Wert (G-18493)

AUTOMOTIVE SVCS, EXC REPAIR: Carwash, Automatic

Allied Car Wash Inc ....E 513 559-1733
  Cincinnati (G-2927)
Elliott Auto Bath Inc.......................E 513 422-3700
  Middletown (G-14299)
Expresso Car Wash Systems Inc ....E 419 866-7099
  Toledo (G-17720)
Falls Supersonic Car Wash Inc ....E 330 928-1657
  Cuyahoga Falls (G-9093)
JKL Development Company ....E 937 390-0358
  Springfield (G-17057)
North Lima Dairy Queen Inc...............E 330 549-3220
  North Lima (G-15273)
Robert Stough Ventures Corp ....E 419 882-4073
  Toledo (G-18011)
Royal Car Wash Inc ....E 513 385-2777
  Cincinnati (G-4404)
Royal Sheen Service Center ....E 330 966-7200
  Canton (G-2464)
Standard Oil Company ....E 330 530-8049
  Girard (G-11301)

AUTOMOTIVE SVCS, EXC REPAIR: Carwash, Self-Service

Coates Car Care Inc ....E 330 652-4180
  Niles (G-15152)

AUTOMOTIVE SVCS, EXC REPAIR: Truck Wash

Blue Beacon of Hubbard Inc..............E 330 534-4419
  Hubbard (G-11941)
Blue Beacon USA LP II ....E 330 534-4419
  Hubbard (G-11942)
Blue Beacon USA LP II ....E 419 643-8146
  Beaverdam (G-1267)
Blue Beacon USA LP II ....E 937 437-5533
  New Paris (G-14940)
Truckomat Corporation ....E 740 467-2818
  Hebron (G-11725)

AUTOMOTIVE SVCS, EXC REPAIR: Washing & Polishing

3 B Ventures LLC ....E 419 236-9461
  Lima (G-12590)
Car Wash ....E 216 662-6289
  Cleveland (G-5121)
Car Wash Plus Ltd ....E 513 683-4228
  Cincinnati (G-3114)
Expresso Car Wash Systems Inc ....D 419 536-7540
  Toledo (G-17719)
John Atwood Inc ....E 440 777-4147
  North Olmsted (G-15294)

Johnnys Carwash ....D 513 474-6603
  Cincinnati (G-3825)
Klean A Kar Inc ....E 614 221-3145
  Columbus (G-7910)
Mikes Carwash Inc ....C 513 677-4700
  Loveland (G-13013)
Moo Moo North Hamilton LLC ....D 614 751-9274
  Etna (G-10611)
Mr Magic Carnegie Inc ....E 440 461-7572
  Beachwood (G-1084)
Napoleon Wash-N-Fill Inc ....C 419 422-7216
  Findlay (G-10947)
Red Carpet Car Wash Inc ....E 330 477-5772
  Canton (G-2451)
Sharonville Car Wash ....E 513 769-4219
  Cincinnati (G-4464)
Waterway Gas & Wash Company ....E 330 995-2900
  Aurora (G-851)
Yund Inc ....E 330 837-9358
  Massillon (G-13738)

AUTOMOTIVE SVCS, EXC RPR/CARWASHES: High Perf Auto Rpr/Svc

Chesrown Oldsmobile Cadillac ....E 740 366-7373
  Granville (G-11337)
Steve Austin Auto Group ....E 937 592-3015
  Bellefontaine (G-1368)

AUTOMOTIVE TOWING & WRECKING SVC

Precision Coatings Systems ....E 937 642-4727
  Marysville (G-13523)
Pro-Tow Inc....................................E 614 444-8697
  Columbus (G-8466)
Scotts Towing Co ....E 419 729-7888
  Toledo (G-18022)
Star Leasing Co...............................D 614 278-9999
  Columbus (G-8687)
Westfall Towing LLC ....E 740 371-5185
  Marietta (G-13401)
World Trck Towing Recovery Inc..........E 330 723-1116
  Seville (G-16693)

AUTOMOTIVE TOWING SVCS

Abers Garage Inc ....E 419 281-5500
  Ashland (G-644)
Arlington Towing Inc ....E 614 488-2006
  Columbus (G-6971)
Atlas Towing Service ....E 513 451-1854
  Cincinnati (G-2999)
B & D Auto & Towing Inc...................E 440 237-3737
  North Royalton (G-15347)
Beaverdam Fleet Services Inc ....E 419 643-8880
  Beaverdam (G-1266)
Broad & James Inc ....E 614 231-8697
  Columbus (G-7075)
Charlie Towing Service Inc ....E 440 234-5300
  Berea (G-1417)
Dutys Towing ....E 614 252-3336
  Columbus (G-7479)
Eastland Crane Service Inc ....E 614 868-9750
  Columbus (G-7490)
Eitel Towing Service Inc ....E 614 877-4139
  Orient (G-15619)
Englewood Truck Inc ....E 937 836-5109
  Clayton (G-4857)
Genicon Inc ....E 419 491-4478
  Swanton (G-17398)
Jo Lynn Inc ....D 419 994-3204
  Loudonville (G-12958)
Madison Motor Service Inc ....E 419 332-0727
  Fremont (G-11085)
Maines Collision Repr & Bdy Sp ....D 937 322-4618
  Springfield (G-17066)
Richs Towing & Service Inc ....E 440 234-3435
  Middleburg Heights (G-14257)
Rustys Towing Service Inc ....D 614 491-6288
  Columbus (G-8562)
Sandys Auto & Truck Svc Inc ....D 937 461-4980
  Moraine (G-14694)
Sandys Towing ....E 937 461-4980
  Moraine (G-14695)
Shamrock Towing Inc ....E 614 882-3555
  Westerville (G-19209)
Southwood Auto Sales ....E 330 788-8822
  Youngstown (G-20214)
Sprandel Enterprises Inc...................E 513 777-6622
  West Chester (G-19011)
Spurlock Truck Service ....E 937 268-6100
  Dayton (G-9787)

Steve S Towing and Recovery ....E 513 422-0254
  Middletown (G-14332)

AUTOMOTIVE TRANSMISSION REPAIR SVC

Ohio Transmission Corporation ....E 614 342-6247
  Columbus (G-8358)
W W Williams Company LLC ....D 614 228-5000
  Dublin (G-10368)
W W Williams Company LLC ....E 330 225-7751
  Brunswick (G-1945)

AUTOMOTIVE UPHOLSTERY SHOPS

Kallas Enterprises Inc ....E 330 253-6893
  Akron (G-297)

AUTOMOTIVE WELDING SVCS

Brown Industrial Inc ....E 937 693-3838
  Botkins (G-1708)
Industry Products Co ....B 937 778-0585
  Piqua (G-16011)
Perkins Motor Service Ltd..................E 440 277-1256
  Lorain (G-12938)
R K Industries Inc ....D 419 523-5001
  Ottawa (G-15666)
Rose City Manufacturing Inc ....D 937 325-5561
  Springfield (G-17106)
Turn-Key Industrial Svcs LLC ....D 614 274-1128
  Columbus (G-8787)

AUTOMOTIVE: Seat Frames, Metal

Alex Products Inc ....C 419 399-4500
  Paulding (G-15790)

AVIATION PROPELLER & BLADE REPAIR SVCS

Standrdaero Component Svcs Inc ....A 513 618-9588
  Cincinnati (G-4535)

AVIATION SCHOOL

Jet Mintenance Consulting Corp..........E 937 205-2406
  Wilmington (G-19625)

BABYSITTING BUREAU

Carol Scudere.................................E 614 839-4357
  New Albany (G-14848)
Jack & Jill Babysitting Svc ....E 513 731-5261
  Cincinnati (G-3797)

BADGES, WHOLESALE

Raco Industries LLC ....D 513 984-2101
  Blue Ash (G-1636)

BAGS: Plastic

Dayton Industrial Drum Inc ....E 937 253-8933
  Dayton (G-9167)

BAGS: Plastic, Made From Purchased Materials

Ampac Holdings LLC.......................A 513 671-1777
  Cincinnati (G-2955)
Atlapac Corp...................................D 614 252-2121
  Columbus (G-6995)

BAGS: Shopping, Made From Purchased Materials

Ampac Holdings LLC.......................A 513 671-1777
  Cincinnati (G-2955)

BAIL BONDING SVCS

A-1 Bail Bonds Inc ....E 937 372-2400
  Xenia (G-19887)

BAKERIES, COMMERCIAL: On Premises Baking Only

Amish Door Inc ....B 330 359-5464
  Wilmot (G-19657)
Buns of Delaware Inc.......................E 740 363-2867
  Delaware (G-9956)
Klosterman Baking Co ....D 513 242-1004
  Cincinnati (G-3880)

Kroger Co .....C 740 335-4030
Wshngtn CT Hs (G-19877)
Mustard Seed Health Fd Mkt Inc ....E 440 519-3663
Solon (G-16875)
Osmans Pies Inc .....E 330 607-9083
Stow (G-17222)
Schwebel Baking Company .....C 440 248-1500
Solon (G-16895)
Thurns Bakery & Deli .....E 614 221-9246
Columbus (G-8753)
White Castle System Inc .....B 614 228-5781
Columbus (G-8896)

BAKERIES: On Premises Baking & Consumption

Aladdins Baking Company Inc ....E ... 216 861-0317
Cleveland (G-4925)
Buns of Delaware Inc .....E 740 363-2867
Delaware (G-9956)
Mapleside Valley LLC .....D 330 225-5576
Brunswick (G-1937)
Michaels Bakery Inc .....E 216 351-7530
Cleveland (G-5978)
Mocha House Inc .....E 330 392-3020
Warren (G-18731)
Osmans Pies Inc .....E 330 607-9083
Stow (G-17222)
Servatii Inc .....D 513 271-5040
Cincinnati (G-4456)
Standard Oil Company .....E 330 530-8049
Girard (G-11301)
Thurns Bakery & Deli .....E 614 221-9246
Columbus (G-8753)
Troyers Home Pantry .....E 330 698-4182
Apple Creek (G-621)

BAKERY PRDTS: Cookies & crackers

Norcia Bakery .....E 330 454-1077
Canton (G-2419)
Osmans Pies Inc .....E 330 607-9083
Stow (G-17222)

BAKERY PRDTS: Pretzels

Ditsch Usa LLC .....E 513 782-8888
Cincinnati (G-3433)

BAKERY PRDTS: Wholesalers

Aladdins Baking Company Inc ....E ... 216 861-0317
Cleveland (G-4925)
Alfred Nickles Bakery Inc .....E 419 332-6418
Fremont (G-11057)
Bagel Place Inc .....E 419 885-1000
Toledo (G-17604)
Bimbo Bakeries Usa Inc .....E 614 868-7565
Columbus (G-7038)
Busken Bakery Inc .....D 513 871-2114
Cincinnati (G-3097)
Ditsch Usa LLC .....E 513 782-8888
Cincinnati (G-3433)
Dutch Cntry Apple Dmplings Inc ....D 330 683-0646
Orrville (G-15629)
Dutchman Hospitality Group Inc ....C 614 873-3414
Plain City (G-16050)
Interbake Foods LLC .....C 614 294-4931
Columbus (G-7833)
Interbake Foods LLC .....A 614 294-4931
Columbus (G-7834)
Klosterman Baking Co .....D 513 242-1004
Cincinnati (G-3880)
Made From Scratch Inc .....E 614 873-3344
Plain City (G-16058)
Michaels Bakery Inc .....E 216 351-7530
Cleveland (G-5978)
Michaels Gourmet Catering .....E 419 698-2988
Toledo (G-17912)
Osmans Pies Inc .....E 330 607-9083
Stow (G-17222)
Perfection Bakeries Inc .....D 937 492-2220
Sidney (G-16793)
Skallys Old World Bakery Inc .....E 513 931-1411
Cincinnati (G-4491)
Thurns Bakery & Deli .....E 614 221-9246
Columbus (G-8753)
Troyers Home Pantry .....E 330 698-4182
Apple Creek (G-621)

BAKERY: Wholesale Or Wholesale & Retail Combined

Calvary Christian Ch of Ohio .....E 740 828-9000
Frazeysburg (G-11048)
Norcia Bakery .....E 330 454-1077
Canton (G-2419)

BAKING PAN GLAZING & CLEANING SVCS

Cmbb LLC .....C 937 652-2151
Urbana (G-18428)
Russell T Bundy Associates Inc ....D 937 652-2151
Urbana (G-18444)

BALLET PRODUCTION SVCS

Ballet Metropolitan Inc .....C 614 229-4860
Columbus (G-7016)
Ohio Chamber Ballet .....E 330 972-7900
Akron (G-356)

BANKS: Commercial, NEC

Croghan Bancshares Inc .....D 419 794-9399
Maumee (G-13778)
Farm Credit Mid-America .....E 740 441-9312
Albany (G-510)
Farmers Savings Bank .....E 330 648-2441
Spencer (G-16954)
First Merchants Bank .....E 614 486-9000
Columbus (G-7587)
FNB Corporation .....D 330 425-1818
Twinsburg (G-18267)
Huntington Capital I .....C 614 480-4038
Columbus (G-7782)
Huntington Insurance Inc .....E 419 429-4627
Findlay (G-10925)
Huntington National Bank .....C 513 762-1860
Cincinnati (G-3742)
Huntington National Bank .....E 330 742-7013
Youngstown (G-20072)
Huntington National Bank .....E 330 343-6611
Dover (G-10083)
Huntington National Bank .....E 740 773-2681
Chillicothe (G-2792)
Huntington National Bank .....E 614 480-4293
Columbus (G-7786)
Huntington National Bank .....E 740 452-8444
Zanesville (G-20319)
Huntington National Bank .....B 614 480-4293
Columbus (G-7787)
Huntington National Bank .....E 740 695-3323
Saint Clairsville (G-16489)
Huntington National Bank .....E 419 226-8200
Lima (G-12662)
Huntington National Bank .....E 216 621-1717
Cleveland (G-5724)
Huntington National Bank .....E 216 515-6401
Cleveland (G-5725)
Huntington National Bank .....E 419 782-5050
Defiance (G-9918)
Jpmorgan Chase Bank Nat Assn ....E 614 759-8955
Reynoldsburg (G-16311)
Jpmorgan Chase Bank Nat Assn ....E 513 784-0770
Cincinnati (G-3838)
Jpmorgan Chase Bank Nat Assn ....E 330 364-7242
New Philadelphia (G-14968)
Jpmorgan Chase Bank Nat Assn ....E 740 382-7362
Marion (G-13426)
Jpmorgan Chase Bank Nat Assn ....E 330 650-0476
Hudson (G-11989)
Jpmorgan Chase Bank Nat Assn ....B 843 679-3653
Columbus (G-7873)
Jpmorgan Chase Bank Nat Assn ....E 330 325-7855
Randolph (G-16231)
Jpmorgan Chase Bank Nat Assn ....E 614 920-4182
Canal Winchester (G-2111)
Jpmorgan Chase Bank Nat Assn ....E 614 834-3120
Pickerington (G-15960)
Jpmorgan Chase Bank Nat Assn ....E 614 853-2999
Galloway (G-11221)
Jpmorgan Chase Bank Nat Assn ....E 614 248-3315
Powell (G-16199)
Jpmorgan Chase Bank Nat Assn ....E 740 657-8906
Lewis Center (G-12547)
Jpmorgan Chase Bank Nat Assn ....E 216 524-0600
Seven Hills (G-16676)
Jpmorgan Chase Bank Nat Assn ....E 440 277-1038
Lorain (G-12909)
Jpmorgan Chase Bank Nat Assn ....E 330 722-6626
Medina (G-13961)

MB Financial Inc .....D 937 283-2027
Wilmington (G-19634)
PNC Bank National Association ....C 330 742-4426
Youngstown (G-20162)
PNC Bank National Association ....C 330 562-9700
Aurora (G-839)
Raymond James Fincl Svcs Inc ....E 419 586-5121
Celina (G-2608)
Republic Bank .....B 513 793-7666
Blue Ash (G-1644)
UBS Financial Services Inc .....E 440 414-2740
Westlake (G-19416)
Wesbanco Inc .....E 614 208-7298
Columbus (G-8888)
Westfield Bank Fsb .....E 800 368-8930
Westfield Center (G-19309)

BANKS: Federal Reserve

Federal Rsrve Bnk of Cleveland ....A ... 216 579-2000
Cleveland (G-5523)

BANKS: Federal Reserve Branches

Federal Rsrve Bnk of Cleveland ....C ... 513 721-4787
Cincinnati (G-3539)

BANKS: Mortgage & Loan

American Eagle Mortgage Co LLC ....E ... 440 988-2900
Lorain (G-12879)
Amerifirst Financial Corp .....D 216 452-5120
Lakewood (G-12335)
Ameristate Bancorp Inc .....E 330 965-9551
Youngstown (G-19955)
Bank England Mortgage Corp .....D 440 327-5626
North Ridgeville (G-15321)
Chase Manhattan Mortgage Corp ....A ... 614 422-6900
Columbus (G-7181)
Equitable Mortgage Corporation ....E ... 614 764-1232
Columbus (G-7524)
Fairway Independent Mrtg Corp ....E ... 614 930-6552
Columbus (G-7556)
Farm Credit Mid-America .....E 740 441-9312
Albany (G-510)
Fifth Third Bank of Sthrn OH .....E 937 840-5353
Hillsboro (G-11839)
First Day Fincl Federal Cr Un .....E 937 222-4546
Dayton (G-9435)
First Federal Bank of Midwest ....E ... 419 695-1055
Delphos (G-10026)
First Ohio Banc & Lending Inc ....B ... 216 642-8900
Cleveland (G-5537)
First Ohio Home Finance Inc .....E 937 322-3396
Springfield (G-17039)
FNB Corporation .....D 330 425-1818
Twinsburg (G-18267)
Liberty Mortgage Company Inc ....E ... 614 224-4000
Columbus (G-7971)
M/I Homes Inc .....B 614 418-8000
Columbus (G-8006)
MB Financial Inc .....E 937 283-2027
Wilmington (G-19634)
National City Mortgage Inc .....A 937 910-1200
Miamisburg (G-14196)
Nations Lending Corporation .....E 440 842-4817
Westlake (G-19377)
Pgim Inc .....E 419 331-6604
Lima (G-12721)
PNC Mortgage Company .....D 412 762-2000
Miamisburg (G-14207)
Precision Funding Corp .....E 330 405-1313
Twinsburg (G-18306)
Priority Mortgage Corp .....E 614 431-1141
Worthington (G-19837)
Sunrise Mortgage Services Inc ....D 614 989-5412
Gahanna (G-11148)
Third Federal Savings .....E 440 885-4900
Cleveland (G-6523)
Vinton County Nat Bnk McArthur ....E ... 740 596-2525
Mc Arthur (G-13892)
Wells Fargo Home Mortgage Inc ....E ... 614 781-8847
Dublin (G-10373)

BANKS: National Commercial

Bank of America .....C 614 882-4319
Westerville (G-19148)
Century National Bank .....E 740 454-2521
Zanesville (G-20292)
Century National Bank .....E 800 548-3557
Zanesville (G-20293)

SERVICES

Champaign National Bank Urbana ....E 937 653-1100
Urbana *(G-18424)*
Champaign National Bank Urbana ....E 614 798-1321
Dublin *(G-10168)*
Chase Equipment Finance Inc ....C 800 678-2601
Columbus *(G-6807)*
Chase Equipment Finance Inc ....C 614 213-2246
Columbus *(G-6808)*
Citizens Nat Bnk of Bluffton ....E 419 358-8040
Bluffton *(G-1690)*
Citizens Nat Bnk of Bluffton ....E 419 224-0400
Lima *(G-12612)*
Citizens Nat Bnk Urbana Ohio ....E 937 653-1200
Urbana *(G-18427)*
Citizens National Bank ....E 740 472-1696
Woodsfield *(G-19672)*
Civista Bank ....E 419 744-3100
Norwalk *(G-15427)*
Colonial Banc Corp ....E 937 456-5544
Eaton *(G-10439)*
Congressional Bank ....E 614 441-9230
Columbus *(G-7348)*
Consumers Bancorp Inc ....C 330 868-7701
Minerva *(G-14517)*
Consumers National Bank ....E 330 868-7701
Minerva *(G-14518)*
Credit First NA ....C 216 362-5000
Brookpark *(G-1894)*
Croghan Bancshares Inc ....D 419 794-9399
Maumee *(G-13778)*
Eastern Ohio P-16 ....E 330 675-7623
Warren *(G-18705)*
Fairfield National Bank ....E 740 653-7242
Lancaster *(G-12400)*
Farmers Bank & Savings Co Inc ....E 740 992-0088
Pomeroy *(G-16094)*
Farmers National Bank ....C 330 533-3341
Canfield *(G-2137)*
Farmers National Bank ....D 330 544-7447
Niles *(G-15156)*
Farmers National Bank ....C 330 682-1010
Orrville *(G-15631)*
Farmers National Bank ....D 330 682-1030
Orrville *(G-15632)*
First Capital Bancshares Inc ....D 740 775-6777
Chillicothe *(G-2779)*
First Citizens Nat Bnk Inc ....E 419 294-2351
Upper Sandusky *(G-18407)*
First Commonwealth Bank ....E 740 548-3340
Delaware *(G-9974)*
First Commonwealth Bank ....E 740 369-0048
Delaware *(G-9975)*
First Commonwealth Bank ....E 614 336-2280
Powell *(G-16194)*
First Financial Bancorp ....C 513 551-5640
Cincinnati *(G-3555)*
First Financial Bank ....E 513 979-5800
Cincinnati *(G-3556)*
First Nat Bnk of Nelsonville ....E 740 753-1941
Nelsonville *(G-14831)*
First National Bank Bellevue ....E 419 483-7340
Bellevue *(G-1378)*
First National Bank of Pandora ....E 419 384-3221
Pandora *(G-15751)*
First National Bank of Waverly ....E 740 947-2136
Waverly *(G-18818)*
First National Bank PA ....E 330 747-0292
Youngstown *(G-20038)*
First National Bnk of Dennison ....E 740 922-2532
Dennison *(G-10049)*
FNB Corporation ....C 330 721-7484
Medina *(G-13939)*
FNB Corporation ....E 440 439-2200
Cleveland *(G-5550)*
FNB Corporation ....D 330 425-1818
Twinsburg *(G-18267)*
Futura Banc Corp ....D 937 653-1167
Urbana *(G-18434)*
Greenville National Bank ....E 937 548-1114
Greenville *(G-11383)*
Huntington Bancshares Inc ....C 614 480-8300
Columbus *(G-7781)*
Huntington National Bank ....A 330 996-6300
Akron *(G-271)*
Huntington National Bank ....A 330 384-7201
Akron *(G-272)*
Huntington National Bank ....E 330 384-7092
Akron *(G-273)*
Huntington National Bank ....D 614 480-8300
Columbus *(G-7788)*
Huntington National Bank ....E 330 343-6611
Dover *(G-10083)*
Huntington National Bank ....E 740 452-8444
Zanesville *(G-20319)*
Huntington National Bank ....C 513 762-1860
Cincinnati *(G-3742)*
Huntington National Bank ....E 740 773-2681
Chillicothe *(G-2792)*
Huntington National Bank ....E 419 226-8200
Lima *(G-12662)*
Huntington Technology Finance ....C 614 480-5169
Columbus *(G-7789)*
Icx Corporation ....E 330 656-3611
Cleveland *(G-5733)*
Jpmorgan Chase Bank Nat Assn ....E 614 248-2410
Reynoldsburg *(G-16312)*
Jpmorgan Chase Bank Nat Assn ....E 614 476-1910
Columbus *(G-7870)*
Jpmorgan Chase Bank Nat Assn ....E 513 221-1040
Cincinnati *(G-3836)*
Jpmorgan Chase Bank Nat Assn ....E 419 358-4055
Bluffton *(G-1692)*
Jpmorgan Chase Bank Nat Assn ....E 513 985-5120
Cincinnati *(G-3837)*
Jpmorgan Chase Bank Nat Assn ....A 740 363-8032
Delaware *(G-9992)*
Jpmorgan Chase Bank Nat Assn ....E 419 394-2358
Saint Marys *(G-16526)*
Jpmorgan Chase Bank Nat Assn ....E 419 294-4944
Upper Sandusky *(G-18408)*
Jpmorgan Chase Bank Nat Assn ....E 740 676-2671
Bellaire *(G-1334)*
Jpmorgan Chase Bank Nat Assn ....E 330 972-1905
Cuyahoga Falls *(G-9104)*
Jpmorgan Chase Bank Nat Assn ....E 513 985-5350
Milford *(G-14399)*
Jpmorgan Chase Bank Nat Assn ....E 513 595-6450
Cincinnati *(G-3839)*
Jpmorgan Chase Bank Nat Assn ....E 440 442-7800
Cleveland *(G-5805)*
Jpmorgan Chase Bank Nat Assn ....E 330 972-1735
New Franklin *(G-14910)*
Jpmorgan Chase Bank Nat Assn ....E 330 287-5101
Wooster *(G-19733)*
Jpmorgan Chase Bank Nat Assn ....E 440 352-5491
Perry *(G-15823)*
Jpmorgan Chase Bank Nat Assn ....E 419 424-7570
Findlay *(G-10929)*
Jpmorgan Chase Bank Nat Assn ....A 937 534-8218
Dayton *(G-9530)*
Jpmorgan Chase Bank Nat Assn ....E 330 287-5101
Wooster *(G-19734)*
Jpmorgan Chase Bank Nat Assn ....E 419 946-3015
Mount Gilead *(G-14727)*
Jpmorgan Chase Bank Nat Assn ....E 419 586-6668
Celina *(G-2596)*
Jpmorgan Chase Bank Nat Assn ....B 440 352-5969
Painesville *(G-15717)*
Jpmorgan Chase Bank Nat Assn ....E 330 545-2551
Girard *(G-11290)*
Jpmorgan Chase Bank Nat Assn ....E 440 286-6111
Chardon *(G-2699)*
Jpmorgan Chase Bank Nat Assn ....E 330 972-1915
Akron *(G-295)*
Jpmorgan Chase Bank Nat Assn ....E 330 759-1750
Youngstown *(G-20088)*
Jpmorgan Chase Bank Nat Assn ....E 419 424-7512
Findlay *(G-10930)*
Jpmorgan Chase Bank Nat Assn ....D 614 248-5800
Westerville *(G-19267)*
Jpmorgan Chase Bank Nat Assn ....E 740 374-2263
Marietta *(G-13341)*
Jpmorgan Chase Bank Nat Assn ....E 614 248-7505
Westerville *(G-19268)*
Jpmorgan Chase Bank Nat Assn ....C 614 248-5800
Westerville *(G-19269)*
Jpmorgan Chase Bank Nat Assn ....E 419 739-3600
Wapakoneta *(G-18647)*
Jpmorgan Chase Bank Nat Assn ....E 614 759-8955
Reynoldsburg *(G-16311)*
Keybanc Capital Markets Inc ....B 800 553-2240
Cleveland *(G-5826)*
Keybank National Association ....B 800 539-2968
Cleveland *(G-5827)*
Keybank National Association ....E 216 689-8481
Cleveland *(G-5828)*
Kingston National Bank Inc ....E 740 642-2191
Kingston *(G-12316)*
Lcnb National Bank ....D 513 932-1414
Lebanon *(G-12478)*
Lcnb National Bank ....D 937 456-5544
Eaton *(G-10450)*
Merchants National Bank ....E 937 393-1134
Hillsboro *(G-11851)*
Merrill Lynch Business ....E 513 791-5700
Blue Ash *(G-1611)*
National City Mortgage ....E 614 401-5030
Dublin *(G-10286)*
One Main Financial Services ....C 419 841-0785
Toledo *(G-17963)*
Pandora Bancshares Inc ....E 419 384-3221
Pandora *(G-15754)*
Park National Bank ....C 740 349-8451
Newark *(G-15089)*
Park National Bank ....E 614 228-0063
Columbus *(G-8420)*
Park National Bank ....C 740 349-8451
Newark *(G-15090)*
Park National Bank ....E 937 324-6800
Springfield *(G-17094)*
Peoples Bancorp Inc ....E 740 373-3155
Marietta *(G-13367)*
Peoples Bank ....E 937 748-0067
Springboro *(G-16980)*
Peoples Bank ....C 937 382-1441
Wilmington *(G-19640)*
Peoples Bank ....E 740 439-2767
Cambridge *(G-2080)*
Peoples Bank National Assn ....E 937 746-5733
Franklin *(G-11037)*
PNC Bank National Association ....C 330 375-8342
Akron *(G-387)*
PNC Bank National Association ....E 740 349-8431
Newark *(G-15092)*
PNC Bank National Association ....E 419 621-2930
Sandusky *(G-16632)*
PNC Bank National Association ....C 330 854-0974
Canal Fulton *(G-2096)*
PNC Bank National Association ....B 419 259-5466
Toledo *(G-17981)*
PNC Bank National Association ....C 330 742-4426
Youngstown *(G-20162)*
PNC Bank National Association ....C 330 562-9700
Aurora *(G-839)*
Second National Bank ....E 937 548-2122
Greenville *(G-11395)*
Standing Stone National Bank ....E 740 653-5115
Lancaster *(G-12438)*
State Bank and Trust Company ....E 419 485-5521
Montpelier *(G-14618)*
The First Central National Bnk ....E 937 663-4186
Saint Paris *(G-16534)*
The Liberty Nat Bankof Ada ....E 419 673-1217
Kenton *(G-12288)*
United Bank National Assn ....E 419 562-3040
Bucyrus *(G-2003)*
Unity National Bank ....E 937 773-0752
Piqua *(G-16033)*
US Bank National Association ....A 513 632-4234
Cincinnati *(G-4738)*
US Bank National Association ....E 740 353-4151
Portsmouth *(G-16178)*
US Bank National Association ....A 513 979-1000
Cincinnati *(G-4739)*
US Bank National Association ....E 513 458-2844
Cincinnati *(G-4740)*
US Bank National Association ....D 937 873-7845
Fairborn *(G-10685)*
US Bank National Association ....E 937 335-8351
Troy *(G-18236)*
US Bank National Association ....E 937 498-1131
Sidney *(G-16803)*
Waterford Bank National Assn ....D 419 720-3900
Toledo *(G-18147)*
Wells Fargo Bank National Assn ....D 513 424-6640
Middletown *(G-14339)*

BANKS: State Commercial

Andover Bancorp Inc ....E 440 293-7605
Andover *(G-603)*
Apple Creek Banking Co (inc) ....E 330 698-2631
Apple Creek *(G-617)*
Buckeye Community Bank ....E 440 233-8800
Lorain *(G-12888)*
Chemical Bank ....E 440 779-0807
North Olmsted *(G-15281)*
Chemical Bank ....D 330 314-1380
Youngstown *(G-19987)*
Citizens Bank National Assn ....D 330 580-1913
Canton *(G-2255)*

SERVICES SECTION | BARBER SHOPS

Citizens Bnk of Logan Ohio Inc ... E ... 740 380-2561
Logan *(G-12833)*
Civista Bank ... E ... 419 744-3100
Norwalk *(G-15427)*
CNB Bank ... D ... 419 562-7040
Bucyrus *(G-1983)*
Commercial Svgs Bank Millersbu ... E ... 330 674-9015
Millersburg *(G-14466)*
Crogan Colonial Bank ... E ... 419 483-2541
Bellevue *(G-1375)*
CSB Bancorp Inc ... E ... 330 674-9015
Millersburg *(G-14473)*
Farmers Citizens Bank ... E ... 419 562-7040
Bucyrus *(G-1990)*
Farmers National Bank ... D ... 330 544-7447
Niles *(G-15156)*
Federal Home Ln Bnk Cincinnati ... D ... 513 852-5719
Cincinnati *(G-3537)*
Fifth Third Bank ... C ... 513 574-4457
Cincinnati *(G-3547)*
Fifth Third Bank ... C ... 440 984-2402
Amherst *(G-587)*
Fifth Third Bank ... D ... 513 579-5203
Cincinnati *(G-3549)*
Fifth Third Bank of NW Ohio ... B ... 419 259-7820
Toledo *(G-17734)*
First Federal Bank of Midwest ... E ... 419 695-1055
Delphos *(G-10026)*
First Financial Bank ... C ... 877 322-9530
Cincinnati *(G-3557)*
First National Bank PA ... E ... 330 747-0292
Youngstown *(G-20038)*
First State Bank ... E ... 937 695-0331
Winchester *(G-19661)*
Fort Jennings State Bank ... E ... 419 286-2527
Fort Jennings *(G-10983)*
Henry County Bank ... E ... 419 599-1065
Napoleon *(G-14808)*
Hometown Bank ... E ... 330 673-9827
Kent *(G-12236)*
Huntington National Bank ... E ... 330 742-7013
Youngstown *(G-20072)*
Huntington National Bank ... E ... 740 695-3323
Saint Clairsville *(G-16489)*
Huntington National Bank ... E ... 419 782-5050
Defiance *(G-9918)*
Independence Bank ... E ... 216 447-1444
Cleveland *(G-5742)*
Jpmorgan Chase Bank Nat Assn ... A ... 614 436-3055
Columbus *(G-6818)*
Jpmorgan Chase Bank Nat Assn ... E ... 513 826-2317
Blue Ash *(G-1591)*
Jpmorgan Chase Bank Nat Assn ... E ... 216 781-2127
Columbus *(G-7871)*
Jpmorgan Chase Bank Nat Assn ... E ... 740 423-4111
Belpre *(G-1405)*
Jpmorgan Chase Bank Nat Assn ... E ... 614 248-5391
Columbus *(G-7872)*
Jpmorgan Chase Bank Nat Assn ... E ... 614 248-2083
Columbus *(G-7874)*
Jpmorgan Chase Bank Nat Assn ... E ... 216 781-4437
Cleveland *(G-5806)*
Jpmorgan Chase Bank Nat Assn ... E ... 614 759-8955
Reynoldsburg *(G-16311)*
Keybank National Association ... B ... 800 539-2968
Cleveland *(G-5827)*
Liberty Savings Bank FSB ... C ... 937 382-1000
Wilmington *(G-19629)*
Mechanics Bank ... E ... 419 524-0831
Mansfield *(G-13213)*
North Valley Bank ... E ... 740 452-7920
Zanesville *(G-20347)*
Northwest Bank ... B ... 330 342-4018
Hudson *(G-12000)*
Northwest Ohio Chapter Cfma ... E ... 419 891-1040
Maumee *(G-13824)*
Ohio Valley Bank Company ... C ... 740 446-2631
Gallipolis *(G-11207)*
Ohio Valley Bank Company ... E ... 740 446-2631
Gallipolis *(G-11209)*
Peoples Bank ... C ... 740 373-3155
Marietta *(G-13368)*
Peoples Bank ... E ... 740 286-6773
Wellston *(G-18854)*
Portage Community Bank Inc ... D ... 330 296-8090
Ravenna *(G-16254)*
Savings Bank ... E ... 740 474-3191
Circleville *(G-4848)*
The Liberty Nat Bankof Ada ... E ... 419 673-1217
Kenton *(G-12288)*
The Middlefield Banking Co ... E ... 440 632-1666
Middlefield *(G-14277)*
The Peoples Bank Co Inc ... E ... 419 678-2385
Coldwater *(G-6766)*
Unified Bank ... E ... 740 633-0445
Martins Ferry *(G-13479)*
Union Bank Company ... E ... 740 387-2265
Marion *(G-13467)*
Wayne Savings Community Bank ... D ... 330 264-5767
Wooster *(G-19780)*
Wesbanco Inc ... E ... 740 532-0263
Ironton *(G-12167)*
Wesbanco Bank Inc ... D ... 740 425-1927
Barnesville *(G-980)*
Wesbanco Bank Inc ... E ... 513 741-5766
Cincinnati *(G-4778)*

BANQUET HALL FACILITIES

A Tara Tiffanys Property ... E ... 330 448-0778
Brookfield *(G-1851)*
Assembly Center ... E ... 800 582-1099
Monroe *(G-14560)*
Banquets Unlimited ... E ... 859 689-4000
Cincinnati *(G-3017)*
Brown Derby Roadhouse ... E ... 330 528-3227
Hudson *(G-11968)*
Buffalo Jacks ... E ... 937 473-2524
Covington *(G-9046)*
Buns of Delaware Inc ... E ... 740 363-2867
Delaware *(G-9956)*
Camden FLS Rcption Cnfrnce Ctr ... E ... 419 448-7699
Tiffin *(G-17511)*
Carrie Cerino Restaurants Inc ... C ... 440 237-3434
Cleveland *(G-5129)*
Cheers Chalet ... E ... 740 654-9036
Lancaster *(G-12378)*
City Life Inc ... E ... 216 523-5899
Cleveland *(G-5186)*
City of Beavercreek ... D ... 937 320-0742
Beavercreek *(G-1141)*
City of Centerville ... D ... 937 438-3585
Dayton *(G-9302)*
City of Vandalia ... E ... 937 890-1300
Vandalia *(G-18517)*
Cleveland Metroparks ... C ... 216 661-6500
Cleveland *(G-5267)*
Connor Concepts Inc ... D ... 937 291-1661
Dayton *(G-9317)*
Coshocton Village Inn Suites ... E ... 740 622-9455
Coshocton *(G-9010)*
Deyor Performing Arts Center ... E ... 330 744-4269
Youngstown *(G-20017)*
Dinos Catering Inc ... E ... 440 943-1010
Wickliffe *(G-19455)*
Farm Inc ... E ... 513 922-7020
Cincinnati *(G-3532)*
Findlay Inn & Conference Ctr ... D ... 419 422-5682
Findlay *(G-10904)*
German Family Society Inc ... E ... 330 678-8229
Kent *(G-12234)*
Grandview Ht Ltd Partnr Ohio ... D ... 937 766-5519
Springfield *(G-17043)*
Guys Party Center ... E ... 330 724-6373
Akron *(G-247)*
Haribol Haribol Inc ... E ... 330 339-7731
New Philadelphia *(G-14963)*
Heatherwoode Golf Course ... C ... 937 748-3222
Springboro *(G-16969)*
Iacominis Papa Joes Inc ... D ... 330 923-7999
Akron *(G-274)*
Kinane Inc ... D ... 513 459-0177
Mason *(G-13605)*
Kitchen Katering Inc ... E ... 216 481-8080
Euclid *(G-10647)*
Kohler Foods Inc ... E ... 937 291-3600
Dayton *(G-9550)*
La Villa Cnference Banquet Ctr ... E ... 216 265-9305
Cleveland *(G-5844)*
Lees Roby Inc ... E ... 330 872-0983
Newton Falls *(G-15139)*
Leos La Piazza Inc ... E ... 937 339-5553
Troy *(G-18210)*
Little Miami River Catering Co ... E ... 937 848-2464
Bellbrook *(G-1341)*
Lorain Party Center ... E ... 440 282-5599
Lorain *(G-12923)*
Mackil Inc ... E ... 937 833-3310
Brookville *(G-1915)*
Makoy Center Inc ... E ... 614 777-1211
Hilliard *(G-11787)*
Mandalay Inc ... E ... 937 294-6600
Moraine *(G-14671)*
Mason Family Resorts LLC ... B ... 513 339-0141
Mason *(G-13615)*
Michaels Inc ... D ... 440 357-0384
Mentor *(G-14085)*
Mocha House Inc ... E ... 330 392-3020
Warren *(G-18731)*
Mustard Seed Health Fd Mkt Inc ... E ... 440 519-3663
Solon *(G-16875)*
New Jersey Aquarium LLC ... D ... 614 414-7300
Columbus *(G-8186)*
Occasions Party Centre ... E ... 330 882-5113
New Franklin *(G-14911)*
Old Barn Out Back Inc ... D ... 419 999-3989
Lima *(G-12711)*
Pines Golf Club ... E ... 330 684-1414
Orrville *(G-15644)*
Raymond Recepton House ... E ... 614 276-6127
Columbus *(G-8490)*
Refectory Restaurant Inc ... E ... 614 451-9774
Columbus *(G-8501)*
Riverside Cmnty Urban Redev ... C ... 330 929-3000
Cuyahoga Falls *(G-9120)*
Roscoe Village Foundation ... D ... 740 622-2222
Coshocton *(G-9026)*
Sam BS Restaurant ... E ... 419 353-2277
Bowling Green *(G-1748)*
Sauder Village ... B ... 419 446-2541
Archbold *(G-638)*
Snpj Recreation Farm ... E ... 440 256-3423
Willoughby *(G-19573)*
Spagnas ... E ... 740 376-9245
Marietta *(G-13383)*
The Oaks Lodge ... E ... 330 769-2601
Chippewa Lake *(G-2838)*
Toris Station ... E ... 513 829-7815
Fairfield *(G-10791)*
Twin Haven Reception Hall ... E ... 330 425-1616
Twinsburg *(G-18331)*
Valley Hospitality Inc ... E ... 740 374-9660
Marietta *(G-13395)*
Villa Milano Inc ... E ... 614 882-2058
Columbus *(G-8851)*
Vulcan Machinery Corporation ... E ... 330 376-6025
Akron *(G-491)*
Winking Lizard Inc ... D ... 330 467-1002
Peninsula *(G-15816)*
Winking Lizard Inc ... D ... 330 220-9944
Brunswick *(G-1948)*

BAR

Bass Lake Tavern Inc ... D ... 440 285-3100
Chardon *(G-2688)*
Bpo Elks of USA ... E ... 740 622-0794
Coshocton *(G-9000)*
Brothers Properties Corp ... C ... 513 381-3000
Cincinnati *(G-3081)*
Elms Country Club Inc ... E ... 330 833-2668
North Lawrence *(G-15258)*
Hyatt Corporation ... B ... 614 463-1234
Columbus *(G-7791)*
Louisville Frternal Order of E ... E ... 330 875-2113
Louisville *(G-12968)*
Loyal Oak Golf Course Inc ... E ... 330 825-2904
Barberton *(G-960)*
Mohawk Golf Club ... E ... 419 447-5876
Tiffin *(G-17525)*
Northeast Cincinnati Hotel LLC ... C ... 513 459-9800
Mason *(G-13623)*
OBannon Creek Golf Club ... E ... 513 683-5657
Loveland *(G-13019)*
Springfield Country Club Co ... E ... 937 399-4215
Springfield *(G-17118)*
Waterfront & Associates Inc ... B ... 859 581-1414
Cincinnati *(G-4770)*

BARBER SHOPS

Attractions ... E ... 740 592-5600
Athens *(G-771)*
Head Quarters Inc ... E ... 440 233-8508
Lorain *(G-12906)*
Lucas Metropolitan Hsing Auth ... D ... 419 259-9457
Toledo *(G-17869)*
Mfh Inc ... E ... 937 435-4701
Dayton *(G-9611)*
Ricks Hair Center ... E ... 330 545-5120
Girard *(G-11299)*

SERVICES

BARGES BUILDING & REPAIR

McGinnis Inc..............................C...... 740 377-4391
South Point (G-16940)

McNational Inc..........................E...... 740 377-4391
South Point (G-16941)

Superior Marine Ways Inc ....C...... 740 894-6224
Proctorville (G-16219)

BARS: Concrete Reinforcing, Fabricated Steel

Gateway Concrete Forming Svcs....D...... 513 353-2000
Miamitown (G-14241)

Ohio Bridge Corporation.............C...... 740 432-6334
Cambridge (G-2079)

Smith Brothers Erection Inc ....E...... 740 373-3575
Marietta (G-13382)

BASKETS, WHOLESALE

Potter Inc ....E...... 419 636-5624
Bryan (G-1970)

BATTERY CHARGERS

TL Industries Inc ....C...... 419 666-8144
Northwood (G-15410)

BEADS, WHOLESALE

J L Swaney Inc ....E...... 740 884-4450
Chillicothe (G-2795)

BEARINGS & PARTS Ball

Federal-Mogul Powertrain LLC.......C...... 740 432-2393
Cambridge (G-2067)

BEAUTY & BARBER SHOP EQPT

Aluminum Line Products Company ..D...... 440 835-8880
Westlake (G-19316)

Carroll Hills Industries Inc ....D...... 330 627-5524
Carrollton (G-2563)

BEAUTY CULTURE SCHOOL

Yearwood Corporation ....E...... 937 223-3572
Dayton (G-9889)

BEAUTY SALONS

Calico Court.............................E...... 740 455-2541
Zanesville (G-20286)

Changes Hair Designers Inc ....E...... 614 846-6666
Columbus (G-6806)

Ecotage ....E...... 513 782-2229
Cincinnati (G-3484)

Flux A Salon By Hazelton ....E...... 419 841-5100
Perrysburg (G-15866)

G E G Enterprises Inc ....E...... 330 494-9160
Canton (G-2320)

Head Quarters Inc ....E...... 440 233-8508
Lorain (G-12906)

Intl Europa Salon & Spa ....E...... 216 292-6969
Cleveland (G-5766)

JC Penney Corporation Inc...........B...... 330 633-7700
Akron (G-288)

Kenneths Hair Salons & Day Sp.....B...... 614 457-7712
Columbus (G-7893)

Kerr House Inc ....E...... 419 832-1733
Grand Rapids (G-11327)

Laser Hair Removal Center ....D...... 937 433-7536
Dayton (G-9559)

Mark Luikart Inc ....E...... 330 339-9141
New Philadelphia (G-14973)

Mfh Inc ....E...... 937 435-4701
Dayton (G-9611)

Mfh Inc ....D...... 937 435-4701
Dayton (G-9612)

Mitchells Salon & Day Spa ....C...... 513 793-0900
West Chester (G-18973)

Mitchells Salon & Day Spa ....E...... 513 772-3200
Cincinnati (G-4062)

Mzf Inc ....E...... 216 464-3910
Cleveland (G-6032)

Rometrics Too Hair Nail Gllery ....E...... 440 808-1391
Westlake (G-19402)

Salon Alexandre Inc ....E...... 513 207-8406
West Chester (G-19078)

Salon Ware Inc ....E...... 330 665-2244
Copley (G-8972)

Tanos Salon.............................E...... 216 831-7880
Cleveland (G-6498)

Tara Flaherty ....E...... 419 565-1334
Mansfield (G-13250)

BED & BREAKFAST INNS

Alexander House Inc ....E...... 513 523-4569
Oxford (G-15672)

Bass Lake Tavern Inc ....D...... 440 285-3100
Chardon (G-2688)

Eastlake Lodging LLC ....E...... 440 953-8000
Eastlake (G-10429)

Emmett Dan House Ltd Partnr ....E...... 740 392-6886
Mount Vernon (G-14764)

Riders 1812 Inn ....E...... 440 354-0922
Painesville (G-15738)

Spread Eagle Tavern Inc ....E...... 330 223-1583
Hanoverton (G-11658)

Town House Motor Lodge Corp......E...... 740 452-4511
Zanesville (G-20367)

BEDDING & BEDSPRINGS STORES

Cinmar LLC.............................C...... 513 603-1000
West Chester (G-18888)

BEDDING, BEDSPREADS, BLANKETS & SHEETS: Comforters & Quilts

Aunties Attic ....E...... 740 548-5059
Lewis Center (G-12528)

BEER & ALE WHOLESALERS

Cdc Management Co ....C...... 614 781-0216
Columbus (G-7146)

Dayton Heidelberg Distrg Co ....C...... 614 308-0400
Columbus (G-7423)

Dayton Heidelberg Distrg Co ....C...... 419 666-9783
Perrysburg (G-15855)

Donzells Flower & Grdn Ctr Inc ......E...... 330 724-0550
Akron (G-191)

Glazers Distributors Ohio Inc ....E...... 440 542-7000
Solon (G-16852)

Southern Glazers Wine and Sp.......D...... 330 422-9463
Streetsboro (G-17271)

Southern Glzers Dstrs Ohio LLC......D...... 614 552-7900
Columbus (G-8664)

BEER & ALE, WHOLESALE: Beer & Other Fermented Malt Liquors

Anheuser-Busch LLC ....C...... 513 381-3927
Cincinnati (G-2970)

Anheuser-Busch LLC ....D...... 330 438-2036
Canton (G-2189)

Bellas Co ....E...... 740 598-4171
Mingo Junction (G-14527)

Beverage Distributors Inc ....E...... 216 431-1600
Cleveland (G-5061)

Bonbright Distributors Inc ....C...... 937 222-1001
Dayton (G-9258)

Brown Distributing Inc ....D...... 740 349-7999
Newark (G-15017)

Cavalier Distributing Company ......D...... 513 247-9222
Blue Ash (G-1520)

Central Beverage Group Ltd ....C...... 614 294-3555
Lewis Center (G-12532)

City Beverage Company ....E...... 419 782-7065
Defiance (G-9906)

Columbus Distributing Company......B...... 614 846-1000
Columbus (G-7275)

Columbus Distributing Company......E...... 740 726-2211
Waldo (G-18629)

Dayton Heidelberg Distrg Co ....C...... 937 222-8692
Moraine (G-14643)

Dayton Heidelberg Distrg Co ....C...... 216 520-2626
Cleveland (G-5412)

Dayton Heidelberg Distrg Co ....C...... 419 666-9783
Perrysburg (G-15856)

Dayton Heidelberg Distrg Co ....C...... 937 220-6450
Moraine (G-14645)

Dayton Heidelberg Distrg Co ....D...... 513 421-5000
Cincinnati (G-3406)

Dickerson Distributing Company .....D...... 513 539-8483
Monroe (G-14565)

Goodman Beverage Co Inc ....D...... 440 787-2255
Lorain (G-12905)

Heidelberg Distributing Co ....E...... 614 308-0400
Columbus (G-7734)

BEER, WINE & LIQUOR STORES: Beer, Packaged

Dayton Heidelberg Distrg Co ....C...... 937 220-6450
Moraine (G-14645)

BEER, WINE & LIQUOR STORES: Wine

Iacominis Papa Joes Inc ....D...... 330 923-7999
Akron (G-274)

Larosas Inc ....A...... 513 347-5660
Cincinnati (G-3911)

BELTING: Plastic

Polychem Corporation ....D...... 419 547-1400
Clyde (G-6750)

BELTS: Seat, Automotive & Aircraft

Tk Holdings Inc ....E...... 937 778-9713
Piqua (G-16031)

BEVERAGE STORES

P-Americas LLC ....D...... 216 252-7377
Cleveland (G-6156)

Superior Beverage Group Ltd.........D...... 614 294-3555
Lewis Center (G-12562)

Superior Beverage Group Ltd.........C...... 440 703-4580
Solon (G-16904)

BEVERAGES, ALCOHOLIC: Near Beer

Georgetown Vineyards Inc............E...... 740 435-3222
Cambridge (G-2069)

BEVERAGES, ALCOHOLIC: Wines

Ferrante Wine Farm Inc ....E...... 440 466-8466
Geneva (G-11240)

BEVERAGES, BEER & ALE, WHOLESALE: Ale

Esber Beverage Company ....E...... 330 456-4361
Canton (G-2306)

Hanson Distributing Co Inc ....D...... 419 435-3214
Fostoria (G-11004)

BEVERAGES, NONALCOHOLIC: Bottled & canned soft drinks

Abbott Laboratories....................A...... 614 624-3191
Columbus (G-6851)

Borden Dairy Co Cincinnati LLC ......C...... 513 948-8811
Cincinnati (G-3068)

Heritage Beverage Company LLC ....D...... 440 255-5550
Mentor (G-14060)

Hill Distributing Company ....D...... 614 276-6533
Dublin (G-10242)

House of La Rose Cleveland..........C...... 440 746-7500
Brecksville (G-1783)

Jetro Cash and Carry Entps LLC .....D...... 216 525-0101
Cleveland (G-5794)

Knall Beverage Inc ....D...... 216 252-2500
Cleveland (G-5834)

Litter Distributing Co Inc ....D...... 740 774-2831
Chillicothe (G-2802)

M & A Distributing Co Inc ....E...... 440 703-4580
Solon (G-16868)

Matesich Distributing Co ....D...... 740 349-8686
Newark (G-15065)

Nwo Beverage Inc ....E...... 419 725-2162
Northwood (G-15403)

Ohio Valley Wine Company ....D...... 513 771-9370
Cincinnati (G-4161)

R L Lipton Distributing LLC ....D...... 800 321-6553
Austintown (G-860)

R L Lipton Distributing Co ....D...... 216 475-4150
Maple Heights (G-13292)

Rhinegeist LLC ....D...... 513 381-1367
Cincinnati (G-4368)

Superior Beverage Company Inc .....D...... 440 703-4580
Solon (G-16903)

The Maple City Ice Company ....E...... 419 668-2531
Norwalk (G-15457)

Treu House of Munch Inc ....E...... 419 666-7770
Northwood (G-15412)

Warsteiner Importers Agency ....E...... 513 942-9872
West Chester (G-19034)

G & J Pepsi-Cola Bottlers Inc ....E 740 774-2148
  Chillicothe (G-2782)
P-Americas LLC ....E 419 227-3541
  Lima (G-12716)
Pepsi-Cola Metro Btlg Co Inc ....B 330 963-0426
  Twinsburg (G-18304)

BEVERAGES, NONALCOHOLIC: Carbonated

G & J Pepsi-Cola Bottlers Inc ....B 740 354-9191
  Franklin Furnace (G-11045)
P-Americas LLC ....C 330 746-7652
  Youngstown (G-20149)

BEVERAGES, NONALCOHOLIC: Carbonated, Canned & Bottled, Etc

Central Coca-Cola Btlg Co Inc ....C 419 476-6622
  Toledo (G-17643)
Coca-Cola Bottling Co Cnsld ....D 937 878-5000
  Dayton (G-9311)
G & J Pepsi-Cola Bottlers Inc ....D 740 593-3366
  Athens (G-781)

BEVERAGES, NONALCOHOLIC: Flavoring extracts & syrups, nec

Abbott Laboratories ....A 614 624-3191
  Columbus (G-6851)
Agrana Fruit Us Inc ....C 937 693-3821
  Botkins (G-1706)

BEVERAGES, NONALCOHOLIC: Soft Drinks, Canned & Bottled, Etc

American Bottling Company ....D 614 237-4201
  Columbus (G-6913)
G & J Pepsi-Cola Bottlers Inc ....D 740 452-2721
  Zanesville (G-20309)
Pepsi-Cola Metro Btlg Co Inc ....B 937 461-4664
  Dayton (G-9690)

BEVERAGES, WINE & DISTILLED ALCOHOLIC, WHOLESALE: Wine

August Food & Wine LLC ....E 513 421-2020
  Cincinnati (G-3003)
Bellas Co ....E 740 598-4171
  Mingo Junction (G-14527)
Dayton Heidelberg Distrg Co ....C 614 308-0400
  Columbus (G-7423)
Dayton Heidelberg Distrg Co ....C 937 220-6450
  Moraine (G-14645)
Goodman Beverage Co Inc ....D 440 787-2255
  Lorain (G-12905)
H Dennert Distributing Corp ....C 513 871-7272
  Cincinnati (G-3666)
M & M Wine Cellar Inc ....E 330 536-6450
  Lowellville (G-13041)
Mid-Ohio Wines Inc ....E 440 989-1011
  Lorain (G-12927)
Ohio Valley Wine Company ....D 513 771-9370
  Cincinnati (G-4161)
R L Lipton Distributing Co ....D 216 475-4150
  Maple Heights (G-13292)
Southern Glazers Wine and Sp ....D 330 422-9463
  Streetsboro (G-17271)
Southern Glazers Wine and Sp ....D 513 755-7082
  Fairfield (G-10786)
Southern Glzers Dstrs Ohio LLC ....D 614 552-7900
  Columbus (G-8664)
Superior Beverage Company Inc ....D 440 703-4580
  Solon (G-16903)
Vanguard Wines LLC ....D 614 291-3493
  Columbus (G-8844)
Vintage Wine Distributor Inc ....E 614 876-2580
  Columbus (G-8852)
Wine Trends Inc ....E 216 520-2626
  Independence (G-12141)

BEVERAGES, WINE/DISTILLED ALCOH, WHOL: Brandy/Brandy Spirits

Fredericks Wine & Dine ....E 216 581-5299
  Cleveland (G-5576)

BIBLE CAMPS

Sheldon Harry E Calvary Camp ....D 440 593-4381
  Conneaut (G-8958)

BICYCLE SHOPS

Zide Sport Shop of Ohio Inc ....D 740 373-6446
  Marietta (G-13403)

BILLIARD & POOL PARLORS

Cloverleaf Bowling Center Inc ....E 216 524-4833
  Cleveland (G-5308)

BILLIARD EQPT & SPLYS WHOLESALERS

Dtv Inc ....E 216 226-5465
  Mayfield Heights (G-13873)

BILLIARD TABLE REPAIR SVCS

Dtv Inc ....E 216 226-5465
  Mayfield Heights (G-13873)

BILLING & BOOKKEEPING SVCS

APS Medical Billing ....D 419 866-1804
  Toledo (G-17597)
Billing Connection Inc ....E 740 964-0043
  Reynoldsburg (G-16285)
Cbiz Med MGT Professionals Inc ....E 614 771-2222
  Hilliard (G-11754)
Change Hlth Prac MGT Solns Grp ....E 937 291-7850
  Miamisburg (G-14151)
Cincinnati Medical Billing Svc ....E 513 965-8041
  Cincinnati (G-3253)
Compensation Programs of Ohio ....E 330 652-9821
  Youngstown (G-20005)
Comprehensive Med Data MGT LLC .....D 614 717-9840
  Powell (G-16191)
Doctors Consulting Service ....E 614 793-1980
  Dublin (G-10201)
E T Financial Service Inc ....E 937 716-1726
  Trotwood (G-18193)
Emergency Medical Svcs Billing ....E 216 664-2598
  Cleveland (G-5474)
Healthpro Medical Billing Inc ....D 419 223-2717
  Lima (G-12657)
Kennedy Group Enterprises Inc ....E 440 879-0078
  Strongsville (G-17320)
MBI Solutions Inc ....C 937 619-4000
  Dayton (G-9592)
MD Business Solutions Inc ....E 513 872-4500
  Blue Ash (G-1606)
Medic Management Group LLC ....D 330 670-5316
  Akron (G-329)
Medical Account Services Inc ....E 937 297-6072
  Moraine (G-14675)
Medical Care PSC Inc ....E 513 281-4400
  Cincinnati (G-3993)
Medical Care Reimbursement ....E 513 281-4400
  Cincinnati (G-3994)
Medicount Management Inc ....E 513 772-4465
  Cincinnati (G-3997)
Midwest Emergency Services LLC ....E 586 294-2700
  Fairlawn (G-10841)
Nationwide Childrens Hospital ....E 330 253-5200
  Akron (G-343)
Northcoast Healthcare MGT ....C 216 591-2000
  Beachwood (G-1087)
Ohio Bell Telephone Company ....A 216 822-3439
  Cleveland (G-6115)
Pioneer Physicians Networking ....E 330 633-6601
  Tallmadge (G-17484)
Quadax Inc ....E 330 759-4600
  Youngstown (G-20170)
Quadax Inc ....C 440 777-6300
  Middleburg Heights (G-14256)
Quadax Inc ....E 614 882-1200
  Westerville (G-19296)
Radiology Assoc Canton Inc ....E 330 363-2842
  Canton (G-2450)
Real Property Management Inc ....E 614 766-6500
  Dublin (G-10320)
Specialty Medical Services ....E 440 245-8010
  Lorain (G-12943)
Terry J Reppa & Associates ....E 440 888-8533
  Cleveland (G-6516)
Village of Byesville ....E 740 685-5901
  Byesville (G-2026)

BINDING SVC: Books & Manuals

A-A Blueprint Co Inc ....E 330 794-8803
  Akron (G-13)
AGS Custom Graphics Inc ....D 330 963-7770
  Macedonia (G-13058)

Bindery & Spc Pressworks Inc ....D 614 873-4623
  Plain City (G-16046)
Black River Group Inc ....D 419 524-6699
  Mansfield (G-13142)
Consoldated Graphics Group Inc ....C 216 881-9191
  Cleveland (G-5335)
Copley Ohio Newspapers Inc ....C 330 364-5577
  New Philadelphia (G-14951)
Fedex Office & Print Svcs Inc ....E 937 436-0677
  Dayton (G-9431)
Hecks Direct Mail & Prtg Svc ....E 419 697-3505
  Toledo (G-17797)
Hopewell Industries Inc ....D 740 622-3563
  Coshocton (G-9018)
Monco Enterprises Inc ....A 937 461-0034
  Dayton (G-9642)
Ohio Laminating & Binding Inc ....E 614 771-4868
  Hilliard (G-11802)
Quick Tab II Inc ....D 419 448-6622
  Tiffin (G-17533)
R T Industries Inc ....C 937 335-5784
  Troy (G-18224)
Repro Acquisition Company LLC ....E 216 738-3800
  Cleveland (G-6309)
Tj Metzgers Inc ....D 419 861-8611
  Toledo (G-18066)
Traxium LLC ....E 330 572-8200
  Stow (G-17236)
Youngstown ARC Engraving Co ....E 330 793-2471
  Youngstown (G-20254)

BINDING SVC: Pamphlets

Macke Brothers Inc ....D 513 771-7500
  Cincinnati (G-3956)

BINGO HALL

David Barber Civic Center ....E 740 498-4383
  Newcomerstown (G-15129)
Our Lady Prptul Hlp Cnmty Bngo ....E 513 742-3200
  Cincinnati (G-4191)

BIOFEEDBACK CENTERS

First Call For Help Inc ....E 419 599-1660
  Napoleon (G-14805)
Sleep Care Inc ....E 614 901-8989
  Columbus (G-8652)

BIOLOGICAL PRDTS: Exc Diagnostic

Bio-Blood Components Inc ....E 614 294-3183
  Columbus (G-7039)
EMD Millipore Corporation ....C 513 631-0445
  Norwood (G-15462)
Perkinelmer Hlth Sciences Inc ....E 330 825-4525
  Akron (G-378)

BIRTH CONTROL CLINIC

Planned Prnthood of Mhning Vly ....E 330 788-6506
  Youngstown (G-20158)

BLASTING SVC: Sand, Metal Parts

Industrial Mill Maintenance ....E 330 746-1155
  Youngstown (G-20078)

BLOCK & BRICK: Sand Lime

R W Sidley Incorporated ....E 440 352-9343
  Painesville (G-15735)

BLOCKS: Standard, Concrete Or Cinder

Hanson Aggregates East LLC ....E 740 773-2172
  Chillicothe (G-2784)
J P Sand & Gravel Company ....E 614 497-0083
  Lockbourne (G-12822)
Koltcz Concrete Block Co ....E 440 232-3630
  Bedford (G-1287)
National Lime and Stone Co ....E 614 497-0083
  Lockbourne (G-12823)
Quality Block & Supply Inc ....E 330 364-4411
  Mount Eaton (G-14723)
Snyder Concrete Products Inc ....E 937 885-5176
  Moraine (G-14697)
Stocker Sand & Gravel Co ....E 740 254-4635
  Gnadenhutten (G-11312)

SERVICES

BLOOD BANK

Bio-Blood Components Inc ....E 614 294-3183
Columbus (G-7039)
Biolife Plasma Services LP ....E 419 224-0117
Lima (G-12608)
Biomat Usa Inc ....E 419 531-3332
Toledo (G-17614)
Csl Plasma Inc ....D 937 331-9186
Dayton (G-9342)
Csl Plasma Inc ....D 216 398-0440
Cleveland (G-5385)
Foundation For Communit ....C 937 461-3450
Dayton (G-9446)
Lifeshare Cmnty Blood Svcs Inc ....E 440 322-6159
Elyria (G-10527)
Lifeshare Community Blood Svcs ....E 440 322-6573
Elyria (G-10528)

BLOOD DONOR STATIONS

American National Red Cross ....E 614 334-0425
Columbus (G-6933)
Csl Plasma Inc ....D 330 535-4338
Akron (G-175)

BLOOD RELATED HEALTH SVCS

24 - Seven Home Hlth Care LLC ......E 614 794-0325
Hilliard (G-11737)
Black Stone Cincinnati LLC ....E 937 773-8573
Piqua (G-15997)
Blood Services Centl Ohio Reg ....C 614 253-7981
Columbus (G-7048)
Cardinal Health Inc ....C 614 473-0786
Columbus (G-7120)
Carespring Health Care MGT LLC ....E 513 943-4000
Loveland (G-12981)
Central Ohio Poison Center ....E 800 222-1222
Columbus (G-7161)
County of Carroll ....E 330 627-4866
Carrollton (G-2564)
Diverscare Healthcare Svcs Inc ......E 513 867-4100
Hamilton (G-11591)
Engaged Health Care Bus Svcs ....E 614 457-8180
Columbus (G-7516)
First Choice Medical Staffing ....D 513 631-5656
Cincinnati (G-3554)
Health Data MGT Solutions Inc ....D 216 595-1232
Beachwood (G-1062)
Health Partners Western Ohio ....E 419 679-5994
Kenton (G-12282)
Horizon Home Health Care ....E 937 264-3155
Vandalia (G-18529)
Kindred Healthcare Inc ....E 513 336-0178
Mason (G-13606)
Maxim Healthcare Services Inc ....D 740 772-4100
Chillicothe (G-2804)
Ohio State University ....D 614 257-5200
Columbus (G-8314)
Peregrine Health Services Inc ....D 419 586-4135
Celina (G-2606)
Signature Healthcare LLC ....D 330 372-1977
Warren (G-18743)
Taylor Murtis Human Svcs Sys ....C 216 283-4400
Cleveland (G-6502)
Toledo Clinic Inc ....C 419 865-3111
Holland (G-11919)
Unity Health Network LLC ....E 330 655-3820
Hudson (G-12010)
Unity Health Network LLC ....D 330 923-5899
Cuyahoga Falls (G-9135)
Unity Health Network LLC ....E 330 633-7782
Tallmadge (G-17497)
Wheeling Hospital Inc ....D 740 676-4623
Bellaire (G-1336)

BLOWERS & FANS

A A S Amels Sheet Meta L Inc ....E 330 793-9326
Youngstown (G-19943)
Kirk Williams Company Inc ....D 614 875-9023
Grove City (G-11445)
Langdon Inc ....E 513 733-5955
Cincinnati (G-3909)
Ohio Blow Pipe Company ....E 216 681-7379
Cleveland (G-6116)
Pcy Enterprises Inc ....E 513 241-5566
Cincinnati (G-4219)
Tosoh America Inc ....B 614 539-8622
Grove City (G-11478)

BLUEPRINTING SVCS

American Reprographics Co LLC ......E 614 224-5149
Columbus (G-6936)
ARC Document Solutions Inc ....D 216 281-1234
Cleveland (G-5003)
Cannell Graphics LLC ....E 614 781-9760
Columbus (G-7110)
Franklin Imaging Llc ....E 614 885-6894
Columbus (G-7618)
Key Blue Prints Inc ....E 614 228-3285
Columbus (G-7898)
Profile Digital Printing LLC ....E 937 866-4241
Dayton (G-9719)
Queen City Reprographics ....C 513 326-2300
Cincinnati (G-4321)

BOARDING SCHOOL

Marsh Foundation ....E 419 238-1695
Van Wert (G-18484)
Society of The Transfiguration ....E 513 771-7462
Cincinnati (G-4501)

BOAT BUILDING & REPAIR

Don Wartko Construction Co ....D 330 673-5252
Kent (G-12229)

BOAT DEALERS

Bob Pulte Chevrolet Inc ....E 513 932-0303
Lebanon (G-12453)
S B S Transit Inc ....B 440 288-2222
Lorain (G-12942)

BOAT DEALERS: Motor

Sima Marine Sales Inc ....E 440 269-3200
Willoughby (G-19572)
South Shore Marine Services ....E 419 433-5798
Huron (G-12033)

BOAT REPAIR SVCS

Superior Marine Ways Inc ....C 740 894-6224
Proctorville (G-16219)

BOAT YARD: Boat yards, storage & incidental repair

Containerport Group Inc ....E 513 771-0275
West Chester (G-18896)
Erie Island Resort and Marina ....E 419 734-9117
Warren (G-18707)
Sandusky Harbor Marina Inc ....E 419 627-1201
Sandusky (G-16638)
Tack-Anew Inc ....E 419 734-4212
Port Clinton (G-16119)

BODIES: Truck & Bus

Hendrickson International Corp ....D 740 929-5600
Hebron (G-11714)
Joseph Industries Inc ....D 330 528-0091
Streetsboro (G-17258)
Youngstown-Kenworth Inc ....D 330 534-9761
Hubbard (G-11952)

BOILER & HEATING REPAIR SVCS

Babcock & Wilcox Company ....A 330 753-4511
Barberton (G-944)
Columbs/Worthington Htg AC Inc .....E 614 771-5381
Columbus (G-7252)
Honeywell International Inc ....D 216 459-6053
Cleveland (G-5702)
Nbw Inc ....E 216 377-1700
Cleveland (G-6051)
Rmf Nooter Inc ....D 419 727-1970
Toledo (G-18009)
Smith & Oby Service Co ....E 440 735-5322
Bedford (G-1306)

BOILER REPAIR SHOP

Norris Brothers Co Inc ....C 216 771-2233
Cleveland (G-6074)
Osterfeld Champion Service ....E 937 254-8437
Dayton (G-9679)

BOND & MORTGAGE COMPANIES

Rapid Mortgage Company ....E 937 748-8888
Cincinnati (G-4338)
Realty Corporation of America ....E 216 522-0020
Cleveland Heights (G-6722)
Residential Finance Corp ....B 614 324-4700
Columbus (G-8520)

BOOK STORES

Barbour Publishing Inc ....E 740 922-1321
Uhrichsville (G-18339)
Friends of The Lib Cyahoga FLS ....C 330 928-2117
Cuyahoga Falls (G-9097)
Mile Inc ....D 614 794-2203
Worthington (G-19829)
Province of St John The Baptis ....D 513 241-5615
Cincinnati (G-4301)
University of Cincinnati ....E 513 556-4200
Cincinnati (G-4714)

BOOK STORES: Religious

Emerge Ministries Inc ....E 330 865-8351
Akron (G-203)

BOOKS, WHOLESALE

Afit Ls Usaf ....E 937 255-3636
Dayton (G-9154)
Barbour Publishing Inc ....E 740 922-1321
Uhrichsville (G-18339)
CSS Publishing Co Inc ....E 419 227-1818
Lima (G-12627)
Ed Map Inc ....D 740 753-3439
Nelsonville (G-14830)
H & M Patch Company ....D 614 339-8950
Columbus (G-7706)
Hubbard Company ....E 419 784-4455
Defiance (G-9917)
Indico LLC ....D 440 775-7777
Oberlin (G-15505)
Mackin Book Company ....E 330 854-0099
Massillon (G-13706)
Media Source Inc ....D 614 873-7635
Plain City (G-16060)
Scholastic Book Fairs Inc ....D 513 714-1000
West Chester (G-18998)
Zaner-Bloser Inc ....D 614 486-0221
Columbus (G-8935)

BOTANICAL GARDENS

Cleveland Metroparks ....C 216 661-6500
Cleveland (G-5267)

BOTTLED GAS DEALERS: Propane

Hearthstone Utilities Inc ....D 440 974-3770
Cleveland (G-5679)
Litter Bob Fuel & Heating Co ....E 740 773-2196
Chillicothe (G-2801)
Youngstown Propane Inc ....E 330 792-6571
Youngstown (G-20266)

BOTTLED WATER DELIVERY

K & R Distributors Inc ....E 937 864-5495
Fairborn (G-10677)
Pro-Kleen Industrial Svcs Inc ....E 740 689-1886
Lancaster (G-12427)

BOTTLES: Plastic

Phoenix Technologies Intl LLC ....E 419 353-7738
Bowling Green (G-1744)

BOUTIQUE STORES

Artistic Dance Enterprises ....E 614 761-2882
Columbus (G-6974)

BOWLING CENTERS

Midway Bowling Lanes Inc ....E 330 762-7477
Cuyahoga Falls (G-9114)
Skylane LLC ....E 330 527-9999
Garrettsville (G-11230)
Sortino Management & Dev Co ....E 419 626-6761
Sandusky (G-16643)
Toledo Sports Center Inc ....E 419 693-0687
Toledo (G-18099)

Westgate Lanes Incorporated...............E 419 229-3845
  Lima (G-12783)

BOWLING EQPT & SPLY STORES

Chillicothe Bowling Lanes Inc............E 740 773-3300
  Chillicothe (G-2759)

BOWLING EQPT & SPLYS

Done-Rite Bowling Service Co ....E 440 232-3280
  Bedford (G-1278)

BOXES & CRATES: Rectangular, Wood

Cima Inc.............................E 513 382-8976
  Hamilton (G-11577)

BOXES & SHOOK: Nailed Wood

Quadco Rehabilitation Ctr Inc ....B 419 682-1011
  Stryker (G-17370)

BOXES: Corrugated

BDS Packaging Inc ....D 937 643-0530
  Moraine (G-14624)
Cambridge Packaging Inc ....E 740 432-3351
  Cambridge (G-2055)
Westrock Cp LLC ....D 770 448-2193
  Wshngtn CT Hs (G-19886)

BOXES: Wooden

Lefco Worthington LLC ....E 216 432-4422
  Cleveland (G-5860)

BOYS' CAMPS

Ohio Camp Cherith Inc ....E 330 725-4202
  Medina (G-13984)

BOYS' TOWNS

Friars Club Inc ....D 513 488-8777
  Cincinnati (G-3594)
Twelve Inc ....E 330 837-3555
  Massillon (G-13733)
Village Network ....C 330 264-0650
  Wooster (G-19776)

BRAKES & BRAKE PARTS

Hebco Products Inc ....A 419 562-7987
  Bucyrus (G-1992)

BRASS FOUNDRY, NEC

Anchor Bronze and Metals Inc ....E 440 549-5653
  Cleveland (G-4976)

BRASS GOODS, WHOLESALE

Andrew Distribution Inc ....B 614 824-3123
  Columbus (G-6948)

BRAZING SVCS

Paulo Products Company ....E 440 942-0153
  Willoughby (G-19561)

BRAZING: Metal

HI Tecmetal Group Inc ....E 440 946-2280
  Willoughby (G-19528)

BRICK, STONE & RELATED PRDTS WHOLESALERS

CCI Supply Inc.......................C 440 953-0045
  Mentor (G-14026)
Glen-Gery Corporation ....D 419 468-4890
  Galion (G-11176)
Hamilton-Parker Company ....D 614 358-7800
  Columbus (G-7713)
Kuhlman Corporation ....E 419 897-6000
  Maumee (G-13808)
Modern Builders Supply Inc ....D 330 726-7000
  Youngstown (G-20131)
Modern Builders Supply Inc ....C 419 241-3961
  Toledo (G-17922)
R W Sidley Incorporated ....E 330 793-7374
  Youngstown (G-20176)
Sidwell Materials Inc..................C 740 849-2394
  Zanesville (G-20361)

Stamm Contracting Co Inc...............E 330 274-8230
  Mantua (G-13276)
Stone Coffman Company LLC ....E 614 861-4668
  Gahanna (G-11147)

BRIDAL SHOPS

Emmys Bridal Inc.....................E 419 628-7555
  Minster (G-14532)

BROACHING MACHINES

Ohio Broach & Machine Company ....E 440 946-1040
  Willoughby (G-19557)

BROADCASTING & COMMS EQPT: Antennas, Transmitting/Comms

Central USA Wireless LLC ....E 513 469-1500
  Cincinnati (G-3159)

BROADCASTING STATIONS, RADIO: Educational

Dayton Public School District.............D 937 542-3000
  Dayton (G-9379)
Lorain City School District ....E 440 233-2239
  Lorain (G-12913)
Marietta College ....E 740 376-4790
  Marietta (G-13350)

BROADCASTING STATIONS, RADIO: Exc Music Format

Ohio University ....E 740 593-1771
  Athens (G-796)

BROADCASTING STATIONS, RADIO: Music Format

Ashtabula Broadcasting Station ....E 440 993-2126
  Ashtabula (G-706)
CBS Radio Inc ....D 513 699-5105
  Cincinnati (G-3136)
Cincinnati Public Radio Inc ....E 513 241-8282
  Cincinnati (G-3262)
Cumulus Broadcasting LLC ....D 330 783-1000
  Youngstown (G-20012)
D A Peterson Inc ....E 330 821-1111
  Alliance (G-529)
Iheartcommunications Inc ....E 419 529-2211
  Mansfield (G-13185)
Southeastern Ohio Brdcstg Sys ....E 740 452-5431
  Zanesville (G-20363)
Southeastern Ohio TV Sys ....E 740 452-5431
  Zanesville (G-20364)

BROADCASTING STATIONS, RADIO: Rock Music

Rubber City Radio Group................D 330 869-9800
  Akron (G-412)

BROADCASTING STATIONS, RADIO: Sports

Fairborn Sftball Offcials Assn ....E 937 902-9920
  Dayton (G-9425)

BROADCASTING STATIONS, TELEVISION: Translator Station

Gray Television Group Inc ....D 419 531-1313
  Toledo (G-17768)
Ohio State University...................C 614 292-4510
  Columbus (G-8312)

BROKERS & DEALERS: Mortgages, Buying & Selling

Equity Resources Inc ....D 513 518-6318
  Cincinnati (G-3512)
Southwest Financial Svcs Ltd ....C 513 621-6699
  Cincinnati (G-4505)
The Cadle Company ....C 330 872-0918
  Newton Falls (G-15141)
Van Dyk Mortgage Corporation ....E 513 429-2122
  Mason (G-13653)

BROKERS & DEALERS: Securities

Citigroup Global Markets Inc.............E 419 842-5383
  Toledo (G-17653)

Columbus Metro Federal Cr Un ....E 614 239-0210
  Columbus (G-7297)
Corporate Fin Assoc of Clumbus ....D 614 457-9219
  Columbus (G-7374)
Ifs Financial Services Inc ....E 513 362-8000
  Westerville (G-19264)
Keybanc Capital Markets Inc ....B 800 553-2240
  Cleveland (G-5826)
Kidney & Hypertension Cons ....E 330 649-9400
  Canton (G-2367)
MAI Capital Management LLC ....E 216 920-4913
  Cleveland (G-5897)
Merrill Lynch Pierce Fenner ....E 614 225-3152
  Columbus (G-8059)
Merrill Lynch Pierce Fenner ....D 740 335-2930
  Wshngtn CT Hs (G-19879)
Merrill Lynch Pierce Fenner ....E 614 225-3197
  Springfield (G-17081)
Merrill Lynch Pierce Fenner ....C 513 579-3600
  Cincinnati (G-4036)
Merrill Lynch Pierce Fenner ....E 330 702-0535
  Canfield (G-2148)
Merrill Lynch Pierce Fenner ....E 330 670-2400
  Bath (G-1017)
Nationwide Inv Svcs Corp ....D 614 249-7111
  Columbus (G-8157)
Ohio Department of Commerce ....E 614 644-7381
  Columbus (G-8237)
Shane Security Services Inc ....E 330 757-4001
  Poland (G-16088)
UBS Financial Services Inc ....E 513 792-2146
  Cincinnati (G-4662)
UBS Financial Services Inc ....E 614 460-6559
  Columbus (G-8793)
UBS Financial Services Inc ....E 513 792-2100
  Cincinnati (G-4663)
Valmark Financial Group LLC ....D 330 576-1234
  Akron (G-483)
Wells Fargo Clearing Svcs LLC ....E 216 378-2722
  Cleveland (G-6661)

BROKERS & DEALERS: Security

Bowers Insurance Agency Inc ....E 330 638-6146
  Cortland (G-8984)
Citigroup Global Markets Inc ....D 860 291-4181
  Beavercreek (G-1210)
Citigroup Global Markets Inc ....D 513 579-8300
  Cincinnati (G-3296)
Huntington Insurance Inc ....E 614 480-3800
  Columbus (G-7783)
Mc Cloy Financial Services ....D 614 457-6233
  Columbus (G-8042)
Merrill Lynch Pierce Fenner ....E 614 475-2798
  Columbus (G-8060)
Merrill Lynch Pierce Fenner ....E 740 452-3681
  Zanesville (G-20330)
Merrill Lynch Pierce Fenner ....E 937 847-4000
  Miamisburg (G-14189)
Merrill Lynch Pierce Fenner ....E 614 225-3000
  Columbus (G-8061)
Merrill Lynch Pierce Fenner ....E 330 670-2400
  Akron (G-331)
Merrill Lynch Pierce Fenner ....C 216 363-6500
  Cleveland (G-5959)
Merrill Lynch Pierce Fenner ....D 330 670-2400
  Akron (G-332)
Merrill Lynch Pierce Fenner ....E 614 825-0350
  Columbus (G-6824)
Merrill Lynch Pierce Fenner ....E 216 292-8000
  Cleveland (G-5960)
Merrill Lynch Pierce Fenner ....E 330 497-6600
  Canton (G-2401)
Merrill Lynch Pierce Fenner ....E 330 655-2312
  Hudson (G-11995)
Morgan Stanley ....E 440 835-6750
  Westlake (G-19376)
Morgan Stanley & Co LLC ....E 614 798-3100
  Dublin (G-10282)
O N Equity Sales Company ....A 513 794-6794
  Montgomery (G-14597)
UBS Financial Services Inc ....E 937 428-1300
  Dayton (G-9827)
UBS Financial Services Inc ....E 614 442-6240
  Columbus (G-8794)
UBS Financial Services Inc ....E 937 223-3141
  Miamisburg (G-14232)
Valmark Securities Inc ....E 330 576-1234
  Akron (G-484)
Wunderlich Securities Inc ....E 440 646-1400
  Cleveland (G-6694)

S
E
R
V
I
C
E
S

BROKERS & DEALERS: Stock

Citigroup Global Markets Inc ....E 440 617-2000
Cleveland *(G-5183)*

Merrill Lynch Pierce Fenner ....E 419 891-2091
Perrysburg *(G-15893)*

Merrill Lynch Pierce Fenner ....E 330 702-7300
Canfield *(G-2147)*

Morgan Stanley ....E 216 523-3000
Cleveland *(G-6010)*

Morgan Stanley ....D 614 473-2086
Columbus *(G-8102)*

Morgan Stnley Smith Barney LLC ....E 216 360-4900
Cleveland *(G-6011)*

Ross Sinclaire & Assoc LLC ....E 513 381-3939
Cincinnati *(G-4396)*

Sirak Financial Services Inc ....D 330 493-0642
Canton *(G-2477)*

UBS Financial Services Inc ....E 513 576-5000
Cincinnati *(G-4661)*

UBS Financial Services Inc ....D 419 318-5525
Sylvania *(G-17461)*

UBS Financial Services Inc ....E 216 831-3400
Cleveland *(G-6560)*

Wells Fargo Clearing Svcs LLC ....E 614 764-2040
Dublin *(G-10372)*

Wells Fargo Clearing Svcs LLC ....E 614 221-8371
Columbus *(G-8885)*

Wells Fargo Clearing Svcs LLC ....E 419 356-3272
Toledo *(G-18150)*

Wells Fargo Clearing Svcs LLC ....E 440 835-9250
Westlake *(G-19422)*

Wells Fargo Clearing Svcs LLC ....E 419 720-9700
Toledo *(G-18151)*

Wells Fargo Clearing Svcs LLC ....D 216 574-7300
Cleveland *(G-6662)*

BROKERS' SVCS

Gateway Distribution Inc ....E 513 891-4477
Cincinnati *(G-3604)*

Knisely Inc ....D 330 343-5812
Dover *(G-10085)*

Shamrock Companies Inc ....D 440 899-9510
Westlake *(G-19405)*

Shredded Bedding Corporation ....E 740 893-3567
Centerburg *(G-2616)*

BROKERS, MARINE TRANSPORTATION

Alpha Freight Systems Inc ....D 800 394-9001
Hudson *(G-11965)*

Complete Qlty Trnsp Sltons LLC ....E 513 914-4882
Cincinnati *(G-3344)*

Containerport Group Inc ....D 440 333-1330
Cleveland *(G-5342)*

Ringler Feedlots LLC ....E 419 253-5300
Marengo *(G-13304)*

BROKERS: Business

Corporate Fin Assoc of Clumbus ....D 614 457-9219
Columbus *(G-7374)*

BROKERS: Food

Acosta Inc ....D 440 498-7370
Solon *(G-16815)*

Advantage Sales & Mktg LLC ....D 513 841-0500
Blue Ash *(G-1500)*

Advantage Waypoint LLC ....E 248 919-3144
Twinsburg *(G-18241)*

Atlantic Fish & Distrg Co ....E 330 454-1307
Canton *(G-2197)*

Cantrell Oil Company ....E 937 695-8003
Winchester *(G-19660)*

Chas G Buchy Packing Company ....E 800 762-1060
Cincinnati *(G-3172)*

Euclid Fish Company ....D 440 951-6448
Mentor *(G-14044)*

General Mills Inc ....D 513 770-0558
Mason *(G-13585)*

Impact Sales Inc ....D 937 274-1905
Dayton *(G-9513)*

Kcbs LLC ....E 513 421-9422
Cincinnati *(G-3849)*

Keystone Foods LLC ....C 419 843-3009
Toledo *(G-17839)*

Mpf Sales and Mktg Group LLC ....C 513 793-6241
Blue Ash *(G-1616)*

Novelart Manufacturing Company ....D 513 351-7700
Cincinnati *(G-4136)*

Queensgate Food Group LLC ....D 513 721-5503
Cincinnati *(G-4325)*

R G Sellers Company ....E 937 299-1545
Moraine *(G-14691)*

Shaker Valley Foods Inc ....E 216 961-8600
Cleveland *(G-6403)*

Spartannash Company ....A 937 599-1110
Bellefontaine *(G-1366)*

Spartannash Company ....B 419 228-3141
Lima *(G-12744)*

Spartannash Company ....D 513 793-6300
Cincinnati *(G-4510)*

Sygma Network Inc ....C 614 771-3801
Columbus *(G-8723)*

Total Wholesale Inc ....E 216 361-5757
Cleveland *(G-6535)*

US Foods Inc ....C 330 963-6789
Twinsburg *(G-18334)*

US Foods Inc ....A 614 539-7993
West Chester *(G-19096)*

Valley Wholesale Foods Inc ....E 740 354-5216
Portsmouth *(G-16180)*

Vendors Supply Inc ....E 513 755-2111
West Chester *(G-19030)*

BROKERS: Loan

Appalachian Development Corp ....D 740 374-9436
Marietta *(G-13313)*

Best Reward Credit Union ....E 216 367-8000
Cleveland *(G-5059)*

Board of Dir of Wittenbe ....E 937 327-6310
Springfield *(G-17000)*

Caliber Home Loans Inc ....E 937 435-5363
Dayton *(G-9272)*

Clyde-Findlay Area Cr Un Inc ....E 419 547-7781
Clyde *(G-6742)*

Columbus Metro Federal Cr Un ....E 614 239-0210
Columbus *(G-7298)*

Directions Credit Union Inc ....E 419 524-7113
Mansfield *(G-13167)*

Firefighters Cmnty Cr Un Inc ....E 216 621-4644
Cleveland *(G-5527)*

Firelands Federal Credit Union ....E 419 483-4180
Bellevue *(G-1377)*

First Merchants Bank ....E 614 486-9000
Columbus *(G-7587)*

Fremont Federal Credit Union ....C 419 334-4434
Fremont *(G-11076)*

George W Mc Cloy ....E 614 457-6233
Columbus *(G-7661)*

Guardian Savings Bank ....E 513 942-3535
West Chester *(G-18938)*

Guardian Savings Bank ....E 513 528-8787
Cincinnati *(G-3661)*

Henry County Bank ....E 419 599-1065
Napoleon *(G-14808)*

Nationstar Mortgage LLC ....D 614 985-9500
Columbus *(G-8142)*

Ohio Equity Fund Inc ....E 614 469-1797
Columbus *(G-8254)*

Osgood State Bank (inc) ....E 419 582-2681
Osgood *(G-15653)*

Precision Funding Corp ....E 330 405-1313
Twinsburg *(G-18306)*

Second National Bank ....E 937 548-2122
Greenville *(G-11395)*

Seven Seventeen Credit Un Inc ....C 330 372-8100
Warren *(G-18741)*

Seven Seventeen Credit Un Inc ....E 330 372-8100
Warren *(G-18742)*

State Bank and Trust Company ....E 419 783-8950
Defiance *(G-9941)*

The Peoples Savings and Ln Co ....E 937 653-1600
Urbana *(G-18445)*

BROKERS: Mortgage, Arranging For Loans

Commonwealth Financial Svcs ....E 440 449-7709
Cleveland *(G-5321)*

Equity Consultants LLC ....D 330 659-7600
Seven Hills *(G-16674)*

Forest City Residential Dev ....E 216 621-6060
Cleveland *(G-5561)*

Manhattan Mortgage Group Ltd ....D 614 933-8955
Blacklick *(G-1482)*

Multi-Fund Inc ....E 216 750-2331
Cleveland *(G-6024)*

Nations Lending Corporation ....D 440 842-4817
Independence *(G-12102)*

Premiere Service Mortgage Corp ....E 513 546-9895
West Chester *(G-18984)*

Randall Mortgage Services ....C 614 336-7948
Dublin *(G-10318)*

Real Estate Mortgage Corp ....D 440 356-5373
Chagrin Falls *(G-2653)*

Sibcy Cline Mortgage Services ....E 513 984-6776
Cincinnati *(G-4478)*

Trio Limited ....E 614 898-5463
Columbus *(G-8784)*

Union Mortgage Services Inc ....E 614 457-4815
Columbus *(G-8799)*

Welles Bowen Realty Inc ....D 419 535-0011
Toledo *(G-18149)*

William D Taylor Sr Inc ....D 614 653-6683
Etna *(G-10621)*

BROKERS: Printing

Pxp Ohio ....E 614 575-4242
Reynoldsburg *(G-16324)*

Veritiv Pubg & Print MGT Inc ....E 330 650-5522
Hudson *(G-12011)*

BROKERS: Security

Charles Schwab & Co Inc ....E 330 908-4478
Richfield *(G-16349)*

Charles Schwab Corporation ....E 440 617-2301
Westlake *(G-19330)*

Charles Schwab Corporation ....E 216 291-9333
Cleveland *(G-5170)*

Deutsche Bank Securities Inc ....E 440 237-0188
Broadview Heights *(G-1831)*

Linsalata Capital Partners Fun ....C 440 684-1400
Cleveland *(G-5873)*

Merrill Lynch Pierce Fenner ....E 513 562-2100
Cincinnati *(G-4037)*

Merrill Lynch Pierce Fenner ....E 614 798-4354
Dublin *(G-10278)*

Morgan Stanley ....E 513 721-2000
Cincinnati *(G-4074)*

Nationwide Life Insur Co Amer ....A 800 688-5177
Columbus *(G-8158)*

Raymond James Fincl Svcs Inc ....E 419 586-5121
Celina *(G-2608)*

Robert W Baird & Co Inc ....E 216 737-7330
Cleveland *(G-6334)*

The Huntington Investment Co ....E 614 480-3600
Columbus *(G-8744)*

The Huntington Investment Co ....E 513 351-2555
Cincinnati *(G-4593)*

Wells Fargo Clearing Svcs LLC ....E 513 241-9900
Cincinnati *(G-4776)*

Westmnster Fncl Securities Inc ....E 937 898-5010
Dayton *(G-9878)*

BROOMS & BRUSHES

Mill Rose Laboratories Inc ....E 440 974-6730
Mentor *(G-14086)*

Stephen M Trudick ....E 440 834-1891
Burton *(G-2019)*

BROOMS & BRUSHES: Household Or Indl

Mill-Rose Company ....C 440 255-9171
Mentor *(G-14087)*

BUCKETS: Plastic

Impact Products LLC ....C 419 841-2891
Toledo *(G-17818)*

BUILDING & OFFICE CLEANING SVCS

Ashland Cleaning LLC ....E 419 281-1747
Ashland *(G-647)*

August Groh & Sons Inc ....E 513 821-0090
Cincinnati *(G-3004)*

Corporate Cleaning Inc ....E 614 203-6051
Columbus *(G-7371)*

High-TEC Industrial Services ....C 937 667-1772
Tipp City *(G-17558)*

Image By J & K LLC ....B 888 667-6929
Maumee *(G-13802)*

Living Matters LLC ....E 866 587-8074
Cleveland *(G-5876)*

BUILDING & STRUCTURAL WOOD MEMBERS

Carter-Jones Lumber Company ....C 330 674-9060
Millersburg *(G-14463)*

Holmes Lumber & Bldg Ctr Inc..............C 330 674-9060
  Millersburg *(G-14475)*

BUILDING CLEANING & MAINTENANCE SVCS

A 1 Janitorial Cleaning Svc ....E 513 932-8003
  Lebanon *(G-12446)*
ABM Facility Services Inc ....E 859 767-4393
  Cincinnati *(G-2898)*
Advanced Facilities Maint Corp............E 614 389-3495
  Columbus *(G-6874)*
Akron Public School Maint Svcs............D 330 761-2640
  Akron *(G-51)*
Allen-Keith Construction Co............D 330 266-2220
  Canton *(G-2178)*
Atlantis Co Inc ....D 888 807-3272
  Cleveland *(G-5020)*
Ats Group LLC ....C 216 744-5757
  Solon *(G-16824)*
Belfor USA Group Inc ....E 513 860-3111
  West Chester *(G-19043)*
C & K Industrial Services Inc............D 216 642-0055
  Independence *(G-12052)*
C M S Enterprises Inc ....E 740 653-1940
  Lancaster *(G-12374)*
Camco Inc............E 740 477-3682
  Circleville *(G-4827)*
Caveney Inc ....D 330 497-4600
  North Canton *(G-15192)*
Columbus Public School Dst............B 614 365-5043
  Columbus *(G-7307)*
Complete Building Maint LLC............E 513 235-7511
  Cincinnati *(G-3343)*
Contract Lumber Inc............D 614 751-1109
  Columbus *(G-7365)*
County of Cuyahoga............A 216 443-6954
  Cleveland *(G-5366)*
Custom Maint ....D 330 793-2523
  Youngstown *(G-20013)*
Dempsey Inc............D 330 758-2309
  Youngstown *(G-20016)*
Emcor Facilities Services Inc ....D 888 846-9462
  Cincinnati *(G-3492)*
Environment Control of Greater............D 614 868-9788
  Columbus *(G-7521)*
Feecorp Industrial Services............C 740 533-1445
  Ironton *(G-12152)*
G7 Services Inc ....E 937 256-3473
  Dayton *(G-9455)*
Green Impressions LLC ....E 440 240-8508
  Sheffield Village *(G-16734)*
Harrison Industries Inc............D 740 942-2988
  Cadiz *(G-2029)*
Heco Operations Inc ....E 614 888-5700
  Worthington *(G-19813)*
High Power Inc ....E 937 667-1772
  Tipp City *(G-17557)*
Hopewell Industries Inc............D 740 622-3563
  Coshocton *(G-9018)*
J Rutledge Enterprises Inc............E 502 241-4100
  Cincinnati *(G-3796)*
Jacob Real Estate Services ....E 216 687-0500
  Cleveland *(G-5777)*
John O Bostock Jr............E 937 263-8540
  Dayton *(G-9528)*
Kettering City School District............D 937 297-1990
  Dayton *(G-9537)*
Kleman Services LLC ....E 419 339-0871
  Lima *(G-12671)*
Lake Side Building Maintenance............E 216 589-9900
  Cleveland *(G-5848)*
Mrap LLC ....E 614 545-3190
  Columbus *(G-8117)*
N Services Inc............D 513 793-2000
  Blue Ash *(G-1619)*
Northpointe Property MGT LLC............C 614 579-9712
  Columbus *(G-8204)*
Promanco Inc ....E 740 374-2120
  Marietta *(G-13373)*
Psp Operations Inc ....E 614 888-5700
  Worthington *(G-19838)*
Putman Janitorial Service Inc............E 513 942-1900
  West Chester *(G-19074)*
Restoration Resources Inc ....E 330 650-4486
  Hudson *(G-12004)*
Richland Newhope Industries............C 419 774-4400
  Mansfield *(G-13237)*
ServiceMaster By Sidwell Inc ....E 740 687-1077
  Lancaster *(G-12434)*

Shining Company LLC ....C 614 588-4115
  Columbus *(G-8634)*
Sr Improvements Services LLC ....E 567 207-6488
  Vickery *(G-18575)*
Star Inc............C 740 354-1517
  Portsmouth *(G-16174)*
Suburban Maintenance & Contrs ....E 440 237-7765
  North Royalton *(G-15369)*
T & L Enterprises Inc ....E 440 234-5900
  Berea *(G-1439)*
T N C Construction Inc............E 614 554-5330
  Grove City *(G-11476)*
Tdg Facilities LLC............C 513 834-6105
  Blue Ash *(G-1655)*
Trg Maintenance LLC............A 614 891-4850
  Westerville *(G-19214)*
Ultimate Building Maintenance............D 330 369-9771
  Warren *(G-18763)*
United Scoto Senior Activities ....E 740 354-6672
  Portsmouth *(G-16176)*
University of Cincinnati............E 513 556-6381
  Cincinnati *(G-4707)*
Ward & Werner Co ....C 614 885-0741
  Worthington *(G-19858)*
White Glove Executive Services............E 614 226-2553
  Grove City *(G-11488)*

BUILDING CLEANING SVCS

Ace Building Maintenance LLC ....E 614 471-2223
  Columbus *(G-6864)*
Beneficial Building Services............D 330 848-2556
  Akron *(G-94)*
Circle Building Services Inc............D 614 228-6090
  Columbus *(G-7202)*
DCS Sanitation Management Inc ....E 513 891-4980
  Cincinnati *(G-3407)*
Guardian Care Services............E 614 436-8500
  Columbus *(G-7700)*
Leadec Corp............E 513 731-3590
  Blue Ash *(G-1597)*
Lucas Building Mainenance LLC............A 740 479-1800
  Ironton *(G-12162)*
MPW Industrial Services Inc ....E 440 277-9072
  Lorain *(G-12928)*
Quality Clg Svc of NW Ohio ....D 419 335-9105
  Wauseon *(G-18809)*
Stout Lori Cleaning & Such ....E 419 637-7644
  Gibsonburg *(G-11279)*
W David Maupin Inc............E 419 389-0458
  Toledo *(G-18141)*

BUILDING COMPONENT CLEANING SVCS

MPW Industrial Services Inc............D 330 454-1898
  Canton *(G-2410)*
Professional Restoration Svc ....E 330 825-1803
  Medina *(G-13989)*

BUILDING COMPONENTS: Structural Steel

Frederick Steel Company LLC............D 513 821-6400
  Cincinnati *(G-3586)*
GL Nause Co Inc ....E 513 722-9500
  Loveland *(G-12996)*
J&J Precision Machine Ltd ....D 330 923-5783
  Cuyahoga Falls *(G-9103)*
Mound Technologies Inc ....E 937 748-2937
  Springboro *(G-16977)*
Turn-Key Industrial Svcs LLC............D 614 274-1128
  Columbus *(G-8787)*
Universal Fabg Cnstr Svcs Inc ....D 614 274-1128
  Columbus *(G-8815)*
Wernli Realty Inc............D 937 258-7878
  Beavercreek *(G-1240)*

BUILDING INSPECTION SVCS

A2z Field Services LLC ....E 614 873-0211
  Plain City *(G-16041)*
Inspection Group Incorporated ....E 614 891-3606
  Westerville *(G-19175)*
Quality Control Inspection ....D 440 359-1900
  Cleveland *(G-6269)*
Technical Assurance Inc ....E 440 953-3147
  Willoughby *(G-19575)*

BUILDING MAINTENANCE SVCS, EXC REPAIRS

AMF Facility Services Inc............E 800 991-2273
  Dayton *(G-9232)*

Blanchard Valley Health System ....A 419 423-4500
  Findlay *(G-10871)*
Butchko Electric Inc ....E 440 985-3180
  Amherst *(G-582)*
G J Goudreau & Co............E 216 351-5233
  Cleveland *(G-5586)*
Lima Sheet Metal Machine & Mfg ....E 419 229-1161
  Lima *(G-12687)*
Louderback Fmly Invstments Inc ....E 937 845-1762
  New Carlisle *(G-14893)*

BUILDING PRDTS & MATERIALS DEALERS

Carter-Jones Lumber Company ....A 330 673-6000
  Kent *(G-12219)*
Carter-Jones Lumber Company ....C 330 674-9060
  Millersburg *(G-14463)*
CCI Supply Inc............C 440 953-0045
  Mentor *(G-14026)*
Clays Heritage Carpet Inc ....E 330 497-1280
  Canton *(G-2257)*
Contract Lumber Inc............C 740 964-3147
  Pataskala *(G-15783)*
Contract Lumber Inc............D 614 751-1109
  Columbus *(G-7365)*
Contractors Materials Company ....E 513 733-3000
  Cincinnati *(G-3353)*
D C Curry Lumber Company ....E 330 264-5223
  Dundee *(G-10383)*
Daniels Lumber Co Inc ....D 330 533-2211
  Canfield *(G-2135)*
Do It Best Corp............C 330 725-3859
  Medina *(G-13933)*
Famous Enterprises Inc ....E 419 478-0343
  Toledo *(G-17726)*
Holmes Lumber & Bldg Ctr Inc............C 330 674-9060
  Millersburg *(G-14475)*
Hull Builders Supply Inc............E 440 967-3159
  Vermilion *(G-18553)*
J & B Equipment & Supply Inc ....D 419 884-1155
  Mansfield *(G-13188)*
Judy Mills Company Inc ....E 513 271-4241
  Cincinnati *(G-3841)*
K M B Inc............E 330 889-3451
  Bristolville *(G-1826)*
Khempco Bldg Sup Co Ltd Partnr............D 740 549-0465
  Delaware *(G-9993)*
Lang Stone Company Inc............D 614 235-4099
  Columbus *(G-7951)*
Lowes Home Centers LLC............C 216 351-4723
  Cleveland *(G-5882)*
Lowes Home Centers LLC............C 419 739-1300
  Wapakoneta *(G-18649)*
Lowes Home Centers LLC ....C 440 392-0027
  Mentor *(G-14078)*
Lowes Home Centers LLC............C 330 245-4300
  Akron *(G-322)*
Lowes Home Centers LLC............C 330 965-4500
  Youngstown *(G-20101)*
Lowes Home Centers LLC............C 937 854-8200
  Dayton *(G-9577)*
Mentor Lumber and Supply Co............C 440 255-8814
  Mentor *(G-14082)*
Modern Builders Supply Inc ....E 216 273-3605
  Cleveland *(G-6004)*
Stamm Contracting Co Inc............E 330 274-8230
  Mantua *(G-13276)*

BUILDING SCALES MODELS

3-D Technical Services Company..........E 937 746-2901
  Franklin *(G-11020)*

BUILDINGS & COMPONENTS: Prefabricated Metal

Hoge Lumber Company ....E 419 753-2263
  New Knoxville *(G-14917)*

BUILDINGS, PREFABRICATED: Wholesalers

Real America Inc ....B 216 261-1177
  Cleveland *(G-6289)*

BUILDINGS: Farm & Utility

Morton Buildings Inc ....D 419 675-2311
  Kenton *(G-12285)*

BUILDINGS: Prefabricated, Metal

Enclosure Suppliers LLC ....E 513 782-3900
  Cincinnati *(G-3496)*

BUILDINGS: Prefabricated, Wood

Morton Buildings Inc ....D 419 675-2311
Kenton (G-12285)
Vinyl Design Corporation ....E 419 283-4009
Holland (G-11925)

BURGLAR ALARM MAINTENANCE & MONITORING SVCS

Area Wide Protective Inc ....E 513 321-9889
Fairfield (G-10696)
Guardian Protection Svcs Inc ....D 513 422-5319
West Chester (G-18937)
Integrated Protection Svcs Inc ....D 513 631-5505
Cincinnati (G-3770)
Johnson Cntrls SEC Sltions LLC ....C 330 497-0850
Canton (G-2362)
Johnson Cntrls SEC Sltions LLC ....D 440 262-1084
Brecksville (G-1786)
Johnson Cntrls SEC Sltions LLC ....C 561 988-3600
Dublin (G-10260)
Johnson Cntrls SEC Sltions LLC ....E 419 243-8400
Maumee (G-13806)
Mills Security Alarm Systems ....E 513 921-4600
Cincinnati (G-4058)
Ohio Valley Integration Svcs ....E 937 492-0008
Sidney (G-16790)
Research & Investigation Assoc ....E 419 526-1299
Mansfield (G-13234)
State Alarm Inc ....E 888 726-8111
Youngstown (G-20217)
United States Protective ....E 216 475-8550
Independence (G-12135)
Vector Security Inc ....E 440 466-7233
Geneva (G-11249)
Vector Security Inc ....E 330 726-9841
Canfield (G-2164)

BURIAL VAULTS: Concrete Or Precast Terrazzo

Mack Industries ....C 419 353-7081
Bowling Green (G-1740)

BURLAP WHOLESALERS

Dayton Bag & Burlap Co ....C 937 258-8000
Dayton (G-9355)

BUS BARS: Electrical

Schneider Electric Usa Inc ....D 513 755-5000
West Chester (G-18997)

BUS CHARTER SVC: Local

A T V Inc ....C 614 252-5060
Columbus (G-6848)
Charter Vans Inc ....E 937 898-4043
Vandalia (G-18513)
Croswell of Williamsburg LLC ....E 513 724-2206
Williamsburg (G-19492)
Cusa LI Inc ....C 216 267-8810
Brookpark (G-1895)
Cuyahoga Marketing Service ....E 440 526-5350
Cleveland (G-5400)
Firstgroup America Inc ....D 513 241-2200
Cincinnati (G-3566)
Lakefront Lines Inc ....D 513 829-8290
Fairfield (G-10746)
Lakefront Lines Inc ....C 216 267-8810
Brookpark (G-1900)
Marfre Inc ....C 513 321-3377
Cincinnati (G-3969)
Precious Cargo Transportation ....E 440 564-8039
Newbury (G-15124)
Queen City Transportation LLC ....B 513 941-8700
Cincinnati (G-4322)
S B S Transit Inc ....B 440 288-2222
Lorain (G-12942)
Transit Service Company ....E 330 782-3343
Youngstown (G-20223)

BUS CHARTER SVC: Long-Distance

Buckeye Charter Service Inc ....D 419 222-2455
Lima (G-12610)
Buckeye Charter Service Inc ....E 937 879-3000
Dayton (G-9264)
Croswell of Williamsburg LLC ....E 513 724-2206
Williamsburg (G-19492)

Croswell of Williamsburg LLC ....D 800 782-8747
Dayton (G-9340)
Cusa LI Inc ....C 216 267-8810
Brookpark (G-1895)
Cuyahoga Marketing Service ....E 440 526-5350
Cleveland (G-5400)
Garfield Hts Coach Line Inc ....D 440 232-4550
Chagrin Falls (G-2646)
Greyhound Lines Inc ....E 614 221-0577
Columbus (G-7697)
Hat White Management LLC ....E 800 525-7967
Akron (G-255)
Lakefront Lines Inc ....C 216 267-8810
Brookpark (G-1900)
Lakefront Lines Inc ....E 419 537-0677
Toledo (G-11848)
Lakefront Lines Inc ....E 614 476-1113
Columbus (G-7944)
Pioneer Trails Inc ....E 330 674-1234
Millersburg (G-14487)
Put In Bay Transportation ....E 419 285-4855
Put In Bay (G-16228)
Queen City Transportation LLC ....B 513 941-8700
Cincinnati (G-4322)
S B S Transit Inc ....B 440 288-2222
Lorain (G-12942)
Starforce National Corporation ....C 513 979-3600
Cincinnati (G-4540)
Sutton Motor Coach Tours Inc ....E 330 726-2800
Youngstown (G-20219)
Tesco-Transportation Eqp Sls ....E 419 836-2835
Oregon (G-15610)

BUS TERMINALS & SVC FACILITIES

Lakota Local School District ....C 513 777-2150
Liberty Township (G-12582)
Meigs Local School District ....E 740 742-2990
Middleport (G-14282)
Ottawa County Transit Board ....E 419 898-7433
Oak Harbor (G-15477)

BUSES: Wholesalers

Tesco-Transportion Eqp Sls ....E 419 836-2835
Oregon (G-15610)

BUSHINGS & BEARINGS

McNeil Industries Inc ....E 440 951-7756
Painesville (G-15726)

BUSINESS ACTIVITIES: Non-Commercial Site

Ability Works Inc ....C 419 626-1048
Sandusky (G-16572)
Adventure Cmbat Operations LLC ....E 330 818-1029
Canton (G-2175)
Buckeye Mechanical Contg Inc ....D 740 282-0089
Toronto (G-18181)
Burgess & Niple-Heapy LLC ....D 614 459-2050
Columbus (G-7099)
Calvin Lanier ....E 937 952-4221
Dayton (G-9273)
Evanston Bulldogs Youth Footba ....E 513 254-9500
Cincinnati (G-3518)
Franklin Cnty Bd Commissioners ....E 614 525-3322
Columbus (G-7604)
Fx Facility Group LLC ....E 513 639-2509
Cincinnati (G-3598)
Haven Financial Enterprise ....E 800 265-2401
Cleveland (G-5667)
Hochstedler Construction Ltd ....E 740 427-4880
Gambier (G-11224)
Improvedge LLC ....E 614 793-1738
Powell (G-16197)
Industrial Insul Coatings LLC ....E 800 506-1399
Girard (G-11288)
Jason Wilson ....E 937 604-8209
Tipp City (G-17561)
Kns Financial Inc ....E 800 215-1136
Toledo (G-17842)
L Van & Associates Corporation ....E 419 208-9145
Toledo (G-17846)
Legacy Industrial Services LLC ....E 606 584-8953
Ripley (G-16400)
Lions Gate SEC Solutions Inc ....E 440 539-8382
Euclid (G-10648)
Ltd Productions LLC ....D 440 688-1905
Cleveland (G-5885)

McConnell Excavating Ltd ....E 440 774-4578
Oberlin (G-15508)
McDonalds 3490 ....E 330 762-7747
Akron (G-326)
Microanalysis Society Inc ....B 614 256-8063
Hilliard (G-11797)
Miencorp Inc ....E 330 978-8511
Niles (G-15159)
Mt Washington Care Center Inc ....C 513 231-4561
Cincinnati (G-4083)
P3 Infrastructure Inc ....A 330 686-1129
Stow (G-17223)
Platinum Prestige Property ....E 614 705-2251
Columbus (G-8453)
Pmwi LLC ....D 614 975-5004
Hilliard (G-11806)
Popper & Associates Msrp LLC ....E 614 798-8991
Dublin (G-10309)
Quality Lines Inc ....C 740 815-1165
Findlay (G-10957)
Reliable Polymer Services LP ....E 800 321-0954
Wadsworth (G-18614)
Richard Allen Group LLC ....D 614 623-2654
Powell (G-16206)
Roy J Miller ....E 330 674-2405
Millersburg (G-14490)
Service Pronet Inc ....E 614 874-4300
Columbus (G-8623)
Shotstop Ballistics LLC ....E 330 686-0020
Stow (G-17230)
Snapblox Hosted Solutions LLC ....E 866 524-7707
Cincinnati (G-4498)
Soundtrack Printing ....C 330 606-7117
Cuyahoga Falls (G-9124)
Stamper Staffing LLC ....E 937 938-7010
Kettering (G-12300)
Superior Abrasives LLC ....E 937 278-9123
Vandalia (G-18542)
Tim Mundy ....E 937 862-8686
Spring Valley (G-16959)
Tm Capture Services LLC ....D 937 728-1781
Beavercreek (G-1238)
Top Tier Soccer LLC ....E 937 903-6114
Dayton (G-9816)
Tri County Tower Service ....E 330 538-9874
North Jackson (G-15255)
Turtles Envmtl Abatement Co ....E 614 603-9439
Columbus (G-8790)
Vigilant Global Trade Svcs LLC ....E 260 417-1825
Shaker Heights (G-16719)

BUSINESS FORMS WHOLESALERS

American Future Systems Inc ....E 330 394-1555
Warren (G-18662)
GBS Corp ....C 330 494-5330
North Canton (G-15206)
Optimum System Products Inc ....E 614 885-4464
Westerville (G-19288)
Shamrock Companies Inc ....D 440 899-9510
Westlake (G-19405)

BUSINESS FORMS: Printed, Manifold

Custom Products Corporation ....D 440 528-7100
Solon (G-16842)
Eleet Cryogenics Inc ....E 330 874-4009
Bolivar (G-1702)
GBS Corp ....C 330 494-5330
North Canton (G-15206)

BUSINESS MACHINE REPAIR, ELECTRIC

Blakemans Valley Off Eqp Inc ....E 330 729-1000
Youngstown (G-19965)
Blue Technologies Inc ....E 330 499-9300
Canton (G-2215)
Leppo Inc ....C 330 633-3999
Tallmadge (G-17480)
Modern Office Methods Inc ....D 513 791-0909
Blue Ash (G-1613)
Modern Office Methods Inc ....E 614 891-3693
Westerville (G-19281)
NCR Corporation ....D 330 497-7300
Canton (G-2417)
Ohio Business Machines LLC ....E 216 485-2000
Cleveland (G-6117)
Toshiba Amer Bus Solutions Inc ....E 216 642-7555
Cleveland (G-6533)

BUSINESS SUPPORT SVCS

Beheydts Auto Wrecking............E....... 330 658-6109
Doylestown *(G-10108)*
Dennis & Carol Liederbach............E....... 256 582-6200
Northfield *(G-15377)*
Eventions Ltd............E....... 216 952-9898
Cleveland *(G-5496)*
Notoweega Nation Inc............D....... 740 777-1480
Logan *(G-12851)*
Stark County Federation of Con............E....... 330 268-1652
Canton *(G-2492)*
Streamline Technical Svcs LLC............D....... 614 441-7448
Lockbourne *(G-12825)*

BUSINESS TRAINING SVCS

International Association of............E....... 330 628-3012
Canton *(G-2357)*

BUTTER WHOLESALERS

Hillandale Farms Corporation............E....... 330 724-3199
Akron *(G-262)*

CABINETS: Entertainment

Kraftmaid Trucking Inc............D....... 440 632-2531
Middlefield *(G-14271)*

CABINETS: Entertainment Units, Household, Wood

Progressive Furniture Inc............E....... 419 446-4500
Archbold *(G-635)*

CABINETS: Kitchen, Wood

Brower Products Inc............D....... 937 563-1111
Cincinnati *(G-3082)*
Carter-Jones Lumber Company............C....... 330 674-9060
Millersburg *(G-14463)*
Hattenbach Company............D....... 216 881-5200
Cleveland *(G-5666)*
Holmes Lumber & Bldg Ctr Inc............C....... 330 674-9060
Millersburg *(G-14475)*
Online Mega Sellers Corp............D....... 888 384-6468
Toledo *(G-17964)*
Riverside Cnstr Svcs Inc............E....... 513 723-0900
Cincinnati *(G-4380)*

CABINETS: Office, Wood

Hoge Lumber Company............E....... 419 753-2263
New Knoxville *(G-14917)*

CABINETS: Show, Display, Etc, Wood, Exc Refrigerated

Hattenbach Company............D....... 216 881-5200
Cleveland *(G-5666)*

CABLE & OTHER PAY TELEVISION DISTRIBUTION

Armstrong Utilities Inc............E....... 330 758-6411
North Lima *(G-15262)*
ASC of Cincinnati Inc............E....... 513 886-7100
Lebanon *(G-12450)*
C T Wireless............D....... 937 653-2208
Urbana *(G-18420)*
Conneaut Telephone Company............E....... 440 593-7140
Conneaut *(G-8953)*
Ohio News Network............D....... 614 460-3700
Columbus *(G-8275)*
Verizon Communications Inc............C....... 440 892-4504
Westlake *(G-19420)*

CABLE & PAY TELEVISION SVCS: Closed Circuit

State Alarm Inc............E....... 888 726-8111
Youngstown *(G-20217)*

CABLE & PAY TELEVISION SVCS: Direct Broadcast Satellite

Dish Network Corporation............D....... 614 534-2001
Hilliard *(G-11761)*
Satcom Service LLC............D....... 614 863-6470
Reynoldsburg *(G-16331)*

CABLE & PAY TELEVISION SVCS: Multipoint Distribution Sys/MDS

Fulfillment Technologies LLC............C....... 513 346-3100
West Chester *(G-19055)*

CABLE TELEVISION

Block Communications Inc............B....... 419 724-2539
Northwood *(G-15389)*
Chillicothe Telephone Company............C....... 740 772-8200
Chillicothe *(G-2767)*
Coaxial Communications of Sout............D....... 513 797-4400
Columbus *(G-7238)*
Comcast Cble Cmmunications LLC............C....... 503 372-9144
Steubenville *(G-17149)*
Comcast Corporation............D....... 740 633-3437
Bridgeport *(G-1815)*
Comcast Spotlight............E....... 440 617-2280
Westlake *(G-19335)*
Comcast Spotlight Inc............B....... 216 575-8016
Cleveland *(G-5315)*
Cox Cable Cleveland Area Inc............C....... 216 676-8300
Cleveland *(G-5374)*
Cox Communications Inc............D....... 216 712-4500
Parma *(G-15763)*
Doylestown Communications............E....... 330 658-7000
Doylestown *(G-10111)*
Erie County Cablevision Inc............E....... 419 627-0800
Sandusky *(G-16600)*
Insight Communications of Co............C....... 614 236-1200
Columbus *(G-7825)*
Marrik Dish Company LLC............E....... 419 475-6538
Toledo *(G-17895)*
Massillon Cable TV Inc............D....... 330 833-4134
Massillon *(G-13710)*
Pioneer North America Inc............E....... 614 771-1050
Columbus *(G-8448)*
Spectrum MGT Holdg Co LLC............D....... 614 481-5408
Columbus *(G-8669)*
Spectrum MGT Holdg Co LLC............D....... 740 455-9705
Zanesville *(G-20365)*
Spectrum MGT Holdg Co LLC............D....... 330 856-2343
Warren *(G-18745)*
Spectrum MGT Holdg Co LLC............D....... 419 386-0040
Port Clinton *(G-16118)*
Spectrum MGT Holdg Co LLC............D....... 740 762-0291
Chillicothe *(G-2829)*
Spectrum MGT Holdg Co LLC............D....... 513 469-1112
Cincinnati *(G-4513)*
Spectrum MGT Holdg Co LLC............E....... 614 344-4159
Columbus *(G-8670)*
Spectrum MGT Holdg Co LLC............D....... 937 552-5760
Springfield *(G-17114)*
Spectrum MGT Holdg Co LLC............D....... 740 200-3385
Athens *(G-803)*
Spectrum MGT Holdg Co LLC............D....... 614 503-4153
Hilliard *(G-11816)*
Spectrum MGT Holdg Co LLC............D....... 440 319-3271
Ashtabula *(G-756)*
Spectrum MGT Holdg Co LLC............D....... 419 775-9292
Mansfield *(G-13245)*
Spectrum MGT Holdg Co LLC............E....... 330 208-9028
Akron *(G-437)*
Spectrum MGT Holdg Co LLC............D....... 937 684-8891
Dayton *(G-9783)*
Spectrum MGT Holdg Co LLC............E....... 740 772-7809
Lancaster *(G-12437)*
Spectrum MGT Holdg Co LLC............D....... 937 294-6800
Dayton *(G-9784)*
Spectrum MGT Holdg Co LLC............D....... 937 306-6082
Piqua *(G-16029)*
Time Warner Cable Entps LLC............A....... 614 255-6289
Columbus *(G-8754)*
Time Warner Cable Entps LLC............A....... 513 489-5000
Blue Ash *(G-1658)*
Time Warner Cable Entps LLC............E....... 614 481-5072
Columbus *(G-8755)*
Time Warner Cable Inc............E....... 614 236-1200
Columbus *(G-8756)*
Time Warner Cable Inc............D....... 440 366-0416
Elyria *(G-10567)*
Time Warner Cable Inc............D....... 419 331-1111
Lima *(G-12763)*
Time Warner Cable Inc............D....... 614 481-5050
Columbus *(G-8757)*
Time Warner Cable Inc............E....... 330 800-3874
Akron *(G-470)*
Time Warner Cable Inc............A....... 614 481-5000
Columbus *(G-8758)*

Time Warner Cable Inc............D....... 330 494-9200
Canton *(G-2511)*
Time Warner Cable Inc............E....... 330 633-9203
Youngstown *(G-20222)*
Time Warner Cable Inc............D....... 513 489-5000
Blue Ash *(G-1660)*
Time Warner Cable Inc............E....... 937 471-1572
Eaton *(G-10462)*
Time Warner Cable Inc............D....... 513 523-6333
Oxford *(G-15690)*
Time Warner Cable Inc............D....... 937 483-5152
Troy *(G-18230)*
Time Warner Cable Inc............D....... 937 667-8302
Tipp City *(G-17567)*
Time Warner Cable Inc............D....... 937 492-4145
Sidney *(G-16802)*
TSC Television Inc............D....... 419 941-6001
Wapakoneta *(G-18658)*
USI Cable Corp............E....... 937 606-2636
Piqua *(G-16036)*

CABLE WIRING SETS: Battery, Internal Combustion Engines

Noco Company............B....... 216 464-8131
Solon *(G-16879)*

CABLE: Noninsulated

Microplex Inc............E....... 330 498-0600
North Canton *(G-15220)*

CABS, FOR HIRE: Horse Drawn

Age Line Inc............E....... 216 941-9990
Cleveland *(G-4912)*
Total Transportation Trckg Inc............E....... 216 398-6090
Cleveland *(G-6534)*

CAFES

Covelli Family Ltd Partnership............E....... 330 856-3176
Warren *(G-18694)*
Howley Bread Group Ltd............D....... 440 808-1600
Westlake *(G-19352)*

CAFETERIAS

Westgate Lanes Incorporated............E....... 419 229-3845
Lima *(G-12783)*

CALENDARS, WHOLESALE

Gordon Bernard Company LLC............E....... 513 248-7600
Milford *(G-14393)*

CALIBRATING SVCS, NEC

Raitz Inc............E....... 513 769-1200
Cincinnati *(G-4336)*

CAMERA & PHOTOGRAPHIC SPLYS STORES

Collins KAO Inc............E....... 513 948-9000
Cincinnati *(G-3329)*
KAO Collins Inc............D....... 513 948-9000
Cincinnati *(G-3847)*

CAMPGROUNDS

Big Broth and Big Siste of Cen............E....... 614 839-2447
Columbus *(G-7034)*
Clare-Mar Camp Inc............E....... 440 647-3318
New London *(G-14931)*
Dayton Tall Timbers Resort............E....... 937 833-3888
Brookville *(G-1913)*
Elbe Properties............A....... 513 489-1955
Cincinnati *(G-3485)*
Real America Inc............B....... 216 261-1177
Cleveland *(G-6289)*

CAMPSITES

Great Miami Valley YMCA............E....... 513 867-0600
Hamilton *(G-11603)*

CANDLES

Gorant Chocolatier LLC............C....... 330 726-8821
Boardman *(G-1698)*

SERVICES

CANDLES: Wholesalers

White Barn Candle Co ....A 614 856-6000
  Reynoldsburg (G-16338)

CANDY & CONFECTIONS: Chocolate Covered Dates

Walnut Creek Chocolate Company ....E 330 893-2995
  Walnut Creek (G-18632)

CANDY & CONFECTIONS: Cough Drops, Exc Pharmaceutical Preps

Amerisource Health Svcs LLC ....D 614 492-8177
  Columbus (G-6941)

CANDY, NUT & CONFECTIONERY STORE: Popcorn, Incl Caramel Corn

Drc Holdings Inc ....E 419 230-0188
  Pandora (G-15750)

CANDY, NUT & CONFECTIONERY STORES: Candy

Gorant Chocolatier LLC ....C 330 726-8821
  Boardman (G-1698)
Robert E McGrath Inc ....E 440 572-7747
  Strongsville (G-17341)
Walnut Creek Chocolate Company ....E 330 893-2995
  Walnut Creek (G-18632)

CANDY, NUT & CONFECTIONERY STORES: Produced For Direct Sale

Cleveland Soc For The Blind ....C 216 791-8118
  Cleveland (G-5288)

CANDY: Chocolate From Cacao Beans

Walnut Creek Chocolate Company ....E 330 893-2995
  Walnut Creek (G-18632)

CANNED SPECIALTIES

Abbott Laboratories ....A 614 624-3191
  Columbus (G-6851)
Bittersweet Inc ....D 419 875-6986
  Whitehouse (G-19444)
Skyline Chili Inc ....C 513 874-1188
  Fairfield (G-10785)

CANS: Fiber

Sonoco Products Company ....D 937 429-0040
  Beavercreek Township (G-1263)

CANVAS PRDTS

Samsel Rope & Marine Supply Co ....E 216 241-0333
  Cleveland (G-6370)

CANVAS PRDTS: Convertible Tops, Car/Boat, Fm Purchased Mtrl

Crown Dielectric Inds Inc ....C 614 224-5161
  Columbus (G-7397)

CANVAS PRDTS: Shades, Made From Purchased Materials

Lumenomics Inc ....E 614 798-3500
  Lewis Center (G-12550)

CAR LOADING SVCS

Ameripro Logistics LLC ....E 410 375-3469
  Dayton (G-9231)

CAR WASH EQPT

Giant Industries Inc ....E 419 531-4600
  Toledo (G-17762)

CAR WASHES

Beheydts Auto Wrecking ....E 330 658-6109
  Doylestown (G-10108)
Bp ....E 216 731-3826
  Euclid (G-10625)
Consumer Foods ....E 440 284-5972
  Elyria (G-10493)

Covington Car Wash Inc ....E 513 831-6164
  Milford (G-14382)
Henderson Road Rest Systems ....E 614 442-3310
  Columbus (G-7739)
Lawnview Industries Inc ....C 937 653-5217
  Urbana (G-18438)
Napoleon Wash-N-Fill Inc ....D 419 592-0851
  Napoleon (G-14814)
Sax 5th Ave Car Wash Inc ....E 614 486-9093
  Columbus (G-8594)
Susan A Smith Crystal Care ....E 419 747-2666
  Butler (G-2022)

CARBON & GRAPHITE PRDTS, NEC

Applied Sciences Inc ....E 937 766-2020
  Cedarville (G-2579)
GE Aviation Systems LLC ....B 937 898-5881
  Vandalia (G-18524)
Graftech Holdings Inc ....B 216 676-2000
  Independence (G-12077)
Mill-Rose Company ....C 440 255-9171
  Mentor (G-14087)

CARBON PAPER & INKED RIBBONS

Pubco Corporation ....D 216 881-5300
  Cleveland (G-6268)

CARDS: Beveled

Cott Systems Inc ....D 614 847-4405
  Columbus (G-7379)

CARNIVAL & AMUSEMENT PARK EQPT WHOLESALERS

Majestic Manufacturing Inc ....E 330 457-2447
  New Waterford (G-15005)

CARPET & RUG CLEANING PLANTS

C M S Enterprises Inc ....E 740 653-1940
  Lancaster (G-12374)
Farrow Cleaners Co ....E 216 561-2355
  Cleveland (G-5514)
Martin Carpet Cleaning Company ....E 614 443-4655
  Columbus (G-8031)

CARPET & UPHOLSTERY CLEANING SVCS

Allen-Keith Construction Co ....D 330 266-2220
  Canton (G-2178)
Americas Floor Source LLC ....E 216 342-4929
  Bedford Heights (G-1316)
C&C Clean Team Enterprises LLC ....C 513 321-5100
  Cincinnati (G-3102)
Icon Environmental Group LLC ....E 513 426-6767
  Milford (G-14396)
Image By J & K LLC ....B 888 667-6929
  Maumee (G-13802)
New Albany Cleaning Services ....E 614 855-9990
  New Albany (G-14863)
Ohio Building Service Inc ....E 513 761-0268
  Cincinnati (G-4151)
Springfeld Unfrm-Linen Sup Inc ....D 937 323-5544
  Springfield (G-17116)
Sunset Carpet Cleaning ....E 937 836-5531
  Englewood (G-10602)
Teasdale Fenton Carpet Cleanin ....E 513 797-0900
  Cincinnati (G-4578)
Widmers LLC ....C 513 321-5100
  Cincinnati (G-4795)

CARPET & UPHOLSTERY CLEANING SVCS: Carpet/Furniture, On Loc

Arslanian Bros Crpt Rug Clg Co ....E 216 271-6888
  Warrensville Heights (G-18776)
Carpet Services Plus Inc ....E 330 458-2409
  Canton (G-2246)
Lazar Brothers Inc ....E 440 585-9333
  Wickliffe (G-19468)
Merlene Enterprises Inc ....E 440 593-6771
  Conneaut (G-8956)
Miles Cleaning Services Inc ....D 330 633-8562
  Cleveland (G-5992)
Samron Inc ....E 330 782-6539
  Youngstown (G-20203)
Stanley Steemer Intl Inc ....C 614 764-2007
  Dublin (G-10341)

Stanley Steemer Intl Inc ....E 419 227-1212
  Lima (G-12754)
Stanley Steemer Intl Inc ....E 513 771-0213
  Cincinnati (G-4536)
Stanley Steemer Intl Inc ....E 614 652-2241
  Dublin (G-10342)
Stanley Stemer of Akron Canton ....E 330 785-5005
  Coventry Township (G-9043)
Velco Inc ....E 513 772-4226
  Cincinnati (G-4752)
Wiggins Clg & Crpt Svc Inc ....D 937 279-9080
  Dayton (G-9881)

CARPET & UPHOLSTERY CLEANING SVCS: On Customer Premises

D & J Master Clean Inc ....D 614 847-1181
  Columbus (G-7406)
Marks Cleaning Service Inc ....E 330 725-5702
  Medina (G-13968)

CARTONS: Egg, Molded Pulp, Made From Purchased Materials

Tekni-Plex Inc ....E 419 491-2399
  Holland (G-11918)

CASH REGISTERS WHOLESALERS

Business Data Systems Inc ....E 330 633-1221
  Tallmadge (G-17470)

CASINO HOTELS & MOTELS

Hollywood Casino Toledo ....D 419 661-5200
  Toledo (G-17804)
Horseshoe Cleveland MGT LLC ....E 216 297-4777
  Cleveland (G-5709)
Jack Cincinnati Casino LLC ....E 513 252-0777
  Cincinnati (G-3798)

CASTINGS: Commercial Investment, Ferrous

B W Grinding Co ....E 419 923-1376
  Lyons (G-13056)
Howmet Corporation ....E 757 825-7086
  Newburgh Heights (G-15114)

CASTINGS: Die, Aluminum

Akron Foundry Co ....C 330 745-3101
  Akron (G-40)
Seilkop Industries Inc ....E 513 761-1035
  Cincinnati (G-4448)
Yoder Industries Inc ....C 937 278-5769
  Dayton (G-9890)

CASTINGS: Die, Nonferrous

Empire Brass Co ....E 216 431-6565
  Cleveland (G-5477)
Yoder Industries Inc ....C 937 278-5769
  Dayton (G-9890)

CASTINGS: Machinery, Aluminum

Enprotech Industrial Tech LLC ....C 216 883-3220
  Cleveland (G-5482)

CASTINGS: Precision

Akron Foundry Co ....C 330 745-3101
  Akron (G-40)

CATALOG & MAIL-ORDER HOUSES

Cornerstone Brands Group Inc ....A 513 603-1000
  West Chester (G-18899)
Janell Inc ....E 513 489-9111
  Blue Ash (G-1589)

CATALOG SALES

Amerimark Holdings LLC ....B 440 325-2000
  Cleveland (G-4969)
Cinmar LLC ....C 513 603-1000
  West Chester (G-18888)

CATALYSTS: Chemical

BASF Catalysts LLC ....D 216 360-5005
  Cleveland (G-5039)

CATAPULTS

Universal Fabg Cnstr Svcs Inc ....D 614 274-1128
  Columbus *(G-8815)*

CATERERS

A Tara Tiffanys Property ....E 330 448-0778
  Brookfield *(G-1851)*
AVI Food Systems Inc ....C 330 372-6000
  Warren *(G-18677)*
Bagel Place Inc ....E 419 885-1000
  Toledo *(G-17604)*
Black Tie Affair Inc ....E 330 345-8333
  Wooster *(G-19691)*
Fredericks Wine & Dine ....E 216 581-5299
  Cleveland *(G-5576)*
Kitchen Katering Inc ....E 216 481-8080
  Euclid *(G-10647)*
Kohler Foods Inc ....E 937 291-3600
  Dayton *(G-9550)*
Little Miami River Catering Co ....E 937 848-2464
  Bellbrook *(G-1341)*
Lmt Enterprises Maumee Inc ....E 419 891-7325
  Maumee *(G-13810)*
Lorain Party Center ....E 440 282-5599
  Lorain *(G-12923)*
Made From Scratch Inc ....E 614 873-3344
  Plain City *(G-16058)*
Michaels Gourmet Catering ....E 419 698-2988
  Toledo *(G-17912)*
Mustard Seed Health Fd Mkt Inc ....E 440 519-3663
  Solon *(G-16875)*
Pine Brook Golf Club Inc ....E 440 748-2939
  Grafton *(G-11319)*
Sycamore Lake Inc ....C 440 729-9775
  Chesterland *(G-2746)*
Twin Haven Reception Hall ....E 330 425-1616
  Twinsburg *(G-18331)*
Winking Lizard Inc ....D 330 467-1002
  Peninsula *(G-15816)*

CEMENT & CONCRETE RELATED PRDTS & EQPT: Bituminous

Mesa Industries Inc ....D 513 321-2950
  Cincinnati *(G-4038)*

CEMENT ROCK: Crushed & Broken

R W Sidley Incorporated ....E 440 352-9343
  Painesville *(G-15736)*

CEMENT: Hydraulic

Huron Cement Products Company ....E 419 433-4161
  Huron *(G-12026)*

CEMETERIES

Catholic Association of The Di ....D 216 641-7575
  Cleveland *(G-5131)*
Catholic Cemeteries ....E 614 491-2751
  Lockbourne *(G-12810)*
Catholic Diocese of Cleveland ....E 216 267-2850
  Cleveland *(G-5135)*
City of Cleveland ....E 216 348-7210
  Cleveland *(G-5196)*
Stonemor Partners LP ....E 330 491-8001
  Canton *(G-2501)*
Stonemor Partners LP ....E 937 866-4135
  Dayton *(G-9794)*

CEMETERIES: Real Estate Operation

Arlington Memorial Grdns Assn ....E 513 521-7003
  Cincinnati *(G-2987)*
Green Haven Memorial Gardens ....E 330 533-6811
  Canfield *(G-2139)*
Ottawa Hills Memorial Park ....E 419 539-0218
  Ottawa Hills *(G-15668)*
Roman Cthlic Docese Youngstown ....E 330 792-4721
  Youngstown *(G-20191)*
Stonemor Partners LP ....E 330 425-8128
  Twinsburg *(G-18325)*
Sunset Memorial Park Assn ....E 440 777-0450
  North Olmsted *(G-15313)*

CEMETERY ASSOCIATION

Green Lawn Cemetery Assn ....E 614 444-1123
  Columbus *(G-7695)*

Miami Valley Memory Grdns Assn ....E 937 885-7779
  Dayton *(G-9624)*
Spring Grove Cmtry & Arboretum ....D 513 681-7526
  Cincinnati *(G-4517)*
Sunset Hills Cemetery Corp ....E 330 494-2051
  Canton *(G-2503)*
Toledo Memorial Pk & Mausoleum ....E 419 882-7151
  Sylvania *(G-17460)*

CEMETERY MEMORIAL DEALERS

Maza Inc ....E 614 760-0003
  Plain City *(G-16059)*

CERAMIC FLOOR & WALL TILE WHOLESALERS

Accco Inc ....E 740 697-2005
  Roseville *(G-16453)*
Clay Burley Products Co ....E 740 452-3633
  Roseville *(G-16454)*
Virginia Tile Company ....E 216 741-8400
  Brooklyn Heights *(G-1886)*

CHAINS: Power Transmission

US Tsubaki Power Transm LLC ....C 419 626-4560
  Sandusky *(G-16653)*

CHAMBERS OF COMMERCE

Canton Reg Cham of Comm Fdn ....E 330 456-7253
  Canton *(G-2241)*
Chamber Commerce New Carlisle ....E 937 845-3911
  New Carlisle *(G-14889)*
Cincinnati USA Rgional Chamber ....D 513 579-3100
  Cincinnati *(G-3274)*
Dayton Area Chamber Commerce ....E 937 226-1444
  Dayton *(G-9353)*
Greater Cleveland Partnership ....D 216 621-3300
  Cleveland *(G-5637)*
Greater Columbus Chmbr Commrce ......E 614 221-1321
  Columbus *(G-7692)*
Ohio Chamber of Commerce ....E 614 228-4201
  Columbus *(G-8232)*
Youngstown-Warren Reg Chamber ....E 330 744-2131
  Youngstown *(G-20267)*

CHARGE ACCOUNT SVCS

Medigistics Inc ....E 614 430-5700
  Columbus *(G-8054)*

CHARTER FLYING SVC

Jilco Industries Inc ....E 330 698-0280
  Kidron *(G-12306)*

CHASSIS: Motor Vehicle

Falls Stamping & Welding Co ....C 330 928-1191
  Cuyahoga Falls *(G-9092)*

CHECK CASHING SVCS

Allied Cash Holdings LLC ....D 305 371-3141
  Cincinnati *(G-2928)*
Buckeye Check Cashing Inc ....C 614 798-5900
  Dublin *(G-10152)*
Cashland Financial Svcs Inc ....E 937 253-7842
  Dayton *(G-9284)*
Checksmart Financial Company ....E 614 798-5900
  Dublin *(G-10170)*
CNG Financial Corporation ....B 513 336-7735
  Cincinnati *(G-3316)*
Community Choice Financial Inc ....D 440 602-9922
  Willoughby *(G-19515)*
Community Choice Financial Inc ....D 614 798-5900
  Dublin *(G-10185)*
Southwstern PCF Spclty Fin Inc ....E 513 336-7735
  Cincinnati *(G-4508)*

CHECK CLEARING SVCS

Chemical Bank ....D 330 965-5806
  Youngstown *(G-19986)*
Huntington National Bank ....D 614 480-0067
  Columbus *(G-7785)*
Huntington National Bank ....D 614 336-4620
  Dublin *(G-10249)*
National Consumer Coop Bnk ....E 937 393-4246
  Hillsboro *(G-11852)*

CHECK VALIDATION SVCS

Security Check LLC ....C 614 944-5788
  Columbus *(G-8615)*

CHEESE WHOLESALERS

Coblentz Distributing Inc ....E 330 852-2888
  Walnut Creek *(G-18631)*
Great Lakes Cheese Co Inc ....B 440 834-2500
  Hiram *(G-11865)*
Lori Holding Co ....E 740 342-3230
  New Lexington *(G-14920)*
Siemer Distributing Company ....E 740 342-3230
  New Lexington *(G-14928)*
Troyer Cheese Inc ....E 330 893-2479
  Millersburg *(G-14497)*

CHEMICAL CLEANING SVCS

Bleachtech LLC ....E 216 921-1980
  Seville *(G-16683)*
Chemical Solvents Inc ....E 216 741-9310
  Cleveland *(G-5173)*
Sparkle Wash of Lima ....E 419 224-9274
  Lima *(G-12743)*

CHEMICAL PROCESSING MACHINERY & EQPT

Guild Associates Inc ....D 614 798-8215
  Dublin *(G-10236)*

CHEMICAL SPLYS FOR FOUNDRIES

Atotech USA Inc ....D 216 398-0550
  Cleveland *(G-5022)*

CHEMICALS & ALLIED PRDTS WHOLESALERS, NEC

Airgas Usa LLC ....E 513 563-8070
  Cincinnati *(G-2916)*
Akrochem Corporation ....E 330 535-2108
  Barberton *(G-938)*
Ashland LLC ....C 614 839-4503
  Dublin *(G-10138)*
Ashland LLC ....C 614 790-3333
  Dublin *(G-10139)*
Avalon Foodservice Inc ....D 330 854-4551
  Canal Fulton *(G-2092)*
Bleachtech LLC ....E 216 921-1980
  Seville *(G-16683)*
Calvary Industries Inc ....D 513 874-1113
  Fairfield *(G-10706)*
Cimcool Industrial Pdts LLC ....D 888 246-2665
  Cincinnati *(G-3216)*
Dubois Chemicals Inc ....C 513 731-6350
  Cincinnati *(G-3447)*
Dupont Inc ....E 937 268-3411
  Dayton *(G-9398)*
Emerald Hilton Davis LLC ....D 513 841-0057
  Cincinnati *(G-3493)*
Flow Polymers LLC ....C 216 249-4900
  Cleveland *(G-5549)*
Formlabs Ohio Inc ....E 419 837-9783
  Millbury *(G-14448)*
GFS Chemicals Inc ....D 740 881-5501
  Columbus *(G-7667)*
Hillside Maint Sup Co Inc ....E 513 751-4100
  Cincinnati *(G-3708)*
Imcd Us LLC ....E 216 228-8900
  Lakewood *(G-12348)*
Koch Industries LLC ....D 330 488-1651
  East Canton *(G-10387)*
Maines Paper & Food Svc Inc ....E 216 643-7500
  Bedford *(G-1291)*
Polymer Additives Holdings Inc ....C 216 875-7200
  Independence *(G-12108)*
Rde System Corp ....C 513 933-8000
  Lebanon *(G-12496)*
Skidmore Sales & Distrg Co Inc ....E 513 755-4200
  West Chester *(G-19009)*
Struktol Company America LLC ....C 330 928-5188
  Stow *(G-17233)*
T&L Global Management LLC ....D 614 586-0303
  Columbus *(G-8727)*
The Mau-Sherwood Supply Co ....E 330 405-1200
  Twinsburg *(G-18326)*
Tricor Industrial Inc ....D 330 264-3299
  Wooster *(G-19773)*

Univar Inc........................E....... 440 510-1259
Eastlake (G-10435)
VWR Chemicals LLC...............E....... 330 425-2522
Aurora (G-847)
Zep Inc...........................E....... 440 239-1580
Cleveland (G-6713)

CHEMICALS & ALLIED PRDTS, WHOL: Chemicals, Swimming Pool/Spa

Rhiel Supply Co Inc...............E....... 330 799-7777
Austintown (G-861)

CHEMICALS & ALLIED PRDTS, WHOL: Food Additives/Preservatives

Mitsubshi Intl Fd Ingrdnts Inc....E....... 614 652-1111
Dublin (G-10281)

CHEMICALS & ALLIED PRDTS, WHOL: Gases, Compressed/Liquefied

Matheson Tri-Gas Inc..............E....... 614 771-1311
Hilliard (G-11788)

CHEMICALS & ALLIED PRDTS, WHOLESALE: Adhesives

Rudolph Brothers & Co.............E....... 614 833-0707
Canal Winchester (G-2118)

CHEMICALS & ALLIED PRDTS, WHOLESALE: Alkalines & Chlorine

Ashland LLC.......................D....... 614 232-8510
Columbus (G-6977)
Ashland LLC.......................E....... 614 276-6144
Columbus (G-6978)
Ashland LLC.......................D....... 216 961-4690
Cleveland (G-5012)
Ashland LLC.......................E....... 216 883-8200
Cleveland (G-5013)
Ashland LLC.......................D....... 419 289-9588
Ashland (G-652)

CHEMICALS & ALLIED PRDTS, WHOLESALE: Anti-Corrosion Prdts

Electro Prime Group LLC...........D....... 419 476-0100
Toledo (G-17710)

CHEMICALS & ALLIED PRDTS, WHOLESALE: Caustic Soda

National Colloid Company..........E....... 740 282-1171
Steubenville (G-17168)

CHEMICALS & ALLIED PRDTS, WHOLESALE: Chemicals, Indl

Budenheim Usa Inc.................E....... 614 345-2400
Columbus (G-7093)
Chemical Services Inc.............E....... 937 898-5566
Dayton (G-9295)
Chemical Solvents Inc.............D....... 216 741-9310
Cleveland (G-5174)
CL Zimmerman Delaware LLC.........E....... 513 860-9300
West Chester (G-18890)
Custom Chemical Solutions.........E....... 800 291-1057
Loveland (G-12987)
Eliokem Inc.......................D....... 330 734-1100
Fairlawn (G-10824)
Galaxy Associates Inc.............E....... 513 731-6350
Cincinnati (G-3600)
Lanxess Corporation...............C....... 440 279-2367
Chardon (G-2701)
Nexeo Solutions LLC...............E....... 330 405-0461
Twinsburg (G-18301)
Nexeo Solutions LLC...............D....... 330 405-0461
Whipple (G-19442)
Palmer Holland Inc................D....... 440 686-2300
North Olmsted (G-15304)
Rwc Inc...........................E....... 614 890-0600
Westerville (G-19208)
Sea-Land Chemical Co..............D....... 440 871-7887
Westlake (G-19404)
Tembec Btlsr Inc..................E....... 419 244-5856
Toledo (G-18063)
Tosoh America Inc.................B....... 614 539-8622
Grove City (G-11478)

Univar USA Inc....................C....... 513 714-5264
West Chester (G-19095)
Univar USA Inc....................E....... 419 666-7880
Walbridge (G-18626)
Univar USA Inc....................E....... 330 425-4330
Twinsburg (G-18333)
Univar USA Inc....................E....... 513 870-4050
Hamilton (G-11653)
Univar USA Inc....................D....... 440 238-8550
Strongsville (G-17356)
Young Chemical Co LLC.............E....... 330 486-4210
Twinsburg (G-18338)

CHEMICALS & ALLIED PRDTS, WHOLESALE: Chemicals, Indl & Heavy

Harwick Standard Dist Corp........D....... 330 798-9300
Akron (G-253)
Industrial Chemical Corp..........E....... 330 725-0800
Medina (G-13953)

CHEMICALS & ALLIED PRDTS, WHOLESALE: Compressed Gas

Airgas Inc........................D....... 937 222-8312
Moraine (G-14619)
Airgas Usa LLC....................B....... 216 642-6600
Independence (G-12042)

CHEMICALS & ALLIED PRDTS, WHOLESALE: Concrete Additives

Sika Corporation..................D....... 740 387-9224
Marion (G-13459)

CHEMICALS & ALLIED PRDTS, WHOLESALE: Detergent/Soap

Anatrace Products LLC.............E....... 419 740-6600
Maumee (G-13751)
Chemical Solvents Inc.............E....... 216 741-9310
Cleveland (G-5173)
Cr Brands Inc.....................D....... 513 860-5039
West Chester (G-18905)

CHEMICALS & ALLIED PRDTS, WHOLESALE: Detergents

Procter & Gamble Distrg LLC.......B....... 513 945-7960
Cincinnati (G-4291)
Procter & Gamble Distrg LLC.......C....... 937 387-5189
Union (G-18351)
Washing Systems LLC...............C....... 800 272-1974
Loveland (G-13032)

CHEMICALS & ALLIED PRDTS, WHOLESALE: Dry Ice

D & D Investment Co...............E....... 614 272-6567
Columbus (G-7405)

CHEMICALS & ALLIED PRDTS, WHOLESALE: Essential Oils

Cantrell Oil Company..............E....... 937 695-8003
Winchester (G-19660)

CHEMICALS & ALLIED PRDTS, WHOLESALE: Glue

Gorilla Glue Company..............E....... 513 271-3300
Cincinnati (G-3627)

CHEMICALS & ALLIED PRDTS, WHOLESALE: Oxygen

Americas Best Medical Eqp Co......E....... 330 928-0884
Akron (G-71)
Braden Med Services Inc...........E....... 740 732-2356
Caldwell (G-2036)
Medi Home Health Agency Inc.......E....... 740 266-3977
Steubenville (G-17165)

CHEMICALS & ALLIED PRDTS, WHOLESALE: Plastics Film

Multi-Plastics Inc................D....... 740 548-4894
Lewis Center (G-12552)

CHEMICALS & ALLIED PRDTS, WHOLESALE: Plastics Materials, NEC

Alro Steel Corporation............E....... 419 720-5300
Toledo (G-17586)
Alro Steel Corporation............E....... 614 878-7271
Columbus (G-6905)
Plastics R Unique Inc.............E....... 330 334-4820
Wadsworth (G-18613)

CHEMICALS & ALLIED PRDTS, WHOLESALE: Plastics Prdts, NEC

Bprex Plastic Packaging Inc.......C....... 419 423-3271
Findlay (G-10882)
F B Wright Co Cincinnati...........E....... 513 874-9100
West Chester (G-18921)
Polymer Packaging Inc.............D....... 330 832-2000
Massillon (G-13720)
Queen City Polymers Inc...........E....... 513 779-0990
West Chester (G-18989)
Surreal Entertainment LLC.........E....... 330 262-5277
Wooster (G-19772)
Tahoma Enterprises Inc............D....... 330 745-9016
Barberton (G-969)
Tahoma Rubber & Plastics Inc......D....... 330 745-9016
Barberton (G-970)

CHEMICALS & ALLIED PRDTS, WHOLESALE: Plastics Sheets & Rods

HP Manufacturing Company Inc......D....... 216 361-6500
Cleveland (G-5721)
Ilpea Industries Inc..............C....... 330 562-2916
Aurora (G-830)

CHEMICALS & ALLIED PRDTS, WHOLESALE: Plastics, Basic Shapes

Checker Notions Company Inc.......D....... 419 893-3636
Maumee (G-13770)

CHEMICALS & ALLIED PRDTS, WHOLESALE: Resins

Florline Group Inc................E....... 330 830-3380
Massillon (G-13682)
Hexpol Compounding LLC............C....... 440 834-4644
Burton (G-2016)
Polyone Corporation...............D....... 440 930-1000
Avon Lake (G-926)

CHEMICALS & ALLIED PRDTS, WHOLESALE: Resins, Plastics

Cannon Group Inc..................E....... 614 890-0343
Westerville (G-19230)

CHEMICALS & ALLIED PRDTS, WHOLESALE: Rubber, Synthetic

Mantaline Corporation.............D....... 330 274-2264
Mantua (G-13273)

CHEMICALS & ALLIED PRDTS, WHOLESALE: Salts & Polishes, Indl

Cargill Incorporated..............D....... 440 716-4664
North Olmsted (G-15278)

CHEMICALS & ALLIED PRDTS, WHOLESALE: Sanitation Preparations

Bonded Chemicals Inc..............E....... 614 777-9240
Columbus (G-7053)
Joshen Paper & Packaging Co.......C....... 216 441-5600
Cleveland (G-5804)

CHEMICALS & ALLIED PRDTS, WHOLESALE: Sealants

Applied Indus Tech - Dixie Inc....C....... 216 426-4000
Cleveland (G-4995)
Applied Industrial Tech Inc.......B....... 216 426-4000
Cleveland (G-4996)
United McGill Corporation.........E....... 614 829-1200
Groveport (G-11546)

(G-0000) Company's Geographic Section entry number

CHEMICALS & ALLIED PRDTS, WHOLESALE: Spec Clean/Sanitation

Dawnchem Inc ....E 440 943-3332
Willowick (G-19597)

Midwest Industrial Supply Inc ....E 800 321-0699
Toledo (G-17914)

Texo International Inc ....D 513 731-6350
Norwood (G-15463)

CHEMICALS & ALLIED PRDTS, WHOLESALE: Syn Resin, Rub/Plastic

Flex Technologies Inc ....E 330 897-6311
Baltic (G-934)

Kraton Polymers US LLC ....B 740 423-7571
Belpre (G-1407)

Phoenix Technologies Intl LLC ....E 419 353-7738
Bowling Green (G-1744)

Polyone Corporation ....D 440 930-1000
North Baltimore (G-15179)

CHEMICALS, AGRICULTURE: Wholesalers

Waterworks America Inc ....C 440 526-4815
Cleveland (G-6655)

CHEMICALS: Agricultural

Hawthorne Hydroponics LLC ....D 480 777-2000
Marysville (G-13501)

CHEMICALS: Aluminum Compounds

Gayston Corporation ....C 937 743-6050
Miamisburg (G-14173)

CHEMICALS: Bleaching Powder, Lime Bleaching Compounds

Bleachtech LLC ....E 216 921-1980
Seville (G-16683)

CHEMICALS: High Purity, Refined From Technical Grade

Heraeus Precious Metals North ....E 937 264-1000
Vandalia (G-18525)

CHEMICALS: Inorganic, NEC

Borchers Americas Inc ....D 440 899-2950
Westlake (G-19323)

Calvary Industries Inc ....D 513 874-1113
Fairfield (G-10706)

National Colloid Company ....E 740 282-1171
Steubenville (G-17168)

Univar USA Inc ....C 513 714-5264
West Chester (G-19095)

CHEMICALS: Isotopes, Radioactive

Aldrich Chemical ....D 937 859-1808
Miamisburg (G-14138)

CHEMICALS: NEC

Aldrich Chemical ....D 937 859-1808
Miamisburg (G-14138)

Ashland LLC ....C 614 790-3333
Dublin (G-10139)

Borchers Americas Inc ....D 440 899-2950
Westlake (G-19323)

Cargill Incorporated ....C 216 651-7200
Cleveland (G-5127)

Cincinnati - Vulcan Company ....D 513 242-5300
Cincinnati (G-3219)

EMD Millipore Corporation ....C 513 631-0445
Norwood (G-15462)

Flexsys America LP ....D 330 666-4111
Akron (G-225)

Formlabs Ohio Inc ....E 419 837-9783
Millbury (G-14448)

Fuchs Lubricants Co ....E 330 963-0400
Twinsburg (G-18270)

Hexpol Compounding LLC ....C 440 834-4644
Burton (G-2016)

Lubrizol Advanced Mtls Inc ....E 440 933-0400
Avon Lake (G-923)

Morton Salt Inc ....C 330 925-3015
Rittman (G-16407)

National Colloid Company ....E 740 282-1171
Steubenville (G-17168)

New Vulco Mfg & Sales Co LLC ....D 513 242-2672
Cincinnati (G-4109)

Noco Company ....B 216 464-8131
Solon (G-16879)

Polymer Additives Holdings Inc ....C 216 875-7200
Independence (G-12108)

Rhenium Alloys Inc ....D 440 365-7388
North Ridgeville (G-15340)

State Industrial Products Corp ....B 877 747-6986
Cleveland (G-6458)

Teknol Inc ....E 937 264-0190
Dayton (G-9808)

Univar USA Inc ....C 513 714-5264
West Chester (G-19095)

CHEMICALS: Organic, NEC

Alco-Chem Inc ....E 330 253-3535
Akron (G-63)

Aldrich Chemical ....D 937 859-1808
Miamisburg (G-14138)

Borchers Americas Inc ....D 440 899-2950
Westlake (G-19323)

Heraeus Precious Metals North ....E 937 264-1000
Vandalia (G-18525)

National Colloid Company ....E 740 282-1171
Steubenville (G-17168)

Univar USA Inc ....C 513 714-5264
West Chester (G-19095)

CHICKEN SLAUGHTERING & PROCESSING

V H Cooper & Co Inc ....C 419 375-4116
Fort Recovery (G-10994)

CHILD & YOUTH SVCS, NEC

A Better Choice Child Care LLC ....E 614 268-8503
Columbus (G-6847)

Applewood Centers Inc ....D 216 696-6815
Cleveland (G-4991)

Applewood Centers Inc ....D 216 521-6511
Cleveland (G-4992)

Applewood Centers Inc ....E 440 324-1300
Lorain (G-12882)

Applewood Centers Inc ....D 216 741-2241
Cleveland (G-4993)

Board of Delaware County ....D 740 201-3600
Lewis Center (G-12530)

Brook Beech ....C 216 831-2255
Cleveland (G-5086)

Catholic Charities Corporation ....E 419 289-1903
Ashland (G-663)

Center For Families & Children ....D 216 432-7200
Cleveland (G-5150)

Child Focus Inc ....E 513 732-8800
Batavia (G-986)

Child Focus Inc ....D 513 752-1555
Cincinnati (G-3180)

Child Focus Inc ....D 937 444-1613
Mount Orab (G-14739)

Childrens Advocacy Center ....E 740 432-6581
Cambridge (G-2058)

Childrens HM of Cncinnati Ohio ....C 513 272-2800
Cincinnati (G-3182)

Childrens Hosp Med Ctr Akron ....E 330 633-2055
Tallmadge (G-17471)

County of Adams ....E 937 544-5067
West Union (G-19135)

County of Allen ....E 419 227-8590
Lima (G-12624)

County of Allen ....E 419 996-7050
Lima (G-12626)

County of Ashtabula ....D 440 998-1811
Ashtabula (G-733)

County of Clark ....E 937 327-1700
Springfield (G-17025)

County of Clinton ....E 937 382-2449
Wilmington (G-19619)

County of Coshocton ....D 740 622-1020
Coshocton (G-9012)

County of Cuyahoga ....A 216 432-2621
Cleveland (G-5370)

County of Hamilton ....E 513 821-6946
Cincinnati (G-3373)

County of Huron ....D 419 663-5437
Norwalk (G-15432)

County of Logan ....E 937 599-7290
Bellefontaine (G-1352)

County of Marion ....E 740 389-2317
Marion (G-13415)

County of Montgomery ....D 937 224-5437
Dayton (G-9332)

County of Tuscarawas ....E 330 343-0099
New Philadelphia (G-14954)

County of Wayne ....E 330 287-5600
Wooster (G-19718)

Crawford County Children Svcs ....E 419 562-1200
Bucyrus (G-1988)

Family & Child Abuse ....E 419 244-3053
Toledo (G-17723)

For Specialized Alternatives ....D 419 695-8010
Delphos (G-10027)

Franklin Cnty Bd Commissioners ....B 614 462-3275
Columbus (G-7607)

Franklin Cnty Bd Commissioners ....B 614 229-7100
Columbus (G-7609)

Grove Cy Chrstn Child Care Ctr ....E 614 875-2551
Grove City (G-11438)

Hancock Job & Family Services ....D 419 424-7022
Findlay (G-10919)

Juvenile Court Cnty Muskingum ....E 740 453-0351
Zanesville (G-20322)

Kinnect ....E 216 692-1161
Cleveland (G-5833)

Lawrence Cnty Bd Dev Dsblties ....E 740 377-2356
South Point (G-16938)

Lighthouse Youth Services Inc ....E 513 221-3350
Cincinnati (G-3931)

Miami County Childrens Svcs Bd ....E 937 335-4103
Troy (G-18213)

National Exchange Club Foundat ....E 419 535-3232
Toledo (G-17930)

Ohioguidestone ....E 440 234-2006
Berea (G-1434)

Providence House Inc ....E 216 651-5982
Cleveland (G-6263)

Safely Home Inc ....E 440 232-9310
Bedford (G-1304)

Services On Mark Inc ....E 614 846-5400
Worthington (G-19848)

Simply Youth LLC ....D 330 284-2537
Canton (G-2476)

Specialized Alternatives For F ....C 216 295-7239
Shaker Heights (G-16714)

Specialized Alternatives For F ....C 419 222-1527
Lima (G-12746)

Specialized Alternatives For F ....E 419 695-8010
Delphos (G-10035)

Sylvania Community Svcs Ctr ....E 419 885-2451
Sylvania (G-17454)

University of Cincinnati ....D 513 556-3803
Cincinnati (G-4726)

Wood County Chld Svcs Assn ....E 419 352-7588
Bowling Green (G-1752)

Youth Advocate Services ....E 614 258-9927
Columbus (G-8932)

CHILD DAY CARE SVCS

Abacus Child Care Centers Inc ....E 330 773-4200
Akron (G-14)

Abilities First Foundation Inc ....D 513 423-9496
Middletown (G-14285)

Action For Children Inc ....E 614 224-0222
Columbus (G-6868)

Akron Summit Cmnty Action Agcy ....D 330 733-2290
Akron (G-57)

Angel Care Inc ....E 440 736-7267
Brecksville (G-1768)

Angels On Earth Child Care Co ....E 216 476-8100
Cleveland (G-4979)

Arlitt Child Development Ctr ....D 513 556-3802
Cincinnati (G-2988)

Bay Village City School Dst ....E 440 617-7330
Cleveland (G-5043)

Beavercreek YMCA ....D 937 426-9622
Dayton (G-9246)

Bethlehem Lutheran Ch Parma ....E 440 845-2230
Cleveland (G-5060)

Board Man Frst Untd Methdst Ch ....E 330 758-4527
Youngstown (G-19968)

Bright Horizons Chld Ctrs LLC ....E 614 566-4847
Columbus (G-7067)

Brunswick City Schools ....A 330 225-7731
Brunswick (G-1921)

Canton Country Day School ....E 330 453-8279
Canton (G-2231)

Carol Scudere ....E 614 839-4357
New Albany (G-14848)

S E R V I C E S

Catholic Social Svc Miami Vly ....E 937 223-7217
Dayton *(G-9287)*
Chal-Ron LLC ....E 216 383-9050
Cleveland *(G-5166)*
Child Care Resource Center ....E 216 575-0061
Cleveland *(G-5177)*
Child Focus Inc ....D 937 444-1613
Mount Orab *(G-14739)*
Childrens Rehabilitation Ctr ....E 330 856-2107
Warren *(G-18683)*
Christian Missionary Alliance ....E 614 457-4085
Columbus *(G-7195)*
City of Lakewood ....E 216 226-0080
Cleveland *(G-5206)*
Cleveland Child Care Inc ....E 216 631-3211
Cleveland *(G-5233)*
Cleveland Mus Schl Settlement ....C 216 421-5806
Cleveland *(G-5280)*
Columbus Christian Center Inc ....E 614 416-9673
Columbus *(G-7266)*
Columbus Day Care Center ....E 614 269-8980
Columbus *(G-7274)*
Columbus Montessori Education ....E 614 231-3790
Columbus *(G-7299)*
Consolidated Learning Ctrs Inc ....C 614 791-0050
Dublin *(G-10189)*
Council For Economic Opport ....D 216 696-9077
Cleveland *(G-5355)*
Council On Rur Svc Prgrams Inc ....E 937 773-0773
Piqua *(G-16002)*
County of Athens ....D 740 592-3061
Athens *(G-774)*
County of Guernsey ....E 740 439-5555
Cambridge *(G-2060)*
County of Mercer ....D 419 586-2369
Celina *(G-2591)*
Creative Center For Children ....E 513 867-1118
Hamilton *(G-11588)*
Creative Childrens World LLC ....E 513 336-7799
Mason *(G-13570)*
Creative Playrooms Inc ....E 440 572-9365
Strongsville *(G-17294)*
Creative Playrooms Inc ....E 440 349-9111
Solon *(G-16841)*
Creme De La Creme Colorado Inc ....E 513 459-4300
Mason *(G-13571)*
Days of Discovery ....E 937 862-4465
Spring Valley *(G-16958)*
Diocese of Toledo ....E 419 243-7255
Toledo *(G-17702)*
Dover City Schools ....D 330 343-8880
Dover *(G-10073)*
Early Childhood Learning Commu ....D 614 451-6418
Columbus *(G-7488)*
East End Neighborhood Hse Assn ....E 216 791-9378
Cleveland *(G-5456)*
Elderly Day Care Center ....E 419 228-2688
Lima *(G-12632)*
Epworth Preschool and Daycare ....E 740 387-1062
Marion *(G-13419)*
Erie Huron Cac Headstart Inc ....E 419 663-2623
Norwalk *(G-15434)*
Family YMCA of LANcstr&fairfld ....D 740 277-7373
Lancaster *(G-12403)*
Findlay Y M C A Child Dev ....E 419 422-3174
Findlay *(G-10908)*
First Apostolic Church ....E 419 885-4888
Toledo *(G-17738)*
First Assembly Child Care ....E 419 529-6501
Mansfield *(G-13176)*
First Baptist Day Care Center ....E 216 371-9394
Cleveland *(G-5530)*
First Community Church ....E 614 488-0681
Columbus *(G-7583)*
First Community Church ....E 614 488-0681
Columbus *(G-7584)*
First Fruits Child Dev Ctr I ....E 216 862-4715
Euclid *(G-10635)*
Four Oaks Early Intervention ....E 937 562-6779
Xenia *(G-19900)*
Frans Child Care-Mansfield ....C 419 775-2500
Mansfield *(G-13178)*
Galion Community Center YMCA ....E 419 468-7754
Galion *(G-11173)*
Gearity Early Child Care Ctr ....E 216 371-7356
Cleveland *(G-5601)*
Geary Family YMCA Fostria ....E 419 435-6608
Fostoria *(G-11002)*
Genesis Healthcare ....A 937 875-4604
Troy *(G-18203)*
Genesis Healthcare System ....E 740 453-4959
Zanesville *(G-20311)*
Gethsemane Lutheran Church ....E 614 885-4319
Columbus *(G-7666)*
Grace Baptist Church ....E 937 652-1133
Urbana *(G-18435)*
Grace Brthren Ch Columbus Ohio ....C 614 888-7733
Westerville *(G-19168)*
Great Expectations D CA Center ....E 330 782-9500
Youngstown *(G-20054)*
Great Miami Valley YMCA ....A 513 887-0001
Hamilton *(G-11602)*
Great Miami Valley YMCA ....C 513 892-9622
Fairfield Township *(G-10808)*
Great Miami Valley YMCA ....D 513 887-0014
Hamilton *(G-11604)*
Great Miami Valley YMCA ....D 513 868-9622
Hamilton *(G-11605)*
Great Miami Valley YMCA ....D 513 829-3091
Fairfield *(G-10732)*
Hardin County Family YMCA ....E 419 673-6131
Kenton *(G-12279)*
Health Care Plus ....C 614 340-7587
Westerville *(G-19170)*
Highland County Family YMCA ....E 937 840-9622
Hillsboro *(G-11842)*
Horizon Education Centers ....E 440 458-5115
Elyria *(G-10517)*
Huber Heights YMCA ....D 937 236-9622
Dayton *(G-9508)*
Independence Local Schools ....E 216 642-5865
Independence *(G-12083)*
Israel Adath ....E 513 793-1800
Cincinnati *(G-3789)*
Just 4 Kidz Childcare ....E 440 285-2221
Chardon *(G-2700)*
Kangaroo Pouch Daycare Inc ....E 440 473-4725
Cleveland *(G-5812)*
Kids R Kids 1 Ohio Inc ....E 513 398-9944
Mason *(G-13604)*
Kindercare Learning Ctrs LLC ....E 513 961-3164
Cincinnati *(G-3872)*
Kingdom Kids Inc ....E 513 851-6400
Hamilton *(G-11620)*
Ladan Learning Center ....E 614 426-4306
Columbus *(G-7942)*
Lake County YMCA ....C 440 352-3303
Painesville *(G-15718)*
Lake County YMCA ....C 440 946-1160
Willoughby *(G-19538)*
Lake County YMCA ....E 440 259-2724
Perry *(G-15824)*
Lake County YMCA ....D 440 428-5125
Madison *(G-13099)*
Lakewood Catholic Academy ....E 216 521-4352
Lakewood *(G-12351)*
Lawrence Cnty Bd Dev Dsblities ....E 740 377-2356
South Point *(G-16938)*
Le Chaperon Rouge ....E 440 934-0296
Avon *(G-892)*
Le Chaperon Rouge Company ....E 440 899-9477
Westlake *(G-19368)*
Life Center Adult Day Care ....E 614 866-7212
Reynoldsburg *(G-16316)*
Lima Family YMCA ....E 419 223-6045
Lima *(G-12680)*
Little Lambs Childrens Center ....E 614 471-9269
Gahanna *(G-11132)*
Madison Local School District ....B 419 589-2600
Mansfield *(G-13201)*
Medcentral Health System ....E 419 526-8043
Mansfield *(G-13217)*
Merrick House ....E 216 771-5077
Cleveland *(G-5958)*
Miami Valley Hospital ....E 937 224-3916
Dayton *(G-9621)*
Mini University Inc ....D 513 275-5184
Oxford *(G-15685)*
Mk Childcare Warsaw Ave LLC ....E 513 922-6279
Cincinnati *(G-4064)*
Mlm Childcare LLC ....E 513 623-8243
Cincinnati *(G-4065)*
My First Days Daycare LLC ....E 419 466-3354
Toledo *(G-17927)*
My Place Child Care ....E 740 349-3505
Newark *(G-15078)*
N & C Active Learning LLC ....E 937 545-1342
Beavercreek *(G-1172)*
Nanaeles Day Care Inc ....E 216 991-6139
Cleveland *(G-6035)*
National Benevolent Associatio ....D 216 476-0333
Cleveland *(G-6037)*
Neighborhood House ....D 614 252-4941
Columbus *(G-8169)*
New Bgnnngs Assembly of God Ch ....E 614 497-2658
Columbus *(G-8184)*
New Dawn Health Care Inc ....C 330 343-5521
Dover *(G-10090)*
New Life Christian Center ....E 740 687-1572
Lancaster *(G-12422)*
Noahs Ark Child Dev Ctr ....E 513 988-0921
Trenton *(G-18189)*
Northfield Presbt Day Care Ctr ....E 330 467-4411
Northfield *(G-15384)*
Northwest Child Development An ....E 937 559-9565
Dayton *(G-9660)*
Oak Creek United Church ....E 937 434-3941
Dayton *(G-9663)*
Ohio Dept of Job & Fmly Svcs ....C 614 466-1213
Columbus *(G-8247)*
Ohio State University ....D 614 292-4453
Columbus *(G-8311)*
Ohioguidestone ....E 440 234-2006
Berea *(G-1434)*
Our Lady of Bethlehem Schools ....E 614 459-8285
Columbus *(G-8404)*
Pike County YMCA ....E 740 947-8862
Waverly *(G-18822)*
Precious Angels Lrng Ctr Inc ....E 440 886-1919
Cleveland *(G-6225)*
Presbyterian Child Center ....E 740 852-3190
London *(G-12873)*
Professional Maint of Columbus ....B 513 579-1762
Cincinnati *(G-4293)*
Promedica Health Systems Inc ....A 567 585-7454
Toledo *(G-17993)*
R & J Investment Co Inc ....C 440 934-5204
Avon *(G-902)*
Ravenna Assembly of God Inc ....E 330 297-1493
Ravenna *(G-16260)*
Robert A Kaufmann Inc ....E 216 663-1150
Maple Heights *(G-13293)*
Ross County YMCA ....D 740 772-4340
Chillicothe *(G-2823)*
Saint James Day Care Center ....E 513 662-2287
Cincinnati *(G-4425)*
Saint Johns Villa ....C 330 627-4662
Carrollton *(G-2576)*
Sandusky Area YMCA Foundation ....E 419 621-9622
Sandusky *(G-16637)*
Santas Hide Away Hollow Inc ....E 440 632-5000
Middlefield *(G-14276)*
Seton Catholic School Hudson ....E 330 342-4200
Hudson *(G-12005)*
Sharonville Mthdist Wkdays Nrs ....E 513 563-8278
Cincinnati *(G-4465)*
Sisters of Notre D ....E 419 471-0170
Toledo *(G-18035)*
Something Special Lrng Ctr Inc ....E 419 422-1400
Findlay *(G-10960)*
Springfield Family Y M C A ....D 937 323-3781
Springfield *(G-17119)*
St Marys City Board Education ....D 419 394-2616
Saint Marys *(G-16533)*
St Stephen United Church Chrst ....E 419 624-1814
Sandusky *(G-16644)*
St Stephens Community House ....D 614 294-6347
Columbus *(G-8680)*
St Thomas Episcopal Church ....E 513 831-6908
Terrace Park *(G-17500)*
Success Kidz 24-Hr Enrchmt Ctr ....E 614 419-2276
Columbus *(G-8708)*
Sycamore Board of Education ....D 513 489-3937
Cincinnati *(G-4560)*
Sylvania Community Svcs Ctr ....E 419 885-2451
Sylvania *(G-17454)*
Troy Christian School ....D 937 339-5692
Troy *(G-18233)*
U C Child Care Center Inc ....E 513 961-2825
Cincinnati *(G-4659)*
Ucc Childrens Center ....E 513 217-5501
Middletown *(G-14356)*
United Rehabilitation Services ....D 937 233-1230
Dayton *(G-9832)*
United States Enrichment Corp ....A 740 897-2457
Piketon *(G-15990)*
University of Akron ....E 330 972-8210
Akron *(G-480)*
Upper Arlington City Schl Dst ....E 614 487-5133
Columbus *(G-8824)*

Vermilion Family YMCA.........................E 440 967-4208
  Vermilion (G-18563)
West Liberty Care Center Inc ....C 937 465-5065
  West Liberty (G-19122)
West Ohio Cmnty Action Partnr ....C 419 227-2586
  Lima (G-12782)
West Ohio Conference of ....E 937 773-5313
  Piqua (G-16038)
West Shore Child Care Center ....E 440 333-2040
  Cleveland (G-6667)
Westerville-Worthington Learni............E 614 891-4105
  Westerville (G-19306)
Wright State University ....E 937 775-4070
  Dayton (G-9192)
Y M C A Central Stark County ....E 330 305-5437
  Canton (G-2539)
Y M C A Central Stark County ....E 330 875-1611
  Louisville (G-12975)
Y M C A Central Stark County ....E 330 877-8933
  Uniontown (G-18392)
Y M C A Central Stark County ....E 330 830-6275
  Massillon (G-13736)
Y M C A Central Stark County ....E 330 498-4082
  Canton (G-2540)
Y M C A of Ashland Ohio Inc ....D 419 289-0626
  Ashland (G-700)
YMCA ....E 330 823-1930
  Alliance (G-558)
YMCA of Clermont County Inc ....E 513 724-9622
  Batavia (G-1016)
YMCA of Massillon ....E 330 879-0800
  Navarre (G-14826)
Young Mens Christian ....B 513 932-1424
  Lebanon (G-12516)
Young Mens Christian Assn ....D 740 373-2250
  Marietta (G-13402)
Young Mens Christian Assn ....E 419 238-0443
  Van Wert (G-18498)
Young Mens Christian Assoc ....E 330 724-1255
  Akron (G-508)
Young Mens Christian Assoc ....A 330 376-1335
  Akron (G-509)
Young Mens Christian Assoc ....D 419 523-5233
  Ottawa (G-15667)
Young Mens Christian Assoc ....E 937 228-9622
  Dayton (G-9895)
Young Mens Christian Assoc ....C 937 223-5201
  Springboro (G-16990)
Young Mens Christian Assoc ....E 419 729-8135
  Toledo (G-18167)
Young Mens Christian Assoc ....C 614 871-9622
  Grove City (G-11491)
Young Mens Christian Assoc ....E 937 223-5201
  Dayton (G-9892)
Young Mens Christian Assoc ....D 330 923-5223
  Cuyahoga Falls (G-9141)
Young Mens Christian Assoc ....E 330 467-8366
  Macedonia (G-13091)
Young Mens Christian Assoc ....E 330 784-0408
  Akron (G-507)
Young Mens Christian Assoc ....C 614 416-9622
  Gahanna (G-11152)
Young Mens Christian Assoc ....C 614 334-9622
  Hilliard (G-11832)
Young Mens Christian Assoc ....E 937 312-1810
  Dayton (G-9893)
Young Mens Christian Assoc ....E 614 539-1770
  Urbancrest (G-18453)
Young Mens Christian Assoc ....D 614 252-3166
  Columbus (G-8929)
Young Mens Christian Assoc ....E 937 593-9001
  Bellefontaine (G-1370)
Young Mens Christian Associat ....E 513 731-0115
  Cincinnati (G-4813)
Young Mens Christian Associat ....C 513 474-1400
  Cincinnati (G-4814)
Young Mens Christian Associat ....C 513 791-5000
  Blue Ash (G-1685)
Young Mens Christian Associat ....D 513 241-9622
  Cincinnati (G-4815)
Young Mens Christian Associat ....D 513 923-4466
  Cincinnati (G-4816)
Young Mens Christian Associat ....E 419 474-3995
  Toledo (G-18169)
Young Mens Christian Associat ....D 419 866-9622
  Maumee (G-13871)
Young Mens Christian Associat ....C 419 475-3496
  Toledo (G-18170)
Young Mens Christian Associat ....D 419 691-3523
  Oregon (G-15615)

Young Mens Christian Mt Vernon ....D 740 392-9622
  Mount Vernon (G-14794)
Young MNS Chrstn Assn Clveland ....E 216 521-8400
  Lakewood (G-12364)
Young MNS Chrstn Assn Clveland ....E 216 731-7454
  Cleveland (G-6703)
Young MNS Chrstn Assn Clveland ....D 440 285-7543
  Chardon (G-2726)
Young MNS Chrstn Assn Grter NY ....D 740 392-9622
  Mount Vernon (G-14795)
Young Womens Christian ....D 419 241-3235
  Toledo (G-18172)
Young Womens Christian ....E 419 238-6639
  Van Wert (G-18499)
Young Womens Christian Assn ....D 614 224-9121
  Columbus (G-8931)
Young Womens Christian Associ ....E 216 881-6878
  Cleveland (G-6705)
Young Womns Chrstn Assc Canton ....D 330 453-0789
  Canton (G-2543)
YWCA Dayton ....D 937 461-5550
  Dayton (G-9896)
YWCA Mahoning Valley ....E 330 746-6361
  Youngstown (G-20269)
YWCA of Greater Cincinnati ....D 513 241-7090
  Cincinnati (G-4817)
YWCA Shelter & Housing Network ....E 937 222-6333
  Dayton (G-9897)
Znm Wecare Corporation ....E 740 548-2022
  Delaware (G-10018)

CHILD GUIDANCE SVCS

Child Adlscent Behavioral Hlth ....D 330 433-6075
  Canton (G-2250)
Comprehensive Cmnty Child Care ....E 513 221-0033
  Cincinnati (G-3345)
County of Cuyahoga ....E 216 443-5100
  Cleveland (G-5365)
Mercy Health - St ....E 419 696-7465
  Oregon (G-15600)
Richland County Child Support ....E 419 774-5700
  Mansfield (G-13235)

CHILD RESTRAINT SEATS, AUTOMOTIVE, WHOLESALE

Recaro Child Safety LLC ....E 248 904-1570
  Cincinnati (G-4344)
TS Tech Americas Inc ....E 740 593-5958
  Athens (G-808)
TS Tech Americas Inc ....B 614 575-4100
  Reynoldsburg (G-16334)

CHILDBIRTH PREPARATION CLINIC

American National Red Cross ....E 330 469-6403
  Warren (G-18663)
Family Birth Center Lima Mem ....E 419 998-4570
  Lima (G-12636)
London Health & Rehab Ctr LLC ....C 740 852-3100
  London (G-12865)
Mercy Health ....E 937 323-4585
  Springfield (G-17073)
Molina Healthcare Inc ....B 216 606-1400
  Independence (G-12099)
Primary Cr Ntwrk Prmr Hlth Prt ....E 513 204-5785
  Mason (G-13629)
Saber Healthcare Group LLC ....C 440 352-0788
  Painesville (G-15739)
Sports Medicine Grant Inc ....E 614 461-8199
  Pickerington (G-15968)
Wheeling Hospital Inc ....D 740 671-0850
  Shadyside (G-16699)

CHILDREN'S & INFANTS' CLOTHING STORES

Abercrombie & Fitch Trading Co ....E 614 283-6500
  New Albany (G-14839)

CHILDREN'S AID SOCIETY

Cleveland Municipal School Dst ....D 216 521-6511
  Cleveland (G-5278)
Feed Lucas County Children Inc ....D 419 260-1556
  Toledo (G-17732)
Franklin Cnty Bd Commissioners ....C 614 275-2571
  Columbus (G-7605)
Homes For Kids of Ohio Inc ....E 330 544-8005
  Niles (G-15157)

Prokids Inc ....E 513 281-2000
  Cincinnati (G-4297)
Scioto County Ohio ....E 740 456-4164
  New Boston (G-14882)

CHILDREN'S BOARDING HOME

One Way Farm of Fairfield Inc ....E 513 829-3276
  Fairfield (G-10765)

CHILDREN'S DANCING SCHOOL

Artistic Dance Enterprises ....E 614 761-2882
  Columbus (G-6974)

CHILDREN'S HOME

Christian Chld HM Ohio Inc ....D 330 345-7949
  Wooster (G-19700)
County of Richland ....C 419 774-4100
  Mansfield (G-13155)
County of Wayne ....D 330 345-5340
  Wooster (G-19717)
Hill Manor Enterprises ....E 614 567-7134
  Groveport (G-11517)
Mid-Western Childrens Home ....E 513 877-2141
  Pleasant Plain (G-16074)
Necco Center ....D 740 534-1386
  Pedro (G-15800)
Pathway Caring For Children ....D 330 493-0083
  Canton (G-2435)
Saint Joseph Orphanage ....D 513 741-3100
  Cincinnati (G-4427)

CHINAWARE WHOLESALERS

Ghp II LLC ....B 740 681-6825
  Lancaster (G-12406)

CHIROPRACTORS' OFFICES

Active Chiropractic ....E 440 893-8800
  Chagrin Falls (G-2637)
Healthquest Blanchester Inc ....E 937 783-4535
  Blanchester (G-1487)
Lbi Starbucks DC 3 ....C 614 415-6363
  Columbus (G-7960)

CHOCOLATE, EXC CANDY FROM BEANS: Chips, Powder, Block, Syrup

Gorant Chocolatier LLC ....C 330 726-8821
  Boardman (G-1698)
Malleys Candies Inc ....C 216 529-6262
  Cleveland (G-5903)
Robert E McGrath Inc ....E 440 572-7747
  Strongsville (G-17341)

CHURCHES

Epworth Preschool and Daycare ....E 740 387-1062
  Marion (G-13419)
First Christian Church ....E 330 445-2700
  Canton (G-2313)
Salvation Army ....E 937 528-5100
  Dayton (G-9747)

CIRCUIT BOARD REPAIR SVCS

Mid-Ohio Electric Co ....E 614 274-8000
  Columbus (G-8076)

CLAIMS ADJUSTING SVCS

Crawford & Company ....E 440 243-8710
  Cleveland (G-5375)
S & S Halthcare Strategies Ltd ....C 513 772-8866
  Cincinnati (G-4420)

CLEANING & DESCALING SVC: Metal Prdts

Carpe Diem Industries LLC ....E 419 358-0129
  Bluffton (G-1689)
Carpe Diem Industries LLC ....D 419 659-5639
  Columbus Grove (G-8940)
Chemical Solvents Inc ....E 216 741-9310
  Cleveland (G-5173)

CLEANING & DYEING PLANTS, EXC RUGS

A One Fine Dry Cleaners Inc ....D 513 351-2663
  Cincinnati (G-2892)
Apc2 Inc ....D 513 231-5540
  Cincinnati (G-2972)

Caskey Cleaning Co ....D...... 614 443-7448
  Columbus (G-7132)
Dee Jay Cleaners Inc ....E...... 216 731-7060
  Euclid (G-10630)
Dublin Cleaners Inc ....D...... 614 764-9934
  Columbus (G-7474)
La France South Inc ....E...... 330 782-1400
  Youngstown (G-20095)
Miles Cleaning Services Inc ....D...... 330 633-8562
  Cleveland (G-5992)
Rockwood Dry Cleaners Corp ....E...... 614 471-3700
  Gahanna (G-11142)
Rondinelli Company Inc ....D...... 330 726-7643
  Youngstown (G-20194)
Widmers LLC ....C...... 513 321-5100
  Cincinnati (G-4795)

CLEANING EQPT: Commercial

MPW Industrial Svcs Group Inc ....D...... 740 927-8790
  Hebron (G-11719)

CLEANING EQPT: Floor Washing & Polishing, Commercial

Image By J & K LLC ....B...... 888 667-6929
  Maumee (G-13802)

CLEANING OR POLISHING PREPARATIONS, NEC

Ohio Auto Supply Company ....E...... 330 454-5105
  Canton (G-2424)

CLEANING PRDTS: Sanitation Preps, Disinfectants/Deodorants

Tranzonic Companies ....C...... 216 535-4300
  Richmond Heights (G-16395)

CLEANING PRDTS: Specialty

Rose Products and Services Inc ....E...... 614 443-7647
  Columbus (G-8551)

CLEANING SVCS

Akil Incorporated ....E...... 419 625-0857
  Sandusky (G-16573)
Akron Area Commercial Cleaning ....E...... 330 434-0767
  Akron (G-26)
Corporate Cleaning Inc ....E...... 614 203-6051
  Columbus (G-7371)
French Company LLC ....D...... 330 963-4344
  Twinsburg (G-18269)
House Calls LLC ....E...... 513 841-9800
  Cincinnati (G-3732)
Inner-Space Cleaning Corp ....C...... 440 646-0701
  Cleveland (G-5755)
Lance A1 Cleaning Services LLC ....D...... 614 370-0550
  Columbus (G-7948)
Liberty Casting Company LLC ....E...... 740 363-1941
  Delaware (G-9996)
Med Clean ....C...... 614 207-3317
  Columbus (G-8050)
Mid-American Clg Contrs Inc ....C...... 937 859-6222
  Dayton (G-9631)
Mispace Inc ....E...... 614 626-2602
  Columbus (G-8091)
Oregon Clean Energy Center ....E...... 419 566-9466
  Oregon (G-15604)
Premier Cleaning Services Inc ....E...... 513 831-2492
  Milford (G-14426)
Steven H Byerly Inc ....E...... 614 882-0092
  Columbus (G-8699)

CLEANING SVCS: Industrial Or Commercial

A B M Inc ....E...... 419 421-2292
  Findlay (G-10862)
Ajax Commercial Cleaning Inc ....D...... 330 928-4543
  Cuyahoga Falls (G-9067)
Any Domest Work Inc ....D...... 440 845-9911
  Cleveland (G-4986)
Blue Chip 2000 Coml Clg Inc ....B...... 513 561-2999
  Cincinnati (G-3061)
Butterfield Co Inc ....D...... 330 832-1282
  Massillon (G-13666)
Carrara Companies Inc ....D...... 330 659-2800
  Richfield (G-16348)
Champion Clg Specialists Inc ....E...... 513 871-2333
  Cincinnati (G-3167)

Control Cleaning Solutions ....E...... 330 220-3333
  Brunswick (G-1925)
Cummins Facility Services LLC ....B...... 740 726-9800
  Prospect (G-16222)
Environment Ctrl Beachwood Inc ....D...... 330 405-6201
  Twinsburg (G-18260)
Essentialprofile1corp ....E...... 614 805-4794
  Columbus (G-7535)
Four Corners Cleaning Inc ....E...... 330 644-0834
  Barberton (G-952)
Galaxie Industrial Svcs LLC ....E...... 330 503-2334
  Youngstown (G-20042)
Industrial Air Control Inc ....E...... 330 772-6422
  Hubbard (G-11947)
Metropolitan Envmtl Svcs Inc ....D...... 614 771-1881
  Hilliard (G-11793)
Milford Coml Clg Svcs Inc ....E...... 513 575-5678
  Milford (G-14411)
MPW Industrial Services Inc ....A...... 800 827-8790
  Hebron (G-11718)
MPW Industrial Services Inc ....D...... 740 774-5251
  Chillicothe (G-2805)
MPW Industrial Services Inc ....E...... 937 644-0200
  East Liberty (G-10393)
MPW Industrial Svcs Group Inc ....D...... 740 927-8790
  Hebron (G-11719)
New Albany Cleaning Services ....E...... 614 855-9990
  New Albany (G-14863)
Ohio State University ....A...... 614 292-6158
  Columbus (G-8352)
Professional Hse Clg Svcs Inc ....E...... 440 729-7866
  Chesterland (G-2743)
R K Hydro-Vac Inc ....E...... 937 773-8600
  Piqua (G-16026)
Schenker Inc ....E...... 419 491-1055
  Swanton (G-17404)
TNT Power Wash Inc ....E...... 614 662-3110
  Groveport (G-11541)
TNT Power Wash Inc ....E...... 614 662-3110
  Groveport (G-11542)
Toledo Building Services Co ....A...... 419 241-3101
  Toledo (G-18075)
Tri Tech Service Systems Inc ....C...... 937 787-4664
  Somerville (G-16919)
Two Men & A Vacuum LLC ....D...... 614 300-7970
  Columbus (G-8791)
Vadakin Inc ....E...... 740 373-7518
  Marietta (G-13394)
Wiggins Clg & Crpt Svc Inc ....D...... 937 279-9080
  Dayton (G-9881)

CLEARINGHOUSE ASSOCIATIONS: Bank Or Check

Nationwide Biweekly ADM Inc ....C...... 937 376-5800
  Xenia (G-19921)
Ptc Holdings Inc ....B...... 216 771-6960
  Cleveland (G-6267)

CLOTHING & ACCESS, WOMEN, CHILD & INFANT, WHSLE: Sportswear

Brennan-Eberly Team Sports Inc ....E...... 419 865-8326
  Holland (G-11876)

CLOTHING & ACCESS, WOMEN, CHILDREN & INFANT, WHOL: Handbags

Atrium Buying Corporation ....D...... 740 966-8200
  Blacklick (G-1474)
R G Barry Corporation ....D...... 614 864-6400
  Pickerington (G-15966)

CLOTHING & ACCESS, WOMEN, CHILDREN & INFANT, WHOL: Uniforms

Cintas Corporation No 1 ....A...... 513 459-1200
  Mason (G-13556)
Cintas Sales Corporation ....B...... 513 459-1200
  Cincinnati (G-3295)
Lion-Vallen Ltd Partnership ....E...... 937 898-1949
  Dayton (G-9571)

CLOTHING & ACCESS: Costumes, Theatrical

Costume Specialists Inc ....E...... 614 464-2115
  Columbus (G-7378)

CLOTHING & ACCESS: Hospital Gowns

Standard Textile Co Inc ....B...... 513 761-9256
  Cincinnati (G-4533)

CLOTHING & FURNISHINGS, MEN'S & BOYS', WHOLESALE: Gloves

Safety Solutions Inc ....D...... 614 799-9900
  Columbus (G-8578)

CLOTHING & FURNISHINGS, MEN'S & BOYS', WHOLESALE: Uniforms

Cintas Corporation No 1 ....A...... 513 459-1200
  Mason (G-13556)
Cintas Sales Corporation ....B...... 513 459-1200
  Cincinnati (G-3295)
Lion-Vallen Ltd Partnership ....E...... 937 898-1949
  Dayton (G-9571)
Standard Textile Co Inc ....B...... 513 761-9256
  Cincinnati (G-4533)
Walter F Stephens Jr Inc ....E...... 937 746-0521
  Franklin (G-11041)

CLOTHING & FURNISHINGS, MENS & BOYS, WHOL: Sportswear/Work

Brennan-Eberly Team Sports Inc ....E...... 419 865-8326
  Holland (G-11876)

CLOTHING & FURNISHINGS, MENS & BOYS, WHOLESALE: Apprl Belts

J Peterman Company LLC ....E...... 888 647-2555
  Blue Ash (G-1588)

CLOTHING STORES, NEC

Schneider Saddlery LLC ....E...... 440 543-2700
  Chagrin Falls (G-2682)

CLOTHING STORES: Dancewear

Artistic Dance Enterprises ....E...... 614 761-2882
  Columbus (G-6974)

CLOTHING STORES: Designer Apparel

K Amalia Enterprises Inc ....D...... 614 733-3800
  Plain City (G-16056)

CLOTHING STORES: Formal Wear

American Commodore Tu ....D...... 216 291-4601
  Cleveland (G-4950)
Rondinellis Tuxedo ....E...... 330 726-7768
  Youngstown (G-20195)

CLOTHING STORES: Lingerie & Corsets, Underwear

Pure Romance LLC ....D...... 513 248-8656
  Cincinnati (G-4306)

CLOTHING STORES: T-Shirts, Printed, Custom

Soundtrack Printing ....C...... 330 606-7117
  Cuyahoga Falls (G-9124)
TSC Apparel LLC ....D...... 513 771-1138
  Cincinnati (G-4651)

CLOTHING/ACCESS, WOMEN, CHILDREN/INFANT, WHOL: Hosp Gowns

Philips Medical Systems Clevel ....B...... 440 247-2652
  Cleveland (G-6203)

CLOTHING/FURNISHINGS, MEN/BOY, WHOL: Furnishings, Exc Shoes

R G Barry Corporation ....D...... 614 864-6400
  Pickerington (G-15966)

CLOTHING: Caps, Baseball

Barbs Graffiti Inc ....E...... 216 881-5550
  Cleveland (G-5036)

CLOTHING: Hospital, Men's

Standard Textile Co Inc ....B 513 761-9256
Cincinnati *(G-4533)*

CLOTHING: T-Shirts & Tops, Knit

E Retailing Associates LLC ....D 614 300-5785
Columbus *(G-7486)*

CLOTHING: Uniforms & Vestments

Walter F Stephens Jr Inc ....E 937 746-0521
Franklin *(G-11041)*

CLOTHING: Uniforms, Ex Athletic, Women's, Misses' & Juniors'

Cintas Corporation ....A 513 459-1200
Cincinnati *(G-3291)*
Cintas Corporation ....D 513 631-5750
Cincinnati *(G-3292)*
Cintas Corporation No 2 ....D 330 966-7800
Canton *(G-2254)*
Standard Textile Co Inc ....B 513 761-9256
Cincinnati *(G-4533)*

CLOTHING: Uniforms, Military, Men/Youth, Purchased Materials

Vgs Inc ....C 216 431-7800
Cleveland *(G-6627)*

CLOTHING: Uniforms, Work

Cintas Corporation ....D 513 631-5750
Cincinnati *(G-3292)*
Cintas Corporation ....A 513 459-1200
Cincinnati *(G-3291)*
Cintas Corporation No 2 ....D 330 966-7800
Canton *(G-2254)*
Cintas Sales Corporation ....B 513 459-1200
Cincinnati *(G-3295)*
Vgs Inc ....C 216 431-7800
Cleveland *(G-6627)*

CLUTCHES, EXC VEHICULAR

Logan Clutch Corporation ....E 440 808-4258
Cleveland *(G-5879)*

COAL & OTHER MINERALS & ORES WHOLESALERS

Graphel Corporation ....C 513 779-6166
West Chester *(G-18934)*
Tosoh America Inc ....B 614 539-8622
Grove City *(G-11478)*

COAL MINING SERVICES

Coal Services Inc ....D 740 795-5220
Powhatan Point *(G-16214)*
Harrison County Coal Company ....E 740 338-3100
Saint Clairsville *(G-16488)*
Ohio Valley Resources Inc ....E 740 795-5220
Saint Clairsville *(G-16499)*
Peabody Coal Company ....B 740 450-2420
Zanesville *(G-20353)*
Suncoke Energy Nc ....E 513 727-5571
Middletown *(G-14333)*

COAL MINING SVCS: Bituminous, Contract Basis

Ohio Valley Transloading Co ....A 740 795-4967
Saint Clairsville *(G-16500)*

COAL MINING: Anthracite

Coal Services Inc ....D 740 795-5220
Powhatan Point *(G-16214)*

COAL MINING: Bituminous & Lignite Surface

J & D Mining Inc ....E 330 339-4935
New Philadelphia *(G-14967)*
Murray American Energy Inc ....A 740 338-3100
Saint Clairsville *(G-16496)*

COAL MINING: Bituminous Coal & Lignite-Surface Mining

Coal Services Inc ....D 740 795-5220
Powhatan Point *(G-16214)*
Ohio Valley Coal Company ....B 740 926-1351
Saint Clairsville *(G-16498)*
Rosebud Mining Company ....E 740 768-2097
Bergholz *(G-1444)*

COAL MINING: Bituminous Underground

Coal Services Inc ....D 740 795-5220
Powhatan Point *(G-16214)*
Rosebud Mining Company ....E 740 658-4217
Freeport *(G-11055)*
Rosebud Mining Company ....E 740 768-2097
Bergholz *(G-1444)*
Rosebud Mining Company ....E 740 922-9122
Uhrichsville *(G-18343)*
Western KY Coal Resources LLC ....B 740 338-3100
Saint Clairsville *(G-16510)*

COAL MINING: Bituminous, Strip

B&N Coal Inc ....D 740 783-3575
Dexter City *(G-10059)*
Oxford Mining Company Inc ....D 740 342-7666
New Lexington *(G-14924)*
Rosebud Mining Company ....E 740 922-9122
Uhrichsville *(G-18343)*
Sands Hill Coal Hauling Co Inc ....C 740 384-4211
Hamden *(G-11553)*

COAL MINING: Bituminous, Surface, NEC

Marietta Coal Co. ....E 740 695-2197
Saint Clairsville *(G-16494)*

COAL MINING: Lignite, Surface, NEC

Nacco Industries Inc ....E 440 229-5151
Cleveland *(G-6034)*

COATING SVC: Aluminum, Metal Prdts

SH Bell Company ....E 412 963-9910
East Liverpool *(G-10417)*

COATING SVC: Metals & Formed Prdts

Howmet Corporation ....E 757 825-7086
Newburgh Heights *(G-15114)*

COATING SVC: Metals, With Plastic Or Resins

Corrotec Inc ....E 937 325-3585
Springfield *(G-17021)*
Godfrey & Wing Inc ....E 330 562-1440
Aurora *(G-828)*

COATINGS: Epoxy

Master Builders LLC ....E 216 831-5500
Beachwood *(G-1076)*

COCKTAIL LOUNGE

Akron Management Corp ....B 330 644-8441
Akron *(G-48)*
Al-Mar Lanes ....E 419 352-4637
Bowling Green *(G-1713)*
Avalon Inn Services Inc ....C 330 856-1900
Warren *(G-18674)*
Bramarjac Inc ....E 419 884-3434
Mansfield *(G-13144)*
Capri Bowling Lanes Inc ....E 937 832-4000
Dayton *(G-9276)*
Carrie Cerino Restaurants Inc ....C 440 237-3434
Cleveland *(G-5129)*
Chillicothe Bowling Lanes Inc ....E 740 773-3300
Chillicothe *(G-2759)*
City Life Inc ....E 216 523-5899
Cleveland *(G-5186)*
Columbus Square Bowling Palace ....E 614 895-1122
Columbus *(G-7316)*
Corporate Exchange Hotel Assoc ....C 614 890-8600
Columbus *(G-7373)*
Eastbury Bowling Center ....E 330 452-3700
Canton *(G-2294)*
Holiday Lanes Inc ....E 614 861-1600
Columbus *(G-7760)*

Interstate Lanes of Ohio Ltd ....E 419 666-2695
Rossford *(G-16462)*
Island Service Company ....C 419 285-3695
Put In Bay *(G-16226)*
McPaul Corp ....E 419 447-6313
Tiffin *(G-17523)*
Paul A Ertel ....D 216 696-8888
Cleveland *(G-6183)*
Pike Run Golf Club Inc ....E 419 538-7000
Ottawa *(G-15664)*
Poelking Lanes Inc ....E 937 299-5573
Dayton *(G-9697)*
R P L Corporation ....C 937 335-0021
Troy *(G-18223)*
Rainbow Lanes Inc ....E 614 491-7155
Columbus *(G-8487)*
Riverside Cmnty Urban Redev ....C 330 929-3000
Cuyahoga Falls *(G-9120)*
Sb Hotel LLC ....E 614 793-2244
Dublin *(G-10329)*
Stonehedge Enterprises Inc ....E 330 928-2161
Akron *(G-442)*
The Oaks Lodge ....E 330 769-2601
Chippewa Lake *(G-2838)*
Town House Motor Lodge Corp ....E 740 452-4511
Zanesville *(G-20367)*
Victory Lanes Inc ....E 937 323-8684
Springfield *(G-17130)*
Wedgewood Lanes Inc ....E 330 792-1949
Youngstown *(G-20241)*

COFFEE SVCS

Filterfresh Coffee Service Inc ....E 513 681-8911
West Chester *(G-19053)*
K & R Distributors Inc ....E 937 864-5495
Fairborn *(G-10677)*
Sanese Services Inc ....B 614 436-1234
Warren *(G-18739)*
Walter Alexander Entps Inc ....E 513 841-1100
Cincinnati *(G-4769)*

COIN COUNTERS

Garda CL Technical Svcs Inc ....E 937 294-4099
Moraine *(G-14660)*

COIN OPERATED LAUNDRIES & DRYCLEANERS

Super Laundry Inc ....E 614 258-5147
Columbus *(G-8713)*

COIN-OPERATED LAUNDRY

American Sales Inc ....E 937 253-9520
Dayton *(G-9159)*
Fox Cleaners Inc ....D 937 276-4171
Dayton *(G-9447)*
St Clair 60 Minute Clrs Inc ....E 740 695-3100
Saint Clairsville *(G-16506)*

COIN-OPERATED LAUNDRY MACHINE ROUTES

Joseph S Mischell ....E 513 542-9800
Cincinnati *(G-3834)*

COINS, WHOLESALE

United States Commemrtv Art GA ....E 330 494-5504
Canton *(G-2521)*

COLLECTION AGENCIES

Allied Interstate LLC ....D 715 386-1810
Columbus *(G-6898)*
Axcess Rcvery Cr Solutions Inc ....E 513 229-6700
Cincinnati *(G-3011)*
Dfs Corporate Services LLC ....B 614 777-7020
Hilliard *(G-11760)*
Guardian Water & Power Inc ....D 614 291-3141
Columbus *(G-7703)*
Head Mercantile Co Inc ....D 440 847-2700
Westlake *(G-19349)*
Innovtive Cllectn Concepts Inc ....E 513 489-5500
Blue Ash *(G-1584)*
Macys Cr & Customer Svcs Inc ....A 513 398-5221
Mason *(G-13613)*
Medical Administrators Inc ....E 440 899-2229
Westlake *(G-19372)*

SERVICES

Spartan Asset Rcvery Group Inc ....D 786 930-0188
Cincinnati (G-4509)

COLLECTION AGENCY, EXC REAL ESTATE

Apelles LLC ....E 614 899-7322
Columbus (G-6957)

C & S Associates Inc ....E 440 461-9661
Highland Heights (G-11732)

Celco Ltd ....E 330 655-7000
Hudson (G-11969)

Choice Recovery Inc ....D 614 358-9900
Columbus (G-7193)

Controlled Credit Corporation ....E 513 921-2600
Cincinnati (G-3354)

Credit Adjustments Inc ....D 419 782-3709
Defiance (G-9908)

Credit Bur Collectn Svcs Inc ....E 614 223-0688
Columbus (G-7388)

Credit Bur Collectn Svcs Inc ....E 937 496-2577
Dayton (G-9338)

Estate Information Svcs LLC ....D 614 729-1700
Gahanna (G-11119)

Fidelity Properties Inc ....E 330 821-9700
Alliance (G-531)

Finance System of Toledo Inc ....E 419 578-4300
Toledo (G-17735)

First Federal Credit Control ....E 216 360-2000
Cleveland (G-5534)

General Audit Corp ....E 419 993-2900
Lima (G-12642)

General Revenue Corporation ....B 513 469-1472
Mason (G-13586)

HMC Group Inc ....E 440 847-2720
Westlake (G-19350)

Hs Financial Group LLC ....E 440 871-8484
Westlake (G-19353)

JP Recovery Services Inc ....D 440 331-2200
Rocky River (G-16438)

McCarthy Burgess & Wolff Inc ....C 440 735-5100
Bedford (G-1292)

Media Collections Inc ....D 216 831-5626
Twinsburg (G-18297)

Medical Care PSC Inc ....E 513 281-4400
Cincinnati (G-3993)

National Entp Systems Inc ....C 440 542-1360
Solon (G-16876)

Ncs Incorporated ....D 440 684-9455
Cleveland (G-6052)

Oriana House Inc ....C 419 447-1444
Tiffin (G-17531)

PRC Medical LLC ....D 330 493-9004
Cuyahoga Falls (G-9118)

Receivable MGT Svcs Corp ....D 330 659-1000
Richfield (G-16373)

Recovery One LLC ....D 614 336-4207
Columbus (G-8496)

Reliant Capital Solutions LLC ....C 614 452-6100
Gahanna (G-11141)

Revenue Assistance Corporation ......C 216 763-2100
Cleveland (G-6317)

Rossman ....E 614 523-4150
New Albany (G-14872)

Security Check LLC ....E 614 944-5788
Columbus (G-8615)

Tek-Collect Incorporated ....E 614 299-2766
Columbus (G-8736)

United Collection Bureau Inc ....C 419 866-6227
Toledo (G-18117)

United Collection Bureau Inc ....E 419 866-6227
Maumee (G-13864)

COLLEGE, EXC JUNIOR

Baldwin Wallace University ....E 440 826-2285
Berea (G-1413)

Kenyon College ....E 740 427-2202
Gambier (G-11225)

Marietta College ....E 740 376-4790
Marietta (G-13350)

Oberlin College ....C 440 775-8519
Oberlin (G-15513)

University of Toledo ....A 419 383-4000
Toledo (G-18127)

University of Toledo ....A 419 383-3759
Toledo (G-18129)

COLLEGES, UNIVERSITIES & PROFESSIONAL SCHOOLS

Antioch University ....D 937 769-1366
Yellow Springs (G-19938)

Aultman Hospital ....A 330 452-9911
Canton (G-2202)

Cleveland Clinic Lerner Colleg ....D 216 445-3853
Cleveland (G-5249)

Ohio State University ....B 614 292-3238
Columbus (G-8333)

Ohio State University ....E 614 292-4453
Columbus (G-8311)

Ohio State University ....A 614 293-2494
Columbus (G-8318)

Ohio State University ....C 614 292-6251
Columbus (G-8337)

Ohio State University ....E 614 293-8333
Columbus (G-8346)

COLOR SEPARATION: Photographic & Movie Film

Tj Metzgers Inc ....D 419 861-8611
Toledo (G-18066)

COMBINATION UTILITIES, NEC

City of Lorain ....C 440 204-2500
Lorain (G-12891)

City of Painesville ....B 440 392-5795
Painesville (G-15700)

Jersey Central Pwr & Light Co ....E 330 315-6713
Fairlawn (G-10836)

Ohio Edison Company ....C 740 671-2900
Shadyside (G-16697)

Universal Green Energy Solutio ....E 844 723-7768
Reynoldsburg (G-16335)

University of Cincinnati ....D 513 558-1799
Cincinnati (G-4719)

COMBINED ELEMENTARY & SECONDARY SCHOOLS, PRIVATE

Christian Schools Inc ....D 330 857-7311
Kidron (G-12305)

East Dayton Christian School ....E 937 252-5400
Dayton (G-9172)

Laurel School ....C 216 464-1441
Cleveland (G-5857)

Open Door Christian School ....D 440 322-6386
Elyria (G-10551)

COMMERCIAL & INDL SHELVING WHOLESALERS

Cbf Industries Inc ....E 216 229-9300
Bedford (G-1271)

Ebo Inc ....E 216 229-9300
Bedford (G-1279)

COMMERCIAL & OFFICE BUILDINGS RENOVATION & REPAIR

Advanced Intgrted Slutions LLC ....E 313 724-8600
Blue Ash (G-1497)

Airko Inc ....E 440 333-0133
Cleveland (G-4922)

Apex Restoration Contrs Ltd ....E 513 489-1795
Cincinnati (G-2974)

Arnolds Home Improvement LLC ....E 734 847-9600
Toledo (G-17600)

Belfor USA Group Inc ....E 330 916-6468
Peninsula (G-15809)

Brackett Builders Inc ....E 937 339-7505
Troy (G-18197)

Burge Building Co Inc ....E 440 245-6871
Lorain (G-12889)

Canton Floors Inc ....E 330 492-1121
Canton (G-2233)

CFS Construction Inc ....E 513 559-4500
Cincinnati (G-3163)

Daugherty Construction Inc ....E 216 731-9444
Euclid (G-10628)

Disaster Reconstruction Inc ....E 440 918-1523
Eastlake (G-10428)

Fryman-Kuck General Contrs Inc ....E 937 274-2892
Dayton (G-9452)

Icon Environmental Group LLC ....E 513 426-6767
Milford (G-14396)

James Hunt Construction Co Inc ....E 513 721-0559
Cincinnati (G-3807)

Jeffrey Carr Construction Inc ....E 330 879-5210
Massillon (G-13701)

M-A Building and Maint Co ....E 216 391-5577
Independence (G-12096)

Mattlin Construction Inc ....E 513 598-5402
Cleves (G-6733)

Mc Meechan Construction Co ....E 216 581-9373
Cleveland (G-5928)

Mural & Son Inc ....E 216 267-3322
Cleveland (G-6025)

Oliver House Rest Complex ....D 419 243-1302
Toledo (G-17960)

Plevniak Construction Inc ....E 330 718-1600
Youngstown (G-20159)

Ram Construction Services of ....D 513 297-1857
West Chester (G-18990)

Residence Artists Inc ....E 440 286-8822
Chardon (G-2710)

Residntial Coml Rnovations Inc ....E 330 815-1476
Clinton (G-6737)

Smb Construction Co Inc ....E 419 269-1473
Toledo (G-18038)

Swartz Enterprises Inc ....E 419 331-1024
Lima (G-12758)

Trisco Systems Incorporated ....C 419 339-9912
Lima (G-12769)

VIP Restoration Inc ....E 216 426-9500
Cuyahoga Falls (G-9136)

Wingler Construction Corp ....E 614 626-8546
Columbus (G-8910)

COMMERCIAL ART & GRAPHIC DESIGN SVCS

Don Drumm Studios & Gallery ....E 330 253-6840
Akron (G-190)

Exhibitpro Inc ....E 614 885-9541
New Albany (G-14853)

Fx Digital Media Inc ....E 216 241-4040
Cleveland (G-5584)

General Theming Contrs LLC ....C 614 252-6342
Columbus (G-7655)

Graffiti Inc ....D 216 881-5550
Cleveland (G-5621)

Innovtive Crtive Solutions LLC ....E 614 491-9638
Groveport (G-11520)

Mlp Interent Enterprises LLC ....E 614 917-8705
Mansfield (G-13224)

Sfc Graphics Inc ....E 419 255-1283
Toledo (G-18027)

Visual Art Graphic Services ....E 330 274-2775
Mantua (G-13278)

Whitespace Design Group Inc ....E 330 762-9320
Akron (G-501)

Young Mens Christian Associat ....C 513 791-5000
Blue Ash (G-1685)

COMMERCIAL ART & ILLUSTRATION SVCS

Fisher Design Inc ....E 513 417-8235
Cincinnati (G-3570)

ONeil & Associates Inc ....B 937 865-0800
Miamisburg (G-14201)

COMMERCIAL CONTAINERS WHOLESALERS

Kaufman Container Company ....C 216 898-2000
Cleveland (G-5817)

COMMERCIAL EQPT & SPLYS, WHOLESALE: Price Marking

Century Marketing Corporation ....C 419 354-2591
Bowling Green (G-1727)

COMMERCIAL EQPT WHOLESALERS, NEC

Acorn Distributors Inc ....E 614 294-6444
Columbus (G-6867)

AVI Food Systems Inc ....E 740 452-9363
Zanesville (G-20279)

Bakemark USA LLC ....D 513 870-0880
West Chester (G-18872)

Cleveland Coin Mch Exch Inc ....D 847 842-6310
Willoughby (G-19514)

CMC Daymark Corporation ....C 419 354-2591
Bowling Green (G-1728)

General Data Company Inc ....C 513 752-7978
Cincinnati (G-2853)

Restaurant Equippers Inc ....E 614 358-6622
Columbus (G-8526)

Shearer Farm Inc ....E 419 465-4622
Monroeville (G-14590)

Sprayworks Equipment Group LLC ......E 330 587-4141
Canton *(G-2483)*

COMMERCIAL EQPT, WHOLESALE: Bakery Eqpt & Splys

Cmbb LLC...C 937 652-2151
Urbana *(G-18428)*
Russell T Bundy Associates Inc............D 937 652-2151
Urbana *(G-18444)*

COMMERCIAL EQPT, WHOLESALE: Coffee Brewing Eqpt & Splys

Access Catalog Company LLC............E 440 572-5377
Strongsville *(G-17279)*

COMMERCIAL EQPT, WHOLESALE: Comm Cooking & Food Svc Eqpt

Business Data Systems Inc ....E 330 633-1221
Tallmadge *(G-17470)*
Captive-Aire Systems Inc.......................E 614 777-7378
Gahanna *(G-11111)*
Carroll Manufacturing & Sales..............E 440 937-3900
Avon *(G-871)*
Harry C Lobalzo & Sons Inc...................E 330 666-6758
Akron *(G-251)*
Nemco Inc..D 419 542-7751
Hicksville *(G-11730)*
Quality Supply Co...................................E 937 890-6114
Cincinnati *(G-4310)*
S S Kemp & Company ....C 216 271-7062
Cleveland *(G-6357)*
Vulcan Feg ....D 937 332-2763
Troy *(G-18239)*
Wasserstrom Company ....B 614 228-6525
Columbus *(G-8878)*

COMMERCIAL EQPT, WHOLESALE: Restaurant, NEC

Burkett and Sons Inc.............................E 419 242-7377
Perrysburg *(G-15844)*
Globe Food Equipment Company ....E 937 299-5493
Moraine *(G-14662)*
ITW Food Equipment Group LLC ....A 937 332-2396
Troy *(G-18208)*
John H Kappus Co ....E 216 367-6677
Cleveland *(G-5799)*
N Wasserstrom & Sons Inc ....C 614 228-5550
Columbus *(G-8126)*
Restaurant Depot LLC ....E 513 542-3000
Cincinnati *(G-4364)*
Restaurant Depot LLC ....E 614 272-6670
Columbus *(G-8525)*
Specialty Equipment Sales Co ....E 216 351-2559
Brooklyn Heights *(G-1882)*
The Cottingham Paper Co ....E 614 294-6444
Columbus *(G-8742)*
Trimark Usa LLC ....D 216 271-7700
Cleveland *(G-6549)*
Zink Foodservice Group.........................E 800 492-7400
Columbus *(G-8937)*

COMMERCIAL EQPT, WHOLESALE: Scales, Exc Laboratory

Brechbuhler Scales Inc ....E 330 458-3060
Canton *(G-2217)*
Filing Scale Company Inc ....E 330 425-3092
Twinsburg *(G-18266)*

COMMERCIAL EQPT, WHOLESALE: Teaching Machines, Electronic

Productivity Qulty Systems Inc.............E 937 885-2255
Dayton *(G-9717)*

COMMERCIAL EQPT, WHOLESALE: Vending Machines, Coin-Operated

Dtv Inc...E 216 226-5465
Mayfield Heights *(G-13873)*

COMMERCIAL PHOTOGRAPHIC STUDIO

Childers Photography ....E 937 256-0501
Dayton *(G-9165)*
Ideal Image Inc ....D 937 832-1660
Englewood *(G-10590)*

COMMERCIAL PRINTING & NEWSPAPER PUBLISHING COMBINED

Copley Ohio Newspapers Inc ....C 330 364-5577
New Philadelphia *(G-14951)*
Dispatch Printing Company...................C 740 548-5331
Lewis Center *(G-12541)*

COMMODITIES SAMPLING SVC

US Protection Service LLC ....D 513 422-7910
Cincinnati *(G-4742)*

COMMODITY CONTRACT POOL OPERATORS

Roulston Research Corp.........................E 216 431-3000
Cleveland *(G-6343)*

COMMODITY CONTRACTS BROKERS, DEALERS

Merrill Lynch Pierce Fenner ....E 937 847-4000
Miamisburg *(G-14189)*
Merrill Lynch Pierce Fenner ....D 330 670-2400
Akron *(G-332)*
Wells Fargo Clearing Svcs LLC ....D 216 574-7300
Cleveland *(G-6662)*

COMMODITY INVESTORS

Lti Inc ....D 614 278-7777
Columbus *(G-7996)*

COMMON SAND MINING

Stocker Sand & Gravel Co ....E 740 254-4635
Gnadenhutten *(G-11312)*
Welch Holdings Inc...............................E 513 353-3220
Cincinnati *(G-4774)*

COMMUNICATIONS CARRIER: Wired

Verizon Business Global LLC ....E 614 219-2317
Hilliard *(G-11826)*
Verizon Select Services Inc...................E 908 559-2054
North Royalton *(G-15370)*

COMMUNICATIONS EQPT REPAIR & MAINTENANCE

Consolidated Communications ....E 330 896-3905
Canton *(G-2266)*
Mobilcomm Inc ....D 513 742-5555
Cincinnati *(G-4066)*
Professional Telecom Svcs ....E 513 232-7700
Cincinnati *(G-4294)*

COMMUNICATIONS EQPT WHOLESALERS

Bear Communications Inc......................E 216 642-1670
Independence *(G-12049)*
Clercom Inc ....D 513 724-6101
Williamsburg *(G-19491)*
Commercial Electronics Inc...................E 740 281-0180
Newark *(G-15023)*
Communications III Inc..........................E 614 901-7720
Westerville *(G-19244)*
Consolidated Communications ....E 330 896-3905
Canton *(G-2266)*
Midwest Digital Inc................................D 330 966-4744
North Canton *(G-15222)*
Quasonix Inc ....E 513 942-1287
West Chester *(G-18988)*
Sound Com Corporation ....D 440 234-2604
Berea *(G-1437)*
Winncom Technologies Corp ....E 440 498-9510
Solon *(G-16916)*

COMMUNICATIONS SVCS

Centre Communications Corp................E 440 454-3262
Beavercreek *(G-1209)*
Htp Inc...E 614 885-1272
Columbus *(G-6816)*
Mack Communications LLC ....E 330 347-4020
Youngstown *(G-20103)*
Stg Communication Services Inc ....E 330 482-0500
Columbiana *(G-6792)*
University of Cincinnati..........................A 513 556-5087
Cincinnati *(G-4711)*

Wireless Source Entps LLC....................E 419 266-5556
Bowling Green *(G-1751)*

COMMUNICATIONS SVCS: Cellular

ABC Phones North Carolina Inc ....E 440 290-4262
Mentor On The Lake *(G-14128)*
ABC Phones North Carolina Inc ....E 440 319-3654
Ashtabula *(G-703)*
ABC Phones North Carolina Inc ....E 330 752-0009
Macedonia *(G-13057)*
ABC Phones North Carolina Inc ....E 440 328-4331
Sheffield Village *(G-16731)*
Aka Wireless Inc ....E 440 572-5777
Strongsville *(G-17282)*
Aka Wireless Inc ....E 216 213-8040
Hartville *(G-11682)*
AT&T Corp ....D 937 320-9648
Beavercreek *(G-1203)*
AT&T Corp ....D 614 798-3898
Dublin *(G-10140)*
AT&T Corp ....D 614 539-0165
Grove City *(G-11407)*
AT&T Corp ....D 740 455-3042
Zanesville *(G-20278)*
AT&T Corp ....D 740 549-4546
Lewis Center *(G-12525)*
AT&T Corp ....D 330 665-3100
Akron *(G-80)*
AT&T Corp ....D 440 951-5309
Willoughby *(G-19507)*
AT&T Corp ....D 614 575-3044
Columbus *(G-6991)*
AT&T Corp ....D 614 851-2400
Columbus *(G-6992)*
AT&T Corp ....D 513 741-1700
Cincinnati *(G-2993)*
AT&T Corp ....D 330 723-1717
Medina *(G-13911)*
AT&T Corp ....E 330 505-4200
Niles *(G-15145)*
AT&T Inc ....E 937 320-9648
Beavercreek *(G-1204)*
AT&T Mobility LLC ....E 614 291-2500
Columbus *(G-6994)*
AT&T Mobility LLC ....C 330 565-5000
Youngstown *(G-19957)*
AT&T Mobility LLC ....E 440 846-3232
Strongsville *(G-17287)*
AT&T Mobility LLC ....E 216 382-0825
Cleveland *(G-5018)*
AT&T Mobility LLC ....E 419 516-0602
Lima *(G-12603)*
AT&T Mobility LLC ....E 513 381-6800
Cincinnati *(G-2995)*
AT&T Mobility LLC ....E 937 439-4900
Centerville *(G-2622)*
AT&T Services Inc.................................C 937 456-2330
Eaton *(G-10437)*
Cellco Partnership ....B 614 560-2000
Dublin *(G-10162)*
Cellco Partnership ....D 513 923-2700
Cincinnati *(G-3143)*
Cellco Partnership ....D 330 823-7758
Alliance *(G-523)*
Cellco Partnership ....D 419 333-1009
Fremont *(G-11061)*
Cellco Partnership ....D 740 652-9540
Lancaster *(G-12377)*
Cellco Partnership ....D 740 695-3600
Saint Clairsville *(G-16482)*
Cellco Partnership ....D 740 432-7785
Cambridge *(G-2057)*
Cellco Partnership ....D 330 376-8275
Akron *(G-122)*
Cellco Partnership ....D 513 755-1666
West Chester *(G-18883)*
Cellco Partnership ....D 513 697-1190
Cincinnati *(G-3144)*
Cellco Partnership ....D 440 934-0576
Avon *(G-872)*
Cellco Partnership ....D 419 381-1726
Toledo *(G-17640)*
Cellco Partnership ....C 216 765-1444
Beachwood *(G-1042)*
Cellco Partnership ....D 440 998-3111
Ashtabula *(G-724)*
Cellco Partnership ....D 513 422-3437
Middletown *(G-14345)*
Cellco Partnership ....D 740 588-0018
Zanesville *(G-20289)*

SERVICES

COMMUNICATIONS SVCS: Cellular

Cellco Partnership ....E 513 688-1300
Cincinnati (G-3145)
Cellco Partnership ....E 419 424-2351
Findlay (G-10886)
Cellco Partnership ....D 419 897-9133
Maumee (G-13768)
Cellco Partnership ....E 440 953-1155
Mentor (G-14027)
Cellco Partnership ....E 440 646-9625
Cleveland (G-5147)
Cellco Partnership ....E 440 846-8881
Strongsville (G-17289)
Cellco Partnership ....E 740 397-6609
Mount Vernon (G-14752)
Cellco Partnership ....E 614 459-7200
Columbus (G-7148)
Cellco Partnership ....E 937 429-4000
Beavercreek (G-1138)
Cellco Partnership ....E 513 671-2200
Cincinnati (G-3146)
Cellco Partnership ....E 513 697-0222
Cincinnati (G-3147)
Cellco Partnership ....E 419 843-2995
Toledo (G-17641)
Cellco Partnership ....E 330 493-7979
Canton (G-2247)
Cellco Partnership ....E 216 573-5880
Independence (G-12056)
Cellco Partnership ....D 937 578-0022
Marysville (G-13489)
Cellco Partnership ....D 440 542-9631
Solon (G-16834)
Cellco Partnership ....D 330 626-0524
Streetsboro (G-17248)
Cellco Partnership ....D 330 308-0549
New Philadelphia (G-14948)
Cellco Partnership ....D 614 793-8989
Dublin (G-10163)
Cellco Partnership ....E 440 324-9479
Elyria (G-10486)
Cellco Partnership ....E 614 793-8989
Dublin (G-10164)
Cellco Partnership ....D 614 277-2900
Grove City (G-11418)
Cellco Partnership ....E 740 522-6446
Newark (G-15021)
Cellco Partnership ....D 330 345-6465
Wooster (G-19698)
Cellco Partnership ....E 330 722-6622
Medina (G-13916)
Cellco Partnership ....E 440 984-5200
Amherst (G-583)
Cellco Partnership ....E 740 450-1525
Zanesville (G-20290)
Cellular Sales Knoxville Inc ....E 614 322-9975
Columbus (G-7149)
Diamond Company Inc ....C 937 374-1111
Xenia (G-19898)
Nextel Communications Inc .....E 513 891-9200
Cincinnati (G-4113)
Nextel Communications Inc .....D 614 801-9267
Grove City (G-11458)
Nextel Partners Operating Corp ....E 330 305-1365
North Canton (G-15223)
Nextel Partners Operating Corp ....E 419 380-2000
Toledo (G-17941)
Sprint Spectrum LP ....E 614 575-5500
Columbus (G-8675)
Sprint Spectrum LP ....E 614 428-2300
Columbus (G-8677)
Supermedia LLC ....D 740 369-2391
Marion (G-13462)
Verizon Communications Inc ...C 330 334-1268
Wadsworth (G-18617)
Verizon Communications Inc ...C 440 892-4504
Westlake (G-19420)
Verizon New York Inc ....E 614 301-2498
Hilliard (G-11827)
Verizon Wireless ....E 330 963-1300
Twinsburg (G-18336)
Verizon Wireless Inc ....D 937 434-2355
Dayton (G-9853)
Wireless Center Inc ....B 216 503-3777
Cleveland (G-6686)

COMMUNICATIONS SVCS: Data

A M Communications Ltd ....E 419 528-3051
Vandalia (G-18500)
Allied Communications Corp ....E 614 275-2075
Columbus (G-6896)

Brand Technologies Inc ....E 419 873-6600
Perrysburg (G-15841)
Calvert Wire & Cable Corp ......E 216 433-7600
Cleveland (G-5115)
Communication Svc For Deaf Inc ....C 937 299-0917
Moraine (G-14635)
Inet Interactive LLC ....E 513 322-5600
West Chester (G-18947)
Jay Blue Communications ....E 216 661-2828
Cleveland (G-5783)
Oovoo LLC ....D 917 515-2074
Kettering (G-12298)
Springdot Inc ....E 513 542-4000
Cincinnati (G-4523)
Time Warner Cable Inc ....E 513 354-1100
Blue Ash (G-1659)
Velocity Grtest Phone Ever Inc ....B 419 868-9983
Holland (G-11924)

COMMUNICATIONS SVCS: Electronic Mail

Maximum Communications Inc ....E 513 489-3414
Cincinnati (G-3981)

COMMUNICATIONS SVCS: Internet Connectivity Svcs

1 Community ....E 216 923-2272
Cleveland (G-4863)
4mybenefits Inc ....E 513 891-6648
Blue Ash (G-1494)
At T Broadband & Intern ....E 614 839-4271
Columbus (G-6988)
Broadvox LLC ....E 216 373-4600
Cleveland (G-5083)
Buckeye Telesystem Inc ....C 419 724-9898
Northwood (G-15390)
Community Isp Inc ....E 419 867-6060
Toledo (G-17672)
Datzap LLC ....E 330 785-2100
Akron (G-181)
Dct Telecom Group Inc ....E 440 892-0300
Westlake (G-19339)
Great Lakes Telcom Ltd ....E 330 629-8848
Youngstown (G-20055)
Intellinet Corporation ....D 216 289-4100
Cleveland (G-5759)
Intgrted Bridge Communications ....E 513 381-1380
Cincinnati (G-3782)
Level 3 Telecom LLC ....E 234 542-6279
Akron (G-311)
Level 3 Telecom LLC ....E 513 841-0000
Cincinnati (G-3919)
Premier System Integrators Inc ....D 513 217-7294
Middletown (G-14323)
Raco Wireless LLC ....E 513 870-6480
Blue Ash (G-1637)
Revolution Group Inc ....E 614 212-1111
Westerville (G-19207)
Skycasters LLC ....E 330 785-2100
Akron (G-431)
Time Warner Cable Inc ....E 330 800-3874
Akron (G-470)
TSC Communications Inc ....E 419 739-2200
Wapakoneta (G-18657)
West Central Ohio Internet ......E 419 229-2645
Lima (G-12779)

COMMUNICATIONS SVCS: Internet Host Svcs

Advanced Cmpt Connections LLC ....E 419 668-4080
Norwalk (G-15424)
Construction Biddingcom LLC ....E 440 716-4087
North Olmsted (G-15284)
Infotelecom Holdings LLC ....B 216 373-4811
Cleveland (G-5753)
Jumplinecom Inc ....E 614 859-1170
Columbus (G-7877)
Link Iq LLC ....E 859 983-6080
Dayton (G-9569)
Making Evrlasting Memories LLC ....E 513 864-0100
Cincinnati (G-3964)
Massillon Cable TV Inc ....D 330 833-4134
Massillon (G-13710)
Oxcyon Inc ....E 440 239-3345
Cleveland (G-6152)
Profit Recovery of Ohio ....C 440 243-1743
Cleveland (G-6240)
Roundtable Online Learning LLC ....E 440 220-5252
Chagrin Falls (G-2680)

Tremor LLC ....E 513 983-1100
Blue Ash (G-1662)

COMMUNICATIONS SVCS: Nonvocal Message

Stratacache Inc ....C 937 224-0485
Dayton (G-9796)

COMMUNICATIONS SVCS: Online Svc Providers

Armstrong Utilities Inc ....E 740 894-3886
South Point (G-16928)
C T Wireless ....D 937 653-2208
Urbana (G-18420)
Com Net Inc ....D 419 739-3100
Wapakoneta (G-18639)
F+w Media Inc ....B 513 531-2690
Blue Ash (G-1559)
Primax Marketing Group ....E 513 443-2797
Cincinnati (G-4279)
Suite 224 Internet ....E 440 593-7113
Conneaut (G-8959)

COMMUNICATIONS SVCS: Radio Pager Or Beeper

Twin Comm Inc ....E 740 774-4701
Marietta (G-13390)

COMMUNICATIONS SVCS: Signal Enhancement Network Svcs

Cincinnati Voice and Data ....D 513 683-4127
Loveland (G-12983)
Telcom Construction Svcs Inc ....D 330 239-6900
Medina (G-14010)
Vox Mobile ....E 800 536-9030
Independence (G-12139)

COMMUNICATIONS SVCS: Telegram

AT&T Corp ....A 513 629-5000
Cincinnati (G-2994)

COMMUNICATIONS SVCS: Telephone Or Video

AVI-Spl Employee ....E 937 836-4787
Englewood (G-10579)

COMMUNICATIONS SVCS: Telephone, Broker

J E Davis Corporation ....E 440 377-4700
Sheffield Village (G-16735)
Rxp Ohio LLC ....D 614 937-2844
Columbus (G-8564)

COMMUNICATIONS SVCS: Telephone, Data

AT&T Datacomm LLC ....E 614 223-5799
Westerville (G-19225)
Connect Call Global LLC ....E 513 348-1800
Mason (G-13567)
Mvd Communications LLC ....D 513 683-4711
Mason (G-13621)
Quanexus Inc ....E 937 885-7272
Dayton (G-9722)
Swn Communications Inc ....E 877 698-3262
Dayton (G-9803)

COMMUNICATIONS SVCS: Telephone, Local

Alltel Communications Corp ......D 740 349-8551
Newark (G-15008)
Champaign Telephone Company ....E 937 653-4000
Urbana (G-18426)
Chillicothe Telephone Company ....C 740 772-8200
Chillicothe (G-2767)
Chillicothe Telephone Company ....D 740 772-8361
Chillicothe (G-2768)
Cincinnati Bell Tele Co LLC ......C 513 565-9402
Cincinnati (G-3228)
Conneaut Telephone Company ....E 440 593-7140
Conneaut (G-8953)
Deliass Assets Corp ....D 614 891-0101
Westerville (G-19248)
Doylestown Telephone Company ....E 330 658-2121
Doylestown (G-10113)

Doylestown Telephone Company..........E 330 658-6666
Doylestown (G-10114)

Horizon Telcom Inc.........................B 740 772-8200
Chillicothe (G-2791)

Verizon North Inc.........................E 740 942-2566
Cadiz (G-2033)

COMMUNICATIONS SVCS: Telephone, Local & Long Distance

Alltel Communications Corp................E 330 656-8000
Chardon (G-2686)

AT&T Corp....................................C 330 752-7776
Akron (G-81)

AT&T Corp....................................C 216 672-0809
Cleveland (G-5017)

AT&T Services Inc.........................C 937 456-2330
Eaton (G-10437)

Block Communications Inc................B 419 724-2539
Northwood (G-15389)

Centurylink Inc.............................A 614 215-4223
Dublin (G-10167)

Cincinnati Bell Inc.........................D 513 397-9900
Cincinnati (G-3226)

Ohio Bell Telephone Company............A 216 822-3439
Cleveland (G-6115)

Round Room LLC...........................E 330 880-0660
Massillon (G-13726)

Round Room LLC...........................E 937 429-2230
Beavercreek (G-1184)

Sprint Communications Co LP............E 419 725-2444
Toledo (G-18043)

Sprint Spectrum LP.........................E 440 686-2600
North Olmsted (G-15311)

Sprint Spectrum LP.........................E 614 575-5500
Columbus (G-8675)

Sprint Spectrum LP.........................E 614 793-2500
Columbus (G-8676)

Sprint Spectrum LP.........................E 614 428-2300
Columbus (G-8677)

Sprint Spectrum LP.........................E 330 470-4614
Canton (G-2484)

Verizon Business Global LLC.............E 614 219-2317
Hilliard (G-11826)

Verizon Communications Inc.............C 330 334-1268
Wadsworth (G-18617)

Verizon Communications Inc.............C 440 892-4504
Westlake (G-19420)

COMMUNICATIONS SVCS: Telephone, Long Distance

AT&T Corp....................................A 513 629-5000
Cincinnati (G-2994)

First Communications LLC................E 330 835-2323
Fairlawn (G-10830)

First Communications LLC................D 330 835-2323
Fairlawn (G-10831)

Marietta College...........................E 740 376-4790
Marietta (G-13350)

MCI Communications Svcs Inc...........B 216 265-9953
Cleveland (G-5934)

MCI Communications Svcs Inc...........B 440 635-0418
Chardon (G-2704)

Mitel (delaware) Inc.......................E 513 733-8000
West Chester (G-18974)

Png Telecommunications Inc.............D 513 942-7900
Cincinnati (G-4260)

Professional Telecom Svcs................E 513 232-7700
Cincinnati (G-4294)

Xo Communications LLC...................E 216 619-3200
Cleveland (G-6698)

COMMUNICATIONS SVCS: Telephone, Voice

Pearl Interactive Network Inc............B 614 258-2943
Columbus (G-8432)

COMMUNICATIONS SVCS: Television Antenna Construction & Rent

Armstrong Utilities Inc...................E 740 894-3886
South Point (G-16928)

COMMUNITY ACTION AGENCY

Abcd Inc....................................E 330 455-6385
Canton (G-2171)

Adams & Brown Counties Economi.......E 937 695-0316
Winchester (G-19659)

Adams & Brown Counties Economi.......C 937 378-6041
Georgetown (G-11260)

Akron Cmnty Svc Ctr Urban Leag.......E 234 542-4141
Akron (G-33)

Akron Summit Cmnty Action Agcy.......B 330 376-7730
Akron (G-58)

Ashtabula County Commnty Actn.........D 440 997-5957
Ashtabula (G-713)

Clinton County Community Actn..........D 937 382-8365
Wilmington (G-19610)

Clinton County Community Actn..........E 937 382-5624
Wilmington (G-19611)

Community Action Commission...........E 419 626-6540
Sandusky (G-16591)

Community Action Program Corp.........B 740 373-3745
Marietta (G-13319)

Community Action Program Corp.........E 740 373-6016
Marietta (G-13320)

Community Action Program Inc...........D 937 382-0225
Wilmington (G-19616)

Council On Rur Svc Prgrams Inc.........E 937 492-8787
Sidney (G-16769)

Council On Rur Svc Prgrams Inc.........E 937 778-5220
Piqua (G-16001)

Council On Rur Svc Prgrams Inc.........E 937 773-0773
Piqua (G-16002)

County of Montgomery.....................E 937 225-4192
Dayton (G-9325)

Hancock Hardin Wyandot Putnam.......C 419 423-3755
Findlay (G-10918)

Hockingthensperry Cmnty Action.........C 740 767-4500
Glouster (G-11310)

Jackson-Vinton Cmnty Action............D 740 384-3722
Wellston (G-18852)

Jefferson Cnty Cmmnty Action............C 740 282-0971
Steubenville (G-17159)

Leads Inc....................................E 740 349-8606
Newark (G-15049)

Lorain County Community Action.........E 440 245-2009
Lorain (G-12918)

Miami Cnty Cmnty Action Cuncil.........E 937 335-7921
Troy (G-18212)

Miami Valley Community Action..........D 937 222-1009
Dayton (G-9617)

Neighborhood Progress Inc................E 216 830-2770
Cleveland (G-6054)

Northwestrn OH Communty Action......C 419 784-2150
Defiance (G-9932)

Ohio Citizen Action.........................E 216 861-5200
Cleveland (G-6119)

Ohio Hrtland Cmnty Action Comm........E 740 387-1039
Marion (G-13450)

Ohio Hrtland Cmnty Action Comm........E 419 468-5121
Galion (G-11180)

Ross County Community....................D 740 702-7222
Chillicothe (G-2819)

Stark County Cmnty Action Agcy.........C 330 454-1676
Canton (G-2491)

Stark County Cmnty Action Agcy.........E 330 821-5977
Alliance (G-553)

Tri-County Community Act..................E 740 385-6812
Logan (G-12857)

West Ohio Cmnty Action Partnr...........C 419 227-2586
Lima (G-12782)

COMMUNITY CENTER

Canton Jewish Community Center........D 330 452-6444
Canton (G-2236)

Chmc Cmnty Hlth Svcs Netwrk...........A 513 636-8778
Cincinnati (G-3196)

City of Brecksville.........................D 440 526-4109
Brecksville (G-1775)

City of Independence.......................E 216 524-7373
Cleveland (G-5204)

Clintonville Beechwold Communi.........E 614 268-3539
Columbus (G-7230)

Community Services Inc....................D 937 667-8631
Tipp City (G-17553)

County of Guernsey.........................D 740 432-2381
Cambridge (G-2062)

Don Bosco Community Center Inc........E 816 421-3160
Cleveland (G-5438)

East Toledo Family Center................D 419 691-1429
Toledo (G-17708)

Hudson City Engineering Dept............E 330 342-1770
Hudson (G-11982)

Impact Community Action.................E 614 252-2799
Columbus (G-7802)

Jewish Cmnty Ctr of Toledo...............D 419 885-4485
Sylvania (G-17434)

Jewish Fdrtion of Grter Dayton............D 937 837-2651
Dayton (G-9525)

Mahoning Youngstown Community.......D 330 747-7921
Youngstown (G-20112)

Merrick House..............................E 216 771-5077
Cleveland (G-5958)

Salem Community Center Inc.............D 330 332-5885
Salem (G-16559)

Shaw Jewish Community Center.........C 330 867-7850
Akron (G-427)

St Pauls Community Center...............D 419 255-5520
Toledo (G-18046)

St Stephens Community House...........D 614 294-6347
Columbus (G-8680)

Taylor Murtis Human Svcs Sys...........D 216 281-7192
Cleveland (G-6504)

Taylor Murtis Human Svcs Sys...........D 216 283-4400
Cleveland (G-6503)

COMMUNITY CENTERS: Adult

Area Agency On Aging Planni.............C 800 258-7277
Dayton (G-9239)

Area Agency On Aging Dst 7 Inc..........C 800 582-7277
Rio Grande (G-16399)

Area Agency On Aging Dst 7 Inc..........E 740 446-7000
Gallipolis (G-11185)

Area Office On Aging of Nwstrn...........D 419 382-0624
Toledo (G-17599)

Ashtabula County Commnty Actn.........D 440 593-6441
Conneaut (G-8949)

Ashtabula Job and Family Svcs...........D 440 994-2020
Ashtabula (G-718)

Brown Cnty Snior Ctzen Council..........E 937 378-6603
Georgetown (G-11262)

Canton Christian Home Inc................C 330 456-0004
Canton (G-2228)

Care & Share of Erie Count................D 419 624-1411
Sandusky (G-16581)

Central OH Area Agency On Agng.........C 614 645-7250
Columbus (G-7156)

Cincinnati Area Senior Svcs...............C 513 721-4330
Cincinnati (G-3222)

City of Bucyrus..............................E 419 562-3050
Bucyrus (G-1982)

City of Canal Winchester..................E 614 837-8276
Canal Winchester (G-2107)

City of Lakewood...........................E 216 521-1515
Lakewood (G-12338)

City of Parma................................E 440 888-4514
Cleveland (G-5213)

Clermont Senior Services Inc.............C 513 724-1255
Batavia (G-992)

Community Caregivers......................D 330 533-3427
Youngstown (G-19999)

Crawford County Council On Agi.........E 419 562-3050
Bucyrus (G-1989)

Cuyahoga County...........................D 216 420-6750
Cleveland (G-5393)

Day Share Ltd...............................E 513 451-1100
Cincinnati (G-3405)

Delhi Township.............................D 513 922-0060
Cincinnati (G-3419)

Direction Home Akron Canton AR........D 330 896-9172
Uniontown (G-18367)

Elderly United of Springfield..............D 937 323-4948
Springfield (G-17033)

Episcopal Retirement Homes Inc.........E 513 271-9610
Cincinnati (G-3508)

Family Senior Care Inc....................E 740 441-1428
Gallipolis (G-11191)

Gerlach John J Center For Sen...........E 614 566-5858
Columbus (G-7663)

Hardin Cnty Cncil On Aging Inc...........E 419 673-1102
Kenton (G-12277)

Haven Bhavioral Healthcare Inc..........B 937 234-0100
Dayton (G-9487)

Kettering Recreation Center..............E 937 296-2587
Dayton (G-9542)

Lake County Council On Aging............E 440 205-8111
Mentor (G-14071)

Lyman W Liggins Urban Affairs...........D 419 385-2532
Toledo (G-17875)

Mercy Health Partners.....................B 513 451-8900
Cincinnati (G-4031)

Miami Valley Community Action..........D 937 548-8143
Greenville (G-11390)

Middltown Area Senior Citizens..........D 513 423-1734
Middletown (G-14311)

Mount Carmel Health.......................C 614 234-8170
Columbus (G-8112)

SERVICES

Muskingum Cnty Ctr For Seniors.........E 740 454-9761
  Zanesville (G-20333)
Muskingum County Ohio ....D 740 452-0678
  Zanesville (G-20335)
Ohio District 5 Area ....C 419 522-5612
  Ontario (G-15567)
Older Wiser Life Services LLC............E 330 659-2111
  Richfield (G-16370)
Olmsted Residence Corporation ....C 440 235-7100
  Olmsted Twp (G-15539)
Pickaway County Community Acti.........E 740 477-1655
  Circleville (G-4841)
Pro Seniors Inc ....E 513 345-4160
  Cincinnati (G-4288)
Senior Resource Connection.................C 937 223-8246
  Dayton (G-9759)
Senior Star Management Company ......B 513 271-1747
  Cincinnati (G-4453)
Sourcepoint......................................D 740 363-6677
  Delaware (G-10008)
Sycamore Senior Center ....D 513 984-1234
  Blue Ash (G-1654)
Tuscarawas County Commitee...........D 330 364-6611
  Dover (G-10104)
United Scoto Senior Activities............E 740 354-6672
  Portsmouth (G-16176)
Vantage Aging ....D 330 253-4597
  Akron (G-486)
Vasconcellos Inc ....E 513 576-1250
  Milford (G-14442)
Village of Groveport ....E 614 830-2060
  Groveport (G-11549)
Western Reserve Area Agency ....C 216 621-0303
  Cleveland (G-6673)
Western Reserve Area Agency ....E 216 621-0303
  Cleveland (G-6674)
Wood County Committee On Aging ....E 419 353-5661
  Bowling Green (G-1753)

COMMUNITY CENTERS: Youth

Cincinnati Youth Collaborative.............E 513 475-4165
  Cincinnati (G-3275)
Crittenton Family Services...................E 614 251-0103
  Columbus (G-7394)
Directions For Youth Families ....E 614 258-8043
  Columbus (G-7447)
Directions For Youth Families ....E 614 694-0203
  Columbus (G-7448)
Fairborn YMCA ....E 937 754-9622
  Fairborn (G-10674)
Focus On Youth Inc ....E 513 644-1030
  West Chester (G-18925)
KElly Youth Services Inc ....E 513 761-0700
  Cincinnati (G-3856)
Lighthouse Youth Services Inc.............D 513 221-1017
  Cincinnati (G-3929)
Lighthouse Youth Services Inc.............D 740 634-3094
  Bainbridge (G-931)
Marion Family YMCA ....D 740 725-9622
  Marion (G-13437)
Muskingum County Adult and CHI........E 740 849-2344
  Zanesville (G-20334)
New Horizon Youth Center Co ....E 740 782-0092
  Bethesda (G-1456)
Sheakley Cente ....E 513 487-7106
  Cincinnati (G-4466)
Young Mens Christian Assn.................D 330 744-8411
  Youngstown (G-20253)
Youth Services Ohio Department ....C 419 875-6965
  Liberty Center (G-12576)

COMMUNITY COLLEGE

Key Career Place...............................D 216 987-3029
  Cleveland (G-5825)

COMMUNITY DEVELOPMENT GROUPS

Barberton Jaycees.............................E 330 745-3733
  Barberton (G-946)
Columbus Urban League Inc ....E 614 257-6300
  Columbus (G-7320)
Community Imprv Corp Nble Cnty ....D 740 509-0248
  Caldwell (G-2037)
Economic & Cmnty Dev Inst Inc ....E 614 559-0104
  Columbus (G-7500)
Famicos Foundation ....E 216 791-6476
  Cleveland (G-5509)
Greater Cleveland Food Bnk Inc ....C 216 738-2265
  Cleveland (G-5635)

Guernsey County Cmnty Dev Corp.......E 740 439-0020
  Cambridge (G-2071)
Habitat For Humanity..........................E 216 429-1299
  Cleveland (G-5654)
Karamu House Inc ....E 216 795-7070
  Cleveland (G-5815)
Lifeservices Development Corp ....E 440 257-3866
  Mentor (G-14077)
Lutheran Metropolitan Ministry ....C 216 658-4638
  Cleveland (G-5890)
Montpelier Senior Center ....E 419 485-3218
  Montpelier (G-14616)
National Affrdbl Hsing Tr Inc ....E 614 451-9929
  Columbus (G-8128)
Neighborhood Development Svcs ....E 330 296-2003
  Ravenna (G-16250)
Randall R Leab ....E 330 689-6263
  Ashland (G-685)
REM-Ohio Inc ....E 440 986-3337
  South Amherst (G-16922)
Salvation Army ....D 800 728-7825
  Columbus (G-8588)
Senior Independence...........................D 330 873-3468
  Fairlawn (G-10850)
Tipp-Monroe Community Svcs Inc ....E 937 667-8631
  Tipp City (G-17569)
United Labor Agency Inc ....C 216 664-3446
  Cleveland (G-6574)
University of Tledo Foundation ....E 419 530-7730
  Toledo (G-18124)
University Settlement Inc ....E 216 641-8948
  Cleveland (G-6603)
Urban League of Greater Southw..........D 513 281-9955
  Cincinnati (G-4733)
Westcare Ohio Inc ....E 937 259-1898
  Dayton (G-9876)

COMMUNITY SVCS EMPLOYMENT TRAINING PROGRAM

Community Action Organization ....C 740 354-7541
  Portsmouth (G-16132)
Goodwill Inds Rhbilitation Ctr ....C 330 454-9461
  Canton (G-2330)
Gw Business Solutions LLC................C 740 645-9861
  Newark (G-15039)
Licking-Knox Goodwill Inds Inc ....D 740 345-9861
  Newark (G-15061)
Marion Cnty Bd Dev Dsabilities............E 740 387-1035
  Marion (G-13435)
Ohio Dept of Job & Fmly Svcs.............E 614 752-9494
  Columbus (G-8246)
Project Rebuild Inc ....E 330 639-1559
  Canton (G-2441)
Vocational Guidance Services..............A 216 431-7800
  Cleveland (G-6639)

COMMUNITY THEATER PRODUCTION SVCS

Licking County Players Inc ....E 740 349-2287
  Newark (G-15054)
The In Cincinnati Playhouse ....D 513 421-3888
  Cincinnati (G-4594)

COMMUTATORS: Electronic

Ra Consultants LLC...........................E 513 469-6600
  Blue Ash (G-1635)

COMPACT DISCS OR CD'S, WHOLESALE

Telarc International Corp ....E 216 464-2313
  Beachwood (G-1111)

COMPOST

Kurtz Bros Compost Services ....E 330 864-2621
  Akron (G-306)
Werlor Inc ....E 419 784-4285
  Defiance (G-9946)

COMPRESSORS, AIR CONDITIONING: Wholesalers

Air Systems of Ohio Inc ....E 216 741-1700
  Brooklyn Heights (G-1865)
Best Aire Compressor Service ....D 419 726-0055
  Millbury (G-14446)
Diversified Air Systems Inc.................E 330 784-3366
  Akron (G-188)

COMPRESSORS: Air & Gas, Including Vacuum Pumps

Finishmaster Inc ....D 614 228-4328
  Columbus (G-7578)

COMPRESSORS: Repairing

A P O Holdings Inc.............................D 330 650-1330
  Hudson (G-11960)
Best Aire Compressor Service ....D 419 726-0055
  Millbury (G-14446)
Diversified Air Systems Inc.................E 330 784-3366
  Akron (G-188)
National Compressor Svcs LLC ....E 419 868-4980
  Holland (G-11900)

COMPRESSORS: Wholesalers

A P O Holdings Inc.............................D 330 650-1330
  Hudson (G-11960)
Air Systems of Ohio Inc ....E 216 741-1700
  Brooklyn Heights (G-1865)
Atlas Machine and Supply Inc ....E 502 584-7262
  West Chester (G-19041)
Becker Pumps Corporation ....E 330 928-9966
  Cuyahoga Falls (G-9074)
Breathing Air Systems Inc ....E 614 864-1235
  Reynoldsburg (G-16286)
General Electric Intl Inc ....E 330 963-2066
  Twinsburg (G-18273)
Industrial Air Centers Inc ....E 614 274-9171
  Columbus (G-7812)

COMPUTER & COMPUTER SOFTWARE STORES

Computer Helper Publishing ....E 614 939-9094
  Columbus (G-7345)
Datavantage Corporation ....B 440 498-4414
  Cleveland (G-5406)
Great Lakes Computer Corp ....D 440 937-1100
  Avon (G-883)
Harley-Dvidson Dlr Systems Inc............D 216 573-1393
  Cleveland (G-5661)
Micro Center Inc................................B 614 850-3000
  Hilliard (G-11794)
Micro Electronics Inc ....D 614 334-1430
  Columbus (G-8071)
Office World Inc ....E 419 991-4694
  Lima (G-12791)
Ohio Business Machines LLC ....E 216 485-2000
  Cleveland (G-6117)
Resource One Cmpt Systems Inc ....D 614 485-4800
  Worthington (G-19844)
Virtual Technologies Group ....E 419 991-4694
  Lima (G-12794)

COMPUTER & COMPUTER SOFTWARE STORES: Peripheral Eqpt

Cbts Technology Solutions LLC............B 513 841-2287
  Cincinnati (G-3137)
Microman Inc ....E 614 923-8000
  Dublin (G-10280)
Personalized Data Corporation ....E 216 289-2200
  Cleveland (G-6198)

COMPUTER & COMPUTER SOFTWARE STORES: Personal Computers

Micro Center Online Inc.......................C 614 326-8500
  Columbus (G-8069)
Micro Electronics Inc ....D 614 850-3500
  Hilliard (G-11796)
Micro Electronics Inc ....C 440 449-7000
  Cleveland (G-5979)
Micro Electronics Inc ....C 513 782-8500
  Cincinnati (G-4048)
Micro Electronics Inc ....B 614 850-3000
  Hilliard (G-11795)

COMPUTER & COMPUTER SOFTWARE STORES: Software & Access

Information Builders Inc ....E 513 891-2338
  Montgomery (G-14595)
Provantage LLC ....D 330 494-3781
  North Canton (G-15228)
S & P Solutions Inc............................C 440 918-9111
  Willoughby Hills (G-19593)

COMPUTER & COMPUTER SOFTWARE STORES: Software, Bus/Non-Game

Etransmedia Technology Inc ....E ... 724 743-5960
Columbus (G-7539)

Retalix Inc ....C ... 937 384-2277
Miamisburg (G-14212)

Stratacache Inc ....C ... 937 224-0485
Dayton (G-9796)

COMPUTER & DATA PROCESSING EQPT REPAIR & MAINTENANCE

Datatech Depot (east) Inc ....E ... 513 860-5651
West Chester (G-18908)

Decisionone Corporation ....E ... 614 883-0228
Urbancrest (G-18448)

Efix Computer Repair & Svc LLC ......E ... 937 985-4447
Kettering (G-12292)

Positive Bus Solutions Inc ....D ... 513 772-2255
Cincinnati (G-4265)

Realm Technologies LLC ....E ... 513 297-3095
Lebanon (G-12497)

COMPUTER & OFFICE MACHINE MAINTENANCE & REPAIR

Bpi Infrmtion Systems Ohio Inc ....E ... 440 717-4112
Brecksville (G-1771)

Bsl - Applied Laser Tech LLC ....E ... 216 663-8181
Cleveland (G-5097)

Butler County of Ohio ....E ... 513 887-3418
Hamilton (G-11571)

Cincinnati Copiers Inc ....C ... 513 769-0606
Blue Ash (G-1525)

Cincinnati Voice and Data ....D ... 513 683-4127
Loveland (G-12983)

County of Montgomery ....B ... 937 496-3103
Dayton (G-9333)

CTS Construction Inc ....D ... 513 489-8290
Cincinnati (G-3385)

Diebold Nixdorf Incorporated ....D ... 513 682-6216
Hamilton (G-11590)

DMC Technology Group ....E ... 419 535-2900
Toledo (G-17703)

Enterprise Data Management Inc ....E ... 513 791-7272
Blue Ash (G-1554)

Evanhoe & Associates Inc ....E ... 937 235-2995
Dayton (G-9173)

Fiserv Solutions LLC ....C ... 412 577-3000
Dublin (G-10228)

Government Acquisitions Inc ....E ... 513 721-8700
Cincinnati (G-3628)

Intelligent Information Inc ....E ... 513 860-4233
West Chester (G-19061)

Northcoast Duplicating Inc ....C ... 216 573-6681
Cleveland (G-6087)

Park Place Technologies LLC ....E ... 603 617-7123
Cleveland (G-6169)

Park Place Technologies LLC ....B ... 610 544-0571
Mayfield Heights (G-13879)

Park Place Technologies LLC ....C ... 877 778-8707
Mayfield Heights (G-13880)

Perry Pro Tech Inc ....D ... 419 228-1360
Lima (G-12720)

Pomeroy It Solutions Sls Inc ....E ... 440 717-1364
Brecksville (G-1798)

Resource One Cmpt Systems Inc ....D ... 614 485-4800
Worthington (G-19844)

Sjn Data Center LLC ....E ... 513 386-7871
Cincinnati (G-4488)

Systems Alternatives Intl ....E ... 419 891-1100
Maumee (G-13860)

Uptime Corporation ....E ... 216 661-1655
Brooklyn Heights (G-1885)

Vertiv Corporation ....C ... 614 841-6400
Westerville (G-19215)

Wellington Technologies Inc ....E ... 440 238-4377
Westlake (G-19421)

Xerox Corporation ....D ... 216 642-7806
Cleveland (G-6697)

COMPUTER DATA ESCROW SVCS

Speedeon Data LLC ....E ... 440 264-2100
Cleveland (G-6446)

COMPUTER FACILITIES MANAGEMENT SVCS

Ability Network Inc ....E ... 513 943-8888
Cincinnati (G-2840)

Change Hlth Prac MGT Solns Grp ....E ... 937 291-7850
Miamisburg (G-14151)

City of Cleveland ....E ... 216 664-2941
Cleveland (G-5192)

Computer Sciences Corporation ....E ... 937 904-5113
Dayton (G-9166)

Computer Sciences Corporation ....C ... 614 801-2343
Grove City (G-11421)

Dedicated Tech Services Inc ....E ... 614 309-0059
Dublin (G-10197)

Dyn Marine Services Inc ....E ... 937 427-2663
Beavercreek (G-1149)

E&I Solutions LLC ....E ... 937 912-0288
Beavercreek (G-1150)

Evanhoe & Associates Inc ....E ... 937 235-2995
Dayton (G-9173)

General Electric Company ....C ... 513 583-3500
Cincinnati (G-3610)

Jjr Solutions LLC ....E ... 937 912-0288
Beavercreek (G-1159)

Jyg Innovations LLC ....E ... 937 630-3858
Dayton (G-9531)

Selecttech Services Corp ....C ... 937 438-9905
Centerville (G-2633)

Technical Assurance Inc ....E ... 440 953-3147
Willoughby (G-19575)

COMPUTER GRAPHICS SVCS

Clubessential LLC ....E ... 800 448-1475
Blue Ash (G-1530)

Great Lakes Publishing Company ....D ... 216 771-2833
Cleveland (G-5630)

Hyperquake LLC ....E ... 513 563-6555
Cincinnati (G-3748)

Interact One Inc ....E ... 513 469-7042
Blue Ash (G-1585)

International Data MGT Inc ....E ... 330 869-8500
Fairlawn (G-10835)

Karcher Group Inc ....E ... 330 493-6141
North Canton (G-15215)

Kuno Creative Group LLC ....E ... 440 225-4144
Avon (G-891)

Service Pronet Inc ....E ... 614 874-4300
Columbus (G-8623)

Universal Enterprises Inc ....C ... 419 529-3500
Ontario (G-15577)

COMPUTER INTERFACE EQPT: Indl Process

Keithley Instruments LLC ....C ... 440 248-0400
Solon (G-16864)

COMPUTER PERIPHERAL EQPT REPAIR & MAINTENANCE

Ascendtech Inc ....E ... 216 458-1101
Willoughby (G-19506)

Great Lakes Computer Corp ....D ... 440 937-1100
Avon (G-883)

Mt Business Technologies Inc ....C ... 419 529-6100
Mansfield (G-13225)

COMPUTER PERIPHERAL EQPT, NEC

Government Acquisitions Inc ....E ... 513 721-8700
Cincinnati (G-3628)

Parker-Hannifin Corporation ....D ... 513 831-2340
Milford (G-14419)

Systemax Manufacturing Inc ....C ... 937 368-2300
Dayton (G-9805)

Tech Pro Inc ....E ... 330 923-3546
Akron (G-466)

COMPUTER PERIPHERAL EQPT, WHOLESALE

Advanced Cmpt Connections LLC ....E ... 419 668-4080
Norwalk (G-15424)

Advantech Corporation ....D ... 513 742-8895
Blue Ash (G-1501)

Ascendtech Inc ....E ... 216 458-1101
Willoughby (G-19506)

Cincinnati Bell Techno ....D ... 513 841-6700
Cincinnati (G-3227)

Cisco Systems Inc ....D ... 614 764-4987
Dublin (G-10174)

Cranel Incorporated ....D ... 614 431-8000
Columbus (G-6811)

Global Gvrnment Edcatn Sltions ....D ... 937 368-2308
Dayton (G-9462)

Legrand North America LLC ....B ... 937 224-0639
Dayton (G-9561)

Manatron Inc ....E ... 937 431-4000
Beavercreek (G-1228)

Meyer Hill Lynch Corporation ....E ... 419 897-9797
Maumee (G-13821)

Micro Center Online Inc ....C ... 614 326-8500
Columbus (G-8069)

Micro Electronics Inc ....D ... 614 334-1430
Columbus (G-8071)

Micro Electronics Inc ....B ... 614 850-3000
Hilliard (G-11795)

Micro Electronics Inc ....D ... 614 850-3500
Hilliard (G-11796)

Micro Electronics Inc ....C ... 440 449-7000
Cleveland (G-5979)

Micro Electronics Inc ....E ... 513 782-8500
Cincinnati (G-4048)

Microplex Inc ....E ... 330 498-0600
North Canton (G-15220)

Park Place International LLC ....D ... 877 991-1991
Chagrin Falls (G-2677)

Pomeroy It Solutions Sls Inc ....E ... 440 717-1364
Brecksville (G-1798)

Systemax Manufacturing Inc ....C ... 937 368-2300
Dayton (G-9805)

COMPUTER PERIPHERAL EQPT: Decoders

Harris Mackessy & Brennan ....C ... 614 221-6831
Westerville (G-19169)

COMPUTER PROGRAMMING SVCS

Aclara Technologies LLC ....C ... 440 528-7200
Solon (G-16814)

Advanced Prgrm Resources Inc ....E ... 614 761-9994
Dublin (G-10119)

American Systems Cnsulting Inc ....D ... 614 282-7180
Dublin (G-10134)

Btas Inc ....C ... 937 431-9431
Beavercreek (G-1135)

Camgen Ltd ....E ... 330 204-8636
Canal Winchester (G-2105)

Care Information Systems LLC ....D ... 614 496-4338
Dublin (G-10160)

Cengage Learning Inc ....B ... 513 229-1000
Mason (G-13552)

Centergrid LLC ....E ... 513 712-1212
Hamilton (G-11574)

Cimx LLC ....E ... 513 248-7700
Cincinnati (G-3217)

Coleman Professional Svcs Inc ....C ... 330 673-1347
Kent (G-12223)

Command Alkon Incorporated ....E ... 614 799-0600
Dublin (G-10183)

Computer Helper Publishing ....E ... 614 939-9094
Columbus (G-7345)

County of Montgomery ....B ... 937 496-3103
Dayton (G-9333)

Datavantage Corporation ....B ... 440 498-4414
Cleveland (G-5406)

Devcare Solutions Ltd ....E ... 614 221-2277
Columbus (G-7439)

Dexxxon Digital Storage Inc ....E ... 740 548-7179
Lewis Center (G-12538)

Distribution Data Incorporated ....E ... 216 362-3009
Brookpark (G-1896)

DMC Technology Group ....E ... 419 535-2900
Toledo (G-17703)

Drb Systems LLC ....D ... 330 645-3299
Akron (G-195)

Drs Signal Technologies Inc ....E ... 937 429-7470
Beavercreek (G-1148)

Dynamite Technologies LLC ....D ... 614 538-0095
Columbus (G-7481)

Eclipse Blind Systems Inc ....C ... 330 296-0112
Ravenna (G-16242)

Eliassen Group LLC ....E ... 781 205-8100
Blue Ash (G-1550)

Epsilon ....E ... 513 248-2882
Milford (G-14387)

Exodus Integrity Service ....D ... 440 918-0140
Willoughby (G-19522)

First Data Gvrnmnt Solutns Inc ....C ... 513 489-9599
Blue Ash (G-1563)

Gb Liquidating Company Inc ....E ... 513 248-7600
Milford (G-14391)

SERVICES

Gracie Plum Investments Inc..........E...... 740 355-9029
Portsmouth (G-16141)
Harley-Dvidson Dlr Systems Inc......D...... 216 573-1393
Cleveland (G-5661)
Indecon Solutions LLC..........E...... 614 799-1850
Dublin (G-10254)
Indigo Group..........E...... 513 557-8794
Liberty Twp (G-12587)
Infor (us) Inc..........B...... 678 319-8000
Columbus (G-7816)
Jyg Innovations LLC..........E...... 937 630-3858
Dayton (G-9531)
Lifecycle Solutions Jv LLC..........D...... 937 938-1321
Beavercreek (G-1167)
Mapsys Inc..........E...... 614 255-7258
Columbus (G-8014)
Office World Inc..........E...... 419 991-4694
Lima (G-12791)
Ohio University..........D...... 740 593-1000
Athens (G-795)
Pegasus Technical Services Inc..........E...... 513 793-0094
Cincinnati (G-4223)
Rainbow Data Systems Inc..........E...... 937 431-8000
Beavercreek (G-1180)
Resource International Inc..........C...... 614 823-4949
Columbus (G-8523)
Roadtrippers Inc..........E...... 917 688-9887
Cincinnati (G-4387)
Sawdey Solution Services Inc..........E...... 937 490-4060
Beavercreek (G-1236)
Seapine Software Inc..........E...... 513 754-1655
Mason (G-13636)
Seifert & Group Inc..........D...... 330 833-2700
Massillon (G-13727)
Staid Logic LLC..........E...... 309 807-0575
Columbus (G-8682)
Sumaria Systems Inc..........D...... 937 429-6070
Beavercreek (G-1188)
Tata America Intl Corp..........B...... 513 677-6500
Milford (G-14435)
Tech Mahindra (americas) Inc..........D...... 216 912-2002
Cleveland (G-6508)
Tradeglobal LLC..........D...... 866 345-5835
West Chester (G-19092)
Tyco International MGT Co LLC..........E...... 888 787-8324
Cincinnati (G-4658)
Vediscovery LLC..........E...... 216 241-3443
Cleveland (G-6622)
Ventech Solutions Inc..........D...... 614 757-1167
Columbus (G-6837)
Yashco Systems Inc..........E...... 614 467-4600
Hilliard (G-11831)

COMPUTER PROGRAMMING SVCS: Custom

Cbiz Operations Inc..........D...... 216 447-9000
Cleveland (G-5140)
Critical Business Analysis Inc..........E...... 419 874-0800
Perrysburg (G-15852)
Digiknow Inc..........E...... 888 482-4455
Cleveland (G-5422)
Erp Analysts Inc..........B...... 614 718-9222
Dublin (G-10220)
Evanhoe & Associates Inc..........E...... 937 235-2995
Dayton (G-9173)
Horizon Payroll Services Inc..........B...... 937 434-8244
Dayton (G-9506)
Sordyl & Associates Inc..........E...... 419 866-6811
Maumee (G-13854)
Strategic Data Systems Inc..........E...... 513 772-7374
Cincinnati (G-4549)

COMPUTER RELATED MAINTENANCE SVCS

Ascendtech Inc..........E...... 216 458-1101
Willoughby (G-19506)
Atos It Solutions and Svcs Inc..........B...... 513 336-1000
Mason (G-13543)
Creek Technologies Company..........C...... 937 272-4581
Beavercreek (G-1142)
Dedicated Tech Services Inc..........E...... 614 309-0059
Dublin (G-10197)
Digital Controls Corporation..........D...... 513 746-8118
Miamisburg (G-14166)
Digital Management Inc..........D...... 240 223-4800
Mason (G-13573)
E&I Solutions LLC..........E...... 937 912-0288
Beavercreek (G-1150)
Echo-Tape LLC..........E...... 614 892-3246
Columbus (G-7498)
Fhc Enterprises LLC..........E...... 614 271-3513
Columbus (G-7574)

Greentree Group Inc..........D...... 937 490-5500
Dayton (G-9477)
Jjr Solutions LLC..........E...... 937 912-0288
Beavercreek (G-1159)
Jyg Innovations LLC..........E...... 937 630-3858
Dayton (G-9531)
Laketec Communications Inc..........E...... 440 892-2001
North Olmsted (G-15295)
Link Iq LLC..........E...... 859 983-6080
Dayton (G-9569)
Plus One Communications LLC..........B...... 330 255-4500
Akron (G-386)
Staid Logic LLC..........E...... 309 807-0575
Columbus (G-8682)
Top Gun Sales Performance Inc..........E...... 513 770-0870
Mason (G-13647)
Vana Solutions LLC..........E...... 937 242-6399
Beavercreek (G-1194)
Ventech Solutions Inc..........E...... 614 757-1167
Columbus (G-6837)
Wolters Kluwer Clinical Drug..........D...... 330 650-6506
Hudson (G-12014)

COMPUTER RELATED SVCS, NEC

PC Connection Services..........D...... 937 382-4800
Wilmington (G-19639)

COMPUTER SOFTWARE DEVELOPMENT

Alien Technology LLC..........C...... 408 782-3900
Miamisburg (G-14139)
Astute Inc..........E...... 614 508-6100
Columbus (G-6986)
Auto Des Sys Inc..........E...... 614 488-7984
Upper Arlington (G-18394)
Billback Systems LLC..........E...... 937 433-1844
Dayton (G-9253)
Briteskies LLC..........E...... 216 369-3600
Cleveland (G-5081)
Business Equipment Co Inc..........E...... 513 948-1500
Cincinnati (G-3096)
Cincom Intrnational Operations..........B...... 513 612-2300
Cincinnati (G-3285)
Cloudroute LLC..........E...... 216 373-4601
Cleveland (G-5307)
Clubessential LLC..........E...... 800 448-1475
Blue Ash (G-1530)
Cochin Technologies LLC..........E...... 440 941-4856
Avon (G-878)
Commercial Time Sharing Inc..........E...... 330 644-3059
Akron (G-148)
Comtech Global Inc..........D...... 614 796-1148
Columbus (G-7347)
Connectivity Systems Inc..........E...... 740 420-5400
Williamsport (G-19498)
CT Logistics Inc..........C...... 216 267-1636
Cleveland (G-5387)
Dassault Systemes Simulia Corp..........E...... 513 275-1430
Mason (G-13572)
Dedicated Tech Services Inc..........E...... 614 309-0059
Dublin (G-10197)
Digitek Software Inc..........E...... 614 764-8875
Lewis Center (G-12540)
Diskcopy Duplication Services..........E...... 440 460-0800
Cleveland (G-5427)
Dizer Corp..........E...... 440 368-0200
Painesville (G-15709)
Dotloop LLC..........D...... 513 257-0550
Cincinnati (G-3441)
Eci Macola/Max LLC..........C...... 978 539-6186
Dublin (G-10213)
Einstruction Corporation..........D...... 330 746-3015
Youngstown (G-20027)
Electronic Registry Systems..........E...... 513 771-7330
Cincinnati (G-3489)
Everyone Counts Inc..........E...... 858 427-4673
Cleveland (G-5498)
Fastems LLC..........E...... 513 779-4614
West Chester (G-18922)
Flairsoft Ltd..........E...... 614 888-0700
Columbus (G-7594)
Gannett Media Tech Intl..........E...... 513 665-3777
Cincinnati (G-3602)
Health Care Dataworks Inc..........D...... 614 255-5400
Columbus (G-7724)
Henry Call Inc..........C...... 216 433-5609
Cleveland (G-5684)
Ils Technology LLC..........E...... 800 695-8650
Cleveland (G-5738)
Incubit LLC..........D...... 740 362-1401
Delaware (G-9988)

Inet Interactive LLC..........E...... 513 322-5600
West Chester (G-18947)
Infovision 21 Inc..........E...... 614 761-8844
Dublin (G-10256)
Integrated Telehealth Inc..........E...... 216 373-2221
Hudson (G-11985)
Intelligrated Systems Inc..........A...... 866 936-7300
Mason (G-13598)
Intelligrated Systems LLC..........A...... 513 701-7300
Mason (G-13599)
International Technegroup Inc..........D...... 513 576-3900
Milford (G-14397)
Iq Innovations LLC..........E...... 614 222-0882
Columbus (G-7841)
Irth Solutions Inc..........E...... 614 459-2328
Columbus (G-7843)
Isqft Inc..........C...... 513 645-8004
Cincinnati (G-3788)
Keithley Instruments LLC..........C...... 440 248-0400
Solon (G-16864)
Kiwiplan Inc..........E...... 513 554-1500
Cincinnati (G-3878)
Knowledge MGT Interactive Inc..........E...... 614 224-0664
Columbus (G-7919)
Leader Technologies Inc..........E...... 614 890-1986
Lewis Center (G-12549)
Leidos Inc..........E...... 937 431-2270
Beavercreek (G-1164)
Liberty Comm Sftwr Sltions Inc..........E...... 614 318-5000
Columbus (G-7970)
Lisnr Inc..........E...... 513 322-8400
Cincinnati (G-3938)
London Computer Systems Inc..........D...... 513 583-0840
Cincinnati (G-3942)
Main Sequence Technology Inc..........E...... 440 946-5214
Mentor On The Lake (G-14129)
Marshall Information Svcs LLC..........E...... 614 430-0355
Columbus (G-8030)
Matrix Pointe Software LLC..........E...... 216 333-1263
Westlake (G-19371)
Mirifex Systems LLC..........C...... 440 891-1210
Cleveland (G-6001)
Morphick Inc..........E...... 844 506-6774
Blue Ash (G-1615)
Mri Software LLC..........C...... 800 321-8770
Solon (G-16874)
MSI International LLC..........E...... 330 869-6459
Cleveland (G-6022)
Neumeric Technologies Corp..........D...... 248 204-0652
Westerville (G-19190)
New Innovations Inc..........E...... 330 899-9954
Uniontown (G-18380)
Noble Technologies Corp..........E...... 330 287-1530
Wooster (G-19752)
Northwods Cnslting Prtners Inc..........C...... 614 781-7800
Dublin (G-10292)
Nsb Retail Systems Inc..........D...... 614 840-1421
Lewis Center (G-12554)
Ntt Data Inc..........D...... 513 794-1400
Cincinnati (G-4137)
Parker-Hannifin Corporation..........D...... 513 831-2340
Milford (G-14419)
Patterson Pope Inc..........D...... 513 891-4430
Cincinnati (G-4213)
Plumbline Solutions Inc..........E...... 419 581-2963
Findlay (G-10954)
Positive Bus Solutions Inc..........D...... 513 772-2255
Cincinnati (G-4265)
Primax Marketing Group..........E...... 513 443-2797
Cincinnati (G-4279)
Productivity Qulty Systems Inc..........E...... 937 885-2255
Dayton (G-9717)
Qvidian Corporation..........E...... 513 631-1155
Blue Ash (G-1634)
Retalix Usa Inc..........C...... 937 384-2277
Miamisburg (G-14213)
Rippe & Kingston Systems Inc..........D...... 513 977-4578
Cincinnati (G-4375)
Sadler-Necamp Financial Svcs..........E...... 513 489-5477
Cincinnati (G-4421)
Sanctuary Software Studio Inc..........E...... 330 666-9690
Fairlawn (G-10847)
Sap America Inc..........E...... 513 762-7630
Cincinnati (G-4433)
Scientific Forming Tech Corp..........E...... 614 451-8330
Columbus (G-8610)
Shoptech Industrial Sftwr..........D...... 513 985-9900
Cincinnati (G-4471)
Siemens Product Life Mgmt Sftw..........D...... 513 576-2400
Milford (G-14431)

Software Answers Inc ....E 440 526-0095
   Brecksville **(G-1806)**
Srinsoft Inc ....E 614 893-6535
   Dublin **(G-10339)**
Streamlink Software Inc ....E 216 377-5500
   Cleveland **(G-6473)**
Sumtotal Systems LLC ....C 352 264-2800
   Columbus **(G-8711)**
Sunstorm Games LLC ....E 216 403-4820
   Beachwood **(G-1109)**
Systems Evolution Inc ....D 513 459-1992
   Cincinnati **(G-4564)**
Thinkware Incorporated ....E 513 598-3300
   Cincinnati **(G-4600)**
Timeware Inc ....E 330 963-2700
   Twinsburg **(G-18327)**
TOA Technologies Inc ....D 216 360-8106
   Beachwood **(G-1112)**
Tour De Force Inc ....E 419 425-4800
   Findlay **(G-10970)**
Triad Governmental Systems ....E 937 376-5446
   Xenia **(G-19930)**
Virtual Hold Technology LLC ....D 330 670-2200
   Akron **(G-489)**
Widepint Intgrted Sltions Corp ....E 614 410-1587
   Columbus **(G-8901)**

COMPUTER SOFTWARE DEVELOPMENT & APPLICATIONS

Acadia Solutions Inc ....E 614 505-6135
   Dublin **(G-10118)**
Advantage Technology Group ....E 513 563-3560
   West Chester **(G-18860)**
Aktion Associates Incorporated ....E 419 893-7001
   Maumee **(G-13747)**
Alonovus Corp ....D 330 674-2300
   Millersburg **(G-14454)**
Assured Information SEC Inc ....D 937 427-9720
   Beavercreek **(G-1127)**
Batch Labs Inc ....D 216 901-9366
   Cleveland **(G-5041)**
Camgen Ltd ....D 330 204-8636
   Cleveland **(G-5116)**
Cott Systems Inc ....D 614 847-4405
   Columbus **(G-7379)**
Crosschx Inc ....D 800 501-3161
   Columbus **(G-7395)**
Deemsys Inc ....D 614 322-9928
   Gahanna **(G-11117)**
Flexnova Inc ....E 216 288-6961
   Broadview Heights **(G-1833)**
Foresight Corporation ....E 614 791-1600
   Dublin **(G-10230)**
Fortis North Canton LLC ....E 330 682-5984
   North Canton **(G-15204)**
Fraternal Order of Eagles BR ....E 419 636-7812
   Bryan **(G-1957)**
Frontier Technology Inc ....E 937 429-3302
   Beavercreek Township **(G-1248)**
Fund Evaluation Group LLC ....E 513 977-4400
   Cincinnati **(G-3597)**
Gatesair Inc ....D 513 459-3400
   Mason **(G-13583)**
Hab Inc ....E 608 785-7650
   Solon **(G-16856)**
Imflux Inc ....E 513 488-1017
   Hamilton **(G-11611)**
Inreality LLC ....E 513 218-9603
   Cincinnati **(G-3763)**
Jjr Solutions LLC ....E 937 912-0288
   Beavercreek **(G-1159)**
Keystone Technology Cons ....E 330 666-6200
   Akron **(G-302)**
Kmi Inc ....E 614 326-6304
   Columbus **(G-7914)**
Lakeland Foundation ....E 440 525-7094
   Willoughby **(G-19541)**
Marxent Labs LLC ....D 937 999-5005
   Kettering **(G-12297)**
Mitosis LLC ....E 937 557-3440
   Dayton **(G-9640)**
Montpelier Exempted Vlg Schl ....D 419 485-3676
   Montpelier **(G-14615)**
Raco Wireless LLC ....E 513 870-6480
   Blue Ash **(G-1637)**
Saec/Kinetic Vision Inc ....C 513 793-4959
   Cincinnati **(G-4422)**
Service Pronet Inc ....E 614 874-4300
   Columbus **(G-8623)**

Solutions Through Innovative T ....D 937 320-9994
   Beavercreek **(G-1187)**
T-Cetra LLC ....E 877 956-2359
   Dublin **(G-10352)**

COMPUTER SOFTWARE SYSTEMS ANALYSIS & DESIGN: Custom

22nd Century Technologies Inc ....C 866 537-9191
   Beavercreek **(G-1121)**
Big Red Rooster ....E 614 255-0200
   Columbus **(G-7036)**
Cdo Technologies Inc ....D 937 258-0022
   Dayton **(G-9164)**
Certified SEC Solutions Inc ....E 216 785-2986
   Independence **(G-12057)**
Click4care Inc ....D 614 431-3700
   Powell **(G-16188)**
Commsys Inc ....E 937 220-4990
   Moraine **(G-14634)**
Diversified Systems Inc ....E 614 476-9939
   Westerville **(G-19249)**
Edaptive Computing Inc ....D 937 433-0477
   Dayton **(G-9408)**
Fascor Inc ....E 513 421-1777
   Cincinnati **(G-3533)**
Genomoncology LLC ....E 216 496-4216
   Cleveland **(G-5605)**
Gensuite LLC ....E 513 774-1000
   Mason **(G-13587)**
Itcube LLC ....D 513 891-7300
   Blue Ash **(G-1587)**
Lap Technology LLC ....E 937 415-5794
   Dayton **(G-9558)**
Logic Soft Inc ....D 614 884-5544
   Dublin **(G-10274)**
Manifest Solutions Corp ....D 614 930-2800
   Upper Arlington **(G-18401)**
Odyssey Consulting Services ....E 614 523-4248
   Columbus **(G-8226)**
Oeconnection LLC ....D 888 776-5792
   Richfield **(G-16367)**
Online Mega Sellers Corp ....D 888 384-6468
   Toledo **(G-17964)**
Path Robotics Inc ....E 330 808-2788
   Cleveland **(G-6181)**
Primatech Inc ....E 614 841-9800
   Columbus **(G-8462)**
Systems Alternatives Intl ....E 419 891-1100
   Maumee **(G-13860)**
Tridec Technologies LLC ....E 937 938-8160
   Huber Heights **(G-11959)**
Unicon International Inc ....C 614 861-7070
   Columbus **(G-8798)**
Wtw Delaware Holdings LLC ....C 216 937-4000
   Cleveland **(G-6693)**

COMPUTER SOFTWARE WRITERS

Holo Pundits Inc ....E 614 707-5225
   Dublin **(G-10244)**
Pcms Datafit Inc ....D 513 587-3100
   Blue Ash **(G-1629)**

COMPUTER SOFTWARE WRITERS: Freelance

Boundless Flight Inc ....E 440 610-3683
   Rocky River **(G-16424)**

COMPUTER STORAGE DEVICES, NEC

EMC Corporation ....E 216 606-2000
   Independence **(G-12069)**

COMPUTER SYSTEM SELLING SVCS

Infotelecom Holdings LLC ....B 216 373-4811
   Cleveland **(G-5753)**
Velocity Grtest Phone Ever Inc ....B 419 868-9983
   Holland **(G-11924)**

COMPUTER SYSTEMS ANALYSIS & DESIGN

Honeywell International Inc ....D 513 745-7200
   Cincinnati **(G-3724)**
Northrop Grumman Systems Corp .....E 937 429-6450
   Beavercreek **(G-1232)**
Peerless Technologies Corp ....D 937 490-5000
   Beavercreek Township **(G-1257)**
Sytronics Inc ....E 937 431-6100
   Beavercreek **(G-1189)**

Teknobility LLC ....E 216 255-9433
   Medina **(G-14009)**

COMPUTER TERMINALS

Parker-Hannifin Corporation ....D 513 831-2340
   Milford **(G-14419)**

COMPUTER TRAINING SCHOOLS

Pomeroy It Solutions Sls Inc ....E 440 717-1364
   Brecksville **(G-1798)**

COMPUTER-AIDED DESIGN SYSTEMS SVCS

Pegasus Technical Services Inc ....E 513 793-0094
   Cincinnati **(G-4223)**

COMPUTER-AIDED ENGINEERING SYSTEMS SVCS

Thinkpath Engineering Svcs LLC ......E 937 291-8374
   Miamisburg **(G-14229)**
Twism Enterprises LLC ....E 513 800-1098
   Cincinnati **(G-4657)**

COMPUTERS, NEC

Ascendtech Inc ....E 216 458-1101
   Willoughby **(G-19506)**
Parker-Hannifin Corporation ....D 513 831-2340
   Milford **(G-14419)**
Systemax Manufacturing Inc ....C 937 368-2300
   Dayton **(G-9805)**
Teradata Operations Inc ....D 937 242-4030
   Miamisburg **(G-14228)**

COMPUTERS, NEC, WHOLESALE

Arrow Globl Asset Dspstion Inc ....D 614 328-4100
   Gahanna **(G-11110)**
Office World Inc ....E 419 991-4694
   Lima **(G-12791)**
Pcm Sales Inc ....E 501 342-1000
   Cleveland **(G-6185)**
Pcm Sales Inc ....C 513 842-3500
   Blue Ash **(G-1628)**
Pcm Sales Inc ....E 740 548-2222
   Lewis Center **(G-12558)**
Vecmar Corporation ....E 440 953-1119
   Mentor **(G-14121)**
Virtual Technologies Group ....E 419 991-4694
   Lima **(G-12794)**

COMPUTERS, PERIPHERAL & SOFTWARE, WHOLESALE: Word Processing

Blue Technologies Inc ....E 330 499-9300
   Canton **(G-2215)**
Gordon Flesch Company Inc ....E 419 884-2031
   Mansfield **(G-13179)**

COMPUTERS, PERIPHERALS & SOFTWARE, WHOLESALE: Printers

Bsl - Applied Laser Tech LLC ....E 216 663-8181
   Cleveland **(G-5097)**
Raco Industries LLC ....D 513 984-2101
   Blue Ash **(G-1636)**

COMPUTERS, PERIPHERALS & SOFTWARE, WHOLESALE: Software

Avid Technologies Inc ....E 330 487-0770
   Twinsburg **(G-18248)**
Canon Solutions America Inc ....D 937 260-4495
   Miamisburg **(G-14148)**
Commercial Time Sharing Inc ....E 330 644-3059
   Akron **(G-148)**
Computer Helper Publishing ....E 614 939-9094
   Columbus **(G-7345)**
Dolbey Systems Inc ....E 440 392-9900
   Painesville **(G-15710)**
Eci Macola/Max LLC ....C 978 539-6186
   Dublin **(G-10213)**
Enhanced Software Inc ....E 877 805-8388
   Columbus **(G-7518)**
Environmental Systems Research .....D 614 933-8698
   Columbus **(G-7522)**
GBS Corp ....E 330 797-2700
   Youngstown **(G-20046)**

Government Acquisitions Inc ....E 513 721-8700
Cincinnati **(G-3628)**

Indico LLC ....D 440 775-7777
Oberlin **(G-15505)**

Insight Direct Usa Inc ....D 614 456-0423
Columbus **(G-7826)**

Isqft Inc ....C 513 645-8004
Cincinnati **(G-3788)**

Kiwiplan Inc ....E 513 554-1500
Cincinnati **(G-3878)**

Manatron Sabre Systems and Svc ....D 937 431-4000
Beavercreek **(G-1229)**

Mediquant Inc ....E 440 746-2300
Brecksville **(G-1789)**

Mitel (delaware) Inc ....E 513 733-8000
West Chester **(G-18974)**

Positive Bus Solutions Inc ....D 513 772-2255
Cincinnati **(G-4265)**

Quilalea Corporation ....E 330 487-0777
Richfield **(G-16372)**

Software Solutions Inc ....E 513 932-6667
Lebanon **(G-12504)**

Total Loop Inc ....D 888 614-5667
Uniontown **(G-18388)**

Transcriptiongear Inc ....E 888 834-2392
Painesville **(G-15743)**

COMPUTERS, PERIPHERALS & SOFTWARE, WHOLESALE: Terminals

Business Data Systems Inc ....E 330 633-1221
Tallmadge **(G-17470)**

CONCERT MANAGEMENT SVCS

Ovations ....E 216 687-9292
Cleveland **(G-6149)**

CONCRETE BUILDING PRDTS WHOLESALERS

Janell Inc ....E 513 489-9111
Blue Ash **(G-1589)**

CONCRETE CURING & HARDENING COMPOUNDS

Master Builders LLC ....E 216 831-5500
Beachwood **(G-1076)**

Sika Corporation ....D 740 387-9224
Marion **(G-13459)**

CONCRETE PRDTS

Baxter Burial Vault Service ....E 513 641-1010
Cincinnati **(G-3024)**

Hanson Aggregates East LLC ....E 740 773-2172
Chillicothe **(G-2784)**

Hanson Concrete Products Ohio ....E 614 443-4846
Columbus **(G-7716)**

Hilltop Basic Resources Inc ....E 513 621-1500
Cincinnati **(G-3709)**

Huron Cement Products Company ....E 419 433-4161
Huron **(G-12026)**

K M B Inc ....E 330 889-3451
Bristolville **(G-1826)**

Lang Stone Company Inc ....D 614 235-4099
Columbus **(G-7951)**

Orrville Trucking & Grading Co ....E 330 682-4010
Orrville **(G-15641)**

Pawnee Maintenance Inc ....D 740 373-6861
Marietta **(G-13366)**

Snyder Concrete Products Inc ....E 937 885-5176
Moraine **(G-14697)**

Tri County Concrete Inc ....E 330 425-4464
Twinsburg **(G-18328)**

CONCRETE: Asphaltic, Not From Refineries

Shelly Materials Inc ....D 740 246-6315
Thornville **(G-17506)**

CONCRETE: Dry Mixture

Smith Concrete Co ....E 740 373-7441
Dover **(G-10101)**

CONCRETE: Ready-Mixed

Central Ready Mix LLC ....E 513 402-5001
Cincinnati **(G-3157)**

D W Dickey and Son Inc ....D 330 424-1441
Lisbon **(G-12799)**

G Big Inc ....E 740 867-5758
Chesapeake **(G-2729)**

Hanson Aggregates East LLC ....E 740 773-2172
Chillicothe **(G-2784)**

Hanson Aggregates East LLC ....E 937 587-2671
Peebles **(G-15802)**

Hilltop Basic Resources Inc ....E 513 621-1500
Cincinnati **(G-3709)**

Hull Builders Supply Inc ....E 440 967-3159
Vermilion **(G-18553)**

Huron Cement Products Company ....E 419 433-4161
Huron **(G-12026)**

Joe McClelland Inc ....E 740 452-3036
Zanesville **(G-20321)**

K M B Inc ....E 330 889-3451
Bristolville **(G-1826)**

Kuhlman Corporation ....C 419 897-6000
Maumee **(G-13808)**

Mecco Inc ....E 513 422-3651
Middletown **(G-14307)**

National Lime and Stone Co ....E 419 423-3400
Findlay **(G-10948)**

Orrville Trucking & Grading Co ....E 330 682-4010
Orrville **(G-15641)**

Phillips Companies ....E 937 426-5461
Beavercreek Township **(G-1258)**

Phillips Ready Mix Co ....D 937 426-5151
Beavercreek Township **(G-1259)**

Quality Block & Supply Inc ....E 330 364-4411
Mount Eaton **(G-14723)**

R W Sidley Incorporated ....E 330 793-7374
Youngstown **(G-20176)**

Smith Concrete Co ....E 740 373-7441
Dover **(G-10101)**

Stamm Contracting Co Inc ....E 330 274-8230
Mantua **(G-13276)**

Terminal Ready-Mix Inc ....E 440 288-0181
Lorain **(G-12947)**

Tri County Concrete Inc ....E 330 425-4464
Twinsburg **(G-18328)**

W G Lockhart Construction Co ....D 330 745-6520
Akron **(G-492)**

CONDENSERS: Heat Transfer Eqpt, Evaporative

Hydro-Dyne Inc ....E 330 832-5076
Massillon **(G-13696)**

CONES, PYROMETRIC: Earthenware

Orton Edward Jr Crmic Fndation ....E 614 895-2663
Westerville **(G-19197)**

CONFECTIONERY PRDTS WHOLESALERS

Albert Guarnieri & Co ....D 330 794-9834
Hudson **(G-11962)**

EBY-Brown Company LLC ....C 937 324-1036
Springfield **(G-17032)**

JE Carsten Company ....E 330 794-4440
Hudson **(G-11987)**

Lobby Shoppes Inc ....C 937 324-0002
Springfield **(G-17063)**

Novelart Manufacturing Company ....D 513 351-7700
Cincinnati **(G-4136)**

The Anter Brothers Company ....E 216 252-4555
Cleveland **(G-6519)**

Tiffin Paper Company ....E 419 447-2121
Tiffin **(G-17544)**

CONFECTIONS & CANDY

Malleys Candies Inc ....E 216 529-6262
Cleveland **(G-5903)**

Nestle Usa Inc ....E 513 576-4930
Loveland **(G-13015)**

CONFINEMENT SURVEILLANCE SYS MAINTENANCE & MONITORING SVCS

Macair Aviation LLC ....E 937 347-1302
Xenia **(G-19919)**

CONNECTORS: Electronic

Powell Electrical Systems Inc ....D 330 966-1750
Canton **(G-2438)**

CONSERVATION PROGRAMS ADMINISTRATION SVCS

City of Cleveland ....E 216 348-7210
Cleveland **(G-5196)**

Natural Resources Ohio Dept ....E 614 265-6948
Columbus **(G-8162)**

Natural Resources Ohio Dept ....D 419 938-5411
Perrysville **(G-15942)**

Natural Resources Ohio Dept ....E 614 265-6852
Columbus **(G-8163)**

CONSTRUCTION & MINING MACHINERY WHOLESALERS

Advanced Specialty Products ....D 419 882-6528
Bowling Green **(G-1712)**

Ag-Pro Ohio LLC ....D 740 450-7446
Zanesville **(G-20273)**

Cope Farm Equipment Inc ....E 330 821-5867
Alliance **(G-528)**

E T B Ltd ....E 740 373-6686
Marietta **(G-13326)**

Ebony Construction Co ....E 419 841-3455
Sylvania **(G-17421)**

Equipment Maintenance Inc ....E 513 353-3518
Cleves **(G-6728)**

Findlay Implement Co ....E 419 424-0471
Findlay **(G-10903)**

Hartville Hardware Inc ....C 330 877-4690
Hartville **(G-11688)**

Kuester Implement Company Inc ....E 740 944-1502
Bloomingdale **(G-1490)**

Lefeld Implement Inc ....E 419 678-2375
Coldwater **(G-6761)**

Mesa Industries Inc ....D 513 321-2950
Cincinnati **(G-4038)**

Ohio Machinery Co ....E 330 874-1003
Bolivar **(G-1705)**

Seal Aftermarket Products LLC ....D 419 355-1200
Fremont **(G-11094)**

Shearer Farm Inc ....E 330 345-9023
Wooster **(G-19768)**

Shearer Farm Inc ....E 419 465-4622
Monroeville **(G-14590)**

Shetlers Sales & Service Inc ....E 330 760-3358
Copley **(G-8975)**

Simpson Strong-Tie Company Inc ....C 614 876-8060
Columbus **(G-8645)**

Stone Products Inc ....E 800 235-6088
Canton **(G-2500)**

CONSTRUCTION EQPT REPAIR SVCS

Hans Truck and Trlr Repr Inc ....E 216 581-0046
Cleveland **(G-5660)**

Leppo Inc ....E 330 456-2930
Canton **(G-2376)**

Mine Equipment Services LLC ....E 740 936-5427
Sunbury **(G-17390)**

Ohio Machinery Co ....E 330 530-9010
Girard **(G-11295)**

TNT Equipment Company ....E 614 882-1549
Columbus **(G-8761)**

Vermeer Sales & Service Inc ....E 330 723-8383
Medina **(G-14012)**

CONSTRUCTION EQPT: Cranes

Terex Utilities Inc ....D 513 539-9770
Monroe **(G-14584)**

CONSTRUCTION EQPT: Roofing Eqpt

Dimensional Metals Inc ....D 740 927-3633
Reynoldsburg **(G-16299)**

CONSTRUCTION MATERIALS, WHOLESALE: Aggregate

Arrowhead Transport Co ....E 330 638-2900
Cortland **(G-8983)**

Bruder Inc ....E 216 791-9800
Maple Heights **(G-13282)**

Digeronimo Aggregates LLC ....E 216 524-2950
Independence **(G-12067)**

Martin Marietta Materials Inc ....E 513 829-6446
Fairfield **(G-10750)**

Martin Marietta Materials Inc ....E 614 871-6708
Grove City **(G-11451)**

CONSTRUCTION MATERIALS, WHOLESALE: Air Ducts, Sheet Metal

American Warming and Vent ....D....... 419 288-2703
Bradner *(G-1763)*

CONSTRUCTION MATERIALS, WHOLESALE: Awnings

Schneider Home Equipment Co ....E....... 513 522-1200
Cincinnati *(G-4438)*

CONSTRUCTION MATERIALS, WHOLESALE: Block, Concrete & Cinder

Allega Recycled Mtls & Sup Co ....E....... 216 447-0814
Cleveland *(G-4937)*
Quality Block & Supply Inc ....E....... 330 364-4411
Mount Eaton *(G-14723)*

CONSTRUCTION MATERIALS, WHOLESALE: Brick, Exc Refractory

Snyder Concrete Products Inc ....E....... 937 885-5176
Moraine *(G-14697)*

CONSTRUCTION MATERIALS, WHOLESALE: Building Stone

C & B Buck Bros Asp Maint LLC ....E....... 419 536-7325
Toledo *(G-17633)*
Lang Stone Company Inc ....D....... 614 235-4099
Columbus *(G-7951)*

CONSTRUCTION MATERIALS, WHOLESALE: Building Stone, Granite

Direct Import Home Decor Inc ....E....... 216 898-9758
Cleveland *(G-5424)*
Indus Trade & Technology LLC ....E....... 614 527-0257
Columbus *(G-7811)*
Jainco International Inc ....C....... 440 519-0100
Solon *(G-16863)*
Justice & Co Inc ....E....... 330 225-6000
Medina *(G-13962)*
Micro Construction LLC ....E....... 740 862-0751
Baltimore *(G-937)*

CONSTRUCTION MATERIALS, WHOLESALE: Building Stone, Marble

Konkus Marble & Granite Inc ....C....... 614 876-4000
Columbus *(G-7921)*
Maza Inc ....E....... 614 760-0003
Plain City *(G-16059)*

CONSTRUCTION MATERIALS, WHOLESALE: Building, Exterior

Allied Building Products Corp ....E....... 216 362-1764
Cleveland *(G-4938)*
Bennett Supply of Ohio LLC ....E....... 800 292-5577
Macedonia *(G-13062)*
Bluelinx Corporation ....E....... 330 794-1141
Akron *(G-101)*
Boise Cascade Company ....E....... 740 382-6766
Marion *(G-13406)*
Francis-Schulze Co ....E....... 937 295-3941
Russia *(G-16466)*
Hd Supply Inc ....E....... 614 771-4849
Groveport *(G-11516)*
Koch Aluminum Mfg Inc ....E....... 419 625-5956
Sandusky *(G-16622)*
Lowes Home Centers LLC ....C....... 216 351-4723
Cleveland *(G-5882)*
Lowes Home Centers LLC ....C....... 419 739-1300
Wapakoneta *(G-18649)*
Lowes Home Centers LLC ....C....... 937 235-2920
Dayton *(G-9574)*
Lowes Home Centers LLC ....C....... 740 574-6200
Wheelersburg *(G-19435)*
Lowes Home Centers LLC ....C....... 330 665-9356
Akron *(G-321)*
Lowes Home Centers LLC ....C....... 330 829-2700
Alliance *(G-538)*
Lowes Home Centers LLC ....C....... 937 599-4000
Bellefontaine *(G-1357)*
Lowes Home Centers LLC ....C....... 419 420-7531
Findlay *(G-10935)*
Lowes Home Centers LLC ....C....... 330 832-1901
Massillon *(G-13704)*
Lowes Home Centers LLC ....C....... 513 741-0585
Cincinnati *(G-3945)*
Lowes Home Centers LLC ....C....... 614 433-9957
Columbus *(G-6822)*
Lowes Home Centers LLC ....C....... 740 389-9737
Marion *(G-13430)*
Lowes Home Centers LLC ....C....... 740 450-5500
Zanesville *(G-20326)*
Lowes Home Centers LLC ....C....... 513 598-7050
Cincinnati *(G-3946)*
Lowes Home Centers LLC ....C....... 614 769-9940
Reynoldsburg *(G-16317)*
Lowes Home Centers LLC ....C....... 614 853-6200
Columbus *(G-7990)*
Lowes Home Centers LLC ....C....... 440 937-3500
Avon *(G-893)*
Lowes Home Centers LLC ....C....... 513 445-1000
South Lebanon *(G-16926)*
Lowes Home Centers LLC ....B....... 216 831-2860
Bedford *(G-1290)*
Lowes Home Centers LLC ....C....... 937 327-6000
Springfield *(G-17065)*
Lowes Home Centers LLC ....C....... 419 331-3598
Lima *(G-12693)*
Lowes Home Centers LLC ....C....... 740 681-3464
Lancaster *(G-12413)*
Lowes Home Centers LLC ....C....... 614 659-0530
Dublin *(G-10275)*
Lowes Home Centers LLC ....C....... 614 238-2601
Columbus *(G-7991)*
Lowes Home Centers LLC ....C....... 740 522-0003
Newark *(G-15063)*
Lowes Home Centers LLC ....C....... 740 773-7777
Chillicothe *(G-2803)*
Lowes Home Centers LLC ....C....... 440 998-6555
Ashtabula *(G-745)*
Lowes Home Centers LLC ....B....... 513 753-5094
Cincinnati *(G-2861)*
Lowes Home Centers LLC ....C....... 614 497-6170
Columbus *(G-7992)*
Lowes Home Centers LLC ....C....... 513 731-6127
Cincinnati *(G-3947)*
Lowes Home Centers LLC ....C....... 330 287-2261
Wooster *(G-19742)*
Lowes Home Centers LLC ....C....... 937 339-2544
Troy *(G-18211)*
Lowes Home Centers LLC ....C....... 440 392-0027
Mentor *(G-14078)*
Lowes Home Centers LLC ....C....... 440 942-2759
Willoughby *(G-19546)*
Lowes Home Centers LLC ....C....... 740 374-2151
Marietta *(G-13345)*
Lowes Home Centers LLC ....C....... 419 874-6758
Perrysburg *(G-15891)*
Lowes Home Centers LLC ....C....... 330 626-2980
Streetsboro *(G-17259)*
Lowes Home Centers LLC ....C....... 419 389-9464
Toledo *(G-17864)*
Lowes Home Centers LLC ....C....... 419 843-9758
Toledo *(G-17865)*
Lowes Home Centers LLC ....C....... 614 447-2851
Columbus *(G-7993)*
Lowes Home Centers LLC ....C....... 330 245-4300
Akron *(G-322)*
Lowes Home Centers LLC ....C....... 513 965-3280
Milford *(G-14402)*
Lowes Home Centers LLC ....C....... 330 908-2750
Northfield *(G-15382)*
Lowes Home Centers LLC ....C....... 419 470-2491
Toledo *(G-17866)*
Lowes Home Centers LLC ....C....... 513 336-9741
Mason *(G-13612)*
Lowes Home Centers LLC ....C....... 937 498-8400
Sidney *(G-16785)*
Lowes Home Centers LLC ....C....... 740 699-3000
Saint Clairsville *(G-16493)*
Lowes Home Centers LLC ....C....... 330 920-9280
Stow *(G-17218)*
Lowes Home Centers LLC ....C....... 740 589-3750
Athens *(G-791)*
Lowes Home Centers LLC ....C....... 740 393-5350
Mount Vernon *(G-14779)*
Lowes Home Centers LLC ....C....... 937 547-2400
Greenville *(G-11389)*
Lowes Home Centers LLC ....C....... 330 335-1900
Wadsworth *(G-18606)*
Lowes Home Centers LLC ....C....... 937 347-4000
Xenia *(G-19918)*
Lowes Home Centers LLC ....C....... 440 239-2630
Strongsville *(G-17324)*
Lowes Home Centers LLC ....C....... 513 755-4300
West Chester *(G-18966)*
Lowes Home Centers LLC ....C....... 513 671-2093
Cincinnati *(G-3948)*
Lowes Home Centers LLC ....C....... 440 331-1027
Rocky River *(G-16440)*
Lowes Home Centers LLC ....C....... 330 677-3040
Kent *(G-12247)*
Lowes Home Centers LLC ....C....... 419 747-1920
Ontario *(G-15559)*
Lowes Home Centers LLC ....C....... 330 339-1936
New Philadelphia *(G-14971)*
Lowes Home Centers LLC ....C....... 440 985-5700
Lorain *(G-12924)*
Lowes Home Centers LLC ....C....... 419 447-4101
Tiffin *(G-17521)*
Lowes Home Centers LLC ....C....... 937 578-4440
Marysville *(G-13511)*
Lowes Home Centers LLC ....C....... 440 324-5004
Elyria *(G-10531)*
Lowes Home Centers LLC ....C....... 937 438-4900
Dayton *(G-9575)*
Lowes Home Centers LLC ....C....... 937 427-1110
Beavercreek *(G-1168)*
Lowes Home Centers LLC ....C....... 937 848-5600
Dayton *(G-9576)*
Lowes Home Centers LLC ....C....... 614 529-5900
Hilliard *(G-11786)*
Lowes Home Centers LLC ....C....... 513 737-3700
Hamilton *(G-11625)*
Lowes Home Centers LLC ....C....... 419 355-0221
Fremont *(G-11084)*
Lowes Home Centers LLC ....C....... 419 624-6000
Sandusky *(G-16625)*
Lowes Home Centers LLC ....C....... 419 782-9000
Defiance *(G-9926)*
Lowes Home Centers LLC ....C....... 330 609-8000
Warren *(G-18725)*
Lowes Home Centers LLC ....C....... 740 894-7120
South Point *(G-16939)*
Lowes Home Centers LLC ....C....... 513 727-3900
Middletown *(G-14305)*
Lowes Home Centers LLC ....C....... 330 497-2720
Canton *(G-2381)*
Lowes Home Centers LLC ....C....... 740 266-3500
Steubenville *(G-17164)*
Lowes Home Centers LLC ....C....... 330 965-4500
Youngstown *(G-20101)*
Lowes Home Centers LLC ....C....... 937 383-7000
Wilmington *(G-19630)*
Lowes Home Centers LLC ....C....... 937 854-8200
Dayton *(G-9577)*
Lowes Home Centers LLC ....C....... 614 476-7100
Columbus *(G-7994)*
Marsh Building Products Inc ....E....... 937 222-3321
Dayton *(G-9586)*
Northwest Bldg Resources Inc ....E....... 419 286-5400
Fort Jennings *(G-10984)*
Orrville Trucking & Grading Co ....E....... 330 682-4010
Orrville *(G-15641)*
Palmer-Donavin Mfg Co ....D....... 614 277-2777
Urbancrest *(G-18451)*
Ply-Trim South Inc ....E....... 330 799-7876
Youngstown *(G-20161)*
Schneider Home Equipment Co ....E....... 513 522-1200
Cincinnati *(G-4438)*
Style Crest Inc ....B....... 419 332-7369
Fremont *(G-11099)*
Usavinyl LLC ....E....... 614 771-4805
Groveport *(G-11547)*

CONSTRUCTION MATERIALS, WHOLESALE: Building, Interior

Meyer Decorative Surfaces USA ....E....... 800 776-3900
Hudson *(G-11996)*

CONSTRUCTION MATERIALS, WHOLESALE: Ceiling Systems & Prdts

D & S Crtive Cmmunications Inc ....E....... 419 524-4312
Mansfield *(G-13164)*
Eger Products Inc ....D....... 513 753-4200
Amelia *(G-572)*

SERVICES

CONSTRUCTION MATERIALS, WHOLESALE: Cement

Boral Resources LLC ....D....... 740 622-8042
  Coshocton (G-8999)
Huron Cement Products Company ....E 419 433-4161
  Huron (G-12026)

CONSTRUCTION MATERIALS, WHOLESALE: Ceramic, Exc Refractory

Mees Distributors Inc ....E....... 513 541-2311
  Cincinnati (G-4002)

CONSTRUCTION MATERIALS, WHOLESALE: Door Frames

Huttig Building Products Inc ....E 614 492-8248
  Obetz (G-15526)
Mae Holding Company ....E 513 751-2424
  Cincinnati (G-3959)
Provia Holdings Inc ....C....... 330 852-4711
  Sugarcreek (G-17379)

CONSTRUCTION MATERIALS, WHOLESALE: Doors, Garage

Dayton Door Sales Inc ....E....... 937 253-9181
  Dayton (G-9364)
Graf and Sons Inc ....E....... 614 481-2020
  Columbus (G-7683)
North Shore Door Co Inc ....E....... 800 783-6112
  Elyria (G-10547)

CONSTRUCTION MATERIALS, WHOLESALE: Drywall Materials

Drywall Barn Inc ....E 330 750-6155
  Youngstown (G-20022)
Gms Inc ....E 937 222-4444
  Dayton (G-9463)
J & B Equipment & Supply Inc ....D 419 884-1155
  Mansfield (G-13188)
L & W Supply Corporation ....E 614 276-6391
  Columbus (G-7932)
L & W Supply Corporation ....E 513 723-1150
  Cincinnati (G-3899)
Robinson Insulation Co Inc ....E 937 323-9599
  Springfield (G-17102)

CONSTRUCTION MATERIALS, WHOLESALE: Eavestroughing, Part/Sply

Apco Industries Inc ....D....... 614 224-2345
  Columbus (G-6956)

CONSTRUCTION MATERIALS, WHOLESALE: Glass

Cleveland Glass Block Inc ....E 216 531-6363
  Cleveland (G-5256)
Cleveland Glass Block Inc ....E 614 252-5888
  Columbus (G-7225)
Harmon Inc ....E 513 645-1550
  West Chester (G-18942)
Medina Glass Block Inc ....E 330 239-0239
  Medina (G-13974)
Olde Towne Windows Inc ....E 419 626-9613
  Milan (G-14364)

CONSTRUCTION MATERIALS, WHOLESALE: Gravel

Westfall Aggregate & Mtls Inc ....D....... 740 420-9090
  Circleville (G-4852)

CONSTRUCTION MATERIALS, WHOLESALE: Hardboard

Kansas City Hardwood Corp ....E 913 621-1975
  Lakewood (G-12349)

CONSTRUCTION MATERIALS, WHOLESALE: Joists

Marysville Steel Inc ....E....... 937 642-5971
  Marysville (G-13515)

CONSTRUCTION MATERIALS, WHOLESALE: Lime Building Prdts

Mintek Resources Inc ....E 937 431-0218
  Beavercreek (G-1171)

CONSTRUCTION MATERIALS, WHOLESALE: Lime, Exc Agricultural

Mid-Ohio Valley Lime Inc ....E 740 373-1006
  Marietta (G-13360)

CONSTRUCTION MATERIALS, WHOLESALE: Limestone

Hull Builders Supply Inc ....E 440 967-3159
  Vermilion (G-18553)
Pinney Dock & Transport LLC ....E 440 964-7186
  Ashtabula (G-752)

CONSTRUCTION MATERIALS, WHOLESALE: Masons' Materials

Koltcz Concrete Block Co ....E 440 232-3630
  Bedford (G-1287)

CONSTRUCTION MATERIALS, WHOLESALE: Metal Buildings

Six C Fabrication Inc ....D....... 330 296-5594
  Ravenna (G-16267)

CONSTRUCTION MATERIALS, WHOLESALE: Millwork

Bluelinx Corporation ....E 513 874-6770
  West Chester (G-19045)
Carter-Jones Companies Inc ....C....... 330 674-0047
  Millersburg (G-14462)
Clem Lumber and Distrg Co ....D....... 330 821-2130
  Alliance (G-526)
Milliken Millwork Inc ....D....... 513 874-6771
  West Chester (G-19069)

CONSTRUCTION MATERIALS, WHOLESALE: Molding, All Materials

Toledo Molding & Die Inc ....D....... 419 692-6022
  Delphos (G-10036)

CONSTRUCTION MATERIALS, WHOLESALE: Pallets, Wood

Pallet Distributors Inc ....C....... 888 805-9670
  Lakewood (G-12359)

CONSTRUCTION MATERIALS, WHOLESALE: Particleboard

Litco International Inc ....E 330 539-5433
  Vienna (G-18581)

CONSTRUCTION MATERIALS, WHOLESALE: Prefabricated Structures

Morton Buildings Inc ....D....... 419 675-2311
  Kenton (G-12285)
Palmer-Donavin Mfg Co ....E 419 692-5000
  Delphos (G-10032)
Will-Burt Company ....B....... 330 682-7015
  Orrville (G-15649)
Will-Burt Company ....E 330 682-7015
  Orrville (G-15650)

CONSTRUCTION MATERIALS, WHOLESALE: Roof, Asphalt/Sheet Metal

Beacon Sales Acquisition Inc ....C....... 330 425-3359
  Twinsburg (G-18250)

CONSTRUCTION MATERIALS, WHOLESALE: Roofing & Siding Material

Allied Building Products Corp ....E 513 784-9090
  Cincinnati (G-2926)
Allied Building Products Corp ....E 614 488-0717
  Columbus (G-6895)
Associated Materials LLC ....E 614 985-4611
  Columbus (G-6983)

Associated Materials LLC ....B 330 929-1811
  Cuyahoga Falls (G-9070)
Associated Materials Group Inc ....E 330 929-1811
  Cuyahoga Falls (G-9071)
Associated Mtls Holdings LLC ....A 330 929-1811
  Cuyahoga Falls (G-9072)
Modern Builders Supply Inc ....E 937 222-2627
  Dayton (G-9641)
Palmer-Donavin Mfg Co ....C 800 652-1234
  Columbus (G-8416)

CONSTRUCTION MATERIALS, WHOLESALE: Sand

Acme Company ....D 330 758-2313
  Poland (G-16079)
Columbus Coal & Lime Co ....E 614 224-9241
  Columbus (G-7269)
Kenmore Construction Co Inc ....C 330 762-8936
  Akron (G-299)
Sylvester Materials Co ....C 419 841-3874
  Sylvania (G-17457)

CONSTRUCTION MATERIALS, WHOLESALE: Septic Tanks

Valicor Environmental Svcs LLC ....D 513 733-4666
  Monroe (G-14586)

CONSTRUCTION MATERIALS, WHOLESALE: Sewer Pipe, Clay

Sewer Rodding Equipment Co ....E 419 991-2065
  Lima (G-12739)

CONSTRUCTION MATERIALS, WHOLESALE: Siding, Exc Wood

Apco Industries Inc ....D 614 224-2345
  Columbus (G-6956)
Modern Builders Supply Inc ....E 216 273-3605
  Cleveland (G-6004)
Norandex Bldg Mtls Dist Inc ....A 330 656-8924
  Hudson (G-11999)
Vinyl Design Corporation ....E 419 283-4009
  Holland (G-11925)

CONSTRUCTION MATERIALS, WHOLESALE: Stone, Crushed Or Broken

Proterra Inc ....E 216 383-8449
  Wickliffe (G-19474)

CONSTRUCTION MATERIALS, WHOLESALE: Trim, Sheet Metal

Dublin Millwork Co Inc ....E 614 889-7776
  Dublin (G-10211)

CONSTRUCTION MATERIALS, WHOLESALE: Veneer

Milestone Ventures LLC ....E 317 908-2093
  Newark (G-15072)
T J Ellis Enterprises Inc ....E 419 999-5026
  Lima (G-12761)

CONSTRUCTION MATERIALS, WHOLESALE: Windows

Allied Building Products Corp ....E 513 784-9090
  Cincinnati (G-2926)
Associated Materials LLC ....B 330 929-1811
  Cuyahoga Falls (G-9070)
Associated Materials Group Inc ....E 330 929-1811
  Cuyahoga Falls (G-9071)
Associated Mtls Holdings LLC ....A 330 929-1811
  Cuyahoga Falls (G-9072)
Gunton Corporation ....C 216 831-2420
  Cleveland (G-5647)
Olde Towne Windows Inc ....E 419 626-9613
  Milan (G-14364)
Pella Corporation ....D 513 948-8480
  Cincinnati (G-4224)
Window Factory of America ....D 440 439-3050
  Bedford (G-1314)

(G-0000) Company's Geographic Section entry number

CONSTRUCTION MATLS, WHOL: Lumber, Rough, Dressed/Finished

Acord Rk Lumber Company ....E 740 289-3761
Piketon (G-15970)

Adkins Timber Products Inc ....E 740 984-2768
Beverly (G-1459)

Appalachia Wood Inc ....E 740 596-2551
Mc Arthur (G-13889)

Appalachian Hardwood Lumber Co ......E 440 232-6767
Cleveland (G-4990)

Baillie Lumber Co LP.........................E 419 462-2000
Galion (G-11168)

Brenneman Lumber Co ....E 740 397-0573
Mount Vernon (G-14750)

Carter-Jones Companies Inc ....E 330 673-6100
Kent (G-12217)

Carter-Jones Lumber Company ....C 330 673-6100
Kent (G-12218)

Carter-Jones Lumber Company ....A 330 673-6000
Kent (G-12219)

Contract Lumber Inc ....D 614 751-1109
Columbus (G-7365)

Eagle Hardwoods Inc ....E 330 339-8838
Newcomerstown (G-15130)

Gross Lumber Inc ....E 330 683-2055
Apple Creek (G-619)

Hartzell Hardwoods Inc ....D 937 773-7054
Piqua (G-16006)

J McCoy Lumber Co Ltd ....E 937 587-3423
Peebles (G-15803)

Keim Lumber Company ....E 330 893-2251
Baltic (G-935)

Khempco Bldg Sup Co Ltd Partnr........D 740 549-0465
Delaware (G-9993)

Lumberjacks Inc ....E 330 762-2401
Akron (G-323)

Mentor Lumber and Supply Co ....C 440 255-8814
Mentor (G-14082)

Nilco LLC ....E 888 248-5151
Hartville (G-11695)

Nilco LLC ....E 330 538-3386
North Jackson (G-15249)

Paxton Hardwoods LLC ....E 513 984-8200
Cincinnati (G-4216)

Premier Construction Company ....E 513 874-2611
Fairfield (G-10771)

Price Woods Products Inc ....E 513 722-1200
Loveland (G-13021)

Stephen M Trudick ....E 440 834-1891
Burton (G-2019)

Tri-State Forest Products Inc................E 937 323-6325
Springfield (G-17127)

Wappoo Wood Products Inc ....E 937 492-1166
Sidney (G-16805)

CONSTRUCTION MATLS, WHOLESALE: Soil Erosion Cntrl Fabrics

Efficient Services Ohio Inc...................E 330 627-4440
Carrollton (G-2568)

CONSTRUCTION MTRLS, WHOL: Exterior Flat Glass, Plate/Window

Anderson Glass Co Inc ....E 614 476-4877
Columbus (G-6947)

CONSTRUCTION SAND MINING

J P Sand & Gravel Company.................E 614 497-0083
Lockbourne (G-12822)

Lakeside Sand & Gravel Inc ....E 330 274-2569
Mantua (G-13271)

Mecco Inc..E 513 422-3651
Middletown (G-14307)

National Lime and Stone Co ....E 614 497-0083
Lockbourne (G-12823)

CONSTRUCTION SITE PREPARATION SVCS

Edwards Land Clearing Inc...................E 440 988-4477
Amherst (G-585)

Great Lakes Crushing Ltd ....E 440 944-5500
Wickliffe (G-19461)

Landscping Rclmtion Spcialists............E 330 339-4900
New Philadelphia (G-14970)

Miller Logging Inc ....E 330 279-4721
Holmesville (G-11932)

CONSTRUCTION: Agricultural Building

Witmers Inc ....E 330 427-2147
Salem (G-16567)

CONSTRUCTION: Airport Runway

Crp Contracting..................................D 614 338-8501
Columbus (G-7398)

Nas Ventures ....D 614 338-8501
Columbus (G-8127)

CONSTRUCTION: Apartment Building

Abco Contracting LLC ....E 419 973-4772
Toledo (G-17580)

Ahv Development LLC ....D 614 890-1440
Westerville (G-19143)

Bernard Busson Builder ....E 330 929-4926
Akron (G-95)

Community Management Corp...............D 513 761-6339
Cincinnati (G-3341)

Donald R Kenney & Company ....D 614 540-2404
Westerville (G-19159)

Etech-Systems LLC ....D 216 221-6600
Lakewood (G-12342)

Forest City Residential Dev ....E 216 621-6060
Cleveland (G-5561)

G J Goudreau & Co ....E 216 351-5233
Cleveland (G-5586)

Homewood Corporation ....C 614 898-7200
Columbus (G-7771)

K-Y Residential Coml Indus Dev ....D 330 448-4055
Brookfield (G-1852)

Lemmon & Lemmon Inc ....C 330 497-8686
North Canton (G-15218)

National Housing Corporation ....E 614 481-8106
Columbus (G-8134)

Schroeder Company ....E 419 473-3139
Toledo (G-18021)

Showe Builders Inc ....E 614 481-8106
Columbus (G-8636)

Snavely Building Company ....E 440 585-9091
Chagrin Falls (G-2654)

Towne Building Group Inc ....D 513 381-8696
Cincinnati (G-4614)

Woda Construction Inc ....E 614 396-3200
Columbus (G-8912)

CONSTRUCTION: Athletic Field

Scg Fields LLC ....E 440 546-1200
Brecksville (G-1804)

Sports Surfaces Cnstr LLC ....E 440 546-1200
Brecksville (G-1807)

CONSTRUCTION: Bridge

A P OHoro Company...........................D 330 759-9317
Youngstown (G-19944)

Aecom Energy & Cnstr Inc ....B 216 622-2300
Cleveland (G-4906)

Akil Incorporated ....E 419 625-0857
Sandusky (G-16573)

Armstrong Steel Erectors Inc ....E 740 345-4503
Newark (G-15012)

Becdir Construction Company ....E 330 547-2134
Berlin Center (G-1449)

Brumbaugh Construction Inc ....E 937 692-5107
Arcanum (G-623)

Clayton Railroad Cnstr LLC ....E 937 549-2952
West Union (G-19134)

Colas Solutions Inc............................E 513 272-5348
Cincinnati (G-3321)

Complete General Cnstr Co ....C 614 258-9515
Columbus (G-7342)

E S Wagner Company ....D 419 691-8651
Oregon (G-15592)

Eagle Bridge Co ....D 937 492-5654
Sidney (G-16775)

J & J Schlaegel Inc ....E 937 652-2045
Urbana (G-18437)

Kokosing Construction Co Inc ....C 614 228-1029
Westerville (G-19270)

MBC Holdings Inc ....E 419 445-1015
Archbold (G-632)

National Engrg & Contg Co..................A 440 238-3331
Cleveland (G-6044)

Ohio Bridge Corporation ....C 740 432-6334
Cambridge (G-2079)

Prus Construction Company ....C 513 321-7774
Cincinnati (G-4303)

Righter Co Inc ....E 614 272-9700
Columbus (G-8531)

Righter Construction Svcs Inc ....E 614 272-9700
Columbus (G-8532)

Ruhlin Company ....C 330 239-2800
Sharon Center (G-16724)

Sunesis Construction Company ....E 513 326-6000
West Chester (G-19014)

Velotta Company ....E 330 239-1211
Sharon Center (G-16727)

Westpatrick Corp ....E 614 875-8200
Columbus (G-8891)

CONSTRUCTION: Commercial & Institutional Building

A2 Services LLC.................................D 440 466-6611
Geneva (G-11236)

Adena Corporation ....C 419 529-4456
Ontario (G-15542)

Aecom Energy & Cnstr Inc..................C 419 698-6277
Oregon (G-15582)

Behal Sampson Dietz Inc ....E 614 464-1933
Columbus (G-7025)

Boak & Sons Inc.................................C 330 793-5646
Youngstown (G-19967)

Burkshire Construction Company ....E 440 885-9700
Cleveland (G-5103)

Canaan Companies Inc ....E 419 842-8373
Toledo (G-17634)

Cocca Development Ltd ....D 330 729-1010
Youngstown (G-19993)

Colaianni Construction Inc ....E 740 769-2362
Dillonvale (G-10062)

Columbus City Trnsp Div ....E 614 645-3182
Columbus (G-7267)

Combs Interior Specialties Inc ....E 937 879-2047
Fairborn (G-10665)

Corna Kokosing Construction Co ....C 614 901-8844
Westerville (G-19247)

Dynamic Structures Inc.......................E 330 892-0164
New Waterford (G-15004)

Fairfield Homes Inc ....E 614 873-3533
Plain City (G-16053)

Ferguson Construction Company ....D 937 274-1173
Dayton (G-9432)

Foti Contracting LLC ....C 330 656-3454
Wickliffe (G-19460)

G III Reitter Walls LLC ....E 614 545-4444
Columbus (G-7638)

Gilbane Building Company ....E 614 948-4000
Columbus (G-7668)

L Jack Ruscilli ....E 614 876-9484
Columbus (G-7936)

Luke Theis Enterprises Inc ....D 419 422-2040
Findlay (G-10936)

M&W Construction Entps LLC ....E 419 227-2000
Lima (G-12697)

MI - De - Con Inc ....D 740 532-2277
Ironton (G-12164)

Miller-Valentine Construction ....D 937 293-0900
Dayton (G-9637)

Mpower Inc ....E 614 783-0478
Gahanna (G-11136)

Nordmann Roofing Co Inc ....E 419 691-5737
Toledo (G-17944)

Nyman Construction Co ....E 216 475-7800
Cleveland (G-6108)

Oberer Development Co ....E 937 910-0851
Miamisburg (G-14199)

Righter Co Inc ....E 614 272-9700
Columbus (G-8531)

Righter Construction Svcs Inc ....E 614 272-9700
Columbus (G-8532)

Rudolph Libbe Inc...............................C 419 241-5000
Walbridge (G-18624)

Shelly and Sands Inc ....D 740 859-2104
Rayland (G-16273)

Shelly and Sands Inc ....E 614 444-5100
Columbus (G-8632)

Skanska USA Building Inc ....E 513 421-0082
Cincinnati (G-4492)

Tab Construction Company Inc ....E 330 454-5228
Canton (G-2506)

Tri State Corporation ....E 513 763-0215
Cincinnati (G-4631)

Universal Development MGT Inc ....E 330 759-7017
Girard (G-11303)

Whiting-Turner Contracting Co ....B 614 459-6515
Worthington (G-19861)

Whiting-Turner Contracting Co ....D 440 449-9200
Cleveland (G-6681)

CONSTRUCTION: Commercial & Office Building, New

A & A Wall Systems Inc ....E 513 489-0086
Cincinnati (G-2887)

A P & P Dev & Cnstr Co ....D 330 833-8886
Massillon (G-13658)

AA Boos & Sons Inc ....D 419 691-2329
Oregon (G-15580)

Adolph Johnson & Son Co ....E 330 544-8900
Mineral Ridge (G-14508)

Albert M Higley Co LLC ....C 216 861-2050
Cleveland (G-4926)

Alvada Const Inc ....E 419 595-4224
Alvada (G-560)

Amsdell Construction Inc ....C 216 458-0670
Cleveland (G-4974)

Armcorp Construction Inc ....E 419 778-7024
Celina (G-2583)

Austin Building and Design Inc ....E 440 544-2600
Cleveland (G-5023)

B & B Contrs & Developers Inc ....D 330 270-5020
Youngstown (G-19960)

Becker Construction Inc ....E 937 859-8308
Dayton (G-9247)

Bogner Construction Company ....D 330 262-6730
Wooster (G-19693)

Brocon Construction Inc ....E 614 871-7300
Grove City (G-11412)

Brumbaugh Construction Inc ....E 937 692-5107
Arcanum (G-623)

C Tucker Cope & Assoc Inc ....E 330 482-4472
Columbiana (G-6782)

Calvary Contracting Inc ....E 937 754-0300
Tipp City (G-17550)

Camargo Construction Company ....E 513 248-1500
Cincinnati (G-3107)

Campbell Construction Inc ....D 330 262-5186
Wooster (G-19696)

Cedarwood Construction Company ....E 330 836-9971
Akron (G-121)

Chaney Roofing Maintenance ....E 419 639-2761
Clyde (G-6741)

Cincinnati Coml Contg LLC ....E 513 561-6633
Cincinnati (G-3235)

Cm-Gc LLC ....E 513 527-4141
Cincinnati (G-3313)

Conger Construction Group Inc ....E 513 932-1206
Lebanon (G-12456)

Construction One Inc ....E 614 961-1140
Columbus (G-7353)

Continental RE Companies ....C 614 221-1800
Columbus (G-7361)

Corporate Cleaning Inc ....E 614 203-6051
Columbus (G-7371)

Crapsey & Gillis Contractors ....E 513 891-6333
Loveland (G-12985)

Crock Construction Co ....E 740 732-2306
Caldwell (G-2038)

D & G Focht Construction Co ....E 419 732-2412
Port Clinton (G-16105)

DAG Construction Co Inc ....E 513 542-8597
Cincinnati (G-3397)

Dan Marchetta Cnstr Co Inc ....E 330 668-4800
Akron (G-180)

Danis Building Construction Co ....B 937 228-1225
Miamisburg (G-14159)

Daytep Inc ....E 937 456-5860
Eaton (G-10442)

DE Huddleston Inc ....E 740 773-2130
Chillicothe (G-2776)

Deerfield Construction Co Inc ....E 513 984-4096
Loveland (G-12990)

Desalvo Construction Company ....E 330 759-8145
Hubbard (G-11944)

DKM Construction Inc ....E 740 289-3006
Piketon (G-15974)

Donleys Inc ....C 216 524-6800
Cleveland (G-5440)

Douglas Company ....E 419 865-8600
Holland (G-11883)

Dugan & Meyers Construction Co ....C 513 891-4300
Blue Ash (G-1546)

Dugan & Meyers Construction Co ....E 614 257-7430
Columbus (G-6812)

Dugan & Meyers Interests Inc ....E 513 891-4300
Blue Ash (G-1547)

Dunlop and Johnston Inc ....E 330 220-2700
Valley City (G-18461)

Elford Inc ....C 614 488-4000
Columbus (G-7511)

Enterprise Construction Inc ....E 440 349-3443
Solon (G-16845)

Equity Inc ....E 614 802-2900
Hilliard (G-11766)

Ernest Fritsch ....E 614 436-5995
Columbus (G-7530)

Exxcel Project Management LLC ....E 614 621-4500
Columbus (G-7549)

Feick Contractors Inc ....E 419 625-3241
Sandusky (G-16603)

Ferguson Construction Company ....C 937 498-2243
Sidney (G-16777)

Finneytown Contracting Corp ....E 513 482-2700
Cincinnati (G-3552)

Fiorilli Construction Co Inc ....E 216 696-5845
Medina (G-13938)

Fleming Construction Co ....E 740 494-2177
Prospect (G-16223)

Floyd P Bucher & Son Inc ....E 419 867-8792
Toledo (G-17745)

Ford Development Corp ....E 513 772-1521
Cincinnati (G-3577)

Fortney & Weygandt Inc ....E 440 716-4000
North Olmsted (G-15288)

Foti Construction Company LLP ....E 440 347-0728
Wickliffe (G-19459)

Fred Olivieri Construction Co ....E 330 494-1007
North Canton (G-15205)

G J Goudreau & Co ....E 216 351-5233
Cleveland (G-5586)

Gold Star Insulation L P ....E 614 221-3241
Columbus (G-7676)

Gowdy Partners LLC ....E 614 488-4424
Columbus (G-7682)

Grae-Con Construction Inc ....E 740 282-6830
Steubenville (G-17157)

Greater Dayton Cnstr Ltd ....D 937 426-3577
Beavercreek (G-1220)

Gutknecht Construction Company ....E 614 532-5410
Columbus (G-7705)

H A Dorsten Inc ....E 419 628-2327
Minster (G-14535)

Hal Homes Inc ....E 513 984-5360
Blue Ash (G-1574)

Hanlin-Rainaldi Construction ....E 614 436-4204
Columbus (G-7715)

Higgins Building Company Inc ....E 740 439-5553
Cambridge (G-2074)

Homan Inc ....E 419 925-4349
Maria Stein (G-13307)

Hughes & Knollman Construction ....D 614 237-6167
Columbus (G-7778)

Hummel Construction Company ....D 330 274-8584
Ravenna (G-16246)

Ideal Company Inc ....E 937 836-8683
Clayton (G-4858)

Ingle-Barr Inc ....C 740 702-6117
Chillicothe (G-2793)

Interstate Construction Inc ....E 614 539-1188
Grove City (G-11444)

Ivan Weaver Construction Co ....E 330 695-3461
Fredericksburg (G-11051)

J & F Construction and Dev Inc ....E 419 562-6662
Bucyrus (G-1995)

J D Williamson Cnstr Co Inc ....D 330 633-1258
Tallmadge (G-17478)

Jhi Group Inc ....C 419 465-4611
Monroeville (G-14589)

JJO Construction Inc ....E 440 255-1515
Mentor (G-14067)

JKL Construction Inc ....E 513 553-3333
New Richmond (G-14995)

Justice & Business Svcs LLC ....E 740 423-5005
Belpre (G-1406)

Kapp Construction Inc ....E 937 324-0134
Springfield (G-17059)

Kenny Obayashi Joint Venture V ....C 703 969-0611
Akron (G-300)

Knoch Corporation ....D 330 244-1440
Canton (G-2370)

Kokosing Construction Co Inc ....C 614 228-1029
Westerville (G-19270)

Krumroy-Cozad Cnstr Corp ....D 330 376-4136
Akron (G-305)

L Brands Store Dsgn Cnstr Inc ....C 614 415-7000
Columbus (G-7934)

Lathrop Company Inc ....E 419 893-7000
Toledo (G-17849)

Lm Constrction Trry Lvrini Inc ....E 740 695-9604
Saint Clairsville (G-16492)

Mark-L Inc ....E 614 863-8832
Gahanna (G-11134)

McDonalds Design & Build Inc ....E 419 782-4191
Defiance (G-9928)

McNerney & Son Inc ....E 419 666-0200
Toledo (G-17899)

MCR Services Inc ....E 614 421-0860
Columbus (G-8047)

Messer Construction Co ....E 513 672-5000
Cincinnati (G-4039)

Messer Construction Co ....D 614 275-0141
Columbus (G-8062)

Mid-Continent Construction Co ....E 440 439-6100
Oakwood Village (G-15491)

Midland Contracting Inc ....E 440 439-4571
Cleveland (G-5985)

Midwest Contracting Inc ....E 419 866-4560
Holland (G-11897)

Midwest Roofing & Furnace Co ....E 614 252-5241
Columbus (G-8084)

Miles-Mcclellan Cnstr Co Inc ....E 614 487-7744
Columbus (G-8086)

Miller Contracting Group Inc ....E 419 453-3825
Ottoville (G-15670)

Miller Industrial Svc Team Inc ....D 513 877-2708
Pleasant Plain (G-16075)

Monarch Construction Company ....C 513 351-6900
Cincinnati (G-4070)

Mowry Construction & Engrg Inc ....E 419 289-2262
Ashland (G-682)

Mullett Company ....E 440 564-9000
Newbury (G-15123)

Murphy Contracting Co ....E 330 743-8915
Youngstown (G-20133)

National Housing Corporation ....E 614 481-8106
Columbus (G-8134)

Ozanne Construction Co Inc ....E 216 696-2876
Cleveland (G-6153)

Pepper Cnstr Co Ohio LLC ....E 614 793-4477
Dublin (G-10307)

Peterson Construction Company ....C 419 941-2233
Wapakoneta (G-18652)

Prestige Interiors Inc ....E 330 425-1690
Twinsburg (G-18307)

Property Estate Management LLC .....C 513 684-0418
Cincinnati (G-4298)

QBS Inc ....E 330 821-8801
Alliance (G-544)

Quantum Construction Company ....E 513 351-6903
Cincinnati (G-4311)

R A Hermes Inc ....E 513 251-5200
Cincinnati (G-4329)

R L Fortney Management Inc ....C 440 716-4000
North Olmsted (G-15307)

Ray Fogg Building Methods Inc ....E 216 351-7976
Cleveland (G-6287)

Renier Construction Corp ....E 614 866-4580
Columbus (G-8514)

Retail Renovations Inc ....E 330 334-4501
Wadsworth (G-18615)

Romanelli & Hughes Building Co ....E 614 891-2042
Westerville (G-19299)

Ruhlin Company ....C 330 239-2800
Sharon Center (G-16724)

Ruscilli Construction Co Inc ....D 614 876-9484
Columbus (G-8560)

Schirmer Construction Co ....E 440 716-4900
North Olmsted (G-15309)

Schnippel Construction Inc ....E 937 693-3831
Botkins (G-1709)

Scs Construction Services Inc ....E 513 929-0260
Cincinnati (G-4441)

Season Contractors Inc ....E 440 717-0188
Broadview Heights (G-1845)

Shook Construction Co ....D 440 838-5400
Dayton (G-9763)

Simonson Construction Svcs Inc ....D 419 281-8299
Ashland (G-691)

Site Worx LLC ....D 513 229-0295
Lebanon (G-12503)

Smith Construction Group Inc ....E 937 426-0500
Beavercreek Township (G-1262)

Spieker Company ....E 419 872-7000
Perrysburg (G-15924)

Stanley Miller Construction Co ....E 330 484-2229
East Sparta (G-10424)

Studer-Obringer Inc ....E 419 492-2121
New Washington (G-15003)

Sunrush Construction Co Inc ....E 740 775-1300
Chillicothe (G-2830)

T O J Inc ....E 440 352-1900
Mentor (G-14114)

Tri-Con Incorporated ....E 513 530-9844
Blue Ash (G-1663)

Trubuilt Construction Svcs LLC ....E 614 279-4800
Columbus (G-8785)

Turner Construction Company ....E 216 522-1180
Cleveland (G-6556)

Turner Construction Company ....D 513 363-0883
Cincinnati (G-4653)

Turner Construction Company ....D 614 984-3000
Columbus (G-8788)

Turner Construction Company ....C 513 721-4224
Cincinnati (G-4652)

Tusing Builders Ltd ....E 419 465-3100
Monroeville (G-14591)

Twok General Co ....E 740 417-9195
Delaware (G-10011)

Union Industrial Contractors ....E 440 998-7871
Ashtabula (G-757)

Universal Contracting Corp ....E 513 482-2700
Cincinnati (G-4694)

Van Tassel Construction Corp ....E 419 873-0188
Perrysburg (G-15931)

Wallick Construction LLC ....E 614 863-4640
New Albany (G-14876)

Weaver Custom Homes Inc ....E 330 264-5444
Wooster (G-19781)

Welty Building Company Ltd ....D 330 867-2400
Fairlawn (G-10855)

West Roofing Systems Inc ....E 800 356-5748
Lagrange (G-12327)

Wise Services Inc ....E 937 854-0281
Dayton (G-9883)

Woodward Construction Inc ....E 513 247-9241
Blue Ash (G-1682)

CONSTRUCTION: Commercial & Office Buildings, Prefabricated

Wenco Inc ....C 937 849-6002
New Carlisle (G-14899)

CONSTRUCTION: Concrete Patio

Architctural Con Solutions Inc ....E 614 940-5399
Columbus (G-6968)

CONSTRUCTION: Condominium

Dixon Builders & Developers ....D 513 887-6400
West Chester (G-18915)

Dugan & Meyers Construction Co ....C 513 891-4300
Blue Ash (G-1546)

Dugan & Meyers Interests Inc ....E 513 891-4300
Blue Ash (G-1547)

Hills Communities Inc ....C 513 984-0300
Blue Ash (G-1579)

Superior Kraft Homes LLC ....D 740 947-7710
New Boston (G-14884)

T O J Inc ....E 440 352-1900
Mentor (G-14114)

CONSTRUCTION: Curb

Charles H Hamilton Co ....D 513 683-2442
Maineville (G-13113)

CONSTRUCTION: Dams, Waterways, Docks & Other Marine

Aecom Energy & Cnstr Inc ....B 216 622-2300
Cleveland (G-4906)

Jacobs Constructors Inc ....D 419 226-1344
Lima (G-12667)

Kokosing Industrial Inc ....B 614 212-5700
Westerville (G-19273)

Sunesis Environmental LLC ....D 513 326-6000
Fairfield (G-10788)

CONSTRUCTION: Drainage System

Ohio Irrigation Lawn Sprinkler ....E 937 432-9911
Dayton (G-9670)

CONSTRUCTION: Electric Power Line

Main Lite Electric Co Inc ....E 330 369-8333
Warren (G-18726)

CONSTRUCTION: Elevated Highway

Fryman-Kuck General Contrs Inc ....E 937 274-2892
Dayton (G-9452)

CONSTRUCTION: Fire Station

Valley View Fire Dept ....E 216 524-7200
Cleveland (G-6619)

CONSTRUCTION: Food Prdts Manufacturing or Packing Plant

Refrigeration Systems Company ....D 614 263-0913
Columbus (G-8502)

Resers Fine Foods Inc ....E 216 231-7112
Cleveland (G-6313)

CONSTRUCTION: Garage

Alpine Structures LLC ....E 330 359-5708
Dundee (G-10382)

CONSTRUCTION: Gas Main

Fishel Company ....C 937 233-2268
Dayton (G-9439)

Majaac Inc ....E 419 636-5678
Bryan (G-1962)

CONSTRUCTION: Golf Course

Buckeye Landscape Service Inc ....D 614 866-0088
Blacklick (G-1475)

M T Golf Course Managment Inc ....E 513 923-1188
Cincinnati (G-3955)

CONSTRUCTION: Grain Elevator

Agridry LLC ....E 419 459-4399
Edon (G-10470)

CONSTRUCTION: Greenhouse

Ludy Greenhouse Mfg Corp ....D 800 255-5839
New Madison (G-14937)

Rough Brothers Mfg Inc ....D 513 242-0310
Cincinnati (G-4402)

CONSTRUCTION: Guardrails, Highway

Lake Erie Construction Co ....C 419 668-3302
Norwalk (G-15441)

M P Dory Co ....D 614 444-2138
Columbus (G-8004)

Paul Peterson Company ....E 614 486-4375
Columbus (G-8427)

Pdk Construction Inc ....E 740 992-6451
Pomeroy (G-16096)

Security Fence Group Inc ....E 513 681-3700
Cincinnati (G-4444)

CONSTRUCTION: Heavy

Kokosing Construction Co Inc ....E 440 323-9346
Elyria (G-10522)

CONSTRUCTION: Heavy Highway & Street

A P OHoro Company ....D 330 759-9317
Youngstown (G-19944)

Becdir Construction Company ....E 330 547-2134
Berlin Center (G-1449)

Canton Public Works ....E 330 489-3030
Canton (G-2240)

City of Cuyahoga Falls ....E 330 971-8030
Cuyahoga Falls (G-9083)

City of Westerville ....E 614 901-6500
Westerville (G-19236)

Colas Solutions Inc ....E 513 272-5348
Cincinnati (G-3321)

Cook Paving and Cnstr Co ....E 216 267-7705
Independence (G-12062)

County of Delaware ....D 740 833-2400
Delaware (G-9963)

County of Monroe ....E 740 472-0760
Woodsfield (G-19673)

County of Portage ....D 330 296-6411
Ravenna (G-16238)

County of Shelby ....E 937 498-7244
Sidney (G-16770)

Double Z Construction Company ....D 614 274-9334
Columbus (G-7468)

Franklin Cnty Bd Commissioners ....C 614 462-3030
Columbus (G-7603)

Fred A Nemann Co ....E 513 467-9400
Cincinnati (G-3585)

Hardin County Engineer ....E 419 673-2232
Kenton (G-12278)

Northstar Asphalt Inc ....E 330 497-0936
North Canton (G-15224)

Queen City Blacktop Company ....E 513 251-8400
Cincinnati (G-4312)

R D Jergens Contractors Inc ....D 937 669-9799
Vandalia (G-18539)

Samples Chuck-General Contr ....E 419 586-1434
Celina (G-2610)

Shelly Company ....D 330 425-7861
Twinsburg (G-18320)

Smalls Asphalt Paving Inc ....E 740 427-4096
Gambier (G-11227)

Tab Construction Company Inc ....E 330 454-5228
Canton (G-2506)

Township of Copley ....D 330 666-1853
Copley (G-8978)

Tri State Corporation ....E 513 763-0215
Cincinnati (G-4631)

Trucco Construction Co Inc ....D 740 417-9010
Delaware (G-10010)

Unicustom Inc ....E 513 874-9806
Fairfield (G-10795)

W G Lockhart Construction Co ....D 330 745-6520
Akron (G-492)

CONSTRUCTION: Hospital

Messer Construction Co ....D 513 242-1541
Cincinnati (G-4040)

CONSTRUCTION: Hotel & Motel, New

Amsdell Construction Inc ....C 216 458-0670
Cleveland (G-4974)

Messer Construction Co ....D 513 242-1541
Cincinnati (G-4040)

CONSTRUCTION: Indl Building & Warehouse

Adolph Johnson & Son Co ....E 330 544-8900
Mineral Ridge (G-14508)

Akron Public Schools ....B 330 761-1660
Akron (G-52)

Al Neyer LLC ....D 513 271-6400
Cincinnati (G-2918)

Allen-Keith Construction Co ....D 330 266-2220
Canton (G-2178)

Bell Hensley Inc ....E 937 498-1718
Sidney (G-16761)

Bilfinger Westcon Inc ....E 330 818-9734
Canton (G-2212)

Boak & Sons Inc ....C 330 793-5646
Youngstown (G-19967)

Chemsteel Construction Company ....E 440 234-3930
Middleburg Heights (G-14249)

Compak Inc ....E 419 207-8888
Ashland (G-668)

Continental Building Company ....D 614 221-1800
Columbus (G-7356)

Continental RE Companies ....C 614 221-1800
Columbus (G-7361)

Corna Kokosing Construction Co ....C 614 901-8844
Westerville (G-19247)

Danis Building Construction Co ....B 937 228-1225
Miamisburg (G-14159)

Dawn Incorporated ....D 330 652-7711
Warren (G-18700)

Deerfield Construction Co Inc ....E 513 984-4096
Loveland (G-12990)

DKM Construction Inc ....E 740 289-3006
Piketon (G-15974)

Dunlop and Johnston Inc ....E 330 220-2700
Valley City (G-18461)

Dynamic Structures Inc ....E 330 892-0164
New Waterford (G-15004)

Enerfab Inc ....B 513 641-0500
Cincinnati (G-3498)

Hammond Construction Inc ....D 330 455-7039
Canton (G-2335)

Helm and Associates Inc ....E 419 893-1480
Maumee (G-13799)

SERVICES

J & F Construction and Dev Inc............E...... 419 562-6662
Bucyrus *(G-1995)*

Jack Gibson Construction Co.............D...... 330 394-5280
Warren *(G-18717)*

Kapp Construction Inc.............E...... 937 324-0134
Springfield *(G-17059)*

Kramer & Feldman Inc.............E...... 513 821-7444
Cincinnati *(G-3889)*

Lathrop Company Inc.............E...... 419 893-7000
Toledo *(G-17849)*

Lcs Inc.............E...... 419 678-8600
Saint Henry *(G-16516)*

Lepi Enterprises Inc.............D...... 740 453-2980
Zanesville *(G-20324)*

Link Construction Group Inc.............E...... 937 292-7774
Bellefontaine *(G-1354)*

Lm Constrction Trry Lvrini Inc.............E...... 740 695-9604
Saint Clairsville *(G-16492)*

Luke Theis Enterprises Inc.............D...... 419 422-2040
Findlay *(G-10936)*

M&W Construction Entps LLC.............E...... 419 227-2000
Lima *(G-12697)*

McTech Corp.............E...... 216 391-7700
Cleveland *(G-5938)*

Messer Construction Co.............D...... 937 291-1300
Dayton *(G-9609)*

Messer Construction Co.............D...... 513 242-1541
Cincinnati *(G-4040)*

Mike Coates Cnstr Co Inc.............C...... 330 652-0190
Niles *(G-15160)*

Monarch Construction Company.............C...... 513 351-6900
Cincinnati *(G-4070)*

Nyman Construction Co.............E...... 216 475-7800
Cleveland *(G-6108)*

Ors Nasco Inc.............E...... 918 781-5300
West Chester *(G-19071)*

Pawnee Maintenance Inc.............D...... 740 373-6861
Marietta *(G-13366)*

Pepper Cnstr Co Ohio LLC.............E...... 614 793-4477
Dublin *(G-10307)*

Protective Coatings Inc.............E...... 937 275-7711
Dayton *(G-9721)*

Quantum Construction Company.............E...... 513 351-6903
Cincinnati *(G-4311)*

Registered Contractors Inc.............E...... 440 205-0873
Mentor *(G-14102)*

Righter Construction Svcs Inc.............E...... 614 272-9700
Columbus *(G-8532)*

Robertson Cnstr Svcs Inc.............D...... 740 929-1000
Heath *(G-11708)*

Rudolph/Libbe Companies Inc.............D...... 419 241-5000
Walbridge *(G-18625)*

Skanska USA Building Inc.............E...... 513 421-0082
Cincinnati *(G-4492)*

Stamm Contracting Co Inc.............E...... 330 274-8230
Mantua *(G-13276)*

Star Builders Inc.............E...... 440 986-5951
Amherst *(G-599)*

Structural Building Systems.............D...... 330 656-9353
Hudson *(G-12007)*

Studer-Obringer Inc.............E...... 419 492-2121
New Washington *(G-15003)*

Technical Assurance Inc.............E...... 440 953-3147
Willoughby *(G-19575)*

Tri State Corporation.............E...... 513 763-0215
Cincinnati *(G-4631)*

Whiting-Turner Contracting Co.............D...... 440 449-9200
Cleveland *(G-6681)*

CONSTRUCTION: Indl Building, Prefabricated

Wenco Inc.............C...... 937 849-6002
New Carlisle *(G-14899)*

CONSTRUCTION: Indl Buildings, New, NEC

AA Boos & Sons Inc.............D...... 419 691-2329
Oregon *(G-15580)*

Adena Corporation.............C...... 419 529-4456
Ontario *(G-15542)*

Aecom Energy & Cnstr Inc.............B...... 216 622-2300
Cleveland *(G-4906)*

Albert M Higley Co LLC.............C...... 216 861-2050
Cleveland *(G-4926)*

Austin Building and Design Inc.............C...... 440 544-2600
Cleveland *(G-5023)*

Ayrshire Inc.............E...... 440 286-9507
Chardon *(G-2687)*

B & B Contrs & Developers Inc.............D...... 330 270-5020
Youngstown *(G-19960)*

Beem Construction Inc.............E...... 937 693-3176
Botkins *(G-1707)*

Ben D Imhoff Inc.............E...... 330 683-4498
Orrville *(G-15625)*

Burkshire Construction Company.............E...... 440 885-9700
Cleveland *(G-5103)*

Butt Construction Company Inc.............E...... 937 426-1313
Dayton *(G-9163)*

C Tucker Cope & Assoc Inc.............D...... 330 482-4472
Columbiana *(G-6782)*

Canaan Companies Inc.............E...... 419 842-8373
Toledo *(G-17634)*

Central Ohio Building Co Inc.............E...... 614 475-6392
Columbus *(G-7157)*

Chapman Industrial Cnstr Inc.............D...... 330 343-1632
Louisville *(G-12961)*

D & G Focht Construction Co.............E...... 419 732-2412
Port Clinton *(G-16105)*

DE Huddleston Inc.............E...... 740 773-2130
Chillicothe *(G-2776)*

Delventhal Company.............E...... 419 244-5570
Millbury *(G-14447)*

Desalvo Construction Company.............E...... 330 759-8145
Hubbard *(G-11944)*

Dotson Company.............E...... 419 877-5176
Whitehouse *(G-19446)*

Dugan & Meyers Construction Co.............C...... 513 891-4300
Blue Ash *(G-1546)*

Dugan & Meyers Construction Co.............E...... 614 257-7430
Columbus *(G-6812)*

Dugan & Meyers Interests Inc.............E...... 513 891-4300
Blue Ash *(G-1547)*

Elford Inc.............C...... 614 488-4000
Columbus *(G-7511)*

Equity Inc.............E...... 614 802-2900
Hilliard *(G-11766)*

Exxcel Project Management LLC.............E...... 614 621-4500
Columbus *(G-7549)*

Ferguson Construction Company.............C...... 937 498-2243
Sidney *(G-16777)*

Ferguson Construction Company.............D...... 937 274-1173
Dayton *(G-9432)*

Fleming Construction Co.............E...... 740 494-2177
Prospect *(G-16223)*

Floyd P Bucher & Son Inc.............E...... 419 867-8792
Toledo *(G-17745)*

Fortney & Weygandt Inc.............E...... 440 716-4000
North Olmsted *(G-15288)*

Geis Construction Inc.............D...... 330 528-3500
Streetsboro *(G-17253)*

H A Dorsten Inc.............E...... 419 628-2327
Minster *(G-14535)*

Head Inc.............E...... 614 338-8501
Columbus *(G-7723)*

Higgins Building Company Inc.............E...... 740 439-5553
Cambridge *(G-2074)*

Hume Supply Inc.............E...... 419 991-5751
Lima *(G-12661)*

Justice & Business Svcs LLC.............E...... 740 423-5005
Belpre *(G-1406)*

Knoch Corporation.............D...... 330 244-1440
Canton *(G-2370)*

Kokosing Construction Co Inc.............E...... 614 228-1029
Westerville *(G-19270)*

McDonalds Design & Build Inc.............E...... 419 782-4191
Defiance *(G-9928)*

McNerney & Son Inc.............E...... 419 666-0200
Toledo *(G-17899)*

Mel Lanzer Co.............E...... 419 592-2801
Napoleon *(G-14811)*

Mid-Continent Construction Co.............E...... 440 439-6100
Oakwood Village *(G-15491)*

Miles-Mcclellan Cnstr Co Inc.............E...... 614 487-7744
Columbus *(G-8086)*

Miller-Valentine Construction.............D...... 937 293-0900
Dayton *(G-9637)*

Mowry Construction & Engrg Inc.............E...... 419 289-2262
Ashland *(G-682)*

Mullett Company.............E...... 440 564-9000
Newbury *(G-15123)*

Murphy Contracting Co.............E...... 330 743-8915
Youngstown *(G-20133)*

Nicolozakes Trckg & Cnstr Inc.............E...... 740 432-5648
Cambridge *(G-2078)*

Norris Brothers Co Inc.............C...... 216 771-2233
Cleveland *(G-6074)*

Palmetto Construction Svcs LLC.............E...... 614 503-7150
Columbus *(G-8417)*

QBS Inc.............E...... 330 821-8801
Alliance *(G-544)*

R G Smith Company.............E...... 419 524-4778
Mansfield *(G-13231)*

Ray Fogg Building Methods Inc.............E...... 216 351-7976
Cleveland *(G-6287)*

Rudolph Libbe Inc.............C...... 419 241-5000
Walbridge *(G-18624)*

Ruhlin Company.............C...... 330 239-2800
Sharon Center *(G-16724)*

Ruscilli Construction Co Inc.............D...... 614 876-9484
Columbus *(G-8560)*

Schirmer Construction Co.............E...... 440 716-4900
North Olmsted *(G-15309)*

Schnippel Construction Inc.............E...... 937 693-3831
Botkins *(G-1709)*

Simmons Brothers Corporation.............E...... 330 722-1415
Medina *(G-14001)*

Spieker Company.............E...... 419 872-7000
Perrysburg *(G-15924)*

Standard Contg & Engrg Inc.............D...... 440 243-1001
Brookpark *(G-1906)*

Stanley Miller Construction Co.............E...... 330 484-2229
East Sparta *(G-10424)*

Sunrush Construction Co Inc.............E...... 740 775-1300
Chillicothe *(G-2830)*

Suresite Consulting Group LLC.............E...... 216 593-0400
Beachwood *(G-1110)*

Testa Enterprises Inc.............E...... 330 926-9060
Cuyahoga Falls *(G-9130)*

Troy Built Building LLC.............D...... 419 425-1093
Findlay *(G-10971)*

Turner Construction Company.............C...... 513 721-4224
Cincinnati *(G-4652)*

TWC Concrete Services LLC.............D...... 513 771-8192
Cincinnati *(G-4656)*

Union Industrial Contractors.............E...... 440 998-7871
Ashtabula *(G-757)*

Universal Contracting Corp.............E...... 513 482-2700
Cincinnati *(G-4694)*

Williams Bros Builders Inc.............E...... 440 365-3261
Elyria *(G-10575)*

CONSTRUCTION: Indl Plant

Babcock & Wilcox Company.............A...... 330 753-4511
Barberton *(G-944)*

Danis Companies.............B...... 937 228-1225
Miamisburg *(G-14160)*

ISI Systems Inc.............E...... 740 942-0050
Cadiz *(G-2030)*

Jack Gibson Construction Co.............D...... 330 394-5280
Warren *(G-18717)*

Pae & Associates Inc.............E...... 937 833-0013
Dayton *(G-9682)*

Tri-America Contractors Inc.............E...... 740 574-0148
Wheelersburg *(G-19441)*

Whiting-Turner Contracting Co.............D...... 440 449-9200
Cleveland *(G-6681)*

CONSTRUCTION: Institutional Building

Aecom Energy & Cnstr Inc.............B...... 216 622-2300
Cleveland *(G-4906)*

Ben D Imhoff Inc.............E...... 330 683-4498
Orrville *(G-15625)*

Butt Construction Company Inc.............E...... 937 426-1313
Dayton *(G-9163)*

Central Ohio Building Co Inc.............E...... 614 475-6392
Columbus *(G-7157)*

Head Inc.............E...... 614 338-8501
Columbus *(G-7723)*

J & R Associates.............A...... 440 250-4080
Brookpark *(G-1898)*

Mike Coates Cnstr Co Inc.............C...... 330 652-0190
Niles *(G-15160)*

CONSTRUCTION: Irrigation System

Riepenhoff Landscape Ltd.............E...... 614 876-4683
Hilliard *(G-11813)*

CONSTRUCTION: Land Preparation

Independence Excavating Inc.............E...... 216 524-1700
Independence *(G-12082)*

Jacobs Constructors Inc.............E...... 513 595-7900
Cincinnati *(G-3800)*

Petro Environmental Tech.............E...... 513 489-6789
Cincinnati *(G-4237)*

Todd Alspaugh & Associates.............E...... 419 476-8126
Toledo *(G-18071)*

CONSTRUCTION: Marine

Aquarius Marine LLC ....E 614 875-8200
Columbus *(G-6961)*

J Way Leasing Ltd ....E 440 934-1020
Avon *(G-887)*

McDermott International Inc ....C 740 687-4292
Lancaster *(G-12415)*

CONSTRUCTION: Multi-Family Housing

Al Neyer LLC ....D 513 271-6400
Cincinnati *(G-2918)*

Fairfield Homes Inc ....E 740 653-3583
Lancaster *(G-12396)*

GCI Construction LLC ....E 216 831-6100
Beachwood *(G-1061)*

Iacovetta Builders Inc ....E 614 272-6464
Columbus *(G-7797)*

Kopf Construction Corporation ....C 440 933-6908
Avon Lake *(G-921)*

Runyon & Sons Roofing Inc ....D 440 974-6810
Mentor *(G-14105)*

Schnippel Construction Inc ....E 937 693-3831
Botkins *(G-1709)*

CONSTRUCTION: Multi-family Dwellings, New

Douglas Construction Company ....E 419 865-8600
Holland *(G-11884)*

Fc 1346 LLC ....E 330 864-8170
Akron *(G-216)*

I & M J Gross Company ....E 440 237-1681
Cleveland *(G-5731)*

Interstate Construction Inc ....E 614 539-1188
Grove City *(G-11444)*

Lifestyle Communities Ltd ....D 614 918-2000
Columbus *(G-7976)*

Snavely Development Company ....E 440 585-9091
Chagrin Falls *(G-2655)*

Turner Construction Company ....C 513 721-4224
Cincinnati *(G-4652)*

CONSTRUCTION: Nonresidential Buildings, Custom

Gem Interiors Inc ....E 513 831-6535
Milford *(G-14392)*

CONSTRUCTION: Oil & Gas Line & Compressor Station

A Crano Excavating Inc ....E 330 630-1061
Akron *(G-11)*

Don Wartko Construction Co ....D 330 673-5252
Kent *(G-12229)*

Six C Fabrication Inc ....D 330 296-5594
Ravenna *(G-16267)*

CONSTRUCTION: Oil & Gas Pipeline Construction

Bluefoot Industrial LLC ....E 740 314-5299
Steubenville *(G-17141)*

J B Express Inc ....D 740 702-9830
Chillicothe *(G-2794)*

Mid-Ohio Contracting Inc ....C 330 343-2925
Dover *(G-10089)*

Mid-Ohio Pipeline Company Inc ....E 419 884-3772
Mansfield *(G-13222)*

Russell Hawk Enterprises Inc ....E 330 343-4612
Dover *(G-10097)*

Southtown Heating & Cooling ....E 937 320-9900
Moraine *(G-14699)*

Vallejo Company ....E 216 741-3933
Cleveland *(G-6616)*

CONSTRUCTION: Pharmaceutical Manufacturing Plant

Liebel-Flarsheim Company LLC ....C 513 761-2700
Cincinnati *(G-3926)*

CONSTRUCTION: Pipeline, NEC

AAA Flexible Pipe Cleaning ....E 216 341-2900
Cleveland *(G-4887)*

ABC Piping Co ....E 216 398-4000
Brooklyn Heights *(G-1863)*

Aecom Energy & Cnstr Inc ....B 216 622-2300
Cleveland *(G-4906)*

Bolt Construction Inc ....D 330 549-0349
Youngstown *(G-19970)*

Enviro-Flow Companies Ltd ....E 740 453-7980
Zanesville *(G-20306)*

H & W Contractors Inc ....D 330 833-0982
Massillon *(G-13691)*

Mannon Pipeline LLC ....E 740 643-1534
Willow Wood *(G-19595)*

Miller Pipeline LLC ....B 937 506-8837
Tipp City *(G-17562)*

Miller Pipeline LLC ....B 614 777-8377
Hilliard *(G-11799)*

Quality Lines Inc ....C 740 815-1165
Findlay *(G-10957)*

R & R Pipeline Inc ....D 740 345-3692
Newark *(G-15094)*

Teasdale Fenton Carpet Cleanin ......C 513 797-0900
Cincinnati *(G-4578)*

CONSTRUCTION: Power & Communication Transmission Tower

Broadband Express LLC ....D 419 536-9127
Toledo *(G-17626)*

Microwave Leasing Services LLC .....E 614 308-5433
Columbus *(G-8072)*

Thayer Pwr Comm Line Cnstr LLC ....D 330 922-4950
Cuyahoga Falls *(G-9131)*

Thayer Pwr Comm Line Cnstr LLC ....E 740 927-0021
Pataskala *(G-15788)*

CONSTRUCTION: Power Plant

Babcock & Wilcox Cnstr Co Inc ....D 330 860-6301
Barberton *(G-943)*

Enerfab Inc ....B 513 641-0500
Cincinnati *(G-3498)*

Siemens Energy Inc ....B 740 393-8897
Mount Vernon *(G-14790)*

CONSTRUCTION: Railroad & Subway

E S Wagner Company ....D 419 691-8651
Oregon *(G-15592)*

CONSTRUCTION: Railway Roadbed

Amtrac of Ohio Inc ....D 330 683-7206
Orrville *(G-15622)*

Delta Railroad Cnstr Inc ....D 440 992-2997
Ashtabula *(G-736)*

Fritz-Rumer-Cooke Co Inc ....E 614 444-8844
Columbus *(G-7630)*

Railworks Track Services Inc ....B 330 538-2261
North Jackson *(G-15253)*

CONSTRUCTION: Refineries

Toledo Refining Company LLC ....C 419 698-6600
Oregon *(G-15611)*

W Pol Contracting Inc ....E 330 325-7177
Ravenna *(G-16270)*

CONSTRUCTION: Religious Building

Midwest Church Cnstr Ltd ....E 419 874-0838
Perrysburg *(G-15894)*

CONSTRUCTION: Residential, Nec

Advocate Property Servic ....E 330 952-1313
Medina *(G-13906)*

Asbuilt Construction Ltd ....E 937 550-4900
Franklin *(G-11022)*

Behal Sampson Dietz Inc ....E 614 464-1933
Columbus *(G-7025)*

Central Ohio Contractors Inc ....D 740 369-7700
Delaware *(G-9958)*

Cy Schwieterman Inc ....E 419 753-2566
Wapakoneta *(G-18641)*

D C Curry Lumber Company ....E 330 264-5223
Dundee *(G-10383)*

Danis Industrial Cnstr Co ....D 937 228-1225
Miamisburg *(G-14161)*

Dr Michael J Hulit ....E 330 863-7173
Malvern *(G-13122)*

Endeavor Construction Ltd ....E 513 469-1900
Pleasant Plain *(G-16073)*

Equity Central LLC ....E 614 861-7777
Gahanna *(G-11118)*

Fairfield Homes Inc ....C 614 873-3533
Plain City *(G-16053)*

G III Reitter Walls LLC ....E 614 545-4444
Columbus *(G-7638)*

Great Lakes Contractors LLC ....E 216 631-7777
Cleveland *(G-5626)*

Greater Dayton Cnstr Ltd ....E 937 426-3577
Beavercreek *(G-1220)*

Habitat For Humanity-Midohio ....E 614 422-4828
Columbus *(G-7708)*

Installed Building Pdts Inc ....C 614 221-3399
Columbus *(G-7828)*

L R G Inc ....D 937 890-0510
Dayton *(G-9553)*

Lake Erie Home Repair ....E 419 871-0687
Norwalk *(G-15442)*

Mv Residential Cnstr Inc ....A 513 588-1000
Cincinnati *(G-4087)*

Oberer Development Co ....E 937 910-0851
Miamisburg *(G-14199)*

Oberer Residential Cnstr ....C 937 278-0851
Miamisburg *(G-14200)*

Otterbein Snior Lfstyle Chices ....B 513 933-5400
Lebanon *(G-12492)*

Pivotek LLC ....E 513 372-6205
Milford *(G-14424)*

Property Estate Management LLC ......E 513 684-0418
Cincinnati *(G-4298)*

Pulte Homes Inc ....D 330 239-1587
Medina *(G-13991)*

Rockford Homes Inc ....D 614 785-0015
Columbus *(G-6834)*

Strawser Construction Inc ....E 614 276-5501
Columbus *(G-8705)*

Topmind/Planex Construction ....E 248 719-0474
Middletown *(G-14338)*

Transcon Builders Inc ....E 440 439-3400
Cleveland *(G-6540)*

Upgrade Homes ....E 614 975-8532
Columbus *(G-8822)*

Wirtzberger Enterprises Corp ....E 440 428-1901
Madison *(G-13110)*

CONSTRUCTION: Restaurant

Restaurant Specialties Inc ....E 614 885-9707
Sunbury *(G-17394)*

CONSTRUCTION: School Building

Jack Gibson Construction Co ....D 330 394-5280
Warren *(G-18717)*

CONSTRUCTION: Sewer Line

A P OHoro Company ....D 330 759-9317
Youngstown *(G-19944)*

Adleta Inc ....E 513 554-1469
Cincinnati *(G-2908)*

Bitzel Excavating Inc ....E 330 477-9653
Canton *(G-2214)*

Cook Paving and Cnstr Co ....E 216 267-7705
Independence *(G-12062)*

Darby Creek Excavating Inc ....D 740 477-8600
Circleville *(G-4831)*

E S Wagner Company ....E 419 691-8651
Oregon *(G-15592)*

Fleming Construction Co ....E 740 494-2177
Prospect *(G-16223)*

George J Igel & Co Inc ....A 614 445-8421
Columbus *(G-7659)*

H M Miller Construction Co ....D 330 628-4811
Mogadore *(G-14549)*

Jack Conie & Sons Corp ....D 614 291-5931
Columbus *(G-7852)*

Kokosing Construction Co Inc ....C 614 228-1029
Westerville *(G-19270)*

Larry Smith Contractors Inc ....E 513 367-0218
Cleves *(G-6732)*

Maintenance Unlimited Inc ....E 440 238-1162
Strongsville *(G-17325)*

Marucci and Gaffney Excvtg Co ....E 330 743-8170
Youngstown *(G-20117)*

Mike Enyart & Sons Inc ....D 740 523-0235
South Point *(G-16943)*

Municpal Cntrs Saling Pdts Inc ....E 513 482-3300
Cincinnati *(G-4085)*

National Engrg & Contg Co ....A 440 238-3331
Cleveland *(G-6044)*

Nerone & Sons Inc ....E 216 662-2235
Cleveland *(G-6057)*

Rla Investments Inc ....E 513 554-1470
Cincinnati (G-4384)

Sunesis Environmental LLC ....D 513 326-6000
Fairfield (G-10788)

Todd Alspaugh & Associates..........E 419 476-8126
Toledo (G-18071)

Wenger Excavating Inc ....E 330 837-4767
Dalton (G-9148)

Zemba Bros Inc ....E 740 452-1880
Zanesville (G-20388)

CONSTRUCTION: Shopping Center & Mall

Arbor Construction Co ....E 216 360-8989
Cleveland (G-5000)

Eckinger Construction Company ....E 330 453-2566
Canton (G-2296)

Etech-Systems LLC ....D 216 221-6600
Lakewood (G-12342)

K-Y Residential Coml Indus Dev ....D 330 448-4055
Brookfield (G-1852)

R B Development Company Inc..........B 513 829-8100
Fairfield (G-10772)

CONSTRUCTION: Silo, Agricultural

Marietta Silos LLC..........E 740 373-2822
Marietta (G-13356)

CONSTRUCTION: Single-Family Housing

50 X 20 Holding Company Inc..........E 740 238-4262
Belmont (G-1394)

50 X 20 Holding Company Inc..........E 330 865-4663
Akron (G-10)

Alexander and Bebout Inc..........D 419 238-9567
Van Wert (G-18471)

Asplundh Construction Corp ....C 614 532-5224
Columbus (G-6980)

Bernard Busson Builder ....E 330 929-4926
Akron (G-95)

Brayman Construction Corp ....E 740 237-0000
Ironton (G-12146)

Brock & Associates Builders..........E 330 757-7150
Youngstown (G-19975)

Buckeye Cmnty Hope Foundation ....D 614 942-2014
Columbus (G-7087)

Burkhart Trucking Inc ....E 740 896-2244
Lowell (G-13037)

Cleveland Construction Inc ....E 440 255-8000
Mason (G-13563)

Columbus Drywall & Insulation ....D 614 257-0257
Columbus (G-7276)

Columbus Drywall Inc ....E 614 257-0257
Columbus (G-7277)

Combs Interior Specialties Inc ....D 937 879-2047
Fairborn (G-10665)

Cork Inc..........E 614 253-8400
Columbus (G-7370)

Cy Schwieterman Inc ....E 419 753-2566
Wapakoneta (G-18641)

Design Homes & Development Co ....E 937 438-3667
Dayton (G-9389)

Dominion Homes Inc ....D 614 356-5000
Dublin (G-10202)

Dublin Building Systems Co ....E 614 760-5831
Dublin (G-10204)

Elite Home Remodeling Inc ....E 614 785-6700
Columbus (G-7512)

Endeavor Construction Ltd ....E 513 469-1900
Pleasant Plain (G-16073)

Equity Central LLC..........E 614 861-7777
Gahanna (G-11118)

Evans Construction ....E 330 305-9355
North Canton (G-15201)

Fetters Construction Inc ....C 419 542-0944
Hicksville (G-11727)

G & G Concrete Cnstr LLC ....E 614 475-4151
Columbus (G-7637)

GCI Construction LLC ....E 216 831-6100
Beachwood (G-1061)

Goettle Co ....D 513 825-8100
Cincinnati (G-3622)

Great Lakes Companies Inc ....C 513 554-0720
Cincinnati (G-3643)

Great Traditions Homes ....E 513 759-7444
West Chester (G-18935)

Hochstedler Construction Ltd ....E 740 427-4880
Gambier (G-11224)

Homes America Inc..........E 614 848-8551
Columbus (G-7766)

Hoppes Construction LLC ....E 580 310-0090
Malvern (G-13124)

Investmerica limited ....D 216 618-3296
Chagrin Falls (G-2650)

J A A Interior & Coml Cnstr ....E 216 431-7633
Cleveland (G-5769)

Jtf Construction Inc ....D 513 860-9835
Fairfield (G-10740)

Kokosing Construction Co Inc ....E 440 323-9346
Elyria (G-10522)

Lei Cbus LLC ....E 614 302-8830
Worthington (G-19823)

M M Construction ....E 513 553-0106
Bethel (G-1453)

Manufactured Housing Entps Inc..........C 419 636-4511
Bryan (G-1963)

Miller Contracting Group Inc ....E 419 453-3825
Ottoville (G-15670)

Miracle Renovations ....E 513 371-0750
Cincinnati (G-4060)

Moyer Industries Inc ....E 937 832-7283
Clayton (G-4860)

Nasco Roofing and Cnstr Inc..........E 330 746-3566
Youngstown (G-20135)

New NV Co LLC ....E 330 896-7611
Uniontown (G-18381)

Nhs - Totco Inc ....E 419 691-2900
Toledo (G-17942)

Northern Style Cnstr LLC ....D 330 412-9594
Akron (G-352)

Nrp Contractors LLC ....E 216 475-8900
Cleveland (G-6102)

Oberer Development Co ....E 937 910-0851
Miamisburg (G-14199)

Pirhl Contractors LLC ....E 216 378-9690
Cleveland (G-6214)

RE Middleton Cnstr LLC ....E 513 398-9255
Mason (G-13632)

Registered Contractors Inc ....E 440 205-0873
Mentor (G-14102)

Rycon Construction Inc ....D 440 481-3770
Parma (G-15774)

Shoupes Constuction ....E 937 352-6457
Xenia (G-19926)

Sws Environmental Services ....E 254 629-1718
Findlay (G-10967)

Tusing Builders Ltd ....E 419 465-3100
Monroeville (G-14591)

Two-X Engners Constructers LLC ....E 330 995-0592
Aurora (G-845)

Vibo Construction Inc ....E 614 210-6780
Dublin (G-10365)

CONSTRUCTION: Single-family Housing, New

50 X 20 Holding Company Inc..........D 330 478-4500
Canton (G-2168)

A & R Builders Ltd ....E 330 893-2111
Millersburg (G-14453)

Allan Hunter Construction LLC ....E 330 634-9882
Akron (G-65)

Bob Webb Builders Inc..........E 740 548-5577
Lewis Center (G-12531)

Brady Homes Inc ....E 440 937-6255
Avon (G-867)

C V Perry & Co ....E 614 221-4131
Columbus (G-7105)

Crapsey & Gillis Contractors ....E 513 891-6333
Loveland (G-12985)

Crock Construction Co..........E 740 732-2306
Caldwell (G-2038)

Dan Marchetta Cnstr Co Inc ....E 330 668-4800
Akron (G-180)

Daugherty Construction Inc..........E 216 731-9444
Euclid (G-10628)

David W Milliken ....E 740 998-5023
Frankfort (G-11018)

Dayton Roof & Remodeling Co ....E 937 224-7667
Beavercreek (G-1146)

Dixon Builders & Developers ....D 513 887-6400
West Chester (G-18915)

Dold Homes Inc..........E 419 874-2535
Perrysburg (G-15860)

Drees Company ....E 330 899-9554
Uniontown (G-18368)

E A Zicka Co ....E 513 451-1440
Cincinnati (G-3464)

Enterprise Construction Inc ....E 440 349-3443
Solon (G-16845)

Etech-Systems LLC ....D 216 221-6600
Lakewood (G-12342)

Gold Star Insulation L P ....E 614 221-3241
Columbus (G-7676)

Greater Dayton Cnstr Ltd ....D 937 426-3577
Beavercreek (G-1220)

H&H Custom Homes LLC ....E 419 994-4070
Loudonville (G-12956)

Hersh Construction Inc ....E 330 877-1515
Hartville (G-11690)

HMS Construction & Rental Co ....D 330 628-4811
Mogadore (G-14551)

Hoge Lumber Company ....E 419 753-2263
New Knoxville (G-14917)

Ivan Weaver Construction Co ....E 330 695-3461
Fredericksburg (G-11051)

J W Enterprises Inc..........E 740 774-4500
Chillicothe (G-2796)

Joshua Investment Company Inc ....E 614 428-5555
Columbus (G-7869)

K Hovnanian Summit Homes LLC ....E 330 454-4048
Canton (G-2364)

Kf Construction and Excvtg LLC..........E 419 547-7555
Clyde (G-6747)

Kopf Construction Corporation ....C 440 933-6908
Avon Lake (G-921)

Lemmon & Lemmon Inc ....C 330 497-8686
North Canton (G-15218)

Luke Theis Enterprises Inc ....D 419 422-2040
Findlay (G-10936)

Maronda Homes Inc Florida..........D 937 472-3907
Eaton (G-10451)

Marous Brothers Cnstr Inc..........B 440 951-3904
Willoughby (G-19550)

Miller Homes of Kidron LLC ....E 330 857-0161
Kidron (G-12309)

Nvr Inc..........E 440 933-7734
Avon (G-898)

Nvr Inc ....E 440 584-4200
Kent (G-12252)

Nvr Inc ....E 440 639-0525
Painesville (G-15729)

Nvr Inc ....E 513 494-0167
South Lebanon (G-16927)

Nvr Inc ....E 440 584-4250
Brecksville (G-1794)

Oberer Residential Cnstr..........C 937 278-0851
Miamisburg (G-14200)

Park Group Co of America Inc ....E 440 238-9440
Strongsville (G-17338)

Petros Homes Inc ....E 440 546-9000
Cleveland (G-6202)

Phil Wagler Construction Inc ....E 330 899-0316
Uniontown (G-18382)

R A Hermes Inc ....E 513 251-5200
Cincinnati (G-4329)

Residence Artists Inc ....E 440 286-8822
Chardon (G-2710)

Robert Lucke Homes Inc ....E 513 683-3300
Cincinnati (G-4392)

Rockford Homes Inc ....D 614 785-0015
Columbus (G-6834)

Romanelli & Hughes Building Co ....E 614 891-2042
Westerville (G-19299)

Season Contractors Inc..........E 440 717-0188
Broadview Heights (G-1845)

Simonson Construction Svcs Inc..........D 419 281-8299
Ashland (G-691)

Snavely Building Company..........E 440 585-9091
Chagrin Falls (G-2654)

Snavely Development Company ....E 440 585-9091
Chagrin Falls (G-2655)

Society Handicapped Citz Medin ....D 330 722-1710
Medina (G-14003)

Steel Valley Construction Co ....E 330 392-8391
Warren (G-18746)

Towne Development Group Ltd ....E 513 381-8696
Cincinnati (G-4615)

Trimat Construction Inc..........E 740 388-9515
Bidwell (G-1470)

Trinity Home Builders Inc ....E 614 889-7830
Columbus (G-8783)

Weaver Custom Homes Inc..........E 330 264-5444
Wooster (G-19781)

Wh Midwest LLC ....C 330 896-7611
Uniontown (G-18390)

Woda Construction Inc ....E 614 396-3200
Columbus (G-8912)

CONSTRUCTION: Steel Buildings

Ferrous Metal Transfer ....E 216 671-8500
  Brooklyn (G-1861)
J & J General Maintenance Inc ....E 740 533-9729
  Ironton (G-12158)
Maco Construction Services..................E 330 482-4472
  Columbiana (G-6789)

CONSTRUCTION: Street Sign Installation & Mntnce

A & A Safety Inc.......................................E 513 943-6100
  Amelia (G-563)

CONSTRUCTION: Street Surfacing & Paving

Barbicas Construction Co......................E 330 733-9101
  Akron (G-86)
Barrett Paving Materials Inc..................C 513 271-6200
  Middletown (G-14343)
Camargo Construction Company.........E 513 248-1500
  Cincinnati (G-3107)
Image Pavement Maintenance..............E 937 833-9200
  Brookville (G-1914)
Lash Paving Inc ....D 740 635-4335
  Bridgeport (G-1818)
Lyndco Inc ....E 740 671-9098
  Shadyside (G-16696)
Maintenance Systerms of N Ohio ......E 440 323-1291
  Elyria (G-10532)
Moyer Industries Inc ....E 937 832-7283
  Clayton (G-4860)
Ohio Paving & Cnstr Co Inc ....E 440 975-8929
  Willoughby (G-19559)
Perrysburg Rsdntial Seal Cting ....E 419 872-7325
  Perrysburg (G-15904)
Pinnacle Paving & Sealing Inc ....E 513 474-4900
  Milford (G-14423)
Precision Paving Inc.............................E 419 499-7283
  Milan (G-14366)
Rack Seven Paving Co Inc.....................E 513 271-4863
  Cincinnati (G-4334)
Rick Eplion Paving................................E 740 446-3000
  Gallipolis (G-11214)
S & K Asphalt & Concrete ....E 330 848-6284
  Akron (G-414)
Sheedy Paving Inc ....E 614 252-2111
  Columbus (G-8631)
Shelly Company ....E 740 441-1714
  Circleville (G-4849)
Shelly Materials Inc.............................E 740 666-5841
  Ostrander (G-15655)

CONSTRUCTION: Svc Station

Duncan Oil Co ....E 937 426-5945
  Dayton (G-9171)

CONSTRUCTION: Swimming Pools

Aquarian Pools Inc ....E 513 576-9771
  Loveland (G-12978)
Buckeye Pool Inc ....E 937 434-7916
  Dayton (G-9266)
Burnett Pools Inc ....E 330 372-1725
  Cortland (G-8985)
High-Tech Pools Inc ....E 440 979-5070
  North Olmsted (G-15292)
Metropolitan Pool Service Co ....E 216 741-9451
  Parma (G-15768)
Ohio Pools & Spas Inc..........................E 330 494-7755
  Canton (G-2428)

CONSTRUCTION: Telephone & Communication Line

Fishel Company ....D 614 274-8100
  Columbus (G-7588)
Fishel Company ....D 614 850-4400
  Columbus (G-7590)
Gudenkauf Corporation ....C 614 488-1776
  Columbus (G-7704)
Kenneth G Myers Cnstr Co Inc ....D 419 639-2051
  Green Springs (G-11354)
O C I Construction Co Inc ....E 440 338-3166
  Novelty (G-15465)
Parallel Technologies Inc ....D 614 798-9700
  Dublin (G-10304)

CONSTRUCTION: Tennis Court

C & B Buck Bros Asp Maint LLC ....E 419 536-7325
  Toledo (G-17633)
Image Pavement Maintenance..............E 937 833-9200
  Brookville (G-1914)

CONSTRUCTION: Transmitting Tower, Telecommunication

Dynamic Construction Inc ....D 740 927-8898
  Pataskala (G-15785)
Sky Climber Twr Solutions LLC ....E 740 203-3900
  Delaware (G-10007)
Stg Communication Services Inc ....E 330 482-0500
  Columbiana (G-6793)
Tri County Tower Service ....E 330 538-9874
  North Jackson (G-15255)

CONSTRUCTION: Tunnel

K M & M ....C 216 651-3333
  Cleveland (G-5811)

CONSTRUCTION: Utility Line

Adams-Robinson Enterprises Inc ....C 937 274-5318
  Dayton (G-9208)
Boone Coleman Construction Inc ....E 740 858-6661
  Portsmouth (G-16126)
Charles H Hamilton Co ....D 513 683-2442
  Maineville (G-13113)
City of Dayton......................................E 937 333-3725
  Dayton (G-9304)
City of Englewood ....E 937 836-2434
  Englewood (G-10582)
County of Clermont ....E 513 732-7970
  Batavia (G-994)
County of Delaware ....E 740 833-2240
  Delaware (G-9962)
County of Union ....D 937 645-4145
  Marysville (G-13492)
Dave Sugar Excavating LLC ....E 330 542-1100
  Petersburg (G-15943)
Davey Resource Group Inc ....E 859 630-9879
  Cincinnati (G-3401)
Ford Development Corp ....D 513 772-1521
  Cincinnati (G-3577)
Fred A Nemann Co ....E 513 467-9400
  Cincinnati (G-3585)
Kokosing Industrial Inc ....B 614 212-5700
  Westerville (G-19273)
Mark Schaffer Excvtg Trckg Inc..........D 419 668-5990
  Norwalk (G-15443)
Nelson Stark Company ....C 513 489-0866
  Cincinnati (G-4106)
North Bay Construction Inc ....E 440 835-1898
  Westlake (G-19380)
Ots-NJ LLC ....D 732 833-0600
  Butler (G-2021)
Sunesis Construction Company ....C 513 326-6000
  West Chester (G-19014)
Tribute Contracting & Cons LLC ....E 740 451-1010
  South Point (G-16946)

CONSTRUCTION: Warehouse

Amsdell Construction Inc ....C 216 458-0670
  Cleveland (G-4974)
Genco of Lebanon Inc ....A 330 837-0561
  Massillon (G-13688)
Koroseal Interior Products LLC............E 855 753-5474
  Marietta (G-13343)

CONSTRUCTION: Waste Disposal Plant

Apex Environmental LLC ....D 740 543-4389
  Amsterdam (G-600)
Uranium Disposition Svcs LLC ....C 740 289-3620
  Piketon (G-15991)

CONSTRUCTION: Waste Water & Sewage Treatment Plant

A P OHoro Company ....D 330 759-9317
  Youngstown (G-19944)
Fryman-Kuck General Contrs Inc ....E 937 274-2892
  Dayton (G-9452)
Kirk Bros Co Inc ....D 419 595-4020
  Alvada (G-561)
Kokosing Construction Co Inc ....C 614 228-1029
  Westerville (G-19270)

Peterson Construction Company.........C 419 941-2233
  Wapakoneta (G-18652)
Platinum Restoration Inc......................E 440 327-0699
  Elyria (G-10556)
Shook Construction Co ....D 440 838-5400
  Dayton (G-9763)
Ulliman Schutte Cnstr LLC ....B 937 247-0375
  Miamisburg (G-14233)

CONSTRUCTION: Water & Sewer Line

Fabrizi Trucking & Pav Co Inc ....C 330 483-3291
  Cleveland (G-5504)
J & J General Maintenance Inc ....E 740 533-9729
  Ironton (G-12158)
Kirk Bros Co Inc ....D 419 595-4020
  Alvada (G-561)

CONSTRUCTION: Water Main

Brock & Sons Inc ....E 513 874-4555
  Fairfield (G-10701)
Digioia/Suburban Excvtg LLC ....C 440 237-1978
  North Royalton (G-15353)
Inliner American Inc.............................E 614 529-6440
  Hilliard (G-11778)
Miracle Plumbing & Heating Co ....E 330 477-2402
  Canton (G-2406)

CONSULTING SVC: Actuarial

Wtw Delaware Holdings LLC ....C 216 937-4000
  Cleveland (G-6693)

CONSULTING SVC: Business, NEC

Accenture LLP.......................................C 216 685-1435
  Cleveland (G-4898)
Accenture LLP.......................................C 614 629-2000
  Columbus (G-6861)
Accessrn Inc ....D 419 698-1988
  Maumee (G-13746)
Acrt Services Inc ....A 330 945-7500
  Stow (G-17188)
Actionlink LLC ....A 888 737-8757
  Akron (G-18)
American Health Group Inc...................D 419 891-1212
  Maumee (G-13750)
Apple Growth Partners Inc...................D 330 867-7350
  Akron (G-76)
Ardent Technologies Inc ....C 937 312-1345
  Dayton (G-9238)
Ashtabula Cnty Eductl Svc Ctr ....D 440 576-4085
  Ashtabula (G-709)
Attentn Web Administrtr Marjon ....D 513 708-9888
  Franklin (G-11023)
Avantia Inc ....E 216 901-9366
  Cleveland (G-5027)
B2b Power Partners ....E 614 309-6964
  Galena (G-11155)
Bbs & Associates Inc ....E 330 665-5227
  Akron (G-89)
Biorx LLC ....C 866 442-4679
  Cincinnati (G-3051)
Bkd LLP ....D 513 621-8300
  Cincinnati (G-3053)
Bright Horizons Chld Ctrs LLC.............E 614 227-0550
  Columbus (G-7066)
Calabresem Racek & Markos Inc...........E 216 696-5442
  Cleveland (G-5113)
Capital City Indus Systems LLC............E 614 519-5047
  Put In Bay (G-16224)
Cardinal Maintenance & Svc Co ....C 330 252-0282
  Akron (G-118)
Cash Flow Solutions Inc ....D 513 524-2320
  Oxford (G-15676)
Cbiz Inc ....D 330 644-2044
  Uniontown (G-18361)
Cbiz Operations Inc ....E 216 447-9000
  Cleveland (G-5140)
Cbiz Risk & Advisory Svcs LLC ....E 216 447-9000
  Cleveland (G-5141)
Cgh-Global Technologies LLC...............E 800 376-0655
  Cincinnati (G-3165)
Check It Out 4 Me LLC ....E 513 568-4269
  Cincinnati (G-3173)
Cincinnati Cnslting Consortium ....E 513 233-0011
  Cincinnati (G-3234)
Clermont County Gen Hlth Dst ....C 513 732-7499
  Batavia (G-989)
Composite Tech Amer Inc ....E 330 562-5201
  Cleveland (G-5332)

Connaissance Consulting LLC ....C 614 289-5200
  Columbus (G-7349)
Corbus LLC ....D 937 226-7724
  Dayton (G-9321)
Corporate Ladder Search ....E 330 776-4390
  Uniontown (G-18364)
Dan-Ray Construction LLC ....E 216 518-8484
  Cleveland (G-5404)
Dancor Inc ....E 614 340-2155
  Columbus (G-7414)
Datavantage Corporation ....B 440 498-4414
  Cleveland (G-5406)
Dedicated Technologies Inc ....E 614 460-3200
  Columbus (G-7427)
Deemsys Inc ....D 614 322-9928
  Gahanna (G-11117)
Deloitte & Touche LLP ....B 513 784-7100
  Cincinnati (G-3420)
Deloitte Consulting LLP ....C 937 223-8821
  Dayton (G-9387)
E Retailing Associates LLC ....D 614 300-5785
  Columbus (G-7486)
Educational Solutions Co ....D 614 989-4588
  Columbus (G-7504)
Enviroscience Inc ....C 330 688-0111
  Stow (G-17202)
Excellence In Motivation Inc ....C 763 445-3000
  Dayton (G-9420)
General Electric Company ....C 513 583-3626
  Mason (G-13584)
Gunning & Assocaites Marketing ....E 513 688-1370
  Cincinnati (G-3663)
Halley Consulting Group LLC ....E 614 899-7325
  Westerville (G-19258)
Healthquest Blanchester Inc ....E 937 783-4535
  Blanchester (G-1487)
Homeland Defense Solutions ....E 513 333-7800
  Cincinnati (G-3723)
Humantics Innovative Solutions ....E 567 265-5200
  Huron (G-12025)
Illumination Works LLC ....D 937 938-1321
  Beavercreek (G-1157)
Image Consulting Services Inc ....E 440 951-9919
  Cleveland (G-5739)
Impact Medical Mgt Group ....E 440 365-7014
  Elyria (G-10519)
Improvedge LLC ....E 614 793-1738
  Powell (G-16197)
Infoverity Inc ....E 614 310-1709
  Dublin (G-10255)
Integrated Solutions and ....E 513 826-1932
  Dayton (G-9516)
Jennings & Associates ....E 740 369-4426
  Delaware (G-9991)
Juice Technologies Inc ....E 800 518-5576
  Columbus (G-7875)
Kemper Company ....D 440 846-1100
  Strongsville (G-17319)
Kennedy Group Enterprises Inc ....E 440 879-0078
  Strongsville (G-17320)
Key Office Services ....E 419 747-9749
  Mansfield (G-13193)
Ladder Man Inc ....E 614 784-1120
  Wooster (G-19740)
Landrum & Brown Incorporated ....E 513 530-5333
  Blue Ash (G-1595)
Lateef Elmin Mhammad Inv Group ....D 937 450-3388
  Springfield (G-17060)
Legacy Consultant Pharmacy ....E 336 760-1670
  Bedford (G-1288)
Lextant Corporation ....E 614 228-9711
  Columbus (G-7969)
Mannik & Smith Group Inc ....C 419 891-2222
  Maumee (G-13812)
Nugrowth Solutions LLC ....E 800 747-9273
  Columbus (G-8215)
Occupational Health Services ....E 937 492-7296
  Sidney (G-16788)
Ohio Utilities Protection Svc ....D 800 311-3692
  North Jackson (G-15250)
Ply-Trim Enterprises Inc ....E 330 799-7876
  Youngstown (G-20160)
Qwaide Enterprises LLC ....E 614 209-0551
  New Albany (G-14868)
Resolvit Resources LLC ....E 513 619-5900
  Cincinnati (G-4362)
Resolvit Resources LLC ....D 703 564-2100
  Cincinnati (G-4363)
RJ Runge Company Inc ....E 419 740-5781
  Port Clinton (G-16116)

Romitech Inc ....E 937 297-9529
  Dayton (G-9739)
Saloma Intl Co Since 1978 ....E 440 941-1527
  Akron (G-417)
Seifert & Group Inc ....D 330 833-2700
  Massillon (G-13727)
Service Corps Retired Execs ....E 330 379-3163
  Akron (G-424)
Six Disciplines LLC ....E 419 424-6647
  Findlay (G-10959)
Smith & English II Inc ....E 513 697-9300
  Loveland (G-13029)
Software Support Group Inc ....E 216 566-0555
  Shaker Heights (G-16713)
Sordyl & Associates Inc ....E 419 866-6811
  Maumee (G-13854)
Status Solutions LLC ....E 866 846-7272
  Westerville (G-19211)
Stout Risius Ross LLC ....E 216 685-5000
  Cleveland (G-6471)
Summit Solutions Inc ....E 937 291-4333
  Dayton (G-9799)
Systems Evolution Inc ....E 513 459-1992
  Cincinnati (G-4563)
Techsolve Inc ....E 513 948-2000
  Cincinnati (G-4581)
Tipharah Group Corp ....E 937 430-6266
  Dayton (G-9814)
Tipharah Group Corp ....E 937 430-6266
  Dayton (G-9815)
Towe & Associates Inc ....E 937 275-0900
  West Milton (G-19127)
Tribute Contracting & Cons LLC ....E 740 451-1010
  South Point (G-16946)
Truechoicepack Corp ....E 937 630-3832
  Mason (G-13651)
Uc Health Llc ....E 513 475-7630
  West Chester (G-19021)
Unique Home Solutions Inc ....E 800 800-1971
  Hinckley (G-11861)
US Home Center LLC ....E 614 737-9000
  Columbus (G-8834)
Vans Express Inc ....E 216 224-5388
  Hinckley (G-11863)
Weber Obrien Ltd ....E 419 885-8338
  Sylvania (G-17463)
William Sydney Druen ....E 614 444-7655
  Columbus (G-8905)
Wtb Inc ....E 216 298-1895
  Cleveland (G-6692)
Yashco Systems Inc ....E 614 467-4600
  Hilliard (G-11831)

CONSULTING SVC: Computer

1 Edi Source Inc ....C 440 519-7800
  Solon (G-16812)
Advanced Prgrm Resources Inc ....E 614 761-9994
  Dublin (G-10119)
Advantage Technology Group ....E 513 563-3560
  West Chester (G-18860)
Affiliated Resource Group Inc ....D 614 889-6555
  Dublin (G-10121)
American Bus Solutions Inc ....D 614 888-2227
  Lewis Center (G-12522)
Attevo Inc ....D 216 928-2800
  Beachwood (G-1032)
Baseline Consulting LLC ....D 440 336-5382
  Cleveland (G-5038)
Bcg Systems That Work Inc ....E 330 864-4816
  Akron (G-90)
Cache Next Generation LLC ....D 614 850-9444
  Hilliard (G-11752)
Capgemini America Inc ....B 678 427-6642
  Dayton (G-9274)
Cbiz Operations Inc ....D 216 447-9000
  Cleveland (G-5140)
Cbts Technology Solutions LLC ....B 513 841-2287
  Cincinnati (G-3137)
Cgi Technologies Solutions Inc ....C 216 687-1480
  Cleveland (G-5163)
Cgi Technologies Solutions Inc ....D 614 228-2245
  Columbus (G-7173)
Cgi Technologies Solutions Inc ....D 614 880-2200
  Columbus (G-6805)
Cincinnati Bell Inc ....D 513 397-9900
  Cincinnati (G-3226)
Cincinnati Bell Techno ....D 513 841-6700
  Cincinnati (G-3227)
Cincom Systems Inc ....E 513 389-2344
  Cincinnati (G-3287)

Comptech Computer Tech Inc ....E 937 228-2667
  Dayton (G-9314)
CSRA LLC ....B 937 429-9774
  Beavercreek (G-1143)
Datacomm Tech ....E 614 755-5100
  Reynoldsburg (G-16296)
Datafield Inc ....C 614 847-9600
  Worthington (G-19803)
DMC Technology Group ....E 419 535-2900
  Toledo (G-17703)
E2b Teknologies Inc ....E 440 352-4700
  Chardon (G-2693)
Einstruction Corporation ....D 330 746-3015
  Youngstown (G-20027)
Enterprise Data Management Inc ....E 513 791-7272
  Blue Ash (G-1554)
Enterprise Systems Sftwr LLC ....E 419 841-3179
  Sylvania (G-17423)
Entrust Solutions LLC ....E 614 504-4900
  Columbus (G-7519)
Forsythe Technology LLC ....D 513 697-5100
  Cincinnati (G-3578)
Franklin Cmpt Svcs Group Inc ....E 614 431-3327
  New Albany (G-14854)
Genesis Corp ....E 614 934-1211
  Columbus (G-7657)
Girard Technologies Inc ....E 330 783-2495
  Youngstown (G-20050)
GP Strategies Corporation ....E 513 583-8810
  Cincinnati (G-3629)
Infovision 21 Inc ....E 614 761-8844
  Dublin (G-10256)
Integrated Solutions and ....E 513 826-1932
  Dayton (G-9516)
International Bus Mchs Corp ....B 917 406-7400
  Beavercreek (G-1158)
Itelligence Inc ....C 513 956-2000
  Cincinnati (G-3790)
Jaekle Group Inc ....E 330 405-9353
  Macedonia (G-13076)
Kristi Britton ....E 614 868-7612
  Reynoldsburg (G-16315)
Leading Edje LLC ....E 614 636-3353
  Dublin (G-10268)
Maxim Technologies Inc ....E 614 457-6325
  Hilliard (G-11789)
Mt Business Technologies Inc ....C 419 529-6100
  Mansfield (G-13225)
Natural Resources Ohio Dept ....E 614 265-6852
  Columbus (G-8163)
Navigtor MGT Prtners Ltd Lblty ....E 614 796-0090
  Columbus (G-8164)
Netsmart Technologies Inc ....E 440 942-4040
  Solon (G-16877)
Netwave Corporation ....E 614 850-6300
  Dublin (G-10289)
Oasis Systems Inc ....E 937 426-1295
  Beavercreek Township (G-1256)
Ohio State University ....C 614 292-4843
  Columbus (G-8313)
Onx USA LLC ....D 440 569-2300
  Cleveland (G-6136)
Prime Prodata Inc ....E 330 497-2578
  North Canton (G-15227)
Quanexus Inc ....E 937 885-7272
  Dayton (G-9722)
Quest Def Systems Slutions Inc ....D 860 573-5950
  Cincinnati (G-4326)
R Dorsey & Company Inc ....E 614 486-8900
  Worthington (G-19840)
R Square Inc ....E 216 328-2077
  Cleveland (G-6274)
Rainbow Data Systems Inc ....E 937 431-8000
  Beavercreek (G-1180)
Revolution Group Inc ....D 614 212-1111
  Westerville (G-19207)
Rippe & Kingston Systems Inc ....D 513 977-4578
  Cincinnati (G-4375)
Rockwell Automation Ohio Inc ....D 513 576-6151
  Milford (G-14428)
Roundtower Technologies LLC ....D 513 247-7900
  Cincinnati (G-4403)
Snapblox Hosted Solutions LLC ....E 866 524-7707
  Cincinnati (G-4498)
Sophisticated Systems Inc ....D 614 418-4600
  Columbus (G-8660)
Sudhi Infomatics Inc ....E 614 882-7309
  Westerville (G-19212)
Technology Recovery Group Ltd ....D 440 250-9970
  Westlake (G-19412)

Techsoft Systems Inc ....E 513 772-5010
Cincinnati *(G-4580)*

Teksystems Inc ....E 216 606-3600
Independence *(G-12129)*

Teksystems Inc ....E 513 719-3950
Cincinnati *(G-4583)*

Telligen Tech Inc ....E 614 934-1554
Columbus *(G-8739)*

Teradata Operations Inc ....D 937 242-4030
Miamisburg *(G-14228)*

Unicon International Inc ....C 614 861-7070
Columbus *(G-8798)*

Vital Resources Inc ....E 440 614-5150
Huron *(G-12034)*

Vitalyst ....D 216 201-9070
Cleveland *(G-6637)*

Warnock Tanner & Assoc Inc ....E 419 897-6999
Maumee *(G-13867)*

Web Yoga Inc ....E 937 428-0000
Dayton *(G-9870)*

Wolcott Group ....E 330 666-5900
Medina *(G-14015)*

XA Technologies LLC ....E 330 787-7846
Youngstown *(G-20250)*

Zin Technologies Inc ....C 440 625-2200
Middleburg Heights *(G-14267)*

CONSULTING SVC: Data Processing

American Systems Cnsulting Inc ....D 614 282-7180
Dublin *(G-10134)*

Cincinnati Training Trml Svcs ....D 513 563-4474
Cincinnati *(G-3273)*

Definitive Solutions Co Inc ....D 513 719-9100
Cincinnati *(G-3417)*

Diversified Systems Inc ....E 614 476-9939
Westerville *(G-19249)*

Illumination Works LLC ....D 937 938-1321
Beavercreek *(G-1157)*

Indecon Solutions LLC ....E 614 799-1850
Dublin *(G-10254)*

Interactive Bus Systems Inc ......E 513 984-2205
Cincinnati *(G-3775)*

Professonal Data Resources Inc ....C 513 792-5100
Blue Ash *(G-1633)*

Qbase LLC ....E 888 458-0345
Beavercreek *(G-1179)*

S & P Solutions Inc ....C 440 918-9111
Willoughby Hills *(G-19593)*

CONSULTING SVC: Educational

Barbara S Desalvo Inc ....E 513 729-2111
Cincinnati *(G-3019)*

Hobsons Inc ....C 513 891-5444
Cincinnati *(G-3714)*

CONSULTING SVC: Engineering

ACC Automation Co Inc ....E 330 928-3821
Akron *(G-15)*

Advanced Engrg Solutions Inc ....D 937 743-6990
Springboro *(G-16960)*

Aecom Global II LLC ....E 937 233-1230
Dayton *(G-9210)*

Aecom Global II LLC ....D 216 523-5600
Cleveland *(G-4910)*

Alexander & Associates Co ....C 513 731-7800
Cincinnati *(G-2920)*

Alphaport Inc ....E 216 619-2400
Cleveland *(G-4941)*

Alt & Witzig Engineering Inc ....E 513 777-9890
West Chester *(G-18865)*

Amg Inc ....E 937 260-4646
Dayton *(G-9233)*

Avid Technologies Inc ....E 330 487-0770
Twinsburg *(G-18248)*

Azimuth Corporation ....E 937 256-8571
Beavercreek Township *(G-1243)*

BBC&m Engineering Inc ....D 614 793-2226
Dublin *(G-10142)*

Bbs Professional Corporation ....E 614 888-3100
Columbus *(G-7022)*

Bertec Corporation ....E 614 543-0962
Columbus *(G-7029)*

Black & Veatch Corporation ....E 614 473-0921
Columbus *(G-7044)*

Brilligent Solutions Inc ....E 937 879-4148
Fairborn *(G-10664)*

BSI Engineering LLC ....C 513 201-3100
Cincinnati *(G-3085)*

Burgess & Niple Inc ....B 502 254-2344
Columbus *(G-7098)*

Burgess & Niple Inc ....D 440 354-9700
Painesville *(G-15696)*

Burgess & Niple Inc ....C 513 579-0042
Cincinnati *(G-3089)*

Burgess & Niple-Heapy LLC ....D 614 459-2050
Columbus *(G-7099)*

Cbc Engineers & Associates Ltd ....E 937 428-6150
Dayton *(G-9288)*

CDM Smith Inc ....D 740 897-2937
Piketon *(G-15972)*

Cec Combustion Safety LLC ....E 216 749-2992
Brookpark *(G-1893)*

Ch2m Hill Inc ....D 513 243-5070
Cincinnati *(G-3166)*

Ch2m Hill Inc ....E 614 888-3100
Columbus *(G-7176)*

Cha Consulting Inc ....C 216 443-1700
Cleveland *(G-5165)*

Chemstress Consultant Company ....C 330 535-5591
Akron *(G-126)*

Choice One Engineering Corp .....E 937 497-0200
Sidney *(G-16764)*

Circuits & Cables Inc ....E 937 415-2070
Vandalia *(G-18514)*

Clarkdietrich Engineering Serv ....D 513 870-1100
West Chester *(G-18892)*

Clear Vision Engineering LLC .....E 419 478-7151
Toledo *(G-17664)*

Cmta Inc ....C 502 326-3085
Cincinnati *(G-3314)*

County of Athens ....E 740 593-5514
Athens *(G-773)*

County of Champaign ....E 937 653-4848
Urbana *(G-18430)*

CT Consultants Inc ....E 513 791-1700
Blue Ash *(G-1543)*

Ctl Engineering Inc ....C 614 276-8123
Columbus *(G-7404)*

Curtiss-Wright Controls ....E 937 252-5601
Fairborn *(G-10667)*

DCS Corporation ....E 937 306-7180
Beavercreek Township *(G-1247)*

Dlz American Drilling Inc ....E 614 888-0040
Columbus *(G-7459)*

Dlz National Inc ....E 614 888-0040
Columbus *(G-7461)*

Dlz Ohio Inc ....C 614 888-0040
Columbus *(G-7462)*

Dlz Ohio Inc ....E 330 923-0401
Akron *(G-189)*

E & A Pedco Services Inc ....D 513 782-4920
Cincinnati *(G-3461)*

E-Technologies Group LLC ....D 513 771-7271
West Chester *(G-18917)*

Engineering Design and Testing ....D 440 239-0362
Cleveland *(G-5481)*

Engisystems Inc ....D 513 229-8860
Mason *(G-13577)*

Essig Research Inc ....E 513 942-7100
West Chester *(G-19050)*

Evans Mechwart Ham ....B 614 775-4500
New Albany *(G-14852)*

Fishbeck Thmpson Carr Hber Inc ....E 513 469-2370
Blue Ash *(G-1564)*

Forte Indus Eqp Systems Inc......E 513 398-2800
Mason *(G-13581)*

Fosdick & Hilmer Inc ....D 513 241-5640
Cincinnati *(G-3581)*

Frontier Technology Inc ....E 937 429-3302
Beavercreek Township *(G-1248)*

Gannett Fleming Inc ....E 614 794-9424
Westerville *(G-19257)*

Gbc Design Inc ....E 330 283-6870
Akron *(G-232)*

Global Risk Consultants Corp .....E 440 746-8861
Brecksville *(G-1781)*

Glowe-Smith Industrial Inc ....C 330 638-5088
Vienna *(G-18579)*

Hammontree & Associates Ltd ....E 330 499-8817
Canton *(G-2336)*

Hawa Incorporated......................E 614 451-1711
Columbus *(G-7718)*

Hntb Corporation ....E 216 522-1140
Cleveland *(G-5697)*

Horn Electric Company ....E 330 364-7784
Dover *(G-10082)*

Hull & Associates Inc ....E 614 793-8777
Dublin *(G-10247)*

Hull & Associates Inc ....E 419 385-2018
Toledo *(G-17812)*

HWH Archtcts-Ngnrs-Plnners Inc..........D 216 875-4000
Cleveland *(G-5727)*

Ibi Group Engrg Svcs USA Inc .....E 513 942-3141
Cincinnati *(G-3749)*

Ibi Group Engrg Svcs USA Inc .....D 614 818-4900
Westerville *(G-19263)*

Iet Inc ....E 419 385-1233
Toledo *(G-17816)*

Ijus LLC ....D 614 470-9882
Gahanna *(G-11126)*

Illumination Works LLC ....D 937 938-1321
Beavercreek *(G-1157)*

Innovtive Sltons Unlimited LLC ....E 740 289-3282
Piketon *(G-15978)*

J R Johnson Engineering Inc ....E 440 234-9972
Cleveland *(G-5772)*

Jacobs Engineering Group Inc .....E 513 595-7500
Cincinnati *(G-3801)*

Jacobs Engineering Group Inc .....D 513 595-7500
Cincinnati *(G-3802)*

Jetson Engineering ....E 513 965-5999
Cincinnati *(G-3813)*

Jones & Henry Engineers Ltd ......E 419 473-9611
Toledo *(G-17832)*

Kemron Environmental Svcs Inc ....D 740 373-4071
Marietta *(G-13342)*

Keuchel & Associates Inc ....D 330 945-9455
Cuyahoga Falls *(G-9108)*

Kevin Kennedy Associates Inc ....E 317 536-7000
Columbus *(G-7897)*

Kleingers Group Inc ....E 513 779-7851
West Chester *(G-18957)*

Louis Perry & Associates Inc .....C 330 334-1585
Wadsworth *(G-18605)*

M Consultants LLC ....E 614 839-4639
Westerville *(G-19277)*

M Retail Engineering Inc ....E 614 818-2323
Westerville *(G-19278)*

Macaulay-Brown Inc ....B 937 426-3421
Beavercreek *(G-1227)*

Majidzadeh Enterprises Inc ....E 614 823-4949
Columbus *(G-8011)*

Mannik & Smith Group Inc ....C 419 891-2222
Maumee *(G-13812)*

Mannik & Smith Group Inc ....E 740 942-4222
Cadiz *(G-2031)*

Maval Industries LLC ....C 330 405-1600
Twinsburg *(G-18296)*

McGill Smith Punshon Inc...........E 513 759-0004
Cincinnati *(G-3987)*

Metamateria Partners LLC ....E 614 340-1690
Columbus *(G-8063)*

Michael Baker Intl Inc ....E 614 418-1773
Columbus *(G-8068)*

Michael Benza and Assoc Inc .....E 440 526-4206
Brecksville *(G-1790)*

Middough Inc...............................B 216 367-6000
Cleveland *(G-5983)*

Modern Tech Solutions Inc ....D 937 426-9025
Beavercreek Township *(G-1254)*

Ms Consultants Inc ....C 330 744-5321
Youngstown *(G-20132)*

Ms Consultants Inc ....E 614 898-7100
Columbus *(G-8118)*

Ms Consultants Inc ....E 216 522-1926
Cleveland *(G-6021)*

Nexus Engineering Group LLC.....E 216 404-7867
Cleveland *(G-6067)*

On-Power Inc ....E 513 228-2100
Lebanon *(G-12489)*

Osborn Engineering Company .....D 216 861-2020
Cleveland *(G-6145)*

P E Systems Inc ....D 937 258-0141
Dayton *(G-9185)*

Pakteem Technical Services ....D 513 772-1515
Cincinnati *(G-4197)*

Pegasus Technical Services Inc ....E 513 793-0094
Cincinnati *(G-4223)*

Peterman Associates Inc ....E 419 722-9566
Findlay *(G-10953)*

Phoenix Group Holding Co ....C 937 704-9850
Springboro *(G-16981)*

Pioneer Solutions LLC ....E 216 383-3400
Euclid *(G-10652)*

Poggemeyer Design Group Inc ....E 419 748-7438
Mc Clure *(G-13893)*

Power Engineers Incorporated ....E 513 326-1500
Cincinnati *(G-4266)*

Power Engineers Incorporated ....E.... 234 678-9875
Akron (G-392)
Power System Engineering Inc ....E.... 740 568-9220
Marietta (G-13372)
Process Plus LLC ....C.... 513 742-7590
Cincinnati (G-4290)
Professional Service Inds Inc ....E.... 614 876-8000
Columbus (G-8470)
Professional Service Inds Inc ....D.... 216 447-1335
Cleveland (G-6239)
Quality Aero Inc ....E.... 614 436-1609
Worthington (G-19839)
Quilalea Corporation ....E.... 330 487-0777
Richfield (G-16372)
Resource International ....D.... 513 769-6998
Blue Ash (G-1646)
Resource International Inc ....C.... 614 823-4949
Columbus (G-8523)
River Consulting LLC ....D.... 614 797-2480
Columbus (G-8534)
Rovisys Company ....C.... 330 562-8600
Aurora (G-842)
S&Me Inc ....D.... 614 793-2226
Dublin (G-10326)
Safran Humn Rsrces Support Inc ....D.... 513 552-3230
Cincinnati (G-4423)
Sandusky County Engr & Hwy Gar ....E.... 419 334-9731
Fremont (G-11093)
Sawdey Solution Services Inc ....E.... 937 490-4060
Beavercreek (G-1236)
Scheeser Buckley Mayfield LLC ....E.... 330 896-4664
Uniontown (G-18385)
Schomer Glaus Pyle ....D.... 614 210-0751
Columbus (G-8604)
Schomer Glaus Pyle ....B.... 330 572-2100
Akron (G-420)
Schomer Glaus Pyle ....D.... 330 645-2131
Coventry Township (G-9042)
Schooley Caldwell Associates ....D.... 614 628-0300
Columbus (G-8607)
Sea Ltd ....D.... 614 888-4160
Columbus (G-8614)
Sebesta Inc ....E.... 216 351-7621
Parma (G-15775)
Shaffer Pomeroy Ltd ....E.... 419 756-7302
Mansfield (G-13242)
Sierra Lobo Inc ....E.... 419 332-7101
Fremont (G-11095)
Sigma Technologies Ltd ....E.... 419 874-9262
Perrysburg (G-15921)
Sponseller Group Inc ....E.... 419 861-3000
Holland (G-11915)
Stantec Consulting Svcs Inc ....E.... 216 621-2407
Cleveland (G-6455)
Stilson & Associates Inc ....E.... 614 847-0300
Columbus (G-8700)
Strand Associates Inc ....E.... 513 861-5600
Cincinnati (G-4548)
Strand Associates Inc ....E.... 614 835-0460
Groveport (G-11540)
Stress Engineering Svcs Inc ....D.... 513 336-6701
Mason (G-13641)
Sumaria Systems Inc ....D.... 937 429-6070
Beavercreek (G-1188)
Technical Consultants Inc ....E.... 513 521-2696
Cincinnati (G-4579)
Terracon Consultants Inc ....C.... 513 321-5816
Cincinnati (G-4586)
Terracon Consultants Inc ....E.... 614 863-3113
Gahanna (G-11150)
Thelen Associates Inc ....E.... 513 825-4350
Cincinnati (G-4598)
Thomas L Miller ....D.... 740 374-3041
Marietta (G-13385)
Transystems Corporation ....E.... 614 433-7800
Columbus (G-8775)
Transystems Corporation ....E.... 216 861-1780
Cleveland (G-6545)
Tri-Tech Associates Inc ....E.... 937 306-1630
Dayton (G-9821)
Ttl Associates Inc ....C.... 419 241-4556
Toledo (G-18111)
Utility Technologies Intl Corp ....E.... 614 879-7624
Groveport (G-11548)
Varo Engineers Inc ....D.... 513 729-9313
West Chester (G-19029)
Varo Engineers Inc ....E.... 740 587-2228
Granville (G-11349)
W E Quicksall and Assoc Inc ....E.... 330 339-6676
New Philadelphia (G-14988)
Wood Environment & ....E.... 513 489-6611
Blue Ash (G-1681)
Zin Technologies Inc ....C.... 440 625-2200
Middleburg Heights (G-14267)

CONSULTING SVC: Executive Placement & Search

Abacus Corporation ....B.... 614 367-7000
Reynoldsburg (G-16278)
Accountants To You LLC ....E.... 513 651-2855
Cincinnati (G-2902)
Alexander Mann Solutions Corp ....B.... 216 336-6756
Cleveland (G-4928)
American Bus Personnel Svcs ....E.... 513 770-3300
Mason (G-13539)
Chad Downing ....E.... 614 532-5127
Columbus (G-7177)
Daily Services LLC ....C.... 614 431-5100
Columbus (G-7411)
Diversity Search Group LLC ....B.... 614 352-2988
Columbus (G-7455)
Endevis LLc ....E.... 419 482-4848
Toledo (G-17715)
Experis Us Inc ....E.... 614 223-2300
Columbus (G-7547)
Fast Switch Ltd ....B.... 614 336-1122
Dublin (G-10226)
First Diversity Staffing Group ....B.... 937 323-4114
Springfield (G-17038)
Global Exec Slutions Group LLC ....E.... 330 666-3354
Akron (G-237)
Global Tchnical Recruiters Inc ....E.... 216 251-9560
Westlake (G-19344)
Global Tchnical Recruiters Inc ....D.... 440 365-1670
Westlake (G-19345)
Jacor LLC ....A.... 330 441-4182
Medina (G-13958)
Job Center LLC ....E.... 440 499-1000
Elyria (G-10521)
Kforce Inc ....E.... 216 643-8141
Independence (G-12085)
Management Recruiters Intl Inc ....E.... 614 252-6200
Columbus (G-8012)
Management Recruiters Intl Inc ....D.... 440 543-1284
Chagrin Falls (G-2672)
Marvel Consultants ....E.... 216 292-2855
Cleveland (G-5918)
National Staffing Group Ltd ....E.... 440 546-0800
Brecksville (G-1791)
Pps Holding LLC ....D.... 513 985-6400
Cincinnati (G-4267)
Psychpros Inc ....E.... 513 651-9500
Cincinnati (G-4304)
R E Richards Inc ....E.... 330 499-1001
Canton (G-2448)
Robert Half International Inc ....D.... 937 224-7376
Dayton (G-9738)
Robert Half International Inc ....D.... 330 629-9494
Youngstown (G-20188)
Robert Half International Inc ....D.... 614 221-1544
Columbus (G-8542)
Rvet Operating LLC ....E.... 513 683-5020
Loveland (G-13025)
S & H Risner Inc ....D.... 937 778-8563
Piqua (G-16027)
Tech Center Inc ....E.... 330 762-6212
Akron (G-465)
Telecmmnctons Stffing Slutions ....E.... 614 799-9300
Dublin (G-10355)
Thinkpath Engineering Svcs LLC ....E.... 937 291-8374
Miamisburg (G-14229)
Trak Staffing Services Inc ....E.... 513 333-4199
Cincinnati (G-4625)
Trustaff Management Inc ....A.... 513 272-3999
Blue Ash (G-1668)
Vector Technical Inc ....C.... 440 946-8800
Willoughby (G-19581)
Willory LLC ....E.... 330 576-5486
Bath (G-1020)

CONSULTING SVC: Financial Management

Ameriprise Financial Svcs Inc ....E.... 614 934-4057
Dublin (G-10135)
Axa Advisors LLC ....D.... 216 621-7715
Cleveland (G-5029)
B&F Capital Markets Inc ....E.... 216 472-2700
Cleveland (G-5032)
Bodine Perry LLC ....E.... 330 702-8100
Canfield (G-2131)
Boenning & Scattergood Inc ....E.... 614 336-8851
Powell (G-16186)
Budros Ruhlin & Roe Inc ....E.... 614 481-6900
Columbus (G-7094)
Chapman & Chapman Inc ....E.... 440 934-4102
Avon (G-874)
Commercial Debt Cunseling Corp ....D.... 614 848-9800
Columbus (G-7326)
Consumer Credit Counseling Ser ....E.... 800 254-4100
Cleveland (G-5341)
First Command Fincl Plg Inc ....E.... 937 429-4490
Beavercreek (G-1218)
General Fncl Tax Cnsulting LLC ....E.... 888 496-2679
Cincinnati (G-2854)
Hanson McClain Inc ....E.... 513 469-7500
Cincinnati (G-3680)
Kaiser Consulting LLC ....E.... 614 378-5361
Powell (G-16200)
Kelley Companies ....D.... 330 668-6100
Copley (G-8967)
Km2 Solutions LLC ....B.... 610 213-1408
Columbus (G-7913)
Lang Financial Group Inc ....E.... 513 699-2966
Blue Ash (G-1596)
Lincoln Fincl Advisors Corp ....D.... 614 888-6516
Columbus (G-7980)
Lpl Financial Holdings Inc ....B.... 513 772-2592
Cincinnati (G-3950)
MB Financial Inc ....D.... 937 283-2027
Wilmington (G-19634)
Mc Cloy Financial Services ....D.... 614 457-6233
Columbus (G-8042)
Merrill Lynch Pierce Fenner ....D.... 614 225-3000
Columbus (G-8061)
Merrill Lynch Pierce Fenner ....E.... 330 655-2312
Hudson (G-11995)
Neighborhood Development Svcs ....E.... 330 296-2003
Ravenna (G-16250)
Oppenheimer & Co Inc ....E.... 513 723-9200
Cincinnati (G-4176)
Pension Corporation America ....E.... 513 281-3366
Cincinnati (G-4226)
Raymond James Fincl Svcs Inc ....E.... 513 287-6777
Cincinnati (G-4340)
Real Estate Capital Fund LLC ....E.... 216 491-3990
Cleveland (G-6290)
Royalton Financial Group ....E.... 440 582-3020
Cleveland (G-6347)
Skylight Financial Group LLC ....E.... 216 621-5680
Cleveland (G-6413)
Support Fincl Resources Inc ....E.... 800 444-5465
Centerville (G-2634)
Truepoint Inc ....E.... 513 792-6648
Blue Ash (G-1667)
Upper Valley Financial Inc ....E.... 937 381-0054
Piqua (G-16035)
Weber Obrien Ltd ....E.... 419 885-8338
Sylvania (G-17463)

CONSULTING SVC: Human Resource

Acloche LLC ....E.... 888 608-0889
Columbus (G-6865)
Barrett & Associates Inc ....E.... 330 928-2323
Cuyahoga Falls (G-9073)
Devry University Inc ....C.... 614 251-6969
Columbus (G-7443)
Hr Butler LLC ....E.... 614 923-2900
Dublin (G-10246)
Institute For Human Services ....E.... 614 251-6000
Columbus (G-7830)
Kroger Refill Center ....E.... 614 333-5017
Columbus (G-7929)
Peopleworks Dev of Hr LLC ....E.... 419 636-4637
Bryan (G-1969)
Sheakley Unicomp Inc ....C.... 513 771-2277
Cincinnati (G-4467)
Sheakley-Uniservice Inc ....C.... 513 771-2277
Cincinnati (G-4468)
State of Ohio ....D.... 614 466-3455
Columbus (G-8693)
Synergy Consulting Group Inc ....E.... 330 899-9301
Uniontown (G-18387)

CONSULTING SVC: Management

Accelerant Technologies LLC ....D.... 419 236-8768
Genoa (G-11251)
Advanced Prgrm Resources Inc ....E.... 614 761-9994
Dublin (G-10119)
Armada Ltd ....D.... 614 505-7256
Powell (G-16184)

(G-0000) Company's Geographic Section entry number

AT&T Government Solutions Inc D 937 306-3030
Beavercreek *(G-1128)*

Atlas Advisors LLC E 888 282-0873
Columbus *(G-6996)*

Attevo Inc D 216 928-2800
Beachwood *(G-1032)*

Austin Building and Design Inc C 440 544-2600
Cleveland *(G-5023)*

Azimuth Corporation E 937 256-8571
Beavercreek Township *(G-1243)*

Backoffice Associates LLC D 419 660-4600
Norwalk *(G-15425)*

Baxter Hodell Donnelly Preston C 513 271-1634
Cincinnati *(G-3025)*

Benchmark Technologies Corp E 419 843-6691
Toledo *(G-17611)*

Bionetics Corporation E 757 873-0900
Heath *(G-11702)*

Burke Inc C 513 241-5663
Cincinnati *(G-3090)*

C H Dean Inc D 937 222-9531
Beavercreek *(G-1136)*

Cbiz Inc C 216 447-9000
Cleveland *(G-5139)*

Center For Health Affairs D 800 362-2628
Cleveland *(G-5152)*

Clgt Solutions LLC E 740 920-4795
Granville *(G-11338)*

Commquest Services Inc C 330 455-0374
Canton *(G-2261)*

Comprehensive Hr Solutions LLC E 513 771-2277
Cincinnati *(G-3346)*

Comprehensive Logistics Co Inc E 330 233-2627
Avon Lake *(G-914)*

Dayton Foundation Inc E 937 222-0410
Dayton *(G-9365)*

Dedicated Tech Services Inc E 614 309-0059
Dublin *(G-10197)*

Deloitte & Touche LLP D 937 223-8821
Dayton *(G-9386)*

Deloitte & Touche LLP C 216 589-1300
Cleveland *(G-5415)*

Deloitte & Touche LLP B 513 784-7100
Cincinnati *(G-3420)*

Deloitte Consulting LLP C 937 223-8821
Dayton *(G-9387)*

Delta Energy LLC E 614 761-3603
Dublin *(G-10198)*

Digital Controls Corporation D 513 746-8118
Miamisburg *(G-14166)*

Diversified Systems Inc E 614 476-9939
Westerville *(G-19249)*

Djd Express Inc D 740 676-7464
Shadyside *(G-16694)*

Duke Energy Ohio Inc C 513 421-9500
Cincinnati *(G-3453)*

Duncan Falls Assoc D 740 674-7105
Duncan Falls *(G-10381)*

Enterprise Data Management Inc E 513 791-7272
Blue Ash *(G-1554)*

Financial Design Group Inc E 419 843-4737
Toledo *(G-17736)*

Focus Solutions Inc C 513 376-8349
Cincinnati *(G-3575)*

Forest City Enterprises LP D 216 621-6060
Cleveland *(G-5558)*

Garretyson Frm Resolution Grp C 513 794-0400
Loveland *(G-12995)*

Gbq Consulting LLC D 614 221-1120
Columbus *(G-7651)*

Genesis Corp E 614 934-1211
Columbus *(G-7657)*

GP Strategies Corporation E 513 583-8810
Cincinnati *(G-3629)*

Greentree Group Inc D 937 490-5500
Dayton *(G-9477)*

H T V Industries Inc D 216 514-0060
Cleveland *(G-5652)*

Halley Consulting Group LLC E 614 899-7325
Westerville *(G-19258)*

Harris Mackessy & Brennan C 614 221-6831
Westerville *(G-19169)*

HDR Engineering Inc E 614 839-5770
Columbus *(G-7722)*

Health and Safety Sciences LLC E 513 488-1952
Fairfield Township *(G-10809)*

Henry Call Inc C 216 433-5609
Cleveland *(G-5684)*

HJ Ford Associates Inc C 937 429-9711
Beavercreek *(G-1155)*

I T E LLC D 513 576-6200
Loveland *(G-13000)*

Innovative Technologies Corp D 937 252-2145
Dayton *(G-9179)*

Integra Realty Resources - Cin B 513 561-2305
Cincinnati *(G-3769)*

Integrated Prj Resources LLC E 330 272-0998
Salem *(G-16549)*

Iron Mountain Info MGT LLC C 440 248-0999
Solon *(G-16862)*

Island Hospitality MGT LLC E 614 864-8844
Columbus *(G-7847)*

J G Martin Inc D 216 491-1584
Cleveland *(G-5771)*

Jersey Central Pwr & Light Co E 330 315-6713
Fairlawn *(G-10836)*

Jonathon R Johnson & Assoc E 216 932-6529
Cleveland *(G-5802)*

Jyg Innovations LLC E 937 630-3858
Dayton *(G-9531)*

Kingsley Gate Partners LLC D 216 400-9880
Independence *(G-12086)*

Knowledgeworks Foundation E 513 241-1422
Cincinnati *(G-3884)*

Level Seven D 216 524-9055
Independence *(G-12088)*

Managed Technology Svcs LLC D 937 247-8915
Miamisburg *(G-14186)*

Matrix Claims Management Inc D 513 351-1222
Cincinnati *(G-3980)*

McKinsey & Company Inc D 216 274-4000
Cleveland *(G-5936)*

Med-Pass Incorporated E 937 438-8884
Dayton *(G-9599)*

Medco Health Solutions Inc A 614 822-2000
Dublin *(G-10276)*

Medical Account Services Inc E 937 297-6072
Moraine *(G-14675)*

Merrill Lynch Pierce Fenner E 937 847-4000
Miamisburg *(G-14189)*

Merrill Lynch Pierce Fenner D 330 670-2400
Akron *(G-332)*

Nationwide Rtrment Sltions Inc C 614 854-8300
Dublin *(G-10287)*

Navigtor MGT Prtners Ltd Lblty E 614 796-0090
Columbus *(G-8164)*

Northwest Country Place Inc D 440 488-2700
Willoughby *(G-19556)*

Ohio Custodial Maintenance C 614 443-1232
Columbus *(G-8235)*

Ohio State University E 614 728-8100
Columbus *(G-8338)*

One10 LLC D 763 445-3000
Dayton *(G-9676)*

OR Colan Associates LLC E 440 827-6116
Cleveland *(G-6140)*

Park International Theme Svcs E 513 381-6131
Cincinnati *(G-4203)*

Pcs Cost E 216 771-1090
Cleveland *(G-6186)*

Perduco Group Inc E 937 401-0271
Beavercreek *(G-1175)*

Phoenix Cosmopolitan Group LLC E 814 746-4863
Avon *(G-901)*

Piasans Mill Inc E 419 448-0100
Tiffin *(G-17532)*

Power Management Inc E 937 222-2909
Dayton *(G-9701)*

Professnal Mint Cincinnati Inc A 513 579-1161
Cincinnati *(G-4295)*

Quick Solutions Inc C 614 825-8000
Westerville *(G-19205)*

Rahim Inc E 216 621-8977
Cleveland *(G-6283)*

Redwood Living Inc C 216 360-9441
Independence *(G-12112)*

Residential Hm Assn of Marion C 740 387-9999
Marion *(G-13455)*

Risk International Svcs Inc E 216 255-3400
Fairlawn *(G-10844)*

RMS of Ohio Inc B 440 617-6605
Westlake *(G-19401)*

Rpf Consulting LLC E 678 494-8030
Cincinnati *(G-4406)*

Ruralogic Inc D 419 630-0500
Beachwood *(G-1103)*

Sacs Cnslting Training Ctr Inc E 330 255-1101
Akron *(G-415)*

Safelite Solutions LLC A 614 210-9000
Columbus *(G-8577)*

Schrudder Prfmce Group LLC E 513 652-7675
West Chester *(G-18999)*

SEI - Cincinnati LLC D 513 459-1992
Cincinnati *(G-4447)*

Signet Management Co Ltd C 330 762-9102
Akron *(G-428)*

Silver Spruce Holding LLC E 937 259-1200
Dayton *(G-9770)*

Sodexo Inc E 330 425-0709
Twinsburg *(G-18321)*

SSS Consulting Inc E 937 259-1200
Dayton *(G-9788)*

Sun Valley Infosys LLC D 937 267-6435
Springfield *(G-17121)*

Terry J Reppa & Associates E 440 888-8533
Cleveland *(G-6516)*

Trinity Health Corporation E 419 448-3124
Tiffin *(G-17545)*

University of Dayton C 937 255-3141
Dayton *(G-9836)*

University of Dayton C 937 229-3913
Dayton *(G-9841)*

Vand Corp E 216 481-3788
Cleveland *(G-6620)*

Vediscovery LLC E 216 241-3443
Cleveland *(G-6622)*

William Thomas Group Inc D 800 582-3107
Cincinnati *(G-4797)*

Willowood Care Center C 330 225-3156
Brunswick *(G-1947)*

Worthington Public Library C 614 807-2626
Worthington *(G-19862)*

Wpmi Inc E 440 392-2171
Mentor *(G-14127)*

CONSULTING SVC: Marketing Management

2060 Digital LLC E 513 699-5012
Cincinnati *(G-2878)*

Adept Marketing Outsourced LLC E 614 452-4011
Columbus *(G-6871)*

Advanced Computer Graphics E 513 936-5060
Blue Ash *(G-1496)*

Ake Marketing E 440 232-1661
Bedford *(G-1268)*

Alonovus Corp D 330 674-2300
Millersburg *(G-14454)*

Applied Marketing Services E 440 716-9962
Westlake *(G-19317)*

Archway Marketing Services Inc C 440 572-0725
Strongsville *(G-17286)*

Babcox Media Inc D 330 670-1234
Akron *(G-85)*

Brandmuscle Inc C 216 464-4342
Cleveland *(G-5074)*

Catalina Marketing Corporation E 513 564-8200
Cincinnati *(G-3131)*

Claritas LLC E 513 739-6869
Cincinnati *(G-3300)*

Coho Creative LLC E 513 751-7500
Cincinnati *(G-3320)*

Communica Inc E 419 244-7766
Toledo *(G-17671)*

Concordia Properties LLC E 513 671-0120
Cincinnati *(G-3349)*

Contract Marketing Inc D 440 639-9100
Mentor *(G-14034)*

Corbus LLC D 937 226-7724
Dayton *(G-9321)*

Cornerstone Brands Group Inc A 513 603-1000
West Chester *(G-18899)*

Cosmic Concepts Ltd D 614 228-1104
Columbus *(G-7377)*

D L Ryan Companies LLC E 614 436-6558
Westerville *(G-19156)*

Davis 5 Star Holdings LLC E 954 470-8456
Springfield *(G-17029)*

Direct Options Inc E 513 779-4416
West Chester *(G-18913)*

Dunnhumby Inc D 513 579-3400
Cincinnati *(G-3456)*

Efficient Collaborative Retail D 440 498-0500
Solon *(G-16843)*

Epipheo Incorporated E 888 687-7620
Cincinnati *(G-3506)*

Fahlgren Inc D 614 383-1500
Columbus *(G-7553)*

Fathom Seo LLC D 614 291-8456
Columbus *(G-7565)*

Fathom Seo LLC D 216 525-0510
Cleveland *(G-5517)*

Frankes Wood Products LLC ....E 937 642-0706
Marysville (G-13497)
Gund Sports Marketing Llc ....E 216 420-2000
Cleveland (G-5646)
Hafenbrack Mktg Cmmnctions Inc ....E 937 424-8950
Dayton (G-9482)
Hmt Associates Inc ....E 216 369-0109
Broadview Heights (G-1836)
Ilead LLC ....E 440 846-2346
Strongsville (G-17315)
Innerworkings Inc ....E 513 984-9500
Cincinnati (G-3762)
Inquiry Systems Inc ....E 614 464-3800
Columbus (G-7824)
Ipsos-Asi LLC ....D 513 872-4300
Cincinnati (G-3785)
ITM Marketing Inc ....C 740 295-3575
Coshocton (G-9019)
Language Logic ....E 513 241-9112
Cincinnati (G-3910)
Madison Avenue Mktg Group Inc ....E 419 473-9000
Toledo (G-17878)
Mas International Mktg LLC ....D 614 446-2003
Columbus (G-8033)
Nsa Technologies LLC ....C 330 576-4600
Akron (G-353)
Ologie LLC ....D 614 221-1107
Columbus (G-8372)
Pat Henry Group LLC ....E 216 447-0831
Milford (G-14420)
Patientpint Hosp Solutions LLC ....C 513 936-6800
Cincinnati (G-4209)
Patientpint Ntwrk Slutions LLC ....D 513 936-6800
Cincinnati (G-4210)
Patientpoint LLC ....E 513 936-6800
Cincinnati (G-4211)
Pitmark Services Inc ....E 330 876-2217
Kinsman (G-12319)
Quotient Technology Inc ....E 513 229-8659
Mason (G-13631)
R D D Inc ....C 216 781-5858
Cleveland (G-6273)
R P Marketing Public Relations ....E 419 241-2221
Holland (G-11909)
Resource Ventures Ltd ....D 614 621-2888
Columbus (G-8524)
Revlocal Inc ....D 740 392-9246
Mount Vernon (G-14786)
SCI Direct LLC ....A 330 494-5504
North Canton (G-15232)
Smart Harbor LLC ....E 800 295-4519
Columbus (G-8653)
Sumner Solutions Inc ....E 513 531-6382
Cincinnati (G-4553)
Universal Marketing Group LLC ....D 419 720-9696
Toledo (G-18123)
Weber Partners Ltd ....E 614 222-6806
Columbus (G-8882)
Young and Associates Inc ....E 330 678-0524
Kent (G-12270)

CONSULTING SVC: New Business Start Up

Dari Pizza Enterprises II Inc ....C 419 534-3000
Maumee (G-13780)
Ingleside Investments Inc ....E 614 221-1025
Columbus (G-7818)

CONSULTING SVC: Online Technology

Blue Chip Consulting Group LLC ....E 216 503-6001
Seven Hills (G-16672)
Cadre Computer Resources Co ....E 513 762-7350
Cincinnati (G-3103)
Cardinal Solutions Group Inc ....D 513 984-6700
Cincinnati (G-3118)
Cbiz Technologies LLC ....E 216 447-9000
Independence (G-12055)
Cisco Systems Inc ....A 937 427-4264
Beavercreek (G-1140)
Comresource Inc ....E 614 221-6348
Columbus (G-7346)
Datalysys LLC ....E 614 495-0260
Dublin (G-10196)
Dayhuff Group LLC ....E 614 854-9999
Worthington (G-19804)
E-Mek Technologies LLC ....D 937 424-3163
Dayton (G-9399)
Entrypoint Consulting LLC ....D 216 674-9070
Cleveland (G-5484)
Enviro It LLC ....E 614 453-0709
Columbus (G-7520)

Estreamz Inc ....E 513 278-7836
Cincinnati (G-3516)
Everest Technologies Inc ....E 614 436-3120
Worthington (G-19808)
Fit Technologies LLC ....E 216 583-5000
Cleveland (G-5540)
Genesis Corp ....D 330 597-4100
Akron (G-234)
Great Nthrn Cnsulting Svcs Inc ....E 614 890-9999
Columbus (G-7689)
Information Control Co LLC ....B 614 523-3070
Columbus (G-7817)
Integrity Information Tech Inc ....E 937 846-1769
New Carlisle (G-14891)
International Association of ....E 330 628-3012
Canton (G-2357)
Intralot Inc ....E 440 268-2900
Strongsville (G-17316)
Itelligence Outsourcing Inc ....D 513 956-2000
Cincinnati (G-3791)
Lan Solutions Inc ....E 513 469-6500
Blue Ash (G-1594)
Lanco Global Systems Inc ....D 937 660-8090
Dayton (G-9557)
Leadership Circle LLC ....E 801 518-2980
Whitehouse (G-19450)
Lightwell Inc ....E 614 310-2700
Dublin (G-10272)
London Computer Systems Inc ....D 513 583-0840
Cincinnati (G-3942)
Main Sail LLC ....D 216 472-5100
Cleveland (G-5898)
Myca Mltmdia Trning Sltons LLC ....E 513 544-2379
Blue Ash (G-1618)
Nova Technology Solutions LLC ....E 937 426-2596
Beavercreek (G-1173)
Optimum Technology Inc ....E 614 785-1110
Columbus (G-8380)
Perceptis LLC ....C 216 458-4122
Cleveland (G-6194)
Phoenix Systems Group Inc ....E 330 726-6500
Youngstown (G-20156)
Platinum Technologies ....E 216 926-1080
Akron (G-385)
Recker Consulting LLC ....D 513 924-5500
Cincinnati (G-4345)
Regent Systems Inc ....E 937 640-8010
Dayton (G-9729)
Resolvit Resources LLC ....E 703 734-3330
Cincinnati (G-4361)
Sjn Data Center LLC ....E 513 386-7871
Cincinnati (G-4488)
Sogeti USA LLC ....E 614 847-4477
Westerville (G-19210)
Sogeti USA LLC ....D 937 433-3334
Dayton (G-9773)
Sogeti USA LLC ....C 937 291-8100
Miamisburg (G-14223)
Sogeti USA LLC ....E 216 654-2230
Cleveland (G-6419)
Sogeti USA LLC ....E 513 824-3000
Blue Ash (G-1651)
Sonit Systems LLC ....E 419 446-2151
Archbold (G-640)
Strategic Systems Inc ....C 614 717-4774
Dublin (G-10343)
United Software Group Inc ....C 614 791-3223
Dublin (G-10358)
Vertical Knowledge LLC ....E 216 920-7790
Chagrin Falls (G-2658)

CONSULTING SVC: Personnel Management

Patrick Mahoney ....E 614 292-5766
Columbus (G-8426)
Selection MGT Systems Inc ....D 513 522-8764
Cincinnati (G-4450)

CONSULTING SVC: Productivity Improvement

Productivity Qulty Systems Inc ....E 937 885-2255
Dayton (G-9717)

CONSULTING SVC: Sales Management

Tm Capture Services LLC ....D 937 728-1781
Beavercreek (G-1238)

CONSULTING SVC: Telecommunications

Acadia Solutions Inc ....E 614 505-6135
Dublin (G-10118)
American Broadband Telecom Co ....E 419 824-5800
Toledo (G-17587)
Communications III Inc ....E 614 901-7720
Westerville (G-19244)
CTS Construction Inc ....D 513 489-8290
Cincinnati (G-3385)
Massillon Cable TV Inc ....D 330 833-4134
Massillon (G-13710)
Neutral Telecom Corporation ....D 440 377-4700
North Ridgeville (G-15338)
Tangoe Us Inc ....D 614 842-9918
Columbus (G-8730)
Turnkey Network Solutions LLC ....E 614 876-9944
Columbus (G-8789)
Twism Enterprises LLC ....E 513 800-1098
Cincinnati (G-4657)
Uts Inc ....E 513 332-9000
Cincinnati (G-4746)

CONSULTING SVCS, BUSINESS: Agricultural

Feg Consulting LLC ....E 412 224-2263
Blue Ash (G-1560)

CONSULTING SVCS, BUSINESS: City Planning

City of Coshocton ....D 740 622-1763
Coshocton (G-9001)
Poggemeyer Design Group Inc ....C 419 244-8074
Bowling Green (G-1746)
Schooley Caldwell Associates ....D 614 628-0300
Columbus (G-8607)
Toledo Metro Area Cncl Gvrnmnt ....E 419 241-9155
Toledo (G-18090)

CONSULTING SVCS, BUSINESS: Communications

A M Communications Ltd ....D 419 528-3051
Galion (G-11165)
Interactive Solutions Intl LLC ....E 513 619-5100
Cincinnati (G-3776)
Mediadvertiser Company ....E 513 651-0265
Fayetteville (G-10858)
Nas Rcrtment Cmmunications LLC ....C 216 478-0300
Cleveland (G-6036)
Northeast Ohio Communic ....D 330 399-2700
Warren (G-18735)
Pro Ed Communications Inc ....E 216 595-7919
Cleveland (G-6238)

CONSULTING SVCS, BUSINESS: Economic

Miami Valley Regional Plg Comm ....E 937 223-6323
Dayton (G-9625)
Port Grter Cincinnati Dev Auth ....E 513 621-3000
Cincinnati (G-4263)
Team NEO ....E 216 363-5400
Cleveland (G-6507)

CONSULTING SVCS, BUSINESS: Employee Programs Administration

Bravo Wellness LLC ....C 216 658-9500
Cleveland (G-5075)
Compmanagement Health Systems ......D 614 766-5223
Dublin (G-10188)
Employee Benefit Management ....E 614 766-5800
Dublin (G-10217)
Incentisoft Solutions LLC ....D 877 562-4461
Cleveland (G-5741)
Klais and Company Inc ....E 330 867-8443
Fairlawn (G-10839)
Nationwide Rtrment Sltions Inc ....C 614 854-8300
Dublin (G-10287)
Sequent Inc ....D 614 436-5880
Columbus (G-6836)
Simplifi Eso LLC ....C 614 635-8679
Columbus (G-8644)

CONSULTING SVCS, BUSINESS: Energy Conservation

Eco Engineering Inc ....D 513 985-8300
Cincinnati (G-3483)

Hoskins International LLC ....E 419 628-6015
Minster (G-14536)
Nationwide Energy Partners LLC ......E 614 918-2031
Columbus (G-8153)
Northern Indus Enrgy Dev Inc ....D 330 498-9130
Canton (G-2422)

CONSULTING SVCS, BUSINESS: Environmental

Acrt Inc ....E 800 622-2562
Stow (G-17187)
Aecom ....D 513 651-3440
Cincinnati (G-2914)
Air Compliance Testing Inc ....E 216 525-0900
Cleveland (G-4916)
Allied Environmental Svcs Inc ....E 419 227-4004
Lima (G-12599)
Als Group Usa Corp ....E 513 733-5336
Blue Ash (G-1503)
American Envmtl Group Ltd ....B 330 659-5930
Richfield (G-16344)
Arcadis US Inc ....D 419 473-1121
Toledo (G-17598)
Bjaam Environmental Inc ....E 330 854-5300
Canal Fulton (G-2093)
Bureau Veritas North Amer Inc ....E 330 252-5100
Akron (G-115)
CDM SMITH INC ....E 614 847-8340
Columbus (G-7147)
Clinton-Carvell Inc ....E 614 351-8858
Columbus (G-7229)
Coact Associates Ltd ....E 866 646-4400
Toledo (G-17666)
Ecs Holdco Inc ....E 614 433-0170
Worthington (G-19805)
Emergency Response & Trnng ....E 440 349-2700
Solon (G-16844)
Envirnmental Resources MGT Inc ......E 216 593-5200
Beachwood (G-1055)
Envirnmental Resources MGT Inc ......E 513 830-9030
Blue Ash (G-1556)
Environmental Quality MGT ....D 513 825-7500
Cincinnati (G-3502)
Environmental Solutions ....E 513 451-1777
Cincinnati (G-3503)
Enviroserve Inc ....C 330 966-0910
North Canton (G-15200)
Floyd Browne Group Inc ....E 740 363-6792
Delaware (G-9977)
Grace Consulting Inc ....E 440 647-6672
Wellington (G-18841)
Heritage Envmtl Svcs LLC ....E 419 729-1321
Toledo (G-17802)
Hull & Associates Inc ....E 614 793-8777
Dublin (G-10247)
Hzw Environmental Cons LLC ....E 800 804-8484
Mentor (G-14062)
Icon Environmental Group LLC ....E 513 426-6767
Milford (G-14396)
Interdyne Corporation ....E 419 229-8192
Lima (G-12666)
Kemron Environmental Svcs Inc ....D 740 373-4071
Marietta (G-13342)
Lawhon and Associates Inc ....E 614 481-8600
Columbus (G-7958)
On Site Instruments LLC ....E 614 846-1900
Lewis Center (G-12555)
Orin Group LLC ....E 330 630-3937
Akron (G-369)
Pinnacle Environmental Cons ....E 513 533-1823
Cincinnati (G-4250)
Safety-Kleen Systems Inc ....E 513 563-0931
Fairfield (G-10777)
Tetra Tech Inc ....E 513 251-2730
Cincinnati (G-4588)
Ttl Associates Inc ....C 419 241-4556
Toledo (G-18111)
Vahalla Company Inc ....E 216 326-2245
Cleveland (G-6615)

CONSULTING SVCS, BUSINESS: Indl Development Planning

Big Red Rooster ....E 614 255-0200
Columbus (G-7036)

CONSULTING SVCS, BUSINESS: Lighting

Jones Group Interiors Inc ....E 330 253-9180
Akron (G-294)

Warstler Brothers Landscaping ....E 330 492-9500
Canton (G-2531)

CONSULTING SVCS, BUSINESS: Safety Training Svcs

ABC Fire Inc ....E 440 237-6677
North Royalton (G-15346)
Alice Training Institute LLC ....D 330 661-0106
Medina (G-13908)
Kirila Fire Trning Fclties Inc ....E 724 854-5207
Brookfield (G-1854)
Mission Essntial Personnel LLC ....C 614 416-2345
New Albany (G-14859)

CONSULTING SVCS, BUSINESS: Sys Engnrg, Exc Computer/Prof

Aecom Global II LLC ....D 419 774-9862
Delta (G-10040)
Centric Consulting LLC ....E 888 781-7567
Dayton (G-9290)
Cohesion Consulting LLC ....D 513 587-7700
Blue Ash (G-1533)
Construction Resources Inc ....E 440 248-9800
Cleveland (G-5339)
Controlsoft Inc ....E 440 443-3900
Cleveland (G-5346)
Devcare Solutions Ltd ....E 614 221-2277
Columbus (G-7439)
Ellipse Solutions LLC ....E 937 312-1547
Dayton (G-9413)
Flexential Corp ....D 513 645-2900
Hamilton (G-11595)
Gleaming Systems LLC ....E 614 348-7475
Lewis Center (G-12543)
Indecon Solutions LLC ....E 614 799-1850
Dublin (G-10254)
Jyg Innovations LLC ....E 937 630-3858
Dayton (G-9531)
Primatech Inc ....E 614 841-9800
Columbus (G-8462)
Sadler-Necamp Financial Svcs ....E 513 489-5477
Cincinnati (G-4421)
Sawdey Solution Services Inc ....E 937 490-4060
Beavercreek (G-1236)
Shotstop Ballistics LLC ....E 330 686-0020
Stow (G-17230)
Sjn Data Center LLC ....E 513 386-7871
Cincinnati (G-4488)

CONSULTING SVCS, BUSINESS: Systems Analysis & Engineering

Industrial Vibrations Cons ....D 513 932-4678
Lebanon (G-12472)
Interactive Engineering Corp ....E 330 239-6888
Medina (G-13956)
Lumenance LLC ....E 319 541-6811
Columbus (G-7997)
Oracle Systems Corporation ....D 216 328-9100
Beachwood (G-1093)

CONSULTING SVCS, BUSINESS: Test Development & Evaluation

Benchmark Technologies Corp ....E 419 843-6691
Toledo (G-17611)
Root Inc ....D 419 874-0077
Sylvania (G-17448)

CONSULTING SVCS, BUSINESS: Testing, Educational Or Personnel

Clgt Solutions LLC ....E 740 920-4795
Granville (G-11338)
Envision Corporation ....D 513 772-5437
Cincinnati (G-3504)

CONSULTING SVCS, BUSINESS: Traffic

Celebrity Security Inc ....E 216 671-6425
Cleveland (G-5146)
City of Akron ....E 330 375-2851
Akron (G-138)
Its Traffic Systems Inc ....D 440 892-4500
Westlake (G-19359)

CONSULTING SVCS, BUSINESS: Urban Planning & Consulting

Buckeye Hills-Hck Vly Reg Dev ....D 740 373-0087
Marietta (G-13317)
Emersion Design LLC ....E 513 841-9100
Cincinnati (G-3494)
Flavik Village Development ....E 216 429-1182
Cleveland (G-5544)
Lorain Cnty Elderly Hsing Corp ....D 440 288-1600
Lorain (G-12915)
Northeast Ohio Areawide ....E 216 621-3055
Cleveland (G-6091)
Ohio Housing Finance Agency ....B 614 466-7970
Columbus (G-8268)
Star County Home Consortium ....E 330 451-7395
Canton (G-2486)
Trumbull Housing Dev Corp ....E 330 369-1533
Warren (G-18757)

CONSULTING SVCS: Nuclear

Accelerant Technologies LLC ....D 419 236-8768
Genoa (G-11251)

CONSULTING SVCS: Physics

Central Ohio Primary Care ....E 614 882-0708
Westerville (G-19235)

CONSULTING SVCS: Psychological

Coleman Professional Svcs Inc ....C 330 673-1347
Kent (G-12223)
Psychology Consultants Inc ....E 330 764-7916
Medina (G-13990)

CONSULTING SVCS: Scientific

Centric Consulting LLC ....E 513 791-3061
Cincinnati (G-3160)
Civil & Environmental Cons Inc ....E 419 724-5281
Toledo (G-17661)
National Valuation Consultants ....E 513 929-4100
Cincinnati (G-4096)

CONSUMER BUYING SVCS

Best Upon Request Corp Inc ....D 513 605-7800
Cincinnati (G-3044)

CONSUMER CREDIT REPORTING BUREAU

Cbc Companies Inc ....D 614 538-6100
Columbus (G-7142)
Cbcinnovis International Inc ....E 614 222-4343
Columbus (G-7143)
Innovis Data Solutions Inc ....E 614 222-4343
Columbus (G-7823)

CONSUMER PURCHASING SVCS

Administrative Svcs Ohio Dept ....D 614 466-5090
Columbus (G-6872)

CONTAINERS: Cargo, Wood

Frankes Wood Products LLC ....E 937 642-0706
Marysville (G-13497)

CONTAINERS: Corrugated

Buckeye Boxes Inc ....E 614 274-8484
Columbus (G-7085)
JIT Packaging Inc ....E 330 562-8080
Aurora (G-831)
Systems Pack Inc ....E 330 467-5729
Macedonia (G-13083)

CONTAINERS: Metal

Sabco Industries Inc ....E 419 531-5347
Toledo (G-18016)
Westrock Cp LLC ....D 770 448-2193
Wshngtn CT Hs (G-19886)

CONTAINERS: Plastic

Hendrickson International Corp ....D 740 929-5600
Hebron (G-11714)
Ilpea Industries Inc ....C 330 562-2916
Aurora (G-830)
Plastics R Unique Inc ....E 330 334-4820
Wadsworth (G-18613)

SERVICES

CONTAINERS: Shipping, Bombs, Metal Plate

Industrial Repair & Mfg Inc ....D....... 419 822-4232
  Delta (G-10045)

CONTAINERS: Shipping, Wood

Frankes Wood Products LLC...............E....... 937 642-0706
  Marysville (G-13497)

CONTAINMENT VESSELS: Reactor, Metal Plate

FSRc Tanks Inc ....E....... 234 221-2015
  Bolivar (G-1703)

CONTRACTOR: Dredging

Metropolitan Envmtl Svcs Inc ....D....... 614 771-1881
  Hilliard (G-11793)

CONTRACTOR: Framing

Castle Construction Co Inc ....E....... 419 289-1122
  Ashland (G-662)
Contract Lumber Inc................................C....... 740 964-3147
  Pataskala (G-15783)
Dynamic Structures Inc ....E....... 330 892-0164
  New Waterford (G-15004)
Metal Framing Enterprises LLC...........E....... 216 433-7080
  Cleveland (G-5962)
Season Contractors Inc ....E....... 440 717-0188
  Broadview Heights (G-1845)

CONTRACTOR: Rigging & Scaffolding

AM Industrial Group LLC ....E....... 216 433-7171
  Brookpark (G-1890)
J R Mead Industrial Contrs ....E....... 614 891-4466
  Galena (G-11160)
Janson Industries ....D....... 330 455-7029
  Canton (G-2360)
Sws Equipment Services Inc ....E....... 330 806-2767
  Akron (G-462)

CONTRACTORS: Access Control System Eqpt

Frontier Security LLC ....E....... 937 247-2824
  Miamisburg (G-14172)
Northwestern Ohio SEC Systems ....E....... 419 227-1655
  Lima (G-12708)
Yeck Brothers Company ....E....... 937 294-4000
  Moraine (G-14708)

CONTRACTORS: Access Flooring System Installation

American Star Painting Co LLC.............E....... 740 373-5634
  Marietta (G-13311)
Axis Interior Systems Inc ....E....... 513 642-0039
  West Chester (G-18870)
Corporate Floors Inc..............................E....... 216 475-3232
  Cleveland (G-5350)
OK Interiors Corp....................................C....... 513 742-3278
  Cincinnati (G-4164)

CONTRACTORS: Acoustical & Ceiling Work

Certanteed Gyps Ciling Mfg Inc............E....... 800 233-8990
  Aurora (G-824)
Fairfield Insul & Drywall LLC ....E....... 740 654-8811
  Lancaster (G-12398)
Frank Novak & Sons Inc ....D....... 216 475-2495
  Cleveland (G-5573)
OK Interiors Corp....................................C....... 513 742-3278
  Cincinnati (G-4164)
Sports Facility Acoustics Inc ....E....... 440 323-1400
  Elyria (G-10565)
T and D Interiors Incorporated ....E....... 419 331-4372
  Lima (G-12760)
Valley Acoustics Inc ....E....... 330 799-1894
  Youngstown (G-20234)

CONTRACTORS: Acoustical & Insulation Work

Immaculate Interiors ....E....... 440 324-9300
  Elyria (G-10518)
Omni Fireproofing Co LLC.....................D....... 513 870-9115
  West Chester (G-18980)

R E Kramig & Co Inc..............................C....... 513 761-4010
  Cincinnati (G-4330)

CONTRACTORS: Artificial Turf Installation

Motz Group Inc..E....... 513 533-6452
  Cincinnati (G-4077)

CONTRACTORS: Asbestos Removal & Encapsulation

AAA Amrican Abatement Asb Corp ......D....... 216 281-9400
  Cleveland (G-4886)
Allied Environmental Svcs Inc...............E....... 419 227-4004
  Lima (G-12599)
Cardinal Environmental Svc Inc ....E....... 330 252-0220
  Akron (G-117)
Central Insulation Systems Inc ....E....... 513 242-0600
  Cincinnati (G-3155)
Daniel A Terreri & Sons Inc ....E....... 330 538-2950
  Youngstown (G-20014)
Keen & Cross Envmtl Svcs Inc ....E....... 513 674-1700
  Cincinnati (G-3851)
Lepi Enterprises Inc...............................D....... 740 453-2980
  Zanesville (G-20324)
Pedersen Insulation Company ....E....... 614 471-3788
  Columbus (G-8434)
Precision Environmental Co ....B....... 216 642-6040
  Independence (G-12109)
Priority 1 Construction Svcs ....E....... 513 922-0203
  Cincinnati (G-4282)

CONTRACTORS: Asphalt

B G Trucking & Construction.................E....... 234 759-3440
  North Lima (G-15266)
Barbicas Construction Co.......................E....... 330 733-9101
  Akron (G-86)
Brown County Asphalt Inc ....E....... 937 446-2481
  Georgetown (G-11264)
Cook Paving and Cnstr Co ....E....... 216 267-7705
  Independence (G-12062)
Depuy Paving Inc ....E....... 614 272-0256
  Columbus (G-7437)
Freisthler Paving Inc..............................E....... 937 498-4802
  Sidney (G-16779)
Geddis Paving & Excavating Inc ....E....... 419 536-8501
  Toledo (G-17757)
George Kuhn Enterprises Inc ....E....... 614 481-8838
  Columbus (G-7660)
J K Enterprises Inc ....E....... 614 481-8838
  Columbus (G-7850)
Jennite Co...E....... 419 531-1791
  Toledo (G-17830)
Lucas County Asphalt Inc ....E....... 419 476-0705
  Toledo (G-17867)
Maintenance Systerms of N Ohio...........E....... 440 323-1291
  Elyria (G-10532)
Miller Yount Paving Inc..........................E....... 330 372-4408
  Cortland (G-8991)
Northstar Asphalt Inc ....E....... 330 497-0936
  North Canton (G-15224)
Pavement Protectors Inc ....E....... 614 875-9989
  Grove City (G-11464)
Perrin Asphalt Co Inc ....D....... 330 253-1020
  Akron (G-379)
Premier Asphalt Paving Co Inc ....E....... 440 237-6600
  North Royalton (G-15364)
Prus Construction Company ....C....... 513 321-7774
  Cincinnati (G-4303)
Queen City Blacktop Company ....E....... 513 251-8400
  Cincinnati (G-4312)
S & K Asphalt & Concrete ....E....... 330 848-6284
  Akron (G-414)
Smalls Asphalt Paving Inc ....E....... 740 427-4096
  Gambier (G-11227)
Tallmadge Asphalt & Pav Co Inc ....D....... 330 677-0000
  Kent (G-12262)
Tri-Mor Corp ....C....... 330 963-3101
  Twinsburg (G-18329)
Wenger Asphalt Inc.................................E....... 330 837-4767
  Dalton (G-9147)

CONTRACTORS: Awning Installation

Apco Aluminum Awning Co ....E....... 614 334-2726
  Columbus (G-6955)

CONTRACTORS: Banking Machine Installation & Svc

Diebold Incorporated.............................C....... 330 588-3619
  Canton (G-2285)
Diebold Nixdorf Incorporated ....D....... 513 682-6216
  Hamilton (G-11590)

CONTRACTORS: Bathtub Refinishing

Sayles Company LLC ....E....... 614 801-0432
  Columbus (G-8595)
Thiels Replacement Systems Inc ....D....... 419 289-6139
  Ashland (G-694)

CONTRACTORS: Boiler Maintenance Contractor

Arise Incorporated ....E....... 440 746-8860
  Brecksville (G-1770)
Park Corporation.....................................B....... 216 267-4870
  Cleveland (G-6163)
Prout Boiler Htg & Wldg Inc ....E....... 330 744-0293
  Youngstown (G-20167)

CONTRACTORS: Boiler Setting

Nbw Inc ....E....... 216 377-1700
  Cleveland (G-6051)

CONTRACTORS: Bricklaying

Duer Construction Co Inc ....D....... 330 848-9930
  Akron (G-197)
Giambrone Masonry Inc ....D....... 216 475-1200
  Hudson (G-11980)
International Masonry Inc ....D....... 614 469-8338
  Columbus (G-7837)
Jess Hauer Masonry Inc.........................E....... 513 521-2178
  Cincinnati (G-3812)
Kurzhals Inc..E....... 513 941-4624
  Cincinnati (G-3896)
Medhurst Mason Contractors Inc...........C....... 440 543-8885
  Chagrin Falls (G-2674)
Zavarella Brothers Cnstr Co ....E....... 440 232-2243
  Cleveland (G-6711)

CONTRACTORS: Bridge Painting

Apbn Inc..E....... 724 964-8252
  Campbell (G-2090)
Liberty Maintenance Inc ....D....... 330 755-7711
  Youngstown (G-20099)
Liberty-Alpha III JV ....E....... 330 755-7711
  Campbell (G-2091)
North Star Painting Co Inc ....E....... 330 743-2333
  Youngstown (G-20141)

CONTRACTORS: Building Eqpt & Machinery Installation

Allied Erct & Dismantling Co ....C....... 330 744-0808
  Youngstown (G-19951)
CTS Construction Inc ....D....... 513 489-8290
  Cincinnati (G-3385)
Nbw Inc ....E....... 216 377-1700
  Cleveland (G-6051)
North Bay Construction Inc ....E....... 440 835-1898
  Westlake (G-19380)
Schindler Elevator Corporation..............E....... 614 573-2777
  Columbus (G-8599)

CONTRACTORS: Building Fireproofing

Northwest Firestop Inc ....E....... 419 517-4777
  Toledo (G-17948)
Omni Fireproofing Co LLC.....................D....... 513 870-9115
  West Chester (G-18980)
Thermal Solutions Inc ....D....... 740 886-2861
  Proctorville (G-16220)

CONTRACTORS: Building Sign Installation & Mntnce

Archer Corporation ....E....... 330 455-9995
  Canton (G-2193)
Brilliant Electric Sign Co Ltd ....D....... 216 741-3800
  Brooklyn Heights (G-1866)
Danite Holdings Ltd ....E....... 614 444-3333
  Columbus (G-7416)
Gus Holthaus Signs Inc.........................E....... 513 861-0060
  Cincinnati (G-3664)

Identitek Systems Inc ....D 330 832-9844
   Massillon (G-13697)

Lighting Maint Harmon Sign ....D .. 419 841-6658
   Toledo (G-17855)

Palazzo Brothers Electric Inc..............E .. 419 668-1100
   Norwalk (G-15451)

United-Maier Signs Inc ....D .. 513 681-6600
   Cincinnati (G-4690)

CONTRACTORS: Building Site Preparation

Gradient Corporation............................E .. 513 779-0000
   Cincinnati (G-3631)

Rudzik Excavating Inc ....E .. 330 755-1540
   Struthers (G-17367)

CONTRACTORS: Cable Laying

Edgar Trent Cnstr Co LLC.....................D .. 419 683-4939
   Crestline (G-9054)

South Shore Cable Cnstr Inc ....D .. 440 816-0033
   Cleveland (G-6424)

Universal Recovery Systems.................D .. 614 299-0184
   Columbus (G-8817)

Wachter Inc..C .. 513 777-0701
   West Chester (G-19099)

CONTRACTORS: Cable Splicing Svcs

Buckeye Cable Systems Inc ....E .. 419 724-2539
   Toledo (G-17631)

CONTRACTORS: Cable TV Installation

Broadband Express LLC ....E .. 513 834-8085
   Cincinnati (G-3076)

Broadband Express LLC ....E .. 614 823-6464
   Westerville (G-19149)

Broadband Express LLC ....D .. 419 536-9127
   Toledo (G-17626)

Cable TV Services Inc...........................E .. 440 816-0033
   Cleveland (G-5112)

Dss Installations Ltd..............................E .. 513 761-7000
   Cincinnati (G-3446)

Precision Broadbnd Installatns ....C .. 614 523-2917
   Westerville (G-19201)

Primetech Communications Inc ....D .. 513 942-6000
   West Chester (G-18986)

CONTRACTORS: Caisson Drilling

Parks Drilling Company ....E .. 614 761-7707
   Dublin (G-10305)

Scherzinger Drilling Inc ....E .. 513 738-2000
   Harrison (G-11676)

CONTRACTORS: Carpentry Work

Airko Inc..E .. 440 333-0133
   Cleveland (G-4922)

Brock & Associates Builders................E .. 330 757-7150
   Youngstown (G-19975)

Combs Interior Specialties Inc ....D .. 937 879-2047
   Fairborn (G-10665)

Command Roofing Co ....C .. 937 298-1155
   Moraine (G-14633)

Competitive Interiors Inc......................C .. 330 297-1281
   Ravenna (G-16237)

Hgc Construction Co ....D .. 513 861-8866
   Cincinnati (G-3700)

J & B Equipment & Supply Inc ....D .. 419 884-1155
   Mansfield (G-13188)

Marous Brothers Cnstr Inc....................B .. 440 951-3904
   Willoughby (G-19550)

Mjr-Construction Co ....E .. 216 523-8050
   Cleveland (G-6002)

Ohio Builders Resources LLC ....E .. 614 865-0306
   Westerville (G-19194)

Overhead Door Co- Cincinnati..............C .. 513 346-4000
   West Chester (G-18981)

Premier Construction Company ....E .. 513 874-2611
   Fairfield (G-10771)

Riverside Cnstr Svcs Inc.......................E .. 513 723-0900
   Cincinnati (G-4380)

Roger Kreps Drywall & Plst Inc ....D .. 330 726-6090
   Youngstown (G-20190)

Valley Acoustics Inc ....E .. 330 799-1894
   Youngstown (G-20234)

CONTRACTORS: Carpentry, Cabinet & Finish Work

Builders Firstsource Inc.......................E .. 937 898-1358
   Vandalia (G-18510)

Casegoods Inc ....E .. 330 825-2461
   Barberton (G-949)

Countertop Alternatives Inc ....E .. 937 254-3334
   Dayton (G-9324)

Mammana Custom Woodworking Inc ...E .. 216 581-9059
   Maple Heights (G-13289)

Schlabach Wood Design Inc ....E .. 330 897-2600
   Baltic (G-936)

CONTRACTORS: Carpentry, Cabinet Building & Installation

Forum Manufacturing Inc......................E .. 937 349-8685
   Milford Center (G-14445)

CONTRACTORS: Carpet Laying

Dominguez Inc ....E .. 513 425-9955
   Monroe (G-14566)

Legacy Commercial Flooring Ltd ....B .. 614 476-1043
   Columbus (G-7962)

Marble Restoration Inc ....D .. 419 865-9000
   Maumee (G-13813)

Patellas Floor Center Inc......................E .. 330 758-4099
   Youngstown (G-20152)

Progressive Flooring Svcs Inc ....E .. 614 868-9005
   Etna (G-10619)

Schoch Tile & Carpet Inc......................E .. 513 922-3466
   Cincinnati (G-4439)

Stedman Floor Co Inc ....E .. 614 836-3190
   Groveport (G-11539)

CONTRACTORS: Ceramic Floor Tile Installation

JD Music Tile Co ....E .. 740 420-9611
   Circleville (G-4837)

Weiffenbach Marble & Tile Co ....E .. 937 832-7055
   Englewood (G-10605)

CONTRACTORS: Chimney Construction & Maintenance

Able Company Ltd Partnership ....D 614 444-7663
   Columbus (G-6853)

Ray St Clair Roofing Inc ....E 513 874-1234
   Fairfield (G-10773)

CONTRACTORS: Closet Organizers, Installation & Design

Organized Living Ltd ....C .. 513 674-5484
   Cincinnati (G-4182)

Ptmj Enterprises ....C .. 440 543-8000
   Solon (G-16886)

CONTRACTORS: Coating, Caulking & Weather, Water & Fire

American Star Painting Co LLC.............E 740 373-5634
   Marietta (G-13311)

Canaan Companies Inc ....E .. 419 842-8373
   Toledo (G-17634)

Capital Fire Protection Co ....E .. 614 279-9448
   Columbus (G-7112)

Central Fire Protection Co Inc ....E .. 937 322-0713
   Springfield (G-17006)

M T Golf Course Managmnt Inc ....E .. 513 923-1188
   Cincinnati (G-3955)

Midwest Industrial Supply Inc ....E .. 800 321-0699
   Toledo (G-17914)

OCP Contractors Inc..............................E .. 419 865-7168
   Holland (G-11903)

Prime Polymers Inc................................E .. 330 662-4200
   Medina (G-13988)

Regency Roofing Companies Inc..........E .. 330 468-1021
   Macedonia (G-13081)

CONTRACTORS: Commercial & Office Building

Abco Contracting LLC............................E .. 419 973-4772
   Toledo (G-17580)

Al Neyer LLC ....D .. 513 271-6400
   Cincinnati (G-2918)

Berlin Construction Ltd..........................E .. 330 893-2003
   Millersburg (G-14458)

Boyas Excavating Inc ....E .. 216 524-3620
   Cleveland (G-5072)

Brenmar Construction Inc.....................D .. 740 286-2151
   Jackson (G-12169)

Cattrell Companies Inc ....D .. 740 537-2481
   Toronto (G-18183)

Cleveland Construction Inc ....E .. 440 255-8000
   Mentor (G-14031)

Cleveland Construction Inc ....E .. 740 927-9000
   Columbus (G-7224)

Cleveland Construction Inc ....E .. 440 255-8000
   Mason (G-13563)

Da Vinci Group Inc ....E .. 614 419-2393
   Reynoldsburg (G-16295)

Delventhal Company ....E .. 419 244-5570
   Millbury (G-14447)

Design Homes & Development Co ....E .. 937 438-3667
   Dayton (G-9389)

Dotson Company ....E .. 419 877-5176
   Whitehouse (G-19446)

Dugan & Meyers LLC.............................C .. 513 891-4300
   Blue Ash (G-1548)

Early Construction Co ....E .. 740 894-5150
   South Point (G-16933)

Goliath Contracting Ltd..........................E .. 614 568-7878
   Reynoldsburg (G-16306)

Great Lakes Contractors LLC ....E .. 216 631-7777
   Cleveland (G-5626)

Hammond Construction Inc...................D .. 330 455-7039
   Canton (G-2335)

J&H Rnfrcing Strl Erectors Inc ....C .. 740 355-0141
   Portsmouth (G-16151)

Kramer & Feldman Inc...........................E .. 513 821-7444
   Cincinnati (G-3889)

L R G Inc ....D .. 937 890-0510
   Dayton (G-9553)

Link Construction Group Inc ....E .. 937 292-7774
   Bellefontaine (G-1354)

Mel Lanzer Co...E .. 419 592-2801
   Napoleon (G-14811)

Muha Construction Inc ....E .. 937 435-0678
   Dayton (G-9647)

Multicon Builders Inc.............................E .. 614 241-2070
   Columbus (G-8121)

Multicon Builders Inc.............................E .. 614 463-1142
   Columbus (G-8122)

N Cook Inc ....E .. 513 275-9872
   Cincinnati (G-4089)

Ohio Maint & Renovation Inc ....E .. 330 315-3101
   Akron (G-360)

Ohio Technical Services Inc ....E .. 614 372-0829
   Columbus (G-8356)

Palmetto Construction Svcs LLC ....E .. 614 503-7150
   Columbus (G-8417)

Pivotek LLC ....E .. 513 372-6205
   Milford (G-14424)

Quandel Construction Group Inc ....E .. 717 657-0909
   Westerville (G-19297)

Reece-Campbell Inc...............................D .. 513 542-4600
   Cincinnati (G-4349)

Registered Contractors Inc...................E .. 440 205-0873
   Mentor (G-14102)

Rudolph/Libbe Companies Inc ....D .. 419 241-5000
   Walbridge (G-18625)

Runyon & Sons Roofing Inc ....D .. 440 974-6810
   Mentor (G-14105)

Rupp/Rosebrock Inc ....E .. 419 533-7999
   Liberty Center (G-12575)

Snavely Building Company ....E .. 440 585-9091
   Chagrin Falls (G-2654)

Stamm Contracting Co Inc ....E .. 330 274-8230
   Mantua (G-13276)

Star Builders Inc ....E .. 440 986-5951
   Amherst (G-599)

Stockmeister Enterprises Inc ....E .. 740 286-1619
   Jackson (G-12179)

T Allen Inc ....E .. 440 234-2366
   Berea (G-1440)

Watertown Steel Company LLC.............E .. 740 749-3512
   Waterford (G-18787)

Williams Bros Builders Inc.....................E .. 440 365-3261
   Elyria (G-10575)

Winsupply Inc..D .. 937 294-5331
   Moraine (G-14707)

Xtreme Contracting Ltd ....E .. 614 568-7030
   Reynoldsburg (G-16341)

Employee Codes: A=Over 500 employees, B=251-500
C=101-250, D=51-100, E=25-50

CONTRACTORS: Communications Svcs

Gatesair Inc ....D 513 459-3400
Mason (G-13583)

Legrand North America LLC ....B 937 224-0639
Dayton (G-9561)

Legrand North America LLC ....C 937 224-0639
Dayton (G-9562)

Professional Telecom Svcs ....E 513 232-7700
Cincinnati (G-4294)

Telecom Expertise Inds Inc ....D 937 548-5254
Greenville (G-11397)

Telephone & Cmpt Contrs Inc...........E 419 726-8142
Toledo (G-18062)

US Communications and Elc Inc ....D 440 519-0880
Cleveland (G-6610)

Zenith Systems LLC ....B 216 587-9510
Cleveland (G-6712)

CONTRACTORS: Computer Installation

Advanced Service Tech LLC ....E 937 435-4376
Miamisburg (G-14137)

Intercnnect Cbling Netwrk Svcs ....E 440 891-0465
Berea (G-1428)

Pomeroy It Solutions Sls Inc ....E 440 717-1364
Brecksville (G-1798)

Staley Inc ....E 614 552-2333
Plain City (G-16067)

CONTRACTORS: Concrete

21st Century Con Cnstr Inc ....E 216 362-0900
Cleveland (G-4870)

Adleta Inc ....E 513 554-1469
Cincinnati (G-2908)

Aerodynamic Concrete & Cnstr...........E 330 906-7477
Akron (G-21)

Atlas Construction Company ....D 614 475-4705
Columbus (G-6998)

B & D Concrete Footers Inc ....E 740 964-2294
Etna (G-10612)

Baker Concrete Cnstr Inc ....A 513 539-4000
Monroe (G-14561)

Berlin Contractors ....E 330 893-2904
Berlin (G-1445)

Bradcorp Ohio II LLC ....E 513 671-3300
Fairfield (G-10700)

Ceco Concrete Cnstr Del LLC...........D 513 874-6953
West Chester (G-18881)

Cem-Base Inc ....E 330 963-3101
Twinsburg (G-18251)

Cincinnati Asphalt Corporation ....D 513 367-0250
Cleves (G-6726)

Concrete Coring Company Inc ....E 937 864-7325
Enon (G-10607)

Cornerstone Concrete Cnstr Inc ....E 937 442-2805
Sardinia (G-16658)

Donley Concrete Cutting ....D 614 834-0300
Pickerington (G-15956)

DOT Diamond Core Drilling Inc ....E 440 322-6466
Elyria (G-10502)

Dwyer Concrete Lifting Inc ....E 614 501-0998
Groveport (G-11508)

E&I Construction LLC ....E 513 421-2045
Cincinnati (G-3466)

Elastizell Systems Inc...........E 937 298-1313
Moraine (G-14652)

Engineered Con Structures Corp ....E 216 520-2000
Cleveland (G-5480)

Formwork Services LLC...........E 513 539-4000
Monroe (G-14567)

G Big Inc ....E 740 867-5758
Chesapeake (G-2729)

Gardner Cement Contractors ....D 419 389-0768
Toledo (G-17756)

Gironda Vito & Bros Inc ....E 330 630-9399
Akron (G-235)

H & R Concrete Inc ....E 937 885-2910
Dayton (G-9480)

Hanson Concrete Products Ohio ....E 614 443-4846
Columbus (G-7716)

Hovest Construction ....E 419 456-3426
Ottawa (G-15659)

Ivan Law Inc ....E 330 533-5000
Youngstown (G-20084)

Jostin Construction Inc...........E 513 559-9390
Cincinnati (G-3835)

Keim Concrete LLC ....E 330 264-5313
Wooster (G-19736)

L & I Custom Walls Inc ....E 513 683-2045
Loveland (G-13005)

Latorre Concrete Cnstr Inc ....E 614 257-1401
Columbus (G-7956)

Lavy Concrete Construction ....E 937 606-4754
Covington (G-9047)

Lithko Contracting LLC ....C 513 564-2000
West Chester (G-18963)

Lockhart Concrete Co ....D 330 745-6520
Akron (G-319)

Mattlin Construction Inc...........E 513 598-5402
Cleves (G-6733)

Milcon Concrete Inc ....E 937 339-6274
Troy (G-18216)

Modern Day Concrete Cnstr ....E 513 738-1026
Harrison (G-11674)

MPW Construction Services ....E 440 647-6661
Wellington (G-18844)

Norris Brothers Co Inc ....C 216 771-2233
Cleveland (G-6074)

Northeast Concrete & Cnstr...........D 614 898-5728
Westerville (G-19191)

Ohio Paving Group LLC ....E 216 475-1700
Cleveland (G-6122)

Platform Cement Inc ....E 440 602-9750
Mentor (G-14097)

R W Sidley Incorporated ....E 440 352-9343
Painesville (G-15735)

Shelly and Sands Inc ....E 614 444-5100
Columbus (G-8632)

Shelly and Sands Inc ....E 740 453-0721
Zanesville (G-20360)

Spano Brothers Cnstr Co ....E 330 645-1544
Akron (G-436)

Spaulding Construction Co Inc ....D 330 494-1776
Canton (G-2481)

Spillman Company ....E 614 444-2184
Columbus (G-8672)

Staarmann Concrete Inc...........E 513 756-9191
Hamilton (G-11643)

Stamm Contracting Co Inc ....E 330 274-8230
Mantua (G-13276)

Standard Contg & Engrg Inc ....D 440 243-1001
Brookpark (G-1906)

Thompson Concrete Ltd ....B 740 756-7256
Carroll (G-2558)

Towne Construction Svcs LLC ....C 513 561-3700
Batavia (G-1012)

Triple Q Foundations Co Inc ....E 513 932-3121
Lebanon (G-12511)

Trucco Construction Co Inc ....E 740 417-9010
Delaware (G-10010)

Tscs Inc ....E 419 644-3921
Metamora (G-14133)

U S A Concrete Specialists ....E 330 482-9150
Columbiana (G-6794)

Vandra Bros Construction Inc ....E 440 232-3030
Cleveland (G-6621)

Wasiniak Construction Inc ....D 419 668-8624
Norwalk (G-15459)

CONTRACTORS: Concrete Pumping

Akron Concrete Corp...........E 330 864-1188
Akron (G-35)

Foor Concrete Co Inc ....D 740 513-4346
Delaware (G-9978)

H & M Precision Concrete LLC ....E 937 547-0012
Greenville (G-11385)

Newcomer Concrete Services Inc ....D 419 668-2789
Norwalk (G-15445)

North Coast Concrete Inc...........E 216 642-1114
Cleveland (G-6076)

Phillips Companies ....E 937 426-5461
Beavercreek Township (G-1258)

Phillips Ready Mix Co...........D 937 426-5151
Beavercreek Township (G-1259)

Scioto-Darby Concrete Inc...........E 614 876-3114
Hilliard (G-11814)

Signature Concrete Inc...........E 937 723-8435
Dayton (G-9769)

Williams Concrete Cnstr Co Inc ....E 330 745-6388
Norton (G-15423)

CONTRACTORS: Concrete Reinforcement Placing

J & B Interests Inc...........D 513 874-1722
West Chester (G-18950)

Midwest Reinforcing Contrs ....E 937 390-8998
Springfield (G-17085)

CONTRACTORS: Concrete Repair

Independence Excavating Inc...........E 216 524-1700
Independence (G-12082)

Lithko Restoration Tech LLC...........D 513 863-5500
Monroe (G-14575)

Lithko Restoration Tech LLC...........E 614 221-0711
Columbus (G-7984)

Ohio Con Sawing & Drlg Inc ....E 419 841-1330
Sylvania (G-17440)

Ohio Con Sawing & Drlg Inc ....E 614 252-1122
Columbus (G-8233)

Prime Polymers Inc ....E 330 662-4200
Medina (G-13988)

Suburban Maint & Cnstr Inc ....E 440 237-7765
North Royalton (G-15368)

CONTRACTORS: Concrete Structure Coating, Plastic

Paulo Products Company ....E 440 942-0153
Willoughby (G-19561)

Systems Jay LLC Nanogate...........A 419 524-3778
Mansfield (G-13248)

CONTRACTORS: Construction Caulking

American International Cnstr...........E 440 243-5535
Berea (G-1411)

Coon Caulking & Sealants Inc ....D 330 875-2100
Louisville (G-12964)

Hummel Industries Incorporated ....E 513 242-1321
Cincinnati (G-3741)

Master Builders LLC ....E 216 831-5500
Beachwood (G-1076)

Terrafirm Construction LLC ....E 913 433-2998
Columbus (G-8740)

CONTRACTORS: Construction Site Cleanup

Early Construction Co ....E 740 894-5150
South Point (G-16933)

Extreme Detail Clg Cnstr Svcs ....E 419 392-3243
Toledo (G-17721)

MRM Construction Inc...........E 740 388-0079
Gallipolis (G-11205)

CONTRACTORS: Construction Site Metal Structure Coating

Bogie Industries Inc Ltd ....E 330 745-3105
Akron (G-102)

Carpe Diem Industries LLC...........D 419 659-5639
Columbus Grove (G-8940)

Carpe Diem Industries LLC...........E 419 358-0129
Bluffton (G-1689)

Chemsteel Construction Company ....E 440 234-3930
Middleburg Heights (G-14249)

L B Foster Company ....E 330 652-1461
Mineral Ridge (G-14510)

CONTRACTORS: Core Drilling & Cutting

Barr Engineering Incorporated...........E 614 714-0299
Columbus (G-7019)

CONTRACTORS: Countertop Installation

Countertop Alternatives Inc...........E 937 254-3334
Dayton (G-9324)

Crafted Surface and Stone LLC...........E 440 658-3799
Bedford Heights (G-1321)

Modlich Stoneworks Inc...........E 614 276-2848
Columbus (G-8094)

CONTRACTORS: Demolition, Building & Other Structures

B & B Wrecking & Excvtg Inc ....E 216 429-1700
Cleveland (G-5031)

C & J Contractors Inc ....E 216 391-5700
Cleveland (G-5109)

Daniel A Terreri & Sons Inc ....E 330 538-2950
Youngstown (G-20014)

Eslich Wrecking Company ....E 330 488-8300
Louisville (G-12967)

Independence Excavating Inc...........E 216 524-1700
Independence (G-12082)

JS Paris Excavating Inc...........E 330 538-3048
North Jackson (G-15247)

Marucci and Gaffney Excvtg Co ....E 330 743-8170
Youngstown (G-20117)

Miller Brothers Cnstr Dem LLC ....E 513 257-1082
  Oxford *(G-15684)*
ORourke Wrecking Company ....D 513 871-1400
  Cincinnati *(G-4184)*
S G Loewendick and Sons Inc............E 614 539-2582
  Grove City *(G-11467)*
Sidwell Materials Inc ....C 740 849-2394
  Zanesville *(G-20361)*

CONTRACTORS: Diamond Drilling & Sawing

Curtiss-Wright Flow Control ....D 513 735-2538
  Batavia *(G-995)*
Safety Grooving & Grinding LP ....E 419 592-8666
  Napoleon *(G-14817)*

CONTRACTORS: Directional Oil & Gas Well Drilling Svc

Warren Drilling Co Inc ....C 740 783-2775
  Dexter City *(G-10060)*

CONTRACTORS: Drapery Track Installation

Style-Line Incorporated ....E 614 291-0600
  Columbus *(G-8707)*

CONTRACTORS: Driveway

American Coatings Corporation............E 614 335-1000
  Plain City *(G-16043)*
Cox Paving Inc ....D 937 780-3075
  Wshngtn CT Hs *(G-19867)*
Image Pavement Maintenance............E 937 833-9200
  Brookville *(G-1914)*

CONTRACTORS: Drywall

Anstine Drywall Inc ....E 330 784-3867
  Akron *(G-75)*
Apex Interiors Inc ....E 330 327-2226
  Avon *(G-862)*
Architectural Intr Restoration ....E 216 241-2255
  Cleveland *(G-5006)*
Blackstar Drywall Inc ....E 614 242-4242
  Sunbury *(G-17383)*
Cincinnati Drywall Inc............E 513 321-7322
  Cincinnati *(G-3240)*
Clubhouse Pub N Grub ....E 440 884-2582
  Cleveland *(G-5310)*
Columbus Drywall & Insulation ....D 614 257-0257
  Columbus *(G-7276)*
Columbus Drywall Inc ....E 614 257-0257
  Columbus *(G-7277)*
Compass Construction Inc ....E 614 761-7800
  Dublin *(G-10186)*
Competitive Interiors Inc............C 330 297-1281
  Ravenna *(G-16237)*
Construction Systems Inc............D 614 252-0708
  Columbus *(G-7354)*
Dayton Walls & Ceilings Inc ....D 937 277-0531
  Dayton *(G-9384)*
Halker Drywall Inc ....E 419 646-3679
  Columbus Grove *(G-8941)*
Hughes & Knollman Construction ....D 614 237-6167
  Columbus *(G-7778)*
Integrity Wall & Ceiling Inc............E 419 381-1855
  Toledo *(G-17823)*
Knollman Construction LLC ....C 614 841-0130
  Columbus *(G-7918)*
Larry L Minges ....E 513 738-4901
  Hamilton *(G-11622)*
M & S Drywall Inc ....E 513 738-1510
  Harrison *(G-11673)*
Newark Drywall Inc ....E 740 763-3572
  Nashport *(G-14820)*
OCP Contractors Inc............E 419 865-7168
  Holland *(G-11903)*
Porter Drywall Inc ....D 614 890-2111
  Westerville *(G-19293)*
Roger Kreps Drywall & Plst Inc ....D 330 726-6090
  Youngstown *(G-20190)*
Ron Kreps Drywall Plst Compang ....E 330 726-8252
  Youngstown *(G-20193)*
Roricks Inc ....E 330 497-6888
  Canton *(G-2463)*
Valley Interior Systems Inc ....E 937 890-7319
  Dayton *(G-9847)*
Valley Interior Systems Inc ....B 513 961-0400
  Cincinnati *(G-4747)*
Valley Interior Systems Inc ....C 614 351-8440
  Columbus *(G-8840)*

CONTRACTORS: Earthmoving

Jack Conie & Sons Corp ....D 614 291-5931
  Columbus *(G-7852)*

CONTRACTORS: Electric Power Systems

Columbia Energy Group............A 614 460-4683
  Columbus *(G-7247)*
Dovetail Construction Co Inc............E 740 592-1800
  Cleveland *(G-5445)*

CONTRACTORS: Electrical

Acpi Systems Inc ....E 513 738-3840
  Hamilton *(G-11554)*
AE Electric Inc ....E 419 392-8468
  Grand Rapids *(G-11324)*
Aetna Building Maintenance Inc............B 614 476-1818
  Columbus *(G-6881)*
Akron Foundry Co ....E 330 745-3101
  Barberton *(G-939)*
Allcan Global Services Inc ....E 513 825-1655
  Cincinnati *(G-2924)*
American Electric Power Co Inc............E 740 295-3070
  Coshocton *(G-8998)*
AMS Construction Inc ....C 513 398-6689
  Maineville *(G-13112)*
AMS Construction Inc ....E 513 794-0410
  Loveland *(G-12977)*
Apollo Heating and AC Inc ....E 513 271-3600
  Cincinnati *(G-2975)*
Atlas Industrial Contrs LLC ....B 614 841-4500
  Columbus *(G-7000)*
Bay Mechanical & Elec Corp............D 440 282-6816
  Lorain *(G-12885)*
Buckeye Cable Systems Inc ....E 419 724-2539
  Toledo *(G-17631)*
Cincinnati Voice and Data ....D 513 683-4127
  Loveland *(G-12983)*
Copp Systems Inc ....E 937 228-4188
  Dayton *(G-9320)*
CTS Construction Inc ....E 513 489-8290
  Cincinnati *(G-3385)*
Dynamic Currents Corp............E 419 861-2036
  Holland *(G-11885)*
Enviroserve Inc ....C 330 966-0910
  North Canton *(G-15200)*
Excel Electrical Contractor ....E 740 965-3795
  Worthington *(G-19809)*
Fishel Company ....D 614 850-4400
  Columbus *(G-7590)*
General Electric Company ....D 330 256-5331
  Cuyahoga Falls *(G-9099)*
General Electric Company ....E 614 527-1078
  Hilliard *(G-11768)*
General Electric Company ....C 513 583-3500
  Cincinnati *(G-3610)*
Helm and Associates Inc............E 419 893-1480
  Maumee *(G-13799)*
Horizon Mechanical and Elec ....E 419 529-2738
  Mansfield *(G-13183)*
Ies Infrstrcture Solutions LLC ....E 330 830-3500
  Massillon *(G-13698)*
Industrial Power Systems Inc............C 419 531-3121
  Rossford *(G-16461)*
Insight Communications of Co............C 614 236-1200
  Columbus *(G-7825)*
John A Becker Co ....E 614 272-8800
  Columbus *(G-7861)*
Lake Horry Electric ....D 440 808-8791
  Chagrin Falls *(G-2651)*
Lippincott Plumbing-Heating AC ....E 419 222-0856
  Lima *(G-12689)*
Nationwide Energy Partners LLC ....E 614 918-2031
  Columbus *(G-8153)*
North Electric Inc ....E 216 331-4141
  Cleveland *(G-6077)*
O D Miller Electric Co Inc ....E 330 875-1651
  Louisville *(G-12969)*
Ohio Power Company ....E 888 216-3523
  Canton *(G-2429)*
Ohio Power Company ....E 419 443-4634
  Tiffin *(G-17529)*
RJ Runge Company Inc ....E 419 740-5781
  Port Clinton *(G-16116)*
Rmf Nooter Inc ....D 419 727-1970
  Toledo *(G-18009)*
Robinson Htg Air-Conditioning ....E 513 422-6812
  Middletown *(G-14326)*
Schneder Elc Bldngs Amrcas Inc............D 513 398-9800
  Lebanon *(G-12499)*

Shawntech Communications Inc............E 937 898-4900
  Miamisburg *(G-14220)*
Southtown Heating & Cooling ....E 937 320-9900
  Moraine *(G-14699)*
Star Dist & Manufacturring LLC ....D 513 860-3573
  West Chester *(G-19083)*
Superior Group ....C 614 488-8035
  Columbus *(G-8714)*
Timmerman John P Heating AC Co......E 419 229-4015
  Lima *(G-12764)*

CONTRACTORS: Electronic Controls Installation

Controls Inc ....E 330 239-4345
  Medina *(G-13923)*
Industrial Comm & Sound Inc............E 614 276-8123
  Cincinnati *(G-3759)*

CONTRACTORS: Energy Management Control

Hoskins International LLC ....E 419 628-6015
  Minster *(G-14536)*
Mc Phillips Plbg Htg & AC Co ....E 216 481-1400
  Cleveland *(G-5929)*
Siemens Energy Inc............B 740 393-8897
  Mount Vernon *(G-14790)*

CONTRACTORS: Epoxy Application

Flow-Liner Systems Ltd ....E 800 348-0020
  Zanesville *(G-20308)*
Ohio Concrete Resurfacing Inc ....E 440 786-9100
  Bedford *(G-1297)*

CONTRACTORS: Erection & Dismantling, Poured Concrete Forms

Ceco Concrete Cnstr Del LLC ....D 513 874-6953
  West Chester *(G-18881)*
Stachler Concrete Inc............E 419 678-3867
  Saint Henry *(G-16517)*

CONTRACTORS: Excavating

Allard Excavation LLC ....D 740 778-2242
  South Webster *(G-16950)*
Anderzack-Pitzen Cnstr Inc ....E 419 553-7015
  Metamora *(G-14132)*
Bansal Construction Inc............E 513 874-5410
  Fairfield *(G-10698)*
Bontrager Excavating Co Inc............E 330 499-8775
  Uniontown *(G-18358)*
Boyas Excavating Inc ....E 216 524-3620
  Cleveland *(G-5072)*
Burkhart Excavating Inc............E 740 896-3312
  Lowell *(G-13036)*
C & J Contractors Inc ....E 216 391-5700
  Cleveland *(G-5109)*
Camargo Construction Company............E 513 248-1500
  Cincinnati *(G-3107)*
Charles F Jergens Cnstr Inc ....E 937 233-1830
  Dayton *(G-9293)*
Charles Jergens Contractor............E 937 233-1830
  Dayton *(G-9294)*
Cincinnati Asphalt Corporation............D 513 367-0250
  Cleves *(G-6726)*
D B Bentley Inc............E 440 352-8495
  Painesville *(G-15707)*
Dave Sugar Excavating LLC ....E 330 542-1100
  Petersburg *(G-15943)*
Digioia/Suburban Excvtg LLC ....D 440 237-1978
  North Royalton *(G-15353)*
Don Wartko Construction Co ....D 330 673-5252
  Kent *(G-12229)*
Elite Excavating Company Inc............E 419 683-4200
  Mansfield *(G-13172)*
Eslich Wrecking Company ....E 330 488-8300
  Louisville *(G-12967)*
Fechko Excavating LLC ....D 330 722-2890
  Medina *(G-13937)*
Fishel Company ....C 937 233-2268
  Dayton *(G-9439)*
Ford Development Corp............D 513 772-1521
  Cincinnati *(G-3577)*
Geddis Paving & Excavating Inc ....E 419 536-8501
  Toledo *(G-17757)*
GMC Excavation & Trucking............E 419 468-0121
  Galion *(G-11177)*

SERVICES

Goettle Holding Company Inc..............C...... 513 825-8100
   Cincinnati (G-3623)
Ground Tech Inc..............................E...... 330 270-0700
   Youngstown (G-20058)
H & R Concrete Inc.........................E...... 937 885-2910
   Dayton (G-9480)
Hardrock Excavating LLC ....D...... 330 792-9524
   Youngstown (G-20060)
Independence Excavating Inc............E...... 216 524-1700
   Independence (G-12082)
Indian Nation Inc ....E...... 740 532-6143
   North Canton (G-15212)
John F Gallagher Plumbing Co ....E...... 440 946-4256
   Eastlake (G-10430)
JS Bova Excavating LLC ....E...... 234 254-4040
   Struthers (G-17365)
Kelchner Inc.................................C...... 937 704-9890
   Springboro (G-16971)
Law Excavating Inc.........................E...... 740 745-3420
   Saint Louisville (G-16519)
Layton Inc....................................E...... 740 349-7101
   Newark (G-15048)
Luburgh Inc..................................E...... 740 452-3668
   Zanesville (G-20327)
Menke Bros Construction Co ....E...... 419 286-2086
   Delphos (G-10031)
Metropolitan Envmtl Svcs Inc............D...... 614 771-1881
   Hilliard (G-11793)
Mike Enyart & Sons Inc ....D...... 740 523-0235
   South Point (G-16943)
Mike George Excavating ....E...... 419 855-4147
   Genoa (G-11259)
Mike Pusateri Excavating Inc............E...... 330 385-5221
   East Liverpool (G-10407)
Miller Yount Paving Inc....................E...... 330 372-4408
   Cortland (G-8991)
Modern Poured Walls Inc ....D...... 440 647-6661
   Wellington (G-18843)
Nelson Stark Company.....................C...... 513 489-0866
   Cincinnati (G-4106)
Ohio Heavy Equipment Lsg LLC ....E...... 513 965-6600
   Fairfield (G-10764)
Osborne Co..................................D...... 440 942-7000
   Mentor (G-14094)
Phillips Ready Mix Co.......................D...... 937 426-5151
   Beavercreek Township (G-1259)
Rack & Ballauer Excvtg Co Inc..........E...... 513 738-7000
   Hamilton (G-11635)
Ray Bertolini Trucking Co ....E...... 330 867-0666
   Akron (G-397)
Rbm Environmental and Cnstr ....E...... 419 693-5840
   Oregon (G-15607)
S E T Inc.....................................E...... 330 536-6724
   Lowellville (G-13043)
Schumm Richard A Plbg & Htg............E...... 419 238-4994
   Van Wert (G-18488)
Siler Excavation Services ....E...... 513 400-8628
   Milford (G-14432)
Sisler Heating & Cooling Inc..............E...... 330 722-7101
   Medina (G-14002)
Spano Brothers Cnstr Co ....E...... 330 645-1544
   Akron (G-436)
Stahlheber & Sons Inc.....................E...... 513 726-4446
   Hamilton (G-11644)
Standard Contg & Engrg Inc..............D...... 440 243-1001
   Brookpark (G-1906)
Star-Ex Inc..................................E...... 937 473-2397
   Covington (G-9048)
Stonegate Construction Inc...............D...... 740 423-9170
   Belpre (G-1410)
Sws Environmental Services ....E...... 254 629-1718
   Findlay (G-10967)
Thompson Concrete Ltd ....B...... 740 756-7256
   Carroll (G-2558)
Todd Alspaugh & Associates.............E...... 419 476-8126
   Toledo (G-18071)
Trimat Construction Inc....................E...... 740 388-9515
   Bidwell (G-1470)
Utter Construction Inc ....C...... 513 876-2246
   Bethel (G-1455)
Vandalia Blacktop Seal Coating ....E...... 937 454-0571
   Dayton (G-9850)

CONTRACTORS: Exterior Concrete Stucco

Reitter Stucco Inc ....E...... 614 291-2212
   Columbus (G-8508)
Reitter Wall Systems Inc ....D...... 614 545-4444
   Columbus (G-8509)

CONTRACTORS: Exterior Painting

Mrap LLC ....E...... 614 545-3190
   Columbus (G-8117)
Reilly Painting Co ....E...... 216 371-8160
   Cleveland Heights (G-6723)
RI Painting and Mfg Inc ....E...... 937 968-5526
   Union City (G-18354)

CONTRACTORS: Fence Construction

Allied Builders Inc.........................E...... 937 226-0311
   Dayton (G-9215)
Alumina Rling Cstm Ir Wrks Inc ....E...... 513 353-1116
   Cleves (G-6724)
Deerfield Farms ....E...... 330 584-4715
   Deerfield (G-9903)
Mills Fence Co Inc..........................E...... 513 631-0333
   Cincinnati (G-4057)
Security Fence Group Inc ....E...... 513 681-3700
   Cincinnati (G-4444)
Southway Fence Company ....E...... 330 477-5251
   Canton (G-2480)

CONTRACTORS: Fiber Optic Cable Installation

Elect General Contractors Inc ....E...... 740 420-3437
   Circleville (G-4833)
Newcome Corp...............................E...... 614 848-5688
   Columbus (G-6826)
Taylor Telecommunications Inc...........D...... 330 628-5501
   Mogadore (G-14557)
Universal Recovery Systems...............D...... 614 299-0184
   Columbus (G-8817)

CONTRACTORS: Fire Detection & Burglar Alarm Systems

ABC Fire Inc ....E...... 440 237-6677
   North Royalton (G-15346)
D B A Inc ....E...... 513 541-6600
   Cincinnati (G-3394)
GA Business Purchaser LLC ....D...... 419 255-8400
   Toledo (G-17752)
Gene Ptacek Son Fire Eqp Inc ....E...... 216 651-8300
   Cleveland (G-5602)
Gillmore Security Systems Inc ....E...... 440 232-1000
   Cleveland (G-5608)
Habitec Security Inc.......................D...... 419 537-6768
   Holland (G-11887)
Koorsen Fire & Security Inc ....E...... 937 324-9405
   Vandalia (G-18530)
Megacity Fire Protection Inc ....E...... 937 335-0775
   Dayton (G-9605)
Paladin Protective Systems Inc...........E...... 216 441-6500
   Cleveland (G-6158)
Protech Security Inc ....E...... 330 499-3555
   Canton (G-2442)
Research & Investigation Assoc ....E...... 419 526-1299
   Mansfield (G-13234)
Riverside Electric Inc......................E...... 513 936-0100
   Cincinnati (G-4381)
Shiver Security Systems Inc ....E...... 513 719-4000
   Mason (G-13639)
Simplex Time Recorder LLC...............E...... 800 746-7539
   West Chester (G-19007)
Simplex Time Recorder LLC...............D...... 937 291-0355
   Miamisburg (G-14221)
Southeast Security Corporation ....E...... 330 239-4600
   Sharon Center (G-16726)
State Alarm Inc ....E...... 888 726-8111
   Youngstown (G-20217)
Vector Security Inc.........................E...... 440 466-7233
   Geneva (G-11249)
Vector Security Inc.........................E...... 330 726-9841
   Canfield (G-2164)

CONTRACTORS: Fire Sprinkler System Installation Svcs

ABC Fire Inc ....E...... 440 237-6677
   North Royalton (G-15346)
Eckert Fire Protection Systems...........E...... 513 948-1030
   Cincinnati (G-3481)
Fire Guard LLC ....E...... 740 625-5181
   Sunbury (G-17388)
Johnson Controls ....D...... 513 874-1227
   West Chester (G-18953)
Johnson Controls ....D...... 614 717-9079
   Dublin (G-10261)

Johnson Controls ....C...... 440 268-1160
   Strongsville (G-17317)
Vulcan Enterprises Inc ....E...... 419 396-3535
   Carey (G-2549)

CONTRACTORS: Floor Laying & Other Floor Work

Andover Floor Covering....................E...... 440 293-5339
   Newbury (G-15118)
Centimark Corporation.....................C...... 330 920-3560
   Stow (G-17194)
Clays Heritage Carpet Inc ....E...... 330 497-1280
   Canton (G-2257)
Cleveland Construction Inc ....E...... 440 255-8000
   Mentor (G-14031)
Cleveland Construction Inc ....E...... 740 927-9000
   Columbus (G-7224)
Command Carpet ....D...... 330 673-7404
   Kent (G-12224)
Company Inc ....E...... 216 431-2334
   Cleveland (G-5329)
Done-Rite Bowling Service Co ....E...... 440 232-3280
   Bedford (G-1278)
Florline Group Inc ....E...... 330 830-3380
   Massillon (G-13682)
OCP Contractors Inc.......................E...... 419 865-7168
   Holland (G-11903)
Preferred Acquisition Co LLC ....D...... 216 587-0957
   Cleveland (G-6229)
Prime Polymers Inc.........................E...... 330 662-4200
   Medina (G-13988)
Protective Coatings Inc ....E...... 937 275-7711
   Dayton (G-9721)
Regal Carpet Center Inc ....E...... 216 475-1844
   Cleveland (G-6296)
Rite Rug Co ....E...... 937 318-9197
   Fairborn (G-10681)
Samron Inc ....E...... 330 782-6539
   Youngstown (G-20203)
T and D Interiors Incorporated ....E...... 419 331-4372
   Lima (G-12760)
Tremco Incorporated ....B...... 216 292-5000
   Beachwood (G-1114)
W R Shepherd Inc ....E...... 614 889-2896
   Powell (G-16212)

CONTRACTORS: Flooring

Technical Construction Spc ....E...... 330 929-1088
   Cuyahoga Falls (G-9129)

CONTRACTORS: Food Concessions

Lobby Shoppes Inc.........................C...... 937 324-0002
   Springfield (G-17063)
Swim Incorporated ....E...... 614 885-1619
   Worthington (G-19855)

CONTRACTORS: Food Svcs Eqpt Installation

Kens Beverage Inc..........................E...... 513 874-8200
   Fairfield (G-10743)

CONTRACTORS: Foundation & Footing

Arledge Construction Inc ....E...... 614 732-4258
   Columbus (G-6969)
Central Ohio Poured Walls Inc ....E...... 614 889-0505
   Dublin (G-10166)
Cleveland Concrete Cnstr Inc ....D...... 216 741-3954
   Brooklyn Heights (G-1868)
Day Precision Wall Inc.....................E...... 513 353-2999
   Cleves (G-6727)
Gateway Concrete Forming Svcs ....D...... 513 353-2000
   Miamitown (G-14241)
Goettle Holding Company Inc.............C...... 513 825-8100
   Cincinnati (G-3623)
Halcomb Concrete Construction ....E...... 513 829-3576
   Fairfield (G-10733)
Hayes Concrete Construction ....E...... 513 648-9400
   Cincinnati (G-3685)
Hoyer Poured Walls Inc ....E...... 937 642-6148
   Marysville (G-13507)
J & D Home Improvement Inc ....D...... 740 927-0722
   Reynoldsburg (G-16310)
Lithko Contracting LLC ....C...... 614 733-0300
   Plain City (G-16057)
Lithko Contracting LLC ....D...... 513 863-5100
   Monroe (G-14574)
Menke Bros Construction Co ....E...... 419 286-2086
   Delphos (G-10031)

Metcon Ltd ....E 937 447-9200
  Bradford (*G-1762*)
Modern Poured Walls Inc ....D 440 647-6661
  Wellington (*G-18843*)
Shepherd Excavating Inc ....D 614 889-1115
  Dublin (*G-10333*)
Sowder Concrete Corporation ....E 937 890-1633
  Dayton (*G-9780*)

CONTRACTORS: Foundation Building

J & D Home Improvement Inc ....D 740 927-0722
  Reynoldsburg (*G-16310*)
Mural & Son Inc ....E 216 267-3322
  Cleveland (*G-6025*)
Ohio State Home Services Inc ....D 614 850-5600
  Hilliard (*G-11803*)
Protective Coatings Inc ....E 937 275-7711
  Dayton (*G-9721*)

CONTRACTORS: Fountain Installation

Lawn Management Sprinkler Co ....E 513 272-3808
  Cincinnati (*G-3913*)

CONTRACTORS: Garage Doors

Dortronic Service Inc ....E 216 739-3667
  Cleveland (*G-5443*)
Graf and Sons Inc ....E 614 481-2020
  Columbus (*G-7683*)
Nofziger Door Sales Inc ....C 419 337-9900
  Wauseon (*G-18808*)
Overhead Door Corporation ....D 330 674-7015
  Mount Hope (*G-14738*)
Overhead Inc ....E 419 476-7811
  Toledo (*G-17967*)

CONTRACTORS: Gas Field Svcs, NEC

Clearfield Ohio Holdings Inc ....D 740 947-5121
  Waverly (*G-18816*)
Stingray Pressure Pumping LLC ......E 405 648-4177
  Belmont (*G-1396*)

CONTRACTORS: General Electric

A J Goulder Electric Co ....E 440 942-4026
  Willoughby (*G-19501*)
Abbott Electric ....D 330 452-6601
  Canton (*G-2170*)
Accurate Electric Cnstr Inc ....C 614 863-1844
  Reynoldsburg (*G-16279*)
Aero Electrical Contractors ....E 614 834-8181
  Canal Winchester (*G-2103*)
Aey Electric Inc ....E 330 792-5745
  Youngstown (*G-19949*)
All Phase Power and Ltg Inc ....E 419 624-9640
  Sandusky (*G-16574*)
American Electric Power Co Inc ....E 614 716-1000
  Columbus (*G-6918*)
Archiable Electric Company ....D 513 621-1307
  Cincinnati (*G-2982*)
Area Energy & Electric Inc ....E 937 642-0386
  Marysville (*G-13483*)
Area Energy & Electric Inc ....C 937 498-4784
  Sidney (*G-16759*)
Atkins & Stang Inc ....D 513 242-8300
  Cincinnati (*G-2997*)
Atlas Electrical Construction ....E 440 323-5418
  Elyria (*G-10480*)
B & J Electrical Company Inc ....E 513 351-7100
  Cincinnati (*G-3014*)
Bansal Construction Inc ....E 513 874-5410
  Fairfield (*G-10698*)
Banta Electrical Contrs Inc ....E 513 353-4446
  Cleves (*G-6725*)
BCU Electric Inc ....E 419 281-8944
  Ashland (*G-656*)
Beacon Electric Company ....E 513 851-0711
  Cincinnati (*G-3029*)
Becdel Controls Incorporated ....E 330 652-1386
  Niles (*G-15147*)
Benevento Enterprises Inc ....D 216 621-5890
  Cleveland (*G-5054*)
Berwick Electric Company ....E 614 834-2301
  Canal Winchester (*G-2104*)
Biz Com Electric Inc ....E 513 961-7200
  Cincinnati (*G-3052*)
Bodie Electric Inc ....E 419 435-3672
  Fostoria (*G-10997*)
Bp-Ls-Pt Co ....D 614 841-4500
  Columbus (*G-7057*)

Brennan Electric LLC ....E 513 353-2229
  Miamitown (*G-14240*)
Bryan Electric Inc ....E 740 695-9834
  Saint Clairsville (*G-16481*)
Busy Bee Electric Inc ....E 513 353-3553
  Hooven (*G-11934*)
Butchko Electric Inc ....E 440 985-3180
  Amherst (*G-582*)
Calvin Electric LLC ....E 937 670-2558
  Arcanum (*G-624*)
Capital City Electric LLC ....E 614 933-8700
  New Albany (*G-14847*)
Carey Electric Co ....E 937 669-3399
  Vandalia (*G-18512*)
Cattrell Companies Inc ....D 740 537-2481
  Toronto (*G-18183*)
Chapel Electric Co LLC ....E 937 222-2290
  Dayton (*G-9291*)
Claypool Electric Inc ....C 740 653-5683
  Lancaster (*G-12381*)
Cochran Electric Inc ....E 614 847-0035
  Powell (*G-16189*)
Colgan-Davis Inc ....E 419 893-6116
  Maumee (*G-13771*)
Commercial Electric Pdts Corp ....E 216 241-2886
  Cleveland (*G-5318*)
Converse Electric Inc ....D 614 808-4377
  Grove City (*G-11422*)
Corporate Electric Company LLC ......E 330 331-7517
  Barberton (*G-951*)
Countryside Electric Inc ....D 614 478-7960
  Columbus (*G-7380*)
Craftsman Electric Inc ....D 513 891-4426
  Cincinnati (*G-3377*)
D C Minnick Contracting Ltd ....E 937 322-1012
  Springfield (*G-17028*)
D E Williams Electric Inc ....E 440 543-1222
  Chagrin Falls (*G-2644*)
Darana Hybrid Inc ....E 513 785-7540
  Hamilton (*G-11589*)
Davis H Elliot Cnstr Co Inc ....C 937 847-8025
  Miamisburg (*G-14162*)
Davis Pickering & Company Inc ....D 740 373-5896
  Marietta (*G-13324*)
Delta Electrical Contrs Ltd ....E 513 421-7744
  Cincinnati (*G-3421*)
Denier Electric Co Inc ....C 513 738-2641
  Harrison (*G-11665*)
Denier Electric Co Inc ....E 614 338-4664
  Grove City (*G-11425*)
DIA Electric Inc ....E 513 281-0783
  Cincinnati (*G-3427*)
Dillard Electric Inc ....E 937 836-5381
  Union (*G-18350*)
Dynalectric Company ....E 614 529-7500
  Columbus (*G-7480*)
Dynamic Mechanical Systems ....E 513 858-6722
  Fairfield (*G-10720*)
E S I Inc ....D 513 454-3741
  West Chester (*G-19048*)
Efficient Electric Corp ....E 614 552-0200
  Columbus (*G-7510*)
Electric Connection Inc ....D 614 436-1121
  Westerville (*G-19252*)
Electrical Corp America Inc ....D 440 245-3007
  Lorain (*G-12903*)
Enertech Electrical Inc ....E 330 536-2131
  Lowellville (*G-13040*)
Erb Electric Co ....C 740 633-5055
  Bridgeport (*G-1816*)
Fishel Company ....D 614 274-8100
  Columbus (*G-7588*)
Fowler Electric Co ....D 440 735-2385
  Bedford (*G-1281*)
Fresch Electric Inc ....E 419 626-2535
  Sandusky (*G-16609*)
Frey Electric Inc ....D 513 385-0700
  Cincinnati (*G-3593*)
Garber Electrical Contrs Inc ....E 937 771-5202
  Englewood (*G-10587*)
Gateway Electric Incorporated ....C 216 518-5500
  Cleveland (*G-5594*)
Gem Electric ....E 440 286-6200
  Chardon (*G-2697*)
Gem Industrial Inc ....D 419 666-6554
  Walbridge (*G-18622*)
Goodin Electric Inc ....E 740 522-3113
  Newark (*G-15038*)
Gorjanc Comfort Services Inc ....E 440 449-4411
  Cleveland (*G-5617*)

Harrington Electric Company ....D 216 361-5101
  Cleveland (*G-5662*)
Hatzel & Buehler Inc ....E 740 420-3088
  Circleville (*G-4834*)
Hilscher-Clarke Electric Co ....E 330 452-9806
  Canton (*G-2345*)
Hilscher-Clarke Electric Co ....D 740 622-5557
  Coshocton (*G-9017*)
Indrolect Co ....E 513 821-4788
  Cincinnati (*G-3758*)
Instrmntation Ctrl Systems Inc ....E 513 662-2600
  Cincinnati (*G-3765*)
J & J General Maintenance Inc ....E 740 533-9729
  Ironton (*G-12158*)
J W Didado Electric Inc ....C 330 374-0070
  Akron (*G-284*)
Jess Howard Electric Company ....C 614 864-2167
  Blacklick (*G-1481*)
Jims Electric Inc ....E 440 327-8800
  North Ridgeville (*G-15331*)
Joe Dickey Electric Inc ....D 330 549-3976
  North Lima (*G-15270*)
John H Cooper Elec Contg Co ....E 513 471-9900
  Cincinnati (*G-3823*)
John P Novatny Electric Co ....E 330 630-8900
  Akron (*G-293*)
JZE Electric Inc ....C 440 243-7600
  Cleveland (*G-5810*)
Kal Electric Inc ....E 740 593-8720
  Athens (*G-788*)
Kastle Electric Co LLC ....D 937 254-2681
  Moraine (*G-14666*)
Kastle Electric Company ....C 937 254-2681
  Moraine (*G-14667*)
Kastle Electric Company ....E 513 360-2901
  Monroe (*G-14572*)
Kastle Technologies Co LLC ....E 513 360-2901
  Monroe (*G-14573*)
Kastle Technologies Co LLC ....E 614 433-9860
  Columbus (*G-7885*)
Kathman Electric Co Inc ....E 513 353-3365
  Cleves (*G-6729*)
Kenmarc Inc ....E 513 541-2791
  Cincinnati (*G-3859*)
Kidron Electric Inc ....E 330 857-2871
  Kidron (*G-12308*)
Kraft Electrical Contg Inc ....E 513 467-0500
  Cincinnati (*G-3888*)
Kween Industries Inc ....E 513 932-2293
  Lebanon (*G-12477*)
Laibe Electric Co ....D 419 724-8200
  Toledo (*G-17847*)
Lake Erie Electric Inc ....D 440 835-5565
  Westlake (*G-19366*)
Lake Erie Electric Inc ....E 330 724-1241
  Akron (*G-308*)
Lake Erie Electric Inc ....E 419 529-4611
  Ontario (*G-15558*)
Lin R Rogers Elec Contrs Inc ....B 614 876-9336
  Hilliard (*G-11785*)
Lowry Controls Inc ....E 513 583-0182
  Loveland (*G-13009*)
M & L Electric Inc ....E 937 833-5154
  Lewisburg (*G-12570*)
Main Lite Electric Co Inc ....E 330 369-8333
  Warren (*G-18726*)
Mayers Electric Co Inc ....C 513 272-2900
  Cincinnati (*G-3982*)
McClintock Electric Inc ....E 330 264-6380
  Wooster (*G-19743*)
McKeever & Niekamp Elc Inc ....E 937 431-9363
  Beavercreek (*G-1169*)
MDU Resources Group Inc ....E 937 424-2550
  Moraine (*G-14673*)
Miller Cable Company ....D 419 639-2091
  Green Springs (*G-11355*)
New River Electrical Corp ....E 614 891-1142
  Westerville (*G-19285*)
Ngn Electric Corp ....E 330 923-2777
  Brecksville (*G-1793*)
Northeast Ohio Electric LLC ....B 216 587-9510
  Cleveland (*G-6093*)
Northwest Electrical Contg Inc ....E 419 865-4757
  Holland (*G-11901*)
Ohio Valley Elec Svcs LLC ....D 513 771-2410
  Blue Ash (*G-1623*)
Osterwisch Company Inc ....D 513 791-3282
  Cincinnati (*G-4189*)
Oyer Electric Inc ....D 740 773-2828
  Chillicothe (*G-2809*)

S E R V I C E S

Palazzo Brothers Electric Inc..........E 419 668-1100
  Norwalk (G-15451)
Penn-Ohio Electrical Company ....E 330 448-1234
  Masury (G-13742)
Perram Electric Inc ....E 330 239-2661
  Wadsworth (G-18612)
Positive Electric Inc ....E 937 428-0606
  Dayton (G-9700)
Precision Electrical Services ....E 740 474-4490
  Circleville (G-4846)
Proline Electric Inc ....E 740 687-4571
  Lancaster (G-12428)
Queen City Electric Inc ....E 513 591-2600
  Cincinnati (G-4313)
R & R Wiring Contractors Inc ....E 513 752-6304
  Batavia (G-1007)
R J Martin Elec Svcs Inc ....D 216 662-7100
  Bedford Heights (G-1326)
Rapier Electric Inc ....D 513 868-9087
  Hamilton (G-11636)
Reddy Electric Co ....C 937 372-8205
  Xenia (G-19922)
Regent Electric Inc ....D 419 476-8333
  Toledo (G-17998)
Reliable Contractors Inc ....D 937 433-0262
  Dayton (G-9730)
Reynolds Electric Company Inc ....D 419 228-5448
  Lima (G-12731)
Roehrenbeck Electric Inc ....E 614 443-9709
  Columbus (G-8545)
Romanoff Electric Inc ....C 614 755-4500
  Gahanna (G-11143)
Romanoff Electric Co LLC ....B 937 640-7925
  Toledo (G-18013)
Royal Electric Cnstr Corp ....E 614 253-6600
  Columbus (G-8556)
Ruhl Electric Co ....E 330 823-7230
  Alliance (G-551)
S & E Electric Inc ....E 330 425-7866
  Twinsburg (G-18315)
Sabroske Electric Inc ....E 419 332-6444
  Fremont (G-11092)
Safeway Electric Company Inc ....E 614 443-7672
  Columbus (G-8579)
Saturn Electric Inc ....E 937 278-2580
  Dayton (G-9752)
Security Fence Group Inc ....E 513 681-3700
  Cincinnati (G-4444)
Servall Electric Company Inc ....E 513 771-5584
  Cincinnati (G-4455)
Settle Muter Electric Ltd ....C 614 866-7554
  Columbus (G-8625)
Sidney Electric Company ....D 419 222-1109
  Sidney (G-16799)
Smink Electric Inc ....E 440 322-5518
  Elyria (G-10563)
South Shore Electric Inc ....E 440 366-6289
  Elyria (G-10564)
Speelman Electric Inc ....D 330 633-1410
  Tallmadge (G-17488)
Studebaker Electric Company ....D 937 890-9510
  Dayton (G-9797)
T & B Electric Ltd ....E 740 881-5696
  Ostrander (G-15656)
T J Williams Electric Co ....E 513 738-5366
  Harrison (G-11677)
Thompson Electric Inc ....C 330 686-2300
  Munroe Falls (G-14799)
Transtar Electric Inc ....D 419 385-7573
  Toledo (G-18108)
Tri Area Electric Co Inc ....E 330 744-0151
  Youngstown (G-20225)
Triec Electrical Services Inc ....D 937 323-3721
  Springfield (G-17128)
Unicustom Inc ....E 513 874-9806
  Fairfield (G-10795)
United Electric Company Inc ....E 502 459-5242
  Cincinnati (G-4679)
US Utility Electrical Svcs ....E 419 837-9753
  Perrysburg (G-15930)
USI Inc ....E 513 954-4561
  Cleves (G-6735)
Valley Electrical Cnsld Inc ....C 330 539-4044
  Girard (G-11304)
Vaughn Industries LLC ....B 419 396-3900
  Carey (G-2548)
Vaughn Industries LLC ....E 740 548-7100
  Lewis Center (G-12566)
Vec Inc ....E 330 539-4044
  Girard (G-11305)

VIP Electric Company ....E 440 255-0180
  Mentor (G-14123)
W W Schaub Electric Co ....E 330 494-3560
  Canton (G-2530)
Wachter Inc ....C 513 777-0701
  West Chester (G-19099)
Wagner Industrial Electric Inc ....E 937 298-7481
  Moraine (G-14705)
Wells Brothers Inc ....E 937 394-7559
  Anna (G-611)
Westfield Electric Inc ....E 419 862-0078
  Gibsonburg (G-11280)
Wood Electric Inc ....D 330 339-7002
  New Philadelphia (G-14989)
Woolace Electric Corp ....E 419 428-3161
  Stryker (G-17372)
X F Construction Svcs Inc ....E 614 575-2700
  Columbus (G-8923)
Zender Electric ....E 419 436-1538
  Fostoria (G-11015)

CONTRACTORS: Glass Tinting, Architectural & Automotive

AGC Automotive Americas ....D 937 599-3131
  Bellefontaine (G-1343)

CONTRACTORS: Glass, Glazing & Tinting

A E D Inc ....E 419 661-9999
  Northwood (G-15388)
Advanced Auto Glass Inc ....E 412 373-6675
  Akron (G-19)
AGC Automotive Americas ....D 937 599-3131
  Bellefontaine (G-1343)
Anderson Aluminum Corporation ....D 614 476-4877
  Columbus (G-6946)
E J Robinson Glass Co ....E 513 242-9250
  Cincinnati (G-3465)
J & B Equipment & Supply Inc ....E 419 884-1155
  Mansfield (G-13188)
Lakeland Glass Co ....E 440 277-4527
  Lorain (G-12912)
Lorain Glass Co Inc ....D 440 277-6004
  Lorain (G-12920)
Medina Glass Block Inc ....E 330 239-0239
  Medina (G-13974)
Modern Glass Pnt & Tile Co Inc ....E 740 454-1253
  Zanesville (G-20332)
Pioneer Cldding Glzing Systems ....E 216 816-4242
  Cleveland (G-6213)
Pioneer Cldding Glzing Systems ....E 513 583-5925
  Mason (G-13627)
R C Hemm Glass Shops Inc ....E 937 773-5591
  Piqua (G-16025)
Richardson Glass Service Inc ....E 740 366-5090
  Newark (G-15096)
Ryans All-Glass Incorporated ....E 513 771-4440
  Cincinnati (G-4417)
Thomas Glass Company Inc ....E 614 268-8611
  Worthington (G-19856)
Toledo Glass LLC ....E 419 241-3151
  Toledo (G-18084)
United GL & Panl Systems Inc ....E 330 244-9745
  Canton (G-2518)
Wiechart Enterprises Inc ....E 419 227-0027
  Lima (G-12784)

CONTRACTORS: Gutters & Downspouts

Apco Industries Inc ....D 614 224-2345
  Columbus (G-6956)
Durable Slate Co ....E 216 751-0151
  Shaker Heights (G-16707)
Leaffilter North LLC ....C 330 655-7950
  Hudson (G-11994)
Mid-America Gutters Inc ....E 513 671-4000
  West Chester (G-19067)
Mollett Seamless Gutter Co ....E 513 825-0500
  West Chester (G-18976)
Thiels Replacement Systems Inc ....D 419 289-6139
  Ashland (G-694)

CONTRACTORS: Heating & Air Conditioning

Aggressive Mechanical Inc ....E 614 443-3280
  Columbus (G-6884)
Allied Restaurant Svc Ohio Inc ....E 419 589-4759
  Mansfield (G-13134)
Area Energy & Electric Inc ....C 937 498-4784
  Sidney (G-16759)

Dave Pinkerton ....E 740 477-8888
  Chillicothe (G-2775)
Del Monde Inc ....E 859 371-7780
  Miamisburg (G-14165)
Drake State Air ....E 937 472-3740
  Eaton (G-10443)
Ellerbrock Heating & AC ....E 419 782-1834
  Defiance (G-9912)
Engineering Excellence ....D 972 535-3756
  Blue Ash (G-1553)
HEat Ttal Fclty Slutions Inc ....E 740 965-3005
  Galena (G-11159)
Horizon Mechanical and Elec ....E 419 529-2738
  Mansfield (G-13183)
J Feldkamp Design Build Ltd ....E 513 870-0601
  Cincinnati (G-3795)
Johnson Controls Inc ....E 614 895-6600
  Westerville (G-19266)
R & R Hvac Systems ....E 419 861-0266
  Holland (G-11907)
Schibi Heating & Cooling Corp ....E 513 385-3344
  Cincinnati (G-4436)
Service Experts Htg & AC LLC ....E 937 426-3444
  Springfield (G-17112)
Service Experts Htg & AC LLC ....E 513 489-3361
  Blue Ash (G-1650)
Service Experts Htg & AC LLC ....E 614 859-6993
  Columbus (G-8622)
Wenger Temperature Control ....E 614 586-4016
  Columbus (G-8887)

CONTRACTORS: Heating Systems Repair & Maintenance Svc

American Air Furnace Company ....D 614 876-1702
  Grove City (G-11404)
Emcor Fclities Svcs N Amer Inc ....D 614 430-5078
  Columbus (G-7513)
Thompson Heating & Cooling ....E 513 242-4450
  Cincinnati (G-4605)
Thompson Heating Corporation ....D 513 769-7696
  Cincinnati (G-4606)

CONTRACTORS: Highway & Street Construction, General

Aecom Energy & Cnstr Inc ....B 216 622-2300
  Cleveland (G-4906)
Altruism Society Inc ....D 877 283-4001
  Beachwood (G-1028)
Beaver Constructors Inc ....D 330 478-2151
  Canton (G-2210)
Brock & Sons Inc ....E 513 874-4555
  Fairfield (G-10701)
Cincinnati Fill Inc ....E 513 242-7526
  Cincinnati (G-3244)
D B Bentley Inc ....E 440 352-8495
  Painesville (G-15707)
D G M Inc ....D 740 226-1950
  Beaver (G-1120)
Don S Cisle Contractor Inc ....E 513 867-1400
  Hamilton (G-11592)
Erie Construction Group Inc ....E 419 625-7374
  Sandusky (G-16599)
Ferrous Metal Transfer ....E 216 671-8500
  Brooklyn (G-1861)
Fryman-Kuck General Contrs Inc ....E 937 274-2892
  Dayton (G-9452)
Independence Excavating Inc ....E 216 524-1700
  Independence (G-12082)
J A Donadee Corporation ....E 330 533-3305
  Canfield (G-2144)
J&B Steel Erectors Inc ....E 513 874-1722
  West Chester (G-18951)
K West Group LLC ....C 972 722-3874
  Perrysburg (G-15884)
Kenmore Construction Co Inc ....C 330 762-8936
  Akron (G-299)
Kenmore Construction Co Inc ....E 330 832-8888
  Massillon (G-13702)
Kokosing Construction Co Inc ....C 614 228-1029
  Westerville (G-19270)
Kokosing Construction Co Inc ....E 614 228-1029
  Westerville (G-19271)
Kokosing Inc ....D 614 212-5700
  Westerville (G-19272)
McDaniels Cnstr Corp Inc ....D 614 252-5852
  Columbus (G-8043)
Nerone & Sons Inc ....E 216 662-2235
  Cleveland (G-6057)

Perk Company Inc ....E 216 391-1444
   Cleveland *(G-6195)*

R B Jergens Contractors Inc ....D 937 669-9799
   Vandalia *(G-18538)*

Ray Bertolini Trucking Co ....E 330 867-0666
   Akron *(G-397)*

Ruhlin Company ....C 330 239-2800
   Sharon Center *(G-16724)*

Spieker Company ....E 419 872-7000
   Perrysburg *(G-15924)*

Stonegate Construction Inc ....D 740 423-9170
   Belpre *(G-1410)*

Sunesis Construction Company ....C 513 326-6000
   West Chester *(G-19014)*

Trafftech Inc ....E 216 361-8808
   Cleveland *(G-6538)*

Tucson Inc ....E 330 339-4935
   New Philadelphia *(G-14985)*

Velotta Company ....E 330 239-1211
   Sharon Center *(G-16727)*

Virginia Ohio-West Excvtg Co ....C 740 676-7464
   Shadyside *(G-16698)*

Waltek Inc ....E 614 469-0156
   Columbus *(G-8873)*

Westpatrick Corp ....E 614 875-8200
   Columbus *(G-8891)*

CONTRACTORS: *Highway & Street Paving*

Akil Incorporated ....E 419 625-0857
   Sandusky *(G-16573)*

Allied Paving Inc ....E 419 666-3100
   Holland *(G-11869)*

Armor Paving & Sealing ....E 614 751-6900
   Reynoldsburg *(G-16284)*

Butler Asphalt Co LLC ....E 937 890-1141
   Vandalia *(G-18511)*

Chemcote Inc ....C 614 792-2683
   Dublin *(G-10171)*

City of Lima ....E 419 221-5165
   Lima *(G-12613)*

City of Norwalk ....E 419 663-6715
   Norwalk *(G-15426)*

Columbus Asphalt Paving Inc ....E 614 759-9800
   Gahanna *(G-11113)*

Cunningham Paving Company ....E 216 581-8600
   Bedford *(G-1275)*

Decorative Paving Company ....E 513 576-1222
   Loveland *(G-12989)*

Ebony Construction Co ....E 419 841-3455
   Sylvania *(G-17421)*

Erie Blacktop Inc ....E 419 625-7374
   Sandusky *(G-16598)*

Fabrizi Trucking & Pav Co Inc ....C 330 483-3291
   Cleveland *(G-5504)*

Hicon Inc ....D 513 242-3612
   Cincinnati *(G-3701)*

J K Meurer Corp ....E 513 831-7500
   Loveland *(G-13003)*

Ken Heiberger Paving Inc ....D 614 837-0290
   Canal Winchester *(G-2112)*

Kirila Contractors Inc ....D 330 448-4055
   Brookfield *(G-1853)*

Kokosing Construction Inc ....A 330 263-4168
   Wooster *(G-19739)*

MBC Holdings Inc ....E 419 445-1015
   Archbold *(G-632)*

Miller Bros Const Inc ....E 419 445-1015
   Archbold *(G-633)*

Neff Paving Ltd ....E 740 453-3063
   Zanesville *(G-20345)*

Premier Asphalt Paving Co Inc ....E 440 237-6600
   North Royalton *(G-15364)*

R T Vernal Paving Inc ....E 330 549-3189
   North Lima *(G-15274)*

Scot Burton Contractors LLC ....E 440 564-1011
   Newbury *(G-15125)*

Shelly and Sands Inc ....E 614 444-5100
   Columbus *(G-8632)*

Shelly and Sands Inc ....D 419 529-8455
   Ontario *(G-15572)*

Shelly and Sands Inc ....E 740 453-0721
   Zanesville *(G-20360)*

Shelly Company ....E 419 396-7641
   Carey *(G-2547)*

Superior Paving & Materials ....E 330 499-5849
   Canton *(G-2504)*

Terminal Ready-Mix Inc ....E 440 288-0181
   Lorain *(G-12947)*

Vandalia Blacktop Seal Coating ....E 937 454-0571
   Dayton *(G-9850)*

CONTRACTORS: *Highway & Street Resurfacing*

K & M Construction Company ....C 330 723-3681
   Medina *(G-13963)*

Prime Polymers Inc ....E 330 662-4200
   Medina *(G-13988)*

CONTRACTORS: *Home & Office Intrs Finish, Furnish/Remodel*

Lorad LLC ....E 216 265-2862
   Westlake *(G-19370)*

Omni Construction Company Inc ....E 216 514-6664
   Beachwood *(G-1091)*

Ram Restoration LLC ....E 937 347-7418
   Dayton *(G-9726)*

Wmk LLC ....E 440 951-4335
   Mentor *(G-14125)*

CONTRACTORS: *Hotel, Motel/Multi-Family Home Renovtn/Remodel*

Cardinal Builders Inc ....E 614 237-1000
   Columbus *(G-7119)*

CFS Construction Inc ....E 513 559-4500
   Cincinnati *(G-3163)*

Ram Restoration LLC ....E 937 347-7418
   Dayton *(G-9726)*

CONTRACTORS: *Hydraulic Eqpt Installation & Svcs*

North Bay Construction Inc ....E 440 835-1898
   Westlake *(G-19380)*

CONTRACTORS: *Hydronics Heating*

Jackson Comfort Systems Inc ....E 330 468-3111
   Northfield *(G-15381)*

CONTRACTORS: *Indl Building Renovation, Remodeling & Repair*

Belfor USA Group Inc ....E 330 916-6468
   Peninsula *(G-15809)*

Cm-Gc LLC ....E 513 527-4141
   Cincinnati *(G-3313)*

DAG Construction Co Inc ....E 513 542-8597
   Cincinnati *(G-3397)*

Farrow Cleaners Co ....E 216 561-2355
   Cleveland *(G-5514)*

Fryman-Kuck General Contrs Inc ....E 937 274-2892
   Dayton *(G-9452)*

Grunwell-Cashero Co ....E 419 476-2426
   Toledo *(G-17774)*

Icon Environmental Group LLC ....E 513 426-6767
   Milford *(G-14396)*

Ingle-Barr Inc ....C 740 702-6117
   Chillicothe *(G-2793)*

Maintenance Unlimited Inc ....E 440 238-1162
   Strongsville *(G-17325)*

Matt Construction Services ....D 216 641-0030
   Cleveland *(G-5923)*

Mc Meechan Construction Co ....E 216 581-9373
   Cleveland *(G-5928)*

McGraw/Kokosing Inc ....B 614 212-5700
   Monroe *(G-14576)*

Miencorp Inc ....E 330 978-8511
   Niles *(G-15159)*

Mural & Son Inc ....E 216 267-3322
   Cleveland *(G-6025)*

Ram Construction Services of ....D 513 297-1857
   West Chester *(G-18990)*

Reinnovations Contracting Inc ....E 330 505-9035
   Mineral Ridge *(G-14511)*

Tradesmen Group Inc ....E 614 799-0889
   Plain City *(G-16070)*

Trisco Systems Incorporated ....C 419 339-9912
   Lima *(G-12769)*

Universal Fabg Cnstr Svcs Inc ....D 614 274-1128
   Columbus *(G-8815)*

Van Tassel Construction Corp ....E 419 873-0188
   Perrysburg *(G-15931)*

CONTRACTORS: *Insulation Installation, Building*

All Construction Services Inc ....E 330 225-1653
   Brunswick *(G-1918)*

Alloyd Insulation Co Inc ....E 937 890-7900
   Dayton *(G-9218)*

Boak & Sons Inc ....C 330 793-5646
   Youngstown *(G-19967)*

Buckholz Wall Systems LLC ....E 614 870-1775
   Hilliard *(G-11751)*

Builder Services Group Inc ....E 614 263-9378
   Columbus *(G-7095)*

Builder Services Group Inc ....E 513 942-2204
   Hamilton *(G-11560)*

Central Insulation Systems Inc ....E 513 242-0600
   Cincinnati *(G-3155)*

Community Action Comsn Belmont ....E 740 695-0293
   Saint Clairsville *(G-16483)*

Edwards Mooney & Moses ....D 614 351-1439
   Columbus *(G-7505)*

Global Insulation Inc ....E 330 479-3100
   Canton *(G-2327)*

Industrial Insul Coatings LLC ....E 800 506-1399
   Girard *(G-11288)*

Installed Building Pdts II LLC ....D 626 812-6070
   Columbus *(G-7827)*

Installed Building Pdts LLC ....E 614 308-9900
   Columbus *(G-7829)*

Installed Building Pdts LLC ....E 330 798-9640
   Akron *(G-278)*

Installed Building Pdts LLC ....E 419 662-4524
   Northwood *(G-15396)*

Insulating Sales Co Inc ....E 513 742-2600
   Cincinnati *(G-3766)*

Liberty Insulation Co Inc ....D 513 621-0108
   Beavercreek *(G-1166)*

M K Moore & Sons Inc ....E 937 236-1812
   Dayton *(G-9579)*

Pedersen Insulation Company ....E 614 471-3788
   Columbus *(G-8434)*

Priority 1 Construction Svcs ....E 513 922-0203
   Cincinnati *(G-4282)*

Rak Corrosion Control Inc ....E 440 985-2171
   Amherst *(G-596)*

Robinson Insulation Co Inc ....E 937 323-9599
   Springfield *(G-17102)*

Roofing By Insulation Inc ....E 937 315-5024
   New Carlisle *(G-14896)*

Sandel Corp ....E 614 475-5898
   Gahanna *(G-11144)*

Thermal Solutions Inc ....D 513 742-2836
   Fairfield *(G-10790)*

Thermal Solutions Inc ....D 740 886-2861
   Proctorville *(G-16220)*

Thermo-TEC Insulation Inc ....E 216 663-3842
   Euclid *(G-10659)*

Truteam LLC ....E 513 942-2204
   Hamilton *(G-11649)*

Unified Cnstr Systems Ltd ....E 330 773-2511
   Akron *(G-475)*

CONTRACTORS: *Kitchen & Bathroom Remodeling*

Bathroom Alternatives Inc ....E 937 434-1984
   Dayton *(G-9245)*

Cardinal Builders Inc ....E 614 237-1000
   Columbus *(G-7119)*

Complete Services Inc ....E 513 770-5575
   Mason *(G-13566)*

Erie Construction Mid-West Inc ....E 937 898-4688
   Dayton *(G-9417)*

Hughes Kitchens and Bath LLC ....E 330 455-5269
   Canton *(G-2351)*

Korman Construction Corp ....E 614 274-2170
   Columbus *(G-7924)*

CONTRACTORS: *Lighting Conductor Erection*

Maxwell Lightning Protection ....E 937 228-7250
   Dayton *(G-9590)*

CONTRACTORS: *Lighting Syst*

Brush Contractors Inc ....D 614 850-8500
   Columbus *(G-7083)*

Cls Facilities MGT Svcs Inc ....E 440 602-4600
   Mentor *(G-14032)*

Lawn Management Sprinkler Co ....E 513 272-3808
   Cincinnati *(G-3913)*

Quebe Holdings Inc ....D 937 222-2290
   Dayton *(G-9723)*

Wireless Environment LLC ....E 216 455-0192
   Mayfield Village *(G-13888)*

S E R V I C E S

CONTRACTORS: Lightweight Steel Framing Installation

OCP Contractors Inc ....E 419 865-7168
Holland *(G-11903)*

CONTRACTORS: Machine Rigging & Moving

Atlas Industrial Contrs LLC ....B ... 614 841-4500
Columbus *(G-7000)*

Canton Erectors Inc ....E 330 453-7363
Canton *(G-2232)*

Fenton Rigging & Contg Inc ....C 513 631-5500
Cincinnati *(G-3542)*

Hensley Industries Inc ....E 513 769-6666
Cincinnati *(G-3698)*

Myers Machinery Movers Inc ....E 614 871-5052
Grove City *(G-11455)*

Piqua Steel Co ....D 937 773-3632
Piqua *(G-16020)*

Sk Rigging Co Inc ....E 513 771-7766
Cincinnati *(G-4490)*

Standard Contg & Engrg Inc ....D 440 243-1001
Brookpark *(G-1906)*

CONTRACTORS: Machinery Dismantling

J R Mead Industrial Contrs ....E 614 891-4466
Galena *(G-11160)*

CONTRACTORS: Machinery Installation

A and A Mllwright Rigging Svcs .....E 513 396-6212
Cincinnati *(G-2888)*

Expert Crane Inc ....E 216 451-9900
Cleveland *(G-5502)*

Gem Industrial Inc ....D 419 666-6554
Walbridge *(G-18622)*

Glt Inc ....E 937 395-0508
Moraine *(G-14663)*

Grubb Construction Inc ....E 419 293-2316
Mc Comb *(G-13894)*

Hy-Tek Material Handling Inc ....D 614 497-2500
Columbus *(G-7790)*

Industrial Power Systems Inc ....C 419 531-3121
Rossford *(G-16461)*

Intertec Corporation ....B 419 537-9711
Toledo *(G-17824)*

Norris Brothers Co Inc ....C 216 771-2233
Cleveland *(G-6074)*

Spallinger Millwright Svc Co..........E 419 225-5830
Lima *(G-12742)*

Tesar Industrial Contrs Inc...........E 216 741-8008
Cleveland *(G-6517)*

CONTRACTORS: Maintenance, Parking Facility Eqpt

Purple Marlin Inc ....E 440 323-1291
Elyria *(G-10557)*

CONTRACTORS: Marble Installation, Interior

Cleveland Marble Mosaic Co ....C 216 749-2840
Cleveland *(G-5265)*

Cutting Edge Countertops Inc ....E 419 873-9500
Perrysburg *(G-15853)*

Legacy Ntral Stone Srfaces LLC .....E 419 420-7440
Findlay *(G-10934)*

T H Winston Company ....E 513 271-2123
Cincinnati *(G-4566)*

CONTRACTORS: Marble Masonry, Exterior

Cleveland Marble Mosaic Co ....C 216 749-2840
Cleveland *(G-5265)*

CONTRACTORS: Masonry & Stonework

Albert Freytag Inc ....E 419 628-2018
Minster *(G-14531)*

Bama Masonry Inc ....E 440 834-4175
Burton *(G-2014)*

Beaver Constructors Inc ....D 330 478-2151
Canton *(G-2210)*

Benchmark Masonry Contractors ....D 937 228-1225
Middletown *(G-14292)*

Buckner and Sons Masonry Inc ....E 614 279-9777
Columbus *(G-7092)*

Canaan Companies Inc ....E 419 842-8373
Toledo *(G-17634)*

Centennial Prsrvtion Group LLC ....E 614 238-0730
Columbus *(G-7150)*

Empire Masonry Company Inc ....D 440 230-2800
North Royalton *(G-15354)*

F B and S Masonry Inc ....E 330 608-3442
Silver Lake *(G-16807)*

Foti Construction Company LLP ....E 440 347-0728
Wickliffe *(G-19459)*

Hester Masonry Co Inc ....E 937 890-2283
Vandalia *(G-18528)*

Hicon Inc ....D 513 242-3612
Cincinnati *(G-3701)*

Hovest Construction ....E 419 456-3426
Ottawa *(G-15659)*

Hummel Industries Incorporated.......E 513 242-1321
Cincinnati *(G-3741)*

Industrial First Inc ....C 216 991-8605
Bedford *(G-1286)*

Karst & Sons Inc ....E 614 501-9530
Reynoldsburg *(G-16313)*

Miter Masonry Contractors ....E 513 821-3334
Arlington Heights *(G-643)*

Pioneer Cldding Glzing Systems ....E 216 816-4242
Cleveland *(G-6213)*

Quality Masonry Company Inc ....E 740 387-6720
Marion *(G-13453)*

S A Storer and Sons Company ....D 419 843-3133
Sylvania *(G-17450)*

Spartan Construction Co Inc ....E 419 389-1854
Monclova *(G-14559)*

Steven H Byerly Inc ....E 614 882-0092
Columbus *(G-8699)*

Warren Guillard Bricklayers ....E 330 633-3855
Tallmadge *(G-17499)*

Wasiniak Construction Inc ....D 419 668-8624
Norwalk *(G-15459)*

Whitaker Masonry Inc ....E 330 225-7970
Brunswick *(G-1946)*

William Kerfoot Masonry Inc ....E 330 772-6460
Burghill *(G-2010)*

CONTRACTORS: Mechanical

A J Stockmeister Inc ....E 740 286-2106
Jackson *(G-12168)*

Advanced Mechanical Svcs Inc ....E 937 879-7426
Fairborn *(G-10662)*

Ayers-Sterrett Inc ....E 419 238-5480
Van Wert *(G-18473)*

Ayrshire Inc ....D 440 992-0743
Ashtabula *(G-721)*

Bayes Inc ....E 419 661-3933
Perrysburg *(G-15835)*

Brewer-Garrett Co ....C 440 243-3535
Middleburg Heights *(G-14248)*

Buckeye Mechanical Contg Inc ....E 740 282-0089
Toronto *(G-18181)*

Cahill Corporation ....E 330 724-1224
Uniontown *(G-18359)*

Campbell Inc ....E 419 476-4444
Northwood *(G-15391)*

Cattrell Companies Inc ....D 740 537-2481
Toronto *(G-18183)*

Chemsteel Construction Company ....E 440 234-3930
Middleburg Heights *(G-14249)*

Clearcreek Construction ....E 740 420-3568
Stoutsville *(G-17186)*

Coleman Spohn Corporation ....E 216 431-8070
Cleveland *(G-5311)*

Commercial Hvac Inc ....E 513 396-6100
Cincinnati *(G-3338)*

Complete Mechanical Svcs LLC.......D 513 489-3080
Blue Ash *(G-1536)*

Debra-Kuempel Inc ....E 513 271-6500
Cincinnati *(G-3414)*

Dimech Services Inc ....E 419 727-0111
Toledo *(G-17701)*

Dunbar Mechanical Inc ....D 734 856-6601
Toledo *(G-17706)*

Edwards Electrical & Mech ....E 614 485-2003
Columbus *(G-7507)*

Enerfab Inc ....B 513 641-0500
Cincinnati *(G-3498)*

Energy MGT Specialists Inc ....E 216 676-9045
Cleveland *(G-5479)*

Enervise Incorporated ....E 513 761-6000
Blue Ash *(G-1552)*

Enervise Incorporated ....E 614 885-9800
Columbus *(G-7515)*

Envirnmental Engrg Systems Inc ....E 937 228-6492
Dayton *(G-9415)*

Excellence Alliance Group Inc..........E 513 619-4800
Cincinnati *(G-3524)*

Farber Corporation ....E 614 294-1626
Columbus *(G-7561)*

Fowler Electric Co......................D 440 735-2385
Bedford *(G-1281)*

G Mechanical Inc.......................E 614 844-6750
Columbus *(G-7639)*

Gem Industrial Inc......................D...... 419 666-6554
Walbridge *(G-18622)*

Greer & Whitehead Cnstr Inc ....E 513 202-1757
Harrison *(G-11668)*

Guenther Mechanical Inc ....C...... 419 289-6900
Ashland *(G-674)*

Industrial Power Systems Inc ....C 419 531-3121
Rossford *(G-16461)*

Jarvis Mechanical Constrs Inc ....E 513 831-0055
Milford *(G-14398)*

John F Gallagher Plumbing Co ....E 440 946-4256
Eastlake *(G-10430)*

Julian Speer Co ....D 614 261-6331
Columbus *(G-7876)*

Kirk Williams Company Inc ....E 614 875-9023
Grove City *(G-11445)*

Kuempel Service Inc ....E 513 271-6500
Cincinnati *(G-3894)*

Limbach Company LLC ....C 614 299-2175
Columbus *(G-7978)*

Lochard Inc ....D 937 492-8811
Sidney *(G-16784)*

Marlin Mechanical LLC ....E 800 669-2645
Cleveland *(G-5910)*

Mechancal/Industrial Contg Inc ....E 513 489-8282
Cincinnati *(G-3991)*

Mechanical Cnstr Managers LLC ....C 937 274-1987
Dayton *(G-9597)*

Mechanical Systems Dayton Inc ....D 937 254-3235
Dayton *(G-9181)*

Mid-Ohio Mechanical Inc ....E 740 587-3362
Granville *(G-11346)*

Monroe Mechanical Incorporated.......E 513 539-7555
Monroe *(G-14577)*

Osterfeld Champion Service ....E 937 254-8437
Dayton *(G-9679)*

Premier Rstrtion Mech Svcs LLC ....E 513 420-1600
Middletown *(G-14322)*

Process Construction Inc ....D 513 251-2211
Cincinnati *(G-4289)*

R Kelly Inc ....E 513 631-8488
Cincinnati *(G-4331)*

Regal Plumbing & Heating Co ....E 937 492-2894
Sidney *(G-16795)*

Relmec Mechanical LLC ....C 216 391-1030
Cleveland *(G-6302)*

Rmf Nooter Inc ....D 419 727-1970
Toledo *(G-18009)*

RPC Mechanical Services ....C 513 733-1641
Cincinnati *(G-4405)*

Sauer Group Inc ....C 614 853-2500
Columbus *(G-8592)*

Sauer Incorporated ....D 614 853-2500
Columbus *(G-8593)*

Schmid Mechanical Co ....E 614 261-6331
Columbus *(G-8601)*

Schweizer Dipple Inc ....D 440 786-8090
Cleveland *(G-6378)*

Scioto Services LLc ....E 937 644-0888
Marysville *(G-13527)*

Sexton Industrial Inc ....C 513 530-5555
West Chester *(G-19080)*

Speer Industries Incorporated ....C 614 261-6331
Columbus *(G-8671)*

The Peck-Hannaford Briggs Co ....D 513 681-4600
Cincinnati *(G-4595)*

Tilton Corporation ....C 419 227-6421
Lima *(G-12762)*

TP Mechanical Contractors Inc ....C 614 253-8556
Columbus *(G-8768)*

Trame Mechanical Inc..................E 937 258-1000
Dayton *(G-9820)*

Trep Ltd.................................E 419 717-5624
Napoleon *(G-14818)*

Triton Services Inc ....C 513 679-6800
Mason *(G-13650)*

Vaughn Industries LLC ....B 419 396-3900
Carey *(G-2548)*

Vaughn Industries LLC ....E 740 548-7100
Lewis Center *(G-12566)*

Warner Mechanical Corporation.......E 419 332-7116
Fremont *(G-11106)*

Western Reserve Mechanical Inc ....E 330 652-3888
Niles *(G-15175)*

York-Mahoning Mech Contrs Inc ....D 330 788-7011
Youngstown (G-20252)

CONTRACTORS: Millwrights

Hgc Construction Co ....D 513 861-8866
Cincinnati (G-3700)

K F T Inc ....D 513 241-5910
Cincinnati (G-3843)

Orbit Movers & Erectors Inc ....E 937 277-8080
Dayton (G-9677)

CONTRACTORS: Mosaic Work

Midwest Mosaic Inc ....E 419 377-3894
Toledo (G-17915)

CONTRACTORS: Multi-Family Home Remodeling

Garland Group Inc ....E 614 294-4411
Columbus (G-7650)

Klingbeil Management Group Co ....E 614 220-8900
Columbus (G-7911)

Oliver House Rest Complex ....D 419 243-1302
Toledo (G-17960)

Residntial Coml Rnovations Inc ....E 330 815-1476
Clinton (G-6737)

Rubber City Realty Inc..........................D 330 745-9034
Akron (G-413)

Safeguard Properties MGT LLC ....A 216 739-2900
Cleveland (G-6362)

CONTRACTORS: Nonresidential Building Design & Construction

Hi-Five Development Svcs Inc...............E 513 336-9280
Mason (G-13594)

Wenger Temperature Control ....E 614 586-4016
Columbus (G-8887)

CONTRACTORS: Office Furniture Installation

Corporate Environments of Ohio ....E 614 358-3375
Columbus (G-7372)

Custom Fabricators Inc ....E 216 831-2266
Cleveland (G-5391)

Jtc Contracting Inc ....E 216 635-0745
Cleveland (G-5807)

Lincoln Moving & Storage Co ....D 216 741-5500
Cleveland (G-5871)

Modular Systems Technicians ....E 216 459-2630
Cleveland (G-6005)

P-N-D Communications Inc....................E 419 683-1922
Crestline (G-9059)

Wegman Construction Company ....E 513 381-1111
Cincinnati (G-4773)

CONTRACTORS: Oil & Gas Field Fire Fighting Svcs

Cgh-Global Emerg Mngmt Strateg ....E 800 376-0655
Cincinnati (G-2843)

CONTRACTORS: Oil & Gas Field Geological Exploration Svcs

New World Energy Resources..............B 740 344-4087
Newark (G-15081)

CONTRACTORS: Oil & Gas Field Geophysical Exploration Svcs

Dlz Ohio Inc ....C 614 888-0040
Columbus (G-7462)

CONTRACTORS: Oil & Gas Well Casing Cement Svcs

Terra Star Inc.......................................E 405 200-1336
Waynesburg (G-18830)

CONTRACTORS: Oil & Gas Well Drilling Svc

Eclipse Resources - Ohio LLC..............E 740 452-4503
Zanesville (G-20303)

J D Drilling Co ....E 740 949-2512
Racine (G-16229)

Kilbarger Construction Inc....................C 740 385-6019
Logan (G-12843)

Qes Pressure Control LLC ....E 740 489-5721
Lore City (G-12953)

Stratagraph Ne Inc ....E 740 373-3091
Marietta (G-13384)

Victor McKenzie Drilling Co ....E 740 453-0834
Zanesville (G-20372)

CONTRACTORS: Oil & Gas Well Flow Rate Measurement Svcs

Fts International Inc..............................A 330 754-2375
East Canton (G-10386)

CONTRACTORS: Oil & Gas Well On-Site Foundation Building Svcs

Greer & Whitehead Cnstr Inc ....E 513 202-1757
Harrison (G-11668)

CONTRACTORS: Oil & Gas Well Redrilling

Decker Drilling Inc ....E 740 749-3939
Vincent (G-18585)

CONTRACTORS: Oil Field Haulage Svcs

Fishburn Tank Truck Service ....D 419 253-6031
Marengo (G-13303)

CONTRACTORS: Oil Field Mud Drilling Svcs

Kelchner Inc ....C 937 704-9890
Springboro (G-16971)

CONTRACTORS: Oil Sampling Svcs

Bdi Inc ....C 216 642-9100
Cleveland (G-5045)

CONTRACTORS: Oil/Gas Field Casing, Tube/Rod Running, Cut/Pull

Varco LP...E 440 277-8696
Lorain (G-12950)

CONTRACTORS: Oil/Gas Well Construction, Rpr/Dismantling Svcs

Ingle-Barr Inc.......................................C 740 702-6117
Chillicothe (G-2793)

Siler Excavation Services ....E 513 400-8628
Milford (G-14432)

CONTRACTORS: On-Site Welding

Burdens Machine & Welding ....E 740 345-9246
Newark (G-15019)

Lefeld Welding & Stl Sups Inc ....E 419 678-2397
Coldwater (G-6762)

Marsam Metalfab Inc............................E 330 405-1520
Twinsburg (G-18295)

Quality Fabricated Metals Inc ....E 330 332-7008
Salem (G-16555)

Six C Fabrication Inc ....D 330 296-5594
Ravenna (G-16267)

CONTRACTORS: Ornamental Metal Work

Architectural Metal Erectors ....E 513 242-5106
Cincinnati (G-2983)

CONTRACTORS: Paint & Wallpaper Stripping

Decoating Inc ....E 419 347-9191
Shelby (G-16745)

CONTRACTORS: Painting & Wall Covering

A & A Safety Inc ....E 513 943-6100
Amelia (G-563)

Cummins Building Maint Inc..................D 740 726-9800
Prospect (G-16221)

David W Steinbach Inc ....E 330 497-5959
Canton (G-2279)

National Electro-Coatings Inc...............D 216 898-0080
Cleveland (G-6043)

Performance Painting LLC ....E 440 735-3340
Oakwood Village (G-15492)

CONTRACTORS: Painting, Commercial

American Star Painting Co LLC..............E 740 373-5634
Marietta (G-13311)

August Groh & Sons Inc ....E 513 821-0090
Cincinnati (G-3004)

Dennis Todd Painting Inc ....E 614 879-7952
West Jefferson (G-19106)

Ionno Properties s Corp ....E 330 479-9267
Dennison (G-10051)

Johnson & Fischer Inc ....E 614 276-8868
Columbus (G-7862)

Muha Construction Inc ....E 937 435-0678
Dayton (G-9647)

Napoleon Machine LLC ....E 419 591-7010
Napoleon (G-14813)

Painting Company ....C 614 873-1334
Plain City (G-16063)

Preferred Acquisition Co LLC................D 216 587-0957
Cleveland (G-6229)

South Town Painting Inc ....E 937 847-1600
Miamisburg (G-14225)

Unique Construction Svcs Inc ....E 513 608-1363
Blue Ash (G-1673)

W F Bolin Company Inc ....E 614 276-6397
Columbus (G-8868)

Yerman & Young Painting Inc ....E 330 861-0022
Barberton (G-973)

CONTRACTORS: Painting, Commercial, Exterior

Allstate Painting & Contg Co ....D 330 220-5533
Brunswick (G-1919)

Barbara Gheens Painting Inc.................E 740 949-0405
Long Bottom (G-12877)

Costello Pntg Bldg Restoration.............E 513 321-3326
Cincinnati (G-3366)

Dependable Painting Co ....E 216 431-4470
Cleveland (G-5417)

Mike Morris ....E 330 767-4122
Brewster (G-1811)

CONTRACTORS: Painting, Commercial, Interior

Frank Novak & Sons Inc ....D 216 475-2495
Cleveland (G-5573)

Lou Ritenour Decorators Inc ....D 330 425-3232
Twinsburg (G-18294)

Masterpiece Painting Company ....E 330 395-9900
Warren (G-18727)

Protective Coatings Inc ....E 937 275-7711
Dayton (G-9721)

CONTRACTORS: Painting, Indl

A B Industrial Coatings ....E 614 228-0383
Columbus (G-6846)

Eagle Industrial Painting LLC ....E 330 866-5965
Magnolia (G-13111)

Flamos Enterprises Inc ....E 330 478-0009
Canton (G-2315)

Gpc Contracting Company ....E 740 264-6060
Steubenville (G-17156)

Industrial Mill Maintenance ....E 330 746-1155
Youngstown (G-20078)

P & W Painting Contractors Inc ....E 419 698-2209
Toledo (G-17969)

Vimas Painting Company Inc ....E 330 536-2222
Lowellville (G-13044)

CONTRACTORS: Painting, Residential

Cipriano Painting ....E 440 892-1827
Cleveland (G-5181)

Classic Papering & Painting ....E 614 221-0505
Columbus (G-7221)

Commercial Painting Inc ....E 614 298-9963
Worthington (G-19799)

Kendrick-Mollenauer Pntg Co...............E 614 443-7037
Columbus (G-7892)

Lehn Painting Inc ....E 513 732-1515
Batavia (G-1003)

Perry Interiors Inc ....E 513 761-9333
Batavia (G-1006)

Residence Artists Inc ....E 440 286-8822
Chardon (G-2710)

CONTRACTORS: Parking Facility Eqpt Installation

Signature Control Systems LLC............E 614 864-2222
Columbus (G-8639)

Employee Codes: A=Over 500 employees, B=251-500
C=101-250, D=51-100, E=25-50   2019 Harris Ohio
Services Directory   1391

CONTRACTORS: Parking Lot Maintenance

Camco Inc ....E 740 477-3682
  Circleville (G-4827)
Image Pavement Maintenance ....E 937 833-9200
  Brookville (G-1914)

CONTRACTORS: Patio & Deck Construction & Repair

Bzak Landscaping Inc ....E 513 831-0907
  Milford (G-14375)
Deerfield Farms ....E 330 584-4715
  Deerfield (G-9903)
North Branch Nursery Inc ....E 419 287-4679
  Pemberville (G-15805)
Olde Towne Windows Inc ....E 419 626-9613
  Milan (G-14364)
Services On Deck Inc ....E 513 759-2854
  Liberty Township (G-12585)
Shade Tree Cool Living LLC ....E 614 844-5990
  Columbus (G-8626)

CONTRACTORS: Pavement Marking

Aero-Mark Inc ....E 330 995-0100
  Streetsboro (G-17244)
Gradient Corporation ....E 513 779-0000
  Cincinnati (G-3631)
Kneisel Contracting Corp ....E 513 615-8816
  Cincinnati (G-3882)
Mark Dura Inc ....E 330 995-0883
  Aurora (G-836)

CONTRACTORS: Pile Driving

Goettle Holding Company Inc ....C 513 825-8100
  Cincinnati (G-3623)
Righter Construction Svcs Inc ....E 614 272-9700
  Columbus (G-8532)

CONTRACTORS: Pipe & Boiler Insulating

M K Moore & Sons Inc ....E 937 236-1812
  Dayton (G-9579)
Priority III Contracting Inc ....E 513 922-0203
  Cincinnati (G-4283)
R E Kramig & Co Inc ....C 513 761-4010
  Cincinnati (G-4330)

CONTRACTORS: Pipe Laying

Steelial Wldg Met Fbrction Inc ....E 740 669-5300
  Vinton (G-18586)

CONTRACTORS: Plastering, Plain or Ornamental

Cleveland Construction Inc ....E 440 255-8000
  Mentor (G-14031)
Cleveland Construction Inc ....E 740 927-9000
  Columbus (G-7224)
Lm Constrction Trry Lvrini Inc................E 740 695-9604
  Saint Clairsville (G-16492)
Synthetic Stucco Corporation ....E 513 897-9227
  Waynesville (G-18836)
Western Reserve Interiors Inc ....E 216 447-1081
  Cleveland (G-6676)

CONTRACTORS: Plumbing

A AAA H Jacks Plumbing Htg Co ....E 440 946-1166
  Wickliffe (G-19453)
A-1 Advanced Plumbing Inc ....E 614 873-0548
  Plain City (G-16040)
A-Team LLC ....E 216 271-7223
  Cleveland (G-4885)
ABC Piping Co ....E 216 398-4000
  Brooklyn Heights (G-1863)
Adelmos Electric Sewer Clg Co...............E 216 641-2301
  Brooklyn Heights (G-1864)
American Residential Svcs LLC ....D 216 561-8880
  Cleveland (G-4964)
American Residential Svcs LLC ....E 888 762-7752
  Columbus (G-6937)
Applied Mechanical Systems Inc ....D 513 825-1800
  Cincinnati (G-2976)
ARS Rescue Rooter Inc ....E 440 842-8494
  Cleveland (G-5009)
Aztec Plumbing Inc ....E 513 732-3320
  Milford (G-14373)
Bay Mechanical & Elec Corp...................D....... 440 282-6816
  Lorain (G-12885)

Bellman Plumbing Inc ....E 440 324-4477
  Elyria (G-10481)
Best Plumbing Limited ....E 614 855-1919
  New Albany (G-14843)
Blue Chip Plumbing Inc...........................D 513 941-4010
  Cincinnati (G-3062)
Brady Plumbing & Heating Inc ....E 440 324-4261
  Elyria (G-10484)
Bruner Corporation ....C 614 334-9000
  Hilliard (G-11749)
Crawford Mechanical Svcs Inc ....D 614 478-9424
  Columbus (G-7385)
D C Minnick Contracting Ltd ....E 937 322-1012
  Springfield (G-17028)
Dar Plumbing..E 614 445-8243
  Columbus (G-7417)
Diewald & Pope Inc................................E 614 861-6160
  Reynoldsburg (G-16298)
Dival Inc ....D 216 831-4200
  Warrensville Heights (G-18777)
Dynamic Mechanical Systems ....E 513 858-6722
  Fairfield (G-10720)
Eaton Plumbing Inc................................E 614 891-7005
  Westerville (G-19251)
Ecoplumbers Inc ....E 614 299-9903
  Hilliard (G-11765)
Enviro-Flow Companies Ltd ....E 740 453-7980
  Zanesville (G-20306)
Flickinger Piping Company Inc ....E 330 364-4224
  Dover (G-10078)
Freeland Contracting Co ....E 614 443-2718
  Columbus (G-7623)
Glennco Systems Inc..............................E 740 353-4328
  Portsmouth (G-16140)
Grabill Plumbing & Heating ....E 330 756-2075
  Beach City (G-1024)
Gross Plumbing Incorporated ....E 440 324-9999
  Elyria (G-10514)
H & M Plumbing Co.................................E 614 491-4880
  Columbus (G-7707)
Houston Dick Plbg & Htg Inc ....E 740 763-3961
  Newark (G-15043)
J & D Home Improvement Inc ....D....... 740 927-0722
  Reynoldsburg (G-16310)
Jeff Plumber Inc.....................................E 330 940-2600
  Akron (G-289)
Ken Neyer Plumbing Inc.........................C 513 353-3311
  Cleves (G-6730)
Komar Plumbing Co ....E 330 758-5073
  Youngstown (G-20094)
Lippincott Plumbing-Heating AC............E 419 222-0856
  Lima (G-12689)
Mansfield Plumbing Pdts LLC ....E 330 496-2301
  Big Prairie (G-1472)
Marvin W Mielke Inc...............................E 330 725-8845
  Medina (G-13969)
Mc Phillips Plbg Htg & AC Co ....E 216 481-1400
  Cleveland (G-5929)
Mechanical Construction Co ....E 740 353-5668
  Portsmouth (G-16154)
Midwestern Plumbing Service ....E 513 753-0050
  Cincinnati (G-4051)
Mj Baumann Co Inc.................................D....... 614 759-7100
  Columbus (G-8092)
Muetzel Plumbing & Heating Co.............D 614 299-7700
  Columbus (G-8120)
Nelson Stark Company ....C 513 489-0866
  Cincinnati (G-4106)
Neptune Plumbing & Heating Co.............D 216 475-9100
  Cleveland (G-6056)
Northern Ohio Plumbing Co ....E 440 951-3370
  Eastlake (G-10433)
Northern Plumbing Systems.....................E....... 513 831-5111
  Goshen (G-11313)
Perry Kelly Plumbing Inc.........................E 513 528-6554
  Cincinnati (G-4232)
Peterman Plumbing and Htg Inc..............E 330 364-4497
  Dover (G-10093)
Pioneer Pipe Inc.....................................A....... 740 376-2400
  Marietta (G-13370)
Piper Plumbing Inc ....E 330 274-0160
  Mantua (G-13275)
Professional Plumbing Services ....E 740 454-1066
  Zanesville (G-20356)
Queen City Mechanicals Inc ....E 513 353-1430
  Cincinnati (G-4316)
Rapid Plumbing Inc.................................D....... 513 575-1509
  Loveland (G-13023)
Roman Plumbing Company ....D....... 330 455-5155
  Canton (G-2462)

Ron Johnson Plumbing and Htg ....E 419 433-5365
  Norwalk (G-15455)
Roto-Rooter Development Co..................D 513 762-6690
  Cincinnati (G-4398)
Roto-Rooter Services Company ....D 513 762-6690
  Cincinnati (G-4400)
S&D/Osterfeld Mech Contrs Inc ....E 937 277-1700
  Dayton (G-9746)
Schmid Mechanical Inc ....E 330 264-3633
  Wooster (G-19765)
Slagle Mechanical Contractors ....E 937 492-4151
  Sidney (G-16801)
Standard Plumbing & Heating Co ....D 330 453-5150
  Canton (G-2485)
Steel Valley Construction Co ....E 330 392-8391
  Warren (G-18746)
Steingass Mechanical Contg ....E 330 725-6090
  Medina (G-14005)
Thomas J Dyer Company ....C 513 321-8100
  Cincinnati (G-4602)
U S A Plumbing Company ....E 614 882-6402
  Columbus (G-8792)
Wells Brothers Inc.................................D....... 937 394-7559
  Anna (G-611)
West Jefferson Plumbing Htg ....E 614 879-9606
  West Jefferson (G-19113)
Whisler Plumbing & Heating Inc..............E 330 833-2875
  Massillon (G-13735)
Whitt Inc ....E 513 753-7707
  Amelia (G-577)
Wilkes & Company Inc ....E 419 433-2325
  Huron (G-12035)

CONTRACTORS: Pollution Control Eqpt Installation

McGill Airclean LLC ....D 614 829-1200
  Columbus (G-8045)

CONTRACTORS: Post Disaster Renovations

Belfor USA Group Inc ....E 513 860-3111
  West Chester (G-19043)
C M S Enterprises Inc ....E 740 653-1940
  Lancaster (G-12374)
Design Rstrtion Reconstruction ....E 330 563-0010
  North Canton (G-15196)
Disaster Reconstruction Inc ....E 440 918-1523
  Eastlake (G-10428)
Stanley Stemer of Akron Canton.............E 330 785-5005
  Coventry Township (G-9043)

CONTRACTORS: Power Generating Eqpt Installation

Clopay Corporation ....C....... 800 282-2260
  Mason (G-13564)

CONTRACTORS: Precast Concrete Struct Framing & Panel Placing

Frameco Inc ....E 216 433-7080
  Cleveland (G-5570)
Henry Gurtzweiler Inc............................D 419 729-3955
  Toledo (G-17801)
Vmi Group Inc ....D....... 330 405-4146
  Macedonia (G-13088)

CONTRACTORS: Prefabricated Window & Door Installation

Advance Door Company ....E 216 883-2424
  Cleveland (G-4903)
Burbank Inc ....E 419 698-3434
  Toledo (G-17632)
Dayton Door Sales Inc ....E 937 253-9181
  Dayton (G-9364)
Erie Construction Mid-West Inc ....E 419 472-4200
  Toledo (G-17716)
Midwest Curtainwalls Inc ....D 216 641-7900
  Cleveland (G-5989)
OK Interiors Corp ....C 513 742-3278
  Cincinnati (G-4164)
Ray St Clair Roofing Inc ....E 513 874-1234
  Fairfield (G-10773)
Regency Windows Corporation ....D 330 963-4077
  Twinsburg (G-18310)
Ryans All-Glass Incorporated ....E 513 771-4440
  Cincinnati (G-4417)
Thiels Replacement Systems Inc............D 419 289-6139
  Ashland (G-694)

Window Factory of America.................D...... 440 439-3050
Bedford **(G-1314)**

CONTRACTORS: Process Piping

Lucas Plumbing & Heating Inc..........E...... 440 282-4567
Lorain **(G-12925)**
United Group Services Inc.................C...... 800 633-9690
West Chester **(G-19094)**

CONTRACTORS: Refractory or Acid Brick Masonry

Allen Refractories Company................C...... 740 927-8000
Pataskala **(G-15782)**
Onex Construction Inc........................E...... 330 995-9015
Streetsboro **(G-17264)**

CONTRACTORS: Refrigeration

All Temp Refrigeration Inc ....E...... 419 692-5016
Delphos **(G-10019)**
Dickson Industrial Park Inc.................E...... 740 377-9162
South Point **(G-16931)**
Hattenbach Company..........................D...... 216 881-5200
Cleveland **(G-5666)**
Morrison Inc......................................E...... 740 373-5869
Marietta **(G-13361)**
North East Mechanical Inc ....E...... 440 871-7525
Westlake **(G-19381)**
Wadsworth Service Inc........................E...... 419 861-8181
Middleburg Heights **(G-14265)**

CONTRACTORS: Resilient Floor Laying

River City Furniture LLC ....D...... 513 612-7303
West Chester **(G-18994)**

CONTRACTORS: Roof Repair

Eastside Roofg Restoration Co............E...... 513 471-0434
Cincinnati **(G-3479)**
Ohio & Indiana Roofing.......................E...... 937 339-8768
Troy **(G-18218)**

CONTRACTORS: Roofing

1st Choice Roofing Company...............E...... 216 227-7755
Cleveland **(G-4868)**
Able Company Ltd Partnership ....D...... 614 444-7663
Columbus **(G-6853)**
Able Roofing LLC................................E...... 614 444-7663
Columbus **(G-6854)**
Advanced Industrial Roofg Inc............D...... 330 837-1999
Massillon **(G-13660)**
AH Sturgill Roofing Inc.......................E...... 937 254-2955
Dayton **(G-9155)**
Architectural Systems Inc...................D...... 614 873-2057
Plain City **(G-16044)**
Atlas Roofing Company ....E...... 330 467-7683
Cleveland **(G-5021)**
Aw Farrell Son Inc.............................E...... 513 334-0715
Milford **(G-14372)**
B & B Roofing Inc ....E...... 740 772-4759
Chillicothe **(G-2757)**
Beck Company ....E...... 216 883-0909
Cleveland **(G-5050)**
Boak & Sons Inc.................................C...... 330 793-5646
Youngstown **(G-19967)**
Bruns Building & Dev Corp Inc ....D...... 419 925-4095
Saint Henry **(G-16515)**
Building Technicians Corp...................E...... 440 466-1651
Geneva **(G-11237)**
Burbank Inc.......................................E...... 419 698-3434
Toledo **(G-17632)**
Burns & Scalo Roofing Co Inc.............E...... 740 383-4639
Marion **(G-13408)**
Campeon Roofg & Waterproofing.........E...... 513 271-8972
Cincinnati **(G-3112)**
Centimark Corporation.......................E...... 614 536-1960
Reynoldsburg **(G-16288)**
Centimark Corporation.......................E...... 937 704-9909
Franklin **(G-11026)**
Chaney Roofing Maintenance..............E...... 419 639-2761
Clyde **(G-6741)**
Chemcote Roofing Company................D...... 614 792-2683
Dublin **(G-10172)**
Command Roofing Co ....C...... 937 298-1155
Moraine **(G-14633)**
Contract Lumber Inc...........................C...... 740 964-3147
Pataskala **(G-15783)**
Custom Seal Inc.................................E...... 419 334-1020
Fremont **(G-11068)**

Dahm Brothers Company Inc ....E...... 937 461-5627
Dayton **(G-9343)**
Dalton Roofing Co..............................D...... 513 871-2800
Cincinnati **(G-3398)**
Damschroder Roofing Inc....................E...... 419 332-5000
Fremont **(G-11069)**
Daugherty Construction Inc ....E...... 216 731-9444
Euclid **(G-10628)**
Deer Park Roofing Inc ....E...... 513 891-9151
Cincinnati **(G-3416)**
Diamond Roofing Systems LLP............E...... 330 856-2500
Warren **(G-18701)**
Division 7 Inc.....................................E...... 740 965-1970
Galena **(G-11157)**
Dun Rite Home Improvement Inc ....E...... 330 650-5322
Macedonia **(G-13068)**
Durable Slate Co................................D...... 614 299-5522
Columbus **(G-7478)**
Feazel Roofing Company.....................E...... 614 898-7663
Westerville **(G-19164)**
Fred Christen & Sons Company ....D...... 419 243-4161
Toledo **(G-17747)**
Frost Roofing Inc ....D...... 419 739-2701
Wapakoneta **(G-18643)**
Harold J Becker Company Inc ....E...... 614 279-1414
Beavercreek **(G-1222)**
Hart Roofing Inc.................................E...... 330 452-4055
Canton **(G-2341)**
Hicks Roofing Inc...............................E...... 330 364-7737
New Philadelphia **(G-14964)**
Hinckley Roofing Inc ....E...... 330 722-7663
Medina **(G-13949)**
Holland Roofing Inc............................E...... 330 963-0237
Twinsburg **(G-18280)**
Holland Roofing Inc............................E...... 614 430-3724
Columbus **(G-7761)**
Hwz Contracting LLC..........................D...... 513 671-3300
West Chester **(G-18945)**
Industrial Energy Systems Inc.............E...... 216 267-9590
Cleveland **(G-5747)**
K & W Roofing Inc..............................E...... 740 927-3122
Etna **(G-10616)**
Kelley Brothers Roofing Inc.................D...... 513 829-7717
Fairfield **(G-10742)**
Kerkan Roofing Inc.............................D...... 513 821-0556
Cincinnati **(G-3863)**
Korman Construction Corp..................E...... 614 274-2170
Columbus **(G-7924)**
M&W Construction Entps LLC..............E...... 419 227-2000
Lima **(G-12697)**
Meade Construction Inc ....E...... 740 694-5525
Lexington **(G-12574)**
Midwest Roofing & Furnace Co ....E...... 614 252-5241
Columbus **(G-8084)**
Moisture Guard Corporation.................E...... 330 928-7200
Stow **(G-17220)**
Molloy Roofing Company.....................E...... 513 791-7400
Blue Ash **(G-1614)**
N F Mansuetto & Sons Inc...................E...... 740 633-7320
Martins Ferry **(G-13477)**
Nasco Roofing and Cnstr Inc...............E...... 330 746-3566
Youngstown **(G-20135)**
Nations Roof of Ohio LLC ....E...... 937 439-4160
Springboro **(G-16978)**
Nordmann Roofing Co Inc ....E...... 419 691-5737
Toledo **(G-17944)**
Northern Ohio Roofg Shtmtl Inc...........E...... 440 322-8262
Elyria **(G-10549)**
Phinney Industrial Roofing ....D...... 614 308-9000
Columbus **(G-8445)**
Preferred Roofing Ohio Inc ....E...... 216 587-0957
Cleveland **(G-6231)**
Preferred Roofing Services LLC............E...... 216 587-0957
Cleveland **(G-6232)**
Promanco Inc.....................................E...... 740 374-2120
Marietta **(G-13373)**
R & B Contractors LLC........................E...... 513 738-0954
Shandon **(G-16721)**
Ray St Clair Roofing Inc......................E...... 513 874-1234
Fairfield **(G-10773)**
Regency Roofing Companies Inc..........E...... 330 468-1021
Macedonia **(G-13081)**
Richland Co & Associates Inc ....E...... 419 782-0141
Defiance **(G-9937)**
Roofing By Insulation Inc....................E...... 937 315-5024
New Carlisle **(G-14896)**
Roth Bros Inc.....................................C...... 330 793-5571
Youngstown **(G-20197)**
Simon Roofing and Shtmtl Corp..........C...... 330 629-7392
Youngstown **(G-20212)**

T & F Systems Inc..............................D...... 216 881-3525
Cleveland **(G-6492)**
Tecta America Corp............................D...... 419 447-1716
Tiffin **(G-17541)**
Tecta America Zero Company LLC........D...... 513 541-1848
Cincinnati **(G-4582)**
Terik Roofing Inc................................E...... 330 785-0060
Coventry Township **(G-9044)**
Tremco Incorporated ....B...... 216 292-5000
Beachwood **(G-1114)**
Tycor Roofing Inc...............................E...... 330 452-8150
Canton **(G-2516)**
Valley Roofing LLC.............................E...... 513 831-9444
Milford **(G-14441)**
Weatherproofing Tech Inc ....D...... 216 292-5000
Beachwood **(G-1117)**
West Roofing Systems Inc...................E...... 800 356-5748
Lagrange **(G-12327)**
Wm Kramer and Sons Inc....................D...... 513 353-1142
Cleves **(G-6736)**
Wolfes Roofing Inc.............................E...... 419 666-6233
Walbridge **(G-18628)**

CONTRACTORS: Safety & Security Eqpt

Genric Inc...B...... 937 553-9250
Marysville **(G-13500)**
Guardian Protection Svcs Inc..............E...... 330 797-1570
Youngstown **(G-20059)**
Mills Security Alarm Systems...............E...... 513 921-4600
Cincinnati **(G-4058)**
Simplex Time Recorder LLC.................E...... 513 874-1227
West Chester **(G-19081)**

CONTRACTORS: Sandblasting Svc, Building Exteriors

Aerco Sandblasting Company..............E...... 419 224-2464
Lima **(G-12593)**
Allstate Painting & Contg Co ....D...... 330 220-5533
Brunswick **(G-1919)**
Euclid Indus Maint Clg Contrs.............C...... 216 361-0288
Cleveland **(G-5493)**
Flamos Enterprises Inc ....E...... 330 478-0009
Canton **(G-2315)**
Ionno Properties s Corp......................E...... 330 479-9267
Dennison **(G-10051)**
Rak Corrosion Control Inc ....E...... 440 985-2171
Amherst **(G-596)**
Universal Fabg Cnstr Svcs Inc.............D...... 614 274-1128
Columbus **(G-8815)**

CONTRACTORS: Septic System

Accurate Mechanical Inc.....................E...... 740 681-1332
Lancaster **(G-12368)**
Mack Industries.................................C...... 419 353-7081
Bowling Green **(G-1740)**
Nieman Plumbing Inc..........................D...... 513 851-5588
Cincinnati **(G-4119)**
Zemba Bros Inc..................................E...... 740 452-1880
Zanesville **(G-20388)**

CONTRACTORS: Sheet Metal Work, NEC

All-Type Welding & Fabrication ....E...... 440 439-3990
Cleveland **(G-4936)**
Anchor Metal Processing Inc................E...... 216 362-1850
Cleveland **(G-4978)**
Avon Lake Sheet Metal Co ....E...... 440 933-3505
Avon Lake **(G-910)**
Budde Sheet Metal Works Inc..............E...... 937 224-0868
Dayton **(G-9268)**
Detmer & Sons Inc.............................E...... 937 879-2373
Fairborn **(G-10671)**
Dimensional Metals Inc ....D...... 740 927-3633
Reynoldsburg **(G-16299)**
Ducts Inc..E...... 216 391-2400
Cleveland **(G-5448)**
Eckstein Roofing Company..................E...... 513 941-1511
Cincinnati **(G-3482)**
Franck and Fric Incorporated..............D...... 216 524-4451
Cleveland **(G-5572)**
Geauga Mechanical Company..............D...... 440 285-2000
Chardon **(G-2696)**
Global Insulation Inc..........................E...... 330 479-3100
Canton **(G-2327)**
Hickey Metal Fabrication Roofg............E...... 330 337-9329
Salem **(G-16546)**
J A Guy Inc..E...... 937 642-3415
Marysville **(G-13508)**

SERVICES

Kirk & Blum Manufacturing Co..............C...... 513 458-2600
  Cincinnati (G-3875)
Mechanical Cnstr Managers LLC..............C...... 937 274-1987
  Dayton (G-9597)
Mechanical Construction Co.................E...... 740 353-5668
  Portsmouth (G-16154)
National Blanking LLC.......................E...... 419 385-0636
  Toledo (G-17928)
Ontario Mechanical LLC.....................E...... 419 529-2578
  Ontario (G-15569)
Pcy Enterprises Inc..........................E...... 513 241-5566
  Cincinnati (G-4219)
Quality Electrical & Mech Inc.................E...... 419 294-3591
  Lima (G-12726)
Slagle Mechanical Contractors..............E...... 937 492-4151
  Sidney (G-16801)
Tendon Manufacturing Inc...................E...... 216 663-3200
  Cleveland (G-6512)
Tilton Corporation..........................C...... 419 227-6421
  Lima (G-12762)
York-Mahoning Mech Contrs Inc.............D...... 330 788-7011
  Youngstown (G-20252)

CONTRACTORS: Sheet metal Work, Architectural

Ameridian Specialty Services...............E...... 513 769-0150
  Cincinnati (G-2952)

CONTRACTORS: Shoring & Underpinning

Boyas Excavating Inc........................E...... 216 524-3620
  Cleveland (G-5072)
Goettle Holding Company Inc................C...... 513 825-8100
  Cincinnati (G-3623)

CONTRACTORS: Sidewalk

Cioffi & Son Construction....................E...... 330 794-9448
  Akron (G-132)

CONTRACTORS: Siding

Airko Inc....................................E...... 440 333-0133
  Cleveland (G-4922)
Cardinal Builders Inc........................E...... 614 237-1000
  Columbus (G-7119)
Champion Opco LLC..........................B...... 513 327-7338
  Cincinnati (G-3168)
Erie Construction Mid-West Inc..............E...... 419 472-4200
  Toledo (G-17716)
Erie Construction Mid-West Inc..............E...... 937 898-4688
  Dayton (G-9417)
Holmes Siding Contractors...................D...... 330 674-2867
  Millersburg (G-14476)
Industrial First Inc..........................C...... 216 991-8605
  Bedford (G-1286)
Olde Towne Windows Inc.....................E...... 419 626-9613
  Milan (G-14364)
Regency Windows Corporation................D...... 330 963-4077
  Twinsburg (G-18310)
Summit Enterprises Contg Corp..............E...... 513 426-1623
  Lebanon (G-12507)

CONTRACTORS: Single-Family Home Fire Damage Repair

AAA Standard Services Inc..................D...... 419 535-0274
  Toledo (G-17578)
Belfor USA Group Inc........................E...... 330 916-6468
  Peninsula (G-15809)
Clarke Contractors Corp.....................E...... 513 285-7844
  West Chester (G-18893)
Davis Paul Restoration Dayton...............E...... 937 436-3411
  Moraine (G-14639)
Farris Enterprises Inc........................E...... 614 367-9611
  Worthington (G-19810)
Farrow Cleaners Co..........................E...... 216 561-2355
  Cleveland (G-5514)
Icon Environmental Group LLC...............E...... 513 426-6767
  Milford (G-14396)
Smb Construction Co Inc.....................E...... 419 269-1473
  Toledo (G-18038)

CONTRACTORS: Single-family Home General Remodeling

1522 Hess Street LLC.......................E...... 614 291-6876
  Columbus (G-6840)
Airko Inc....................................E...... 440 333-0133
  Cleveland (G-4922)

Apco Industries Inc..........................D...... 614 224-2345
  Columbus (G-6956)
Apex Restoration Contrs Ltd..................E...... 513 489-1795
  Cincinnati (G-2974)
Arnolds Home Improvement LLC..............E...... 734 847-9600
  Toledo (G-17600)
Behal Sampson Dietz Inc.....................E...... 614 464-1933
  Columbus (G-7025)
Berlin Construction Ltd.......................E...... 330 893-2003
  Millersburg (G-14458)
Brian-Kyles Construction Inc..................E...... 440 242-0298
  Lorain (G-12887)
Burge Building Co Inc........................E...... 440 245-6871
  Lorain (G-12889)
Cardinal Builders Inc........................E...... 614 237-1000
  Columbus (G-7119)
Community Improvement Corp.................E...... 440 466-4675
  Geneva (G-11238)
Craftsmen Restoration LLC...................E...... 877 442-3424
  Akron (G-168)
Disaster Reconstruction Inc..................E...... 440 918-1523
  Eastlake (G-10428)
Dry It Rite LLC..............................E...... 614 295-8135
  Columbus (G-7472)
Edrich Supply Co............................E...... 440 238-9440
  Strongsville (G-17299)
Erie Construction Mid-West Inc..............E...... 937 898-4688
  Dayton (G-9417)
Handy Hubby................................E...... 419 754-1150
  Toledo (G-17777)
Harrison Construction Inc.....................E...... 740 373-7000
  Marietta (G-13333)
Hometown Improvement Co...................E...... 614 846-1060
  Columbus (G-7767)
Improve It Home Remodeling.................C...... 614 297-5121
  Columbus (G-7804)
Ingle-Barr Inc...............................E...... 740 702-6117
  Chillicothe (G-2793)
J & D Home Improvement Inc.................D...... 740 927-0722
  Reynoldsburg (G-16310)
J Russell Construction........................E...... 330 633-6462
  Tallmadge (G-17479)
Jack Gray...................................D...... 216 688-0466
  Cincinnati (G-3799)
Midwest Roofing & Furnace Co...............E...... 614 252-5241
  Columbus (G-8084)
Mural & Son Inc.............................E...... 216 267-3322
  Cleveland (G-6025)
Neals Construction Company..................E...... 513 489-7700
  Cincinnati (G-4101)
Nextt Corp..................................E...... 513 813-6398
  Cincinnati (G-4115)
Nrp Group LLC..............................D...... 216 475-8900
  Cleveland (G-6103)
Rubber City Realty Inc.......................D...... 330 745-9034
  Akron (G-413)
Sure Home Improvments LLC..................E...... 614 586-0610
  Columbus (G-8720)
Swartz Enterprises Inc.......................E...... 419 331-1024
  Lima (G-12758)
Toth Renovation LLC.........................E...... 614 542-9683
  Columbus (G-8764)
Wingler Construction Corp....................E...... 614 626-8546
  Columbus (G-8910)
Zinz Cnstr & Restoration.....................E...... 330 332-7939
  Youngstown (G-20270)

CONTRACTORS: Skylight Installation

Scs Construction Services Inc................E...... 513 929-0260
  Cincinnati (G-4441)

CONTRACTORS: Solar Energy Eqpt

Dovetail Construction Co Inc..................E...... 740 592-1800
  Cleveland (G-5445)

CONTRACTORS: Sound Eqpt Installation

Eighth Day Sound Systems Inc................E...... 440 995-2647
  Cleveland (G-5469)
Live Technologies LLC.......................D...... 614 278-7777
  Columbus (G-7986)

CONTRACTORS: Special Trades, NEC

Brown Contracting & Dev LLC.................E...... 419 341-3939
  Port Clinton (G-16100)
Central Ohio Custom Contg LLC...............E...... 614 579-4971
  Mount Vernon (G-14753)
Multi Cntry SEC Slutions Group................E...... 216 973-0291
  Cleveland (G-6023)

Toledo Area Insulator Wkrs Jac...............D...... 419 531-5911
  Toledo (G-18073)
Trinity Contracting Inc.......................D...... 614 905-4410
  Columbus (G-8780)

CONTRACTORS: Specialized Public Building

Forest City Residential Dev...................E...... 216 621-6060
  Cleveland (G-5561)

CONTRACTORS: Spraying, Nonagricultural

Resource International Inc....................C...... 614 823-4949
  Columbus (G-8523)

CONTRACTORS: Sprinkler System

Supply Network Inc..........................E...... 614 527-5800
  Columbus (G-8715)

CONTRACTORS: Steam Cleaning, Building Exterior

TNT Mobile Powerwash Inc...................E...... 614 402-7474
  Canal Winchester (G-2121)

CONTRACTORS: Stone Masonry

Casagrande Masonry Inc.....................E...... 740 964-0781
  New Albany (G-14849)
Lang Masonry Contractors Inc................D...... 740 749-3512
  Waterford (G-18786)
S P S & Associates Inc.......................E...... 330 283-4267
  Silver Lake (G-16808)
Van Ness Stone Inc..........................E...... 440 564-1111
  Newbury (G-15127)

CONTRACTORS: Storage Tank Erection, Metal

Columbiana Boiler Company LLC..............E...... 330 482-3373
  Columbiana (G-6784)
Daniel A Terreri & Sons Inc...................E...... 330 538-2950
  Youngstown (G-20014)
FSRc Tanks Inc.............................E...... 234 221-2015
  Bolivar (G-1703)
Mid Atlantic Stor Systems Inc.................D...... 740 335-2019
  Wshngtn CT Hs (G-19880)

CONTRACTORS: Store Fixture Installation

Goliath Contracting Ltd.......................E...... 614 568-7878
  Reynoldsburg (G-16306)

CONTRACTORS: Structural Iron Work, Structural

Columbus Steel Erectors Inc..................E...... 614 876-5050
  Columbus (G-7317)
Forest City Erectors Inc......................D...... 330 425-2345
  Twinsburg (G-18268)
Foundation Steel LLC........................D...... 419 402-4241
  Swanton (G-17397)
J&H Rnfrcing Strl Erectors Inc................C...... 740 355-0141
  Portsmouth (G-16151)
Orbit Movers & Erectors Inc..................E...... 937 277-8080
  Dayton (G-9677)
Sofco Erectors Inc...........................C...... 513 771-1600
  Cincinnati (G-4502)

CONTRACTORS: Structural Steel Erection

Akron Erectors Inc..........................E...... 330 745-7100
  Akron (G-39)
Black Swamp Steel Inc.......................E...... 419 867-8050
  Holland (G-11873)
Dublin Building Systems Co...................E...... 614 760-5831
  Dublin (G-10204)
Evers Welding Co Inc........................E...... 513 385-7352
  Cincinnati (G-3521)
Frederick Steel Company LLC.................D...... 513 821-6400
  Cincinnati (G-3586)
GL Nause Co Inc............................E...... 513 722-9500
  Loveland (G-12996)
Hovest Construction.........................E...... 419 456-3426
  Ottawa (G-15659)
Industrial First Inc..........................C...... 216 991-8605
  Bedford (G-1286)
Kelley Steel Erectors Inc.....................D...... 440 232-1573
  Cleveland (G-5821)
Legacy Industrial Services LLC................E...... 606 584-8953
  Ripley (G-16400)

Marysville Steel Inc	E	937 642-5971
Marysville (G-13515)		
Mason Steel Erecting Inc	E	440 439-1040
Cleveland (G-5921)		
Mohawk RE-Bar Services Inc	E	440 268-0780
Strongsville (G-17334)		
Mound Technologies Inc	E	937 748-2937
Springboro (G-16977)		
Northbend Archtctural Pdts Inc	D	513 577-7988
Cincinnati (G-4128)		
Ontario Mechanical LLC	E	419 529-2578
Ontario (G-15569)		
R&F Erectors Inc	E	513 574-8273
Cincinnati (G-4333)		
Reading Rock Residential LLC	E	513 874-4770
West Chester (G-19075)		
Rittman Inc	D	330 927-6855
Rittman (G-16409)		
Sawyer Steel Erectors Inc	E	419 867-8050
Holland (G-11910)		
Seneca Steel Erectors Inc	E	740 385-0517
Logan (G-12853)		
Smith Brothers Erection Inc	E	740 373-3575
Marietta (G-13382)		
Stein Inc	D	216 883-4277
Cleveland (G-6464)		

CONTRACTORS: Svc Station Eqpt

Empaco Equipment Corporation	E	330 659-9393
Richfield (G-16354)		

CONTRACTORS: Svc Station Eqpt Installation, Maint & Repair

Industrial Fiberglass Spc Inc	E	937 222-9000
Dayton (G-9514)		
X F Construction Svcs Inc	E	614 575-2700
Columbus (G-8923)		

CONTRACTORS: Tile Installation, Ceramic

OCP Contractors Inc	E	419 865-7168
Holland (G-11903)		
Southwestern Tile and MBL Co	E	614 464-1257
Columbus (G-8667)		

CONTRACTORS: Trenching

Maintenance Unlimited Inc	E	440 238-1162
Strongsville (G-17325)		
Mollett Seamless Gutter Co	E	513 825-0500
West Chester (G-18976)		

CONTRACTORS: Tuck Pointing & Restoration

American International Cnstr	E	440 243-5535
Berea (G-1411)		
Kapton Caulking & Building	E	440 526-0670
Cleveland (G-5814)		
Lencyk Masonry Co Inc	E	330 729-9780
Youngstown (G-20098)		
Platinum Restoration Inc	E	440 327-0699
Elyria (G-10556)		
Technical Construction Spc	E	330 929-1088
Cuyahoga Falls (G-9129)		
VIP Restoration Inc	E	216 426-9500
Cuyahoga Falls (G-9136)		

CONTRACTORS: Underground Utilities

Amboy Contractors LLc	D	419 644-2111
Metamora (G-14131)		
American Boring Inc	E	740 969-8000
Carroll (G-2555)		
Anderzack-Pitzen Cnstr Inc	E	419 553-7015
Metamora (G-14132)		
Capitol Tunneling Inc	E	614 444-0255
Columbus (G-7117)		
Finlaw Construction Inc	E	330 889-2074
Bristolville (G-1825)		
Fishel Company	C	614 850-9012
Columbus (G-7589)		
Geotex Construction Svcs Inc	E	614 444-5690
Columbus (G-7662)		
Gleason Construction Co Inc	D	419 865-7480
Holland (G-11886)		
Gradient Corporation	E	513 779-0000
Cincinnati (G-3631)		
Great Lakes Crushing Ltd	E	440 944-5500
Wickliffe (G-19461)		

J Daniel & Company Inc	D	513 575-3100
Loveland (G-13002)		
JS Bova Excavating LLC	E	234 254-4040
Struthers (G-17365)		
Ohio Utilities Protection Svc	D	800 311-3692
North Jackson (G-15250)		
Precision Pipeline Svcs LLC	E	740 652-1679
Lancaster (G-12426)		
R D Jergens Contractors Inc	D	937 669-9799
Vandalia (G-18539)		
Terrace Construction Co Inc	D	216 739-3170
Cleveland (G-6515)		
Trucco Construction Co Inc	C	740 417-9010
Delaware (G-10010)		
Underground Utilities Inc	D	419 465-2587
Monroeville (G-14592)		
Usic Locating Services LLC	E	419 874-9988
North Baltimore (G-15180)		
Usic Locating Services LLC	D	513 554-0456
Cincinnati (G-4745)		
Utilicon Corporation	E	216 391-8500
Cleveland (G-6614)		
Woodward Excavating Co	E	614 866-4384
Reynoldsburg (G-16340)		

CONTRACTORS: Ventilation & Duct Work

A A S Amels Sheet Meta L Inc	E	330 793-9326
Youngstown (G-19943)		
Feldkamp Enterprises Inc	E	513 347-4500
Cincinnati (G-3540)		
Franck and Fric Incorporated	D	216 524-4451
Cleveland (G-5572)		
Jacobs Mechanical Co	C	513 681-6800
Cincinnati (G-3803)		
Sisler Heating & Cooling Inc	E	330 722-7101
Medina (G-14002)		
TH Martin Inc	D	216 741-2020
Cleveland (G-6518)		

CONTRACTORS: Wall Covering

Clubhouse Pub N Grub	E	440 884-2582
Cleveland (G-5310)		

CONTRACTORS: Wall Covering, Commercial

Cleveland Construction Inc	E	440 255-8000
Mason (G-13563)		

CONTRACTORS: Warm Air Heating & Air Conditioning

A A Astro Service Inc	D	216 459-0363
Cleveland (G-4873)		
A To Zoff Co Inc	E	330 733-7902
Akron (G-12)		
Accurate Heating & Cooling	E	740 775-5005
Chillicothe (G-2749)		
Accurate Mechanical Inc	E	740 353-4328
Wheelersburg (G-19427)		
Accurate Mechanical Inc	E	937 382-1436
Wilmington (G-19602)		
Air Comfort Systems Inc	E	216 587-4125
Cleveland (G-4915)		
Air Conditioning Entps Inc	E	440 729-0900
Cleveland (G-4917)		
Air-Temp Climate Control Inc	E	216 579-1552
Cleveland (G-4918)		
Aire-Tech Inc	E	614 836-5670
Groveport (G-11492)		
Airtron LP	D	614 274-2345
Columbus (G-6888)		
All About Heating Cooling	E	513 621-4620
Cincinnati (G-2921)		
American Mechanical Group Inc	E	614 575-3720
Columbus (G-6930)		
Apollo Heating and AC Inc	E	513 271-3600
Cincinnati (G-2975)		
Apple Heating Inc	E	440 997-1212
Barberton (G-941)		
Arco Heating & AC Co	E	216 663-3211
Solon (G-16821)		
Ashland Comfort Control Inc	E	419 281-0144
Ashland (G-650)		
Atlas Capital Services Inc	D	614 294-7373
Columbus (G-6997)		
Bachmans Inc	E	513 943-5300
Batavia (G-983)		
Bay Furnace Sheet Metal Co	E	440 871-3777
Westlake (G-19320)		

Blind & Son LLC	D	330 753-7711
Barberton (G-948)		
Brennan & Associates Inc	E	216 391-4822
Cleveland (G-5076)		
Burrier Service Company Inc	E	440 946-6019
Mentor (G-14023)		
Castle Heating & Air Inc	E	216 696-3940
Solon (G-16833)		
Century Mech Solutions Inc	E	513 681-5700
Cincinnati (G-3161)		
Cincinnati Air Conditioning Co	D	513 721-5622
Cincinnati (G-3220)		
Colonial Heating & Cooling Co	E	614 837-6100
Pickerington (G-15953)		
Columbs/Worthington Htg AC Inc	E	614 771-5381
Columbus (G-7252)		
Columbus Heating & Vent Co	C	614 274-1177
Columbus (G-7286)		
Comfort Systems USA Ohio Inc	E	440 703-1600
Bedford (G-1273)		
Commercial Comfort Systems Inc	E	419 481-4444
Perrysburg (G-15849)		
Corcoran and Harnist Htg & AC	E	513 921-2227
Cincinnati (G-3361)		
Crane Heating & AC Co	E	513 641-4700
Cincinnati (G-3378)		
Crown Heating & Cooling Inc	D	330 499-4988
Uniontown (G-18365)		
Custom AC & Htg Co	D	614 552-4822
Gahanna (G-11116)		
David R White Services Inc	E	740 594-8381
Athens (G-775)		
Detmer & Sons Inc	E	937 879-2373
Fairborn (G-10671)		
Dooley Heating and AC LLC	E	614 278-9944
Columbus (G-7467)		
Drake State Air Systems Inc	E	937 472-0640
Eaton (G-10444)		
Falls Heating & Cooling Inc	D	330 929-8777
Cuyahoga Falls (G-9090)		
Favret Company	D	614 488-5211
Columbus (G-7566)		
Fitzenrider Inc	E	419 784-0828
Defiance (G-9915)		
Geauga Mechanical Company	D	440 285-2000
Chardon (G-2696)		
Gene Tolliver Corp	D	440 324-7727
Medina (G-13941)		
General Temperature Ctrl Inc	E	614 837-3888
Canal Winchester (G-2109)		
Genes Refrigeration Htg & AC	E	330 723-4104
Medina (G-13942)		
Gilbert Heating & AC	E	419 625-8875
Sandusky (G-16610)		
Gorjanc Comfort Services Inc	E	440 449-4411
Cleveland (G-5617)		
Gundlach Sheet Metal Works Inc	D	419 626-4525
Sandusky (G-16614)		
Gundlach Sheet Metal Works Inc	E	419 734-7351
Port Clinton (G-16108)		
Haslett Heating & Cooling Inc	E	614 299-2133
Dublin (G-10239)		
Havsco Inc	E	440 439-8900
Bedford (G-1284)		
Helm and Associates Inc	E	419 893-1480
Maumee (G-13799)		
Imperial Heating and Coolg Inc	D	440 498-1788
Solon (G-16860)		
Inloes Mechanical Inc	E	513 896-9499
Hamilton (G-11612)		
J A Guy Inc	E	937 642-3415
Marysville (G-13508)		
J F Bernard Inc	E	330 785-3830
Akron (G-283)		
J W Geopfert Co Inc	E	330 762-2293
Akron (G-285)		
Jennings Heating Company Inc	E	330 784-1286
Akron (G-290)		
Jonle Co Inc	E	513 662-2282
Cincinnati (G-3831)		
K Company Incorporated	C	330 773-5125
Coventry Township (G-9037)		
Kessler Heating & Cooling	E	614 837-9961
Canal Winchester (G-2113)		
Kidron Electric Inc	E	330 857-2871
Kidron (G-12308)		
Kusan Inc	E	614 262-1818
Columbus (G-7931)		
Lakes Heating and AC	E	330 644-7811
Coventry Township (G-9038)		

Employee Codes: A=Over 500 employees, B=251-500
C=101-250, D=51-100, E=25-50

2019 Harris Ohio
Services Directory

1395

SERVICES

Langdon Inc ....E 513 733-5955
Cincinnati (G-3909)

Limbach Company LLC ....E 614 299-2175
Columbus (G-7977)

Luxury Heating Co ....D 440 366-0971
Sheffield Village (G-16738)

M&M Heating & Cooling Inc ....D 419 243-3005
Toledo (G-17876)

McAfee Heating & AC Co Inc .....E 937 438-1976
Dayton (G-9593)

Metal Masters Inc ....E 330 343-3515
Dover (G-10088)

Metro Heating and AC Co ....E 614 777-1237
Hilliard (G-11792)

Midwest Roofing & Furnace Co ....E 614 252-5241
Columbus (G-8084)

Miracle Plumbing & Heating Co ...E 330 477-2402
Canton (G-2406)

Noron Inc ....E 419 726-2677
Toledo (G-17947)

Ohio Heating & AC Inc ....E 614 863-6666
Columbus (G-8264)

Osterwisch Company Inc ....D 513 791-3282
Cincinnati (G-4189)

Overcashier and Horst Htg & AC ..E 419 841-3333
Sylvania (G-17441)

P K Wadsworth Heating & Coolg ...E 440 248-4821
Solon (G-16880)

Peck-Hannaford Briggs Svc Corp ..D 513 681-1200
Cincinnati (G-4220)

Perfection Group Inc ....C 513 772-7545
Cincinnati (G-4230)

Perfection Services Inc ....E 513 772-7545
Cincinnati (G-4231)

Pre-Fore Inc ....E 740 467-2206
Millersport (G-14503)

Quality Electrical & Mech Inc ....E 419 294-3591
Lima (G-12726)

Recker and Boerger Inc ....D 513 942-9663
West Chester (G-19076)

Reupert Heating and AC Co Inc ...E 513 922-5050
Cincinnati (G-4365)

Robinson Htg Air-Conditioning ....E 513 422-6812
Middletown (G-14326)

Roth Bros Inc ....C 330 793-5571
Youngstown (G-20197)

Sals Heating and Cooling Inc .....E 216 676-4949
Cleveland (G-6366)

Schmids Service Now Inc ....E 330 264-2040
Wooster (G-19766)

Schneller Heating and AC Co ......E 859 341-1200
Cincinnati (G-2867)

Schumm Richard A Plbg & Htg .....E 419 238-4994
Van Wert (G-18488)

Service Experts LLC ....E 330 577-3918
Akron (G-425)

Smith & Oby Company ....D 440 735-5333
Walton Hills (G-18638)

Smith & Oby Service Co ....E 440 735-5322
Bedford (G-1306)

Smylie One Heating & Cooling .....E 440 449-4328
Bedford (G-1307)

Southtown Heating & Cooling ......E 937 320-9900
Moraine (G-14699)

Superior Mechanical Svcs Inc .....E 937 259-0082
Dayton (G-9187)

Tanner Heating & AC Inc ....E 937 299-2500
Moraine (G-14701)

Timmerman John P Heating AC Co ...E 419 229-4015
Lima (G-12764)

Trane Inc ....E 440 946-7823
Cleveland (G-6539)

Universal Enterprises Inc ....C 419 529-3500
Ontario (G-15577)

V M Systems Inc ....D 419 535-1044
Toledo (G-18133)

Volpone Enterprises Inc ....E 440 969-1141
Ashtabula (G-759)

Watkins Mechanical Inc ....E 937 748-0220
Springboro (G-16987)

Willis One Hour Heating & AC ......D 513 752-2512
Cincinnati (G-2875)

Wojos Heating & AC Inc ....E 419 693-3220
Northwood (G-15415)

CONTRACTORS: Water Well Drilling

Collector Wells Intl Inc ....E 614 888-6263
Columbus (G-7246)

Moodys of Dayton Inc ....E 614 443-3898
Miamisburg (G-14194)

CONTRACTORS: Water Well Servicing

Ohio Drilling Company ....E 330 832-1521
Massillon (G-13718)

CONTRACTORS: Waterproofing

Adelmos Electric Sewer Clg Co .....E 216 641-2301
Brooklyn Heights (G-1864)

Basement Systems Ohio Inc ....C 330 423-4430
Twinsburg (G-18249)

Burbank Inc ....E 419 698-3434
Toledo (G-17632)

Daniels Basement Waterproofing ...E 440 965-4332
Berlin Heights (G-1450)

Gem City Waterproofing ....E 937 220-6800
Dayton (G-9457)

Harold J Becker Company Inc ......E 614 279-1414
Beavercreek (G-1222)

J & D Home Improvement Inc ......D 740 927-0722
Reynoldsburg (G-16310)

Jaco Waterproofing LLC ....E 513 738-0084
Fairfield (G-10739)

Kapton Caulking & Building ....E 440 526-0670
Cleveland (G-5814)

Mural & Son Inc ....E 216 267-3322
Cleveland (G-6025)

Ohio State Home Services Inc .....C 330 467-1055
Macedonia (G-13079)

Ohio State Home Services Inc .....E 614 850-5600
Hilliard (G-11803)

Paul Peterson Company ....E 614 486-4375
Columbus (G-8427)

Ram Construction Services ....E 440 740-0100
Broadview Heights (G-1844)

Ram Construction Services of ......D 513 297-1857
West Chester (G-18990)

Riverfront Diversified Inc ....D 513 874-7200
West Chester (G-18995)

Rusk Industries Inc ....D 419 841-6055
Toledo (G-18015)

Suburban Maint & Cnstr Inc ......E 440 237-7765
North Royalton (G-15368)

U S A Waterproofing Inc ....E 330 425-2440
Twinsburg (G-18332)

Unified Cnstr Systems Ltd ....E 330 773-2511
Akron (G-475)

CONTRACTORS: Window Treatment Installation

Pucher Paint Co Inc ....E 440 234-0991
Berea (G-1435)

Vwc Liquidation Company LLC ......C 330 372-6776
Warren (G-18767)

CONTRACTORS: Windows & Doors

Door Shop & Service Inc ....E 614 423-8043
Westerville (G-19160)

Fortune Brands Windows Inc ......C 614 532-3500
Columbus (G-7602)

Traichal Construction Company .....E 800 255-3667
Niles (G-15172)

Youngstown Automatic Door Co .....E 330 747-3135
Youngstown (G-20258)

CONTRACTORS: Wood Floor Installation & Refinishing

Cincinnati Floor Company Inc ......E 513 641-4500
Cincinnati (G-3245)

Continental Office Furn Corp ....C 614 262-5010
Columbus (G-7358)

Frank Novak & Sons Inc ....D 216 475-2495
Cleveland (G-5573)

Hoover & Wells Inc ....C 419 691-9220
Toledo (G-17807)

K H F Inc ....E 330 928-0694
Cuyahoga Falls (G-9106)

Schumacher & Co Inc ....E 859 655-9000
Milford (G-14430)

CONTRACTORS: Wrecking & Demolition

Allgeier & Son Inc ....E 513 574-3735
Cincinnati (G-2925)

Allied Erct & Dismantling Co ......E 330 744-0808
Youngstown (G-19951)

Aztec Services Group Inc ....D 513 541-2002
Cincinnati (G-3012)

Bladecutters Lawn Service Inc .....E 937 274-3861
Dayton (G-9255)

Boyas Excavating Inc ....E 216 524-3620
Cleveland (G-5072)

Charles F Jergens Cnstr Inc ....E 937 233-1830
Dayton (G-9293)

Cook Paving and Cnstr Co ....E 216 267-7705
Independence (G-12062)

Dave Sugar Excavating LLC ....E 330 542-1100
Petersburg (G-15943)

Fluor-Bwxt Portsmouth LLC ....A 866 706-6992
Piketon (G-15975)

Mark Schaffer Excvtg Trckg Inc ...D 419 668-5990
Norwalk (G-15443)

Mosier Industrial Services ....E 419 683-4000
Crestline (G-9058)

Ray Bertolini Trucking Co ....E 330 867-0666
Akron (G-397)

Rnw Holdings Inc ....E 330 792-0600
Youngstown (G-20187)

Sunesis Environmental LLC ....D 513 326-6000
Fairfield (G-10788)

CONTROL EQPT: Electric

Controls Inc ....E 330 239-4345
Medina (G-13923)

CONTROL EQPT: Noise

Tech Products Corporation ....E 937 438-1100
Miamisburg (G-14227)

CONTROL PANELS: Electrical

Innovative Controls Corp ....D 419 691-6684
Toledo (G-17821)

Instrmntation Ctrl Systems Inc .....E 513 662-2600
Cincinnati (G-3765)

Panelmatic Inc ....E 330 782-8007
Youngstown (G-20151)

Scott Fetzer Company ....C 216 267-9000
Cleveland (G-6379)

CONTROLS & ACCESS: Indl, Electric

Corrotec Inc ....E 937 325-3585
Springfield (G-17021)

Filnor Inc ....E 330 821-8731
Alliance (G-532)

PMC Systems Limited ....E 330 538-2268
North Jackson (G-15252)

CONTROLS: Environmental

Alan Manufacturing Inc ....E 330 262-1555
Wooster (G-19684)

Babcock & Wilcox Company ....A 330 753-4511
Barberton (G-944)

Cincinnati Air Conditioning Co .....D 513 721-5622
Cincinnati (G-3220)

Hunter Defense Tech Inc ....E 216 438-6111
Solon (G-16859)

Peco II Inc ....D 614 431-0694
Columbus (G-8433)

Pepperl + Fuchs Inc ....C 330 425-3555
Twinsburg (G-18302)

Schneder Elc Bldngs Amrcas Inc ...D 513 398-9800
Lebanon (G-12499)

CONTROLS: Relay & Ind

Chandler Systems Incorporated .....D 888 363-9434
Ashland (G-666)

Command Alkon Incorporated ......D 614 799-0600
Dublin (G-10183)

Curtiss-Wright Controls ....E 937 252-5601
Fairborn (G-10667)

GE Aviation Systems LLC ....B 937 898-5881
Vandalia (G-18524)

Hite Parts Exchange Inc ....E 614 272-5115
Columbus (G-7756)

Innovative Controls Corp ....D 419 691-6684
Toledo (G-17821)

Peco II Inc ....D 614 431-0694
Columbus (G-8433)

Pepperl + Fuchs Inc ....C 330 425-3555
Twinsburg (G-18302)

Schneider Electric Usa Inc ....D 513 755-5000
West Chester (G-18997)

Stock Fairfield Corporation ....C 440 543-6000
Chagrin Falls (G-2684)

CONVALESCENT HOME

Bel Air Care Center ....D....... 330 821-3939
Alliance (G-518)
Birchaven Village ....C....... 419 424-3000
Findlay (G-10869)
Boy-Ko Management Inc ....E....... 513 677-4900
Loveland (G-12979)
Brewster Parke Inc ....D....... 330 767-4179
Brewster (G-1809)
Brookview Healthcare Ctr ....D....... 419 784-1014
Defiance (G-9905)
Chcc Home Health Care ....E....... 330 759-4069
Austintown (G-857)
Country Club Center Homes Inc.......D....... 330 343-6351
Dover (G-10071)
Dublin Geriatric Care Co LP ....E....... 614 761-1188
Dublin (G-10207)
Elms Retirement Village Inc ....D....... 440 647-2414
Wellington (G-18840)
Gaslite Villa Convalescent Ctr ......D....... 330 494-4500
Canal Fulton (G-2095)
Golden Living LLC ....D....... 419 599-4070
Napoleon (G-14807)
Golden Living LLC ....D....... 419 227-2154
Lima (G-12644)
Golden Living LLC ....C....... 440 247-4200
Chagrin Falls (G-2647)
Golden Living LLC ....C....... 614 861-6666
Columbus (G-7678)
Golden Living LLC ....C....... 440 256-8100
Willoughby (G-19527)
Golden Living LLC ....C....... 330 297-5781
Ravenna (G-16244)
Golden Living LLC ....C....... 330 762-6486
Akron (G-239)
Golden Living LLC ....D....... 330 335-1558
Wadsworth (G-18596)
Golden Living LLC ....D....... 330 725-3393
Medina (G-13944)
Heath Nursing Care Center ....C....... 740 522-1171
Newark (G-15040)
Hospice of The Western Reserve ....D....... 440 357-5833
Willoughby Hills (G-19589)
J E F Inc ....D....... 513 921-4130
Cincinnati (G-3794)
Laurel Health Care Company ....C....... 614 885-0408
Worthington (G-19821)
Lcd Home Health Agency LLC ....E....... 513 497-0441
Hamilton (G-11623)
Lima Cnvlscent HM Fndation Inc ....C....... 419 227-5450
Lima (G-12677)
Marymount Health Care Systems ......E....... 216 332-1100
Cleveland (G-5919)
National Church Residences ....C....... 614 451-2151
Columbus (G-8130)
Nentwick Convalescent Home...........C....... 330 385-5001
East Liverpool (G-10409)
Ohio Presbt Retirement Svcs ....C....... 937 415-5666
Dayton (G-9673)
Ohio Valley Manor Inc ....C....... 937 392-4318
Ripley (G-16401)
Provider Services Inc ....D....... 614 888-2021
Columbus (G-8476)
Rae-Ann Enterprises Inc ....D....... 440 249-5092
Cleveland (G-6280)
RMS of Ohio Inc ....E....... 513 841-0990
Cincinnati (G-4386)
Salutary Providers Inc ....C....... 440 964-8446
Ashtabula (G-753)
Senior Care Inc ....E....... 937 291-3211
Miamisburg (G-14217)
Senior Lifestyle Corporation ....D....... 513 777-4457
West Chester (G-19002)
University Hospitals Health ....E....... 440 285-4040
Chardon (G-2722)
Vienna Enterprises Inc ....E....... 937 568-4524
South Vienna (G-16949)
Wedgewood Estates ....E....... 419 756-7400
Mansfield (G-13262)
Whetstone Care Center LLC ....C....... 614 457-1100
Columbus (G-8895)
Whetstone Care Center LLC ....C....... 740 474-6036
Circleville (G-4853)
Whispering Hills Care Center ....E....... 740 392-3982
Mount Vernon (G-14792)

CONVALESCENT HOMES

3g Operating Company LLC ....B....... 440 944-9400
Parma (G-15758)

Altenheim Foundation Inc ....E....... 440 238-3361
Strongsville (G-17284)
Altercare of Bucyrus Inc ....C....... 419 562-7644
Bucyrus (G-1976)
Altercare of Mentor Center ....C....... 440 953-4421
Mentor (G-14017)
Altercare of Millersburg ....D....... 330 674-4444
Millersburg (G-14455)
American Nursing Care Inc ....D....... 513 576-0262
Milford (G-14371)
American Nursing Care Inc ....D....... 419 228-0888
Lima (G-12601)
Anderson Healthcare Ltd ....D....... 513 474-6200
Cincinnati (G-2959)
Andover Vlg Retirement Cmnty ....C....... 440 293-5416
Andover (G-604)
Aurora Manor Ltd Partnership ....B....... 330 562-5000
Aurora (G-818)
Austin Woods Nursing Center ....C....... 330 792-7681
Youngstown (G-19958)
Autumn Aegis Inc ....D....... 440 282-6768
Lorain (G-12883)
Autumn Hills Care Center Inc ....C....... 330 652-2053
Niles (G-15146)
Beacon of Light Ltd ....E....... 419 531-9060
Toledo (G-17608)
Beechwood Terrace Care Ctr Inc.......C....... 513 578-6200
Cincinnati (G-3036)
Bellbrook Rhbltتion Healthcare ....D....... 937 848-8421
Bellbrook (G-1338)
Bethany Nursing Home Inc ....E....... 330 492-7171
Canton (G-2211)
Blossom Hills Nursing Home..........D....... 440 635-5567
Huntsburg (G-12017)
Braeview Manor Inc ....C....... 216 486-9300
Cleveland (G-5073)
Brecksville Leasing Co LLC ....C....... 330 659-6166
Richfield (G-16347)
Brenn Field Nursing Center ....C....... 330 683-4075
Orrville (G-15626)
Brentwood Life Care Company ......C....... 330 468-2273
Northfield (G-15375)
Briar Hl Hlth Care Rsdence Inc ....D....... 440 632-5241
Middlefield (G-14269)
Briarwood Ltd ....D....... 330 688-1828
Stow (G-17193)
Bryden Place Inc ....E....... 614 258-6623
Beachwood (G-1038)
Burlington House Inc ....D....... 513 851-7888
Cincinnati (G-3093)
Canton Assisted Living ....C....... 330 492-7131
Canton (G-2227)
Care One LLC ....C....... 937 236-6707
Dayton (G-9277)
Carington Health Systems ....B....... 513 732-6500
Batavia (G-985)
Carington Health Systems ....C....... 513 961-8881
Cincinnati (G-3124)
Carington Health Systems ....C....... 937 743-2754
Franklin (G-11025)
Caritas Inc ....E....... 419 332-2589
Fremont (G-11060)
Carlisle Health Care Inc ....E....... 937 746-2662
Carlisle (G-2551)
Carriage Inn of Cadiz Inc ....E....... 740 942-8084
Cadiz (G-2027)
Carriage Inn of Trotwood Inc ....C....... 937 854-1180
Trotwood (G-18192)
Carriage Inn of Trotwood Inc ....D....... 937 277-0505
Dayton (G-9281)
Carriage Inn Retirement Cmnty ......C....... 937 278-0404
Dayton (G-9282)
Carroll Health Care Center ....C....... 330 627-5501
Carrollton (G-2562)
Casto Health Care ....D....... 419 884-6400
Mansfield (G-13148)
Catherines Care Center Inc ....D....... 740 282-3605
Steubenville (G-17146)
Centerburg Two LLC ....D....... 740 625-5774
Centerburg (G-2614)
CHS Miami Valley Inc ....E....... 330 204-1040
Sidney (G-16765)
Chs-Norwood Inc ....C....... 513 351-7007
Cincinnati (G-3215)
Church of God Retirement Cmnty........E....... 513 422-5600
Middletown (G-14295)
Cincinnati Senior Care LLC ....E....... 513 272-0600
Cincinnati (G-3266)
City View Nursing & Rehab LLC ....C....... 216 361-1414
Cleveland (G-5218)

Clermont Care Inc ....C....... 513 831-1770
Milford (G-14381)
Coal Grove Long Term Care Inc ....D....... 740 532-0449
Ironton (G-12151)
Columbus Clny For Elderly Care........C....... 614 891-5055
Westerville (G-19239)
Communi Care Inc ....E....... 419 382-2200
Toledo (G-17670)
Communicare Health Svcs Inc ....C....... 937 399-9217
Springfield (G-17018)
Community Skilled Health Care........C....... 330 373-1160
Warren (G-18689)
Consulate Management Co LLC ....C....... 419 683-3255
Crestline (G-9052)
Country Club Center Homes Inc.......D....... 330 343-6351
Dover (G-10071)
Country Club Center II Ltd ....C....... 740 397-2350
Mount Vernon (G-14756)
Country Court Ltd ....C....... 740 397-4125
Mount Vernon (G-14757)
County of Erie ....C....... 419 627-8733
Huron (G-12024)
County of Ottawa ....C....... 419 898-6459
Oak Harbor (G-15470)
County of Sandusky ....D....... 419 334-2602
Fremont (G-11066)
Covenant Care Ohio Inc ....D....... 419 898-5506
Port Clinton (G-16104)
Covenant Care Ohio Inc ....D....... 937 526-5570
Versailles (G-18569)
Covington Snf Inc ....E....... 330 426-2920
East Palestine (G-10419)
Crandall Medical Center Inc ....C....... 330 938-6126
Sebring (G-16668)
Crestmont Nursing Home N Corp ....C....... 216 228-9550
Lakewood (G-12340)
Crestmont Nursing Home N Corp ....D....... 216 228-9550
Lakewood (G-12341)
Crestview Ridge Nursing ....E....... 937 393-6700
Hillsboro (G-11836)
Crystal Care Center Portsmouth........E....... 740 354-6619
Portsmouth (G-16134)
Crystal Care Centers Inc ....C....... 419 281-9595
Ashland (G-670)
Crystal Care Centers Inc ....E....... 419 747-2666
Mansfield (G-13161)
Crystal Care Centers Inc ....D....... 419 747-2666
Mansfield (G-13162)
D James Incorporated ....C....... 513 574-4550
Cincinnati (G-3395)
Danridge Nursing Home Inc ....D....... 330 746-5157
Youngstown (G-20015)
DMD Management Inc ....E....... 330 405-6040
Twinsburg (G-18258)
Doylestown Health Care Center........C....... 330 658-1533
Doylestown (G-10112)
Eaglewood Care Center ....C....... 937 399-7195
Springfield (G-17031)
East Carroll Nursing Home ....D....... 330 627-6900
Carrollton (G-2567)
East Water Leasing Co LLC ....D....... 419 278-6921
Deshler (G-10057)
Eastside Multi Care Inc ....C....... 216 662-3343
Maple Heights (G-13286)
Embassy Healthcare Inc ....D....... 513 868-6500
Fairfield (G-10724)
Emery Leasing Co LLC ....B....... 216 475-8880
Cleveland (G-5476)
Fairport Enterprises Inc ....C....... 330 830-9988
Massillon (G-13680)
Falling Leasing Co LLC ....C....... 440 238-1100
Strongsville (G-17303)
Falls Village Retirement Cmnty ....D....... 330 945-9797
Cuyahoga Falls (G-9094)
Four Seasons Washington LLC........D....... 740 895-6101
Wshngtn CT Hs (G-19873)
Franklin Shcp Inc ....D....... 440 614-0160
Columbus (G-7619)
Friendship Vlg of Clumbus Ohio........D....... 614 890-8287
Columbus (G-7628)
Front Leasing Co LLC ....C....... 440 243-4000
Berea (G-1427)
Gables At Green Pastures ....C....... 937 642-3893
Marysville (G-13498)
Gables Care Center Inc ....C....... 740 937-2900
Hopedale (G-11936)
Gallipolis Care LLC ....C....... 740 446-7112
Gallipolis (G-11194)
Garden Manor Extended Care Cen........C....... 513 420-5972
Middletown (G-14300)

SERVICES

Gardens At Wapakoneta..............E...... 419 738-0725
  Wapakoneta (G-18644)
Gaymont Nursing Homes Inc.........D...... 419 668-8258
  Norwalk (G-15439)
GFS Leasing Inc.........................D...... 330 877-2666
  Hartville (G-11687)
Glendale Place Care Center LLC.........E...... 513 771-1779
  Cincinnati (G-3619)
Glendora Health Care Center.........D...... 330 264-0912
  Wooster (G-19723)
Golden Living LLC.......................D...... 419 227-2154
  Lima (G-12644)
Good Shepard Village LLC.............D...... 937 322-1911
  Springfield (G-17042)
Good Shepherd Home For Aged.........C...... 614 228-5200
  Ashland (G-673)
Grace Brethren Village Inc.............E...... 937 836-4011
  Englewood (G-10589)
Greenbrier Senior Living Cmnty.........C...... 440 888-5900
  Cleveland (G-5641)
Guardian Elder Care LLC...............C...... 330 549-0898
  North Lima (G-15269)
Hamlet Village In Chagrin FLS.........D...... 216 263-6033
  Chagrin Falls (G-2649)
Hampton Woods Nursing Ctr Inc.........E...... 330 707-1400
  Poland (G-16084)
Hanover House Inc.......................C...... 330 837-1741
  Massillon (G-13692)
Harborside Clveland Ltd Partnr.........C...... 440 526-4770
  Broadview Heights (G-1835)
Hcf Management Inc.....................D...... 419 999-2010
  Lima (G-12652)
Hcf of Bowl Green Care Ctr Inc.........D...... 419 352-7558
  Bowling Green (G-1735)
Hcf of Court House Inc.................C...... 740 335-9290
  Wshngtn CT Hs (G-19874)
Hcf of Crestview Inc...................D...... 937 426-5033
  Beavercreek (G-1223)
Hcf of Fox Run Inc.....................D...... 419 424-0832
  Findlay (G-10921)
Hcf of Piqua Inc.......................D...... 937 773-0040
  Piqua (G-16008)
Hcf of Roselawn Inc...................C...... 419 647-4115
  Spencerville (G-16956)
Hcf of Shawnee Inc.....................D...... 419 999-2055
  Lima (G-12655)
Hcf of Van Wert Inc...................D...... 419 999-2010
  Van Wert (G-18479)
Hcf of Wapakoneta Inc.................D...... 419 738-3711
  Wapakoneta (G-18645)
Hcr Manorcare Med Svcs Fla LLC.........D...... 513 233-0831
  Cincinnati (G-3689)
Hcr Manorcare Med Svcs Fla LLC.........C...... 419 252-5500
  Portsmouth (G-16142)
Hcr Manorcare Med Svcs Fla LLC.........C...... 419 531-2127
  Toledo (G-17786)
Hcr Manorcare Med Svcs Fla LLC.........C...... 330 753-5005
  Barberton (G-954)
Hcr Manorcare Med Svcs Fla LLC.........C...... 513 561-4111
  Cincinnati (G-3690)
Hcr Manorcare Med Svcs Fla LLC.........C...... 614 882-1511
  Westerville (G-19260)
Hcr Manorcare Med Svcs Fla LLC.........D...... 330 668-6889
  Akron (G-257)
Hcr Manorcare Med Svcs Fla LLC.........C...... 419 252-5500
  Toledo (G-17787)
Hcr Manorcare Med Svcs Fla LLC.........C...... 216 251-3300
  Cleveland (G-5670)
Hcr Manorcare Med Svcs Fla LLC.........D...... 440 473-0090
  Cleveland (G-5671)
Hcr Manorcare Med Svcs Fla LLC.........C...... 216 486-2300
  Cleveland (G-5672)
Hcr Manorcare Med Svcs Fla LLC.........C...... 937 436-9700
  Centerville (G-2627)
Hcr Manorcare Med Svcs Fla LLC.........C...... 419 691-3088
  Oregon (G-15597)
Hcr Manorcare Med Svcs Fla LLC.........E...... 440 808-9275
  Westlake (G-19348)
Hcr Manorcare Med Svcs Fla LLC.........C...... 513 591-0400
  Cincinnati (G-3691)
Health Care Rtrement Corp Amer.........C...... 419 252-5500
  Toledo (G-17789)
Health Care Rtrement Corp Amer.........D...... 740 286-5026
  Jackson (G-12174)
Health Care Rtrement Corp Amer.........D...... 740 373-8920
  Marietta (G-13335)
Health Care Rtrement Corp Amer.........C...... 937 429-1106
  Dayton (G-9175)
Health Care Rtrement Corp Amer.........D...... 614 882-3782
  Westerville (G-19261)

Health Care Rtrement Corp Amer.........D...... 937 599-5123
  Bellefontaine (G-1353)
Health Care Rtrement Corp Amer.........D...... 614 464-2273
  Columbus (G-7725)
Health Care Rtrement Corp Amer.........C...... 937 390-0005
  Springfield (G-17044)
Health Care Rtrement Corp Amer.........D...... 740 894-3287
  South Point (G-16936)
Health Care Rtrement Corp Amer.........D...... 937 393-5766
  Hillsboro (G-11841)
Health Care Rtrement Corp Amer.........D...... 937 773-9346
  Piqua (G-16009)
Health Care Rtrement Corp Amer.........C...... 937 866-8885
  Miamisburg (G-14176)
Health Care Rtrement Corp Amer.........C...... 419 878-8523
  Waterville (G-18789)
Heartlnd-Riverview S Pt OH LLC.........D...... 740 894-3287
  South Point (G-16937)
Heather Knoll Retirement Vlg.........C...... 330 688-8600
  Tallmadge (G-17476)
Hempstead Manor.......................C...... 740 354-8150
  Portsmouth (G-16145)
Hennis Nursing Home...................C...... 330 364-8849
  Dover (G-10081)
Highbanks Care Center LLC.............D...... 614 888-2021
  Columbus (G-7747)
Hill Side Plaza.......................D...... 216 486-6300
  Cleveland (G-5689)
Hillspring Health Care Center.........E...... 937 748-1100
  Springboro (G-16970)
Hilty Memorial Home Inc...............C...... 419 384-3218
  Pandora (G-15753)
Hooberry Associates Inc...............D...... 330 872-1991
  Newton Falls (G-15137)
Huron Health Care Center Inc.........C...... 419 433-4990
  Huron (G-12027)
Huston Nursing Home...................D...... 740 384-3485
  Hamden (G-11552)
Isabelle Ridgway Care Ctr Inc.........C...... 614 252-4931
  Columbus (G-7846)
Ivy Health Care Inc...................C...... 513 251-2557
  Cincinnati (G-3792)
Jennings Eliza Home Inc...............C...... 216 226-0282
  Cleveland (G-5788)
Jma Healthcare LLC.....................C...... 440 439-7976
  Cleveland (G-5977)
Kenwood Ter Hlth Care Ctr Inc.........C...... 513 793-2255
  Cincinnati (G-3861)
Kimes Convalescent Center.............E...... 740 593-3391
  Athens (G-789)
Kindred Nursing Centers E LLC.........D...... 614 276-8222
  Columbus (G-7905)
Kindred Nursing Centers E LLC.........C...... 614 837-9666
  Canal Winchester (G-2114)
Kindred Nursing Centers E LLC.........C...... 314 631-3000
  Pickerington (G-15961)
Kindred Nursing Centers E LLC.........C...... 502 596-7300
  Logan (G-12844)
King Tree Leasing Co LLC.............D...... 937 278-0723
  Dayton (G-9548)
Kingston Healthcare Company.........C...... 419 289-3859
  Ashland (G-677)
Lancia Nursing Home Inc...............E...... 740 695-4404
  Saint Clairsville (G-16491)
Laurel Healthcare.....................C...... 419 782-7879
  Defiance (G-9925)
Levering Management Inc...............B...... 740 397-3897
  Mount Vernon (G-14778)
Levering Management Inc...............D...... 419 756-4747
  Mansfield (G-13198)
Liberty Nrsing Ctr of Jmestown.........D...... 937 675-3311
  Jamestown (G-12188)
Liberty Nrsing Ctr Rvrside LLC.........D...... 513 557-3621
  Cincinnati (G-3924)
Liberty Nursing Center.................E...... 937 836-5143
  Englewood (G-10593)
Life Care Centers America Inc.........C...... 440 365-5200
  Elyria (G-10524)
Life Care Centers America Inc.........C...... 440 871-3030
  Westlake (G-19369)
Life Care Centers America Inc.........D...... 614 889-6320
  Columbus (G-7972)
Lincoln Crawford Nrsg/Rehab CT.........E...... 513 861-2044
  Cincinnati (G-3932)
Lincoln Park Associates II LP.........C...... 937 297-4300
  Dayton (G-9568)
Locust Ridge Nursing Home Inc.........C...... 937 444-2920
  Williamsburg (G-19494)
Lodge Care Center Inc.................C...... 513 683-9966
  Loveland (G-13007)

Lorantffy Care Center Inc.............D...... 330 666-2631
  Copley (G-8969)
Loveland Health Care Center.........C...... 513 605-6000
  Loveland (G-13008)
Lutheran Senior City Inc...............B...... 614 228-5200
  Columbus (G-8000)
Lynnhaven Xii LLC.....................C...... 419 756-7111
  Mansfield (G-13200)
Manleys Manor Nursing Home Inc.........C...... 419 424-0402
  Findlay (G-10937)
Manor Care of America Inc.............C...... 330 867-8530
  Akron (G-325)
Manor Care of America Inc.............C...... 330 492-7835
  Canton (G-2386)
Manor Care of America Inc.............C...... 440 779-6900
  North Olmsted (G-15296)
Manor Care of America Inc.............C...... 440 951-5551
  Willoughby (G-19548)
Manor Care of America Inc.............C...... 440 345-9300
  North Royalton (G-15362)
Mansfield Memorial Homes LLC.........C...... 419 774-5100
  Mansfield (G-13209)
Maple Knoll Communities Inc.........E...... 513 524-7990
  Oxford (G-15679)
Maple Knoll Communities Inc.........A...... 513 782-2400
  Cincinnati (G-3967)
Maplewood Nursing Center Inc.........E...... 740 383-2126
  Marion (G-13431)
Mason Health Care Center.............D...... 513 398-2881
  Mason (G-13616)
Masonic Healthcare Inc.................B...... 937 525-3001
  Springfield (G-17067)
Mayfair Nursing Care Centers.........D...... 614 889-6320
  Columbus (G-8041)
Mayflower Nursing Home Inc.............C...... 330 492-7131
  Canton (G-2393)
Mc Auley Center.......................C...... 937 653-5432
  Urbana (G-18439)
McClellan Management Inc...............C...... 419 855-7755
  Genoa (G-11258)
Meadow Wind Hlth Care Ctr Inc.........C...... 330 833-2026
  Massillon (G-13714)
Meadowbrook Manor of Hartford.........D...... 330 772-5253
  Fowler (G-11016)
Medina Meadows.......................D...... 330 725-1550
  Medina (G-13977)
Medina Medical Investors Ltd.........C...... 330 483-3131
  Medina (G-13978)
Megco Management Inc.................C...... 330 874-9999
  Bolivar (G-1704)
Mill Creek Nursing.....................E...... 419 468-4046
  Galion (G-11179)
Mill Manor Nursing Home Inc.........E...... 440 967-6614
  Vermilion (G-18558)
Mt Washington Care Center Inc.........C...... 513 231-4561
  Cincinnati (G-4083)
Multicare Management Group.........C...... 513 868-6500
  Fairfield (G-10759)
Muskingum County Ohio.................D...... 740 454-1911
  Zanesville (G-20336)
New Albany Care Center LLC.............C...... 614 855-8866
  Columbus (G-8183)
Newark Care Center LLC.................D...... 740 366-2321
  Newark (G-15082)
Newcomerstown Progress Corp.........C...... 740 498-5165
  Newcomerstown (G-15134)
Nightingale Holdings LLC...............B...... 330 645-0200
  Akron (G-346)
Normandy Manor of Rocky River.........C...... 440 333-5401
  Rocky River (G-16443)
Northpoint Senior Services LLC.........C...... 740 373-3597
  Marietta (G-13363)
Northpoint Senior Services LLC.........D...... 513 248-1655
  Milford (G-14414)
Oak Creek Terrace Inc.................C...... 937 439-1454
  Dayton (G-9662)
Oak Health Care Investors.............D...... 740 397-3200
  Mount Vernon (G-14784)
October Enterprises Inc...............C...... 937 456-9535
  Eaton (G-10456)
Ohiohealth Corporation.................A...... 614 788-8860
  Columbus (G-8362)
Omni Manor Inc.........................C...... 330 545-1550
  Girard (G-11297)
Omni Manor Inc.........................C...... 330 793-5648
  Youngstown (G-20148)
Parkview Manor Inc.....................C...... 419 243-5191
  Toledo (G-17972)
Pickaway Manor Inc.....................C...... 740 474-5400
  Circleville (G-4844)

(G-0000) Company's Geographic Section entry number

Piketon Nursing Center Inc.................D....... 740 289-4074
Piketon *(G-15986)*

Pleasant View Nursing Home ....D...... 330 745-6028
Barberton *(G-961)*

Progressive Green Meadows LLC........C....... 330 875-1456
Louisville *(G-12971)*

Quaker Heights Nursing HM Inc ....D....... 513 897-6050
Waynesville *(G-18835)*

R & J Investment Co Inc.....................C....... 440 934-5204
Avon *(G-902)*

Rcr East Inc.......................................C....... 513 793-2090
Cincinnati *(G-4341)*

Rcr East Inc.......................................C....... 513 231-8292
Cincinnati *(G-4342)*

Rivers Bend Health Care LLC ....D....... 740 894-3476
South Point *(G-16945)*

Royal Oak Nrsing Rhbltttion Ctr ....D....... 440 884-9191
Cleveland *(G-6346)*

Saber Healthcare Group LLC ....C....... 937 779-4150
West Union *(G-19138)*

Saber Healthcare Group LLC ....E....... 216 292-5706
Bedford *(G-1303)*

Saber Healthcare Group LLC ....B....... 740 852-3100
London *(G-12874)*

Sarah Jane Living Center Ltd ....E....... 419 692-6618
Delphos *(G-10034)*

Sensi Care 3 ....E....... 440 323-6310
Elyria *(G-10562)*

Shg Whitehall Holdings LLC.............C....... 614 501-8271
Columbus *(G-8633)*

Sisters Od Saint Joseph of SAI ....B....... 216 531-7426
Euclid *(G-10656)*

Solon Pnte At Emrald Ridge LLC ....E....... 440 498-3000
Solon *(G-16900)*

South Broadway.................................D....... 330 339-2151
New Philadelphia *(G-14981)*

Springhills LLC ....C....... 937 274-1400
Dayton *(G-9786)*

St Catherines Care Centers O.............C....... 419 435-8112
Fostoria *(G-11013)*

St Catherines Care Ctr Findlay ....C....... 419 422-3978
Findlay *(G-10962)*

Summitt Ohio Leasing Co LLC ....C....... 937 436-2273
Dayton *(G-9800)*

Sunbridge Care Enterprises Inc ....D....... 740 653-8630
Lancaster *(G-12439)*

Sunbridge Circleville ....E....... 740 477-1695
Circleville *(G-4851)*

Sunrise Healthcare Group LLC ....C....... 216 662-3343
Maple Heights *(G-13299)*

Swanton Hlth Care Rtrement Ctr ....D....... 419 825-1145
Swanton *(G-17407)*

Trinity Healthcare Corporation ....C....... 513 489-2444
Cincinnati *(G-4648)*

Twin Maples Nursing Home ....E....... 740 596-5955
Mc Arthur *(G-13891)*

Uhrichsville Health Care Ctr ....D....... 740 922-2208
Uhrichsville *(G-18346)*

United Church Homes Inc ....C....... 513 922-1440
Cincinnati *(G-4677)*

United Church Homes Inc ....C....... 330 854-4177
Canal Fulton *(G-2099)*

United Church Homes Inc ....C....... 937 426-8481
Beavercreek *(G-1239)*

Van Rue Incorporated.......................C....... 419 238-0715
Van Wert *(G-18491)*

Vancrest Ltd ....C....... 419 695-2871
Delphos *(G-10038)*

Vancrest Ltd ....C....... 419 749-2194
Convoy *(G-8962)*

Vancrest Ltd ....D....... 937 456-3010
Eaton *(G-10465)*

Village Green Healthcare Ctr ....C....... 937 548-1993
Greenville *(G-11399)*

Volunters Amer Care Facilities ....C....... 419 447-7151
Tiffin *(G-17546)*

Volunters Amer Care Facilities ....C....... 419 334-9521
Fremont *(G-11103)*

Vrable Healthcare Inc.......................E....... 614 545-5500
Columbus *(G-8864)*

Walton Manor Health Care Ctr ....C....... 440 439-4433
Cleveland *(G-6652)*

Water Leasing Co LLC ....C....... 440 285-9400
Chardon *(G-2725)*

Wessell Generations Inc ....C....... 440 775-1491
Oberlin *(G-15521)*

West View Manor Inc ....C....... 330 264-8640
Wooster *(G-19782)*

Whetstone Care Center LLC ....C....... 614 875-7700
Grove City *(G-11487)*

Whetstone Care Center LLC ....C....... 614 457-1100
Columbus *(G-8895)*

Whetstone Care Center LLC ....C....... 740 474-6036
Circleville *(G-4853)*

Willowood Care Center ....C....... 330 225-3156
Brunswick *(G-1947)*

Womens Welsh Clubs of America ....D....... 440 331-0420
Rocky River *(G-16449)*

Wood County Ohio ....C....... 419 353-8411
Bowling Green *(G-1756)*

Woodland Country Manor Inc ....E....... 513 523-4449
Somerville *(G-16920)*

Xenia East Management Systems ....D....... 937 372-4495
Xenia *(G-19936)*

Zandex Inc ....C....... 740 676-8381
Shadyside *(G-16700)*

Zandex Health Care Corporation ....C....... 740 454-9747
Zanesville *(G-20380)*

CONVENIENCE STORES

Duncan Oil Co ....E....... 937 426-5945
Dayton *(G-9171)*

Holland Oil Company.........................D....... 330 835-1815
Akron *(G-266)*

Standard Oil Company ....D....... 330 530-8049
Girard *(G-11301)*

Ta Operating LLC ....B....... 440 808-9100
Westlake *(G-19411)*

Travelcenters America Inc ....A....... 440 808-9100
Westlake *(G-19413)*

CONVENTION & TRADE SHOW SVCS

Akron-Summit Convention ....E....... 330 374-7560
Akron *(G-62)*

City of North Olmsted ....E....... 440 777-0678
North Olmsted *(G-15283)*

Columbus Bride ....D....... 614 888-4567
Columbus *(G-7263)*

Convention & Vistors Bureau of..........E....... 216 875-6603
Cleveland *(G-5347)*

Greater Cincinnati Cnvntn/Vstr ....E....... 513 621-2142
Cincinnati *(G-3650)*

I-X Center Corporation ....C....... 216 265-2675
Cleveland *(G-5732)*

Jbjs Acquisitions LLC ....E....... 513 769-0393
Cincinnati *(G-3810)*

Miami University ....D....... 513 529-6911
Oxford *(G-15681)*

Nexxtshow Exposition Svcs LLC ....E....... 877 836-3131
Cincinnati *(G-4116)*

Wiegands Lake Park Inc ....E....... 440 338-5795
Novelty *(G-15467)*

CONVERTERS: Data

Cisco Systems Inc ....A....... 937 427-4264
Beavercreek *(G-1140)*

CONVERTERS: Phase Or Rotary, Electrical

Electric Service Co Inc ....E....... 513 271-6387
Cincinnati *(G-3487)*

CONVEYOR SYSTEMS

Power-Pack Conveyor Company...........E....... 440 975-9955
Willoughby *(G-19563)*

CONVEYOR SYSTEMS: Belt, General Indl Use

Mine Equipment Services LLC ....E....... 740 936-5427
Sunbury *(G-17390)*

CONVEYOR SYSTEMS: Robotic

Grob Systems Inc ....C....... 419 358-9015
Bluffton *(G-1691)*

CONVEYORS & CONVEYING EQPT

Alba Manufacturing Inc ....D....... 513 874-0551
Fairfield *(G-10694)*

Allied Fabricating & Wldg Co ....E....... 614 751-6664
Columbus *(G-6897)*

Dillin Engineered Systems Corp ....E....... 419 666-6789
Perrysburg *(G-15859)*

Grasan Equipment Company Inc ....D....... 419 526-4440
Mansfield *(G-13180)*

Innovative Controls Corp ....D....... 419 691-6684
Toledo *(G-17821)*

Intelligrated Systems Inc ....A....... 866 936-7300
Mason *(G-13598)*

Intelligrated Systems LLC ....A....... 513 701-7300
Mason *(G-13599)*

Intelligrated Systems Ohio LLC ....A....... 513 701-7300
Mason *(G-13600)*

Pfpc Enterprises Inc ....B....... 513 941-6200
Cincinnati *(G-4240)*

Siemens Industry Inc ....E....... 440 526-2770
Brecksville *(G-1805)*

Stock Fairfield Corporation ....C....... 440 543-6000
Chagrin Falls *(G-2684)*

CONVEYORS: Overhead

K F T Inc...D....... 513 241-5910
Cincinnati *(G-3843)*

COOKING & FOOD WARMING EQPT: Commercial

High-TEC Industrial Services.................C....... 937 667-1772
Tipp City *(G-17558)*

Lima Sheet Metal Machine & Mfg ....E....... 419 229-1161
Lima *(G-12687)*

COPPER ORE MINING

Warrenton Copper LLC ....E....... 636 456-3488
Cleveland *(G-6654)*

COPY MACHINES WHOLESALERS

Andrew Belmont Sargent ....E....... 513 769-7800
Cincinnati *(G-2965)*

Blakemans Valley Off Eqp Inc.............E....... 330 729-1000
Youngstown *(G-19965)*

Blue Technologies Inc ....C....... 216 271-4800
Cleveland *(G-5066)*

Blue Technologies Inc ....E....... 330 499-9300
Canton *(G-2215)*

Canon Solutions America Inc ....D....... 937 260-4495
Miamisburg *(G-14148)*

Document Solutions Ohio LLC ....E....... 614 846-2400
Columbus *(G-7465)*

Graphic Entps Off Slutions Inc ....D....... 800 553-6616
North Canton *(G-15208)*

Meritech Inc ....D....... 216 459-8333
Cleveland *(G-5956)*

Mt Business Technologies Inc.............C....... 419 529-6100
Mansfield *(G-13225)*

Office Products Toledo Inc ....E....... 419 865-7001
Holland *(G-11904)*

Visual Edge Technology Inc ....C....... 330 494-9694
Canton *(G-2528)*

CORRECTIONAL FACILITY OPERATIONS

Community Education Ctrs Inc ....B....... 330 424-4065
Lisbon *(G-12797)*

Corecivic Inc.....................................B....... 330 746-3777
Youngstown *(G-20011)*

Correction Commission NW Ohio ....C....... 419 428-3800
Stryker *(G-17369)*

Franklin Community Base Correc..........D....... 614 525-4600
Columbus *(G-7615)*

Licking Muskingum Cmnty Correc.......E....... 740 349-6980
Newark *(G-15058)*

Management & Training Corp ....C....... 801 693-2600
Conneaut *(G-8955)*

Neocap/Cbcf ....E....... 330 675-2669
Warren *(G-18733)*

CORRECTIONAL INSTITUTIONS

Ohio Dept Rhbilitation Corectn ....B....... 614 274-9000
Columbus *(G-8248)*

CORRECTIONAL INSTITUTIONS, GOVERNMENT: Detention Center

County of Ross ....E....... 740 773-4169
Chillicothe *(G-2772)*

CORRECTIONAL INSTITUTIONS, GOVERNMENT: Prison, government

Youth Services Ohio Department ....C....... 419 875-6965
Liberty Center *(G-12576)*

SERVICES

CORRECTIONAL INSTITUTIONS, GOVERNMENT: State

Rehabltation Corectn Ohio Dept ....D 614 752-0800
Columbus (G-8507)

CORRESPONDENCE SCHOOLS

Zaner-Bloser Inc..................................D 614 486-0221
Columbus (G-8935)

CORRUGATED PRDTS: Boxes, Partition, Display Items, Sheet/Pad

Kennedy Mint Inc ....D 440 572-3222
Cleveland (G-5824)

COSMETIC PREPARATIONS

Universal Packg Systems Inc ....B 513 732-2000
Batavia (G-1013)
Universal Packg Systems Inc ....B 513 674-9400
Cincinnati (G-4695)
Universal Packg Systems Inc ....E 513 735-4777
Batavia (G-1014)

COSMETICS & TOILETRIES

Luminex Home Decor...........................A 513 563-1113
Blue Ash (G-1601)
Nehemiah Manufacturing Co LLC ....E 513 351-5700
Cincinnati (G-4102)

COSMETICS WHOLESALERS

Cosmax USA Inc Cosmax USA Corp ....E 440 600-5738
Solon (G-16839)

COSMETOLOGIST

Salon Hazelton ....E 419 874-9404
Perrysburg (G-15917)
Soto Salon & Spa ....E 419 872-5555
Perrysburg (G-15922)
Star Beauty Plus LLC ....E 216 662-9750
Maple Heights (G-13298)

COSMETOLOGY & PERSONAL HYGIENE SALONS

Beauty Bar LLC...................................E 419 537-5400
Toledo (G-17609)
M C Hair Consultants Inc ....E 234 678-3987
Cuyahoga Falls (G-9110)
Marios International Spa & Ht................C 330 562-5141
Aurora (G-835)
Mato Inc ....E 440 729-9008
Chesterland (G-2740)
Pure Concept Salon Inc ....E 513 770-2120
Mason (G-13630)
Pure Concept Salon Inc ....D 513 794-0202
Cincinnati (G-4305)
Vlp Inc ....E 330 758-8811
Youngstown (G-20238)

COSMETOLOGY SCHOOL

Creative Images College of B ....E 937 478-7922
Dayton (G-9337)
Nurtur Holdings LLC ....E 614 487-3033
Loveland (G-13016)
Nutur Holdings LLC ....C 513 576-9333
Loveland (G-13017)
Skyland Columbus LLC........................E 614 478-0922
Columbus (G-8651)

COUNCIL FOR SOCIAL AGENCY

Adams Cnty Snior Ctzens Cuncil ....E 937 544-7459
West Union (G-19130)
ARC Industries Incorporated O ....E 614 836-6050
Groveport (G-11495)
Council On Aging of Southweste ....C 513 721-1025
Cincinnati (G-3368)
Fairfield Cnty Job & Fmly Svcs ....D 800 450-8845
Lancaster (G-12391)
Fairfield County ....D 740 653-4060
Lancaster (G-12393)
Jewish Edcatn Ctr of Cleveland ....D 216 371-0446
Cleveland Heights (G-6720)

COUNTER & SINK TOPS

Crafted Surface and Stone LLC...........E 440 658-3799
Bedford Heights (G-1321)

COUNTERS & COUNTING DEVICES

Aclara Technologies LLC ....C 440 528-7200
Solon (G-16814)
Commercial Electric Pdts Corp ....E 216 241-2886
Cleveland (G-5318)

COUNTRY CLUBS

American Golf Corporation....................E 419 726-9353
Toledo (G-17588)
American Golf Corporation....................E 419 693-1991
Toledo (G-17589)
Athens Golf & Country Club ....E 740 592-1655
Athens (G-767)
Avalon Golf & Country Club ....D 330 539-5008
Vienna (G-18577)
Avon Oaks Country Club ....D 440 892-0660
Avon (G-863)
Beechmont Inc ....D 216 831-9100
Cleveland (G-5051)
Bel-Wood Country Club Inc ....E 513 899-3361
Morrow (G-14714)
Belmont Country Club ....D 419 666-1472
Perrysburg (G-15837)
Belmont Hills Country Club ....D 740 695-2181
Saint Clairsville (G-16477)
Brook Plum Country Club ....E 419 625-5394
Sandusky (G-16578)
Brookside Country Club Inc ....D 330 477-6505
Canton (G-2218)
Brookside Golf & Cntry CLB Co ....C 614 889-2581
Columbus (G-7081)
Browns Run Country Club ....D 513 423-6291
Middletown (G-14294)
Buckeye Golf Club Co Inc ....E 419 636-6984
Bryan (G-1953)
Camargo Club ....D 513 561-9292
Cincinnati (G-3106)
Cambridge Country Club Company ....E 740 439-2744
Byesville (G-2023)
Cambridge Country Club Corp ....E 740 432-2107
Byesville (G-2024)
Catawba-Cleveland Dev Corp ....D 419 797-4424
Port Clinton (G-16101)
Chagrin Valley Country Club Co............D 440 248-4310
Chagrin Falls (G-2641)
Chagrin Valley Hunt Club ....D 440 423-4414
Gates Mills (G-11234)
Chillicothe Country Club Co ....E 740 775-0150
Chillicothe (G-2761)
Cincinnati Country Club ....D 513 533-5200
Cincinnati (G-3236)
Cleveland Skating Club........................D 216 791-2800
Cleveland (G-5287)
Clovernook Country Club ....D 513 521-0333
Cincinnati (G-3312)
Club At Hillbrook Inc ....E 440 247-4940
Chagrin Falls (G-2643)
Clubcorp Usa Inc ....E 330 724-4444
Akron (G-145)
Clubcorp Usa Inc ....E 216 851-2582
Cleveland (G-5309)
Coldstream Country Club ....E 513 231-3900
Cincinnati (G-3322)
Columbia Hills Country CLB Inc............E 440 236-5051
Columbia Station (G-6773)
Columbus Country Club ....E 614 861-0800
Columbus (G-7272)
Corporex Realty & Inv LLC ....B 859 292-5500
Cincinnati (G-3364)
Country Club Inc ....C 216 831-9200
Cleveland (G-5359)
Country Club At Muirfield Vlg ....E 614 764-1714
Dublin (G-10190)
Country Club of Hudson ....E 330 650-1188
Hudson (G-11974)
Country Club of North ....E 937 374-5000
Xenia (G-19895)
County of Perry ....E 740 342-0416
New Lexington (G-14918)
Dayton Country Club Company..............D 937 294-3352
Dayton (G-9360)
Dayton Mdowbrook Cntry CLB LLC.......D 937 836-5186
Clayton (G-4856)
Dry Run Limited Partnership ....E 513 561-9119
Cincinnati (G-3445)

Elms Country Club Inc ....E 330 833-2668
North Lawrence (G-15258)
Elms of Massillon Inc ....E 330 833-2668
North Lawrence (G-15259)
Elyria Country Club Company ....C 440 322-6391
Elyria (G-10505)
Fairlawn Country Club Company ....D 330 836-5541
Akron (G-208)
Findlay Country Club............................E 419 422-9263
Findlay (G-10902)
Five Seasons Spt Cntry CLB Inc ....D 513 842-1188
Cincinnati (G-3573)
Five Seasons Spt Cntry CLB Inc ....D 937 848-9200
Dayton (G-9441)
Five Seasons Spt Cntry CLB Inc ....D 440 899-4555
Cleveland (G-5541)
Four Bridges Country Club Ltd ....D 513 759-4620
Liberty Township (G-12581)
Glenmoor Country Club Inc ....C 330 966-3600
Canton (G-2326)
Golf Course Maintenance ....D 330 262-9141
Wooster (G-19724)
Grove Walnut Country Club Inc.............E 937 253-3109
Dayton (G-9174)
Hawthorne Valley Country Club ....D 440 232-1400
Bedford (G-1285)
Hillbrook Club Inc ....E 440 247-4940
Cleveland (G-5690)
Hyde Park Golf & Country Club.............D 513 321-3721
Cincinnati (G-3743)
Inverness Club ....D 419 578-9000
Toledo (G-17825)
Kenwood Country Club Inc...................C 513 527-3590
Cincinnati (G-3860)
Kirtland Country Club Company ....D 440 942-4400
Willoughby (G-19534)
Lake Front II Inc ....E 330 337-8033
Salem (G-16551)
Lakes Golf & Country Club Inc ....E 614 882-2582
Westerville (G-19178)
Lakewood Country Club Company ....D 440 871-0400
Cleveland (G-5851)
Lenau Park ....E 440 235-2646
Olmsted Twp (G-15537)
Losantiville Country Club ....D 513 631-4133
Cincinnati (G-3943)
Maketewah Country Club Company ....D 513 242-9333
Cincinnati (G-3963)
Marietta Country Club Inc ....E 740 373-7722
Marietta (G-13351)
Marion Country Club Company..............E 740 387-0974
Marion (G-13436)
Mayfield Sand Ridge Club ....D 216 381-0826
Cleveland (G-5924)
Medallion Club ....C 614 794-6999
Westerville (G-19185)
Montgomery Swim & Tennis Club ....E 513 793-6433
Montgomery (G-14596)
Moraine Country Club ....E 937 294-6200
Dayton (G-9644)
Moundbuilders Country Club Co............D 740 344-4500
Newark (G-15076)
N C R Employee Benefit Assn ....C 937 299-3571
Dayton (G-9651)
New Albany Country Club Comm A ....E 614 939-8500
New Albany (G-14864)
New Wembley LLC...............................E 440 543-8171
Chagrin Falls (G-2675)
Opcc LLC ....D 904 276-7660
Johnstown (G-12202)
Oxford Country Club Inc ....E 513 524-0801
Oxford (G-15686)
Piqua Country Club Holding Co ....E 937 773-7744
Piqua (G-16017)
Portage Country Club Company ....D 330 836-8565
Akron (G-389)
Progressive Fishing Assn ....D 419 877-9909
Whitehouse (G-19451)
Raintree Country Club Inc ....E 330 699-3232
Uniontown (G-18384)
Shady Hollow Cntry CLB Co Inc ....D 330 832-1581
Massillon (G-13729)
Shaker Heights Country Club Co ....C 216 991-3324
Shaker Heights (G-16712)
Shawnee Country Club.........................D 419 227-7177
Lima (G-12740)
Silver Lake Country Club ....D 330 688-6066
Silver Lake (G-16809)
Silver Lake Management Corp...............C 330 688-6066
Silver Lake (G-16810)

Snow Hill Country Club Inc................E....... 937 987-2491
New Vienna (G-14999)

Springfield Country Club Co................E....... 937 399-4215
Springfield (G-17118)

Steubenville Country Club Inc.............D....... 740 264-0521
Steubenville (G-17172)

Sycamore Creek Country Club.........C....... 937 748-0791
Springboro (G-16985)

Sylvania Country Club........................D....... 419 392-0530
Sylvania (G-17455)

Terrace Park Country Club Inc...........D....... 513 965-4061
Milford (G-14436)

Tippecanoe Country Club Inc.............E....... 330 758-7518
Canfield (G-2161)

Toledo Club..D....... 419 243-2200
Toledo (G-18081)

Troy Country Club Inc.........................E....... 937 335-5691
Troy (G-18234)

Turtle Golf Management Ltd................E....... 614 882-5920
Westerville (G-19303)

Union Country Club.............................E....... 330 343-5544
Dover (G-10105)

Walden Company Ltd..........................C....... 330 562-7145
Aurora (G-849)

Wedgewood Golf & Country Club........C....... 614 793-9600
Powell (G-16213)

Western Hills Country Club.................D....... 513 922-0011
Cincinnati (G-4789)

Westwood Country Club Company......D....... 440 331-3016
Rocky River (G-16448)

Wetherngton Golf Cntry CLB Inc.........D....... 513 755-2582
West Chester (G-19036)

Weymouth Valley Inc...........................E....... 440 498-8888
Solon (G-16915)

Wooster Country Club Inc....................E....... 330 263-1890
Wooster (G-19785)

York Temple Country Club Inc.............E....... 614 885-5459
Columbus (G-8925)

Youngstown Country Club...................D....... 330 759-1040
Youngstown (G-20261)

Zanesville Country Club......................E....... 740 452-2726
Zanesville (G-20382)

COURIER OR MESSENGER SVCS

Dash Logistics Inc..............................E....... 937 382-9110
Wilmington (G-19621)

Logistics Inc.......................................E....... 419 478-1514
Toledo (G-17856)

Rush Package Delivery Inc..................D....... 937 297-6182
Dayton (G-9743)

Six Sigma Logistics Inc.......................E....... 440 666-6026
Vermilion (G-18559)

Trumbull Special Courier Inc...............E....... 330 841-0074
Warren (G-18761)

COURIER SVCS, AIR: Letter Delivery, Private

Abx Air Inc..B....... 937 382-5591
Wilmington (G-19600)

Abx Air Inc..A....... 937 366-2282
Wilmington (G-19601)

Federal Express Corporation...............E....... 800 463-3339
Lima (G-12640)

Federal Express Corporation...............D....... 800 463-3339
Vandalia (G-18522)

Fedex Ground Package Sys Inc...........E....... 800 463-3339
Richfield (G-16356)

United Parcel Service Inc....................D....... 614 385-9100
Columbus (G-8805)

COURIER SVCS, AIR: Package Delivery, Private

Federal Express Corporation...............E....... 800 463-3339
Mansfield (G-13174)

Federal Express Corporation...............B....... 614 492-6106
Columbus (G-7568)

Federal Express Corporation...............C....... 800 463-3339
Northwood (G-15393)

Federal Express Corporation...............C....... 800 463-3339
Columbus (G-7569)

Federal Express Corporation...............C....... 800 463-3339
Columbus (G-7570)

Federal Express Corporation...............E....... 800 463-3339
Canton (G-2311)

Fedex Ground Package Sys Inc...........E....... 800 463-3339
Chillicothe (G-2778)

COURIER SVCS, AIR: Parcel Delivery, Private

Federal Express Corporation...............D....... 937 898-3474
Vandalia (G-18523)

COURIER SVCS: Air

Air Transport Svcs Group Inc..............D....... 937 382-5591
Wilmington (G-19603)

Ames Material Services Inc.................A....... 937 382-5591
Wilmington (G-19606)

Dhl Express (usa) Inc.........................E....... 614 865-8325
Westerville (G-19157)

Dhl Express (usa) Inc.........................E....... 800 225-5345
Lockbourne (G-12813)

Federal Express Corporation...............D....... 800 463-3339
Miamisburg (G-14170)

Fedex Corporation..............................E....... 440 234-0315
Cleveland (G-5524)

Fedex Corporation..............................E....... 614 801-0953
Grove City (G-11431)

Fedex Smartpost Inc...........................D....... 800 463-3339
Grove City (G-11433)

Garda CL Technical Svcs Inc..............E....... 937 294-4099
Moraine (G-14660)

Lgstx Services Inc..............................E....... 866 931-2337
Wilmington (G-19627)

Prime Time Enterprises Inc.................E....... 440 891-8855
Cleveland (G-6236)

United Parcel Service Inc OH..............D....... 419 222-7399
Lima (G-12772)

United Parcel Service Inc OH..............C....... 330 339-6281
New Philadelphia (G-14987)

United Parcel Service Inc OH..............D....... 419 782-3552
Defiance (G-9945)

United States Cargo & Courier.............E....... 216 325-0483
Cleveland (G-6579)

COURIER SVCS: Ground

City Dash LLC....................................C....... 513 562-2000
Cincinnati (G-3298)

Federal Express Corporation...............D....... 800 463-3339
Miamisburg (G-14170)

Federal Express Corporation...............D....... 937 898-3474
Vandalia (G-18523)

Fedex Freight Corporation...................E....... 800 521-3505
Lima (G-12641)

Fedex Ground Package Sys Inc...........B....... 800 463-3339
Toledo (G-17731)

Firelands Security Services.................E....... 419 627-0562
Sandusky (G-16606)

Keller Logistics Group Inc...................B....... 419 784-4805
Defiance (G-9922)

Prime Time Enterprises Inc.................E....... 440 891-8855
Cleveland (G-6236)

Priority Dispatch Inc...........................E....... 216 332-9852
Solon (G-16885)

Robert M Neff Inc...............................D....... 614 444-1562
Columbus (G-8543)

SMS Transport LLC............................E....... 937 813-8897
Dayton (G-9772)

United Parcel Service Inc OH..............B....... 740 363-0636
Delaware (G-10013)

United States Cargo & Courier.............E....... 216 325-0483
Cleveland (G-6579)

COURIER SVCS: Package By Vehicle

Barberton Laundry & Cleaning.............D....... 330 825-6911
Barberton (G-947)

City Taxicab & Transfer Co..................E....... 440 992-2156
Ashtabula (G-727)

Clockwork Logistics Inc.......................E....... 216 587-5371
Garfield Heights (G-11228)

Elite Expediting Corp..........................D....... 614 279-1181
Worthington (G-19806)

Fed Ex Rob Carpenter.........................E....... 419 260-1889
Maumee (G-13790)

Federal Express Corporation...............B....... 614 492-6106
Columbus (G-7568)

Fedex Ground Package Sys Inc...........E....... 330 244-1534
Canton (G-2312)

Fedex Ground Package Sys Inc...........C....... 800 463-3339
Richfield (G-16357)

Palmer Express Incorporated..............E....... 440 942-3333
Willoughby (G-19560)

Stat Express Delivery LLC...................E....... 614 880-7828
Worthington (G-19853)

United Parcel Service Inc....................D....... 937 859-2314
West Carrollton (G-18857)

United Parcel Service Inc....................E....... 800 742-5877
Chillicothe (G-2833)

United Parcel Service Inc....................E....... 614 431-0600
Columbus (G-8806)

United Parcel Service Inc....................E....... 440 846-6000
Strongsville (G-17355)

United Parcel Service Inc OH..............C....... 419 747-3080
Mansfield (G-13259)

United Parcel Service Inc OH..............C....... 740 373-0772
Marietta (G-13393)

United Parcel Service Inc OH..............A....... 419 891-6776
Maumee (G-13865)

United Parcel Service Inc OH..............C....... 614 841-7159
Columbus (G-8807)

United Parcel Service Inc OH..............C....... 800 742-5877
Zanesville (G-20370)

United Parcel Service Inc OH..............D....... 419 891-6841
Toledo (G-18119)

United Parcel Service Inc OH..............D....... 419 782-3552
Defiance (G-9945)

United Parcel Service Inc OH..............C....... 937 382-0658
Wilmington (G-19652)

United Parcel Service Inc OH..............E....... 800 742-5877
Youngstown (G-20232)

COURIER SVCS: Parcel By Vehicle

Centaur Mail Inc.................................E....... 419 887-5857
Maumee (G-13769)

United Parcel Service Inc....................B....... 440 826-2591
Cleveland (G-6576)

United Parcel Service Inc OH..............C....... 513 852-6135
Cincinnati (G-4683)

United Parcel Service Inc OH..............C....... 800 742-5877
Cleveland (G-6577)

United Parcel Service Inc OH..............D....... 419 222-7399
Lima (G-12772)

United Parcel Service Inc OH..............C....... 440 826-3320
Wooster (G-19775)

United Parcel Service Inc OH..............C....... 419 424-9494
Findlay (G-10972)

United Parcel Service Inc OH..............C....... 330 545-0177
Girard (G-11302)

United Parcel Service Inc OH..............D....... 440 275-3301
Austinburg (G-854)

United Parcel Service Inc OH..............C....... 330 339-6281
New Philadelphia (G-14987)

United Parcel Service Inc OH..............C....... 740 598-4293
Brilliant (G-1824)

United Parcel Service Inc OH..............E....... 740 592-4570
Athens (G-809)

United Parcel Service Inc OH..............E....... 740 968-3508
Saint Clairsville (G-16508)

United Parcel Service Inc OH..............C....... 330 478-1007
Canton (G-2520)

United Parcel Service Inc OH..............C....... 419 586-8556
Celina (G-2613)

United Parcel Service Inc OH..............C....... 513 241-5289
Cincinnati (G-4684)

United Parcel Service Inc OH..............C....... 614 383-4580
Marion (G-13472)

United Parcel Service Inc OH..............C....... 513 782-4000
Cincinnati (G-4685)

United Parcel Service Inc OH..............D....... 513 241-5316
Cincinnati (G-4686)

United Parcel Service Inc OH..............C....... 419 872-0211
Perrysburg (G-15928)

United Parcel Service Inc OH..............C....... 614 272-8500
Obetz (G-15531)

United Parcel Service Inc OH..............D....... 513 863-1681
Hamilton (G-11651)

United Parcel Service Inc OH..............C....... 937 773-4762
Piqua (G-16032)

COURT REPORTING SVCS

Ace-Merit LLC....................................E....... 513 241-3200
Cincinnati (G-2904)

Mehler and Hagestrom Inc..................E....... 216 621-4984
Cleveland (G-5948)

National Service Information................E....... 740 387-6806
Marion (G-13448)

COURTS

County of Hamilton.............................C....... 513 552-1200
Cincinnati (G-3370)

County of Logan.................................E....... 937 599-7252
Bellefontaine (G-1349)

County of Summit...............................C....... 330 643-2943
Akron (G-163)

Supreme Court United States ....E 419 213-5800
  Toledo *(G-18057)*
Supreme Court United States ....E 513 564-7575
  Cincinnati *(G-4558)*
Supreme Court United States ....E 216 357-7300
  Cleveland *(G-6487)*

COURTS OF LAW: County Government

Butler County of Ohio ....E 513 887-3090
  Hamilton *(G-11570)*

COURTS OF LAW: Federal

6th Circuit Court ....E 614 719-3100
  Dayton *(G-9196)*

COURTS OF LAW: Local

Butler County of Ohio ....D 513 887-3282
  Hamilton *(G-11561)*

COURTS OF LAW: State

Supreme Court of Ohio ....E 937 898-3996
  Vandalia *(G-18543)*

COVERS: Automobile Seat

Crown Dielectric Inds Inc ....C 614 224-5161
  Columbus *(G-7397)*

CRANE & AERIAL LIFT SVCS

American Crane Inc ....E 614 496-2268
  Reynoldsburg *(G-16281)*
Bay Mechanical & Elec Corp ....D 440 282-6816
  Lorain *(G-12885)*
Crane 1 Services Inc ....E 937 704-9900
  Miamisburg *(G-14157)*
Division 7 Inc ....E 740 965-1970
  Galena *(G-11157)*
In Terminal Services Corp ....E 216 518-8407
  Maple Heights *(G-13288)*
Pollock Research & Design Inc ....E 330 332-3300
  Salem *(G-16554)*

CRANES & MONORAIL SYSTEMS

Emh Inc ....E 330 220-8600
  Valley City *(G-18462)*

CRANES: Indl Plant

Hiab USA Inc ....D 419 482-6000
  Perrysburg *(G-15874)*

CRANES: Indl Truck

Venturo Manufacturing Inc ....E 513 772-8448
  Cincinnati *(G-4754)*

CRANES: Overhead

ACC Automation Co Inc ....E 330 928-3821
  Akron *(G-15)*

CRANKSHAFTS & CAMSHAFTS: Machining

Atlas Industries Inc ....B 419 637-2117
  Tiffin *(G-17509)*
Napoleon Machine LLC ....E 419 591-7010
  Napoleon *(G-14813)*

CREATIVE SVCS: Advertisers, Exc Writers

Digital Color Intl LLC ....E 330 762-6959
  Akron *(G-187)*

CREDIT & OTHER FINANCIAL RESPONSIBILITY INSURANCE

Progressive Corporation ....B 440 461-5000
  Cleveland *(G-6247)*

CREDIT AGENCIES: Federal & Federally Sponsored

Columbus Metro Federal Cr Un ....E 614 239-0210
  Columbus *(G-7297)*
Columbus Metro Federal Cr Un ....E 614 239-0210
  Columbus *(G-7298)*
Federal Home Ln Bnk Cincinnati ....A 513 852-7500
  Cincinnati *(G-3536)*

CREDIT AGENCIES: Federal Home Loan Mortgage Corporation

Hanna Holdings Inc ....E 440 971-5600
  North Royalton *(G-15358)*

CREDIT AGENCIES: National Consumer Cooperative Bank

National Cooperative Bank NA ....D 937 393-4246
  Hillsboro *(G-11853)*

CREDIT BUREAUS

Cbc Companies Inc ....E 614 222-4343
  Columbus *(G-7141)*
Credit Infonet Inc ....E 866 218-1003
  Dayton *(G-9339)*
Kreller Bus Info Group Inc ....E 513 723-8900
  Cincinnati *(G-3891)*
Open Online LLC ....E 614 481-6999
  Columbus *(G-8376)*
Pasco Inc ....B 330 650-0613
  Hudson *(G-12001)*

CREDIT CARD PROCESSING SVCS

Relentless Recovery Inc ....D 216 621-8333
  Cleveland *(G-6300)*
Sears Roebuck and Co ....C 440 845-0120
  Cleveland *(G-6385)*

CREDIT CARD SVCS

Alliance Data Systems Corp ....B 614 729-5000
  Westerville *(G-19219)*
Alliance Data Systems Corp ....C 614 729-5800
  Reynoldsburg *(G-16280)*
Banc Certified Merch Svcs LLC ....E 614 850-2740
  Hilliard *(G-11744)*
Best Payment Solutions Inc ....E 630 321-0117
  Symmes Twp *(G-17465)*
Citicorp Credit Services Inc ....B 212 559-1000
  Columbus *(G-7204)*
Dfs Corporate Services LLC ....B 614 777-7020
  Hilliard *(G-11760)*
Heartland Payment Systems LLC ....D 513 518-6125
  Loveland *(G-12998)*
Jpmorgan Chase Bank Nat Assn ....E 614 436-3055
  Columbus *(G-6818)*
Macys Cr & Customer Svcs Inc ....E 513 881-9950
  West Chester *(G-18967)*
Macys Cr & Customer Svcs Inc ....A 513 398-5221
  Mason *(G-13613)*
Npc Group Inc ....E 312 627-6000
  Symmes Twp *(G-17466)*
Solupay Consulting Inc ....D 216 535-9016
  Twinsburg *(G-18322)*
Worldpay Inc ....C 513 900-5250
  Symmes Twp *(G-17467)*

CREDIT INST, SHORT-TERM BUSINESS: Financing Dealers

Lakewood Acceptance Corp ....E 216 658-1234
  Cleveland *(G-5850)*

CREDIT INSTITUTIONS, SHORT-TERM BUS: Buying Install Notes

Sherman Financial Group LLC ....E 513 707-3000
  Cincinnati *(G-4470)*
Unifund Ccr LLC ....D 513 489-8877
  Blue Ash *(G-1671)*
Unifund Corporation ....E 513 489-8877
  Blue Ash *(G-1672)*

CREDIT INSTITUTIONS, SHORT-TERM BUS: Wrkg Capital Finance

Business Backer LLC ....E 513 792-6866
  Cincinnati *(G-3095)*
Preferred Capital Lending Inc ....E 216 472-1391
  Cleveland *(G-6230)*

CREDIT INSTITUTIONS: Personal

Caliber Home Loans Inc ....E 937 435-5363
  Dayton *(G-9272)*
Citizens Capital Markets Inc ....E 216 589-0900
  Cleveland *(G-5184)*

Education Loan Servicing Corp ....D 216 706-8130
  Cleveland *(G-5467)*
Farm Credit Mid-America ....E 740 441-9312
  Albany *(G-510)*
General Revenue Corporation ....B 513 469-1472
  Mason *(G-13586)*
Macys Cr & Customer Svcs Inc ....A 513 398-5221
  Mason *(G-13613)*
PNC Bank National Association ....D 440 546-6760
  Brecksville *(G-1797)*
Security Nat Auto Accptnce LLC ....C 513 459-8118
  Mason *(G-13637)*
Student Loan Strategies LLC ....E 513 645-5400
  Cincinnati *(G-4550)*
Tebo Financial Services Inc ....E 234 207-2500
  Canton *(G-2507)*

CREDIT INSTITUTIONS: Short-Term Business

Ally Financial Inc ....E 330 533-7300
  Canfield *(G-2130)*
General Electric Company ....C 440 255-0930
  Mentor *(G-14050)*
General Electric Company ....E 937 534-2000
  Dayton *(G-9459)*
General Electric Company ....A 937 534-6920
  Dayton *(G-9458)*
Morgan Stanley ....E 330 670-4600
  Akron *(G-341)*
Scott Fetzer Financial Group ....E 440 892-3000
  Cleveland *(G-6380)*

CREDIT UNIONS: Federally Chartered

Advantage Credit Union Inc ....E 419 529-5603
  Ontario *(G-15543)*
American Chem Soc Fderal Cr Un ....A 614 447-3675
  Columbus *(G-6914)*
Aur Group Financial Credit Un ....E 513 737-0508
  Hamilton *(G-11558)*
Aurgroup Financial Credit Un ....D 513 942-4422
  Fairfield *(G-10697)*
B F G Federal Credit Union ....D 330 374-2990
  Akron *(G-84)*
Bayer Heritage Federal Cr Un ....C 740 929-2015
  Hebron *(G-11710)*
Best Reward Credit Union ....E 216 367-8000
  Cleveland *(G-5059)*
Bmi Federal Credit Union ....D 614 707-4000
  Dublin *(G-10147)*
Bmi Federal Credit Union ....D 614 298-8527
  Columbus *(G-7049)*
C E S Credit Union Inc ....E 740 397-1136
  Mount Vernon *(G-14751)*
Canton School Employees Fed Cr ....E 330 452-9801
  Canton *(G-2243)*
Century Federal Credit Union ....E 216 535-3600
  Cleveland *(G-5159)*
Chaco Credit Union Inc ....E 513 785-3500
  Hamilton *(G-11576)*
Cincinnati Central Cr Un Inc ....D 513 241-2050
  Cincinnati *(G-3232)*
Cinco Credit Union ....E 513 281-9988
  Cincinnati *(G-3284)*
Cinfed Federal Credit Union ....D 513 333-3800
  Cincinnati *(G-3290)*
Clyde-Findlay Area Cr Un Inc ....E 419 547-7781
  Clyde *(G-6742)*
Columbus Municipal Employees ....E 614 224-8890
  Columbus *(G-7300)*
Corporate One Federal Cr Un ....D 614 825-9314
  Columbus *(G-6810)*
Day Air Credit Union Inc ....E 937 643-2160
  Dayton *(G-9348)*
Day-Met Credit Union Inc ....E 937 236-2562
  Moraine *(G-14640)*
Desco Federal Credit Union ....D 740 354-7791
  Portsmouth *(G-16135)*
Dover Phila Federal Credit Un ....E 330 364-8874
  Dover *(G-10076)*
Fairview Hlth Sys Fderal Cr Un ....A 216 476-7000
  Cleveland *(G-5507)*
Firelands Federal Credit Union ....E 419 483-4180
  Bellevue *(G-1377)*
First Day Fincl Federal Cr Un ....E 937 222-4546
  Dayton *(G-9435)*
First Miami Student Credit Un ....E 513 529-1251
  Oxford *(G-15677)*
Fremont Federal Credit Union ....C 419 334-4434
  Fremont *(G-11076)*

General Electric Credit Union ....D 513 243-4328
Cincinnati **(G-3612)**
Glass City Federal Credit Un ....E 419 887-1000
Maumee **(G-13797)**
Honda Federal Credit Union ....E 937 642-6000
Marysville **(G-13503)**
Lima Superior Federal Cr Un ....C 419 223-9746
Lima **(G-12688)**
Miami University ....E 513 529-1251
Oxford **(G-15682)**
Midwest Cmnty Federal Cr Un ....E 419 782-9856
Defiance **(G-9931)**
Ohio Catholic Federal Cr Un ....E 216 663-6800
Cleveland **(G-6118)**
Ohio Educational Credit Union ....E 216 621-6296
Seven Hills **(G-16678)**
Ohio Healthcare Federal Cr Un ....E 614 737-6034
Dublin **(G-10297)**
River Valley Credit Union Inc ....E 937 859-1970
Miamisburg **(G-14214)**
Saint Francis De Sales Church ....E 440 884-2319
Cleveland **(G-6364)**
School Employees Lorain County ....E 440 324-3400
Elyria **(G-10561)**
Sun Federal Credit Union ....E 800 786-0945
Maumee **(G-13856)**
Sun Federal Credit Union ....D 419 537-0200
Toledo **(G-18052)**
Superior Credit Union Inc ....E 419 738-4512
Wapakoneta **(G-18654)**
Telhio Credit Union Inc ....E 614 221-3233
Columbus **(G-8737)**
Telhio Credit Union Inc ....E 614 221-3233
Columbus **(G-8738)**
True Core Federal Credit Union ....E 740 345-6608
Newark **(G-15104)**
Vacationland Federal Credit Un ....E 440 967-5155
Sandusky **(G-16654)**

CREDIT UNIONS: State Chartered

Aur Group Financial Credit Un ....E 513 737-0508
Hamilton **(G-11558)**
C E S Credit Union Inc ....E 740 892-3323
Utica **(G-18454)**
Cuso Corporation ....D 513 984-2876
Cincinnati **(G-3390)**
Kemba Credit Union Inc ....D 513 762-5070
West Chester **(G-18955)**
Midusa Credit Union ....D 513 420-8640
Middletown **(G-14313)**
Midusa Credit Union ....D 513 420-8640
Middletown **(G-14351)**
Taleris Credit Union Inc ....E 216 739-2300
Independence **(G-12128)**

CREMATORIES

Cremation Service Inc ....E 216 861-2334
Cleveland **(G-5378)**

CRISIS CENTER

Community Center ....D 330 746-7721
Youngstown **(G-20000)**
Crisis Intervention & Rcvy Ctr ....D 330 455-9407
Canton **(G-2272)**
Huckleberry House ....D 614 294-5553
Columbus **(G-7777)**
Sioto Paintsville Mental Hlth ....E 740 775-1260
Chillicothe **(G-2826)**

CRISIS INTERVENTION CENTERS

Community Counseling Services ....E 419 468-8211
Bucyrus **(G-1984)**
Crisis Intvntn Ctr Stark Cnty ....D 330 452-9812
Canton **(G-2273)**
Help Hotline Crisis Center ....E 330 747-5111
Youngstown **(G-20064)**
Help Line of Dlware Mrrow Cnty ....E 740 369-3316
Delaware **(G-9984)**
Rape Information & Counseling ....E 330 782-3936
Youngstown **(G-20177)**
Scioto Pnt Vly Mental Hlth Ctr ....E 740 335-6935
Wshngtn CT Hs **(G-19883)**

CRUDE PETROLEUM & NATURAL GAS PRODUCTION

AB Resources LLC ....E 440 922-1098
Brecksville **(G-1766)**

Kenoil Inc ....E 330 262-1144
Wooster **(G-19738)**

CRUDE PETROLEUM & NATURAL GAS PRODUCTION

City of Lancaster ....E 740 687-6670
Lancaster **(G-12380)**
M3 Midstream LLC ....D 740 945-1170
Scio **(G-16663)**

CRUDE PETROLEUM PRODUCTION

Alliance Petroleum Corporation ....D 330 493-0440
Canton **(G-2180)**
Belden & Blake Corporation ....E 330 602-5551
Dover **(G-10066)**
Chevron Ae Resources LLC ....E 330 654-4343
Deerfield **(G-9902)**
Columbia Energy Group ....A 614 460-4683
Columbus **(G-7247)**
Gulfport Energy Corporation ....E 740 251-0407
Saint Clairsville **(G-16487)**
Koch Knight LLC ....D 330 488-1651
East Canton **(G-10387)**
Xto Energy Inc ....D 740 671-9901
Bellaire **(G-1337)**

CRYSTAL GOODS, WHOLESALE

Gia USA Inc ....E 216 831-8678
Cleveland **(G-5606)**

CUPS: Paper, Made From Purchased Materials

Ricking Paper and Specialty Co ....E 513 825-3551
Cincinnati **(G-4372)**

CURTAIN & DRAPERY FIXTURES: Poles, Rods & Rollers

Lumenomics Inc ....E 614 798-3500
Lewis Center **(G-12550)**

CURTAIN WALLS: Building, Steel

Scs Construction Services Inc ....E 513 929-0260
Cincinnati **(G-4441)**

CURTAINS: Window, From Purchased Materials

Style-Line Incorporated ....E 614 291-0600
Columbus **(G-8707)**

CUSTODIAL SVCS: School, Contract Basis

Logan-Hocking School District ....E 740 385-7844
Logan **(G-12848)**
Toledo Public Schools ....D 419 243-6422
Toledo **(G-18095)**

CUSTOMIZING SVCS

1157 Design Concepts LLC ....E 937 497-1157
Sidney **(G-16755)**

CUSTOMS CLEARANCE OF FREIGHT

Comprehensive Logistics Co Inc ....E 800 734-0372
Youngstown **(G-20008)**

CUT STONE & STONE PRODUCTS

Brower Products Inc ....D 937 563-1111
Cincinnati **(G-3082)**
Lang Stone Company Inc ....D 614 235-4099
Columbus **(G-7951)**
National Lime and Stone Co ....D 419 562-0771
Bucyrus **(G-1997)**
National Lime and Stone Co ....C 419 396-7671
Carey **(G-2545)**

CUTLERY

Npk Construction Equipment Inc ....D 440 232-7900
Bedford **(G-1295)**

CYLINDER & ACTUATORS: Fluid Power

Eaton-Aeroquip Llc ....D 419 891-7775
Maumee **(G-13782)**

Hydraulic Parts Store Inc ....E 330 364-6667
New Philadelphia **(G-14966)**
Hydraulic Specialists Inc ....E 740 922-3343
Midvale **(G-14358)**
Robeck Fluid Power Co ....D 330 562-1140
Aurora **(G-840)**
Steel Eqp Specialists Inc ....D 330 823-8260
Alliance **(G-555)**
Swagelok Company ....C 440 349-5934
Solon **(G-16905)**

CYLINDERS: Pressure

Gayston Corporation ....C 937 743-6050
Miamisburg **(G-14173)**

Convents

Ursuline Convent Sacred Heart ....E 419 531-8990
Toledo **(G-18131)**

DAIRY PRDTS STORE: Ice Cream, Packaged

Austintown Dairy Inc ....E 330 629-6170
Youngstown **(G-19959)**

DAIRY PRDTS STORES

Discount Drug Mart Inc ....C 330 725-2340
Medina **(G-13931)**
Hans Rothenbuhler & Son Inc ....E 440 632-6000
Middlefield **(G-14270)**
J V Hansel Inc ....E 330 716-0806
Warren **(G-18716)**
S and S Gilardi Inc ....D 740 397-2751
Mount Vernon **(G-14788)**
United Dairy Farmers Inc ....C 513 396-8700
Cincinnati **(G-4678)**
Youngs Jersey Dairy Inc ....B 937 325-0629
Yellow Springs **(G-19941)**

DAIRY PRDTS WHOLESALERS: Fresh

Auburn Dairy Products Inc ....E 614 488-2536
Columbus **(G-7001)**
Barkett Fruit Co Inc ....E 330 364-6645
Dover **(G-10065)**
Borden Dairy Co Cincinnati LLC ....C 513 948-8811
Cincinnati **(G-3068)**
Euclid Fish Company ....D 440 951-6448
Mentor **(G-14044)**
Hans Rothenbuhler & Son Inc ....E 440 632-6000
Middlefield **(G-14270)**
Hillcrest Egg & Cheese Co ....D 216 361-4625
Cleveland **(G-5691)**
Instantwhip Foods Inc ....E 330 688-8825
Stow **(G-17213)**
Instantwhip-Columbus Inc ....E 614 871-9447
Grove City **(G-11443)**
Prairie Farms Dairy Inc ....D 937 235-5930
Huber Heights **(G-11958)**
S and S Gilardi Inc ....D 740 397-2751
Mount Vernon **(G-14788)**
Smithfoods Orrville Inc ....D 330 683-8710
Orrville **(G-15648)**
Sysco Cincinnati LLC ....B 513 563-6300
Cincinnati **(G-4562)**
US Foods Inc ....A 614 539-7993
West Chester **(G-19096)**
Weaver Bros Inc ....D 937 526-3907
Versailles **(G-18573)**

DAIRY PRDTS: Butter

Dairy Farmers America Inc ....E 330 670-7800
Medina **(G-13929)**

DAIRY PRDTS: Cheese

Dairy Farmers America Inc ....E 330 670-7800
Medina **(G-13929)**

DAIRY PRDTS: Dietary Supplements, Dairy & Non-Dairy Based

Instantwhip-Columbus Inc ....E 614 871-9447
Grove City **(G-11443)**

DAIRY PRDTS: Frozen Desserts & Novelties

Louis Trauth Dairy LLC ....B 859 431-7553
West Chester **(G-19064)**
Robert E McGrath Inc ....E 440 572-7747
Strongsville **(G-17341)**

Springdale Ice Cream Beverage...........E...... 513 699-4984
  Cincinnati *(G-4522)*
Youngs Jersey Dairy Inc....................B...... 937 325-0629
  Yellow Springs *(G-19941)*

DAIRY PRDTS: Ice Cream & Ice Milk

United Dairy Farmers Inc ....C...... 513 396-8700
  Cincinnati *(G-4678)*

DAIRY PRDTS: Milk, Condensed & Evaporated

Hans Rothenbuhler & Son Inc ....E...... 440 632-6000
  Middlefield *(G-14270)*

DAIRY PRDTS: Milk, Fluid

Dairy Farmers America Inc ....E...... 330 670-7800
  Medina *(G-13929)*
Louis Trauth Dairy LLC ....B...... 859 431-7553
  West Chester *(G-19064)*

DAIRY PRDTS: Milk, Processed, Pasteurized, Homogenized/Btld

Borden Dairy Co Cincinnati LLC ....C...... 513 948-8811
  Cincinnati *(G-3068)*
United Dairy Farmers Inc ....C...... 513 396-8700
  Cincinnati *(G-4678)*

DAIRY PRDTS: Natural Cheese

Great Lakes Cheese Co Inc..................B...... 440 834-2500
  Hiram *(G-11865)*
Hans Rothenbuhler & Son Inc ....E...... 440 632-6000
  Middlefield *(G-14270)*
Miceli Dairy Products Co.....................D...... 216 791-6222
  Cleveland *(G-5975)*

DAIRY PRDTS: Whipped Topping, Exc Frozen Or Dry Mix

Auburn Dairy Products Inc ....E...... 614 488-2536
  Columbus *(G-7001)*
Instantwhip-Columbus Inc ....E...... 614 871-9447
  Grove City *(G-11443)*

DANCE HALL OR BALLROOM OPERATION

Eldora Enterprises Inc.........................E...... 937 338-3815
  New Weston *(G-15007)*
Piqua Country Club Holding Co ....E...... 937 773-7744
  Piqua *(G-16017)*

DANCE HALL SVCS

Applause Talent Presentation................E...... 513 844-6788
  Hamilton *(G-11557)*

DANCE INSTRUCTOR & SCHOOL

Truenorth Cultural Arts ....E...... 440 949-5200
  Avon Lake *(G-928)*

DATA ENTRY SVCS

Cache Next Generation LLC ....D...... 614 850-9444
  Hilliard *(G-11752)*
Coleman Professional Svcs Inc.............C...... 330 628-2275
  Akron *(G-147)*
Coleman Professional Svcs Inc.............C...... 330 673-1347
  Kent *(G-12223)*
Lake Data Center Inc ....D...... 440 944-2020
  Wickliffe *(G-19467)*

DATA PROCESSING & PREPARATION SVCS

Btas Inc ....C...... 937 431-9431
  Beavercreek *(G-1135)*
Cbc Companies Inc..............................D...... 614 538-6100
  Columbus *(G-7142)*
Central Command Inc ....E...... 330 723-2062
  Columbia Station *(G-6771)*
City of Cleveland ....D...... 216 664-2430
  Cleveland *(G-5194)*
Cleveland State University....................E...... 216 687-3786
  Cleveland *(G-5289)*
Datatrak International Inc ....E...... 440 443-0082
  Mayfield Heights *(G-13872)*
Definitive Solutions Co Inc ....D...... 513 719-9100
  Cincinnati *(G-3417)*

Eliassen Group LLC............................E...... 781 205-8100
  Blue Ash *(G-1550)*
Enterprise Data Management Inc ....E...... 513 791-7272
  Blue Ash *(G-1554)*
Expedata LLC.....................................E...... 937 439-6767
  Dayton *(G-9423)*
Gracie Plum Investments Inc...............E...... 740 355-9029
  Portsmouth *(G-16141)*
Illumination Works LLC.......................D...... 937 938-1321
  Beavercreek *(G-1157)*
Infovision 21 Inc.................................E...... 614 761-8844
  Dublin *(G-10256)*
Lou-Ray Associates Inc ....E...... 330 220-1999
  Brunswick *(G-1936)*
Mast Technology Services Inc..............A...... 614 415-7000
  Columbus *(G-8036)*
Medical Mutual Services LLC...............C...... 440 878-4800
  Strongsville *(G-17331)*
Midland Council Governments ....E...... 330 264-6047
  Wooster *(G-19745)*
Mri Software LLC................................C...... 800 321-8770
  Solon *(G-16874)*
Racksquared LLC................................E...... 614 737-8812
  Columbus *(G-8483)*
Rgis LLC ....D...... 248 651-2511
  Reynoldsburg *(G-16328)*
Sedlak Management Consultants ....E...... 216 206-4700
  Cleveland *(G-6391)*
Sumaria Systems Inc ....E...... 937 429-6070
  Beavercreek *(G-1188)*
Thinkware Incorporated ....E...... 513 598-3300
  Cincinnati *(G-4600)*
Vediscovery LLC.................................E...... 216 241-3443
  Cleveland *(G-6622)*

DATA PROCESSING SVCS

1st All File Recovery Usa ....E...... 800 399-7150
  Shaker Heights *(G-16701)*
Aero Fulfillment Services Corp ....D...... 800 225-7145
  Mason *(G-13536)*
Alliance Data Systems Corp ....B...... 614 729-4000
  Columbus *(G-6894)*
Automatic Data Processing Inc.............C...... 216 447-1980
  Independence *(G-12048)*
Automatic Data Processing Inc.............E...... 614 895-7700
  Westerville *(G-19226)*
Change Hlthcare Operations LLC ....E...... 330 405-0001
  Hudson *(G-11970)*
Change Hlthcare Operations LLC ....E...... 216 589-5878
  Cleveland *(G-5168)*
Checkfree Services Corporation ....A...... 614 564-3000
  Dublin *(G-10169)*
Cincinnati Bell Inc..............................E...... 513 397-9900
  Cincinnati *(G-3226)*
Concentrix Cvg Corporation.................A...... 513 723-7000
  Cincinnati *(G-3348)*
Convergys Gvrnment Sltions LLC ....D...... 513 723-7006
  Cincinnati *(G-3359)*
County of Cuyahoga............................C...... 216 443-8011
  Cleveland *(G-5364)*
Csi Complete Inc.................................E...... 800 343-0641
  Plain City *(G-16048)*
Ctrac Inc..E...... 440 572-1000
  Cleveland *(G-5388)*
Decisionone Corporation ....E...... 614 883-0228
  Urbancrest *(G-18448)*
Early Express Services Inc ....E...... 937 223-5801
  Dayton *(G-9400)*
Enterprise Services LLC.......................D...... 740 423-9501
  Belpre *(G-1402)*
Fiserv Inc...E...... 412 577-3326
  Dublin *(G-10227)*
Integrated Data Services Inc................E...... 937 656-5496
  Dayton *(G-9515)*
Integrated Marketing Tech Inc ....D...... 330 225-3550
  Brunswick *(G-1933)*
Midwest Tape LLC..............................B...... 419 868-9370
  Holland *(G-11898)*
Northwest Ohio Computer Assn ....D...... 419 267-5565
  Archbold *(G-634)*
Office World Inc ....E...... 419 991-4694
  Lima *(G-12791)*
Quadax Inc...E...... 614 882-1200
  Westerville *(G-19296)*
Rurbanc Data Services Inc...................D...... 419 782-2530
  Defiance *(G-9938)*
Sourcelink Ohio LLC ....C...... 937 885-8000
  Miamisburg *(G-14224)*
Speedeon Data LLC ....E...... 440 264-2100
  Cleveland *(G-6446)*

Worldpay LLC.....................................B...... 877 713-5964
  Symmes Twp *(G-17468)*

DATABASE INFORMATION RETRIEVAL SVCS

Ecommerce LLC..................................D...... 800 861-9394
  Columbus *(G-7499)*
Lexisnexis Group ....C...... 937 865-6800
  Miamisburg *(G-14185)*
One Source Technology LLC ....E...... 216 420-1700
  Cleveland *(G-6134)*
Title First Agency Inc ....E...... 614 224-9207
  Columbus *(G-8759)*

DATING SVCS

Great Southern Video Inc ....E...... 216 642-8855
  Cleveland *(G-5632)*

DEBT COUNSELING OR ADJUSTMENT SVCS: Individuals

Consumer Credit Coun........................E...... 614 552-2222
  Gahanna *(G-11115)*

DECORATIVE WOOD & WOODWORK

77 Coach Supply Ltd ....E...... 330 674-1454
  Millersburg *(G-14452)*

DEGREASING MACHINES

Crowne Group LLC..............................D...... 216 589-0198
  Cleveland *(G-5383)*

DELIVERY SVCS, BY VEHICLE

Blood Courier Inc................................E...... 216 251-3050
  Cleveland *(G-5063)*
Capitol Express Entps Inc....................D...... 614 279-2819
  Columbus *(G-7116)*
Direct Express Delivery Svc ....E...... 513 541-0600
  Cincinnati *(G-3431)*
Dyno Nobel Transportation ....E...... 740 439-5050
  Cambridge *(G-2065)*
Early Express Services Inc ....E...... 937 223-5801
  Dayton *(G-9400)*
Fedex Ground Package Sys Inc ....C...... 412 859-2653
  Steubenville *(G-17154)*
Fedex Ground Package Sys Inc ....B...... 800 463-3339
  Toledo *(G-17731)*
Fedex Ground Package Sys Inc ....D...... 513 942-4330
  West Chester *(G-19052)*
Hc Transport Inc.................................E...... 513 574-1800
  Cincinnati *(G-3687)*
James Air Cargo Inc ....E...... 440 243-9095
  Cleveland *(G-5779)*
Masur Trucking Inc ....E...... 513 860-9600
  Cincinnati *(G-3978)*
Midway Delivery Service ....E...... 216 391-0700
  Cleveland *(G-5988)*
Prestige Delivery Systems LLC ....E...... 614 836-8980
  Groveport *(G-11531)*
Priority Dispatch Inc ....E...... 513 791-3900
  Blue Ash *(G-1631)*
Priority Dispatch Inc ....E...... 216 332-9852
  Solon *(G-16885)*
Quick Delivery Service Inc ....E...... 330 453-3709
  Canton *(G-2447)*
R & M Delivery ....E...... 740 574-2113
  Franklin Furnace *(G-11047)*
Rainbow Express Inc...........................D...... 614 444-5600
  Columbus *(G-8485)*
Rapid Delivery Service Co Inc ....E...... 513 733-0500
  Cincinnati *(G-4337)*
Rush Package Delivery Inc ....E...... 937 224-7874
  Dayton *(G-9742)*
Rush Package Delivery Inc ....D...... 937 297-6182
  Dayton *(G-9743)*
Rush Package Delivery Inc ....E...... 513 771-7874
  Cincinnati *(G-4413)*
Thomas Transport Delivery Inc ....E...... 330 908-3100
  Macedonia *(G-13084)*
Top Dawg Group LLC ....E...... 216 398-1066
  Brooklyn Heights *(G-1883)*
Total Package Express Inc ....E...... 513 741-5500
  Cincinnati *(G-4611)*
Veritas Enterprises Inc ....E...... 513 578-2748
  Cincinnati *(G-2874)*
Wright Brothers Aero Inc ....E...... 937 454-8475
  Dayton *(G-9887)*

DENTAL EQPT & SPLYS

Dental Ceramics Inc ....E 330 523-5240
Richfield *(G-16353)*

Dresch Tolson Dental Labs ....D 419 842-6730
Sylvania *(G-17420)*

United Dental Laboratories ....E 330 253-1810
Tallmadge *(G-17496)*

Wbc Group LLC ....D 866 528-2144
Hudson *(G-12012)*

DENTAL EQPT & SPLYS WHOLESALERS

Benco Dental Supply Co ....D 513 874-2990
Cincinnati *(G-3040)*

Benco Dental Supply Co ....D 614 761-1053
Dublin *(G-10144)*

Benco Dental Supply Co ....D 317 845-5356
West Chester *(G-19044)*

Cardinal Health 301 LLC ....A 614 757-5000
Dublin *(G-10159)*

Dentronix Inc ....E 330 916-7300
Cuyahoga Falls *(G-9086)*

Henry Schein Inc ....E 440 349-0891
Cleveland *(G-5685)*

Professional Sales Associates ....E 330 299-7343
Seville *(G-16687)*

DENTAL EQPT & SPLYS: Orthodontic Appliances

Dentronix Inc ....E 330 916-7300
Cuyahoga Falls *(G-9086)*

DENTISTS' OFFICES & CLINICS

C Ted Forsberg ....E 440 992-3145
Ashtabula *(G-723)*

Concorde Therapy Group Inc ....C 330 493-4210
Canton *(G-2264)*

Dental One Inc ....E 216 584-1000
Independence *(G-12066)*

Dental Servics of Ohio Daniel ....D 614 863-2222
Reynoldsburg *(G-16297)*

Dr Michael J Hulit ....E 330 863-7173
Malvern *(G-13122)*

Health Smile Center ....E 440 992-2700
Ashtabula *(G-739)*

Lima Dental Assoc Risolvato Lt ....E 419 228-4036
Lima *(G-12679)*

Metro Health Dental Associates ....E 216 778-4982
Cleveland *(G-5964)*

Metrohealth System ....E 216 957-1500
Cleveland *(G-5970)*

Ohio State University ....D 614 292-2751
Columbus *(G-8350)*

R P Cunningham DDS Inc ....E 614 885-2022
Worthington *(G-19841)*

DEPARTMENT STORES

Centro Properties Group LLC ....E 440 324-6610
Elyria *(G-10487)*

DEPARTMENT STORES: Non-Discount

JC Penney Corporation Inc ....B 330 633-7700
Akron *(G-288)*

DEPARTMENT STORES: Surplus & Salvage

Glen Surplus Sales Inc ....E 419 347-1212
Shelby *(G-16746)*

Goodwill Inds Centl Ohio Inc ....B 614 294-5181
Columbus *(G-7679)*

Public Safety Ohio Department ....E 937 335-6209
Troy *(G-18222)*

DEPOSIT INSURANCE

American Mutl Share Insur Corp ....E 614 764-1900
Dublin *(G-10133)*

Excess Share Insurance Corp ....E 614 764-1900
Dublin *(G-10222)*

DESALTER KITS: Sea Water

Luxfer Magtech Inc ....E 513 772-3066
Cincinnati *(G-3952)*

DESIGN SVCS, NEC

ADS Manufacturing Ohio LLC ....D 513 217-4502
Middletown *(G-14286)*

Bollin & Sons Inc ....E 419 693-6573
Toledo *(G-17618)*

Controls Inc ....E 330 239-4345
Medina *(G-13923)*

Dasher Lawless Automation LLC ....E 855 755-7275
Warren *(G-18699)*

Elevar Design Group Inc ....E 513 721-0600
Cincinnati *(G-3490)*

Emersion Design LLC ....E 513 841-9100
Cincinnati *(G-3494)*

Lindsey Cnstr & Design Inc ....E 330 785-9931
Akron *(G-316)*

Loth Inc ....E 513 554-4900
Cincinnati *(G-3944)*

Snl Designs Ltd ....E 440 247-2344
Chagrin Falls *(G-2656)*

DESIGN SVCS: Commercial & Indl

Design Central Inc ....E 614 890-0202
Columbus *(G-7438)*

Electrovations Inc ....E 330 274-3558
Aurora *(G-826)*

Hanco International ....D 330 456-9407
Canton *(G-2338)*

Ies Systems Inc ....E 330 533-6683
Canfield *(G-2143)*

Military Resources LLC ....E 330 263-1040
Wooster *(G-19746)*

Military Resources LLC ....D 330 309-9970
Wooster *(G-19747)*

New Path International LLC ....E 614 410-3974
Powell *(G-16204)*

North Bay Construction Inc ....E 440 835-1898
Westlake *(G-19380)*

Polaris Automation Inc ....D 614 431-0170
Lewis Center *(G-12560)*

Priority Designs Inc ....D 614 337-9979
Columbus *(G-8463)*

R and J Corporation ....E 440 871-6009
Westlake *(G-19394)*

Ultra Tech Machinery Inc ....E 330 929-5544
Cuyahoga Falls *(G-9134)*

DESIGN SVCS: Computer Integrated Systems

Aclara Technologies LLC ....C 440 528-7200
Solon *(G-16814)*

Advanced Service Tech LLC ....E 937 435-4376
Miamisburg *(G-14137)*

Afidence Inc ....E 513 234-5822
Mason *(G-13537)*

Assured Information SEC Inc ....D 937 427-9720
Beavercreek *(G-1127)*

Attevo Inc ....D 216 928-2800
Beachwood *(G-1032)*

Baxter Hodell Donnelly Preston ....C 513 271-1634
Cincinnati *(G-3025)*

Bpi Infrmtion Systems Ohio Inc ....E 440 717-4112
Brecksville *(G-1771)*

Cdo Technologies Inc ....D 937 258-0022
Dayton *(G-9164)*

Cincinnati Training Trml Svcs ....D 513 563-4474
Cincinnati *(G-3273)*

Cincom Intrnational Operations ....B 513 612-2300
Cincinnati *(G-3285)*

Concentrix Cvg Corporation ....A 513 723-7000
Cincinnati *(G-3348)*

Cott Systems Inc ....D 614 847-4405
Columbus *(G-7379)*

Definitive Solutions Co Inc ....D 513 719-9100
Cincinnati *(G-3417)*

Document Tech Systems Ltd ....E 330 928-5311
Cuyahoga Falls *(G-9088)*

E&I Solutions LLC ....E 937 912-0288
Beavercreek *(G-1150)*

Matrix Management Solutions ....E 330 470-3700
Canton *(G-2392)*

Microman Inc ....E 614 923-8000
Dublin *(G-10280)*

Natural Resources Ohio Dept ....E 614 265-6852
Columbus *(G-8163)*

Northrop Grumman Technical ....C 937 320-3100
Beavercreek Township *(G-1255)*

Ohio State University ....E 614 728-8100
Columbus *(G-8338)*

Pcms Datafit Inc ....D 513 587-3100
Blue Ash *(G-1629)*

Pomeroy It Solutions Sls Inc ....E 937 439-9682
Dayton *(G-9698)*

Pomeroy It Solutions Sls Inc ....E 440 717-1364
Brecksville *(G-1798)*

Presidio Infrastructure ....E 614 381-1400
Dublin *(G-10310)*

Rainbow Data Systems Inc ....E 937 431-8000
Beavercreek *(G-1180)*

Reynolds and Reynolds Company ....A 937 485-2000
Kettering *(G-12299)*

Rovisys Building Tech LLC ....E 330 954-7600
Aurora *(G-841)*

Sgi Matrix LLC ....D 937 438-9033
Miamisburg *(G-14219)*

Software Solutions Inc ....E 513 932-6667
Lebanon *(G-12504)*

Sogeti USA LLC ....E 614 847-4477
Westerville *(G-19210)*

Suite 224 Internet ....E 440 593-7113
Conneaut *(G-8959)*

Sumaria Systems Inc ....D 937 429-6070
Beavercreek *(G-1188)*

Tata America Intl Corp ....B 513 677-6500
Milford *(G-14435)*

Tsi Inc ....E 419 468-1855
Galion *(G-11184)*

Wescom Solutions Inc ....E 513 831-1207
Milford *(G-14443)*

DETECTIVE & ARMORED CAR SERVICES

Aset Corporation ....E 937 890-8881
Vandalia *(G-18504)*

Home State Protective Svcs LLC ....E 513 253-3095
Cincinnati *(G-3722)*

Infinite SEC Solutions LLC ....E 419 720-5678
Toledo *(G-17820)*

Safeguard Properties LLC ....A 216 739-2900
Cleveland *(G-6361)*

Seven Secured Inc ....E 281 362-2887
Strongsville *(G-17342)*

Veteran Security Patrol Co ....E 937 222-7333
Dayton *(G-9855)*

DETECTIVE AGENCY

Acrux Investigation Agency ....B 937 842-5780
Lakeview *(G-12332)*

Cefaratti Investigation & Prcs ....E 216 696-1161
Cleveland *(G-5145)*

Key II Security Inc ....E 937 339-8530
Troy *(G-18209)*

Marshall & Associates Inc ....E 513 683-6396
Loveland *(G-13011)*

DETECTIVE SVCS

Atlantis Co Inc ....D 888 807-3272
Cleveland *(G-5020)*

Securitas SEC Svcs USA Inc ....D 513 639-7615
Cincinnati *(G-4443)*

DETOXIFICATION CENTERS, OUTPATIENT

Ryan Sheridan ....E 330 270-2380
Youngstown *(G-20201)*

DIAGNOSTIC SUBSTANCES

Perkinelmer Hlth Sciences Inc ....E 330 825-4525
Akron *(G-378)*

Thermo Fisher Scientific Inc ....C 800 871-8909
Oakwood Village *(G-15495)*

DICE & DICE CUPS

Container Graphics Corp ....D 419 531-5133
Toledo *(G-17678)*

DIES & TOOLS: Special

Acro Tool & Die Company ....D 330 773-5173
Akron *(G-17)*

Athens Mold and Machine Inc ....D 740 593-6613
Athens *(G-768)*

Custom Machine Inc ....E 419 986-5122
Tiffin *(G-17515)*

General Tool Company ....C 513 733-5500
Cincinnati *(G-3616)*

Mtd Holdings Inc ....B 330 225-2600
Valley City *(G-18467)*

Seilkop Industries Inc ....E 513 761-1035
Cincinnati *(G-4448)*

DIET & WEIGHT REDUCING CENTERS

Diet Center Worldwide Inc ....E 330 665-5861
Akron **(G-186)**

Formu3 International Inc ....E 330 668-1461
Akron **(G-227)**

DIETICIANS' OFFICES

Dietary Solutions Inc ....E 614 985-6567
Lewis Center **(G-12539)**

DIODES: Light Emitting

Ceso Inc ....D 937 435-8584
Miamisburg **(G-14150)**

DIRECT SELLING ESTABLISHMENTS: Appliances, House-To-House

Central Repair Service Inc ....E 513 943-0500
Point Pleasant **(G-16078)**

DIRECT SELLING ESTABLISHMENTS: Telemarketing

Mas International Mktg LLC ....D 614 446-2003
Columbus **(G-8033)**

Universal Marketing Group LLC ....D 419 720-9696
Toledo **(G-18123)**

DISASTER SVCS

A-Team LLC ....E 216 271-7223
Cleveland **(G-4885)**

American Red Cross..........................D 513 579-3000
Cincinnati **(G-2950)**

Christian Aid Ministries.....................E 330 893-2428
Millersburg **(G-14465)**

DISC JOCKEYS

Rock House Entrmt Group Inc ....C 440 232-7625
Oakwood Village **(G-15493)**

DISCOUNT DEPARTMENT STORES

Target Stores Inc ....C 614 279-4224
Columbus **(G-8731)**

Walmart Inc................................C 937 399-0370
Springfield **(G-17133)**

Walmart Inc................................B 740 286-8203
Jackson **(G-12182)**

DISINFECTING SVCS

DCS Sanitation Management Inc...........D 513 891-4980
Cincinnati **(G-3407)**

DISKETTE DUPLICATING SVCS

Arszman & Lyons LLC ....E 513 527-4900
Blue Ash **(G-1508)**

Evanhoe & Associates Inc ....E 937 235-2995
Dayton **(G-9173)**

DISPLAY FIXTURES: Wood

Ptmj Enterprises ....C 440 543-8000
Solon **(G-16886)**

DISPLAY ITEMS: Solid Fiber, Made From Purchased Materials

Digital Color Intl LLC ....E 330 762-6959
Akron **(G-187)**

DOCK EQPT & SPLYS, INDL

Tmt Inc ....C 419 592-1041
Perrysburg **(G-15926)**

DOCUMENT DESTRUCTION SVC

Cdd LLC ....B 905 829-2794
Mason **(G-13551)**

P C Workshop Inc ....D 419 399-4805
Paulding **(G-15795)**

Recycling Services Inc ....E 419 381-7762
Maumee **(G-13842)**

Shred-It USA LLC...........................D 847 288-0377
Fairfield **(G-10781)**

Shred-It USA LLC...........................E 800 697-4733
Fairfield **(G-10782)**

TDS Document Management Ltd..........E 614 367-9633
Columbus **(G-8734)**

Weaver Industries Inc ....C 330 745-2400
Akron **(G-499)**

DOCUMENT STORAGE SVCS

Allied Infotech Corporation ....D 330 745-8529
Akron **(G-66)**

Cintas Corporation No 2.....................D 440 838-8611
Cleveland **(G-5180)**

DOLOMITE: Crushed & Broken

Covia Holdings Corporation ....D 440 214-3284
Independence **(G-12063)**

DOMESTIC HELP SVCS

Carol Scudere..............................E 614 839-4357
New Albany **(G-14848)**

Franklin Cnty Crt Common Pleas..........E 614 525-5775
Columbus **(G-7612)**

Larue Enterprises Inc ....E 937 438-5711
Beavercreek **(G-1225)**

Super Shine Inc ....E 513 423-8999
Middletown **(G-14334)**

DOMICILIARY CARE FACILITY

Brookdale Deer Park.........................D 513 745-7600
Cincinnati **(G-3077)**

Judson ....D 216 791-2004
Cleveland **(G-5808)**

DOOR & WINDOW REPAIR SVCS

Advance Door Company ....E 216 883-2424
Cleveland **(G-4903)**

Dortronic Service Inc ....E 216 739-3667
Cleveland **(G-5443)**

Marsh Building Products Inc ....E 937 222-3321
Dayton **(G-9586)**

Southern Ohio Door Contrls Inc............E 513 353-4793
Miamitown **(G-14243)**

Thomas Door Controls Inc ....E 614 263-1756
Columbus **(G-8746)**

DOORS & WINDOWS WHOLESALERS: All Materials

American Warming and Vent ....D 419 288-2703
Bradner **(G-1763)**

Gorell Enterprises Inc ....B 724 465-1800
Streetsboro **(G-17254)**

Mason Structural Steel Inc..................D 440 439-1040
Walton Hills **(G-18637)**

Modern Builders Supply Inc ....E 513 531-1000
Cincinnati **(G-4069)**

Norandex Bldg Mtls Dist Inc ....A 330 656-8924
Hudson **(G-11999)**

Southern Ohio Door Contrls Inc............E 513 353-4793
Miamitown **(G-14243)**

Traichal Construction Company............E 800 255-3667
Niles **(G-15172)**

DOORS & WINDOWS: Storm, Metal

Champion Opco LLC ....B 513 327-7338
Cincinnati **(G-3168)**

DOORS: Garage, Overhead, Metal

Clopay Corporation ....C 800 282-2260
Mason **(G-13564)**

DOORS: Garage, Overhead, Wood

Clopay Corporation ....C 800 282-2260
Mason **(G-13564)**

DOORS: Glass

Scs Construction Services Inc ....E 513 929-0260
Cincinnati **(G-4441)**

DOORS: Wooden

Khempco Bldg Sup Co Ltd Partnr..........D 740 549-0465
Delaware **(G-9993)**

S R Door Inc ....C 740 927-3558
Hebron **(G-11723)**

DRAFTING SPLYS WHOLESALERS

Key Blue Prints Inc ....D 614 228-3285
Columbus **(G-7898)**

Queen City Reprographics..................C 513 326-2300
Cincinnati **(G-4321)**

DRAFTING SVCS

Seifert Technologies Inc ....D 330 833-2700
Massillon **(G-13728)**

DRAGSTRIP OPERATION

National Hot Rod Association ....C 740 928-5706
Hebron **(G-11722)**

DRAPERIES & CURTAINS

Accent Drapery Co Inc ....E 614 488-0741
Columbus **(G-6860)**

Janson Industries ....D 330 455-7029
Canton **(G-2360)**

Vocational Services Inc ....C 216 431-8085
Cleveland **(G-6640)**

DRAPERIES & DRAPERY FABRICS, COTTON

Lumenomics Inc............................E 614 798-3500
Lewis Center **(G-12550)**

DRAPERIES: Plastic & Textile, From Purchased Materials

Standard Textile Co Inc ....B 513 761-9256
Cincinnati **(G-4533)**

DRAPERY & UPHOLSTERY STORES: Draperies

Accent Drapery Co Inc ....E 614 488-0741
Columbus **(G-6860)**

Farrow Cleaners Co ....E 216 561-2355
Cleveland **(G-5514)**

DRAPES & DRAPERY FABRICS, FROM MANMADE FIBER

Lumenomics Inc............................E 614 798-3500
Lewis Center **(G-12550)**

DRIED FRUITS WHOLESALERS

Ohio Hickory Harvest Brand Pro...........E 330 644-6266
Coventry Township **(G-9040)**

DRINKING PLACES: Alcoholic Beverages

A C Management Inc ....E 440 461-9200
Cleveland **(G-4876)**

B & I Hotel Management LLC ....C 330 995-0200
Aurora **(G-819)**

Best Western Columbus N Hotel ....E 614 888-8230
Columbus **(G-7030)**

Bird Enterprises LLC ....E 330 674-1457
Millersburg **(G-14460)**

Breezy Point Ltd Partnership................E 330 995-0600
Aurora **(G-822)**

Broad Street Hotel Assoc LP ....D 614 861-0321
Columbus **(G-7076)**

Cambridge Country Club Company ....E 740 439-2744
Byesville **(G-2023)**

Ch Relty Iv/Clmbus Partners LP............D 614 885-3334
Columbus **(G-7174)**

Claire De Leigh Corp ....E 614 459-6575
Columbus **(G-7216)**

Cleveland Airport Hospitality ....D 440 871-6000
Westlake **(G-19333)**

Clubhouse Pub N Grub ....E 440 884-2582
Cleveland **(G-5310)**

Columbus Airport Ltd Partnr ....C 614 475-7551
Columbus **(G-7253)**

Columbus Country Club.....................E 614 861-0800
Columbus **(G-7272)**

Commonwealth Hotels LLC ....C 614 790-9000
Dublin **(G-10184)**

Epiqurian Inns ....D 614 885-2600
Worthington **(G-19807)**

Fairlawn Associates Ltd ....C 330 867-5000
Fairlawn **(G-10826)**

Fairlawn Country Club Company ....D 330 836-5541
Akron **(G-208)**

Fat Jacks Pizza II Inc ....E 419 227-1813
Lima *(G-12639)*
Findlay Country Club ....E 419 422-9263
Findlay *(G-10902)*
First Hotel Associates LP ....D 614 228-3800
Columbus *(G-7586)*
Gallipolis Hospitality Inc ....E 740 446-0090
Gallipolis *(G-11195)*
Grandview Ht Ltd Partnr Ohio ....D 937 766-5519
Springfield *(G-17043)*
Granville Hospitality Llc ....D 740 587-3333
Granville *(G-11342)*
Hit Portfolio I Misc Trs LLC ....C 614 228-1234
Columbus *(G-7753)*
Hotel 50 S Front Opco L P ....D 614 885-3334
Columbus *(G-7774)*
Lodging Industry Inc ....E 440 323-7488
Sandusky *(G-16624)*
Madison Route 20 LLC ....E 440 358-7888
Painesville *(G-15723)*
Marriott Hotel Services Inc ....C 216 252-5333
Cleveland *(G-5911)*
Mayfield Sand Ridge Club ....D 216 381-0826
Cleveland *(G-5924)*
Medallion Club ....C 614 794-6999
Westerville *(G-19185)*
Natural Resources Ohio Dept ....D 419 938-5411
Perrysville *(G-15942)*
Ohio State Parks Inc ....D 513 664-3504
College Corner *(G-6768)*
Ohio State University ....B 614 292-3238
Columbus *(G-8333)*
Park Hotels & Resorts Inc ....B 216 464-5950
Cleveland *(G-6166)*
Quail Hollow Management Inc ....D 440 639-4000
Painesville *(G-15734)*
Ridgehills Hotel Ltd Partnr ....D 440 585-0600
Wickliffe *(G-19475)*
River Road Hotel Corp ....E 614 267-7461
Columbus *(G-8535)*
S P S Inc ....E 937 339-7801
Troy *(G-18228)*
Saw Mill Creek Ltd ....C 419 433-3800
Huron *(G-12030)*
Summit Associates Inc ....D 216 831-3300
Cleveland *(G-6475)*
Tartan Fields Golf Club Ltd ....D 614 792-0900
Dublin *(G-10353)*
Union Club Company ....D 216 621-4230
Cleveland *(G-6564)*
Westgate Limited Partnership ....C 419 535-7070
Toledo *(G-18155)*
Weymouth Valley Inc ....E 440 498-8888
Solon *(G-16915)*
Wyndham International Inc ....E 330 666-9300
Copley *(G-8980)*

DRINKING PLACES: Bars & Lounges

Plaz-Way Inc ....E 330 264-9025
Wooster *(G-19759)*
Rhinegeist LLC ....D 513 381-1367
Cincinnati *(G-4368)*
Valley Hospitality Inc ....E 740 374-9660
Marietta *(G-13395)*

DRINKING PLACES: Tavern

16 Bit Bar ....E 513 381-1616
Cincinnati *(G-2876)*
Island House Inc ....E 419 734-0100
Port Clinton *(G-16110)*
Mahalls 20 Lanes ....E 216 521-3280
Cleveland *(G-5895)*
Marcus Theatres Corporation ....D 614 436-9818
Columbus *(G-8018)*
Northland Lanes Inc ....E 419 224-1961
Lima *(G-12707)*
Roscoe Village Foundation ....D 740 622-2222
Coshocton *(G-9026)*
Snows Lakeside Tavern ....E 513 954-5626
Cincinnati *(G-4499)*

DRIVE-A-WAY AUTOMOBILE SVCS

Cronins Inc ....E 513 851-5900
Cincinnati *(G-3380)*

DRUG ABUSE COUNSELOR, NONTREATMENT

Hocking College Addc ....E 740 541-2221
Glouster *(G-11309)*

DRUG CLINIC, OUTPATIENT

Amethyst Inc ....D 614 242-1284
Columbus *(G-6943)*
Central Commnty Hlth Brd of Ha ....E 513 559-2981
Cincinnati *(G-3154)*
Clermont Recovery Center Inc ....E 513 735-8100
Batavia *(G-991)*
Community Action Against Addic ....E 216 881-0765
Cleveland *(G-5323)*

DRUG STORES

Ancillary Medical Investments ....E 937 456-5520
Eaton *(G-10436)*
City of Wooster ....A 330 263-8100
Wooster *(G-19705)*
Columbus Prescr Phrms Inc ....C 614 294-1600
Westerville *(G-19243)*
Discount Drug Mart Inc ....C 330 725-2340
Medina *(G-13931)*
Discount Drug Mart Inc ....E 330 343-7700
Dover *(G-10072)*
Garys Pharmacy Inc ....E 937 456-5777
Eaton *(G-10446)*
George W Arensberg Phrm Inc ....E 740 344-2195
Newark *(G-15036)*
Giant Eagle Inc ....D 330 364-5301
Dover *(G-10079)*
Guernsey Health Enterprises ....A 740 439-3561
Cambridge *(G-2072)*
Joseph A Girgis MD Inc ....E 440 930-6095
Sheffield Village *(G-16737)*
Kaiser-Wells Inc ....E 419 668-7651
Norwalk *(G-15440)*
Kroger Co ....C 937 294-7210
Dayton *(G-9551)*
Kunkel Pharmaceuticals Inc ....E 513 231-1943
Cincinnati *(G-3895)*
Medical Service Company ....D 440 232-3000
Bedford *(G-1293)*
Omnicare Phrm of Midwest LLC ....D 513 719-2600
Cincinnati *(G-4171)*
Shr Management Resources Corp ....E 937 274-1546
Dayton *(G-9764)*
St Lukes Hospital ....D 419 893-5911
Maumee *(G-13855)*
Trumbull-Mahoning Med Group ....D 330 372-8800
Cortland *(G-8995)*
Walgreen Co ....E 937 433-5314
Dayton *(G-9864)*
Walgreen Co ....E 614 236-8622
Columbus *(G-8869)*
Walgreen Co ....E 330 677-5650
Kent *(G-12267)*
Walgreen Co ....E 330 745-2674
Barberton *(G-971)*
Walgreen Co ....E 937 396-1358
Kettering *(G-12303)*
Walgreen Co ....E 937 781-9561
Dayton *(G-9865)*
Walgreen Co ....E 330 733-4237
Akron *(G-494)*
Walgreen Co ....E 937 277-6022
Dayton *(G-9866)*
Walgreen Co ....E 740 368-9380
Delaware *(G-10015)*
Walgreen Co ....E 614 336-0431
Dublin *(G-10369)*
Walgreen Co ....E 937 859-3879
Miamisburg *(G-14235)*
Walgreen Co ....E 330 928-5444
Cuyahoga Falls *(G-9139)*
Ziks Family Pharmacy 100 ....E 937 225-9350
Dayton *(G-9898)*

DRUGS & DRUG PROPRIETARIES, WHOL: Biologicals/Allied Prdts

Butler Animal Health Sup LLC ....E 614 718-2000
Columbus *(G-7100)*
Butler Animal Health Sup LLC ....C 614 761-9095
Dublin *(G-10154)*
Columbus Serum Company ....C 614 444-5211
Columbus *(G-7313)*

DRUGS & DRUG PROPRIETARIES, WHOLESALE

F Dohmen Co ....C 614 757-5000
Dublin *(G-10223)*
MSA Group Inc ....B 614 334-0400
Columbus *(G-8119)*
Omnicare Phrm of Midwest LLC ....D 513 719-2600
Cincinnati *(G-4171)*
Pharmed Corporation ....C 440 250-5400
Westlake *(G-19391)*

DRUGS & DRUG PROPRIETARIES, WHOLESALE: Antiseptics

Beiersdorf Inc ....C 513 682-7300
West Chester *(G-19042)*

DRUGS & DRUG PROPRIETARIES, WHOLESALE: Biotherapeutics

Imagepace LLC ....B 513 579-9911
Cincinnati *(G-3753)*

DRUGS & DRUG PROPRIETARIES, WHOLESALE: Blood Plasma

Biolife Plasma Services LP ....D 419 425-8680
Findlay *(G-10868)*

DRUGS & DRUG PROPRIETARIES, WHOLESALE: Druggists' Sundries

Mimrx Co Inc ....B 614 850-6672
Columbus *(G-8088)*
Riser Foods Company ....D 216 292-7000
Bedford Heights *(G-1327)*
Samuels Products Inc ....E 513 891-4456
Blue Ash *(G-1649)*

DRUGS & DRUG PROPRIETARIES, WHOLESALE: Medicinals/Botanicals

Gem Edwards Inc ....D 330 342-8300
Hudson *(G-11979)*

DRUGS & DRUG PROPRIETARIES, WHOLESALE: Patent Medicines

Institutional Care Pharmacy ....D 419 447-6216
Tiffin *(G-17520)*
Teva Womens Health Inc ....C 513 731-9900
Cincinnati *(G-4589)*

DRUGS & DRUG PROPRIETARIES, WHOLESALE: Pharmaceuticals

American Regent Inc ....D 614 436-2222
Hilliard *(G-11741)*
Amerisourcebergen Corporation ....C 610 727-7000
Columbus *(G-6942)*
Amerisourcebergen Corporation ....D 614 497-3665
Lockbourne *(G-12808)*
Amerisourcebergen Drug Corp ....D 614 409-0741
Lockbourne *(G-12809)*
Biorx LLC ....C 866 442-4679
Cincinnati *(G-3051)*
Braden Med Services Inc ....E 740 732-2356
Caldwell *(G-2036)*
Butler Animal Hlth Holdg LLC ....E 614 761-9095
Dublin *(G-10155)*
Capital Wholesale Drug Company ....D 614 297-8225
Columbus *(G-7114)*
Cardinal Health Inc ....A 614 757-5000
Dublin *(G-10156)*
Cardinal Health Inc ....D 614 497-9552
Obetz *(G-15524)*
Cardinal Health Inc ....E 614 409-6770
Groveport *(G-11499)*
Cardinal Health Inc ....D 614 757-7690
Columbus *(G-7121)*
Cardinal Health 414 LLC ....E 419 867-1077
Holland *(G-11877)*
Cardinal Health 414 LLC ....E 937 438-1888
Moraine *(G-14632)*
Discount Drug Mart Inc ....C 330 725-2340
Medina *(G-13931)*
Equitas Health Inc ....E 937 424-1440
Dayton *(G-9416)*

S
E
R
V
I
C
E
S

Evergreen Pharmaceutical LLC ....B 513 719-2600
Cincinnati (G-3519)

Evergreen Phrm Cal Inc ....B 513 719-2600
Cincinnati (G-3520)

Greenfield Hts Oper Group LLC ....E 312 877-1153
Lima (G-12648)

Heartland Healthcare Svcs LLC ....C 419 535-8435
Toledo (G-17794)

Keysource Acquisition LLC ....E 513 469-7881
Cincinnati (G-3865)

Kroger Co ....B 614 898-3200
Westerville (G-19274)

Masters Drug Company Inc ....B 800 982-7922
Lebanon (G-12484)

McKesson Corporation ....C 740 636-3500
Wshngtn CT Hs (G-19878)

Medpace Inc ....A 513 579-9911
Cincinnati (G-4000)

Mhc Medical Products LLC ....E 877 358-4342
Fairfield (G-10757)

Ncs Healthcare of Ohio LLC ....E 330 364-5011
Wadsworth (G-18609)

Ncs Healthcare of Ohio LLC ....E 614 534-0400
Columbus (G-8167)

Neighborcare Inc ....A 513 719-2600
Cincinnati (G-4103)

Omnicare Inc ....C 513 719-2600
Cincinnati (G-4168)

Omnicare Distribution Ctr LLC ....D 419 720-8200
Cincinnati (G-4169)

Orchard Phrm Svcs LLC ....C 330 491-4200
North Canton (G-15225)

Pca-Corrections LLC ....E 614 297-8244
Columbus (G-8430)

Prescription Supply Inc ....D 419 661-6600
Northwood (G-15405)

Remedi Seniorcare of Ohio LLC ....E 800 232-4239
Troy (G-18227)

River City Pharma ....E 513 870-1680
Fairfield (G-10775)

Robert J Matthews Company ....D 330 834-3000
Massillon (G-13724)

Schaaf Drugs LLC ....E 419 879-4327
Lima (G-12736)

Specialized Pharmacy Svcs LLC ....E 513 719-2600
Cincinnati (G-4511)

Superior Care Pharmacy Inc ....C 513 719-2600
Cincinnati (G-4556)

Triplefin LLC ....D 855 877-5346
Blue Ash (G-1665)

Westhaven Services Co LLC ....B 419 661-2200
Perrysburg (G-15935)

DRUGS & DRUG PROPRIETARIES, WHOLESALE: Vitamins & Minerals

Basic Drugs Inc ....E 937 898-4010
Vandalia (G-18507)

Mitsubshi Intl Fd Ingrdnts Inc ....E 614 652-1111
Dublin (G-10281)

Physicians Weight Ls Ctr Amer ....E 330 666-7952
Akron (G-382)

Raisin Rack Inc ....E 614 882-5886
Westerville (G-19298)

Suarez Corporation Industries ....D 330 494-4282
Canton (G-2502)

Wbc Group LLC ....D 866 528-2144
Hudson (G-12012)

DRYCLEANING & LAUNDRY SVCS: Commercial & Family

Buckeye Launderer and Clrs LLC ....D 419 592-2941
Sylvania (G-17413)

Dee Jay Cleaners Inc ....E 216 731-7060
Euclid (G-10630)

Economy Linen & Towel Svc Inc ....C 740 454-6888
Zanesville (G-20304)

Evergreen Cooperative Ldry Inc ....E 216 268-3548
Cleveland (G-5497)

George Gardner ....D 419 636-4277
Bryan (G-1958)

Heights Laundry & Dry Cleaning ....E 216 932-9666
Cleveland Heights (G-6718)

Midwest Laundry Inc ....D 513 563-5560
Cincinnati (G-4050)

DRYCLEANING PLANTS

Aramark Unf & Career AP LLC ....D 937 223-6667
Dayton (G-9236)

Edco Cleaners Inc ....E 330 477-3357
Canton (G-2297)

Farrow Cleaners Co ....E 216 561-2355
Cleveland (G-5514)

Fox Cleaners Inc ....D 937 276-4171
Dayton (G-9447)

George Gardner ....D 419 636-4277
Bryan (G-1958)

Heights Laundry & Dry Cleaning ....E 216 932-9666
Cleveland Heights (G-6718)

Kimmel Cleaners Inc ....D 419 294-1959
Upper Sandusky (G-18410)

Kramer Enterprises Inc ....E 419 422-7924
Findlay (G-10932)

Midwest Laundry Inc ....D 513 563-5560
Cincinnati (G-4050)

Quality Cleaners of Ohio Inc ....E 330 688-5616
Stow (G-17226)

Rentz Corp ....E 937 434-2774
Dayton (G-9732)

Sunset Carpet Cleaning ....E 937 836-5531
Englewood (G-10602)

DRYCLEANING SVC: Collecting & Distributing Agency

Pierce Cleaners Inc ....E 614 888-4225
Columbus (G-8446)

St Clair 60 Minute Clrs Inc ....E 740 695-3100
Saint Clairsville (G-16506)

DRYCLEANING SVC: Drapery & Curtain

Dutchess Dry Cleaners ....E 330 759-9382
Youngstown (G-20023)

Heider Cleaners Inc ....E 937 298-6631
Dayton (G-9494)

Velco Inc ....E 513 772-4226
Cincinnati (G-4752)

DRYERS & REDRYERS: Indl

Agridry LLC ....E 419 459-4399
Edon (G-10470)

DUCTS: Sheet Metal

Controls and Sheet Metal Inc ....E 513 721-3610
Cincinnati (G-3355)

Langdon Inc ....E 513 733-5955
Cincinnati (G-3909)

United McGill Corporation ....E 614 829-1200
Groveport (G-11546)

DURABLE GOODS WHOLESALERS, NEC

U-Haul Neighborhood Dealer -Ce ....E 419 929-3724
New London (G-14936)

DYES & PIGMENTS: Organic

Hexpol Compounding LLC ....C 440 834-4644
Burton (G-2016)

EARTH SCIENCE SVCS

ASC Group Inc ....E 614 268-2514
Columbus (G-6976)

Diproinduca (usa) Limited LLC ....D 330 722-4442
Medina (G-13930)

Gray & Pape Inc ....E 513 287-7700
Cincinnati (G-3635)

Superior Envmtl Sltons SES Inc ....B 513 874-6910
West Chester (G-19086)

EATING PLACES

5901 Pfffer Rd Htels Sites LLC ....D 513 793-4500
Blue Ash (G-1495)

A C Management Inc ....E 440 461-9200
Cleveland (G-4876)

Akron Management Corp ....B 330 644-8441
Akron (G-48)

Americas Best Value Inn ....E 419 626-9890
Sandusky (G-16575)

Avalon Foodservice Inc ....C 330 854-4551
Canal Fulton (G-2092)

AVI Food Systems Inc ....E 740 452-9363
Zanesville (G-20279)

B & I Hotel Management LLC ....D 330 995-0200
Aurora (G-819)

Bel-Wood Country Club Inc ....D 513 899-3361
Morrow (G-14714)

Best Western Columbus N Hotel ....E 614 888-8230
Columbus (G-7030)

Bob Mor Inc ....C 419 485-5555
Montpelier (G-14607)

Brandywine Country Club Inc ....E 330 657-2525
Peninsula (G-15810)

Breezy Point Ltd Partnership ....E 330 995-0600
Aurora (G-822)

Broad Street Hotel Assoc LP ....D 614 861-0321
Columbus (G-7076)

Brothers Properties Corp ....E 513 381-3000
Cincinnati (G-3081)

Buehler Food Markets Inc ....C 330 364-3079
Dover (G-10068)

Buns of Delaware Inc ....E 740 363-2867
Delaware (G-9956)

Buxton Inn Inc ....E 740 587-0001
Granville (G-11335)

Cambridge Country Club Company ....E 740 439-2744
Byesville (G-2023)

Cameron Mitchell Rest LLC ....E 614 621-3663
Columbus (G-7108)

Canterbury Golf Club Inc ....D 216 561-1914
Cleveland (G-5119)

Capri Bowling Lanes Inc ....E 937 832-4000
Dayton (G-9276)

Ch Relty Iv/Clmbus Partners LP ....D 614 885-3334
Columbus (G-7174)

Charter Hotel Group Ltd Partnr ....E 216 772-4538
Mentor (G-14028)

Cheers Chalet ....E 740 654-9036
Lancaster (G-12378)

Chgc Inc ....D 330 225-6122
Valley City (G-18459)

Circling Hills Golf Course ....E 513 367-5858
Harrison (G-11664)

City of Centerville ....D 937 438-3585
Dayton (G-9302)

Cleveland Airport Hospitality ....D 440 871-6000
Westlake (G-19333)

Cleveland Crowne Plaza Airport ....E 440 243-4040
Cleveland (G-5251)

Cleveland Racquet Club Inc ....D 216 831-2155
Cleveland (G-5282)

Cleveland Rest Oper Ltd Partnr ....C 216 328-1121
Cleveland (G-5285)

Clintonville Community Mkt ....E 614 261-3663
Columbus (G-7231)

Clubhouse Pub N Grub ....E 440 884-2582
Cleveland (G-5310)

Columbus Airport Ltd Partnr ....C 614 475-7551
Columbus (G-7253)

Columbus Country Club ....E 614 861-0800
Columbus (G-7272)

Columbus Museum of Art ....D 614 221-6801
Columbus (G-7301)

Commodore Prry Inns Suites LLC ....D 419 732-2645
Port Clinton (G-16102)

Commonwealth Hotels LLC ....C 614 790-9000
Dublin (G-10184)

Corporate Exchange Hotel Assoc ....C 614 890-8600
Columbus (G-7373)

Coshocton Bowling Center ....E 740 622-6332
Coshocton (G-9004)

Country Club of Hudson ....E 330 650-1188
Hudson (G-11974)

Crossgate Lanes Inc ....E 513 891-0310
Blue Ash (G-1542)

Dinos Catering Inc ....E 440 943-1010
Wickliffe (G-19455)

Dixie Management II Inc ....D 937 832-1234
Englewood (G-10585)

Emmett Dan House Ltd Partnr ....E 740 392-6886
Mount Vernon (G-14764)

Fairlawn Country Club Company ....D 330 836-5541
Akron (G-208)

Farm Inc ....E 513 922-7020
Cincinnati (G-3532)

Ferrante Wine Farm Inc ....E 440 466-8466
Geneva (G-11240)

Findlay Country Club ....E 419 422-9263
Findlay (G-10902)

Findlay Inn & Conference Ctr ....D 419 422-5682
Findlay (G-10904)

First Hotel Associates LP ....D 614 228-3800
Columbus (G-7586)

Fox Den Fairways Inc ....E 330 678-6792
Stow (G-17206)

Fred W Albrecht Grocery Co ....C 330 645-6222
Coventry Township (G-9034)

Gallipolis Hospitality Inc ....E 740 446-0090
   Gallipolis (G-11195)

Glenlaurel Inc ....E 740 385-4070
   Rockbridge (G-16413)

Golden Lamb ....C 513 932-5065
   Lebanon (G-12468)

Grandview Ht Ltd Partnr Ohio ....D 937 766-5519
   Springfield (G-17043)

Green Township Hospitality LLC...........B 513 574-6000
   Cincinnati (G-3656)

Grizzly Golf Center Inc ....B 513 398-5200
   Mason (G-13590)

Guys Party Center................................E 330 724-6373
   Akron (G-247)

Hauck Hospitality LLC ....D 513 563-8330
   Cincinnati (G-3684)

Heritage Golf Club Ltd Partnr ....D 614 777-1690
   Hilliard (G-11773)

Hit Portfolio I Misc Trs LLC.................C 216 575-1234
   Cleveland (G-5694)

Hit Portfolio I Misc Trs LLC.................C 614 228-1234
   Columbus (G-7753)

Hotel 50 S Front Opco L P ....D 614 885-3334
   Columbus (G-7774)

I-X Center Corporation ....C 216 265-2675
   Cleveland (G-5732)

Iacominis Papa Joes Inc ....D 330 923-7999
   Akron (G-274)

Ice Land USA Ltd ....D 440 268-2800
   Strongsville (G-17314)

Island Service Company ....C 419 285-3695
   Put In Bay (G-16226)

Jackson I-94 Ltd Partnership...............E 614 793-2244
   Dublin (G-10259)

Kinane Inc ....D 513 459-0177
   Mason (G-13605)

Lancaster Country Club ....D 740 654-3535
   Lancaster (G-12411)

Madison Route 20 LLC ....E 440 358-7888
   Painesville (G-15723)

Mahoning Country Club Inc ....D 330 545-2517
   Girard (G-11294)

Maplecrst Asistd Lvg Intl Ordr.............E 419 562-4988
   Bucyrus (G-1996)

Mapleside Valley LLC ....D 330 225-5576
   Brunswick (G-1937)

Marion Country Club Company ....E 740 387-0974
   Marion (G-13436)

Marriott Hotel Services Inc..................C 216 252-5333
   Cleveland (G-5911)

Mayfield Sand Ridge Club....................D 216 381-0826
   Cleveland (G-5924)

McPaul Corp ....E 419 447-6313
   Tiffin (G-17523)

Medallion Club ....C 614 794-6999
   Westerville (G-19185)

Mohawk Golf Club................................E 419 447-5876
   Tiffin (G-17525)

N C R Employee Benefit Assn ....C 937 299-3571
   Dayton (G-9651)

Natural Resources Ohio Dept ....D 419 938-5411
   Perrysville (G-15942)

Ohio State Parks Inc ....C 513 664-3504
   College Corner (G-6768)

Ohio State University...........................B 614 292-3238
   Columbus (G-8333)

Park Hotels & Resorts Inc ....B 216 464-5950
   Cleveland (G-6166)

Pike Run Golf Club Inc ....E 419 538-7000
   Ottawa (G-15664)

Pines Golf Club ....E 330 684-1414
   Orrville (G-15644)

Piqua Country Club Holding Co ....E 937 773-7744
   Piqua (G-16017)

Playhouse Square Foundation ....C 216 615-7500
   Cleveland (G-6217)

Quail Hollow Management Inc ....D 440 639-4000
   Painesville (G-15734)

Rcwc Col Inc..D 614 564-9344
   Columbus (G-8493)

Riders 1812 Inn ....E 440 354-0922
   Painesville (G-15738)

Ridgehills Hotel Ltd Partnr...................D 440 585-0600
   Wickliffe (G-19475)

Rockwell Springs Trout Club ....E 419 684-7971
   Clyde (G-6751)

S & S Management Inc ....E 567 356-4151
   Wapakoneta (G-18653)

Saint Johns Villa ....C 330 627-4662
   Carrollton (G-2576)

Sanese Services Inc ....B 614 436-1234
   Warren (G-18739)

Saw Mill Creek Ltd ....C 419 433-3800
   Huron (G-12030)

Sawmill Creek Resort Ltd....................C 419 433-3800
   Huron (G-12031)

Seagate Hospitality Group LLC.............E 216 252-7700
   Cleveland (G-6383)

Shady Hollow Cntry CLB Co Inc............D 330 832-1581
   Massillon (G-13729)

Shawnee Country Club ....D 419 227-7177
   Lima (G-12740)

Silver Lake Country Club ....D 330 688-6066
   Silver Lake (G-16809)

Six Continents Hotels Inc ....C 513 563-8330
   Cincinnati (G-4487)

Skallys Old World Bakery Inc ....E 513 931-1411
   Cincinnati (G-4491)

Sortino Management & Dev Co ....E 419 626-6761
   Sandusky (G-16643)

Spread Eagle Tavern Inc ....E 330 223-1583
   Hanoverton (G-11658)

Springfield Country Club Co ....E 937 399-4215
   Springfield (G-17118)

Stranahan Theatre Trust......................D 419 381-8851
   Toledo (G-18050)

Summit Associates Inc ....E 216 831-3300
   Cleveland (G-6475)

Ta Operating LLC ....B 440 808-9100
   Westlake (G-19411)

Tartan Fields Golf Club Ltd ....D 614 792-0900
   Dublin (G-10353)

Tiki Bowling Lanes Inc ....E 740 654-4513
   Lancaster (G-12442)

Tippecanoe Country Club Inc ....E 330 758-7518
   Canfield (G-2161)

Tom Tise Golf Professional...................D 937 836-5186
   Clayton (G-4862)

Travelcenters America Inc ....A 440 808-9100
   Westlake (G-19413)

Travelcenters of America LLC ....D 330 769-2053
   Lodi (G-12829)

Trepanier Daniels & Trepanier ....D 740 286-1288
   Jackson (G-12180)

Union Club Company ....D 216 621-4230
   Cleveland (G-6564)

United Scoto Senior Activities ....E 740 354-6672
   Portsmouth (G-16176)

University of Cincinnati.........................A 513 556-6381
   Cincinnati (G-4707)

Vermilion Boat Club Inc ....E 440 967-6634
   Vermilion (G-18562)

Wadsworth Galaxy Rest Inc ....D 330 334-3663
   Wadsworth (G-18618)

Walden Club ....D 330 995-7162
   Aurora (G-848)

Walden Company Ltd ....C 330 562-7145
   Aurora (G-849)

Weymouth Valley Inc ....E 440 498-8888
   Solon (G-16915)

Wyndham International Inc ....E 330 666-9300
   Copley (G-8980)

York Temple Country Club Inc ....E 614 885-5459
   Columbus (G-8925)

Youngstown Country Club.....................D 330 759-1040
   Youngstown (G-20261)

ECONOMIC PROGRAMS ADMINISTRATION SVCS, NEC

National Weather Service......................E 937 383-0031
   Wilmington (G-19636)

National Weather Service......................E 216 265-2370
   Cleveland (G-6050)

National Weather Service......................E 419 522-1375
   Mansfield (G-13226)

EDUCATIONAL PROGRAM ADMINISTRATION, GOVERNMENT: County

County of Lucas...................................D 419 385-6021
   Toledo (G-17685)

Cuyahoga County ....D 216 265-3030
   Cleveland (G-5394)

EDUCATIONAL PROGRAM ADMINISTRATION, GOVERNMENT: State

Ohio Department of Education ....E 740 289-2908
   Piketon (G-15980)

EDUCATIONAL PROGRAMS ADMINISTRATION SVCS

County of Hamilton..............................C 513 552-1200
   Cincinnati (G-3370)

EDUCATIONAL SVCS

3c Technologies Inc.............................D 419 868-8999
   Holland (G-11868)

A+ Solutions LLC ....E 216 896-0111
   Beachwood (G-1025)

Allen County Eductl Svc Ctr ....D 419 222-1836
   Lima (G-12595)

Aset Corporation..................................E 937 890-8881
   Vandalia (G-18504)

Heartbeats To City Inc ....E 330 452-4524
   Canton (G-2342)

Iq Innovations LLC ....E 614 222-0882
   Columbus (G-7841)

Knowledgeworks Foundation ....E 513 241-1422
   Cincinnati (G-3884)

Lakeland Foundation ....E 440 525-7094
   Willoughby (G-19541)

Microanalysis Society Inc ....B 614 256-8063
   Hilliard (G-11797)

Osu Nephrology Medical Ctr.................E 614 293-8300
   Columbus (G-8392)

Rev1 Ventures ....E 614 487-3700
   Columbus (G-8529)

Roundtable Online Learning LLC...........E 440 220-5252
   Chagrin Falls (G-2680)

W T C S A Headstart Niles Ctr..............E 330 652-0338
   Niles (G-15173)

EDUCATIONAL SVCS, NONDEGREE GRANTING: Continuing Education

Columbus Montessori Education ....E 614 231-3790
   Columbus (G-7299)

Deemsys Inc ....D 614 322-9928
   Gahanna (G-11117)

Great Oaks Inst Tech Creer Dev ....D 513 613-3657
   Cincinnati (G-3644)

Great Oaks Inst Tech Creer Dev ....E 513 771-8840
   Cincinnati (G-3645)

Lake Erie Nature & Science Ctr ....E 440 871-2900
   Bay Village (G-1022)

EGG WHOLESALERS

Ballas Egg Products Corp.....................D 614 453-0386
   Zanesville (G-20280)

Barkett Fruit Co Inc.............................E 330 364-6645
   Dover (G-10065)

C W Egg Products LLC.........................E 419 375-5800
   Fort Recovery (G-10987)

Cooper Frms Spring Madow Farms ......E 419 375-4119
   Rossburg (G-16458)

Hillandale Farms Inc ....E 740 968-3597
   Flushing (G-10979)

Hillandale Farms Corporation ....E 330 724-3199
   Akron (G-262)

Hillcrest Egg & Cheese Co....................E 216 361-4625
   Cleveland (G-5691)

Ohio Fresh Eggs LLC ....E 740 893-7200
   Croton (G-9065)

Ohio Fresh Eggs LLC ....E 937 354-2233
   Mount Victory (G-14796)

R W Sauder Inc....................................E 330 359-5440
   Winesburg (G-19666)

ELECTRIC & OTHER SERVICES COMBINED

City of Columbus ....C 614 645-7627
   Columbus (G-7205)

Cliffs Minnesota Minerals Co.................A 216 694-5700
   Cleveland (G-5303)

Dayton Power and Light Company ....D 937 549-2641
   Manchester (G-13128)

Dayton Power and Light Company ....D 937 331-4123
   Moraine (G-14647)

Dayton Power and Light Company ....C 937 331-4063
   Dayton (G-9168)

Dayton Power and Light Company ....E 937 331-3032
   Miamisburg (G-14163)

Duke Energy Kentucky Inc ....C 704 594-6200
   Cincinnati (G-3449)

Duke Energy Ohio Inc...........................D 704 382-3853
   Cincinnati (G-3450)

Medical Center Co (inc)........................E 216 368-4256
   Cleveland (G-5942)

Employee Codes: A=Over 500 employees, B=251-500
C=101-250, D=51-100, E=25-50   2019 Harris Ohio
Services Directory   1409

S E R V I C E S

Stockport Mill Country Inn Inc..............E 740 559-2822
  Stockport *(G-17183)*

ELECTRIC FENCE CHARGERS

Agratronix LLC..............................E 330 562-2222
  Streetsboro *(G-17245)*

ELECTRIC MOTOR REPAIR SVCS

3-D Service Ltd..............................C 330 830-3500
  Massillon *(G-13656)*
Fenton Bros Electric Co ....E 330 343-0093
  New Philadelphia *(G-14959)*
Horner Industrial Services Inc ....E 937 390-6667
  Springfield *(G-17047)*
Integrated Power Services LLC ....E 513 863-8816
  Hamilton *(G-11615)*
Kiemle-Hankins Company ....E 419 661-2430
  Perrysburg *(G-15886)*
M & R Electric Motor Svc Inc ....E 937 222-6282
  Dayton *(G-9578)*
Magnetech Industrial Svcs Inc ....C 330 830-3500
  Massillon *(G-13708)*
Matlock Electric Co Inc ....E 513 731-9600
  Cincinnati *(G-3979)*
Mid-Ohio Electric Co.........................E 614 274-8000
  Columbus *(G-8076)*
National Electric Coil Inc ....B 614 488-1151
  Columbus *(G-8131)*
Shoemaker Electric Company ....E 614 294-5626
  Columbus *(G-8635)*
Whelco Industrial Ltd ....E 419 873-6134
  Perrysburg *(G-15936)*

ELECTRIC POWER DISTRIBUTION TO CONSUMERS

Adams Rural Electric Coop Inc ....E 937 544-2305
  West Union *(G-19132)*
American Electric Power Co Inc ....E 419 420-3011
  Findlay *(G-10864)*
American Electric Power Co Inc ....E 740 594-1988
  Athens *(G-763)*
American Electric Power Co Inc............C 330 438-7024
  Canton *(G-2184)*
American Electric Power Co Inc............D 614 351-3715
  Columbus *(G-6917)*
American Electric Power Co Inc ....E 740 384-7981
  Wellston *(G-18847)*
American Electric Power Co Inc ....E 330 580-5085
  Canton *(G-2185)*
American Electric Power Co Inc............E 740 598-4164
  Brilliant *(G-1819)*
American Electric Pwr Svc Corp ....B 614 716-1000
  Columbus *(G-6919)*
Appalachian Power Company ....C 614 716-1000
  Columbus *(G-6958)*
Buckeye Rural Elc Coop Inc ....E 740 379-2025
  Patriot *(G-15789)*
Butler Rural Electric Coop ....E 513 867-4400
  Oxford *(G-15674)*
Carroll Electric Coop Inc ....E 330 627-2116
  Carrollton *(G-2560)*
Cinergy Corp ....A 513 421-9500
  Cincinnati *(G-3289)*
City of Cuyahoga Falls ....E 330 971-8000
  Cuyahoga Falls *(G-9080)*
Cleveland Elc Illuminating Co..............D 440 953-7650
  Painesville *(G-15702)*
Columbus Southern Power Co ....D 614 716-1000
  Columbus *(G-7314)*
Consolidated Electric Coop ....E 740 363-2641
  Delaware *(G-9961)*
Consolidated Electric Coop Inc ....D 419 947-3055
  Mount Gilead *(G-14725)*
Duke Energy Ohio Inc ....D 704 382-3853
  Cincinnati *(G-3450)*
Firstenergy Corp ....A 800 736-3402
  Akron *(G-221)*
Firstenergy Solutions Corp..................E 800 736-3402
  Akron *(G-223)*
Frontier Power Company ....E 740 622-6755
  Coshocton *(G-9015)*
Guernsy-Muskingum Elc Coop Inc ......E 740 826-7661
  New Concord *(G-14900)*
Hancock-Wood Electric Coop Inc ....E 419 257-3241
  North Baltimore *(G-15177)*
Hearthstone Utilities Inc ....D 440 974-3770
  Cleveland *(G-5679)*
Holmes-Wayne Electric Coop ....E 330 674-1055
  Millersburg *(G-14477)*

Indiana Michigan Power Company........C 614 716-1000
  Columbus *(G-7807)*
Jersey Central Pwr & Light Co ....A 440 546-8609
  Brecksville *(G-1785)*
Jersey Central Pwr & Light Co ....D 216 479-1132
  Cleveland *(G-5792)*
Licking Rural Electrification ....D 740 892-2071
  Utica *(G-18456)*
Mid-Ohio Energy Cooperative ....E 419 568-5321
  Kenton *(G-12284)*
North Central Elc Coop Inc ....E 800 426-3072
  Attica *(G-814)*
Paulding-Putnam Electric Coop............E 419 399-5015
  Paulding *(G-15798)*
Pennsylvania Power Company ....C 800 720-3600
  Akron *(G-376)*
Pioneer Rural Electric Coop ....D 800 762-0997
  Piqua *(G-16016)*
Public Service Company Okla ....C 614 716-1000
  Columbus *(G-8479)*
South Central Power Company ....E 740 474-6045
  Circleville *(G-4850)*
South Central Power Company ....D 740 653-4422
  Lancaster *(G-12436)*
South Central Power Company ....D 614 837-4351
  Canal Winchester *(G-2120)*
South Central Power Company ....E 740 425-4018
  Barnesville *(G-979)*
Toledo Edison Company ....E 800 447-3333
  Akron *(G-471)*
Toledo Edison Company ....D 419 249-5364
  Holland *(G-11920)*
Union Rural Electric Coop Inc ....E 937 642-1826
  Marysville *(G-13535)*

ELECTRIC POWER GENERATION: Fossil Fuel

City of Painesville ....E 440 392-5954
  Painesville *(G-15699)*
Dayton Power and Light Company ....B 937 549-2641
  Manchester *(G-13127)*
Dayton Power and Light Company ....E 937 549-2641
  Manchester *(G-13128)*
Vistra Energy Corp ....E 513 467-4900
  North Bend *(G-15183)*
Walleye Power LLC.............................D 567 298-7400
  Oregon *(G-15614)*

ELECTRIC POWER, COGENERATED

AEP Dresden Plant ....E 740 450-1964
  Dresden *(G-10115)*

ELECTRIC SERVICES

AEP Energy Partners Inc.......................E 614 716-1000
  Columbus *(G-6877)*
AEP Energy Services Inc ....B 614 583-2900
  Columbus *(G-6878)*
AEP Power Marketing Inc....................A 614 716-1000
  Columbus *(G-6880)*
American Electric Power Co Inc ....E 740 829-4129
  Conesville *(G-8947)*
American Electric Power Co Inc ....E 419 998-5106
  Lima *(G-12600)*
American Electric Power Co Inc ....E 614 856-2750
  Columbus *(G-6916)*
American Electric Pwr Svc Corp ....E 614 582-1742
  Columbus *(G-6920)*
Appalachian Power Company ....D 330 438-7102
  Canton *(G-2192)*
Butterfly Inc ....E 440 892-7777
  Independence *(G-12051)*
Cardinal Operating Company ....C 740 598-4164
  Brilliant *(G-1821)*
City of Dublin.....................................E 614 410-4750
  Dublin *(G-10175)*
City of Hudson Village ....D 330 650-1052
  Hudson *(G-11973)*
City of Toledo....................................D 419 245-1800
  Toledo *(G-17654)*
City of Westerville ....E 614 901-6700
  Westerville *(G-19237)*
Columbus Southern Power Co ....D 740 829-2378
  Conesville *(G-8948)*
Dayton Power and Light Company ....D 937 331-4123
  Moraine *(G-14647)*
Duke Energy Beckjord LLC.................A 513 287-2561
  Cincinnati *(G-3448)*
Duke Energy Ohio Inc ....C 800 544-6900
  Cincinnati *(G-3451)*

Duke Energy Ohio Inc ....E 513 287-1120
  Cincinnati *(G-3452)*
Duke Energy Ohio Inc ....E 513 467-5000
  New Richmond *(G-14994)*
Duquesne Light Company ....C 330 385-6103
  East Liverpool *(G-10401)*
Dynegy Zimmer LLC...........................E 713 767-0483
  Moscow *(G-14720)*
Energy Cooperative Inc ....E 740 348-1206
  Newark *(G-15031)*
First Energy Linde ....D 330 384-4959
  Akron *(G-220)*
Firstenergy Corp ....E 419 321-7114
  Oak Harbor *(G-15472)*
Firstenergy Nuclear Oper Co ....A 800 646-0400
  Akron *(G-222)*
Gavin AEP Plant ....E 740 925-3166
  Cheshire *(G-2735)*
Great Lakes Energy ....E 440 582-4662
  Broadview Heights *(G-1834)*
Igs Solar LLC....................................E 844 447-7652
  Dublin *(G-10253)*
Jersey Central Pwr & Light Co ....D 440 994-8271
  Ashtabula *(G-744)*
Jersey Central Pwr & Light Co ....D 419 366-2915
  Sandusky *(G-16619)*
Jersey Central Pwr & Light Co ....E 330 315-6713
  Fairlawn *(G-10836)*
Jersey Central Pwr & Light Co ....C 740 537-6308
  Stratton *(G-17242)*
Jersey Central Pwr & Light Co ....E 216 432-6330
  Cleveland *(G-5791)*
Jersey Central Pwr & Light Co ....D 330 336-9884
  Wadsworth *(G-18601)*
Jersey Central Pwr & Light Co ....D 440 953-7651
  Painesville *(G-15716)*
National Gas & Oil Corporation ....E 740 344-2102
  Newark *(G-15079)*
Nisource Inc ....E 614 460-4878
  Columbus *(G-8190)*
Ohio Edison Company ....C 330 740-7754
  Youngstown *(G-20143)*
Ohio Edison Company ....C 330 336-9880
  Wadsworth *(G-18610)*
Ohio Power Company ....C 614 716-1000
  Columbus *(G-8279)*
Ohio Power Company ....D 740 695-7800
  Saint Clairsville *(G-16497)*
Pennsylvania Electric Company............D 800 545-7741
  Akron *(G-375)*
Vistra Energy Corp ....E 513 467-5289
  Moscow *(G-14721)*
Volunteer Energy Services Inc ....E 614 856-3128
  Pickerington *(G-15969)*

ELECTRIC SVCS, NEC Power Broker

Ohio Valley Electric Corp ....D 740 289-7225
  Piketon *(G-15982)*

ELECTRIC SVCS, NEC Power Transmission

Reliability First Corporation.................E 216 503-0600
  Cleveland *(G-6301)*

ELECTRIC SVCS, NEC: Power Generation

AEP Generating Company ....A 614 223-1000
  Columbus *(G-6879)*
American Electric Power Co Inc............E 740 779-5261
  Chillicothe *(G-2756)*
American Municipal Power Inc.............C 614 540-1111
  Columbus *(G-6931)*
Buckeye Power Inc ....B 740 598-6534
  Brilliant *(G-1820)*
Buckeye Power Inc ....E 614 781-0573
  Columbus *(G-7089)*
City of Hamilton ....D 513 785-7450
  Hamilton *(G-11580)*
Cleveland Elc Illuminating Co..............D 800 589-3101
  Akron *(G-143)*
Dayton Power and Light Company ....C 937 331-4063
  Dayton *(G-9168)*
Dayton Power and Light Company ....E 937 331-3032
  Miamisburg *(G-14163)*
DPL Inc ....E 937 331-4063
  Dayton *(G-9170)*
Echogen Power Systems Del Inc ....E 234 542-4379
  Akron *(G-201)*
Jersey Central Pwr & Light Co ....C 800 736-3402
  Akron *(G-291)*

Jersey Central Pwr & Light Co ....D 937 327-1218
  Springfield *(G-17056)*
Jersey Central Pwr & Light Co ....D 440 326-3222
  Elyria *(G-10520)*
Metropolitan Edison Company ....C 800 736-3402
  Akron *(G-336)*
NRG Power Midwest LP ....D 440 930-6401
  Avon Lake *(G-925)*
NRG Power Midwest LP ....D 330 505-4327
  Niles *(G-15165)*
Ohio Edison Company ....C 800 736-3402
  Akron *(G-358)*
Ohio Edison Company ....C 740 671-2900
  Shadyside *(G-16697)*
Ohio Valley Electric Corp ....D 740 289-7200
  Piketon *(G-15981)*
Southwestern Electric Power Co..........C 614 716-1000
  Columbus *(G-8666)*
Toledo Edison Company ....E 419 321-8488
  Oak Harbor *(G-15479)*

ELECTRICAL APPARATUS & EQPT WHOLESALERS

Belting Company of Cincinnati..............E 937 498-2104
  Sidney *(G-16762)*
Best Lighting Products Inc ....D 740 964-0063
  Etna *(G-10613)*
Bostwick-Braun Company ....D 419 259-3600
  Toledo *(G-17620)*
Cincinnati Belt and Transm...................D 513 621-9050
  Cincinnati *(G-3229)*
Dickman Supply Inc ....C 937 492-6166
  Sidney *(G-16773)*
Dickman Supply Inc ....E 937 492-6166
  Greenville *(G-11375)*
Dxp Enterprises Inc ....E 513 242-2227
  Cincinnati *(G-3459)*
Eaton Corporation ....E 614 839-4387
  Columbus *(G-7495)*
Eaton Corporation ....E 888 402-1915
  Cleveland *(G-5463)*
Filnor Inc ....E 330 821-8731
  Alliance *(G-532)*
Hubbell Power Systems Inc ....D 330 335-2361
  Wadsworth *(G-18600)*
Hughes Corporation ....E 440 238-2550
  Strongsville *(G-17312)*
Johnson Cntrls SEC Sltions LLC ....D 440 262-1084
  Brecksville *(G-1786)*
Kirk Key Interlock Company LLC ....E 330 833-8223
  North Canton *(G-15217)*
Laughlin Music & Vending Svc ....E 740 593-7778
  Athens *(G-790)*
Major Electronix Corp...........................E 440 942-0054
  Eastlake *(G-10431)*
Monarch Electric Service Co ....D 216 433-7800
  Cleveland *(G-6006)*
New Haven Estates Inc..........................E 419 933-2181
  New Haven *(G-14916)*
Newark Electronics Corporation ....C 330 523-4912
  Richfield *(G-16366)*
Ohio Rural Electric Coops Inc ....E 614 846-5757
  Columbus *(G-8283)*
Powell Electrical Systems Inc................D 330 966-1750
  Canton *(G-2438)*
Schneider Electric Usa Inc....................D 513 755-5000
  West Chester *(G-18997)*
Siemens Industry Inc............................D 614 846-9540
  Worthington *(G-19849)*
Siemens Industry Inc............................D 513 742-5590
  Cincinnati *(G-4480)*
Simplex Time Recorder LLC ....E 513 874-1227
  West Chester *(G-19081)*
Thomas Door Controls Inc ....E 614 263-1756
  Columbus *(G-8746)*
W W Williams Company LLC ....E 419 837-5067
  Perrysburg *(G-15932)*
Wesco Distribution Inc ....E 937 228-9668
  Dayton *(G-9874)*
Wolff Bros Supply Inc............................E 419 425-8511
  Findlay *(G-10976)*
Wolff Bros Supply Inc............................E 330 786-4140
  Akron *(G-503)*
Wright State University ....A 937 775-3333
  Beavercreek *(G-1199)*

ELECTRICAL APPLIANCES, TELEVISIONS & RADIOS WHOLESALERS

Lowes Home Centers LLC ....C 216 351-4723
  Cleveland *(G-5882)*
Lowes Home Centers LLC ....C 419 739-1300
  Wapakoneta *(G-18649)*
Lowes Home Centers LLC ....C 937 235-2920
  Dayton *(G-9574)*
Lowes Home Centers LLC ....C 740 574-6200
  Wheelersburg *(G-19435)*
Lowes Home Centers LLC ....C 330 665-9356
  Akron *(G-321)*
Lowes Home Centers LLC ....C 330 829-2700
  Alliance *(G-538)*
Lowes Home Centers LLC ....C 937 599-4000
  Bellefontaine *(G-1357)*
Lowes Home Centers LLC ....C 419 420-7531
  Findlay *(G-10935)*
Lowes Home Centers LLC ....C 330 832-1901
  Massillon *(G-13704)*
Lowes Home Centers LLC ....C 513 741-0585
  Cincinnati *(G-3945)*
Lowes Home Centers LLC ....C 614 433-9957
  Columbus *(G-6822)*
Lowes Home Centers LLC ....C 740 389-9737
  Marion *(G-13430)*
Lowes Home Centers LLC ....C 740 450-5500
  Zanesville *(G-20326)*
Lowes Home Centers LLC ....C 513 598-7050
  Cincinnati *(G-3946)*
Lowes Home Centers LLC ....C 614 769-9940
  Reynoldsburg *(G-16317)*
Lowes Home Centers LLC ....C 614 853-6200
  Columbus *(G-7990)*
Lowes Home Centers LLC ....C 440 937-3500
  Avon *(G-893)*
Lowes Home Centers LLC ....C 513 445-1000
  South Lebanon *(G-16926)*
Lowes Home Centers LLC ....B 216 831-2860
  Bedford *(G-1290)*
Lowes Home Centers LLC ....C 937 327-6000
  Springfield *(G-17065)*
Lowes Home Centers LLC ....C 419 331-3598
  Lima *(G-12693)*
Lowes Home Centers LLC ....C 740 681-3464
  Lancaster *(G-12413)*
Lowes Home Centers LLC ....C 614 659-0530
  Dublin *(G-10275)*
Lowes Home Centers LLC ....C 614 238-2601
  Columbus *(G-7991)*
Lowes Home Centers LLC ....C 740 522-0003
  Newark *(G-15063)*
Lowes Home Centers LLC ....C 740 773-7777
  Chillicothe *(G-2803)*
Lowes Home Centers LLC ....C 440 998-6555
  Ashtabula *(G-745)*
Lowes Home Centers LLC ....B 513 753-5094
  Cincinnati *(G-2861)*
Lowes Home Centers LLC ....C 614 497-6170
  Columbus *(G-7992)*
Lowes Home Centers LLC ....C 513 731-6127
  Cincinnati *(G-3947)*
Lowes Home Centers LLC ....C 330 287-2261
  Wooster *(G-19742)*
Lowes Home Centers LLC ....C 937 339-2544
  Troy *(G-18211)*
Lowes Home Centers LLC ....C 440 392-0027
  Mentor *(G-14078)*
Lowes Home Centers LLC ....C 440 942-2759
  Willoughby *(G-19546)*
Lowes Home Centers LLC ....C 740 374-2151
  Marietta *(G-13345)*
Lowes Home Centers LLC ....C 419 874-6758
  Perrysburg *(G-15891)*
Lowes Home Centers LLC ....C 330 626-2980
  Streetsboro *(G-17259)*
Lowes Home Centers LLC ....C 419 389-9464
  Toledo *(G-17864)*
Lowes Home Centers LLC ....C 419 843-9758
  Toledo *(G-17865)*
Lowes Home Centers LLC ....C 614 447-2851
  Columbus *(G-7993)*
Lowes Home Centers LLC ....C 330 245-4300
  Akron *(G-322)*
Lowes Home Centers LLC ....C 513 965-3280
  Milford *(G-14402)*
Lowes Home Centers LLC ....C 330 908-2750
  Northfield *(G-15382)*
Lowes Home Centers LLC ....C 419 470-2491
  Toledo *(G-17866)*

Lowes Home Centers LLC ....C 513 336-9741
  Mason *(G-13612)*
Lowes Home Centers LLC ....C 937 498-8400
  Sidney *(G-16785)*
Lowes Home Centers LLC ....C 740 699-3000
  Saint Clairsville *(G-16493)*
Lowes Home Centers LLC ....C 330 920-9280
  Stow *(G-17218)*
Lowes Home Centers LLC ....C 740 589-3750
  Athens *(G-791)*
Lowes Home Centers LLC ....C 740 393-5350
  Mount Vernon *(G-14779)*
Lowes Home Centers LLC ....C 937 547-2400
  Greenville *(G-11389)*
Lowes Home Centers LLC ....C 330 335-1900
  Wadsworth *(G-18606)*
Lowes Home Centers LLC ....C 937 347-4000
  Xenia *(G-19918)*
Lowes Home Centers LLC ....C 440 239-2630
  Strongsville *(G-17324)*
Lowes Home Centers LLC ....C 513 755-4300
  West Chester *(G-18966)*
Lowes Home Centers LLC ....C 513 671-2093
  Cincinnati *(G-3948)*
Lowes Home Centers LLC ....C 440 331-1027
  Rocky River *(G-16440)*
Lowes Home Centers LLC ....C 330 677-3040
  Kent *(G-12247)*
Lowes Home Centers LLC ....C 419 747-1920
  Ontario *(G-15559)*
Lowes Home Centers LLC ....C 330 339-1936
  New Philadelphia *(G-14971)*
Lowes Home Centers LLC ....C 440 985-5700
  Lorain *(G-12924)*
Lowes Home Centers LLC ....C 419 447-4101
  Tiffin *(G-17521)*
Lowes Home Centers LLC ....C 937 578-4440
  Marysville *(G-13511)*
Lowes Home Centers LLC ....C 937 438-4900
  Dayton *(G-9575)*
Lowes Home Centers LLC ....C 937 427-1110
  Beavercreek *(G-1168)*
Lowes Home Centers LLC ....C 937 848-5600
  Dayton *(G-9576)*
Lowes Home Centers LLC ....C 614 529-5900
  Hilliard *(G-11786)*
Lowes Home Centers LLC ....C 513 737-3700
  Hamilton *(G-11625)*
Lowes Home Centers LLC ....C 419 355-0221
  Fremont *(G-11084)*
Lowes Home Centers LLC ....C 419 624-6000
  Sandusky *(G-16625)*
Lowes Home Centers LLC ....C 419 782-9000
  Defiance *(G-9926)*
Lowes Home Centers LLC ....C 330 609-8000
  Warren *(G-18725)*
Lowes Home Centers LLC ....C 740 894-7120
  South Point *(G-16939)*
Lowes Home Centers LLC ....C 513 727-3900
  Middletown *(G-14305)*
Lowes Home Centers LLC ....C 330 497-2720
  Canton *(G-2381)*
Lowes Home Centers LLC ....C 740 266-3500
  Steubenville *(G-17164)*
Lowes Home Centers LLC ....C 330 965-4500
  Youngstown *(G-20101)*
Lowes Home Centers LLC ....C 937 383-7000
  Wilmington *(G-19630)*
Lowes Home Centers LLC ....C 937 854-8200
  Dayton *(G-9577)*
Lowes Home Centers LLC ....C 614 476-7100
  Columbus *(G-7994)*
Mobilcomm Inc ....D 513 742-5555
  Cincinnati *(G-4066)*
Panasonic Corp North America ....D 513 770-9294
  Mason *(G-13625)*
Panasonic Corp North America ....E 201 392-6872
  Troy *(G-18221)*
RPC Electronics Inc..............................E 877 522-7927
  Cleveland *(G-6348)*

ELECTRICAL CONSTRUCTION MATERIALS WHOLESALERS

John A Becker Co ....D 937 226-1341
  Dayton *(G-9527)*
Johnson Electric Supply Co ....E 513 421-3700
  Cincinnati *(G-3828)*
Westfield Electric Inc............................E 419 862-0078
  Gibsonburg *(G-11280)*

SERVICES

ELECTRICAL CURRENT CARRYING WIRING DEVICES

GE Aviation Systems LLC ....B 937 898-5881
Vandalia *(G-18524)*

Legrand North America LLC ....B 937 224-0639
Dayton *(G-9561)*

Simpson Strong-Tie Company Inc .....C 614 876-8060
Columbus *(G-8645)*

Watteredge LLC ....D 440 933-6110
Avon Lake *(G-929)*

ELECTRICAL DISCHARGE MACHINING, EDM

Morris Technologies Inc ....C 513 733-1611
Cincinnati *(G-4075)*

ELECTRICAL EQPT & SPLYS

Akron Foundry Co ....E 330 745-3101
Barberton *(G-939)*

Circle Prime Manufacturing ....E 330 923-0019
Cuyahoga Falls *(G-9079)*

Commercial Electric Pdts Corp ....E 216 241-2886
Cleveland *(G-5318)*

Corrpro Companies Inc ....E 330 723-5082
Medina *(G-13924)*

Hannon Company ....D 330 456-4728
Canton *(G-2339)*

Kiemle-Hankins Company ....E 419 661-2430
Perrysburg *(G-15886)*

Kraft Electrical Contg Inc ....E 614 836-9300
Groveport *(G-11526)*

Matlock Electric Co Inc ....E 513 731-9600
Cincinnati *(G-3979)*

Philips Medical Systems Clevel ....B 440 247-2652
Cleveland *(G-6203)*

Powell Electrical Systems Inc ....D 330 966-1750
Canton *(G-2438)*

Riverside Drives Inc ....E 216 362-1211
Cleveland *(G-6329)*

Wesco Distribution Inc ....E 419 666-1670
Northwood *(G-15414)*

ELECTRICAL EQPT FOR ENGINES

Sumitomo Elc Wirg Systems Inc ....E 937 642-7579
Marysville *(G-13531)*

ELECTRICAL EQPT REPAIR & MAINTENANCE

Amko Service Company ....E 330 364-8857
Midvale *(G-14357)*

Ascendtech Inc ....E 216 458-1101
Willoughby *(G-19506)*

Boeing Company ....E 740 788-4000
Newark *(G-15014)*

Ce Power Engineered Svcs LLC ....D 513 563-6150
Cincinnati *(G-3139)*

Ce Power Holdings Inc ....D 513 563-6150
Cincinnati *(G-3140)*

City of Wadsworth ....E 330 334-1581
Wadsworth *(G-18592)*

Electric Motor Tech LLC ....E 513 821-9999
Cincinnati *(G-3486)*

Enprotech Industrial Tech LLC ....C 216 883-3220
Cleveland *(G-5482)*

Fosbel Inc ....C 216 362-3900
Cleveland *(G-5565)*

General Electric Company ....D 216 883-1000
Cleveland *(G-5603)*

High Line Corporation ....E 330 848-8800
Akron *(G-261)*

J-C-R Tech Inc ....E 937 783-2296
Blanchester *(G-1488)*

Narrow Way Custom Technology ....E 937 743-1611
Carlisle *(G-2553)*

Ohio Machinery Co ....E 740 453-0563
Zanesville *(G-20348)*

Rubber City Machinery Corp ....E 330 434-3500
Akron *(G-411)*

Star Dist & Manufacturring LLC ....D 513 860-3573
West Chester *(G-19083)*

Steel Eqp Specialists Inc ....D 330 823-8260
Alliance *(G-555)*

Terex Utilities Inc ....D 513 539-9770
Monroe *(G-14584)*

Wauseon Machine & Mfg Inc ....D 419 337-0940
Wauseon *(G-18812)*

ELECTRICAL EQPT REPAIR SVCS

Electrical Appl Repr Svc Inc ....E 216 459-8700
Brooklyn Heights *(G-1870)*

Fak Group Inc ....E 440 498-8465
Solon *(G-16848)*

Internash Global Svc Group LLC ....D 513 772-0430
West Chester *(G-19062)*

Kiemle-Hankins Company ....E 419 661-2430
Perrysburg *(G-15886)*

Magnetech Industrial Svcs Inc ....D 330 830-3500
Massillon *(G-13707)*

S D Myers Inc ....C 330 630-7000
Tallmadge *(G-17486)*

ELECTRICAL EQPT: Automotive, NEC

Electra Sound Inc ....D 216 433-9600
Parma *(G-15766)*

ELECTRICAL GOODS, WHOLESALE: Alarms & Signaling Eqpt

Research & Investigation Assoc ....E 419 526-1299
Mansfield *(G-13234)*

ELECTRICAL GOODS, WHOLESALE: Boxes & Fittings

Akron Electric Inc ....D 330 745-8891
Akron *(G-37)*

Akron Foundry Co ....C 330 745-3101
Akron *(G-40)*

Osburn Associates Inc ....E 740 385-5732
Logan *(G-12852)*

ELECTRICAL GOODS, WHOLESALE: Burglar Alarm Systems

GA Business Purchaser LLC ....D 419 255-8400
Toledo *(G-17752)*

State Alarm Inc ....E 888 726-8111
Youngstown *(G-20217)*

ELECTRICAL GOODS, WHOLESALE: Cable Conduit

Legrand North America LLC ....B 937 224-0639
Dayton *(G-9561)*

ELECTRICAL GOODS, WHOLESALE: Closed Circuit Television Or TV

Asset Protection Corporation ....E 419 531-3400
Toledo *(G-17601)*

ELECTRICAL GOODS, WHOLESALE: Connectors

Ladd Distribution LLC ....D 937 438-2646
Kettering *(G-12296)*

ELECTRICAL GOODS, WHOLESALE: Electrical Appliances, Major

C C Mitchell Supply Company ....E 440 526-2040
Cleveland *(G-5110)*

Danby Products Inc ....E 419 425-8627
Findlay *(G-10895)*

Don Walter Kitchen Distrs ....E 330 793-9338
Youngstown *(G-20021)*

Rieman Arszman Cstm Distrs Inc ....E 513 874-5444
Fairfield *(G-10774)*

ELECTRICAL GOODS, WHOLESALE: Electrical Entertainment Eqpt

Mas Inc ....E 330 659-3333
Richfield *(G-16362)*

ELECTRICAL GOODS, WHOLESALE: Electronic Parts

Airborn Electronics Inc ....E 330 245-2630
Akron *(G-25)*

Allied Enterprises Inc ....E 440 808-8760
Westlake *(G-19314)*

Arrow Electronics Inc ....D 800 722-5273
Solon *(G-16822)*

Arrow Electronics Inc ....D 440 498-6400
Solon *(G-16823)*

Avnet Inc ....E 440 479-3607
Eastlake *(G-10427)*

Avnet Inc ....E 440 349-7600
Beachwood *(G-1033)*

Funai Service Corporation ....E 614 409-2600
Groveport *(G-11514)*

Koehlke Components Inc ....E 937 435-5435
Franklin *(G-11034)*

Major Electronix Corp ....E 440 942-0054
Eastlake *(G-10431)*

McM Electronics Inc ....D 937 434-0031
Dayton *(G-9596)*

Mendelson Electronics Co Inc ....E 937 461-3525
Dayton *(G-9606)*

Newark Corporation ....B 330 523-4457
Richfield *(G-16365)*

Newark Electronics Corporation ....C 330 523-4912
Richfield *(G-16366)*

Pepperl + Fuchs Americas Inc ....D 330 425-3555
Twinsburg *(G-18303)*

REM Electronics Supply Co Inc ....E 330 373-1300
Warren *(G-18738)*

Schuster Electronics Inc ....E 330 425-8134
Twinsburg *(G-18319)*

ELECTRICAL GOODS, WHOLESALE: Facsimile Or Fax Eqpt

Donnellon Mc Carthy Inc ....E 937 299-0200
Moraine *(G-14649)*

Gordon Flesch Company Inc ....E 419 884-2031
Mansfield *(G-13179)*

Ricoh Usa Inc ....D 513 984-9898
Sharonville *(G-16730)*

Visual Edge Technology Inc ....C 330 494-9694
Canton *(G-2528)*

ELECTRICAL GOODS, WHOLESALE: Fire Alarm Systems

Gene Ptacek Son Fire Eqp Inc ....E 216 651-8300
Cleveland *(G-5602)*

ELECTRICAL GOODS, WHOLESALE: Generators

Buckeye Power Sales Co Inc ....E 937 346-8322
Moraine *(G-14628)*

Western Branch Diesel Inc ....E 330 454-8800
Canton *(G-2534)*

ELECTRICAL GOODS, WHOLESALE: Intercommunication Eqpt

Copp Systems Inc ....E 937 228-4188
Dayton *(G-9320)*

ELECTRICAL GOODS, WHOLESALE: Light Bulbs & Related Splys

Handl-It Inc ....D 440 439-9400
Bedford *(G-1283)*

ELECTRICAL GOODS, WHOLESALE: Lighting Fittings & Access

Technical Consumer Pdts Inc ....B 800 324-1496
Aurora *(G-844)*

ELECTRICAL GOODS, WHOLESALE: Lighting Fixtures, Comm & Indl

Cls Facilities MGT Svcs Inc ....E 440 602-4600
Mentor *(G-14032)*

ELECTRICAL GOODS, WHOLESALE: Mobile telephone Eqpt

Cellco Partnership ....E 440 779-1313
North Olmsted *(G-15279)*

Shawntech Communications Inc ....E 937 898-4900
Miamisburg *(G-14220)*

ELECTRICAL GOODS, WHOLESALE: Modems, Computer

Enviro It LLC ....E 614 453-0709
Columbus *(G-7520)*

ELECTRICAL GOODS, WHOLESALE: Motor Ctrls, Starters & Relays

Winkle Electric Company Inc..............E......330 744-5303
　Youngstown (G-20249)

ELECTRICAL GOODS, WHOLESALE: Motors

Ametek Tchnical Indus Pdts Inc...........D......330 677-3754
　Kent (G-12214)
Electric Motor Tech LLC...................E......513 821-9999
　Cincinnati (G-3486)
Horner Industrial Services Inc............E......937 390-6667
　Springfield (G-17047)
M & R Electric Motor Svc Inc.............E......937 222-6282
　Dayton (G-9578)
Matlock Electric Co Inc..................E......513 731-9600
　Cincinnati (G-3979)
Mid-Ohio Electric Co.....................E......614 274-8000
　Columbus (G-8076)
Professional Electric Pdts Co............E......419 269-3790
　Toledo (G-17989)
Shoemaker Electric Company...............E......614 294-5626
　Columbus (G-8635)
WW Grainger Inc..........................E......614 276-5231
　Columbus (G-8921)
WW Grainger Inc..........................E......513 563-7100
　Blue Ash (G-1683)

ELECTRICAL GOODS, WHOLESALE: Paging & Signaling Eqpt

Pager Plus One Inc.......................C......513 748-3788
　Milford (G-14417)

ELECTRICAL GOODS, WHOLESALE: Radio Parts & Access, NEC

Comproducts Inc..........................D......614 276-5552
　Columbus (G-7344)
P & R Communications Svc Inc.............E......937 222-0861
　Dayton (G-9680)

ELECTRICAL GOODS, WHOLESALE: Security Control Eqpt & Systems

Aysco Security Consultants Inc...........E......330 733-8183
　Kent (G-12215)
Convergint Technologies LLC..............C......513 771-1717
　Cincinnati (G-3357)
Honeywell International Inc...............E......614 717-2270
　Columbus (G-7772)
Mace Personal Def & SEC Inc..............E......440 424-5321
　Cleveland (G-5893)

ELECTRICAL GOODS, WHOLESALE: Semiconductor Devices

Avnet Inc................................E......614 865-1400
　Columbus (G-7006)

ELECTRICAL GOODS, WHOLESALE: Sound Eqpt

Audio-Technica US Inc....................D......330 686-2600
　Stow (G-17191)
C A E C Inc..............................E......614 337-1091
　Columbus (G-7102)
Electra Sound Inc........................D......216 433-9600
　Parma (G-15766)

ELECTRICAL GOODS, WHOLESALE: Telephone & Telegraphic Eqpt

Acadia Solutions Inc.....................E......614 505-6135
　Dublin (G-10118)
Acuative Corporation.....................D......440 202-4500
　Strongsville (G-17280)
AT&T Corp................................E......330 505-4200
　Niles (G-15145)
Cellco Partnership.......................E......330 722-6622
　Medina (G-13916)
Diamond Company Inc......................C......937 374-1111
　Xenia (G-19898)
E-Cycle LLC..............................D......614 832-7032
　Hilliard (G-11763)
Wurtec Incorporated......................D......419 726-1066
　Toledo (G-18164)

ELECTRICAL GOODS, WHOLESALE: Telephone Eqpt

ABC Appliance Inc........................E......419 693-4414
　Oregon (G-15581)
Famous Industries Inc....................E......330 535-1811
　Akron (G-214)
Midwest Communications Inc...............D......800 229-4756
　North Canton (G-15221)
Mitel (delaware) Inc.....................E......513 733-8000
　West Chester (G-18974)
Neteam Systems LLC.......................D......330 523-5100
　Cleveland (G-6058)
Polycom Inc..............................E......937 245-1853
　Englewood (G-10597)
Pro Oncall Technologies LLC..............D......513 489-7660
　Cincinnati (G-4287)
Tele-Solutions Inc.......................E......330 782-2888
　Youngstown (G-20221)
Teletronic Services Inc..................E......216 778-6500
　Strongsville (G-17351)
Warwick Communications Inc...............E......216 787-0300
　Broadview Heights (G-1850)

ELECTRICAL GOODS, WHOLESALE: Vacuum Cleaners, Household

Royal Appliance Mfg Co...................C......440 996-2000
　Cleveland (G-6344)

ELECTRICAL GOODS, WHOLESALE: Washing Machines

Whirlpool Corporation....................D......419 423-6097
　Findlay (G-10975)
Whirlpool Corporation....................C......740 383-7122
　Marion (G-13473)

ELECTRICAL GOODS, WHOLESALE: Wire & Cable

Afc Cable Systems Inc....................D......740 435-3340
　Cambridge (G-2047)
Anixter Inc..............................E......513 881-4600
　West Chester (G-18868)
Associated Mtls Holdings LLC.............A......330 929-1811
　Cuyahoga Falls (G-9072)
Calvert Wire & Cable Corp................E......216 433-7600
　Cleveland (G-5115)
Multilink Inc............................C......440 366-6966
　Elyria (G-10540)
Nimers & Woody II Inc....................D......937 898-2060
　Vandalia (G-18533)
Noco Company.............................B......216 464-8131
　Solon (G-16879)
Scott Fetzer Company.....................C......216 267-9000
　Cleveland (G-6379)
Sumitomo Elc Wirg Systems Inc............E......937 642-7579
　Marysville (G-13531)

ELECTRICAL GOODS, WHOLESALE: Wire & Cable, Ctrl & Sig

Signature Control Systems LLC............E......614 864-2222
　Columbus (G-8639)
Winkle Industries Inc....................D......330 823-9730
　Alliance (G-557)

ELECTRICAL GOODS, WHOLESALE: Wire & Cable, Electronic

Iewc Corp................................E......440 835-5601
　Westlake (G-19356)
TPC Wire & Cable Corp....................D......800 521-7935
　Macedonia (G-13085)

ELECTRICAL HOUSEHOLD APPLIANCE REPAIR

Alco-Chem Inc............................E......330 833-8551
　Canton (G-2177)
Central Repair Service Inc...............E......513 943-0500
　Point Pleasant (G-16078)
Household Centralized Svc Inc............E......419 474-5754
　Toledo (G-17809)

ELECTRICAL MEASURING INSTRUMENT REPAIR & CALIBRATION SVCS

Instrmntation Ctrl Systems Inc...........E......513 662-2600
　Cincinnati (G-3765)
Tegam Inc................................E......440 466-6100
　Geneva (G-11246)

ELECTRICAL SPLYS

Accurate Mechanical Inc..................E......740 681-1332
　Lancaster (G-12368)
Consolidated Elec Distrs Inc.............E......614 445-8871
　Columbus (G-7351)
Dickman Supply Inc.......................D......937 492-6166
　Sidney (G-16774)
Edison Equipment.........................E......614 883-5710
　Columbus (G-7501)
Fenton Bros Electric Co..................E......330 343-0093
　New Philadelphia (G-14959)
Furbay Electric Supply Co................E......330 454-3033
　Canton (G-2319)
Graybar Electric Company Inc.............E......216 573-6144
　Cleveland (G-5625)
Graybar Electric Company Inc.............D......513 719-7400
　Cincinnati (G-3637)
Graybar Electric Company Inc.............E......614 486-4391
　Columbus (G-7688)
Graybar Electric Company Inc.............E......330 799-3220
　Youngstown (G-20053)
Gross Electric Inc.......................E......419 537-1818
　Toledo (G-17773)
H Leff Electric Company..................C......216 325-0941
　Cleveland (G-5651)
John A Becker Co.........................D......513 771-2550
　Cincinnati (G-3822)
John A Becker Co.........................E......614 272-8800
　Columbus (G-7861)
Loeb Electric Company....................D......614 294-6351
　Columbus (G-7987)
Mars Electric Company....................D......440 946-2250
　Cleveland (G-5913)
McNaughton-Mckay Elc Ohio Inc............D......614 476-2800
　Columbus (G-8046)
McNaughton-Mckay Elc Ohio Inc............E......419 422-2984
　Findlay (G-10941)
McNaughton-Mckay Elc Ohio Inc............E......419 891-0262
　Maumee (G-13820)
Noland Company...........................C......937 396-7980
　Moraine (G-14684)
Rexel Usa Inc............................E......216 778-6400
　Cleveland (G-6318)
Rexel Usa Inc............................D......440 248-3800
　Solon (G-16892)
Rexel Usa Inc............................E......419 625-6761
　Sandusky (G-16636)
Rexel Usa Inc............................E......614 771-7373
　Hilliard (G-11812)
Richards Electric Sup Co Inc.............C......513 242-8800
　Cincinnati (G-4370)
Sabroske Electric Inc....................E......419 332-6444
　Fremont (G-11092)
Schneider Electric Usa Inc...............E......440 526-9070
　Richfield (G-16378)
Wesco Distribution Inc...................E......216 741-0441
　Cleveland (G-6665)
Wolff Bros Supply Inc....................E......330 264-5900
　Wooster (G-19784)

ELECTRODES: Thermal & Electrolytic

De Nora Tech LLC.........................D......440 710-5300
　Painesville (G-15708)
Graphel Corporation......................C......513 779-6166
　West Chester (G-18934)

ELECTROMEDICAL EQPT

Viewray Technologies Inc.................D......440 703-3210
　Oakwood Village (G-15496)

ELECTROMETALLURGICAL PRDTS

Rhenium Alloys Inc.......................D......440 365-7388
　North Ridgeville (G-15340)

ELECTRONIC EQPT REPAIR SVCS

Automation & Control Tech Ltd............E......419 661-6400
　Perrysburg (G-15834)
Electric Service Co Inc..................E......513 271-6387
　Cincinnati (G-3487)

S
E
R
V
I
C
E
S

Ohio State University.................................A 614 292-6158
Columbus (G-8352)

Sage Sustainable Elec LLC.................E 844 472-4373
Columbus (G-8581)

Vertiv Corporation.................................D 614 841-6104
Columbus (G-8848)

Vertiv Corporation.................................A 614 888-0246
Columbus (G-8847)

ELECTRONIC PARTS & EQPT WHOLESALERS

21st Century Solutions Ltd ....E 877 439-5377
Miamisburg (G-14134)

Access Catalog Company LLC..........E 440 572-5377
Strongsville (G-17279)

Agilysys Inc ....E 440 519-6262
Solon (G-16816)

Cincinnati Voice and Data.................D 513 683-4127
Loveland (G-12983)

Cornerstone Controls Inc ....E 937 263-6429
Dayton (G-9322)

DSI Systems Inc ....E 614 871-1456
Grove City (G-11429)

Exonic Systems LLC ....E 330 315-3100
Akron (G-207)

Fox International Limited Inc ....E 216 454-1001
Beachwood (G-1058)

Graybar Electric Company Inc ....E 216 573-6144
Cleveland (G-5625)

Hughes Corporation ....E 440 238-2550
Strongsville (G-17313)

Keithley Instruments Intl Corp..........B 440 248-0400
Cleveland (G-5819)

Mark Feldstein & Assoc Inc ....E 419 867-9500
Sylvania (G-17437)

McM Electronics Inc ....D 888 235-4692
Centerville (G-2630)

Mega Techway Inc..............................C 440 605-0700
Cleveland (G-5947)

Mobilcomm Inc ....D 513 742-5555
Cincinnati (G-4066)

Pepperl + Fuchs Inc ....C 330 425-3555
Twinsburg (G-18302)

RPC Electronics Inc ....E 440 461-4700
Highland Heights (G-11736)

Standex Electronics Inc ....D 513 871-3777
Cincinnati (G-4534)

Western Tradewinds Inc ....E 937 859-4300
Miamisburg (G-14238)

Wholesale House Inc ....D 419 542-1315
Hicksville (G-11731)

ELECTRONIC SHOPPING

Ampersand Group LLC ....E 330 379-0044
Akron (G-73)

E Retailing Associates LLC ....D 614 300-5785
Columbus (G-7486)

Midwest Tape LLC...............................B 419 868-9370
Holland (G-11898)

ELEMENTARY & SECONDARY PRIVATE DENOMINATIONAL SCHOOLS

Catholic Diocese of Columbus ....D 614 276-5263
Columbus (G-7138)

Joseph and Florence Mandel...............D 216 464-4055
Beachwood (G-1070)

Our Lady of Bethlehem Schools ....E 614 459-8285
Columbus (G-8404)

Saint Cecilia Church ....E 614 878-5353
Columbus (G-8583)

ELEMENTARY & SECONDARY SCHOOLS, COMBINED CATHOLIC

Troy Christian School ....D 937 339-5692
Troy (G-18233)

ELEMENTARY & SECONDARY SCHOOLS, PRIVATE NEC

Christian Heartland School ....C 330 482-2331
Columbiana (G-6783)

Christian Perry Pre School ....E 330 477-7262
Canton (G-2252)

Christian Wooster School ....E 330 345-6436
Wooster (G-19701)

Fairmount Montessori Assn ....E 216 321-7571
Cleveland (G-5505)

First Apostolic Church ....E 419 885-4888
Toledo (G-17738)

Jewish Day Schl Assoc Grtr Clv............D 216 763-1400
Pepper Pike (G-15819)

New Hope Christian Academy ....E 740 477-6427
Circleville (G-4838)

Nightingale Montessori Inc ....E 937 324-0336
Springfield (G-17089)

Ruffing Montessori School ....E 440 333-2250
Rocky River (G-16445)

Seton Catholic School Hudson ....E 330 342-4200
Hudson (G-12005)

Zion Christian School ....E 330 792-4066
Youngstown (G-20271)

ELEMENTARY & SECONDARY SCHOOLS, PUBLIC

Boardman Local Schools ....D 330 726-3409
Youngstown (G-19969)

Brunswick City Schools ....A 330 225-7731
Brunswick (G-1921)

Clermont North East School Dst ....E 513 625-8283
Batavia (G-990)

Cleveland Municipal School Dst ....B 216 838-0000
Cleveland (G-5276)

Cleveland Municipal School Dst ....E 216 838-8700
Cleveland (G-5277)

Dover City Schools ....D 330 343-8880
Dover (G-10073)

Independence Local Schools ....E 216 642-5865
Independence (G-12083)

Kettering City School District...............D 937 499-1770
Dayton (G-9538)

Lakewood City School District ....E 216 529-4400
Lakewood (G-12352)

Madison Local School District ....B 419 589-2600
Mansfield (G-13201)

Montpelier Exempted Vlg Schl ....D 419 485-3676
Montpelier (G-14615)

Northwest Local School Dst ....D 513 923-1000
Cincinnati (G-4131)

St Marys City Board Education ....E 419 394-1116
Saint Marys (G-16532)

St Marys City Board Education ....D 419 394-2616
Saint Marys (G-16533)

Sycamore Board of Education...............D 513 489-3937
Cincinnati (G-4560)

ELEMENTARY & SECONDARY SCHOOLS, SPECIAL EDUCATION

Ashtabula Cnty Eductl Svc Ctr ....D 440 576-4085
Ashtabula (G-709)

Brown Co Ed Service Center ....D 937 378-6118
Georgetown (G-11263)

Positive Education Program ....E 216 227-2730
Cleveland (G-6223)

Positive Education Program ....E 440 471-8200
Cleveland (G-6224)

ELEMENTARY SCHOOLS, CATHOLIC

Cardinal Pacelli School ....B 513 321-1048
Cincinnati (G-3117)

St Patrick Church Inc...........................E 937 335-2833
Troy (G-18229)

St Pauls Catholic Church ....E 330 724-1263
Akron (G-439)

ELEMENTARY SCHOOLS, PRIVATE

Canton Country Day School ....E 330 453-8279
Canton (G-2231)

Discovery School.................................E 419 756-8880
Mansfield (G-13169)

Hudson Montessori Association ....E 330 650-0424
Hudson (G-11983)

Lillian and Betty Ratner Schl ....E 216 464-0033
Cleveland (G-5870)

New School Inc ....E 513 281-7999
Cincinnati (G-4108)

Old Trail School.................................D 330 666-1118
Bath (G-1018)

Samkel Inc ....E 614 491-3270
Columbus (G-8589)

West Side Montessori...........................D 419 866-1931
Toledo (G-18154)

ELEMENTARY SCHOOLS, PUBLIC

Bay Village City School Dst ....E 440 617-7330
Cleveland (G-5043)

Columbus Public School Dst ....E 614 365-5456
Columbus (G-7306)

Delaware City School District ....E 740 363-5901
Delaware (G-9967)

Kettering City School District ....D 937 297-1990
Dayton (G-9537)

Lima City School District ....E 419 996-3450
Lima (G-12676)

Lincolnview Local Schools ....C 419 968-2226
Van Wert (G-18483)

Logan-Hocking School District ....E 740 385-7844
Logan (G-12848)

Upper Arlington City Schl Dst ....E 614 487-5133
Columbus (G-8824)

ELEVATOR: Grain, Storage Only

Consolidated Grain & Barge Co ....E 513 941-4805
Cincinnati (G-3351)

Consolidated Grain & Barge Co ....D 419 785-1941
Defiance (G-9907)

Deerfield Farms Service Inc ....D 330 584-4715
Deerfield (G-9904)

ELEVATORS & EQPT

Otis Elevator Company ....D 216 573-2333
Cleveland (G-6147)

Schindler Elevator Corporation ....E 419 861-5900
Holland (G-11912)

ELEVATORS WHOLESALERS

Otis Elevator Company ....E 614 777-6500
Columbus (G-8402)

Schindler Elevator Corporation ....E 614 573-2777
Columbus (G-8599)

Thyssenkrupp Elevator Corp ....E 440 717-0080
Broadview Heights (G-1848)

Thyssenkrupp Elevator Corp ....D 513 241-0222
Cincinnati (G-4608)

Thyssenkrupp Elevator Corp ....E 614 895-8930
Westerville (G-19302)

Wurtec Incorporated ....D 419 726-1066
Toledo (G-18164)

ELEVATORS: Automobile

Dasher Lawless Automation LLC.........E 855 755-7275
Warren (G-18699)

ELEVATORS: Installation & Conversion

Otis Elevator Company ....D 513 531-7888
Cincinnati (G-4190)

Otis Elevator Company ....D 216 573-2333
Cleveland (G-6147)

Thyssenkrupp Elevator Corp ....E 513 241-6000
Cincinnati (G-4609)

Thyssenkrupp Elevator Corp ....E 614 895-8930
Westerville (G-19302)

EMBROIDERING & ART NEEDLEWORK FOR THE TRADE

McCc Sportswear Inc...........................E 513 583-9210
West Chester (G-19065)

EMBROIDERING SVC

Zimmer Enterprises Inc........................E 937 428-1057
Dayton (G-9899)

EMBROIDERY ADVERTISING SVCS

Evolution Crtive Solutions LLC ....E 513 681-4450
Cincinnati (G-3523)

Screen Works Inc................................E 937 264-9111
Dayton (G-9754)

EMERGENCY & RELIEF SVCS

Altruism Society Inc ....D 877 283-4001
Beachwood (G-1028)

American National Red Cross ....E 330 535-6131
Akron (G-70)

American National Red Cross ....E 614 436-3862
Lewis Center (G-12523)

American National Red Cross ....E 614 473-3783
Gahanna (G-11109)

American National Red Cross ....E 800 448-3543
Columbus (G-6932)

American National Red Cross ....E 740 344-2510
Newark (G-15010)

American National Red Cross ....E 419 524-0311
Mansfield (G-13136)

Ansonia Area Emergency Service ....E 937 337-2651
Ansonia (G-612)

Cgh-Global Emerg Mngmt Strateg ....E 800 376-0655
Cincinnati (G-2843)

Community Ems District ....E 330 527-4100
Garrettsville (G-11229)

Counseling Center Huron County ....E 419 663-3737
Norwalk (G-15430)

County of Holmes ....E 330 674-1926
Millersburg (G-14467)

County of Mercer ....E 419 678-8071
Coldwater (G-6757)

Firelands Regional Health Sys ....E 419 663-3737
Norwalk (G-15435)

Mercy Health..A 440 233-1000
Lorain (G-12926)

Oriana House Inc ....D 330 996-7730
Akron (G-367)

Saline Township ....E 330 532-2195
Hammondsville (G-11657)

Trumball Cnty Fire Chiefs Assn ....D 330 675-6602
Warren (G-18753)

EMERGENCY SHELTERS

Battered Womens Shelter ....E 330 723-3900
Medina (G-13912)

Battered Womens Shelter ....D 330 374-0740
Akron (G-88)

Beatitude House ....E 440 992-0265
Ashtabula (G-722)

Choices For Vctims Dom Volence.........E 614 224-6617
Worthington (G-19798)

Domestic Violence Project Inc ....E 330 445-2000
Canton (G-2289)

Faith Mission Inc ....E 614 224-6617
Columbus (G-7557)

Harbor House Inc ....E 740 498-7213
New Philadelphia (G-14960)

Homefull..D 937 293-1945
Dayton (G-9503)

Light of Hearts Villa ....D 440 232-1991
Cleveland (G-5869)

Tender Mercies Inc...............................D 513 721-8666
Cincinnati (G-4585)

Tri County Help Center Inc....................E 740 695-5441
Saint Clairsville (G-16507)

Young Womens Christian ....D 419 241-3235
Toledo (G-18172)

EMPLOYEE LEASING SVCS

Cbiz Inc ....C 216 447-9000
Cleveland (G-5139)

Columbiana Service Company LLC ....D 330 482-5511
Columbiana (G-6785)

D C Transportation Service....................C 440 237-0900
North Royalton (G-15351)

Focus Solutions Inc..............................C 513 376-8349
Cincinnati (G-3575)

Hr Services Inc....................................E 419 224-2462
Lima (G-12660)

Innovtive Sltons Unlimited LLC ....E 740 289-3282
Piketon (G-15978)

JB Management Inc ....D 419 841-2596
Toledo (G-17829)

Paradigm Industrial LLC ....E 937 224-4415
Dayton (G-9685)

Prueter Enterprises Ltd ....C 419 872-5343
Perrysburg (G-15907)

Sequent Inc..D 614 436-5880
Columbus (G-6836)

Verified Person Inc...............................E 901 767-6121
Independence (G-12136)

EMPLOYMENT AGENCY SVCS

A-1 Healthcare Staffing LLC ....C 216 862-0906
Cleveland (G-4884)

A-1 Healthcare Staffing LLC ....D 216 862-0906
Lakewood (G-12334)

Abilities First Foundation Inc ....D 513 423-9496
Middletown (G-14285)

Alliance Solutions Group LLC ....E 216 503-1690
Independence (G-12044)

Amotec Inc...E 440 250-4600
Cleveland (G-4973)

Aspen Community Living ....C 614 880-6000
Columbus (G-6979)

Atterro Inc...E 800 938-9675
Cincinnati (G-3002)

B & B Employment Resource LLC ....E 513 370-5542
Cincinnati (G-3013)

Blanchard Valley Industries ....D 419 422-6386
Findlay (G-10874)

Cardinalcommerce Corporation ....E 877 352-8444
Mentor (G-14025)

Career Cnnctions Staffing Svcs ....E 440 471-8210
Westlake (G-19326)

Careworks of Ohio Inc ....B 614 792-1085
Dublin (G-10161)

Cleveland Job Corps Center ....E 216 541-2500
Cleveland (G-5264)

Cnsld Humacare- Employee MGT ....E 513 605-3522
Cincinnati (G-3317)

Compass Professional Svcs LLC...........D 216 705-2233
Columbus (G-7339)

Corporate Ladder Search ....E 330 776-4390
Uniontown (G-18364)

County of Guernsey..............................D 740 432-2381
Cambridge (G-2062)

County of Huron ....D 419 668-8126
Norwalk (G-15431)

County of Wayne ....E 330 264-5060
Wooster (G-19716)

Csu/Career Services Center ....E 216 687-2233
Cleveland (G-5386)

Ctpartners Exec Search Inc ....D 216 464-8710
Beachwood (G-1049)

Custom Staffing Inc ....E 419 221-3097
Lima (G-12629)

Damascus Staffing LLC........................D 513 954-8941
Maineville (G-13114)

Dawson Resources................................B 614 274-8900
Columbus (G-7421)

Discover Training Inc............................D 614 871-0010
Grove City (G-11426)

Diversfied Emplyee Sltions Inc.............B 330 764-4125
Medina (G-13932)

E & L Premier Corporation ....C 330 836-9901
Fairlawn (G-10823)

Employbridge Holding Company ....C 419 874-7125
Toledo (G-17713)

Exodus Integrity Service ....D 440 918-0140
Willoughby (G-19522)

First Choice Med Staff of Ohio ....D 419 521-2700
Mansfield (G-13177)

First Choice Medical Staffing................B 216 521-2222
Cleveland (G-5532)

Goodwill Industries Inc ....E 330 724-6995
Akron (G-240)

Greater Dyton Rgnal Trnst Auth ....A 937 425-8400
Dayton (G-9475)

Gus Perdikakis Associates ....D 513 583-0900
Cincinnati (G-3665)

Heitmeyer Group LLC...........................B 614 573-5571
Westerville (G-19171)

HJ Ford Associates Inc ....C 937 429-9711
Beavercreek (G-1155)

Horizon Personnel Resources ....C 440 585-0031
Wickliffe (G-19464)

Horizons Employment Svcs LLC............B 419 254-9644
Toledo (G-17808)

Hospice of Darke County Inc ....E 419 678-4808
Coldwater (G-6759)

Hr Services Inc....................................E 419 224-2462
Lima (G-12660)

Human Resources Services....................E 740 587-3484
Westerville (G-19173)

I-Force LLC..C 614 431-5100
Columbus (G-7796)

Integrity Enterprizes ....E 216 289-8801
Euclid (G-10645)

Its Technologies Inc.............................D 419 842-2100
Holland (G-11890)

Job1usa Inc ....D 419 255-5005
Toledo (G-17831)

Key Career Place ....D 216 987-3029
Cleveland (G-5825)

Kforce Inc ....E 614 436-4027
Columbus (G-7900)

Kilgore Group Inc.................................E 513 684-3721
Cincinnati (G-3868)

Lane Wood Industries ....B 419 352-5059
Bowling Green (G-1739)

Mancan Inc..A 440 884-9675
Strongsville (G-17326)

Mid Ohio Employment Services ....E 419 747-5466
Ontario (G-15564)

Midwest Emergency Services LLC........E 586 294-2700
Fairlawn (G-10841)

Murtech Consulting LLC ....D 216 328-8580
Cleveland (G-6026)

Nurses Heart Med Staffing LLC ....E 614 648-5111
Columbus (G-8217)

Ohio Dept of Job & Fmly Svcs ....D 330 484-5402
Akron (G-357)

Ohio State University ....A 614 293-2494
Columbus (G-8318)

Onestaff Inc ....E 859 815-1345
Cincinnati (G-4175)

Pathway Inc ....E 419 242-7304
Toledo (G-17974)

Pearl Interactive Network Inc ....B 614 258-2943
Columbus (G-8432)

Prn Nurse Inc.......................................B 614 864-9292
Columbus (G-8464)

Professional Data Resources Inc...........C 513 792-5100
Blue Ash (G-1633)

Promedica Physcn Cntinuum Svcs........C 419 824-7200
Sylvania (G-17444)

PSI Associates Inc ....B 330 425-8474
Twinsburg (G-18308)

Randstad Professional Us LP ....E 513 792-6658
Blue Ash (G-1638)

Randstad Technologies LLC..................E 614 436-0961
Columbus (G-6832)

Randstad Technologies LLC..................D 216 520-0206
Independence (G-12111)

Rightthing LLC.....................................B 419 420-1830
Findlay (G-10958)

Rkpl Inc ....D 419 224-2121
Lima (G-12732)

Robert Half International Inc ....E 216 621-4253
Cleveland (G-6332)

Rumpf Corporation ....E 419 255-5005
Toledo (G-18014)

Safegard Bckgrund Screening LLC ....C 216 370-7345
Cleveland (G-6360)

Seifert & Group Inc ....D 330 833-2700
Massillon (G-13727)

Tailored Management Services ....C 614 859-1500
Columbus (G-8729)

Telamon Corporation ....E 937 254-2004
Dayton (G-9809)

Tradesmen Services LLC ....D 440 349-3432
Macedonia (G-13087)

Tradesource Inc ....C 216 801-4944
Parma (G-15778)

Wtw Delaware Holdings LLC ....C 216 937-4000
Cleveland (G-6693)

EMPLOYMENT SVCS: Labor Contractors

Advantage Resourcing Amer Inc ....E 781 472-8900
Cincinnati (G-2912)

Alliance Legal Solutions LLC ....D 216 525-0100
Independence (G-12043)

Belflex Staffing Network LLC................C 513 488-8588
Cincinnati (G-3038)

Construction Labor Contrs LLC ....D 614 932-9937
Columbus (G-7352)

Mj-6 LLC..E 419 517-7725
Toledo (G-17920)

Per Diem Nurse Staffing LLT ....E 419 878-8880
Waterville (G-18791)

Robert Half International Inc.................D 614 602-0505
Dublin (G-10324)

Staffmark Investment LLC ....C 513 651-3600
Cincinnati (G-4529)

Stearns Companies LLC ....E 419 422-0241
Findlay (G-10963)

Tradesmen International LLC ....C 419 502-9140
Sandusky (G-16649)

Tradesmen International LLC ....D 513 771-1115
Blue Ash (G-1661)

Tradesmen International LLC ....C 440 349-3432
Macedonia (G-13086)

Tradesource Inc ....C 614 824-3883
Columbus (G-8771)

United Steelworkers ....E 440 244-1358
Lorain (G-12949)

EMPLOYMENT SVCS: Nurses' Registry

A-1 Nursing Care Inc ....C 614 268-3800
Columbus (G-6850)

SERVICES

Accentcare Home Health Cal Inc....C.... 740 387-4568
Circleville (G-4822)
Alternate Solutions First LLC....C.... 937 298-1111
Dayton (G-9223)
Assured Health Care Inc....E.... 937 294-2803
Dayton (G-9242)
Blanchard Valley Health System....D.... 419 424-3000
Findlay (G-10872)
Carestar Inc....C.... 513 618-8300
Cincinnati (G-3122)
Childrens Home Care Dayton....D.... 937 641-4663
Dayton (G-9296)
Collier Nursing Service Inc....C.... 513 791-4357
Montgomery (G-14594)
Community Hlth Prfssionals Inc....C.... 419 238-9223
Van Wert (G-18475)
Community Hlth Prfssionals Inc....D.... 419 586-6266
Celina (G-2590)
Community Home Care....E.... 330 971-7011
Cuyahoga Falls (G-9084)
County of Holmes....E.... 330 674-5035
Millersburg (G-14468)
Dedicated Nursing Assoc Inc....D.... 937 886-4559
Miamisburg (G-14164)
Dedicated Nursing Assoc Inc....E.... 866 450-5550
Cincinnati (G-3415)
Dedicated Nursing Assoc Inc....E.... 877 411-8350
Galloway (G-11219)
Dedicated Nursing Assoc Inc....E.... 877 547-9144
Parma (G-15765)
Dedicated Nursing Assoc Inc....C.... 888 465-6929
Beavercreek (G-1214)
Epilogue Inc....D.... 440 582-5555
North Royalton (G-15355)
Firstat Nursing Services....D.... 216 295-1500
Cleveland (G-5538)
Health Care Plus....C.... 614 340-7587
Westerville (G-19170)
Home Care Network Inc....D.... 937 435-1142
Dayton (G-9498)
Interim Halthcare Columbus Inc....E.... 330 836-5571
Fairlawn (G-10834)
Medi Home Health Agency Inc....E.... 740 266-3977
Steubenville (G-17165)
Medical Solutions LLC....D.... 513 936-3468
Blue Ash (G-1607)
Nurses Care Inc....E.... 513 791-0233
Cincinnati (G-4141)
P E Miller & Assoc....D.... 614 231-4743
Columbus (G-8407)
Personal Touch HM Care IPA Inc....E.... 937 456-4447
Eaton (G-10458)
Private Practice Nurses Inc....E.... 216 481-1305
Cleveland (G-6237)
Prn Health Services Inc....D.... 513 792-2217
Cincinnati (G-4286)
St Ritas Medical Center....C.... 419 538-7025
Lima (G-12751)
Talemed LLC....B.... 513 774-7300
Loveland (G-13031)
Taylors Staffing LLC....D.... 740 446-3305
Pomeroy (G-16098)
Ulrich Professional Group....E.... 330 673-9501
Kent (G-12265)
Vishnia & Associates Inc....D.... 330 929-5512
Cuyahoga Falls (G-9137)

ENGINEERING HELP SVCS

Belcan LLC....A.... 513 985-7777
Blue Ash (G-1509)
Belcan LLC....A.... 513 645-1509
West Chester (G-18875)
Belcan LLC....A.... 513 891-0972
Blue Ash (G-1510)
Belcan LLC....A.... 513 217-4562
Middletown (G-14291)
Belcan LLC....A.... 740 393-8888
Mount Vernon (G-14749)
Belcan LLC....D.... 513 891-0972
Solon (G-16827)
Belcan Corporation....A.... 614 224-6080
Columbus (G-7026)
Belcan Svcs Group Ltd Partnr....C.... 513 891-0972
Blue Ash (G-1512)
Belcan Svcs Group Ltd Partnr....D.... 937 859-8880
Miamisburg (G-14144)
Prestige Technical Svcs Inc....E.... 513 779-6800
West Chester (G-18985)
Top Echelon Contracting Inc....B.... 330 454-3508
Canton (G-2514)

ENGINEERING SVCS

7nt Enterprises LLC....E.... 614 961-2026
Miamisburg (G-14135)
Adaptive Corporation....E.... 440 257-7460
Hudson (G-11961)
Advantage Aerotech Inc....E.... 614 759-8329
Columbus (G-6875)
Aecom Energy & Cnstr Inc....D.... 216 523-5600
Cleveland (G-4909)
Airgas Usa LLC....C.... 440 232-1590
Cleveland (G-4921)
Alfons Haar Inc....E.... 937 560-2031
Springboro (G-16961)
American Electric Pwr Svc Corp....B.... 614 716-1000
Columbus (G-6919)
American Rock Mechanics Inc....E.... 330 963-0550
Twinsburg (G-18243)
Aptim Corp....E.... 513 782-4700
Cincinnati (G-2977)
Aptiv Services Us LLC....B.... 330 373-7666
Warren (G-18667)
Austin Building and Design Inc....C.... 440 544-2600
Cleveland (G-5023)
B&N Coal Inc....D.... 740 783-3575
Dexter City (G-10059)
Belcan LLC....A.... 513 891-0972
Blue Ash (G-1510)
Belcan Corporation....C.... 513 277-3100
Cincinnati (G-3037)
Belcan Engineering Group LLC....A.... 513 891-0972
Blue Ash (G-1511)
Bendix Coml Vhcl Systems LLC....B.... 440 329-9000
Elyria (G-10482)
BHF Incorporated....E.... 740 945-6410
Scio (G-16662)
Booz Allen Hamilton Inc....E.... 937 429-5580
Beavercreek (G-1134)
Boral Resources LLC....D.... 740 622-8042
Coshocton (G-8999)
Bowen Engineering Corporation....C.... 614 536-0273
Columbus (G-7055)
Brewer-Garrett Co....C.... 440 243-3535
Middleburg Heights (G-14248)
Butler County of Ohio....D.... 513 867-5744
Hamilton (G-11569)
Cbre Heery Inc....E.... 216 781-1313
Cleveland (G-5143)
Circle Prime Manufacturing....E.... 330 923-0019
Cuyahoga Falls (G-9079)
City of Akron....D.... 330 375-2355
Akron (G-136)
City of Delphos....E.... 419 695-4010
Delphos (G-10021)
City of Sandusky....D.... 419 627-5829
Sandusky (G-16584)
City of Toledo....D.... 419 936-2275
Toledo (G-17660)
Coal Services Inc....D.... 740 795-5220
Powhatan Point (G-16214)
Corrpro Companies Inc....E.... 330 723-5082
Medina (G-13924)
County Engineers Office....E.... 740 702-3130
Chillicothe (G-2771)
County of Brown....E.... 937 378-6456
Georgetown (G-11267)
County of Coshocton....E.... 740 622-2135
Coshocton (G-9011)
County of Crawford....E.... 419 562-7731
Bucyrus (G-1987)
County of Delaware....D.... 740 833-2400
Delaware (G-9963)
County of Erie....E.... 419 627-7710
Sandusky (G-16596)
County of Fayette....E.... 740 335-1541
Wshngtn CT Hs (G-19866)
County of Fulton....E.... 419 335-3816
Wauseon (G-18797)
County of Gallia....E.... 740 446-4009
Gallipolis (G-11189)
County of Lorain....E.... 440 326-5884
Elyria (G-10497)
County of Lucas....D.... 419 213-2892
Holland (G-11879)
County of Madison....E.... 740 852-9404
London (G-12863)
County of Montgomery....D.... 937 854-4576
Dayton (G-9327)
County of Perry....E.... 740 342-2191
New Lexington (G-14919)
County of Portage....D.... 330 296-6411
Ravenna (G-16238)
County of Richland....E.... 419 774-5591
Mansfield (G-13158)
County of Stark....C.... 330 477-6781
Canton (G-2269)
County of Summit....C.... 330 643-2850
Akron (G-164)
County of Union....E.... 937 645-3018
Marysville (G-13490)
County of Washington....E.... 740 376-7430
Marietta (G-13321)
CTI Engineers Inc....D.... 330 294-5996
Akron (G-176)
Custom Materials Inc....D.... 440 543-8284
Chagrin Falls (G-2663)
Cuyahoga County....A.... 216 348-3800
Cleveland (G-5396)
Design Knowledge Company....D.... 937 320-9244
Beavercreek (G-1147)
Dizer Corp....E.... 440 368-0200
Painesville (G-15709)
Dkmp Consulting Inc....C.... 614 733-0979
Plain City (G-16049)
Dlhbowles Inc....B.... 330 478-2503
Canton (G-2288)
Dlr Group Inc....D.... 216 522-1350
Cleveland (G-5433)
Dlz Construction Services Inc....E.... 614 888-0040
Columbus (G-7460)
Donald E Didion II....E.... 419 483-2226
Bellevue (G-1376)
Earl Twinam....E.... 740 820-2654
Portsmouth (G-16137)
Early Construction Co....E.... 740 894-5150
South Point (G-16933)
Elevar Design Group Inc....E.... 513 721-0600
Cincinnati (G-3490)
Emh Inc....E.... 330 220-8600
Valley City (G-18462)
Enprotech Industrial Tech LLC....C.... 216 883-3220
Cleveland (G-5482)
Equity Engineering Group Inc....D.... 216 283-9519
Shaker Heights (G-16708)
Fed/Matrix A Joint Venture LLC....E.... 863 665-6363
Dayton (G-9429)
Fishel Company....D.... 614 850-4400
Columbus (G-7590)
Fishel Company....D.... 614 274-8100
Columbus (G-7588)
Futura Design Service Inc....E.... 937 890-5252
Dayton (G-9453)
Garmann/Miller & Assoc Inc....E.... 419 628-4240
Minster (G-14533)
GE Aviation Systems LLC....D.... 937 474-9397
Dayton (G-9456)
General Electric Intl Inc....C.... 617 443-3000
Cincinnati (G-3614)
Greene County....E.... 937 562-7500
Xenia (G-19903)
Gus Perdikakis Associates....D.... 513 583-0900
Cincinnati (G-3665)
HDR Engineering Inc....E.... 614 839-5770
Columbus (G-7722)
Hokuto USA Inc....E.... 614 782-6200
Grove City (G-11442)
Hunter Defense Tech Inc....E.... 216 438-6111
Solon (G-16859)
Hydro-Dyne Inc....E.... 330 832-5076
Massillon (G-13696)
Icr Inc....D.... 513 900-7007
Mason (G-13596)
Infoscitex Corporation....E.... 937 429-9008
Beavercreek Township (G-1249)
Innovative Controls Corp....D.... 419 691-6684
Toledo (G-17821)
Innovtive Sltons Unlimited LLC....D.... 740 289-3282
Piketon (G-15979)
Interbrand Design Forum LLC....C.... 513 421-2210
Cincinnati (G-3777)
Jacobs Constructors Inc....D.... 419 226-1344
Lima (G-12667)
Jdi Group Inc....D.... 419 725-7161
Maumee (G-13805)
Jjr Solutions LLC....E.... 937 912-0288
Beavercreek (G-1159)
Jobes Henderson & Assoc Inc....E.... 740 344-5451
Newark (G-15045)
K&K Technical Group Inc....C.... 513 202-1300
Harrison (G-11672)

Kendall Holdings Ltd...............E...... 614 486-4750
  Columbus (G-7891)
Kenexis Consulting Corporation..........E...... 614 451-7031
  Upper Arlington (G-18400)
Keyw Corporation ....E...... 937 702-9512
  Beavercreek (G-1162)
Knox County Engineer ....E...... 740 397-1590
  Mount Vernon (G-14774)
KZF Bwsc Joint Venture ....E...... 513 621-6211
  Cincinnati (G-3897)
KZF Design Inc...............D...... 513 621-6211
  Cincinnati (G-3898)
L3 Aviation Products Inc ....E...... 614 825-2001
  Columbus (G-7938)
Logan County Engineering Off...............E...... 937 592-2791
  Bellefontaine (G-1355)
Mahoning County...............C...... 330 799-1581
  Youngstown (G-20106)
Manufacturing Services Intl ....E...... 937 299-9922
  Dayton (G-9583)
Matrix Research Inc ....D...... 937 427-8433
  Beavercreek (G-1230)
Matrix Technologies Inc ....D...... 419 897-7200
  Maumee (G-13816)
Micro Industries Corporation...............D...... 740 548-7878
  Westerville (G-19279)
Mistras Group Inc ....D...... 330 244-1541
  Canton (G-2407)
Mkc Associates Inc ....E...... 740 657-3202
  Powell (G-16203)
Modal Shop Inc ....D...... 513 351-9919
  Cincinnati (G-4067)
Moody-Nolan Inc...............C...... 614 461-4664
  Columbus (G-8101)
Muskingum County Ohio ....E...... 740 453-0381
  Zanesville (G-20337)
Neteam Systems LLC ....E...... 330 523-5100
  Cleveland (G-6058)
New Path International LLC ....E...... 614 410-3974
  Powell (G-16204)
Northrop Grumman Technical ....C...... 937 320-3100
  Beavercreek Township (G-1255)
Ohio Blow Pipe Company ....E...... 216 681-7379
  Cleveland (G-6116)
Ohio Structures Inc...............E...... 330 533-0084
  Canfield (G-2154)
Onyx Creative Inc...............D...... 216 223-3200
  Cleveland (G-6137)
Peco II Inc ....D...... 614 431-0694
  Columbus (G-8433)
Pmwi LLC...............D...... 614 975-5004
  Hilliard (G-11806)
Polaris Automation Inc...............D...... 614 431-0170
  Lewis Center (G-12560)
Providence Rees Inc ....E...... 614 833-6231
  Columbus (G-8474)
Racaza International LLC ....E...... 614 973-9266
  Dublin (G-10317)
RAD-Con Inc...............E...... 440 871-5720
  Lakewood (G-12361)
Safran Power Usa LLC ....C...... 330 487-2000
  Twinsburg (G-18316)
Seifert & Group Inc ....D...... 330 833-2700
  Massillon (G-13727)
Sgi Matrix LLC...............D...... 937 438-9033
  Miamisburg (G-14219)
Slick Automated Solutions Inc ....E...... 567 247-1080
  Ontario (G-15573)
Society Plastics Engineers Inc ....C...... 419 287-4898
  Pemberville (G-15807)
Stantec Arch & Engrg PC ....E...... 216 454-2150
  Cleveland (G-6451)
Stantec Arch & Engrg PC ....E...... 614 486-4383
  Columbus (G-8683)
Stantec Architecture Inc ....E...... 216 454-2150
  Cleveland (G-6453)
Stantec Consulting Svcs Inc ....E...... 216 454-2150
  Cleveland (G-6454)
Stantec Consulting Svcs Inc ....D...... 513 842-8200
  Cincinnati (G-4537)
Stantec Consulting Svcs Inc ....C...... 614 486-4383
  Columbus (G-8684)
Sumitomo Elc Wirg Systems Inc ....E...... 937 642-7579
  Marysville (G-13532)
Sunpower Inc ....D...... 740 594-2221
  Athens (G-804)
Superior Mechanical Svcs Inc ....E...... 937 259-0082
  Dayton (G-9187)
Technical Assurance Inc ....E...... 440 953-3147
  Willoughby (G-19575)

Telecom Expertise Inds Inc...............D...... 937 548-5254
  Greenville (G-11397)
Thermal Treatment Center Inc ....E...... 216 881-8100
  Cleveland (G-6521)
Transcore Its LLC...............E...... 440 243-2222
  Cleveland (G-6541)
Triad Engineering & Contg Co ....E...... 440 786-1000
  Cleveland (G-6548)
Trumbull County Engineering ....D...... 330 675-2640
  Warren (G-18755)
Tsi Inc...............E...... 419 468-1855
  Galion (G-11184)
Turnkey Network Solutions LLC...............E...... 614 876-9944
  Columbus (G-8789)
U S Army Corps of Engineers...............D...... 740 269-2681
  Uhrichsville (G-18345)
U S Army Corps of Engineers...............D...... 740 767-3527
  Glouster (G-11311)
U S Army Corps of Engineers...............D...... 513 684-3048
  Cincinnati (G-4660)
Universal Technology Corp ....D...... 937 426-2808
  Beavercreek (G-1193)
University of Akron ....D...... 330 972-6008
  Akron (G-479)
University of Cincinnati ....D...... 513 556-3732
  Cincinnati (G-4717)
URS Group Inc ....D...... 216 622-2300
  Cleveland (G-6609)
URS Group Inc ....C...... 614 464-4500
  Columbus (G-8831)
URS Group Inc ....D...... 513 651-3440
  Cincinnati (G-4737)
URS-Smith Group VA Idiq Joint ....E...... 614 464-4500
  Columbus (G-8832)
US Tech Arospc Engrg Corp ....D...... 330 455-1181
  Canton (G-2524)
Wastren Advantage Inc ....E...... 970 254-1277
  Piketon (G-15993)
Weastec Incorporated ....E...... 614 734-9645
  Dublin (G-10371)
Wilkris Company ....E...... 513 271-9344
  Terrace Park (G-17501)

ENGINEERING SVCS: Acoustical

L&T Technology Services Ltd...............E...... 732 688-4402
  Dublin (G-10266)
Straight 72 Inc ....D...... 740 943-5730
  Marysville (G-13530)

ENGINEERING SVCS: Aviation Or Aeronautical

Argus International Inc...............E...... 513 852-5110
  Cincinnati (G-2986)
GE Aviation Systems LLC...............B...... 937 898-5881
  Vandalia (G-18524)
Jacobs Technology Inc ....E...... 937 429-5056
  Beavercreek Township (G-1250)
Optis Solutions ....E...... 513 948-2070
  Cincinnati (G-4178)
Quest Global Services-Na Inc...............D...... 860 787-1600
  Cincinnati (G-4328)
Reps Resource LLC...............E...... 513 874-0500
  West Chester (G-18991)
Vantage Partners LLC...............E...... 216 925-1302
  Brookpark (G-1908)

ENGINEERING SVCS: Civil

Barr Engineering Incorporated...............E...... 614 714-0299
  Columbus (G-7019)
Bayer & Becker Inc ....E...... 513 492-7401
  Mason (G-13545)
Bramhall Engrg & Surveying Co ....E...... 440 934-7878
  Avon (G-868)
Brumbaugh Engrg Surveying LLC ....E...... 937 698-3000
  West Milton (G-19126)
Ceso Inc ....D...... 937 435-8584
  Miamisburg (G-14150)
Civil & Environmental Cons Inc...............E...... 513 985-0226
  Milford (G-14380)
County Engineering Office ....E...... 419 334-9731
  Fremont (G-11064)
County of Hamilton ....D...... 513 946-4250
  Cincinnati (G-3371)
CT Consultants Inc ....C...... 440 951-9000
  Mentor (G-14038)
Design Homes & Development Co ....E...... 937 438-3667
  Dayton (G-9389)
Dj Neff Enterprises Inc ....E...... 440 884-3100
  Cleveland (G-5432)

Dynamix Engineering Ltd...............D...... 614 443-1178
  Columbus (G-7482)
Dynotec Inc...............E...... 614 880-7320
  Columbus (G-7483)
E P Ferris & Associates Inc ....E...... 614 299-2999
  Columbus (G-7485)
Engineering Associates Inc ....E...... 330 345-6556
  Wooster (G-19722)
Euthenics Inc...............D...... 440 260-1555
  Strongsville (G-17302)
Feller Finch & Associates Inc ....E...... 419 893-3680
  Maumee (G-13791)
Hockaden & Associates Inc ....E...... 614 252-0993
  Columbus (G-7757)
Jack A Hamilton & Assoc Inc ....E...... 740 968-4947
  Flushing (G-10980)
Johnson Mirmiran Thompson Inc ....E...... 614 714-0270
  Columbus (G-7863)
Johnson Mirmiran Thompson Inc ....E...... 614 714-0270
  Blue Ash (G-1590)
Johnson Mirmiran Thompson Inc ....E...... 614 714-0270
  Cleveland (G-5801)
Kleingers Group Inc...............E...... 614 882-4311
  Westerville (G-19177)
KS Associates Inc ....D...... 440 365-4730
  Elyria (G-10523)
Land Design Consultants...............E...... 440 255-8463
  Mentor (G-14075)
Michael Baker Intl Inc ....C...... 330 453-3110
  Canton (G-2402)
Michael Baker Intl Inc ....E...... 412 269-6300
  Cleveland (G-5976)
Natural Resources Ohio Dept ....E...... 614 265-6948
  Columbus (G-8162)
Northast Ohio Rgonal Sewer Dst ....D...... 216 961-2187
  Cleveland (G-6083)
Pollock Research & Design Inc ....E...... 330 332-3300
  Salem (G-16554)
Prime Ae Group Inc ....D...... 614 839-0250
  Columbus (G-6831)
Ra Consultants LLC...............E...... 513 469-6600
  Blue Ash (G-1635)
Richard L Bowen & Assoc Inc ....D...... 216 491-9300
  Cleveland (G-6321)
Sands Decker Cps Llc ....E...... 614 459-6992
  Columbus (G-8590)
Schomer Glaus Pyle ....E...... 216 518-5544
  Cleveland (G-6376)
T J Neff Holdings Inc ....E...... 440 884-3100
  Cleveland (G-6494)
Wade Trim ....E...... 216 363-0300
  Cleveland (G-6648)
Woolpert Inc ....E...... 614 476-6000
  Columbus (G-8915)

ENGINEERING SVCS: Construction & Civil

Intren Inc...............E...... 815 482-0651
  Cincinnati (G-3784)

ENGINEERING SVCS: Electrical Or Electronic

Acpi Systems Inc ....E...... 513 738-3840
  Hamilton (G-11554)
Camgen Ltd ....E...... 330 204-8636
  Canal Winchester (G-2105)
Denmark Consultants Inc...............E...... 513 530-9984
  Cincinnati (G-3422)
Electrol Systems Inc ....E...... 513 942-7777
  Cincinnati (G-3488)
Electrovations Inc ....E...... 330 274-3558
  Aurora (G-826)
Global Military Expert Co ....E...... 800 738-9795
  Beavercreek (G-1219)
High Voltage Maintenance Corp ....E...... 937 278-0811
  Dayton (G-9496)
I T E LLC...............D...... 513 576-6200
  Loveland (G-13000)
Karpinski Engineering Inc...............D...... 216 391-3700
  Cleveland (G-5816)
L-3 Cmmncations Nova Engrg Inc ....C...... 877 282-1168
  Mason (G-13608)
Mid-Ohio Electric Co...............E...... 614 274-8000
  Columbus (G-8076)
Nu Waves Ltd ....D...... 513 360-0800
  Middletown (G-14315)
Peters Tschantz & Assoc Inc ....E...... 330 666-3702
  Akron (G-381)
Phantom Technical Services Inc ....E...... 614 868-9920
  Columbus (G-8444)

PMC Systems Limited ....E 330 538-2268
North Jackson (G-15252)
Pyramid Control Systems Inc ....E 513 679-7400
Cincinnati (G-4307)
Stock Fairfield Corporation ....C 440 543-6000
Chagrin Falls (G-2684)
Thermaltech Engineering Inc ....E 513 561-2271
Cincinnati (G-4599)
TL Industries Inc ....C 419 666-8144
Northwood (G-15410)

ENGINEERING SVCS: Energy conservation

Accelerant Technologies LLC ....D 419 236-8768
Genoa (G-11251)

ENGINEERING SVCS: Fire Protection

Cgh-Global Emerg Mngmt Strateg ...E 800 376-0655
Cincinnati (G-2843)

ENGINEERING SVCS: Heating & Ventilation

Cetek Ltd ....E 216 362-3900
Cleveland (G-5161)
County of Wayne ....D 330 287-5500
Wooster (G-19719)

ENGINEERING SVCS: Industrial

Crowne Group LLC ....D 216 589-0198
Cleveland (G-5383)
HJ Ford Associates Inc ....C 937 429-9711
Beavercreek (G-1155)
Industrial Origami Inc ....E 440 260-0000
Cleveland (G-5748)
Jedson Engineering Inc ....D 513 965-5999
Cincinnati (G-3811)
Los Alamos Technical Assoc Inc ......E 614 508-1200
Westerville (G-19275)
Production Design Services Inc ....D 937 866-3377
Dayton (G-9716)
Technology House Ltd ....E 440 248-3025
Streetsboro (G-17274)

ENGINEERING SVCS: Machine Tool Design

Invotec Engineering Inc ....D 937 886-3232
Miamisburg (G-14177)
Youngstown Plastic Tooling ....E 330 782-7222
Youngstown (G-20265)

ENGINEERING SVCS: Mechanical

Chipmatic Tool & Machine Inc ....D 419 862-2737
Elmore (G-10472)
Dillin Engineered Systems Corp ......E 419 666-6789
Perrysburg (G-15859)
Jdrm Engineering Inc ....E 419 824-2400
Sylvania (G-17432)
Juice Technologies Inc ....E 800 518-5576
Columbus (G-7875)
Karpinski Engineering Inc ....E 614 430-9820
Columbus (G-6821)
Mechanical Support Svcs Inc ....E 614 777-8808
Hilliard (G-11790)
Morris Technologies Inc ....C 513 733-1611
Cincinnati (G-4075)
R E Warner & Associates Inc ....D 440 835-9400
Westlake (G-19395)
Saec/Kinetic Vision Inc ....C 513 793-4959
Cincinnati (G-4422)
Shotstop Ballistics LLC ....E 330 686-0020
Stow (G-17230)
Techsolve Inc ....D 513 948-2000
Cincinnati (G-4581)
Thinkpath Engineering Svcs LLC ......E 937 291-8374
Miamisburg (G-14229)
Twism Enterprises LLC ....E 513 800-1098
Cincinnati (G-4657)

ENGINEERING SVCS: Mining

Kucera International Inc ....D 440 975-4230
Willoughby (G-19536)

ENGINEERING SVCS: Pollution Control

Neundorfer Inc ....E 440 942-8990
Willoughby (G-19555)

ENGINEERING SVCS: Professional

Brown and Caldwell ....E 614 410-6144
Columbus (G-7082)
Capano & Associates LLC ....E 513 403-6000
Liberty Township (G-12578)
Eaton-Aeroquip Llc ....D 419 891-7775
Maumee (G-13782)
Metcalf & Eddy Inc ....E 216 910-2000
Cleveland (G-5963)
Poggemeyer Design Group Inc ....C 419 244-8074
Bowling Green (G-1746)
Primatech Inc ....E 614 841-9800
Columbus (G-8462)
Prisma Integration Corp ....E 330 545-8690
Girard (G-11298)
TEC Engineering Inc ....E 513 771-8828
Mason (G-13644)
Thorson Baker & Assoc Inc ....C 330 659-6688
Richfield (G-16380)
URS Group Inc ....D 330 836-9111
Akron (G-481)
Wheaton & Sprague Engineering ......E 330 923-5560
Stow (G-17239)

ENGINEERING SVCS: Sanitary

Aecom Technical Services Inc ....E 937 233-1898
Batavia (G-982)
Arcadis US Inc ....D 330 434-1995
Akron (G-78)
Atc Group Services LLC ....D 513 771-2112
Cincinnati (G-2996)
Johnson Mirmiran Thompson Inc ......E 614 714-0270
Columbus (G-7864)
Macdonald Mott LLC ....E 216 535-3640
Cleveland (G-5892)
Medina County Sanitary ....E 330 273-3610
Medina (G-13972)

ENGINEERING SVCS: Structural

County of Hancock ....E 419 422-7433
Findlay (G-10893)
Emersion Design LLC ....E 513 841-9100
Cincinnati (G-3494)
RCT Engineering Inc ....E 561 684-7534
Beachwood (G-1099)
Ssoe Inc ....E 330 821-7198
Alliance (G-552)
Steven Schaefer Associates Inc ....D 513 542-3300
Cincinnati (G-4547)
Technical Construction Spc ....E 330 929-1088
Cuyahoga Falls (G-9129)
Thp Limited Inc ....E 513 241-3222
Cincinnati (G-4607)

ENGINES: Internal Combustion, NEC

Cummins Bridgeway Columbus LLC ...D 614 771-1000
Hilliard (G-11758)
Cummins Inc ....E 614 771-1000
Hilliard (G-11759)
Western Branch Diesel Inc ....E 330 454-8800
Canton (G-2534)

ENGRAVING SVCS

Enesco Properties LLC ....A 440 473-2000
Highland Heights (G-11733)

ENTERTAINERS & ENTERTAINMENT GROUPS

Adventure Cmbat Operations LLC ......E 330 818-1029
Canton (G-2175)
Bird Enterprises LLC ....E 330 674-1457
Millersburg (G-14460)
Catholic Diocese of Columbus ....D 614 276-5263
Columbus (G-7138)
Columbus Association For The P ....D 614 469-0939
Columbus (G-7260)
Henrys King Touring Company ....E 330 628-1886
Mogadore (G-14550)
Ingram Entrmt Holdings Inc ....E 419 662-3132
Perrysburg (G-15879)
J S P A Inc ....E 407 957-6664
Columbus (G-7851)
Know Theatre of Cincinnati ....E 513 300-5669
Cincinnati (G-3883)
Muskingum Vly Symphonic Winds ......E 740 826-8095
New Concord (G-14901)

Northeast Ohio Dukes

Northeast Ohio Dukes ....E 330 360-0968
Warren (G-18736)
Philo Band Boosters ....E 740 221-3023
Zanesville (G-20354)
Radio Seaway Inc ....E 216 916-6100
Cleveland (G-6277)
Sliddy Ent LLC ....E 419 376-1797
Toledo (G-18037)

ENTERTAINMENT PROMOTION SVCS

Playhouse Square Foundation ....D 216 771-4444
Cleveland (G-6218)

ENTERTAINMENT SVCS

A To Z Golf Managment Co ....E 937 434-4911
Dayton (G-9200)
Food Concepts Intl Inc ....D 513 336-7449
Mason (G-13579)
Fountain Square MGT Group LLC ......E 513 621-4400
Cincinnati (G-3582)
Rcwc Col Inc ....D 614 564-9344
Columbus (G-8493)
Run Jump-N-Play ....E 513 701-7529
Blue Ash (G-1648)
Zink Calls ....E 419 732-6171
Port Clinton (G-16120)

ENVELOPES

Ampac Holdings LLC ....A 513 671-1777
Cincinnati (G-2955)
Envelope Mart of Ohio Inc ....E 440 365-8177
Elyria (G-10512)
Pac Worldwide Corporation ....D 800 610-9367
Middletown (G-14319)
Western States Envelope Co ....D 419 666-7480
Walbridge (G-18627)

ENVELOPES WHOLESALERS

EMI Enterprises Inc ....E 419 666-0012
Northwood (G-15392)
Envelope Mart of North E Ohio ....E 440 322-8862
Elyria (G-10511)
Envelope Mart of Ohio Inc ....E 440 365-8177
Elyria (G-10512)
Pac Worldwide Corporation ....D 800 610-9367
Middletown (G-14319)
Western States Envelope Co ....D 419 666-7480
Walbridge (G-18627)

ENVIR QLTY PROG ADMN, GOV: Land, Minl & Wildlif Consv, State

Natural Resources Ohio Dept ....E 419 394-3611
Saint Marys (G-16528)
Ohio Dept Natural Resources ....E 740 869-3124
Mount Sterling (G-14746)

ENVIRON QUALITY PROGS ADMIN, GOVT: Sanitary Engineering

Mahoning County ....E 330 793-5514
Youngstown (G-20105)

ENVIRON QUALITY PROGS ADMIN, GOVT: Water Control & Quality

City of Lakewood ....E 216 252-4322
Cleveland (G-5205)

ENVIRONMENTAL QUALITY PROGS ADMIN, GOVT: Recreational

City of Cleveland ....E 216 621-4231
Cleveland (G-5193)
County of Hancock ....E 419 425-7275
Findlay (G-10894)

ENVIRONMENTAL QUALITY PROGS ADMIN, GOVT: Waste Mgmt

Poggemeyer Design Group Inc ....E 419 748-7438
Mc Clure (G-13893)

ENZYMES

Mp Biomedicals LLC ....C 440 337-1200
Solon (G-16873)

EQUIPMENT & VEHICLE FINANCE LEASING COMPANIES

PNC Equipment Finance LLC ....D...... 513 421-9191
Cincinnati **(G-4259)**
Summit Funding Group Inc..............D...... 513 489-1222
Mason **(G-13642)**

EQUIPMENT: Rental & Leasing, NEC

Ahern Rentals Inc ....E...... 440 498-0869
Solon **(G-16817)**
All Erection & Crane Rental ....C...... 216 524-6550
Cleveland **(G-4930)**
All Erection & Crane Rental ....D...... 216 524-6550
Cleveland **(G-4931)**
All Temp Refrigeration Inc ....E...... 419 692-5016
Delphos **(G-10019)**
Ayrshire Inc ....D...... 440 992-0743
Ashtabula **(G-721)**
Baker Equipment and Mtls Ltd ....E...... 513 422-6697
Monroe **(G-14562)**
Baker Vehicle Systems Inc..............E...... 330 467-2250
Macedonia **(G-13061)**
Budco Group Inc ....E...... 513 621-6111
Cincinnati **(G-3086)**
Budget Dumpster LLC ....E...... 866 284-6164
Westlake **(G-19325)**
De Nora Tech LLC ....D...... 440 710-5300
Painesville **(G-15708)**
Elliott Tool Technologies Ltd ....D...... 937 253-6133
Dayton **(G-9412)**
Fifth Third Equipment Fin Co ....E...... 800 972-3030
Cincinnati **(G-3550)**
Filing Scale Company Inc ....E...... 330 425-3092
Twinsburg **(G-18266)**
Garda CL Great Lakes Inc ....B...... 561 939-7000
Columbus **(G-7647)**
Gordon Brothers Inc......................E...... 800 331-7611
Salem **(G-16545)**
Great Lakes Crushing Ltd ....E...... 440 944-5500
Wickliffe **(G-19461)**
J Way Leasing Ltd ....E...... 440 934-1020
Avon **(G-887)**
JBK Group Inc ....E...... 216 901-0000
Cleveland **(G-5784)**
M & L Leasing Co ....E...... 330 343-8910
Mineral City **(G-14506)**
Mapleview Farms Inc......................E...... 419 826-3671
Swanton **(G-17401)**
MH Logistics Corp ....E...... 330 425-2476
Hudson **(G-11997)**
Miami Industrial Trucks Inc ....D...... 937 293-4194
Moraine **(G-14677)**
Millers Rental and Sls Co Inc ....E...... 216 642-1447
Cleveland **(G-5997)**
Mitel (delaware) Inc ....E...... 513 733-8000
West Chester **(G-18974)**
Ohio Machinery Co ....C...... 419 874-7975
Perrysburg **(G-15897)**
Piqua Steel Co ....D...... 937 773-3632
Piqua **(G-16020)**
Rent-N-Roll ....D...... 513 528-6929
Cincinnati **(G-4359)**
Rumpke Waste Inc ....C...... 937 548-1939
Greenville **(G-11393)**
S and R Leasing ....E...... 330 276-3061
Millersburg **(G-14491)**
Sunbelt Rentals Inc ....E...... 216 362-0300
Cleveland **(G-6477)**
Thomas Do-It Center Inc ....D...... 740 446-2002
Gallipolis **(G-11215)**
Towlift Inc ....C...... 216 749-6800
Brooklyn Heights **(G-1884)**
U Haul Co of Northwestern Ohio ....E...... 419 478-1101
Toledo **(G-18114)**
United Rentals North Amer Inc..........E...... 800 877-3687
Perrysburg **(G-15929)**
Valley Industrial Trucks Inc ....E...... 330 788-4081
Youngstown **(G-20235)**
Vincent Ltg Systems Co Inc ....E...... 216 475-7600
Solon **(G-16912)**
Winner Aviation Corporation ....D...... 330 856-5000
Vienna **(G-18584)**
Yockey Group Inc ....E...... 513 899-2188
Morrow **(G-14719)**

ETCHING SVC: Metal

Woodrow Manufacturing Co ....E...... 937 399-9333
Springfield **(G-17137)**

EXCAVATING MACHINERY & EQPT WHOLESALERS

Fabco Inc ....D...... 419 427-0872
Findlay **(G-10899)**

EXECUTIVE OFFICES: Federal, State & Local

Attentn Web Administrtr Marjon..........D...... 513 708-9888
Franklin **(G-11023)**
City of Euclid ....E...... 216 289-2800
Cleveland **(G-5200)**
City of Kent ....D...... 330 678-8105
Kent **(G-12222)**

EXHIBITORS, ITINERANT, MOTION PICTURE

AMC Entertainment Inc ....E...... 614 429-0100
Columbus **(G-6912)**
American Multi-Cinema Inc...............D...... 614 801-9130
Grove City **(G-11406)**
American Multi-Cinema Inc...............E...... 614 889-0580
Dublin **(G-10132)**
B and D Investment Partnership ....E...... 937 233-6698
Dayton **(G-9244)**
Carmike Cinemas Inc......................E...... 740 264-1680
Steubenville **(G-17143)**
Danbarry Linemas Inc ....E...... 740 779-6115
Chillicothe **(G-2774)**

EXPLOSIVES

Viking Explosives LLC ....E...... 218 263-8845
Cleveland **(G-6630)**

EXPLOSIVES, EXC AMMO & FIREWORKS WHOLESALERS

D W Dickey and Son Inc ....D...... 330 424-1441
Lisbon **(G-12799)**
Viking Explosives LLC ....E...... 218 263-8845
Cleveland **(G-6630)**
Wampum Hardware Co......................E...... 740 685-2585
Salesville **(G-16569)**
Wampum Hardware Co......................E...... 419 273-2542
Forest **(G-10982)**

EXTENDED CARE FACILITY

A L K Inc.....................................D...... 740 369-8741
Delaware **(G-9947)**
Aristocrat W Nursing Hm Corp ....C...... 440 835-0660
Cleveland **(G-5007)**
Arlington Court Nursing ....C...... 614 545-5502
Upper Arlington **(G-18393)**
Broadview Nursing Home Inc ....C...... 216 661-5084
Parma **(G-15761)**
Brookdale Snior Lving Cmmnties ....E...... 330 249-1071
Austintown **(G-856)**
Chillicothe Long Term Care ....C...... 740 773-6161
Chillicothe **(G-2763)**
Country Pointe Skilled Nursing ....E...... 330 264-7881
Wooster **(G-19714)**
Crestview Manor Nursing Home ....C...... 740 654-2634
Lancaster **(G-12386)**
Crestview Manor Nursing Home ....C...... 740 654-2634
Lancaster **(G-12387)**
Diverscare Healthcare Svcs Inc.........E...... 937 278-8211
Dayton **(G-9392)**
Ezra Health Care Inc ....C...... 440 498-3000
Beachwood **(G-1056)**
Fairlawn Opco LLC ....D...... 502 429-8062
Fairlawn **(G-10827)**
Flower Hospital ....B...... 419 824-1000
Sylvania **(G-17425)**
Franklin Blvd Nursing HM Inc.............C...... 216 651-1600
Cleveland **(G-5574)**
Golden Years Nursing Home Inc ....E...... 513 893-0471
Hamilton **(G-11601)**
Governors Village LLC ....E...... 440 449-8788
Cleveland **(G-5618)**
Havar Inc ....E...... 740 373-7175
Marietta **(G-13334)**
Hcf of Briarwood Inc......................C...... 419 678-2311
Coldwater **(G-6758)**
Hcr Manorcare Med Svcs Fla LLC ....E...... 513 745-9600
Cincinnati **(G-3688)**
Heritage Park Rehabilita ....C...... 937 437-2311
New Paris **(G-14943)**
House of Loreto ....D...... 330 453-8137
Canton **(G-2349)**

Lakewood Health Care Center ....C...... 216 226-3103
Lakewood **(G-12355)**
Liberty Nursing Home Inc ....D...... 937 376-2121
Xenia **(G-19917)**
Madison Care Inc ....D...... 440 428-1492
Madison **(G-13102)**
Manor Care Inc ....D...... 419 252-5500
Toledo **(G-17880)**
Manor Care of America Inc ....D...... 440 543-6766
Chagrin Falls **(G-2673)**
McKinley Life Care Center LLC ....D...... 330 456-1014
Canton **(G-2396)**
McV Health Care Facilities ....C...... 513 398-1486
Mason **(G-13617)**
Meigs Center Ltd...........................C...... 740 992-6472
Middleport **(G-14281)**
Minerva Elder Care Inc ....E...... 330 868-4147
Minerva **(G-14521)**
Pebble Creek Cnvlscnt Ctr ....C...... 330 645-0200
Akron **(G-372)**
Ridge Pleasant Valley Inc ....C...... 440 845-0200
Cleveland **(G-6325)**
Rolling Hlls Rhab Wellness Ctr ....C...... 330 225-9121
Brunswick **(G-1939)**
Rose Ln Hlth Rhabilitation Inc...........C...... 330 833-3174
Massillon **(G-13725)**
Springview Manor Nursing Home ....E...... 419 227-3661
Lima **(G-12748)**
Tri County Extended Care Ctr............C...... 513 829-3555
Fairfield **(G-10793)**
Weber Health Care Center Inc ....C...... 440 647-2088
Wellington **(G-18845)**
West Park Retirement Community ....C...... 513 451-8900
Cincinnati **(G-4783)**

EXTERMINATING & FUMIGATING SVCS

Orkin LLC....................................E...... 614 888-5811
Columbus **(G-8386)**
Steve Shaffer ....E...... 614 276-6355
Columbus **(G-8698)**

EYEGLASSES

Essilor Laboratories Amer Inc ....E...... 614 274-0840
Columbus **(G-7537)**
Toledo Optical Laboratory Inc ....D...... 419 248-3384
Toledo **(G-18094)**

FABRIC STORES

Jo-Ann Stores Holdings Inc ....D...... 888 739-4120
Hudson **(G-11988)**
Zincks In Berlin Inc ....C...... 330 893-2071
Berlin **(G-1447)**

FABRICS: Broadwoven, Synthetic Manmade Fiber & Silk

Owens Corning Sales LLC ....B...... 740 587-3562
Granville **(G-11347)**

FABRICS: Metallized

Laserflex Corporation......................D...... 614 850-9600
Hilliard **(G-11783)**

FABRICS: Trimmings

Bates Metal Products Inc ....D...... 740 498-8371
Port Washington **(G-16121)**
Brown Cnty Bd Mntal Rtardation..........E...... 937 378-4891
Georgetown **(G-11261)**
Fedex Office & Print Svcs Inc ....E...... 614 898-0000
Westerville **(G-19255)**
General Theming Contrs LLC ....C...... 614 252-6342
Columbus **(G-7655)**
Hunt Products Inc ....E...... 440 667-2457
Newburgh Heights **(G-15115)**
Screen Works Inc ....E...... 937 264-9111
Dayton **(G-9754)**
Tendon Manufacturing Inc ....E...... 216 663-3200
Cleveland **(G-6512)**
Woodrow Manufacturing Co ....E...... 937 399-9333
Springfield **(G-17137)**

FABRICS: Woven, Narrow Cotton, Wool, Silk

Keuchel & Associates Inc ....E...... 330 945-9455
Cuyahoga Falls **(G-9108)**
Samsel Rope & Marine Supply Co ....E...... 216 241-0333
Cleveland **(G-6370)**

Employee Codes: A=Over 500 employees, B=251-500
C=101-250, D=51-100, E=25-50   2019 Harris Ohio
Services Directory   1419

SERVICES

FACIAL SALONS

Karen Funke Inc...................................E...... 216 464-4311
  Beachwood **(G-1072)**

Phyllis At Madison..............................E...... 513 321-1300
  Cincinnati **(G-4245)**

FACILITIES SUPPORT SVCS

Aramark Facility Services LLC.........E...... 216 687-5000
  Cleveland **(G-4998)**

Cuyahoga County Convention Fac.....D...... 216 928-1600
  Cleveland **(G-5398)**

Firstgroup America Inc.....................D...... 513 241-2200
  Cincinnati **(G-3566)**

Four Seasons Environmental Inc.........B...... 513 539-2978
  Monroe **(G-14568)**

Franklin Cnty Bd Commissioners......C...... 614 462-3800
  Columbus **(G-7606)**

L B & B Associates Inc......................E...... 216 451-2672
  Cleveland **(G-5842)**

MPW Industrial Svcs Group Inc.........D...... 740 927-8790
  Hebron **(G-11719)**

North Bay Construction Inc..............440 835-1898
  Westlake **(G-19380)**

Selecttech Services Corp..................C...... 937 438-9905
  Centerville **(G-2633)**

Serco Inc...E...... 937 331-4180
  Moraine **(G-14696)**

Space Management Inc......................E...... 937 254-6622
  Dayton **(G-9781)**

Technical Assurance Inc...................E...... 440 953-3147
  Willoughby **(G-19575)**

Wastren - Energx Mission.................C...... 740 897-3724
  Piketon **(G-15992)**

Wastren Advantage Inc......................E...... 970 254-1277
  Piketon **(G-15993)**

FACILITY RENTAL & PARTY PLANNING SVCS

Black Tie Affair Inc............................E...... 330 345-8333
  Wooster **(G-19691)**

Camargo Rental Center Inc................E...... 513 271-6510
  Cincinnati **(G-3109)**

Goldfish Swim School........................E...... 216 364-9090
  Warrensville Heights **(G-18778)**

Queens Tower Restaurant Inc...........E...... 513 251-6467
  Cincinnati **(G-4324)**

FAMILY COUNSELING SVCS

Allwell Behavioral Health Svcs.........E...... 740 439-4428
  Cambridge **(G-2049)**

Center For Families & Children.........E...... 216 252-5800
  Cleveland **(G-5151)**

Cincinnati Ctr/Psychoanalysis.........E...... 513 961-8484
  Cincinnati **(G-3237)**

Consolidated Care Inc........................E...... 937 465-8065
  West Liberty **(G-19119)**

Consolidated Care Inc........................E...... 937 465-8065
  West Liberty **(G-19120)**

County of Paulding............................E...... 419 399-3636
  Paulding **(G-15793)**

Develpmntal Dsblties Ohio Dept.......C...... 513 732-9200
  Batavia **(G-996)**

Emerge Counseling Service..............E...... 330 865-8351
  Akron **(G-202)**

Far West Center................................E...... 440 835-6212
  Westlake **(G-19342)**

Frs Counseling Inc.............................E...... 937 393-0585
  Hillsboro **(G-11840)**

Oneeighty Inc....................................D...... 330 263-6021
  Wooster **(G-19756)**

Southast Cmnty Mental Hlth Ctr......E...... 614 444-0800
  Columbus **(G-8662)**

Summit Cnty Dept Job Fmly Svcs......D...... 330 643-8200
  Akron **(G-456)**

Westark Family Services Inc..............E...... 330 832-5043
  Massillon **(G-13734)**

FAMILY OR MARRIAGE COUNSELING

Compass Family and Cmnty Svcs......E...... 330 743-9275
  Youngstown **(G-20002)**

Compass Family and Cmnty Svcs......D...... 330 743-9275
  Youngstown **(G-20003)**

Trillium Family Solutions Inc............D...... 330 454-7066
  Cuyahoga Falls **(G-9133)**

FAMILY PLANNING CENTERS

Noble Cnty Nble Cnty Cmmsoners.....E...... 740 732-4958
  Caldwell **(G-2043)**

FAMILY PLANNING CLINIC

Family Planning Center.....................E...... 740 439-3340
  Cambridge **(G-2066)**

Fulton County Health Dept................E...... 419 337-0915
  Wauseon **(G-18804)**

Planned Parenthood Association......E...... 937 226-0780
  Dayton **(G-9694)**

Planned Parenthood NW Ohio Inc.....E...... 419 255-1115
  Toledo **(G-17980)**

Planned Parenthood of SW OH.........E...... 513 721-7635
  Cincinnati **(G-4252)**

Planned Prenthood Greater Ohio......E...... 614 224-2235
  Columbus **(G-8452)**

Planned Prenthood Greater Ohio......E...... 330 535-2671
  Akron **(G-384)**

Planned Prenthood Greater Ohio......E...... 216 961-8804
  Bedford Heights **(G-1324)**

Planned Prenthood Greater Ohio......E...... 330 788-2487
  Youngstown **(G-20157)**

FAMILY SVCS AGENCY

Box 21 Rescue Squad Inc..................E...... 937 223-2821
  Dayton **(G-9260)**

Catholic Social Svc Miami Vly...........E...... 937 223-7217
  Dayton **(G-9287)**

Commquest Services Inc...................C...... 330 455-0374
  Canton **(G-2261)**

Community Action Comm Pike CNT.....C...... 740 289-2371
  Piketon **(G-15973)**

Community Action Comm Pike CNT.....E...... 740 961-4011
  Portsmouth **(G-16131)**

Community Action Comm Pike CNT.....E...... 740 286-2826
  Jackson **(G-12172)**

County of Geauga...............................D...... 440 564-2246
  Chardon **(G-2691)**

Couple To Couple Leag Intl Inc.........E...... 513 471-2000
  Cincinnati **(G-3374)**

Goodrich Gnnett Nghborhood Ctr.....E...... 216 432-1717
  Cleveland **(G-5614)**

Greenleaf Family Center....................E...... 330 376-9494
  Akron **(G-245)**

Jewish Family Service of...................E...... 513 469-1188
  Cincinnati **(G-3815)**

Jewish Family Services Associa.........B...... 216 292-3999
  Cleveland **(G-5795)**

Lifespan Incorporated......................D...... 513 868-3210
  Hamilton **(G-11624)**

New Horizon Youth Family Ctr.........E...... 740 687-0835
  Lancaster **(G-12421)**

Salvation Army.................................E...... 937 528-5100
  Dayton **(G-9747)**

FARM & GARDEN MACHINERY WHOLESALERS

Bzak Landscaping Inc........................E...... 513 831-0907
  Milford **(G-14375)**

Clarke Power Services Inc................D...... 513 771-2200
  Cincinnati **(G-3302)**

Fackler Country Gardens Inc............E...... 740 522-3128
  Granville **(G-11341)**

Gardner-Connell LLC.........................E...... 614 456-4000
  Columbus **(G-7649)**

Hull Bros Inc....................................E...... 419 375-2827
  Fort Recovery **(G-10992)**

Kenn-Feld Group LLC........................E...... 419 678-2375
  Coldwater **(G-6760)**

Krystowski Tractor Sales Inc............E...... 440 647-2015
  Wellington **(G-18842)**

Pax Steel Products Inc.......................E...... 419 678-1481
  Coldwater **(G-6764)**

Streacker Tractor Sales Inc..............E...... 419 422-6973
  Findlay **(G-10965)**

Wellington Implement Co Inc............E...... 440 647-3725
  Wellington **(G-18846)**

Western Tradewinds Inc....................E...... 937 859-4300
  Miamisburg **(G-14238)**

FARM MACHINERY REPAIR SVCS

Apple Farm Service Inc.....................E...... 937 526-4851
  Covington **(G-9045)**

Cope Farm Equipment Inc.................E...... 330 821-5867
  Alliance **(G-528)**

Witmers Inc.......................................E...... 330 427-2147
  Salem **(G-16567)**

FARM PRDTS, RAW MATERIAL, WHOLESALE: Tobacco & Tobacco Prdts

Altria Group Distribution Co.............C...... 804 274-2000
  Mason **(G-13538)**

FARM PRDTS, RAW MATERIALS, WHOLESALE: Farm Animals

Hills Supply Inc.................................E...... 740 477-8994
  Circleville **(G-4835)**

FARM PRDTS, RAW MATERIALS, WHOLESALE: Hides

Inland Products Inc...........................E...... 614 443-3425
  Columbus **(G-7819)**

FARM SPLY STORES

Centerra Co-Op.................................E...... 419 281-2153
  Ashland **(G-665)**

Granville Milling Co...........................E...... 740 587-0221
  Granville **(G-11343)**

FARM SPLYS WHOLESALERS

A M Leonard Inc................................D...... 937 773-2694
  Piqua **(G-15994)**

Alabama Farmers Coop Inc................E...... 419 655-2289
  Cygnet **(G-9142)**

Andersons Inc...................................C...... 419 893-5050
  Maumee **(G-13754)**

Archbold Elevator Inc.......................E...... 419 445-2451
  Archbold **(G-626)**

Centerra Co-Op.................................E...... 800 362-9598
  Jefferson **(G-12190)**

Champaign Landmark Inc..................E...... 937 652-2135
  Urbana **(G-18423)**

Farmers Elev Grn & Sply Assoc.........E...... 419 653-4132
  New Bavaria **(G-14879)**

Gardner-Connell LLC.........................E...... 614 456-4000
  Columbus **(G-7649)**

Granville Milling Co...........................E...... 740 587-0221
  Granville **(G-11343)**

Jiffy Products America Inc.................E...... 440 282-2818
  Lorain **(G-12908)**

Phillips Ready Mix Co........................D...... 937 426-5151
  Beavercreek Township **(G-1259)**

Sunrise Cooperative Inc....................E...... 419 683-7340
  Crestline **(G-9060)**

Sunrise Cooperative Inc....................E...... 937 323-7536
  Springfield **(G-17122)**

Sunrise Cooperative Inc....................B...... 937 575-6780
  Piqua **(G-16030)**

United States Dept Agriculture.........D...... 419 626-8439
  Sandusky **(G-16652)**

FARM SPLYS, WHOLESALE: Feed

Cooper Farms Inc.............................D...... 419 375-4116
  Fort Recovery **(G-10989)**

Gerber Feed Service Inc....................E...... 330 857-4421
  Dalton **(G-9145)**

K M B Inc..E...... 330 889-3451
  Bristolville **(G-1826)**

Mennel Milling Company....................E...... 740 385-6824
  Logan **(G-12849)**

Mennel Milling Company....................D...... 740 385-6824
  Logan **(G-12850)**

Premier Feeds LLC............................E...... 937 584-2411
  Wilmington **(G-19641)**

Sunrise Cooperative Inc....................E...... 937 462-8341
  South Charleston **(G-16925)**

Sunrise Cooperative Inc....................E...... 937 382-1633
  Wilmington **(G-19650)**

FARM SPLYS, WHOLESALE: Flower & Field Bulbs

Express Seed Company.......................D...... 440 774-2259
  Oberlin **(G-15502)**

FARM SPLYS, WHOLESALE: Garden Splys

Berns Grnhse & Grdn Ctr Inc............E...... 513 423-5306
  Middletown **(G-14293)**

Bfg Supply Co Llc.............................E...... 440 834-1883
  Burton **(G-2015)**

Do Cut Sales & Service Inc ....E 330 533-9878
Warren *(G-18703)*

FARM SPLYS, WHOLESALE: Greenhouse Eqpt & Splys

Mac Kenzie Nursery Supply Inc ....E 440 259-3517
Perry *(G-15825)*

FARM SPLYS, WHOLESALE: Herbicides

Noxious Vegetation Control Inc ....D 614 486-8994
Ashville *(G-762)*

FARM SPLYS, WHOLESALE: Seed, Grass

Lesco Inc ....C 216 706-9250
Cleveland *(G-5865)*

FASTENERS WHOLESALERS

Fastener Corp of America Inc ....E 440 835-5100
Westlake *(G-19343)*

FASTENERS: Metal

Midwest Motor Supply Co ....C 800 233-1294
Columbus *(G-8082)*

FASTENERS: Notions, NEC

Midwest Motor Supply Co ....C 800 233-1294
Columbus *(G-8082)*

FEDERAL SAVINGS & LOAN ASSOCIATIONS

Belmont Federal Sav & Ln Assn ....E 740 676-1165
Bellaire *(G-1331)*
Century National Bank ....E 740 455-7330
Zanesville *(G-20294)*
Chemical Bank ....E 513 232-0800
Cincinnati *(G-3176)*
Chemical Bank ....E 440 926-2191
Grafton *(G-11316)*
Chemical Bank ....E 330 314-1395
Poland *(G-16082)*
Chemical Bank ....E 440 323-7451
Elyria *(G-10488)*
Chemical Bank ....D 330 298-0510
Ravenna *(G-16235)*
Cheviot Mutual Holding Company ....D 513 661-0457
Cincinnati *(G-3179)*
Cincinnatus Savings & Loan ....E 513 661-6903
Cincinnati *(G-3281)*
Citizens Federal Sav & Ln Assn ....E 937 593-0015
Bellefontaine *(G-1348)*
Fairfield Federal Sav Ln Assn ....E 740 653-3863
Lancaster *(G-12395)*
Ffd Financial Corporation ....D 330 364-7777
Dover *(G-10077)*
First Fdral Sav Ln Assn Galion ....E 419 468-1518
Galion *(G-11170)*
First Fdral Sav Ln Assn Lkwood ....C 216 221-7300
Lakewood *(G-12343)*
First Fdral Sav Ln Assn Lorain ....D 440 282-6188
Lorain *(G-12904)*
First Fdral Sav Ln Assn Newark ....E 740 345-3494
Newark *(G-15033)*
First Fdral Sving Ln Assn Dlta ....E 419 822-3131
Delta *(G-10043)*
First Federal Bank of Midwest ....E 419 782-5015
Defiance *(G-9914)*
First Federal Bank of Midwest ....E 419 695-1055
Delphos *(G-10026)*
First Federal Bank of Midwest ....D 419 855-8326
Genoa *(G-11253)*
First Federal Bank of Ohio ....D 419 468-1518
Galion *(G-11171)*
Greenville Federal ....E 937 548-4158
Greenville *(G-11381)*
Harrison Building and Ln Assn ....E 513 367-2015
Harrison *(G-11669)*
Liberty Capital Inc ....D 937 382-1000
Wilmington *(G-19628)*
New York Community Bank ....E 440 734-7040
North Olmsted *(G-15300)*
New York Community Bank ....E 216 741-7333
Cleveland *(G-6063)*
New York Community Bank ....A 216 736-3480
Cleveland *(G-6064)*
Peoples Bancorp Inc ....D 740 574-9100
Wheelersburg *(G-19437)*

Peoples Bancorp Inc ....D 513 793-2422
Cincinnati *(G-4228)*
Peoples Bank ....D 740 354-3177
Portsmouth *(G-16157)*
Peoples Federal Sav & Ln Assn ....E 937 492-6129
Sidney *(G-16791)*
Peoples Savings and Loan Co...............E 419 562-6896
Bucyrus *(G-2000)*
Peoples-Sidney Financial Corp ....E 937 492-6129
Sidney *(G-16792)*
Richwood Banking Company ....E 937 390-0470
Springfield *(G-17101)*
Talmer Bank and Trust ....E 330 726-3396
Canfield *(G-2159)*
Third Federal Savings ....B 800 844-7333
Cleveland *(G-6522)*
Third Federal Savings ....E 440 716-1865
North Olmsted *(G-15314)*
Third Federal Savings ....E 440 843-6300
Cleveland *(G-6524)*

FEDERAL SAVINGS BANKS

Guardian Savings Bank......................E 513 942-3535
West Chester *(G-18938)*
Union Savings Bank ....D 937 434-1254
Dayton *(G-9829)*
Wesbanco Inc ....E 740 532-0263
Ironton *(G-12167)*

FENCING DEALERS

Able Contracting Group Inc ....E 440 951-0880
Painesville *(G-15691)*
Mills Fence Co Inc ....E 513 631-0333
Cincinnati *(G-4057)*
Usavinyl LLC ....E 614 771-4805
Groveport *(G-11547)*

FENCING: Chain Link

Richards Whl Fence Co Inc..................E 330 773-0423
Akron *(G-407)*

FERRALLOY ORES, EXC VANADIUM

Rhenium Alloys Inc...........................D 440 365-7388
North Ridgeville *(G-15340)*

FERTILIZER MINERAL MINING

Everris NA Inc ....E 614 726-7100
Dublin *(G-10221)*

FERTILIZER, AGRICULTURAL: Wholesalers

Andersons Agriculture Group LP ....E 419 893-5050
Maumee *(G-13756)*
Deerfield Farms Service Inc.................D 330 584-4715
Deerfield *(G-9904)*
Hanby Farms Inc ....E 740 763-3554
Nashport *(G-14819)*
Morral Companies LLC.......................E 740 465-3251
Morral *(G-14713)*
Ohigro Inc ....E 740 726-2429
Waldo *(G-18630)*
S & D Application LLC ....E 419 288-3660
Wayne *(G-18826)*

FERTILIZERS: NEC

Ohigro Inc ....E 740 726-2429
Waldo *(G-18630)*

FERTILIZERS: Phosphatic

Andersons Inc ....C 419 893-5050
Maumee *(G-13754)*

FIBER & FIBER PRDTS: Synthetic Cellulosic

Flexsys America LP ....D 330 666-4111
Akron *(G-225)*

FIBER OPTICS

Jason Wilson...................................E 937 604-8209
Tipp City *(G-17561)*

FIELD WAREHOUSING SVCS

Frankes Unlimited Inc........................E 937 642-0706
Marysville *(G-13496)*
Penske Logistics LLC.........................E 419 547-2615
Clyde *(G-6749)*

Truechoicepack Corp ....E 937 630-3832
Mason *(G-13651)*

FILE FOLDERS

GBS Corp..C 330 494-5330
North Canton *(G-15206)*

FILM & SHEET: Unsuppported Plastic

Ampac Holdings LLC ....A 513 671-1777
Cincinnati *(G-2955)*
General Data Company Inc ....C 513 752-7978
Cincinnati *(G-2853)*
Industry Products Co ....B 937 778-0585
Piqua *(G-16011)*
Polyone Corporation ....D 440 930-1000
Avon Lake *(G-926)*

FILM: Rubber

B D G Wrap-Tite Inc ....D 440 349-5400
Solon *(G-16826)*

FILTER ELEMENTS: Fluid & Hydraulic Line

Two M Precision Co Inc ....E 440 946-2120
Willoughby *(G-19578)*

FILTERS

Hunter Defense Tech Inc ....E 216 438-6111
Solon *(G-16859)*
Swift Filters Inc ....E 440 735-0995
Oakwood Village *(G-15494)*

FILTERS & SOFTENERS: Water, Household

Enting Water Conditioning Inc ....E 937 294-5100
Moraine *(G-14653)*

FINANCIAL INVESTMENT ACTIVITIES, NEC: Security Transfer

Flex Fund Inc...................................E 614 766-7000
Dublin *(G-10229)*

FINANCIAL INVESTMENT ADVICE

Ameriprise Financial Svcs Inc ....E 614 934-4057
Dublin *(G-10135)*
Ameriprise Financial Svcs Inc ....D 614 846-8723
Worthington *(G-19793)*
Brown WD General Agency Inc ....D 216 241-5840
Cleveland *(G-5094)*
Carnegie Capital Asset MGT LLC ....E 216 595-1349
Cleveland *(G-5128)*
CNG Financial Corp ....A 513 336-7735
Cincinnati *(G-3315)*
Cw Financial LLC ....B 941 907-9490
Beachwood *(G-1050)*
Direct Maintenance LLC ....E 330 744-5211
Youngstown *(G-20018)*
Financial Engines Inc ....E 330 726-3100
Boardman *(G-1697)*
Fiserv Solutions LLC..........................C 412 577-3000
Dublin *(G-10228)*
Ifs Financial Services Inc ....E 513 362-8000
Westerville *(G-19264)*
Kemba Financial Credit Un Inc ....D 614 235-2395
Columbus *(G-7889)*
Lang Financial Group Inc ....E 513 699-2966
Blue Ash *(G-1596)*
Lassiter Corporation..........................E 216 391-4800
Cleveland *(G-5856)*
Merrill Lynch Pierce Fenner ....C 216 363-6500
Cleveland *(G-5959)*
Merrill Lynch Pierce Fenner ....E 937 847-4000
Miamisburg *(G-14189)*
Merrill Lynch Pierce Fenner ....D 614 225-3000
Columbus *(G-8061)*
Merrill Lynch Pierce Fenner ....D 330 670-2400
Akron *(G-332)*
Morgan Stanley ....D 614 473-2086
Columbus *(G-8102)*
Morgan Stanley ....E 513 721-2000
Cincinnati *(G-4074)*
Mt Washington Care Center Inc............C 513 231-4561
Cincinnati *(G-4083)*
Stepstone Group Real Estate LP............E 216 522-0330
Cleveland *(G-6467)*
Stonehenge Capital Company LLC ....E 614 246-2456
Columbus *(G-8701)*

S E R V I C E S

FINANCIAL SVCS

1 Financial Corporation ....E 513 936-1400
Blue Ash *(G-1493)*

6200 Rockside LLC ....D 216 642-8004
Cleveland *(G-4872)*

Allstate Insurance Company ....E 330 650-2917
Hudson *(G-11963)*

Ampersand Group LLC ....E 330 379-0044
Akron *(G-73)*

Banc One Services Corporation ....A 614 248-5800
Columbus *(G-6800)*

Bdo Usa LLP ....E 513 592-2400
Cincinnati *(G-3027)*

Business Backer LLC ....E 513 792-6866
Cincinnati *(G-3095)*

Cbiz Inc ....C 216 447-9000
Cleveland *(G-5139)*

Cincinnati Financial Corp ....A 513 870-2000
Fairfield *(G-10710)*

Citizens Financial Svcs Inc ....D 513 385-3200
Cincinnati *(G-3297)*

Cleveland Clinic Foundation ....B 216 444-5000
Cleveland *(G-5239)*

Collections Acquisition Co LLC ....C 614 944-5788
Columbus *(G-7245)*

Credit First National Assn ....B 216 362-5300
Cleveland *(G-5377)*

E T Financial Service Inc ....E 937 716-1726
Trotwood *(G-18193)*

Facts Management Company ....E 440 892-4272
Westlake *(G-19340)*

Fnb Inc ....E 740 922-2532
Dennison *(G-10050)*

FNB Corporation ....D 330 425-1818
Twinsburg *(G-18267)*

Horter Investment MGT LLC ....E 513 984-9933
Cincinnati *(G-3727)*

Landmark America Inc ....E 330 372-6800
Warren *(G-18721)*

Liberty Healthshare Inc ....E 855 585-4237
Canton *(G-2377)*

Nationwide General Insur Co ....D 614 249-7111
Columbus *(G-8156)*

Reliance Financial Services NA ....E 419 783-8007
Defiance *(G-9936)*

Restaurant Finance Corporation ....D 614 764-3100
Dublin *(G-10321)*

Ryder Last Mile Inc ....D 866 711-3129
New Albany *(G-14873)*

Sparkbase Inc ....E 216 867-0877
Cleveland *(G-6442)*

Springleaf Fincl Holdings LLC ....A 419 334-9748
Fremont *(G-11097)*

Sterling Buying Group LLC ....E 513 564-9000
Cincinnati *(G-4543)*

UBS Financial Services Inc ....E 330 655-8319
Hudson *(G-12009)*

UBS Financial Services Inc ....E 440 414-2740
Westlake *(G-19416)*

UBS Financial Services Inc ....E 419 624-6800
Sandusky *(G-16650)*

UBS Financial Services Inc ....E 740 336-7823
Marietta *(G-13391)*

Uhhs/Csahs - Cuyahoga Inc ....D 440 746-3401
Cleveland *(G-6561)*

Unirush LLC ....D 866 766-2229
Blue Ash *(G-1674)*

Zebu Compliance Solutions LLC ....E 740 355-9029
Portsmouth *(G-16182)*

FINGERPRINTING SVCS

Donty Horton HM Care Dhhc LLC .....E 513 463-3442
Cincinnati *(G-3440)*

FINISHING SVCS

One Main Financial Services ....C 419 841-0785
Toledo *(G-17963)*

FIRE ALARM MAINTENANCE & MONITORING SVCS

ABC Fire Inc ....E 440 237-6677
North Royalton *(G-15346)*

The Cadle Company ....C 330 872-0918
Newton Falls *(G-15141)*

William D Taylor Sr Inc ....D 614 653-6683
Etna *(G-10621)*

Gene Ptacek Son Fire Eqp Inc ....E 216 651-8300
Cleveland *(G-5602)*

Gillmore Security Systems Inc ....E 440 232-1000
Cleveland *(G-5608)*

Koorsen Fire & Security Inc ....E 937 324-9405
Vandalia *(G-18530)*

Metro Safety and Security LLC ....D 614 792-2770
Columbus *(G-8064)*

FIRE CONTROL EQPT REPAIR SVCS, MILITARY

Fire Foe Corp ....E 330 759-9834
Girard *(G-11287)*

FIRE EXTINGUISHER SVC

Abco Fire LLC ....E 800 875-7200
Cincinnati *(G-2896)*

Abco Holdings LLC ....D 216 433-7200
Cleveland *(G-4892)*

Koorsen Fire & Security Inc ....E 937 324-9405
Vandalia *(G-18530)*

Megacity Fire Protection Inc ....E 937 335-0775
Dayton *(G-9605)*

Silco Fire Protection Company ....E 330 535-4343
Akron *(G-429)*

FIRE EXTINGUISHERS, WHOLESALE

3s Incorporated ....E 513 202-5070
Harrison *(G-11659)*

Abco Fire Protection Inc ....E 800 875-7200
Cleveland *(G-4891)*

Gene Ptacek Son Fire Eqp Inc ....E 216 651-8300
Cleveland *(G-5602)*

Koorsen Fire & Security Inc ....E 614 878-2228
Columbus *(G-7923)*

FIRE LOSS APPRAISAL

Root Insurance Company ....C 866 980-9431
Columbus *(G-8549)*

FIRE OR BURGLARY RESISTIVE PRDTS

Donald E Didion II ....E 419 483-2226
Bellevue *(G-1376)*

FIRE PROTECTION EQPT

A-1 Sprinkler Company Inc ....D 937 859-6198
Miamisburg *(G-14136)*

Action Coupling & Eqp Inc ....D 330 279-4242
Holmesville *(G-11928)*

FIRE PROTECTION SVCS: Contracted

AA Fire Protection LLC ....E 440 327-0060
Elyria *(G-10475)*

Abco Fire LLC ....D 216 433-7200
Cleveland *(G-4890)*

Bst & G Joint Fire District ....E 740 965-3841
Sunbury *(G-17384)*

City of Solon ....E 440 248-6939
Solon *(G-16836)*

City of Wooster ....E 330 263-5266
Wooster *(G-19704)*

Colerain Volunteer Fire Co ....E 740 738-0735
Dillonvale *(G-10063)*

Greentown Volunteer Fire Dept ....E 330 494-3002
Uniontown *(G-18372)*

J Schoen Enterprises Inc ....E 419 536-0970
Toledo *(G-17828)*

FIRE PROTECTION, EXC CONTRACT

ADT Security ....D 440 397-5751
Strongsville *(G-17281)*

FIRE PROTECTION, GOVERNMENT: County

County of Holmes ....E 330 674-1926
Millersburg *(G-14467)*

FIRE PROTECTION, GOVERNMENT: Fire Department, Volunteer

Leroy Twp Fire Dept ....E 440 254-4124
Painesville *(G-15722)*

Richland Township Fire Dept ....E 740 536-7313
Rushville *(G-16465)*

FIRE PROTECTION, GOVERNMENT: Local

City of Whitehall ....E 614 237-5478
Columbus *(G-7213)*

City of Willoughby Hills ....E 440 942-7207
Willoughby Hills *(G-19587)*

Township of Chester ....E 440 729-9951
Chesterland *(G-2747)*

FIREARMS & AMMUNITION, EXC SPORTING, WHOLESALE

Keidel Supply Company Inc ....E 513 351-1600
Cincinnati *(G-3852)*

Rk Family Inc ....B 740 389-2674
Marion *(G-13457)*

Rk Family Inc ....B 419 355-8230
Fremont *(G-11090)*

Rk Family Inc ....B 330 264-5475
Wooster *(G-19761)*

Rk Family Inc ....B 513 934-0015
Lebanon *(G-12498)*

Vinifera Imports Ltd ....E 440 942-9463
Mentor *(G-14122)*

FIREARMS, EXC SPORTING, WHOLESALE

Southern Ohio Gun Distrs Inc ....E 513 932-8148
Lebanon *(G-12505)*

FIREWOOD, WHOLESALE

Bladecutters Lawn Service Inc ....E 937 274-3861
Dayton *(G-9255)*

FIREWORKS SHOPS

Miller Fireworks Company Inc ....E 419 865-7329
Holland *(G-11899)*

FIREWORKS: Wholesalers

Miller Fireworks Company Inc ....E 419 865-7329
Holland *(G-11899)*

FISH & SEAFOOD WHOLESALERS

101 River Inc ....E 440 352-6343
Grand River *(G-11331)*

Farm House Food Distrs Inc ....E 216 791-6948
Cleveland *(G-5513)*

Omega Sea LLC ....E 440 639-2372
Painesville *(G-15731)*

Sherwood Food Distributors LLC ......B 216 662-6794
Maple Heights *(G-13296)*

FISH, PACKAGED FROZEN: Wholesalers

King Kold Inc ....E 937 836-2731
Englewood *(G-10592)*

Produce One Inc ....D 931 253-4749
Dayton *(G-9715)*

FISHING CAMPS

Rockwell Springs Trout Club ....E 419 684-7971
Clyde *(G-6751)*

FITTINGS & ASSEMBLIES: Hose & Tube, Hydraulic Or Pneumatic

Ohio Hydraulics Inc ....E 513 771-2590
Cincinnati *(G-4155)*

FITTINGS: Pipe

Parker-Hannifin Corporation ....B 937 456-5571
Eaton *(G-10457)*

Parker-Hannifin Corporation ....C 614 279-7070
Columbus *(G-8421)*

SSP Fittings Corp ....C 330 425-4250
Twinsburg *(G-18323)*

FLAT GLASS: Construction

S R Door Inc ....C 740 927-3558
Hebron *(G-11723)*

FLEA MARKET

Ferguson Hills Inc ....D 513 539-4497
Dayton *(G-9433)*

Hrm Enterprises Inc ....C 330 877-9353
Hartville *(G-11691)*

Rainbow Flea Market Inc ....E 614 291-3133
  Columbus **(G-8486)**

FLIGHT TRAINING SCHOOLS

Abx Air Inc ....B 937 382-5591
  Wilmington **(G-19600)**

FLOATING DRY DOCKS

Pinney Dock & Transport LLC ....E 440 964-7186
  Ashtabula **(G-752)**

FLOOR COVERING STORES

Americas Floor Source LLC..................E 216 342-4929
  Bedford Heights **(G-1316)**
Command Carpet ....D 330 673-7404
  Kent **(G-12224)**
Modern Glass Pnt & Tile Co Inc............E 740 454-1253
  Zanesville **(G-20332)**
Rite Rug Co ....E 614 478-3365
  Columbus **(G-8533)**
Samron Inc ....E 330 782-6539
  Youngstown **(G-20203)**
Schoch Tile & Carpet Inc....................E 513 922-3466
  Cincinnati **(G-4439)**

FLOOR COVERING STORES: Carpets

Americas Floor Source LLC..................D 614 808-3915
  Columbus **(G-6940)**
Andover Floor Covering.......................E 440 293-5339
  Newbury **(G-15118)**
Clays Heritage Carpet Inc ....E 330 497-1280
  Canton **(G-2257)**
Farrow Cleaners Co ....E 216 561-2355
  Cleveland **(G-5514)**
Marble Restoration Inc ....D 419 865-9000
  Maumee **(G-13813)**
Patellas Floor Center Inc ....E 330 758-4099
  Youngstown **(G-20152)**
Regal Carpet Center Inc ....E 216 475-1844
  Cleveland **(G-6296)**
Regency Windows Corporation.............D 330 963-4077
  Twinsburg **(G-18310)**
Rite Rug Co ....E 937 318-9197
  Fairborn **(G-10681)**
Stanley Steemer Intl Inc ....C 614 764-2007
  Dublin **(G-10341)**

FLOOR COVERING STORES: Floor Tile

JP Flooring Systems Inc ....E 513 346-4300
  West Chester **(G-18954)**
Justice & Co Inc ....E 330 225-6000
  Medina **(G-13962)**

FLOOR COVERING: Plastic

Armaly LLC ....E 740 852-3621
  London **(G-12859)**

FLOOR COVERINGS WHOLESALERS

Americas Floor Source LLC..................D 614 808-3915
  Columbus **(G-6940)**
D & S Crtive Cmmunications Inc...........E 419 524-4312
  Mansfield **(G-13164)**
Pfpc Enterprises Inc ....B 513 941-6200
  Cincinnati **(G-4240)**

FLOOR WAXING SVCS

Stanley Stemer of Akron Canton ....E 330 785-5005
  Coventry Township **(G-9043)**

FLORIST: Flowers, Fresh

Circle S Farms Inc..............................E 614 878-9462
  Grove City **(G-11420)**
Gears Garden Center Inc.....................E 513 931-3800
  Cincinnati **(G-3606)**
Gs Ohio Inc ....D 614 885-5350
  Powell **(G-16196)**
Hirts Greenhouse Inc..........................E 440 238-8200
  Strongsville **(G-17310)**
HJ Benken Flor & Greenhouses ....D 513 891-1040
  Cincinnati **(G-3713)**
Kens Flower Shop Inc ....E 419 841-9590
  Perrysburg **(G-15885)**
Lowes Grnhse & Gift Sp Inc ....E 440 543-5123
  Chagrin Falls **(G-2670)**

Oberers Flowers Inc ....E 937 223-1253
  Dayton **(G-9665)**
Rosby Brothers Inc ....E 216 351-0850
  Cleveland **(G-6339)**
Scarffs Nursery Inc ....C 937 845-3130
  New Carlisle **(G-14897)**
Wickline Landscaping Inc ....E 937 372-0521
  Xenia **(G-19933)**

FLORIST: Plants, Potted

Maria Gardens LLC ....E 440 238-7637
  Strongsville **(G-17328)**
Park Cincinnati Board ....D 513 421-4086
  Cincinnati **(G-4201)**

FLORISTS

Buehler Food Markets Inc ....C 330 364-3079
  Dover **(G-10068)**
Fred W Albrecht Grocery Co ....C 330 645-6222
  Coventry Township **(G-9034)**
Made From Scratch Inc ....E 614 873-3344
  Plain City **(G-16058)**
Wilsons Hillview Farm Inc ....E 740 763-2873
  Newark **(G-15110)**

FLORISTS' SPLYS, WHOLESALE

New Diamond Line Cont Corp ....E 330 644-9993
  Coventry Township **(G-9039)**

FLOTATION COMPANIES: Securities

Cowen and Company LLC ....E 440 331-3531
  Rocky River **(G-16429)**

FLOWERS & FLORISTS' SPLYS WHOLESALERS

Autograph Inc....................................E 216 881-1911
  Cleveland **(G-5024)**
Cottage Gardens Inc...........................D 440 259-2900
  Perry **(G-15822)**
Darice Inc ....C 440 238-9150
  Strongsville **(G-17297)**
Dummen Group ....E 614 850-9551
  Columbus **(G-7475)**
Flowerland Garden Centers ....E 440 439-8636
  Oakwood Village **(G-15489)**
Giant Eagle Inc ....D 330 364-5301
  Dover **(G-10079)**
North Branch Nursery Inc ....E 419 287-4679
  Pemberville **(G-15805)**
Scarffs Nursery Inc ....C 937 845-3130
  New Carlisle **(G-14897)**
Schmidt Bros Inc ....E 419 826-3671
  Swanton **(G-17406)**

FLOWERS & NURSERY STOCK, WHOLESALE

August Corso Sons Inc ....C 419 626-0765
  Sandusky **(G-16576)**
Lcn Holdings Inc ....E 440 259-5571
  Madison **(G-13101)**
Mac Kenzie Nursery Supply Inc............E 440 259-3517
  Perry **(G-15825)**
Rentokil North America Inc ....E 614 837-0099
  Groveport **(G-11534)**

FLOWERS, ARTIFICIAL, WHOLESALE

Flower Factory Inc ....D 614 275-6220
  Columbus **(G-7598)**

FLOWERS, FRESH, WHOLESALE

Claprood Roman J Co ....E 614 221-5515
  Columbus **(G-7217)**
Denver Wholesale Florists Co ....E 419 241-7241
  Toledo **(G-17698)**
Gs Ohio Inc ....D 614 885-5350
  Powell **(G-16196)**
Kens Flower Shop Inc ....E 419 841-9590
  Perrysburg **(G-15885)**
Oberers Flowers Inc ....E 937 223-1253
  Dayton **(G-9665)**

FLUID POWER PUMPS & MOTORS

Aerocontrolex Group Inc......................D 440 352-6182
  Painesville **(G-15692)**

Eaton-Aeroquip Llc.............................D 419 891-7775
  Maumee **(G-13782)**
Giant Industries Inc ....E 419 531-4600
  Toledo **(G-17762)**
Hite Parts Exchange Inc ....E 614 272-5115
  Columbus **(G-7756)**
Hydraulic Parts Store Inc ....E 330 364-6667
  New Philadelphia **(G-14966)**
Ingersoll-Rand Company ....E 419 633-6800
  Bryan **(G-1960)**
Pfpc Enterprises Inc ....B 513 941-6200
  Cincinnati **(G-4240)**
Robeck Fluid Power Co ....D 330 562-1140
  Aurora **(G-840)**

FLUID POWER VALVES & HOSE FITTINGS

Alkon Corporation ....D 419 355-9111
  Fremont **(G-11058)**
Eaton-Aeroquip Llc.............................E 419 891-7775
  Maumee **(G-13782)**
Hydraulic Parts Store Inc ....E 330 364-6667
  New Philadelphia **(G-14966)**
Parker-Hannifin Corporation.................B 937 456-5571
  Eaton **(G-10457)**
SSP Fittings Corp ....C 330 425-4250
  Twinsburg **(G-18323)**
Superior Products LLC ....D 216 651-9400
  Cleveland **(G-6484)**
Superior Products Llc ....D 216 651-9400
  Cleveland **(G-6483)**

FLUXES

Bluefoot Industrial LLC ....E 740 314-5299
  Steubenville **(G-17141)**

FOAMS & RUBBER, WHOLESALE

Johnson Bros Rubber Co Inc ....D 419 853-4122
  West Salem **(G-19128)**
Johnson Bros Rubber Co Inc ....E 419 752-4814
  Greenwich **(G-11402)**
Tahoma Enterprises Inc ....D 330 745-9016
  Barberton **(G-969)**
Tahoma Rubber & Plastics Inc ....D 330 745-9016
  Barberton **(G-970)**

FOIL & LEAF: Metal

A J Oster Foils LLC.............................D 330 823-1700
  Alliance **(G-512)**

FOOD PRDTS, CANNED: Chili

Gold Star Chili Inc ....E 513 231-4541
  Cincinnati **(G-3624)**

FOOD PRDTS, CANNED: Ethnic

Troyer Cheese Inc ....E 330 893-2479
  Millersburg **(G-14497)**

FOOD PRDTS, CANNED: Fruits

Louis Trauth Dairy LLC ....B 859 431-7553
  West Chester **(G-19064)**

FOOD PRDTS, CANNED: Tomatoes

Hirzel Canning Company ....D 419 693-0531
  Northwood **(G-15395)**

FOOD PRDTS, CONFECTIONERY, WHOLESALE: Candy

Gorant Chocolatier LLC ....C 330 726-8821
  Boardman **(G-1698)**
Gummer Wholesale Inc ....D 740 928-0415
  Heath **(G-11704)**
Robert E McGrath Inc ....E 440 572-7747
  Strongsville **(G-17341)**

FOOD PRDTS, CONFECTIONERY, WHOLESALE: Nuts, Salted/Roasted

Ohio Hickory Harvest Brand Pro ....E 330 644-6266
  Coventry Township **(G-9040)**
Tarrier Foods Corp ....E 614 876-8594
  Columbus **(G-8732)**

FOOD PRDTS, CONFECTIONERY, WHOLESALE: Potato Chips

Jones Potato Chip Co ....E 419 529-9424
  Mansfield *(G-13191)*

FOOD PRDTS, CONFECTIONERY, WHOLESALE: Snack Foods

Frito-Lay North America Inc ....C 513 759-1000
  West Chester *(G-18927)*
Frito-Lay North America Inc ....D 513 874-0112
  West Chester *(G-19054)*
Frito-Lay North America Inc ....C 216 491-4000
  Cleveland *(G-5583)*
Frito-Lay North America Inc ....E 937 224-8716
  Dayton *(G-9451)*
Frito-Lay North America Inc ....E 330 786-6000
  Akron *(G-230)*
Grippo Foods Inc ....E 513 923-1900
  Cincinnati *(G-3658)*
Mike-Sells Potato Chip Co ....E 937 228-9400
  Dayton *(G-9635)*
S-L Distribution Company LLC ....D 740 676-6932
  Bellaire *(G-1335)*
Shearers Foods LLC ....A 330 834-4030
  Massillon *(G-13730)*
Snyders-Lance Inc ....C 419 289-0787
  Ashland *(G-692)*

FOOD PRDTS, CONFECTIONERY, WHOLESALE: Syrups, Fountain

Multi-Flow Dispensers Ohio Inc ....D 216 641-0200
  Brooklyn Heights *(G-1876)*

FOOD PRDTS, DAIRY, WHOLESALE: Milk & Cream, Fluid

Instantwhip-Akron Inc ....E 614 488-2536
  Stow *(G-17214)*
Louis Trauth Dairy LLC ....B 859 431-7553
  West Chester *(G-19064)*

FOOD PRDTS, FISH & SEAFOOD, WHOLESALE: Fresh

Midwest Seafood Inc ....D 937 746-8856
  Springboro *(G-16975)*

FOOD PRDTS, FISH & SEAFOOD, WHOLESALE: Frozen, Unpackaged

Sherwood Food Distributors LLC ....D 216 662-8000
  Maple Heights *(G-13295)*

FOOD PRDTS, FISH & SEAFOOD, WHOLESALE: Seafood

Ocean Wide Seafood Company ....E 937 610-5740
  Cincinnati *(G-4146)*
Riser Foods Company ....D 216 292-7000
  Bedford Heights *(G-1327)*
Ritchies Food Distributors Inc ....E 740 443-6303
  Piketon *(G-15988)*

FOOD PRDTS, FROZEN: NEC

King Kold Inc ....E 937 836-2731
  Englewood *(G-10592)*
Skyline Chili Inc ....C 513 874-1188
  Fairfield *(G-10785)*

FOOD PRDTS, FRUITS & VEG, FRESH, WHOL: Banana Ripening Svc

Z Produce Co Inc ....E 614 224-4373
  Columbus *(G-8934)*

FOOD PRDTS, FRUITS & VEGETABLES, FRESH, WHOLESALE

Al Peake & Sons Inc ....E 419 243-9284
  Toledo *(G-17584)*
Anselmo Rssis Premier Prod Ltd ....E 800 229-5517
  Cleveland *(G-4983)*
Caruso Inc ....C 513 860-9200
  Cincinnati *(G-3127)*
Chariott Foods Inc ....E 419 243-1101
  Toledo *(G-17648)*

Chefs Garden Inc ....C 419 433-4947
  Huron *(G-12022)*
Del Monte Fresh Produce NA Inc ....E 614 527-7398
  Columbus *(G-7431)*
Dno Inc ....D 614 231-3601
  Columbus *(G-7463)*
Dole Fresh Vegetables Inc ....C 937 525-4300
  Springfield *(G-17030)*
Economy Prod Vegetable Co Inc ....E 216 431-2800
  Cleveland *(G-5466)*
Farris Produce Inc ....E 330 837-4607
  Massillon *(G-13681)*
Hillcrest Egg & Cheese Co ....D 216 361-4625
  Cleveland *(G-5691)*
Joe Lasita & Sons Inc ....E 513 241-5288
  Cincinnati *(G-3821)*
Midwest Fresh Foods Inc ....E 614 469-1492
  Columbus *(G-8081)*
Miles Farmers Market Inc ....C 440 248-5222
  Solon *(G-16872)*
Powell Company Ltd ....D 419 228-3552
  Lima *(G-12723)*
Produce One Inc ....D 931 253-4749
  Dayton *(G-9715)*
Sirna & Sons Inc ....C 330 298-2222
  Ravenna *(G-16266)*
Spartannash Company ....E 513 793-6300
  Cincinnati *(G-4510)*

FOOD PRDTS, FRUITS & VEGETABLES, FRESH, WHOLESALE: Potatoes

Mrs Dennis Potato Farm Inc ....E 419 335-2778
  Wauseon *(G-18807)*

FOOD PRDTS, FRUITS & VEGETABLES, FRESH, WHOLESALE: Vegetable

Barkett Fruit Co Inc ....E 330 364-6645
  Dover *(G-10065)*
JES Foods Inc ....E 216 883-8987
  Cleveland *(G-5793)*

FOOD PRDTS, FRUITS & VEGETABLES, FRESH, WHOLESALE: Vegetable

Cabbage Inc ....E 440 899-9171
  Vermilion *(G-18551)*
Freshway Foods Inc ....C 937 498-4664
  Sidney *(G-16780)*
Greenline Foods Inc ....D 419 354-1149
  Bowling Green *(G-1732)*

FOOD PRDTS, MEAT & MEAT PRDTS, WHOLESALE: Brokers

Tsg-Cincinnati LLC ....D 513 793-6241
  Blue Ash *(G-1669)*

FOOD PRDTS, MEAT & MEAT PRDTS, WHOLESALE: Cured Or Smoked

Troyer Cheese Inc ....E 330 893-2479
  Millersburg *(G-14497)*

FOOD PRDTS, MEAT & MEAT PRDTS, WHOLESALE: Fresh

Blue Ribbon Meats Inc ....D 216 631-8850
  Cleveland *(G-5064)*
Carles Bratwurst Inc ....E 419 562-7741
  Bucyrus *(G-1981)*
Dutch Creek Foods Inc ....E 330 852-2631
  Sugarcreek *(G-17378)*
Hillcrest Egg & Cheese Co ....D 216 361-4625
  Cleveland *(G-5691)*
Jetro Cash and Carry Entps LLC ....D 216 525-0101
  Cleveland *(G-5794)*
Kenosha Beef International Ltd ....C 614 771-1330
  Columbus *(G-7894)*
Landes Fresh Meats Inc ....E 937 836-3613
  Clayton *(G-4859)*
Lori Holding Co ....E 740 342-3230
  New Lexington *(G-14920)*
Marshallville Packing Co Inc ....E 330 855-2871
  Marshallville *(G-13474)*
Northern Frozen Foods Inc ....C 440 439-0600
  Cleveland *(G-6096)*
Produce One Inc ....D 931 253-4749
  Dayton *(G-9715)*

Ritchies Food Distributors Inc ....E 740 443-6303
  Piketon *(G-15988)*
S and S Gilardi Inc ....D 740 397-2751
  Mount Vernon *(G-14788)*
Sherwood Food Distributors LLC ....D 216 662-8000
  Maple Heights *(G-13295)*
Sherwood Food Distributors LLC ....B 216 662-6794
  Maple Heights *(G-13296)*
Siemer Distributing Company ....E 740 342-3230
  New Lexington *(G-14928)*
Spartannash Company ....E 513 793-6300
  Cincinnati *(G-4510)*
Tasty Pure Food Company ....E 330 434-8141
  Akron *(G-464)*

FOOD PRDTS, MEAT & MEAT PRDTS, WHOLESALE: Lard

Boars Head Provisions Co Inc ....B 614 662-5300
  Groveport *(G-11497)*

FOOD PRDTS, POULTRY, WHOLESALE: Live/Dressed/Frozen, Unpkgd

Di Feo & Sons Poultry Inc ....E 330 564-8172
  Akron *(G-185)*
Sherwood Food Distributors LLC ....D 216 662-8000
  Maple Heights *(G-13295)*

FOOD PRDTS, WHOL: Canned Goods, Fruit, Veg, Seafood/Meats

Avalon Foodservice Inc ....C 330 854-4551
  Canal Fulton *(G-2092)*
Food Distributors Inc ....E 740 439-2764
  Cambridge *(G-2068)*
Hillcrest Egg & Cheese Co ....D 216 361-4625
  Cleveland *(G-5691)*
Mattingly Foods Inc ....C 740 454-0136
  Zanesville *(G-20329)*
Northern Frozen Foods Inc ....C 440 439-0600
  Cleveland *(G-6096)*
Peck Distributors Inc ....E 216 587-6814
  Maple Heights *(G-13291)*
Powell Company Ltd ....D 419 228-3552
  Lima *(G-12723)*
Produce One Inc ....D 931 253-4749
  Dayton *(G-9715)*
Ritchies Food Distributors Inc ....E 740 443-6303
  Piketon *(G-15988)*
Z Produce Co Inc ....E 614 224-4373
  Columbus *(G-8934)*

FOOD PRDTS, WHOLESALE: Baking Splys

Bakemark USA LLC ....D 513 870-0880
  West Chester *(G-18872)*
Cassanos Inc ....E 937 294-8400
  Dayton *(G-9285)*

FOOD PRDTS, WHOLESALE: Beverage Concentrates

Flavorfresh Dispensers Inc ....E 216 641-0200
  Brooklyn Heights *(G-1871)*

FOOD PRDTS, WHOLESALE: Beverages, Exc Coffee & Tea

Esber Beverage Company ....E 330 456-4361
  Canton *(G-2306)*
G & J Pepsi-Cola Bottlers Inc ....D 740 593-3366
  Athens *(G-781)*
Knall Beverage Inc ....D 216 252-2500
  Cleveland *(G-5834)*
Louis Trauth Dairy LLC ....B 859 431-7553
  West Chester *(G-19064)*
Superior Beverage Group Ltd ....D 614 294-3555
  Lewis Center *(G-12562)*
Superior Beverage Group Ltd ....C 440 703-4580
  Solon *(G-16904)*

FOOD PRDTS, WHOLESALE: Chocolate

Walnut Creek Chocolate Company ......E 330 893-2995
  Walnut Creek *(G-18632)*

FOOD PRDTS, WHOLESALE: Coffee & Tea

Staufs Coffee Roasters II Inc ....E 614 487-6050
  Columbus *(G-8696)*

FOOD PRDTS, WHOLESALE: Coffee, Green Or Roasted

Berardis Fresh Roast Inc ....E 440 582-4303
North Royalton (G-15348)

Coffee Break Corporation ....E 513 841-1100
Cincinnati (G-3318)

FOOD PRDTS, WHOLESALE: Corn

Hanby Farms Inc ....E 740 763-3554
Nashport (G-14819)

Pioneer Hi-Bred Intl Inc ....E 419 748-8051
Grand Rapids (G-11328)

FOOD PRDTS, WHOLESALE: Dried or Canned Foods

Tarrier Foods Corp........................E 614 876-8594
Columbus (G-8732)

FOOD PRDTS, WHOLESALE: Grain Elevators

Archbold Elevator Inc.....................E 419 445-2451
Archbold (G-626)

Barnets Inc ....E 937 452-3275
Camden (G-2088)

Deerfield Farms Service Inc ....D 330 584-4715
Deerfield (G-9904)

Farmers Elev Grn & Sply Assoc ....E 419 653-4132
New Bavaria (G-14879)

Fort Recovery Equity Inc.................C 419 375-4119
Fort Recovery (G-10991)

FOOD PRDTS, WHOLESALE: Grains

Andersons Inc..............................C 419 893-5050
Maumee (G-13754)

Andersons Marathon Ethanol LLC ....E 937 316-3700
Greenville (G-11365)

Bunge North America Foundation........D 419 692-6010
Delphos (G-10020)

Champaign Landmark Inc ....E 937 652-2135
Urbana (G-18423)

Consolidated Grain & Barge Co ....D 419 785-1941
Defiance (G-9907)

Cooper Hatchery Inc......................C 419 594-3325
Oakwood (G-15483)

Granville Milling Co ....E 740 587-0221
Granville (G-11343)

Hansen-Mueller Co ....E 419 729-5535
Toledo (G-17778)

Heritage Cooperative Inc.................D 419 294-2371
West Mansfield (G-19125)

Mercer Landmark Inc ....E 419 586-7443
Celina (G-2602)

Sunrise Cooperative Inc ....B 937 575-6780
Piqua (G-16030)

FOOD PRDTS, WHOLESALE: Health

Natural Foods Inc.........................E 419 537-1713
Toledo (G-17934)

FOOD PRDTS, WHOLESALE: Juices

M & M Wine Cellar Inc....................E 330 536-6450
Lowellville (G-13041)

Ohio Citrus Juices Inc....................E 614 539-0030
Grove City (G-11463)

FOOD PRDTS, WHOLESALE: Molasses, Indl

Interntional Molasses Corp Ltd ....E 937 276-7980
Dayton (G-9519)

FOOD PRDTS, WHOLESALE: Natural & Organic

Clintonville Community Mkt...............E 614 261-3663
Columbus (G-7231)

FOOD PRDTS, WHOLESALE: Pizza Splys

Ohio Pizza Products Inc ....D 937 294-6969
Monroe (G-14578)

Rdp Foodservice Ltd ....D 614 261-5661
Hilliard (G-11811)

Wasserstrom Company ....E 614 228-6525
Columbus (G-8879)

FOOD PRDTS, WHOLESALE: Salt, Edible

Morton Salt Inc ....C 330 925-3015
Rittman (G-16407)

FOOD PRDTS, WHOLESALE: Sandwiches

Veritas Enterprises Inc ....E 513 578-2748
Cincinnati (G-2874)

FOOD PRDTS, WHOLESALE: Spaghetti

Osf International Inc ....D 513 942-6620
Fairfield (G-10767)

FOOD PRDTS, WHOLESALE: Specialty

Antonio Sofo Son Importing Co ....C 419 476-4211
Toledo (G-17596)

Atlantic Foods Corp........................D 513 772-3535
Cincinnati (G-2998)

Cleveland Sysco Inc ....A 216 201-3000
Cleveland (G-5290)

Euro Usa Inc ....D 216 714-0500
Cleveland (G-5495)

Leo A Dick & Sons Co ....D 330 452-5010
Canton (G-2374)

National Marketshare Group ....E 513 921-0800
Cincinnati (G-4094)

Sherwood Food Distributors LLC ....B 216 662-6794
Maple Heights (G-13296)

Troyer Cheese Inc ....E 330 893-2479
Millersburg (G-14497)

FOOD PRDTS, WHOLESALE: Starch

G & J Pepsi-Cola Bottlers Inc ....E 740 774-2148
Chillicothe (G-2782)

FOOD PRDTS, WHOLESALE: Water, Mineral Or Spring, Bottled

Distillata Company.........................D 216 771-2900
Cleveland (G-5428)

Hill Distributing Company ....D 614 276-6533
Dublin (G-10242)

Magnetic Springs Water Company........D 614 421-1780
Columbus (G-8009)

FOOD PRDTS, WHOLESALE: Wine Makers' Eqpt & Splys

Wine-Art of Ohio Inc ....E 330 678-7733
Kent (G-12269)

FOOD PRDTS: Dried & Dehydrated Fruits, Vegetables & Soup Mix

Hirzel Canning Company ....D 419 693-0531
Northwood (G-15395)

FOOD PRDTS: Eggs, Processed

Ballas Egg Products Corp.................D 614 453-0386
Zanesville (G-20280)

Fort Recovery Equity Inc..................C 419 375-4119
Fort Recovery (G-10991)

Ohio Fresh Eggs LLC ....C 740 893-7200
Croton (G-9065)

FOOD PRDTS: Eggs, Processed, Frozen

Cal-Maine Foods Inc ....E 937 968-4874
Union City (G-18352)

FOOD PRDTS: Flour & Other Grain Mill Products

Hansen-Mueller Co ....E 419 729-5535
Toledo (G-17778)

Pioneer Hi-Bred Intl Inc ....E 419 748-8051
Grand Rapids (G-11328)

FOOD PRDTS: Mixes, Flour

General Mills Inc ....D 513 770-0558
Mason (G-13585)

FOOD PRDTS: Potato & Corn Chips & Similar Prdts

Robert E McGrath Inc ....E 440 572-7747
Strongsville (G-17341)

FOOD PRDTS: Potato Chips & Other Potato-Based Snacks

Ballreich Bros Inc ....C 419 447-1814
Tiffin (G-17510)

Jones Potato Chip Co......................E 419 529-9424
Mansfield (G-3191)

Mike-Sells Potato Chip Co ....E 937 228-9400
Dayton (G-9635)

FOOD PRDTS: Poultry, Processed, Frozen

Martin-Brower Company LLC ....B 513 773-2301
West Chester (G-18971)

FOOD PRDTS: Preparations

Agrana Fruit Us Inc ....C 937 693-3821
Botkins (G-1706)

Ballreich Bros Inc ....C 419 447-1814
Tiffin (G-17510)

Dole Fresh Vegetables Inc ....C 937 525-4300
Springfield (G-17030)

Freshway Foods Inc ....C 937 498-4664
Sidney (G-16780)

Gold Star Chili Inc.........................E 513 231-4541
Cincinnati (G-3624)

Hiland Group Incorporated ....D 330 499-8404
Canton (G-2344)

Ohio Hickory Harvest Brand Pro ....E 330 644-6266
Coventry Township (G-9040)

Tarrier Foods Corp........................E 614 876-8594
Columbus (G-8732)

FOOD PRDTS: Salads

Barkett Fruit Co Inc........................E 330 364-6645
Dover (G-10065)

Dno Inc ....D 614 231-3601
Columbus (G-7463)

Sandridge Food Corporation ....C 330 725-8883
Medina (G-13999)

FOOD PRDTS: Sugar

Domino Foods Inc..........................D 216 432-3222
Cleveland (G-5437)

FOOD PRDTS: Turkey, Processed, NEC

Cooper Hatchery Inc......................C 419 594-3325
Oakwood (G-15483)

FOOD PRODUCTS MACHINERY

Harry C Lobalzo & Sons Inc ....E 330 666-6758
Akron (G-251)

Innovative Controls Corp ....D 419 691-6684
Toledo (G-17821)

ITW Food Equipment Group LLC ....A 937 332-2396
Troy (G-18208)

Lima Sheet Metal Machine & Mfg ....E 419 229-1161
Lima (G-12687)

N Wasserstrom & Sons Inc ....C 614 228-5550
Columbus (G-8126)

Norse Dairy Systems Inc ....C 614 294-4931
Columbus (G-8195)

R and J Corporation ....E 440 871-6009
Westlake (G-19394)

Winston Products LLC ....D 440 478-1418
Cleveland (G-6685)

Wolf Machine Company ....C 513 791-5194
Blue Ash (G-1679)

FOOD STORES: Convenience, Chain

Convenient Food Mart Inc................E 800 860-4844
Mentor (G-14035)

Lykins Companies Inc ....E 513 831-8820
Milford (G-14403)

Travelcenters of America LLC ....D 330 769-2053
Lodi (G-12829)

United Dairy Farmers Inc ....C 513 396-8700
Cincinnati (G-4678)

FOOD STORES: Convenience, Independent

1st Stop Inc.................................E 937 695-0318
Winchester (G-19658)

SERVICES

FOOD STORES: Delicatessen

Bagel Place Inc..............................E...... 419 885-1000
   Toledo (G-17604)

Michaels Bakery Inc.........................E...... 216 351-7530
   Cleveland (G-5978)

Weilands Fine Meats Inc.....................E...... 614 267-9910
   Columbus (G-8883)

FOOD STORES: Grocery, Chain

Aldi Inc..D...... 330 273-7351
   Hinckley (G-11857)

Fred W Albrecht Grocery Co..................C...... 330 666-6781
   Akron (G-229)

Sack n Save Inc..............................E...... 740 382-2464
   Marion (G-13458)

FOOD STORES: Grocery, Independent

Buehler Food Markets Inc....................C...... 330 364-3079
   Dover (G-10068)

Carfagnas Incorporated......................E...... 614 846-6340
   Columbus (G-7127)

Sommers Market LLC.........................D...... 330 352-7470
   Hartville (G-11699)

FOOD STORES: Supermarket, More Than 100K Sq Ft, Hypermrkt

Walmart Inc....................................C...... 937 399-0370
   Springfield (G-17133)

Walmart Inc....................................B...... 740 286-8203
   Jackson (G-12182)

FOOD STORES: Supermarkets

Giant Eagle Inc...............................D...... 330 364-5301
   Dover (G-10079)

FOOD STORES: Supermarkets, Chain

Jo Lynn Inc....................................D...... 419 994-3204
   Loudonville (G-12958)

Kroger Co......................................C...... 513 782-3300
   Cincinnati (G-3892)

Kroger Co......................................C...... 740 335-4030
   Wshngtn CT Hs (G-19877)

Kroger Co......................................C...... 937 294-7210
   Dayton (G-9551)

Kroger Co......................................B...... 614 898-3200
   Westerville (G-19274)

Kroger Co......................................D...... 740 363-4398
   Delaware (G-9994)

Kroger Co......................................C...... 614 759-2745
   Columbus (G-7928)

Kroger Co......................................B...... 937 376-7962
   Xenia (G-19916)

Kroger Co......................................D...... 937 848-5990
   Dayton (G-9552)

Riser Foods Company........................D...... 216 292-7000
   Bedford Heights (G-1327)

Spartannash Company........................D...... 513 793-6300
   Cincinnati (G-4510)

FOOD STORES: Supermarkets, Independent

Farm House Food Distrs Inc.................E...... 216 791-6948
   Cleveland (G-5513)

Fisher Foods Marketing Inc..................C...... 330 497-3000
   North Canton (G-15203)

Lofinos Inc....................................D...... 937 431-1662
   Dayton (G-9572)

Mary C Enterprises Inc.......................D...... 937 253-6169
   Dayton (G-9588)

FOOTWEAR, WHOLESALE: Athletic

Brennan-Eberly Team Sports Inc...........E...... 419 865-8326
   Holland (G-11876)

FOOTWEAR, WHOLESALE: Shoes

Drew Ventures Inc............................E...... 740 653-4271
   Lancaster (G-12390)

Ebuys Inc......................................E...... 858 831-0839
   Columbus (G-7496)

Georgia-Boot Inc.............................D...... 740 753-1951
   Nelsonville (G-14832)

Lehigh Outfitters LLC........................C...... 740 753-1951
   Nelsonville (G-14834)

Safety Solutions Inc..........................D...... 614 799-9900
   Columbus (G-8578)

FOOTWEAR, WHOLESALE: Slippers, House

R G Barry Corporation.......................D...... 614 864-6400
   Pickerington (G-15966)

FOREIGN CURRENCY EXCHANGE

Bannockburn Global Forex LLC.............E...... 513 386-7400
   Cincinnati (G-3016)

FORGINGS

Edward W Daniel LLC........................E...... 440 647-1960
   Wellington (G-18839)

US Tsubaki Power Transm LLC...............C...... 419 626-4560
   Sandusky (G-16653)

FORGINGS: Iron & Steel

S&V Industries Inc...........................E...... 330 666-1986
   Medina (G-13997)

FORGINGS: Nonferrous

Edward W Daniel LLC........................E...... 440 647-1960
   Wellington (G-18839)

FORGINGS: Plumbing Fixture, Nonferrous

Mansfield Plumbing Pdts LLC................A...... 419 938-5211
   Perrysville (G-15941)

FORMS: Concrete, Sheet Metal

Efco Corp.....................................E...... 614 876-1226
   Columbus (G-7509)

FOUNDRIES: Aluminum

Akron Foundry Co............................C...... 330 745-3101
   Akron (G-40)

Akron Foundry Co............................E...... 330 745-3101
   Barberton (G-939)

Aluminum Line Products Company..........D...... 440 835-8880
   Westlake (G-19316)

Yoder Industries Inc..........................C...... 937 278-5769
   Dayton (G-9890)

FOUNDRIES: Brass, Bronze & Copper

National Bronze Mtls Ohio Inc...............E...... 440 277-1226
   Lorain (G-12929)

FOUNDRIES: Nonferrous

Technology House Ltd.......................E...... 440 248-3025
   Streetsboro (G-17274)

Yoder Industries Inc..........................C...... 937 278-5769
   Dayton (G-9890)

FOUNDRIES: Steel

B-Tek Scales LLC............................C...... 330 471-8900
   Canton (G-2208)

Worthington Industries Inc...................C...... 513 539-9291
   Monroe (G-14587)

Worthngton Stelpac Systems LLC...........C...... 614 438-3205
   Columbus (G-8919)

FOUNDRY MACHINERY & EQPT

Equipment Manufacturers Intl...............E...... 216 651-6700
   Cleveland (G-5488)

FRAMES & FRAMING WHOLESALE

Culver Art & Frame Co.......................E...... 740 548-6868
   Lewis Center (G-12536)

Hobby Lobby Stores Inc.....................E...... 330 686-1508
   Stow (G-17209)

FRANCHISES, SELLING OR LICENSING

Cassanos Inc.................................E...... 937 294-8400
   Dayton (G-9285)

Clark Brands LLC............................A...... 330 723-9886
   Medina (G-13920)

Convenient Food Mart Inc...................E...... 800 860-4844
   Mentor (G-14035)

Covelli Family Ltd Partnership...............E...... 330 856-3176
   Warren (G-18694)

Diet Center Worldwide Inc...................E...... 330 665-5861
   Akron (G-186)

East of Chicago Pizza Inc....................E...... 419 225-7116
   Lima (G-12630)

Epcon Cmmnties Franchising Inc............D...... 614 761-1010
   Dublin (G-10218)

Escape Enterprises Inc.......................E...... 614 224-0300
   Columbus (G-7533)

Gold Star Chili Inc............................E...... 513 231-4541
   Cincinnati (G-3624)

Gosh Enterprises Inc.........................E...... 614 923-4700
   Columbus (G-7681)

Howley Bread Group Ltd......................D...... 440 808-1600
   Westlake (G-19352)

Larosas Inc....................................A...... 513 347-5660
   Cincinnati (G-3911)

Marcos Inc....................................C...... 419 885-4844
   Toledo (G-17894)

McDonalds Corporation......................E...... 614 682-1128
   Columbus (G-8044)

Moto Franchise Corporation.................E...... 937 291-1900
   Dayton (G-9646)

Ohio Valley Acquisition Inc...................B...... 513 553-0768
   Cincinnati (G-4159)

Petland Inc....................................E...... 740 775-2464
   Chillicothe (G-2811)

Physicians Weight Ls Ctr Amer..............E...... 330 666-7952
   Akron (G-382)

Premier Broadcasting Co Inc.................E...... 614 866-0700
   Columbus (G-8458)

Red Robin Gourmet Burgers Inc.............D...... 330 305-1080
   Canton (G-2452)

ServiceMaster of Defiance Inc...............E...... 419 784-5570
   Defiance (G-9940)

Skyline Chili Inc...............................C...... 513 874-1188
   Fairfield (G-10785)

Stanley Steemer Intl Inc......................E...... 614 764-2007
   Dublin (G-10341)

Ta Operating LLC.............................B...... 440 808-9100
   Westlake (G-19411)

Travelcenters of America LLC................B...... 724 981-9464
   Westlake (G-19414)

Tuffy Associates Corp........................E...... 419 865-6900
   Toledo (G-18112)

United Mercantile Corporation...............E...... 513 831-1300
   Milford (G-14440)

Wendys Company.............................B...... 614 764-3100
   Dublin (G-10374)

Wendys Restaurants LLC....................C...... 614 764-3100
   Dublin (G-10375)

FREIGHT CAR LOADING & UNLOADING SVCS

Precision Vhcl Solutions LLC.................E...... 513 651-9444
   Cincinnati (G-4268)

FREIGHT CONSOLIDATION SVCS

Dayton Freight Lines Inc.....................D...... 937 236-4880
   Dayton (G-9366)

FREIGHT FORWARDING ARRANGEMENTS

Blood Courier Inc.............................E...... 216 251-3050
   Cleveland (G-5063)

C & M Express Logistics Inc..................E...... 440 350-0802
   Painesville (G-15697)

Ceva Freight LLC.............................E...... 216 898-6765
   Cleveland (G-5162)

Ceva Logistics LLC...........................B...... 614 482-5000
   Groveport (G-11501)

Ceva Logistics US Inc........................E...... 614 482-5107
   Columbus (G-7172)

CH Robinson Freight Svcs Ltd...............E...... 440 234-7811
   Cleveland (G-5164)

Colonial Courier Service Inc..................E...... 419 891-0922
   Maumee (G-13773)

Contech Trckg & Logistics LLC...............D...... 513 645-7000
   West Chester (G-18897)

Dhl Supply Chain (usa).......................D...... 614 836-1265
   Groveport (G-11507)

Distribution Data Incorporated...............E...... 216 362-3009
   Brookpark (G-1896)

Eckel Logistics Inc............................E...... 419 349-3118
   Perrysburg (G-15862)

Exel Freight Connect Inc......................D...... 855 393-5378
   Columbus (G-7544)

Exel Global Logistics Inc.....................D...... 440 243-5900
   Cleveland (G-5500)

Exel Inc..D...... 740 929-2113
   Hebron (G-11713)

Exel Inc..D...... 800 426-8434
   Lockbourne (G-12816)

Exel N Amercn Logistics Inc..................C...... 800 272-1052
   Westerville (G-19253)

Expeditors Intl Wash Inc	E	614 492-9840
Lockbourne (G-12817)		
Freight Rite Inc	E	419 478-7400
Toledo (G-17748)		
GKN Freight Services Inc	E	419 232-5623
Van Wert (G-18478)		
Global Transportation Services	E	614 409-0770
Reynoldsburg (G-16305)		
Martin Logistics Inc	D	330 456-8000
Canton (G-2391)		
Nippon Express USA Inc	D	614 801-5695
Grove City (G-11459)		
Nissin Intl Trnspt USA Inc	D	937 644-2644
Marysville (G-13520)		
Noramco Transport Corp	E	513 245-9050
Cincinnati (G-4122)		
Nutrition Trnsp Svcs LLC	C	937 962-2661
Lewisburg (G-12571)		
Overland Xpress LLC	E	513 528-1158
Cincinnati (G-4193)		
Roadrunner Trnsp Systems Inc	E	330 920-4101
Peninsula (G-15812)		
Ryan Logistics Inc	D	937 642-4158
Marysville (G-13526)		
SMS Transport LLC	E	937 813-8897
Dayton (G-9772)		
Tazmanian Freight Fwdg Inc	E	216 265-7881
Middleburg Heights (G-14260)		
Tgs International Inc	E	330 893-4828
Millersburg (G-14495)		
Tier One Distribution LLC	D	937 323-6325
Springfield (G-17126)		
Tjm Express Inc	E	216 385-4164
Berea (G-1441)		
Tpg Noramco LLC	E	513 245-9050
Cincinnati (G-4624)		
Transfreight Inc	E	937 332-0366
Troy (G-18232)		
TV Minority Company Inc	E	937 832-9350
Englewood (G-10603)		
USF Holland LLC	C	216 941-4340
Cleveland (G-6612)		
World Ex Shipg Trnsp Fwdg Svcs	E	440 826-5055
Middleburg Heights (G-14266)		

FREIGHT FORWARDING ARRANGEMENTS: Domestic

Ardmore Power Logistics LLC	E	216 502-0640
Westlake (G-19318)		
Ceva Freight LLC	D	614 482-5100
Groveport (G-11500)		
Exel Global Logistics Inc	E	614 409-4500
Columbus (G-7545)		
IHS Enterprise Inc	C	216 588-9078
Independence (G-12081)		
Innovative Logistics Group Inc	E	937 832-9350
Englewood (G-10591)		
Krakowski Trucking Inc	E	330 722-7935
Medina (G-13966)		
Omni Interglobal Inc	E	216 239-3833
Cleveland (G-6131)		

FREIGHT FORWARDING ARRANGEMENTS: Foreign

Concord Express Inc	E	718 656-7821
Groveport (G-11503)		
Dash Services LLC	D	216 273-9133
Cleveland (G-5405)		
Elite Transportation Svcs LLC	E	330 769-5830
Seville (G-16684)		
Expeditors Intl Wash Inc	D	440 243-9900
Cleveland (G-5501)		
Schenker Inc	E	419 866-6390
Swanton (G-17405)		

FREIGHT HANDLING SVCS: Air

Exel Inc	B	614 865-8500
Westerville (G-19163)		
James Air Cargo Inc	E	440 243-9095
Cleveland (G-5779)		

FREIGHT TRANSPORTATION ARRANGEMENTS

A Plus Expediting & Logistics	E	937 424-0220
Dayton (G-9199)		
Airnet Systems Inc	C	614 409-4900
Columbus (G-6886)		

Bleckmann USA LLC	E	740 809-2645
Johnstown (G-12197)		
CH Robinson Company Inc	E	614 933-5100
Columbus (G-7175)		
Containerport Group Inc	D	216 692-3124
Euclid (G-10627)		
Cos Express Inc	D	614 276-9000
Columbus (G-7376)		
County of Medina	E	330 723-9670
Medina (G-13927)		
Craig Transportation Co	E	419 874-7981
Maumee (G-13777)		
Dick Lavy Trucking Inc	C	937 448-2104
Bradford (G-1761)		
DSV Solutions LLC	D	740 989-1200
Little Hocking (G-12807)		
Exel Inc	B	614 662-9247
Groveport (G-11511)		
Faf Inc	B	800 496-4696
Groveport (G-11512)		
Faro Services Inc	C	614 497-1700
Groveport (G-11513)		
FCA US LLC	D	419 729-5959
Toledo (G-17729)		
Fedex Custom Critical Inc	B	800 463-3339
Uniontown (G-18369)		
Fedex Freight Corporation	B	800 521-3505
Lima (G-12641)		
Fedex Freight Corporation	C	800 728-8190
Northwood (G-15394)		
Fedex Supply Chain	C	614 491-1518
Lockbourne (G-12819)		
Fedex Truckload Brokerage Inc	C	800 463-3339
Uniontown (G-18370)		
Globaltranz Enterprises Inc	C	513 745-0138
Blue Ash (G-1571)		
Hub City Terminals Inc	D	440 779-2226
Westlake (G-19354)		
Hub City Terminals Inc	E	419 217-5200
Toledo (G-17811)		
Jarrett Logistics Systems Inc	C	330 682-0099
Orrville (G-15636)		
JB Hunt Transport Svcs Inc	A	614 335-6681
Columbus (G-7855)		
Keller Logistics Group Inc	E	866 276-9486
Defiance (G-9923)		
Lesaint Logistics LLC	D	513 988-0101
Trenton (G-18188)		
Logikor LLC	E	513 762-7678
Cincinnati (G-3941)		
Mid Ohio Vly Bulk Trnspt Inc	E	740 373-2481
Marietta (G-13359)		
Millwood Inc	E	330 393-4400
Vienna (G-18582)		
Millwood Natural LLC	C	330 393-4400
Vienna (G-18583)		
Moving Solutions Inc	D	440 946-9300
Mentor (G-14090)		
Newark Parcel Service Company	E	614 253-3777
Columbus (G-8187)		
Packship Usa Inc	D	330 682-7225
Orrville (G-15643)		
Ray Hamilton Companies	E	513 641-5400
Blue Ash (G-1640)		
Regional Express Inc	D	516 458-3514
Richfield (G-16374)		
Rk Express International LLC	D	513 574-2400
Cincinnati (G-4383)		
Rondy Fleet Services Inc	C	330 745-9016
Barberton (G-965)		
Stack Container Service Inc	D	216 531-7555
Euclid (G-10657)		
Total Quality Logistics LLC	E	513 831-2600
Cincinnati (G-4612)		
Trans-Continental Systems Inc	E	513 769-4774
Cincinnati (G-4626)		
Trx Great Plains Inc	D	855 259-9259
Cleveland (G-6551)		
United States Cargo & Courier	E	614 449-2854
Columbus (G-8810)		
US Expediting Logistics LLC	E	937 235-1014
Vandalia (G-18547)		
Verst Group Logistics Inc	E	513 772-2494
Cincinnati (G-4757)		
William R Morse	E	440 352-2600
Painesville (G-15748)		
Wnb Group LLC	E	513 641-5400
Cincinnati (G-4801)		
Wright Distribution Ctrs Inc	E	419 227-7621
Lima (G-12785)		

Xpo Intermodal Inc	D	614 923-1400
Dublin (G-10377)		
Xpo Stacktrain LLC	E	614 923-1400
Dublin (G-10379)		
Yrc Inc	E	913 344-5174
Copley (G-8982)		
Zipline Logistics LLC	E	888 469-4754
Columbus (G-8938)		

FROZEN FRUITS WHOLESALERS

Powell Company Ltd	D	419 228-3552
Lima (G-12723)		

FRUIT & VEGETABLE MARKETS

Circle S Farms Inc	E	614 878-9462
Grove City (G-11420)		
Euclid Fish Company	D	440 951-6448
Mentor (G-14044)		

FRUIT STANDS OR MARKETS

Mapleside Valley LLC	D	330 225-5576
Brunswick (G-1937)		
Miles Farmers Market Inc	C	440 248-5222
Solon (G-16872)		
Vermilion Farm Market	E	440 967-9666
Vermilion (G-18564)		

FRUITS & VEGETABLES WHOLESALERS: Fresh

Bowman Organic Farms Ltd	E	740 246-3936
Thornville (G-17504)		
Circle S Farms Inc	E	614 878-9462
Grove City (G-11420)		
Sanfillipo Produce Co Inc	E	614 237-3300
Columbus (G-8591)		
US Foods Inc	A	614 539-7993
West Chester (G-19096)		
Vermilion Farm Market	E	440 967-9666
Vermilion (G-18564)		

FUEL OIL DEALERS

Aim Leasing Company	D	330 759-0438
Girard (G-11282)		
Bazell Oil Co Inc	E	740 385-5420
Logan (G-12831)		
Centerra Co-Op	E	419 281-2153
Ashland (G-665)		
Cincinnati - Vulcan Company	D	513 242-5300
Cincinnati (G-3219)		
Circleville Oil Co	D	740 474-7568
Circleville (G-4828)		
Cuyahoga Landmark Inc	E	440 238-3900
Strongsville (G-17295)		
Duncan Oil Co	E	937 426-5945
Dayton (G-9171)		
Energy Cooperative Inc	E	740 348-1206
Newark (G-15031)		
Lykins Oil Company	E	513 831-8820
Milford (G-14404)		
Mighty Mac Investments Inc	E	937 335-2928
Troy (G-18215)		
New Vulco Mfg & Sales Co LLC	D	513 242-2672
Cincinnati (G-4109)		
Santmyer Oil Co Inc	D	330 262-6501
Wooster (G-19764)		
The Columbia Oil Co.	E	513 868-8700
Liberty Twp (G-12589)		
Uil Inc	E	440 543-5195
Chagrin Falls (G-2685)		

FUND RAISING ORGANIZATION, NON-FEE BASIS

Air Frce Museum Foundation Inc	E	937 258-1218
Dayton (G-9158)		
Catholic Charities Corporation	E	216 939-3713
Cleveland (G-5132)		
Catholic Charities Corporation	E	216 268-4006
Cleveland (G-5133)		
Catholic Charities Corporation	E	419 289-1903
Ashland (G-663)		
Catholic Charities Corporation	E	216 334-2900
Cleveland (G-5134)		
Childrens Hospital Foundation	E	614 355-0888
Columbus (G-7189)		
Cincinnati Institute Fine Arts	E	513 871-2787
Cincinnati (G-3251)		

S
E
R
V
I
C
E
S

City of Columbus ....D 614 645-3072
Columbus (G-7208)

Cleveland Jewish Federation ....C 216 593-2900
Cleveland (G-5263)

Colonial Senior Services Inc ....C 513 856-8600
Hamilton (G-11582)

Columbus Jewish Federation ....E 614 237-7686
Columbus (G-7290)

Daybreak Inc ....E 937 395-4600
Dayton (G-9349)

Epilepsy Cncl/Grter Cincinnati ....E 513 721-2905
Cincinnati (G-3505)

Epilepsy Cntr of Nrthwstrn OH ....D 419 867-5950
Maumee (G-13786)

Fidelity Charitable Gift Fund ....C 800 952-4438
Cincinnati (G-3544)

Fort Hamilton Hosp Foundation ....B 513 867-5492
Hamilton (G-11596)

Greene County Career Center ....E 937 372-6941
Xenia (G-19906)

Interact For Health ....E 513 458-6600
Cincinnati (G-3774)

Medill Elemntary Sch of Volntr ....E 740 687-7352
Lancaster (G-12417)

National Multiple Sclerosis ....E 330 759-9066
Youngstown (G-20139)

Nationwide Childrens Hospital ....C 614 722-2700
Columbus (G-8143)

Orphan Foundation of America ....E 571 203-0270
Beachwood (G-1094)

Playhouse Square Holdg Co LLC ....C 216 771-4444
Cleveland (G-6219)

Sharon Twnship Frfighters Assn ....E 330 239-4992
Sharon Center (G-16725)

United Way Central Ohio Inc ....D 614 227-2700
Columbus (G-8814)

United Way Greater Stark Cnty ....E 330 491-0445
Canton (G-2523)

United Way of Summit County ....E 330 762-7601
Akron (G-477)

FUNDRAISING SVCS

Bbs & Associates Inc ....E 330 665-5227
Akron (G-89)

Board of Dir of Wittenbe ....E 937 327-6231
Springfield (G-16999)

Chapel HI Chrstn Schl Endwmnt ....D 330 929-1901
Cuyahoga Falls (G-9078)

Clovernook Center For The Bli ....C 513 522-3860
Cincinnati (G-3311)

Innovairre Communications LLC ....D 330 869-8500
Fairlawn (G-10833)

Lighthouse Youth Services Inc ....D 513 861-1111
Cincinnati (G-3930)

Miami University ....D 513 529-1230
Oxford (G-15683)

Ohio Presbyterian Rtr Svcs ....E 614 888-7800
Columbus (G-8281)

White Oak Investments Inc ....D 614 491-1000
Columbus (G-8897)

FUNERAL HOME

Cole Selby Funeral Inc ....E 330 856-4695
Vienna (G-18578)

Cummings and Davis Fnrl HM Inc ....E 216 541-1111
Cleveland (G-5389)

Davidson Becker Inc ....E 330 755-2111
Struthers (G-17363)

Domajaparo Inc ....E 513 742-3600
Cincinnati (G-3438)

E F Boyd & Son Inc ....E 216 791-0770
Cleveland (G-5453)

Ferfolia Funeral Homes Inc ....E 216 663-4222
Northfield (G-15379)

Keller Ochs Koch Inc ....E 419 332-8288
Fremont (G-11082)

Lucas Funeral Homes Inc ....E 419 294-1985
Upper Sandusky (G-18411)

Martin Altmeyer Funeral Home ....E 330 385-3650
East Liverpool (G-10406)

Newcomer Funeral Svc Group Inc ....B 513 521-1971
Cincinnati (G-4111)

Paul R Young Funeral Homes ....E 513 521-9303
Cincinnati (G-4214)

Rutherford Funeral Home Inc ....E 614 451-0593
Columbus (G-8563)

Spring Grove Funeral Homes Inc ....C 513 681-7526
Cincinnati (G-4518)

FUNERAL HOMES & SVCS

Cremation Service Inc ....E 216 621-6222
Cleveland (G-5379)

FUNGICIDES OR HERBICIDES

Scotts Company LLC ....B 937 644-0011
Marysville (G-13528)

FURNACES & OVENS: Indl

Hannon Company ....D 330 456-4728
Canton (G-2339)

RAD-Con Inc ....E 440 871-5720
Lakewood (G-12361)

United McGill Corporation ....E 614 829-1200
Groveport (G-11546)

FURNACES: Indl, Electric

Ajax Tocco Magnethermic Corp ....C 330 372-8511
Warren (G-18661)

FURNACES: Warm Air, Electric

Columbus Heating & Vent Co ....C 614 274-1177
Columbus (G-7286)

FURNITURE & CABINET STORES: Custom

Professonal Laminate Mllwk Inc ....E 513 891-7858
Milford (G-14427)

FURNITURE REFINISHING SVCS

Soft Touch Wood LLC ....E 330 545-4204
Girard (G-11300)

FURNITURE REPAIR & MAINTENANCE SVCS

Business Furniture LLC ....E 937 293-1010
Dayton (G-9271)

Everybodys Inc ....E 937 293-1010
Moraine (G-14654)

FURNITURE STORES

Beacon Company ....E 330 733-8322
Akron (G-92)

Big Sandy Furniture Inc ....D 740 574-2113
Franklin Furnace (G-11043)

Big Sandy Furniture Inc ....E 740 894-4242
Chesapeake (G-2727)

Big Sandy Furniture Inc ....E 740 354-3193
Portsmouth (G-16125)

Big Sandy Furniture Inc ....E 740 775-4244
Chillicothe (G-2758)

Columbus AAA Corp ....E 614 889-2840
Dublin (G-10181)

Dtv Inc ....E 216 226-5465
Mayfield Heights (G-13873)

Patterson Pope Inc ....D 513 891-4430
Cincinnati (G-4213)

S&D Farms Inc ....E 419 859-3785
Mount Cory (G-14722)

Workshops of David T Smith ....E 513 932-2472
Morrow (G-14718)

FURNITURE STORES: Office

Cbf Industries Inc ....E 216 229-9300
Bedford (G-1271)

Corporate Environments of Ohio ....E 614 358-3375
Columbus (G-7372)

Ebo Inc ....E 216 229-9300
Bedford (G-1279)

Loth Inc ....D 614 487-4000
Columbus (G-7989)

Recycled Systems Furniture Inc ....E 614 880-9110
Worthington (G-19842)

River City Furniture LLC ....D 513 612-7303
West Chester (G-18994)

Thomas W Ruff and Company ....B 800 828-0234
Columbus (G-8747)

Trimble Engineering & Cnstr ....E 937 233-8921
Dayton (G-9823)

FURNITURE STORES: Outdoor & Garden

Harrison Industries Inc ....D 740 942-2988
Cadiz (G-2029)

FURNITURE WHOLESALERS

Big Lots Stores Inc ....A 614 278-6800
Columbus (G-7035)

Cornerstone Brands Inc ....A 513 603-1000
West Chester (G-18898)

Federated Logistics ....E 937 294-3074
Moraine (G-14656)

Friends Service Co Inc ....D 419 427-1704
Findlay (G-10910)

Indepndence Office Bus Sup Inc ....D 216 398-8880
Cleveland (G-5746)

La-Z-Boy Incorporated ....C 614 478-0898
Columbus (G-7939)

McNerney & Son Inc ....E 419 666-0200
Toledo (G-17899)

Mill Distributors Inc ....D 330 995-9200
Aurora (G-837)

Sauder Woodworking Co ....A 419 446-2711
Archbold (G-639)

Staples Inc ....E 614 472-2014
Columbus (G-8685)

Veritas Enterprises Inc ....E 513 578-2748
Cincinnati (G-2874)

Workshops of David T Smith ....E 513 932-2472
Morrow (G-14718)

FURNITURE, OFFICE: Wholesalers

American Interiors Inc ....E 419 324-0365
Toledo (G-17590)

Apg Office Furnishings Inc ....E 216 621-4590
Cleveland (G-4989)

Business Furniture LLC ....E 937 293-1010
Dayton (G-9271)

Cbf Industries Inc ....E 216 229-9300
Bedford (G-1271)

Continental Office Furn Corp ....C 614 262-5010
Columbus (G-7358)

Ebo Inc ....E 216 229-9300
Bedford (G-1279)

Everybodys Inc ....E 937 293-1010
Moraine (G-14654)

Jones Group Interiors Inc ....E 330 253-9180
Akron (G-294)

King Business Interiors Inc ....E 614 430-0020
Columbus (G-7906)

Loth Inc ....D 614 487-4000
Columbus (G-7989)

Office Furniture Resources Inc ....E 216 781-8200
Cleveland (G-6113)

Regency Seating Inc ....E 330 848-3700
Akron (G-400)

S P Richards Company ....E 614 497-2270
Obetz (G-15529)

Seagate Office Products Inc ....E 419 861-6161
Holland (G-11913)

Springfield Business Eqp Co ....E 937 322-3828
Springfield (G-17117)

W B Mason Co Inc ....D 216 267-5000
Cleveland (G-6644)

Wasserstrom Company ....B 614 228-6525
Columbus (G-8878)

FURNITURE, PUBLIC BUILDING: Wholesalers

Custom Fabricators Inc ....E 216 831-2266
Cleveland (G-5391)

FURNITURE, WHOLESALE: Bedsprings

Mantua Manufacturing Co ....C 800 333-8333
Solon (G-16870)

FURNITURE, WHOLESALE: Filing Units

Central Business Equipment Co ....E 513 891-4430
Cincinnati (G-3150)

Patterson Pope Inc ....D 513 891-4430
Cincinnati (G-4213)

FURNITURE, WHOLESALE: Tables, Occasional

Progressive Furniture Inc ....E 419 446-4500
Archbold (G-635)

FURNITURE: Bed Frames & Headboards, Wood

Progressive Furniture Inc ....E 419 446-4500
Archbold (G-635)

FURNITURE: Frames, Box Springs Or Bedsprings, Metal

Mantua Manufacturing Co ....C 800 333-8333
Solon (G-16870)

FURNITURE: Household, Upholstered, Exc Wood Or Metal

Bulk Carrier Trnsp Eqp Co ....E 330 339-3333
New Philadelphia (G-14947)

FURNITURE: Household, Wood

Diversified Products & Svcs ....C 740 393-6202
Mount Vernon (G-14763)
Ken Harper ....C 740 439-4452
Byesville (G-2025)
Vocational Services Inc ....C 216 431-8085
Cleveland (G-6640)

FURNITURE: Institutional, Exc Wood

Soft Touch Wood LLC ....E 330 545-4204
Girard (G-11300)
Yanfeng US Automotive ....D 419 662-4905
Northwood (G-15416)

FURNITURE: Mattresses & Foundations

Walter F Stephens Jr Inc ....E 937 746-0521
Franklin (G-11041)

FURNITURE: Office, Exc Wood

Casco Mfg Solutions Inc ....D 513 681-0003
Cincinnati (G-3129)
National Electro-Coatings Inc ....D 216 898-0080
Cleveland (G-6043)
Recycled Systems Furniture Inc ....E 614 880-9110
Worthington (G-19842)

FURNITURE: Office, Wood

National Electro-Coatings Inc ....D 216 898-0080
Cleveland (G-6043)
Symatic Inc ....E 330 225-1510
Brunswick (G-1941)

FURNITURE: Play Pens, Children's, Wood

Western & Southern Lf Insur Co ....A 513 629-1800
Cincinnati (G-4786)

FURNITURE: Upholstered

Sauder Woodworking Co ....A 419 446-2711
Archbold (G-639)

FUTURES ADVISORY SVCS

Richard Allen Group LLC ....D 614 623-2654
Powell (G-16206)

GAMES & TOYS: Child Restraint Seats, Automotive

Recaro Child Safety LLC ....E 248 904-1570
Cincinnati (G-4344)

GARAGE DOOR REPAIR SVCS

Dayton Door Sales Inc ....E 937 253-9181
Dayton (G-9364)

GARMENT: Pressing & cleaners' agents

C&C Clean Team Enterprises LLC ....C 513 321-5100
Cincinnati (G-3102)

GAS & OIL FIELD EXPLORATION SVCS

Alliance Petroleum Corporation ....D 330 493-0440
Canton (G-2180)
Antero Resources Corporation ....D 740 760-1000
Marietta (G-13312)
Bakerwell Inc ....D 614 898-7590
Westerville (G-19146)

Belden & Blake Corporation ....E 330 602-5551
Dover (G-10066)
Chevron Ae Resources LLC ....E 330 654-4343
Deerfield (G-9902)
Enervest Ltd ....D 330 877-6747
Hartville (G-11685)
Husky Marketing and Supply Co ....E 614 210-2300
Dublin (G-10250)
Precision Geophysical Inc ....E 330 674-2198
Millersburg (G-14488)
Range Rsurces - Appalachia LLC ....E 330 866-3301
Dover (G-10094)
Triad Energy Corporation ....E 740 374-2940
Marietta (G-13387)
True North Energy LLC ....E 440 442-0060
Mayfield Heights (G-13883)

GAS & OIL FIELD SVCS, NEC

Timothy Sinfield ....E 740 685-3684
Pleasant City (G-16072)

GAS & OTHER COMBINED SVCS

Dayton Power and Light Company ....D 937 549-2641
Manchester (G-13128)
Dayton Power and Light Company ....E 937 331-3032
Miamisburg (G-14163)
Dayton Power and Light Company ....D 937 331-4123
Moraine (G-14647)
Duke Energy Kentucky Inc ....E 704 594-6200
Cincinnati (G-3449)
G & O Resources Ltd ....D 330 253-2525
Akron (G-231)
Heritage Cooperative Inc ....D 419 294-2371
West Mansfield (G-19125)
National Gas & Oil Corporation ....E 740 344-2102
Newark (G-15079)

GAS FIELD MACHINERY & EQPT

Jet Rubber Company ....E 330 325-1821
Rootstown (G-16450)

GAS PRODUCTION & DISTRIBUTION: Liq Petroleum, Distrib-Mains

Heritage Cooperative Inc ....D 419 294-2371
West Mansfield (G-19125)

GAS STATIONS

Bp ....E 216 731-3826
Euclid (G-10625)
Buehler Food Markets Inc ....C 330 364-3079
Dover (G-10068)
Free Enterprises Incorporated ....D 330 722-2031
Medina (G-13940)
Holland Oil Company ....D 330 835-1815
Akron (G-266)
Travelcenters of America LLC ....D 330 769-2053
Lodi (G-12829)
Triumph Energy Corporation ....E 513 367-9900
Harrison (G-11679)

GAS STATIONS WITH CONVENIENCE STORES

Trep Ltd ....E 419 717-5624
Napoleon (G-14818)

GAS SYSTEM CONVERSION SVCS

Compliant Healthcare Tech LLC ....E 216 255-9607
Cleveland (G-5331)

GASES: Acetylene

Delille Oxygen Company ....E 614 444-1177
Columbus (G-7432)

GASES: Indl

National Gas & Oil Corporation ....E 740 344-2102
Newark (G-15079)
Wright Brothers Inc ....E 513 731-2222
Cincinnati (G-4807)

GASKETS

Industry Products Co ....B 937 778-0585
Piqua (G-16011)
Ohio Gasket and Shim Co Inc ....E 330 630-0626
Akron (G-359)

GASKETS & SEALING DEVICES

Federal-Mogul Powertrain LLC ....C 740 432-2393
Cambridge (G-2067)
Ishikawa Gasket America Inc ....C 419 353-7300
Bowling Green (G-1738)

GASOLINE FILLING STATIONS

Calvary Christian Ch of Ohio ....E 740 828-9000
Frazeysburg (G-11048)
Convenient Food Mart Inc ....E 800 860-4844
Mentor (G-14035)
Cuyahoga Landmark Inc ....E 440 238-3900
Strongsville (G-17295)
Giles Marathon Inc ....E 440 974-8815
Mentor (G-14051)
Irace Inc ....E 330 836-7247
Akron (G-281)
Mighty Mac Investments Inc ....E 937 335-2928
Troy (G-18215)
Napoleon Wash-N-Fill Inc ....D 419 592-0851
Napoleon (G-14814)
Sines Inc ....E 440 352-6572
Painesville (G-15740)
Standard Oil Company ....E 330 530-8049
Girard (G-11301)
Ta Operating LLC ....B 440 808-9100
Westlake (G-19411)
Travelcenters America Inc ....A 440 808-9100
Westlake (G-19413)
True North Energy LLC ....E 440 442-0060
Mayfield Heights (G-13883)
True North Energy LLC ....E 877 245-9336
Brecksville (G-1808)
United Dairy Farmers Inc ....C 513 396-8700
Cincinnati (G-4678)

GASOLINE WHOLESALERS

Cuyahoga Landmark Inc ....E 440 238-3900
Strongsville (G-17295)
Duncan Oil Co ....E 937 426-5945
Dayton (G-9171)
Free Enterprises Incorporated ....D 330 722-2031
Medina (G-13940)
Holland Oil Company ....D 330 835-1815
Akron (G-266)
Krebs Steve BP Oil Co ....E 513 641-0150
Cincinnati (G-3890)
Lykins Companies Inc ....E 513 831-8820
Milford (G-14403)
Lykins Oil Company ....E 513 831-8820
Milford (G-14404)
Marathon Petroleum Company LP ....B 330 479-5688
Canton (G-2387)
Marathon Petroleum Company LP ....E 614 274-1125
Columbus (G-8015)
Marathon Petroleum Company LP ....E 513 932-6007
Lebanon (G-12483)
Marathon Petroleum Corporation ....B 419 422-2121
Findlay (G-10938)
Mplx Terminals LLC ....E 440 526-4653
Cleveland (G-6017)
Mplx Terminals LLC ....E 330 479-5539
Canton (G-2409)
Mplx Terminals LLC ....E 504 252-8064
Heath (G-11706)
Nzr Retail of Toledo Inc ....D 419 724-0005
Toledo (G-17955)
The Columbia Oil Co ....D 513 868-8700
Liberty Twp (G-12589)
True North Energy LLC ....E 877 245-9336
Brecksville (G-1808)

GATES: Ornamental Metal

Mound Technologies Inc ....E 937 748-2937
Springboro (G-16977)

GEARS: Power Transmission, Exc Auto

Forge Industries Inc ....A 330 782-8301
Youngstown (G-20040)

GENERAL COUNSELING SVCS

Access Counseling Services LLC ....C 513 649-8008
Middletown (G-14341)
Adena Health System ....E 740 779-4888
Chillicothe (G-2754)
Ben El Child Development Ctr ....E 937 465-0010
Urbana (G-18419)

Bobby Tripodi Foundation Inc ....E 216 524-3787
  Independence *(G-12050)*

Cambridge Counseling Center ....C 740 450-7790
  Zanesville *(G-20287)*

Catholic Charities Corporation ....E 216 939-3713
  Cleveland *(G-5132)*

Center For Families & Children ....E 440 888-0300
  Cleveland *(G-5149)*

Clermont Counseling Center ....E 513 345-8555
  Cincinnati *(G-3305)*

Clermont Counseling Center ....E 513 947-7000
  Amelia *(G-571)*

Cleveland Center For Etng Dsor ....E 216 765-2535
  Beachwood *(G-1045)*

College Now Grter Clveland Inc ....D 216 241-5587
  Cleveland *(G-5312)*

Compdrug ....E 614 224-4506
  Columbus *(G-7340)*

Comprehensive Services Inc ....E 614 442-0664
  Columbus *(G-7343)*

Directions For Youth Families ....E 614 294-2661
  Columbus *(G-7449)*

Emerge Ministries Inc ....E 330 865-8351
  Akron *(G-203)*

F R S Connections ....E 937 393-9662
  Hillsboro *(G-11838)*

Friend To Friend Program ....E 216 861-1838
  Cleveland *(G-5581)*

Marion Area Counseling Ctr ....C 740 387-5210
  Marion *(G-13434)*

Mental Health & Recovery Ctr...............C 937 383-3031
  Wilmington *(G-19635)*

Mercy Health ....E 440 324-0400
  Elyria *(G-10536)*

Mid-Ohio Psychological Svcs Inc............D 740 687-0042
  Lancaster *(G-12419)*

Midwest Behavioral Care Ltd ....E 937 454-0092
  Dayton *(G-9632)*

North East Ohio Health Svcs ....D 216 831-6466
  Beachwood *(G-1086)*

Northland Brdg Franklin Cnty...............E 614 846-2588
  Columbus *(G-8201)*

Pastoral Counseling Svc Summit...............C 330 996-4600
  Akron *(G-371)*

Pressley Ridge Pryde ....E 513 559-1402
  Cincinnati *(G-4275)*

Ryan Sheridan ....E 330 270-2380
  Youngstown *(G-20201)*

Santantonio Diana and Assoc ....E 440 323-5121
  Elyria *(G-10560)*

Scioto Pnt Vly Mental Hlth Ctr...............C 740 775-1260
  Chillicothe *(G-2825)*

Southast Cmnty Mental Hlth Ctr...............E 614 293-9613
  Worthington *(G-19850)*

Syntero Inc ....E 614 889-5722
  Dublin *(G-10350)*

Talbert House Health ....E 513 541-7577
  Cincinnati *(G-4575)*

Townhall 2 ....E 330 678-3006
  Kent *(G-12263)*

Tuscarawas County Help ME Grow ....E 330 339-3493
  New Philadelphia *(G-14986)*

GENERAL ECONOMIC PROGRAM ADMINISTRATION, GOVERNMENT: State

Ohio Department of Commerce.............C 614 728-8400
  Columbus *(G-8238)*

GENERAL MERCHANDISE, NONDURABLE, WHOLESALE

Aurora Wholesalers LLC ....D 440 248-5200
  Solon *(G-16825)*

Buy Below Retail Inc ....E 216 292-7805
  Cleveland *(G-5108)*

Clercom Inc ....D 513 724-6101
  Williamsburg *(G-19491)*

Hammacher Schlemmer & Co Inc ....C 513 860-4570
  West Chester *(G-18941)*

Harold Tatman & Sons Entps Inc ....E 740 655-2880
  Kingston *(G-12315)*

Hays Enterprises Inc ....E 330 392-2278
  Warren *(G-18711)*

Hi-Way Distributing Corp Amer ....D 330 645-6633
  Coventry Township *(G-9035)*

ICM Distributing Company Inc ....E 234 212-3030
  Twinsburg *(G-18281)*

Merchandise Inc ....D 513 353-2200
  Miamitown *(G-14242)*

Riser Foods Company...............D 216 292-7000
  Bedford Heights *(G-1327)*

Trademark Global LLC ....D 440 960-6200
  Lorain *(G-12948)*

X-S Merchandise Inc ....E 216 524-5620
  Independence *(G-12142)*

GERIATRIC RESIDENTIAL CARE FACILITY

Advanced Geriatric Education & ....E 888 393-9799
  Loveland *(G-12976)*

Antwerp Mnor Asssted Lving LLC ....E 419 258-1500
  Antwerp *(G-613)*

C I E Inc.................B 419 986-5566
  Burgoon *(G-2011)*

College Park Inc ....E 740 623-4607
  Coshocton *(G-9002)*

First Community Village ....B 614 324-4455
  Columbus *(G-7585)*

Glen Wesley Inc ....D 614 888-7492
  Columbus *(G-7673)*

Grace Hospice LLC ....C 440 826-0350
  Cleveland *(G-5619)*

Hcf Management Inc ....C 419 999-2055
  Lima *(G-12653)*

Lindley Inn ....E 740 797-9701
  The Plains *(G-17503)*

Oakleaf Village Ltd ....D 614 431-1739
  Columbus *(G-8222)*

Sattlerpearson Inc.................E 419 698-3822
  Northwood *(G-15406)*

United Church Homes Inc ....C 937 426-8481
  Beavercreek *(G-1239)*

Washington Manor Inc ....E 937 433-3441
  Dayton *(G-9867)*

West View Manor Inc ....C 330 264-8640
  Wooster *(G-19782)*

Whitehouse Operator LLC ....D 419 877-5338
  Whitehouse *(G-19452)*

GERIATRIC SOCIAL SVCS

Adams Cnty Snior Ctzens Cuncil ....E 937 544-7459
  West Union *(G-19130)*

Aultman Hospital ....A 330 363-6262
  Canton *(G-2204)*

City of Highland Heights ....D 440 461-2441
  Cleveland *(G-5202)*

Concordia Care ....C 216 791-3580
  Cleveland *(G-5333)*

Otterbein Snior Lfstyle Chices ....C 419 394-2366
  Saint Marys *(G-16530)*

Wesley Community Services LLC ....D 513 661-2777
  Cincinnati *(G-4779)*

GIFT SHOP

Amish Door Inc ....B 330 359-5464
  Wilmot *(G-19657)*

Auxiliary St Lukes Hospital.................E 419 893-5911
  Maumee *(G-13759)*

Bennett Enterprises Inc.................E 419 874-3111
  Perrysburg *(G-15838)*

Columbus Zoological Park Assn ....C 614 645-3400
  Powell *(G-16190)*

Dutch Heritage Farms Inc ....E 330 893-3232
  Berlin *(G-1446)*

Dutchman Hospitality Group Inc...............C 614 873-3414
  Plain City *(G-16050)*

Enesco Properties LLC ....A 440 473-2000
  Highland Heights *(G-11733)*

Golden Lamb ....C 513 932-5065
  Lebanon *(G-12468)*

Gs Ohio Inc.................D 614 885-5350
  Powell *(G-16196)*

H & M Patch Company ....D 614 339-8950
  Columbus *(G-7706)*

Hrm Enterprises Inc.................C 330 877-9353
  Hartville *(G-11691)*

Lowes Grnhse & Gift Sp Inc ....E 440 543-5123
  Chagrin Falls *(G-2670)*

Mapleside Valley LLC ....D 330 225-5576
  Brunswick *(G-1937)*

Park Cincinnati Board ....E 513 421-4086
  Cincinnati *(G-4201)*

Sauder Village ....B 419 446-2541
  Archbold *(G-638)*

Thirty-One Gifts LLC.................A 614 414-4300
  Columbus *(G-8745)*

Waterbeds n Stuff Inc ....E 614 871-1171
  Grove City *(G-11483)*

Youngs Jersey Dairy Inc ....B 937 325-0629
  Yellow Springs *(G-19941)*

GIFT, NOVELTY & SOUVENIR STORES: Party Favors

J V Hansel Inc.................E 330 716-0806
  Warren *(G-18716)*

GIFTS & NOVELTIES: Wholesalers

Ameri Interntl Trade Grp Inc ....E 419 586-6433
  Celina *(G-2582)*

Aunties Attic ....E 740 548-5059
  Lewis Center *(G-12528)*

Dollar Paradise ....E 216 432-0421
  Cleveland *(G-5436)*

Dwa Mrkting Prmtional Pdts LLC ....E 216 476-0635
  Strongsville *(G-17298)*

Esc and Company Inc.................E 614 794-0568
  Columbus *(G-7532)*

Flower Factory Inc ....D 614 275-6220
  Columbus *(G-7598)*

K & M International Inc ....D 330 425-2550
  Twinsburg *(G-18286)*

M & M Wintergreens Inc ....D 216 398-1288
  Cleveland *(G-5891)*

Mark Feldstein & Assoc Inc ....E 419 867-9500
  Sylvania *(G-17437)*

Nannicola Wholesale Co ....D 330 799-0888
  Youngstown *(G-20134)*

Par International Inc ....E 614 529-1300
  Obetz *(G-15528)*

Waterbeds n Stuff Inc ....E 614 871-1171
  Grove City *(G-11483)*

GIRLS CAMPS

Archdiocese of Cincinnati.................E 513 729-1725
  Cincinnati *(G-2980)*

Camp Pinecliff Inc.................D 614 236-5698
  Columbus *(G-7109)*

GLASS FABRICATORS

AGC Automotive Americas ....D 937 599-3131
  Bellefontaine *(G-1343)*

Anderson Glass Co Inc ....E 614 476-4877
  Columbus *(G-6947)*

Enclosure Suppliers LLC ....E 513 782-3900
  Cincinnati *(G-3496)*

Fuyao Glass America Inc ....C 937 496-5777
  Dayton *(G-9454)*

Ghp II LLC ....B 740 681-6825
  Lancaster *(G-12406)*

Rumpke Transportation Co LLC...............C 513 242-4600
  Cincinnati *(G-4410)*

GLASS PRDTS, FROM PURCHASED GLASS: Windshields

Safelite Group Inc ....A 614 210-9000
  Columbus *(G-8576)*

GLASS PRDTS, PRESSED OR BLOWN: Glass Fibers, Textile

Owens Corning Sales LLC...............A 419 248-8000
  Toledo *(G-17968)*

GLASS PRDTS, PRESSED OR BLOWN: Glassware, Novelty

Mosser Glass Incorporated.................E 740 439-1827
  Cambridge *(G-2077)*

GLASS STORES

Cleveland Glass Block Inc ....E 216 531-6363
  Cleveland *(G-5256)*

Cleveland Glass Block Inc ....E 614 252-5888
  Columbus *(G-7225)*

Lorain Glass Co Inc ....D 440 277-6004
  Lorain *(G-12920)*

Medina Glass Block Inc.................E 330 239-0239
  Medina *(G-13974)*

R C Hemm Glass Shops Inc.................E 937 773-5591
  Piqua *(G-16025)*

GLASS, AUTOMOTIVE: Wholesalers

Fuyao Glass America Inc ....C 937 496-5777
Dayton *(G-9454)*

GLASS: Fiber

Industrial Fiberglass Spc Inc ....E 937 222-9000
Dayton *(G-9514)*

GLASS: Flat

Schodorf Truck Body & Eqp Co ....E 614 228-6793
Columbus *(G-8603)*

GLASS: Pressed & Blown, NEC

Anderson Glass Co Inc ....E 614 476-4877
Columbus *(G-6947)*

GLASS: Structural

Continental GL Sls & Inv Group ....B 614 679-1201
Powell *(G-16192)*

GLASSWARE STORES

Mosser Glass Incorporated...................E 740 439-1827
Cambridge *(G-2077)*

GLASSWARE, NOVELTY, WHOLESALE

Mosser Glass Incorporated...................E 740 439-1827
Cambridge *(G-2077)*

GLOVES: Work

West Chester Holdings LLC...................C 800 647-1900
Cincinnati *(G-4781)*

GO-CART DEALERS

Goofy Golf Inc ....E 419 625-1308
Sandusky *(G-16612)*

GOLF CARTS: Powered

Kmj Leasing Ltd ....E 614 871-3883
Orient *(G-15620)*

GOLF CARTS: Wholesalers

Century Equipment Inc ....E 419 865-7400
Toledo *(G-17645)*
Century Equipment Inc.........................E 216 292-6911
Cleveland *(G-5158)*

GOLF COURSES: Public

797 Elks Golf Club Inc ....E 937 382-2666
Wilmington *(G-19599)*
A To Z Golf Managment Co ....E 937 434-4911
Dayton *(G-9200)*
Aboutgolf Limited ....D 419 482-9095
Maumee *(G-13745)*
American Golf Corporation...................E 740 965-5122
Galena *(G-11154)*
American Golf Corporation...................E 419 693-1991
Toledo *(G-17589)*
Amix Inc ....E 513 539-7220
Middletown *(G-14288)*
Ashland Golf Club...............................E 419 289-2917
Ashland *(G-651)*
Aston Oaks Golf Club..........................E 513 467-0070
North Bend *(G-15181)*
Avalon Golf & Country Club ....D 330 539-5008
Vienna *(G-18577)*
Avalon Lakes Golf Inc ....E 330 856-8898
Warren *(G-18675)*
Avon Properties Inc ....E 440 934-6217
Avon *(G-864)*
Avondale Golf Club..............................E 440 934-4398
Avon *(G-865)*
Bayview Retirees Golf Course...............D 419 726-8081
Toledo *(G-17607)*
Beckett Ridge Country Club ....D 513 874-2710
West Chester *(G-18873)*
Black Diamond Golf Course ....E 330 674-6110
Millersburg *(G-14461)*
Blackbrook Country Club Inc................E 440 951-0010
Mentor *(G-14022)*
Bramarjac Inc ....E 419 884-3434
Mansfield *(G-13144)*
Brandywine Country Club Inc ....E 330 657-2525
Peninsula *(G-15810)*

Brentwood Golf Club Inc......................E 440 322-9254
Sheffield Village *(G-16733)*
Bw Enterprises Inc ....E 937 568-9660
South Charleston *(G-16923)*
Cambridge Country Club Company ......E 740 439-2744
Byesville *(G-2023)*
Caravon Golf Company Ltd ....D 440 937-6018
Avon *(G-870)*
Championship Management Co ....D 740 524-4653
Sunbury *(G-17385)*
Chardon Lakes Golf Course Inc ....E 440 285-4653
Chardon *(G-2689)*
Chgc Inc ....D 330 225-6122
Valley City *(G-18459)*
Chippewa Golf Corp ....E 330 658-2566
Doylestown *(G-10109)*
Circling Hills Golf Course ....E 513 367-5858
Harrison *(G-11664)*
City of Akron ....E 330 864-0020
Akron *(G-134)*
City of Beavercreek ....D 937 320-0742
Beavercreek *(G-1141)*
City of Blue Ash ....E 513 745-8577
Blue Ash *(G-1528)*
City of Cuyahoga Falls ....E 330 971-8416
Cuyahoga Falls *(G-9081)*
City of Miamisburg ....E 937 866-4653
Miamisburg *(G-14153)*
City of Parma ....E 440 885-8876
Cleveland *(G-5212)*
City of Pickerington ....E 614 645-8474
Pickerington *(G-15951)*
City of Vandalia ....E 937 890-1300
Vandalia *(G-18517)*
City of Westlake ....E 440 835-6442
Westlake *(G-19332)*
City of Willoughby ....E 440 953-4280
Willoughby *(G-19513)*
Cleveland Metroparks..........................D 440 526-4285
Brecksville *(G-1776)*
Cleveland Metroparks..........................D 440 232-7184
Cleveland *(G-5271)*
Cleveland Metroparks..........................D 440 331-1070
Cleveland *(G-5272)*
Columbus Frkln Cnty Pk ....E 614 861-3193
Reynoldsburg *(G-16293)*
Columbus Zoological Park Assn ....C 614 645-3400
Powell *(G-16190)*
Creekside Golf Ltd ....E 513 785-2999
Fairfield Township *(G-10806)*
Creekside Ltd LLC ....D 513 583-4977
Loveland *(G-12986)*
Crooked Tree Golf Course ....E 513 398-3933
Cincinnati *(G-3381)*
Cumberland Trail Golf CLB Crse ....E 740 964-9336
Etna *(G-10614)*
Darby Creek Golf Course Inc ....E 937 349-7491
Marysville *(G-13494)*
Dorlon Golf Club ....E 440 236-8234
Columbia Station *(G-6774)*
E J Links Co The Inc............................E 440 235-0501
Olmsted Twp *(G-15535)*
Emerald Woods Golf Course ....E 440 236-8940
Columbia Station *(G-6775)*
Fox Den Fairways Inc ....E 330 678-6792
Stow *(G-17206)*
Ganzfair Investment Inc ....E 614 792-6630
Delaware *(G-9980)*
Gc At Stonelick Hills ....E 513 735-4653
Batavia *(G-1000)*
Golf Club of Dublin LLC ....E 614 792-3825
Dublin *(G-10235)*
Grizzly Golf Center Inc ....B 513 398-5200
Mason *(G-13590)*
Hawkins Markets Inc...........................E 330 435-4611
Creston *(G-9061)*
Heatherwoode Golf Course ....C 937 748-3222
Springboro *(G-16969)*
Heritage Golf Club Ltd Partnr ....D 614 777-1690
Hilliard *(G-11773)*
Hickory Woods Golf Course Inc ....E 513 575-3900
Loveland *(G-12999)*
Homestead Golf Course Inc ....E 937 698-4876
Tipp City *(G-17559)*
Indian Ridge Golf Club L L C ....E 513 524-4653
Oxford *(G-15678)*
Joe McClelland Inc.............................E 740 452-3036
Zanesville *(G-20321)*
Kinsale Golf & Fitnes CLB LLC ....C 740 881-6500
Powell *(G-16202)*

Link & Reneissance Inc ....E 440 235-0501
Olmsted Twp *(G-15538)*
Links At Windy Knoll LLC ....D 937 631-3744
Springfield *(G-17062)*
Locust Hills Golf Inc ....E 937 265-5152
Springfield *(G-17064)*
Loyal Oak Golf Course Inc ....E 330 825-2904
Barberton *(G-960)*
Madison Route 20 LLC ....E 440 358-7888
Painesville *(G-15723)*
Mahoning Country Club Inc ....E 330 545-2517
Girard *(G-11294)*
Mayfair Country Club Inc ....D 330 699-2209
Uniontown *(G-18378)*
Meadowlake Corporation ....E 330 492-2010
Canton *(G-2397)*
Mental Memorial Golf Course ....E 614 645-8453
Galloway *(G-11222)*
Miami Valley Golf Club ....D 937 278-7381
Dayton *(G-9618)*
Michael Brothers Inc...........................E 419 332-5716
Fremont *(G-11087)*
Mill Creek Golf Course Corp ....E 740 666-7711
Ostrander *(G-15654)*
Mill Creek Metropolitan Park ....D 330 740-7112
Youngstown *(G-20130)*
Mohican Hills Golf Club Inc ....E 419 368-4700
Jeromesville *(G-12193)*
Moundbuilders Country Club Co ....D 740 344-4500
Newark *(G-15076)*
Norwalk Golf Properties Inc ....E 419 668-8535
Norwalk *(G-15450)*
Ohio State Parks Inc ....D 513 664-3504
College Corner *(G-6768)*
Park Arrowhead Golf Club Inc ....E 419 628-2444
Minster *(G-14539)*
Pine Brook Golf Club Inc ....E 440 748-2939
Grafton *(G-11319)*
Pine Hills Golf Club Inc ....E 330 225-4477
Hinckley *(G-11860)*
Pines Golf Club ....E 330 684-1414
Orrville *(G-15644)*
Quail Hollow Management Inc ....D 440 639-4000
Painesville *(G-15734)*
Rawiga Country Club Inc ....D 330 336-2220
Seville *(G-16688)*
Reserve Run Golf Club LLC ....D 330 758-1017
Poland *(G-16087)*
River Greens Golf Course Inc ....E 740 545-7817
West Lafayette *(G-19116)*
Sable Creek Golf Course Inc ....E 330 877-9606
Hartville *(G-11697)*
Scioto Reserve Inc ....D 740 881-9082
Powell *(G-16208)*
Scioto Reserve Inc ....E 740 881-6500
Powell *(G-16209)*
Shady Hollow Cntry CLB Co Inc............D 330 832-1581
Massillon *(G-13729)*
Shaker Run Golf Club ....D 513 727-0007
Lebanon *(G-12500)*
Silver Lake Country Club ....D 330 688-6066
Silver Lake *(G-16809)*
Split Rock Golf Club Inc ....E 614 877-9755
Orient *(G-15621)*
Spring Hills Golf Club ....E 330 825-2439
New Franklin *(G-14912)*
Sugarbush Golf Inc.............................E 330 527-4202
Garrettsville *(G-11231)*
Table Rock Golf Club Inc ....E 740 625-6859
Centerburg *(G-2617)*
Tamaron Golf LLC ....E 419 474-5067
Toledo *(G-18058)*
TW Recreational Services ....E 419 836-1466
Oregon *(G-15613)*
Valleywood Golf Club Inc ....E 419 826-3991
Swanton *(G-17409)*
Vieira Inc ....E 937 599-3221
Bellefontaine *(G-1369)*
Wicked Woods Gulf Club Inc ....E 440 564-7960
Newbury *(G-15128)*
Win Tamer Corporation ....E 330 637-2881
Cortland *(G-8996)*
Wmvh LLC ....D 513 425-7886
Middletown *(G-14340)*
Yankee Run Golf Course ....D 330 448-8096
Brookfield *(G-1858)*

GOLF DRIVING RANGES

797 Elks Golf Club Inc ....E 937 382-2666
Wilmington *(G-19599)*

SERVICES

Bramarjac Inc .....E..... 419 884-3434
Mansfield (G-13144)
Creekside Golf Dome .....E..... 330 545-5000
Girard (G-11286)
Darby Creek Golf Course Inc .....E..... 937 349-7491
Marysville (G-13494)
Hamilton County Parks District .....E..... 513 825-3701
Cincinnati (G-3676)
Youngs Jersey Dairy Inc .....B..... 937 325-0629
Yellow Springs (G-19941)

GOLF EQPT

Golf Galaxy Golfworks Inc .....C..... 740 328-4193
Newark (G-15037)

GOLF GOODS & EQPT

797 Elks Golf Club Inc .....E..... 937 382-2666
Wilmington (G-19599)
Akron Management Corp .....B..... 330 644-8441
Akron (G-48)
Avon Properties Inc .....E..... 440 934-6217
Avon (G-864)
Beckett Ridge Country Club .....D..... 513 874-2710
West Chester (G-18873)
Bramarjac Inc .....E..... 419 884-3434
Mansfield (G-13144)
Darby Creek Golf Course Inc .....E..... 937 349-7491
Marysville (G-13494)
Delaware Golf Club Inc .....E..... 740 362-2582
Delaware (G-9969)
Fox Den Fairways Inc .....E..... 330 678-6792
Stow (G-17206)
Grizzly Golf Center Inc .....B..... 513 398-5200
Mason (G-13590)
Lancaster Country Club .....D..... 740 654-3535
Lancaster (G-12411)
Links At Windy Knoll LLC .....E..... 937 631-3744
Springfield (G-17062)
Loyal Oak Golf Course Inc .....E..... 330 825-2904
Barberton (G-960)
OBannon Creek Golf Club .....E..... 513 683-5657
Loveland (G-13019)
Park Arrowhead Golf Club Inc .....E..... 419 628-2444
Minster (G-14539)
Pine Brook Golf Club Inc .....E..... 440 748-2939
Grafton (G-11319)
Tippecanoe Country Club Inc .....E..... 330 758-7518
Canfield (G-2161)
Walden Club .....D..... 330 995-7162
Aurora (G-848)

GOURMET FOOD STORES

Antonio Sofo Son Importing Co .....C..... 419 476-4211
Toledo (G-17596)
Gust Gallucci Co .....E..... 216 881-0045
Cleveland (G-5648)
Mustard Seed Health Fd Mkt Inc .....E..... 440 519-3663
Solon (G-16875)
Staufs Coffee Roasters II Inc .....E..... 614 487-6050
Columbus (G-8696)

GOVERNMENT, EXECUTIVE OFFICES: City & Town Managers' Offices

City of Compassion .....D..... 419 422-7800
Findlay (G-10888)
City of Louisville .....E..... 330 875-3321
Louisville (G-12962)
City of Oberlin .....E..... 440 775-1531
Oberlin (G-15499)
City of Wellston .....D..... 740 384-2428
Wellston (G-18848)
Delhi Township .....D..... 513 922-0060
Cincinnati (G-3419)
Granger Township .....E..... 330 239-2111
Medina (G-13945)
Township of Fowler .....D..... 330 637-2653
Fowler (G-11017)
Village of Antwerp .....E..... 419 258-7422
Antwerp (G-615)
Village of Coldwater .....D..... 419 678-2685
Coldwater (G-6767)
Village of Cuyahoga Heights .....C..... 216 641-7020
Cleveland (G-6631)

GOVERNMENT, EXECUTIVE OFFICES: County Supervisor/Exec Office

Alpha Group of Delaware Inc .....D..... 614 222-1855
Columbus (G-6903)
Alpha Group of Delaware Inc .....D..... 740 368-5810
Delaware (G-9951)
Alpha Group of Delaware Inc .....E..... 740 368-5820
Delaware (G-9952)
Bedford Township .....E..... 740 992-2117
Middleport (G-14280)
Butler County of Ohio .....C..... 513 887-3728
Fairfield Township (G-10803)
Butler County Bd of Mental RE .....C..... 513 785-2870
Fairfield Township (G-10805)
Butler County Board of Develop .....E..... 513 867-5913
Fairfield (G-10703)
Clermont County Community Svcs .....E..... 513 732-2277
Batavia (G-988)
County of Athens .....E..... 740 593-5514
Athens (G-773)
County of Athens .....D..... 740 592-3061
Athens (G-774)
County of Auglaize .....D..... 419 629-2419
New Bremen (G-14886)
County of Brown .....E..... 937 378-6104
Georgetown (G-11268)
County of Coshocton .....D..... 740 622-1020
Coshocton (G-9012)
County of Erie .....D..... 419 433-0617
Milan (G-14360)
County of Erie .....E..... 419 627-8733
Huron (G-12024)
County of Erie .....C..... 419 626-6781
Sandusky (G-16595)
County of Erie .....E..... 419 627-7710
Sandusky (G-16596)
County of Gallia .....D..... 740 446-3222
Gallipolis (G-11187)
County of Gallia .....E..... 740 446-2665
Gallipolis (G-11188)
County of Guernsey .....E..... 740 439-5555
Cambridge (G-2060)
County of Holmes .....E..... 330 279-2801
Holmesville (G-11929)
County of Holmes .....E..... 330 674-5916
Millersburg (G-14470)
County of Holmes .....E..... 330 674-1015
Millersburg (G-14471)
County of Holmes .....E..... 330 674-1111
Millersburg (G-14472)
County of Huron .....D..... 419 668-8126
Norwalk (G-15431)
County of Huron .....D..... 419 663-5437
Norwalk (G-15432)
County of Lucas .....C..... 419 213-3000
Toledo (G-17680)
County of Lucas .....C..... 419 213-4700
Toledo (G-17681)
County of Lucas .....B..... 419 213-8999
Toledo (G-17682)
County of Madison .....D..... 740 852-9404
London (G-12863)
County of Marion .....D..... 740 387-1035
Marion (G-13416)
County of Marion .....E..... 740 387-6688
Marion (G-13413)
County of Marion .....E..... 740 389-2317
Marion (G-13415)
County of Medina .....E..... 330 723-9553
Medina (G-13925)
County of Medina .....D..... 330 995-5243
Medina (G-13926)
County of Medina .....E..... 330 723-9670
Medina (G-13927)
County of Mercer .....E..... 419 586-5106
Celina (G-2592)
County of Montgomery .....E..... 937 225-4010
Dayton (G-9329)
County of Ottawa .....E..... 419 898-7433
Oak Harbor (G-15469)
County of Ottawa .....E..... 419 898-6459
Oak Harbor (G-15470)
County of Ottawa .....E..... 419 898-2089
Oak Harbor (G-15471)
County of Pickaway .....D..... 740 474-7588
Circleville (G-4830)
County of Richland .....E..... 419 774-5676
Mansfield (G-13153)
County of Richland .....C..... 419 774-4100
Mansfield (G-13155)

County of Richland .....C..... 419 774-5400
Mansfield (G-13156)
County of Richland .....E..... 419 774-5591
Mansfield (G-13158)
County of Richland .....B..... 419 774-4200
Mansfield (G-13159)
County of Stark .....E..... 330 477-3609
Massillon (G-13674)
County of Summit .....D..... 330 643-2300
Akron (G-162)
County of Summit .....C..... 330 643-2850
Akron (G-164)
County of Trumbull .....D..... 330 675-2640
Warren (G-18692)
County of Tuscarawas .....E..... 330 343-0099
New Philadelphia (G-14954)
County of Union .....E..... 937 645-3018
Marysville (G-13490)
County of Wayne .....D..... 330 262-1786
Wooster (G-19715)
County of Wayne .....D..... 330 345-5340
Wooster (G-19717)
County of Williams .....C..... 419 636-4508
Bryan (G-1956)
Franklin Cnty Bd Commissioners .....C..... 614 462-3030
Columbus (G-7603)
Jackson-Vinton Cmnty Action .....E..... 740 384-3722
Wellston (G-18852)
Jefferson Cnty Cmmnty Action .....C..... 740 282-0971
Steubenville (G-17159)
Mahoning County .....D..... 330 797-2837
Youngstown (G-20107)
Noble Cnty Nble Cnty Cmmsoners .....E..... 740 732-4958
Caldwell (G-2043)
North Point Eductl Svc Ctr .....E..... 440 967-0904
Huron (G-12028)
Oriana House Inc .....D..... 330 535-8116
Akron (G-366)
R T Industries Inc .....C..... 937 339-8313
Troy (G-18225)
Scioto County Ohio .....E..... 740 456-4164
New Boston (G-14882)
Wood County Ohio .....C..... 419 353-8411
Bowling Green (G-1756)

GOVERNMENT, EXECUTIVE OFFICES: Local

City of Aurora .....D..... 330 562-8662
Aurora (G-825)
City of Montgomery .....D..... 513 891-2424
Montgomery (G-14593)

GOVERNMENT, EXECUTIVE OFFICES: Mayors'

City of Akron .....D..... 330 375-2355
Akron (G-136)
City of Akron .....E..... 330 375-2851
Akron (G-138)
City of Canal Winchester .....E..... 614 837-8276
Canal Winchester (G-2107)
City of Cuyahoga Falls .....E..... 330 971-8416
Cuyahoga Falls (G-9081)
City of Kenton .....E..... 419 674-4850
Kenton (G-12273)
City of Marion .....D..... 740 382-1479
Marion (G-13412)
City of New Philadelphia .....E..... 330 339-2121
New Philadelphia (G-14950)
City of Norwalk .....E..... 419 663-6715
Norwalk (G-15426)
City of Perrysburg .....E..... 419 872-8020
Perrysburg (G-15848)
City of Portsmouth .....E..... 740 353-5419
Portsmouth (G-16129)
City of Sandusky .....E..... 419 627-5907
Sandusky (G-16585)
City of Toledo .....D..... 419 245-1800
Toledo (G-17654)
City of Toledo .....A..... 419 245-1001
Toledo (G-17655)
City of Toledo .....C..... 419 936-2924
Toledo (G-17657)
City of Wadsworth .....E..... 330 334-1581
Wadsworth (G-18592)
City of Wilmington .....E..... 937 382-7961
Wilmington (G-19608)
City of Wooster .....E..... 330 263-5266
Wooster (G-19704)
City of Youngstown .....E..... 330 742-8749
Youngstown (G-19992)

Township of Copley ....D....... 330 666-1853
Copley *(G-8978)*

GOVERNMENT, GENERAL: Administration

Butler County of Ohio.................D....... 513 887-3282
Hamilton *(G-11561)*
City of Cleveland ....D....... 216 664-2430
Cleveland *(G-5194)*
Employment Relations Board.................E....... 513 863-0828
Hamilton *(G-11594)*
Supreme Court of Ohio ....E....... 614 387-9800
Columbus *(G-8718)*
Workers Compensation Ohio Bur .... A 800 644-6292
Columbus *(G-8917)*

GOVERNMENT, GENERAL: Administration, County

County of Perry *(G-14918)*.................E....... 740 342-0416
New Lexington
County of Tuscarawas.................D....... 330 339-7791
New Philadelphia *(G-14955)*

GOVERNMENT, GENERAL: Administration, State

Natural Resources Ohio Dept.................E....... 614 265-6948
Columbus *(G-8162)*
Transportation Ohio Department.............E....... 614 275-1300
Columbus *(G-8774)*

GOVERNMENT, GENERAL: Supply Agency

Emergency Medical Svcs Billing ....E....... 216 664-2598
Cleveland *(G-5474)*

GOVERNMENT, LEGISLATIVE BODIES: County

County of Lucas.................E....... 419 213-4500
Toledo *(G-17684)*

GOVERNMENT, LEGISLATIVE BODIES: County Commissioner

County of Clermont ....E....... 513 732-7661
Batavia *(G-993)*

GOVERNMENT, LEGISLATIVE BODIES: Legislative Assembly

Ohio Consumers Counsel ....E....... 614 466-8574
Columbus *(G-8234)*

GOVERNMENT, LEGISLATIVE BODIES: Town Council

Town of Canal Fulton.................E....... 330 854-9448
Canal Fulton *(G-2098)*

GRADING SVCS

D&M Carter LLC.................E....... 513 831-8843
Miamiville *(G-14245)*
Great Lakes Crushing Ltd ....E....... 440 944-5500
Wickliffe *(G-19461)*

GRAIN & FIELD BEANS WHOLESALERS

Consolidated Grain & Barge Co ....E....... 513 941-4805
Cincinnati *(G-3351)*

GRANITE: Crushed & Broken

Martin Marietta Materials Inc.................E....... 513 701-1140
West Chester *(G-18970)*

GRANITE: Cut & Shaped

Cutting Edge Countertops Inc.............E....... 419 873-9500
Perrysburg *(G-15853)*

GRANTMAKING FOUNDATIONS

Altruism Society Inc ....D....... 877 283-4001
Beachwood *(G-1028)*
Golden Endings Golden Ret Resc.......E....... 614 486-0773
Columbus *(G-7677)*
Miami Valley Community Action.......D....... 937 222-1009
Dayton *(G-9617)*
Shawnee Weekday Early Lrng Ctr ....E....... 419 991-4806
Lima *(G-12793)*

GRAPHIC ARTS & RELATED DESIGN SVCS

Academy Graphic Comm Inc.................E....... 216 661-2550
Cleveland *(G-4897)*
Adcom Group Inc.................C....... 216 574-9100
Cleveland *(G-4901)*
Art-American Printing Plates ....E....... 216 241-4420
Cleveland *(G-5010)*
Container Graphics Corp ....D....... 419 531-5133
Toledo *(G-17678)*
Coyne Graphic Finishing Inc ....E....... 740 397-6232
Mount Vernon *(G-14759)*
Edward Howard & Co ....E....... 216 781-2400
Cleveland *(G-5468)*
Evolution Crtive Solutions LLC ....E....... 513 681-4450
Cincinnati *(G-3523)*
Fitch Inc ....D....... 614 885-3453
Columbus *(G-7591)*
Graphic Publications Inc ....E....... 330 674-2300
Millersburg *(G-14474)*
Haney Inc.................D....... 513 561-1441
Cincinnati *(G-3679)*
Interbrand Hulefeld Inc.................D....... 513 421-2210
Cincinnati *(G-3778)*
Libby Prszyk Kthman Hldngs Inc ....B....... 513 241-6401
Cincinnati *(G-3923)*
Mitosis LLC.................E....... 937 557-3440
Dayton *(G-9640)*
Mueller Art Cover & Binding Co ....E....... 440 238-3303
Strongsville *(G-17335)*
Northeast Scene Inc ....E....... 216 241-7550
Cleveland *(G-6095)*
Real Art Design Group Inc ....E....... 937 223-9955
Dayton *(G-9728)*
Suntwist Corp.................D....... 800 935-3534
Maple Heights *(G-13300)*
Taylor Made Graphics.................E....... 440 882-6318
Cleveland *(G-6501)*
Third Dimension Inc ....E....... 877 926-3223
Geneva *(G-11247)*

GRAPHITE MINING SVCS

Graftech Holdings Inc.................B....... 216 676-2000
Independence *(G-12077)*

GRAVEL MINING

Fleming Construction Co ....E....... 740 494-2177
Prospect *(G-16223)*
Stansley Mineral Resources Inc ....E....... 419 843-2813
Sylvania *(G-17453)*
Watson Gravel Inc.................D....... 513 863-0070
Hamilton *(G-11654)*

GREASES & INEDIBLE FATS, RENDERED

Inland Products Inc.................E....... 614 443-3425
Columbus *(G-7819)*

GREENHOUSES: Prefabricated Metal

Ludy Greenhouse Mfg Corp.................D....... 800 255-5839
New Madison *(G-14937)*
Rough Brothers Mfg Inc.................D....... 513 242-0310
Cincinnati *(G-4402)*

GREETING CARD SHOPS

AG Interactive Inc ....C....... 216 889-5000
Cleveland *(G-4911)*
Garys Pharmacy Inc ....E....... 937 456-5777
Eaton *(G-10446)*
Gorant Chocolatier LLC ....C....... 330 726-8821
Boardman *(G-1698)*
Mohun Health Care Center.................E....... 614 416-6132
Columbus *(G-8095)*

GRINDING SVC: Precision, Commercial Or Indl

Micro Products Co Inc.................D....... 440 943-0258
Willoughby Hills *(G-19591)*
Universal Grinding Corporation ....E....... 216 631-9410
Cleveland *(G-6581)*

GROCERIES WHOLESALERS, NEC

American Bottling Company.................D....... 614 237-4201
Columbus *(G-6913)*
Brothers Trading Co Inc ....C....... 937 746-1010
Springboro *(G-16964)*

Central Coca-Cola Btlg Co Inc.................C....... 419 476-6622
Toledo *(G-17643)*
Dayton Heidelberg Distrg Co ....C....... 937 220-6450
Moraine *(G-14645)*
EBY-Brown Company LLC ....C....... 937 324-1036
Springfield *(G-17032)*
Frito-Lay North America Inc.................C....... 216 491-4000
Cleveland *(G-5583)*
Frito-Lay North America Inc ....D....... 419 893-8171
Maumee *(G-13794)*
G & J Pepsi-Cola Bottlers Inc ....B....... 740 354-9191
Franklin Furnace *(G-11045)*
G & J Pepsi-Cola Bottlers Inc ....D....... 740 452-2721
Zanesville *(G-20309)*
Gordon Food Service Inc ....E....... 419 747-1212
Ontario *(G-15550)*
Gordon Food Service Inc ....E....... 419 225-8983
Lima *(G-12646)*
Gordon Food Service Inc ....E....... 216 573-4900
Cleveland *(G-5616)*
Gust Gallucci Co ....E....... 216 881-0045
Cleveland *(G-5648)*
Hiland Group Incorporated ....D....... 330 499-8404
Canton *(G-2344)*
Luxfer Magtech Inc ....E....... 513 772-3066
Cincinnati *(G-3952)*
Maines Paper & Food Svc Inc ....E....... 216 643-7500
Bedford *(G-1291)*
Norcia Bakery ....D....... 330 454-1077
Canton *(G-2419)*
P-Americas LLC ....C....... 330 746-7652
Youngstown *(G-20149)*
Pepsi-Cola Metro Btlg Co Inc ....B....... 937 461-4664
Dayton *(G-9690)*
Pepsi-Cola Metro Btlg Co Inc.................B....... 330 963-0426
Twinsburg *(G-18304)*
R L Lipton Distributing Co ....D....... 216 475-4150
Maple Heights *(G-13292)*
Schwebel Baking Company ....C....... 440 248-1500
Solon *(G-16895)*
Servatii Inc ....D....... 513 271-5040
Cincinnati *(G-4456)*
Skidmore Sales & Distrg Co Inc ....C....... 513 755-4200
West Chester *(G-19009)*
Skyline Chili Inc ....C....... 513 874-1188
Fairfield *(G-10785)*
Sygma Network Inc ....C....... 614 734-2500
Dublin *(G-10349)*
Sysco Cincinnati LLC ....B....... 513 563-6300
Cincinnati *(G-4562)*
Tiffin Paper Company ....E....... 419 447-2121
Tiffin *(G-17544)*
US Foods Inc ....C....... 330 963-6789
Twinsburg *(G-18334)*
US Foods Inc ....A....... 614 539-7993
West Chester *(G-19096)*

GROCERIES, GENERAL LINE WHOLESALERS

Albert Guarnieri & Co ....D....... 330 794-9834
Hudson *(G-11962)*
Anderson and Dubose Inc ....D....... 440 248-8800
Warren *(G-18665)*
Blue Line Distribution.................E....... 614 497-9610
Groveport *(G-11496)*
Brothers Trading Co Inc ....C....... 937 746-1010
Springboro *(G-16964)*
Circle S Farms Inc.................E....... 614 878-9462
Grove City *(G-11420)*
Dwa Mrkting Prmtional Pdts LLC ....E....... 216 476-0635
Strongsville *(G-17298)*
EBY-Brown Company LLC ....C....... 937 324-1036
Springfield *(G-17032)*
Food Sample Express LLc ....D....... 330 225-3550
Brunswick *(G-1930)*
Forths Foods Inc.................E....... 740 886-9769
Proctorville *(G-16216)*
Gordon Food Service Inc ....E....... 440 953-1785
Mentor *(G-14052)*
Greeneview Foods LLC ....E....... 937 675-4161
Jamestown *(G-12187)*
Gummer Wholesale Inc.................D....... 740 928-0415
Heath *(G-11704)*
Hillandale Farms Corporation.................E....... 330 724-3199
Akron *(G-262)*
J V Hansel Inc.................E....... 330 716-0806
Warren *(G-18716)*
Jetro Cash and Carry Entps LLC..........D....... 216 525-0101
Cleveland *(G-5794)*

SERVICES

John Zidian Co Inc ....D 330 743-6050
Youngstown (G-20086)

Kroger Co ....D 740 363-4398
Delaware (G-9994)

Kroger Co ....C 614 759-2745
Columbus (G-7928)

Kroger Co ....B 937 376-7962
Xenia (G-19916)

Kroger Co ....D 937 848-5990
Dayton (G-9552)

Lakes Venture LLC ....D 614 681-7050
Worthington (G-19819)

Larosas Inc ....A 513 347-5660
Cincinnati (G-3911)

Mattingly Foods Inc ....C 740 454-0136
Zanesville (G-20329)

Mds Foods Inc ....E 330 879-9780
Navarre (G-14823)

Meadowbrook Meat Company Inc .....C 614 771-9660
Columbus (G-8049)

Mountain Foods Inc ....E 440 286-7177
Chardon (G-2705)

Nestle Usa Inc ....E 513 576-4930
Loveland (G-13015)

Ovations Food Services LP ....D 513 419-7254
Cincinnati (G-4192)

Physicians Weight Ls Ctr Amer ....E 330 666-7952
Akron (G-382)

Pollak Distributing Co Inc ....E 216 851-9911
Euclid (G-10653)

Reinhart Foodservice LLC ....C 513 421-9184
Cincinnati (G-4353)

Restaurant Depot LLC ....E 216 525-0101
Cleveland (G-6316)

Ricking Paper and Specialty Co ...E 513 825-3551
Cincinnati (G-4372)

Riser Foods Company ....D 216 292-7000
Bedford Heights (G-1327)

Sandridge Food Corporation ....C 330 725-8883
Medina (G-13999)

Sherwood Food Distributors LLC ...B 216 662-6794
Maple Heights (G-13296)

Sommers Market LLC ....D 330 352-7470
Hartville (G-11699)

Spartannash Company ....D 419 998-2562
Lima (G-12745)

Spartannash Company ....D 937 599-1110
Bellefontaine (G-1367)

Sysco Central Ohio Inc ....B 614 272-0658
Columbus (G-8725)

Tasty Pure Food Company ....E 330 434-8141
Akron (G-464)

Tusco Grocers Inc ....D 740 922-8721
Dennison (G-10054)

Wrightway Fd Svc Rest Sup Inc ....E 419 222-7911
Lima (G-12786)

GROUP DAY CARE CENTER

A CCS Day Care Centers Inc ....E 513 841-2227
Cincinnati (G-2891)

Agj Kidz LLC ....E 937 350-1001
Centerville (G-2618)

All About Kids Daycare N ....E 330 494-8700
North Canton (G-15187)

Anderson Little ....E 513 474-7800
Cincinnati (G-2962)

Annas Child Care Lrng Ctr Inc .....D 937 667-1903
Tipp City (G-17549)

Aultman Hospital ....E 330 452-2273
Canton (G-2205)

Bright Horizons Chld Ctrs LLC .....E 614 754-7023
Columbus (G-7064)

Bright Horizons Chld Ctrs LLC .....E 614 566-9322
Columbus (G-7065)

Bright Horizons Chld Ctrs LLC .....E 330 375-7633
Akron (G-107)

Brooksedge Day Care Center ....E 614 529-0077
Hilliard (G-11748)

Centerville Child Development .....E 937 434-5949
Dayton (G-9289)

Champons In Making Daycare LLC ...E 937 728-4886
Wilmington (G-19607)

Child Dev Ctr Jackson Cnty ....E 740 286-3995
Jackson (G-12171)

Children First Inc ....E 614 466-0945
Columbus (G-7187)

Christian Perry Pre School ....E 330 477-7262
Canton (G-2252)

Early Learning Tree Chld Ctr ....D 937 276-3221
Dayton (G-9401)

Edwards Creative Learning Ctr .....E 614 492-8977
Columbus (G-7506)

Epworth United Methodist Ch ......D 740 387-1062
Marion (G-13420)

Friend-Ship Child Care Ctr LLC .....E 330 484-2051
Canton (G-2318)

Future Advantage Inc ....E 330 686-7707
Stow (G-17207)

Giggles & Wiggles Inc ....E 740 574-4536
Wheelersburg (G-19434)

Gingerbread Inc ....E 513 793-4122
Blue Ash (G-1569)

Goddard School ....E 614 920-9810
Canal Winchester (G-2110)

Hilty Child Care Center ....E 419 384-3220
Pandora (G-15752)

Hopes Drams Childcare Lrng Ctr ....E 330 793-8260
Youngstown (G-20068)

Jewish Day Schl Assoc Grtr Clv ....D 216 763-1400
Pepper Pike (G-15819)

Jolly Tots Too Inc ....E 614 471-0688
Columbus (G-7865)

Kandy Kane Childrens Lrng Ctr .....E 330 864-6642
Akron (G-298)

Kare A Lot ....E 614 298-8933
Columbus (G-7880)

Kare A Lot Infnt Tddlr Dev Ctr .....E 614 481-7532
Columbus (G-7881)

Kiddie Kollege Inc ....E 440 327-5435
North Ridgeville (G-15332)

Kids Ahead Inc ....E 330 628-7404
Mogadore (G-14552)

Kids Country ....E 330 899-0909
Uniontown (G-18375)

Kids World ....E 614 473-9229
Columbus (G-7903)

Kids-Play Inc ....E 330 896-2400
Uniontown (G-18376)

Kidz By Riverside Inc ....E 330 392-0700
Warren (G-18719)

Kinder Kare Day Nursery ....E 740 886-6905
Proctorville (G-16218)

Kindercare Education LLC ....E 513 896-4769
Fairfield Township (G-10812)

Kindercare Education LLC ....E 330 405-5556
Twinsburg (G-18289)

Kindercare Education LLC ....E 440 442-3360
Cleveland (G-5830)

Kindercare Learning Ctrs Inc ....E 937 435-2353
Dayton (G-9545)

Kindercare Learning Ctrs Inc ....E 614 888-9696
Worthington (G-19817)

Kindercare Learning Ctrs LLC ....E 440 248-5437
Solon (G-16865)

Kindercare Learning Ctrs LLC ....E 513 771-8787
Cincinnati (G-3871)

Kindercare Learning Ctrs LLC ....E 740 549-0264
Lewis Center (G-12548)

Kindercare Learning Ctrs LLC ....E 440 442-8067
Cleveland (G-5831)

Kindercare Learning Ctrs LLC ....E 614 866-4446
Reynoldsburg (G-16314)

Kindercare Learning Ctrs LLC ....E 614 759-6622
Columbus (G-7904)

Kindercare Learning Ctrs LLC ....E 513 791-4712
Cincinnati (G-3873)

Kindertown Educational Centers ....E 859 344-8802
Cleves (G-6731)

Kozmic Korner ....E 330 494-4148
Canton (G-2371)

Little Drmers Big Blievers LLC ......E 614 824-4666
Columbus (G-7985)

M J J B Ltd ....E 937 748-4414
Springboro (G-16973)

McKinley Early Childhood Ctr ....E 330 454-4800
Canton (G-2395)

McKinley Early Childhood Ctr ....E 330 252-2552
Akron (G-327)

Medina Advantage Inc ....E 330 723-8697
Medina (G-13970)

Ministerial Day Care-Headstart .....E 216 881-6924
Cleveland (G-5998)

Miss Pats Day Care Center ....E 440 729-8255
Chesterland (G-2742)

Morrow County Child Care Ctr ......D 419 946-5007
Mount Gilead (G-14728)

Oberlin Early Childhood Center .....E 440 774-8193
Oberlin (G-15516)

Powell Enterprises Inc ....E 614 882-0111
Westerville (G-19200)

Rainbow Station Day Care Inc ......E 614 759-8667
Pickerington (G-15967)

Something Special Lrng Ctr Inc .....E 419 878-4190
Waterville (G-18792)

Sunny Day Academy LLC ....E 614 718-1717
Dublin (G-10344)

Van Wert County Day Care Inc ......E 419 238-9918
Van Wert (G-18492)

Wenzler Daycare Learning Ctr ....E 937 435-8200
Dayton (G-9873)

Wesley Educ Cntr For Chldrn ....E 513 569-1840
Cincinnati (G-4780)

West Chester Chrstn Chld ....E 513 777-6300
West Chester (G-19035)

Wise Choices In Learning Ltd ....E 440 324-6056
Elyria (G-10576)

Young Services Inc ....E 419 704-2009
Toledo (G-18171)

GROUP FOSTER HOME

Akron Summit Cmnty Action Agcy ...C 330 572-8532
Akron (G-56)

Commons of Providence ....D 419 624-1171
Sandusky (G-16590)

County of Lorain ....C 440 329-5340
Elyria (G-10501)

Help Foundation Inc ....E 216 486-5258
Cleveland (G-5683)

Mended Reeds Home ....E 740 533-1883
Ironton (G-12163)

Oasis Thrptic Fster Care Ntwrk .....E 740 698-0340
Albany (G-511)

GROUP HOSPITALIZATION PLANS

Anthem Insurance Companies Inc ....E 330 492-2151
Canton (G-2191)

Aultcare Corp ....B 330 363-6360
Canton (G-2198)

Kelley Companies ....D 330 668-6100
Copley (G-8967)

Nextrx LLC ....A 317 532-6000
Mason (G-13622)

Ohio Health Choice Inc ....D 800 554-0027
Cleveland (G-6120)

United Healthcare Ohio Inc ....D 216 694-4080
Cleveland (G-6573)

United Healthcare Ohio Inc ....B 614 410-7000
Columbus (G-8801)

GUARD PROTECTIVE SVCS

Cal Crim Inc ....C 513 563-5500
Trenton (G-18187)

Community Crime Patrol ....E 614 247-1765
Columbus (G-7329)

Darke County Sheriffs Patrol ....D 937 548-3399
Greenville (G-11372)

Highway Patrol ....E 740 354-2888
Lucasville (G-13051)

Metro Safety and Security LLC ......D 614 792-2770
Columbus (G-8064)

Public Safety Ohio Department .....E 419 768-3955
Mount Gilead (G-14734)

Shane Security Services Inc ....D 330 757-4001
Poland (G-16088)

GUARD SVCS

1st Advnce SEC Invstgtions Inc .....E 937 317-4433
Dayton (G-9194)

American Svcs & Protection LLC .....D 614 884-0177
Columbus (G-6939)

Area Wide Protective Inc ....E 513 321-9889
Fairfield (G-10696)

Falu Corporation ....E 502 641-8106
Cincinnati (G-3528)

Metropolitan Security Svcs Inc ......B 330 253-6459
Akron (G-337)

NASA-Trmi Group Inc ....D 937 387-6517
Dayton (G-9652)

Official Investigations Inc ....D 844 263-3424
Cincinnati (G-4149)

Ohio Tctcal Enfrcment Svcs LLC .....D 614 989-9485
Columbus (G-8355)

Rmi International Inc ....D 937 642-5032
Marysville (G-13525)

Start-Black Servicesjv LLC ....D 740 598-4891
Mingo Junction (G-14529)

Whitestone Group Inc ....B 614 501-7007
Reynoldsburg (G-16339)

GYMNASTICS INSTRUCTION

Christian Twigs Gymnastics CLB.........E...... 937 866-8356
Dayton (G-9299)
Cincinnati Gymnastics Academy ....E...... 513 860-3082
Fairfield (G-10711)
Flytz Gymnastics Inc ....E...... 330 926-2900
Cuyahoga Falls (G-9096)
Gymnastic World Inc ....E...... 440 526-2970
Cleveland (G-5649)
Integrity Global Marketing LLC............E...... 330 492-9989
Canton (G-2356)
Integrity Gymnstics Chrleading............E...... 614 733-0818
Plain City (G-16055)

HAIRDRESSERS

Alsan Corporation.............................D...... 330 385-3636
East Liverpool (G-10396)
Anthony David Salon & Spa................E...... 440 233-8570
Lorain (G-12881)
Attractions ....E...... 740 592-5600
Athens (G-771)
Bella Capelli Inc ....E...... 440 899-1225
Westlake (G-19322)
Castilian & Co...................................E...... 937 836-9671
Englewood (G-10581)
Dana Lauren Salon & Spa ....E...... 440 262-1092
Broadview Heights (G-1830)
David Scott Salon ....E...... 440 734-7595
North Olmsted (G-15285)
Edge Hair Design & Spa ....E...... 330 477-2300
Canton (G-2298)
Frank Santo LLC ....E...... 216 831-9374
Pepper Pike (G-15817)
Hair Forum ....E...... 513 245-0800
Cincinnati (G-3673)
Hair Shoppe Inc ....D...... 330 497-1651
Canton (G-2334)
Hairy Cactus Salon Inc ....E...... 513 771-9335
West Chester (G-18940)
Jbj Enterprises Inc ....E...... 440 992-6051
Ashtabula (G-743)
John Rbrts Hair Studio Spa Inc ....D...... 216 839-1430
Cleveland (G-5800)
L A Hair Force ....E...... 419 756-3101
Mansfield (G-13196)
Marios International Spa & Ht..............E...... 440 845-7373
Cleveland (G-5908)
Michael A Garcia Salon ....E...... 614 235-1605
Columbus (G-8067)
Mitchells Salon & Day Spa ....D...... 513 793-0900
Cincinnati (G-4061)
Noggins Hair Design Inc ....E...... 513 474-4405
Cincinnati (G-4121)
P JS Hair Styling Shoppe ....E...... 440 333-1244
Cleveland (G-6155)
Paragon Salons Inc...........................E...... 513 683-6700
Cincinnati (G-4200)
Philip Icuss Jr ....E...... 740 264-4647
Steubenville (G-17169)
Reflections Hair Studio Inc ....E...... 330 725-5782
Medina (G-13995)
Salon La ....E...... 513 784-1700
Cincinnati (G-4428)
Shamas Ltd ....E...... 419 872-9908
Perrysburg (G-15920)
Sheer Professionals Inc ....E...... 330 345-8666
Wooster (G-19769)
Urban Oassis Inc ....E...... 614 766-9946
Dublin (G-10361)

HALFWAY GROUP HOME, PERSONS WITH SOCIAL OR PERSONAL PROBLEMS

Alvis Inc ....C...... 614 252-1788
Columbus (G-6907)
Lutheran Home ....D...... 419 724-1414
Toledo (G-17870)
Midwest Health Services Inc...............C...... 330 828-0779
Massillon (G-13716)

HALFWAY HOME FOR DELINQUENTS & OFFENDERS

Womens Recovery Center ....E...... 937 562-2400
Xenia (G-19934)

HAND TOOLS, NEC: Wholesalers

Elliott Tool Technologies Ltd ....D...... 937 253-6133
Dayton (G-9412)

HANDYMAN SVCS

Sr Improvements Services LLC.............E...... 567 207-6488
Vickery (G-18575)

HANGARS & OTHER AIRCRAFT STORAGE FACILITIES

Winner Aviation Corporation ....D...... 330 856-5000
Vienna (G-18584)

HARDWARE

Action Coupling & Eqp Inc..................D...... 330 279-4242
Holmesville (G-11928)
Edward W Daniel LLC.........................E...... 440 647-1960
Wellington (G-18839)
First Francis Company Inc ....E...... 440 352-8927
Painesville (G-15714)
Gateway Concrete Forming Svcs...........D...... 513 353-2000
Miamitown (G-14241)
Hebco Products Inc ....A...... 419 562-7987
Bucyrus (G-1992)
Ohio Hydraulics Inc ....E...... 513 771-2590
Cincinnati (G-4155)
Samsel Rope & Marine Supply Co ....E...... 216 241-0333
Cleveland (G-6370)
Summers Acquisition Corp ....E...... 216 941-7700
Cleveland (G-6474)

HARDWARE & BUILDING PRDTS: Plastic

Associated Materials LLC ....B...... 330 929-1811
Cuyahoga Falls (G-9070)
Associated Materials Group Inc ....E...... 330 929-1811
Cuyahoga Falls (G-9071)
Associated Mtls Holdings LLC ....A...... 330 929-1811
Cuyahoga Falls (G-9072)
Gorell Enterprises Inc.......................B...... 724 465-1800
Streetsboro (G-17254)
Style Crest Enterprises Inc ....D...... 419 355-8586
Fremont (G-11100)

HARDWARE & EQPT: Stage, Exc Lighting

Janson Industries ....D...... 330 455-7029
Canton (G-2360)

HARDWARE STORES

Ace Hardware Corporation ....C...... 440 333-4223
Rocky River (G-16421)
Ace Rental Place ....D...... 937 642-2891
Marysville (G-13482)
Carter-Jones Lumber Company ....D...... 330 784-5441
Akron (G-119)
Daniels Lumber Co Inc ....D...... 330 533-2211
Canfield (G-2135)
Do Cut Sales & Service Inc ....E...... 330 533-9878
Warren (G-18703)
Do It Best Corp ....C...... 330 725-3859
Medina (G-13933)
Famous Enterprises Inc ....E...... 216 529-1010
Cleveland (G-5511)
Hartville Hardware Inc ....C...... 330 877-4690
Hartville (G-11688)
Lochard Inc.......................................D...... 937 492-8811
Sidney (G-16784)
Matco Tools Corporation ....B...... 330 929-4949
Stow (G-17219)
Nilco LLC ....E...... 888 248-5151
Hartville (G-11695)
Thomas Do-It Center Inc ....D...... 740 446-2002
Gallipolis (G-11215)

HARDWARE STORES: Door Locks & Lock Sets

Bass Security Services Inc ....C...... 216 755-1200
Bedford Heights (G-1317)

HARDWARE STORES: Pumps & Pumping Eqpt

Best Aire Compressor Service ....D...... 419 726-0055
Millbury (G-14446)

HARDWARE STORES: Tools

Slaters Inc..E...... 740 654-2204
Lancaster (G-12435)
Tool Testing Lab Inc ....E...... 937 898-5696
Tipp City (G-17570)

HARDWARE WHOLESALERS

Ace Hardware Corporation ....C...... 440 333-4223
Rocky River (G-16421)
Atlas Bolt & Screw Company LLC........C...... 419 289-6171
Ashland (G-653)
Barnes Group Inc ....E...... 419 891-9292
Maumee (G-13760)
Do Cut Sales & Service Inc ....E...... 330 533-9878
Warren (G-18703)
F & M Mafco Inc................................C...... 513 367-2151
Harrison (G-11666)
Gemini Advertising Associates ....D...... 513 896-3541
Hamilton (G-11600)
GMI Holdings Inc ....D...... 330 794-0846
Akron (G-238)
Hd Supply Facilities Maint Ltd ....E...... 440 542-9188
Solon (G-16857)
Hillman Companies Inc ....D...... 513 851-4900
Cincinnati (G-3703)
Hillman Companies Inc ....B...... 513 851-4900
Cincinnati (G-3704)
Hillman Companies Inc ....B...... 513 851-4900
Cincinnati (G-3705)
Hillman Group Inc ....C...... 513 851-4900
Cincinnati (G-3706)
Khempco Bldg Sup Co Ltd Partnr........D...... 740 549-0465
Delaware (G-9993)
Mae Holding Company ....E...... 513 751-2424
Cincinnati (G-3959)
Matco Tools Corporation ....B...... 330 929-4949
Stow (G-17219)
Menard Inc ....E...... 419 726-4029
Toledo (G-17903)
Norwood Hardware & Supply Co..........E...... 513 733-1175
Cincinnati (G-4134)
Ohashi Technica USA Inc ....E...... 740 965-5115
Sunbury (G-17393)
Reitter Stucco Inc ....E...... 614 291-2212
Columbus (G-8508)
Serv-A-Lite Products Inc ....C...... 309 762-7741
Cincinnati (G-4454)
The Mau-Sherwood Supply Co ....E...... 330 405-1200
Twinsburg (G-18326)
Waxman Industries Inc ....C...... 440 439-1830
Cleveland (G-6657)
Ziegler Bolt & Parts Co ....D...... 330 478-2542
Canton (G-2544)

HARDWARE, WHOLESALE: Bolts

Hodell-Natco Industries Inc ....E...... 773 472-2305
Cleveland (G-5699)
Mid-State Bolt and Nut Co Inc ....E...... 614 253-8631
Columbus (G-8078)

HARDWARE, WHOLESALE: Builders', NEC

Akron Hardware Consultants Inc ....E...... 330 644-7167
Akron (G-47)
Bostwick-Braun Company ....D...... 419 259-3600
Toledo (G-17620)
Do It Best Corp ....C...... 330 725-3859
Medina (G-13933)
La Force Inc......................................D...... 614 875-2545
Grove City (G-11446)
LE Smith Company ....D...... 419 636-4555
Bryan (G-1961)
Mazzella Holding Company Inc ....D...... 513 772-4466
Cleveland (G-5926)

HARDWARE, WHOLESALE: Casters & Glides

Waxman Consumer Pdts Group Inc......D...... 440 439-1830
Cleveland (G-6656)
Waxman Consumer Pdts Group Inc......D...... 614 491-0500
Groveport (G-11551)

HARDWARE, WHOLESALE: Garden Tools, Hand

A M Leonard Inc................................D...... 937 773-2694
Piqua (G-15994)

HARDWARE, WHOLESALE: Nuts

Facil North America Inc......................C...... 330 487-2500
Twinsburg (G-18265)
Omni Fasteners Inc............................E...... 440 838-1800
Broadview Heights (G-1842)

SERVICES

HARDWARE, WHOLESALE: Power Tools & Access

Noco Company ....B 216 464-8131
Solon (G-16879)

Saw Service and Supply Company ....E 216 252-5600
Cleveland (G-6372)

TTI Floor Care North Amer Inc.............B 440 996-2000
Solon (G-16909)

WW Grainger Inc ....E 614 276-5231
Columbus (G-8921)

HARDWARE, WHOLESALE: Saw Blades

Country Saw and Knife Inc ....E 330 332-1611
Salem (G-16540)

HARDWARE, WHOLESALE: Screws

Brighton-Best Intl Inc ....E 440 238-1350
Strongsville (G-17288)

HARDWARE: Rubber

Reynolds Industries Inc ....E 330 889-9466
West Farmington (G-19102)

HARNESS ASSEMBLIES: Cable & Wire

Microplex Inc ....E 330 498-0600
North Canton (G-15220)

HEAD START CENTER, EXC IN CONJUNCTION WITH SCHOOL

Butler County Eductl Svc Ctr...............E 513 737-2817
Hamilton (G-11568)

Child Care Resources Inc ....D 740 454-6251
Zanesville (G-20295)

Child Dvlpmnt Cncl of Frnkln ....D 614 221-1709
Columbus (G-7185)

Child Dvlpmnt Cncl of Frnkln ....E 614 416-5178
Columbus (G-7186)

Child Focus Inc ....E 513 752-1555
Cincinnati (G-3180)

Clinton County Community Actn..........E 937 382-5624
Wilmington (G-19611)

Community Action Comsn Belmont......D 740 676-0800
Bellaire (G-1332)

Community Action Comsn Belmont......E 740 695-0293
Saint Clairsville (G-16483)

Corporation For OH Appalachian ....E 330 364-8882
New Philadelphia (G-14953)

Coshocton County Head Start ....E 740 622-3667
Coshocton (G-9006)

Council For Economic Opport ....C 216 736-2934
Cleveland (G-5357)

Council of Ecnmc Opprtnts of G ....E 216 651-5154
Cleveland (G-5358)

Council On Rur Svc Prgrams Inc ....D 937 452-1090
Camden (G-2089)

Council On Rur Svc Prgrams Inc ....E 937 492-8787
Sidney (G-16769)

Crossroads Lake County Adole ....E 440 358-7370
Painesville (G-15706)

Hamilton County Eductl Svc Ctr..........D 513 674-4200
Cincinnati (G-3675)

Harcatus Tri-County Community ....D 330 602-5442
New Philadelphia (G-14962)

Knox County Head Start Inc ....E 740 397-1344
Mount Vernon (G-14775)

Lorain County Community Action........E 440 246-0480
Lorain (G-12919)

Louis Stokes Head Start ....E 216 295-0854
Cleveland (G-5881)

Marion Head Start Center ....E 740 382-6858
Marion (G-13442)

Miami Vly Child Dev Ctrs Inc ....D 937 226-5664
Dayton (G-9628)

Miami Vly Child Dev Ctrs Inc ....E 937 228-1644
Dayton (G-9629)

Migrant Head Start ....E 937 846-0699
New Carlisle (G-14894)

Pickaway County Community Acti ....E 740 474-7411
Circleville (G-4840)

Pike County Head Start Inc ....D 740 289-2371
Piketon (G-15985)

Portage Private Industry ....D 330 297-7795
Ravenna (G-16259)

Pulaski Head Start ....E 419 636-8862
Bryan (G-1972)

Scioto County C A O Headstart ....E 740 354-3333
Portsmouth (G-16166)

South- Western City School Dst ....D 614 801-8438
Grove City (G-11472)

Spanish American Committee ....E 216 961-2100
Cleveland (G-6441)

W S O S Community A ....E 419 729-8035
Toledo (G-18142)

W S O S Community A ....D 419 333-6068
Fremont (G-11104)

W S O S Community A ....D 419 334-8511
Fremont (G-11105)

Wsos Child Development Program ....E 419 334-8511
Fremont (G-11107)

HEALTH & ALLIED SERVICES, NEC

Cardinal Healthcare ....E 954 202-1883
Columbus (G-7123)

Celtic Healthcare Ne Ohio Inc.............E 724 742-4360
Youngstown (G-19983)

Central Clinic Outpatient Svcs ....D 513 558-9005
Cincinnati (G-3151)

Clinic5 ....E 614 598-9960
Columbus (G-7227)

Consulate Management Co LLC ....D 740 259-5536
Lucasville (G-13047)

District Board Health Mahoning ....E 330 270-2855
Youngstown (G-20019)

Divine Healthcare Services LLC ....E 614 899-6767
Columbus (G-7456)

Franklin County Adamh Board ....E 614 224-1057
Columbus (G-7616)

Greater Clvland Halthcare Assn ....D 216 696-6900
Cleveland (G-5640)

Heartspring Home Hlth Care LLC ....D 937 531-6920
Dayton (G-9493)

Madison Cnty Lndon Cy Hlth Dst ....E 740 852-3065
London (G-12867)

Medical Arts Physician Center ....D 216 431-1500
Cleveland (G-5941)

Metro Health System ....D 330 669-2249
Smithville (G-16811)

Novus Clinic ....E 330 630-9699
Tallmadge (G-17483)

Regensis Stna Training Program ....E 614 849-0115
Columbus (G-8506)

Seneca County Ems ....C 419 447-0266
Tiffin (G-17536)

Trihealth Hf LLC ....E 513 398-3445
Mason (G-13649)

TVC Home Health Care ....E 330 755-1110
Youngstown (G-20229)

HEALTH & WELFARE COUNCIL

City of Columbus ....D 614 645-7417
Columbus (G-7209)

Concord ....E 614 882-9338
Westerville (G-19245)

HEALTH CLUBS

Akron General Medical Center.............C 330 665-8000
Akron (G-46)

Beechmont Racquet Club Inc ....E 513 528-5700
Cincinnati (G-3033)

Centerville Fitness Inc ....E 937 291-7990
Centerville (G-2623)

Fitworks Holding LLC ....E 330 688-2329
Stow (G-17205)

Fitworks Holding LLC ....E 513 923-9931
Cincinnati (G-3571)

Fitworks Holding LLC ....E 440 333-4141
Rocky River (G-16433)

Fitworks Holding LLC ....E 513 531-1500
Cincinnati (G-3572)

Flexeco Incorporated ....E 216 812-3304
Cleveland (G-5545)

Holzer Clinic LLC ....E 740 446-5412
Gallipolis (G-11199)

Kinsale Golf & Fitnes CLB LLC ....C 740 881-6500
Powell (G-16202)

Life Time Inc ....C 614 428-6000
Columbus (G-7973)

Life Time Fitness Inc ....C 952 229-7158
Dublin (G-10271)

New Carlisle Spt & Fitnes Ctr ....E 937 846-1000
New Carlisle (G-14895)

Oid Associates ....E 330 666-3161
Akron (G-363)

Southwest General Health Ctr ....D 440 816-4202
Cleveland (G-6430)

T O J Inc ....E 440 352-1900
Mentor (G-14114)

TLC Health Wellness & Fitness ....E 330 527-4852
Garrettsville (G-11232)

Wyandotte Athletic Club ....E 614 861-6303
Columbus (G-8922)

HEALTH FOOD & SUPPLEMENT STORES

Cornucopia Inc ....E 216 521-4600
Lakewood (G-12339)

Raisin Rack Inc ....E 614 882-5886
Westerville (G-19298)

HEALTH INSURANCE CARRIERS

Aultcare Insurance Company ....B 330 363-6360
Canton (G-2199)

Blue Cross & Blue Shield Mich.............A 330 783-3841
Youngstown (G-19966)

Caresource Management Group Co......A 937 224-3300
Dayton (G-9278)

Caresource Management Group Co......E 614 221-3370
Hilliard (G-11753)

Caresource Management Group Co......A 937 224-3300
Dayton (G-9279)

Cincinnati Equitable Insur Co ....E 513 621-1826
Cincinnati (G-3242)

Dawson Companies ....D 440 333-9000
Richfield (G-16352)

Summa Insurance Company Inc ....B 800 996-8411
Akron (G-453)

Superior Dental Care Inc ....E 937 438-0283
Dayton (G-9802)

HEALTH MAINTENANCE ORGANIZATION: Insurance Only

1-888 Ohio Comp LLC ....D 216 426-0646
Cleveland (G-4864)

Aetna Health California Inc ....E 614 933-6000
New Albany (G-14841)

Aetna Life Insurance Company ....E 330 659-8000
Richfield (G-16342)

Amerigroup Ohio Inc ....E 513 733-2300
Blue Ash (G-1504)

Benefit Services Inc ....D 330 666-0337
Copley (G-8963)

Caresource Management Group Co......A 216 839-1001
Cleveland (G-5126)

Family Health Plan Inc ....C 419 241-6501
Toledo (G-17724)

Health Plan of Ohio Inc ....C 330 837-6880
Massillon (G-13693)

Healthspan Integrated Care ....E 440 937-2350
Avon (G-885)

Healthspan Integrated Care ....E 440 572-1000
Cleveland (G-5678)

Humana Health Plan Ohio Inc ....D 513 784-5200
Cincinnati (G-3739)

Humana Inc ....E 330 877-5464
Hartville (G-11692)

Humana Inc ....E 216 328-2047
Independence (G-12080)

Humana Inc ....E 614 210-1038
Dublin (G-10248)

Oxford Blazer Company Inc ....E 614 792-2220
Dublin (G-10302)

Promedica Health Systems Inc............A 567 585-7454
Toledo (G-17993)

Uc Health Llc ....E 513 585-7600
Cincinnati (G-4665)

United Healthcare Ohio Inc ....C 513 603-6200
Cincinnati (G-4680)

Unitedhealth Group Inc ....B 513 603-6200
Cincinnati (G-4691)

HEALTH PRACTITIONERS' OFFICES, NEC

Central Ohio Sleep Medicine ....E 614 475-6700
Westerville (G-19153)

Occupational Health Services ....E 937 492-7296
Sidney (G-16788)

Stephen R Saddemi MD ....E 419 578-7200
Toledo (G-18047)

Youngstown Ohio Otpatient Svcs ....E 330 884-2020
Youngstown (G-20264)

HEALTH SCREENING SVCS

Advantage Imaging LLC ....E 216 292-9998
Beachwood (G-1027)

Cols Health & Wellness Testing ....E 614 839-2781
Westerville (G-19238)

County of Clark ....D 937 390-5600
Springfield (G-17022)

Life Line Screening Amer Ltd ....C 216 581-6556
Independence (G-12091)

Life Line Screening Amer Ltd ....C 216 581-6556
Independence (G-12092)

Ohio State University ....D 614 292-0110
Columbus (G-8324)

P N P Inc ....D 330 386-1231
East Liverpool (G-10415)

Peregrine Health Services Inc ....D 419 298-2321
Edgerton (G-10469)

Proactive Occptnal Mdicine Inc ....E 740 574-8728
Wheelersburg (G-19439)

Renaissance Home Health Care ....D 216 662-8702
Bedford (G-1301)

Ryan Sheridan ....E 330 270-2380
Youngstown (G-20201)

HEALTH SYSTEMS AGENCY

City of Portsmouth ....E 740 353-5153
Portsmouth (G-16128)

County of Medina ....D 330 995-5243
Medina (G-13926)

Far West Center ....E 440 835-6212
Westlake (G-19342)

Health Partners Western Ohio ....D 419 221-3072
Lima (G-12656)

Integrated Services of Appala ....D 740 594-6807
Athens (G-786)

Licking County Aging Program ....D 740 345-0821
Newark (G-15052)

Occupational Health Link ....E 614 885-0039
Columbus (G-8224)

Pike Cnty Adult Activities Ctr ....E 740 947-7503
Waverly (G-18820)

Pilot Dogs Incorporated ....E 614 221-6367
Columbus (G-8447)

Prevent Blindness - Ohio ....E 614 464-2020
Columbus (G-8460)

Solidarity Health Network Inc ....E 216 831-1220
Cleveland (G-6420)

Wood County Ohio ....D 419 353-6914
Bowling Green (G-1757)

HEARING TESTING SVCS

Cincinnati Speech Hearing Ctr ....E 513 221-0527
Cincinnati (G-3268)

HEAT TREATING: Metal

AM Castle & Co ....D 330 425-7000
Bedford (G-1269)

Carpe Diem Industries LLC ....E 419 358-0129
Bluffton (G-1689)

Carpe Diem Industries LLC ....D 419 659-5639
Columbus Grove (G-8940)

Clifton Steel Company ....D 216 662-6111
Maple Heights (G-13283)

Euclid Heat Treating Co ....D 216 481-8444
Euclid (G-10632)

Gerdau Macsteel Atmosphere Ann ....D 330 478-0314
Canton (G-2325)

HI Tecmetal Group Inc ....E 440 373-5101
Wickliffe (G-19463)

Lapham-Hickey Steel Corp ....E 614 443-4881
Columbus (G-7952)

Miller Consolidated Industries ....C 937 294-2681
Moraine (G-14678)

Northwind Industries Inc ....E 216 433-0666
Cleveland (G-6099)

Samuel Steel Pickling Company ....D 330 963-3777
Twinsburg (G-18317)

Thermal Treatment Center Inc ....E 216 881-8100
Cleveland (G-6521)

HEATERS: Room & Wall, Including Radiators

Hunter Defense Tech Inc ....E 216 438-6111
Solon (G-16859)

HEATING & AIR CONDITIONING EQPT & SPLYS WHOLESALERS

Airtron LP ....D 614 274-2345
Columbus (G-6888)

Buckeye Heating and AC Sup Inc ....E 216 831-0066
Bedford Heights (G-1318)

Controls and Sheet Metal Inc ....E 513 721-3610
Cincinnati (G-3355)

Copeland Access + Inc ....E 937 498-3802
Sidney (G-16768)

Daikin Applied Americas Inc ....E 763 553-5009
Dayton (G-9344)

Famous Enterprises Inc ....E 419 478-0343
Toledo (G-17726)

Hamilton-Parker Company ....D 614 358-7800
Columbus (G-7713)

Honeywell International Inc ....D 216 459-6053
Cleveland (G-5702)

Honeywell International Inc ....E 614 717-2270
Columbus (G-7772)

Lennox Industries Inc ....E 614 871-3017
Grove City (G-11447)

Luxury Heating Co ....D 440 366-0971
Sheffield Village (G-16738)

Monroe Mechanical Incorporated ....E 513 539-7555
Monroe (G-14577)

Robertson Heating Sup Co Ohio ....E 800 433-9532
Alliance (G-545)

Robertson Htg Sup Clumbus Ohio ....C 330 821-9180
Alliance (G-548)

Style Crest Inc ....C 419 332-7369
Fremont (G-11098)

Style Crest Inc ....B 419 332-7369
Fremont (G-11099)

Style Crest Enterprises Inc ....E 419 355-8586
Fremont (G-11100)

Wadsworth-Slawson Inc ....E 216 391-7263
Perrysburg (G-15934)

Wolff Bros Supply Inc ....E 330 786-4140
Akron (G-503)

Yanfeng US Automotive ....D 419 662-4905
Northwood (G-15416)

HEATING EQPT & SPLYS

Trumbull Manufacturing Inc ....D 330 393-6624
Warren (G-18759)

HELP SUPPLY SERVICES

Advantage Tchncal Rsurcing Inc ....B 513 651-1111
Cincinnati (G-2913)

Amerimed Inc ....E 513 942-3670
West Chester (G-18866)

Ashtabula Stevedore Company ....E 440 964-7186
Ashtabula (G-720)

Aspen Community Living ....C 614 880-6000
Columbus (G-6979)

Belflex Staffing Network LLC ....C 513 488-8588
Cincinnati (G-3038)

CPC Logistics Inc ....D 513 874-5787
Fairfield (G-10715)

Edge Plastics Inc ....E 419 522-6696
Mansfield (G-13171)

Firstat Nursing Services ....D 216 295-1500
Cleveland (G-5538)

Innovtive Sltons Unlimited LLC ....D 740 289-3282
Piketon (G-15979)

MPW Industrial Services Inc ....D 937 644-0200
East Liberty (G-10393)

Nursing Resources Corp ....C 419 333-3000
Maumee (G-13825)

Ohio Dept of Job & Fmly Svcs ....E 419 334-3891
Fremont (G-11089)

P E Miller & Associates Inc ....D 614 231-4743
Columbus (G-8408)

Professional Transportation ....C 419 661-0576
Walbridge (G-18623)

Rkpl Inc ....D 419 224-2121
Lima (G-12732)

Taylors Staffing LLC ....D 740 446-3305
Pomeroy (G-16098)

Volt Management Corp ....D 513 791-2600
Cincinnati (G-4764)

HELPING HAND SVCS, INCLUDING BIG BROTHER, ETC

Big Broth and Big Siste of Cen ....E 614 839-2447
Columbus (G-7034)

Cleaners Extraordinaire Inc ....D 937 324-8488
Springfield (G-17015)

HIGHWAY & STREET MAINTENANCE SVCS

Able Contracting Group Inc ....E 440 951-0880
Painesville (G-15691)

Belmont County of Ohio ....E 740 695-1580
Saint Clairsville (G-16476)

C J & L Construction Inc ....E 513 769-3600
Cincinnati (G-3099)

City of Aurora ....D 330 562-8662
Aurora (G-825)

City of Avon ....E 440 937-5740
Avon (G-876)

City of Brecksville ....E 440 526-1384
Brecksville (G-1774)

City of Euclid ....E 216 289-2800
Cleveland (G-5200)

City of Kent ....D 330 678-8105
Kent (G-12222)

City of North Ridgeville ....E 440 327-8326
North Ridgeville (G-15326)

City of North Royalton ....E 440 582-3002
Cleveland (G-5210)

City of Portsmouth ....E 740 353-5419
Portsmouth (G-16129)

City of Streetsboro ....E 330 626-2856
Streetsboro (G-17250)

City of Willoughby ....D 440 953-4111
Willoughby (G-19511)

County of Ashtabula ....E 440 576-2816
Jefferson (G-12191)

County of Clinton ....E 937 382-2078
Wilmington (G-19620)

County of Holmes ....E 330 674-5076
Millersburg (G-14469)

County of Seneca ....E 419 447-3863
Tiffin (G-17513)

County of Summit ....C 330 643-2860
Akron (G-165)

County of Trumbull ....E 330 675-2640
Warren (G-18692)

Eaton Construction Co Inc ....D 740 474-3414
Circleville (G-4832)

George Kuhn Enterprises Inc ....E 614 481-8838
Columbus (G-7660)

J K Enterprises Inc ....D 614 481-8838
Columbus (G-7850)

Ohio Department Transportation ....C 740 363-1251
Delaware (G-9999)

Ohio Department Transportation ....E 937 548-3015
Greenville (G-11391)

Ohio Department Transportation ....E 419 738-4214
Wapakoneta (G-18651)

Ohio Department Transportation ....E 330 533-4351
Canfield (G-2153)

Ohio Tpk & Infrastructure Comm ....E 419 826-4831
Swanton (G-17403)

Ohio Tpk & Infrastructure Comm ....C 440 234-2081
Berea (G-1433)

Ohio Tpk & Infrastructure Comm ....E 440 234-2081
Richfield (G-16369)

Springboro Service Center ....E 937 748-0020
Springboro (G-16984)

Transportation Ohio Department ....E 740 773-3191
Chillicothe (G-2832)

Turnpike and Infrastructure Co ....D 330 527-2169
Windham (G-19664)

HIGHWAY BRIDGE OPERATION

Johnson Mirmiran Thompson Inc ....D 614 714-0270
Columbus (G-7863)

HISTORICAL SOCIETY

Anderson Twnship Hstorical Soc ....E 513 231-2114
Cincinnati (G-2964)

National Underground Railroad ....D 513 333-7500
Cincinnati (G-4095)

New London Area Historical Soc ....D 419 929-3674
New London (G-14933)

Western Reserve Historical Soc ....D 216 721-5722
Cleveland (G-6675)

HOBBY & CRAFT SPLY STORES

Jo-Ann Stores Holdings Inc ....D 888 739-4120
Hudson (G-11988)

SERVICES

HOBBY, TOY & GAME STORES: Arts & Crafts & Splys

Darice Inc ....C....... 440 238-9150
  Strongsville *(G-17297)*
Hobby Lobby Stores Inc....................E....... 330 686-1508
  Stow *(G-17209)*

HOBBY, TOY & GAME STORES: Toys & Games

Heaven Bound Ascensions...................E....... 330 633-3288
  Tallmadge *(G-17477)*

HOGS WHOLESALERS

Kalmbach Pork Finishing LLC.............D....... 419 294-3838
  Upper Sandusky *(G-18409)*
Robert Winner Sons Inc ....E....... 419 582-4321
  Yorkshire *(G-19942)*

HOLDING COMPANIES, NEC

AWH Holdings Inc ....D...... 513 241-2614
  Cincinnati *(G-3008)*
Bleux Holdings LLC ....E...... 859 414-5060
  Cincinnati *(G-3056)*
Going Home Medical Holding Co ....E...... 305 340-1034
  Strongsville *(G-17306)*
M J S Holding ....E...... 614 410-2512
  Columbus *(G-8003)*

HOLDING COMPANIES: Banks

Community Invstors Bancorp Inc ....E..... 419 562-7055
  Bucyrus *(G-1985)*
Comunibanc Corp ....D..... 419 599-1065
  Napoleon *(G-14802)*
First Capital Bancshares Inc ....D...... 740 775-6777
  Chillicothe *(G-2779)*
Genbanc ....E..... 419 855-8381
  Genoa *(G-11254)*
Greenville National Bancorp................E..... 937 548-1114
  Greenville *(G-11382)*
Muskingum Vly Bancshares Inc ....E..... 740 984-2381
  Beverly *(G-1464)*
Portage Bancshares Inc ....D...... 330 296-8090
  Ravenna *(G-16253)*

HOLDING COMPANIES: Investment, Exc Banks

Ampac Holdings LLC ....A..... 513 671-1777
  Cincinnati *(G-2955)*
Aprecia Pharmaceuticals Co ....C....... 513 864-4107
  Blue Ash *(G-1506)*
Betco Corporation ....C....... 419 241-2156
  Bowling Green *(G-1719)*
Ce Power Holdings Inc ....D...... 513 563-6150
  Cincinnati *(G-3140)*
Drb Holdings LLC ....D...... 330 645-3299
  Akron *(G-194)*
Drt Holdings Inc ....D...... 937 298-7391
  Dayton *(G-9395)*
Elyria Foundry Holdings LLC ....B....... 440 322-4657
  Elyria *(G-10506)*
Entelco Corporation ....D...... 419 872-4620
  Maumee *(G-13785)*
Global Graphene Group Inc ....E..... 937 331-9884
  Dayton *(G-9461)*
Jo-Ann Stores Holdings Inc ....D...... 888 739-4120
  Hudson *(G-11988)*
Lion Group Inc ....D...... 937 898-1949
  Dayton *(G-9570)*
Liqui-Box International Inc..................D...... 614 888-9280
  Columbus *(G-7983)*
Mssl Consolidated Inc ....B....... 330 766-5510
  Warren *(G-18732)*
Nationwide Life Insur Co Amer...........A...... 800 688-5177
  Columbus *(G-8158)*
Norse Dairy Systems Inc ....C....... 614 294-4931
  Columbus *(G-8195)*
Nri Global Inc...................................E..... 905 790-2828
  Delta *(G-10048)*
Ocr Services Corporation ....C....... 513 719-2600
  Cincinnati *(G-4148)*
Pet Food Holdings Inc ....D...... 419 394-3374
  Saint Marys *(G-16531)*
Pf Holdings LLC ....D...... 740 549-3558
  Lewis Center *(G-12559)*
PMC Acquisitions Inc ....D...... 419 429-0042
  Findlay *(G-10955)*

Premix Holding Company ....B 330 666-3751
  Fairlawn *(G-10843)*
Qsr Parent Co ....A...... 330 425-8472
  Twinsburg *(G-18309)*
Sca Acquisitions Inc ....A...... 216 777-2750
  Seven Hills *(G-16680)*
Towne Investment Company LP...........D...... 513 381-8696
  Cincinnati *(G-4616)*
Wasserstrom Holdings Inc ....C....... 614 228-6525
  Columbus *(G-8880)*

HOLDING COMPANIES: Personal, Exc Banks

A and S Ventures Inc ....E...... 419 376-3934
  Toledo *(G-17575)*
Amrstrong Distributors Inc ....E...... 419 483-4840
  Bellevue *(G-1371)*
Eci Macola/Max Holding LLC ....E...... 614 410-2712
  Dublin *(G-10214)*
Global Cnsld Holdings Inc ....D...... 513 703-0965
  Mason *(G-13588)*
Hartzell Industries Inc ....E...... 937 773-6295
  Piqua *(G-16007)*
Jbo Holding Company ....C....... 216 367-8787
  Cleveland *(G-5785)*
Washington Court Hse Holdg LLC ....E...... 614 873-7733
  Wshngtn CT Hs *(G-19885)*

HOLDING COMPANIES: Public Utility

Nwo Resources Inc ....C....... 419 636-1117
  Bryan *(G-1965)*

HOME CENTER STORES

Apco Industries Inc...........................D...... 614 224-2345
  Columbus *(G-6956)*
Builders Firstsource Inc ....E...... 513 874-9950
  Cincinnati *(G-3087)*
Home Depot USA Inc ....C....... 614 523-0600
  Columbus *(G-7762)*
Home Depot USA Inc ....C....... 330 965-4790
  Boardman *(G-1699)*
Home Depot USA Inc ....C....... 330 497-1810
  Canton *(G-2347)*
Home Depot USA Inc ....C....... 513 688-1654
  Cincinnati *(G-3719)*
Home Depot USA Inc ....C....... 330 922-3448
  Cuyahoga Falls *(G-9100)*
Home Depot USA Inc ....C....... 937 312-9053
  Dayton *(G-9499)*
Home Depot USA Inc ....C....... 937 312-9076
  Dayton *(G-9500)*
Home Depot USA Inc ....C....... 216 692-2780
  Euclid *(G-10642)*
Home Depot USA Inc ....C....... 216 676-9969
  Cleveland *(G-5700)*
Home Depot USA Inc ....C....... 216 581-6611
  Maple Heights *(G-13287)*
Home Depot USA Inc ....C....... 937 431-7346
  Beavercreek *(G-1156)*
Home Depot USA Inc ....C....... 330 245-0280
  Akron *(G-268)*
Home Depot USA Inc ....C....... 937 837-1551
  Dayton *(G-9501)*
Home Depot USA Inc ....C....... 216 297-1303
  Cleveland Heights *(G-6719)*
Home Depot USA Inc ....C....... 513 661-2413
  Cincinnati *(G-3720)*
Home Depot USA Inc ....C....... 513 887-1450
  Fairfield Township *(G-10810)*
Home Depot USA Inc ....C....... 419 476-4573
  Toledo *(G-17805)*
Home Depot USA Inc ....C....... 440 357-0428
  Mentor *(G-14061)*
Home Depot USA Inc ....C....... 513 631-1705
  Cincinnati *(G-3721)*
Home Depot USA Inc ....C....... 440 684-1343
  Highland Heights *(G-11734)*
Home Depot USA Inc ....C....... 419 537-1920
  Toledo *(G-17806)*
Home Depot USA Inc ....C....... 614 878-9150
  Columbus *(G-7763)*
Home Depot USA Inc ....C....... 440 826-9092
  Strongsville *(G-17311)*
Home Depot USA Inc ....C....... 614 939-5036
  Columbus *(G-7764)*
Home Depot USA Inc ....D...... 440 937-2240
  Avon *(G-886)*
Home Depot USA Inc ....C....... 614 577-1601
  Reynoldsburg *(G-16309)*

Home Depot USA Inc ....C....... 330 220-2654
  Brunswick *(G-1932)*
Home Depot USA Inc ....C....... 419 626-6493
  Sandusky *(G-16616)*
Home Depot USA Inc ....C....... 614 876-5558
  Hilliard *(G-11776)*
Home Depot USA Inc ....C....... 440 324-7222
  Elyria *(G-10515)*
Home Depot USA Inc ....C....... 419 529-0015
  Ontario *(G-15552)*
Home Depot USA Inc ....C....... 216 251-3091
  Cleveland *(G-5701)*
Lowes Home Centers LLC ....C....... 937 235-2920
  Dayton *(G-9574)*
Lowes Home Centers LLC ....C....... 740 574-6200
  Wheelersburg *(G-19435)*
Lowes Home Centers LLC ....C....... 330 665-9356
  Akron *(G-321)*
Lowes Home Centers LLC ....C....... 330 829-2700
  Alliance *(G-538)*
Lowes Home Centers LLC ....C....... 937 599-4000
  Bellefontaine *(G-1357)*
Lowes Home Centers LLC ....C....... 419 420-7531
  Findlay *(G-10935)*
Lowes Home Centers LLC ....C....... 330 832-1901
  Massillon *(G-13704)*
Lowes Home Centers LLC ....C....... 513 741-0585
  Cincinnati *(G-3945)*
Lowes Home Centers LLC ....C....... 614 433-9957
  Columbus *(G-6822)*
Lowes Home Centers LLC ....C....... 740 389-9737
  Marion *(G-13430)*
Lowes Home Centers LLC ....C....... 740 450-5500
  Zanesville *(G-20326)*
Lowes Home Centers LLC ....C....... 513 598-7050
  Cincinnati *(G-3946)*
Lowes Home Centers LLC ....C....... 614 769-9940
  Reynoldsburg *(G-16317)*
Lowes Home Centers LLC ....C....... 614 853-6200
  Columbus *(G-7990)*
Lowes Home Centers LLC ....C....... 440 937-3500
  Avon *(G-893)*
Lowes Home Centers LLC ....C....... 513 445-1000
  South Lebanon *(G-16926)*
Lowes Home Centers LLC ....B....... 216 831-2860
  Bedford *(G-1290)*
Lowes Home Centers LLC ....C....... 937 327-6000
  Springfield *(G-17065)*
Lowes Home Centers LLC ....C....... 419 331-3598
  Lima *(G-12693)*
Lowes Home Centers LLC ....C....... 740 681-3464
  Lancaster *(G-12413)*
Lowes Home Centers LLC ....C....... 614 659-0530
  Dublin *(G-10275)*
Lowes Home Centers LLC ....C....... 614 238-2601
  Columbus *(G-7991)*
Lowes Home Centers LLC ....C....... 740 522-0003
  Newark *(G-15063)*
Lowes Home Centers LLC ....C....... 740 773-7777
  Chillicothe *(G-2803)*
Lowes Home Centers LLC ....C....... 440 998-6555
  Ashtabula *(G-745)*
Lowes Home Centers LLC ....B....... 513 753-5094
  Cincinnati *(G-2861)*
Lowes Home Centers LLC ....C....... 614 497-6170
  Columbus *(G-7992)*
Lowes Home Centers LLC ....C....... 513 731-6127
  Cincinnati *(G-3947)*
Lowes Home Centers LLC ....C....... 330 287-2261
  Wooster *(G-19742)*
Lowes Home Centers LLC ....C....... 937 339-2544
  Troy *(G-18211)*
Lowes Home Centers LLC ....C....... 440 942-2759
  Willoughby *(G-19546)*
Lowes Home Centers LLC ....C....... 740 374-2151
  Marietta *(G-13345)*
Lowes Home Centers LLC ....C....... 419 874-6758
  Perrysburg *(G-15891)*
Lowes Home Centers LLC ....C....... 330 626-2980
  Streetsboro *(G-17259)*
Lowes Home Centers LLC ....C....... 419 389-9464
  Toledo *(G-17864)*
Lowes Home Centers LLC ....C....... 419 843-9758
  Toledo *(G-17865)*
Lowes Home Centers LLC ....C....... 614 447-2851
  Columbus *(G-7993)*
Lowes Home Centers LLC ....C....... 513 965-3280
  Milford *(G-14402)*
Lowes Home Centers LLC ....C....... 330 908-2750
  Northfield *(G-15382)*

Lowes Home Centers LLC ....C...... 419 470-2491
  Toledo **(G-17866)**
Lowes Home Centers LLC ....C...... 513 336-9741
  Mason **(G-13612)**
Lowes Home Centers LLC ....C...... 937 498-8400
  Sidney **(G-16785)**
Lowes Home Centers LLC ....C...... 740 699-3000
  Saint Clairsville **(G-16493)**
Lowes Home Centers LLC ....C...... 330 920-9280
  Stow **(G-17218)**
Lowes Home Centers LLC ....C...... 740 589-3750
  Athens **(G-791)**
Lowes Home Centers LLC ....C...... 740 393-5350
  Mount Vernon **(G-14779)**
Lowes Home Centers LLC ....C...... 937 547-2400
  Greenville **(G-11389)**
Lowes Home Centers LLC ....C...... 330 335-1900
  Wadsworth **(G-18606)**
Lowes Home Centers LLC ....C...... 937 347-4000
  Xenia **(G-19918)**
Lowes Home Centers LLC ....C...... 440 239-2630
  Strongsville **(G-17324)**
Lowes Home Centers LLC ....C...... 513 755-4300
  West Chester **(G-18966)**
Lowes Home Centers LLC ....C...... 513 671-2093
  Cincinnati **(G-3948)**
Lowes Home Centers LLC ....C...... 440 331-1027
  Rocky River **(G-16440)**
Lowes Home Centers LLC ....C...... 330 677-3040
  Kent **(G-12247)**
Lowes Home Centers LLC ....C...... 419 747-1920
  Ontario **(G-15559)**
Lowes Home Centers LLC ....C...... 330 339-1936
  New Philadelphia **(G-14971)**
Lowes Home Centers LLC ....C...... 440 985-5700
  Lorain **(G-12924)**
Lowes Home Centers LLC ....C...... 419 447-4101
  Tiffin **(G-17521)**
Lowes Home Centers LLC ....C...... 937 578-4440
  Marysville **(G-13511)**
Lowes Home Centers LLC ....C...... 440 324-5004
  Elyria **(G-10531)**
Lowes Home Centers LLC ....C...... 937 438-4900
  Dayton **(G-9575)**
Lowes Home Centers LLC ....C...... 937 427-1110
  Beavercreek **(G-1168)**
Lowes Home Centers LLC ....C...... 937 848-5600
  Dayton **(G-9576)**
Lowes Home Centers LLC ....C...... 614 529-5900
  Hilliard **(G-11786)**
Lowes Home Centers LLC ....C...... 513 737-3700
  Hamilton **(G-11625)**
Lowes Home Centers LLC ....C...... 419 355-0221
  Fremont **(G-11084)**
Lowes Home Centers LLC ....C...... 419 624-6000
  Sandusky **(G-16625)**
Lowes Home Centers LLC ....C...... 419 782-9000
  Defiance **(G-9926)**
Lowes Home Centers LLC ....C...... 330 609-8000
  Warren **(G-18725)**
Lowes Home Centers LLC ....C...... 740 894-7120
  South Point **(G-16939)**
Lowes Home Centers LLC ....C...... 513 727-3900
  Middletown **(G-14305)**
Lowes Home Centers LLC ....C...... 330 497-2720
  Canton **(G-2381)**
Lowes Home Centers LLC ....C...... 740 266-3500
  Steubenville **(G-17164)**
Lowes Home Centers LLC ....C...... 937 383-7000
  Wilmington **(G-19630)**
Lowes Home Centers LLC ....C...... 614 476-7100
  Columbus **(G-7994)**
Menard Inc............................C...... 937 630-3550
  Miamisburg **(G-14187)**
Menard Inc............................C...... 513 737-2204
  Fairfield Township **(G-10813)**

HOME FOR THE DESTITUTE

Caracole Inc..........................E...... 513 761-1480
  Cincinnati **(G-3115)**
Volunteers America Ohio & Ind ....C...... 614 253-6100
  Columbus **(G-8859)**

HOME FOR THE EMOTIONALLY DISTURBED

Adriel School Inc.....................D...... 937 465-0010
  West Liberty **(G-19117)**
Bellefaire Jewish Chld Bur.........B...... 216 932-2800
  Shaker Heights **(G-16703)**
Buckeye Ranch Inc.................D...... 614 384-7700
  Columbus **(G-7090)**

Buckeye Ranch Inc.................C...... 614 875-2371
  Grove City **(G-11416)**
Community Support Services Inc ......C...... 330 253-9388
  Akron **(G-153)**
Ohioguidestone........................E...... 440 234-2006
  Berea **(G-1434)**
United Methodist Childrens ....C...... 614 885-5020
  Columbus **(G-8804)**

HOME FOR THE MENTALLY HANDICAPPED

Abilities First Foundation Inc ....D...... 513 423-9496
  Middletown **(G-14285)**
Alternative Residences Two ....C...... 740 526-0514
  Saint Clairsville **(G-16468)**
Alternative Residences Two ....E...... 330 453-0200
  Canton **(G-2183)**
Ashtabula County Residential I ....E...... 440 593-6404
  Conneaut **(G-8950)**
Assoc Dvlpmtly Disabled ....E...... 614 486-4361
  Westerville **(G-19222)**
Assoc Dvlpmtly Disabled ....E...... 614 447-0606
  Columbus **(G-6982)**
Bastin Home Inc.....................E...... 513 734-2662
  Bethel **(G-1452)**
Bittersweet Inc.......................D...... 419 875-6986
  Whitehouse **(G-19444)**
Cincinnatis Optimum RES Envir ....C...... 513 771-2673
  Cincinnati **(G-3280)**
Community Hsing Netwrk Dev Co ....C...... 614 487-6700
  Columbus **(G-7332)**
Community Living Experiences ....E...... 614 588-0320
  Columbus **(G-7333)**
County of Auglaize ....D...... 419 629-2419
  New Bremen **(G-14886)**
County of Holmes ....E...... 330 279-2801
  Holmesville **(G-11929)**
County of Lorain ....E...... 440 329-3734
  Elyria **(G-10495)**
Eastwood Residential Living ....E...... 440 417-0608
  Madison **(G-13095)**
ECHO Residential Support ....E...... 614 210-0944
  Columbus **(G-7497)**
Erie Residential Living Inc ....E...... 419 625-0060
  Sandusky **(G-16601)**
Evant ....E...... 330 920-1517
  Stow **(G-17203)**
Firelands Regional Health Sys ....E...... 419 448-9440
  Tiffin **(G-17518)**
Franklin County Residential S ....B...... 614 844-5847
  Worthington **(G-19811)**
G & D Alternative Living Inc ....E...... 937 446-2803
  Sardinia **(G-16659)**
Hopewell ....E...... 440 693-4074
  Mesopotamia **(G-14130)**
Horizons Tuscarawas/Carroll.........E...... 330 262-4183
  Wooster **(G-19729)**
Josina Lott Foundation ....E...... 419 866-9013
  Toledo **(G-17833)**
Ladd Inc..............................E...... 513 861-4089
  Cincinnati **(G-3906)**
McElvain Group Home.................E...... 419 589-6697
  Mansfield **(G-13212)**
Miami Vly Hsing Oprtunties Inc ....C...... 937 263-4449
  Dayton **(G-9630)**
Muskingum Residentials Inc.........E...... 740 453-5350
  Zanesville **(G-20340)**
Network Housing 2005 Inc ....D...... 614 487-6700
  Columbus **(G-8178)**
New Avenues To Independence ....E...... 888 853-8905
  Ashtabula **(G-748)**
New Nghbors Rsdential Svcs Inc ....E...... 937 717-5731
  Springfield **(G-17088)**
Ohio Department of Health ....B...... 419 447-1450
  Tiffin **(G-17528)**
Phoenix Residential Ctrs Inc ....E...... 440 428-9082
  Madison **(G-13107)**
Portage County Board ....E...... 330 297-6209
  Ravenna **(G-16256)**
R T Industries Inc ....C...... 937 335-5784
  Troy **(G-18224)**
Residential Home For The Devlp ....C...... 740 622-9778
  Coshocton **(G-9025)**
Residential Home For The Devlp ....E...... 740 452-5133
  Zanesville **(G-20358)**
Residential Management Systems ....E...... 614 880-6014
  Worthington **(G-19843)**
Rhc Inc...............................C...... 513 389-7501
  Cincinnati **(G-4367)**
Saint Johns Villa ....C...... 330 627-4662
  Carrollton **(G-2576)**

Second Phase Inc ....E...... 330 797-9930
  Youngstown **(G-20206)**
Society Handicapped Citz Medin ....E...... 330 722-1900
  Seville **(G-16689)**
Sociey For Handicapped Citizen ....C...... 330 725-7041
  Seville **(G-16690)**
T/R Rsdntial Care Fclities Inc ....E...... 740 754-2600
  Dresden **(G-10116)**
Tri County Mental Health Svcs ....C...... 740 592-3091
  Athens **(G-806)**
Wynn-Reeth Inc.......................E...... 419 639-2094
  Green Springs **(G-11357)**

HOME FOR THE MENTALLY RETARDED

Alexson Services Inc ....B...... 513 874-0423
  Fairfield **(G-10695)**
Anne Grady Corporation ....C...... 419 380-8985
  Holland **(G-11872)**
Ardmore Inc..........................C...... 330 535-2601
  Akron **(G-79)**
Butler County Bd of Mental RE.........E...... 513 785-2815
  Hamilton **(G-11567)**
Butler County Bd of Mental RE.........E...... 513 785-2870
  Fairfield Township **(G-10805)**
Butler County Board of Develop ....E...... 513 867-5913
  Fairfield **(G-10703)**
Champaign Residential Svcs Inc.........E...... 937 653-1320
  Urbana **(G-18425)**
Choices In Community Living ....C...... 937 898-3655
  Dayton **(G-9298)**
Clark County Board of Developm.........C...... 937 328-5200
  Springfield **(G-17011)**
Community Hbilitation Svcs Inc ....E...... 234 334-4288
  Akron **(G-151)**
Concepts In Community Living ....E...... 740 393-0055
  Mount Vernon **(G-14755)**
County of Cuyahoga ....C...... 216 241-8230
  Cleveland **(G-5367)**
County of Lorain ....E...... 440 282-3074
  Lorain **(G-12900)**
County of Richland ....D...... 419 774-4300
  Mansfield **(G-13152)**
Develpmntal Dsblties Ohio Dept ....B...... 419 385-0231
  Toledo **(G-17699)**
Develpmntal Dsblties Ohio Dept ....C...... 330 544-2231
  Columbus **(G-7440)**
Eastwood Residential Living ....E...... 440 428-1588
  Madison **(G-13096)**
Friends of Good Shepherd Manor.........D...... 740 289-2861
  Lucasville **(G-13049)**
Gateways To Better Living Inc ....E...... 330 480-9870
  Youngstown **(G-20043)**
Gateways To Better Living Inc ....E...... 330 270-0952
  Youngstown **(G-20044)**
Gateways To Better Living Inc ....E...... 330 797-1764
  Canfield **(G-2138)**
Gateways To Better Living Inc ....E...... 330 792-2854
  Youngstown **(G-20045)**
Gentlebrook Inc......................C...... 330 877-3694
  Hartville **(G-11686)**
Hattie Larlham Center For ....C...... 330 274-2272
  Mantua **(G-13267)**
Hattie Larlham Center For ....D...... 330 274-2272
  Mantua **(G-13268)**
Manfield Living Center Ltd ....E...... 419 512-1711
  Mansfield **(G-13203)**
Mount Aloysius Corp ....C...... 740 342-3343
  New Lexington **(G-14921)**
New Avenues To Independence ....D...... 216 481-1907
  Cleveland **(G-6060)**
New Avenues To Independence ....E...... 216 671-8224
  Cleveland **(G-6061)**
Opportunity Homes Inc ....E...... 330 424-1411
  Lisbon **(G-12805)**
REM-Ohio Inc.........................E...... 937 335-8267
  Troy **(G-18226)**
REM-Ohio Inc.........................D...... 330 644-9730
  Coventry Township **(G-9041)**
REM-Ohio Inc.........................D...... 614 367-1370
  Reynoldsburg **(G-16325)**
Renaissance House Inc ....E...... 419 663-1316
  Norwalk **(G-15454)**
Residential Hm Assn of Marion ....C...... 740 387-9999
  Marion **(G-13455)**
Residential Inc.......................E...... 740 342-4158
  New Lexington **(G-14927)**
Scioto Residential Services ....E...... 740 353-0288
  Portsmouth **(G-16168)**
Sunshine Communities ....B...... 419 865-0251
  Maumee **(G-13857)**

SERVICES

Threshold Residential Svcs Inc ....C 330 426-4553
  East Palestine (G-10422)
Toward Independence Inc ....C 937 376-3996
  Xenia (G-19929)
Wiley Homes Inc ....D 419 535-3988
  Toledo (G-18157)

HOME FOR THE MENTALLY RETARDED, EXC SKILLED OR INTERMEDIATE

Boyds Kinsman Home Inc ....E 330 876-5581
  Kinsman (G-12318)
Brookside Extended Care Center ....C 513 398-1020
  Mason (G-13547)
Buckeye Community Services Inc ....C 740 941-1639
  Waverly (G-18815)
Columbus Ctr For Humn Svcs Inc ....E 614 245-8180
  New Albany (G-14850)
Columbus Ctr For Humn Svcs Inc ....C 614 641-2904
  Columbus (G-7273)
Community Concepts Inc ....C 513 398-8181
  Mason (G-13565)
Consumer Support Services Inc ....B 740 788-8257
  Newark (G-15024)
County of Richland ....B 419 774-4200
  Mansfield (G-13159)
County of Wood ....B 419 686-6951
  Portage (G-16122)
East Carroll Nursing Home ....D 330 627-6900
  Carrollton (G-2567)
Echoing Hills Village Inc ....E 937 237-7881
  Dayton (G-9407)
Echoing Hills Village Inc ....D 440 986-3085
  South Amherst (G-16921)
Heinzerling Foundation ....C 614 272-8888
  Columbus (G-7735)
Heinzerling Foundation ....A 614 272-2000
  Columbus (G-7736)
Kingston Healthcare Company ....C 440 967-1800
  Vermilion (G-18555)
Minamyer Residential Mr/Dd Svc ....E 614 802-0190
  Columbus (G-8089)
On-Call Nursing Inc ....D 216 577-8890
  Lakewood (G-12358)
Stewart Lodge Inc ....D 440 417-1898
  Madison (G-13109)
United Cerebral Palsy ....D 216 381-9993
  Cleveland (G-6569)

HOME FOR THE PHYSICALLY HANDICAPPED

Brighter Horizons Residential ....E 440 417-1751
  Madison (G-13093)
County of Hancock ....E 419 422-6387
  Findlay (G-10891)

HOME FURNISHINGS WHOLESALERS

American Frame Corporation ....E 419 893-5595
  Maumee (G-13748)
Bostwick-Braun Company ....D 419 259-3600
  Toledo (G-17620)
Interdesign Inc ....B 440 248-0136
  Solon (G-16861)
Marketing Results Ltd ....E 614 575-9300
  Columbus (G-8021)
National Marketshare Group ....E 513 921-0800
  Cincinnati (G-4094)
Norwood Hardware & Supply Co ....E 513 733-1175
  Cincinnati (G-4134)
Old Time Pottery Inc ....D 513 825-5211
  Cincinnati (G-4167)
Old Time Pottery Inc ....D 440 842-1244
  Cleveland (G-6128)
Old Time Pottery Inc ....D 614 337-1258
  Columbus (G-8370)

HOME HEALTH CARE SVCS

1st Class Home Health Care Ser ....E 216 678-0213
  Northfield (G-15371)
A Touch of Grace Inc ....D 567 560-2350
  Mansfield (G-13131)
A-1 Nursing Care Inc ....C 614 268-3800
  Columbus (G-6850)
Ability Matters LLC ....E 614 214-9652
  Hilliard (G-11739)
Above & Beyond Caregivers LLC ....E 614 478-1700
  Columbus (G-6855)

Accentcare Home Health Cal Inc ....C 740 387-4568
  Circleville (G-4822)
Addus Homecare Corporation ....A 866 684-0385
  Wintersville (G-19667)
Advance Home Care LLC ....D 614 436-3611
  Columbus (G-6873)
Advance Home Care LLC ....D 937 723-6335
  Dayton (G-9209)
Advantage Home Health Svcs Inc ....E 330 491-8161
  North Canton (G-15184)
All About Home Care Svcs LLC ....E 937 222-2980
  Dayton (G-9214)
All Heart Home Care LLC ....E 419 298-0034
  Edgerton (G-10466)
All Hearts Home Health Care ....E 440 342-2026
  Cleveland (G-4933)
Almost Family Inc ....E 614 457-1900
  Columbus (G-6900)
Almost Family Inc ....E 330 724-7545
  Akron (G-67)
Almost Family Inc ....E 216 464-0443
  Cleveland (G-4939)
Alpine Nursing Care ....E 216 650-6295
  Cleveland (G-4942)
Alternate Sltions Private Duty ....D 937 298-1111
  Dayton (G-9222)
Alternate Solutions First LLC ....C 937 298-1111
  Dayton (G-9223)
Alternative Home Care & Stffng ....E 513 794-0571
  Cincinnati (G-2934)
Alternative Home Health Care ....E 513 794-0555
  Cincinnati (G-2935)
Altimate Care LLC ....E 614 794-9600
  Columbus (G-6906)
Amandacare Inc ....C 614 884-8880
  Columbus (G-6908)
Amedisys Inc ....E 740 373-8549
  Marietta (G-13309)
Amenity Home Health Care LLC ....E 513 931-3689
  Cincinnati (G-2937)
American Nursing Care Inc ....E 513 731-4600
  Cincinnati (G-2947)
American Nursing Care Inc ....E 937 438-3844
  Dayton (G-9228)
American Nursing Care Inc ....D 419 228-0888
  Lima (G-12601)
American Nursing Care Inc ....E 740 452-0569
  Zanesville (G-20276)
Angel Above Byond Hm Hlth Svcs ....E 513 553-9955
  Cincinnati (G-2967)
Angels 4 Life LLC ....E 513 474-5683
  Cincinnati (G-2968)
Angels In Waiting Home Care ....E 440 946-0349
  Mentor (G-14018)
Angels Visiting ....D 419 298-0034
  Edgerton (G-10467)
Answercare LLC ....E 855 213-1511
  Canton (G-2190)
Arcadia Services Inc ....D 330 869-9520
  Akron (G-77)
Arcadia Services Inc ....D 937 912-5800
  Beavercreek (G-1126)
Area Agency On Aging Planni ....C 800 258-7277
  Dayton (G-9239)
Area Office On Aging of Nwstrn ....D 419 382-0624
  Toledo (G-17599)
Arlingworth Home Health Inc ....E 614 659-0961
  Dublin (G-10137)
Around Clock Home Care ....D 440 350-2547
  Painesville (G-15694)
ASAP Homecare Inc ....D 330 674-3306
  Millersburg (G-14456)
ASAP Homecare Inc ....D 330 491-0700
  Canton (G-2195)
ASAP Homecare Inc ....E 330 334-7027
  Wadsworth (G-18590)
ASAP Homecare Inc ....C 330 263-4733
  Wooster (G-19688)
Ashtabula Rgional Hm Hlth Svcs ....D 440 992-4663
  Ashtabula (G-719)
Assured Health Care Inc ....E 937 294-2803
  Dayton (G-9242)
Atrium Health System ....D 937 499-5606
  Middletown (G-14342)
B & L Agency LLC ....E 740 373-8272
  Marietta (G-13314)
Benjamin Rose Institute ....D 216 791-8000
  Cleveland (G-5057)
Bethesda Hospital Association ....A 740 454-4000
  Zanesville (G-20281)

Beyond The Horizons Home Healt ....E 608 630-0617
  Columbus (G-7033)
Black Stone Cincinnati LLC ....D 937 424-1370
  Moraine (G-14626)
Black Stone Cincinnati LLC ....E 513 924-1370
  Cincinnati (G-3054)
Blanchard Valley Health System ....D 419 424-3000
  Findlay (G-10872)
Braden Med Services Inc ....E 740 732-2356
  Caldwell (G-2036)
Bradley Bay Assisted Living ....E 440 871-4509
  Bay Village (G-1021)
Bridgeshome Health Care ....D 330 764-1000
  Medina (G-13913)
Brightstar Healthcare ....E 513 321-4688
  Blue Ash (G-1516)
Brook Haven Home Health Care ....E 937 833-6945
  Brookville (G-1910)
Brookdale Senior Living Commun ....E 937 548-6800
  Greenville (G-11367)
Buckeye Hills-Hck Vly Reg Dev ....E 740 373-6400
  Reno (G-16276)
Buckeye Home Health Care ....E 513 791-6446
  Blue Ash (G-1517)
Buckeye Home Health Care ....E 937 291-3780
  Dayton (G-9265)
Buckeye Home Healthcare Inc ....E 614 776-3372
  Westerville (G-19229)
Buckeye Homecare Services Inc ....D 216 321-9300
  Cleveland (G-5098)
Buckeye Rsdntial Solutions LLC ....D 330 235-9183
  Ravenna (G-16233)
C K of Cincinnati Inc ....E 513 752-5533
  Cincinnati (G-3100)
C R G Health Care Systems ....E 330 498-8107
  Niles (G-15148)
Capital Health Homecare ....E 740 264-8815
  Steubenville (G-17142)
Capital Senior Living Corp ....C 330 748-4204
  Macedonia (G-13064)
Caprice Health Care Inc ....C 330 965-9200
  North Lima (G-15267)
Caregivers Health Network Inc ....D 513 662-3400
  Cincinnati (G-3121)
Carestar Inc ....C 513 618-8300
  Cincinnati (G-3122)
Caring Hands Inc ....C 330 821-6310
  Alliance (G-521)
Caring Hearts Home Health Care ....B 513 339-1237
  Mason (G-13548)
Carl Mills ....D 740 282-2382
  Toronto (G-18182)
Central Star ....C 419 756-9449
  Ontario (G-15545)
Chcc Home Health Care ....E 330 759-4069
  Austintown (G-857)
Chestnut Hill Management Co ....D 614 855-3700
  Columbus (G-7183)
CHI Health At Home ....D 513 576-0262
  Milford (G-14376)
Childrens Home Care Dayton ....D 937 641-4663
  Dayton (G-9296)
Childrens Home Care Group ....B 330 543-5000
  Akron (G-129)
Childrens Homecare Services ....C 614 355-1100
  Columbus (G-7188)
Circle J Home Health Care ....D 330 482-0877
  Salineville (G-16570)
City of Wooster ....E 330 263-8636
  Wooster (G-19703)
Clovvr LLC ....E 740 653-2224
  Lancaster (G-12382)
Columbus Behavioral Health LLC ....E 732 747-1800
  Columbus (G-7262)
Comfort Healthcare ....E 216 281-9999
  Cleveland (G-5317)
Community Caregivers ....E 330 725-9800
  Wadsworth (G-18593)
Community Concepts Inc ....C 513 398-8181
  Mason (G-13565)
Community Health Systems Inc ....D 330 841-9011
  Warren (G-18688)
Community Home Care ....E 330 971-7011
  Cuyahoga Falls (G-9084)
Companions of Ashland LLC ....E 419 281-2273
  Ashland (G-669)
Compassionate In Home Care ....E 614 888-5683
  Worthington (G-19800)
Concord Hlth Rhabilitation Ctr ....E 740 574-8441
  Wheelersburg (G-19432)

Consumer Support Services Inc	C	330 652-8800	
Niles *(G-15153)*			
Consumer Support Services Inc	B	740 788-8257	
Newark *(G-15024)*			
Continued Care Inc	E	419 222-2273	
Lima *(G-12618)*			
Continuum Home Care Inc	E	440 964-3332	
Ashtabula *(G-730)*			
Cori Care Inc	D	614 848-4357	
Columbus *(G-7369)*			
Cottages of Clayton	E	937 280-0300	
Dayton *(G-9323)*			
County of Knox	E	740 392-2200	
Mount Vernon *(G-14758)*			
County of Washington	E	740 373-2028	
Marietta *(G-13322)*			
County of Williams	E	419 485-3141	
Montpelier *(G-14612)*			
Covenant Home Health Care LLC	E	614 465-2017	
Columbus *(G-7382)*			
Covington Square Senior APT	E	740 623-4603	
Coshocton *(G-9013)*			
Crawford Cnty Shared Hlth Svcs	E	419 468-7985	
Galion *(G-11169)*			
Dacas Nursing Systems Inc	C	330 884-2530	
Warren *(G-18698)*			
Daugwood Inc	E	937 429-9465	
Beavercreek *(G-1144)*			
Daynas Homecare LLC	E	216 323-0323	
Maple Heights *(G-13285)*			
Dayton Hospice Incorporated	B	937 256-4490	
Dayton *(G-9369)*			
Dayton Hospice Incorporated	C	513 422-0300	
Franklin *(G-11027)*			
Decahealth Inc	D	866 908-3514	
Toledo *(G-17696)*			
Detox Health Care Corp Ohio	B	513 742-6310	
Cincinnati *(G-3424)*			
Dillon Holdings LLC	C	513 942-5600	
West Chester *(G-18911)*			
Discount Drug Mart Inc	C	330 725-2340	
Medina *(G-13931)*			
Diversified Health Management	E	614 338-8888	
Columbus *(G-7454)*			
Eldercare Services Inst LLC	D	216 791-8000	
Cleveland *(G-5470)*			
Ember Home Care	B	740 922-6968	
Uhrichsville *(G-18341)*			
Emh Regional Homecare Agency	E	440 329-7519	
Elyria *(G-10509)*			
Enhanced Homecare Medina Inc	E	330 952-2331	
Medina *(G-13934)*			
Every Child Succeeds	C	513 636-2830	
Cincinnati *(G-3522)*			
Everyday Homecare	E	937 444-1672	
Mount Orab *(G-14740)*			
Exclusive Homecare Services	D	937 236-6750	
Dayton *(G-9421)*			
Fairfield Community Health Ctr	E	740 277-6043	
Lancaster *(G-12392)*			
Fairhope Hospice and Palliativ	D	740 654-7077	
Lancaster *(G-12402)*			
Faithful Companions Inc	E	440 255-4357	
Mentor *(G-14046)*			
Family Senior Care Inc	E	740 441-1428	
Gallipolis *(G-11191)*			
Family Service of NW Ohio	D	419 321-6455	
Toledo *(G-17725)*			
Fidelity Health Care	B	937 208-6400	
Moraine *(G-14657)*			
First Choice Medical Staffing	D	419 861-2722	
Toledo *(G-17739)*			
First Community Hlth Svcs LLC	E	937 247-0400	
Dayton *(G-9434)*			
First Community Village	B	614 324-4455	
Columbus *(G-7585)*			
Fns Inc	E	740 775-5463	
Chillicothe *(G-2781)*			
Frencor Inc	D	330 332-1203	
Salem *(G-16544)*			
Gamble Elzbeth Dcness HM Assn	A	513 751-4224	
Cincinnati *(G-3601)*			
Good Samaritan Hosp Cincinnati	E	513 569-6251	
Cincinnati *(G-3625)*			
Graceworks Lutheran Services	B	937 436-6850	
Dayton *(G-9468)*			
Great Lakes Home Hlth Svcs Inc	E	888 260-9835	
Toledo *(G-17769)*			
Great Lakes Home Hlth Svcs Inc	E	888 260-9835	
Akron *(G-244)*			

Great Lakes Home Hlth Svcs Inc	E	888 260-9835	
Mentor *(G-14055)*			
Guardian Angls Home Hlth Svcs	D	419 517-7797	
Sylvania *(G-17428)*			
Hamilton Homecare Inc	E	614 221-0022	
Columbus *(G-7712)*			
Hastings Home Health Ctr Inc	E	216 898-3300	
Medina *(G-13947)*			
Hattie Larlham Community Svcs	E	330 274-2272	
Mantua *(G-13270)*			
Hcr Manorcare Med Svcs Fla LLC	D	513 233-0831	
Cincinnati *(G-3689)*			
Healing Touch Healthcare	E	937 610-5555	
Dayton *(G-9489)*			
Health & HM Care Concepts Inc	E	740 383-4968	
Marion *(G-13423)*			
Health Care Facility MGT LLC	D	513 489-7100	
Blue Ash *(G-1576)*			
Health Care Plus	C	614 340-7587	
Westerville *(G-19170)*			
Healthcare Circle Inc	D	440 331-7347	
Strongsville *(G-17308)*			
Healthcare Holdings Inc	D	513 530-1600	
Blue Ash *(G-1577)*			
Healthlinx Inc	E	513 402-2018	
Cincinnati *(G-3695)*			
Healthsource of Ohio Inc	E	937 981-7707	
Greenfield *(G-11363)*			
Healthy Life HM Healthcare LLC	E	614 865-3368	
Columbus *(G-7727)*			
Heart To Heart Home Health	E	330 335-9999	
Wadsworth *(G-18598)*			
Heartland Home Care LLC	E	614 433-0423	
Columbus *(G-7731)*			
Heartland Hospice Services LLC	D	614 433-0423	
Columbus *(G-7732)*			
Heartland Hospice Services LLC	E	740 351-0575	
Portsmouth *(G-16144)*			
Heartland Hospice Services LLC	D	740 259-0281	
Lucasville *(G-13050)*			
Heartland Hospice Services LLC	E	419 531-0440	
Perrysburg *(G-15872)*			
Heartland Hospice Services LLC	E	937 299-6980	
Dayton *(G-9492)*			
Heartland Hospice Services LLC	D	216 901-1464	
Independence *(G-12079)*			
Heavenly Home Health	E	740 859-4735	
Rayland *(G-16272)*			
Helping Hands Health Care Inc	C	513 755-4181	
West Chester *(G-19059)*			
Heritage Day Health Centers	E	614 451-2151	
Columbus *(G-7744)*			
Heritage Health Care Services	D	419 222-2404	
Lima *(G-12659)*			
Heritage Health Care Services	C	419 867-2002	
Maumee *(G-13800)*			
Heritage Home Health Care	E	440 333-1925	
Rocky River *(G-16435)*			
Highpoint Home Healthcare Agcy	E	330 491-1805	
Canton *(G-2343)*			
Home Care Relief Inc	D	216 692-2270	
Euclid *(G-10641)*			
Home Helper Direct Link	D	330 865-5730	
Akron *(G-269)*			
Home Helpers	D	937 393-8600	
Hillsboro *(G-11847)*			
Home Instead Senior Care	D	330 334-4664	
Wadsworth *(G-18599)*			
Home Instead Senior Care	E	740 393-2500	
Mount Vernon *(G-14767)*			
Home Instead Senior Care	D	330 729-1233	
Youngstown *(G-20066)*			
Home Instead Senior Care	D	614 432-8524	
Upper Arlington *(G-18398)*			
Homecare Service Inc	E	513 655-5022	
Blue Ash *(G-1582)*			
Homereach Inc	C	614 566-0850	
Worthington *(G-19816)*			
Hope Homes Inc	E	330 688-4935	
Stow *(G-17210)*			
Horizon HM Hlth Care Agcy LLC	E	614 279-2933	
Columbus *(G-7773)*			
Hospice Cincinnati Inc	E	513 862-1100	
Cincinnati *(G-3728)*			
Hospice Cincinnati Inc	D	513 891-7700	
Cincinnati *(G-3729)*			
Hospice of Genesis Health	E	740 454-5381	
Zanesville *(G-20318)*			
Hospice of Knox County	E	740 397-5188	
Mount Vernon *(G-14768)*			

Hospice of Memorial Hospita L	E	419 334-6626	
Clyde *(G-6745)*			
Hospice of Miami County Inc	E	937 335-5191	
Troy *(G-18207)*			
Hospice of Miami Valley LLC	E	937 521-1444	
Springfield *(G-17048)*			
Hospice of North Central Ohio	E	419 524-9200	
Ontario *(G-15553)*			
Hospice of North Central Ohio	E	419 281-7107	
Ashland *(G-675)*			
Hospice of The Western Reserve	D	330 800-2240	
Medina *(G-13951)*			
Hospice of The Western Reserve	D	440 997-6619	
Ashtabula *(G-740)*			
Hospice of The Western Reserve	C	216 227-9048	
Cleveland *(G-5714)*			
Hospice Southwest Ohio Inc	D	513 770-0820	
Cincinnati *(G-3730)*			
Huntsey Corporation	E	614 568-5030	
Westerville *(G-19174)*			
In Home Health LLC	E	419 531-0440	
Toledo *(G-17819)*			
In Home Health LLC	E	513 831-5800	
Cincinnati *(G-3754)*			
In Home Health LLC	E	419 355-9209	
Fremont *(G-11081)*			
Independent Living of Ohio	E	937 323-8400	
Springfield *(G-17051)*			
Infinity Health Services Inc	D	440 614-0145	
Westlake *(G-19357)*			
Infusion Partners Inc	E	513 396-6060	
Cincinnati *(G-3761)*			
Inter Healt Care of Cambr Zane	E	614 436-9404	
Columbus *(G-7832)*			
Inter Healt Care of Cambr Zane	E	513 984-1110	
Cincinnati *(G-3773)*			
Inter Healt Care of North OH I	D	740 453-5130	
Zanesville *(G-20320)*			
Inter Healt Care of North OH I	E	419 422-5328	
Findlay *(G-10927)*			
Interim Halthcare Columbus Inc	E	330 836-5571	
Fairlawn *(G-10834)*			
Interim Halthcare Columbus Inc	A	740 349-8700	
Newark *(G-15044)*			
Interim Healthcare	D	740 354-5550	
Portsmouth *(G-16150)*			
Interim Healthcare of Dayton	B	937 291-5330	
Dayton *(G-9518)*			
Interim Healthcare SE Ohio Inc	D	740 373-3800	
Marietta *(G-13339)*			
International Healthcare Corp	D	513 731-3338	
Cincinnati *(G-3779)*			
Jag Healthcare Inc	A	440 385-4370	
Rocky River *(G-16437)*			
Joint Township Home Health	E	419 394-3335	
Saint Marys *(G-16525)*			
Kaiser-Wells Inc	E	419 668-7651	
Norwalk *(G-15440)*			
Khc Inc	D	740 775-5463	
Chillicothe *(G-2797)*			
Labelle Hmhealth Care Svcs LLC	D	440 842-3005	
Cleveland *(G-5845)*			
Labelle Hmhealth Care Svcs LLC	D	740 392-1405	
Mount Vernon *(G-14777)*			
Laurie Ann Home Health Care	E	330 872-7512	
Newton Falls *(G-15138)*			
Lifecare Alliance	C	614 278-3130	
Columbus *(G-7974)*			
Lighthouse Medical Staffing	D	614 937-6259	
Hilliard *(G-11784)*			
Little Miami Home Care Inc	E	513 248-8988	
Milford *(G-14401)*			
Living Assistance Services	D	330 733-1532	
Tallmadge *(G-17481)*			
Love N Comfort Home Care	E	740 450-7658	
Zanesville *(G-20325)*			
Loving Care Hospice Inc	E	740 852-7755	
London *(G-12866)*			
Loving Hands Home Care Inc	E	330 792-7032	
Youngstown *(G-20100)*			
Lutheran Social Services of	E	614 228-5200	
Worthington *(G-19826)*			
Mahoning Vly Infusioncare Inc	D	330 759-9487	
Youngstown *(G-20111)*			
Majastan Group LLC	D	216 231-6400	
Cleveland *(G-5900)*			
Manor Care Inc	D	419 252-5500	
Toledo *(G-17880)*			
Maple Knoll Communities Inc	A	513 782-2400	
Cincinnati *(G-3967)*			

Maplecrst Asistd Lvg Intl Ordr ....E 419 562-4988
  Bucyrus **(G-1996)**
Marymount Hospital Inc ....B 216 581-0500
  Cleveland **(G-5920)**
Mch Services Inc ....C 260 432-9699
  Dayton **(G-9595)**
Med America Hlth Systems Corp ....A 937 223-6192
  Dayton **(G-9598)**
Medcentral Health System ....E 419 526-8442
  Mansfield **(G-13214)**
Medcorp Inc ....D 419 727-7000
  Toledo **(G-17900)**
Medcorp Inc ....C 419 425-9700
  Findlay **(G-10942)**
Medi Home Health Agency Inc ....E 740 266-3977
  Steubenville **(G-17165)**
Medi Home Health Agency Inc ....E 740 441-1779
  Gallipolis **(G-11204)**
Medlink of Ohio Inc ....B 216 751-5900
  Cleveland **(G-5944)**
Memorial Hospital ....E 419 547-6419
  Clyde **(G-6748)**
Menorah Park Center For Senio ....D 330 867-2143
  Cuyahoga Falls **(G-9112)**
Mercer Cnty Joint Townshp Hosp ....E 419 584-0143
  Celina **(G-2600)**
Mid Ohio Home Health Ltd ....E 419 529-3883
  Ontario **(G-15565)**
Mircale Health Care ....C 614 237-7702
  Columbus **(G-8090)**
Mount Crmel Hospice Evrgrn Ctr ....D 614 234-0200
  Columbus **(G-8115)**
Multicare Home Health Services ....D 216 731-8900
  Euclid **(G-10649)**
Nationwide Childrens Hospital ....E 614 355-8300
  Westerville **(G-19188)**
Nationwide Health MGT LLC ....D 440 888-8888
  Parma **(G-15769)**
NC Hha Inc ....D 216 593-7750
  Elyria **(G-10542)**
NCR At Home Health & Wellness ....D 614 451-2151
  Columbus **(G-8166)**
New Life Hospice Inc ....E 440 934-1458
  Lorain **(G-12930)**
New Life Hospice Inc ....D 440 934-1458
  Lorain **(G-12931)**
Nightingale Home Healthcare ....E 614 408-0104
  Dublin **(G-10291)**
Nurses Care Inc ....D 513 424-1141
  Miamisburg **(G-14198)**
Nursing Resources Corp ....C 419 333-3000
  Maumee **(G-13825)**
Odyssey Healthcare Inc ....C 614 414-0500
  Gahanna **(G-11138)**
Ohio North E Hlth Systems Inc ....E 330 747-9551
  Youngstown **(G-20146)**
Ohio Senior Home Hlth Care LLC ....D 614 470-6070
  Columbus **(G-8286)**
Ohio Valley Home Care LLC ....E 330 385-2333
  East Liverpool **(G-10412)**
Ohio Valley Home Health Inc ....E 740 249-4219
  Athens **(G-800)**
Ohio Valley Home Health Inc ....D 740 441-1393
  Gallipolis **(G-11210)**
Ohiohealth Corporation ....A 614 788-8860
  Columbus **(G-8362)**
Omni Park Health Care LLC ....C 216 289-8963
  Euclid **(G-10651)**
Omnicare Inc ....C 513 719-2600
  Cincinnati **(G-4168)**
On-Call Nursing Inc ....D 216 577-8890
  Lakewood **(G-12358)**
Open Arms Health Systems Llc ....E 614 385-8354
  Columbus **(G-8375)**
Option Care Enterprises Inc ....C 513 576-8400
  Milford **(G-14415)**
Option Care Infusion Svcs Inc ....E 614 431-6453
  Columbus **(G-8381)**
Option Care Infusion Svcs Inc ....D 513 576-8400
  Milford **(G-14416)**
P E Miller & Assoc ....D 614 231-4743
  Columbus **(G-8407)**
P E Miller & Associates Inc ....D 614 231-4743
  Columbus **(G-8408)**
Palladium Healthcare LLC ....C 216 644-4383
  Cleveland **(G-6159)**
Paramount Support Service ....D 740 526-0540
  Saint Clairsville **(G-16501)**
Parkside Care Corporation ....D 440 286-2273
  Chardon **(G-2707)**

Passion To Heal Healthcare ....E 216 849-0180
  Cleveland **(G-6179)**
Paula Jo Moore ....E 330 894-2910
  Kensington **(G-12211)**
Personal Touch HM Care IPA Inc ....C 216 986-0885
  Cleveland **(G-6197)**
Personal Touch HM Care IPA Inc ....C 513 868-2272
  Hamilton **(G-11632)**
Personal Touch HM Care IPA Inc ....D 513 984-9600
  Cincinnati **(G-4233)**
Personal Touch HM Care IPA Inc ....D 614 227-6952
  Columbus **(G-8442)**
Personal Touch HM Care IPA Inc ....A 330 263-1112
  Wooster **(G-19758)**
Phoenix Homes Inc ....E 419 692-2421
  Delphos **(G-10033)**
Physicians Choice Inc ....E 513 844-1608
  Liberty Twp **(G-12588)**
Preferred Medical Group Inc ....C 404 403-8310
  Beachwood **(G-1096)**
Premier Care ....D 614 431-0599
  Worthington **(G-19836)**
Premier Health Partners ....A 937 499-9596
  Dayton **(G-9704)**
Premierfirst Home Health Care ....E 614 443-3110
  Columbus **(G-8459)**
Prime Home Care LLC ....E 419 535-1414
  Toledo **(G-17988)**
Private HM Care Foundation Inc ....D 513 662-8999
  Cincinnati **(G-4285)**
Prome Conti Care Serv Corpo ....A 419 885-1715
  Sylvania **(G-17443)**
Protem Homecare LLC ....E 216 663-8188
  Cleveland **(G-6261)**
Putnam Cnty Homecare & Hospice ....D 419 523-4449
  Ottawa **(G-15665)**
Quality Care Nursing Svcs LLC ....C 740 377-9095
  South Point **(G-16944)**
Quantum Health Inc ....D 614 846-4318
  Columbus **(G-8481)**
R & F Inc ....E 419 868-2909
  Holland **(G-11906)**
Rainbow Residentials LLC ....E 330 819-4202
  Tallmadge **(G-17485)**
Reflektions Ltd ....E 614 560-6994
  Delaware **(G-10003)**
REM Corp ....E 740 828-2601
  Frazeysburg **(G-11050)**
RES-Care Inc ....E 740 782-1476
  Bethesda **(G-1457)**
RES-Care Inc ....D 440 729-2432
  Chesterland **(G-2744)**
RES-Care Inc ....E 513 858-4550
  West Chester **(G-18992)**
Rescare Ohio Inc ....E 740 867-4568
  Chesapeake **(G-2732)**
Right At Home ....D 937 291-2244
  Springboro **(G-16983)**
Right At Home LLC ....D 614 734-1110
  Columbus **(G-6833)**
RMS of Ohio Inc ....D 937 291-3622
  Dayton **(G-9737)**
Ross County Health District ....C 740 775-1114
  Chillicothe **(G-2820)**
RWS Enterprises LLC ....D 513 598-6770
  Cincinnati **(G-4416)**
Rx Home Health Care Inc ....D 216 295-0056
  Cleveland **(G-6352)**
Salo Inc ....D 614 436-9404
  Columbus **(G-8585)**
Salo Inc ....A 740 964-2904
  Pataskala **(G-15787)**
Sand Run Supports LLC ....E 330 256-2127
  Fairlawn **(G-10848)**
Sar Enterprises LLC ....D 419 472-8181
  Toledo **(G-18019)**
Schroer Properties Inc ....D 330 498-8200
  North Canton **(G-15231)**
Sdx Home Care Operations LLC ....D 937 322-6288
  Springfield **(G-17109)**
Senior Care Management Inc ....D 419 578-7000
  Toledo **(G-18024)**
Senior Independence ....E 330 744-5071
  Youngstown **(G-20207)**
Senior Independence ....D 330 873-3468
  Fairlawn **(G-10850)**
Senior Independence Adult ....E 513 539-2697
  Monroe **(G-14583)**
Senior Select Home Health Care ....E 330 665-4663
  Copley **(G-8973)**

Serenity HM Hlathcare Svcs LLC ....D 937 222-0002
  Dayton **(G-9760)**
Simone Health Management Inc ....E 614 224-1347
  Columbus **(G-8643)**
Source Diagnostics LLC ....D 440 542-9481
  Solon **(G-16901)**
Southern Care Inc ....E 419 774-0555
  Ontario **(G-15574)**
Special Touch Homecare LLC ....E 937 549-1843
  Manchester **(G-13129)**
St Augustine Manor ....B 440 888-7722
  Parma **(G-15777)**
St Augustine Towers ....E 216 634-7444
  Cleveland **(G-6447)**
St Ritas Medical Center ....C 419 538-7025
  Lima **(G-12751)**
Summit Acres Inc ....D 740 732-2364
  Caldwell **(G-2044)**
Sunshine Homecare ....E 419 207-9900
  Ashland **(G-693)**
Supportcare Inc ....E 614 889-5837
  Dublin **(G-10346)**
Supreme Touch Home Health Svcs ....D 614 783-1115
  Columbus **(G-8719)**
Svh Holdings LLC ....D 844 560-7775
  Columbus **(G-8722)**
Synergy Homecare ....E 937 610-0555
  Dayton **(G-9804)**
Think-Ability LLC ....E 419 589-2238
  Mansfield **(G-13253)**
Tk Homecare Llc ....E 419 517-7000
  Toledo **(G-18067)**
TLC Home Health Care Inc ....E 740 732-5211
  Caldwell **(G-2045)**
Toledo District Nurses Assn ....C 419 255-0983
  Sylvania **(G-17458)**
Toledo Hospital ....C 419 291-2273
  Sylvania **(G-17459)**
Trusted Homecare Solutions ....E 937 506-7063
  Dayton **(G-9825)**
Tsk Assisted Living Services ....E 330 297-2000
  Ravenna **(G-16269)**
Uahs Heather Hill Home Health ....E 440 285-5098
  Chardon **(G-2719)**
Union Hospital Home Hlth Care ....E 330 343-6909
  Dover **(G-10107)**
United Home Health Services ....D 614 880-8686
  Columbus **(G-8802)**
Unity I Home Healthcare LLC ....E 740 351-0500
  Portsmouth **(G-16177)**
Universal Health Care Svcs Inc ....C 614 547-0282
  Columbus **(G-8816)**
Universal Nursing Services ....E 330 434-7318
  Akron **(G-478)**
University Hospitals Cleveland ....D 216 844-4663
  Cleveland **(G-6594)**
University Hospitals He ....B 216 844-4663
  Cleveland **(G-6596)**
University Mednet ....B 216 383-0100
  Euclid **(G-10660)**
Ussa Inc ....E 740 354-6672
  Portsmouth **(G-16179)**
Viaquest Behavioral Health LLC ....E 614 339-0868
  Dublin **(G-10363)**
VIP Homecare Inc ....D 330 929-2838
  Akron **(G-488)**
Visions Matter LLC ....D 513 934-1934
  Lebanon **(G-12513)**
Visiting Nurse Associat ....C 513 345-8000
  Cincinnati **(G-4761)**
Vistacare USA Inc ....E 614 975-3230
  Columbus **(G-8856)**
Vrable III Inc ....D 740 446-7150
  Bidwell **(G-1471)**
Western Reserve Area Agency ....C 216 621-0303
  Cleveland **(G-6673)**
Ziks Family Pharmacy 100 ....E 937 225-9350
  Dayton **(G-9898)**

HOME IMPROVEMENT & RENOVATION CONTRACTOR AGENCY

Eagle Industries Ohio Inc ....E 513 247-2900
  Fairfield **(G-10721)**
Kinetic Renovations LLC ....E 937 321-1576
  Xenia **(G-19915)**
Longworth Enterprises Inc ....B 513 738-4663
  West Chester **(G-18965)**
Menard Inc ....C 614 501-1654
  Columbus **(G-8056)**

Teasdale Fenton Carpet Cleanin ....C....... 513 797-0900
Cincinnati **(G-4578)**

HOMEBUILDERS & OTHER OPERATIVE BUILDERS

American Prservation Bldrs LLC ....D....... 216 236-2007
Cleveland **(G-4963)**
Dixon Builders & Developers ....D....... 513 887-6400
West Chester **(G-18915)**
Glencoe Restoration Group LLC ....E....... 330 752-1244
Akron **(G-236)**
M/I Homes of Austin LLC ....E....... 614 418-8000
Columbus **(G-8007)**
Mainthia Technologies Inc ....D....... 216 433-2198
Cleveland **(G-5899)**
Multicon Construction Co ....E....... 614 351-2683
Columbus **(G-8123)**
Nvr Inc ....C....... 513 202-0323
Harrison **(G-11675)**
Nvr Inc ....C....... 937 529-7000
Dayton **(G-9661)**

HOMEFURNISHING STORES: Fireplaces & Wood Burning Stoves

Overhead Inc ....E....... 419 476-7811
Toledo **(G-17967)**
Southtown Heating & Cooling ....E....... 937 320-9900
Moraine **(G-14699)**

HOMEFURNISHING STORES: Lighting Fixtures

Gross Electric Inc ....E....... 419 537-1818
Toledo **(G-17773)**
Mars Electric Company ....D....... 440 946-2250
Cleveland **(G-5913)**

HOMEFURNISHING STORES: Metalware

Scs Construction Services Inc ....E....... 513 929-0260
Cincinnati **(G-4441)**

HOMEFURNISHING STORES: Pottery

Workshops of David T Smith ....E....... 513 932-2472
Morrow **(G-14718)**

HOMEFURNISHINGS & SPLYS, WHOLESALE: Decorative

Dwa Mrkting Prmtional Pdts LLC ....E....... 216 476-0635
Strongsville **(G-17298)**
Luminex Home Decor ....A....... 513 563-1113
Blue Ash **(G-1601)**
Ten Thusand Villages Cleveland ....E....... 216 575-1058
Cleveland **(G-6510)**

HOMEFURNISHINGS, WHOLESALE: Blankets

Mill Distributors Inc ....D....... 330 995-9200
Aurora **(G-837)**

HOMEFURNISHINGS, WHOLESALE: Blinds, Venetian

Style-Line Incorporated ....E....... 614 291-0600
Columbus **(G-8707)**

HOMEFURNISHINGS, WHOLESALE: Carpets

Business Furniture LLC ....E....... 937 293-1010
Dayton **(G-9271)**
Dealers Supply North Inc ....E....... 614 274-6285
Lockbourne **(G-12812)**
Everybodys Inc ....E....... 937 293-1010
Moraine **(G-14654)**
Ohio Valley Flooring Inc ....D....... 513 271-3434
Cincinnati **(G-4160)**
Regal Carpet Center Inc ....E....... 216 475-1844
Cleveland **(G-6296)**
State Crest Carpet & Flooring............E....... 440 232-3980
Bedford **(G-1309)**

HOMEFURNISHINGS, WHOLESALE: Draperies

Accent Drapery Co Inc ....E....... 614 488-0741
Columbus **(G-6860)**

Lumenomics Inc...............................E....... 614 798-3500
Lewis Center **(G-12550)**

HOMEFURNISHINGS, WHOLESALE: Grills, Barbecue

Hayward Distributing Co ....E....... 614 272-5953
Columbus **(G-7720)**

HOMEFURNISHINGS, WHOLESALE: Kitchenware

Famous Distribution Inc ....D....... 330 762-9621
Akron **(G-210)**
G G Marck & Associates Inc ....E....... 419 478-0900
Toledo **(G-17751)**
Pottery Barn Inc ....E....... 614 478-3154
Columbus **(G-8456)**
Walter F Stephens Jr Inc ....E....... 937 746-0521
Franklin **(G-11041)**
World Tableware Inc ....D....... 419 325-2608
Toledo **(G-18161)**

HOMEFURNISHINGS, WHOLESALE: Pottery

Original Hartstone Pottery Inc.............E....... 740 452-9999
Zanesville **(G-20350)**
Workshops of David T Smith ....E....... 513 932-2472
Morrow **(G-14718)**

HOMEFURNISHINGS, WHOLESALE: Rugs

Cinmar LLC.......................................C....... 513 603-1000
West Chester **(G-18888)**

HOMEFURNISHINGS, WHOLESALE: Wood Flooring

JP Flooring Systems Inc ....E....... 513 346-4300
West Chester **(G-18954)**

HOMES FOR THE ELDERLY

Abbewood Limited Partnership............E....... 440 366-8980
Elyria **(G-10476)**
Aleph Home & Senior Care Inc ....D....... 216 382-7689
Cleveland **(G-4927)**
Aspen Woodside Village ....D....... 440 439-8666
Cleveland **(G-5014)**
Berea Lake Towers Inc ....E....... 440 243-9050
Berea **(G-1415)**
Browning Mesonic Community ....E....... 419 878-4055
Waterville **(G-18788)**
Caritas Inc.......................................E....... 419 332-2589
Fremont **(G-11060)**
Carriage Crt Mrysvlle Ltd Prtn ....E....... 937 642-2202
Marysville **(G-13487)**
Clark Memorial Home Assn ....E....... 937 399-4262
Springfield **(G-17013)**
County of Allen ....C....... 419 221-1103
Lima **(G-12622)**
County of Logan ....C....... 937 592-2901
Bellefontaine **(G-1351)**
Eastgate Village ....E....... 513 753-4400
Cincinnati **(G-2852)**
Episcopal Retirement Homes Inc ....E....... 513 271-9610
Cincinnati **(G-3508)**
Episcopal Retirement Homes Inc ....E....... 513 561-6363
Cincinnati **(G-3509)**
Episcopal Retirement Homes Inc ....E....... 513 871-2090
Cincinnati **(G-3510)**
Fairways ....D....... 440 943-2050
Wickliffe **(G-19458)**
Feridean Commons LLC ....E....... 614 898-7488
Westerville **(G-19165)**
Friendship Vlg of Clumbus Ohio ....C....... 614 890-8282
Columbus **(G-7629)**
Glenwood Community Inc ....E....... 740 376-9555
Marietta **(G-13330)**
Harrison Co County Home ....E....... 740 942-3573
Cadiz **(G-2028)**
Helen Purcell Home ....E....... 740 453-1745
Zanesville **(G-20317)**
Inn At Christine Valley ....E....... 330 270-3347
Youngstown **(G-20082)**
J & R Associates ....A....... 440 250-4080
Brookpark **(G-1898)**
Kent Ridge At Golden Pond Ltd ....D....... 330 677-4040
Kent **(G-12241)**
Kingston Healthcare Company............D....... 740 389-2311
Marion **(G-13427)**

Kingston Rsdnce Perrysburg LLC ....D....... 419 872-6200
Perrysburg **(G-15887)**
Lakeside Manor Inc ....E....... 330 549-2545
North Lima **(G-15271)**
Life Enriching Communities ....E....... 513 719-3510
Loveland **(G-13006)**
Mason Health Care Center ....D....... 513 398-2881
Mason **(G-13616)**
New Dawn Health Care Inc ....C....... 330 343-5521
Dover **(G-10090)**
North Shore Retirement Cmnty ....E....... 419 798-8203
Lakeside **(G-12330)**
Oakleaf Toledo Ltd Partnership ....E....... 419 885-3934
Toledo **(G-17956)**
Ohio Department of Aging ....D....... 614 466-5500
Columbus **(G-8236)**
Ohio Living ....C....... 513 681-4230
Cincinnati **(G-4156)**
Ohio Living ....B....... 440 942-4342
Willoughby **(G-19558)**
Orrvilla Retirement Community............E....... 330 683-4455
Orrville **(G-15638)**
Otterbein Homes ....D....... 513 933-5439
Lebanon **(G-12490)**
Otterbein Snior Lfstyle Chices ....E....... 513 260-7690
Middletown **(G-14352)**
Otterbein Snior Lfstyle Chices ....B....... 513 933-5400
Lebanon **(G-12492)**
Otterbein Snior Lfstyle Chices ....E....... 419 943-4376
Leipsic **(G-12520)**
Otterbein Snior Lfstyle Chices ....C....... 419 645-5114
Cridersville **(G-9063)**
Paisley House For Aged Women ....E....... 330 799-9431
Youngstown **(G-20150)**
Paul Dennis ....E....... 440 746-8600
Brecksville **(G-1795)**
Premier Estates 525 LLC ....D....... 513 631-6800
Cincinnati **(G-4272)**
Premier Estates 526 LLC ....D....... 513 922-1440
Cincinnati **(G-4273)**
Pristine Senior Living ....D....... 513 471-8667
Cincinnati **(G-4284)**
Pristine Snior Lving Englewood ....C....... 937 836-5143
Englewood **(G-10599)**
SEM Villa Inc...................................E....... 513 831-3262
Loveland **(G-13026)**
Senior Care Inc.................................E....... 937 372-1530
Xenia **(G-19925)**
Senior Care Inc.................................E....... 937 291-3211
Miamisburg **(G-14217)**
Senior Lifestyle Corporation ....D....... 513 777-4457
West Chester **(G-19002)**
Senior Lifestyle Evergreen Ltd ....C....... 513 948-2308
Cincinnati **(G-4452)**
Sisters of Little ....E....... 513 281-8001
Cincinnati **(G-4486)**
Sisters of Mercy ....E....... 419 332-8208
Fremont **(G-11096)**
St Luke Lutheran Community ....E....... 330 868-5600
Minerva **(G-14525)**
Sunrise Senior Living Inc ....E....... 614 846-6500
Worthington **(G-19854)**
Sunrise Senior Living Inc ....D....... 440 895-2383
Rocky River **(G-16446)**
Sunrise Senior Living LLC ....E....... 614 718-2062
Dublin **(G-10345)**
Sunset House Inc...............................C....... 419 536-4645
Toledo **(G-18055)**
Sunset Rtrment Communities Inc ....D....... 419 724-1200
Ottawa Hills **(G-15669)**
Terre Forme Enterprises Inc ....E....... 330 847-6800
Mineral Ridge **(G-14513)**
United Church Homes Inc ....D....... 740 376-5600
Marietta **(G-13392)**
United Church Homes Inc ....C....... 513 922-1440
Cincinnati **(G-4677)**
Uvmc Nursing Care Inc ....C....... 937 667-7500
Tipp City **(G-17572)**
Wesleyan Village ....B....... 440 284-9000
Elyria **(G-10573)**
Widows Home of Dayton Ohio............D....... 937 252-1661
Dayton **(G-9880)**
Womens Welsh Clubs of America ....D....... 440 331-0420
Rocky River **(G-16449)**
Zandex Inc ....E....... 740 452-2087
Zanesville **(G-20374)**

HOSE: Automobile, Rubber

Myers Industries Inc ....E....... 330 253-5592
Akron **(G-342)**

SERVICES

HOSE: Flexible Metal

First Francis Company Inc ....E 440 352-8927
Painesville *(G-15714)*

HOSES & BELTING: Rubber & Plastic

Allied Fabricating & Wldg Co ....E 614 751-6664
Columbus *(G-6897)*

Eaton-Aeroquip Llc ....D 419 891-7775
Maumee *(G-13782)*

Goodyear Tire & Rubber Company ......A 330 796-2121
Akron *(G-242)*

Watteredge LLC ....D 440 933-6110
Avon Lake *(G-929)*

HOSPITAL EQPT REPAIR SVCS

Providian Med Field Svc LLC ....E 440 833-0460
Highland Heights *(G-11735)*

HOSPITALS: AMA Approved Residency

Marion General Hospital Inc ....D 740 383-8400
Marion *(G-13440)*

Trinity Hospital Twin City ....B 740 922-2800
Dennison *(G-10053)*

HOSPITALS: Cancer

Arthur G James Cancer Hospital ....E 614 293-3300
Columbus *(G-6973)*

Mercy Health Anderson Hospital ....E 513 624-4025
Cincinnati *(G-4026)*

Metrohealth System ....C 216 957-2100
Cleveland *(G-5972)*

Parma Clinic Cancer Center ....E 440 743-4747
Cleveland *(G-6176)*

HOSPITALS: Children's

Childrens Hosp Med Ctr Akron ....A 330 308-5432
New Philadelphia *(G-14949)*

Childrens Hosp Med Ctr Akron ....E 330 629-6085
Youngstown *(G-19988)*

Childrens Hosp Med Ctr Akron ....A 330 543-1000
Akron *(G-130)*

Childrens Hosp Med Ctr Akron ....E 330 543-8004
Akron *(G-131)*

Childrens Hospital Medical Ctr ....A 513 636-6036
Cincinnati *(G-2844)*

Childrens Hospital Medical Ctr ....A 513 636-4200
Cincinnati *(G-3190)*

Childrens Hospital Medical Ctr ....E 513 636-6800
Mason *(G-13554)*

Dayton Childrens Hospital ....A 937 641-3000
Dayton *(G-9358)*

Metrohealth System ....E 216 778-3867
Cleveland *(G-5971)*

Nationwide Childrens Hospital ....C 614 722-2700
Columbus *(G-8143)*

Nationwide Childrens Hospital ....E 330 253-5200
Akron *(G-343)*

Nationwide Childrens Hospital ....A 614 722-2000
Columbus *(G-8146)*

Nationwide Childrens Hospital ....E 614 355-8300
Westerville *(G-19188)*

Nationwide Childrens Hospital ....B 614 722-8200
Columbus *(G-8147)*

Nationwide Childrens Hospital ....A 614 864-9216
Pickerington *(G-15964)*

Nationwide Childrens Hospital ....E 614 355-0802
Columbus *(G-8148)*

Nationwide Childrens Hospital ....B 614 355-9200
Columbus *(G-8150)*

Nationwide Childrens Hospital ....B 614 355-8000
Columbus *(G-8151)*

HOSPITALS: Chronic Disease

Stein Hospice Services Inc ....B 800 625-5269
Sandusky *(G-16647)*

Stein Hospice Services Inc ....D 419 663-3222
Norwalk *(G-15456)*

HOSPITALS: Hospital, Professional Nursing School

Kettering Medical Center ....E 937 298-4331
Kettering *(G-12295)*

Kettering Medical Center ....E 937 384-8750
Dayton *(G-9541)*

Mount Carmel Health ....A 614 234-5000
Columbus *(G-8111)*

HOSPITALS: Medical & Surgical

Acute Care Specialty Hospital ....A 330 363-4860
Canton *(G-2172)*

Adams County Regional Med Ctr ....C 937 386-3001
Seaman *(G-16665)*

Adena Health System ....C 740 779-7500
Wshngtn CT Hs *(G-19863)*

Ado Health Services Inc ....D 330 629-2888
Youngstown *(G-19946)*

Affiliates In Oral & Maxlofcl ....E 513 829-8080
Fairfield *(G-10693)*

Akron City Hospital Inc ....A 330 253-5046
Akron *(G-32)*

Akron General Medical Center ....C 330 344-1980
Akron *(G-44)*

Akron General Medical Center ....C 330 344-1444
Akron *(G-45)*

Akron General Medical Center ....C 330 665-8000
Akron *(G-46)*

Akron Radiology Inc ....E 330 375-3043
Akron *(G-53)*

Allianalce Hospitalist Group ....E 330 823-5626
Alliance *(G-514)*

Alliance Citizens Health Assn ....A 330 596-6000
Alliance *(G-515)*

Anesthesiology Consultant Inc ....E 614 566-9983
Columbus *(G-6949)*

Ashtabula County Medical Ctr ....A 440 997-2262
Ashtabula *(G-715)*

Ashtabula County Medical Ctr ....A 440 997-6960
Ashtabula *(G-716)*

Atrium Medical Center ....E 513 420-5013
Middletown *(G-14289)*

Aultman Health Foundation ....C 330 305-6999
Canton *(G-2200)*

Aultman Health Foundation ....A 330 682-3010
Orrville *(G-15624)*

Aultman Hospital ....A 330 452-9911
Canton *(G-2202)*

Aultman Hospital ....B 330 452-9911
Canton *(G-2203)*

Aultman Hospital ....A 330 363-6262
Canton *(G-2204)*

Aultman Hospital ....A 330 452-2273
Canton *(G-2205)*

Aultman North Inc ....E 330 305-6999
Canton *(G-2207)*

Auxiliary Bd Fairview Gen Hosp ....A 216 476-7000
Cleveland *(G-5026)*

Barberton Healthcare Group LLC ....E 330 615-3717
Wadsworth *(G-18591)*

Bay Park Community Hospital ....D 567 585-9600
Toledo *(G-17606)*

Beavercreek Medical Center ....D 937 558-3000
Beavercreek *(G-1132)*

Beavercreek Medical Center ....D 937 558-3000
Beavercreek *(G-1133)*

Beckett Springs LLC ....E 513 942-9500
West Chester *(G-18874)*

Bellevue Hospital ....B 419 483-4040
Bellevue *(G-1373)*

Bellevue Hospital ....B 419 547-0074
Bellevue *(G-1374)*

Belmont Bhc Pines Hospital Inc ....C 330 759-2700
Youngstown *(G-19964)*

Belmont Community Hospital ....B 740 671-1200
Bellaire *(G-1330)*

Bethesda Hospital Inc ....E 513 894-8888
Fairfield Township *(G-10801)*

Bethesda Hospital Inc ....A 513 569-6100
Cincinnati *(G-3047)*

Bethesda Hospital Inc ....A 513 745-1111
Cincinnati *(G-3048)*

Bethesda Hospital Inc ....A 513 563-1505
Cincinnati *(G-3049)*

Bethesda Hospital Association ....A 740 454-4000
Zanesville *(G-20281)*

Blanchard Vly Rgional Hlth Ctr ....C 419 427-0809
Findlay *(G-10878)*

Blue Chp Srgcl Ctr Ptns LLC ....D 513 561-8900
Cincinnati *(G-3063)*

Bon Secours Health System ....E 740 966-3116
Johnstown *(G-12198)*

Bridgeshome Health Care ....E 330 764-1000
Medina *(G-13913)*

Brown Memorial Hospital ....B 440 593-1131
Conneaut *(G-8952)*

Bucyrus Community Hospital LLC ....D 419 562-4677
Bucyrus *(G-1980)*

Butler Cnty Ancillary Svcs LLC ....E 513 454-1400
Fairfield Township *(G-10804)*

Caep-Dunlap LLC ....E 330 456-2695
Canton *(G-2224)*

Canton Altman Emrgncy Physcans ......E 330 456-2695
Canton *(G-2226)*

Center For Health Affairs ....D 800 362-2628
Cleveland *(G-5152)*

Center For Spinal Disorders ....E 419 383-4878
Toledo *(G-17642)*

Change Healthcare Tech Enabled ....D 614 566-5861
Columbus *(G-7179)*

Charles Mercy Hlth-St Hospita ....D 419 696-7200
Oregon *(G-15587)*

Chester West Medical Center ....A 513 298-3000
West Chester *(G-18885)*

Childrens Hosp Med Ctr Akron ....A 330 425-3344
Twinsburg *(G-18252)*

Childrens Hosp Med Ctr Akron ....E 330 676-1020
Kent *(G-12220)*

Childrens Hosp Med Ctr Akron ....A 330 308-5432
New Philadelphia *(G-14949)*

Childrens Hospital ....E 513 636-4051
Cincinnati *(G-3183)*

Childrens Hospital Medical Ctr ....A 513 541-4500
Cincinnati *(G-3184)*

Childrens Hospital Medical Ctr ....A 513 803-9600
Liberty Township *(G-12580)*

Childrens Hospital Medical Ctr ....E 513 636-4200
Cincinnati *(G-3185)*

Childrens Hospital Medical Ctr ....A 513 803-1751
Cincinnati *(G-3186)*

Childrens Hospital Medical Ctr ....A 513 636-4200
Cincinnati *(G-3187)*

Childrens Hospital Medical Ctr ....A 513 636-4366
Cincinnati *(G-3188)*

Childrens Hospital Medical Ctr ....A 513 636-8778
Cincinnati *(G-3193)*

Chirst Hospital Surgery Center ....E 513 272-3448
Cincinnati *(G-3195)*

Christ Hospital ....C 513 347-2300
Cincinnati *(G-3198)*

Christ Hospital ....E 513 721-8272
Cincinnati *(G-3199)*

Christ Hospital ....E 513 564-4000
Cincinnati *(G-3200)*

Christ Hospital ....C 513 561-7809
Cincinnati *(G-3201)*

Christ Hospital ....C 513 564-1340
Cincinnati *(G-3203)*

Christ Hospital ....E 513 651-0094
Cincinnati *(G-3204)*

Christ Hospital ....B 513 272-3448
Cincinnati *(G-3205)*

Christ Hospital ....E 513 585-0050
Cincinnati *(G-3206)*

Christ Hospital ....C 513 755-4700
West Chester *(G-18886)*

Christ Hospital ....D 513 631-3300
Cincinnati *(G-3208)*

Christ Hospital ....D 513 351-0800
Cincinnati *(G-3209)*

Christ Hospital ....C 513 791-5200
Cincinnati *(G-3210)*

Christ Hospital Spine Surgery ....E 513 619-5899
Cincinnati *(G-3211)*

City Hospital Association ....A 330 385-7200
East Liverpool *(G-10399)*

City of Wooster ....A 330 263-8100
Wooster *(G-19705)*

Cleveland Clinic Foundation ....A 216 636-8335
Cleveland *(G-5236)*

Cleveland Clinic Foundation ....A 440 282-6669
Lorain *(G-12892)*

Cleveland Clinic Foundation ....A 800 223-2273
Cleveland *(G-5240)*

Cleveland Clinic Foundation ....D 419 609-2812
Sandusky *(G-16587)*

Cleveland Clinic Foundation ....A 216 444-5755
Cleveland *(G-5241)*

Cleveland Clinic Foundation ....A 440 327-1050
North Ridgeville *(G-15327)*

Cleveland Clinic Foundation ....A 216 448-0116
Beachwood *(G-1046)*

Cleveland Clinic Foundation ....A 440 986-4000
Broadview Heights *(G-1827)*

Cleveland Clinic Foundation ....D 216 444-5757
Cleveland *(G-5245)*

Cleveland Clinic Foundation..............A 216 444-2200
Cleveland (G-5246)

Cleveland Clinic Foundation..............E 330 287-4930
Wooster (G-19707)

Cleveland Clinic Foundation..............D 216 444-2820
Cleveland (G-5237)

Cleveland Clinic Foundation..............D 440 988-5651
Lorain (G-12893)

Cleveland Clinic Health System ....E 440 449-4500
Cleveland (G-5247)

Cleveland Clinic Health System ....E 216 692-7555
Cleveland (G-5248)

Clevelnd Clnc Hlth Systm East ....E 330 287-4830
Wooster (G-19709)

Clevelnd Clnc Hlth Systm East ....E 330 468-0190
Northfield (G-15376)

Clinical Research Center....................D 513 636-4412
Cincinnati (G-3308)

Clinton Memorial Hospital...................A 937 382-6611
Wilmington (G-19613)

Columbia-Csa/Hs Greater Canton .....A 330 489-1000
Canton (G-2260)

Community Health Ptnrs Reg Fou.......A 440 960-4000
Lorain (G-12896)

Community Hospital of Bedford...........B 440 735-3900
Bedford (G-1274)

Community Hospitals ....B 419 636-1131
Bryan (G-1954)

Community Hsptals Wllness Ctrs ....D 419 485-3154
Montpelier (G-14611)

Community Hsptals Wllness Ctrs ....D 419 445-2015
Archbold (G-629)

Community Hsptals Wllness Ctrs ....C 419 636-1131
Bryan (G-1955)

Community Mercy Hlth Partners ....E 937 523-6670
Springfield (G-17019)

Copc Hospitals ....E 614 268-8164
Columbus (G-7368)

County of Holmes ....C 330 674-1015
Millersburg (G-14471)

Dayton Osteopathic Hospital ....A 937 762-1629
Dayton (G-9374)

Deaconess Hospital of Cincinna ....D 513 559-2100
Cincinnati (G-3410)

Defiance Hospital Inc.........................B 419 782-6955
Defiance (G-9911)

Delphos Ambulatory Care Center ....E 419 692-2662
Delphos (G-10024)

Doctors Hospital Cleveland Inc...........C 740 753-7300
Nelsonville (G-14829)

Elmwood of Green Springs Ltd ....D 419 639-2626
Green Springs (G-11352)

Encompass Health Corporation ....E 205 970-4869
Springfield (G-17034)

Euclid Hospital ....D 216 531-9000
Euclid (G-10633)

Fairfield Medical Center ....A 740 687-8000
Lancaster (G-12399)

Fairview Hospital ....E 216 476-7000
Cleveland (G-5508)

Fairview Hospital ....D 440 871-1063
Westlake (G-19341)

Fayette County Memorial Hosp ....C 740 335-1210
Wshngtn CT Hs (G-19871)

Firelands Regional Health Sys ....A 419 557-7400
Sandusky (G-16604)

Firelands Regional Health Sys ....E 419 332-5524
Fremont (G-11072)

Fisher-Titus Medical Center...............A 419 668-8101
Norwalk (G-15438)

Flower Hospital ....A 419 824-1444
Sylvania (G-17426)

Fort Hamilton Hospital ....D 513 867-2000
Hamilton (G-11597)

Fort Hmltn-Hghes Hlthcare Corp ....A 513 867-2000
Hamilton (G-11598)

Fulton County Health Center ....C 419 335-2017
Wauseon (G-18801)

Fulton County Health Center ....A 419 335-2015
Wauseon (G-18803)

G M A Surgery Inc ....E 937 429-7350
Beavercreek (G-1153)

Gamble Elzbeth Dcness HM Assn ......A 513 751-4224
Cincinnati (G-3601)

Garden II Leasing Co LLC ....D 419 381-0037
Toledo (G-17755)

Genesis Healthcare System ....A 740 454-5000
Zanesville (G-20310)

Glenmont..E 614 876-0084
Hilliard (G-11769)

Good Samaritan Hosp Cincinnati.........E 513 569-6251
Cincinnati (G-3625)

Grace Hospital ....D 216 476-2704
Cleveland (G-5620)

Grace Hospital ....D 216 687-1500
Bedford (G-1282)

Grace Hospital ....D 216 687-4013
Amherst (G-588)

Grady Memorial Hospital ....E 740 615-1000
Delaware (G-9982)

Greene Oaks ....D 937 352-2800
Xenia (G-19909)

Greenfield Area Medical Ctr ....D 937 981-9400
Greenfield (G-11361)

Guernsey Health Systems...................A 740 439-3561
Cambridge (G-2073)

H B Magruder Memorial Hospital ....A 419 734-4539
Port Clinton (G-16109)

Hardin Memorial Hospital...................D 419 673-0761
Kenton (G-12281)

Hcl of Dayton Inc...............................C 937 384-8300
Miamisburg (G-14175)

Health Care Specialists ....E 740 454-4530
Zanesville (G-20316)

Henry County Hospital Inc ....B 419 592-4015
Napoleon (G-14809)

Hillcrest Hospital Auxiliary ....D 440 449-4500
Cleveland (G-5692)

Holzer Health System ....E 740 446-5060
Gallipolis (G-11200)

Holzer Hospital Foundation ....A 740 446-5000
Gallipolis (G-11201)

Holzer Hospital Foundation ....B 740 446-5000
Gallipolis (G-11202)

Holzer Medical Ctr - Jackson ....B 740 288-4625
Jackson (G-12375)

Hometown Urgent Care ....C 937 342-9520
Springfield (G-17045)

Hospice of Genesis Health ....E 740 454-5381
Zanesville (G-20318)

Hospice of Southern Ohio ....D 740 356-2567
Portsmouth (G-16148)

Humana Inc ....A 330 498-0537
Canton (G-2352)

Internal Medicine of Akron ....E 330 376-2728
Akron (G-279)

Jewish Hospital LLC...........................D 513 686-3000
Cincinnati (G-3817)

Jewish Hospital Cincinnati Inc ....A 513 686-3303
Cincinnati (G-3818)

Joel Pomerene Memorial Hosp ....B 330 674-1015
Millersburg (G-14480)

Joint Township Dst Mem Hosp ....D 419 394-9959
Saint Marys (G-16523)

Joint Township Dst Mem Hosp ....B 419 394-3335
Saint Marys (G-16524)

Kettering Adventist Healthcare ....E 937 426-0049
Beavercreek (G-1160)

Kettering Adventist Healthcare ....D 937 534-4651
Moraine (G-14668)

Kettering Adventist Healthcare ....D 937 298-3399
Kettering (G-12294)

Kettering Adventist Healthcare ....D 937 878-8644
Fairborn (G-10678)

Kettering Adventist Healthcare ....E 937 401-6306
Centerville (G-2629)

Kettering Adventist Healthcare ....E 937 294-1658
Dayton (G-9532)

Kettering Adventist Healthcare ....D 937 298-4331
Dayton (G-9533)

Kettering Adventist Healthcare ....D 937 762-1361
Miamisburg (G-14179)

Kettering Adventist Healthcare ....E 937 298-4331
Dayton (G-9534)

Kettering Adventist Healthcare ....D 937 395-8816
Miamisburg (G-14180)

Kettering Medical Center....................D 937 702-4000
Beavercreek (G-1161)

Kettering Medical Center....................B 937 866-0551
Miamisburg (G-14181)

Kettering Medical Center....................E 937 298-4331
Dayton (G-9539)

Kettering Medical Center....................E 937 299-0099
Dayton (G-9540)

Kindred Healthcare Inc ....D 937 222-5963
Dayton (G-9546)

Kindred Healthcare Inc ....D 937 222-5963
Dayton (G-9547)

Kindred Hospital Central Ohio.............E 419 526-0777
Lima (G-12670)

Knox Community Hosp Foundation......E 740 393-9814
Mount Vernon (G-14772)

Knox Community Hospital ....A 740 393-9000
Mount Vernon (G-14773)

Lake Hospital System Inc....................A 440 953-9600
Willoughby (G-19539)

Lake Hospital System Inc....................A 440 632-3024
Middlefield (G-14272)

Lakewood Hospital Association ....A 216 529-7160
Lakewood (G-12356)

Lakewood Hospital Association ....E 216 228-5437
Cleveland (G-5852)

Licking Memorial Hospital ....D 740 348-4137
Newark (G-15057)

Life Line Screening ....D 216 581-6556
Independence (G-12090)

Lima Memorial Hospital......................D 419 228-3335
Lima (G-12683)

Lima Memorial Hospital La ....E 419 738-5151
Wapakoneta (G-18648)

Lima Memorial Joint Oper Co ....A 419 228-5165
Lima (G-12684)

Lodi Community Hospital ....C 330 948-1222
Lodi (G-12827)

Lutheran Medical Center ....B 216 696-4300
Solon (G-16867)

Madison Family Health Corp...............C 740 845-7000
London (G-12868)

Madison Medical Campus ....E 440 428-6800
Madison (G-13104)

Manor Care Inc ....D 419 252-5500
Toledo (G-17880)

Marietta Memorial Hospital ....B 740 401-0362
Belpre (G-1408)

Marietta Memorial Hospital ....A 740 374-1400
Marietta (G-13354)

Marietta Memorial Hospital ....E 740 373-8549
Marietta (G-13355)

Marion Gen Social Work Dept ....E 740 383-8788
Marion (G-13438)

Marion General Hosp HM Hlth ....E 740 383-8770
Marion (G-13439)

Mary Rutan Hospital..........................A 937 592-4015
Bellefontaine (G-1359)

Marymount Hospital Inc ....B 216 581-0500
Cleveland (G-5920)

Marysvlle Ohio Srgical Ctr LLC ....D 937 642-6622
Marysville (G-13516)

Massillon Health System LLC ....A 330 837-7200
Massillon (G-13712)

McCullough-Hyde Mem Hosp Inc ....B 513 523-2111
Oxford (G-15680)

McCullough-Hyde Mem Hosp Inc ....B 513 863-2215
Hamilton (G-11628)

Med America Hlth Systems Corp ....A 937 223-6192
Dayton (G-9598)

Medcath Intermediate Holdings ....B 937 221-8016
Dayton (G-9600)

Medcentral Health System ....E 419 526-8900
Ontario (G-15562)

Medcentral Health System ....E 419 526-8442
Mansfield (G-13214)

Medcentral Health System ....D 419 526-8000
Mansfield (G-13215)

Medcentral Health System ....D 419 526-8970
Mansfield (G-13216)

Medcentral Health System ....C 419 683-1040
Crestline (G-9057)

Medcentral Health System ....E 419 342-5015
Shelby (G-16747)

Medcentral Health System ....E 419 526-8043
Mansfield (G-13217)

Medical Associates of Mid-Ohio ....E 419 289-1331
Ashland (G-680)

Medical Center At Elizabeth Pl ....C 937 223-6237
Dayton (G-9601)

Medina Hospital ....E 330 723-3117
Medina (G-13975)

Medone Hospital Physicians ....E 314 255-6900
Columbus (G-8055)

Memorial Hospital...............................B 419 334-6657
Fremont (G-11086)

Memorial Hospital...............................E 419 547-6419
Clyde (G-6748)

Memorial Hospital Union County ....C 937 644-1001
Marysville (G-13518)

Mental Health and Addi Serv ....C 614 752-0333
Columbus (G-8058)

Mercer Cnty Joint Townshp Hosp ....B 419 678-2341
Coldwater (G-6763)

SERVICES

Company	Location	Code	Phone
Mercer Cnty Joint Townshp Hosp	Celina *(G-2601)*	E	419 586-1611
Mercy Franciscan Hosp Mt Airy	Cincinnati *(G-4008)*	A	513 853-5101
Mercy Frncscan Hosp Wstn Hills	Cincinnati *(G-4009)*	A	513 389-5000
Mercy Hamilton Hospital	Fairfield *(G-10753)*	E	513 603-8600
Mercy Health	Youngstown *(G-20122)*	C	330 729-1372
Mercy Health	Cincinnati *(G-4010)*	E	513 686-5392
Mercy Health	Mount Orab *(G-14742)*	D	513 981-4700
Mercy Health	Cincinnati *(G-4011)*	D	513 639-0250
Mercy Health	Cincinnati *(G-4012)*	C	513 981-5750
Mercy Health	Lagrange *(G-12325)*	E	440 355-4206
Mercy Health	Springfield *(G-17074)*	D	937 390-1700
Mercy Health	Cincinnati *(G-4013)*	C	513 639-2800
Mercy Health	Cincinnati *(G-4014)*	D	513 232-7100
Mercy Health	Amherst *(G-593)*	E	440 988-1009
Mercy Health	Urbana *(G-18440)*	E	937 653-3445
Mercy Health	Cincinnati *(G-4015)*	D	561 358-1619
Mercy Health	Cincinnati *(G-4016)*	D	513 981-5463
Mercy Health	Avon *(G-895)*	E	440 937-4600
Mercy Health	North Ridgeville *(G-15335)*	E	440 327-7372
Mercy Health	Cincinnati *(G-4018)*	E	513 639-2800
Mercy Health	Cincinnati *(G-4019)*	D	513 979-2999
Mercy Health	Fairfield *(G-10755)*	E	513 870-7008
Mercy Health	Youngstown *(G-20124)*	C	330 746-7211
Mercy Health	Springfield *(G-17076)*	D	937 328-8700
Mercy Health	Oberlin *(G-15511)*	D	440 774-6800
Mercy Health	Cincinnati *(G-4023)*	E	513 741-8200
Mercy Health	Youngstown *(G-20123)*	E	330 792-7418
Mercy Health	Lorain *(G-12926)*	A	440 233-1000
Mercy Health - St	Oregon *(G-15600)*	E	419 696-7465
Mercy Health - St R	Lima *(G-12702)*	A	419 227-3361
Mercy Health - Tiffin Hosp LLC	Tiffin *(G-17524)*	C	419 455-7000
Mercy Health Anderson Hospital	Cincinnati *(G-4024)*	A	513 624-4500
Mercy Health Anderson Hospital	Cincinnati *(G-4025)*	E	513 624-1950
Mercy Health Anderson Hospital	Cincinnati *(G-4026)*	E	513 624-4025
Mercy Health Cincinnati LLC	Cincinnati *(G-4027)*	D	513 952-5000
Mercy Health Partners	Cincinnati *(G-4028)*	D	513 233-2444
Mercy Health Partners	Cincinnati *(G-4029)*	D	513 389-5000
Mercy Health Partners	Cincinnati *(G-4030)*	C	513 853-5101
Mercy Health Partners	Blue Ash *(G-1610)*	D	513 981-5056
Mercy Health Partners	Cincinnati *(G-4032)*	D	513 686-4800
Mercy Health Sys - Nthrn Reg	Toledo *(G-17908)*	B	419 251-1359
Mercy Hlth - Clermont Hosp LLC	Batavia *(G-1004)*	D	513 732-8200
Mercy Hlth St Vincent Med LLC	Toledo *(G-17909)*	A	419 251-3232
Mercy Hospital of Defiance	Defiance *(G-9929)*	C	419 782-8444
Mercy Medical Center	Springfield *(G-17080)*	A	937 390-5000
Mercy Medical Center Inc	Canton *(G-2399)*	D	330 649-4380
Mercy Medical Center Inc	Canton *(G-2400)*	E	330 489-1000
Metrohealth System	Cleveland *(G-5970)*	E	216 957-1500
Metrohealth System	Beachwood *(G-1080)*	E	216 765-0733
Metrohealth System	Westlake *(G-19373)*	E	216 957-3200
Metrohealth System	Beachwood *(G-1081)*	E	216 591-0523
Miami Valley Hospital	Dayton *(G-9619)*	C	937 436-5200
Miami Valley Hospital	Vandalia *(G-18531)*	A	937 208-7065
Miami Valley Hospital	Dayton *(G-9620)*	A	937 208-8000
Mid-Ohio Heart Clinic Inc	Mansfield *(G-13221)*	E	419 524-8151
Mill Pond Family Physicians	Cuyahoga Falls *(G-9115)*	E	330 928-3111
Morrow County Hospital	Mount Gilead *(G-14731)*	B	419 949-3085
Morrow County Hospital	Mount Gilead *(G-14732)*	B	419 946-5015
Mount Carmel East Hospital	Columbus *(G-8110)*	A	614 234-6000
Mount Carmel Health	New Albany *(G-14860)*	E	614 855-4878
Mount Carmel Health	Westerville *(G-19283)*	D	614 234-0100
Mount Carmel Health System	Columbus *(G-8113)*	A	614 234-6000
Mount Carmel Health System	New Albany *(G-14861)*	E	614 775-6600
Nationwide Childrens Hospital	Columbus *(G-8144)*	B	614 722-5750
Nationwide Childrens Hospital	Columbus *(G-8145)*	A	614 722-2000
Nationwide Childrens Hospital	Cincinnati *(G-2862)*	B	513 636-6000
Nationwide Childrens Hospital	Columbus *(G-8149)*	B	614 355-8100
Neuroscience Center Inc	Columbus *(G-8182)*	D	614 293-8930
New Albany Surgery Center LLC	New Albany *(G-14867)*	C	614 775-1616
New Lfcare Hspitals Dayton LLC	Miamisburg *(G-14197)*	B	937 384-8300
Niagara Health Corporation	Columbus *(G-8189)*	C	614 898-4000
Norwalk Area Hlth Systems Inc	Norwalk *(G-15448)*	A	419 668-8101
Ohio Osteopathic Hospital Assn	Columbus *(G-8278)*	E	614 299-2107
Ohio State Univ Wexner Med Ctr	Columbus *(G-8292)*	A	614 293-8000
Ohio State Univ Wexner Med Ctr	Columbus *(G-8293)*	C	614 366-3687
Ohio State University	Columbus *(G-8300)*	A	614 257-3000
Ohio State University	Columbus *(G-8302)*	C	614 293-8750
Ohio State University	Columbus *(G-8343)*	E	614 293-8419
Ohio State University	Columbus *(G-8345)*	E	614 293-8196
Ohio State University	Columbus *(G-8346)*	E	614 293-8333
Ohio State University	Columbus *(G-8347)*	A	614 293-8000
Ohio Valley Medical Center LLC	Springfield *(G-17093)*	D	937 521-3900
Ohiohealth Corporation	Columbus *(G-8359)*	C	614 566-5456
Ohiohealth Corporation	Dublin *(G-10299)*	B	614 544-8000
Ohiohealth Corporation	Columbus *(G-8360)*	C	614 566-2124
Ohiohealth Corporation	Columbus *(G-8362)*	A	614 788-8860
Ohiohealth Corporation	Columbus *(G-8363)*	D	614 566-5977
Ohiohealth Corporation	Columbus *(G-8364)*	C	614 566-9000
Ohiohealth Corporation	Columbus *(G-8365)*	C	614 566-4800
Ohiohealth Research Institute	Columbus *(G-8367)*	E	614 566-4297
Ohiohlth Rverside Methdst Hosp	Columbus *(G-8368)*	A	614 566-5000
Orrville Hospital Foundation	Orrville *(G-15640)*	C	330 684-4700
Osu Nephrology Medical Ctr	Columbus *(G-8392)*	E	614 293-8300
Parma Community General Hosp	Parma *(G-15771)*	A	440 743-3000
Physician Hospital Alliance	Miamisburg *(G-14205)*	E	937 558-3456
Pine Hills Continuing Care Ctr	Nelsonville *(G-14835)*	E	740 753-1931
Poison Information Center	Cincinnati *(G-4262)*	E	513 636-5111
Promedica Defiance Regional	Defiance *(G-9935)*	E	419 783-6802
Promedica Health Systems Inc	Toledo *(G-17993)*	A	567 585-7454
Rchp - Wilmington LLC	Wilmington *(G-19643)*	D	937 382-6611
Regency Hospital Cincinnati	Cincinnati *(G-4350)*	E	513 862-4700
Research Institute At Nation	Columbus *(G-8518)*	C	614 722-2700
Richmond Medical Center	Richmond Heights *(G-16394)*	B	440 585-6500
Robinson Health System Inc	Ravenna *(G-16262)*	E	330 678-4100
Robinson Health System Inc	Ravenna *(G-16263)*	A	330 297-0811
Robinson Health System Inc	Kent *(G-12257)*	E	330 297-0811
Robinson Memorial Hospital	Streetsboro *(G-17268)*	E	330 626-3455
Salem Community Hospital	Salem *(G-16560)*	A	330 332-1551
Samaritan Health Partners	Dayton *(G-9749)*	A	937 208-8400
Samaritan N Surgery Ctr Ltd	Englewood *(G-10600)*	E	937 567-6100
Samaritan Professional Corp	Ashland *(G-688)*	E	419 289-0491
Samaritan Regional Health Sys	Ashland *(G-689)*	E	419 281-1330
Samaritan Regional Health Sys	Ashland *(G-690)*	B	419 289-0491
Select Medical Corporation	Cleveland *(G-6394)*	C	216 983-8030
Select Medical Corporation	Akron *(G-422)*	D	330 761-7500
Select Specialty Hosp Columbus	Columbus *(G-8618)*	D	614 291-8467
Select Specialty Hospital	Cincinnati *(G-4449)*	D	513 862-4700
Select Speclty Hospi- Colmbus	Columbus *(G-8619)*	C	614 293-6931
Shelby County Mem Hosp Assn	Sidney *(G-16797)*	A	937 498-2311
Shelby County Mem Hosp Assn	Sidney *(G-16798)*	D	937 492-9591
Sheltering Arms Hospital Found	Athens *(G-802)*	B	740 592-9300
Shriners Hspitals For Children	Cincinnati *(G-4473)*	B	513 872-6000
Sisters of Mrcy of Wllard Ohio	Willard *(G-19488)*	C	419 964-5000
Southern Ohio Medical Center	Portsmouth *(G-16171)*	C	740 354-5000
Southern Ohio Medical Center	Portsmouth *(G-16172)*	E	740 356-5000
Southern Ohio Medical Center	Portsmouth *(G-16173)*	A	740 354-5000
Southstern Ohio Rgonal Med Ctr	Cambridge *(G-2083)*	E	740 439-3561
Southwest Cmnty Hlth Systems	Cleveland *(G-6428)*	A	440 816-8000
Southwest General Health Ctr	Cleveland *(G-6430)*	D	440 816-4202
Southwest General Health Ctr	Strongsville *(G-17347)*	C	440 816-4900
Southwest General Health Ctr	Cleveland *(G-6431)*	D	440 816-8200
Southwest General Health Ctr	Cleveland *(G-6432)*	A	440 816-8000
Southwest General Health Ctr	Cleveland *(G-6433)*	E	440 816-8005
Southwest General Med Group	Middleburg Heights *(G-14259)*	A	440 816-8000
Southwest Healthcare of Brown	Georgetown *(G-11275)*	D	937 378-7800

Southwest Internal Medicine ....E 440 816-2777
  Cleveland *(G-6434)*

Specialty Hosp Cleveland Inc ....D 216 592-2830
  Cleveland *(G-6443)*

St Anne Mercy Hospital ....E 419 407-2663
  Toledo *(G-18045)*

St Ritas Medical Center ....E 419 538-6288
  Glandorf *(G-11307)*

St Vincent Charity Med Ctr................A 216 861-6200
  Cleveland *(G-6450)*

Steward Trumbull Mem Hosp Inc ....A 330 841-9011
  Warren *(G-18748)*

Suburban Pediatrics Inc...................E 440 498-0065
  Shaker Heights *(G-16715)*

Summa Health ....A 330 873-1518
  Akron *(G-443)*

Summa Health ....A 330 836-9023
  Akron *(G-444)*

Summa Health ....B 330 252-0095
  Akron *(G-445)*

Summa Health ....B 330 926-0384
  Cuyahoga Falls *(G-9126)*

Summa Health ....E 330 630-9726
  Tallmadge *(G-17489)*

Summa Health ....D 330 753-3649
  Barberton *(G-967)*

Summa Health ....C 330 375-3315
  Akron *(G-446)*

Summa Health ....E 330 688-4531
  Stow *(G-17234)*

Summa Health ....B 330 864-8060
  Akron *(G-447)*

Summa Health Center Lk Medina ......E 330 952-0014
  Medina *(G-14006)*

Summa Health System ....D 330 535-7319
  Akron *(G-448)*

Summa Health System ....E 330 375-3000
  Akron *(G-449)*

Summa Health System ....A 330 334-1504
  Wadsworth *(G-18616)*

Summa Health System ....D 330 375-3584
  Akron *(G-450)*

Summa Health System ....C 330 375-3315
  Akron *(G-451)*

Summa Health System ....E 330 375-3000
  Akron *(G-452)*

Summa Health System ....A 330 615-3000
  Barberton *(G-968)*

Surgery and Gynecology Inc ....E 614 294-1603
  Columbus *(G-8721)*

Sylvania Franciscan Health ....E 419 882-8373
  Maumee *(G-13859)*

Taussig Cancer Center ....E 866 223-8100
  Cleveland *(G-6500)*

Toledo Hospital ....D 419 291-8701
  Toledo *(G-18087)*

Trihealth Inc ....E 513 569-6111
  Cincinnati *(G-4638)*

Trihealth Evendale Hospital ....C 513 454-2222
  Cincinnati *(G-4640)*

Trinity Health System ....B 740 283-7000
  Steubenville *(G-17179)*

Trinity Health System ....A 740 264-8000
  Steubenville *(G-17177)*

Trinity Health System ....E 740 264-8101
  Steubenville *(G-17178)*

Trinity Hospital Holding Co ....A 740 264-8000
  Steubenville *(G-17180)*

Trinity West......................................A 740 264-8000
  Steubenville *(G-17181)*

Tripoint Medical Center ....A 440 375-8100
  Painesville *(G-15744)*

Triumph Hospital Mansfield ....E 419 526-0777
  Mansfield *(G-13255)*

Uc Health Llc ....E 513 584-8600
  Cincinnati *(G-4667)*

Uhhs Westlake Medical Center ....C 440 250-2070
  Westlake *(G-19417)*

Uhhs-Memorial Hosp of Geneva........C 440 466-1141
  Geneva *(G-11248)*

Union Hospital Association ....D 330 343-3311
  Dover *(G-10106)*

University Hospitals ....B 216 593-5500
  Cleveland *(G-6587)*

University Hospitals ....E 216 536-3020
  Cleveland *(G-6588)*

University Hospitals ....A 440 285-6000
  Chardon *(G-2721)*

University Hospitals ....A 216 767-8900
  Shaker Heights *(G-16717)*

University Hospitals ....A 440 743-3000
  Parma *(G-15779)*

University Hospitals ....E 216 844-6400
  Cleveland *(G-6589)*

University Hospitals ....E 216 767-8500
  Cleveland *(G-6591)*

University Hospitals Cleveland ....A 216 844-1000
  Cleveland *(G-6592)*

University Hospitals Cleveland ....A 440 205-5755
  Mentor *(G-14119)*

University Hospitals Cleveland ....A 216 844-1000
  Cleveland *(G-6593)*

University Hospitals Cleveland ....D 216 844-4663
  Cleveland *(G-6594)*

University Hospitals Cleveland ....A 216 844-3323
  Shaker Heights *(G-16718)*

University Hospitals Cleveland ....D 216 342-5556
  Beachwood *(G-1116)*

University Hospitals Cleveland ....A 216 844-3528
  Cleveland *(G-6595)*

University Hospitals Health Sy ....E 216 844-4663
  Cleveland *(G-6597)*

University Hospitals St John ....A 440 835-8000
  Westlake *(G-19419)*

University of Cincinnati ....E 513 584-4396
  Cincinnati *(G-4710)*

University of Cincinnati ....E 513 584-1000
  Cincinnati *(G-4725)*

University Surgeons Inc ....A 216 844-3021
  Cleveland *(G-6605)*

Universty of Cincinnti Medcl C ....E 513 584-1000
  Cincinnati *(G-4730)*

Uvmc Management Corporation........D 937 440-4000
  Troy *(G-18237)*

VA Medical Center Automated RE .....E 740 772-7118
  Chillicothe *(G-2835)*

Van Wert County Hospital Assn ....D 419 238-2390
  Van Wert *(G-18494)*

Van Wert Medical Services Ltd ....B 419 238-7727
  Van Wert *(G-18496)*

Vibra Healthcare LLC......................D 330 675-5555
  Warren *(G-18766)*

Wayne Healthcare ....B 937 548-1141
  Greenville *(G-11400)*

Wheeling Hospital Inc.......................D 740 942-4116
  Cadiz *(G-2035)*

Wood County Hospital Assoc............A 419 354-8900
  Bowling Green *(G-1754)*

Wright Center ....E 216 382-1868
  Cleveland *(G-6691)*

Wyandot Memorial Hospital..............C 419 294-4991
  Upper Sandusky *(G-18416)*

HOSPITALS: Medical School Affiliated With Nursing

Adena Health System ....E 740 779-7201
  Chillicothe *(G-2750)*

Adena Health System ....A 740 779-7360
  Chillicothe *(G-2751)*

Adena Health System ....C 740 420-3000
  Circleville *(G-4824)*

Adena Health System ....C 937 981-9444
  Greenfield *(G-11358)*

Adena Health System ....E 740 779-8995
  Chillicothe *(G-2752)*

Adena Health System ....E 740 779-4801
  Chillicothe *(G-2753)*

Christ Hospital ....B 513 688-1111
  Cincinnati *(G-3202)*

Christ Hospital ....A 513 585-2000
  Cincinnati *(G-3207)*

Community Hlth Ptnr Reg Hlth S........A 440 960-4000
  Lorain *(G-12897)*

Regency Hospital Toledo LLC ....E 419 318-5700
  Sylvania *(G-17445)*

HOSPITALS: Medical School Affiliated with Residency

Doctors Ohiohealth Corporation ....A 614 544-5424
  Columbus *(G-7464)*

Ohiohealth Corporation ....E 614 566-5414
  Columbus *(G-8366)*

HOSPITALS: Medical School Affiliation

Cleveland Clinic Lerner Colleg ....D 216 445-3853
  Cleveland *(G-5249)*

Ohio State University ....E 614 293-8158
  Columbus *(G-8323)*

Ohio State University ....C 614 292-6251
  Columbus *(G-8337)*

University Hospitals ....B 440 250-2001
  Westlake *(G-19418)*

University of Cincinnati ....E 513 584-7522
  Cincinnati *(G-4704)*

University of Cincinnati ....E 513 584-1000
  Cincinnati *(G-4723)*

University of Toledo ....B 419 383-4229
  Toledo *(G-18130)*

HOSPITALS: Mental Retardation

Astoria Place Columbus LLC.............D 614 228-5900
  Columbus *(G-6985)*

Blanchard Vly Residential Ctr............D 419 422-6503
  Findlay *(G-10877)*

Bridges To Independence Inc ....E 740 375-5533
  Marion *(G-13407)*

CHS-Lake Erie Inc ....C 440 964-8446
  Ashtabula *(G-726)*

Columbus Area ....D 614 251-6561
  Columbus *(G-7255)*

County of Montgomery ....B 937 264-0460
  Dayton *(G-9328)*

County of Perry ....E 740 342-0416
  New Lexington *(G-14918)*

Creative Foundations Inc ....E 614 832-2121
  Mount Vernon *(G-14760)*

Echoing Hills Village Inc ....C 740 327-2311
  Warsaw *(G-18783)*

Logan Healthcare Leasing LLC ....E 216 367-1214
  Logan *(G-12847)*

Mental Rtrdtion Preble Cnty Bd..........D 937 456-5891
  Eaton *(G-10453)*

Pleasant Hill Leasing LLC ....C 740 289-2394
  Piketon *(G-15987)*

Ridge Murray Prod Ctr Oberlin ....E 440 774-7400
  Oberlin *(G-15519)*

Siffrin Residential Assn ....C 330 799-8932
  Youngstown *(G-20211)*

Union Christel Manor Inc ....E 937 968-6265
  Union City *(G-18356)*

Winchester Place Leasing LLC..........D 614 834-2273
  Canal Winchester *(G-2127)*

HOSPITALS: Mental, Exc For The Mentally Retarded

Adriel School Inc..............................D 937 465-0010
  West Liberty *(G-19117)*

Cambridge Behavioral Hospital..........C 740 432-4906
  Cambridge *(G-2052)*

Central Commnty Hlth Brd of Ha........D 513 559-2000
  Cincinnati *(G-3152)*

Central Commnty Hlth Brd of Ha........D 513 559-2000
  Cincinnati *(G-3153)*

County of Paulding ....E 419 399-3636
  Paulding *(G-15793)*

Eastway Corporation ....C 937 496-2000
  Dayton *(G-9404)*

Eastway Corporation ....C 937 531-7000
  Dayton *(G-9405)*

Mental Hlth Serv For CL & Mad ....E 937 390-7980
  Springfield *(G-17071)*

Mental Hlth Serv For CL & Mad ....C 937 399-9500
  Springfield *(G-17072)*

Mental Hlth Serv For CL & Mad ....E 740 852-6256
  London *(G-12871)*

Rehab Continuum Inc........................E 513 984-8070
  Blue Ash *(G-1643)*

Rescue Incorporated ....C 419 255-9585
  Toledo *(G-18004)*

HOSPITALS: Orthopedic

Crystal Clnic Orthpdic Ctr LLC............D 330 668-4040
  Akron *(G-173)*

Crystal Clnic Orthpdic Ctr LLC............D 330 535-3396
  Akron *(G-174)*

Northwest Ohio Orthopedic & Sp........C 419 427-1984
  Findlay *(G-10950)*

Trihealth Os LLC ....D 513 791-6611
  Montgomery *(G-14604)*

HOSPITALS: Professional Nursing School With AMA Residency

Toledo Hospital ....A 419 291-4000
  Toledo *(G-18086)*

Employee Codes: A=Over 500 employees, B=251-500
C=101-250, D=51-100, E=25-50
       2019 Harris Ohio
       Services Directory
       1447

HOSPITALS: Psychiatric

Belmont Bhc Pines Hospital Inc...........C...... 330 759-2700
Youngstown *(G-19964)*

Bethesda Hospital Association ....A...... 740 454-4000
Zanesville *(G-20281)*

Bhc Fox Run Hospital Inc ....C...... 740 695-2131
Saint Clairsville *(G-16479)*

Center For Addiction Treatment ....D...... 513 381-6672
Cincinnati *(G-3148)*

Develpmntal Dsblties Ohio Dept ....A...... 740 446-1642
Gallipolis *(G-11190)*

Develpmntal Dsblties Ohio Dept ....B...... 614 272-0509
Columbus *(G-7441)*

Focus Healthcare of Ohio LLC ....E...... 419 891-9333
Maumee *(G-13793)*

Heartland Bhavioral Healthcare...........B...... 330 833-3135
Massillon *(G-13695)*

Laurelwood Hospital ....B...... 440 953-3000
Willoughby *(G-19543)*

Marymount Hospital Inc ....B...... 216 581-0500
Cleveland *(G-5920)*

Mental Health and Addi Serv ....C...... 419 381-1881
Toledo *(G-17904)*

Mental Health and Addi Serv ....B...... 513 948-3600
Cincinnati *(G-4006)*

Mental Health and Addi Serv ....D...... 614 752-0333
Columbus *(G-8057)*

Mental Health and Addi Serv ....B...... 330 467-7131
Northfield *(G-15383)*

Mercy Health ....A...... 440 233-1000
Lorain *(G-12926)*

Oglethorpe Middlepoint LLC ....E...... 419 968-2950
Middle Point *(G-14247)*

Ohio Hospital For Psychiatry ....E...... 877 762-9026
Columbus *(G-8267)*

Southast Cmnty Mental Hlth Ctr ....E...... 614 444-0800
Columbus *(G-8662)*

St Ritas Medical Center ....E...... 419 226-9067
Lima *(G-12749)*

HOSPITALS: Rehabilitation, Alcoholism

Center For Addiction Treatment ....D...... 513 381-6672
Cincinnati *(G-3148)*

Community Counseling Services...........E...... 419 468-8211
Bucyrus *(G-1984)*

Crossroads Center ....C...... 513 475-5300
Cincinnati *(G-3382)*

Frs Counseling Inc ....E...... 937 393-0585
Hillsboro *(G-11840)*

Health Recovery Services Inc ....C...... 740 592-6720
Athens *(G-783)*

Marietta Memorial Hospital ....A...... 740 374-1400
Marietta *(G-13354)*

Maryhaven Inc ....B...... 614 449-1530
Columbus *(G-8032)*

McKinley Hall Inc ....E...... 937 328-5300
Springfield *(G-17068)*

Morrow County Council On Drugs ....E...... 419 947-4055
Mount Gilead *(G-14729)*

Oriana House Inc ....C...... 216 361-9655
Cleveland *(G-6143)*

Parkside Behavioral Healthcare ....E...... 614 471-2552
Gahanna *(G-11140)*

Select Spclty Hspital-Akron LLC ....D...... 330 761-7500
Akron *(G-423)*

Southast Cmnty Mental Hlth Ctr ....E...... 614 444-0800
Columbus *(G-8662)*

Talbert House ....D...... 513 684-7968
Cincinnati *(G-4574)*

Transitional Living Inc ....D...... 513 863-6383
Fairfield Township *(G-10815)*

Youngstown Committee On Alchol ....D...... 330 744-1181
Youngstown *(G-20260)*

HOSPITALS: Rehabilitation, Drug Addiction

Akron Gen Edwin Shaw Rhbltion..........D...... 330 375-1300
Fairlawn *(G-10816)*

Alcohol Drug Addction & Mental ....E...... 937 443-0416
Dayton *(G-9213)*

Behavral Cnnctions WD Cnty Inc ....E...... 419 352-5387
Bowling Green *(G-1717)*

Compass Corp For Recovery Svcs ....D...... 419 241-8827
Toledo *(G-17673)*

County of Stark ....E...... 330 455-6644
Canton *(G-2270)*

Firelands Regional Health Sys ....E...... 419 332-5524
Fremont *(G-11072)*

Glenbeigh ....E...... 440 563-3400
Rock Creek *(G-16411)*

Glenbeigh Health Sources Inc ....C...... 440 951-7000
Rock Creek *(G-16412)*

Lorain County Alcohol and Drug ....E...... 440 989-4900
Lorain *(G-12917)*

Mental Health & Recovery Ctr ....E...... 937 383-3031
Wilmington *(G-19635)*

Oriana House Inc ....D...... 330 996-7730
Akron *(G-367)*

Pike Cnty Recovery Council Inc ....E...... 740 835-8437
Waverly *(G-18821)*

Recovery Works Healing Ctr LLC ....E...... 937 384-0580
West Carrollton *(G-18856)*

Scioto Pnt Vly Mental Hlth Ctr ....E...... 740 335-6935
Wshngtn CT Hs *(G-19883)*

Southwest General Health Ctr ....D...... 440 816-8200
Cleveland *(G-6431)*

Syntero Inc ....E...... 614 889-5722
Dublin *(G-10350)*

Talbert House ....E...... 513 751-7747
Cincinnati *(G-4571)*

HOSPITALS: Specialty, NEC

Affiliates In Oral & Maxlofcl ....E...... 513 829-8080
Fairfield *(G-10693)*

Affiliates In Oral & Maxlofcl ....E...... 513 829-8080
West Chester *(G-18862)*

Anderson Healthcare Ltd ....D...... 513 474-6200
Cincinnati *(G-2959)*

Arthur G James Cance ....A...... 614 293-4878
Columbus *(G-6972)*

Aultman Hospital ....A...... 330 452-9911
Canton *(G-2202)*

Aultman Hospital ....B...... 330 452-9911
Canton *(G-2203)*

Charity Hospice Inc ....E...... 740 264-2280
Steubenville *(G-17147)*

Community Care Hospice ....E...... 937 382-5400
Wilmington *(G-19617)*

Covenant Care Ohio Inc ....D...... 937 878-7046
Fairborn *(G-10666)*

Encompass Health Corporation ....C...... 513 418-5600
Cincinnati *(G-3497)*

Greenbrier Senior Living Cmnty.............C...... 440 888-5900
Cleveland *(G-5641)*

Hcr Manorcare Med Svcs Fla LLC ....C...... 614 882-1511
Westerville *(G-19260)*

HealthSouth ....E...... 937 424-8200
Dayton *(G-9491)*

Hospice of Central Ohio........................C...... 740 344-0311
Newark *(G-15042)*

Hospice of Miami Valley LLC ....E...... 937 521-1444
Springfield *(G-17048)*

Hospice of Middletown ....E...... 513 424-2273
Middletown *(G-14302)*

Hospice of The Valley Inc......................D...... 330 788-1992
Youngstown *(G-20069)*

Hospice of The Western Reserve ....D...... 330 800-2240
Medina *(G-13951)*

Liberty Nrsing Ctr Rvrside LLC ....D...... 513 557-3621
Cincinnati *(G-3924)*

Lutheran Medical Center ....B...... 216 696-4300
Solon *(G-16867)*

Medcath Intermediate Holdings..............B...... 937 221-8016
Dayton *(G-9600)*

Mercy Health.......................................E...... 419 226-9064
Lima *(G-12701)*

Newark Sleep Diagnostic Center ....E...... 740 522-9499
Newark *(G-15087)*

Nord Center Associates Inc ....E...... 440 233-7232
Lorain *(G-12935)*

Ohio State University ....E...... 614 293-4925
Columbus *(G-8348)*

Salvation Army ....D...... 330 773-3331
Akron *(G-418)*

Stein Hospice Services Inc ....D...... 419 447-0475
Sandusky *(G-16645)*

Stein Hospice Services Inc ....D...... 419 502-0019
Sandusky *(G-16646)*

Trinity Health Corporation......................B...... 614 846-5420
Columbus *(G-8781)*

Twin Oaks Care Center Inc.....................E...... 419 524-1205
Mansfield *(G-13258)*

University Hospitals Cleveland ....A...... 216 844-1000
Cleveland *(G-6593)*

University Hospitals Health ....E...... 440 285-4040
Chardon *(G-2722)*

University Mednet ....B...... 216 383-0100
Euclid *(G-10660)*

Uvmc Nursing Care Inc ....C...... 937 473-2075
Covington *(G-9049)*

Vibra Hosp Mahoning Vly LLC................D...... 330 726-5000
Youngstown *(G-20237)*

Whetstone Care Center LLC ....C...... 614 875-7700
Grove City *(G-11487)*

HOSPITALS: Substance Abuse

Cambridge Behavioral Hospital..............C...... 740 432-4906
Cambridge *(G-2052)*

Cornell Companies Inc..........................E...... 419 747-3322
Shelby *(G-16744)*

Laurelwood Hospital ....B...... 440 953-3000
Willoughby *(G-19543)*

Ohio Department Youth Services ....E...... 740 881-3337
Columbus *(G-8244)*

Stella Maris Inc....................................E...... 216 781-0550
Cleveland *(G-6465)*

HOTEL: Franchised

21c Cincinnati LLC................................D...... 513 578-6600
Cincinnati *(G-2879)*

Amitel Rockside Ltd Partnr......................E...... 216 520-1450
Cleveland *(G-4972)*

Avalon Inn Services Inc.........................C...... 330 856-1900
Warren *(G-18674)*

Boulevard Motel Corp.............................E...... 440 234-3131
Cleveland *(G-5070)*

CER Hotels LLC....................................E...... 330 422-1855
Streetsboro *(G-17249)*

Chillicothe Motel LLC ....E...... 740 773-3903
Chillicothe *(G-2764)*

Columbus Worthington Hospitali.............D...... 614 885-3334
Columbus *(G-7321)*

Comfort Inn ....E...... 740 454-4144
Zanesville *(G-20297)*

Doubletree Guest Suites Dayton ....D...... 937 436-2400
Miamisburg *(G-14167)*

Hardage Hotels I LLC............................E...... 614 766-7762
Dublin *(G-10238)*

Hyatt Corporation ....B...... 614 463-1234
Columbus *(G-7791)*

Levis Commons Hotel LLC ....D...... 419 873-3573
Perrysburg *(G-15889)*

Lieben Wooster LP ....E...... 330 390-5722
Millersburg *(G-14481)*

Mansfield Hotel Partnership ....D...... 419 529-1000
Mansfield *(G-13207)*

Msk Hospitality Inc ....E...... 513 771-0370
Cincinnati *(G-4080)*

Newark Management Partners LLC..........D...... 740 322-6455
Newark *(G-15084)*

Nf II Cleveland Op Co LLC ....E...... 216 443-9043
Cleveland *(G-6068)*

Rama Inc ....E...... 614 473-9888
Columbus *(G-8488)*

Riverside Cmnty Urban Redev ....C...... 330 929-3000
Cuyahoga Falls *(G-9120)*

Rockside Hospitality LLC........................D...... 216 524-0700
Independence *(G-12115)*

S & S Management Inc ....E...... 567 356-4151
Wapakoneta *(G-18653)*

Sage Hospitality Resources LLC..............D...... 513 771-2080
Cincinnati *(G-4424)*

Sojourn Lodging Inc ....E...... 330 422-1855
Streetsboro *(G-17270)*

TownePlace Suites By Marriott.................E...... 513 774-0610
Cincinnati *(G-4621)*

West Montrose Properties ....D...... 330 867-4013
Fairlawn *(G-10856)*

HOTELS & MOTELS

50 S Front LLC ....D...... 614 224-4600
Columbus *(G-6843)*

506 Phelps Holdings LLC........................E...... 513 651-1234
Cincinnati *(G-2883)*

5901 Pfffer Rd Htels Sites LLC ....D...... 513 793-4500
Blue Ash *(G-1495)*

631 South Main Street Dev LLC...............D...... 419 423-0631
Findlay *(G-10861)*

AIR Management Group LLC :.................D...... 330 856-1900
Warren *(G-18660)*

Airport Core Hotel LLC...........................C...... 614 536-0500
Columbus *(G-6887)*

AK Group Hotels Inc..............................E...... 937 372-9921
Xenia *(G-19888)*

Amitel Beachwood Ltd Partnr..................E...... 216 831-3030
Cleveland *(G-4971)*

Ap/Aim Dublin Suites Trs LLC.................D...... 614 790-9000
Dublin *(G-10136)*

Ashford Trs Lessee LLC ....E 937 436-2400	Drury Hotels Company LLC ....E 614 798-8802	Island House Inc ....E 419 734-0100
Miamisburg *(G-14142)*	Dublin *(G-10203)*	Port Clinton *(G-16110)*
At Hospitality LLC ....D 513 527-9962	Drury Hotels Company LLC ....E 513 336-0108	Jagi Springhill LLC ....E 216 264-4190
Cincinnati *(G-2992)*	Mason *(G-13575)*	Independence *(G-12084)*
Bennett Enterprises Inc ....B 419 874-3111	Drury Hotels Company LLC ....E 614 221-7008	Kribha LLC ....E 740 788-8991
Perrysburg *(G-15838)*	Columbus *(G-7471)*	Newark *(G-15046)*
Best Western Executive Inn ....E 330 794-1050	Drury Hotels Company LLC ....E 937 454-5200	Legacy Village Hospitality LLC ....D 216 382-3350
Akron *(G-97)*	Dayton *(G-9396)*	Cleveland *(G-5861)*
Best Wooster Inc ....E 330 264-7750	Drury Hotels Company LLC ....E 513 771-5601	Liberty Ctr Lodging Assoc LLC ....E 608 833-4100
Wooster *(G-19690)*	Cincinnati *(G-3444)*	Liberty Township *(G-12583)*
Beverly Hills Inn La Llc ....E 859 494-9151	Drury Hotels Company LLC ....E 614 798-8802	Lq Management LLC ....E 614 866-6456
Aberdeen *(G-1)*	Grove City *(G-11428)*	Reynoldsburg *(G-16318)*
Broad Street Hotel Assoc LP ....D 614 861-0321	Durga Llc ....D 513 771-2080	Lq Management LLC ....E 513 771-0300
Columbus *(G-7076)*	Cincinnati *(G-3457)*	Cincinnati *(G-3951)*
Brothers Properties Corp ....C 513 381-3000	Epiqurian Inns ....D 614 885-2600	Lq Management LLC ....E 216 447-1133
Cincinnati *(G-3081)*	Worthington *(G-19807)*	Cleveland *(G-5883)*
Buffalo-Gtb Associates LLC ....E 216 831-3735	First Hotel Associates LP ....D 614 228-3800	Lq Management LLC ....E 216 251-8500
Beachwood *(G-1040)*	Columbus *(G-7586)*	Cleveland *(G-5884)*
Buxton Inn Inc ....E 740 587-0001	Gallipolis Hospitality Inc ....E 740 446-0090	March Investors Ltd ....E 740 373-5353
Granville *(G-11335)*	Gallipolis *(G-11195)*	Marietta *(G-13346)*
Ca-Mj Hotel Associates Ltd ....D 330 494-6494	Gateway Hospitality Group Inc ....C 330 405-9800	Marcus Hotels Inc ....E 614 228-3800
Canton *(G-2223)*	Twinsburg *(G-18271)*	Columbus *(G-8016)*
Cambria Green Management LLC ....D 330 899-1263	Geeta Hospitality Inc ....E 937 642-3777	Marios International Spa & Ht ....C 330 562-5141
Uniontown *(G-18360)*	Marysville *(G-13499)*	Aurora *(G-835)*
Canton Hotel Holdings Inc ....E 330 492-1331	Glidden House Associates Ltd ....E 216 231-8900	Marriott Hotel Services Inc ....C 216 252-5333
Canton *(G-2234)*	Cleveland *(G-5610)*	Cleveland *(G-5911)*
Canus Hospitality LLC ....E 937 323-8631	Golden Lamb ....C 513 932-5065	Marriott International Inc ....E 330 484-0300
Springfield *(G-17003)*	Lebanon *(G-12468)*	Canton *(G-2390)*
Carol Burton Management LLC ....E 419 666-5120	Grand Heritage Hotel Portland ....E 440 734-4477	McPaul Corp ....E 419 447-6313
Toledo *(G-17638)*	North Olmsted *(G-15291)*	Tiffin *(G-17523)*
CD Block K Hotel LLC ....E 440 871-3100	Grand View Inn Inc ....D 740 377-4388	Meander Inn Inc ....E 330 544-2378
Westlake *(G-19328)*	South Point *(G-16934)*	Youngstown *(G-20120)*
Ch Relty Iv/Clmbus Partners LP ....D 614 885-3334	Granville Hospitality Llc ....D 740 587-3333	Meander Inn Incorporated ....E 330 544-0660
Columbus *(G-7174)*	Granville *(G-11342)*	Youngstown *(G-20121)*
Charter Hotel Group Ltd Partnr ....E 216 772-4538	Green Township Hospitality LLC ....B 513 574-6000	Moody Nat Cy Dt Clumbus Mt LLC ....D 614 228-3200
Mentor *(G-14028)*	Cincinnati *(G-3656)*	Columbus *(G-8100)*
Cherry Valley Lodge ....E 740 788-1200	Hampton Inn & Suite Inc ....E 440 234-0206	Moody Nat Cy Willoughby Mt LLC ....E 440 530-1100
Newark *(G-15022)*	Middleburg Heights *(G-14253)*	Willoughby *(G-19551)*
Cincinnati Netherland Ht LLC ....B 513 421-9100	Haribol Haribol Inc ....E 330 339-7731	Natural Resources Ohio Dept ....E 419 938-5411
Cincinnati *(G-3259)*	New Philadelphia *(G-14963)*	Perrysville *(G-15942)*
Cincinnatian Hotel ....C 513 381-3000	Hauck Hospitality LLC ....D 513 563-8330	Northern Tier Hospitality LLC ....D 570 888-7711
Cincinnati *(G-3279)*	Cincinnati *(G-3684)*	Westlake *(G-19383)*
Cleveland Airport Hospitality ....D 440 871-6000	Hawkeye Hotels Inc ....E 614 782-8292	Ntk Hotel Group II LLC ....D 614 559-2000
Westlake *(G-19333)*	Grove City *(G-11440)*	Columbus *(G-8212)*
Cleveland Bchwood Hsptlity LLC ....D 216 464-5950	Hdi Ltd ....C 937 224-0800	Oakwood Hospitality Corp ....E 440 786-1998
Beachwood *(G-1044)*	Dayton *(G-9488)*	Bedford *(G-1296)*
Cleveland Crowne Plaza Airport ....E 440 243-4040	Hilton Garden Inn Beavercreek ....D 937 458-2650	Oberlin College ....D 440 935-1475
Cleveland *(G-5251)*	Dayton *(G-9177)*	Oberlin *(G-15515)*
Cleveland Westlake ....E 440 892-0333	Hilton Grdn Inn Clmbus Polaris ....E 614 846-8884	Oh-16 Clvlnd Arprt S Prprty Su ....E 440 243-8785
Westlake *(G-19334)*	Columbus *(G-6814)*	Middleburg Heights *(G-14255)*
Cmp I Blue Ash Owner LLC ....E 513 733-4334	Hilton Grdn Inn Columbus Arprt ....D 614 231-2869	Ohio State University ....E 614 247-4000
Blue Ash *(G-1531)*	Columbus *(G-7752)*	Columbus *(G-8310)*
Cmp I Columbus I Owner LLC ....E 614 764-9393	Hilton Polaris ....E 614 885-1600	Park Hotels & Resorts Inc ....C 216 447-0020
Dublin *(G-10177)*	Columbus *(G-6815)*	Cleveland *(G-6165)*
Cmp I Columbus II Owner LLC ....E 614 436-7070	Hit Portfolio I Hil Trs LLC ....E 614 235-0717	Park Hotels & Resorts Inc ....E 513 421-9100
Columbus *(G-7236)*	Dublin *(G-10243)*	Cincinnati *(G-4202)*
Cni Thl Ops LLC ....E 937 890-6112	Hit Portfolio I Misc Trs LLC ....C 216 575-1234	Park Hotels & Resorts Inc ....B 216 464-5950
Dayton *(G-9310)*	Cleveland *(G-5694)*	Cleveland *(G-6166)*
Cni Thl Ops LLC ....E 614 791-8675	Hit Portfolio I Misc Trs LLC ....E 614 228-1234	Playhouse Square Foundation ....C 216 615-7500
Dublin *(G-10179)*	Columbus *(G-7753)*	Cleveland *(G-6217)*
Columbus Airport Ltd Partnr ....C 614 475-7551	Hit Portfolio I Trs LLC ....E 614 846-4355	Primary Dayton Innkeepers LLC ....E 937 938-9550
Columbus *(G-7253)*	Columbus *(G-7754)*	Dayton *(G-9711)*
Columbus Easton Hotel LLC ....D 614 414-5000	Hit Swn Trs LLC ....E 614 228-3200	R & K Gorby LLC ....E 419 222-0004
Columbus *(G-7279)*	Columbus *(G-7755)*	Lima *(G-12728)*
Columbus Easton Hotel LLC ....E 614 383-2005	Honey Run Retreats LLC ....E 330 674-0011	Radisson Hotel Cleve ....E 440 734-5060
Columbus *(G-7280)*	Millersburg *(G-14478)*	North Olmsted *(G-15308)*
Columbus Hotel Partners ....E 513 891-1066	Hoster Hotels LLC ....E 419 931-8900	Renaissance Hotel Operating Co ....A 216 696-5600
Blue Ash *(G-1534)*	Perrysburg *(G-15876)*	Cleveland *(G-6305)*
Columbus Leasing LLC ....D 614 885-1885	Hotel 1100 Carnegie Opco L P ....D 216 658-6400	Residence Inn By Marriott Beav ....E 937 427-3914
Columbus *(G-7292)*	Cleveland *(G-5715)*	Beavercreek *(G-1182)*
Commodore Prry Inns Suites LLC ....D 419 732-2645	Hotel 75 E State Opco L P ....E 614 365-4500	River Road Hotel Corp ....E 614 267-7461
Port Clinton *(G-16102)*	Columbus *(G-7776)*	Columbus *(G-8535)*
Commonwealth Hotels LLC ....C 614 790-9000	Hyatt Regency Columbus ....B 614 463-1234	Rose Gracias ....E 614 785-0001
Dublin *(G-10184)*	Columbus *(G-7792)*	Columbus *(G-8550)*
Concord Hamiltonian Rvrfrnt Ho ....D 513 896-6200	Ihg Management (maryland) LLC ....C 614 461-4100	S & S Management Inc ....E 937 382-5858
Hamilton *(G-11586)*	Columbus *(G-7810)*	Wilmington *(G-19647)*
Continental GL Sls & Inv Group ....B 614 679-1201	Independent Hotel Partners LLC ....D 216 524-0700	S & S Management Inc ....E 937 235-2000
Powell *(G-16192)*	Cleveland *(G-5745)*	Dayton *(G-9745)*
Corporate Exchange Hotel Assoc ....C 614 890-8600	Indus Newark Hotel LLC ....D 740 322-6455	S P S Inc ....E 937 339-7801
Columbus *(G-7373)*	Columbus *(G-7810)*	Troy *(G-18228)*
Courtyard By Marriott Dayton ....E 937 220-9060	Integrated CC LLC ....E 216 707-4132	Seagate Hospitality Group LLC ....E 216 252-7700
Dayton *(G-9335)*	Cleveland *(G-5757)*	Cleveland *(G-6383)*
Courtyard Management Corp ....E 216 901-9988	Integrity Hotel Group ....C 937 224-0800	Select Hotels Group LLC ....E 513 754-0003
Cleveland *(G-5373)*	Dayton *(G-9517)*	Mason *(G-13638)*
CPX Canton Airport LLC ....C 330 305-0500	Intercntnntal Ht Group Rsurces ....D 216 707-4300	Select Hotels Group LLC ....E 216 328-1060
North Canton *(G-15194)*	Cleveland *(G-5760)*	Cleveland *(G-6393)*
Crowne Plaza Toledo ....D 419 241-1411	Intercontinental Hotels Group ....E 216 707-4100	Select Hotels Group LLC ....E 614 799-1913
Toledo *(G-17689)*	Cleveland *(G-5761)*	Dublin *(G-10332)*
DB&p Logistics Inc ....E 614 491-4035	Island Hospitality MGT LLC ....E 614 864-8844	Shaker House ....D 216 991-6000
Columbus *(G-7424)*	Columbus *(G-7847)*	Cleveland *(G-6402)*

Shiv Hotels LLC ....E 740 374-8190	Lowes Home Centers LLC ....C 513 598-7050	Lowes Home Centers LLC ....C 419 747-1920
Marietta *(G-13381)*	Cincinnati *(G-3946)*	Ontario *(G-15559)*
Signature Boutique Hotel LP ....E 216 595-0900	Lowes Home Centers LLC ....C 614 769-9940	Lowes Home Centers LLC ....C 330 339-1936
Beachwood *(G-1106)*	Reynoldsburg *(G-16317)*	New Philadelphia *(G-14971)*
Six Continents Hotels Inc ....C 513 563-8330	Lowes Home Centers LLC ....C 614 853-6200	Lowes Home Centers LLC ....C 440 985-5700
Cincinnati *(G-4487)*	Columbus *(G-7990)*	Lorain *(G-12924)*
Skyline Clvland Rnaissance LLC ......D 216 696-5600	Lowes Home Centers LLC ....C 440 937-3500	Lowes Home Centers LLC ....C 419 447-4101
Cleveland *(G-6414)*	Avon *(G-893)*	Tiffin *(G-17521)*
Sonesta Intl Hotels Corp ....C 614 791-8554	Lowes Home Centers LLC ....C 513 445-1000	Lowes Home Centers LLC ....C 937 578-4440
Dublin *(G-10337)*	South Lebanon *(G-16926)*	Marysville *(G-13511)*
Sree Hotels LLC ....E 513 354-2430	Lowes Home Centers LLC ....B 216 831-2860	Lowes Home Centers LLC ....C 440 324-5004
Cincinnati *(G-4525)*	Bedford *(G-1290)*	Elyria *(G-10531)*
Summit Hotel ....D 513 527-9900	Lowes Home Centers LLC ....C 937 327-6000	Lowes Home Centers LLC ....C 937 438-4900
Cincinnati *(G-4552)*	Springfield *(G-17065)*	Dayton *(G-9575)*
Sunrise Hospitality Inc ....D 419 332-7650	Lowes Home Centers LLC ....C 419 331-3598	Lowes Home Centers LLC ....C 937 427-1110
Fremont *(G-11102)*	Lima *(G-12693)*	Beavercreek *(G-1168)*
Synergy Hotels LLC ....E 614 492-9000	Lowes Home Centers LLC ....C 740 681-3464	Lowes Home Centers LLC ....C 937 848-5600
Obetz *(G-15530)*	Lancaster *(G-12413)*	Dayton *(G-9576)*
Toledo Inns Inc ....E 440 243-4040	Lowes Home Centers LLC ....C 614 659-0530	Lowes Home Centers LLC ....C 614 529-5900
Cleveland *(G-6531)*	Dublin *(G-10275)*	Hilliard *(G-11786)*
Valley Hospitality Inc ....E 740 374-9660	Lowes Home Centers LLC ....C 614 238-2601	Lowes Home Centers LLC ....C 513 737-3700
Marietta *(G-13395)*	Columbus *(G-7991)*	Hamilton *(G-11625)*
Visicon Inc ....D 937 879-2696	Lowes Home Centers LLC ....C 740 522-0003	Lowes Home Centers LLC ....C 419 355-0221
Fairborn *(G-10687)*	Newark *(G-15063)*	Fremont *(G-11084)*
Westgate Limited Partnership ....C 419 535-7070	Lowes Home Centers LLC ....C 740 773-7777	Lowes Home Centers LLC ....C 419 624-6000
Toledo *(G-18155)*	Chillicothe *(G-2803)*	Sandusky *(G-16625)*
Wm Columbus Hotel LLC ....C 614 228-3800	Lowes Home Centers LLC ....C 440 998-6555	Lowes Home Centers LLC ....C 419 782-9000
Columbus *(G-8911)*	Ashtabula *(G-745)*	Defiance *(G-9926)*
Wph Cincinnati LLC ....C 513 771-2080	Lowes Home Centers LLC ....B 513 753-5094	Lowes Home Centers LLC ....C 330 609-8000
Cincinnati *(G-4806)*	Cincinnati *(G-2861)*	Warren *(G-18725)*
	Lowes Home Centers LLC ....C 614 497-6170	Lowes Home Centers LLC ....C 740 894-7120
## HOTLINE	Columbus *(G-7992)*	South Point *(G-16939)*
	Lowes Home Centers LLC ....C 513 731-6127	Lowes Home Centers LLC ....C 513 727-3900
Battle Bullying Hotline Inc ....D 216 731-1976	Cincinnati *(G-3947)*	Middletown *(G-14305)*
Cleveland *(G-5042)*	Lowes Home Centers LLC ....C 330 287-2261	Lowes Home Centers LLC ....C 330 497-2720
Chagrin Valley Dispatch ....E 440 247-7321	Wooster *(G-19742)*	Canton *(G-2381)*
Bedford *(G-1272)*	Lowes Home Centers LLC ....C 937 339-2544	Lowes Home Centers LLC ....C 740 266-3500
City of Willoughby Hills ....E 440 942-7207	Troy *(G-18211)*	Steubenville *(G-17164)*
Willoughby Hills *(G-19587)*	Lowes Home Centers LLC ....C 440 392-0027	Lowes Home Centers LLC ....C 330 965-4500
Option Line ....E 614 586-1380	Mentor *(G-14078)*	Youngstown *(G-20101)*
Columbus *(G-8382)*	Lowes Home Centers LLC ....C 440 942-2759	Lowes Home Centers LLC ....C 937 383-7000
	Willoughby *(G-19546)*	Wilmington *(G-19630)*
## HOUSEHOLD APPLIANCE PARTS:	Lowes Home Centers LLC ....C 740 374-2151	Lowes Home Centers LLC ....C 937 854-8200
### Wholesalers	Marietta *(G-13345)*	Dayton *(G-9577)*
	Lowes Home Centers LLC ....C 419 874-6758	Lowes Home Centers LLC ....C 614 476-7100
Dayton Appliance Parts Co ....E 937 224-0487	Perrysburg *(G-15891)*	Columbus *(G-7994)*
Dayton *(G-9352)*	Lowes Home Centers LLC ....C 330 626-2980	Sears Roebuck and Co................E 330 629-7700
Merc Acquisitions Inc ....E 216 925-5918	Streetsboro *(G-17259)*	Youngstown *(G-20205)*
Twinsburg *(G-18298)*	Lowes Home Centers LLC ....C 419 389-9464	Staufs Coffee Roasters II Inc ....E 614 487-6050
V and V Appliance Parts Inc ....C 330 743-5144	Toledo *(G-17864)*	Columbus *(G-8696)*
Youngstown *(G-20233)*	Lowes Home Centers LLC ....C 419 843-9758	Tracy Refrigeration Inc ....E 419 223-4786
	Toledo *(G-17865)*	Lima *(G-12766)*
## HOUSEHOLD APPLIANCE REPAIR SVCS	Lowes Home Centers LLC ....C 614 447-2851	
	Columbus *(G-7993)*	## HOUSEHOLD APPLIANCE STORES: Air
Sears Roebuck and Co................E 330 629-7700	Lowes Home Centers LLC ....C 330 245-4300	## Cond Rm Units, Self-Contnd
Youngstown *(G-20205)*	Akron *(G-322)*	
Tracy Refrigeration Inc ....E 419 223-4786	Lowes Home Centers LLC ....C 513 965-3280	Robertson Htg Sup Aliance Ohio ......C 330 821-9180
Lima *(G-12766)*	Milford *(G-14402)*	Alliance *(G-546)*
	Lowes Home Centers LLC ....C 330 908-2750	
## HOUSEHOLD APPLIANCE STORES	Northfield *(G-15382)*	## HOUSEHOLD APPLIANCE STORES:
	Lowes Home Centers LLC ....C 419 470-2491	### Appliance Parts
Appliance Recycl Ctrs Amer Inc.......D 614 876-8771	Toledo *(G-17866)*	
Hilliard *(G-11742)*	Lowes Home Centers LLC ....C 513 336-9741	Dayton Appliance Parts Co ....E 937 224-0487
Hull Bros Inc ....E 419 375-2827	Mason *(G-13612)*	Dayton *(G-9352)*
Fort Recovery *(G-10992)*	Lowes Home Centers LLC ....C 937 498-8400	
Lowes Home Centers LLC ....C 216 351-4723	Sidney *(G-16785)*	## HOUSEHOLD APPLIANCE STORES: Electric
Cleveland *(G-5882)*	Lowes Home Centers LLC ....C 740 699-3000	
Lowes Home Centers LLC ....C 419 739-1300	Saint Clairsville *(G-16493)*	Captive-Aire Systems Inc ....E 614 777-7378
Wapakoneta *(G-18649)*	Lowes Home Centers LLC ....C 330 920-9280	Gahanna *(G-11111)*
Lowes Home Centers LLC ....C 937 235-2920	Stow *(G-17218)*	Morrison Inc ....E 740 373-5869
Dayton *(G-9574)*	Lowes Home Centers LLC ....C 740 589-3750	Marietta *(G-13361)*
Lowes Home Centers LLC ....C 740 574-6200	Athens *(G-791)*	Schmids Service Now Inc ....E 330 264-2040
Wheelersburg *(G-19435)*	Lowes Home Centers LLC ....C 740 393-5350	Wooster *(G-19766)*
Lowes Home Centers LLC ....C 330 665-9356	Mount Vernon *(G-14779)*	Thompson Heating Corporation..........D 513 769-7696
Akron *(G-321)*	Lowes Home Centers LLC ....C 937 547-2400	Cincinnati *(G-4606)*
Lowes Home Centers LLC ....C 330 829-2700	Greenville *(G-11389)*	
Alliance *(G-538)*	Lowes Home Centers LLC ....C 330 335-1900	## HOUSEHOLD APPLIANCE STORES: Electric
Lowes Home Centers LLC ....C 937 599-4000	Wadsworth *(G-18606)*	## Household, Major
Bellefontaine *(G-1357)*	Lowes Home Centers LLC ....C 937 347-4000	
Lowes Home Centers LLC ....C 419 420-7531	Xenia *(G-19918)*	Big Sandy Furniture Inc ....E 740 775-4244
Findlay *(G-10935)*	Lowes Home Centers LLC ....C 440 239-2630	Chillicothe *(G-2758)*
Lowes Home Centers LLC ....C 330 832-1901	Strongsville *(G-17324)*	Recker and Boerger Inc................D 513 942-9663
Massillon *(G-13704)*	Lowes Home Centers LLC ....C 513 755-4300	West Chester *(G-19076)*
Lowes Home Centers LLC ....C 513 741-0585	West Chester *(G-18966)*	
Cincinnati *(G-3945)*	Lowes Home Centers LLC ....C 513 671-2093	## HOUSEHOLD APPLIANCE STORES: Gas
Lowes Home Centers LLC ....C 614 433-9957	Cincinnati *(G-3948)*	## Appliances
Columbus *(G-6822)*	Lowes Home Centers LLC ....C 440 331-1027	
Lowes Home Centers LLC ....C 740 389-9737	Rocky River *(G-16440)*	Big Sandy Furniture Inc ....E 740 354-3193
Marion *(G-13430)*	Lowes Home Centers LLC ....C 330 677-3040	Portsmouth *(G-16125)*
Lowes Home Centers LLC ....C 740 450-5500	Kent *(G-12247)*	Big Sandy Furniture Inc ....D 740 574-2113
Zanesville *(G-20326)*		Franklin Furnace *(G-11043)*

HOUSEHOLD FURNISHINGS, NEC

Casco Mfg Solutions Inc ....D 513 681-0003
Cincinnati *(G-3129)*

HOUSEKEEPING & MAID SVCS

Carol Scudere ....E 614 839-4357
New Albany *(G-14848)*

Larue Enterprises Inc ....E 937 438-5711
Beavercreek *(G-1225)*

Maids Home Service of Cincy ....E 513 396-6900
Cincinnati *(G-3961)*

Molly Maid of Lorain County ....E 440 327-0000
Elyria *(G-10539)*

The Maids ....D 440 735-6243
Bedford Heights *(G-1328)*

HOUSES: Fraternity & Sorority

Alpha CHI Omega ....E 614 291-3871
Columbus *(G-6901)*

Ohio State University ....E 614 294-2635
Columbus *(G-8336)*

Sigma CHI Frat ....E 614 297-8783
Columbus *(G-8638)*

HOUSES: Lodging, Organization

Air Force US Dept of ....D 937 257-6068
Dayton *(G-9157)*

Rockwell Springs Trout Club ....E 419 684-7971
Clyde *(G-6751)*

HOUSES: Rooming & Boarding

Lodging First LLC ....E 614 792-2770
Dublin *(G-10273)*

HOUSEWARE STORES

Provantage LLC ....D 330 494-3781
North Canton *(G-15228)*

HOUSEWARES, ELECTRIC: Cooking Appliances

Nacco Industries Inc ....E 440 229-5151
Cleveland *(G-6034)*

HOUSING AUTHORITY OPERATOR

County of Allen ....E 419 228-6065
Lima *(G-12621)*

HOUSING PROGRAM ADMIN, GOVT: Housing Authority, Nonoperating

Akron Metropolitan Hsing Auth ....C 330 920-1652
Stow *(G-17189)*

HOUSING PROGRAM ADMINISTRATION, GOVT: Planning & Development

City of Toledo ....D 419 245-1400
Toledo *(G-17658)*

HOUSING PROGRAMS ADMINISTRATION SVCS

Trumbull Housing Dev Corp ....D 330 369-1533
Warren *(G-18757)*

HUMAN RESOURCE, SOCIAL WORK & WELFARE ADMINISTRATION SVCS

Ohio Department of Aging ....D 614 466-5500
Columbus *(G-8236)*

Ohio Dept of Job & Fmly Svcs ....C 614 466-1213
Columbus *(G-8247)*

Ohio Pub Employees Rtrement Sys ....B 614 228-8471
Columbus *(G-8282)*

School Employees Retirement ....C 614 222-5853
Columbus *(G-8606)*

HUMANE SOCIETIES

Animal Protective League ....E 216 771-4616
Cleveland *(G-4982)*

City of Brunswick ....C 330 225-9144
Brunswick *(G-1924)*

Franklin Cnty Bd Commissioners ....E 614 462-4360
Columbus *(G-7611)*

Hamilton County Society ....E 513 541-6100
Cincinnati *(G-3677)*

Ohio School Boards Association ....E 614 540-4000
Columbus *(G-8284)*

Pheasants Forever Inc ....E 567 454-6319
Pettisville *(G-15944)*

HYDRAULIC EQPT REPAIR SVC

Boc Water Hydraulics Inc ....E 330 332-4444
Salem *(G-16539)*

Cincinnati Hydraulic Svc Inc ....E 513 874-0540
West Chester *(G-18887)*

Dover Hydraulics Inc ....D 330 364-1617
Dover *(G-10074)*

Hydraulic Specialists Inc ....E 740 922-3343
Midvale *(G-14358)*

Ohio Machinery Co ....E 330 874-1003
Bolivar *(G-1705)*

Perkins Motor Service Ltd ....E 440 277-1256
Lorain *(G-12938)*

ICE

Home City Ice Company ....E 614 836-2877
Groveport *(G-11518)*

Lori Holding Co ....E 740 342-3230
New Lexington *(G-14920)*

ICE CREAM & ICES WHOLESALERS

United Dairy Farmers Inc ....C 513 396-8700
Cincinnati *(G-4678)*

ICE WHOLESALERS

Home City Ice Company ....E 614 836-2877
Groveport *(G-11518)*

Lori Holding Co ....E 740 342-3230
New Lexington *(G-14920)*

Siemer Distributing Company ....E 740 342-3230
New Lexington *(G-14928)*

IGNEOUS ROCK: Crushed & Broken

Great Lakes Crushing Ltd ....E 440 944-5500
Wickliffe *(G-19461)*

INCUBATORS & BROODERS: Farm

Chick Master Incubator Company ....C 330 722-5591
Medina *(G-13917)*

INDL & PERSONAL SVC PAPER WHOLESALERS

Avalon Foodservice Inc ....C 330 854-4551
Canal Fulton *(G-2092)*

Buckeye Boxes Inc ....E 614 274-8484
Columbus *(G-7085)*

Buckeye Paper Co Inc ....E 330 477-5925
Canton *(G-2220)*

Bunzl Usa Inc ....E 513 891-9010
Blue Ash *(G-1518)*

Commerce Paper Company ....E 419 241-9101
Toledo *(G-17669)*

Dawnchem Inc ....E 440 943-3332
Willowick *(G-19597)*

Dayton Industrial Drum Inc ....E 937 253-8933
Dayton *(G-9167)*

Deufol Worldwide Packaging LLC ....D 440 232-1100
Bedford *(G-1276)*

Deufol Worldwide Packaging LLC ....D 414 967-8000
Fairfield *(G-10717)*

Food Distributors Inc ....E 740 439-2764
Cambridge *(G-2068)*

I Supply Co ....C 937 878-5240
Fairborn *(G-10676)*

J V Hansel Inc ....E 330 716-0806
Warren *(G-18716)*

Keystone Foods LLC ....C 419 843-3009
Toledo *(G-17839)*

Maines Paper & Food Svc Inc ....E 216 643-7500
Bedford *(G-1291)*

Millcraft Group LLC ....D 216 441-5500
Cleveland *(G-5993)*

Millcraft Paper Company ....C 216 441-5505
Cleveland *(G-5994)*

Millcraft Paper Company ....E 614 675-4800
Columbus *(G-8087)*

Millcraft Paper Company ....E 216 441-5500
Cleveland *(G-5995)*

Peck Distributors Inc ....E 216 587-6814
Maple Heights *(G-13291)*

Pollak Distributing Co Inc ....E 216 851-9911
Euclid *(G-10653)*

Ranpak Corp ....C 440 354-4445
Concord Township *(G-8944)*

Sysco Cincinnati LLC ....B 513 563-6300
Cincinnati *(G-4562)*

The Cincinnati Cordage Ppr Co ....E 513 242-3600
Cincinnati *(G-4590)*

The Cottingham Paper Co ....E 614 294-6444
Columbus *(G-8742)*

Veritiv Operating Company ....E 513 242-0800
Fairfield *(G-10798)*

Veritiv Operating Company ....E 614 251-7100
Grove City *(G-11480)*

Veritiv Operating Company ....E 216 573-7400
Independence *(G-12137)*

Veritiv Operating Company ....C 513 285-0999
Fairfield *(G-10799)*

INDL & PERSONAL SVC PAPER, WHOL: Bags, Paper/Disp Plastic

Atlapac Corp ....D 614 252-2121
Columbus *(G-6995)*

Berk Enterprises Inc ....D 330 369-1192
Warren *(G-18679)*

Cannon Group Inc ....E 614 890-0343
Westerville *(G-19230)*

Joshen Paper & Packaging Co ....C 216 441-5600
Cleveland *(G-5804)*

North American Plas Chem Inc ....E 330 627-2210
Carrollton *(G-2573)*

Ricking Paper and Specialty Co ....E 513 825-3551
Cincinnati *(G-4372)*

INDL & PERSONAL SVC PAPER, WHOL: Boxes, Corrugtd/Solid Fiber

Impressive Packaging Inc ....E 419 368-6808
Hayesville *(G-11701)*

JIT Packaging Inc ....E 330 562-8080
Aurora *(G-831)*

Lynk Packaging Inc ....E 330 562-8080
Aurora *(G-833)*

Westrock Cp LLC ....D 770 448-2193
Wshngtn CT Hs *(G-19886)*

INDL & PERSONAL SVC PAPER, WHOL: Paper, Wrap/Coarse/Prdts

Alco-Chem Inc ....E 330 833-8551
Canton *(G-2177)*

M Conley Company ....C 330 456-8243
Canton *(G-2383)*

Mailender Inc ....D 513 942-5453
West Chester *(G-18968)*

Millcraft Paper Company ....E 937 222-7829
Dayton *(G-9636)*

Ohio & Michigan Paper Company ....E 419 666-1500
Perrysburg *(G-15896)*

Polymer Packaging Inc ....D 330 832-2000
Massillon *(G-13720)*

Tiffin Paper Company ....E 419 447-2121
Tiffin *(G-17544)*

INDL & PERSONAL SVC PAPER, WHOLESALE: Disposable

Acorn Distributors Inc ....E 614 294-6444
Columbus *(G-6867)*

INDL & PERSONAL SVC PAPER, WHOLESALE: Paper Tubes & Cores

Espt Liquidation Inc ....D 330 698-4711
Apple Creek *(G-618)*

Precision Products Group Inc ....D 330 698-4711
Apple Creek *(G-620)*

Sonoco Products Company ....D 937 429-0040
Beavercreek Township *(G-1263)*

INDL & PERSONAL SVC PAPER, WHOLESALE: Patterns, Paper

Millers Textile Services Inc ....D 419 738-3552
Wapakoneta *(G-18650)*

SERVICES

INDL & PERSONAL SVC PAPER, WHOLESALE: Press Sensitive Tape

Tape Products Company ....D 513 489-8840
Cincinnati (G-4577)

INDL & PERSONAL SVC PAPER, WHOLESALE: Shipping Splys

Mast Logistics Services Inc ....C 614 415-7500
Columbus (G-8035)
Systems Pack Inc ....E 330 467-5729
Macedonia (G-13083)

INDL & PERSONAL SVC PAPER, WHOLESALE: Towels, Paper

Aci Industries Converting Ltd ....E 740 368-4160
Delaware (G-9949)

INDL CONTRACTORS: Exhibit Construction

Benchmark Craftsman Inc ....E 330 975-4214
Seville (G-16682)

INDL DIAMONDS WHOLESALERS

Chardon Tool & Supply Co Inc ....E 440 286-6440
Chardon (G-2690)

INDL EQPT CLEANING SVCS

Industrial Air Control Inc ....D 330 772-6422
Hubbard (G-11947)
MPW Container Management Corp ....D 216 362-8400
Cleveland (G-6018)
National Heat Exch Clg Corp ....E 330 482-0893
Youngstown (G-20137)

INDL EQPT SVCS

3-D Service Ltd ....C 330 830-3500
Massillon (G-13656)
Commercial Electric Pdts Corp ....E 216 241-2886
Cleveland (G-5318)
Dayton Industrial Drum Inc ....E 937 253-8933
Dayton (G-9167)
Famous Enterprises Inc ....E 330 762-9621
Akron (G-212)
Forge Industries Inc ....A 330 782-8301
Youngstown (G-20040)
GL Nause Co Inc ....E 513 722-9500
Loveland (G-12996)
Graphic Systems Services Inc ....E 937 746-0708
Springboro (G-16967)
Grob Systems Inc ....C 419 358-9015
Bluffton (G-1691)
Henry P Thompson Company ....E 513 248-3200
Milford (G-14394)
Industrial Parts & Service Co ....E 330 966-5025
Canton (G-2355)
Magnetech Industrial Svcs Inc ....C 330 830-3500
Massillon (G-13708)
Miami Industrial Trucks Inc ....D 937 293-4194
Moraine (G-14677)
Obr Cooling Towers Inc ....E 419 243-3443
Rossford (G-16463)
Primetals Technologies USA LLC ....E 419 929-1554
New London (G-14935)
Quintus Technologies LLC ....E 614 891-2732
Lewis Center (G-12561)
Raymond Storage Concepts Inc ....D 513 891-7290
Blue Ash (G-1641)
Reladyne LLC ....E 513 489-6000
Cincinnati (G-4355)
Scott Fetzer Company ....E 440 892-3000
Westlake (G-19403)
Siemens Industry Inc ....E 800 879-8079
Lebanon (G-12502)
Ssi Fabricated Inc ....E 513 217-3535
Middletown (G-14330)
Team Industrial Services Inc ....E 440 498-9494
Cleveland (G-6506)
Towlift Inc ....D 614 851-1001
Columbus (G-8765)
Towlift Inc ....E 419 666-1333
Northwood (G-15411)
Transforce Inc ....E 513 860-4402
West Chester (G-19019)
US Molding Machinery Co Inc ....E 440 918-1701
Willoughby (G-19580)

Walker National Inc ....E 614 492-1614
Columbus (G-8870)
Winelco Inc ....E 513 755-8050
West Chester (G-19038)

INDL GASES WHOLESALERS

Airgas Inc ....B 440 632-1758
Middlefield (G-14268)
Airgas Merchant Gases LLC ....B 800 242-0105
Cleveland (G-4920)
Airgas Safety Inc ....E 513 942-1465
Hamilton (G-11555)
Airgas Usa LLC ....D 440 786-2864
Oakwood Village (G-15485)

INDL HELP SVCS

Diversified Labor Support LLC ....B 440 234-3090
Cleveland (G-5430)

INDL MACHINERY & EQPT WHOLESALERS

2828 Clinton Inc ....E 216 241-7157
Leetonia (G-12517)
Addisonmckee Inc ....C 513 228-7000
Lebanon (G-12448)
Aerocontrolex Group Inc ....D 440 352-6182
Painesville (G-15692)
Alkon Corporation ....D 419 355-9111
Fremont (G-11058)
Alkon Corporation ....E 614 799-6650
Dublin (G-10126)
Ats Systems Oregon Inc ....B 541 738-0932
Lewis Center (G-12527)
Best & Donovan N A Inc ....E 513 791-9180
Blue Ash (G-1513)
Bevcorp LLC ....D 440 954-3500
Willoughby (G-19508)
Bionix Safety Technologies Ltd ....E 419 727-0552
Toledo (G-17615)
Blastmaster Holdings Usa LLC ....D 877 725-2781
Columbus (G-7047)
Bostwick-Braun Company ....D 419 259-3600
Toledo (G-17620)
Brown Industrial Inc ....E 937 693-3838
Botkins (G-1708)
Casey Equipment Corporation ....E 330 750-1005
Struthers (G-17360)
Cecil I Walker Machinery Co ....E 740 286-7566
Jackson (G-12170)
Columbus Equipment Company ....E 513 771-3922
Cincinnati (G-3330)
CPI - Cnstr Polymers Inc ....E 330 861-5200
North Canton (G-15193)
Ctm Integration Incorporated ....E 330 332-1800
Salem (G-16541)
Dxp Enterprises Inc ....E 513 242-2227
Cincinnati (G-3459)
EMI Corp ....D 937 596-5511
Jackson Center (G-12183)
Equipment Manufacturers Intl ....E 216 651-6700
Cleveland (G-5488)
Esec Corporation ....E 614 875-3732
Grove City (G-11430)
Feintool Equipment Corporation ....E 513 791-1118
Blue Ash (G-1561)
Freeman Manufacturing & Sup Co ......E 440 934-1902
Avon (G-881)
Ged Holdings Inc ....C 330 963-5401
Twinsburg (G-18272)
General Electric Company ....E 513 530-7107
Blue Ash (G-1567)
Glavin Industries Inc ....E 440 349-0049
Solon (G-16851)
Great Lakes Water Treatment ....E 216 464-8292
Cleveland (G-5631)
Hannon Company ....D 330 456-4728
Canton (G-2339)
Hendrickson International Corp ....D 740 929-5600
Hebron (G-11714)
Industrial Financial Svcs Inc ....E 614 777-0000
Columbus (G-7813)
Intelligrated Systems Inc ....A 866 936-7300
Mason (G-13598)
Intelligrated Systems Ohio LLC ....A 513 701-7300
Mason (G-13600)
Jed Industries Inc ....E 440 639-9973
Grand River (G-11332)
Jr Engineering Inc ....C 330 848-0960
Barberton (G-957)

Kolbus America Inc ....E 216 931-5100
Cleveland (G-5837)
Kyocera SGS Precision Tools ....E 330 688-6667
Munroe Falls (G-14797)
Linden Industries Inc ....E 330 928-4064
Cuyahoga Falls (G-9109)
LNS America Inc ....D 513 528-5674
Cincinnati (G-2860)
Maple Mountain Industries Inc ....C 330 948-2510
Lodi (G-12828)
Marcy Industries Company LLC ....E 740 943-2343
Marion (G-13433)
Met-Chem Inc ....E 216 881-7900
Cleveland (G-5961)
Midwest Industrial Supply Inc ....D 330 456-3121
Canton (G-2404)
Mine Equipment Services LLC ....E 740 936-5427
Sunbury (G-17390)
Minerva Welding and Fabg Inc ....E 330 868-7731
Minerva (G-14522)
Multi Products Company ....E 330 674-5981
Millersburg (G-14484)
Nordson Corporation ....B 440 985-4496
Amherst (G-594)
Park Corporation ....B 216 267-4870
Cleveland (G-6163)
Parker-Hannifin Corporation ....E 216 896-3000
Cleveland (G-6170)
Pfpc Enterprises Inc ....B 513 941-6200
Cincinnati (G-4240)
Pines Manufacturing Inc ....E 440 835-5553
Westlake (G-19392)
Power-Pack Conveyor Company ....E 440 975-9955
Willoughby (G-19563)
Primetals Technologies USA LLC ....E 419 929-1554
New London (G-14935)
Prospect Mold & Die Company ....D 330 929-3311
Cuyahoga Falls (G-9119)
Reid Asset Management Company ......E 216 642-3223
Cleveland (G-6298)
Rubber City Machinery Corp ....E 330 434-3500
Akron (G-411)
Samuel Strapping Systems Inc ....D 740 522-2500
Heath (G-11709)
Select Industries Corp ....E 937 233-9191
Dayton (G-9758)
Shawcor Pipe Protection LLC ....E 513 683-7800
Loveland (G-13027)
Shearer Farm Inc ....E 440 237-4806
North Royalton (G-15367)
Siemens Industry Inc ....E 440 526-2770
Brecksville (G-1805)
Stolle Machinery Company LLC ....E 330 493-0444
Canton (G-2498)
Stolle Machinery Company LLC ....D 330 453-2015
North Canton (G-15235)
Super Systems Inc ....E 513 772-0060
Cincinnati (G-4555)
T J Automation Inc ....E 419 267-5687
Archbold (G-641)
Union Supply Group Inc ....E 614 409-1444
Groveport (G-11545)
Venturo Manufacturing Inc ....E 513 772-8448
Cincinnati (G-4754)
W W Williams Company LLC ....E 419 837-5067
Perrysburg (G-15932)
Wardjet LLC ....D 330 677-9100
Tallmadge (G-17498)
Western Tradewinds Inc ....E 937 859-4300
Miamisburg (G-14238)
Wilkris Company ....E 513 271-9344
Terrace Park (G-17501)
Winelco Inc ....E 513 755-8050
West Chester (G-19038)
WW Grainger Inc ....E 513 563-7100
Blue Ash (G-1683)
Xigent Automation Systems Inc ....D 740 548-3700
Lewis Center (G-12567)

INDL MACHINERY REPAIR & MAINTENANCE

A and A Millwright Rigging Svcs ....E 513 396-6212
Cincinnati (G-2888)
Ajax Tocco Magnethermic Corp ....C 330 372-8511
Warren (G-18661)
Applied Industrial Tech Inc ....B 216 426-4000
Cleveland (G-4996)
Cecil I Walker Machinery Co ....E 740 286-7566
Jackson (G-12170)
Cleveland Jsm Inc ....D 440 876-3050
Strongsville (G-17291)

Cleveland Pump Repr & Svcs LLC ....E 330 963-3100
  Twinsburg (G-18254)
Convergint Technologies LLC ....C 513 771-1717
  Cincinnati (G-3357)
Elmco Engineering Oh Inc ....E 419 238-1100
  Van Wert (G-18477)
Emsco Inc ....E 330 830-7125
  Massillon (G-13677)
Emsco Inc ....E 330 833-5600
  Massillon (G-13678)
Estabrook Corporation ....E 440 234-8566
  Berea (G-1424)
Expert Crane Inc ....E 216 451-9900
  Cleveland (G-5502)
General Plastex Inc ....E 330 745-7775
  Barberton (G-953)
Industrial Repair & Mfg Inc ....D 419 822-4232
  Delta (G-10045)
J&J Precision Machine Ltd ....D 330 923-5783
  Cuyahoga Falls (G-9103)
Laserflex Corporation ....D 614 850-9600
  Hilliard (G-11783)
Lucas Precision LLC ....E 216 451-5588
  Cleveland (G-5887)
Mmic Inc ....D 513 697-0445
  Loveland (G-13014)
Monarch Electric Service Co ....D 216 433-7800
  Cleveland (G-6006)
OKL Can Line Inc ....E 513 825-1655
  Cincinnati (G-4166)
Paradigm Industrial LLC ....E 937 224-4415
  Dayton (G-9685)
Patriot Indus Contg Svcs LLC ....E 513 248-8222
  Milford (G-14421)
S & S Inc ....E 216 383-1880
  Cleveland (G-6354)
SMS Group Inc ....E 330 426-4126
  East Palestine (G-10421)
Steel Eqp Specialists Inc ....D 330 823-8260
  Alliance (G-555)
Towlift Inc ....C 216 749-6800
  Brooklyn Heights (G-1884)
Victory Machine and Fab ....E 937 693-3171
  Sidney (G-16804)
Williams Super Service Inc ....E 330 733-7750
  East Sparta (G-10425)
Winkle Industries Inc ....D 330 823-9730
  Alliance (G-557)
Wood Graphics Inc ....E 513 771-6300
  Cincinnati (G-4804)

INDL PROCESS INSTRUMENTS: Controllers, Process Variables

Schneider Electric Usa Inc ....D 513 755-5000
  West Chester (G-18997)

INDL SPLYS WHOLESALERS

3b Holdings Inc ....D 800 791-7124
  Cleveland (G-4871)
Alkon Corporation ....E 614 799-6650
  Dublin (G-10126)
All Ohio Threaded Rod Co Inc ....E 216 426-1800
  Cleveland (G-4935)
Alro Steel Corporation ....E 419 720-5300
  Toledo (G-17586)
Alro Steel Corporation ....E 614 878-7271
  Columbus (G-6905)
Applied Mint Sups Slutions LLC ....E 216 456-3600
  Strongsville (G-17285)
Blackhawk Industries ....E 918 610-4719
  Brunswick (G-1920)
Bordner and Associates Inc ....E 614 552-6905
  Columbus (G-7054)
Brand Energy & Infrastructure ....E 419 324-1305
  Toledo (G-17623)
Ci Disposition Co ....E 216 587-5200
  Brooklyn Heights (G-1867)
Cornerstone Controls Inc ....E 937 263-6429
  Dayton (G-9322)
Cornwell Quality Tools Company ....D 330 628-2627
  Mogadore (G-14545)
Cornwell Quality Tools Company ....E 330 335-2933
  Wadsworth (G-18594)
Dolin Supply Co ....E 304 529-4171
  South Point (G-16932)
Duramax Marine LLC ....D 440 834-5400
  Hiram (G-11864)
Dynatech Systems Inc ....E 440 365-1774
  Elyria (G-10503)

Eagle Industrial Truck Mfg LLC ....E 734 442-1000
  Swanton (G-17396)
Edward W Daniel LLC ....E 440 647-1960
  Wellington (G-18839)
Ellison Technologies Inc ....E 310 323-2121
  Hamilton (G-11593)
Fcx Performance Inc ....E 614 324-6050
  Columbus (G-7567)
Flodraulic Group Incorporated ....E 614 276-8141
  Columbus (G-7597)
General Factory Sups Co Inc ....E 513 681-6300
  Cincinnati (G-3615)
Ges Graphite Inc ....E 216 658-6660
  Parma (G-15767)
Great Lakes Textiles Inc ....E 440 914-1122
  Solon (G-16854)
Hd Supply Facilities Maint Ltd ....E 440 542-9188
  Solon (G-16857)
JIT Packaging Inc ....E 330 562-8080
  Aurora (G-831)
Kaman Corporation ....E 330 468-1811
  Macedonia (G-13077)
Lancaster Commercial Pdts LLC ....E 740 286-5081
  Columbus (G-7945)
Lawrence Industries Inc ....C 216 518-7000
  Cleveland (G-5858)
Liberty Casting Company LLC ....E 740 363-1941
  Delaware (G-9996)
Logan Clutch Corporation ....E 440 808-4258
  Cleveland (G-5879)
Macomb Group Inc ....E 419 666-6899
  Northwood (G-15398)
Mazzella Holding Company Inc ....D 513 772-4466
  Cleveland (G-5926)
McWane Inc ....B 740 622-6651
  Coshocton (G-9022)
Megacity Fire Protection Inc ....E 937 335-0775
  Dayton (G-9605)
Merchandise Inc ....E 513 353-2200
  Miamitown (G-14242)
Mill-Rose Company ....C 440 255-9171
  Mentor (G-14087)
Motion Industries Inc ....E 513 860-8400
  West Chester (G-19070)
New Haven Estates Inc ....E 419 933-2181
  New Haven (G-14916)
Noland Company ....C 937 396-7980
  Moraine (G-14684)
Precision Supply Company Inc ....D 330 225-5530
  Brunswick (G-1938)
Riten Industries ....D 740 335-5353
  Wshngtn CT Hs (G-19881)
Samsel Rope & Marine Supply Co ....E 216 241-0333
  Cleveland (G-6370)
Samuel Strapping Systems Inc ....D 740 522-2500
  Heath (G-11709)
Scioto Services Llc ....E 937 644-0888
  Marysville (G-13527)
Selinsky Force LLC ....D 330 477-4527
  Canton (G-2473)
SSP Fittings Corp ....C 330 425-4250
  Twinsburg (G-18323)
Stark Industrial LLC ....D 330 493-9773
  North Canton (G-15234)
Tricor Metals ....D 330 264-3299
  Wooster (G-19774)
Watteredge LLC ....D 440 933-6110
  Avon Lake (G-929)
Wesco Distribution Inc ....E 419 666-1670
  Northwood (G-15414)
Wesco Distribution Inc ....E 216 741-0441
  Cleveland (G-6665)
Wesco Distribution Inc ....E 937 228-9668
  Dayton (G-9874)
Winsupply Inc ....D 937 294-5331
  Moraine (G-14707)
Wulco Inc ....D 513 679-2600
  Cincinnati (G-4808)
WW Grainger Inc ....C 330 425-8387
  Macedonia (G-13090)

INDL SPLYS, WHOL: Fasteners, Incl Nuts, Bolts, Screws, Etc

Afc Industries Inc ....E 513 874-7456
  Fairfield (G-10692)
Andre Corporation 574 293-0207
  Mason (G-13540)
Atlas Bolt & Screw Company LLC ....C 419 289-6171
  Ashland (G-653)

Chandler Products LLC ....E 216 481-4400
  Cleveland (G-5167)
Earnest Machine Products Co ....E 440 895-8400
  Rocky River (G-16431)
Facil North America Inc ....C 330 487-2500
  Twinsburg (G-18265)
Great Lakes Fasteners Inc ....E 330 425-4488
  Twinsburg (G-18276)
J & J Entps Westerville Inc ....E 614 898-5997
  Sunbury (G-17389)
Mid-State Bolt and Nut Co Inc ....E 614 253-8631
  Columbus (G-8078)
Midwest Fasteners Inc ....D 937 866-0463
  Miamisburg (G-14193)
R L Morrissey & Assoc Inc ....E 440 498-3730
  Solon (G-16889)
Stafast Products Inc ....E 440 357-5546
  Painesville (G-15741)
State Industrial Products Corp ....E 216 861-6363
  Cleveland (G-6459)
Supply Technologies LLC ....C 440 947-2100
  Cleveland (G-6485)
Tricor Industrial Inc ....D 330 264-3299
  Wooster (G-19773)
Ziegler Bolt & Parts Co ....D 330 478-2542
  Canton (G-2544)

INDL SPLYS, WHOLESALE: Abrasives

American Producers Sup Co Inc ....D 740 373-5050
  Marietta (G-13310)
ARC Abrasives Inc ....D 800 888-4885
  Troy (G-18194)
Mirka USA Inc ....D 330 963-6421
  Twinsburg (G-18299)

INDL SPLYS, WHOLESALE: Abrasives & Adhesives

Evans Adhesive Corporation ....E 614 451-2665
  Columbus (G-7540)
Permatex Inc ....E 440 914-3100
  Solon (G-16882)

INDL SPLYS, WHOLESALE: Adhesives, Tape & Plasters

Gorilla Glue Company ....E 513 271-3300
  Cincinnati (G-3627)

INDL SPLYS, WHOLESALE: Barrels, New Or Reconditioned

Sabco Industries Inc ....E 419 531-5347
  Toledo (G-18016)

INDL SPLYS, WHOLESALE: Bearings

Applied Industrial Tech Inc ....B 216 426-4000
  Cleveland (G-4996)
Bearing Distributors Inc ....C 216 642-9100
  Cleveland (G-5048)
Bearing Technologies Ltd ....D 440 937-4770
  Avon (G-866)
Belting Company of Cincinnati ....C 513 621-9050
  Cincinnati (G-3039)
Federal-Mogul Powertrain LLC ....C 740 432-2393
  Cambridge (G-2067)
Forge Industries Inc ....A 330 782-8301
  Youngstown (G-20040)
Miba Bearings US LLC ....B 740 962-4242
  McConnelsville (G-13902)
North Coast Bearings LLC ....E 440 930-7600
  Avon (G-896)
Timken Company ....C 330 471-2121
  Canton (G-2512)
Timken Company ....D 234 262-3000
  Niles (G-15171)
Timken Corporation ....E 330 471-3378
  North Canton (G-15239)

INDL SPLYS, WHOLESALE: Bins & Containers, Storage

Creative Plastic Concepts LLC ....D 419 927-9588
  Sycamore (G-17410)

INDL SPLYS, WHOLESALE: Bottler Splys

Tolco Corporation ....D 419 241-1113
  Toledo (G-18072)

SERVICES

INDL SPLYS, WHOLESALE: Drums, New Or Reconditioned

Dayton Industrial Drum Inc ....E 937 253-8933
Dayton (G-9167)

INDL SPLYS, WHOLESALE: Electric Tools

WW Grainger Inc ....E 614 276-5231
Columbus (G-8921)

INDL SPLYS, WHOLESALE: Fasteners & Fastening Eqpt

Ors Nasco Inc ....E 918 781-5300
West Chester (G-19071)

INDL SPLYS, WHOLESALE: Filters, Indl

Air Supply Co ....E 704 732-8034
Twinsburg (G-18242)

INDL SPLYS, WHOLESALE: Fittings

Faster Inc ....E 419 868-8197
Maumee (G-13789)
Otp Holding LLC ....E 614 342-6123
Columbus (G-8403)
Superior Products LLC ....D 216 651-9400
Cleveland (G-6484)
Superior Products Llc ....D 216 651-9400
Cleveland (G-6483)

INDL SPLYS, WHOLESALE: Gaskets

Ishikawa Gasket America Inc ....C 419 353-7300
Bowling Green (G-1738)

INDL SPLYS, WHOLESALE: Gaskets & Seals

Buckeye Rubber & Packing Co ....E 216 464-8900
Beachwood (G-1039)

INDL SPLYS, WHOLESALE: Hydraulic & Pneumatic Pistons/Valves

Alkon Corporation ....D 419 355-9111
Fremont (G-11058)
Clippard Instrument Lab Inc ....C 513 521-4261
Cincinnati (G-3309)
Fischer Pump & Valve Company ....E 513 583-4800
Loveland (G-12994)

INDL SPLYS, WHOLESALE: Knives, Indl

C B Mfg & Sls Co Inc ....D 937 866-5986
Miamisburg (G-14147)

INDL SPLYS, WHOLESALE: Mill Splys

Allied Supply Company Inc ....E 937 224-9833
Dayton (G-9216)
Vallen Distribution Inc ....D 513 942-9100
West Chester (G-19028)

INDL SPLYS, WHOLESALE: Plastic, Pallets

Pallet Distributors Inc ....C 888 805-9670
Lakewood (G-12359)

INDL SPLYS, WHOLESALE: Power Transmission, Eqpt & Apparatus

Binkelman Corporation ....E 419 537-9333
Toledo (G-17613)
Commercial Electric Pdts Corp ....E 216 241-2886
Cleveland (G-5318)
Great Lakes Power Products Inc ....D 440 951-5111
Mentor (G-14056)
Ohio Transmission Corporation ....C 614 342-6247
Columbus (G-8357)
Ohio Transmission Corporation ....E 419 468-7866
Galion (G-11181)

INDL SPLYS, WHOLESALE: Rubber Goods, Mechanical

Advanced Elastomer Systems LP ....C 800 352-7866
Akron (G-20)
Jet Rubber Company ....E 330 325-1821
Rootstown (G-16450)
Mullins International Sls Corp ....D 937 233-4213
Dayton (G-9648)

Summers Acquisition Corp ....E 216 941-7700
Cleveland (G-6474)

INDL SPLYS, WHOLESALE: Seals

Datwyler Sling Sltions USA Inc ....D 937 387-2800
Vandalia (G-18519)
Mc Neal Industries Inc ....E 440 721-0400
Painesville (G-15724)
McNeil Industries Inc ....E 440 951-7756
Painesville (G-15726)
Roger Zatkoff Company ....E 248 478-2400
Twinsburg (G-18313)

INDL SPLYS, WHOLESALE: Signmaker Eqpt & Splys

Sign Source USA Inc ....D 419 224-1130
Lima (G-12741)

INDL SPLYS, WHOLESALE: Tools

B W Grinding Co ....E 419 923-1376
Lyons (G-13056)
File Sharpening Company Inc ....E 937 376-8268
Xenia (G-19899)
H & D Steel Service Inc ....E 440 237-3390
North Royalton (G-15357)
Pennsylvania Tl Sls & Svc Inc ....D 330 758-0845
Youngstown (G-20153)

INDL SPLYS, WHOLESALE: Tools, NEC

Lute Supply Inc ....E 740 353-1447
Portsmouth (G-16153)

INDL SPLYS, WHOLESALE: Valves & Fittings

A-T Controls Inc ....E 513 530-5175
West Chester (G-19039)
Crane Pumps & Systems Inc ....B 937 773-2442
Piqua (G-16003)
Eagle Equipment Corporation ....E 937 746-0510
Franklin (G-11028)
Famous Distribution Inc ....D 330 762-9621
Akron (G-210)
Lakeside Supply Co ....E 216 941-6800
Cleveland (G-5849)
Main Line Supply Co Inc ....E 937 254-6910
Dayton (G-9581)
MRC Global (us) Inc ....E 419 324-0039
Toledo (G-17925)
MRC Global (us) Inc ....E 513 489-6922
West Chester (G-18977)
Ruthman Pump and Engineering ....E 937 783-2411
Blanchester (G-1489)
Shan-Rod Inc ....E 419 588-2066
Berlin Heights (G-1451)
Swagelok Company ....E 440 542-1250
Solon (G-16906)
The Mau-Sherwood Supply Co ....E 330 405-1200
Twinsburg (G-18326)
Victory White Metal Company ....D 216 271-1400
Cleveland (G-6628)

INDL TOOL GRINDING SVCS

Seilkop Industries Inc ....E 513 761-1035
Cincinnati (G-4448)

INDL TRUCK REPAIR SVCS

All Lift Service Company Inc ....E 440 585-1542
Willoughby (G-19503)
Fallsway Equipment Co Inc ....C 330 633-6000
Akron (G-209)
Sharron Group Inc ....E 614 873-5856
Plain City (G-16066)
Terex Utilities Inc ....E 614 444-7373
Etna (G-10620)
Toyota Industries N Amer Inc ....E 937 237-0976
Dayton (G-9819)

INDOOR PARKING SVCS

Yark Automotive Group Inc ....A 419 841-7771
Toledo (G-18166)

INDUSTRIAL & COMMERCIAL EQPT INSPECTION SVCS

Argus International Inc ....E 513 852-1010
Cincinnati (G-2985)

Cec Combustion Safety LLC ....E 216 749-2992
Brookpark (G-1893)
Orbit Industries Inc ....D 440 243-3311
Cleveland (G-6141)
Predictive Service LLC ....D 866 772-6770
Cleveland (G-6227)
Quintus Technologies LLC ....E 614 891-2732
Lewis Center (G-12561)
Reid Asset Management Company ....E 216 642-3223
Cleveland (G-6298)

INFORMATION BUREAU SVCS

County of Clermont ....E 513 732-7661
Batavia (G-993)
National Service Information ....E 740 387-6806
Marion (G-13448)
Ohio Consumers Counsel ....E 614 466-8574
Columbus (G-8234)
Provato LLC ....E 440 546-0768
Brecksville (G-1800)

INFORMATION RETRIEVAL SERVICES

AGS Custom Graphics Inc ....D 330 963-7770
Macedonia (G-13058)
Cobalt Group Inc ....D 614 876-4013
Hilliard (G-11756)
Com Net Inc ....D 419 739-3100
Wapakoneta (G-18639)
Community Isp Inc ....E 419 867-6060
Toledo (G-17672)
Hkm Drect Mkt Cmmnications Inc ....C 216 651-9500
Cleveland (G-5696)
Innovative Technologies Corp ....D 937 252-2145
Dayton (G-9179)
Intellicorp Records Inc ....D 216 450-5200
Beachwood (G-1067)
Medical Mutual Services LLC ....C 440 878-4800
Strongsville (G-17331)
Png Telecommunications Inc ....D 513 942-7900
Cincinnati (G-4260)
Relx Inc ....B 937 865-6800
Miamisburg (G-14209)
Repro Acquisition Company LLC ....E 216 738-3800
Cleveland (G-6309)
Salvagedata Recovery LLC ....E 914 600-2434
Cleveland (G-6367)
Seifert & Group Inc ....D 330 833-2700
Massillon (G-13727)
TSC Communications Inc ....E 419 739-2200
Wapakoneta (G-18657)
Verisk Crime Analytics Inc ....E 614 865-6000
Worthington (G-19857)
Verizon Business Global LLC ....E 614 219-2317
Hilliard (G-11826)
Webmd Health Corp ....E 330 425-3241
Twinsburg (G-18337)

INFORMATION SVCS: Consumer

Action For Children Inc ....E 614 224-0222
Columbus (G-6868)
Child & Elder Care Insights ....E 440 356-2900
Rocky River (G-16426)
Informa Business Media Inc ....E 216 696-7000
Cleveland (G-5751)
Research Associates Inc ....D 440 892-1000
Cleveland (G-6312)

INNS

B & I Hotel Management LLC ....C 330 995-0200
Aurora (G-819)
Bird Enterprises LLC ....E 330 674-1457
Millersburg (G-14460)
Chimneys Inn ....E 937 567-7850
Dayton (G-9297)
Fairlawn Associates Ltd ....C 330 867-5000
Fairlawn (G-10826)
Fmw Rri Opco LLC ....E 614 744-2659
Columbus (G-7599)
Frog & Toad Inc ....E 419 877-1180
Whitehouse (G-19447)
Glenlaurel Inc ....E 740 385-4070
Rockbridge (G-16413)
Hotel 2345 LLC ....E 614 766-7762
Dublin (G-10245)
Indus Airport Hotels I LLC ....D 614 231-2869
Columbus (G-7809)
Indus Hilliard Hotel LLC ....E 614 334-1800
Hilliard (G-11777)

2019 Harris Ohio
Services Directory

(G-0000) Company's Geographic Section entry number

Inn At Marietta Ltd ....D 740 373-9600
  Marietta (G-13338)
Pacific Heritg Inn Polaris LLC...........E 614 880-9080
  Columbus (G-6829)
R & H Service Inc ....E 330 626-2888
  Streetsboro (G-17267)
Rukh Boardman Properties LLC ....D 330 726-5472
  Youngstown (G-20198)
Sar Biren ....E 419 865-0407
  Maumee (G-13848)
Stockport Mill Country Inn Inc...........E 740 559-2822
  Stockport (G-17183)
Tharaldson Hospitality MGT ....E 513 947-9402
  Cincinnati (G-2872)
Zincks Inn ....E 330 893-6600
  Berlin (G-1448)

INSECTICIDES & PESTICIDES

Scotts Miracle-Gro Company................B 937 644-0011
  Marysville (G-13529)

INSPECTION & TESTING SVCS

Acuren Inspection Inc ....E 937 228-9729
  Dayton (G-9207)
Biotest Pharmaceuticals Corp..........E 419 819-3068
  Bowling Green (G-1720)
Catsi Inc ....E 800 922-0468
  Wheelersburg (G-19429)
Csa Amrica Tstg Crtfcation LLC..........B 216 524-4990
  Independence (G-12064)
James Ray Lozier ....E 419 884-2656
  Mansfield (G-13190)
Mistras Group Inc ....E 419 227-4100
  Lima (G-12704)
National Board of Boiler ....D 614 888-8320
  Columbus (G-8129)
Servicelink Field Services LLC..........A 440 424-0058
  Solon (G-16896)
Vista Industrial Packaging LLC ....D 800 454-6117
  Columbus (G-8855)

INSPECTION SVCS, TRANSPORTATION

Pti Qlity Cntnment Sltions LLC.............D 313 304-8677
  Toledo (G-17994)

INSTRUMENTS, MEASURING & CNTRL: Testing, Abrasion, Etc

Standards Testing Labs Inc ....D 330 833-8548
  Massillon (G-13731)

INSTRUMENTS, MEASURING & CONTROLLING: Cable Testing

Multilink Inc ....C 440 366-6966
  Elyria (G-10540)

INSTRUMENTS: Analytical

Bionix Safety Technologies Ltd...........E 419 727-0552
  Toledo (G-17615)
Dentronix Inc ....E 330 916-7300
  Cuyahoga Falls (G-9086)
Orton Edward Jr Crmic Fndation ....E 614 895-2663
  Westerville (G-19197)
Reid Asset Management Company ....E 216 642-3223
  Cleveland (G-6298)
Teledyne Instruments Inc ....E 513 229-7000
  Mason (G-13645)
Teledyne Tekmar Company..............E 513 229-7000
  Mason (G-13646)

INSTRUMENTS: Eye Examination

Eye Surgery Center Ohio Inc ....E 614 228-3937
  Columbus (G-7550)

INSTRUMENTS: Indl Process Control

Airmate Company ....D 419 636-3184
  Bryan (G-1950)
Alpha Technologies Svcs LLC............D 330 745-1641
  Hudson (G-11966)
Chandler Systems Incorporated..........D 888 363-9434
  Ashland (G-666)
Ingersoll-Rand Company ....E 419 633-6800
  Bryan (G-1960)
Innovative Controls Corp ....D 419 691-6684
  Toledo (G-17821)

Parker-Hannifin Corporation.................A 216 531-3000
  Cleveland (G-6171)
Production Design Services Inc ....D 937 866-3377
  Dayton (G-9716)
Stock Fairfield Corporation.................C 440 543-6000
  Chagrin Falls (G-2684)

INSTRUMENTS: Measurement, Indl Process

Command Alkon Incorporated ....D 614 799-0600
  Dublin (G-10183)

INSTRUMENTS: Measuring & Controlling

Aclara Technologies LLC ....C 440 528-7200
  Solon (G-16814)
AT&T Government Solutions Inc..........D 937 306-3030
  Beavercreek (G-1128)
Bionix Safety Technologies Ltd...........E 419 727-0552
  Toledo (G-17615)
Matrix Research Inc ....D 937 427-8433
  Beavercreek (G-1230)
Super Systems Inc.........................E 513 772-0060
  Cincinnati (G-4555)
Tech Pro Inc ....E 330 923-3546
  Akron (G-466)
Tech Products Corporation................D 937 438-1100
  Miamisburg (G-14227)
Tegam Inc ....E 440 466-6100
  Geneva (G-11246)
Teledyne Instruments Inc ....E 513 229-7000
  Mason (G-13645)
Teledyne Tekmar Company................E 513 229-7000
  Mason (G-13646)

INSTRUMENTS: Measuring Electricity

Aclara Technologies LLC ....C 440 528-7200
  Solon (G-16814)
Hughes Corporation ....E 440 238-2550
  Strongsville (G-17312)
Orton Edward Jr Crmic Fndation ....E 614 895-2663
  Westerville (G-19197)
Tech Pro Inc.................................E 330 923-3546
  Akron (G-466)

INSTRUMENTS: Measuring, Electrical Energy

Drs Signal Technologies Inc ....E 937 429-7470
  Beavercreek (G-1148)

INSTRUMENTS: Medical & Surgical

Applied Medical Technology Inc..........E 440 717-4000
  Brecksville (G-1769)
Casco Mfg Solutions Inc ....D 513 681-0003
  Cincinnati (G-3129)
Dentronix Inc ....E 330 916-7300
  Cuyahoga Falls (G-9086)
General Data Company Inc ....C 513 752-7978
  Cincinnati (G-2853)
Morris Technologies Inc ....C 513 733-1611
  Cincinnati (G-4075)
Synergy Health North Amer Inc...........D 513 398-6406
  Mason (G-13643)
Thermo Fisher Scientific Inc..............C 800 871-8909
  Oakwood Village (G-15495)

INSTRUMENTS: Power Measuring, Electrical

TTI Floor Care North Amer Inc.............B 440 996-2000
  Solon (G-16909)

INSTRUMENTS: Test, Electrical, Engine

Nu-Di Products Co Inc ....D 216 251-9070
  Cleveland (G-6106)

INSTRUMENTS: Test, Electronic & Electric Measurement

Bionix Safety Technologies Ltd...........E 419 727-0552
  Toledo (G-17615)
Keithley Instruments LLC ....C 440 248-0400
  Solon (G-16864)
Keithley Instruments Intl Corp.............B 440 248-0400
  Cleveland (G-5819)
Speelman Electric Inc ....D 330 633-1410
  Tallmadge (G-17488)

INSTRUMENTS: Test, Electronic & Electrical Circuits

Hannon Company ....D 330 456-4728
  Canton (G-2339)

INSULATION & CUSHIONING FOAM: Polystyrene

Austin Foam Plastics Inc ....E 614 921-0824
  Columbus (G-7003)

INSULATION MATERIALS WHOLESALERS

Alpine Insulation I LLC ....A 614 221-3399
  Columbus (G-6904)
CCI Supply Inc..............................C 440 953-0045
  Mentor (G-14026)
Great Lakes Textiles Inc ....E 440 914-1122
  Solon (G-16854)
Installed Building Pdts Inc ....C 614 221-3399
  Columbus (G-7828)
R E Kramig & Co Inc ....C 513 761-4010
  Cincinnati (G-4330)

INSULATION: Fiberglass

Owens Corning Sales LLC.................A 419 248-8000
  Toledo (G-17968)

INSULATORS & INSULATION MATERIALS: Electrical

Eger Products Inc ....D 513 753-4200
  Amelia (G-572)

INSURANCE AGENCIES & BROKERS

American Modrn Insur Group Inc..........C 800 543-2644
  Amelia (G-568)
Gallagher Bassett Services................E 614 764-7616
  Dublin (G-10233)
George W Mc Cloy ....D 614 457-6233
  Columbus (G-7661)
Life Insurance Mktg Co Inc ....E 330 867-1707
  Akron (G-313)
LP Insurance Services LLC...............C 877 369-5121
  Solon (G-16866)
MetLife Auto HM Insur Agcy Inc..........A 815 266-5301
  Dayton (G-9610)
Metropolitan Life Insur Co ....D 614 792-1463
  Dublin (G-10279)
New York Life Insurance Co...............C 216 520-1345
  Independence (G-12103)
New York Life Insurance Co...............D 513 621-9999
  Cincinnati (G-4110)
New York Life Insurance Co...............D 216 221-1100
  Lakewood (G-12357)
NI of Ky Inc ....E 740 689-9876
  Lancaster (G-12423)
NI of Ky Inc ....E 216 643-7100
  Rocky River (G-16442)
Progressive Spclty Ins Agcy Inc..........C 440 461-5000
  Cleveland (G-6241)
Progressive Casualty Insur Co ....E 440 683-8164
  Cleveland (G-6243)
Progressive Corporation....................A 800 925-2886
  Cleveland (G-6246)
Progressive Premier Insurance ....C 440 461-5000
  Cleveland (G-6254)
Rick Allman ....E 330 699-1660
  Canton (G-2461)
Seymour & Associates ....E 419 517-7079
  Maumee (G-13850)
State Farm General Insur Co ....D 740 364-5000
  Newark (G-15100)
State Farm Life Insurance Co ....D 937 276-1900
  Dayton (G-9791)
State Farm Mutl Auto Insur Co ....D 419 873-0100
  Perrysburg (G-15925)
State Farm Mutl Auto Insur Co ....D 216 621-3723
  Cleveland (G-6456)
State Farm Mutl Auto Insur Co ....A 614 775-2001
  New Albany (G-14875)
State Farm Mutl Auto Insur Co ....A 740 364-5000
  Newark (G-15101)
State Farm Mutl Auto Insur Co ....D 216 321-1422
  Cleveland (G-6457)
Uct Property Inc ....E 614 228-3276
  Columbus (G-8795)
United Insurance Company Amer ....E 513 771-6771
  Cincinnati (G-4681)

SERVICES

INSURANCE AGENTS, NEC

A A Hammersmith Insurance Inc ....E 330 832-7411
Massillon (G-13657)

A-1 General Insurance Agency ....D 216 986-3000
Cleveland (G-4883)

AAA Cincinnati Insurance Svc ....E 513 345-5600
Cincinnati (G-2895)

AAA Club Alliance Inc ....C 937 427-5884
Beavercreek (G-1123)

Aba Insurance Services Inc ....D 800 274-5222
Shaker Heights (G-16702)

Allan Peace & Associates Inc ....E 513 579-1700
Cincinnati (G-2923)

Allen Gardiner Deroberts ....E 614 221-1500
Columbus (G-6892)

Allstate Insurance Company ....E 330 650-2917
Hudson (G-11963)

Althans Insurance Agency Inc ....E 440 247-6422
Chagrin Falls (G-2638)

American Family Home Insur Co ......D 513 943-7100
Amelia (G-565)

American Fidelity Assurance Co ....A 800 437-1011
Columbus (G-6921)

American Highways Insur Agcy ....C 330 659-8900
Richfield (G-16345)

American Income Life Insur Co ....D 440 582-0040
Cleveland (G-4954)

American Insur Administrators ....E 614 486-5388
Dublin (G-10131)

American Intl Group Inc ....C 216 479-8800
Cleveland (G-4955)

Ameriprise Financial Svcs Inc ....D 614 846-8723
Worthington (G-19793)

Archer-Meek-Weiler Agency Inc ......E 614 212-1009
Westerville (G-19145)

Art Hauser Insurance Inc ....D 513 745-9200
Cincinnati (G-2990)

Auto-Owners Insurance Company ....D 937 432-6740
Miamisburg (G-14143)

Auto-Owners Life Insurance Co ....D 419 227-1452
Lima (G-12604)

Axa Advisors LLC ....E 513 762-7700
Cincinnati (G-3010)

Beecher Carlson Insur Svcs LLC ......D 330 726-8177
Youngstown (G-19962)

Bowers Insurance Agency Inc ....E 330 638-6146
Cortland (G-8984)

Brands Insurance Agency Inc ....E 513 777-7775
West Chester (G-18878)

Britton-Gallagher & Assoc Inc ....D 216 658-7100
Cleveland (G-5082)

Brooks & Stafford Co ....E 216 696-3000
Cleveland (G-5089)

Bruce Klinger ....E 419 473-2270
Toledo (G-17630)

Brunswick Companies ....D 330 864-8800
Cleveland (G-5095)

Buren Insurance Group Inc ....E 419 281-8060
Ashland (G-661)

Cai/Insurance Agency Inc ....E 513 221-1140
Cincinnati (G-3104)

Clark Theders Insurance Agency .....E 513 779-2800
West Chester (G-18891)

Cobos Insurance Centre LLC ....E 440 324-3732
Elyria (G-10491)

Combined Insurance Co Amer ....D 614 210-6209
Columbus (G-7323)

Cornerstone Broker Ins Svcs AG ......E 513 241-7675
Cincinnati (G-3363)

Cumberland Mutl Fire Insur Co ....E 419 525-4443
Mansfield (G-13163)

Employers Mutual Casualty Co ....D 513 221-6010
Blue Ash (G-1551)

Erie Indemnity Company ....D 330 433-6300
Canton (G-2303)

Executive Insurance Agency ....E 330 576-1234
Akron (G-205)

Explorer Rv Insurance Agcy Inc ......C 330 659-8900
Richfield (G-16355)

F W Arnold Agency Co Inc ....E 330 832-1556
Massillon (G-13679)

Fedeli Group Inc ....D 216 328-8080
Cleveland (G-5520)

First Acceptance Corporation ....E 614 237-9700
Columbus (G-7580)

Freedom Specialty Insurance Co .....C 614 249-1545
Columbus (G-7622)

Galt Enterprises Inc ....E 216 464-6744
Moreland Hills (G-14710)

German Mutual Insurance Co ....E 419 599-3993
Napoleon (G-14806)

Grange Indemnity Insurance Co ......D 614 445-2900
Columbus (G-7685)

Hanover Insurance Company ....D 614 408-9000
Dublin (G-10237)

Hanover Insurance Company ....E 513 829-4555
Fairfield (G-10734)

Hartford Fire Insurance Co ....E 216 447-1000
Cleveland (G-5664)

Home and Farm Insurance Co ....D 937 778-5000
Piqua (G-16010)

Hummel Group Inc ....E 330 683-1050
Orrville (G-15635)

Huntington Insurance Inc ....C 419 720-7900
Toledo (G-17813)

Huntington Insurance Inc ....E 614 480-3800
Columbus (G-7783)

Huntington Insurance Inc ....E 330 262-6611
Wooster (G-19732)

Huntington Insurance Inc ....D 614 899-8500
Columbus (G-7784)

Huntington Insurance Inc ....D 330 674-2931
Millersburg (G-14479)

Huntington Insurance Inc ....E 330 430-1300
Canton (G-2353)

Hylant Administrative Services ....E 419 255-1020
Toledo (G-17814)

Hylant Group Inc ....E 513 985-2400
Cincinnati (G-3747)

Hylant Group Inc ....E 614 932-1200
Dublin (G-10251)

Hylant Group Inc ....E 419 255-1020
Toledo (G-17815)

Hylant Group Inc ....D 216 447-1050
Cleveland (G-5730)

Hylant-Maclean Inc ....E 614 932-1200
Dublin (G-10252)

James B Oswald Company ....E 330 723-3637
Medina (G-13959)

Knight Crockett Miller Ins ....E 419 254-2400
Toledo (G-17841)

Lang Financial Group Inc ....E 513 699-2966
Blue Ash (G-1596)

Lighthouse Insurance Group LLC .....D 216 503-2439
Independence (G-12093)

Louieville Title Agncy For Nrt ....D 419 248-4611
Toledo (G-17861)

Mc Cloy Financial Services ....D 614 457-6233
Columbus (G-8042)

McGohan/Brabender Agency Inc .....D 937 293-1600
Moraine (G-14672)

Medical Benefits Mutl Lf Insur ....C 740 522-8425
Newark (G-15069)

Medical Mutual of Ohio ....D 440 878-4800
Strongsville (G-17330)

Medical Mutual of Ohio ....B 216 292-0400
Beachwood (G-1078)

Motorists Mutual Insurance Co ....E 440 779-8900
North Olmsted (G-15299)

National Auto Care Corporation ......D 800 548-1875
Westerville (G-19187)

National General Insurance ....B 212 380-9462
Cleveland (G-6045)

Nationwide Corporation ....A 330 452-8705
Canton (G-2415)

Nationwide Life Insur Co Amer ....A 800 688-5177
Columbus (G-8158)

Nationwide Mutl Fire Insur Co ....E 614 249-7111
Columbus (G-8159)

Nationwide Mutual Insurance Co .....C 402 420-6153
Grove City (G-11457)

Nationwide Mutual Insurance Co .....A 330 489-5000
Canton (G-2416)

Neace Assoc Insur Agcy of Ohio ......E 614 224-0772
Columbus (G-8168)

New England Life Insurance Co ....E 614 457-6233
Columbus (G-8185)

NI of Ky Inc ....E 614 224-0772
Columbus (G-8192)

Norman-Spencer Agency Inc ....E 800 543-3248
Dayton (G-9659)

Ohio National Life Assurance ....E 513 794-6100
Montgomery (G-14600)

Phelan Insurance Agency Inc ....E 800 843-3069
Versailles (G-18570)

Postema Insurance & Investment .....E 419 782-2500
Defiance (G-9934)

R L King Insurance Agency ....E 419 255-9947
Holland (G-11908)

Rankin & Rankin Inc ....E 740 452-7575
Zanesville (G-20357)

Rick Blazing Insurance Agency ....E 513 677-8300
Cincinnati (G-4371)

Schauer Group Incorporated ....E 330 453-7721
Canton (G-2471)

Schwendeman Agency Inc ....E 740 373-6793
Marietta (G-13378)

Sedgwick CMS Holdings Inc ....A 800 825-6755
Dublin (G-10331)

Seibert-Keck Insurance Agency ....D 330 867-3140
Fairlawn (G-10849)

Self-Funded Plans Inc ....E 216 566-1455
Cleveland (G-6395)

Selman & Company ....D 440 646-9336
Cleveland (G-6396)

Stammen Insurance Agency LLC .....E 419 586-7500
Celina (G-2611)

Steele W W Jr Agency Inc ....E 330 453-7721
Canton (G-2497)

Stolly Insurance Agency Inc ....E 419 227-2570
Lima (G-12756)

Todd Associates Inc ....D 440 461-1101
Beachwood (G-1113)

Travelers Property Cslty Corp ....E 513 639-5300
Cincinnati (G-4630)

Travelers Property Cslty Corp ....C 216 643-2100
Cleveland (G-6546)

United Agencies Inc ....E 216 696-8044
Cleveland (G-6565)

United Insurance Company Amer .....E 419 531-4289
Toledo (G-18118)

Usi Inc ....D 419 243-1191
Toledo (G-18132)

USI Insurance Services Nat Inc ....E 614 228-5565
Columbus (G-8837)

USI Midwest LLC ....C 513 852-6300
Cincinnati (G-4744)

Vision Service Plan ....E 614 471-7511
Columbus (G-8854)

W P Dolle LLC ....E 513 421-6515
Cincinnati (G-4767)

Wabe Maquaw Holdings Inc ....D 419 243-1191
Toledo (G-18144)

Wallace & Turner Insurance Inc ....E 937 324-8492
Springfield (G-17131)

Western & Southern Lf Insur Co ....E 234 380-4525
Hudson (G-12013)

William D Taylor Sr Inc ....E 614 653-6683
Etna (G-10621)

Wilmared Inc ....E 513 891-6615
Loveland (G-13035)

INSURANCE BROKERS, NEC

American Risk Services LLC ....E 513 772-3712
Cincinnati (G-2951)

AON Consulting Inc ....E 614 436-8100
Columbus (G-6952)

AON Consulting Inc ....D 614 847-4670
Columbus (G-6953)

AON Consulting Inc ....E 216 621-8100
Cleveland (G-4987)

AON Risk Svcs Northeast Inc ....A 216 621-8100
Cleveland (G-4988)

Arthur J Gallagher & Co ....E 513 977-3100
Cincinnati (G-2991)

Benefit ADM Agcy LLC ....E 614 791-1143
Dublin (G-10145)

CSC Insurance Agency Inc ....D 614 895-2000
Westerville (G-19154)

Forge Industries Inc ....A 330 782-8301
Youngstown (G-20040)

Hyatt Legal Plans Inc ....D 216 241-0022
Cleveland (G-5729)

Insurance Intermediaries Inc ....D 614 846-1111
Columbus (G-7831)

Kellison & Co ....D 216 464-5160
Cleveland (G-5822)

Marsh & McLennan Agency LLC ....E 513 248-4888
Loveland (G-13010)

Marsh & McLennan Agency LLC ....C 937 228-4135
Dayton (G-9585)

Marsh USA Inc ....B 216 937-1700
Cleveland (G-5914)

Marsh USA Inc ....D 513 287-1600
Cincinnati (G-3976)

Marsh USA Inc ....D 614 227-6200
Columbus (G-8029)

Marsh USA Inc ....D 216 830-8000
Cleveland (G-5915)

Ohio Mutual Insurance Company..........C 419 562-3011
Bucyrus *(G-1999)*
Richfield Financial Group Inc ....E 440 546-4288
Brecksville *(G-1802)*
Stephens-Matthews Mktg Inc..............E 740 984-8011
Beverly *(G-1466)*

INSURANCE CARRIERS: Automobile

American Commerce Insurance Co ......C 614 272-6951
Columbus *(G-6915)*
Artisan and Truckers Cslty Co ....A 440 461-5000
Cleveland *(G-5011)*
Grange Mutual Casualty Company ....A 614 445-2900
Columbus *(G-7687)*
Great American Insurance Co ....A 513 369-5000
Cincinnati *(G-3639)*
Mountain Laurel Assurance Co ....C 440 461-5000
Cleveland *(G-6015)*
Ohio Casualty Insurance Co.................C 513 867-3000
Hamilton *(G-11631)*
Ohio Indemnity Company ....E 614 228-1601
Columbus *(G-8269)*
Progressive Casualty Insur Co............D 440 603-4033
Cleveland *(G-6244)*
Progressive Express Insur Co...............A 440 461-5000
Cleveland *(G-6248)*
Progressive Grdn State Insur ....C 440 461-5000
Cleveland *(G-6250)*
Progressive Select Insur Co ....B 440 461-5000
Cleveland *(G-6256)*
Progressive Vehicle Service Co ....C 440 461-5000
Cleveland *(G-6258)*
Progressive West Insurance Co ....B 440 446-5100
Cleveland *(G-6259)*
Safe Auto Insurance Company ....C 740 472-1900
Woodsfield *(G-19678)*
Safe Auto Insurance Group Inc ....D 614 231-0200
Columbus *(G-8572)*
Verti Insurance Company ....D 844 448-3784
Columbus *(G-8845)*

INSURANCE CARRIERS: Bank Deposit

American Contrs Indemnity Co ....E 513 688-0800
Cincinnati *(G-2938)*

INSURANCE CARRIERS: Dental

Dcp Holding Company ....D 513 554-1100
Sharonville *(G-16728)*
Medical Mutual of Ohio..........................A 216 687-7000
Cleveland *(G-5943)*

INSURANCE CARRIERS: Direct Accident & Health

1-888 Ohio Comp LLC ....D 216 426-0646
Cleveland *(G-4864)*
American Financial Group Inc ....C 513 579-2121
Cincinnati *(G-2943)*
J P Farley Corporation ....E 440 250-4300
Westlake *(G-19360)*
James B Oswald Company ....E 330 723-3637
Medina *(G-13959)*
Medical Bnfits Admnstrtors Inc ....D 740 522-8425
Newark *(G-15070)*
Progressive Casualty Insur Co.............A 440 461-5000
Mayfield Village *(G-13886)*
Signature Healthcare LLC.....................C 440 232-1800
Bedford *(G-1305)*
State Farm Mutl Auto Insur Co ....A 614 775-2001
New Albany *(G-14875)*
Transamerica Premier Lf Insur ....E 614 488-5983
Columbus *(G-8773)*

INSURANCE CARRIERS: Hospital & Medical

Anthem Insurance Companies Inc ....D 614 438-3542
Columbus *(G-6799)*
Aultman Hospital ....A 330 363-6262
Canton *(G-2204)*
Centene Corporation.............................C 513 469-4500
Blue Ash *(G-1523)*
Clinical Research Center.......................D 513 636-4412
Cincinnati *(G-3308)*
Close To Home Health Care Ctr............E 614 932-9013
Dublin *(G-10176)*
Community Insurance Company ....E 859 282-7888
Cincinnati *(G-3340)*
Custom Design Benefits Inc ....E 513 598-2929
Cincinnati *(G-3391)*

Deaconess Associations Inc ....B 513 559-2100
Cincinnati *(G-3409)*
Ebso Inc ....E 419 423-3823
Findlay *(G-10898)*
Ebso Inc ....E 440 262-1133
Cleveland *(G-5464)*
Firelands Regional Health Sys ....C 419 626-7400
Sandusky *(G-16605)*
Healthspan Integrated Care ....D 216 362-2000
Cleveland *(G-5675)*
Healthspan Integrated Care ....E 216 524-7377
Cleveland *(G-5676)*
Healthspan Integrated Care ....E 216 621-5600
Cleveland *(G-5677)*
Healthspan Integrated Care ....E 330 767-3436
Brewster *(G-1810)*
Healthspan Integrated Care ....E 330 486-2800
Twinsburg *(G-18278)*
Healthspan Integrated Care ....E 330 877-4018
Hartville *(G-11689)*
Healthspan Integrated Care ....E 330 334-1549
Wadsworth *(G-18597)*
Healthspan Integrated Care ....E 216 362-2277
Lakewood *(G-12346)*
J P Farley Corporation ....E 440 250-4300
Westlake *(G-19360)*
Medical Mutual of Ohio..........................B 419 473-7100
Toledo *(G-17902)*
Metrohealth System ....E 216 778-3867
Cleveland *(G-5971)*
Miami Valley Hospitalist Group ....D 937 208-8394
Dayton *(G-5175)*
Molina Healthcare Inc ....A 800 642-4168
Columbus *(G-8096)*

INSURANCE CARRIERS: Life

21st Century Financial Inc ....E 330 668-9065
Akron *(G-9)*
Allstate Insurance Company..................E 330 650-2917
Hudson *(G-11963)*
Alpha Investment Partnership ....D 513 621-1826
Cincinnati *(G-2931)*
American Financial Group Inc ....C 513 579-2121
Cincinnati *(G-2943)*
American Security Insurance Co...........E 937 327-7700
Springfield *(G-16995)*
Ameritas Life Insurance Corp...............E 513 595-2334
Cincinnati *(G-2953)*
Bankers Life & Casualty Co ....E 614 987-0590
Columbus *(G-6801)*
Cigna Corporation ....C 216 642-1700
Independence *(G-12058)*
Cincinnati Life Insurance Co ....A 513 870-2000
Fairfield *(G-10713)*
Colonial Lf Accident Insur Co...............B 614 793-8622
Dublin *(G-10180)*
Columbus Financial Gr ....E 614 785-5100
Columbus *(G-6809)*
Family Heritg Lf Insur Co Amer ....E 440 922-5200
Broadview Heights *(G-1832)*
Guardian Life Insur Co of Amer............E 513 579-1114
Cincinnati *(G-3660)*
Howard Hanna Smythe Cramer ....D 330 725-4137
Medina *(G-13952)*
J P Farley Corporation ....E 440 250-4300
Westlake *(G-19360)*
Kelley Companies..................................D 330 668-6100
Copley *(G-8967)*
Lafayette Life Insurance Co ....C 800 443-8793
Cincinnati *(G-3907)*
Loyal American Life Insur Co ....C 800 633-6752
Cincinnati *(G-3949)*
Massachusetts Mutl Lf Insur Co...........E 513 579-8555
Cincinnati *(G-3977)*
Massachusetts Mutl Lf Insur Co...........E 216 592-7359
Cleveland *(G-5922)*
Motorists Life Insurance Co...................E 614 225-8211
Columbus *(G-8106)*
Nationwide Financial Svcs Inc..............C 614 249-7111
Columbus *(G-8155)*
Nationwide General Insur Co.................D 614 249-7111
Columbus *(G-8156)*
Northwestern Mutl Lf Insur Co ....E 614 221-5287
Columbus *(G-8209)*
Ohio Pia Service Corporation ....E 614 552-8000
Gahanna *(G-11139)*
Penn Mutual Life Insurance Co ....E 330 668-9065
Akron *(G-374)*
State Farm Mutl Auto Insur Co ....A 614 775-2001
New Albany *(G-14875)*

Summa Insurance Company Inc ....B 800 996-8411
Akron *(G-453)*
Transamerica Premier Lf Insur ....E 216 524-1436
Independence *(G-12133)*
Ulysses Caremark Holding Corp ....C 440 542-4214
Solon *(G-16910)*
UNUM Life Insurance Co Amer ....E 614 807-2500
Columbus *(G-8821)*
Voya Financial Inc.................................E 614 431-5000
Columbus *(G-8863)*
Western & Southern Lf Insur Co ....E 614 277-4800
Grove City *(G-11486)*
Western & Southern Lf Insur Co ....E 330 792-6818
Youngstown *(G-20242)*
Western & Southern Lf Insur Co ....E 937 435-1964
Miamisburg *(G-14237)*
Western & Southern Lf Insur Co ....A 513 629-1800
Cincinnati *(G-4786)*
Western & Southern Lf Insur Co ....E 234 380-4525
Hudson *(G-12013)*

INSURANCE CARRIERS: Pet, Health

Hartville Group Inc ....E 330 484-8166
Akron *(G-252)*
Ohio Farmers Insurance Company ....C 330 484-5660
Canton *(G-2425)*

INSURANCE CARRIERS: Property & Casualty

Affiliated FM Insurance Co.....................E 216 362-4820
North Olmsted *(G-15276)*
American Empire Surplus Lines ....E 513 369-3000
Cincinnati *(G-2939)*
American Financial Group Inc ....C 513 579-2121
Cincinnati *(G-2943)*
American Modern Home Insur Co ....D 513 943-7100
Amelia *(G-566)*
American Select Insurance Co...............A 330 887-0101
Westfield Center *(G-19307)*
American Western Home Insur Co ....B 513 943-7100
Amelia *(G-569)*
Central Mutual Insurance Co ....B 419 238-1010
Van Wert *(G-18474)*
Factory Mutual Insurance Co.................D 513 742-9516
Cincinnati *(G-3527)*
Foremost Insurance Company ....D 216 674-7000
Independence *(G-12075)*
Grange Mutual Casualty Company ....E 513 671-3722
Cincinnati *(G-3633)*
Great American Insurance Co ....D 513 603-2570
Fairfield *(G-10731)*
Home and Farm Insurance Co ....D 937 778-5000
Piqua *(G-16010)*
James B Oswald Company ....E 330 723-3637
Medina *(G-13959)*
Lancer Insurance Company ....E 440 473-1634
Cleveland *(G-5854)*
Liberty Mutual Insurance Co..................D 614 864-4100
Gahanna *(G-11131)*
Liberty Mutual Insurance Co..................D 513 984-0550
Fairfield *(G-10747)*
Motorists Mutual Insurance Co ....E 330 896-9311
Uniontown *(G-18379)*
National Continental Insur Co ....B 631 320-2405
Cleveland *(G-6041)*
National Interstate Corp ....D 330 659-8900
Richfield *(G-16363)*
National Interstate Insur Co ....D 330 659-8900
Richfield *(G-16364)*
Nationwide General Insur Co.................D 614 249-7111
Columbus *(G-8156)*
Ohio Farmers Insurance Company ....A 800 243-0210
Westfield Center *(G-19308)*
Ohio National Life Insur Co....................D 513 794-6100
Montgomery *(G-14601)*
Progressive Advanced Insur Co.............C 440 461-5000
Cleveland *(G-6242)*
Progressive Casualty Insur Co..............E 440 683-8164
Cleveland *(G-6243)*
Progressive Choice Insur Co ....B 440 461-5000
Cleveland *(G-6245)*
Progressive Freedom Insur Co...............C 440 461-5000
Cleveland *(G-6249)*
Progressive Max Insurance Co ....E 330 533-8733
Youngstown *(G-20165)*
Progressive Northwestern Insur ....E 440 461-5000
Cleveland *(G-6251)*
Progressive Paloverde Insur Co ....C 440 461-5000
Cleveland *(G-6252)*

S
E
R
V
I
C
E
S

Progressive Rsc Inc.................................C....... 440 461-5000
Cleveland (G-6255)

Progressive Universal Insur Co..............C....... 440 461-5000
Cleveland (G-6257)

State Auto Financial Corp ....D....... 614 464-5000
Columbus (G-8691)

Wayne Mutual Insurance Co ....E....... 330 345-8100
Wooster (G-19778)

Zurich American Insurance Co.................E....... 216 328-9400
Independence (G-12143)

INSURANCE CARRIERS: Title

A R E A Title Agency Inc ....E....... 419 242-5485
Toledo (G-17576)

Barristers of Ohio LLC ....D....... 330 898-5600
Warren (G-18678)

Chicago Title Insurance Co ....E....... 216 241-6045
Cleveland (G-5175)

First Amrcn Cash Advnce SC LLC ....D....... 330 644-9144
Akron (G-219)

Howard Hanna Smythe Cramer ....D....... 330 725-4137
Medina (G-13952)

Louisvlle Title Agcy For NW OH ....D....... 419 248-4611
Toledo (G-17862)

Mortgage Information Services ....D....... 216 514-7480
Cleveland (G-6012)

Northwest Hts Title Agcy LLC ....E....... 614 451-6313
Columbus (G-8206)

Northwest Ttl Agy of OH MI In ....D....... 419 241-8195
Toledo (G-17951)

Omega Title Agency LLC ....D....... 330 436-0600
Stow (G-17221)

Service Center Title Agency ....E....... 937 312-3080
Dayton (G-9761)

Southern Title of Ohio Ltd ....E....... 419 525-4600
Mansfield (G-13244)

Sterling Land Title Agency ....E....... 513 755-3700
West Chester (G-19013)

Stewart Advnced Land Title Ltd ....E....... 513 753-2800
Cincinnati (G-2870)

INSURANCE CARRIERS: Worker's Compensation

Amtrust North America Inc ....C....... 216 328-6100
Cleveland (G-4975)

Broadspire Services Inc ....E....... 614 436-8990
Columbus (G-7077)

Liberty Mutual Insurance Co....................E....... 614 855-6193
Westerville (G-19183)

Occupational Health Link ....E....... 614 885-0039
Columbus (G-8224)

Ohio Casualty Insurance Co ....A....... 800 843-6446
Fairfield (G-10763)

Seven Hills Fireman Assn ....E....... 216 524-3321
Seven Hills (G-16681)

Workers Compensation Ohio Bur ....A....... 800 644-6292
Columbus (G-8917)

INSURANCE CLAIM ADJUSTERS, NOT EMPLOYED BY INSURANCE COMPANY

Insurance Claims MGT Inc ....C....... 937 328-4300
Springfield (G-17053)

Ohic Insurance Company.........................D....... 614 221-7777
Columbus (G-8227)

Sedgwick CMS Holdings Inc ....A....... 614 658-0900
Hilliard (G-11815)

Summit Claim Services LLC ....D....... 330 706-9898
New Franklin (G-14915)

Supreme Court of Ohio ....E....... 614 387-9800
Columbus (G-8718)

York Risk Services Group Inc ....E....... 440 863-2500
Cleveland (G-6700)

INSURANCE CLAIM PROCESSING, EXC MEDICAL

Amtrust North America Inc ....C....... 216 328-6100
Cleveland (G-4975)

Envision Phrm Svcs LLC ....B....... 330 405-8080
Twinsburg (G-18263)

Grange Mutual Casualty Company ....E....... 614 337-4400
Cleveland (G-5622)

Harrington Health Services Inc...............C....... 614 212-7000
Westerville (G-19259)

Infoquest Information Services ....E....... 614 761-3003
Columbus (G-7815)

Safelite Group Inc ....A....... 614 210-9000
Columbus (G-8576)

INSURANCE EDUCATION SVCS

Keybank National Association ....C....... 216 813-0000
Cleveland (G-5829)

INSURANCE INFORMATION & CONSULTING SVCS

Business Admnstrators Cons Inc ....E....... 614 863-8780
Reynoldsburg (G-16287)

Chapman & Chapman Inc ....E....... 440 934-4102
Avon (G-874)

Gallagher Benefit Services Inc ....E....... 216 623-2600
Cleveland (G-5590)

Pasco Inc ....B....... 330 650-0613
Hudson (G-12001)

Paul Moss LLC ....E....... 216 765-1580
Solon (G-16881)

INSURANCE RESEARCH SVCS

Strategic Research Group Inc ....E....... 614 220-8860
Columbus (G-8704)

Ues Metals Group ....E....... 937 255-9340
Beavercreek (G-1191)

INSURANCE: Agents, Brokers & Service

Ability Network Inc...................................E....... 513 943-8888
Cincinnati (G-2840)

Advanced Group Corp ....E....... 216 431-8800
Cleveland (G-4904)

AFLAC Incorporated................................C....... 614 410-1696
Columbus (G-6882)

All America Insurance Company ....B....... 419 238-1010
Van Wert (G-18472)

Allstate Insurance Company ....D....... 330 656-6000
Hudson (G-11964)

Alternative Care Mgt Systems ....E....... 614 761-0035
Dublin (G-10127)

American Gen Lf Insur Co Del ....E....... 513 762-7807
Cincinnati (G-2944)

American Title of Ohio LLC ....E....... 303 868-2250
Cleveland (G-4968)

Anthem Midwest Inc ....A....... 614 433-8350
Mason (G-13541)

Brown & Brown of Ohio LLC ....C....... 419 874-1974
Perrysburg (G-15842)

Careworks of Ohio Inc.............................B....... 614 792-1085
Dublin (G-10161)

Cincinnati Casualty Company ....D....... 513 870-2000
Fairfield (G-10709)

Cincinnati Equitable Insur Co ....E....... 440 349-2210
Solon (G-16835)

Columbus Life Insurance Co ....D....... 513 361-6700
Cincinnati (G-3331)

Compmanagement Inc ....E....... 614 376-5300
Dublin (G-10187)

Corporate Health Benefits.......................E....... 740 348-1401
Newark (G-15027)

Corporate Plans Inc ....E....... 440 542-7800
Solon (G-16838)

Defense Info Systems Agcy ....C....... 614 692-4433
Columbus (G-7430)

Ebso Inc ....E....... 419 423-3823
Findlay (G-10898)

Employee Benefit Management...............E....... 614 766-5800
Dublin (G-10217)

Erie Insurance Exchange ....D....... 614 430-8530
Columbus (G-7528)

Farmers Financial Services ....E....... 937 424-0643
Beavercreek (G-1217)

Farmers Group Inc ....E....... 330 467-6575
Northfield (G-15378)

Farmers Group Inc ....E....... 614 766-6005
Columbus (G-7562)

Farmers Group Inc ....E....... 614 799-3200
Columbus (G-7563)

Farmers Group Inc ....E....... 216 750-4010
Independence (G-12073)

Farmers Insurance of Columbus ....B....... 614 799-3200
Columbus (G-7564)

Federal Insurance Company ....E....... 216 687-1700
Cleveland (G-5521)

Federal Insurance Company ....D....... 513 721-0601
Cincinnati (G-3538)

Financial Design Group Inc ....E....... 419 843-4737
Toledo (G-17736)

First Acceptance Corporation ....E....... 937 778-8888
Piqua (G-16004)

First Acceptance Corporation ....E....... 513 741-0811
Cincinnati (G-3553)

First Acceptance Corporation ....E....... 614 492-1446
Columbus (G-7581)

First Acceptance Corporation ....E....... 330 792-7181
Youngstown (G-20037)

First Acceptance Corporation ....E....... 614 853-3344
Columbus (G-7582)

First Defiance Financial Corp ....E....... 419 353-8611
Bowling Green (G-1731)

Geico General Insurance Co ....B....... 513 794-3426
Cincinnati (G-3607)

Grange Life Insurance Company ....E....... 800 445-3030
Columbus (G-7686)

Great American Advisors Inc ....E....... 513 357-3300
Cincinnati (G-3638)

Guardian Business Services ....E....... 614 416-6090
Columbus (G-7699)

Huntington Insurance Inc ....E....... 216 206-1787
Cleveland (G-5723)

Huntington Insurance Inc ....E....... 330 337-9933
Salem (G-16548)

International Healthcare Corp...................D....... 513 731-3338
Cincinnati (G-3779)

Leonard Insur Svcs Agcy Inc ....E....... 330 266-1904
Canton (G-2375)

Licking Memorial Hlth Systems...............A....... 220 564-4000
Newark (G-15056)

Luce Smith & Scott Inc ....E....... 440 746-1700
Brecksville (G-1788)

Masters Agency Inc ....E....... 330 805-5985
Wadsworth (G-18607)

Motorists Mutual Insurance Co ....E....... 937 435-5540
Columbus (G-8108)

Nationwide Corporation ....E....... 614 249-7111
Columbus (G-8152)

Nationwide Corporation ....B....... 614 277-5103
Grove City (G-11456)

Nationwide Mutual Insurance Co ....E....... 614 948-4153
Westerville (G-19189)

Nationwide Mutual Insurance Co ....E....... 614 430-3047
Lewis Center (G-12553)

Nationwide Rtrment Sltions Inc ....C....... 614 854-8300
Dublin (G-10287)

Northwestern Mutl Lf Insur Co ....D....... 513 366-3600
Cincinnati (G-4132)

Northwstern Ohio Admnistrators ....E....... 419 248-2401
Holland (G-11902)

Ohio Indemnity Company ....E....... 614 228-1601
Columbus (G-8269)

Old Rpblic Ttle Nthrn Ohio LLC...............B....... 216 524-5700
Independence (G-12106)

Progressive Casualty Insur Co................A....... 440 461-5000
Mayfield Village (G-13886)

Prudential Insur Co of Amer ....E....... 513 612-6400
Cincinnati (G-4302)

Prudential Insur Co of Amer ....E....... 330 896-7200
Uniontown (G-18383)

Prudential Insur Co of Amer ....E....... 440 684-4409
Cleveland (G-6264)

Prudential Insur Co of Amer ....E....... 419 893-6227
Maumee (G-13836)

Rod Lightning Mutual Insur Co ....B....... 330 262-9060
Wooster (G-19762)

Royalton Financial Group ....E....... 440 582-3020
Cleveland (G-6347)

Safe Auto Insurance Company ....B....... 614 231-0200
Columbus (G-8571)

Safe Auto Insurance Group Inc ....D....... 614 231-0200
Columbus (G-8572)

Sbm Business Services Inc ....E....... 330 396-7000
Akron (G-419)

Sirak-Moore Insurance Agcy Inc ....E....... 330 493-3211
Canton (G-2478)

Smart...C....... 216 228-9400
North Olmsted (G-15310)

State Automobile Mutl Insur Co ....A....... 833 724-3577
Columbus (G-8692)

The Sheakley Group Inc ....E....... 513 771-2277
Cincinnati (G-4596)

United Insurance Company Amer ....E....... 216 514-1904
Beachwood (G-1115)

United Ohio Insurance Company ....C....... 419 562-3011
Bucyrus (G-2004)

Utica National Insurance Group ....E....... 614 823-5300
Columbus (G-8838)

Valmark Financial Group LLC..................D....... 330 576-1234
Akron (G-483)

Voya Financial Inc ....E....... 614 431-5000
Columbus (G-8863)

Western & Southern Lf Insur Co ....E....... 419 524-1800
Ontario (G-15579)

Willis of Ohio Inc ....E 614 457-7000
Columbus *(G-8907)*

Workers Compensation Ohio Bur ....A 800 644-6292
Columbus *(G-8916)*

York Risk Services Group Inc ....C 866 391-9675
Dublin *(G-10380)*

INTEGRATED CIRCUITS, SEMICONDUCTOR NETWORKS, ETC

Leidos Inc ....D 937 431-2270
Beavercreek *(G-1164)*

INTERCOMMUNICATIONS SYSTEMS:
Electric

Quasonix Inc ....E 513 942-1287
West Chester *(G-18988)*

INTERIOR DECORATING SVCS

Flamos Enterprises Inc ....E 330 478-0009
Canton *(G-2315)*

Karlsberger Companies ....C 614 461-9500
Columbus *(G-7883)*

Pucher Paint Co Inc ....E 440 234-0991
Berea *(G-1435)*

INTERIOR DESIGN SVCS, NEC

Interbrand Design Forum LLC ....C 513 421-2210
Cincinnati *(G-3777)*

Interior Supply Cincinnati LLC ....E 614 424-6611
Columbus *(G-7835)*

Onyx Creative Inc ....D 216 223-3200
Cleveland *(G-6137)*

Rdl Architects Inc ....E 216 752-4300
Cleveland *(G-6288)*

Rite Rug Co ....E 614 478-3365
Columbus *(G-8533)*

River City Furniture LLC ....D 513 612-7303
West Chester *(G-18994)*

Vocon Design Inc ....D 216 588-0800
Cleveland *(G-6641)*

INTERIOR DESIGNING SVCS

Chute Gerdeman Inc ....D 614 469-1001
Columbus *(G-7198)*

CIP International Inc ....D 513 874-9925
West Chester *(G-18889)*

Collaborative Inc ....E 419 242-7405
Toledo *(G-17667)*

E & A Pedco Services Inc ....D 513 782-4920
Cincinnati *(G-3461)*

Jones Group Interiors Inc ....E 330 253-9180
Akron *(G-294)*

Michael Schuster Associates ....E 513 241-5666
Cincinnati *(G-4047)*

Ohio Design Centre ....D 216 831-1245
Beachwood *(G-1090)*

INTERMEDIATE CARE FACILITY

10 Wilmington Place ....D 937 253-1010
Dayton *(G-9193)*

A Provide Care Inc ....C 330 828-2278
Dalton *(G-9143)*

Alexson Services Inc ....B 513 874-0423
Fairfield *(G-10695)*

Algart Health Care Inc ....D 216 631-1550
Cleveland *(G-4929)*

Alpha Nursing Homes Inc ....D 740 345-9197
Newark *(G-15009)*

Alpha Nursing Homes Inc ....D 740 622-2074
Coshocton *(G-8997)*

Altercare Inc ....C 330 335-2555
Wadsworth *(G-18588)*

Altercare Nobles Pond Inc ....D 330 834-4800
Canton *(G-2182)*

Alternative Residences Two ....C 740 526-0514
Saint Clairsville *(G-16468)*

Alternative Residences Two ....E 330 453-0200
Canton *(G-2183)*

American Retirement Corp ....D 216 291-6140
Cleveland *(G-4965)*

Amherst Manor Nursing Home ....D 440 988-4415
Amherst *(G-581)*

Anchor Lodge Nursing Home Inc ....C 440 244-2019
Lorain *(G-12880)*

Anne Grady Corporation ....C 419 380-8985
Holland *(G-11872)*

Apostolic Christian Home Inc ....D 330 927-1010
Rittman *(G-16403)*

Arbors At Clide Asssted Living ....E 419 547-7746
Clyde *(G-6738)*

Arbors East LLC ....D 614 575-9003
Columbus *(G-6963)*

Arlington Care Ctr ....D 740 344-0303
Newark *(G-15011)*

Arlington Court Nursing ....C 614 545-5502
Upper Arlington *(G-18393)*

Baptist Home and Center ....C 513 662-5880
Cincinnati *(G-3018)*

Bel Air Care Center ....D 330 821-3939
Alliance *(G-518)*

Bittersweet Inc ....D 419 875-6986
Whitehouse *(G-19444)*

Blossom Hills Nursing Home ....C 440 635-5567
Huntsburg *(G-12017)*

Bluesky Healthcare Inc ....C 330 345-9050
Wooster *(G-19692)*

Braeview Manor Inc ....C 216 486-9300
Cleveland *(G-5073)*

Brethren Care Inc ....C 419 289-0803
Ashland *(G-659)*

Brewster Parke Inc ....D 330 767-4179
Brewster *(G-1809)*

Brook Willow Chrstn Cmmunities ....D 614 885-3300
Columbus *(G-7079)*

Brookville Enterprises Inc ....B 937 833-2133
Brookville *(G-1911)*

Butler County of Ohio ....C 513 887-3728
Fairfield Township *(G-10803)*

Butler County Board of Develop ....C 513 867-5913
Fairfield *(G-10703)*

C R G Health Care Systems ....E 330 498-8107
Niles *(G-15148)*

Camargo Manor Inc ....D 513 605-3000
Cincinnati *(G-3108)*

Canton Assisted Living ....C 330 492-7131
Canton *(G-2227)*

Caprice Health Care Inc ....C 330 965-9200
North Lima *(G-15267)*

Cardinal Retirement Village ....E 330 928-7888
Cuyahoga Falls *(G-9076)*

Carington Health Systems ....C 937 743-2754
Franklin *(G-11025)*

Carriage Crt Mrysvlle Ltd Prtn ....E 937 642-2202
Marysville *(G-13487)*

Carroll Golden Age Retreat ....E 330 627-4665
Carrollton *(G-2561)*

Carroll Health Care Center ....C 330 627-5501
Carrollton *(G-2562)*

Center Ridge Nursing Home Inc ....C 440 808-5500
North Ridgeville *(G-15324)*

Chelmsford Apartments Ltd ....E 419 389-0800
Toledo *(G-17649)*

Childs Investment Co ....C 330 837-2100
Massillon *(G-13669)*

Choices In Community Living ....C 937 898-3655
Dayton *(G-9298)*

Church of God Retirement Cmnty ....C 513 422-5600
Middletown *(G-14295)*

Columbus Area Integrated Healt ....D 614 252-0711
Columbus *(G-7257)*

Commons of Providence ....D 419 624-1171
Sandusky *(G-16590)*

Communicare Health Svcs Inc ....D 419 394-7611
Saint Marys *(G-16521)*

Concord Health Care Inc ....E 330 759-2357
Youngstown *(G-20009)*

Congregate Living of America ....E 937 393-6700
Hillsboro *(G-11834)*

Congregate Living of America ....D 513 899-2801
Morrow *(G-14716)*

Consulate Healthcare Inc ....E 419 865-1248
Maumee *(G-13775)*

Consulate Management Co LLC ....D 440 237-7966
Cleveland *(G-5340)*

Country Club Center Homes Inc ....D 330 343-6351
Dover *(G-10071)*

Country Club Center II Ltd ....C 740 397-2350
Mount Vernon *(G-14756)*

Country Club Retirement Center ....C 740 671-9330
Bellaire *(G-1333)*

County of Lorain ....E 440 282-3074
Lorain *(G-12900)*

County of Shelby ....C 937 492-6900
Sidney *(G-16771)*

County of Wood ....B 419 686-6951
Portage *(G-16122)*

Covenant Care Ohio Inc ....D 937 878-7046
Fairborn *(G-10666)*

Cridersville Health Care Ctr ....E 419 645-4468
Cridersville *(G-9062)*

Crystal Care Centers Inc ....E 419 747-2666
Mansfield *(G-13161)*

Crystalwood Inc ....D 513 605-1000
Cincinnati *(G-3383)*

Dayspring Health Care Center ....C 937 864-5800
Fairborn *(G-10670)*

Deaconess Long Term Care of MI ....A 513 487-3600
Cincinnati *(G-3412)*

Dearth Management Company ....C 419 253-0144
Marengo *(G-13302)*

Develpmntal Dsblties Ohio Dept ....A 740 446-1642
Gallipolis *(G-11190)*

Develpmntal Dsblties Ohio Dept ....B 614 272-0509
Columbus *(G-7441)*

Dover Nursing Center ....D 330 364-4436
Dover *(G-10075)*

Doylestown Health Care Center ....C 330 658-1533
Doylestown *(G-10112)*

Eagle Creek Hlthcare Group Inc ....E 937 544-5531
West Union *(G-19136)*

Earley & Ross Ltd ....D 740 634-3301
Sabina *(G-16467)*

East Galbraith Nursing Home ....C 513 984-5220
Cincinnati *(G-3472)*

Eastern Star Hm of Cyhoga Cnty ....C 216 761-0170
Cleveland *(G-5459)*

Ebenezer Road Corp ....C 513 941-0099
Cincinnati *(G-3480)*

Echoing Hills Village Inc ....D 440 989-1400
Lorain *(G-12902)*

Edgewood Manor of Wellston ....E 740 384-5611
Wellston *(G-18849)*

Elms Retirement Village Inc ....D 440 647-2414
Wellington *(G-18840)*

Fairmont Nursing Home Inc ....D 440 338-8220
Newbury *(G-15120)*

Falls Village Retirement Cmnty ....D 330 945-9797
Cuyahoga Falls *(G-9094)*

Fisher-Titus Medical Center ....E 419 668-4228
Norwalk *(G-15437)*

Fisher-Titus Medical Center ....A 419 668-8101
Norwalk *(G-15438)*

Flower Hospital ....B 419 824-1000
Sylvania *(G-17425)*

Fort Austin Ltd Partnership ....C 440 892-4200
Cleveland *(G-5564)*

Foundations Hlth Solutions Inc ....D 440 793-0200
North Olmsted *(G-15289)*

Franciscan At St Leonard ....B 937 433-0480
Dayton *(G-9448)*

Friends of Good Shepherd Manor ....D 740 289-2861
Lucasville *(G-13049)*

Furney Group Home ....E 419 389-0152
Toledo *(G-17750)*

Garbry Ridge Assisted Living ....E 937 778-9385
Piqua *(G-16005)*

Gaslite Villa Convalescent Ctr ....D 330 494-4500
Canal Fulton *(G-2095)*

Gateway Health Care Center ....C 216 486-4949
Cleveland *(G-5595)*

Gaymont Nursing Homes Inc ....D 419 668-8258
Norwalk *(G-15439)*

Generation Health & Rehab Cntr ....D 740 344-9465
Newark *(G-15035)*

Gillette Nursing Home Inc ....D 330 372-1960
Warren *(G-18710)*

Golden Living LLC ....D 419 227-2154
Lima *(G-12644)*

Golden Living LLC ....C 614 861-6666
Columbus *(G-7678)*

Golden Living LLC ....C 330 297-5781
Ravenna *(G-16244)*

Golden Living LLC ....D 330 335-1558
Wadsworth *(G-18596)*

Good Shepherd Home ....C 419 937-1801
Fostoria *(G-11003)*

Greens of Lyndhurst The Inc ....C 440 460-1000
Cleveland *(G-5643)*

Guardian Elde ....D 419 225-9040
Lima *(G-12649)*

Guernsey Health Systems ....A 740 439-3561
Cambridge *(G-2073)*

Harborside Sylvania LLC ....D 419 882-1875
Sylvania *(G-17429)*

Hattie Larlham Center For ....C 330 274-2272
Mantua *(G-13267)*

SERVICES

Healthcare Facility MGT LLC ....C 330 836-7953
Akron (G-258)

Healthcare Management Cons ....E 419 363-2193
Rockford (G-16416)

Heinzerling Foundation ....C 614 272-8888
Columbus (G-7735)

Hempstead Manor ....C 740 354-8150
Portsmouth (G-16145)

Hennis Nursing Home ....C 330 364-8849
Dover (G-10081)

Heritage Park Rehabilita ....E 937 437-2311
New Paris (G-14943)

Hill Side Plaza ....D 216 486-6300
Cleveland (G-5689)

Home Echo Club Inc ....C 614 864-1718
Pickerington (G-15958)

Horn Nursing and Rehab Center ....D 330 262-2951
Wooster (G-19730)

Humility House ....D 330 505-0144
Youngstown (G-20070)

Indian Hlls Hlthcare Group Inc ....A 216 486-8880
Euclid (G-10644)

Inn At Marietta Ltd ....D 740 373-9600
Marietta (G-13338)

Isabelle Ridgway Care Ctr Inc ....C 614 252-4931
Columbus (G-7846)

Jennings Eliza Home Inc ....C 216 226-0282
Cleveland (G-5788)

Jennings Ctr For Older Adults ....B 216 581-2900
Cleveland (G-5789)

Judson ....D 216 791-2004
Cleveland (G-5808)

Kendal At Oberlin ....C 440 775-0094
Oberlin (G-15506)

Kindred Healthcare Oper Inc ....D 740 545-6355
West Lafayette (G-19115)

Kindred Healthcare Operating ....D 419 877-5338
Whitehouse (G-19449)

Kingston Healthcare Company ....D 419 824-4200
Sylvania (G-17435)

Lakeside Manor Inc ....E 330 549-2545
North Lima (G-15271)

Laurels of Hillsboro ....D 937 393-1925
Hillsboro (G-11849)

Levering Management Inc ....D 740 369-6400
Delaware (G-9995)

Lexington Court Care Center ....D 419 884-2000
Mansfield (G-13199)

Liberty Nursing Center ....E 937 836-5143
Englewood (G-10593)

Liberty Nursing Center of Thre ....C 513 941-0787
Cincinnati (G-3925)

Liberty Nursing of Willard ....D 419 935-0148
Willard (G-19483)

Liberty Residence II ....E 330 334-3262
Wadsworth (G-18603)

Life Care Centers America Inc ....C 330 483-3131
Valley City (G-18464)

Lifeservices Development Corp ....E 440 257-3866
Mentor (G-14077)

Light of Hearts Villa ....D 440 232-1991
Cleveland (G-5869)

Lincoln Park Associates II LP ....C 937 297-4300
Dayton (G-9568)

Longmeadow Care Center Inc ....C 330 297-5781
Ravenna (G-16249)

Luther Home of Mercy ....B 419 836-3918
Williston (G-19500)

Lutheran Home ....B 440 871-0090
Cleveland (G-5889)

Lutheran Village At Wolf Creek ....C 419 861-2233
Holland (G-11893)

Lynnhaven V LLC ....D 440 272-5600
Windsor (G-19665)

Main Street Terrace Care Ctr ....D 740 653-8767
Lancaster (G-12414)

Manorcare of Willoughby Inc ....C 419 252-5500
Toledo (G-17893)

Mansfield Memorial Homes LLC ....C 419 774-5100
Mansfield (G-13209)

Maple Knoll Communities Inc ....A 513 782-2400
Cincinnati (G-3967)

McClellan Management Inc ....C 419 855-7755
Genoa (G-11258)

McV Health Care Facilities ....C 513 398-1486
Mason (G-13617)

Mennonite Memorial Home ....B 419 358-1015
Bluffton (G-1693)

Mill Manor Nursing Home Inc ....E 440 967-6614
Vermilion (G-18558)

Mill Run Care Center LLC ....D 614 527-3000
Hilliard (G-11798)

Mount Aloysius Corp ....C 740 342-3343
New Lexington (G-14921)

Muskingum County Ohio ....D 740 454-1911
Zanesville (G-20336)

New Dawn Health Care Inc ....C 330 343-5521
Dover (G-10090)

New Hope & Horizons ....E 513 761-7999
Cincinnati (G-4107)

North Hills Management Company ......D 740 450-9999
Zanesville (G-20346)

Northpoint Senior Services LLC ....C 740 373-3597
Marietta (G-13363)

Northpoint Senior Services LLC ....D 513 248-1655
Milford (G-14414)

Norwood Health Care Center LLC ....D 513 351-0153
Cincinnati (G-4135)

Oak Health Care Investors ....D 740 397-3200
Mount Vernon (G-14784)

October Enterprises Inc ....C 937 456-9535
Eaton (G-10456)

Ohio Eastern Star Home ....C 740 397-1706
Mount Vernon (G-14785)

Ohio Living ....C 513 681-4230
Cincinnati (G-4156)

Ohio Living ....B 614 224-1651
Columbus (G-8271)

Ohio Presbt Retirement Svcs ....B 330 746-2944
Youngstown (G-20147)

Ohio Presbt Retirement Svcs ....C 513 539-7391
Monroe (G-14579)

Ohio Presbt Retirement Svcs ....B 937 498-2391
Sidney (G-16789)

Ohio Valley Manor Inc ....C 937 392-4318
Ripley (G-16401)

Olmsted Manor Nursing Home ....C 440 250-4080
North Olmsted (G-15302)

Orchard Villa Inc ....C 419 697-4100
Oregon (G-15603)

Orion Care Services LLC ....C 216 752-3600
Cleveland (G-6144)

Otterbein Portage Valley Inc ....C 888 749-4950
Pemberville (G-15806)

Otterbein Snior Lfstyle Chices ....B 513 933-5400
Lebanon (G-12492)

Park Creek Rtirement Cmnty Inc ....E 440 842-5100
Cleveland (G-6164)

Parkview Manor Inc ....D 937 296-1550
Englewood (G-10595)

Parma Care Center Inc ....C 216 661-6800
Cleveland (G-6175)

Personacare of Ohio Inc ....C 440 357-1311
Painesville (G-15733)

Pickaway Manor Inc ....C 740 474-5400
Circleville (G-4844)

Pleasant Lake Nursing Home ....B 440 842-2273
Cleveland (G-6221)

Rae-Ann Holdings Inc ....D 440 871-0500
Westlake (G-19397)

Raeann Inc ....D 440 466-5733
Geneva (G-11245)

Renaissance House Inc ....D 419 626-1110
Sandusky (G-16634)

Rescare Ohio Inc ....E 513 724-1177
Williamsburg (G-19496)

Residence of Chardon ....D 440 286-2277
Chardon (G-2711)

Rest Haven Nursing Home Inc ....C 937 548-1138
Greenville (G-11392)

Ridge Pleasant Valley Inc ....C 440 845-0200
Cleveland (G-6325)

Ridgewood At Friendship Vlg ....E 614 890-8285
Columbus (G-8530)

Rivers Bend Health Care LLC ....D 740 894-3476
South Point (G-16945)

Roman Cthlic Docese Youngstown ......C 330 875-5562
Louisville (G-12973)

Rose Mary Johanna Grassell ....C 216 481-4823
Cleveland (G-6340)

Royal Manor Health Care Inc ....E 216 752-3600
Cleveland (G-6345)

Saint Johns Villa ....C 330 627-4662
Carrollton (G-2576)

Salutary Providers Inc ....C 440 964-8446
Ashtabula (G-753)

Samaritan Care Center & Villa ....C 330 725-4123
Medina (G-13998)

Sarah Moore Hlth Care Ctr Inc ....D 740 362-9641
Delaware (G-10005)

Sateri Home Inc ....D 330 758-8106
Youngstown (G-20204)

Senior Care Inc ....D 330 721-2000
Medina (G-14000)

Sensi Care 3 ....E 440 323-6310
Elyria (G-10562)

Sisters of Little ....C 216 464-1222
Warrensville Heights (G-18780)

Sisters of Little ....C 513 281-8001
Cincinnati (G-4486)

Society Handicapped Citz Medin ....E 330 722-1900
Seville (G-16689)

Sociey For Handicapped Citizen ....C 330 725-7041
Seville (G-16690)

Spring Meadow Extended Care Ce ....D 419 866-6124
Holland (G-11916)

Spring Meadow Extended Care Ce ....E 419 866-6124
Mansfield (G-13246)

St Augustine Corporation ....B 216 939-7600
Lakewood (G-12363)

Stratford Commons Inc ....C 440 914-0900
Solon (G-16902)

Summit Acres Inc ....C 740 732-2364
Caldwell (G-2044)

Summit Facility Operations LLC ....D 330 633-0555
Tallmadge (G-17490)

Sunbridge Healthcare LLC ....D 740 342-5161
New Lexington (G-14929)

Sunset House Inc ....C 419 536-4645
Toledo (G-18055)

Sunshine Communities ....B 419 865-0251
Maumee (G-13857)

Swanton Hlth Care Rtrement Ctr ....E 419 825-1145
Swanton (G-17407)

The Maria-Joseph Center ....B 937 278-2692
Dayton (G-8914)

The Villa At Lake MGT Co ....D 440 599-1999
Conneaut (G-8960)

Twilight Gardens Healthcare ....E 419 668-2086
Norwalk (G-15458)

Twin Maples Nursing Home ....E 740 596-5955
Mc Arthur (G-13891)

Twin Pines Retreat Care Center ....E 330 688-5553
Stow (G-17237)

United Cerebral Palsy ....D 216 381-9993
Cleveland (G-6569)

United Church Homes Inc ....C 937 878-0262
Fairborn (G-10684)

United Church Homes Inc ....D 740 286-7551
Jackson (G-12181)

United Church Homes Inc ....C 513 922-1440
Cincinnati (G-4677)

United Church Homes Inc ....C 937 426-8481
Beavercreek (G-1239)

United Church Homes Inc ....C 419 294-4973
Upper Sandusky (G-18414)

University Hospitals Health ....E 440 285-4040
Chardon (G-2722)

University Manor Hlth Care Ctr ....C 216 721-1400
Cleveland (G-6599)

Vancare Inc ....C 937 898-4202
Vandalia (G-18549)

Vienna Enterprises Inc ....E 937 568-4524
South Vienna (G-16949)

Volunters Amer Care Facilities ....C 419 225-9040
Lima (G-12774)

Walnut Hills Inc ....C 330 852-2457
Walnut Creek (G-18633)

Washington Manor Inc ....E 937 433-3441
Dayton (G-9867)

Weber Health Care Center Inc ....C 440 647-2088
Wellington (G-18845)

Wedgewood Estates ....E 419 756-7400
Mansfield (G-13262)

Wellington Place LLC ....D 440 734-9933
North Olmsted (G-15316)

Wesley Ridge Inc ....C 614 759-0023
Reynoldsburg (G-16337)

West Liberty Care Center Inc ....C 937 465-5065
West Liberty (G-19122)

Western Rsrve Msonic Cmnty Inc ....C 330 721-3000
Medina (G-14014)

Wexner Heritage Village ....B 614 231-4900
Columbus (G-8894)

Willow Brook Chrstn Cmmunities ....C 740 369-0048
Delaware (G-10016)

Windsor House Inc ....C 330 549-9259
Columbiana (G-6796)

Windsor Medical Center Inc ....D 330 499-8300
Canton (G-2536)

Woodside Village Care Center ....D 419 947-2015
  Mount Gilead *(G-14736)*
Zandex Inc ....E 740 695-3281
  Saint Clairsville *(G-16512)*
Zandex Inc ....E 740 454-1400
  Zanesville *(G-20373)*
Zandex Inc ....C 740 872-0809
  New Concord *(G-14905)*
Zandex Inc ....C 740 454-9769
  Zanesville *(G-20375)*
Zandex Inc ....E 740 695-7233
  Saint Clairsville *(G-16513)*
Zandex Health Care Corporation ....C 740 452-4636
  Zanesville *(G-20377)*
Zandex Health Care Corporation ....C 740 454-9769
  Zanesville *(G-20378)*
Zandex Health Care Corporation ....E 740 454-1400
  Zanesville *(G-20379)*
Zandex Health Care Corporation ....D 740 454-1400
  Johnstown *(G-12206)*
Zandex Health Care Corporation ....C 740 454-1400
  New Concord *(G-14906)*
Zandex Health Care Corporation ....C 740 454-9747
  Zanesville *(G-20380)*

INTERMEDIATE INVESTMENT BANKS

Lancaster Pollard Mrtg Co LLC ....D 614 224-8800
  Columbus *(G-7947)*
N C B International Department ....D 216 488-7990
  Cleveland *(G-6033)*

INVENTORY COMPUTING SVCS

Accurate Inventory and C ....B 800 777-9414
  Columbus *(G-6863)*
Canton Inventory Service ....E 330 453-1633
  Canton *(G-2235)*
Merchant Data Service Inc ....C 937 847-6585
  Miamisburg *(G-14188)*
Rgis LLC ....D 216 447-1744
  Independence *(G-12114)*
Rgis LLC ....D 330 799-1566
  Youngstown *(G-20186)*
Rgis LLC ....D 248 651-2511
  Reynoldsburg *(G-16328)*
Rgis LLC ....D 330 896-9802
  Akron *(G-406)*
Rgis LLC ....C 513 772-5990
  Cincinnati *(G-4366)*

INVESTMENT ADVISORY SVCS

American Money Management Corp .....E 513 579-2592
  Cincinnati *(G-2946)*
Ameriprise Financial Svcs Inc ....E 330 494-9300
  Akron *(G-72)*
Bartlett & Co LLC ....D 513 621-4612
  Cincinnati *(G-3023)*
Centaurus Financial Inc ....D 419 756-9747
  Mansfield *(G-13149)*
Crestview Partners II Gp LP ....B 216 898-2400
  Brooklyn *(G-1860)*
Diamond Hill Capital MGT Inc ....E 614 255-3333
  Columbus *(G-7444)*
Diamond Hill Funds ....E 614 255-3333
  Columbus *(G-7445)*
Eubel Brady Suttman Asset Mgt ....E 937 291-1223
  Miamisburg *(G-14169)*
Financial Plnners of Cleveland ....E 440 473-1115
  Cleveland *(G-5526)*
Fort Wash Inv Advisors Inc ....D 513 361-7600
  Cincinnati *(G-3579)*
Fund Evaluation Group LLC ....E 513 977-4400
  Cincinnati *(G-3597)*
Hanson McClain Inc ....E 513 469-7500
  Cincinnati *(G-3680)*
Jpmorgan Inv Advisors Inc ....A 614 248-5800
  Columbus *(G-6820)*
Lancaster Pollard Mrtg Co LLC ....D 614 224-8800
  Columbus *(G-7947)*
Lincoln Fincl Advisors Corp ....E 216 765-7400
  Beachwood *(G-1074)*
MAI Capital Management LLC ....D 216 920-4800
  Cleveland *(G-5896)*
Oak Associates Ltd ....E 330 666-5263
  Akron *(G-354)*
Parkwood Corporation ....E 216 875-6500
  Cleveland *(G-6174)*
Red Capital Partners LLC ....D 614 857-1400
  Columbus *(G-8498)*

Roulston & Company Inc ....E 216 431-3000
  Cleveland *(G-6342)*
S&P Global Inc ....C 614 835-2444
  Groveport *(G-11536)*
S&P Global Inc ....C 330 482-9544
  Leetonia *(G-12519)*
Standard Retirement Svcs Inc ....C 440 808-2724
  Westlake *(G-19409)*
Stratos Wealth Partners Ltd ....D 440 519-2500
  Beachwood *(G-1108)*
Summit Financial Strategies ....E 614 885-1115
  Columbus *(G-8710)*
Westminster Financial Company ....E 937 898-5010
  Dayton *(G-9877)*

INVESTMENT BANKERS

Brown Gibbons Lang & Co LLC ....E 216 241-2800
  Cleveland *(G-5092)*
Cadle Company II Inc ....C 330 872-0918
  Newton Falls *(G-15136)*
Jpmorgan Chase Bank Nat Assn ....A 614 436-3055
  Columbus *(G-6818)*
Lancaster Pollard & Co LLC ....E 614 224-8800
  Columbus *(G-7946)*
R B C Apollo Equity Partners ....E 216 875-2626
  Cleveland *(G-6272)*
Riversidecompanycom ....E 216 344-1040
  Cleveland *(G-6330)*

INVESTMENT CLUBS

Rightway Investments LLC ....E 216 854-7697
  Twinsburg *(G-18312)*

INVESTMENT COUNSELORS

C H Dean Inc ....D 937 222-9531
  Beavercreek *(G-1136)*
Johnson Trust Co ....C 513 598-8859
  Cincinnati *(G-3830)*
Mc Cormack Advisors Intl ....E 216 522-1200
  Cincinnati *(G-5927)*
Meeder Asset Management Inc ....D 614 760-2112
  Dublin *(G-10277)*
Sena Weller Rohs Williams ....E 513 241-6443
  Cincinnati *(G-4451)*

INVESTMENT FIRM: General Brokerage

Cincinnati Financial Corp ....A 513 870-2000
  Fairfield *(G-10710)*
Haven Financial Enterprise ....E 800 265-2401
  Cleveland *(G-5667)*
Hbi Payments Ltd ....D 614 944-5788
  Columbus *(G-7721)*
Jdel Inc ....E 614 436-2418
  Columbus *(G-7856)*
Morgan Stanley & Co LLC ....E 614 228-0600
  Columbus *(G-8103)*
Red Capital Markets LLC ....C 614 857-1400
  Columbus *(G-8497)*
Stateco Financial Services ....C 614 464-5000
  Columbus *(G-8695)*
Western & Southern Lf Insur Co ....A 513 629-1800
  Cincinnati *(G-4786)*
Western Southern Mutl Holdg Co ....A 866 832-7719
  Cincinnati *(G-4791)*
Western Sthern Fincl Group Inc ....A 866 832-7719
  Cincinnati *(G-4792)*

INVESTMENT FUNDS, NEC

Rockbridge Capital LLC ....E 614 246-2400
  Columbus *(G-8544)*
Rockwood Equity Partners LLC ....E 216 342-1760
  Cleveland *(G-6337)*

INVESTMENT FUNDS: Open-Ended

James Advantage Funds ....E 937 426-7640
  Xenia *(G-19913)*
Stonehenge Fincl Holdings Inc ....D 614 246-2500
  Columbus *(G-8702)*

INVESTMENT OFFICES: Management, Closed-End

National Housing Tr Ltd Partnr ....E 614 451-9929
  Columbus *(G-8135)*

INVESTMENT OFFICES: Money Market Mutual

Jpmorgan High Yield Fund ....E 614 248-7017
  Columbus *(G-6819)*
Victory Capital Management Inc ....C 216 898-2400
  Brooklyn *(G-1862)*

INVESTMENT RESEARCH SVCS

Cleveland Research Company LLC ....E 216 649-7250
  Cleveland *(G-5284)*
Longbow Research LLC ....D 216 986-0700
  Independence *(G-12095)*

INVESTORS, NEC

Arthur Middleton Capital Holdn ....C 330 966-3033
  Canton *(G-2194)*
Camelot Realty Investments ....E 740 357-5291
  Lucasville *(G-13045)*
Capital Investment Group Inc ....E 513 241-5090
  Cincinnati *(G-3113)*
Ctd Investments LLC ....E 614 570-9949
  Columbus *(G-7403)*
K M Clemens DDS Inc ....E 419 228-4036
  Lima *(G-12668)*
McM Capital Partners ....B 216 514-1840
  Beachwood *(G-1077)*
Natl City Coml Capitol LLC ....E 513 455-9746
  Cincinnati *(G-4098)*
Newmark & Company RE Inc ....E 216 453-3000
  Cleveland *(G-6065)*
Oakdale Estates II Inv LLC ....E 216 520-1250
  West Union *(G-19137)*
Rjb Acquisitions LLC ....E 513 314-2711
  Cincinnati *(G-4382)*
Shancliff Investments Ltd ....E 330 883-5560
  West Chester *(G-19003)*
Shields Capital Corporation ....C 216 767-1340
  Beachwood *(G-1104)*
Styx Acquisition LLC ....A 330 264-9900
  Wooster *(G-19770)*
Superior Street Partners LLC ....D 216 862-0058
  Shaker Heights *(G-16716)*
The Huntington Investment Co ....E 513 351-2555
  Cincinnati *(G-4593)*
Wings Investors Company Ltd ....E 513 241-5800
  Cincinnati *(G-4799)*
Ws One Investment Usa LLC ....D 855 895-3728
  Aurora *(G-852)*

INVESTORS: Real Estate, Exc Property Operators

Blackbird Capital Group LLC ....C 513 762-7890
  Cincinnati *(G-3055)*
Ibi Group Engrg Svcs USA Inc ....D 614 818-4900
  Westerville *(G-19263)*
Jpmorgan Chase Bank Nat Assn ....A 614 436-3055
  Columbus *(G-6818)*
Klingbeil Capital MGT LLC ....D 614 396-4919
  Worthington *(G-19818)*

IRON ORE MINING

Cleveland-Cliffs Inc ....D 216 694-5700
  Cleveland *(G-5299)*
Cliffs Minnesota Minerals Co ....A 216 694-5700
  Cleveland *(G-5303)*
The Cleveland-Cliffs Iron Co ....C 216 694-5700
  Cleveland *(G-6520)*
Tilden Mining Company LC ....A 216 694-5700
  Cleveland *(G-6530)*
Wabush Mines Cliffs Mining Co ....A 216 694-5700
  Cleveland *(G-6647)*

IRON ORES

International Steel Group ....C 330 841-2800
  Warren *(G-18715)*

IRRIGATION EQPT WHOLESALERS

Wolf Creek Company Inc ....D 937 854-2694
  Dayton *(G-9884)*

IRRIGATION SYSTEMS, NEC Water Distribution Or Sply Systems

City of Dayton ....D 937 333-7138
  Dayton *(G-9307)*

SERVICES

JANITORIAL & CUSTODIAL SVCS

AAA Standard Services Inc ....D 419 535-0274
  Toledo (G-17578)
ABM Janitorial Services Inc ....C 216 861-1199
  Cleveland (G-4894)
ABM Janitorial Services Inc ....C 513 731-1418
  Cincinnati (G-2899)
Absolute Cleaning Services ....D 440 542-1742
  Solon (G-16813)
Academic Support Services LLC ....E 740 274-6138
  Columbus (G-6857)
Access Cleaning Service Inc ....E 937 276-2605
  Dayton (G-9204)
Aetna Building Maintenance Inc ....B 614 476-1818
  Columbus (G-6881)
Aetna Building Maintenance Inc ....C 866 238-6201
  Dayton (G-9211)
All Pro Cleaning Services Inc ....D 440 519-0055
  Solon (G-16819)
Alpha & Omega Bldg Svcs Inc ....E 513 429-5082
  Blue Ash (G-1502)
Alpha & Omega Bldg Svcs Inc ....E 937 298-2125
  Dayton (G-9219)
American Maintenance Svcs Inc ....E 330 744-3400
  Youngstown (G-19954)
Anchor Cleaning Contractors ....E 216 961-7343
  Cleveland (G-4977)
Apex Environmental Svcs LLC ....D 513 772-2739
  Cincinnati (G-2973)
Aramark Facility Services LLC ....E 216 687-5000
  Cleveland (G-4998)
Ashland Cleaning LLC ....E 419 281-1747
  Ashland (G-648)
Basol Maintenance Service Inc ....D 419 422-0946
  Findlay (G-10867)
Bkg Services Inc ....E 614 476-1800
  Columbus (G-7043)
Buckeye Commercial Cleaning ....E 614 866-4700
  Pickerington (G-15949)
Cardinal Maintenance & Svc Co ....C 330 252-0282
  Akron (G-118)
Clean All Services Inc ....C 937 498-4146
  Sidney (G-16766)
Clean Break Inc ....E 330 638-5648
  Warren (G-18684)
Clean Care Inc ....C 419 725-2100
  Toledo (G-17663)
Cleaner Carpet & Jantr Inc ....E 513 469-2070
  Mason (G-13562)
CMS Business Services LLC ....D 740 687-0577
  Lancaster (G-12383)
Coleman Professional Svcs Inc ....C 330 673-1347
  Kent (G-12223)
Commercial Cleaning Solutions ....E 937 981-4870
  Greenfield (G-11359)
Crystal Clear Bldg Svcs Inc ....D 440 439-2288
  Oakwood Village (G-15488)
Csi International Inc ....A 614 781-1571
  Worthington (G-19802)
Cummins Building Maint Inc ....D 740 726-9800
  Prospect (G-16221)
Custom Cleaning and Maint ....E 440 946-7028
  Willoughby (G-19517)
Custom Cleaning Service LLC ....E 440 774-1222
  Oberlin (G-15500)
Custom Maid Cleaning Services ....E 513 351-6571
  Cincinnati (G-3392)
D & J Master Clean Inc ....D 614 847-1181
  Columbus (G-7406)
Dave & Barb Enterprises Inc ....D 513 553-0050
  New Richmond (G-14992)
Dependable Cleaning Contrs ....D 440 953-9191
  Willoughby (G-19518)
Dove Building Services Inc ....D 614 299-4700
  Columbus (G-7469)
Dublin Coml Property Svcs Inc ....E 419 732-6732
  Port Clinton (G-16106)
Environment Ctrl of Miami Cnty ....D 937 669-9900
  Tipp City (G-17556)
Euclid Indus Maint Clg Contrs ....C 216 361-0288
  Cleveland (G-5493)
Executive Management Services ....C 419 529-8800
  Ontario (G-15549)
Extreme Detail Clg Cnstr Svcs ....E 419 392-3243
  Toledo (G-17721)
Facility Svc Maint Systems Inc ....D 513 422-7060
  Middletown (G-14347)
Family Entertainment Services ....D 740 286-8587
  Jackson (G-12173)

Gca Services Group Inc ....D 800 422-8760
  Cleveland (G-5598)
General Building Maintenance ....D 330 682-2238
  Orrville (G-15633)
General Services Cleaning Co ....E 614 840-0562
  Columbus (G-7654)
George Gardner ....D 419 636-4277
  Bryan (G-1958)
Gsf North American Jantr Svc ....C 513 733-1451
  West Chester (G-19057)
Heits Building Svcs Cnkd LLC ....D 855 464-3487
  Cincinnati (G-3697)
Inovative Facility Svcs LLC ....B 419 861-1710
  Maumee (G-13803)
Ivory Services Inc ....E 216 344-3094
  Cleveland (G-5768)
J B M Cleaning & Supply Co ....E 330 837-8805
  Massillon (G-13700)
J V Janitorial Services Inc ....E 216 749-1150
  Cleveland (G-5774)
Jancoa Janitorial Services Inc ....E 513 351-7200
  Cincinnati (G-3808)
Jani-Source LLC ....E 740 374-6298
  Marietta (G-13340)
Janitorial Services Inc ....B 216 341-8601
  Cleveland (G-5781)
Jantech Building Services Inc ....C 216 661-6102
  Brooklyn Heights (G-1872)
Jdd Inc ....E 216 464-8855
  Cleveland (G-5786)
Jenkins Enterprises LLC ....E 513 752-7896
  Cincinnati (G-2857)
Jordan Kyli Enterprises Inc ....E 216 256-3773
  Westlake (G-19361)
K & L Floormasters LLC ....D 330 493-0869
  Canton (G-2363)
K & M Kleening Service Inc ....E 614 737-3750
  Groveport (G-11525)
Kellermyer Bergensons Svcs LLC .....D 419 867-4300
  Maumee (G-13807)
Kelli Woods Management Inc ....C 419 478-1200
  Toledo (G-17838)
Ktm Enterprises Inc ....E 937 548-8357
  Greenville (G-11388)
Mapp Building Service LLC ....E 513 253-3990
  Blue Ash (G-1602)
Marks Cleaning Service Inc ....E 330 725-5702
  Medina (G-13968)
Mathews Josiah ....E 567 204-8818
  Lima (G-12699)
Mid-American Clg Contrs Inc ....C 419 429-6222
  Findlay (G-10945)
Mid-American Clg Contrs Inc ....D 419 229-3899
  Lima (G-12703)
Mid-American Clg Contrs Inc ....C 614 291-7170
  Columbus (G-8074)
Mougianis Industries Inc ....D 740 264-6372
  Steubenville (G-17167)
Nicholas D Starr Inc ....C 419 229-3192
  Lima (G-12706)
North Coast Sales ....E 440 632-0793
  Middlefield (G-14274)
Nortone Service Inc ....E 740 527-2057
  Buckeye Lake (G-1975)
Ohio Building Service Inc ....E 513 761-0268
  Cincinnati (G-4151)
Ohio Custodial Maintenance ....C 614 443-1232
  Columbus (G-8235)
Perry Contract Services Inc ....D 614 274-4350
  Columbus (G-8440)
Priority Building Services Inc ....D 937 233-7030
  Beavercreek Township (G-1260)
Pro Care Janitor Supply ....E 937 778-2275
  Piqua (G-16024)
Pro-Touch Inc ....C 614 586-0303
  Columbus (G-8465)
Professional Maint Dayton ....D 937 461-5259
  Dayton (G-9718)
Professional Maint of Columbus ....C 614 443-6528
  Columbus (G-8469)
Professional Maint of Columbus ....B 513 579-1762
  Cincinnati (G-4293)
Professnal Mint Cincinnati Inc ....A 513 579-1161
  Cincinnati (G-4295)
Quality Assured Cleaning Inc ....D 614 798-1505
  Columbus (G-8480)
Quality Cleaning Systems LLC ....E 330 567-2050
  Shreve (G-16754)
R T Industries Inc ....C 937 335-5784
  Troy (G-18224)

Rde System Corp ....C 513 933-8000
  Lebanon (G-12496)
Rde System Corporation ....D 513 933-8000
  Dayton (G-9727)
Red Carpet Janitorial Service ....B 513 242-7575
  Cincinnati (G-4347)
Romaster Corp ....D 330 825-1945
  Norton (G-15422)
Rwk Services Inc ....E 440 526-2144
  Cleveland (G-6351)
Saftek Industrial Service Inc ....E 937 667-1772
  Tipp City (G-17566)
Scioto Services Llc ....E 937 644-0888
  Marysville (G-13527)
Seaway Sponge & Chamois Co ....E 419 691-4694
  Toledo (G-18023)
Service Master Co ....E 330 864-7300
  Eastlake (G-10434)
ServiceMaster By Steinbach ....E 330 497-5959
  Canton (G-2474)
ServiceMaster of Defiance Inc ....D 419 784-5570
  Defiance (G-9940)
Starlight Enterprises Inc ....C 330 339-2020
  New Philadelphia (G-14983)
Super Shine Inc ....E 513 423-8999
  Middletown (G-14334)
T&L Global Management LLC ....C 614 586-0303
  Columbus (G-8727)
Turn Around Group Inc ....D 330 372-0064
  Warren (G-18762)
Twin Cedars Services Inc ....D 513 932-0399
  Lebanon (G-12512)
Wells & Sons Janitorial Svc ....E 937 878-4375
  Fairborn (G-10690)
Wj Service Co Inc ....E 330 372-5040
  Warren (G-18773)
York Building Maintenance Inc ....C 216 398-8100
  Cleveland (G-6699)
Youngstown Window Cleaning Co ......C 330 743-3880
  Girard (G-11306)

JANITORIAL EQPT & SPLYS WHOLESALERS

Acorn Distributors Inc ....E 614 294-6444
  Columbus (G-6867)
Airgas Usa LLC ....B 216 642-6600
  Independence (G-12042)
Alco-Chem Inc ....E 330 253-3535
  Akron (G-63)
Alco-Chem Inc ....E 330 833-8551
  Canton (G-2177)
Clean Innovations ....E 614 299-1187
  Columbus (G-7222)
Envirochemical Inc ....E 440 287-2200
  Solon (G-16846)
Friends Service Co Inc ....D 419 427-1704
  Findlay (G-10910)
H P Products Corporation ....D 513 683-8553
  Cincinnati (G-3667)
Hillside Maint Sup Co Inc ....E 513 751-4100
  Cincinnati (G-3708)
I Supply Co ....C 937 878-5240
  Fairborn (G-10676)
Impact Products LLC ....C 419 841-2891
  Toledo (G-17818)
M Conley Company ....C 330 456-8243
  Canton (G-2383)
National Marketshare Group ....E 513 921-0800
  Cincinnati (G-4094)
Phillips Supply Company ....D 513 579-1762
  Cincinnati (G-4242)
Powell Company Ltd ....D 419 228-3552
  Lima (G-12723)
Pro-Touch Inc ....C 614 586-0303
  Columbus (G-8465)
Rhiel Supply Co Inc ....E 330 799-7777
  Austintown (G-861)
Rose Products and Services Inc ....E 614 443-7647
  Columbus (G-8551)
Seaway Sponge & Chamois Co ....E 419 691-4694
  Toledo (G-18023)
ServiceMaster of Defiance Inc ....D 419 784-5570
  Defiance (G-9940)
The Cottingham Paper Co ....E 614 294-6444
  Columbus (G-8742)

JEWELRY APPAREL

Marfo Company ....D 614 276-3352
  Columbus (G-8019)

JEWELRY REPAIR SVCS

Sdr Services LLC ....E 513 625-0695
  Goshen *(G-11315)*

JEWELRY STORES

Equity Diamond Brokers Inc.................E 513 793-4760
  Cincinnati *(G-3511)*

JEWELRY, WHOLESALE

Equity Diamond Brokers Inc.................E 513 793-4760
  Cincinnati *(G-3511)*
Marfo Company ....D 614 276-3352
  Columbus *(G-8019)*

JIGS & FIXTURES

Jergens Inc..C 216 486-5540
  Cleveland *(G-5790)*

JOB COUNSELING

Butler County of Ohio........................E 513 785-6500
  Hamilton *(G-11563)*
Linking Employment Abilities.............E 216 696-2716
  Cleveland *(G-5872)*

JOB TRAINING & VOCATIONAL REHABILITATION SVCS

A W S Inc ....D 216 941-8800
  Cleveland *(G-4882)*
Abilities First Foundation Inc ....D 513 423-9496
  Middletown *(G-14285)*
Alpha Group of Delaware Inc..............E 740 368-5820
  Delaware *(G-9952)*
Anne Grady Corporation.....................E 419 867-7501
  Holland *(G-11871)*
ARC Industries Incorporated O ....B 614 836-0700
  Groveport *(G-11494)*
Cleveland Christian Home Inc.............C 216 671-0977
  Cleveland *(G-5234)*
Collins Career Center ....D 740 867-6641
  Chesapeake *(G-2728)*
County of Geauga................................D 440 564-2246
  Chardon *(G-2691)*
County of Hancock ....E 419 422-6387
  Findlay *(G-10891)*
County of Lake.....................................A 440 350-5100
  Mentor *(G-14036)*
County of Lake.....................................D 440 269-2193
  Willoughby *(G-19516)*
County of Marion ....D 740 387-1035
  Marion *(G-13416)*
County of Mercer ....D 419 586-2369
  Celina *(G-2591)*
County of Montgomery.........................B 937 225-4804
  Dayton *(G-9330)*
County of Stark....................................D 330 484-4814
  Canton *(G-2267)*
Dayton Urban League..........................E 937 226-1513
  Dayton *(G-9383)*
Deepwood Industries Inc.....................C 440 350-5231
  Mentor *(G-14040)*
Findaway World LLC ....D 440 893-0808
  Solon *(G-16849)*
Goodwill Idstrs Grtr Clvlnd L ....E 440 783-1168
  Strongsville *(G-17307)*
Goodwill Industries Inc.......................E 330 724-6995
  Akron *(G-240)*
Great Oaks Inst Tech Creer Dev ....D 513 613-3657
  Cincinnati *(G-3644)*
Great Oaks Inst Tech Creer Dev ....E 513 771-8840
  Cincinnati *(G-3645)*
Handson Central Ohio Inc...................E 614 221-2255
  Columbus *(G-7714)*
Hockingthensperry Cmnty Action ....C 740 767-4500
  Glouster *(G-11310)*
Holmes County Board of Dd.................D 330 674-8045
  Holmesville *(G-11930)*
Integrated Services of Appala ....D 740 594-6807
  Athens *(G-786)*
Ironton and Lawrence County ....B 740 532-3534
  Ironton *(G-12155)*
Joe and Jill Lewis Inc ....D 937 718-8829
  Dayton *(G-9526)*
Matco Industries Inc ....E 740 852-7054
  London *(G-12870)*
Mickis Creative Options Inc.................E 419 526-4254
  Mansfield *(G-13220)*

Pickaway Diversfied Industries ....D 740 474-1522
  Circleville *(G-4842)*
Richland Newhope Industries...............E 419 774-4200
  Mansfield *(G-13238)*
Richland Newhope Industries...............D 419 774-4496
  Mansfield *(G-13239)*
Richland Newhope Industries...............C 419 774-4400
  Mansfield *(G-13237)*
Ridge Murray Prod Ctr Oberlin ....E 440 774-7400
  Oberlin *(G-15519)*
Southeast Diversified Inds...................D 740 432-4241
  Cambridge *(G-2082)*
TAC Industries Inc ....C 937 328-5200
  Springfield *(G-17124)*
United Disability Services Inc.............C 330 374-1169
  Akron *(G-476)*
Vgs Inc ....C 216 431-7800
  Cleveland *(G-6627)*
Vision & Vocational Services...............E 614 294-5571
  Columbus *(G-8853)*
Vocational Services Inc ....C 216 431-8085
  Cleveland *(G-6640)*
Waycraft Inc ....D 419 562-3321
  Bucyrus *(G-2006)*
Weaver Industries Inc..........................E 330 379-3660
  Akron *(G-497)*
Weaver Industries Inc..........................C 330 666-5114
  Akron *(G-498)*
Wood County Ohio ....E 419 352-5059
  Bowling Green *(G-1758)*
Zanesville Welfare Organizatio ....B 740 450-6060
  Zanesville *(G-20386)*
Zepf Center ....E 419 213-5627
  Toledo *(G-18177)*

JOB TRAINING SVCS

Akron Blind Center & Workshop..........D 330 253-2555
  Akron *(G-29)*
Butler County Bd of Mental RE.............C 513 785-2870
  Fairfield Township *(G-10805)*
County of Crawford ....D 419 562-0015
  Bucyrus *(G-1986)*
County of Holmes.................................E 330 674-1111
  Millersburg *(G-14472)*
Goodwill Inds Centl Ohio Inc................B 614 294-5181
  Columbus *(G-7679)*
Goodwill Inds Centl Ohio Inc................E 614 274-5296
  Columbus *(G-7680)*
GP Strategies Corporation....................E 513 583-8810
  Cincinnati *(G-3629)*
Miami University ....B 513 727-3200
  Middletown *(G-14308)*
Ohio State University............................D 614 292-4353
  Columbus *(G-8316)*
Portage Private Industry ....D 330 297-7795
  Ravenna *(G-16259)*
Spanish American Committee ....E 216 961-2100
  Cleveland *(G-6441)*
Star Inc...C 740 354-1517
  Portsmouth *(G-16174)*
Step By Step Emplyment Trining ....E 440 967-9042
  Vermilion *(G-18560)*
W S O S Community A...........................E 419 639-2802
  Green Springs *(G-11356)*
W S O S Community A...........................D 419 334-8511
  Fremont *(G-11105)*
W S O S Community A...........................D 419 333-6068
  Fremont *(G-11104)*
Workforce Initiative Assn.....................E 330 433-9675
  Canton *(G-2537)*

JUICE, FROZEN: Wholesalers

Mattingly Foods Inc ....C 740 454-0136
  Zanesville *(G-20329)*

JUNIOR HIGH SCHOOLS, PUBLIC

Ashland City School District.................E 419 289-7967
  Ashland *(G-646)*

JUNIOR OR SENIOR HIGH SCHOOLS, NEC

Adams Cnty /Ohio Vly Schl Dst.............D 937 544-2951
  West Union *(G-19129)*

JUVENILE CORRECTIONAL FACILITIES

Bellmont County ....E 740 695-9750
  Saint Clairsville *(G-16471)*
County of Richland ....D 419 774-5578
  Mansfield *(G-13157)*

County of Ross ....E 740 773-4169
  Chillicothe *(G-2772)*
County of Summit ....C 330 643-2943
  Akron *(G-163)*
Five County Joint Juvenile Det.............E 937 642-1015
  Marysville *(G-13495)*
Franklin Cnty Bd Commissioners.........E 614 462-3429
  Columbus *(G-7608)*
Lighthouse Youth Services Inc.............D 740 634-3094
  Bainbridge *(G-931)*
Multi County Juvenile Det Ctr...............E 740 652-1525
  Lancaster *(G-12420)*

JUVENILE CORRECTIONAL HOME

Medina Cnty Jvnile Dtntion Ctr............E 330 764-8408
  Medina *(G-13971)*
Multi-Cnty Jvnile Attntion Sys ....D 330 484-6471
  Canton *(G-2412)*

KEY DUPLICATING SHOP

Hillman Companies Inc ....B 513 851-4900
  Cincinnati *(G-3705)*

KIDNEY DIALYSIS CENTERS

Alomie Dialysis LLC ....E 740 941-1688
  Waverly *(G-18813)*
Amelia Davita Dialysis Center ....E 513 797-0713
  Amelia *(G-564)*
Barrington Dialysis LLC ....E 740 346-2740
  Steubenville *(G-17140)*
Basin Dialysis LLC..............................E 937 643-2337
  Kettering *(G-12291)*
Beck Dialysis LLC ....E 513 422-6879
  Middletown *(G-14290)*
Bio-Mdcal Applcations Ohio Inc...........E 937 279-3120
  Trotwood *(G-18191)*
Bio-Mdcal Applcations Ohio Inc...........E 419 874-3447
  Perrysburg *(G-15839)*
Bio-Mdcal Applcations Ohio Inc...........E 614 538-1060
  Columbus *(G-7040)*
Bio-Mdcal Applcations Ohio Inc...........E 330 376-4905
  Akron *(G-98)*
Bio-Mdcal Applcations Ohio Inc...........E 419 774-0180
  Mansfield *(G-13141)*
Bio-Mdcal Applcations Ohio Inc...........E 330 896-6311
  Uniontown *(G-18357)*
Bio-Mdcal Applcations Ohio Inc...........E 614 338-8202
  Columbus *(G-7041)*
Bio-Mdical Applications RI Inc.............E 740 389-4111
  Marion *(G-13405)*
Center For Dlysis Cre of Cnfld..............E 330 702-3040
  Canfield *(G-2133)*
Centers For Dialysis Care Inc ....C 216 295-7000
  Shaker Heights *(G-16705)*
Columbus Med Partners LLC................E 614 538-1060
  Columbus *(G-7295)*
Columbus-Rna-Davita LLC ....E 614 985-1732
  Columbus *(G-7322)*
Community Dialysis Center ....E 216 295-7000
  Cleveland *(G-5325)*
Community Dialysis Center ....E 216 229-6170
  Cleveland *(G-5326)*
Community Dialysis Center ....E 330 609-0370
  Warren *(G-18687)*
Community Dialysis Center ....B 216 295-7000
  Shaker Heights *(G-16706)*
Community Dialysis Ctr Mentor ....E 440 255-5999
  Mentor *(G-14033)*
Court Dialysis LLC...............................E 740 773-3733
  Chillicothe *(G-2773)*
Crestview Health Care Center...............D 740 695-2500
  Saint Clairsville *(G-16485)*
Davita Healthcare Partners Inc ....E 216 961-6498
  Cleveland *(G-5410)*
Davita Healthcare Partners Inc ....E 440 353-0114
  North Ridgeville *(G-15328)*
Davita Inc..E 513 939-1110
  Fairfield *(G-10716)*
Davita Inc..E 216 712-4700
  Rocky River *(G-16430)*
Davita Inc..E 440 891-5645
  Cleveland *(G-5411)*
Davita Inc..E 740 376-2622
  Marietta *(G-13325)*
Davita Inc..E 937 456-1174
  Eaton *(G-10441)*
Davita Inc..E 330 494-2091
  Canton *(G-2280)*

Davita Inc ....E 216 525-0990
Independence (G-12065)

Davita Inc ....E 937 879-0433
Fairborn (G-10669)

Davita Inc ....E 937 426-6475
Beavercreek (G-1145)

Davita Inc ....E 937 435-4030
Dayton (G-9346)

Davita Inc ....E 937 376-1453
Xenia (G-19897)

Davita Inc ....E 440 293-6028
Andover (G-605)

Davita Inc ....E 513 784-1800
Cincinnati (G-3403)

Davita Inc ....E 740 401-0607
Belpre (G-1401)

Davita Inc ....E 330 335-2300
Wadsworth (G-18595)

Davita Inc ....E 440 251-6237
Madison (G-13094)

Davita Inc ....E 615 341-6311
Georgetown (G-11270)

Davita Inc ....E 330 733-1861
Akron (G-182)

Davita Inc ....E 419 697-2191
Oregon (G-15589)

Davita Inc ....E 513 624-0400
Cincinnati (G-3404)

Dayton Regional Dialysis Inc .....E 937 898-5526
Dayton (G-9380)

Desoto Dialysis LLC ....E 419 691-1514
Oregon (G-15590)

Dialysis Center of Dayton East ....E 937 252-1867
Dayton (G-9390)

Dialysis Clinic Inc ....D 513 281-0091
Cincinnati (G-3428)

Dialysis Clinic Inc ....E 740 351-0596
Portsmouth (G-16136)

Dialysis Clinic Inc ....E 513 777-0855
West Chester (G-18910)

Dialysis Clinic Inc ....E 740 264-6687
Steubenville (G-17151)

Dialysis Specialists Fairfield ......E 513 863-6331
Fairfield (G-10718)

Dome Dialysis LLC ....E 614 882-1734
Westerville (G-19250)

DSI East ....E 330 733-1861
Akron (G-196)

Dva Healthcare - South ....E 513 347-0444
Cincinnati (G-3458)

Dva Renal Healthcare Inc ....E 740 454-2911
Zanesville (G-20302)

Fort Dialysis LLC ....E 330 837-7730
Massillon (G-13683)

Fresenius Med Care Butler Cty .....E 513 737-1415
Hamilton (G-11599)

Fresenius Med Care Hldings Inc ....E 216 267-1451
Cleveland (G-5578)

Fresenius Med Care Hldings Inc ....E 800 881-5101
Columbus (G-7624)

Fresenius Med Care Milford LLC ....E 513 248-1690
Milford (G-14389)

Fresenius Medical Care Vro LLC ....E 614 875-2349
Grove City (G-11435)

Fresenius Usa Inc ....E 330 837-2575
Massillon (G-13684)

Fresenius Usa Inc ....E 419 691-2475
Oregon (G-15595)

Fresenius Usa Inc ....E 440 734-7474
North Olmsted (G-15290)

Goza Dialysis LLC ....E 513 738-0276
Fairfield (G-10730)

Greater Columbus Regional ....D 614 228-9114
Columbus (G-7693)

Greenfield Health Systems Corp ....E 419 389-9681
Toledo (G-17771)

Hemodialysis Services Inc ....E 216 378-2691
Beachwood (G-1063)

Heyburn Dialysis LLC ....E 614 876-3610
Hilliard (G-11774)

Innovative Dialysis ....E 419 473-9900
Toledo (G-17822)

Isd Renal Inc ....D 330 375-6848
Akron (G-282)

Kidney Center of Bexley LLC ....D 614 231-2200
Columbus (G-7902)

Kidney Center Partnership ....D 330 799-1150
Youngstown (G-20090)

Kidney Group Inc ....E 330 746-1488
Youngstown (G-20091)

Kidney Services W Centl Ohio ....E 419 227-0918
Lima (G-12669)

Kinswa Dialysis LLC ....E 419 332-0310
Fremont (G-11083)

Lakeshore Dialysis LLC ....E 937 278-0516
Dayton (G-9555)

Lory Dialysis LLC ....E 740 522-2955
Newark (G-15062)

Mahoney Dialysis LLC ....E 937 642-0676
Marysville (G-13512)

Manzano Dialysis LLC ....E 937 879-0433
Fairborn (G-10680)

Mesilla Dialysis LLC ....E 937 484-4600
Urbana (G-18441)

Morro Dialysis LLC ....E 937 865-0633
Miamisburg (G-14195)

Mount Carmel E Dialysis Clnc ....E 614 322-0433
Columbus (G-8109)

Ohio Renal Care Group LLC ....D 440 974-3459
Mentor (G-14092)

Ohio Renal Care Group LLC ....E 330 928-4511
Cuyahoga Falls (G-9116)

Pendster Dialysis LLC ....E 937 237-0769
Huber Heights (G-11956)

Renal Life Link Inc ....E 937 383-3338
Wilmington (G-19644)

Seneca Dialysis LLC ....D 419 443-1051
Tiffin (G-17538)

Steele Dialysis LLC ....E 419 462-1028
Galion (G-11182)

Tonka Bay Dialysis LLC ....E 740 375-0849
Marion (G-13464)

Total Renal Care Inc ....E 937 294-6711
Kettering (G-12301)

Total Renal Care Inc ....E 937 252-1867
Dayton (G-9817)

Trinity Health Corporation ....B 614 846-5420
Columbus (G-8781)

Vogel Dialysis LLC ....E 614 834-3564
Canal Winchester (G-2124)

Wakoni Dialysis LLC ....E 937 294-7188
Moraine (G-14706)

Wallowa Dialysis LLC ....E 419 747-4039
Ontario (G-15578)

Wauseon Dialysis LLC ....E 419 335-0695
Wauseon (G-18811)

KINDERGARTEN

Akron Metropolitan Hsing Auth .....C 330 920-1652
Stow (G-17189)

Colonial Senior Services Inc ....C 513 856-8600
Hamilton (G-11582)

Colonial Senior Services Inc ....C 513 867-4006
Hamilton (G-11583)

Hanna Perkins School ....E 216 991-4472
Shaker Heights (G-16709)

J&B Sprafka Enterprises Inc ....E 330 733-4212
Akron (G-286)

Montessori Community School ....E 740 344-9411
Newark (G-15074)

Royal Redeemer Lutheran Church ...E 440 237-7958
North Royalton (G-15365)

St Francis De Sales Church ....D 740 345-9874
Newark (G-15099)

Twinbrook Hills Baptist Church .....E 513 863-3107
Hamilton (G-11650)

Whitehall City Schools ....E 614 417-5680
Columbus (G-8898)

KITCHEN CABINET STORES, EXC CUSTOM

Brower Products Inc ....D 937 563-1111
Cincinnati (G-3082)

Creative Products Inc ....E 419 866-5501
Holland (G-11880)

Lumberjacks Inc ....E 330 762-2401
Akron (G-323)

Schlabach Wood Design Inc ....E 330 897-2600
Baltic (G-936)

Thiels Replacement Systems Inc ....D 419 289-6139
Ashland (G-694)

KITCHEN CABINETS WHOLESALERS

Brower Products Inc ....D 937 563-1111
Cincinnati (G-3082)

Clark Son Actn Liquidation Inc ......E 330 837-9710
Canal Fulton (G-2094)

Direct Import Home Decor Inc ......E 216 898-9758
Cleveland (G-5424)

Don Walter Kitchen Distrs ....E 330 793-9338
Youngstown (G-20021)

Keidel Supply Company Inc ....E 513 351-1600
Cincinnati (G-3852)

Lute Supply Inc ....E 740 353-1447
Portsmouth (G-16153)

Professonal Laminate Mllwk Inc .....E 513 891-7858
Milford (G-14427)

Sims-Lohman Inc ....E 513 651-3510
Cincinnati (G-4483)

KITCHEN TOOLS & UTENSILS WHOLESALERS

Creative Products Inc ....E 419 866-5501
Holland (G-11880)

Newell Brands Inc ....C 419 662-2225
Bowling Green (G-1741)

KITCHENWARE STORES

Nacco Industries Inc ....E 440 229-5151
Cleveland (G-6034)

Pottery Barn Inc ....E 614 478-3154
Columbus (G-8456)

Wasserstrom Company ....B 614 228-6525
Columbus (G-8878)

KNIVES: Agricultural Or indl

C B Mfg & Sls Co Inc ....D 937 866-5986
Miamisburg (G-14147)

LABELS: Paper, Made From Purchased Materials

CMC Daymark Corporation ....C 419 354-2591
Bowling Green (G-1728)

General Data Company Inc ....C 513 752-7978
Cincinnati (G-2853)

LABOR RESOURCE SVCS

Integrated Marketing Tech Inc ......D 330 225-3550
Brunswick (G-1933)

Medsearch Staffing Svcs Inc ....E 440 243-6363
Cleveland (G-5946)

Staffmark Holdings Inc ....D 513 651-1111
Cincinnati (G-4528)

Stage Works ....E 513 522-3118
Cincinnati (G-4530)

LABOR UNION

American Federation of Gov ....E 513 861-6047
Cincinnati (G-2941)

Brotherhood of Locomotive Engi .....E 740 345-0978
Newark (G-15016)

Cleveland Teachers Union Inc ....E 216 861-7676
Cleveland (G-5292)

Healthcare and Social ....E 614 461-1199
Columbus (G-7726)

International Chem Wkrs Cr Un ....E 330 926-1444
Akron (G-280)

International Union United Au ....E 216 447-6080
Cleveland (G-5764)

International Union United Au ....D 513 897-4939
Waynesville (G-18833)

International Union United Au ....D 513 563-1252
Cincinnati (G-3780)

International Union United Au ....E 419 893-4677
Maumee (G-13804)

Interntional Assn Firefighters ....E 330 823-5222
Alliance (G-535)

Licking Knox Labor Council ....D 740 345-1765
Newark (G-15055)

Local Union 856 Uaw Bldg Corp .....E 330 733-6231
Akron (G-318)

National Assn Ltr Carriers ....E 419 289-8359
Ashland (G-683)

National Assn Ltr Carriers ....D 419 693-8392
Northwood (G-15400)

Ohio Assn Pub Schl Employees ......E 614 890-4770
Columbus (G-8228)

Ohio Assn Pub Schl Employees ......D 937 253-5100
Dayton (G-9183)

Ohio Assn Pub Schl Employees ......D 330 659-7335
Richfield (G-16368)

Ohio Civil Service Employees A ......D 614 865-4700
Westerville (G-19195)

Ohio Education Association ....D 614 485-6000
Columbus (G-8250)

Ohio Education Association ....D 614 228-4526
Columbus **(G-8251)**

Ohio Lbrers Frnge Bneft Prgram ....E 614 898-9006
Westerville **(G-19287)**

Ohio Operating Engineers Apprn ....E 614 487-6531
Columbus **(G-8276)**

Smart...C 216 228-9400
North Olmsted **(G-15310)**

Union Cnstr Wkrs Hlth Plan ....E 419 248-2401
Holland **(G-11923)**

United Fd & Coml Wkrs Intl Un ....E 216 241-2828
Broadview Heights **(G-1849)**

United Fd Coml Wkrs Local 880 ....E 216 241-5930
Cleveland **(G-6571)**

United Food & Commercial Wkr ....E 330 452-4850
Canton **(G-2517)**

United Food and Coml Wkrs ....D 937 665-0075
Dayton **(G-9831)**

United Food Comml Wrkrs Un ....E 614 235-3635
Columbus **(G-8800)**

United Steelworkers ....E 740 772-5988
Chillicothe **(G-2834)**

United Steelworkers ....C 740 928-0157
Newark **(G-15105)**

United Steelworkers ....E 440 979-1050
North Olmsted **(G-15315)**

United Steelworkers ....E 419 238-7980
Van Wert **(G-18490)**

United Steelworkers ....E 740 633-0899
Martins Ferry **(G-13480)**

United Steelworkers ....E 440 244-1358
Lorain **(G-12949)**

United Steelworkers ....E 440 354-2328
Painesville **(G-15746)**

United Steelworkers ....E 614 272-8609
Columbus **(G-8812)**

United Steelworkers ....E 740 622-8860
Coshocton **(G-9030)**

United Steelworkers of America ....C 330 493-7721
Canton **(G-2522)**

LABORATORIES, TESTING: Automobile Proving & Testing Ground

Ohio Department Transportation ....D 614 275-1324
Columbus **(G-8242)**

Transportation Ohio Department ....E 614 275-1300
Columbus **(G-8774)**

LABORATORIES, TESTING: Food

Agrana Fruit Us Inc ....C 937 693-3821
Botkins **(G-1706)**

Daymark Food Safety Systems ....C 419 353-2458
Bowling Green **(G-1729)**

Food Safety Net Services Ltd ....E 614 274-2070
Columbus **(G-7601)**

Nestle Usa Inc ....D 614 526-5300
Dublin **(G-10288)**

Silliker Laboratories Ohio Inc ....E 614 486-0150
Columbus **(G-8640)**

LABORATORIES, TESTING: Hazardous Waste

Aqua Tech Envmtl Labs Inc ....E 740 389-5991
Marion **(G-13404)**

Envirite of Ohio Inc ....E 330 456-6238
Canton **(G-2302)**

LABORATORIES, TESTING: Hydrostatic

US Tubular Products Inc ....D 330 832-1734
North Lawrence **(G-15260)**

LABORATORIES, TESTING: Industrial Sterilization

Isomedix Operations Inc ....E 614 836-5757
Groveport **(G-11521)**

Isomedix Operations Inc ....C 440 354-2600
Mentor **(G-14064)**

LABORATORIES, TESTING: Metallurgical

Bowser-Morner Inc ....E 419 691-4800
Toledo **(G-17621)**

Ctl Engineering Inc ....C 614 276-8123
Columbus **(G-7404)**

Element Mtrls Tchnlgy Hntngtn ....E 216 643-1208
Cleveland **(G-5472)**

J T Adams Co ....E 216 641-3290
Cleveland **(G-5773)**

Metcut Research Associates Inc ....D 513 271-5100
Cincinnati **(G-4041)**

LABORATORIES, TESTING: Pollution

Grace Consulting Inc ....E 440 647-6672
Wellington **(G-18841)**

Ohio Rver Vly Wtr Snttion Comm ....E 513 231-7719
Cincinnati **(G-4158)**

Shaw Group Inc ....A 937 593-2022
Bellefontaine **(G-1365)**

LABORATORIES, TESTING: Prdt Certification, Sfty/Performance

Juice Technologies Inc ....E 800 518-5576
Columbus **(G-7875)**

Tool Testing Lab Inc ....E 937 898-5696
Tipp City **(G-17570)**

LABORATORIES, TESTING: Product Testing

Bwi North America Inc ....E 937 212-2892
Moraine **(G-14630)**

Certified Pressure Testing LLC ....E 740 374-2071
Marietta **(G-13318)**

Cliff North Consultants Inc ....E 513 251-4930
Cincinnati **(G-3306)**

Glowe-Smith Industrial Inc ....C 330 638-5088
Vienna **(G-18579)**

McCloy Engineering LLC ....E 513 984-4112
Fairfield **(G-10752)**

Smithers Quality Assessments ....E 330 762-4231
Akron **(G-433)**

Smithers Rapra Inc ....E 330 297-1495
Ravenna **(G-16268)**

Smithers Rapra Inc ....D 330 762-7441
Akron **(G-434)**

Smithers Tire & Auto Testng TX ....E 330 762-7441
Akron **(G-435)**

Standard Laboratories Inc ....E 513 422-1088
Middletown **(G-14331)**

Wallover Enterprises Inc ....E 440 238-9250
Strongsville **(G-17358)**

LABORATORIES, TESTING: Product Testing, Safety/Performance

Bionetics Corporation ....E 757 873-0900
Heath **(G-11702)**

Chemsultants International Inc ....E 440 974-3080
Mentor **(G-14029)**

Plastic Technologies Inc ....D 419 867-5400
Holland **(G-11905)**

Standards Testing Labs Inc ....D 330 833-8548
Massillon **(G-13731)**

Tool Testing Lab Inc ....D 937 898-5696
Tipp City **(G-17571)**

LABORATORIES, TESTING: Soil Analysis

Analytical Pace Services LLC ....E 937 832-8242
Englewood **(G-10578)**

Brookside Laboratories Inc ....E 419 977-2766
New Bremen **(G-14885)**

Testamerica Laboratories Inc ....C 800 456-9396
North Canton **(G-15237)**

Testamerica Laboratories Inc ....E 513 733-5700
Cincinnati **(G-4587)**

LABORATORIES, TESTING: Water

Enviroscience Inc ....C 330 688-0111
Stow **(G-17202)**

MPW Industrial Services Inc ....E 740 345-2431
Newark **(G-15077)**

National Testing Laboratories ....E 440 449-2525
Cleveland **(G-6049)**

LABORATORIES: Biological

Medpace Inc ....A 513 366-3220
Cincinnati **(G-3999)**

Stembanc Inc ....E 440 332-4279
Chardon **(G-2717)**

LABORATORIES: Biological Research

Asymmetric Technologies LLC ....E 614 725-5310
Columbus **(G-6987)**

Biosortia Pharmaceuticals Inc.............E 614 636-4850
Dublin **(G-10146)**

Edison Biotechnology Institute ....E 740 593-4713
Athens **(G-779)**

Mp Biomedicals LLC...........................C 440 337-1200
Solon **(G-16873)**

Stembanc Inc ....E 440 332-4279
Chardon **(G-2717)**

LABORATORIES: Biotechnology

Battelle Memorial Institute ....D 937 258-6717
Beavercreek **(G-1129)**

Charles River Laboratories Inc.............C 419 647-4196
Spencerville **(G-16955)**

Childrens Hospital Medical Ctr ....A 513 636-4200
Cincinnati **(G-3190)**

EMD Millipore Corporation ....C 513 631-0445
Norwood **(G-15462)**

Medpace Inc ....A 513 579-9911
Cincinnati **(G-4000)**

Renovo Neural Inc ....E 216 445-4202
Cleveland **(G-6307)**

Ues Inc ....C 937 426-6900
Beavercreek **(G-1190)**

LABORATORIES: Blood Analysis

Cols Health & Wellness Testing ....E 614 839-2781
Westerville **(G-19238)**

Laboratory Corporation America ....E 614 475-7852
Columbus **(G-7940)**

Laboratory Corporation America ....E 440 838-0404
Cleveland **(G-5847)**

Ridgepark Medical Associates ....E 216 749-8256
Cleveland **(G-6326)**

LABORATORIES: Commercial Nonphysical Research

AK Steel Corporation...........................C 513 425-6541
Middletown **(G-14287)**

Applied Research Assoc Inc ....E 937 873-8166
Dayton **(G-9235)**

I T E LLC ....D 513 576-6200
Loveland **(G-13000)**

Icon Government ....B 330 278-2343
Hinckley **(G-11859)**

Infocision Management Corp ....B 330 544-1400
Youngstown **(G-20081)**

Integer Holdings Corporation ....E 216 937-2800
Cleveland **(G-5756)**

Ipsos-Asi LLC....................................D 513 872-4300
Cincinnati **(G-3785)**

Power Management Inc ....E 937 222-2909
Dayton **(G-9701)**

Sytronics Inc ....E 937 431-6100
Beavercreek **(G-1189)**

LABORATORIES: Dental

Classic Dental Labs Inc.......................E 614 443-0328
Columbus **(G-7220)**

State Valley Dental Center....................E 330 920-8060
Cuyahoga Falls **(G-9125)**

LABORATORIES: Dental & Medical X-Ray

Alliance Imaging Inc ....C 330 493-5100
Canton **(G-2179)**

Associated Imaging Corporation ....E 419 517-0500
Toledo **(G-17602)**

Berkebile Russell & Associates ....E 440 989-4480
Lorain **(G-12886)**

Dayton Medical Imaging.......................D 937 439-0390
Dayton **(G-9372)**

Mount Carmel Imaging & Therapy........E 614 234-8080
Columbus **(G-8114)**

Regional Imaging Cons Corp ....E 330 726-9006
Youngstown **(G-20179)**

Trident USA Health Svcs LLC ....E 614 888-2226
Columbus **(G-8779)**

X-Ray Industries Inc ....E 216 642-0100
Cleveland **(G-6696)**

LABORATORIES: Dental, Artificial Teeth Production

Health Smile Center............................E 440 992-2700
Ashtabula **(G-739)**

Sentage Corporation ....E 937 865-5900
Miamisburg **(G-14218)**

SERVICES

LABORATORIES: Dental, Crown & Bridge Production

Dental Ceramics Inc ....E 330 523-5240
Richfield (G-16353)
Doling & Associates Dental Lab ....E 937 254-0075
Dayton (G-9393)
Dresch Tolson Dental Labs ....D 419 842-6730
Sylvania (G-17420)
National Dentex LLC ....E 216 671-0577
Cleveland (G-6042)
Roe Dental Laboratory Inc ....D 216 663-2233
Independence (G-12116)

LABORATORIES: Dental, Denture Production

Greater Cincinnati Dental Labs ....E 513 385-4222
Cincinnati (G-3651)
United Dental Laboratories ....E 330 253-1810
Tallmadge (G-17496)

LABORATORIES: Electronic Research

Promerus LLC ....E 440 922-0300
Brecksville (G-1799)
Steiner Eoptics Inc ....D 937 426-2341
Miamisburg (G-14226)

LABORATORIES: Environmental Research

ASC Group Inc ....E 614 268-2514
Columbus (G-6976)
Conwed Plas Acquisition V LLC ....D 440 926-2607
Akron (G-157)
Hydrogeologic Inc ....E 330 463-3303
Hudson (G-11984)
Midwest Optoelectronics LLC ....C 419 724-0565
Toledo (G-17916)
Terracon Consultants Inc ....E 614 863-3113
Gahanna (G-11150)

LABORATORIES: Medical

Ameripath Cincinnati Inc ....E 513 745-8330
Blue Ash (G-1505)
Arbor View Family Medicine Inc ....E 740 687-3386
Lancaster (G-12371)
Blossom Nursing & Rehab Center ....C 330 337-3033
Salem (G-16538)
Brook Haven Home Health Care ....E 937 833-6945
Brookville (G-1910)
Cellular Technology Limited ....E 216 791-5084
Shaker Heights (G-16704)
Childrens Hospital Medical Ctr ....E 513 636-6400
Fairfield (G-10708)
Cleveland Heartlab Inc ....D 866 358-9828
Cleveland (G-5258)
Compunet Clinical Labs LLC ....D 937 427-2655
Beavercreek (G-1211)
Compunet Clinical Labs LLC ....D 937 342-0015
Springfield (G-17020)
Compunet Clinical Labs LLC ....C 937 296-0844
Moraine (G-14636)
Compunet Clinical Labs LLC ....B 937 208-3555
Dayton (G-9315)
Dna Diagnostics Center Inc ....C 513 881-7800
Fairfield (G-10719)
Drew Medical Inc ....E 407 363-6700
Hudson (G-11976)
Drs Hill & Thomas Co ....E 440 944-8887
Cleveland (G-5446)
Gloria Gadmack Do ....C 216 363-2353
Cleveland (G-5611)
Heart To Heart Home Health ....E 330 335-9999
Wadsworth (G-18598)
Labcare ....E 330 753-3649
Barberton (G-958)
Labone Inc ....A 513 585-9000
Cincinnati (G-3903)
Laboratory Corporation America ....E 440 951-6841
Willoughby (G-19537)
Laboratory Corporation America ....E 440 328-3275
Mansfield (G-13197)
Laboratory Corporation America ....E 440 205-8299
Mentor (G-14070)
Maternohio Clinical Assoicates ....E 614 457-7660
Columbus (G-8038)
Medcentral Workable ....E 419 526-8444
Ontario (G-15563)
Mercy Health Youngstown LLC ....A 330 729-1420
Youngstown (G-20125)

Monroe Family Health Center ....E 740 472-0757
Woodsfield (G-19677)
Mp Biomedicals LLC ....C 440 337-1200
Solon (G-16873)
Nationwide Childrens Hospital ....C 614 722-2700
Columbus (G-8143)
Northeast OH Neighborhood Heal ....C 216 231-7700
Cleveland (G-6090)
Shared PET Imaging Llc ....C 330 491-0480
Canton (G-2475)
Southwest Urology LLC ....E 440 845-0900
Cleveland (G-6435)
St Lukes Hospital ....A 419 441-1002
Waterville (G-18793)
St Ritas Medical Center ....D 419 226-9229
Lima (G-12750)
Standards Testing Labs Inc ....D 330 833-8548
Massillon (G-13731)
Summa Health ....D 330 753-3649
Barberton (G-967)
Summa Health ....E 330 688-4531
Stow (G-17234)
Superior Medical Care Inc ....E 440 282-7420
Lorain (G-12946)
University of Cincinnati ....E 513 558-4444
Cincinnati (G-4708)
University of Cincinnati ....C 513 558-5439
Cincinnati (G-4713)

LABORATORIES: Medical Pathology

Bayless Pathmark Inc ....E 440 274-2494
Cleveland (G-5044)
Consultants Laboratory Medici ....E 419 535-9629
Toledo (G-17677)
Lima Pathology Associates Labs ....E 419 226-9595
Lima (G-12685)
Oncodiagnostic Laboratory Inc ....E 216 861-5846
Cleveland (G-6132)
Osu Pathology Services LLC ....D 614 247-6461
Columbus (G-8394)
Pathology Laboratories Inc ....C 419 255-4600
Toledo (G-17973)
Vet Path Services Inc ....E 513 469-0777
Mason (G-13654)

LABORATORIES: Noncommercial Research

Advantage Aerotech Inc ....E 614 759-8329
Columbus (G-6875)
American Cancer Society East ....B 888 227-6446
Dublin (G-10129)
Benjamin Rose Institute ....D 216 791-8000
Cleveland (G-5055)
Dayton Foundation Inc ....E 937 222-0410
Dayton (G-9365)
Ofeq Institute Inc ....E 440 943-1497
Wickliffe (G-19472)
Ohio Aerospace Institute ....D 440 962-3000
Cleveland (G-6114)
Ohio State University ....D 614 292-1681
Columbus (G-8308)
Ohio Technical College Inc ....E 216 881-1700
Cleveland (G-6124)
University of Dayton ....A 937 229-2919
Dayton (G-9837)

LABORATORIES: Physical Research, Commercial

Alcatel-Lucent USA Inc ....B 614 860-2000
Dublin (G-10124)
Alliance Imaging Inc ....C 330 493-5100
Canton (G-2179)
Antioch University ....D 937 769-1366
Yellow Springs (G-19938)
Applied Research Assoc Inc ....E 937 435-1016
Columbus (G-6959)
Arthur G James Cance ....A 614 293-4878
Columbus (G-6972)
Azimuth Corporation ....E 937 256-8571
Beavercreek Township (G-1243)
BASF Catalysts LLC ....D 216 360-5005
Cleveland (G-5039)
Borchers Americas Inc ....D 440 899-2950
Westlake (G-19323)
Bridgestone Research LLC ....A 330 379-7570
Akron (G-106)
Brilligent Solutions Inc ....E 937 879-4148
Fairborn (G-10664)
Champion Spark Plug Company ....D 419 535-2567
Toledo (G-17647)

Chemimage Filter Tech LLC ....E 330 686-2829
Stow (G-17195)
Circle Prime Manufacturing ....E 330 923-0019
Cuyahoga Falls (G-9079)
Cleveland F E S Center ....D 216 231-3257
Cleveland (G-5254)
Ctl Engineering Inc ....C 614 276-8123
Columbus (G-7404)
Curtiss-Wright Controls ....E 937 252-5601
Fairborn (G-10667)
Defense Research Assoc Inc ....E 937 431-1644
Dayton (G-9169)
Edison Welding Institute Inc ....C 614 688-5000
Columbus (G-7502)
Ensafe Inc ....E 513 621-7233
West Chester (G-18918)
Flexsys America LP ....D 330 666-4111
Akron (G-225)
Fram Group Operations LLC ....D 419 661-6700
Perrysburg (G-15867)
Illumination Research Inc ....E 513 774-9531
Mason (G-13597)
Kemron Environmental Svcs Inc ....D 740 373-4071
Marietta (G-13342)
Kenmore Research Company ....D 330 297-1407
Ravenna (G-16248)
Laboratory Corporation America ....A 614 336-3993
Dublin (G-10267)
Leidos Inc ....B 858 826-6000
Columbus (G-7965)
Leidos Inc ....B 937 431-2220
Beavercreek (G-1165)
Leidos Engineering LLC ....D 330 405-9810
Twinsburg (G-18292)
Leidos Technical Services Inc ....D 513 672-8400
West Chester (G-19063)
Lindner Clinical Trial Center ....E 513 585-1777
Cincinnati (G-3935)
Lyondell Chemical Company ....D 513 530-4000
Cincinnati (G-3953)
Modern Tech Solutions Inc ....D 937 426-9025
Beavercreek Township (G-1254)
Muskingum Starlight Industries ....D 740 453-4622
Zanesville (G-20342)
Nationwide Childrens Hospital ....C 614 722-2700
Columbus (G-8143)
Natural Resources Ohio Dept ....E 614 265-6852
Columbus (G-8163)
Nsa Technologies LLC ....C 330 576-4600
Akron (G-353)
Omnova Solutions Inc ....D 330 794-6300
Akron (G-364)
Owens Corning Sales LLC ....B 740 587-3562
Granville (G-11347)
Pen Brands LLC ....E 216 447-1199
Brooklyn Heights (G-1878)
Plastic Technologies Inc ....D 419 867-5400
Holland (G-11905)
Potter Technologies LLC ....D 419 380-8404
Toledo (G-17983)
Q Labs LLC ....C 513 471-1300
Cincinnati (G-4309)
Rogosin Institute Inc ....E 937 374-3116
Xenia (G-19924)
Schneller LLC ....D 330 673-1299
Kent (G-12258)
Sensation Research ....E 513 602-1611
Maineville (G-13118)
Sunpower Inc ....D 740 594-2221
Athens (G-804)
Sytronics Inc ....E 937 431-6100
Beavercreek (G-1189)
University of Cincinnati ....E 513 556-5511
Cincinnati (G-4709)
Wyle Laboratories Inc ....C 937 320-2712
Beavercreek (G-1242)

LABORATORIES: Testing

Cadx Systems Inc ....D 937 431-1464
Beavercreek (G-1137)
Connie Parks ....E 330 759-8334
Hubbard (G-11943)
Ecg Scanning & Medical Svcs ....E 888 346-5837
Moraine (G-14651)
Laboratory Corporation America ....E 937 383-6964
Wilmington (G-19626)
Laboratory Corporation America ....E 330 865-3624
Akron (G-307)
Laboratory Corporation America ....E 614 882-6278
Columbus (G-7941)

(G-0000) Company's Geographic Section entry number

Laboratory Corporation America ....E 513 242-6800
Cincinnati (G-3904)

Laboratory Corporation America ....E 937 866-8188
Miamisburg (G-14184)

Laboratory Corporation America ....A 614 336-3993
Dublin (G-10267)

Laboratory Corporation America ....E 440 884-1591
Cleveland (G-5846)

Laboratory Corporation America ....E 740 522-2034
Newark (G-15047)

Laboratory Corporation America ....E 330 686-0194
Stow (G-17216)

Laboratory of Dermatopathology ....E 937 434-2351
Dayton (G-9554)

Medical Diagnostic Lab Inc ....E 440 333-1375
Avon (G-894)

Medpace Bioanalytical Labs LLC ....E 513 366-3260
Cincinnati (G-4001)

Suburban Medical Laboratory ....C 330 929-7992
Euclid (G-10658)

Triad Group Inc ....D 419 228-8800
Lima (G-12768)

University of Cincinnati ....D 513 584-5331
Cincinnati (G-4716)

Zak Enterprises Ltd ....D 216 261-9700
Euclid (G-10661)

LABORATORIES: Testing

Acuren Inspection Inc ....E 513 671-7073
Cincinnati (G-2906)

Advanced Testing Lab Inc ....C 513 489-8447
Blue Ash (G-1498)

Advanced Testing MGT Group Inc ....C 513 489-8447
Blue Ash (G-1499)

Akzo Nobel Coatings Inc ....E 614 294-3361
Columbus (G-6890)

Als Group Usa Corp ....E 513 733-5336
Blue Ash (G-1503)

Als Services Usa Corp ....D 513 582-8277
West Chester (G-18864)

Als Services Usa Corp ....E 604 998-5311
Cleveland (G-4943)

Atc Group Services LLC ....D 513 771-2112
Cincinnati (G-2996)

Balancing Company Inc ....E 937 898-9111
Vandalia (G-18506)

Barr Engineering Incorporated ....E 614 714-0299
Columbus (G-7019)

Bayless Pathmark Inc ....E 440 274-2494
Cleveland (G-5044)

Bwi Chassis Dynamics NA Inc ....E 937 455-5230
Moraine (G-14629)

Clinton-Carvell Inc ....E 614 351-8858
Columbus (G-7229)

Csa America Inc ....D 216 524-4990
Cleveland (G-5384)

Curtiss-Wright Flow Control ....D 513 528-7900
Cincinnati (G-2847)

Curtiss-Wright Flow Ctrl Corp ....D 513 528-7900
Cincinnati (G-2848)

Electro-Analytical Inc ....E 440 951-3514
Mentor (G-14043)

Element Cincinnati ....E 513 984-4112
Fairfield (G-10722)

Element Mtls Tech Cncnnati Inc ....E 513 771-2536
Fairfield (G-10723)

Emlab P&K LLC ....D 330 497-9396
North Canton (G-15199)

Firstenergy Nuclear Oper Co ....D 440 604-9836
Cleveland (G-5539)

Fram Group Operations LLC ....D 419 661-6700
Perrysburg (G-15867)

General Electric Company ....C 937 587-2631
Peebles (G-15801)

Gentherm Medical LLC ....D 513 326-5252
Cincinnati (G-3618)

Godfrey & Wing Inc ....E 330 562-1440
Aurora (G-828)

Grl Engineers Inc ....E 216 831-6131
Solon (G-16855)

High Voltage Maintenance Corp ....E 937 278-0811
Dayton (G-9496)

Idexx Laboratories Inc ....D 330 629-6076
Youngstown (G-20075)

Intertek Testing Svcs NA Inc ....E 614 279-8090
Columbus (G-7840)

Kemron Environmental Svcs Inc ....D 740 373-4071
Marietta (G-13342)

Kenmore Research Company ....D 330 297-1407
Ravenna (G-16248)

Landing Gear Test Facility ....E 937 255-5740
Dayton (G-9180)

Lexamed ....E 419 693-5307
Toledo (G-17852)

Mercy Health ....E 330 841-4406
Warren (G-18729)

Mistras Group Inc ....D 419 836-5904
Millbury (G-14450)

Mistras Group Inc ....E 740 788-9188
Heath (G-11705)

North Amercn Science Assoc Inc ....C 419 666-9455
Northwood (G-15401)

Northast Ohio Rgonal Sewer Dst ....C 216 641-6000
Cleveland (G-6084)

Nsl Analytical Services Inc ....D 216 438-5200
Cleveland (G-6105)

Nucon International Inc ....E 614 846-5710
Columbus (G-8213)

Omega Laboratories Inc ....D 330 628-5748
Mogadore (G-14553)

Pace Analytical Services Inc ....E 614 486-5421
Dublin (G-10303)

Professional Service Inds Inc ....E 614 876-8000
Columbus (G-8470)

Q Labs LLC ....C 513 471-1300
Cincinnati (G-4309)

Reid Asset Management Company ....E 216 642-3223
Cleveland (G-6298)

Resource International Inc ....E 614 823-4949
Columbus (G-8523)

Rev1 Ventures ....E 614 487-3700
Columbus (G-8529)

S D Myers Inc ....C 330 630-7000
Tallmadge (G-17486)

Sample Machining Inc ....E 937 258-3338
Dayton (G-9750)

SD Myers LLC ....C 330 630-7000
Tallmadge (G-17487)

Sensation Research ....E 513 602-1611
Maineville (G-13118)

Summit Environmental Tech Inc ....D 330 253-8211
Cuyahoga Falls (G-9127)

Testamerica Laboratories Inc ....D 937 294-6856
Moraine (G-14702)

US Inspection Services Inc ....E 937 660-9879
Dayton (G-9844)

US Inspection Services Inc ....E 513 671-7073
Cincinnati (G-4741)

Wyle Laboratories Inc ....E 937 912-3470
Beavercreek (G-1201)

X-Ray Industries Inc ....E 216 642-0100
Cleveland (G-6696)

Yoder Industries Inc ....C 937 278-5769
Dayton (G-9890)

LABORATORIES: Ultrasound

Amerathon LLC ....B 513 752-7300
Cincinnati (G-2841)

Mercy Health Youngstown LLC ....A 330 746-7211
Youngstown (G-20126)

Proscan Imaging LLC ....D 513 281-3400
Cincinnati (G-4299)

Stork Studios Inc ....E 419 841-7766
Toledo (G-18049)

Womens Centers-Dayton ....E 937 228-2222
Dayton (G-9885)

LABORATORY APPARATUS & FURNITURE

Chemsultants International Inc ....E 440 974-3080
Mentor (G-14029)

Dentronix Inc ....E 330 916-7300
Cuyahoga Falls (G-9086)

Ies Systems Inc ....E 330 533-6683
Canfield (G-2143)

Philips Medical Systems Clevel...........B 440 247-2652
Cleveland (G-6203)

Tech Pro Inc ....E 330 923-3546
Akron (G-466)

Teledyne Instruments Inc ....E 513 229-7000
Mason (G-13645)

Teledyne Tekmar Company ....E 513 229-7000
Mason (G-13646)

LABORATORY EQPT, EXC MEDICAL: Wholesalers

Perkinelmer Hlth Sciences Inc ....E 330 825-4525
Akron (G-378)

Teledyne Instruments Inc ....E 513 229-7000
Mason (G-13645)

Teledyne Tekmar Company ....E 513 229-7000
Mason (G-13646)

LABORATORY EQPT: Clinical Instruments Exc Medical

Cellular Technology Limited ....E 216 791-5084
Shaker Heights (G-16704)

LABORATORY INSTRUMENT REPAIR SVCS

Tech Pro Inc ....E 330 923-3546
Akron (G-466)

LADDERS: Metal

Bauer Corporation ....E 800 321-4760
Wooster (G-19689)

LAMINATED PLASTICS: Plate, Sheet, Rod & Tubes

Applied Medical Technology Inc ....E 440 717-4000
Brecksville (G-1769)

Ilpea Industries Inc ....C 330 562-2916
Aurora (G-830)

LAMINATING SVCS

Conversion Tech Intl Inc ....E 419 924-5566
West Unity (G-19140)

Kent Adhesive Products Co ....D 330 678-1626
Kent (G-12239)

Ohio Laminating & Binding Inc ....E 614 771-4868
Hilliard (G-11802)

United Art and Education Inc ....E 800 322-3247
Dayton (G-9830)

LAND SUBDIVIDERS & DEVELOPERS: Commercial

Al Neyer LLC ....D 513 271-6400
Cincinnati (G-2918)

C V Perry & Co ....E 614 221-4131
Columbus (G-7105)

Cardida Corporation ....E 740 439-4359
Kimbolton (G-12311)

Coral Company ....E 216 932-8822
Cleveland (G-5349)

Creekside II LLC ....E 614 280-4000
Columbus (G-7389)

Duke Realty Corporation ....D 513 651-3900
Mason (G-13576)

Eagle Realty Group LLC ....E 513 361-7700
Cincinnati (G-3469)

Forest City Washington LLC ....E 261 621-6060
Cleveland (G-5562)

Goodman Properties Inc ....E 740 264-7781
Steubenville (G-17155)

Highland Som Development ....E 330 528-3500
Streetsboro (G-17256)

Laurel Development Corporation ....E 614 794-8800
Westerville (G-19179)

Multicon Builders Inc ....E 614 241-2070
Columbus (G-8121)

Multicon Builders Inc ....E 614 463-1142
Columbus (G-8122)

Oberer Development Co ....E 937 910-0851
Miamisburg (G-14199)

Ostendorf-Morris Properties ....D 216 861-7200
Cleveland (G-6146)

Phillips Edison & Company LLC ....E 513 554-1110
Cincinnati (G-4241)

Req/Jqh Holdings Inc ....E 513 891-1066
Blue Ash (G-1645)

Robert L Stark Enterprises Inc ....E 216 292-0242
Cleveland (G-6333)

Slavic Village Development ....E 216 429-1182
Cleveland (G-6415)

Sommerset Development Ltd ....C 440 286-6194
Chardon (G-2715)

Southgate Corp ....E 740 522-2151
Newark (G-15098)

Sunrise Land Co ....E 216 621-6060
Cleveland (G-6478)

T O J Inc ....E 440 352-1900
Mentor (G-14114)

The Daimler Group Inc ....E 614 488-4424
Columbus (G-8743)

Visconsi Companies Ltd ....E 216 464-5550
Cleveland (G-6634)

SERVICES

Zaremba Group Incorporated ....E 216 221-6600
Cleveland **(G-6708)**
Zaremba Group LLC ....C 216 221-6600
Lakewood **(G-12366)**

LAND SUBDIVIDERS & DEVELOPERS: Residential

Breezy Point Ltd Partnership...............C 440 247-3363
Solon **(G-16828)**
Columbus Housing Partnr Inc ....D 614 221-8889
Columbus **(G-7289)**
Forrer Development Ltd ....E 937 431-6489
Dayton **(G-9445)**
Towne Development Group Ltd ....E 513 381-8696
Cincinnati **(G-4615)**
Wryneck Development LLC ....E 419 354-2535
Bowling Green **(G-1760)**

LAND SUBDIVISION & DEVELOPMENT

Carnegie Management & Dev Corp ....E 440 892-6800
Westlake **(G-19327)**
Carter-Jones Companies Inc ....E 330 673-6100
Kent **(G-12217)**
Edwards Land Company ....E 614 241-2070
Columbus **(G-7508)**
Equity Inc ....E 614 802-2900
Hilliard **(G-11766)**
Forest City Enterprises LP ....B 216 621-6060
Cleveland **(G-5553)**
Forest Cy Residential MGT Inc ....C 216 621-6060
Cleveland **(G-5563)**
George J Igel & Co Inc ....A 614 445-8421
Columbus **(G-7659)**
Great Traditions Dev Group Inc ....E 513 563-4070
Cincinnati **(G-3646)**
Henkle-Schueler & Associates ....E 513 932-6070
Lebanon **(G-12471)**
Jack Gray ....D 216 688-0466
Cincinnati **(G-3799)**
Lha Developments ....E 330 785-3219
Akron **(G-312)**
Lt Land Development LLC ....E 937 382-0072
Wilmington **(G-19631)**
Magnum Management Corporation.......A 419 627-2334
Sandusky **(G-16626)**
Midwestern Plumbing Service ....E 513 753-0050
Cincinnati **(G-4051)**
Miller-Vlentine Operations Inc ....E 937 293-0900
Dayton **(G-9638)**
Miller-Vlentine Operations Inc ....A 513 771-0900
Dayton **(G-9639)**
Mv Residential Development LLC ....E 937 293-0900
Moraine **(G-14682)**
Nationwide Rlty Investors Ltd ....E 614 857-2330
Columbus **(G-8161)**
North American Properties Inc ....E 513 721-2744
Cincinnati **(G-4125)**
Piatt Park Ltd Partnership...................D 513 381-8696
Cincinnati **(G-4246)**
Pizzuti Builders LLC ....E 614 280-4000
Columbus **(G-8449)**
Pizzuti Inc ....E 614 280-4000
Columbus **(G-8450)**
Rama Tika Developers LLC..................E 419 806-6446
Mansfield **(G-13232)**
Richland Mall Shopping Ctr ....E 419 529-4003
Mansfield **(G-13236)**
Rockford Homes Inc ....D 614 785-0015
Columbus **(G-6834)**
Sawyer Realtors ....E 513 423-6521
Middletown **(G-14327)**
Seg of Ohio Inc ....E 614 414-7300
Columbus **(G-8617)**
Signature Associates Inc ....E 419 244-7505
Toledo **(G-18034)**
Soho Development Company ....D 614 207-3261
Johnstown **(G-12203)**
TP Mechanical Contractors Inc ....A 513 851-8881
Cincinnati **(G-4623)**
Urban Retail Properties LLC ....E 513 346-4482
Cincinnati **(G-4736)**
Wallick Enterprises Inc......................D 614 863-4640
New Albany **(G-14877)**
Warren Housing Development ....D 330 369-1533
Warren **(G-18770)**
Windsor Companies ....E 740 653-8822
Lancaster **(G-12445)**

LANGUAGE SCHOOLS

Cincilingua Inc ....E 513 721-8782
Cincinnati **(G-3218)**

LAUNDRIES, EXC POWER & COIN-OPERATED

Central Ohio Medical Textiles ....C 614 453-9274
Columbus **(G-7159)**
Clean Living Laundry LLC ....E 513 569-0439
Cincinnati **(G-3304)**
Springfeld Unfrm-Linen Sup Inc ....D 937 323-5544
Springfield **(G-17116)**

LAUNDRY & DRYCLEANER AGENTS

Apc2 Inc ....D 513 231-5540
Cincinnati **(G-2972)**

LAUNDRY & DRYCLEANING SVCS, EXC COIN-OPERATED: Pickup

R & E Joint Venture Inc ....E 614 891-9404
Westerville **(G-19206)**

LAUNDRY & GARMENT SVCS, NEC: Accy/Non-Garment Cleaning/Rpr

Van Dyne-Crotty Co ....E 614 684-0048
Columbus **(G-8842)**

LAUNDRY & GARMENT SVCS, NEC: Garment Alteration & Repair

Quality Cleaners of Ohio Inc...............E 330 688-5616
Stow **(G-17226)**

LAUNDRY & GARMENT SVCS, NEC: Garment Making, Alter & Repair

G&K Services LLC ....B 952 912-5500
Mason **(G-13582)**
Pins & Needles Inc............................E 440 243-6400
Cleveland **(G-6212)**

LAUNDRY SVC: Mat & Rug Sply

Kimmel Cleaners Inc ....D 419 294-1959
Upper Sandusky **(G-18410)**

LAUNDRY SVC: Safety Glove Sply

Brent Industries Inc ....E 419 382-8693
Toledo **(G-17624)**

LAUNDRY SVC: Work Clothing Sply

Unifirst Corporation...........................E 614 575-9999
Blacklick **(G-1483)**

LAUNDRY SVCS: Indl

Aramark Unf & Career AP LLC.............C 614 445-8341
Columbus **(G-6962)**
Aramark Unf & Career AP LLC.............C 216 341-7400
Cleveland **(G-4999)**
Cintas Corporation ....D 330 821-2220
Alliance **(G-524)**
Cintas Corporation No 2 ....D 614 878-7313
Columbus **(G-7201)**
Cintas Corporation No 2 ....C 614 860-9152
Blacklick **(G-1477)**
Duckworth Enterprises LLC.................E 614 575-2900
Reynoldsburg **(G-16301)**
Midwest Laundry Inc ....D 513 563-5560
Cincinnati **(G-4050)**
Morgan Services Inc ....E 419 243-2214
Toledo **(G-17924)**
Springfeld Unfrm-Linen Sup Inc ....D 937 323-5544
Springfield **(G-17116)**
Unifirst Corporation...........................D 216 658-6900
Independence **(G-12134)**

LAWN & GARDEN EQPT

Mtd Holdings Inc ....B 330 225-2600
Valley City **(G-18467)**
Power Distributors LLC ....D 614 876-3533
Columbus **(G-8457)**
Scotts Company LLC.........................B 937 644-0011
Marysville **(G-13528)**

LAWN & GARDEN EQPT STORES

Carmichael Equipment Inc ....E 740 446-2412
Bidwell **(G-1467)**
Equipment Maintenance Inc ....E 513 353-3518
Cleves **(G-6728)**
Hull Bros Inc ....E 419 375-2827
Fort Recovery **(G-10992)**
Supers Landscaping Inc ....E 440 775-0027
Oberlin **(G-15520)**

LAWN MOWER REPAIR SHOP

Altaquip LLC ....E 513 674-6464
Harrison **(G-11660)**
Supers Landscaping Inc ....E 440 775-0027
Oberlin **(G-15520)**

LEASING & RENTAL SVCS: Cranes & Aerial Lift Eqpt

A and A Millwright Rigging Svcs ....E 513 396-6212
Cincinnati **(G-2888)**
All Aerials LLC ....E 330 659-9600
Richfield **(G-16343)**
All Crane Rental Corp........................D 614 261-1800
Columbus **(G-6891)**
All Erection Crane Rentl Corp ....E 216 524-6550
Cleveland **(G-4932)**
American Crane Inc ....E 614 496-2268
Reynoldsburg **(G-16281)**
Canton Erectors Inc ....E 330 453-7363
Canton **(G-2232)**
Capital City Group Inc ....E 419 931-6757
Oregon **(G-15586)**
Eastland Crane Service Inc ....E 614 868-9750
Columbus **(G-7490)**
General Crane Rental LLC ....E 330 908-0001
Macedonia **(G-13070)**
Jeffers Crane Service Inc ....D 419 693-0421
Oregon **(G-15599)**
Kelley Steel Erectors Inc ....D 440 232-1573
Cleveland **(G-5821)**
Midwest Equipment Co ....E 216 441-1400
Cleveland **(G-5990)**
Piqua Steel Co ....D 937 773-3632
Piqua **(G-16020)**
United Rentals North Amer Inc ....E 800 877-3687
Perrysburg **(G-15929)**

LEASING & RENTAL SVCS: Earth Moving Eqpt

Malavite Excavating Inc......................E 330 484-1274
East Sparta **(G-10423)**

LEASING & RENTAL SVCS: Oil Field Eqpt

Eleet Cryogenics Inc ....E 330 874-4009
Bolivar **(G-1702)**

LEASING & RENTAL: Computers & Eqpt

Information Builders Inc......................E 513 891-2338
Montgomery **(G-14595)**
Pomeroy It Solutions Sls Inc ....E 440 717-1364
Brecksville **(G-1798)**

LEASING & RENTAL: Construction & Mining Eqpt

1st Choice LLC.................................D 877 564-6658
Cleveland **(G-4867)**
All Erection & Crane Rental ....C 216 524-6550
Cleveland **(G-4930)**
All Erection & Crane Rental ....D 216 524-6550
Cleveland **(G-4931)**
Bluefoot Industrial LLC ....E 740 314-5299
Steubenville **(G-17141)**
Bobcat Enterprises Inc.......................D 513 874-8945
West Chester **(G-18877)**
Cecil I Walker Machinery Co ....E 740 286-7566
Jackson **(G-12170)**
Charles Jergens Contractor.................E 937 233-1830
Dayton **(G-9294)**
Columbus Equipment Company ....E 614 437-0352
Columbus **(G-7281)**
Columbus Equipment Company ....E 614 443-6541
Columbus **(G-7282)**
Construction Eqp & Sup Ltd ....E 419 625-7192
Sandusky **(G-16593)**

Dolin Supply Co ....E 304 529-4171
South Point (G-16932)
Efco Corp ....E 614 876-1226
Columbus (G-7509)
F & M Mafco Inc ....C 513 367-2151
Harrison (G-11666)
H M Miller Construction Co ....D 330 628-4811
Mogadore (G-14549)
Holt Rental Services ....E 513 771-0515
Cincinnati (G-3716)
Indian Nation Inc ....E 740 532-6143
North Canton (G-15212)
JBK Group Inc ....E 216 901-0000
Cleveland (G-5784)
Lefeld Welding & Stl Sups Inc ....E 419 678-2397
Coldwater (G-6762)
Leppo Inc ....E 330 456-2930
Canton (G-2376)
Leppo Inc ....C 330 633-3999
Tallmadge (G-17480)
Ohio Machinery Co ....E 330 530-9010
Girard (G-11295)
Ohio Machinery Co ....C 440 526-6200
Broadview Heights (G-1840)
Phillips Ready Mix Co ....D 937 426-5151
Beavercreek Township (G-1259)
Pollock Research & Design Inc ......E 330 332-3300
Salem (G-16554)
RELAM Inc ....E 440 232-3354
Solon (G-16891)
Sommerset Development Ltd ....C 440 286-6194
Chardon (G-2715)
Sunbelt Rentals Inc ....E 216 362-0300
Cleveland (G-6477)
TNT Equipment Company ....E 614 882-1549
Columbus (G-8761)
Towlift Inc ....E 419 666-1333
Northwood (G-15411)
Trimble Engineering & Cnstr ....E 937 233-8921
Dayton (G-9823)

LEASING & RENTAL: Medical Machinery & Eqpt

American Home Health Care Inc ......E 614 237-1133
Columbus (G-6925)
Ancillary Medical Investments ......E 937 456-5520
Eaton (G-10436)
Apria Healthcare LLC ....E 614 351-5920
Columbus (G-6960)
Apria Healthcare LLC ....E 216 485-1180
Cleveland (G-4997)
Apria Healthcare LLC ....D 419 471-1919
Maumee (G-13758)
Boardman Medical Supply Co ....C 330 545-6700
Girard (G-11283)
Braden Med Services Inc ....E 740 732-2356
Caldwell (G-2036)
Cornerstone Med Svcs Midwest ......E 513 554-0222
Blue Ash (G-1537)
Cornerstone Medical Associates ......E 330 374-0229
Akron (G-159)
Cornerstone Medical Services ....E 513 554-0222
Blue Ash (G-1538)
Fairfield Medical Center ....A 740 687-8000
Lancaster (G-12399)
Fortec Medical Inc ....E 330 463-1265
Hudson (G-11978)
Fortec Medical Inc ....E 513 742-9100
Cincinnati (G-3580)
Medical Service Company ....D 440 232-3000
Bedford (G-1293)
Medical Specialties Distrs LLC ......E 440 232-0320
Oakwood Village (G-15490)
Mercy Health - St R ....A 419 227-3361
Lima (G-12702)
Millers Rental and Sls Co Inc ....D 330 753-8600
Akron (G-339)
Sateri Home Inc ....D 330 758-8106
Youngstown (G-20204)
Seeley Enterprises Company ....E 440 293-6600
Andover (G-608)
Seeley Medical Oxygen Co ....E 440 255-7163
Andover (G-609)
Toledo Medical Equipment Co ....E 419 866-7120
Maumee (G-13862)

LEASING & RENTAL: Mobile Home Sites

Mercelina Mobile Home Park ....D 419 586-5407
Celina (G-2599)

Park Management Specialist ....D 419 893-4879
Maumee (G-13831)

LEASING & RENTAL: Office Machines & Eqpt

Gordon Flesch Company Inc ....E 419 884-2031
Mansfield (G-13179)
Modern Office Methods Inc ....D 513 791-0909
Blue Ash (G-1613)
Office Products Toledo Inc ....E 419 865-7001
Holland (G-11904)
Ricoh Usa Inc ....D 513 984-9898
Sharonville (G-16730)

LEASING & RENTAL: Other Real Estate Property

Baker Bnngson Rlty Auctioneers ......E 419 547-7777
Clyde (G-6740)
Bessemer and Lake Erie RR Co ....C 440 593-1102
Conneaut (G-8951)
Catawba-Cleveland Dev Corp ....D 419 797-4424
Port Clinton (G-16101)
Cutler Real Estate Inc ....E 614 339-4664
Dublin (G-10194)
Darfus ....E 740 380-1710
Logan (G-12834)
Employers Mutual Casualty Co ......D 513 221-6010
Blue Ash (G-1551)
Etb University Properties LLC ....C 440 826-2212
Berea (G-1425)
Fairlawn Associates Ltd ....C 330 867-5000
Fairlawn (G-10826)
Hertz Clvland 600 Superior LLC ......E 310 584-8108
Cleveland (G-5687)
J & E LLC ....E 513 241-0429
Cincinnati (G-3793)
Midway Realty Company ....E 440 324-2404
Elyria (G-10538)
Ohio Living ....A 330 638-2420
Cortland (G-8993)
Sami S Rafidi ....C 330 799-9508
Youngstown (G-20202)
Select Hotels Group LLC ....E 513 754-0003
Mason (G-13638)
Stranahan Theatre Trust ....E 419 381-8851
Toledo (G-18050)
Weston Inc ....E 440 349-9001
Solon (G-16914)

LEASING & RENTAL: Trucks, Indl

All Lift Service Company Inc ....E 440 585-1542
Willoughby (G-19503)
Bluefoot Industrial LLC ....E 740 314-5299
Steubenville (G-17141)
Bobcat of Dayton Inc ....E 937 293-3176
Moraine (G-14627)
Brennan Industrial Truck Co ....E 419 867-6000
Holland (G-11875)
Fallsway Equipment Co Inc ....C 330 633-6000
Akron (G-209)

LEASING & RENTAL: Trucks, Without Drivers

E H Schmidt Executive ....D 419 874-4331
Perrysburg (G-15861)
Graham Chevrolet-Cadillac Co ....D 419 989-4012
Ontario (G-15551)
Hogan Truck Leasing Inc ....E 513 454-3500
Fairfield (G-10736)
Interstate Truckway Inc ....D 513 542-5500
Cincinnati (G-3781)
Kempthorn Motors Inc ....C 800 451-3877
Canton (G-2365)
Krieger Ford Inc ....C 614 888-3320
Columbus (G-7927)
McCluskey Chevrolet Inc ....C 513 761-1111
Cincinnati (G-3986)
Miami Valley Intl Trcks Inc ....D 513 733-8500
Cincinnati (G-4045)
Montrose Ford Inc ....D 330 666-0711
Fairlawn (G-10842)
Northern Management & Leasing ......D 216 676-4600
Cleveland (G-6097)
Penske Truck Leasing Co LP ....E 513 771-7701
Cincinnati (G-4227)
Predator Trucking Company ....E 330 530-0712
Mc Donald (G-13897)
Premier Truck Sls & Rentl Inc ....E 800 825-1255
Cleveland (G-6234)

Rouen Chrysler Plymouth Dodge ......E 419 837-6228
Woodville (G-19683)
Roush Equipment Inc ....C 614 882-1535
Westerville (G-19300)
Rush Truck Centers Ohio Inc ....D 513 733-8500
Cincinnati (G-4414)
Rush Truck Centers Ohio Inc ....A 419 224-6045
Lima (G-12735)
Schoner Chevrolet Inc ....E 330 877-6731
Hartville (G-11698)
South East Chevrolet Co ....E 440 585-9300
Willoughby Hills (G-19594)
U Haul Co of Northwestern Ohio ......E 419 478-1101
Toledo (G-18114)
U-Haul Neighborhood Dealer -Ce ......E 419 929-3724
New London (G-14936)
Vin Devers ....C 888 847-9535
Sylvania (G-17462)
Voss Auto Network Inc ....E 937 428-2447
Dayton (G-9860)
White Family Companies Inc ....C 937 222-3701
Dayton (G-9879)

LEASING & RENTAL: Utility Trailers & RV's

Brown Gibbons Lang Ltd Ptrship ......E 216 241-2800
Cleveland (G-5093)
Ryder Truck Rental Inc ....E 614 846-6780
Columbus (G-8567)
U-Haul Neighborhood Dealer -Ce ......E 419 929-3724
New London (G-14936)

LEASING: Passenger Car

1106 West Main Inc ....E 330 673-2122
Kent (G-12212)
Albert Mike Leasing Inc ....C 513 563-1400
Cincinnati (G-2919)
Auto Center USA Inc ....E 513 683-4900
Cincinnati (G-3006)
Beechmont Ford Inc ....C 513 752-6611
Cincinnati (G-2842)
Bob Pulte Chevrolet Inc ....E 513 932-0303
Lebanon (G-12453)
Bobb Automotive Inc ....E 614 853-3000
Columbus (G-7052)
Brondes All Makes Auto Leasing ......D 419 887-1511
Maumee (G-13767)
Brondes Ford ....D 419 473-1411
Toledo (G-17627)
Brown Motor Sales Co ....E 419 531-0151
Toledo (G-17629)
Budget Rent A Car System Inc ....E 937 898-1396
Vandalia (G-18509)
Carcorp Inc ....C 877 857-2801
Columbus (G-7118)
Chesrown Oldsmobile GMC Inc ....E 614 846-3040
Columbus (G-7182)
City Yellow Cab Company ....E 330 253-3141
Akron (G-140)
Classic Buick Olds Cadillac ....D 440 639-4500
Painesville (G-15701)
Clerac LLC ....E 440 345-3999
Strongsville (G-17290)
Columbus SAI Motors LLC ....E 614 851-3273
Columbus (G-7312)
Dave White Chevrolet Inc ....E 419 885-4444
Sylvania (G-17417)
Dunning Motor Sales Inc ....E 740 439-4465
Cambridge (G-2064)
E H Schmidt Executive ....D 419 874-4331
Perrysburg (G-15861)
Ed Schmidt Chevrolet Inc ....D 419 897-8600
Maumee (G-13783)
Ed Tomko Chryslr Jep Dge Inc ....C 440 835-5900
Avon Lake (G-916)
Enterprise Holdings Inc ....E 937 879-0023
Blue Ash (G-1555)
Germain On Scarborough LLC ....C 614 868-0300
Columbus (G-7665)
Graham Chevrolet-Cadillac Co ....D 419 989-4012
Ontario (G-15551)
Greenwoods Hubbard Chevy-Olds ......E 330 568-4335
Hubbard (G-11946)
Grogans Towne Chrysler Inc ....E 419 476-0761
Toledo (G-17772)
Hidy Motors Inc ....D 937 426-9564
Dayton (G-9176)
Jake Sweeney Automotive Inc ....E 513 782-2800
Cincinnati (G-3805)
Jim Brown Chevrolet Inc ....C 440 255-5511
Mentor (G-14065)

SERVICES

Joe Dodge Kidd Inc ....E 513 752-1804
Cincinnati (G-2858)

Kempthorn Motors Inc ....C 800 451-3877
Canton (G-2365)

Kent Automotive Inc ....E 330 678-5520
Kent (G-12240)

Kerns Chevrolet-Buick-Gmc Inc ....E 419 586-5131
Celina (G-2597)

Kerry Ford Inc ....D 513 671-6400
Cincinnati (G-3864)

Kings Toyota Inc ....D 513 583-4333
Cincinnati (G-3874)

Klaben Family Dodge Inc ....E 330 673-9971
Kent (G-12244)

Klaben Lincoln Ford Inc ....D 330 673-3139
Kent (G-12246)

Krieger Ford Inc ....C 614 888-3320
Columbus (G-7927)

Lakewood Chrysler-Plymouth ....E 216 521-1000
Brookpark (G-1901)

Lang Chevrolet Co ....D 937 426-2313
Beavercreek Township (G-1253)

Lariche Subaru Inc ....D 419 422-1855
Findlay (G-10933)

Lavery Chevrolet-Buick Inc ....E 330 823-1100
Alliance (G-537)

Lebanon Chrysler - Plymuth Inc ....E 513 932-2717
Lebanon (G-12480)

Lima Auto Mall Inc ....D 419 993-6000
Lima (G-12675)

Lincoln Mrcury Kings Auto Mall ....C 513 683-3800
Cincinnati (G-3933)

Mathews Dodge Chrysler Jeep ....E 740 389-2341
Marion (G-13444)

Mathews Kennedy Ford L-M Inc ....D 740 387-3673
Marion (G-13445)

Mc Daniel Motor Co (Inc) ....E 740 389-2355
Marion (G-13446)

McCluskey Chevrolet Inc ....C 513 761-1111
Cincinnati (G-3986)

Medina World Cars Inc ....E 330 725-4901
Strongsville (G-17332)

Merrick Chevrolet Co ....D 440 878-6700
Strongsville (G-17333)

Montrose Ford Inc ....D 330 666-0711
Fairlawn (G-10842)

Mullinax Ford North Canton Inc ....C 330 238-3206
Canton (G-2411)

Nick Mayer Lincoln-Mercury Inc ....E 440 835-3700
Westlake (G-19379)

Northgate Chrysler Jeep Inc ....D 513 385-3900
Cincinnati (G-4129)

Oregon Ford Inc ....E 419 698-4444
Oregon (G-15605)

Partners Auto Group Bdford Inc ....D 440 439-2323
Bedford (G-1299)

Ron Marhofer Automall Inc ....E 330 923-5059
Cuyahoga Falls (G-9122)

Rouen Chrysler Plymouth Dodge ....E 419 837-6228
Woodville (G-19683)

Roush Equipment Inc ....C 614 882-1535
Westerville (G-19300)

Saturn of Toledo Inc ....E 419 841-9070
Toledo (G-18020)

Schoner Chevrolet Inc ....E 330 877-6731
Hartville (G-11698)

Sonic Automotive ....D 614 870-8200
Columbus (G-8658)

Sonic Automotive-1495 Automall ....E 614 317-4326
Columbus (G-8659)

Sorbir Inc ....D 440 449-1000
Cleveland (G-6421)

South East Chevrolet Co ....E 440 585-9300
Willoughby Hills (G-19594)

Spitzer Auto World Amherst ....D 440 988-4444
Amherst (G-598)

Sunnyside Toyota Inc ....D 440 777-9911
North Olmsted (G-15312)

Tansky Motors Inc ....E 650 322-7069
Logan (G-12855)

Team Rahal of Dayton Inc ....E 937 438-3800
Dayton (G-9807)

Tom Ahl Chryslr-Plymouth-Dodge ....C 419 227-0202
Lima (G-12765)

Toyota of Bedford ....D 440 439-8600
Bedford (G-1310)

Van Devere Inc ....D 330 253-6137
Akron (G-485)

Vin Devers ....C 888 847-9535
Sylvania (G-17462)

Yark Automotive Group Inc ....A 419 841-7771
Toledo (G-18166)

LEASING: Railroad Property

Feridean Group Inc ....E 614 898-7488
Westerville (G-19166)

LEASING: Residential Buildings

Birchaven Village ....B 419 424-3000
Findlay (G-10870)

Cincinnati Metro Hsing Auth ....E 513 421-8190
Cincinnati (G-3255)

Cincinnati Metro Hsing Auth ....E 513 333-0670
Cincinnati (G-3256)

Cwb Property Managment Inc ....E 614 793-2244
Dublin (G-10195)

J & R Associates ....A 440 250-4080
Brookpark (G-1898)

Kent Place Housing ....D 614 942-2020
Columbus (G-7896)

L and M Investment Co ....E 740 653-3583
Lancaster (G-12409)

North Park Care Center LLC ....D 440 250-4080
Brookpark (G-1904)

Norwalk Golf Properties Inc ....E 419 668-8535
Norwalk (G-15450)

Original Partners Ltd Partnr ....C 513 381-8696
Cincinnati (G-4183)

Our House Inc ....E 440 835-2110
Westlake (G-19390)

Towne Properties Assoc Inc ....E 513 874-3737
Cincinnati (G-4620)

Westview-Youngstown Ltd ....D 330 799-2787
Youngstown (G-20245)

LEATHER & CUT STOCK WHOLESALERS

Leather Gallery Inc ....E 513 312-1722
Lebanon (G-12479)

LEATHER GOODS, EXC FOOTWEAR, GLOVES, LUGGAGE/BELTING, WHOL

B D G Wrap-Tite Inc ....D 440 349-5400
Solon (G-16826)

LEATHER GOODS: Coin Purses

Hamilton Manufacturing Corp ....E 419 867-4858
Holland (G-11888)

LEATHER, LEATHER GOODS & FURS, WHOLESALE

Millennium Leather LLC ....E 201 541-7121
Mason (G-13620)

LEGAL & TAX SVCS

Barnett Associates Inc ....D 516 877-2860
Hilliard (G-11745)

LEGAL AID SVCS

Advoctes For Bsic Lgal Eqality ....E 419 255-0814
Toledo (G-17583)

Community Legal Aid Services ....E 330 725-1231
Medina (G-13921)

Community Legal Aid Services ....D 330 535-4191
Akron (G-152)

Legal Aid Society Cincinnati ....D 513 241-9400
Cincinnati (G-3917)

Legal Aid Society of Cleveland ....D 216 861-5500
Cleveland (G-5863)

Legal Aid Society of Columbus ....D 614 737-0139
Columbus (G-7964)

Legal Aid Western Ohio Inc ....E 419 724-0030
Toledo (G-17851)

Litigation Management Inc ....B 440 484-2000
Mayfield Heights (G-13876)

Toledo Legal Aid Society ....E 419 720-3048
Toledo (G-18089)

LEGAL COUNSEL & PROSECUTION: Attorney General's Office

Bricker & Eckler LLP ....C 513 870-6700
Cincinnati (G-3073)

LEGAL COUNSEL & PROSECUTION: County Government

County of Richland ....E 419 774-5676
Mansfield (G-13153)

LEGAL COUNSEL & PROSECUTION: Local Government

City of Columbus ....E 614 645-6624
Columbus (G-7211)

LEGAL COUNSEL & PROSECUTION: Public Prosecutors' Office

County of Portage ....E 330 297-3850
Ravenna (G-16240)

LEGAL OFFICES & SVCS

American Title Services Inc ....E 330 652-1609
Niles (G-15144)

Arthur Middleton Capital Holdn ....E 330 966-9000
North Canton (G-15190)

Baker & Hostetler LLP ....C 614 228-1541
Columbus (G-7014)

Bigmar Inc ....E 740 966-5800
Johnstown (G-12196)

Bolotin Law Offices ....E 419 424-9800
Findlay (G-10881)

Butler County of Ohio ....E 513 887-3090
Hamilton (G-11570)

City of Columbus ....E 614 645-6624
Columbus (G-7211)

City of Lakewood ....C 216 529-6170
Cleveland (G-5207)

Cleveland Metro Bar Assn ....E 216 696-3525
Cleveland (G-5266)

Cleveland Teachers Union Inc ....E 216 861-7676
Cleveland (G-5292)

County of Portage ....E 330 297-3850
Ravenna (G-16240)

Criminal Jstice Crdnting Cncil ....E 567 200-6850
Toledo (G-17688)

Executives Agencies ....E 614 466-2980
Columbus (G-7543)

Fairfield Federal Sav Ln Assn ....E 740 653-3863
Lancaster (G-12395)

Franklin Cnty Bd Commissioners ....C 614 462-3194
Columbus (G-7610)

General Audit Corp ....E 419 993-2900
Lima (G-12642)

Jefferson Medical Co ....E 216 443-9000
Cleveland (G-5787)

Lawrence Cnty Hstorical Museum ....E 740 532-1222
Ironton (G-12161)

Litigation Support Svcs Inc ....E 513 241-5605
Cincinnati (G-3940)

Marshall & Associates Inc ....E 513 683-6396
Loveland (G-13011)

Morris Schneider Wittstadt LLC ....E 440 942-5168
Willoughby (G-19552)

National Service Information ....E 740 387-6806
Marion (G-13448)

Northwest Ttl Agy of OH MI In ....D 419 241-8195
Toledo (G-17951)

Ohio Disability Rights Law Pol ....E 614 466-7264
Columbus (G-8249)

Ohio State Bar Association ....E 614 487-2050
Columbus (G-8288)

Opers Legal Dept ....E 614 227-0550
Columbus (G-8377)

Pappas Leah ....E 614 621-7007
Columbus (G-8419)

Recovery One LLC ....D 614 336-4207
Columbus (G-8496)

Shared Services LLC ....D 513 821-4278
Cincinnati (G-4463)

Sottile & Barile LLC ....E 513 345-0592
Loveland (G-13030)

Supreme Court of Ohio ....E 937 898-3996
Vandalia (G-18543)

United Scoto Senior Activities ....E 740 354-6672
Portsmouth (G-16176)

Zaremba Group Incorporated ....E 216 221-6600
Cleveland (G-6708)

Zaremba Group LLC ....C 216 221-6600
Lakewood (G-12366)

LEGAL SVCS: Administrative & Government Law

Butler County of Ohio..................D...... 513 887-3282
  Hamilton (G-11561)
Village of Strasburg..................E...... 330 878-7115
  Strasburg (G-17241)

LEGAL SVCS: Bankruptcy Law

Epiq Systems Inc..................C...... 513 794-0400
  Loveland (G-12993)
Law Offices of John D Clunk C..........D...... 330 436-0300
  Stow (G-17217)

LEGAL SVCS: Criminal Law

Bonezzi Swtzer Polito Hupp Lpa..........E...... 216 875-2767
  Cleveland (G-5068)

LEGAL SVCS: Debt Collection Law

Value Recovery Group Inc..................E...... 614 324-5959
  Columbus (G-8841)

LEGAL SVCS: General Practice Attorney or Lawyer

Allen Khnle Stovall Neuman LLP..........E...... 614 221-8500
  Columbus (G-6893)
Altick & Corwin Co Lpa..................E...... 937 223-1201
  Dayton (G-9225)
American Financial Corporation..........D...... 513 579-2121
  Cincinnati (G-2942)
Anspach Meeks Ellenberger LLP..........E...... 614 745-8350
  Columbus (G-6951)
Anspach Meeks Ellenberger LLP..........E...... 419 447-6181
  Toledo (G-17595)
Auman Mahan & Furry A Legal..........E...... 937 223-6003
  Dayton (G-9243)
Bailey Cavalieri LLC..................D...... 614 221-3258
  Columbus (G-7013)
Baker & Hostetler LLP..................B...... 216 861-7587
  Cleveland (G-5033)
Baker & Hostetler LLP..................B...... 216 621-0200
  Cleveland (G-5034)
Baker & Hostetler LLP..................E...... 513 929-3400
  Cincinnati (G-3015)
Baker Dblkar Beck Wley Mathews..........E...... 330 499-6000
  Canton (G-2209)
Bavan & Associates..................E...... 330 650-0088
  Northfield (G-15374)
Benesch Friedlander Coplan &..........E...... 614 223-9300
  Columbus (G-7027)
Bieser Greer & Landis LLP..................E...... 937 223-3277
  Dayton (G-9250)
Bordas & Bordas Pllc..................E...... 740 695-8141
  Saint Clairsville (G-16480)
Bricker & Eckler LLP..................C...... 513 870-6700
  Cincinnati (G-3073)
Bruce M Allman..................D...... 513 352-6712
  Cincinnati (G-3083)
Buckingham Dlttle Brroughs LLC..........D...... 330 492-8717
  Canton (G-2222)
Burke Manley Lpa..................E...... 513 721-5525
  Cincinnati (G-3092)
Butler Cincione and Dicuccio..........E...... 614 221-3151
  Columbus (G-7101)
Calfee Halter & Griswold LLP..........B...... 216 831-2732
  Cleveland (G-5114)
Calfee Halter & Griswold LLP..........C...... 513 693-4880
  Cincinnati (G-3105)
Calfee Halter & Griswold LLP..........E...... 614 621-1500
  Columbus (G-7106)
Calfee Halgerr Griswold LLC..........E...... 614 621-7003
  Columbus (G-7107)
Carlile Patchen & Murphy LLP..........D...... 614 228-6135
  Columbus (G-7128)
Chamberlain Hr..................C...... 216 589-9280
  Avon (G-873)
City of Marion..................D...... 740 382-1479
  Marion (G-13412)
Cohen Todd Kite Stanford LLC..........E...... 513 205-7286
  Cincinnati (G-3319)
Connor Evans Hafenstein LLP..........E...... 614 464-2025
  Columbus (G-7350)
Cors & Bassett LLC..................D...... 513 852-8200
  Cincinnati (G-3365)
County of Montgomery..................C...... 937 225-5623
  Dayton (G-9331)
County of Ottawa..................C...... 419 898-6459
  Oak Harbor (G-15470)

County of Ottawa..................E...... 419 898-2089
  Oak Harbor (G-15471)
Dagger Johnston Miller..................E...... 740 653-6464
  Lancaster (G-12388)
Dana & Pariser Attys..................E...... 614 253-1010
  Columbus (G-7413)
David L Barth Lwyr..................D...... 513 852-8228
  Cincinnati (G-3402)
Dinn Hochman and Potter LLC..........E...... 440 446-1100
  Cleveland (G-5423)
Dinsmore & Shohl LLP..................B...... 513 977-8200
  Cincinnati (G-3430)
Douglass & Associates Co Lpa..........E...... 216 362-7777
  Cleveland (G-5444)
Duane Morris LLP..................E...... 202 577-3075
  Cleveland (G-5447)
Duane Morris LLP..................E...... 937 424-7086
  Columbus (G-7473)
Dungan & Lefevre Co Lpa..................E...... 937 339-0511
  Troy (G-18200)
Dworken & Bernstein Co Lpa..........E...... 216 861-4211
  Cleveland (G-5451)
Dworken & Bernstein Co Lpa..........E...... 440 352-3391
  Painesville (G-15711)
Eastman & Smith Ltd..................C...... 419 241-6000
  Toledo (G-17709)
Elizabeth H Farbman..................E...... 330 744-5211
  Youngstown (G-20028)
Elk & Elk Co Lpa..................D...... 800 355-6446
  Mayfield Heights (G-13874)
Elliott Heller Maas Morrow Lpa..........E...... 330 792-6611
  Youngstown (G-20029)
Flanagan Lberman Hoffman Swaim.....E...... 937 223-5200
  Dayton (G-9442)
Freeze/Arnold A Freund Legal..........D...... 937 222-2424
  Dayton (G-9450)
Friedberg Meyers Roman..................E...... 216 831-0042
  Cleveland (G-5579)
Friedman Domiano Smith Co Lpa..........E...... 216 621-0070
  Cleveland (G-5580)
Frost Brown Todd LLC..................B...... 513 651-6800
  Cincinnati (G-3596)
Frost Brown Todd LLC..................E...... 614 464-1211
  Columbus (G-7631)
Fuller & Henry Ltd..................E...... 419 247-2500
  Toledo (G-17749)
Gallagher Sharp..................C...... 216 241-5310
  Cleveland (G-5591)
Gallon Takacs Boissoneault & S..........D...... 419 843-2001
  Toledo (G-17753)
Gottlieb Johnson Beam Dal P..........E...... 740 452-7555
  Zanesville (G-20313)
Harris & Burgin..................E...... 513 891-3270
  Blue Ash (G-1575)
Hawkins & Co Lpa Ltd..................E...... 216 861-1365
  Cleveland (G-5668)
Heller Maas Moro & Magill..........E...... 330 393-6602
  Youngstown (G-20063)
Heyman Ralph E Attorney At Law..........D...... 937 449-2820
  Dayton (G-9495)
International Paper Compa..................D...... 513 248-6000
  Loveland (G-13001)
Jackson Kelly Pllc..................D...... 330 252-9060
  Akron (G-287)
James C Sass Atty..................E...... 419 843-3545
  Swanton (G-17400)
James L Jacobson..................E...... 937 223-1130
  Dayton (G-9523)
Javitch Block LLC..................D...... 216 623-0000
  Columbus (G-7854)
Jeffrey W Smith..................E...... 740 532-9000
  Ironton (G-12159)
Jones Day Limited Partnership..........C...... 614 469-3939
  Columbus (G-7866)
Katz Teller Brant Hild Co Lpa..........D...... 513 721-4532
  Cincinnati (G-3848)
Keating Muething & Klekamp Pll..........B...... 513 579-6400
  Cincinnati (G-3850)
Kegler Brown Hl Ritter Co Lpa..........C...... 614 462-5400
  Columbus (G-7886)
Kegler Brown Hl Ritter Co Lpa..........D...... 216 586-6650
  Cleveland (G-5818)
Kelley & Ferraro LLP..................E...... 216 575-0777
  Cleveland (G-5820)
Kelly Farrish Lpa..................E...... 513 621-8700
  Cincinnati (G-3855)
Kenneth Zerrusen..................D...... 330 869-9007
  Fairlawn (G-10838)
Kohnen & Patton..................E...... 513 381-0656
  Cincinnati (G-3885)

Krugliak Wilkins Grifiyhd &..........E...... 330 364-3472
  New Philadelphia (G-14969)
Levine Arnold S Law Offices..........E...... 513 241-6748
  Cincinnati (G-3922)
Levy & Associates LLC..................E...... 614 898-5200
  Columbus (G-7967)
Lewis P C Jackson..................E...... 216 750-0404
  Independence (G-12089)
Lindhorst & Dreidame Co Lpa..........D...... 513 421-6630
  Cincinnati (G-3934)
LLP Ziegler Metzger..................E...... 216 781-5470
  Cleveland (G-5877)
Magolius Margolius & Assoc Lpa..........D...... 216 621-2034
  Cleveland (G-5894)
Maguire & Schneider LLP..................E...... 614 224-1222
  Columbus (G-8010)
Mazanec Raskin & Ryder Co Lpa..........D...... 440 248-7906
  Cleveland (G-5925)
Micha Ltd..................E...... 740 653-6464
  Lancaster (G-12418)
Miller Cnfeld Pddock Stone PLC..........D...... 513 394-5252
  Cincinnati (G-4053)
Murray & Murray Co Lpa..................E...... 419 624-3000
  Sandusky (G-16627)
Nicola Gudbranson & Cooper LLC..........E...... 216 621-7227
  Cleveland (G-6069)
Peter M Kostoff..................D...... 330 849-6681
  Akron (G-380)
Peterj Brodhead..................E...... 216 696-3232
  Cleveland (G-6201)
Porter Wrght Morris Arthur LLP..........E...... 513 381-4700
  Cincinnati (G-4264)
Reese Pyle Drake & Meyer..................E...... 740 345-3431
  Newark (G-15095)
Reimer Law Co..................C...... 440 600-5500
  Solon (G-16890)
Reminger Co LPA..................D...... 614 228-1311
  Columbus (G-8513)
Renner Kenner Grieve Bobak..........E...... 330 376-1242
  Akron (G-402)
Rennie & Jonson Montgomery..........E...... 513 241-4722
  Cincinnati (G-4358)
Rich Crites & Dittmer LLC..................E...... 614 228-5822
  Dublin (G-10322)
Rickerier and Eckler..................E...... 513 870-6565
  West Chester (G-18993)
Ritter & Randolph LLC..................E...... 513 381-5700
  Cincinnati (G-4376)
Robbins Kelly Patterson Tucker..........E...... 513 721-3330
  Cincinnati (G-4388)
Rose & Dobyns An Ohio Partnr..........E...... 740 335-4700
  Wshngtn CT Hs (G-19882)
Rose & Dobyns An Ohio Partnr..........D...... 937 382-2838
  Wilmington (G-19646)
Roth Blair Roberts..................E...... 330 744-5211
  Youngstown (G-20196)
Schimpf Ginocchio Mullins Lpa..........E...... 513 977-5570
  Cincinnati (G-4437)
Scott D Phillips..................E...... 513 870-8200
  West Chester (G-19000)
Sebaly Shillito & Dyer Lpa..................E...... 937 222-2500
  Dayton (G-9755)
Seeley Svdge Ebert Gourash Lpa..........E...... 216 566-8200
  Cleveland (G-6392)
Shapiro Shapiro & Shapiro..........E...... 216 927-2030
  Cleveland (G-6404)
Shindler Neff Holmes Schlag..........E...... 419 243-6281
  Toledo (G-18030)
Siegel Siegel J & Jennings Co..........E...... 216 763-1004
  Beachwood (G-1105)
Smith Rolfes & Skazdahl Lpa..........E...... 513 579-0080
  Cincinnati (G-4495)
Spengler Nathanson PLL..................D...... 419 241-2201
  Toledo (G-18041)
Tafaro John..................E...... 513 381-0656
  Cincinnati (G-4567)
Thompson Hine LLP..................C...... 614 469-3200
  Columbus (G-8749)
Thompson Hine LLP..................C...... 614 469-3200
  Columbus (G-8750)
Thompson Hine LLP..................C...... 937 443-6859
  Miamisburg (G-14230)
Thos A Lupica..................D...... 419 252-6298
  Toledo (G-18064)
Tucker Ellis LLP..................D...... 720 897-4400
  Cleveland (G-6553)
Tucker Ellis LLP..................C...... 216 592-5000
  Cleveland (G-6554)
Tucker Ellis LLP..................D...... 614 358-9717
  Columbus (G-8786)

SERVICES

Ulmer & Berne LLP	D	513 698-5000
Cincinnati (G-4669)		
Ulmer & Berne LLP	C	513 698-5058
Cincinnati (G-4671)		
Ulmer & Berne LLP	E	614 229-0000
Columbus (G-8796)		
Walter Haverfield LLP	D	216 781-1212
Cleveland (G-6650)		
Wegman Hessler Vanderburg	D	216 642-3342
Cleveland (G-6658)		
Weiner Keith D Co L P A Inc	E	216 771-6500
Cleveland (G-6659)		
Wiles Boyle Burkholder &	D	614 221-5216
Columbus (G-8902)		
Wood Herron & Evans LLP	E	513 241-2324
Cincinnati (G-4802)		
Wood & Lamping LLP	D	513 852-6000
Cincinnati (G-4803)		
Young & Alexander Co Lpa	D	937 224-9291
Dayton (G-9891)		
Zeiger Tigges & Little LLP	E	614 365-9900
Columbus (G-8936)		

LEGAL SVCS: General Practice Law Office

Agee Clymer Mtchll & Prtman	E	614 221-3318
Columbus (G-6883)		
Barkan & Neff Co Lpa	E	614 221-4221
Columbus (G-7018)		
Brennan Manna & Diamond LLC	E	330 253-5060
Akron (G-105)		
Bricker & Eckler LLP	B	614 227-2300
Columbus (G-7063)		
Brouse McDowell Lpa	E	216 830-6830
Cleveland (G-5090)		
Brown and Margolius Co Lpa	E	216 621-2034
Cleveland (G-5091)		
Buckingham Dlttle Brroughs LLC	C	330 376-5300
Akron (G-114)		
Buckingham Dlttle Brroughs LLC	D	216 621-5300
Cleveland (G-5099)		
Carpenter Lipps & Leland LLP	E	614 365-4100
Columbus (G-7130)		
Cavitch Familo & Durkin Co Lpa	E	216 621-7860
Cleveland (G-5138)		
Climaco Lefkwtz Peca Wlcox &	D	216 621-8484
Cleveland (G-5305)		
Coolidge Law	D	937 223-8177
Dayton (G-9318)		
Coolidge Wall Co LPA	C	937 223-8177
Dayton (G-9319)		
Crabbe Brown & James LLP	E	614 229-4587
Columbus (G-7384)		
Critchfeld Crtchfield Johnston	D	330 264-4444
Wooster (G-19720)		
Davis Young A Legal Prof Assn	E	216 348-1700
Cleveland (G-5409)		
Day Ketterer Ltd	D	330 455-0173
Canton (G-2281)		
E S Gallon & Associates	E	937 586-3100
Moraine (G-14650)		
Ernest V Thomas Jr	E	513 961-5311
Cincinnati (G-3514)		
Faulkner Grmhsen Keister Shenk	E	937 492-1271
Sidney (G-16776)		
Fay Sharpe LLP	D	216 363-9000
Cleveland (G-5518)		
Firm Hahn Law	E	614 221-0240
Columbus (G-7579)		
Gallagher Gams Pryor Tallan	E	614 228-5151
Columbus (G-7645)		
Green Haines Sgambati Lpa	E	330 743-5101
Youngstown (G-20056)		
Hahmooeser & Parks	E	330 864-5550
Cleveland (G-5655)		
Hahn Loeser & Parks LLP	C	216 621-0150
Cleveland (G-5656)		
Hammond Law Group LLC	E	513 381-2011
Cincinnati (G-3678)		
Hoglund Chwlkowski Mrozik Pllc	C	330 252-8009
Akron (G-265)		
Horenstein Nicho & Blume A L	E	937 224-7200
Dayton (G-9505)		
Ice Miller LLP	D	614 462-2700
Columbus (G-7798)		
Isaac Brant Ledman Teetor LLP	D	614 221-2121
Columbus (G-7844)		
Isaac Wiles Burkholder & Teeto	E	614 221-5216
Columbus (G-7845)		
Jackson Kohrman & Pll Krantz	D	216 696-8700
Cleveland (G-5776)		

Janik LLP	D	440 838-7600
Cleveland (G-5780)		
Javitch Block LLC	E	513 381-3051
Cincinnati (G-3809)		
Javitch Block LLC	C	216 623-0000
Cleveland (G-5782)		
Jones Day Limited Partnership	A	216 586-3939
Cleveland (G-5803)		
Jones Law Group LLC	E	614 545-9998
Columbus (G-7867)		
Joseph R Harrison Company Lpa	E	330 666-6900
Barberton (G-956)		
Kademenos Wisehart Hines	E	419 524-6011
Mansfield (G-13192)		
Kendis & Associates Co Lpa	E	216 579-1818
Cleveland (G-5823)		
Krugliak Wilkins Grifiyhd &	D	330 497-0700
Canton (G-2372)		
Lane Alton & Horst LLC	E	614 228-6885
Columbus (G-7949)		
Larrimer & Larrimer LLC	E	614 221-7548
Columbus (G-7954)		
Laurito & Laurito LLC	E	937 743-4878
Dayton (G-9560)		
Law Offces Rbert A Schrger Lpa	E	614 824-5731
Columbus (G-7957)		
Lerner Sampson & Rothfuss	B	513 241-3100
Cincinnati (G-3918)		
Lewis P C Jackson	E	937 306-6304
Beavercreek (G-1226)		
Littler Mendelson PC	D	216 696-7600
Cleveland (G-5875)		
Luper Neidental & Logan A Leg	E	614 221-7663
Columbus (G-7998)		
Lyons Doughty & Veldhuis PC	E	614 229-3888
Columbus (G-8001)		
Manchester Bennett Towers & Ul	E	330 743-1171
Youngstown (G-20115)		
Manley Deas & Kochalski LLC	D	614 220-5611
Columbus (G-8013)		
Mannion & Gray Co LpA	E	216 344-9422
Cleveland (G-5905)		
Marshall & Melhorn LLC	E	419 249-7100
Toledo (G-17896)		
McCaslin Imbus & Mccaslin Lpa	E	513 421-4646
Cincinnati (G-3985)		
MCDONALD HOPKINS LLC	C	216 348-5400
Cleveland (G-5931)		
Millikin and Fitton Law Firm	E	513 829-6700
Hamilton (G-11629)		
Nadler Nadler & Burdman Co Lpa	E	330 533-6195
Canfield (G-2152)		
Nicholas E Davis	E	937 228-2838
Dayton (G-9657)		
Nurenberg Plevin Heller	D	440 423-0750
Cleveland (G-6107)		
OConnor Acciani & Levy LLC	E	513 241-7111
Cincinnati (G-4147)		
Palmer Volkema Thomas Inc	E	614 221-4400
Columbus (G-8415)		
Pearne & Gordon LLP	E	216 579-1700
Cleveland (G-6187)		
Pickrel Schaeffer Ebeling Lpa	E	937 223-1130
Dayton (G-9692)		
Porter Wrght Morris Arthur LLP	D	216 443-2506
Cleveland (G-6222)		
Porter Wrght Morris Arthur LLP	E	937 449-6810
Dayton (G-9699)		
Rathbone Group LLC	D	800 870-5521
Cleveland (G-6286)		
Reisenfeld & Assoc Lpa LLC	C	513 322-7000
Cincinnati (G-4354)		
Reminger Co LPA	E	513 721-1311
Cincinnati (G-4356)		
Rendigs Fry Kiely & Dennis LLP	D	513 381-9200
Cincinnati (G-4357)		
Renner Otto Boiselle & Sklar	E	216 621-1113
Cleveland (G-6306)		
Roderick Linton Belfance LLP	E	330 434-3000
Akron (G-409)		
Roetzel and Andress A Legal P	E	330 376-2700
Akron (G-410)		
Roetzel and Andress A Legal P	E	216 623-0150
Cleveland (G-6338)		
Shumaker Loop & Kendrick LLP	C	419 241-9000
Toledo (G-18033)		
Spangenberg Shibley Liber LLP	E	216 215-7445
Cleveland (G-6440)		
Stagnaro Saba Patterson Co Lpa	E	513 533-2700
Cincinnati (G-4531)		

Stark Knoll	E	330 376-3300
Akron (G-441)		
Sweeney Robert E Co Lpa	E	216 696-0606
Cleveland (G-6490)		
Taft Stettinius Hollister LLP	B	513 381-2838
Cincinnati (G-4569)		
Taft Stettinius Hollister LLP	D	614 221-4000
Columbus (G-8728)		
Taft Stettinius Hollister LLP	D	216 241-3141
Cleveland (G-6497)		
Thompson Hine LLP	B	216 566-5500
Cleveland (G-6526)		
Thrasher Dinsmore & Dolan	E	440 285-2242
Chardon (G-2718)		
Ulmer & Berne LLP	B	216 583-7000
Cleveland (G-6563)		
Ulmer & Berne LLP	D	513 698-5000
Cincinnati (G-4670)		
Vorys Sater Seymour Pease LLP	E	216 479-6100
Cleveland (G-6643)		
Warner Dennehey Marshall	D	216 912-3787
Cleveland (G-6653)		
Weltman Weinberg & Reis Co Lpa	E	216 739-5100
Brooklyn Heights (G-1888)		
Weltman Weinberg & Reis Co Lpa	C	216 685-1000
Cleveland (G-6663)		
Weltman Weinberg & Reis Co Lpa	E	614 801-2600
Grove City (G-11485)		
Weltman Weinberg & Reis Co Lpa	C	513 723-2200
Cincinnati (G-4777)		
Weltman Weinberg & Reis Co Lpa	C	216 459-8633
Cleveland (G-6664)		
Wickens Hrzer Pnza Cook Btista	D	440 695-8000
Avon (G-905)		
Wong Margaret W Assoc Co Lpa	E	313 527-9989
Cleveland (G-6688)		

LEGAL SVCS: Labor & Employment Law

Freking Betz	E	513 721-1975
Cincinnati (G-3592)		
Jurus Stanley R Atty At Law	E	614 486-0297
Columbus (G-7878)		
Larrimer & Larrimer LLC	E	419 222-6266
Columbus (G-7953)		
National Labor Relations Board	E	216 522-3716
Cleveland (G-6047)		
Ross Brittain Schonberg Lpa	E	216 447-1551
Independence (G-12119)		
Scott Scriven & Wahoff LLP	E	614 222-8686
Columbus (G-8613)		
Smith Peter Kalail Co Lpa	E	216 503-5055
Independence (G-12124)		
Zashin & Rich Co LPA	E	216 696-4441
Cleveland (G-6710)		

LEGAL SVCS: Real Estate Law

Carlisle McNellie Rini Kram	E	216 360-7200
Beachwood (G-1041)		

LEGAL SVCS: Specialized Law Offices, Attorney

County of Lucas	C	419 213-4700
Toledo (G-17681)		
Frantz Ward LLP	C	216 515-1660
Cleveland (G-5575)		
Harrington Hoppe Mitchell Ltd	E	330 744-1111
Youngstown (G-20061)		
OBrien Law Firm Company Lpa	E	216 685-7500
Westlake (G-19384)		
Reminger Co LPA	C	216 687-1311
Cleveland (G-6304)		
Reminger Co LPA	D	419 254-1311
Toledo (G-18001)		
Squire Patton Boggs (us) LLP	E	513 361-1200
Cincinnati (G-4524)		
Wilmer Cutler Pick Hale Dorr	B	937 395-2100
Dayton (G-9882)		

LEGISLATIVE BODIES: Federal, State & Local

County of Auglaize	C	419 738-3816
Wapakoneta (G-18640)		

LEGITIMATE LIVE THEATER PRODUCERS

Columbus Association For The P	A	614 469-1045
Columbus (G-7259)		

Columbus Association For The P ....D 614 469-0939
Columbus (G-7260)
Little Theater Off Broadway ....E 614 875-3919
Grove City (G-11450)
Xenia Area Cmnty Theater Inc ....D 937 372-0516
Xenia (G-19935)

LESSORS: Farm Land

Mapleview Farms Inc ....E 419 826-3671
Swanton (G-17401)

LESSORS: Landholding Office

James Lafontaine ....E 740 474-5052
Circleville (G-4836)
Mwa Enterprises Ltd ....E 419 599-3835
Napoleon (G-14812)

LIABILITY INSURANCE

American Commerce Insurance Co ......C 614 272-6951
Columbus (G-6915)

LIFE INSURANCE AGENTS

Brown WD General Agency Inc ....D 216 241-5840
Cleveland (G-5094)
Carriage Town Chrysler Plymuth ....D 740 369-9611
Delaware (G-9957)
Savage and Associates Inc..................C 419 475-8665
Maumee (G-13849)
Union Security Insurance Co ....E 513 621-1924
Cincinnati (G-4674)
United American Insurance Co.............E 440 265-9200
Strongsville (G-17354)
Western & Southern Lf Insur Co ....E 440 324-2626
Elyria (G-10574)
Western & Southern Lf Insur Co ....E 330 825-9935
Barberton (G-972)
Western & Southern Lf Insur Co ....E 740 653-3210
Lancaster (G-12444)
Western & Southern Lf Insur Co ....E 513 891-0777
Loveland (G-13034)
Western & Southern Lf Insur Co ....E 614 898-1066
Columbus (G-6838)
Western & Southern Lf Insur Co ....E 937 773-5303
Piqua (G-16039)
Western & Southern Lf Insur Co ....E 937 399-7696
Springfield (G-17135)
Western & Southern Lf Insur Co ....E 740 354-2848
Portsmouth (G-16181)
Western & Southern Lf Insur Co ....E 937 393-1969
Hillsboro (G-11855)

LIFE INSURANCE CARRIERS

American Income Life Insur Co ....D 440 582-0040
Cleveland (G-4954)
Cincinnati Financial Corp......................A 513 870-2000
Fairfield (G-10710)
Columbus Life Insurance Co ....D 513 361-6700
Cincinnati (G-3331)
Employers Mutual Casualty Co ....D 513 221-6010
Blue Ash (G-1551)
Great American Life Insur Co ....E 513 357-3300
Cincinnati (G-3640)
Midland-Guardian Co............................A 513 943-7100
Amelia (G-575)
Nationwide Mutual Insurance Co ....A 614 249-7111
Columbus (G-8160)
Ohio Casualty Insurance Co ....A 800 843-6446
Fairfield (G-10763)
Transamerica Premier Lf Insur ....E 614 488-5983
Columbus (G-8773)
United American Insurance Co.............E 440 265-9200
Strongsville (G-17354)
United Omaha Life Insurance Co ....E 216 573-6900
Cleveland (G-6575)

LIFE INSURANCE: Fraternal Organizations

American Mutual Life Assn...................E 216 531-1900
Cleveland (G-4960)

LIFE INSURANCE: Mutual Association

Irongate Inc..C 937 433-3300
Centerville (G-2628)
Ohio Nat Mutl Holdings Inc ....A 513 794-6100
Montgomery (G-14598)
Ohio National Fincl Svcs Inc.................A 513 794-6100
Montgomery (G-14599)

Union Central Life Insur Co ....A 866 696-7478
Cincinnati (G-4673)

LIFEGUARD SVC

Cincinnati Pool Management Inc...........A 513 777-1444
Cincinnati (G-3261)
Metropolitan Pool Service Co ....E 216 741-9451
Parma (G-15768)

LIGHTING EQPT: Motor Vehicle

Federal-Mogul Powertrain LLC ....C 740 432-2393
Cambridge (G-2067)

LIGHTING FIXTURES WHOLESALERS

Capital Lighting Inc...............................D 614 841-1200
Columbus (G-6802)
Current Lighting Solutions LLC ....E 800 435-4448
Cleveland (G-5390)
Hinkley Lighting Inc ....D 440 653-5500
Avon Lake (G-920)
Lighting Services Inc ....E 330 405-4879
Twinsburg (G-18293)
LSI Industries Inc ....C 913 281-1100
Blue Ash (G-1600)
Venture Lighting Intl Inc ....D 800 451-2606
Twinsburg (G-18335)
Vincent Ltg Systems Co Inc.................E 216 475-7600
Solon (G-16912)

LIGHTING FIXTURES, NEC

Current Lighting Solutions LLC ....E 800 435-4448
Cleveland (G-5390)
Will-Burt Company ....B 330 682-7015
Orrville (G-15649)

LIGHTING FIXTURES: Indl & Commercial

Best Lighting Products Inc ....D 740 964-0063
Etna (G-10613)
LSI Industries Inc ....C 913 281-1100
Blue Ash (G-1600)

LIGHTING FIXTURES: Motor Vehicle

Grimes Aerospace Company ....B 937 484-2001
Urbana (G-18436)

LIGHTING MAINTENANCE SVC

Ermc II LP ....E 513 424-8517
Middletown (G-14346)
Sylvania Lighting Svcs Corp ....E 440 742-8208
Solon (G-16907)

LIME

Hanson Aggregates East LLC ....E 937 587-2671
Peebles (G-15802)
Hanson Aggregates East LLC ....D 419 483-4390
Castalia (G-2578)
National Lime and Stone Co ....C 419 396-7671
Carey (G-2545)
Piqua Materials Inc ....E 937 773-4824
Piqua (G-16019)
Shelly Materials Inc ....E 740 666-5841
Ostrander (G-15655)

LIME ROCK: Ground

National Lime and Stone Co ....C 419 396-7671
Carey (G-2545)

LIMESTONE: Crushed & Broken

Acme Company ....D 330 758-2313
Poland (G-16079)
Allgeier & Son Inc ....E 513 574-3735
Cincinnati (G-2925)
Carmeuse Lime Inc ....E 419 638-2511
Millersville (G-14504)
Carmeuse Lime Inc ....E 419 986-5200
Bettsville (G-1458)
Chesterhill Stone Co.............................C 740 849-2338
East Fultonham (G-10388)
Hanson Aggregates East LLC ....E 937 587-2671
Peebles (G-15802)
Hanson Aggregates East LLC ....E 937 442-6009
Winchester (G-19662)
Lang Stone Company Inc......................D 614 235-4099
Columbus (G-7951)

Martin Marietta Materials Inc................D 513 353-1400
North Bend (G-15182)
Martin Marietta Materials Inc................E 513 701-1140
West Chester (G-18970)
National Lime and Stone Co ....E 740 548-4206
Delaware (G-9997)
National Lime and Stone Co ....E 419 423-3400
Findlay (G-10948)
National Lime and Stone Co ....D 419 562-0771
Bucyrus (G-1997)
Omya Industries Inc ....D 513 387-4600
Blue Ash (G-1625)
Shelly Materials Inc ....E 740 666-5841
Ostrander (G-15655)
Shelly Materials Inc ....D 740 246-6315
Thornville (G-17506)
Sidwell Materials Inc ....C 740 849-2394
Zanesville (G-20361)
Stoneco Inc...E 419 393-2555
Oakwood (G-15484)
White Rock Quarry L P ....A 419 855-8388
Clay Center (G-4855)

LIMESTONE: Dimension

National Lime and Stone Co ....D 419 562-0771
Bucyrus (G-1997)
Stoneco Inc...D 419 422-8854
Findlay (G-10964)

LIMESTONE: Ground

Conag Inc..E 419 394-8870
Saint Marys (G-16522)
Hanson Aggregates East LLC ....D 419 483-4390
Castalia (G-2578)
Piqua Materials Inc ....E 937 773-4824
Piqua (G-16019)
Piqua Materials Inc ....D 513 771-0820
Cincinnati (G-4251)
Wagner Quarries Company ....E 419 625-8141
Sandusky (G-16655)

LIMOUSINE SVCS

A1 Mr Limo Inc ....E 440 943-5466
Wickliffe (G-19454)
Aladdins Enterprises Inc.......................E 614 891-3440
Westerville (G-19218)
American Livery Service Inc ....E 216 221-9330
Cleveland (G-4956)
Capital Transportation Inc.....................C 614 258-0400
Columbus (G-7113)
Cleveland Auto Livery Inc ....E 216 421-1101
Cleveland (G-5231)
Eastern Horizon Inc ....E 614 253-7000
Columbus (G-7489)
Eric Boeppler Fmly Ltd Partnr ....D 513 336-8108
Fairfield (G-10725)
Fab Limousines Inc ....E 330 792-6700
Youngstown (G-20033)
First Class Limos Inc ....E 440 248-1114
Cleveland (G-5533)
Gold Cross Limousine Service ....E 330 757-3053
Struthers (G-17364)
Henderson Road Rest Systems............E 614 442-3310
Columbus (G-7739)
Hopkin Arprt Lmsine Shttle Svc ....E 216 267-8282
Cleveland (G-5703)
Hopkins Airport Limousine Svc ....C 216 267-8810
Cleveland (G-5704)
Jls Enterprises Inc ....E 513 769-1888
West Chester (G-18952)
Lakefront Lines Inc...............................E 419 537-0677
Toledo (G-17848)
Northwest Limousine Inc ....E 440 322-5804
Elyria (G-10550)
Precious Cargo Transportation ....E 440 564-8039
Newbury (G-15124)
Shima Limousine Services Inc ....E 440 918-6400
Mentor (G-14109)

LINEN SPLY SVC

Aramark Unf & Career AP LLC..............C 216 341-7400
Cleveland (G-4999)
Midwest Laundry Inc ....D 513 563-5560
Cincinnati (G-4050)
Morgan Services Inc ....E 419 243-2214
Toledo (G-17924)
Morgan Services Inc ....C 216 241-3107
Cleveland (G-6009)

SERVICES

Morgan Services Inc ....D 937 223-5241
Dayton (G-9645)

Nucentury Textile Services LLC ....D 419 241-2267
Toledo (G-17952)

Ohio Textile Service Inc ....E 740 450-4900
Zanesville (G-20349)

Springfeld Unfrm-Linen Sup Inc ......D 937 323-5544
Springfield (G-17116)

Synergy Health North Amer Inc ......D 513 398-6406
Mason (G-13643)

Van Dyne-Crotty Co ....E 440 248-6935
Solon (G-16911)

LINEN SPLY SVC: Apron

G&K Services LLC ....B 952 912-5500
Mason (G-13582)

LINEN SPLY SVC: Towel

Kimmel Cleaners Inc ....D 419 294-1959
Upper Sandusky (G-18410)

Superior Linen & AP Svcs Inc ......D 513 751-1345
Cincinnati (G-4557)

LINEN SPLY SVC: Uniform

Aramark Unf & Career AP LLC ......D 937 223-6667
Dayton (G-9236)

Aramark Unf & Career AP LLC ......C 614 445-8341
Columbus (G-6962)

Barberton Laundry & Cleaning ......D 330 825-6911
Barberton (G-947)

Buckeye Linen Service Inc ....D 740 345-4046
Newark (G-15018)

Cintas Corporation No 1 ....A 513 459-1200
Mason (G-13556)

Cintas Corporation No 2 ....D 614 878-7313
Columbus (G-7201)

Cintas Corporation No 2 ....D 440 352-4003
Painesville (G-15698)

Cintas Corporation No 2 ....E 740 687-6230
Lancaster (G-12379)

Cintas Corporation No 2 ....C 614 860-9152
Blacklick (G-1477)

Cintas Corporation No 2 ....C 513 965-0800
Milford (G-14379)

Economy Linen & Towel Svc Inc ......C 740 454-6888
Zanesville (G-20304)

Kramer Enterprises Inc ....D 419 422-7924
Findlay (G-10932)

Millers Textile Services Inc ....D 419 738-3552
Wapakoneta (G-18650)

Millers Textile Services Inc ....E 614 262-1206
Springfield (G-17086)

Paris Cleaners Inc ....C 330 296-3300
Ravenna (G-16252)

Unifirst Corporation ....E 614 575-9999
Blacklick (G-1483)

Unifirst Corporation ....D 937 746-0531
Franklin (G-11040)

Van Dyne-Crotty Co ....E 614 684-0048
Columbus (G-8842)

Van Dyne-Crotty Co ....C 614 491-3903
Columbus (G-8843)

LIQUEFIED PETROLEUM GAS DEALERS

Valvoline Inc ....D 513 451-1753
Cincinnati (G-4748)

LIQUEFIED PETROLEUM GAS WHOLESALERS

Centerra Co-Op ....E 800 362-9598
Jefferson (G-12190)

Centerra Co-Op ....E 419 281-2153
Ashland (G-665)

Hearthstone Utilities Inc ....D 440 974-3770
Cleveland (G-5679)

Youngstown Propane Inc ....E 330 792-6571
Youngstown (G-20266)

LIQUIDATORS

Midwest Liquidators Inc ....E 614 433-7355
Worthington (G-19828)

Sb Capital Group LLC ....E 516 829-2400
Columbus (G-8597)

LIVESTOCK WHOLESALERS, NEC

Hord Livestock Company Inc ....E 419 562-0277
Bucyrus (G-1994)

LOADS: Electronic

TL Industries Inc ....C 419 666-8144
Northwood (G-15410)

LOGGING

Appalachia Wood Inc ....E 740 596-2551
Mc Arthur (G-13889)

Miller Logging Inc ....E 330 279-4721
Holmesville (G-11932)

LOOSELEAF BINDERS

Mueller Art Cover & Binding Co ......E 440 238-3303
Strongsville (G-17335)

LOTIONS OR CREAMS: Face

Beiersdorf Inc ....C 513 682-7300
West Chester (G-19042)

LUBRICATING OIL & GREASE WHOLESALERS

Applied Indus Tech - Dixie Inc ......C 216 426-4000
Cleveland (G-4995)

Blue Star Lubrication Tech LLC ......E 847 285-1888
Cincinnati (G-3064)

Northeast Lubricants Ltd ....E 216 478-0507
Cleveland (G-6088)

Specialty Lubricants Corp ....E 330 425-2567
Macedonia (G-13082)

LUGGAGE & LEATHER GOODS STORES: Leather, Exc Luggage & Shoes

Leather Gallery Inc ....E 513 312-1722
Lebanon (G-12479)

LUMBER & BLDG MATLS DEALER, RET: Garage Doors, Sell/Install

Dayton Door Sales Inc ....E 937 253-9181
Dayton (G-9364)

Overhead Door Co- Cincinnati ......C 513 346-4000
West Chester (G-18981)

Overhead Inc ....E 419 476-7811
Toledo (G-17967)

LUMBER & BLDG MATRLS DEALERS, RET: Bath Fixtures, Eqpt/Sply

Bathroom Alternatives Inc ....E 937 434-1984
Dayton (G-9245)

Xtreme Contracting Ltd ....E 614 568-7030
Reynoldsburg (G-16341)

LUMBER & BLDG MATRLS DEALERS, RETAIL: Doors, Wood/Metal

Koch Aluminum Mfg Inc ....E 419 625-5956
Sandusky (G-16622)

Nofziger Door Sales Inc ....C 419 337-9900
Wauseon (G-18808)

LUMBER & BLDG MTRLS DEALERS, RET: Planing Mill Prdts/Lumber

Keim Lumber Company ....E 330 893-2251
Baltic (G-935)

LUMBER & BUILDING MATERIAL DEALERS, RETAIL: Roofing Material

Johns Manville Corporation ....D 419 784-7000
Defiance (G-9921)

LUMBER & BUILDING MATERIALS DEALER, RET: Door & Window Prdts

Daugherty Construction Inc ....E 216 731-9444
Euclid (G-10628)

Dun Rite Home Improvement Inc ......E 330 650-5322
Macedonia (G-13068)

Erie Construction Mid-West Inc ......E 937 898-4688
Dayton (G-9417)

Fortune Brands Windows Inc ......C 614 532-3500
Columbus (G-7602)

Olde Towne Windows Inc ....E 419 626-9613
Milan (G-14364)

Schneider Home Equipment Co ......E 513 522-1200
Cincinnati (G-4438)

Window Factory of America ....D 440 439-3050
Bedford (G-1314)

LUMBER & BUILDING MATERIALS DEALER, RET: Masonry Matls/Splys

B G Trucking & Construction ....E 234 759-3440
North Lima (G-15266)

Koltcz Concrete Block Co ....E 440 232-3630
Bedford (G-1287)

Mack Industries ....C 419 353-7081
Bowling Green (G-1740)

Maza Inc ....E 614 760-0003
Plain City (G-16059)

Stone Coffman Company LLC ......E 614 861-4668
Gahanna (G-11147)

LUMBER & BUILDING MATERIALS DEALERS, RETAIL: Brick

Bruder Inc ....E 216 791-9800
Maple Heights (G-13282)

Columbus Coal & Lime Co ....E 614 224-9241
Columbus (G-7269)

Hamilton-Parker Company ....D 614 358-7800
Columbus (G-7713)

LUMBER & BUILDING MATERIALS DEALERS, RETAIL: Cement

Huron Cement Products Company ......E 419 433-4161
Huron (G-12026)

LUMBER & BUILDING MATERIALS DEALERS, RETAIL: Countertops

Modlich Stoneworks Inc ....E 614 276-2848
Columbus (G-8094)

LUMBER & BUILDING MATERIALS DEALERS, RETAIL: Siding

Marsh Building Products Inc ....E 937 222-3321
Dayton (G-9586)

Regency Windows Corporation ......D 330 963-4077
Twinsburg (G-18310)

LUMBER & BUILDING MATERIALS DEALERS, RETAIL: Tile, Ceramic

Pucher Paint Co Inc ....E 440 234-0991
Berea (G-1435)

LUMBER & BUILDING MATERIALS RET DEALERS: Millwork & Lumber

Carter-Jones Companies Inc ....E 330 673-6100
Kent (G-12217)

LUMBER & BUILDING MATLS DEALERS, RET: Concrete/Cinder Block

Allega Recycled Mtls & Sup Co ......E 216 447-0814
Cleveland (G-4937)

LUMBER & BUILDING MTRLS DEALERS, RET: Insulation Mtrl, Bldg

Alpine Insulation I LLC ....A 614 221-3399
Columbus (G-6904)

Installed Building Pdts Inc ....C 614 221-3399
Columbus (G-7828)

Installed Building Pdts LLC ....E 419 662-4524
Northwood (G-15396)

LUMBER: Dimension, Hardwood

J McCoy Lumber Co Ltd ....E 937 587-3423
Peebles (G-15803)

Stephen M Trudick ....E 440 834-1891
Burton (G-2019)

LUMBER: Fiberboard

Frankes Wood Products LLC ....E 937 642-0706
  Marysville (G-13497)

LUMBER: Hardwood Dimension & Flooring Mills

Baillie Lumber Co LP ....E 419 462-2000
  Galion (G-11168)
Carter-Jones Lumber Company ....C 330 674-9060
  Millersburg (G-14463)
Gross Lumber Inc ....E 330 683-2055
  Apple Creek (G-619)
Hartzell Hardwoods Inc ....D 937 773-7054
  Piqua (G-16006)
Holmes Lumber & Bldg Ctr Inc ....C 330 674-9060
  Millersburg (G-14475)
Wappoo Wood Products Inc ....E 937 492-1166
  Sidney (G-16805)

LUMBER: Plywood, Hardwood

Sims-Lohman Inc ....E 513 651-3510
  Cincinnati (G-4483)
Wappoo Wood Products Inc ....E 937 492-1166
  Sidney (G-16805)

LUMBER: Plywood, Softwood

Wappoo Wood Products Inc ....E 937 492-1166
  Sidney (G-16805)

LUMBER: Treated

Appalachia Wood Inc ....E 740 596-2551
  Mc Arthur (G-13889)

LUMBER: Veneer, Hardwood

Hartzell Industries Inc ....D 937 773-6295
  Piqua (G-16007)

LUNCHROOMS & CAFETERIAS

Dari Pizza Enterprises II Inc ....C 419 534-3000
  Maumee (G-13780)

MACHINE PARTS: Stamped Or Pressed Metal

Abbott Tool Inc ....E 419 476-6742
  Toledo (G-17579)

MACHINE SHOPS

All-Type Welding & Fabrication ....E 440 439-3990
  Cleveland (G-4936)
Jed Industries Inc ....E 440 639-9973
  Grand River (G-11332)
Metcut Research Associates Inc ....D 513 271-5100
  Cincinnati (G-4041)
Neff Machinery and Supplies ....E 740 454-0128
  Zanesville (G-20344)

MACHINE TOOL ACCESS: Cutting

Container Graphics Corp ....D 419 531-5133
  Toledo (G-17678)
Kyocera SGS Precision Tools ....E 330 688-6667
  Munroe Falls (G-14797)

MACHINE TOOL ACCESS: Diamond Cutting, For Turning, Etc

Chardon Tool & Supply Co Inc ....E 440 286-6440
  Chardon (G-2690)

MACHINE TOOL ACCESS: Drill Bushings, Drilling Jig

Jergens Inc ....C 216 486-5540
  Cleveland (G-5790)

MACHINE TOOL ACCESS: Tools & Access

Imco Carbide Tool Inc ....D 419 661-6313
  Perrysburg (G-15877)

MACHINE TOOLS & ACCESS

Johnson Bros Rubber Co Inc ....E 419 752-4814
  Greenwich (G-11402)
Matvest Inc ....E 614 487-8720
  Columbus (G-8040)

Ohio Broach & Machine Company ....E 440 946-1040
  Willoughby (G-19557)
Production Design Services Inc ....D 937 866-3377
  Dayton (G-9716)
Setco Sales Company ....D 513 941-5110
  Cincinnati (G-4457)
Stark Industrial LLC ....E 330 493-9773
  North Canton (G-15234)

MACHINE TOOLS, METAL CUTTING: Home Workshop

H & D Steel Service Inc ....E 440 237-3390
  North Royalton (G-15357)

MACHINE TOOLS, METAL CUTTING: Sawing & Cutoff

AM Industrial Group LLC ....E 216 433-7171
  Brookpark (G-1890)
Lawrence Industries Inc ....C 216 518-7000
  Cleveland (G-5858)

MACHINE TOOLS, METAL CUTTING: Tool Replacement & Rpr Parts

Cardinal Builders Inc ....E 614 237-1000
  Columbus (G-7119)
J-C-R Tech Inc ....E 937 783-2296
  Blanchester (G-1488)

MACHINE TOOLS, METAL FORMING: Bending

Addisonmckee Inc ....C 513 228-7000
  Lebanon (G-12448)
Pines Manufacturing Inc ....E 440 835-5553
  Westlake (G-19392)

MACHINE TOOLS, METAL FORMING: Marking

Monode Marking Products Inc ....D 440 975-8802
  Mentor (G-14089)

MACHINE TOOLS, METAL FORMING: Mechanical, Pneumatic Or Hyd

Compass Systems & Sales LLC ....D 330 733-2111
  Norton (G-15418)

MACHINE TOOLS: Metal Cutting

Acro Tool & Die Company ....D 330 773-5173
  Akron (G-17)
Carter Manufacturing Co Inc ....E 513 398-7303
  Mason (G-13550)
Elliott Tool Technologies Ltd ....D 937 253-6133
  Dayton (G-9412)
J and S Tool Incorporated ....E 216 676-8330
  Cleveland (G-5770)

MACHINE TOOLS: Metal Forming

Anderson & Vreeland Inc ....D 419 636-5002
  Bryan (G-1952)
Elliott Tool Technologies Ltd ....D 937 253-6133
  Dayton (G-9412)
Howmet Corporation ....E 757 825-7086
  Newburgh Heights (G-15114)
J and S Tool Incorporated ....E 216 676-8330
  Cleveland (G-5770)
Scotts Miracle-Gro Company ....B 937 644-0011
  Marysville (G-13529)

MACHINERY & EQPT FINANCE LEASING

Ohio Machinery Co ....C 440 526-6200
  Broadview Heights (G-1840)
Reynolds and Reynolds Company ....A 937 485-2000
  Kettering (G-12299)
Ricoh Usa Inc ....D 513 984-9898
  Sharonville (G-16730)

MACHINERY & EQPT, AGRICULTURAL, WHOL: Farm Eqpt Parts/Splys

Myers Equipment Corporation ....E 330 533-5556
  Canfield (G-2151)
Rk Family Inc ....B 513 737-0436
  Hamilton (G-11639)

Schmidt Machine Company ....E 419 294-3814
  Upper Sandusky (G-18412)

MACHINERY & EQPT, AGRICULTURAL, WHOLESALE: Agricultural, NEC

Apple Farm Service Inc ....E 937 526-4851
  Covington (G-9045)
Speck Sales Incorporated ....E 419 353-8312
  Bowling Green (G-1749)

MACHINERY & EQPT, AGRICULTURAL, WHOLESALE: Dairy

Roger Shawn Houck ....E 513 933-0563
  Oregonia (G-15617)

MACHINERY & EQPT, AGRICULTURAL, WHOLESALE: Farm Implements

Cahall Bros Inc ....E 937 378-4439
  Georgetown (G-11265)
Crouse Implement ....E 740 892-2086
  Utica (G-18455)
Evolution Ag LLC ....E 740 363-1341
  Plain City (G-16052)
Farmers Equipment Inc ....E 419 339-7000
  Lima (G-12638)
Farmers Equipment Inc ....E 419 339-7000
  Urbana (G-18432)
Homier & Sons Inc ....E 419 596-3965
  Continental (G-8961)
Shearer Farm Inc ....E 419 529-6160
  Ontario (G-15571)

MACHINERY & EQPT, AGRICULTURAL, WHOLESALE: Hydroponic

Hawthorne Hydroponics LLC ....D 480 777-2000
  Marysville (G-13501)

MACHINERY & EQPT, AGRICULTURAL, WHOLESALE: Landscaping Eqpt

Dta Inc ....E 419 529-2920
  Ontario (G-15548)
Kenmar Lawn & Grdn Care Co LLC ......E 330 239-2924
  Medina (G-13965)

MACHINERY & EQPT, AGRICULTURAL, WHOLESALE: Lawn

Hayward Distributing Co ....E 614 272-5953
  Columbus (G-7720)
Lesco Inc ....C 216 706-9250
  Cleveland (G-5865)

MACHINERY & EQPT, AGRICULTURAL, WHOLESALE: Lawn & Garden

Bostwick-Braun Company ....D 419 259-3600
  Toledo (G-17620)
Buckeye Supply Company ....E 740 452-3641
  Zanesville (G-20285)
Ohio Irrigation Lawn Sprinkler ....E 937 432-9911
  Dayton (G-9670)

MACHINERY & EQPT, AGRICULTURAL, WHOLESALE: Livestock Eqpt

Coughlin Chevrolet Inc ....E 740 852-1122
  London (G-12862)
Fort Recovery Equipment Inc ....E 419 375-1006
  Fort Recovery (G-10990)

MACHINERY & EQPT, AGRICULTURAL, WHOLESALE: Tractors

Shearer Farm Inc ....E 440 237-4806
  North Royalton (G-15367)

MACHINERY & EQPT, INDL, WHOL: Brewery Prdts Mfrg, Commercial

D M I Distribution Inc ....E 765 584-3234
  Columbus (G-7410)
Staufs Coffee Roasters II Inc ....E 614 487-6050
  Columbus (G-8696)

Employee Codes: A=Over 500 employees, B=251-500
C=101-250, D=51-100, E=25-50   2019 Harris Ohio
Services Directory   1475

MACHINERY & EQPT, INDL, WHOL: Controlling Instruments/Access

Innovative Enrgy Solutions LLC ....E 937 228-3044
  Hamilton *(G-11613)*
Modal Shop Inc ....D 513 351-9919
  Cincinnati *(G-4067)*
Rilco Industrial Controls Inc ....E 513 530-0055
  Cincinnati *(G-4374)*

MACHINERY & EQPT, INDL, WHOL: Environ Pollution Cntrl, Air

Questar Solutions LLC ....E 330 966-2070
  North Canton *(G-15229)*

MACHINERY & EQPT, INDL, WHOLESALE: Cement Making

Spillman Company ....E 614 444-2184
  Columbus *(G-8672)*

MACHINERY & EQPT, INDL, WHOLESALE: Chemical Process

Aldrich Chemical ....D 937 859-1808
  Miamisburg *(G-14138)*

MACHINERY & EQPT, INDL, WHOLESALE: Conveyor Systems

Alba Manufacturing Inc ....D 513 874-0551
  Fairfield *(G-10694)*
E F Bavis & Associates Inc ....E 513 677-0500
  Maineville *(G-13115)*
Vargo Inc ....E 614 876-1163
  Hilliard *(G-11825)*

MACHINERY & EQPT, INDL, WHOLESALE: Cranes

Expert Crane Inc ....E 216 451-9900
  Cleveland *(G-5502)*
Hiab USA Inc ....D 419 482-6000
  Perrysburg *(G-15874)*
Tiffin Loader Crane Company ....D 419 448-8156
  Tiffin *(G-17543)*
Venco Venturo Industries LLC ....E 513 772-8448
  Cincinnati *(G-4753)*

MACHINERY & EQPT, INDL, WHOLESALE: Dairy Prdts Manufacturing

Heritage Equipment Company ....E 614 873-3941
  Plain City *(G-16054)*
Rodem Inc ....E 513 922-6140
  Cincinnati *(G-4394)*

MACHINERY & EQPT, INDL, WHOLESALE: Drilling Bits

Dickman Supply Inc ....C 937 492-6166
  Sidney *(G-16773)*
Dickman Supply Inc ....E 937 492-6166
  Greenville *(G-11375)*

MACHINERY & EQPT, INDL, WHOLESALE: Engines & Parts, Diesel

Clarke Power Services Inc ....E 937 684-4402
  Huber Heights *(G-11953)*
Cummins Bridgeway Columbus LLC ....D 614 771-1000
  Hilliard *(G-11758)*
Cummins Inc ....E 614 771-1000
  Hilliard *(G-11759)*
Cummins Inc ....E 513 563-6670
  West Chester *(G-18907)*
Detroit Diesel Corporation ....B 330 430-4300
  Canton *(G-2284)*
Fluid Mechanics LLC ....E 216 362-7800
  Avon Lake *(G-917)*
W W Williams Company LLC ....E 330 534-1161
  Hubbard *(G-11951)*
W W Williams Company LLC ....D 800 336-6651
  West Chester *(G-19098)*
W W Williams Company LLC ....E 330 225-7751
  Brunswick *(G-1945)*
Western Branch Diesel Inc ....E 330 454-8800
  Canton *(G-2534)*

MACHINERY & EQPT, INDL, WHOLESALE: Engines, Gasoline

Gardner Inc ....C 614 456-4000
  Columbus *(G-7648)*

MACHINERY & EQPT, INDL, WHOLESALE: Engs & Parts, Air-Cooled

Power Distributors LLC ....D 614 876-3533
  Columbus *(G-8457)*

MACHINERY & EQPT, INDL, WHOLESALE: Fans

WW Grainger Inc ....E 614 276-5231
  Columbus *(G-8921)*

MACHINERY & EQPT, INDL, WHOLESALE: Food Manufacturing

R and J Corporation ....E 440 871-6009
  Westlake *(G-19394)*
Sentinel Fluid Controls LLC ....E 419 478-9086
  Toledo *(G-18025)*

MACHINERY & EQPT, INDL, WHOLESALE: Food Product Manufacturng

Bettcher Industries Inc ....C 440 965-4422
  Wakeman *(G-18619)*

MACHINERY & EQPT, INDL, WHOLESALE: Heat Exchange

Sgl Carbon Technic LLC ....E 440 572-3600
  Strongsville *(G-17343)*

MACHINERY & EQPT, INDL, WHOLESALE: Hoists

Pennsylvania Tl Sls & Svc Inc ....D 330 758-0845
  Youngstown *(G-20153)*

MACHINERY & EQPT, INDL, WHOLESALE: Hydraulic Systems

Argo-Hytos Inc ....A 419 353-6070
  Bowling Green *(G-1714)*
Bosch Rexroth Corporation ....E 614 527-7400
  Grove City *(G-11409)*
Eaton Corporation ....B 216 523-5000
  Beachwood *(G-1054)*
Eaton Corporation ....B 216 920-2000
  Cleveland *(G-5462)*
Fluid Line Products Inc ....C 440 946-9470
  Willoughby *(G-19525)*
Genesis Rescue Systems ....E 937 293-6240
  Kettering *(G-12293)*
Hydraulic Parts Store Inc ....E 330 364-6667
  New Philadelphia *(G-14966)*
JWF Technologies Llc ....E 513 769-9611
  Fairfield *(G-10741)*
Ohio Hydraulics Inc ....E 513 771-2590
  Cincinnati *(G-4155)*
R & M Fluid Power Inc ....E 330 758-2766
  Youngstown *(G-20173)*
Robeck Fluid Power Co ....D 330 562-1140
  Aurora *(G-840)*
Scott Industrial Systems Inc ....D 937 233-8146
  Dayton *(G-9753)*
System Seals Inc ....D 440 735-0200
  Cleveland *(G-6491)*
Triad Technologies LLC ....E 937 832-2861
  Vandalia *(G-18544)*
V & P Hydraulic Products LLC ....D 740 203-3600
  Delaware *(G-10014)*

MACHINERY & EQPT, INDL, WHOLESALE: Indl Machine Parts

Double A Trailer Sales Inc ....E 419 692-7626
  Delphos *(G-10025)*

MACHINERY & EQPT, INDL, WHOLESALE: Instruments & Cntrl Eqpt

Fcx Performance Inc ....E 614 324-6050
  Columbus *(G-7567)*

Neff Group Distributors Inc ....E 440 835-7010
  Westlake *(G-19378)*
Simco Supply Co ....E 614 253-1999
  Columbus *(G-8641)*
South Shore Controls Inc ....E 440 259-2500
  Perry *(G-15828)*

MACHINERY & EQPT, INDL, WHOLESALE: Lift Trucks & Parts

Crown Equipment Corporation ....A 419 629-2311
  New Bremen *(G-14887)*
Crown Equipment Corporation ....D 419 629-2311
  New Bremen *(G-14888)*
Fastener Industries Inc ....E 440 891-2031
  Berea *(G-1426)*
Joseph Industries Inc ....D 330 528-0091
  Streetsboro *(G-17258)*
Newtown Nine Inc ....D 440 781-0623
  Macedonia *(G-13078)*
North Coast Lift Trck Ohio LLC ....D 419 836-2100
  Curtice *(G-9066)*
Towlift Inc ....D 614 851-1001
  Columbus *(G-8765)*
Toyota Industries N Amer Inc ....E 937 237-0976
  Dayton *(G-9819)*
Toyota Material Hdlg Ohio Inc ....D 216 328-0970
  Independence *(G-12132)*
Williams Super Service Inc ....E 330 733-7750
  East Sparta *(G-10425)*

MACHINERY & EQPT, INDL, WHOLESALE: Machine Tools & Access

Absolute Machine Tools Inc ....D 440 839-9696
  Lorain *(G-12878)*
AM Industrial Group LLC ....E 216 433-7171
  Brookpark *(G-1890)*
Eurolink Inc ....E 740 392-1549
  Mount Vernon *(G-14765)*
Gosiger Inc ....C 937 228-5174
  Dayton *(G-9466)*
Gosiger Inc ....D 937 228-5174
  Dayton *(G-9467)*
Imco Carbide Tool Inc ....D 419 661-6313
  Perrysburg *(G-15877)*
J and S Tool Incorporated ....E 216 676-8330
  Cleveland *(G-5770)*
Jergens Inc ....C 216 486-5540
  Cleveland *(G-5790)*
Neff Machinery and Supplies ....E 740 454-0128
  Zanesville *(G-20344)*
Precision Supply Company Inc ....D 330 225-5530
  Brunswick *(G-1938)*
Salvagnini America Inc ....E 513 874-8284
  Hamilton *(G-11641)*
Wolf Machine Company ....C 513 791-5194
  Blue Ash *(G-1679)*
Yoder Machinery Sales Company ....E 419 865-5555
  Holland *(G-11927)*

MACHINERY & EQPT, INDL, WHOLESALE: Machine Tools & Metalwork

Ellison Technologies Inc ....E 440 546-1920
  Brecksville *(G-1780)*

MACHINERY & EQPT, INDL, WHOLESALE: Measure/Test, Electric

Dreier & Maller Inc ....E 614 575-0065
  Reynoldsburg *(G-16300)*

MACHINERY & EQPT, INDL, WHOLESALE: Noise Control

Tech Products Corporation ....E 937 438-1100
  Miamisburg *(G-14227)*

MACHINERY & EQPT, INDL, WHOLESALE: Packaging

Alfons Haar Inc ....E 937 560-2031
  Springboro *(G-16961)*
Bollin & Sons Inc ....E 419 693-6573
  Toledo *(G-17618)*
S & S Inc ....E 216 383-1880
  Cleveland *(G-6354)*
Tape Products Company ....D 513 489-8840
  Cincinnati *(G-4577)*

Tripack LLC ....E 513 248-1255
 Milford **(G-14439)**

MACHINERY & EQPT, INDL, WHOLESALE: Paper Manufacturing

Goettsch International Inc......................E 513 563-6500
 Blue Ash **(G-1572)**
Industrial Maint Svcs Inc ....E 440 729-2068
 Chagrin Falls **(G-2669)**

MACHINERY & EQPT, INDL, WHOLESALE: Petroleum Industry

C H Bradshaw Co......................................E 614 871-2087
 Grove City **(G-11417)**

MACHINERY & EQPT, INDL, WHOLESALE: Plastic Prdts Machinery

IMS Company ....D 440 543-1615
 Chagrin Falls **(G-2668)**
Nfm/Welding Engineers Inc ....E 330 837-3868
 Massillon **(G-13717)**
Sumitomo Demag Plstc Machinery ....E 440 876-8960
 Strongsville **(G-17350)**

MACHINERY & EQPT, INDL, WHOLESALE: Pneumatic Tools

Tomita USA Inc.......................................E 614 873-6509
 Plain City **(G-16069)**

MACHINERY & EQPT, INDL, WHOLESALE: Processing & Packaging

Equipment Depot Ohio Inc....................E 513 934-2121
 Lebanon **(G-12464)**
Veritiv Operating Company ....D 216 901-5700
 Cleveland **(G-6623)**

MACHINERY & EQPT, INDL, WHOLESALE: Propane Conversion

KA Bergquist Inc....................................E 419 865-4196
 Toledo **(G-17835)**

MACHINERY & EQPT, INDL, WHOLESALE: Pulverizing

Maag Automatik Inc ....E 330 677-2225
 Kent **(G-12248)**

MACHINERY & EQPT, INDL, WHOLESALE: Recycling

Gateway Products Recycling Inc ....E 216 341-8777
 Cleveland **(G-5596)**

MACHINERY & EQPT, INDL, WHOLESALE: Robots

Remtec Engineering ....E 513 860-4299
 Mason **(G-13635)**

MACHINERY & EQPT, INDL, WHOLESALE: Safety Eqpt

A & A Safety Inc.....................................E 513 943-6100
 Amelia **(G-563)**
Cintas Corporation ....A 513 459-1200
 Cincinnati **(G-3291)**
Cintas Corporation ....D 513 631-5750
 Cincinnati **(G-3292)**
Cintas Corporation No 2 ....A 513 459-1200
 Mason **(G-13557)**
Cintas Corporation No 2 ....A 513 459-1200
 Mason **(G-13558)**
Impact Products LLC ....C 419 841-2891
 Toledo **(G-17818)**
M Conley Company ....C 330 456-8243
 Canton **(G-2383)**
Paul Peterson Company.........................E 614 486-4375
 Columbus **(G-8427)**
Safety Solutions Inc..............................D 614 799-9900
 Columbus **(G-8578)**
Safety Today Inc ....E 614 409-7200
 Grove City **(G-11468)**
US Safetygear Inc ....E 330 898-1344
 Warren **(G-18764)**

MACHINERY & EQPT, INDL, WHOLESALE: Tanks, Storage

Cleveland Tank & Supply Inc ....E 216 771-8265
 Cleveland **(G-5291)**
Tank Leasing Corp ....E 330 339-3333
 New Philadelphia **(G-14984)**

MACHINERY & EQPT, INDL, WHOLESALE: Woodworking

Woodcraft Supply LLC ....D 513 407-8371
 Cincinnati **(G-4805)**

MACHINERY & EQPT, WHOLESALE: Construction & Mining, Ladders

Bauer Corporation ....E 800 321-4760
 Wooster **(G-19689)**
Dover Investments Inc...........................E 440 235-5511
 Olmsted Falls **(G-15533)**

MACHINERY & EQPT, WHOLESALE: Construction, Cranes

American Crane Inc ....E 614 496-2268
 Reynoldsburg **(G-16281)**
Reco Equipment Inc ....E 740 619-8071
 Belmont **(G-1395)**

MACHINERY & EQPT, WHOLESALE: Construction, General

Columbus Equipment Company ....E 614 437-0352
 Columbus **(G-7281)**
Columbus Equipment Company ....E 513 771-3922
 Cincinnati **(G-3330)**
Columbus Equipment Company ....E 330 659-6681
 Richfield **(G-16351)**
Columbus Equipment Company ....E 614 443-6541
 Columbus **(G-7282)**
D&M Sales & Solutions LLC ....E 937 667-8713
 Tipp City **(G-17554)**
F & M Mafco Inc.....................................C 513 367-2151
 Harrison **(G-11666)**
Janell Inc...E 513 489-9111
 Blue Ash **(G-1589)**
K & M Contracting Ohio Inc ....E 330 759-1090
 Girard **(G-11292)**
Leppo Inc...C 330 633-3999
 Tallmadge **(G-17480)**
Murphy Tractor & Eqp Co Inc ....E 513 772-3232
 Cincinnati **(G-4086)**
Npk Construction Equipment Inc ....D 440 232-7900
 Bedford **(G-1295)**
Ohio Machinery Co ....C 419 874-7975
 Perrysburg **(G-15897)**
Ohio Machinery Co ....E 740 942-4626
 Cadiz **(G-2032)**
Ohio Machinery Co ....E 330 478-6525
 Canton **(G-2427)**
Ohio Machinery Co ....E 740 453-0563
 Zanesville **(G-20348)**
Ohio Machinery Co ....C 513 771-0515
 Cincinnati **(G-4157)**
Ohio Machinery Co ....B 614 878-2287
 Columbus **(G-8273)**
Ohio Machinery Co ....D 440 526-0520
 Broadview Heights **(G-1841)**
Ohio Machinery Co ....D 937 335-7660
 Troy **(G-18220)**
Ohio Machinery Co ....C 330 530-9010
 Girard **(G-11295)**
Ohio Machinery Co ....C 440 526-6200
 Broadview Heights **(G-1840)**
Southeastern Equipment Co Inc ....C 614 889-1073
 Dublin **(G-10338)**
TNT Equipment Company ....E 614 882-1549
 Columbus **(G-8761)**
Wrench Ltd Company ....D 740 654-5304
 Carroll **(G-2559)**

MACHINERY & EQPT, WHOLESALE: Contractors Materials

American Producers Sup Co Inc ....D 740 373-5050
 Marietta **(G-13310)**
Bobcat Enterprises Inc..........................D 513 874-8945
 West Chester **(G-18877)**

Carmichael Equipment Inc....................E 740 446-2412
 Bidwell **(G-1467)**
Cecil I Walker Machinery Co ....E 740 286-7566
 Jackson **(G-12170)**
Richard Goettle Inc................................D 513 825-8100
 Cincinnati **(G-4369)**
Vermeer Sales & Service Inc ....E 330 723-8383
 Medina **(G-14012)**

MACHINERY & EQPT, WHOLESALE: Drilling, Wellpoints

Yoder Drilling and Geothermal ....E 330 852-4342
 Sugarcreek **(G-17381)**

MACHINERY & EQPT, WHOLESALE: Logging

Baker & Sons Equipment Co ....E 740 567-3317
 Lewisville **(G-12573)**

MACHINERY & EQPT, WHOLESALE: Masonry

EZ Grout Corporation Inc.......................E 740 962-2024
 Malta **(G-13121)**

MACHINERY & EQPT, WHOLESALE: Oil Field Eqpt

Belden & Blake Corporation ....E 330 602-5551
 Dover **(G-10066)**

MACHINERY & EQPT, WHOLESALE: Road Construction & Maintenance

Terry Asphalt Materials Inc ....E 513 874-6192
 Hamilton **(G-11646)**

MACHINERY & EQPT: Electroplating

Corrotec Inc..E 937 325-3585
 Springfield **(G-17021)**

MACHINERY & EQPT: Farm

Intertec Corporation ....B 419 537-9711
 Toledo **(G-17824)**

MACHINERY & EQPT: Gas Producers, Generators/Other Rltd Eqpt

Applied Marketing Services....................E 440 716-9962
 Westlake **(G-19317)**

MACHINERY CLEANING SVCS

Burch Hydro Inc......................................E 740 694-9146
 Fredericktown **(G-11052)**

MACHINERY, MAILING: Postage Meters

Pitney Bowes Inc ....D 203 426-7025
 Brecksville **(G-1796)**
Pitney Bowes Inc ....D 740 374-5535
 Marietta **(G-13371)**

MACHINERY, METALWORKING: Assembly, Including Robotic

Hunter Defense Tech Inc ....E 216 438-6111
 Solon **(G-16859)**

MACHINERY, METALWORKING: Cutting & Slitting

Ged Holdings Inc ....C 330 963-5401
 Twinsburg **(G-18272)**

MACHINERY, OFFICE: Paper Handling

Symatic Inc...E 330 225-1510
 Brunswick **(G-1941)**

MACHINERY, PACKAGING: Wrapping

Samuel Strapping Systems Inc ....D 740 522-2500
 Heath **(G-11709)**

MACHINERY, WOODWORKING: Pattern Makers'

Seilkop Industries Inc............................E 513 761-1035
 Cincinnati **(G-4448)**

SERVICES

MACHINERY/EQPT, INDL, WHOL: Cleaning, High Press, Sand/Steam

Contract Sweepers & Eqp Co ....E 614 221-7441
Columbus (G-7366)
Tom Langhals ....E 419 659-5629
Columbus Grove (G-8942)

MACHINERY: Ammunition & Explosives Loading

Military Resources LLC ....E 330 263-1040
Wooster (G-19746)
Military Resources LLC ....D 330 309-9970
Wooster (G-19747)

MACHINERY: Assembly, Exc Metalworking

Remtec Engineering ....E 513 860-4299
Mason (G-13635)

MACHINERY: Automotive Related

Wauseon Machine & Mfg Inc ....D 419 337-0940
Wauseon (G-18812)

MACHINERY: Binding

Baumfolder Corporation ....E 937 492-1281
Sidney (G-16760)

MACHINERY: Bottling & Canning

OKL Can Line Inc ....E 513 825-1655
Cincinnati (G-4166)

MACHINERY: Construction

Grasan Equipment Company Inc ....D 419 526-4440
Mansfield (G-13180)
Kaffenbarger Truck Eqp Co ....E 513 772-6800
Cincinnati (G-3846)
Npk Construction Equipment Inc ....D 440 232-7900
Bedford (G-1295)
Pubco Corporation ....D 216 881-5300
Cleveland (G-6268)

MACHINERY: Custom

Alfons Haar Inc ....E 937 560-2031
Springboro (G-16961)
Cleveland Jsm Inc ....D 440 876-3050
Strongsville (G-17291)
East End Welding Company ....C 330 677-6000
Kent (G-12230)
Enprotech Industrial Tech LLC ....C 216 883-3220
Cleveland (G-5482)
Interscope Manufacturing Inc ....E 513 423-8866
Middletown (G-14303)
Invotec Engineering Inc ....D 937 886-3232
Miamisburg (G-14177)
Narrow Way Custom Technology ....E 937 743-1611
Carlisle (G-2553)
Sample Machining Inc ....E 937 258-3338
Dayton (G-9750)
Steel Eqp Specialists Inc ....D 330 823-8260
Alliance (G-555)

MACHINERY: Folding

Baumfolder Corporation ....E 937 492-1281
Sidney (G-16760)

MACHINERY: Glassmaking

Ged Holdings Inc ....C 330 963-5401
Twinsburg (G-18272)
Intertec Corporation ....B 419 537-9711
Toledo (G-17824)
J & S Industrial Mch Pdts Inc ....D 419 691-1380
Toledo (G-17827)

MACHINERY: Logging Eqpt

Buck Equipment Inc ....E 614 539-3039
Grove City (G-11414)

MACHINERY: Metalworking

Addisonmckee Inc ....C 513 228-7000
Lebanon (G-12448)
Ctm Integration Incorporated ....E 330 332-1800
Salem (G-16541)

Pines Manufacturing Inc ....E 440 835-5553
Westlake (G-19392)
South Shore Controls Inc ....E 440 259-2500
Perry (G-15828)

MACHINERY: Mining

Kaffenbarger Truck Eqp Co ....E 513 772-6800
Cincinnati (G-3846)
Npk Construction Equipment Inc ....D 440 232-7900
Bedford (G-1295)

MACHINERY: Packaging

Ctm Integration Incorporated ....E 330 332-1800
Salem (G-16541)
Millwood Natural LLC ....C 330 393-4400
Vienna (G-18583)
Norse Dairy Systems Inc ....C 614 294-4931
Columbus (G-8195)

MACHINERY: Plastic Working

Linden Industries Inc ....E 330 928-4064
Cuyahoga Falls (G-9109)
Vulcan Machinery Corporation ....E 330 376-6025
Akron (G-491)
Youngstown Plastic Tooling ....E 330 782-7222
Youngstown (G-20265)

MACHINERY: Printing Presses

Graphic Systems Services Inc ....E 937 746-0708
Springboro (G-16967)

MACHINERY: Recycling

Grasan Equipment Company Inc ....D 419 526-4440
Mansfield (G-13180)

MACHINERY: Road Construction & Maintenance

Forge Industries Inc ....A 330 782-8301
Youngstown (G-20040)
Power-Pack Conveyor Company ....E 440 975-9955
Willoughby (G-19563)

MACHINERY: Rubber Working

Rubber City Machinery Corp ....E 330 434-3500
Akron (G-411)

MACHINERY: Textile

Wolf Machine Company ....C 513 791-5194
Blue Ash (G-1679)

MACHINERY: Wire Drawing

EZ Grout Corporation Inc ....E 740 962-2024
Malta (G-13121)

MAGAZINES, WHOLESALE

Windy Hill Ltd Inc ....D 216 391-4800
Cleveland (G-6684)

MAGNETS: Permanent

Walker National Inc ....E 614 492-1614
Columbus (G-8870)
Winkle Industries Inc ....D 330 823-9730
Alliance (G-557)

MAIL PRESORTING SVCS

Pitney Bowes Presort Svcs Inc ....E 513 860-3607
West Chester (G-19072)

MAIL-ORDER HOUSE, NEC

American Frame Corporation ....E 419 893-5595
Maumee (G-13748)
Schneider Saddlery LLC ....E 440 543-2700
Chagrin Falls (G-2682)

MAIL-ORDER HOUSES: Arts & Crafts Eqpt & Splys

Craft Wholesalers Inc ....C 740 964-6210
Groveport (G-11504)

MAIL-ORDER HOUSES: Automotive Splys & Eqpt

Jegs Automotive Inc ....C 614 294-5050
Delaware (G-9990)

MAIL-ORDER HOUSES: Books, Exc Book Clubs

Pure Romance LLC ....D 513 248-8656
Cincinnati (G-4306)

MAIL-ORDER HOUSES: Cheese

K & R Distributors Inc ....E 937 864-5495
Fairborn (G-10677)

MAIL-ORDER HOUSES: Computer Software

Provantage LLC ....D 330 494-3781
North Canton (G-15228)

MAIL-ORDER HOUSES: Computers & Peripheral Eqpt

PC Connection Sales Corp ....C 937 382-4800
Wilmington (G-19638)
Systemax Manufacturing Inc ....C 937 368-2300
Dayton (G-9805)

MAIL-ORDER HOUSES: Educational Splys & Eqpt

Bendon Inc ....D 419 207-3600
Ashland (G-657)

MAIL-ORDER HOUSES: Food

Gem Edwards Inc ....D 330 342-8300
Hudson (G-11979)

MAIL-ORDER HOUSES: Gift Items

H & M Patch Company ....D 614 339-8950
Columbus (G-7706)

MAILBOX RENTAL & RELATED SVCS

Ngm Inc ....E 513 821-7363
Cincinnati (G-4118)
United Parcel Service Inc ....E 440 243-3344
Middleburg Heights (G-14263)
United Parcel Service Inc OH ....B 740 363-0636
Delaware (G-10013)
United Parcel Service Inc OH ....B 614 277-3300
Urbancrest (G-18452)

MAILING & MESSENGER SVCS

Richardson Printing Corp ....D 740 373-5362
Marietta (G-13377)
United Parcel Service Inc OH ....B 216 676-4560
Cleveland (G-6578)
United Parcel Service Inc OH ....B 614 870-4111
Columbus (G-8808)

MAILING LIST: Compilers

Brothers Publishing Co LLC ....E 937 548-3330
Greenville (G-11368)
Haines & Company Inc ....C 330 494-9111
North Canton (G-15210)

MAILING SVCS, NEC

Aero Fulfillment Services Corp ....D 800 225-7145
Mason (G-13536)
Angstrom Graphics Inc Midwest ....E 330 225-8950
Cleveland (G-4981)
Bindery & Spc Pressworks Inc ....D 614 873-4623
Plain City (G-16046)
Blue Chip Mailing Services Inc ....E 513 541-4800
Blue Ash (G-1514)
Bpm Realty Inc ....E 614 221-6811
Columbus (G-7058)
Case Western Reserve Univ ....E 216 368-2560
Cleveland (G-5130)
Centurion of Akron Inc ....D 330 645-6699
Copley (G-8964)
Ctrac Inc ....E 440 572-1000
Cleveland (G-5388)
Dayton Mailing Services Inc ....E 937 222-5056
Dayton (G-9371)

Directconnectgroup Ltd ....A 216 281-2866
Cleveland (G-5425)
Early Express Services Inc ....E 937 223-5801
Dayton (G-9400)
Fine Line Graphics Corp ....C 614 486-0276
Columbus (G-7577)
Hkm Drect Mkt Cmmnications Inc .....C 216 651-9500
Cleveland (G-5696)
J C Direct Mail Inc ....C 614 836-4848
Groveport (G-11522)
Literature Fulfillment Svcs ....E 513 774-8600
Blue Ash (G-1598)
Macke Brothers Inc ....D 513 771-7500
Cincinnati (G-3956)
Macys Cr & Customer Svcs Inc ....D 513 881-9950
West Chester (G-18967)
Mail It Corp ....E 419 249-4848
Toledo (G-17879)
Patented Acquisition Corp ....C 937 353-2299
Miamisburg (G-14203)
Postal Mail Sort Inc ....E 330 747-1515
Youngstown (G-20164)
Power Management Inc ....E 937 222-2909
Dayton (G-9701)
Presort America Ltd ....D 614 836-5120
Groveport (G-11530)
W C National Mailing Corp ....B 614 836-5703
Groveport (G-11550)
Weekleys Mailing Service Inc ....D 440 234-4325
Berea (G-1443)
Yeck Brothers Company ....E 937 294-4000
Moraine (G-14708)

MANAGEMENT CONSULTING SVCS:
Administrative

Facilities MGT Solutions LLC ....E 513 639-2230
Cincinnati (G-3526)
Incentisoft Solutions LLC ....D 877 562-4461
Cleveland (G-5741)
Klingbeil Management Group Co ....E 614 220-8900
Columbus (G-7911)
National Administative Svc LLC ....E 614 358-3607
Dublin (G-10285)
Ride Share Information ....E 513 621-6300
Cincinnati (G-4373)

MANAGEMENT CONSULTING SVCS:
Automation & Robotics

Clear Vision Engineering LLC ....E 419 478-7151
Toledo (G-17664)
Motion Controls Robotics Inc ....E 419 334-5886
Fremont (G-11088)
Remtec Automation LLC ....E 877 759-8151
Mason (G-13634)
Robex LLC ....D 419 270-0770
Perrysburg (G-15914)
Wirefree Home Automation ....E 440 247-8978
Chagrin Falls (G-2661)

MANAGEMENT CONSULTING SVCS:
Banking & Finance

Banc Amer Prctice Slutions Inc ....C 614 794-8247
Westerville (G-19147)
Kings Medical Company ....C 330 653-3968
Hudson (G-11991)
Nationwide Financial Svcs Inc ....C 614 249-7111
Columbus (G-8155)
Trinity Credit Counseling Inc ....E 513 769-0621
Cincinnati (G-4647)

MANAGEMENT CONSULTING SVCS:
Business

5me LLC ....E 513 719-1600
Cincinnati (G-2839)
Accenture LLP ....C 216 685-1435
Cleveland (G-4898)
Accenture LLP ....C 614 629-2000
Columbus (G-6861)
Accenture LLP ....D 513 455-1000
Cincinnati (G-2900)
Accenture LLP ....D 513 651-2444
Cincinnati (G-2901)
Accurate Inventory and C ....B 800 777-9414
Columbus (G-6863)
Advocate Solutions LLC ....E 614 444-5144
Columbus (G-6876)

Arysen Inc ....D 440 230-4400
Independence (G-12047)
Avatar Management Services ....E 330 963-3900
Macedonia (G-13059)
Btas Inc ....C 937 431-9431
Beavercreek (G-1135)
Corporate Fin Assoc of Clumbus ....D 614 457-9219
Columbus (G-7374)
Dayton Aerospace Inc ....C 937 426-4300
Beavercreek Township (G-1246)
DE Foxx & Associates Inc ....B 513 621-5522
Cincinnati (G-3408)
Dental One Inc ....E 216 584-1000
Independence (G-12066)
Enabling Partners LLC ....E 440 878-9418
Strongsville (G-17301)
Engaged Health Care Bus Svcs ....E 614 457-8180
Columbus (G-7516)
Epiphany Management Group LLC .....E 330 706-4056
Akron (G-204)
Ernst & Young LLP ....C 614 224-5678
Columbus (G-7531)
Ernst & Young LLP ....C 513 612-1400
Cincinnati (G-3515)
Excellence Alliance Group Inc ....E 513 619-4800
Cincinnati (G-3524)
Finit Group LLC..............................D 513 793-4648
Cincinnati (G-3551)
Incubit LLC ....D 740 362-1401
Delaware (G-9988)
Industry Insights Inc ....E 614 389-2100
Columbus (G-7814)
Kalypso LP ....D 216 378-4290
Beachwood (G-1071)
Marsh Berry & Company Inc ....E 440 354-3230
Beachwood (G-1075)
McKinsey & Company Inc ....E 216 274-4000
Cleveland (G-5935)
Normandy Group LLC ....E 513 745-0990
Blue Ash (G-1622)
Orbit Systems Inc ....E 614 504-8011
Lewis Center (G-12556)
Organizational Horizons Inc ....E 614 268-6013
Worthington (G-19832)
Phoenix Resource Network LLC ....E 800 990-4948
Cincinnati (G-4244)
Projetech Inc ....E 513 481-4900
Cincinnati (G-4296)
Provenitfinance LLC ....E 888 958-1060
Pickerington (G-15965)
Racksquared LLC ....E 614 737-8812
Columbus (G-8483)
Root Inc ....D 419 874-0077
Sylvania (G-17448)
Scrogginsgrear Inc ....C 513 672-4281
Cincinnati (G-4440)
Smith & English II Inc ....E 513 697-9300
Loveland (G-13029)
Smithers Group Inc ....D 330 762-7441
Akron (G-432)
Smithers Rapra Inc ....D 330 762-7441
Akron (G-434)
Solenis LLC ....E 614 336-1101
Dublin (G-10336)
Surgere Inc ....E 330 526-7971
North Canton (G-15236)
Tacg LLC ....C 937 203-8201
Beavercreek (G-1237)
Versatex LLC ....E 513 639-3119
Cincinnati (G-4755)

MANAGEMENT CONSULTING SVCS:
Business Planning & Organizing

Equity Resources Inc ....D 513 518-6318
Cincinnati (G-3512)
First Data Gvrnment Sltions LP ....D 513 489-9599
Blue Ash (G-1562)
Techncal Sltons Spcialists Inc ....E 513 792-8930
Blue Ash (G-1656)
Total Marketing Resources LLC ....E 330 220-1275
Brunswick (G-1943)
Tsg Resources Inc ....A 330 498-8200
North Canton (G-15241)

MANAGEMENT CONSULTING SVCS:
Compensation & Benefits Planning

Corporate Plans Inc ....E 440 542-7800
Solon (G-16838)

Findley Inc ....D 419 255-1360
Toledo (G-17737)
Frank Gates Service Company ....B 614 793-8000
Dublin (G-10231)
Group Management Services Inc ....E 330 659-0100
Richfield (G-16359)
Independent Evaluators Inc ....D 419 872-5650
Perrysburg (G-15878)
Mercer (us) Inc ....E 513 632-2600
Cincinnati (G-4007)
Parman Group Inc ....E 513 673-0077
Columbus (G-8424)
Progressive Entps Holdings Inc ....A 614 794-3300
Westerville (G-19204)
Rx Options LLC..............................D 330 405-8080
Twinsburg (G-18314)
The Sheakley Group Inc ....E 513 771-2277
Cincinnati (G-4596)
Wtw Delaware Holdings LLC ....C 216 937-4000
Cleveland (G-6693)

MANAGEMENT CONSULTING SVCS:
Construction Project

Critical Business Analysis Inc ....E 419 874-0800
Perrysburg (G-15852)
Smoot Construction Co Ohio ....E 614 253-9000
Columbus (G-8657)

MANAGEMENT CONSULTING SVCS:
Corporation Organizing

Comex North America Inc ....D 303 307-2100
Cleveland (G-5316)

MANAGEMENT CONSULTING SVCS:
Distribution Channels

Trilogy Fulfillment LLC ....E 614 491-0553
Groveport (G-11543)

MANAGEMENT CONSULTING SVCS: Food & Beverage

AVI Food Systems Inc ....C 330 372-6000
Warren (G-18677)

MANAGEMENT CONSULTING SVCS: Foreign Trade

Bannockburn Global Forex LLC ....E 513 386-7400
Cincinnati (G-3016)

MANAGEMENT CONSULTING SVCS:
Franchising

Its Financial LLC ....D 937 425-6889
Beavercreek (G-1224)
Producer Group LLC ....E 440 871-7700
Rocky River (G-16444)

MANAGEMENT CONSULTING SVCS: General

Career Partners Intl LLC ....A 919 401-4260
Columbus (G-7126)
Murtech Consulting LLC ....D 216 328-8580
Cleveland (G-6026)
Oncall LLC ....D 513 381-4320
Cincinnati (G-4173)
Paragon Consulting Inc ....E 440 684-3101
Cleveland (G-6160)
Paragon Tec Inc ....D 216 361-5555
Cleveland (G-6161)
Pope & Associates Inc ....E 513 671-1277
West Chester (G-18983)
Turtle Golf Management Ltd ....E 614 882-5920
Westerville (G-19303)
Xzamcorp ....E 330 629-2218
Perry (G-15830)

MANAGEMENT CONSULTING SVCS:
Hospital & Health

Acuity Healthcare LP ....D 740 283-7499
Steubenville (G-17139)
Alternative Care Mgt Systems ....E 614 761-0035
Dublin (G-10127)
American Health Group Inc ....D 419 891-1212
Maumee (G-13750)
Beacon of Light Ltd ....E 419 531-9060
Toledo (G-17608)

Change Hlth Prac MGT Solns Grp........E 937 291-7850
  Miamisburg *(G-14151)*
Chattree and Associates Inc ....D 216 831-1494
  Cleveland *(G-5172)*
East Way Behavioral Hlth Care...........C 937 222-4900
  Dayton *(G-9403)*
Emerald Health Network Inc ....D 216 479-2030
  Fairlawn *(G-10825)*
First Choice Medical Staffing.............E 419 626-9740
  Sandusky *(G-16608)*
Germain & Co Inc ....E 937 885-5827
  Dayton *(G-9460)*
Healthcomp Inc ....D 216 696-6900
  Cleveland *(G-5674)*
Integra Group Inc ....E 513 326-5600
  Cincinnati *(G-3767)*
Malik Punam ....D 513 636-1333
  Cincinnati *(G-3965)*
Medical Recovery Systems Inc ....D 513 872-7000
  Cincinnati *(G-3995)*
Medisync Midwest Ltd Lblty Co ....D 513 533-1199
  Cincinnati *(G-3998)*
Ohic Insurance Company ....D 614 221-7777
  Columbus *(G-8227)*
Ohiohealth Corporation ....D 614 566-3500
  Columbus *(G-8361)*
Patient Account MGT Svcs LLC ....E 614 575-0044
  Columbus *(G-8425)*
Plus Management Services Inc ....C 419 225-9018
  Lima *(G-12722)*
PSI Supply Chain Solutions LLC ....E 614 389-4717
  Dublin *(G-10313)*
Regent Systems Inc...........E 937 640-8010
  Dayton *(G-9729)*
Spirit Women Health Netwrk LLC..........E 561 544-2004
  Cincinnati *(G-2869)*
Touchstone Group Assoc LLC ....E 513 791-1717
  Cincinnati *(G-4613)*
United Audit Systems Inc...........C 513 723-1122
  Cincinnati *(G-4675)*
Vernon F Glaser & Associates ....E 937 298-5536
  Dayton *(G-9854)*
Wellington Group LLC...........E 216 525-2200
  Independence *(G-12140)*

MANAGEMENT CONSULTING SVCS: Industrial & Labor

Mancan Inc ....A 440 884-9675
  Strongsville *(G-17326)*

MANAGEMENT CONSULTING SVCS: Industry Specialist

Brentley Institute Inc ....E 216 225-0087
  Cleveland *(G-5078)*
Carol Scudere ....E 614 839-4357
  New Albany *(G-14848)*
Chemsultants International Inc ....E 440 974-3080
  Mentor *(G-14029)*
Dealers Group Limited ....E 440 352-4970
  Beachwood *(G-1052)*
Dedicated Technologies Inc...........D 614 460-3200
  Columbus *(G-7427)*
Protiviti Inc ....E 216 696-6010
  Cleveland *(G-6262)*
Triad Oil & Gas Engineering ....D 740 374-2940
  Marietta *(G-13388)*

MANAGEMENT CONSULTING SVCS: Information Systems

3sg Plus LLC ....E 614 652-0019
  Columbus *(G-6797)*
Fusion Alliance LLC ....E 614 852-8000
  Westerville *(G-19167)*
Fusion Alliance LLC ....E 513 563-8444
  Blue Ash *(G-1565)*
Jjr Solutions LLC ....E 937 912-0288
  Beavercreek *(G-1159)*
Kennedy Group Enterprises Inc ....E 440 879-0078
  Strongsville *(G-17320)*
Tek Systems ....D 614 789-6200
  Dublin *(G-10354)*
Vartek Services Inc ....E 937 438-3550
  Dayton *(G-9852)*

MANAGEMENT CONSULTING SVCS: Maintenance

County of Marion ....E 740 382-0624
  Marion *(G-13417)*
Hamilton Parks Conservancy ....E 513 785-7055
  Hamilton *(G-11608)*

MANAGEMENT CONSULTING SVCS: Management Engineering

Johnson Mirmiran Thompson Inc ....D 614 714-0270
  Columbus *(G-7863)*
Shotstop Ballistics LLC...........E 330 686-0020
  Stow *(G-17230)*

MANAGEMENT CONSULTING SVCS: Manufacturing

Impact Ceramics LLC ....E 440 554-3624
  Cleveland *(G-5740)*
Midwest Mfg Solutions LLC ....E 513 381-7200
  West Chester *(G-19068)*
Ply-Trim Enterprises Inc...........E 330 799-7876
  Youngstown *(G-20160)*
Techsolve Inc ....D 513 948-2000
  Cincinnati *(G-4581)*

MANAGEMENT CONSULTING SVCS: Merchandising

Merchandising Services Co ....D 866 479-8246
  Blue Ash *(G-1608)*

MANAGEMENT CONSULTING SVCS: New Products & Svcs

Akron Centl Engrv Mold Mch Inc..........E 330 794-8704
  Akron *(G-30)*

MANAGEMENT CONSULTING SVCS: Planning

Aeea LLC ....E 330 497-5304
  Canton *(G-2176)*
Interbrand Design Forum LLC ....C 513 421-2210
  Cincinnati *(G-3777)*
Karlsberger Companies ....C 614 461-9500
  Columbus *(G-7883)*
National City Cmnty Dev Corp ....C 216 575-2000
  Cleveland *(G-6039)*
Ohio-Kentucky-Indiana Regional ....E 513 621-6300
  Cincinnati *(G-4162)*
Retail Forward Inc...........E 614 355-4000
  Columbus *(G-8527)*
Sedlak Management Consultants.........E 216 206-4700
  Cleveland *(G-6391)*
Shp Leading Design ....D 513 381-2112
  Cincinnati *(G-4472)*

MANAGEMENT CONSULTING SVCS: Public Utilities

United States Enrichment Corp...........A 740 897-2331
  Piketon *(G-15989)*
United States Enrichment Corp...........A 740 897-2457
  Piketon *(G-15990)*

MANAGEMENT CONSULTING SVCS: Quality Assurance

Safety Resources Company Ohio ....E 330 477-1100
  Canton *(G-2469)*
Smithers Quality Assessments ....E 330 762-4231
  Akron *(G-433)*

MANAGEMENT CONSULTING SVCS: Real Estate

0714 Inc...........E 440 327-2123
  North Ridgeville *(G-15318)*
Chartwell Group LLC ....E 216 360-0009
  Cleveland *(G-5171)*
Classic Real Estate Co ....E 937 393-3416
  Hillsboro *(G-11833)*
Hanna Commercial LLC ....D 216 861-7200
  Cleveland *(G-5659)*
Homelife Companies Inc ....E 740 369-1297
  Delaware *(G-9986)*

Ohio Equities LLC...........E 614 207-1805
  Columbus *(G-8252)*
Signature Associates Inc ....E 419 244-7505
  Toledo *(G-18034)*
Stepstone Group Real Estate LP.........E 216 522-0330
  Cleveland *(G-6467)*
Toni & Marie Bader ....E 937 339-3621
  Troy *(G-18231)*

MANAGEMENT CONSULTING SVCS: Restaurant & Food

Columbus Public School Dst ....E 614 365-5000
  Columbus *(G-7308)*
L and C Soft Serve Inc ....E 330 364-3823
  Dover *(G-10086)*
Thomas and King Inc ....C 614 527-0571
  Hilliard *(G-11821)*

MANAGEMENT CONSULTING SVCS: Retail Trade Consultant

Melo International Inc ....B 440 519-0526
  Cleveland *(G-5951)*
Sb Capital Acquisitions LLC ....A 614 443-4080
  Columbus *(G-8596)*

MANAGEMENT CONSULTING SVCS: Training & Development

1st Advnce SEC Invstgtions Inc ....E 937 317-4433
  Dayton *(G-9194)*
Automotive Events Inc ....E 440 356-1383
  Rocky River *(G-16423)*
D L A Training Center ....D 614 692-5986
  Columbus *(G-7409)*
Dayton Digital Media Inc ....E 937 223-8335
  Dayton *(G-9362)*
Global Military Expert Co ....E 800 738-9795
  Beavercreek *(G-1219)*
Honda of America Mfg Inc ....C 937 644-0724
  Marysville *(G-13505)*
Leidos Inc ....D 937 431-2270
  Beavercreek *(G-1164)*
Miami University ....B 513 727-3200
  Middletown *(G-14308)*

MANAGEMENT CONSULTING SVCS: Transportation

Ardmore Power Logistics LLC ....E 216 502-0640
  Westlake *(G-19318)*
Ascent Global Logistics Holdin...........E 800 689-6255
  Hudson *(G-11967)*
Comprehensive Logistics Co Inc ....E 330 793-0504
  Youngstown *(G-20007)*
CPC Logistics Inc ....D 513 874-5787
  Fairfield *(G-10715)*
Distribution Data Incorporated ....E 216 362-3009
  Brookpark *(G-1896)*
First Transit Inc ....B 513 241-2200
  Cincinnati *(G-3564)*
Jarrett Logistics Systems Inc ....C 330 682-0099
  Orrville *(G-15636)*
Landrum & Brown Incorporated ....E 513 530-5333
  Blue Ash *(G-1595)*
Ryder Last Mile Inc ....E 614 801-0621
  Columbus *(G-8566)*
TV Minority Company Inc ....E 937 832-9350
  Englewood *(G-10603)*
Universal Transportation Syste..........C 513 829-1287
  Fairfield *(G-10796)*

MANAGEMENT SERVICES

Aim Integrated Logistics Inc...........B 330 759-0438
  Girard *(G-11281)*
Allcan Global Services Inc ....E 513 825-1655
  Cincinnati *(G-2924)*
American Med ....B 330 762-8999
  Akron *(G-69)*
Apollo Property Management LLC ....E 216 468-0050
  Beachwood *(G-1030)*
Babcock & Wilcox Company ....A 330 753-4511
  Barberton *(G-944)*
Benchmark Technologies Corp ....E 419 843-6691
  Toledo *(G-17611)*
Benjamin Rose Institute ....D 216 791-3580
  Cleveland *(G-5056)*
Bernard Busson Builder...........E 330 929-4926
  Akron *(G-95)*

(G-0000) Company's Geographic Section entry number

Company	Code	Phone
Bridgepoint Risk MGT LLC .... Maumee (G-13766)	E	419 794-1075
Brown Co Ed Service Center .... Georgetown (G-11263)	D	937 378-6118
Cardinal Health Inc .... Dublin (G-10156)	A	614 757-5000
Cardinal Health Inc .... Obetz (G-15524)	D	614 497-9552
Careworks of Ohio Inc .... Dublin (G-10161)	B	614 792-1085
Cargotec Services USA Inc .... Perrysburg (G-15846)	D	419 482-6000
Cbre Heery Inc .... Cleveland (G-5143)	E	216 781-1313
Cdc Management Co .... Columbus (G-7146)	C	614 781-0216
CFM Religion Pubg Group LLC .... Cincinnati (G-3162)	E	513 931-4050
Clermont North East School Dst .... Batavia (G-990)	E	513 625-8283
Cleveland Clinic Foundation........... Cleveland (G-5236)	A	216 636-8335
Cleveland Clinic Foundation........... Sandusky (G-16587)	D	419 609-2812
Cleveland Health Network .... Cleveland (G-5257)	E	216 986-1100
Clk Multi-Family MGT LLC .... Columbus (G-7232)	C	614 891-0011
Coal Services Inc .... Powhatan Point (G-16214)	E	740 795-5220
Colonial Senior Services Inc........... Hamilton (G-11582)	C	513 856-8600
Colonial Senior Services Inc........... Hamilton (G-11583)	C	513 867-4006
Colonial Senior Services Inc........... Hamilton (G-11584)	C	513 844-8004
Comprehensive Managed Care Sys........... Cincinnati (G-3347)	E	513 533-0021
Constellations Enterprise LLC .... Youngstown (G-20010)	C	330 740-8208
Consulate Management Co LLC........... Crestline (G-9051)	A	419 683-3436
Crawford & Company .... Warren (G-18695)	E	330 652-3296
Crescent Park Corporation .... West Chester (G-18906)	C	513 759-7000
Crestwood Mgmt LLC .... Cleveland (G-5381)	D	440 484-2400
Cypress Communications Inc .... Cleveland (G-5402)	C	404 965-7248
Cypress Companies Inc .... Akron (G-179)	E	330 849-6500
Dave Commercial Ground MGT........... North Royalton (G-15352)	E	440 237-5394
Dayton Foundation Inc .... Dayton (G-9365)	E	937 222-0410
Dearth Management Company........... Columbus (G-7426)	C	614 847-1070
Dhl Supply Chain (usa) .... Toledo (G-17700)	E	419 727-4318
Distribution Data Incorporated .... Brookpark (G-1896)	E	216 362-3009
Education Innovations Intl LLC .... Dublin (G-10215)	C	614 339-3676
Eleet Cryogenics Inc .... Bolivar (G-1702)	E	330 874-4009
Erie Indemnity Company .... Canton (G-2303)	D	330 433-6300
Excellence In Motivation Inc........... Dayton (G-9420)	C	763 445-3000
Executive Jet Management Inc .... Cincinnati (G-3525)	B	513 979-6600
Facilities Kahn Management........... Dayton (G-9424)	E	313 202-7607
FC Schwendler LLC .... Akron (G-217)	E	330 733-8715
First Services Inc .... Cincinnati (G-3559)	A	513 241-2200
First Transit Inc .... Cincinnati (G-3564)	B	513 241-2200
Fisher Foods Marketing Inc .... North Canton (G-15203)	C	330 497-3000
Flat Rock Care Center .... Flat Rock (G-10978)	E	419 483-7330
Focus Solutions Inc .... Cincinnati (G-3575)	C	513 376-8349
Folkers Management Corporation........... Cincinnati (G-3576)	E	513 421-0230
Foseco Management Inc .... Cleveland (G-5567)	B	440 826-4548

Company	Code	Phone
Franklin & Seidelmann LLC .... Beachwood (G-1060)	D	216 255-5700
French Company LLC .... Twinsburg (G-18269)	D	330 963-4344
Frito-Lay North America Inc .... Maumee (G-13794)	D	419 893-8171
Genesis Technology Partners .... Cincinnati (G-3617)	E	513 585-5800
Gentlebrook Inc .... Hartville (G-11686)	C	330 877-3694
Grote Enterprises LLC .... Cincinnati (G-3659)	D	513 731-5700
Hanger Prosthetics & .... Tallmadge (G-17475)	E	330 633-9807
Helmsman Management Svcs LLC .... Cleveland (G-7738)	D	614 478-8282
Hmshost Corporation .... Clyde (G-6744)	C	419 547-8667
Holzer Clinic LLC .... Gallipolis (G-11197)	A	740 446-5411
Ideal Setech LLC .... Defiance (G-9919)	E	419 782-5522
Illinois Tool Works Inc .... Blue Ash (G-1583)	E	513 891-7485
Illumetek Corp .... Cuyahoga Falls (G-9101)	E	330 342-7582
Imflux Inc .... Hamilton (G-11611)	E	513 488-1017
Infinite Shares LLC .... Mentor (G-14063)	E	216 317-1601
Infocision Management Corp........... Dayton (G-9178)	C	937 259-2400
Instantwhip-Columbus Inc .... Grove City (G-11443)	E	614 871-9447
Intergrated Consulting .... Bedford Heights (G-1323)	E	216 214-7547
Investek Management Svcs F/C .... Perrysburg (G-15880)	E	419 873-1236
Island Service Company .... Put In Bay (G-16226)	E	419 285-3695
J A G Black Gold Management Co .... Lockbourne (G-12821)	D	614 565-3246
Jake Sweeney Automotive Inc........... Cincinnati (G-3805)	C	513 782-2800
Juice Technologies Inc........... Columbus (G-7875)	E	800 518-5576
Kappa House Corp of Delta .... Upper Arlington (G-18399)	E	614 487-9461
Klingbeil Capital MGT LLC .... Worthington (G-19818)	D	614 396-4919
Kroger Co .... Cincinnati (G-3892)	C	513 782-3300
Kurtz Bros Compost Services .... Akron (G-306)	E	330 864-2621
Leadec Corp .... Blue Ash (G-1597)	E	513 731-3590
Leatherman Nursing Ctrs Corp .... Wadsworth (G-18602)	A	330 336-6684
Legacy Village Management Off .... Cleveland (G-5862)	E	216 382-3871
Levering Management Inc .... Chesterville (G-2748)	E	419 768-2401
Levering Management Inc........... Marion (G-13429)	D	740 387-9545
Licking-Knox Goodwill Inds Inc .... Newark (G-15061)	D	740 345-9861
Lincolnview Local Schools .... Van Wert (G-18483)	E	419 968-2226
Lott Industries Incorporated .... Toledo (G-17859)	A	419 534-4980
Lutheran Housing Services Inc .... Toledo (G-17872)	E	419 861-4990
M A Folkes Company Inc........... Hamilton (G-11626)	E	513 785-4200
Marsh Berry & Company Inc........... Beachwood (G-1075)	E	440 354-3230
MD Business Solutions Inc........... Blue Ash (G-1606)	E	513 872-4500
Med America Hlth Systems Corp........... Dayton (G-9598)	A	937 223-6192
Michael Baker Intl Inc .... Canton (G-2402)	C	330 453-3110
Michael Baker Intl Inc .... Cleveland (G-5976)	E	412 269-6300
Ministerial Day Care-Headstart........... Cleveland (G-5976)	E	216 881-6924
National Heritg Academies Inc .... Dayton (G-9653)	D	937 223-2889
National Heritg Academies Inc .... Cincinnati (G-4092)	D	513 251-6000

Company	Code	Phone
National Heritg Academies Inc .... Toledo (G-17931)	D	419 269-2247
National Heritg Academies Inc .... Cincinnati (G-4093)	D	513 751-5555
National Heritg Academies Inc .... Toledo (G-17932)	D	419 531-3285
National Heritg Academies Inc .... Dayton (G-9654)	D	937 235-5498
National Heritg Academies Inc .... Dayton (G-9655)	D	937 278-6671
National Heritg Academies Inc .... Euclid (G-10650)	D	216 731-0127
National Heritg Academies Inc .... Cleveland (G-6046)	D	216 451-1725
National Heritg Academies Inc .... Youngstown (G-20138)	D	330 792-4806
Nexstep Healthcare LLC .... Cleveland (G-6066)	E	216 797-4040
Niederst Management Ltd .... Cleveland (G-6070)	E	440 331-8800
Northcoast Healthcare MGT........... Beachwood (G-1087)	C	216 591-2000
Novotec Recycling LLC .... Columbus (G-8210)	E	614 231-8326
Ohio Department of Education .... Piketon (G-15980)	E	740 289-2908
Omnicare Management Company........... Cincinnati (G-4170)	A	513 719-1535
P I & I Motor Express Inc........... Masury (G-13741)	C	330 448-4035
Parkops Columbus LLC .... Columbus (G-8423)	B	877 499-9155
Perduco Group Inc........... Beavercreek (G-1175)	E	937 401-0271
Pk Management LLC........... Richmond Heights (G-16392)	C	216 472-1870
Plus Management Services Inc .... Lima (G-12722)	E	419 225-9018
Premier Management Co Inc .... Chesapeake (G-2731)	E	740 867-2144
Professional Transit Mgt .... Loveland (G-13022)	E	513 677-6000
Promedica Health Systems Inc........... Toledo (G-17993)	A	567 585-7454
Promedica Physcn Cntinuum Svcs........... Sylvania (G-17444)	C	419 824-7200
Resource International Inc........... Columbus (G-8523)	E	614 823-4949
Revolution Group Inc .... Westerville (G-19207)	E	614 212-1111
Ricco Enterprises Incorporated .... Cleveland (G-6319)	E	216 883-7775
Richland Mall Shopping Ctr .... Mansfield (G-13236)	E	419 529-4003
Ross Consolidated Corp .... Grafton (G-11320)	D	440 748-5800
Safeguard Properties LLC........... Cleveland (G-6361)	A	216 739-2900
Salvation Army .... Tiffin (G-17535)	D	419 447-2252
Sears Roebuck and Co........... Cincinnati (G-4442)	E	513 741-6422
Signature Inc .... Dublin (G-10334)	C	614 734-0010
Skanska USA Building Inc .... Cincinnati (G-4492)	C	513 421-0082
Sleep Network Inc .... Toledo (G-18036)	D	419 535-9282
Smg Holdings Inc .... Columbus (G-8654)	E	614 827-2500
Ssoe Inc .... Alliance (G-552)	E	330 821-7198
Stat Integrated Tech Inc .... Chardon (G-2716)	E	440 286-7663
Sylvania Franciscan Health .... Maumee (G-13859)	E	419 882-8373
TAC Industries Inc .... Springfield (G-17123)	B	937 328-5200
The Sheakley Group Inc .... Cincinnati (G-4596)	E	513 771-2277
Trinity Hospital Holding Co .... Steubenville (G-17180)	A	740 264-8000
Uc Health Llc .... Cincinnati (G-4667)	E	513 584-8600
United Telemanagement Corp .... Dayton (G-9833)	E	937 454-1888
University Hospitals .... Cleveland (G-6590)	D	216 844-8797
University Hospitals Cleveland .... Cleveland (G-6595)	E	216 844-3528

SERVICES

Vance Property Management LLC........D 419 887-1878
Toledo (G-18136)
Verst Group Logistics Inc ....E 513 772-2494
Cincinnati (G-4757)
Voc Works Ltd ....D...... 614 760-3515
Dublin (G-10366)
Western Management Inc ....E 216 941-3333
Cleveland (G-6672)
Wings Investors Company Ltd ....E 513 241-5800
Cincinnati (G-4799)

MANAGEMENT SVCS, FACILITIES SUPPORT: Environ Remediation

Alco Inc ....E 740 527-2991
Logan (G-12830)
Aztec Services Group Inc ....E 513 541-2002
Cincinnati (G-3012)
Environmental Specialists Inc ....E 740 788-8134
Newark (G-15032)
Enviroserve Inc ....C 330 966-0910
North Canton (G-15200)
Midwest Environmental Inc ....E 419 382-9200
Perrysburg (G-15895)
Southside Envmtl Group LLC..........E 330 299-0027
Niles (G-15170)

MANAGEMENT SVCS, FACILITIES SUPPORT: Jails, Privately Ops

Correctons Comm Sthastern Ohio........D 740 753-4060
Nelsonville (G-14828)

MANAGEMENT SVCS: Administrative

Advocare Inc ....D 216 514-1451
Cleveland (G-4905)
Arthur Middleton Capital Holdn............E 330 966-9000
North Canton (G-15190)
Aultcomp Inc ....E 330 830-4919
Massillon (G-13664)
Bravo Wellness LLC ....C 216 658-9500
Cleveland (G-5075)
City of Youngstown ....B 330 742-8700
Youngstown (G-19991)
County of Cuyahoga ....B 216 443-7181
Cleveland (G-5369)
County of Morrow ....E 419 946-2618
Mount Gilead (G-14726)
Help Foundation Inc ....D 216 432-4810
Euclid (G-10638)
Lineage Logistics LLC ....E 937 328-3349
Springfield (G-17061)
McR LLC ....D 937 879-5055
Beavercreek (G-1170)
Midwest Tape LLC ....B 419 868-9370
Holland (G-11898)
Nationwide General Insur Co ....D 614 249-7111
Columbus (G-8156)
Netjets Aviation Inc ....E 614 239-5501
Gahanna (G-11137)
Parker-Hannifin Intl Corp ....B 216 896-3000
Cleveland (G-6172)
Providence Medical Group Inc ....D 937 297-8999
Moraine (G-14689)
Salvation Army ....C 330 773-3331
Akron (G-418)
Standard Retirement Svcs Inc ....E 440 808-2724
Westlake (G-19409)
Sterling Medical Corporation ....C 513 984-1800
Cincinnati (G-4546)
Thomas Rosser ....C 614 890-2900
Westerville (G-19301)
Tm Capture Services LLC ....D 937 728-1781
Beavercreek (G-1238)
University of Cincinnati ....E 513 556-4200
Cincinnati (G-4714)
University of Cincinnati ....C 513 558-4231
Cincinnati (G-4715)
Village of Valley View ....C 216 524-6511
Cleveland (G-6632)

MANAGEMENT SVCS: Business

3c Technologies Inc ....D 419 868-8999
Holland (G-11868)
Camden Management Inc ....E 513 383-1635
Cincinnati (G-3110)
Dimensionmark Ltd ....E 513 305-3525
West Chester (G-18912)

Early Learning Tree Chld Ctr ....D 937 293-7907
Dayton (G-9402)
EDM Management Inc ....E 330 726-5790
Youngstown (G-20026)
Hat White Management LLC ....E 800 525-7967
Akron (G-255)
Integra Ohio Inc ....B 513 378-5214
Cincinnati (G-3768)
Jeff Wyler Automotive Fmly Inc........E 513 752-7450
Cincinnati (G-2855)
Kaiser Logistics LLC ....D 937 534-0213
Monroe (G-14571)
Kross Acquisition Company LLC ......E 513 554-0555
Loveland (G-13004)
Mfbusiness Group ....E 216 510-0717
Cleveland (G-5974)
Ohio Cllbrtive Lrng Sltons Inc ....E 216 595-5289
Beachwood (G-1089)
Omnicare Purch Ltd Partner Inc........C 800 990-6664
Cincinnati (G-4172)
Osu Internal Medicine LLC ....D 614 293-0080
Dublin (G-10301)
Providence Health Partners LLC ......E 937 297-8999
Moraine (G-14688)
Quality Supply Chain Co-Op Inc ......E 614 764-3124
Dublin (G-10314)
Rev1 Ventures ....E 614 487-3700
Columbus (G-8529)
RMS of Ohio Inc ....B 440 617-6605
Westlake (G-19401)
Roundstone Management Ltd ....E 440 617-0333
Lakewood (G-12362)
Safran Power Usa LLC ....C 330 487-2000
Twinsburg (G-18316)
St George & Co Inc ....E 330 733-7528
Akron (G-438)
Viaquest Inc ....E 614 889-5837
Dublin (G-10362)
Vora Ventures LLC ....C 513 792-5100
Blue Ash (G-1676)
Walnut Ridge Management ....D 234 678-3900
Akron (G-495)
Zarcal Zanesville LLC ....D 216 226-2132
Lakewood (G-12365)

MANAGEMENT SVCS: Circuit, Motion Picture Theaters

Continntal Mssage Solution Inc ....D 614 224-4534
Columbus (G-7364)

MANAGEMENT SVCS: Construction

Aecom Global II LLC.......................D 216 523-5600
Cleveland (G-4910)
Ameridian Specialty Services...........E 513 769-0150
Cincinnati (G-2952)
Baxter Hodell Donnelly Preston ......C 513 271-1634
Cincinnati (G-3025)
Cedarwood Construction Company ......D 330 836-9971
Akron (G-121)
Chemstress Consultant Company ......C 330 535-5591
Akron (G-126)
Collins Assoc Tchncal Svcs Inc........C 740 574-2320
Wheelersburg (G-19430)
Contech-Gdcg ....E 937 426-3577
Beavercreek (G-1212)
Cook Paving and Cnstr Co ....E 216 267-7705
Independence (G-12062)
Core Resources Inc ....C 513 731-1771
Cincinnati (G-3362)
DE Foxx & Associates Inc ....B 513 621-5522
Cincinnati (G-3408)
Eclipse Co LLC ....E 440 552-9400
Cleveland (G-5465)
Elford Inc ....C 614 488-4000
Columbus (G-7511)
Fx Facility Group LLC ....E 513 639-2509
Cincinnati (G-3598)
G Stephens Inc ....D 614 227-0304
Columbus (G-7640)
Gilbane Building Company ....E 614 948-4000
Columbus (G-7668)
Hammond Construction Inc..............D 330 455-7039
Canton (G-2335)
Hemandez Cnstr Svcs Inc...............E 330 796-0500
Akron (G-259)
Hills Developers Inc ....C 513 984-0300
Blue Ash (G-1580)
Ingle-Barr Inc ....C 740 702-6117
Chillicothe (G-2793)

Innovative Architectural ....E 614 416-0614
Columbus (G-7820)
Jack Gibson Construction Co ....D 330 394-5280
Warren (G-18717)
Lathrop Company Inc ....E 419 893-7000
Toledo (G-17849)
McDaniels Cnstr Corp Inc ....D 614 252-5852
Columbus (G-8043)
Megen Construction Company Inc......E 513 742-9191
Cincinnati (G-4003)
Quality Control Inspection ....D 440 359-1900
Cleveland (G-6269)
Quandel Construction Group Inc ......E 717 657-0909
Westerville (G-19297)
Renier Construction Corp ....E 614 866-4580
Columbus (G-8514)
Richard L Bowen & Assoc Inc ....D 216 491-9300
Cleveland (G-6321)
RJ Runge Company Inc ....E 419 740-5781
Port Clinton (G-16116)
Ruscilli Construction Co Inc.............D 614 876-9484
Columbus (G-8560)
Simonson Construction Svcs Inc......D 419 281-8299
Ashland (G-691)
Technical Consultants Inc ....E 513 521-2696
Cincinnati (G-4579)
Triversity Construction Co LLC ....E 513 733-0046
Cincinnati (G-4650)
Ttl Associates Inc ....E 419 241-4556
Toledo (G-18111)

MANAGEMENT SVCS: Financial, Business

Bailey Associates ....C 614 760-7752
Columbus (G-7012)
Critical Business Analysis Inc ....E 419 874-0800
Perrysburg (G-15852)
Dco LLC ....B 419 931-9086
Perrysburg (G-15857)
Hill Barth & King LLC ....E 330 758-8613
Canfield (G-2140)

MANAGEMENT SVCS: Hospital

Acuity Healthcare LP ....D 740 283-7499
Steubenville (G-17139)
Blanchard Valley Health System ....A 419 423-4500
Findlay (G-10871)
Blanchard Valley Health System ....D 419 424-3000
Findlay (G-10872)
Carespring Health Care MGT LLC ......E 513 943-4000
Loveland (G-12981)
Carington Health Systems ....E 513 682-2700
Hamilton (G-11573)
Cincinnati Health Network Inc ....E 513 961-0600
Cincinnati (G-3248)
Clevelan Clinic Hlth Sys W Reg........B 216 518-3444
Cleveland (G-5225)
Clevelan Clinic Hlth Sys W Reg........A 216 476-7000
Cleveland (G-5226)
Clevelan Clinic Hlth Sys W Reg........E 216 476-7606
Cleveland (G-5227)
Clevelan Clinic Hlth Sys W Reg........E 216 476-7007
Cleveland (G-5228)
Communicare Health Svcs Inc ....E 513 530-1654
Blue Ash (G-1535)
Community Mercy Hlth Partners ......C 937 653-5432
Urbana (G-18429)
Comprehensive Health Care ....A 440 329-7500
Elyria (G-10492)
Corporate Health Dimensions ....E 740 775-6119
Chillicothe (G-2770)
Emp Management Group Ltd............D 330 493-4443
Canton (G-2301)
Gcha ....D 216 696-6900
Cleveland (G-5599)
Harborside Healthcare Corp ....D 937 436-6155
Dayton (G-9486)
Healthscope Benefits Inc ....E 614 797-5200
Westerville (G-19262)
Hospitalists MGT Group LLC............A 866 464-7497
Canton (G-2348)
Jtd Health Systems Inc ....A 419 394-3335
Saint Marys (G-16527)
Licking Memorial Hlth Systems ....A 220 564-4000
Newark (G-15056)
Mary Rtan Hlth Assn Logan Cnty ......E 937 592-4015
Bellefontaine (G-1358)
Marymount Health Care Systems ......E 216 332-1100
Cleveland (G-5919)
Mercy Franciscan Hosp Mt Airy ......A 513 853-5101
Cincinnati (G-4008)

Niagara Health Corporation ....C 614 898-4000
Columbus (G-8189)

Permedion Inc ....D 614 895-9900
Westerville (G-19198)

Renaissance House Inc ....D 419 626-1110
Sandusky (G-16634)

Sterling Medical Corporation 513 984-1800
Cincinnati (G-4545)

Trihealth Inc ....E 513 929-0020
Cincinnati (G-4635)

Trihealth Inc ....E 513 865-1111
Cincinnati (G-4636)

Trihealth Inc ....E 513 569-6777
Cincinnati (G-4637)

Trihealth Inc ....E 513 891-1627
Blue Ash (G-1664)

Trihealth Inc ....E 513 569-6111
Cincinnati (G-4638)

Trihealth Inc ....E 513 871-2340
Cincinnati (G-4639)

Trihealth Inc ....C 513 985-0900
Montgomery (G-14603)

Trinity Health System ....C 740 283-7848
Steubenville (G-17176)

Trinity Health System ....A 740 264-8000
Steubenville (G-17177)

Trinity Health System 740 264-8101
Steubenville (G-17178)

Uc Health Llc ....C 513 298-3000
West Chester (G-19023)

Uc Health Llc ....A 513 585-6000
Cincinnati (G-4668)

University Hospitals ....A 216 767-8900
Shaker Heights (G-16717)

University Hospitals ....A 440 743-3000
Parma (G-15779)

MANAGEMENT SVCS: Hotel Or Motel

American Hospitality Group Inc ....A 330 336-6684
Wadsworth (G-18589)

Atlantic Hospitality & MGT LLC ....E 216 454-5450
Beachwood (G-1031)

Chu Management Co Inc ....E 330 725-4571
Medina (G-13919)

Cmp I Owner-T LLC ....E 614 764-9393
Dublin (G-10178)

Cmp I Owner-T LLC ....E 614 436-7070
Columbus (G-7237)

Cmp I Owner-T LLC ....E 513 733-4334
Blue Ash (G-1532)

Crestline Hotels & Resorts LLC ....E 614 846-4355
Columbus (G-7390)

Crestline Hotels & Resorts LLC ....E 513 489-3666
Blue Ash (G-1541)

M&C Hotel Interests Inc ....E 440 543-1331
Chagrin Falls (G-2671)

MEI Hotels Incorporated ....C 216 589-0441
Cleveland (G-5949)

Rama Tika Developers LLC ....E 419 806-6446
Mansfield (G-13232)

Rbp Atlanta LLC ....D 614 246-2522
Columbus (G-8491)

Regal Hospitality LLC ....E 614 436-0004
Columbus (G-8504)

Req/Jqh Holdings Inc ....D 513 891-1066
Blue Ash (G-1645)

Select Hotels Group LLC ....E 513 754-0003
Mason (G-13638)

Tjm Clmbus LLC Tjm Clumbus LLC ....D 614 885-1885
Columbus (G-8760)

Tudor Arms Mstr Subtenant LLC ....D 216 696-6611
Cleveland (G-6555)

MANAGEMENT SVCS: Nursing & Personal Care Facility

Alternative Home Health Care ....E 513 794-0555
Cincinnati (G-2935)

Balanced Care Corporation ....E 330 908-1166
Northfield (G-15373)

Balanced Care Corporation ....E 937 372-7205
Xenia (G-19892)

Christian Benevolent Assn ....B 513 931-5000
Cincinnati (G-3212)

Deaconess Long Term Care Inc ....D 513 861-0400
Cincinnati (G-3411)

DMD Management Inc ....C 440 944-9400
Wickliffe (G-19456)

DMD Management Inc ....E 216 898-8399
Cleveland (G-5434)

Healthcare Management Cons.............E 419 363-2193
Rockford (G-16416)

Holzer Senior Care Center ....E 740 446-5001
Bidwell (G-1469)

HRP Capital Inc ....E 419 865-3111
Holland (G-11889)

Kerrington Health Systems Inc.............C 513 863-0360
Fairfield Township (G-10811)

Kettcor Inc ....B 937 458-4949
Miamisburg (G-14178)

Kingston Healthcare Company ....E 419 247-2880
Toledo (G-17840)

Laurel Health Care Company ....E 614 888-4553
Worthington (G-19820)

Laurel Health Care Company ....C 614 885-0408
Worthington (G-19821)

Nursing Care MGT Amer Inc ....D 740 927-9888
Pataskala (G-15786)

Nursing Care MGT Amer Inc ....D 513 793-5092
Cincinnati (G-4142)

Omnicare Inc ....C 513 719-2600
Cincinnati (G-4168)

Saber Healthcare Group LLC ....E 216 292-5706
Bedford (G-1303)

Salem Healthcare MGT LLC ....E 330 332-1588
Salem (G-16561)

St Augustine Corporation ....B 216 939-7600
Lakewood (G-12363)

Westminster Management Company ....C 614 274-5154
Columbus (G-8890)

Windsor House Inc ....E 440 834-0544
Burton (G-2020)

MANAGEMENT SVCS: Restaurant

Authentic Food LLC............................E 740 369-0377
Delaware (G-9954)

Bistro Off Broadway ....E 937 316-5000
Greenville (G-11366)

Bon Appetit Management Co ....E 614 823-1880
Westerville (G-19227)

Cameron Mitchell Rest LLC ....E 614 621-3663
Columbus (G-7108)

D J- Seve Group Inc ....E 614 888-6600
Lewis Center (G-12537)

Das Dutch Kitchen Inc ....D 330 683-0530
Dalton (G-9144)

T K Edwards LLC ....E 614 406-8064
Columbus (G-8726)

V Westaar Inc ....E 740 803-2803
Lewis Center (G-12565)

Wadsworth Galaxy Rest Inc ....E 330 334-3663
Wadsworth (G-18618)

MANAGERS: Athletes

International Management Group...........B 216 522-1200
Cleveland (G-5762)

International Mdsg Corp ....B 216 522-1200
Cleveland (G-5763)

MANPOWER POOLS

Diversified Employment Grp II.............E 513 428-6525
Cincinnati (G-3435)

Patrick Staffing Inc ....E 937 743-5585
Franklin (G-11036)

MANPOWER TRAINING

Esc of Cuyahoga County ....D 216 524-3000
Independence (G-12071)

Ohio State University...........................D 614 292-7788
Columbus (G-8319)

Riverview Industries Inc ....C 419 898-5250
Oak Harbor (G-15478)

MANUFACTURING INDUSTRIES, NEC

Ace Assembly Packaging Inc ....E 330 866-9117
Waynesburg (G-18827)

MARBLE, BUILDING: Cut & Shaped

Heritage Marble of Ohio Inc ....E 614 436-1464
Columbus (G-7745)

MARINAS

Catawba-Cleveland Dev Corp ....D 419 797-4424
Port Clinton (G-16101)

Island Service Company ....C 419 285-3695
Put In Bay (G-16226)

S B S Transit Inc................................B 440 288-2222
Lorain (G-12942)

Saw Mill Creek Ltd ....C 419 433-3800
Huron (G-12030)

Sima Marine Sales Inc ....E 440 269-3200
Willoughby (G-19572)

Tappan Lake Marina Inc ....E 740 269-2031
Scio (G-16664)

Vermilion Boat Club Inc ....E 440 967-6634
Vermilion (G-18562)

MARINE CARGO HANDLING SVCS

A-1 Quality Labor Services LLC ....E 513 353-0173
Cincinnati (G-2893)

Consolidated Grain & Barge Co ....E 513 941-4805
Cincinnati (G-3351)

Marietta Industrial Entps Inc................D 740 373-2252
Marietta (G-13353)

McGinnis Inc ....C 740 377-4391
South Point (G-16940)

McGinnis Inc ....E 513 941-8070
Cincinnati (G-3988)

McNational Inc....................................E 740 377-4391
South Point (G-16941)

Toledo-Lucas County Port Auth ....E 419 243-8251
Toledo (G-18103)

MARINE CARGO HANDLING SVCS: Loading

Hofstetter Orran Inc ....E 330 683-8070
Orrville (G-15634)

MARINE CARGO HANDLING SVCS: Loading & Unloading

Bellaire Harbor Service LLC ....E 740 676-4305
Bellaire (G-1329)

MARINE CARGO HANDLING SVCS: Marine Terminal

Cincinnati Bulk Terminals LLC ....E 513 621-4800
Cincinnati (G-3231)

Reserve Ftl LLC ....E 440 519-1768
Twinsburg (G-18311)

Tidewater River Rail Oper LLC ....D 817 659-0091
Steubenville (G-17174)

MARINE SPLYS WHOLESALERS

Mazzella Holding Company Inc ....D 513 772-4466
Cleveland (G-5926)

MARINE SVC STATIONS

Island Service Company ....C 419 285-3695
Put In Bay (G-16226)

MARKETS: Meat & fish

Euclid Fish Company ....D 440 951-6448
Mentor (G-14044)

Weilands Fine Meats Inc ....E 614 267-9910
Columbus (G-8883)

MARKING DEVICES: Embossing Seals & Hand Stamps

System Seals Inc................................E 440 735-0200
Cleveland (G-6491)

MARKING DEVICES: Screens, Textile Printing

Marathon Mfg & Sup Co ....D 330 343-2656
New Philadelphia (G-14972)

MARRIAGE BUREAU

Cuyahoga County ....D 216 443-8920
Cleveland (G-5397)

MARTIAL ARTS INSTRUCTION

Cincinnati Tae Kwon Do Inc.................E 513 271-6900
Cincinnati (G-3272)

MASSAGE PARLOR & STEAM BATH SVCS

Healthquest Blanchester Inc.................E 937 783-4535
Blanchester (G-1487)

SERVICES

MASSAGE PARLORS

G E G Enterprises Inc ....E 330 477-3133
Canton *(G-2321)*
Irish Envy LLC ....E 440 808-8000
Westlake *(G-19358)*
Mark Luikart Inc ....E 330 339-9141
New Philadelphia *(G-14973)*
Massage Envy ....E 440 878-0500
Strongsville *(G-17329)*

MATERIALS HANDLING EQPT WHOLESALERS

Agrinomix LLC ....E 440 774-2981
Oberlin *(G-15497)*
Andersen & Associates Inc ....E 330 425-8500
Twinsburg *(G-18244)*
Bobcat of Dayton Inc ....E 937 293-3176
Moraine *(G-14627)*
Bohl Crane Inc ....D 419 476-7525
Toledo *(G-17616)*
Bohl Equipment Company ....D 419 476-7525
Toledo *(G-17617)*
Brennan Industrial Truck Co ....E 419 867-6000
Holland *(G-11875)*
Burns Industrial Equipment Inc ....E 330 425-2476
Macedonia *(G-13063)*
Decker Equipment Company Inc ....E 866 252-4395
Cleveland *(G-5414)*
Devirsified Material Handling ....E 419 865-8025
Holland *(G-11882)*
Equipment Depot Ohio Inc ....E 513 934-2121
Lebanon *(G-12463)*
Equipment Depot Ohio Inc ....E 513 891-0600
Blue Ash *(G-1557)*
Esec Corporation ....E 330 799-1536
Youngstown *(G-20030)*
Fairborn Equipment Company Inc ....D 419 209-0760
Upper Sandusky *(G-18406)*
Federal Machinery & Eqp Co ....E 800 652-2466
Cleveland *(G-5522)*
Forte Indus Eqp Systems Inc ....E 513 398-2800
Mason *(G-13581)*
Great Lakes Power Products Inc ....D 440 951-5111
Mentor *(G-14056)*
Hgr Industrial Surplus Inc ....E 216 486-4567
Euclid *(G-10639)*
Hy-Tek Material Handling Inc ....D 614 497-2500
Columbus *(G-7790)*
Industrial Parts & Service Co ....E 330 966-5025
Canton *(G-2355)*
Intelligrated Systems LLC ....A 513 701-7300
Mason *(G-13599)*
Iwi Incorporated ....E 440 585-5900
Wickliffe *(G-19466)*
Kmh Systems Inc ....E 513 469-9400
Cincinnati *(G-3881)*
McCormick Equipment Co Inc ....E 513 677-8888
Loveland *(G-13012)*
Mh Equipment Company ....E 937 890-6800
Dayton *(G-9613)*
Mh Equipment Company ....E 614 871-1571
Grove City *(G-11452)*
Mh Equipment Company ....D 513 681-2200
Cincinnati *(G-4043)*
MH Logistics Corp ....D 513 681-2200
West Chester *(G-19066)*
MH Logistics Corp ....E 330 425-2476
Hudson *(G-11997)*
Miami Industrial Trucks Inc ....D 937 293-4194
Moraine *(G-14677)*
Miami Industrial Trucks Inc ....E 419 424-0042
Findlay *(G-10944)*
Mid-Ohio Forklifts Inc ....E 330 633-1230
Akron *(G-338)*
Midlands Millroom Supply Inc ....E 330 453-9100
Canton *(G-2403)*
Newtown Nine Inc ....E 330 376-7741
Akron *(G-345)*
Ohio Transmission Corporation ....C 614 342-6247
Columbus *(G-8357)*
R&M Materials Handling Inc ....E 937 328-5100
Springfield *(G-17099)*
Raymond Storage Concepts Inc ....D 513 891-7290
Blue Ash *(G-1641)*
Rde System Corp ....C 513 933-8000
Lebanon *(G-12496)*
Total Fleet Solutions LLC ....E 419 868-8853
Holland *(G-11921)*

Towlift Inc ....C 216 749-6800
Brooklyn Heights *(G-1884)*
Towlift Inc ....E 419 666-1333
Northwood *(G-15411)*
Towlift Inc ....E 419 531-6110
Toledo *(G-18106)*
Toyota Industrial Eqp Dlr ....E 419 865-8025
Holland *(G-11922)*
Toyota Industries N Amer Inc ....E 513 779-7500
West Chester *(G-19018)*
Valley Industrial Trucks Inc ....E 330 788-4081
Youngstown *(G-20235)*
Willis Day Management Inc ....E 419 476-8000
Toledo *(G-18159)*

MATS OR MATTING, NEC: Rubber

Durable Corporation ....D 800 537-1603
Norwalk *(G-15433)*

MATS, MATTING & PADS: Auto, Floor, Exc Rubber Or Plastic

Crown Dielectric Inds Inc ....C 614 224-5161
Columbus *(G-7397)*

MATS, MATTING & PADS: Nonwoven

Durable Corporation ....D 800 537-1603
Norwalk *(G-15433)*
Tranzonic Companies ....C 216 535-4300
Richmond Heights *(G-16395)*

MEAL DELIVERY PROGRAMS

Casleo Corporation ....E 614 252-6508
Columbus *(G-7133)*
Clossman Catering Incorporated ....E 513 942-7744
Hamilton *(G-11581)*
Licking County Aging Program ....D 740 345-0821
Newark *(G-15052)*
Meals On Wheels-Older Adult Al ....E 740 681-5050
Lancaster *(G-12416)*
Mid-Ohio Foodbank ....C 614 317-9400
Grove City *(G-11453)*
Mobile Meals ....D 330 376-7717
Akron *(G-340)*
Mobile Meals of Salem Inc ....E 330 332-2160
Salem *(G-16553)*
Tom Paige Catering Company ....E 216 431-4236
Cleveland *(G-6532)*
Trinity Action Partnership ....E 937 456-2800
Eaton *(G-10463)*

MEAT & MEAT PRDTS WHOLESALERS

Carfagnas Incorporated ....E 614 846-6340
Columbus *(G-7127)*
Fresh Mark Inc ....B 330 832-7491
Massillon *(G-13687)*
Fresh Mark Inc ....B 330 834-3669
Massillon *(G-13685)*
Hillandale Farms Corporation ....E 330 724-3199
Akron *(G-262)*
Hormel Foods Corp Svcs LLC ....E 513 563-0211
Cincinnati *(G-3726)*
Meadowbrook Meat Company Inc ....C 614 771-9660
Columbus *(G-8049)*
Pioneer Packing Co ....D 419 352-5283
Bowling Green *(G-1745)*
Robert Winner Sons Inc ....E 419 582-4321
Yorkshire *(G-19942)*
Tri-State Beef Co Inc ....E 513 579-1722
Cincinnati *(G-4633)*
Weilands Fine Meats Inc ....E 614 267-9910
Columbus *(G-8883)*

MEAT CUTTING & PACKING

Fresh Mark Inc ....B 330 834-3669
Massillon *(G-13685)*
King Kold Inc ....E 937 836-2731
Englewood *(G-10592)*
Marshallville Packing Co Inc ....E 330 855-2871
Marshallville *(G-13474)*
Robert Winner Sons Inc ....E 419 582-4321
Yorkshire *(G-19942)*
Shaker Valley Foods Inc ....E 216 961-8600
Cleveland *(G-6403)*
Tri-State Beef Co Inc ....E 513 579-1722
Cincinnati *(G-4633)*

MEAT MARKETS

Carles Bratwurst Inc ....E 419 562-7741
Bucyrus *(G-1981)*
Landes Fresh Meats Inc ....E 937 836-3613
Clayton *(G-4859)*
Marshallville Packing Co Inc ....E 330 855-2871
Marshallville *(G-13474)*
Mary C Enterprises Inc ....D 937 253-6169
Dayton *(G-9588)*
Rubin Erb ....E 330 852-4423
Sugarcreek *(G-17380)*
S and S Gilardi Inc ....D 740 397-2751
Mount Vernon *(G-14788)*

MEAT PRDTS: Cooked Meats, From Purchased Meat

King Kold Inc ....E 937 836-2731
Englewood *(G-10592)*

MEAT PRDTS: Frozen

Martin-Brower Company LLC ....B 513 773-2301
West Chester *(G-18971)*

MEAT PRDTS: Pork, From Slaughtered Meat

V H Cooper & Co Inc ....C 419 375-4116
Fort Recovery *(G-10994)*

MEAT PRDTS: Prepared Beef Prdts From Purchased Beef

Fresh Mark Inc ....B 330 834-3669
Massillon *(G-13685)*

MEAT PROCESSED FROM PURCHASED CARCASSES

A To Z Portion Ctrl Meats Inc ....E 419 358-2926
Bluffton *(G-1686)*
Fresh Mark Inc ....B 330 832-7491
Massillon *(G-13687)*
Kenosha Beef International Ltd ....C 614 771-1330
Columbus *(G-7894)*
Marshallville Packing Co Inc ....E 330 855-2871
Marshallville *(G-13474)*
Robert Winner Sons Inc ....E 419 582-4321
Yorkshire *(G-19942)*
Tri-State Beef Co Inc ....E 513 579-1722
Cincinnati *(G-4633)*
White Castle System Inc ....B 614 228-5781
Columbus *(G-8896)*

MEATS, PACKAGED FROZEN: Wholesalers

A To Z Portion Ctrl Meats Inc ....E 419 358-2926
Bluffton *(G-1686)*
Blue Ribbon Meats Inc ....D 216 631-8850
Cleveland *(G-5064)*
White Castle System Inc ....B 614 228-5781
Columbus *(G-8896)*

MEDIA BUYING AGENCIES

Ctv Media Inc ....E 614 848-5800
Powell *(G-16193)*
Elyria-Lorain Broadcasting Co ....E 440 322-3761
Elyria *(G-10508)*
Empower Mediamarketing Inc ....C 513 871-7779
Cincinnati *(G-3495)*
Harmon Media Group ....E 330 478-5325
Canton *(G-2340)*

MEDICAL & HOSPITAL EQPT WHOLESALERS

Americas Best Medical Eqp Co ....E 330 928-0884
Akron *(G-71)*
Amerimed Inc ....E 513 942-3670
West Chester *(G-18866)*
Assuramed Inc ....E 330 963-6998
Twinsburg *(G-18246)*
Biorx LLC ....C 866 442-4679
Cincinnati *(G-3051)*
Cardinal Health 100 Inc ....B 614 757-5000
Dublin *(G-10157)*
Cardinal Health 200 LLC ....E 440 349-1247
Cleveland *(G-5122)*
Cintas Corporation No 2 ....D 513 459-1200
Mason *(G-13559)*

Clinical Specialties Inc ....C...... 614 659-6580
  Columbus (G-7228)
Concordnce Hlthcare Sltons LLC ....D... 419 455-2153
  Tiffin (G-17512)
CT Medical Electronics Co ....E....... 440 526-3551
  Broadview Heights (G-1829)
Dermamed Coatings Company LLC ....E 330 634-9449
  Tallmadge (G-17474)
Espt Liquidation Inc ....D...... 330 698-4711
  Apple Creek (G-618)
Full Range Rehab LLC ....E 513 330-5995
  West Chester (G-19056)
Institutional Care Pharmacy ....D...... 419 447-6216
  Tiffin (G-17520)
Lake Erie Med Surgical Sup Inc ....E....... 734 847-3847
  Holland (G-11892)
Modern Medical Inc ....C...... 800 547-3330
  Westerville (G-19186)
O E Meyer Co ....C....... 419 625-1256
  Sandusky (G-16631)
Ohio State University ....E 614 293-8588
  Columbus (G-8328)
Omnicare Inc ....C...... 513 719-2600
  Cincinnati (G-4168)
Pharmed Corporation ....C...... 440 250-5400
  Westlake (G-19391)
Precision Products Group Inc ....D...... 330 698-4711
  Apple Creek (G-620)
Wbc Group LLC ....D...... 866 528-2144
  Hudson (G-12012)
Ziks Family Pharmacy 100 ....E 937 225-9350
  Dayton (G-9898)

MEDICAL & SURGICAL SPLYS: Bandages & Dressings

Beiersdorf Inc ....C...... 513 682-7300
  West Chester (G-19042)

MEDICAL & SURGICAL SPLYS: Clothing, Fire Resistant & Protect

West Chester Holdings LLC ....C...... 800 647-1900
  Cincinnati (G-4781)

MEDICAL & SURGICAL SPLYS: Hosiery, Support

Julius Zorn Inc ....D...... 330 923-4999
  Cuyahoga Falls (G-9105)

MEDICAL CENTERS

Big Run Urgent Care Center ....E 614 871-7130
  Grove City (G-11408)
Center For Urologic Health LLC ....E 330 375-0924
  Akron (G-124)
Childrens Hospital Medical Ctr ....A 513 803-9600
  Liberty Township (G-12580)
Cleveland Clinic Foundation ....B 216 448-4325
  Cleveland (G-5242)
Cleveland Clinic Foundation ....A 216 636-8335
  Cleveland (G-5236)
Cleveland Clinic Foundation ....D...... 419 609-2812
  Sandusky (G-16587)
Clinton Memorial Hospital ....E 937 283-2273
  Wilmington (G-19615)
Community Health Partners Regi ....E 440 960-4000
  Lorain (G-12895)
Dayton Eye Surgery Center ....E 937 431-9531
  Beavercreek (G-1213)
Dignity Health ....C...... 330 493-4944
  Canton (G-2287)
Equitas Health Inc ....D...... 614 340-6700
  Columbus (G-7526)
Eye Inst of Northwestern OH In ....E 419 865-3866
  Toledo (G-17722)
Fauster-Cameron Inc ....B 419 784-1414
  Defiance (G-9913)
Fisher-Titus Medical Center ....C...... 419 663-6464
  Norwalk (G-15436)
Hometown Urgent Care ....C...... 614 263-4400
  Columbus (G-7768)
Hometown Urgent Care ....C...... 330 505-9400
  Warren (G-18712)
Hometown Urgent Care ....C...... 614 272-1100
  Columbus (G-7770)
Hometown Urgent Care ....C...... 937 236-8630
  Dayton (G-9504)
Hometown Urgent Care ....C...... 937 322-6222
  Springfield (G-17046)

Hometown Urgent Care ....C...... 330 629-2300
  Youngstown (G-20067)
Hometown Urgent Care ....D...... 740 363-3133
  Delaware (G-9987)
Hometown Urgent Care ....C...... 937 252-2000
  Wooster (G-19728)
Hometown Urgent Care ....D...... 513 831-5900
  Milford (G-14395)
Hometown Urgent Care ....C...... 937 342-9520
  Springfield (G-17045)
Joseph A Girgis MD Inc ....E 440 930-6095
  Sheffield Village (G-16737)
Kaiser Foundation Hospitals ....A 330 633-8400
  Akron (G-296)
Kaiser Foundation Hospitals ....A 216 524-7377
  Avon (G-889)
Kaiser Foundation Hospitals ....A 800 524-7377
  Cleveland Heights (G-6721)
Kaiser Foundation Hospitals ....A 800 524-7377
  Brooklyn Heights (G-1874)
Kaiser Foundation Hospitals ....A 216 524-7377
  Strongsville (G-17318)
Kaiser Foundation Hospitals ....A 330 486-2800
  Twinsburg (G-18287)
Labcare ....E 330 753-3649
  Barberton (G-958)
Lake Hospital System Inc ....A 440 632-3024
  Middlefield (G-14272)
Life Line Screening ....D...... 216 581-6556
  Independence (G-12090)
Midwest Cmnty Hlth Assoc Inc ....C...... 419 633-4034
  Bryan (G-1964)
Miller-Valentine Construction ....D...... 937 293-0900
  Dayton (G-9637)
Northwest Ohio Urgent Care Inc ....E 419 720-7363
  Toledo (G-17950)
Ohio State Univ Wexner Med Ctr ....C...... 614 293-2663
  Columbus (G-8291)
Ohio State University ....A 614 366-3692
  Columbus (G-8295)
Ohio State University ....A 614 293-3860
  Columbus (G-8309)
Ohio University ....D...... 740 593-2195
  Athens (G-798)
Osu Emergency Medicine LLC ....D...... 614 947-3700
  Columbus (G-8391)
Osu Physical Medicine LLC ....E 614 366-6398
  Columbus (G-8395)
Portsmouth Hospital Corp ....A 740 991-4000
  Portsmouth (G-16159)
Richmond Medical Center ....B 440 585-6500
  Richmond Heights (G-16394)
Riverview Health Institute ....E 937 222-5390
  Dayton (G-9736)
Saras Garden ....D...... 419 335-7272
  Wauseon (G-18810)
Southwest General Health Ctr ....C...... 440 816-4900
  Strongsville (G-17347)
St Ritas Medical Center ....E 419 996-5895
  Lima (G-12753)
Superior Med LLC ....E 740 439-8839
  Cambridge (G-2084)
Toledo Hospital ....A 419 291-4000
  Toledo (G-18086)
Tri State Urlogic Svcs PSC Inc ....C...... 513 841-7400
  Cincinnati (G-4632)
Trinity Hospital Twin City ....B 740 922-2800
  Dennison (G-10053)
Trumbull-Mahoning Med Group ....D...... 330 372-8800
  Cortland (G-8995)
Uc Health Llc ....E 513 475-7777
  West Chester (G-19024)
Uc Health Llc ....D...... 513 475-7500
  West Chester (G-19025)
University Suburban Health Ctr ....C...... 216 382-8920
  Cleveland (G-6604)
Veterans Affairs US Dept ....A 937 268-6511
  Dayton (G-9856)
Veterans Health Administration ....A 740 773-1141
  Chillicothe (G-2836)
Veterans Health Administration ....A 513 861-3100
  Cincinnati (G-4759)
Veterans Health Adminstration ....A 216 791-3800
  Cleveland (G-6625)
Wood Health Company LLC ....D...... 419 353-7069
  Bowling Green (G-1759)

MEDICAL EQPT REPAIR SVCS, NON-ELECTRIC

Equipment MGT Svc & Repr Inc ....E 937 383-1052
  Wilmington (G-19622)
Precision Endoscopy Amer Inc ....E 410 527-9598
  Stow (G-17224)
United Technical Support Svcs ....E 330 562-3330
  Aurora (G-846)

MEDICAL FIELD ASSOCIATION

American Ceramic Society ....E 614 890-4700
  Westerville (G-19144)
American Cllege Crdlgy Fndtion ....E 614 442-5950
  Dublin (G-10130)
American National Red Cross ....D...... 937 399-3872
  Springfield (G-16993)
American Society For Nondstctv ....E 614 274-6003
  Columbus (G-6938)
Breathing Association ....E 614 457-4570
  Columbus (G-7061)
Central Hospital Services Inc ....D...... 216 696-6900
  Cleveland (G-5154)
Columbus Med Assn Foundation ....E 614 240-7420
  Columbus (G-7294)
Dnv GL Healthcare Usa Inc ....E 281 396-1610
  Milford (G-14385)
Greater Cleveland Hosp Assn ....D...... 216 696-6900
  Cleveland (G-5636)
Ohio State Medical Association ....D...... 614 527-6762
  Dublin (G-10298)
Wingspan Care Group ....E 216 932-2800
  Shaker Heights (G-16720)

MEDICAL HELP SVCS

Arcadia Services Inc ....D...... 330 869-9520
  Akron (G-77)
Arcadia Services Inc ....D...... 937 912-5800
  Beavercreek (G-1126)
Central Ohio Hospitalists ....E 614 255-6900
  Columbus (G-7158)
CHI Health At Home ....E 513 576-0262
  Milford (G-14377)
Dedicated Nursing Assoc Inc ....E 866 450-5550
  Cincinnati (G-3415)
Dedicated Nursing Assoc Inc ....E 877 411-8350
  Galloway (G-11219)
Dedicated Nursing Assoc Inc ....E 877 547-9144
  Parma (G-15765)
Dedicated Nursing Assoc Inc ....C...... 888 465-6929
  Beavercreek (G-1214)
Emp Holdings Ltd ....A 330 493-4443
  Canton (G-2300)
Frontline National LLC ....D...... 513 528-7823
  Milford (G-14390)
Heartland Employment Svcs LLC ....A 419 252-5500
  Toledo (G-17792)
Interim Hlthcare Columbus Inc ....E 330 836-5571
  Fairlawn (G-10834)
Locum Medical Group LLC ....D...... 216 464-2125
  Independence (G-12094)
Maxim Healthcare Services Inc ....D...... 216 606-3000
  Independence (G-12097)
Maxim Healthcare Services Inc ....D...... 614 986-3001
  Gahanna (G-11135)
Medport Inc ....D...... 216 244-6832
  Cleveland (G-5945)
Msstaff LLC ....C...... 419 868-8536
  Toledo (G-17926)
Neo-Pet LLC ....E 440 893-9949
  Cleveland (G-6055)
Physician Staffing Inc ....B 440 542-5000
  Cleveland (G-6209)
Prn Nurse Inc ....B 614 864-9292
  Columbus (G-8464)
Quadax Inc ....E 330 759-4600
  Youngstown (G-20170)
Salo Inc ....A 740 623-2331
  Coshocton (G-9027)
Township of Chester ....E 440 729-9951
  Chesterland (G-2747)

MEDICAL INSURANCE CLAIM PROCESSING: Contract Or Fee Basis

Central Bnfits Admnstrtors Inc ....D...... 614 797-5200
  Westerville (G-19232)
Health Design Plus Inc ....D...... 330 656-1072
  Hudson (G-11981)

Optumrx Inc..............................A   614 794-3300
  Westerville (G-19196)
Qualchoice Inc..........................B   330 656-1231
  Beachwood (G-1098)

MEDICAL RESCUE SQUAD

Harter Ventures Inc...................D   419 224-4075
  Lima (G-12651)
Leroy Twp Fire Dept...................E   440 254-4124
  Painesville (G-15722)
Metrohealth System...................E   216 957-5000
  Cleveland (G-5966)

MEDICAL SVCS ORGANIZATION

Aksm/Genesis Medical Svcs Inc.........E   614 447-0281
  Columbus (G-6889)
Broadspire Services Inc...............E   614 436-8990
  Columbus (G-7077)
Community and Rural Hlth Svcs.........D   419 334-8943
  Fremont (G-11063)
Excelas LLC...........................E   440 442-7310
  Cleveland (G-5499)
F R S Connections.....................E   937 393-9662
  Hillsboro (G-11838)
First Choice Med Staff of Ohio........D   330 867-1409
  Fairlawn (G-10829)
Good Night Medical Ohio LLC...........E   614 384-7433
  Columbus (G-6813)
Hopewell Health Centers Inc...........E   740 596-5249
  Mc Arthur (G-13890)
Joint Emergency Med Svc Inc...........E   937 746-3471
  Franklin (G-11033)
Larlham Care Hattie Group.............D   330 274-2272
  Mantua (G-13272)
Lifecenter Organ Donor Network........E   513 558-5555
  Cincinnati (G-3927)
Lifestges Smrtan Ctr For Women........E   937 277-8988
  Dayton (G-9566)
Mercy Health..........................E   440 324-0400
  Elyria (G-10536)
Mount Crmel Hospice Evrgrn Ctr........D   614 234-0200
  Columbus (G-8115)
Mutual Health Services Company........D   216 687-7000
  Cleveland (G-6030)
Mvhe Inc..............................E   937 499-8211
  Dayton (G-9650)
Northast Ohio Med Rserve Corps........E   216 789-6653
  Broadview Heights (G-1839)
Northeast OH Neighborhood Heal........E   216 231-7700
  Cleveland (G-6089)
Northeast OH Neighborhood Heal........C   216 231-7700
  Cleveland (G-6090)
Ohio Health Physician Group...........D   740 594-8819
  Athens (G-793)
Ohio Kepro Inc........................E   216 447-9604
  Seven Hills (G-16679)
Ohio State University.................D   614 293-8074
  Columbus (G-8349)
P C Vpa...............................E   440 826-0500
  Cleveland (G-6154)
Palestine Chld Relief Fund............D   330 678-2645
  Kent (G-12253)
Prosperity Care Service...............E   614 430-8626
  Columbus (G-8473)
Spryance Inc..........................E   678 808-0600
  Toledo (G-18044)
Sterling Medical Associates...........D   513 984-1800
  Cincinnati (G-4544)
Summacare Inc.........................B   330 996-8410
  Akron (G-455)
University Womens Healthcare..........E   937 208-2948
  Dayton (G-9842)

MEDICAL TRAINING SERVICES

East Way Behavioral Hlth Care.........C   937 222-4900
  Dayton (G-9403)

MEDICAL X-RAY MACHINES & TUBES WHOLESALERS

Alpha Imaging LLC.....................E   440 953-3800
  Willoughby (G-19504)
Riverain Technologies LLC.............E   937 425-6811
  Miamisburg (G-14215)

MEDICAL, DENTAL & HOSP EQPT, WHOLESALE: X-ray Film & Splys

Philips Medical Systems Clevel........B   440 247-2652
  Cleveland (G-6203)

MEDICAL, DENTAL & HOSPITAL EQPT, WHOL: Dentists' Prof Splys

Perio Inc.............................E   614 791-1207
  Dublin (G-10308)

MEDICAL, DENTAL & HOSPITAL EQPT, WHOL: Hospital Eqpt & Splys

Jones Metal Products Company..........E   740 545-6341
  West Lafayette (G-19114)
Phoenix Resource Network LLC..........E   800 990-4948
  Cincinnati (G-4244)

MEDICAL, DENTAL & HOSPITAL EQPT, WHOL: Hosptl Eqpt/Furniture

American Home Health Care Inc.........E   614 237-1133
  Columbus (G-6925)
Apria Healthcare LLC..................D   419 471-1919
  Maumee (G-13758)
Braden Med Services Inc...............E   740 732-2356
  Caldwell (G-2036)
Garys Pharmacy Inc....................E   937 456-5777
  Eaton (G-10446)
Gem Edwards Inc.......................D   330 342-8300
  Hudson (G-11979)

MEDICAL, DENTAL & HOSPITAL EQPT, WHOL: Physician Eqpt/Splys

Radebaugh-Fetzer Company..............E   440 878-4700
  Strongsville (G-17340)

MEDICAL, DENTAL & HOSPITAL EQPT, WHOL: Surgical Eqpt & Splys

Cardinal Health Inc...................A   614 757-5000
  Dublin (G-10156)
Cardinal Health Inc...................D   614 497-9552
  Obetz (G-15524)
Columbus Prescr Phrms Inc.............C   614 294-1600
  Westerville (G-19243)
Community Srgl Sply Toms Rvr..........C   216 475-8440
  Cleveland (G-5328)
Haag-Streit USA Inc...................E   513 336-7255
  Mason (G-13591)
Haag-Streit USA Inc...................E   513 336-7255
  Mason (G-13592)
Kunkel Pharmaceuticals Inc............E   513 231-1943
  Cincinnati (G-3895)

MEDICAL, DENTAL & HOSPITAL EQPT, WHOLESALE: Artificial Limbs

Blatchford Inc........................D   937 291-3636
  Miamisburg (G-14145)
Pel LLC...............................E   216 267-5775
  Cleveland (G-6191)

MEDICAL, DENTAL & HOSPITAL EQPT, WHOLESALE: Diagnostic, Med

Hitachi Hlthcare Americas Corp........B   330 425-1313
  Twinsburg (G-18279)
Thermo Fisher Scientific Inc..........C   800 871-8909
  Oakwood Village (G-15495)
Tosoh America Inc.....................B   614 539-8622
  Grove City (G-11478)

MEDICAL, DENTAL & HOSPITAL EQPT, WHOLESALE: Med Eqpt & Splys

Advanced Medical Equipment Inc........E   937 534-1080
  Kettering (G-12290)
Advantage Appliance Services..........C   330 498-8101
  Canton (G-2174)
Ardus Medical Inc.....................D   855 592-7387
  Blue Ash (G-1507)
Asd Specialty Healthcare LLC..........D   513 682-3600
  West Chester (G-18869)
Biotech Medical Inc...................A   330 494-5504
  Canton (G-2213)

Bound Tree Medical LLC................D   614 760-5000
  Dublin (G-10149)
Cando Pharmaceutical..................E   513 354-2694
  Loveland (G-12980)
Cardinal Health 200 LLC...............C   614 491-0050
  Columbus (G-7122)
Centura Inc...........................E   216 593-0226
  Cleveland (G-5156)
Community Srgl Sply Toms Rvr..........C   614 307-2975
  Columbus (G-7338)
Compass Health Brands Corp............C   800 947-1728
  Middleburg Heights (G-14250)
Cornerstone Medical Associates........E   330 374-0229
  Akron (G-159)
Demarius Corporation..................E   760 957-5500
  Dublin (G-10199)
Ethicon Endo-Surgery Inc..............A   513 337-7000
  Blue Ash (G-1558)
Ferno-Washington Inc..................C   877 733-0911
  Wilmington (G-19623)
Gulf South Medical Supply Inc.........E   614 501-9080
  Gahanna (G-11123)
Hardy Diagnostics.....................D   937 550-2768
  Springboro (G-16968)
Homereach Inc.........................E   614 566-0850
  Lewis Center (G-12545)
Julius Zorn Inc.......................D   330 923-4999
  Cuyahoga Falls (G-9105)
Keysource Acquisition LLC.............E   513 469-7881
  Cincinnati (G-3865)
Lima Medical Supplies Inc.............E   419 226-9581
  Lima (G-12682)
M & R Fredericktown Ltd Inc...........E   440 801-1563
  Akron (G-324)
Marquis Mobility Inc..................D   330 497-5373
  Canton (G-2389)
McKesson Medical-Surgical Inc.........C   614 539-2600
  Urbancrest (G-18450)
McKesson Medical-Surgical Top.........E   513 985-0525
  Cincinnati (G-3989)
Medline Diamed LLC....................E   330 484-1450
  Canton (G-2398)
Medpace Inc...........................A   513 579-9911
  Cincinnati (G-4000)
Mill Rose Laboratories Inc............E   440 974-6730
  Mentor (G-14086)
Mobility Revolution LLC...............E   909 980-2259
  Cleveland (G-6003)
Neighborcare Inc......................A   513 719-2600
  Cincinnati (G-4103)
Nightngl-Alan Med Eqp Svcs LLC........E   513 247-8200
  Blue Ash (G-1621)
Partssource Inc.......................C   330 562-9900
  Aurora (G-838)
Pdi Communication Systems Inc.........D   937 743-6010
  Springboro (G-16979)
Radiometer America Inc................D   440 871-8900
  Westlake (G-19396)
Sarnova Inc...........................D   614 760-5000
  Dublin (G-10328)
Seeley Medical Oxygen Co..............E   440 255-7163
  Andover (G-609)
Seneca Medical LLC....................C   419 447-0236
  Tiffin (G-17539)
Therapy Support Inc...................D   513 469-6999
  Blue Ash (G-1657)
Tri-Anim Health Services Inc..........E   614 760-5000
  Dublin (G-10357)
Twin Med LLC..........................E   440 973-4555
  Middleburg Heights (G-14262)
United Seating & Mobility LLC.........E   567 302-4000
  Maumee (G-13866)
United States Endoscopy...............C   440 639-4494
  Mentor (G-14118)

MEDICAL, DENTAL & HOSPITAL EQPT, WHOLESALE: Medical Lab

Sourceone Healthcare Tech Inc.........C   440 701-1200
  Mentor (G-14111)

MEDICAL, DENTAL & HOSPITAL EQPT, WHOLESALE: Orthopedic

S L Klabunde Corp.....................E   614 508-6012
  Columbus (G-8570)

MEDICAL, DENTAL & HOSPITAL EQPT, WHOLESALE: Safety

Safety Today Inc ....E 614 409-7200
Grove City *(G-11468)*

MEDICAL, DENTAL & HOSPITAL EQPT, WHOLESALE: Therapy

Vieway Technologies Inc ....D 440 703-3210
Oakwood Village *(G-15496)*

MEDICAL, DENTAL/HOSPITAL EQPT, WHOL: Tech Aids, Handicapped

Siffrin Residential Assn ....C 330 799-8932
Youngstown *(G-20211)*

MEDICAL, DENTAL/HOSPITAL EQPT, WHOL: Veterinarian Eqpt/Sply

Butler Animal Health Sup LLC ....C 614 761-9095
Dublin *(G-10154)*
Butler Animal Hlth Holdg LLC ....E 614 761-9095
Dublin *(G-10155)*

MEMBER ORGS, CIVIC, SOCIAL & FRATERNAL: Bars & Restaurants

Feldys ....D 513 474-2212
Cincinnati *(G-3541)*
S R Restaurant Corp ....E 216 781-6784
Cleveland *(G-6356)*

MEMBERSHIP HOTELS

Cincinnati Fifth Street Ht LLC ....D 513 579-1234
Cincinnati *(G-3243)*

MEMBERSHIP ORGANIZATIONS, BUSINESS: Community Affairs & Svcs

Altruism Society Inc ....D 877 283-4001
Beachwood *(G-1028)*
Bnai Brith Hillel Fdn At Osu ....E 614 294-4797
Columbus *(G-7050)*
Canton Rgnal Chmber of Cmmerce ......E 330 456-7253
Canton *(G-2242)*
In His Prsence Ministries Intl ....E 614 516-1812
Columbus *(G-7805)*
Oak Harbor Lions Club ....E 419 898-3828
Oak Harbor *(G-15475)*
Saint Mary Parish ....D 440 285-7051
Chardon *(G-2712)*

MEMBERSHIP ORGANIZATIONS, BUSINESS: Contractors' Association

Builders Exchange Inc ....E 216 393-6300
Cleveland *(G-5102)*
Home Bldrs Assn Grter Cncnnati ....D 513 851-6300
Cincinnati *(G-3717)*

MEMBERSHIP ORGANIZATIONS, BUSINESS: Merchants' Association

Westfield Belden Village ....E 330 494-5490
Canton *(G-2535)*

MEMBERSHIP ORGANIZATIONS, BUSINESS: Public Utility Assoc

City of Circleville ....E 740 477-8255
Circleville *(G-4829)*
Energy Cooperative Inc ....E 740 348-1206
Newark *(G-15031)*
Ohio Utilities Protection Svc ....D 800 311-3692
North Jackson *(G-15250)*
Village of Versailles ....E 937 526-4191
Versailles *(G-18572)*

MEMBERSHIP ORGANIZATIONS, CIVIC, SOCIAL/FRAT: Boy Scout Org

Boy Scouts of America ....E 513 961-2336
Cincinnati *(G-3069)*
Boy Scuts Amer - Lk Erie Cncil ....E 216 861-6060
Cleveland *(G-5071)*
Boys & Girls Club of Toledo ....E 419 241-4258
Toledo *(G-17622)*

Heart of OH Cncl Bsa ....E 740 389-4615
Marion *(G-13424)*
Heart of OH Cncl Bsa ....E 419 522-8300
Mansfield *(G-13182)*
Simon Knton Cncil Byscuts Amer ....E 614 436-7200
Columbus *(G-8642)*

MEMBERSHIP ORGANIZATIONS, CIVIC, SOCIAL/FRAT: Rec Assoc

Bluffton Family Recreation ....E 419 358-6978
Bluffton *(G-1688)*
Geary Family YMCA Fostria ....E 419 435-6608
Fostoria *(G-11002)*
Parks Recreation Division ....E 937 496-7135
Dayton *(G-9687)*
Young Mens Christian Assn ....D 740 373-2250
Marietta *(G-13402)*
Young Mens Christian Assoc ....A 330 376-1335
Akron *(G-509)*
Young Mens Christian Assoc ....E 419 523-5233
Ottawa *(G-15667)*

MEMBERSHIP ORGANIZATIONS, CIVIC, SOCIAL/FRAT: Social Assoc

Family Motor Coach Assn Inc ....C 513 474-3622
Cincinnati *(G-3530)*
Natio Assoc For The Advan of ....E 330 782-9777
Youngstown *(G-20136)*
Optimist International ....D 419 238-5086
Van Wert *(G-18485)*
The For National Association ....E 937 470-1059
Dayton *(G-9811)*
YMCA of Ashtabula County Inc ....D 440 997-5321
Ashtabula *(G-760)*

MEMBERSHIP ORGANIZATIONS, CIVIC, SOCIAL/FRAT: Youth Orgs

Boys & Girls Club of Columbus ....E 614 221-8830
Columbus *(G-7056)*
Boys & Girls Clubs Grtr Cinc ....D 513 421-8909
Cincinnati *(G-3070)*
Cafaro Co ....E 330 652-6980
Niles *(G-15149)*
Chester West YMCA ....E 513 779-3917
Liberty Township *(G-12579)*
Clevelnd Clnc Hlth Systm East ....E 216 761-3300
Cleveland *(G-5300)*
Communities In Schools ....D 614 268-2472
Columbus *(G-7328)*
Community Action Columbiana CT ....E 330 385-7251
East Liverpool *(G-10400)*
County of Cuyahoga ....D 216 443-7265
Cleveland *(G-5371)*
County of Darke ....E 937 526-4488
Versailles *(G-18568)*
Fairborn YMCA ....E 937 754-9622
Fairborn *(G-10674)*
Family YMCA of LANcstr&fairfld ....D 740 277-7373
Lancaster *(G-12403)*
Fayette County Family YMCA ....D 740 335-0477
Wshngtn CT Hs *(G-19870)*
Findlay Y M C A Child Dev ....E 419 422-3174
Findlay *(G-10908)*
For Evers Kids LLC ....E 330 258-9014
Akron *(G-226)*
Frans Child Care-Mansfield ....C 419 775-2500
Mansfield *(G-13178)*
Friends of Art For Cultural ....E 614 888-9929
Columbus *(G-7627)*
Galion Community Center YMCA ....E 419 468-7754
Galion *(G-11173)*
Great Miami Valley YMCA ....D 513 217-5501
Middletown *(G-14348)*
Great Miami Valley YMCA ....A 513 887-0001
Hamilton *(G-11602)*
Great Miami Valley YMCA ....C 513 892-9622
Fairfield Township *(G-10808)*
Great Miami Valley YMCA ....E 513 867-0600
Hamilton *(G-11603)*
Great Miami Valley YMCA ....D 513 887-0014
Hamilton *(G-11604)*
Great Miami Valley YMCA ....D 513 868-9622
Hamilton *(G-11605)*
Great Miami Valley YMCA ....E 513 829-3091
Fairfield *(G-10732)*
Hardin County Family YMCA ....E 419 673-6131
Kenton *(G-12279)*

Highland County Family YMCA ....E 937 840-9622
Hillsboro *(G-11842)*
Huber Heights YMCA ....D 937 236-9622
Dayton *(G-9508)*
Lake County YMCA ....C 440 352-3303
Painesville *(G-15718)*
Lake County YMCA ....C 440 946-1160
Willoughby *(G-19538)*
Lake County YMCA ....E 440 259-2724
Perry *(G-15824)*
Lake County YMCA ....D 440 428-5125
Madison *(G-13099)*
Lorain Cnty Bys Girls CLB Inc ....D 440 775-2582
Lorain *(G-12914)*
Marion Family YMCA ....D 740 725-9622
Marion *(G-13437)*
Miami Co YMCA Child Care ....E 937 778-5241
Piqua *(G-16013)*
Orrville Boys and Girls Club ....E 330 683-4888
Orrville *(G-15639)*
Pike County YMCA ....E 740 947-8862
Waverly *(G-18822)*
Ross County YMCA ....D 740 772-4340
Chillicothe *(G-2823)*
Sandusky Area YMCA Foundation ....E 419 621-9622
Sandusky *(G-16637)*
Sidney-Shelby County YMCA ....E 937 492-9134
Sidney *(G-16800)*
Springfield Family Y M C A ....E 937 323-3781
Springfield *(G-17119)*
Springfield Little Tigers Foot ....D 330 549-2359
Youngstown *(G-20215)*
Sycamore Board of Education ....E 513 489-3937
Cincinnati *(G-4560)*
The Boys and Girls Club of ....E 330 773-3375
Akron *(G-468)*
Ucc Childrens Center ....E 513 217-5501
Middletown *(G-14356)*
Vermilion Family YMCA ....E 440 967-4208
Vermilion *(G-18563)*
Wapakoneta YMCA ....D 419 739-9622
Wapakoneta *(G-18659)*
Y M C A Central Stark County ....E 330 305-5437
Canton *(G-2539)*
Y M C A Central Stark County ....E 330 875-1611
Louisville *(G-12975)*
Y M C A Central Stark County ....E 330 877-8933
Uniontown *(G-18392)*
Y M C A Central Stark County ....D 330 830-6275
Massillon *(G-13736)*
Y M C A Central Stark County ....E 330 498-4082
Canton *(G-2540)*
Y M C A of Ashland Ohio Inc ....D 419 289-0626
Ashland *(G-700)*
YMCA ....E 330 823-1930
Alliance *(G-558)*
YMCA of Clermont County Inc ....E 513 724-9622
Batavia *(G-1016)*
YMCA of Massillon ....E 330 879-0800
Navarre *(G-14826)*
YMCA of Sandusky Ohio Inc ....E 419 621-9622
Sandusky *(G-16657)*
Young Mens Christian ....B 513 932-1424
Lebanon *(G-12516)*
Young Mens Christian Assn ....,E 419 332-9622
Fremont *(G-11108)*
Young Mens Christian Assn ....D 330 744-8411
Youngstown *(G-20253)*
Young Mens Christian Assn ....E 419 238-0443
Van Wert *(G-18498)*
Young Mens Christian Assoc ....C 614 491-0980
Lockbourne *(G-12826)*
Young Mens Christian Assoc ....E 419 729-8135
Toledo *(G-18167)*
Young Mens Christian Assoc ....C 614 871-9622
Grove City *(G-11491)*
Young Mens Christian Assoc ....E 937 223-5201
Dayton *(G-9892)*
Young Mens Christian Assoc ....D 330 923-5223
Cuyahoga Falls *(G-9141)*
Young Mens Christian Assoc ....E 330 467-8366
Macedonia *(G-13091)*
Young Mens Christian Assoc ....E 330 784-0408
Akron *(G-507)*
Young Mens Christian Assoc ....D 740 477-1661
Circleville *(G-4854)*
Young Mens Christian Assoc ....C 614 885-4252
Columbus *(G-8927)*
Young Mens Christian Assoc ....E 330 724-1255
Akron *(G-508)*

S E R V I C E S

Young Mens Christian Assoc.............C....... 614 416-9622
Gahanna *(G-11152)*
Young Mens Christian Assoc.............C....... 614 334-9622
Hilliard *(G-11832)*
Young Mens Christian Assoc.............E....... 937 312-1810
Dayton *(G-9893)*
Young Mens Christian Assoc.............E....... 614 539-1770
Urbancrest *(G-18453)*
Young Mens Christian Assoc.............D....... 614 276-8224
Columbus *(G-8928)*
Young Mens Christian Assoc.............D....... 513 932-3756
Oregonia *(G-15618)*
Young Mens Christian Assoc.............C....... 614 252-3166
Columbus *(G-8929)*
Young Mens Christian Assoc.............D....... 937 426-9622
Dayton *(G-9894)*
Young Mens Christian Assoc.............E....... 937 228-9622
Dayton *(G-9895)*
Young Mens Christian Assoc.............C....... 937 223-5201
Springboro *(G-16990)*
Young Mens Christian Assoc.............E....... 614 878-7269
Columbus *(G-8930)*
Young Mens Christian Assoc.............E....... 937 593-9001
Bellefontaine *(G-1370)*
Young Mens Christian Assoc.............C....... 614 834-9622
Canal Winchester *(G-2129)*
Young Mens Christian Assoc.............D....... 330 264-3131
Wooster *(G-19789)*
Young Mens Christian Associat.............C....... 419 475-3496
Toledo *(G-18168)*
Young Mens Christian Associat.............C....... 419 794-7304
Maumee *(G-13870)*
Young Mens Christian Associat.............D....... 513 521-7112
Cincinnati *(G-4812)*
Young Mens Christian Associat.............C....... 419 251-9622
Perrysburg *(G-15938)*
Young Mens Christian Associat.............E....... 513 731-0115
Cincinnati *(G-4813)*
Young Mens Christian Associat.............C....... 513 791-5000
Blue Ash *(G-1685)*
Young Mens Christian Associat.............C....... 513 474-1400
Cincinnati *(G-4814)*
Young Mens Christian Associat.............D....... 513 241-9622
Cincinnati *(G-4815)*
Young Mens Christian Associat.............D....... 513 923-4466
Cincinnati *(G-4816)*
Young Mens Christian Associat.............E....... 419 474-3995
Toledo *(G-18169)*
Young Mens Christian Associat.............D....... 419 866-9622
Maumee *(G-13871)*
Young Mens Christian Associat.............C....... 419 475-3496
Toledo *(G-18170)*
Young Mens Christian Associat.............D....... 419 691-3523
Oregon *(G-15615)*
Young Mens Christian Mt Vernon.............D....... 740 392-9622
Mount Vernon *(G-14794)*
Young Mens Christn Assn Shelby.............D....... 419 347-1312
Shelby *(G-16751)*
Young MNS Christn Assn Findlay.............D....... 419 422-4424
Findlay *(G-10977)*
Young MNS Chrstn Assn Clveland.............E....... 216 521-8400
Lakewood *(G-12364)*
Young MNS Chrstn Assn Clveland.............E....... 216 941-4654
Cleveland *(G-6702)*
Young MNS Chrstn Assn Clveland.............E....... 216 731-7454
Cleveland *(G-6703)*
Young MNS Chrstn Assn Clveland.............D....... 216 382-4300
Cleveland *(G-6704)*
Young MNS Chrstn Assn Clveland.............D....... 440 285-7543
Chardon *(G-2726)*
Young MNS Chrstn Assn Clveland.............D....... 440 808-8150
Westlake *(G-19426)*
Young MNS Chrstn Assn Grter NY.............D....... 740 392-9622
Mount Vernon *(G-14795)*
Young Wns Chrstn Assn Canton.............D....... 330 453-7644
Canton *(G-2542)*
Young Womens Christian.............E....... 419 238-6639
Van Wert *(G-18499)*
Young Womens Christian Assn.............D....... 614 224-9121
Columbus *(G-8931)*
Young Womens Christian Associ.............E....... 216 881-6878
Cleveland *(G-6705)*
Young Womns Chrstn Assc Canton.............D....... 330 453-0789
Canton *(G-2543)*
Young Womns Chrstn Assc Lima.............E....... 419 241-3230
Toledo *(G-18173)*
YWCA Dayton.............................E....... 937 461-5550
Dayton *(G-9896)*
YWCA Mahoning Valley.............E....... 330 746-6361
Youngstown *(G-20269)*

YWCA of Greater Cincinnati.............D....... 513 241-7090
Cincinnati *(G-4817)*
YWCA of Hamilton.............E....... 513 856-9800
Hamilton *(G-11655)*
YWCA Shelter & Housing Network.............E....... 937 222-6333
Dayton *(G-9897)*

MEMBERSHIP ORGANIZATIONS, LABOR UNIONS & SIMILAR: Trade

Amalgamated Transit Union.............E....... 216 861-3350
Cleveland *(G-4945)*
Painters District Council 6.............D....... 440 239-4575
Cleveland *(G-6157)*
Painters Local Union 555.............D....... 740 353-1431
Portsmouth *(G-16156)*
United Steelworkers.............E....... 513 793-0272
Cincinnati *(G-4687)*

MEMBERSHIP ORGANIZATIONS, NEC: Amateur Sports Promotion

Sporty Events.............E....... 440 342-5046
Chesterland *(G-2745)*

MEMBERSHIP ORGANIZATIONS, NEC: Art Council

Eastern Mumee Bay Arts Council.............E....... 419 690-5718
Oregon *(G-15593)*
Jeanne B McCoy Comm.............E....... 614 245-4701
New Albany *(G-14857)*

MEMBERSHIP ORGANIZATIONS, NEC: Automobile Owner Association

AAA Allied Group Inc.............B....... 513 762-3301
Cincinnati *(G-2894)*
AAA Club Alliance Inc.............D....... 419 843-1200
Toledo *(G-17577)*
AAA Miami Valley.............D....... 937 224-2896
Dayton *(G-9201)*
AAA South Central Ohio Inc.............E....... 740 354-5614
Portsmouth *(G-16123)*
Akron Automobile Association.............D....... 330 762-0631
Akron *(G-28)*
American Motorcycle Assn.............D....... 614 856-1900
Pickerington *(G-15945)*
Buckeye Drag Racing Assn LLC.............E....... 419 562-0869
Bucyrus *(G-1978)*
Columbus Landmarks Foundation.............E....... 614 221-0227
Columbus *(G-7291)*
Massillon Automobile Club.............E....... 330 833-1084
Massillon *(G-13709)*
Ohio Automobile Club.............C....... 614 431-7901
Worthington *(G-19831)*

MEMBERSHIP ORGANIZATIONS, NEC: Charitable

Akron-Canton Regional Foodbank.............E....... 330 535-6900
Akron *(G-61)*
American National Red Cross.............D....... 937 399-3872
Springfield *(G-16993)*
Applewood Centers Inc.............D....... 216 696-6815
Cleveland *(G-4991)*
Ardmore Inc.............C....... 330 535-2601
Akron *(G-79)*
Athletes In Action Sports.............D....... 937 352-1000
Xenia *(G-19891)*
Auxiliary St Lukes Hospital.............E....... 419 893-5911
Maumee *(G-13759)*
Battelle Memorial Institute.............A....... 614 424-6424
Columbus *(G-7020)*
Broken Arrow Inc.............E....... 419 562-3480
Bucyrus *(G-1977)*
Brunswick Food Pantry Inc.............E....... 330 225-0395
Brunswick *(G-1922)*
Carol A & Ralp V H US B Fdn Tr.............E....... 513 632-4426
Cincinnati *(G-3125)*
Cincinnati Health Network Inc.............E....... 513 961-0600
Cincinnati *(G-3248)*
Cincinnati Humn Relations Comm.............E....... 513 352-3237
Cincinnati *(G-3249)*
City of Compassion.............D....... 419 422-7800
Findlay *(G-10888)*
Cleveland America Scores.............E....... 216 881-7988
Cleveland *(G-5230)*
Cliffs Cleveland Foundation.............E....... 216 694-5700
Cleveland *(G-5302)*

Community Dev For All People.............E....... 614 445-7342
Columbus *(G-7330)*
Conserv For Cyhg Vlly Nat Prk.............D....... 330 657-2909
Peninsula *(G-15811)*
Council For Economic Opport.............D....... 216 476-3201
Cleveland *(G-5354)*
County of Summit Board of Mntl.............A....... 330 634-8100
Akron *(G-167)*
Downtown Akron Partnership Inc.............E....... 330 374-7676
Akron *(G-193)*
East Akron Neighborhood Dev.............E....... 330 773-6838
Akron *(G-200)*
Elizabeths New Life Center Inc.............D....... 937 226-7414
Dayton *(G-9411)*
Fairfield Industries Inc.............E....... 740 409-1539
Carroll *(G-2557)*
First Capital Enterprises Inc.............D....... 740 773-2166
Chillicothe *(G-2780)*
Free & Accepted Masons.............D....... 419 822-3736
Delta *(G-10044)*
Gideons International.............E....... 513 932-2857
Lebanon *(G-12467)*
Goodwill Inds Centl Ohio Inc.............E....... 740 439-7000
Cambridge *(G-2070)*
Granger Township.............E....... 330 239-2111
Medina *(G-13945)*
Hadassah Dayton Chapter.............E....... 937 275-0227
Dayton *(G-9481)*
Hearing Spch Deaf Ctr Grtr Cnc.............E....... 513 221-0527
Cincinnati *(G-3696)*
Heartbeats To City Inc.............E....... 330 452-4524
Canton *(G-2342)*
Kids In Need Foundation.............E....... 937 296-1230
Moraine *(G-14669)*
Koinonia Homes Inc.............B....... 216 588-8777
Cleveland *(G-5835)*
Kroger Co Foundation.............E....... 513 762-4000
Cincinnati *(G-3893)*
Leo Yannenoff Jewish Community.............C....... 614 231-2731
Columbus *(G-7966)*
Licking Valley Lions Club.............C....... 740 763-3733
Newark *(G-15060)*
Marysville Food Pantry.............E....... 937 644-3248
Marysville *(G-13514)*
Mid-Ohio Foodbank.............C....... 614 317-9400
Grove City *(G-11453)*
Nami of Preble County Ohio.............E....... 937 456-4947
Eaton *(G-10455)*
Northast Ohio Sstnble Cmmnties.............D....... 216 410-7698
Akron *(G-349)*
Ohio Academy of Science.............E....... 614 488-2228
Dublin *(G-10296)*
Ohio Federation of Soil and WA.............E....... 614 784-1900
Reynoldsburg *(G-16323)*
Parma Community General Hosp.............B....... 440 743-4280
Parma *(G-15772)*
Pepper Pike Club Company Inc.............D....... 216 831-9400
Cleveland *(G-6193)*
Recovery Center.............E....... 740 687-4500
Lancaster *(G-12429)*
Ridgeville Community Choir.............E....... 419 267-3820
Ridgeville Corners *(G-16398)*
Royal Arch Masons of Ohio.............E....... 419 762-5565
Napoleon *(G-14816)*
Ruritan.............E....... 330 542-2308
New Springfield *(G-14997)*
School Choice Ohio Inc.............E....... 614 223-1555
Columbus *(G-8605)*
Seneca RE ADS Ind Fostoria Div.............C....... 419 435-0729
Fostoria *(G-11012)*
Team NEO.............E....... 216 363-5400
Cleveland *(G-6507)*
Wapakoneta YMCA.............D....... 419 739-9622
Wapakoneta *(G-18659)*
White Gorilla Corporation.............E....... 202 384-6486
Hilliard *(G-11830)*
Womens Civic Club Grove City.............E....... 614 871-0145
Grove City *(G-11489)*
Youngstown Neighborhood Dev.............E....... 330 480-0423
Youngstown *(G-20263)*
Zanesville Welfare Organizatio.............B....... 740 450-6060
Zanesville *(G-20386)*

MEMBERSHIP ORGANIZATIONS, NEC: Food Co-Operative

Heights Emergency Food Center.............D....... 216 381-0707
Cleveland *(G-5682)*

MEMBERSHIP ORGANIZATIONS, NEC: Historical Club

Dayton Society Natural History ....E 513 932-4421
  Oregonia **(G-15616)**

Niles Historical Society ....D 330 544-2143
  Niles **(G-15162)**

MEMBERSHIP ORGANIZATIONS, NEC: Personal Interest

Affinion Group LLC...........................A 614 895-1803
  Westerville **(G-19217)**

Carmen Steering Committee..................E 330 756-2066
  Navarre **(G-14822)**

Ethnic Voice of America ....E 440 845-0922
  Cleveland **(G-5492)**

Frazeysburg Lions Club Inc ....E 740 828-2313
  Frazeysburg **(G-11049)**

Shoreby Club Inc ....D 216 851-2587
  Cleveland **(G-6406)**

Sons of Un Vtrans of Civil War ....D 740 992-6144
  Middleport **(G-14283)**

Volunteers of America NW Ohio ....E 419 248-3733
  Toledo **(G-18140)**

MEMBERSHIP ORGANIZATIONS, PROF: Education/Teacher Assoc

Aauw Action Fund Inc ....E 330 833-0520
  Massillon **(G-13659)**

Association For Middle Lvl Edu ....E 614 895-4730
  Westerville **(G-19223)**

Buckeye Assn Schl Admnstrators ....E 614 846-4080
  Columbus **(G-7084)**

MEMBERSHIP ORGANIZATIONS, PROFESSIONAL: Accounting Assoc

Ohio Soc of Crtif Pub Accntnts ....D 614 764-2727
  Columbus **(G-8287)**

MEMBERSHIP ORGANIZATIONS, PROFESSIONAL: Health Association

Clark County Combined Hlth Dst ....D 937 390-5600
  Springfield **(G-17012)**

Cleveland Health Network....................E 216 986-1100
  Cleveland **(G-5257)**

Columbus Medical Association ....E 614 240-7410
  Columbus **(G-7296)**

Consortium For Hlthy & Immunzd........D 216 201-2001
  Cleveland **(G-5336)**

Dayton Anthem ....D 937 428-8000
  Dayton **(G-9351)**

Geauga County Health District.............E 440 279-1940
  Chardon **(G-2695)**

Jefferson Behavioral Hlth Sys ....C 740 264-7751
  Steubenville **(G-17158)**

Ohio Department of Health ....C 614 466-1521
  Columbus **(G-8240)**

Ohio Health Council ....D 614 221-7614
  Columbus **(G-8262)**

Ohio Hospital Association ....D 614 221-7614
  Columbus **(G-8266)**

MEMBERSHIP ORGANIZATIONS, REL: Christian & Reformed Church

Calvary Christian Ch of Ohio ....E 740 828-9000
  Frazeysburg **(G-11048)**

MEMBERSHIP ORGANIZATIONS, RELIGIOUS: Apostolic Church

First Apostolic Church ....E 419 885-4888
  Toledo **(G-17738)**

MEMBERSHIP ORGANIZATIONS, RELIGIOUS: Assembly Of God Church

New Bgnnngs Assembly of God Ch......E 614 497-2658
  Columbus **(G-8154)**

Tri County Assembly of God.................E 513 874-8575
  Fairfield **(G-10792)**

MEMBERSHIP ORGANIZATIONS, RELIGIOUS: Baptist Church

Grace Baptist Church ....E 937 652-1133
  Urbana **(G-18435)**

Twinbrook Hills Baptist Church............E 513 863-3107
  Hamilton **(G-11650)**

MEMBERSHIP ORGANIZATIONS, RELIGIOUS: Brethren Church

Grace Brthren Ch Columbus Ohio ....C 614 888-7733
  Westerville **(G-19168)**

MEMBERSHIP ORGANIZATIONS, RELIGIOUS: Catholic Church

Catholic Diocese of Cleveland..............E 419 289-7224
  Ashland **(G-664)**

Our Lady of Bethlehem Schools ....E 614 459-8285
  Columbus **(G-8404)**

Saint Francis De Sales Church.............E 440 884-2319
  Cleveland **(G-6364)**

Saint Mary Parish...............................D 440 285-7051
  Chardon **(G-2712)**

St Francis De Sales Church ....D 740 345-9874
  Newark **(G-15099)**

St Patrick Church Inc..........................E 937 335-2833
  Troy **(G-18229)**

St Pauls Catholic Church ....E 330 724-1263
  Akron **(G-439)**

MEMBERSHIP ORGANIZATIONS, RELIGIOUS: Church Of Christ

Oak Creek United Church ....E 937 434-3941
  Dayton **(G-9663)**

Pilgrim United Church Christ.................E 513 574-4208
  Cincinnati **(G-4248)**

St Stephen United Church Chrst ....E 419 624-1814
  Sandusky **(G-16644)**

MEMBERSHIP ORGANIZATIONS, RELIGIOUS: Church Of God

Salem Church of God Inc ....E 937 836-6500
  Clayton **(G-4861)**

MEMBERSHIP ORGANIZATIONS, RELIGIOUS: Community Church

First Community Church........................E 614 488-0681
  Columbus **(G-7583)**

First Community Church........................E 740 385-3827
  Logan **(G-12835)**

First Community Church........................E 614 488-0681
  Columbus **(G-7584)**

Oesterlen-Services For Youth................C 937 399-6101
  Springfield **(G-17091)**

MEMBERSHIP ORGANIZATIONS, RELIGIOUS: Lutheran Church

Bethlehem Lutheran Ch Parma ....E 440 845-2230
  Cleveland **(G-5060)**

Gethsemane Lutheran Church ....E 614 885-4319
  Columbus **(G-7666)**

Royal Redeemer Lutheran Church........E 440 237-7958
  North Royalton **(G-15365)**

Upper Arlington Lutheran Ch ....E 614 451-3736
  Columbus **(G-8825)**

MEMBERSHIP ORGANIZATIONS, RELIGIOUS: Methodist Church

Board Man Frst Untd Methdst Ch........E 330 758-4527
  Youngstown **(G-19968)**

Epworth United Methodist Ch................D 740 387-1062
  Marion **(G-13420)**

Sharonville Mthdist Wkdays Nrs ....E 513 563-8278
  Cincinnati **(G-4465)**

United Methodist Community Ctr..........E 330 743-5149
  Canfield **(G-2162)**

West Ohio Conference of ....E 937 773-5313
  Piqua **(G-16038)**

West Ohio Conference of ....E 614 844-6200
  Worthington **(G-19859)**

MEMBERSHIP ORGANIZATIONS, RELIGIOUS: Nonchurch

Sisters of Charity of Cinc ....D 513 347-5200
  Mount Saint Joseph **(G-14744)**

MEMBERSHIP ORGANIZATIONS, RELIGIOUS: Pentecostal Church

New Life Christian Center ....E 740 687-1572
  Lancaster **(G-12422)**

Ravenna Assembly of God Inc ....E 330 297-1493
  Ravenna **(G-16260)**

MEMBERSHIP ORGANIZATIONS, RELIGIOUS: Presbyterian Church

Lebanon Presbyterian Church...............E 513 932-0369
  Lebanon **(G-12482)**

Wsos Child Development Program ....E 419 334-8511
  Fremont **(G-11107)**

MEMBERSHIP ORGS, CIVIC, SOCIAL & FRAT: Comm Member Club

Columbus Maennerchor........................E 614 444-3531
  Columbus **(G-7293)**

Jewish Community Center Inc...............D 513 761-7500
  Cincinnati **(G-3814)**

O S U Faculty Club..............................E 614 292-2262
  Columbus **(G-8220)**

Tiffin Cmnty YMCA Rcration Ctr...........D 419 447-8711
  Tiffin **(G-17542)**

Young Mens Christian Assoc.................D 937 836-9622
  Englewood **(G-10606)**

MEMBERSHIP ORGS, CIVIC, SOCIAL & FRAT: Dwelling-Related

Cincinnati Scholar House LP.................E 513 559-0048
  Cincinnati **(G-3265)**

The For Cincinnati Association ....D 513 744-3344
  Cincinnati **(G-4591)**

MEMBERSHIP ORGS, CIVIC, SOCIAL & FRAT: Girl Scout

Buckeye Trils Girl Scout Cncil...............E 937 275-7601
  Dayton **(G-9267)**

Girl Scouts Lake Erie Council................E 330 864-9933
  Macedonia **(G-13071)**

Girl Scouts North East Ohio ....D 216 481-1313
  Cleveland **(G-5609)**

Girl Scouts North East Ohio ....D 330 864-9933
  Macedonia **(G-13072)**

Girl Scouts of The US Amer ....C 614 487-8101
  Columbus **(G-7669)**

Girl Scouts of Western Ohio ....E 513 489-1025
  Blue Ash **(G-1570)**

Girl Scouts of Western Ohio ....E 567 225-3557
  Toledo **(G-17763)**

Girl Scuts Appleseed Ridge Inc ....E 419 225-4085
  Lima **(G-12643)**

Girl Scuts Ohios Heartland Inc..............D 614 340-8820
  Columbus **(G-7670)**

Girl Scuts Wstn Ohio Tledo Div............E 419 243-8216
  Toledo **(G-17764)**

Western Rsrve Girl Scout Cncil..............E 330 864-9933
  Macedonia **(G-13089)**

MEMBERSHIP ORGS, CIVIC, SOCIAL & FRATERNAL: Civic Assoc

Akron Roundtable................................E 330 247-8682
  Cuyahoga Falls **(G-9068)**

Benevolent/Protectv Order Elks............E 440 357-6943
  Painesville **(G-15695)**

Cleveland Botanical Garden ....E 216 721-1600
  Cleveland **(G-5232)**

Cuyahoga County AG Soc ....E 440 243-0090
  Berea **(G-1421)**

Easter Seals Nothern Ohio Inc...............C 440 324-6600
  Lorain **(G-12901)**

Farmersville Fire Assn Inc ....E 937 696-2863
  Farmersville **(G-10857)**

Greater Cnncnati Crime Stopper ....E 859 468-1310
  Cincinnati **(G-3655)**

Grove City Community Club ....E 614 875-6074
  Grove City **(G-11437)**

Employee Codes: A=Over 500 employees, B=251-500
C=101-250, D=51-100, E=25-50   2019 Harris Ohio
Services Directory   1489

SERVICES

Independent Order Odd Fellows ....E 740 548-5038
   Lewis Center **(G-12546)**

International Assn Lions ....E 740 986-6502
   Williamsport **(G-19499)**

International Ordr of Rnbow Fo ....E 419 862-3009
   Elmore **(G-10473)**

International Un Elev Constrs ....C 614 291-5859
   Columbus **(G-7838)**

Kiwanis International Inc ....E 740 385-5887
   Logan **(G-12845)**

Lima Family YMCA ....E 419 223-6045
   Lima **(G-12680)**

Lions Club International Inc ....E 330 424-3490
   Lisbon **(G-12803)**

Moose International Inc ....E 513 422-6776
   Middletown **(G-14314)**

Ohio Masonic Retirement Vlg ....D 937 525-1743
   Springfield **(G-17092)**

Order of Symposiarchs America ....E 740 387-9713
   Marion **(G-13452)**

Port Clnton Bpo Elks Ldge 1718 ....E 419 734-1900
   Port Clinton **(G-16114)**

Urban Leagu of Greater Clevlnd ....E 216 622-0999
   Cleveland **(G-6606)**

Wesley Community Center Inc ....E 937 263-3556
   Dayton **(G-9875)**

YMCA of Massillon ....E 330 837-5116
   Massillon **(G-13737)**

MEMBERSHIP ORGS, CIVIC, SOCIAL & FRATERNAL: Condo Assoc

2444 Mdson Rd Cndo Owners Assn ......E 513 871-0100
   Cincinnati **(G-2880)**

Brandywine Master Assn ....D 419 866-0135
   Maumee **(G-13765)**

Owners Management ....E 440 439-3800
   Cleveland **(G-6151)**

Saxon House Condo ....D 440 333-8675
   Cleveland **(G-6373)**

Three Village Condominium ....E 440 461-1483
   Cleveland **(G-6527)**

MEMBERSHIP ORGS, CIVIC, SOCIAL & FRATERNAL: Protection

Cleveland Municipal School Dst ....D 216 459-4200
   Cleveland **(G-5275)**

Division Drnking Ground Waters ....D 614 644-2752
   Columbus **(G-7457)**

The Nature Conservancy ....E 614 717-2770
   Dublin **(G-10356)**

Western Rsrve Land Conservancy ......E 440 729-9621
   Chagrin Falls **(G-2660)**

MEMBERSHIP ORGS, CIVIC, SOCIAL & FRATERNAL: Singing Society

Cleveland Heights Highschool ....E 216 691-5452
   Cleveland **(G-5259)**

MEMBERSHIP ORGS, CIVIC, SOCIAL & FRATERNAL: University Club

Aerie Frtnrl Order Egles 2875 ....E 419 433-4611
   Huron **(G-12019)**

Beta Theta PI Fraternity ....E 513 523-7591
   Oxford **(G-15673)**

Delta Gamma Fraternity ....E 614 487-5599
   Upper Arlington **(G-18397)**

Delta Kappa Gamma Society ....E 419 586-6016
   Celina **(G-2593)**

Gamma PHI Beta Sorority Alpha ....D 937 324-3436
   Springfield **(G-17041)**

Grand Aerie of The Fraternal ....E 614 883-2200
   Grove City **(G-11436)**

International Frat of Del ....E 330 922-5959
   Cuyahoga Falls **(G-9102)**

Kappa Kappa Gamma Foundation ......E 614 228-6515
   Dublin **(G-10263)**

Sigma CHI Frat ....E 614 297-8783
   Columbus **(G-8638)**

MEMBERSHIP ORGS, CIVIC, SOCIAL/FRAT: Educator's Assoc

Junior Achvment Mhning Vly Inc ......E 330 539-5268
   Girard **(G-11291)**

Ohio State University ....E 614 688-5721
   Columbus **(G-8329)**

MEMBERSHIP ORGS, LABOR UNIONS/SIMILAR: Employees' Assoc

American Federation of State ....E 937 461-9983
   Dayton **(G-9227)**

Humaserve Hr LLC ....E 513 605-3522
   Cincinnati **(G-3740)**

MEMBERSHIP ORGS, RELIGIOUS: Non-Denominational Church

Columbus Christian Center Inc ....E 614 416-9673
   Columbus **(G-7266)**

Haven Rest Ministries Inc ....D 330 535-1563
   Akron **(G-256)**

In His Prsence Ministries Intl ....E ...., 614 516-1812
   Columbus **(G-7805)**

MEMBERSHIP SPORTS & RECREATION CLUBS

Akron Womans City Club Inc ....E 330 762-6261
   Akron **(G-59)**

Alano Club Inc ....D 419 335-6211
   Wauseon **(G-18796)**

Armco Association Park ....E 513 695-3980
   Lebanon **(G-12449)**

Avondale Golf Club ....E 440 934-4398
   Avon **(G-865)**

Boys & Girls CLB Hamilton Inc ....E 513 893-0071
   Hamilton **(G-11559)**

Chagrin Valley Athletic Club ....D 440 543-5141
   Chagrin Falls **(G-2662)**

Cincinnati Sports Mall Inc ....D 513 527-4000
   Cincinnati **(G-3269)**

City of Sylvania ....E 419 885-1167
   Sylvania **(G-17415)**

Cleveland Hts Tigers Youth Spo ......E 216 906-4168
   Cleveland **(G-5260)**

Columbus Club Co ....E 614 224-4131
   Columbus **(G-7268)**

Dayton Toro Motorcycle Club ....D 937 723-9133
   Dayton **(G-9382)**

Fairfield Tempo Club ....E 513 863-2081
   Fairfield **(G-10727)**

Family YMCA of LANcstr&fairfld ....C 740 654-0616
   Lancaster **(G-12404)**

Fitworks Holding LLC ....E 440 333-4141
   Rocky River **(G-16433)**

Ganzfair Investment Inc ....E 614 792-6630
   Delaware **(G-9980)**

General Electric Employees ....E 513 243-2129
   Cincinnati **(G-3613)**

Geneva Area Recreational ....E 440 466-1002
   Geneva **(G-11242)**

German Family Society Inc ....E 330 678-8229
   Kent **(G-12234)**

Grove City Community Club ....E 614 875-6074
   Grove City **(G-11437)**

Heritage Golf Club Ltd Partnr ....D 614 777-1690
   Hilliard **(G-11773)**

M&C Hotel Interests Inc ....E 440 543-1331
   Chagrin Falls **(G-2671)**

Marietta Bantam Baseball Leag ......E 740 350-9844
   Marietta **(G-13348)**

Miami Rifle Pistol Club ....D 513 732-9943
   Milford **(G-14409)**

National Exchange Club ....E 419 535-3232
   Toledo **(G-17929)**

New Albany Athc Booster CLB ....E 614 413-8325
   New Albany **(G-14862)**

Newlex Classic Riders Inc ....D 740 342-3885
   New Lexington **(G-14923)**

Oakland Pk Cnservation CLB Inc ....D 614 989-8739
   Dublin **(G-10294)**

Oberlin College ....C 440 775-8519
   Oberlin **(G-15513)**

Ohio Automobile Club ....E 614 277-1310
   Grove City **(G-11462)**

Ohio Automobile Club ....E 513 870-0951
   West Chester **(G-18978)**

Safari Club International ....E 440 247-8614
   North Ridgeville **(G-15342)**

Salt Fork Resort Club Inc ....A 740 498-8116
   Kimbolton **(G-12312)**

Sandusky Rotary Club Charitabl ......E 419 625-1707
   Huron **(G-12029)**

Scioto Reserve Inc ....D 740 881-9082
   Powell **(G-16208)**

Tiffin Cmnty YMCA Rcration Ctr ....D 419 447-8711
   Tiffin **(G-17542)**

Tom Tise Golf Professional ....D 937 836-5186
   Clayton **(G-4862)**

Vermilion Family YMCA ....E 440 967-4208
   Vermilion **(G-18563)**

Vertical Adventures Inc ....D 614 888-8393
   Columbus **(G-8846)**

YMCA of Ashtabula County Inc ....D 440 997-5321
   Ashtabula **(G-760)**

Young Mens Christian Assn ....E 419 332-9622
   Fremont **(G-11108)**

Young Mens Christian Assn ....D 330 744-8411
   Youngstown **(G-20253)**

Young Mens Christian Assoc ....D 740 477-1661
   Circleville **(G-4854)**

Young Mens Christian Assoc ....E 937 426-9622
   Dayton **(G-9894)**

Young Mens Christian Assoc ....D 330 264-3131
   Wooster **(G-19789)**

Young Mens Christian Assoc ....E 937 836-9622
   Englewood **(G-10606)**

Young Mens Christian Assoc ....E 937 228-9622
   Dayton **(G-9895)**

Young Mens Christian Assoc ....C 937 223-5201
   Springboro **(G-16990)**

Young Mens Christian Assoc ....E 614 834-9622
   Canal Winchester **(G-2129)**

Young Mens Christian Associat ....D 513 521-7112
   Cincinnati **(G-4812)**

Young Mens Christian Associat ....E 513 731-0115
   Cincinnati **(G-4813)**

Young Mens Christian Associat ....C 513 474-1400
   Cincinnati **(G-4814)**

Young Mens Christian Associat ....E 513 791-5000
   Blue Ash **(G-1685)**

Young Mens Christn Assn Shelby ......D 419 347-1312
   Shelby **(G-16751)**

Young MNS Christn Assn Findlay ......D 419 422-4424
   Findlay **(G-10977)**

Young MNS Chrstn Assn Clveland ......D 216 382-4300
   Cleveland **(G-6704)**

Young MNS Chrstn Assn Clveland ......E 216 941-4654
   Cleveland **(G-6702)**

MEN'S & BOYS' CLOTHING STORES

Abercrombie & Fitch Trading Co ....E 614 283-6500
   New Albany **(G-14839)**

For Women Like Me Inc ....E 407 848-7339
   Chagrin Falls **(G-2645)**

J Peterman Company LLC ....E 888 647-2555
   Blue Ash **(G-1588)**

MEN'S & BOYS' CLOTHING WHOLESALERS, NEC

Abercrombie & Fitch Trading Co ....E 614 283-6500
   New Albany **(G-14839)**

For Women Like Me Inc ....E 407 848-7339
   Chagrin Falls **(G-2645)**

K Amalia Enterprises Inc ....D 614 733-3800
   Plain City **(G-16056)**

Mast Industries Inc ....C 614 415-7000
   Columbus **(G-8034)**

Mast Industries Inc ....D 614 856-6000
   Reynoldsburg **(G-16319)**

McCc Sportswear Inc ....E 513 583-9210
   West Chester **(G-19065)**

MGF Sourcing Us LLC ....D 614 904-3300
   Columbus **(G-8066)**

Rassak LLC ....E 513 791-9453
   Cincinnati **(G-4339)**

Rondinellis Tuxedo ....E 330 726-7768
   Youngstown **(G-20195)**

West Chester Holdings LLC ....C 800 647-1900
   Cincinnati **(G-4781)**

MEN'S & BOYS' SPORTSWEAR WHOLESALERS

Barbs Graffiti Inc ....D 216 881-5550
   Cleveland **(G-5035)**

Barbs Graffiti Inc ....E 216 881-5550
   Cleveland **(G-5036)**

Gymnastic World Inc ....E 440 526-2970
   Cleveland **(G-5649)**

Heritage Sportswear Inc ....D 740 928-7771
   Hebron **(G-11715)**

R & A Sports Inc ....E 216 289-2254
   Euclid **(G-10654)**

MENTAL HEALTH CLINIC, OUTPATIENT

A W S Inc ....D....... 216 941-8800
Cleveland *(G-4882)*
A+ Solutions LLC ....E....... 216 896-0111
Beachwood *(G-1025)*
Access Ohio ....E....... 614 367-7700
Columbus *(G-6862)*
Alcohol Drug Addction & Mental ....E....... 937 443-0416
Dayton *(G-9213)*
Allwell Behavioral Health Svcs ....E....... 740 454-9766
Zanesville *(G-20274)*
Allwell Behavioral Health Svcs ....E....... 740 439-4428
Cambridge *(G-2049)*
Alta Care Group Inc ....E....... 330 793-2487
Youngstown *(G-19952)*
Alternative Paths Inc ....E....... 330 725-9195
Medina *(G-13909)*
Ambulatory Care Solutions LLC ....C....... 740 695-3721
Saint Clairsville *(G-16469)*
Bayshore Counseling Svc Inc ....E....... 419 626-9156
Sandusky *(G-16577)*
Beacon Health ....C....... 440 354-9924
Mentor *(G-14021)*
Behavorial Healthcare ....C....... 740 522-8477
Newark *(G-15013)*
Behavral Cnnctions WD Cnty Inc ....C....... 419 352-5387
Bowling Green *(G-1718)*
Belmont Bhc Pines Hospital Inc ....C....... 330 759-2700
Youngstown *(G-19964)*
Bhc Fox Run Hospital Inc ....C....... 740 695-2131
Saint Clairsville *(G-16479)*
Blick Clinic Inc ....C....... 330 762-5425
Akron *(G-99)*
Blick Clinic Inc ....D....... 330 762-5425
Akron *(G-100)*
Butler Bhavioral Hlth Svcs Inc ....E....... 513 896-7887
Hamilton *(G-11564)*
Center 5 ....D....... 330 379-5900
Akron *(G-123)*
Center For Families & Children ....E....... 216 252-5800
Cleveland *(G-5151)*
Center For Individual and Fmly ....C....... 419 522-4357
Mansfield *(G-13150)*
Central Ohio Mental Health Ctr ....C....... 740 368-7831
Delaware *(G-9959)*
Child Adlscent Behavioral Hlth ....E....... 330 454-7917
Canton *(G-2249)*
Child Focus Inc ....D....... 513 752-1555
Cincinnati *(G-3180)*
Coleman Professional Svcs Inc ....C....... 330 673-1347
Kent *(G-12223)*
Coleman Professional Svcs Inc ....D....... 330 296-8313
Ravenna *(G-16236)*
Columbus Area ....D....... 614 251-6561
Columbus *(G-7255)*
Columbus Area Inc ....E....... 614 252-0711
Columbus *(G-7256)*
Columbus Area Integrated Healt ....D....... 614 252-0711
Columbus *(G-7257)*
Community Counseling Services ....E....... 419 468-8211
Bucyrus *(G-1984)*
Community Counslng Ctr Ashtabu ....D....... 440 998-4210
Ashtabula *(G-729)*
Community Mental Healthcare ....E....... 330 343-1811
Dover *(G-10070)*
Community Solutions Assn ....E....... 330 394-9090
Warren *(G-18690)*
Community Support Services Inc ....C....... 330 253-9388
Akron *(G-153)*
Community Support Services Inc ....D....... 330 253-9675
Akron *(G-154)*
Community Support Services Inc ....D....... 330 733-6203
Akron *(G-155)*
Compass Community Health ....E....... 740 355-7102
Portsmouth *(G-16133)*
Comprehensive Behavioral Hlth ....E....... 330 797-4050
Youngstown *(G-20006)*
Comprehensive Counseling Svc ....E....... 513 424-0921
Middletown *(G-14297)*
Consolidated Care Inc ....E....... 937 465-8065
West Liberty *(G-19120)*
Cornerstone Support Services ....D....... 330 339-7850
New Philadelphia *(G-14952)*
Counseling Center Huron County ....E....... 419 663-3737
Norwalk *(G-15430)*
Counseling Source Inc ....E....... 513 984-9838
Blue Ash *(G-1539)*
County of Allen ....E....... 419 221-1226
Lima *(G-12625)*
County of Geauga ....C....... 440 286-6264
Chesterland *(G-2738)*
County of Hamilton ....B....... 513 598-2965
Cincinnati *(G-3372)*
Craig and Frances Lindner Cent ....C....... 513 536-4673
Mason *(G-13569)*
Crossroads Lake County Adole ....C....... 440 255-1700
Mentor *(G-14037)*
Darke Cnty Mental Hlth Clinic ....E....... 937 548-1635
Greenville *(G-11371)*
Day-Mont Bhvoral Hlth Care Inc ....D....... 937 222-8111
Moraine *(G-14641)*
East Way Behavioral Hlth Care ....C....... 937 222-4900
Dayton *(G-9403)*
Emerge Counseling Service ....E....... 330 865-8351
Akron *(G-202)*
Empowered For Excellence ....E....... 567 316-7253
Toledo *(G-17714)*
Equitas Health Inc ....E....... 614 926-4132
Columbus *(G-7525)*
Equitas Health Inc ....D....... 614 299-2437
Columbus *(G-7527)*
F R S Connections ....E....... 937 393-9662
Hillsboro *(G-11838)*
Family Rsource Ctr NW Ohio Inc ....E....... 419 222-1168
Lima *(G-12637)*
Family Rsource Ctr NW Ohio Inc ....E....... 419 422-8616
Findlay *(G-10900)*
Firelands Regional Health Sys ....E....... 419 332-5524
Fremont *(G-11072)*
Foundtion Behavioral Hlth Svcs ....E....... 419 584-1000
Celina *(G-2595)*
Frs Counseling Inc ....E....... 937 393-0585
Hillsboro *(G-11840)*
Fulton County Health Center ....E....... 419 337-8661
Wauseon *(G-18802)*
Greater Cincinnati Behavioral ....C....... 513 354-7000
Walnut Hills *(G-18634)*
Harbor ....D....... 419 479-3233
Toledo *(G-17779)*
Harbor ....D....... 419 241-6191
Toledo *(G-17780)*
Harbor ....E....... 800 444-3353
Toledo *(G-17781)*
Health Partners Health Clinic ....E....... 937 645-8488
Marysville *(G-13502)*
Hopewell Health Centers Inc ....C....... 740 385-8468
Logan *(G-12840)*
Hopewell Health Centers Inc ....E....... 740 773-1006
Chillicothe *(G-2789)*
Hopewell Health Centers Inc ....E....... 740 385-6594
Logan *(G-12841)*
Integrated Youth Services Inc ....E....... 937 427-3837
Springfield *(G-17054)*
Ironton and Lawrence County ....B....... 740 532-3534
Ironton *(G-12155)*
Jac-Lin Manor ....D....... 419 994-5700
Loudonville *(G-12957)*
Lorain County Board ....E....... 440 329-3734
Elyria *(G-10530)*
Lutheran Social ....E....... 419 229-2222
Lima *(G-12696)*
Main Place Inc ....E....... 740 345-6246
Newark *(G-15064)*
Maumee Valley Guidance Center ....E....... 419 782-8856
Defiance *(G-9927)*
Mental Health and Addi Serv ....E....... 740 594-5000
Athens *(G-792)*
Mental Health and Addi Serv ....C....... 614 752-0333
Columbus *(G-8058)*
Mental Health Services ....E....... 216 623-6555
Cleveland *(G-5953)*
Mental Hlth Serv For CL & Mad ....E....... 740 852-6256
London *(G-12871)*
Mid-Ohio Psychlogical Svcs Inc ....D....... 740 687-0042
Lancaster *(G-12419)*
Midwest Behavioral Care Ltd ....E....... 937 454-0092
Dayton *(G-9632)*
Moundbuilders Guidance Ctr Inc ....E....... 740 397-0442
Mount Vernon *(G-14782)*
Nationwide Childrens Hospital ....B....... 614 355-8000
Columbus *(G-8151)*
Netcare Corporation ....D....... 614 274-9500
Columbus *(G-8171)*
Norcare Enterprises Inc ....B....... 440 233-7232
Lorain *(G-12932)*
Nord Center ....E....... 440 233-7232
Lorain *(G-12933)*
Nord Center Associates Inc ....C....... 440 233-7232
Lorain *(G-12934)*
North Cntl Mntal Hlth Svcs Inc ....D....... 614 227-6865
Columbus *(G-8198)*
North Community Counseling Ctr ....D....... 614 846-2588
Columbus *(G-8199)*
Northwest Mental Health Svcs ....E....... 614 457-7876
Columbus *(G-8207)*
Portage Path Behavorial Health ....D....... 330 253-3100
Akron *(G-390)*
Portage Path Behavorial Health ....D....... 330 762-6110
Akron *(G-391)*
Psy-Care Inc ....E....... 330 856-6663
Warren *(G-18737)*
Psychlgcal Behavioral Cons LLC ....E....... 216 456-8123
Beachwood *(G-1097)*
Ravenwood Mental Health Center ....E....... 440 632-5355
Middlefield *(G-14275)*
Ravenwood Mental Hlth Ctr Inc ....C....... 440 285-3568
Chardon *(G-2709)*
Recovery Resources ....E....... 216 431-4131
Cleveland *(G-6292)*
Samaritan Behavioral Health ....E....... 937 276-8333
Dayton *(G-9748)*
Scioto Pnt Vly Mental Hlth Ctr ....E....... 740 335-6935
Wshngtn CT Hs *(G-19883)*
Scioto Pnt Vly Mental Hlth Ctr ....C....... 740 775-1260
Chillicothe *(G-2825)*
Signature Health Inc ....B....... 440 953-9999
Willoughby *(G-19571)*
South Community Inc ....C....... 937 293-8300
Moraine *(G-14698)*
South Community Inc ....E....... 937 252-0100
Dayton *(G-9775)*
Southast Cmnty Mental Hlth Ctr ....C....... 614 225-0980
Columbus *(G-8661)*
Southast Cmnty Mental Hlth Ctr ....E....... 614 445-6832
Columbus *(G-8663)*
Southast Cmnty Mental Hlth Ctr ....E....... 614 293-9613
Worthington *(G-19850)*
Southast Cmnty Mental Hlth Ctr ....E....... 614 444-0800
Columbus *(G-8662)*
St Aloysius Services Inc ....E....... 513 482-1745
Cincinnati *(G-4526)*
St Ritas Medical Center ....E....... 419 226-9067
Lima *(G-12749)*
Stark County Board of Developm ....A....... 330 477-5200
Canton *(G-2490)*
Syntero Inc ....E....... 614 889-5722
Dublin *(G-10350)*
Taylor Murtis Human Svcs Sys ....D....... 216 283-4400
Cleveland *(G-6503)*
Taylor Murtis Human Svcs Sys ....D....... 216 283-4400
Cleveland *(G-6505)*
Taylor Murtis Human Svcs Sys ....D....... 216 281-7192
Cleveland *(G-6504)*
Thompkins Child Adlescent Svcs ....D....... 740 622-4470
Coshocton *(G-9028)*
Tri County Mental Health Svcs ....C....... 740 592-3091
Athens *(G-806)*
Tri County Mental Health Svcs ....D....... 740 594-5045
Athens *(G-807)*
Trihealth Inc ....E....... 513 569-6777
Cincinnati *(G-4637)*
Unison Behavioral Health Group ....C....... 419 693-0631
Toledo *(G-18115)*
Unison Bhvioral Hlth Group Inc ....D....... 419 214-4673
Toledo *(G-18116)*
Westwood Behavioral Health Ctr ....E....... 419 238-3434
Van Wert *(G-18497)*
Woodland Centers Inc ....D....... 740 446-5500
Gallipolis *(G-11217)*
Zepf Center ....E....... 419 255-4050
Toledo *(G-18175)*
Zepf Center ....D....... 419 841-7701
Toledo *(G-18176)*
Zepf Center ....E....... 419 213-5627
Toledo *(G-18177)*
Zepf Center ....E....... 419 255-4050
Toledo *(G-18178)*
Zepf Center ....E....... 419 213-5627
Toledo *(G-18179)*

MENTAL HEALTH PRACTITIONERS' OFFICES

Crisis Intervention & Rcvy Ctr ....D....... 330 455-9407
Canton *(G-2272)*
Layh & Associates ....E....... 937 767-9171
Yellow Springs *(G-19940)*
Netcare Corporation ....E....... 614 274-9500
Columbus *(G-8172)*

SERVICES

Employee Codes: A=Over 500 employees, B=251-500
C=101-250, D=51-100, E=25-50
2019 Harris Ohio
Services Directory
1491

MERCHANDISING MACHINE OPERATORS:

Vending

AVI Food Systems Inc ....C 330 372-6000
Warren (G-18677)

AVI Food Systems Inc ....E 740 452-9363
Zanesville (G-20279)

Dtv Inc ....E 216 226-5465
Mayfield Heights (G-13873)

S & B Enterprises LLC ....E 740 753-2646
Nelsonville (G-14836)

METAL & STEEL PRDTS: Abrasive

Tomson Steel Company ....E 513 420-8600
Middletown (G-14337)

METAL COMPONENTS: Prefabricated

Pioneer Cldding Glzing Systems ....E 216 816-4242
Cleveland (G-6213)

METAL CUTTING SVCS

Gerdau Macsteel Atmosphere Ann ....D 330 478-0314
Canton (G-2325)

Independent Steel Company LLC ....E 330 225-7741
Valley City (G-18463)

Laserflex Corporation ....D 614 850-9600
Hilliard (G-11783)

Perfect Cut-Off Inc ....E 440 943-0000
Wickliffe (G-19473)

Scot Industries Inc ....E 330 262-7585
Wooster (G-19767)

METAL FABRICATORS: Architechtural

A & G Manufacturing Co Inc ....E 419 468-7433
Galion (G-11164)

Bauer Corporation ....E 800 321-4760
Wooster (G-19689)

Blevins Metal Fabrication Inc ....E 419 522-6082
Mansfield (G-13143)

Debra-Kuempel Inc ....D 513 271-6500
Cincinnati (G-3414)

GL Nause Co Inc ....E 513 722-9500
Loveland (G-12996)

Graber Metal Works Inc ....E 440 237-8422
North Royalton (G-15356)

Langdon Inc ....E 513 733-5955
Cincinnati (G-3909)

Modern Builders Supply Inc ....C 419 241-3961
Toledo (G-17922)

Spillman Company ....E 614 444-2184
Columbus (G-8672)

Triangle Precision Industries ....D 937 299-6776
Dayton (G-9822)

Viking Fabricators Inc ....E 740 374-5246
Marietta (G-13397)

Wright Brothers Inc ....E 513 731-2222
Cincinnati (G-4807)

METAL FABRICATORS: Plate

A A S Amels Sheet Meta L Inc ....E 330 793-9326
Youngstown (G-19943)

A & G Manufacturing Co Inc ....E 419 468-7433
Galion (G-11164)

AM Castle & Co ....D 330 425-7000
Bedford (G-1269)

Babcock & Wilcox Company ....A 330 753-4511
Barberton (G-944)

Bico Akron Inc ....D 330 794-1716
Mogadore (G-14543)

Blevins Metal Fabrication Inc ....E 419 522-6082
Mansfield (G-13143)

Breitinger Company ....C 419 526-4255
Mansfield (G-13145)

C & R Inc ....E 614 497-1130
Groveport (G-11498)

Curtiss-Wright Flow Ctrl Corp ....D 513 528-7900
Cincinnati (G-2848)

Debra-Kuempel Inc ....D 513 271-6500
Cincinnati (G-3414)

Efco Corp ....E 614 876-1226
Columbus (G-7509)

General Tool Company ....C 513 733-5500
Cincinnati (G-3616)

GL Nause Co Inc ....E 513 722-9500
Loveland (G-12996)

Graber Metal Works Inc ....E 440 237-8422
North Royalton (G-15356)

Jergens Inc ....C 216 486-5540
Cleveland (G-5790)

Kendall Holdings Ltd ....E 614 486-4750
Columbus (G-7891)

Kirk & Blum Manufacturing Co ....C 513 458-2600
Cincinnati (G-3875)

Langdon Inc ....E 513 733-5955
Cincinnati (G-3909)

Lapham-Hickey Steel Corp ....E 614 443-4881
Columbus (G-7952)

Long-Stanton Mfg Company ....E 513 874-8020
West Chester (G-18964)

Nbw Inc ....E 216 377-1700
Cleveland (G-6051)

Pcy Enterprises Inc ....E 513 241-5566
Cincinnati (G-4219)

Pioneer Pipe Inc ....A 740 376-2400
Marietta (G-13370)

Prout Boiler Htg & Wldg Inc ....E 330 744-0293
Youngstown (G-20167)

Schweizer Dipple Inc ....D 440 786-8090
Cleveland (G-6378)

St Lawrence Holdings LLC ....E 330 562-9000
Maple Heights (G-13297)

Swagelok Company ....D 440 349-5934
Solon (G-16905)

Triangle Precision Industries ....D 937 299-6776
Dayton (G-9822)

Viking Fabricators Inc ....E 740 374-5246
Marietta (G-13397)

Will-Burt Company ....E 330 682-7015
Orrville (G-15650)

Will-Burt Company ....B 330 682-7015
Orrville (G-15649)

METAL FABRICATORS: Sheet

A A S Amels Sheet Meta L Inc ....E 330 793-9326
Youngstown (G-19943)

A & C Welding Inc ....E 330 762-4777
Peninsula (G-15808)

A & G Manufacturing Co Inc ....E 419 468-7433
Galion (G-11164)

Acro Tool & Die Company ....D 330 773-5173
Akron (G-17)

Akron Foundry Co ....E 330 745-3101
Barberton (G-939)

Alan Manufacturing Inc ....E 330 262-1555
Wooster (G-19684)

Alro Steel Corporation ....E 419 720-5300
Toledo (G-17586)

Alro Steel Corporation ....E 614 878-7271
Columbus (G-6905)

AM Castle & Co ....D 330 425-7000
Bedford (G-1269)

American Frame Corporation ....E 419 893-5595
Maumee (G-13748)

Anchor Metal Processing Inc ....E 216 362-1850
Cleveland (G-4978)

Avon Lake Sheet Metal Co ....E 440 933-3505
Avon Lake (G-910)

Bayloff Stmped Pdts Knsman Inc ....D 330 876-4511
Kinsman (G-12317)

Blevins Metal Fabrication Inc ....E 419 522-6082
Mansfield (G-13143)

Bogie Industries Inc Ltd ....D 330 745-3101
Akron (G-102)

Breitinger Company ....C 419 526-4255
Mansfield (G-13145)

Budde Sheet Metal Works Inc ....E 937 224-0868
Dayton (G-9268)

C-N-D Industries Inc ....D 330 478-8811
Massillon (G-13667)

Dimensional Metals Inc ....D 740 927-3633
Reynoldsburg (G-16299)

Ducts Inc ....E 216 391-2400
Cleveland (G-5448)

Dynamic Weld Corporation ....D 419 582-2900
Osgood (G-15652)

First Francis Company Inc ....E 440 352-8927
Painesville (G-15714)

Franck and Fric Incorporated ....D 216 524-4451
Cleveland (G-5572)

Gaspar Inc ....D 330 477-2222
Canton (G-2322)

General Tool Company ....C 513 733-5500
Cincinnati (G-3616)

GL Nause Co Inc ....E 513 722-9500
Loveland (G-12996)

Graber Metal Works Inc ....E 440 237-8422
North Royalton (G-15356)

Gundlach Sheet Metal Works Inc ....D 419 626-4525
Sandusky (G-16614)

Industrial Mill Maintenance ....E 330 746-1155
Youngstown (G-20078)

Jacobs Mechanical Co ....C 513 681-6800
Cincinnati (G-3803)

Kirk Williams Company Inc ....D 614 875-9023
Grove City (G-11445)

Lima Sheet Metal Machine & Mfg ....E 419 229-1161
Lima (G-12687)

Long-Stanton Mfg Company ....E 513 874-8020
West Chester (G-18964)

M H EBY Inc ....E 614 879-6901
West Jefferson (G-19110)

Marsam Metalfab Inc ....E 330 405-1520
Twinsburg (G-18295)

McWane Inc ....B 740 622-6651
Coshocton (G-9022)

N Wasserstrom & Sons Inc ....E 614 228-5550
Columbus (G-8126)

Norstar Aluminum Molds Inc ....D 440 632-0853
Middlefield (G-14273)

Northwind Industries Inc ....E 216 433-0666
Cleveland (G-6099)

Ohio Blow Pipe Company ....E 216 681-7379
Cleveland (G-6116)

Ohio Steel Sheet & Plate Inc ....E 800 827-2401
Hubbard (G-11949)

Pcy Enterprises Inc ....E 513 241-5566
Cincinnati (G-4219)

Precision Mtal Fabrication Inc ....D 937 235-9261
Dayton (G-9702)

Precision Steel Services Inc ....D 419 476-5702
Toledo (G-17984)

Precision Welding Corporation ....E 216 524-6110
Cleveland (G-6226)

Schweizer Dipple Inc ....D 440 786-8090
Cleveland (G-6378)

Steelial Wldg Met Fbrction Inc ....E 740 669-5300
Vinton (G-18586)

Tendon Manufacturing Inc ....E 216 663-3200
Cleveland (G-6512)

Tilton Corporation ....C 419 227-6421
Lima (G-12762)

TL Industries Inc ....C 419 666-8144
Northwood (G-15410)

Triangle Precision Industries ....D 937 299-6776
Dayton (G-9822)

Tricor Industrial Inc ....D 330 264-3299
Wooster (G-19773)

Universal Steel Company ....D 216 883-4972
Cleveland (G-6583)

V M Systems Inc ....D 419 535-1044
Toledo (G-18133)

Will-Burt Company ....B 330 682-7015
Orrville (G-15649)

Ysd Industries Inc ....D 330 792-6521
Youngstown (G-20268)

METAL MINING SVCS

Alloy Metal Exchange LLC ....E 216 478-0200
Bedford Heights (G-1315)

Hopedale Mining LLC ....E 740 937-2225
Hopedale (G-11937)

METAL SERVICE CENTERS & OFFICES

A J Oster Foils LLC ....D 330 823-1700
Alliance (G-512)

Advanced Graphite Machining US ....E 216 658-6521
Parma (G-15759)

All Foils Inc ....D 440 572-3645
Strongsville (G-17283)

Alumalloy Metalcasting Company ....D 440 930-2222
Avon Lake (G-907)

Aluminum Line Products Company ....D 440 835-8880
Westlake (G-19316)

American Consolidated Inds Inc ....E 216 587-8000
Cleveland (G-4951)

American Tank & Fabricating Co ....C 216 252-1500
Cleveland (G-4967)

Atlas Bolt & Screw Company LLC ....C 419 289-6171
Ashland (G-653)

Boston Retail Products Inc ....D 330 744-8100
Youngstown (G-19971)

Chatham Steel Corporation ....E 740 377-9310
South Point (G-16929)

Concast Metal Products Co ....D 440 965-4455
Wakeman (G-18620)

Diamond Metals Dist Inc ....E 216 898-7900
Cleveland (G-5421)

Fisher Cast Steel Products Inc ....E 614 879-8325
West Jefferson (G-19108)
Graber Metal Works Inc ....E 440 237-8422
North Royalton (G-15356)
Jsw Steel USA Ohio Inc ....C 740 535-8172
Mingo Junction (G-14528)
Modern Welding Co Ohio Inc ....E 740 344-9425
Newark (G-15073)
New Technology Steel LLC ....D 419 385-0636
Toledo (G-17939)
Ohio Metal Processing Inc ....E 740 286-6457
Jackson (G-12178)
Ohio Steel Sheet & Plate Inc ....E 800 827-2401
Hubbard (G-11949)
Panacea Products Corporation ....E 614 850-7000
Columbus (G-8418)
Samuel Steel Pickling Company ....D 330 963-3777
Twinsburg (G-18317)
Singer Steel Company ....E 330 562-7200
Streetsboro (G-17269)
SL Wellspring LLC ....D 513 948-2339
Cincinnati (G-4494)
Special Metals Corporation ....B 216 755-3030
Warrensville Heights (G-18781)
The Mansfield Strl & Erct Co ....E 419 522-5911
Mansfield (G-13251)
Thyssenkrupp Materials NA Inc ....E 937 898-7400
Miamisburg (G-14231)
Tricor Industrial Inc ....D 330 264-3299
Wooster (G-19773)
Watteredge LLC ....D 440 933-6110
Avon Lake (G-929)
Worthington Industries Inc ....C 513 539-9291
Monroe (G-14587)
Worthngton Stelpac Systems LLC ....C 614 438-3205
Columbus (G-8919)

METAL SLITTING & SHEARING

Laser Craft Inc ....E 440 327-4300
North Ridgeville (G-15333)
Metal Shredders Inc ....E 937 866-0777
Miamisburg (G-14190)
Ohio Metal Processing Inc ....E 740 286-6457
Jackson (G-12178)
Ohio Steel Slitters Inc ....E 330 477-6741
Canton (G-2432)
Samuel Steel Pickling Company ....D 330 963-3777
Twinsburg (G-18317)

METAL STAMPING, FOR THE TRADE

Acro Tool & Die Company ....D 330 773-5173
Akron (G-17)
Andre Corporation ....E 574 293-0207
Mason (G-13540)
Bayloff Stmped Pdts Knsman Inc ....D 330 876-4511
Kinsman (G-12317)
Falls Stamping & Welding Co ....C 330 928-1191
Cuyahoga Falls (G-9092)
Ohio Gasket and Shim Co Inc ....E 330 630-0626
Akron (G-359)
Pentaflex Inc ....C 937 325-5551
Springfield (G-17096)
Supply Technologies LLC ....C 440 947-2100
Cleveland (G-6485)

METAL STAMPINGS: Patterned

Seilkop Industries Inc ....E 513 761-1035
Cincinnati (G-4448)

METALS SVC CENTERS & WHOL: Semifinished Prdts, Iron/Steel

Voestlpine Precision Strip LLC ....E 330 220-7800
Brunswick (G-1944)

METALS SVC CENTERS & WHOL: Structural Shapes, Iron Or Steel

Blackburns Fabrication Inc ....E 614 875-0784
Columbus (G-7046)

METALS SVC CENTERS & WHOLESALERS: Cable, Wire

Radix Wire Co ....D 216 731-9191
Cleveland (G-6279)

METALS SVC CENTERS & WHOLESALERS: Casting, Rough,Iron/Steel

Ferralloy Inc ....E 440 250-1900
Cleveland (G-5525)

METALS SVC CENTERS & WHOLESALERS: Concrete Reinforcing Bars

Contractors Materials Company ....E 513 733-3000
Cincinnati (G-3353)

METALS SVC CENTERS & WHOLESALERS: Copper

Anchor Bronze and Metals Inc ....E 440 549-5653
Cleveland (G-4976)
National Bronze Mtls Ohio Inc ....E 440 277-1226
Lorain (G-12929)

METALS SVC CENTERS & WHOLESALERS: Ferroalloys

Howmet Corporation ....E 757 825-7086
Newburgh Heights (G-15114)

METALS SVC CENTERS & WHOLESALERS: Ferrous Metals

All Metal Sales Inc ....E 440 617-1234
Westlake (G-19312)

METALS SVC CENTERS & WHOLESALERS: Flat Prdts, Iron Or Steel

H & D Steel Service Inc ....E 440 237-3390
North Royalton (G-15357)
Major Metals Company ....E 419 886-4600
Mansfield (G-13202)
National Metal Trading LLC ....E 440 487-9771
Willoughby (G-19553)

METALS SVC CENTERS & WHOLESALERS: Foundry Prdts

Shells Inc ....D 330 808-5558
Copley (G-8974)

METALS SVC CENTERS & WHOLESALERS: Iron & Steel Prdt, Ferrous

Fpt Cleveland LLC ....C 216 441-3800
Cleveland (G-5569)
Heidtman Steel Products ....A 419 691-4646
Toledo (G-17799)

METALS SVC CENTERS & WHOLESALERS: Nonferrous Sheets, Etc

Shadco Inc ....E 310 217-8777
Toronto (G-18185)
Thyssenkrupp Materials NA Inc ....C 440 234-7500
Cleveland (G-6529)
Thyssenkrupp Onlinemetals LLC ....E 206 285-8603
Northwood (G-15408)

METALS SVC CENTERS & WHOLESALERS: Pipe & Tubing, Steel

Earle M Jorgensen Company ....D 330 425-1500
Twinsburg (G-18259)
L B Industries Inc ....E 330 750-1002
Struthers (G-17366)
McWane Inc ....B 740 622-6651
Coshocton (G-9022)

METALS SVC CENTERS & WHOLESALERS: Plates, Metal

Loveman Steel Corporation ....D 440 232-6200
Bedford (G-1289)

METALS SVC CENTERS & WHOLESALERS: Rope, Wire, Exc Insulated

Mazzella Holding Company Inc ....D 513 772-4466
Cleveland (G-5926)
Samsel Rope & Marine Supply Co ....E 216 241-0333
Cleveland (G-6370)

METALS SVC CENTERS & WHOLESALERS: Sheets, Galvanized/Coated

Witt Glvnzing - Cincinnati Inc ....E 513 871-5700
Cincinnati (G-4800)

METALS SVC CENTERS & WHOLESALERS: Sheets, Metal

Atlas Steel Products Co ....D 330 425-1600
Twinsburg (G-18247)
Majestic Steel Usa Inc ....C 440 786-2666
Cleveland (G-5902)

METALS SVC CENTERS & WHOLESALERS: Stampings, Metal

R L Morrissey & Assoc Inc ....E 440 498-3730
Solon (G-16889)

METALS SVC CENTERS & WHOLESALERS: Steel

Albco Sales Inc ....E 330 424-9446
Lisbon (G-12795)
Alro Steel Corporation ....E 330 929-4660
Cuyahoga Falls (G-9069)
Alro Steel Corporation ....D 513 769-9999
Cincinnati (G-2932)
Alro Steel Corporation ....E 419 720-5300
Toledo (G-17586)
Alro Steel Corporation ....E 614 878-7271
Columbus (G-6905)
Alro Steel Corporation ....E 937 253-6121
Dayton (G-9221)
AM Castle & Co ....E 330 425-7000
Bedford (G-1269)
American Posts LLC ....E 419 720-0652
Toledo (G-17593)
Associated Steel Company Inc ....E 216 475-8000
Cleveland (G-5015)
Avalon Precision Cast Co LLC ....C 216 362-4100
Brookpark (G-1891)
Benjamin Steel Company Inc ....E 937 233-1212
Springfield (G-16998)
Benjamin Steel Company Inc ....E 419 229-8045
Lima (G-12605)
Benjamin Steel Company Inc ....E 419 522-5500
Mansfield (G-13140)
Bico Akron Inc ....D 330 794-1716
Mogadore (G-14543)
Burger Iron Company ....C 330 794-1716
Mogadore (G-14544)
Butler Processing Inc ....E 513 874-1400
Hamilton (G-11572)
Central Steel and Wire Company ....C 513 242-2233
Cincinnati (G-3158)
Chapel Steel Corp ....E 800 570-7674
Bedford Heights (G-1319)
Cincinnati Steel Products Co ....E 513 871-4444
Cincinnati (G-3270)
Clifton Steel Company ....D 216 662-6111
Maple Heights (G-13283)
Clinton Aluminum Dist Inc ....C 330 882-6743
New Franklin (G-14907)
Cme Acquisitions LLC ....E 216 464-4480
Twinsburg (G-18255)
Coilplus Inc ....D 614 866-1338
Columbus (G-7242)
Coilplus Inc ....E 937 322-4455
Springfield (G-17016)
Coilplus Inc ....D 937 778-8884
Piqua (G-16000)
Contractors Steel Company ....E 330 425-3050
Twinsburg (G-18256)
Earle M Jorgensen Company ....E 513 771-3223
Cincinnati (G-3470)
Efco Corp ....E 614 876-1226
Columbus (G-7509)
F I L US Inc ....E 440 248-9500
Solon (G-16847)
Fay Industries Inc ....D 440 572-5030
Strongsville (G-17304)
Flack Steel LLC ....E 216 456-0700
Cleveland (G-5542)
Freedom Steel Inc ....E 440 266-6800
Mentor (G-14048)
Greer Steel Company ....C 330 343-8811
Dover (G-10080)

Employee Codes: A=Over 500 employees, B=251-500
C=101-250, D=51-100, E=25-50

2019 Harris Ohio
Services Directory

SERVICES

1493

Haverhill Coke Company LLC .... D 740 355-9819
　Franklin Furnace **(G-11046)**
Heidtman Steel Products Inc .... D 216 641-6995
　Cleveland **(G-5681)**
Heidtman Steel Products Inc .... D 419 385-0636
　Toledo **(G-17800)**
Holub Iron & Steel Company .... E 330 252-5655
　Akron **(G-267)**
Hynes Industries Inc .... C 330 799-3221
　Youngstown **(G-20073)**
Independent Steel Company LLC .... E 330 225-7741
　Valley City **(G-18463)**
Infra-Metals Co .... E 740 353-1350
　Portsmouth **(G-16149)**
Is Acquisition Inc .... E 440 287-0150
　Streetsboro **(G-17257)**
Jade-Sterling Steel Co Inc .... E 330 425-3141
　Twinsburg **(G-18285)**
Joseph T Ryerson & Son Inc .... E 513 896-4600
　Hamilton **(G-11618)**
Kloeckner Metals Corporation .... D 513 769-4000
　Cincinnati **(G-3879)**
Lapham-Hickey Steel Corp .... E 614 443-4881
　Columbus **(G-7952)**
Latrobe Spcialty Mtls Dist Inc .... D 330 609-5137
　Vienna **(G-18580)**
Liberty Steel Industries Inc .... E 330 372-6363
　Warren **(G-18724)**
Liberty Steel Products Inc .... E 330 538-2236
　North Jackson **(G-15248)**
Liberty Steel Products Inc .... C 330 534-7998
　Hubbard **(G-11948)**
Master-Halco Inc .... E 513 869-7600
　Fairfield **(G-10751)**
Metals USA Crbn Flat Rlled Inc .... D 937 882-6354
　Springfield **(G-17082)**
Metals USA Flat Rlled Cntl Inc .... E 618 451-4700
　Wooster **(G-19744)**
Miami Valley Steel Service Inc .... C 937 773-7127
　Piqua **(G-16014)**
Mid-America Steel Corp .... E 800 282-3466
　Cleveland **(G-5982)**
Mid-West Materials Inc .... E 440 259-5200
　Perry **(G-15826)**
Miller Consolidated Industries .... C 937 294-2681
　Moraine **(G-14678)**
Monarch Steel Company Inc .... E 216 587-8000
　Cleveland **(G-6007)**
New Technology Steel LLC .... E 419 385-0636
　Toledo **(G-17940)**
Northstar Alloys & Machine Co .... E 440 234-3069
　Berea **(G-1431)**
Ohio-Kentucky Steel Corp .... E 937 743-4600
　Franklin **(G-11035)**
Olympic Steel Inc .... D 216 292-3800
　Cleveland **(G-6129)**
Olympic Steel Inc .... D 216 292-3800
　Cleveland **(G-6130)**
Olympic Steel Inc .... E 440 287-0150
　Streetsboro **(G-17263)**
Olympic Steel Inc .... C 216 292-3800
　Bedford **(G-1298)**
Parker Steel International Inc .... E 419 473-2481
　Maumee **(G-13832)**
Phoenix Corporation .... E 513 727-4763
　Middletown **(G-14320)**
Phoenix Steel Service Inc .... E 216 332-0600
　Cleveland **(G-6206)**
Precesion Finning Bending Inc .... E 330 382-9351
　East Liverpool **(G-10416)**
Precision Steel Services Inc .... D 419 476-5702
　Toledo **(G-17984)**
Quality Steels Corp .... E 937 294-4133
　Moraine **(G-14690)**
Remelt Sources Incorporated .... E 216 289-4555
　Cleveland **(G-6303)**
Samuel Son & Co (usa) Inc .... D 419 470-7070
　Toledo **(G-18018)**
Scot Industries Inc .... E 330 262-7585
　Wooster **(G-19767)**
Scott Steel LLC .... E 937 552-9670
　Piqua **(G-16028)**
Select Steel Inc .... E 330 652-1756
　Niles **(G-15169)**
Specialty Steel Co Inc .... E 800 321-8500
　Cleveland **(G-6444)**
St Lawrence Holdings LLC .... E 330 562-9000
　Maple Heights **(G-13297)**
Stark Metal Sales Inc .... E 330 823-7383
　Alliance **(G-554)**

Steel Plate LLC .... E 888 894-8818
　Twinsburg **(G-18324)**
Steel Warehouse Cleveland LLC .... E 888 225-3760
　Cleveland **(G-6461)**
Steel Warehouse Company LLC .... E 216 206-2800
　Cleveland **(G-6462)**
Steel Warehouse of Ohio LLC .... D 888 225-3760
　Cleveland **(G-6463)**
Steelsummit Holdings Inc .... E 513 825-8550
　Cincinnati **(G-4542)**
Symcox Grinding & Steele Co .... E 330 678-1080
　Kent **(G-12261)**
Thomas Steel Strip Corporation .... B 330 841-6429
　Warren **(G-18751)**
Thyssenkrupp Materials NA Inc .... D 216 883-8100
　Independence **(G-12131)**
Tomson Steel Company .... E 513 420-8600
　Middletown **(G-14337)**
United Performance Metals Inc .... E 513 860-6500
　Hamilton **(G-11652)**
United Steel Service LLC .... C 330 448-4057
　Brookfield **(G-1857)**
Universal Steel Company .... D 216 883-4972
　Cleveland **(G-6583)**
Van Pelt Corporation .... E 513 242-6000
　Cincinnati **(G-4750)**
Waelzholz North America LLC .... E 216 267-5500
　Cleveland **(G-6649)**
Westfield Steel Inc .... E 937 322-2414
　Springfield **(G-17136)**
William Wood .... E 740 543-4052
　Bloomingdale **(G-1491)**

METALS SVC CENTERS & WHOLESALERS: Strip, Metal

Three D Metals Inc .... D 330 220-0451
　Valley City **(G-18470)**

METALS SVC CENTERS & WHOLESALERS: Tubing, Metal

Industrial Tube and Steel Corp .... E 330 474-5530
　Kent **(G-12237)**
Swagelok Company .... D 440 349-5934
　Solon **(G-16905)**

METALS SVC CNTRS & WHOL: Metal Wires, Ties, Cables/Screening

Tylinter Inc .... D 800 321-6188
　Mentor **(G-14117)**

METALS SVC CTRS & WHOLESALERS: Aluminum Bars, Rods, Etc

Gnw Aluminum Inc .... E 330 821-7955
　Alliance **(G-533)**
Metal Conversions Ltd .... E 419 525-0011
　Mansfield **(G-13219)**
Timken Corporation .... E 330 471-3378
　North Canton **(G-15239)**
Tri-State Aluminium .... E 419 666-0100
　Toledo **(G-18109)**

METALS: Primary Nonferrous, NEC

Aci Industries Ltd .... E 740 368-4160
　Delaware **(G-9948)**
Rhenium Alloys Inc .... D 440 365-7388
　North Ridgeville **(G-15340)**

METALWORK: Miscellaneous

Watteredge LLC .... D 440 933-6110
　Avon Lake **(G-929)**
Will-Burt Company .... E 330 682-7015
　Orrville **(G-15650)**
Will-Burt Company .... B 330 682-7015
　Orrville **(G-15649)**

METER READERS: Remote

Bermex Inc .... B 330 945-7500
　Stow **(G-17192)**
Guardian Water & Power Inc .... D 614 291-3141
　Columbus **(G-7703)**
Matvest Inc .... E 614 487-8720
　Columbus **(G-8040)**
US Bronco Services Inc .... E 513 829-9880
　Fairfield **(G-10797)**

MGMT CONSULTING SVCS: Matls, Incl Purch, Handle & Invntry

Global Cnsld Holdings Inc .... D 513 703-0965
　Mason **(G-13588)**
Lesaint Logistics LLC .... D 513 988-0101
　Trenton **(G-18188)**
Marketing Indus Solutions Corp .... E 513 703-0965
　Mason **(G-13614)**
Midwest Motor Supply Co .... C 800 233-1294
　Columbus **(G-8082)**
Top Echelon Contracting Inc .... B 330 454-3508
　Canton **(G-2514)**

MGT SVCS, FACIL SUPPT: Base Maint Or Provide Personnel

City of Xenia .... E 937 376-7260
　Xenia **(G-19894)**
County of Miami .... E 937 335-1314
　Troy **(G-18199)**
Greene County .... E 937 562-7800
　Xenia **(G-19905)**
Henry Call Inc .... C 216 433-5609
　Cleveland **(G-5684)**

MICROFILM EQPT WHOLESALERS

Schenker Inc .... D 614 257-8365
　Lockbourne **(G-12824)**

MICROFILM SVCS

High Line Corporation .... E 330 848-8800
　Akron **(G-261)**

MILITARY INSIGNIA

Gayston Corporation .... C 937 743-6050
　Miamisburg **(G-14173)**

MILK, FLUID: Wholesalers

Austintown Dairy Inc .... E 330 629-6170
　Youngstown **(G-19959)**

MILLING: Cereal Flour, Exc Rice

Mennel Milling Company .... D 740 385-6824
　Logan **(G-12850)**
Mennel Milling Company .... E 740 385-6824
　Logan **(G-12849)**

MILLWORK

Carter-Jones Lumber Company .... C 330 674-9060
　Millersburg **(G-14463)**
Door Fabrication Services Inc .... E 937 454-9207
　Vandalia **(G-18520)**
Dublin Millwork Co Inc .... E 614 889-7776
　Dublin **(G-10211)**
Holmes Lumber & Bldg Ctr Inc .... C 330 674-9060
　Millersburg **(G-14475)**
Judy Mills Company Inc .... E 513 271-4241
　Cincinnati **(G-3841)**
Riverside Cnstr Svcs Inc .... E 513 723-0900
　Cincinnati **(G-4380)**
Stephen M Trudick .... E 440 834-1891
　Burton **(G-2019)**

MINE & QUARRY SVCS: Nonmetallic Minerals

M G Q Inc .... E 419 992-4236
　Tiffin **(G-17522)**

MINERALS: Ground or Treated

Acme Company .... D 330 758-2313
　Poland **(G-16079)**
Edw C Levy Co .... E 419 822-8286
　Delta **(G-10042)**
EMD Millipore Corporation .... C 513 631-0445
　Norwood **(G-15462)**
Pioneer Sands LLC .... E 740 659-2241
　Glenford **(G-11308)**
Pioneer Sands LLC .... E 740 599-7773
　Howard **(G-11940)**

MINIATURE GOLF COURSES

Goofy Golf II Inc .... D 419 732-6671
　Port Clinton **(G-16107)**

Recreational Golf Inc ....E 513 677-0347
Loveland *(G-13024)*

Stonehedge Enterprises Inc ....E 330 928-2161
Akron *(G-442)*

Three D Golf LLC ....E 513 732-0295
Batavia *(G-1011)*

MINING MACHINES & EQPT: Crushers, Stationary

Grasan Equipment Company Inc ....D 419 526-4440
Mansfield *(G-13180)*

MISC FINAN INVEST ACTIVITY: Mutual Fund, Ind Salesperson

Ameriprise Financial Svcs Inc ....D 614 846-8723
Worthington *(G-19793)*

Axa Advisors LLC ....C 614 985-3015
Columbus *(G-7007)*

Nationwide Fin Inst Dis Agency ....D 614 249-6825
Columbus *(G-8154)*

Ultimus Fund Solutions LLC..................E 513 587-3400
Cincinnati *(G-4672)*

MIXTURES & BLOCKS: Asphalt Paving

Barrett Paving Materials Inc...................C 513 271-6200
Middletown *(G-14343)*

Hy-Grade Corporation ....E 216 341-7711
Cleveland *(G-5728)*

Image Pavement Maintenance.................E 937 833-9200
Brookville *(G-1914)*

Mplx Terminals LLC ....B 330 479-5539
Canton *(G-2409)*

Shelly and Sands Inc ....D 740 859-2104
Rayland *(G-16273)*

Sidwell Materials Inc.............................C 740 849-2394
Zanesville *(G-20361)*

Smalls Asphalt Paving Inc ....E 740 427-4096
Gambier *(G-11227)*

Stoneco Inc..E 419 393-2555
Oakwood *(G-15484)*

MOBILE HOME REPAIR SVCS

Sirpilla Recrtl Vhcl Ctr Inc.....................D 330 494-2525
Akron *(G-430)*

MOBILE HOMES, EXC RECREATIONAL

Manufactured Housing Entps Inc..........C 419 636-4511
Bryan *(G-1963)*

MODELS

Morris Technologies Inc.........................C 513 733-1611
Cincinnati *(G-4075)*

MODELS: General, Exc Toy

3-D Technical Services Company..........E 937 746-2901
Franklin *(G-11020)*

MOLDED RUBBER PRDTS

Datwyler Sling Sltions USA Inc ....D 937 387-2800
Vandalia *(G-18519)*

Jet Rubber Company ....E 330 325-1821
Rootstown *(G-16450)*

MOLDING COMPOUNDS

Flex Technologies Inc ....E 330 897-6311
Baltic *(G-934)*

MOLDS: Indl

Akron Centl Engrv Mold Mch Inc...........E 330 794-8704
Akron *(G-30)*

MOLDS: Plastic Working & Foundry

Eger Products Inc ....D 513 753-4200
Amelia *(G-572)*

Prospect Mold & Die Company...............D 330 929-3311
Cuyahoga Falls *(G-9119)*

MONEY ORDER ISSUANCE SVCS

Sack n Save Inc ....E 740 382-2464
Marion *(G-13458)*

MONTESSORI CHILD DEVELOPMENT CENTER

All Around Children Montessori ....E 330 928-1444
Stow *(G-17190)*

Bay Village Montessori Inc ....E 440 871-8773
Westlake *(G-19321)*

Canton Montessori Association ....E 330 452-0148
Canton *(G-2238)*

Creative Playroom ....D 216 475-6464
Cleveland *(G-5376)*

Creative Playroom ....E 440 248-3100
Solon *(G-16840)*

Fairmount Montessori Assn ....E 216 321-7571
Cleveland *(G-5505)*

Lillian and Betty Ratner Schl ....E 216 464-0033
Cleveland *(G-5870)*

Montessori High School Assn ....E 216 421-3033
Cleveland *(G-6008)*

Nightingale Montessori Inc ....E 937 324-0336
Springfield *(G-17089)*

Ruffing Montessori School ....E 440 333-2250
Rocky River *(G-16445)*

West Side Montessori..............................E 419 866-1931
Toledo *(G-18154)*

Westlake Mntsr Schl & Chld Dv.............E 440 835-5858
Westlake *(G-19425)*

MOPS: Floor & Dust

Impact Products LLC ....C 419 841-2891
Toledo *(G-17818)*

MORTGAGE BANKERS

American Midwest Mortgage Corp.......E 440 882-5210
Cleveland *(G-4958)*

Broadview Mortgage Company ....D 614 854-7000
Powell *(G-16187)*

Chase Manhattan Mortgage Corp.........C 614 422-7982
Columbus *(G-7180)*

Fairway Independent Mrtg Corp ....D 513 367-6344
Harrison *(G-11667)*

First Union Banc Corp ....E 330 896-1222
Uniontown *(G-18371)*

Firstmerit Mortgage Corp......................D 330 478-3400
Canton *(G-2314)*

Hallmark Home Mortgage LLC..............E 614 568-1960
Columbus *(G-7711)*

Huntington National Bank ....C 513 762-1860
Cincinnati *(G-3742)*

Huntington National Bank ....D 740 773-2681
Chillicothe *(G-2792)*

Huntington National Bank ....E 419 226-8200
Lima *(G-12662)*

Jpmorgan Chase Bank Nat Assn ....A 614 436-3055
Columbus *(G-6818)*

Lancaster Pollard Mrtg Co LLC ....D 614 224-8800
Columbus *(G-7947)*

Liberty Capital Services LLC ....E 614 505-0620
Worthington *(G-19824)*

Mortgage Now Inc ....E 800 245-1050
Cleveland *(G-6013)*

Nations Lending Corporation ....D 440 842-4817
Independence *(G-12102)*

Nationstar Mortgage LLC ....D 614 985-9500
Columbus *(G-8142)*

Nfgm Inc ....D 800 236-2600
Dublin *(G-10290)*

Northern Ohio Investment Co ....D 419 885-8300
Sylvania *(G-17438)*

Old Rpblic Ttle Nthrn Ohio LLC.............B 216 524-5700
Independence *(G-12106)*

Primero Home Loans LLC.......................D 877 959-2921
Dublin *(G-10312)*

Quicken Loans Inc ....E 216 586-8900
Cleveland *(G-6270)*

Security Savings Mortgage Corp ....D 330 455-2833
Canton *(G-2472)*

Sibcy Cline Inc ....D 513 777-8100
West Chester *(G-19005)*

Sirva Mortgage Inc ....D 800 531-3837
Independence *(G-12121)*

Union Home Mortgage Corp ....E 440 234-4300
Strongsville *(G-17353)*

MORTGAGE COMPANIES: Urban

G & G Investment LLC............................D 513 984-0300
Blue Ash *(G-1566)*

MOTEL

1st Stop Inc ....E 937 695-0318
Winchester *(G-19658)*

Alsan Corporation ....D 330 385-3636
East Liverpool *(G-10396)*

Commodore Resorts Inc ....E 419 285-3101
Port Clinton *(G-16103)*

Detroit Westfield LLC ....D 330 666-4131
Akron *(G-184)*

East End Ro Burton Inc ....E 440 942-2742
Willoughby *(G-19519)*

Econo Lodge ....D 419 627-8000
Sandusky *(G-16597)*

Elbe Properties ....A 513 489-1955
Cincinnati *(G-3485)*

He Hari Inc ....D 614 436-0700
Worthington *(G-19812)*

Motel 6 Operating LP ....E 614 431-2525
Columbus *(G-8104)*

Motel Investments Marietta Inc ....E 740 374-8190
Marietta *(G-13362)*

R P L Corporation...................................C 937 335-0021
Troy *(G-18223)*

South Beach Resort ....E 419 798-4900
Lakeside Marblehead *(G-12331)*

Westlake Marriott ....E 440 892-6887
Westlake *(G-19424)*

MOTION PICTURE & VIDEO DISTRIBUTION

Nunn Productions LLC ....E 614 695-5350
Columbus *(G-8216)*

Technicolor Thomson Group ....C 937 383-6000
Wilmington *(G-19651)*

Zebo Productions ....D 937 339-0397
Troy *(G-18240)*

MOTION PICTURE & VIDEO PRODUCTION SVCS

Fastball Spt Productions LLC.................E 440 746-8000
Cleveland *(G-5516)*

Province of St John The Baptis ....D 513 241-5615
Cincinnati *(G-4301)*

Shalom Ministries Intl Inc......................E 614 504-6052
Plain City *(G-16065)*

MOTION PICTURE DISTRIBUTION SVCS

Technicolor Thomson Group ....C 937 383-6000
Wilmington *(G-19651)*

MOTION PICTURE PRODUCTION & DISTRIBUTION

Mills/James Inc......................................C 614 777-9933
Hilliard *(G-11800)*

MOTION PICTURE PRODUCTION & DISTRIBUTION: Television

Estreamz Inc..E 513 278-7836
Cincinnati *(G-3516)*

Fox Television Stations Inc....................C 216 431-8888
Cleveland *(G-5568)*

MOTION PICTURE PRODUCTION ALLIED SVCS

Mills/James Inc......................................C 614 777-9933
Hilliard *(G-11800)*

Signal Productions Inc ....E 323 382-0000
Cleveland *(G-6409)*

University of Dayton ....C 937 229-5432
Dayton *(G-9838)*

MOTOR INN

Dino Persichetti....................................E 330 821-9600
Alliance *(G-530)*

MOTOR SCOOTERS & PARTS

Dco LLC..B 419 931-9086
Perrysburg *(G-15857)*

MOTOR VEHICLE ASSEMBLY, COMPLETE: Autos, Incl Specialty

Brookville Roadster Inc ....E 937 833-4605
Brookville *(G-1912)*

Employee Codes: A=Over 500 employees, B=251-500
C=101-250, D=51-100, E=25-50   2019 Harris Ohio
Services Directory   1495

SERVICES

P C Workshop Inc ....D...... 419 399-4805
Paulding (G-15795)
Weastec Incorporated ....E...... 614 734-9645
Dublin (G-10371)

MOTOR VEHICLE ASSEMBLY, COMPLETE: Fire Department Vehicles

Sutphen Corporation ....C...... 800 726-7030
Dublin (G-10347)

MOTOR VEHICLE DEALERS: Automobiles, New & Used

1106 West Main Inc ....E...... 330 673-2122
Kent (G-12212)
Advantage Ford Lincoln Mercury ....E...... 419 334-9751
Fremont (G-11056)
Affordable Cars & Finance Inc ....E...... 440 777-2424
North Olmsted (G-15277)
Aladdins Enterprises Inc ....E...... 614 891-3440
Westerville (G-19218)
Allstate Trk Sls of Estrn OH ....E...... 330 339-5555
New Philadelphia (G-14945)
Arch Abraham Susuki Ltd ....E...... 440 934-6001
Elyria (G-10479)
Auto Center USA Inc ....E...... 513 683-4900
Cincinnati (G-3006)
Bauman Chrysler Jeep Dodge ....E...... 419 332-8291
Fremont (G-11059)
Beechmont Ford Inc ....C...... 513 752-6611
Cincinnati (G-2842)
Beechmont Motors Inc ....E...... 513 388-3883
Cincinnati (G-3031)
Beechmont Toyota Inc ....D...... 513 388-3800
Cincinnati (G-3034)
Bill Delord Autocenter Inc ....D...... 513 932-3000
Lebanon (G-12452)
Bob Pulte Chevrolet Inc ....E...... 513 932-0303
Lebanon (G-12453)
Bob-Boyd Ford Inc ....D...... 614 860-0606
Lancaster (G-12372)
Bobb Automotive Inc ....E...... 614 853-3000
Columbus (G-7052)
Bobby Layman Cadillac GMC Inc ....E...... 740 654-9590
Carroll (G-2556)
Bowling Green Lncln-Mrcury Inc ....E...... 419 352-2553
Bowling Green (G-1722)
Brentlinger Enterprises ....C...... 614 889-2571
Dublin (G-10150)
Broadvue Motors Inc ....D...... 440 845-6000
Cleveland (G-5084)
Brondes Ford ....D...... 419 473-1411
Toledo (G-17627)
Busam Fairfield LLC ....E...... 513 771-8100
Fairfield (G-10702)
Cain Motors Inc ....E...... 330 494-5588
Canton (G-2225)
Carcorp Inc ....C...... 877 857-2801
Columbus (G-7118)
Cascade Group Inc ....E...... 330 929-1861
Cuyahoga Falls (G-9077)
Central Cadillac Limited ....D...... 216 861-5800
Cleveland (G-5153)
Chesrown Oldsmobile Cadillac ....E...... 740 366-7373
Granville (G-11337)
Chesrown Oldsmobile GMC Inc ....E...... 614 846-3040
Columbus (G-7182)
Chuck Nicholson Pntc-GMC Trcks ....E...... 330 343-7781
Dover (G-10069)
Classic Buick Olds Cadillac ....D...... 440 639-4500
Painesville (G-15701)
Classic International Inc ....D...... 440 975-1222
Mentor (G-14030)
Cole-Valley Motor Co ....D...... 330 372-1665
Warren (G-18685)
Columbus SAI Motors LLC ....E...... 614 851-3273
Columbus (G-7312)
Coughlin Chevrolet Inc ....E...... 740 852-1122
London (G-12862)
Coughlin Chevrolet Inc ....D...... 740 964-9191
Pataskala (G-15784)
Coughlin Chevrolet Toyota Inc ....D...... 740 366-1381
Newark (G-15028)
Crestmont Cadillac Corporation ....E...... 216 831-5300
Cleveland (G-5380)
Cronins Inc ....E...... 513 851-5900
Cincinnati (G-3380)
Dan Tobin Pontiac Buick GMC ....D...... 614 889-6300
Columbus (G-7412)

Dave Dnnis Chrysler Jeep Dodge ....D...... 937 429-5566
Beavercreek Township (G-1245)
Dave Knapp Ford Lincoln Inc ....E...... 937 547-3000
Greenville (G-11373)
Dave White Chevrolet Inc ....C...... 419 885-4444
Sylvania (G-17417)
Decosky Motor Holdings Inc ....E...... 740 397-9122
Mount Vernon (G-14762)
Diane Sauer Chevrolet Inc ....D...... 330 373-1600
Warren (G-18702)
Don Wood Inc ....D...... 740 593-6641
Athens (G-776)
Don Wood Inc ....D...... 740 593-6641
Athens (G-777)
Donley Ford-Lincoln Inc ....E...... 419 281-3673
Ashland (G-672)
Donnell Ford-Lincoln ....E...... 330 332-0031
Salem (G-16542)
Dons Automotive Group LLC ....E...... 419 337-3010
Wauseon (G-18799)
Dons Brooklyn Chevrolet Inc ....E...... 216 741-1500
Cleveland (G-5441)
Doug Bigelow Chevrolet Inc ....D...... 330 644-7500
Akron (G-192)
Doug Marine Motors Inc ....E...... 740 335-3700
Wshngtn CT Hs (G-19869)
Downtheroad Inc ....E...... 740 452-4579
Zanesville (G-20300)
Downtown Ford Lincoln Inc ....D...... 330 456-2781
Canton (G-2290)
Dunning Motor Sales Inc ....E...... 740 439-4465
Cambridge (G-2064)
Dutro Ford Lincoln-Mercury Inc ....D...... 740 452-6334
Zanesville (G-20301)
Ed Mullinax Ford LLC ....C...... 440 984-2431
Amherst (G-584)
Ed Schmidt Auto Inc ....C...... 419 874-4331
Perrysburg (G-15863)
Ed Schmidt Chevrolet Inc ....D...... 419 897-8600
Maumee (G-13783)
Ed Tomko Chryslr Jep Dge Inc ....E...... 440 835-5900
Avon Lake (G-616)
Falls Motor City Inc ....E...... 330 929-3066
Cuyahoga Falls (G-9091)
Family Ford Lincoln Inc ....D...... 740 373-9127
Marietta (G-13328)
Fred Martin Nissan LLC ....E...... 330 644-8888
Akron (G-228)
Gene Stevens Auto & Truck Ctr ....E...... 419 429-2000
Findlay (G-10913)
George P Ballas Buick GMC Trck ....D...... 419 535-1000
Toledo (G-17760)
Germain Ford LLC ....C...... 614 889-7777
Columbus (G-7664)
Germain On Scarborough LLC ....C...... 614 868-0300
Columbus (G-7665)
Graham Chevrolet-Cadillac Co ....D...... 419 989-4012
Ontario (G-15551)
Greenwood Chevrolet Inc ....C...... 330 270-1299
Youngstown (G-20057)
Greenwoods Hubbard Chevy-Olds ....E...... 330 568-4335
Hubbard (G-11946)
Greg Ford Sweet Inc ....E...... 440 593-7714
North Kingsville (G-15257)
Grogans Towne Chrysler Inc ....D...... 419 476-0761
Toledo (G-17772)
Guess Motors Inc ....E...... 866 890-0522
Carrollton (G-2571)
Haydocy Automotive Inc ....D...... 614 279-8880
Columbus (G-7719)
Herrnstein Chrysler Inc ....D...... 740 773-2203
Chillicothe (G-2786)
Hidy Motors Inc ....E...... 937 426-9564
Dayton (G-9176)
Hoss II Inc ....E...... 937 669-4300
Tipp City (G-17560)
Hoss Value Cars & Trucks Inc ....E...... 937 428-2400
Dayton (G-9507)
I-75 Pierson Automotive Inc ....E...... 513 424-1881
Middletown (G-14350)
Jerry Haag Motors Inc ....E...... 937 402-2090
Hillsboro (G-11848)
Jim Brown Chevrolet Inc ....C...... 440 255-5511
Mentor (G-14065)
Jim Keim Ford ....D...... 614 888-3333
Columbus (G-7859)
Joe Dodge Kidd Inc ....E...... 513 752-1804
Cincinnati (G-2858)
Joseph Chevrolet Oldsmobile Co ....C...... 513 741-6700
Cincinnati (G-3833)

Joyce Buick Inc ....E...... 419 529-3211
Ontario (G-15557)
Kempthorn Motors Inc ....C...... 800 451-3877
Canton (G-2365)
Kent Automotive Inc ....E...... 330 678-5520
Kent (G-12240)
Kerns Chevrolet-Buick-Gmc Inc ....E...... 419 586-5131
Celina (G-2597)
Kerry Ford Inc ....D...... 513 671-6400
Cincinnati (G-3864)
Kings Cove Automotive LLC ....D...... 513 677-0177
Fairfield (G-10744)
Kings Toyota Inc ....D...... 513 583-4333
Cincinnati (G-3874)
Klaben Family Dodge Inc ....D...... 330 673-9971
Kent (G-12244)
Klaben Lincoln Ford Inc ....D...... 330 673-3139
Kent (G-12246)
Knox Auto LLC ....E...... 330 701-5266
Mount Vernon (G-14771)
Krieger Ford Inc ....C...... 614 888-3320
Columbus (G-7927)
Lakewood Chrysler-Plymouth ....E...... 216 521-1000
Brookpark (G-1901)
Lane Chevrolet ....D...... 937 426-2313
Beavercreek Township (G-1252)
Lang Chevrolet Co ....D...... 937 426-2313
Beavercreek Township (G-1253)
Laria Chevrolet-Buick Inc ....E...... 330 925-2015
Rittman (G-16406)
Lariche Subaru Inc ....D...... 419 422-1855
Findlay (G-10933)
Lavery Chevrolet-Buick Inc ....E...... 330 823-1100
Alliance (G-537)
Lebanon Chrysler - Plymouth Inc ....E...... 513 932-2717
Lebanon (G-12480)
Leikin Motor Companies Inc ....D...... 440 946-6900
Willoughby (G-19544)
Liberty Ford Southwest Inc ....D...... 440 888-2600
Cleveland (G-5867)
Lima Auto Mall Inc ....D...... 419 993-6000
Lima (G-12675)
Lincoln Mrcury Kings Auto Mall ....C...... 513 683-3800
Cincinnati (G-3933)
Lindsey Accura Inc ....E...... 800 980-8199
Columbus (G-7981)
Man-Tansky Inc ....E...... 740 454-2512
Zanesville (G-20328)
Mark Thomas Ford Inc ....E...... 330 638-1010
Cortland (G-8989)
Martin Chevrolet Inc ....E...... 937 849-1381
Dayton (G-9587)
Mathews Dodge Chrysler Jeep ....E...... 740 389-2341
Marion (G-13444)
Mathews Ford Inc ....D...... 740 522-2181
Newark (G-15066)
Mathews Kennedy Ford L-M Inc ....D...... 740 387-3673
Marion (G-13445)
Matia Motors Inc ....E...... 440 365-7311
Elyria (G-10534)
Mc Daniel Motor Co (Inc) ....E...... 740 389-2355
Marion (G-13446)
McCluskey Chevrolet Inc ....E...... 513 761-1111
Cincinnati (G-3986)
Medina World Cars Inc ....E...... 330 725-4901
Strongsville (G-17332)
Merrick Body Shop ....E...... 440 243-6700
Berea (G-1430)
Merrick Chevrolet Co ....D...... 440 878-6700
Strongsville (G-17333)
Mike Castrucci Ford ....C...... 513 831-7010
Milford (G-14410)
Montrose Ford Inc ....D...... 330 666-0711
Fairlawn (G-10842)
Montrose Sheffield LLC ....E...... 440 934-6699
Sheffield Village (G-16740)
Morris Cadillac Buick GMC ....D...... 440 327-4181
North Olmsted (G-15298)
Mullinax East LLC ....D...... 440 296-3020
Wickliffe (G-19470)
Mullinax Ford North Canton Inc ....C...... 330 238-3206
Canton (G-2411)
Nassief Automotive Inc ....E...... 440 997-5151
Austinburg (G-853)
Nick Mayer Lincoln-Mercury Inc ....E...... 440 835-3700
Westlake (G-19379)
Northern Automotive Inc ....E...... 614 436-2001
Columbus (G-8200)
Northgate Chrysler Jeep Inc ....D...... 513 385-3900
Cincinnati (G-4129)

2019 Harris Ohio
Services Directory

(G-0000) Company's Geographic Section entry number

Oregon Ford Inc ....C 419 698-4444
  Oregon (G-15605)
Partners Auto Group Bdford Inc ....D 440 439-2323
  Bedford (G-1299)
Paul Hrnchar Ford-Mercury Inc ....E 330 533-3673
  Canfield (G-2155)
Pete Baur Buick Gmc Inc ....E 440 238-5600
  Cleveland (G-6200)
Progrssive Oldsmobile Cadillac ....E 330 833-8585
  Massillon (G-13721)
Ricart Ford Inc ....B 614 836-5321
  Groveport (G-11535)
Ron Marhofer Automall Inc ....B 330 835-6707
  Cuyahoga Falls (G-9121)
Ron Marhofer Automall Inc ....E 330 923-5059
  Cuyahoga Falls (G-9122)
Rouen Chrysler Plymouth Dodge ....E 419 837-6228
  Woodville (G-19683)
Roush Equipment Inc ....C 614 882-1535
  Westerville (G-19300)
Rush Motor Sales Inc ....E 614 471-9980
  Columbus (G-8561)
Saturn of Toledo Inc ....E 419 841-9070
  Toledo (G-18020)
Schoner Chevrolet Inc ....E 330 877-6731
  Hartville (G-11698)
Sharpnack Chvrlet Bick Cdillac ....D 419 935-0194
  Willard (G-19487)
Sims Buick-G M C Truck Inc ....D 330 372-3500
  Warren (G-18744)
Slimans Sales & Service Inc ....E 440 988-4484
  Amherst (G-597)
Sonic Automotive ....D 614 870-8200
  Columbus (G-8658)
Sonic Automotive-1495 Automall ....E 614 317-4326
  Columbus (G-8659)
Sorbir Inc ....D 440 449-1000
  Cleveland (G-6421)
South East Chevrolet Co ....E 440 585-9300
  Willoughby Hills (G-19594)
Spires Motors Inc. ....E 614 771-2345
  Hilliard (G-11817)
Spitzer Auto World Amherst ....D 440 988-4444
  Amherst (G-598)
Spitzer Chevrolet Company ....E 330 966-9524
  Canton (G-2482)
Spitzer Chevrolet Inc ....D 330 467-4141
  Northfield (G-15386)
Stoddard Imported Cars Inc. ....D 440 951-1040
  Mentor (G-14112)
Stratton Chevrolet Co ....E 330 537-3151
  Beloit (G-1398)
Stykemain Pntiac-Buick-Gmc Ltd ....D 419 784-5252
  Defiance (G-9942)
Sunnyside Toyota Inc ....D 440 777-9911
  North Olmsted (G-15312)
Surfside Motors Inc ....E 419 462-1746
  Galion (G-11183)
Tansky Motors Inc. ....E 650 322-7069
  Logan (G-12855)
Taylor Chevrolet Inc. ....C 740 653-2091
  Lancaster (G-12440)
Tbn Acquisition LLC ....D 740 653-2091
  Lancaster (G-12441)
Team Rahal of Dayton Inc ....E 937 438-3800
  Dayton (G-9807)
Tom Ahl Chryslr-Plymouth-Dodge ....C 419 227-0202
  Lima (G-12765)
Toyota of Bedford ....D 440 439-8600
  Bedford (G-1310)
Trader Buds Westside Dodge ....D 614 272-0000
  Columbus (G-8770)
Transitworks LLC ....D 330 861-1118
  Richfield (G-16381)
Transmerica Svcs Technical Sup ....E 740 282-3695
  Steubenville (G-17175)
Valentine Buick Gmc Inc ....D 937 878-7371
  Fairborn (G-10686)
Valley Ford Truck Inc ....D 216 524-2400
  Cleveland (G-6617)
Van Devere Inc ....D 330 253-6137
  Akron (G-485)
Village Motors Inc ....D 330 674-2055
  Millersburg (G-14498)
Vin Devers ....C 888 847-9535
  Sylvania (G-17462)
Volvo BMW Dyton Evans Volkswag ....E 937 890-6200
  Dayton (G-9859)
Voss Auto Network Inc ....E 937 428-2447
  Dayton (G-9860)

Voss Chevrolet Inc ....C 937 428-2500
  Dayton (G-9862)
Voss Dodge ....E 937 435-7800
  Dayton (G-9863)
Voss Toyota Inc ....E 937 431-2100
  Beavercreek (G-1195)
Wagner Lincoln-Mercury Inc ....E 419 435-8131
  Carey (G-2550)
Walker Auto Group Inc ....D 937 433-4950
  Miamisburg (G-14236)
Warner Buick-Nissan Inc ....E 419 423-7161
  Findlay (G-10974)
White Family Companies Inc ....C 937 222-3701
  Dayton (G-9879)
Whites Service Center Inc ....E 937 653-5279
  Urbana (G-18446)
Yark Automotive Group Inc ....A 419 841-7771
  Toledo (G-18166)
Young Truck Sales Inc ....E 330 477-6271
  Canton (G-2541)
Zanesville Chevrolet Cadillac ....E 740 452-3611
  Zanesville (G-20381)

MOTOR VEHICLE DEALERS: Cars, Used Only

Afford-A-Car Inc ....E 937 235-2700
  Tipp City (G-17548)
Albert Mike Leasing Inc ....C 513 563-1400
  Cincinnati (G-2919)
Brims Imports ....E 419 674-4137
  Kenton (G-12272)
Coughlin Chevrolet Inc. ....E 740 852-1122
  London (G-12862)
Hertz Corporation ....E 937 890-2721
  Vandalia (G-18526)
Kenton Auto and Truck Wrecking ....E 419 673-8234
  Kenton (G-12283)
May Jim Auto Sales LLC ....E 419 422-9797
  Findlay (G-10940)
Merrick Body Shop ....E 440 243-6700
  Berea (G-1430)
Midwest Motors Inc. ....E 330 758-5800
  Youngstown (G-20128)
Montpelier Auto Auction Ohio ....C 419 485-1691
  Montpelier (G-14614)
Stricker Bros Inc ....E 513 732-1152
  Batavia (G-1010)
Volunteers America Ohio & Ind ....C 614 253-6100
  Columbus (G-8859)
Voss Auto Network Inc ....B 937 433-1444
  Dayton (G-9861)

MOTOR VEHICLE DEALERS: Pickups & Vans, Used

Life Star Rescue Inc ....E 419 238-2507
  Van Wert (G-18482)

MOTOR VEHICLE DEALERS: Pickups, New & Used

Palmer Trucks Inc ....E 937 235-3318
  Dayton (G-9683)

MOTOR VEHICLE DEALERS: Trucks, Tractors/Trailers, New & Used

Abers Garage Inc ....E 419 281-5500
  Ashland (G-644)
Allied Truck Parts Co ....E 330 477-8127
  Canton (G-2181)
Benedict Enterprises Inc ....E 513 539-9216
  Monroe (G-14563)
Fallsway Equipment Co Inc ....C 330 633-6000
  Akron (G-209)
Freightliner Trcks of Cncinnati ....E 513 772-7171
  Cincinnati (G-3591)
Hans Truck and Trlr Repr Inc ....E 216 581-0046
  Cleveland (G-5660)
Hill Intl Trcks NA LLC ....D 330 386-6440
  East Liverpool (G-10404)
Mansfield Truck Sls & Svc Inc ....E 419 522-9811
  Mansfield (G-13211)
Mizar Motors Inc. ....D 419 729-2400
  Toledo (G-17919)
R & R Inc ....E 330 799-1536
  Youngstown (G-20174)
R & R Truck Sales Inc ....E 330 784-5881
  Akron (G-395)

Rumpke/Kenworth Contract ....D 740 774-5111
  Chillicothe (G-2824)
Steubenville Truck Center Inc. ....E 740 282-2711
  Steubenville (G-17173)
Stoops Frghtlnr-Qlity Trlr Inc ....E 937 236-4092
  Dayton (G-9795)
Stoops of Lima Inc ....C 419 228-4334
  Lima (G-12757)
Truck Country Indiana Inc ....C 419 228-4334
  Lima (G-12770)

MOTOR VEHICLE PARTS & ACCESS: Body Components & Frames

Frontier Tank Center Inc ....E 330 659-3888
  Richfield (G-16358)

MOTOR VEHICLE PARTS & ACCESS: Booster Cables, Jump-Start

Noco Company ....B 216 464-8131
  Solon (G-16879)

MOTOR VEHICLE PARTS & ACCESS: Clutches

Westfield Steel Inc ....D 937 322-2414
  Springfield (G-17136)

MOTOR VEHICLE PARTS & ACCESS: Engines & Parts

Fram Group Operations LLC ....D 419 661-6700
  Perrysburg (G-15867)
Hite Parts Exchange Inc ....E 614 272-5115
  Columbus (G-7756)
Keihin Thermal Tech Amer Inc ....B 740 869-3000
  Mount Sterling (G-14745)

MOTOR VEHICLE PARTS & ACCESS: Fuel Systems & Parts

Interstate Diesel Service Inc ....B 216 881-0015
  Cleveland (G-5765)

MOTOR VEHICLE PARTS & ACCESS: Mufflers, Exhaust

Faurecia Emissions Control Sys ....C 812 341-2000
  Toledo (G-17727)

MOTOR VEHICLE PARTS & ACCESS: Power Steering Eqpt

Maval Industries LLC ....C 330 405-1600
  Twinsburg (G-18296)

MOTOR VEHICLE PARTS & ACCESS: Pumps, Hydraulic Fluid Power

Eaton Corporation ....B 216 523-5000
  Beachwood (G-1054)
Eaton Corporation ....B 216 920-2000
  Cleveland (G-5462)

MOTOR VEHICLE PARTS & ACCESS: Wiring Harness Sets

G S Wiring Systems Inc ....B 419 423-7111
  Findlay (G-10911)
Sumitomo Elc Wirg Systems Inc ....E 937 642-7579
  Marysville (G-13531)

MOTOR VEHICLE RACING & DRIVER SVCS

Brush Creek Motorsports ....E 937 515-1353
  West Union (G-19133)
Team Rahal Inc ....D 614 529-7000
  Hilliard (G-11820)

MOTOR VEHICLE SPLYS & PARTS WHOLESALERS: New

Ace Truck Body Inc ....E 614 871-3100
  Grove City (G-11403)
Beechmont Ford Inc ....C 513 752-6611
  Cincinnati (G-2842)
Beechmont Motors Inc ....E 513 388-3883
  Cincinnati (G-3031)

Beechmont Toyota Inc ....D 513 388-3800
Cincinnati (G-3034)

Faurecia Emissions Control Sys ....C 812 341-2000
Toledo (G-17727)

G S Wiring Systems Inc ....B 419 423-7111
Findlay (G-10911)

General Motors LLC ....C 513 874-0535
West Chester (G-18931)

General Motors LLC ....C 513 603-6600
West Chester (G-18932)

Goodyear Tire & Rubber Company ....A 330 796-2121
Akron (G-242)

Jr Engineering Inc ....C 330 848-0960
Barberton (G-957)

Lower Great Lakes Kenworth Inc ....E 419 874-3511
Perrysburg (G-15890)

Luk-Aftermarket Service Inc ....D 330 273-4383
Valley City (G-18466)

Mac Trailer Manufacturing Inc ....C 330 823-9900
Alliance (G-540)

Neff Machinery and Supplies ....E 740 454-0128
Zanesville (G-20344)

Nk Parts Industries Inc ....E 937 493-4651
Sidney (G-16787)

Pat Young Service Co Inc ....E 440 891-1550
Avon (G-899)

Pioneer Automotive Tech Inc ....C 937 746-2293
Springboro (G-16982)

Shrader Tire & Oil Inc ....E 419 472-2128
Toledo (G-18032)

Tk Holdings Inc ....E 937 778-9713
Piqua (G-16031)

Truckomat Corporation ....E 740 467-2818
Hebron (G-11725)

Western Tradewinds Inc ....E 937 859-4300
Miamisburg (G-14238)

MOTOR VEHICLE SPLYS & PARTS WHOLESALERS: Used

Beheydts Auto Wrecking ....E 330 658-6109
Doylestown (G-10108)

Dales Truck Parts Inc ....E 937 766-2551
Cedarville (G-2580)

General Motors LLC ....C 513 603-6600
West Chester (G-18932)

Mac Trailer Manufacturing Inc ....C 330 823-9900
Alliance (G-540)

Nk Parts Industries Inc ....E 937 493-4651
Sidney (G-16787)

MOTOR VEHICLE: Shock Absorbers

Thyssenkrupp Bilstein Amer Inc ....C 513 881-7600
Hamilton (G-11647)

MOTOR VEHICLES & CAR BODIES

Bobbart Industries Inc ....E 419 350-5477
Sylvania (G-17412)

Comprehensive Logistics Co Inc ....E 330 793-0504
Youngstown (G-20007)

Honda of America Mfg Inc ....C 937 644-0724
Marysville (G-13505)

MOTOR VEHICLES, WHOLESALE: Ambulances

Life Star Rescue Inc ....E 419 238-2507
Van Wert (G-18482)

MOTOR VEHICLES, WHOLESALE: Commercial

Interstate Truckway Inc ....D 513 542-5500
Cincinnati (G-3781)

Sharron Group Inc ....E 614 873-5856
Plain City (G-16066)

MOTOR VEHICLES, WHOLESALE: Trailers, Truck, New & Used

Bulk Carrier Trnsp Eqp Co ....E 330 339-3333
New Philadelphia (G-14947)

Great Dane Columbus Inc ....E 614 876-0666
Hilliard (G-11770)

M H EBY Inc ....E 614 879-6901
West Jefferson (G-19110)

Mac Manufacturing Inc ....A 330 823-9900
Alliance (G-539)

Mac Manufacturing Inc ....C 330 829-1680
Salem (G-16552)

Mac Trailer Manufacturing Inc ....C 330 823-9900
Alliance (G-540)

MOTOR VEHICLES, WHOLESALE: Truck bodies

Ace Truck Body Inc ....E 614 871-3100
Grove City (G-11403)

Brown Industrial Inc ....E 937 693-3838
Botkins (G-1708)

Buckeye Truck Equipment Inc ....E 614 299-1136
Columbus (G-7091)

Schodorf Truck Body & Eqp Co ....E 614 228-6793
Columbus (G-8603)

Venco Venturo Industries LLC ....E 513 772-8448
Cincinnati (G-4753)

MOTOR VEHICLES, WHOLESALE: Truck tractors

Bulldawg Holdings LLC ....E 419 423-3131
Findlay (G-10885)

Helton Enterprises Inc ....E 419 423-4180
Findlay (G-10922)

Peterbilt of Cincinnati ....E 513 772-1740
Cincinnati (G-4235)

Peterbilt of Northwest Ohio ....E 419 423-3441
Findlay (G-10952)

MOTOR VEHICLES, WHOLESALE: Trucks, commercial

Bob Sumerel Tire Co Inc ....E 513 792-6600
Cincinnati (G-3065)

Cerni Motor Sales Inc ....D 330 652-9917
Youngstown (G-19984)

Esec Corporation ....E 330 799-1536
Youngstown (G-20030)

Esec Corporation ....E 614 875-3732
Grove City (G-11430)

Freightlner Trcks of Cncinnati ....E 513 772-7171
Cincinnati (G-3591)

Fyda Freightliner Youngstown ....D 330 797-0224
Youngstown (G-20041)

Kenworth of Cincinnati Inc ....D 513 771-5831
Cincinnati (G-3862)

Liberty Ford Southwest Inc ....D 440 888-2600
Cleveland (G-5867)

Lower Great Lakes Kenworth Inc ....E 419 874-3511
Perrysburg (G-15890)

Mansfield Truck Sls & Svc Inc ....E 419 522-9811
Mansfield (G-13211)

Nollenberger Truck Center ....E 419 837-5996
Stony Ridge (G-17185)

R & R Inc ....E 330 799-1536
Youngstown (G-20174)

R & R Truck Sales Inc ....E 330 784-5881
Akron (G-395)

Stoops of Lima Inc ....C 419 228-4334
Lima (G-12757)

Tri-State Trailer Sales Inc ....E 412 747-7777
West Chester (G-19093)

Truck Country Indiana Inc ....C 419 228-4334
Lima (G-12770)

Whites Service Center Inc ....E 937 653-5279
Urbana (G-18446)

Youngstown-Kenworth Inc ....E 330 534-9761
Hubbard (G-11952)

MOTOR VEHICLES, WHOLESALE: Vans, commercial

State Park Motors Inc ....E 740 264-3113
Steubenville (G-17170)

MOTORCYCLE DEALERS

AD Farrow LLC ....E 614 228-6353
Columbus (G-6869)

Adventure Harley Davidson ....E 330 343-2295
Dover (G-10064)

Damarc Inc ....E 330 454-6171
Canton (G-2278)

Mid-Ohio Harley-Davidson Inc ....E 937 322-3590
Springfield (G-17084)

Valley Harley Davidson Co ....E 740 695-9591
Belmont (G-1397)

Wholecycle Inc ....E 330 929-8123
Peninsula (G-15815)

MOTORCYCLE DEALERS

Carcorp Inc ....C 877 857-2801
Columbus (G-7118)

Sonic Automotive-1495 Automall ....E 614 317-4326
Columbus (G-8659)

South E Harley Davidson Sls Co ....E 440 439-5300
Cleveland (G-6422)

MOTORCYCLE PARTS & ACCESS DEALERS

Freedom Harley-Davidson Inc ....E 330 494-2453
Canton (G-2317)

MOTORCYCLE REPAIR SHOPS

AD Farrow LLC ....E 614 228-6353
Columbus (G-6869)

Adventure Harley Davidson ....E 330 343-2295
Dover (G-10064)

Damarc Inc ....E 330 454-6171
Canton (G-2278)

Freedom Harley-Davidson Inc ....E 330 494-2453
Canton (G-2317)

Mid-Ohio Harley-Davidson Inc ....E 937 322-3590
Springfield (G-17084)

No Cages Harley-Davidson ....E 614 764-2453
Plain City (G-16062)

Randy L Fork Inc ....E 419 891-1230
Maumee (G-13841)

Valley Harley Davidson Co ....E 740 695-9591
Belmont (G-1397)

MOTORCYCLES: Wholesalers

Ktm North America Inc ....D 855 215-6360
Amherst (G-591)

Wholecycle Inc ....E 330 929-8123
Peninsula (G-15815)

MOTORS: Electric

Ametek Tchnical Indus Pdts Inc ....D 330 677-3754
Kent (G-12214)

Hannon Company ....D 330 456-4728
Canton (G-2339)

MOTORS: Generators

City Machine Technologies Inc ....E 330 740-8186
Youngstown (G-19990)

GE Aviation Systems LLC ....B 937 898-5881
Vandalia (G-18524)

General Electric Company ....D 216 883-1000
Cleveland (G-5603)

MOVIE THEATERS, EXC DRIVE-IN

AMC Entertainment Inc ....E 614 846-6575
Columbus (G-6910)

AMC Entertainment Inc ....E 614 428-5716
Columbus (G-6911)

AMC Entertainment Inc ....E 216 749-0260
Brooklyn (G-1859)

American Multi-Cinema Inc ....E 216 749-0260
Cleveland (G-4959)

American Multi-Cinema Inc ....E 440 331-2826
Rocky River (G-16422)

Cincinnati Museum Center ....B 513 287-7000
Cincinnati (G-3258)

Cinemark Usa Inc ....E 330 965-2335
Youngstown (G-19989)

Cinemark Usa Inc ....C 216 447-8820
Cleveland (G-5179)

Cinemark Usa Inc ....E 330 908-1005
Macedonia (G-13065)

Cinemark Usa Inc ....E 419 589-7300
Ontario (G-15546)

Cinemark Usa Inc ....E 614 538-0403
Columbus (G-7199)

Cinemark Usa Inc ....E 330 497-9118
Canton (G-2253)

Cinemark Usa Inc ....E 614 527-3773
Hilliard (G-11755)

Cinemark Usa Inc ....E 614 471-7620
Gahanna (G-11112)

Cinemark Usa Inc ....E 330 345-2610
Wooster (G-19702)

Cinemark Usa Inc ....E 614 529-8547
Columbus (G-7200)

Drc Holdings Inc ....E 419 230-0188
Pandora (G-15750)

Great Eastern Theatre Company ....D 419 691-9668
Oregon (G-15596)

M E Theaters Inc ....E 937 596-6424
Jackson Center (G-12184)

Marcus Theatres Corporation ....E 614 759-6500
Pickerington (G-15963)

Marcus Theatres Corporation ....D 614 436-9818
Columbus (G-8018)

National Amusements Inc ....E 513 699-1500
Milford (G-14413)

National Amusements Inc ....E 513 699-1500
Cincinnati (G-4090)

National Amusements Inc ....D 419 215-3095
Maumee (G-13823)

Ohio Light Opera ....D 330 263-2345
Wooster (G-19753)

Quincy Amusements Inc ....E 419 874-2154
Perrysburg (G-15909)

Regal Cinemas Inc ....E 614 853-0850
Columbus (G-8503)

Regal Cinemas Inc ....E 330 723-4416
Medina (G-13996)

Regal Cinemas Inc ....E 440 975-8820
Willoughby (G-19566)

Regal Cinemas Inc ....E 937 431-9418
Beavercreek (G-1181)

Regal Cinemas Inc ....E 440 934-3356
Elyria (G-10558)

Regal Cinemas Inc ....E 330 666-9373
Akron (G-398)

Regal Cinemas Inc ....E 440 871-4546
Westlake (G-19399)

Regal Cinemas Inc ....E 330 758-0503
Youngstown (G-20178)

Regal Cinemas Inc ....E 330 633-7668
Akron (G-399)

Regal Cinemas Corporation...................E 513 770-0713
Mason (G-13633)

Regal Cinemas Corporation...................E 440 720-0500
Richmond Heights (G-16393)

Regal Cinemas Inc ....E 440 891-9845
Cleveland (G-6297)

Seminole Theater Co LLC ....E 440 934-6998
Avon Lake (G-927)

Theatre Management Corporation ....E 513 723-1180
Cincinnati (G-4597)

MOVING SVC & STORAGE: Local

Bell Moving and Storage Inc.................E 513 942-7500
Fairfield (G-10699)

Brendamour Moving & Stor Inc ....D 800 354-9715
Cincinnati (G-3071)

Corrigan Moving Systems-Ann AR ....E 419 874-2900
Perrysburg (G-15850)

Greater Dayton Mvg & Stor Co ....E 937 235-0011
Dayton (G-9471)

Lewis & Michael Inc ....E 937 252-6683
Dayton (G-9564)

Midfitz Inc ....E 216 663-8816
Cleveland (G-5984)

Mitchell & Sons Moving & Stor.............E 419 289-3311
Ashland (G-681)

Planes Moving & Storage Inc.................C 513 759-6000
West Chester (G-18982)

Rollins Moving and Storage Inc ....E 937 525-4013
Springfield (G-17105)

Security Storage Co Inc ....D 513 961-2700
Cincinnati (G-4445)

Tersher Corporation ....D 440 439-8383
Strongsville (G-17352)

University Moving & Storage Co ....E 248 615-7000
West Chester (G-19027)

Vance Property Management LLC ....D 419 467-9548
Toledo (G-18135)

MOVING SVC: Local

Accelerated Moving & Stor Inc ....E 614 836-1007
Columbus (G-6859)

All My Sons Moving & Storge of...........E 614 405-7202
Hilliard (G-11740)

Continental Office Furn Corp.................E 614 781-0080
Columbus (G-7359)

Corrigan Moving Systems-Ann AR ....E 419 874-2900
Perrysburg (G-15850)

Custom Movers Services Inc ....E 330 564-0507
Stow (G-17196)

Dearman Moving & Storage Co ....E 419 524-3456
Mansfield (G-13166)

Drivers On Call LLC ....C 330 867-5193
Norton (G-15419)

E & V Ventures Inc ....E 330 794-6683
Akron (G-198)

Greater Dayton Mvg & Stor Co ....E 937 235-0011
Dayton (G-9471)

Leaders Moving Company ....E 614 785-9595
Worthington (G-19822)

Nest Tenders Limited ....D 614 901-1570
Columbus (G-8170)

Nicholas Carney-Mc Inc ....E 440 243-8560
Sheffield Village (G-16741)

Northcoast Moving Enterprising ....D 440 943-3900
Wickliffe (G-19471)

SDS Earth Moving Inc ....E 330 358-2132
Diamond (G-10061)

Two Men & Truck Inc ....E 419 882-1002
Toledo (G-18113)

Wnb Group LLC ....E 513 641-5400
Cincinnati (G-4801)

MOVING SVC: Long-Distance

Accelerated Moving & Stor Inc ....E 614 836-1007
Columbus (G-6859)

Awrs LLC ....E 888 611-2292
Cincinnati (G-3009)

Corrigan Moving Systems-Ann AR ....E 419 874-2900
Perrysburg (G-15850)

Exel Holdings (usa) Inc ....C 614 865-8500
Westerville (G-19161)

Greater Dayton Mvg & Stor Co ....E 937 235-0011
Dayton (G-9471)

Lewis & Michael Inc ....E 937 252-6683
Dayton (G-9564)

Locker Moving & Storage Inc ....E 330 784-0477
Canton (G-2380)

Midfitz Inc ....E 216 663-8816
Cleveland (G-5984)

Mitchell & Sons Moving & Stor.............E 419 289-3311
Ashland (G-681)

New World Van Lines Ohio Inc ....E 614 836-5720
Groveport (G-11527)

Planes Mvg & Stor Co Columbus ....D 614 777-9090
Columbus (G-8451)

Rollins Moving and Storage Inc ....E 937 525-4013
Springfield (G-17105)

Shetler Moving & Stor of Ohio..............E 513 755-0700
West Chester (G-19004)

Tersher Corporation ....D 440 439-8383
Strongsville (G-17352)

Van Howards Lines Inc.........................E 937 235-0007
Dayton (G-9848)

Van Mayberrys & Storage Inc ....E 937 298-8800
Moraine (G-14704)

Van Mills Lines Inc ....C 440 846-0200
Strongsville (G-17357)

Van Stevens Lines Inc ....E 419 729-8871
Toledo (G-18134)

MULTI-SVCS CENTER

Salvation Army ....D 614 252-7171
Columbus (G-8587)

Salvation Army ....D 859 255-5791
Cincinnati (G-4429)

Salvation Army ....D 800 728-7825
Columbus (G-8588)

Skyview Baptist Ranch Inc ....E 330 674-7511
Millersburg (G-14493)

MUSEUMS

Akron Art Museum ....D 330 376-9185
Akron (G-27)

Akron Childrens Museum ....E 330 396-6103
Akron (G-31)

Ark Foundation of Dayton.....................E 937 256-2759
Dayton (G-9240)

Belpre Historical Society.......................E 740 423-7588
Belpre (G-1399)

Butler Institute American Art ....E 330 743-1711
Youngstown (G-19979)

Chagrin Falls Historical Soc ....E 440 247-4695
Chagrin Falls (G-2640)

Cincinnati Institute Fine Arts ....E 513 241-0343
Cincinnati (G-3252)

Cincinnati Museum Association...............C 513 721-5204
Cincinnati (G-3257)

Cleveland Hungarian Heritg Soc ....E 216 523-3900
Cleveland (G-5261)

Clevelnd Museum of Natural His...........D 216 231-4600
Cleveland (G-5301)

Dayton Art Institute.............................D 937 223-5277
Dayton (G-9354)

Dayton History ....C 937 293-2841
Dayton (G-9368)

Dayton Intl Peace Museum ....E 937 227-3223
Dayton (G-9370)

Dayton Society Natural History ....D 937 275-7431
Dayton (G-9381)

Dayton Society Natural History ....E 513 932-4421
Oregonia (G-15616)

Delaware County Historical Soc.............D 740 369-3831
Delaware (G-9968)

Franklin County Historical Soc..............C 614 228-2674
Columbus (G-7617)

Great Lakes Museum of Science.............C 216 694-2000
Cleveland (G-5629)

Kingwood Center ....E 419 522-0211
Mansfield (G-13194)

Lawrence Cnty Hstorical Museum ....E 740 532-1222
Ironton (G-12161)

Museum Cntmprary Art Cleveland ....E 216 421-8671
Cleveland (G-6027)

Norhteast Ohio Museum ....E 330 336-7657
Medina (G-13981)

Ohio Historical Society.........................C 614 297-2300
Columbus (G-8265)

Rock and Roll of Fame and Muse...........D 216 781-7625
Cleveland (G-6336)

Rthrford B Hayes Prsdntial Ctr ....E 419 332-2081
Fremont (G-11091)

Salem Historical Soc Museum ....E 330 337-6733
Salem (G-16562)

Sauder Village ....B 419 446-2541
Archbold (G-638)

Stan Hywet Hall and Grdns Inc.............D 330 836-5533
Akron (G-440)

Stark Cnty Historical Soc Inc ....E 330 455-7043
Canton (G-2489)

Taft Museum of Art..............................E 513 241-0343
Cincinnati (G-4568)

Toledo Museum of Art..........................C 419 255-8000
Toledo (G-18092)

Toledo Science Center ....E 419 244-2674
Toledo (G-18096)

Western Reserve Historical Soc..............D 330 666-3711
Bath (G-1019)

MUSEUMS & ART GALLERIES

Arts and Exhibitions Intl LLC.................D 330 995-9300
Streetsboro (G-17246)

Cincinnati Museum Center.....................B 513 287-7000
Cincinnati (G-3258)

Greater Andrson Premotes Peace...........E 513 588-8391
Cincinnati (G-3647)

MUSIC BROADCASTING SVCS

N Safe Sound Security Inc ....E 888 317-7233
Millersburg (G-14485)

National Weather Service ....E 937 383-0031
Wilmington (G-19636)

MUSIC RECORDING PRODUCER

Telarc International Corp.......................E 216 464-2313
Beachwood (G-1111)

MUSIC SCHOOLS

Phillis Wheatley..................................E 216 391-4443
Cleveland (G-6204)

MUSICAL INSTRUMENTS & ACCESS: NEC

Belco Works Inc ....B 740 695-0500
Saint Clairsville (G-16470)

Hanser Music Group Inc ....D 859 817-7100
West Chester (G-19058)

MUSICAL INSTRUMENTS WHOLESALERS

Hanser Music Group Inc ....D 859 817-7100
West Chester (G-19058)

MUSICIAN

Toledo Swiss Singers ....E 419 693-4110
Oregon (G-15612)

MUTUAL ACCIDENT & HEALTH ASSOCIATIONS

Union Central Life Insur Co ....A 866 696-7478
   Cincinnati *(G-4673)*

MUTUAL FUND MANAGEMENT

Mutual Shareholder Svcs LLC ....E 440 922-0067
   Broadview Heights *(G-1838)*

NAIL SALONS

Attitudes New Inc................................E 330 856-1143
   Warren *(G-18669)*
Brenwood Inc ....E 740 452-7533
   Zanesville *(G-20283)*
Casals Hair Salon Inc ....E 330 533-6766
   Canfield *(G-2132)*
Definitions of Design Inc.....................E 419 891-0188
   Maumee *(G-13781)*
Esbi International Salon ....E 330 220-3724
   Brunswick *(G-1929)*
Intrigue Salon & Day Spa ....E 330 493-7003
   Canton *(G-2358)*
Kristie Warner ....E 330 650-4450
   Hudson *(G-11992)*
Le Nails ....E 440 846-1866
   Cleveland *(G-5859)*
Paragon Salons Inc ....E 513 651-4600
   Cincinnati *(G-4199)*
Picasso For Nail LLC ....E 440 308-4470
   Solon *(G-16883)*
Reves Salon & Spa ....E 419 885-1140
   Sylvania *(G-17447)*
Uptown Hair Studio Inc ....E 937 832-2111
   Englewood *(G-10604)*
Walmart Inc ....C 937 399-0370
   Springfield *(G-17133)*

NATIONAL SECURITY FORCES

Defense Fin & Accounting Svc ....A 614 693-6700
   Columbus *(G-7429)*

NATIONAL SECURITY, GOVERNMENT: Air Force

Air Force US Dept of............................B 937 656-2354
   Dayton *(G-9156)*
Air Force US Dept of............................D 937 257-6068
   Dayton *(G-9157)*
Army & Air Force Exchange Svc ....C 937 257-2928
   Dayton *(G-9160)*
Army & Air Force Exchange Svc ....A 937 257-7736
   Dayton *(G-9161)*
US Dept of the Air Force ....D 937 257-0837
   Dayton *(G-9190)*
US Dept of the Air Force ....B 937 255-5150
   Dayton *(G-9191)*

NATIONAL SECURITY, GOVERNMENT: Army

U S Army Corps of Engineers ....D 513 684-3048
   Cincinnati *(G-4660)*

NATIONAL SECURITY, GOVERNMENT: National Guard

National Guard Ohio.............................D 614 492-3166
   Columbus *(G-8132)*

NATIONAL SECURITY, GOVERNMENT: Navy

United States Dept of Navy ....E 937 938-3926
   Dayton *(G-9189)*

NATURAL GAS DISTRIBUTION TO CONSUMERS

Bay State Gas Company ....B 614 460-4292
   Columbus *(G-7021)*
Cinergy Corp ....A 513 421-9500
   Cincinnati *(G-3289)*
City of Lancaster ....E 740 687-6670
   Lancaster *(G-12380)*
City of Toledo ....D 419 245-1800
   Toledo *(G-17654)*
Columbia Gas of Ohio Inc ....E 614 460-6000
   Columbus *(G-7248)*
Columbia Gas of Ohio Inc ....D 440 891-2458
   Cleveland *(G-5314)*

Columbia Gas of Ohio Inc....................E 419 435-7725
   Findlay *(G-10890)*
Columbia Gas of Ohio Inc....................E 740 264-5577
   Steubenville *(G-17148)*
Columbia Gas of Ohio Inc....................C 614 481-1000
   Columbus *(G-7249)*
Columbia Gas of Ohio Inc....................D 419 539-6046
   Toledo *(G-17668)*
Delta Energy LLC ....E 614 761-3603
   Dublin *(G-10198)*
Duke Energy Ohio Inc.........................D 704 382-3853
   Cincinnati *(G-3450)*
East Ohio Gas Company ....A 800 362-7557
   Cleveland *(G-5457)*
East Ohio Gas Company ....C 330 742-8121
   Youngstown *(G-20024)*
East Ohio Gas Company ....B 330 266-2169
   New Franklin *(G-14909)*
East Ohio Gas Company ....C 330 477-9411
   Canton *(G-2291)*
East Ohio Gas Company ....E 216 736-6959
   Cleveland *(G-5458)*
East Ohio Gas Company ....E 216 736-6120
   Ashtabula *(G-737)*
East Ohio Gas Company ....D 330 499-2501
   Canton *(G-2292)*
East Ohio Gas Company ....C 330 478-1700
   Canton *(G-2293)*
East Ohio Gas Company ....C 216 736-6917
   Wickliffe *(G-19457)*
Energy Cooperative Inc ....E 740 348-1206
   Newark *(G-15031)*
Hearthstone Utilities Inc.....................D 440 974-3770
   Cleveland *(G-5679)*
National Gas & Oil Corporation ....E 740 344-2102
   Newark *(G-15079)*
National Gas & Oil Corporation ....E 740 454-7252
   Zanesville *(G-20343)*
National Gas Oil Corp ....E 740 348-1243
   Hebron *(G-11721)*
Nwo Resources Inc ....C 419 636-1117
   Bryan *(G-1965)*
Ohio Gas Company ....E 419 636-1117
   Bryan *(G-1966)*
Stand Energy Corporation ....E 513 621-1113
   Cincinnati *(G-4532)*

NATURAL GAS PRODUCTION

Interstate Gas Supply Inc ....D 614 659-5000
   Dublin *(G-10258)*
M3 Midstream LLC ....E 330 679-5580
   Salineville *(G-16571)*
M3 Midstream LLC ....E 330 223-2220
   Kensington *(G-12210)*
M3 Midstream LLC ....E 740 431-4168
   Dennison *(G-10052)*
Williams Partners LP ....C 330 966-3674
   North Canton *(G-15244)*

NATURAL GAS TRANSMISSION

Belden & Blake Corporation ....E 330 602-5551
   Dover *(G-10066)*
Columbia Energy Group........................A 614 460-4683
   Columbus *(G-7247)*
Columbia Gas Transmission LLC ....E 614 460-4704
   Columbus *(G-7251)*
Consumers Gas Cooperative................E 330 682-4144
   Orrville *(G-15627)*
Dominion Energy Transm Inc ....E 513 932-5793
   Lebanon *(G-12460)*
Duke Energy Ohio Inc.........................D 704 382-3853
   Cincinnati *(G-3450)*
Kinder Mrgan Lqds Trminals LLC ....E 513 841-0500
   Cincinnati *(G-3870)*
Koch Knight LLC ....D 330 488-1651
   East Canton *(G-10387)*
National Gas & Oil Corporation ....E 740 344-2102
   Newark *(G-15079)*
National Gas & Oil Corporation ....E 740 454-7252
   Zanesville *(G-20343)*
Ohio Gas Company ....E 419 636-3642
   Bryan *(G-1967)*
Texas Eastern Transmission LP ....E 513 932-1816
   Lebanon *(G-12510)*

NATURAL GAS TRANSMISSION & DISTRIBUTION

Aspire Energy of Ohio LLC...................E 330 682-7726
   Orrville *(G-15623)*

Columbia Gas Transmission LLC.........E 740 432-1612
   Cambridge *(G-2059)*
Dayton Power and Light Company ....D 937 331-4123
   Moraine *(G-14647)*
East Ohio Gas Company ....C 330 478-1700
   Canton *(G-2293)*
National Gas & Oil Corporation ....E 740 454-7252
   Zanesville *(G-20343)*

NATURAL GASOLINE PRODUCTION

Husky Marketing and Supply Co ....E 614 210-2300
   Dublin *(G-10250)*

NATURAL RESOURCE PRESERVATION SVCS

City of Toledo ....E 419 936-2875
   Toledo *(G-17656)*
Miami Conservancy District ....E 937 223-1271
   Dayton *(G-9614)*
Miami County Park District ....E 937 335-6273
   Troy *(G-18214)*

NAUTICAL & NAVIGATIONAL INSTRUMENT REPAIR SVCS

Inertial Airline Services Inc ....E 440 995-6555
   Cleveland *(G-5749)*

NAUTICAL REPAIR SVCS

Riverside Marine Inds Inc.....................D 419 729-1621
   Toledo *(G-18008)*

NAVIGATIONAL SYSTEMS & INSTRUMENTS

Cedar Elec Holdings Corp.....................D 773 804-6288
   West Chester *(G-18882)*

NEIGHBORHOOD CENTER

Friendly Inn Settlement House ....E 216 431-7656
   Cleveland *(G-5582)*
Gladden Community House....................E 614 221-7801
   Columbus *(G-7671)*
Phillis Wheatley ....E 216 391-4443
   Cleveland *(G-6204)*
Seven Hlls Neighborhood Houses ....D 513 407-5362
   Cincinnati *(G-4460)*

NEIGHBORHOOD DEVELOPMENT GROUP

Gc Neighborhood Ctrs Assoc Inc ....C 216 298-4440
   Cleveland *(G-5597)*
Neighborhood Hsg Servs Toledo ....E 419 691-2900
   Toledo *(G-17936)*

NEPHELINE SYENITE MINING

Covia Holdings Corporation ....D 440 214-3284
   Independence *(G-12063)*

NETS: Launderers & Dyers

TAC Industries Inc ....B 937 328-5200
   Springfield *(G-17123)*

NEW & USED CAR DEALERS

Albert Mike Leasing Inc ....C 513 563-1400
   Cincinnati *(G-2919)*
Genicon Inc ....E 419 491-4478
   Swanton *(G-17398)*
Jake Sweeney Automotive Inc...............C 513 782-2800
   Cincinnati *(G-3805)*
Jeff Wyler Automotive Fmly Inc.............E 513 752-7450
   Cincinnati *(G-2855)*
Nollenberger Truck Center ....E 419 837-5996
   Stony Ridge *(G-17185)*

NEWS SYNDICATES

Ohio News Network ....D 614 460-3700
   Columbus *(G-8275)*

NEWSPAPERS & PERIODICALS NEWS REPORTING SVCS

Associated Press ....E 614 885-3444
   Columbus *(G-6984)*

NEWSSTAND

Sandusky Register................................E..... 419 625-5500
  Sandusky (G-16640)

NONCURRENT CARRYING WIRING DEVICES

Akron Foundry Co................................E..... 330 745-3101
  Barberton (G-939)
Vertiv Energy Systems Inc..................A...... 440 288-1122
  Lorain (G-12951)
Zekelman Industries Inc.......................C..... 740 432-2146
  Cambridge (G-2087)

NONMETALLIC MINERALS DEVELOPMENT & TEST BORING SVC

Barr Engineering Incorporated............E...... 614 714-0299
  Columbus (G-7019)

NOTARIES PUBLIC

Official Investigations Inc ....D..... 844 263-3424
  Cincinnati (G-4149)
Passprt Accept Fclty Mansfld P ....C....... 419 755-4621
  Mansfield (G-13230)

NOVELTIES, PAPER, WHOLESALE

Gummer Wholesale Inc........................D..... 740 928-0415
  Heath (G-11704)

NOVELTY SHOPS

Top Tier Soccer LLC............................E..... 937 903-6114
  Dayton (G-9816)

NURSERIES & LAWN & GARDEN SPLY STORE, RET: Lawn/Garden Splys

Garick LLC..E..... 937 462-8350
  South Charleston (G-16924)
Gears Garden Center Inc......................E..... 513 931-3800
  Cincinnati (G-3606)
McCallisters Landscaping & Sup ....E..... 440 259-3348
  Painesville (G-15725)
R B Stout Inc..E..... 330 666-8811
  Akron (G-396)
Tersigni Cargill Entps LLC....................E..... 330 351-0942
  Stow (G-17235)
Thomsons Landscaping.........................E..... 740 374-9353
  Marietta (G-13386)

NURSERIES & LAWN & GARDEN SPLY STORES, RETAIL

Lesco Inc...C...... 216 706-9250
  Cleveland (G-5865)
Lockes Garden Center Inc.....................E..... 440 774-6981
  Oberlin (G-15507)
Straders Garden Centers Inc.................C...... 614 889-1314
  Columbus (G-8703)

NURSERIES & LAWN & GARDEN SPLY STORES, RETAIL: Fertilizer

Centerra Co-Op....................................E...... 419 281-2153
  Ashland (G-665)
Centerra Co-Op....................................E...... 800 362-9598
  Jefferson (G-12190)
Heritage Cooperative Inc......................D...... 419 294-2371
  West Mansfield (G-19125)
K M B Inc...E..... 330 889-3451
  Bristolville (G-1826)
Ohigro Inc..E...... 740 726-2429
  Waldo (G-18630)

NURSERIES & LAWN & GARDEN SPLY STORES, RETAIL: Top Soil

Bladecutters Lawn Service Inc.............E....... 937 274-3861
  Dayton (G-9255)

NURSERIES & LAWN/GARDEN SPLY STORE, RET: Lawnmowers/Tractors

Do Cut Sales & Service Inc ....E..... 330 533-9878
  Warren (G-18703)
Findlay Implement Co............................E..... 419 424-0471
  Findlay (G-10903)
Shearer Farm Inc..................................E..... 440 237-4806
  North Royalton (G-15367)

Shetlers Sales & Service Inc.................E..... 330 760-3358
  Copley (G-8975)
Tri Green Interstate Equipment ....E..... 614 879-7731
  London (G-12876)
Tuttle Landscaping & Grdn Ctr..............E..... 419 756-7555
  Mansfield (G-13257)

NURSERIES & LAWN/GARDEN SPLY STORES, RET: Garden Splys/Tools

Barnes Nursery Inc..............................E..... 800 421-8722
  Huron (G-12021)
Berns Grnhse & Grdn Ctr Inc................E..... 513 423-5306
  Middletown (G-14293)
Bfg Supply Co Llc.................................E..... 440 834-1883
  Burton (G-2015)
Fackler Country Gardens Inc.................E..... 740 522-3128
  Granville (G-11341)
Knollwood Florists Inc..........................E..... 937 426-0861
  Beavercreek (G-1163)

NURSERIES/LAWN/GARDEN SPLY STORES, RET: Hydroponic Eqpt/Sply

Naragon Companies Inc........................E..... 330 745-7700
  Norton (G-15420)

NURSERIES/LAWN/GRDN SPLY STORE, RET: Nursery Stck, Seed/Bulb

Dennis Top Soil & Landscaping ....E..... 419 865-5656
  Toledo (G-17697)
Grandmas Gardens Inc.........................E..... 937 885-2973
  Waynesville (G-18831)
Oakland Nursery Inc.............................E..... 614 268-3834
  Columbus (G-8221)
Seed Consultants Inc............................E..... 740 333-8644
  Wshngtn CT Hs (G-19884)
Wickline Landscaping Inc......................E..... 937 372-0521
  Xenia (G-19933)

NURSERY & GARDEN CENTERS

August Corso Sons Inc.........................C...... 419 626-0765
  Sandusky (G-16576)
Bzak Landscaping Inc...........................E..... 513 831-0907
  Milford (G-14375)
Dawes Arboretum ....E..... 740 323-2355
  Newark (G-15030)
Greenleaf Landscapes Inc.....................D..... 740 373-1639
  Marietta (G-13332)
Gs Ohio Inc...D..... 614 885-5350
  Powell (G-16196)
HJ Benken Flor & Greenhouses.............D..... 513 891-1040
  Cincinnati (G-3713)
Kuester Implement Company Inc ....E..... 740 944-1502
  Bloomingdale (G-1490)
North Branch Nursery Inc ....E..... 419 287-4679
  Pemberville (G-15805)
Scarffs Nursery Inc ....C...... 937 845-3130
  New Carlisle (G-14897)
Siebenthaler Company ....D..... 937 427-4110
  Dayton (G-9767)
Wade & Gatton Nurseries.......................D..... 419 883-3191
  Bellville (G-1393)
White Pond Gardens Inc ....E..... 330 836-2727
  Akron (G-500)

NURSERY SCHOOLS

Goddard School.....................................E..... 513 271-6311
  Cincinnati (G-3621)
Lebanon Presbyterian Church...............E..... 513 932-0369
  Lebanon (G-12482)
Montessori Community School ....E..... 740 344-9411
  Newark (G-15074)
Nurtury ....E..... 330 723-1800
  Medina (G-13983)
Play Time Day Nursery Inc.....................E..... 513 385-8281
  Cincinnati (G-4254)
Scribes & Scrbblr Chld Dev Ctr..............E..... 440 884-5437
  Cleveland (G-6382)
Tiny Tots Day Nursery ....E..... 330 755-6473
  Struthers (G-17368)

NURSERY STOCK, WHOLESALE

Beroske Farms & Greenhouse Inc.........E..... 419 826-4547
  Delta (G-10041)
C M Brown Nurseries Inc.......................E..... 440 259-5403
  Perry (G-15820)

Davis Tree Farm & Nursery Inc.............E..... 330 483-3324
  Valley City (G-18460)
Dennis Top Soil & Landscaping ....E..... 419 865-5656
  Toledo (G-17697)
North Coast Perennials Inc...................E..... 440 428-1277
  Madison (G-13105)
Rusty Oak Nursery Ltd..........................E..... 330 225-7704
  Valley City (G-18468)
Siebenthaler Company ....D..... 937 427-4110
  Dayton (G-9767)
Thorsens Greenhouse LLC.....................E..... 740 363-5069
  Delaware (G-10009)

NURSING & PERSONAL CARE FACILITIES, NEC

Csi Managed Care Inc..........................D..... 440 717-1700
  Brecksville (G-1778)
Guardian Elder Care Columbus.............D..... 614 868-9306
  Columbus (G-7701)
Hampton Woods Nursing Ctr Inc ....E..... 330 707-1400
  Poland (G-16084)
Niles Residential Care LLC...................D..... 216 727-3996
  Niles (G-15164)
Pristine Senior Living of.........................D..... 419 935-0148
  Willard (G-19486)
Sumner On Ridgewood ....E..... 330 664-1360
  Copley (G-8977)
Windsorwood Place Inc..........................E..... 740 623-4600
  Coshocton (G-9031)

NURSING CARE FACILITIES: Skilled

10 Wilmington Place ....D..... 937 253-1010
  Dayton (G-9193)
204 W Main Street Oper Co LLC............D..... 419 929-1563
  New London (G-14930)
5440 Charlesgate Rd Oper LLC ....D..... 937 236-6707
  Dayton (G-9195)
A M Mc Gregor Home ....B..... 216 851-8200
  Cleveland (G-4878)
A Provide Care Inc ....C..... 330 828-2278
  Dalton (G-9143)
Adams County Manor.............................D..... 937 544-2205
  West Union (G-19131)
Adena NH LLC.......................................E..... 740 546-3620
  Adena (G-7)
Ahf Ohio Inc..D..... 330 725-4123
  Medina (G-13907)
Ahf Ohio Inc..D..... 740 532-6188
  Ironton (G-12144)
Ahf Ohio Inc..D..... 614 760-8870
  Dublin (G-10122)
Ahf Ohio Inc..D..... 937 256-4663
  Dayton (G-9212)
Ahf/Central States Inc...........................D..... 615 383-3570
  Dublin (G-10123)
Alexson Services Inc.............................B..... 513 874-0423
  Fairfield (G-10695)
Alpha Nursing Homes Inc......................D..... 740 345-9197
  Newark (G-15009)
Altercare Inc...C..... 330 335-2555
  Wadsworth (G-18588)
Altercare Inc...E..... 440 327-5285
  North Ridgeville (G-15320)
Altercare Nobles Pond Inc ....D..... 330 834-4800
  Canton (G-2182)
Altercare of Louisville Center ....E..... 330 875-4224
  Louisville (G-12959)
Amedisys Inc ....E..... 740 373-8549
  Marietta (G-13309)
American Eagle Hlth Care Svcs.............C..... 440 428-5103
  Madison (G-13092)
American Nursing Care Inc....................E..... 513 731-4600
  Cincinnati (G-2947)
American Nursing Care Inc....................D..... 513 245-1500
  Cincinnati (G-2948)
American Nursing Care Inc....................E..... 937 438-3844
  Dayton (G-9228)
American Nursing Care Inc....................C..... 614 847-0555
  Zanesville (G-20275)
American Retirement Corp ....D..... 216 291-6140
  Cleveland (G-4965)
American Retirement Corp ....D..... 216 321-6331
  Cleveland (G-4966)
Anchor Lodge Nursing Home Inc...........C..... 440 244-2019
  Lorain (G-12880)
Anna Maria of Aurora Inc ....C..... 330 562-6171
  Aurora (G-815)
Anna Maria of Aurora Inc ....D..... 330 562-3120
  Aurora (G-816)

SERVICES

Apostolic Christian Home Inc .... D 330 927-1010
Rittman (G-16403)

Appalachian Respite Care Ltd .... D 740 984-4262
Beverly (G-14623)

April Enterprises Inc .... B 937 293-7703
Moraine (G-14623)

Arbors East LLC .... C 614 575-9003
Columbus (G-6963)

Arbors West LLC .... D 614 879-7661
West Jefferson (G-19103)

Aristocrat W Nursing Hm Corp .... C 216 252-7730
Cleveland (G-5008)

Arlington Care Ctr .... C 740 344-0303
Newark (G-15011)

Ashley Enterprises LLC .... D 330 726-5790
Boardman (G-1695)

Ashley Place Health Care Inc .... C 330 793-3010
Youngstown (G-19956)

Assisted Living Concepts LLC .... E 419 586-2484
Celina (G-2584)

Assisted Living Concepts LLC .... E 419 224-6327
Lima (G-12602)

Assumption Village .... C 330 549-2434
North Lima (G-15264)

Astoria Healthcare Group LLC .... B 937 855-2363
Germantown (G-11276)

Astoria Place of Clyde LLC .... D 419 547-9595
Clyde (G-6739)

Balanced Care Corporation .... E 330 908-1166
Northfield (G-15373)

Balanced Care Corporation .... E 937 372-7205
Xenia (G-19892)

Baltic Health Care Corp .... D 330 897-4311
Baltic (G-933)

Baptist Home and Center .... C 513 662-5880
Cincinnati (G-3018)

Barnesville Healthcare Rehab .... D 740 425-3648
Barnesville (G-974)

Bath Manor Limited Partnership .... E 330 836-1006
Akron (G-87)

Beechwood Home .... C 513 321-9294
Cincinnati (G-3035)

Bel Air Care Center .... D 330 821-3939
Alliance (G-518)

Bellevue Healthcare Group LLC .... E 419 483-6225
Bellevue (G-1372)

Belmont County Home .... D 740 695-4925
Saint Clairsville (G-16472)

Belmore Leasing Co LLC .... C 216 268-3600
Cleveland (G-5053)

Bentley Leasing Co LLC .... A 330 337-9503
Salem (G-16536)

Best Care Nrsing Rhbltttion Ctr .... C 740 574-2558
Wheelersburg (G-19428)

Bethesda Foundation Inc .... E 513 569-6575
Cincinnati (G-3046)

Biorx LLC .... C 866 442-4679
Cincinnati (G-3051)

Birchaven Village .... B 419 424-3000
Findlay (G-10870)

Blossom Nursing & Rehab Center .... C 330 337-3033
Salem (G-16538)

Blue Ash Healthcare Group Inc .... E 513 793-3362
Cincinnati (G-3060)

Blue Creek Healthcare LLC .... D 419 877-5338
Whitehouse (G-19445)

Bluesky Healthcare Inc .... C 330 345-9050
Wooster (G-19692)

Brethren Care Inc .... C 419 289-0803
Ashland (G-659)

Brewster Parke Inc .... D 330 767-4179
Brewster (G-1809)

Briarfield Manor LLC .... C 330 270-3468
Youngstown (G-19973)

Broadview NH LLC .... D 614 337-1066
Columbus (G-7078)

Brook Willow Chrstn Cmmunities .... D 614 885-3300
Columbus (G-7079)

Brookdale Senior Living Inc .... E 614 336-3677
Dublin (G-10151)

Brookdale Senior Living Inc .... D 937 203-8596
Beavercreek Township (G-1264)

Brookdale Senior Living Inc .... E 216 321-6331
Cleveland (G-5087)

Brookdale Senior Living Inc .... D 419 422-8657
Findlay (G-10883)

Brookview Healthcare Ctr .... D 419 784-1014
Defiance (G-9905)

Brookville Enterprises Inc .... B 937 833-2133
Brookville (G-1911)

Bryant Eliza Village .... B 216 361-6141
Cleveland (G-5096)

Bryant Health Center Inc .... C 740 532-6188
Ironton (G-12147)

Burchwood Care Center .... E 513 868-3300
Fairfield Township (G-10802)

Butler County of Ohio .... C 513 887-3728
Fairfield Township (G-10803)

C Micah Rand Inc .... C 513 605-2000
Cincinnati (G-3101)

Camargo Manor Inc .... D 513 605-3000
Cincinnati (G-3108)

Cambridge Home Healthcare .... C 740 432-6191
Cambridge (G-2053)

Cambridge NH LLC .... D 740 432-7717
Cambridge (G-2054)

Camillus Villa Inc .... D 440 236-5091
Columbia Station (G-6770)

Canterbury Vlla Oprations Corp .... D 330 821-4000
Alliance (G-520)

Capital Health Services Inc .... E 937 278-0404
Dayton (G-9275)

Caprice Health Care Inc .... C 330 965-9200
North Lima (G-15267)

Careserve .... C 740 454-4000
Zanesville (G-20288)

Careserve Inc .... C 740 962-3761
McConnelsville (G-13899)

Carington Health Systems .... E 513 682-2700
Hamilton (G-11573)

Carriage Court Company Inc .... E 740 654-4422
Lancaster (G-12376)

Carriage Inn of Bowerston Inc .... D 740 269-8001
Bowerston (G-1710)

Carriage Inn of Steubenville .... C 740 264-7161
Steubenville (G-17145)

Castle Nursing Homes Inc .... C 330 674-0015
Millersburg (G-14464)

Center Ridge Nursing Home Inc .... C 440 808-5500
North Ridgeville (G-15324)

CHI Living Communities .... D 567 455-0414
Toledo (G-17651)

Childs Investment Co .... D 330 837-2100
Massillon (G-13669)

Chillicothe Long Term Care .... C 513 793-8804
Cincinnati (G-3194)

Chillicothe Opco LLC .... D 740 772-5900
Chillicothe (G-2765)

Christian Worthington Vlg Inc .... E 614 846-6076
Columbus (G-7196)

CHS Norwood Inc .... D 513 242-1360
Cincinnati (G-3214)

CHS of Bowerston Oper Co Inc .... D 937 277-0505
Dayton (G-9300)

Clifton Care Center Inc .... C 513 530-1600
Cincinnati (G-3307)

Clime Leasing Co LLC .... D 614 276-4400
Columbus (G-7226)

Clovernook Inc .... C 513 605-4000
Cincinnati (G-3310)

Colonial Manor Health Care Ctr .... C 419 994-4191
Loudonville (G-12955)

Columbus Alzheimers Care Ctr .... C 614 459-7050
Columbus (G-7254)

Communicare Health Svcs Inc .... D 440 234-0454
Berea (G-1420)

Communicare Health Svcs Inc .... D 330 726-3700
Youngstown (G-19996)

Communicare Health Svcs Inc .... D 419 485-8307
Montpelier (G-14610)

Communicare Health Svcs Inc .... E 330 454-6508
Canton (G-2262)

Communicare Health Svcs Inc .... C 877 366-5306
Wintersville (G-19669)

Communicare Health Svcs Inc .... D 740 264-1155
Steubenville (G-17150)

Communicare Health Svcs Inc .... D 330 792-7799
Youngstown (G-19997)

Communicare Health Svcs Inc .... D 330 792-5511
Youngstown (G-19998)

Communicare Health Svcs Inc .... D 330 454-2152
Canton (G-2263)

Communicare Health Svcs Inc .... D 330 630-9780
Tallmadge (G-17472)

Communicare Health Svcs Inc .... D 419 394-7611
Saint Marys (G-16521)

Community Hlth Prfssionals Inc .... E 419 634-7443
Ada (G-3)

Community Mercy Hlth Partners .... C 937 653-5432
Urbana (G-18429)

Concord Care Center of Toledo .... D 419 385-6616
Toledo (G-17676)

Concord Health Care Inc .... E 330 759-2357
Youngstown (G-20009)

Concord Health Care Inc .... E 419 626-5373
Sandusky (G-16592)

Concord Hlth Rhabilitation Ctr .... E 740 574-8441
Wheelersburg (G-19432)

Congregate Living of America .... D 513 899-2801
Morrow (G-14716)

Congregate Living of America .... D 937 393-6700
Hillsboro (G-11834)

Consulate Healthcare Inc .... E 419 865-1248
Maumee (G-13775)

Consulate Management Co LLC .... D 330 837-1001
Massillon (G-13673)

Consulate Management Co LLC .... D 419 886-3922
Bellville (G-1389)

Consulate Management Co LLC .... D 440 237-7966
Cleveland (G-5340)

Consulate Management Co LLC .... D 419 867-7926
Maumee (G-13776)

Consulate Management Co LLC .... D 740 259-2351
Lucasville (G-13046)

Continent Hlth Co Cortland LLC .... E 330 637-7906
Cortland (G-8986)

Contining Hlthcare Sltions Inc .... D 440 466-1181
Geneva (G-11239)

Copley Health Center Inc .... C 330 666-0980
Copley (G-8965)

Cortland Healthcare Group Inc .... C 330 638-4015
Cortland (G-8987)

Coshocton Opco LLC .... D 740 622-1220
Coshocton (G-9008)

Cottingham Retirement Cmnty .... C 513 563-3600
Cincinnati (G-3367)

Country Club Retirement Center .... C 740 671-9330
Bellaire (G-1333)

Country Mdow Fclty Oprtons LLC .... D 419 886-3922
Bellville (G-1390)

County of Allen .... C 419 221-1103
Lima (G-12622)

County of Logan .... C 937 592-2901
Bellefontaine (G-1351)

County of Lucas .... D 419 385-6021
Toledo (G-17685)

County of Marion .... D 740 389-4624
Marion (G-13414)

County of Monroe .... D 740 472-0144
Woodsfield (G-19674)

County of Shelby .... C 937 492-6900
Sidney (G-16771)

County of Van Wert .... E 419 968-2141
Middle Point (G-14246)

County of Williams .... C 419 636-4508
Bryan (G-1956)

Covenant Care Ohio Inc .... C 419 531-4201
Toledo (G-17687)

Covenant Care Ohio Inc .... D 937 378-0188
Georgetown (G-11269)

Covenant Care Ohio Inc .... D 937 399-5551
Springfield (G-17026)

Covenant Care Ohio Inc .... D 937 878-7046
Fairborn (G-10666)

Crestline Nursing Home Inc .... E 419 683-3255
Crestline (G-9053)

Crestview Health Care Center .... D 740 695-2500
Saint Clairsville (G-16485)

Cridersville Health Care Ctr .... E 419 645-4468
Cridersville (G-9062)

Crotinger Nursing Home Inc .... D 937 968-5284
Union City (G-18353)

Day Spring Health Care Corp .... D 740 984-4262
Beverly (G-1462)

Dayspring Health Care Center .... C 937 864-5800
Fairborn (G-10670)

Dayton Dmh Inc .... C 937 436-2273
Dayton (G-9363)

Dayton Nwborn Care Spclsts Inc .... A 937 641-3329
Dayton (G-9373)

Deaconess Long Term Care of MI .... A 513 487-3600
Cincinnati (G-3412)

Dearth Management Company .... C 419 253-0144
Marengo (G-13302)

Dearth Management Company .... E 740 389-1214
Marion (G-13418)

Dearth Management Company .... C 330 339-3595
New Philadelphia (G-14956)

Dedicated Nursing Assoc Inc .... C 888 465-6929
Beavercreek (G-1214)

Dedicated Nursing Assoc Inc	E	866 450-5550
Cincinnati (G-3415)		
Dedicated Nursing Assoc Inc	E	877 411-8350
Galloway (G-11219)		
Dedicated Nursing Assoc Inc	E	877 547-9144
Parma (G-15765)		
Delaware Opco LLC	D	502 429-8062
Delaware (G-9970)		
Diverscare Healthcare Svcs Inc	E	513 271-7010
Cincinnati (G-3434)		
Diversicare Leasing Corp	D	615 771-7575
Wheelersburg (G-19433)		
Diversicare of Avon LLC	C	440 937-6201
Avon (G-879)		
Diversicare of Mansfield LLC	D	419 529-6447
Ontario (G-15547)		
DMD Management Inc	A	216 371-3600
Cleveland (G-5435)		
Doctors Hospital Cleveland Inc	C	740 753-7300
Nelsonville (G-14829)		
Dover Nursing Center	D	330 364-4436
Dover (G-10075)		
Drake Center LLC	A	513 418-2500
Cincinnati (G-3442)		
Dublin Geriatric Care Co LP	E	614 761-1188
Dublin (G-10207)		
Eagle Creek Hlthcare Group Inc	D	937 544-5531
West Union (G-19136)		
East Galbraith Nursing Home	C	513 984-5220
Cincinnati (G-3472)		
Eastern Star Hm of Cyhoga Cnty	D	216 761-0170
Cleveland (G-5459)		
Eastgate Health Care Center	C	513 752-3710
Cincinnati (G-2850)		
Eaton Gardens Rehabilitation A	D	937 456-5537
Eaton (G-10445)		
Ebenezer Road Corp	C	513 941-0099
Cincinnati (G-3480)		
Echoing Hills Village Inc	D	937 854-5151
Dayton (G-9406)		
Echoing Hills Village Inc	D	440 989-1400
Lorain (G-12902)		
Edgewood Manor of Lucasville	C	740 259-5536
Lucasville (G-13048)		
Elms Retirement Village Inc	D	440 647-2414
Wellington (G-18840)		
Elmwood Center Inc	D	419 639-2626
Green Springs (G-11351)		
Embassy Autumnwood MGT LLC	D	330 927-2060
Rittman (G-16405)		
Emeritus Corporation	D	440 201-9200
Cleveland (G-5475)		
Encore Healthcare LLC	C	330 769-2015
Seville (G-16685)		
Episcopal Retirement Homes Inc	E	513 271-9610
Cincinnati (G-3508)		
Es3 Management Inc	D	440 593-6266
Conneaut (G-8954)		
Euclid Health Care Inc	C	513 561-4105
Cincinnati (G-3517)		
Evangelical Lutheran	D	419 365-5115
Arlington (G-642)		
Fairchild MD Leasing Co LLC	C	330 678-4912
Kent (G-12232)		
Fairhope Hospice and Palliativ	D	740 654-7077
Lancaster (G-12402)		
Fairmont Nursing Home Inc	D	440 338-8220
Newbury (G-15120)		
First Community Village	B	614 324-4455
Columbus (G-7585)		
First Louisville Arden LLC	E	419 252-5500
Toledo (G-17740)		
First Richmond Corp	D	937 783-4949
Blanchester (G-1486)		
Five Star Senior Living Inc	D	614 451-6793
Columbus (G-7592)		
Fountainhead Nursing Home Inc	E	740 354-9113
Franklin Furnace (G-11044)		
Franciscan Care Ctr Sylvania	C	419 882-2087
Toledo (G-17746)		
Franciscan Sisters of Chicago	C	440 843-7800
Cleveland (G-5571)		
Friendly Nursing Home Inc	E	937 855-2363
Franklin (G-11029)		
Friends Health Care Assn	C	937 767-7363
Yellow Springs (G-19939)		
Friendship Vlg of Clumbus Ohio	C	614 890-8282
Columbus (G-7629)		
Friendship Vlg of Dublin Ohio	C	614 764-1600
Dublin (G-10232)		

Fulton County Health Center	C	419 335-2017
Wauseon (G-18801)		
Gahanna Health Care Center	E	614 475-7222
Columbus (G-7643)		
Galion Community Hospital	B	419 468-4841
Galion (G-11174)		
Gateway Family House	E	216 531-5400
Euclid (G-10636)		
Gateway Health Care Center	E	216 486-4949
Cleveland (G-5595)		
Generation Health & Rehab Cntr	D	740 344-9465
Newark (G-15035)		
Generation Health Corp	C	614 337-1066
Columbus (G-7656)		
GFS Leasing Inc	D	330 296-6415
Kent (G-12235)		
Gibsonburg Health Llc	C	419 637-2104
Gibsonburg (G-11278)		
Gillette Nursing Home Inc	D	330 372-1960
Warren (G-18710)		
Glen Wesley Inc	D	614 888-7492
Columbus (G-7673)		
Glenn View Manor Inc	C	330 652-9901
Mineral Ridge (G-14509)		
Glenward Inc	C	513 863-3100
Fairfield Township (G-10807)		
Golden Living LLC	D	419 599-4070
Napoleon (G-14807)		
Golden Living LLC	C	330 762-6486
Akron (G-239)		
Golden Living LLC	D	330 725-3393
Medina (G-13944)		
Golden Living LLC	C	614 861-6666
Columbus (G-7678)		
Golden Living LLC	C	330 297-5781
Ravenna (G-16244)		
Golden Living LLC	D	330 335-1558
Wadsworth (G-18596)		
Good Shepherd Home	C	419 937-1801
Fostoria (G-11003)		
Graceworks Lutheran Services	A	937 433-2140
Dayton (G-9469)		
Greenbrier Senior Living Cmnty	D	440 888-0400
Cleveland (G-5642)		
Greens of Lyndhurst The Inc	C	440 460-1000
Cleveland (G-5643)		
Hackensack Meridian Health Inc	D	513 792-9697
Cincinnati (G-3670)		
Harborside Clveland Ltd Partnr	D	440 871-5900
Westlake (G-19347)		
Harborside Healthcare Corp	C	419 825-1111
Swanton (G-17399)		
Harborside Healthcare NW Ohio	C	419 636-5071
Bryan (G-1959)		
Harborside Pointe Place LLC	C	419 727-7870
Toledo (G-17782)		
Harborside Sylvania LLC	D	419 882-1875
Sylvania (G-17429)		
Harborside Troy LLC	D	937 335-7161
Troy (G-18205)		
Hcf Management Inc	D	740 289-2394
Piketon (G-15977)		
Hcf Management Inc	D	419 435-8112
Fostoria (G-11005)		
Hcf Management Inc	D	419 999-2055
Lima (G-12653)		
Hcf of Bowling Green Inc	B	419 352-4694
Bowling Green (G-1736)		
Hcf of Lima Inc	D	419 999-2010
Lima (G-12654)		
Hcf of Perrysburg Inc	D	419 874-0306
Perrysburg (G-15870)		
Hcr Manor Care Svc Fla III Inc	E	419 252-5500
Toledo (G-17785)		
Hcr Manorcare Med Svcs Fla LLC	D	440 887-1442
North Royalton (G-15360)		
Health Care Opportunities Inc	C	513 932-0300
Lebanon (G-12469)		
Health Care Opportunities Inc	E	513 932-4861
Lebanon (G-12470)		
Health Care Retirement Corp	B	419 252-5500
Toledo (G-17788)		
Health Care Rtrement Corp Amer	D	419 474-6021
Toledo (G-17790)		
Health Care Rtrement Corp Amer	D	419 562-9907
Bucyrus (G-1991)		
Health Care Rtrement Corp Amer	C	937 298-8084
Dayton (G-9490)		
Health Care Rtrement Corp Amer	D	937 456-5537
Eaton (G-10447)		

Health Care Rtrement Corp Amer	D	740 773-5000
Chillicothe (G-2785)		
Health Care Rtrement Corp Amer	C	740 354-4505
Portsmouth (G-16143)		
Health Care Rtrement Corp Amer	C	440 946-1912
Mentor (G-14059)		
Health Care Rtrement Corp Amer	D	740 635-4600
Bridgeport (G-1817)		
Health Care Rtrement Corp Amer	D	419 874-3578
Perrysburg (G-15871)		
Health Care Rtrement Corp Amer	C	937 548-3141
Greenville (G-11386)		
Health Care Rtrement Corp Amer	E	419 337-3050
Wauseon (G-18806)		
Health Care Rtrement Corp Amer	C	513 751-0880
Cincinnati (G-3692)		
Healthcare Facility MGT LLC	D	419 382-2200
Toledo (G-17791)		
Healthcare Facility MGT LLC	C	330 836-7953
Akron (G-258)		
Healthcare Walton Group LLC	C	440 439-4433
Cleveland (G-5673)		
Heartland Fort Myers Fl LLC	E	419 252-5500
Toledo (G-17793)		
Heath Nursing Care Center	C	740 522-1171
Newark (G-15040)		
Heatherhill Care Communities	E	440 285-4040
Chardon (G-2698)		
Hgcc of Allentown Inc	C	419 252-5500
Toledo (G-17803)		
Hickory Creek Healthcare	D	419 542-7795
Hicksville (G-11728)		
Hickory Health Care Inc	D	330 762-6486
Akron (G-260)		
Hill View Retirement Center	C	740 354-3135
Portsmouth (G-16146)		
Hillandale Healthcare Inc	C	513 813-5595
West Chester (G-18943)		
Holzer Senior Care Center	E	740 446-5001
Bidwell (G-1469)		
Home Echo Club Inc	C	614 864-1718
Pickerington (G-15958)		
Home The Friends Inc	C	513 897-6050
Waynesville (G-18832)		
Homestead II Healthcare Group	B	440 352-0788
Painesville (G-15715)		
Horizon Health Management LLC	D	513 793-5220
Cincinnati (G-3725)		
Horn Nursing and Rehab Center	D	330 262-2951
Wooster (G-19730)		
Hospice Cincinnati Inc	E	513 862-1100
Cincinnati (G-3728)		
Hospice Cincinnati Inc	D	513 891-7700
Cincinnati (G-3729)		
Hospice of Genesis Health	E	740 454-5381
Zanesville (G-20318)		
Hospice of North Central Ohio	E	419 281-7107
Ashland (G-675)		
Hospice of The Western Reserve	D	440 951-8692
Willoughby Hills (G-19588)		
Hosser Assisted Living	E	740 286-8785
Jackson (G-12176)		
Huffman Health Care Inc	C	937 476-1000
Dayton (G-9510)		
Humility House	D	330 505-0144
Youngstown (G-20070)		
Hyde Park Health Center	E	513 272-0600
Cincinnati (G-3744)		
I Vrable Inc	C	614 545-5500
Columbus (G-7795)		
Independence Care Community	D	419 435-8505
Fostoria (G-11007)		
Indian Hlls Hlthcare Group Inc	A	216 486-8880
Euclid (G-10644)		
J W J Investments Inc	C	419 643-3161
Delphos (G-10028)		
Jackson County Hlth Facilities	D	740 384-0722
Wellston (G-18851)		
Jacobs Dwelling Nursing Home	E	740 824-3635
Coshocton (G-9020)		
Jennings Eliza Senior Care	A	216 226-5000
Olmsted Twp (G-15536)		
Jennings Ctr For Older Adults	B	216 581-2900
Cleveland (G-5789)		
Jewish Fdrtion of Grter Dayton	D	937 837-2651
Dayton (G-9525)		
Jewish Home of Cincinnati	B	513 754-3100
Mason (G-13603)		
Jo Lin Health Center Inc	C	740 532-0860
Ironton (G-12160)		

SERVICES

Joint Township Dst Mem Hosp..............B...... 419 394-3335
Saint Marys *(G-16524)*
Judson Care Center Inc........................E...... 513 662-5880
Cincinnati *(G-3840)*
Karl Hc LLC...B...... 614 846-5420
Columbus *(G-7882)*
Kendal At Granville.................................C...... 740 321-0400
Granville *(G-11344)*
Kendal At Oberlin....................................C...... 440 775-0094
Oberlin *(G-15506)*
Kindred Healthcare Inc............................D...... 937 222-5963
Dayton *(G-9546)*
Kindred Healthcare Oper Inc..................D...... 740 545-6355
West Lafayette *(G-19115)*
Kindred Healthcare Oper Inc..................C...... 740 439-4437
Cambridge *(G-2075)*
Kindred Healthcare Operating................C...... 330 762-0901
Akron *(G-303)*
Kindred Healthcare Operating................D...... 419 877-5338
Whitehouse *(G-19449)*
Kindred Nursing Centers E LLC.............C...... 740 772-5900
Chillicothe *(G-2798)*
Kindred Nursing Centers E LLC.............C...... 513 932-0105
Lebanon *(G-12475)*
Kingston Healthcare Company...............C...... 937 866-9089
Miamisburg *(G-14183)*
Kingston Healthcare Company...............C...... 440 967-1800
Vermilion *(G-18555)*
Kingston Rsdnce Perrysburg LLC..........D...... 419 872-6200
Perrysburg *(G-15887)*
Lancia Nursing Home Inc........................E...... 740 264-7101
Steubenville *(G-17162)*
Larchwood Health Group LLC...............E...... 216 941-6100
Cleveland *(G-5855)*
Laurel Health Care Company.................D...... 740 264-5042
Steubenville *(G-17163)*
Laurel Health Care Company.................D...... 614 794-8800
Westerville *(G-19180)*
Laurel Health Care Company.................C...... 614 888-4553
Worthington *(G-19820)*
Laurel Health Care Company.................C...... 614 885-0408
Worthington *(G-19821)*
Laurel Hlth Care Battle Creek.................E...... 614 794-8800
Westerville *(G-19181)*
Laurel Hlth Care of Mt Plasant...............D...... 614 794-8800
Westerville *(G-19182)*
Laurel Lk Retirement Cmnty Inc.............B...... 330 650-0681
Hudson *(G-11993)*
Laurels of Hillsboro.................................D...... 937 393-1925
Hillsboro *(G-11849)*
Leader Nuring & Rehabilitation..............C...... 419 252-5718
Toledo *(G-17850)*
Lebanon Nursing & Rehab Ctr................D...... 513 932-1121
Lebanon *(G-12481)*
Levering Management Inc.......................D...... 740 387-9545
Marion *(G-13429)*
Levering Management Inc.......................D...... 740 369-6400
Delaware *(G-9995)*
Lexington Court Care Center..................D...... 419 884-2000
Mansfield *(G-13199)*
Liberty Health Care Center Inc...............E...... 937 296-1550
Bellbrook *(G-1340)*
Liberty Nursing of Willard.......................D...... 419 935-0148
Willard *(G-19483)*
Life Care Centers America Inc................C...... 330 483-3131
Valley City *(G-18464)*
Lima Cnvlscent HM Fndation Inc...........C...... 419 227-5450
Lima *(G-12677)*
Livin Care Alter of Kirke Inc...................E...... 740 927-3209
Kirkersville *(G-12320)*
Living Care Alternatives..........................E...... 740 927-3209
Kirkersville *(G-12321)*
Logan Health Care Center......................C...... 740 385-2155
Logan *(G-12846)*
Longterm Lodging Inc.............................C...... 614 224-0614
Columbus *(G-7988)*
Lost Creek Health Care...........................B...... 419 225-9040
Lima *(G-12692)*
Lutheran Home..B...... 440 871-0090
Cleveland *(G-5889)*
Lutheran Scial Svcs Centl Ohio...............C...... 419 289-3523
Ashland *(G-678)*
Lutheran Village At Wolf Creek...............C...... 419 861-2233
Holland *(G-11893)*
Lynnhaven V LLC.....................................C...... 440 272-5600
Windsor *(G-19665)*
Madeira Health Care Center....................C...... 513 561-4105
Cincinnati *(G-3957)*
Main Street Terrace Care Ctr..................D...... 740 653-8767
Lancaster *(G-12414)*

Mallard Cove Senior Dev LLC..................C...... 513 772-6655
Cincinnati *(G-3966)*
Manor Care Nursing Center.....................E...... 419 252-5500
Toledo *(G-17881)*
Manor Care of Boynton Beach.................C...... 419 252-5500
Toledo *(G-17882)*
Manor Care of Kansas Inc.......................D...... 419 252-5500
Toledo *(G-17883)*
Manor Care of North Olmsted..................B...... 419 252-5500
Toledo *(G-17884)*
Manor Care of Plantation Inc...................C...... 419 252-5500
Toledo *(G-17885)*
Manor Care of York North Inc..................C...... 419 252-5500
Toledo *(G-17886)*
Manor Care Wilmington Inc......................E...... 419 252-5500
Toledo *(G-17887)*
Manor Care York (south) Inc....................C...... 419 252-5500
Toledo *(G-17888)*
Manor Cr-Mprial Rchmond VA LLC.........D...... 419 252-5000
Toledo *(G-17889)*
Manorcare Health Services LLC..............E...... 419 252-5500
Toledo *(G-17890)*
Manorcare Health Svcs VA Inc.................D...... 419 252-5500
Toledo *(G-17891)*
Manorcare of Kingston Court...................C...... 419 252-5500
Toledo *(G-17892)*
Manorcare of Willoughby Inc....................C...... 419 252-5500
Toledo *(G-17893)*
Mansfield Opco LLC..................................D...... 502 429-8062
Mansfield *(G-13210)*
Marietta Center For Health &...................C...... 740 373-1867
Marietta *(G-13349)*
Marion Manor...D...... 740 387-9545
Marion *(G-13443)*
Marymount Hospital Inc............................B...... 216 581-0500
Cleveland *(G-5920)*
McGregor Senior Ind Hsing......................D...... 216 851-8200
Cleveland *(G-5933)*
McKinley Hall Inc.......................................E...... 937 328-5300
Springfield *(G-17068)*
Mennonite Memorial Home.......................E...... 419 358-7654
Bluffton *(G-1694)*
Mennonite Memorial Home.......................B...... 419 358-1015
Bluffton *(G-1693)*
Menorah Park Center For Senio...............A...... 216 831-6500
Cleveland *(G-5952)*
Mentor Way Nursing & Rehab Cen...........C...... 440 255-9309
Mentor *(G-14084)*
Mercy Health West Park............................C...... 513 451-8900
Cincinnati *(G-4033)*
Mercy St Theresa Center Inc....................C...... 513 271-7010
Cincinnati *(G-4035)*
Merit House LLC..C...... 419 478-5131
Toledo *(G-17911)*
Merit Leasing Co LLC................................C...... 216 261-9592
Cleveland *(G-5955)*
Mff Somerset LLC......................................E...... 216 752-5600
Shaker Heights *(G-16710)*
Mill Run Care Center LLC..........................D...... 614 527-3000
Hilliard *(G-11798)*
Mkjb Inc...C...... 513 851-8400
West Chester *(G-18975)*
Montefiore Home.......................................B...... 216 360-9080
Beachwood *(G-1083)*
Mount Vernon NH LLC................................E...... 740 392-1099
Mount Vernon *(G-14783)*
Multi-Care Inc..D...... 440 352-0788
Painesville *(G-15728)*
Muskingum Vly Nrsing Rhblttion..............D...... 740 984-4262
Beverly *(G-1465)*
Myocare Nursing Home Inc........................C...... 216 252-7555
Cleveland *(G-6031)*
National Church Residences......................C...... 614 451-2151
Columbus *(G-8130)*
Ncop LLC...D...... 419 599-4070
Napoleon *(G-14815)*
Nentwick Convalescent Home...................C...... 330 385-5001
East Liverpool *(G-10409)*
New Dawn Health Care Inc.........................C...... 330 343-5521
Dover *(G-10090)*
New Life Hospice Inc...................................E...... 440 934-1458
Lorain *(G-12930)*
New Life Hospice Inc...................................D...... 440 934-1458
Lorain *(G-12931)*
Newark Leasing LLC....................................C...... 740 344-0357
Newark *(G-15083)*
Newark NH LLC..D...... 740 345-9197
Newark *(G-15085)*
Newcomerstown Development Inc...........C...... 740 498-5165
Newcomerstown *(G-15133)*

Northpoint Senior Services LLC...............D...... 740 369-9614
Delaware *(G-9998)*
Norwalk Area Hlth Systems Inc...............A...... 419 668-8101
Norwalk *(G-15448)*
Norwood Health Care Center LLC............D...... 513 351-0153
Cincinnati *(G-4135)*
Nursing Care MGT Amer Inc....................C...... 419 385-3958
Toledo *(G-17953)*
Nursing Care MGT Amer Inc....................D...... 740 927-9888
Pataskala *(G-15786)*
Nursing Care MGT Amer Inc....................D...... 513 793-5092
Cincinnati *(G-4142)*
Oak Grove Manor Inc................................C...... 419 589-6222
Mansfield *(G-13227)*
Oak Health Care Investors.......................E...... 614 794-8800
Westerville *(G-19193)*
Oakhill Manor Care Center.......................C...... 330 875-5060
Louisville *(G-12970)*
Oaks of West Kettering Inc......................C...... 937 293-1152
Dayton *(G-9664)*
Oaktree LLC...D...... 513 598-8000
Cincinnati *(G-4145)*
Ohio Department Veterans Svcs..............A...... 614 644-0898
Columbus *(G-8243)*
Ohio Eastern Star Home...........................C...... 740 397-1706
Mount Vernon *(G-14785)*
Ohio Living...B...... 614 224-1651
Columbus *(G-8271)*
Ohio Living...C...... 513 681-4230
Cincinnati *(G-4156)*
Ohio Presbt Retirement Svcs...................B...... 330 746-2944
Youngstown *(G-20147)*
Ohio Presbt Retirement Svcs...................C...... 330 867-2150
Akron *(G-361)*
Ohio Presbt Retirement Svcs...................B...... 937 498-2391
Sidney *(G-16789)*
Ohio Presbt Retirement Svcs...................C...... 513 539-7391
Monroe *(G-14579)*
Ohio Valley Manor Inc..............................C...... 937 392-4318
Ripley *(G-16401)*
Ohioguidestone...E...... 440 234-2006
Berea *(G-1434)*
Olmsted Manor Nursing Home.................C...... 440 250-4080
North Olmsted *(G-15302)*
Olmsted Mnor Rtrment Cmnty Ltd...........E...... 440 779-8886
North Olmsted *(G-15303)*
Orchard Villa Inc..C...... 419 697-4100
Oregon *(G-15603)*
Orion Care Services LLC...........................C...... 216 752-3600
Cleveland *(G-6144)*
Otterbein Lebanon......................................E...... 513 933-5465
Lebanon *(G-12491)*
Otterbein Portage Valley Inc.....................C...... 888 749-4950
Pemberville *(G-15806)*
Otterbein Snior Lfstyle Chices..................B...... 513 933-5400
Lebanon *(G-12492)*
Otterbein Snior Lfstyle Chices..................C...... 419 645-5114
Cridersville *(G-9063)*
Otterbein Snior Lfstyle Chices..................C...... 513 260-7690
Middletown *(G-14352)*
Otterbein Snior Lfstyle Chices..................C...... 419 394-2366
Saint Marys *(G-16530)*
Ovm Investment Group LLC......................C...... 937 392-0145
Ripley *(G-16402)*
Parkcliffe Development.............................D...... 419 381-9447
Toledo *(G-17971)*
Parkview Manor Inc....................................D...... 937 296-1550
Englewood *(G-10595)*
Parma Care Center Inc...............................C...... 216 661-6800
Cleveland *(G-6175)*
Peregrine Health Services Inc...................D...... 330 823-9005
Alliance *(G-543)*
Phyllis Wheatley Assn Dev........................E...... 216 391-4443
Cleveland *(G-6208)*
Pleasant Lake Nursing Home.....................B...... 440 842-2273
Cleveland *(G-6221)*
Pleasant Ridge Care Center Inc.................C...... 513 631-1310
Cincinnati *(G-4255)*
Premier Estates 521 LLC...........................D...... 765 288-2488
Cincinnati *(G-4271)*
Premier Health Care MGT Inc....................E...... 248 644-5522
Blue Ash *(G-1630)*
Progressive Macedonia LLC......................E...... 330 908-1260
Macedonia *(G-13080)*
Progressive Park LLC.................................C...... 330 434-4514
Cleveland *(G-6253)*
Quality Care Nursing Svcs LLC..................C...... 740 377-9095
South Point *(G-16944)*
R & F Inc..E...... 419 868-2909
Holland *(G-11906)*

Rae-Ann Holdings Inc...............D...... 440 871-5181
Cleveland (G-6281)

Rae-Ann Holdings Inc...............D...... 440 871-0500
Westlake (G-19397)

Rae-Ann Suburban Inc..............C...... 440 871-5181
Westlake (G-19398)

Raeann Inc...............................E...... 440 871-5181
Cleveland (G-6282)

Raeann Inc...............................D...... 440 466-5733
Geneva (G-11245)

Rapids Nursing Homes Inc.........E...... 216 292-5706
Grand Rapids (G-11329)

Red Carpet Health Care Center.....C...... 740 439-4401
Cambridge (G-2081)

Regency Leasing Co LLC............B...... 614 542-3100
Columbus (G-8505)

Rescare Ohio Inc......................E...... 740 625-6873
Centerburg (G-2615)

Rest Haven Nursing Home Inc......C...... 937 548-1138
Greenville (G-11392)

Riverside Care Center LLC..........D...... 740 962-5303
Mc Connelsville (G-13895)

Rocky River Leasing Co LLC........C...... 440 243-5688
Berea (G-1436)

Roman Cthlic Docese Youngstown....C...... 330 875-5562
Louisville (G-12973)

Rosary Care Center...................D...... 419 824-3600
Sylvania (G-17449)

Rossford Grtric Care Ltd Prtnr.......C...... 614 459-0445
Columbus (G-8554)

Royal Manor Health Care Inc........E...... 216 752-3600
Cleveland (G-6345)

Royce Leasing Co LLC................D...... 740 354-1240
Portsmouth (G-16165)

Rwdop LLC.............................C...... 330 666-3776
Fairlawn (G-10845)

Saber Healthcare Group LLC........E...... 440 546-0643
Brecksville (G-1803)

Saber Healthcare Group LLC........E...... 216 486-5736
Euclid (G-10655)

Saber Healthcare Group LLC........E...... 216 662-3343
Maple Heights (G-13294)

Saber Healthcare Group LLC........E...... 937 826-3351
Woodstock (G-19680)

Saber Healthcare Group LLC........E...... 419 484-1111
Grand Rapids (G-11330)

Salem Community Hospital..........A...... 330 332-1551
Salem (G-16560)

Salutary Providers Inc...............C...... 440 964-8446
Ashtabula (G-753)

Samaritan Care Center & Villa......D...... 330 725-4123
Medina (G-13998)

Sanctuary At Tuttle Crossing........D...... 614 408-0182
Dublin (G-10327)

Sanctuary At Wilmington Place.....D...... 937 256-4663
Dayton (G-9751)

Sateri Home Inc.......................D...... 330 758-8106
Youngstown (G-20204)

Schoenbrunn Healthcare.............D...... 330 339-3595
New Philadelphia (G-14980)

Schroer Properties Inc...............D...... 740 687-5100
Lancaster (G-12433)

Schroer Properties Inc...............C...... 440 357-7900
Mentor (G-14106)

Select Spclty Hsptal-Akron LLC.....D...... 330 761-7500
Akron (G-423)

Semma Enterprises Inc..............C...... 513 863-7775
Middletown (G-14328)

Senior Care Inc........................E...... 937 372-1530
Xenia (G-19925)

Senior Care Inc........................E...... 937 291-3211
Miamisburg (G-14217)

Shelby County Mem Hosp Assn......D...... 937 492-9591
Sidney (G-16798)

Shepherd of The Valley Luthera.....D...... 330 530-4038
Youngstown (G-20209)

Shepherd of The Valley Luthera.....C...... 330 726-9061
Youngstown (G-20210)

Sienna Hills Nursing & Rehab.......E...... 740 546-3013
Adena (G-8)

Singleton Health Care Center.......E...... 216 231-0076
Cleveland (G-6410)

Sisters of Charity of Cinc............D...... 513 347-5200
Mount Saint Joseph (G-14744)

Sisters of Little.......................C...... 216 464-1222
Warrensville Heights (G-18780)

Sisters of Little.......................C...... 419 698-4331
Oregon (G-15608)

Slovene Home For The Aged.........C...... 216 486-0268
Cleveland (G-6417)

Snf Wadsworth LLC..................D...... 330 336-3472
Solon (G-16898)

Somerset NH LLC.....................D...... 740 743-2924
Somerset (G-16918)

Southbrook Health Care Ctr Inc.....C...... 937 322-3436
Springfield (G-17113)

Sprenger Enterprises Inc............A...... 440 244-2019
Lorain (G-12945)

Spring Meadow Extended Care Ce....D...... 419 866-6124
Holland (G-11916)

Springhills LLC.......................D...... 513 424-9999
Middletown (G-14355)

St Augustine Corporation............B...... 216 939-7600
Lakewood (G-12363)

St Edward Home.......................C...... 330 668-2828
Fairlawn (G-10851)

St Joseph Leasing Co LLC...........C...... 513 530-1654
Blue Ash (G-1652)

Stone Crossing Assisted Living......C...... 330 492-7131
Canton (G-2499)

Stow Opco LLC........................D...... 502 429-8062
Stow (G-17232)

Streetsboro Opco LLC................D...... 502 429-8062
Streetsboro (G-17273)

Summit Facility Operations LLC.....D...... 330 633-0555
Tallmadge (G-17492)

Sumner Home For The Aged Inc.....C...... 330 666-2952
Copley (G-8976)

Sun Healthcare Group Inc............C...... 419 784-1450
Defiance (G-9943)

Sunbrdge Marion Hlth Care Corp....D...... 740 389-6306
Marion (G-13461)

Sunbridge Healthcare LLC...........C...... 740 342-5161
New Lexington (G-14929)

Sunrise Connecticut Avenue Ass....E...... 614 451-6766
Columbus (G-8712)

Sunrise Manor Convalescent Ctr....D...... 513 797-5144
Amelia (G-576)

Sunrise Senior Living Inc............C...... 937 438-0054
Dayton (G-9801)

Sunrise Senior Living Inc............E...... 614 418-9775
Gahanna (G-11149)

Sunrise Senior Living Inc............D...... 440 895-2383
Rocky River (G-16446)

Sunrise Senior Living Inc............D...... 440 808-0074
Westlake (G-19410)

Sunrise Senior Living Inc............E...... 216 751-0930
Cleveland (G-6479)

Sunrise Senior Living Inc............D...... 614 457-3500
Upper Arlington (G-18402)

Sunrise Senior Living Inc............E...... 614 846-6500
Worthington (G-19854)

Sunrise Senior Living LLC...........D...... 937 836-9617
Englewood (G-10601)

Sunrise Senior Living LLC...........E...... 330 262-1615
Wooster (G-19771)

Sunrise Senior Living LLC...........E...... 419 425-3440
Findlay (G-10966)

Sunrise Senior Living LLC...........E...... 330 707-1313
Poland (G-16090)

Sunrise Senior Living LLC...........E...... 513 729-5233
Cincinnati (G-4554)

Sunrise Senior Living LLC...........D...... 330 929-8500
Cuyahoga Falls (G-9128)

Sunrise Senior Living LLC...........E...... 216 447-8909
Cleveland (G-6480)

Sunrise Senior Living LLC...........E...... 513 893-9000
Hamilton (G-11645)

Sunset Mnor Hlthcare Group Inc....E...... 216 795-5710
Cleveland (G-6481)

Swa Inc................................C...... 440 243-7888
Cleveland (G-6489)

Swan Pnte Fclty Operations LLC.....D...... 419 867-7926
Maumee (G-13858)

Tender Nursing Care..................E...... 614 856-3508
Reynoldsburg (G-16332)

The Maria-Joseph Center.............B...... 937 278-2692
Dayton (G-9812)

Thornville NH LLC....................D...... 740 246-5253
Thornville (G-17507)

Tlevay Inc.............................C...... 419 385-3958
Toledo (G-18070)

Toledo Opco LLC......................D...... 502 429-8062
Toledo (G-18093)

Traditions At Bath Rd Inc.............D...... 330 929-6272
Cuyahoga Falls (G-9132)

Traditions At Stygler Road...........E...... 614 475-8778
Columbus (G-8772)

Trilogy Health Services LLC.........D...... 419 935-6511
Willard (G-19489)

Trilogy Healthcare Allen LLC........D...... 419 643-3161
Delphos (G-10037)

Trilogy Healthcare Putnam LLC.....C...... 419 532-2961
Kalida (G-12207)

Trilogy Rehab Services LLC.........A...... 740 452-3000
Zanesville (G-20368)

Trinity Health Corporation...........B...... 614 846-5420
Columbus (G-8781)

Twilight Gardens Healthcare.........E...... 419 668-2086
Norwalk (G-15458)

Twin Oaks Care Center Inc..........E...... 419 524-1205
Mansfield (G-13258)

U C M Residential Services..........D...... 937 643-3757
Union City (G-18355)

United Church Homes Inc............D...... 740 382-4885
Marion (G-13471)

United Church Homes Inc............C...... 419 621-1900
Sandusky (G-16651)

United Church Homes Inc............C...... 937 878-0262
Fairborn (G-10684)

United Church Homes Inc............D...... 740 376-5600
Marietta (G-13392)

United Church Homes Inc............D...... 740 286-7551
Jackson (G-12181)

University Hospitals Health..........E...... 440 285-4040
Chardon (G-2722)

University Manor Healthcare.........C...... 216 721-1400
Cleveland (G-6598)

University Manor Hlth Care Ctr......C...... 216 721-1400
Cleveland (G-6599)

Uvmc Management Corporation.....D...... 937 440-4000
Troy (G-18237)

Uvmc Nursing Care Inc..............C...... 937 440-7663
Troy (G-18238)

Uvmc Nursing Care Inc..............C...... 937 667-7500
Tipp City (G-17572)

Uvmc Nursing Care Inc..............C...... 937 473-2075
Covington (G-9049)

V Clew LLC............................E...... 740 687-2273
Lancaster (G-12443)

V Vrable Inc...........................C...... 614 545-5500
Columbus (G-8839)

Valley Hospice Inc....................E...... 740 859-5041
Rayland (G-16274)

Valley View Alzhimers Care Ctr.....D...... 740 998-2948
Frankfort (G-11019)

Vancare Inc...........................C...... 937 898-4202
Vandalia (G-18549)

Vancrest Apts.........................E...... 419 695-7335
Delphos (G-10039)

Vancrest Health Care Center.........D...... 419 264-0700
Holgate (G-11867)

Vienna Enterprises Inc...............E...... 937 568-4524
South Vienna (G-16949)

Vista Centre...........................D...... 330 424-5852
Lisbon (G-12806)

Volunters Amer Care Facilities.......C...... 419 225-9040
Lima (G-12774)

Vrable II Inc...........................D...... 614 545-5502
Columbus (G-8865)

Vrable IV Inc..........................D...... 614 545-5502
Columbus (G-8866)

Walnut Hills Inc......................C...... 330 852-2457
Walnut Creek (G-18633)

Washington Manor Inc...............C...... 937 433-3441
Dayton (G-9867)

Waterville Care LLC..................D...... 419 878-3901
Waterville (G-18795)

Waverly Care Center Inc.............E...... 740 947-2113
Waverly (G-18824)

Wayside Farms Inc...................D...... 330 666-7716
Peninsula (G-15814)

West Liberty Care Center Inc........C...... 937 465-5065
West Liberty (G-19122)

West Side Dtscher Fruen Verein.....B...... 440 238-3361
Strongsville (G-17359)

Western Hills Care Center...........C...... 513 941-0099
Cincinnati (G-4788)

Western Rsrve Msonic Cmnty Inc...C...... 330 721-3000
Medina (G-14014)

Wexner Heritage Village.............B...... 614 231-4900
Columbus (G-8894)

Wickliffe Country Place Ltd..........C...... 440 944-9400
Wickliffe (G-19478)

Widows Home of Dayton Ohio.......D...... 937 252-1661
Dayton (G-9880)

Willow Brook Chrstn Cmmunities....C...... 740 369-0048
Delaware (G-10016)

Wilmington Halthcare Group Inc....D...... 937 382-1621
Wilmington (G-19653)

Employee Codes: A=Over 500 employees, B=251-500
C=101-250, D=51-100, E=25-50

SERVICES

Windsong Healthcare Group LLC ....E 216 292-5706
Akron (G-502)
Windsor House Inc ....D....... 330 743-1393
Youngstown (G-20248)
Windsor House Inc ....D....... 330 482-1375
Columbiana (G-6795)
Windsor House Inc ....C....... 330 549-9259
Columbiana (G-6796)
Windsor House Inc ....C....... 330 759-7858
Youngstown (G-20247)
Windsor House Inc ....E....... 440 834-0544
Burton (G-2020)
Windsor Medical Center Inc ....' 330 499-8300
Canton (G-2536)
Woodland Assisted Living Resi ....E 614 755-7591
Columbus (G-8914)
Woodlands Healthcare Group LLC ......D 330 297-4564
Ravenna (G-16271)
Woodsfield Opco LLC ....D....... 502 429-8062
Woodsfield (G-19679)
Woodside Village Care Center ....D....... 419 947-2015
Mount Gilead (G-14736)
Woodstock Healthcare Group Inc ....E 937 826-3351
Woodstock (G-19681)
Wyant Leasing Co LLC ....B....... 330 836-7953
Akron (G-505)
Xenia West Management Systems ......D....... 937 372-8081
Xenia (G-19937)
Yorkland Health Care Inc ....D....... 614 751-2525
Columbus (G-8926)
Youngstown Area Jwish Fdration ....D....... 330 746-1076
Youngstown (G-20257)
Zandex Inc ....E....... 740 454-1400
Zanesville (G-20373)
Zandex Inc ....C....... 740 872-0809
New Concord (G-14905)
Zandex Inc ....C....... 740 454-9769
Zanesville (G-20375)
Zandex Inc ....C....... 740 695-7233
Saint Clairsville (G-16513)
Zandex Inc ....D....... 740 967-1111
Johnstown (G-12205)
Zandex Inc ....D....... 740 454-6823
Zanesville (G-20376)
Zandex Health Care Corporation ......C....... 740 452-4636
Zanesville (G-20377)
Zandex Health Care Corporation ......C....... 740 454-9769
Zanesville (G-20378)
Zandex Health Care Corporation ......C....... 740 695-7233
Saint Clairsville (G-16514)
Zandex Health Care Corporation ......C....... 740 454-1400
New Concord (G-14906)
Zandex Health Care Corporation ......E....... 740 454-1400
Zanesville (G-20379)
Zanesville NH LLC ....D....... 740 452-4351
Zanesville (G-20384)

NURSING HOME, EXC SKILLED & INTERMEDIATE CARE FACILITY

Accurate Healthcare Inc ....E....... 513 208-6988
West Chester (G-19040)
Alpha Nursing Homes Inc ....D....... 740 622-2074
Coshocton (G-8997)
Antioch Cnnction Canton MI LLC ......E....... 614 531-9285
Pickerington (G-15947)
Antioch Salem Fields Frederick ....E....... 614 531-9285
Pickerington (G-15948)
Apostolic Christian Home Inc ....D....... 330 927-1010
Rittman (G-16403)
Arbors West LLC ....D....... 614 879-7661
West Jefferson (G-19103)
Blue Ash Healthcare Group Inc ....E....... 513 793-3362
Cincinnati (G-3060)
Bristol Village Homes ....E....... 740 947-2118
Waverly (G-18814)
Brookdale Senior Living Inc ....D....... 855 308-2438
Cincinnati (G-3078)
Brookdale Senior Living Inc ....E....... 513 745-9292
Cincinnati (G-3079)
Brookdale Senior Living Inc ....D....... 330 666-7011
Akron (G-110)
Brookdale Senior Living Inc ....E....... 440 892-4200
Westlake (G-19324)
Brookdale Senior Living Inc ....D....... 513 745-7600
Cincinnati (G-3080)
Bryant Health Center Inc ....C....... 740 532-6188
Ironton (G-12147)
Center Ridge Nursing Home Inc ....C....... 440 808-5500
North Ridgeville (G-15324)

Columbus Alzheimers Care Ctr ....C....... 614 459-7050
Columbus (G-7254)
Concord Hlth Rhabilitation Ctr ....E....... 740 574-8441
Wheelersburg (G-19432)
Consulate Management Co LLC ....D....... 740 259-2351
Lucasville (G-13046)
Country Acres of Wayne County ....E....... 330 698-2031
Wooster (G-19713)
Country Club Retirement Center ....D....... 440 992-0022
Ashtabula (G-731)
Country Club Retirement Center ....D....... 740 671-9330
Bellaire (G-1333)
Country Meadow Care Center LLC ......E....... 419 886-3922
Bellville (G-1391)
County of Auglaize ....C....... 419 738-3816
Wapakoneta (G-18640)
County of Henry ....C....... 419 592-8075
Napoleon (G-14803)
County of Shelby ....C....... 937 492-6900
Sidney (G-16771)
County of Wyandot ....D....... 419 294-1714
Upper Sandusky (G-18404)
Deaconess Long Term Care of MI ....A....... 513 487-3600
Cincinnati (G-3412)
Dobbins Nursing Home Inc ....C....... 513 553-4139
New Richmond (G-14993)
East Galbraith Health Care Ctr ....C....... 513 984-5220
Cincinnati (G-3471)
Elizabeth Scott Inc ....C....... 419 865-3002
Maumee (G-13784)
Encore Healthcare LLC ....C....... 330 769-2015
Seville (G-16685)
Evangelical Lutheran ....D....... 419 365-5115
Arlington (G-642)
First Choice Medical Staffing ....C....... 216 521-2222
Cleveland (G-5531)
First Community Village ....B....... 614 324-4455
Columbus (G-7585)
Gillette Associates LP ....D....... 330 372-1960
Warren (G-18709)
H C F Inc ....C....... 740 289-2528
Piketon (G-15976)
H C R Corp ....D....... 419 472-0076
Toledo (G-17776)
Harborside Healthcare NW Ohio ....C....... 419 636-5071
Bryan (G-1959)
Hardin County Home ....D....... 419 673-0961
Kenton (G-12280)
Harrison Pavilion ....E....... 513 662-5800
Cincinnati (G-3682)
Hcf of Findlay Inc ....D....... 419 999-2010
Findlay (G-10920)
Hcf of Fox Run Inc ....D....... 419 424-0832
Findlay (G-10921)
Hcf of Washington Inc ....E....... 419 999-2010
Wshngtn CT Hs (G-19875)
Hospice Tuscarawas County Inc ....C....... 330 343-7605
New Philadelphia (G-14965)
J W J Investments Inc ....C....... 419 643-3161
Delphos (G-10028)
Jacobs Dwelling Nursing Home ....E....... 740 824-3635
Coshocton (G-9049)
Jennings Ctr For Older Adults ....B....... 216 581-2900
Cleveland (G-5789)
Kingston Healthcare Company ....E....... 419 247-2880
Toledo (G-17840)
Levering Management Inc ....D....... 740 369-6400
Delaware (G-9995)
Levering Management Inc ....D....... 419 768-2401
Chesterville (G-2748)
Lincoln Park Associates II LP ....C....... 937 297-4300
Dayton (G-9568)
Maplewood At Bath Creek LLC ....D....... 234 208-9872
Cuyahoga Falls (G-9111)
Marion Manor ....D....... 740 387-9545
Marion (G-13443)
Mercer Residential Services ....E....... 419 586-4709
Celina (G-2603)
Mercy Health West Park ....C....... 513 451-8900
Cincinnati (G-4033)
Mikouis Enterprise Inc ....D....... 330 424-1418
Lisbon (G-12804)
Mill Run Care Center LLC ....D....... 614 527-3000
Hilliard (G-11798)
Mkjb Inc ....D....... 513 851-8400
West Chester (G-18975)
Mohun Health Care Center ....E....... 614 416-6132
Columbus (G-8095)
Morning View Delaware Inc ....C....... 740 965-3984
Sunbury (G-17391)

New Concord Health Center ....C....... 740 826-4135
New Concord (G-14902)
Norwood Health Care Center LLC ......D....... 513 351-0153
Cincinnati (G-4135)
Nursing Care MGT Amer Inc ....D....... 740 927-9888
Pataskala (G-15786)
Nursing Care MGT Amer Inc ....D....... 513 793-5092
Cincinnati (G-4142)
Oakwood Health Care Svcs Inc ....C....... 440 439-7976
Cleveland (G-6109)
Orchard Villa Inc ....C....... 419 697-4100
Oregon (G-15603)
Otterbein Snior Lfstyle Chices ....C....... 513 260-7690
Middletown (G-14352)
Overlook House ....E....... 216 795-3550
Cleveland (G-6150)
Park Haven Inc ....E....... 440 992-9441
Ashtabula (G-751)
Partners of City View LLC ....C....... 216 361-1414
Cleveland (G-6177)
Rae-Ann Holdings Inc ....D....... 440 871-0500
Westlake (G-19397)
Rae-Ann Holdings Inc ....D....... 440 871-5181
Cleveland (G-6281)
Regency Park ....D....... 330 682-2273
Orrville (G-15645)
Regency Park Nursing & Rehab ....D....... 330 682-2273
Orrville (G-15646)
Residence At Kensington Place ....C....... 513 863-4218
Hamilton (G-11638)
Roselawn Health Services Corp ....E....... 330 823-0618
Alliance (G-550)
Samaritan Care Center & Villa ....D....... 330 725-4123
Medina (G-13998)
Sarah Moore Hlth Care Ctr Inc ....D....... 740 362-9641
Delaware (G-10005)
Schoenbrunn Healthcare ....D....... 330 339-3595
New Philadelphia (G-14980)
Serenity Center Inc ....C....... 614 891-1111
Columbus (G-8621)
Shiloh Group ....C....... 937 833-2219
Brookville (G-1917)
Society of The Transfiguration ....E....... 513 771-7462
Cincinnati (G-4501)
Steubenville Country CLB Manor ....D....... 740 266-6118
Steubenville (G-17171)
Stratford Commons Inc ....C....... 440 914-0900
Solon (G-16902)
Summit At Park Hills LLC ....E....... 317 462-8048
Fairborn (G-10683)
Sunrise Senior Living Inc ....E....... 614 846-6500
Worthington (G-19854)
Susan A Smith Crystal Care ....E....... 419 747-2666
Butler (G-2022)
The Villa At Lake MGT Co ....D....... 440 599-1999
Conneaut (G-8960)
Traditions At Mill Run ....D....... 614 771-0100
Hilliard (G-11823)
Traditions of Chillicothe ....E....... 740 773-8107
Chillicothe (G-2831)
Uvmc Nursing Care Inc ....C....... 937 473-2075
Covington (G-9049)
Windsor House Inc ....C....... 330 759-7858
Youngstown (G-20247)
Youngstown Area Jwish Fdration ....D....... 330 746-1076
Youngstown (G-20257)
Zandex Health Care Corporation ....C....... 740 695-7233
Saint Clairsville (G-16514)

NUTRITION SVCS

Abbott Laboratories ....A....... 614 624-3191
Columbus (G-6851)
Ironton and Lawrence County ....E....... 740 532-7855
Ironton (G-12156)
Ironton and Lawrence County ....B....... 740 532-3534
Ironton (G-12155)
New Carlisle Spt & Fitnes Ctr ....E....... 937 846-1000
New Carlisle (G-14895)
Ohio State University ....E....... 614 292-5504
Columbus (G-8304)

NUTS: Metal

Facil North America Inc ....C....... 330 487-2500
Twinsburg (G-18265)

OFC/CLINIC OF MED DRS: Special, Phys Or Surgeon, Eye Or ENT

Cei Physicians PSC Inc ....E....... 513 531-2020
Cincinnati (G-3142)

(G-0000) Company's Geographic Section entry number

David M Schneider MD Inc ....E 513 752-5700
Cincinnati (G-2849)
Lca-Vision Inc ....C 513 792-9292
Cincinnati (G-3915)
Ohio Retina Associates Inc................E 330 966-9800
Canton (G-2430)
Surgicenter Ltd ....E 740 522-3937
Newark (G-15102)
System Optics Laser Vision Ctr ....D 330 630-2451
Tallmadge (G-17492)

OFC/CLINIC OF MED DRS: Specl, Phys Or Surgeon, Occup & Indl

Medcentral Health System ....E 419 526-8900
Ontario (G-15562)
Whole Health Management Inc ....C 216 921-8601
Cleveland (G-6682)

OFC/CLINIC, MED DRS: Specl, Phys Or Surgeon, Infect Disease

Central Ohio Primary Care ....D 614 508-0110
Westerville (G-19234)
Ohio State University ....E 614 293-8732
Columbus (G-8321)

OFCS & CLINICS, MEDICAL DRS: Specl, Physician Or Surgn, ENT

Adrian M Schnall MD ....D 216 291-4300
Cleveland (G-4902)
Cincinnati Head and Neck Inc..............E 513 232-3277
Cincinnati (G-3247)
E N T Toledo Inc ....E 419 578-7555
Toledo (G-17707)
Mark E Grosinger ....E 937 382-2000
Wilmington (G-19633)
Nelson & Bold Inc ....E 440 975-1422
Willoughby (G-19554)
Ohio Head & Neck Surgeons Inc ....E 330 492-2844
Canton (G-2426)
Richard J Nelson MD ....E 419 578-7555
Maumee (G-13845)
Southwest Ohio Ent Spclsts Inc ....E 937 496-2600
Dayton (G-9779)
University Otolaryngologists ....E 614 273-2241
Columbus (G-8820)

OFFICE CLEANING OR CHARRING SVCS

Clinton-Carvell Inc ....E 614 351-8858
Columbus (G-7229)
Rcs Enterprises Inc ....D 614 337-8520
Columbus (G-8492)
Scarlet & Gray Cleaning Svc................C 513 661-4483
Cincinnati (G-4434)
Stb Enterprises ....E 330 478-0044
Canton (G-2496)

OFFICE EQPT & ACCESSORY CUSTOMIZING SVCS

Andrew Belmont Sargent ....E 513 769-7800
Cincinnati (G-2965)
Document Imging Spcialists LLC...........E 614 868-9008
Hilliard (G-11762)
Fusion Interior Services Ltd ....E 513 759-4100
West Chester (G-18928)

OFFICE EQPT WHOLESALERS

American Copy Equipment Inc.............C 330 722-9555
Cleveland (G-4952)
Apg Office Furnishings Inc ....E 216 621-4590
Cleveland (G-4989)
Big Lots Stores Inc ....A 614 278-6800
Columbus (G-7035)
Canon Solutions America Inc ....D 216 446-3830
Independence (G-12053)
Collaborative Inc ....E 419 242-7405
Toledo (G-17667)
Comdoc Inc ....C 330 896-2346
Uniontown (G-18363)
David Francis Corporation ....C 216 524-0900
Cleveland (G-5408)
Document Imging Spcialists LLC ....E 614 868-9008
Hilliard (G-11762)
Essendant Co ....C 330 425-4001
Twinsburg (G-18264)

Essendant Co ....D 614 876-7774
Columbus (G-7534)
Friends Service Co Inc ....D 419 427-1704
Findlay (G-10910)
Giesecke & Devrient Amer Inc ....C 330 425-1515
Twinsburg (G-18274)
Lorain Cnty Sty Off Eqp Co Inc ....E 440 960-7070
Amherst (G-592)
M T Business Technologies ....E 440 933-7682
Avon Lake (G-924)
Modern Office Methods Inc ....D 513 791-0909
Blue Ash (G-1613)
Neopost USA Inc ....E 440 526-3196
Brecksville (G-1792)
Office Concepts Inc ....E 419 221-2679
Lima (G-12710)
Office Depot Inc ....E 800 463-3768
Cleveland (G-6112)
Office World Inc ....E 419 991-4694
Lima (G-12791)
Ohio Business Machines LLC ....E 216 485-2000
Cleveland (G-6117)
P-N-D Communications Inc..................E 419 683-1922
Crestline (G-9059)
Perry Pro Tech Inc ....E 419 475-9030
Perrysburg (G-15901)
Perry Pro Tech Inc ....D 419 228-1360
Lima (G-12720)
Ricoh Usa Inc ....D 216 574-9111
Cleveland (G-6324)
Ricoh Usa Inc ....E 330 384-9111
Akron (G-408)
Springfield Business Eqp Co.................E 937 322-3828
Springfield (G-17117)
Symatic Inc ....E 330 225-1510
Brunswick (G-1941)
Tameran Graphic Systems Inc..............E 440 349-7100
Solon (G-16908)
Viking Office Products Inc ....B 513 881-7200
West Chester (G-19032)
W B Mason Co Inc ....D 216 267-5000
Cleveland (G-6644)
Xerox Corporation ....D 740 592-5609
Athens (G-812)
Xerox Corporation ....B 513 554-3200
Blue Ash (G-1684)

OFFICE EQPT, WHOLESALE: Blueprinting

Franklin Imaging Llc ....E 614 885-6894
Columbus (G-7618)

OFFICE EQPT, WHOLESALE: Duplicating Machines

Northcoast Duplicating Inc ....C 216 573-6681
Cleveland (G-6087)

OFFICE EQPT, WHOLESALE: Photocopy Machines

Comdoc Inc ....E 330 539-4822
Girard (G-11285)
Donnellon Mc Carthy Inc.....................E 937 299-3564
Moraine (G-14648)
Donnellon Mc Carthy Inc.....................E 513 681-3200
Cincinnati (G-3439)
Goodremonts ....E 419 476-1492
Toledo (G-17766)
Gordon Flesch Company Inc ....E 419 884-2031
Mansfield (G-13179)
Graphic Enterprises Inc ....D 800 553-6616
North Canton (G-15207)
Konica Minolta Business Soluti ....E 614 766-7800
Dublin (G-10264)
Konica Minolta Business Soluti ....E 910 990-5837
Cleveland (G-5840)
Konica Minolta Business Soluti ....D 440 546-5795
Broadview Heights (G-1837)
Konica Minolta Business Soluti ....E 419 536-7720
Toledo (G-17843)
Ricoh Usa Inc ....D 513 984-9898
Sharonville (G-16730)
Ricoh Usa Inc ....D 614 310-6500
Worthington (G-19845)
Ricoh Usa Inc ....D 330 523-3900
Richfield (G-16376)
Xerox Corporation ....D 216 642-7806
Cleveland (G-6697)

OFFICE FURNITURE REPAIR & MAINTENANCE SVCS

Recycled Systems Furniture Inc ....E 614 880-9110
Worthington (G-19842)

OFFICE MANAGEMENT SVCS

North Randall Village ....D 216 663-1112
Cleveland (G-6080)
Outreach Professional Svcs Inc............D 216 472-4094
Cleveland (G-6148)
Summit Advantage LLC ....D 330 835-2453
Fairlawn (G-10853)

OFFICE SPLY & STATIONERY STORES

Staples Inc ....E 740 845-5600
London (G-12875)
Staples Inc ....E 614 472-2014
Columbus (G-8685)

OFFICE SPLY & STATIONERY STORES: Office Forms & Splys

Hubbard Company ....E 419 784-4455
Defiance (G-9917)
Lorain Cnty Sty Off Eqp Co Inc ....E 440 960-7070
Amherst (G-592)
Office Depot Inc ....E 800 463-3768
Cleveland (G-6112)
OfficeMax North America Inc ....E 614 899-6186
Westerville (G-19286)
Veritiv Operating Company ....E 419 243-6100
Toledo (G-18137)
Viking Office Products Inc ....B 513 881-7200
West Chester (G-19032)

OFFICE SPLY & STATIONERY STORES: School Splys

United Art and Education Inc................E 800 322-3247
Dayton (G-9830)

OFFICE SPLYS, NEC, WHOLESALE

Essendant Co ....D 330 650-9361
Hudson (G-11977)
Essendant Co ....C 330 425-4001
Twinsburg (G-18264)
Essendant Co ....D 513 942-1354
West Chester (G-19049)
Essendant Co ....D 614 876-7774
Columbus (G-7534)
Indepndence Office Bus Sup Inc...........D 216 398-8880
Cleveland (G-5746)
Powell Company Ltd...........................D 419 228-3552
Lima (G-12723)
S P Richards Company ....E 614 497-2270
Obetz (G-15529)
Seagate Office Products Inc ....E 419 861-6161
Holland (G-11913)
Wasserstrom Company ....B 614 228-6525
Columbus (G-8878)

OFFICES & CLINICS DOCTORS OF MED: Intrnl Med Practitioners

Cardiologist of Clark & Champ.............E 937 323-1404
Springfield (G-17004)
Central Ohio Primary Care ....E 614 882-0708
Westerville (G-19235)
Erieside Medical Group ....E 440 918-6270
Willoughby (G-19521)
Unity Health Network LLC ....E 330 678-7782
Kent (G-12266)

OFFICES & CLINICS DRS OF MED: Psychiatrists/Psychoanalysts

Consolidated Care Inc ....E 937 465-8065
West Liberty (G-19120)

OFFICES & CLINICS HLTH PRACTITNRS: Psychiatric Social Wrkr

Consolidated Care Inc ....E 937 465-8065
West Liberty (G-19120)
Pastoral Counseling Svc Summit...........C 330 996-4600
Akron (G-371)

SERVICES

OFFICES & CLINICS OF DENTISTS: Dental Clinic

Dental Center Northwest Ohio..............E....... 419 422-7664
   Findlay *(G-10897)*
Metrohealth Dept of Dentistry...............E....... 216 778-4739
   Cleveland *(G-5965)*
Smile Brands Inc.................................E....... 419 627-1255
   Sandusky *(G-16642)*
State Valley Dental Center....................E....... 330 920-8060
   Cuyahoga Falls *(G-9125)*
Stow Dental Group Inc.........................E....... 330 688-6456
   Stow *(G-17231)*

OFFICES & CLINICS OF DENTISTS: Dental Surgeon

Ohio State University............................E....... 614 292-5144
   Columbus *(G-8326)*
Oral & Maxillofacial Surgeons ....E....... 419 385-5743
   Toledo *(G-17965)*
Oral & Maxillofacial Surgeons ....E....... 419 471-0300
   Toledo *(G-17966)*

OFFICES & CLINICS OF DENTISTS: Dentists' Office

Advance Implant Dentistry Inc ....E....... 513 271-0821
   Cincinnati *(G-2909)*
Ashtabula Dental Associates..................E....... 440 992-3146
   Ashtabula *(G-717)*
Association of Prosthodontics................E....... 614 885-2022
   Worthington *(G-19794)*
Charles C Smith DDS Inc ....E....... 937 667-2417
   Tipp City *(G-17551)*
Chester West Dental Group Inc...............E....... 513 942-8181
   West Chester *(G-18884)*
Chester West Dentistry ....E....... 330 753-7734
   Akron *(G-127)*
Cincinnati Dental Services.....................E....... 513 753-6446
   Cincinnati *(G-2845)*
Cincinnati Dental Services.....................E....... 513 741-7779
   Cincinnati *(G-3238)*
Cincinnati Dental Services.....................D....... 513 721-8888
   Cincinnati *(G-3239)*
Cincinnati Dental Services.....................E....... 513 774-8800
   Loveland *(G-12982)*
Dental Facility ....E....... 614 292-1472
   Columbus *(G-7436)*
Dental Health Group PA ....E....... 330 630-9222
   Akron *(G-183)*
Dental Health Services ....E....... 330 864-9090
   Fairlawn *(G-10821)*
Donald Bowen and Assoc DDS ....E....... 614 274-0454
   Columbus *(G-7466)*
Eric W Warnock...................................E....... 419 228-2233
   Lima *(G-12633)*
Family Dental Team Inc ....E....... 330 733-7911
   Fairlawn *(G-10828)*
Family Dentistry Inc.............................E....... 513 932-6991
   Lebanon *(G-12465)*
Fixari Family Dental Inc........................E....... 614 866-7445
   Columbus *(G-7593)*
Greiner Dental Association ....E....... 440 255-2600
   Mentor *(G-14057)*
Hopewell Dental Care ....E....... 740 522-5000
   Newark *(G-15041)*
Hudec Dental Associates Inc ....D....... 216 485-5788
   Brecksville *(G-1784)*
Lawrence M Shell DDS ....E....... 614 235-3444
   Columbus *(G-7959)*
Locust Dental Center ....E....... 330 535-7876
   Akron *(G-320)*
Lucas & Clark Family Dentistry ....E....... 937 393-3494
   Hillsboro *(G-11850)*
Mahoning Valley Dental Service ....E....... 330 759-1771
   Youngstown *(G-20109)*
Painesville Dental Group Inc ....E....... 440 354-2183
   Painesville *(G-15732)*
Rahn Dental Group Inc ....E....... 937 435-0324
   Dayton *(G-9725)*
Raymond A Greiner DDS Inc ....E....... 440 951-6688
   Mentor *(G-14100)*
Shelley Elizabeth Blum.........................E....... 440 964-0542
   Ashtabula *(G-755)*
Thomas and Associates ....E....... 330 494-2111
   Canton *(G-2510)*
Thomas E Anderson DDS Inc ....E....... 330 467-6466
   Northfield *(G-15387)*

US Dental Care/M D Gelender................E....... 614 252-3181
   Columbus *(G-8833)*
Van Buren Dental Associates ....E....... 937 253-9115
   Kettering *(G-12302)*

OFFICES & CLINICS OF DENTISTS: Periodontist

Martin Ls DDS Ms ....E....... 513 829-8999
   Fairfield *(G-10749)*

OFFICES & CLINICS OF DENTISTS: Prosthodontist

Ohio State University............................D....... 614 292-5578
   Columbus *(G-8299)*
Ohio State University............................D....... 614 292-1472
   Columbus *(G-8344)*

OFFICES & CLINICS OF DENTISTS: Specialist, Practitioners

Affiliates In Oral & Maxlofcl ....E....... 513 829-8080
   West Chester *(G-18862)*
Equitas Health Inc ....D....... 614 299-2437
   Columbus *(G-7527)*

OFFICES & CLINICS OF DOCTORS OF MEDICINE: Allergist

Allergy & Asthma Inc ....E....... 740 654-8623
   Lancaster *(G-12369)*
Allergy & Asthma Centre Dayton ....E....... 937 435-8999
   Centerville *(G-2621)*
Bernstein Allergy Group Inc ....E....... 513 931-0775
   Cincinnati *(G-3041)*
ENt and Allergy Health Svcs ....E....... 440 779-1112
   North Olmsted *(G-15286)*

OFFICES & CLINICS OF DOCTORS OF MEDICINE: Anesthesiologist

Anesthesia Associates Inc ....E....... 440 350-0832
   Painesville *(G-15693)*
Anesthesiology Assoc of Akron...............E....... 330 344-6401
   Akron *(G-74)*
Anesthesiology Services Netwrk ....E....... 937 208-6173
   Dayton *(G-9234)*
Anesthsia Assoc Cincinnati Inc ....D....... 513 585-0577
   Cincinnati *(G-2966)*
Bel-Park Anesthesia ....E....... 330 480-3658
   Youngstown *(G-19963)*
Cleveland Anesthesia Group ....E....... 216 901-5706
   Independence *(G-12059)*
Kettering Anesthesia Assoc Inc ....D....... 937 298-4331
   Dayton *(G-9535)*
Kevin C McDonnell MD ....D....... 330 344-6401
   Akron *(G-301)*
Midwest Physcans Ansthsia Svcs ....D....... 614 884-0641
   Columbus *(G-8083)*
Russell D Ens Do ....E....... 330 499-5700
   Canton *(G-2467)*
Sabry Hospital ....E....... 216 476-7052
   Cleveland *(G-6359)*
University Anesthesiologists...................E....... 216 844-3777
   Cleveland *(G-6585)*

OFFICES & CLINICS OF DOCTORS OF MEDICINE: Dermatologist

Advanced Dermatology and Skin............E....... 330 965-8760
   Youngstown *(G-19947)*
Associates In Dermatology Inc................E....... 440 249-0274
   Westlake *(G-19319)*
Buckeye Drmtlogy Drmthphthlogy............E....... 614 389-6331
   Dublin *(G-10153)*
Buckeye Drmtlogy Drmthphthlogy............E....... 614 317-9630
   Grove City *(G-11415)*
Center For Srgcal Drmtlogy Inc..............D....... 614 847-4100
   Westerville *(G-19150)*
Dermatlgists of Southwest Ohio ....E....... 937 435-2094
   Dayton *(G-9388)*
H M T Dermatology Inc ....E....... 330 725-0569
   Medina *(G-13946)*
Hmt Dermatology Associates Inc ....E....... 330 725-0569
   Medina *(G-13950)*
Laser Hair Removal Center ....D....... 937 433-7536
   Dayton *(G-9559)*
Patricia A Dickerson MD........................E....... 937 436-1117
   Dayton *(G-9688)*

Univ Dermatology................................D....... 513 475-7630
   Cincinnati *(G-4692)*
University Dermatology Cons..................E....... 513 584-4775
   Cincinnati *(G-4698)*
University Dermatology Cons..................E....... 513 475-7630
   Cincinnati *(G-4699)*
Warren Drmatology Allergies PC.............E....... 330 856-6365
   Warren *(G-18769)*
Westerville Dermatology Inc...................E....... 614 895-0400
   Westerville *(G-19305)*
Wright State Physcans Drmtlogy ....E....... 937 224-7546
   Beavercreek *(G-1198)*

OFFICES & CLINICS OF DOCTORS OF MEDICINE: Dispensary

Kindred Healthcare Inc........................D....... 937 222-5963
   Dayton *(G-9546)*

OFFICES & CLINICS OF DOCTORS OF MEDICINE: Endocrinologist

Endo-Surgical Center Fla LLC.................B....... 440 708-0582
   Chagrin Falls *(G-2664)*
Joslin Diabetes Center Inc ....E....... 937 401-7575
   Dayton *(G-9529)*
Reproductive Gynecology Inc ....E....... 330 452-6010
   Canton *(G-2454)*

OFFICES & CLINICS OF DOCTORS OF MEDICINE: Gastronomist

Columbus Gstrntrlogy Group Inc..........D....... 614 457-1213
   Columbus *(G-7285)*
Consultnts In Gastroenterology ....E....... 440 386-2250
   Painesville *(G-15705)*
Dayton Primary & Urgent Care ....E....... 937 461-0800
   Dayton *(G-9377)*
Digestive Care Inc...............................D....... 937 320-5050
   Beavercreek *(G-1215)*
Digestive Disease Consultants ....E....... 330 225-6468
   Brunswick *(G-1927)*
Endoscopy Center of Dayton..................E....... 937 320-5050
   Beavercreek *(G-1216)*
Gastrntrlogy Assoc Clvland Inc ....E....... 216 593-7700
   Cleveland *(G-5593)*
Gastroenterology Associates ....E....... 330 493-1480
   Canton *(G-2323)*
Greater Cincinnati Gastro Assc...............D....... 513 336-8636
   Cincinnati *(G-3652)*
North Shore Gstrenterology Inc ....E....... 440 808-1212
   Westlake *(G-19382)*
Norwood Endoscopy Center....................E....... 513 731-5600
   Cincinnati *(G-4133)*
Nwo Gastroenterology Assoc Inc ....E....... 419 471-1317
   Toledo *(G-17954)*
Ohio Gstroenterology Group Inc...............E....... 614 754-5500
   Columbus *(G-8260)*
Ohio Gstroenterology Group Inc...............D....... 614 754-5500
   Columbus *(G-8261)*
Promedica GI Physicians LLC.................E....... 419 843-7996
   Toledo *(G-17991)*

OFFICES & CLINICS OF DOCTORS OF MEDICINE: Group Health Assoc

Primecare Sutheastern Ohio Inc ....E....... 740 454-8551
   Zanesville *(G-20355)*

OFFICES & CLINICS OF DOCTORS OF MEDICINE: Gynecologist

Christ Hospital ....E....... 513 564-4000
   Cincinnati *(G-3200)*
Drs Paul Boyles & Kennedy ....E....... 614 734-3347
   Columbus *(G-7470)*
Findlay Womens Care LLC ....E....... 419 420-0904
   Findlay *(G-10907)*
George P Pettit MD Inc ....E....... 740 354-1434
   Portsmouth *(G-16139)*
Gyneclgic Onclgists of Ne Ohio ....E....... 330 384-6041
   Akron *(G-248)*
Marietta Gynecologic Assoc ....D....... 740 374-3622
   Marietta *(G-13352)*
Maumee Ob Gyn Assoc ....E....... 419 891-6201
   Maumee *(G-13819)*
Mercy Health......................................D....... 419 935-0187
   Willard *(G-19484)*
Northern Ohio Med Spclists LLC.............E....... 419 625-2841
   Sandusky *(G-16630)*

Ob-Gyn Specialists Lima Inc ....E 419 227-0610
  Lima (G-12709)
Obstetrics Gynclogy of Reserve ....E 330 666-1166
  Akron (G-355)
Physicians Surgeons For Women ....E 937 323-7340
  Springfield (G-17098)
Primary Cr Ntwrk Prmr Hlth Prt ....D 937 424-9800
  Dayton (G-9710)
Professionals For Womens Hlth...........E 614 268-8800
  Columbus (G-8471)
Reproductive Gynecology Inc ....E 330 375-7722
  Akron (G-403)
Reserve ....E 330 666-1166
  Akron (G-405)
Southwestern Obstetricians & G ....E 614 875-0444
  Grove City (G-11473)
Stark County Womens Clinic Inc...........D 330 493-0313
  Canton (G-2495)
Sunforest Ob Gyn Associates ....E 419 473-6622
  Toledo (G-18053)
University GYN&ob Cnsltnts Inc ....E 614 293-8697
  Columbus (G-8819)
Women Physicans of Ob/Gyn Inc ....E 614 734-3340
  Columbus (G-8913)
Womens Care Inc..................................D 419 756-6000
  Mansfield (G-13263)

OFFICES & CLINICS OF DOCTORS OF MEDICINE: Hematologist

Columbus Oncology Assoc Inc ....D 614 442-3130
  Columbus (G-7304)
Mahoning Vly Hmtlgy Onclgy Aso ...E 330 318-1100
  Youngstown (G-20110)
Medical Onclgy-Hematology Assn ....E 937 223-2183
  Dayton (G-9602)
Ohio Cancer Specialists......................E 419 756-2122
  Mansfield (G-13228)
Trumbull Mem Hosp Foundation ....A 330 841-9376
  Warren (G-18760)

OFFICES & CLINICS OF DOCTORS OF MEDICINE: Med Insurance Plan

American Para Prof Systems Inc..........E 513 531-2900
  Cincinnati (G-2949)
Doctors Ohiohealth Corporation ....A 614 544-5424
  Columbus (G-7464)
Medical Mutual of Ohio.........................E 614 621-4585
  Columbus (G-8053)

OFFICES & CLINICS OF DOCTORS OF MEDICINE: Nephrologist

Dayton Regional Dialysis Inc.................E 937 898-5526
  Dayton (G-9380)
Kidney & Hypertension Center ....E 513 861-0800
  Cincinnati (G-3867)
Kidney Group Inc ....E 330 746-1488
  Youngstown (G-20091)
Riverside Nephrology Assoc Inc ....E 614 538-2250
  Columbus (G-8536)
University of Cincinnati........................E 513 558-5471
  Cincinnati (G-4721)

OFFICES & CLINICS OF DOCTORS OF MEDICINE: Neurologist

Mayfield Clinic Inc...............................D 513 221-1100
  Cincinnati (G-3983)
Neurological Associates Inc ....D 614 544-4455
  Columbus (G-8181)
Neurology Nroscience Assoc Inc..........E 330 572-1011
  Akron (G-344)
Nuerocare Center Inc...........................D 330 494-2917
  Canton (G-2423)
Orthoneuro ....D 614 890-6555
  Columbus (G-8388)
Riverhills Healthcare Inc ....E 513 241-2370
  Cincinnati (G-4378)
Stark County Neurologists Inc ....D 330 494-2097
  Canton (G-2493)
University Neurology Inc.......................D 513 475-8730
  Cincinnati (G-4702)

OFFICES & CLINICS OF DOCTORS OF MEDICINE: Neurosurgeon

Chander M Kohli MD Facs Inc ....E 330 759-6978
  Youngstown (G-19985)

OFFICES & CLINICS OF DOCTORS OF MEDICINE: Obstetrician

Columbus Obsttrcans Gynclgists ....E 614 434-2400
  Columbus (G-7303)
Davue Ob-Gyn Associates Inc...............D 937 277-8988
  Dayton (G-9347)
Greater Cincinnati Ob/Gyn Inc...............D 513 245-3103
  Cincinnati (G-3653)
Metrohealth System ....D 216 778-8446
  Cleveland (G-5969)
Mount Auburn Obstetrics & Gyne ....E 513 241-4774
  Cincinnati (G-4078)
Obstetrics & Gynecology S Inc ....E 937 296-0167
  Dayton (G-9666)
Ohio State University............................E 614 293-4997
  Columbus (G-8317)
Preble County General Hlth Dst ....E 937 472-0087
  Eaton (G-10460)
Primehalth Wns Hlth Specialist ....E 440 918-4630
  Willoughby Hills (G-19592)
Progressive Womens Care ....E 330 629-8466
  Youngstown (G-20166)
Seven Hills Obgyn Associates ....E 513 922-6666
  Cincinnati (G-4458)
Seven Hills Womens Health Ctrs...........C 513 721-3200
  Cincinnati (G-4459)
Women Health Partners ....E 740 363-9021
  Delaware (G-10017)

OFFICES & CLINICS OF DOCTORS OF MEDICINE: Oncologist

Cleveland Clinic Community Onc ....E 216 447-9747
  Independence (G-12060)
Dayton Physicians LLC ....C 937 280-8400
  Dayton (G-9376)
Hope Ctr For Cncer Care Warren ....D 330 856-8600
  Warren (G-18713)
Independence Oncology ....E 216 524-7979
  Cleveland (G-5743)
Mercy Health - Springfield C ....E 937 323-5001
  Springfield (G-17078)
Ohio State University............................A 614 293-5066
  Columbus (G-8342)
Ohio State University............................A 614 257-3000
  Columbus (G-8300)
Oncolgy/Hmatology Care Inc PSC ....D 513 751-2145
  Cincinnati (G-4174)
Trihealth Oncology Inst LLC ....E 513 451-4033
  Cincinnati (G-4645)
University Hospitals Cleveland ....E 440 205-5755
  Mentor (G-14119)
US Oncology Inc ....E 937 352-2140
  Xenia (G-19932)

OFFICES & CLINICS OF DOCTORS OF MEDICINE: Ophthalmologist

Assocted Ctract Laser Surgeons ....E 419 693-4444
  Oregon (G-15583)
Aultman North Inc................................E 330 305-6999
  Canton (G-2207)
Bloomberg Ross MD............................E 740 454-1216
  Zanesville (G-20282)
Canton Ophthalmology Assoc ....E 330 994-1286
  Canton (G-2239)
Cei Physicians Inc ....B 513 984-5133
  Blue Ash (G-1521)
Cei Physicians PSC Inc ....E 513 233-2700
  Cincinnati (G-3141)
Cei Physicians PSC LLC ....C 513 984-5133
  Blue Ash (G-1522)
Eye Care Associates Inc ....D 330 746-7691
  Youngstown (G-20032)
Eye Centers of Ohio Inc ....E 330 966-1111
  North Canton (G-15202)
Eye Centers of Ohio Inc ....E 330 966-1111
  Canton (G-2308)
Fairview Eye Center Inc........................E 440 333-3060
  Cleveland (G-5506)
Kathleen K Karol MD ....D 419 878-7992
  Toledo (G-17837)
Kunesh Eye Center Inc.........................E 937 298-1703
  Oakwood (G-15482)
Midwest Retina Inc..............................E 614 233-9500
  Zanesville (G-20331)
Northast Ohio Eye Surgeons Inc...........E 330 678-0201
  Kent (G-12250)

Northast Ohio Eye Surgeons Inc...........E 330 836-8545
  Akron (G-347)
Northwest Eye Surgeons Inc ....E 614 451-7550
  Columbus (G-8205)
Ohio Eye Alliance.................................E 330 823-1680
  Alliance (G-542)
Ohio Eye Associates Inc ....D 800 423-0694
  Mansfield (G-13229)
Ohio Eye Specialists Inc ....E 800 948-3937
  Chillicothe (G-2807)
Ohio State University............................A 614 293-8116
  Columbus (G-8303)
Ophthalmology Associates of ....E 419 865-3866
  Maumee (G-13828)
Ophthlmic Srgeons Cons of Ohio ....E 614 221-7464
  Columbus (G-8378)
Optivue Inc ....C 419 891-1391
  Oregon (G-15602)
Pajka Eye Center Inc............................E 419 228-7432
  Lima (G-12717)
Regency Park Eye Associates ....E 419 882-0588
  Toledo (G-17997)
Retina Associate of Cleveland ....E 216 831-5700
  Beachwood (G-1100)
Retina Associate of Cleveland ....E 216 221-2878
  Westlake (G-19400)
Retina Group Inc ....E 614 464-3937
  Columbus (G-8528)
Robert Wiley MD Inc ....E 216 621-3211
  Cleveland (G-6335)
Roholt Vision Institute Inc.....................E 330 702-8755
  Canfield (G-2156)
Southern Ohio Eye Assoc LLC...............E 740 773-6347
  Chillicothe (G-2827)
Spectrum Eye Care Inc.........................E 419 423-8665
  Findlay (G-10961)
Summit Opthomology Optical ....E 330 864-8060
  Akron (G-459)
System Optics Csmt Srgcal Arts ....E 330 630-9699
  Tallmadge (G-17491)
TLC Eyecare ....E 419 882-2020
  Toledo (G-18069)
University Ophthalmology Assoc ....E 216 382-8022
  Cleveland (G-6600)
Wooster Ophthalmologists Inc...............E 330 345-7800
  Wooster (G-19787)

OFFICES & CLINICS OF DOCTORS OF MEDICINE: Pathologist

County of Montgomery..........................E 937 225-4156
  Dayton (G-9334)
Southwest Urology LLC ....E 440 845-0900
  Cleveland (G-6435)

OFFICES & CLINICS OF DOCTORS OF MEDICINE: Pediatrician

Anderson Hills Pediatrics Inc ....D 513 232-8100
  Cincinnati (G-2960)
AP Cchmc ....E 513 636-4200
  Cincinnati (G-2971)
Central Ohio Primary Care ....E 614 891-9505
  Westerville (G-19151)
Child & Adolescent Speciality ....E 937 667-7711
  Tipp City (G-17552)
Childrens Hospital Medical Ctr..............A 513 636-8778
  Cincinnati (G-3192)
Childrens Physician Inc ....E 330 494-5600
  Canton (G-2251)
Comprehensive Pediatrics.....................E 440 835-8270
  Westlake (G-19336)
Eastern Hills Pediatric Assoc ....E 513 231-3345
  Cincinnati (G-3476)
Emerald Pediatrics................................E 614 932-5050
  Dublin (G-10216)
Healthsource of Ohio Inc ....E 937 392-4381
  Georgetown (G-11272)
Jon R Dvorak MD ....E 419 872-7700
  Perrysburg (G-15883)
Kiddie West Pediatric Center.................E 614 276-7733
  Columbus (G-7901)
Mid-Ohio Pdiatrics Adolescents ....E 614 899-0000
  Westerville (G-19280)
New Beginnings Pediatrics Inc...............E 419 483-4122
  Bellevue (G-1381)
Ohio Pediatrics Inc ....E 937 299-2339
  Dayton (G-9671)
Ohio Pediatrics Inc ....E 937 299-2743
  Dayton (G-9672)

Pediatric Assoc Cincinnati..............E...... 513 791-1222
Cincinnati **(G-4221)**
Pediatric Assoc of Fairfield.............E...... 513 874-9460
Fairfield **(G-10769)**
Pediatric Assoc of Springfield............D...... 937 328-2320
Springfield **(G-17095)**
Pediatric Associates Inc....................E...... 614 501-7337
Columbus **(G-8435)**
Pediatric Associates of Dayton ....E...... 937 832-7337
Englewood **(G-10596)**
Pediatric Care Inc...........................E...... 513 931-6357
Cincinnati **(G-4222)**
Pediatric Services Inc......................E...... 440 845-1500
Cleveland **(G-6189)**
Pediatrics Assoc of Mt Carmel ....E...... 513 752-3650
Cincinnati **(G-2864)**
Pediatrics of Akron Inc.....................E...... 330 253-7753
Akron **(G-373)**
Pediatrics of Lima Inc......................E...... 419 222-4045
Lima **(G-12719)**
Portage Pediatrics...........................E...... 330 297-8824
Ravenna **(G-16258)**
Primary Care Physicians Assn...........E...... 330 499-9944
Canton **(G-2440)**
Queen City Physicians ....D...... 513 872-2061
Cincinnati **(G-4318)**
Rocking Horse Chld Hlth Ctr ....E...... 937 328-7266
Springfield **(G-17103)**
Suburban Pediatrics Inc....................E...... 513 336-6700
Cincinnati **(G-4551)**
Trihealth G LLC...............................D...... 513 624-5535
Cincinnati **(G-4643)**
University Prmry Care Prctices...........E...... 440 946-7391
Willoughby **(G-19579)**
West Side Pediatrics Inc....................E...... 513 922-8200
Cincinnati **(G-4785)**

OFFICES & CLINICS OF DOCTORS OF MEDICINE: Psychiatric Clinic

Osu Psychiatry LLC..........................E...... 614 794-1818
Columbus **(G-8396)**
Psy-Care Inc...................................E...... 330 856-6663
Warren **(G-18737)**
Psychiatric Solutions Inc...................C...... 440 953-3000
Willoughby **(G-19564)**
Psychiatric Solutions Inc...................C...... 330 759-2700
Youngstown **(G-20169)**
Psychiatric Solutions Inc...................C...... 419 891-9333
Maumee **(G-13837)**
Psychiatric Solutions Inc...................C...... 740 695-2131
Saint Clairsville **(G-16502)**

OFFICES & CLINICS OF DOCTORS OF MEDICINE: Psychiatrist

Rakesh Ranjan MD & Assoc Inc............E...... 216 375-9897
Cleveland **(G-6284)**
Robert E Lubow MD..........................E...... 513 961-8861
Cincinnati **(G-4389)**
University of Toledo.........................D...... 419 534-3770
Toledo **(G-18125)**

OFFICES & CLINICS OF DOCTORS OF MEDICINE: Radiologist

Advocate Radiology Bil......................C...... 614 210-1885
Powell **(G-16183)**
Center For Dagnstc Imaging Inc...........C...... 614 841-0800
Columbus **(G-6803)**
Dayton Medical Imaging.....................D...... 937 439-0390
Dayton **(G-9372)**
Drs Hill & Thomas Co ....E...... 440 944-8887
Cleveland **(G-5446)**
Franklin & Seidelmann Inc.................E...... 216 255-5700
Beachwood **(G-1059)**
Mrp Inc...E...... 513 965-9700
Milford **(G-14412)**
Nuray Radiologists Inc......................E...... 513 965-8059
Cincinnati **(G-4139)**
Osu Radiology LLC...........................E...... 614 293-8315
Columbus **(G-8397)**
Premier Radiology Group Inc..............E...... 937 431-9729
Beavercreek **(G-1177)**
Proscan Imaging LLC........................E...... 513 759-7350
West Chester **(G-18987)**
Radiology Physicians Inc...................E...... 614 717-9840
Delaware **(G-10001)**
Riverside Radiology and....................C...... 614 340-7747
Columbus **(G-8537)**

Uc Health Llc..................................D...... 513 475-7458
West Chester **(G-19020)**
University of Toledo.........................E...... 419 383-5322
Toledo **(G-18128)**
University Radiology Assoc ....D...... 513 475-8760
Cincinnati **(G-4729)**
University Rdlgsts of Clveland.............D...... 216 844-1700
Cleveland **(G-6602)**
Vanguard Imaging Partners ....D...... 937 236-4780
Dayton **(G-9851)**

OFFICES & CLINICS OF DOCTORS OF MEDICINE: Surgeon

Affiliates In Oral & Maxlofcl ....E...... 513 829-8080
West Chester **(G-18862)**
Akron General Health System ....E...... 330 665-8200
Akron **(G-42)**
Cincinnati Hand Surgery Cons ....E...... 513 961-4263
Cincinnati **(G-3246)**
Crystal Clinic Surgery Ctr Inc ....A...... 330 668-4040
Akron **(G-172)**
Evokes LLC....................................E...... 513 947-8433
Mason **(G-13578)**
Greater Dayton Surgery Ctr LLC ....E...... 937 535-2200
Dayton **(G-9473)**
Mount Carmel Central Ohio ....D...... 614 268-9561
Westerville **(G-19282)**
Neurosurgical Network Inc ....E...... 419 251-1155
Toledo **(G-17938)**
Northast Srgical Assoc of Ohio ....E...... 216 643-2780
Independence **(G-12104)**
Nueterra Holdings LLC......................E...... 614 451-0500
Columbus **(G-8214)**
Osu Surgery LLC..............................E...... 614 293-8116
Columbus **(G-8399)**
Osu Surgery LLC..............................C...... 614 261-1141
Columbus **(G-8400)**
Premier Health Specialists Inc............E...... 937 223-4518
Dayton **(G-9705)**
Provider Physicians Inc ....D...... 614 755-3000
Columbus **(G-8475)**
Queen City General & Vascular ....E...... 513 232-8181
Cincinnati **(G-4314)**
Riverhills Healthcare Inc ....E...... 513 791-6400
Cincinnati **(G-4379)**
Surgery Center Cincinnati LLC............D...... 513 947-1130
Cincinnati **(G-2871)**
Surgery Ctr An Ohio Ltd Partnr ....D...... 440 826-3240
Cleveland **(G-6488)**
Taylor Stn Surgical Ctr Ltd ....D...... 614 751-4466
Columbus **(G-8733)**
Thomas E Rojewski MD Inc ....E...... 740 454-0158
Zanesville **(G-20366)**
Uc Health Llc..................................D...... 513 475-8881
West Chester **(G-19022)**
University of Cncnnati Srgeons ....E...... 513 245-3300
Cincinnati **(G-4727)**
West Central Ohio Group Ltd ....E...... 419 224-7586
Lima **(G-12778)**

OFFICES & CLINICS OF DOCTORS OF MEDICINE: Surgeon, Plastic

A Thomas Dalagiannis MD..................E...... 419 887-7000
Maumee **(G-13744)**
Akron Plastic Surgeons Inc ....E...... 330 253-9161
Akron **(G-50)**
Lawrence A Cervino MD......................E...... 330 668-4065
Akron **(G-309)**
Lu-Jean Feng Clinic LLC......................E...... 216 831-7007
Cleveland **(G-5886)**
Plastic Surgery Group Inc...................E...... 513 791-4440
Cincinnati **(G-4253)**
Reynolds Road Surgical Ctr LLC ....D...... 419 578-7500
Toledo **(G-18006)**

OFFICES & CLINICS OF DOCTORS OF MEDICINE: Urologist

Advanced Urology Inc ....E...... 330 758-9787
Youngstown **(G-19948)**
Bruce R Bracken ....E...... 513 558-3700
Cincinnati **(G-3084)**
Gem City Urologist Inc.......................E...... 937 832-8400
Englewood **(G-10588)**
Northwest Columbus Urology ....E...... 937 342-9260
Springfield **(G-17090)**
Promedica Gnt-Urinary Surgeons ....E...... 419 531-8558
Toledo **(G-17992)**

South Dyton Urlgcal Asscations ....E...... 937 294-1489
Dayton **(G-9777)**
Uhmg Department of Urologist..............E...... 216 844-3009
Cleveland **(G-6562)**
Urological Associates Inc ....E...... 614 221-5189
Columbus **(G-8830)**

OFFICES & CLINICS OF DOCTORS, MEDICINE: Gen & Fam Practice

Adena Pckwy-Ross Fmly Physcans.........E...... 740 779-4500
Chillicothe **(G-2755)**
Alta Partners LLC..............................E...... 440 808-3654
Westlake **(G-19315)**
Barberton Area Family Practice ....E...... 330 615-3205
Barberton **(G-945)**
Blanchard Valley Hospital ....E...... 419 423-4335
Findlay **(G-10873)**
Butler Cnty Cmnty Hlth Cnsrtm.............D...... 513 454-1460
Hamilton **(G-11565)**
Campolo Michael MD ....E...... 740 522-7600
Newark **(G-15020)**
Canal Physician Group.......................E...... 330 344-4000
Akron **(G-116)**
Central Ohio Primary Care ....E...... 614 459-3687
Columbus **(G-7162)**
Central Ohio Primary Care ....E...... 614 451-1551
Columbus **(G-7163)**
Central Ohio Primary Care ....E...... 614 473-1300
Columbus **(G-7165)**
Central Ohio Primary Care ....D...... 614 552-2300
Reynoldsburg **(G-16290)**
Central Ohio Primary Care ....D...... 614 268-8164
Columbus **(G-7166)**
Central Ohio Primary Care ....E...... 614 834-8042
Canal Winchester **(G-2106)**
Central Ohio Primary Care ....D...... 614 540-7339
Worthington **(G-19796)**
Chillicothe Family Physicians ....E...... 740 779-4100
Chillicothe **(G-2762)**
City of Columbus ....E...... 614 645-1600
Columbus **(G-7207)**
Clevelan Clinic Hlth Sys W Reg...........E...... 216 476-7606
Cleveland **(G-5227)**
Clinton Memorial Hospital..................E...... 937 383-3402
Wilmington **(G-19614)**
Comprehensive Health Care Inc...........E...... 419 238-7777
Van Wert **(G-18476)**
Corporate Health Dimensions ....E...... 740 775-6119
Chillicothe **(G-2770)**
Defiance Family Physicians ....E...... 419 785-3281
Defiance **(G-9910)**
Dennis C McCluskey MD & Assoc..........E...... 330 628-2686
Mogadore **(G-14547)**
Doctors Hosp Physcn Svcs LLC............E...... 330 834-4725
Massillon **(G-13675)**
Dublin Family Care Inc.......................E...... 614 761-2244
Dublin **(G-10206)**
Dunlap Family Physicians Inc ....E...... 330 684-2015
Orrville **(G-15628)**
Fallen Timbers Fmly Physicians ....D...... 419 893-3321
Maumee **(G-13788)**
Falls Family Practice Inc ....E...... 330 923-9585
Cuyahoga Falls **(G-9089)**
Family Health Care Center Inc..............E...... 614 274-4171
Columbus **(G-7559)**
Family Medical Group........................E...... 513 389-1400
Cincinnati **(G-3529)**
Family Medicine Center Minerva ....E...... 330 868-4184
Minerva **(G-14519)**
Family Medicine Stark County..............E...... 330 499-5600
Canton **(G-2309)**
Family Physician Associates ....E...... 614 901-2273
Westerville **(G-19254)**
Family Physicians Associates..............E...... 440 442-3866
Cleveland **(G-5510)**
Family Physicians of Coshocton ....E...... 740 622-0332
Coshocton **(G-9014)**
Family Physicians of Gahanna ....E...... 614 471-9654
Columbus **(G-7560)**
Family Practice & Associates ....E...... 937 399-6650
Springfield **(G-17036)**
Family Practice Ctr Salem Inc ....E...... 330 332-9961
Salem **(G-16543)**
First Med Urgent & Fmly Ctr ....E...... 740 756-9238
Lancaster **(G-12405)**
Flowers Family Practice Inc.................E...... 614 277-9631
Grove City **(G-11434)**
Frederick C Smith Clinic Inc ....E...... 740 363-9021
Delaware **(G-9979)**

George G Ellis Jr MD ....E 330 965-0832
Youngstown *(G-20048)*

Grandview Family Practice ....E 740 258-9267
Columbus *(G-7684)*

Healthsource of Ohio Inc ....E 937 981-7707
Greenfield *(G-11363)*

Hillsboro Health Center Inc ....E 937 393-5781
Hillsboro *(G-11846)*

Holzer Clinic LLC ....E 740 886-9403
Proctorville *(G-16217)*

Hopewell Health Centers Inc ....E 740 596-5249
Mc Arthur *(G-13890)*

Institute/Reproductive Health ....E 513 585-2355
Cincinnati *(G-3764)*

Johnson Adams & Protrouski ....E 419 238-6251
Van Wert *(G-18481)*

Lake County Family Practice ....E 440 352-4880
Mentor *(G-14072)*

Medical Diagnostic Lab Inc....................E 440 333-1375
Avon *(G-894)*

Mercy Health ....E 419 492-1300
New Washington *(G-15002)*

Mercy Health ....E 513 985-0741
Cincinnati *(G-4017)*

Metropolitian Family Care Inc................E 614 237-1067
Reynoldsburg *(G-16320)*

Miamisburg Family Practice ....E 937 866-2494
Miamisburg *(G-14192)*

Mt Carmel Medical Group......................E 614 277-9631
Grove City *(G-11454)*

Neighborhood Health Care Inc ....E 216 281-8945
Cleveland *(G-6053)*

New Horizons Surgery Center ....E 740 375-5854
Marion *(G-13449)*

Oakhill Medical Associates ....E 937 599-1411
West Liberty *(G-19121)*

Perrysburg Pediatrics..................E 419 872-7700
Perrysburg *(G-15903)*

Portage Family Medicine ....E 330 626-5566
Streetsboro *(G-17266)*

Premier Health Partners ....D 937 526-3235
Versailles *(G-18571)*

Premier Physicians Centers Inc ....E 440 895-5085
Westlake *(G-19393)*

Primary Cr Ntwrk Prmr Hlth Prt ....E 513 492-5940
Mason *(G-13628)*

Primary Cr Ntwrk Prmr Hlth Prt ....E 937 278-5854
Dayton *(G-9707)*

Primary Cr Ntwrk Prmr Hlth Prt ....D 937 208-9090
Dayton *(G-9708)*

Primary Cr Ntwrk Prmr Hlth Prt ....D 937 208-7000
Beavercreek *(G-1178)*

Primary Cr Ntwrk Prmr Hlth Prt ....E 513 420-5233
Middletown *(G-14354)*

Primary Cr Ntwrk Prmr Hlth Prt ....E 937 226-7085
Dayton *(G-9709)*

Primed ....E 937 435-9013
Dayton *(G-9712)*

Primed Physicians ....E 937 298-8058
Dayton *(G-9713)*

Reading Family Practice ....E 513 563-6934
Cincinnati *(G-4343)*

Reid Physician Associates Inc ....B 937 456-4400
Eaton *(G-10461)*

Richard L Liston MD ....D 937 320-2020
Beavercreek *(G-1235)*

Richard Tomm MD ....D 216 297-3060
Cleveland *(G-6323)*

River Road Family Physicians................E 419 872-7745
Perrysburg *(G-15913)*

Robert Ellis ....E 513 821-0275
Cincinnati *(G-4390)*

Springdale Family Medicine PC..............E 513 771-7213
Cincinnati *(G-4521)*

Summa Health System ....D 330 375-3584
Akron *(G-450)*

Superior Medical Care Inc ....E 440 282-7420
Lorain *(G-12946)*

Talmage N Porter MD ....E 937 435-9013
Dayton *(G-9806)*

Terence Isakov MD ....D 440 449-1014
Cleveland *(G-6513)*

Toledo Hospital ....E 419 291-2051
Toledo *(G-18085)*

Tri County Family Physicians ....E 614 837-6363
Canal Winchester *(G-2122)*

University Family Physicians ....E 513 929-0104
Cincinnati *(G-4700)*

University Family Physicians ....D 513 475-7505
Cincinnati *(G-4701)*

University of Cincinnati.........................E 513 475-8771
Cincinnati *(G-4705)*

Upper Valley Family Care ....E 937 339-5355
Piqua *(G-16034)*

Van Wert County Hospital Assn ....C 419 232-2077
Van Wert *(G-18495)*

Western Family Physicians ....E 513 853-4900
Cincinnati *(G-4787)*

Westshore Prmry Care Assoc Inc ....D 440 934-0276
Sheffield Village *(G-16742)*

Westside Family Practice Inc ....E 614 878-4541
Columbus *(G-8893)*

Wheeling Hospital Inc ....E 740 695-2090
Saint Clairsville *(G-16511)*

Wilmington Medical Associates ....D 937 382-1616
Wilmington *(G-19655)*

OFFICES & CLINICS OF DRS OF MED: Cardiologist & Vascular

Capitol City Cardiology Inc ....E 614 464-0884
Columbus *(G-7115)*

Cardiac Vsclar Thrcic Surgeons...........E 513 421-3494
Cincinnati *(G-3116)*

Cardiologist Clark & Champaign...........E 937 653-8897
Urbana *(G-18421)*

Cardiology Consultants Inc ....D 330 454-8076
Canton *(G-2244)*

Cardiology Ctr of Cincinnati ....E 513 745-9800
Cincinnati *(G-3119)*

Cardiology Specialists Inc ....E 330 297-6110
Ravenna *(G-16234)*

Cardiovascular Associates Inc ....E 330 747-6446
Youngstown *(G-19981)*

Cardiovascular Clinic Inc ....D 440 882-0075
Cleveland *(G-5124)*

Cardiovascular Consultants Inc ....D 330 454-8076
Canton *(G-2245)*

Cardiovascular Medicine Assoc ....E 440 816-2708
Cleveland *(G-5125)*

Central Ohio Surgical Assoc ....E 614 222-8000
Columbus *(G-7168)*

Columbus Cardiology Cons Inc ....C 614 224-2281
Columbus *(G-7264)*

Columbus Cardiology Cons Inc ....C 614 224-2281
Columbus *(G-7265)*

Cranley Surgical Associates ....E 513 961-4335
Cincinnati *(G-3379)*

Dayton Cardiology Consultants ....E 937 223-3053
Dayton *(G-9356)*

Dayton Heart Center Inc ....D 937 277-4274
Dayton *(G-9367)*

Greater Cin Cardi Consults In ....E 513 751-4222
Cincinnati *(G-3649)*

Hans Zwart MD & Associates ....E 937 433-4183
Dayton *(G-9485)*

Heart Care ....E 614 533-5000
Gahanna *(G-11124)*

Heart Center of N Eastrn Ohio ....E 330 758-7703
Youngstown *(G-20062)*

Heart Specialists of Ohio ....E 614 538-0527
Columbus *(G-7729)*

Middltown Crdvscular Assoc Inc ....E 513 217-6400
Middletown *(G-14312)*

Midohio Crdiolgy Vascular Cons...........C 614 262-6772
Columbus *(G-8079)*

Mobile Cardiac Imaging LLC.................E 419 251-3711
Toledo *(G-17921)*

North Ohio Heart Center ....D 440 204-4000
Lorain *(G-12936)*

North Ohio Heart Center Inc ....E 440 414-9500
Cleveland *(G-6078)*

North Ohio Heart Center Inc ....E 440 366-3600
Elyria *(G-10545)*

North Ohio Heart Center Inc ....E 440 204-4000
Avon *(G-897)*

North Ohio Heart Center Inc ....E 440 204-4000
Lorain *(G-12937)*

North Ohio Heart Center Inc ....E 440 326-4120
Elyria *(G-10546)*

Northeast Ohio Cardiology Svcs ....E 330 253-8195
Akron *(G-350)*

Northwest Ohio Cardiology Cons ....D 419 842-3000
Toledo *(G-17949)*

Ohio Gstroenterology Group Inc...........E 614 221-8355
Columbus *(G-8259)*

Ohio Heart ....E 513 206-1320
Cincinnati *(G-4152)*

Ohio Heart and Vascular ....E 513 206-1800
Cincinnati *(G-4153)*

Ohio Heart Health Center Inc................C 513 351-9900
Cincinnati *(G-4154)*

Ohio Institute of Cardiac Care ....E 937 322-1700
Dayton *(G-9184)*

Ohio Medical Group..................E 440 414-9400
Westlake *(G-19386)*

Ohio State Univ Wexner Med Ctr ....A 614 293-6255
Columbus *(G-8294)*

Ohio State University ....A 614 293-7417
Columbus *(G-8301)*

Ohio State University ....A 614 293-4967
Columbus *(G-8351)*

Premier Heart Associates Inc ....E 937 832-2425
Dayton *(G-9706)*

Premier Heart Inc ....E 937 832-2425
Englewood *(G-10598)*

Sagar Satyavolu MD ....E 937 323-1404
Springfield *(G-17107)*

Schuster Cardiology..................E 937 866-0637
Miamisburg *(G-14216)*

Toledo Cardiology Cons Inc ....D 419 251-6183
Toledo *(G-18076)*

Toledo Cardiology Inc ....E 419 479-5690
Toledo *(G-18077)*

West Side Cardiology Assoc ....E 440 333-8600
Cleveland *(G-6668)*

West Side Cardiology Assoc ....E 440 333-8600
Cleveland *(G-6669)*

OFFICES & CLINICS OF DRS OF MED: Clinic, Op by Physicians

Access Ohio ....E 614 367-7700
Columbus *(G-6862)*

Ambulatory Medical Care Inc................E 513 831-8555
Milford *(G-14370)*

Ashtabula Clinic Inc..................D 440 997-6980
Ashtabula *(G-708)*

Aultman North Canton Med Group........B 330 433-1200
Canton *(G-2206)*

Axesspointe Cmnty Hlth Ctr Inc ....E 330 724-5471
Akron *(G-83)*

Centers For Dialysis Care Inc ....C 216 295-7000
Shaker Heights *(G-16705)*

Childrens Hospital Medical Ctr...............A 513 636-4200
Cincinnati *(G-3190)*

Christian Community Hlth Svcs ....E 513 381-2247
Cincinnati *(G-3213)*

Cleveland Clinic Cole Eye Inst...............E 216 444-4508
Cleveland *(G-5235)*

Clevelnd Clnc Chagrn Flls Fmly ....E 440 893-9393
Chagrin Falls *(G-2642)*

Columbus Neighborhood Health C ......C 614 445-0685
Columbus *(G-7302)*

Community Action Comm Pike CNT .....E 740 947-7726
Waverly *(G-18817)*

Community Mental Health Svc ....D 740 695-9344
Saint Clairsville *(G-16484)*

County of Delaware ....D 740 203-2040
Delaware *(G-9964)*

Doctors Urgent Care..................E 419 586-1611
Celina *(G-2594)*

Family Hlth Svcs Drke Cnty Inc ....C 937 548-3806
Greenville *(G-11377)*

Five Rivers Health Centers ....E 937 734-6841
Dayton *(G-9440)*

Heart Ohio Family Health Ctrs ....E 614 235-5555
Columbus *(G-7728)*

Holzer Clinic LLC ....C 304 746-3701
Gallipolis *(G-11196)*

Holzer Clinic LLC ....E 740 446-5412
Gallipolis *(G-11199)*

Holzer Clinic LLC ....E 740 589-3100
Athens *(G-785)*

Hometown Urgent Care..................C 937 372-6012
Xenia *(G-19911)*

Jyg Innovations LLC ....E 937 630-3858
Dayton *(G-9531)*

Lifecare Fmly Hlth & Dntl Ctr ....E 330 454-2000
Canton *(G-2378)*

Margaret B Shipley Child Hlth ....E 330 478-6333
Canton *(G-2388)*

Matern Ohio Management Inc ....D 614 457-7660
Columbus *(G-8037)*

Medical Assoc Cambridge Inc ....E 740 439-3515
Cambridge *(G-2076)*

Mercy Health ....E 330 792-7418
Youngstown *(G-20123)*

Mercy Hlth - Clermont Hosp LLC...........D 513 732-8200
Batavia *(G-1004)*

Mercy Hlth St Vincent Med LLC ....A 419 251-0580
   Toledo (G-17910)
Mercy Medical Center Inc ....E 330 627-7641
   Carrollton (G-2572)
Monroe Family Health Center ....E 740 472-0757
   Woodsfield (G-19677)
Norwalk Clinic Inc ....E 419 668-4851
   Norwalk (G-15449)
Oberlin Clinic Inc ....C 440 774-7337
   Oberlin (G-15512)
Ohio Hills Health Services ....D 740 425-5165
   Barnesville (G-978)
Promedica ....D 419 291-3450
   Maumee (G-13834)
Schoenbrunn Healthcare ....D 330 339-3595
   New Philadelphia (G-14980)
Senior Lifestyle Corporation ....E 513 777-4457
   West Chester (G-19002)
Toledo Family Health Center ....D 419 241-1554
   Toledo (G-18083)
Total Renal Care Inc ....E 937 294-6711
   Kettering (G-12301)
University Mednet ....C 440 255-0800
   Mentor (G-14120)
University Mednet ....E 440 285-9079
   Bedford (G-1313)
Veterans Health Administration ....B 740 568-0412
   Marietta (G-13396)
Veterans Health Administration ....B 513 943-3680
   Cincinnati (G-4760)
Veterans Health Administration ....C 614 257-5524
   Columbus (G-8849)
Veterans Health Administration ....B 866 463-0912
   Ashtabula (G-758)
Veterans Health Administration ....B 740 695-9321
   Saint Clairsville (G-16509)
Veterans Health Administration ....D 419 259-2000
   Toledo (G-18138)
Veterans Health Administration ....E 330 740-9200
   Youngstown (G-20236)
Veterans Health Administration ....B 216 939-0699
   Cleveland (G-6626)
Veterans Health Administration ....D 330 489-4600
   Canton (G-2526)
Zepf Center ....E 419 255-4050
   Toledo (G-18178)

OFFICES & CLINICS OF DRS OF MED: Em Med Ctr, Freestanding

Amherst Hospital Association ....C 440 988-6000
   Amherst (G-580)
Emergency Medicine Specialists ....D 937 438-8910
   Dayton (G-9414)
Immediate Health Associates ....E 614 794-0481
   Westerville (G-19265)
Immediate Medical Service Inc ....E 330 823-0400
   Alliance (G-534)
Joint Emergency Med Svc Inc ....E 937 746-3471
   Franklin (G-11033)
Lake Urgent & Family Med Ctr ....E 440 255-6400
   Mentor (G-14074)
Med -Center/Med Partners ....E 440 349-6400
   Cleveland (G-5940)
Mercy Health Youngstown LLC ....A 330 729-1420
   Youngstown (G-20125)
St Ritas Medical Center ....D 419 227-3361
   Lima (G-12752)
Township of Colerain ....C 513 741-7551
   Cincinnati (G-4622)

OFFICES & CLINICS OF DRS OF MED: Health Maint Org Or HMO

Aultman Health Foundation ....E 330 452-9911
   Canton (G-2201)
Blanchard Vly Rgional Hlth Ctr ....C 419 358-9010
   Bluffton (G-1687)
County of Lucas ....C 419 213-4018
   Toledo (G-17683)
Foundations Hlth Solutions Inc ....D 440 793-0200
   North Olmsted (G-15289)
Health Collaborative ....D 513 618-3600
   Cincinnati (G-3694)

OFFICES & CLINICS OF DRS OF MED: Physician/Surgeon, Int Med

Associated Specialists ....E 937 208-7272
   Dayton (G-9241)

Avita Health System ....C 419 468-7059
   Galion (G-11166)
Avita Health System ....C 419 468-4841
   Galion (G-11167)
Blanchard Valley Medical Assoc ....D 419 424-0380
   Findlay (G-10875)
Canyon Medical Center Inc ....E 614 864-6010
   Columbus (G-7111)
Central Ohio Primary Care ....D 614 326-2672
   Westerville (G-19152)
David Lee Grossman MD ....E 419 843-8150
   Toledo (G-17692)
Dayton Childrens Hospital ....E 937 641-3376
   Dayton (G-9357)
Eastern Hill Internal Medicine ....E 513 232-3500
   Cincinnati (G-3475)
Goudy Internal Medicine Inc ....D 419 468-8323
   Galion (G-11178)
Hector A Buch Jr MD ....E 419 227-7399
   Lima (G-12658)
Hickman Cancer Center ....D 419 824-1952
   Sylvania (G-17430)
Internal Mdcine Cons of Clmbus ....E 614 878-6413
   Columbus (G-7836)
Markowitz Rosenberg Assoc Drs ....E 440 646-2200
   Cleveland (G-5909)
Mercy Health ....E 513 248-0100
   Milford (G-14408)
Mercy Medical Associates ....E 513 686-4840
   Cincinnati (G-4034)
Moyal and Petroff MD ....E 440 461-6477
   Cleveland (G-6016)
Occupational Health Services ....E 937 492-7296
   Sidney (G-16788)
Ohio State University ....A 614 293-8045
   Columbus (G-8297)
Premier Integrated Med Assoc ....D 937 291-6813
   Centerville (G-2632)
Queen City Medical Group ....E 513 528-5600
   Cincinnati (G-4317)
Robert E Kose ....E 419 843-7800
   Maumee (G-13847)
Roger S Palutsis MD ....E 330 821-0201
   Alliance (G-549)
Salem Internal Medicine Assoc ....E 330 332-5232
   Salem (G-16563)
Stephen A Rudolph Inc ....E 216 381-1367
   Cleveland (G-6466)
Summit Cnty Internists & Assoc ....E 330 375-3690
   Akron (G-457)
Uc Health Llc ....E 513 584-6999
   Mason (G-13652)
Uc Health Llc ....D 513 475-7880
   Cincinnati (G-4664)
Uc Health Llc ....D 513 648-9077
   Cincinnati (G-4666)
University of Cincinnati ....E 513 475-8524
   Cincinnati (G-4722)
Ushc Physicians Inc ....E 216 382-2036
   Cleveland (G-6613)
Veterinary RFRrl&emer Ctr of ....E 330 665-4996
   Copley (G-8979)

OFFICES & CLINICS OF DRS OF MED: Physician/Surgeon, Phy Med

Barb Linden ....E 440 233-1068
   Lorain (G-12884)
Bucyrus Community Physicians ....D 419 492-2200
   New Washington (G-15000)
Hernando Zegarra ....E 216 831-5700
   Cleveland (G-5686)
Holzer Clinic LLC ....C 304 744-2300
   Gallipolis (G-11198)
Lasik Plus Vision Center ....D 513 794-9964
   Cincinnati (G-3912)
Medical College of Ohio ....E 419 383-7100
   Toledo (G-17901)
Primary Cr Ntwrk Prmr Hlth Prt ....E 937 890-6644
   Vandalia (G-18535)
Wheeling Hospital Inc ....E 740 633-4765
   Martins Ferry (G-13481)

OFFICES & CLINICS OF DRS OF MED: Specialist/Phy, Fertility

Dayton Ob Gyn ....E 937 439-7550
   Centerville (G-2625)

OFFICES & CLINICS OF DRS OF MEDICINE: Geriatric

P C Vpa ....E 937 293-2133
   Moraine (G-14686)

OFFICES & CLINICS OF DRS OF MEDICINE: Med Clinic, Pri Care

3rd Street Community Clinic ....D 419 522-6191
   Mansfield (G-13130)
Belmont Professional Assoc Inc ....C 740 425-5140
   Barnesville (G-977)
Bethesda Hospital Inc ....E 513 563-1505
   Cincinnati (G-3049)
Central Ohio Geriatrics LLC ....E 614 530-4077
   Granville (G-11336)
Community Health & Wellness PA ....D 937 599-1411
   West Liberty (G-19118)
Dayton Physicians LLC ....C 937 547-0563
   Greenville (G-11374)
Equitas Health Inc ....D 614 299-2437
   Columbus (G-7527)
Hometown Urgent Care ....C 614 472-2880
   Columbus (G-7769)
Hometown Urgent Care ....C 614 835-0400
   Groveport (G-11519)
Ironton and Lawrence County ....B 740 532-3534
   Ironton (G-12155)
Lakewood Clveland Fmly Med Ctr ....E 216 227-2162
   Lakewood (G-12353)
Luke Immediate Care Center ....E 419 227-2245
   Lima (G-12695)
Mercy Health ....E 440 366-5577
   North Ridgeville (G-15336)
North Coast Prof Co LLC ....C 419 557-5541
   Sandusky (G-16629)
Primed Premier Integrated Med ....C 937 291-6893
   Dayton (G-9714)
Robinson Memorial Hospital ....E 330 626-3455
   Streetsboro (G-17268)

OFFICES & CLINICS OF DRS OF MEDICINE: Med Insurance Assoc

Ohio Health Group LLC ....E 614 566-0010
   Columbus (G-8263)

OFFICES & CLINICS OF DRS OF MEDICINE: Physician, Orthopedic

Far Oaks Orthopedists Inc ....E 937 433-5309
   Dayton (G-9427)
Hand Ctr At Orthopaedic Inst ....D 937 298-4417
   Dayton (G-9484)
Hand Rehabilitation Associates ....E 330 668-4055
   Akron (G-249)
Joint Implant Surgeons Inc ....E 614 221-6331
   New Albany (G-14858)
Kolczun & Kolczun Orthopedics ....E 440 985-3113
   Lorain (G-12911)
Marysvlle Ohio Srgical Ctr LLC ....A 937 578-4200
   Marysville (G-13517)
Northast Ohio Orthpedics Assoc ....E 330 344-1980
   Akron (G-348)
Northwest Ohio Orthopedics ....E 419 885-2553
   Sylvania (G-17439)
Ohio Orthpd Surgery Inst LLC ....E 614 827-8777
   Columbus (G-8277)
Orthoneuro ....E 614 890-6555
   Westerville (G-19289)
Orthopaedic & Spine Center At ....E 614 468-0300
   Dublin (G-10300)
Orthopaedic Institute Ohio Inc ....D 419 222-6622
   Lima (G-12714)
Orthopaedic Offices Inc ....E 513 221-5500
   Blue Ash (G-1626)
Orthopdic Spt Mdicine Cons Inc ....E 513 777-7714
   Middletown (G-14318)
Orthopedic Assoc of Zanesville ....E 740 454-3273
   Zanesville (G-20351)
Orthopedic Associates ....D 800 824-9861
   Liberty Township (G-12584)
Orthopedic Associates ....E 937 415-9100
   Centerville (G-2631)
Orthopedic Associates Dayton ....E 937 280-4988
   Dayton (G-9678)
Orthopedic Associates Inc ....E 440 892-1440
   Westlake (G-19388)

Orthopedic Cons Cincinnati ....C....... 513 733-8894
Blue Ash *(G-1627)*
Orthopedic Cons Cincinnati ....E....... 513 753-7488
Cincinnati *(G-2863)*
Orthopedic Cons Cincinnati ....E....... 513 232-6677
Cincinnati *(G-4185)*
Orthopedic Cons Cincinnati ....E....... 513 245-2500
Cincinnati *(G-4186)*
Orthopedic Cons Cincinnati ....E....... 513 347-9999
Cincinnati *(G-4187)*
Orthopedic Diagnstc Trtmnt Ctr ....E....... 513 791-6611
Montgomery *(G-14602)*
Orthopedic Diagnstc Trtmnt Ctr ....E....... 513 221-4848
Cincinnati *(G-4188)*
Orthopedic One Inc ....D....... 614 827-8700
Columbus *(G-8389)*
Orthopedic One Inc ....D....... 614 545-7900
Columbus *(G-8390)*
Orthorpdics Mltspcialty Netwrk ....E....... 330 493-1630
Canton *(G-2433)*
Queen Cy Spt Mdcine Rhbltation ....E....... 513 561-1111
Cincinnati *(G-4323)*
Reconstructive Orthopedics ....E....... 513 793-3933
Cincinnati *(G-4346)*
River Vly Orthpdics Spt Mdcine ....E....... 740 687-3346
Lancaster *(G-12431)*
Spectrum Orthpedics Inc Canton ....E....... 330 455-5367
North Canton *(G-15233)*
Summit Hand Center Inc ....E....... 330 668-4055
Akron *(G-458)*
Teater Orthopedic Surgeons ....E....... 330 343-3335
Dover *(G-10103)*
Unity Health Network LLC ....E....... 330 626-0549
Streetsboro *(G-17276)*
University Orthopaedic Cnsltnt ....E....... 513 475-8690
Cincinnati *(G-4728)*
University Orthpedic Assoc Inc ....E....... 216 844-1000
Cleveland *(G-6601)*
Youngstown Orthopaedic Assoc ....E....... 330 726-1466
Canfield *(G-2166)*

OFFICES & CLINICS OF DRS OF MEDICINE: Pulmonary

Pulmonary & Medicine Dayton ....E....... 937 439-3600
Miamisburg *(G-14208)*
Pulmonary Crtcal Care Spcalist ....E....... 419 843-7800
Maumee *(G-13838)*
R I D Inc ....E....... 419 251-4790
Toledo *(G-17996)*
Southwest Cleveland Sleep Ctr ....E....... 440 239-7533
Cleveland *(G-6427)*
University of Cincinnati ....E....... 513 558-4831
Cincinnati *(G-4724)*

OFFICES & CLINICS OF DRS OF MEDICINE: Rheumatology

Columbus Arthritis Center Inc ....E....... 614 486-5200
Columbus *(G-7258)*
Crystal Arthritis Center Inc ....E....... 330 668-4045
Akron *(G-171)*

OFFICES & CLINICS OF DRS OF MEDICINE: Sports Med

Far Oaks Orthopedists Inc ....E....... 937 433-5309
Dayton *(G-9426)*
First Settlement Orthopaedics ....E....... 740 373-8756
Marietta *(G-13329)*
Ohio State University ....D....... 614 293-2222
Columbus *(G-8339)*
OSu Spt Mdcine Physcians Inc ....E....... 614 293-3600
Columbus *(G-8398)*
Sports Care Rehabilitation ....E....... 419 578-7530
Toledo *(G-18042)*

OFFICES & CLINICS OF DRS, MED: Specialized Practitioners

Akron Neonatology Inc ....E....... 330 379-9473
Akron *(G-49)*
Nuerological & Sleep Disorders ....E....... 513 721-7533
Cincinnati *(G-4138)*

OFFICES & CLINICS OF HEALTH PRACTITIONERS: Coroner

County of Cuyahoga ....D....... 216 721-5610
Cleveland *(G-5363)*

OFFICES & CLINICS OF HEALTH PRACTITIONERS: Nurse & Med Asst

Equitas Health Inc ....D....... 614 299-2437
Columbus *(G-7527)*
Inter Healt Care of Cambr Zane ....E....... 513 984-1110
Cincinnati *(G-3773)*
Maxim Healthcare Services Inc ....D....... 740 772-4100
Chillicothe *(G-2804)*
Milan Skilled Nursing LLC ....D....... 216 727-3996
Milan *(G-14362)*
Msstaff LLC ....C....... 419 868-8536
Toledo *(G-17926)*
Tky Associates LLC ....D....... 419 535-7777
Toledo *(G-18068)*

OFFICES & CLINICS OF HEALTH PRACTITIONERS: Nutrition

Herman Bair Enterprise ....E....... 330 262-4449
Wooster *(G-19727)*

OFFICES & CLINICS OF HEALTH PRACTITIONERS: Nutritionist

Central Ohio Nutrition Center ....E....... 614 864-7225
Columbus *(G-7160)*
George W Arensberg Phrm Inc ....E....... 740 344-2195
Newark *(G-15036)*

OFFICES & CLINICS OF HEALTH PRACTITIONERS: Occu Therapist

Chcc Home Health Care ....E....... 330 759-4069
Austintown *(G-857)*
Cincinnati Occupational Therap ....E....... 513 791-5688
Blue Ash *(G-1526)*
Hometown Urgent Care ....C....... 330 629-2300
Youngstown *(G-20067)*
Hometown Urgent Care ....D....... 740 363-3133
Delaware *(G-9987)*
Hometown Urgent Care ....C....... 937 252-2000
Wooster *(G-19728)*
Hometown Urgent Care ....E....... 513 831-5900
Milford *(G-14395)*
Hometown Urgent Care ....C....... 937 342-9520
Springfield *(G-17045)*
Medwork LLC ....D....... 937 449-0800
Dayton *(G-9604)*
Samaritan Regional Health Sys ....E....... 419 281-1330
Ashland *(G-689)*
Therapy In Motion LLC ....C....... 216 459-2846
Independence *(G-12130)*

OFFICES & CLINICS OF HEALTH PRACTITIONERS: Paramedic

City of Blue Ash ....E....... 513 745-8534
Blue Ash *(G-1527)*
Colerain Volunteer Fire Co ....E....... 740 738-0735
Dillonvale *(G-10063)*
Lifeteam Ems Inc ....E....... 330 386-9284
East Liverpool *(G-10405)*
Sandy Creek Joint Fire Dst ....E....... 330 868-5193
Minerva *(G-14524)*

OFFICES & CLINICS OF HEALTH PRACTITIONERS: Physical Therapy

Abilities First Foundation Inc ....D....... 513 423-9496
Middletown *(G-14285)*
Amedisys Inc ....E....... 740 373-8549
Marietta *(G-13309)*
Atrium Medical Center ....E....... 513 420-5013
Middletown *(G-14289)*
Aultman Health Foundation ....B....... 330 875-6050
Louisville *(G-12960)*
Carington Health Systems ....C....... 513 961-8881
Cincinnati *(G-3124)*
Christ Hospital ....B....... 513 688-1111
Cincinnati *(G-3202)*
Concorde Therapy Group Inc ....E....... 330 478-1752
Canton *(G-2265)*
Concorde Therapy Group Inc ....E....... 330 493-4210
Alliance *(G-527)*
Cora Health Services Inc ....E....... 419 221-3004
Lima *(G-12619)*
First Settlement Orthopaedics ....E....... 740 373-8756
Marietta *(G-13329)*

Health Services Inc ....E....... 330 837-7678
Massillon *(G-13694)*
Healthquest Blanchester Inc ....E....... 937 783-4535
Blanchester *(G-1487)*
Hilty Memorial Home Inc ....C....... 419 384-3218
Pandora *(G-15753)*
Holzer Clinic LLC ....E....... 740 886-9403
Proctorville *(G-16217)*
Jewish Home of Cincinnati ....B....... 513 754-3100
Mason *(G-13603)*
Licking Rhabilitation Svcs Inc ....E....... 740 345-2837
Newark *(G-15059)*
Medcentral Health System ....C....... 419 342-5015
Shelby *(G-16747)*
Medcentral Health System ....C....... 419 683-1040
Crestline *(G-9057)*
Mercy Health ....E....... 937 390-5075
Springfield *(G-17077)*
Newcomerstown Progress Corp ....C....... 740 498-5165
Newcomerstown *(G-15134)*
Nexstep Healthcare LLC ....C....... 216 797-4040
Cleveland *(G-6066)*
Ohio HI Point Career Center ....E....... 937 599-3010
Urbana *(G-18442)*
Ohio State University ....A....... 614 366-3692
Columbus *(G-8295)*
Ohio State University ....A....... 614 257-3000
Columbus *(G-8300)*
Orthoneuro ....D....... 614 890-6555
Columbus *(G-8387)*
Prohealth Partners Inc ....E....... 419 491-7150
Perrysburg *(G-15906)*
R & F Inc ....E....... 419 868-2909
Holland *(G-11906)*
Rehab Center ....E....... 330 297-2770
Ravenna *(G-16261)*
Rehab Continuum Inc ....E....... 513 984-8070
Blue Ash *(G-1643)*
Rehabilitation Aquatics ....E....... 419 843-2500
Toledo *(G-17999)*
River Rock Rehabilitation ....E....... 740 382-4035
Marion *(G-13456)*
Selby General Hospital ....C....... 740 568-2037
Marietta *(G-13379)*
Society For Rehabilitation ....E....... 440 209-0135
Mentor *(G-14110)*
Sports Therapy Inc ....E....... 513 671-5841
Cincinnati *(G-4515)*
Sports Therapy Inc ....E....... 513 531-1698
Cincinnati *(G-4516)*
St Lukes Hospital ....A....... 419 441-1002
Waterville *(G-18793)*
Steward Trumbull Mem Hosp Inc ....A....... 330 841-9011
Warren *(G-18748)*
Total Rhabilitation Specialist ....E....... 440 236-8527
Columbia Station *(G-6780)*
Trihealth G LLC ....D....... 513 922-1200
Cincinnati *(G-4644)*
Walnut Hills Physical Therapy ....E....... 614 234-8000
Columbus *(G-8872)*
Wsb Rehabilitation Svcs Inc ....D....... 330 533-1338
Canfield *(G-2165)*

OFFICES & CLINICS OF HEALTH PRACTITIONERS: Physiotherapist

Bellefontaine Physical Therapy ....E....... 937 592-1625
Bellefontaine *(G-1346)*
Concorde Therapy Group Inc ....C....... 330 493-4210
Canton *(G-2264)*
Concorde Therapy Group Inc ....E....... 330 493-4210
Louisville *(G-12963)*
Summa Rehab Hospital LLC ....E....... 330 572-7300
Akron *(G-454)*

OFFICES & CLINICS OF HEALTH PRACTITIONERS: Speech Pathology

United Rehabilitation Services ....D....... 937 233-1230
Dayton *(G-9832)*

OFFICES & CLINICS OF HEALTH PRACTITIONERS: Speech Therapist

A+ Solutions LLC ....E....... 216 896-0111
Beachwood *(G-1025)*
Just In Time Care Inc ....E....... 614 985-3555
Columbus *(G-7879)*

OFFICES & CLINICS OF HEALTH PRACTRS: Clinical Psychologist

Appleseed Cmnty Mntl Hlth Ctr ....E 419 281-3716
  Ashland *(G-645)*

Center For Cognitive and Beh ....E 614 459-4490
  Columbus *(G-7151)*

Childrens Aid Society ....E 216 521-6511
  Cleveland *(G-5178)*

Coleman Professional Svcs Inc............D 330 296-8313
  Ravenna *(G-16236)*

Emerge Counseling Service ....E 330 865-8351
  Akron *(G-202)*

Midwest Behavioral Care Ltd ....E 937 454-0092
  Dayton *(G-9632)*

Ohio State University..........................D 614 292-6741
  Columbus *(G-8325)*

PSI Associates Inc ....B 330 425-8474
  Twinsburg *(G-18308)*

Psycare Inc ....C 330 759-2310
  Youngstown *(G-20168)*

Psychiatric Solutions Inc ....C 440 953-3000
  Willoughby *(G-19564)*

Reverse Center Clinic.........................E 419 885-8800
  Sylvania *(G-17446)*

Summit Psychological Assoc Inc.........E 330 535-8181
  Akron *(G-460)*

Weinstein Donald Jay PHD ....E 216 831-1040
  Painesville *(G-15747)*

OFFICES & CLINICS OF HLTH PRACTITIONERS: Reg/Practical Nurse

Accurate Nurse Staffing ....E 419 475-2424
  Toledo *(G-17581)*

American Nursing Care Inc..................D 740 452-0569
  Zanesville *(G-20276)*

Around Clock Home Care ....D 440 350-2547
  Painesville *(G-15694)*

Medlink of Ohio Inc............................B 216 751-5900
  Cleveland *(G-5944)*

Medlink of Ohio Inc............................B 330 773-9434
  Akron *(G-330)*

Sisters of Mercy Amer Reg Comm ......D 419 696-7203
  Oregon *(G-15609)*

Toledo District Nurses Assn ....C 419 255-0983
  Sylvania *(G-17458)*

OFFICES & CLINICS OF OPTOMETRISTS: Group & Corporate

Sight Resource Corporation ....D 513 942-4423
  West Chester *(G-19006)*

OFFICES & CLINICS OF OPTOMETRISTS: Specialist, Contact Lens

Shawnee Optical Inc............................D 440 997-2020
  Ashtabula *(G-754)*

OFFICES & CLINICS OF OPTOMETRISTS: Specialist, Optometrists

Optivue Inc ....C 419 891-1391
  Oregon *(G-15602)*

Ottivue...D 419 693-4444
  Oregon *(G-15606)*

Thomas R Truitt Od ....E 937 644-8637
  Marysville *(G-13533)*

OIL & GAS FIELD EQPT: Drill Rigs

Buckeye Companies.............................E 740 452-3641
  Zanesville *(G-20284)*

OIL FIELD MACHINERY & EQPT

Multi Products Company.......................E 330 674-5981
  Millersburg *(G-14484)*

OIL FIELD SVCS, NEC

Belden & Blake Corporation ....E 330 602-5551
  Dover *(G-10066)*

Express Energy Svcs Oper LP ....E 740 337-4530
  Toronto *(G-18184)*

Halliburton Energy Svcs Inc ....C 740 617-2917
  Zanesville *(G-20314)*

Stallion Oilfield Cnstr LLC ....E 330 868-2083
  Paris *(G-15757)*

Stratagraph Ne Inc.............................E 740 373-3091
  Marietta *(G-13384)*

Tk Gas Services Inc............................E 740 826-0303
  New Concord *(G-14904)*

U S Weatherford L P ....C 330 746-2502
  Youngstown *(G-20230)*

OIL ROYALTY TRADERS

Exchangebase LLC.............................E 440 331-3600
  Rocky River *(G-16432)*

OILS & GREASES: Blended & Compounded

Chemical Solvents Inc........................E 216 741-9310
  Cleveland *(G-5173)*

Cincinnati - Vulcan Company ....D 513 242-5300
  Cincinnati *(G-3219)*

New Vulco Mfg & Sales Co LLC............D 513 242-2672
  Cincinnati *(G-4109)*

Wallover Enterprises Inc ....E 440 238-9250
  Strongsville *(G-17358)*

OILS & GREASES: Lubricating

Borchers Americas Inc.......................D 440 899-2950
  Westlake *(G-19323)*

Fuchs Lubricants Co ....E 330 963-0400
  Twinsburg *(G-18270)*

R and J Corporation ....E 440 871-6009
  Westlake *(G-19394)*

State Industrial Products Corp ....B 877 747-6986
  Cleveland *(G-6458)*

Triad Energy Corporation.....................E 740 374-2940
  Marietta *(G-13387)*

OILS: Lubricating

Universal Oil Inc.................................E 216 771-4300
  Cleveland *(G-6582)*

OLD AGE ASSISTANCE

Artis Senior Living.............................E 513 229-7450
  Mason *(G-13542)*

Ashland Cnty Council On Aging ....E 419 281-1477
  Ashland *(G-649)*

Bluebird Retirement Community ....E 740 845-1880
  London *(G-12860)*

County of Richland ....E 419 774-5894
  Mansfield *(G-13154)*

Danbury Woods of Wooster..................E 330 264-0355
  Wooster *(G-19721)*

Foundations Hlth Solutions Inc ....D 440 793-0200
  North Olmsted *(G-15289)*

Ganzhorn Suites Inc...........................D 614 356-9810
  Powell *(G-16195)*

Hcr Manorcare Med Svcs Fla LLC ....D 440 887-1442
  North Royalton *(G-15360)*

Hilty Memorial Home Inc ....E 419 384-3218
  Pandora *(G-15753)*

Jackson County Board On Aging...........D 740 286-2909
  Jackson *(G-12177)*

Meigs County Council On Aging ....E 740 992-2161
  Pomeroy *(G-16095)*

Nami of Preble County Ohio ....E 937 456-4947
  Eaton *(G-10455)*

Senior Outreach Services ....E 216 421-6900
  Cleveland *(G-6397)*

Taylor Corporation ....E 419 420-0790
  Findlay *(G-10969)*

OLEFINS

Lyondell Chemical Company ....D 513 530-4000
  Cincinnati *(G-3953)*

ON-LINE DATABASE INFORMATION RETRIEVAL SVCS

Acxiom Corporation ....C 216 520-3181
  Independence *(G-12038)*

Amaxx Inc ....E 614 486-3481
  Dublin *(G-10128)*

Doylestown Communications................E 330 658-7000
  Doylestown *(G-10111)*

Oclc Inc ....A 614 764-6000
  Dublin *(G-10295)*

Simplified Logistics LLC ....E 440 250-8912
  Westlake *(G-19406)*

OPERATIVE BUILDERS: Condominiums

Douglas Construction Company ....E 419 865-8600
  Holland *(G-11884)*

Epcon Cmmnties Franchising Inc.........D 614 761-1010
  Dublin *(G-10218)*

Epcon Communities Inc ....E 614 761-1010
  Dublin *(G-10219)*

OPERATIVE BUILDERS: Townhouse

Nrp Holdings LLC...............................C 216 475-8900
  Cleveland *(G-6104)*

OPERATOR TRAINING, COMPUTER

Advanced Service Tech LLC ....E 937 435-4376
  Miamisburg *(G-14137)*

Babbage-Simmel & Assoc Inc ....E 614 481-6555
  Columbus *(G-7010)*

S & P Solutions Inc ....C 440 918-9111
  Willoughby Hills *(G-19593)*

OPERATOR: Apartment Buildings

12000 Edgewater Drive LLC................D 216 520-1250
  Lakewood *(G-12333)*

A P & P Dev & Cnstr Co ....D 330 833-8886
  Massillon *(G-13658)*

Akron Metropolitan Hsing Auth ....C 330 920-1652
  Stow *(G-17189)*

Allen Metropolitan Hsing Auth ....E 419 228-6065
  Lima *(G-12598)*

Alliance Towers LLC ....A 330 823-1063
  Alliance *(G-517)*

Alpha PHI Alpha Homes Inc ....D 330 376-2115
  Akron *(G-68)*

Andrews Apartments Ltd ....C 440 946-3600
  Willoughby *(G-19505)*

Arbor Park Phase Two Assoc ....E 561 998-0700
  Cleveland *(G-5001)*

Arbor Pk Phase Three Assoc LP ....E 561 998-0700
  Cleveland *(G-5002)*

Azalea Alabama Investment LLC..........D 216 520-1250
  Cleveland *(G-5030)*

Barcus Company Inc...........................E 614 451-9000
  Columbus *(G-7017)*

Belmont Metro Hsing Auth...................E 740 633-5085
  Martins Ferry *(G-13476)*

Biltmore Apartments Ltd ....D 937 461-9695
  Dayton *(G-9254)*

Brethren Care Inc...............................C 419 289-0803
  Ashland *(G-659)*

Brodhead Village Ltd ....D 614 863-4640
  New Albany *(G-14845)*

Buckeye Cmnty Eighty One LP ....E 614 942-2020
  Columbus *(G-7086)*

Buckeye Cmnty Thirty Five LP ....D 614 942-2020
  Akron *(G-112)*

Buckingham Management LLC ....C 844 361-5559
  Perrysburg *(G-15843)*

Burton Carol Management ....E 216 464-5130
  Cleveland *(G-5104)*

Cassady Vlg Aprtments Ohio LLC ....D 216 520-1250
  Columbus *(G-7136)*

Chelmsford Apartments Ltd ....E 419 389-0800
  Toledo *(G-17649)*

Cincinnati Metro Hsing Auth.................E 513 421-2642
  Cincinnati *(G-3254)*

Cincinnati Metro Hsing Auth.................E 513 333-0670
  Cincinnati *(G-3256)*

City of Akron ....D 330 564-4075
  Akron *(G-133)*

Commons of Providence.......................D 419 624-1171
  Sandusky *(G-16590)*

Community Prpts Ohio III LLC...............D 614 253-0984
  Columbus *(G-7334)*

Community Prpts Ohio MGT Svcs ....D 614 253-0984
  Columbus *(G-7335)*

Creative Living Housing Corp ....E 614 421-1226
  Columbus *(G-7387)*

Crestview Manor Nursing Home............C 740 654-2634
  Lancaster *(G-12386)*

Cwb Property Managment Inc ....E 614 793-2244
  Dublin *(G-10195)*

Ea Vica Co ....E 513 481-3500
  Cincinnati *(G-3467)*

Eaglewood Care Center.......................C 937 399-7195
  Springfield *(G-17031)*

Edward Rose Associates Inc ....E 513 752-2727
  Batavia *(G-998)*

(G-0000) Company's Geographic Section entry number

Emerald Dev Ecnomic Netwrk Inc.........D....... 216 961-9690
Cleveland *(G-5473)*
Englewood Square Ltd........................D....... 937 836-4117
Englewood *(G-10586)*
Equity Residential Properties...............E....... 216 861-2700
Cleveland *(G-5489)*
Fairfield Homes Inc..............................E....... 740 653-3583
Lancaster *(G-12397)*
Fairfield Homes Inc..............................C....... 614 873-3533
Plain City *(G-16053)*
Fay Limited Partnership.......................E....... 513 542-8333
Cincinnati *(G-3534)*
Fay Limited Partnership.......................E....... 513 241-1911
Cincinnati *(G-3535)*
Fieldstone Limited Partnership.............C....... 937 293-0900
Moraine *(G-14658)*
Fish Creek Plaza Ltd............................D....... 330 688-0450
Stow *(G-17204)*
Forest City Enterprises LP...................B....... 216 621-6060
Cleveland *(G-5553)*
FTM Associates LLC.............................D....... 614 846-1834
Columbus *(G-7632)*
G J Goudreau Operating Co..................E....... 216 741-7524
Cleveland *(G-5587)*
Galion East Ohio I LP...........................D....... 216 520-1250
Galion *(G-11175)*
Garland Group Inc................................E....... 614 294-4411
Columbus *(G-7650)*
Giffin Management Group Inc...............E....... 330 758-4695
Youngstown *(G-20049)*
Glen Wesley Inc...................................D....... 614 888-7492
Columbus *(G-7673)*
Gms Management Co Inc.......................E....... 216 766-6000
Cleveland *(G-5612)*
Goldberg Companies Inc.......................E....... 216 475-2600
Cleveland *(G-5613)*
Hcf Management Inc.............................D....... 419 999-2010
Lima *(G-12652)*
Highland Village Ltd Partnr..................D....... 614 863-4640
New Albany *(G-14856)*
Hills Property Management Inc..............D....... 513 984-0300
Blue Ash *(G-1581)*
Holland Management Inc.......................B....... 330 239-4474
Sharon Center *(G-16722)*
Horizon House Apartments LLC.............D....... 740 354-6393
Portsmouth *(G-16147)*
Huber Investment Corporation..............E....... 937 233-1122
Dayton *(G-9509)*
Iacovetta Builders Inc..........................E....... 614 272-6464
Columbus *(G-7797)*
Indian Hills Senior Community..............E....... 216 486-7700
Euclid *(G-10643)*
Interntional Towers I Ohio Ltd..............D....... 216 520-1250
Youngstown *(G-20083)*
K & D Enterprises Inc...........................E....... 440 946-3600
Willoughby *(G-19531)*
K&D Group Inc.....................................E....... 440 946-3600
Willoughby *(G-19532)*
Kingsbury Tower I Ltd..........................D....... 216 795-3950
Cleveland *(G-5832)*
Klingbeil Multifamilty Fund IV...............D....... 415 398-0106
Columbus *(G-7912)*
Kopf Construction Corporation..............D....... 440 933-0250
Avon Lake *(G-922)*
L W Limited..E....... 513 721-2744
Cincinnati *(G-3901)*
Lakewoods II Ltd..................................D....... 937 254-6141
Dayton *(G-9556)*
Links..E....... 937 644-9988
Marysville *(G-13510)*
Little Bark View Limited........................E....... 216 520-1250
Cleveland *(G-5874)*
Mansfield Memorial Homes...................C....... 419 774-5100
Mansfield *(G-13208)*
Marsol Apartments................................E....... 440 449-5800
Cleveland *(G-5916)*
Menorah Park Center For Senio............A....... 216 831-6500
Cleveland *(G-5952)*
Mercy Health West Park.......................C....... 513 451-8900
Cincinnati *(G-4033)*
Miami Cnty Cmnty Action Cuncil...........E....... 937 335-7921
Troy *(G-18212)*
Millennia Housing MGT Ltd...................E....... 216 520-1250
Cleveland *(G-5996)*
Mrn Limited Partnership.......................E....... 216 589-5631
Cleveland *(G-6019)*
Murray Guttman....................................D....... 513 984-0300
Blue Ash *(G-1617)*
National Church Residences.................C....... 614 451-2151
Columbus *(G-8130)*

National Housing Corporation..............E....... 614 481-8106
Columbus *(G-8134)*
Network Restorations II........................D....... 614 253-0984
Columbus *(G-8179)*
Network Restorations III LLC................D....... 614 253-0984
Columbus *(G-8180)*
New Birch Manor I Assoc LLC..............D....... 330 723-3404
Medina *(G-13980)*
Notre Dame Academy Apartments........E....... 216 707-1590
Cleveland *(G-6100)*
Npa Associates.....................................D....... 614 258-4053
Beachwood *(G-1088)*
Oak Brook Gardens..............................D....... 440 237-3613
North Royalton *(G-15363)*
Oberer Development Co........................E....... 937 910-0851
Miamisburg *(G-14199)*
Ohio Eastern Star Home........................C....... 740 397-1706
Mount Vernon *(G-14785)*
Ohio Presbt Retirement Svcs...............B....... 330 746-2944
Youngstown *(G-20147)*
Oliver House Rest Complex...................D....... 419 243-1302
Toledo *(G-17960)*
Original Partners Ltd Partnr..................C....... 513 381-8696
Cincinnati *(G-4183)*
Otterbein Portage Valley Inc.................C....... 888 749-4950
Pemberville *(G-15806)*
Overbrook Park Ltd..............................D....... 740 773-1159
Chillicothe *(G-2808)*
Owners Management Company............E....... 440 439-3800
Parma *(G-15770)*
Parklane Manor of Akron Inc.................E....... 330 724-3315
Akron *(G-370)*
Paul Dennis..E....... 440 746-8600
Brecksville *(G-1795)*
Phoenix Residential Centers.................D....... 440 887-6097
Cleveland *(G-6205)*
Pickaway County Community Acti.........D....... 740 477-1655
Circleville *(G-4839)*
Pinewood Place Apartments.................A....... 419 243-1413
Toledo *(G-17977)*
Plaza Properties Inc..............................E....... 614 237-3726
Columbus *(G-8455)*
Pleasant Lake Apartments Ltd..............E....... 440 845-2694
Cleveland *(G-6220)*
Power Management Inc.........................E....... 937 222-2909
Dayton *(G-9701)*
Province Kent OH LLC..........................E....... 330 673-3808
Kent *(G-12255)*
Rahf IV Kent LLC..................................E....... 216 621-6060
Kent *(G-12256)*
Real Estate Investors Mgt Inc...............E....... 614 777-2444
Columbus *(G-8494)*
Riverside Commons Ltd Partnr.............D....... 614 863-4640
Reynoldsburg *(G-16329)*
Sateri Home Inc....................................D....... 330 758-8106
Youngstown *(G-20204)*
Sh-91 Limited Partnership....................E....... 330 535-1581
Akron *(G-426)*
Shaker House.......................................D....... 216 991-6000
Cleveland *(G-6402)*
Sherman Thompson Oh Tc LP..............D....... 216 520-1250
Ironton *(G-12166)*
SKW Management LLC........................E....... 937 382-7938
Lynchburg *(G-13055)*
Slaters Inc..E....... 740 654-2204
Lancaster *(G-12435)*
Smb Construction Co Inc......................E....... 419 269-1473
Toledo *(G-18038)*
Smith Tandy Company..........................E....... 614 224-9255
Columbus *(G-8656)*
Spruce Bough Homes LLC....................D....... 614 253-0984
Columbus *(G-8678)*
St Regis Investment LLC......................D....... 216 520-1250
Cleveland *(G-6449)*
Stautberg Family LLC...........................E....... 513 941-5070
Cincinnati *(G-4541)*
Summerfield Homes LLC.......................D....... 614 253-0984
Columbus *(G-8709)*
Summit Management Services Inc........E....... 330 723-0864
Medina *(G-14007)*
Superior Apartments.............................E....... 216 861-6405
Cleveland *(G-6482)*
Tm Wallick Rsdntl Prpts I Ltd...............D....... 614 863-4640
Reynoldsburg *(G-16333)*
Towne Properties Asset MGT...............A....... 513 381-8696
Cincinnati *(G-4617)*
Towne Properties Assoc Inc..................E....... 513 874-3737
Cincinnati *(G-4620)*
Townhomes Management Inc................E....... 614 228-3578
Columbus *(G-8767)*

Transcon Builders Inc...........................E....... 440 439-3400
Cleveland *(G-6540)*
Unite Churc Resid of Oxfor Mis............E....... 740 382-4885
Marion *(G-13469)*
United Church Homes...........................D....... 740 382-4885
Marion *(G-13470)*
United Church Res of Kenton................D....... 740 382-4885
Kenton *(G-12289)*
United Church Residences of................D....... 614 837-2008
Canal Winchester *(G-2123)*
Universal Development MGT Inc...........E....... 330 759-7017
Girard *(G-11303)*
Uptown Rental Properties LLC..............E....... 513 861-9394
Cincinnati *(G-4732)*
Urbancrest Affrdbl Hsing LLC...............D....... 614 228-3578
Columbus *(G-8829)*
Victory Sq Aprtmnts Ltd Partnr............D....... 330 455-8035
Canton *(G-2527)*
Wallace F Ackley Co.............................D....... 614 231-3661
Columbus *(G-8871)*
Walnut Hills Preservation LP................D....... 513 281-1288
Cincinnati *(G-4768)*
Welltower Inc.......................................B....... 419 247-2800
Toledo *(G-18152)*
Westview Apartments Ohio LLC...........B....... 216 520-1250
Youngstown *(G-20244)*
Whitehurst Company............................E....... 419 865-0799
Maumee *(G-13868)*
Zanesville Metro Hsing Auth.................D....... 740 454-9714
Zanesville *(G-20383)*
Zepf Housing Corp One Inc...................C....... 419 531-0019
Toledo *(G-18180)*

OPERATOR: Nonresidential Buildings

Americas Best Value Inn.......................E....... 419 626-9890
Sandusky *(G-16575)*
Best Western Columbus N Hotel...........E....... 614 888-8230
Columbus *(G-7030)*
Canal Road Partners.............................E....... 216 447-0814
Cleveland *(G-5118)*
Cavaliers Holdings LLC.........................C....... 216 420-2000
Cleveland *(G-5136)*
Central Ohio Associates Ltd..................E....... 419 342-2045
Shelby *(G-16743)*
Centro Properties Group LLC................E....... 440 324-6610
Elyria *(G-10487)*
Ch Relty Iv/Clmbus Partners LP............D....... 614 885-3334
Columbus *(G-7174)*
Cincinnati Sports Mall Inc.....................D....... 513 527-4000
Cincinnati *(G-3269)*
City of Cleveland..................................E....... 216 621-4231
Cleveland *(G-5193)*
Columbian Corporation Mantua............E....... 330 274-2576
Mantua *(G-13265)*
Cornerstone Managed Prpts LLC..........E....... 440 263-7708
Lorain *(G-12899)*
Coughlin Holdings Ltd Partnr................E....... 614 847-1002
Worthington *(G-19801)*
Dayton Hcri Place Denver.....................E....... 419 247-2800
Toledo *(G-17693)*
Emmett Dan House Ltd Partnr..............E....... 740 392-6886
Mount Vernon *(G-14764)*
Fairfield Homes Inc..............................C....... 614 873-3533
Plain City *(G-16053)*
Findlay Inn & Conference Ctr...............D....... 419 422-5682
Findlay *(G-10904)*
Forest City Enterprises LP...................B....... 216 621-6060
Cleveland *(G-5553)*
Forest City Enterprises LP...................E....... 216 416-3756
Cleveland *(G-5554)*
Forest City Enterprises LP...................E....... 440 888-8664
Cleveland *(G-5555)*
Forest City Enterprises LP...................E....... 216 416-3780
Cleveland *(G-5556)*
Forest City Enterprises LP...................D....... 216 416-3766
Cleveland *(G-5557)*
Gardner Inc...C....... 614 456-4000
Columbus *(G-7648)*
Glen Arbors Ltd Partnership.................D....... 937 293-0900
Moraine *(G-14661)*
Great Lakes Management Inc..............E....... 216 883-6500
Cleveland *(G-5628)*
Highland Village Ltd Partnr..................D....... 614 863-4640
New Albany *(G-14856)*
Hills Property Management Inc.............D....... 513 984-0300
Blue Ash *(G-1581)*
Hit Portfolio I Misc Trs LLC..................C....... 614 228-1234
Columbus *(G-7753)*
Holland Management Inc......................B....... 330 239-4474
Sharon Center *(G-16722)*

Hotel 50 S Front Opco L P ....D....... 614 885-3334
  Columbus (G-7774)
I-X Center Corporation ....C....... 216 265-2675
  Cleveland (G-5732)
King Group Inc ....E....... 216 831-9330
  Beachwood (G-1073)
L Brands Service Company LLC ....D....... 614 415-7000
  Columbus (G-7933)
Ladera Healthcare Company ....E....... 614 459-1313
  Columbus (G-7943)
Laudan Properties LLC ....E....... 234 212-3225
  Twinsburg (G-18290)
Marion Road Enterprises ....C....... 614 228-6525
  Columbus (G-8020)
Matco Properties Inc ....D....... 440 366-5501
  Elyria (G-10533)
McM General Properties Ltd ....E....... 216 851-8000
  Cleveland (G-5937)
Oak Health Care Investor ....E....... 614 794-8800
  Westerville (G-19192)
Park Cincinnati Board ....D....... 513 421-4086
  Cincinnati (G-4201)
Phil Giessler ....E....... 614 888-0307
  Worthington (G-19835)
Polaris Towne Center LLC ....E....... 614 456-0123
  Columbus (G-6830)
Power Management Inc ....E....... 937 222-2909
  Dayton (G-9701)
Primo Properties LLC ....E....... 330 606-6746
  Austintown (G-859)
Pubco Corporation ....D....... 216 881-5300
  Cleveland (G-6268)
Richard E Jacobs Group LLC ....E....... 440 871-4800
  Cleveland (G-6320)
Sanico Inc ....D....... 440 439-5686
  Cleveland (G-6371)
Saw Mill Creek Ltd ....C....... 419 433-3800
  Huron (G-12030)
Smg Holdings Inc ....C....... 614 827-2500
  Columbus (G-8654)
Three M Associates ....D....... 330 674-9646
  Millersburg (G-14496)
Valley Title & Escro Agency ....E....... 330 392-6171
  Warren (G-18765)
Wernli Realty Inc ....D....... 937 258-7878
  Beavercreek (G-1240)
Zvn Properties Inc ....D....... 330 854-5890
  Canal Fulton (G-2100)

OPHTHALMIC GOODS

Steiner Eoptics Inc ....D....... 937 426-2341
  Miamisburg (G-14226)

OPHTHALMIC GOODS WHOLESALERS

Haag-Streit USA Inc ....C....... 513 336-7255
  Mason (G-13592)
Interstate Optical Co ....D....... 419 529-6800
  Ontario (G-15555)
Walmart Inc ....B....... 740 286-8203
  Jackson (G-12182)

OPHTHALMIC GOODS, NEC, WHOLESALE: Lenses

Toledo Optical Laboratory Inc ....D....... 419 248-3384
  Toledo (G-18094)

OPHTHALMIC GOODS: Lenses, Ophthalmic

Volk Optical Inc ....D....... 440 942-6161
  Mentor (G-14124)

OPTICAL GOODS STORES

Big Sandy Furniture Inc ....D....... 740 574-2113
  Franklin Furnace (G-11043)
Pen Brands LLC ....E....... 216 447-1199
  Brooklyn Heights (G-1878)
Shawnee Optical Inc ....D....... 440 997-2020
  Ashtabula (G-754)
Summit Opthomology Optical ....E....... 330 864-8060
  Akron (G-459)

OPTICAL GOODS STORES: Contact Lenses, Prescription

Arlington Contact Lens Svc Inc ....E....... 614 921-9894
  Columbus (G-6970)
James D Egbert Optometrist ....E....... 937 236-1770
  Huber Heights (G-11955)

OPTICAL INSTRUMENTS & LENSES

Volk Optical Inc ....D....... 440 942-6161
  Mentor (G-14124)

OPTICAL SCANNING SVCS

Aurora Imaging Company ....E....... 614 761-1390
  Dublin (G-10141)
Merchant Data Service Inc ....C....... 937 847-6585
  Miamisburg (G-14188)
Rebiz LLC ....E....... 844 467-3249
  Cleveland (G-6291)
Record Express LLC ....E....... 513 685-7329
  Batavia (G-1008)

OPTOMETRIC EQPT & SPLYS WHOLESALERS

Sight Resource Corporation ....D....... 513 942-4423
  West Chester (G-19006)
Walman Optical Company ....D....... 419 248-3384
  Toledo (G-18145)

OPTOMETRISTS' OFFICES

James D Egbert Optometrist ....E....... 937 236-1770
  Huber Heights (G-11955)
Primary Eyecare Associates ....E....... 937 492-2351
  Sidney (G-16794)
Vision Associates Inc ....D....... 419 578-7598
  Toledo (G-18139)

ORCHESTRAS & BANDS

Blue Water Chamber Orchestra ....E....... 440 781-6215
  Cleveland (G-5067)
Cleveland Phlhrmonic Orchestra ....D....... 216 556-1800
  Rocky River (G-16427)
Columbus Symphony Orchestra ....D....... 614 228-9600
  Columbus (G-7318)

ORGAN BANK

Life Connection of Ohio ....E....... 419 893-4891
  Maumee (G-13809)
Life Connection of Ohio Inc ....E....... 937 223-8223
  Dayton (G-9565)
Lifebanc ....D....... 216 752-5433
  Cleveland (G-5868)

ORGANIZATIONS & UNIONS: Labor

Lake County Local Hazmat ....E....... 440 350-5499
  Mentor (G-14073)
Local 18 IUOE ....E....... 216 432-3131
  Cleveland (G-5878)
Local 911 United Mine Workers ....E....... 740 256-6083
  Gallipolis (G-11203)
Pace International Union ....E....... 419 929-1335
  New London (G-14934)
Pace International Union ....E....... 740 772-2038
  Chillicothe (G-2810)
Pace International Union ....E....... 740 289-2368
  Piketon (G-15983)

ORGANIZATIONS, NEC

Beachwood Prof Fire Fighters C ....E....... 216 292-1968
  Beachwood (G-1035)
Ross County Sportsmen and Wild ....E....... 740 649-9614
  Chillicothe (G-2821)

ORGANIZATIONS: Civic & Social

American Heritage Girls Inc ....D....... 513 771-2025
  Cincinnati (G-2945)
Bowling Green State University ....D....... 419 372-2186
  Bowling Green (G-1724)
Burkhardt Springfield Neighbor ....E....... 937 252-7076
  Dayton (G-9270)
Change Healthcare Tech Enabled ....D....... 614 566-5861
  Columbus (G-7179)
Columbus Foundation ....E....... 614 251-4000
  Columbus (G-7283)
EMs Rams Youth Dev Group Inc ....E....... 216 282-4688
  Cleveland (G-5478)
Help Foundation Inc ....E....... 216 289-7710
  Euclid (G-10637)
Highland Relief Organization ....E....... 614 843-5152
  Columbus (G-7748)
Independence Foundation Inc ....C....... 330 296-2851
  Ravenna (G-16247)

Intercity Amateur Rdo CLB Inc ....E....... 419 989-3429
  Ontario (G-15554)
Izaak Walton League America ....E....... 740 532-2342
  Ironton (G-12157)
Joey Boyle ....E....... 216 273-8317
  Athens (G-787)
Lenau Park ....E....... 440 235-2646
  Olmsted Twp (G-15537)
Lithuanian World Community ....E....... 513 542-0076
  Cincinnati (G-3939)
Miami County Park District ....E....... 937 335-6273
  Troy (G-18214)
Neighborhood Development Svcs ....E....... 330 296-2003
  Ravenna (G-16250)
New Pittsburgh Fire & Rescue F ....E....... 330 264-1230
  Wooster (G-19749)
Ohio Rver Vly Wtr Snttion Comm ....E....... 513 231-7719
  Cincinnati (G-4158)
Salvation Army ....D....... 216 861-8185
  Cleveland (G-6368)
Salvation Army ....D....... 419 447-2252
  Tiffin (G-17535)
Seneca County Firemens Assn ....E....... 419 447-7909
  Tiffin (G-17537)
Seven Hills Fireman Assn ....E....... 216 524-3321
  Seven Hills (G-16681)
Star House Foundation ....E....... 614 826-5868
  Columbus (G-8686)
Towards Employment Inc ....E....... 216 696-5750
  Cleveland (G-6537)
Village of Cuyahoga Heights ....C....... 216 641-7020
  Cleveland (G-6631)
Whitehall Frmens Bnvlence Fund ....E....... 614 237-5478
  Columbus (G-8899)
Wolves Club Inc ....E....... 419 476-4418
  Toledo (G-18160)
York Rite ....E....... 216 751-1417
  Cleveland (G-6701)

ORGANIZATIONS: Educational Research Agency

Cincinnti Educ & RES For Vetrn ....E....... 513 861-3100
  Cincinnati (G-3282)

ORGANIZATIONS: Medical Research

Arthur G James Cance ....A....... 614 293-4878
  Columbus (G-6972)
Childrens Hosp Med Ctr Akron ....E....... 330 633-2055
  Tallmadge (G-17471)
Childrens Hospital Medical Ctr ....E....... 513 636-6100
  Cincinnati (G-3189)
Childrens Hospital Medical Ctr ....A....... 513 636-4200
  Cincinnati (G-3190)
Childrens Hospital Medical Ctr ....E....... 513 636-6400
  Fairfield (G-10708)
Childrens Hospital Medical Ctr ....E....... 513 636-6800
  Mason (G-13554)
Cleveland VA Medical Research ....E....... 216 791-2300
  Cleveland (G-5295)
Kendle International Inc ....E....... 513 763-1414
  Cincinnati (G-3858)
Mp Biomedicals LLC ....C....... 440 337-1200
  Solon (G-16873)
Prologue Research Intl Inc ....D....... 614 324-1500
  Columbus (G-8472)
Research Institute At Nation ....C....... 614 722-2700
  Columbus (G-8518)
Rogosin Institute Inc ....E....... 937 374-3116
  Xenia (G-19924)
United States Dept of Navy ....E....... 937 938-3926
  Dayton (G-9189)
University Hospitals ....D....... 216 844-8797
  Cleveland (G-6590)
US Dept of the Air Force ....B....... 937 255-5150
  Dayton (G-9191)
Wright State University ....E....... 937 298-4331
  Kettering (G-12304)

ORGANIZATIONS: Noncommercial Social Research

American Institute Research ....B....... 614 221-8717
  Columbus (G-6926)
Truenorth Cultural Arts ....E....... 440 949-5200
  Avon Lake (G-928)

ORGANIZATIONS: Physical Research, Noncommercial

Applied Optimization Inc ....C 937 431-5100
Beavercreek (G-1125)

Assured Information SEC Inc ....D 937 427-9720
Beavercreek (G-1127)

Jjr Solutions LLC ....E 937 912-0288
Beavercreek (G-1159)

Ohio State University ....B 330 263-3701
Wooster (G-19755)

Quasonix Inc ....E 513 942-1287
West Chester (G-18988)

Sunpower Inc ....D 740 594-2221
Athens (G-804)

ORGANIZATIONS: Political

County of Richland ....E 419 774-5676
Mansfield (G-13153)

ORGANIZATIONS: Political Campaign

Republican State Central Execu...........E 614 228-2481
Columbus (G-8517)

ORGANIZATIONS: Professional

Akron Council of Engineering ....E 330 535-8835
Akron (G-36)

American Heart Association Inc...........E 614 848-6676
Columbus (G-6923)

Balanced Care Corporation ....E 330 908-1166
Northfield (G-15373)

Center School Association ....D 440 995-7400
Mayfield Village (G-13884)

Community Shelter Board..................E 614 221-9195
Columbus (G-7337)

Deaconis Assocation Inc ....D 419 874-9008
Perrysburg (G-15858)

Dignity Health ....C 330 493-4443
Canton (G-2287)

Emergency Medical Transport.............D 330 484-4000
North Canton (G-15198)

Health Collaborative ....D 513 618-3600
Cincinnati (G-3694)

Lakeside Association ....E 419 798-4461
Lakeside (G-12329)

Monroe County Association For ....D 740 472-1712
Woodsfield (G-19676)

Ohio School Psychologists Assn ....E 614 414-5980
Columbus (G-8285)

Pain Net Inc ....D 614 481-5960
Columbus (G-8414)

Resident Home Association ....D 937 278-0791
Dayton (G-9734)

State of Ohio...............................E 614 466-3834
Grove City (G-11474)

Visiting Nurse Association ....E 216 931-1300
Independence (G-12138)

Warren Twnship Vlntr Fire Dept...........E 740 373-2424
Marietta (G-13399)

ORGANIZATIONS: Religious

Ark Foundation of Dayton..................E 937 256-2759
Dayton (G-9240)

Bnai Brith Hillel Fdn At Osu ....E 614 294-4797
Columbus (G-7050)

Camp Pinecliff Inc.........................D 614 236-5698
Columbus (G-7109)

Cincinnati Gymnastics Academy ....E 513 860-3082
Fairfield (G-10711)

Comfort Inn ....E 740 454-4144
Zanesville (G-20297)

Community Ambulance Service ....D 740 454-6800
Zanesville (G-20298)

Cyo & Community Services Inc............E 330 762-2961
Akron (G-178)

First Assembly Child Care ....E 419 529-6501
Mansfield (G-13176)

Heartbeat International Inc................E 614 885-7577
Columbus (G-7730)

Mideast Baptist Conference...............E 440 834-8984
Burton (G-2018)

Ohio State Univ Alumni Assn ....D 614 292-2200
Columbus (G-8290)

Overlook House ....E 216 795-3550
Cleveland (G-6150)

Pastoral Care Management Svcs ....E 513 205-1398
Cincinnati (G-4207)

Pillar of Fire ....E 513 542-1212
Cincinnati (G-4249)

Ross County YMCA ....D 740 772-4340
Chillicothe (G-2823)

Saint Cecilia Church ....E 614 878-5353
Columbus (G-8583)

Salvation Army ....D 216 861-8185
Cleveland (G-6368)

Sheldon Harry E Calvary Camp...........D 440 593-4381
Conneaut (G-8958)

Sidney-Shelby County YMCA ....E 937 492-9134
Sidney (G-16800)

Society of The Transfiguration ....E 513 771-7462
Cincinnati (G-4501)

United Church Homes Inc.................C 419 294-4973
Upper Sandusky (G-18414)

Wapakoneta YMCA ....D 419 739-9622
Wapakoneta (G-18659)

West Side Ecumenical Ministry ....C 216 325-9369
Cleveland (G-6671)

Windsor Medical Center Inc...............D 330 499-8300
Canton (G-2536)

Young Mens Christian Assoc..............D 937 836-9622
Englewood (G-10606)

Young Mens Christian Assoc..............C 614 834-9622
Canal Winchester (G-2129)

Young MNS Chrstn Assn Clveland ....D 440 808-8150
Westlake (G-19426)

ORGANIZATIONS: Research Institute

American Heart Assn Ohio Vly ....E 216 791-7500
Cleveland (G-4953)

American Institute Research ....B 614 310-8982
Columbus (G-6927)

Applied Research Solutions Inc ....D 937 912-6100
Beavercreek (G-1202)

Barrett Center For Cancer Prev ....D 513 558-3200
Cincinnati (G-3022)

Charles River Labs Ashland LLC ....C 419 282-8700
Ashland (G-667)

Macaulay-Brown Inc ....B 937 426-3421
Beavercreek (G-1227)

Nationwide Childrens Hospital ....A 614 722-2000
Columbus (G-8146)

Ohio State University ....E 614 292-5990
Columbus (G-8335)

Riverside Research Institute...............D 937 431-3810
Beavercreek (G-1183)

University of Dayton ....C 937 229-2113
Dayton (G-9839)

University of Dayton ....B 937 229-3822
Dayton (G-9840)

ORGANIZATIONS: Scientific Research Agency

Cornerstone Research Group Inc ....C 937 320-1877
Miamisburg (G-14155)

Universities Space Res Assn ....E 216 368-0750
Cleveland (G-6584)

ORGANIZATIONS: Veterans' Membership

American Legion............................D 330 488-0119
East Canton (G-10385)

American Legion............................E 440 834-8621
Burton (G-2013)

American Legion Post ....D 330 393-9858
Southington (G-16952)

Amvets Post No 6 Inc ....D 330 833-5935
Massillon (G-13662)

Commodore Denig Post No 83 ....E 419 625-3274
Sandusky (G-16589)

Disabled American Veterans...............E 330 875-5795
Louisville (G-12965)

Disabled American Veterans...............B 419 526-0203
Mansfield (G-13168)

Disabled American Veterans...............B 330 364-1204
New Philadelphia (G-14957)

Disabled American Veterans...............B 740 367-7973
Cheshire (G-2733)

Genoa Legion Post 324 ....E 419 855-7049
Genoa (G-11256)

Ohio Dept Amvet Svc Foundation.........D 614 431-6990
Columbus (G-8245)

Veterans Fgn Wars Post 2850 ....D 216 631-2585
Cleveland (G-6624)

Vietnam Veterans America Inc............E 330 877-6017
Hartville (G-11700)

ORPHANAGE

Saint Joseph Orphanage..................D 513 231-5010
Cincinnati (G-4426)

ORTHODONTIST

Orthodontic Associates LLC ....E 419 229-8771
Lima (G-12713)

Orthodontic Association ....E 419 523-4014
Ottawa (G-15662)

Osu Orthodontic Clinic ....E 614 292-1058
Columbus (G-8393)

Smile Development Inc ....E 419 882-7187
Sylvania (G-17451)

OUTDOOR PARKING SVCS

Falcon Transport Co ....D 330 793-1345
Youngstown (G-20035)

OUTREACH PROGRAM

Area Agency On Aging Reg 9 Inc ....D 740 439-4478
Cambridge (G-2050)

Beth-El Agape Christian Center ....E 614 445-0674
Columbus (G-7032)

Bryant Eliza Village........................B 216 361-6141
Cleveland (G-5096)

First Community Village ....B 614 324-4455
Columbus (G-7585)

Lutheran Scial Svcs Centl Ohio...........E 419 289-3523
Worthington (G-19825)

Menorah Park Center For Senio ....A 216 831-6500
Cleveland (G-5952)

Ross Cnty Cmmittee For Elderly ....E 740 773-3544
Chillicothe (G-2817)

WEBa Outreach Food Pantry ....E 740 543-3227
Amsterdam (G-602)

OXYGEN TENT SVCS

Angels Home Care LLC ....E 419 947-9373
Mount Gilead (G-14724)

PACKAGE DESIGN SVCS

Austin Foam Plastics Inc ....E 614 921-0824
Columbus (G-7003)

Diversipak Inc..............................C 513 321-7884
Cincinnati (G-3436)

Marsh Inc ....E 513 421-1234
Cincinnati (G-3975)

Nottingham-Spirk Des ....E 216 800-5782
Cleveland (G-6101)

Univenture Inc..............................D 937 645-4600
Dublin (G-10359)

PACKAGED FROZEN FOODS WHOLESALERS, NEC

Anderson and Dubose Inc ....D 440 248-8800
Warren (G-18665)

Avalon Foodservice Inc ....C 330 854-4551
Canal Fulton (G-2092)

Best Express Foods Inc ....D 513 531-2378
Cincinnati (G-3043)

Euclid Fish Company ....D 440 951-6448
Mentor (G-14044)

Food Distributors Inc......................E 740 439-2764
Cambridge (G-2068)

Gordon Food Service Inc ....E 419 747-1212
Ontario (G-15550)

Gordon Food Service Inc ....E 419 225-8983
Lima (G-12646)

Gordon Food Service Inc ....E 216 573-4900
Cleveland (G-5616)

Hillcrest Egg & Cheese Co ....D 216 361-4625
Cleveland (G-5691)

Instantwhip Foods Inc ....E 330 688-8825
Stow (G-17213)

Jetro Cash and Carry Entps LLC..........D 216 525-0101
Cleveland (G-5794)

Koch Meat Co Inc..........................B 513 874-3500
Fairfield (G-10745)

Lori Holding Co ....E 740 342-3230
New Lexington (G-14920)

Maines Paper & Food Svc Inc ....E 216 643-7500
Bedford (G-1291)

Northern Frozen Foods Inc ....C 440 439-0600
Cleveland (G-6096)

Peck Distributors Inc ....E 216 587-6814
Maple Heights (G-13291)

SERVICES

Pinata Foods Inc ....E 216 281-8811
Cleveland (G-6211)

Ritchies Food Distributors Inc ....E 740 443-6303
Piketon (G-15988)

Sherwood Food Distributors LLC ....B 216 662-6794
Maple Heights (G-13296)

Spartannash Company ....D 513 793-6300
Cincinnati (G-4510)

Swd Corporation ....E 419 227-2436
Lima (G-12759)

Sysco Central Ohio Inc ....B 614 272-0658
Columbus (G-8725)

Tasty Pure Food Company ....E 330 434-8141
Akron (G-464)

US Foods Inc ....A 614 539-7993
West Chester (G-19096)

Z Produce Co Inc ....E 614 224-4373
Columbus (G-8934)

PACKAGING & LABELING SVCS

Accel Inc ....C 614 656-1100
New Albany (G-14840)

Ace Assembly Packaging Inc ....E 330 866-9117
Waynesburg (G-18827)

Advanced Specialty Products ....D 419 882-6528
Bowling Green (G-1712)

Alternative Services Inc ....E 419 861-2121
Holland (G-11870)

Avery Dennison Corporation ....C 440 534-6000
Mentor (G-14020)

Baumfolder Corporation ....E 937 492-1281
Sidney (G-16760)

BDS Packaging Inc ....D 937 643-0530
Moraine (G-14624)

Corporate Support Inc ....E 419 221-3838
Lima (G-12620)

Crescent Park Corporation ....C 513 759-7000
West Chester (G-18906)

Custom Pkg & Inspecting Inc ....E 330 399-8961
Warren (G-18697)

Custom Products Corporation ....D 440 528-7100
Solon (G-16842)

Custom-Pak Inc ....D 330 725-0800
Medina (G-13928)

Domino Foods Inc ....D 216 432-3222
Cleveland (G-5437)

Express Packaging Ohio Inc ....B 740 498-4700
Newcomerstown (G-15131)

First Choice Packaging Inc ....C 419 333-4100
Fremont (G-11073)

Freudenberg-Nok General Partnr ....B 419 499-2502
Milan (G-14361)

Future Poly Tech Inc ....E 614 942-1209
Columbus (G-7636)

Garda CL Great Lakes Inc ....B 561 939-7000
Columbus (G-7647)

General Electric Company ....A 937 534-6920
Dayton (G-9458)

Hunt Products Inc ....E 440 667-2457
Newburgh Heights (G-15115)

Industrial Chemical Corp ....E 330 725-0800
Medina (G-13953)

J & B Systems Company Inc ....C 513 732-2000
Batavia (G-1002)

Keller Logistics Group Inc ....E 866 276-9486
Defiance (G-9923)

King Tut Logistics LLC ....E 614 538-0509
Columbus (G-7908)

Lawnview Industries Inc ....C 937 653-5217
Urbana (G-18438)

M A Folkes Company Inc ....E 513 785-4200
Hamilton (G-11626)

M P & A Fibers Inc ....E 440 926-1074
Grafton (G-11318)

Metzenbaum Sheltered Inds Inc ....C 440 729-1919
Chesterland (G-2741)

Midwest Tape LLC ....B 419 868-9370
Holland (G-11898)

Miller Products Inc ....E 330 238-4200
Alliance (G-541)

Nelson Packaging Company Inc ....D 419 229-3471
Lima (G-12705)

Ohio Gasket and Shim Co Inc ....E 330 630-0626
Akron (G-359)

Packship Usa Inc ....D 330 682-7225
Orrville (G-15643)

Pactiv LLC ....C 614 771-5400
Columbus (G-8410)

Pak Lab ....E 513 735-4777
Batavia (G-1005)

Pandora Manufacturing Llc ....D 419 384-3241
Ottawa (G-15663)

Project Packaging Inc ....E 216 451-7878
Cleveland (G-6260)

Raco Industries LLC ....D 513 984-2101
Blue Ash (G-1636)

Richland Newhope Industries ....E 419 774-4400
Mansfield (G-13237)

Rudolph Brothers & Co ....E 614 833-0707
Canal Winchester (G-2118)

Sonoco Prtective Solutions Inc ....E 937 890-7628
Dayton (G-9774)

Specialty Lubricants Corp ....E 330 425-2567
Macedonia (G-13082)

Systems Pack Inc ....E 330 467-5729
Macedonia (G-13083)

T W I International Inc ....C 440 439-1830
Cleveland (G-6496)

Tekni-Plex Inc ....E 419 491-2399
Holland (G-11918)

Teva Womens Health Inc ....C 513 731-9900
Cincinnati (G-4589)

Third Dimension Inc ....E 877 926-3223
Geneva (G-11247)

Univenture Inc ....D 937 645-4600
Dublin (G-10359)

Univenture Inc ....E 937 645-4600
Dublin (G-10360)

Universal Packg Systems Inc ....B 513 732-2000
Batavia (G-1013)

Universal Packg Systems Inc ....E 513 735-4777
Batavia (G-1014)

Universal Packg Systems Inc ....B 513 674-9400
Cincinnati (G-4695)

Weaver Industries Inc ....C 330 379-3606
Akron (G-496)

Weaver Industries Inc ....E 330 379-3660
Akron (G-497)

Weaver Industries Inc ....C 330 666-5114
Akron (G-498)

Welch Packaging Group Inc ....C 614 870-2000
Columbus (G-8884)

PACKAGING MATERIALS, INDL: Wholesalers

Mauser Usa LLC ....E 740 397-1762
Mount Vernon (G-14781)

Process Pump & Seal Inc ....E 513 988-7000
Trenton (G-18190)

PACKAGING MATERIALS, WHOLESALE

A-Roo Company LLC ....D 440 238-8850
Strongsville (G-17278)

Avery Dennison Corporation ....C 440 534-6000
Mentor (G-14020)

Bag-Pack Inc ....E 513 346-3900
West Chester (G-18871)

Bprex Closures LLC ....D 812 424-2904
Maumee (G-13764)

Cambridge Packaging Inc ....E 740 432-3351
Cambridge (G-2055)

Century Marketing Corporation ....C 419 354-2591
Bowling Green (G-1727)

Compass Packaging LLC ....E 330 274-2001
Mantua (G-13266)

Custom Products Corporation ....D 440 528-7100
Solon (G-16842)

Diversified Products & Svcs ....C 740 393-6202
Mount Vernon (G-14763)

Eastgate Graphics LLC ....E 513 228-5522
Lebanon (G-12461)

First 2 Market Products LLC ....E 419 874-5444
Perrysburg (G-15865)

G R B Inc ....D 800 628-9195
West Chester (G-18929)

Global-Pak Inc ....E 330 482-1993
Lisbon (G-12802)

Gpax Ltd ....E 614 501-7622
Reynoldsburg (G-16307)

Graham Packaging Holdings Co ....E 419 628-1070
Minster (G-14534)

Graham Packg Plastic Pdts Inc ....E 419 423-3271
Findlay (G-10914)

Impressive Packaging Inc ....E 419 368-6808
Hayesville (G-11701)

Inno-Pak LLC ....E 740 363-0090
Delaware (G-9989)

Innovtive Lbling Solutions Inc ....D 513 860-2457
Hamilton (G-11614)

Jlt Packaging Cincinnati Inc ....D 513 933-0250
Lebanon (G-12474)

Kapstone Container Corporation ....C 330 562-6111
Aurora (G-832)

Liqui-Box Corporation ....E 614 888-9280
Columbus (G-7982)

Mid-States Packaging Inc ....E 937 843-3243
Lewistown (G-12572)

Pac Worldwide Corporation ....E 800 535-0039
Cincinnati (G-4196)

Pacific MGT Holdings LLC ....E 440 324-3339
Elyria (G-10552)

Packaging & Pads R Us LLC ....E 419 499-2905
Milan (G-14365)

Pactiv LLC ....E 614 777-4019
Columbus (G-8411)

Pakmark LLC ....E 513 285-1040
Fairfield (G-10768)

Plastipak Packaging Inc ....C 330 725-0205
Medina (G-13987)

Printpack Inc ....C 513 891-7886
Cincinnati (G-4281)

Questar Solutions LLC ....E 330 966-2070
North Canton (G-15229)

Rosemark Paper Inc ....D 614 443-0303
Columbus (G-8552)

Rrp Packaging ....E 419 666-6119
Perrysburg (G-15915)

S & S Inc ....E 216 383-1880
Cleveland (G-6354)

Samuel Strapping Systems Inc ....D 740 522-2500
Heath (G-11709)

Scioto Packaging Inc ....E 614 491-1500
Columbus (G-8612)

Ship-Paq Inc ....E 513 860-0700
Fairfield (G-10780)

SJS Packaging Group Inc ....E 513 841-1351
Cincinnati (G-4489)

Skybox Packaging LLC ....D 419 525-7209
Mansfield (G-13243)

Star Packaging Inc ....E 614 564-9936
Columbus (G-8688)

Sterling Paper Co ....E 614 443-0303
Columbus (G-8697)

Storopack Inc ....E 513 874-0314
West Chester (G-19084)

Superior Packaging Toledo LLC ....E 419 380-3335
Toledo (G-18056)

Systems Pack Inc ....E 330 467-5729
Macedonia (G-13083)

Third Dimension Inc ....E 877 926-3223
Geneva (G-11247)

US Safetygear Inc ....E 330 898-1344
Warren (G-18764)

Welch Packaging LLC ....E 937 223-3958
Dayton (G-9872)

Welch Packaging Group Inc ....C 419 726-3491
Toledo (G-18148)

Welch Packaging Group Inc ....D 216 447-9800
Cleveland (G-6660)

PACKAGING MATERIALS: Paper

Bollin & Sons Inc ....E 419 693-6573
Toledo (G-17618)

Custom Products Corporation ....D 440 528-7100
Solon (G-16842)

Hunt Products Inc ....E 440 667-2457
Newburgh Heights (G-15115)

Kapstone Container Corporation ....C 330 562-6111
Aurora (G-832)

Norse Dairy Systems Inc ....C 614 294-4931
Columbus (G-8195)

Springdot Inc ....D 513 542-4000
Cincinnati (G-4523)

Storopack Inc ....E 513 874-0314
West Chester (G-19084)

PACKAGING MATERIALS: Plastic Film, Coated Or Laminated

Universal Packg Systems Inc ....B 513 732-2000
Batavia (G-1013)

Universal Packg Systems Inc ....B 513 674-9400
Cincinnati (G-4695)

Universal Packg Systems Inc ....E 513 735-4777
Batavia (G-1014)

PACKAGING MATERIALS: Polystyrene Foam

Skybox Packaging LLC ....D 419 525-7209
Mansfield (G-13243)

Storopack Inc ....E 513 874-0314
West Chester (G-19084)

Truechoicepack Corp ....E 937 630-3832
  Mason (G-13651)

PACKAGING: Blister Or Bubble Formed, Plastic

Truechoicepack Corp ....E 937 630-3832
  Mason (G-13651)

PACKING & CRATING SVC

Bates Metal Products Inc ....D 740 498-8371
  Port Washington (G-16121)
Crescent Park Corporation ....C 513 759-7000
  West Chester (G-18906)
Deufol Worldwide Packaging LLC ......D 440 232-1100
  Bedford (G-1276)
Deufol Worldwide Packaging LLC ......D 414 967-8000
  Fairfield (G-10717)
Impact Fulfillment Svcs LLC ....C 614 262-8911
  Columbus (G-7803)
Lefco Worthington LLC ....E 216 432-4422
  Cleveland (G-5860)
Morral Companies LLC ....E 740 465-3251
  Morral (G-14713)
Packship Usa Inc ....D 330 682-7225
  Orrville (G-15643)
Southeast Diversified Inds ....D 740 432-4241
  Cambridge (G-2082)
Sugar Creek Packing Co ....E 513 551-5255
  Blue Ash (G-1653)
Vista Industrial Packaging LLC ....D 800 454-6117
  Columbus (G-8855)

PACKING & CRATING SVCS: Containerized Goods For Shipping

Containerport Group Inc ....E 440 333-1330
  Columbus (G-7355)

PACKING SVCS: Shipping

Amerisource Health Svcs LLC ....D 614 492-8177
  Columbus (G-6941)
Flick Lumber Co Inc ....E 419 468-6278
  Galion (G-11172)
Hcg Inc ....E 513 539-9269
  Monroe (G-14569)
Inquiry Systems Inc ....E 614 464-3800
  Columbus (G-7824)
McNerney & Associates LLC ....E 513 241-9951
  Cincinnati (G-3990)
Reynolds Industries Inc ....E 330 889-9466
  West Farmington (G-19102)
Star Packaging Inc ....E 614 564-9936
  Columbus (G-8688)

PADS: Athletic, Protective

Soccer Centre Owners Ltd ....E 419 893-5425
  Maumee (G-13853)

PAGING SVCS

Answering Service Inc ....E 440 473-1200
  Cleveland (G-4984)
Maximum Communications Inc ....E 513 489-3414
  Cincinnati (G-3981)
TSC Communications Inc ....E 419 739-2200
  Wapakoneta (G-18657)

PAINT STORE

Comex North America Inc ....D 303 307-2100
  Cleveland (G-5316)
Miller Bros Wallpaper Company ....E 513 231-4470
  Cincinnati (G-4052)
Modern Glass Pnt & Tile Co Inc ....E 740 454-1253
  Zanesville (G-20332)

PAINTING SVC: Metal Prdts

Carpe Diem Industries LLC ....D 419 659-5639
  Columbus Grove (G-8940)
Carpe Diem Industries LLC ....E 419 358-0129
  Bluffton (G-1689)
Herbert E Orr Company ....E 419 399-4866
  Paulding (G-15794)
Precision Coatings Systems ....E 937 642-4727
  Marysville (G-13523)
Tendon Manufacturing Inc ....E 216 663-3200
  Cleveland (G-6512)

PAINTS & ADDITIVES

Comex North America Inc ....D 303 307-2100
  Cleveland (G-5316)
Continental Products Company ....E 216 531-0710
  Cleveland (G-5344)

PAINTS & ALLIED PRODUCTS

Akzo Nobel Coatings Inc ....C 614 294-3361
  Columbus (G-6890)
Bollin & Sons Inc ....E 419 693-6573
  Toledo (G-17618)
Fuchs Lubricants Co ....E 330 963-0400
  Twinsburg (G-18270)
Hexpol Compounding LLC ....C 440 834-4644
  Burton (G-2016)
Hoover & Wells Inc ....E 419 691-9220
  Toledo (G-17807)
Matrix Sys Auto Finishes LLC ....D 248 668-8135
  Massillon (G-13713)
Teknol Inc ....D 937 264-0190
  Dayton (G-9808)
Tremco Incorporated ....B 216 292-5000
  Beachwood (G-1114)

PAINTS, VARNISHES & SPLYS WHOLESALERS

Carlisle Fluid Tech Inc ....E 419 825-5186
  Toledo (G-17637)
Continental Products Company ....E 216 531-0710
  Cleveland (G-5344)
Finishmaster Inc ....D 614 228-4328
  Columbus (G-7578)
Teknol Inc ....D 937 264-0190
  Dayton (G-9808)

PAINTS, VARNISHES & SPLYS, WHOLESALE: Paints

Comex North America Inc ....D 303 307-2100
  Cleveland (G-5316)
Matrix Sys Auto Finishes LLC ....D 248 668-8135
  Massillon (G-13713)
Miller Bros Wallpaper Company ....E 513 231-4470
  Cincinnati (G-4052)
Systems Jay LLC Nanogate ....E 419 747-6639
  Mansfield (G-13249)

PALLET REPAIR SVCS

Spartan Supply Co Inc ....E 513 932-6954
  Lebanon (G-12506)

PALLETIZERS & DEPALLETIZERS

Intelligrated Systems Ohio LLC ....A 513 701-7300
  Mason (G-13600)

PALLETS & SKIDS: Wood

Belco Works Inc ....B 740 695-0500
  Saint Clairsville (G-16470)
Brookhill Center Industries ....C 419 876-3932
  Ottawa (G-15657)
Ken Harper ....C 740 439-4452
  Byesville (G-2025)
Quadco Rehabilitation Center ....D 419 445-1950
  Archbold (G-636)
Quadco Rehabilitation Ctr Inc ....B 419 682-1011
  Stryker (G-17370)
Richland Newhope Industries ....C 419 774-4400
  Mansfield (G-13237)

PALLETS: Plastic

Myers Industries Inc ....D 330 253-5592
  Akron (G-342)

PALLETS: Wooden

Gross Lumber Inc ....E 330 683-2055
  Apple Creek (G-619)
JIT Packaging Inc ....E 330 562-8080
  Aurora (G-831)
Litco International Inc ....E 330 539-5433
  Vienna (G-18581)

PANELS: Building, Wood

Premier Construction Company ....E 513 874-2611
  Fairfield (G-10771)

PAPER & BOARD: Die-cut

Hunt Products Inc ....E 440 667-2457
  Newburgh Heights (G-15115)
Kent Adhesive Products Co ....D 330 678-1626
  Kent (G-12239)
Springdot Inc ....D 513 542-4000
  Cincinnati (G-4523)

PAPER CONVERTING

Buckeye Paper Co Inc ....E 330 477-5925
  Canton (G-2220)
Kent Adhesive Products Co ....D 330 678-1626
  Kent (G-12239)
Millcraft Group LLC ....D 216 441-5500
  Cleveland (G-5993)

PAPER PRDTS: Napkins, Sanitary, Made From Purchased Material

Tranzonic Companies ....C 216 535-4300
  Richmond Heights (G-16395)

PAPER PRDTS: Sanitary

Giant Industries Inc ....E 419 531-4600
  Toledo (G-17762)

PAPER PRDTS: Towels, Napkins/Tissue Paper, From Purchd Mtrls

Aci Industries Converting Ltd ....E 740 368-4160
  Delaware (G-9949)

PAPER, WHOLESALE: Fine

Catalyst Paper (usa) Inc ....E 937 528-3800
  Dayton (G-9286)
Millcraft Paper Company ....E 937 222-7829
  Dayton (G-9636)
Veritiv Pubg & Print MGT Inc ....E 330 650-5522
  Hudson (G-12011)

PAPER, WHOLESALE: Printing

Millcraft Group LLC ....D 216 441-5500
  Cleveland (G-5993)
Millcraft Paper Company ....C 216 441-5505
  Cleveland (G-5994)
Millcraft Paper Company ....E 614 675-4800
  Columbus (G-8087)
Millcraft Paper Company ....E 216 441-5500
  Cleveland (G-5995)
Ohio & Michigan Paper Company ....E 419 666-1500
  Perrysburg (G-15896)
Rosemark Paper Inc ....D 614 443-0303
  Columbus (G-8552)
Sterling Paper Co ....E 614 443-0303
  Columbus (G-8697)
The Cincinnati Cordage Ppr Co ....E 513 242-3600
  Cincinnati (G-4590)

PAPER: Adhesive

Bollin & Sons Inc ....E 419 693-6573
  Toledo (G-17618)
Kent Adhesive Products Co ....D 330 678-1626
  Kent (G-12239)

PAPER: Cloth, Lined, Made From Purchased Materials

Tekni-Plex Inc ....E 419 491-2399
  Holland (G-11918)

PAPER: Coated & Laminated, NEC

Giesecke & Devrient Amer Inc ....C 330 425-1515
  Twinsburg (G-18274)
Ohio Laminating & Binding Inc ....E 614 771-4868
  Hilliard (G-11802)

PAPER: Wrapping & Packaging

Polymer Packaging Inc ....D 330 832-2000
  Massillon (G-13720)
Welch Packaging Group Inc ....C 614 870-2000
  Columbus (G-8884)

PAPERBOARD

Norse Dairy Systems Inc ....C 614 294-4931
  Columbus (G-8195)

Employee Codes: A=Over 500 employees, B=251-500
C=101-250, D=51-100, E=25-50

2019 Harris Ohio
Services Directory

1519

SERVICES

Pactiv LLC ....C 614 771-5400
Columbus (G-8410)

PARKING GARAGE

ABM Parking Services Inc ....E 330 747-7678
Youngstown (G-19945)
Amherst Exempted Vlg Schools ....E 440 988-2633
Amherst (G-579)
City of Garfield Heights ....E 216 475-1107
Cleveland (G-5201)
City of Parma ....D 440 885-8983
Cleveland (G-5211)
City of Portsmouth ....E 740 353-3459
Portsmouth (G-16130)
County of Holmes ....E 330 674-5916
Millersburg (G-14470)
Kwik Parking ....E 419 246-0454
Toledo (G-17844)
Ohio Department Transportation ....E 330 637-5951
Cortland (G-8992)
Park-N-Go Inc ....E 937 890-7275
Dayton (G-9686)
Parking Company America Inc ....E 216 265-0500
Cleveland (G-6173)
Parking Company America Inc ....E 513 381-2179
Cincinnati (G-4205)
Sp Plus Corporation ....E 216 687-0141
Cleveland (G-6437)
USA Parking Systems Inc ....D 216 621-9255
Cleveland (G-6611)

PARKING LOTS

ABM Parking Services Inc ....E 937 461-2113
Dayton (G-9203)
ABM Parking Services Inc ....E 216 621-6600
Cleveland (G-4895)
Central Parking System Inc ....E 513 381-2621
Cincinnati (G-3156)
Park n Fly Inc ....E 404 264-1000
Cleveland (G-6167)
Park Place Management Inc ....E 216 362-1080
Cleveland (G-6168)
Parking Company America Inc ....B 513 241-0415
Cincinnati (G-4204)
Prestige Valet Inc ....D 513 871-4220
Cincinnati (G-4277)
Shaias Parking Inc ....E 216 621-0328
Cleveland (G-6401)
Sp Plus Corporation ....D 216 444-2255
Cleveland (G-6436)
Sp Plus Corporation ....D 216 267-7275
Cleveland (G-6438)
Sp Plus Corporation ....D 216 267-5030
Cleveland (G-6439)

PARKING LOTS & GARAGES

Allpro Parking Ohio LLC ....E 614 221-9696
Columbus (G-6899)
Asv Services LLC ....E 216 797-1701
Euclid (G-10623)
City of Lakewood ....D 216 941-1116
Cleveland (G-5208)
Republic Parking System Inc ....E 937 415-0016
Vandalia (G-18540)
Sharps Valet Parking ....E 513 863-1777
Fairfield (G-10779)
Southwood Auto Sales ....E 330 788-8822
Youngstown (G-20214)

PAROLE OFFICE

Ohio Dept Rhbilitation Corectn ....B 614 274-9000
Columbus (G-8248)
Rehabltation Corectn Ohio Dept ....D 614 752-0800
Columbus (G-8507)

PARTITIONS & FIXTURES: Except Wood

3-D Technical Services Company ....E 937 746-2901
Franklin (G-11020)
HP Manufacturing Company Inc ....D 216 361-6500
Cleveland (G-5721)
Panacea Products Corporation ....E 614 850-7000
Columbus (G-8418)

PARTITIONS WHOLESALERS

Door Fabrication Services Inc ....E 937 454-9207
Vandalia (G-18520)

OK Interiors Corp ....C 513 742-3278
Cincinnati (G-4164)

PARTITIONS: Wood & Fixtures

Brower Products Inc ....D 937 563-1111
Cincinnati (G-3082)
Creative Products Inc ....E 419 866-5501
Holland (G-11880)
Diversified Products & Svcs ....C 740 393-6202
Mount Vernon (G-14763)
LE Smith Company ....D 419 636-4555
Bryan (G-1961)
Symatic Inc ....E 330 225-1510
Brunswick (G-1941)

PARTS: Metal

Clifton Steel Company ....D 216 662-6111
Maple Heights (G-13283)

PARTY & SPECIAL EVENT PLANNING SVCS

Cec Entertainment Inc ....D 937 439-1108
Miamisburg (G-14149)
Cincinnati Circus Company LLC ....D 513 921-5454
Cincinnati (G-3233)
Eventions Ltd ....E 216 952-9898
Cleveland (G-5496)
Excel Decorators Inc ....E 614 522-0056
Columbus (G-7541)
Fun Day Events LLC ....E 740 549-9000
Gahanna (G-11121)
Kiddie Party Company LLC ....E 440 273-7680
Mayfield Heights (G-13875)
Pure Romance LLC ....D 513 248-8656
Cincinnati (G-4306)

PASSENGER AIRLINE SVCS

American Airlines Inc ....E 216 706-0702
Cleveland (G-4947)
American Airlines Inc ....D 937 454-7472
Vandalia (G-18501)
American Airlines Inc ....E 937 890-6668
Vandalia (G-18502)
Champlain Enterprises LLC ....C 440 779-4588
North Olmsted (G-15280)
Delta Air Lines Inc ....D 614 239-4440
Columbus (G-7434)
Envoy Air Inc ....D 614 231-4391
Columbus (G-7523)
Psa Airlines Inc ....D 937 454-9338
Vandalia (G-18536)
Psa Airlines Inc ....C 937 454-1116
Vandalia (G-18537)
United Airlines Inc ....E 937 454-2009
Vandalia (G-18546)
United Airlines Inc ....C 216 501-4700
Cleveland (G-6566)

PATENT OWNERS & LESSORS

Cleveland Rest Oper Ltd Partnr ....C 216 328-1121
Cleveland (G-5285)

PATIENT MONITORING EQPT WHOLESALERS

Clinical Technology Inc ....E 440 526-0160
Brecksville (G-1777)

PATROL SVCS: Electric Transmission Or Gas Lines

City of Cleveland ....E 216 664-3922
Cleveland (G-5198)

PATTERNS: Indl

Freeman Manufacturing & Sup Co ....E 440 934-1902
Avon (G-881)
Shells Inc ....D 330 808-5558
Copley (G-8974)

PAYROLL SVCS

Advance Payroll Funding Ltd ....C 216 831-8900
Beachwood (G-1026)
Ahola Corporation ....D 440 717-7620
Brecksville (G-1767)
Chard Snyder & Associates LLC ....C 513 459-9997
Mason (G-13553)

Hr Butler LLC ....E 614 923-2900
Dublin (G-10246)
Humaserve Hr LLC ....E 513 605-3522
Cincinnati (G-3740)
Kent State University ....D 330 672-2607
Kent (G-12242)
Paychex Inc ....E 614 781-6143
Worthington (G-19833)
Paychex Inc ....C 330 342-0530
Hudson (G-12002)
Paychex Inc ....E 513 727-9182
Middletown (G-14353)
Paychex Inc ....D 800 939-2462
Lima (G-12718)
Paychex Inc ....D 614 210-0400
Dublin (G-10306)
Paycom Software Inc ....A 888 678-0796
Cincinnati (G-4217)
Paycor Inc ....E 614 985-6140
Worthington (G-19834)
Paycor Inc ....E 216 447-7913
Cleveland (G-6184)
Paycor Inc ....C 513 381-0505
Cincinnati (G-4218)
Payroll Services Unlimited ....E 740 653-9581
Lancaster (G-12425)
Sheakley-Uniservice Inc ....C 513 771-2277
Cincinnati (G-4468)
Top Echelon Contracting Inc ....B 330 454-3508
Canton (G-2514)

PENSION & RETIREMENT PLAN CONSULTANTS

Cbiz Inc ....D 330 644-2044
Uniontown (G-18361)
Financial Plnners of Cleveland ....E 440 473-1115
Cleveland (G-5526)
Nationwide Financial Svcs Inc ....C 614 249-7111
Columbus (G-8155)
Noble-Davis Consulting Inc ....E 440 519-0850
Solon (G-16878)
Producer Group LLC ....E 440 871-7700
Rocky River (G-16444)
Sirak Financial Services Inc ....D 330 493-0642
Canton (G-2477)

PENSION FUNDS

Nationwide Rtrment Sltions Inc ....C 614 854-8300
Dublin (G-10287)
Ohio Pub Emplyees Rtrement Sys ....B 614 228-8471
Columbus (G-8282)
State Tchers Rtrement Sys Ohio ....C 614 227-4090
Columbus (G-8694)

PERFORMING ARTS CENTER PRODUCTION SVCS

Beck Center For Arts ....C 216 521-2540
Cleveland (G-5049)
Deyor Performing Arts Center ....E 330 744-4269
Youngstown (G-20017)
Playhouse Square Holdg Co LLC ....C 216 771-4444
Cleveland (G-6219)

PERIODICALS, WHOLESALE

Findaway World LLC ....D 440 893-0808
Solon (G-16849)

PERSONAL APPEARANCE SVCS

Engle Management Group ....D 513 232-9729
Cincinnati (G-3499)
Life Time Inc ....C 614 428-6000
Columbus (G-7973)
Mercy Health ....E 419 407-3990
Toledo (G-17906)
Ussa Inc ....E 740 354-6672
Portsmouth (G-16179)

PERSONAL CARE FACILITY

Adams County Manor ....D 937 544-2205
West Union (G-19131)
Asana Hospice Cleveland LLC ....E 419 903-0300
Berea (G-1412)
Brookdale Senior Living Inc ....E 740 373-9600
Marietta (G-13316)
Brown Memorial Home Inc ....D 740 474-6238
Circleville (G-4826)

(G-0000) Company's Geographic Section entry number

Childrens Forever Haven Inc ....E 440 652-6749
  North Royalton (G-15349)
Co Open Options Inc ....E 513 932-0724
  Lebanon (G-12455)
Concord Hlth Rhabilitation Ctr ....E 740 574-8441
  Wheelersburg (G-19432)
Cred-Kap Inc ....D 330 755-1466
  Struthers (G-17362)
Cypress Hospice LLC ....E 440 973-0250
  Berea (G-1422)
Dearth Management Company ....E 740 389-1214
  Marion (G-13418)
Dearth Management Company ....C 614 847-1070
  Columbus (G-7426)
Dearth Management Company ....C 330 339-3595
  New Philadelphia (G-14956)
Elmwood Center Inc ....D 419 639-2581
  Green Springs (G-11350)
Emeritus Corporation ....E 330 342-0934
  Stow (G-17201)
Emeritus Corporation ....E 614 836-5990
  Groveport (G-11509)
Grace Hospice LLC ....C 513 458-5545
  Cincinnati (G-3630)
Grace Hospice LLC ....C 937 293-1381
  Moraine (G-14664)
Grace Hospice LLC ....C 216 288-7413
  Mentor (G-14054)
Greater Arms Holistic Health ....E 513 970-2767
  Cincinnati (G-3648)
Heritage Professional Services ....E 740 456-8245
  New Boston (G-14880)
Hospice of Darke County Inc ....E 937 548-2999
  Greenville (G-11387)
Hospice of Hamilton ....E 513 895-1270
  Hamilton (G-11610)
Hospice of Hope Inc ....D 937 444-4900
  Mount Orab (G-14741)
Hospice of Miami Valley LLC ....E 937 458-6028
  Xenia (G-19912)
Hospice of Northwest Ohio ....B 419 661-4001
  Perrysburg (G-15875)
Hospice of Ohio LLC ....D 440 286-2500
  Cleveland (G-5710)
Hospice of The Western Reserve ....E 440 787-2080
  Lorain (G-12907)
Hospice of The Western Reserve ....C 216 383-2222
  Cleveland (G-5712)
Hospice of The Western Reserve ....D 800 707-8922
  Cleveland (G-5713)
Inn At Univ Vlg MGT Co LLC ....E 330 837-3000
  Massillon (G-13699)
Inner City Nursing Home ....C 216 795-1363
  Cleveland (G-5754)
Judson Care Center Inc ....E 513 662-5880
  Cincinnati (G-3840)
Living Care Altrntves of Utica ....E 740 892-3414
  Utica (G-18457)
Lutheran Memorial Home Inc................D 419 502-5700
  Toledo (G-17873)
Mary Scott Nursing Home Inc..............D 937 278-0761
  Dayton (G-9589)
Meigs Center Ltd ....C 740 992-6472
  Middleport (G-14281)
Mercer Residential Svcs Inc ....D 419 586-4709
  Celina (G-2604)
Mercy Health..C 937 390-9665
  Springfield (G-17075)
On-Call Nursing Inc ....D 216 577-8890
  Lakewood (G-12358)
Perio Inc ....E 614 791-1207
  Dublin (G-10308)
Pleasant View Nursing Home ....E 330 848-5028
  Barberton (G-962)
Queen City Hospice LLC ....E 513 510-4406
  Cincinnati (G-4315)
Singleton Health Care Center ....E 216 231-0076
  Cleveland (G-6410)
St Luke Lutheran Community ....D 330 644-3914
  New Franklin (G-14913)
St Luke Lutheran Community ....D 330 644-3914
  New Franklin (G-14914)
Stein Hospice Services Inc ....D 419 663-3222
  Norwalk (G-15456)
Vitas Healthcare Corporation ....D 513 742-6310
  Cincinnati (G-4762)
Voiers Enterprises Inc ....E 740 259-2838
  Mc Dermott (G-13896)
West Park Retirement Community ....C 513 451-8900
  Cincinnati (G-4783)

Zandex Inc ....D 740 967-1111
  Johnstown (G-12205)
Zandex Inc ....D 740 454-6823
  Zanesville (G-20376)
Zandex Health Care Corporation ....C 740 695-7233
  Saint Clairsville (G-16514)
Zusman Community Hospice ....E 614 559-0350
  Columbus (G-8939)

PERSONAL CREDIT INSTITUTIONS: Auto Loans, Incl Insurance

Central Credit Corp ....D 614 856-5840
  Reynoldsburg (G-16289)

PERSONAL CREDIT INSTITUTIONS: Consumer Finance Companies

Dfs Corporate Services LLC ....E 614 283-2499
  New Albany (G-14851)
Howard Hanna Smythe Cramer ....D 330 725-4137
  Medina (G-13952)
Security National Bank & Tr Co ....C 937 324-6800
  Springfield (G-17110)
United Consumer Fincl Svcs Co ....D 440 835-3230
  Cleveland (G-6570)

PERSONAL CREDIT INSTITUTIONS: Finance Licensed Loan Co's, Sm

Homeland Credit Union Inc ....E 740 775-3331
  Chillicothe (G-2788)

PERSONAL CREDIT INSTITUTIONS: Financing, Autos, Furniture

722 Redemption Funding Inc................E 513 679-8302
  Cincinnati (G-2885)
Affordable Cars & Finance Inc ....E 440 777-2424
  North Olmsted (G-15277)
Mtd Holdings Inc ....B 330 225-2600
  Valley City (G-18467)

PERSONAL CREDIT INSTITUTIONS: Install Sales Finance

General Electric Company ....A 330 433-5163
  Canton (G-2324)

PERSONAL DOCUMENT & INFORMATION SVCS

3sg Plus LLC ....E 614 652-0019
  Columbus (G-6797)
Cintas Document Management LLC .....E 800 914-1960
  Mason (G-13560)
Continntal Mssage Solution Inc ....D 614 224-4534
  Columbus (G-7364)
Humility of Mary Info Systems.............D 330 884-6600
  Youngstown (G-20071)
Public Safety Ohio Department ....A 614 752-7600
  Columbus (G-8478)

PERSONAL FINANCIAL SVCS

Hkt Teleservices Inc...........................C 614 652-6300
  Grove City (G-11441)
Nelson Financial Group ....E 513 686-7800
  Dayton (G-9182)

PERSONAL INVESTIGATION SVCS

Employeescreeniq Inc ....D 216 514-2800
  Independence (G-12070)
Human Resource Profile Inc ....E 513 388-4300
  Cincinnati (G-3738)
Sterling Infosystems Inc ....E 216 685-7600
  Independence (G-12125)
Tricor Emplyment Screening Ltd...........E 800 818-5116
  Berea (G-1442)

PERSONAL SHOPPING SVCS

Intelisol Inc ....D 614 409-0052
  Lockbourne (G-12820)

PERSONAL SVCS

City of Rocky River ....E 440 356-5630
  Cleveland (G-5215)

PERSONAL SVCS, NEC

Cabin Restaurant ....E 330 562-9171
  Aurora (G-823)

PEST CONTROL IN STRUCTURES SVCS

All Gone Termite & Pest Ctrl ....E 513 874-7500
  West Chester (G-18863)
General Pest Control Company ....E 216 252-7140
  Cleveland (G-5604)
Rentokil North America Inc ....E 216 328-0700
  Brooklyn Heights (G-1880)
Terminix Intl Coml Xenia ....E 513 539-7846
  Middletown (G-14336)

PEST CONTROL SVCS

J T Eaton & Co Inc ....E 330 425-7801
  Twinsburg (G-18283)
Rentokil North America Inc ....E 330 797-9090
  Youngstown (G-20180)
Rentokil North America Inc ....E 216 328-0700
  Brooklyn Heights (G-1879)
Rentokil North America Inc ....E 614 837-0099
  Canal Winchester (G-2117)
Scotts Miracle-Gro Company ....B 937 644-0011
  Marysville (G-13529)
Terminix Intl Co Ltd Partnr ....E 513 942-6670
  Fairfield (G-10789)
Terminix Intl Co Ltd Partnr ....E 216 518-1091
  Cleveland (G-6514)
Terminix Intl Co Ltd Partnr ....E 419 868-8290
  Maumee (G-13861)
Terminix Intl Co Ltd Partnr ....E 513 539-7846
  Middletown (G-14335)
Terminix Intl Co Ltd Partnr ....E 978 744-2402
  Canton (G-2509)

PET & PET SPLYS STORES

Anark Inc..E 513 825-7387
  Cincinnati (G-2958)
Petsmart Inc ....E 513 336-0365
  Mason (G-13626)
Red Dog Pet Resort & Spa ....E 513 733-3647
  Cincinnati (G-4348)

PET FOOD WHOLESALERS

Butler Animal Hlth Holdg LLC ....E 614 761-9095
  Dublin (G-10155)

PET SPLYS

Miraclecorp Products ....D 937 293-9994
  Moraine (G-14680)

PET SPLYS WHOLESALERS

Columbus Serum Company ....C 614 444-5211
  Columbus (G-7313)
IAMS Company ....D 937 962-7782
  Lewisburg (G-12568)
Petland Inc ....E 740 775-2464
  Chillicothe (G-2811)
Wolverton Inc ....E 330 220-3320
  Brunswick (G-1949)

PETROLEUM & PETROLEUM PRDTS, WHOL Svc Station Splys, Petro

X F Construction Svcs Inc ....E 614 575-2700
  Columbus (G-8923)

PETROLEUM & PETROLEUM PRDTS, WHOLESALE Crude Oil

Afm East Archwood Oil Inc..................E 330 786-1000
  Akron (G-23)
Bd Oil Gathering Corp ....E 740 374-9355
  Marietta (G-13315)
Lyden Oil Company ....E 330 792-1100
  Youngstown (G-20102)
Vesco Oil Corporation ....E 614 367-1412
  Blacklick (G-1484)

PETROLEUM & PETROLEUM PRDTS, WHOLESALE Diesel Fuel

Hightowers Petroleum Company ....E 513 423-4272
  Middletown (G-14349)

Employee Codes: A=Over 500 employees, B=251-500
C=101-250, D=51-100, E=25-50   2019 Harris Ohio
Services Directory   1521

S E R V I C E S

Knisely Inc ....D...... 330 343-5812
Dover (G-10085)

PETROLEUM & PETROLEUM PRDTS, WHOLESALE Fuel Oil

Bazell Oil Co Inc ....E...... 740 385-5420
Logan (G-12831)
Coolants Plus Inc ....E...... 513 892-4000
Hamilton (G-11587)
D W Dickey and Son Inc ....D...... 330 424-1441
Lisbon (G-12799)
Hartland Petroleum LLC ....E...... 740 452-3115
Zanesville (G-20315)
Heartland Petroleum LLC ....E...... 614 441-4001
Columbus (G-7733)
Mighty Mac Investments Inc ....E...... 937 335-2928
Troy (G-18215)
Santmyer Oil Co Inc ....D...... 330 262-6501
Wooster (G-19764)
Sines Inc ....E...... 440 352-6572
Painesville (G-15740)

PETROLEUM & PETROLEUM PRDTS, WHOLESALE: Bulk Stations

Cincinnati - Vulcan Company ....D...... 513 242-5300
Cincinnati (G-3219)
Englefield Inc ....D...... 740 452-2707
Zanesville (G-20305)
New Vulco Mfg & Sales Co LLC ....D...... 513 242-2672
Cincinnati (G-4109)
Universal Oil Inc ....E...... 216 771-4300
Cleveland (G-6582)

PETROLEUM PRDTS WHOLESALERS

Champaign Landmark Inc ....E...... 937 652-2135
Urbana (G-18423)
Circleville Oil Co ....D...... 740 474-7568
Circleville (G-4828)
Clay Distributing Co ....E...... 419 426-3051
Attica (G-813)
Koch Knight LLC ....D...... 330 488-1651
East Canton (G-10387)
Lyden Oil Company ....D...... 330 832-7800
Massillon (G-13705)
Melzers Fuel Service Inc ....E...... 800 367-0203
Painesville (G-15727)
Mplx Terminals LLC ....E...... 513 451-0485
Cincinnati (G-4079)
Shrader Tire & Oil Inc ....E...... 419 472-2128
Toledo (G-18032)
Travelcenters of America LLC ....D...... 330 793-4426
Youngstown (G-20224)
Triumph Energy Corporation ....E...... 513 367-9900
Harrison (G-11679)
Ull Inc ....E...... 440 543-5195
Chagrin Falls (G-2685)

PHARMACEUTICALS

Abbott Laboratories ....A...... 614 624-3191
Columbus (G-6851)
American Regent Inc ....D...... 614 436-2222
Hilliard (G-11741)
Amerisourcebergen Corporation ....D...... 614 497-3665
Lockbourne (G-12808)
Bigmar Inc ....E...... 740 966-5800
Johnstown (G-12196)
Biorx LLC ....C...... 866 442-4679
Cincinnati (G-3051)
Mp Biomedicals LLC ....C...... 440 337-1200
Solon (G-16873)
Omnicare Phrm of Midwest LLC ....D...... 513 719-2600
Cincinnati (G-4171)
River City Pharma ....D...... 513 870-1680
Fairfield (G-10775)
Teva Womens Health Inc ....C...... 513 731-9900
Cincinnati (G-4589)

PHARMACEUTICALS: Mail-Order Svc

Catamaran Home Dlvry Ohio Inc ....D...... 440 930-5520
Avon Lake (G-911)
Medco Health Solutions Inc ....A...... 614 822-2000
Dublin (G-10276)
Nextrx LLC ....A...... 317 532-6000
Mason (G-13622)

PHARMACIES & DRUG STORES

Buehler Food Markets Inc ....C...... 330 364-3079
Dover (G-10068)
Fred W Albrecht Grocery Co ....C...... 330 645-6222
Coventry Township (G-9034)
Fred W Albrecht Grocery Co ....C...... 330 666-6781
Akron (G-229)
Institutional Care Pharmacy ....D...... 419 447-6216
Tiffin (G-17520)
Kroger Co ....C...... 614 759-2745
Columbus (G-7928)
Marc Glassman Inc ....C...... 330 995-9246
Aurora (G-834)
Modern Medical Inc ....C...... 800 547-3330
Westerville (G-19186)
Neighborcare Inc ....A...... 513 719-2600
Cincinnati (G-4103)
Northeast OH Neighborhood Heal ....E...... 216 231-7700
Cleveland (G-6090)
Target Stores Inc ....C...... 614 279-4224
Columbus (G-8731)
Walmart Inc ....B...... 740 286-8203
Jackson (G-12182)

PHOSPHATES

Scotts Company LLC ....B...... 937 644-0011
Marysville (G-13528)

PHOTOCOPY MACHINE REPAIR SVCS

Comdoc Inc ....C...... 330 896-2346
Uniontown (G-18363)
Woodhull LLC ....E...... 937 294-5311
Springboro (G-16989)
Xerox Corporation ....E...... 419 418-6500
Toledo (G-18165)
Xerox Corporation ....D...... 216 642-7806
Cleveland (G-6697)

PHOTOCOPY MACHINES

Xerox Corporation ....B...... 513 554-3200
Blue Ash (G-1684)

PHOTOCOPY SPLYS WHOLESALERS

Ricoh Usa Inc ....D...... 513 984-9898
Sharonville (G-16730)

PHOTOCOPYING & DUPLICATING SVCS

A-A Blueprint Co Inc ....E...... 330 794-8803
Akron (G-13)
ARC Document Solutions Inc ....E...... 513 326-2300
Cincinnati (G-2979)
ARC Document Solutions Inc ....E...... 937 277-7930
Dayton (G-9237)
Fedex Office & Print Svcs Inc ....E...... 440 946-6353
Willoughby (G-19523)
Fedex Office & Print Svcs Inc ....E...... 937 436-0677
Dayton (G-9431)
Fedex Office & Print Svcs Inc ....E...... 614 621-1100
Columbus (G-7572)
Fedex Office & Print Svcs Inc ....E...... 614 898-0000
Westerville (G-19255)
Fedex Office & Print Svcs Inc ....E...... 216 292-2679
Beachwood (G-1057)
Mike Rennie ....E...... 513 830-0020
Dayton (G-9634)
Ricoh Usa Inc ....E...... 513 984-9898
Sharonville (G-16730)
TMR Inc ....C...... 330 220-8564
Brunswick (G-1942)

PHOTOENGRAVING SVC

Youngstown ARC Engraving Co ....E...... 330 793-2471
Youngstown (G-20254)

PHOTOFINISHING LABORATORIES

Buckeye Prof Imaging Inc ....E...... 800 433-1292
Canton (G-2221)
Digico Imaging Inc ....D...... 614 239-5200
Columbus (G-7446)
Discount Drug Mart Inc ....E...... 330 343-7700
Dover (G-10072)
Kroger Co ....C...... 937 294-7210
Dayton (G-9551)
Marco Photo Service Inc ....D...... 419 529-9010
Ontario (G-15561)

Solar Imaging LLC ....E...... 614 626-8536
Gahanna (G-11145)
Target Stores Inc ....C...... 614 279-4224
Columbus (G-8731)
Walgreen Co ....E...... 937 433-5314
Dayton (G-9864)
Walgreen Co ....E...... 614 236-8622
Columbus (G-8869)
Walgreen Co ....E...... 330 677-5650
Kent (G-12267)
Walgreen Co ....E...... 330 745-2674
Barberton (G-971)
Walgreen Co ....E...... 937 396-1358
Kettering (G-12303)
Walgreen Co ....E...... 937 781-9561
Dayton (G-9865)
Walgreen Co ....E...... 330 733-4237
Akron (G-494)
Walgreen Co ....E...... 937 277-6022
Dayton (G-9866)
Walgreen Co ....E...... 740 368-9380
Delaware (G-10015)
Walgreen Co ....E...... 614 336-0431
Dublin (G-10369)
Walgreen Co ....E...... 937 859-3879
Miamisburg (G-14235)
Walgreen Co ....E...... 330 928-5444
Cuyahoga Falls (G-9139)

PHOTOFINISHING LABORATORIES

Buehler Food Markets Inc ....C...... 330 364-3079
Dover (G-10068)
Fred W Albrecht Grocery Co ....C...... 330 645-6222
Coventry Township (G-9034)
Fred W Albrecht Grocery Co ....C...... 330 666-6781
Akron (G-229)
Marc Glassman Inc ....C...... 330 995-9246
Aurora (G-834)

PHOTOGRAMMATIC MAPPING SVCS

Aerocon Photogrammetric Svcs ....E...... 440 946-6277
Willoughby (G-19502)
Kucera International Inc ....D...... 440 975-4230
Willoughby (G-19536)

PHOTOGRAPH DEVELOPING & RETOUCHING SVCS

Vista Color Imaging Inc ....E...... 216 651-2830
Brooklyn Heights (G-1887)

PHOTOGRAPHIC EQPT & SPLYS WHOLESALERS

Collins KAO Inc ....E...... 513 948-9000
Cincinnati (G-3329)
KAO Collins Inc ....D...... 513 948-9000
Cincinnati (G-3847)
Technicolor Thomson Group ....C...... 937 383-6000
Wilmington (G-19651)

PHOTOGRAPHY SVCS: Commercial

AG Interactive Inc ....C...... 216 889-5000
Cleveland (G-4911)
Interphace Phtgrphy Cmmnctions ....E...... 254 289-6270
Amelia (G-573)
Marsh Inc ....E...... 513 421-1234
Cincinnati (G-3975)
Queen City Reprographics ....C...... 513 326-2300
Cincinnati (G-4321)
Rapid Mortgage Company ....E...... 937 748-8888
Cincinnati (G-4338)
Woodard Photographic Inc ....E...... 419 483-3364
Bellevue (G-1386)
Youngstown ARC Engraving Co ....E...... 330 793-2471
Youngstown (G-20254)

PHOTOGRAPHY SVCS: Portrait Studios

Pam Johnsonident ....D...... 419 946-4551
Mount Gilead (G-14733)
Universal Technology Corp ....D...... 937 426-2808
Beavercreek (G-1193)

PHOTOGRAPHY SVCS: School

Lifetouch Nat Schl Studios Inc ....E...... 419 483-8200
Bellevue (G-1380)

Lifetouch Nat Schl Studios Inc ....E 330 497-1291
  Canton (G-2379)
Lifetouch Nat Schl Studios Inc ....E 513 772-2110
  Cincinnati (G-3928)
Woodard Photographic Inc ....E 419 483-3364
  Bellevue (G-1386)

PHOTOGRAPHY SVCS: Still Or Video

Childers Photography ....E 937 256-0501
  Dayton (G-9165)
Lifetouch Inc ....E 419 435-2646
  Fostoria (G-11008)
Lifetouch Inc ....E 937 298-6275
  Dayton (G-9567)
Peters Main Street Photography ....E 740 852-2731
  London (G-12872)
Rapid Mortgage Company ....E 937 748-8888
  Cincinnati (G-4338)
Ripcho Studio ....E 216 631-0664
  Cleveland (G-6327)
Royal Color Inc ....B 440 234-1337
  Bellevue (G-1385)
Usam Inc ....D 330 244-8782
  Canton (G-2525)

PHOTOGRAPHY: Aerial

Aerocon Photogrammetric Svcs ....E 440 946-6277
  Willoughby (G-19502)
Kucera International Inc ....D 440 975-4230
  Willoughby (G-19536)

PHOTOTYPESETTING SVC

Tj Metzgers Inc ....D 419 861-8611
  Toledo (G-18066)

PHYSICAL EXAMINATION & TESTING SVCS

Brecksvlle Hlthcare Group Inc ....D 440 546-0643
  Brecksville (G-1772)
Fairfield Diagnstc Imaging LLC ....E 740 654-7559
  Lancaster (G-12394)
Ohio North E Hlth Systems Inc ....E 330 747-9551
  Youngstown (G-20146)

PHYSICAL EXAMINATION SVCS, INSURANCE

Alveo Health LLC ....E 513 557-3502
  Cincinnati (G-2936)

PHYSICAL FITNESS CENTERS

Avalon Holdings Corporation ....D 330 856-8800
  Warren (G-18673)
B & I Hotel Management LLC ....C 330 995-0200
  Aurora (G-819)
Bennett Enterprises Inc ....B 419 874-3111
  Perrysburg (G-15838)
Best Western Columbus N Hotel ....E 614 888-8230
  Columbus (G-7030)
Breezy Point Ltd Partnership ....E 330 995-0600
  Aurora (G-822)
Broad Street Hotel Assoc LP ....D 614 861-0321
  Columbus (G-7076)
Carroll Properties ....E 513 398-8075
  Mason (G-13549)
Chalk Box Get Fit LLC ....E 440 992-9619
  Ashtabula (G-725)
Chillicothe Motel LLC ....E 740 773-3903
  Chillicothe (G-2764)
Chillicothe Racquet Club ....E 740 773-4928
  Chillicothe (G-2766)
City of Brecksville ....D 440 526-4109
  Brecksville (G-1775)
Columbus Country Club ....E 614 861-0800
  Columbus (G-7272)
Coshocton Village Inn Suites ....E 740 622-9455
  Coshocton (G-9010)
Courtyard Ltd ....E 513 777-5530
  West Chester (G-18902)
Emh Regional Medical Center ....D 440 988-6800
  Avon (G-880)
Family YMCA of LANcstr&fairfld ....C 740 654-0616
  Lancaster (G-12404)
Family YMCA of LANcstr&fairfld ....D 740 277-7373
  Lancaster (G-12403)
Findlay Country Club ....E 419 422-9263
  Findlay (G-10902)
Findlay Y M C A Child Dev ....E 419 422-3174
  Findlay (G-10908)

Fitness International LLC ....E 513 298-0134
  West Chester (G-18924)
Fitness International LLC ....E 419 482-7740
  Maumee (G-13792)
Frans Child Care-Mansfield ....C 419 775-2500
  Mansfield (G-13178)
Galion Community Center YMCA ....E 419 468-7754
  Galion (G-11173)
Geeta Hospitality Inc ....E 937 642-3777
  Marysville (G-13499)
General Electric Company ....E 513 243-9404
  Cincinnati (G-3611)
Grandview Ht Ltd Partnr Ohio ....D 937 766-5519
  Springfield (G-17043)
Great Miami Valley YMCA ....A 513 887-0001
  Hamilton (G-11602)
Great Miami Valley YMCA ....C 513 892-9622
  Fairfield Township (G-10808)
Great Miami Valley YMCA ....E 513 887-0014
  Hamilton (G-11604)
Great Miami Valley YMCA ....D 513 868-9622
  Hamilton (G-11605)
Great Miami Valley YMCA ....D 513 829-3091
  Fairfield (G-10732)
Grooveryde Cle ....E 323 595-1701
  Cleveland (G-5644)
Hardin County Family YMCA ....E 419 673-6131
  Kenton (G-12279)
Highland County Family YMCA ....E 937 840-9622
  Hillsboro (G-11842)
Huber Heights YMCA ....D 937 236-9622
  Dayton (G-9508)
Island Hospitality MGT LLC ....E 614 864-8844
  Columbus (G-7847)
Jto Club Corp ....D 440 352-1900
  Mentor (G-14068)
Kettering Recreation Center ....E 937 296-2587
  Dayton (G-9542)
Lake County YMCA ....C 440 352-3303
  Painesville (G-15718)
Lake County YMCA ....C 440 946-1160
  Willoughby (G-19538)
Lake County YMCA ....E 440 259-2724
  Perry (G-15824)
Lake County YMCA ....D 440 428-5125
  Madison (G-13099)
Lima Family YMCA ....E 419 223-6045
  Lima (G-12680)
Mansfield Hotel Partnership ....D 419 529-1000
  Mansfield (G-13207)
Medallion Club ....C 614 794-6999
  Westerville (G-19185)
Midwest Fitness LLC ....E 216 965-5694
  Westlake (G-19374)
N C R Employee Benefit Assn ....C 937 299-3571
  Dayton (G-9651)
Ohio State University ....E 614 293-2800
  Columbus (G-8298)
Ohio State University ....B 614 292-3238
  Columbus (G-8333)
Pike County YMCA ....E 740 947-8862
  Waverly (G-18822)
Queen City Racquet Club LLC ....D 513 771-2835
  Cincinnati (G-4320)
Redefine Enterprises LLC ....E 330 952-2024
  Medina (G-13994)
Ross County YMCA ....D 740 772-4340
  Chillicothe (G-2823)
S P S Inc ....E 937 339-7801
  Troy (G-18228)
Scioto Reserve Inc ....D 740 881-9082
  Powell (G-16208)
Select Hotels Group LLC ....E 614 799-1913
  Dublin (G-10332)
Shady Hollow Cntry CLB Co Inc ....D 330 832-1581
  Massillon (G-13729)
Springfield Family Y M C A ....D 937 323-3781
  Springfield (G-17119)
Swim Incorporated ....E 614 885-1619
  Worthington (G-19855)
Sycamore Board of Education ....D 513 489-3937
  Cincinnati (G-4560)
Synergy Hotels LLC ....E 614 492-9000
  Obetz (G-15530)
Tippecanoe Country Club Inc ....D 330 758-7518
  Canfield (G-2161)
Tom Tise Golf Professional ....D 937 836-5186
  Clayton (G-4862)
Ucc Childrens Center ....E 513 217-5501
  Middletown (G-14356)

Vermilion Family YMCA ....E 440 967-4208
  Vermilion (G-18563)
Washington Township Mntgomery ......C 937 433-0130
  Dayton (G-9868)
Y M C A Central Stark County ....E 330 305-5437
  Canton (G-2539)
Y M C A Central Stark County ....E 330 875-1611
  Louisville (G-12975)
Y M C A Central Stark County ....E 330 877-8933
  Uniontown (G-18392)
Y M C A Central Stark County ....E 330 830-6275
  Massillon (G-13736)
Y M C A Central Stark County ....E 330 498-4082
  Canton (G-2540)
Y M C A of Ashland Ohio Inc ....D 419 289-0626
  Ashland (G-700)
YMCA ....E 330 823-1930
  Alliance (G-558)
YMCA ....D 937 653-9622
  Urbana (G-18447)
YMCA of Clermont County Inc ....E 513 724-9622
  Batavia (G-1016)
YMCA of Massillon ....D 513 879-0800
  Navarre (G-14826)
Young Mens Christian ....B 513 932-1424
  Lebanon (G-12516)
Young Mens Christian Assn ....E 419 238-0443
  Van Wert (G-18498)
Young Mens Christian Assoc ....E 419 729-8135
  Toledo (G-18167)
Young Mens Christian Assoc ....C 614 871-9622
  Grove City (G-11491)
Young Mens Christian Assoc ....E 937 223-5201
  Dayton (G-9892)
Young Mens Christian Assoc ....D 330 923-5223
  Cuyahoga Falls (G-9141)
Young Mens Christian Assoc ....E 330 467-8366
  Macedonia (G-13091)
Young Mens Christian Assoc ....D 330 784-0408
  Akron (G-507)
Young Mens Christian Assoc ....C 614 416-9622
  Gahanna (G-11152)
Young Mens Christian Assoc ....C 614 334-9622
  Hilliard (G-11832)
Young Mens Christian Assoc ....E 937 312-1810
  Dayton (G-9893)
Young Mens Christian Assoc ....E 614 539-1770
  Urbancrest (G-18453)
Young Mens Christian Assoc ....E 614 252-3166
  Columbus (G-8929)
Young Mens Christian Assoc ....E 937 593-9001
  Bellefontaine (G-1370)
Young Mens Christian Assoc ....D 740 477-1661
  Circleville (G-4854)
Young Mens Christian Assoc ....D 330 264-3131
  Wooster (G-19789)
Young Mens Christian Assoc ....E 937 228-9622
  Dayton (G-9895)
Young Mens Christian Assoc ....C 937 223-5201
  Springboro (G-16990)
Young Mens Christian Assoc ....C 614 834-9622
  Canal Winchester (G-2129)
Young Mens Christian Associat ....D 513 241-9622
  Cincinnati (G-4815)
Young Mens Christian Associat ....D 513 923-4466
  Cincinnati (G-4816)
Young Mens Christian Associat ....E 419 474-3995
  Toledo (G-18169)
Young Mens Christian Associat ....D 419 866-9622
  Maumee (G-13871)
Young Mens Christian Associat ....C 419 475-3496
  Toledo (G-18170)
Young Mens Christian Associat ....E 419 691-3523
  Oregon (G-15615)
Young Mens Christian Associat ....C 513 474-1400
  Cincinnati (G-4814)
Young Mens Christian Mt Vernon ......D 740 392-9622
  Mount Vernon (G-14794)
Young Mens Christn Assn Shelby ....D 419 347-1312
  Shelby (G-16751)
Young MNS Christn Assn Findlay ....D 419 422-4424
  Findlay (G-10977)
Young MNS Chrstn Assn Clveland ....E 216 521-8400
  Lakewood (G-12364)
Young MNS Chrstn Assn Clveland ....E 216 731-7454
  Cleveland (G-6703)
Young MNS Chrstn Assn Clveland ....D 440 285-7543
  Chardon (G-2726)
Young MNS Chrstn Assn Clveland ....D 216 382-4300
  Cleveland (G-6704)

SERVICES

Young MNS Chrstn Assn Clveland........D...... 440 808-8150
Westlake *(G-19426)*

Young MNS Chrstn Assn Grter NY ....D...... 740 392-9622
Mount Vernon *(G-14795)*

Young Womens Christian ....E...... 419 238-6639
Van Wert *(G-18499)*

Young Womens Christian Assn.............D...... 614 224-9121
Columbus *(G-8931)*

Young Womens Christian Associ...........E...... 216 881-6878
Cleveland *(G-6705)*

Young Womns Chrstn Assc Canton.......D...... 330 453-0789
Canton *(G-2543)*

YWCA Dayton ....D...... 937 461-5550
Dayton *(G-9896)*

YWCA Mahoning Valley ....E...... 330 746-6361
Youngstown *(G-20269)*

YWCA of Greater Cincinnati ....D...... 513 241-7090
Cincinnati *(G-4817)*

YWCA Shelter & Housing Network.......E...... 937 222-6333
Dayton *(G-9897)*

PHYSICAL FITNESS CLUBS WITH TRAINING EQPT

Aussiefit I LLC..................................E...... 614 755-4400
Columbus *(G-7002)*

Compel Fitness LLC ....C...... 216 965-5694
Cincinnati *(G-3342)*

Fitness International LLC ....E...... 937 427-0700
Beavercreek *(G-1152)*

L A Fitness Intl LLC ....E...... 937 439-2795
Washington Township *(G-18785)*

W T Sports Inc ....E...... 740 654-0035
Dublin *(G-10367)*

PHYSICIANS' OFFICES & CLINICS: Medical

American Hlth Ntwrk & Fmly PRC........E...... 419 524-2212
Mansfield *(G-13135)*

Brian Brocker Dr ....E...... 330 747-9215
Youngstown *(G-19972)*

Cardinal Orthopaedic Group Inc ....E...... 614 759-1186
Columbus *(G-7124)*

Christopher C Kaeding ....E...... 614 293-3600
Columbus *(G-7197)*

Cleveland Clinic Foundation................E...... 330 287-4930
Wooster *(G-19707)*

Clyo Internal Medicine Inc.................D...... 937 435-5857
Centerville *(G-2624)*

Digestive Specialists Inc ....E...... 937 534-7330
Dayton *(G-9391)*

Elizabeth Place Holdings LLC ....E...... 323 300-3700
Dayton *(G-9410)*

Family Physicians Inc........................E...... 330 494-7099
Canton *(G-2310)*

Fisher-Titus Medical Center ....D...... 440 839-2226
Wakeman *(G-18621)*

Frederick C Smith Clinic Inc ....B...... 740 383-7000
Marion *(G-13421)*

Health Works Mso Inc........................E...... 740 368-5366
Delaware *(G-9983)*

Holzer Clinic LLC ....A...... 740 446-5411
Gallipolis *(G-11197)*

HRP Capital Inc ....E...... 419 865-3111
Holland *(G-11889)*

Medical Arts Physician Center ....D...... 216 431-1500
Cleveland *(G-5941)*

Medical Group Associates Inc ....E...... 740 283-4773
Steubenville *(G-17166)*

Midwest Allergy Associates................E...... 614 846-5944
Columbus *(G-8080)*

My Community Health Center ....E...... 330 363-6242
Canton *(G-2413)*

Northeast Family Health Care..............E...... 330 630-2332
Tallmadge *(G-17482)*

Ob Gyn Associates of Lancaster ....E...... 740 653-5088
Lancaster *(G-12424)*

Obstetrics & Gynecology Assoc ....D...... 513 221-3800
Fairfield *(G-10762)*

Ohio State University ....B...... 614 293-8133
Columbus *(G-8340)*

Osup Community Outreach LLC ....E...... 614 685-1542
Columbus *(G-8401)*

Pioneer Physicians Networking ....E...... 330 633-6601
Tallmadge *(G-17484)*

Public Safety Ohio Department ....E...... 937 335-6209
Troy *(G-18222)*

Russell Weisman Jr MD ....C...... 216 844-3127
Cleveland *(G-6350)*

Somc Foundation Inc ....D...... 740 356-5000
Portsmouth *(G-16170)*

South Dayton Acute Care Cons............E...... 937 433-8990
Dayton *(G-9776)*

Southwest Family Physicians ....E...... 440 816-2750
Cleveland *(G-6429)*

Stark Medical Specialties Inc ....E...... 330 837-1111
Massillon *(G-13732)*

Toledo Clinic Inc ....B...... 419 473-3561
Toledo *(G-18078)*

Trihealth G LLC ....D...... 513 732-0700
Cincinnati *(G-4641)*

University Eye Surgeons ....C...... 614 293-5635
Columbus *(G-8818)*

PHYSICIANS' OFFICES & CLINICS: Medical doctors

A-1 Healthcare Staffing LLC ....C...... 216 862-0906
Cleveland *(G-4884)*

A-1 Healthcare Staffing LLC ....D...... 216 862-0906
Lakewood *(G-12334)*

American Health Network Inc ....E...... 614 794-4500
Columbus *(G-6922)*

American Hlth Netwrk Ohio LLC ....E...... 614 794-4500
Columbus *(G-6924)*

Arlington Contact Lens Svc Inc............E...... 614 921-9894
Columbus *(G-6970)*

Ashtabula County Medical Ctr ....C...... 440 997-6960
Ashtabula *(G-716)*

Belmont Bhc Pines Hospital Inc...........C...... 330 759-2700
Youngstown *(G-19964)*

Bio-Mdical Applications RI Inc ....E...... 740 389-4111
Marion *(G-13405)*

Cardio Thoracic Surgery ....E...... 614 293-4509
Columbus *(G-7125)*

Cardiologist ....D...... 440 882-0075
Cleveland *(G-5123)*

Central Ohio Primary Care ....E...... 614 818-9550
Westerville *(G-19233)*

Central Ohio Primary Care ....E...... 614 442-7550
Columbus *(G-7167)*

Charles L Maccallum MD Inc ....E...... 330 655-2161
Hudson *(G-11971)*

Chester West Dentistry ....E...... 330 753-7734
Akron *(G-127)*

Childrens Hosp Med Ctr Akron ....E...... 330 543-8004
Akron *(G-131)*

Childrens Hospital Medical Ctr ....E...... 513 636-6800
Mason *(G-13554)*

Christ Hospital ....C...... 513 561-7809
Cincinnati *(G-3201)*

Christian Healthcare ....E...... 330 848-1511
Barberton *(G-950)*

City of Whitehall ....E...... 614 237-5478
Columbus *(G-7213)*

Clevelan Clinic Hlth Sys W Reg............D...... 216 476-7007
Cleveland *(G-5228)*

Cleveland Preterm ....E...... 216 991-4577
Cleveland *(G-5281)*

Coleman Professional Svcs Inc............C...... 330 673-1347
Kent *(G-12223)*

Compass Community Health ....E...... 740 355-7102
Portsmouth *(G-16133)*

Concorde Therapy Group Inc ....E...... 330 493-4210
Alliance *(G-527)*

Covenant Care Ohio Inc ....D...... 937 526-5570
Versailles *(G-18569)*

Crossroads Lake County Adole ....C...... 440 255-1700
Mentor *(G-14037)*

Davis Eye Center...............................E...... 330 923-5676
Cuyahoga Falls *(G-9085)*

Emergency Medical Group Inc ....E...... 419 866-6009
Toledo *(G-17712)*

Emergency Services Inc......................E...... 614 224-6420
Columbus *(G-7514)*

Emp Management Group Ltd ....D...... 330 493-4443
Canton *(G-2301)*

Eric Hasemeier Do ....E...... 740 594-7979
Athens *(G-780)*

Eye Surgery Center Ohio Inc ....E...... 614 228-3937
Columbus *(G-7550)*

Fairview Hospital ....E...... 216 476-7000
Cleveland *(G-5508)*

Family Health Partners Inc..................E...... 419 935-0196
Willard *(G-19480)*

Family Health Plan Inc........................C...... 419 241-6501
Toledo *(G-17724)*

Far Oaks Orthopedists Inc ....E...... 937 298-0452
Vandalia *(G-18521)*

Fortunefavorsthe Bold LLC ....E...... 216 469-2845
Lakewood *(G-12344)*

Fresenius Medical Care.......................E...... 614 855-3677
Gahanna *(G-11120)*

Good Samaritan Hosp Cincinnati ....E...... 513 569-6251
Cincinnati *(G-3625)*

GTE Internet ....D...... 614 508-6000
Columbus *(G-7698)*

Gw Sutherland MD ....E...... 419 578-7200
Toledo *(G-17775)*

Herzig-Krall Medical Group ....E...... 513 896-9595
Fairfield *(G-10735)*

Home Health Connection Inc ....E...... 614 839-4545
Worthington *(G-19815)*

Kaiser Foundation Hospitals ....A...... 440 350-3614
Concord Township *(G-8943)*

Kaiser Foundation Hospitals ....A...... 216 524-7377
Brooklyn Heights *(G-1873)*

Kaiser Foundation Hospitals ....E...... 800 524-7377
North Canton *(G-15214)*

Kaiser Foundation Hospitals ....A...... 800 524-7377
Medina *(G-13964)*

Kaiser Foundation Hospitals ....A...... 800 524-7377
Fairlawn *(G-10837)*

Kaiser Foundation Hospitals ....A...... 800 524-7377
Mentor *(G-14069)*

Kaiser Foundation Hospitals ....A...... 800 524-7377
Kent *(G-12238)*

Kaiser Foundation Hospitals ....A...... 216 524-7377
Rocky River *(G-16439)*

Kentucky Heart Institute Inc ....E...... 740 353-8100
Portsmouth *(G-16152)*

Lakewood Hospital Association ....E...... 216 228-5437
Cleveland *(G-5852)*

Layh & Associates ....E...... 937 767-9171
Yellow Springs *(G-19940)*

Libbey Inc ....A...... 419 671-6000
Toledo *(G-17853)*

Lifestges Smrtan Ctr For Women ....E...... 937 277-8988
Dayton *(G-9566)*

Luis F Soto MD..................................E...... 330 649-9400
Canton *(G-2382)*

Lutheran Medical Center ....B...... 216 696-4300
Solon *(G-16867)*

Magnum Medical Overseas JV LLC ......D...... 979 848-8169
Cincinnati *(G-3960)*

Mammovan Inc ....E...... 330 726-2064
Youngstown *(G-20114)*

MBC Cardiologist Inc..........................D...... 937 223-4461
Dayton *(G-9591)*

Mercer Cnty Joint Townshp Hosp ....E...... 419 586-1611
Celina *(G-2601)*

Mercy Health.....................................E...... 513 829-1700
Fairfield *(G-10754)*

Mercy Health.....................................E...... 513 686-8100
Blue Ash *(G-1609)*

Mercy Health.....................................E...... 440 336-2239
Elyria *(G-10535)*

Mercy Health.....................................E...... 440 775-1881
Oberlin *(G-15509)*

Mercy Health.....................................E...... 440 934-8344
Sheffield Village *(G-16739)*

Mercy Health.....................................E...... 440 967-8713
Vermilion *(G-18557)*

Mercy Health.....................................D...... 513 233-6736
Cincinnati *(G-4020)*

Mercy Health.....................................D...... 419 251-2659
Toledo *(G-17905)*

Mercy Health.....................................E...... 513 924-8200
Cincinnati *(G-4021)*

Mercy Health.....................................E...... 513 339-0800
Mason *(G-13618)*

Mercy Health.....................................E...... 513 585-9600
Cincinnati *(G-4022)*

Mercy Health.....................................E...... 419 475-4666
Toledo *(G-17907)*

Mercy Health.....................................E...... 419 264-5800
Holgate *(G-11866)*

Mercy Professional Care ....E...... 330 832-2280
Massillon *(G-13715)*

Metro Health System ....D...... 330 669-2249
Smithville *(G-16811)*

Mvhe Inc...E...... 937 499-8211
Dayton *(G-9650)*

National Guard Ohio ....D...... 614 492-3166
Columbus *(G-8132)*

National Rgstry Emrgncy Mdcl ....E...... 614 888-4484
Columbus *(G-8138)*

Northeast OH Neighborhood Heal.........C...... 216 231-7700
Cleveland *(G-6090)*

Ohio Minority Medical.........................E...... 513 400-5011
East Liverpool *(G-10411)*

Ohio North E Hlth Systems Inc ....E 330 747-9551
  Youngstown *(G-20145)*

Ohio University ....E 740 593-1660
  Athens *(G-799)*

Orthoneuro ....D 614 890-6555
  Columbus *(G-8387)*

Pain Control Consultants Inc ....E 614 430-5727
  Columbus *(G-8413)*

Pain Net Inc ....D 614 481-5960
  Columbus *(G-8414)*

Physicians Care of Marietta ....D 740 373-2519
  Marietta *(G-13369)*

Physicians In Family Practice ....E 440 775-1881
  Oberlin *(G-15517)*

Premier Health Group LLC ....E 937 535-4100
  Dayton *(G-9703)*

Primary Care Nursing Services ....D 614 764-0960
  Dublin *(G-10311)*

Primary Cr Ntwrk Prmr Hlth Prt ....E 937 743-5965
  Franklin *(G-11038)*

Primary Eyecare Associates ....E 937 492-2351
  Sidney *(G-16794)*

Promedica Health Systems Inc ....E 419 891-6201
  Maumee *(G-13835)*

Queen City Physicians Ltd ....E 513 791-6992
  Cincinnati *(G-4319)*

Rehab Continuum Inc ....E 513 984-8070
  Blue Ash *(G-1643)*

Robert F Arrom Md Inc ....E 513 893-4107
  Fairfield *(G-10776)*

Robinson Health System Inc ....A 330 297-0811
  Ravenna *(G-16263)*

Shawneespring Hlth Cre Cntr Rl ....B 513 943-4000
  Loveland *(G-13028)*

Signature Healthcare LLC ....C 440 232-1800
  Bedford *(G-1305)*

Southast Cmnty Mental Hlth Ctr ....C 614 225-0980
  Columbus *(G-8661)*

Southern Ohio Wns Cancer Prj ....D 740 775-7332
  Chillicothe *(G-2828)*

Summa Health System ....E 330 375-3000
  Akron *(G-452)*

Summa Health System ....C 330 375-3315
  Akron *(G-451)*

Thomas L Stover Inc ....E 330 665-8060
  Mogadore *(G-14558)*

Toledo Clinic Inc ....C 419 841-1600
  Toledo *(G-18080)*

Tri County Mental Health Svcs ....C 740 592-3091
  Athens *(G-806)*

Trihealth Inc ....E 513 891-1627
  Blue Ash *(G-1664)*

Trihealth G LLC ....E 513 346-5000
  Cincinnati *(G-4642)*

Trihealth G LLC ....D 513 922-1200
  Cincinnati *(G-4644)*

Trihealth Inc ....C 513 985-0900
  Montgomery *(G-14603)*

Trinity Health System ....B 740 283-7000
  Steubenville *(G-17179)*

Union Hospital Association ....D 330 343-3311
  Dover *(G-10106)*

United Health Network Ltd ....E 330 492-2102
  Canton *(G-2519)*

University Hospitals ....A 216 767-8900
  Shaker Heights *(G-16717)*

University Hospitals ....A 440 743-3000
  Parma *(G-15779)*

University Hospitals ....D 216 844-8797
  Cleveland *(G-6590)*

University Hospitals Cleveland ....D 216 342-5556
  Beachwood *(G-1116)*

University Medical Assoc Inc ....C 740 593-0753
  Athens *(G-810)*

University of Cincinnati ....E 513 558-4194
  Cincinnati *(G-4703)*

University of Cincinnati ....B 513 558-1200
  Cincinnati *(G-4706)*

University of Toledo ....E 419 383-3556
  Toledo *(G-18126)*

US Dept of the Air Force ....D 937 257-0837
  Dayton *(G-9190)*

Volk Optical Inc ....D 440 942-6161
  Mentor *(G-14124)*

West Park Family Physician ....E 419 472-1124
  Toledo *(G-18153)*

Yeater Alene K MD ....E 740 348-4694
  Newark *(G-15112)*

PHYSICIANS' OFFICES & CLINICS:
Osteopathic

Access Ohio ....E 614 367-7700
  Columbus *(G-6862)*

Adena Health System ....E 740 779-7201
  Chillicothe *(G-2750)*

Allergy & Asthma Centre Dayton ....E 937 435-8999
  Centerville *(G-2621)*

Christ Hospital ....C 513 561-7809
  Cincinnati *(G-3201)*

Davis Eye Center ....E 330 923-5676
  Cuyahoga Falls *(G-9085)*

Doctors Hospital Health Center ....E 614 544-0101
  Grove City *(G-11427)*

Eric Hasemeier Do ....E 740 594-7979
  Athens *(G-780)*

Family Practice Center Inc ....E 330 682-3075
  Orrville *(G-15630)*

Grandview Family Practice ....E 740 258-9267
  Columbus *(G-7684)*

Hometown Urgent Care ....C 937 372-6012
  Xenia *(G-19911)*

Internal Mdcine Cons of Clmbus ....E 614 878-6413
  Columbus *(G-7836)*

Medical and Surgical Assoc ....E 740 522-7600
  Newark *(G-15068)*

Mercy Health ....E 419 264-5800
  Holgate *(G-11866)*

Metro Health System ....D 330 669-2249
  Smithville *(G-16811)*

Michael G Lawley ....E 513 793-3933
  Cincinnati *(G-4046)*

Physicians In Family Practice ....E 440 775-1881
  Oberlin *(G-15517)*

R I D Inc ....E 419 251-4790
  Toledo *(G-17996)*

Sports Medicine Grant Inc ....D 614 461-8174
  Columbus *(G-8673)*

Ulrich Professional Group ....E 330 673-9501
  Kent *(G-12265)*

PICTURE FRAMING SVCS, CUSTOM

American Frame Corporation ....E 419 893-5595
  Maumee *(G-13748)*

American Frame Corporation ....E 419 893-5595
  Maumee *(G-13749)*

PIECE GOODS, NOTIONS & DRY GOODS, WHOL: Textiles, Woven

Welspun Usa Inc ....E 614 945-5100
  Grove City *(G-11484)*

PIECE GOODS, NOTIONS & DRY GOODS, WHOL: Yard Goods, Woven

Zincks In Berlin Inc ....E 330 893-2071
  Berlin *(G-1447)*

PIECE GOODS, NOTIONS & DRY GOODS, WHOLESALE: Fabrics

Miami Corporation ....E 800 543-0448
  Cincinnati *(G-4044)*

PIECE GOODS, NOTIONS & DRY GOODS, WHOLESALE: Tape, Textile

Great Lakes Textiles Inc ....E 440 914-1122
  Solon *(G-16854)*

PIECE GOODS, NOTIONS/DRY GOODS, WHOL: Drapery Mtrl, Woven

Style-Line Incorporated ....E 614 291-0600
  Columbus *(G-8707)*

PIECE GOODS, NOTIONS/DRY GOODS, WHOL: Sewing Splys/Notions

Checker Notions Company Inc ....D 419 893-3636
  Maumee *(G-13770)*

R S Sewing Inc ....E 330 478-3360
  Canton *(G-2449)*

PILOT SVCS: Aviation

Constant Aviation LLC ....C 800 440-9004
  Cleveland *(G-5338)*

Jet Mintenance Consulting Corp ....E 937 205-2406
  Wilmington *(G-19625)*

Macair Aviation LLC ....E 937 347-1302
  Xenia *(G-19919)*

Netjets Assn Shred Arcft Plots ....D 614 532-0555
  Columbus *(G-8173)*

Waypoint Aviation LLC ....E 800 769-4765
  Cincinnati *(G-4771)*

PIPE & FITTING: Fabrication

Atlas Industrial Contrs LLC ....B 614 841-4500
  Columbus *(G-7000)*

Contractors Steel Company ....E 330 425-3050
  Twinsburg *(G-18256)*

Crest Bending Inc ....E 419 492-2108
  New Washington *(G-15001)*

Elliott Tool Technologies Ltd ....D 937 253-6133
  Dayton *(G-9412)*

Kings Welding and Fabg Inc ....E 330 738-3592
  Mechanicstown *(G-13905)*

Phillips Mfg and Tower Co ....D 419 347-1720
  Shelby *(G-16749)*

Rbm Environmental and Cnstr ....E 419 693-5840
  Oregon *(G-15607)*

Rhenium Alloys Inc ....D 440 365-7388
  North Ridgeville *(G-15340)*

Scot Industries Inc ....E 330 262-7585
  Wooster *(G-19767)*

SSP Fittings Corp ....C 330 425-4250
  Twinsburg *(G-18323)*

Swagelok Company ....D 440 349-5934
  Solon *(G-16905)*

Tilton Corporation ....C 419 227-6421
  Lima *(G-12762)*

Tri-America Contractors Inc ....E 740 574-0148
  Wheelersburg *(G-19441)*

Unison Industries LLC ....B 904 667-9904
  Dayton *(G-9188)*

United Group Services Inc ....C 800 633-9690
  West Chester *(G-19094)*

Zekelman Industries Inc ....C 740 432-2146
  Cambridge *(G-2087)*

PIPE & FITTINGS: Cast Iron

McWane Inc ....B 740 622-6651
  Coshocton *(G-9022)*

PIPE FITTINGS: Plastic

Lenz Inc ....E 937 277-9364
  Dayton *(G-9563)*

Osburn Associates Inc ....E 740 385-5732
  Logan *(G-12852)*

PIPE SECTIONS, FABRICATED FROM PURCHASED PIPE

Kottler Metal Products Co Inc ....E 440 946-7473
  Willoughby *(G-19535)*

Pioneer Pipe Inc ....A 740 376-2400
  Marietta *(G-13370)*

PIPE: Seamless Steel

Zekelman Industries Inc ....C 740 432-2146
  Cambridge *(G-2087)*

PIPELINE & POWER LINE INSPECTION SVCS

Dreier & Maller Inc ....E 614 575-0065
  Reynoldsburg *(G-16300)*

PIPELINE TERMINAL FACILITIES:
Independent

Brothers Auto Transport LLC ....E 330 824-0082
  Warren *(G-18681)*

CSX Corporation ....A 614 242-3932
  Columbus *(G-7402)*

CT Logistics Inc ....C 216 267-1636
  Cleveland *(G-5387)*

Dayton Freight Lines Inc ....C 419 589-0350
  Mansfield *(G-13165)*

Fidelitone Inc ....E 440 260-6523
  Middleburg Heights *(G-14252)*

Haggerty Logistics Inc ....E 734 713-9800
  Cincinnati *(G-3671)*

Health Care Logistics Inc ....D 800 848-1633
  Galloway *(G-11220)*

SERVICES

Hogan Services Inc ....E 614 491-8402
  Columbus *(G-7758)*
Jarrells Moving & Transport Co ....E 330 952-1240
  Medina *(G-13960)*
Lake Local Board of Education ....B 330 877-9383
  Hartville *(G-11694)*
Mkm Distribution Services Inc ....D 330 549-9670
  North Lima *(G-15272)*
PAm Transportation Svcs Inc ....B 330 270-7900
  North Jackson *(G-15251)*
Schenker Inc ....E 614 662-7217
  Groveport *(G-11537)*
Schroeder Associates Inc ....E 419 258-5075
  Antwerp *(G-614)*
Secure Trnsp Co Ohio LLC ....E 800 856-9994
  Worthington *(G-19847)*
Woodruff Enterprises Inc ....E 937 399-9300
  Springfield *(G-17138)*

PIPELINES, EXC NATURAL GAS: Gasoline, Common Carriers

Integrity Kokosing Pipeline Sv ....C 740 694-6315
  Fredericktown *(G-11054)*

PIPELINES: Crude Petroleum

Bluefoot Industrial LLC ....E 740 314-5299
  Steubenville *(G-17141)*
Marathon Pipe Line LLC ....C 419 422-2121
  Findlay *(G-10939)*
Mplx LP ....E 419 421-2414
  Findlay *(G-10946)*
Ohio Oil Gathering Corporation ....E 740 828-2892
  Nashport *(G-14821)*

PIPELINES: Natural Gas

Columbia Gas Transmission LLC ....E 614 460-6000
  Columbus *(G-7250)*
Columbia Gas Transmission LLC ....E 740 397-8242
  Mount Vernon *(G-14754)*
Columbia Gas Transmission LLC ....E 740 892-2552
  Homer *(G-11933)*
Columbia Gulf Transmission LLC ....E 740 746-9105
  Sugar Grove *(G-17373)*
Eureka Midstream LLC ....E 740 868-1325
  Marietta *(G-13327)*
Utica East Ohio Midstream LLC ....A 740 431-4168
  Dennison *(G-10056)*

PIPELINES: Refined Petroleum

Buckeye Pipe Line Services Co ....E 419 698-8770
  Oregon *(G-15584)*
Marathon Pipe Line LLC ....C 419 422-2121
  Findlay *(G-10939)*
Mplx LP ....E 419 421-2414
  Findlay *(G-10946)*
Three Rivers Energy LLC ....E 740 623-3035
  Coshocton *(G-9029)*

PIPES & TUBES: Steel

Alro Steel Corporation ....E 937 253-6121
  Dayton *(G-9221)*
Benjamin Steel Company Inc ....E 937 233-1212
  Springfield *(G-16998)*
Crest Bending Inc ....E 419 492-2108
  New Washington *(G-15001)*
Major Metals Company ....E 419 886-4600
  Mansfield *(G-13202)*
Phillips Mfg and Tower Co ....D 419 347-1720
  Shelby *(G-16749)*
Unison Industries LLC ....B 904 667-9904
  Dayton *(G-9188)*

PIPES OR FITTINGS: Sewer, Clay

Superior Clay Corp ....D 740 922-4122
  Uhrichsville *(G-18344)*

PISTONS & PISTON RINGS

Federal-Mogul Powertrain LLC ....C 740 432-2393
  Cambridge *(G-2067)*

PLANETARIUMS

Lake Erie Nature & Science Ctr ....E 440 871-2900
  Bay Village *(G-1022)*

PLANNING & DEVELOPMENT ADMIN, GOVT: Urban & Community, Local

City of Columbus ....D 614 645-8270
  Columbus *(G-7210)*

PLANNING & DEVELOPMENT ADMIN, GOVT: Urban/Community, County

Cuyahoga County ....A 216 348-3800
  Cleveland *(G-5396)*

PLANNING & DEVELOPMENT ADMINISTRATION, GOVT: County Agency

City of Berea ....E 440 826-5853
  Berea *(G-1418)*

PLANTING MACHINERY & EQPT WHOLESALERS

Agrinomix LLC ....E 440 774-2981
  Oberlin *(G-15497)*

PLANTS, POTTED, WHOLESALE

Express Seed Company ....D 440 774-2259
  Oberlin *(G-15502)*
Maria Gardens LLC ....E 440 238-7637
  Strongsville *(G-17328)*
Plantscaping Inc ....D 216 367-1200
  Cleveland *(G-6216)*
Straders Garden Centers Inc ....E 614 889-1314
  Columbus *(G-8703)*

PLAQUES: Picture, Laminated

Lawnview Industries Inc ....C 937 653-5217
  Urbana *(G-18438)*

PLASMAPHEROUS CENTER

Biolife Plasma Services LP ....D 419 425-8680
  Findlay *(G-10868)*
Csl Plasma Inc ....D 614 267-4982
  Columbus *(G-7401)*

PLASTIC COLORING & FINISHING

Ampacet Corporation ....E 513 247-5400
  Cincinnati *(G-2956)*

PLASTIC PRDTS REPAIR SVCS

Integrity Processing LLC ....E 330 285-6937
  Barberton *(G-955)*

PLASTICS FILM & SHEET

Clopay Corporation ....C 800 282-2260
  Mason *(G-13564)*
PMC Acquisitions Inc ....D 419 429-0042
  Findlay *(G-10955)*

PLASTICS MATERIAL & RESINS

Flexsys America LP ....D 330 666-4111
  Akron *(G-225)*
Freeman Manufacturing & Sup Co ......E 440 934-1902
  Avon *(G-881)*
Kraton Polymers US LLC ....B 740 423-7571
  Belpre *(G-1407)*
Lubrizol Advanced Mtls Inc ....E 440 933-0400
  Avon Lake *(G-923)*
Polymer Packaging Inc ....D 330 832-2000
  Massillon *(G-13720)*
Tembec Btlsr Inc ....E 419 244-5856
  Toledo *(G-18063)*

PLASTICS MATERIALS, BASIC FORMS & SHAPES WHOLESALERS

Advanced Elastomer Systems LP ....C 800 352-7866
  Akron *(G-20)*
Ampacet Corporation ....E 513 247-5400
  Cincinnati *(G-2956)*
Blade-Tech Industries Inc ....D 877 331-5793
  Streetsboro *(G-17247)*
Polymershapes LLC ....E 937 877-1903
  Tipp City *(G-17564)*

PLASTICS PROCESSING

Ball Bounce and Sport Inc ....B 419 289-9310
  Ashland *(G-654)*
HP Manufacturing Company Inc ....D 216 361-6500
  Cleveland *(G-5721)*
Samuel Strapping Systems Inc ....D 740 522-2500
  Heath *(G-11709)*
Tahoma Enterprises Inc ....D 330 745-9016
  Barberton *(G-969)*
Tahoma Rubber & Plastics Inc ....D 330 745-9016
  Barberton *(G-970)*

PLASTICS SHEET: Packing Materials

Kapstone Container Corporation ....C 330 562-6111
  Aurora *(G-832)*

PLASTICS: Cast

S&V Industries Inc ....E 330 666-1986
  Medina *(G-13997)*

PLASTICS: Extruded

Eclipse Blind Systems Inc ....C 330 296-0112
  Ravenna *(G-16242)*

PLASTICS: Injection Molded

Dlhbowles Inc ....B 330 478-2503
  Canton *(G-2288)*
Lancaster Commercial Pdts LLC ....E 740 286-5081
  Columbus *(G-7945)*
Queen City Polymers Inc ....E 513 779-0990
  West Chester *(G-18989)*
US Molding Machinery Co Inc ....E 440 918-1701
  Willoughby *(G-19580)*

PLASTICS: Molded

U S Development Corp ....E 330 673-6900
  Kent *(G-12264)*

PLASTICS: Polystyrene Foam

A K Athletic Equipment Inc ....E 614 920-3069
  Canal Winchester *(G-2102)*
Armaly LLC ....E 740 852-3621
  London *(G-12859)*
Myers Industries Inc ....E 330 253-5592
  Akron *(G-342)*

PLASTICS: Thermoformed

First Choice Packaging Inc ....C 419 333-4100
  Fremont *(G-11073)*

PLATE WORK: For Nuclear Industry

Curtiss-Wright Flow Control ....D 513 735-2538
  Batavia *(G-995)*

PLATES

Amos Media Company ....C 937 498-2111
  Sidney *(G-16758)*
Anderson & Vreeland Inc ....D 419 636-5002
  Bryan *(G-1952)*
Art-American Printing Plates ....E 216 241-4420
  Cleveland *(G-5010)*
Wood Graphics Inc ....E 513 771-6300
  Cincinnati *(G-4804)*

PLATES: Sheet & Strip, Exc Coated Prdts

Major Metals Company ....E 419 886-4600
  Mansfield *(G-13202)*

PLATING & POLISHING SVC

A J Oster Foils LLC ....D 330 823-1700
  Alliance *(G-512)*
D-G Custom Chrome LLC ....D 513 531-1881
  Cincinnati *(G-3396)*
Electro Prime Group LLC ....E 419 476-0100
  Toledo *(G-17710)*
Micro Products Co Inc ....D 440 943-0258
  Willoughby Hills *(G-19591)*
Samuel Steel Pickling Company ....D 330 963-3777
  Twinsburg *(G-18317)*
Scot Industries Inc ....E 330 262-7585
  Wooster *(G-19767)*
Worthington Industries Inc ....C 513 539-9291
  Monroe *(G-14587)*

Yoder Industries Inc.............................C 937 278-5769
Dayton **(G-9890)**

PLEATING & STITCHING SVC

Barbs Graffiti Inc...............................E 216 881-5550
Cleveland **(G-5036)**

Shamrock Companies Inc....................D 440 899-9510
Westlake **(G-19405)**

PLUMBING & HEATING EQPT & SPLY, WHOLESALE: Hydronic Htg Eqpt

Accurate Mechanical Inc....................E 740 681-1332
Lancaster **(G-12368)**

Habegger Corporation........................D 513 612-4700
Cincinnati **(G-3669)**

Industrial Controls Distrs LLC.............E 513 733-5200
West Chester **(G-18946)**

Morrow Control and Supply Inc...........E 330 452-9791
Canton **(G-2408)**

Palmer-Donavin Mfg Co......................E 419 692-5000
Delphos **(G-10032)**

Ssi Fabricated Inc..............................E 513 217-3535
Middletown **(G-14330)**

United Atmtc Htng Spply of Clv...........E 216 621-5571
Cleveland **(G-6567)**

PLUMBING & HEATING EQPT & SPLYS WHOLESALERS

Famous Distribution Inc.....................D 330 762-9621
Akron **(G-210)**

Famous Distribution Inc.....................E 330 434-5194
Akron **(G-211)**

Famous Enterprises Inc.....................E 330 762-9621
Akron **(G-212)**

Famous II Inc....................................D 330 762-9621
Akron **(G-213)**

Famous Industries Inc.......................E 330 535-1811
Akron **(G-215)**

Ferguson Enterprises Inc...................E 513 771-6566
West Chester **(G-18923)**

Gordon Brothers Inc..........................E 800 331-7611
Salem **(G-16545)**

Habegger Corporation........................E 330 499-4328
North Canton **(G-15209)**

Mussun Sales Inc..............................E 216 431-5088
Cleveland **(G-6029)**

New Haven Estates Inc.......................E 419 933-2181
New Haven **(G-14916)**

Noland Company................................C 937 396-7980
Moraine **(G-14684)**

Oatey Supply Chain Svcs Inc..............C 216 267-7100
Cleveland **(G-6110)**

Rexel Usa Inc....................................E 419 625-6761
Sandusky **(G-16636)**

Robertson Heating Sup Co Ohio...........E 800 433-9532
Alliance **(G-545)**

The Famous Manufacturing Co.............E 330 762-9621
Akron **(G-469)**

Trumbull Industries Inc......................E 330 393-6624
Warren **(G-18758)**

Trumbull Manufacturing Inc................D 330 393-6624
Warren **(G-18759)**

Waxman Consumer Pdts Group Inc.......D 440 439-1830
Cleveland **(G-6656)**

Waxman Industries Inc.......................C 440 439-1830
Cleveland **(G-6657)**

Wolff Bros Supply Inc.........................E 330 400-5990
Sandusky **(G-16656)**

Wolff Bros Supply Inc.........................E 330 786-4140
Akron **(G-503)**

PLUMBING & HEATING EQPT & SPLYS, WHOL: Fireplaces, Prefab

L B Brunk & Sons Inc.........................E 330 332-0359
Salem **(G-16550)**

Mason Structural Steel Inc..................D 440 439-1040
Walton Hills **(G-18637)**

Reading Rock Residential LLC..............E 513 874-4770
West Chester **(G-19075)**

PLUMBING & HEATING EQPT & SPLYS, WHOL: Pipe/Fitting, Plastic

Corrosion Fluid Products Corp.............E 248 478-0100
Columbus **(G-7375)**

PLUMBING & HEATING EQPT & SPLYS, WHOL: Plumbing Fitting/Sply

Eastway Supplies Inc.........................E 614 252-3650
Columbus **(G-7494)**

Edelman Plumbing Supply Inc.............E 216 591-0150
Bedford Heights **(G-1322)**

Empire Brass Co................................E 216 431-6565
Cleveland **(G-5477)**

Famous Enterprises Inc.....................E 330 938-6350
Sebring **(G-16669)**

Ferguson Enterprises Inc...................E 614 876-8555
Hilliard **(G-11767)**

Hajoca Corporation............................E 216 447-0050
Cleveland **(G-5657)**

Keidel Supply Company Inc.................E 513 351-1600
Cincinnati **(G-3852)**

Lakeside Supply Co............................E 216 941-6800
Cleveland **(G-5849)**

Lute Supply Inc.................................E 740 353-1447
Portsmouth **(G-16153)**

Mansfield Plumbing Pdts LLC..............A 419 938-5211
Perrysville **(G-15941)**

Maumee Plumbing & Htg Sup Inc.........E 419 874-7991
Perrysburg **(G-15892)**

Parker-Hannifin Corporation................B 937 456-5571
Eaton **(G-10457)**

Parker-Hannifin Corporation................C 614 279-7070
Columbus **(G-8421)**

Pickrel Brothers Inc...........................E 937 461-5960
Dayton **(G-9691)**

River Plumbing Inc............................E 440 934-3720
Avon **(G-903)**

Robertson Htg Sup Aliance Ohio..........C 330 821-9180
Alliance **(G-546)**

Robertson Htg Sup Canton Ohio...........E 330 821-9180
Alliance **(G-547)**

Trumbull Industries Inc......................D 330 270-7800
Youngstown **(G-20226)**

Waxman Consumer Pdts Group Inc.......D 614 491-0500
Groveport **(G-11551)**

Winsupply Inc...................................E 937 865-0796
Miamisburg **(G-14239)**

Winsupply Inc...................................D 937 294-5331
Moraine **(G-14707)**

Wolff Bros Supply Inc.........................E 419 425-8511
Findlay **(G-10976)**

Wolff Bros Supply Inc.........................E 330 264-5900
Wooster **(G-19784)**

Woodhill Supply Inc...........................E 440 269-1100
Willoughby **(G-19585)**

Worly Plumbing Supply Inc.................D 614 445-1000
Columbus **(G-8918)**

Zekelman Industries Inc.....................C 740 432-2146
Cambridge **(G-2087)**

PLUMBING & HEATING EQPT & SPLYS, WHOL: Plumbng/Heatng Valves

Dayton Windustrial Co.......................E 937 461-2603
Dayton **(G-9385)**

Famous Industries Inc.......................E 330 535-1811
Akron **(G-214)**

PLUMBING & HEATING EQPT & SPLYS, WHOL: Water Purif Eqpt

Chandler Systems Incorporated...........D 888 363-9434
Ashland **(G-666)**

Enting Water Conditioning Inc..............E 937 294-5100
Moraine **(G-14653)**

Wayne/Scott Fetzer Company..............C 800 237-0987
Harrison **(G-11680)**

PLUMBING FIXTURES

Empire Brass Co................................E 216 431-6565
Cleveland **(G-5477)**

Mansfield Plumbing Pdts LLC..............A 419 938-5211
Perrysville **(G-15941)**

Trumbull Manufacturing Inc................D 330 393-6624
Warren **(G-18759)**

Waxman Industries Inc.......................C 440 439-1830
Cleveland **(G-6657)**

Zekelman Industries Inc.....................C 740 432-2146
Cambridge **(G-2087)**

PLUMBING FIXTURES: Plastic

Bobbart Industries Inc.......................E 419 350-5477
Sylvania **(G-17412)**

Mansfield Plumbing Pdts LLC..............E 330 496-2301
Big Prairie **(G-1472)**

Mansfield Plumbing Pdts LLC..............A 419 938-5211
Perrysville **(G-15941)**

PLUMBING FIXTURES: Vitreous

Mansfield Plumbing Pdts LLC..............A 419 938-5211
Perrysville **(G-15941)**

PODIATRISTS' OFFICES

Ankle and Foot Care Center.................E 330 385-2413
East Liverpool **(G-10397)**

Foot & Ankle Care Center....................E 937 492-1211
Sidney **(G-16778)**

Medicine Midwest LLC........................D 513 533-1199
Cincinnati **(G-3996)**

Medicine Midwest LLC........................E 937 435-8786
Dayton **(G-9603)**

Toledo Clinic Inc...............................D 419 381-9977
Toledo **(G-18079)**

Unity Health Network LLC...................E 330 626-0549
Streetsboro **(G-17276)**

POLICE PROTECTION

ADT Security.....................................D 440 397-5751
Strongsville **(G-17281)**

City of Toledo....................................E 419 936-2875
Toledo **(G-17656)**

Metrohealth System...........................E 216 957-5000
Cleveland **(G-5966)**

POLICE PROTECTION: Local Government

City of Lakewood...............................C 216 529-6170
Cleveland **(G-5207)**

Township of Fowler............................D 330 637-2653
Fowler **(G-11017)**

POLICE PROTECTION: Sheriffs' Office

County of Montgomery........................D 937 225-4192
Dayton **(G-9325)**

POLICE PROTECTION: State Highway Patrol

Greene County...................................E 937 562-7500
Xenia **(G-19903)**

Public Safety Ohio Department.............E 937 335-6209
Troy **(G-18222)**

POLICYHOLDERS' CONSULTING SVCS

Alex N Sill Company...........................E 216 524-9999
Seven Hills **(G-16671)**

POLITICAL ACTION COMMITTEES

Republican Headquarters.....................E 330 343-6131
Dover **(G-10096)**

POLYETHYLENE CHLOROSULFONATED RUBBER

Lyondell Chemical Company................D 513 530-4000
Cincinnati **(G-3953)**

POLYVINYLIDENE CHLORIDE RESINS

Great Lakes Textiles Inc.....................E 440 914-1122
Solon **(G-16854)**

POSTERS, WHOLESALE

Scholastic Book Fairs Inc...................D 513 714-1000
West Chester **(G-18998)**

POULTRY & POULTRY PRDTS WHOLESALERS

Borden Dairy Co Cincinnati LLC...........C 513 948-8811
Cincinnati **(G-3068)**

Euclid Fish Company..........................D 440 951-6448
Mentor **(G-14044)**

Koch Meat Co Inc..............................B 513 874-3500
Fairfield **(G-10745)**

Sysco Cincinnati LLC.........................B 513 563-6300
Cincinnati **(G-4562)**

POULTRY & SMALL GAME SLAUGHTERING & PROCESSING

Cal-Maine Foods Inc ....E 937 337-9576
Rossburg (G-16457)
Koch Meat Co Inc ....B 513 874-3500
Fairfield (G-10745)
Ohio Fresh Eggs LLC ....E 937 354-2233
Mount Victory (G-14796)
Weaver Bros Inc ....D 937 526-3907
Versailles (G-18573)

POWDER: Metal

Bogie Industries Inc Ltd ....E 330 745-3105
Akron (G-102)

POWER MOWERS WHOLESALERS

Century Equipment Inc ....E 419 865-7400
Toledo (G-17645)
Century Equipment Inc ....E 513 285-1800
Hamilton (G-11575)
Century Equipment Inc ....E 216 292-6911
Cleveland (G-5158)

POWER SUPPLIES: Transformer, Electronic Type

Electric Service Co Inc ....E 513 271-6387
Cincinnati (G-3487)

POWER TOOL REPAIR SVCS

Saw Service and Supply Company ....E 216 252-5600
Cleveland (G-6372)

POWER TRANSMISSION EQPT WHOLESALERS

ABB Inc ....C 614 818-6300
Westerville (G-19142)
Applied Indus Tech - CA LLC .....B 216 426-4000
Cleveland (G-4994)
Belting Company of Cincinnati ...C 513 621-9050
Cincinnati (G-3039)
Riverside Drives Inc ....E 216 362-1211
Cleveland (G-6329)
Stock Fairfield Corporation .....C 440 543-6000
Chagrin Falls (G-2684)

POWER TRANSMISSION EQPT: Mechanical

City Machine Technologies Inc ...E 330 740-8186
Youngstown (G-19990)
General Electric Company ....D 216 883-1000
Cleveland (G-5603)
Hite Parts Exchange Inc ....E 614 272-5115
Columbus (G-7756)
Western Branch Diesel Inc ....E 330 454-8800
Canton (G-2534)

POWER TRANSMISSION EQPT: Vehicle

Adelmans Truck Parts Corp ....E 330 456-0206
Canton (G-2173)

PRACTICAL NURSING SCHOOL

Lcd Home Health Agency LLC ......E 513 497-0441
Hamilton (G-11623)

PRECIPITATORS: Electrostatic

McGill Airclean LLC ....D 614 829-1200
Columbus (G-8045)
Neundorfer Inc ....E 440 942-8990
Willoughby (G-19555)
United McGill Corporation ....E 614 829-1200
Groveport (G-11546)

PRESCHOOL CENTERS

1 Amazing Place Co ....E 419 420-0424
Findlay (G-10860)
A & D Daycare and Learning Ctr ..E 937 263-4447
Dayton (G-9197)
A Better Child Care Corp ....E 513 353-5437
Cincinnati (G-2889)
A Childs Place Nursery School ...D 330 493-1333
Canton (G-2169)
A New Beginning Preschool ....D 216 531-7465
Cleveland (G-4879)

ABC Child Care & Learning Ctr ...E 440 964-8799
Ashtabula (G-702)
Academy Kids Learning Ctr Inc ...E 614 258-5437
Columbus (G-6858)
Adams Cnty /Ohio Vly Schl Dst ...D 937 544-2951
West Union (G-19129)
Ajm Worthington Inc ....E 614 888-5800
Worthington (G-19791)
All About Kids ....E 937 885-7480
Centerville (G-2620)
All For Kids Inc ....E 740 435-8050
Cambridge (G-2048)
Allen County Eductl Svc Ctr .....D 419 222-1836
Lima (G-12595)
Amandas Playroom Inc ....E 330 296-3934
Ravenna (G-16232)
Ashland City School District ....E 419 289-7967
Ashland (G-646)
Assoc Dvlpmtly Disabled ....E 614 447-0606
Columbus (G-6982)
Bailey & Long Inc ....E 614 937-9435
Columbus (G-7011)
Beachwood City Schools ....D 216 464-2600
Beachwood (G-1034)
Beavercreek Church of Nazarene ..E 937 426-0079
Beavercreek (G-1131)
Bombeck Family Learning Center ..E 937 229-2158
Dayton (G-9257)
Bowling Green Coop Nurs Schl ....E 419 352-8675
Bowling Green (G-1721)
Bright Beginnings ....E 937 748-2612
Springboro (G-16963)
Brownstone Private Child Care ...E 216 221-1470
Lakewood (G-12337)
Butler County Bd of Mental RE ...E 513 785-2815
Hamilton (G-11567)
Campbell Family Childcare Inc ...E 614 855-4780
New Albany (G-14846)
Canton City School District .....E 330 456-3167
Canton (G-2229)
Cardinal Pacelli School ....B 513 321-1048
Cincinnati (G-3117)
Child Focus Learning Center .....E 513 528-7224
Cincinnati (G-3181)
Childrens Discovery Center ......E 419 861-1060
Holland (G-11878)
Childtime Childcare Inc ....E 330 723-8697
Medina (G-13918)
Childvine Inc ....E 937 748-1260
Springboro (G-16965)
Chippewa School District ....E 330 658-4868
Doylestown (G-10110)
Christian Heartland School ......C 330 482-2331
Columbiana (G-6783)
Christian Rivertree School ......E 330 494-1860
Massillon (G-13670)
Christian Schools Inc ....D 330 857-7311
Kidron (G-12305)
Christian Wooster School ....E 330 345-6436
Wooster (G-19701)
Cincinnati Early Learning Ctr ...E 513 961-2690
Cincinnati (G-3241)
Cincinnati Early Learning Ctr ...E 513 367-2129
Harrison (G-11663)
Colerain Dry Rdge Chldcare Ltd ..E 513 923-4300
Cincinnati (G-3328)
Colonial Senior Services Inc ....C 513 867-4006
Hamilton (G-11583)
Colonial Senior Services Inc ....C 513 856-8600
Hamilton (G-11582)
Columbus Public School Dst ......E 614 365-5456
Columbus (G-7306)
Dakota Girls LLC ....E 614 801-2558
Grove City (G-11424)
Delth Corporation ....E 440 255-7655
Mentor (G-14041)
Discovery School ....C 419 756-8880
Mansfield (G-13169)
Dublin Latchkey Inc ....D 614 793-0871
Dublin (G-10209)
Dublin Learning Academy ....E 614 761-1800
Dublin (G-10210)
Early Childhood Enrichment Ctr ..E 216 991-9761
Cleveland (G-5455)
Early Learning Tree Chld Ctr ....D 937 293-7907
Dayton (G-9402)
East Dayton Christian School ....E 937 252-5400
Dayton (G-9172)
Enrichment Center of Wishing W ..D 440 237-5000
Cleveland (G-5483)

Fairborn St Luke Untd Mthdst ....E 937 878-5042
Fairborn (G-10673)
Family Lrng Ctr At Sentinel .....E 419 448-5079
Tiffin (G-17517)
First Christian Church ....E 330 445-2700
Canton (G-2313)
First School Corp ....E 937 433-3455
Dayton (G-9437)
Flying Colors Public Preschool ..E 740 349-1629
Newark (G-15034)
For Kids Sake Inc ....E 330 726-6878
Youngstown (G-20039)
Goddard School ....E 513 697-9663
Loveland (G-12997)
Goddard School of Avon ....E 440 934-3300
Avon (G-882)
Goddard School of Twinsburg .....E 330 487-0394
Twinsburg (G-18275)
Golden Key Ctr For Excptnl Chl ..E 330 493-4400
Canton (G-2328)
Hanna Perkins School ....E 216 991-4472
Shaker Heights (G-16709)
Hewlettco Inc ....E 440 238-4600
Strongsville (G-17309)
Horizon Education Centers ....E 440 322-0288
Elyria (G-10516)
Hudson Montessori Association ...E 330 650-0424
Hudson (G-11983)
Hyde Park Play School ....E 513 631-2095
Cincinnati (G-3746)
Ironton and Lawrence County .....B 740 532-3534
Ironton (G-12155)
J Nan Enterprises LLC ....E 330 653-3766
Hudson (G-11986)
J&B Sprafka Enterprises Inc .....E 330 733-4212
Akron (G-286)
Joseph and Florence Mandel ......D 216 464-4055
Beachwood (G-1070)
Kiddle Korral ....E 419 626-9082
Sandusky (G-16621)
Kids First Learning Centers .....D 440 235-2500
Olmsted Falls (G-15534)
Kids Kastle Day Care ....E 419 586-0903
Celina (G-2598)
Kids R Kids 2 Ohio ....E 513 860-3197
West Chester (G-18956)
Kids R Kids Schools Qulty Lrng ..E 937 748-1260
Springboro (G-16972)
Kids-Play Inc ....E 330 896-2400
Canton (G-2368)
Kidstown LLC ....E 330 502-4484
Youngstown (G-20092)
Kinder Garden School ....E 513 791-4300
Blue Ash (G-1592)
Kindercare Education LLC ....E 614 337-2035
Gahanna (G-11128)
Krieger Enterprises Inc ....E 513 573-9132
Mason (G-13607)
Lakewood Community Care Center ..E 216 226-0080
Lakewood (G-12354)
Laurel School ....C 216 464-1441
Cleveland (G-5857)
Learning Tree Childcare Ctr .....E 419 229-5484
Lima (G-12790)
Leo Yannenoff Jewish Community ..C 614 231-2731
Columbus (G-7966)
Liberty Bible Academy Assn ......E 513 754-1234
Mason (G-13610)
Logan Housing Corp Inc ....D 937 592-2009
Bellefontaine (G-1356)
Louisville Child Care Center ....E 330 875-4303
Uniontown (G-18377)
Madison Local School District ...E 440 428-5111
Madison (G-13103)
Merry Moppets Early Learning ....E 614 529-1730
Hilliard (G-11791)
Miami Valley School ....E 937 434-4444
Dayton (G-9626)
Miami Vly Child Dev Ctrs Inc ....C 937 325-2559
Springfield (G-17083)
Mini University Inc ....C 937 426-1414
Beavercreek (G-1231)
New Hope Christian Academy ......E 740 477-6427
Circleville (G-4838)
New School Inc ....E 513 281-7999
Cincinnati (G-4108)
Nichalex Inc ....E 330 726-1422
Youngstown (G-20140)
Noahs Ark Creative Care ....E 740 323-3664
Newark (G-15088)

Noahs Ark Learning Center ....E 740 965-1668
Sunbury (G-17392)

Nobel Learning Center ....E 740 732-4722
Caldwell (G-2042)

North Broadway Childrens Ctr ....E 614 262-6222
Columbus (G-8197)

Northside Baptst Child Dev Ctr ....E 513 932-5642
Lebanon (G-12487)

Northwest Local School Dst ....D 513 923-1000
Cincinnati (G-4131)

Old Trail School ....D 330 666-1118
Bath (G-1018)

Open Door Christian School ....D ..., 440 322-6386
Elyria (G-10551)

Ourday At Messiah Preschool ....E 614 882-4416
Westerville (G-19290)

Oxford Blazer Company Inc ....E 614 792-2220
Dublin (G-10302)

P J & R J Connection Inc ....E 513 398-2777
Mason (G-13624)

Paulding Exempted Vlg Schl Dst ....C 419 594-3309
Paulding (G-15797)

Pilgrim United Church Christ ....E 513 574-4208
Cincinnati (G-4248)

Playtime Preschool LLC ....E 614 975-1005
Columbus (G-8454)

Pride -N- Joy Preschool Inc ....E 740 522-3338
Newark (G-15093)

Primrose School At Golf Vlg ....E 740 881-5830
Powell (G-16205)

Primrose School At Polaris ....E 614 899-2588
Westerville (G-19203)

Primrose School of Symmes ....E 513 697-6970
Cincinnati (G-4280)

Ready Set Grow ....E 614 855-5100
New Albany (G-14870)

Royal Redeemer Lutheran Church ......E 440 237-7958
North Royalton (G-15365)

Saint Cecilia Church ....E 614 878-5353
Columbus (G-8583)

Salem Church of God Inc ....E 937 836-6500
Clayton (G-4861)

Samkel Inc ....E 614 491-3270
Columbus (G-8589)

Sisters of Notre Dame of Chard..........E 440 279-0575
Chardon (G-2714)

Smoky Row Childrens Center ....E 614 766-2122
Powell (G-16211)

Southside Learning & Dev Ctr ....E 614 444-1529
Columbus (G-8665)

St Francis De Sales Church ....D 740 345-9874
Newark (G-15099)

St Patrick Church Inc ....E 937 335-2833
Troy (G-18229)

St Pauls Catholic Church ....E 330 724-1263
Akron (G-439)

T L C Child Development Center ....E 330 655-2797
Hudson (G-12008)

T M C Systems LLC ....E 440 740-1234
Broadview Heights (G-1847)

Tri County Assembly of God...............E 513 874-8575
Fairfield (G-10792)

Twinbrook Hills Baptist Church...........E 513 863-3107
Hamilton (G-11650)

Upper Arlington Lutheran Ch ....E 614 451-3736
Columbus (G-8825)

Valentour Education Inc ....E 937 434-5949
Dayton (G-9846)

Wee Care Daycare............................E 330 856-1313
Warren (G-18771)

Wee Care Learning Center ....E 937 454-9363
Dayton (G-9871)

Whitehall City Schools ....E 614 417-5680
Columbus (G-8898)

Willoughby Montessori Day Schl ....E 440 942-5602
Willoughby (G-19584)

Zion Christian School ....E 330 792-4066
Youngstown (G-20271)

PRESSED FIBER & MOLDED PULP PRDTS, EXC FOOD PRDTS

Vista Industrial Packaging LLC ....D 800 454-6117
Columbus (G-8855)

PRINTED CIRCUIT BOARDS

Circle Prime Manufacturing ....E 330 923-0019
Cuyahoga Falls (G-9079)

Interactive Engineering Corp ....E 330 239-6888
Medina (G-13956)

Metzenbaum Sheltered Inds Inc...........C 440 729-1919
Chesterland (G-2741)

PRINTERS' SVCS: Folding, Collating, Etc

Bookmasters Inc ....C 419 281-1802
Ashland (G-658)

Document Concepts Inc.....................E 330 575-5685
North Canton (G-15197)

Patented Acquisition Corp ....C 937 353-2299
Miamisburg (G-14203)

Printing Services ....E 440 708-1999
Chagrin Falls (G-2678)

PRINTING & WRITING PAPER WHOLESALERS

Veritiv Operating Company ....C 419 243-6100
Toledo (G-18137)

PRINTING MACHINERY

Anderson & Vreeland Inc ....D 419 636-5002
Bryan (G-1952)

Wood Graphics Inc ....E 513 771-6300
Cincinnati (G-4804)

PRINTING MACHINERY, EQPT & SPLYS: Wholesalers

Anderson & Vreeland Inc ....D 419 636-5002
Bryan (G-1952)

Esko-Graphics Inc ....D 937 454-1721
Miamisburg (G-14168)

General Data Company Inc ....C 513 752-7978
Cincinnati (G-2853)

Heidelberg USA Inc...........................E 937 492-1281
Sidney (G-16782)

Hirsch International Holdings...............C 513 733-4111
Cincinnati (G-3710)

Monode Marking Products Inc.............D 440 975-8802
Mentor (G-14089)

PRINTING TRADES MACHINERY & EQPT REPAIR SVCS

Hall Contracting Services Inc ....D 440 930-0050
Avon Lake (G-919)

Industrial Maint Svcs Inc....................E 440 729-2068
Chagrin Falls (G-2669)

PRINTING, COMMERCIAL: Labels & Seals, NEC

Century Marketing Corporation.............C 419 354-2591
Bowling Green (G-1727)

PRINTING, COMMERCIAL: Literature, Advertising, NEC

Bottomline Ink Corporation ....E 419 897-8000
Perrysburg (G-15840)

PRINTING, COMMERCIAL: Music, Sheet, NEC

Lorenz Corporation............................D 937 228-6118
Dayton (G-9573)

PRINTING, COMMERCIAL: Screen

Glavin Industries Inc..........................E 440 349-0049
Solon (G-16851)

Innovtive Crtive Solutions LLC.............E 614 491-9638
Groveport (G-11520)

Kaufman Container Company ....C 216 898-2000
Cleveland (G-5817)

PRINTING, LITHOGRAPHIC: Calendars

Novelty Advertising Co Inc ....E 740 622-3113
Coshocton (G-9024)

PRINTING, LITHOGRAPHIC: Calendars & Cards

Gb Liquidating Company Inc ....E 513 248-7600
Milford (G-14391)

PRINTING, LITHOGRAPHIC: Forms & Cards, Business

Optimum System Products Inc.............E 614 885-4464
Westerville (G-19288)

PRINTING, LITHOGRAPHIC: Forms, Business

Quick Tab II Inc.................................D 419 448-6622
Tiffin (G-17533)

PRINTING, LITHOGRAPHIC: Offset & photolithographic printing

Hecks Direct Mail & Prtg Svc ....E 419 661-6028
Toledo (G-17798)

Kennedy Mint Inc ....D 440 572-3222
Cleveland (G-5824)

Power Management Inc.......................E 937 222-2909
Dayton (G-9701)

PRINTING, LITHOGRAPHIC: On Metal

Queen City Reprographics....................C 513 326-2300
Cincinnati (G-4321)

PRINTING: Books

Hubbard Company..............................E 419 784-4455
Defiance (G-9917)

PRINTING: Commercial, NEC

Advanced Specialty Products ....D 419 882-6528
Bowling Green (G-1712)

Aero Fulfillment Services Corp ....D 800 225-7145
Mason (G-13536)

AGS Custom Graphics Inc ....D 330 963-7770
Macedonia (G-13058)

Bindery & Spc Pressworks Inc.............D 614 873-4623
Plain City (G-16046)

Bollin & Sons Inc ....E 419 693-6573
Toledo (G-17618)

Consoldated Graphics Group Inc..........C 216 881-9191
Cleveland (G-5335)

Custom Products Corporation ....D 440 528-7100
Solon (G-16842)

Dayton Mailing Services Inc ....E 937 222-5056
Dayton (G-9371)

Evolution Crtive Solutions LLC ....E 513 681-4450
Cincinnati (G-3523)

Fedex Office & Print Svcs Inc..............E 614 898-0000
Westerville (G-19255)

Gb Liquidating Company Inc ....E 513 248-7600
Milford (G-14391)

GBS Corp...C 330 494-5330
North Canton (G-15206)

General Data Company Inc ....C 513 752-7978
Cincinnati (G-2853)

General Theming Contrs LLC ....C 614 252-6342
Columbus (G-7655)

Haines & Company Inc ....C 330 494-9111
North Canton (G-15210)

Hecks Direct Mail & Prtg Svc ....E 419 697-3505
Toledo (G-17797)

Hkm Drect Mkt Cmmnications Inc.........C 216 651-9500
Cleveland (G-5696)

Mlp Interent Enterprises LLC................E 614 917-8705
Mansfield (G-13224)

Profile Digital Printing LLC ....E 937 866-4241
Dayton (G-9719)

Springdot Inc....................................D 513 542-4000
Cincinnati (G-4523)

Tj Metzgers Inc.................................D 419 861-8611
Toledo (G-18066)

Youngstown ARC Engraving Co............E 330 793-2471
Youngstown (G-20254)

PRINTING: Flexographic

Samuels Products Inc ....E 513 891-4456
Blue Ash (G-1649)

PRINTING: Gravure, Color

Fx Digital Media Inc ....E 216 241-4040
Cleveland (G-5584)

PRINTING: Gravure, Rotogravure

Shamrock Companies Inc....................D 440 899-9510
Westlake (G-19405)

SERVICES

PRINTING: Laser

Marketing Comm Resource Inc .... D 440 484-3010
  Willoughby (G-19549)

PRINTING: Letterpress

A-A Blueprint Co Inc .... E 330 794-8803
  Akron (G-13)

Eci Macola/Max LLC .... C 978 539-6186
  Dublin (G-10213)

Traxium LLC .... E 330 572-8200
  Stow (G-17236)

PRINTING: Lithographic

Black River Group Inc .... D 419 524-6699
  Mansfield (G-13142)

Bookmasters Inc .... C 419 281-1802
  Ashland (G-658)

Century Marketing Corporation ...... C 419 354-2591
  Bowling Green (G-1727)

Digital Color Intl LLC .... E 330 762-6959
  Akron (G-187)

Directconnectgroup Ltd .... A 216 281-2866
  Cleveland (G-5425)

Edwards Electrical & Mech .... E 614 485-2003
  Columbus (G-7507)

Gordon Bernard Company LLC .... E 513 248-7600
  Milford (G-14393)

Haines & Company Inc .... C 330 494-9111
  North Canton (G-15210)

Hkm Drect Mkt Cmmnications Inc ... C 216 651-9500
  Cleveland (G-5696)

McNerney & Associates LLC .... E 513 241-9951
  Cincinnati (G-3990)

Printing Services .... E 440 708-1999
  Chagrin Falls (G-2678)

Profile Digital Printing LLC .... E 937 866-4241
  Dayton (G-9719)

Province of St John The Baptis ...... D 513 241-5615
  Cincinnati (G-4301)

Sandusky Newspapers Inc .... C 419 625-5500
  Sandusky (G-16639)

Sourcelink Ohio LLC .... C 937 885-8000
  Miamisburg (G-14224)

Visual Art Graphic Services .... E 330 274-2775
  Mantua (G-13278)

Woodrow Manufacturing Co .... E 937 399-9333
  Springfield (G-17137)

PRINTING: Offset

A-A Blueprint Co Inc .... E 330 794-8803
  Akron (G-13)

Academy Graphic Comm Inc .... E 216 661-2550
  Cleveland (G-4897)

AGS Custom Graphics Inc .... D 330 963-7770
  Macedonia (G-13058)

Angstrom Graphics Inc Midwest ..... B 216 271-5300
  Cleveland (G-4980)

Bindery & Spc Pressworks Inc .... D 614 873-4623
  Plain City (G-16046)

Bpm Realty Inc .... E 614 221-6811
  Columbus (G-7058)

Consoldated Graphics Group Inc ..... C 216 881-9191
  Cleveland (G-5335)

Copley Ohio Newspapers Inc .... C 330 364-5577
  New Philadelphia (G-14951)

Fine Line Graphics Corp .... C 614 486-0276
  Columbus (G-7577)

Galaxy Balloons Incorporated .... C 216 476-3360
  Cleveland (G-5589)

Hecks Direct Mail & Prtg Svc .... E 419 697-3505
  Toledo (G-17797)

Hubbard Company .... E 419 784-4455
  Defiance (G-9917)

Repro Acquisition Company LLC ..... E 216 738-3800
  Cleveland (G-6309)

Richardson Printing Corp .... D 740 373-5362
  Marietta (G-13377)

Springdot Inc .... D 513 542-4000
  Cincinnati (G-4523)

Tj Metzgers Inc .... D 419 861-8611
  Toledo (G-18066)

Traxium LLC .... E 330 572-8200
  Stow (G-17236)

Youngstown ARC Engraving Co ...... E 330 793-2471
  Youngstown (G-20254)

PRINTING: Photolithographic

Friends Service Co Inc .... D 419 427-1704
  Findlay (G-10910)

PRINTING: Screen, Fabric

R & A Sports Inc .... E 216 289-2254
  Euclid (G-10654)

PRINTING: Screen, Manmade Fiber & Silk, Broadwoven Fabric

Evolution Crtive Solutions LLC .... E 513 681-4450
  Cincinnati (G-3523)

PRIVATE INVESTIGATOR SVCS

Celebrity Security Inc .... E 216 671-6425
  Cleveland (G-5146)

Cooperate Screening Services .... E 440 816-0500
  Cleveland (G-5348)

Corporate Screening Svcs Inc .... D 440 816-0500
  Cleveland (G-5351)

D B A Inc .... E 513 541-6600
  Cincinnati (G-3394)

Info Trak Incorporated .... E 419 747-9296
  Mansfield (G-13186)

Jefferson Invstgtors Scurities .... D 740 283-3681
  Steubenville (G-17160)

Kreller Bus Info Group Inc .... E 513 723-8900
  Cincinnati (G-3891)

Professional Investigating .... D 614 228-7422
  Columbus (G-8468)

Sterling Infosystems Inc .... E 216 685-7600
  Independence (G-12125)

PROBATION OFFICE

6th Circuit Court .... E 614 719-3100
  Columbus (G-6844)

6th Circuit Court .... E 614 719-3100
  Dayton (G-9196)

County of Cuyahoga .... A 419 399-8260
  Paulding (G-15792)

County of Erie .... C 419 626-6781
  Sandusky (G-16595)

County of Lorain .... E 440 326-4700
  Elyria (G-10496)

County of Preble .... E 937 456-2085
  Eaton (G-10440)

County of Summit .... D 330 643-2300
  Akron (G-162)

County of Summit .... B 330 643-7217
  Akron (G-166)

County of Tuscarawas .... D 330 339-7791
  New Philadelphia (G-14955)

Supreme Court United States .... E 419 213-5800
  Toledo (G-18057)

Supreme Court United States .... D 614 719-3107
  Columbus (G-8717)

Supreme Court United States .... E 513 564-7575
  Cincinnati (G-4558)

Supreme Court United States .... E 216 357-7300
  Cleveland (G-6487)

Wood County Ohio .... C 419 354-9201
  Bowling Green (G-1755)

PRODUCT STERILIZATION SVCS

Sotera Health LLC .... D 440 262-1410
  Broadview Heights (G-1846)

Steriltek Inc .... E 615 627-0241
  Painesville (G-15742)

PROFESSIONAL DANCE SCHOOLS

Ballet Metropolitan Inc .... C 614 229-4860
  Columbus (G-7016)

PROFESSIONAL EQPT & SPLYS, WHOLESALE: Bank

Diebold Incorporated .... C 330 588-3619
  Canton (G-2285)

Diebold Nixdorf Incorporated .... D 513 682-6216
  Hamilton (G-11590)

Diebold Self Service Systems .... A 330 490-5099
  Canton (G-2286)

Hamilton Safe Products Co Inc .... E 614 268-5530
  Hilliard (G-11771)

Panini North America Inc .... E 937 291-2195
  Dayton (G-9684)

PROFESSIONAL EQPT & SPLYS, WHOLESALE: Engineers', NEC

Franklin Imaging Llc .... E 614 885-6894
  Columbus (G-7618)

S&V Industries Inc .... E 330 666-1986
  Medina (G-13997)

US Tsubaki Power Transm LLC .... C 419 626-4560
  Sandusky (G-16653)

PROFESSIONAL EQPT & SPLYS, WHOLESALE: Optical Goods

Champion Optical Network .... E 216 831-1800
  Beachwood (G-1043)

Essilor Laboratories Amer Inc .... E 614 274-0840
  Columbus (G-7537)

Shawnee Optical Inc .... D 440 997-2020
  Ashtabula (G-754)

PROFESSIONAL EQPT & SPLYS, WHOLESALE: Precision Tools

Monarch Steel Company Inc .... E 216 587-8000
  Cleveland (G-6007)

PROFESSIONAL INSTRUMENT REPAIR SVCS

Cleveland Electric Labs Co .... E 800 447-2207
  Twinsburg (G-18253)

PROFESSIONAL SCHOOLS

Cleveland Municipal School Dst ...... D 216 459-4200
  Cleveland (G-5275)

PROFESSIONAL STANDARDS REVIEW BOARDS

Chesapeake Research Review LLC ... E 410 884-2900
  Cincinnati (G-3178)

William I Notz .... E 614 292-3154
  Columbus (G-8904)

PROFILE SHAPES: Unsupported Plastics

Alkon Corporation .... E 614 799-6650
  Dublin (G-10126)

Bobbart Industries Inc .... E 419 350-5477
  Sylvania (G-17412)

HP Manufacturing Company Inc ...... D 216 361-6500
  Cleveland (G-5721)

PROGRAM ADMINISTRATION, GOVERNMENT: Social & Human Resources

County of Cuyahoga .... D 216 443-7265
  Cleveland (G-5371)

Cuyahoga County .... D 216 420-6750
  Cleveland (G-5393)

Cuyahoga County .... D 216 443-8920
  Cleveland (G-5397)

PROGRAM ADMINISTRATION, GOVERNMENT: Social & Manpower, State

Ohio Dept of Job & Fmly Svcs .... E 419 334-3891
  Fremont (G-11089)

Ohio Dept of Job & Fmly Svcs .... E 614 752-9494
  Columbus (G-8246)

Ohio Dept of Job & Fmly Svcs .... D 330 484-5402
  Akron (G-357)

Ohio Rehabilitation Svcs Comm ...... E 330 643-3080
  Akron (G-362)

PROGRAM ADMINISTRATION, GOVT: Social & Manpower, County

Clinton County Dept Jobs/Fmly .... D 937 382-0963
  Wilmington (G-19612)

County of Cuyahoga .... E 216 443-5100
  Cleveland (G-5365)

County of Cuyahoga .... D 216 681-4433
  Cleveland (G-5368)

Cuyahoga County .... A 216 431-4500
  Cleveland (G-5395)

PROMOTION SVCS

Fast Traxx Promotions LLC ....E 740 767-3740
Millfield (G-14505)
Marsh Inc ....E 513 421-1234
Cincinnati (G-3975)
Midway Mall Merchants Assoc ....E 440 244-1245
Elyria (G-10537)
Quotient Technology Inc ....E 513 229-8659
Mason (G-13631)

PROOFREADING SVCS

Robert Erney ....E 312 788-9005
Brookpark (G-1905)

PROPERTY & CASUALTY INSURANCE AGENTS

Cincinnati Financial Corp......................A 513 870-2000
Fairfield (G-10710)
McGowan & Company Inc ....D 800 545-1538
Cleveland (G-5932)
National Interstate Corp ....D 330 659-8900
Richfield (G-16363)
Ohio Farmers Insurance Company ......A 800 243-0210
Westfield Center (G-19308)
Ohio Farmers Insurance Company ......C 330 484-5660
Canton (G-2425)
Ohio Farmers Insurance Company ......D 614 848-6174
Columbus (G-6828)
Schiff John J & Thomas R & Co ....E 513 870-2580
Fairfield (G-10778)
Westfield Services Inc ....E 614 796-7700
Columbus (G-6839)

PROPERTY DAMAGE INSURANCE

Carrara Companies Inc ....D 330 659-2800
Richfield (G-16348)
Factory Mutual Insurance Co...............C 440 779-0651
North Olmsted (G-15287)
Midland Company ....A 513 947-5503
Amelia (G-574)
Ohio Fair Plan Undwrt Assn ....E 614 839-6446
Columbus (G-8257)
Personal Service Insurance Co ....B 800 282-9416
Columbus (G-8441)
Platinum Restoration Contrs ....E 440 327-0699
Elyria (G-10555)
Progressive Corporation ....B 440 461-5000
Cleveland (G-6247)

PUBLIC FINANCE, TAX & MONETARY POLICY OFFICES, GOVT: State

Ohio Department of Commerce.............E 614 644-7381
Columbus (G-8237)

PUBLIC FINANCE, TAXATION & MONETARY POLICY OFFICES

City of Cleveland..................................E 216 664-2620
Cleveland (G-5195)

PUBLIC HEALTH PROGRAM ADMIN, GOVT: Health Statistics Ctr

County of Cuyahoga.............................C 216 443-8011
Cleveland (G-5364)
County of Cuyahoga.............................A 216 443-6954
Cleveland (G-5366)

PUBLIC HEALTH PROGRAM ADMIN, GOVT: Mental Health Agency

County of Carroll...................................E 330 627-7651
Carrollton (G-2565)
County of Cuyahoga.............................C 216 241-8230
Cleveland (G-5367)
County of Hamilton ....B 513 742-1576
Cincinnati (G-3369)
County of Hamilton ....B 513 598-2965
Cincinnati (G-3372)
County of Paulding ....E 419 399-3636
Paulding (G-15793)
County of Stark ....D 330 484-4814
Canton (G-2267)
Mental Health and Addi Serv ....C 419 381-1881
Toledo (G-17904)

Mental Health and Addi Serv ....B 513 948-3600
Cincinnati (G-4006)
Mental Health and Addi Serv ....D 614 752-0333
Columbus (G-8057)
Mental Health and Addi Serv ....B 330 467-7131
Northfield (G-15383)

PUBLIC HEALTH PROGRAM ADMINISTRATION, GOVERNMENT: County

Clermont County Gen Hlth Dst ....E 513 732-7499
Batavia (G-989)
County of Cuyahoga.............................D 216 721-5610
Cleveland (G-5363)
County of Holmes ....E 330 674-5035
Millersburg (G-14468)
County of Knox ....E 740 392-2200
Mount Vernon (G-14758)
County of Summit ....A 330 634-8193
Tallmadge (G-17473)
County of Union ....D 937 645-6733
Marysville (G-13491)
County of Williams ....E 419 485-3141
Montpelier (G-14612)
Wood County Ohio ....D 419 353-6914
Bowling Green (G-1757)

PUBLIC HEALTH PROGRAM ADMINISTRATION, GOVERNMENT: Local

City of Columbus ....D 614 645-7417
Columbus (G-7209)

PUBLIC HEALTH PROGRAM ADMINISTRATION, GOVERNMENT: State

Develpmntal Dsblties Ohio Dept ....B 419 385-0231
Toledo (G-17699)
Develpmntal Dsblties Ohio Dept ....C 330 544-2231
Columbus (G-7440)
Develpmntal Dsblties Ohio Dept ....C 937 233-8108
Columbus (G-7442)
Develpmntal Dsblties Ohio Dept ....E 513 732-9200
Batavia (G-996)
Develpmntal Dsblties Ohio Dept ....A 740 446-1642
Gallipolis (G-11190)
Develpmntal Dsblties Ohio Dept ....B 614 272-0509
Columbus (G-7441)
Mental Health and Addi Serv ....E 740 594-5000
Athens (G-792)
Ohio Department of Health ....D 937 285-6250
Dayton (G-9668)
Ohio Department of Health ....B 419 447-1450
Tiffin (G-17528)
Opportunities For Ohioans ....E 513 852-3260
Cincinnati (G-4177)

PUBLIC HEALTH PROGRAM ADMINISTRATION, GOVT: Child Health

Champaign Cnty Board of Dd................E 937 653-5217
Urbana (G-18422)
County of Cuyahoga.............................A 216 432-2621
Cleveland (G-5370)

PUBLIC HEALTH PROGRAMS ADMINISTRATION SVCS

City of Akron ....D 330 564-4075
Akron (G-133)
City of Columbus ....E 614 645-1600
Columbus (G-7207)
City of Columbus ....D 614 645-3072
Columbus (G-7208)
County of Hamilton ....E 513 821-6946
Cincinnati (G-3373)
Mental Health and Addi Serv ....C 614 752-0333
Columbus (G-8058)
Ohio Department of Health ....C 614 466-1521
Columbus (G-8240)
Ohio Department of Health ....A 614 438-1255
Columbus (G-8241)

PUBLIC LIBRARY

Worthington Public Library...................C 614 807-2626
Worthington (G-19862)

PUBLIC ORDER & SAFETY ACTIVITIES, NEC

ADT Security ....D 440 397-5751
Strongsville (G-17281)

PUBLIC ORDER & SAFETY OFFICES, GOVERNMENT: County

County of Cuyahoga.............................D 216 475-7066
Cleveland (G-5362)

PUBLIC ORDER & SAFETY OFFICES, GOVT: Emergency Mgmt Office

City of Cleveland..................................B 216 664-2555
Cleveland (G-5189)

PUBLIC RELATIONS & PUBLICITY SVCS

Dix & Eaton Incorporated.....................E 216 241-0405
Cleveland (G-5431)
Domestic Relations ....E 937 225-4063
Dayton (G-9394)
Edward Howard & Co ....E 216 781-2400
Cleveland (G-5468)
Fahlgren Inc..D 614 383-1500
Columbus (G-7553)
Paul Werth Associates Inc ....E 614 224-8114
Columbus (G-8429)
United States Trotting Assn ....D 614 224-2291
Columbus (G-8811)
Ver-A-Fast Corp ....E 440 331-0250
Rocky River (G-16447)

PUBLIC RELATIONS SVCS

Babbage-Simmel & Assoc Inc ....E 614 481-6555
Columbus (G-7010)
City of Cleveland Heights......................E 216 291-2323
Cleveland Heights (G-6716)
Code One Communications Inc.............E 614 338-0321
Columbus (G-7240)
County of Guernsey...............................D 800 307-8422
Cambridge (G-2061)
County of Logan ....E 937 599-7252
Bellefontaine (G-1349)
Forwith Logistics LLC ....E 513 386-8310
Milford (G-14388)
L Brands Service Company LLC ....D 614 415-7000
Columbus (G-7933)
Marcus Thomas Llc ....D 330 793-3000
Youngstown (G-20116)
Ohio State University.............................E 614 293-3737
Columbus (G-8330)
Whitespace Design Group Inc ....E 330 762-9320
Akron (G-501)

PUBLIC WELFARE CENTER

Belmont County of Ohio........................E 740 695-3813
Saint Clairsville (G-16474)
County of Brown ....E 937 378-6104
Georgetown (G-11268)
County of Clark ....C 937 327-1700
Springfield (G-17023)
County of Geauga.................................D 440 285-9141
Chardon (G-2692)
County of Huron....................................D 419 668-8126
Norwalk (G-15431)
County of Marion...................................E 740 387-6688
Marion (G-13413)
Dayton Urban League ....E 937 226-1513
Dayton (G-9383)
Greene County ....C 937 562-6000
Xenia (G-19904)
Stark Cnty Dept Job Fmly Svcs ....B 330 451-8400
Canton (G-2488)
Vantage Aging ....A 440 324-3588
Elyria (G-10569)

PUBLISHERS: Book

Bookmasters Inc ....C 419 281-1802
Ashland (G-658)
Hubbard Company ....E 419 784-4455
Defiance (G-9917)
Precision Metalforming Assn ....E 216 241-1482
Independence (G-12110)
Province of St John The Baptis ....D 513 241-5615
Cincinnati (G-4301)
Tgs International Inc ....E 330 893-4828
Millersburg (G-14495)

SERVICES

Zaner-Bloser Inc...................................D...... 614 486-0221
  Columbus (G-8935)

PUBLISHERS: Books, No Printing

Asm International.................................D...... 440 338-5151
  Novelty (G-15464)
Bendon Inc...D...... 419 207-3600
  Ashland (G-657)
CSS Publishing Co Inc.........................E...... 419 227-1818
  Lima (G-12627)
F+w Media Inc.....................................B...... 513 531-2690
  Blue Ash (G-1559)
Golf Galaxy Golfworks Inc.....................C...... 740 328-4193
  Newark (G-15037)
Relx Inc...E...... 937 865-6800
  Miamisburg (G-14210)
Wolters Kluwer Clinical Drug.................D...... 330 650-6506
  Hudson (G-12014)

PUBLISHERS: Magazines, No Printing

Amos Media Company ....C...... 937 498-2111
  Sidney (G-16758)
CFM Religion Pubg Group LLC...............E...... 513 931-4050
  Cincinnati (G-3162)
Columbus Bride....................................D...... 614 888-4567
  Columbus (G-7263)
F+w Media Inc.....................................B...... 513 531-2690
  Blue Ash (G-1559)
Great Lakes Publishing Company...........D...... 216 771-2833
  Cleveland (G-5630)
Province of St John The Baptis..............D...... 513 241-5615
  Cincinnati (G-4301)

PUBLISHERS: Miscellaneous

Alonovus Corp.....................................D...... 330 674-2300
  Millersburg (G-14454)
Amos Media Company ....C...... 937 498-2111
  Sidney (G-16758)
AT&T Corp..A...... 614 223-8236
  Columbus (G-6990)
Gb Liquidating Company Inc..................E...... 513 248-7600
  Milford (G-14391)
Gordon Bernard Company LLC...............E...... 513 248-7600
  Milford (G-14393)
L M Berry and Company........................A...... 937 296-2121
  Moraine (G-14670)
Lexisnexis Group..................................E...... 937 865-6800
  Miamisburg (G-14185)
Province of St John The Baptis..............D...... 513 241-5615
  Cincinnati (G-4301)

PUBLISHERS: Music, Sheet

Lorenz Corporation...............................D...... 937 228-6118
  Dayton (G-9573)

PUBLISHERS: Newspaper

B G News...E...... 419 372-2601
  Bowling Green (G-1715)
Franklin Communications Inc.................D...... 614 459-9769
  Columbus (G-7614)
Iheartcommunications Inc.....................D...... 419 223-2060
  Lima (G-12664)
Northeast Scene Inc.............................E...... 216 241-7550
  Cleveland (G-6095)
Ohio News Network................................D...... 614 460-3700
  Columbus (G-8275)
Sandusky Newspapers Inc.....................C...... 419 625-5500
  Sandusky (G-16639)

PUBLISHERS: Newspapers, No Printing

American City Bus Journals Inc.............E...... 937 528-4400
  Dayton (G-9226)
Brothers Publishing Co LLC...................E...... 937 548-3330
  Greenville (G-11368)
Crain Communications Inc.....................D...... 330 836-9180
  Akron (G-169)

PUBLISHERS: Periodical, With Printing

American Ceramic Society.....................E...... 614 890-4700
  Westerville (G-19144)

PUBLISHERS: Periodicals, Magazines

AGS Custom Graphics Inc.....................D...... 330 963-7770
  Macedonia (G-13058)
Crain Communications Inc.....................D...... 330 836-9180
  Akron (G-169)

PUBLISHERS: Periodicals, No Printing

Agri Communicators Inc........................E...... 614 273-0465
  Columbus (G-6885)
Asm International.................................D...... 440 338-5151
  Novelty (G-15464)
C & S Associates Inc............................E...... 440 461-9661
  Highland Heights (G-11732)
Graphic Publications Inc.......................E...... 330 674-2300
  Millersburg (G-14474)
Lorenz Corporation...............................D...... 937 228-6118
  Dayton (G-9573)
Northeast Scene Inc.............................E...... 216 241-7550
  Cleveland (G-6095)

PUBLISHERS: Technical Manuals

ONeil & Associates Inc.........................B...... 937 865-0800
  Miamisburg (G-14201)

PUBLISHERS: Telephone & Other Directory

B G News...E...... 419 372-2601
  Bowling Green (G-1715)

PUBLISHERS: Trade journals, No Printing

Relx Inc...E...... 937 865-6800
  Miamisburg (G-14210)

PUBLISHING & BROADCASTING: Internet Only

Deemsys Inc..D...... 614 322-9928
  Gahanna (G-11117)

PUBLISHING & PRINTING: Books

McGraw-Hill School Education H............B...... 419 207-7400
  Ashland (G-679)
World Harvest Church Inc.......................B...... 614 837-1990
  Canal Winchester (G-2128)

PUBLISHING & PRINTING: Directories, NEC

Haines & Company Inc..........................C...... 330 494-9111
  North Canton (G-15210)

PUBLISHING & PRINTING: Magazines: publishing & printing

Family Motor Coach Assn Inc.................C...... 513 474-3622
  Cincinnati (G-3530)

PUBLISHING & PRINTING: Newspapers

Amos Media Company ....C...... 937 498-2111
  Sidney (G-16758)

PUBLISHING & PRINTING: Trade Journals

Ohio Association Realtors Inc.................E...... 614 228-6675
  Columbus (G-8230)

PULP MILLS

Rumpke Transportation Co LLC...............C...... 513 242-4600
  Cincinnati (G-4410)
Waste Parchment Inc.............................E...... 330 674-6868
  Millersburg (G-14499)

PUMPS

Eaton-Aeroquip Llc..............................D...... 419 891-7775
  Maumee (G-13782)
General Electric Company ....D...... 216 883-1000
  Cleveland (G-5603)
Giant Industries Inc.............................E...... 419 531-4600
  Toledo (G-17762)
Ingersoll-Rand Company ....E...... 419 633-6800
  Bryan (G-1960)
Tolco Corporation.................................D...... 419 241-1113
  Toledo (G-18072)

PUMPS & PARTS: Indl

Cima Inc...E...... 513 382-8976
  Hamilton (G-11577)

PUMPS & PUMPING EQPT REPAIR SVCS

Compak Inc...E...... 419 207-8888
  Ashland (G-668)

PUMPS & PUMPING EQPT WHOLESALERS

Buckeye Supply Company ....E...... 740 452-3641
  Zanesville (G-20285)
Corrosion Fluid Products Corp ....E...... 248 478-0100
  Columbus (G-7375)
Estabrook Corporation..........................E...... 440 234-8566
  Berea (G-1424)
Fischer Pump & Valve Company..............E...... 513 583-4800
  Loveland (G-12994)
Giant Industries Inc.............................E...... 419 531-4600
  Toledo (G-17762)
Graco Ohio Inc.....................................D...... 330 494-1313
  Canton (G-2331)
Henry P Thompson Company ....E...... 513 248-3200
  Milford (G-14394)
Nelsen Corporation...............................E...... 330 745-6000
  Norton (G-15421)
Ohio Transmission Corporation ....E...... 419 468-7866
  Galion (G-11181)
Process Pump & Seal Inc.......................E...... 513 988-7000
  Trenton (G-18190)

PUMPS: Domestic, Water Or Sump

Wayne/Scott Fetzer Company.................C...... 800 237-0987
  Harrison (G-11680)

PUMPS: Measuring & Dispensing

Tolco Corporation.................................D...... 419 241-1113
  Toledo (G-18072)

PUMPS: Oil Well & Field

General Electric Intl Inc.......................E...... 330 963-2066
  Twinsburg (G-18273)

PURCHASING SVCS

City of Cleveland.................................E...... 216 664-2620
  Cleveland (G-5195)
Neighborcare Inc..................................A...... 513 719-2600
  Cincinnati (G-4103)

QUARTZ CRYSTAL MINING SVCS

Covia Holdings Corporation....................D...... 440 214-3284
  Independence (G-12063)

RACE TRACK OPERATION

Raceway Foods Inc...............................E...... 513 932-2457
  Lebanon (G-12495)
Stonehedge Enterprises Inc...................E...... 330 928-2161
  Akron (G-442)

RACETRACKS: Auto

Eldora Enterprises Inc..........................E...... 937 338-3815
  New Weston (G-15007)
Fast Traxx Promotions LLC.....................E...... 740 767-3740
  Millfield (G-14505)
Kil Kare Inc...D...... 937 429-2961
  Xenia (G-19914)

RACETRACKS: Horse

Pnk (ohio) LLC.....................................A...... 513 232-8000
  Cincinnati (G-4261)
River Downs Turf Club Inc......................E...... 513 232-8000
  Cincinnati (G-4377)
Scioto Downs Inc..................................A...... 614 295-4700
  Columbus (G-8611)
Thistledown Inc....................................C...... 216 662-8600
  Cleveland (G-6525)

RACKS: Display

Bates Metal Products Inc.......................D...... 740 498-8371
  Port Washington (G-16121)

RADIO & TELEVISION COMMUNICATIONS EQUIPMENT

Gatesair Inc..D...... 513 459-3400
  Mason (G-13583)
Jason Wilson.......................................E...... 937 604-8209
  Tipp City (G-17561)

RADIO & TELEVISION OR TV ANNOUNCING SVCS

Dispatch Productions Inc.................D....... 614 460-3700
Columbus (G-7452)

RADIO & TELEVISION REPAIR

Office World Inc ....E....... 419 991-4694
Lima (G-12791)

RADIO BROADCASTING & COMMUNICATIONS EQPT

Circle Prime Manufacturing ....E....... 330 923-0019
Cuyahoga Falls (G-9079)

RADIO BROADCASTING STATIONS

Alpha Media LLC............................E....... 937 294-5858
Dayton (G-9220)
Bonneville International Corp.............D....... 513 699-5102
Cincinnati (G-3067)
Bowling Green State University ....D....... 419 372-8657
Bowling Green (G-1723)
CBS Corporation...........................C....... 513 749-1035
Cincinnati (G-3135)
CBS Radio Inc ....E....... 216 861-0100
Cleveland (G-5144)
Cd1025 ....E....... 614 221-9923
Columbus (G-7145)
City Casters ....E....... 937 224-1137
Dayton (G-9301)
Cumulus Broadcasting LLC..............E....... 850 243-7676
Cincinnati (G-3387)
Cumulus Media Inc ....D....... 419 725-5700
Toledo (G-17690)
Cumulus Media Inc ....D....... 513 241-9898
Cincinnati (G-3388)
Cumulus Media Inc ....D....... 419 240-1000
Toledo (G-17691)
Educational and Community Rdo ....E....... 513 724-3939
Batavia (G-997)
Elyria-Lorain Broadcasting Co ....E....... 440 322-3761
Elyria (G-10507)
Family Stations Inc ....E....... 330 783-9986
Youngstown (G-20036)
Findlay Publishing Company ....E....... 419 422-4545
Findlay (G-10905)
Franklin Communications Inc............D....... 614 451-2191
Columbus (G-7613)
Franklin Communications Inc............D....... 614 459-9769
Columbus (G-7614)
Hubbard Radio Cincinnati LLC..........D....... 513 699-5102
Cincinnati (G-3737)
Iheartcommunications Inc ....E....... 419 625-1010
Sandusky (G-16618)
Iheartcommunications Inc ....E....... 937 224-1137
Dayton (G-9511)
Iheartcommunications Inc ....D....... 614 486-6101
Columbus (G-7799)
Iheartcommunications Inc ....C....... 937 224-1137
Dayton (G-9512)
Iheartcommunications Inc ....C....... 513 241-1550
Cincinnati (G-3750)
Iheartcommunications Inc ....E....... 440 992-9700
Ashtabula (G-742)
Iheartcommunications Inc ....C....... 216 520-2600
Cleveland (G-5736)
Iheartcommunications Inc ....E....... 419 289-2605
Ashland (G-676)
Iheartcommunications Inc ....D....... 330 965-0057
Youngstown (G-20076)
Iheartcommunications Inc ....E....... 216 409-9673
Cleveland (G-5737)
Iheartcommunications Inc ....B....... 513 763-5500
Cincinnati (G-3751)
Iheartcommunications Inc ....D....... 419 782-9336
Defiance (G-9920)
Iheartcommunications Inc ....D....... 419 223-2060
Lima (G-12664)
Ingleside Investments Inc ....E....... 614 221-1025
Columbus (G-7818)
Johnny Appleseed Broadcasting ....E....... 419 529-5900
Ontario (G-15556)
Kent State University ....E....... 330 672-3114
Kent (G-12243)
Maverick Media ....E....... 419 331-1600
Lima (G-12700)
Media-Com Inc ....E....... 330 673-2323
Kent (G-12249)

Miami Valley Broadcasting Corp ....C....... 937 259-2111
Dayton (G-9616)
North American Broadcasting ....D....... 614 481-7800
Columbus (G-8196)
Ohio State University.......................C....... 614 292-4510
Columbus (G-8312)
Ohio University ....E....... 740 593-1771
Athens (G-797)
Pillar of Fire ....E....... 513 542-1212
Cincinnati (G-4249)
Public Broadcasting Found NW ....D....... 419 380-4600
Toledo (G-17995)
Radio Promotions ....C....... 513 381-5000
Cincinnati (G-4335)
Radio Seaway Inc ....E....... 216 916-6100
Cleveland (G-6277)
Radiohio Incorporated.....................D....... 614 460-3850
Columbus (G-8484)
Saga Communications Neng Inc ....D....... 614 451-2191
Columbus (G-8580)
Salem Media Group Inc ....D....... 216 901-0921
Cleveland (G-6365)
Sandusky Newspapers Inc................E....... 419 625-5500
Sandusky (G-16639)
Sunrise Television Corp ....E....... 419 244-2197
Toledo (G-18054)
Urban One Inc ....D....... 216 579-1111
Cleveland (G-6607)
Urban One Inc ....E....... 513 749-1009
Cincinnati (G-4734)
Urban One Inc ....E....... 614 487-1444
Columbus (G-8828)
Urban One Inc ....D....... 216 861-0100
Cleveland (G-6608)
Urban One Inc ....E....... 513 679-6000
Cincinnati (G-4735)
W H O T Inc.................................D....... 330 783-1000
Youngstown (G-20239)
W K H R Radio ....E....... 440 708-0915
Bainbridge (G-932)
W M V O 1300 AM ....E....... 740 397-1000
Mount Vernon (G-14791)
Weol ....E....... 440 236-9283
Elyria (G-10571)
Wqio 93q Request ....E....... 740 392-9370
Mount Vernon (G-14793)
Wqmx Love Fund ....D....... 330 869-9800
Akron (G-504)
Wrwk 1065 ....E....... 419 725-5700
Toledo (G-18162)
Wzrx ....E....... 419 223-2060
Lima (G-12787)
Xavier University ....E....... 513 745-3335
Cincinnati (G-4810)

RADIO COMMUNICATIONS: Airborne Eqpt

Quasonix Inc ....E....... 513 942-1287
West Chester (G-18988)

RADIO COMMUNICATIONS: Carrier Eqpt

L-3 Cmmncations Nova Engrg Inc ....C....... 877 282-1168
Mason (G-13608)

RADIO REPAIR & INSTALLATION SVCS

Comproducts Inc ....D....... 614 276-5552
Columbus (G-7344)

RADIO REPAIR SHOP, NEC

P & R Communications Svc Inc...........E....... 937 222-0861
Dayton (G-9680)
Staley Technologies Inc ....E....... 330 339-2898
New Philadelphia (G-14982)

RADIO, TELEVISION & CONSUMER ELECTRONICS STORES: Eqpt, NEC

Audio-Technica US Inc ....D....... 330 686-2600
Stow (G-17191)

RADIO, TV & CONSUMER ELEC STORES: Automotive Sound Eqpt

C A E C Inc..................................E....... 614 337-1091
Columbus (G-7102)
Electra Sound Inc..........................D....... 216 433-9600
Parma (G-15766)
Hi-Way Distributing Corp Amer ....D....... 330 645-6633
Coventry Township (G-9035)

Jim Hayden Inc.............................D....... 513 563-8828
Cincinnati (G-3819)

RADIO, TV & CONSUMER ELEC STORES: High Fidelity Stereo Eqpt

ABC Appliance Inc ....E....... 419 693-4414
Oregon (G-15581)

RADIO, TV/CONSUMER ELEC STORES: Antennas, Satellite Dish

Dss Installations Ltd.......................E....... 513 761-7000
Cincinnati (G-3446)

RADIOS WHOLESALERS

W W W M ....E....... 419 240-1055
Toledo (G-18143)

RAILROAD CAR CUSTOMIZING SVCS

Consolidated Rail Corporation ....D....... 440 786-3014
Macedonia (G-13066)
Transco Railway Products Inc ....E....... 419 726-3383
Toledo (G-18107)

RAILROAD CAR RENTING & LEASING SVCS

Andersons Inc ....C....... 419 893-5050
Maumee (G-13754)
Djj Holding Corporation ....C....... 513 621-8770
Cincinnati (G-3437)

RAILROAD CAR REPAIR SVCS

Andersons Inc ....C....... 419 893-5050
Maumee (G-13754)
Jk-Co LLC ....E....... 419 422-5240
Findlay (G-10928)

RAILROAD CARGO LOADING & UNLOADING SVCS

Ahoy Transport LLC ....E....... 740 596-0536
Creola (G-9050)
All American Trnsp Svcs LLC..............E....... 419 589-7433
Ontario (G-15544)
Alstom Signaling Operation LLC..........B....... 513 552-6485
Cincinnati (G-2933)
American Linehaul Corporation ....E....... 614 409-8568
Columbus (G-6929)
Ashtabula Chemical Corp ....E....... 440 998-0100
Ashtabula (G-707)
Coldliner Express Inc ....D....... 614 570-0836
Columbus (G-7243)
Great Lakes Cold Logistics ....E....... 216 520-0930
Independence (G-12078)
Hoc Transport Company ....E....... 330 630-0100
Akron (G-264)
Kettering City School District..............D....... 937 499-1770
Dayton (G-9538)
Midwest Trmnals Tledo Intl Inc ....E....... 419 698-8171
Toledo (G-17918)
Multi Flow Transport Inc...................E....... 216 641-0200
Brooklyn Heights (G-1875)
Nye F A & Sons Enterprises...............E....... 419 986-5400
Tiffin (G-17527)
Ohio State University.......................E....... 614 292-6122
Columbus (G-8332)
Parsec Inc ....E....... 513 621-6111
Cincinnati (G-4206)
Total Quality Logistics LLC.................E....... 800 580-3101
Centerville (G-2635)
Total Quality Logistics LLC.................E....... 800 580-3101
West Chester (G-19017)
Universal Transportation Syste ....E....... 513 539-9491
Monroe (G-14585)
Water Transport LLC ....E....... 740 937-2199
Hopedale (G-11938)
Wmk Inc ....E....... 630 782-1900
Richfield (G-16384)
World Trck Towing Recovery Inc..........E....... 330 723-1116
Seville (G-16693)

RAILROAD EQPT

Amsted Industries Incorporated..........C....... 614 836-2323
Groveport (G-11493)
Buck Equipment Inc ....E....... 614 539-3039
Grove City (G-11414)

Johnson Bros Rubber Co Inc ....E 419 752-4814
   Greenwich (G-11402)
L B Foster Company ....E 330 652-1461
   Mineral Ridge (G-14510)

RAILROAD EQPT & SPLYS WHOLESALERS

A & K Railroad Materials Inc ....E 419 537-9470
   Toledo (G-17574)
Amsted Industries Incorporated ....C 614 836-2323
   Groveport (G-11493)
Buck Equipment Inc ....E 614 539-3039
   Grove City (G-11414)
Djj Holding Corporation ....C 513 621-8770
   Cincinnati (G-3437)
Ysd Industries Inc ....D 330 792-6521
   Youngstown (G-20268)

RAILROAD EQPT: Cars, Rebuilt

Jk-Co LLC ....E 419 422-5240
   Findlay (G-10928)

RAILROAD MAINTENANCE & REPAIR SVCS

Andersons Inc ....E 419 891-6634
   Maumee (G-13753)
R W Godbey Railroad Services ....E 513 651-3800
   Cincinnati (G-4332)
Tmt Inc ....C 419 592-1041
   Perrysburg (G-15926)

RAILROAD SWITCHING & TERMINAL SVCS

Ashland Railway Inc ....E 419 525-2822
   Mansfield (G-13137)
National Railroad Pass Corp ....E 419 246-0159
   Toledo (G-17933)

RAILROADS: Long Haul

Ann Arbor Railroad Inc ....E 419 726-4181
   Toledo (G-17594)
Ashland Railway Inc ....E 419 525-2822
   Mansfield (G-13137)
Cleveland Works Railway Co ....D 216 429-7267
   Cleveland (G-5297)
Cliffs Resources Inc ....C 216 694-5700
   Cleveland (G-5304)
Columbus & Ohio River RR Co ....D 740 622-8092
   Coshocton (G-9003)
CSX Corporation ....C 419 225-4121
   Lima (G-12628)
CSX Corporation ....C 419 933-5027
   Willard (G-19479)
CSX Transportation Inc ....E 440 992-0871
   Ashtabula (G-735)
CSX Transportation Inc ....E 513 369-5514
   Cincinnati (G-3384)
CSX Transportation Inc ....E 937 642-2221
   Marysville (G-13493)
CSX Transportation Inc ....E 419 257-1225
   North Baltimore (G-15176)
CSX Transportation Inc ....E 513 422-2031
   Middletown (G-14298)
CSX Transportation Inc ....D 419 697-2323
   Oregon (G-15588)
Illinois & Midland RR Inc ....D 217 670-1242
   Columbus (G-7801)
Indiana & Ohio Central RR ....C 740 385-3127
   Logan (G-12842)
Indiana & Ohio Rail Corp ....E 513 860-1000
   Cincinnati (G-3756)
Indiana & Ohio Rail Corp ....E 419 229-1010
   Lima (G-12665)
Indiana & Ohio Railway Company ....D 513 860-1000
   Cincinnati (G-3757)
Nimishillen & Tuscarawas LLC ....E 330 438-5821
   Canton (G-2418)
Norfolk Southern Corporation ....D 419 436-2408
   Fostoria (G-11009)
Norfolk Southern Corporation ....D 614 251-2684
   Columbus (G-8193)
Norfolk Southern Corporation ....E 419 381-5505
   Toledo (G-17945)
Norfolk Southern Corporation ....D 419 254-1562
   Toledo (G-17946)
Norfolk Southern Corporation ....E 440 992-2274
   Ashtabula (G-749)
Norfolk Southern Corporation ....D 440 992-2215
   Ashtabula (G-750)
Norfolk Southern Corporation ....E 216 362-6087
   Cleveland (G-6071)

Norfolk Southern Corporation ....E 419 529-4574
   Ontario (G-15566)
Norfolk Southern Corporation ....E 419 483-1423
   Bellevue (G-1382)
Norfolk Southern Corporation ....E 419 485-3510
   Montpelier (G-14617)
Norfolk Southern Corporation ....E 216 518-8407
   Maple Heights (G-13290)
Norfolk Southern Corporation ....E 216 362-6087
   Cleveland (G-6072)
Norfolk Southern Corporation ....D 740 353-4529
   Portsmouth (G-16155)
Norfolk Southern Corporation ....E 937 297-5420
   Moraine (G-14685)
Norfolk Southern Corporation ....D 513 977-3246
   Cincinnati (G-4123)
Norfolk Southern Corporation ....E 740 574-8491
   Wheelersburg (G-19436)
Norfolk Southern Railway Co ....D 440 439-1827
   Bedford (G-1294)
Ohi-Rail Corp ....E 740 765-5083
   Richmond (G-16386)
Republic N&T Railroad Inc ....C 330 438-5826
   Canton (G-2455)
Wheeling & Lake Erie Rlwy Co ....B 330 767-3401
   Brewster (G-1812)

REAL ESTATE AGENCIES & BROKERS

Allen Est Mangement Ltd ....E 419 526-6505
   Mansfield (G-13133)
Altobelli Realestate ....E 330 652-0200
   Niles (G-15143)
Best Realty Inc ....E 513 932-3948
   Lebanon (G-12451)
Big Hill Realty Corp ....D 937 426-4420
   Beavercreek (G-1206)
C V Perry & Co ....E 614 221-4131
   Columbus (G-7105)
Chartwell Group LLC ....E 216 360-0009
   Cleveland (G-5171)
Coldwell Banker ....E 513 321-9944
   Cincinnati (G-3323)
Comey & Shepherd LLC ....E 513 489-2100
   Cincinnati (G-3332)
Comey & Shepherd LLC ....E 513 321-4343
   Cincinnati (G-3333)
Continental Realty Ltd ....E 614 221-6260
   Columbus (G-7362)
Cutler Real Estate ....D 330 499-9922
   North Canton (G-15195)
Cutler Real Estate ....E 330 688-2100
   Stow (G-17198)
Cutler Real Estate ....D 330 492-7230
   Canton (G-2277)
Cutler Real Estate Inc ....E 614 339-4664
   Dublin (G-10194)
Ddr Corp ....E 216 755-5547
   Canton (G-2282)
Deed Realty Co ....E 330 225-5220
   Brunswick (G-1926)
Deerfield Estates Inc ....E 440 838-1400
   Brecksville (G-1779)
Di Salle Real Estate Co ....E 419 885-4475
   Sylvania (G-17418)
Eaton Group GMAC Real Estate ....E 330 726-9999
   Warren (G-18706)
Garland Group Inc ....E 614 294-4411
   Columbus (G-7650)
Hanna Holdings Inc ....E 440 971-5600
   North Royalton (G-15358)
Hanna Holdings Inc ....D 330 707-1000
   Poland (G-16085)
Her Inc ....E 614 239-7400
   Columbus (G-7742)
Her Inc ....E 614 878-4734
   Columbus (G-7743)
Her Inc ....C 614 890-7400
   Westerville (G-19172)
Howard Hanna Smythe Cramer ....E 440 237-8888
   North Royalton (G-15361)
Howard Hanna Smythe Cramer ....E 330 345-2244
   Wooster (G-19731)
Howard Hanna Smythe Cramer ....E 440 248-3000
   Solon (G-16858)
Howard Hanna Smythe Cramer ....E 800 656-7356
   Canfield (G-2142)
Howard Hanna Smythe Cramer ....E 216 831-0210
   Beachwood (G-1064)
Howard Hanna Smythe Cramer ....D 216 447-4477
   Akron (G-270)

Howard Hanna Smythe Cramer ....E 330 468-6833
   Macedonia (G-13074)
Howard Hanna Smythe Cramer ....D 330 725-4137
   Medina (G-13952)
Howard Hanna Smythe Cramer ....E 440 835-2800
   Cleveland (G-5717)
Howard Hanna Smythe Cramer ....E 330 686-1166
   Stow (G-17212)
Howard Hanna Smythe Cramer ....E 440 248-3380
   Cleveland (G-5718)
Howard Hanna Smythe Cramer ....D 216 831-9310
   Pepper Pike (G-15818)
Howard Hanna Smythe Cramer ....E 330 562-6188
   Aurora (G-829)
Howard Hanna Smythe Cramer ....E 440 428-1818
   Madison (G-13097)
Howard Hanna Smythe Cramer ....E 330 493-6555
   Canton (G-2350)
Howard Hanna Smythe Cramer ....E 440 526-1800
   Cleveland (G-5719)
Howard Hanna Smythe Cramer ....E 330 896-3333
   Uniontown (G-18374)
Irongate Inc ....D 937 432-3432
   Dayton (G-9522)
Jacobs Real Estate Services ....E 216 514-9830
   Beachwood (G-1068)
Joseph Schmidt Realty Inc ....E 330 225-6688
   Brunswick (G-1934)
Kramer & Kramer Inc ....E 937 456-1101
   Eaton (G-10448)
Lee & Associates Inc ....E 614 923-3300
   Dublin (G-10269)
Lenz Inc ....E 937 277-9364
   Dayton (G-9563)
Lewis Price Realty Co ....E 330 856-1911
   Warren (G-18723)
Mendelson Realty Ltd ....E 937 461-3525
   Dayton (G-9607)
National Realty Services Inc ....E 614 798-0971
   Columbus (G-8136)
Noneman Real Estate Company ....E 419 531-4020
   Toledo (G-17943)
NOR Corp ....E 440 366-0099
   Elyria (G-10544)
North Star Realty Incorporated ....E 513 737-1700
   Fairfield (G-10761)
Phil Giessler ....E 614 888-0307
   Worthington (G-19835)
Phillips Edison & Company LLC ....E 513 554-1110
   Cincinnati (G-4241)
Randolph and Associates RE ....E 614 269-8418
   Columbus (G-8489)
Real Estate Capital Fund LLC ....E 216 491-3990
   Cleveland (G-6290)
Real Estate Showcase ....E 740 389-2000
   Marion (G-13454)
Real Living Title Agency Ltd ....E 440 974-7810
   Painesville (G-15737)
Robert F Lindsay Co ....D 419 476-6221
   Toledo (G-18010)
Ron Neff Real Estate ....E 740 773-4670
   Chillicothe (G-2816)
Rubber City Realty Inc ....D 330 745-9034
   Akron (G-413)
Rybac Inc ....E 614 228-3578
   Columbus (G-8565)
Sibcy Cline Inc ....E 937 610-3404
   Dayton (G-9766)
Sibcy Cline Inc ....E 513 385-3330
   Fairfield (G-10783)
Sibcy Cline Inc ....D 513 829-0044
   Fairfield (G-10784)
Sibcy Cline Inc ....D 513 793-2700
   Cincinnati (G-4476)
Sibcy Cline Inc ....E 513 931-7700
   Cincinnati (G-4477)
Star One Holdings Inc ....E 513 300-6663
   Cincinnati (G-4539)
Steve Brown ....D 937 436-2700
   Dayton (G-9793)
Stouffer Realty Inc ....E 330 835-4900
   Fairlawn (G-10852)
Townhomes Management Inc ....E 614 228-3578
   Columbus (G-8767)
U S Associates Realty Inc ....E 216 663-3400
   Cleveland (G-6557)
West Shell Gale Schnetzer ....E 513 683-3833
   Loveland (G-13033)
Williams Homes LLC ....E 419 472-1005
   Toledo (G-18158)

Zaremba LLC ....D...... 216 221-6600
Cleveland *(G-6709)*

REAL ESTATE AGENCIES: Buying

Cutler and Associates Inc ....E...... 330 493-9323
Canton *(G-2276)*
Mrap LLC ....E...... 614 545-3190
Columbus *(G-8117)*
Sawmill Road Management Co LLC......E...... 937 342-9071
Springfield *(G-17108)*

REAL ESTATE AGENCIES: Commercial

Adena Commercial LLC ....E...... 614 436-9800
Columbus *(G-6798)*
Bellwether Entp RE Capitl LLC ....E...... 216 820-4500
Cleveland *(G-5052)*
Carnegie Companies Inc ....E...... 440 232-2300
Solon *(G-16831)*
Cassidy Trley Coml RE Svcs Inc ....E...... 513 771-2580
Cincinnati *(G-3130)*
Cbre Inc.......................................D...... 513 369-1300
Cincinnati *(G-3134)*
Cbre Inc.......................................E...... 216 687-1800
Cleveland *(G-5142)*
Cbre Inc.......................................E...... 614 419-7429
Blacklick *(G-1476)*
Cbre Inc.......................................D...... 614 438-5488
Columbus *(G-7144)*
Classic Real Estate Co ....E...... 937 393-3416
Hillsboro *(G-11833)*
Cushman & Wakefield Inc ....E...... 937 222-7884
Moraine *(G-14638)*
Eastgate Professional Off Pk V ....E...... 513 943-0050
Cincinnati *(G-2851)*
Ellis Richard CB Reichle Klein ....E...... 419 861-1100
Toledo *(G-17711)*
Giammarco Properties LLC ....E...... 419 885-4844
Toledo *(G-17761)*
Hadler Realty Company.....................E...... 614 457-6650
Columbus *(G-7709)*
Knoxbi Company LLC ....D...... 440 892-6800
Westlake *(G-19365)*
Marcus Mllchap RE Inv Svcs Inc ....E...... 614 360-9800
Columbus *(G-8017)*
Midland Atlantic Prpts LLC ....E...... 513 792-5000
Cincinnati *(G-4049)*
Mv Land Development Company ....B...... 937 293-0900
Dayton *(G-9649)*
Northpointe Plaza ....D...... 614 744-2229
Columbus *(G-8203)*
Ohio Equities LLC..........................D...... 614 469-0058
Columbus *(G-8253)*
Signature Associates Inc ....E...... 419 244-7505
Toledo *(G-18034)*
West Shell Commercial Inc ....D...... 513 721-4200
Cincinnati *(G-4784)*

REAL ESTATE AGENCIES: Leasing & Rentals

Blossom Hill Elderly Housing L..........D...... 330 385-4310
East Liverpool *(G-10398)*
Coffman Family Partnership ....E...... 614 864-5400
Columbus *(G-7241)*
Inc/Ballew A Head Joint Ventr ....D...... 614 338-5801
Columbus *(G-7806)*
Lt Land Development LLC ....E...... 937 382-0072
Wilmington *(G-19631)*
Nwd Arena District II LLC ....E...... 614 857-2330
Columbus *(G-8219)*
Pfh Partners LLC ....E...... 513 241-5800
Cincinnati *(G-4239)*
Triad PII ....E...... 740 374-2940
Marietta *(G-13389)*
Triangle Office Park LLC ....E...... 513 563-7555
Cincinnati *(G-4634)*

REAL ESTATE AGENCIES: Multiple Listing Svc

Sweeney Team Inc ....E...... 513 241-3400
Cincinnati *(G-4559)*

REAL ESTATE AGENCIES: Rental

Brg Realty Group LLC ....C...... 513 936-5960
Cincinnati *(G-3072)*
Green Springs Residential Ltd ....C...... 419 639-2581
Green Springs *(G-11353)*
Millennia Housing MGT Ltd...............E...... 216 520-1250
Cleveland *(G-5996)*

Neyer Real Estate MGT LLC................E...... 513 618-6000
Cincinnati *(G-4117)*
Tom Properties LLC ....D...... 614 781-0055
Columbus *(G-8762)*
Valley View Place ....C...... 740 454-7720
Zanesville *(G-20371)*
Village Communities LLC..................C...... 614 540-2400
Westerville *(G-19216)*

REAL ESTATE AGENCIES: Residential

1440 Corporation Inc ....E...... 513 424-2421
Middletown *(G-14284)*
AA Green Realty Inc ....E...... 419 352-5331
Bowling Green *(G-1711)*
Baur Leo Century 21 Realty ....E...... 440 585-2300
Willowick *(G-19596)*
Beyond 2000 Realty Inc ....E...... 440 842-7200
Cleveland *(G-5062)*
Big Hill Realty Corp ....C...... 937 435-1177
Dayton *(G-9251)*
Big Hill Realty Corp ....E...... 937 429-2200
Beavercreek *(G-1207)*
Capital Partners Realty LLC...............E...... 614 888-1000
Worthington *(G-19795)*
Carleton Realty Inc ....E...... 740 653-5200
Lancaster *(G-12375)*
Century 21 Elite Performance ....E...... 937 438-8221
Spring Valley *(G-16957)*
Century 21 Trammell Odonnell ....D...... 440 888-6800
Cleveland *(G-5157)*
Century 21-Joe Walker & Assoc ....E...... 614 899-1400
Columbus *(G-6804)*
Coldwell Banker First Place RE...........D...... 330 726-8161
Poland *(G-16083)*
Coldwell Banker King Thompson.........D...... 614 759-0808
Pickerington *(G-15952)*
Coldwell Banker West Shell ....E...... 513 829-4000
West Chester *(G-18894)*
Coldwell Banker West Shell ....D...... 513 922-9400
Cincinnati *(G-3324)*
Coldwell Banker West Shell ....D...... 513 385-9300
Cincinnati *(G-3325)*
Coldwell Banker West Shell ....D...... 513 777-7900
West Chester *(G-18895)*
Coldwell Banker West Shell ....E...... 513 271-7200
Cincinnati *(G-3326)*
Coldwell Bnkr Hritg Rltors LLC ....E...... 937 304-8500
Dayton *(G-9312)*
Coldwell Bnkr Hritg Rltors LLC ....E...... 937 748-5500
Springboro *(G-16966)*
Coldwell Bnkr Hritg Rltors LLC ....E...... 937 434-7600
Dayton *(G-9313)*
Coldwell Bnkr Hritg Rltors LLC ....E...... 937 426-6060
Beavercreek Township *(G-1244)*
Coldwell Bnkr Hritg Rltors LLC ....E...... 937 890-2200
Vandalia *(G-18518)*
Comey & Shepherd LLC ....E...... 513 231-2800
Cincinnati *(G-3334)*
Comey & Shepherd LLC ....E...... 513 891-4444
Cincinnati *(G-3335)*
Cutler Real Estate ....C...... 330 836-9141
Fairlawn *(G-10820)*
Cutler Real Estate ....D...... 330 733-7575
Ravenna *(G-16241)*
Danberry Co ....D...... 419 866-8888
Maumee *(G-13779)*
David Campbell ....E...... 937 266-7064
Dayton *(G-9345)*
Equity Central LLC ....E...... 614 861-7777
Gahanna *(G-11118)*
Flex Realty ....E...... 419 841-6208
Toledo *(G-17743)*
Geneva Chervenic Realty Inc.............D...... 330 686-8400
Stow *(G-17208)*
Hanna Holdings Inc ....E...... 440 933-6195
Avon *(G-884)*
Henkle-Schueler & Associates ....E...... 513 932-6070
Lebanon *(G-12471)*
Her Inc ....E...... 614 240-7400
Columbus *(G-7740)*
Her Inc ....E...... 614 221-7400
Columbus *(G-7741)*
Her Inc ....D...... 614 888-7400
Worthington *(G-19814)*
Her Inc ....D...... 614 864-7400
Pickerington *(G-15957)*
Her Inc ....C...... 614 889-7400
Dublin *(G-10240)*
Her Inc ....E...... 614 771-7400
Hilliard *(G-11772)*

Hoeting Inc ....D...... 513 451-4800
Cincinnati *(G-3715)*
Howard Hanna Smythe Cramer ....C...... 216 447-4477
Cleveland *(G-5716)*
Howard Hanna Smythe Cramer ....E...... 440 333-6500
Rocky River *(G-16436)*
Howard Hanna Smythe Cramer ....E...... 440 282-8002
Amherst *(G-590)*
Howard Hanna Smythe Cramer ....E...... 440 516-4444
Willoughby *(G-19530)*
Howard Hanna Smythe Cramer ....E...... 216 751-8550
Beachwood *(G-1065)*
Hunter Realty Inc ....E...... 216 831-2911
Cleveland *(G-5722)*
Hunter Realty Inc ....E...... 440 466-9177
Geneva *(G-11243)*
Irongate Inc ....E...... 937 433-3300
Centerville *(G-2628)*
J W Enterprises Inc.........................E...... 740 774-4500
Chillicothe *(G-2796)*
Jordan Realtors Inc ....E...... 513 791-0281
Cincinnati *(G-3832)*
Joseph Walker Inc ....E...... 614 895-3840
Columbus *(G-6817)*
Karam & Simon Realty Inc ....E...... 330 929-0707
Cuyahoga Falls *(G-9107)*
Keller Williams Advisors LLC ....E...... 513 766-9200
Cincinnati *(G-3853)*
Keller Williams Advisory Rlty ....E...... 513 372-6500
Cincinnati *(G-3854)*
Keller Williams Classic Pro ....D...... 614 451-8500
Columbus *(G-7888)*
Keller Williams Rlty M Walker ....E...... 330 571-2020
Stow *(G-17215)*
Key Realty Ltd ....C...... 419 270-7445
Holland *(G-11891)*
Lakeside Realty LLC ....E...... 330 793-4200
Youngstown *(G-20096)*
Lucien Realty..................................D...... 440 331-8500
Cleveland *(G-5888)*
Mall Realty Inc ....E...... 937 866-3700
Dayton *(G-9582)*
Maryann McEowen............................D...... 330 638-6385
Cortland *(G-8990)*
Mc Mahon Realestate Co..................E...... 740 344-2250
Newark *(G-15067)*
Miller-Vintine Partners Ltd Lc ....E...... 513 588-1000
Cincinnati *(G-4055)*
Murwood Real Estate Group LLC ....E...... 216 839-5500
Beachwood *(G-1085)*
Noakes Rooney Rlty & Assoc Co ....E...... 419 423-4861
Findlay *(G-10949)*
North Wood Realty ....E...... 330 423-0837
Youngstown *(G-20142)*
North Wood Realty ....E...... 330 856-3915
Warren *(G-18734)*
Nrt Commercial Utah LLC ....D...... 614 239-0808
Columbus *(G-8211)*
Nrt Commercial Utah LLC ....E...... 614 889-0808
Dublin *(G-10293)*
Platinum RE Professionals LLC ....E...... 440 942-2100
Willoughby *(G-19562)*
Preferred Real Estate Group ....E...... 513 533-4111
Cincinnati *(G-4269)*
Prudential Calhoon Co Realtors ....E...... 614 777-1000
Hilliard *(G-11808)*
Prudential Lucien Realty ....E...... 216 226-4673
Lakewood *(G-12360)*
Prudential Select Properties ....D...... 440 255-1111
Mentor *(G-14098)*
Prudential Welsh Realty ....E...... 440 974-3100
Mentor *(G-14099)*
Re/Max ....E...... 937 477-4997
Beavercreek *(G-1234)*
Re/Max Consultant Group.................D...... 614 855-2822
New Albany *(G-14869)*
RE/Max Experts Realty ....E...... 330 364-7355
Dover *(G-10095)*
RE/Max Real Estate Experts ....E...... 440 255-6505
Mentor *(G-14101)*
Real Estate II Inc ....E...... 937 390-3119
Springfield *(G-17100)*
Remax Homesource ....E...... 440 951-2500
Willoughby *(G-19567)*
REO Network Inc ....E...... 740 374-8900
Marietta *(G-13376)*
Residential One Realty Inc................E...... 614 436-9830
Columbus *(G-8521)*
Roediger Realty Inc ....E...... 937 322-0352
Springfield *(G-17104)*

S E R V I C E S

Rolls Realty ....E 614 792-5662
Powell (G-16207)
Saxton Real Estate Co ....D 614 875-2327
Grove City (G-11469)
Sibcy Cline Inc ....E 513 752-4000
Cincinnati (G-2868)
Sibcy Cline Inc ....D 513 793-2121
Cincinnati (G-4474)
Sibcy Cline Inc ....D 513 984-4100
Cincinnati (G-4475)
Sibcy Cline Inc ....D 513 777-8100
West Chester (G-19005)
Sibcy Cline Inc ....D 513 677-1830
Mason (G-13640)
Sibcy Cline Inc ....E 937 429-2101
Beavercreek (G-1186)
Sibcy Cline Inc ....D 513 932-6334
Lebanon (G-12501)
Star One Holdings Inc ....E 513 474-9100
Cincinnati (G-4538)
Star One Holdings Inc ....E 513 779-9500
West Chester (G-19012)
Sue Smedley ....E 937 399-5155
Springfield (G-17120)
Sweeney Team Inc ....E 513 934-0700
Lebanon (G-12508)
Tiger 2010 LLC ....E 330 236-5100
North Canton (G-15238)
Tom Baier & Assoc Inc ....E 330 497-3115
Canton (G-2513)
Ward Realestate Inc ....E 419 281-2000
Ashland (G-698)
Welles Bowen Realty Inc ....D 419 535-0011
Toledo (G-18149)
Western Reserve Realty LLC ....E 440 247-3707
Chagrin Falls (G-2659)
Wilbur Realty Inc ....E 330 673-5883
Kent (G-12268)
William Zamarelli Realtors ....E 330 856-2299
Warren (G-18772)
Y Town Realty Inc ....E 330 743-8844
Youngstown (G-20251)
Yocum Realty Company ....E 419 222-3040
Lima (G-12788)

REAL ESTATE AGENCIES: Selling

Plus Realty Cincinnati Inc ....E 513 575-4500
Milford (G-14425)
Richard H Freyhof ....E 937 653-5837
Urbana (G-18443)

REAL ESTATE AGENTS & MANAGERS

0714 Inc ....E 440 327-2123
North Ridgeville (G-15318)
2780 Airport Drive LLC ....E 513 563-7555
Cincinnati (G-2881)
36 E Seventh LLC ....E 513 699-2279
Cincinnati (G-2882)
Abco Contracting LLC ....E 419 973-4772
Toledo (G-17580)
Allen Metro Hsing MGT Dev Corp ....E 419 228-6065
Lima (G-12597)
American Title Services Inc ....E 330 652-1609
Niles (G-15144)
Amsdell Construction Inc ....C 216 458-0670
Cleveland (G-4974)
Arena Management Holdings LLC ....A 513 421-4111
Cincinnati (G-2984)
Blue Ash Distribution Ctr LLC ....E 513 699-2279
Cincinnati (G-3059)
Buckeye Cmnty Twenty Six LP ....E 614 942-2020
Columbus (G-7088)
Capital Senior Living ....E 440 356-5444
Rocky River (G-16425)
Cincinnati Coml Contg LLC ....E 513 561-6633
Cincinnati (G-3235)
Communicare Health Svcs Inc ....D 330 792-7799
Youngstown (G-19997)
Communicare Health Svcs Inc ....D 419 394-7611
Saint Marys (G-16521)
Communicare Health Svcs Inc ....D 330 792-5511
Youngstown (G-19998)
Communicare Health Svcs Inc ....C 330 454-2152
Canton (G-2263)
Communicare Health Svcs Inc ....D 330 630-9780
Tallmadge (G-17472)
Connor Group A RE Inv Firm LLC ....B 937 434-3095
Miamisburg (G-14154)
Crawford Hoying Ltd ....C 614 335-2020
Dublin (G-10192)
Croxton Realty Company ....E 330 492-1697
Canton (G-2275)
Cushman & Wakefield Inc ....E 513 631-1121
Norwood (G-15461)
Cutler and Associates Inc ....D 330 896-1680
Akron (G-177)
Cutler and Associates Inc ....E 330 688-2100
Stow (G-17197)
Cwb Property Managment Inc ....E 614 793-2244
Dublin (G-10195)
Darfus ....E 740 380-1710
Logan (G-12834)
Dari Pizza Enterprises II Inc ....C 419 534-3000
Maumee (G-13780)
Design Homes & Development Co ....E 937 438-3667
Dayton (G-9389)
Duke Realty Corporation ....D 513 651-3900
Mason (G-13576)
E A Zicka Co ....E 513 451-1440
Cincinnati (G-3464)
Echoing Hills Village Inc ....C 740 327-2311
Warsaw (G-18783)
Elden Properties Ltd Partnr ....E 440 967-0521
Vermilion (G-18552)
Essex Healthcare Corporation ....E 614 416-0600
Columbus (G-7536)
Fairfield Homes Inc ....C 614 873-3533
Plain City (G-16053)
Fay Limited Partnership ....E 513 241-1911
Cincinnati (G-3535)
Fc Continental Landlord LLC ....A 216 621-6060
Cleveland (G-5519)
Fujiyama International Inc ....E 614 891-2224
Columbus (G-7633)
Gideon ....D 800 395-6014
Cleveland (G-5607)
Greene Town Center LLC ....D 937 490-4990
Beavercreek (G-1221)
Hmshost Corporation ....C 419 547-8667
Clyde (G-6744)
Home Town Realtors LLC ....D 937 890-9111
Dayton (G-9502)
Homelife Companies Inc ....E 740 369-1297
Delaware (G-9986)
Hunt Club LLC ....E 419 885-4647
Sylvania (G-17431)
Integra Cncinnati/Columbus Inc ....E 614 764-8040
Dublin (G-10257)
Irongate Inc ....E 937 298-6000
Dayton (G-9521)
Jacob Real Estate Services ....E 216 687-0500
Cleveland (G-5777)
Jobar Enterprise Inc ....E 216 561-5184
Cleveland (G-5798)
Jones Lang Lsalle Americas Inc ....E 216 447-5276
Brecksville (G-1787)
Kwik Parking ....E 419 246-0454
Toledo (G-17844)
Linn Street Holdings LLC ....E 513 699-8825
Cincinnati (G-3936)
Longwood Phase One Assoc LP ....E 561 998-0700
Cleveland (G-5880)
Meadowbrook Mall Company ....E 330 747-2661
Youngstown (G-20119)
Midwest Liquidators Inc ....E 614 433-7355
Worthington (G-19828)
Miller-Valentine Partners Ltd ....E 513 588-1000
Cincinnati (G-4054)
Mri Software LLC ....C 800 321-8770
Solon (G-16874)
National Church Residences ....C 614 451-2151
Columbus (G-8130)
Nationwide Mutual Insurance Co ....A 614 249-7111
Columbus (G-8160)
Neighborhood Properties Inc ....E 419 473-2604
Toledo (G-17937)
Newmark & Company RE Inc ....E 216 453-3000
Cleveland (G-6065)
Nisbet Corporation ....C 513 563-1111
Cincinnati (G-4120)
Normandy Office Associates ....D 513 381-8696
Cincinnati (G-4124)
Oak Brook Gardens ....D 440 237-3613
North Royalton (G-15363)
Oberer Residential Cnstr ....C 937 278-0851
Miamisburg (G-14200)
One Lincoln Park ....D 937 298-0594
Dayton (G-9675)
Owners Management Company ....E 440 439-3800
Parma (G-15770)
Petros Homes Inc ....E 440 546-9000
Cleveland (G-6202)
Port Lawrence Title and Tr Co ....E 419 244-4605
Toledo (G-17982)
R A Hermes Inc ....E 513 251-5200
Cincinnati (G-4329)
Residential Hm Assn of Marion ....C 740 387-9999
Marion (G-13455)
Richland Mall Shopping Ctr ....E 419 529-4003
Mansfield (G-13236)
Sami S Rafidi ....C 330 799-9508
Youngstown (G-20202)
Sawyer Realtors ....E 513 423-6521
Middletown (G-14327)
Siena Springs II ....E 513 639-2800
Dayton (G-9768)
Skye Development Company LLC ....E 216 223-0160
Cleveland (G-6412)
Springcar Company LLC ....E 440 892-6800
Westlake (G-19408)
Sterling Heights Gsa Prpts Ltd ....E 419 609-7000
Sandusky (G-16648)
Towne Properties Assoc Inc ....E 513 874-3737
Cincinnati (G-4620)
U S Title Agency Inc ....E 216 621-1424
Cleveland (G-6559)
Ufcw 75 Real Estate Corp ....D 937 677-0075
Dayton (G-9828)
University Circle Incorporated ....E 216 791-3900
Cleveland (G-6586)
Visconsi Companies Ltd ....E 216 464-5550
Cleveland (G-6634)
Washington Square Apartments ....E 740 349-8353
Newark (G-15107)
Your Home Court Advantage LLC ....E 330 364-6602
New Philadelphia (G-14990)
Zaremba Zanesville LLC ....E 216 221-6600
Lakewood (G-12367)

REAL ESTATE APPRAISERS

Al-Mar Lanes ....E 419 352-4637
Bowling Green (G-1713)
Appraisal Research Corporation ....C 419 423-3582
Findlay (G-10865)
Baker Bnngson Rlty Auctioneers ....E 419 547-7777
Clyde (G-6740)
Calabresem Racek & Markos Inc ....E 216 696-5442
Cleveland (G-5113)
Manatron Sabre Systems and Svc ....D 937 431-4000
Beavercreek (G-1229)
Martin + WD Apprisal Group Ltd ....E 419 241-4998
Toledo (G-17897)
Mortgage Information Services ....D 216 514-7480
Cleveland (G-6012)
Stickelman Schneider Assoc LLC ....E 513 475-6000
Fairborn (G-10682)

REAL ESTATE AUCTION

Butler County of Ohio ....D 513 887-3154
Hamilton (G-11562)

REAL ESTATE ESCROW AGENCIES

Real Living Title Agency Ltd ....D 614 459-7400
Columbus (G-8495)
Resource Title Agency Inc ....D 216 520-0050
Cleveland (G-6315)
Resource Title Nat Agcy Inc ....D 216 520-0050
Independence (G-12113)

REAL ESTATE INVESTMENT TRUSTS

Bre Ddr Parker Pavilions LLC ....E 216 755-6451
Beachwood (G-1036)
Ddr Corp ....E 614 785-6445
Columbus (G-7425)
Ddr Tucson Spectrum I LLC ....E 216 755-5500
Beachwood (G-1051)
Forest City Realty Trust Inc ....E 216 621-6060
Cleveland (G-5560)
Investmerica limited ....D 216 618-3296
Chagrin Falls (G-2650)
Morelia Consultants LLC ....D 513 469-1500
Cincinnati (G-4072)
Moskowitz Family Ltd ....C 513 729-2300
Cincinnati (G-4076)
Site Centers Corp ....C 216 755-5500
Beachwood (G-1107)

REAL ESTATE MANAGERS: Cemetery

City of Willoughby ....B...... 440 953-4111
  Willoughby (G-19512)
Township of Fowler ....D...... 330 637-2653
  Fowler (G-11017)

REAL ESTATE MANAGERS: Condominium

Brookwood Management Company ......E...... 330 497-6565
  Canton (G-2219)
Hidden Lake Condominiums ....D...... 614 488-1131
  Columbus (G-7746)

REAL ESTATE MANAGERS: Cooperative Apartment

Erhal Inc ....E...... 513 272-5555
  Cincinnati (G-3513)
Waldon Management Corp ....E...... 330 792-7688
  Youngstown (G-20240)

REAL ESTATE OPERATORS, EXC DEVEL: Prprty, Auditorium/Theater

Ohio State University.....................A...... 614 688-3939
  Columbus (G-8296)

REAL ESTATE OPERATORS, EXC DEVELOPERS: Apartment Hotel

D & S Properties ....E...... 614 224-6663
  Columbus (G-7407)
E A Zicka Co ....E...... 513 451-1440
  Cincinnati (G-3464)
Forest City Properties LLC ....C...... 216 621-6060
  Cleveland (G-5559)
Intown Suites Management Inc ....E...... 937 433-9038
  Dayton (G-9520)
Islander Company.....................E...... 440 243-0593
  Cleveland (G-5767)
L S C Service Corp.....................E...... 216 521-7260
  Lakewood (G-12350)
Oakwood Management Company ....E...... 740 774-3570
  Chillicothe (G-2806)
Olentangy Village Associates ....E...... 614 515-4680
  Columbus (G-8371)
Washington Square Apartments ....E...... 740 349-8353
  Newark (G-15107)

REAL ESTATE OPERATORS, EXC DEVELOPERS: Auditorium & Hall

Assembly Center.....................E...... 800 582-1099
  Monroe (G-14560)
Catholic Diocese of Cleveland...............E...... 419 289-7224
  Ashland (G-664)
Hall Nazareth Inc ....D...... 419 832-2900
  Grand Rapids (G-11325)
Makoy Center Inc ....E...... 614 777-1211
  Hilliard (G-11787)
Musical Arts Association ....C...... 216 231-7300
  Cleveland (G-6028)
Rootstown Township ....E...... 330 296-8240
  Ravenna (G-16265)
Stranahan Theatre Trust ....D...... 419 381-8851
  Toledo (G-18050)
Waterfront & Associates Inc ....B...... 859 581-1414
  Cincinnati (G-4770)

REAL ESTATE OPERATORS, EXC DEVELOPERS: Commercial/Indl Bldg

127 PS Fee Owner LLC.....................D...... 216 520-1250
  Cleveland (G-4865)
Ad Investments LLC ....E...... 614 857-2340
  Columbus (G-6870)
American Maritime Officers ....E...... 419 255-3940
  Toledo (G-17591)
Anderson Jeffery R RE Inc.....................E...... 513 241-5800
  Cincinnati (G-2961)
Ashtabula Chemical Corp ....E...... 440 998-0100
  Ashtabula (G-707)
At Holdings Corporation ....A...... 216 692-6000
  Cleveland (G-5016)
Barcus Company Inc ....E...... 614 451-9000
  Columbus (G-7017)
C M Limited ....E...... 614 888-4567
  Columbus (G-7103)
Cararo Co Inc ....E...... 330 652-6980
  Niles (G-15150)

Carew Realty Inc ....E...... 513 241-3888
  Cincinnati (G-3123)
Carnegie Management & Dev Corp .....E...... 440 892-6800
  Westlake (G-19327)
Casto Communities Cnstr Ltd ....B...... 614 228-8545
  Columbus (G-7137)
Coldwell Bnkr Hrtg Rltors LLC ....E...... 937 434-7600
  Dayton (G-9313)
Compco Land Company ....D...... 330 482-0200
  Youngstown (G-20004)
Continental Properties ....B...... 614 221-1800
  Columbus (G-7360)
Court Stret Center Associates.....................E...... 513 241-0415
  Cincinnati (G-3375)
Daniel Maury Construction Co ....E...... 513 984-4096
  Loveland (G-12988)
Duke Realty Corporation ....D...... 614 932-6000
  Dublin (G-10212)
Equity Residential Properties ....E...... 216 861-2700
  Cleveland (G-5489)
F H Bonn ....E...... 937 323-7024
  Springfield (G-17035)
Fairlawn Associates Ltd ....C...... 330 867-5000
  Fairlawn (G-10826)
Garland/Dbs Inc ....C...... 216 641-7500
  Cleveland (G-5592)
Gms Management Co Inc ....E...... 216 766-6000
  Cleveland (G-5612)
Goldberg Companies Inc ....E...... 216 475-2600
  Cleveland (G-5613)
Goodall Properties Ltd ....E...... 513 621-5522
  Cincinnati (G-3626)
Graham Investment Co.....................D...... 740 382-0902
  Marion (G-13422)
Greater Clumbus Convention Ctr ....D...... 614 827-2500
  Columbus (G-7691)
Hadler-Zimmerman Inc ....E...... 614 457-6650
  Columbus (G-7710)
Hoty Enterprises Inc ....E...... 419 609-7000
  Sandusky (G-16617)
Islander Company.....................E...... 440 243-0593
  Cleveland (G-5767)
Jacobs Real Estate Services ....E...... 216 514-9830
  Beachwood (G-1068)
Jade Investments.....................E...... 330 425-3141
  Twinsburg (G-18284)
Judy Mills Company Inc ....E...... 513 271-4241
  Cincinnati (G-3841)
Jvc Sports Corp ....E...... 330 726-1757
  Youngstown (G-20089)
King James Group IV Ltd ....E...... 440 250-1851
  Westlake (G-19363)
King James Park Ltd ....E...... 440 835-1100
  Westlake (G-19364)
Kohr Royer Griffith Dev Co LLC ....E...... 614 228-2471
  Columbus (G-7920)
L and M Investment Co.....................E...... 740 653-3583
  Lancaster (G-12409)
Lewis Price Realty Co ....E...... 330 856-1911
  Warren (G-18723)
Lmt Enterprises Maumee Inc ....E...... 419 891-7325
  Maumee (G-13810)
M & L Leasing Co ....E...... 330 343-8910
  Mineral City (G-14506)
Majestic Steel Properties Inc ....D...... 440 786-2666
  Cleveland (G-5901)
Manleys Manor Nursing Home Inc ....C...... 419 424-0402
  Findlay (G-10937)
Meadowbrook Mall Company ....E...... 330 747-2661
  Youngstown (G-20119)
MEI Hotels Incorporated ....C...... 216 589-0441
  Cleveland (G-5949)
Mendelson Realty Ltd ....E...... 937 461-3525
  Dayton (G-9607)
Miller-Valentine Partners ....C...... 937 293-0900
  Moraine (G-14679)
Olentangy Village Associates ....E...... 614 515-4680
  Columbus (G-8371)
Oliver House Rest Complex ....D...... 419 243-1302
  Toledo (G-17960)
Park Corporation ....B...... 216 267-4870
  Cleveland (G-6163)
Reed Hartman Corporate Center ....E...... 513 984-3030
  Blue Ash (G-1642)
Ricco Enterprises Incorporated ....E...... 216 883-7775
  Cleveland (G-6319)
Robinson Investments Ltd ....E...... 937 593-1849
  Bellefontaine (G-1362)
Roemer Land Investment Co ....E...... 419 475-5151
  Toledo (G-18012)

Rose Properties Inc ....E...... 216 881-6000
  Cleveland (G-6341)
Southwest Associates ....C...... 440 243-7888
  Cleveland (G-6426)
Ted Graham ....E...... 740 223-3509
  Marion (G-13463)
The C-Z Company ....E...... 740 432-6334
  Cambridge (G-2085)
Thompson Hall & Jordan Fnrl HM .....E...... 513 761-8881
  Cincinnati (G-4604)
U S Development Corp ....E...... 330 673-6900
  Kent (G-12264)
United Fd Coml Wkrs Local 880 ....E...... 216 241-5930
  Cleveland (G-6571)
Universal Veneer Mill Corp ....C...... 740 522-1147
  Newark (G-15106)
Visconsi Management Inc ....E...... 216 464-5550
  Cleveland (G-6635)
Waldon Management Corp ....E...... 330 792-7688
  Youngstown (G-20240)
Washington PRI ....C...... 614 621-9000
  Columbus (G-8875)
Weston Inc ....E...... 440 349-9000
  Cleveland (G-6679)
White & Chambers Partnership ....E...... 740 594-8381
  Athens (G-811)
Whitford Woods Co Inc ....E...... 440 693-4344
  Middlefield (G-14279)
Wickliffe Associates Partnr ....E...... 440 585-3505
  Wickliffe (G-19477)
Willis Day Management Inc ....E...... 419 476-8000
  Toledo (G-18159)
Zucker Building Company ....D...... 216 861-7114
  Cleveland (G-6714)

REAL ESTATE OPERATORS, EXC DEVELOPERS: Property, Retail

Friedman Management Company ....D...... 614 224-2424
  Columbus (G-7626)
Washington Prime Group Inc ....D...... 614 621-9000
  Columbus (G-8877)

REAL ESTATE OPERATORS, EXC DEVELOPERS: Residential Hotel

Aurora Hotel Partners LLC.....................E...... 330 562-0767
  Aurora (G-817)
Northeast Cincinnati Hotel LLC.....................C...... 513 459-9800
  Mason (G-13623)
Westgate Limited Partnership ....C...... 419 535-7070
  Toledo (G-18155)

REAL ESTATE OPERATORS, EXC DEVELOPERS: Retirement Hotel

Baptist Home and Center ....C...... 513 662-5880
  Cincinnati (G-3018)
Brookdale Lving Cmmunities Inc ....E...... 330 666-4545
  Akron (G-109)
Brookdale Senior Living Inc ....E...... 330 262-1615
  Wooster (G-19695)
C I E Inc.....................B...... 419 986-5566
  Burgoon (G-2011)
Capital Senior Living Corp ....C...... 419 874-2564
  Perrysburg (G-15845)
Capital Senior Living Corp ....C...... 216 289-9800
  Richmond Heights (G-16388)
Capital Senior Living Corp ....C...... 513 829-6200
  Fairfield (G-10707)
Cardinal Retirement Village ....E...... 330 928-7888
  Cuyahoga Falls (G-9076)
Claremont Retirement Village ....D...... 614 761-2011
  Columbus (G-7218)
Copeland Oaks ....B...... 330 938-1050
  Sebring (G-16666)
Copeland Oaks ....E...... 330 938-6126
  Sebring (G-16667)
Creative Living Inc ....E...... 614 421-1131
  Columbus (G-7386)
Ebenezer Road Corp ....C...... 513 941-0099
  Cincinnati (G-3480)
Episcopal Retirement Homes ....D...... 513 271-9610
  Cincinnati (G-3507)
Evangelical Retirement ....C...... 937 837-5581
  Dayton (G-9419)
Fort Austin Ltd Partnership ....C...... 440 892-4200
  Cleveland (G-5564)
Gemini Properties ....E...... 419 531-9211
  Toledo (G-17758)

Gemini Properties ....E 614 764-2800
Dublin *(G-10234)*

Harvest Facility Holdings LP ....E 419 472-7115
Toledo *(G-17784)*

Harvest Facility Holdings LP ....E 440 268-9555
Cleveland *(G-5665)*

Hilltop Village ....E 216 261-8383
Cleveland *(G-5693)*

Judson ....D 216 791-2004
Cleveland *(G-5808)*

Kensington Place Inc ....E 614 252-5276
Columbus *(G-7895)*

Kettering Medical Center.................D 937 866-2984
Miamisburg *(G-14182)*

Menorah Park Center For Senio ....E 216 831-6515
Beachwood *(G-1079)*

Mulberry Garden A L S ....E 330 630-3980
Munroe Falls *(G-14798)*

Neighborhood Properties Inc ....E 419 473-2604
Toledo *(G-17937)*

Northwesterly Ltd ....E 216 228-2266
Cleveland *(G-6098)*

Oakleaf Toledo Ltd Partnership ....E 419 885-3934
Toledo *(G-17956)*

Ohio Living ....B 614 224-1651
Columbus *(G-8271)*

Olmsted Mnor Rtrment Cmnty Ltd ....E 440 779-8886
North Olmsted *(G-15303)*

One Lincoln Park ....D 937 298-0594
Dayton *(G-9675)*

Orrvilla Inc ....E 330 683-4455
Orrville *(G-15637)*

Primrose Rtrment Cmmnities LLC ....E 419 224-1200
Lima *(G-12724)*

Saint Edward Housing Corp ....E 330 668-2828
Fairlawn *(G-10846)*

Senior Lifestyle Corporation ....D 513 777-4457
West Chester *(G-19002)*

Shepherd of The Valley Luthera ....E 330 726-7110
Poland *(G-16089)*

South Franklin Circle.......................C 440 247-1300
Chagrin Falls *(G-2683)*

Sunpoint Senior Living Hamlet..........E 440 247-4200
Chagrin Falls *(G-2657)*

Sunset Rtrment Communities Inc ....D 419 724-1200
Ottawa Hills *(G-15669)*

Wallick Construction Co ....E 937 399-7009
Springfield *(G-17132)*

Westlake Village Inc........................C 440 892-4200
Cleveland *(G-6678)*

Windsorwood Place Inc ....E 740 623-4600
Coshocton *(G-9031)*

REAL ESTATE OPERATORS, EXC DEVELOPERS: Shopping Ctr

Easton Town Center LLC ....C 614 337-2560
Columbus *(G-7493)*

Mall Park Southern ....D 330 758-4511
Youngstown *(G-20113)*

REAL ESTATE OPERATORS, EXC DEVELOPERS: Shopping Ctr, Commnty

Chapel Hill Management Inc ....D 330 633-7100
Akron *(G-125)*

Glimcher Realty Trust......................E 614 861-3232
Columbus *(G-7674)*

Raf Celina LLC ....E 216 464-6626
Celina *(G-2607)*

REAL ESTATE OPS, EXC DEVELOPER: Residential Bldg, 4 Or Less

Huber Investment Corporation ....E 937 233-1122
Dayton *(G-9509)*

Rv Properties LLC ....E 330 928-7888
Cuyahoga Falls *(G-9123)*

REALTY INVESTMENT TRUSTS

845 Yard Street LLC ....D 614 857-2330
Columbus *(G-6845)*

Washington Prime Group LP ....A 614 621-9000
Columbus *(G-8876)*

Washington Prime Group Inc ....D 614 621-9000
Columbus *(G-8877)*

RECLAIMED RUBBER: Reworked By Manufacturing Process

Tahoma Enterprises Inc ....D 330 745-9016
Barberton *(G-969)*

Tahoma Rubber & Plastics Inc ....D 330 745-9016
Barberton *(G-970)*

RECOVERY SVCS: Solvents

Safety-Kleen Systems Inc ....D 740 929-3532
Hebron *(G-11724)*

RECREATIONAL & SPORTING CAMPS

Columbus Frkln Cnty Pk ....E 614 891-0700
Westerville *(G-19242)*

Community Services Inc ....D 937 667-8631
Tipp City *(G-17553)*

Echoing Hills Village Inc ....D 740 594-3541
Athens *(G-778)*

Echoing Hills Village Inc ....C 740 327-2311
Warsaw *(G-18783)*

Echoing Hills Village Inc ....D 937 854-5151
Dayton *(G-9406)*

Echoing Hills Village Inc ....E 937 237-7881
Dayton *(G-9407)*

Echoing Hills Village Inc ....E 440 989-1400
Lorain *(G-12902)*

Echoing Hills Village Inc ....E 440 986-3085
South Amherst *(G-16921)*

First Community Church....................E 740 385-3827
Logan *(G-12835)*

Lutheran Outdr Ministries OH ....E 614 890-2267
Westerville *(G-19276)*

Mideast Baptist Conference ....E 440 834-8984
Burton *(G-2018)*

Procamps Inc ....E 513 745-5855
Blue Ash *(G-1632)*

Salvation Army ....D 330 735-2671
Carrollton *(G-2577)*

Young Mens Christian Assoc ....C 614 885-4252
Columbus *(G-8927)*

RECREATIONAL CAMPS

Ohio F F A Camps Inc ....E 330 627-2208
Carrollton *(G-2574)*

West Ohio Conference of ....E 614 844-6200
Worthington *(G-19859)*

RECREATIONAL DAY CAMPS

J&B Sprafka Enterprises Inc.............E 330 733-4212
Akron *(G-286)*

Leo Yannenoff Jewish Community ....C 614 231-2731
Columbus *(G-7966)*

RECREATIONAL SPORTING EQPT REPAIR SVCS

All American Sports Corp ....A 440 366-8225
North Ridgeville *(G-15319)*

Capitol Varsity Sports Inc ....E 513 523-4126
Oxford *(G-15675)*

RECREATIONAL VEHICLE DEALERS

Clare-Mar Camp Inc ....E 440 647-3318
New London *(G-14931)*

L B Brunk & Sons Inc ....E 330 332-0359
Salem *(G-16550)*

Surfside Motors Inc ....E 419 462-1746
Galion *(G-11183)*

RECREATIONAL VEHICLE PARKS

Parks Recreation Athens ....E 740 592-0046
Athens *(G-801)*

RECREATIONAL VEHICLE PARKS & CAMPGROUNDS

Muskingum Wtrshed Cnsrvncy Dst ......E 330 343-6780
Mineral City *(G-14507)*

Natural Resources Ohio Dept ....E 419 394-3611
Saint Marys *(G-16528)*

RECYCLABLE SCRAP & WASTE MATERIALS WHOLESALERS

Aci Industries Ltd ....E 740 368-4160
Delaware *(G-9948)*

Ascendtech Inc ....E 216 458-1101
Willoughby *(G-19506)*

Imperial Alum - Minerva LLC ....D 330 868-7765
Minerva *(G-14520)*

Mauser Usa LLC ....E 740 397-1762
Mount Vernon *(G-14780)*

Midwest Iron and Metal Co...............D 937 222-5992
Dayton *(G-9633)*

Omnisource LLC ....E 419 227-3411
Lima *(G-12712)*

PSC Metals Inc ....E 330 455-0212
Canton *(G-2443)*

Rnw Holdings Inc ....E 330 792-0600
Youngstown *(G-20187)*

Shredded Bedding Corporation ....E 740 893-3567
Centerburg *(G-2616)*

Tms International LLC ....E 419 747-5500
Mansfield *(G-13254)*

REFERRAL SVCS, PERSONAL & SOCIAL PROBLEMS

Caracole Inc ....E 513 761-1480
Cincinnati *(G-3115)*

Clinton County Board of Dd ....E 937 382-7519
Wilmington *(G-19609)*

Country Neighbor Program Inc ....E 440 437-6311
Orwell *(G-15651)*

Info Line Inc ....E 330 252-8064
Akron *(G-275)*

Pregnancy Care of Cincinnati............E 513 487-7777
Cincinnati *(G-4270)*

REFINERS & SMELTERS: Aluminum

Imco Recycling of Ohio LLC ....C 740 922-2373
Uhrichsville *(G-18342)*

REFINERS & SMELTERS: Lead, Secondary

Victory White Metal Company ....E 216 271-1400
Cleveland *(G-6629)*

REFINERS & SMELTERS: Nonferrous Metal

A J Oster Foils LLC.........................D 330 823-1700
Alliance *(G-512)*

Aci Industries Ltd ....E 740 368-4160
Delaware *(G-9948)*

City Scrap & Salvage Co ....C 330 753-5051
Akron *(G-139)*

Fpt Cleveland LLC ....C 216 441-3800
Cleveland *(G-5569)*

Franklin Iron & Metal Corp ....C 937 253-8184
Dayton *(G-9449)*

Garden Street Iron & Metal ....E 513 853-3700
Cincinnati *(G-3603)*

I H Schlezinger Inc.........................E 614 252-1188
Columbus *(G-7794)*

Metal Shredders Inc ....E 937 866-0777
Miamisburg *(G-14190)*

Metalico Akron Inc ....E 330 376-1400
Akron *(G-333)*

Midwest Iron and Metal Co...............D 937 222-5992
Dayton *(G-9633)*

National Bronze Mtls Ohio Inc ....E 440 277-1226
Lorain *(G-12929)*

Precision Strip Inc ....C 419 674-4186
Kenton *(G-12286)*

R L S Corporation ....E 740 773-1440
Chillicothe *(G-2812)*

Rm Advisory Group Inc ....E 513 242-2100
Cincinnati *(G-4385)*

Rnw Holdings Inc ....E 330 792-0600
Youngstown *(G-20187)*

Rumpke Transportation Co LLC ....C 513 242-4600
Cincinnati *(G-4410)*

Thyssenkrupp Materials NA Inc ....D 216 883-8100
Independence *(G-12131)*

W R G Inc ....E 216 351-8494
Cleveland *(G-6645)*

REFINING: Petroleum

Aecom Energy & Cnstr Inc................C 419 698-6277
Oregon *(G-15582)*

Koch Knight LLC..........................D.......330 488-1651
  East Canton *(G-10387)*

Marathon Petroleum Corporation.........B.....419 422-2121
  Findlay *(G-10938)*

REFRACTORIES: Nonclay

Martin Marietta Materials Inc.................E.....513 701-1140
  West Chester *(G-18970)*

REFRACTORY MATERIALS WHOLESALERS

Allen Refractories Company.................C.....740 927-8000
  Pataskala *(G-15782)*

REFRIGERATION & HEATING EQUIPMENT

A A S Amels Sheet Meta L Inc...........E.....330 793-9326
  Youngstown *(G-19943)*

Anatrace Products LLC....................E.....419 740-6600
  Maumee *(G-13751)*

REFRIGERATION EQPT & SPLYS WHOLESALERS

Allied Supply Company Inc.................E.....937 224-9833
  Dayton *(G-9216)*

Buckeye Heating and AC Sup Inc ....E.....216 831-0066
  Bedford Heights *(G-1318)*

Controls Center Inc.......................D.....513 772-2665
  Cincinnati *(G-3356)*

Gordon Brothers Inc......................E.....800 331-7611
  Salem *(G-16545)*

WW Grainger Inc..........................E.....614 276-5231
  Columbus *(G-8921)*

REFRIGERATION EQPT & SPLYS, WHOL: Refrig Units, Motor Veh

Scotts Towing Co.........................E.....419 729-7888
  Toledo *(G-18022)*

REFRIGERATION EQPT & SPLYS, WHOLESALE: Commercial Eqpt

Hattenbach Company......................D.....216 881-5200
  Cleveland *(G-5666)*

REFRIGERATION REPAIR SVCS

Dickson Industrial Park Inc................E.....740 377-9162
  South Point *(G-16931)*

Refrigeration Systems Company ....D.....614 263-0913
  Columbus *(G-8502)*

Roto-Rooter Services Company ....D.....513 541-3840
  Cincinnati *(G-4401)*

Transport Specialists Inc.................E.....513 771-2220
  Cincinnati *(G-4628)*

REFRIGERATION SVC & REPAIR

Electrical Appl Repr Svc Inc ....E.....216 459-8700
  Brooklyn Heights *(G-1870)*

Gardiner Service Company LLC...........C.....440 248-3400
  Solon *(G-16850)*

Honeywell International Inc................D.....216 459-6053
  Cleveland *(G-5702)*

REFUGEE SVCS

Community Refugee & Immigation ....D.....614 235-5747
  Columbus *(G-7336)*

REFUSE SYSTEMS

Boral Resources LLC ....D.....740 622-8042
  Coshocton *(G-8999)*

City of Dayton...........................C.....937 333-4860
  Dayton *(G-9303)*

City of Elyria............................D.....440 366-2211
  Elyria *(G-10489)*

City of Lakewood........................E.....216 252-4322
  Cleveland *(G-5205)*

City of Perrysburg.......................E.....419 872-8020
  Perrysburg *(G-15848)*

Clean Harbors Envmtl Svcs Inc...........E.....513 681-6242
  Cincinnati *(G-3303)*

County of Portage.......................E.....330 297-3670
  Ravenna *(G-16239)*

Liquid Wste Solidification LLC ....E.....440 285-4648
  Chardon *(G-2703)*

Metalico Akron Inc......................E.....330 376-1400
  Akron *(G-333)*

Republic Services Inc....................E.....216 741-4013
  Cleveland *(G-6310)*

Republic Services Inc....................E.....567 712-6634
  Lima *(G-12729)*

Republic Services Inc....................E.....937 492-3470
  Sidney *(G-16796)*

Rls Disposal Company Inc................E.....740 773-1440
  Chillicothe *(G-2815)*

Safety-Kleen Systems Inc.................D.....740 929-3532
  Hebron *(G-11724)*

T C Rumpke Waste Collection ....E.....513 385-7627
  Cincinnati *(G-4565)*

Waste Management Ohio Inc..............E.....440 201-1235
  Solon *(G-16913)*

Waste Management Ohio Inc..............E.....614 382-6342
  Canal Winchester *(G-2125)*

Waste Management Ohio Inc..............D.....740 345-1212
  Newark *(G-15108)*

Waste Management Ohio Inc..............D.....614 833-5290
  Canal Winchester *(G-2126)*

Waste Management Ohio Inc..............E.....440 285-6767
  Geneva *(G-11250)*

Waste Management Ohio Inc..............E.....419 221-2029
  Lima *(G-12777)*

REGULATION & ADMIN, GOVT: Public Svc Commission, Exc Transp

City of Westerville......................E.....614 901-6500
  Westerville *(G-19236)*

REGULATION & ADMINISTRATION, GOVT: Transp Dept, Nonoperating

City of Hamilton ....E.....513 785-7551
  Hamilton *(G-11578)*

REGULATORS: Power

Vertiv Corporation.......................A.....614 888-0246
  Columbus *(G-8847)*

REHABILITATION CENTER, OUTPATIENT TREATMENT

Aaris Therapy Group Inc.................E.....330 505-1606
  Niles *(G-15142)*

Aurora Manor Ltd Partnership.............E.....330 562-5000
  Aurora *(G-818)*

Brecksvle Halthcare Group Inc............D.....440 546-0643
  Brecksville *(G-1772)*

Cancer Ntwk of W Cent ....E.....419 226-9085
  Lima *(G-12611)*

Childrens Rehabilitation Ctr ....D.....330 856-2107
  Warren *(G-18683)*

Cleveland Treatment Center ....E.....216 861-4246
  Cleveland *(G-5294)*

Concept Rehab Inc.......................D.....419 843-6002
  Toledo *(G-17675)*

Country Meadow Care Center LLC........E.....419 886-3922
  Bellville *(G-1391)*

County of Carroll........................E.....330 627-7651
  Carrollton *(G-2565)*

Easter Seal Society of ....D.....330 743-1168
  Youngstown *(G-20025)*

Education Alternatives ....D.....216 332-9360
  Brookpark *(G-1897)*

Fieldstone Farm Therapeutic Rl ....E.....440 708-0013
  Chagrin Falls *(G-2666)*

Hcf of Roselawn Inc.....................C.....419 647-4115
  Spencerville *(G-16956)*

Heartland Rhblitation Svcs Inc............D.....419 537-0764
  Toledo *(G-17796)*

Heartlnd-Riverview S Pt OH LLC..........E.....740 894-3287
  South Point *(G-16937)*

Hill Manor 1 Inc.........................E.....740 972-3227
  Columbus *(G-7750)*

Kindred Healthcare Oper Inc..............D.....740 545-6355
  West Lafayette *(G-19115)*

Kindred Nursing Centers E LLC...........C.....502 596-7300
  Logan *(G-12844)*

Lorain County Alcohol and Drug...........E.....440 989-4900
  Lorain *(G-12917)*

Manor Care of Kansas Inc................D.....419 252-5500
  Toledo *(G-17883)*

Marca Terrace Widows ....D.....937 252-1661
  Dayton *(G-9584)*

Marietta Center For Health & ....C.....740 373-1867
  Marietta *(G-13349)*

Medcentral Health System ....C.....419 683-1040
  Crestline *(G-9057)*

Meigs Center Ltd.........................C.....740 992-6472
  Middleport *(G-14281)*

Melrose Rehab LLC......................E.....419 424-9625
  Findlay *(G-10943)*

Metrohealth System......................D.....216 778-8446
  Cleveland *(G-5969)*

Midwest Rehab Inc......................D.....419 692-3405
  Ada *(G-5)*

Ohio State University.....................A.....614 257-3000
  Columbus *(G-8300)*

Opportunities For Ohioans ....E.....513 852-3260
  Cincinnati *(G-4177)*

Peak Performance Center Inc ....E.....440 838-5600
  Broadview Heights *(G-1843)*

Peregrine Health Services Inc ....D.....330 823-9005
  Alliance *(G-543)*

Piqua Village Rehab LLC..................E.....937 773-9537
  Piqua *(G-16022)*

Recovery Center ....E.....740 687-4500
  Lancaster *(G-12429)*

Rehab Center ....E.....330 297-2770
  Ravenna *(G-16261)*

Rehab Medical Inc.......................D.....513 381-3740
  Cincinnati *(G-4351)*

Rehabcare Group MGT Svcs Inc ....E.....740 779-6732
  Chillicothe *(G-2814)*

Rehabcare Group MGT Svcs Inc ....D.....740 356-6160
  Portsmouth *(G-16163)*

Rehablttion Ctr At Mrietta Mem ....D.....740 374-1407
  Marietta *(G-13375)*

Society For Rehabilitation.................E.....440 209-0135
  Mentor *(G-14110)*

Summit Acres Inc........................C.....740 732-2364
  Caldwell *(G-2044)*

Sunbrdge Marion Hlth Care Corp.........D.....740 389-6306
  Marion *(G-13461)*

Theratrust ....E.....740 345-7688
  Newark *(G-15103)*

Trihealth G LLC.........................E.....513 346-5000
  Cincinnati *(G-4642)*

Ultimate Rehab Ltd ....D.....513 563-8777
  Blue Ash *(G-1670)*

United Disability Services Inc.............C.....330 374-1169
  Akron *(G-476)*

United Rehabilitation Services ....E.....937 233-1230
  Dayton *(G-9832)*

Wsb Rehabilitation Svcs Inc...............A.....330 847-7819
  Warren *(G-18774)*

REHABILITATION CTR, RESIDENTIAL WITH HEALTH CARE INCIDENTAL

Amedisys Inc............................E.....740 373-8549
  Marietta *(G-13309)*

Cherry St Mission Ministries...............E.....419 242-5141
  Toledo *(G-17650)*

City Mission ....D.....216 431-3510
  Cleveland *(G-5187)*

Community Corrections Assn ....D.....330 744-5143
  Youngstown *(G-20001)*

Compdrug..............................D.....614 224-4506
  Columbus *(G-7340)*

Comprehensive Addiction Svc Sy.........D.....419 241-8827
  Toledo *(G-17674)*

Contining Hlthcare Sltions Inc.............E.....216 772-1105
  Middleburg Heights *(G-14251)*

Crestview Health Care Center.............D.....740 695-2500
  Saint Clairsville *(G-16485)*

Foundations Hlth Solutions Inc............D.....440 793-0200
  North Olmsted *(G-15289)*

Harbor ....D.....419 241-6191
  Toledo *(G-17780)*

Health Recovery Services Inc.............C.....740 592-6720
  Athens *(G-783)*

Hitchcock Center For Women Inc ....E.....216 421-0662
  Cleveland *(G-5695)*

Interval Brotherhood Homes ....D.....330 644-4095
  Coventry Township *(G-9036)*

Jo Lin Health Center Inc..................C.....740 532-0860
  Ironton *(G-12160)*

New Directions Inc......................D.....216 591-0324
  Cleveland *(G-6062)*

Rchp - Wilmington LLC...................D.....937 382-6611
  Wilmington *(G-19643)*

Rose Mary Johanna Grassell.............C.....216 481-4823
  Cleveland *(G-6340)*

Toledo Hospital ....C.....419 291-2273
  Sylvania *(G-17459)*

United Cerebral Palsy ....E.....216 791-8363
  Cleveland *(G-6568)*

United Cerebral Palsy ....D 216 381-9993
Cleveland **(G-6569)**

United Cerebral Palsy Gr Cinc ....E 513 221-4606
Cincinnati **(G-4676)**

REHABILITATION SVCS

A Renewed Mind ....D 419 214-0606
Perrysburg **(G-15831)**

A W S Inc ....E 216 486-0600
Euclid **(G-10622)**

Adena NH LLC ....E 740 546-3620
Adena **(G-7)**

Akron General Medical Center ....D 330 344-6000
Akron **(G-43)**

Arbor Rehabilitation & Healtcr ....B 440 423-0206
Gates Mills **(G-11233)**

Beeghly Oaks Operating LLC ....C 330 884-2300
Boardman **(G-1696)**

Brookdale Place Wooster LLC ....E 330 262-1615
Wooster **(G-19694)**

Carriage Inn of Cadiz Inc ....E 740 942-8084
Cadiz **(G-2027)**

City Mission ....D 216 431-3510
Cleveland **(G-5187)**

Clark County Board of Developm ....E 937 328-2675
Springfield **(G-17009)**

Clovernook Center For The Bli ....C 513 522-3860
Cincinnati **(G-3311)**

Community Drug Board Inc ....D 330 996-5114
Akron **(G-150)**

Coshocton Drug Alcohol Council ....E 740 622-0033
Coshocton **(G-9007)**

County of Ashtabula ....C 440 224-2157
Ashtabula **(G-732)**

Diverscare Healthcare Svcs Inc ....E 937 278-8211
Dayton **(G-9392)**

Goodwill Inds Rhbilitation Ctr ....C 330 454-9461
Canton **(G-2330)**

Harrison Pavilion ....E 513 662-5800
Cincinnati **(G-3682)**

Hcf Management Inc ....C 740 289-2394
Piketon **(G-15977)**

Hcf of Roselawn Inc ....C 419 647-4115
Spencerville **(G-16956)**

Hearing Spch Deaf Ctr Grtr Cnc ....E 513 221-0527
Cincinnati **(G-3696)**

James Powers ....E 614 566-9397
Columbus **(G-7853)**

Liberty Nursing Center of Thre ....C 513 941-0787
Cincinnati **(G-3925)**

Miami Vly Jvnile Rhbltion Ctr ....E 937 562-4000
Xenia **(G-19920)**

Ohio Department of Health ....A 614 438-1255
Columbus **(G-8241)**

Ohio State University ....A 614 366-3692
Columbus **(G-8295)**

Rehab Resources ....E 513 474-4123
Cincinnati **(G-4352)**

Southeastern Rehabilitation ....E 740 679-2111
Salesville **(G-16568)**

Talbert House ....E 513 541-0127
Cincinnati **(G-4570)**

Talbert House ....D 513 872-5863
Cincinnati **(G-4573)**

Trihealth Rehabilitation Hosp ....C 513 601-0600
Cincinnati **(G-4646)**

REINSURANCE CARRIERS: Accident & Health

American Modern Home Svc Co ....E 513 943-7100
Amelia **(G-567)**

Employers Mutual Casualty Co ....D 513 221-6010
Blue Ash **(G-1551)**

REINSURANCE CARRIERS: Surety

Progressive Casualty Insur Co ....A 440 461-5000
Mayfield Village **(G-13886)**

State Automobile Mutl Insur Co ....A 833 724-3577
Columbus **(G-8692)**

RELOCATION SVCS

Dwellworks LLC ....D 216 682-4200
Cleveland **(G-5450)**

Sirva Inc ....E 216 606-4000
Independence **(G-12120)**

Sirva Relocation LLC ....B 216 606-4000
Independence **(G-12122)**

Wegman Construction Company ....E 513 381-1111
Cincinnati **(G-4773)**

REMOTE DATABASE INFORMATION RETRIEVAL SVCS

Mirifex Systems LLC ....C 440 891-1210
Cleveland **(G-6001)**

RENT-A-CAR SVCS

Avis Administration ....D 937 898-2581
Vandalia **(G-18505)**

Budget Rent A Car System Inc ....D 216 267-2080
Cleveland **(G-5101)**

Cartemp USA Inc ....C 440 715-1000
Solon **(G-16832)**

Clerac LLC ....E 440 345-3999
Strongsville **(G-17290)**

Crawford Group Inc ....D 419 873-7360
Perrysburg **(G-15851)**

Dealers Group Limited ....E 440 352-4970
Beachwood **(G-1052)**

Enterprise Holdings Inc ....D 614 866-1480
Reynoldsburg **(G-16303)**

Enterprise Holdings Inc ....E 937 879-0023
Blue Ash **(G-1555)**

Falls Motor City Inc ....E 330 929-3066
Cuyahoga Falls **(G-9091)**

Geo Byers Sons Holding Inc ....E 614 239-1084
Columbus **(G-7658)**

George P Ballas Buick GMC Trck ....D 419 535-1000
Toledo **(G-17760)**

Hertz Corporation ....D 216 267-8900
Cleveland **(G-5688)**

Hertz Corporation ....E 513 533-3161
Cincinnati **(G-3699)**

Hertz Corporation ....E 937 890-2721
Vandalia **(G-18526)**

Hertz Corporation ....D 937 898-5806
Vandalia **(G-18527)**

National Rental (us) Inc ....E 937 890-0100
Vandalia **(G-18532)**

National Rental (us) Inc ....E 614 239-3270
Columbus **(G-8137)**

Precision Coatings Systems ....E 937 642-4727
Marysville **(G-13523)**

Rental Concepts Inc ....E 216 525-3870
Cleveland **(G-6308)**

Schoner Chevrolet Inc ....E 330 877-6731
Hartville **(G-11698)**

Thrifty Rent-A-Car System Inc ....E 440 842-1660
Cleveland **(G-6528)**

U Save Auto Rental ....E 330 925-2015
Rittman **(G-16410)**

RENTAL CENTERS: Furniture

Aarons Inc ....E 216 251-4500
Cleveland **(G-4889)**

Aarons Inc ....E 937 778-3577
Piqua **(G-15995)**

Aarons Inc ....E 216 587-2745
Maple Heights **(G-13279)**

Beacon Company ....E 330 733-8322
Akron **(G-92)**

Cort Business Services Corp ....D 513 759-8181
West Chester **(G-18900)**

RENTAL CENTERS: Party & Banquet Eqpt & Splys

A B C Rental Center East Inc ....E 216 475-8240
Cleveland **(G-4874)**

All Occasions Event Rental ....E 513 563-0600
Cincinnati **(G-2922)**

Camargo Rental Center Inc ....E 513 271-6510
Cincinnati **(G-3109)**

Columbus AAA Corp ....C 614 889-2840
Dublin **(G-10181)**

Jbjs Acquisitions LLC ....E 513 769-0393
Cincinnati **(G-3810)**

Made From Scratch Inc ....E 614 873-3344
Plain City **(G-16058)**

Maloney & Associates Inc ....E 330 479-7084
Canton **(G-2384)**

Prime Time Party Rental Inc ....E 937 296-9262
Moraine **(G-14687)**

RENTAL CENTERS: Tools

Black Swamp Equipment LLC ....E 419 445-0030
Archbold **(G-627)**

Bnd Rentals Inc ....E 937 898-5061
Vandalia **(G-18508)**

Chase Phipps ....E 330 754-0467
Canton **(G-2248)**

Home Depot USA Inc ....C 614 523-0600
Columbus **(G-7762)**

Home Depot USA Inc ....C 330 965-4790
Boardman **(G-1699)**

Home Depot USA Inc ....C 330 497-1810
Canton **(G-2347)**

Home Depot USA Inc ....C 513 688-1654
Cincinnati **(G-3719)**

Home Depot USA Inc ....C 330 922-3448
Cuyahoga Falls **(G-9100)**

Home Depot USA Inc ....C 937 312-9053
Dayton **(G-9499)**

Home Depot USA Inc ....C 937 312-9076
Dayton **(G-9500)**

Home Depot USA Inc ....C 216 692-2780
Euclid **(G-10642)**

Home Depot USA Inc ....C 216 676-9969
Cleveland **(G-5700)**

Home Depot USA Inc ....C 216 581-6611
Maple Heights **(G-13287)**

Home Depot USA Inc ....C 937 431-7346
Beavercreek **(G-1156)**

Home Depot USA Inc ....C 330 245-0280
Akron **(G-268)**

Home Depot USA Inc ....C 937 837-1551
Dayton **(G-9501)**

Home Depot USA Inc ....C 216 297-1303
Cleveland Heights **(G-6719)**

Home Depot USA Inc ....C 513 661-2413
Cincinnati **(G-3720)**

Home Depot USA Inc ....C 513 887-1450
Fairfield Township **(G-10810)**

Home Depot USA Inc ....C 419 476-4573
Toledo **(G-17805)**

Home Depot USA Inc ....C 440 357-0428
Mentor **(G-14061)**

Home Depot USA Inc ....C 513 631-1705
Cincinnati **(G-3721)**

Home Depot USA Inc ....C 440 684-1343
Highland Heights **(G-11734)**

Home Depot USA Inc ....C 419 537-1920
Toledo **(G-17806)**

Home Depot USA Inc ....C 614 878-9150
Columbus **(G-7763)**

Home Depot USA Inc ....C 440 826-9092
Strongsville **(G-17311)**

Home Depot USA Inc ....C 614 939-5036
Columbus **(G-7764)**

Home Depot USA Inc ....D 440 937-2240
Avon **(G-886)**

Home Depot USA Inc ....C 614 577-1601
Reynoldsburg **(G-16309)**

Home Depot USA Inc ....C 330 220-2654
Brunswick **(G-1932)**

Home Depot USA Inc ....C 419 626-6493
Sandusky **(G-16616)**

Home Depot USA Inc ....C 614 876-5558
Hilliard **(G-11776)**

Home Depot USA Inc ....C 440 324-7222
Elyria **(G-10515)**

Home Depot USA Inc ....C 419 529-0015
Ontario **(G-15552)**

Home Depot USA Inc ....C 216 251-3091
Cleveland **(G-5701)**

Janell Inc ....E 513 489-9111
Blue Ash **(G-1589)**

RENTAL SVCS: Aircraft

Flight Options Inc ....B 216 261-3880
Richmond Heights **(G-16389)**

Flight Options LLC ....C 216 261-3500
Cleveland **(G-5547)**

Flight Options Intl Inc ....E 216 261-3500
Richmond Heights **(G-16390)**

Netjets Inc ....E 614 239-5500
Columbus **(G-8174)**

RENTAL SVCS: Appliance

Rent-A-Center Inc ....D 330 337-1107
Salem **(G-16557)**

Rent-A-Center Inc ....D 419 382-8585
Toledo **(G-18002)**

RENTAL SVCS: Audio-Visual Eqpt & Sply

Bkg Holdings LLC............................E....... 614 252-7455
   Columbus *(G-7042)*

Cleveland Corporate Svcs Inc ....C....... 216 397-1492
   Cleveland *(G-5250)*

Colortone Audio Visual ....E....... 216 928-1530
   Cleveland *(G-5313)*

Live Technologies LLC ....D....... 614 278-7777
   Columbus *(G-7986)*

Northeast Projections Inc ....E....... 216 514-5023
   Cleveland *(G-6094)*

Prestige Audio Visual Inc ....D....... 513 641-1600
   Cincinnati *(G-4276)*

Rentech Solutions Inc ....D....... 216 398-1111
   Willoughby *(G-19568)*

RENTAL SVCS: Beach & Water Sports Eqpt

Ohio Dept Natural Resources ....E....... 740 869-3124
   Mount Sterling *(G-14746)*

Paul A Ertel ....D....... 216 696-8888
   Cleveland *(G-6183)*

Stockport Mill Country Inn Inc ....E....... 740 559-2822
   Stockport *(G-17183)*

RENTAL SVCS: Bicycle

Island Bike Rental Inc..........................E....... 419 285-2016
   Put In Bay *(G-16225)*

RENTAL SVCS: Business Machine & Electronic Eqpt

Comdoc Inc ....C....... 330 896-2346
   Uniontown *(G-18363)*

David Francis Corporation.....................C....... 216 524-0900
   Cleveland *(G-5408)*

Diane Sauer Chevrolet Inc ....D....... 330 373-1600
   Warren *(G-18702)*

Pitney Bowes Inc ....D....... 203 426-7025
   Brecksville *(G-1796)*

Pitney Bowes Inc ....D....... 740 374-5535
   Marietta *(G-13371)*

Setiawan Associates LLC ....E....... 614 285-5815
   Columbus *(G-8624)*

RENTAL SVCS: Clothing

Barberton Laundry & Cleaning ....D....... 330 825-6911
   Barberton *(G-947)*

Emmys Bridal Inc..................................E....... 419 628-7555
   Minster *(G-14532)*

RENTAL SVCS: Costume

Costume Specialists Inc.........................E....... 614 464-2115
   Columbus *(G-7378)*

RENTAL SVCS: Dress Suit

American Commodore Tu ....D....... 216 291-4601
   Cleveland *(G-4950)*

RENTAL SVCS: Electronic Eqpt, Exc Computers

Continuum Inc ....E....... 614 891-9200
   Westerville *(G-19246)*

Fern Exposition Services LLC.................E....... 513 621-6111
   Cincinnati *(G-3543)*

Modal Shop Inc ....D....... 513 351-9919
   Cincinnati *(G-4067)*

Warwick Communications Inc ....E....... 216 787-0300
   Broadview Heights *(G-1850)*

RENTAL SVCS: Golf Cart, Power

South E Harley Davidson Sls Co ....E....... 440 439-5300
   Cleveland *(G-6422)*

RENTAL SVCS: Home Cleaning & Maintenance Eqpt

Equipment Depot Ohio Inc.....................E....... 513 934-2121
   Lebanon *(G-12464)*

Stout Lori Cleaning & Such ....E....... 419 637-7644
   Gibsonburg *(G-11279)*

Two Men & A Vacuum LLC ....D....... 614 300-7970
   Columbus *(G-8791)*

RENTAL SVCS: Invalid Splys

Americas Best Medical Eqp Co ....E....... 330 928-0884
   Akron *(G-71)*

Pharmerica Long-Term Care Inc.............E....... 330 425-4450
   Twinsburg *(G-18305)*

RENTAL SVCS: Mobile Communication Eqpt

Mobilcomm Inc ....D....... 513 742-5555
   Cincinnati *(G-4066)*

RENTAL SVCS: Office Facilities & Secretarial Svcs

Renaissance Hotel Operating Co ....A....... 216 696-5600
   Cleveland *(G-6305)*

RENTAL SVCS: Oil Eqpt

Grady Rentals LLC................................E....... 330 627-2022
   Carrollton *(G-2570)*

RENTAL SVCS: Sound & Lighting Eqpt

HEat Ttal Fclty Slutions Inc....................E....... 740 965-3005
   Galena *(G-11159)*

RENTAL SVCS: Sporting Goods, NEC

Daves Running Shop Inc........................E....... 567 525-4767
   Findlay *(G-10896)*

RENTAL SVCS: Stores & Yards Eqpt

Ace Rental Place ....D....... 937 642-2891
   Marysville *(G-13482)*

E T B Ltd ....E....... 740 373-6686
   Marietta *(G-13326)*

RENTAL SVCS: Television

Countryside Rentals Inc.........................E....... 740 634-2666
   Bainbridge *(G-930)*

RENTAL SVCS: Tent & Tarpaulin

Advanced Tenting Solutions...................E....... 216 291-3300
   Newbury *(G-15117)*

Baker Bnngson Rlty Auctioneers...........E....... 419 547-7777
   Clyde *(G-6740)*

ONeil Awning and Tent Inc ....D....... 614 837-6352
   Canal Winchester *(G-2115)*

RENTAL SVCS: Trailer

A Duie Pyle Inc ....D....... 330 342-7750
   Streetsboro *(G-17243)*

Ample Trailer Leasing & Sales...............E....... 513 563-2550
   Cincinnati *(G-2957)*

Benedict Enterprises Inc........................E....... 513 539-9216
   Monroe *(G-14563)*

E & J Trailer Leasing Inc ....E....... 513 563-7366
   Cincinnati *(G-3462)*

E & J Trailer Sales & Service ....E....... 513 563-2550
   Cincinnati *(G-3463)*

Eleet Cryogenics Inc.............................E....... 330 874-4009
   Bolivar *(G-1702)*

Ryder Truck Rental Inc ....E....... 513 772-0223
   Cincinnati *(G-4419)*

Transport Services Inc ....D....... 440 582-4900
   Cleveland *(G-6543)*

U Haul Co of Northwestern Ohio ....E....... 419 478-1101
   Toledo *(G-18114)*

RENTAL SVCS: Tuxedo

Rondinelli Company Inc ....D....... 330 726-7643
   Youngstown *(G-20194)*

Rondinellis Tuxedo ....E....... 330 726-7768
   Youngstown *(G-20195)*

RENTAL SVCS: Vending Machine

Cuyahoga Vending Co Inc......................B....... 216 663-1457
   Maple Heights *(G-13284)*

Multi-Flow Dispensers Ohio Inc ....D....... 216 641-0200
   Brooklyn Heights *(G-1876)*

RENTAL SVCS: Video Disk/Tape, To The General Public

Emerge Ministries Inc............................E....... 330 865-8351
   Akron *(G-203)*

RENTAL SVCS: Work Zone Traffic Eqpt, Flags, Cones, Etc

A & A Safety Inc....................................E....... 513 943-6100
   Amelia *(G-563)*

American Roadway Logistics Inc............E....... 330 659-2003
   Richfield *(G-16346)*

Paul Peterson Company.........................E....... 614 486-4375
   Columbus *(G-8427)*

Paul Peterson Safety Div Inc ....E....... 614 486-4375
   Columbus *(G-8428)*

RENTAL: Passenger Car

Afford-A-Car Inc ....E....... 937 235-2700
   Tipp City *(G-17548)*

Budget Rent A Car System Inc ....E....... 937 898-1396
   Vandalia *(G-18509)*

Crawford Group Inc ....D....... 330 665-5432
   Akron *(G-170)*

Edison Local School District ....E....... 740 543-4011
   Amsterdam *(G-601)*

Leikin Motor Companies Inc ....D....... 440 946-6900
   Willoughby *(G-19544)*

Lincoln Mrcury Kings Auto Mall ....C....... 513 683-3800
   Cincinnati *(G-3933)*

Schmidt Daily Rental Inc........................D....... 419 874-4331
   Perrysburg *(G-15919)*

Spitzer Chevrolet Company....................E....... 330 966-9524
   Canton *(G-2482)*

Taylor Chevrolet Inc..............................C....... 740 653-2091
   Lancaster *(G-12440)*

RENTAL: Portable Toilet

Miller & Co Portable Toil Svcs ....E....... 330 453-9472
   Canton *(G-2405)*

Pro-Kleen Industrial Svcs Inc ....E....... 740 689-1886
   Lancaster *(G-12427)*

Rumpke Transportation Co LLC...............E....... 937 461-0004
   Dayton *(G-9740)*

Superr-Spdie Portable Svcs Inc ....E....... 330 733-9000
   Akron *(G-461)*

Waids Rainbow Rental Inc ....E....... 216 524-3736
   Akron *(G-493)*

Waste Management Ohio Inc ....D....... 800 343-6047
   Fairborn *(G-10688)*

RENTAL: Trucks, With Drivers

Aim Integrated Logistics Inc...................B....... 330 759-0438
   Girard *(G-11281)*

Aim Leasing Company ....D....... 330 759-0438
   Girard *(G-11282)*

Expeditus Transport LLC ....E....... 419 464-9450
   Sylvania *(G-17424)*

Hirzel Transfer Co ....E....... 419 287-3288
   Pemberville *(G-15804)*

J M Towning Inc ....E....... 614 876-7335
   Hilliard *(G-11779)*

Professional Drivers GA Inc ....E....... 614 529-8282
   Columbus *(G-8467)*

T R L Inc...C....... 330 448-4071
   Brookfield *(G-1856)*

RENTAL: Video Tape & Disc

Mile Inc ....C....... 614 252-6724
   Columbus *(G-8085)*

Mile Inc...D....... 614 794-2203
   Worthington *(G-19829)*

REPOSSESSION SVCS

G Robert Toney & Assoc Inc...................E....... 216 391-1900
   Cleveland *(G-5588)*

Interscope Manufacturing Inc..................E....... 513 423-8866
   Middletown *(G-14303)*

Millennium Cpitl Recovery Corp..............E....... 330 528-1450
   Hudson *(G-11998)*

REPRODUCTION SVCS: Video Tape Or Disk

Litigation Support Svcs Inc ....E....... 513 241-5605
   Cincinnati *(G-3940)*

Technicolor Thomson Group ....C....... 937 383-6000
   Wilmington *(G-19651)*

RESEARCH & DEVELOPMENT SVCS, COMMERCIAL: Engineering Lab

Applied Research Assoc Inc ....E....... 937 873-8166
   Dayton *(G-9235)*

S E R V I C E S

Employee Codes: A=Over 500 employees, B=251-500
C=101-250, D=51-100, E=25-50   2019 Harris Ohio
Services Directory   1541

Morris Technologies Inc................C...... 513 733-1611
Cincinnati *(G-4075)*
Quest Global Services-Na Inc...........D...... 513 563-8855
Cincinnati *(G-4327)*
Quest Global Services-Na Inc...........D...... 860 787-1600
Cincinnati *(G-4328)*
Zin Technologies Inc....................C...... 440 625-2200
Middleburg Heights *(G-14267)*

RESEARCH, DEV & TESTING SVCS, COMM: Chem Lab, Exc Testing

Guild Associates Inc...................D...... 614 798-8215
Dublin *(G-10236)*
Heraeus Precious Metals North..........E...... 937 264-1000
Vandalia *(G-18525)*
Ohio State University..................C...... 614 688-8220
Columbus *(G-8331)*
U S Laboratories Inc..................E...... 440 248-1223
Cleveland *(G-6558)*

RESEARCH, DEVELOPMENT & TEST SVCS, COMM: Business Analysis

Scanner Applications LLC..............E...... 513 248-5588
Milford *(G-14429)*

RESEARCH, DEVELOPMENT & TEST SVCS, COMM: Cmptr Hardware Dev

Aktion Associates Incorporated..........E...... 419 893-7001
Maumee *(G-13747)*

RESEARCH, DEVELOPMENT & TEST SVCS, COMM: Research, Exc Lab

Alphamicron Inc......................E...... 330 676-0648
Kent *(G-12213)*
Ohio State University..................E...... 614 292-9404
Columbus *(G-8341)*

RESEARCH, DEVELOPMENT & TESTING SVCS, COMM: Agricultural

Champaign Premium Grn Growers......E...... 937 826-3003
Milford Center *(G-14444)*
Ohio State University..................A...... 330 263-3700
Wooster *(G-19754)*
Ohio State University..................E...... 330 263-3725
Canton *(G-2431)*

RESEARCH, DEVELOPMENT & TESTING SVCS, COMM: Bus Economic Sve

Illumination Research Inc..............E...... 513 774-9531
Mason *(G-13597)*
Jobsohio.............................D...... 614 224-6446
Columbus *(G-7860)*

RESEARCH, DEVELOPMENT & TESTING SVCS, COMM: Natural Resource

Work Connections Intl LLC............E...... 419 448-4655
Tiffin *(G-17547)*

RESEARCH, DEVELOPMENT & TESTING SVCS, COMM: Research Lab

Akron Rubber Dev Lab Inc.............D...... 330 794-6600
Akron *(G-54)*
American Showa Inc..................E...... 740 965-4040
Sunbury *(G-17382)*
Applied Sciences Inc..................E...... 937 766-2020
Cedarville *(G-2579)*
Firstenergy Nuclear Oper Co............D...... 440 604-9836
Cleveland *(G-5539)*
PPG Architectural Finishes Inc..........B...... 440 826-5100
Strongsville *(G-17339)*

RESEARCH, DEVELOPMENT & TESTING SVCS, COMM: Sociological

Klein Associates Inc..................E...... 937 873-8166
Fairborn *(G-10679)*

RESEARCH, DEVELOPMENT & TESTING SVCS, COMMERCIAL: Business

Business Research Services.............E...... 216 831-5200
Cleveland *(G-5106)*

Lindner Clinical Trial Center............E...... 513 585-1777
Cincinnati *(G-3935)*

RESEARCH, DEVELOPMENT & TESTING SVCS, COMMERCIAL: Economic

Mahoning Youngstown Community......D...... 330 747-7921
Youngstown *(G-20112)*
Ohio State University..................D...... 614 442-7300
Columbus *(G-8320)*

RESEARCH, DEVELOPMENT & TESTING SVCS, COMMERCIAL: Education

Canton Med Educatn Foundation.........E...... 330 363-6783
Canton *(G-2237)*
Ohio State University..................D...... 740 376-7431
Marietta *(G-13364)*
Ohio State University..................D...... 740 593-2657
Athens *(G-794)*
Ohio State University..................D...... 614 292-4353
Columbus *(G-8316)*
Ohio State University..................D...... 614 292-5491
Columbus *(G-8305)*
University of Cincinnati................E...... 513 556-4054
Cincinnati *(G-4712)*

RESEARCH, DEVELOPMENT & TESTING SVCS, COMMERCIAL: Energy

Phycal Inc...........................E...... 440 460-2477
Cleveland *(G-6207)*

RESEARCH, DEVELOPMENT & TESTING SVCS, COMMERCIAL: Food

R & D Nestle Center Inc...............C...... 937 642-7015
Marysville *(G-13524)*
R & D Nestle Center Inc...............D...... 440 349-5757
Solon *(G-16888)*

RESEARCH, DEVELOPMENT & TESTING SVCS, COMMERCIAL: Medical

Applied Medical Technology Inc..........E...... 440 717-4000
Brecksville *(G-1769)*
Center For Eating Disorders.............E...... 614 896-8222
Columbus *(G-7153)*
Concord Biosciences LLC..............D...... 440 357-3200
Painesville *(G-15704)*
Icon Government......................B...... 330 278-2343
Hinckley *(G-11859)*
North Amercn Science Assoc Inc.........C...... 419 666-9455
Northwood *(G-15401)*
North Amercn Science Assoc Inc.........C...... 419 666-9455
Northwood *(G-15402)*
Syneos Health LLC...................C...... 513 381-5550
Cincinnati *(G-4561)*

RESEARCH, DEVELOPMENT & TESTING SVCS, COMMERCIAL: Physical

Atk Space Systems Inc.................E...... 937 490-4121
Beavercreek *(G-1205)*
Battelle Memorial Institute..............A...... 614 424-6424
Columbus *(G-7020)*
Battelle Memorial Institute..............B...... 614 424-5435
West Jefferson *(G-19104)*
Battelle Memorial Institute..............C...... 614 424-5435
West Jefferson *(G-19105)*
Charles Rver Labs Clveland Inc..........D...... 216 332-1665
Cleveland *(G-5169)*
Ftech R&D North America Inc............D...... 937 339-2777
Troy *(G-18202)*
Leidos Inc...........................E...... 330 405-9810
Twinsburg *(G-18291)*
Leidos Inc...........................D...... 937 431-2270
Beavercreek *(G-1164)*
Lubrizol Advanced Mtls Inc.............E...... 440 933-0400
Avon Lake *(G-923)*
Olon Ricerca Bioscience LLC............D...... 440 357-3300
Painesville *(G-15730)*
Velocys Inc..........................D...... 614 733-3300
Plain City *(G-16071)*

RESEARCH, DVLPT & TEST SVCS, COMM: Mkt Analysis or Research

8451 LLC............................C...... 513 632-1020
Cincinnati *(G-2886)*

Assistnce In Mktg Columbus Inc.........E...... 614 583-2100
Columbus *(G-6981)*
Burke Inc............................D...... 513 576-5700
Milford *(G-14374)*
Burke Inc............................C...... 513 241-5663
Cincinnati *(G-3090)*
Convergys Cstmer MGT Group Inc......B...... 513 723-6104
Cincinnati *(G-3358)*
Creative Marketing Enterprises.........D...... 419 867-4444
Sylvania *(G-17416)*
Deskey Associates Inc.................D...... 513 721-6800
Cincinnati *(G-3423)*
Directions Research Inc................C...... 513 651-2990
Cincinnati *(G-3432)*
Fields Marketing Research Inc...........D...... 513 821-6266
Cincinnati *(G-3545)*
Freedonia Publishing LLC..............D...... 440 684-9600
Cleveland *(G-5577)*
Friedman-Swift Associates Inc...........D...... 513 772-9200
Cincinnati *(G-3595)*
Gfk Custom Research LLC..............C...... 513 562-1507
Blue Ash *(G-1568)*
Great Lakes Mktg Assoc Inc............E...... 419 534-4700
Toledo *(G-17770)*
Honda R&D Americas Inc..............E...... 937 644-0439
Raymond *(G-16275)*
Intelliq Health.......................D...... 513 489-8838
Cincinnati *(G-3772)*
Ipsos-Insight LLC....................C...... 513 552-1100
Cincinnati *(G-3786)*
Leidos Inc...........................B...... 937 431-2220
Beavercreek *(G-1165)*
Maritzcx Research LLC.................B...... 419 725-4000
Maumee *(G-13815)*
Market Inquiry Llc....................E...... 513 794-1088
Blue Ash *(G-1603)*
Marketing Research Svcs Inc............D...... 513 772-7580
Cincinnati *(G-3970)*
Marketing Research Svcs Inc............D...... 513 579-1555
Cincinnati *(G-3971)*
Marketvision Research Inc..............E...... 513 603-6340
West Chester *(G-18969)*
Marketvision Research Inc..............D...... 513 791-3100
Blue Ash *(G-1604)*
Nielsen Consumer Insights Inc..........D...... 513 489-9000
Blue Ash *(G-1620)*
Northrop Grumman Technical............C...... 937 320-3100
Beavercreek Township *(G-1255)*
Opinions Ltd.........................E...... 440 893-0300
Chagrin Falls *(G-2652)*
Osborn Marketing Research Corp........E...... 440 871-1047
Westlake *(G-19389)*
Parker Marketing Research LLC..........C...... 513 248-8100
Milford *(G-14418)*
Q Fact Marketing Research Inc...........C...... 513 891-2271
Cincinnati *(G-4308)*
Ritter & Associates Inc.................E...... 419 535-5757
Maumee *(G-13846)*
SSS Consulting Inc....................E...... 937 259-1200
Dayton *(G-9788)*
Tns North America Inc.................D...... 513 621-7887
Cincinnati *(G-4610)*
Various Views Research Inc.............D...... 513 489-9000
Blue Ash *(G-1675)*
Wolf Sensory Inc.....................E...... 513 891-9100
Blue Ash *(G-1680)*

RESEARCH, DVLPT & TESTING SVCS, COMM: Mkt, Bus & Economic

Bionetics Corporation.................E...... 757 873-0900
Heath *(G-11702)*
National Rgstry Emrgncy Mdcl...........E...... 614 888-4484
Columbus *(G-8138)*

RESEARCH, DVLPT & TESTING SVCS, COMM: Survey, Mktg

Orc International Inc...................E...... 419 893-0029
Maumee *(G-13829)*

RESIDENTIAL CARE FOR CHILDREN

Nickolas Rsidential Trtmnt Ctr...........E...... 937 496-7100
Dayton *(G-9658)*

RESIDENTIAL CARE FOR THE HANDICAPPED

Ability Ctr of Greater Toledo............E...... 419 517-7123
Sylvania *(G-17411)*

Basinger Lfe Enhncmnt Sprt Svc ....D...... 614 557-5461
  Marysville *(G-13484)*
Donty Horton HM Care Dhhc LLC ....E...... 513 463-3442
  Cincinnati *(G-3440)*
Flat Rock Care Center ....C...... 419 483-7330
  Flat Rock *(G-10978)*
New England Rms Inc ....E...... 401 384-6759
  Worthington *(G-19830)*
Pine Ridge Pine Vllg Resdntl H ....E...... 513 724-3460
  Williamsburg *(G-19495)*
Residential Management Systems ....E...... 419 222-8806
  Lima *(G-12730)*
Residential Management Systems ....D...... 419 255-6060
  Maumee *(G-13843)*
St Vincent Family Centers ....C...... 614 252-0731
  Columbus *(G-8681)*
Stonewood Residential Inc ....E...... 216 267-9777
  Cleveland *(G-6470)*

RESIDENTIAL MENTAL HEALTH & SUBSTANCE ABUSE FACILITIES

A&L Home Care & Training Ctr ....C...... 740 886-7623
  Proctorville *(G-16215)*
Ahf Ohio Inc ....D...... 330 725-4123
  Medina *(G-13907)*
Ahf Ohio Inc ....D...... 614 760-8870
  Dublin *(G-10122)*
Ahf Ohio Inc ....D...... 937 256-4663
  Dayton *(G-9212)*
American Nursing Care Inc ....C...... 614 847-0555
  Zanesville *(G-20275)*
Archdiocese of Cincinnati ....E...... 513 231-5010
  Cincinnati *(G-2981)*
Assisted Living Concepts LLC ....E...... 740 450-2744
  Zanesville *(G-20277)*
Atria Senior Living Inc ....E...... 513 923-3711
  Cincinnati *(G-3001)*
Broadway Care Ctr Mple Hts LLC ....E...... 216 662-0551
  Beachwood *(G-1037)*
Brookdale Lving Cmmunities Inc ....D...... 614 734-1000
  Columbus *(G-7080)*
Brookdale Senior Living Inc ....D...... 513 229-3155
  Mason *(G-13546)*
Brookdale Senior Living Inc ....D...... 614 277-1200
  Grove City *(G-11413)*
Brookdale Senior Living Inc ....D...... 614 794-2499
  Westerville *(G-19228)*
Brookdale Senior Living Inc ....D...... 330 723-5825
  Medina *(G-13914)*
Brookdale Senior Living Inc ....D...... 937 738-7342
  Marysville *(G-13485)*
Cardinal Retirement Village ....E...... 330 928-7888
  Cuyahoga Falls *(G-9076)*
Carriage Court Company Inc ....E...... 740 654-4422
  Lancaster *(G-12376)*
Carriage House Assisted Living ....E...... 740 264-7667
  Steubenville *(G-17144)*
Childrens Cmprhensive Svcs Inc ....D...... 419 589-5511
  Mansfield *(G-13151)*
Choices For Vctims Dom Violence ....D...... 614 258-6080
  Columbus *(G-7194)*
Church of God Retirement Cmnty ....C...... 513 422-5600
  Middletown *(G-14295)*
Cleveland Christian Home Inc ....C...... 216 671-0977
  Cleveland *(G-5234)*
Cleveland Municipal School Dst ....C...... 216 459-9818
  Cleveland *(G-5279)*
Close To Home III ....E...... 740 534-1100
  Ironton *(G-12150)*
Community Assisted Living Inc ....E...... 740 653-2575
  Lancaster *(G-12385)*
Cornell Companies Inc ....C...... 419 747-3322
  Shelby *(G-16744)*
County of Hancock ....D...... 419 424-7050
  Findlay *(G-10892)*
Crossroads Center ....C...... 513 475-5300
  Cincinnati *(G-3382)*
Crystalwood Inc ....D...... 513 605-1000
  Cincinnati *(G-12738)*
D-R Training Center & Workshop ....C...... 419 289-0470
  Ashland *(G-671)*
Deaconess Long Term Care of MI ....A...... 513 487-3600
  Cincinnati *(G-3412)*
Domestic Violence Project Inc ....E...... 330 445-2000
  Canton *(G-2289)*
Drake Development Inc ....D...... 513 418-4370
  Cincinnati *(G-3443)*
Echoing Hills Village Inc ....D...... 740 594-3541
  Athens *(G-778)*

Echoing Hills Village Inc ....C...... 740 327-2311
  Warsaw *(G-18783)*
Emeritus Corporation ....E...... 330 477-5727
  Canton *(G-2299)*
Emeritus Corporation ....E...... 440 269-8600
  Willoughby *(G-19520)*
Extended Family Concepts Inc ....D...... 330 966-2555
  Canton *(G-2307)*
First Mental Retardation Corp ....E...... 937 262-3077
  Dayton *(G-9436)*
Friedman Vlg Retirement Cmnty ....E...... 419 443-1540
  Tiffin *(G-17519)*
Furney Group Home ....E...... 419 389-0152
  Toledo *(G-17750)*
Garden Manor Extended Care Cen ....C...... 513 420-5972
  Middletown *(G-14300)*
Gardens Western Reserve Inc ....D...... 330 928-4500
  Cuyahoga Falls *(G-9098)*
Gerspacher Companies ....E...... 330 725-1596
  Medina *(G-13943)*
Greenbrier Senior Living Cmnty ....D...... 440 888-0400
  Cleveland *(G-5642)*
Harmony Home Care Inc ....E...... 440 877-1977
  North Royalton *(G-15359)*
Havar Inc ....D...... 740 594-3533
  Athens *(G-782)*
Heinzerling Foundation ....A...... 614 272-2000
  Columbus *(G-7736)*
Hill Manor 1 Inc ....E...... 740 972-3227
  Columbus *(G-7750)*
Hocking Vly Cmnty Rsdntial Ctr ....E...... 740 753-4400
  Nelsonville *(G-14833)*
House of New Hope ....E...... 740 345-5437
  Saint Louisville *(G-16518)*
Judson ....D...... 216 791-2555
  Cleveland *(G-5809)*
Kingston Healthcare Company ....D...... 419 824-4200
  Sylvania *(G-17435)*
Larchwood Health Group LLC ....E...... 216 941-6100
  Cleveland *(G-5855)*
Lutheran Homes Society Inc ....E...... 419 724-1525
  Toledo *(G-17871)*
Lutheran Village At Wolf Creek ....C...... 419 861-2233
  Holland *(G-11893)*
Maple Knoll Communities Inc ....E...... 513 524-7990
  Oxford *(G-15679)*
Mulberry Garden A L S ....E...... 330 630-3980
  Munroe Falls *(G-14798)*
National Benevolent Associatio ....D...... 216 476-0333
  Cleveland *(G-6037)*
National Mentor Inc ....E...... 216 525-1885
  Cleveland *(G-6048)*
Newark Resident Homes Inc ....D...... 740 345-7231
  Newark *(G-15086)*
North Cntl Mntal Hlth Svcs Inc ....D...... 614 227-6865
  Columbus *(G-8198)*
North Hills Management Company ....D...... 740 450-9999
  Zanesville *(G-20346)*
Northgate Pk Retirement Cmnty ....D...... 513 923-3711
  Cincinnati *(G-4130)*
Oesterlen-Services For Youth ....C...... 937 399-6101
  Springfield *(G-17091)*
Otterbein Snior Lfstyle Chices ....C...... 419 394-2366
  Saint Marys *(G-16530)*
Parkcliffe Development ....D...... 419 381-9447
  Toledo *(G-17971)*
Providence House Inc ....E...... 216 651-5982
  Cleveland *(G-6263)*
Rehablttion Ctr At Mrietta Mem ....D...... 740 374-1407
  Marietta *(G-13375)*
RES-Care Inc ....E...... 740 526-0285
  Saint Clairsville *(G-16504)*
Rescue Incorporated ....C...... 419 255-9585
  Toledo *(G-18004)*
Second Mental Retardation ....E...... 937 262-3077
  Dayton *(G-9756)*
Select Spclty Hsptal-Akron LLC ....D...... 330 761-7500
  Akron *(G-423)*
Senior Care Inc ....E...... 419 516-4788
  Lima *(G-12338)*
Shalom House Inc ....E...... 614 239-1999
  Columbus *(G-8629)*
Shurmer Place At Altenheim ....E...... 440 238-9001
  Strongsville *(G-17346)*
Society For Handicapped Citzns ....E...... 937 746-4201
  Carlisle *(G-2554)*
Southeast Cmnty Mental Hlth Ctr ....C...... 614 225-0980
  Columbus *(G-8661)*
St Edward Home ....C...... 330 668-2828
  Fairlawn *(G-10851)*

Stone Gardens ....D...... 216 292-0070
  Cleveland *(G-6469)*
Style Crest Inc ....B...... 419 332-7369
  Fremont *(G-11099)*
Summerville Senior Living Inc ....D...... 440 354-5499
  Mentor *(G-14113)*
Sunrise Senior Living Inc ....E...... 614 418-9775
  Gahanna *(G-11149)*
Sunrise Senior Living LLC ....E...... 330 262-1615
  Wooster *(G-19771)*
Sunrise Senior Living LLC ....E...... 419 425-3440
  Findlay *(G-10966)*
Sunrise Senior Living LLC ....E...... 216 447-8909
  Cleveland *(G-6480)*
Traditions At Bath Rd Inc ....C...... 330 929-6272
  Cuyahoga Falls *(G-9132)*
Trilogy Health Services LLC ....D...... 419 935-6511
  Willard *(G-19489)*
Wallick Construction Co ....E...... 937 399-7009
  Springfield *(G-17132)*
Wesleyan Senior Living ....C...... 440 284-9000
  Elyria *(G-10572)*
Wood County Chld Svcs Assn ....D...... 419 352-7588
  Bowling Green *(G-1752)*
Zandex Health Care Corporation ....C...... 740 454-1400
  New Concord *(G-14906)*

RESIDENTIAL MENTALLY HANDICAPPED FACILITIES

599 W Main Corporation ....E...... 440 466-5901
  Geneva *(G-11235)*
Angels 4 Life LLC ....E...... 513 474-5683
  Cincinnati *(G-2968)*
Beeghly Oaks Operating LLC ....C...... 330 884-2300
  Boardman *(G-1696)*
Boyds Kinsman Home Inc ....E...... 330 876-5581
  Kinsman *(G-12318)*
Center For Eating Disorders ....E...... 614 896-8222
  Columbus *(G-7153)*
Childrens Forever Haven Inc ....E...... 440 250-9182
  Westlake *(G-19331)*
County of Montgomery ....B...... 937 264-0460
  Dayton *(G-9328)*
Elmwood Center Inc ....D...... 419 447-6885
  Tiffin *(G-17516)*
Filling Memorial Home of Mercy ....B...... 419 592-6451
  Napoleon *(G-14804)*
Foundations ....D...... 937 437-2311
  New Paris *(G-14942)*
Harbor ....E...... 800 444-3353
  Toledo *(G-17781)*
Leeda Services Inc ....E...... 330 392-6006
  Warren *(G-18722)*
Mental Health Service ....E...... 937 399-9500
  Springfield *(G-17070)*
Miami Valley Hsing Assn I Inc ....E...... 937 263-4449
  Dayton *(G-9623)*
North Point Eductl Svc Ctr ....E...... 440 967-0904
  Huron *(G-12028)*
Palm Crest East Inc ....E...... 440 322-0726
  Elyria *(G-10553)*
Places Inc ....D...... 937 461-4300
  Dayton *(G-9693)*
RES-Care Inc ....E...... 740 968-0181
  Flushing *(G-10981)*
RES-Care Inc ....E...... 330 627-7552
  Carrollton *(G-2575)*
RES-Care Inc ....E...... 740 941-1178
  Waverly *(G-18823)*
RES-Care Inc ....E...... 419 435-6620
  Fostoria *(G-11010)*
RES-Care Inc ....D...... 740 446-7549
  Gallipolis *(G-11213)*
RES-Care Inc ....E...... 330 453-4144
  Canton *(G-2457)*
Residential Concepts Inc ....E...... 513 724-6067
  Williamsburg *(G-19497)*
St Joseph Infant Maternity Hm ....C...... 513 563-2520
  Cincinnati *(G-4527)*
Supportcare Inc ....C...... 216 446-2650
  Independence *(G-12126)*
Triad Residential ....E...... 419 482-0711
  Maumee *(G-13863)*
Vista Centre ....D...... 330 424-5852
  Lisbon *(G-12806)*
Voca of Ohio ....E...... 419 435-5836
  Fostoria *(G-11014)*
Warren County Board Devlpmntal ....E...... 513 925-1813
  Lebanon *(G-12514)*

SERVICES

Willglo Services Inc ....E 614 443-3020
Columbus (G-8903)

RESIDENTIAL REMODELERS

Dun Rite Home Improvement Inc ....E 330 650-5322
Macedonia (G-13068)
Hays & Sons Construction Inc ....E 513 671-9110
Cincinnati (G-3686)
Menard Inc ....C 937 630-3550
Miamisburg (G-14187)
Menard Inc ....C 513 737-2204
Fairfield Township (G-10813)
Ohio Builders Resources LLC ....E 614 865-0306
Westerville (G-19194)
Ram Restoration LLC ....E 937 347-7418
Dayton (G-9726)
Residntial Coml Rnovations Inc ....E 330 815-1476
Clinton (G-6737)
Runyon & Sons Roofing Inc ....D 440 974-6810
Mentor (G-14105)
US Home Center LLC ....E 614 737-9000
Columbus (G-8834)

RESINS: Custom Compound Purchased

Flex Technologies Inc ....E 330 897-6311
Baltic (G-934)
Freeman Manufacturing & Sup Co ......E 440 934-1902
Avon (G-881)
Hexpol Compounding LLC ....C 440 834-4644
Burton (G-2016)
Polyone Corporation ....D 440 930-1000
Avon Lake (G-926)
Polyone Corporation ....D 440 930-1000
North Baltimore (G-15179)

RESORT HOTEL: Franchised

Aurora Hotel Partners LLC ....E 330 562-0767
Aurora (G-817)
Columbus Hotel Partnership LLC ....D 614 890-8600
Columbus (G-7288)
Seal Mayfield LLC ....E 440 684-4100
Mayfield Heights (G-13881)

RESORT HOTELS

Cardida Corporation ....E 740 439-4359
Kimbolton (G-12311)
Cedar Point Park LLC ....D 419 627-2500
Sandusky (G-16583)
Coshocton Village Inn Suites ....E 740 622-9455
Coshocton (G-9010)
Crefiii Waramaug ....D 937 322-3600
Springfield (G-17027)
Findlay Inn & Conference Ctr ....D 419 422-5682
Findlay (G-10904)
Great Bear Lodge Sandusky LLC ......B 419 609-6000
Sandusky (G-16613)
Hide-A-Way Hills Club ....E 740 746-9589
Sugar Grove (G-17374)
Home2 By Hilton ....E 513 422-3454
West Chester (G-18944)
Hopkins Partners ....C 216 267-1500
Cleveland (G-5705)
Hotel 50 S Front Opco LP ....D 614 228-4600
Columbus (G-7775)
Lmn Development LLC ....D 419 433-7200
Sandusky (G-16623)
Mad River Mountain Resort ....E 937 303-3646
Zanesfield (G-20272)
Olshan Hotel Management Inc ....E 614 416-8000
Columbus (G-8374)
Qh Management Company LLC ....D 440 497-1100
Concord Twp (G-8946)
Salt Fork Resort Club Inc ....A 740 498-8116
Kimbolton (G-12312)
Sawmill Creek Resort Ltd ....C 419 433-3800
Huron (G-12031)

RESPIRATORY THERAPY CLINIC

Genesis Respiratory Svcs Inc ....C 740 354-4363
Portsmouth (G-16138)

REST HOME, WITH HEALTH CARE INCIDENTAL

Benjamin Rose Institute ....D 216 791-3580
Cleveland (G-5056)
Bradley Bay Assisted Living ....E 440 871-4509
Bay Village (G-1021)

County of Medina ....E 330 723-9553
Medina (G-13925)
Laurel Lk Retirement Cmnty Inc ....B 330 650-0681
Hudson (G-11993)
Ohio Living ....E 614 888-7800
Columbus (G-8272)
Ohio Presbt Retirement Svcs ....C 513 539-7391
Monroe (G-14579)
Roman Cthlic Docese Youngstown ....C 330 875-5562
Louisville (G-12973)
Ursuline Convent Sacred Heart ....E 419 531-8990
Toledo (G-18131)

RESTAURANT EQPT REPAIR SVCS

Cov-Ro Inc ....E 330 856-3176
Warren (G-18693)
Harry C Lobalzo & Sons Inc ....E 330 666-6758
Akron (G-251)
Kens Beverage Inc ....E 513 874-8200
Fairfield (G-10743)

RESTAURANTS: Fast Food

Escape Enterprises Inc ....E 614 224-0300
Columbus (G-7533)
Fortis North Canton LLC ....E 330 682-5984
North Canton (G-15204)
Marcus Theatres Corporation ....D 614 436-9818
Columbus (G-8018)
Winking Lizard Inc ....D 330 220-9944
Brunswick (G-1948)

RESTAURANTS:Full Svc, American

Aurora Hotel Partners LLC ....E 330 562-0767
Aurora (G-817)
Bass Lake Tavern Inc ....D 440 285-3100
Chardon (G-2688)
Beverly Hills Inn La Llc ....E 859 494-9151
Aberdeen (G-1)
City Life Inc ....E 216 523-5899
Cleveland (G-5186)
Concord Dayton Hotel II LLC ....E 937 223-1000
Dayton (G-9316)
Connor Concepts Inc ....D 937 291-1661
Dayton (G-9317)
Crefiii Waramaug ....D 937 322-3600
Springfield (G-17027)
Durga Llc ....D 513 771-2080
Cincinnati (G-3457)
Elms Country Club Inc ....E 330 833-2668
North Lawrence (G-15258)
Epiqurian Inns ....E 614 885-2600
Worthington (G-19807)
Henderson Road Rest Systems ....E 614 442-3310
Columbus (G-7739)
Hillbrook Club Inc ....E 440 247-4940
Cleveland (G-5690)
Hrm Enterprises Inc ....C 330 877-9353
Hartville (G-11691)
Mackil Inc ....E 937 833-3310
Brookville (G-1915)
Northeast Cincinnati Hotel LLC ....C 513 459-9800
Mason (G-13623)
Oberlin College ....D 440 935-1475
Oberlin (G-15515)
Paul A Ertel ....D 216 696-8888
Cleveland (G-6183)
River Road Hotel Corp ....E 614 267-7461
Columbus (G-8535)
Sam BS Restaurant ....E 419 353-2277
Bowling Green (G-1748)
Stockport Mill Country Inn Inc ....E 740 559-2822
Stockport (G-17183)
Town House Motor Lodge Corp ....E 740 452-4511
Zanesville (G-20367)
Travelcenters of America LLC ....A 440 808-9100
Westlake (G-19415)

RESTAURANTS:Full Svc, Diner

Hyatt Corporation ....B 614 463-1234
Columbus (G-7791)

RESTAURANTS:Full Svc, Ethnic Food

Tappan Lake Marina Inc ....E 740 269-2031
Scio (G-16664)

RESTAURANTS:Full Svc, Family

Bistro Off Broadway ....E 937 316-5000
Greenville (G-11366)
Buffalo Jacks ....E 937 473-2524
Covington (G-9046)
Mason Family Resorts LLC ....B 513 339-0141
Mason (G-13615)
R P L Corporation ....C 937 335-0021
Troy (G-18223)
Sb Hotel LLC ....E 614 793-2244
Dublin (G-10329)
Valley Hospitality Inc ....E 740 374-9660
Marietta (G-13395)

RESTAURANTS:Full Svc, Family, Chain

Bennett Enterprises Inc ....B 419 874-3111
Perrysburg (G-15838)
Dino Persichetti ....E 330 821-9600
Alliance (G-530)
Fairlawn Associates Ltd ....C 330 867-5000
Fairlawn (G-10826)
Island House Inc ....E 419 734-0100
Port Clinton (G-16110)
Red Robin Gourmet Burgers Inc ....D 330 305-1080
Canton (G-2452)
Roscoe Village Foundation ....D 740 622-2222
Coshocton (G-9026)
Skylane LLC ....E 330 527-9999
Garrettsville (G-11230)
Skyline Chili Inc ....C 513 874-1188
Fairfield (G-10785)

RESTAURANTS:Full Svc, Family, Independent

AK Group Hotels Inc ....E 937 372-9921
Xenia (G-19888)
Alsan Corporation ....D 330 385-3636
East Liverpool (G-10396)
Amish Door Inc ....B 330 359-5464
Wilmot (G-19657)
Bird Enterprises LLC ....E 330 674-1457
Millersburg (G-14460)
Cherry Valley Lodge ....E 740 788-1200
Newark (G-15022)
Detroit Westfield LLC ....D 330 666-4131
Akron (G-184)
Granville Hospitality Llc ....D 740 587-3333
Granville (G-11342)
Lees Roby Inc ....E 330 872-0983
Newton Falls (G-15139)
Louisville Frternal Order of E ....E 330 875-2113
Louisville (G-12968)
Moundbuilders Country Club Co ....D 740 344-4500
Newark (G-15076)
Old Barn Out Back Inc ....D 419 999-3989
Lima (G-12711)
Riverside Cmnty Urban Redev ....C 330 929-3000
Cuyahoga Falls (G-9120)
Sauder Village ....B 419 446-2541
Archbold (G-638)
Shoreby Club Inc ....D 216 851-2587
Cleveland (G-6406)
The Oaks Lodge ....E 330 769-2601
Chippewa Lake (G-2838)

RESTAURANTS:Full Svc, French

Refectory Restaurant Inc ....E 614 451-9774
Columbus (G-8501)

RESTAURANTS:Full Svc, Italian

Cabin Restaurant ....E 330 562-9171
Aurora (G-823)
Carrie Cerino Restaurants Inc ....C 440 237-3434
Cleveland (G-5129)
Dutchman Hospitality Group Inc ....C 614 873-3414
Plain City (G-16050)
Leos La Piazza Inc ....E 937 339-5553
Troy (G-18210)
Marios International Spa & Ht ....C 330 562-5141
Aurora (G-835)
Queens Tower Restaurant Inc ....E 513 251-6467
Cincinnati (G-4324)
Spagnas ....E 740 376-9245
Marietta (G-13383)

RESTAURANTS:Full Svc, Mexican

Food Concepts Intl Inc ....D.... 513 336-7449
Mason (G-13579)

RESTAURANTS:Full Svc, Seafood

James Lafontaine..................................E 740 474-5052
Circleville (G-4836)

RESTAURANTS:Full Svc, Steak

Brown Derby Roadhouse ....E 330 528-3227
Hudson (G-11968)

RESTAURANTS:Full Svc, Steak & Barbecue

101 River Inc ....E 440 352-6343
Grand River (G-11331)

RESTAURANTS:Limited Svc, Box Lunch Stand

Sand Ridge Golf Club ....D.... 440 285-8088
Chardon (G-2713)

RESTAURANTS:Limited Svc, Carry-Out Only, Exc Pizza

Tony Packos Toledo LLC ....D.... 419 691-6054
Toledo (G-18105)

RESTAURANTS:Limited Svc, Chicken

Travelcenters of America LLC ....B 724 981-9464
Westlake (G-19414)

RESTAURANTS:Limited Svc, Coffee Shop

Fairfield Industries Inc ....E 740 409-1539
Carroll (G-2557)
Mocha House Inc ....E 330 392-3020
Warren (G-18731)

RESTAURANTS:Limited Svc, Fast-Food, Chain

D J- Seve Group Inc ....E 614 888-6600
Lewis Center (G-12537)
McDonalds Corporation ....E 614 682-1128
Columbus (G-8044)
Pam Johnsonident ....D.... 419 946-4551
Mount Gilead (G-14733)
Wendys Company ....B 614 764-3100
Dublin (G-10374)
Wendys Restaurants LLC ....C 614 764-3100
Dublin (G-10375)
White Castle System Inc ....B 614 228-5781
Columbus (G-8896)

RESTAURANTS:Limited Svc, Fast-Food, Independent

McDonalds 3490....................................E 330 762-7747
Akron (G-326)
Skateworld Inc.......................................E 937 294-4032
Dayton (G-9771)

RESTAURANTS:Limited Svc, Grill

Gosh Enterprises Inc ....E 614 923-4700
Columbus (G-7681)
OBannon Creek Golf Club......................E 513 683-5657
Loveland (G-13019)
Rivals Sports Grille LLC ....E 216 267-0005
Middleburg Heights (G-14258)
Waterfront & Associates Inc ....B 859 581-1414
Cincinnati (G-4770)

RESTAURANTS:Limited Svc, Ice Cream Stands Or Dairy Bars

North Lima Dairy Queen Inc...................E 330 549-3220
North Lima (G-15273)
Strike Zone Inc ....D.... 440 235-4420
Olmsted Twp (G-15541)
Youngs Jersey Dairy Inc ....B 937 325-0629
Yellow Springs (G-19941)

RESTAURANTS:Limited Svc, Lunch Counter

Bpo Elks of USA....................................E 740 622-0794
Coshocton (G-9000)

RESTAURANTS:Limited Svc, Pizza

Claire De Leigh Corp ....E 614 459-6575
Columbus (G-7216)
Georgetown Vineyards Inc.....................E 740 435-3222
Cambridge (G-2069)
Premier Broadcasting Co Inc ....E 614 866-0700
Columbus (G-8458)

RESTAURANTS:Limited Svc, Pizzeria, Chain

Cassanos Inc...E 937 294-8400
Dayton (G-9285)
Cec Entertainment Inc ....D.... 937 439-1108
Miamisburg (G-14149)
East of Chicago Pizza Inc......................E 419 225-7116
Lima (G-12630)
Larosas Inc..A...... 513 347-5660
Cincinnati (G-3911)
Marcos Inc...E 419 885-4844
Toledo (G-17894)

RESTAURANTS:Limited Svc, Pizzeria, Independent

Fat Jacks Pizza II Inc ....E 419 227-1813
Lima (G-12639)

RESTAURANTS:Ltd Svc, Ice Cream, Soft Drink/Fountain Stands

David W Milliken....................................E 740 998-5023
Frankfort (G-11018)

RESTROOM CLEANING SVCS

Corporate Cleaning Inc ....E 614 203-6051
Columbus (G-7371)
Image By J & K LLC...............................B 888 667-6929
Maumee (G-13802)
Living Matters LLC.................................E 866 587-8074
Cleveland (G-5876)

RETAIL BAKERY: Bagels

Bagel Place Inc......................................E 419 885-1000
Toledo (G-17604)

RETAIL BAKERY: Bread

Busken Bakery Inc.................................D.... 513 871-2114
Cincinnati (G-3097)
Covelli Family Ltd Partnership ....E 330 856-3176
Warren (G-18694)
Norcia Bakery ....E 330 454-1077
Canton (G-2419)
Schwebel Baking Company ....C 440 248-1500
Solon (G-16895)

RETAIL FIREPLACE STORES

Youngstown Propane Inc ....E 330 792-6571
Youngstown (G-20266)

RETAIL LUMBER YARDS

Carter-Jones Lumber Company ....C 330 673-6100
Kent (G-12218)
Carter-Jones Lumber Company ....D.... 330 784-5441
Akron (G-119)
Fifth Avenue Lumber Co ....D.... 614 294-0068
Columbus (G-7575)
Gms Inc...E 937 222-4444
Dayton (G-9463)
L & W Supply Corporation ....E 513 723-1150
Cincinnati (G-3899)
Thomas Do-It Center Inc ....D.... 740 446-2002
Gallipolis (G-11215)

RETAIL STORES: Alarm Signal Systems

Guardian Protection Svcs Inc.................E 330 797-1570
Youngstown (G-20059)
Northwestern Ohio SEC Systems ....E 419 227-1655
Lima (G-12708)
Research & Investigation Assoc ....E 419 526-1299
Mansfield (G-13234)
State Alarm Inc ....E 888 726-8111
Youngstown (G-20217)

RETAIL STORES: Alcoholic Beverage Making Eqpt & Splys

Gene Ptacek Son Fire Eqp Inc...............E 216 651-8300
Cleveland (G-5602)

RETAIL STORES: Audio-Visual Eqpt & Splys

Cleveland Corporate Svcs Inc ....C 216 397-1492
Cleveland (G-5250)
Findaway World LLC ....D.... 440 893-0808
Solon (G-16849)

RETAIL STORES: Business Machines & Eqpt

Blakemans Valley Off Eqp Inc................E 330 729-1000
Youngstown (G-19965)
Cincinnati Copiers Inc ....C 513 769-0606
Blue Ash (G-1525)
Modern Office Methods Inc....................E 614 891-3693
Westerville (G-19281)
Toshiba Amer Bus Solutions Inc ....E 216 642-7555
Cleveland (G-6533)

RETAIL STORES: Christmas Lights & Decorations

Donzells Flower & Grdn Ctr Inc..............E 330 724-0550
Akron (G-191)
McCoy Landscape Services Inc ....E 740 375-2730
Marion (G-13447)

RETAIL STORES: Cleaning Eqpt & Splys

Jani-Source LLC ....E 740 374-6298
Marietta (G-13340)

RETAIL STORES: Communication Eqpt

Cellco Partnership ....D.... 330 345-6465
Wooster (G-19698)
Mobilcomm Inc.......................................D.... 513 742-5555
Cincinnati (G-4066)
Professional Telecom Svcs....................E 513 232-7700
Cincinnati (G-4294)
Shawntech Communications Inc............E 937 898-4900
Miamisburg (G-14220)

RETAIL STORES: Concrete Prdts, Precast

J B M Cleaning & Supply Co...................E 330 837-8805
Massillon (G-13700)

RETAIL STORES: Educational Aids & Electronic Training Mat

Bendon Inc...D.... 419 207-3600
Ashland (G-657)

RETAIL STORES: Electronic Parts & Eqpt

Ctd Investments LLC ....E 614 570-9949
Columbus (G-7403)
Mendelson Electronics Co Inc................E 937 461-3525
Dayton (G-9606)

RETAIL STORES: Farm Eqpt & Splys

Ag-Pro Ohio LLC....................................D.... 740 450-7446
Zanesville (G-20273)
Ag-Pro Ohio LLC....................................C 614 879-6620
London (G-12858)
Carmichael Equipment Inc.....................E 740 446-2412
Bidwell (G-1467)
Cope Farm Equipment Inc ....E 330 821-5867
Alliance (G-528)
Hull Bros Inc..E 419 375-2827
Fort Recovery (G-10992)
Krystowski Tractor Sales Inc..................E 440 647-2015
Wellington (G-18842)
Streacker Tractor Sales Inc....................E 419 422-6973
Findlay (G-10965)
Witmers Inc..E 330 427-2147
Salem (G-16567)

RETAIL STORES: Farm Machinery, NEC

Homan Inc..E 419 925-4349
Maria Stein (G-13307)
Kuester Implement Company Inc............E 740 944-1502
Bloomingdale (G-1490)
Lefeld Implement Inc ....E 419 678-2375
Coldwater (G-6761)

SERVICES

Shearer Farm Inc ....E 419 529-6160
  Ontario (G-15571)

RETAIL STORES: Fiberglass Materials, Exc Insulation

Romitech Inc ....E 937 297-9529
  Dayton (G-9739)

RETAIL STORES: Fire Extinguishers

Koorsen Fire & Security Inc ....E 937 324-9405
  Vandalia (G-18530)

RETAIL STORES: Hair Care Prdts

G E G Enterprises Inc ....E 330 477-3133
  Canton (G-2321)
Mark Luikart Inc ....E 330 339-9141
  New Philadelphia (G-14973)
Salon Hazelton ....E 419 874-9404
  Perrysburg (G-15917)

RETAIL STORES: Hearing Aids

Nelson & Bold Inc ....E 440 975-1422
  Willoughby (G-19554)
United Rehabilitation Services ....D 937 233-1230
  Dayton (G-9832)
University Otolaryngologists ....E 614 273-2241
  Columbus (G-8820)

RETAIL STORES: Hospital Eqpt & Splys

Boardman Medical Supply Co ....C 330 545-6700
  Girard (G-11283)
Garys Pharmacy Inc ....E 937 456-5777
  Eaton (G-10446)
Health Services Inc ....E 330 837-7678
  Massillon (G-13694)
Millers Rental and Sls Co Inc ....D 330 753-8600
  Akron (G-339)

RETAIL STORES: Ice

D & D Investment Co ....E 614 272-6567
  Columbus (G-7405)
Home City Ice Company ....E 614 836-2877
  Groveport (G-11518)

RETAIL STORES: Medical Apparatus & Splys

Advanced Medical Equipment Inc ....E 937 534-1080
  Kettering (G-12290)
American Home Health Care Inc ....E 614 237-1133
  Columbus (G-6925)
Amerimed Inc ....E 513 942-3670
  West Chester (G-18866)
Apria Healthcare LLC ....E 216 485-1180
  Cleveland (G-4997)
Fairfield Medical Center ....A 740 687-8000
  Lancaster (G-12399)
Genesis Respiratory Svcs Inc ....C 740 354-4363
  Portsmouth (G-16138)
Modern Medical Inc ....C 800 547-3330
  Westerville (G-19186)
Sarnova Inc ....D 614 760-5000
  Dublin (G-10328)
Sateri Home Inc ....D 330 758-8106
  Youngstown (G-20204)
Seeley Enterprises Company ....E 440 293-6600
  Andover (G-608)
Toledo Medical Equipment Co ....E 419 866-7120
  Maumee (G-13862)
University Mednet ....B 216 383-0100
  Euclid (G-10660)

RETAIL STORES: Mobile Telephones & Eqpt

Aka Wireless Inc ....E 216 213-8040
  Hartville (G-11682)
Cellco Partnership ....E 440 953-1155
  Mentor (G-14027)
Cellco Partnership ....E 440 646-9625
  Cleveland (G-5147)
Cellco Partnership ....E 440 846-8881
  Strongsville (G-17289)
Cellco Partnership ....E 740 397-6609
  Mount Vernon (G-14752)
Cellco Partnership ....E 614 459-7200
  Columbus (G-7148)
Cellco Partnership ....E 937 429-4000
  Beavercreek (G-1138)

Cellco Partnership ....E 513 671-2200
  Cincinnati (G-3146)
Cellco Partnership ....E 513 697-0222
  Cincinnati (G-3147)
Cellco Partnership ....E 740 522-6446
  Newark (G-15021)
Commercial Electronics Inc ....E 740 281-0180
  Newark (G-15023)
Diamond Company Inc ....C 937 374-1111
  Xenia (G-19898)
Magic Industries Inc ....E 614 759-8422
  Columbus (G-8008)

RETAIL STORES: Orthopedic & Prosthesis Applications

Blatchford Inc ....D 937 291-3636
  Miamisburg (G-14145)
Hanger Prosthetics & ....E 330 633-9807
  Tallmadge (G-17475)
Unity Health Network LLC ....E 330 626-0549
  Streetsboro (G-17276)

RETAIL STORES: Pet Food

Petsmart Inc ....E 513 752-8463
  Cincinnati (G-2865)
Petsmart Inc ....E 937 236-1335
  Huber Heights (G-11957)
Petsmart Inc ....D 614 418-9389
  Columbus (G-8443)
Petsmart Inc ....E 330 922-4114
  Cuyahoga Falls (G-9117)
Petsmart Inc ....E 330 629-2479
  Youngstown (G-20154)
Petsmart Inc ....E 330 544-1499
  Niles (G-15167)
Petsmart Inc ....E 614 497-3001
  Groveport (G-11529)
Petsmart Inc ....E 440 974-1100
  Mentor (G-14096)

RETAIL STORES: Pet Splys

Miraclecorp Products ....D 937 293-9994
  Moraine (G-14680)
Petsmart Inc ....E 513 248-4954
  Milford (G-14422)

RETAIL STORES: Photocopy Machines

ABC Appliance Inc ....E 419 693-4414
  Oregon (G-15581)
Donnellon Mc Carthy Inc ....E 937 299-0200
  Moraine (G-14649)
Woodhull LLC ....E 937 294-5311
  Springboro (G-16989)

RETAIL STORES: Picture Frames, Ready Made

Darice Inc ....C 440 238-9150
  Strongsville (G-17297)

RETAIL STORES: Plumbing & Heating Splys

Ferguson Enterprises Inc ....E 614 876-8555
  Hilliard (G-11767)
Gross Plumbing Incorporated ....E 440 324-9999
  Elyria (G-10514)
Horizon Mechanical and Elec ....E 419 529-2738
  Mansfield (G-13183)
Robertson Htg Sup Aliance Ohio ....C 330 821-9180
  Alliance (G-546)
Southtown Heating & Cooling ....E 937 320-9900
  Moraine (G-14699)

RETAIL STORES: Police Splys

Walter F Stephens Jr Inc ....E 937 746-0521
  Franklin (G-11041)

RETAIL STORES: Religious Goods

Christian Aid Ministries ....E 330 893-2428
  Millersburg (G-14465)

RETAIL STORES: Safety Splys & Eqpt

Paul Peterson Safety Div Inc ....E 614 486-4375
  Columbus (G-8428)

RETAIL STORES: Technical Aids For The Handicapped

Wmk LLC ....E 440 951-4335
  Mentor (G-14125)

RETAIL STORES: Telephone & Communication Eqpt

Cellco Partnership ....E 419 843-2995
  Toledo (G-17641)
Cellco Partnership ....E 440 779-1313
  North Olmsted (G-15279)
High Line Corporation ....E 330 848-8800
  Akron (G-261)
Jacobs Telephone Contrs Inc ....E 614 527-8977
  Hilliard (G-11780)
Maximum Communications Inc ....E 513 489-3414
  Cincinnati (G-3981)

RETAIL STORES: Telephone Eqpt & Systems

C T Wireless ....D 937 653-2208
  Urbana (G-18420)
Cellco Partnership ....D 419 333-1009
  Fremont (G-11061)
Cellco Partnership ....E 419 424-2351
  Findlay (G-10886)
Cellco Partnership ....D 419 897-9133
  Maumee (G-13768)
Cellco Partnership ....E 330 493-7979
  Canton (G-2247)
Cellco Partnership ....E 216 573-5880
  Independence (G-12056)
Cellco Partnership ....E 614 793-8989
  Dublin (G-10164)
Chillicothe Telephone Company ....D 740 772-8361
  Chillicothe (G-2768)
Spectrum Networks Inc ....E 513 697-2000
  Cincinnati (G-4514)
Twin Comm Inc ....E 740 774-4701
  Marietta (G-13390)

RETAIL STORES: Theatrical Eqpt & Splys

Vincent Ltg Systems Co Inc ....E 216 475-7600
  Solon (G-16912)

RETAIL STORES: Tropical Fish

RMS Aquaculture Inc ....E 216 433-1340
  Cleveland (G-6331)

RETAIL STORES: Typewriters & Business Machines

Perry Pro Tech Inc ....D 419 228-1360
  Lima (G-12720)

RETAIL STORES: Water Purification Eqpt

Enting Water Conditioning Inc ....E 937 294-5100
  Moraine (G-14653)
Gordon Brothers Inc ....E 800 331-7611
  Salem (G-16545)
Great Lakes Water Treatment ....E 216 464-8292
  Cleveland (G-5631)

RETAIL STORES: Welding Splys

Albright Welding Supply Co Inc ....E 330 264-2021
  Wooster (G-19685)

RETIREMENT COMMUNITIES WITH NURSING

Berea Lk Twers Rtirement Cmnty ....E 440 243-9050
  Berea (G-1416)
Briarwood Ltd ....D 330 688-1828
  Stow (G-17193)
Brookdale Lving Cmmunities Inc ....E 937 399-1216
  Springfield (G-17002)
Brookdale Senior Living Commun ....E 330 829-0180
  Alliance (G-519)
Brookdale Senior Living Commun ....E 937 203-8443
  Beavercreek (G-1208)
Brookdale Senior Living Commun ....E 937 548-6800
  Greenville (G-11367)
Brookdale Senior Living Inc ....E 419 756-5599
  Mansfield (G-13146)
Brookdale Snior Lving Cmmnties ....E 740 366-0005
  Newark (G-15015)

Brookdale Snior Lving Cmmnties ....E 937 832-8500
Englewood (G-10580)

Brookdale Snior Lving Cmmnties ....E 419 354-5300
Bowling Green (G-1726)

Brookdale Snior Lving Cmmnties ....E 740 681-9903
Lancaster (G-12373)

Brookdale Snior Lving Cmmnties ....E 419 423-4440
Findlay (G-10884)

Brookdale Snior Lving Cmmnties ....E 330 249-1071
Austintown (G-856)

Brookdale Snior Lving Cmmnties ....E 419 756-5599
Mansfield (G-13147)

Brookdale Snior Lving Cmmnties ....E 937 773-0500
Piqua (G-15998)

Brookdale Snior Lving Cmmnties ....E 330 793-0085
Youngstown (G-19976)

Capital Senior Living ....E 440 356-5444
Rocky River (G-16425)

Carroll Golden Age Retreat ....E 330 627-4665
Carrollton (G-2561)

Countryview Assistant Living ....E 740 489-5351
Lore City (G-12952)

Crystal Care Centers Inc ....D 419 747-2666
Mansfield (G-13162)

Crystalwood Inc ....D 513 605-1000
Cincinnati (G-3383)

Friendship Vlg of Dublin Ohio ....C 614 764-1600
Dublin (G-10232)

Gardens Western Reserve Inc ....D 330 342-9100
Streetsboro (G-17252)

Guernsey Health Enterprises.................A 740 439-3561
Cambridge (G-2072)

Hamlet Village In Chagrin FLS ....D 440 247-4200
Chagrin Falls (G-2648)

Hospice of North Central Ohio ....E 419 281-7107
Ashland (G-675)

Inn At Hillenvale Ltd ....D 740 392-8245
Mount Vernon (G-14769)

Judson Palmer Home Corp ....E 419 422-9656
Findlay (G-10931)

Koinonia Homes Inc ....D 216 351-5361
Cleveland (G-5836)

Lutheran Memorial Home Inc................D 419 502-5700
Toledo (G-17873)

Lutheran Village At Wolf Creek..............C 419 861-2233
Holland (G-11893)

McV Health Care Facilities ....C 513 398-1486
Mason (G-13617)

Medina Medical Investors Ltd ....C 330 483-3131
Medina (G-13978)

Miami Valley Urgent Care ....E 937 252-2000
Dayton (G-9627)

Minford Retirement Center LLC............E 740 820-2821
Minford (G-14526)

Mt Healthy Christian Home Inc ....C 513 931-5000
Cincinnati (G-4081)

North Park Retirement Cmnty................E 216 267-0555
Cleveland (G-6079)

Ohio Presbt Retirement Svcs ....B 937 498-2391
Sidney (G-16789)

Olmsted Manor Retirement Prpts.........E 440 250-4080
Westlake (G-19387)

Red Carpet Health Care Center ....C 740 439-4401
Cambridge (G-2081)

Rest Haven Nursing Home Inc ....C 937 548-1138
Greenville (G-11392)

Royalton Senior Living Inc.....................E 440 582-4111
North Royalton (G-15366)

Sunrise Senior Living Inc ....D 614 457-3500
Upper Arlington (G-18402)

Valley View Alzhimers Care Ctr ....D 740 998-2948
Frankfort (G-11019)

Western Rsrve Msonic Cmnty Inc ....C 330 721-3000
Medina (G-14014)

Williamsburg of Cincinnati Mgt ....C 513 948-2308
Cincinnati (G-4798)

Zandex Health Care Corporation ....E 740 454-1400
Zanesville (G-20379)

Zandex Health Care Corporation ....D 740 454-1400
Johnstown (G-12206)

Zandex Health Care Corporation ....C 740 454-9747
Zanesville (G-20380)

REUPHOLSTERY & FURNITURE REPAIR

OfficeMax North America Inc ....E 614 899-6186
Westerville (G-19286)

RIDING APPAREL STORES

Schneider Saddlery LLC ....E 440 543-2700
Chagrin Falls (G-2682)

RIDING STABLES

Fieldstone Farm Therapeutic RI ....E 440 708-0013
Chagrin Falls (G-2666)

Foxridge Farms Corp ....E 740 965-1369
Galena (G-11158)

Valley Riding ....E 216 267-2525
Cleveland (G-6618)

ROBOTS: Assembly Line

Advanced Design Industries Inc ....E 440 277-4141
Sheffield Village (G-16732)

Ats Systems Oregon Inc ....B 541 738-0932
Lewis Center (G-12527)

Production Design Services Inc..............D 937 866-3377
Dayton (G-9716)

RODS: Steel & Iron, Made In Steel Mills

American Posts LLC ....E 419 720-0652
Toledo (G-17593)

ROLL FORMED SHAPES: Custom

Hynes Industries Inc ....C 330 799-3221
Youngstown (G-20073)

Ontario Mechanical LLC ....E 419 529-2578
Ontario (G-15569)

ROLLING MILL MACHINERY

Addisonmckee Inc ....C 513 228-7000
Lebanon (G-12448)

Enprotech Industrial Tech LLC..............C 216 883-3220
Cleveland (G-5482)

Kottler Metal Products Co Inc................E 440 946-7473
Willoughby (G-19535)

Park Corporation ....B 216 267-4870
Cleveland (G-6163)

Pines Manufacturing Inc ....E 440 835-5553
Westlake (G-19392)

Steel Eqp Specialists Inc ....D 330 823-8260
Alliance (G-555)

Wauseon Machine & Mfg Inc ....D 419 337-0940
Wauseon (G-18812)

ROOFING MATERIALS: Asphalt

Garland/Dbs Inc ....C 216 641-7500
Cleveland (G-5592)

Tremco Incorporated ....B 216 292-5000
Beachwood (G-1114)

ROOFING MATERIALS: Sheet Metal

Interstate Contractors LLC ....E 513 372-5393
Mason (G-13601)

Oatey Supply Chain Svcs Inc ....C 216 267-7100
Cleveland (G-6110)

ROOMING & BOARDING HOUSES: Dormitory, Commercially Operated

A M Management Inc ....E 937 426-6500
Beavercreek (G-1122)

RUBBER

Flexsys America LP ....D 330 666-4111
Akron (G-225)

Kraton Polymers US LLC ....B 740 423-7571
Belpre (G-1407)

Mondo Polymer Technologies Inc..........E 740 376-9396
Reno (G-16277)

RUBBER PRDTS: Mechanical

Datwyler Sling Sltions USA Inc ....D 937 387-2800
Vandalia (G-18519)

Frankes Wood Products LLC..................E 937 642-0706
Marysville (G-13497)

Johnson Bros Rubber Co Inc ....D 419 853-4122
West Salem (G-19128)

Mantaline Corporation ....D 330 274-2264
Mantua (G-13273)

Midlands Millroom Supply Inc ....E 330 453-9100
Canton (G-2403)

RUBBER PRDTS: Reclaimed

Flexsys America LP ....D 330 666-4111
Akron (G-225)

Lanxess Corporation ....C 440 279-2367
Chardon (G-2701)

RUBBER, CRUDE, WHOLESALE

Two Happy Frogs Incorporated ....E 330 633-1666
Tallmadge (G-17495)

SADDLERY STORES

Schneider Saddlery LLC ....E 440 543-2700
Chagrin Falls (G-2682)

SAFETY EQPT & SPLYS WHOLESALERS

ABC Fire Inc ....E 440 237-6677
North Royalton (G-15346)

Abco Fire LLC ....E 800 875-7200
Cincinnati (G-2896)

Abco Holdings LLC ....D 216 433-7200
Cleveland (G-4892)

Safety Today Inc ....E 614 409-7200
Grove City (G-11468)

Union Tank Car Company ....C 419 864-7216
Marion (G-13468)

West Chester Holdings LLC ....E 800 647-1900
Cincinnati (G-4781)

SAFETY INSPECTION SVCS

Flight Services & Systems Inc...............D 216 328-0090
Cleveland (G-5548)

SALES PROMOTION SVCS

Automotive Events Inc ....E 440 356-1383
Rocky River (G-16423)

Campbell Sales Company ....E 513 697-2900
Cincinnati (G-3111)

D L Ryan Companies LLC ....E 614 436-6558
Westerville (G-19156)

Nugrowth Solutions LLC ....E 800 747-9273
Columbus (G-8215)

RA Staff Company Inc ....E 440 891-9900
Cleveland (G-6276)

Universal Veneer Sales Corp ....E 740 522-2000
Granville (G-11348)

SALT MINING: Common

Cargill Incorporated ....C 216 651-7200
Cleveland (G-5127)

SAND & GRAVEL

Barrett Paving Materials Inc...................C 513 271-6200
Middletown (G-14343)

Covia Holdings Corporation ....D 440 214-3284
Independence (G-12063)

FML Resin LLC ....E 440 214-3200
Independence (G-12074)

Hanson Aggregates East LLC ....E 740 773-2172
Chillicothe (G-2784)

Hilltop Basic Resources Inc...................E 513 621-1500
Cincinnati (G-3709)

Joe McClelland Inc................................E 740 452-3036
Zanesville (G-20321)

Kenmore Construction Co Inc ....E 330 832-8888
Massillon (G-13702)

Martin Marietta Materials Inc.................E 513 701-1140
West Chester (G-18970)

National Lime and Stone Co ....C 419 396-7671
Carey (G-2545)

Oeder Carl E Sons Sand & Grav............E 513 494-1238
Lebanon (G-12488)

Phillips Ready Mix Co............................D 937 426-5151
Beavercreek Township (G-1259)

Pioneer Sands LLC ....E 740 599-7773
Howard (G-11940)

Rjw Trucking Company Ltd....................E 740 363-5343
Delaware (G-10004)

Shelly and Sands Inc ....E 740 453-0721
Zanesville (G-20360)

Shelly Materials Inc ....D 740 246-6315
Thornville (G-17506)

Smith Concrete Co................................E 740 373-7441
Dover (G-10101)

Tri County Concrete Inc ....E 330 425-4464
Twinsburg (G-18328)

SAND MINING

Carl E Oeder Sons Sand & Grav............E 513 494-1555
Lebanon (G-12454)

SAND MINING

Central Ready Mix LLC..........E...... 513 402-5001
Cincinnati *(G-3157)*

Osborne Materials Company........E...... 440 357-7026
Grand River *(G-11333)*

Small Sand & Gravel Inc..........E...... 740 427-3130
Gambier *(G-11226)*

SAND: Hygrade

Fairmount Minerals LLC..........C...... 269 926-9450
Independence *(G-12072)*

Pioneer Sands LLC..........E...... 740 659-2241
Glenford *(G-11308)*

Pioneer Sands LLC..........E...... 740 599-7773
Howard *(G-11940)*

SANDBLASTING SVC: Building Exterior

Feecorp Corporation..........E...... 614 837-3010
Canal Winchester *(G-2108)*

Industrial Waste Control Inc..........D...... 330 270-9900
Youngstown *(G-20079)*

Mc Fadden Construction Inc..........E...... 419 668-4165
Norwalk *(G-15444)*

Mike Morris..........E...... 330 767-4122
Brewster *(G-1811)*

Mrap LLC..........E...... 614 545-3190
Columbus *(G-8117)*

Northpointe Property MGT LLC..........E...... 614 579-9712
Columbus *(G-8204)*

SANDSTONE: Dimension

Irg Operating LLC..........E...... 440 963-4008
Vermilion *(G-18554)*

SANITARY SVC, NEC

City of Lima..........B...... 419 221-5294
Lima *(G-12614)*

City of Toledo..........C...... 419 936-2924
Toledo *(G-17657)*

Cuyahoga County Sani Engrg Svc..........C...... 216 443-8211
Cleveland *(G-5399)*

Northast Ohio Rgonal Sewer Dst..........C...... 216 641-3200
Cleveland *(G-6082)*

Wastren Advantage Inc..........E...... 970 254-1277
Piketon *(G-15993)*

SANITARY SVCS: Disease Control

Ohio State University..........E...... 614 293-8732
Columbus *(G-8327)*

SANITARY SVCS: Environmental Cleanup

AST Environmental Inc..........E...... 937 743-0002
Springboro *(G-16962)*

Chemtron Corporation..........E...... 440 937-6348
Avon *(G-875)*

Diproinduca (usa) Limited LLC..........D...... 330 722-4442
Medina *(G-13930)*

Environment Control of Greater..........D...... 614 868-9788
Columbus *(G-7521)*

Interdyne Corporation..........E...... 419 229-8192
Lima *(G-12666)*

Los Alamos Technical Assoc Inc..........E...... 614 508-1200
Westerville *(G-19275)*

Samsel Rope & Marine Supply Co..........E...... 216 241-0333
Cleveland *(G-6370)*

Superior Envmtl Solutions LLC..........C...... 513 874-8355
West Chester *(G-19087)*

SANITARY SVCS: Hazardous Waste, Collection & Disposal

Avalon Holdings Corporation..........D...... 330 856-8800
Warren *(G-18673)*

Clean Harbors Envmtl Svcs Inc..........D...... 216 429-2402
Cleveland *(G-5222)*

Clean Harbors Envmtl Svcs Inc..........D...... 216 429-2401
Cleveland *(G-5223)*

Clean Harbors Envmtl Svcs Inc..........E...... 740 929-3532
Hebron *(G-11711)*

Clean Hrbors Es Indus Svcs Inc..........C...... 937 425-0512
Dayton *(G-9308)*

Envirosafe Services of Ohio..........E...... 419 698-3500
Oregon *(G-15594)*

Triad Transport Inc..........E...... 614 491-9497
Columbus *(G-8777)*

Waste Management Ohio Inc..........E...... 419 547-7791
Vickery *(G-18576)*

SANITARY SVCS: Incinerator, Operation Of

County of Montgomery..........E...... 937 781-3046
Moraine *(G-14637)*

Ross Consolidated Corp..........D...... 440 748-5800
Grafton *(G-11320)*

Ross Incineration Services Inc..........C...... 440 366-2000
Grafton *(G-11321)*

SANITARY SVCS: Medical Waste Disposal

Browning-Ferris Industries LLC..........D...... 330 393-0385
Warren *(G-18682)*

Stericycle Inc..........D...... 330 393-0370
Warren *(G-18747)*

Stericycle Inc..........E...... 419 729-1934
Toledo *(G-18048)*

SANITARY SVCS: Oil Spill Cleanup

Cousins Waste Control LLC..........D...... 419 726-1500
Toledo *(G-17686)*

SANITARY SVCS: Refuse Collection & Disposal Svcs

Allied Waste Systems Inc..........E...... 937 268-8110
Dayton *(G-9217)*

BFI Waste Services LLC..........E...... 800 437-1123
Salem *(G-16537)*

Browning-Ferris Industries LLC..........E...... 440 786-9390
Solon *(G-16830)*

Buckeye Waste Industries Inc..........E...... 330 645-9900
Coventry Township *(G-9033)*

Builders Trash Service..........E...... 614 444-7060
Columbus *(G-7096)*

Cecos International Inc..........E...... 513 724-6114
Williamsburg *(G-19490)*

Central Ohio Contractors Inc..........D...... 740 369-7700
Delaware *(G-9958)*

Industrial Waste Control Inc..........D...... 330 270-9900
Youngstown *(G-20079)*

Kimble Companies Inc..........D...... 330 963-5493
Twinsburg *(G-18288)*

R & R Sanitation Inc..........E...... 330 325-2311
Mogadore *(G-14555)*

Republic Services Inc..........E...... 330 536-8013
Lowellville *(G-13042)*

Republic Services Inc..........E...... 419 626-2454
Sandusky *(G-16635)*

Republic Services Inc..........D...... 216 741-4013
Cleveland *(G-6311)*

Republic Services Inc..........E...... 440 458-5191
Elyria *(G-10559)*

Republic Services Inc..........E...... 330 830-9050
Massillon *(G-13722)*

Republic Services Inc..........E...... 330 793-7676
Youngstown *(G-20183)*

Republic Services Inc..........E...... 440 774-4060
Oberlin *(G-15518)*

Republic Services Inc..........E...... 513 554-0237
Cincinnati *(G-4360)*

Republic Services Inc..........E...... 937 268-8110
Dayton *(G-9733)*

Republic Services Inc..........D...... 740 969-4487
Columbus *(G-8516)*

Republic Services Inc..........E...... 800 247-3644
Massillon *(G-13723)*

Republic Services Inc..........E...... 800 331-0988
Gallipolis *(G-11212)*

Republic Services Inc..........E...... 419 396-3581
Carey *(G-2546)*

Republic Services Inc..........E...... 419 635-2367
Port Clinton *(G-16115)*

Rumpke Transportation Co LLC..........E...... 937 461-0004
Dayton *(G-9740)*

Rumpke Waste Inc..........D...... 937 378-4126
Georgetown *(G-11274)*

Waste Management Ohio Inc..........E...... 440 286-7116
Chardon *(G-2724)*

Waste Management Ohio Inc..........C...... 800 343-6047
Fairborn *(G-10689)*

SANITARY SVCS: Rubbish Collection & Disposal

Big O Refuse Inc..........E...... 740 344-7544
Granville *(G-11334)*

Republic Services Inc..........E...... 614 308-3000
Columbus *(G-8515)*

Republic Services Inc..........E...... 419 726-9465
Toledo *(G-18003)*

Sidwell Materials Inc..........C...... 740 849-2394
Zanesville *(G-20361)*

Waste Management Ohio Inc..........E...... 866 797-9018
North Jackson *(G-15256)*

Waste Management Ohio Inc..........D...... 866 409-4671
Northwood *(G-15413)*

SANITARY SVCS: Sanitary Landfill, Operation Of

American Landfill Inc..........E...... 330 866-3265
Waynesburg *(G-18828)*

Browning-Ferris Inds of Ohio..........D...... 330 536-8013
Lowellville *(G-13039)*

Browning-Ferris Industries Inc..........E...... 513 899-2942
Morrow *(G-14715)*

Central Ohio Contractors Inc..........E...... 614 539-2579
Grove City *(G-11419)*

County of Erie..........D...... 419 433-0617
Milan *(G-14360)*

Republic Services Inc..........E...... 937 593-3566
Bellefontaine *(G-1361)*

Republic Services Inc..........E...... 419 925-4592
Celina *(G-2609)*

Republic Services Inc..........E...... 330 793-7676
Youngstown *(G-20181)*

Republic Services Inc..........E...... 330 793-7676
Youngstown *(G-20182)*

Republic Services Inc..........E...... 419 636-5109
Bryan *(G-1973)*

Rumpke Sanitary Landfill Inc..........C...... 513 851-0122
Cincinnati *(G-4409)*

Solid Waste Auth Centl Ohio..........C...... 614 871-5100
Grove City *(G-11471)*

Spring Grove Rsrce Rcovery Inc..........D...... 513 681-6242
Cincinnati *(G-4519)*

SANITARY SVCS: Sewage Treatment Facility

City of Canton..........E...... 330 489-3080
Canton *(G-2256)*

City of Xenia..........E...... 937 376-7271
Xenia *(G-19893)*

SANITARY SVCS: Toxic Or Hazardous Waste Cleanup

Petro Environmental Tech..........E...... 513 489-6789
Cincinnati *(G-4237)*

SANITARY SVCS: Waste Materials, Disposal At Sea

Waste Management Ohio Inc..........E...... 800 910-2831
Wooster *(G-19777)*

SANITARY SVCS: Waste Materials, Recycling

Allied Waste Industries LLC..........E...... 440 774-3100
Oberlin *(G-15498)*

Appliance Recycl Ctrs Amer Inc..........D...... 614 876-8771
Hilliard *(G-11742)*

Athens-Hcking Cnty Recycl Ctrs..........E...... 740 594-5312
Athens *(G-770)*

Atlas Recycling Inc..........E...... 800 837-1520
Warren *(G-18668)*

B & B Plastics Recyclers Inc..........C...... 614 409-2880
Columbus *(G-7009)*

Caraustar Industries Inc..........E...... 937 298-9969
Moraine *(G-14631)*

Chemtron Corporation..........E...... 440 937-6348
Avon *(G-875)*

City of Cleveland Heights..........E...... 216 691-7300
Cleveland *(G-5199)*

Clean Water Environmental LLC..........E...... 937 268-6501
Dayton *(G-9309)*

Clm Pallet Recycling Inc..........E...... 614 272-5761
Columbus *(G-7233)*

Counts Container Corporation..........E...... 216 433-4336
Cleveland *(G-5360)*

Crispin Iron & Metal Co LLC..........E...... 740 616-6213
Granville *(G-11340)*

Eco Global Corp..........E...... 419 363-2681
Rockford *(G-16414)*

Envirite of Ohio Inc..........E...... 330 456-6238
Canton *(G-2302)*

Environmental Enterprises Inc..........D...... 513 541-1823
Cincinnati *(G-3501)*

Envision Waste Services LLC..........D...... 216 831-1818
Cleveland *(G-5487)*

Fpt Cleveland LLC ....C 216 441-3800
  Cleveland (G-5569)
Fultz & Son Inc ....E 419 547-9365
  Clyde (G-6743)
Garden Street Iron & Metal ....E 513 853-3700
  Cincinnati (G-3603)
Gateway Products Recycling Inc ......E 216 341-8777
  Cleveland (G-5596)
Grasan Equipment Company Inc ......D 419 526-4440
  Mansfield (G-13180)
Greenstar Mid-America LLC ....E 330 784-1167
  Akron (G-246)
Hpj Industries Inc ....E 419 278-1000
  Deshler (G-10058)
Hpj Industries Inc ....D 419 278-1000
  North Baltimore (G-15178)
I-Tran Inc ....E 330 659-0801
  Richfield (G-16360)
Imco Recycling of Ohio LLC ....C 740 922-2373
  Uhrichsville (G-18342)
In-Plas Recycling Inc ....E 513 541-9800
  Cincinnati (G-3755)
Interstate Shredding LLC ....E 330 545-5477
  Girard (G-11289)
Jasar Recycling Inc ....D 864 233-5421
  East Palestine (G-10420)
Jee Foods ....E 513 917-1712
  Hamilton (G-11617)
M W Recycling LLC ....E 440 753-5400
  Mayfield Heights (G-13877)
Metal Management Ohio Inc ....E 419 782-7791
  Defiance (G-9930)
Miles Alloy Inc ....E 216 245-8893
  Cleveland (G-5991)
Milliron Recycling Inc ....D 419 747-6522
  Mansfield (G-13223)
Mondo Polymer Technologies Inc ....E 740 376-9396
  Reno (G-16277)
Montgomery Iron & Paper Co Inc .....D 937 222-4059
  Dayton (G-9643)
Novotec Recycling LLC ....E 614 231-8326
  Columbus (G-8210)
Pinnacle Recycling LLC ....E 330 745-3700
  Akron (G-383)
Plastic Recycling Tech Inc ....E 937 615-9286
  Piqua (G-16023)
Plastic Recycling Tech Inc ....E 419 238-9395
  Van Wert (G-18486)
Polychem Corporation ....D 419 547-1400
  Clyde (G-6750)
Royal Paper Stock Company Inc .....D 614 851-4714
  Columbus (G-8557)
Royal Paper Stock Company Inc .....E 513 870-5780
  West Chester (G-19077)
Rpg Inc ....D 419 289-2757
  Ashland (G-687)
RSR Partners LLC ....B 440 248-3991
  Solon (G-16894)
Rumpke Cnsld Companies Inc ....C 513 738-0800
  Hamilton (G-11640)
Rumpke Transportation Co LLC ....C 513 242-4600
  Cincinnati (G-4410)
Rumpke Waste Inc ....C 937 548-1939
  Greenville (G-11393)
Rumpke Waste Inc ....D 513 242-4401
  Cincinnati (G-4412)
Shredded Bedding Corporation ....E 740 893-3567
  Centerburg (G-2616)
Veolia Es Tchncal Slutions LLC ....D 937 859-6101
  Miamisburg (G-14234)
Vexor Technology Inc ....E 330 721-9773
  Medina (G-14013)
Waste Parchment Inc ....E 330 674-6868
  Millersburg (G-14499)

SANITATION CHEMICALS & CLEANING AGENTS

Alco-Chem Inc ....E 330 253-3535
  Akron (G-63)
Cincinnati - Vulcan Company ....D 513 242-5300
  Cincinnati (G-3219)
EMD Millipore Corporation ....C 513 631-0445
  Norwood (G-15462)
Fuchs Lubricants Co ....E 330 963-0400
  Twinsburg (G-18270)
National Colloid Company ....E 740 282-1171
  Steubenville (G-17168)
New Vulco Mfg & Sales Co LLC ....D 513 242-2672
  Cincinnati (G-4109)

State Industrial Products Corp ....B 877 747-6986
  Cleveland (G-6458)
Tolco Corporation ....D 419 241-1113
  Toledo (G-18072)
Tremco Incorporated ....B 216 292-5000
  Beachwood (G-1114)
Univar USA Inc ....C 513 714-5264
  West Chester (G-19095)

SATELLITES: Communications

Great Lakes Telcom Ltd ....E 330 629-8848
  Youngstown (G-20055)

SAVINGS & LOAN ASSOCIATIONS, NOT FEDERALLY CHARTERED

Harrison Building and Ln Assn ....E 513 367-2015
  Harrison (G-11669)
Home Savings Bank ....D 330 499-1900
  North Canton (G-15211)
Huntington National Bank ....E 740 335-3771
  Wshngtn CT Hs (G-19876)
The Peoples Savings and Ln Co ....B 937 653-1600
  Urbana (G-18445)
Union Savings Bank ....D 937 434-1254
  Dayton (G-9829)

SAVINGS INSTITUTIONS: Federally Chartered

Eagle Financial Bancorp Inc ....E 513 574-0700
  Cincinnati (G-3468)
First Defiance Financial Corp ....E 419 353-8611
  Bowling Green (G-1731)
First Financial Bancorp ....C 513 551-5640
  Cincinnati (G-3555)
Guardian Savings Bank ....E 513 528-8787
  Cincinnati (G-3661)
Peoples Bancorp Inc ....E 740 947-4372
  Waverly (G-18819)
Peoples Bancorp Inc ....E 513 271-9100
  Cincinnati (G-4229)
Wayne Savings Bancshares Inc ....C 330 264-5767
  Wooster (G-19779)

SAVINGS INSTITUTIONS: Not Federally Chartered

Resolute Bank ....D 419 868-1750
  Maumee (G-13844)

SAW BLADES

Dynatech Systems Inc ....E 440 365-1774
  Elyria (G-10503)
J and S Tool Incorporated ....E 216 676-8330
  Cleveland (G-5770)

SAWING & PLANING MILLS

Appalachia Wood Inc ....E 740 596-2551
  Mc Arthur (G-13889)
Baillie Lumber Co LP ....E 419 462-2000
  Galion (G-11168)
Gross Lumber Inc ....E 330 683-2055
  Apple Creek (G-619)
Hartzell Hardwoods Inc ....D 937 773-7054
  Piqua (G-16006)
Sawmill Road Management Co LLC ....E 937 342-9071
  Springfield (G-17108)
Stephen M Trudick ....E 440 834-1891
  Burton (G-2019)
Wappoo Wood Products Inc ....E 937 492-1166
  Sidney (G-16805)

SCAFFOLDING WHOLESALERS

Brandsafway Services LLC ....E 513 860-2626
  West Chester (G-18879)

SCALE REPAIR SVCS

Brechbuhler Scales Inc ....E 330 458-3060
  Canton (G-2217)
Filing Scale Company Inc ....E 330 425-3092
  Twinsburg (G-18266)

SCHOOL BUS SVC

Akron School Trnsp Svcs ....D 330 761-1390
  Akron (G-55)

Anthony Wayne Local Schools ....D 419 877-0451
  Whitehouse (G-19443)
Beachwood City Schools ....E 216 464-6609
  Cleveland (G-5047)
Benton-Carroll-Salem ....E 419 898-6214
  Oak Harbor (G-15468)
Berea B O E Trnsp Dept ....D 216 898-8300
  Berea (G-1414)
Boardman Local Schools ....D 330 726-3409
  Youngstown (G-19969)
Canton City School District ....D 330 456-6710
  Canton (G-2230)
Chillicothe City School Dst ....E 740 775-2936
  Chillicothe (G-2760)
Clark Shawnee Schl Transprtn ....E 937 328-5382
  Springfield (G-17014)
Cleveland Municipal School Dst ....B 216 634-7005
  Cleveland (G-5273)
Cleveland Municipal School Dst ....B 216 432-4600
  Cleveland (G-5274)
Community Bus Services Inc ....E 330 369-6060
  Warren (G-18686)
Dublin City Schools ....C 614 764-5926
  Dublin (G-10205)
First Group Investment Partnr ....D 513 241-2200
  Cincinnati (G-3558)
First Student Inc ....D 513 531-6888
  Cincinnati (G-3560)
First Student Inc ....E 937 645-0201
  Dayton (G-9438)
First Student Inc ....D 513 761-6100
  Cincinnati (G-3561)
First Student Inc ....B 513 761-5136
  Cincinnati (G-3562)
First Student Inc ....E 419 382-9915
  Toledo (G-17741)
First Student Inc ....E 513 241-2200
  Cincinnati (G-3563)
Firstgroup America Inc ....E 513 241-2200
  Cincinnati (G-3566)
Firstgroup America Inc ....B 513 419-8611
  Cincinnati (G-3567)
Firstgroup America Inc ....E 513 241-2200
  Cincinnati (G-3568)
Firstgroup Usa Inc ....B 513 241-2200
  Cincinnati (G-3569)
Gahanna-Jefferson Pub Schl Dst ......D 614 751-7581
  Columbus (G-7644)
Geneva Area City School Dst ....E 440 466-2684
  Geneva (G-11241)
Lakota Local School District ....C 513 777-2150
  Liberty Township (G-12582)
Lima City School District ....E 419 996-3450
  Lima (G-12676)
Mahoning County ....D 330 797-2837
  Youngstown (G-20107)
Marfre Inc ....C 513 321-3377
  Cincinnati (G-3969)
Massillon City School Bus Gar ....E 330 830-1849
  Massillon (G-13711)
Mentor Exempted Vlg Schl Dst ....C 440 974-5260
  Mentor (G-14080)
Miamisburg City School Dst ....D 937 866-1283
  Miamisburg (G-14191)
Middletown School Vhcl Svc Ctr ....D 513 420-4568
  Middletown (G-14310)
New Albany Plain Loc SC Transp ....E 614 855-2033
  New Albany (G-14866)
North Canton City School Dst ....D 330 497-5615
  Canton (G-2420)
Northmont Service Center ....D 937 832-5050
  Englewood (G-10594)
Ontario Local School District ....E 419 529-3814
  Ontario (G-15568)
Palmer Express Incorporated ....E 440 942-3333
  Willoughby (G-19560)
Pauls Bus Service Inc ....E 513 851-5089
  Cincinnati (G-4215)
Perry Transportation Dept ....E 440 259-3005
  Perry (G-15827)
Perrysburg Board of Education ....E 419 874-3127
  Perrysburg (G-15902)
Peterman ....E 513 722-2229
  Goshen (G-11314)
Petermann ....E 513 539-0324
  Monroe (G-14580)
Petermann Ltd ....D 330 653-3323
  Hudson (G-12003)
Petermann Northeast LLC ....A 513 351-7383
  Cincinnati (G-4236)

Queen City Transportation LLC ....B 513 941-8700
Cincinnati *(G-4322)*
S B S Transit Inc ....B 440 288-2222
Lorain *(G-12942)*
SC Madison Bus Garage ....D 419 589-3373
Mansfield *(G-13241)*
Streetsboro Board Education ....E 330 626-4909
Streetsboro *(G-17272)*
Suburban Transportation Co Inc ....E 440 846-9291
Brunswick *(G-1940)*
Vermilion Board of Education ....E 440 204-1700
Vermilion *(G-18561)*
Washington Local Schools ....D 419 473-8356
Toledo *(G-18146)*

SCHOOL FOR PHYSICALLY HANDICAPPED, NEC

North Point Eductl Svc Ctr ....E 440 967-0904
Huron *(G-12028)*

SCHOOL FOR RETARDED, NEC

Abilities First Foundation Inc ....D 513 423-9496
Middletown *(G-14285)*
D-R Training Center & Workshop ....C 419 289-0470
Ashland *(G-671)*
Mental Rtrdtion Preble Cnty Bd ....D 937 456-5891
Eaton *(G-10453)*
Whetstone Industries Inc ....E 419 947-9222
Mount Gilead *(G-14735)*

SCHOOL SPLYS, EXC BOOKS: Wholesalers

Euclid City Schools ....D 216 261-2900
Euclid *(G-10631)*
ICM Distributing Company Inc ....E 234 212-3030
Twinsburg *(G-18281)*
Lorenz Corporation ....D 937 228-6118
Dayton *(G-9573)*
Zaner-Bloser Inc ....D 614 486-0221
Columbus *(G-8935)*

SCHOOLS & EDUCATIONAL SVCS, NEC

Key Career Place ....D 216 987-3029
Cleveland *(G-5825)*

SCHOOLS: Elementary & Secondary

First School Corp ....E 937 433-3455
Dayton *(G-9437)*
Flying Colors Public Preschool ....E 740 349-1629
Newark *(G-15034)*
Grace Baptist Church ....E 937 652-1133
Urbana *(G-18435)*
Interval Brotherhood Homes ....D 330 644-4095
Coventry Township *(G-9036)*
Medill Elemntary Sch of Volntr ....E 740 687-7352
Lancaster *(G-12417)*
Miami Valley School ....E 937 434-4444
Dayton *(G-9626)*
Midland Council Governments ....E 330 264-6047
Wooster *(G-19745)*
Northwest Ohio Computer Assn ....D 419 267-5565
Archbold *(G-634)*
Ohio School Psychologists Assn ....E 614 414-5980
Columbus *(G-8285)*
Ohio University ....D 740 593-2195
Athens *(G-798)*
Paulding Exempted Vlg Schl Dst ....C 419 594-3309
Paulding *(G-15797)*
Ravenna Assembly of God Inc ....E 330 297-1493
Ravenna *(G-16260)*
Young Services Inc ....E 419 704-2009
Toledo *(G-18171)*

SCHOOLS: Vocational, NEC

Great Oaks Inst Tech Creer Dev ....D 513 613-3657
Cincinnati *(G-3644)*
Great Oaks Inst Tech Creer Dev ....E 513 771-8840
Cincinnati *(G-3645)*

SCRAP & WASTE MATERIALS, WHOLESALE: Auto Wrecking For Scrap

Brims Imports ....E 419 674-4137
Kenton *(G-12272)*
Diver Steel City Auto Crushers ....E 330 744-5083
Youngstown *(G-20020)*

Kenton Auto and Truck Wrecking ....E 419 673-8234
Kenton *(G-12283)*

SCRAP & WASTE MATERIALS, WHOLESALE: Ferrous Metal

Agmet LLC ....E 440 439-7400
Cleveland *(G-4913)*
Agmet LLC ....E 216 662-6939
Maple Heights *(G-13280)*
Allen County Recyclers Inc ....E 419 223-5010
Lima *(G-12596)*
Byer Steel Recycling Inc ....E 513 948-0300
Cincinnati *(G-3098)*
City Scrap & Salvage Co ....E 330 753-5051
Akron *(G-139)*
Cohen Electronics Inc ....D 513 425-6911
Middletown *(G-14296)*
Djj Holding Corporation ....C 513 621-8770
Cincinnati *(G-3437)*
Fpt Cleveland LLC ....C 216 441-3800
Cleveland *(G-5569)*
Franklin Iron & Metal Corp ....C 937 253-8184
Dayton *(G-9449)*
Harry Rock & Company ....E 330 644-3748
Cleveland *(G-5663)*
Holub Iron & Steel Company ....E 330 252-5655
Akron *(G-267)*
I H Schlezinger Inc ....E 614 252-1188
Columbus *(G-7794)*
Metalico Akron Inc ....E 330 376-1400
Akron *(G-333)*
Niles Iron & Metal Company LLC ....E 330 652-2262
Niles *(G-15163)*
Omnisource LLC ....D 419 537-1631
Toledo *(G-17961)*
Omnisource LLC ....E 419 784-5669
Defiance *(G-9933)*
Omnisource LLC ....E 419 394-3351
Saint Marys *(G-16529)*
Omnisource LLC ....C 419 537-9400
Toledo *(G-17962)*
PSC Metals - Wooster LLC ....D 330 264-8956
Wooster *(G-19760)*
Reserve Ftl LLC 773 721-8740
Canton *(G-2459)*
River Recycling Entps Ltd ....E 216 459-2100
Cleveland *(G-6328)*
Rm Advisory Group Inc ....E 513 242-2100
Cincinnati *(G-4385)*
Unico Alloys & Metals Inc ....D 614 299-0545
Columbus *(G-8797)*
Wilmington Iron and Met Co Inc ....E 937 382-3867
Wilmington *(G-19654)*

SCRAP & WASTE MATERIALS, WHOLESALE: Junk & Scrap

Slesnick Iron & Metal Co ....E 330 453-8475
Canton *(G-2479)*

SCRAP & WASTE MATERIALS, WHOLESALE: Metal

Carpenter Metal Solutions Inc ....E 330 829-2771
Alliance *(G-522)*
Diproinduca (usa) Limited LLC ....D 330 722-4442
Medina *(G-13930)*
G-Cor Automotive Corp ....E 614 443-6735
Columbus *(G-7641)*
PSC Metals Inc ....E 614 299-4175
Columbus *(G-8477)*
PSC Metals Inc ....D 234 208-2331
Barberton *(G-963)*
PSC Metals Inc ....E 330 745-4437
Barberton *(G-964)*
PSC Metals Inc ....E 330 484-7610
Canton *(G-2444)*
PSC Metals Inc ....E 216 341-3400
Cleveland *(G-6266)*
R L S Corporation ....E 740 773-1440
Chillicothe *(G-2812)*
Scrap Yard LLC ....E 216 271-5825
Cleveland *(G-6381)*

SCRAP & WASTE MATERIALS, WHOLESALE: Nonferrous Metals Scrap

Legend Smelting and Recycl Inc ....D 740 928-0139
Hebron *(G-11716)*

M & M Metals International Inc ....E 513 221-4411
Cincinnati *(G-3954)*
Muskingum Iron & Metal Co ....E 740 452-9351
Zanesville *(G-20338)*
Quantum Metals Inc ....E 513 573-0144
Lebanon *(G-12494)*
W R G Inc ....E 216 351-8494
Cleveland *(G-6645)*

SCRAP & WASTE MATERIALS, WHOLESALE: Paper

Associated Paper Stock Inc ....E 330 549-5311
North Lima *(G-15263)*
Hamilton Scrap Processors ....E 513 863-3474
Hamilton *(G-11609)*

SCRAP & WASTE MATERIALS, WHOLESALE: Rags

Intex Supply Company ....E 216 535-4300
Richmond Heights *(G-16391)*
PSC Metals Inc ....A 330 879-5001
Navarre *(G-14824)*

SCRAP & WASTE MATERIALS, WHOLESALE: Rubber Scrap

Frankes Wood Products LLC ....E 937 642-0706
Marysville *(G-13497)*

SCRAP STEEL CUTTING

Geneva Liberty Steel Ltd ....E 330 740-0103
Youngstown *(G-20047)*
Toledo Shredding LLC ....E 419 698-1153
Toledo *(G-18097)*

SCREW MACHINE PRDTS

Hebco Products Inc ....A 419 562-7987
Bucyrus *(G-1992)*
Superior Products Llc ....D 216 651-9400
Cleveland *(G-6483)*

SCREWS: Metal

General Plastex Inc ....E 330 745-7775
Barberton *(G-953)*

SEALANTS

Teknol Inc ....D 937 264-0190
Dayton *(G-9808)*
Tremco Incorporated ....B 216 292-5000
Beachwood *(G-1114)*

SEALING COMPOUNDS: Sealing, synthetic rubber or plastic

Technical Rubber Company Inc ....B 740 967-9015
Johnstown *(G-12204)*

SEARCH & NAVIGATION SYSTEMS

Boeing Company ....E 740 788-4000
Newark *(G-15014)*
Grimes Aerospace Company ....B 937 484-2001
Urbana *(G-18436)*

SEARCH & RESCUE SVCS

Richland Township Fire Dept ....E 740 536-7313
Rushville *(G-16465)*

SEAT BELTS: Automobile & Aircraft

Tk Holdings Inc ....E 937 778-9713
Piqua *(G-16031)*

SECRETARIAL SVCS

Chase Transcriptions Inc ....E 330 650-0539
Hudson *(G-11972)*
Premier Transcription Service ....E 513 741-1800
Cincinnati *(G-4274)*

SECURE STORAGE SVC: Document

Briar-Gate Realty Inc ....E 614 299-2122
Grove City *(G-11410)*
Briar-Gate Realty Inc ....D 614 299-2121
Grove City *(G-11411)*

High Line Corporation ....E 330 848-8800
Akron *(G-261)*
Infostore LLC ....E 216 749-4636
Cleveland *(G-5752)*
Iron Mountain Incorporated ....D 513 874-3535
West Chester *(G-18948)*
Iron Mountain Incorporated ....D 614 801-0151
Urbancrest *(G-18449)*
Iron Mountain Info MGT LLC ....E 513 297-3268
Cincinnati *(G-3787)*
Iron Mountain Info MGT LLC ....E 513 942-7300
Hamilton *(G-11616)*
Iron Mountain Info MGT LLC ....E 513 297-1906
West Chester *(G-18949)*
Iron Mountain Info MGT LLC ....E 614 840-9321
Columbus *(G-7842)*
Iron Mountain Info MGT LLC ....C 440 248-0999
Solon *(G-16862)*
Iron Mountain Info MGT LLC ....E 513 247-2183
Blue Ash *(G-1586)*
Ray Hamilton Companies ....E 513 641-5400
Blue Ash *(G-1640)*

SECURE STORAGE SVC: Household & Furniture

Andreas Furniture Company ....E 330 852-2494
Sugarcreek *(G-17376)*
Great Value Storage ....E 614 848-8420
Columbus *(G-7690)*

SECURITY DEVICES

Aysco Security Consultants Inc ....E 330 733-8183
Kent *(G-12215)*

SECURITY EQPT STORES

Gem Edwards Inc ....D 330 342-8300
Hudson *(G-11979)*
Lucas Funeral Homes Inc ....E 419 294-1985
Upper Sandusky *(G-18411)*

SECURITY GUARD SVCS

1st Advnce SEC Invstgtions Inc ....D 937 210-9010
Dayton *(G-9153)*
1st Choice Security Inc ....C 513 381-6789
Cincinnati *(G-2877)*
Allied Security LLC ....B 513 771-3776
Cincinnati *(G-2929)*
Alliedbarton Security Svcs LLC ....C 614 225-9061
Worthington *(G-19792)*
Alliedbarton Security Svcs LLC ....E 419 874-9005
Rossford *(G-16459)*
Alpha Security LLC ....D 330 406-2181
Poland *(G-16080)*
Anderson SEC & Fire Systems ....E 937 294-1478
Moraine *(G-14620)*
Anderson Security Inc ....D 937 294-1478
Moraine *(G-14621)*
Andy Frain Services Inc ....B 419 897-7909
Maumee *(G-13757)*
Awp Inc ....A 330 677-7401
North Canton *(G-15191)*
Danson Inc ....C 513 948-0066
Cincinnati *(G-3400)*
Deacon 10 ....D 216 731-4000
Euclid *(G-10629)*
Dusk To Dawn Protective Svcs ....E 330 837-9992
Massillon *(G-13676)*
Elite Isg ....E 937 668-6858
Dayton *(G-9409)*
Firelands Security Services ....E 419 627-0562
Sandusky *(G-16606)*
G4s Secure Solutions (usa) ....C 513 874-0941
Cincinnati *(G-3599)*
G4s Secure Solutions USA Inc ....C 614 322-5100
Columbus *(G-7642)*
Genric Inc ....B 937 553-9250
Marysville *(G-13500)*
Guardsmark LLC ....C 513 851-5523
Cincinnati *(G-3662)*
Guardsmark LLC ....E 419 229-9300
Lima *(G-12650)*
Job1usa Inc ....D 419 255-5005
Toledo *(G-17831)*
McKeen Security Inc ....D 740 699-1301
Saint Clairsville *(G-16495)*
Merchants Scrty Srvc of Dayton ....B 937 256-9373
Dayton *(G-9608)*

Metropolitan Security Svcs Inc ....A 216 298-4076
Cleveland *(G-5973)*
Moonlight Security Inc ....D 937 252-1600
Moraine *(G-14681)*
Ohio Entertainment Security ....D 937 325-7216
South Vienna *(G-16948)*
Ohio Support Services Corp ....E 614 443-0291
Columbus *(G-8353)*
Patrol Urban Services LLC ....E 614 620-4672
Westerville *(G-19291)*
Pennington International Inc ....E 513 631-2130
Cincinnati *(G-4225)*
Pls Protective Services ....E 513 521-3581
Cincinnati *(G-4256)*
R C Enterprises Inc ....D 330 782-2111
Youngstown *(G-20175)*
R-Cap Security LLC ....C 216 761-6355
Cleveland *(G-6275)*
Rumpf Corporation ....E 419 255-5005
Toledo *(G-18014)*
Ryno 24 Inc ....E 440 946-7700
Willoughby *(G-19569)*
Sam-Tom Inc ....C 216 426-7752
Cleveland *(G-6369)*
Securitas SEC Svcs USA Inc ....C 216 431-3139
Cleveland *(G-6388)*
Securitas SEC Svcs USA Inc ....C 937 224-7432
Dayton *(G-9757)*
Securitas SEC Svcs USA Inc ....C 614 871-6051
Grove City *(G-11470)*
Securitas SEC Svcs USA Inc ....A 440 887-6800
Cleveland *(G-6389)*
Securitas SEC Svcs USA Inc ....C 216 503-2021
Cleveland *(G-6390)*
Shield Security Service ....E 330 650-2001
Hudson *(G-12006)*
St Moritz Security Svcs Inc ....D 330 270-5922
Youngstown *(G-20216)*
St Moritz Security Svcs Inc ....E 614 351-8798
Worthington *(G-19852)*
Tenable Protective Svcs Inc ....A 216 361-0002
Cleveland *(G-6511)*
Tenable Protective Svcs Inc ....A 513 741-3560
Cincinnati *(G-4584)*
US Protection Service LLC ....D 513 422-7910
Cincinnati *(G-4742)*
US Security Associates Inc ....C 513 381-7033
Cincinnati *(G-4743)*
US Security Associates Inc ....C 937 454-9035
Vandalia *(G-18548)*
US Security Holdings Inc ....D 614 488-6110
Columbus *(G-8835)*
Veteran Security Patrol Co ....E 513 381-4482
Cincinnati *(G-4758)*
Whittguard Security Services ....E 440 288-7233
Avon *(G-904)*
Willo Security Inc ....C 614 481-9456
Columbus *(G-8908)*
Willo Security Inc ....E 440 953-9191
Willoughby *(G-19582)*

SECURITY PROTECTIVE DEVICES MAINTENANCE & MONITORING SVCS

Johnson Cntrls SEC Sltions LLC ....E 513 277-4966
Cincinnati *(G-3826)*
Koorsen Fire & Security Inc ....E 419 526-2212
Mansfield *(G-13195)*
Securitas Electronic SEC Inc ....C 855 331-0359
Uniontown *(G-18386)*
Security Investments LLC ....D 614 441-4601
Columbus *(G-8616)*

SECURITY SYSTEMS SERVICES

ADT Security ....D 440 397-5751
Strongsville *(G-17281)*
American Svcs & Protection LLC ....D 614 884-0177
Columbus *(G-6939)*
Anderson Security Inc ....D 937 294-1478
Moraine *(G-14621)*
Asset Protection Corporation ....E 419 531-3400
Toledo *(G-17601)*
Bass Security Services Inc ....E 216 755-1200
Bedford Heights *(G-1317)*
Brawnstone Security LLC ....D 330 800-9006
Canton *(G-2216)*
Brentley Institute Inc ....E 216 225-0087
Cleveland *(G-5078)*
Bureau Workers Compensation ....E 614 466-5109
Pickerington *(G-15950)*

D B A Inc ....E 513 541-6600
Cincinnati *(G-3394)*
Electra Sound Inc ....C 216 433-1050
Cleveland *(G-5471)*
GA Business Purchaser LLC ....D 419 255-8400
Toledo *(G-17752)*
Genric Inc ....B 937 553-9250
Marysville *(G-13500)*
Guardian Protection Svcs Inc ....E 330 797-1570
Youngstown *(G-20059)*
Henley & Assoc SEC Group LLC ....E 614 378-3727
Blacklick *(G-1479)*
Honeywell International Inc ....E 614 717-2270
Columbus *(G-7772)*
Integrted Prcision Systems Inc ....E 330 963-0064
Twinsburg *(G-18282)*
Jenne Inc ....C 440 835-0040
Avon *(G-888)*
Koorsen Fire & Security Inc ....E 614 878-2228
Columbus *(G-7922)*
Kst Security Inc ....E 614 878-2228
Columbus *(G-7930)*
Northwestern Ohio SEC Systems ....E 419 227-1655
Lima *(G-12708)*
OGara Group Inc ....C 513 338-0660
Cincinnati *(G-4150)*
Ohio Tctcal Enfrcment Svcs LLC ....D 614 989-9485
Columbus *(G-8355)*
Protech Security Inc ....E 330 499-3555
Canton *(G-2442)*
Safe-N-Sound Security Inc ....D 330 491-1148
Millersburg *(G-14492)*
Safeguard Properties LLC ....A 216 739-2900
Cleveland *(G-6361)*
Securestate LLC ....E 216 927-0115
Cleveland *(G-6387)*
Sievers Security Systems Inc ....E 216 383-1234
Cleveland *(G-6408)*
Tacg LLC ....C 937 203-8201
Beavercreek *(G-1237)*
Universal Green Energy Solutio ....E 844 723-7768
Reynoldsburg *(G-16335)*
Vigilant Defense ....E 513 309-0672
West Chester *(G-19031)*
Wj Service Co Inc ....E 330 372-5040
Warren *(G-18773)*

SECURITY UNDERWRITERS

Old Rpblic Ttle Nthrn Ohio LLC ....B 216 524-5700
Independence *(G-12106)*

SELF-HELP GROUP HOME

Madison House Inc ....E 740 845-0145
London *(G-12869)*
Rescare Ohio Inc ....E 330 479-9841
Canton *(G-2458)*
Rescare Ohio Inc ....E 513 724-1177
Williamsburg *(G-19496)*
Rescare Ohio Inc ....D 513 829-8992
Hamilton *(G-11637)*

SELF-HELP ORGANIZATION, NEC

Positive Education Program ....E 216 227-2730
Cleveland *(G-6223)*

SELF-PROPELLED AIRCRAFT DEALER

Lane Aviation Corporation ....C 614 237-3747
Columbus *(G-7950)*
McKinley Air Transport Inc ....E 330 497-6956
Canton *(G-2394)*

SEMICONDUCTOR CIRCUIT NETWORKS

Micro Industries Corporation ....D 740 548-7878
Westerville *(G-19279)*

SEMICONDUCTORS & RELATED DEVICES

CPC Logistics Inc ....D 513 874-5787
Fairfield *(G-10715)*
Pepperl + Fuchs Inc ....C 330 425-3555
Twinsburg *(G-18302)*

SENIOR HIGH SCHOOLS, PUBLIC

Ashtabula Area City School Dst ....E 440 992-1221
Ashtabula *(G-705)*
Edison Local School District ....E 740 543-4011
Amsterdam *(G-601)*

SERVICES

SEPTIC TANK CLEANING SVCS

Pro-Kleen Industrial Svcs Inc ....E 740 689-1886
Lancaster (G-12427)

SERVICE STATION EQPT REPAIR SVCS

Petro-Com Corp ....E 440 327-6900
North Ridgeville (G-15339)

SERVICES, NEC

Chp AP Shared Services ....E 513 981-6704
Cincinnati (G-3197)
Linemaster Services LLC ....E 614 507-9945
Grove City (G-11449)
Mid Ohio Emergency Svcs LLC ....E 614 566-5070
Columbus (G-8073)
P & D Removal Service ....E 513 226-7687
Cincinnati (G-4194)

SETTLEMENT HOUSE

Deepwood Industries Inc ....C 440 350-5231
Mentor (G-14040)

SEWAGE & WATER TREATMENT EQPT

De Nora Tech LLC ....D 440 710-5300
Painesville (G-15708)
Flow-Liner Systems Ltd ....E 800 348-0020
Zanesville (G-20308)

SEWAGE FACILITIES

Belmont County of Ohio ....C 740 695-3144
Saint Clairsville (G-16473)
City of Akron ....E 330 375-2666
Akron (G-137)
City of Avon Lake ....E 440 933-6226
Avon Lake (G-912)
City of Columbus ....D 614 645-3248
Lockbourne (G-12811)
City of Dayton ....D 937 333-1837
Dayton (G-9305)
City of Findlay ....E 419 424-7179
Findlay (G-10889)
City of Hamilton ....E 513 785-7551
Hamilton (G-11578)
City of Hamilton ....E 513 868-5971
Hamilton (G-11579)
City of Kent ....D 330 678-8105
Kent (G-12222)
City of Lima ....E 419 221-5175
Lima (G-12615)
City of Lorain ....C 440 204-2500
Lorain (G-12891)
City of Sandusky ....E 419 627-5907
Sandusky (G-16585)
City of Toledo ....C 419 936-2924
Toledo (G-17657)
City of Toledo ....D 419 245-1800
Toledo (G-17654)
City of Westerville ....E 614 901-6500
Westerville (G-19236)
City of Zanesville ....E 740 455-0641
Zanesville (G-20296)
Clermont Cnty Wtr Rsources Dept ....D 513 732-7970
Batavia (G-987)
County of Lorain ....D 440 329-5584
Elyria (G-10494)
County of Stark ....A 330 451-2303
Canton (G-2268)
County of Warren ....D 513 925-1377
Lebanon (G-12459)
Metropolitan Sewer District ....A 513 244-1300
Cincinnati (G-4042)
New Lexington City of ....E 740 342-1633
New Lexington (G-14922)
Northast Ohio Rgonal Sewer Dst ......C 216 641-6000
Cleveland (G-6084)
Northast Ohio Rgonal Sewer Dst ......D 216 531-4892
Cleveland (G-6085)
Northast Ohio Rgonal Sewer Dst ......C 216 641-3200
Cleveland (G-6082)
Northwestern Water & Sewer Dst ......E 419 354-9090
Bowling Green (G-1742)

SEWER CLEANING & RODDING SVC

AAA Pipe Cleaning Corporation ....C 216 341-2900
Cleveland (G-4888)

Adelmos Electric Sewer Clg Co ....E 216 641-2301
Brooklyn Heights (G-1864)
Chemed Corporation ....D 513 762-6690
Cincinnati (G-3175)
Dreier & Maller Inc ....E 614 575-0065
Reynoldsburg (G-16300)
J and J Environmental Inc ....E 513 398-4521
Mason (G-13602)
Mr Rooter Plumbing Corporation ....E 419 625-4444
Independence (G-12100)
Nurotoco Massachusetts Inc ....C 513 762-6690
Cincinnati (G-4140)
Roto Rt Inc ....C 513 762-6690
Cincinnati (G-4397)
Roto-Rooter Development Co ....D 513 762-6690
Cincinnati (G-4398)
Roto-Rooter Group Inc ....C 513 762-6690
Cincinnati (G-4399)
Roto-Rooter Services Company ....E 614 238-8006
Columbus (G-8555)
Roto-Rooter Services Company ....D 513 762-6690
Cincinnati (G-4400)
Roto-Rooter Services Company ....D 513 541-3840
Cincinnati (G-4401)
Roto-Rooter Services Company ....E 216 429-1928
Solon (G-16893)
Tfh-Eb Inc ....D 614 253-7246
Columbus (G-8741)

SEWING CONTRACTORS

Piqua Industrial Cut & Sew ....E 937 773-7397
Piqua (G-16018)

SEWING MACHINE STORES

Pins & Needles Inc ....E 440 243-6400
Cleveland (G-6212)

SEWING, NEEDLEWORK & PIECE GOODS STORE: Quilting Matls/Splys

Checker Notions Company Inc ....D 419 893-3636
Maumee (G-13770)

SEWING, NEEDLEWORK & PIECE GOODS STORES: Knitting Splys

Pins & Needles Inc ....E 440 243-6400
Cleveland (G-6212)

SHAPES & PILINGS, STRUCTURAL: Steel

Brenmar Construction Inc ....D 740 286-2151
Jackson (G-12169)

SHEET METAL SPECIALTIES, EXC STAMPED

Allied Fabricating & Wldg Co ....E 614 751-6664
Columbus (G-6897)
C & R Inc ....E 614 497-1130
Groveport (G-11498)
Kirk & Blum Manufacturing Co ....C 513 458-2600
Cincinnati (G-3875)

SHEETING: Laminated Plastic

Schneller LLC ....D 330 673-1299
Kent (G-12258)

SHELTERED WORKSHOPS

Ability Works Inc ....C 419 626-1048
Sandusky (G-16572)
Alpha Group of Delaware Inc ....D 614 222-1855
Columbus (G-6903)
Alpha Group of Delaware Inc ....D 740 368-5810
Delaware (G-9951)
Angeline Industries Inc ....E 419 294-4488
Upper Sandusky (G-18403)
ARC Industries Incorporated O ....C 614 479-2500
Columbus (G-6964)
ARC Industries Incorporated O ....B 614 436-4800
Columbus (G-6965)
ARC Industries Incorporated O ....B 614 864-2406
Columbus (G-6966)
ARC Industries Incorporated O ....B 614 267-1207
Columbus (G-6967)
Atco Inc ....C 740 592-6659
Athens (G-765)
Belco Works Inc ....B 740 695-0500
Saint Clairsville (G-16470)

Brookhill Center Industries ....C 419 876-3932
Ottawa (G-15657)
Brown Cnty Bd Mntal Rtardation ......E 937 378-4891
Georgetown (G-11261)
Capabilities Inc ....E 419 394-0003
Saint Marys (G-16520)
Carroll Hills Industries Inc ....D 330 627-5524
Carrollton (G-2563)
Cincinnati Assn For The Blind ....C 513 221-8558
Cincinnati (G-3223)
CLI Incorporated ....C 419 668-8840
Norwalk (G-15429)
County of Hamilton ....B 513 742-1576
Cincinnati (G-3369)
County of Sandusky ....D 419 637-2243
Fremont (G-11065)
County of Seneca ....C 419 435-0729
Fostoria (G-10999)
Cuyahoga County ....D 216 265-3030
Cleveland (G-5394)
D-R Training Center & Workshop ......C 419 289-0470
Ashland (G-671)
Easter Seals Tristate LLC ....C 513 281-2316
Cincinnati (G-3473)
Employment Development Inc ....C 330 424-7711
Lisbon (G-12800)
Fairhaven Sheltered Workshop ....C 330 652-1116
Niles (G-15154)
Fairhaven Sheltered Workshop ....C 330 847-7275
Warren (G-18708)
Fairhaven Sheltered Workshop ....C 330 505-3644
Niles (G-15155)
First Capital Enterprises Inc ....D 740 773-2166
Chillicothe (G-2780)
Gallco Inc ....D 740 446-3775
Gallipolis (G-11192)
Goodwill Industries ....E 330 264-1300
Wooster (G-19725)
Greene Inc ....D 937 562-4200
Xenia (G-19907)
Harco Industries Inc ....E 419 674-4159
Kenton (G-12276)
Harrison Industries Inc ....D 740 942-2988
Cadiz (G-2029)
Hocking Valley Industries Inc ....D 740 385-2118
Logan (G-12838)
Hopewell Industries Inc ....D 740 622-3563
Coshocton (G-9018)
Hunter Defense Tech Inc ....E 216 438-6111
Solon (G-16859)
J-Vac Industries Inc ....D 740 384-2155
Wellston (G-18850)
Ken Harper ....C 740 439-4452
Byesville (G-2025)
Knox New Hope Industries Inc ....C 740 397-4601
Mount Vernon (G-14776)
Licco Inc ....C 740 522-8345
Newark (G-15050)
Lorain County Board ....E 440 329-3734
Elyria (G-10530)
Lott Industries Incorporated ....B 419 476-2516
Toledo (G-17858)
Lott Industries Incorporated ....B 419 891-5215
Maumee (G-13811)
Lott Industries Incorporated ....A 419 534-4980
Toledo (G-17859)
Lott Industries Incorporated ....B 419 534-4980
Toledo (G-17860)
Lynn Hope Industries Inc ....D 330 674-8045
Holmesville (G-11931)
Marca Industries Inc ....E 740 387-1035
Marion (G-13432)
Marion Goodwill Industries ....E 740 387-7023
Marion (G-13441)
Medina County Sheltered Inds ....B 330 334-4491
Wadsworth (G-18608)
Meigs Industries Inc ....E 740 992-6681
Syracuse (G-17469)
Metzenbaum Sheltered Inds Inc ....C 440 729-1919
Chesterland (G-2741)
Monco Enterprises Inc ....A 937 461-0034
Dayton (G-9642)
Muskingum Starlight Industries ....C 740 453-4622
Zanesville (G-20341)
Nick Amster Inc ....C 330 264-9667
Wooster (G-19750)
Portage Industries Inc ....C 330 296-3996
Ravenna (G-16257)
Production Services Unlimited ....D 513 695-1658
Lebanon (G-12493)

R T Industries Inc ....C 937 339-8313
  Troy (G-18225)
R T Industries Inc ....C 937 335-5784
  Troy (G-18224)
Ross Training Center Inc ....D 937 592-0025
  Bellefontaine (G-1363)
RTC Industries Inc ....E 937 592-0534
  Bellefontaine (G-1364)
Sandco Industries ....C 419 334-9090
  Clyde (G-6752)
Stark County Board of Developm ....A 330 477-5200
  Canton (G-2490)
Starlight Enterprises Inc ....C 330 339-2020
  New Philadelphia (G-14983)
Tri-State Industries Inc ....C 740 532-0406
  Coal Grove (G-6756)
U-Co Industries Inc ....D 937 644-3021
  Marysville (G-13534)
Wasco Inc ....E 740 373-3418
  Marietta (G-13400)
Zanesvlle Welfre Orgnztn/Goodw ...E 740 450-6060
  Zanesville (G-20387)

SHIMS: Metal

Ohio Gasket and Shim Co Inc ....E 330 630-0626
  Akron (G-359)

SHIPBUILDING & REPAIR

Great Lakes Group ....C 216 621-4854
  Cleveland (G-5627)
Tack-Anew Inc ....E 419 734-4212
  Port Clinton (G-16119)

SHIPPING AGENTS

Garys Pharmacy Inc ....E 937 456-5777
  Eaton (G-10446)
Innovel Solutions Inc ....D 614 878-2092
  Columbus (G-7821)
Innovel Solutions Inc ....A 614 492-5304
  Columbus (G-7822)
Tersher Corporation ....D 440 439-8383
  Strongsville (G-17352)
World Shipping Inc ....E 440 356-7676
  Cleveland (G-6690)
Xpo Intermodal Solutions Inc ....A 614 923-1400
  Dublin (G-10378)

SHOE STORES: Men's

Cov-Ro Inc ....E 330 856-3176
  Warren (G-18693)
Lehigh Outfitters LLC ....C 740 753-1951
  Nelsonville (G-14834)

SHOES & BOOTS WHOLESALERS

M & R Fredericktown Ltd Inc ....E 440 801-1563
  Akron (G-324)

SHOES: Men's

Georgia-Boot Inc ....D 740 753-1951
  Nelsonville (G-14832)

SHOES: Plastic Or Rubber

Georgia-Boot Inc ....D 740 753-1951
  Nelsonville (G-14832)

SHOES: Women's

Georgia-Boot Inc ....D 740 753-1951
  Nelsonville (G-14832)

SHOPPING CART REPAIR SVCS

Hays Enterprises Inc ....E 330 392-2278
  Warren (G-18711)
Omni Cart Services Inc ....C 440 205-8363
  Mentor (G-14093)

SHOPPING CENTERS & MALLS

Cbl & Associates Prpts Inc ....E 513 424-8517
  Middletown (G-14344)
Easton Town Center II LLC ....D 614 416-7000
  Columbus (G-7492)
First Interstate Properties ....E 216 381-2900
  Cleveland (G-5536)
Forest City Properties LLC ....C 216 621-6060
  Cleveland (G-5559)

Glemsure Realty Trust ....E 740 522-6620
  Heath (G-11703)
Goodman Properties Inc ....E 740 264-7781
  Steubenville (G-17155)
Kingsmason Properties Ltd ....E 513 932-6010
  Lebanon (G-12476)
Lima Mall Inc ....E 419 331-6255
  Lima (G-12681)
Lofinos Inc ....D 937 431-1662
  Dayton (G-9572)
Mills Corporation ....E 513 671-2882
  Cincinnati (G-4056)
Quincy Mall Inc ....E 614 228-5331
  Columbus (G-8482)
Schottenstein Realty LLC ....E 614 445-8461
  Columbus (G-8609)
Simon Property Group ....E 614 717-9300
  Dublin (G-10335)
United Management Inc ....D 614 228-5331
  Columbus (G-8803)
Zaremba LLC ....D 216 221-6600
  Cleveland (G-6709)

SIDING: Plastic

Style Crest Inc ....B 419 332-7369
  Fremont (G-11099)

SIGN PAINTING & LETTERING SHOP

General Theming Contrs LLC ....C 614 252-6342
  Columbus (G-7655)
Toledo Sign Company Inc ....E 419 244-4444
  Toledo (G-18098)

SIGNALS: Traffic Control, Electric

Area Wide Protective Inc ....E 513 321-9889
  Fairfield (G-10696)
Paul Peterson Company ....E 614 486-4375
  Columbus (G-8427)
Security Fence Group Inc ....E 513 681-3700
  Cincinnati (G-4444)

SIGNS & ADVERTISING SPECIALTIES

A & A Safety Inc ....E 513 943-6100
  Amelia (G-563)
Archer Corporation ....E 330 455-9995
  Canton (G-2193)
Bates Metal Products Inc ....D 740 498-8371
  Port Washington (G-16121)
Belco Works Inc ....B 740 695-0500
  Saint Clairsville (G-16470)
Brown Cnty Bd Mntal Rtardation ....E 937 378-4891
  Georgetown (G-11261)
Galaxy Balloons Incorporated ....C 216 476-3360
  Cleveland (G-5589)
Glavin Industries Inc ....E 440 349-0049
  Solon (G-16851)
HP Manufacturing Company Inc ....D 216 361-6500
  Cleveland (G-5721)
Identitek Systems Inc ....D 330 832-9844
  Massillon (G-13697)
Orange Barrel Media LLC ....E 614 294-4898
  Columbus (G-8383)
Sabco Industries Inc ....E 419 531-5347
  Toledo (G-18016)
Screen Works Inc ....E 937 264-9111
  Dayton (G-9754)
Sign America Incorporated ....E 740 765-5555
  Richmond (G-16387)
Sign Source USA Inc ....D 419 224-1130
  Lima (G-12741)

SIGNS & ADVERTISING SPECIALTIES: Signs

Kessler Sign Company ....E 740 453-0668
  Zanesville (G-20323)
Paul Peterson Safety Div Inc ....E 614 486-4375
  Columbus (G-8428)

SIGNS & ADVERTSG SPECIALTIES: Displays/Cutouts Window/Lobby

BDS Packaging Inc ....D 937 643-0530
  Moraine (G-14624)
Benchmark Craftsman Inc ....E 330 975-4214
  Seville (G-16682)

SIGNS, ELECTRICAL: Wholesalers

Sign America Incorporated ....E 740 765-5555
  Richmond (G-16387)

SIGNS, EXC ELECTRIC, WHOLESALE

Dualite Sales & Service Inc ....C 513 724-7100
  Williamsburg (G-19493)

SIGNS: Electrical

Brilliant Electric Sign Co Ltd ....D 216 741-3800
  Brooklyn Heights (G-1866)
Danite Holdings Ltd ....E 614 444-3333
  Columbus (G-7416)
Gus Holthaus Signs Inc ....E 513 861-0060
  Cincinnati (G-3664)
United-Maier Signs Inc ....D 513 681-6600
  Cincinnati (G-4690)

SILICA MINING

Covia Holdings Corporation ....D 440 214-3284
  Independence (G-12063)

SILK SCREEN DESIGN SVCS

Galaxy Balloons Incorporated ....C 216 476-3360
  Cleveland (G-5589)
Screen Works Inc ....E 937 264-9111
  Dayton (G-9754)
Woodrow Manufacturing Co ....E 937 399-9333
  Springfield (G-17137)

SKATING RINKS: Roller

Edgewood Skate Arena ....E 419 331-0647
  Lima (G-12631)
Ohio Skate Inc ....E 419 476-2808
  Toledo (G-17958)
Skate Town U S A ....E 513 874-9855
  West Chester (G-19008)
Skateworld Inc ....E 937 294-4032
  Dayton (G-9771)
United Skates America Inc ....E 440 944-5300
  Wickliffe (G-19476)

SKI LODGE

Sycamore Lake Inc ....C 440 729-9775
  Chesterland (G-2746)

SKILL TRAINING CENTER

Capano & Associates LLC ....E 513 403-6000
  Liberty Township (G-12578)

SNACK & NONALCOHOLIC BEVERAGE BARS

Chillicothe Bowling Lanes Inc ....E 740 773-3300
  Chillicothe (G-2759)
Freeway Lanes Bowl Group LLC ....E 440 946-5131
  Mentor (G-14049)
Holiday Lanes Inc ....E 614 861-1600
  Columbus (G-7760)
Loyal Oak Golf Course Inc ....E 330 825-2904
  Barberton (G-960)
Plaz-Way Inc ....E 330 264-9025
  Wooster (G-19759)
Roseland Lanes Inc ....D 440 439-0097
  Bedford (G-1302)
Stonehedge Enterprises Inc ....E 330 928-2161
  Akron (G-442)

SNOW PLOWING SVCS

Bauer Lawn Maintenance Inc ....E 419 893-5296
  Maumee (G-13761)
Bladecutters Lawn Service Inc ....E 937 274-3861
  Dayton (G-9255)
C & B Buck Bros Asp Maint LLC ....E 419 536-7325
  Toledo (G-17633)
Dun Rite Home Improvement Inc ....E 330 650-5322
  Macedonia (G-13068)
Green Impressions LLC ....E 440 240-8508
  Sheffield Village (G-16734)
Greenscapes Landscape Company ....D 614 837-1869
  Columbus (G-7696)
H A M Landscaping Inc ....E 216 663-6666
  Cleveland (G-5650)
Mc Clurg & Creamer Inc ....E 419 866-7080
  Holland (G-11896)

SERVICES

Ohio Irrigation Lawn Sprinkler ....E 937 432-9911
  Dayton (G-9670)
Paramount Lawn Service Inc ....E 513 984-5200
  Loveland (G-13020)
Schill Landscaping and Lawn CA ....D 440 327-3030
  North Ridgeville (G-15343)
Supers Landscaping Inc ....E 440 775-0027
  Oberlin (G-15520)
T L C Landscaping Inc ....E 440 248-4852
  Cleveland (G-6495)
T O J Inc ....E 440 352-1900
  Mentor (G-14114)
Warstler Brothers Landscaping ....E 330 492-9500
  Canton (G-2531)
Yardmaster of Columbus Inc ....E 614 863-4510
  Blacklick (G-1485)
Z Snow Removal Inc ....E 513 683-7719
  Maineville (G-13120)

SOAPS & DETERGENTS

Cincinnati - Vulcan Company ....D 513 242-5300
  Cincinnati (G-3219)
Cr Brands Inc ....D 513 860-5039
  West Chester (G-18905)
New Vulco Mfg & Sales Co LLC ....D 513 242-2672
  Cincinnati (G-4109)
Washing Systems LLC ....C 800 272-1974
  Loveland (G-13032)

SOCIAL CHANGE ASSOCIATION

Community Action Columbiana CT ....D 330 424-7221
  Lisbon (G-12796)
Community Re-Entry Inc ....E 216 696-2717
  Cleveland (G-5327)
Provider Services Inc ....D 614 888-2021
  Columbus (G-8476)

SOCIAL CLUBS

Hide-A-Way Hills Club ....E 740 746-9589
  Sugar Grove (G-17374)
Leo Yannenoff Jewish Community ....C 614 231-2731
  Columbus (G-7966)
Minature Society Cincinnati ....D 513 931-9708
  Cincinnati (G-4059)
Toledo Club ....D 419 243-2200
  Toledo (G-18081)
Tusco Imaa Chapter No 602 ....E 330 878-7369
  Strasburg (G-17240)
Union Club Company ....D 216 621-4230
  Cleveland (G-6564)
University Club Inc ....E 513 721-2600
  Cincinnati (G-4697)
Youngstown Club ....E 330 744-3111
  Youngstown (G-20259)

SOCIAL SERVICES INFORMATION EXCHANGE

City of Warrensville Heights ....E 216 587-1230
  Cleveland (G-5217)
Greene Cnty Chld Svc Brd Frbrn ....D 937 878-1415
  Xenia (G-19901)
Lifeline Systems Company ....E 330 762-5627
  Akron (G-314)
Med Assist Prgram of Info Line ....E 330 762-0609
  Akron (G-328)

SOCIAL SERVICES, NEC

Columbus Surgical Center LLP ....E 614 932-9503
  Dublin (G-10182)
GE Reuter Stokes ....D 216 749-6332
  Cleveland (G-5600)
Neighborhood Health Care Inc ....E 513 221-4949
  Cincinnati (G-4104)
Shafer Confession ....E 419 399-4662
  Paulding (G-15799)
St Jude Social Concern Hot ....D 440 365-7971
  Elyria (G-10566)
W T C S A Headstart Niles Ctr ....E 330 652-0338
  Niles (G-15173)

SOCIAL SVCS CENTER

Aids Tskfrce Grter Clvland Inc ....D 216 357-3131
  Cleveland (G-4914)
American Cancer Society East ....E 800 227-2345
  Cleveland (G-4949)
American National Red Cross ....C 419 382-2707
  Toledo (G-17592)

American National Red Cross ....E 937 376-3111
  Xenia (G-19889)
American Red Cross of Grtr Col ....E 614 253-7981
  Columbus (G-6935)
Ashtabula County Community ....C 440 997-1721
  Ashtabula (G-714)
Bedford Township ....E 740 992-2117
  Middleport (G-14280)
Bridgeway Inc ....B 216 688-4114
  Cleveland (G-5079)
Catholic Charities Corporation ....B 330 723-9615
  Medina (G-13915)
Catholic Charities of Southwst ....D 937 325-8715
  Springfield (G-17005)
Catholic Charities of SW Ohio ....D 513 241-7745
  Cincinnati (G-3132)
Catholic Diocese of Columbus ....E 614 221-5891
  Columbus (G-7139)
Catholic Social Services Inc ....D 614 221-5891
  Columbus (G-7140)
Central Cmnty Hse of Columbus ....E 614 253-7267
  Columbus (G-7155)
Childrens Hunger Alliance ....E 614 341-7700
  Columbus (G-7190)
Cleveland Christian Home Inc ....C 216 671-0977
  Cleveland (G-5234)
Commu Act Comm of Fayette Cnty ....D 740 335-7282
  Wshngtn CT Hs (G-19865)
Community Action Comsn Belmont ....E 740 695-0293
  Saint Clairsville (G-16483)
Community Action Organization ....C 740 354-7541
  Portsmouth (G-16132)
Community Action Program Comm ....C 740 653-1711
  Lancaster (G-12384)
Community Action-Wayne/Medina ....D 330 264-8677
  Wooster (G-19710)
Consumer Support Services Inc ....D 740 522-5464
  Newark (G-15025)
County of Allen ....C 419 228-2120
  Lima (G-12623)
County of Lorain ....E 440 329-3734
  Elyria (G-10495)
County of Lorain ....D 440 284-1830
  Elyria (G-10498)
County of Richland ....E 419 774-5400
  Mansfield (G-13156)
County of Warren ....E 513 695-1420
  Lebanon (G-12457)
County of Washington ....D 740 373-5513
  Marietta (G-13323)
Creative Foundations Inc ....D 740 362-5102
  Delaware (G-9965)
Develpmntal Dsblties Ohio Dept ....C 937 233-8108
  Columbus (G-7442)
East End Neighborhood Hse Assn ....E 216 791-9378
  Cleveland (G-5456)
Easter Seals Center ....E 614 228-5523
  Hilliard (G-11764)
Fairborn Fish ....E 937 879-1313
  Fairborn (G-10672)
Faith Mission Inc ....E 614 224-6617
  Columbus (G-7558)
Family Service ....E 513 381-6300
  Cincinnati (G-3531)
Family Service Association ....E 937 222-9481
  Moraine (G-14655)
Family Service of NW Ohio ....D 419 321-6455
  Toledo (G-17725)
Free Store/Food Bank Inc ....E 513 482-4526
  Cincinnati (G-3588)
Freestore Foodbank Inc ....E 513 482-4500
  Cincinnati (G-3590)
Fulton County Senior Center ....E 419 337-9299
  Wauseon (G-18805)
Furniture Bank Central Ohio ....E 614 272-9544
  Columbus (G-7635)
G M N Tri Cnty Comnuty Action ....C 740 732-2388
  Caldwell (G-2039)
Godman Guild ....E 614 294-5476
  Columbus (G-7675)
Grace Resurrection Association ....E 937 548-2595
  Greenville (G-11380)
Greater Cincinnati Behavioral ....D 513 755-2203
  Walnut Hills (G-18635)
Greene Cnty Combined Hlth Dst ....D 937 374-5600
  Xenia (G-19902)
Handson Central Ohio Inc ....E 614 221-2255
  Columbus (G-7714)
Harcatus Tri-County Community ....E 740 922-0933
  New Philadelphia (G-14961)

HighInd Cnty Commnty Action or ....E 937 393-3060
  Hillsboro (G-11845)
Hockingthensperry Cmnty Action ....E 740 385-6813
  Logan (G-12839)
Homeless Families Foundation ....E 614 461-9427
  Columbus (G-7765)
Inside Out ....D 937 525-7880
  Springfield (G-17052)
Jewish Community Ctr Cleveland ....C 216 831-0700
  Beachwood (G-1069)
Jewish Family Services ....D 614 231-1890
  Columbus (G-7858)
Jewish Family Services Associa ....E 216 292-3999
  Cleveland (G-5796)
Jewish Fderation of Cincinnati ....E 513 985-1500
  Cincinnati (G-3816)
Kno-Ho-Co- Ashland Community A ....C 740 622-9801
  Coshocton (G-9021)
Leeda Services Inc ....C 330 325-1560
  Rootstown (G-16451)
Living In Family Environment ....D 614 475-5305
  Gahanna (G-11133)
Miami Valley Community Action ....E 937 456-2800
  Eaton (G-10454)
Nick Amster Inc ....D 330 264-9667
  Wooster (G-19751)
Ohio Association of Foodbanks ....E 614 221-4336
  Columbus (G-8229)
Ohioguidestone ....C 440 260-8900
  Cleveland (G-6126)
Pathway Inc ....E 419 242-7304
  Toledo (G-17974)
Pathways of Central Ohio ....E 740 345-6166
  Newark (G-15091)
Personal & Fmly Counseling Svc ....E 330 343-8171
  New Philadelphia (G-14976)
Pickaway County Community Acti ....D 740 477-1655
  Circleville (G-4839)
Pickaway County Community Acti ....E 740 474-7411
  Circleville (G-4840)
Pump House Ministries ....E 419 207-3900
  Ashland (G-684)
Rescue Mission of Mahoning Val ....D 330 744-5485
  Youngstown (G-20184)
Rescue Mission of Mahoning Val ....E 330 744-5485
  Youngstown (G-20185)
Royal Redeemer Lutheran Church ....E 440 237-7958
  North Royalton (G-15365)
Santa Maria Community Svcs Inc ....E 513 557-2720
  Cincinnati (G-4432)
Spanish American Committee ....E 216 961-2100
  Cleveland (G-6441)
St Vincent Family Centers ....C 614 252-0731
  Columbus (G-8681)
Support To At Risk Teens ....E 216 696-5507
  Cleveland (G-6486)
Tarry House Inc ....E 330 253-6689
  Akron (G-463)
Tasc of Northwest Ohio Inc ....E 419 242-9955
  Toledo (G-18060)
Taylor Murtis Human Svcs Sys ....D 216 283-4400
  Cleveland (G-6505)
The Foodbank Inc ....E 937 461-0265
  Dayton (G-9810)
Trumbull County One Stop ....D 330 675-2000
  Warren (G-18756)
Ussa Inc ....E 740 354-6672
  Portsmouth (G-16179)
Volunteers America Ohio & Ind ....C 614 253-6100
  Columbus (G-8859)
Volunters of Amer Greater Ohio ....D 216 541-9000
  Cleveland (G-6642)
Volunters of Amer Greater Ohio ....E 614 263-9134
  Columbus (G-8862)
West Ohio Cmnty Action Partnr ....C 419 227-2586
  Lima (G-12781)
West Side Community House ....E 216 771-7297
  Cleveland (G-6670)
Westcare Ohio Inc ....E 937 259-1898
  Dayton (G-9876)
Woodlnds Srving Centl Ohio Inc ....E 740 349-7051
  Newark (G-15111)
Youngstown Area Jwish Fdration ....C 330 746-3251
  Youngstown (G-20256)
Youngstown Neighborhood Dev ....E 330 480-0423
  Youngstown (G-20263)

SOCIAL SVCS, HANDICAPPED

Achievement Ctrs For Children ....D 216 292-9700
  Cleveland (G-4899)

Alexson Services Inc ....E 614 889-5837
  Dublin (G-10125)
ARC Industries Incorporated O ....B 614 836-0700
  Groveport (G-11494)
Athens County Board of Dev ....D 740 594-3539
  Athens (G-766)
Board Mental Retardation Dvlpm ....E 740 472-1712
  Woodsfield (G-19671)
Bridges To Independence Inc ....C 740 362-1996
  Delaware (G-9955)
Broken Arrow Inc ....E 419 562-3480
  Bucyrus (G-1977)
Catholic Residential Service ....E 513 784-0400
  Cincinnati (G-3133)
Champaign Residential Services ....E 614 481-5550
  Columbus (G-7178)
Columbus Speech & Hearing Ctr ....D 614 263-5151
  Columbus (G-7315)
County of Union ....D 937 645-6733
  Marysville (G-13491)
Free Store/Food Bank Inc ....E 513 241-1064
  Cincinnati (G-3589)
Licking County Board of Mrdd ....C 740 349-6588
  Newark (G-15053)
Matco Industries Inc ....E 740 852-7054
  London (G-12870)
Murray Ridge Production Center ....B 440 329-3734
  Elyria (G-10541)
Opportunities For Ohioans ....E 614 438-1200
  Columbus (G-8379)
Ottawa County Board M R D D ....E 419 734-6650
  Oak Harbor (G-15476)
Outreach Community Living Svcs ....E 330 263-0862
  Wooster (G-19757)
Pickaway Diversified ....E 740 474-1522
  Circleville (G-4843)
Portage County Board ....D 330 678-2400
  Ravenna (G-16255)
Sechkar Company ....E 740 385-8900
  Nelsonville (G-14837)
Self Reliance Inc ....E 937 525-0809
  Springfield (G-17111)
Siffrin Residential Assn ....C 330 799-8932
  Youngstown (G-20211)
Society For Handicapped Citzns ....E 937 746-4201
  Carlisle (G-2554)
United Disability Services Inc ....C 330 374-1169
  Akron (G-476)
Upreach LLC ....B 614 442-7702
  Columbus (G-8827)
Venture Productions Inc ....D 937 544-2823
  West Union (G-19139)
Whetstone Industries Inc ....E 419 947-9222
  Mount Gilead (G-14735)

SOCIAL SVCS: Individual & Family

Ability Works Inc ....C 419 626-1048
  Sandusky (G-16572)
Absolute Care Management Llc ....E 614 846-8053
  Columbus (G-6856)
Access Inc ....E 330 535-2999
  Akron (G-16)
Achievement Ctrs For Children ....E 440 250-2520
  Westlake (G-19310)
Action For Children Inc ....E 614 224-0222
  Columbus (G-6868)
Akron General Foundation ....E 330 344-6888
  Akron (G-41)
All Star Training Club ....E 330 352-5602
  Akron (G-64)
Allwell Behavioral Health Svcs ....E 740 454-9766
  Zanesville (G-20274)
Alternative Paths Inc ....E 330 725-9195
  Medina (G-13909)
American National Red Cross ....E 216 303-5476
  Parma (G-15760)
American National Red Cross ....E 937 631-9315
  Springfield (G-16994)
American Red Cross ....E 937 222-0124
  Dayton (G-9230)
Archdiocese of Cincinnati ....E 937 323-6507
  Springfield (G-16996)
Ashtabula Community Counseling ....D 440 998-6032
  Ashtabula (G-710)
Ashtabula County Commnty Actn ....D 440 576-6911
  Jefferson (G-12189)
Assoc Dvlpmtly Disabled ....E 614 486-4361
  Westerville (G-19222)
Avalon Foodservice Inc ....C 330 854-4551
  Canal Fulton (G-2092)

Beavercreek YMCA ....D 937 426-9622
  Dayton (G-9246)
Behavioral Treatments ....E 614 558-1968
  Hilliard (G-11746)
Behavral Cnnctions WD Cnty Inc ....E 419 872-2419
  Perrysburg (G-15836)
Bellefaire Jewish Chld Bur ....B 216 932-2800
  Shaker Heights (G-16703)
Belmont County of Ohio ....D 740 695-0460
  Saint Clairsville (G-16475)
Benjamin Rose Institute ....D 216 791-8000
  Cleveland (G-5057)
Benjamin Rose Institute ....D 216 791-3580
  Cleveland (G-5056)
Blanchard Vlly Crt Case Mngmnt ....D 419 422-6387
  Findlay (G-10876)
Blick Clinic Inc ....C 330 762-5425
  Akron (G-99)
Brenn Field Nursing Center ....C 330 683-4075
  Orrville (G-15626)
Butler County of Ohio ....C 513 887-3728
  Fairfield Township (G-10803)
Casto Health Care ....D 419 884-6400
  Mansfield (G-13148)
Catholic Charities Corporation ....E 216 268-4006
  Cleveland (G-5133)
Catholic Chrties Regional Agcy ....D 330 744-3320
  Youngstown (G-19982)
Center For Cognitv Behav Psych ....E 614 459-4490
  Columbus (G-7152)
Center For Families & Children ....E 216 932-9497
  Cleveland Heights (G-6715)
Center For Individual and Fmly ....E 419 522-4357
  Mansfield (G-13150)
Champaign Cnty Board of Dd ....E 937 653-5217
  Urbana (G-18422)
Childrens Cmprhensive Svcs Inc ....E 419 589-5511
  Mansfield (G-13151)
Childrens Homecare Services ....C 614 355-1100
  Columbus (G-7188)
Choices For Vctims Dom Volence ....E 614 258-6080
  Columbus (G-7194)
Christian Chld HM Ohio Inc ....D 330 345-7949
  Wooster (G-19700)
Cincinnati-Hmltn Cnty Comm Act ....C 513 569-1840
  Cincinnati (G-3276)
Cincinnati-Hmltn Cnty Comm Act ....C 513 569-4510
  Cincinnati (G-3277)
Cincinnati-Hmltn Cnty Comm Act ....C 513 354-3900
  Cincinnati (G-3278)
Cincysmiles Foundation Inc ....E 513 621-0248
  Cincinnati (G-3288)
Circle Health Services ....E 216 721-4010
  Cleveland (G-5182)
City Gospel Mission ....E 513 241-5525
  Cincinnati (G-3299)
Clermont County Community Svcs ....E 513 732-2277
  Batavia (G-988)
Community Action Program Corp ....E 740 373-6016
  Marietta (G-13320)
Community Solutions Assn ....E 330 394-9090
  Warren (G-18690)
Concord ....E 614 882-9338
  Westerville (G-19245)
Consumer Support Services Inc ....B 740 788-8257
  Newark (G-15024)
Consumer Support Services Inc ....D 330 764-4785
  Medina (G-13922)
Corporation For OH Appalachian ....E 740 594-8499
  Athens (G-772)
Council For Economic Opport ....D 216 696-9077
  Cleveland (G-5355)
Council On Aging of Southweste ....C 513 721-1025
  Cincinnati (G-3368)
Council On Rur Svc Prgrams Inc ....E 937 773-0773
  Piqua (G-16002)
Counseling Ctr Wayne Holmes CT ....C 330 264-9029
  Wooster (G-19712)
County of Clark ....B 937 327-1700
  Springfield (G-17024)
County of Columbiana ....C 330 424-1386
  Lisbon (G-12798)
County of Cuyahoga ....D 216 681-4433
  Cleveland (G-5368)
County of Darke ....E 937 526-4488
  Versailles (G-18568)
County of Guernsey ....E 740 439-6681
  Cambridge (G-2063)
County of Hamilton ....B 513 742-1576
  Cincinnati (G-3369)

County of Highland ....E 937 393-4278
  Hillsboro (G-11835)
County of Holmes ....E 330 674-1111
  Millersburg (G-14472)
County of Lake ....D 440 269-2193
  Willoughby (G-19516)
County of Lucas ....C 419 213-3000
  Toledo (G-17680)
County of Lucas ....B 419 213-8999
  Toledo (G-17682)
County of Mercer ....E 419 586-5106
  Celina (G-2592)
County of Montgomery ....B 937 224-5437
  Dayton (G-9326)
County of Montgomery ....E 937 225-4804
  Dayton (G-9330)
County of Ottawa ....E 419 898-2089
  Oak Harbor (G-15471)
County of Pickaway ....E 740 474-7588
  Circleville (G-4830)
County of Richland ....C 419 774-4100
  Mansfield (G-13155)
County of Summit ....A 330 634-8193
  Tallmadge (G-17473)
Creative Diversified Services ....E 937 376-7810
  Xenia (G-19896)
Crossroads Lake County Adole ....C 440 255-1700
  Mentor (G-14037)
Cuyahoga County ....A 216 431-4500
  Cleveland (G-5395)
Cyo & Community Services Inc ....E 330 762-2961
  Akron (G-178)
Defiance Cnty Bd Commissioners ....E 419 782-3233
  Defiance (G-9909)
Developmental Disabilities ....D 513 732-7015
  Owensville (G-15671)
Easter Seal Society of ....D 330 743-1168
  Youngstown (G-20025)
Easter Seals Metro Chicago Inc ....E 419 332-3016
  Fremont (G-11071)
Easter Seals Tristate ....C 513 985-0515
  Blue Ash (G-1549)
Easter Seals Tristate LLC ....C 513 475-6791
  Cincinnati (G-3474)
Eastway Corporation ....C 937 496-2000
  Dayton (G-9404)
Echoing Hills Village Inc ....C 740 327-2311
  Warsaw (G-18783)
Equitas Health Inc ....D 614 299-2437
  Columbus (G-7527)
Fairfld Ctr For Disablts & CER ....E 740 653-1186
  Lancaster (G-12401)
Family Cmnty Svcs Portage Cnty ....C 330 297-0078
  Ravenna (G-16243)
Family YMCA of LANcstr&fairfld ....D 740 277-7373
  Lancaster (G-12403)
Fayette Progressive Industries ....E 740 335-7453
  Wshngtn CT Hs (G-19872)
Findlay Y M C A Child Dev ....E 419 422-3174
  Findlay (G-10908)
Frans Child Care-Mansfield ....C 419 775-2500
  Mansfield (G-13178)
Galion Community Center YMCA ....E 419 468-7754
  Galion (G-11173)
Gallia-Meigs Community Action ....E 740 367-7341
  Cheshire (G-2734)
Girl Scuts Appleseed Ridge Inc ....E 419 225-4085
  Lima (G-12643)
Golden String Inc ....E 330 503-3894
  Youngstown (G-20052)
Good Smaritan Netwrk Ross Cnty ....E 740 774-6303
  Chillicothe (G-2783)
Goodwill Industries Inc ....E 330 724-6995
  Akron (G-240)
Goodwill Industries of Erie ....E 419 625-4744
  Sandusky (G-16611)
Goodwill Industries of Erie ....D 419 334-7566
  Fremont (G-11079)
Graceworks Lutheran Services ....C 937 433-2110
  Dayton (G-9470)
Great Miami Valley YMCA ....A 513 887-0001
  Hamilton (G-11602)
Great Miami Valley YMCA ....C 513 892-9622
  Fairfield Township (G-10808)
Great Miami Valley YMCA ....D 513 887-0014
  Hamilton (G-11604)
Great Miami Valley YMCA ....D 513 868-9622
  Hamilton (G-11605)
Great Miami Valley YMCA ....D 513 829-3091
  Fairfield (G-10732)

SERVICES

Greater Cleveland Food Bnk Inc .... C 216 738-2265	Ohio Hrtland Cmnty Action Comm .... E 419 468-5121	West Ohio Cmnty Action Partnr .... C 419 227-2586
Cleveland (G-5635)	Galion (G-11180)	Lima (G-12782)
Hardin County Family YMCA .... E 419 673-6131	Pastoral Care Management Svcs .... E 513 205-1398	West Side Ecumenical Ministry .... C 216 325-9369
Kenton (G-12279)	Cincinnati (G-4207)	Cleveland (G-6671)
Hattie Larlham Center For .... C 330 274-2272	Pathway 2 Hope Inc .... E 866 491-3040	Y M C A Central Stark County .... E 330 305-5437
Mantua (G-13267)	Cincinnati (G-4208)	Canton (G-2539)
Havar Inc .... D 740 594-3533	Pathways Inc .... D 440 918-1000	Y M C A Central Stark County .... E 330 875-1611
Athens (G-782)	Mentor (G-14095)	Louisville (G-12975)
Haven Rest Ministries Inc .... D 330 535-1563	Pike County YMCA .... E 740 947-8862	Y M C A Central Stark County .... E 330 877-8933
Akron (G-256)	Waverly (G-18822)	Uniontown (G-18392)
Healing Hrts Cunseling Ctr Inc .... E 419 528-5993	Planned Parenthood Association .... E 937 226-0780	Y M C A Central Stark County .... E 330 830-6275
Mansfield (G-13181)	Dayton (G-9694)	Massillon (G-13736)
Heap Home Energy Assistance .... D 419 626-6540	Portsmouth Metro Housing Auth .... E 740 354-4547	Y M C A Central Stark County .... E 330 498-4082
Sandusky (G-16615)	Portsmouth (G-16161)	Canton (G-2540)
Highland County Family YMCA .... E 937 840-9622	Pressley Ridge Foundation .... A 513 752-4548	Y M C A of Ashland Ohio Inc .... D 419 289-0626
Hillsboro (G-11842)	Cincinnati (G-2866)	Ashland (G-700)
Hockingthensperry Cmnty Action ...... C 740 767-4500	Pressley Ridge Foundation .... E 513 737-0400	YMCA .... D 937 653-9622
Glouster (G-11310)	Hamilton (G-11633)	Urbana (G-18447)
Home Instead Senior Care .... D 330 334-4664	Private Duty Services Inc .... C 419 238-3714	YMCA .... E 330 823-1930
Wadsworth (G-18599)	Van Wert (G-18487)	Alliance (G-558)
Hospice of Knox County .... E 740 397-5188	Rocking Horse Chld Hlth Ctr .... E 937 328-7266	YMCA of Clermont County Inc .... E 513 724-9622
Mount Vernon (G-14768)	Springfield (G-17103)	Batavia (G-1016)
Hospice of The Valley Inc .... D 330 788-1992	Ronald McDonald Hse Grtr Cinci .... E 513 636-7642	YMCA of Massillon .... E 330 879-0800
Youngstown (G-20069)	Cincinnati (G-4395)	Navarre (G-14826)
Hospice of The Western Reserve .... D 440 997-6619	Ross County Children Svcs Ctr .... D 740 773-2651	Young Mens Christian .... B 513 932-1424
Ashtabula (G-740)	Chillicothe (G-2818)	Lebanon (G-12516)
Huber Heights YMCA .... E 937 236-9622	Ross County YMCA .... D 740 772-4340	Young Mens Christian Assn .... E 419 332-9622
Dayton (G-9508)	Chillicothe (G-2823)	Fremont (G-11108)
Inn At Medina Limited LLC .... D 330 723-0110	Salvation Army .... D 513 762-5600	Young Mens Christian Assn .... E 419 238-0443
Medina (G-13954)	Cincinnati (G-4430)	Van Wert (G-18498)
Integrated Services of Appala .... D 740 594-6807	Salvation Army .... D 216 861-8185	Young Mens Christian Assoc .... C 614 885-4252
Athens (G-786)	Cleveland (G-6368)	Columbus (G-8927)
Interfaith Hosptlty Ntwrk of W .... D 513 934-5250	Sateri Home Inc .... D 330 758-8106	Young Mens Christian Assoc .... D 614 276-8224
Lebanon (G-12473)	Youngstown (G-20204)	Columbus (G-8928)
Lake County YMCA .... C 440 352-3303	Seamans Services .... E 216 621-4107	Young Mens Christian Assoc .... C 614 834-9622
Painesville (G-15718)	Cleveland (G-6384)	Canal Winchester (G-2129)
Lake County YMCA .... C 440 946-1160	Sickle Cell Awaremess Grp .... E 513 281-4450	Young Mens Christian Assoc .... E 419 729-8135
Willoughby (G-19538)	Cincinnati (G-4479)	Toledo (G-18167)
Lake County YMCA .... E 440 259-2724	Sidney-Shelby County YMCA .... E 937 492-9134	Young Mens Christian Assoc .... C 614 871-9622
Perry (G-15824)	Sidney (G-16800)	Grove City (G-11491)
Lake County YMCA .... D 440 428-5125	Society of St Vincent De Paul .... E 513 421-2273	Young Mens Christian Assoc .... E 937 223-5201
Madison (G-13099)	Cincinnati (G-4500)	Dayton (G-9892)
Leads Inc .... E 740 349-8606	Southstern Ohio Rgional Fd Ctr .... E 740 385-6813	Young Mens Christian Assoc .... D 330 923-5223
Newark (G-15049)	Logan (G-12854)	Cuyahoga Falls (G-9141)
Licco Inc .... C 740 522-8345	Springfield Family Y M C A .... D 937 323-3781	Young Mens Christian Assoc .... E 330 467-8366
Newark (G-15050)	Springfield (G-17119)	Macedonia (G-13091)
Lifecare Hospice .... E 330 264-4899	St Joseph Infant Maternity Hm .... C 513 563-2520	Young Mens Christian Assoc .... E 330 784-0408
Wooster (G-19741)	Cincinnati (G-4527)	Akron (G-507)
Lifecare Hospice .... D 330 336-6595	St Vincent De Paul Scl Svs .... D 937 222-7349	Young Mens Christian Assoc .... C 614 416-9622
Wadsworth (G-18604)	Dayton (G-9789)	Gahanna (G-11152)
Lima Family YMCA .... E 419 223-6045	Sunshine Communities .... B 419 865-0251	Young Mens Christian Assoc .... C 614 334-9622
Lima (G-12680)	Maumee (G-13857)	Hilliard (G-11832)
Lucas County Board of Developm ...... D 419 380-4000	Sycamore Board of Education .... D 513 489-3937	Young Mens Christian Assoc .... E 937 312-1810
Toledo (G-17868)	Cincinnati (G-4560)	Dayton (G-9893)
Maco Inc .... E 740 472-5445	Tasc New Town LLC .... E 419 242-9955	Young Mens Christian Assoc .... E 614 539-1770
Woodsfield (G-19675)	Toledo (G-18059)	Urbancrest (G-18453)
Mahoning County .... D 330 797-2837	Tasc of Southeast Ohio .... D 740 594-2276	Young Mens Christian Assoc .... D 614 252-3166
Youngstown (G-20107)	Athens (G-805)	Columbus (G-8929)
Marsh Foundation .... E 419 238-1695	Tcn Behavioral Health Svcs Inc .... C 937 376-8700	Young Mens Christian Assoc .... C 937 223-5201
Van Wert (G-18484)	Xenia (G-19927)	Springboro (G-16990)
Masco Inc .... E 330 797-2904	Transformation Network .... E 419 207-1188	Young Mens Christian Assoc .... E 937 593-9001
Youngstown (G-20118)	Ashland (G-695)	Bellefontaine (G-1370)
Miami Valley Community Action .... D 937 222-1009	Tri-County Community Act .... E 740 385-6812	Young Mens Christian Associat .... D 513 241-9622
Dayton (G-9617)	Logan (G-12857)	Cincinnati (G-4815)
Miracle Spirtl Retrst Orgnsizn .... E 216 324-4287	Twelve Inc .... E 330 837-3555	Young Mens Christian Associat .... D 513 923-4466
Cleveland (G-6000)	Massillon (G-13733)	Cincinnati (G-4816)
Mound Builders Guidance Center ...... D 740 522-2828	Ucc Childrens Center .... E 513 217-5501	Young Mens Christian Associat .... E 419 474-3995
Newark (G-15075)	Middletown (G-14356)	Toledo (G-18169)
Mt Washington Care Center Inc .... C 513 231-4561	United Rehabilitation Services .... D 937 233-1230	Young Mens Christian Associat .... D 419 866-9622
Cincinnati (G-4083)	Dayton (G-9832)	Maumee (G-13871)
National Youth Advocate Progra .... E 740 349-7511	United Way Greater Cincinnati .... D 513 762-7100	Young Mens Christian Associat .... C 419 475-3496
Newark (G-15080)	Cincinnati (G-4689)	Toledo (G-18170)
National Youth Advocate Progra .... E 614 487-8758	United Way of Greater Toledo .... D 419 254-4742	Young Mens Christian Associat .... D 419 691-3523
Columbus (G-8139)	Toledo (G-18122)	Oregon (G-15615)
National Youth Advocate Progra .... D 614 252-6927	United Way of The Greater Dayt .... E 937 225-3060	Young Mens Christian Mt Vernon ...... D 740 392-9622
Columbus (G-8140)	Dayton (G-9834)	Mount Vernon (G-14794)
Neighborhood House .... D 614 252-4941	Vermilion Family YMCA .... E 440 967-4208	Young MNS Chrstn Assn Clveland ...... E 216 941-4654
Columbus (G-8169)	Vermilion (G-18563)	Cleveland (G-6702)
Northwest Mental Health Svcs .... E 614 457-7876	Volunteers of America NW Ohio .... E 419 248-3733	Young MNS Chrstn Assn Clveland ...... D 440 808-8150
Columbus (G-8207)	Toledo (G-18140)	Westlake (G-19426)
Northwestrn OH Communty Action ..... C 419 784-2150	Volunters of Amer Greater Ohio .... E 614 861-8551	Young MNS Chrstn Assn Clveland ...... E 216 521-8400
Defiance (G-9932)	Columbus (G-8860)	Lakewood (G-12364)
Ohio Department of Health .... B 330 792-2397	Volunters of Amer Greater Ohio .... C 614 372-3120	Young MNS Chrstn Assn Clveland ...... E 216 731-7454
Austintown (G-858)	Columbus (G-8861)	Cleveland (G-6703)
Ohio Department of Health .... B 614 645-3621	Volunters of Amer Greater Ohio .... E 419 524-5013	Young MNS Chrstn Assn Clveland ...... D 440 285-7543
Columbus (G-8239)	Mansfield (G-13261)	Chardon (G-2726)
Ohio Department of Health .... D 937 285-6250	Volunters of America Cntl Ohio .... D 614 801-1655	Young MNS Chrstn Assn Grter NY ...... D 740 392-9622
Dayton (G-9668)	Grove City (G-11481)	Mount Vernon (G-14795)
Ohio Dept of Job & Fmly Svcs .... C 614 466-1213	W S O S Community A .... D 419 333-6068	Young Womens Christian .... E 419 238-6639
Columbus (G-8247)	Fremont (G-11104)	Van Wert (G-18499)

Young Womens Christian Assn..............D...... 614 224-9121
Columbus *(G-8931)*

Young Womens Christian Associ........E...... 216 881-6878
Cleveland *(G-6705)*

Young Womns Chrstn Assc Canton........D...... 330 453-0789
Canton *(G-2543)*

Youngstown Area Jwish Fdration........D...... 330 746-1076
Youngstown *(G-20257)*

Youngstown Committee On Alchol........D...... 330 744-1181
Youngstown *(G-20260)*

Youth Mntrng & At Rsk Intrvntn........E...... 216 324-2451
Richmond Heights *(G-16396)*

YWCA Dayton..................................D...... 937 461-5550
Dayton *(G-9896)*

YWCA Mahoning Valley..................E...... 330 746-6361
Youngstown *(G-20269)*

YWCA of Greater Cincinnati...........D...... 513 241-7090
Cincinnati *(G-4817)*

YWCA Shelter & Housing Network........E...... 937 222-6333
Dayton *(G-9897)*

SOCIAL WORKER

Four County Family Center.............E...... 800 693-6000
Wauseon *(G-18800)*

Mental Hlth Serv For CL & Mad........E...... 937 390-7980
Springfield *(G-17071)*

Preble County Council On Aging........E...... 937 456-4947
Eaton *(G-10459)*

SOFT DRINKS WHOLESALERS

Akron Coca-Cola Bottling Co...........A...... 330 784-2653
Akron *(G-34)*

Bellas Co....................................E...... 740 598-4171
Mingo Junction *(G-14527)*

Coca-Cola Bottling Co Cnsld...........D...... 937 878-5000
Dayton *(G-9311)*

P-Americas LLC.............................E...... 419 227-3541
Lima *(G-12716)*

P-Americas LLC.............................D...... 216 252-7377
Cleveland *(G-6156)*

Pepsi-Cola Metro Btlg Co Inc..........D...... 937 328-6750
Springfield *(G-17097)*

Pepsi-Cola Metro Btlg Co Inc..........E...... 330 336-3553
Wadsworth *(G-18611)*

Pepsi-Cola Metro Btlg Co Inc..........E...... 440 323-5524
Elyria *(G-10554)*

SOFTWARE PUBLISHERS: Application

Advanced Prgrm Resources Inc..........E...... 614 761-9994
Dublin *(G-10119)*

Delta Media Group Inc.................E...... 330 493-0350
Canton *(G-2283)*

Gracie Plum Investments Inc...........E...... 740 355-9029
Portsmouth *(G-16141)*

Hyland Software Inc....................A...... 440 788-5000
Westlake *(G-19355)*

Microsoft Corporation.................E...... 614 719-5900
Columbus *(G-6825)*

Microsoft Corporation.................E...... 216 986-1440
Cleveland *(G-5980)*

Microsoft Corporation.................D...... 513 339-2800
Mason *(G-13619)*

Mim Software Inc.......................E...... 216 896-9798
Beachwood *(G-1082)*

Preemptive Solutions LLC..............D...... 440 443-7200
Cleveland *(G-6228)*

Rivals Sports Grille LLC................E...... 216 267-0005
Middleburg Heights *(G-14258)*

Sanctuary Software Studio Inc.........E...... 330 666-9690
Fairlawn *(G-10847)*

Software Solutions Inc.................E...... 513 932-6667
Lebanon *(G-12504)*

SOFTWARE PUBLISHERS: Business & Professional

Agile Global Solutions Inc.............E...... 916 655-7745
Independence *(G-12041)*

Air Force US Dept of...................B...... 937 656-2354
Dayton *(G-9156)*

Cincom Systems Inc....................C...... 513 459-1470
Mason *(G-13555)*

Clinicl Otcms Mngmnt Syst LLC..........D...... 330 650-9900
Broadview Heights *(G-1828)*

Infoaccessnet LLC......................E...... 216 328-0100
Cleveland *(G-5750)*

Mapsys Inc.............................E...... 614 255-7258
Columbus *(G-8014)*

Netsmart Technologies Inc.............E...... 440 942-4040
Solon *(G-16877)*

Nextmed Systems Inc...................E...... 216 674-0511
Cincinnati *(G-4114)*

Ohio Cllbrtive Lrng Sltons Inc........E...... 216 595-5289
Beachwood *(G-1089)*

Onx USA LLC...........................D...... 440 569-2300
Cleveland *(G-6136)*

Oracle Corporation....................C...... 513 826-5632
Beavercreek *(G-1174)*

Parallel Technologies Inc.............D...... 614 798-9700
Dublin *(G-10304)*

Patriot Software LLC..................D...... 877 968-7147
Canton *(G-2436)*

Rebiz LLC.............................E...... 844 467-3249
Cleveland *(G-6291)*

Tmw Systems Inc.......................C...... 216 831-6606
Mayfield Heights *(G-13882)*

Turning Technologies LLC..............C...... 330 746-3015
Youngstown *(G-20228)*

Workspeed Management LLC..............E...... 917 369-9025
Solon *(G-16917)*

Zipscene LLC..........................D...... 513 201-5174
Cincinnati *(G-4819)*

SOFTWARE PUBLISHERS: Education

Flypaper Studio Inc...................E...... 602 801-2208
Cincinnati *(G-3574)*

Skillsoft Corporation.................D...... 216 524-5200
Independence *(G-12123)*

SOFTWARE PUBLISHERS: Home Entertainment

Estreamz Inc..........................E...... 513 278-7836
Cincinnati *(G-3516)*

SOFTWARE PUBLISHERS: NEC

Auto Des Sys Inc......................E...... 614 488-7984
Upper Arlington *(G-18394)*

Besttransportcom Inc..................E...... 614 888-2378
Columbus *(G-7031)*

Cimx LLC..............................E...... 513 248-7700
Cincinnati *(G-3217)*

Citynet Ohio LLC......................E...... 614 364-7881
Columbus *(G-7214)*

Creative Microsystems Inc.............D...... 937 836-4499
Englewood *(G-10583)*

Dakota Software Corporation...........D...... 216 765-7100
Cleveland *(G-5403)*

Datatrak International Inc............D...... 440 443-0082
Mayfield Heights *(G-13872)*

Digital Controls Corporation..........D...... 513 746-8118
Miamisburg *(G-14166)*

Drb Systems LLC.......................C...... 330 645-3299
Akron *(G-195)*

Eci Macola/Max LLC....................C...... 978 539-6186
Dublin *(G-10213)*

Edict Systems Inc.....................E...... 937 429-4288
Beavercreek *(G-1151)*

Einstruction Corporation..............D...... 330 746-3015
Youngstown *(G-20027)*

EMC Corporation.......................E...... 216 606-2000
Independence *(G-12069)*

Esko-Graphics Inc.....................D...... 937 454-1721
Miamisburg *(G-14168)*

Explorys Inc..........................D...... 216 767-4700
Cleveland *(G-5503)*

Finastra USA Corporation..............E...... 937 435-2335
Miamisburg *(G-14171)*

Flexnova Inc..........................E...... 216 288-6961
Cleveland *(G-5546)*

Foundation Software Inc...............D...... 330 220-8383
Strongsville *(G-17305)*

Hab Inc...............................E...... 608 785-7650
Solon *(G-16856)*

Honeywell International Inc............D...... 513 745-7200
Cincinnati *(G-3724)*

Juniper Networks Inc..................D...... 614 932-1432
Dublin *(G-10262)*

Matrix Management Solutions...........C...... 330 470-3700
Canton *(G-2392)*

Open Text Inc.........................E...... 614 658-3588
Hilliard *(G-11804)*

Oracle Systems Corporation............E...... 513 826-6000
Beachwood *(G-1092)*

Patrick J Burke & Co..................E...... 513 455-8200
Cincinnati *(G-4212)*

Peco II Inc...........................D...... 614 431-0694
Columbus *(G-8433)*

Quest Software Inc....................D...... 614 336-9223
Dublin *(G-10315)*

Retalix Inc...........................C...... 937 384-2277
Miamisburg *(G-14212)*

Revolution Group Inc..................D...... 614 212-1111
Westerville *(G-19207)*

Sigmatek Systems LLC..................D...... 513 674-0005
Cincinnati *(G-4481)*

Software Management Group.............E...... 513 618-2165
Cincinnati *(G-4504)*

Starwin Industries LLC................E...... 937 293-8568
Dayton *(G-9790)*

Symantec Corporation..................D...... 216 643-6700
Independence *(G-12127)*

Tata America Intl Corp................B...... 513 677-6500
Milford *(G-14435)*

Thinkware Incorporated................D...... 513 598-3300
Cincinnati *(G-4600)*

Triad Governmental Systems............E...... 937 376-5446
Xenia *(G-19930)*

Virtual Hold Technology LLC............D...... 330 670-2200
Akron *(G-489)*

SOFTWARE PUBLISHERS: Operating Systems

Seapine Software Inc..................E...... 513 754-1655
Mason *(G-13636)*

SOFTWARE PUBLISHERS: Publisher's

Exponentia US Inc.....................E...... 614 944-5103
Columbus *(G-7548)*

Nsa Technologies LLC..................C...... 330 576-4600
Akron *(G-353)*

SOFTWARE TRAINING, COMPUTER

Critical Business Analysis Inc........E...... 419 874-0800
Perrysburg *(G-15852)*

SOLDERS

Victory White Metal Company...........D...... 216 271-1400
Cleveland *(G-6628)*

SORORITY HOUSES

Alpha Epsilon PHI.....................E...... 614 294-5243
Columbus *(G-6902)*

CHI Omega Sorority....................E...... 937 325-9323
Springfield *(G-17007)*

SOUND EFFECTS & MUSIC PRODUCTION: Motion Picture

Live Technologies LLC.................D...... 614 278-7777
Columbus *(G-7986)*

SOUND RECORDING STUDIOS

Recording Workshop....................E...... 740 663-1000
Chillicothe *(G-2813)*

SOYBEAN PRDTS

Pioneer Hi-Bred Intl Inc..............E...... 419 748-8051
Grand Rapids *(G-11328)*

Schlessman Seed Co....................E...... 419 499-2572
Milan *(G-14367)*

SPACE VEHICLE EQPT

Curtiss-Wright Controls...............E...... 937 252-5601
Fairborn *(G-10667)*

General Electric Company..............B...... 513 977-1500
Cincinnati *(G-3608)*

Grimes Aerospace Company..............B...... 937 484-2001
Urbana *(G-18436)*

Sunpower Inc..........................D...... 740 594-2221
Athens *(G-804)*

SPARK PLUGS: Internal Combustion Engines

Fram Group Operations LLC.............D...... 419 661-6700
Perrysburg *(G-15867)*

SPAS

Alsan Corporation.....................D...... 330 385-3636
East Liverpool *(G-10396)*

SERVICES

Bellazio Salon & Day Spa............E 937 432-6722
Dayton (G-9249)
Changes Hair Designers Inc 614 846-6666
Columbus (G-6806)
Jbentley Studio & Spa LLC.........D..... 614 790-8828
Powell (G-16198)
Karen Funke Inc......................E 216 464-4311
Beachwood (G-1072)
Kerr House Inc.......................E 419 832-1733
Grand Rapids (G-11327)
Kristie Warner ....E 330 650-4450
Hudson (G-11992)
Marios International Spa & Ht.........E 330 562-5141
Aurora (G-835)
Mitchells Salon & Day Spa.........D..... 513 793-0900
Cincinnati (G-4061)
Mitchells Salon & Day Spa.........D..... 513 731-0600
Cincinnati (G-4063)
Paragon Salons Inc..................E 513 574-7610
Cincinnati (G-4198)
Spa Fitness Centers Inc ....E 419 476-6018
Toledo (G-18040)
Tuscany Spa Salon ....E 513 489-8872
Cincinnati (G-4655)
Uptown Hair Studio Inc ....E 937 832-2111
Englewood (G-10604)

SPECIAL EDUCATION SCHOOLS, PRIVATE

Adriel School Inc....................D..... 937 465-0010
West Liberty (G-19117)
Education Alternatives ....D..... 216 332-9360
Brookpark (G-1897)
Muskingum Starlight Industries ....D..... 740 453-4622
Zanesville (G-20342)
Oesterlen-Services For Youth.........C..... 937 399-6101
Springfield (G-17091)

SPECIAL EDUCATION SCHOOLS, PUBLIC

Belmont County of Ohio..............D..... 740 695-0460
Saint Clairsville (G-16475)

SPECIAL EVENTS DECORATION SVCS

Camargo Rental Center Inc...........E 513 271-6510
Cincinnati (G-3109)
Convivo Network LLC.................E 216 631-9000
Rocky River (G-16428)

SPECIALIZED LIBRARIES

Western Reserve Historical Soc...........D....... 216 721-5722
Cleveland (G-6675)

SPECIALTY FOOD STORES: Eggs & Poultry

Di Feo & Sons Poultry Inc ....E 330 564-8172
Akron (G-185)

SPECIALTY FOOD STORES: Health & Dietetic Food

Garys Pharmacy Inc ....E 937 456-5777
Eaton (G-10446)

SPECIALTY FOOD STORES: Juices, Fruit Or Vegetable

M & M Wine Cellar Inc................E 330 536-6450
Lowellville (G-13041)

SPECIALTY OUTPATIENT CLINICS, NEC

Akron General Medical Center.........C..... 330 665-8000
Akron (G-46)
American Kidney Stone MGT Ltd ....E 800 637-5188
Columbus (G-6928)
Anazao Community Partners ....E 330 264-9597
Wooster (G-19687)
Appleseed Cmnty Mntal Hlth Ctr ......E 419 281-3716
Ashland (G-645)
Best Care Nrsing Rhbltion Ctr.........C..... 740 574-2558
Wheelersburg (G-19428)
Bridgeway Inc........................B...... 216 688-4114
Cleveland (G-5079)
Caprice Health Care Inc..............C..... 330 965-9200
North Lima (G-15267)
Center For Addiction Treatment ....D..... 513 381-6672
Cincinnati (G-3148)
Central Commnty Hlth Brd of Ha ......D..... 513 559-2000
Cincinnati (G-3152)

CHI Health At Home ....E 513 576-0262
Milford (G-14377)
Childrens Hospital Medical Ctr ....E....... 513 636-6100
Cincinnati (G-3189)
Childrens Hospital Medical Ctr ....E....... 513 636-6800
Mason (G-13554)
Christ Hospital Spine Surgery ....E...... 513 619-5899
Cincinnati (G-3211)
Cleveland Clinic Foundation ....D....... 440 988-5651
Lorain (G-12893)
Clevelnd Clnc Hlth Systm East ....E...... 330 287-4830
Wooster (G-19709)
Clevelnd Clnc Hlth Systm East ....E...... 330 468-0190
Northfield (G-15376)
Clinton County Board of Dd ....E 937 382-7519
Wilmington (G-19609)
Clinton Memorial Hospital ....E 937 383-3402
Wilmington (G-19614)
Community Assesment and Treatm ....D..... 216 441-0200
Cleveland (G-5324)
Community Health Centers Ohio........D..... 216 831-1494
Beachwood (G-1047)
Community Mental Health Svc ....D..... 740 695-9344
Saint Clairsville (G-16484)
Comprehensive Addiction Svc Sy ......D..... 419 241-8827
Toledo (G-17674)
Crossroads Center ....C..... 513 475-5300
Cincinnati (G-3382)
Eastway Corporation ....C..... 937 531-7000
Dayton (G-9405)
HCA Holdings Inc ....D..... 440 826-3240
Cleveland (G-5669)
Healthsource of Ohio Inc ....E 513 707-1997
Batavia (G-1001)
Healthsource of Ohio Inc ....E 937 981-7707
Greenfield (G-11363)
Hope Ctr For Cncer Care Warren ......D..... 330 856-8600
Warren (G-18713)
Hospice of Darke County Inc ....E 419 678-4808
Coldwater (G-6759)
Mahoning Vly Hmtlgy Onclgy Aso ......E 330 318-1100
Youngstown (G-20110)
Marion Area Counseling Ctr ....C..... 740 387-5210
Marion (G-13434)
McKinley Hall Inc ....E 937 328-5300
Springfield (G-17068)
Medcentral Health System ....E 419 526-8442
Mansfield (G-13214)
Mercy Healthplexm LLC...............E 513 870-7101
Fairfield (G-10756)
Mercy Medical Center Inc ....E 330 627-7641
Carrollton (G-2572)
Met Group ....E 330 864-1916
Fairlawn (G-10840)
Metrohealth System ....E 216 957-5000
Cleveland (G-5966)
Neighborhood Health Asso ....D..... 419 720-7883
Toledo (G-17935)
Neighborhood House ....D..... 614 252-4941
Columbus (G-8169)
North East Ohio Health Svcs ....D..... 216 831-6466
Beachwood (G-1086)
Northpoint Senior Services LLC........D..... 740 369-9614
Delaware (G-9998)
Odyssey Healthcare Inc ....E 937 298-2800
Dayton (G-9667)
Ohio Heart Institute Inc ....E 330 747-6446
Youngstown (G-20144)
Oral & Maxillofacial Surgeons ....E 419 385-5743
Toledo (G-17965)
Pain Management Associates Inc ......E 937 252-2000
Dayton (G-9186)
Plastic Surgery Group Inc ....E 513 791-4440
Cincinnati (G-4253)
Positive Education Program ....E 440 471-8200
Cleveland (G-6224)
Pregnancy Care of Cincinnati ....E 513 487-7777
Cincinnati (G-4270)
Rescue Incorporated ....C..... 419 255-9585
Toledo (G-18004)
Robinson Health System Inc ....E 330 678-4100
Ravenna (G-16262)
Shr Management Resources Corp ......E 937 274-1546
Dayton (G-9764)
Springfeld Rgnal Otpatient Ctr ....E 937 390-8310
Springfield (G-17115)
St Vincent Family Centers ....C..... 614 252-0731
Columbus (G-8681)
Summa Health System ....C..... 330 375-3315
Akron (G-451)

Surgicenter of Mansfield..............E 419 774-9410
Mansfield (G-13247)
Tcn Behavioral Health Svcs Inc........C..... 937 376-8700
Xenia (G-19927)
Univ Dermatology ....D..... 513 475-7630
Cincinnati (G-4692)
University Mednet ....C..... 440 255-0800
Mentor (G-14120)
University of Cincinnati ....C..... 513 584-3200
Cincinnati (G-4720)
University Radiology Assoc ....D..... 513 475-8760
Cincinnati (G-4729)
Upper Arlington Surgery Center ....E 614 442-6515
Columbus (G-8826)
Wendt-Bristol Health Services ....E 614 403-9966
Columbus (G-8886)
West End Health Center Inc ....E 513 621-2726
Cincinnati (G-4782)
Wood County Chld Svcs Assn ....D..... 419 352-7588
Bowling Green (G-1752)

SPECULATIVE BUILDERS: Multi-Family Housing

Bernard Busson Builder...............E 330 929-4926
Akron (G-95)

SPECULATIVE BUILDERS: Single-Family Housing

Dold Homes Inc......................E 419 874-2535
Perrysburg (G-15860)
M/I Homes Inc.......................B...... 614 418-8000
Columbus (G-8006)
Phil Wagler Construction Inc ....E 330 899-0316
Uniontown (G-18382)
Plus Realty Cincinnati Inc ....E 513 575-4500
Milford (G-14425)
Weaver Custom Homes Inc ....E 330 264-5444
Wooster (G-19781)
Zicka Walker Builders Ltd ....E 513 247-3500
Cincinnati (G-4818)

SPEECH DEFECT CLINIC

Cincinnati Speech Hearing Ctr ....E 513 221-0527
Cincinnati (G-3268)
Youngstown Hearing Speech Ctr ......E 330 726-8391
Youngstown (G-20262)

SPEED CHANGERS

Great Lakes Power Products Inc...........D 440 951-5111
Mentor (G-14056)

SPICE & HERB STORES

Gold Star Chili Inc....................E 513 231-4541
Cincinnati (G-3624)

SPONGES, ANIMAL, WHOLESALE

Armaly LLC..........................E 740 852-3621
London (G-12859)

SPORTING & RECREATIONAL GOODS & SPLYS WHOLESALERS

4th and Goal Distribution LLC ....E 440 212-0769
Burbank (G-2008)
AB Marketing LLC....................E 513 385-6158
Fairfield (G-10691)
Air Venturi Ltd ....D..... 216 292-2570
Solon (G-16818)
Coachs Sports Corner Inc.............E 419 609-3737
Sandusky (G-16588)
Dwa Mrkting Prmtional Pdts LLC ......E 216 476-0635
Strongsville (G-17298)
Kohlmyer Sporting Goods Inc ....E 440 277-8296
Lorain (G-12910)
Mc Gregor Family Enterprises.........E 513 583-0040
Cincinnati (G-3984)
R & A Sports Inc.....................E 216 289-2254
Euclid (G-10654)
Schneider Saddlery LLC ....E 440 543-2700
Chagrin Falls (G-2682)
Willow and Cane LLC ....E 609 280-1150
Springboro (G-16988)
Wilson Sporting Goods Co ....C..... 419 634-9901
Ada (G-6)
Zebec of North America Inc ....E 513 829-5533
Fairfield (G-10800)

Zide Sport Shop of Ohio Inc ....D...... 740 373-6446
Marietta (G-13403)

SPORTING & RECREATIONAL GOODS, WHOL: Water Slides, Rec Park

Cherry Valley Lodge ....E...... 740 788-1200
Newark (G-15022)
Durga Llc ....D...... 513 771-2080
Cincinnati (G-3457)
Lmn Development LLC ....D...... 419 433-7200
Sandusky (G-16623)

SPORTING & RECREATIONAL GOODS, WHOLESALE: Athletic Goods

Brennan-Eberly Team Sports Inc ....E....... 419 865-8326
Holland (G-11876)
Riddell Inc ....E....... 440 366-8225
North Ridgeville (G-15341)

SPORTING & RECREATIONAL GOODS, WHOLESALE: Boat Access & Part

Miami Corporation ....E....... 800 543-0448
Cincinnati (G-4044)

SPORTING & RECREATIONAL GOODS, WHOLESALE: Bowling

Beaver-Vu Bowl ....E....... 937 426-6771
Beavercreek (G-1130)
Done-Rite Bowling Service Co ....E....... 440 232-3280
Bedford (G-1278)
Micnan Inc ....E....... 330 920-6200
Cuyahoga Falls (G-9113)

SPORTING & RECREATIONAL GOODS, WHOLESALE: Fitness

21st Century Health Spa Inc ....E....... 419 476-5585
Toledo (G-17573)
Ball Bounce and Sport Inc ....B....... 419 289-9310
Ashland (G-654)
Suarez Corporation Industries ....D....... 330 494-4282
Canton (G-2502)

SPORTING & RECREATIONAL GOODS, WHOLESALE: Golf

Golf Galaxy Golfworks Inc ....C....... 740 328-4193
Newark (G-15037)

SPORTING & RECREATIONAL GOODS, WHOLESALE: Gymnasium

A K Athletic Equipment Inc ....E....... 614 920-3069
Canal Winchester (G-2102)

SPORTING FIREARMS WHOLESALERS

Aspc Corp ....C....... 937 593-7010
Bellefontaine (G-1345)

SPORTING GOODS

Galaxy Balloons Incorporated ....C....... 216 476-3360
Cleveland (G-5589)
Mc Alarney Pool Spas and Blld ....E....... 740 373-6698
Marietta (G-13357)
Zebec of North America Inc ....E....... 513 829-5533
Fairfield (G-10800)

SPORTING GOODS STORES, NEC

Al-Mar Lanes ....E....... 419 352-4637
Bowling Green (G-1713)
Bigelow Corporation ....E....... 937 339-3315
Troy (G-18196)
Cambridge Country Club Company ......E....... 740 439-2744
Byesville (G-2023)
Coachs Sports Corner Inc ....E....... 419 609-3737
Sandusky (G-16588)
Columbus Country Club ....E....... 614 861-0800
Columbus (G-7272)
Daves Running Shop Inc ....E....... 567 525-4767
Findlay (G-10896)
Emerald Woods Golf Course ....E....... 440 236-8940
Columbia Station (G-6775)
Hawthorne Valley Country Club ....D....... 440 232-1400
Bedford (G-1285)

Heritage Golf Club Ltd Partnr ....D...... 614 777-1690
Hilliard (G-11773)
Kohlmyer Sporting Goods Inc ....E...... 440 277-8296
Lorain (G-12910)
Madison Route 20 LLC ....E...... 440 358-7888
Painesville (G-15723)
Mahoning Country Club Inc ....E...... 330 545-2517
Girard (G-11294)
Mayfield Sand Ridge Club ....E...... 216 381-0826
Cleveland (G-5924)
Mc Gregor Family Enterprises ....E...... 513 583-0040
Cincinnati (G-3984)
Meadowlake Corporation ....E...... 330 492-2010
Canton (G-2397)
Medallion Club ....C...... 614 794-6999
Westerville (G-19185)
Moundbuilders Country Club Co ....D...... 740 344-4500
Newark (G-15076)
Pines Golf Club ....E...... 330 684-1414
Orrville (G-15644)
Quail Hollow Management Inc ....D...... 440 639-4000
Painesville (G-15734)
Sand Ridge Golf Club ....D...... 440 285-8088
Chardon (G-2713)
Shady Hollow Cntry CLB Co Inc ....D...... 330 832-1581
Massillon (G-13729)
Silver Lake Country Club ....D...... 330 688-6066
Silver Lake (G-16809)
Springfield Country Club Co ....E...... 937 399-4215
Springfield (G-17118)
Tartan Fields Golf Club Ltd ....D...... 614 792-0900
Dublin (G-10353)
Yankee Run Golf Course ....D...... 330 448-8096
Brookfield (G-1858)
Youngstown Country Club ....D...... 330 759-1040
Youngstown (G-20261)

SPORTING GOODS STORES: Firearms

Pyramyd Air Ltd ....E...... 216 896-0893
Solon (G-16887)

SPORTING GOODS STORES: Gymnasium Eqpt, NEC

Chalk Box Get Fit LLC ....E...... 440 992-9619
Ashtabula (G-725)

SPORTING GOODS STORES: Pool & Billiard Tables

Burnett Pools Inc ....E...... 330 372-1725
Cortland (G-8985)

SPORTING GOODS STORES: Skating Eqpt

Ohio Skate Inc ....E...... 419 476-2808
Toledo (G-17958)

SPORTING GOODS STORES: Specialty Sport Splys, NEC

Capitol Varsity Sports Inc ....E...... 513 523-4126
Oxford (G-15675)

SPORTING GOODS STORES: Tennis Goods & Eqpt

Tennis Unlimited Inc ....E...... 330 928-8763
Akron (G-467)

SPORTS APPAREL STORES

Chalk Box Get Fit LLC ....E...... 440 992-9619
Ashtabula (G-725)
Gymnastic World Inc ....E...... 440 526-2970
Cleveland (G-5649)

SPORTS CLUBS, MANAGERS & PROMOTERS

Ap23 Sports Complex LLC ....E...... 614 452-0760
Columbus (G-6954)
Five Seasons Spt Cntry CLB Inc ....D...... 937 848-9200
Dayton (G-9441)
Windwood Swim & Tennis Club ....E...... 513 777-2552
West Chester (G-19037)

SPORTS TEAMS & CLUBS: Baseball

Alliance Hot Stove Baseball L ....E...... 330 823-7034
Alliance (G-516)

Cascia LLC ....E....... 440 975-8085
Willoughby (G-19509)
Cincinnati Reds LLC ....C....... 513 765-7000
Cincinnati (G-3263)
Cincinnati Reds LLC ....D....... 513 765-7923
Cincinnati (G-3264)
Cleveland Indians Baseball Com ....D....... 216 420-4487
Cleveland (G-5262)
Dayton Prof Basbal CLB LLC ....E....... 937 228-2287
Dayton (G-9378)
Palisdes Bsbal A Cal Ltd Prtnr ....C....... 330 505-0000
Niles (G-15166)
Toledo Mud Hens Basbal CLB Inc ....D....... 419 725-4367
Toledo (G-18091)

SPORTS TEAMS & CLUBS: Basketball

Cavaliers Holdings LLC ....C....... 216 420-2000
Cleveland (G-5136)

SPORTS TEAMS & CLUBS: Football

Cincinnati Bengals Inc ....C....... 513 621-3550
Cincinnati (G-3230)
Cleveland Browns Football LLC ....C....... 440 891-5000
Berea (G-1419)
National Football Museum Inc ....E....... 330 456-8207
Canton (G-2414)
Ohio High School Football Coac ....E....... 419 673-1286
Etna (G-10618)

SPORTS TEAMS & CLUBS: Ice Hockey

Colhoc Limited Partnership ....C....... 614 246-4625
Columbus (G-7244)

SPORTS TEAMS & CLUBS: Soccer

Columbus Team Soccer LLC ....E....... 614 447-1301
Columbus (G-7319)
Crew Soccer Stadium LLC ....E....... 614 447-2739
Columbus (G-7392)
Wall2wall Soccer LLC ....E....... 513 573-9898
Mason (G-13655)

SPRAYS: Self-Defense

Mace Personal Def & SEC Inc ....E....... 440 424-5321
Cleveland (G-5893)

SPRINGS: Steel

Hendrickson International Corp ....D....... 740 929-5600
Hebron (G-11714)

SPRINGS: Wire

Barnes Group Inc ....E....... 419 891-9292
Maumee (G-13760)

SPRINKLING SYSTEMS: Fire Control

Fire Foe Corp ....E....... 330 759-9834
Girard (G-11287)

STADIUM EVENT OPERATOR SERVICES

Phoenix ....D....... 513 721-8901
Cincinnati (G-4243)

STAFFING, EMPLOYMENT PLACEMENT

56 Plus Management LLC ....E....... 937 323-4114
Springfield (G-16991)
Advantage Rn LLC ....D....... 866 301-4045
West Chester (G-18859)
Allcan Global Services Inc ....E....... 513 825-1655
Cincinnati (G-2924)
Berns Oneill SEC & Safety LLC ....E....... 330 374-9133
Akron (G-96)
Custom Halthcare Proffessional ....E....... 216 381-1010
Cleveland (G-5392)
Dawson Resources ....E....... 614 255-1400
Columbus (G-7420)
Dedicated Technologies Inc ....D....... 614 460-3200
Columbus (G-7427)
Employment Network ....E....... 440 324-5244
Elyria (G-10510)
Gallery Holdings LLC ....D....... 773 693-6220
Independence (G-12076)
Professional Contract Systems ....C....... 513 469-8800
Cincinnati (G-4292)
Reserves Network Inc ....E....... 440 779-1400
Cleveland (G-6314)

S
E
R
V
I
C
E
S

Robert Half International Inc .... D 513 563-0770
  Blue Ash (G-1647)

Robert Half International Inc .... D 614 221-8326
  Columbus (G-8541)

Robert Half International Inc .... D 513 621-8367
  Cincinnati (G-4391)

Siffrin Residential Assn .... C 330 799-8932
  Youngstown (G-20211)

Staffmark Holdings Inc .... D 513 651-1111
  Cincinnati (G-4528)

Wood County Ohio .... E 419 352-5059
  Bowling Green (G-1758)

Work Solutions Group LLC .... E 440 205-8297
  Mentor (G-14126)

Youth Opportunities Unlimited .... E 216 566-5445
  Cleveland (G-6706)

STAINLESS STEEL

Latrobe Spcialty Mtls Dist Inc .... D 330 609-5137
  Vienna (G-18580)

STAMPINGS: Automotive

Falls Stamping & Welding Co .... C 330 928-1191
  Cuyahoga Falls (G-9092)

Honda of America Mfg Inc .... C 937 644-0724
  Marysville (G-13505)

R K Industries Inc .... D 419 523-5001
  Ottawa (G-15666)

STAMPINGS: Metal

Bates Metal Products Inc .... D 740 498-8371
  Port Washington (G-16121)

Breitinger Company .... C 419 526-4255
  Mansfield (G-13145)

Long-Stanton Mfg Company .... E 513 874-8020
  West Chester (G-18964)

Matco Tools Corporation .... B 330 929-4949
  Stow (G-17219)

Mid-America Steel Corp .... E 800 282-3466
  Cleveland (G-5982)

Mtd Holdings Inc .... B 330 225-2600
  Valley City (G-18467)

Northwind Industries Inc .... E 216 433-0666
  Cleveland (G-6099)

Quality Fabricated Metals Inc .... E 330 332-7008
  Salem (G-16555)

Scott Fetzer Company .... C 216 267-9000
  Cleveland (G-6379)

STATE CREDIT UNIONS, NOT FEDERALLY CHARTERED

Atomic Credit Union Inc .... E 740 289-5060
  Piketon (G-15971)

Buckeye State Credit Union .... D 330 253-9197
  Akron (G-113)

C E S Credit Union Inc .... E 561 203-5443
  Loudonville (G-12954)

Cme Federal Credit Union .... E 614 224-4388
  Columbus (G-7235)

Credit Union of Ohio Inc .... E 614 487-6650
  Hilliard (G-11757)

Directions Credit Union Inc .... D 419 720-4769
  Sylvania (G-17419)

Directions Credit Union Inc .... E 419 524-7113
  Mansfield (G-13167)

Erie Shores Credit Union Inc .... E 419 897-8110
  Maumee (G-13787)

Firefighters Cmnty Cr Un Inc .... E 216 621-4644
  Cleveland (G-5527)

Greater Cincinnati Credit Un .... D 513 559-1234
  Mason (G-13589)

Hancock Federal Credit Union .... E 419 420-0338
  Findlay (G-10917)

Homeland Credit Union Inc .... D 740 775-3024
  Chillicothe (G-2787)

Homeland Credit Union Inc .... E 740 775-3331
  Chillicothe (G-2788)

Kemba Financial Credit Union .... D 614 235-2395
  Columbus (G-7890)

Seven Seventeen Credit Un Inc .... C 330 372-8100
  Warren (G-18741)

Seven Seventeen Credit Un Inc .... E 330 372-8100
  Warren (G-18742)

Sun Federal Credit Union .... D 419 537-0200
  Toledo (G-18052)

Universal 1 Credit Union Inc .... D 800 762-9555
  Dayton (G-9835)

Wright-Patt Credit Union Inc .... B 937 912-7000
  Beavercreek (G-1200)

STATE SAVINGS BANKS, NOT FEDERALLY CHARTERED

Belmont Savings Bank .... E 740 695-0140
  Saint Clairsville (G-16478)

Fort Jennings State Bank .... E 419 286-2527
  Fort Jennings (G-10983)

Geauga Savings Bank .... E 440 564-9441
  Newbury (G-15121)

United Community Fincl Corp .... C 330 742-0500
  Youngstown (G-20231)

STATIONARY & OFFICE SPLYS, WHOL: Computer/Photocopying Splys

Canon Solutions America Inc .... E 216 750-2980
  Independence (G-12054)

Dexxxon Digital Storage Inc .... E 740 548-7179
  Lewis Center (G-12538)

Med-Pass Incorporated .... E 937 438-8884
  Dayton (G-9599)

STATIONARY & OFFICE SPLYS, WHOLESALE: Laser Printer Splys

Electronic Printing Pdts Inc .... E 330 689-3930
  Stow (G-17200)

STATIONARY & OFFICE SPLYS, WHOLESALE: Stationery

Business Stationery LLC .... D 216 514-1192
  Cleveland (G-5107)

Ohio & Michigan Paper Company .... E 419 666-1500
  Perrysburg (G-15896)

STATIONERY & OFFICE SPLYS WHOLESALERS

AW Faber-Castell Usa Inc .... D 216 643-4660
  Cleveland (G-5028)

Friends Service Co Inc .... E 419 427-1704
  Findlay (G-10910)

Pfg Ventures LP .... D 216 520-8400
  Independence (G-12107)

Quick Tab II Inc .... D 419 448-6622
  Tiffin (G-17533)

Signal Office Supply Inc .... E 513 821-2280
  Cincinnati (G-4482)

Staples Inc .... E 740 845-5600
  London (G-12875)

W B Mason Co Inc .... D 216 267-5000
  Cleveland (G-6644)

STEAM HEATING SYSTEMS SPLY SVCS

Akron Energy Systems LLC .... D 330 374-0600
  Akron (G-38)

STEAM SPLY SYSTEMS SVCS INCLUDING GEOTHERMAL

Cleveland Thermal LLC .... E 216 241-3636
  Cleveland (G-5293)

STEAM, HEAT & AIR CONDITIONING DISTRIBUTION SVC

Brewer-Garrett Co .... C 440 243-3535
  Middleburg Heights (G-14248)

Honeywell International Inc .... D 216 459-6053
  Cleveland (G-5702)

Medical Center Co (inc) .... E 216 368-4256
  Cleveland (G-5942)

STEEL FABRICATORS

A & G Manufacturing Co Inc .... E 419 468-7433
  Galion (G-11164)

Albert Freytag Inc .... E 419 628-2018
  Minster (G-14531)

Allied Fabricating & Wldg Co .... E 614 751-6664
  Columbus (G-6897)

Alro Steel Corporation .... E 937 253-6121
  Dayton (G-9221)

Ameridian Specialty Services .... E 513 769-0150
  Cincinnati (G-2952)

Arctech Fabricating Inc .... E 937 525-9353
  Springfield (G-16997)

Bauer Corporation .... E 800 321-4760
  Wooster (G-19689)

Blackburns Fabrication Inc .... E 614 875-0784
  Columbus (G-7046)

Blevins Metal Fabrication Inc .... E 419 522-6082
  Mansfield (G-13143)

Breitinger Company .... C 419 526-4255
  Mansfield (G-13145)

Buck Equipment Inc .... E 614 539-3039
  Grove City (G-11414)

C-N-D Industries Inc .... E 330 478-8811
  Massillon (G-13667)

Clifton Steel Company .... D 216 662-6111
  Maple Heights (G-13283)

Continental GL Sls & Inv Group .... B 614 679-1201
  Powell (G-16192)

County of Lake .... D 440 269-2193
  Willoughby (G-19516)

Curtiss-Wright Flow Control .... D 513 528-7900
  Cincinnati (G-2847)

Debra-Kuempel Inc .... E 513 271-6500
  Cincinnati (G-3414)

Emh Inc .... E 330 220-8600
  Valley City (G-18462)

Evers Welding Co Inc .... E 513 385-7352
  Cincinnati (G-3521)

Franck and Fric Incorporated .... D 216 524-4451
  Cleveland (G-5572)

George Steel Fabricating Inc .... E 513 932-2887
  Lebanon (G-12466)

Graber Metal Works Inc .... E 440 237-8422
  North Royalton (G-15356)

Hanson Concrete Products Ohio .... E 614 443-4846
  Columbus (G-7716)

Hynes Industries Inc .... C 330 799-3221
  Youngstown (G-20073)

Industrial Mill Maintenance .... E 330 746-1155
  Youngstown (G-20078)

Kings Welding and Fabg Inc .... E 330 738-3592
  Mechanicstown (G-13905)

Kottler Metal Products Co Inc .... E 440 946-7473
  Willoughby (G-19535)

Langdon Inc .... E 513 733-5955
  Cincinnati (G-3909)

Lapham-Hickey Steel Corp .... E 614 443-4881
  Columbus (G-7952)

Laserflex Corporation .... D 614 850-9600
  Hilliard (G-11783)

Lefeld Welding & Stl Sups Inc .... E 419 678-2397
  Coldwater (G-6762)

Marsam Metalfab Inc .... E 330 405-1520
  Twinsburg (G-18295)

Marysville Steel Inc .... E 937 642-5971
  Marysville (G-13515)

Mason Structural Steel Inc .... D 440 439-1040
  Walton Hills (G-18637)

McWane Inc .... B 740 622-6651
  Coshocton (G-9022)

Northwind Industries Inc .... E 216 433-0666
  Cleveland (G-6099)

Ohio Structures Inc .... E 330 533-0084
  Canfield (G-2154)

Pcy Enterprises Inc .... E 513 241-5566
  Cincinnati (G-4219)

Pioneer Pipe Inc .... A 740 376-2400
  Marietta (G-13370)

Precision Steel Services Inc .... D 419 476-5702
  Toledo (G-17984)

Precision Welding Corporation .... E 216 524-6110
  Cleveland (G-6226)

Rbm Environmental and Cnstr .... E 419 693-5840
  Oregon (G-15607)

Rittman Inc .... D 330 927-6855
  Rittman (G-16409)

St Lawrence Holdings LLC .... E 330 562-9000
  Maple Heights (G-13297)

Steel Eqp Specialists Inc .... D 330 823-8260
  Alliance (G-555)

Steelial Wldg Met Fbrction Inc .... E 740 669-5300
  Vinton (G-18586)

The Mansfield Strl & Erct Co .... E 419 522-5911
  Mansfield (G-13251)

Tilton Corporation .... C 419 227-6421
  Lima (G-12762)

Tri-America Contractors Inc .... E 740 574-0148
  Wheelersburg (G-19441)

Triangle Precision Industries .... D 937 299-6776
  Dayton (G-9822)

Viking Fabricators Inc ....E 740 374-5246
　Marietta (G-13397)
Wauseon Machine & Mfg Inc ....D 419 337-0940
　Wauseon (G-18812)
Worthington Industries Inc ....C 513 539-9291
　Monroe (G-14587)
Ysd Industries Inc ....D 330 792-6521
　Youngstown (G-20268)

STEEL MILLS

Alba Manufacturing Inc ....D 513 874-0551
　Fairfield (G-10694)
Alro Steel Corporation ....E 937 253-6121
　Dayton (G-9221)
Benjamin Steel Company Inc ....E 937 233-1212
　Springfield (G-16998)
C & R Inc ....E 614 497-1130
　Groveport (G-11498)
Contractors Steel Company ....E 330 425-3050
　Twinsburg (G-18256)
Franklin Iron & Metal Corp ....C 937 253-8184
　Dayton (G-9449)
Garden Street Iron & Metal ....E 513 853-3700
　Cincinnati (G-3603)
International Steel Group ....C 330 841-2800
　Warren (G-18715)
Lapham-Hickey Steel Corp ....E 614 443-4881
　Columbus (G-7952)
McWane Inc ....B 740 622-6651
　Coshocton (G-9022)
Metals USA Crbn Flat Rlled Inc ......D 937 882-6354
　Springfield (G-17082)
Mid-America Steel Corp ....E 800 282-3466
　Cleveland (G-5982)
Pioneer Pipe Inc ....A 740 376-2400
　Marietta (G-13370)
Precision Strip Inc ....D 937 667-6255
　Tipp City (G-17565)
Samuel Steel Pickling Company .....D 330 963-3777
　Twinsburg (G-18317)
Worthington Industries Inc ....C 513 539-9291
　Monroe (G-14587)
Zekelman Industries Inc ....C 740 432-2146
　Cambridge (G-2087)

STEEL, COLD-ROLLED: Flat Bright, From Purchased Hot-Rolled

Geneva Liberty Steel Ltd ....E 330 740-0103
　Youngstown (G-20047)

STEEL, COLD-ROLLED: Sheet Or Strip, From Own Hot-Rolled

Matandy Steel & Metal Pdts LLC ....D 513 844-2277
　Hamilton (G-11627)

STEEL, HOT-ROLLED: Sheet Or Strip

Ohio Steel Sheet & Plate Inc ....E 800 827-2401
　Hubbard (G-11949)

STEEL: Cold-Rolled

All Ohio Threaded Rod Co Inc ....E 216 426-1800
　Cleveland (G-4935)
Alro Steel Corporation ....E 937 253-6121
　Dayton (G-9221)
Benjamin Steel Company Inc ....E 937 233-1212
　Springfield (G-16998)
Independent Steel Company LLC ....E 330 225-7741
　Valley City (G-18463)
Mid-America Steel Corp ....E 800 282-3466
　Cleveland (G-5982)

STEVEDORING SVCS

Midwest Trmnals Tledo Intl Inc ......E 419 897-6868
　Toledo (G-17917)

STITCHING SVCS: Custom

Blue Chip Mailing Services Inc ....E 513 541-4800
　Blue Ash (G-1514)

STONE: Dimension, NEC

Heritage Marble of Ohio Inc ....E 614 436-1464
　Columbus (G-7745)

STONEWARE PRDTS: Pottery

Clay Burley Products Co ....E 740 452-3633
　Roseville (G-16454)

STORE FIXTURES, EXC REFRIGERATED: Wholesalers

Hubert Company LLC ....B 513 367-8600
　Harrison (G-11670)
Takkt America Holding Inc ....C 513 367-8600
　Harrison (G-11678)

STORE FIXTURES: Wood

CIP International Inc ....D 513 874-9925
　West Chester (G-18889)

STORES: Auto & Home Supply

Abraham Ford LLC ....E 440 233-7402
　Elyria (G-10477)
Albert Mike Leasing Inc ....C 513 563-1400
　Cincinnati (G-2919)
Beechmont Ford Inc ....C 513 752-6611
　Cincinnati (G-2842)
Brown Motor Sales Co ....D 419 531-0151
　Toledo (G-17629)
Cascade Group Inc ....E 330 929-1861
　Cuyahoga Falls (G-9077)
Chesrown Oldsmobile GMC Inc ......E 614 846-3040
　Columbus (G-7182)
Coughlin Chevrolet Inc ....E 740 964-9191
　Pataskala (G-15784)
Coughlin Chevrolet Toyota Inc ....D 740 366-1381
　Newark (G-15028)
Cronins Inc ....E 513 851-5900
　Cincinnati (G-3380)
Dave Knapp Ford Lincoln Inc ....E 937 547-3000
　Greenville (G-11373)
Doug Marine Motors Inc ....E 740 335-3700
　Wshngtn CT Hs (G-19869)
Ed Schmidt Auto Inc ....C 419 874-4331
　Perrysburg (G-15863)
Germain On Scarborough LLC ....E 614 868-0300
　Columbus (G-7665)
Haydocy Automotive Inc ....D 614 279-8880
　Columbus (G-7719)
Jerry Haag Motors Inc ....E 937 402-2090
　Hillsboro (G-11848)
Joe Dodge Kidd Inc ....E 513 752-1804
　Cincinnati (G-2858)
Kent Automotive Inc ....E 330 678-5520
　Kent (G-12240)
Kerry Ford Inc ....D 513 671-6400
　Cincinnati (G-3864)
KOI Enterprises Inc ....E 513 357-2400
　Cincinnati (G-3886)
Lebanon Chrysler - Plymuth Inc .....E 513 932-2717
　Lebanon (G-12480)
Leikin Motor Companies Inc ....D 440 946-6900
　Willoughby (G-19544)
Matia Motors Inc ....E 440 365-7311
　Elyria (G-10534)
Medina World Cars Inc ....E 330 725-4901
　Strongsville (G-17332)
Rush Truck Centers Ohio Inc ....D 513 733-8500
　Cincinnati (G-4414)
Rush Truck Centers Ohio Inc ....D 419 224-6045
　Lima (G-12735)
Sonic Automotive ....D 614 870-8200
　Columbus (G-8658)
Sunnyside Toyota Inc ....D 440 777-9911
　North Olmsted (G-15312)
Tansky Motors Inc ....E 650 322-7069
　Logan (G-12855)
Walker Auto Group Inc ....D 937 433-4950
　Miamisburg (G-14236)

STUDIOS: Artists & Artists' Studios

American National Red Cross ....E 216 431-3152
　Cleveland (G-4962)
County of Logan ....E 937 599-4221
　Bellefontaine (G-1350)
Daily Services LLC ....C 740 326-6130
　Mount Vernon (G-14761)
Lighthouse Youth Services Inc ....D 513 861-1111
　Cincinnati (G-3930)
Marsden Holding LLC ....D 440 973-7774
　Middleburg Heights (G-14254)

Pcm Inc ....E 614 854-1399
　Lewis Center (G-12557)
Quantech Services Inc ....C 937 490-8461
　Beavercreek Township (G-1261)
Vantage Aging ....A 330 785-9770
　Akron (G-487)

STUDIOS: Sculptor's

Don Drumm Studios & Gallery ....E 330 253-6840
　Akron (G-190)

STUDS & JOISTS: Sheet Metal

Matandy Steel & Metal Pdts LLC ....D 513 844-2277
　Hamilton (G-11627)

SUB-LESSORS: Real Estate

Schottenstein Realty LLC ....E 614 445-8461
　Columbus (G-8609)

SUBSCRIPTION FULFILLMENT SVCS: Magazine, Newspaper, Etc

Ebsco Industries Inc ....B 330 478-0281
　Canton (G-2295)
Inquiry Systems Inc ....E 614 464-3800
　Columbus (G-7824)

SUBSTANCE ABUSE CLINICS, OUTPATIENT

Christian Chld HM Ohio Inc ....D 330 345-7949
　Wooster (G-19700)
Community Behavioral Hlth Inc ....C 513 887-8500
　Hamilton (G-11585)
Community Drug Board Inc ....D 330 315-5590
　Akron (G-149)
County of Cuyahoga ....E 216 443-7035
　Cleveland (G-5361)
Family Recovery Center Inc ....E 330 424-1468
　Lisbon (G-12801)
Legacy Freedom Treatment Ctr ......E 614 741-2100
　Columbus (G-7963)
Lorain County Alcohol and Drug .....D 440 246-0109
　Lorain (G-12916)
Maryhaven Inc ....E 937 644-9192
　Marysville (G-13513)
Meridian Healthcare ....D 330 797-0070
　Youngstown (G-20127)
Philio Inc ....E 419 531-5544
　Toledo (G-17976)
Project C U R E Inc ....E 937 262-3500
　Dayton (G-9720)
Recovery Resources ....D 216 431-4131
　Cleveland (G-6293)

SUBSTANCE ABUSE COUNSELING

Anazao Community Partners ....E 330 264-9597
　Wooster (G-19687)
Community Drug Board Inc ....D 330 315-5590
　Akron (G-149)
Oriana House Inc ....A 330 374-9610
　Akron (G-365)
Oriana House Inc ....C 330 643-2171
　Akron (G-368)
Quest Recovery Prevention Svcs .....C 330 453-8252
　Canton (G-2446)
Talbert House ....E 513 541-1184
　Cincinnati (G-4572)
Talbert House ....D 513 933-9304
　Lebanon (G-12509)

SUMMER CAMPS, EXC DAY & SPORTS INSTRUCTIONAL

Camp Patmos Inc ....E 419 746-2214
　Kelleys Island (G-12209)
Classroom Antics Inc ....E 800 595-3776
　North Royalton (G-15350)
Friars Club Inc ....D 513 488-8777
　Cincinnati (G-3594)
Scribes & Scrbblr Chld Dev Ctr ....E 440 884-5437
　Cleveland (G-6382)
Skyview Baptist Ranch Inc ....E 330 674-7511
　Millersburg (G-14493)
Young Mens Christian Assoc ....D 513 932-3756
　Oregonia (G-15618)

SERVICES

SUPERMARKETS & OTHER GROCERY STORES

Discount Drug Mart Inc ....C 330 725-2340
Medina (G-13931)
Forths Foods Inc ....E 740 886-9769
Proctorville (G-16216)
Fred W Albrecht Grocery Co ....C 330 645-6222
Coventry Township (G-9034)
Heights Emergency Food Center ....D 216 381-0707
Cleveland (G-5682)
J V Hansel Inc ....E 330 716-0806
Warren (G-18716)
Yund Inc ....E 330 837-9358
Massillon (G-13738)

SURGICAL APPLIANCES & SPLYS

Cardinal Health Inc ....A 614 757-5000
Dublin (G-10156)
Dentronix Inc ....E 330 916-7300
Cuyahoga Falls (G-9086)
Doling & Associates Dental Lab ....E 937 254-0075
Dayton (G-9393)
Jones Metal Products Company .....E 740 545-6341
West Lafayette (G-19114)
Philips Medical Systems Clevel .....B 440 247-2652
Cleveland (G-6203)

SURGICAL EQPT: See Also Instruments

Ethicon Endo-Surgery Inc ....A 513 337-7000
Blue Ash (G-1558)
Mill-Rose Company ....C 440 255-9171
Mentor (G-14087)

SURGICAL INSTRUMENT REPAIR SVCS

Mobile Instr Svc & Repr Inc ....C 937 592-5025
Bellefontaine (G-1360)

SURVEYING & MAPPING: Land Parcels

7nt Enterprises LLC ....E 614 961-2026
Miamisburg (G-14135)
American Electric Pwr Svc Corp ....B 614 716-1000
Columbus (G-6919)
ASC Group Inc ....E 614 268-2514
Columbus (G-6976)
Barr Engineering Incorporated ......E 614 714-0299
Columbus (G-7019)
Bayer & Becker Inc ....E 513 492-7297
Mason (G-13544)
Bayer & Becker Inc ....E 513 492-7401
Mason (G-13545)
Bramhall Engrg & Surveying Co ....E 440 934-7878
Avon (G-868)
Choice One Engineering Corp ......E 937 497-0200
Sidney (G-16764)
CT Consultants Inc ....C 440 951-9000
Mentor (G-14038)
CT Consultants Inc ....E 513 791-1700
Blue Ash (G-1543)
Ctl Engineering Inc ....C 614 276-8123
Columbus (G-7404)
Division of Geological Survey ....E 614 265-6576
Columbus (G-7458)
Dj Neff Enterprises Inc ....E 440 884-3100
Cleveland (G-5432)
Dlz Ohio Inc ....C 614 888-0040
Columbus (G-7462)
E P Ferris & Associates Inc ....E 614 299-2999
Columbus (G-7485)
Evans Mechwart Ham ....B 614 775-4500
New Albany (G-14852)
Feller Finch & Associates Inc ....E 419 893-3680
Maumee (G-13791)
Garcia Surveyors Inc ....E 419 877-0400
Whitehouse (G-19448)
Hammontree & Associates Ltd ......E 330 499-8817
Canton (G-2336)
Jack A Hamilton & Assoc Inc ....E 740 968-4947
Flushing (G-10980)
Jobes Henderson & Assoc Inc ....E 740 344-5451
Newark (G-15045)
Kleingers Group Inc ....D 513 779-7851
West Chester (G-18957)
KS Associates Inc ....D 440 365-4730
Elyria (G-10523)
Kucera International Inc ....D 440 975-4230
Willoughby (G-19536)

Land Design Consultants ....E 440 255-8463
Mentor (G-14075)
McGill Smith Punshon Inc ....E 513 759-0004
Cincinnati (G-3987)
McSteen & Associates Inc ....E 440 585-9800
Wickliffe (G-19469)
Penetrating R Ground ....E 419 843-9804
Toledo (G-17975)
Peterman Associates Inc ....E 419 722-9566
Findlay (G-10953)
Poggemeyer Design Group Inc .....E 419 748-7438
Mc Clure (G-13893)
Poggemeyer Design Group Inc .....C 419 244-8074
Bowling Green (G-1746)
R E Warner & Associates Inc ....D 440 835-9400
Westlake (G-19395)
Resource International Inc ....C 614 823-4949
Columbus (G-8523)
Sands Decker Cps Llc ....E 614 459-6992
Columbus (G-8590)
T J Neff Holdings Inc ....E 440 884-3100
Cleveland (G-6494)
Usic Locating Services LLC ....C 330 733-9393
Akron (G-482)
Wade Trim ....E 216 363-0300
Cleveland (G-6648)

SVC ESTABLISHMENT EQPT & SPLYS WHOLESALERS

Century Equipment Inc ....E 513 285-1800
Hamilton (G-11575)
Lute Supply Inc ....E 740 353-1447
Portsmouth (G-16153)
Mark Humrichouser ....E 614 324-5231
Westerville (G-19184)
Rde System Corp ....C 513 933-8000
Lebanon (G-12496)
Sally Beauty Supply LLC ....C 937 548-7684
Greenville (G-11394)
Sally Beauty Supply LLC ....C 614 278-1691
Columbus (G-8584)

SVC ESTABLISHMENT EQPT, WHOL: Cleaning & Maint Eqpt & Splys

Dawnchem Inc ....E 440 943-3332
Willowick (G-19597)
Hd Supply Facilities Maint Ltd ....E 440 542-9188
Solon (G-16857)
Mansfield City Building Maint ....E 419 755-9698
Mansfield (G-13205)
Mapp Building Service LLC ....E 513 253-3990
Blue Ash (G-1602)
Mougianis Industries Inc ....D 740 264-6372
Steubenville (G-17167)
Tranzonic Companies ....C 216 535-4300
Richmond Heights (G-16395)

SVC ESTABLISHMENT EQPT, WHOL: Concrete Burial Vaults & Boxes

Baxter Burial Vault Service ....E 513 641-1010
Cincinnati (G-3024)

SVC ESTABLISHMENT EQPT, WHOL: Laundry/Dry Cleaning Eqpt/Sply

Norm Sharlotte Inc ....E 336 788-7705
Fairfield (G-10760)

SVC ESTABLISHMENT EQPT, WHOLESALE : Barber Shop Eqpt & Splys

Fredrics Corporation ....C 513 874-2226
West Chester (G-18926)

SVC ESTABLISHMENT EQPT, WHOLESALE: Beauty Parlor Eqpt & Sply

MSA Group Inc ....B 614 334-0400
Columbus (G-8119)
North Central Sales Inc ....E 216 481-2418
Cleveland (G-6075)
Perio Inc ....E 614 791-1207
Dublin (G-10308)
Salon Ware Inc ....E 330 665-2244
Copley (G-8972)

SVC ESTABLISHMENT EQPT, WHOLESALE: Firefighting Eqpt

A-1 Sprinkler Company Inc ....D 937 859-6198
Miamisburg (G-14136)
Action Coupling & Eqp Inc ....D 330 279-4242
Holmesville (G-11928)
Brakefire Incorporated ....E 330 535-4343
Akron (G-103)
Finley Fire Equipment Co ....E 740 962-4328
McConnelsville (G-13900)
Fox International Limited Inc ....E 216 454-1001
Beachwood (G-1058)
Sutphen Corporation ....C 800 726-7030
Dublin (G-10347)

SVC ESTABLISHMENT EQPT, WHOLESALE: Laundry Eqpt & Splys

American Sales Inc ....E 937 253-9520
Dayton (G-9159)
Laughlin Music & Vending Svc ......E 740 593-7778
Athens (G-790)

SVC ESTABLISHMENT EQPT, WHOLESALE: Restaurant Splys

Captive-Aire Systems Inc ....E 614 777-7378
Gahanna (G-11111)
Commercial Parts & Ser ....D 614 221-0057
Columbus (G-7327)
Martin-Brower Company LLC ....B 513 773-2301
West Chester (G-18971)
Rdp Foodservice Ltd ....D 614 261-5661
Hilliard (G-11811)
Wasserstrom Company ....B 614 228-6525
Columbus (G-8878)

SVC ESTABLISHMENT EQPT, WHOLESALE: Vending Machines & Splys

Cleveland Coin Mch Exch Inc ....D 847 842-6310
Willoughby (G-19514)
Shaffer Distributing Company ....D 614 421-6800
Columbus (G-8628)

SWIMMING INSTRUCTION

Goldfish Swim School ....E 216 364-9090
Warrensville Heights (G-18778)

SWIMMING POOL & HOT TUB CLEANING & MAINTENANCE SVCS

Buckeye Pool Inc ....E 937 434-7916
Dayton (G-9266)
Hastings Water Works Inc ....E 440 832-7700
Brecksville (G-1782)
Marcums Don Pool Care Inc ....E 513 561-7050
Cincinnati (G-3968)
Metropolitan Pool Service Co ....E 216 741-9451
Parma (G-15768)

SWIMMING POOL SPLY STORES

Burnett Pools Inc ....E 330 372-1725
Cortland (G-8985)
Marcums Don Pool Care Inc ....E 513 561-7050
Cincinnati (G-3968)
Metropolitan Pool Service Co ....E 216 741-9451
Parma (G-15768)

SWIMMING POOLS, EQPT & SPLYS: Wholesalers

Competitor Swim Products Inc ......D 800 888-7946
Columbus (G-7341)
Emsco ....E 440 238-2100
Strongsville (G-17300)
Mc Alarney Pool Spas and Blld .....E 740 373-6698
Marietta (G-13357)
Metropolitan Pool Service Co ....E 216 741-9451
Parma (G-15768)

SWITCHES: Thermostatic

Great Lakes Management Inc ....E 216 883-6500
Cleveland (G-5628)

SWITCHGEAR & SWITCHBOARD APPARATUS

General Electric Company ....D 216 883-1000
Cleveland (G-5603)

Schneider Electric Usa Inc ....D 513 755-5000
West Chester (G-18997)

SYMPHONY ORCHESTRA

Cincinnati Symphony Orchestra ......C 513 621-1919
Cincinnati (G-3271)

Dayton Performing Arts Aliance ....D 937 224-3521
Dayton (G-9375)

Musical Arts Association ....C 216 231-7300
Cleveland (G-6028)

Southeastern Ohio Symphony Orc ....E 740 826-8197
New Concord (G-14903)

SYNAGOGUES

Israel Adath ....E 513 793-1800
Cincinnati (G-3789)

SYRUPS, DRINK

Central Coca-Cola Btlg Co Inc ....C 419 476-6622
Toledo (G-17643)

Slush Puppie ....D 513 771-0940
West Chester (G-19082)

SYSTEMS ENGINEERING: Computer Related

Devcare Solutions Ltd ....E 614 221-2277
Columbus (G-7439)

Leidos Inc ....D 937 431-2270
Beavercreek (G-1164)

Telligen Tech Inc ....E 614 934-1554
Columbus (G-8739)

Ventech Solutions Inc ....D 614 757-1167
Columbus (G-6837)

SYSTEMS INTEGRATION SVCS

Advanced Prgrm Resources Inc ....E 614 761-9994
Dublin (G-10119)

Altamira Technologies Corp ....C 937 490-4804
Beavercreek (G-1124)

Ats Carolina Inc ....D 803 324-9300
Lewis Center (G-12526)

Axia Consulting Inc ....D 614 675-4050
Columbus (G-7008)

Commercial Time Sharing Inc ....E 330 644-3059
Akron (G-148)

Commsys Inc ....E 937 220-4990
Moraine (G-14634)

Creative Microsystems Inc ....D 937 836-4499
Englewood (G-10583)

Dyncorp ....C 513 942-6500
West Chester (G-18916)

Dyncorp ....D 513 569-7415
Cincinnati (G-3460)

Millenium Control Systems LLC ....E 440 510-0050
Eastlake (G-10432)

Northern Datacomm Corp ....E 330 665-0344
Akron (G-351)

Sterling Buying Group LLC ....E 513 564-9000
Cincinnati (G-4543)

Systemax Manufacturing Inc ....C 937 368-2300
Dayton (G-9805)

Tyco International MGT Co LLC ....E 888 787-8324
Cincinnati (G-4658)

SYSTEMS INTEGRATION SVCS: Local Area Network

Acadia Solutions Inc ....E 614 505-6135
Dublin (G-10118)

Cisco Systems Inc ....C 330 523-2000
Richfield (G-16350)

Dedicated Tech Services Inc ....E 614 309-0059
Dublin (G-10197)

Juniper Networks Inc ....D 614 932-1432
Dublin (G-10262)

Manifest Solutions Corp ....D 614 930-2800
Upper Arlington (G-18401)

United Technical Support Svcs ....D 330 562-3330
Streetsboro (G-17275)

SYSTEMS INTEGRATION SVCS: Office Computer Automation

Presidio Infrastructure ....D 419 241-8303
Toledo (G-17986)

SYSTEMS SOFTWARE DEVELOPMENT SVCS

Aisling Enterprises LLC ....E 937 203-1757
Centerville (G-2619)

Brandmuscle Inc ....C 216 464-4342
Cleveland (G-5074)

Cincinnati Bell Inc ....D 513 397-9900
Cincinnati (G-3226)

Cincom Systems Inc ....B 513 612-2300
Cincinnati (G-3286)

Courtview Justice Solutions ....E 330 497-0033
Canton (G-2271)

Deemsys Inc ....D 614 322-9928
Gahanna (G-11117)

Drb Systems LLC ....C 330 645-3299
Akron (G-195)

Easy2 Technologies Inc ....E 216 479-0482
Cleveland (G-5461)

ID Networks Inc ....E 440 992-0062
Ashtabula (G-741)

Infor (us) Inc ....B 678 319-8000
Columbus (G-7816)

Knotice LLC ....D 800 801-4194
Akron (G-304)

Online Mega Sellers Corp ....D 888 384-6468
Toledo (G-17964)

Onx Entrprise Solutions US Inc ....D 440 569-2300
Mayfield Heights (G-13878)

Robots and Pencils LP ....D 587 350-4095
Beachwood (G-1101)

Rockwell Automation Ohio Inc ....D 513 576-6151
Milford (G-14428)

Soaring Eagle Inc ....E 330 385-5579
East Liverpool (G-10418)

Talx Corporation ....E 614 527-9404
Hilliard (G-11819)

TABULATING SVCS

Personalized Data Corporation ....E 216 289-2200
Cleveland (G-6198)

TAGS & LABELS: Paper

Century Marketing Corporation ....C 419 354-2591
Bowling Green (G-1727)

TANK & BOILER CLEANING SVCS

C & W Tank Cleaning Company ....D 419 691-1995
Oregon (G-15585)

Rbm Environmental and Cnstr ....E 419 693-5840
Oregon (G-15607)

TANK REPAIR & CLEANING SVCS

Amko Service Company ....E 330 364-8857
Midvale (G-14357)

Ohio Hydraulics Inc ....E 513 771-2590
Cincinnati (G-4155)

Sabco Industries Inc ....E 419 531-5347
Toledo (G-18016)

TANK REPAIR SVCS

C H Bradshaw Co ....E 614 871-2087
Grove City (G-11417)

Corrotec Inc ....E 937 325-3585
Springfield (G-17021)

Frontier Tank Center Inc ....E 330 659-3888
Richfield (G-16358)

TANKS: Cryogenic, Metal

Amko Service Company ....E 330 364-8857
Midvale (G-14357)

Eleet Cryogenics Inc ....E 330 874-4009
Bolivar (G-1702)

TANKS: Lined, Metal

Modern Welding Co Ohio Inc ....E 740 344-9425
Newark (G-15073)

TANKS: Standard Or Custom Fabricated, Metal Plate

Enerfab Inc ....B 513 641-0500
Cincinnati (G-3498)

Gaspar Inc ....D 330 477-2222
Canton (G-2322)

TANNING SALONS

Attractions ....E 740 592-5600
Athens (G-771)

Noggins Hair Design Inc ....E 513 474-4405
Cincinnati (G-4121)

Super Tan ....E 330 722-2799
Medina (G-14008)

TAPES: Pressure Sensitive

Beiersdorf Inc ....C 513 682-7300
West Chester (G-19042)

TAX RETURN PREPARATION SVCS

Barnes Wendling Cpas Inc ....E 216 566-9000
Cleveland (G-5037)

Colonial Banc Corp ....E 937 456-5544
Eaton (G-10439)

Damon Tax Service ....E 513 574-9087
Cincinnati (G-3399)

Delaneys Tax Accunting Svc Ltd ....E 513 248-2829
Milford (G-14384)

Deloitte & Touche LLP ....B 513 784-7100
Cincinnati (G-3420)

Dw Together LLC ....E 330 225-8200
Brunswick (G-1928)

E T Financial Service Inc ....E 937 716-1726
Trotwood (G-18193)

H & R Block ....E 419 352-9467
Bowling Green (G-1733)

H & R Block Inc ....E 330 345-1040
Wooster (G-19726)

H & R Block Inc ....E 513 868-1818
Hamilton (G-11606)

H&R Block Inc ....E 440 282-4288
Amherst (G-589)

H&R Block Inc ....E 216 861-1185
Cleveland (G-5653)

Hometown Urgent Care ....C 330 629-2300
Youngstown (G-20067)

Hometown Urgent Care ....D 740 363-3133
Delaware (G-9987)

Hometown Urgent Care ....C 937 252-2000
Wooster (G-19728)

Jennings & Associates ....E 740 369-4426
Delaware (G-9991)

Phillip Mc Guire ....E 740 482-2701
Nevada (G-14838)

Regional Income Tax Agency ....C 800 860-7482
Brecksville (G-1801)

Skoda Minotti Holdings LLC ....E 440 449-6800
Cleveland (G-6411)

Village of Coldwater ....D 419 678-2685
Coldwater (G-6767)

TAXI CABS

Americab Inc ....E 216 429-1134
Cleveland (G-4946)

City Taxicab & Transfer Co ....E 440 992-2156
Ashtabula (G-727)

City Yellow Cab Company ....E 330 253-3141
Akron (G-140)

Columbus Green Cabs Inc ....E 614 444-4444
Columbus (G-7284)

Independent Radio Taxi Inc ....E 330 746-8844
Youngstown (G-20077)

Knox Area Transit ....E 740 392-7433
Mount Vernon (G-14770)

Pickaway County Community Acti ....D 740 477-1655
Circleville (G-4839)

Shamrock Taxi Ltd ....E 614 263-8294
Columbus (G-8630)

United Garage & Service Corp ....D 216 623-1550
Cleveland (G-6572)

Westlake Cab Service ....D 440 331-5000
Cleveland (G-6677)

TECHNICAL & TRADE SCHOOLS, NEC

Recording Workshop ....E 740 663-1000
Chillicothe (G-2813)

TECHNICAL INSTITUTE

Cleveland Municipal School Dst..........D..... 216 459-4200
Cleveland (G-5275)

TECHNICAL MANUAL PREPARATION SVCS

ONeil & Associates Inc...............B...... 937 865-0800
Miamisburg (G-14201)

TECHNICAL WRITING SVCS

Thinkpath Engineering Svcs LLC..........E..... 937 291-8374
Miamisburg (G-14229)

TELECOMMUNICATION EQPT REPAIR SVCS, EXC TELEPHONES

AT&T Corp ....A..... 614 223-8236
Columbus (G-6990)
Jersey Central Pwr & Light Co ....E...... 419 321-7207
Oak Harbor (G-15473)
Vertiv Energy Systems Inc ....A..... 440 288-1122
Lorain (G-12951)

TELECOMMUNICATION SYSTEMS & EQPT

DTE Inc.......................................E...... 419 522-3428
Mansfield (G-13170)
Mitel (delaware) Inc ....E...... 513 733-8000
West Chester (G-18974)
Peco II Inc...................................D..... 614 431-0694
Columbus (G-8433)
Vertiv Energy Systems Inc ....A..... 440 288-1122
Lorain (G-12951)

TELECOMMUNICATIONS CARRIERS & SVCS: Wired

AT&T Corp ....D..... 330 337-3505
Salem (G-16535)
AT&T Corp ....D..... 614 223-5318
Westerville (G-19224)
AT&T Corp ....C...... 614 271-8911
Powell (G-16185)
AT&T Corp ....D..... 614 223-6513
Columbus (G-6989)
AT&T Corp ....C...... 937 372-9945
Xenia (G-19890)
AT&T Corp ....D..... 614 337-3902
Columbus (G-6993)
AT&T Corp ....A..... 614 223-8236
Columbus (G-6990)
AT&T Mobility LLC ....E...... 614 291-2500
Columbus (G-6994)
Cass Information Systems Inc ....E...... 614 839-4503
Columbus (G-7134)
Cellco Partnership ....E...... 440 984-5200
Amherst (G-583)
Cellco Partnership ....E...... 740 450-1525
Zanesville (G-20290)
Cinciti BI Etd Trts LLC ....D..... 513 397-0963
Cincinnati (G-3283)
Cox Communications Inc ....D..... 937 222-5700
Dayton (G-9336)
Cox Ohio Telcom LLC ....D..... 216 535-3500
Parma (G-15764)
Cypress Communications Inc ....C...... 404 965-7248
Cleveland (G-5402)
Echo 24 Inc.................................E...... 740 964-7081
Reynoldsburg (G-16302)
Kraft Electrical Contg Inc.................E...... 614 836-9300
Groveport (G-11526)
Kraftmaid Trucking Inc....................D..... 440 632-2531
Middlefield (G-14271)
Level 3 Communications Inc ....E...... 330 256-8999
Akron (G-310)
Level 3 Telecom LLC ....E...... 513 841-0000
Cincinnati (G-3920)
Level 3 Telecom LLC ....E...... 513 682-7806
West Chester (G-18960)
Level 3 Telecom LLC ....E...... 513 682-7806
West Chester (G-18961)
Level 3 Telecom LLC ....E...... 513 682-7806
West Chester (G-18962)
Level 3 Telecom LLC ....E...... 513 841-0000
Cincinnati (G-3921)
Morelia Group LLC ....E...... 513 469-1500
Cincinnati (G-4073)
Ohio State University.......................E...... 614 292-6291
Columbus (G-8322)

Qwest Corporation..........................D..... 614 793-9258
Dublin (G-10316)
Rxp Wireless LLC ....E...... 330 264-1500
Wooster (G-19763)
Southerntier Telecom ....E...... 614 505-6365
Worthington (G-19851)
Spectrum Networks Inc ....E...... 513 697-2000
Cincinnati (G-4514)
TSC Television Inc ....D..... 419 941-6001
Wapakoneta (G-18658)
TW Telecom Inc ....E...... 234 542-6279
Akron (G-474)
United Telephone Company Ohio ....B...... 419 227-1660
Lima (G-12773)
Verizon Bus Netwrk Svcs Inc ....E...... 513 897-1501
Waynesville (G-18837)
Vox Mobile ....E...... 800 536-9030
Independence (G-12139)

TELECOMMUNICATIONS CARRIERS & SVCS: Wireless

Alltel Communications Corp................D..... 740 349-8551
Newark (G-15008)
AT&T Corp ....A..... 513 629-5000
Cincinnati (G-2994)
Horizon Pcs Inc ....C...... 740 772-8200
Chillicothe (G-2790)
Lima Radio Hospital Inc ....E...... 419 229-6010
Lima (G-12686)

TELEMARKETING BUREAUS

Alorica Customer Care Inc..................A..... 216 525-3311
Cleveland (G-4940)
American Publishers LLC ....D..... 419 626-0623
Huron (G-12020)
Ameridial Inc ....B...... 800 445-7128
Canton (G-2188)
Ameridial Inc ....D..... 330 479-8044
North Canton (G-15188)
Ameridial Inc ....B...... 330 497-4888
North Canton (G-15189)
Ameridial Inc ....D..... 330 339-7222
New Philadelphia (G-14946)
Ameridial Inc ....D..... 330 868-2000
Minerva (G-14515)
Convergys Cstmer MGT Group Inc.......B...... 513 723-6104
Cincinnati (G-3358)
Dialamerica Marketing Inc ....C...... 330 836-5293
Fairlawn (G-10822)
Dialamerica Marketing Inc ....C...... 440 234-4410
Cleveland (G-5420)
Fox International Limited Inc ....E...... 216 454-1001
Beachwood (G-1058)
Hkt Teleservices Inc.........................C...... 614 652-6300
Grove City (G-11441)
Incept Corporation ....C...... 330 649-8000
Canton (G-2354)
Infocision Management Corp................B...... 330 668-1411
Akron (G-276)
Infocision Management Corp................B...... 330 726-0872
Youngstown (G-20080)
Infocision Management Corp................D..... 419 529-8685
Mansfield (G-13187)
Infocision Management Corp................B...... 330 668-6615
Akron (G-277)
Infocision Management Corp................B...... 330 544-1400
Youngstown (G-20081)
R D D Inc....................................C...... 216 781-5858
Cleveland (G-6273)
Rdi Corporation ....D..... 513 524-3320
Oxford (G-15688)
S&P Data Ohio LLC ....B...... 216 965-0018
Cleveland (G-6358)
Startek Inc...................................C...... 419 528-7801
Ontario (G-15576)
Summit Advantage LLC ....D..... 330 835-2453
Fairlawn (G-10853)
Telinx Solutions LLC ....E...... 330 819-0657
Medina (G-14011)
Tpusa Inc ....B...... 330 374-1232
Akron (G-472)
Tpusa Inc ....A..... 614 621-5512
Columbus (G-8769)
Triplefin LLC ....E...... 513 794-9870
Blue Ash (G-1666)

TELEPHONE ANSWERING SVCS

Academy Answering Service Inc...........E...... 440 442-8500
Cleveland (G-4896)

Answering Service Inc.......................E...... 440 473-1200
Cleveland (G-4984)
Carol Reese ....E...... 513 347-0252
Cincinnati (G-3126)
Continental Business Services ....E...... 614 224-4534
Columbus (G-7357)
Maximum Communications Inc ....E...... 513 489-3414
Cincinnati (G-3981)
Perceptionist Inc ....E...... 614 384-7500
Westerville (G-19292)
Tan Products ....E...... 513 288-9264
Cincinnati (G-4576)
Telemessaging Services Inc ....E...... 440 845-5400
Cleveland (G-6509)
Twin Comm Inc...............................E...... 740 774-4701
Marietta (G-13390)

TELEPHONE COUNSELING SVCS

Southeast Cmnty Mental Hlth Ctr..........E...... 614 445-6832
Columbus (G-8663)

TELEPHONE EQPT INSTALLATION

Chapel-Romanoff Tech LLC ....E...... 937 222-9840
Dayton (G-9292)
Mitel (delaware) Inc ....E...... 513 733-8000
West Chester (G-18974)
Rei Telecom Inc ....E...... 614 255-3100
Canal Winchester (G-2116)
Tele-Solutions Inc ....E...... 330 782-2888
Youngstown (G-20221)

TELEPHONE EQPT: NEC

Commercial Electric Pdts Corp ....E...... 216 241-2886
Cleveland (G-5318)

TELEPHONE SET REPAIR SVCS

Cellco Partnership ....E...... 440 779-1313
North Olmsted (G-15279)
DTE Inc.......................................E...... 419 522-3428
Mansfield (G-13170)
Jacobs Telephone Contrs Inc ....E...... 614 527-8977
Hilliard (G-11780)
Mmi-Cpr LLC ....E...... 216 674-0645
Independence (G-12098)
Professional Telecom Svcs..................E...... 513 232-7700
Cincinnati (G-4294)

TELEPHONE SVCS

Citigroup Inc ....B...... 740 548-0594
Delaware (G-9960)
Pathway House LLC ....E...... 872 223-9797
Cleveland (G-6182)
Republic Telcom Worldwide LLC ....D..... 330 244-8285
North Canton (G-15230)
Republic Telcom Worldwide LLC ....C...... 330 966-4586
Canton (G-2456)
Spectrum Networks Inc ....E...... 513 697-2000
Cincinnati (G-4514)
Toms Installation Co Inc ....E...... 419 584-1218
Celina (G-2612)

TELEVISION BROADCASTING STATIONS

Barrington Toledo LLC ....E...... 419 535-0024
Toledo (G-17605)
Bowling Green State University ....E...... 419 372-2700
Bowling Green (G-1725)
Dispatch Printing Company ....A..... 614 461-5000
Columbus (G-7451)
Dispatch Printing Company ....C...... 740 548-5331
Lewis Center (G-12541)
Fox Television Stations Inc ....C...... 216 431-8888
Cleveland (G-5568)
Gray Media Group Inc ....C...... 216 367-7300
Cleveland (G-5624)
Gray Media Group Inc ....C...... 513 421-1919
Cincinnati (G-3636)
Greater Cincinnati TV Educ Fnd ....D..... 513 381-4033
Cincinnati (G-3654)
Greater Dayton Public TV....................D..... 937 220-1600
Dayton (G-9472)
Ideastream ....C...... 216 916-6100
Cleveland (G-5734)
Iheartcommunications Inc ....C...... 216 520-2600
Cleveland (G-5736)
Johnny Appleseed Broadcasting ....E...... 419 529-5900
Ontario (G-15556)

(G-0000) Company's Geographic Section entry number

Lima Communications Corp ....D 419 228-8835
Lima (G-12678)
Nexstar Broadcasting Inc ....C 614 263-4444
Columbus (G-8188)
Nexstar Broadcasting Inc ....D 937 293-2101
Moraine (G-14683)
Northastern Eductl TV Ohio Inc ....E 330 677-4549
Kent (G-12251)
Ohio News Network ....D 216 367-7493
Cleveland (G-6121)
Ohio University ....E 740 593-1771
Athens (G-796)
Ohio University ....E 740 593-1771
Athens (G-797)
Ohio/Oklahoma Hearst TV Inc ....C 513 412-5000
Cincinnati (G-4163)
Public Broadcasting Found NW ....D 419 380-4600
Toledo (G-17995)
Sinclair Broadcast Group Inc ....E 513 641-4400
Cincinnati (G-4484)
Sinclair Broadcast Group Inc ....D 513 641-4400
Cincinnati (G-4485)
Sinclair Media II Inc ....C 614 481-6666
Columbus (G-8646)
Sinclair Media II Inc ....C 614 481-6666
Columbus (G-8647)
Sinclair Media II Inc ....D 614 481-6666
Columbus (G-8648)
Southeastern Ohio TV Sys ....E 740 452-5431
Zanesville (G-20364)
Sunrise Television Corp ....C 937 293-2101
Moraine (G-14700)
Sunrise Television Corp ....D 740 282-9999
Mingo Junction (G-14530)
Sunrise Television Corp ....E 419 244-2197
Toledo (G-18054)
Tegna Inc ....C 419 248-1111
Toledo (G-18061)
Thinktv Network ....E 937 220-1600
Dayton (G-9813)
Toledo Television Investors LP ....E 419 535-0024
Toledo (G-18100)
W B N X T V 55 ....E 330 922-5500
Cuyahoga Falls (G-9138)
W L W TT V 5 ....C 513 412-5000
Cincinnati (G-4766)
Wbns Tv Inc ....C 614 460-3700
Columbus (G-8881)
Wfmj Television Inc ....C 330 744-8611
Youngstown (G-20246)
Wfts ....C 216 431-5555
Cleveland (G-6680)
Wfts ....C 513 721-9900
Cincinnati (G-4794)
Winston Brdcstg Netwrk Inc ....E 330 928-5711
Cuyahoga Falls (G-9140)
Wkyc-Tv Inc ....C 216 344-3300
Cleveland (G-6687)
Wupw LLC ....E 419 244-3600
Toledo (G-18163)
Wwst Corporation LLC ....A 330 264-5122
Wooster (G-19788)

TELEVISION FILM PRODUCTION SVCS

For Women Like Me Inc ....E 407 848-7339
Cleveland (G-5551)
For Women Like Me Inc ....E 407 848-7339
Chagrin Falls (G-2645)
Greater Cincinnati TV Educ Fnd ....D 513 381-4033
Cincinnati (G-3654)

TELEVISION REPAIR SHOP

Electra Sound Inc ....C 216 433-1050
Cleveland (G-5471)
Electra Sound Inc ....D 216 433-9600
Parma (G-15766)
Household Centralized Svc Inc ....E 419 474-5754
Toledo (G-17809)
Sunrise Television Corp ....D 740 282-9999
Mingo Junction (G-14530)

TEMPORARY HELP SVCS

A B S Temps Inc ....E 937 252-9888
Dayton (G-9198)
Acloche LLC ....E 888 608-0889
Columbus (G-6865)
Act I Temporaries Findlay Inc ....B 419 423-0713
Findlay (G-10863)

Adecco Usa Inc ....E 419 720-0111
Toledo (G-17582)
Ado Staffing Inc ....E 419 222-8395
Lima (G-12592)
Advantage Human Resourcing Inc ....D 318 324-8060
Cincinnati (G-2911)
Aerotek Inc ....E 330 517-7330
Akron (G-22)
Aerotek Inc ....E 216 573-5520
Independence (G-12040)
Alliance Solutions Group LLC ....E 216 503-1690
Independence (G-12044)
Alternate Solutions Healthcare ....D 937 299-1111
Dayton (G-9224)
Area Temps Inc ....A 216 227-8200
Lakewood (G-12336)
Area Temps Inc ....E 216 781-5350
Independence (G-12046)
Area Temps Inc ....A 216 518-2000
Maple Heights (G-13281)
Atterro Inc ....E 800 938-9675
Cincinnati (G-3002)
Belcan Svcs Group Ltd Partnr ....C 937 586-5053
Dayton (G-9248)
Callos Resource LLC ....E 330 788-3033
Youngstown (G-19980)
Cima Inc ....E 513 382-8976
Hamilton (G-11577)
Custom Staffing Inc ....E 419 221-3097
Lima (G-12629)
Dawson Resources ....E 614 255-1400
Columbus (G-7420)
Doepker Group Inc ....E 419 355-1409
Fremont (G-11070)
E & L Premier Corporation ....C 330 836-9901
Fairlawn (G-10823)
Emily Management Inc ....D 440 354-6713
Painesville (G-15712)
Everstaff LLC ....E 440 992-0238
Mentor (G-14045)
Flex Temp Employment Services ....C 419 355-9675
Fremont (G-11074)
Flex-Team Inc ....B 330 745-3838
Akron (G-224)
Health Carousel LLC ....D 866 665-4544
Cincinnati (G-3693)
Heiser Staffing Services LLC ....E 614 800-4188
Columbus (G-7737)
Horizon Personnel Resources ....C 440 585-0031
Wickliffe (G-19464)
Interim Halthcare Columbus Inc ....E 614 888-3130
Gahanna (G-11127)
Its Technologies Inc ....D 419 842-2100
Holland (G-11890)
Job1usa Inc ....D 419 255-5005
Toledo (G-17831)
Kilgore Group Inc ....E 513 684-3721
Cincinnati (G-3868)
Lee Personnel Inc ....E 513 744-6780
Cincinnati (G-3916)
Medlink of Ohio Inc ....B 330 773-9434
Akron (G-330)
Minute Men Inc ....D 216 426-2225
Cleveland (G-5999)
Pontoon Solutions Inc ....D 855 881-1533
Maumee (G-13833)
Preferred Temporary Services ....E 330 494-5502
Canton (G-2439)
Production Design Services Inc ....D 937 866-3377
Dayton (G-9716)
Randstad Professionals Us LLC ....E 419 893-2400
Maumee (G-13840)
Randstad Professionals Us LP ....E 513 791-8600
Blue Ash (G-1639)
Renhill Stffing Srvces-America ....E 419 254-2800
Perrysburg (G-15912)
Reserves Network Inc ....E 440 779-1400
Cleveland (G-6314)
Rumpf Corporation ....E 419 255-5005
Toledo (G-18014)
Select Staffing ....D 513 247-9772
West Chester (G-19001)
Sfn Group Inc ....E 419 727-4104
Toledo (G-18028)
Spherion of Lima Inc ....A 419 224-8367
Lima (G-12747)
Trueblue Inc ....E 740 282-1079
Steubenville (G-17182)
Wayne Industries Inc ....E 937 548-6025
Greenville (G-11401)

TEN PIN CENTERS

Al-Mar Lanes ....E 419 352-4637
Bowling Green (G-1713)
AMF Bowling Centers Inc ....E 330 725-4548
Medina (G-13910)
AMF Bowling Centers Inc ....E 614 889-0880
Columbus (G-6944)
Beaver-Vu Bowl ....E 937 426-6771
Beavercreek (G-1130)
Big Western Operating Co Inc ....E 614 274-1169
Columbus (G-7037)
Bigelow Corporation ....E 937 339-3315
Troy (G-18196)
Bowlero Corp ....E 440 327-1190
North Ridgeville (G-15322)
Brookpark Freeway Lanes LLC ....E 216 267-2150
Cleveland (G-5088)
Capri Bowling Lanes Inc ....E 937 832-4000
Dayton (G-9276)
Cherry Grove Sports Center ....E 513 232-7199
Cincinnati (G-3177)
Chillicothe Bowling Lanes Inc ....E 740 773-3300
Chillicothe (G-2759)
Cloverleaf Bowling Center Inc ....E 216 524-4833
Cleveland (G-5308)
Columbus Square Bowling Palace ....E 614 895-1122
Columbus (G-7316)
Coshocton Bowling Center ....E 740 622-6332
Coshocton (G-9004)
Crossgate Lanes Inc ....E 513 891-0310
Blue Ash (G-1542)
East Mentor Recreation Inc ....E 440 354-2000
Mentor (G-14042)
Eastbury Bowling Center ....E 330 452-3700
Canton (G-2294)
Eastland Lanes Inc ....E 614 868-9866
Columbus (G-7491)
Freeway Lanes Bowl Group LLC ....E 440 946-5131
Mentor (G-14049)
Holiday Lanes Inc ....E 614 861-1600
Columbus (G-7760)
Interstate Lanes of Ohio Ltd ....E 419 666-2695
Rossford (G-16462)
Madison Bowl Inc ....E 513 271-2700
Cincinnati (G-3958)
Mahalls 20 Lanes ....E 216 521-3280
Cleveland (G-5895)
Northland Lanes Inc ....E 419 224-1961
Lima (G-12707)
Olmsted Lanes Inc ....E 440 777-6363
North Olmsted (G-15301)
Park Centre Lanes Inc ....E 330 499-0555
Canton (G-2434)
Plaz-Way Inc ....E 330 264-9025
Wooster (G-19759)
Poelking Bowling Centers ....E 937 435-3855
Dayton (G-9696)
Poelking Lanes Inc ....D 937 299-5573
Dayton (G-9697)
Rainbow Lanes Inc ....E 614 491-7155
Columbus (G-8487)
Rebman Recreation Inc ....E 440 282-6761
Lorain (G-12941)
Roseland Lanes Inc ....D 440 439-0097
Bedford (G-1302)
Sequoia Pro Bowl ....E 614 885-7043
Columbus (G-8620)
Stonehedge Enterprises Inc ....E 330 928-2161
Akron (G-442)
Suburban Gala Lanes Inc ....E 419 468-7488
Bucyrus (G-2001)
Thompson Capri Lanes Inc ....E 614 888-3159
Columbus (G-8748)
Tiki Bowling Lanes Inc ....E 740 654-4513
Lancaster (G-12442)
United Sttes Bowl Congress Inc ....D 440 327-0102
North Ridgeville (G-15344)
Victory Lanes Inc ....E 937 323-8684
Springfield (G-17130)
Wedgewood Lanes Inc ....E 330 792-1949
Youngstown (G-20241)

TENANT SCREENING SVCS

Acxiom Info SEC Svcs Inc ....B 216 685-7600
Independence (G-12039)

TERMITE CONTROL SVCS

Ohio Exterminating Co Inc ....E 614 294-6311
Columbus (G-8256)

SERVICES

Scherzinger Corp ....D 513 531-7848
Cincinnati (G-4435)

TEST BORING SVCS: Nonmetallic Minerals

Longyear Company ....E 740 373-2190
Marietta (G-13344)

TEST BORING, METAL MINING

Hahs Factory Outlet ....E 330 405-4227
Twinsburg (G-18277)

TESTERS: Gas, Exc Indl Process

Compliant Healthcare Tech LLC ....E 216 255-9607
Cleveland (G-5331)

TESTING SVCS

Alpha Technologies Svcs LLC ....D 330 745-1641
Hudson (G-11966)
Cliff North Consultants Inc ....E 513 251-4930
Cincinnati (G-3306)
Keyw Corporation ....E 937 702-9512
Beavercreek (G-1162)
Orton Edward Jr Crmic Fndation ......E 614 895-2663
Westerville (G-19197)
Smithers Quality Assessments ....E 330 762-4231
Akron (G-433)
Solar Testing Laboratories Inc ....C 216 741-7007
Brooklyn Heights (G-1881)
South Central Ohio Eductl Ctr ....C 740 456-0517
New Boston (G-14883)
SSS Consulting Inc ....E 937 259-1200
Dayton (G-9788)

TEXTILE & APPAREL SVCS

Affinity Specialty Apparel Inc ....D 866 548-8434
Fairborn (G-10663)

THEATER COMPANIES

Cincinnati Opera Association ....E 513 768-5500
Cincinnati (G-3260)
Cincinnati Shakespeare Company ....E 513 381-2273
Cincinnati (G-3267)
Shadoart Productions Inc ....D 614 416-7625
Columbus (G-8627)

THEATRICAL PRODUCERS & SVCS

City of Cleveland ....D 216 664-6800
Cleveland (G-5197)
Funny Bone Comedy Club & Cafe ....E 614 471-5653
Columbus (G-7634)
International Management Group ....B 216 522-1200
Cleveland (G-5762)
Interntonal Aliance Thea Stage ....E 440 734-4883
North Olmsted (G-15293)
Ohio Light Opera ....D 330 263-2345
Wooster (G-19753)
Rock and Roll of Fame and Muse .....D 216 781-7625
Cleveland (G-6336)
Stranahan Theatre Trust ....D 419 381-8851
Toledo (G-18050)

THERMOCOUPLES: Indl Process

Cleveland Electric Labs Co ....E 800 447-2207
Twinsburg (G-18253)

THERMOPLASTIC MATERIALS

Polyone Corporation ....D 440 930-1000
Avon Lake (G-926)

TICKET OFFICES & AGENCIES: Theatrical

Events On Top ....E 330 757-3786
Youngstown (G-20031)

TICKET OFFICES & AGENCIES: Travel

Delta Air Lines Inc ....E 216 265-2400
Cleveland (G-5416)

TIRE & TUBE REPAIR MATERIALS, WHOLESALE

Myers Industries Inc ....E 330 253-5592
Akron (G-342)
Technical Rubber Company Inc ....B 740 967-9015
Johnstown (G-12204)

TIRE CORD & FABRIC

ARC Abrasives Inc ....D 800 888-4885
Troy (G-18194)

TIRE DEALERS

Best One Tire & Svc Lima Inc ....E 419 229-2380
Lima (G-12606)
Bob Sumerel Tire Co Inc ....E 937 235-0062
Dayton (G-9256)
Bridgestone Ret Operations LLC ....E 330 929-3391
Cuyahoga Falls (G-9075)
Conrads Tire Service Inc ....E 216 941-3333
Cleveland (G-5334)
Dayton Marshall Tire Sales Co ....E 937 293-8330
Moraine (G-14646)
Grismer Tire Company ....E 937 643-2526
Centerville (G-2626)
Millersburg Tire Service Inc ....E 330 674-1085
Millersburg (G-14483)
Monro Inc ....E 440 835-2393
Westlake (G-19375)
North Gateway Tire Co Inc ....E 330 725-8473
Medina (G-13982)
QT Equipment Company ....D 330 724-3055
Akron (G-394)
Sines Inc ....E 440 352-6572
Painesville (G-15740)
Speck Sales Incorporated ....E 419 353-8312
Bowling Green (G-1749)
Ziegler Tire and Supply Co ....E 330 353-1499
Massillon (G-13739)

TIRE INNER-TUBES

Goodyear Tire & Rubber Company ....A 330 796-2121
Akron (G-242)

TIRE RECAPPING & RETREADING

Bob Sumerel Tire Co Inc ....E 937 235-0062
Dayton (G-9256)
Bob Sumerel Tire Co Inc ....E 614 527-9700
Columbus (G-7051)
Bridgestone Ret Operations LLC ....E 513 367-7888
Harrison (G-11662)
Bridgestone Ret Operations LLC ....E 419 586-1600
Celina (G-2585)
Goodyear Tire & Rubber Company ....E 440 735-9910
Walton Hills (G-18636)
Goodyear Tire & Rubber Company ....A 330 796-2121
Akron (G-242)
Liberty Tire Recycling LLC ....E 614 871-8097
Grove City (G-11448)

TIRE SUNDRIES OR REPAIR MATERIALS: Rubber

Technical Rubber Company Inc ....B 740 967-9015
Johnstown (G-12204)

TIRES & TUBES WHOLESALERS

American Kenda Rbr Indus Ltd ....E 866 536-3287
Reynoldsburg (G-16283)
Bob Sumerel Tire Co Inc ....E 614 527-9700
Columbus (G-7051)
Dealer Tire LLC ....B 216 432-0088
Cleveland (G-5413)
Hercules Tire & Rubber Company .....D 419 425-6400
Findlay (G-10923)
Joseph Russo ....E 440 748-2690
Grafton (G-11317)
Rush Truck Centers Ohio Inc ....D 513 733-8500
Cincinnati (G-4414)
Rush Truck Centers Ohio Inc ....E 419 224-6045
Lima (G-12735)
Shrader Tire & Oil Inc ....E 419 472-2128
Toledo (G-18032)
Shrader Tire & Oil Inc ....E 614 445-6601
Columbus (G-8637)
Tire Waste Transport Inc ....B 419 363-2681
Rockford (G-16417)
W D Tire Warehouse Inc ....E 614 461-8944
Columbus (G-8867)

TIRES & TUBES, WHOLESALE: Automotive

Belle Tire Distributors Inc ....E 419 473-1393
Toledo (G-17610)
Bob Sumerel Tire Co Inc ....E 513 792-6600
Cincinnati (G-3065)

Capital Tire Inc ....E 419 241-5111
Toledo (G-17635)
Capital Tire Inc ....E 419 865-7151
Toledo (G-17636)
Conrads Tire Service Inc ....E 216 941-3333
Cleveland (G-5334)
Dayton Marshall Tire Sales Co ....E 937 293-8330
Moraine (G-14646)
Grismer Tire Company ....E 937 643-2526
Centerville (G-2626)
Hankook Tire America Corp ....E 330 896-6199
Uniontown (G-18373)
K & M Tire Inc ....C 419 695-1061
Delphos (G-10029)
K & M Tire Inc ....E 419 695-1060
Delphos (G-10030)
Millersburg Tire Service Inc ....E 330 674-1085
Millersburg (G-14483)
North Gateway Tire Co Inc ....E 330 725-8473
Medina (G-13982)
Reville Tire Co ....D 330 468-1900
Northfield (G-15385)
Speck Sales Incorporated ....E 419 353-8312
Bowling Green (G-1749)
Stoney Hollow Tire Inc ....D 740 635-5200
Martins Ferry (G-13478)
Thyssenkrupp Bilstein Amer Inc ......D 513 881-7600
Hamilton (G-11648)

TIRES & TUBES, WHOLESALE: Truck

Best One Tire & Svc Lima Inc ....E 419 229-2380
Lima (G-12606)
Central Ohio Bandag LP ....E 740 454-9728
Zanesville (G-20291)
Ziegler Tire and Supply Co ....E 330 353-1499
Massillon (G-13739)

TITLE & TRUST COMPANIES

A R E A Title Agency Inc ....E 419 242-5485
Toledo (G-17576)
Commerce Title Agcy Youngstown ...E 330 743-1171
Youngstown (G-19995)
First Fincl Title Agcy of Ohio ....E 216 664-1920
Cleveland (G-5535)
Intitle Agency Inc ....D 513 241-8780
Cincinnati (G-3783)
Lakeside Title Escrow Agcy Inc ....E 216 503-5600
Westlake (G-19367)
Landsel Title Agency Inc ....E 614 337-1928
Gahanna (G-11130)
Security Title Guarantee Agcy ....C 513 651-3393
Cincinnati (G-4446)
Sterling Land Title Agency ....E 937 438-2000
Dayton (G-9792)
Talon Title Agency LLC ....E 614 818-0500
Westerville (G-19213)
Valley Title & Escrow Agency ....E 440 632-9833
Middlefield (G-14278)

TITLE ABSTRACT & SETTLEMENT OFFICES

American Title Services Inc ....E 330 652-1609
Niles (G-15144)
County of Delaware ....E 740 657-3945
Lewis Center (G-12535)
Search 2 Close Columbus Ltd ....E 614 389-5353
Powell (G-16210)

TITLE INSURANCE AGENTS

Accurate Group Holdings Inc ....D 216 520-1740
Independence (G-12037)
Nations Title Agency of Ohio ....E 614 839-3848
Columbus (G-8141)

TITLE INSURANCE: Real Estate

Accurate Group Holdings Inc ....D 216 520-1740
Independence (G-12037)
Chicago Title Insurance Co ....D 330 873-9393
Akron (G-128)
Fidelity National Fincl Inc ....E 614 865-1562
Westerville (G-19256)
First American Equity Ln Svcs ....C 800 221-8683
Cleveland (G-5528)
First American Title Insur Co ....E 216 241-1278
Cleveland (G-5529)
First American Title Insur Co ....E 419 625-8505
Sandusky (G-16607)
First American Title Insur Co ....E 740 450-0006
South Zanesville (G-16951)

Landsel Title Agency Inc .... E 614 337-1928
Gahanna (G-11130)
Lawyers Title Cincinnati Inc .... D 513 421-1313
Cincinnati (G-3914)
Midland Title Security Inc .... D 216 241-6045
Cleveland (G-5986)
Ohio Bar Title Insurance Co .... D 614 310-8098
Columbus (G-6827)
Ohio Real Title Agency LLC .... E 216 373-9900
Cleveland (G-6123)
Port Lawrence Title and Tr Co .... E 419 244-4605
Toledo (G-17982)
Resource Title Agency Inc .... D 216 520-0050
Cleveland (G-6315)
Resource Title Nat Agcy Inc .... D 216 520-0050
Independence (G-12113)
Stewart Title Company .... E 440 520-7130
Willoughby (G-19574)
Title First Agency Inc .... E 614 224-9207
Columbus (G-8759)
U S Title Agency Inc .... E 216 621-1424
Cleveland (G-6559)
Valmer Land Title Agency .... E 614 860-0005
Reynoldsburg (G-16336)
Valmer Land Title Agency .... E 614 875-7001
Grove City (G-11479)

TITLE SEARCH COMPANIES

Real Living Title Agency Ltd .... D 614 459-7400
Columbus (G-8495)
Weston Inc .... E 440 349-9000
Cleveland (G-6679)

TOBACCO & PRDTS, WHOLESALE: Cigarettes

Core-Mark Ohio .... C 650 589-9445
Solon (G-16837)
Dittman-Adams Company .... E 513 870-7530
West Chester (G-18914)
EBY-Brown Company LLC .... C 937 324-1036
Springfield (G-17032)
Gummer Wholesale Inc .... D 740 928-0415
Heath (G-11704)
JE Carsten Company .... E 330 794-4440
Hudson (G-11987)

TOBACCO & TOBACCO PRDTS WHOLESALERS

Albert Guarnieri & Co .... D 330 794-9834
Hudson (G-11962)
Jetro Cash and Carry Entps LLC .... D 216 525-0101
Cleveland (G-5794)
Novelart Manufacturing Company .... D 513 351-7700
Cincinnati (G-4136)
Swd Corporation .... E 419 227-2436
Lima (G-12759)
The Anter Brothers Company .... E 216 252-4555
Cleveland (G-6519)

TOILETRIES, COSMETICS & PERFUME STORES

Big Sandy Furniture Inc .... D 740 574-2113
Franklin Furnace (G-11043)
Kenneths Hair Salons & Day Sp .... B 614 457-7712
Columbus (G-7893)

TOILETRIES, WHOLESALE: Hair Preparations

G E G Enterprises Inc .... E 330 477-3133
Canton (G-2321)
ICM Distributing Company Inc .... E 234 212-3030
Twinsburg (G-18281)

TOILETRIES, WHOLESALE: Razor Blades

American Cutting Edge Inc .... C 937 866-5986
Miamisburg (G-14140)

TOILETRIES, WHOLESALE: Toiletries

Nehemiah Manufacturing Co LLC .... E 513 351-5700
Cincinnati (G-4102)
Walter F Stephens Jr Inc .... E 937 746-0521
Franklin (G-11041)

TOILETS, PORTABLE, WHOLESALE

Superr-Spdie Portable Svcs Inc .... E 330 733-9000
Akron (G-461)

TOLL BRIDGE OPERATIONS

Magnum Management Corporation .... A 419 627-2334
Sandusky (G-16626)

TOLL ROAD OPERATIONS

Ohio Tpk & Infrastructure Comm .... C 440 234-2081
Berea (G-1432)

TOOL REPAIR SVCS

Lawrence Industries Inc .... C 216 518-7000
Cleveland (G-5858)
Pennsylvania TI Sls & Svc Inc .... D 330 758-0845
Youngstown (G-20153)

TOOLS: Hand

Acme Company .... D 330 758-2313
Poland (G-16079)
Cornwell Quality Tools Company .... D 330 628-2627
Mogadore (G-14545)
File Sharpening Company Inc .... E 937 376-8268
Xenia (G-19899)
J and S Tool Incorporated .... E 216 676-8330
Cleveland (G-5770)
Matco Tools Corporation .... B 330 929-4949
Stow (G-17219)
Sewer Rodding Equipment Co .... E 419 991-2065
Lima (G-12739)

TOOLS: Hand, Plumbers'

Calvin Lanier .... E 937 952-4221
Dayton (G-9273)

TOOLS: Hand, Power

Huron Cement Products Company .... E 419 433-4161
Huron (G-12026)
Ingersoll-Rand Company .... E 419 633-6800
Bryan (G-1960)
Npk Construction Equipment Inc .... D 440 232-7900
Bedford (G-1295)
Sewer Rodding Equipment Co .... E 419 991-2065
Lima (G-12739)
Wolf Machine Company .... C 513 791-5194
Blue Ash (G-1679)

TOUR OPERATORS

Tours of Black Heritage Inc .... D 440 247-2737
Cleveland (G-6536)

TOURIST INFORMATION BUREAU

Dayton Cvb .... E 937 226-8211
Dayton (G-9361)
Greatr Columbus Conventn & Vis .... E 614 221-6623
Columbus (G-7694)

TOURIST LODGINGS

Sauder Haritage Inn .... E 419 445-6408
Archbold (G-637)
TW Recreational Services Inc .... E 440 564-9144
Newbury (G-15126)

TOWELS: Fabric & Nonwoven, Made From Purchased Materials

Lawnview Industries Inc .... C 937 653-5217
Urbana (G-18438)

TOWERS: Cooling, Sheet Metal

Obr Cooling Towers Inc .... E 419 243-3443
Rossford (G-16463)

TOWING & TUGBOAT SVC

A M & O Towing Inc .... E 330 385-0639
Negley (G-14827)

TOWING SVCS: Marine

Great Lakes Group .... C 216 621-4854
Cleveland (G-5627)

TOYS

AW Faber-Castell Usa Inc .... D 216 643-4660
Cleveland (G-5028)

TOYS & HOBBY GOODS & SPLYS, WHOLESALE: Arts/Crafts Eqpt/Sply

AW Faber-Castell Usa Inc .... D 216 643-4660
Cleveland (G-5028)
Craft Wholesalers Inc .... C 740 964-6210
Groveport (G-11504)
Flower Factory Inc .... D 614 275-6220
Columbus (G-7598)
K & K Interiors Inc .... D 419 627-0039
Sandusky (G-16620)
Lamrite West Inc .... E 440 268-0634
Strongsville (G-17323)

TOYS & HOBBY GOODS & SPLYS, WHOLESALE: Balloons, Novelty

Galaxy Balloons Incorporated .... C 216 476-3360
Cleveland (G-5589)

TOYS & HOBBY GOODS & SPLYS, WHOLESALE: Bingo Games & Splys

Lancaster Bingo Company Inc .... D 740 681-4759
Lancaster (G-12410)
Nannicola Wholesale Co .... D 330 799-0888
Youngstown (G-20134)

TOYS & HOBBY GOODS & SPLYS, WHOLESALE: Educational Toys

Bendon Inc .... D 419 207-3600
Ashland (G-657)

TOYS & HOBBY GOODS & SPLYS, WHOLESALE: Toys & Games

Closeout Distribution Inc .... A 614 278-6800
Columbus (G-7234)
CSC Distribution Inc .... E 614 278-6800
Columbus (G-7400)
R and G Enterprises of Ohio .... E 440 845-6870
Cleveland (G-6271)

TOYS & HOBBY GOODS & SPLYS, WHOLESALE: Toys, NEC

Ball Bounce and Sport Inc .... E 419 759-3838
Dunkirk (G-10384)
Ball Bounce and Sport Inc .... B 419 289-9310
Ashland (G-654)
Ball Bounce and Sport Inc .... E 419 289-9310
Ashland (G-655)
ICM Distributing Company Inc .... E 234 212-3030
Twinsburg (G-18281)
K & M International Inc .... D 330 425-2550
Twinsburg (G-18286)
National Marketshare Group .... E 513 921-0800
Cincinnati (G-4094)
Pyramyd Air Ltd .... E 216 896-0893
Solon (G-16887)

TOYS & HOBBY GOODS & SPLYS, WHOLESALE: Video Games

Mas Inc .... E 330 659-3333
Richfield (G-16362)

TOYS, HOBBY GOODS & SPLYS WHOLESALERS

Ball Bounce and Sport Inc .... E 614 662-5381
Columbus (G-7015)
Dwa Mrkting Prmtional Pdts LLC .... E 216 476-0635
Strongsville (G-17298)
Lamrite West Inc .... C 440 238-9150
Strongsville (G-17321)
Neil Kravitz Group Sales Inc .... E 513 961-8697
Cincinnati (G-4105)

TRADE SHOW ARRANGEMENT SVCS

Affinity Disp Expositions Inc .... C 513 771-2339
Cincinnati (G-2915)
Definitive Solutions Co Inc .... D 513 719-9100
Cincinnati (G-3417)

SERVICES

Exhibitpro Inc ....E 614 885-9541
New Albany (G-14853)

Relx Inc ....E 937 865-6800
Miamisburg (G-14210)

TRAFFIC CONTROL FLAGGING SVCS

Traffic Ctrl Safety Svcs LLC ....E 330 904-2732
Alliance (G-556)

TRAILERS & PARTS: Truck & Semi's

Mac Manufacturing Inc ....A 330 823-9900
Alliance (G-539)

Mac Manufacturing Inc ....C 330 829-1680
Salem (G-16552)

Mac Trailer Manufacturing Inc ....C 330 823-9900
Alliance (G-540)

TRAILERS & TRAILER EQPT

Interstate Truckway Inc ....E 614 771-1220
Columbus (G-7839)

TRAILERS: Bodies

East Manufacturing Corporation ....B 330 325-9921
Randolph (G-16230)

TRAILERS: Semitrailers, Truck Tractors

Nelson Manufacturing Company ....D 419 523-5321
Ottawa (G-15660)

TRAINING SCHOOL FOR DELINQUENTS

County of Hamilton ....C 513 552-1200
Cincinnati (G-3370)

TRANS PROG REG & ADMIN, GOVT: Motor Vehicle Licensing & Insp

Butler County of Ohio........................D 513 887-3282
Hamilton (G-11561)

Public Safety Ohio Department ....A 614 752-7600
Columbus (G-8478)

TRANSFORMERS: Electric

Schneider Electric Usa Inc ....D 513 755-5000
West Chester (G-18997)

TRANSFORMERS: Furnace, Electric

Ajax Tocco Magnethermic Corp ....C 330 372-8511
Warren (G-18661)

TRANSFORMERS: Power Related

Fishel Company ....D 614 850-4400
Columbus (G-7590)

General Electric Company ....D 216 883-1000
Cleveland (G-5603)

Hannon Company ....D 330 456-4728
Canton (G-2339)

Matlock Electric Co Inc ....E 513 731-9600
Cincinnati (G-3979)

TRANSLATION & INTERPRETATION SVCS

Advanced Translation/Cnsltng ....E 440 716-0820
Westlake (G-19311)

Ceiba Enterprises Incorporated ....C 614 818-3220
Westerville (G-19231)

Cincilingua Inc ....E 513 721-8782
Cincinnati (G-3218)

Clgt Solutions LLC ....E 740 920-4795
Granville (G-11338)

Conversa Language Center Inc ....E 513 651-5679
Cincinnati (G-3360)

Mission Essntial Personnel LLC ....C 614 416-2345
New Albany (G-14859)

Vocalink Inc ....B 937 223-1415
Dayton (G-9858)

TRANSPORTATION AGENTS & BROKERS

ABF Freight System Inc ....C 419 525-0118
Mansfield (G-13132)

Bnsf Logistics LLC ....E 937 526-3141
Versailles (G-18566)

Bolt Express LLC ....D 419 729-6698
Toledo (G-17619)

Commercial Traffic Company ....C 216 267-2000
Cleveland (G-5319)

Commercial Traffic Company ....D 216 267-2000
Cleveland (G-5320)

Freshway Foods Inc ....C 937 498-4664
Sidney (G-16781)

Haid Acquisitions LLC........................D 513 941-8700
Cincinnati (G-3672)

J B Express Inc ....D 740 702-9830
Chillicothe (G-2794)

Reliable Trnsp Solutions LLC ....E 937 378-2700
Georgetown (G-11273)

Shoreline Transportation Inc ....C 440 878-2000
Strongsville (G-17345)

Taylor Logistics Inc ....E 513 771-1850
West Chester (G-19090)

Triple T Transport Inc ....D 740 657-3244
Lewis Center (G-12563)

United Parcel Service Inc OH...............B 740 363-0636
Delaware (G-10013)

TRANSPORTATION ARRANGEMENT SVCS, PASSENGER: Carpool/Vanpool

Daugwood Inc ....E 937 429-9465
Beavercreek (G-1144)

Rush Expediting Inc ....E 937 885-0894
Dayton (G-9741)

TRANSPORTATION ARRANGEMENT SVCS, PASSENGER: Tours, Conducted

Newport Walking Tours LLC ....E 859 951-8560
Cincinnati (G-4112)

Trolley Tours of Cleveland ....E 216 771-4484
Cleveland (G-6550)

TRANSPORTATION BROKERS: Truck

Advance Trnsp Systems Inc ....E 513 818-4311
Cincinnati (G-2910)

Ameri-Line Inc ....E 440 316-4500
Columbia Station (G-6769)

American Marine Express Inc ....E 216 268-3005
Cleveland (G-4957)

Burd Brothers Inc ....E 513 708-7787
Dayton (G-9269)

Colonial Courier Service Inc ....E 419 891-0922
Maumee (G-13772)

Esj Carrier Corporation ....E 513 728-7388
Fairfield (G-10726)

Freedom Enterprises Inc ....E 419 675-1192
Kenton (G-12275)

Garner Trucking Inc ....C 419 422-5742
Findlay (G-10912)

Integrity Ex Logistics LLC ....B 888 374-5138
Cincinnati (G-3771)

J Rayl Transport Inc ....E 330 940-1668
Euclid (G-10646)

Kgbo Holdings Inc ....E 513 831-2600
Cincinnati (G-2859)

Nationwide Transport Llc ....E 513 554-0203
Cincinnati (G-4097)

Ohio Transport Inc ....E 216 741-8000
Cleveland (G-6125)

Pride Transportation Inc ....E 419 424-2145
Findlay (G-10956)

Schneider Nat Carriers Inc ....E 740 362-6910
Delaware (G-10006)

Total Package Express Inc ....E 513 741-5500
Cincinnati (G-4611)

Total Quality Logistics LLC ....E 513 831-2600
Milford (G-14437)

Total Quality Logistics LLC ....C 513 831-2600
Milford (G-14438)

Total Quality Logistics LLC ....B 513 831-2600
Cincinnati (G-2873)

TRANSPORTATION EPQT & SPLYS, WHOL: Aircraft Engs/Eng Parts

Aim Mro Holdings Inc ....D 513 831-2938
Miamiville (G-14244)

TRANSPORTATION EPQT & SPLYS, WHOLESALE: Tanks & Tank Compnts

Eleet Cryogenics Inc ....E 330 874-4009
Bolivar (G-1702)

TRANSPORTATION EQPT & SPLYS WHOLESALERS, NEC

Greenfield Products Inc ....D 937 981-2696
Greenfield (G-11362)

Schuster Electronics Inc ....E 330 425-8134
Twinsburg (G-18319)

TRANSPORTATION EQUIPMENT, NEC

Cleveland Wheels ....D 440 937-6211
Avon (G-877)

TRANSPORTATION INSPECTION SVCS

Argus International Inc ....E 513 852-1010
Cincinnati (G-2985)

TRANSPORTATION PROG REG & ADMIN, GOVT: Bureau, Public Roads

Transportation Ohio Department...........E 740 773-3191
Chillicothe (G-2832)

TRANSPORTATION PROGRAM REGULATION & ADMIN GOVT: Local

City of Lima ....E 419 221-5165
Lima (G-12613)

TRANSPORTATION PROGRAM REGULATION & ADMIN, GOVT: Federal

National Railroad Pass Corp.................E 419 246-0159
Toledo (G-17933)

TRANSPORTATION PROGRAM REGULATION & ADMIN, GOVT: State

Ohio Department Transportation...........C 740 363-1251
Delaware (G-9999)

Ohio Department Transportation...........E 937 548-3015
Greenville (G-11391)

Ohio Department Transportation...........E 419 738-4214
Wapakoneta (G-18651)

Ohio Department Transportation...........D 614 275-1324
Columbus (G-8242)

Ohio Department Transportation...........E 330 533-4351
Canfield (G-2153)

Ohio Department Transportation...........E 330 637-5951
Cortland (G-8992)

TRANSPORTATION PROGRAMS REGULATION & ADMINISTRATION SVCS

Ohio Tpk & Infrastructure Comm ....E 419 826-4831
Swanton (G-17403)

Ohio Tpk & Infrastructure Comm ....C 440 234-2081
Berea (G-1433)

Ohio Tpk & Infrastructure Comm ....E 440 234-2081
Richfield (G-16369)

Turnpike and Infrastructure Co ....D 330 527-2169
Windham (G-19664)

TRANSPORTATION SVCS, AIR, NONSCHEDULED: Air Cargo Carriers

Airnet Systems Inc............................C 614 409-4900
Columbus (G-6886)

TRANSPORTATION SVCS, NEC

Access Home Care LLC ....E 937 224-9991
Dayton (G-9205)

Bob Evans Transportation ....A 937 322-4447
Springfield (G-17001)

Euclid SC Transportation ....D 216 797-7600
Cleveland (G-5494)

Genox Transportation Inc ....E 419 837-2023
Perrysburg (G-15868)

Jti Transportation Inc ....E 419 661-9360
Stony Ridge (G-17184)

Marietta Transfer Company ....E 740 896-3565
Lowell (G-13038)

Mikesell Transportation Broker ....E 937 996-5731
Arcanum (G-625)

Niese Transport Inc ....E 419 523-4400
Ottawa (G-15661)

Nobel County Engineers Office ....E 740 732-4400
Caldwell (G-2041)

OH St Trans Dist 02 Outpost.................E 419 693-8870
  Northwood (G-15404)
School Transportation.........................E 937 855-3897
  Germantown (G-11277)
Village Transport Corp ....C 440 461-5000
  Cleveland (G-6633)
Williams Freight Logistics ....E 614 333-9173
  Columbus (G-8906)

TRANSPORTATION SVCS, WATER: Boat Cleaning

Ship Shape Marine Inc........................E 419 734-1554
  Port Clinton (G-16117)
South Shore Marine Services ....E 419 433-5798
  Huron (G-12033)

TRANSPORTATION SVCS, WATER: Canal Barge Operations

Consolidated Grain & Barge Co ....E 513 941-4805
  Cincinnati (G-3351)

TRANSPORTATION SVCS, WATER: Cleaning

MPW Industrial Water Svcs Inc ....C 800 827-8790
  Hebron (G-11720)

TRANSPORTATION SVCS, WATER: Intracoastal, Freight

Midland Company ....A 513 947-5503
  Amelia (G-574)

TRANSPORTATION SVCS: Airport

Charter Vans Inc.................................E 937 898-4043
  Vandalia (G-18513)
City of Wilmington ....E 937 382-7961
  Wilmington (G-19608)
Led Transportation ....E 330 484-2772
  Canton (G-2373)
Park-N-Go Inc ....E 937 890-7275
  Dayton (G-9686)

TRANSPORTATION SVCS: Airport, Regular Route

Sutton Motor Coach Tours Inc..............E 330 726-2800
  Youngstown (G-20219)

TRANSPORTATION SVCS: Bus Line Operations

Allen Cnty Regional Trnst Auth ....E 419 222-2782
  Lima (G-12594)
Central Ohio Transit Authority.............C 614 275-5800
  Columbus (G-7169)
Central Ohio Transit Authority.............A 614 275-5800
  Columbus (G-7170)
Greater Dyton Rgnal Trnst Auth ....D 937 425-8310
  Dayton (G-9474)
Metro Regional Transit Auth ....B 330 762-0341
  Akron (G-334)
Southwest OH Trans Auth....................A 513 621-4455
  Cincinnati (G-4506)
Southwest OH Trans Auth....................A 513 632-7511
  Cincinnati (G-4507)
Toledo Area Rgional Trnst Auth ....D 419 243-7433
  Toledo (G-18074)
Western Reserve Transit Auth..............D 330 744-8431
  Youngstown (G-20243)

TRANSPORTATION SVCS: Bus Line, Interstate

Greyhound Lines Inc ....E 513 421-7442
  Cincinnati (G-3657)
Muskingum Coach Company..................E 740 622-2545
  Coshocton (G-9023)

TRANSPORTATION SVCS: Maint Facilities, Vehicle Passenger

City of Willoughby ....E 440 942-0215
  Willoughby (G-19510)
Washington Local Schools ....D 419 473-8356
  Toledo (G-18146)

TRANSPORTATION SVCS: Maintenance Facilities, Buses

Hans Truck and Trlr Repr Inc ....E 216 581-0046
  Cleveland (G-5660)
Reynoldsburg City Schools ....E 614 501-1041
  Reynoldsburg (G-16326)

TRANSPORTATION SVCS: Railroad Terminals

Tidewater River Rail Oper LLC ....D 817 659-0091
  Steubenville (G-17174)

TRANSPORTATION SVCS: Railroad, Passenger

Greater Cleveland ....A 216 566-5107
  Cleveland (G-5633)

TRANSPORTATION SVCS: Railroads, Interurban

CSX Transportation Inc ....E 614 898-3651
  Westerville (G-19155)
Illinois Central Railroad Co ....E 419 726-6028
  Toledo (G-17817)

TRANSPORTATION SVCS: Railroads, Steam

Covia Holdings Corporation ....D 440 214-3284
  Independence (G-12063)

TRANSPORTATION SVCS: Rental, Local

Direct Expediting LLC ....E 513 459-0100
  Mason (G-13574)
Universal Work and Power LLC.............E 513 981-1111
  Cincinnati (G-4696)

TRANSPORTATION SVCS: Subway Operation

Laketran ....C 440 350-1000
  Painesville (G-15721)

TRANSPORTATION SVCS: Vanpool Operation

Seneca-Crawford Area Trnsp.................E 419 937-2428
  Tiffin (G-17540)

TRANSPORTATION: Air, Nonscheduled Passenger

Lane Aviation Corporation ....C 614 237-3747
  Columbus (G-7950)

TRANSPORTATION: Air, Nonscheduled, NEC

Netjets Sales Inc ....C 614 239-5500
  Columbus (G-8177)
Options Flight Support Inc...................C 216 261-3500
  Cleveland (G-6139)
Panther II Transportation Inc ....C 800 685-0657
  Medina (G-13985)

TRANSPORTATION: Air, Scheduled Freight

Federal Express Corporation................B 614 492-6106
  Columbus (G-7568)
Flight Express Inc ....D 305 379-8686
  Columbus (G-7596)
United Parcel Service Inc OH................B 740 363-0636
  Delaware (G-10013)

TRANSPORTATION: Air, Scheduled Passenger

American Airlines Inc ....E 216 898-1347
  Cleveland (G-4948)
City of Dayton ....C 937 454-8200
  Vandalia (G-18515)
Distribution and Trnsp Svc Inc............E 937 295-3343
  Fort Loramie (G-10985)
Executive Jet Management Inc ....B 513 979-6600
  Cincinnati (G-3525)
Lane Aviation Corporation ....C 614 237-3747
  Columbus (G-7950)

TRANSPORTATION: Bus Transit Systems

Firstgroup America Inc........................D 513 241-2200
  Cincinnati (G-3566)
Greater Dyton Rgnal Trnst Auth ....A 937 425-8400
  Dayton (G-9476)
Greyhound Lines Inc ....E 614 221-0577
  Columbus (G-7697)
Precious Cargo Transportation ....E 440 564-8039
  Newbury (G-15124)
Stark Area Regional Trnst Auth ....C 330 477-2782
  Canton (G-2487)

TRANSPORTATION: Bus Transit Systems

Columbus Public School Dst.................C 614 365-6542
  Columbus (G-7309)
First Transit Inc ....D 937 652-4175
  Urbana (G-18433)
Metro Regional Transit Auth ....D 330 762-0341
  Akron (G-335)
Mv Transportation Inc ....D 740 681-5086
  Cincinnati (G-4088)

TRANSPORTATION: Deep Sea Foreign Freight

APL Logistics Ltd ....C 440 930-2822
  Avon Lake (G-908)
Toula Industries Ltd LLC ....C 937 689-1818
  Dayton (G-9818)

TRANSPORTATION: Deep Sea Passenger

AAA Allied Group Inc...........................D 513 228-0866
  Lebanon (G-12447)

TRANSPORTATION: Great Lakes Domestic Freight

The Interlake Steamship Co...................E 440 260-6900
  Middleburg Heights (G-14261)

TRANSPORTATION: Local Passenger, NEC

Above & Beyond Caregivers LLC...........E 614 478-1700
  Columbus (G-6855)
Asv Services LLC.................................E 216 797-1701
  Euclid (G-10623)
Catholic Charities of SW Ohio ....D 513 241-7745
  Cincinnati (G-3132)
City of Lakewood ....E 216 521-1288
  Cleveland (G-5209)
Clark County Board of Developm...........D 937 328-5240
  Springfield (G-17010)
Cloverleaf Transport Co ....E 419 599-5015
  Napoleon (G-14801)
Contract Transport Services.................E 216 524-8435
  Cleveland (G-5345)
County of Ottawa ....E 419 898-7433
  Oak Harbor (G-15469)
Cremation Service Inc ....E 216 861-2334
  Cleveland (G-5378)
Critical Life Inc ....E 419 525-0502
  Mansfield (G-13160)
Cusa LI Inc ....C 216 267-8810
  Brookpark (G-1895)
Donty Horton HM Care Dhhc LLC ....E 513 463-3442
  Cincinnati (G-3440)
Firstgroup America Inc........................E 513 241-2200
  Cincinnati (G-3566)
Firstgroup America Inc........................D 513 241-2200
  Cincinnati (G-3568)
Greater Cleveland Regional ....C 216 781-1110
  Cleveland (G-5639)
Guernsey Health Systems......................A 740 439-3561
  Cambridge (G-2073)
Intercoastal Trnsp Systems ....D 513 829-1287
  Fairfield (G-10737)
Lakefront Lines Inc..............................C 216 267-8810
  Brookpark (G-1900)
Lakefront Lines Inc..............................E 614 476-1113
  Columbus (G-7944)
Lakefront Lines Inc..............................D 513 829-8290
  Fairfield (G-10746)
Mahoning County.................................D 330 797-2837
  Youngstown (G-20107)
Muskingum County Ohio ....D 740 452-0678
  Zanesville (G-20335)
Mycity Transporatation Co....................E 216 591-1900
  Shaker Heights (G-16711)

National Express Transit Corp...............D...... 513 322-6214
Cincinnati (G-4091)
Pickaway County Community Acti........D...... 740 477-1655
Circleville (G-4839)
Professional Transportation ....C...... 419 661-0576
Walbridge (G-18623)
Senior Outreach Services.....................E...... 216 421-6900
Cleveland (G-6397)
United Scoto Senior Activities ....E...... 740 354-6672
Portsmouth (G-16176)
Youngstown Area Jwish Fdration ....D...... 330 746-1076
Youngstown (G-20257)

TRANSPORTATION: Passenger Ferries

Kelleys Isle Ferry Boat Lines ....E...... 419 798-9763
Marblehead (G-13301)
Miller Boat Line Inc...............................D...... 419 285-2421
Put In Bay (G-16227)

TRANSPORTATION: Transit Systems, NEC

Anthony Wayne Local Schools ....D...... 419 877-0451
Whitehouse (G-19443)
Butler Cnty Rgional Trnst Auth ....C...... 513 785-5237
Hamilton (G-11566)
City Taxicab & Transfer Co ....E...... 440 992-2156
Ashtabula (G-727)
First Group Investment Partnr...............D...... 513 241-2200
Cincinnati (G-3558)
First Transit Inc ....D...... 513 732-1206
Batavia (G-999)
Firstgroup America Inc..........................D...... 513 241-2200
Cincinnati (G-3566)
Firstgroup America Inc..........................D...... 513 241-2200
Cincinnati (G-3568)
Firstgroup Usa Inc ....B...... 513 241-2200
Cincinnati (G-3569)
Greater Cleveland Regional ....D...... 216 575-3932
Cleveland (G-5638)
Intercoastal Trnsp Systems ....D...... 513 829-1287
Fairfield (G-10737)
Ironton and Lawrence County ....B...... 740 532-3534
Ironton (G-12155)
Ironton and Lawrence County ....E...... 740 532-7855
Ironton (G-12156)
Laidlaw Transit Services Inc ....E...... 513 241-2200
Cincinnati (G-3908)
Lifecare Ambulance Inc.........................E...... 440 323-6111
Elyria (G-10526)
Mv Transportation Inc............................D...... 419 627-0740
Sandusky (G-16628)
Pickaway County Community Acti........D...... 740 477-1655
Circleville (G-4839)
Portage Area Rgonal Trnsp Auth..........D...... 330 678-1287
Kent (G-12254)
South Transportation.............................E...... 216 691-2040
Cleveland (G-6425)
Southeast Area Transit ....E...... 740 454-8574
Zanesville (G-20362)
Stark Area Regional Trnst Auth.............C...... 330 477-2782
Canton (G-2487)
United Scoto Senior Activities ....E...... 740 354-6672
Portsmouth (G-16176)
Universal Transportation Syste.............C...... 513 829-1287
Fairfield (G-10796)
Universal Transportation Syste.............E...... 513 539-9491
Monroe (G-14585)
Universal Work and Power LLC.............E...... 513 981-1111
Cincinnati (G-4696)

TRAVEL AGENCIES

AAA Allied Group Inc.............................E...... 419 228-1022
Lima (G-12591)
AAA Allied Group Inc.............................B...... 513 762-3301
Cincinnati (G-2894)
AAA Miami Valley ....D...... 937 224-2896
Dayton (G-9201)
AAA Shelby County Motor Club ....E...... 937 492-3167
Sidney (G-16756)
Avalon Holdings Corporation ....D...... 330 856-8800
Warren (G-18673)
Maritz Travel Company..........................B...... 660 626-1501
Maumee (G-13814)
Muskingum Coach Company...................E...... 740 622-2545
Coshocton (G-9023)
Pier n Port Travel Inc ....E...... 513 841-9900
Cincinnati (G-4247)
Professional Travel Inc..........................D...... 440 734-8800
North Olmsted (G-15305)

Travel Authority......................................E...... 513 272-2887
Cincinnati (G-4629)

TRAVEL TRAILER DEALERS

Sirpilla Recrtl Vhcl Ctr Inc ....D...... 330 494-2525
Akron (G-430)
Sonic Automotive-1495 Automall ....E...... 614 317-4326
Columbus (G-8659)

TRAVEL TRAILERS & CAMPERS

Capitol City Trailers Inc ....D...... 614 491-2616
Obetz (G-15523)

TRAVELER ACCOMMODATIONS, NEC

1460 Ninth St Assoc Ltd Partnr ....E...... 216 241-6600
Cleveland (G-4866)
16644 Snow Rd LLC...............................E...... 216 676-5200
Brookpark (G-1889)
5 Star Hotel Management IV LP ....D...... 614 431-1819
Columbus (G-6842)
6300 Sharonville Assoc LLC...................C...... 513 489-3636
Cincinnati (G-2884)
A C Management Inc..............................E...... 440 461-9200
Cleveland (G-4876)
Aimbridge Hospitality LLC.....................A...... 330 668-9090
Akron (G-24)
Akron Inn Limited Partnership ....E...... 330 336-7692
Wadsworth (G-18587)
Alliance Hospitality...............................D...... 330 505-2173
Youngstown (G-19950)
Alliance Hospitality Inc..........................E...... 440 951-7333
Mentor (G-14016)
American Prprty-Mnagement Corp ....D...... 330 454-5000
Canton (G-2187)
Americas Best Value Inn ....E...... 419 626-9890
Sandusky (G-16575)
Amish Door Inc ....B...... 330 359-5464
Wilmot (G-19657)
Amitel Beachwood Ltd Partnr.................E...... 216 707-9839
Cleveland (G-4970)
Ap/Aim Indpndnce Sites Trs LLC ....D...... 216 986-9900
Independence (G-12045)
Apple Gate Operating Co Inc ....E...... 330 405-4488
Twinsburg (G-18245)
Army & Air Force Exchange Svc ....C...... 937 257-2928
Dayton (G-9160)
Arvind Sagar Inc ....E...... 614 428-8800
Columbus (G-6975)
Athens OH 1013 LLC..............................E...... 740 589-5839
Athens (G-769)
Avalon Resort and Spa LLC....................D...... 330 856-1900
Warren (G-18676)
Awe Hospitality Group LLC....................C...... 330 888-8836
Macedonia (G-13060)
Bellville Hotel Company.........................E...... 419 886-7000
Bellville (G-1387)
Bennett Enterprises Inc.........................E...... 419 893-1004
Maumee (G-13762)
Best Western Columbus N Hotel............E...... 614 888-8230
Columbus (G-7030)
Bindu Associates LLC............................E...... 440 324-0099
Elyria (G-10483)
Black Sapphire C Columbus Univ ....D...... 614 297-9912
Columbus (G-7045)
Blue-Kenwood LLC.................................E...... 513 469-6900
Blue Ash (G-1515)
Bob Mor Inc ....C...... 419 485-5555
Montpelier (G-14607)
Cabin Restaurant ....E...... 330 562-9171
Aurora (G-823)
Cafaro Peachcreek Co Ltd ....D...... 419 625-6280
Sandusky (G-16579)
Cambridge Associates Ltd ....E...... 740 432-7313
Cambridge (G-2051)
Cambridge Property Investors ....E...... 740 432-7313
Cambridge (G-2056)
Canter Inns Inc ....E...... 740 354-7711
Portsmouth (G-16127)
Carlisle Hotels Inc.................................E...... 614 851-5599
Columbus (G-7129)
Carlson Hotels Ltd Partnership..............D...... 740 386-5451
Marion (G-13409)
Carroll Properties..................................E...... 513 398-8075
Mason (G-13549)
Ceres Enterprises LLC...........................D...... 440 617-9385
Westlake (G-19329)
Claire De Leigh Corp..............................E...... 614 459-6575
Columbus (G-7216)

Clermont Hills Co LLC............................D...... 513 752-4400
Cincinnati (G-2846)
Cleveland East Hotel LLC.......................D...... 216 378-9191
Cleveland (G-5252)
Cleveland S Hospitality LLC....................E...... 216 447-1300
Cleveland (G-5286)
Clinic Care Inc.......................................D...... 216 707-4200
Cleveland (G-5306)
Columbia Properties Lima LLC ....D...... 419 222-0004
Lima (G-12616)
Columbus Concord Ltd Partnr ....E...... 614 228-3200
Columbus (G-7271)
Columbus Easton Hotel LLC....................E...... 614 414-1000
Columbus (G-7278)
Columbus Hospitality ....E...... 614 461-2648
Columbus (G-7287)
Columbus Oh-16 Airport Gahanna..........E...... 614 501-4770
Gahanna (G-11114)
Comfort Inn Northeast............................E...... 513 683-9700
Cincinnati (G-3336)
Comfort Inns ....E...... 614 885-4084
Columbus (G-7325)
Commonwealth Hotels LLC.....................D...... 216 524-5814
Cleveland (G-5322)
Concord Dayton Hotel II LLC...................D...... 937 223-1000
Dayton (G-9316)
Concord Testa Hotel Assoc LLC ....D...... 330 252-9228
Akron (G-156)
Continental/Olentangy Ht LLC.................D...... 614 297-9912
Columbus (G-7363)
Courtyard By Marriott ....E...... 216 765-1900
Cleveland (G-5372)
Courtyard By Marriott ....E...... 513 341-4140
West Chester (G-18901)
Courtyard By Marriott ....E...... 440 871-3756
Westlake (G-19338)
Courtyard By Marriott ....D...... 937 433-3131
Miamisburg (G-14156)
Courtyard By Marriott Rossford ....E...... 419 872-5636
Rossford (G-16460)
Courtyard Management Corp ....E...... 614 475-8530
Columbus (G-7381)
CPX Carrollton Es LLC............................E...... 330 627-1200
Carrollton (G-2566)
Cs Hotels Limited Partnership.................D...... 614 771-8999
Columbus (G-7399)
Cumberland Gap LLC..............................E...... 513 681-9300
Cincinnati (G-3386)
Cwb Property Managmnt Inc ....E...... 614 793-2244
Dublin (G-10195)
Days Inn ....E...... 740 695-0100
Saint Clairsville (G-16486)
Dayton Hotels LLC..................................E...... 937 832-2222
Englewood (G-10584)
Dbp Enterprises LLC...............................E...... 740 513-2399
Sunbury (G-17386)
Dixie Management II Inc ....D...... 937 832-1234
Englewood (G-10585)
Donlen Inc..D...... 216 961-6767
Cleveland (G-5439)
Dublin Hotel Ltd Liability Co...................C...... 513 891-1066
Dublin (G-10208)
Dure Investments LLC ....E...... 419 697-7800
Oregon (G-15591)
Edmond Hotel Investors LLC...................D...... 614 891-2900
Columbus (G-7503)
Fairfeld Inn Stes Clmbus Arprt ....E...... 614 237-2100
Columbus (G-7554)
Fairfield Inn...D...... 614 267-1111
Columbus (G-7555)
Falcon Plaza LLC....................................E...... 419 352-4671
Bowling Green (G-1730)
First Hospitality Company LLC ....E...... 614 864-4555
Reynoldsburg (G-16304)
Goodnight Inn Inc ....E...... 419 334-9551
Fremont (G-11078)
Grandview Ht Ltd Partnr Ohio ....D...... 937 766-5519
Springfield (G-17043)
Hampton Inns LLC..................................E...... 330 492-0151
Canton (G-2337)
Hampton Inns LLC..................................E...... 330 422-0500
Streetsboro (G-17255)
He Hari Inc ....D...... 614 846-6600
Lewis Center (G-12544)
Hilton Garden Inn ....D...... 614 263-7200
Columbus (G-7751)
Hilton Garden Inn Akron ....E...... 330 966-4907
Canton (G-2346)
Hit Portfolio I Misc Trs LLC.....................C...... 513 241-3575
Cincinnati (G-3711)

Hmshost Corporation............C...... 419 547-8667
Clyde *(G-6744)*
Holiday Inn............E...... 419 691-8800
Oregon *(G-15598)*
Holiday Inn Express............E...... 419 332-7700
Fremont *(G-11080)*
Holiday Inn Express............E...... 937 424-5757
Dayton *(G-9497)*
Holiday Inn Express............E...... 614 447-1212
Columbus *(G-7759)*
Host Cincinnati Hotel LLC............C...... 513 621-7700
Cincinnati *(G-3731)*
Hotel 50 S Front Opco L P............D...... 614 885-3334
Columbus *(G-7774)*
Hotel Stow LP............E...... 330 945-9722
Stow *(G-17211)*
Howard Johnson............C...... 513 825-3129
Cincinnati *(G-3733)*
Hst Lessee Cincinnati LLC............C...... 513 852-2702
Cincinnati *(G-3736)*
IA Urban Htels Bchwood Trs LLC............D...... 216 765-8066
Beachwood *(G-1066)*
Indus Airport Hotel II LLC............D...... 614 235-0717
Columbus *(G-7808)*
Inn At Wickliffe LLC............E...... 440 585-0600
Wickliffe *(G-19465)*
Jackson I-94 Ltd Partnership............E...... 614 793-2244
Dublin *(G-10259)*
Jagi Clveland Independence LLC............C...... 216 524-8050
Cleveland *(G-5778)*
Jagi Juno LLC............E...... 513 489-1955
Cincinnati *(G-3804)*
Janus Hotels and Resorts Inc............E...... 513 631-8500
Lewisburg *(G-12569)*
Johnson Howard International............E...... 513 401-8683
Cincinnati *(G-3829)*
Kenyon College............E...... 740 427-2202
Gambier *(G-11225)*
Kiwi Hospitality - Cincinnati............E...... 513 241-8660
Cincinnati *(G-3877)*
Lancaster Host LLC............E...... 740 654-4445
Lancaster *(G-12412)*
Lawnfield Properties LLC............E...... 440 974-3572
Mentor *(G-14076)*
Liberty Ashtabula Holdings............E...... 330 872-6000
Newton Falls *(G-15140)*
Lodging Industry Inc............E...... 440 323-7488
Sandusky *(G-16624)*
Lodging Industry Inc............E...... 419 732-2929
Port Clinton *(G-16112)*
Lodging Industry Inc............E...... 440 324-3911
Elyria *(G-10529)*
M&C Hotel Interests Inc............E...... 937 778-8100
Piqua *(G-16012)*
Mansfield Hotel Partnership............E...... 419 529-2100
Mansfield *(G-13206)*
Marriott............E...... 440 542-2375
Solon *(G-16871)*
Marriott International Inc............C...... 614 861-1400
Columbus *(G-8022)*
Marriott International Inc............C...... 513 487-3800
Cincinnati *(G-3973)*
Marriott International Inc............C...... 513 487-3800
Cincinnati *(G-3974)*
Marriott International Inc............B...... 216 696-9200
Cleveland *(G-5912)*
Marriott International Inc............B...... 614 228-5050
Columbus *(G-8023)*
Marriott International Inc............E...... 614 436-7070
Columbus *(G-8024)*
Marriott International Inc............C...... 614 475-8530
Columbus *(G-8025)*
Marriott International Inc............C...... 614 864-8844
Columbus *(G-8026)*
Marriott International Inc............C...... 614 222-2610
Columbus *(G-8027)*
Marriott International Inc............E...... 614 885-0799
Columbus *(G-8028)*
Marriott International Inc............E...... 330 666-4811
Copley *(G-8970)*
Marriott International Inc............C...... 419 866-1001
Holland *(G-11895)*
Marriott International Inc............E...... 440 716-9977
North Olmsted *(G-15297)*
Marriott International Inc............C...... 513 530-5060
Blue Ash *(G-1605)*
Mason Family Resorts LLC............B...... 513 339-0141
Mason *(G-13615)*
Maumee Lodging Enterprises............D...... 419 865-1380
Maumee *(G-13818)*

Meander Hospitality Group Inc............E...... 330 702-0226
Canfield *(G-2146)*
Meander Hsptality Group II LLC............E...... 330 422-0500
Streetsboro *(G-17260)*
Middletown Innkeepers Inc............E...... 513 942-3440
Fairfield *(G-10758)*
Moti Corporation............E...... 440 734-4500
Cleveland *(G-6014)*
Mrn-Newgar Hotel Ltd............E...... 216 443-1000
Cleveland *(G-6020)*
N P Motel System Inc............E...... 330 339-7731
New Philadelphia *(G-14975)*
Norstar Aluminum Molds Inc............D...... 440 632-0853
Middlefield *(G-14273)*
Northeast Cincinnati Hotel LLC............C...... 513 459-9800
Mason *(G-13623)*
Northland Hotel Inc............E...... 614 885-1601
Columbus *(G-8202)*
Northtown Square Ltd Partnr............E...... 419 691-8911
Oregon *(G-15601)*
Oh-16 Cleveland Westlake............E...... 440 892-4275
Westlake *(G-19385)*
Ohio Inns Inc............E...... 937 440-9303
Troy *(G-18219)*
Ohio State University............B...... 614 292-3238
Columbus *(G-8333)*
Olshan Hotel Management Inc............E...... 614 414-1000
Columbus *(G-8373)*
Optima 777 LLC............E...... 216 771-7700
Cleveland *(G-6138)*
Oxford Hospitality Group Inc............E...... 513 524-0114
Oxford *(G-15687)*
Park Hotels & Resorts Inc............E...... 937 436-2400
Miamisburg *(G-14202)*
Park Inn............E...... 419 241-3000
Toledo *(G-17970)*
Parkins Incorporated............E...... 614 334-1800
Hilliard *(G-11805)*
Peitro Properties Ltd Partnr............E...... 216 328-7777
Cleveland *(G-6190)*
PH Fairborn Ht Owner 2800 LLC............D...... 937 426-7800
Beavercreek *(G-1176)*
Pinecraft Land Holdings LLC............E...... 330 390-5722
Millersburg *(G-14486)*
Polaris Innkeepers Inc............E...... 614 568-0770
Westerville *(G-19199)*
Quail Hollow Management Inc............D...... 440 639-4000
Painesville *(G-15734)*
R & Y Holding............E...... 419 353-3464
Bowling Green *(G-1747)*
Radisson Hotel Cleveland Gtwy............D...... 216 377-9000
Cleveland *(G-6278)*
Red Roof Inns Inc............A...... 614 744-2600
New Albany *(G-14871)*
Red Roof Inns Inc............E...... 614 224-6539
Columbus *(G-8500)*
Red Roof Inns Inc............E...... 440 892-7920
Cleveland *(G-6294)*
Red Roof Inns Inc............E...... 740 695-4057
Saint Clairsville *(G-16503)*
Red Roof Inns Inc............E...... 440 243-5166
Cleveland *(G-6295)*
Renthotel Dayton LLC............D...... 937 461-4700
Dayton *(G-9731)*
Req/Jqh Holdings Inc............D...... 937 432-0000
Miamisburg *(G-14211)*
Residence Inn............E...... 614 222-2610
Columbus *(G-8519)*
Richfield Banquet & Confer............E...... 330 659-6151
Richfield *(G-16375)*
Ridgehills Hotel Ltd Partnr............D...... 440 585-0600
Wickliffe *(G-19475)*
Riverview Hotel LLC............E...... 614 268-8700
Columbus *(G-8538)*
Rlj III - Em Clmbus Lessee LLC............D...... 614 890-8600
Columbus *(G-8539)*
Roce Group LLC............E...... 330 969-2627
Stow *(G-17227)*
Roschmans Restaurant ADM............E...... 419 225-8300
Lima *(G-12734)*
Rossford Hospitality Group Inc............E...... 419 874-2345
Rossford *(G-16464)*
Rukh-Jagi Holdings LLC............D...... 330 494-2770
Canton *(G-2465)*
Sadguru Krupa LLC............E...... 330 644-2111
Akron *(G-416)*
Saw Mill Creek Ltd............C...... 419 433-3800
Huron *(G-12030)*
Sb Hotel LLC............E...... 614 793-2244
Dublin *(G-10329)*

SBS of Canton Jv LLC............E...... 330 966-6620
Canton *(G-2470)*
Shree Shankar LLC............E...... 440 734-4477
Richfield *(G-16379)*
Skyline CM Portfolio LLC............E...... 937 433-3131
Miamisburg *(G-14222)*
Skyline CM Portfolio LLC............E...... 419 866-1001
Holland *(G-11914)*
SM Double Tree Hotel Lake............E...... 216 241-5100
Cleveland *(G-6418)*
Solon Lodging Associates LLC............E...... 440 248-9600
Solon *(G-16899)*
Somnus Corporation............E...... 740 695-3961
Saint Clairsville *(G-16505)*
Son-Rise Hotels Inc............E...... 330 769-4949
Seville *(G-16691)*
Sortino Management & Dev Co............E...... 419 626-6761
Sandusky *(G-16643)*
Spring Hill Suites............E...... 513 381-8300
Cincinnati *(G-4520)*
Star Group Ltd............E...... 614 428-8678
Gahanna *(G-11146)*
Starwood Hotels & Resorts............C...... 614 345-9291
Columbus *(G-8689)*
Starwood Hotels & Resorts............C...... 614 888-8230
Columbus *(G-8690)*
Sterling Lodging LLC............E...... 419 879-4000
Lima *(G-12755)*
Stoney Lodge Inc............D...... 419 837-6409
Millbury *(G-14451)*
Strang Corporation............E...... 216 961-6767
Cleveland *(G-6472)*
Strongsville Lodging Assoc 1............C...... 440 238-8800
Strongsville *(G-17348)*
Summit Associates Inc............D...... 216 831-3300
Cleveland *(G-6475)*
Summit Hotel Trs 144 LLC............E...... 216 443-9043
Cleveland *(G-6476)*
Town Inn Co LLC............D...... 614 221-3281
Columbus *(G-8766)*
Tramz Hotels LLC............D...... 440 975-9922
Willoughby *(G-19577)*
Travelcenters of America LLC............D...... 330 769-2053
Lodi *(G-12829)*
Union Centre Hotel LLC............C...... 513 874-7335
West Chester *(G-19026)*
United Hsptality Solutions LLC............A...... 800 238-0487
Buffalo *(G-2007)*
Uph Holdings LLC............D...... 614 447-9777
Columbus *(G-8823)*
Valleyview Management Co Inc............E...... 419 886-4000
Bellville *(G-1392)*
Vjp Hospitality Ltd............E...... 614 475-8383
Columbus *(G-8858)*
W & H Realty Inc............E...... 513 891-1066
Blue Ash *(G-1677)*
Westpost Columbus LLC............D...... 614 885-1885
Columbus *(G-8892)*
Willoughby Lodging LLC............E...... 440 530-1100
Willoughby *(G-19583)*
Winegardner & Hammons Inc............C...... 614 791-1000
Dublin *(G-10376)*
Winegrdner Hmmons Ht Group LLC............E...... 513 891-1066
Blue Ash *(G-1678)*
Wright Executive Ht Ltd Partnr............C...... 937 283-3200
Wilmington *(G-19656)*
Wright Executive Ht Ltd Partnr............C...... 937 426-7800
Beavercreek *(G-1196)*
Wright Executive Ht Ltd Partnr............C...... 937 429-0600
Beavercreek *(G-1197)*
Wyndham International Inc............E...... 330 666-9300
Copley *(G-8980)*

TRAVELERS' CHECK ISSUANCE SVCS

Jpmorgan Chase Bank Nat Assn............A...... 614 436-3055
Columbus *(G-6818)*

TROPHIES, NEC

Lawnview Industries Inc............C...... 937 653-5217
Urbana *(G-18438)*

TROPHY & PLAQUE STORES

Sporty Events............E...... 440 342-5046
Chesterland *(G-2745)*

TRUCK & BUS BODIES: Ambulance

Life Star Rescue Inc............E...... 419 238-2507
Van Wert *(G-18482)*

SERVICES

TRUCK & BUS BODIES: Truck, Motor Vehicle

Brown Industrial Inc ....E 937 693-3838
Botkins (G-1708)

Kaffenbarger Truck Eqp Co ....C 937 845-3804
New Carlisle (G-14892)

Schodorf Truck Body & Eqp Co ....E 614 228-6793
Columbus (G-8603)

Venco Venturo Industries LLC ....E 513 772-8448
Cincinnati (G-4753)

TRUCK & BUS BODIES: Utility Truck

QT Equipment Company ....E 330 724-3055
Akron (G-394)

TRUCK & FREIGHT TERMINALS & SUPPORT ACTIVITIES

Chieftain Trucking & Excav Inc ....E 216 485-8034
Cleveland (G-5176)

Dayton Freight Lines Inc ....D 937 236-4880
Dayton (G-9366)

Disttech LLC ....D 800 321-3143
Cleveland (G-5429)

Eab Truck Service ....D 216 525-0020
Cleveland (G-5454)

Fedex Freight Corporation ....E 877 661-8956
Mentor (G-14047)

PAm Transportation Svcs Inc ....D 419 935-9501
Willard (G-19485)

Pitt-Ohio Express LLC ....B 216 433-9000
Cleveland (G-6215)

Short Freight Lines Inc ....E 419 729-1691
Toledo (G-18031)

Slay Transportation Co Inc ....C 740 865-2910
Sardis (G-16661)

Stover Transportation Inc ....E 614 777-4184
Hilliard (G-11818)

STS Logistics Inc ....E 419 294-1498
Upper Sandusky (G-18413)

Xpo Logistics Freight Inc ....C 614 876-7100
Columbus (G-8924)

Xpo Logistics Freight Inc ....D 330 896-7300
Uniontown (G-18391)

Yrc Inc ....D 614 878-9281
Columbus (G-8933)

TRUCK BODIES: Body Parts

Kaffenbarger Truck Eqp Co ....E 513 772-6800
Cincinnati (G-3846)

TRUCK BODY SHOP

QT Equipment Company ....E 330 724-3055
Akron (G-394)

Skinner Diesel Services Inc ....E 614 491-8785
Columbus (G-8649)

TRUCK DRIVER SVCS

A Jacobs Inc ....E 614 774-6757
Hilliard (G-11738)

Aldo Peraza ....D 614 804-0403
Galloway (G-11218)

American Bulk Commodities Inc ....C 330 758-0841
Youngstown (G-19953)

Buckeye Leasing Inc ....E 330 758-0841
Youngstown (G-19978)

Hogan Truck Leasing Inc ....E 513 454-3500
Fairfield (G-10736)

Industrial Repair & Mfg Inc ....D 419 822-4232
Delta (G-10045)

S & B Trucking Inc ....E 614 554-4090
Hubbard (G-11950)

Transportation Unlimited Inc ....A 216 426-0088
Cleveland (G-6544)

Tsl Ltd ....A 419 843-3200
Toledo (G-18110)

TRUCK GENERAL REPAIR SVC

Abers Garage Inc ....E 419 281-5500
Ashland (G-644)

Aim Leasing Company ....D 330 759-0438
Girard (G-11282)

Allstate Trk Sls of Estrn OH ....E 330 339-5555
New Philadelphia (G-14945)

American Nat Fleet Svc Inc ....D 216 447-6060
Cleveland (G-4961)

Beaverdam Fleet Services Inc ....E 419 643-8880
Beaverdam (G-1266)

Benedict Enterprises Inc ....E 513 539-9216
Monroe (G-14563)

City of Toledo ....D 419 936-2507
Toledo (G-17659)

Dickinson Fleet Services LLC ....E 513 772-3629
Cincinnati (G-3429)

Fyda Freightliner Youngstown ....D 330 797-0224
Youngstown (G-20041)

Mansfield Truck Sls & Svc Inc ....E 419 522-9811
Mansfield (G-13211)

Midwest Trailer Sales & Svc ....E 513 772-2818
West Chester (G-18972)

Navistar Intl Trnsp Corp ....E 937 390-4242
Springfield (G-17087)

Peterbilt of Cincinnati ....E 513 772-1740
Cincinnati (G-4235)

PGT Trucking Inc ....E 419 943-3437
Leipsic (G-12521)

R & R Inc ....E 330 799-1536
Youngstown (G-20174)

Rebman Truck Service Inc ....E 419 589-8161
Mansfield (G-13233)

Spurlock Truck Service ....E 937 268-6100
Dayton (G-9787)

Stoops Frghtlnr-Qlity Trlr Inc ....E 937 236-4092
Dayton (G-9795)

Ta Operating LLC ....E 440 808-9100
Westlake (G-19411)

Ted Ruck Co Inc ....E 419 738-2613
Wapakoneta (G-18655)

Travelcenters America Inc ....A 440 808-9100
Westlake (G-19413)

Travelcenters of America LLC ....A 440 808-9100
Westlake (G-19415)

W W Williams Company LLC ....E 216 252-9977
Cleveland (G-6646)

W W Williams Company LLC ....E 614 527-9400
Hilliard (G-11828)

W W Williams Company LLC ....E 614 527-9400
Hilliard (G-11829)

Workforce Services Inc ....E 330 484-2566
Canton (G-2538)

TRUCK PAINTING & LETTERING SVCS

Palmer Trucks Inc ....E 937 235-3318
Dayton (G-9683)

TRUCK PARTS & ACCESSORIES: Wholesalers

Adelmans Truck Parts Corp ....E 330 456-0206
Canton (G-2173)

All Lift Service Company Inc ....E 440 585-1542
Willoughby (G-19503)

Allied Truck Parts Co ....E 330 477-8127
Canton (G-2181)

Better Brake Parts Inc ....E 419 227-0685
Lima (G-12607)

Buyers Products Company ....C 440 974-8888
Mentor (G-14024)

Cross Truck Equipment Co Inc ....E 330 477-8151
Canton (G-2274)

Denso International Amer Inc ....B 937 393-6800
Hillsboro (G-11837)

East Manufacturing Corporation ....B 330 325-9921
Randolph (G-16230)

GTM Service Inc ....E 440 944-5099
Wickliffe (G-19462)

Hy-Tek Material Handling Inc ....D 614 497-2500
Columbus (G-7790)

Kaffenbarger Truck Eqp Co ....C 937 845-3804
New Carlisle (G-14892)

Kenworth of Cincinnati Inc ....D 513 771-5831
Cincinnati (G-3862)

Ohio Automotive Supply Co ....E 419 422-1655
Findlay (G-10951)

Perkins Motor Service Ltd ....E 440 277-1256
Lorain (G-12938)

Peterbilt of Cincinnati ....E 513 772-1740
Cincinnati (G-4235)

Power Train Components Inc ....D 419 636-4430
Bryan (G-1971)

Premier Truck Parts Inc ....E 216 642-5000
Cleveland (G-6233)

R & R Inc ....E 330 799-1536
Youngstown (G-20174)

Valley Ford Truck Inc ....D 216 524-2400
Cleveland (G-6617)

W W Williams Company LLC ....D 419 837-5067
Perrysburg (G-15933)

Wz Management Inc ....E 330 628-4881
Akron (G-506)

Young Truck Sales Inc ....E 330 477-6271
Canton (G-2541)

Youngstown-Kenworth Inc ....E 330 534-9761
Hubbard (G-11952)

TRUCK STOPS

Travelcenters of America LLC ....A 440 808-9100
Westlake (G-19415)

Trepanier Daniels & Trepanier ....D 740 286-1288
Jackson (G-12180)

TRUCKING & HAULING SVCS: Baggage Transfer Svcs

Veyance Industrial Svcs Inc ....C 307 682-7855
Fairlawn (G-10854)

TRUCKING & HAULING SVCS: Building Materials

Home Run Inc ....E 800 543-9198
Xenia (G-19910)

TRUCKING & HAULING SVCS: Coal, Local

Robert Neff & Son Inc ....E 740 454-0128
Zanesville (G-20359)

TRUCKING & HAULING SVCS: Contract Basis

A L Smith Trucking Inc ....E 937 526-3651
Versailles (G-18565)

A&R Logistics Inc ....D 614 444-4111
Columbus (G-6849)

ABF Freight System Inc ....D 440 843-4600
Cleveland (G-4893)

ABF Freight System Inc ....E 614 294-3537
Columbus (G-6852)

ABF Freight System Inc ....E 937 236-2210
Dayton (G-9202)

ABF Freight System Inc ....E 513 779-7888
West Chester (G-18858)

ABF Freight System Inc ....E 330 549-3800
North Lima (G-15261)

AG Trucking Inc ....E 937 497-7770
Sidney (G-16757)

All Industrial Group Inc ....E 216 441-2000
Newburgh Heights (G-15113)

Alpha Freight Systems Inc ....D 800 394-9001
Hudson (G-11965)

Ameri-Line Inc ....E 440 316-4500
Columbia Station (G-6769)

Arctic Express Inc ....C 614 876-4008
Hilliard (G-11743)

Arms Trucking Co Inc ....E 800 362-1343
Huntsburg (G-12016)

Awl Transport Inc ....E 330 899-3444
Mantua (G-13264)

B D Transportation Inc ....E 937 773-9280
Piqua (G-15996)

Berlin Transportaion LLC ....E 330 674-3395
Millersburg (G-14459)

Besl Transfer Co ....E 513 242-3456
Cincinnati (G-3042)

Best Way Motor Lines Inc ....C 419 485-8373
Montpelier (G-14606)

Blatt Trucking Co Inc ....E 419 898-0002
Rocky Ridge (G-16419)

Bowling Transportation Inc ....D 419 436-9590
Fostoria (G-10998)

Bulk Transit Corporation ....E 614 873-4632
Plain City (G-16047)

Bulk Transit Corporation ....E 937 497-9573
Sidney (G-16763)

Bulkmatic Transport Company ....E 614 497-2372
Columbus (G-7097)

Burd Brothers Inc ....E 800 538-2873
Batavia (G-984)

By-Line Transit Inc ....E 937 642-2500
Marysville (G-13486)

C&K Trucking LLC ....E 440 657-5249
Elyria (G-10485)

Carry Transport Inc ....E 937 236-0026
Dayton (G-9283)

Cavins Trucking & Garage LLC ....E 419 661-9947
Perrysburg (G-15847)

Chambers Leasing Systems ....E 937 547-9777
Greenville **(G-11369)**

Cimarron Express Inc ....D 419 855-7713
Genoa **(G-11252)**

Clark Trucking Inc ....E 937 642-0335
East Liberty **(G-10390)**

Classic Carriers Inc ....E 937 604-8118
Versailles **(G-18567)**

Cowen Truck Line Inc ....D 419 938-3401
Perrysville **(G-15940)**

Crw Inc ....E 330 264-3785
Shreve **(G-16753)**

D L Belknap Trucking Inc ....D 330 868-7766
Paris **(G-15756)**

Dayton Freight Lines Inc ....E 330 346-0750
Kent **(G-12227)**

Dedicated Transport LLC ....C 216 641-2500
Brooklyn Heights **(G-1869)**

Dick Lavy Trucking Inc ....C 937 448-2104
Bradford **(G-1761)**

Dingledine Trucking Company ....E 937 652-3454
Urbana **(G-18431)**

Dlc Transport Inc ....E 740 282-1763
Steubenville **(G-17152)**

Drew Ag-Transport Inc ....D 937 548-3200
Greenville **(G-11376)**

Dworkin Inc ....E 216 271-5318
Cleveland **(G-5452)**

Erie Trucking Inc ....E 419 625-7374
Sandusky **(G-16602)**

Estes Express Lines Inc ....E 937 237-7536
Huber Heights **(G-11954)**

Estes Express Lines Inc ....D 419 522-2641
Mansfield **(G-13173)**

Estes Express Lines Inc ....D 513 779-9581
West Chester **(G-18920)**

Estes Express Lines Inc ....E 740 401-0410
Belpre **(G-1403)**

F S T Express Inc ....D 614 529-7900
Columbus **(G-7551)**

Fedex Freight Corporation ....E 877 661-8956
Mentor **(G-14047)**

Fedex Ground Package Sys Inc ....C 800 463-3339
Columbus **(G-7571)**

Fedex Ground Package Sys Inc ....B 800 463-3339
Grove City **(G-11432)**

Fetter and Son LLC ....E 740 465-2961
Morral **(G-14711)**

Fetter Son Farms Ltd Lblty Co ....E 740 465-2961
Morral **(G-14712)**

Five Star Trucking Inc ....E 440 953-9300
Willoughby **(G-19524)**

Foodliner Inc ....E 563 451-1047
Dayton **(G-9444)**

Fraley & Schilling Inc ....C 740 598-4118
Brilliant **(G-1822)**

G & S Transfer Inc ....E 330 673-3899
Kent **(G-12233)**

Garner Trucking Inc ....C 419 422-5742
Findlay **(G-10912)**

Globe Trucking Inc ....D 419 727-8307
Toledo **(G-17765)**

Guenther & Sons Inc ....E 513 738-1448
Ross **(G-16456)**

Harris Distributing Co ....E 513 541-4222
Cincinnati **(G-3681)**

Hillsboro Transportation Co ....E 513 772-9223
Cincinnati **(G-3707)**

Hilltrux Tank Lines Inc ....E 330 538-3700
North Jackson **(G-15246)**

Hoosier Express Inc ....E 419 436-9590
Fostoria **(G-11006)**

Hyway Trucking Company ....D 419 423-7145
Findlay **(G-10926)**

J & J Carriers LLC ....E 614 447-2615
Columbus **(G-7849)**

J M T Cartage Inc ....E 330 478-2430
Canton **(G-2359)**

J P Jenks Inc ....E 440 428-4500
Madison **(G-13098)**

J P Transportation Company ....E 513 424-6978
Middletown **(G-14304)**

K & L Trucking Inc ....E 419 822-3836
Delta **(G-10046)**

K-Limited Carrier Ltd ....C 419 269-0002
Toledo **(G-17834)**

Kaplan Trucking Company ....D 216 341-3322
Cleveland **(G-5813)**

Klingshirn & Sons Trucking ....E 937 338-5000
Burkettsville **(G-2012)**

Kmj Leasing Ltd ....E 614 871-3883
Orient **(G-15620)**

Knight-Swift Trnsp Hldings Inc ....D 614 274-5204
Columbus **(G-7917)**

Kuntzman Trucking Inc ....E 330 821-9160
Alliance **(G-536)**

L V Trucking Inc ....E 614 275-4994
Columbus **(G-7937)**

La King Trucking Inc ....E 419 225-9039
Lima **(G-12672)**

Liquid Transport Corp ....E 513 769-4777
Cincinnati **(G-3937)**

Lt Trucking Inc ....E 440 997-5528
Ashtabula **(G-747)**

Luckey Transfer LLC ....D 800 435-4371
Lima **(G-12694)**

Lyden Company ....E 419 868-6800
Toledo **(G-17874)**

Mast Trucking Inc ....D 330 674-8913
Millersburg **(G-14482)**

McFarland Truck Lines Inc ....E 937 854-2200
Dayton **(G-9594)**

McMullen Transportation LLC ....E 937 981-4455
Greenfield **(G-11364)**

Miami Valley Bekins Inc ....E 937 278-4296
Dayton **(G-9615)**

Millis Transfer Inc ....E 513 863-0222
Hamilton **(G-11630)**

Moeller Trucking Inc ....D 419 925-4799
Maria Stein **(G-13308)**

Motor Carrier Service Inc ....C 419 693-6207
Northwood **(G-15399)**

Nationwide Truck Brokers Inc ....E 937 335-9229
Troy **(G-18217)**

Old Dominion Freight Line Inc ....E 937 235-1596
Dayton **(G-9674)**

Old Dominion Freight Line Inc ....E 216 641-5566
Cleveland **(G-6127)**

Otis Wright & Sons Inc ....E 419 227-4400
Lima **(G-12715)**

P & D Transportation Inc ....C 740 454-1221
Zanesville **(G-20352)**

Penske Logistics LLC ....D 216 765-5475
Beachwood **(G-1095)**

PGT Trucking Inc ....E 419 943-3437
Leipsic **(G-12521)**

Piqua Transfer & Storage Co ....D 937 773-3743
Piqua **(G-16021)**

Pitt-Ohio Express LLC ....C 419 726-6523
Toledo **(G-17978)**

Pitt-Ohio Express LLC ....D 513 860-3424
West Chester **(G-19073)**

Pros Freight Corporation ....E 440 543-7555
Chagrin Falls **(G-2679)**

R & L Carriers Inc ....E 419 874-5976
Perrysburg **(G-15911)**

R K Campf Corp ....E 330 332-7089
Salem **(G-16556)**

Robert G Owen Trucking Inc ....E 330 756-1013
Navarre **(G-14825)**

Robert M Neff Inc ....D 614 444-1562
Columbus **(G-8543)**

Roeder Cartage Company Inc ....D 419 221-1600
Lima **(G-12733)**

Ron Burge Trucking Inc ....E 330 624-5373
Burbank **(G-2009)**

Ross Transportation Svcs Inc ....C 440 748-5900
Grafton **(G-11322)**

S & T Truck and Auto Svc Inc ....E 614 272-8163
Columbus **(G-8569)**

Saia Motor Freight Line LLC ....E 419 726-9761
Toledo **(G-18017)**

Saia Motor Freight Line LLC ....E 330 659-4277
Richfield **(G-16377)**

Saia Motor Freight Line LLC ....D 614 870-8778
Columbus **(G-8582)**

Sanfrey Freight Services Inc ....E 330 372-1883
Warren **(G-18740)**

Scheiderer Transport Inc ....D 614 873-5103
Plain City **(G-16064)**

Schindewolf Express Inc ....D 937 585-5919
De Graff **(G-9900)**

Sewell Leasing Corporation ....D 937 382-3847
Wilmington **(G-19648)**

SMS Transport LLC ....E 937 813-8897
Dayton **(G-9772)**

Spader Freight Services Inc ....D 419 547-1117
Clyde **(G-6754)**

Superior Bulk Logistics Inc ....E 513 874-3440
West Chester **(G-19085)**

Thomas E Keller Trucking Inc ....C 419 784-4805
Defiance **(G-9944)**

Thomas Trucking Inc ....E 513 731-8411
Cincinnati **(G-4603)**

Titan Transfer Inc ....D 513 458-4233
West Chester **(G-19016)**

Trans-States Express Inc ....D 513 679-7100
Cincinnati **(G-4627)**

Transport Corp America Inc ....E 330 538-3328
North Jackson **(G-15254)**

U S Xpress Inc ....E 937 328-4100
Springfield **(G-17129)**

U S Xpress Inc ....E 740 363-0700
Delaware **(G-10012)**

U S Xpress Inc ....C 740 452-4153
Zanesville **(G-20369)**

UPS Ground Freight Inc ....C 330 659-6693
Richfield **(G-16382)**

UPS Ground Freight Inc ....E 937 236-4700
Dayton **(G-9843)**

Valley Transportation Inc ....C 419 289-6200
Ashland **(G-696)**

Venezia Transport Service Inc ....E 330 542-9735
New Middletown **(G-14939)**

Vision Express Inc ....E 740 922-8848
Uhrichsville **(G-18348)**

Vitran Express Inc ....D 216 426-8584
Cleveland **(G-6638)**

W L Logan Trucking Company ....C 330 478-1404
Canton **(G-2529)**

Ward Trucking LLC ....E 330 659-6658
Richfield **(G-16383)**

Ward Trucking LLC ....E 614 275-3800
Columbus **(G-8874)**

Werner Enterprises Inc ....E 937 325-5403
Springfield **(G-17134)**

Xpo Logistics Freight Inc ....C 513 870-0044
West Chester **(G-19100)**

Xpo Logistics Freight Inc ....E 419 499-8888
Milan **(G-14368)**

Xpo Logistics Freight Inc ....C 216 433-1000
Parma **(G-15780)**

Xpo Logistics Freight Inc ....E 740 894-3859
South Point **(G-16947)**

Xpo Logistics Freight Inc ....C 330 824-2242
Warren **(G-18775)**

Xpo Logistics Freight Inc ....E 419 294-5728
Upper Sandusky **(G-18418)**

Xpo Logistics Freight Inc ....D 419 666-3022
Perrysburg **(G-15937)**

Xpo Logistics Freight Inc ....D 330 896-7300
Uniontown **(G-18391)**

Xpo Logistics Freight Inc ....E 937 492-3899
Sidney **(G-16806)**

Yowell Transportation Svc Inc ....E 937 294-5933
Moraine **(G-14709)**

Yrc Inc ....D 330 659-4151
Richfield **(G-16385)**

Yrc Inc ....B 419 729-0631
Toledo **(G-18174)**

Yrc Inc ....C 330 665-0274
Copley **(G-8981)**

TRUCKING & HAULING SVCS: Draying, Local, Without Storage

Containerport Group Inc ....D 216 692-3124
Euclid **(G-10627)**

Stack Container Service Inc ....D 216 531-7555
Euclid **(G-10657)**

TRUCKING & HAULING SVCS: Furniture Moving & Storage, Local

Accelerated Moving & Stor Inc ....E 614 836-1007
Columbus **(G-6859)**

Gws FF&E LLC ....E 513 759-6000
West Chester **(G-18939)**

Leaders Moving Company ....E 614 785-9595
Worthington **(G-19822)**

Moving Solutions Inc ....D 440 946-9300
Mentor **(G-14090)**

Ray Hamilton Companies ....E 513 641-5400
Blue Ash **(G-1640)**

River City Furniture LLC ....D 513 612-7303
West Chester **(G-18994)**

Shetler Moving & Stor of Ohio ....E 513 755-0700
West Chester **(G-19004)**

SERVICES

TRUCKING & HAULING SVCS: Furniture, Local W/out Storage

River City Furniture LLC ....D....... 513 612-7303
  West Chester (G-18994)

TRUCKING & HAULING SVCS: Garbage, Collect/Transport Only

BFI Waste Services LLC ....E....... 800 437-1123
  Salem (G-16537)
City of Marion ....D....... 740 382-1479
  Marion (G-13412)
Fultz & Son Inc ....E....... 419 547-9365
  Clyde (G-6743)
R & R Sanitation Inc ....E....... 330 325-2311
  Mogadore (G-14555)
Universal Disposal Inc ....E....... 440 286-3153
  Chardon (G-2720)
Werlor Inc ....E....... 419 784-4285
  Defiance (G-9946)

TRUCKING & HAULING SVCS: Haulage & Cartage, Light, Local

Arrowhead Transport Co ....E....... 330 638-2900
  Cortland (G-8983)
Brookside Holdings LLC ....E....... 419 224-7019
  Lima (G-12609)
Burch Hydro Inc ....E....... 740 694-9146
  Fredericktown (G-11052)
Burch Hydro Trucking Inc ....E....... 740 694-9146
  Fredericktown (G-11053)
Containerport Group Inc ....E....... 440 333-1330
  Columbus (G-7355)
J M T Cartage Inc ....E....... 330 478-2430
  Canton (G-2359)
Montgomery Trucking Company ....E....... 740 384-2138
  Wellston (G-18853)
Nicolozakes Trckg & Cnstr Inc .....E....... 740 432-5648
  Cambridge (G-2078)
Varney Dispatch Inc ....E....... 513 682-4200
  Cincinnati (G-4751)
William Hafer Drayage Inc ....E....... 513 771-5000
  Cincinnati (G-4796)

TRUCKING & HAULING SVCS: Hazardous Waste

American Waste MGT Svcs Inc ......E....... 330 856-8800
  Warren (G-18664)
Cousins Waste Control LLC ....D....... 419 726-1500
  Toledo (G-17686)
Tfh-Eb Inc ....D....... 614 253-7246
  Columbus (G-8741)
Trans Vac Inc ....E....... 419 229-8192
  Lima (G-12767)

TRUCKING & HAULING SVCS: Heavy Machinery, Local

Back In Black Co ....E....... 419 425-5555
  Findlay (G-10866)
Bob Miller Rigging Inc ....E....... 419 422-7477
  Findlay (G-10880)
Tesar Industrial Contrs Inc ....E....... 216 741-8008
  Cleveland (G-6517)

TRUCKING & HAULING SVCS: Heavy, NEC

B & T Express Inc ....D....... 330 549-0000
  North Lima (G-15265)
Cooper Brothers Trucking LLC ......E....... 330 784-1717
  Akron (G-158)
Diamond Heavy Haul Inc ....E....... 330 677-8061
  Kent (G-12228)
Estes Express Lines Inc ....D....... 440 327-3884
  North Ridgeville (G-15329)
Falcon Transport Co ....C....... 330 793-1345
  Youngstown (G-20034)
Ferrous Metal Transfer ....E....... 216 671-8500
  Brooklyn (G-1861)
Golden Hawk Transportation Co ....D....... 419 683-3304
  Crestline (G-9056)
Homan Transportation Inc ....D....... 419 465-2626
  Monroeville (G-14588)
Knight Transportation Inc ....D....... 614 308-4900
  Columbus (G-7916)
L O G Transportation Inc ....E....... 440 891-0850
  Berea (G-1429)

Mizar Motors Inc ....D....... 419 729-2400
  Toledo (G-17919)
Pitt-Ohio Express LLC ....C....... 614 801-1064
  Grove City (G-11465)
R & J Trucking Inc ....D....... 740 374-3050
  Marietta (G-13374)
Richard Wolfe Trucking Inc ....E....... 740 392-2445
  Mount Vernon (G-14787)
Saro Truck Dispatch Inc ....E....... 419 873-1358
  Perrysburg (G-15918)

TRUCKING & HAULING SVCS: Liquid Petroleum, Exc Local

Advantage Tank Lines Inc ....C....... 330 427-1010
  Leetonia (G-12518)
Autumn Industries Inc ....E....... 330 372-5002
  Warren (G-18671)
Kenan Advantage Group Inc ....C....... 800 969-5419
  North Canton (G-15216)
Lykins Transportation Inc ....D....... 513 831-8820
  Milford (G-14405)
Ohio Oil Gathering Corporation .....E....... 740 828-2892
  Nashport (G-14821)

TRUCKING & HAULING SVCS: Liquid, Local

Autumn Industries Inc ....E....... 330 372-5002
  Warren (G-18671)
Drasc Enterprises Inc ....E....... 330 852-3254
  Sugarcreek (G-17377)
Sidle Transit Service Inc ....E....... 330 683-2807
  Orrville (G-15647)

TRUCKING & HAULING SVCS: Live Poultry

Wendel Poultry Service Inc ....E....... 419 375-2439
  Fort Recovery (G-10995)

TRUCKING & HAULING SVCS: Lumber & Timber

Ferrous Metal Transfer ....E....... 216 671-8500
  Brooklyn (G-1861)
Huntley Trucking Co ....E....... 740 385-7615
  New Plymouth (G-14991)

TRUCKING & HAULING SVCS: Machinery, Heavy

Miller Transfer and Rigging Co ......E....... 330 325-2521
  Rootstown (G-16452)
Myers Machinery Movers Inc ....E....... 614 871-5052
  Grove City (G-11455)
Nicolozakes Trckg & Cnstr Inc .....E....... 740 432-5648
  Cambridge (G-2078)
Tesar Industrial Contrs Inc ....E....... 216 741-8008
  Cleveland (G-6517)
Tfi Transportation Inc ....E....... 330 332-4655
  Salem (G-16564)

TRUCKING & HAULING SVCS: Mail Carriers, Contract

44444 LLC ....E....... 330 502-2023
  Austintown (G-855)
G & S Transfer Inc ....E....... 330 673-3899
  Kent (G-12233)
Robert M Neff Inc ....D....... 614 444-1562
  Columbus (G-8543)
Rood Trucking Company Inc ....C....... 330 652-3519
  Mineral Ridge (G-14512)
T&T Enterprises of Ohio Inc ....E....... 513 942-1141
  West Chester (G-19088)
Ted Ruck Co Inc ....E....... 419 738-2613
  Wapakoneta (G-18655)

TRUCKING & HAULING SVCS: Petroleum, Local

Certified Oil Inc ....D....... 614 421-7500
  Columbus (G-7171)
Hilltrux Tank Lines Inc ....E....... 330 965-1103
  Youngstown (G-20065)
Howland Logistics LLC ....E....... 513 469-5263
  Cincinnati (G-3734)
Santmyer Oil Co Inc ....D....... 330 262-6501
  Wooster (G-19764)

TRUCKING & HAULING SVCS: Safe Moving, Local

Ray Hamilton Companies ....E....... 513 641-5400
  Blue Ash (G-1640)

TRUCKING & HAULING SVCS: Trailer/Container On Flat Car

American Power LLC ....E....... 937 235-0418
  Dayton (G-9229)

TRUCKING, AUTOMOBILE CARRIER

Akron Centl Engrv Mold Mch Inc ...E....... 330 794-8704
  Akron (G-30)
Cassens Transport Company ....C....... 937 644-8886
  Marysville (G-13488)
Cassens Transport Company ....C....... 419 727-0520
  Toledo (G-17639)
Cowan Systems LLC ....E....... 330 963-8483
  Twinsburg (G-18257)
CRST International Inc ....D....... 740 599-0008
  Danville (G-9149)
Express Twing Recovery Svc Inc ....E....... 513 881-1900
  West Chester (G-19051)
Jack Cooper Transport Co Inc ....C....... 440 949-2044
  Sheffield Village (G-16736)
Ohio Auto Delivery Inc ....E....... 614 277-1445
  Grove City (G-11461)
Quality Carriers Inc ....E....... 419 222-6800
  Lima (G-12725)
R & L Transfer Inc ....D....... 330 743-3609
  Youngstown (G-20172)
Roseville Motor Express Inc ....E....... 614 921-2121
  Columbus (G-8553)
United Road Services Inc ....D....... 419 837-2703
  Toledo (G-18120)

TRUCKING, DUMP

Aci Const Co Inc ....E....... 419 595-4284
  Alvada (G-559)
Alan Woods Trucking Inc ....E....... 513 738-3314
  Hamilton (G-11556)
American Bulk Commodities Inc .....C....... 330 758-0841
  Youngstown (G-19953)
Berner Trucking ....E....... 419 476-0207
  Toledo (G-17612)
Berner Trucking Inc ....C....... 330 343-5812
  Dover (G-10067)
Burkhart Trucking Inc ....E....... 740 896-2244
  Lowell (G-13037)
Carl E Oeder Sons Sand & Grav .....E....... 513 494-1555
  Lebanon (G-12454)
Coshocton Trucking South Inc ......C....... 740 622-1311
  Coshocton (G-9009)
D & V Trucking Inc ....E....... 330 482-9440
  Columbiana (G-6786)
Dale Ross Trucking Inc ....E....... 937 981-2168
  Greenfield (G-11360)
Daves Sand & Stone Inc ....E....... 419 445-9256
  Wauseon (G-18798)
Edw C Levy Co ....E....... 419 822-8286
  Delta (G-10042)
Forrest Trucking Company ....E....... 614 879-8642
  West Jefferson (G-19109)
James H Alvis Trucking Inc ....E....... 513 623-8121
  Harrison (G-11671)
K R Drenth Trucking Inc ....D....... 708 983-6340
  Cincinnati (G-3844)
Mikes Trucking Ltd ....E....... 614 879-8808
  Galloway (G-11223)
Monesi Trucking & Eqp Repr Inc ....E....... 614 921-9183
  Columbus (G-8097)
R & J Trucking Inc ....E....... 800 262-9365
  Youngstown (G-20171)
R & J Trucking Inc ....D....... 330 758-0841
  Shelby (G-16750)
R & J Trucking Inc ....D....... 740 374-3050
  Marietta (G-13374)
R & J Trucking Inc ....D....... 440 960-1508
  Lorain (G-12939)
R & J Trucking Inc ....E....... 419 837-9937
  Perrysburg (G-15910)
R E Watson Inc ....E....... 513 863-0070
  Hamilton (G-11634)
Ray Bertolini Trucking Co ....E....... 330 867-0666
  Akron (G-397)
Ron Carrocce Trucking Company ....C....... 330 758-0841
  Youngstown (G-20192)

Sebastiani Trucking Inc ....D 330 286-0059
Canfield (G-2158)
Strawser Equipment & Lsg Inc ....D 614 444-2521
Columbus (G-8706)
Wright Material Solutions Ltd ....E 614 530-6999
Columbus (G-8920)
Zeiter Trucking Inc ....E 419 668-2229
Norwalk (G-15460)

TRUCKING, REFRIGERATED: Long-Distance

Continental Express Inc ....B 937 497-2100
Sidney (G-16767)
Crete Carrier Corporation ....C 614 853-4500
Columbus (G-7391)
J & B Leasing Inc of Ohio ....E 419 269-1440
Toledo (G-17826)
Montgomery Trucking Company ....E 740 384-2138
Wellston (G-18853)
P C C Refrigerated Ex Inc ....E 614 754-8929
Columbus (G-8406)
T & L Transport Inc ....E 330 674-0655
Millersburg (G-14494)
Zartran LLC ....D 513 870-4800
Hamilton (G-11656)

TRUCKING: Except Local

1st Carrier Corp ....D 740 477-2587
Circleville (G-4821)
A C Leasing Company ....E 513 771-3676
Cincinnati (G-2890)
Ace Doran Hauling & Rigging Co ....D 513 681-7900
Cincinnati (G-2903)
Advantage Tank Lines Inc ....E 330 491-0474
North Canton (G-15185)
All Pro Freight Systems Inc ....D 440 934-2222
Westlake (G-19313)
As Logistics Inc ....D 513 863-4627
Liberty Township (G-12577)
B & H Industries Inc ....E 419 485-8373
Montpelier (G-14605)
Bantam Leasing Inc ....E 513 734-6696
Amelia (G-570)
Barnets Inc ....E 937 452-3275
Camden (G-2088)
Bell Moving and Storage Inc ....E 513 942-7500
Fairfield (G-10699)
Bestway Transport Co ....E 419 687-2000
Plymouth (G-16076)
Black Horse Carriers Inc ....C 330 225-2250
Hinckley (G-11858)
Blb Transport Inc ....E 740 474-1341
Circleville (G-4825)
Bobs Moraine Trucking Inc ....E 937 746-8420
Franklin (G-11024)
Brendamour Moving & Stor Inc ....D 800 354-9715
Cincinnati (G-3071)
Brent Burris Trucking LLC ....E 419 759-2020
Ada (G-2)
Brookside Holdings LLC ....E 419 925-4457
Maria Stein (G-13306)
Bryan Truck Line Inc ....D 419 485-8373
Montpelier (G-14609)
Building Systems Trnsp Co ....C 740 852-9700
London (G-12861)
Carrier Industries Inc ....B 614 851-6363
Columbus (G-7131)
Century Lines Inc ....E 216 271-0700
Cleveland (G-5160)
Chambers Leasing Systems Corp ....E 419 726-9747
Toledo (G-17646)
Circle S Transport Inc ....E 614 207-2184
Columbus (G-7203)
Circle T Logistics Inc ....E 740 262-5096
Marion (G-13411)
Clayton Weaver Trucking Inc ....E 513 896-6932
Fairfield (G-10714)
Cle Transportation Company ....D 567 805-4008
Norwalk (G-15428)
Cleveland Express Trckg Co Inc ....D 216 348-0922
Cleveland (G-5253)
Competitive Transportation ....E 419 529-5300
Bellville (G-1388)
Concept Freight Service Inc ....E 330 784-1134
New Franklin (G-14908)
Containerport Group Inc ....E 614 539-4601
Columbus (G-7355)
Containerport Group Inc ....E 216 341-4800
Cleveland (G-5343)
Contract Freighters Inc ....A 614 577-0447
Reynoldsburg (G-16294)

Cotter Moving & Storage Co ....E 330 535-5115
Akron (G-161)
Covenant Transport Inc ....D 423 821-1212
Columbus (G-7383)
Cowan Systems LLC ....C 513 769-4774
Cincinnati (G-3376)
Cowan Systems LLC ....C 513 721-6444
West Chester (G-18903)
Coy Brothers Inc ....E 330 533-6864
Canfield (G-2134)
Craig Transportation Co ....E 419 874-7981
Maumee (G-13777)
Crescent Park Corporation ....C 513 759-7000
West Chester (G-18906)
Dart Trucking Company Inc ....E 330 549-0994
North Lima (G-15268)
Daves Sand & Stone Inc ....E 419 445-9256
Wauseon (G-18798)
Davidson Trucking Inc ....E 419 288-2318
Bradner (G-1764)
Dayton Freight Lines Inc ....E 419 661-8600
Perrysburg (G-15854)
Dayton Freight Lines Inc ....E 614 860-1080
Columbus (G-7422)
Dedicated Logistics Inc ....D 513 275-1135
West Chester (G-18909)
Dhl Supply Chain (usa) ....E 614 492-6614
Lockbourne (G-12814)
Dhl Supply Chain (usa) ....E 513 942-1575
Cincinnati (G-3426)
Dill-Elam Inc ....E 513 575-0017
Loveland (G-12991)
Dist-Trans Inc ....E 614 497-1660
Columbus (G-7453)
Distribution and Trnsp Svc Inc ....E 937 295-3343
Fort Loramie (G-10985)
Disttech LLC ....D 800 321-3143
Cleveland (G-5429)
Drasc Enterprises Inc ....E 330 852-3254
Sugarcreek (G-17377)
Elmco Trucking Inc ....E 419 983-2010
Bloomville (G-1492)
Excel Trucking LLC ....E 614 826-1988
Columbus (G-7542)
Exel Inc ....B 614 865-8500
Westerville (G-19163)
Falcon Transport Co ....E 330 793-1345
Youngstown (G-20035)
FANTON Logistics Inc ....D 216 341-2400
Cleveland (G-5512)
Federal Express Corporation ....B 614 492-6106
Columbus (G-7568)
Fedex Freight Corporation ....E 419 729-1755
Toledo (G-17730)
Fedex Freight Corporation ....D 800 344-6448
West Jefferson (G-19107)
Fedex Freight Corporation ....E 800 354-9489
Zanesville (G-20307)
Fedex Ground Package Sys Inc ....D 513 942-4330
West Chester (G-19052)
First Group Investment Partnr ....D 513 241-2200
Cincinnati (G-3558)
Firstenterprises Inc ....B 740 369-5100
Delaware (G-9976)
Firstgroup Usa Inc ....B 513 241-2200
Cincinnati (G-3569)
Fleetmaster Express Inc ....E 419 420-1835
Findlay (G-10909)
Foodliner Inc ....E 937 898-0075
Dayton (G-9443)
Foster Sales & Delivery Inc ....D 740 245-0200
Bidwell (G-1468)
Garber Ag Freight Inc ....E 937 548-8400
Greenville (G-11378)
General Transport Incorporated ....E 330 786-3400
Akron (G-233)
Glm Transport Inc ....E 419 363-2041
Rockford (G-16415)
Global Workplace Solutions LLC ....E 513 759-6000
West Chester (G-18933)
GMC Excavation & Trucking ....E 419 468-0121
Galion (G-11177)
Green Lines Transportation Inc ....E 330 863-2111
Malvern (G-13123)
H O C J Inc ....E 614 539-4601
Grove City (G-11439)
Hillandale Farms Trnsp ....D 740 893-2232
Johnstown (G-12201)
Hofstetter Orran Inc ....E 330 683-8070
Orrville (G-15634)

Horizon Freight System Inc ....E 216 341-7410
Cleveland (G-5706)
Horizon Mid Atlantic Inc ....D 800 480-6829
Cleveland (G-5707)
Horizon South Inc ....D 800 480-6829
Cleveland (G-5708)
Hs Express LLC ....D 419 729-2400
Toledo (G-17810)
HTI - Hall Trucking Inc ....E 419 423-9555
Findlay (G-10924)
Huntley Trucking Co ....E 740 385-7615
New Plymouth (G-14991)
Integres Global Logistics Inc ....D 866 347-2101
Medina (G-13955)
J B Hunt Transport Inc ....C 419 547-2777
Clyde (G-6746)
J T Express Inc ....E 513 727-8185
Monroe (G-14570)
J-Trac Inc ....E 419 524-3456
Mansfield (G-13189)
Jaro Transportation Svcs Inc ....D 330 393-5659
Warren (G-18718)
Jarrells Moving & Transport Co ....D 330 764-4333
Seville (G-16686)
JB Hunt Transport Svcs Inc ....A 614 335-6681
Columbus (G-7855)
Jet Express Inc ....D 937 274-7033
Dayton (G-9524)
K & P Trucking LLC ....E 419 935-8646
Willard (G-19482)
Keystone Freight Corp ....E 614 542-0320
Columbus (G-7899)
KF Express LLC ....E 614 258-8858
Powell (G-16201)
Kllee Trucking Inc ....D 740 867-6454
Chesapeake (G-2730)
Kuhnle Brothers Inc ....C 440 564-7168
Newbury (G-15122)
L A King Trucking Inc ....E 419 727-9398
Toledo (G-17845)
L J Navy Trucking Company ....E 614 754-8929
Columbus (G-7935)
Lincoln Moving & Storage Co ....D 216 741-5500
Cleveland (G-5871)
Logos Logistics Inc ....E 734 304-1777
Toledo (G-17857)
LT Harnett Trucking Inc ....E 440 997-5528
Ashtabula (G-746)
Lykins Companies Inc ....E 513 831-8820
Milford (G-14403)
M & B Trucking Express Corp ....E 440 236-8820
Columbia Station (G-6777)
Maines Collision Repr & Bdy Sp ....D 937 322-4618
Springfield (G-17066)
Mansfield Whsng & Dist Inc ....C 419 522-3510
Ontario (G-15560)
Martin Trnsp Systems Inc ....D 419 726-1348
Toledo (G-17898)
Material Suppliers Inc ....E 419 298-2440
Edgerton (G-10468)
Merchants 5 Star Ltd ....D 740 373-0313
Marietta (G-13358)
Midwest Logistics Systems ....B 419 584-1414
Celina (G-2605)
Moore Transport of Tulsa LLC ....D 419 726-4499
Toledo (G-17923)
Murray Leasing Inc ....C 330 386-4757
East Liverpool (G-10408)
National Highway Equipment Co ....D 614 459-4900
Columbus (G-8133)
National Trnsp Solutions Inc ....D 330 405-2660
Twinsburg (G-18300)
Nick Strimbu Inc ....D 330 448-4046
Brookfield (G-1855)
Nick Strimbu Inc ....D 330 448-4046
Dover (G-10091)
Noramco Transport Corp ....E 513 245-9050
Cincinnati (G-4122)
Oeder Carl E Sons Sand & Grav ....E 513 494-1238
Lebanon (G-12488)
One Way Express Incorporated ....E 440 439-9182
Cleveland (G-6135)
Osborne Trucking Company ....D 513 874-2090
Fairfield (G-10766)
P & D Transportation Inc ....E 614 577-1130
Columbus (G-8405)
P I & I Motor Express Inc ....C 330 448-4035
Masury (G-13741)
PAm Transportation Svcs Inc ....D 419 935-9501
Willard (G-19485)

Panther II Transportation Inc ....C....... 800 685-0657
Medina (G-13985)
Panther Premium Logistics Inc ....B....... 800 685-0657
Medina (G-13986)
Peak Transportation Inc ....D....... 419 874-5201
Perrysburg (G-15899)
Penske Logistics LLC ....D....... 330 626-7623
Streetsboro (G-17265)
Peoples Services Inc ....E....... 330 453-3709
Canton (G-2437)
Pitt-Ohio Express LLC ....D....... 419 729-8173
Toledo (G-17979)
Pitt-Ohio Express LLC ....B....... 216 433-9000
Cleveland (G-6215)
Planes Moving & Storage Inc ....C....... 513 759-6000
West Chester (G-18982)
Platinum Express Inc.............................D....... 937 235-9540
Dayton (G-9695)
Ploger Transportation LLC.....................E....... 419 465-2100
Bellevue (G-1383)
Predator Trucking Company...................E....... 419 849-2601
Woodville (G-19682)
Premium Trnsp Logistics LLC ....D....... 419 861-3430
Toledo (G-17985)
Pride Transportation Inc.........................E....... 419 424-2145
Findlay (G-10956)
R & L Transfer Inc ....C....... 216 531-3324
Norwalk (G-15453)
R & L Transfer Inc ....C....... 330 482-5800
Columbiana (G-6791)
R & S Lines Inc.......................................E....... 419 682-7807
Stryker (G-17371)
R E Watson Inc.......................................E....... 513 863-0070
Hamilton (G-11634)
R+I Pramount Trnsp Systems Inc..........B....... 937 382-1494
Wilmington (G-19642)
Rainbow Express Inc..............................D....... 614 444-5600
Columbus (G-8485)
Ray Bertolini Trucking Co.......................E....... 330 867-0666
Akron (G-397)
RDF Trucking Corporation.......................D....... 440 282-9060
Lorain (G-12940)
Rising Sun Express LLC ....D....... 937 596-6167
Jackson Center (G-12185)
Robert Neff & Son Inc.............................E....... 740 454-0128
Zanesville (G-20359)
Rood Trucking Company Inc ....C....... 330 652-3519
Mineral Ridge (G-14512)
Rrr Express LLC.....................................C....... 800 723-3424
West Chester (G-18996)
Rt80 Express Inc....................................E....... 330 706-0900
Barberton (G-966)
Ryder Last Mile Inc ....D....... 866 711-3129
New Albany (G-14873)
Schneider Nat Carriers Inc.....................E....... 740 362-6910
Delaware (G-10006)
Schneider National Inc ....B....... 419 673-0254
Kenton (G-12287)
Schroeder Associates Inc ....E....... 419 258-5075
Antwerp (G-614)
Security Storage Co Inc ....D....... 513 961-2700
Cincinnati (G-4445)
Shippers Consolidated Dist.....................E....... 216 579-9303
Cleveland (G-6405)
Shoreline Express Inc ....E....... 440 878-3750
Strongsville (G-17344)
Shoreline Transportation Inc ....C....... 440 878-2000
Strongsville (G-17345)
Short Freight Lines Inc............................E....... 419 729-1691
Toledo (G-18031)
Slay Transportation Co Inc ....C....... 740 865-2910
Sardis (G-16661)
Smith Trucking Inc..................................E....... 419 841-8676
Sylvania (G-17452)
Spader Freight Carriers Inc....................D....... 419 547-1117
Clyde (G-6753)
State-Wide Express Inc ....D....... 216 676-4600
Cleveland (G-6460)
Store & Haul Inc.....................................E....... 419 238-4284
Van Wert (G-18489)
Style Crest Transport Inc ....D....... 419 332-7369
Fremont (G-11101)
Swx Enterprises Inc................................E....... 216 676-4600
Brookpark (G-1907)
Thoman Weil Moving & Stor Co ....E....... 513 251-5000
Cincinnati (G-4601)
Three-D Transport Inc.............................E....... 419 924-5368
West Unity (G-19141)
Thyssenkrupp Logistics Inc ....D....... 419 662-1800
Northwood (G-15407)
Tkx Logistics ....E....... 419 662-1800
Northwood (G-15409)
Total Package Express Inc......................E....... 513 741-5500
Cincinnati (G-4611)
Tpg Noramco LLC...................................E....... 513 245-9050
Cincinnati (G-4624)
Transportation Unlimited Inc ....A....... 216 426-0088
Cleveland (G-6544)
Triad Transport Inc.................................E....... 614 491-9497
Columbus (G-8777)
Trio Trucking Inc ....E....... 513 679-7100
Cincinnati (G-4649)
Triple Ladys Agency Inc.........................E....... 330 274-1100
Mantua (G-13277)
UPS Ground Freight Inc ....E....... 330 448-0440
Masury (G-13743)
USF Holland LLC....................................C....... 937 233-7600
Dayton (G-9845)
USF Holland LLC....................................C....... 216 941-4340
Cleveland (G-6612)
Vance Road Enterprises Inc...................E....... 937 268-6953
Dayton (G-9849)
Vitran Express Inc...................................C....... 614 870-2255
Columbus (G-8857)
Wannemacher Enterprises Inc ....D....... 419 225-9060
Lima (G-12775)
William R Morse ....E....... 440 352-2600
Painesville (G-15748)
World Shipping Inc ....E....... 440 356-7676
Cleveland (G-6690)
Xpo Cnw Inc ....C....... 440 716-8971
North Olmsted (G-15317)
Xpo Logistics Freight Inc........................E....... 937 898-9808
Dayton (G-9888)
Xpo Logistics Freight Inc........................E....... 937 364-2361
Hillsboro (G-11856)
Xpo Logistics Freight Inc........................E....... 740 922-5614
Uhrichsville (G-18349)
Xpo Logistics Freight Inc........................C....... 614 876-7100
Columbus (G-8924)
Yrc Inc..D....... 614 878-9281
Columbus (G-8933)
Zone Transportation Co ....D....... 440 324-3544
Elyria (G-10577)

TRUCKING: Local, With Storage

A C Leasing Company ....E....... 513 771-3676
Cincinnati (G-2890)
Abco Contracting LLC.............................E....... 419 973-4772
Toledo (G-17580)
All My Sons Business Dev Corp..............C....... 469 461-5000
Cleveland (G-4934)
All Pro Freight Systems Inc ....D....... 440 934-2222
Westlake (G-19313)
American Way Van and Stor Inc ....E....... 937 898-7294
Vandalia (G-18503)
Arms Trucking Co Inc.............................E....... 800 362-1343
Huntsburg (G-12016)
Atlas Home Moving & Storage................E....... 614 445-8831
Columbus (G-6999)
Bridge Logistics Inc................................E....... 513 874-7444
West Chester (G-19046)
Clark Trucking Inc...................................C....... 937 642-0335
East Liberty (G-10390)
Cleveland Express Trckg Co Inc ....D....... 216 348-0922
Cleveland (G-5253)
Containerport Group Inc ....E....... 216 341-4800
Cleveland (G-5343)
County of Hancock ....E....... 419 422-7433
Findlay (G-10893)
Dhl Supply Chain (usa)...........................E....... 419 727-4318
Toledo (G-17700)
Distribution and Trnsp Svc Inc...............E....... 937 295-3343
Fort Loramie (G-10985)
Getgo Transportation Co LLC.................E....... 419 666-6850
Millbury (G-14449)
Henderson Trucking Inc..........................E....... 740 369-6100
Delaware (G-9985)
J-Trac Inc ....E....... 419 524-3456
Mansfield (G-13189)
King Tut Logistics LLC...........................E....... 614 538-0509
Columbus (G-7908)
Lanes Transfer Inc ....E....... 419 222-8692
Lima (G-12674)
Lewis & Michael Mvg & Stor Co ....E....... 614 275-2997
Columbus (G-7968)
Lincoln Moving & Storage Co.................D....... 216 741-5500
Cleveland (G-5871)
Locker Moving & Storage Inc ....E....... 330 784-0477
Canton (G-2380)
M G Q Inc ....E....... 419 992-4236
Tiffin (G-17522)
Mano Logistics LLC................................E....... 330 454-1307
Canton (G-2385)
Marietta Industrial Entps Inc..................D....... 740 373-2252
Marietta (G-13353)
Miami Valley Bekins Inc..........................E....... 937 278-4296
Dayton (G-9615)
Neighborhood Logistics Co Inc...............E....... 440 466-0020
Geneva (G-11244)
Picklesimer Trucking Inc.........................E....... 937 642-1091
Marysville (G-13522)
Piqua Transfer & Storage Co ....D....... 937 773-3743
Piqua (G-16021)
Planes Mvg & Stor Co Columbus............D....... 614 777-9090
Columbus (G-8451)
Proterra Inc...E....... 216 383-8449
Wickliffe (G-19474)
R K Campf Corp ....E....... 330 332-7089
Salem (G-16556)
Rainbow Express Inc..............................D....... 614 444-5600
Columbus (G-8485)
Rmb Enterprises Inc...............................D....... 513 539-3431
Middletown (G-14325)
Shippers Consolidated Dist....................E....... 216 579-9303
Cleveland (G-6405)
Spears Transf & Expediting Inc..............E....... 937 275-2443
Dayton (G-9782)
State-Wide Express Inc ....D....... 216 676-4600
Cleveland (G-6460)
T & B Transportation Inc ....E....... 330 495-0316
Canton (G-2505)
Taylor Distributing Company...................D....... 513 771-1850
West Chester (G-19089)
Thoman Weil Moving & Stor Co ....E....... 513 251-5000
Cincinnati (G-4601)
Tri Modal Service Inc ....E....... 614 876-6325
Columbus (G-8776)
Van Howards Lines Inc...........................E....... 937 235-0007
Dayton (G-9848)
Van Mayberrys & Storage Inc ....E....... 937 298-8800
Moraine (G-14704)
Van Mills Lines Inc..................................C....... 440 846-0200
Strongsville (G-17357)
Van Stevens Lines Inc ....E....... 419 729-8871
Toledo (G-18134)
William R Morse ....E....... 440 352-2600
Painesville (G-15748)
Willis Day Management Inc....................E....... 419 476-8000
Toledo (G-18159)
Wnb Group LLC ....E....... 513 641-5400
Cincinnati (G-4801)
Wooster Motor Ways Inc ....C....... 330 264-9557
Wooster (G-19786)
Yowell Transportation Svc Inc ....D....... 937 294-5933
Moraine (G-14709)

TRUCKING: Local, Without Storage

1st Carrier Corp......................................D....... 740 477-2587
Circleville (G-4821)
A L Smith Trucking Inc ....E....... 937 526-3651
Versailles (G-18565)
Advantage Tank Lines Inc.......................C....... 330 427-1010
Leetonia (G-12518)
AG Trucking Inc ....E....... 937 497-7770
Sidney (G-16757)
Allan Hunter Construction LLC ....E....... 330 634-9882
Akron (G-65)
Atlantic Coastal Trucking........................C....... 201 438-6500
Delaware (G-9953)
B & H Industries Inc................................E....... 419 485-8373
Montpelier (G-14605)
B & L Transport Inc.................................E....... 866 848-2888
Millersburg (G-14457)
B D Transportation Inc ....E....... 937 773-9280
Piqua (G-15996)
Bell Moving and Storage Inc...................E....... 513 942-7500
Fairfield (G-10699)
Besl Transfer Co ....E....... 513 242-3456
Cincinnati (G-3042)
Best Way Motor Lines Inc ....C....... 419 485-8373
Montpelier (G-14606)
Big Blue Trucking Inc ....E....... 330 372-1421
Warren (G-18680)
Blatt Trucking Co Inc..............................E....... 419 898-0002
Rocky Ridge (G-16419)
Blb Transport Inc ....E....... 740 474-1341
Circleville (G-4825)
Bowling Transportation Inc.....................D....... 419 436-9590
Fostoria (G-10998)

Brookside Holdings LLC........E....... 419 925-4457
Maria Stein *(G-13306)*
Browning-Ferris Industries LLC........D....... 330 393-0385
Warren *(G-18682)*
Bryan Truck Line Inc........D....... 419 485-8373
Montpelier *(G-14609)*
Building Systems Trnsp Co........C....... 740 852-9700
London *(G-12861)*
BWC Trucking Company Inc........E....... 740 532-5188
Ironton *(G-12148)*
C & G Transportation Inc........E....... 419 288-2653
Wayne *(G-18825)*
C-Z Trucking Co........D....... 330 758-2313
Poland *(G-16081)*
Carrier Industries Inc........B....... 614 851-6363
Columbus *(G-7131)*
Century Lines Inc........E....... 216 271-0700
Cleveland *(G-5160)*
Chapin Logistics Inc........E....... 440 327-1360
North Ridgeville *(G-15325)*
Charles D McIntosh Trckg Inc........E....... 937 378-3803
Georgetown *(G-11266)*
Cheeseman LLC........E....... 419 375-4132
Fort Recovery *(G-10988)*
Circle S Transport Inc........E....... 614 207-2184
Columbus *(G-7203)*
City Dash LLC........C....... 513 562-2000
Cincinnati *(G-3298)*
City of Dayton........C....... 937 333-4860
Dayton *(G-9303)*
Clary Trucking Inc........E....... 740 702-4242
Chillicothe *(G-2769)*
Clayton Weaver Trucking Inc........E....... 513 896-6932
Fairfield *(G-10714)*
Competitive Transportation........E....... 419 529-5300
Bellville *(G-1388)*
Continental Express Inc........B....... 937 497-2100
Sidney *(G-16767)*
Continental Transport Inc........E....... 513 360-2960
Monroe *(G-14564)*
Cotter Moving & Storage Co........E....... 330 535-5115
Akron *(G-161)*
Cowen Truck Line Inc........D....... 419 938-3401
Perrysville *(G-15940)*
D&D Trucking and Services Inc........E....... 419 692-3205
Delphos *(G-10023)*
Davidson Trucking Inc........E....... 419 288-2318
Bradner *(G-1764)*
Dedicated Logistics Inc........D....... 513 275-1135
West Chester *(G-18909)*
Dedicated Transport LLC........C....... 216 641-2500
Brooklyn Heights *(G-1869)*
Dill-Elam Inc........E....... 513 575-0017
Loveland *(G-12991)*
Dingledine Trucking Company........E....... 937 652-3454
Urbana *(G-18431)*
Disttech LLC........D....... 800 321-3143
Cleveland *(G-5429)*
DOT Smith LLC........E....... 740 245-5105
Thurman *(G-17508)*
Ed Wilson & Son Trucking Inc........E....... 330 549-9287
New Springfield *(G-14996)*
Emory Rothenbuhler & Sons........E....... 740 458-1432
Beallsville *(G-1119)*
Energy Power Services Inc........E....... 330 343-2312
New Philadelphia *(G-14958)*
Falcon Transport Co........D....... 330 793-1345
Youngstown *(G-20035)*
Federal Express Corporation........C....... 800 463-3339
Bedford *(G-1280)*
Fedex Freight Inc........D....... 330 645-0879
Akron *(G-218)*
Fedex Freight Corporation........E....... 800 354-9489
Zanesville *(G-20307)*
Fedex Ground Package Sys Inc........B....... 800 463-3339
Grove City *(G-11432)*
Findlay Truck Line Inc........D....... 419 422-1945
Findlay *(G-10906)*
First Group Investment Partnr........D....... 513 241-2200
Cincinnati *(G-3558)*
Firstgroup Usa Inc........B....... 513 241-2200
Cincinnati *(G-3569)*
Five Star Trucking Inc........E....... 440 953-9300
Willoughby *(G-19524)*
Forrest Trucking Company........E....... 614 879-7347
London *(G-12864)*
Fraley & Schilling Inc........C....... 740 598-4118
Brilliant *(G-1822)*
Garber Ag Freight Inc........E....... 937 548-8400
Greenville *(G-11378)*
Garner Trucking Inc........C....... 419 422-5742
Findlay *(G-10912)*
Glm Transport Inc........E....... 419 363-2041
Rockford *(G-16415)*
GMC Excavation & Trucking........E....... 419 468-0121
Galion *(G-11177)*
Golden Hawk Inc........D....... 419 683-3304
Crestline *(G-9055)*
H & W Holdings LLC........E....... 800 826-3560
South Point *(G-16935)*
H L C Trucking Inc........D....... 740 676-6181
Shadyside *(G-16695)*
H T I Express........E....... 419 423-9555
Findlay *(G-10915)*
Henderson Trucking Inc........E....... 740 369-6100
Delaware *(G-9985)*
Henderson Turf Farm Inc........E....... 937 748-1559
Franklin *(G-11032)*
Hofstetter Orran Inc........E....... 330 683-8070
Orrville *(G-15634)*
Home Run Inc........E....... 800 543-9198
Xenia *(G-19910)*
Hyway Trucking Company........D....... 419 423-7145
Findlay *(G-10926)*
Imperial Express Inc........E....... 937 399-9400
Springfield *(G-17050)*
Innovative Logistics Svcs Inc........D....... 330 468-6422
Northfield *(G-15380)*
Integrity Ex Logistics LLC........B....... 888 374-5138
Cincinnati *(G-3771)*
International Truck & Eng Corp........A....... 937 390-4045
Springfield *(G-17055)*
J P Jenks Inc........E....... 440 428-4500
Madison *(G-13098)*
J P Transportation Company........E....... 513 424-6978
Middletown *(G-14304)*
J T Express Inc........E....... 513 727-8185
Monroe *(G-14570)*
J-Trac Inc........E....... 419 524-3456
Mansfield *(G-13189)*
Jet Express Inc........D....... 937 274-7033
Dayton *(G-9524)*
John Brown Trucking Inc........E....... 330 758-0841
Youngstown *(G-20085)*
Kace Logistics LLC........D....... 419 273-3388
Toledo *(G-17836)*
Kenan Advantage Group Inc........C....... 800 969-5419
North Canton *(G-15216)*
KF Express LLC........E....... 614 258-8858
Powell *(G-16201)*
Klingshirn & Sons Trucking........E....... 937 338-5000
Burkettsville *(G-2012)*
KMu Trucking & Excvtg Inc........E....... 440 934-1008
Avon *(G-890)*
Knight Transportation Inc........D....... 614 308-4900
Columbus *(G-7916)*
Ktib Inc........E....... 330 722-7935
Medina *(G-13967)*
Kuhnle Brothers Inc........C....... 440 564-7168
Newbury *(G-15122)*
Kuntzman Trucking Inc........E....... 330 821-9160
Alliance *(G-536)*
L V Trucking Inc........E....... 614 275-4994
Columbus *(G-7937)*
Lairson Trucking LLC........E....... 513 894-0452
Hamilton *(G-11621)*
Lesaint Logistics Inc........C....... 513 874-3900
West Chester *(G-18958)*
Locker Moving & Storage Inc........E....... 330 784-0477
Canton *(G-2380)*
LT Harnett Trucking Inc........E....... 440 997-5528
Ashtabula *(G-746)*
M C Trucking Company LLC........E....... 937 584-2486
Wilmington *(G-19632)*
Mail Contractors America Inc........C....... 513 769-5967
Cincinnati *(G-3962)*
Martin Trnsp Systems Inc........D....... 419 726-1348
Toledo *(G-17898)*
Mid America Trucking Company........E....... 216 447-0814
Cleveland *(G-5981)*
Midwest Logistics Systems........B....... 419 584-1414
Celina *(G-2605)*
Moeller Trucking Inc........D....... 419 925-4799
Maria Stein *(G-13308)*
Murray Leasing Inc........C....... 330 386-4757
East Liverpool *(G-10408)*
Mwd Logistics Inc........D....... 440 266-2500
Mentor *(G-14091)*
Myers Machinery Movers Inc........E....... 614 871-5052
Grove City *(G-11455)*
National Highway Equipment Co........D....... 614 459-4900
Columbus *(G-8133)*
National Trnsp Solutions Inc........D....... 330 405-2660
Twinsburg *(G-18300)*
Nb Trucking Inc........E....... 740 335-9331
Washington Court Hou *(G-18784)*
Neighborhood Logistics Co Inc........E....... 440 466-0020
Geneva *(G-11244)*
Northcutt Trucking Inc........E....... 440 458-5139
Elyria *(G-10548)*
Ohio Oil Gathering Corporation........E....... 740 828-2892
Nashport *(G-14821)*
Ohio Transport Corporation........E....... 513 539-0576
Middletown *(G-14316)*
One Way Express Incorporated........E....... 440 439-9182
Cleveland *(G-6135)*
Otis Wright & Sons Inc........E....... 419 227-4400
Lima *(G-12715)*
P & D Transportation Inc........E....... 614 577-1130
Columbus *(G-8405)*
P I & I Motor Express Inc........C....... 330 448-4035
Masury *(G-13741)*
Panther II Transportation Inc........C....... 800 685-0657
Medina *(G-13985)*
Panther Premium Logistics Inc........B....... 800 685-0657
Medina *(G-13986)*
Peak Transportation Inc........D....... 419 874-5201
Perrysburg *(G-15899)*
Peoples Services Inc........E....... 330 453-3709
Canton *(G-2437)*
PGT Trucking Inc........E....... 419 943-3437
Leipsic *(G-12521)*
Pierceton Trucking Co Inc........E....... 740 446-0114
Gallipolis *(G-11211)*
Pitt-Ohio Express LLC........D....... 513 860-3424
West Chester *(G-19073)*
Pitt-Ohio Express LLC........B....... 216 433-9000
Cleveland *(G-6215)*
Powers Equipment........E....... 740 746-8220
Sugar Grove *(G-17375)*
Pride Transportation Inc........E....... 419 424-2145
Findlay *(G-10956)*
Proline Xpress Inc........E....... 440 777-8120
North Olmsted *(G-15306)*
R & L Transfer Inc........C....... 216 531-3324
Norwalk *(G-15453)*
R & L Transfer Inc........C....... 330 482-5800
Columbiana *(G-6791)*
Ramos Trucking Corporation........E....... 216 781-0770
Cleveland *(G-6285)*
Reis Trucking Inc........E....... 513 353-1960
Cleves *(G-6734)*
Reliable Appl Installation Inc........E....... 614 817-1801
Columbus *(G-8511)*
Reliable Appl Installation Inc........E....... 614 246-6840
Columbus *(G-8512)*
Reliable Appl Installation Inc........E....... 330 784-7474
Akron *(G-401)*
Rick Kuntz Trucking Inc........E....... 330 296-9311
Windham *(G-19663)*
Ricketts Excavating Inc........E....... 740 687-0338
Lancaster *(G-12430)*
Rising Sun Express LLC........D....... 937 596-6167
Jackson Center *(G-12185)*
Rjw Trucking Company Ltd........E....... 740 363-5343
Delaware *(G-10004)*
Rmx Freight Systems Inc........E....... 740 849-2374
Roseville *(G-16455)*
Rose Transport Inc........E....... 614 864-4004
Reynoldsburg *(G-16330)*
Ross Consolidated Corp........D....... 440 748-5800
Grafton *(G-11320)*
Rt80 Express Inc........E....... 330 706-0900
Barberton *(G-966)*
Rumpke Waste Inc........D....... 937 378-4126
Georgetown *(G-11274)*
Rumpke Waste Inc........D....... 513 242-4401
Cincinnati *(G-4412)*
Rumpke Waste Inc........C....... 937 548-1939
Greenville *(G-11393)*
S B Morabito Trucking Inc........D....... 216 441-3070
Cleveland *(G-6355)*
Sanfrey Freight Services Inc........E....... 330 372-1883
Warren *(G-18740)*
Schindewolf Express Inc........D....... 937 585-5919
De Graff *(G-9900)*
Schroeder Associates Inc........E....... 419 258-5075
Antwerp *(G-614)*
Sewell Leasing Corporation........D....... 937 382-3847
Wilmington *(G-19648)*

Shoreline Transportation Inc ....C 440 878-2000
   Strongsville (G-17345)
Slay Transportation Co Inc ....C 740 865-2910
   Sardis (G-16661)
Spears Transf & Expediting Inc ....E 937 275-2443
   Dayton (G-9782)
Spring Grove Rsrce Rcovery Inc ....D 513 681-6242
   Cincinnati (G-4519)
State-Wide Express Inc ....D 216 676-4600
   Cleveland (G-6460)
Style Crest Transport Inc ....D 419 332-7369
   Fremont (G-11101)
Su-Jon Enterprises ....E 330 372-1100
   Warren (G-18749)
Sylvester Materials Co ....C 419 841-3874
   Sylvania (G-17457)
Todd A Ruck Inc ....E 614 527-9927
   Hilliard (G-11822)
Trans-States Express Inc ....D 513 679-7100
   Cincinnati (G-4627)
Transmerica Svcs Technical Sup ....E 740 282-3695
   Steubenville (G-17175)
Transportation Unlimited Inc ....A 216 426-0088
   Cleveland (G-6544)
Tricont Trucking Company ....C 614 527-7398
   Columbus (G-8778)
Trio Trucking Inc ....E 513 679-7100
   Cincinnati (G-4649)
Triple Ladys Agency Inc ....E 330 274-1100
   Mantua (G-13277)
Tsm Logistics LLC ....E 419 234-6074
   Rockford (G-16418)
TV Minority Company Inc ....E 937 226-1559
   Dayton (G-9826)
U-Haul Neighborhood Dealer -Ce ....E 419 929-3724
   New London (G-14936)
UPS Ground Freight Inc ....C 330 659-6693
   Richfield (G-16382)
UPS Ground Freight Inc ....E 937 236-4700
   Dayton (G-9843)
USF Holland Inc ....D 740 441-1200
   Gallipolis (G-11216)
USF Holland LLC ....C 937 233-7600
   Dayton (G-9845)
USF Holland LLC ....C 513 874-8960
   West Chester (G-19097)
USF Holland LLC ....C 614 529-9300
   Columbus (G-8836)
USF Holland LLC ....C 216 941-4340
   Cleveland (G-6612)
Vallejo Company ....E 216 741-3933
   Cleveland (G-6616)
Van Howards Lines Inc ....E 937 235-0007
   Dayton (G-9848)
Van Mills Lines Inc ....C 440 846-0200
   Strongsville (G-17357)
Vexor Technology Inc ....E 330 721-9773
   Medina (G-14013)
Vin Devers ....C 888 847-9535
   Sylvania (G-17462)
Vision Express Inc ....E 740 922-8848
   Uhrichsville (G-18348)
W L Logan Trucking Company ....C 330 478-1404
   Canton (G-2529)
Waste Management Ohio Inc ....D 440 201-1235
   Solon (G-16913)
Waste Management Ohio Inc ....C 800 343-6047
   Fairborn (G-10688)
Waste Management Ohio Inc ....E 440 286-7116
   Chardon (G-2724)
Waste Management Ohio Inc ....C 800 343-6047
   Fairborn (G-10689)
Westhafer Trucking Inc ....E 330 698-3030
   Apple Creek (G-622)
Wooster Motor Ways Inc ....C 330 264-9557
   Wooster (G-19786)
Xpo Logistics Freight Inc ....C 513 870-0044
   West Chester (G-19100)
Xpo Logistics Freight Inc ....C 216 433-1000
   Parma (G-15780)
Xpo Logistics Freight Inc ....C 614 876-7100
   Columbus (G-8924)
Xpo Logistics Freight Inc ....D 330 896-7300
   Uniontown (G-18391)
Yrc Inc ....D 330 659-4151
   Richfield (G-16385)
Yrc Inc ....B 419 729-0631
   Toledo (G-18174)
Zemba Bros Inc ....E 740 452-1880
   Zanesville (G-20388)

Zone Transportation Co ....D 440 324-3544
   Elyria (G-10577)

TRUCKING: Long-Distance, Less Than Truckload

City Dash LLC ....C 513 562-2000
   Cincinnati (G-3298)
Dayton Freight Lines Inc ....D 937 236-4880
   Dayton (G-9366)
Estes Express Lines Inc ....C 614 275-6000
   Columbus (G-7538)
Estes Express Lines Inc ....E 419 531-1500
   Toledo (G-17718)
Fedex Freight Inc ....D 330 645-0879
   Akron (G-218)
Fedex Freight Inc ....C 937 233-4826
   Dayton (G-9430)
Fedex Freight Corporation ....E 800 390-0159
   Mansfield (G-13175)
Fedex Freight Corporation ....C 800 521-3505
   Lima (G-12641)
Fedex Freight Corporation ....C 800 728-8190
   Northwood (G-15394)
Franklin Specialty Trnspt Inc ....E 614 529-7900
   Columbus (G-7620)
Old Dominion Freight Line Inc ....E 330 545-8628
   Girard (G-11296)
Old Dominion Freight Line Inc ....E 513 771-1486
   West Chester (G-18979)
Old Dominion Freight Line Inc ....E 419 726-4032
   Toledo (G-17959)
Old Dominion Freight Line Inc ....B 614 491-3903
   Columbus (G-8369)
Partnership LLC ....E 440 471-8310
   Cleveland (G-6178)
USF Holland Inc ....D 740 441-1200
   Gallipolis (G-11216)
USF Holland LLC ....C 513 874-8960
   West Chester (G-19097)
USF Holland LLC ....D 419 354-6633
   Bowling Green (G-1750)
USF Holland LLC ....C 614 529-9300
   Columbus (G-8836)
USF Holland LLC ....C 330 549-2917
   North Lima (G-15275)
Vitran Express Inc ....E 513 771-4894
   West Chester (G-19033)
Yrc Inc ....C 513 874-9320
   West Chester (G-19101)

TRUCKS & TRACTORS: Industrial

Eagle Industrial Truck Mfg LLC ....E 734 442-1000
   Swanton (G-17396)
Forte Indus Eqp Systems Inc ....E 513 398-2800
   Mason (G-13581)
General Electric Company ....B 513 977-1500
   Cincinnati (G-3608)
Pollock Research & Design Inc ....E 330 332-3300
   Salem (G-16554)
Stock Fairfield Corporation ....C 440 543-6000
   Chagrin Falls (G-2684)
Transco Railway Products Inc ....E 419 726-3383
   Toledo (G-18107)
Youngstown-Kenworth Inc ....E 330 534-9761
   Hubbard (G-11952)

TRUCKS, INDL: Wholesalers

All Lift Service Company Inc ....E 440 585-1542
   Willoughby (G-19503)
Cross Truck Equipment Co Inc ....E 330 477-8151
   Canton (G-2274)
Fallsway Equipment Co Inc ....C 330 633-6000
   Akron (G-209)
Rumpke/Kenworth Contract ....D 740 774-5111
   Chillicothe (G-2824)

TRUSSES: Wood, Floor

Khempco Bldg Sup Co Ltd Partnr ....D 740 549-0465
   Delaware (G-9993)

TRUSSES: Wood, Roof

Buckeye Components LLC ....E 330 482-5163
   Columbiana (G-6781)
Thomas Do-It Center Inc ....D 740 446-2002
   Gallipolis (G-11215)

TRUST COMPANIES: National With Deposits, Commercial

Farmers National Bank ....D 330 385-9200
   East Liverpool (G-10403)
First-Knox National Bank ....C 740 399-5500
   Mount Vernon (G-14766)
Huntington National Bank ....E 216 515-6401
   Cleveland (G-5725)
Lcnb National Bank ....E 740 775-6777
   Chillicothe (G-2800)
Lorain National Bank ....C 440 244-6000
   Lorain (G-12922)
Peoples Nat Bnk of New Lxngton ....E 740 342-5111
   New Lexington (G-14925)
PNC Bank National Association ....B 513 721-2500
   Cincinnati (G-4257)
PNC Bank National Association ....E 513 455-9522
   Cincinnati (G-4258)
Security National Bank & Tr Co ....C 740 426-6384
   Newark (G-15097)
Security National Bank & Tr Co ....C 937 324-6800
   Springfield (G-17110)

TRUST COMPANIES: State Accepting Deposits, Commercial

Citizens Bank Company ....E 740 984-2381
   Beverly (G-1461)
Citizens Bank of Ashville Ohio ....E 740 983-2511
   Ashville (G-761)
Civista Bank ....D 419 625-4121
   Sandusky (G-16586)
Croghan Colonial Bank ....E 419 332-7301
   Fremont (G-11067)
Farmers & Merchants State Bank ....C 419 446-2501
   Archbold (G-630)
Fifth Third Bancorp ....D 800 972-3030
   Cincinnati (G-3546)
Fifth Third Bank ....A 513 579-5203
   Cincinnati (G-3548)
Fifth Third Bank ....E 419 259-7820
   Toledo (G-17733)
Fifth Third Bank ....D 330 686-0511
   Cuyahoga Falls (G-9095)
Fifth Third Bank of Sthrn OH ....E 937 840-5353
   Hillsboro (G-11839)
Fifth Third Bnk of Columbus OH ....A 614 744-7553
   Columbus (G-7576)
First Commonwealth Bank ....C 740 657-7000
   Lewis Center (G-12542)
Genoa Banking Company ....E 419 855-8381
   Genoa (G-11255)
Heartland Bank ....E 614 337-4600
   Gahanna (G-11125)
Hicksville Bank Inc ....E 419 542-7726
   Hicksville (G-11729)
Hocking Vly Bnk of Athens Co ....E 740 592-4441
   Athens (G-784)
Killbuck Savings Bank Co Inc ....E 330 276-4881
   Killbuck (G-12310)
Minster Bank ....E 419 628-2351
   Minster (G-14538)
North Side Bank and Trust Co ....D 513 542-7800
   Cincinnati (G-4126)
North Side Bank and Trust Co ....C 513 533-8000
   Cincinnati (G-4127)
Ohio Valley Bank Company ....D 740 446-2168
   Gallipolis (G-11206)
Ohio Valley Bank Company ....E 740 446-1646
   Gallipolis (G-11208)
Old Fort Banking Company ....D 419 447-4790
   Tiffin (G-17530)
Osgood State Bank (inc) ....E 419 582-2681
   Osgood (G-15653)
Richland Trust Company ....D 419 525-8700
   Mansfield (G-13240)
Richwood Banking Company ....E 740 943-2317
   Richwood (G-16397)
Sb Financial Group Inc ....C 419 783-8950
   Defiance (G-9939)
State Bank and Trust Company ....E 419 783-8950
   Defiance (G-9941)
State Bank and Trust Company ....E 419 485-5521
   Montpelier (G-14618)
The Cortland Sav & Bnkg Co ....D 330 637-8040
   Cortland (G-8994)
The Peoples Bank Co Inc ....E 419 678-2385
   Coldwater (G-6765)
Vinton County Nat Bnk McArthur ....E 740 596-2525
   Mc Arthur (G-13892)

TRUST MANAGEMENT SVCS: Charitable

Cleveland Foundation ....D 216 861-3810
  Cleveland (G-5255)
Mercy Health Foundation ....B 937 523-6670
  Springfield (G-17079)

TRUST MANAGEMENT SVCS: Personal Investment

Charles V Francis Trust ....E 513 528-5600
  Cincinnati (G-3170)

TUBE & TUBING FABRICATORS

Benjamin Steel Company Inc ....E 937 233-1212
  Springfield (G-16998)
Parker-Hannifin Corporation ....B 937 456-5571
  Eaton (G-10457)
US Tubular Products Inc ....D 330 832-1734
  North Lawrence (G-15260)

TUBES: Steel & Iron

Crest Bending Inc ....E 419 492-2108
  New Washington (G-15001)
Phillips Mfg and Tower Co ....D 419 347-1720
  Shelby (G-16749)

TUBING: Flexible, Metallic

Wayne Trail Technologies Inc ....D 937 295-2120
  Fort Loramie (G-10986)

TUBING: Plastic

Alkon Corporation ....D 419 355-9111
  Fremont (G-11058)
Dlhbowles Inc ....B 330 478-2503
  Canton (G-2288)

TUGBOAT SVCS

Shelly Materials Inc ....D 740 246-6315
  Thornville (G-17506)

TUNGSTEN MILL PRDTS

Rhenium Alloys Inc ....D 440 365-7388
  North Ridgeville (G-15340)

TURBINES & TURBINE GENERATOR SETS

Pfpc Enterprises Inc ....B 513 941-6200
  Cincinnati (G-4240)
Siemens Energy Inc ....B 740 393-8897
  Mount Vernon (G-14790)

TURBINES: Gas, Mechanical Drive

On-Power Inc ....E 513 228-2100
  Lebanon (G-12489)

TURNKEY VENDORS: Computer Systems

Manatron Inc ....E 937 431-4000
  Beavercreek (G-1228)
Ranac Computer Corporation ....E 317 844-0141
  Moraine (G-14692)

TYPESETTING SVC

A-A Blueprint Co Inc ....E 330 794-8803
  Akron (G-13)
Advanced Translation/Cnsltng ....E 440 716-0820
  Westlake (G-19311)
AGS Custom Graphics Inc ....D 330 963-7770
  Macedonia (G-13058)
Bindery & Spc Pressworks Inc ....D 614 873-4623
  Plain City (G-16046)
Black River Group Inc ....D 419 524-6699
  Mansfield (G-13142)
Bookmasters Inc ....C 419 281-1802
  Ashland (G-658)
Brothers Publishing Co LLC ....E 937 548-3330
  Greenville (G-11368)
Consoldated Graphics Group Inc ....C 216 881-9191
  Cleveland (G-5335)
Copley Ohio Newspapers Inc ....C 330 364-5577
  New Philadelphia (G-14951)
Fedex Office & Print Svcs Inc ....E 937 436-0677
  Dayton (G-9431)
Fedex Office & Print Svcs Inc ....E 614 621-1100
  Columbus (G-7572)

Hecks Direct Mail & Prtg Svc ....E 419 697-3505
  Toledo (G-17797)
Hkm Drect Mkt Cmmnications Inc ....C 216 651-9500
  Cleveland (G-5696)
Quick Tab II Inc ....D 419 448-6622
  Tiffin (G-17533)
Youngstown ARC Engraving Co ....E 330 793-2471
  Youngstown (G-20254)

TYPESETTING SVC: Computer

Wolters Kluwer Clinical Drug ....D 330 650-6506
  Hudson (G-12014)

UNIFORM SPLY SVCS: Indl

Aramark Unf & Career AP LLC ....C 513 533-1000
  Cincinnati (G-2978)
Aramark Unf & Career AP LLC ....D 937 223-6667
  Dayton (G-9236)
Cintas Corporation ....A 513 459-1200
  Cincinnati (G-3291)
Cintas Corporation ....D 513 671-7717
  Cincinnati (G-3293)
Cintas Corporation ....D 513 631-5750
  Cincinnati (G-3292)
Cintas Corporation No 2 ....D 440 746-7777
  Girard (G-11284)
Cintas Corporation No 2 ....D 440 746-7777
  Brecksville (G-1773)
Cintas Corporation No 2 ....C 513 965-0800
  Milford (G-14379)
Cintas Corporation No 2 ....D 330 966-7800
  Canton (G-2254)
Cintas R US Inc ....A 513 459-1200
  Cincinnati (G-3294)
Cintas Sales Corporation ....B 513 459-1200
  Cincinnati (G-3295)
Cintas-Rus LP ....E 513 459-1200
  Mason (G-13561)
G&K Services LLC ....B 952 912-5500
  Mason (G-13582)
G&K Services LLC ....D 937 873-4500
  Fairborn (G-10675)
Leef Bros Inc ....C 952 912-5500
  Mason (G-13609)
Morgan Services Inc ....C 216 241-3107
  Cleveland (G-6009)
Rentwear Inc ....D 330 535-2301
  Canton (G-2453)
Runt Ware & Sanitary Service ....E 330 494-5776
  Canton (G-2466)
Unifirst Corporation ....D 937 746-0531
  Franklin (G-11040)
Van Dyne-Crotty Co ....E 614 684-0048
  Columbus (G-8842)
Van Dyne-Crotty Co ....C 614 491-3903
  Columbus (G-8843)
Van Dyne-Crotty Co ....E 440 248-6935
  Solon (G-16911)

UNIFORM STORES

Affinity Specialty Apparel Inc ....D 866 548-8434
  Fairborn (G-10663)

UNISEX HAIR SALONS

Best Cuts Inc ....E 440 884-6300
  Cleveland (G-5058)
Beverly Hills Inn La Llc ....E 859 494-9151
  Aberdeen (G-1)
Collins Salon Inc ....E 513 683-1700
  Loveland (G-12984)
Cookie Cutters Haircutters ....E 614 522-0220
  Pickerington (G-15955)
Dino Palmieri Beauty Salon ....D 440 498-9411
  Bedford (G-1277)
Englefield Inc ....D 740 323-2077
  Thornville (G-17505)
G E G Enterprises Inc ....E 330 477-3133
  Canton (G-2321)
Image Engineering Inc ....E 513 541-8544
  Cincinnati (G-3752)
Jbentley Studio & Spa LLC ....D 614 790-8828
  Powell (G-16198)
Legrand Services Inc ....E 740 682-6046
  Oak Hill (G-15481)
Merle-Holden Enterprises Inc ....E 216 661-6887
  Cleveland (G-5957)
Michael Christopher Salon Inc ....E 440 449-0999
  Cleveland (G-5977)

Mitchells Salon & Day Spa ....D 513 731-0600
  Cincinnati (G-4063)
PS Lifestyle LLC ....A 440 600-1595
  Cleveland (G-6265)
R L O Inc ....E 937 620-9998
  Dayton (G-9724)
Salon Communication Services ....E 614 233-8500
  Columbus (G-8586)
Z A F Inc ....E 216 291-1234
  Cleveland (G-6707)

UNITED FUND COUNCILS

United Rehabilitation Services ....D 937 233-1230
  Dayton (G-9832)
United Way Greater Cleveland ....C 216 436-2100
  Cleveland (G-6580)
United Way of The Greater Dayt ....E 937 225-3060
  Dayton (G-9834)

UNIVERSITY

Board of Dir of Wittenbe ....E 937 327-6310
  Springfield (G-17000)
Bowling Green State University ....D 419 372-2186
  Bowling Green (G-1724)
Bowling Green State University ....D 419 372-8657
  Bowling Green (G-1723)
Bowling Green State University ....E 419 372-2700
  Bowling Green (G-1725)
Case Western Reserve Univ ....E 216 368-2560
  Cleveland (G-5130)
Cleveland State University ....E 216 687-3786
  Cleveland (G-5289)
Devry University Inc ....C 614 251-6969
  Columbus (G-7443)
Kent State University ....D 330 672-2607
  Kent (G-12242)
Kent State University ....E 330 672-3114
  Kent (G-12243)
Miami University ....B 513 727-3200
  Middletown (G-14308)
Miami University ....D 513 529-6911
  Oxford (G-15681)
Miami University ....E 513 529-1251
  Oxford (G-15682)
Miami University ....D 513 529-1230
  Oxford (G-15683)
Oberlin College ....E 440 775-8500
  Oberlin (G-15514)
Ohio State Univ Wexner Med Ctr ....A 614 293-6255
  Columbus (G-8294)
Ohio State University ....D 614 292-5491
  Columbus (G-8305)
Ohio State University ....C 614 292-4843
  Columbus (G-8313)
Ohio State University ....E 330 263-3725
  Canton (G-2431)
Ohio State University ....E 614 688-5721
  Columbus (G-8329)
Ohio State University ....A 614 688-3939
  Columbus (G-8296)
Ohio State University ....E 614 293-2800
  Columbus (G-8298)
Ohio State University ....D 614 292-5578
  Columbus (G-8299)
Ohio State University ....A 614 293-7417
  Columbus (G-8301)
Ohio State University ....C 614 293-8750
  Columbus (G-8302)
Ohio State University ....A 330 263-3700
  Wooster (G-19754)
Ohio State University ....E 614 292-5504
  Columbus (G-8304)
Ohio State University ....D 740 376-7431
  Marietta (G-13364)
Ohio State University ....E 614 292-4139
  Columbus (G-8306)
Ohio State University ....E 614 292-2624
  Columbus (G-8307)
Ohio State University ....D 614 292-1681
  Columbus (G-8308)
Ohio State University ....D 740 593-2657
  Athens (G-794)
Ohio State University ....A 614 293-3860
  Columbus (G-8309)
Ohio State University ....E 614 247-4000
  Columbus (G-8310)
Ohio State University ....B 330 263-3701
  Wooster (G-19755)
Ohio State University ....D 614 257-5200
  Columbus (G-8314)

S E R V I C E S

Ohio State University............E...... 614 293-4997
Columbus *(G-8317)*

Ohio State University............D...... 614 292-7788
Columbus *(G-8319)*

Ohio State University............D...... 614 442-7300
Columbus *(G-8320)*

Ohio State University............E...... 614 293-8732
Columbus *(G-8321)*

Ohio State University............E...... 614 292-6291
Columbus *(G-8322)*

Ohio State University............E...... 614 293-8158
Columbus *(G-8323)*

Ohio State University............D...... 614 292-0110
Columbus *(G-8324)*

Ohio State University............D...... 614 292-6741
Columbus *(G-8325)*

Ohio State University............E...... 614 292-5144
Columbus *(G-8326)*

Ohio State University............E...... 614 293-8732
Columbus *(G-8327)*

Ohio State University............E...... 614 293-8588
Columbus *(G-8328)*

Ohio State University............E...... 614 293-3737
Columbus *(G-8330)*

Ohio State University............E...... 614 292-6122
Columbus *(G-8332)*

Ohio State University............C...... 614 292-6661
Columbus *(G-8334)*

Ohio State University............C...... 614 292-5990
Columbus *(G-8335)*

Ohio State University............E...... 614 294-2635
Columbus *(G-8336)*

Ohio State University............D...... 614 293-2222
Columbus *(G-8339)*

Ohio State University............B...... 614 293-8133
Columbus *(G-8340)*

Ohio State University............E...... 614 292-9404
Columbus *(G-8341)*

Ohio State University............A...... 614 293-5066
Columbus *(G-8342)*

Ohio State University............E...... 614 293-8419
Columbus *(G-8343)*

Ohio State University............D...... 614 292-1472
Columbus *(G-8344)*

Ohio State University............E...... 614 293-8196
Columbus *(G-8345)*

Ohio State University............A...... 614 293-8000
Columbus *(G-8347)*

Ohio State University............E...... 614 293-4925
Columbus *(G-8348)*

Ohio State University............D...... 614 292-2751
Columbus *(G-8350)*

Ohio University............D...... 740 593-1000
Athens *(G-795)*

Ohio University............E...... 740 593-1660
Athens *(G-799)*

University Hospitals............B...... 440 250-2001
Westlake *(G-19418)*

University of Akron............D...... 330 972-6008
Akron *(G-479)*

University of Akron............E...... 330 972-8210
Akron *(G-480)*

University of Cincinnati............A...... 513 556-6381
Cincinnati *(G-4707)*

University of Cincinnati............E...... 513 556-4054
Cincinnati *(G-4712)*

University of Cincinnati............E...... 513 556-3732
Cincinnati *(G-4717)*

University of Cincinnati............E...... 513 558-4194
Cincinnati *(G-4703)*

University of Cincinnati............E...... 513 584-7522
Cincinnati *(G-4704)*

University of Cincinnati............E...... 513 475-8771
Cincinnati *(G-4705)*

University of Cincinnati............B...... 513 558-1200
Cincinnati *(G-4706)*

University of Cincinnati............E...... 513 558-4444
Cincinnati *(G-4708)*

University of Cincinnati............E...... 513 584-4396
Cincinnati *(G-4710)*

University of Cincinnati............A...... 513 556-5087
Cincinnati *(G-4711)*

University of Cincinnati............C...... 513 558-5439
Cincinnati *(G-4713)*

University of Cincinnati............C...... 513 558-4231
Cincinnati *(G-4715)*

University of Cincinnati............D...... 513 584-5331
Cincinnati *(G-4716)*

University of Cincinnati............C...... 513 556-4603
Cincinnati *(G-4718)*

University of Cincinnati............D...... 513 558-1799
Cincinnati *(G-4719)*

University of Cincinnati............C...... 513 584-3200
Cincinnati *(G-4720)*

University of Cincinnati............E...... 513 558-5471
Cincinnati *(G-4721)*

University of Cincinnati............E...... 513 584-1000
Cincinnati *(G-4723)*

University of Cincinnati............E...... 513 558-4831
Cincinnati *(G-4724)*

University of Cincinnati............E...... 513 584-1000
Cincinnati *(G-4725)*

University of Cincinnati............E...... 513 556-3803
Cincinnati *(G-4726)*

University of Dayton............A...... 937 229-2919
Dayton *(G-9837)*

University of Dayton............C...... 937 255-3141
Dayton *(G-9836)*

University of Dayton............C...... 937 229-2113
Dayton *(G-9839)*

University of Dayton............B...... 937 229-3822
Dayton *(G-9840)*

University of Dayton............C...... 937 229-3913
Dayton *(G-9841)*

University of Toledo............B...... 419 383-4229
Toledo *(G-18130)*

University of Toledo............D...... 419 534-3770
Toledo *(G-18125)*

University of Toledo............E...... 419 383-3556
Toledo *(G-18126)*

University of Toledo............E...... 419 383-5322
Toledo *(G-18128)*

Wright State University............E...... 937 298-4331
Kettering *(G-12304)*

Wright State University............A...... 937 775-3333
Beavercreek *(G-1199)*

Xavier University............E...... 513 745-3335
Cincinnati *(G-4810)*

UPHOLSTERY WORK SVCS

Casco Mfg Solutions Inc............D...... 513 681-0003
Cincinnati *(G-3129)*

USED CAR DEALERS

Abraham Ford LLC............E...... 440 233-7402
Elyria *(G-10477)*

Akron Auto Auction Inc............C...... 330 724-7708
Coventry Township *(G-9032)*

Arch Abraham Susuki Ltd............E...... 440 934-6001
Elyria *(G-10479)*

Auto Center USA Inc............E...... 513 683-4900
Cincinnati *(G-3006)*

Brown Motor Sales Co............E...... 419 531-0151
Toledo *(G-17629)*

Cain Motors Inc............E...... 330 494-5588
Canton *(G-2225)*

Carcorp Inc............C...... 877 857-2801
Columbus *(G-7118)*

Cascade Group Inc............E...... 330 929-1861
Cuyahoga Falls *(G-9077)*

Central Cadillac Limited............D...... 216 861-5800
Cleveland *(G-5153)*

Chesrown Oldsmobile GMC Inc............E...... 614 846-3040
Columbus *(G-7182)*

Chuck Nicholson Pntc-GMC Trcks............E...... 330 343-7781
Dover *(G-10069)*

Columbus Fair Auto Auction Inc............A...... 614 497-2000
Obetz *(G-15525)*

Columbus SAI Motors LLC............E...... 614 851-3273
Columbus *(G-7312)*

Coughlin Chevrolet Toyota Inc............D...... 740 366-1381
Newark *(G-15028)*

Dan Tobin Pontiac Buick GMC............D...... 614 889-6300
Columbus *(G-7412)*

Dave White Chevrolet Inc............C...... 419 885-4444
Sylvania *(G-17417)*

Don Wood Inc............D...... 740 593-6641
Athens *(G-777)*

Donnell Ford-Lincoln............E...... 330 332-0031
Salem *(G-16542)*

Dons Automotive Group LLC............E...... 419 337-3010
Wauseon *(G-18799)*

Doug Bigelow Chevrolet Inc............D...... 330 644-7500
Akron *(G-192)*

Ed Mullinax Ford LLC............C...... 440 984-2431
Amherst *(G-584)*

Ed Schmidt Auto Inc............C...... 419 874-4331
Perrysburg *(G-15863)*

Gene Stevens Auto & Truck Ctr............E...... 419 429-2000
Findlay *(G-10913)*

George P Ballas Buick GMC Trck............D...... 419 535-1000
Toledo *(G-17760)*

Graham Chevrolet-Cadillac Co............D...... 419 989-4012
Ontario *(G-15551)*

Greenwood Chevrolet Inc............C...... 330 270-1299
Youngstown *(G-20057)*

Grogans Towne Chrysler Inc............D...... 419 476-0761
Toledo *(G-17772)*

Jake Sweeney Automotive Inc............C...... 513 782-2800
Cincinnati *(G-3805)*

Jim Keim Ford............D...... 614 888-3333
Columbus *(G-7859)*

Joseph Chevrolet Oldsmobile Co............C...... 513 741-6700
Cincinnati *(G-3833)*

Kempthorn Motors Inc............C...... 800 451-3877
Canton *(G-2365)*

Kent Automotive Inc............E...... 330 678-5520
Kent *(G-12240)*

Kerns Chevrolet-Buick-Gmc Inc............E...... 419 586-5131
Celina *(G-2597)*

Lang Chevrolet Co............D...... 937 426-2313
Beavercreek Township *(G-1253)*

Laria Chevrolet-Buick Inc............E...... 330 925-2015
Rittman *(G-16406)*

Lariche Subaru Inc............D...... 419 422-1855
Findlay *(G-10933)*

Lavery Chevrolet-Buick Inc............E...... 330 823-1100
Alliance *(G-537)*

Lebanon Chrysler - Plymouth Inc............E...... 513 932-2717
Lebanon *(G-12480)*

Leikin Motor Companies Inc............D...... 440 946-6900
Willoughby *(G-19544)*

Lincoln Mrcury Kings Auto Mall............C...... 513 683-3800
Cincinnati *(G-3933)*

Lkq Triplettasap Inc............C...... 330 733-6333
Akron *(G-317)*

Mark Thomas Ford Inc............E...... 330 638-1010
Cortland *(G-8989)*

McCluskey Chevrolet Inc............C...... 513 761-1111
Cincinnati *(G-3986)*

Mike Castrucci Ford............C...... 513 831-7010
Milford *(G-14410)*

Montrose Ford Inc............D...... 330 666-0711
Fairlawn *(G-10842)*

Mullinax East LLC............D...... 440 296-3020
Wickliffe *(G-19470)*

Mullinax Ford North Canton Inc............C...... 330 238-3206
Canton *(G-2411)*

Northern Automotive Inc............E...... 614 436-2001
Columbus *(G-8200)*

Progrssive Oldsmobile Cadillac............E...... 330 833-8585
Massillon *(G-13721)*

Rouen Chrysler Plymouth Dodge............E...... 419 837-6228
Woodville *(G-19683)*

Roush Equipment Inc............C...... 614 882-1535
Westerville *(G-19300)*

Schoner Chevrolet Inc............E...... 330 877-6731
Hartville *(G-11698)*

Skipco Financial Adjusters............D...... 330 854-4800
Canal Fulton *(G-2097)*

Sonic Automotive............E...... 614 870-8200
Columbus *(G-8658)*

Sonic Automotive-1495 Automall............E...... 614 317-4326
Columbus *(G-8659)*

Spitzer Auto World Amherst............D...... 440 988-4444
Amherst *(G-598)*

Spitzer Chevrolet Inc............E...... 330 467-4141
Northfield *(G-15386)*

Sunnyside Toyota Inc............D...... 440 777-9911
North Olmsted *(G-15312)*

Surfside Motors Inc............E...... 419 462-1746
Galion *(G-11183)*

Tansky Motors Inc............E...... 650 322-7069
Logan *(G-12855)*

Toyota of Bedford............D...... 440 439-8600
Bedford *(G-1310)*

Village Motors Inc............D...... 330 674-2055
Millersburg *(G-14498)*

Vin Devers............C...... 888 847-9535
Sylvania *(G-17462)*

Voss Auto Network Inc............E...... 937 428-2447
Dayton *(G-9860)*

Voss Chevrolet Inc............C...... 937 428-2500
Dayton *(G-9862)*

Voss Dodge............E...... 937 435-7800
Dayton *(G-9863)*

Voss Toyota Inc............E...... 937 431-2100
Beavercreek *(G-1195)*

Wagner Lincoln-Mercury Inc............E...... 419 435-8131
Carey *(G-2550)*

USED CLOTHING STORES

Walker Auto Group Inc ....D....... 937 433-4950
  Miamisburg (G-14236)
Warner Buick-Nissan Inc.................E....... 419 423-7161
  Findlay (G-10974)

USED CLOTHING STORES

Goodwill Inds NW Ohio Inc ....D....... 419 255-0070
  Toledo (G-17767)
Goodwill Industries of Erie ....E....... 419 625-4744
  Sandusky (G-16611)
Volunteers America Ohio & Ind ....C....... 614 253-6100
  Columbus (G-8859)

USED MERCHANDISE STORES

Blanchard Valley Hospital ....E....... 419 423-4335
  Findlay (G-10873)
Goodwill Inds Centl Ohio Inc ....E....... 740 439-7000
  Cambridge (G-2070)
Goodwill Inds of Ashtabula ....D....... 440 964-3565
  Ashtabula (G-738)
Goodwill Industries...........................E....... 330 264-1300
  Wooster (G-19725)
Gw Business Solutions LLC ....C....... 740 645-9861
  Newark (G-15039)
Licking-Knox Goodwill Inds Inc ....D....... 740 345-9861
  Newark (G-15061)
Mc Gregor Family Enterprises.............E....... 513 583-0040
  Cincinnati (G-3984)
Salvation Army ....D....... 419 447-2252
  Tiffin (G-17535)
Salvation Army ....C....... 330 773-3331
  Akron (G-418)
Zanesvlle Welfre Orgnztn/Goodw..........E....... 740 450-6060
  Zanesville (G-20387)

USED MERCHANDISE STORES: Clothing & Shoes

Youngstown Area Goodwill Inds ....C....... 330 759-7921
  Youngstown (G-20255)

USED MERCHANDISE STORES: Furniture

Cort Business Services Corp ....D....... 513 759-8181
  West Chester (G-18900)
Marion Goodwill Industries....................E....... 740 387-7023
  Marion (G-13441)

USHER SVC

Dedicated Tech Services Inc.................E....... 614 309-0059
  Dublin (G-10197)

UTILITY PROGRAM ADMINISTRATION & REGULATION, GOVT: Local

City of Columbus ....C....... 614 645-7627
  Columbus (G-7205)

VACATION LODGES

Das Dutch Village Inn ....D....... 330 482-5050
  Columbiana (G-6787)
Ohio State Parks Inc ....D....... 513 664-3504
  College Corner (G-6768)

VACUUM CLEANER STORES

ABC Appliance Inc............................E....... 419 693-4414
  Oregon (G-15581)

VACUUM CLEANERS: Household

Stanley Steemer Intl Inc ....C....... 614 764-2007
  Dublin (G-10341)

VALET PARKING SVCS

Parking Solutions Inc ....A....... 614 469-7000
  Columbus (G-8422)

VALUE-ADDED RESELLERS: Computer Systems

Cameo Solutions Inc ....E....... 513 645-4220
  West Chester (G-18880)
Evanhoe & Associates Inc ....E....... 937 235-2995
  Dayton (G-9173)
Rolta Advizex Technologies LLC..........E....... 216 901-1818
  Independence (G-12117)

Warnock Tanner & Assoc Inc..............E....... 419 897-6999
  Maumee (G-13867)

VALVE REPAIR SVCS, INDL

Kig Enterprises LLC ....E....... 937 263-6429
  Dayton (G-9544)

VALVES & PIPE FITTINGS

Crane Pumps & Systems Inc ....B....... 937 773-2442
  Piqua (G-16003)
Edward W Daniel LLC ....E....... 440 647-1960
  Wellington (G-18839)
Fcx Performance Inc..........................E....... 614 324-6050
  Columbus (G-7567)
Robeck Fluid Power Co ....D....... 330 562-1140
  Aurora (G-840)
Ruthman Pump and Engineering ....E....... 937 783-2411
  Blanchester (G-1489)
Superior Products LLC........................D....... 216 651-9400
  Cleveland (G-6484)
Superior Products Llc ....D....... 216 651-9400
  Cleveland (G-6483)
Swagelok Company ....D....... 440 349-5934
  Solon (G-16905)
Waxman Industries Inc ....D....... 440 439-1830
  Cleveland (G-6657)

VALVES: Aerosol, Metal

Accurate Mechanical Inc.....................E....... 740 681-1332
  Lancaster (G-12368)
J Feldkamp Design Build Ltd...............E....... 513 870-0601
  Cincinnati (G-3795)

VALVES: Aircraft, Hydraulic

Aerocontrolex Group Inc.....................D....... 440 352-6182
  Painesville (G-15692)

VALVES: Indl

Alkon Corporation ....E....... 614 799-6650
  Dublin (G-10126)
Curtiss-Wright Flow Control ....D....... 513 735-2538
  Batavia (G-995)
Curtiss-Wright Flow Control ....D....... 513 528-7900
  Cincinnati (G-2847)
Ruthman Pump and Engineering ....E....... 937 783-2411
  Blanchester (G-1489)
Waxman Industries Inc ....C....... 440 439-1830
  Cleveland (G-6657)

VALVES: Nuclear Power Plant, Ferrous

Alkon Corporation ....D....... 419 355-9111
  Fremont (G-11058)

VAN CONVERSIONS

Wmk LLC ....E....... 440 951-4335
  Mentor (G-14125)

VARIETY STORE MERCHANDISE, WHOLESALE

Glen Surplus Sales Inc ....E....... 419 347-1212
  Shelby (G-16746)
Glow Industries Inc............................E....... 419 872-4772
  Perrysburg (G-15869)

VARIETY STORES

Big Lots Stores Inc ....A....... 614 278-6800
  Columbus (G-7035)
Discount Drug Mart Inc ....C....... 330 725-2340
  Medina (G-13931)
Dollar Paradise ....E....... 216 432-0421
  Cleveland (G-5436)
Glow Industries Inc............................E....... 419 872-4772
  Perrysburg (G-15869)
Marc Glassman Inc ....C....... 330 995-9246
  Aurora (G-834)
Trepanier Daniels & Trepanier ....D....... 740 286-1288
  Jackson (G-12180)

VEGETABLE STANDS OR MARKETS

A Brown & Sons Nursery ....E....... 937 836-5826
  Brookville (G-1909)

VEHICLES: All Terrain

Wholecycle Inc ....E....... 330 929-8123
  Peninsula (G-15815)

VENDING MACHINE OPERATORS: Beverage

Coffee Break Corporation ....E....... 513 841-1100
  Cincinnati (G-3318)

VENDING MACHINE OPERATORS: Food

Sanese Services Inc ....B....... 614 436-1234
  Warren (G-18739)
Walter Alexander Entps Inc ....E....... 513 841-1100
  Cincinnati (G-4769)

VENDING MACHINE OPERATORS: Sandwich & Hot Food

Laughlin Music & Vending Svc.............E....... 740 593-7778
  Athens (G-790)

VENDING MACHINE REPAIR SVCS

Enterprise Vending Inc ....E....... 513 772-1373
  Cincinnati (G-3500)
Serex Corporation ....E....... 330 726-6062
  Youngstown (G-20208)

VENDING MACHINES & PARTS

Giant Industries Inc ....E....... 419 531-4600
  Toledo (G-17762)

VENTILATING EQPT: Metal

Famous Industries Inc ....E....... 330 535-1811
  Akron (G-214)

VENTURE CAPITAL COMPANIES

Rev1 Ventures ....E....... 614 487-3700
  Columbus (G-8529)
Rse Group Inc ....D....... 937 596-6167
  Jackson Center (G-12186)

VESSELS: Process, Indl, Metal Plate

Columbiana Boiler Company LLC........E....... 330 482-3373
  Columbiana (G-6784)

VETERANS AFFAIRS ADMINISTRATION SVCS

Veterans Affairs US Dept.....................A....... 937 268-6511
  Dayton (G-9856)
Veterans Health Administration.............A....... 513 861-3100
  Cincinnati (G-4759)
Veterans Health Administration.............E....... 330 740-9200
  Youngstown (G-20236)

VETERANS' AFFAIRS ADMINISTRATION, GOVERNMENT: Federal

Veterans Health Administration.............B....... 740 568-0412
  Marietta (G-13396)
Veterans Health Administration.............A....... 740 773-1141
  Chillicothe (G-2836)
Veterans Health Administration.............B....... 513 943-3680
  Cincinnati (G-4760)
Veterans Health Administration.............A....... 216 791-3800
  Cleveland (G-6625)
Veterans Health Administration.............C....... 614 257-5524
  Columbus (G-8849)
Veterans Health Administration.............B....... 866 463-0912
  Ashtabula (G-758)
Veterans Health Administration.............B....... 740 695-9321
  Saint Clairsville (G-16509)
Veterans Health Administration.............D....... 419 259-2000
  Toledo (G-18138)
Veterans Health Administration.............B....... 216 939-0699
  Cleveland (G-6626)
Veterans Health Administration.............D....... 330 489-4600
  Canton (G-2526)

VETERINARY PRDTS: Instruments & Apparatus

Suarez Corporation Industries ....D....... 330 494-4282
  Canton (G-2502)

SERVICES

VIDEO & AUDIO EQPT, WHOLESALE

Live Technologies LLC ....D...... 614 278-7777
Columbus (G-7986)

Merchandise Inc ....D...... 513 353-2200
Miamitown (G-14242)

VIDEO PRODUCTION SVCS

Killer Spotscom Inc ....D...... 513 201-1380
Cincinnati (G-3869)

Madison Avenue Mktg Group Inc ....E...... 419 473-9000
Toledo (G-17878)

Mitosis LLC ....E...... 937 557-3440
Dayton (G-9640)

VIDEO REPAIR SVCS

K M T Service ....E...... 614 777-7770
Hilliard (G-11782)

VIDEO TAPE PRODUCTION SVCS

Video Duplication Services Inc ....E...... 614 871-3827
Columbus (G-8850)

World Harvest Church Inc ....B...... 614 837-1990
Canal Winchester (G-2128)

VIDEO TAPE WHOLESALERS, RECORDED

Midwest Tape LLC ....B...... 419 868-9370
Holland (G-11898)

VINYL RESINS, NEC

Polyone Corporation ....D...... 440 930-1000
North Baltimore (G-15179)

VISITING NURSE

A Touch of Grace Inc ....D...... 740 397-7971
Mount Vernon (G-14748)

Accentcare Home Health Cal Inc ....C...... 740 474-7826
Circleville (G-4823)

Advantage Home Health Care ....D...... 800 636-2330
Portsmouth (G-16124)

Alternacare Home Health Inc ....E...... 740 689-1589
Lancaster (G-12370)

Amber Home Care LLC ....E...... 614 523-0668
Columbus (G-6909)

Angels Touch Nursing Care ....E...... 513 661-4111
Cincinnati (G-2969)

Appalachian Community Visi ....D...... 740 594-8226
Athens (G-764)

Apria Healthcare LLC ....E...... 937 291-2842
Miamisburg (G-14141)

B H C Services Inc ....A...... 216 289-5300
Euclid (G-10624)

Bracor Inc ....E...... 216 289-5300
Euclid (G-10626)

Care Connection of Cincinnati ....D...... 513 842-1101
Cincinnati (G-3120)

Caring Hands Home Health Care ....E...... 740 532-9020
Ironton (G-12149)

Chemed Corporation ....D...... 513 762-6690
Cincinnati (G-3175)

Choice Healthcare Limited ....D...... 937 254-6220
Beavercreek (G-1139)

Clearpath HM Hlth Hospice LLC ....D...... 330 784-2162
Akron (G-141)

Colt Enterprises Inc ....E...... 567 336-6062
Maumee (G-13774)

Comfort Keepers ....E...... 419 229-1031
Lima (G-12617)

Comfort Keepers ....E...... 440 721-0100
Painesville (G-15703)

Comfort Keepers Inc ....E...... 937 322-6288
Springfield (G-17017)

Committed To Care Inc ....E...... 513 245-1190
Cincinnati (G-3339)

Community Choice Home Care ....E...... 740 574-9900
Wheelersburg (G-19431)

Community Hlth Prfssionals Inc ....E...... 419 634-7443
Ada (G-3)

Community Hlth Prfssionals Inc ....E...... 419 445-5128
Archbold (G-628)

Community Hlth Prfssionals Inc ....C...... 419 238-9223
Van Wert (G-18475)

Community Hlth Prfssionals Inc ....E...... 419 399-4708
Paulding (G-15791)

Community Hlth Prfssionals Inc ....E...... 419 991-1822
Lima (G-12789)

Community Hlth Prfssionals Inc ....E...... 419 586-1999
Celina (G-2589)

Community Hlth Prfssionals Inc ....D...... 419 586-6266
Celina (G-2590)

Community Hlth Prfssionals Inc ....E...... 419 695-8101
Delphos (G-10022)

Diane Vishnia Rn and Assoc ....D...... 330 929-1113
Cuyahoga Falls (G-9087)

EJq Home Health Care Inc ....D...... 440 323-7004
Elyria (G-10504)

Ember Complete Care ....C...... 740 922-6888
Uhrichsville (G-18340)

Enhanced Home Health Care LLC ....D...... 614 433-7266
Columbus (G-7517)

Excel Health Services LLC ....D...... 614 794-0006
Delaware (G-9973)

Hanson Services Inc ....C...... 216 226-5425
Lakewood (G-12345)

Healing Hands Home Health Ltd ....E...... 740 385-0710
Logan (G-12836)

Health Services Coshocton Cnty ....E...... 740 622-7311
Coshocton (G-9016)

Hillebrand Home Health Inc ....D...... 513 598-6648
Cincinnati (G-3702)

Home Care Advantage ....D...... 330 337-4663
Salem (G-16547)

Home Care Network Inc ....D...... 937 435-1142
Dayton (G-9498)

Homecare Mtters HM Hlth Hspice ....D...... 419 562-2001
Bucyrus (G-1993)

Hospice Care Ohio ....D...... 330 665-1455
Fairlawn (G-10832)

Hospice Caring Way ....D...... 419 238-9223
Van Wert (G-18480)

Hospice of The Western Reserve ....D...... 800 707-8921
Cleveland (G-5711)

Intervention For Peace Inc ....D...... 330 725-1298
Medina (G-13957)

Karopa Incorporate ....E...... 513 860-1616
Hamilton (G-11619)

Lbs International Inc ....D...... 614 866-3688
Pickerington (G-15962)

Loving Family Home Care Inc ....D...... 888 469-2178
Toledo (G-17863)

Marietta Memorial Hospital ....E...... 740 373-8549
Marietta (G-13355)

Northeast Professional Hm Care ....E...... 330 966-2311
Canton (G-2421)

Nurse Medicial Healthcare Svcs ....D...... 614 801-1300
Grove City (G-11460)

Ohio Home Health Care Inc ....E...... 937 853-0271
Dayton (G-9669)

Ohio Valley Home Hlth Svcs Inc ....E...... 330 385-2333
East Liverpool (G-10413)

Ohioans Home Health Care Inc ....D...... 419 843-4422
Perrysburg (G-15898)

Personal Touch HM Care IPA Inc ....E...... 937 456-4447
Eaton (G-10458)

Primary Care Nursing Services ....D...... 614 764-0960
Dublin (G-10311)

Prime Home Care LLC ....E...... 513 340-4183
Maineville (G-13117)

Private Duty Services Inc ....C...... 419 238-3714
Van Wert (G-18487)

Pro Health Care Services Ltd ....E...... 614 856-9111
Groveport (G-11532)

Proactive Occpational Medicine ....E...... 740 574-8728
Wheelersburg (G-19438)

Quality Life Providers LLC ....E...... 614 527-9999
Hilliard (G-11809)

Richard Health Systems LLC ....C...... 419 534-2371
Toledo (G-18007)

Robinson Visitn Nrs Asoc/Hospc ....E...... 330 297-8899
Ravenna (G-16264)

Salem Area Vsiting Nurse Assoc ....E...... 330 332-9986
Salem (G-16558)

Selective Networking Inc ....D...... 740 574-2682
Wheelersburg (G-19440)

Ssth LLC ....D...... 614 884-0793
Columbus (G-8679)

Tky Associates LLC ....D...... 419 535-7777
Toledo (G-18068)

Tri County Visitng Nrs Prvt ....E...... 419 738-7430
Wapakoneta (G-18656)

TVC Home Health Care ....E...... 330 755-1110
Youngstown (G-20229)

Vishnia & Associates Inc ....D...... 330 929-5512
Cuyahoga Falls (G-9137)

Visiting Nrse Assn of Clveland ....B...... 419 281-2480
Ashland (G-697)

Visiting Nrse Assn of Clveland ....E...... 419 522-4969
Mansfield (G-13260)

Visiting Nrse Assn of Mid-Ohio ....E...... 216 931-1300
Cleveland (G-6636)

Visiting Nurse Service Inc ....B...... 330 745-1601
Akron (G-490)

Visiting Nurse Service Inc ....E...... 440 286-9461
Chardon (G-2723)

VISUAL COMMUNICATIONS SYSTEMS

Findaway World LLC ....D...... 440 893-0808
Solon (G-16849)

VOCATIONAL OR TECHNICAL SCHOOLS, PUBLIC

Great Oaks Inst Tech Creer Dev ....D...... 513 613-3657
Cincinnati (G-3644)

VOCATIONAL REHABILITATION AGENCY

A W S Inc ....E...... 216 486-0600
Euclid (G-10622)

Ash Craft Industries Inc ....C...... 440 224-2177
Ashtabula (G-704)

Center of Voctnl Altrntvs Mntl ....D...... 614 294-7117
Columbus (G-7154)

Community Support Services Inc ....C...... 330 253-9388
Akron (G-153)

Cornucopia Inc ....E...... 216 521-4600
Lakewood (G-12339)

County of Cuyahoga ....D...... 216 475-7066
Cleveland (G-5362)

Creative Learning Workshop ....E...... 330 393-5929
Warren (G-18696)

Creative Learning Workshop ....E...... 937 437-0146
New Paris (G-14941)

Easter Seals Tristate ....C...... 513 985-0515
Blue Ash (G-1549)

Food For Good Thought Inc ....E...... 614 447-0424
Columbus (G-7600)

Goodwill Ester Seals Miami Vly ....C...... 937 461-4800
Dayton (G-9464)

Goodwill Idstrs Grtr Clvlnd L ....E...... 216 581-6320
Cleveland (G-5615)

Goodwill Idstrs Grtr Clvlnd L ....D...... 330 454-9461
Canton (G-2329)

Goodwill Inds Centl Ohio Inc ....D...... 740 373-1304
Marietta (G-13331)

Goodwill Inds Centl Ohio Inc ....E...... 740 439-7000
Cambridge (G-2070)

Goodwill Inds NW Ohio Inc ....E...... 419 255-0070
Toledo (G-17767)

Goodwill Inds of Ashtabula ....D...... 440 964-3565
Ashtabula (G-738)

Goodwill Industries of Akron ....C...... 330 724-6995
Akron (G-241)

Goodwill Industries of Lima ....D...... 419 228-4821
Lima (G-12645)

Jewish Family Services ....E...... 614 231-1890
Columbus (G-7858)

L & M Products Inc ....C...... 937 456-7141
Eaton (G-10449)

Marimor Industries Inc ....E...... 419 221-1226
Lima (G-12698)

Murray Ridge Production Center ....B...... 440 329-3734
Elyria (G-10541)

Ohio Rehabilitation Svcs Comm ....E...... 330 643-3080
Akron (G-362)

Perco Inc ....D...... 740 342-5156
New Lexington (G-14926)

Quadco Rehabilitation Center ....D...... 419 445-1950
Archbold (G-636)

Quadco Rehabilitation Ctr Inc ....B...... 419 682-1011
Stryker (G-17370)

Richcreek Bailey Rehabilitatio ....E...... 440 527-8610
Mentor (G-14104)

Spectrum Supportive Services ....E...... 216 875-0460
Cleveland (G-6445)

United Cerebral Palsy ....C...... 216 791-8363
Cleveland (G-6568)

Voc Works Ltd ....D...... 614 760-3515
Dublin (G-10366)

Waycraft Inc ....C...... 419 563-0550
Bucyrus (G-2005)

Youngstown Area Goodwill Inds ....C...... 330 759-7921
Youngstown (G-20255)

VOCATIONAL TRAINING AGENCY

A W S Inc ....C 440 333-1791
Rocky River (G-16420)
A W S Inc ....B 216 749-0356
Cleveland (G-4881)
County of Hardin ....E 419 674-4158
Kenton (G-12274)
Vocational Guidance Services ....E 440 322-1123
Elyria (G-10570)

WALL COVERINGS WHOLESALERS

Fashion Architectural Designs ....D 216 432-1600
Cleveland (G-5515)

WALLPAPER STORE

Pucher Paint Co Inc ....E 440 234-0991
Berea (G-1435)

WALLS: Curtain, Metal

Midwest Curtainwalls Inc ....D 216 641-7900
Cleveland (G-5989)

WAREHOUSING & STORAGE FACILITIES, NEC

Ballreich Bros Inc ....C 419 447-1814
Tiffin (G-17510)
Comprehensive Logistics Co Inc ....E 330 793-0504
Youngstown (G-20007)
Distribution and Trnsp Svc Inc ....E 937 295-3343
Fort Loramie (G-10985)
Exel Holdings (usa) Inc ....C 614 865-8500
Westerville (G-19161)
General Motors LLC ....C 513 603-6600
West Chester (G-18932)
Honda Logistics North Amer Inc ....A 937 642-0335
East Liberty (G-10391)
Interstate Warehousing VA LLC ....D 513 874-6500
Fairfield (G-10738)
Jacobson Warehouse Company Inc .....C 614 314-1091
Obetz (G-15527)
Kitchen Collection LLC ....E 740 773-9150
Chillicothe (G-2799)
Kuhlman Corporation ....C 419 897-6000
Maumee (G-13808)
Lefco Worthington LLC ....E 216 432-4422
Cleveland (G-5860)
Locker Moving & Storage Inc ....E 330 784-0477
Canton (G-2380)
Midwest Express Inc ....A 937 642-0335
East Liberty (G-10392)
Nex Transport Inc ....C 937 645-3761
East Liberty (G-10394)
PC Connection Inc ....C 937 382-4800
Wilmington (G-19637)
Radial South LP ....C 678 584-4047
Groveport (G-11533)
SH Bell Company ....E 412 963-9910
East Liverpool (G-10417)
Ship Shape Marine Inc ....E 419 734-1554
Port Clinton (G-16117)
Target Corporation ....B 614 801-6700
West Jefferson (G-19112)
Vista Industrial Packaging LLC ....D 800 454-6117
Columbus (G-8855)
Warren City Board Education ....E 330 841-2265
Warren (G-18768)
Wooster Motor Ways Inc ....C 330 264-9557
Wooster (G-19786)

WAREHOUSING & STORAGE, REFRIGERATED: Cold Storage Or Refrig

Americold Logistics LLC ....D 330 834-1742
Massillon (G-13661)
Cloverleaf Cold Storage Co ....E 330 833-9870
Massillon (G-13672)
D & D Investment Co ....E 614 272-6567
Columbus (G-7405)
Fresh Mark Inc ....B 330 833-9870
Massillon (G-13686)
Gorbett Enterprises of Solon ....E 440 248-3950
Solon (G-16853)
Interstate Warehousing VA LLC ....D 513 874-6500
Fairfield (G-10738)
RLR Investments LLC ....D 937 382-1494
Wilmington (G-19645)

WAREHOUSING & STORAGE, REFRIGERATED: Frozen Or Refrig Goods

Exel N Amercn Logistics Inc ....C 937 854-7900
Dayton (G-9422)

WAREHOUSING & STORAGE: Automobile, Dead Storage

Auto Warehousing Co Inc ....E 419 727-1534
Toledo (G-17603)

WAREHOUSING & STORAGE: General

A Duie Pyle Inc ....D 330 342-7750
Streetsboro (G-17243)
Aero Fulfillment Services Corp ....D 800 225-7145
Mason (G-13536)
Aero Fulfillment Services Corp ....D 513 874-4112
West Chester (G-18861)
Albring Vending Company ....E 419 726-8059
Toledo (G-17585)
All Pro Freight Systems Inc ....D 440 934-2222
Westlake (G-19313)
Andersons Inc ....C 419 891-6479
Maumee (G-13752)
Andersons Inc ....E 419 893-5050
Maumee (G-13755)
Arett Sales Corp ....D 937 552-2005
Troy (G-18195)
Asw Global LLC ....D 330 733-6291
Mogadore (G-14541)
Asw Global LLC ....D 330 899-1003
Canton (G-2196)
Asw Global LLC ....D 330 798-5184
Mogadore (G-14542)
Building Systems Trnsp Co ....C 740 852-9700
London (G-12861)
Burd Brothers Inc ....E 800 538-2873
Batavia (G-984)
Childrens Hospital Medical Ctr ....A 513 636-4200
Cincinnati (G-3191)
Cloverleaf Cold Storage Co ....C 419 599-5015
Napoleon (G-14800)
Comprehensive Logistics Co Inc ....E 800 734-0372
Youngstown (G-20008)
Containerport Group Inc ....E 216 341-4800
Cleveland (G-5343)
Cotter Mdse Stor of Ohio ....E 330 773-9177
Akron (G-160)
Crescent Park Corporation ....C 513 759-7000
West Chester (G-18906)
Daniel Logistics Inc ....D 614 367-9442
Columbus (G-7415)
Dhl Supply Chain (usa) ....E 419 727-4318
Toledo (G-17700)
Dhl Supply Chain (usa) ....D 513 482-6015
Cincinnati (G-3425)
Dhl Supply Chain (usa) ....E 513 942-1575
Cincinnati (G-3426)
Dhl Supply Chain (usa) ....E 513 745-7445
Blue Ash (G-1545)
Doylestown Telephone Company ....E 330 658-6666
Doylestown (G-10114)
E and P Warehouse Services Ltd ....E 330 898-4800
Warren (G-18704)
Efco Corp ....E 614 876-1226
Columbus (G-7509)
Exel Inc ....D 419 996-7703
Lima (G-12634)
Exel Inc ....D 419 226-5500
Lima (G-12635)
Exel Inc ....E 614 865-8294
Westerville (G-19162)
Exel Inc ....D 740 927-1762
Etna (G-10615)
Exel Inc ....B 614 865-8500
Westerville (G-19163)
Faro Services Inc ....C 614 497-1700
Groveport (G-11513)
First Group Investment Partnr ....D 513 241-2200
Cincinnati (G-3558)
Firstgroup Usa Inc ....B 513 241-2200
Cincinnati (G-3569)
G & J Pepsi-Cola Bottlers Inc ....D 740 593-3366
Athens (G-781)
G & J Pepsi-Cola Bottlers Inc ....E 937 393-5744
Wilmington (G-19624)
Getgo Transportation Co LLC ....E 419 666-6850
Millbury (G-14449)

Handl-It Inc ....C 330 468-0734
Macedonia (G-13073)
Hyperlogistics Group Inc ....E 614 497-0800
Columbus (G-7793)
Impact Fulfillment Svcs LLC ....C 614 262-8911
Columbus (G-7803)
J-Trac Inc ....E 419 524-3456
Mansfield (G-13189)
Keller Warehousing & Dist LLC ....C 419 784-4805
Defiance (G-9924)
Lesaint Logistics LLC ....E 513 874-3900
West Chester (G-18959)
Lewis & Michael Inc ....E 937 252-6683
Dayton (G-9564)
Liberty Insulation Co Inc ....E 513 621-0108
Milford (G-14400)
Mansfield Whsng & Dist Inc ....C 419 522-3510
Ontario (G-15560)
McM Electronics Inc ....D 937 434-0031
Dayton (G-9596)
Midwest Trmnals Tledo Intl Inc ....E 419 897-6868
Toledo (G-17917)
Mwd Logistics Inc ....E 419 342-6253
Shelby (G-16748)
Nifco America Corporation ....C 614 836-8733
Groveport (G-11528)
North Coast Logistics Inc ....E 216 362-7159
Brookpark (G-1903)
Osborne Trucking Company ....D 513 874-2090
Fairfield (G-10766)
Parker-Hannifin Corporation ....D 419 878-7000
Waterville (G-18790)
Peoples Cartage Inc ....E 330 833-8571
Massillon (G-13719)
Peoples Services Inc ....C 330 453-3709
Canton (G-2437)
Piqua Steel Co ....D 937 773-3632
Piqua (G-16020)
Restaurant Equippers Inc ....E 614 358-6622
Columbus (G-8526)
Ryder Last Mile Inc ....E 614 801-0621
Columbus (G-8566)
South E Harley Davidson Sls Co ....E 440 439-3013
Cleveland (G-6423)
Spartan Whse & Dist Co Inc ....D 614 497-1777
Columbus (G-8668)
Surface Combustion Inc ....E 419 878-8444
Waterville (G-18794)
Sygma Network Inc ....B 614 734-2500
Dublin (G-10348)
Synnex Corporation ....E 614 539-6995
Grove City (G-11475)
Taylor Warehouse Corporation ....E 513 771-2956
West Chester (G-19091)
Terminal Warehouse Inc ....D 330 773-2056
Canton (G-2508)
The Maple City Ice Company ....E 419 747-4777
Mansfield (G-13252)
Total Warehousing Services ....D 419 562-2878
Bucyrus (G-2002)
Triple Ladys Agency Inc ....E 330 274-1100
Mantua (G-13277)
TRT Management Corporation ....E 419 661-1233
Perrysburg (G-15927)
Whirlpool Corporation ....C 419 547-2610
Clyde (G-6755)
Willis Day Management Inc ....E 419 476-8000
Toledo (G-18159)
Wright Distribution Ctrs Inc ....E 419 227-7621
Lima (G-12785)

WAREHOUSING & STORAGE: General

Akron Porcelain & Plastics Co ....E 330 745-2159
Barberton (G-940)
Aldi Inc ....D 330 273-7351
Hinckley (G-11857)
AM Industrial Group LLC ....E 216 267-6783
Cleveland (G-4944)
Atotech USA Inc ....D 216 398-0550
Cleveland (G-5022)
Bartram & Sons Groceries ....E 740 532-5216
Ironton (G-12145)
Basista Furniture Inc ....E 216 398-5900
Cleveland (G-5040)
BDS Inc ....E 513 921-8441
Cincinnati (G-3028)
Big Sandy Distribution Inc ....C 740 574-2113
Franklin Furnace (G-11042)
Big Sandy Furniture Inc ....D 740 574-2113
Franklin Furnace (G-11043)

SERVICES

Big Sandy Furniture Inc ....E 740 354-3193
Portsmouth (G-16125)

Big Sandy Furniture Inc ....E 740 775-4244
Chillicothe (G-2758)

Big Sandy Furniture Inc ....E 740 894-4242
Chesapeake (G-2727)

Briar-Gate Realty Inc ....E 614 299-2121
Columbus (G-7062)

Commercial Warehouse & Cartage ....D 614 409-3901
Groveport (G-11502)

Compak Inc ....E 330 345-5666
Wooster (G-19711)

Comprehensive Logistics Co Inc ....C 330 233-0805
Parma (G-15762)

Comprehensive Logistics Co Inc ....E 440 934-0870
Lorain (G-12898)

Cotter Moving & Storage Co ....E 330 535-5115
Akron (G-161)

D & D Investment Co ....E 614 272-6567
Columbus (G-7405)

D M I Distribution Inc ....E 765 584-3234
Columbus (G-7410)

Daikin Applied Americas Inc ....E 763 553-5009
Dayton (G-9344)

Dayton Heidelberg Distrg Co ....C 419 666-9783
Perrysburg (G-15855)

Dedicated Logistics Inc ....D 513 275-1135
West Chester (G-18909)

Dhl Supply Chain (usa) ....D 614 895-1959
Westerville (G-19158)

Dolgencorp LLC ....A 740 588-5700
Zanesville (G-20299)

DSC Logistics LLC ....D 847 390-6800
Toledo (G-17704)

Enterprise Vending Inc ....E 513 772-1373
Cincinnati (G-3500)

Essilor of America Inc ....C 614 492-0888
Groveport (G-11510)

Exel Inc ....E 614 670-6473
Lockbourne (G-12815)

Federal Express Corporation ....B 614 492-6106
Columbus (G-7568)

Fedex Sup Chain Dist Sys Inc ....B 412 820-3700
Lockbourne (G-12818)

Fremont Logistics LLC ....D 419 333-0669
Fremont (G-11077)

Fuchs Lubricants Co ....E 330 963-0400
Twinsburg (G-18270)

Fusion Ceramics Inc ....E 330 627-5821
Carrollton (G-2569)

G & S Metal Products Co Inc ....C 216 831-2388
Cleveland (G-5585)

Gateway Distribution Inc ....E 513 891-4477
Cincinnati (G-3604)

General Motors LLC ....C 513 874-0535
West Chester (G-18931)

GMI Holdings Inc ....D 330 794-0846
Akron (G-238)

Goodwill Ester Seals Miami Vly ....B 937 461-4800
Dayton (G-9465)

Graham Investment Co ....D 740 382-0902
Marion (G-13422)

Great Value Storage ....E 614 848-8420
Columbus (G-7690)

Hofstetter Orran Inc ....E 330 683-8070
Orrville (G-15634)

Home City Ice Company ....C 513 574-1800
Cincinnati (G-3718)

Ieh Auto Parts LLC ....E 216 351-2560
Cleveland (G-5735)

Ingersoll-Rand Company ....E 419 633-6800
Bryan (G-1960)

Inter Distr Svcs of Cleve ....E 330 468-4949
Macedonia (G-13075)

J B Express Inc ....D 740 702-9830
Chillicothe (G-2794)

Jacobson Warehouse Company Inc ....E 614 409-0003
Groveport (G-11523)

Jacobson Warehouse Company Inc ....D 614 497-6300
Groveport (G-11524)

Keller Logistics Group Inc ....E 866 276-9486
Defiance (G-9923)

King Tut Logistics LLC ....E 614 538-0509
Columbus (G-7908)

Kuehne + Nagel Inc ....E 419 635-4051
Port Clinton (G-16111)

Lakota Local School District ....C 513 777-2150
Liberty Township (G-12582)

Lesaint Logistics Inc ....C 513 874-3900
West Chester (G-18958)

Lesaint Logistics LLC ....D 513 988-0101
Trenton (G-18188)

Liverpool Coil Processing Inc ....C 330 558-2600
Valley City (G-18465)

Locker Moving & Storage Inc ....E 330 784-0477
Canton (G-2380)

M A Folkes Company Inc ....E 513 785-4200
Hamilton (G-11626)

Malleys Candies Inc ....E 216 529-6262
Cleveland (G-5903)

Marc Glassman Inc ....C 216 265-7700
Cleveland (G-5906)

Matandy Steel & Metal Pdts LLC ....D 513 844-2277
Hamilton (G-11627)

Menlo Logistics Inc ....D 740 963-1154
Etna (G-10617)

Micro Electronics Inc ....D 614 334-1430
Columbus (G-8071)

Mid State Systems Inc ....D 740 928-1115
Hebron (G-11717)

Mid-Ohio Mechanical Inc ....E 740 587-3362
Granville (G-11346)

Midwest Trmnals Tledo Intl Inc ....E 419 698-8171
Toledo (G-17918)

Millwood Inc ....E 330 393-4400
Vienna (G-18582)

Neighborhood Logistics Co Inc ....E 440 466-0020
Geneva (G-11244)

New Age Logistics LLC ....E 440 439-0846
Cleveland (G-6059)

Odw Logistics Inc ....B 614 549-5000
Columbus (G-8225)

Ohio Desk Co ....E 216 623-0600
Brooklyn Heights (G-1877)

P-Americas LLC ....C 330 746-7652
Youngstown (G-20149)

Parker-Hannifin Corporation ....A 216 531-3000
Cleveland (G-6171)

PC Connection Sales Corp ....C 937 382-4800
Wilmington (G-19638)

Pepsi-Cola Metro Btlg Co Inc ....E 330 336-3553
Wadsworth (G-18611)

Pepsi-Cola Metro Btlg Co Inc ....E 440 323-5524
Elyria (G-10554)

Precision Strip Inc ....D 937 667-6255
Tipp City (G-17565)

Precision Strip Inc ....C 419 628-2343
Minster (G-14540)

Precision Strip Inc ....C 419 674-4186
Kenton (G-12286)

Precision Strip Inc ....D 419 661-1100
Perrysburg (G-15905)

Precision Strip Inc ....D 513 423-4166
Middletown (G-14321)

Prime Time Enterprises Inc ....E 440 891-8855
Cleveland (G-6236)

Reliable Rnners Curier Svc Inc ....E 440 578-1011
Mentor (G-14103)

Restaurant Depot LLC ....E 216 525-0101
Cleveland (G-6316)

Roppe Holding Company ....E 419 435-9335
Fostoria (G-11011)

RR Donnelley & Sons Company ....E 614 539-5527
Grove City (G-11466)

Safelite Fulfillment Inc ....E 614 781-5449
Columbus (G-8573)

Safelite Fulfillment Inc ....E 216 475-7781
Cleveland (G-6363)

Sally Beauty Supply LLC ....C 937 548-7684
Greenville (G-11394)

Sally Beauty Supply LLC ....C 614 278-1691
Columbus (G-8584)

SH Bell Company ....E 412 963-9910
East Liverpool (G-10417)

Specialty Logistics Inc ....E 513 421-2041
Cincinnati (G-4512)

Springfield Cartage LLC ....D 937 222-2120
Dayton (G-9785)

Springs Window Fashions LLC ....D 614 492-6770
Groveport (G-11538)

The C-Z Company ....E 740 432-6334
Cambridge (G-2085)

Tmarzetti Company ....C 614 277-3577
Grove City (G-11477)

Top Dawg Group LLC ....E 216 398-1066
Brooklyn Heights (G-1883)

Twist Inc ....E 937 675-9581
Xenia (G-19931)

United Retail Logistics Svcs ....C 937 332-1500
Troy (G-18235)

Utility Trailer Mfg Co ....E 513 436-2600
Batavia (G-1015)

Ventra Salem LLC ....E 330 337-3240
Salem (G-16565)

Verst Group Logistics Inc ....C 513 782-1725
Cincinnati (G-4756)

Verst Group Logistics Inc ....E 513 772-2494
Cincinnati (G-4757)

Victory White Metal Company ....E 216 271-1400
Cleveland (G-6629)

Walmart Inc ....B 937 843-3681
Belle Center (G-1342)

Wannemacher Enterprises Inc ....D 419 225-9060
Lima (G-12775)

Warehouse Services Group Llc ....E 419 868-6400
Holland (G-11926)

Westway Trml Cincinnati LLC ....E 513 921-8441
Cincinnati (G-4793)

WW Grainger Inc ....C 330 425-8387
Macedonia (G-13090)

WAREHOUSING & STORAGE: Liquid

BDS Inc ....E 513 921-8441
Cincinnati (G-3028)

WAREHOUSING & STORAGE: Miniwarehouse

Public Storage ....E 216 220-7978
Bedford Heights (G-1325)

WAREHOUSING & STORAGE: Refrigerated

Cloverleaf Cold Storage Co ....C 419 599-5015
Napoleon (G-14800)

Crescent Park Corporation ....C 513 759-7000
West Chester (G-18906)

Woodruff Enterprises Inc ....E 937 399-9300
Springfield (G-17138)

WAREHOUSING & STORAGE: Self Storage

Al-Mar Lanes ....E 419 352-4637
Bowling Green (G-1713)

Compass Self Storage LLC ....E 216 458-0670
Cleveland (G-5330)

Fulfillment Technologies LLC ....C 513 346-3100
West Chester (G-19055)

Oatey Supply Chain Svcs Inc ....E 216 267-7100
Cleveland (G-6111)

WAREHOUSING & STORAGE: Textile

Thirty-One Gifts LLC ....A 614 414-4300
Columbus (G-8745)

WARM AIR HEATING & AC EQPT & SPLYS, WHOLESALE Air Filters

Swift Filters Inc ....E 440 735-0995
Oakwood Village (G-15494)

WARM AIR HEATING & AC EQPT & SPLYS, WHOLESALE Furnaces

Famous Distribution Inc ....E 330 434-5194
Akron (G-211)

Famous Distribution Inc ....D 330 762-9621
Akron (G-210)

WARM AIR HEATING & AC EQPT & SPLYS, WHOLESALE Furnaces, Elec

Famous II Inc ....D 330 762-9621
Akron (G-213)

The Famous Manufacturing Co ....E 330 762-9621
Akron (G-469)

WARM AIR HEATING/AC EQPT/SPLYS, WHOL Warm Air Htg Eqpt/Splys

Allied Supply Company Inc ....E 937 224-9833
Dayton (G-9216)

Famous Enterprises Inc ....E 330 762-9621
Akron (G-212)

Famous Enterprises Inc ....E 216 529-1010
Cleveland (G-5511)

Habegger Corporation ....E 513 853-6644
Cincinnati (G-3668)

Lakeside Supply Co ....E 216 941-6800
Cleveland (G-5849)

OEM Parts Outlet ....E 419 472-2237
Toledo *(G-17957)*
Slawson Equipment Co Inc ....E 216 391-7263
Cleveland *(G-6416)*
WW Grainger Inc ....E 614 276-5231
Columbus *(G-8921)*

WARM AIR HEATING/AC EQPT/SPLYS, WHOL: Ventilating Eqpt/Sply

American Hood Systems Inc ....E 440 365-4567
Elyria *(G-10478)*

WARRANTY INSURANCE: Automobile

Dimension Service Corporation ....C 614 226-7455
Dublin *(G-10200)*
Heritage Wrranty Insur Rrg Inc ....D 800 753-5236
Dublin *(G-10241)*

WASHERS: Metal

Andre Corporation ....E 574 293-0207
Mason *(G-13540)*
Atlas Bolt & Screw Company LLC ....C 419 289-6171
Ashland *(G-653)*

WASTE CLEANING SVCS

Bedford Heights City Waste ....E 440 439-5343
Bedford *(G-1270)*

WATCH REPAIR SVCS

Cox Paving Inc ....D 937 780-3075
Wshngtn CT Hs *(G-19867)*

WATCHES & PARTS, WHOLESALE

Toledo Jewelers Supply Co ....E 419 241-4181
Toledo *(G-18088)*

WATER SOFTENER SVCS

Chardon Laboratories Inc ....E 614 860-1000
Reynoldsburg *(G-16291)*
Clearwater Services Inc ....D 330 836-4946
Akron *(G-142)*
Cwm Envronmental Cleveland LLC .....E 216 663-0808
Cleveland *(G-5401)*
Empire One LLC ....E 330 628-9310
Mogadore *(G-14548)*
Hague Water Conditioning Inc ....E 614 482-8121
Groveport *(G-11515)*
Western Rserve Wtr Systems Inc ....D 216 341-9797
Newburgh Heights *(G-15116)*

WATER SOFTENING WHOLESALERS

Hague Water Conditioning Inc ....E 614 482-8121
Groveport *(G-11515)*

WATER SPLY: Irrigation

City of Westerville ....E 614 901-6500
Westerville *(G-19236)*
Pentair Rsdntial Fltration LLC ....E 440 286-4116
Chardon *(G-2708)*
Warstler Brothers Landscaping ....E 330 492-9500
Canton *(G-2531)*

WATER SUPPLY

Aqua Ohio Inc ....E 440 255-3984
Mentor *(G-14019)*
Aqua Ohio Inc ....E 330 832-5764
Massillon *(G-13663)*
Aqua Pennsylvania Inc ....E 614 882-6586
Westerville *(G-19221)*
Belmont County of Ohio ....E 740 695-3144
Saint Clairsville *(G-16473)*
City Alliance Water Sewer Dst ....E 330 823-5216
Alliance *(G-525)*
City of Akron ....E 330 678-0077
Kent *(G-12221)*
City of Akron ....C 330 375-2420
Akron *(G-135)*
City of Avon Lake ....E 440 933-6226
Avon Lake *(G-912)*
City of Celina ....E 419 586-2451
Celina *(G-2588)*
City of Cleveland ....E 216 664-3121
Cleveland *(G-5191)*

City of Cleveland Heights ....E 216 291-5995
Cleveland Heights *(G-6717)*
City of Columbus ....E 614 645-7490
Columbus *(G-7206)*
City of Columbus ....E 614 645-8297
Columbus *(G-7212)*
City of Columbus ....D 614 645-8270
Columbus *(G-7210)*
City of Cuyahoga Falls ....E 330 971-8130
Cuyahoga Falls *(G-9082)*
City of Dayton ....C 937 333-6070
Dayton *(G-9306)*
City of Dayton ....E 937 333-3725
Dayton *(G-9304)*
City of Huron ....D 419 433-5000
Huron *(G-12023)*
City of Lorain ....E 440 288-0281
Lorain *(G-12890)*
City of Lorain ....C 440 204-2500
Lorain *(G-12891)*
City of Massillon ....E 330 833-3304
Massillon *(G-13671)*
City of Toledo ....D 419 245-1800
Toledo *(G-17654)*
City of Troy ....E 937 335-1914
Troy *(G-18198)*
City of Westerville ....E 614 901-6500
Westerville *(G-19236)*
City of Youngstown ....E 330 742-8749
Youngstown *(G-19992)*
Clearwater Services Inc ....D 330 836-4946
Akron *(G-142)*
Cleveland Water Department ....A 216 664-3168
Cleveland *(G-5296)*
County of Licking ....E 740 967-5951
Johnstown *(G-12199)*
County of Warren ....D 513 925-1377
Lebanon *(G-12459)*
Del-Co Water Company Inc ....D 740 548-7746
Delaware *(G-9966)*
East Liverpool Water Dept ....E 330 385-8812
East Liverpool *(G-10402)*
Employment Relations Board ....E 513 863-0828
Hamilton *(G-11594)*
Hecla Water Association ....E 740 533-0526
Ironton *(G-12154)*
Highland County Water Co Inc ....E 937 393-4281
Hillsboro *(G-11844)*
Medical Center Co (inc) ....E 216 368-4256
Cleveland *(G-5942)*
Muskingum Wtrshed Cnsrvncy Dst .....B 330 343-6647
New Philadelphia *(G-14974)*
New Lexington City of ....E 740 342-1633
New Lexington *(G-14922)*
Northast Ohio Rgonal Sewer Dst ....C 216 881-6600
Cleveland *(G-6081)*
Northern Ohio Rural Water ....E 419 668-7213
Norwalk *(G-15446)*
Northwestern Water & Sewer Dst ....E 419 354-9090
Bowling Green *(G-1742)*
Ohio-American Water Co Inc ....E 740 382-3993
Marion *(G-13451)*
Ross County Water Company Inc ....E 740 774-4117
Chillicothe *(G-2822)*
Rural Lorain County Water Auth ....D 440 355-5121
Lagrange *(G-12326)*
Scioto County Region Wtr Dst 1 ....E 740 259-2301
Lucasville *(G-13053)*
Syracuse Water Dept ....E 740 992-7777
Pomeroy *(G-16097)*
The Mahoning Valley Sani Dst ....D 330 799-6315
Mineral Ridge *(G-14514)*
Toledo Cy Pub Utlity Wtr Distr ....C 419 936-2506
Toledo *(G-18082)*
Twin City Water and Sewer Dst ....E 740 922-1460
Dennison *(G-10055)*
Victory White Metal Company ....E 216 271-1400
Cleveland *(G-6629)*

WATER: Distilled

Distillata Company ....D 216 771-2900
Cleveland *(G-5428)*

WATERBEDS & ACCESS STORES

Waterbeds n Stuff Inc ....E 614 871-1171
Grove City *(G-11483)*

WEATHER FORECASTING SVCS

National Weather Service ....E 937 383-0031
Wilmington *(G-19636)*
National Weather Service ....E 216 265-2370
Cleveland *(G-6050)*
National Weather Service ....E 419 522-1375
Mansfield *(G-13226)*

WEDDING CHAPEL: Privately Operated

Delaware Golf Club Inc ....E 740 362-2582
Delaware *(G-9969)*
Hall Nazareth Inc ....D 419 832-2900
Grand Rapids *(G-11325)*

WELDING EQPT & SPLYS WHOLESALERS

Airgas Inc ....B 866 935-3370
Cleveland *(G-4919)*
Airgas Inc ....D 937 222-8312
Moraine *(G-14619)*
Airgas Usa LLC ....E 513 563-8070
Cincinnati *(G-2916)*
Airgas Usa LLC ....B 216 642-6600
Independence *(G-12042)*
Albright Welding Supply Co Inc ....E 330 264-2021
Wooster *(G-19685)*
Daihen Inc ....E 937 667-0800
Tipp City *(G-17555)*
Lefeld Welding & Stl Sups Inc ....E 419 678-2397
Coldwater *(G-6762)*
Matheson Tri-Gas Inc ....E 614 771-1311
Hilliard *(G-11788)*
Nelson Stud Welding Inc ....E 440 250-9242
Elyria *(G-10543)*
O E Meyer Co ....C 419 625-1256
Sandusky *(G-16631)*
Praxair Distribution Inc ....E 330 376-2242
Akron *(G-393)*
Taylor - Winfield Corporation ....D 330 797-0300
Youngstown *(G-20220)*
Weld Plus Inc ....E 513 941-4411
Cincinnati *(G-4775)*
Wright Brothers Inc ....E 513 731-2222
Cincinnati *(G-4807)*

WELDING REPAIR SVC

A & C Welding Inc ....E 330 762-4777
Peninsula *(G-15808)*
A & G Manufacturing Co Inc ....E 419 468-7433
Galion *(G-11164)*
Abbott Tool Inc ....E 419 476-6742
Toledo *(G-17579)*
All-Type Welding & Fabrication ....E 440 439-3990
Cleveland *(G-4936)*
Allied Fabricating & Wldg Co ....E 614 751-6664
Columbus *(G-6897)*
ARC Gas & Supply LLC ....E 216 341-5882
Cleveland *(G-5004)*
Arctech Fabricating Inc ....E 937 525-9353
Springfield *(G-16997)*
Athens Mold and Machine Inc ....D 740 593-6613
Athens *(G-768)*
Bayloff Stmped Pdts Knsman Inc ....D 330 876-4511
Kinsman *(G-12317)*
Blevins Metal Fabrication Inc ....E 419 522-6082
Mansfield *(G-13143)*
Breitinger Company ....C 419 526-4255
Mansfield *(G-13145)*
Byron Products Inc ....D 513 870-9111
Fairfield *(G-10704)*
C & R Inc ....E 614 497-1130
Groveport *(G-11498)*
C-N-D Industries Inc ....E 330 478-8811
Massillon *(G-13667)*
Carter Manufacturing Co Inc ....E 513 398-7303
Mason *(G-13550)*
Chipmatic Tool & Machine Inc ....D 419 862-2737
Elmore *(G-10472)*
Cleveland Jsm Inc ....D 440 876-3050
Strongsville *(G-17291)*
Compton Metal Products Inc ....D 937 382-2403
Wilmington *(G-19618)*
Creative Mold and Machine Inc ....E 440 338-5146
Newbury *(G-15119)*
Crest Bending Inc ....E 419 492-2108
New Washington *(G-15001)*
Custom Machine Inc ....E 419 986-5122
Tiffin *(G-17515)*

SERVICES

Dynamic Weld Corporation ....E 419 582-2900
Osgood (G-15652)
East End Welding Company ....C 330 677-6000
Kent (G-12230)
Falls Stamping & Welding Co ....C 330 928-1191
Cuyahoga Falls (G-9092)
Fosbel Inc ....C 216 362-3900
Cleveland (G-5565)
Fosbel Holding Inc ....E 216 362-3900
Cleveland (G-5566)
Gaspar Inc ....D 330 477-2222
Canton (G-2322)
General Tool Company ....C 513 733-5500
Cincinnati (G-3616)
George Steel Fabricating Inc ....E 513 932-2887
Lebanon (G-12466)
Glenridge Machine Co ....E 440 975-1055
Willoughby (G-19526)
Habco Tool and Dev Co Inc ....E 440 946-5546
Mentor (G-14058)
HI Tecmetal Group Inc ....E 440 946-2280
Willoughby (G-19528)
HI Tecmetal Group Inc ....E 440 373-5101
Wickliffe (G-19463)
Hi-Tek Manufacturing Inc ....C 513 459-1094
Mason (G-13595)
Hobart Bros Stick Electrode ....C 937 332-5375
Troy (G-18206)
J & S Industrial Mch Pdts Inc ....D 419 691-1380
Toledo (G-17827)
Jerl Machine Inc ....D 419 873-0270
Perrysburg (G-15882)
JMw Welding and Mfg ....E 330 484-2428
Canton (G-2361)
K-M-S Industries Inc ....E 440 243-6680
Brookpark (G-1899)
Kings Welding and Fabg Inc ....E 330 738-3592
Mechanicstown (G-13905)
Kottler Metal Products Co Inc ....E 440 946-7473
Willoughby (G-19535)
L B Industries Inc ....E 330 750-1002
Struthers (G-17366)
Laserflex Corporation ....D 614 850-9600
Hilliard (G-11783)
Liberty Casting Company LLC ....E 740 363-1941
Delaware (G-9996)
Lima Sheet Metal Machine & Mfg .....E 419 229-1161
Lima (G-12687)
Long-Stanton Mfg Company ....E 513 874-8020
West Chester (G-18964)
Majestic Tool and Machine Inc ....E 440 248-5058
Solon (G-16869)
Marsam Metalfab Inc ....E 330 405-1520
Twinsburg (G-18295)
Meta Manufacturing Corporation .....E 513 793-6382
Blue Ash (G-1612)
Norman Noble Inc ....C 216 761-2133
Cleveland (G-6073)
Northwind Industries Inc ....E 216 433-0666
Cleveland (G-6099)
Ohio Hydraulics Inc ....E 513 771-2590
Cincinnati (G-4155)
Ohio State University ....E 614 292-4139
Columbus (G-8306)
Pentaflex Inc ....E 937 325-5551
Springfield (G-17096)
Phillips Mfg and Tower Co ....D 419 347-1720
Shelby (G-16749)
Precision Mtal Fabrication Inc ....D 937 235-9261
Dayton (G-9702)
Precision Welding Corporation ....E 216 524-6110
Cleveland (G-6226)
Prout Boiler Htg & Wldg Inc ....E 330 744-0293
Youngstown (G-20167)
Quality Welding Inc ....E 419 483-6067
Bellevue (G-1384)
Quality Wldg & Fabrication LLC ....D 419 225-6208
Lima (G-12727)
Rbm Environmental and Cnstr ....E 419 693-5840
Oregon (G-15607)
Schmidt Machine Company ....E 419 294-3814
Upper Sandusky (G-18412)
Steubenville Truck Center Inc ....E 740 282-2711
Steubenville (G-17173)
Tendon Manufacturing Inc ....E 216 663-3200
Cleveland (G-6512)
Triangle Precision Industries ....D 937 299-6776
Dayton (G-9822)
Two M Precision Co Inc ....E 440 946-2120
Willoughby (G-19578)

Valley Machine Tool Co Inc ....E 513 899-2737
Morrow (G-14717)
Viking Fabricators Inc ....E 740 374-5246
Marietta (G-13397)
Wayne Trail Technologies Inc ....D 937 295-2120
Fort Loramie (G-10986)

WELDING SPLYS, EXC GASES: Wholesalers

Albright Welding Supply Co Inc ....E 330 264-2021
Wooster (G-19685)
Delille Oxygen Company ....E 614 444-1177
Columbus (G-7432)
F & M Mafco Inc ....C 513 367-2151
Harrison (G-11666)

WELDMENTS

American Tank & Fabricating Co ....C 216 252-1500
Cleveland (G-4967)
Loveman Steel Corporation ....D 440 232-6200
Bedford (G-1289)

WELFARE PENSIONS

County of Seneca ....D 419 447-5011
Tiffin (G-17514)

WHEELS

Rocknstarr Holdings LLC ....E 330 509-9086
Youngstown (G-20189)

WHEELS & BRAKE SHOES: Railroad, Cast Iron

Amsted Industries Incorporated ....C 614 836-2323
Groveport (G-11493)

WINDOW & DOOR FRAMES

Midwest Curtainwalls Inc ....D 216 641-7900
Cleveland (G-5989)

WINDOW CLEANING SVCS

Aetna Building Maintenance Inc ....D 937 324-5711
Springfield (G-16992)
Ajax Cleaning Contractors Co ....D 216 881-8484
Cleveland (G-4924)
Clearview Cleaning Contractors ....E 216 621-6688
Cleveland (G-5224)
E Wynn Inc ....E 614 444-5288
Columbus (G-7487)
H & B Window Cleaning Inc ....E 440 934-6158
Avon Lake (G-918)
Ohio Window Cleaning Inc ....D 937 877-0832
Tipp City (G-17563)

WINDOW FRAMES & SASHES: Plastic

Champion Opco LLC ....B 513 327-7338
Cincinnati (G-3168)

WINDOW FRAMES, MOLDING & TRIM: Vinyl

Modern Builders Supply Inc ....C 419 241-3961
Toledo (G-17922)
Owens Corning Sales LLC ....A 419 248-8000
Toledo (G-17968)
Vinyl Design Corporation ....E 419 283-4009
Holland (G-11925)

WINE & DISTILLED ALCOHOLIC BEVERAGES WHOLESALERS

Dayton Heidelberg Distrg Co ....C 419 666-9783
Perrysburg (G-15855)
Esber Beverage Company ....E 330 456-4361
Canton (G-2306)
Glazers Distributors Ohio Inc ....E 440 542-7000
Solon (G-16852)
M & A Distributing Co Inc ....E 440 703-4580
Solon (G-16868)
M & A Distributing Co Inc ....D 614 294-3555
Columbus (G-8002)

WINE CELLARS, BONDED: Wine, Blended

Georgetown Vineyards Inc ....E 740 435-3222
Cambridge (G-2069)

WIRE & WIRE PRDTS

Dolin Supply Co ....E 304 529-4171
South Point (G-16932)
Efco Corp ....E 614 876-1226
Columbus (G-7509)
Gateway Concrete Forming Svcs ....D 513 353-2000
Miamitown (G-14241)
Panacea Products Corporation ....E 614 850-7000
Columbus (G-8418)
Schweizer Dipple Inc ....D 440 786-8090
Cleveland (G-6378)

WIRE FENCING & ACCESS WHOLESALERS

Agratronix LLC ....E 330 562-2222
Streetsboro (G-17245)
Mills Fence Co Inc ....E 513 631-0333
Cincinnati (G-4057)
Richards Whl Fence Co Inc ....E 330 773-0423
Akron (G-407)
Security Fence Group Inc ....E 513 681-3700
Cincinnati (G-4444)

WIRE MATERIALS: Steel

Bayloff Stmped Pdts Knsman Inc ......D 330 876-4511
Kinsman (G-12317)
File Sharpening Company Inc ....E 937 376-8268
Xenia (G-19899)
Noco Company ....B 216 464-8131
Solon (G-16879)

WIRE WINDING OF PURCHASED WIRE

Providence Rees Inc ....E 614 833-6231
Columbus (G-8474)

WIRE, FLAT: Strip, Cold-Rolled, Exc From Hot-Rolled Mills

Hynes Industries Inc ....C 330 799-3221
Youngstown (G-20073)

WIRE: Nonferrous

Electrovations Inc ....E 330 274-3558
Aurora (G-826)
Legrand North America LLC ....B 937 224-0639
Dayton (G-9561)
Radix Wire Co ....D 216 731-9191
Cleveland (G-6279)
Scott Fetzer Company ....C 216 267-9000
Cleveland (G-6379)

WOMEN'S & CHILDREN'S CLOTHING WHOLESALERS, NEC

Abercrombie & Fitch Trading Co ....E 614 283-6500
New Albany (G-14839)
Cheek-O Inc ....E 513 942-4880
Cincinnati (G-3174)
Classic Imports Inc ....E 330 262-5277
Wooster (G-19706)
For Women Like Me Inc ....E 407 848-7339
Chagrin Falls (G-2645)
J Peterman Company LLC ....E 888 647-2555
Blue Ash (G-1588)
Mast Industries Inc ....C 614 415-7000
Columbus (G-8034)
Mast Industries Inc ....D 614 856-6000
Reynoldsburg (G-16319)
McCc Sportswear Inc ....E 513 583-9210
West Chester (G-19065)
MGF Sourcing Us LLC ....D 614 904-3300
Columbus (G-8066)
Rassak LLC ....E 513 791-9453
Cincinnati (G-4339)
West Chester Holdings LLC ....C 800 647-1900
Cincinnati (G-4781)
Zimmer Enterprises Inc ....E 937 428-1057
Dayton (G-9899)

WOMEN'S & GIRLS' SPORTSWEAR WHOLESALERS

Barbs Graffiti Inc ....D 216 881-5550
Cleveland (G-5035)
Barbs Graffiti Inc ....E 216 881-5550
Cleveland (G-5036)
Gymnastic World Inc ....E 440 526-2970
Cleveland (G-5649)

Heritage Sportswear Inc ....D 740 928-7771
Hebron (G-11715)
R & A Sports Inc ....E 216 289-2254
Euclid (G-10654)
TSC Apparel LLC ....D 513 771-1138
Cincinnati (G-4651)

WOMEN'S CLOTHING STORES

Abercrombie & Fitch Trading Co ....E 614 283-6500
New Albany (G-14839)
For Women Like Me Inc ....E 407 848-7339
Chagrin Falls (G-2645)
J Peterman Company LLC ....E 888 647-2555
Blue Ash (G-1588)

WOOD & WOOD BY-PRDTS, WHOLESALE

77 Coach Supply Ltd ....E 330 674-1454
Millersburg (G-14452)
Earth n Wood Products Inc ....E 330 644-1858
Akron (G-199)
Gross Lumber Inc ....E 330 683-2055
Apple Creek (G-619)
Premium Beverage Supply Ltd ....E 614 777-1007
Hilliard (G-11807)

WOOD CHIPS, PRODUCED AT THE MILL

Miller Logging Inc ....E 330 279-4721
Holmesville (G-11932)

WOOD PRDTS: Moldings, Unfinished & Prefinished

J McCoy Lumber Co Ltd ....E 937 587-3423
Peebles (G-15803)

WOOD PRDTS: Mulch, Wood & Bark

Gayston Corporation ....C 937 743-6050
Miamisburg (G-14173)
Scotts Company LLC ....B 937 644-0011
Marysville (G-13528)

WOOD PRDTS: Survey Stakes

Lawnview Industries Inc ....C 937 653-5217
Urbana (G-18438)

WOODWORK & TRIM: Interior & Ornamental

LE Smith Company ....D 419 636-4555
Bryan (G-1961)

WORK EXPERIENCE CENTER

Mary Hmmond Adult Actvties Ctr ....D 740 962-4200
McConnelsville (G-13901)
TAC Industries Inc ....B 937 328-5200
Springfield (G-17123)
Trumbull Cmnty Action Program ....E 330 393-2507
Warren (G-18754)

X-RAY EQPT & TUBES

Philips Medical Systems Clevel ....B 440 247-2652
Cleveland (G-6203)

X-RAY EQPT REPAIR SVCS

Alpha Imaging LLC ....E 440 953-3800
Willoughby (G-19504)

YACHT CLUBS

Atwood Yacht Club Inc ....E 330 735-2135
Sherrodsville (G-16752)
Blennerhassett Yacht Club Inc ....E 740 423-9062
Belpre (G-1400)
Buckeye Lake Yacht Club Inc ....E 740 929-4466
Buckeye Lake (G-1974)
Cleveland Yachting Club Inc ....D 440 333-1155
Cleveland (G-5298)

Mentor Lagoons Yacht Club Inc ....D 440 205-3625
Mentor (G-14081)
Wildwood Yacht Club Inc ....D 216 531-9052
Cleveland (G-6683)

YOUTH CAMPS

Family YMCA of LANcstr&fairfld ....D 740 277-7373
Lancaster (G-12403)
Findlay Y M C A Child Dev ....E 419 422-3174
Findlay (G-10908)
Galion Community Center YMCA ....E 419 468-7754
Galion (G-11173)
Great Miami Valley YMCA ....A 513 887-0001
Hamilton (G-11602)
Great Miami Valley YMCA ....C 513 892-9622
Fairfield Township (G-10808)
Great Miami Valley YMCA ....D 513 887-0014
Hamilton (G-11604)
Great Miami Valley YMCA ....D 513 868-9622
Hamilton (G-11605)
Great Miami Valley YMCA ....D 513 829-3091
Fairfield (G-10732)
Hardin County Family YMCA ....E 419 673-6131
Kenton (G-12279)
Highland County Family YMCA ....E 937 840-9622
Hillsboro (G-11842)
Huber Heights YMCA ....D 937 236-9622
Dayton (G-9508)
Lake County YMCA ....C 440 352-3303
Painesville (G-15718)
Lake County YMCA ....C 440 946-1160
Willoughby (G-19538)
Lake County YMCA ....E 440 259-2724
Perry (G-15824)
Lake County YMCA ....D 440 428-5125
Madison (G-13099)
Pike County YMCA ....E 740 947-8862
Waverly (G-18822)
Red Oak Camp ....E 440 256-0716
Willoughby (G-19565)
Springfield Family Y M C A ....D 937 323-3781
Springfield (G-17119)
Sycamore Board of Education ....D 513 489-3937
Cincinnati (G-4560)
Ucc Childrens Center ....E 513 217-5501
Middletown (G-14356)
Y M C A Central Stark County ....E 330 305-5437
Canton (G-2539)
Y M C A Central Stark County ....E 330 875-1611
Louisville (G-12975)
Y M C A Central Stark County ....E 330 877-8933
Uniontown (G-18392)
Y M C A Central Stark County ....E 330 830-6275
Massillon (G-13736)
Y M C A Central Stark County ....E 330 498-4082
Canton (G-2540)
Y M C A of Ashland Ohio Inc ....D 419 289-0626
Ashland (G-700)
YMCA ....E 330 823-1930
Alliance (G-558)
YMCA of Clermont County Inc ....E 513 724-9622
Batavia (G-1016)
YMCA of Massillon ....E 330 879-0800
Navarre (G-14826)
Young Mens Christian ....B 513 932-1424
Lebanon (G-12516)
Young Mens Christian Assn ....E 419 238-0443
Van Wert (G-18498)
Young Mens Christian Assoc ....E 419 729-8135
Toledo (G-18167)
Young Mens Christian Assoc ....C 614 871-9622
Grove City (G-11491)
Young Mens Christian Assoc ....E 937 223-5201
Dayton (G-9892)
Young Mens Christian Assoc ....D 330 923-5223
Cuyahoga Falls (G-9141)
Young Mens Christian Assoc ....E 330 467-8366
Macedonia (G-13091)
Young Mens Christian Assoc ....E 330 784-0408
Akron (G-507)

Young Mens Christian Assoc ....C 614 416-9622
Gahanna (G-11152)
Young Mens Christian Assoc ....C 614 334-9622
Hilliard (G-11832)
Young Mens Christian Assoc ....E 937 312-1810
Dayton (G-9893)
Young Mens Christian Assoc ....E 614 539-1770
Urbancrest (G-18453)
Young Mens Christian Assoc ....D 614 252-3166
Columbus (G-8929)
Young Mens Christian Assoc ....E 937 593-9001
Bellefontaine (G-1370)
Young Mens Christian Associat ....D 513 241-9622
Cincinnati (G-4815)
Young Mens Christian Associat ....D 513 923-4466
Cincinnati (G-4816)
Young Mens Christian Associat ....E 419 474-3995
Toledo (G-18169)
Young Mens Christian Associat ....D 419 866-9622
Maumee (G-13871)
Young Mens Christian Associat ....C 419 475-3496
Toledo (G-18170)
Young Mens Christian Associat ....D 419 691-3523
Oregon (G-15615)
Young Mens Christian Mt Vernon ....D 740 392-9622
Mount Vernon (G-14794)
Young MNS Chrstn Assn Clveland ....E 216 521-8400
Lakewood (G-12364)
Young MNS Chrstn Assn Clveland ....E 216 731-7454
Cleveland (G-6703)
Young MNS Chrstn Assn Clveland ....D 440 285-7543
Chardon (G-2726)
Young MNS Chrstn Assn Grter NY ....D 740 392-9622
Mount Vernon (G-14795)
Young Womens Christian ....D 419 241-3235
Toledo (G-18172)
Young Womens Christian ....E 419 238-6639
Van Wert (G-18499)
Young Womens Christian Assn ....E 614 224-9121
Columbus (G-8931)
Young Womens Christian Associ ....E 216 881-6878
Cleveland (G-6705)
Young Womns Chrstn Assc Canton ....D 330 453-0789
Canton (G-2543)
YWCA Dayton ....E 937 461-5550
Dayton (G-9896)
YWCA Mahoning Valley ....E 330 746-6361
Youngstown (G-20269)
YWCA of Greater Cincinnati ....E 513 241-7090
Cincinnati (G-4817)
YWCA Shelter & Housing Network ....E 937 222-6333
Dayton (G-9897)

YOUTH SELF-HELP AGENCY

Help ME Grow ....E 419 738-4773
Wapakoneta (G-18646)

ZOOLOGICAL GARDEN, NONCOMMERCIAL

Akron Zoological Park ....E 330 375-2550
Akron (G-60)
Animal Mgt Svcs Ohio Inc ....E 248 398-6533
Port Clinton (G-16099)
Columbus Zoological Park Assn ....C 614 645-3400
Powell (G-16190)
Toledo Zoological Society ....B 419 385-4040
Toledo (G-18102)
Zoological Society Cincinnati ....B 513 281-4700
Cincinnati (G-4820)

ZOOS & BOTANICAL GARDENS

Cleveland Metroparks ....C 216 661-6500
Cleveland (G-5270)
Park Cincinnati Board ....D 513 421-4086
Cincinnati (G-4201)
Stan Hywet Hall and Grdns Inc ....D 330 836-5533
Akron (G-440)